With fold-out map!
JPMGUIDES This Way
AUSTRALIA
JPMGUIDES This Way
PRAGUE
JPMGUIDES This Way
SICILY
JPMGUIDES This Way
RUSSIA
JPMGUIDES This Way
CARIBBEAN ISLANDS
Ideal giveaway for
· tour operators
· airlines
· cruise lines
· travel agents
· coach companies
· conference organizers
More than 70 titles available
JPMGUIDES
WORLDWIDE COVERAGE • HIGHLY READABLE • USER-FRIENDLY POCKET GUIDES
JPM Guides • Av. William-Fraisse 12 • CH-1006 Lausanne
Tel: 0041 21 617 75 61 • Fax: 0041 21 616 12 57 • information@jpmguides.com • www.jpmguides.com

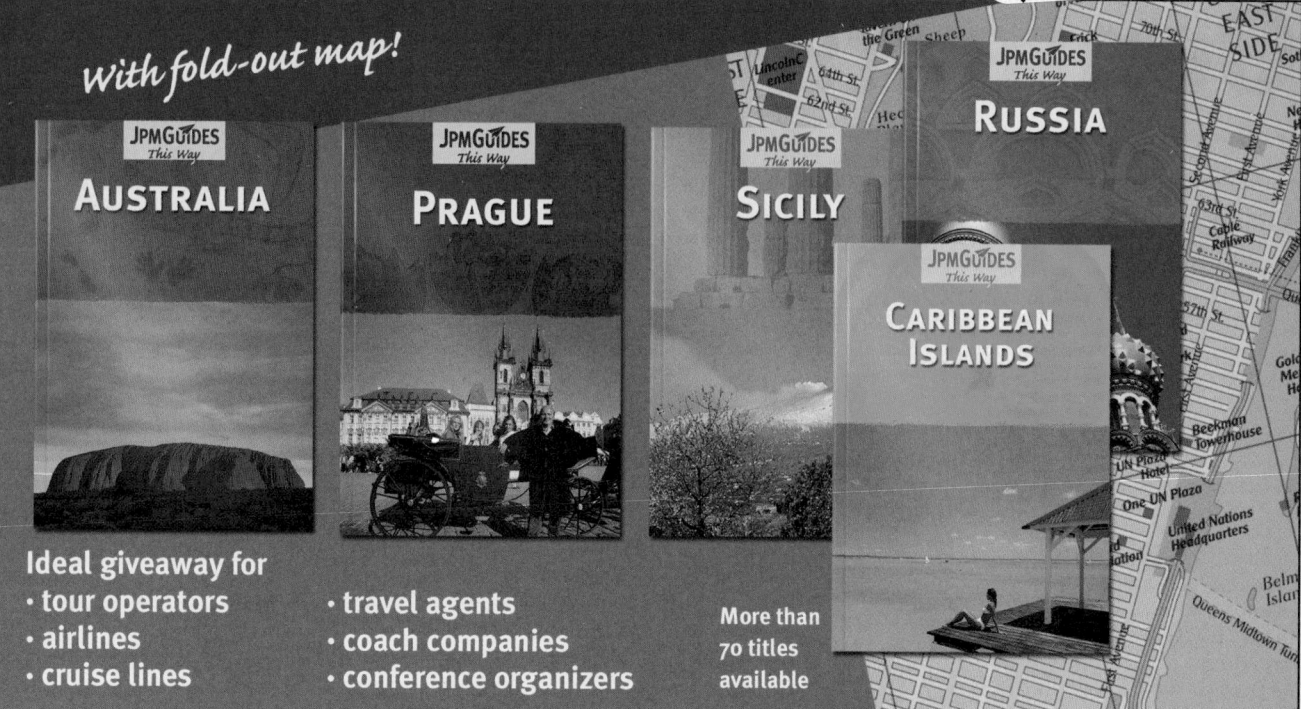

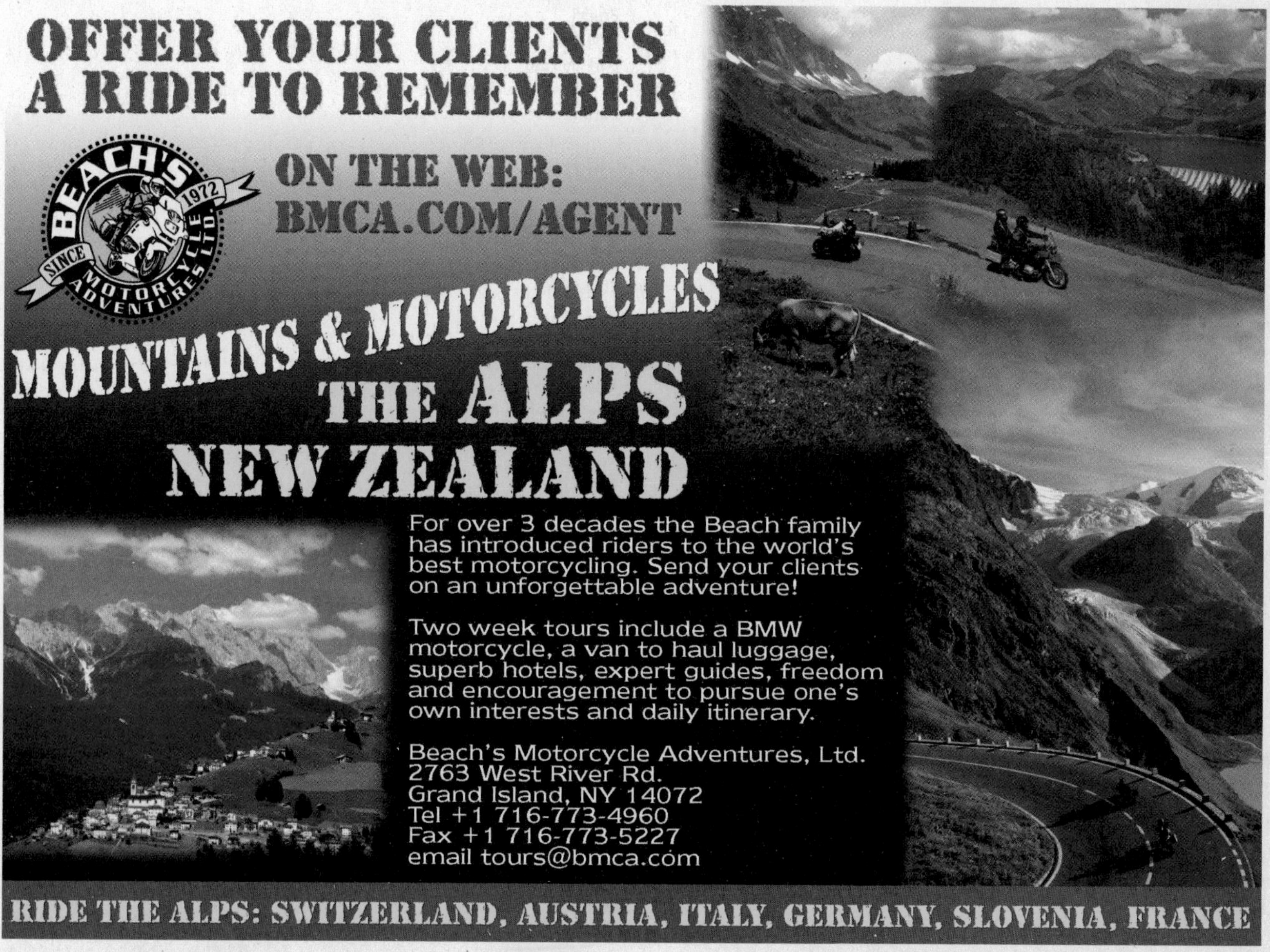
OFFER YOUR CLIENTS A RIDE TO REMEMBER
BEACH'S MOTORCYCLE ADVENTURES LTD. SINCE 1972
ON THE WEB: BMCA.COM/AGENT
MOUNTAINS & MOTORCYCLES
THE ALPS
NEW ZEALAND
For over 3 decades the Beach family has introduced riders to the world's best motorcycling. Send your clients on an unforgettable adventure!
Two week tours include a BMW motorcycle, a van to haul luggage, superb hotels, expert guides, freedom and encouragement to pursue one's own interests and daily itinerary.
Beach's Motorcycle Adventures, Ltd.
2763 West River Rd.
Grand Island, NY 14072
Tel +1 716-773-4960
Fax +1 716-773-5227
email tours@bmca.com
RIDE THE ALPS: SWITZERLAND, AUSTRIA, ITALY, GERMANY, SLOVENIA, FRANCE

Contents

Whether you are a regular subscriber or a first-time user, we trust that you will find the 2006-2007 edition of the *World Travel Guide* concise, accurate and easy to use. Every country in the world is covered in the pages that follow — and in lavish detail. There are hundreds of maps, charts, city plans and colour photographs, as well as over a million words of relevant yet colourful information accessibly presented. No destination, no matter how far flung, obscure or recently emerged, will now be beyond your reach.

Whether you are a travel agent or tourist, a business traveller or conference planner, a librarian or student, you will have frequent questions about the world of travel which require instant and accurate answers. We have spent 25 years researching these for you and the results are spread over the following pages. Globally applicable, meticulously researched and user-friendly, we are sure that the *World Travel Guide* will function as a vital sales and reference tool for your business.

But don't just take our word for it. A glance at the front cover, and the pages at the beginning of the appendices, will demonstrate the strength of the backing and endorsement for the publication from some of the world's leading travel-trade associations.

Every country in the book is listed alphabetically in the contents, from Afghanistan to Zimbabwe, together with the page number on which each country's entry begins. Alternative names of countries are also listed to avoid confusion eg French Polynesia – see Tahiti; Kampuchea – see Cambodia; Ivory Coast – see Côte d'Ivoire. Readers may also discover that smaller destinations may be found within a larger area, eg Bali – see Indonesia; Isle of Man – see United Kingdom; Crete – see Greece; or Dubai – see United Arab Emirates.

For more information on how each country's entry is laid out, see the introduction, 'How to Use this Guide'. For more information on the world, just start turning the pages!

Countries marked in red in the contents have been sponsored by the tourist board or tourism authority to help in the promotion of the destination for business and leisure travel. The presence of such sponsorship should not be taken to imply a different editorial approach.

Contents

PUBLICIS

More and more people are openly declaring their Saxism. No wonder because what Saxony offers ignites passion: the fascinating combination of culture & nature, cities & landscapes far from the beaten track. *For further information visit www.saxonytourism.com or call (503) 227-1750* When will you become a Saxist?

SUCH AN EXPERIENCE OF GERMANY

Contents

See beautiful Scandinavia

OSL✈

Contents

Contents

Mozart: Celebrating a Musical Genius

In **Salzburg** alone there will be some 260 special concerts as well as 55 Masses devoted to Mozart's sacred music. A series of 29 "Best of Mozart" concerts will run throughout the year, and the Salzburg Festival features performances of all 22 of Mozart's operas and musical comedies within a six-week period from late July until the end of August.

The celebrations in **Vienna** are no less impressive. Highlights will be performances of Mozart's last three symphonies conducted by Nikolaus Harnoncourt during the Vienna OsterKlang (Sound of Easter) festival and many of the events during the Vienna Festival Weeks from mid-May to mid-June. Chick Corea, the world-famous jazz pianist, plays Mozart on 1 July, while Fabio Luisi will be conducting the Vienna Symphonic Orchestra as part of a Mozart open-air event on Josefsplatz on 7 July. Throughout the year, Vienna's churches will host performances of Mozart's complete sacred works. Several of the concerts in Vienna will take place in the Schönbrunn Palace, including the Hall of Mirrors, where Mozart himself played.

The 30th Innsbruck Festival Weeks from mid-July to the end of August has *Don Giovanni* and the rarely performed *Il Re Pastore* on the programme, while the **Landestheater in Linz** will show *The Abduction of Seraglio* throughout the year.

Outside of Austria, **Prague**, where Mozart completed Don Giovanni in 1787, has the most comprehensive programme of Mozart anniversary events, with a vast number of performances throughout the year and particularly during the Spring Festival in May and the Prague Music Festival in August.

This year the world is celebrating the 250th anniversary of the birth of one of the greatest musical geniuses who have ever lived, Wolfgang Amadeus Mozart. Arguably the best-loved of all classical composers, he created music so rich and life-affirming that it still moves audiences the world over. On his birthday, 27 January, there were recitals of his works in Moscow, Prague, London, Tokyo, Havana, New York and many other cities. In Salzburg, his birthplace, and Vienna, where he spent some of his happiest years, there have been hundreds of events already this year marking the anniversary.

Goethe - a man not easily impressed - once said that Mozart was "a miracle that cannot be explained", and there certainly is something unfathomable about Mozart and his creative powers. A true child prodigy, he began composing at the age of four and started work on his first symphony aged eight. By the time he had reached 16, Mozart had visited England, Italy, France and Germany, met the leading musical and political figures of the time and had three operas performed in Milan. When he died in 1791, at the age of 35, he had composed over 600 works - and was still working on his *Requiem*.

Mozart achieved an incredible mastery of a wide variety of musical forms, and he was always capable of infusing the most complex musical structures and textures with an unsurpassed clarity of vision and expression.

He was indeed befitting the name Amadeus, meaning "beloved of God".

While popular legend has tended to exaggerate Mozart's miserable circumstances at the time of this death, it is still scarcely believable today that his popularity was waning towards the end of his life - even though he kept churning out operatic masterpieces like *The Marriage of Figaro* (1786), *Don Giovanni* (1787) and *Così fan tutte* (1790). When he died in December 1791, not long after the premiere of *The Magic Flute*, he was heavily in debt and was buried in an unmarked grave.

Mozart features prominently on the musical calendar in most major cities around the world this year, but nowhere is the programme of events quite as busy as in **Austria**.

Among other cities visited by Mozart on his many travels, **Milan** stages *Ascanio in Alba*, a piece of music Mozart wrote for the city when he was 16 years old, at the Teatro alla Scala in October. In late June, the restored Teatro La Fenice in **Venice** will stage *Lucio Silla*, which Mozart composed in 1772.

In **Paris**, there will be performances of *Così fan tutte* and *The Marriage of Figaro*.

In **Utrecht**, the new Vredenburg Music Centre will be offering Mozart chamber concerts throughout 2006, and a Flemish version of *The Magic Flute* is performed at the neo-Classical opera house in **Ghent** in March and April.

Last, but not least, The Barbican in **London** offers a month of Mozart events in June and July, while Mozart's music will also be heard at the Royal Festival Hall throughout the year.

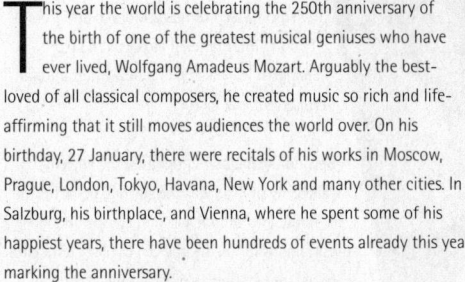

Credit: ©Tourismus Salzburg GmbH

Credit: ©Tourismus Salzburg GmbH

Credit: ©Krafts Foods Österreich

Credit: ©Tourismus Salzburg GmbH

Credit: ©Tourismus Salzburg GmbH

China:

Most first-time visitors will want to experience the ancient temples and palaces of China's grand capital, Beijing (meaning "northern Capital"). In 2005, Beijing received 3.12 million foreign tourists, up 15 per cent on 2004. Its most popular sites include the Forbidden City, Summer Palace Temple of Heaven. Beijing also serves as a base for day trips to the Great Wall of China.

Today, Beijing is undergoing a major pre-Olympic makeover, and some of its cherished attractions are currently being renovated. In addition, some of the world's foremost architects are reinventing its skyline and profile. New hotels, bars and restaurants are opening at a frantic pace, yet - for now - Beijing retains a cultured, refined ambience that contrasts with Shanghai's rollercoaster ride into New China.

Labeled "the world's most happening city" by Time magazine, Shanghai is the nation's largest city and a blueprint for Future China - fusing cutting-edge fashion, fine cuisine and a futuristic skyline with rich history and architecture. Yu Garden, Oriental Pearl Tower, Jade Buddha Temple and People's Square are all popular with tourists, while the historic riverside strip of early 20th-century mansions, known as The Bund, is evolving into an upscale dining and luxury retail destination. Shanghai also boasts the world's fastest passenger train line, the Maglev, which ferries visitors to and from Pudong International airport at 431kph. Shanghai will also open a new international cruise terminal in 2007.

Beyond the major metropolises, the ancient walled city of Xi'an was the starting point for the Silk Route into central Asia and Europe, though is most famous for the nearby Qin Dynasty terracotta warriors - one of China's most-visited attractions. The former capital city of Nanjing (meaning 'southern Capital') offers a wealth of historic treasures, including Ming tombs, former Presidential Palace and the remnants of the longest city wall in the world. The mystical West Lake has inspired painters, poets and

Remember this time and date: 20:08 on 20.08.2008. At that moment, the Olympic flame will be lit in Beijing&s Olympic Stadium and the 2008 Olympic Games will commence. China, like never before, will have what it craves: the world&s unflinching attention.

It is impossible to overstate the importance of hosting the 2008 Games, both for the continued growth of China's economy and one of its strongest and fastest-growing industries: tourism. A country of 1.3 billion people, China (or Zhongguo as it is locally known, meaning "Middle Kingdom") is now a red-hot destination - a mystical, enchanting, fast-changing land that sits at the top of more travel itineraries than ever.

China's inbound tourism market is growing at around 8 per cent per annum, and the World Tourism Organisation predicts that by 2020 it will be the most-visited country on earth. The buzz is already building. China received almost 42 million tourists in 2004, overtaking Italy to become the world's fourth most-visited country.

Flexible Itinerary

Given China's vastness, flexibility is the byword. Tailor-made holidays are the best way to blend enjoyment of its vast lands, varied cuisines, ancient history, tradition and culture with the best of 21st-century China.

Olympic Nation

writers for centuries and is the tourism centrepiece of Hangzhou, one of China's most attractive cities, which sits surrounded by Zhejiang Province's picturesque tea plantations. Visitors might wish to combine Hangzhou with a trip to the serene Chinese water gardens of Suzhou. Both are immortalised in a Chinese proverb: "In heaven there is paradise, on earth there is Suzhou and Hangzhou."

Credit: © Macau

Credit: © Macau Government Tourism Office

Further south, the world's largest Buddha at Leshan and the fabulous mountain scenery and indigenous peoples of Yunnan province provide memorable experiences. Adventure sports enthusiasts can enjoy white-water rafting, climbing and hiking amid spectacular scenery near Yangshuo. Golf fans have several options, including the world's largest course at Mission Hills and the snow-capped mountain backdrop of Lijiang's Jade Dragon Snow Mountain course.

Hong Kong and Macau

Hong Kong and Macau were returned to Chinese rule by the British (1997) and Portugal (1997) respectively, and both are governed by China as Special Administrative Regions (SAR), retaining their own currencies, although the Chinese yuan is widely accepted.

Set around beautiful Victoria Harbour, Hong Kong boasts one of the world's most stunning cityscapes, best viewed, day or night, by taking the funicular railway up to The Peak. An established tourism destination, Hong Kong recorded 23.3 million tourism arrivals (10.8 million international plus 12.8 million mainland Chinese) in 2005, its best ever figures and up 7.1 per cent on 2004. Part of the extra inflow can be attributed to the opening of Disneyland Hong Kong. However, Hong Kong has revamped its tourism image, with new hotel openings by Four Seasons, Mandarin Oriental and boutique property, Jia. Its celebrated dining and shopping scene is also thriving, and the new IFC Two skytower features some of Hong Kong's chicest shops and finest restaurants.

A 45-minute ferry ride from Hong Kong, Macau is shedding its sleepy, sleazy image of yesteryear and reinventing itself as the Las Vegas of Asia. In 2005, it received 18.7 million visitor arrivals, up 12 per cent on 2004. The new harbourside Fisherman's Wharf dining, entertainment and gambling complex is now open and, from 2007, several giant casinos and five-star hotels will open on Cotai, a strip of reclaimed land that links Macau City with the islands of Coloane and Taipa. The historic old heart of Macau remains intact, with fabulous Portuguese colonial architecture, historic ruins and the fascinating Macau Museum. Macau is also becoming a Chinese hub for southeast Asia's fast-growing low-cost airline sector.

Beaches and Boutique Hotels

Hundreds of new hotels are opening across China's cities. International brands like Starwood, InterContinental, Accor, Hyatt, Marriott, Four Seasons, Shangri-La and Hilton are opening state-of-the-art 5-star properties at a rapid pace, giving travellers more options when travelling beyond the main cities of Shanghai, Beijing and Hong Kong.

Resort hotels are popping up across China's premier beach resort, Hainan Island - where the Miss World contest has been hosted each December for the last few years. China's third-largest island offers beautiful beaches, forest hikes, cyling, adventure travel and championship-standard golf courses. It is popular as a weekend break for mainland Chinese and expats and as a honeymoon destination. The largest resort, Halong Bay near Sanya, offers Marriott, Sheraton and Hilton resort hotels, with more to follow in the next two years.

Credit: © Hong Kong Tourism Board

Boutique properties are also catching on, especially in China's scenic hideways. The stunning contemporary design of Commune by the Great Wall 70km (44 miles) northwest of Beijing earned it a special award at the 2002 la Biennale di Venezia, the first ever recognition for Chinese architecture at the famed festival. It has also attracted a host of celebrities, including J Lo and Serena Williams (website: www.commune.com.cn). Located near the historic city of Hanzhou, Fuchun Resort is an elegant lakeside villa resort and golf course set in lush hillside scenery and was rated one of *Conde Nast Traveller*'s best new hotels in the world for 2005 (website: www.fuchunresort.com). Banyan Tree Ringha offers divine Tibetan-themed lodges located in mythical Shangri La country. Wooden balconies frame the breathtaking mountain scenery of Yunnan Province, which inspired James Hilton's seminal novel. In mid-2006, Banyan Tree will open a brand new boutique property near the beautiful town of Liijiang, Yunnan Province (website: www.banyantree.com)

Ecotourism:

Concerns about the impact of tourism on the environment have increased interest in responsible travel.
We pick a selection of global ecotourism projects.

Tourism is the fastest growing industry in the world. Ever more people are travelling, and ever more exotic tourist destinations are being sought out by travellers. But how does this affect local people, environments and species across the globe? What kind of impact does tourism have on fragile ecosystems and indigenous cultures?

Concerns like these have ensured that ecotourism has become one of the fastest growing niches in the travel market over the last couple of decades. It grew out of the nature-based holiday market in the 1980s, and its importance was internationally acknowledged in 2002 when the United Nations celebrated the International Year of Ecotourism. Many global environmental organisations and aid agencies favour ecotourism as a vehicle to sustainable development, and for many countries, ecotourism is not so much seen as a marginal activity intended to finance protection of the environment as a major sector of the national economy. In countries such as Kenya, Ecuador, Nepal, Costa Rica and Madagascar, ecotourism represents a significant part of foreign revenue.

There is not one universally accepted definition of ecotourism but one of the most widely quoted is that of The International Ecotourism Society: 'Responsible travel to natural areas that conserves the environment and sustains the well-being of local people.' Typically, ecotourism focuses on local cultures, wilderness adventures, volunteering and personal education, but increasingly, initiatives by hospitality providers to promote recycling, energy efficiency, water re-use, and the creation of economic opportunities for local communities are seen as an integral part of ecotourism. Some of the finest initiatives within ecotourism turn a bad situation into a good one, for instance by making whale hunters become whale watching guides or by establishing rainforest tourism alternatives to logging. There are also plenty of examples where ecotourism has helped empower indigenous people and channel funds to local communities where the traditional travel industry would have kept it all for itself. Moreover, by providing ethical and environmentally friendly solutions, ecotourism forces other sectors to consider their practices. The cruise industry, for instance, has significantly improved its environmental record in recent years.

Ecotourism does have its critics who tend to regard it as a PR exercise designed to make tourists from rich countries feel less guilty about taking cheap holidays in poor countries. Yet while all ecotourism projects must be considered on their own merits and some may not be as beneficial as others, there is abundant evidence - as well as the testimony of thousands of tourists, environmentalists and local people around the world - that ecotourism in general does make a difference to the environment and to people's lives on the ground.

This is why the sector after more than two decades of growth is still looking very healthy and is likely to continue to expand in the the years ahead.

Below you will find a few examples of great ecotourism destinations and activities.

Discover aboriginal culture in Australia

Uluru - or Ayers Rock - in Australia is a great ecotourism destination offering visitors the chance to learn about the rich culture of the local aboriginal people and experience the area's magic nature. This sacred place was returned to the aboriginal Anangu people in 1985, and they are in charge of all official activities in the area, running the award-winning cultural centre as well as the various guided tours on offer. Uluru not only gives economic resources to the local aboriginal communities; it also gives a sense of pride and dignity to some of the most disadvantaged people in Australia.
Website: www.anangutours.com.au

Credit: © Brigitte Gladstone

Credit: © Ghana Ministry of Tourism

Protect the rainforest in Ghana

When the Kakum National Park in Ghana was established, more than 80 per cent of the rainforest in the area had been lost because of agricultural expansion, growing settlements and timber extraction. The Kakum Canopy Walkway and Visitor's Centre has helped to halt the destruction. It has become a very popular destination, and the centre educates visitors - tens of thousands of schoolchildren among them - about the forest, its biodiversity and its people. In addition to park entrance fees, income generation through the sale of handicrafts, transportation, food, and lodging for tourists has had a substantial effect on the local economy.
Tel: +233 0 42 33278
Website: www.GhanaTourism.gov.gh

Help run an ecolodge in the Bolivian Amazon

Chalalán Ecolodge in the Madidi National Park in the Bolivian Amazon is a joint ecotourism initiative of the rainforest community of San José de Uchupiamonas and Conservation International. Having first been trained to run the ecolodge, the villagers were given full ownership of it five years ago. The lodge provides a much-needed economic alternative to logging, and some 70 families receive regular direct economic benefits from it. They also get indirect benefits from the sale of crafts. In return, visitors have the opportunity to experience some of the richest rainforest in the whole of the Amazon.
Tel/fax: +591 2 434058.

Regenerate mountain villages in Cyprus

SAVE - an abbreviation of 'Support Abandoned Villages and their Environment' - is the name given to a project in Cyprus that seeks to regenerate mountain villages virtually abandoned by young people who have moved to work in the tourist industry along the coast. The project takes holidaymakers on a bus tour into Cyprus' interior, and it has already begun to make a difference to the lives of rural villagers. Visitors are helped to understand more about the island and to make a real contribution to the economic livelihoods of the villagers by visiting their restaurants and cafes and by buying their products.
Website: www.thetravelfoundation.org.uk

a Growing Niche Market

Return baby elephants to the wild in Sri Lanka

Credit: © Mike Daines

The Elephant Transit Home at Udalawe National Park is the only facility in Sri Lanka that is designed to return orphans to their natural home in the wild. As such it poses a dilemma to the ecotourist, for while the transit home, unlike other elephant orphan sanctuaries in Sri Lanka, is seeking to preserve and save wildlife, it also restricts visitor involvement with the young calves in its care. Tourists are welcome to watch the elephants from a short distance at feeding times, but are not generally allowed to come near them or feed them.
Website: www.bornfree.org.uk

Support the training of Maasai school leavers in Kenya

The Koiyaki Guiding School & Wilderness Camp is the first training facility in Africa for young Maasai school leavers as tourist guides for the Maasai Mara ecosystem. The project provides employment opportunities and promotes conservation of Maasai Mara wildlife by helping to convert the region into an economically viable conservation area through tourism. The Wilderness Camp provides exciting safari and wildlife experiences to the general public in an area of unspoilt beauty away from the main tourism routes. The trainee guides are involved in running the camp under the guidance of the manager as part of their work experience.
Website: www.rekero.com/koiyaki

Credit: © Tusk Trust

Join a clean-up patrol in the Gunung Rinjani mountain in Indonesia

The Rinjani Trek Centre in Senaru is a model for ecotourism in Indonesia. The result of a unique partnership between the National Park, the tourism industry and the local communities, its aim is to manage and protect the Rinjani mountain environment and give locals a voice in tourist management and revenue issues. Gunung Rinjani, one of Indonesia's sacred sites, is a forested volcano perfect for trekking to awe-inspiring waterfalls, crater valleys and panoramic ocean views. Twice a month, park staff and local residents join in a clean-up patrol to remove garbage from the mountainside. Almost 200 villagers work as trek guides and porters, while local women produce handicrafts for sale to travellers.
Website: www.lomboksumbawa.com.

Encourage the use of renewable energy at Aspen's ski resort, Colorado, USA

Visiting a ski resort may not sound like the average ecotourism holiday, but ecotourism can be about supporting best practice in regard of environmentally friendly policies, and Aspen Skiing Company is the ski industry's leading resort when it comes to green initiatives and investment in renewable energy. It was the first ski resort to purchase wind power, in 1997, and in 2006 it purchased wind energy certificates to offset 100 per cent of its electricity use. It uses solar energy and has built a 115-kilowatt microhydro plant that serves as a model for renewable generation in alpine communities. And the skiing is great!
Website: www.aspensnowmass.com

Turn poachers into tourist guides in India

The Periyar Tiger Trail is a unique project showing that ecotourism can turn a bad situation into a good one. It is conducted by a team of poachers turned tourist guides and protectors of the forests, and the benefits are many; Not only are they no longer poaching, but they are superb guides with an intimate knowledge of the forests, and they have helped capture other poachers. The trek route passes through hills and valleys with rich vegetation and wildlife. Trekking groups are accompanied by armed forest guards geared to face any emergency situation. Here, one stands a good chance to encounter much indigenous wildlife like Nilgiri langur, giant squirrel, elephant and - who knows? - maybe even the tiger!
Website: www.exploreperiyar.com

Credit: © Ministry of Tourism, India

Learn local handicrafts techniques in Laos

A trip visiting handicraft makers in Laos is a great way of learning about a different way of life and getting to appreciate the importance of local cultures. It is possible to get instruction in local handicraft techniques, and homestays are available in many places. By spending money on local accommodation and food as well as on local craft products visitors contribute to sustain people in their livelihoods. A recommended destination is Ban Natan village near the amazing 7.5km (4 miles) long Kong Lor Cave in the Khammouane Province. It is well known for its intricate cotton weavings that are dyed using natural colours.
Website: www.ecotourismlaos.com

Credit: © Linda McIntosh

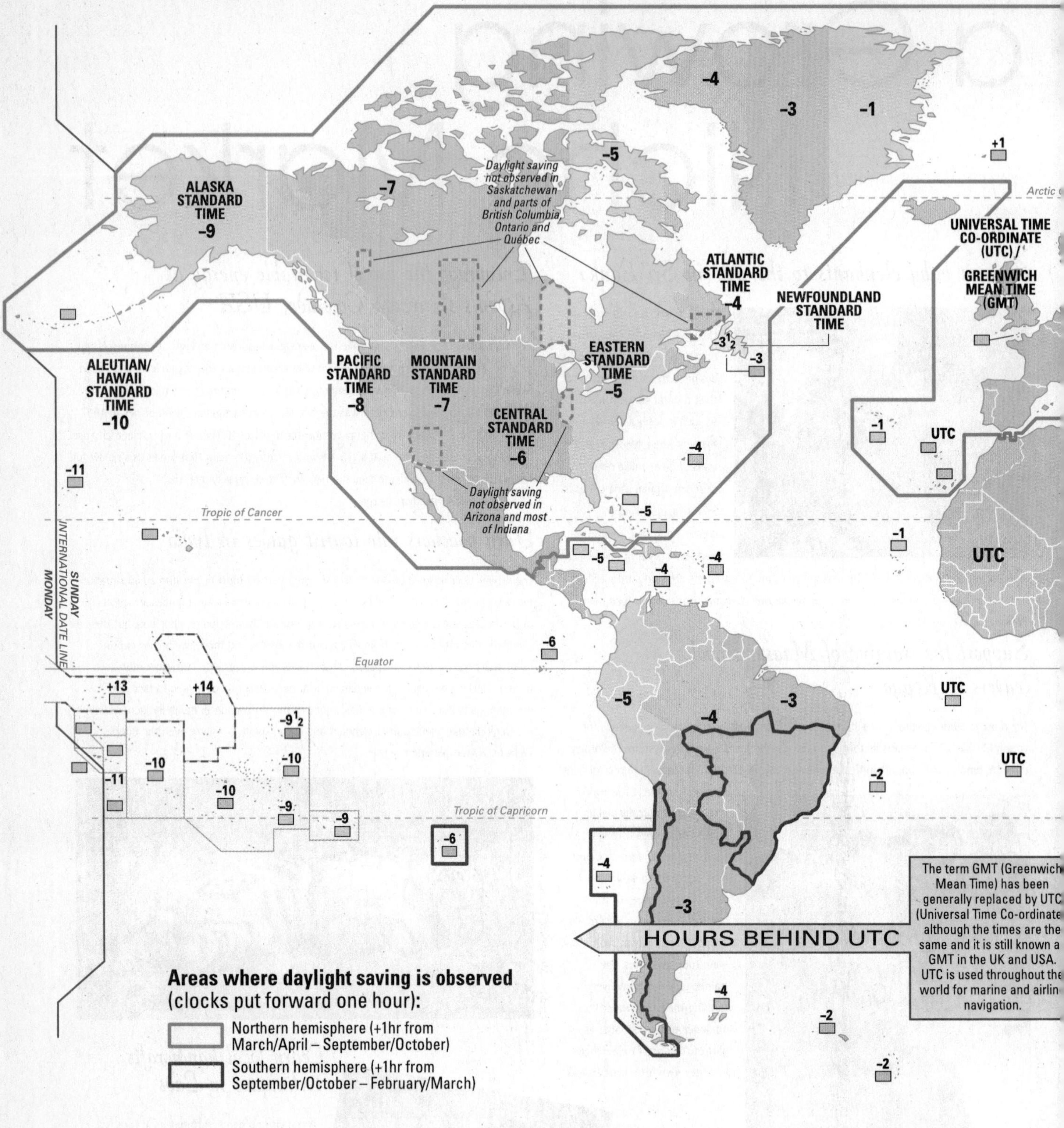

-4

-3 **-1**

+1

-5

Arctic

ALASKA STANDARD TIME -9

-7

Daylight saving not observed in Saskatchewan and parts of British Columbia, Ontario and Québec

ATLANTIC STANDARD TIME -4

NEWFOUNDLAND STANDARD TIME

-3½

-3

UNIVERSAL TIME CO-ORDINATE (UTC) /

GREENWICH MEAN TIME (GMT)

ALEUTIAN/ HAWAII STANDARD TIME -10

PACIFIC STANDARD TIME -8

MOUNTAIN STANDARD TIME -7

EASTERN STANDARD TIME -5

CENTRAL STANDARD TIME -6

-1

UTC

-11

Tropic of Cancer

Daylight saving not observed in Arizona and most of Indiana

-4

-1

UTC

-5

-4

-4

-5

-5

-4

-6

Equator

+13

+14

-5

-3

UTC

-9½

-4

-10

-10

UTC

-11

-10

-9

-2

Tropic of Capricorn

-9

-6

-4

-3

HOURS BEHIND UTC

The term GMT (Greenwich Mean Time) has been generally replaced by UTC (Universal Time Co-ordinate) although the times are the same and it is still known as GMT in the UK and USA. UTC is used throughout the world for marine and airline navigation.

-4

-2

-2

Areas where daylight saving is observed
(clocks put forward one hour):

Northern hemisphere (+1hr from March/April – September/October)

Southern hemisphere (+1hr from September/October – February/March)

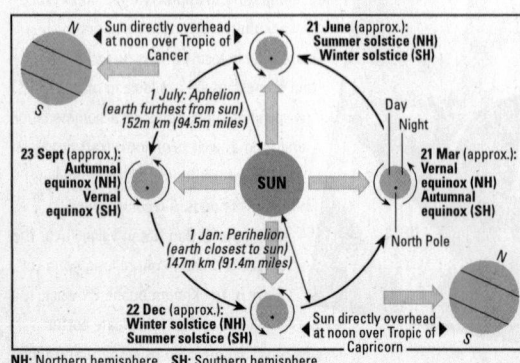

THE SUN AND THE EARTH

N

Sun directly overhead at noon over Tropic of Cancer

S

21 June (approx.):
Summer solstice (NH)
Winter solstice (SH)

1 July: Aphelion (earth furthest from sun) 152m km (94.5m miles)

Day

Night

23 Sept (approx.):
Autumnal equinox (NH)
Vernal equinox (SH)

SUN

21 Mar (approx.):
Vernal equinox (NH)
Autumnal equinox (SH)

1 Jan: Perihelion (earth closest to sun) 147m km (91.4m miles)

North Pole

N

22 Dec (approx.):
Winter solstice (NH)
Summer solstice (SH)

Sun directly overhead at noon over Tropic of Capricorn

S

NH: Northern hemisphere   **SH:** Southern hemisphere

PHASES OF THE MOON

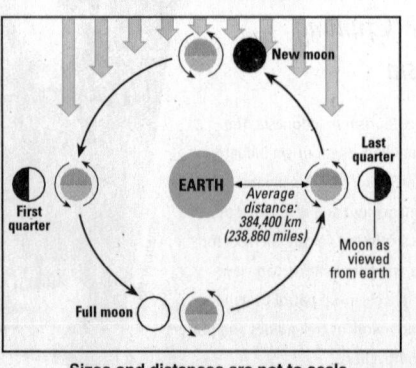

New moon

First quarter

EARTH

Average distance: 384,400 km (238,860 miles)

Last quarter

Moon as viewed from earth

Full moon

Sizes and distances are not to scale

SOLAR ECLIPSE

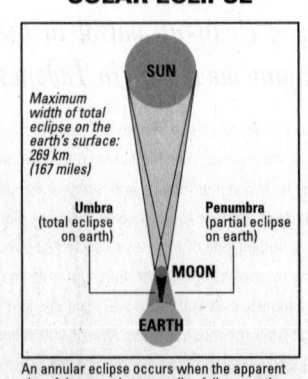

Maximum width of total eclipse on the earth's surface: 269 km (167 miles)

SUN

Umbra (total eclipse on earth)

Penumbra (partial eclipse on earth)

MOON

EARTH

An annular eclipse occurs when the apparent size of the moon is too small to fully cover the disc of the sun, resulting in a ring of sunlight remaining around the moon

24
22
20
18
16
14
12
10
8
6
4
2
0

Hours of daylight

Ja

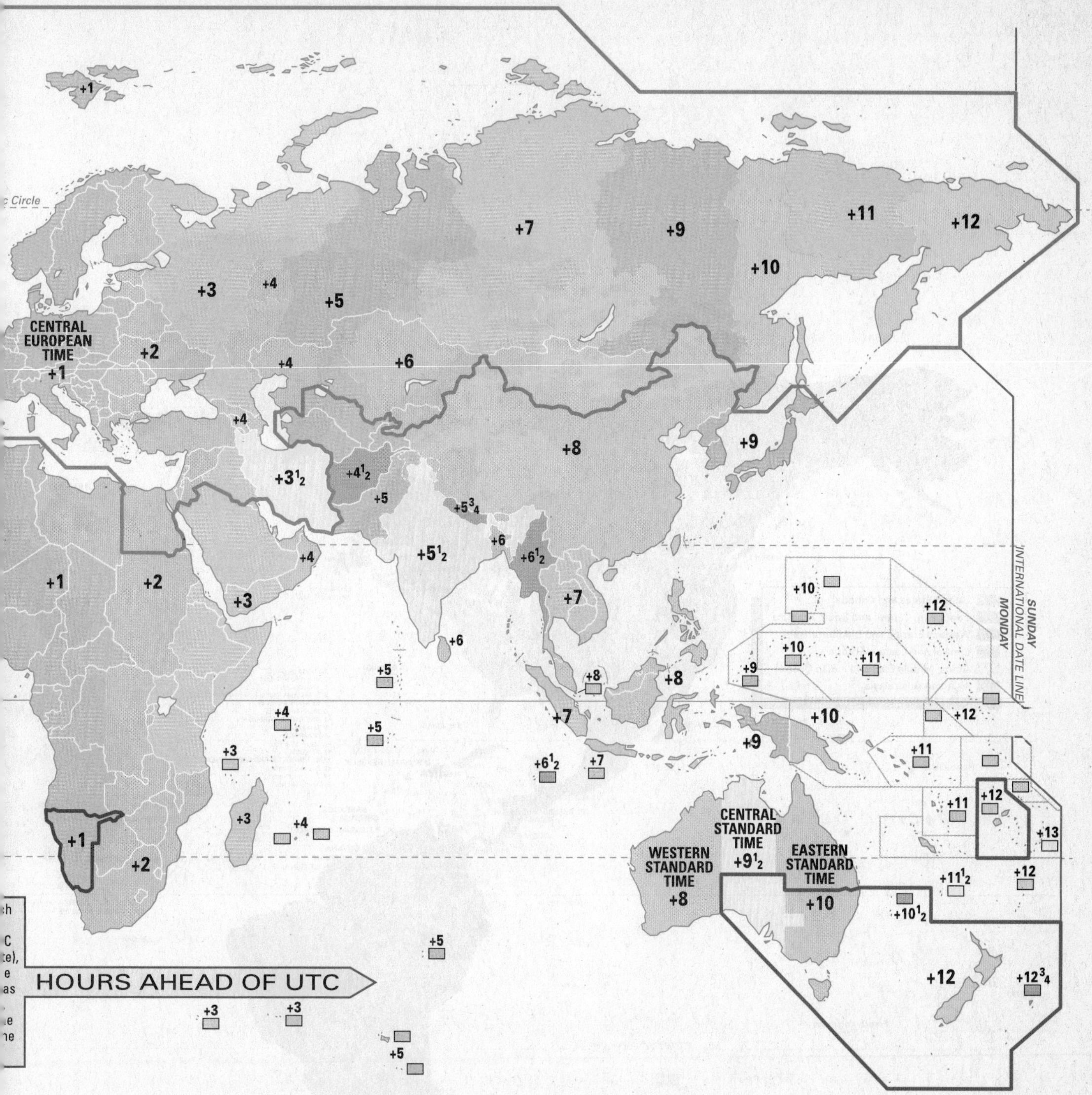

+1

Arctic Circle

+7 +9 +11 +12

+10

+3 +4

+5

CENTRAL
EUROPEAN
TIME
+1

+2

+4 +6

+4

+8 +9

+4

+3½

+4½

+9

+5

+5³⁄₄

+1 +2

+4

+5½

+6

+6½

+8 +8

+10

+12

+3

+5

+6

+7

+10

+11

+9

+5

+9

+8 +8

+10

+12

+4

+5

+7

+11

+3

+6½

+7

+9

+11

+11

+12

+3

+4

+1

+2

CENTRAL
STANDARD
TIME
+9½

WESTERN
STANDARD
TIME
+8

EASTERN
STANDARD
TIME
+10

+13

+11½

+12

+10½

+5

HOURS AHEAD OF UTC

+3 +3

+12

+12³⁄₄

+5

SUNDAY
MONDAY
INTERNATIONAL DATE LINE

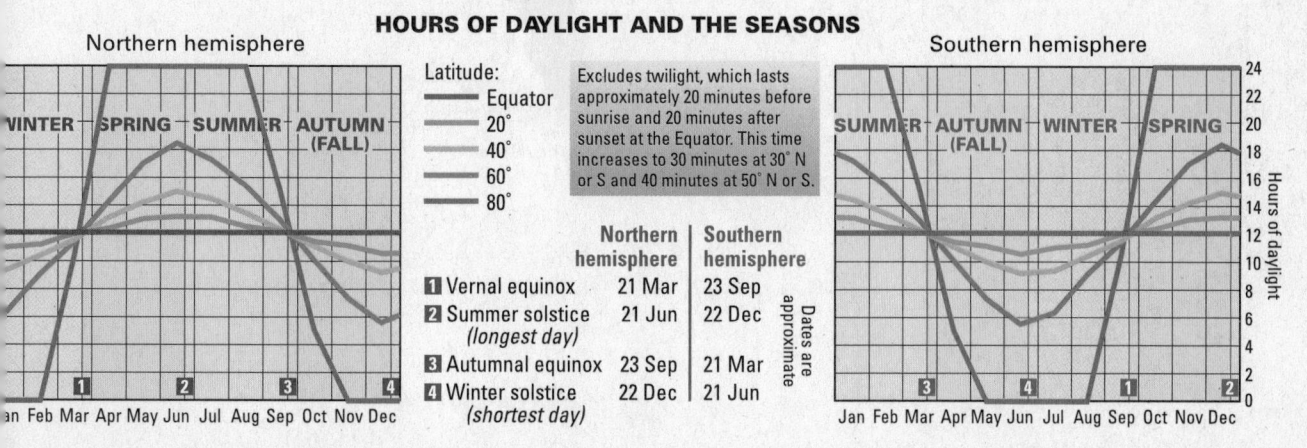

HOURS OF DAYLIGHT AND THE SEASONS

Northern hemisphere

WINTER | SPRING | SUMMER | AUTUMN (FALL)

Jan Feb Mar Apr May Jun Jul Aug Sep Oct Nov Dec

Latitude:
— Equator
— 20°
— 40°
— 60°
— 80°

Excludes twilight, which lasts approximately 20 minutes before sunrise and 20 minutes after sunset at the Equator. This time increases to 30 minutes at 30° N or S and 40 minutes at 50° N or S.

	Northern hemisphere	Southern hemisphere
1 Vernal equinox	21 Mar	23 Sep
2 Summer solstice *(longest day)*	21 Jun	22 Dec
3 Autumnal equinox	23 Sep	21 Mar
4 Winter solstice *(shortest day)*	22 Dec	21 Jun

Dates are approximate

Southern hemisphere

SUMMER | AUTUMN (FALL) | WINTER | SPRING

Jan Feb Mar Apr May Jun Jul Aug Sep Oct Nov Dec

Hours of daylight
24
22
20
18
16
14
12
10
8
6
4
2
0

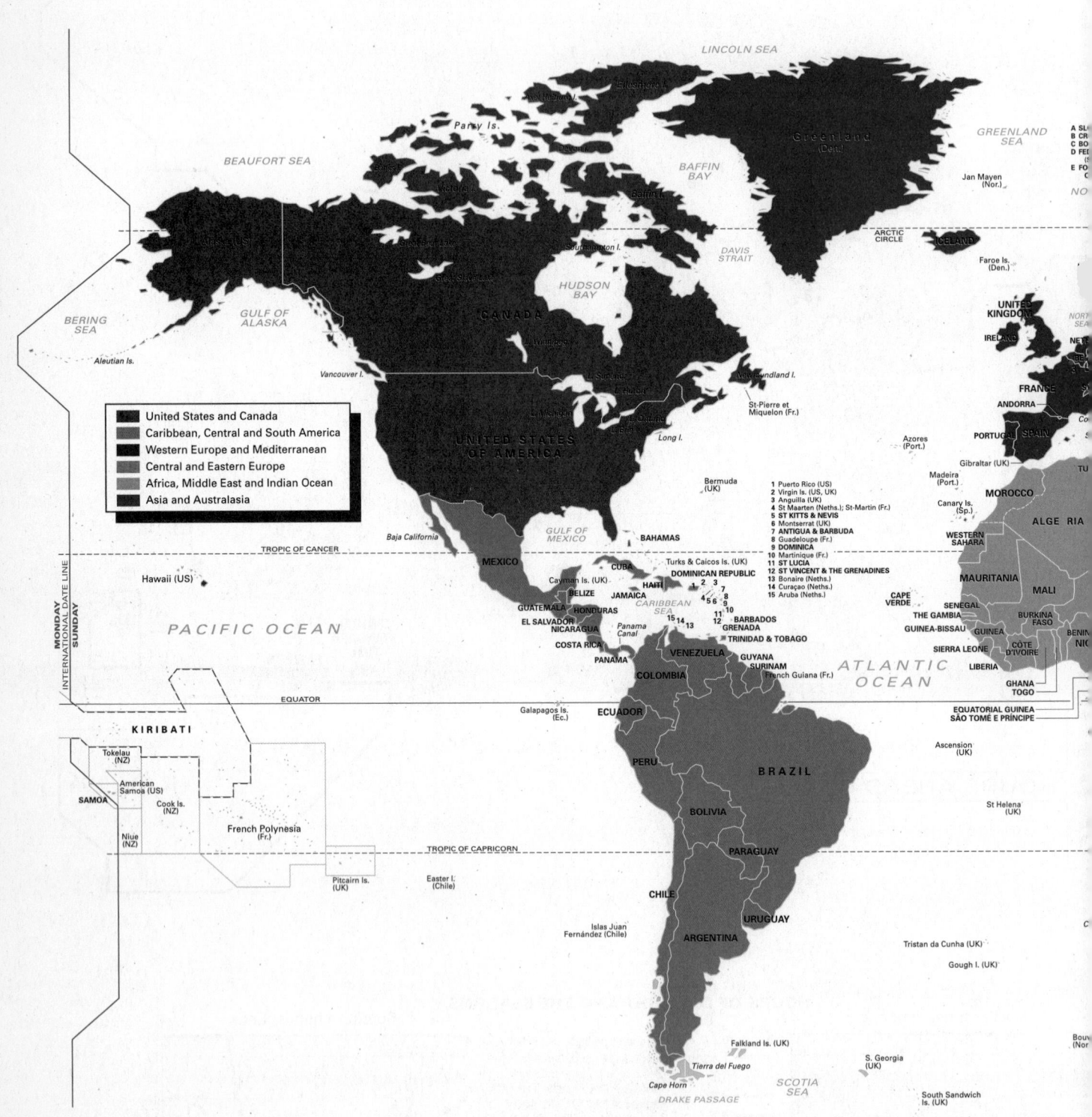

United States and Canada
Caribbean, Central and South America
Western Europe and Mediterranean
Central and Eastern Europe
Africa, Middle East and Indian Ocean
Asia and Australasia

1 Puerto Rico (US)
2 Virgin Is. (US, UK)
3 Anguilla (UK)
4 St Maarten (Neths.); St-Martin (Fr.)
5 ST KITTS & NEVIS
6 Montserrat (UK)
7 ANTIGUA & BARBUDA
8 Guadeloupe (Fr.)
9 DOMINICA
10 Martinique (Fr.)
11 ST LUCIA
12 ST VINCENT & THE GRENADINES
13 Bonaire (Neths.)
14 Curaçao (Neths.)
15 Aruba (Neths.)

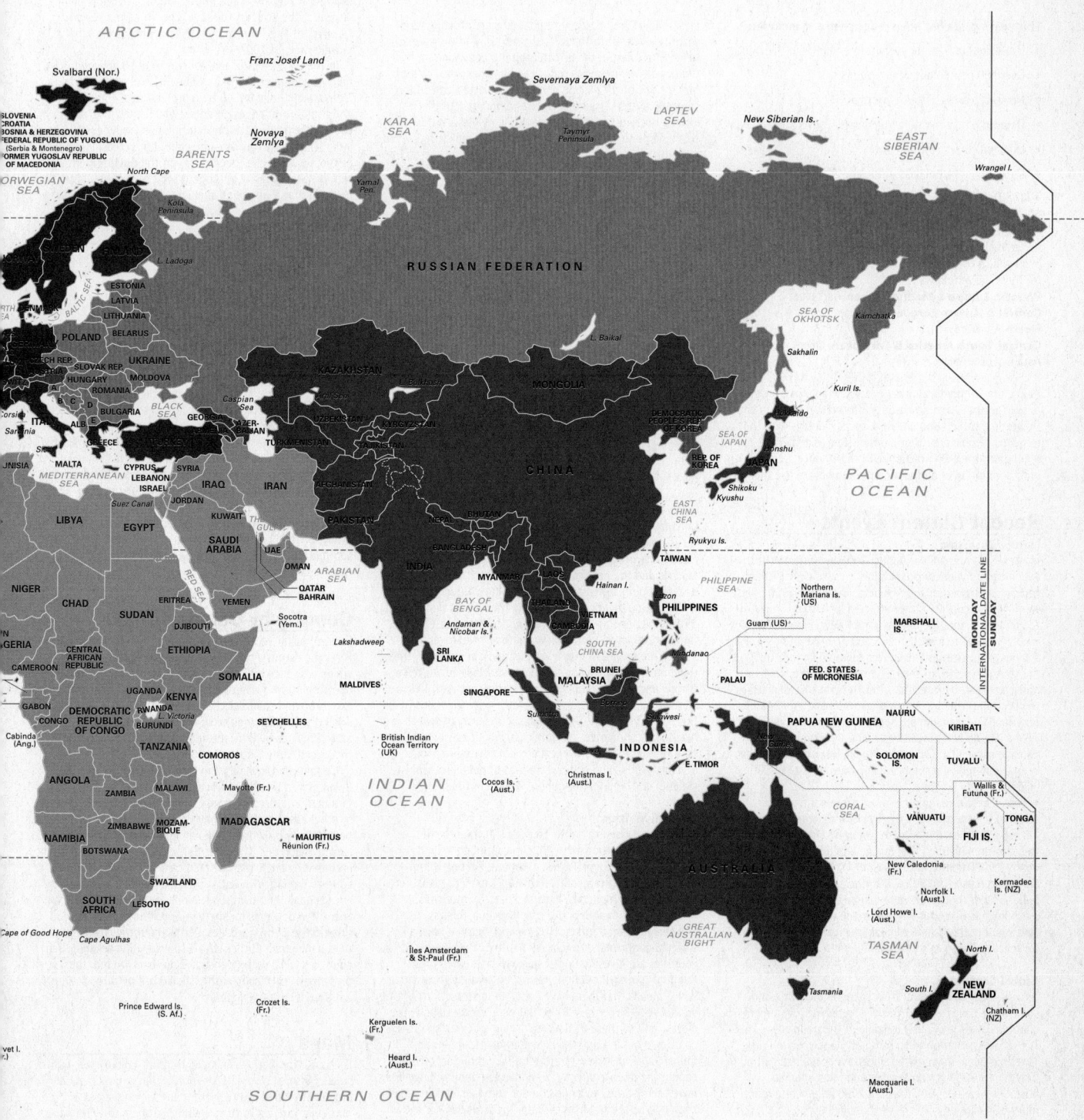

ARCTIC OCEAN

Svalbard (Nor.)

Franz Josef Land

Severnaya Zemlya

SLOVENIA
CROATIA
BOSNIA & HERZEGOVINA
FEDERAL REPUBLIC OF YUGOSLAVIA
(Serbia & Montenegro)
FORMER YUGOSLAV REPUBLIC
OF MACEDONIA

KARA
SEA

LAPTEV
SEA

New Siberian Is.

EAST
SIBERIAN
SEA

Novaya
Zemlya

BARENTS
SEA

Taymyr
Peninsula

Wrangel I.

ORWEGIAN
SEA

North Cape

Yamal
Pen.

Kola
Peninsula

RUSSIAN FEDERATION

SEA OF
OKHOTSK

Kamchatka

L. Ladoga

ESTONIA
LATVIA
LITHUANIA
BELARUS

Sakhalin

RTH
PN
SEA

BALTIC SEA

POLAND

KAZAKHSTAN

L. Balkhash

MONGOLIA

Kuril Is.

Hokkaido

ZECH REP
SLOVAK REP
HUNGARY
ROMANIA

UKRAINE

MOLDOVA

Caspian
Sea

UZBEKISTAN

KYRGYZSTAN

DEMOCRATIC
PEOPLE'S REP
OF KOREA

SEA OF
JAPAN

Honshu

D
BULGARIA

BLACK
SEA

GEORGIA
AZER-
BAIJAN

TURKMENISTAN

CHINA

REP OF
KOREA

JAPAN

PACIFIC
OCEAN

Corsica
Sardinia

ALB
GREECE

TAJIKISTAN

Shikoku
Kyushu

JNISIA

MALTA

MEDITERRANEAN
SEA

CYPRUS
LEBANON
ISRAEL

SYRIA

IRAQ

IRAN

AFGHANISTAN

EAST
CHINA
SEA

LIBYA

EGYPT

SUEZ Canal

JORDAN

KUWAIT

PAKISTAN

NEPAL

BHUTAN

Ryukyu Is.

NIGER

CHAD

SUDAN

SAUDI
ARABIA

THE
GULF

UAE

BAHRAIN

QATAR

OMAN

ARABIAN
SEA

Socotra
(Yem.)

YEMEN

INDIA

BANGLADESH

MYANMAR

TAIWAN

Hainan I.

PHILIPPINE
SEA

Luzon

Northern
Mariana Is.
(US)

MONDAY
INTERNATIONAL DATE LINE
SUNDAY

ERITREA

DJIBOUTI

BAY OF
BENGAL

LAOS

THAILAND

VIETNAM

CAMBODIA

PHILIPPINES

Guam (US)

MARSHALL
IS.

GERIA

CAMEROON

CENTRAL
AFRICAN
REPUBLIC

ETHIOPIA

SOMALIA

Lakshadweep

Andaman &
Nicobar Is.

SRI
LANKA

SOUTH
CHINA SEA

Mindanao

FED. STATES
OF MICRONESIA

PALAU

GABON

DEMOCRATIC
REPUBLIC
OF CONGO

UGANDA

RWANDA

BURUNDI

KENYA

L. Victoria

TANZANIA

MALDIVES

SEYCHELLES

BRITISH Indian
Ocean Territory
(UK)

SINGAPORE

BRUNEI

MALAYSIA

Sumatra

Borneo

Sulawesi

INDONESIA

PAPUA NEW GUINEA

NAURU

KIRIBATI

Cabinda
(Ang.)

COMOROS

INDIAN
OCEAN

Cocos Is.
(Aust.)

Christmas I.
(Aust.)

E. TIMOR

SOLOMON
IS.

TUVALU

ANGOLA

ZAMBIA

MALAWI

Mayotte (Fr.)

MADAGASCAR

MAURITIUS
Réunion (Fr.)

Wallis &
Futuna (Fr.)

CORAL
SEA

VANUATU

FIJI IS.

TONGA

NAMIBIA

ZIMBABWE

MOZAM-
BIQUE

BOTSWANA

SWAZILAND

AUSTRALIA

New Caledonia
(Fr.)

Norfolk I.
(Aust.)

Kermadec
Is. (NZ)

SOUTH
AFRICA

LESOTHO

Cape of Good Hope

Cape Agulhas

Îles Amsterdam
& St-Paul (Fr.)

GREAT
AUSTRALIAN
BIGHT

Lord Howe I.
(Aust.)

TASMAN
SEA

North I.

Prince Edward Is.
(S. Af.)

Crozet Is.
(Fr.)

Kerguelen Is.
(Fr.)

Tasmania

South I.

NEW
ZEALAND

Chatham I.
(NZ)

vet I.
r.)

Heard I.
(Aust.)

Macquarie I.
(Aust.)

SOUTHERN OCEAN

How to Use this Guide

Welcome to the 25th edition of the *World Travel Guide* (2006-2007), which has once again been thoroughly revised and updated.

This year's guide has been redesigned and includes:

- Full-colour entries for every single country in the world
- Over 400 new colour images sourced
- Newly researched health information
- Detailed passport/visa requirements for every destination
- Updated currency information
- Dates of public holidays until June 2007
- Top Things To See & Do

For both ease of reference and to enhance its appearance, the guide is regionally colour-coded. Each country is headed by a coloured box showing which region it belongs to. These are as follows:

Western Europe & Mediterranean: dark blue;
Central & Eastern Europe: light blue;
North America: red;
Central, South America & Caribbean: green;
Asia & Australasia: mauve;
Africa, Middle East & Indian Ocean: orange.

At the time of going to press, every attempt has been made to give accurate and up-to-date information for each entry. However, travellers should check specific details with the respective Embassy or High Commission, as certain regulations are likely to change at short notice. Below is a brief description of all the sections and how to use them.

Recent Current Events

Natural Disasters

The USA was hit badly in August 2005 by Hurricane Katrina, which caused widespread damage in the states of Florida, Louisiana, Mississippi and Alabama. More than 1300 people were killed across the states affected by Katrina - most of them in Louisiana. The population of New Orleans fell from nearly 500,000 to less than 200,000. To make things worse, a series of hurricanes and storms followed. In fact, in 2005, the southern states of the USA experienced the worst hurricane season on record. After Hurricane Katrina struck the US Gulf of Mexico coast in late August 2005, Rita hit Texas and Louisiana in late September 2005, and in October Wilma caused widespread destruction in Florida. The damage caused by Hurricanes Wilma, Rita and Katrina has been estimated by insurance companies to total US$60 billion.

Last year saw many other areas around the world affected by severe weather patterns and natural disasters. A 7.6 magnitude earthquake struck close to Muzaffarabad in Pakistan-administered Kashmir on 8 October 2005 causing nearly 75,000 deaths and devastation that may take a decade to repair. 1400 died in the sector administered by India. Tens of thousands were injured and up to 3 million left homeless. The situation was made worse by the extreme cold weather that followed, making it extremely difficult for relief teams to reach people in remote areas.

Global Conflict

Terrorism remains a major threat around the world and some areas have been adversely affected by Government warnings about travelling to some of the troubled regions. The security situation remains highly dangerous in Iraq. There has been an increased spate of kidnappings. Although British national Norman Kember and two Canadian hostages were released in March 2006 after nearly four months in captivity, several of those kidnapped have been killed. In the meantime, the chaotic trial of Saddam Hussein continues in Baghdad.

Another former dictator, former Serbian Head of State, Slobodan Milosevic, died of a heart attack in his cell in March 2006 in The Hague, where his trial by the international war crimes tribunal was continuing. The uncertainty surrounding the location of his sepulture - he is buried in his home town of Pozarevac - reflects Serbia's inability to decide whether he was a war criminal or a defender of Yugoslavia, singled out for persecution by the West.

7 July 2005 became a black day in the history of the UK when four suicide bombers struck in central London, killing 52 people and injuring 700. The co-ordinated attacks hit the transport system as the morning rush hour drew to a close. The UK immediately responded by reinforcing its security levels. Unfortunately, the next day, in the state of heightened alert in the British capital, electrician Jean Charles de Menezes was shot dead by police who mistook him for one of the suicide bombers who attacked London's transport system. Four attempted bombings took place exactly two weeks after the deadly 7 July blasts but luckily, this time none of the devices exploded and police recovered a wealth of forensic material, leading to several arrests. The heavy police presence that followed the attacks has now somewhat decreased but the country remains under a state of alert as, until all the questions are answered, the concerns over further attacks will not go away.

In Israel, Minister Ariel Sharon, suffered a stroke on 4 January 2006 and, at the time of writing, remains in a coma in a Jerusalem hospital. Ehud Olmert, the deputy Premier, has assumed the powers of Prime Minister since then. Mr Olmert was declared winner of the March 2006 election. The question of Israel's permanent borders still need to be resolved and the situation in the Occupied Territories remains tense. Visitors are still advised to avoid travel along Israel's border with Lebanon, and close to the Israeli side of the Israel/Gaza Strip border. While there was a reduction in the level of violence in 2005, a high threat from terrorism and military activity in Israel and in the Occupied Territories remains. A suicide bomber attacked the Old Central Bus Station in Tel Aviv on 19 January 2006, injuring 14 people.

In 2005 and 2006, the political situation in Nepal remained tense and unpredictable and levels of violence remain high across the country. King Gyanendra sacked his entire Government in February 2005 because he was unhappy with their efforts to stop the Maoist insurgency. He assumed control of the country himself and granted the Nepalese Army greater powers. In November 2005, the Maoists and the political parties announced a 12-point understanding aimed at ending the King's autocratic rule and restoring democracy. Following the Government's refusal to cooperate, the Maoists ended their ceasefire in January 2006 and, with political parties, threatened to disrupt the proposed municipal elections. In response, the Government issued a ban on demonstrations, instituted a curfew and arrested hundreds of political activists. Despite all the major political parties boycotting the elections (with the exception of RPP Thapa) and the majority of seats having no candidates, the municipal elections went ahead on 8 February 2006. Travellers are still advised to avoid demonstrations and large gatherings of people as Maoist violence and attacks throughout Nepal continue.

Medical Matters

Initially contained to South-East Asia, at the time of writing, Austria, Azerbaijan, Bulgaria, Cambodia, China, Croatia, Cyprus, Egypt, France, Germany, Greece, Hong Kong, Indonesia, Italy, India, Iran, Iraq, Japan, Kazakhstan, Laos, Malaysia, Mongolia, Nigeria, Korea (Democratic Republic of), Korea (Republic of), Romania, Russia, Slovenia, Thailand, Turkey, Ukraine and Vietnam have all suffered confirmed outbreaks in poultry or wild birds. Other countries are investigating suspected cases. The World Health Organisation (WHO) has issued an alert phase three, which means that there have been human infections of the virus. As of 13 February 2006, 169 people have caught the disease and of these 91 have died. Human cases have been confirmed in Vietnam, Thailand, Cambodia, Indonesia, China, Iraq and Turkey. As almost all are thought to have caught the disease directly from infected poultry, travellers have been warned to avoid contact with live birds in areas known to be at risk of the disease. The virus has not shown an ability to pass easily between people. However, health officials have raised the alarm over their fears of a global bird flu pandemic.

The French Overseas Territory of Réunion has been affected since the end of 2005, by a serious epidemic of the mosquito-borne *Chikungunya* virus. According to the French Ministry of Health, over 100,000 people have been affected of whom over 70 have died either directly or indirectly as a result of being infected with the virus. Visitors are advised to avoid areas where mosquitoes may be concentrated.

Looking Forward

While Beijing, China is preparing to host the 2008 Olympic Games, which will no doubt hugely boost its tourism sector, London also has ground to celebrate. In 2005, the city won the Olympic bid against close contender Paris, and will host the 2012 Olympic Games. There are no grudges between the two countries though. It has also been announced that London will also host the start of the race, known as the "*Grand Départ*" of the Tour de France, the famous French bicycle race, in 2007.

In the travel sector, eco-tourism is quickly becoming a fast growing niche market. Many players now offer "responsible holidays" to help protect local communities and the natural environment in which they live. This could potentially have devastating consequences for airlines as many tourists are becoming increasingly aware of the negative effects of flying on the environment and climate change. Part of modern society, it is unimaginable to think that flying is on the verge of disappearing, but a better balance between the needs of tourists and the necessity to lower gas emissions and reduce other negative effects of flying will have to be achieved in order to protect our planet. To find out how much CO2 your journey would emit, visit:
www.chooseclimate.org/flying/mapcalc.html.

World Maps

The World Political Map features the colour coding used throughout the guide.

The World Time Zones Map shows the time in each part of the world. All time zones are centred on the Greenwich Meridian, zero degrees longitude. Note that in many countries, some form of Daylight Saving Time/Summertime is observed, during which clocks will be altered to make maximum use of daylight; this is also specified under each country's entry. Many parts of the world are moving towards standard regional Daylight Saving Times (a process associated with the formation of regional trade blocs, similar to the EU); some countries in the Tropics have adopted Daylight Saving Time/Summertime only for commercial reasons.

Country-by-Country Guide

Every officially recognised country in the world is included. For some countries, not all headed sections are relevant, in which case they have been omitted. In others, the amount of information it is necessary to convey has resulted in the extension and subdivision of some sections. The entry for Australia, Canada and the USA is dealt with State by State/Province by Province and includes extended profiles for several States/Provinces.

Certain islands, states and territories do not have their own entry in the World Travel Guide but are instead grouped together; this applies particularly to island groups. In other cases, countries may, correctly or not, be known popularly by more than one name: for example, Sri Lanka/Ceylon and Myanmar/Burma. A further complication is caused by areas that are politically an integral part of a country with its own entry; thus the Balearic and Canary islands have their own subsections at the end of the Spain entry. If in doubt as to where information may be found, refer to the Contents pages. Certain countries have opted to enhance their entries with a sponsorship package; such countries will be set against a colour background. The presence of such sponsorship should not be taken to imply a different editorial approach.

Maps

Each country section is headed by a full-colour map, with a smaller inset showing its location within a more general region. More detailed regional maps showing areas of particular interest to the tourist or business traveller have, where possible, also been introduced. In addition, there are two world maps at the beginning of the book.

For ease of reference, the country's location and time zones, together with details of Daylight Saving Time/Summertime where appropriate, are provided below the map.

Overview

The overview provides readers with background information about the country's history, culture and its past and current political and economic situation. It gives a snapshot of the destination and will help readers to have a better understanding of the country's current position on the world scene and discover its touristic assets.

General Information

Information about each country includes:

- Area, capital and population figures derived from the most reliable and up-to-date official statistics.
- The country's main geographical features.
- Government and Recent History– the type of Government, the date the country gained independence (if applicable), the names of the Head of State and the Head of Government and the dates they were elected and a brief overview of the country's most recent political history.
- Language – the principal official, spoken and understood languages.
- Main religious denominations.
- Electricity, eg voltage, cycles (in Hertz) (where available), and types of plugs used.
- Social conventions (including usual forms of greeting, photography, etc).

Climate

A brief description of the country's climate, including clothing recommendations. The information is supplemented by at least one climate graph.

Communications

Modes of communication available, including telephone, mobile (cellular), Internet and postal services. The country dialling code is given: dialling this code from any other country will connect it with the country in question. Visitors should note that Internet and e-mail access can be problematic in some areas, owing to power cuts and lack of infrastructure. The Media section provides information on the press, radio and TV services available. It lists the most important papers published in the national language(s), TV channels and radio stations as well as some of the main English-language papers published in that country when available.

Passport/Visa

Information is presented by means of a quick-glance table on the passport and visa requirements for British and other EU nationals, as well as Australian, Canadian, Japanese and US nationals. Information, where available, is also given on the types and prices of visas and their validity, where to apply for visas, application requirements, the length of time an application takes to process and the procedures to be followed when renewing visas. There is also information on who to contact if seeking temporary residence. Other relevant information is included where necessary.

In many cases, the same regulations for passports and visas (or other identity documents) apply equally to all countries that are members of a particular international organisation (such as the Commonwealth or the EU). Occasionally, in the notes following the charts, the organisation only, rather than the often-lengthy list of member states, will be referred to. For this reason, a table showing the membership (and contact details) of the Arab League, CIS countries, the Commonwealth, ECOWAS (Economic Community of West African States), the EU and other organisations may be found in the International Organisations section at the back of the book.

In the interest of clarity and brevity, various groups of people who are often exempt from passport and visa requirements have generally not been referred to in the charts or notes. These include holders of seamen's books, UN travel passes, service or diplomatic passports and stateless persons.

Unless otherwise stated in the chart, all travellers should be in possession of a return ticket and/or sufficient funds for the duration of their stay. In many cases they will be required to prove this on arrival in the country, or when they apply for their visa prior to departure.

Note: Although every effort has been made to ensure the accuracy of the information included in this section, entry requirements may be subject to change at short notice. If in doubt, check with the Embassy or High Commission concerned, being sure to state the nature of the visit (eg business, touristic, transit) and the intended length of stay, and to confirm exactly what documentation will be necessary for the application. Remember that transit visas may be required for stopovers.

Entry and other restrictions: Nationals of Israel and Taiwan (China) especially (though not exclusively) may be subject to restrictions when visiting other countries. Travellers whose passports indicate that they have entered these countries may also encounter difficulties. Some countries enforce stricter regulations for those crossing land borders than for those entering by air or sea. Travellers whose passports confer less than full British citizenship may also be subject to additional requirements. In such cases, it is advisable to check with the relevant Embassy or with the Foreign Office well in advance of travel.

Information on passports and visas is provided mainly by Embassies/Consulates and High Commissions. Contact addresses of Embassies/Consulates or other relevant organisations are given in the following order: the name and address of the diplomatic representative of the particular country in the UK and in the USA; If there is no diplomatic representation in the UK or in the USA, the name and address of the diplomatic representative of the particular country in mainland Europe or within the particular country.

British passports: Under the terms of the British Nationality Act 1981, which came into force on 1 January 1983, 'Citizenship of the United Kingdom and Colonies' has been divided into six categories. The three main categories are: British Citizen, for those closely connected with the UK (the holder has automatic right of abode in the UK); British Overseas Territories Citizen, for those with certain specific ties with one or more of the Overseas Territories; and British Overseas Citizen, for those citizens of the UK and Colonies who have not acquired either of the above citizenship. The other three categories are: British Nationals (Overseas), for former British Dependent citizens in Hong Kong who changed their status after the handover of Hong Kong to China in 1997; British Subjects; and British Protected Persons. Since 1 January 1983, no endorsement about immigration status has been necessary on passports issued to British Citizens, as they will automatically be exempt from UK immigration control and have the right to take up employment or to establish business in another member state of the EU.

Visitors should check with the relevant Embassy or High Commission if they have any queries regarding which level of citizenship is necessary to qualify for entry to any country destination without possession of a visa.

All applications and enquiries should be made to the following: Passport Office, Globe House, 89 Eccleston Square, London SW1V 1PN (tel: (0870) 521 0410), who also handle visa requirements relating to British Overseas Territories; or the Home Office Immigration & Nationality Policy Directorate, Lunar House, 40 Wellesley Road, Croydon CR9 2BY (website: www.ind.homeoffice.gov.uk).

The Schengen Agreement: Since March 1995, a 'borderless' region known as the Schengen area has been declared covering the following states: Austria, Belgium, Denmark, Finland, France, Germany, Greece, Iceland, Italy, Luxembourg, The Netherlands, Norway, Portugal, Spain and Sweden.

Schengen countries now issue standard Schengen visas, and nationals holding visas issued by one of the Schengen countries are, in principle, permitted to travel freely within the borders of all 15. However, since Schengen states are still free to decide their own visa requirements, entry regulations may vary and nationals not requiring a visa for one Schengen country may require one for other Schengen countries. This has various practical implications; for example, travellers may be refused entry to a Schengen country for which they do not require a visa if holding onward tickets to a country for which they do. If visiting more than one Schengen country, the traveller should apply for the Schengen visa to the Embassy/Consulate of the first or main country to be visited.

There are three types of Schengen visa: airport transit, transit and short-stay. For stays of over three months, a long-stay visa will be required; this will be valid only in the country of issue.

Western Hemisphere Travel Initiative: The US Intelligence Reform and Terrorism Prevention Act of 2004 requires that by 1 January 2008, travellers to and from the Caribbean, Bermuda, Panama, Mexico and Canada have a passport or other secure, accepted document to enter or re-enter the United States. In order to facilitate the implementation of this requirement, the Administration is proposing to complete it in phases following a proposed timeline, which will be published in the Federal Register in the near future.

This is a change from prior travel requirements and will affect all United States citizens entering the United States from countries within the Western Hemisphere who do not currently possess valid passports. This new requirement will also affect certain foreign nationals who currently are not required to present a passport to travel to the United States. Most Canadian citizens, citizens of the British Overseas Territory of Bermuda, and to a lesser degree, Mexican citizens will be affected by the implementation of this requirement.

In the proposed implementation plan, which is subject to a period of initial public comment, the Initiative will be rolled out in phases, providing as much advance notice as possible to the affected public to enable them to meet the terms of the new guidelines. The proposed timeline will be as follows:

- 31 December 2006 – Requirement applied to all air and sea travel to or from Canada, Mexico, Central and South America, the Caribbean, and Bermuda.

- 31 December 2007 – Requirement extended to all land border crossings as well as air and sea travel.

Money

The entries for each country provide information on currency denominations, currency restrictions, latest exchange rate (at time of publishing) for Sterling and the US Dollar, and banking hours. It must be stressed that figures provided are only a guide.

The denominations of notes and coins given are correct at the time of writing, but new ones may be introduced or old ones withdrawn, particularly in countries with high rates of inflation. In some countries, certain foreign currencies may be accepted instead of, or in addition to, the local currency.

The guide contains a list of global currencies and the three-character currency codes that are generally used to represent them. Often, but not always, this code is the same as the ISO 4217 standard. (The ISO - or International Organization for Standardization - is a worldwide federation of national standards bodies.) In most cases, the currency code is composed of the country's two-character Internet country code plus an extra character to denote the currency unit. These codes are in general industry use to represent the currencies. In some instance, we have also included currency symbols used in everyday life, such as the dollar sign "$", the Pound sign "£", and the Euro sign "€". In most cases, UK Sterling and US Dollar bank notes and traveller's cheques can be exchanged at banks and bureaux de change. In certain countries, some foreign currencies are more readily exchanged than others, and details are included where this is likely to affect a visitor carrying Sterling notes or traveller's cheques. Banks may recommend US Dollars in preference to Pounds Sterling, depending on the exchange rates, and will also be able to offer up-to-date information as to the acceptability of Sterling in a particular country.

It is worth remembering that certain currencies can be reconverted into Sterling only at very disadvantageous rates; others cannot be reconverted at all. In some cases, banknotes of a very low value will not be negotiable in the UK, whilst denominations that are considered too high may attract a less favourable rate of exchange. However, US travellers can expect to get a better rate for US$100 notes than for US$5, but please note that many banks will refuse to exchange US$1 notes. Coins should not be brought back, as UK banks may not be able to exchange them. Some countries prohibit reconversion except at airports or borders, and then only up to a certain limit. It is often advisable to change only the amount needed to cover immediate expenses.

Currency restrictions permitting, it may be advisable to change enough money before travelling to cover practicalities such as taxi fares from the airport, in the event of the airport bank not being open (these banks do not always keep normal banking hours). Visitors should also note that each country has specific Public Holidays (see Public Holidays section).

Information has been given on the acceptability of credit and debit cards.

Most countries permit the unlimited import of foreign currency, although it is often subject to declaration on arrival. In such cases, the export of foreign currency will usually be limited to the amount imported and declared. Some countries insist on the exchange of a certain quantity of foreign currency for each day of the visit; this may need to be done in advance. In some cases, receipts must be kept in order to reconvert surplus local currency on departure; in others, special forms or permits may be required.

Travellers should note that black market transactions are not necessarily favourable, in some cases illegal, and cannot be accounted for (which may cause problems when leaving a country). Changing money on the black market often results in severe punishment (including, in some places, a possible death sentence).

European Monetary Union (EMU) and the Euro: On 1 January 1999, the Euro became the official currency of 11 of the 15 member states of the European Union. Greece adopted the Euro in January 2001. Ten new countries joined the European Union on 1 May 2004 and are set to join the European Monetary Union in the next couple of years: the 10 new countries are Cyprus, Czech Republic, Estonia, Hungary, Latvia, Lithuania, Malta, Poland, Slovak Republic and Slovenia. In all the countries belonging to the Eurozone, it is now possible to use one single currency. The new Euro coins and notes appeared on 1 January 2002. At the time of writing, three of the pre-2004 EU member-states – Denmark, Sweden and the United Kingdom – have not joined the single currency.

Duty Free

All duty free allowances, including differentials for EU and non-EU travellers, are given where applicable, as well as information on prohibited items and any other relevant details. Details given are not necessarily exhaustive and should only be used as a general guide. Further information may be obtained from the appropriate High Commission, Embassy or Tourist Board, HM Customs and Excise or the British Overseas Trade Board.

Following the introduction of the Single European Market in 1993, there are now no legal limits imposed on importing duty-paid tobacco and alcoholic products from one EU country to another. However, travellers may be questioned at customs if they exceed the amounts recommended and may be asked to prove that the goods are for personal consumption only.

Public Holidays

The holidays given are usually those when Government offices, businesses and banks will close. Public holidays are only listed for the January 2006-June 2007 period. Note that the dates for Islamic holidays are approximate, since they must accord with local sightings of the moon; similar variations of dating occur for Buddhist, Chinese and Hindu holidays.

In some cases, official dates for public holidays have not been fixed at the time of writing. Check with the respective Tourist Office, Embassy or High Commission for further details.

Health

Vaccination requirements and/or recommendations are presented in a quick-glance chart. Wherever an immunisation is considered 'advisable', it is strongly recommended that precautions are taken, even though they may not be strictly necessary. Occasionally this advice may conflict with guidance given by the relevant Tourist Board or Embassy, but it is felt that the advice of the Department of Health and the World Health Organization should be heeded, on the principle of safeguarding against even a minimal risk. Where immunisation is required, vaccination should be taken well in advance so that adequate intervals between doses can be maintained: rapid courses do not guarantee the same level of immunisation. Children and pregnant women may require special vaccination procedures. (See the immunisation chart in the Health appendix.)

Information has been compiled from several sources, including the Department of Health, the World Health Organization, the London School of Hygiene and Tropical Medicine and the British Medical Journal (official publication of the British Medical Association).

Travel

This information is divided into sections for International and Internal travel.

International

The name and code of the national airline serving the country is given. If there is no national airline, other airlines flying to the destinations are also provided. In most cases, the approximate flight times from London and other major cities to the main airport are also given; it must be stressed that these figures are approximate and depend on a number of factors. Only top international and national airports are listed. Most of the information is based on the information supplied by airports that participated in the Airports Council International (ACI) annual statistics collection. The listings are based on the total number of passengers arriving and departing and direct transit passengers counted once (source: Airports Council International, World Headquarters, Geneva, Switzerland, website: www.aci.aero).

When available, information on travelling to and from the airport and a list of facilities has also been included.

Information is also supplied on the main international ports. Where applicable, ferry and cruise ports will be mentioned and details given of international ferry services. In cases where a river runs through more than one country, services available from one country to the other will be specified.

Where applicable, the main international rail routes are detailed. The main border crossings and routes between countries are also listed.

Colourful representative icons have been introduced to make it easier for readers to find the relevant means of transport.

Internal

Where appropriate, similar information is given on internal services and ports. This includes information on internal travel by air, sea, river/lake, rail and road, plus urban travel (travel facilities in and around the main cities).

Please note in regards to travelling by road that the validity of a visitor's national driving licence varies from country to country, therefore contact should be made with the motoring club or driver-licensing authority in the country of residence to determine whether or not an International Driving Permit is required. The International Driving Permit cannot be issued outside the country responsible for issuing the holder's national driving licence.

For some countries, a travel times chart has also been included, giving the approximate travel times between the capital and major destinations in the country.

Travel Advice

The latest travel advice has been added. This advice is based on information provided by the Foreign and Commonwealth Office in the UK. It is correct at time of publishing but as the situation can change rapidly, visitors are advised to contact the British Foreign and Commonwealth Office, the US Department of State or the Ministry of Foreign Affairs in their country for the latest travel advice.

British Foreign and Commonwealth Office
Tel: (0845) 850 2829.
Website: www.fco.gov.uk

US Department of State
http://travel.state.gov

Occasionally this advice may conflict with guidance given by the relevant Tourist Board or Embassy, but it is felt that the advice of the British Foreign and Commonwealth Office and the US Department of State should be heeded, on the principle of safeguarding against even a minimal risk.

Accommodation

Details are given on the range of available hotel accommodation, including Government classifications, regulations etc, according to the latest information available at the time of writing. Details of the national hotel association are provided where possible, together with specific information on the national grading system. The national grading system should not be confused with local award schemes such as the AA or Michelin star systems. Information is also included on other types of accommodation, including self-catering, guest houses, camping/caravanning and youth hostels.

Editor's Choice: unusual/fine accommodation has sometimes been included under "Editor's Choice".

Contact details of relevant organisations are given at the end of this section.

Top Things To See

A selection of the country's main tourist sites and most popular resorts are described. Please note that not all attractions could be listed in this section.

Editor's Choice: unusual or impressive sites have sometimes been included under "Editor's Choice".

Top Things To Do

The main activities available in the country concerned are outlined. Please note that not all activities could be listed in this section.

Editor's Choice: unusual or thrilling activities have sometimes been included under "Editor's Choice".

Contact details of relevant organisations are given at the end of this section. Information on Top Things to See and Do is provided mainly by Tourist Boards. Addresses of Tourist Boards and other relevant organisations are given in the following order: the name and address of the country's Tourist Board or other relevant organisations in the UK and in the USA. If there is no Tourist Board in the UK or in the USA, the address of the Tourist Board of the particular country in mainland Europe or within the particular country.

Entertainment

Areas covered in this section include Food & Drink with information on national specialities and national drinks, Nightlife and Shopping.

Business

This section includes key statistics (GDP, main exports and imports and main trade partners) about the country and a brief description of its economy.

Business Etiquette includes the best times to visit, the necessity or otherwise for visiting cards, prior appointments, translation/interpreter services and punctuality, the required style of dress for business meetings and business/office hours.

The National Chamber of Commerce in each country is able to offer detailed commercial advice and information to any prospective business traveller, and contact details, where possible, are listed, plus details of any other relevant organisation(s).

Where applicable, a brief description of the conference/convention facilities within the country is included, along with contact details of the national conference organisation.

Appendices

Travel Trade Associations
A list of associations in the travel and tourism sector.

International Organisations
A list of organisations concerned with world trade and international cooperation, which can be used to supplement the Business section of individual country entries.

Calendar of Events
Dates for major travel-trade events around the world.

Weather
A general introduction to the way in which weather conditions can affect individuals, and supplements the information contained in the Climate section of each country's entry. Information is included on humidity, wind and wind-chill factor, temperature range, precipitation and precautions.

Health
Essential information for anyone travelling abroad, particularly to tropical countries; supplements the information contained in the Health section of individual country entries.

The Disabled Traveller
Designed to provide the travel trade with information relevant to making travel arrangements for people with disabilities. A list of further sources of information/useful organisations is also given.

Religion
These four articles, World of Buddhism, World of Christianity, World of Islam and World of Judaism, are intended to give introductions to religious and cultural attitudes in countries where these religions are practised. They supplement the information contained in the Public Holidays, Social Profiles and Business sections.

Final Note
If there is anything that you would like to see expanded, clarified or included for the first time, or if you come across any information that is no longer accurate, we would be happy to hear from you. Such suggestions will be considered for future editions of the World Travel Guide. Address your suggestions to:

The Editor
World Travel Guide
Columbus Travel Guides
Media House
Azalea Drive
Swanley
Kent BR8 8HU, UK
Tel: (01322) 611474. Fax: (01322) 616323.
E-mail: travel.editorial@nexusmedia.com

COLUMBUS
TRAVEL GUIDES
NEXUS

Afghanistan

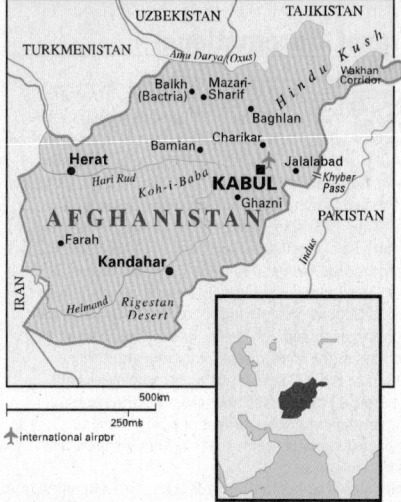

Location: Southwest Asia; northwest part of Indian subcontinent.

Time: GMT + 4.5.

Overview

Because of its strategic position, control of Afghanistan has always been deemed essential to the dominant regional power of the day despite its rugged and forbidding terrain. The rise of a pro-Soviet Communist party in the 1970s, with extensive support from the Soviets, soon gave place to a growing conflict with the country's Islamists and Afghanistan became a key Cold War battleground after thousands of Soviet troops intervened in 1979 to prop up a pro-Communist regime.

Operating from bases in remote mountainous regions and with copious support from the West, the Islamist rebels, known as the 'Mujaheddin', were able to fight the Soviets to a standstill. However, the war inflicted enormous damage on the country, from which it has never recovered.

A new political movement, the Taleban ('students of religion'), with among them Saudi-born Osama bin Laden, led to the withdrawal of the last Red Army troops in February 1989. Soon arguments between the disparate factions within the Mujaheddin were settled with the use of military force and during this period, much of the capital was destroyed. Later, the country was subject to heavy aerial bombardment by the USA following the attacks on the World Trade Center and the Pentagon buildings on 11 September 2001.

The Taleban's own policy decisions, the hostility of an uncomprehending outside world, and other factors – including the worst drought for half a century – combined to isolate the country from the rest of the world. Afghanistan's troubles are far from over; the Taleban are re-emerging as a fighting force in pockets in the south and southeast and much of the country outside Kabul is plagued by local warlords fighting for dominance. The Government continues to rely on the presence of thousands of foreign peace-keeping troops to maintain order.

As a result of years of fighting, Afghanistan has very few tourist attractions to offer today. It is estimated that the capital has only managed to preserve a fraction of its historic past. In Damian, the second- to fifth-century Great Buddhas were destroyed by the Talebans in 2001 to international outcry. Eighty per cent of all roads and bridges have also been destroyed during years of conflict. Travellers are advised against azll but essential travel to Kabul and very strongly advised against all travel to other parts of Afghanistan as the threat to Westerners from terrorist or criminal violence remains high. In addition, there is a widespread danger from mines and unexploded ordnance throughout Afghanistan.

General Information

Note: Very little reliable information is available relating to some of the following sections; much of the infrastructure and services were destroyed or ceased to function in the months of fighting in 2001, and are still in the process of being rebuilt and repaired. Those that were there before were severely limited and old-fashioned due to the years of civil war and occupation that preceded this.

AREA: 652,225 sq km (251,773 sq miles).

POPULATION: 26 million (UN, 2005).

POPULATION DENSITY: 39.8 per sq km.

CAPITAL: Kabul. **Population:** 2.7 million (official estimate 2000).

GEOGRAPHY: Afghanistan is a landlocked country, sharing its borders with Turkmenistan, Uzbekistan and Tajikistan to the north, China to the northeast, Pakistan to the east and south and Iran to the west. On the eastern tip of the Iranian plateau, central Afghanistan is made up of a tangled mass of mountain chains. The Hindu Kush is the highest range, rising to more than 7500m (24,600ft). The Bamian Valley separates the Hindu Kush from Koh-i-Baba, the central mountain range and source of the Helmand River. To the north and southwest of these mountains, alluvial plains provide fertile agricultural soil. To the northeast is Kabul, the capital. The other major cities are Jalalabad, Kandahar, Mazar-i-Sharif and Herat.

GOVERNMENT: Republic. Civil war since 1992. **Head of State:** President Hamid Karzai since December 2001 (officially elected as President in October 2004). **Recent history:** After the defeat of the Taleban in November 2001, the main opposition factions agreed upon the formation of a new interim administration, pending the convening of a *loya jirga* (traditional assembly). This traditional form of assembly, held in mid-2002, brought together representatives of all the major powers in the country and attempted to map out a constitutional future for Afghanistan. The assembly agreed on the appointment of Hamad Karzai as interim Premier but very little else. Hamad Karzai won Afghanistan's first direct Presidential elections in October 2004 despite reports of voting irregularities. The President will serve a five-year term and will implement Afghanistan's new constitution. The first parliamentary and local elections for more than 30 years were held on 18 September 2005. Only about 55 per cent of registered voters cast their ballots, more than 20 per cent down on the previous year's Presidential poll. Many voters said they did not want to vote for candidates they regarded as warlords. There was also evidence that many people found the elections too confusing. The process of counting the results was completed in November 2005. President Hamid Karzai's brother, Abdul Qayyum Karzai, was elected to the lower House of Parliament. The inauguration of the Afghan National Assembly took place on 19 December 2005.

LANGUAGE: The principal languages are Pashto and Dari Persian. Some English and Russian may also be spoken.

RELIGION: Islamic majority (mostly Sunni), with Shi'ite, Hindu and Sikh minorities.

ELECTRICITY: 220 volts AC, 50Hz. Supplies may be seriously affected and powercuts frequent for the foreseeable future.

SOCIAL CONVENTIONS: Outside Kabul, Afghanistan is still very much a tribal society. Religion and traditional customs have a strong influence within the family, and there are strict male and female roles in society. It is considered insulting to show the soles of the feet. Guests may have to share a room as specific accommodation is rarely set aside. Women are advised to wear trousers or long skirts and avoid revealing dress. Homosexuality is illegal. The importation and use of narcotics, alcohol and pork products are forbidden. Handshaking is an acceptable form of greeting, though nose-rubbing and embracing are more traditional. Smoking is a common social habit and tobacco is cheap by European standards. It is a compliment to accept an offered cigarette from your host. **Photography:** Care should be taken when using cameras. Military installations should not be photographed.

Climate

Although occupying the same latitudes as South-Central USA, the mountainous nature of much of Afghanistan produces a far colder climate. Being landlocked, there are considerable differences in temperature between summer and winter, and day and night in lowland regions and in the valleys. The southern lowlands have intensely hot summers and harsh winters.

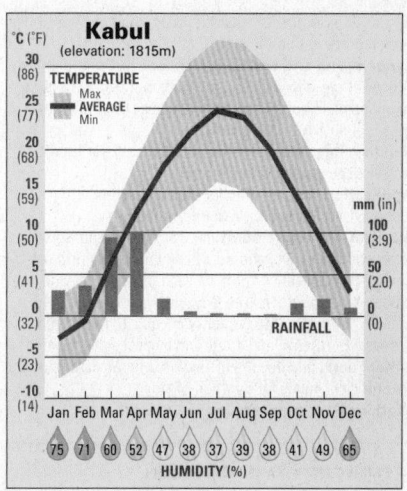

Communications

At the time of writing, no telephone, fax, telex, telegram or postal services are generally available.

Telephone: No IDD. There is generally a severe shortage of lines for operator-connected international calls.

Mobile telephone: There is coverage in cities like Kabul and Herat, and in other small pockets throughout the country.

Internet: The first public Internet service opened in Kabul in late 2003, and several post offices have since been outfitted with Internet connections.

Post: Prior to military action, airmail used to take one week to reach Europe.

MEDIA: Afghanistan's media were seriously restricted under Taleban rule. In late 2001, *Radio Afghanistan* returned to the air in Kabul after the Taleban deserted the capital. One of the first signs of change was the music broadcast over *Radio Afghanistan* for the first time in five years. Days later *Kabul TV* was back on the air, with a woman presenting the news. Afghanistan's newly-invigorated press enjoys freedom of expression, although print runs are small. There is a small band of private radio and TV stations. A law bans media criticism of Islam and other religions.

Press: Newspapers include *Hewad* and *Anis,* two Government-sponsored daily newspapers, *Kabul Times,* an official, English-language newspaper and *Kabul Weekly,* a private, English-language publication.

TV: *Afghanistan Television* is state-run; *Balkh TV* broadcasts from Mazar-e-Sharif; *Aina TV* is private; *Tolu TV* is a Kabul-based private channel.

Radio: Radio stations include *Radio Afghanistan,* a state-run station, *Radio Herat, Radio Khilid Kabul (RKK),* an FM station set up by NGOs, *Arman FM,* a private FM network, in Kabul and other cities and *Azad Afghan Radio,* a private station in Kandahar. Taleban radio re-emerged in April 2005. Relays of foreign radio stations or stations funded from overseas are on the air in Kabul, including the BBC, *Radio France Internationale, Deutsche Welle* and US-funded broadcasts from *Radio Free Afghanistan,* which uses the name *Azadi Radio,* and the *Voice of America,* which brands its Dari and Pashto broadcasts as *Radio Ashna* ("Friend").

Passport/Visa

Note: Please note that travellers are strongly advised by the British Foreign and Commonwealth Office and the US Department of State not to travel to Afghanistan.

	Passport Required?	Visa Required?	Return Ticket Required?
Full British	Yes	Yes	Yes
Australian	Yes	Yes	Yes
Canadian	Yes	Yes	Yes
USA	Yes	Yes	Yes
Other EU	Yes	Yes	Yes
Japanese	Yes	Yes	Yes

Note: *Regulations and requirements may be subject to change at short notice, and you are advised to contact the appropriate diplomatic or consular authority before finalising travel arrangements. Any numbers in the chart refer to the footnotes below.*

Entry restrictions: Women of all nationalities should dress appropriately with a scarf to cover their heads and an overcoat for their bodies.
PASSPORTS: Valid passport required by all.
VISAS: Required by all except the following:
(a) travellers holding a re-entry permit issued by Afghanistan;
(b) transit passengers not leaving the airport and continuing their journey within two hours.
Types of visa and cost: *Single-entry:* £30. *Double-entry:* £40. *Multiple-entry:* £55 (up to three months); £115 (up to six months). Enquiries should be made at the Embassy for details about visiting Afghanistan.
Validity: Three or six months from date of issue. Duration of stay depends on purpose of visit.
Application to: Consulate (or Consular section at Embassy); see *Passport/Visa Information.*
Application requirements: (a) Company or sponsorship letter with name and address of commissioning firm or person. (b) Application form. (c) Valid passport. (d) One passport-size photo. (e) Fee, payable by cash (except when applying by post), postal order or cheque. (f) Registered self-addressed envelope if replying by post. (g) Return or onward ticket and documents required for onward journey. (h) Sufficient funds for duration of stay.
Working days required: Two to five.

PASSPORT/VISA INFORMATION

Embassy of Afghanistan in the UK
31 Princes Gate, London SW7 1QQ, UK
Tel: (020) 7589 8891 *or* 8892 (consular section).
Website: www.afghanembassy.co.uk
Opening hours: Mon-Fri 0900-1600; 0930-1330 (visa applications).

Embassy of Afghanistan in the USA
2341 Wyoming Avenue, NW, Washington DC, 20008, USA
Consular section: 2233 Wisconsin Avenue, Suite 216, NW, Washington DC, 20007, USA
Tel: (202) 483 6410 *or* 298 9125 (consular section).
Website: www.embassyofafghanistan.org

Consulate General of Afghanistan in the USA
360 Lexington Avenue, 11th Floor, New York, NY 10017, USA
Tel: (212) 972 2276/7.
Website: www.afghanconsulateny.org

Money

Currency: Afghani (AFA) = 100 puls. Notes are in denominations of AFA1000, 500, 100, 50, 20, 10, 5, 2 and 1. The US Dollar is also widely accepted.
Credit & debit cards: Travellers should be aware that these are not generally accepted. There is one ATM in the entire country, which dispenses Afghanis. This is located in Kabul (Street 10, Wazir Akbar Khan) and only accepts Visa-branded credit and debit cards between 0830-1900 daily. It is recommended that visitors carry sufficient funds in US dollars.
Traveller's cheques: It is not currently recommended to take traveller's cheques to Afghanistan, since they are not widely accepted and may take up to two months to clear. If necessary, however, to avoid additional exchange rate charges, travellers are advised to take traveller's cheques in US Dollars, Euros or Pounds Sterling.
Currency restrictions: The import and export of local currency (in banknotes and coins) is permitted up to AFA500. The import of foreign currency is unlimited if declared on arrival; export is permitted up to the amount imported and declared.

Banking hours: Generally Sat-Wed 0800-1200 and 1300-1630, Thurs 0800-1330.
Exchange rate indicators:
Rate at time of publishing
£1.00=   AFA75.49
$1.00=   AFA42.78

Duty Free

The following goods may be imported into Afghanistan without incurring customs duty:
A reasonable amount of tobacco products and alcoholic beverages for personal use; any amount of perfume.
Restricted items: The import of film cameras is possible only with a licence. The export of antiquities, carpets, furs and camera film is prohibited without a licence.

Public Holidays

Below are listed Public Holidays for the January 2006-June 2007 period.
2006: Jan 10 Eid-al-Adha (Feast of the Sacrifice). **Feb 9** Ashura (Martyrdom of Imam Hussain). **Feb 22** Mount Arafat Day. **Mar 21** Navruz (Persian New Year). **Apr 11** Roze-Maulud (Birth of the Prophet). **Apr 18** Liberation Day. **Apr 28** Revolution Day; Loss of the Muslim Nation. **May 1** Labour Day. **Aug 19** National Day. **Oct 22-24** Eid al-Fitr (End of Ramadan). **Dec 31** Eid-al-Adha (Feast of the Sacrifice).
2007: Jan 29 Ashura (Martyrdom of Imam Hussein). **Feb** Mount Arafat Day. **Mar** Navruz (Persian New Year). **Apr 1** Roze-Maulud (Birth of the Prophet). **Apr 18** Liberation Day. **Apr 28** Revolution Day; Loss of the Muslim Nation. **May 1** Labour Day.
Note: Muslim festivals are timed according to local sightings of various phases of the moon and the dates given above are approximations. During the lunar month of Ramadan that precedes Eid al-Fitr, Muslims fast during the day and feast at night and normal business patterns may be interrupted. Some disruption may continue into Eid al-Fitr itself. Eid al-Fitr and Eid al-Adha may last up to several days, depending on the region. For more information, see the *World of Islam* appendix.

Health

	Special Precautions?	Certificate Required?
Yellow Fever	Yes	1
Cholera	2	No
Typhoid & Polio	3	N/A
Malaria	4	N/A

Note: *Regulations and requirements may be subject to change at short notice, and you are advised to contact your doctor well in advance of your intended date of departure. Any numbers in the chart refer to the footnotes below.*

1: A yellow fever vaccination certificate is required if arriving within six days of leaving or transiting countries with endemic or infected areas. Travellers arriving from non-endemic zones should note that vaccination is strongly recommended for travel outside urban areas, even if an outbreak of the disease has not been reported and they would normally not require a vaccination certificate to enter the country.
2: Following WHO guidelines issued in 1973, a cholera vaccination certificate is no longer a condition of entry to Afghanistan. However, cholera is considered a risk in this country and precautions are advised. Up-to-date advice should be sought before deciding whether these precautions should include vaccination, as medical opinion is divided over its effectiveness; see the *Health* appendix for further information.
3: Typhoid fever occurs and vaccination is advised. Polio eradication measures were being taken but will have been disrupted by the fighting. Polio should still, therefore, be assumed to be a threat.
4: Malarial risk, primarily in the benign *vivax* form, exists from May to November below 2000m (6562ft). The *falciparum* strain occurs in the south of the country. Chloroquine- and sulfadoxine-pyrimethamine-resistant falciparum has been reported. The recommended prophylaxis is mefloquine, doxycycline or atovaquone/proguanil.
Food & drink: All water should be regarded as being potentially contaminated. Milk is unpasteurised and should be boiled. Powdered or tinned milk is available and is advised, but make sure that it is reconstituted with pure water. Avoid dairy products which are likely to have been made from unboiled milk. Only eat well-cooked meat and fish, preferably served hot. Pork, salad and mayonnaise may carry increased risk. Vegetables should be cooked and fruit peeled.
Other risks: *Cutaneous leishmaniasis* and tick-borne relapsing fever occur in Afghanistan. *Hepatitis A* and *E* are

both present. *Hepatitis B* is endemic. *Typhus* occurs and *trachoma* is common. *Giardiasis* and other waterborne diseases are common. *Respiratory tuberculosis* is common. *Diarrhoeal* disease and other *gastrointestinal* infections are common causes of ill health, especially in hotter months. Outbreaks of *meningococcal disease* have been reported. *Rabies* is present. For those at high risk, vaccination before arrival should be considered. If you are bitten, seek medical advice without delay. For more information, consult the *Health* appendix.
Health care: Medical care was very limited before the 2001 conflict but now medicines are in even shorter supply and many hospitals have been damaged or destroyed. Doctors and hospitals demand immediate cash payment for most services. Medical insurance, covering emergency evacuation, is essential. International aid groups operate in some cities and villages.

Travel - International

AIR:

Afghanistan's national airline is *Ariana Afghan Airlines (FG)* (website: www.flyariana.com). At the time of writing, there are regular flights from Kabul to Ankara and Istanbul (Turkey), Delhi (India), Dubai (UAE), Amristar (India), Tehran (Iran), Frankfurt and Munich (Germany), Moscow (Russian Federation), Urumqi (China), Dushanbe (Tajikistan), Kuwait City (Kuwait), Jeddah (Saudi Arabia), Baku (Azerbaijan) and Sharjah (UAE). *Pakistan International Airlines (PK)* (website: www.piac.com.pk) also flies three times a week from Islamabad to Kabul. There is a United Nations presence in the country, with aid mission flights in operation. For further information, consult a local Embassy or the Foreign and Commonwealth Office. Currently, the FCO advises against its employees (and therefore all travellers should take note) travelling to Afghanistan on *Ariana Airlines* or *Kam Air* due to suspected safety concerns that have not yet been fully addressed and assessed.
Main airports: *Kabul Airport (KBL)* is 16km (10 miles) from the city. The airport was largely destroyed during the conflict at the end of 2001 but has now re-opened for limited international commercial flights as well as military and aid flights. *To/from the airport:* Taxis are available to the city centre (travel time - 30 minutes). *Facilities:* Bank, bar and restaurant.
Departure tax: AfA200. Children under two years of age are exempt.
ROAD:

Overland travel is currently very dangerous in some parts of the country, with rural roads often unpaved, and the official advice is that it should be avoided. Prior to US bombing, buses used to operate along the Asia Highway, which links Afghanistan to Iran and Pakistan. There were also good road links from Mazar-i-Sharif and Herat to the countries in the north. It is, however, now known that 80 per cent of all roads and bridges have been destroyed. It will be a slow process to repair the damage.

Travel - Internal

AIR:

There are limited internal flights; *Kam Air* operates twice-daily flights between Kabul and Herat. **Main airports:** *Kabul Airport (KBL)* is 16km (10 miles) from the city.
ROAD:

Prior to the 2001 conflict, there were over 22,000km (13,000 miles) of roads, some of which were paved. This network has largely been destroyed. Traffic drives on the right. **Documentation:** International Driving Permit required.
URBAN:

Buses, trolleybuses and taxis used to operate in Kabul but often proved unreliable. Since the fighting, some services have resumed, but are less reliable than ever due to the extensive infrastructure and vehicle destruction incurred.

Travel Advice

Travellers are strongly advised against all but essential travel to Kabul and against all travel to other parts of Afghanistan. The Afghan NGO Security Organisation (ANSO) is currently recommending that NGO staff in Kabul should observe a curfew commencing before dark and limit daytime movement to essential (preferably two) vehicle moves only. Unless they have adequate protection ie an armoured vehicle at minimum, it is recommended that travellers follow this advice. Travellers should always ensure car doors are locked and windows closed, and if possible maintain radio or telephone communications to report their movements.

There is reporting to indicate an increased threat of bomb attacks, possibly by suicide bombers, against Western targets in central Kabul and in the vicinity of Kabul airport. The security situation in Afghanistan remains serious and the threat to Westerners from terrorist or criminal violence, including kidnappings, remains high. There have been a number of attacks against the UN, NGOs, ISAF, coalition forces and individuals. Travellers throughout the country, particularly outside Kabul, should keep as low a profile as possible and should reassess their position on a regular basis. Travellers who believe that their visit is essential should seek local advice before undertaking their journey. Information on specific and urgent threats is circulated via the Warden network within Afghanistan. It is therefore important that you register with your Embassy in Kabul on arrival.

There is a widespread danger from mines and unexploded ordnance throughout Afghanistan.

This advice is based on information provided by the Foreign and Commonwealth Office in the UK. It is correct at time of publishing. As the situation can change rapidly, visitors are advised to contact the following organisaions for the latest travel advice.

British Foreign and Commonwealth Office
Tel: (0845) 850 2829.
Website: www.fco.gov.uk

US Department of State
Website: http://travel.state.gov/travel

Accommodation

HOTELS:

In Kabul there are very few hotels, like the Hotel Inter-Continental, that measure up to Western standards. Only basic accommodation is available elsewhere. In some rural areas there may still be hotels run by the provincial authority, but these are of a low standard.

Top Things To See & Do

It should be noted that much of the land in Afghanistan is still mined and, therefore, trips outside urban areas are ill-advised and dangerous.

• Visit Afghanistan's capital, **Kabul**; Although it is estimated that after the fighting in 2001, at least one-third of all public buildings and approximately 40 per cent of the houses were completely destroyed, a few conventional attractions for tourists remain, including: the **Gardens of Babur** and a well-presented museum, and the ancient walls of the citadel **Bala Hissar**. There are plans to re-open the **National Gallery** in the near future.

• If able, it is worth trying to visit the **Valley of Paghman**, 90 minutes by road west of the capital, where the rich had second houses and, to the north, **Karez-i-Amir**, **Charikar** and the **Valley of Chakardara**.

• Visit **Jalalabad**, the capital of the Nangarhar Province, which used to be an attractive winter resort, with many cypress trees and flowering shrubs.

• Best left for travellers prepared to rough it, the **Hindu Kush** is a wild and remote region consisting of two huge mountain ranges. Although travelling by car is possible, the steepness of the routes makes vehicles prone to breakdowns. For those who make the journey, the mountains, valleys and lakes provide stunning scenery. **Bamian** is the main centre. The second- to fifth-century Great Buddhas were destroyed here to international outcry in 2001.

• The Red City (**Shahr-i-Zahak**), 17km (11miles) from Bamian, is the location of the remains of another ancient citadel.

> **TOURIST INFORMATION**
>
> **Ministry of Foreign Affairs**
> Malak Azghar Road, Kabul, Afghanistan
> Tel: (70) 104 005 or (20) 210 0366.
> Website: www.afghanistan-mfa.net

Entertainment

FOOD & DRINK: Indian-style cuisine, based on rice. Most modern restaurants in Kabul offer international cuisine as well as Afghan specialities.
Things to know: Afghan dishes can be very good, but spicy. Vegetarians are not well catered for in Afghanistan. Cutlery is not normally used, and food is eaten with the right hand, often using bread (nan) as a scoop.
National specialities:
• The most common dish is *pulao* - steamed rice with raisins and carrot. This is usually served with a side dish of meat, vegetables or beans.
• The most popular variant is *qabli pulao* (sometimes

mistakenly called *Kabuli pulao*), served with lamb.
• Soup (*shorma*) is common, as are kebabs.
• Afghanistan abounds in seasonal fruit, most notably melons from Mazar-e Sharif and Maimana, grapes and pomegranates from Kandahar and oranges from Jalalabad.
National drinks:
• The most common drink is tea (*chai*).
Tipping: Service is normally included.
SHOPPING: Special purchases include Turkman hats, Kandahar embroidery, Istaff pottery, local glassware from Herat, nomad jewellery, handmade carpets and rugs, Nuristani woodcarving, silkware, brass, copper and silverwork. **Note:** Many craft items may only be exported under licence. **Shopping hours:** Generally Sat-Wed 0800-1200 and 1300-1630, Thurs 0800-1330.

Business

• **GDP:** US$4.6 billion (IMF, January 2005).
• **Main exports:** Fruit, nuts, vegetables and carpets.
• **Main imports:** Capital goods, food, textiles and petroleum products.
• **Main trade partners:** Exports to Pakistan, the EU, India and the Russian Federation; Imports from Pakistan, Japan, Kenya and Korea (Rep).

ECONOMY: Twenty-four years of continuous war completely wrecked the Afghan economy. Reconstruction of the agricultural sector, which accounted for about half of GDP, has been severely hampered by abandonment of farms and the huge number of minefields. Agricultural problems have led to recurring food shortages. Afghanistan has had to rely heavily on foreign aid. Many farmers have come to rely on growing opium as a relatively lucrative cash crop – both the Taleban and now the Karzai Government have attempted to limit production, with mixed success. The industrial sector, which barely functions, was formerly concentrated in mining and some manufacturing. There are significant deposits of natural gas, coal, salt, barite and other ores. The small manufacturing sector produces textiles, chemical fertilisers, leather and plastics. Some trade links have been established with the former Soviet Central Asian republics but Pakistan and Saudi Arabia are now the strongest economic influences in the country. The Karzai Government has applied for membership of the World Trade Organization and is likely to receive observer status. There have also been some positive advancements in recent years: in January 2003, Afghanistan signed a trilateral trade agreement with Iran and India that designated the Iranian port of Chabahar as a major port for Afghanistan. In September 2003, representatives of Afghanistan and its neighbours, China, Iran, Pakistan, Tajikistan, Turkmenistan and Uzbekistan met in Dubai to forge new trade dynamics and foster investment gradually. There seems to have been a genuine attempt to revivify the Afghan economy.
BUSINESS ETIQUETTE: Price bargaining is expected and oral agreements are honoured. Formal wear is expected and meetings should be pre-arranged. **Office hours:** Generally Sat-Wed 0800-1200 and 1300-1630, Thurs 0800-1330.

> **COMMERCIAL INFORMATION**
>
> **Afghan Chamber of Commerce and Industry**
> Mohammad Jan Khan Watt, Kabul, Afghanistan
> Tel: (2) 290 090.
>
> **Federation of Afghan Chambers of Commerce and Industry**
> Daraulaman Wat, Kabul, Afghanistan

Albania

Location: Eastern Europe, Adriatic and Ionian Coast.

Time: GMT + 1 (GMT + 2 from last Sunday in March to last Sunday in October).

Overview

Albania is one of Europe's poorest countries and continues to face severe difficulties adjusting to the new Europe after decades of Stalinist isolation. Only in 1985, after the death of Enver Hoxha, its President, did Albania, began to develop contacts with the outside world. More recently, conditions were worsened by regional political instability and the collapse of 'pyramid' investment schemes in 1997. New components of the economy, such as tourism, which were mostly set up with foreign investment, suffered badly in the wake of the 1997 upheaval. Nonetheless, Albania now enjoys access to funding from the main international donor bodies (IMF, World Bank and EBRD), as well as growing contacts with major European countries, such as Italy and France. Albania hopes to follow the rest of eastern Europe into the European Union.

Despite this, travellers will enjoy Albania's wild and mountainous landscape, with its extensive forests, sandy beaches and many beautiful lakes. Bathed by the Adriatic Sea, the southern coastline remains unspoilt and many activities such as swimming, diving, sailing and fishing can be enjoyed.

General Information

AREA: 27,398 sq km (11,100 sq miles).
POPULATION: 3.14 million (UN estimate 2002).
POPULATION DENSITY: 109.3 per sq km.
CAPITAL: Tirana. **Population:** 519,720 (2001).
GEOGRAPHY: Albania shares borders with Serbia & Montenegro to the north, with Macedonia (Former Yugoslav Republic of) to the northeast, and with Greece to the south; to the west are the Adriatic and Ionian Seas. Most of the country is wild and mountainous, with extensive forests. There are fine sandy beaches and, inland, many beautiful lakes.
GOVERNMENT: Democratic Republic since 1991. **Head of State:** President Alfred Moisiu since 2002.
Head of Government: Prime Minister Sali Berisha since

July 2005. **Recent history:** Following years of Communist ruling, the *Partia Demokratike të Shqipërisë* (DPA – Democratic Party of Albania) won an outright majority in the first democratic elections to the People's Assembly held in March 1992. The DPA leader, Sali Berisha, took over as President. Four years later, the DPA repeated its success and increased its majority. Under the Democrats, the bulk of the economy had been transferred to the private sector by this stage. However, as elsewhere in Eastern Europe, essential legal and regulatory systems were inadequate – where they existed at all. This was especially true of the banking and finance sector, which was replete with highly popular 'pyramid' investment schemes offering absurdly high rates of interest to investors. In January 1997, the collapse of one of the largest schemes triggered violent protests across large parts of the country. During the next two months, with the help of foreign mediation and an Italian-led peacekeeping force, some semblance of normality was gradually restored. Elections were held at the end of June 1997, bringing a comfortable victory for Socialist Fatos Nano, who became Premier. However, Nano was unable to contain the deteriorating economic situation and was forced out of office in September 1998. His replacement, Pandeli Majko, suffered the same fate a year later. The Socialist Party turned to Ilir Meta, who at age 30 became Europe's youngest Premier. Meta survived in office and won the general election in 2001. However, the relative political calm was short-lived. An ever-widening rift between Meta and Nano promoted three Ministers to resign. Eventually, Meta himself resigned and, by early 2002, yet another Premier had failed to reach the end of his allocated tenure. Pandeli Majko became the new Premier and pledged to end in-fighting. Alfred Moisiu became President and fraction seemed to be ebbing. However, yet more upheaval materialised when it was decided that the roles of Premier and Party Chairman should merge, and Nano was appointed this dual title. 2004 and 2005 have both borne witness to angry demonstrations by opposition lambasting Nano's failure to improve living standards in Albania.

Albania's new Prime Minister, Sali Berisha, won a parliamentary vote of confidence in September after pledging that his Government would make tackling corruption and organised crime its overriding priority.

LANGUAGE: The official language is Albanian (Tosk is the official dialect). Some Albanians also speak Italian and English. Greek is widely spoken in the Gjirokastra and Saranda districts in south Albania.

RELIGION: Three religions co-exist in Albania: Islam, Catholicism and Eastern Orthodox Christianity. The majority of the population is Muslim.

ELECTRICITY: 220 volts AC, 50Hz.

SOCIAL CONVENTIONS: Nearly half of the population lives in urban areas, with the rest pursuing a relatively quiet rural existence. Some Albanian characteristics and mannerisms resemble those of the mainland Greeks, most notably in the more rural areas; for instance, a nod of the head means 'no' and shaking one's head means 'yes'. Handshaking is the accepted form of greeting. Albanians should be addressed with *Zoti* (Mr) and *Zonja* (Mrs). The former widespread greeting of *Shoku* (Comrade) has all but disappeared. Small gifts are customary when visiting someone's house, although flowers are not usually given. Any attempt to speak Albanian is greatly appreciated. Visitors

should accept offers of *raki*, coffee or sweets. Dress is generally informal. Bikinis are acceptable on the beach; elsewhere, women are expected to dress modestly although attitudes are becoming increasingly relaxed. Offices and restaurants are often unheated. Visitors should be aware that foreigners tend to be charged a lot more than locals, with this applying to entry fees as well as general merchandise. Smoking is permitted except where the sign *Ndalohet Duhani* or *Ndalohet pirja e duhanit* is displayed. Penalties for drug-related crimes are severe. Homosexuality, although legal, is not fully accepted and discretion should be exercised.

Climate

Temperate climate with warm and dry periods from June to September, cool and wet from October to May. April to June and mid-September to mid-October are the best months for visits. Flash-flooding is possible throughout the year.

Required clothing: Warm clothing and rainwear is advisable for winter. Lightweight for summer.

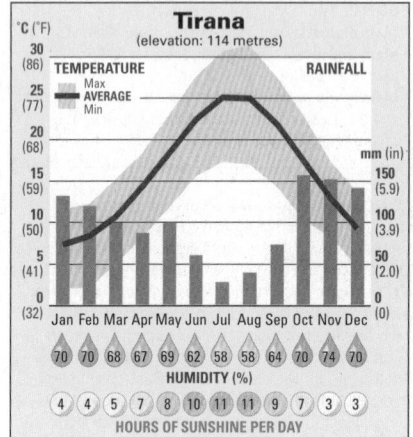

°C (°F) **Tirana** (elevation: 114 metres) **mm (in)**

TEMPERATURE — Max — AVERAGE — Min   RAINFALL

HUMIDITY (%): Jan 70, Feb 70, Mar 68, Apr 67, May 69, Jun 62, Jul 58, Aug 58, Sep 64, Oct 70, Nov 74, Dec 70

HOURS OF SUNSHINE PER DAY: 4, 4, 5, 7, 8, 10, 11, 11, 9, 7, 3, 3

Communications

Telephone: IDD is available to major towns. Country code: 355. City codes: Tirana 42, Durresi 52, Elbasan 545, Shkodra 224, Gjirokastra 726, Korça 824, Kavaja 574. For other regions, international connections are made through the nearest city.

Mobile telephone: Coverage is limited to main towns and coastal areas.

Internet: Internet cafes available in most towns.

Post: All mail to and from Albania is subject to delays. Letters can be sent recorded delivery to avoid loss. There are DHL offices in Tirana and Durres, offering services between Albania and other countries. The postal and telecommunications systems are undergoing extensive modernisation. Post office hours: Mon-Fri 0700-1400 and Sat 0800-1300.

MEDIA: Press: There are now about 400 newspapers and periodicals, many of which are independent. The main newspapers are published daily. *Rilindja Demokratike*, the organ of the ruling Democratic Party, has a circulation of 50,000. English-language newspapers published in Albania include the *Albanian Daily News*. Some Albanian newspapers contain a few pages in English; these include *Gazeta Shqiptare*. Foreign newspapers are on sale in main towns.

TV/Radio: The public broadcaster, *Albanian Radio and TV* (*RTSh*), operates national radio and TV networks. It faces competition from private stations, which have mushroomed since the late 1990s. Political parties, religious groups and state bodies are not allowed to own private TV and radio stations. Many viewers can pick up Italian and Greek TV via terrestrial reception. Radio services from the *BBC, Deutsche Welle, Radio France Internationale, Radio Free Europe* and the *Voice of America* are available on FM or mediumwave (AM).

Passport/Visa

	Passport Required?	Visa Required?	Return Ticket Required?
Full British	Yes	No	Yes
Australian	Yes	No	Yes
Canadian	Yes	No	Yes
USA	Yes	No	Yes
Other EU	Yes	No/1/2	Yes
Japanese	Yes	No	Yes

Note: *Regulations and requirements may be subject to change at short notice, and you are advised to contact the appropriate diplomatic or consular authority before finalising travel arrangements. Any numbers in the chart refer to the footnotes below.*

PASSPORTS: A valid passport is required by all.

VISAS: Required by all except the following for stays of up to 30 days:

(a) nationals of countries referred to in the chart above, except **1.** nationals of Malta who must obtain a visa upon arrival;

(b) nationals of Bulgaria, Croatia, Israel, Korea (Rep), Kosovo, Malaysia, New Zealand, Norway, Romania, San Marino, Switzerland, and Turkey;

(c) transit passengers continuing their journey to a third country by the same or next connecting aircraft provided holding confirmed onward documentation and not leaving the airport.

Note: (a) Nationals of countries listed above pay an entry fee of €10 at Tirana airport or at the border crossing point, except nationals of Israel who must pay €30 and nationals of Poland and the Slovak Republic who may enter without charge. (b) **2.** Nationals of Israel, Macedonia (Former Yugoslav Republic of), Malta and Montenegro can obtain visas on arrival for free (Montenegro), €10 (Macedonia) or €30 (Malta).

Types of visa and cost: Dependent on nationality of applicant and length and purpose of intended stay.

Validity: Duration of visas is individually specified for each visit. The maximum length of stay is three months. Extensions are possible.

Application to: Consulate (or Consular Section at Embassy); see *Passport/Visa Information*.

Application requirements: (a) Application form(s). (b) Valid passport. (c) Two passport-size photos. (d) Sufficient funds to cover duration of stay. (e) Visa fee (cheque only). *Business*: (a)-(d) and, (e) Letter from applicant's company. (f) Invitation from Albanian company.

Working days required: Up to two weeks.

Temporary residence: Application to be made to the Embassy of the Republic of Albania.

PASSPORT/VISA INFORMATION

Embassy of the Republic of Albania in the UK
2nd Floor, 24 Buckingham Gate,
London SW1E 6LB, UK
Tel: (020) 7828 8897.
E-mail: amblonder@hotmail.com
Opening hours: Mon-Fri 0900-1530 (general enquiries); 0900-1200 (consular section).

Embassy of the Republic of Albania in the USA
2100 S Street, NW, Washington, DC 20008, USA
Tel: (202) 223 4942.
Website: www.albaniaembassy.org

Money

Currency: Lek (ALL) = 100 qindarka. Notes are in denominations of ALL5000, 1000, 500, 200 and 100. Coins are in denominations of ALL50, 20, 10, 5, 2 and 1.

Currency exchange: Currency can be exchanged at bureaux de change and banks. US dollars are the preferred foreign currency.

Credit & debit cards: Rarely used. Cash is preferred in nearly all cases. However, American Express, Diners Club and MasterCard are accepted by some banks and hotels.

Traveller's cheques: To avoid additional exchange rate charges, travellers are advised to take traveller's cheques in US Dollars or Euros. They may not always be easily changed in all places.

Currency restrictions: The import and export of local currency is prohibited. The import of foreign currency is unlimited. The export of foreign currency is permitted up to US$5000 or up to the amount declared on arrival.

Banking hours: Mon-Fri 0800-1600.

Exchange rate indicators:
Rate at time of publishing
£1.00= ALL181.79
$1.00= ALL103.01

Duty Free

The following items may be imported into Albania without incurring customs duty:

200 cigarettes or 50 cigars or 250g of tobacco; 1l of spirits or 2l of wine; 250ml of eau de toilette and 50ml of perfume.

Prohibited items: Firearms, ammunition and narcotics. Special export permits are required for precious metals, antiques, national costumes of artistic or folkloric value, books and works of art which form part of the national heritage and culture.

Public Holidays

Below are listed Public Holidays for the January 2006-June 2007 period.

2006: Jan 1 New Year's Day. **Jan 10-13** Greater Bairam

Credit: ©Ministry of Tourism, Culture, Youth and Sports, Albania

(Feast of the Sacrifice). **Apr 14** Good Friday. **Apr 17** Easter Monday. **May 1** May Day. **Oct 22-24** Lesser Bairam (End of Ramadan). **Nov 28** Independence and Liberation Day. **Dec 25** Christmas Day.
2007: Jan 1 New Year's Day. **Jan 10-13** Greater Bairam (Feast of the Sacrifice). **Apr 6** Good Friday. **Apr 9** Easter Monday. **May 1** May Day.
Annual events in Tirana include: *Marie Kraja* (Opera Festival), *Fall in Tirana Festival* and the *Days of New Music Festival*. For information about special events, contact the Embassy (see *Passport/Visa Information*).
Note: Muslim festivals are timed according to local sightings of various phases of the moon and the dates given above are approximations. During the lunar month of Ramadan that precedes Lesser Bairam (Eid al-Fitr), Muslims fast during the day and feast at night and normal business patterns may be interrupted. Some disruption may continue into Lesser Bairam itself. Lesser Bairam and Greater Bairam (Eid al-Adha) may last anything from two to 10 days, depending on the region. For more information, see the *World of Islam* appendix.

Health

	Special Precautions?	Certificate Required?
Yellow Fever	No	1
Cholera	No	No
Typhoid & Polio	2	N/A
Malaria	No	N/A

Note: Regulations and requirements may be subject to change at short notice, and you are advised to contact your doctor well in advance of your intended date of departure. Any numbers in the chart refer to the footnotes below.

1: A yellow fever vaccination certificate is required from travellers over one year of age arriving from or transiting countries with infected areas.
2: Immunisation against typhoid and poliomyelitis is recommended. Typhoid is more common in summer and autumn. Although the last major outbreak of poliomyelitis was in 1996, since when eradication activities have been conducted, a small risk still exists.
Food & drink: Mains water is normally chlorinated and, whilst relatively safe, may cause mild abdominal upsets. Bottled water is advised, especially outside Tirana, and should be used for cleaning teeth, washing food, making ice and, of course, drinking. Drinking water outside main cities and towns is likely to be contaminated and sterilisation is considered essential. Milk is pasteurised and dairy products are safe for consumption. Local meat, poultry, seafood, fruit and vegetables are under the control of sanitary/hygiene authorities and are generally considered safe to eat. Avoid cooked food offered by street traders unless you are sure it is freshly prepared and piping hot.
Other risks: Immunisation against *hepatitis A* and *B* and *tetanus* is recommended. Campers and trekkers should avoid tick bites and consider immunisation against *tick-borne encephalitis*, which has been reported in the north. Long-term visitors should consider immunisation against *diphtheria* and check their BCG status.
Rabies is present. Albania has a particularly large number of stray dogs. For those at high risk, vaccination before arrival should be considered. If you are bitten abroad seek medical advice without delay. For more information, see the *Health* appendix.
Health care: Medical facilities are extremely basic (including accident and emergency) and there is a lack of supplies and doctors. It is not advised that visitors use the dental facilities available. If taking prescribed drugs, the visitor should bring a supply. There are no reciprocal agreements with the UK or USA. However, foreign travellers will be excluded from payment for emergency medical treatment and first aid. International travellers are strongly advised to take out full medical insurance before departure.

Travel - International

AIR:

The national airline is *Albanian Airlines (LV)* (website: www.flyalbanian.com). Established in cooperation with *Tyrolean Airways*, the airline operates services to major European cities.
Approximate flight times: From Tirana to *London* is four to five hours (including stopover times, the shortest being via Zurich, 45 minutes, and via Rome, one to two hours). Other connections are slow. Passengers may travel via a number of cities including Athens, Belgrade, Budapest, Vienna and Zurich.
Main airports: *Mother Tereza (TIA)* is 26km (16 miles) from the capital. *To/from the airport:* An *Albtourist* shuttle runs to the city centre every three hours (travel time - 30 minutes). Taxis are also available. *Facilities:* Small duty free shop, car hire, bank and light refreshments are available.
Departure tax: US$10 is levied on all foreign nationals. Nationals of Albania pay Lk1000.

SEA:

Main ports: *Durres* has ferry connections to Italy (to Bari is about nine hours, to Brindisi and to Trieste is 23 hours, to Ancona is 16 hours). *Vlora* has ferry connections to Bari (travel time - nine hours) and Brindisi (travel time - 18 hours); *Saranda* has a connection with Corfu.
Shen Gjini has ferry connections to Bari. Ferry services are run by *Adriatica Line* (website: www.adriatica.it) and *Agoudimos Lines* (website: www.agoudimos-lines.com), amongst others.

RAIL:

There are no international passenger services at present.

ROAD:

Road links to the Kosovo region are either closed or too dangerous to use, owing to political tensions in the region. There are possible crossings at Hani i Hotit (Podgorica in Montenegro), Bllata (Diber in the Former Yugoslav Republic of Macedonia), Qafa e Thaës (Struga and Ohrid in the Former Yugoslav Republic of Macedonia), Tushemisht (Ohrid in the Former Yugoslav Republic of Macedonia), Gorica (Resnja in the Former Yugoslav Republic of Macedonia), Kapshtica (Florina in Greece) and Kakavija (Ioanina in Greece). **Note:** It is now permitted to travel in a private car. Parking places are generally available near hotels or at other designated areas. **Bus:** There are services to Istanbul, Sofia and Athens.

Travel - Internal

SEA:

A fast ferry service links Durres and Vlora.

RAIL:

Trains are diesel, dilapidated and mostly overcrowded. Services operate from Tirana to Shkodra, Vlora, Fier, Ballsh and Pogradec. There are long-term plans to build railways connecting Pogradec with Kicevo (Macedonia, FYR) and Florina (Greece).

ROAD:

There are around 18,000km (11,250 miles) of roads in Albania, but only 7450km (4656 miles) are considered main roads. Maintained by the State, they are supposed to be suitable for motor vehicles, although only 2850km (1781 miles) are paved and, of those, three-quarters are in very poor condition, with numerous potholes: 4-wheel drive vehicles are recommended. There are strict speed limits according to type of vehicle and type of road as well as within towns. International road signs apply. Traffic drives on the right. Visitors are advised to exercise extreme caution when driving, owing to the poor condition of the roads and the unpredictability of local drivers. Night-time driving should be avoided, as there is no street lighting except in urban areas and major inter-urban arterial routes. In addition, whilst petrol stations are available in urban areas, they are not common in the countryside. Cars should be fully self-sufficient, carrying minor repair equipment since there is no national recovery system. **Documentation:** International Driving Permit and national driving licence are required. A fully comprehensive insurance policy is absolutely essential. **Bus:** This is the main form of transport within Albania. The main routes from Shkodra, Korça, Saranda, Gjirokastra, Peshkopia and Durres to Tirana are operated by private bus companies.

URBAN:

A cheap, flat-fare urban **bus** service operates in the main cities, although the buses are usually crowded. **Taxis** can be found in Tirana in front of the main hotels housing foreigners.
Travel Times: The following chart gives approximate travel times from **Tirana** (in hours and minutes) to other major cities/towns in Albania.

	Road
Durres	1.00
Shkodra	2.30
Vlora	3.00
Korça	4.00

Travel Advice

Travel to the northeast border areas between Albania and Kosovo is advised against because of the very poor condition of the roads and the risk of unexploded ordnance.
Although public security is generally good, particularly in Tirana, the crime rate has risen, especially theft, and visitors should be careful not to display valuables. Passports which allow entry to EU countries without a visa, foreign currency and cameras are mostly at risk, although all possessions should be kept close at hand at all times. Avoid remote areas and streets, especially at night. Gun ownership is widespread. This advice is based on information provided by the Foreign and Commonwealth Office in the UK. It is correct at time of publishing. As the situation can change rapidly, visitors are

Credit: ©Ministry of Tourism, Culture, Youth and Sports, Albania

advised to contact the following organisations for the latest travel advice:

British Foreign and Commonwealth Office
Tel: (0845) 850 2829.
Website: www.fco.gov.uk

US Department of State
Website: http://travel.state.gov/travel

Accommodation

HOTELS:

Albturist runs the state-owned tourist hotels but many others are now privately run and increasing numbers are being built. For further information contact *Albturist* (see *Top Things To Do*). There are two four-star hotels in Tirana - the Hotel Tirana International and the Rogner Hotel Europapark Tirana. Hotels are currently being classified in one of five categories according to the facilities offered.

Top Things To See

- Discover examples of early 19th-century architecture such as the **Ethem-Bey Mosque** (built 1789-1823) and the 35m- (117ft-) high **clocktower** (1830) in the capital city, **Tirana**. The city centre and the Government buildings on **Skanderbeg Square** date back to the Italian era, creating the impression of a provincial Italian town.
- Enjoy the best view over Tirana from the **Martyrs' Cemetery**, which contains the Mother Albania Monument.
- From the **Venetian Tower** at the harbour in **Durres,** the second-largest city in Albania, the medieval **Town Wall** leads to the **Amphitheatre** dating back to the second century BC and containing an early Christian crypt with a rare wall mosaic.
- In Roman times, **Apollonia**, located 12km (7.5 miles) from the city of **Fier**, was a large, prosperous city at the mouth of the **river Vjosa** where there is still much left to be excavated. The **amphitheatre**, a colonnade of shops and several other parts of the Roman city centre are open to the public. There are monuments of **Agonothetes** and **Odeon**, as well as an ancient portico and the **Mosaic House** with a fountain. Unfortunately, some of the statues and other portable objects were removed before 1946 and sent to other countries. Those remaining have been placed in the well-organised **museum** which is to be found on the site of a 13th-century **monastery**. In the courtyard of the monastery is a Byzantine-style church, the **Church of St Mary**, believed to have been built in the 14th century. Not far from Apollonia, on the route to Durres, is the **Monastery of Ardenica**.
- **Vlora** is not only a major port, but of great historical importance, for it was here in 1912 that the Assembly was convened which first proclaimed Albania an Independent state and set up the first national Government, headed by Ismail Qemali. In recognition of this, it was proclaimed a 'Hero City' in 1962. The **Muradiye Mosque** (1538-42) was designed by the famous architect Mimar Sinan whose family originated in Albania. On a hill above the city is the tourist centre **Liria**, which offers panoramic views of the beach and town.
- The ancient town of **Butrint** was once an important centre for the Illyrian tribes. It has been known as a settlement since 1000 BC and has belonged to both the Greek and Roman empires during its long history, leaving a rich legacy. Several sites dating from the first and fourth centuries AD can now be visited, among them a theatre, the **Temple of Aesculapius**, the **Nypheum**, the **Lion Gate**, the **Dionysus Altar**, Roman houses and baths. The **Baptistry**, with a floor of colourful mosaics, is not to be

missed. The nearby tourist site of **Ksamil** offers magnificent views of **Butrint Lake**, the islands and citrus- and olive-tree plantations.

- Standing at the foot of the dramatic Morava mountain near the Greek border, **Korça** is home to the **Mirahor Mosque**, dating back to 1466.
- Visible for miles around, **Kruja** is an attractive medieval town perched on top of a mountain north of Tirana. It was the centre of Albanian resistance to the Ottoman Turks under Skanderbeg, the national hero, and the **Skanderbeg Museum** is to be found inside the recently restored castle. The street leading up to the castle is built in the style of a medieval Turkish bazaar.
- Situated on **Lake Scutari**, which divides Albania from Montenegro, **Shkodra** is dominated by the ruins of the **Fortress of Rozafa**, one of the ancient Illyrian castles, built on a rock hill from which a spectacular panorama of the surrounding countryside, the lake and the **Lead Mosque** can be enjoyed. The **Mesi Bridge**, 8km (5 miles) from Shkodra, is also well worth a visit, as is the **Monument to Gjergj Kastrioti Skanderbeg** at his burial ground in **Lezha**.

Top Things To Do

- With mountains and hills representing two thirds of the Albania's total area, skiing, climbing, trekking, cave exploration (the **Pirrogoshi cave** in the Skrapari area is the largest in Albania) and mountain biking are available in **Dajti, Llogaraja, Dardha, Bozdoveci, Voskopoja, Valbona** and **Thethi**. Skiing is especially popular in **Korça**.
- Enjoy Albania's 450km (280 miles) of coastline and shallow beaches. **Durres** and **Golem** are the largest beaches. Albania's southern coastline remains completely unspoilt. Situated opposite Corfu, **Saranda** is now much visited by daytrippers who come to enjoy this previously inaccessible resort. Various water activities and sports, including beach volley, are popular along most of the Albanian Coast.
- Fish in the **Ohrid Lake** (southeast Albania), the deepest lake of the Balkan Peninsula, renowned for its clear water and rich in alcoran (similar to a trout) and carp.
- Visit **Tirana**'s numerous museums such as the **National Historical Museum**, the **National Art Gallery** and the **Exhibition of Folk Culture**. Tirana's **Pyramid**, which was built as a museum for Enver Hoxha (Albania's former Communist leader), has been turned into an international Cultural Centre. In Tirana, you will also find the **Palace of Culture**, which houses the **Opera** and **Ballet Theatre**, and the **National Library**.
- There is an excellent **Archaeological Museum** in the port of **Durres**, best known for the nearby beach resort of **Durres Plazh**.
- Both **Berat**, known as the 'city of a thousand windows', and **Gjirokastra**, in the far south, have been declared 'Museum Cities'. The **Onufri Museum** in Berat, dedicated to the 16th-century painter and his contemporaries, houses restored icons in an orthodox church. **Gjirokastra** is dominated by the 13th-century **Fortress** which was extended by Ali Pasha in 1811. It now contains the **National Museum of Weapons** (the collection ranges from medieval armour to a shot-down US reconnaissance aircraft (the museum was looted in 1997 but most of the collection is still there) and the view is not to be missed. The surrounding area is renowned for its many mineral springs.
- In **Korça**, visit the **Museum for Medieval Art**, the **Museum of Education** (where the first Albanian school was opened in 1887) and a listed, though decaying, bazaar quarter.

Entertainment

FOOD & DRINK: Private restaurants are appearing rapidly in Albania. In the more popular places, it is necessary to reserve a table and to be punctual. Food is typically Balkan with Turkish influences evident on any menu – byrek, kofte, shish kebab.

National specialities:
- Fërgesë tirane, a hot fried dish of meat, liver, eggs and tomatoes, and tavë kosi or tavë elbasani, a mutton and yoghurt dish.
- The koran, a trout from Lake Ohrid, and the Shkodra carp.
- In summer, tarator, a cold yoghurt and cucumber soup, is particularly refreshing.
- Popular Albanian desserts include oshaf, a fig and sheep's milk pudding, cakes soaked in honey and candied fruits or reçel.

- Guests of honour are quite often presented with a baked sheep's head.
- A favourite in the south is kukurec (stuffed sheep's intestines).
- Continental breakfasts are usually served in hotels, but in the country the Albanian breakfast of pilaf (rice) or paça (a wholesome soup made from animals' innards) may not be to everyone's taste.

National drinks:
- All bars and restaurants serve raki, local red and white wines and different liqueurs.
- The Albanian cognac, with its distinctive aroma, is also popular.
- Many imported drinks can also be found, including Austrian canned beer, Macedonian wine and ouzo from Greece.
- Turkish coffee (kafe Turke) is popular with Albanians, but many bars also serve Italian espresso (ekspres).

Tipping: Previously frowned upon by the authorities, tips are gratefully received in restaurants or for any service provided.

NIGHTLIFE: The most popular form of nightlife is the xhiro, the evening stroll along the main boulevards and squares of each town and village. Cultural life takes the form of theatre, opera and concerts. Discos and games arcades are beginning to appear. Some hotels have taverns with music and dancing.

SHOPPING: Special purchases include carpets, filigree silver and copper, woodcarvings, ceramics and any kind of needlework. Old markets are often worth exploring. Bartering is very much the order of the day for foreigners as well as for locals. Some of the tourist hotels also have shops. **Shopping hours:** Generally Mon-Sat 0800-1200 and 1500-1900 (although regional variations are possible). Many shops are also open Sunday.

Business

ECONOMY: Albania is one of Europe's poorest countries and continues to face severe difficulties adjusting to the new Europe after decades of Stalinist isolation. More recently, conditions were worsened by regional political instability and the collapse of 'pyramid' investment schemes in 1997. Albania is blessed with appreciable natural resources – it is one of the world's largest producers of chromium and boasts reserves of copper, nickel, pyrites and coal. There are also oil deposits, both on and offshore. The agricultural sector, which accounts for 40 per cent of GDP and underwent some upheaval following de-collectivisation, has now settled down with all but a few farming enterprises in the private sector. Export capacity is limited with 80 per cent of agricultural production destined for domestic use. New components of the economy, such as tourism, which were mostly set up with foreign investment, suffered badly in the wake of the 1997 upheaval – a great deal of Albania's hard-won economic progress was destroyed during that period. In the last five years, much of the damage has been restored but the black economy remains a huge influence over Albania, especially in view of the 40 per cent unemployment rate. Nonetheless, Albania has since received steady support from major foreign donors and it was admitted to the World Trade Organization in July 2000 – as much a valuable symbol of international recognition as a potential boost to the economy. The Government hopes to join the EU in around 2010, although most observers consider this highly optimistic.

BUSINESS ETIQUETTE: Punctuality is expected. Business cards are common and European practices are observed. Nodding the head may mean 'No' and shaking it, 'Yes'.

Office hours: Mon-Fri 0800-1600. All offices are closed on Saturday and Sunday.

Algeria

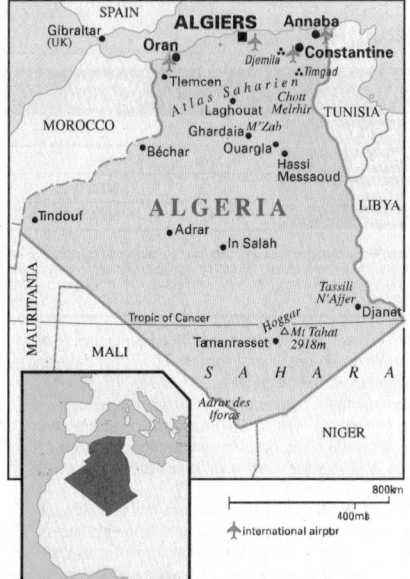

Location: North Africa, Mediterranean Coast.

Time: GMT + 1.

Overview

A large country, Algeria was originally inhabited by the Berbers until the Arabs conquered North Africa in the seventh century. Staying mainly in the mountainous regions, the Berbers resisted the spreading Arab influence, managing to preserve much of their language and culture until the present day. Today, they make up some 20 per cent of the total population.

Part of the Turkish Ottoman empire from the 16th century, Algeria was conquered by the French in 1830. The country was given the status of a département in its own right. The struggle for Independence began in 1954 headed by the National Liberation Front, which came to power on Independence in 1962. In the 1990s, Algerian politics was dominated by the struggle involving the military and Islamic militants. In 1992, a general election won by an Islamic party (FIS - Islamic Salvation Front) was annulled, marking the beginning of a bloody campaign which saw the slaughter of more than 150,000 people. An amnesty in 1999 led many rebels to lay down their arms. Violence has largely abated, although a state of emergency remains in place. In 2001, the Government agreed to a series of demands from the minority Berber community, after months of unrest involving Berber youths pressing for greater cultural and political recognition.

With more than four-fifths of its territory covered by the Sahara desert, the Sahara is Algeria's most striking feature. Relatively inhabited, the area is drawing increasing numbers of tourists. Several flights operate from Algiers, the capital, to Ghardia, Djanet and Tamanrasset, as well as to smaller towns, oases and oil settlements. Algerian oases generally defy the European cliché of a small patch of palms forever threatened by encroaching dunes as they are often fairly large towns with highly organised, walled-in gardens with date palms, and mosques, shops and monuments. Les hommes bleus, blue-robed Touaregs, who are the ancient nomadic inhabitants of the Hoggar Mountains, can be seen making their way in camel caravans around the inscrutable desert.

It should be noted, however, that Algeria faces a serious internal security problem from terrorist insurgency and that travellers by road in northern Algeria are at risk of attack by terrorist groups. It is advised that all travellers be extra cautious with personal security arrangements throughout their stay. All travel to the southeastern provinces of Tamanrasset, Djanet and Illizi is currently advised against.

General Information

AREA: 2,381,741 sq km (919,595 sq miles).
POPULATION: 31 million (2002).
POPULATION DENSITY: 13.0 per sq km.
CAPITAL: Algiers (El Djezaïr). **Population:** 1,519,570 (1998).
GEOGRAPHY: Algeria is situated along the North African coast, bordered to the east by Tunisia and Libya, to the southeast by Niger, to the southwest by Mali, and to the west by Mauritania and Morocco. It is Africa's second-largest country, with 1200km (750 miles) of coastline. Along the coastal strip are the main towns, fertile land, beach resorts and 90 per cent of the population. Further south lies the area of the *Hauts Plateaux*, mountains of up to 2000m (6600ft) covered in cedar, pine and cypress forests with broad arable plains dividing the plateaux. The remaining 85 per cent of the country is the Sahara Desert in its various forms, sustaining only 500,000 people, many of whom are nomadic tribes with goat and camel herds. The oil and minerals boom has created new industrial centres like Hassi Messaoud, which have grown up within previously barely inhabited regions of the northern Sahara. The plains of gravel and sand in the deep south are interrupted by two mountain ranges: the dramatic *Hoggar* massif, rising to almost 3000m (9800ft), and the *Tassili N'Ajjer* or 'Plateau of Chasms'. Both have long been important centres of Tuareg culture.
GOVERNMENT: Republic. Gained independence from France in 1962. **Head of State:** President Abdelaziz Bouteflika since 1999. **Head of Government:** Prime Minister Ahmed Ouyahia since 2003. **Recent history:** In the 1990s, Algerian politics was dominated by the struggle involving the military and Islamic militants. Violence has largely abated, although a state of emergency remains in place. More recently, the Government has also been confronted with agitation from the country's Berber ethnic minority pressing for greater cultural and political recognition. Despite limited concessions to their demands – Tamazight, the Berber tongue, is now recognised as an official national language - Berber protests have continued. Since the beginning of 1999, when President Zéroual announced his intention to step down, several elections have been held in order to bolster the regime's legitimacy. A new Presidential poll was arranged but under such tightly controlled conditions that candidates who initially chose to oppose the official candidate eventually decided to boycott it. Abdelaziz Bouteflika, formerly Algeria's long-standing and respected Foreign Minister, was thus elected unopposed. A Parliamentary election was held in May 2002, which was also subject to a partial boycott and returned the ruling FLN with a working majority in the National Assembly. In 2003, in the general election, Ali Benglis of the FLN also won as Prime Minister. However, this election recorded a low turnout and was marred by violence. In April 2004, Bouteflika emerged as President for a second term with an overwhelming majority, although contentions continued.
LANGUAGE: The official languages are Arabic and Berber (Tamazight), but French is still used for most official and business transactions. Berber (Amazigh) is spoken in the northern mountainous regions of the Kabylias and the Aures and also in the south. In general, English is spoken only in major business or tourist centres.
RELIGION: 99 per cent of the population adhere to Islam.
ELECTRICITY: 220 volts AC, 50Hz. The European two-pin plug is standard.
SOCIAL CONVENTIONS: Courtesy should be adopted with new acquaintances. The provision and acceptance of hospitality are as important a part of Algerian culture as elsewhere in the Arab world. In the main cities, the urban population lives at a frantic pace much akin to European urban dwellers, but in the south and in rural areas people are much more open and friendly. Algerian women are expected to dress modestly in rural areas but this is not necessary in Algiers. Homosexuality is illegal and punishable by imprisonment. Tourist visits should be avoided during Ramadan. For more information, see the *World of Islam* appendix. **Photography:** Military installations and personnel should not be photographed. Visitors are advised to make sure there is nothing that could be of a Governmental or military nature around their prospective photographic subject.

Climate

Summer temperatures are high throughout the country, particularly in the south where it is both very dry and very hot. During this time, road travel is difficult and air travel prone to delay because of sandstorms. Northern cities have high humidity, while those along the coast are cooled by sea breezes. In the winter, the oases of the far south are

pleasant and attract many visitors. The desert temperature drops dramatically at night. North of the Sahara, temperatures are very mild from September to May and vary little between day and night. South of the Sahara, temperatures are pleasant from October to April, but there are great variations between day and night. Coastal towns are prone to storms from the sea. Rainfall is relatively low throughout the country and in the far south it is virtually unknown.
Required clothing: Cotton and linen lightweights for winter months and for evenings in desert areas. Woollens and light rainwear are advised for the winter along the coast and the *Hauts Plateaux*. South of the Sahara, from mid-December to mid-January, temperatures drop and warm clothes are necessary both in the morning and the evening. A mountain sleeping bag is also required when camping.

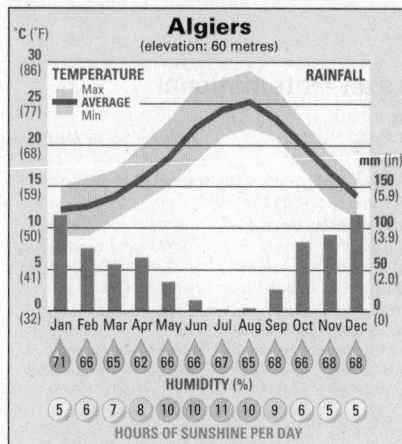

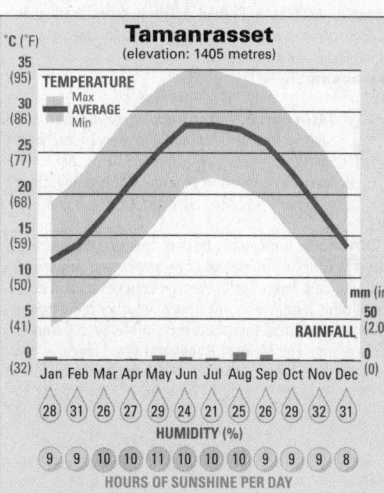

Communications

Telephone: IDD is available. Country code: 213. **Mobile telephone:** Roaming agreements exist but coverage is mostly limited to main towns.
Internet: There are three Internet cafes in Algiers, Constantine and Oran.
Post: Mail posted in any of the main cities along the coast takes three to four days to reach Europe; posted elsewhere, it could take much longer. Parcels sent by surface mail may take up to two months to reach Algeria. Post office hours: Generally Sat-Wed 0800-1700; Thurs 0800-1200; but the main post office in Algiers (5 boulevard Mohamed Khémisti) is open 24 hours.
MEDIA: Algeria's TV and radio stations are state-controlled, but there is a lively private press which is often critical of the authorities. Although there is no overt censorship, legislation sets out prison terms and fines for insulting or defaming the President, MPs, judges and the army.
Press: Daily newspapers are printed in Arabic or French. The main French-language dailies are *El Watan, Liberté, Le Quotidien d'Oran* and *La Tribune. El Khabar* is one of the leading Arabic-language dailies. Another daily, *Horizons*, has an English section.
TV: *Enterprise Nationale de Télévision (ENTV)* is state-run. The use of satellite dishes is widespread; some satellite TV stations, such as *BRTV*, a Berber station based in France, target viewers in Algeria and European channels are widely watched.
Radio: *Algerian Radio*, operated by state-run *Radio-Télévision Algérienne*, runs national Arabic, Berber and French networks and several local stations.

Passport/Visa

	Passport Required?	Visa Required?	Return Ticket Required?
Full British	Yes	Yes	No
Australian	Yes	Yes	No
Canadian	Yes	Yes	No
USA	Yes	Yes	No
Other EU	Yes	Yes	No
Japanese	Yes	Yes	No

Note: Regulations and requirements may be subject to change at short notice, and you are advised to contact the appropriate diplomatic or consular authority before finalising travel arrangements. Any numbers in the chart refer to the footnotes below.

Restricted entry: Entry and transit is refused to holders of Israeli passports.
Note: It is no longer compulsory to import a specific amount of currency for each day of the intended stay. However, all foreign currency imported must be declared and receipts retained for inspection.
PASSPORTS: Passport valid for at least six months required by all.
VISAS: Required by all except the following:
(a) nationals of Libya, Maldives, Mali, Malaysia, Mauritania, Seychelles, Syrian Arab Republic, Tunisia and Yemen for stays of up to three months;
(b) transit passengers continuing their journey by the same or first connecting aircraft within 24 hours provided holding sufficient funds, onward and return documentation and not leaving the airport. If transit exceeds 24 hours, a transit permit for up to 48 hours has to be obtained from airport authorities.
Note: Children under 15 years of age travelling on their parents' passports do not need a visa, although a letter of authorisation is required from the parents or guardian.
Types of visa and cost: *Tourist, Business* and *Transit*. The cost varies according to nationality. For British passport holders, the costs are: *Single-entry:* £28 (US$39); *Multiple-entry:* £35 (US$39; 90 days). Contact the Consulate (or Consular section at Embassy) for details; see *Passport/Visa Information.*
Validity: *Tourist:* approximately 30 days. *Transit:* maximum 48 hours. *Business:* up to 90 days.
Application to: Consulate (see *Passport/Visa Information*).
Application requirements: (a) Two completed application forms. (b) Two passport-size photos. (c) Passport valid for six months. (d) Fee. (e) Letter from current UK employer (and photocopy). (f) Pre-paid special delivery envelope for postal applications. *Tourist:* (a)-(f) and, (g) Letter of invitation from an Algerian national or a hotel booking (accommodation certificate), duly certified by the relevant authorities. Itinerary details will also have to be provided if visiting southern Algeria. *Business:* (a)-(f) and, (g) Letter of invitation from the sponsoring company.
Working days required: Dependent upon nationality, but three (minimum) for British nationals, 10 for postal applications and at peak times.
Temporary residence: Apply to the authorities in Algeria.

PASSPORT/VISA INFORMATION

Embassy of the People's Democratic Republic of Algeria in the UK
54 Holland Park, London W11 3RS, UK
Tel: (020) 7221 7800.
Website: www.consalglond.u-net.com
Opening hours: Mon-Fri 0900-1700.

Algerian Consulate in the UK
6 Hyde Park Gate, London SW7 5EW, UK
Tel: (020) 7589 6885.
Website: www.consalglond.u-net.com
Opening hours: Tues-Sat 0900-1600; Tues-Fri 0930-1200 (visa applications); 1600-1630 (visa collection).

Embassy of the People's Democratic Republic of Algeria in the USA
2118 Kalorama Road, NW, Washington, DC 20008, USA
Tel: (202) 265 2800.
Website: www.algeria-us.org

Money

Currency: Dinar (DZD) = 100 centimes. Notes are in denominations of DZD1000, 500, 200, 100 and 50. Coins are in denominations of DZD100, 50, 20, 10, 5, 2 and 1, and 50, 20, 10, 5 and 1 centimes.
Note: Visitors are strongly advised not to be associated with the black market, which tends to concentrate on the Euro and portable electronics.
Currency exchange: In the past, difficulties have arisen when

trying to exchange currency in Algeria, with only one national bank (*La Banque Extérieure d'Algérie*) able to exchange foreign currency at branches in major business centres. Difficulties are now decreasing and it is possible, for example, to exchange currency at some of the larger hotels. However, the facilities for currency exchange remain quite limited.
Credit & debit cards: Credit cards are generally only accepted in urban areas. Check with your credit or debit card company for details of merchant acceptability and other services that may be available.
Traveller's cheques: Accepted only in top-class (4-star and above) hotels, Government-run craft (souvenir) shops and in certain establishments. To avoid additional exchange rate charges, travellers are advised to take traveller's cheques in US Dollars or Euros.
Currency restrictions: The import and export of local currency is allowed. The import of foreign currency is unlimited, but must be declared on arrival and changed at the nearest bank. The export of foreign currency is permitted up to the amount declared on arrival. The currency declaration and the exchange declaration must be presented upon departure.
Banking hours: Sun-Thurs 0900-1530.
Exchange rate indicators:
Rate at time of publishing

£1.00=	DZD129.88
$1.00=	DZD73.62

Duty Free

The following goods may be imported into Algeria by persons over 17 years of age without incurring customs duty:
200 cigarettes or 50 cigars or 400g of tobacco; 1l of alcoholic beverages; 500ml of Eau de Cologne or 150ml of perfume in opened bottles.
Prohibited items: Gold, firearms, ammunition and narcotics may not be imported or exported. Jewellery, gold and firearms may not be exported.

Public Holidays

Below are listed Public Holidays for the January 2006-June 2007 period.
2006: Jan 1 New Year's Day. **Jan 10** Eid al-Adha (Feast of the Sacrifice). **Jan 31** Islamic New Year. **Feb 9** Ashoura. **Apr 11** Mouloud (Birth of the Prophet). **May 1** Labour Day. **Jun 19** Revolutionary Readjustment. **Jul 5** Independence Day. **Oct 22-24** Eid al-Fitr (End of Ramadan). **Nov 1** Anniversary of the Revolution. **Dec 31** Eid al-Adha (Feast of the Sacrifice).
2007: Jan 1 New Year's Day. **Jan 20** Islamic New Year. **Jan 29** Ashoura. **Apr** Mouloud. **May 1** Labour Day. **Jun 19** Revolutionary Readjustment.
Note: Muslim festivals are timed according to local sightings of various phases of the moon and the dates given above are approximations. The Algerian observance of Ramadan (lasting one lunar month and culminating in the feast days of *Eid al-Fitr*) has recently relaxed, and restaurants and other business centres will be open during the day. However, in the towns and oases of the south where religious observance tends to be more orthodox, some difficulty might be had in finding eating places and getting transport during the daylight hours. For a more detailed description, see the *World of Islam* appendix.

Health

	Special Precautions?	Certificate Required?
Yellow Fever	Yes	1
Cholera	No	No
Typhoid & Polio	2	N/A
Malaria	3	N/A

Note: *Regulations and requirements may be subject to change at short notice, and you are advised to contact your doctor well in advance of your intended date of departure. Any numbers in the chart refer to the footnotes below.*

1: A yellow fever vaccination certificate is required by travellers over one year of age arriving from or leaving endemic or infected areas.
2: It is sometimes advised to get an immunisation course or booster against typhoid and sometimes poliomyelitis.
3: Malaria risk is limited. The benign *vivax* strain has been reported in Ihrir (Illizi Department). The recommended prophylaxis is mosquito bite protection only.
Food & drink: Mains water is normally chlorinated and, whilst relatively safe, may cause mild abdominal upsets. Bottled water is available and is advised for the first few weeks of stay. Drinking water outside main cities and towns is likely to be contaminated and sterilisation is considered essential. Milk is pasteurised and dairy products are safe for consumption. Powdered or tinned milk is available and is advised, but make sure that it is reconstituted with pure water. Local meat, poultry, seafood, fruit and vegetables are generally considered safe to eat.
Other risks: *Hepatitis A* occurs. *Hepatitis B, diphtheria* and *tuberculosis* are all present.
Rabies is present. For those at high risk, vaccination before arrival should be considered. If you are bitten, seek medical help without delay. For more information, consult the *Health* appendix.
Note: In 2003, there were three reported outbreaks of bubonic plague in western Algeria: El Kehailia, south of Oran, and in the areas of Mascara and Sidi Bel Abbes; the last reported case was on July 10 2003.
Health care: Medical insurance is not always valid in Algeria and a medical insurance supplement with specific overseas coverage is recommended. Healthcare facilities are generally of a reasonable standard in the north but more limited in the south. Doctors and hospitals usually ask for immediate cash payment for their services. Emergency cases will be dealt with free of charge.

Travel - International

AIR:
Algeria's national airline is *Air Algérie (AH)* (website: www.airalgerie.dz).
Approximate flight times: From Algiers to *London* is two hours 15 minutes.
Main airports: *Algiers (ALG) (Houari Boumediène)* is 20km (12 miles) east of Algiers. *To/from the airport:* Buses and trains operate to the city from 0600-1900 (travel time - 30 minutes). Taxis are also available. *Facilities:* Bank, bureau de change, left luggage, shops, post office, tourist information, restaurants and car hire.
Oran (ORN) (Es Senia) is 10km (6 miles) from the city. *To/from the airport:* Taxis are available to the city. *Facilities:* Bank, limited catering and car hire.
Annaba (AAE) (Les Salines) is 12km (7.5 miles) from the city. *To/from the airport:* A bus service departs to the city every 30 minutes. Coach service is available on request and taxis are also available. *Facilities:* Restaurant, bank and car hire.
Constantine (CZL) (Ain El Bey) is 9km (6 miles) from the city. *To/from the airport:* There are bus and taxi links with the city. *Facilities:* Limited.
Departure tax: None.
SEA:
Main ports: *Algiers, Annaba, Béjaia, Oran* and *Skikda*. Regular shipping lines serve Algiers from Mediterranean ports. *Algérie Ferries* runs passenger services connecting Algeria to Marseille (France) and Alicante (Spain) (website: www.algerieferries.com).
RAIL:
There is one daily train connecting Algiers with Tunis in Tunisia via Constantine and Annaba. The train has a buffet car and couchettes and a reservation is required for this route. Another daily train runs between Algiers and Marrakech in Morocco. Stops en route are Oran, Fès, Mèknes, Rabat and Casablanca. Reservations are required and a supplement is charged. Air-conditioned coaches and light refreshments/buffet car are available. At present, services are interrupted owing to the closure of the border between Algeria and Morocco and through-trains are not operating.
ROAD:
Owing to border closures, land crossings between Morocco and Algeria are not possible at present. The main road entry points are Maghnia (Morocco), Souk-Ahras, Tebessa and El Kala (Tunisia), Fort Thiriet (Libya), In Guezzam (Niger) and Bordj Mokhtar (Mali). There is a good network of paved roads in the coastal regions and paved roads connect the major towns in the northern Sahara. Further south, the only substantial stretches of paved roads are on the two trans-Saharan 'highways', one of which runs to the west through Reggane and up through Morocco to the coast, while the other runs through Tamanrasset and Djanet on its way to Ghardaia and Algiers. The precise route taken by trans-Saharan travellers often depends on the season. Please note that many desert 'roads' are up to 10km- (6 mile-) wide ribbons of unimproved desert and are suitable only for well-maintained 4-wheel-drive vehicles. **Coach:** Services are run by *Altour* (www.altour.com) and *SNTF* with international routes to Tunisia and Morocco. **Documentation:** International Driving Permit required.

Travel - Internal

AIR:
Air Algérie operates frequent services from Algiers domestic airport (adjacent to Algiers International) to the major business centres of Annaba, Constantine and Oran. Less frequent services run from Algiers, Oran, Constantine and Annaba to the other less important commercial centres and gateway oases such as Ghardaia (six hours from Algiers) and Ouargla, as well as important oil towns such as In Amenas and Hassi Messaoud. Services are generally reliable, but air travel to the far south may be subject to delay during the dry summer months because of sandstorms. Despite this, air is by far the most practical means of transport to the far south for the visitor with limited resources of time; Djanet and Tamanrasset are the oasis gateways to the *Tassili N'Ajjer* and the *Hoggar*, respectively.
Note: The London office of *Air Algérie* (tel: (020) 7487 5903) can provide a timetable of services and prices, make reservations and issue tickets. There is an *Air Algérie* office in every Algerian town which is served by the airline. Reservations and itineraries can be arranged from these offices, but as some of the more isolated offices are not connected by computer, fax or telex, reservations should be confirmed well in advance. Offices are very busy in the major towns.
SEA:
Government ferries service the main coastal ports. **Main ports**: *Algiers, Annaba, Arzew, Béjaia, Djidjelli, Ghazaouet, Mostaganem, Oran* and *Skikda.*
RAIL:
Algerian railways are run by the *Société Nationale des Transports Ferroviaires (SNTF)*. Daily - but fairly slow - services operate in the northern part of the country between Algiers and Oran, Béjaia, Skikda, Annaba and Constantine. The southern routes connect once a day from Annaba to Tebessa via Souk Ahras, Constantine with Touggourt via Biskra (twice a day) and Mohammadia with Bechar.
ROAD:
Road surfaces are reasonably good. All vehicles travelling in the desert should be in good mechanical condition, as breakdown facilities are virtually non-existent. Travellers *must* carry full supplies of water and petrol. Traffic drives on the right. Travel by road (outside Algiers) in northern Algeria should be avoided, especially after dark. **Coach:** Relatively inexpensive coaches, run by the SNTF, link major towns. Services are regular but this mode of travel is not recommended for long journeys, such as travel to the south from the coastal strip. Services leave from the coach stations close to the centres of Algiers and Oran. **Car hire:** Can be arranged at the airport on arrival or in most towns. Many hotels can also arrange car hire. **Documentation:** An International Driving Permit is required. A *carnet de passage* may be required. Cars are allowed entry for three months without duty. Insurance must be purchased at the border. Proof of ownership is essential.
URBAN:
Municipal bus and tram services operate in Algiers, its suburbs and the coastal area. 10-journey *carnets* and daily, weekly or longer duration passes are available. There are also two public lifts and a funicular which lead up to the hill overlooking the old *souk* in Algiers. An underground system is planned (still several years from completion), plus a new tramway with a multi-route system projected to carry upwards of 200,000 daily passenger trips. **Taxi:** It is advised not to use public transport other than taxis recommended by established hotels. All taxis are metered and are plentiful in most cities and major towns, though busy during the early evening in the main cities as many people use them to return home after work. The habit of sharing a taxi is widespread. The amount on the meter is the correct fare, but there are surcharges after dark. Travellers are advised not to use unlicensed taxis, as these are likely to be uninsured.
Travel times: The following chart gives approximate travel times (in hours and minutes) from **Algiers** to other major cities/towns in Algeria.

	Air	Road
Constantine	0.45	4.00
Ghardaia	0.55	6.00
Oran	0.50	4.00
Tlemcen	1.00	6.00

Travel Advice

Travellers are advised against all travel to the southeastern provinces of Tamanrasset, Djanet and Illizi until further notice. The kidnapping of a number of groups of foreign tourists in the desert and mountainous region of southeast Algeria in 2003 underlined the dangers to travellers in that region. There is a continuing threat from terrorism in Algeria. Algeria faces a serious internal security problem from terrorist insurgency. Travellers by road in northern Algeria are at risk of attack by terrorist groups. One of these groups recently issued an explicit threat to target non-Muslims.
If you are planning to travel to Algeria, you should be very careful about your personal security arrangements throughout your visit. Developments in the region could affect the security situation.
Crimes against individuals, such as assaults and muggings, are on the increase in urban areas.
This advice is based on information provided by the Foreign and Commonwealth Office in the UK. It is correct at time of publishing. As the situation can change rapidly, visitors are advised to contact the following organisations for the latest travel advice:

British Foreign and Commonwealth Office
Tel: (0845) 850 2829.
Website: www.fco.gov.uk

US Department of State
Website: http://travel.state.gov/travel

Accommodation

HOTELS: In general, good hotel accommodation in Algeria is limited. The business centres, and in particular Algiers, tend to have either extremely expensive luxury hotels or cheaper hotels primarily suited to the local population visiting on business or for social purposes. Algiers and Oran are full of the cheaper hotels, but they tend to be crowded and difficult to get into, even with a confirmed booking. For assurance on business, reserve rooms only at the best hotels. All hotels are subject to Government regulations and are classified by a star rating: deluxe (**5-star**), second class (**4/3-star**) and tourist class (**2/1-star**).
The Coast: The hotels in the resorts along the Mediterranean coast have increased in number, and many are of a reasonably high standard. Often, the good hotels in these resorts run their own nightclubs. Winter rates for coastal resorts apply from 1 October to 31 May, and summer rates for the remainder of the year.
The Oases: Good hotels in the gateway oases of the mid-south - such as Ghardaia and Ouargla - are few and far between, and during the season (any time other than high summer, which runs from late June to early September), it is vital to book well in advance.
The Far South: Hotels in the very far south are extremely limited. In Tamanrasset, better-class hotels have been built since the oasis became a fashionable winter resort. Room availability is, however, limited.
CAMPING/CARAVANNING: Camping is free on common land or on the beaches but permission from the local authorities is necessary. Campsites with good facilities are found in Ain el-Turk, Annaba and Larhat.
YOUTH HOSTELS: There is a good network of (single sex) youth hostels throughout the country offering accommodation at budget rates.

ACCOMMODATION INFORMATION

Fédération Algérienne des Auberges de Jeunesse
213 Rue Hassiba Ben Bouali, BP 15, El Annasser, Algiers, Algeria
Tel: (21) 678 658/7.

Top Things To See

- **Algiers**, the capital, has been a port since Roman times and many impressive ruins can still be seen, such as those at **Djemila** and **Timgad**, which are all in good condition because of the dry desert climate. Although commercialised by the French in the mid-19th century, Algiers still has a Maghreb feel to it, with many zig-zag alleyways, mosques, a *casbah*, *medersas* (study houses) and the beautiful Turkish houses and palaces much admired by Le Corbusier.
- Within easy reach of Algiers along the coast, **Tipasa** has exceptional Roman, Punic and Christian ruins, and a Numidian mausoleum.
- The **Chiffa Gorges** and **Kabylia** in the mountains provide more rural scenery. Fig and olive groves in summer become ski resorts in the winter.
- The western coast around **Oran**, Algeria's second city, has historic remains and mosques.
- **Tlemcen** was an important imperial city from the 12th to 16th centuries. It stands in the wooded foothills of the **Tellian Atlas** and is a pleasant retreat from the stifling heat of high summer. Sights include the **Grand Mosque**, the **Mansourah Fortress** and the **Almohad ramparts**.
- **Constantine**, to the east, is a natural citadel lying across the **River Rhumnel**. Founded by the Carthaginians, who called it Cirta, it is the oldest continuously inhabited city in Algeria. Sights include the **Ahmed Bey Palace** (one of the most picturesque in the Maghreb) and the **Djamma el-Kebir Mosque**.
- In the east of the M'Zab region is **Ouargla**, referred to as 'the golden key to the desert'. This town is well worth visiting for its *malekite* (an Islamic sect) **minaret**.
- Deeper into the south lies the town of **El Goléa**, referred to as 'the pearl of the desert' or 'the enchanted oasis' because of its luxuriant vegetation and abundant water. The town is dominated by an old *ksar* (fort), whose ruins are well preserved.
- Further south are the **Hoggar Mountains**, an impressive, jagged range reaching as far as Libya and surrounded by desert on all sides. It consists of a plateau made of volcanic rock. Eroded cliffs and granite needles form fascinating shapes in pink, blue or black basalt. At the top of the **Assekreu** nestles the famous refuge of Charles de Foucault at 2800m (9259ft). **Mount Tahat**, which belongs to the **Atakor Massif**, can be seen in the distance, reaching 3000m (9921ft) at its highest point.

Top Things To Do

- Visit Algiers' **Bardo Ethnographic and Local Art Museum** and the **National Museum of Fine Arts**, which are amongst the finest museums in North Africa.
- Within easy reach of Algiers, along the coast, lie some fine resorts. **Zeralda** is a beach resort with a holiday village and a replica nomad village. To the east of Algiers, the **Turquoise Coast** offers rocky coves and long beaches within easy reach of the city, equipped with sports, cruise and watersports facilities. The **Sidi Fredj** peninsula has a marina, an open-air theatre and complete amenities, including sporting facilities.
- Along the coast from **Oran**, which is primarily a business centre and an oil depot, there are a number of resorts, many with well-equipped hotels. Notable beaches to spend some time in include **Ain El Turk**, **Les Andalouses**, **Canastel**, **Kristel**, **Mostaganem** and **Sablettes**.
- The **Sahara** is the most striking and also most forbidding feature of the country. The best way to enter the south is to cross the **El Kautara Gorges** to the south of **Constantine**. The sudden glimpse of the Sahara through the El Kautara Gorges is breathtaking. These gorges are said to separate the winter areas from the land of everlasting summer and are called **Fouur Es Sahra** ('the Sahara's mouth') by the inhabitants. Favourite starting places for exploring the Sahara are **Laghouat**, a town with a geometric plan, or the **M'Zab Valley**, which has seven typical holy towns and is inhabited by a Muslim fundamentalist sect called the Mozabites. Mozabite towns are distinguished by a characteristic minaret with four spires. The most famous among them is **Ghardaia**, coiled within a group of bare, ochre rocks.
- The special feature of the holy town of **Beni-Isguen**, not far from Ghardaia, is its permanent **auction market**.
- Picturesque **Tamanrasset**, situated at the heart of the **Hoggar Mountains**, is a large town with many hotels and restaurants. Tourists often stay in 'Tam' (as it is sometimes called) and use it as a base for touring the Hoggar Mountains or hiking in the open desert to the south and west. It is also a popular winter holiday resort. It is visited regularly by the camel caravans of *les hommes bleus*, blue-robed Touaregs, who are the ancient nomadic inhabitants of this wide region.
- Tour the **Tassili N'Ajjer**, or 'Plateau of Chasms', a vast volcanic plateau crossed by massive gorges gouged out by rivers which have long since dried out or gone underground. The Tassili conceals a whole group of entirely unique **rupestrian paintings** (rock paintings), which spread out over a 130,000 sq km surface (50,000 sq miles)

TOURIST INFORMATION

Office National du Tourisme (ONT)
2 rue Ismail Kerrar, 1600 Algiers, Algeria
Tel: (21) 713 060.
E-mail: ont@wissal.dz

Entertainment

FOOD & DRINK: Traditional Algerian food shows the historic influences of Berber, Arab, Turkish, and French tastes. It can be mild or very spicy and many flavourings are used. Algiers and popular coastal towns have a fair selection of good restaurants, serving mainly French and Italian-style food. Even classic dishes will have an unmistakable Algerian quality. Fish dishes are exceptionally good.
Things to know: The sale of alcohol is not encouraged. Alcohol is only available in more expensive restaurants. There are no licensing hours and hotel bars tend to stay open for as long as there is custom. Algeria produces some good wines but very few of them seem to be served in the country itself. The major hotels may have a reasonable cellar of European wines.
National specialities:
- In the towns, stalls sell *brochettes* (*kebabs*) in French bread and covered in a spicy sauce (if desired). The range of foodstuffs in the south is more limited.
- *Couscous*, a semolina-like pasta made from cracked wheat, is a staple food in Algeria and throughout North Africa.
- Rice is also a popular staple, and chickpea-cakes make a cheap and tasty accompaniment for food.
- Stews like *shakshuka*, with vegetables, and *tajine*, with lamb or chicken, are popular everyday dishes. Sugar or honey can be added to savoury dishes to create a sweet-and-sour taste.
- The traditional diet of desert nomads is based on couscous and the meat of the sheep or goats they herd. When travelling, desert people carry pressed dates or figs, and hard cheese, which keeps for a long time.

National drinks:
- As in much of North Africa and the Middle East, refreshing, golden-coloured mint tea and strong, sweet coffee (sometimes called Turkish coffee) are drunk wherever people gather to talk and relax.
- If available, try *Medea*, *Mansourah* and *Mascara* red wines and *Medea*, *Mascara* and *Lismara* rosés.

Tipping: 10 per cent is usual.
NIGHTLIFE: The main towns offer reasonable entertainment facilities, including hotel restaurants, nightclubs, discos, folk dancing and traditional music. In Algiers and Oran, some cinemas show English and French films.
SHOPPING: Possible souvenirs include leatherware, rugs, copper and brassware, local dresses and jewellery. Berber carpets are beautifully decorated, and from the Sahara comes finely dyed basketwork and primitive-style pottery. Bargaining is customary in street markets and smaller shops. The rue Didouche Mourad is the best shopping street in Algiers. There are two state-run craft centres with fixed prices. One is located at Algiers airport. **Shopping hours:** Sat-Thurs 0900-1200 and 1400-1900. Some shops open on Fridays.

Business

- **GDP:** US$66 billion (2003).
- **Main exports:** Petroleum, natural gas and minerals.
- **Main imports:** Industrial equipment and consumer goods.
- **Main trade partners:** France, Germany, Italy, Spain and USA.

ECONOMY: Petroleum and natural gas are the most important industries in Algeria and account for all but a small fraction of the country's exports. Most of the country is covered by the Sahara Desert and despite investments in the agricultural sector (the main crops being wheat, potatoes, grapes, cereals and citrus fruits), Algeria is far from self-sufficient in foodstuffs and is vulnerable to drought. Most of the fertile land is located in the northern littoral region. The Government has recently completed the process of breaking up state agricultural co-operatives and turning the land over to its occupants. Minerals, principally iron ore and phosphates, are the other major export. The country's principal trading partners are France, Germany, Italy and Spain – it currently supplies a quarter of European natural gas imports. This proportion is likely to increase with the construction of a new pipeline linking coastal terminals to newly developed Saharan gas fields. From Europe, Algeria imports most of its industrial equipment and consumer goods. The IMF and other Western donors have provided loans and aid packages, conditional on liberalising economic reforms and the sale of state-owned industrial assets – the Government has, by and large, been prepared to meet these. As the security crisis has eased in the last few years, economic links between Algeria and the EU have grown. In April 2002, Algeria signed an Association Agreement with the EU, which aimed at boosting both-way trade.
BUSINESS ETIQUETTE: Suits should always be worn in winter months, shirt sleeves during the summer. Prior appointments are necessary for larger business firms. Businesspeople generally speak Arabic or French and, as a great deal of bargaining is necessary, it is rarely convenient to carry out transactions through an interpreter. Patience is always important. Visitors are usually entertained in hotels or restaurants, where Algerian businessmen are rarely accompanied by their wives. Visitors are seldom entertained at home. If visiting during Ramadan (and this should be avoided if possible), care should be taken to observe local custom in public places (for a more detailed description, see the *World of Islam* appendix). **Office hours:** Generally Sat-Wed 0800-1200 and 1300-1600.

COMMERCIAL INFORMATION

Chambre Algérienne de Commerce et d'Industrie
Palais Consulaire, BP 100, 6 boulevard Amilcar Cabral, Place des Martyrs, Algiers, Algeria
Tel: (21) 965 050 or 966 666.
Website: www.caci.dz

American Samoa

A

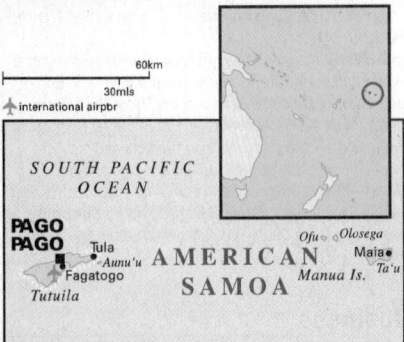

Location: South Pacific.

Time: GMT - 11.

American Samoa is an External Territory of the United States of America, and is represented abroad by US Embassies – see the *USA* section.

Overview

American Samoa is a tropical island paradise in the heart of Polynesia, which has succeeded in keeping the traditional values of old Samoa. It comprises seven islands, including *Ta'u, Olosega* and *Ofu*, known as the *Manu'a* group, which are volcanic in origin and dominated by high peaks. The islands' volcanoes, inactive since 1911, have left an intriguing land formation, including lava tubes to explore. Most people live in villages along the narrow coastal plains, living off the sea and cultivating agriculture in the plains and nearby hills. Half the island chain is still covered with tropical forests and woodlands that are home to wildlife and birds.

US interest in Samoa was prompted by the late-19th century search for a deep-water port in the South Pacific. Control of the islands was eventually divided between the USA and Germany. As Washington had no established apparatus for colonial Government, the US Navy was put in charge. Despite the US presence, island life remained largely unaffected until the 1940s, when American Samoa acquired great strategic importance in the course of the Pacific war and was subject to a huge influx of US Marines.

After the war, the Americans started to encourage the island towards self-government. In 1956, the first indigenous Samoan Governor was appointed, followed a decade later by a new constitution that sought to guarantee the rights of the local inhabitants in matters of land ownership and civil rights. The first full election for the post of Governor was held in 1977.

Traditional Samoan society is based on a chieftain system of hereditary rank, and is known as the Samoan way or *fa'a Samoa*. Despite the inroads of modern, Western civilisation, local cultural institutions are the strongest single influence in American Samoa. The fa'a Samoa way of life stems from the *aiga*, the extended family with a common allegiance to the *matai*, the family chief who regulates the family's activities. Religious institutions are very influential in the community and the village minister is accorded a privileged position, equal in status to a chief. Today, Samoa is still a land where status is more important than material possessions and travellers can be assured that they will feel most welcome.

General Information

AREA: 201 sq km (77.6 sq miles).
POPULATION: 57,291 (2000).
POPULATION DENSITY: 285.0 per sq km.
CAPITAL: Pago Pago. Population: 4,278 (2000).
GEOGRAPHY: American Samoa lies in the Pacific Ocean, approximately 3700km (2300 miles) southwest of Hawaii.

It comprises seven islands: Tutuila, the largest with an area of 53 sq miles; Ofu, Olosega and Ta'u, known as the Manu'a group; and Aunu'u, Rose and Swain's. The Manu'a group is volcanic in origin and dominated by high peaks. Rose and Swain's Islands are uninhabited coral atolls, located to the east and north, respectively, of the other two island groups.
GOVERNMENT: US External Territory (Unincorporated). Gained a measure of self-government in 1977. **Head of State:** President George W Bush since 2001. **Head of Government:** Acting Governor Togiola Tulafono since 2003. **Recent history:** Since World War II, American Samoa has developed into a modern, self-governing political system; The Government is divided into three branches, similar to the United States; The Executive Branch is led by the Governor and Lieutenant Governor, the Legislative Branch is led by the local legislature, consisting of the House of Representatives, who are elected by popular vote and the Senate, who are represented by the village *matai*; The judicial branch is part of the U.S. judicial system, and American Samoa has a non-voting representative elected to the US. Congress.
LANGUAGE: Samoan, but many islanders speak English.
RELIGION: Half of the population are Christian Congregational. There are also Roman Catholics, Latter Day Saints and Protestants, amongst others.
ELECTRICITY: 110V AC, 60Hz. US-style two-pin plugs are in use.
SOCIAL CONVENTIONS: Traditional Samoan society is still bound by very strict customs and, despite the younger generation's dissatisfaction with the old values, they are very much adhered to. The Government issues an official list of behaviour codes for both Samoas. Skimpy shorts or other revealing clothes should be avoided except when swimming or climbing coconut palms, although disapproval of shorts, if they are not *too* short, is on the wane. Samoan social behaviour conforms to strict and rather complicated rituals, to which the visitor will probably be introduced on arrival, and which should be respected. In the early evening hours, even if swimming offshore, be sure to avoid making any noise that could interrupt the Samoans' prayer period. Usually three gongs are sounded. The first is the signal to return to the house, the second is for prayer and the third sounds the all-clear. In some villages, swimming and fishing are forbidden on Sunday. A visitor who happens to be invited to stay in a Samoan household should be mindful of these customs. On leaving, making a gift, a *mea alofa* (literally a 'thing of love') of shirts, belts or dress-length fabrics is most appreciated. Samoans are extremely hospitable and visitors may receive more than one invitation to stay with neighbours. However, it is inappropriate to leave your first hosts before a pre-arranged date.

Climate

Very warm, tropical climate. The heaviest rainfalls are usually between December and April. The climate is best during the winter months, May to September, when there are moderate southeast trade winds. There is a local cyclone season from November to April.
Required clothing: Lightweight cottons and linens through-out the year with warm wrap for cooler winter evenings, and rainwear for the wet season (December to April).

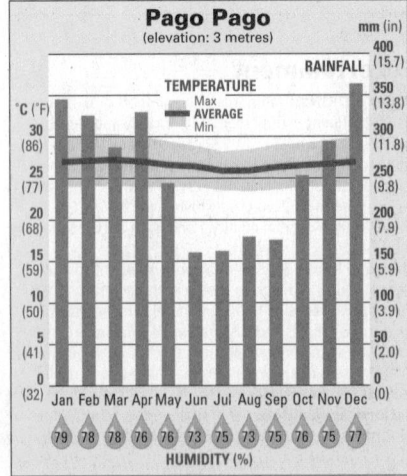

Communications

Telephone: IDD is available. Country code: 684. All outgoing calls must go through the international operator.
Mobile telephone: Roaming agreements do not exist at present.

Internet: Internet cafes exist.
Post: American Samoa is part of the US postal system and the same standard postal rates apply. The main Post office in the Lumana'i Building in Fagatogo is open 24 hours. There are also branches in Leone and Faguita villages, open Mon-Fri 0800-1600 and Sat 0830-1200.
MEDIA: Press: The island's own English-language newspaper is the *News Bulletin*, published from Monday to Friday. The *Samoa Journal and Advertiser* and *Samoa News* are also published in English.
Radio: Music FM stations include *Magik*, *K-Lite* and *Talofa*.

Passport/Visa

	Passport Required?	Visa Required?	Return Ticket Required?
Full British	Yes	No	Yes
Australian	Yes	No	Yes
Canadian	Yes	No	Yes
USA	1	No	Yes
Other EU	Yes	No	Yes
Japanese	Yes	No	Yes

Note: *Regulations and requirements may be subject to change at short notice, and you are advised to contact the appropriate diplomatic or consular authority before finalising travel arrangements. Any numbers in the chart refer to the footnotes below.*

PASSPORTS: Passport valid for at least 60 days beyond period of stay required by all except: **1.** nationals of the USA holding passport or other valid proof of identity (bearing a photograph), a valid onward or return ticket for stays of up to 30 days and proof of sufficient funds for the duration of stay.
Note: Pago Pago is not a port of entry to the USA and passengers proceeding to the USA must comply with the appropriate regulations.
VISAS: Depends on individual case. Advance permission must be obtained from the immigration authorities. Some nationals may be able to enter visa-free.
Note: All nationals must be in possession of a valid passport, documentation for onward travel, sufficient funds to cover their stay and a confirmed accommodation reservation. Advance hotel reservations are required in the absence of a local sponsor.
Application to: US Consulate in plenty of time for prospective visits of more than 30 days (or consular section at US Embassy); see the *USA* section.
Temporary residence: Apply to Immigration Department in Pago Pago.
Passport/Visa Information: American Samoa is an External Territory of the United States of America, and is represented abroad by US Embassies – see the USA section.

Money

Currency: US Dollar (USD; symbol US$) = 100 cents. See the *USA* section for information on denominations, traveller's cheques and exchange rates.
Currency exchange: Exchange facilities are available at the airport and through trade banks. ATMs are located at the banking branches of the Amerika Samoa Bank and the Bank of Hawaii.
Credit & debit cards: American Express is widely accepted whereas MasterCard has more limited use. Check with your credit or debit card company for details of merchant acceptability and other services which may be available.
Traveller's cheques: These are easy to cash, if in US dollars, at most shops and hotels.
Currency restrictions: There are no restrictions on the import and export of local and foreign currencies.
Banking hours: Mon-Fri 0900-1500.

Duty Free

The following items may be imported into American Samoa without incurring customs duty:
200 cigarettes or 50 cigars or 454g of tobacco; one US gallon or five bottles of alcohol; a reasonable amount of perfume.

Public Holidays

Below are listed Public Holidays for the January 2006-June 2007 period.
2006: Jan 1 New Year's Day. **Jan 19** Martin Luther King Day. **Feb 13** Presidents' Day/ Washington's Birthday. **Sep 5** Labour Day. **Oct 10** Columbus Day. **Nov** Thanksgiving Day. **Nov 11** Veterans Day. **Dec 25** Christmas Day.
2007: Jan 1 New Year's Day. **Jan 19** Martin Luther King Day. **Feb 12** Presidents' Day/ Washington's Birthday.

Health

	Special Precautions?	Certificate Required?
Yellow Fever	No	1
Cholera	No	No
Typhoid & Polio	2	N/A
Malaria	No	N/A

Note: *Regulations and requirements may be subject to change at short notice, and you are advised to contact your doctor well in advance of your intended date of departure. Any numbers in the chart refer to the footnotes below.*

1: A yellow fever vaccination certificate is required from travellers over one year of age arriving from - or within six days of transiting - infected areas.
2: Immunisation against typhoid is generally advised.
Food & drink: Mains water is normally chlorinated and, whilst relatively safe, may cause mild abdominal upsets. Bottled water is available and is advised for the first few weeks of the stay. Drinking water outside main cities and towns may be contaminated and sterilisation is advisable. Milk is pasteurised and dairy products are safe for consumption. Local meat, poultry, seafood, fruit and vegetables are generally considered safe to eat.
Other risks: *Hepatitis A* and *B* occur and vaccination is recommended. Outbreaks of *Japanese encephalitis* have been reported, as have epidemics of *dengue fever*.
Health care: There is no reciprocal Health Care Agreement with the UK. Health insurance is strongly recommended for all travellers.

Travel - International

AIR:

The international airline is *Samoa Air (SE)*.
Air passes: The *Polypass* (offered by Polynesian Airlines) allows the holder to fly between the southern Pacific destinations of American Samoa, Fiji, Niue, Samoa, Tahiti and Tonga; Honolulu (Hawaii), Las Vegas, Los Angeles, Oakland, San Francisco, Santa Ana and Seattle in the USA; Adelaide, Brisbane, Canberra, Melbourne and Sydney in Australia; and Auckland, Christchurch and Wellington in New Zealand. The pass is valid for one year. Once a reservation has been made and travel begun, all travel must be completed within a maximum of 45 days. Tickets will be issued against the Polypass by any Polynesian Airlines office (a valid passport is also required). For further information, contact Polynesian Airlines (website: www.polynesianairlines.com).
Approximate flight times: From Pago Pago to *London* is 25 hours, depending on route taken and stopover times. A typical journey would probably involve stopovers in Los Angeles and Honolulu.
Main airports: *Pago Pago (PPG)* is 12km (8 miles) from the city. *To/from the airport:* Buses and taxis are available. Regular scheduled trips are available plus charters and sightseeing. *Facilities:* Duty free shops and a restaurant.
Departure tax: None.
SEA:

Main port: The international port is *Pago Pago (Tuituila)*, which is served by a number of passenger/cruise and cargo lines. Cruise lines include *Orient Line* and *P&O*.

Travel - Internal

AIR:

Samoa Air operates daily scheduled flights to Apia, Maota, Ofu, Olosega and Ta'u carrying up to 18 passengers.
SEA:

Main port: *Pago Pago (Tuituila)*. There is a weekly ferry service from Pago Pago to the Manu'a Islands. A Government-run excursion boat sails regularly around Tutuila, calling at the north coast villages of Afono, Vatia and Fagasa. Contact the local authorities for details.
ROAD:

There are 150km (93 miles) of paved roads and 200km (125 miles) of unpaved or secondary roads throughout the islands. Traffic drives on the right. **Bus:** A local service operates between the airport and the centre of Pago Pago. The *Aiga* bus operates an inexpensive but unscheduled service between Fagatogo and outlying villages. These buses are quaint and are often an 'experience' in themselves, usually lively and decked out in stereo or video systems. **Taxi:** Plentiful; the Government-fixed fares are displayed in all taxis. **Car hire:** Available; local companies impose a minimum age of 21 for drivers. **Documentation:** An International Driving Permit or valid national driving licence will be accepted.

Travel Advice

Most visits to American Samoa are trouble-free but you should be aware of the global risk of indiscriminate international terrorist attacks, which could be against civilian targets, including places frequented by foreigners. This advice is based on information provided by the Foreign and Commonwealth Office in the UK. It is correct at time of publishing. As the situation can change rapidly, visitors are advised to contact the following organisations for the latest travel advice:

British Foreign and Commonwealth Office
Tel: (0845) 850 2829.
Website: www.fco.gov.uk

US Department of State
Website: http://travel.state.gov/travel

Accommodation

HOTELS:

Wide range of motel and hotel accommodation, from international-standard hotels to simple guest houses.
BED & BREAKFAST:
Fale, Fala ma Ti ('Samoan home'). The Office of Tourism will help to make arrangements for visitors who wish to stay in a Samoan household. This will be of particular interest to those who wish to learn more of Samoan customs (see *Top Things To See & Do*).

Top Things To See & Do

• The harbour of **Pago Pago**, made famous by Somerset Maugham's short story, *Rain*, is actually the crater of an extinct volcano.
• The two coral atolls and five volcanic islands that make up American Samoa get twice as much rain as nearby Samoa, which makes American Samoa a lot greener. A number of marked trails lead into the lush interior of the islands, notably to the **National Park of American Samoa**. The visitor centre for the national park is situated in the **Pago Plaza** and the park itself is spread across three islands: **Ofu**, **Ta'u** and **Tutuila**. Of the park's total area of 10,500 acres, about 8000 consist of rainforest. Guided trips to the volcanoes are also possible.
• **Ta'u Island** is considered the birthplace of the Polynesian people and is therefore recognised as a sacred site. **Upolu** in neighbouring Samoa is sometimes visible.
• **Tula Village** is a traditional Samoan settlement. Situated at the far end of the eastern district of Tutuila, it overlooks a coastline of white sandy beaches and reefs that are exposed at low tide.
• **Amanave Village** is in an area renowned for the rugged beauty of its volcanic coastline.
• On the north coast of the island is the **Forbidden Bay**, claimed to be one of the most beautiful in the South Pacific. It can be reached from Fagasa on a trek or a boat trip. The traditional 'turtle and shark' legend is performed in Vaitogi. Mountain excursions are available at nearby **Aoloau**.
• American Samoa has many white sandy beaches offering safe **swimming**, with excellent facilities for **diving**, **snorkelling** and **kayaking**. The **Fagatele Bay National Marine Sanctuary** was established to protect the corals reefs and marine life in the area. Diving equipment can be hired easily and a number of companies provide dive courses and cruises to the best sites. Cruises to neighbouring Samoa are also available, and these can include an overnight stay in a local *Fale* (Samoan home). Surfing can be done at **Alofay Bay**, **Carter Beach** and **Leone Bay**. The surrounding waters offer **game-fishing** for marlin, yellowfin tuna, wahoo and skip jack. Fully-equipped fishing boats can be hired through hotels or tour operators.
• Food and entertainment go hand in hand at the Samoan feast, **fia fia**, where suckling pig, chicken and fish, breadfruit, coconuts and mango are served during performances of traditional dancing.

Entertainment

FOOD & DRINK: Restaurants offer a variety of cuisines, including American, Chinese, Japanese, Italian and Polynesian. There are also various drive-in restaurants.
National specialities:
• The Samoan feast, *fia fia*, consists of suckling pig, chicken, fish, *palusami* (coconut cream wrapped in taro leaves and cooked in the *umu*, or pit oven), breadfruit, coconut, bananas, lime and mango.
National drinks:
• The national drink is *kava*, which is drunk in sacred ceremonies. If you become intimate with Samoans, you may be invited to a genuine *kava* ceremony. If you attend a genuine *kava* ceremony, do not sip until you tip a little *kava* from its coconut shell cup onto the ground immediately in front of you while saying *manuia* (mah-noo-ee-ah), meaning good luck. Do not drain your cup. Leave a little and tip it out before handing the cup back to the server. Remember that drinking *kava* is a solemn, sacred ceremony and should never be confused with a casual round of drinks in Western society. The taste may take a while to acquire. Most places have a 'happy hour' serving cheaper drinks (1630-1830).
Tipping: Not customary.
NIGHTLIFE: There are many nightspots with music and dancing. Samoan *fia fias* – feasting and traditional dancing – are organised regularly by several establishments. Samoan village *fia fias* can be arranged through local tour operators. Visitors are usually welcome at any event in the villages and churches.
SHOPPING: Special purchases include handmade *tapa* cloth, the *puletasi* (women's dress) or *lavalava* (men's costume) made by local dressmakers, shell beads and purses, woodcarvings, woven *laufala* table and floor mats, carved kava bowls, Samoan records and duty free goods.
Shopping hours: Mon-Fri 0800-1700 and Sat 0800-1300.

Business

• **GDP:** Not available.
• **Main exports:** Tuna, fruit and vegetables.
• **Main imports:** Materials for canneries, food and petroleum products.
• **Main trade partners:** Exports to: Samoa, Australia, Japan, New Zealand and Canada; Imports from: Japan, New Zealand, Germany and Australia.

ECONOMY: The economy is based mainly on agriculture and fishing, with two tuna canneries providing employment for almost half the workforce; their output accounts for most of American Samoa's export revenue. Agricultural output is mainly for domestic consumption; a small surplus of fruit and vegetables is exported. Industrial estates have been built in an effort to encourage light industrial development. On these estates, consumer goods, such as handicrafts, soap and perfume, are produced. The tourist industry is growing slowly; Government employment accounts for the bulk of the country's service sector. The Government's economic priorities have been to tackle the lack of infrastructure. Shortage of skilled workers and this lack of infrastructure have combined, along with its remote location, to inhibit American Samoa's economic development. American Samoa is a member of the South Pacific Commission.
BUSINESS ETIQUETTE: Lightweight or tropical suits for business visits. Ties need only be worn for formal occasions.

A B C D E F G H I J K L M N O P Q R S T U V W X Y Z

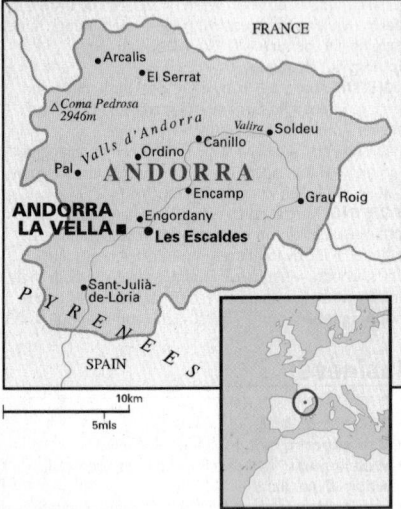

Location: Western Europe, border of France and Spain.

Time: GMT + 1 (GMT + 2 from last Sunday in March to last Sunday in October).

Overview

Almost hidden on the border between France and Spain, the tiny Principality of Andorra is a land of narrow valleys and mountainous landscapes situated in the eastern Pyrenees, bordered by France and Spain. The country is traversed by a main road which runs roughly north-east to south-west, along which most of the settlements are to be found. Many of these are villages or hamlets with Romanesque churches and houses built in the local style; others, off the main road, are even more unspoilt, and provide spectacular views across the rugged countryside.

Andorra is one of the oldest nations in Europe, originally established by Charlemagne as a buffer state against the Iberian muslims. As a result of the *Paretages* of 1278 and 1288, control of the country was split between the Spanish Bishop of Urgell and a nominee appointed by the King of France (initially the Count de Foix) and subsequently by the French emperors and presidents. The country was therefore a co-Principality, with two Heads of State jointly sharing power – the readiness of both sides to compromise allowed this unique arrangement to last intact until the late 20th century. Although the inhabitants of Andorra were not consulted, they were prepared to accept a deal that guaranteed their security and national integrity. With the exception of a brief period during the Napoleonic Wars, Andorra has retained its Independence ever since. The present Andorran constitution, introduced in 1993, formally enshrined Andorra as a Principality.

Today, the mainstay of Andorra's economy is tourism, which accounts for roughly 80 per cent of the Principality's GDP. An estimated 10 million people visit each year, drawn by the winter sports, summer climate and duty free goods. The banking sector also enjoys a tax-haven status.

General Information

AREA: 467.76 sq km (180.6 sq miles).
POPULATION: 67,159 (official estimate 2002).
POPULATION DENSITY: 143.6 per sq km.
CAPITAL: Andorra la Vella. **Population:** 20,724 (2002).
GEOGRAPHY: Andorra is situated in the eastern Pyrenees, bordered by France to the north and east and Spain to the south and west. It is roughly halfway between Barcelona and Toulouse. The landscape consists of gorges and narrow valleys surrounded by mountains. Much of the landscape is forested, but there are several areas of rich pastureland in the valleys. There are four rivers and several mountain lakes. Ski resorts and the spa town of Les Escaldes are Andorra's main attractions.
GOVERNMENT: Principality under the suzerainty of the President of France and the Spanish Bishop of Urgel. **Heads of State:** Co-Princes Joan Enric Vives i Sicilia (Bishop of la Seu d'Urgell) since 2003 and Jacques Chirac (President of France) since 1994. **Head of Government:** Albert Pintat since 2005. **Recent history:** The present Andorran constitution, introduced in 1993, formally enshrined Andorra as a Principality. Administration is in the hands of a General Council with 28 members, four from each of the seven parishes, elected by universal suffrage. The Council elects a President and a Vice-President. Domestic politics are dominated by two parties – the *Uniò Liberal* (UL) and the *Agrupament Nacional Democràtic* (AND). Following a comprehensive victory in the February 1997 poll, at which the UL took 18 of the 28 seats on the *Conseil Général*, a UL Government took office under the leadership of Marc Forné Molné. Four years later, in 2001, the electorate returned the Molné Government for a second term, again with an absolute majority. However, in 2005, Albert Pintat of the Liberal Party became Prime Minister, although not with an absolute majority. Molné lost his seat in the 2005 election but, in any case, was barred by the constitution from standing for a new term.
LANGUAGE: The official language is Catalan. Spanish and French are also spoken.
RELIGION: Roman Catholic.
ELECTRICITY: Sockets: 230 volts AC, 50Hz. Lighting: 125 volts AC.
SOCIAL CONVENTIONS: Normal social courtesies should be extended when visiting someone's home. Handshaking is the accepted form of greeting. Dress is informal and smoking is very common; customs are similar to those of Spain.

Climate

Temperate climate with warm summers and cold winters. Rain falls throughout the year.
Required clothing: Lightweights for the summer and warm mediumweights during winter. Waterproofing is advisable throughout the year.

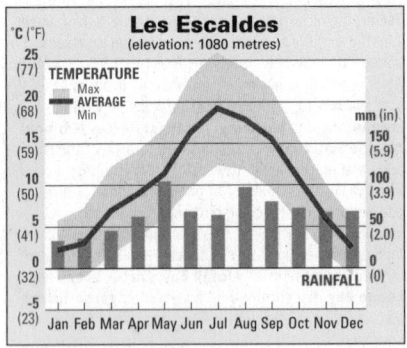

Communications

Telephone: Telephone: Full IDD is available. Country code: 376.
Mobile telephone: Roaming agreements exist with most international mobile companies. Coverage is good.
Internet: Internet cafes available throughout Andorra.
Post: Internal mail services are free; international mail takes about one week within Europe. Post office hours: 0900-1300 and 1500-1700 in Andorra la Vella, otherwise variable.
MEDIA: The Andorran media scene has been partly shaped by the country's proximity to France and Spain. Andorrans have access to broadcasts from both countries, and for many years Andorra was home to Sud Radio, a powerful radio station broadcasting to southwest France. The constitution provides for freedom of speech and of the press.
Press: Andorra has two daily newspapers, the *Diari d'Andorra* and *El Periodic*.
TV: *TVA* is operated by Radio i Televisio d'Andorra.
Radio: Nacional d'Andorra operates *Radio Andorra* and music station *Andorra Musica*; *Radio Valira* and *Andorra 1* are commercial stations.

Passport/Visa

	Passport Required?	Visa Required?	Return Ticket Required?
Full British	Yes	No/2	No
Australian	Yes	No/2	Yes
Canadian	Yes	No/2	Yes
USA	Yes	No/2	Yes
Other EU	Yes/1	No/2	No
Japanese	Yes	No/2	Yes

Note: *Regulations and requirements may be subject to change at short notice, and you are advised to contact the appropriate diplomatic or consular authority before finalising travel arrangements. Any numbers in the chart refer to the footnotes below.*

PASSPORTS: Valid passport required by all except:
1. nationals of France and Spain, providing they hold a valid national ID card.
VISAS: 2. There are no visa requirements for entry into Andorra; however, the relevant regulations for France or Spain should be followed, depending on which country is transited to reach Andorra. Visitors wishing to have their passport stamped with the Andorran coat of arms should apply to the Sindicat d'Initiativa in the capital.
Validity: Stays of up to three months are allowed without a visa.
Temporary residence: Apply in person at the Immigration Office, Carrer de les Boigues-Escaldes-Engordany.

PASSPORT/VISA INFORMATION

Embassy of the Principality of Andorra in the UK
63 Westover Road, London SW18 2RF, UK
Tel: (020) 8874 4806.
Website: www.andorra.ad
Opening hours: Mon-Sat 0900-1700 (by appointment only).
This office also provides tourist information.

Permanent Mission of the Principality of Andorra to the United Nations in the USA
2 United Nations Plaza, 25th Floor, New York, NY 10017, USA
Tel: (212) 750 8064.
Website: www.andorra.ad

Money

Currency: Although most currencies are accepted, the main currency in circulation is the Euro. See the *France* or *Spain* section for further details of exchange rates.
Single European currency (Euro): The Euro is now the official currency of 12 EU member states (including France and Spain). The first Euro coins and notes were introduced in January 2002 and completely replaced the French Franc on 17 February 2002, and the Spanish Peseta on 28 February 2002. Euro (€) = 100 cents. Notes are in denominations of €500, 200, 100, 50, 20, 10 and 5. Coins are in denominations of €2, 1 and 50, 20, 10, 5, 2 and 1 cents.
Currency exchange: Andorran banks and bureaux de change will exchange foreign currency.
Credit & debit cards: American Express, Diners Club, MasterCard and Visa are accepted, as well as Eurocheque cards. Check with your credit or debit card company for details of merchant acceptability and other services which may be available.
Traveller's cheques: To avoid additional exchange rate charges, travellers are advised to take traveller's cheques in Euros, Pounds Sterling and US Dollars.
Currency restrictions: There are no restrictions when entering or exiting the country, but French and Spanish authorities may carry out formalities on departure.
Banking hours: Mon-Fri 0900-1300 and 1500-1700, Sat 0900-1200.
Exchange rates:
Rate at time of publishing
£1.00	€1.46
$1.00	€0.82

Duty Free

Andorra is a duty free zone, but travellers should check French/Spanish regulations as both these countries maintain customs control at the borders.
Prohibited/restricted items: Narcotics, firearms, ammunition, explosives (including fireworks), flick knives, pornography, horror comics, radio transmitters, certain foodstuffs, plants, flowers, animals and birds and items made from endangered species. No works of art can be exported without permission.

Public Holidays

Below are listed Public Holidays for the January 2006-June 2007 period.

2006: Jan 1 New Year's Day. **Jan 6** Epiphany. **Mar 14** Constitution Day. **Apr 14-16** Good Friday to Easter Monday. **May 1** Labour Day. **May 25** Ascension. **Jun 5** Whit Monday. **Jun 24** St John's Day. **Aug 15** Assumption of the Blessed Virgin. **Sep 8** National Day. **Nov 1** All Saints' Day. **Nov 4** St Charles' Day. **Dec 8** Immaculate Conception. **Dec 24** Christmas Eve. **Dec 25-26** Christmas. **Dec 31** New Year's Eve.

2007: Jan 1 New Year's Day. **Jan 6** Epiphany. **Mar 14** Constitution Day. **Apr 6-9** Good Friday to Easter Monday. **May 1** Labour Day. **May 17** Ascension. **May 28** Whit Monday. **Jun 24** St John's Day.

Note: In July, August and September, parishes have their own public holidays, during which festivals are held.

Health

	Special Precautions?	Certificate Required?
Yellow Fever	No	No
Cholera	No	No
Typhoid & Polio	No	N/A
Malaria	No	N/A

Note: *Regulations and requirements may be subject to change at short notice, and you are advised to contact your doctor well in advance of your intended date of departure. Any numbers in the chart refer to the footnotes below.*

Other risks: Visitors should check their *tetanus* immunisation is up to date.

Rabies is present. For those at high risk, vaccination before arrival should be considered. If you are bitten, seek medical help without delay. For more information, consult the *Health* appendix.

Health care: For UK citizens, most health costs are covered by reciprocal health agreements but additional insurance is advised. Visitors should note that as entry to Andorra is usually through France or Spain, the health regulations of these countries should be complied with.

Travel - International

AIR:

Andorra does not have an international airport. **Closest international airports:** *Barcelona (BCN)* in Spain, 225km (140 miles) from Andorra and *Toulouse (TLS)*, in France, 180km (112 miles) from Andorra. For more information on the airports and their facilities, consult the *Spain* and *France* sections. *To/from the airport*: Shared taxis and buses are available.

RAIL:

Routes from Perpignan, Villefranche, Toulouse and Barcelona go to *La Tour de Carol*, 20km (12 miles) from Andorra. The nearest station is *L'Hospitalet*, but buses run from both L'Hospitalet and La Tour de Carol (see *Road* below). Routes from Madrid (Spain) go to *Lleida* and then a connection by coach leads to *La Seu d'Urgell*. Routes from Barcelona (Spain) go to *Puig Cerda* and then a connection by coach leads to *La Seu d'Urgell*.

ROAD:

Mountainous roads exist over the Envalira pass from Perpignan, Tarbes and Toulouse (France); and southwards to Barcelona and Lérida (Spain). Buses run regularly from Barcelona, Tarragona, Valencia and Madrid (Spain); and Toulouse (France). Taxis may also be taken and sharing is common practice to cut costs. **Bus:** The journey from La Tour de Carol takes two hours 20 minutes. From L'Hospitalet the service takes two hours 40 minutes and runs early enough to permit a day-return trip from France. A seasonal service runs from Aix-les-Thermes and services may be available from Seo de Urgel in Spain. *Eurolines*, departing from Victoria Coach Station in London, serves destinations in Andorra. For further information, contact *Eurolines* (tel: (08705) 143 219; website: www.nationalexpress.com/eurolines). Three daily services from Toulousse, five daily from Lleida (Spain) and 15 from Madrid are available for **coach** trips to Andorra.

Travel - Internal

ROAD:

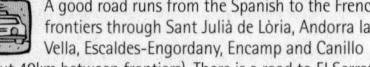

A good road runs from the Spanish to the French frontiers through Sant Julià de Lòria, Andorra la Vella, Escaldes-Engordany, Encamp and Canillo (about 40km between frontiers). There is a road to El Serrat, and a secondary road from Ordino to Canillo, which is usually closed in winter. **Bus:** There are buses and minibuses linking Andorra's villages on the 186km (115 miles) of road. Traffic drives on the right. **Documentation:** National driving licence accepted.

Travel Advice

Most visits to Andorra are trouble-free but you should be aware of the global risk of indiscriminate international terrorist attacks, which could be against civilian targets, including places frequented by foreigners.

This advice is based on information provided by the Foreign and Commonwealth Office in the UK. It is correct at time of publishing. As the situation can change rapidly, visitors are advised to contact the following organisations for the latest travel advice:

British Foreign and Commonwealth Office
Tel: (0845) 850 2829.
Website: www.fco.gov.uk

US Department of State
Website: http://travel.state.gov/travel

Accommodation

HOTELS:

There are hundreds of hotels and guest houses, principally catering for the summer months and ski season, although some stay open all year round. Rooms during the summer months (July to August) should be booked well in advance. Hotels and restaurants are registered with the Tourist Office (*Sindicat d'Initiativa*) and are bound to keep to the registered prices and services. Information on hotels can be obtained from the Andorran Hotel Association (*Unió Hotelera d'Andorra*), Antic Carrer Major, 18 Andorra la Vella (tel: 820 602 *or* 625; website: www.turismeandorra.com).

CAMPING:

There are 13 campsites in Andorra, most of which are close to the main towns and are well signposted. Several have shops and other facilities. There are also facilities for caravans.

EDITOR'S CHOICE: MOUNTAIN REFUGES

Mountain refuges offer cheap and basic accommodation; normally they will have one room available for visitors, and may or may not have a hearth and bunk beds. Enquire locally about locations and prices.

Top Things To See & Do

- **Andorra la Vella**, the country's capital, lies at the junction of two mountain streams. Sights there include a fine 12th-century church and the **Casa de la Vall**, the ancient seat of Government.
- Adjoining the capital is the spa town of **Escaldes-Engordany**, which also has examples of Romanesque architecture. These towns are also the centre of the colourful Andorran local **festival** in early September, in honour of the Virgin of Meritxell. Approximately 18km (11 miles) from Escaldes-Engordany, off the main road, is the hamlet of **El Serrat**, which commands a breathtaking view across the mountains. The town of **Encamp**, between the capital and the French frontier, is also worth a visit.
- There are several **ski resorts** in Andorra, most of which offer good facilities. A bus service picks up skiers from hotels and inns, and takes them to the slopes, returning in the evening. The main centre is **Soldeu**, the first major settlement on the road after the French frontier at Port d'Envalira. Both nursery slopes and skiing for intermediates are available, with a good ski school offering tuition at reasonable prices. There are also ski centres at **Pas de la Casa-Grau Roig**, on the French frontier, and at **Ordino-Arcalis** and **Arinsal-Pal**, all north of Andorra la Vella. Cross-country skiing is available in the resort of **La Rabassa**. Further information can be obtained from Ski Andorra, Edifici les columnes, despatx 14, Andorra la Vella (tel: 805 200; website: www.skiandorra.ad). The Tourist Office (see *Tourist Information*) can provide details on prices and snow conditions.
- Other available activities include **horse riding**, **cycling**, **tennis**, **swimming**, **trout fishing**, **clay-pigeon shooting**, **hiking** and **rock climbing**. **Football**, **rugby**, **basketball**, **motorbike** and **car rallies** are the most popular spectator sports. Examples of high-level sports amenities include the **Gerradells** swimming pool and **Comú Stadium** (Andorra La Vella), the shooting range at **La Rabassa** (at Sant Juliá de Lória) and the **Ice Palace** (Canillo).

TOURIST INFORMATION

Sindicat d'Iniciativa Oficina de Turisme (Tourist Office)
Carrer Dr Vilanova, Andorra la Vella, Andorra
Tel: 820 214.
E-mail: sindicatdiniciativa@andorra.ad

Entertainment

FOOD & DRINK: Cuisine is mainly Catalan, and generally expensive. Quality and prices in restaurants are similar to those in small French and Spanish resort towns.

Things to know:
Alcoholic drinks bought in shops and supermarkets are cheap (Andorra is a duty free zone), but prices in bars can be high. They do, however, stay open late.

National specialities:
- *Coques* (flavoured flat cakes).
- *Trinxat* (a potato and cabbage dish).
- *Truites de carreroles* (a type of mushroom omelette).
- Local sausages and cheese.
- A variety of pork and ham dishes.

Tipping: Service charges are usually included in the bill. Porters and waiters expect a further 10 per cent.

NIGHTLIFE: Andorra's many bars and hotels provide a variety of evening entertainment. Clubs are open during both summer and winter.

SHOPPING: There is duty free shopping for all goods. Petrol, alcohol, cameras and watches can be purchased at low prices. Electrical goods are very good value. **Shopping hours:** Mon-Sat 0930-1330 and 1600-2000, Sun 0930-1330 and 1600-1900. Department stores, Mon-Fri 0930-2000; Sat 0930-2100; Sun 0930-1900.

Business

- **GDP:** US$1.3 billion (2003).
- **Main exports:** Tobacco, furniture and leather goods.
- **Main imports:** Electricity, fuels, food and consumer goods.
- **Main trade partners:** France and Spain.

ECONOMY: Andorra's status as a low tax and duty free zone has led to the development of a major trade in consumer goods. This trade, along with tourism and, more recently, financial services, are now the major components of the Andorran economy. There is a small but thriving agricultural sector farming potatoes, tobacco and livestock. There is also a small mining industry exploiting deposits of lead, iron and alum. The country's hydroelectric power plant supplies about a quarter of domestic needs; Andorra is dependent on imports of electricity and other fuels from France and Spain. Andorra's main trading partners are neighbouring France and Spain. In 1997, the country opened negotiations to join the World Trade Organization. In June 2000, Andorra was identified by the Organization for Economic Cooperation and Development (OECD) – the world's 30 largest economies – as one of 35 'tax havens' whose financial laws are believed to encourage large-scale tax evasion and money-laundering. By March 2002, all but seven of the 35 had introduced measures to meet the OECD demands – Andorra was one of the seven and could now be subject to economic and financial sanctions.

BUSINESS ETIQUETTE: Suits are recommended at all times with white shirt and black shoes. Prior appointments are necessary and meetings tend to be formal. Punctuality is important. Lunch is usually after 1330 and can extend through the afternoon. Although English is quite widely spoken, a knowledge of Spanish/Catalan or French is very useful. **Office hours:** Mon-Fri 0800-1700. Some offices open Mon-Fri 0800-1500 (summer only).

COMMERCIAL INFORMATION

Chamber of Commerce, Industry and Services
c/ Prat de la Creu, 8, Andorra la Vella - CP: AD500, Andorra
Tel: 809 292.
Website: www.ccis.ad

Centre de Congressos i Exposicions (Information on Conferences/Conventions)
Plaça Poble, Andorra la Vella, Andorra
Tel: 861 131.

Angola

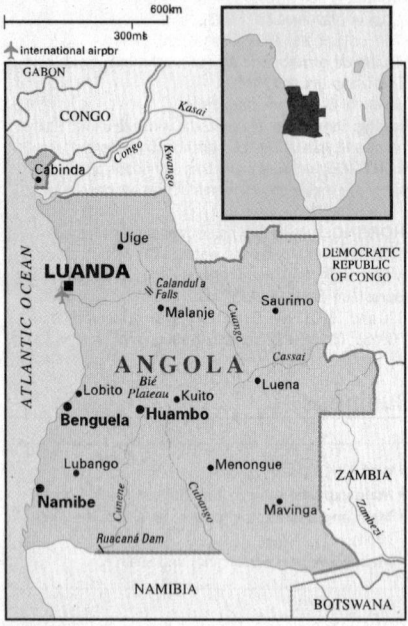

Location: Southwest Africa.

Time: GMT + 1.

Overview

The first Portuguese explorers reached Angola in the 15th century. Opposition to the Portuguese presence was relatively muted until the 1950s – when it did emerge, however, the divisions between the liberation movements laid the foundations for the civil war, which has consumed Angola for most of the past four decades. Although decolonisation was put into effect in November 1975, cold-war politics contributed to this becoming Africa's longest civil war, with an estimated cost of 500,000 lives. Both sides exploited their control of parts of Angola's vast natural resources – oil, in the case of the Government, and diamond mines, in the case of UNITA – to finance their campaigns. The Government side, wearied by the years of fighting, drifted under the leadership of ailing president Dos Santos into inertia and corruption. The biggest losers,

inevitably, were the people of Angola, most of whom were reduced to subsistence agriculture or a marginal urban existence.

A ceasefire was finally achieved in 2002, paving the way for a final political settlement and the people and Government of Angola celebrated their first year of continuous peace for more than a quarter of a century, in April 2003. Although there is still some sporadic fighting, notably between Government forces and separatist groups in the oil-rich Cabinda enclave, most of the country has now embarked upon the monumental task of reconstruction.

However, unless on essential business, it is still not advised to travel to Angola and visitors should contact their local Government travel advice department. It is advised that visitors travel under the auspices of a sponsoring organisation, especially those journeying beyond Luanda. Even those solely visiting Luanda should be aware that Luanda suffers from a high level of street crime. A large proportion of the civil population is armed. Foreign travellers are still advised not to visit the Uige Province (due to an outbreak of the highly contagious Marburg virus), North and South Lunda Provinces (there has been police activity to expel illegal diamond miners) and the interior of the Cabinda Province (there has been an active separatist movement).

General Information

AREA: 1,246,700 sq km (481,354 sq miles).
POPULATION: 14 million (estimate 2003).
POPULATION DENSITY: 11.22 per sq km.
CAPITAL: Luanda. **Population:** 4,000,000 (estimate 2003).
GEOGRAPHY: Angola is bordered by the Democratic Republic of Congo to the north, Zambia to the east, Namibia to the south and the Atlantic Ocean to the west. Mountains rise from the coast, levelling to a plateau which makes up most of the country. The country is increasingly arid towards the south; the far south is on the edge of the Namib Desert. The northern plateau is thickly vegetated. Cabinda is a small enclave to the north of Angola proper, surrounded by the territories of the Democratic Republic of Congo and the Congo. The discovery of large oil deposits off the coast of the enclave has led to it becoming the centre of Angola's foreign business interests. The oil industry is based primarily at Malongo.
GOVERNMENT: Republic. Gained Independence from Portugal in 1975. **Head of State:** President José Eduardo dos Santos since 1979. **Head of Government:** Prime Minister Fernando Dias dos Santos since 2002. **Recent history:** Opposition to the Portuguese, who colonised Angola in the 15th Century, was relatively muted until the 1950s; when it did emerge, however, the divisions between the liberation movements laid the foundations for the civil war, which has consumed Angola for most of the past four decades. In 1976, the *Marxist Popular Movement for the Liberation of Angola* (*MPLA*) formally achieved victory, although it never fully defeated the *National Union for the Total Independence of Angola*, which, with South African support and the dominating leadership of Jonas Savimbi, sustained a continuous and effective guerrilla war in the south and centre of the country. Cold war politics contributed to this becoming Africa's longest civil war, with an estimated cost of 500,000 lives.

But in February 2002, Savimbi was killed during a clash with the Angolan army. Within weeks of his death, military leaders on both sides had signed a ceasefire, paving the way for a final political settlement. This was achieved within weeks and the people and Government of Angola celebrated their first year of continuous peace for more than a quarter of a century in April 2003. Although there is still some sporadic fighting, notably between Government forces and separatist groups in the oil-rich Cabinda enclave, most of the country has now embarked upon the monumental task of reconstruction.

The next Parliamentary elections are scheduled for September 2006, possibly with Presidential elections the following year. In preparation, a package of electoral laws was approved in April 2005, although a new constitution, already six years under debate, has not yet been finalised. It is possible that local Government elections, the first ever, might take place in 2007, although no final decision has been taken.
LANGUAGE: The official language is Portuguese. African languages (Umbundu, Kimbundu, Kikongo and Chokwe being the most common) are spoken by the majority of the population.
RELIGION: Mainly Roman Catholic (51 per cent). There are also other Christian minorities. Local animist beliefs are held by a significant minority.
ELECTRICITY: 220 volts AC, 60Hz. Plugs are of the European-style round two-pin type.
SOCIAL CONVENTIONS: Normal social courtesies should be observed. Drug trafficking or carrying incurs severe penalties. Homosexuality is illegal. **Photography:** It is inadvisable to photograph public places, public buildings or public events. Copies of photography permits should be deposited with the British Embassy; permits should be carried at all times.

Climate

The north of the country is hot and wet during the summer months (November to April); winters are slightly cooler and mainly dry. The south is hot throughout much of the year with a slight decrease in temperature in winter (May to October).
Required clothing: Lightweight cottons and linens throughout the year in the south. Tropical clothing for summers in the north. Nights can be cold, so warm clothing should be taken. Waterproofing is advisable for the rainy season throughout the country.

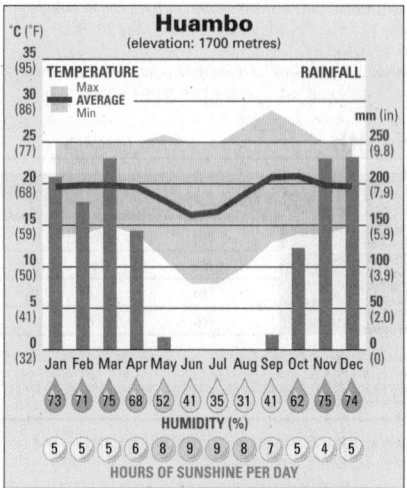

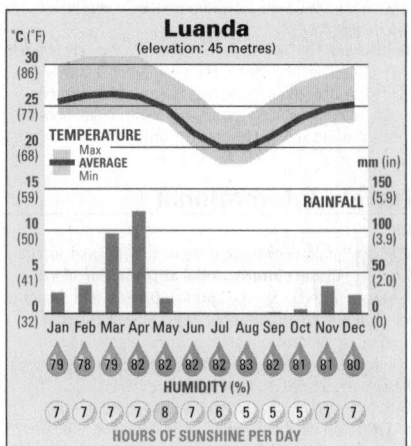

Communications

Telephone: Country code: 244. Until recently, all international calls had to be made through the operator, booking in advance. Direct calls to Luanda (although not to the rest of the country) are increasingly available.
Mobile telephone: Coverage limited to Luanda and the surrounding area.
Internet: There are a few Internet cafes in Luanda.
Post: Airmail between Europe and Angola takes five to 10 days. Surface mail between Europe and Angola takes at least two months. There is a fairly reliable internal service. Most correspondence is by telex.
MEDIA: Government-controlled media are predominant. Angola's only daily newspaper, *Jornal de Angola*, and the terrestrial TV service, *TPA*, are state-owned and carry little criticism of the Government.
Private radio stations operate in the main cities but the state maintains a monopoly in radio broadcasting across much of the country. The constitution provides for freedom of expression but the Government does not always respect this and the few private media outlets are liable to harassment. Pay-TV services are operated by *Multichoice Angola*, and include Brazilian and Portuguese channels.
Press: Newspapers include national daily, Government controlled *Jornal de Angola*, weekly *Angolense*, Luanda-based private weekly *Folha 8*, private weeklies *A Capital*, *Actual* and *Agora*. There are no English-language newspapers.
TV: *Televisao Popular de Angola* (TPA) operates two state-run channels.
Radio: State-run *Radio Nacional de Angola (RNA)* operates *Canal A*, *Radio 5*, *Radio Ngola Yetu*, *Radio FM Stereo* and *Radio Luanda*; *Radio Ecclesia* is a Roman Catholic FM station; *Luanda-Antena Comercial and Radio Morena* (Benguela-based) are private stations.

Passport/Visa

	Passport Required?	Visa Required?	Return Ticket Required?
Full British	Yes	Yes	Yes
Australian	Yes	Yes	Yes
Canadian	Yes	Yes	Yes
USA	Yes	Yes	Yes
Other EU	Yes	Yes	Yes
Japanese	Yes	Yes	Yes

Note: *Regulations and requirements may be subject to change at short notice, and you are advised to contact the appropriate diplomatic or consular authority before finalising travel arrangements. Any numbers in the chart refer to the footnotes below.*

PASSPORTS: Passport valid for at least six months after intended period of stay required by all.

VISAS: Required by all, except:
(a) nationals of the Cape Verde Islands;
(b) transit passengers continuing their journey to a third country by the same or first connecting aircraft without leaving the airport.

Types of visa and cost: *Ordinary, Business* and *Transit*: £40 (single-entry); £80 (double-entry). *Express visa:* £110 (to process visas within two to three days).

Validity: Valid usually for 60 days from date of issue. Permitted length of stay is usually for a maximum of 30 days, but depends on application.

Application to: Consulate (or Consular section at Embassy); see *Passport/Visa Information.*

Application requirements: (a) Valid passport with two blank pages. (b) One application form. (c) Two passport-size photos with applicant's name on back. *Ordinary*: (a)-(c) and, (d) Return ticket. (e) Letter from employer. (f) Recent bank statement. (g) Personal invitation letter from Angola (if sent by an Angolan citizen, must include an authenticated photocopy of their identity card; if sent by a non-Angolan citizen, must include a photocopy of their passport and work/residence visa or residence card). *Business*: (a)-(c) and, (d) Photocopy of the company's Commercial Licence. (e) Photocopy of the company's most recent Industrial Tax receipt. (f) Photocopy of the company's registration. (g) Itinerary (airline or travel agent). *Transit*: (a)-(c) and, (d) Letter from the company *or* return ticket *or* itinerary.

Working days required: Up to 15 for all visa applications, although some visas may take more than one month. There is an express visa service (see above).

Temporary residence: Applications should be made to the Immigration Office in Angola.

PASSPORT/VISA INFORMATION

Embassy of the Republic of Angola in the UK
22 Dorset Street, London W1U 6QY, UK
Tel: (020) 7299 9850 *or* 7487 5125 (consular section).
Website: www.angola.org.uk
Opening hours: Mon-Fri 0900-1600; 0930-1300, closed Wed (consular section).

Embassy of the Republic of Angola in the USA
2100-2108 16th Street, NW, Washington, DC 20009, USA
Tel: (202) 785 1156.
Website: www.angola.org

Money

Currency: Kwanza (AOA) = 100 centimos. Notes are in denominations of AOA100, 50, 10 and 5. Coins are in denominations of AOA1, 2, 5, 10, 20, 50, 100 and 50, 20 and 10 centimos.

Note: The Kwanza was devalued by a factor of 1000 in January 2000 (1 new Kwanza = 1000 old Kwanzas). New banknotes have now been introduced.

Currency exchange: Money should be exchanged at official bureaux de change only, which can be found throughout the country, but particularly in Luanda (changing money on the black market is illegal). US Dollars are also widely accepted. Cash withdrawal is not possible.

Credit & debit cards: Credit cards are not generally accepted. American Express, Diners Club and Visa enjoy limited acceptance. Check with your credit or debit card company for details of merchant acceptability and other services which may be available.

Traveller's cheques: Traveller's cheques are accepted.

Currency restrictions: All imported currency should be declared on arrival. The import of local currency is limited to AOA15,000. The import of foreign currency is unlimited, subject to declaration on arrival. The export of local currency is prohibited. The export of foreign currency is limited to US$5000. Those travelling on return tickets purchased in Angola may export up to the equivalent of US$5000 per year.

Banking hours: Mon-Fri 0845-1600.
Exchange rate indicators:
Rate at time of publishing
£1.00= AOA156.99
$1.00= AOA88.98

Duty Free

The following items may be imported into Angola without incurring customs duty:

400 cigarettes or 500g of cigars or other tobacco products; 2 litres of wine and 1 litre of spirits; 250ml of eau de toilette or 50ml of perfume, aftershave or similar; general items for personal use, gifts or souvenirs up to the value of US$500.

Prohibited items: Firearms and ammunition; pornographic materials; plants originating in infected areas; gaming machines; pure alcohol (denatured); animals without corresponding certificates; dangerous medicines or foodstuffs; fiscal or postal stamps or valuables.

Public Holidays

Below are listed Public Holidays for the January 2006-June 2007 period.

2006: Jan 1 New Year's Day. **Jan 4** Martyrs of the Colonial Repression Day. **Feb 4** Start of Liberation War. **Mar 8** International Women's Day. **Apr 4** Peace and Reconciliation Day. **Apr 14** Good Friday. **Apr 17** Easter Monday. **May 1** Labour Day. **May 25** Africa Day. **Jun 1** International Children's Day. **Sep 17** Nation's Founder and National Hero's Day. **Nov 1** All Soul's Day. **Nov 11** Independence Day. **Dec 25** Christmas Day.
2007: Jan 1 New Year's Day. **Jan 4** Martyrs of the Colonial Repression Day. **Feb 4** Start of Liberation War. **Mar 8** International Women's Day. **Apr 4** Peace and Reconciliation Day. **Apr 6** Good Friday. **Apr 9** Easter Monday. **May 1** Labour Day. **May 25** Africa Day. **Jun 1** International Children's Day.
Note: Holidays falling on a Saturday or Sunday are observed the following Monday.

Health

	Special Precautions?	Certificate Required?
Yellow Fever	Yes	1
Cholera	Yes	2
Typhoid & Polio	3	N/A
Malaria	4	N/A

Note: *Regulations and requirements may be subject to change at short notice, and you are advised to contact your doctor well in advance of your intended date of departure. Any numbers in the chart refer to the footnotes below.*

1: A yellow fever vaccination certificate is required from travellers over one year of age coming from infected areas. Pregnant women and infants under nine months should not be vaccinated and therefore should avoid exposure to infection. Travellers arriving from non-endemic zones should note that vaccination is strongly recommended for travel outside the urban areas, even if an outbreak of the disease has not been reported and they would normally not require a vaccination certificate to enter the country.
2: Following WHO guidelines issued in 1973, a cholera vaccination certificate is no longer a condition of entry to Angola. However, cholera is a serious risk in this country and precautions are essential. Up-to-date advice should be sought before deciding whether these precautions should include vaccination as medical opinion is divided over its effectiveness. For more information, consult the *Health* appendix.
3: Typhoid fever is widespread; poliomyelitis is endemic.
4: Malaria risk, predominantly in the malignant *falciparum* form, exists all year throughout the country, even in urban areas, and is reported to be resistant to chloroquine and sulfadoxine-pyrimethamine. Mefloquine (MEF), doxycycline or malarone are the recommended prophylaxes.
Food & drink: All water should be regarded as being potentially contaminated. Water used for drinking, brushing teeth or making ice should have first been boiled or otherwise sterilised. Milk is unpasteurised and should be boiled. Powdered or tinned milk is available and is advised, but make sure that it is reconstituted with pure water. Avoid dairy products, which are likely to have been made from unboiled milk. Only eat well-cooked meat and fish, preferably served hot. Pork, salad and mayonnaise may carry increased risk. Vegetables should be cooked and fruit peeled.
Other risks: *Hepatitis A* and *E* are widespread, *hepatitis B* is hyperendemic. Many insect-borne diseases, such as *onchocerciasis* (river blindness) and *trypanosomiasis* (sleeping sickness) exist all year throughout the country, including urban areas. *Bilharzia* (schistosomiasis) is present; avoid swimming and paddling in fresh water. Swimming pools which are well chlorinated and maintained are safe.

Meningitis outbreaks occur. *Dengue fever* epidemics occur sporadically; natural foci of *plague* have been reported. Vaccination is advisable for long-staying visitors, who should also consider *hepatitis B* and *diphtheria* vaccines and check their BCG status.
Rabies is present. For those at high risk, vaccination before arrival should be considered. If you are bitten, seek medical advice without delay. For more information, consult the *Health* appendix.
Health care: Full health insurance is essential and should include medical evacuation insurance. There are some hospital facilities in the main towns but, at the moment, adequate medical facilities are virtually non-existent. However, there are some good private clinics in Luanda. Medical treatment is free although often inadequate, and visitors should travel with their own supply of remedies for simple ailments such as stomach upsets, as pharmaceutical supplies are usually difficult to obtain.

Travel - International

AIR:

Angola's national airline is *TAAG Angola Airlines (DT)*.
Approximate flight times: From *London* to *Luanda* is approximately 12 to 13 hours (including stopover in Brussels, Lisbon or Paris).
Main airports: *Luanda (LAD)* is 4km (2.5 miles) from the city. *To/from the airport:* There are no taxis; visitors must be met by their sponsors or use a transport service provided by their hotel. *Facilities:* Restaurant, bar, post office, currency exchange and 24-hour medical facilities with cholera and yellow fever vaccination available.
Departure tax: None.
SEA:

Main ports: *Lobito, Luanda, Malongo* and *Namibe.*

RAIL/ROAD:

Overland routes to neighbouring countries are generally not open, but conditions are subject to frequent change. Driving outside Luanda is not recommended and can be risky. Travellers should contact an Embassy for advice on security along their planned routes. Plans to re-open the Benguela railway seem unlikely to come to fruition until the country has become more stable.

Travel - Internal

AIR:

TAAG Angola Airlines operates flights within Angola. There are scheduled services between major towns. However, aircraft run by this airline may not be properly maintained, and travellers should aim to use flights run by reputable international organisations. Private jets are operated by some Portuguese, French and Italian business interests (trading most notably in oil and diamonds) in the north of the country, particularly to and from the Cabinda enclave, which is only accessible by air. *Air Gemini* and *Sonair* are recommended. Helicopter access to Cabinda is possible as well. Passengers on internal flights must carry official authorisation (*guia de marcha*).
Approximate flight times: From Luanda to *Benguela* and *Cabinda* is 50 minutes, to *Huambo* is one hour, to *Namibe* is one hour 45 minutes and to *Lubango* is one hour 10 minutes.
RAIL:

Owing to the instability of the political situation, rail services are erratic, and tickets hard to purchase. Trains run on three separate routes inland from Luanda: to Malanje (daily) with short branches to Dondo and Golungo Alto; Lobito to Dilolo (the *Benguela Railway*, daily); and Namibe to Menongue (daily). There are no sleeping cars and no air-conditioned services, though food and drink is available on some journeys. Children under three travel free and children aged three to 11 pay half fare.
ROAD:

Traffic drives on the right. Driving outside of Luanda may be risky. Outside major urban areas, unexploded ordnance proves a risk. There were once nearly 8000km (5000 miles) of tarred roads but much of the infrastructure was destroyed in the conflict after 1975. Many roads are unsuitable for travel at present, and local advice should be sought and followed carefully. It is hard to hire a car: taxis are the best way to travel. Car-jacking is a risk. Identity papers must be carried.
Documentation: An International Driving Permit is recommended (or translation of UK licence), although, in theory, visitors may drive with a UK licence for up to 30 days.
URBAN:
Local buses run in Luanda. A flat fare is charged.

Travel Advice

Travellers are advised against all but essential travel to Uige Province where an outbreak of highly contagious Marburg virus has been confirmed, to North and South Lunda Provinces, where there has been police activity to expel illegal diamond miners, and the interior of Cabinda Province, where there is an active separatist movement. All visitors to Angola, and particularly those going beyond Luanda, are advised to travel under the auspices of a sponsoring organisation.

Leisure travel in Angola is not recommended.

The main risk to visitors to Luanda is from the high level of crime.

Travellers should register with their Embassy on arrival, and de-register on departure.

Travellers should be aware of the global risk of indiscriminate international terrorist attacks, which could be against civilian targets, including places frequented by foreigners.

This advice is based on information provided by the Foreign and Commonwealth Office in the UK. It is correct at time of publishing. As the situation can change rapidly, visitors are advised to contact the following organisations for the latest travel advice:

British Foreign and Commonwealth Office
Tel: (0845) 850 2829.
Website: www.fco.gov.uk

US Department of State
Website: http://travel.state.gov/travel

Accommodation

HOTELS:

Many hotels in Angola have recently undergone refurbishment, and have air conditioning, a private bath or shower, a telephone, radio and TV. However, there is a general shortage of accommodation, and it is advisable to book well in advance (at least one month prior to departure); accommodation cannot be booked at the airport. Visitors should also note that accommodation in Luanda is expensive. Further information can also be obtained from the Ministry of Hotels & Tourism. There is also accommodation in Kissama National Park (see *Top Things To See & Do*).

Top Things To See & Do

- In the capital, **Luanda**, the main places to visit are the fortress (containing the **Museum of Armed Forces**) and the **National Museum of Anthropology.**
- The **Humbi-Humbi art gallery**, located at Largo Rainha Ginga 21, offers cultural delights.
- The **Museum of Slavery**, 25km (16 miles) along the coast from Luanda, offers an insight into the history of slavery.
- Luanda itself is built around a bay and there are bathing beaches (the **Ilha** beaches) five minutes from the centre of the city. Approximately 45km (28 miles) south of Luanda is **Palmeirinhas**, a long, deserted beach. The scenery is magnificent, but bathing here is hazardous. Fishing is possible both here and at **Santiago** beach, 45km (28 miles) north of Luanda. **Watersports** are available on the **Mussolo Peninsula**.
- The **Kissama National Park** lies 70km (45 miles) south of Luanda, and is home to a great variety of wild animals. Accommodation is available in bungalows located in the middle of the park, but visitors must bring their own food. The park is closed during the rainy season.
- The **Calandula Waterfalls**, located in the Malanje area, make an impressive spectacle, particularly at the end of the rainy season.
- **Basketball** remains a firm favourite, with Angola having won the African Basketball title on several occasions, attending the Olympics twice.

TOURIST INFORMATION

Ministry of Hotels and Tourism
Largo 4 de Fevereiro, Palácio de Vidro, CP 1242, Luanda, Angola
Tel: (2) 310 899.
Website: www.angola.org

Entertainment

FOOD & DRINK: There are severe food and drink shortages at present. Tables should be booked well in advance in the few restaurants and hotels. Notice needs to be given for extra guests.

National specialities:
- Palm oil beans.
- *Calulu* (dried fish or dried meat layered with fresh fish or fresh meat, onion, tomatoes, okra and sweet potato leaves).
- *Chicken muamba* (seasoned with palm oil hash).
- *Mufete de Cacuso.*
- *Farofa* (cooked with manioc flour).

Tipping: Where service charge is not added to the bill, 10 per cent is acceptable, although tipping is not officially encouraged. Tipping can be in kind (eg cigarettes).

NIGHTLIFE: There are some nightclubs and cinemas in Luanda. Cinema seats should be booked in advance. *The Lenarius*, a gallery, cafe and ball all-in-one, is situated behind the Ministry of Defence and is open from 1600 until late in the evening.

SHOPPING: Traditional handicrafts are sold in the city; shopping is not easy outside the main cities. **Shopping hours:** These can vary, but are generally Mon-Fri 0900-1700.

Business

- **GDP:** US$17 billion (2005 projected).
- **Main exports:** Crude oil and diamonds.
- **Main imports:** Manufactured equipment and food products.
- **Main trade partners:** Portugal, Brazil, France and USA.

ECONOMY: Angola is rich in natural resources, including oil, coffee and diamonds. Despite this, 95 per cent of Angolans live in poverty or extreme poverty. In the years immediately after independence, economic development was stunted by the departure of 700,000 Portuguese colonists, who controlled the Government and most of the economy. Thereafter, a quarter century of civil war reduced the country to ruins. The 2002 peace accord, which brought the war to an end, has allowed reconstruction to begin. In April 2003, the World Bank committed US$100 million to the Angolan reconstruction and rehabilitation programme. However, both the Bank and the IMF were reluctant to release funds until Angola's endemic corruption was curtailed. Agriculture employs over 50 per cent of the population but production has declined so much that, from being a net exporter, Angola now imports over half its food requirements. There has been genuine progress in this area, although the US were not keen to administer food aid after Angola banned genetically modified food products in March 2004, since the US does not make such a distinction and economically gains through the consumption of GM foods. Fishing, which almost ceased to exist, is now being rejuvenated with foreign aid. New oil and gas fields off the shore of Cabinda (an enclave in the north of the country) are being developed. However, Angola has only one refinery and so exports most of its oil in the crude form. The Government is looking to a new cooperative agreement with Algeria and partial privatisation of the state oil firm, Sangol, to boost production and refining capacity. The only other industry of any size is diamond mining. Angola's largest trading partners are Portugal, Brazil, France and the USA, from whom it imports much of its food and almost all its manufactured equipment. Annual growth in 2005 is estimated at 11.7 per cent.

BUSINESS ETIQUETTE: Lightweight suits are recommended. Many Angolan businesspeople dress casually, wearing open-neck shirts. Any dark colours can be worn for social occasions. As Portuguese is the official language, a knowledge of this is an advantage in business transactions; French and Spanish are also useful. There are limited translation services. Avoid June to September as Angolans tend to take their holidays at this time. **Office hours:** Mon-Thurs 0730-1230 and 1430-1830, Fri 1430-1730; some offices open Sat 0830-1230.

COMMERCIAL INFORMATION

Câmara de Comércio e Indústria de Angola (Chamber of Commerce and Industry)
Largo do Kinaxixi 14, 1 Andar, CP 92, Luanda, Angola
Tel: (2) 344 541.
E-mail: ccira@ebonet.net

The US-Angola Chamber of Commerce in the USA
1100 Connecticut Avenue, Suite 1000, NW, Washington, DC 20036, USA
Tel: (202) 223 0540.
Website: www.us-angola.org

Anguilla

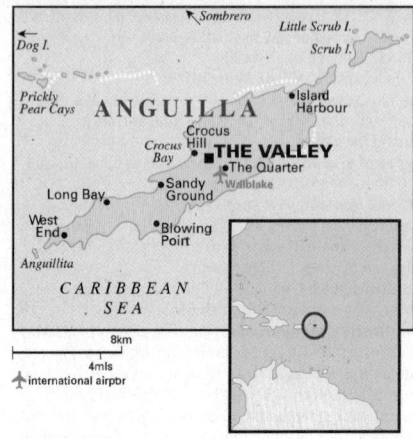

Location: Caribbean, Leeward Islands.

Time: GMT - 4.

Overview

What Anguilla lacks in size, it more than makes up for in that much-sought Caribbean asset: pristine, powdery beaches. Boasting 12 miles (19km) of white coral coastline, Anguilla's calm and polychromatic waters are enough to lure any potential visitor. Anguilla also comprises Sombrero, and numerous other smaller islands and cays, which are even more secluded. Many call Anguilla "tranquillity wrapped in blue". Surrounded by blue skies (Anguilla has an average monthly temperature of 80 degrees Fahrenheit [27 degrees Celsius]) and vivid blue ocean, Anguilla offers the perfect cocktail to absorb and relax in.

For those seeking an altogether different type of cocktail, nothing can beat staring out at a Caribbean sunset while sipping an Anguillan tipple. Those who like their food need not worry either, since restaurants on the island are excellent and offer a mixture of cuisines, with a natural emphasis on seafood. Al fresco dining is everywhere, with roadside barbecues and beachside bistros and grills speckled all about the shoreline. The nightlife is centred on the hotels and the tourist areas and has a relaxed and friendly atmosphere. Accommodation ranges from luxury-class resorts to guest houses, apartments, villas and cottages. Some feature the latest in spa and wellness facilities, services and treatments to further guarantee you unwind. If you ever get bored of relaxing, there are a myriad of activity choices. Many resorts and hotels are situated on the beach and offer boating, snorkelling, fishing and scuba diving equipment for adventurous types. For the culturally minded, Anguilla, despite its diminutive size, has around 15 art galleries to stroll around and observe Anguillan talent. The name *Anguilla* was given to the island by the Spanish and means 'eel', in reference to the island's eel-like shape. It is therefore only apt that Anguilla slips out of any attempts to 'define' its appeal as a destination. Whether in pursuit of adventure, relaxation, romance or vibrancy, Anguilla has it all. It is little wonder that Anguillans are fiercely proud of their island, having first fought their way out of British control in 1967, and then out of a three-island self-governing entity with St Kitts & Nevis, which formally ended in 1980, when Anguilla emerged as an independent British Overseas Territory.

General Information

AREA: Anguilla: 91 sq km (35 sq miles). **Sombrero:** 5 sq km (2 sq miles). **Total:** 96 sq km (37 sq miles).
POPULATION: 11,430 (official estimate 2002).
POPULATION DENSITY: 124.2 per sq km (2002).
CAPITAL: The Valley. **Population:** 1,169 (2001).
GEOGRAPHY: Anguilla, the northernmost of the Leeward Islands, also comprises the island of Sombrero, lying 48km (30 miles) north of Anguilla, and several small islets or cays.

The nearest islands are St Maarten, 8km (5 miles) south of Anguilla, and St Kitts and Nevis, 113km (70 miles) to the southeast. The islands are mainly flat – the highest point, Crocus Hill, is only 60m (213ft) above sea level – with, arguably, some of the best beaches in the world.

GOVERNMENT: United Kingdom Overseas Territory since 1980. **Head of State:** HM Queen Elizabeth II, represented locally by Governor Alan Huckle since 2005. **Head of Government:** Chief Minister Osbourne Fleming since 2000. **Recent history:** Osbourne Fleming was re-elected as Chief Minister in February 2005. There are seven elected seats in Anguilla's assembly - four assembly members are appointed, three by the Governor and one by the ruling party. The assembly is part of the Executive Council, led by the Chief Minister who advises the Governor, who is appointed by the British Monarch, according to the 1982 constitution.

LANGUAGE: English is the official and commercial language. **RELIGION:** Roman Catholic, Anglican, Baptist, Methodist and Moravian, with Hindu, Jewish and Muslim minorities. **ELECTRICITY:** 110/220 volts AC, 60Hz.

SOCIAL CONVENTIONS: The Government is anxious to set limits to the commercialisation of the island and visitors will find that social life is centred on the tourist areas. The atmosphere is relaxed and English customs prevail. Beachwear should be confined to resorts. Topless and nude bathing is prohibited.

Climate

Hot throughout the year, tempered by trade winds in local areas. The average rainfall for the year is 14cm (35in) and the hurricane season is from July to November.
Required clothing: Lightweight cottons throughout the year. Waterproofing is advisable during the rainy season.

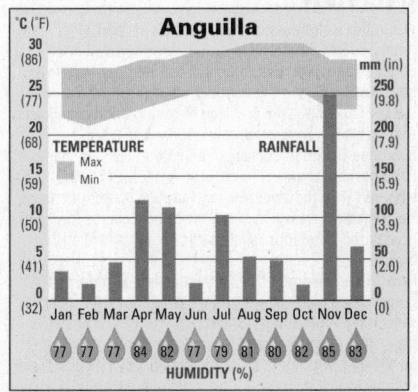

Communications

Telephone: Full IDD is available. Country code: 1 264.
Mobile telephone: Roaming agreements exist with some international phone companies. Coverage is average.
Internet: Available in large cities and resorts. There are some Internet cafes and free Wi-Fi access is available.
Post: Post Office hours: Mon-Fri 0800-1530 and closed at weekends. Airmail to Europe takes from four days to two weeks.
MEDIA: Anguilla enjoys free press.
Press: *The Light* is a weekly newspaper and *Anguilla Life Magazine* is published three times a year. *What We Do In Anguilla*, an official tourism guide, is published monthly.
TV: There is one TV station.
Radio: *Radio Anguilla* is government owned. *Heart Beat Radio* and *Kool FM* are private stations.

Passport/Visa

	Passport Required?	Visa Required?	Return Ticket Required?
Full British	Yes	No	Yes
Australian	Yes	No	Yes
Canadian	Yes	No	Yes
USA	1	No	Yes
Other EU	Yes	No	Yes
Japanese	Yes	No	Yes

Note: *Regulations and requirements may be subject to change at short notice, and you are advised to contact the appropriate diplomatic or consular authority before finalising travel arrangements. Any numbers in the chart refer to the footnotes below.*

PASSPORTS: Passport valid for six months after date of entry into Anguilla required by all except:
1. nationals of the USA with an original birth certificate and official photo ID.
VISAS: Required by all except the following:
(a) nationals of countries referred to in the chart above and nationals of their overseas territories;

(b) citizens of Commonwealth countries (except nationals of Bangladesh, Cameroon, Fiji, The Gambia, Ghana, Guyana, India, Jamaica, Kenya, Maldives, Mauritius, Mozambique, Nigeria, Pakistan, Papua New Guinea, Sierra Leone, Sri Lanka, Tanzania and Uganda who *do* require visas);
(c) nationals of Andorra, Argentina, Bahrain, Bolivia, Brazil, Chile, Costa Rica, East Timor, El Salvador, Guatemala, Honduras, Iceland, Israel, Korea (Rep), Marshall Islands, Mexico, Micronesia (Federated States of), Monaco, Nicaragua, Norway, Panama, Paraguay, San Marino, Switzerland, Uruguay, Vatican City, Venezuela and Zimbabwe.
Note: Nationals of the following countries require Direct Airside Transit Visas (DAVTs) to transit through Anguilla, even if not leaving the airport: Afghanistan, China (PR), Colombia, Congo (Dem Rep), Croatia, Ecuador, Eritrea, Ethiopia, Ghana, Iran, Iraq, Libya, Nigeria, Serbia and Montenegro, Somalia, Sri Lanka, Turkey and Uganda.
Types of visa and cost: *Tourist, Transit* and *Business*: £28.
Note: If applying by post, an extra £4 surcharge is requested for special delivery.
Validity: Three months from date of issue. Extensions can be granted in Anguilla.
Application to: Visa Section at UK Passport Office; see *Passport/Visa Information.*
Application requirements: (a) Valid passport with two blank pages. (b) One application form (AV/BT). (c) Proof of onward or return ticket. (d) Fee payable in cash.
Working days required: Three to four weeks. An extra one to two days may be added if applying by post.
Temporary residence: Persons intending to take up residence and/or employment should contact the Immigration authorities in Anguilla.

PASSPORT/VISA INFORMATION

The UK Passport Service
London Passport Office, Globe House, 89 Eccleston Square, London SW1V 1PN, UK
Tel: (0870) 521 0410 (national advice line) or (020) 7901 2150/1.
Website: www.passport.gov.uk
Opening hours: Mon-Fri 0745-1900, Sat 0915-1515 (passport office); Mon-Fri 0900-1600 (visa section).

Personal callers for visas should go to the agency window in the collection room of the London office.

Money

Currency: Eastern Caribbean Dollar (XCD; symbol EC$) = 100 cents. Notes are in denominations of EC$100, 50, 20, 10 and 5. Coins are in denominations of EC$1, and 25, 10, 5, 2 and 1 cents.
Note: The EC Dollar is tied to the US Dollar.
Currency exchange: Currency may be exchanged in the capital. US dollars are widely accepted and prices quoted are generally in US dollars.
Credit & debit cards: American Express and Visa are widely accepted. Check with your credit or debit card company for details of merchant acceptability and other services which may be available. ATMS are available in major cities.
Traveller's cheques: To avoid additional exchange rate charges, travellers are advised to take traveller's cheques in US Dollars.
Currency restrictions: The import of local and foreign currency is unlimited provided declared upon arrival. The export of local and foreign currency is limited to the amount imported and declared.
Banking hours: Mon-Thurs 0800-1500, Fri 0800-1700.
Exchange rate indicators:
Rate at time of publishing
£1.00=   EC$4.89
$1.00=   EC$2.70

Duty Free

The following goods may be imported into Anguilla without incurring customs duty:
200 cigarettes or 50 cigars or 225g of tobacco; 1.136l of wine or spirits.

Public Holidays

Below are listed Public Holidays for the January 2006-June 2007 period.
2006: Jan 1 New Year's Day. **Apr 14** Good Friday. **Apr 17** Easter Monday. **Apr 30** Queen's Birthday. **May 1** Labour Day. **May 31** Anguilla Day. **Jun 5** Whit Monday.
2007: Jan 1 New Year's Day. **Apr 6** Good Friday. **Apr 9** Easter Monday. **Apr 30** Queen's Official Birthday. **May** Anguilla Day. **May 1** Labour Day. **May 28** Whit Monday.

Health

	Special Precautions?	Certificate Required?
Yellow Fever	No	1
Cholera	No	No
Typhoid & Polio	2	N/A
Malaria	No	N/A

Note: *Regulations and requirements may be subject to change at short notice, and you are advised to contact your doctor well in advance of your intended date of departure. Any numbers in the chart refer to the footnotes below.*

1: A yellow fever vaccination certificate is required from travellers over one year of age arriving from infected areas.
2: Polio vaccination is recommended.
Food & drink: Mains water is normally chlorinated and, whilst relatively safe, may cause mild abdominal upsets. Bottled water is available and is advised. Milk is pasteurised and dairy products are safe for consumption. Local meat, poultry, seafood, fruit and vegetables are generally considered safe to eat.
Other risks: *Tetanus* vaccinations are recommended. *Hepatitis A* and *B, diphtheria* and *dengue fever* occur.
Health care: Primary health services can be obtained from the three private health clinics, where registered nurses provide care for minor emergencies. Family doctors hold clinics twice weekly. Secondary health care can be found at the small hospital located in The Valley. Minor emergency treatment is usually free for UK citizens with proof of UK residence. Health insurance is recommended as costs for other categories of treatment are high.

Travel - International

AIR:
The national airline is *Air Anguilla.*
Approximate flight times: From Anguilla to *London* is eight to 10 hours (including a stopover in Antigua), to *Los Angeles* is 10 hours and to *New York* is six hours.
Main airports: *Wallblake Airport (AXA)* is in The Valley. *To/from the airport:* Transport to the city centre is by taxi (travel time – five minutes). *Facilities:* Limited but disabled facilities, light refreshments and tourist information are available.
Departure tax: US$20. Children: US$10 (five to 11 years of age); children under five years of age are exempt.
SEA:
Main ports: *Blowing Point, Road Bay:* Handles ships of up to 1000 tonnes.
Departure tax: US$3.

Travel - Internal

ROAD:
The road network is good but basic and the main road is asphalt, stretching throughout the 25km (16 miles) length of Anguilla. Unpaved roads lead to beaches. Traffic drives on the left and is restricted to 30-50kph (20-30mph). **Taxis** are available at the airport and seaports with fixed prices to the various hotels. Island tours can be arranged on an individual basis. In addition, there are numerous **car hire** agencies available, including *Avis, Budget, Thrifty* and local agencies. Bicycles and mopeds can also be hired.
Documentation: Visitors must buy a temporary Anguillan licence. This can be issued by the car hire companies or the traffic department in The Valley on presentation of a national driving licence, and currently costs US$20.

Travel Advice

Most visits to Anguilla are trouble-free but you should be aware of the global risk of indiscriminate international terrorist attacks, which could be against civilian targets, including places frequented by foreigners.
This advice is based on information provided by the Foreign and Commonwealth Office in the UK. It is correct at time of publishing. As the situation can change rapidly, visitors are advised to contact the following organisations for the latest travel advice:

British Foreign and Commonwealth Office
Tel: (0845) 850 2829.
Website: www.fco.gov.uk

US Department of State
Website: http://travel.state.gov/travel

A B C D E F G H I J K L M N O P Q R S T U V W X Y Z

Accommodation

HOTELS:

A range of hotels are available throughout Anguilla.

GUEST HOUSES:

These are in frequent supply on Anguilla.

SELF-CATERING:

Villas, Houses and Apartments Rental: These are all available, and visitors can also hire cottages, plus an assortment of mixed-range accommodation.

Note: A government tax of 8 per cent is levied on all hotel bills as well as a 10 per cent service charge.

ACCOMMODATION INFORMATION

Anguilla Hotel and Tourism Association
PO Box 1020, Coronation Avenue, The Valley, Anguilla
Tel: 497 2944.
Website: www.ahta.ai

Entertainment

FOOD & DRINK: Restaurants offer a mixture of Continental, US and Anguillan dishes. Seafoods include lobster, conch and a variety of fish. For a Caribbean island, Anguilla boasts an array of gourmet, gastronomic dining experiences.

National specialities:

• *Salt fish*, usually served shredded and tossed with finely chopped onions, sweet peppers, some oil and a bit of hot pepper, is a traditional breakfast.

• *Spiny lobster bisque*, often served with a side of *rice and peas*.

• *Johnny cakes*, which taste somewhere between bread and cake, are served instead of dinner rolls.

• *Tamarind balls* make a nice sweet and sour treat.

Legal drinking age: The legal age for drinking alcohol in a bar/cafe is 16.

NIGHTLIFE: Anguilla's nightlife is centred around hotels and small local bars offering live music. *Sandy Ground* is the 'hotspot' on Fridays and Saturdays, while the crowds move to Shoal Bay East on Wednesdays and Sundays. Tourists and locals alike dance barefoot.

SHOPPING: There is a national *Arts and Crafts Centre*, and the island-built racing boats are world-famous. Souvenirs will also include shells and small models of island sloops. There are small boutiques offering resort clothing and accessories, swimwear and a gift shop offering international name brands in bone china, crystal and jewellery. **Shopping hours:** Mon-Sat 0900-1700. A few shops open on Sunday.

Business

• **GDP:** US$112 million.
• **Main exports:** Fish, lobster and salt.
• **Main imports:** Fuels, foodstuffs, manufactures, chemicals, trucks and textiles.
• **Main trade partners:** North America (mainly USA) and the Caribbean Region (CARICOM, St Martin/St Maarten and others).

ECONOMY: Industries include fishing and fish processing, salt mining and boat manufacture (both traditional and contemporary crafts) and construction. Most of the island's agricultural produce is, however, for domestic consumption. The service sector, specifically tourism and financial services, are responsible for the great majority of economic output. The financial sector has been damaged by a series of scandals, which, along with growing competition from other Caribbean micro states, has put its future viability in question. Moreover, in June 2000, Anguilla was identified by the Organization for Economic Cooperation and Development (OECD) – the world's 30 largest economies – as one of 35 'tax havens' whose financial laws are believed to encourage large-scale tax evasion and money laundering. It has since taken measures to meet OECD demands, thereby avoiding the threat of economic sanctions. Tourism accounts for approximately 40 per cent of GDP. The Anguillan government receives development aid from the UK and, as an overseas dependency, enjoys the status of an EU Associate Overseas Territory.

BUSINESS ETIQUETTE: Anguilla is a small island with few business opportunities as such; lightweight suits or shirt and tie should be adequate for meetings. **Office hours:** Mon-Fri 0800-1200 and 1300-1600.

COMMERCIAL INFORMATION

Anguilla Chamber of Commerce
PO Box 321, The Valley, Anguilla
Tel: 497 2839.
Website www.anguillachamber.com

Top Things To See

• Explore Anguilla's many idyllic, white coral beaches at a leisurely pace: some of the best beaches are **Rendezvous Bay**, **Shoal Bay**, **Road Bay**, **Maundays Bay**, **Cove Bay**, **Meads Bay** and **Crocus Bay**.

• Pop into the impressive **Wallblake House**, a restored plantation house whose foundations date back to 1787.

• Peer into Anguilla's many grotto-like rock areas and hidden coves, which are dotted all around the island's 30-odd beaches - one to definitely not miss out on is the historic landmark that is **The Fountain**, a huge underground cave with a constant supply of fresh water at **Shoal Bay**.

• Ponder the ruins of the **Dutch Fort**, built in the 1700s and located at **Sandy Hill**, famous as the scene of fierce fighting during the second French invasion of Anguilla in 1796, and gaze upon the well-preserved **Tomb of Governor Richardson** (1679-1742), also in Sandy Hill.

• Take a tour of the **Old Salt Mine and Pumphouse** at Sandy Ground (1000 every Thursday) and see the **Salt Ponds** at **Sandy Ground** and **West End**.

• Visit **Sandy Island**, 15 minutes from Sandy Ground Harbour, or **Sombrero Island**, 48km (30 miles) northwest of Anguilla, which has a picturesque lighthouse, for some relaxing solitude; even smaller sandy cays, such as **Scrub**, **Dog** and **Prickly Pear Islands**, are within reach of Anguilla by powerboat.

• See some more of the Caribbean by taking a day trip to nearby **St Maarten** and **St Barthelémy** by ferry, cruise boat or aeroplane.

Top Things To Do

• Explore scores of deliberately sunken wrecks and award-winning underwater parks that attract schools of fish by **diving** in one of the seven marine parks that Anguilla offers: **Prickly Pear**, a beautiful canyon characterised by ledges and caverns, where nurse sharks can be seen; **Little Bay**, a calm, sheltered site suitable for training and night dives; **Shoal Bay Harbour Reef System**; **Stoney Bay**; **Dog Island**; **Seal Island Reef System** and **Sandy Island**.

• Savour traditional reggae music and cocktails under a luminous full moon at Anguilla's **annual music festival**, *Moonsplash* (website: www.dunepreserve.com).

• Make the most of being surrounded by water by trying any of Anguilla's numerous **watersports** on offer, such as **para-sailing**, **windsurfing** and **water-skiing**, easily organised through Shoal Bay, individual hotels and Anguilla Watersports.

• Penetrate Anguilla's waters: do something you will never forget and **swim with** friendly **dolphins**; go **shore-** or **deep-sea fishing** and discover an abundance of marlin, tuna, swordfish and wahoo.

• **Dance** yourself silly at Anguilla's **annual summer Festival** of fun, and expect to experience everything from Calypso, pageants, street jams, fireworks and **boat races** (Anguilla's national sport).

• Take a **historic tour** of The Valley, available every Tuesday and Thursday (1000-1200), and also enjoy a guided **rainforest tour**.

• Stroll through any of Anguilla's 15 galleries and studios for a bit of **culture**, and consider buying your own water-colour painting for a permanent reminder of your holiday.

• For those who wish to dabble in aesthetics of the self, take a trip to one of Anguilla's (attractively priced) **spas** and be pampered: **Cap Juluca**; **CuisinArt Resort & Spa**; and **Malliouhana Hotel & Spa**.

• Sip a **traditional Caribbean tipple** while gazing at a magnificent **sunset**.

TOURIST INFORMATION

Anguilla Tourist Board in the UK
7A Crealock Street, London SW18 2BS, UK
Tel: (020) 8871 0012.
Website: www.anguilla-vacation.com

Anguilla Tourist Board in the USA
246 Central Avenue, White Plains, NY 10606, USA
Tel: (914) 287 2400.
Website: www.anguilla-vacation.com
PR and marketing agency only; does not provide tourist information.

Antarctica

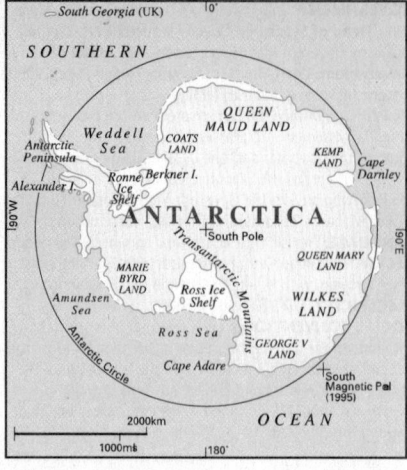

Location: South of 60 degrees latitude.

Time: Strictly speaking, Antarctica operates on GMT + 0 time, but bases and stations in Antarctica tend to keep the time of their home territory.

Overview

Antarctica is not easy to access but that is part of its appeal. Amidst such solitude, adventurous travellers will discover an ethereal landscape that lingers in the memory. Very few have ventured onto the continent and those who do will usually rave about the privilege of gazing upon topography that yields towering mountains, bulky glaciers and luminous, dreamlike icebergs, carved into curious shapes. Perhaps more than anywhere else, Antarctica reminds those who visit it of the awesome (and savage) power of nature. No two travellers will ever see the same icebergs forged in exactly the same form, such is its ephemeral and austere beauty.

However, some argue that Antarctica is changing, and by humanmade causes rather than natural ones. Antarctica is welcoming more tourist-orientated cruises and ferries to the region every year, and facilities are continually developing, with more accommodation, culinary and travel options available. There is now ample opportunity to ascend Mount Erebus, the southernmost active volcano on Earth; to fly via helicopter or venture by boat to penguin colonies; to really make the most of a terrain that teems with wildlife, with a multitude of birds, seals, albatrosses and enormous whales; and so on. Some regard this gradual focus on tourism as disconcerting – many wish to preserve Antarctica in its elemental state and want to avoid any potential environmental damage. However, the focus on tourism is, indeed, gradual, and as long as any visitor is aware of their impact upon the landscape and does their utmost to limit that impact, Antarctica is still a magical experience that most, given the chance, would find hard to resist.

Perhaps the reason behind fascination with Antarctica is its function as a symbol of endurance and survival. It has only been a little over 100 years since humans first occupied the continent (1899) and only nearly 200 years since seafarers first even saw the islands of the Antarctic Peninsula (1819). Before this, the continent was the subject of constant speculation, spoken of in almost mythical terms as *Terra Australia Incognita* – the Unknown Southern Land. Even once known, Antarctica seemed inhospitable and incomprehensible and, in many ways, it still is. But it seems fitting that the continent should be the site for numerous global research stations, proving it remains testament to human endeavour.

General Information

AREA: 13,661,000 sq km (5,274,126 sq miles).
GEOGRAPHY: Antarctica is the largest remaining wilderness on Earth and is still relatively untouched by human impact. It covers an area of 13.6 million sq km around the South Pole and is covered with an ice sheet 4km (2.5 miles) deep. It has no permanent human population other than a small number of personnel at 82 research stations run by 27 different nations.
The main human activity undertaken in Antarctica is scientific research, and it was at the British Halley research station that the hole in the ozone layer was discovered in 1985.
The constitutional position of Antarctica is governed by the

terms of the Antarctic Treaty of 1959 (which came into effect in 1961), which was signed initially by Argentina, Australia, Chile, France, New Zealand, Norway, the UK, Belgium, Japan, South Africa, the USA and the former USSR. The first seven of these countries have historic claims to the ice-bound continent (none of which were - or are - generally recognised) and the Treaty preserves the status quo, neither recognising nor repudiating the old claims, but forbidding their expansion in any way. The terms of the Treaty also forbid, absolutely, the assertion of new claims. The Treaty applies to all land and ice shelves below 60 degrees South. The discovery in 1985 by the British Antarctic Survey of a 'hole' in the ozone layer of the Earth's atmosphere did more than perhaps any other event, bar nuclear accidents, to bring ecology to prominence in the international political agenda. The Antarctic Treaty made no provision for mineral exploitation and in November 1988, an Antarctic Minerals Convention was carefully instigated. This was intended to regulate but not directly prevent the extraction of minerals, and caused much protest from environmental lobbyists. Several nations, led by Australia and France, declined to ratify the Convention.

As a result, in 1991, the Antarctic Treaty nations agreed to add the Environmental Protocol to the Antarctic Treaty, which bans mining and provides for a fully comprehensive regime of environmental protection. The Protocol entered into force in 1998 after ratification by each of the 26 Antarctic Treaty nations.

In May 1994, the International Whaling Commission agreed to the creation of a whale sanctuary around Antarctica below 40 degrees South.

In May 1997, it was suggested by the World Meteorological Organization that the long-term outlook for the ozone layer over the Antarctic was improving. It will take some years for this to be conclusively proved, however. Even depending on a significant reduction of CFCs and other harmful emissions, it is unlikely that the hole will repair itself permanently (if, indeed, it does at all) before 2060 at the earliest.

Scientists from many nations collaborate on research projects in Antarctica. Every summer, about 5000 of them travel to the continent to obtain vital information on the Earth's ecosystem. Antarctica's ice and sediment cores provide insights into how the world's climatic system functioned in the past. Studies of the Antarctic ice sheet help predict future sea levels, knowledge which is crucial to our future given that 50 per cent of the world's population lives in coastal areas. Information on the break up of continents and the interaction between the Sun's wind and the outer limits of the Earth's atmosphere can be gained from studies here.

Climate

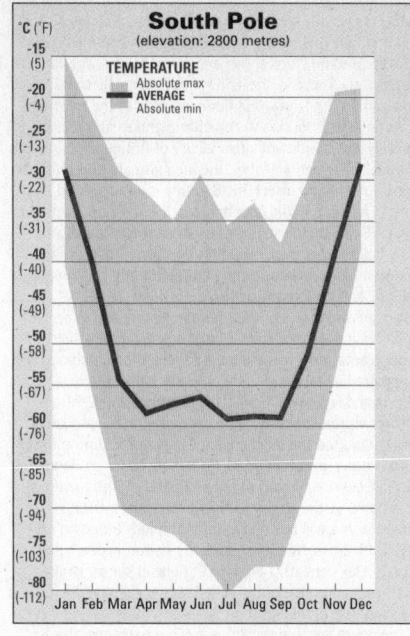

South Pole
(elevation: 2800 metres)

TEMPERATURE
Absolute max
AVERAGE
Absolute min

°C (°F)
-15 (5)
-20 (-4)
-25 (-13)
-30 (-22)
-35 (-31)
-40 (-40)
-45 (-49)
-50 (-58)
-55 (-67)
-60 (-76)
-65 (-85)
-70 (-94)
-75 (-103)
-80 (-112)

Jan Feb Mar Apr May Jun Jul Aug Sep Oct Nov Dec

Top Things To See & Do

• Endure *The Last Marathon* on **King George Island** and run long-distance in sub-zero conditions.
• Take a **cruise/ferry** around some of the most dramatic scenery in the world: most trips depart from Ushuaia (in Argentina) or Punta Arenas (in Chile), and the passage from South America to the Antarctic Peninsula takes approximately two days.
• Be one of the few to observe **polar animals** (including penguins and albatrosses) in their natural environment; grant yourself even better access to emperor penguin colonies by **taking a helicopter**.
• Follow in the footsteps of famous explorers such as Captain RF Scott, and **visit historic sites** dotted throughout Antarctica.
• **Climb Observation Hill**, 30 minutes' ascent from nearby **McMurdo station**, which awards intrepid travellers with magnificent views of **Mount Erebus** and the **Ross Ice**

Shelf, plus the **'Royal Societies' range** across the ice; you will also find here the **Memorial Cross** erected in honour of Captain RF Scott and his polar party.
• **Kayak** up to icebergs for even closer views and, weather permitting, you may even be able to **camp** on the ice.
• Take advantage of some of the best **wildlife viewing** in the world, and spend your time bird-, seal- and **whale watching**.
• Huddle around the **geothermal waters** of **Pendulum Cove** on **Deception Island**.
• Become a budding astronomer: gaze up at the cosmos and delight in an exceptionally **clear night full of stars**.
• Impress your friends by sending them a **postcard from the only post office** in Antarctica, at **Port Lockroy**, which used to be a British station and is now a museum.

TOURIST INFORMATION

British Antarctic Survey in the UK
High Cross, Madingley Road, Cambridge CB3 0ET, UK
Tel: (01223) 221 400.
Website: www.antarctica.ac.uk

International Association of Antarctica Tour Operators in the USA
PO Box 2178, Basalt, CO 81621, USA
Tel: (970) 704 1047
Website: www.iaato.org

Travel Advice

Be aware of the risks posed by the harsh climatic conditions that prevail in Antarctica.

Most visits to Antarctica are trouble-free but you should be aware of the global risk of indiscriminate international terrorist attacks, which could be against civilian targets, including places frequented by foreigners.

This advice is based on information provided by the Foreign and Commonwealth Office in the country-region. It is correct at time of publishing. As the situation can change rapidly, visitors are advised to contact the following organisations for the latest travel advice:

British Foreign and Commonwealth Office
Tel: (0845) 850 2829.
Website: www.fco.gov.uk

US Department of State
Website: http://travel.state.gov/travel

Antigua & Barbuda

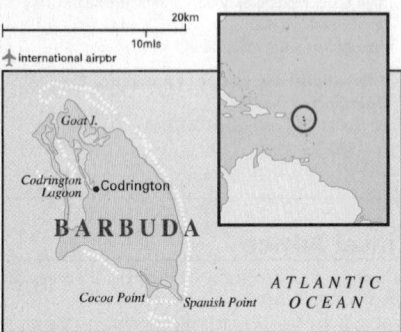

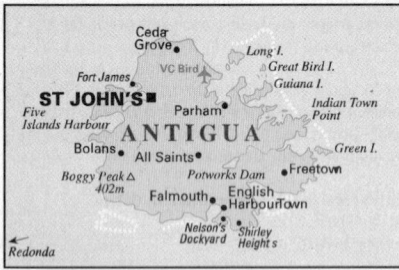

Location: Caribbean, Leeward Islands.

Time: GMT - 4.

Overview

Antiguans claim to have a different beach for every day of the year and their island's many beautiful soft, sandy beaches and coves certainly constitute its main attraction. This is where people come to relax and luxuriate in clear water that sparkles under hot sun. Low-lying and volcanic in origin, Antigua & Barbuda form part of the Leeward Islands group in the northeast Caribbean and have certainly adopted the notoriously 'Caribbean' way of life: this is a place to take things easy, to stroll around markets, gulp the

fresh juices of coconuts and pineapple, and to meet friendly locals with plenty of anecdotes. Unsurprisingly, Antigua & Barbuda's way of life is governed by water, and any visitor will find that their stay is too. The ocean is crammed with crustaceans and tropical fish and offers huge scope for watersports. Those in-the-know will flock to Nelson's Dockyard in the English Harbour, which is at the forefront of Antigua & Barbuda's vast yachting and sailing scene. Unlikely, but should you grow weary of Antigua & Barbuda's nautically-themed activities, the area also abounds with colourful bird and insect life. Barbuda is an unspoiled natural haven for wild deer and exotic birds and boasts the Frigate Bird Sanctuary. There are also national parks and blow holes to discover, including, of course, the Devil's Bridge, a natural phenomenon crafted by the colliding of Atlantic and Caribbean surf.

Antiguans are proud of their human history too, especially as it documents their release from colonization, slavery and sugar plantations. This keenness to remember emancipation is apparent as towns proudly proclaim names such as Liberta and Freetown. Dow's Hill Interpretation Centre ensures visitors are also aware of the economic problems that catapulted the independence movement during the 20th century. In recent years, leadership has been dogged with allegations of corruption, and parts of Antigua are still devastated by the legacy of Hurricane Louis in 1995. However, you will not find many Antiguans brooding on such difficulties. Neither should any visitor: instead, they should relax beneath a brilliant Caribbean sunset whilst quaffing rum punch or ice-cold fruit juice. Shirley Heights is the epicentre of all nighttime activity. With amazing views of the ocean, local music and a sizzling barbeque, this is where you dance the night away. Just as St John's Cathedral has had many incarnations over the years because of reconstruction, the persistent will find that Antigua & Barbuda has just as many incarnations as a destination.

General Information

AREA: Antigua: 280 sq km (108 sq miles); **Barbuda:** 161 sq km (62 sq miles); **Redonda:** 1.6 sq km (0.6 sq miles). **Total:** 441.6 sq km (170.5 sq miles).
POPULATION: 77,426 (2001).
POPULATION DENSITY: 175.3 per sq km.
CAPITAL: St John's. **Population:** 24,000 (UN estimate 2001).
GEOGRAPHY: Antigua & Barbuda comprises three islands; Antigua, Barbuda and Redonda. Low-lying and volcanic in origin, they are part of the Leeward Islands group in the northeast Caribbean. Antigua's coastline curves into a multitude of coves and harbours (they were once volcanic craters) and there are more than 365 beaches of fine white sand, fringed with palms. The island's highest point is Boggy Peak (402m, 1318ft); its capital is St John's. Barbuda lies 40km (25 miles) north of Antigua and is an unspoiled natural haven for wild deer and exotic birds. Its 8km- (5 mile-) long beach is reputed to be among the most beautiful in the world. The island's village capital, Codrington, was named after the Gloucestershire family that once leased Barbuda from the British Crown for the price of 'one fat pig per year if asked for'. There are excellent beaches and the ruins of some of the earliest plantations in the West Indies. The coastal waters are rich with all types of crustaceans and tropical fish. Redonda, the smallest in the group, is little more than an uninhabited rocky islet. It lies 40km (25 miles) southwest of Antigua.
GOVERNMENT: Constitutional monarchy. Gained internal full independence in 1981. **Head of State:** HM Queen Elizabeth II, represented locally by Governor-General Sir James Carlisle since 1993. **Head of Government:** Prime Minister Baldwin Spencer since 2004. **Recent history:** Antigua & Barbuda is a constitutional monarchy, with the British Sovereign as Head of State. The Prime Minister advises on the appointment of the Governor General, who represents the Sovereign. Parliament has supreme legislative power and comprises the Senate, with 17 appointed members, and the House of Representatives, with 17 members directly elected from single-member constituencies. The judiciary is fully autonomous and Antigua and Barbuda shares it with five other Eastern Caribbean states. Barbuda has its own local council with wide-ranging powers. Except for a brief spell in opposition during the 1970s, Vere C Bird and his Antiguan Labour Party (ALP) held power continuously from 1946 – first as Chief Minister, later as Prime Minister – until 1994. He was then replaced by his son, Lester, after the ALP won the March 1994 poll (albeit with a sharply reduced majority). Lester Bird retained the post at the most recent poll, held in March 1999, at which the ALP recovered some of the ground lost five years previously and now holds 12 of the House of Representatives' 17 seats.
LANGUAGE: English is the official language. English *patois* is widely spoken.
RELIGION: Predominantly Anglican but also Methodist, Moravian, Roman Catholic, Pentecostal, Baptist, Seventh Day Adventist and others.

ELECTRICITY: 220/110 volts AC, 60Hz. American-style two-pin plugs. Some hotels also have outlets for 240 volts AC; in this case European-style, two-pin plugs are used.
SOCIAL CONVENTIONS: Dress is informal unless formal dress is specifically requested. It is not acceptable to wear scanty clothing or beachwear in towns or villages. It is an offence for anyone, including children, to dress in camouflage clothing. Relatives and good friends generally embrace. Friends tend to drop by unannounced, but an invitation is necessary for acquaintances or business associates. Although gifts will generally be well received, they are normally only given on celebratory occasions. Flowers are appropriate for dinner parties; bring a bottle only when specifically requested. Smoking is accepted in most public places. Certain homosexual acts are illegal.

Climate

The islands enjoy a very pleasant tropical climate which remains warm and relatively dry throughout the year. Tropical storms and hurricanes may occur between June and November.
Required clothing: Lightweight cottons or linen, with rainwear needed from September to December.

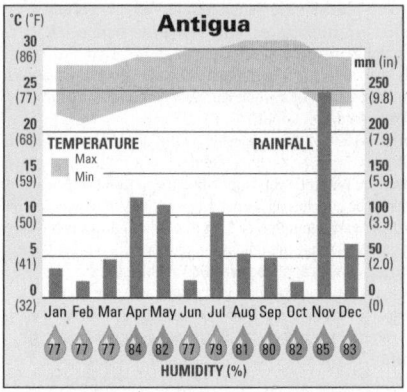

Communications

Telephone: Country code: 1 268.
Mobile telephone: Roaming agreements exist with some international mobile phone companies. Unregistered roaming is available – visitors with TDMA handsets can make calls without registering, provided they can give a credit card number. Coverage is average.
Internet: Available in large cities and resorts.
Post: Post office hours: Mon-Fri 0800-1200 and 1300-1600.
MEDIA: Press: Some newspapers have political or governmental associations. All are in English. The main newspapers are the *Antigua Sun* (which is published twice-weekly) and the *Daily Observer*.
TV: The local TV station is called *ABN* (Antigua & Barbuda Network). Cable television is widely available.
Radio: *Observer Radio* and *ZDK* are commercial broadcasters. *Sun FM* is private and commercial. Some radio stations are owned by political or religious factions.

Passport/Visa

	Passport Required?	Visa Required?	Return Ticket Required?
Full British	Yes	No	Yes
Australian	Yes	No	Yes
Canadian	Yes	No	Yes
USA	Yes	No	Yes
Other EU	Yes	No/1	Yes
Japanese	Yes	No	Yes

Note: *Regulations and requirements may be subject to change at short notice, and you are advised to contact the appropriate diplomatic or consular authority before finalising travel arrangements. Any numbers in the chart refer to the footnotes below.*

PASSPORTS: Passport valid for at least six months beyond period of stay required by all.
VISAS: Required by all except the following for stays of up to six months:
(a) nationals of countries referred to in the chart above,
1. except nationals of Cyprus, Czech Republic, Latvia and the Slovak Republic;
(b) citizens of Commonwealth countries (except nationals of Bangladesh, Cameroon, The Gambia, Ghana, India, Mozambique, Nigeria, Pakistan, Sierra Leone and Sri Lanka, who *do* require a visa);
(c) nationals of Albania, Argentina, Brazil, Bulgaria, Chile,

CIS, Cuba, Korea (Rep), Liechtenstein, Mexico, Monaco, Norway, Peru, Romania, Surinam, Switzerland, Turkey and Venezuela;

(d) transit passengers continuing their journey within 24 hours by the same or next connecting aircraft provided holding valid onward or return documentation and not leaving the airport.

Note: Cruise ship passengers do not require a visa provided that they arrive in Antigua and Barbuda in the morning and depart the same evening.

Types of visa and cost: *Single-entry:* £24. *Multiple-entry:* £28.

Validity: *Single-entry:* Three months from date of issue. *Multiple-entry:* Six months from date of issue. Business visitors can stay as long as their business takes, provided it does not exceed six months.

Application to: Consulate (or Consular Section at Embassy or High Commission); see *Passport/Visa Information.*

Application requirements: (a) One completed application form. (b) One passport-size photo. (c) Passport valid for at least six months. (d) Fee (payable by postal order, international money order or exact cash only [if delivered in person]), with an additional £4 for postal applications. (e) Confirmation of travel (return/onward ticket, letter from travel agent confirming date of travel etc). (f) Confirmation of accommodation or letter of invitation. *Business:* (a)-(f) and, (g) Proof of sufficient funds.

Working days required: Three to five.

Temporary residence: Applications should be made to the Ministry of Foreign Affairs, St John's. However, it is advisable to enquire first at the Embassy or High Commission.

PASSPORT/VISA INFORMATION

Antigua & Barbuda High Commission in the UK
2nd floor, 45 Crawford Place, London W1H 4LP, UK
Tel: (020) 7258 0070.
Website: www.antigua-barbuda.com
Opening hours: Mon-Fri 0930-1230 and 1330-1500; 0900-1730 (telephone enquiries).

Embassy of Antigua & Barbuda in the USA
3216 New Mexico Avenue, NW, Washington, DC 20016, USA
Tel: (202) 362 5122 or 5166.
E-mail: embantbar@aol.com

Money

Currency: Eastern Caribbean Dollar (XCD; symbol EC$) = 100 cents. Notes are in denominations of EC$100, 50, 20, 10 and 5. Coins are in denominations of EC$1, and 50, 25, 10, 5, 2 and 1 cents. US currency is accepted almost everywhere.

Note: The EC Dollar is tied to the US Dollar.

Currency exchange: Although the EC Dollar is tied to the US Dollar, exchange rates will vary at different exchange establishments. There are international banks in St John's, and Sterling and US Dollars can be exchanged at hotels and in the larger shops. ATMs are available in major resorts.

Credit & debit cards: American Express, Diners Club, MasterCard and Visa are accepted. Check with your credit and debit card company for details of merchant acceptability and other services which may be available.

Traveller's cheques: Are widely accepted. They can be exchanged at international banks, hotels and the larger stores. To avoid additional exchange rate charges, travellers are advised to take traveller's cheques in US Dollars.

Currency restrictions: There are no limits on the import of local and foreign currency, provided declared on arrival. The export of local and foreign currency is permitted up to the amount imported and declared.

Banking hours: Mon-Thurs 0800-1300 and 1500-1700; Fri 0800-1200 and 1500-1700 (some banks open until midday on Saturday).

Exchange rate indicators:
Rate at time of publishing
£1.00= EC$4.88
$1.00= EC$2.70

Duty Free

The following items may be imported into Antigua & Barbuda without incurring customs duty:
200 cigarettes or 50 cigars or 225g of tobacco; 1.137l of wine or spirits.

Prohibited items: Firearms, ammunition, weapons and narcotics.

Public Holidays

Below are listed Public Holidays for the January 2006-June 2007 period.
2006: Jan 1 New Year's Day. **Apr 14** Good Friday. **Apr 17** Easter Monday. **May 2** Labour Day. **Jun 5** Whit Monday.

Credit: ©Antigua and Barbuda Tourist Office

Jul 4 Caricom Day. **Aug 7** Carnival Monday. **Aug 8** Carnival Tuesday. **Nov 1** Independence Day. **Dec 9** VC Bird Day. **Dec 25-26** Christmas.
2007: Jan 1 New Year's Day. **Apr 6** Good Friday. **Apr 9** Easter Monday. **May 2** Labour Day. **May 28** Whit Monday.

Health

	Special Precautions?	Certificate Required?
Yellow Fever	No	1
Cholera	No	No
Typhoid & Polio	2	N/A
Malaria	No	N/A

Note: *Regulations and requirements may be subject to change at short notice, and you are advised to contact your doctor well in advance of your intended date of departure. Any numbers in the chart refer to the footnotes below.*

1: A yellow fever certificate is required from travellers aged one year arriving from infected areas.

2: Vaccination against typhoid is sometimes advised.

Food & drink: Mains water is normally chlorinated and, whilst relatively safe, may cause mild abdominal upsets. Bottled water is available and is advised for the first few weeks of the stay. Milk is pasteurised and dairy products are safe for consumption. Local meat, poultry, seafood, fruit and vegetables are generally considered safe to eat.

Other risks: *Hepatitis A* and *dengue fever* may occur. Normal precautions against mosquito bites should be heeded. There is a high prevalence of *HIV/AIDS* in the Caribbean. *Diphtheria, tuberculosis* and *hepatitis B* vaccinations are sometimes recommended.

Health care: Health insurance is strongly recommended as medical treatment is expensive. There are several GPs on the island as well as one hospital and one private clinic. Recompression chambers are on nearby Saba and St Thomas (travel by air ambulance). Please note that the private health clinic, Adelin, will not accept medical travel insurance in payment for treatment. A deposit must be paid of US$4000 by credit card.

Travel - International

AIR:

Many airlines operate to Antigua & Barbuda, including many which operate inter-Caribbean flights. Some require connections.

Approximate flight times: From St John's to *Frankfurt/M* is nine hours 15 minutes, to *London* is eight hours, to *Miami* is three hours, to *New York* is four hours and to *Toronto* is four hours.

Main airports: *VC Bird International (ANU),* formerly Coolidge International, located on the northeast corner of Antigua, is 8km (5 miles) northeast of St John's. The airport

provides access to major international centres, such as Frankfurt/M, London, Miami, Montréal, New York and Toronto, with feeder services to all the Eastern Caribbean islands, the US Virgin Islands and Puerto Rico.

To/from the airport: Taxi services run to the town and hotels on a fixed-fare basis (travel time - 10 to 15 minutes). There is no public transport to or from the airport.

Facilities: Full outgoing duty free shopping, restaurant, bar, 24-hour ATM, post office, car hire and currency exchange.

Departure tax: EC$50 or US$20. EC$35 for nationals of CARICOM countries. EC$25 for nationals of Antigua and Barbuda. Children under 16 are exempt.

SEA:

Main ports: *St John's* has a deep-sea harbour served by cruise liners from the USA, Puerto Rico, the UK, Europe and South America. Many smaller ships sail to other Caribbean islands.

Travel - Internal

AIR:

A small airstrip at Codrington on Barbuda is equipped to handle light aircraft. *Carib Aviation* operates scheduled flights between Antigua and Barbuda (20 minutes' duration, twice daily).

SEA:

Local boats are available for excursions. It usually takes three hours to travel from Antigua to Barbuda. However, the *Barbuda Express* takes 90 minutes and journeys five days per week from St John's.

ROAD:
There are nearly 1000km (600 miles) of roads in the country, most of which are all-weather. Roads are reasonable, although they lack road markings. Few streets are lit at night.

Regulations: The national speed limit is 40mph (64kph) and there is a limit of 20mph (32kph) in built-up areas. Driving is on the left.

Documentation: Valid national driving licence.

Car hire: This can be organised from your home country but is easy to do on arrival. There are several reputable car hire companies on Antigua (some of which also hire out mopeds and bicycles). Hire rates are for the day and there is no mileage or through the car rental agencies on presentation of a valid national driving licence. **Bus:** The bus network is small, and buses are infrequent. **Taxi:** Available everywhere with standardised rates. US Dollars are more readily accepted by taxi drivers. Taxi drivers are also qualified as tour guides for sightseeing trips.

Travel times: The following chart gives approximate travel times (in hours and minutes) from **St John's** to other major towns, resorts or centres in Antigua.

	Road
VC Bird (airport)	0.10
English Harbour	0.35
Jolly Beach	0.20
Shirley Heights	0.35

Antigua & Barbuda

A B C D E F G H I J K L M N O P Q R S T U V W X Y Z

Travel Advice

Most visits to Antigua & Barbuda are trouble-free but you should be aware of the global risk of indiscriminate international terrorist attacks, which could be against civilian targets, including places frequented by foreigners. This advice is based on information provided by the Foreign and Commonwealth Office in the UK. It is correct at time of publishing. As the situation can change rapidly, visitors are advised to contact the following organisations for the latest travel advice:

British Foreign and Commonwealth Office
Tel: (0845) 850 2829.
Website: www.fco.gov.uk

US Department of State
Website: http://travel.state.gov/travel

Accommodation

Note: Accommodation must be booked well in advance during *Tennis Weeks*, *Antigua Sailing Week* and *Carnival* (contact the Tourist Board for further information). No special accommodation facilities exist for students and young travellers and there are no official campsites in Antigua or Barbuda. Sleeping and living on the beaches is not permitted.

HOTELS:
Hotel rates are considerably cheaper in the summer months (May to November). A government tax of 8.5 per cent is added to hotel bills, plus a service charge of 10 per cent. There is no official grading system but there is a wide choice of hotels available ranging from deluxe to standard. A full list of hotels and guest houses, with rates, is available from the Information Office and at VC Bird International Airport in Antigua. Most of the larger hotels in Antigua have rooms with either full air conditioning or with fans and provide a choice of meal plans. The more luxurious establishments offer a large variety of watersports, tennis and evening entertainment. There are three major resort hotels on Barbuda, but accommodation range is more limited.

GUEST HOUSES:
These much cheaper than the hotels and provide basic but clean accommodation, sometimes with meals. There are a number of guest houses on both Antigua and Barbuda.

SELF-CATERING:
Self-catering accommodation is available for the budget-minded.

ACCOMMODATION INFORMATION

Antigua Hotels and Tourist Association
PO Box 454, Island House, Newgate Street, St John's, Antigua
Tel: 462 0374 or 3703.
Website: www.antiguahotels.org

Top Things To See

- Take an excursion to **Great Bird Island** from **Dickenson Bay - glass-bottomed boats** afford leisurely views of the reef, and a **restored pirate ship** also sails around the island and takes passengers for day or evening trips, with food, unlimited drink and entertainment all included.
- **St John's Cathedral** appears on postcards and in almost all visitors' photographs. The church was originally built in 1683, but was replaced by a stone building in 1745. An earthquake destroyed it almost a century later and, in 1845, the cornerstone of the present Anglican cathedral was laid. The figures of St John the Baptist and St John the Divine, erected at the south gate, were supposedly taken from one of Napoleon's ships and brought to the island by a British man-of-war.
- Discover some more of **St John's** gems: the **Museum of Antigua & Barbuda** is housed in the old **Court House** at the corner of **Long** and **Market Streets** and, having been built in 1750, is the oldest building in Antigua. Exhibits explore Antigua's geological origins and political history, the culture of the Arawaks (with a life-sized house) and a model sugar plantation. Be sure not to miss out on their small, interesting gift shop.
- **Indian Town**, one of Antigua's national parks, is at the northeastern point of the island. Breakers roaring in with the full force of the Atlantic behind them have carved **Devil's Bridge** and have created **blow-holes** with foaming surf. Devil's Bridge itself is a must-see visit. Located in the Southeast side of the island, the rough Atlantic Ocean battering against the shoreline has created Devil's Bridge. For those daring enough, walk across the bridge, although this is not advised for safety reasons!
- **Half Moon Bay** is a popular national park, with nearby **Long Bay** protected by a reef and ideal for holidaying families.
- Go see the **lake** that now monopolises the countryside in the centre of Antigua. The result of the **Potworks Dam**, it is Antigua's largest artificial lake, with a capacity of one thousand million gallons.
- **Fig Tree Drive** is a scenic route through the lush tropical hills and picturesque fishing villages along the southwest coast.
- See the **megaliths** at **Greencastle Hill**, said to have been erected for the worship of the Sun God and Moon Goddess.
- Take a trek to the less-developed Barbuda, which has a wilder, more spontaneous beauty, with deserted beaches and heavily wooded interior abounding in birdlife, wild pigs and fallow deer, plus fellow humans at nearby **Codrington**, the main village, that sits on the edge of a lagoon and in which the inhabitants rely largely on the sea for their existence. Here is also the magnificent **Frigate Bird Sanctuary**. In the mating season from September to April, the Frigate bird displays a huge red breast to attract a female mate. This nesting site is one of the most important in the world for these endangered birds.
- For even more desertion and greater eccentricity, stopover at **Redonda**, an uninhabited rocky islet, lying about 56km (35 miles) northeast of Antigua, which was once an important source of phosphates and guano (the remains of some of the mining buildings can still be seen), but for more than a century has had a different claim to fame. In 1865, Redonda was 'claimed' by Matthew Shiell as a kingdom for his son, Philippe. King Philippe I's 'successor', the poet John Gawsworth, appointed many leading literary figures of his day as dukes and duchesses of his kingdom; the lucky peers included JB Priestley, Dylan Thomas and Rebecca West. The current king lives in Sussex, but his subjects are not likely to produce any great works of fiction as they are all either goats, lizards or seabirds. The island is also well known amongst birdwatchers for its small population of burrowing owls, a bird now extinct on Antigua.
- Those wishing to brush up on some British colonial history, should visit **Shirley Heights** and **Fort James**, examples of the efforts made by the British to fortify the colony during the 18th century. Close by is the **cemetery**, containing an **obelisk** commemorating the soldiers of the 54th Regiment.

Top Things To Do

- Go to the **Carnival**, Antigua & Barbuda's 10-day festival of colourful costumes, beauty pageants, talent shows and good music, all in celebration of emancipation (usually in August); the revelry is nonstop and ranges from the Party Monarch and Calypso Monarch competitions to the spectacular Parade of Bands to food fairs and cultural shows.
- Do what the locals do and enjoy the extensive **yachting** and **sailing** facilities on offer: sample yachting events include the **Round the Island Race**, organised by the Antiguan Yacht Club (usually in January) and the **Antigua Classic Yacht Regatta** (usually in April), with all events centred around Nelson's Dockyard, renowned around the world for world-class yacht racing and fun; sample sailing events are the **International Sailing Week** (usually in April), plus smaller regattas held throughout the year, in particular a two-day event at the Jolly Harbour Yacht Club starting on Valentine's Day, a **Cruise Race** in July, and a two-day regatta in November; those preferring to seek out a secluded cove or sheltered beach and anchor for a day of peace and quiet can do so by hiring a **dinghy**.
- Play Antigua & Barbuda's national game, **Warri**, an ancient board ('count and capture') game that was traditionally played using shells placed in cups: a **National Warri Festival** is held every year.
- Get stuck into Antigua & Barbuda's impressive range of **watersports**: equipment is available at some hotels and resorts but is nevertheless cheap and easy to hire throughout Antigua & Barbuda, with **windsurfing**, **water-skiing**, **beachcombing**, **surfing** (especially on Gallery Bay on the northwest coast), **snorkelling** and **scuba diving** on offer, with over 365 beaches to practice in – also convenient if you just fancy a bit of **swimming**!
- **Crab-race**: this eccentric sport is ideal for the very lazy and is staged in certain bars once or twice a week. A punter may win enough to pay for the next round of drinks, but stakes are moderate and the crabs are unlikely to make anyone a millionaire – but most will be playing for the fun, not the prize!
- Be genteel and dabble in the national (modern) game, **cricket**, which is played to the highest international standard. In Viv Richards, Antigua produced one of the finest cricketers the game has ever seen. January is the official start of the cricket season.
- Salivate and haggle over the riot of colourful fruits, vegetables and spices available at one of the best **local markets** in the Caribbean, situated in the south end of town at the junction of Valley and All Saints Roads; if you buy only one item of produce, make it a **pineapple** – Antigua & Barbuda's are considered some of the world's best.
- Quench your thirst with **coconut juice**, brought down straight from the trees and scraped out at its freshest.
- Explore huge **caves** at **Two Foot Bay**: look at ancient cave drawings; climb to the top of the Highland and look out for miles; get expert help and go underground and underwater.
- Stop for a **picnic** in the shade and watch for the **wildlife** amongst the salt ponds and bush safari.

TOURIST INFORMATION

Antigua & Barbuda Tourist Office in the UK
15 Thayer Street, London W1U 3JT, UK
Website: www.antigua-barbuda.com
Opening hours: Mon-Fri 0930-1230 and 1330-1500.

Antigua & Barbuda Department of Tourism and Trade in the USA
610 Fifth Avenue, Suite 311, New York, NY 10020, USA
Tel: (212) 541 4117.
Website: www.antigua-barbuda.org

Entertainment

FOOD & DRINK: Antigua's gastronomic speciality is lobster, with red snapper and occasionally other fish running a close second when available.

Things to know: Larger hotels offer a wide selection of imported meats, vegetables, fruits and cheeses. Casual wear is accepted in all bars and restaurants. There is an 8.5 per cent government tax on most restaurant bills.

National specialities:

- *Fungi and pepperpot*, the national dish, is a hearty vegetable stew with salted meat.
- *Roti* are patties filled with curried potatoes, chicken or beef.
- *Ducana* are sweet potato dumplings often served with saltfish and *chop up* (see below).
- *Chop up* is mashed aubergine, okra and seasoning.
- *Tamarind balls* are the local sweets.
- Popular dishes include barbecued chicken, roast suckling pig, pilaffs, curries and mushrooms.

National drinks:

- *Ting* is a grapefruit drink that is homegrown and sparkling.
- *Wadadli* beer is locally-brewed, light and refreshing.
- Popular ingredients include pineapple, coconut, guavas and mangoes.
- For an alcoholic kick, rum is plentiful; try both dark and light rums (*Cavalier*), and rum punches.
- Imported wines and spirits are available, as well as imported sodas and fruit drinks.

Legal drinking age: 16. There are no licensing restrictions, but excessive consumption of alcohol is frowned upon and further service will be refused.

Tipping: 10 to 15 per cent is included on hotel bills for staff gratuities, plus an 8.5 per cent government tax. Taxi drivers expect 10 per cent of the fare, and dockside and airport porters expect US$0.50-1.00 per bag.

NIGHTLIFE: There is a wide choice of restaurants and bars around main tourist areas. Steel bands, combos and limbo dancers travel around hotels, performing nightly during the high season (November to April). There are five casinos on the island and two nightclubs/discos. Some hotels have their own discos.

SHOPPING: Uniquely Antiguan purchases include straw goods, pottery, *batik* and silk-screen printed fabrics, and jewellery incorporating semi-precious Antiguan stones. English bone china and crystal and French perfumes, watches and table linens are all available at very attractive prices. *Heritage Quay Complex* is a shopping and entertainment complex with 40 duty free shops, a theatre, restaurants and a casino and supper club. It forms part of the newest development in central St John's. **Shopping hours:** Mon-Sat 0800-1200 and 1300-1700, although some shops and chemists do not close for lunch; some shops close at noon on Thursday.

Business

- **GDP:** US$756 million (2003 estimate).
- **Main exports:** Petroleum products, manufactured goods, foodstuffs and livestock, machinery and transport equipment.
- **Main imports:** Food and live animals, machinery, transport equipment, manufactures, chemicals and oil.
- **Main trade partners:** Exports to: OECS, Barbados, Guyana, Trinidad & Tobago, USA; Imports from: USA, UK, Canada and OECS.

ECONOMY: Antigua was one of the first Caribbean islands to actively encourage tourism, beginning in the late 1960s; the late 1980s brought another phase of major development. Tourism and financial services are now the main components of the service sector, which accounts for over three-quarters of the Antiguan economy. Both have suffered problems in recent years – tourism because of repeated hurricanes, finance because of questionable associations with money-laundering operations. For instance, in June 2000, Antigua was identified by the Organization for Economic Cooperation and Development (OECD) – the world's 30 largest economies – as one of 35 'tax havens' whose financial laws are considered inadequate. It must tighten its regime or face sanctions.

Fears of an over-reliance on tourism and finance have led the government to try and diversify the economy into manufacturing, agriculture and fisheries. Local agriculture and fisheries have been promoted to reduce dependency on imported food – a range of fruit and vegetables is now produced and many fish farms have been established. There are numerous light industries producing such items as clothing, paper, furniture and household appliances. A final source of revenue for the government is the rent on two US military bases. However, the difficult period for the hotel industry has seemingly continued despite such efforts. National debts are high - in excess of 130 per cent of GDP. The 2005 budget included cuts to the public service salary, with 2600 jobs from a 13,000 workforce being cut. It was assured that those made redundant would be given assistance in finding employment in the private sector and establishing their own businesses. The Prime Minister and the Cabinet have taken a 10 per cent salary cut. Income tax was also reintroduced for those earning more than EC$3000 (US$1,111) monthly, ranging from a 10 per cent to a 25 per cent tax.

Antigua & Barbuda has large trade and balance of payments deficits and relies heavily on foreign aid.

BUSINESS ETIQUETTE: A lightweight suit, a long- or short-sleeved shirt and a tie are suitable for most business visits. Handshaking is the normal greeting for acquaintances and for formal introductions. Calling cards are expected from people who do not live on the islands.

Office hours: Mon-Fri 0800-1200 and 1300-1630.

Government office hours: Mon-Thurs 0800-1630, Fri 0800-1500.

CONFERENCES/CONVENTIONS: Around 20 per cent of the members of the Antigua Hotels & Tourist Association (see *Accommodation* for details) offer meeting facilities.

COMMERCIAL INFORMATION

Antigua & Barbuda Investment Authority
Redcliffe Street, St John's, Antigua
Tel: 462 1033.
E-mail: ldb@candw.ag

Antigua & Barbuda Chamber of Commerce and Industry Ltd
PO Box 774, Corner of Popeshead Street and North Street, St John's, Antigua
Tel: 462 0743.
E-mail: chamcom@candw.ag

Alexander Parrish (Antigua) Ltd (Information on Conferences/Conventions)
PO Box 45, Travel Department, Redcliffe Street, St John's, Antigua
Tel: 462 0638.
E-mail: apal@candw.ag

Argentina

Location: Southeastern South America.

Time: GMT - 3.

Overview

Argentina is a land of extremes: its hectic urban centres contrast with a staggeringly remote hinterland. The country can be simultaneously hot in one region and cold in another. The one common thread is that the people possess a curiosity, passion and fervour for life - most visible when it comes to football, the national obsession. The Tango, *gauchos* and *estancias* are the country's cliched attractions, but what strikes visitors most is that life here is for living: the fast pace only letting up for the afternoon siesta. Those who think of Argentina and a long list of clichés will also evoke the legendary incidents of Argentina's political past, as immortalised in 'Evita'. A coup in 1943 resulted in the rise of Lieutenant General Peron Sosa as President, who instigated a policy of extreme nationalism and social improvement: the *Peronista* movement. Despite triumphant re-election as President in 1973, he died one year later and his wife, Isabelita Peron, took over, but was dramatically deposed by a military coup in 1976. This legacy of Peron (and his wife) continues to inspire Argentinean politicians and fascinate the popular imagination. The end of the *Peronista* period heralded perhaps the darkest period in Argentinean history. However, the mass discontent of the populace paved the way for improvement in economic circumstances and much-needed retribution for years of repression. What also emerged was a country that may well surprise those with pre-expectations. Argentina is cosmopolitan and modern. Nowhere is this more apparent than in Buenos Aires. Somewhat unfairly referred to as a grimy Paris, Buenos Aires is a sophisticated capital brimming with character and an excellent spot for shopping and watching the world go by. Nightlife is spectacular and restaurants overspill with delectable dishes. You are just as likely to find businesspeople spending cash on the latest fashions as you are to find couples in passionate stages of tango.

But perhaps it is Argentina's natural history that truly astounds. It is so topographically diverse that there is something for everyone: every type of landscape is here in microcosm. National parks teem with wildlife and mountainous vistas, while the colossal Perito Moreno Glacier and Iguazú Falls are natural wonders renowned worldwide. Horse riding, adventure sports and birdwatching are available throughout, and the Andes offer excellent skiing. Endless hiking opportunities are in the south, where Patagonia is stunningly barren and mystifying and the Tierra del Fuego feels like the end of the world. In short, Argentina is a menagerie of delights: vastly unexplored and undiscovered by most tourists, it is an adventure that is waiting to happen.

General Information

AREA: 2,780,400 sq km (1,073,518 sq miles).

POPULATION: 37.48 milion (official estimate 2001).

POPULATION DENSITY: 13.0 per sq km (2001).

CAPITAL: Buenos Aires. **Population:** 2.77 million (official estimate 2001).

GEOGRAPHY: Argentina is situated in South America, east of the Andes, and is bordered by Chile to the west, the Atlantic Ocean to the east and Uruguay, Bolivia, Paraguay and Brazil to the north and northeast. There are four main geographical areas: the Andes, the North and Mesopotamia, the Pampas and Patagonia. The climate and geography of Argentina vary considerably, ranging from the great heat of the Chaco (*El Chaco*), through the pleasant climate of the central Pampas to the sub-Antarctic cold of the Patagonian Sea. Mount Aconcagua soars almost 7000m (23,000ft) and waterfalls at Iguazú stretch around a massive semi-circle, thundering 70m (230ft) to the bed of the Paraná River. In the southwest is a small 'Switzerland' with a string of beautiful icy lakes framed by mountains.

GOVERNMENT: Federal and Democratic Republic. Gained independence from Spain in 1816. Under the amended constitution, which came into force in August 1994, legislative power is in the bicameral *Congreso* (Congress), comprising a 257-member lower house, the *Cámara de Diputados* (Chamber of Deputies), and a 72-member *Senado* (Senate). Members of the Lower House are elected every four years by proportional representation; the Senate is indirectly elected by provincial legislatures and serves a six-year term. Executive power is held by the President, assisted by a Cabinet of Ministers, who is directly elected for a four-year term (renewable once only). **Head of State and Government:** President Néstor Carlos Kirchner since 2003.

Recent history: The last scheduled Presidential election due in October 2003 was eventually brought forward by six months. The left performed badly, as was expected. The surprise was that Carlos Menem was eligible to stand again. With just under 20 per cent of the vote, he took second place behind the official Peronista candidate, Nestor Kirchner. Supporters of other candidates then switched their allegiance to Kirchner, simply to ensure that Menem did not return. Now facing a humiliating defeat in the second round run-off, Menem withdrew, leaving Kirchner to win by default. Kirchner's priority is the economy and the restoration of Argentina's international credibility. Measures towards this include the issue of an international arrest warrant for Menem over allegations of fraud, although these were later cancelled and he has since returned from exile.

LANGUAGE: Spanish is the official language. English is widely spoken with some French and German.

RELIGION: More than 90 per cent Roman Catholic, 2 per cent Protestant with small Muslim and Jewish communities.

ELECTRICITY: 220 volts AC, 50Hz. Lamp fittings are of the screw-type. Plug fittings in older buildings are of the two-pin round type, but some new buildings use the three-pin flat type.

SOCIAL CONVENTIONS: The most common form of greeting between friends is kissing cheeks. When invited to somebody's house it is quite common to take a homemade dish or dessert. Dinner is usually served between 2100-2200. Avoid casual discussion of the Falklands/Malvinas war. Dress is not usually formal, though clothes should be conservative away from the beach. Formal wear is worn for official functions and dinners, particularly in exclusive restaurants. Smoking is prohibited on public transport, in cinemas and theatres.

Climate

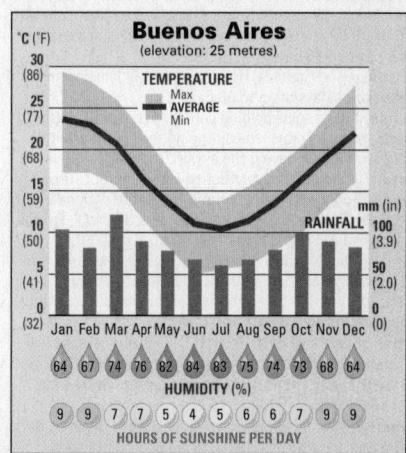

The north is subtropical with rain throughout the year, while the Tierra del Fuego in the south has a sub-arctic climate. The main central area is temperate, but can be hot and humid during summer (December to February) and cool in winter.
Required clothing: European clothes for the main central area. Lightweight cottons and linens in the north. Warm clothes are necessary in the south and during winter months in the central area. Waterproofing is advisable for all areas.

Communications

Telephone: Country code: 54. The system is often overburdened and international calls are expensive. Local calls can be made from public call-boxes, which are located in shops and restaurants and are identifiable by a blue sign outside. Public phones take 1 peso or 50 and 25 centavos coins. Most public telephones accept international phone cards. Reduced tariffs apply from 2200-0800.
Mobile telephone: Roaming agreements exist with some international mobile phone companies. Coverage is good.
Internet: Available in most large cities and resorts.
Post: Airmail to Europe takes between five and 10 days. Surface mail to Europe takes on average 20 to 25 days but can take as long as 50 days, so it is advisable to send everything airmail. Internal postal services are subject to delay. The main post office in Buenos Aires is located in Sarmiento 189 and is open Mon-Fri 0900-1930. Post office hours: Mon-Fri 0800-2000, Sat 0800-1400.
MEDIA: Press: The *Buenos Aires Herald* is the leading English-language newspaper in Latin America. Argentina's principal dailies include *Clarín*, *Crónica*, *El Cronista*, *La Nación*, *Página 12*, *Diario Popular* and *La Prensa*.
TV: There are about 42 TV broadcast stations. After Brazil and Mexico, Argentina has the largest number of TV receivers in the region. Cable TV is prevalent. There are five 'superstations' in Buenos Aires, four of which are privately owned (Channels 2, 9, 11 and 13) and one which remains public (*Channel 7/Argentina Televisora Color*).
Radio: There are about 1000, mostly unlicensed FM radio stations, including the popular *Cristal FM* and *Radio Antena UNO CNN* in Santa Fe. There are about 260 AM and six shortwave radio stations.

Passport/Visa

	Passport Required?	Visa Required?	Return Ticket Required?
Full British	Yes	No	Yes
Australian	Yes	No	Yes
Canadian	Yes	No	Yes
USA	Yes	No	Yes
Other EU	Yes	No	Yes
Japanese	Yes	No	Yes

Note: *Regulations and requirements may be subject to change at short notice, and you are advised to contact the appropriate diplomatic or consular authority before finalising travel arrangements. Any numbers in the chart refer to the footnotes below.*

PASSPORTS: Valid passport required by all except nationals of Brazil, Chile, Paraguay and Uruguay who, for journeys that do not go beyond Argentina and these five countries, may use their national ID cards.
VISAS: Required by all except the following:
(a) nationals of the countries shown in the chart above for stays of up to 90 days;
(b) nationals of Andorra, Barbados, Bolivia, Brazil, Chile, Colombia, Costa Rica, Croatia, Dominican Republic, Ecuador, El Salvador, Guatemala, Guyana, Haiti, Honduras, Hong Kong (SAR), Iceland, Israel, Korea (Rep), Liechtenstein, Macedonia (Former Yugoslav Republic of), Mexico, Monaco, New Zealand, Nicaragua, Norway, Panama, Paraguay, Peru, St Lucia, St Vincent & the Grenadines, San Marino, Serbia & Montenegro, Singapore, South Africa, Switzerland, Trinidad & Tobago, Turkey, Uruguay, Vatican City and Venezuela for stays of up to 90 days;
(c) nationals of Grenada, Hong Kong (BNO), Jamaica and Malaysia for stays of up to 30 days;
(d) transit passengers holding confirmed onward or return tickets for travel provided continuing their journey within six hours and not leaving the airport.
Note: Visa exemptions mentioned above are for *tourist purposes only*. Business exemptions apply to nationals of Australia, Belgium, Brazil, Czech Republic, Denmark, Estonia, Finland, France, Grenada, Guyana, Hong Kong (SAR), Hungary, Iceland, Japan, Korea (Rep), Latvia, Lithuania, Malaysia, Netherlands, New Zealand, Norway, Poland, St Lucia, St Vincent & the Grenadines, Singapore, South Africa, Trinidad & Tobago, the UK and the USA.
Types of visa and cost: *Tourist*: £16.50; *Business*: £27.50. Passengers requiring visas for transit only should still apply for tourist visas. The cost of visas changes monthly with exchange rates.
Validity: Visas are generally valid for stays of up to 90 days. Extensions for a further 180 days are possible for some nationals; contact the Consulate (or consular section at Embassy) for details.
Application to: Consulate, or consular section at Embassy (see *Passport/Visa Information*).
Application requirements: *Tourist*: (a) Valid passport. (b) Application form. (c) One passport photo. (d) Fee; payable by cheque or postal order. (e) Medical certificate stating that the applicant is free of any symptoms of infectious diseases. (f) Return ticket. (g) Proof of sufficient funds (eg bank statement); minimum US$50 per day of stay. (h) Affidavit signed at Consular section by applicant, declaring that applicant has not, in the last 30 days, been to any SARS countries or zones and that they will not travel to them during the validity of the visa. (i) Proof of legal residence in country of residence. *Business*: (a)-(h) and,
(i) Letter of introduction from employer. If visit does not respond to an invitation from company in Argentina, letter must include a paragraph specifying this fact. If visit follows an invitation received from company/person established or residing in Argentina, this application must be submitted by the applicant at the Dirección Nacional de Migraciones (DNM) in Argentina. *Student*: (a)-(e) and, (f) Two additional passport photos. (g) Letter from Argentine university confirming student admission and stating length of stay, legalised by the Ministry of Education. (h) Medical certificate, Birth Certificate, Marriage Certificate (if applicable) and Police Record Certificate, with translations into English, all legalised by the FCO and "Apostille".
(i) Signed declaration that the applicant has no international criminal record.
Working days required: Three days. Applications can be processed in one working day for an additional £22 express service fee. Applications sent by mail may incur additional processing time.
Note: Argentine minors travelling to or from Argentina, if unaccompanied by their parents, must carry their parents' or other legal guardian's authorisation to travel, which must be certified by an Argentine Consul if issued abroad. Fines will be levied if passengers do not comply with immigration requirements and passengers will be deported.
Temporary residence: Applicants for temporary residence, working holidays and long-stay business visits to Argentina should contact the Embassy or Consulate (see *Passport/Visa Information*).

PASSPORT/VISA INFORMATION

Embassy of the Argentine Republic in the UK
65 Brooke Street, London W1K 4AH, UK
Tel: (020) 7318 1300.
Website: www.argentine-embassy-uk.org
Opening hours: Mon-Fri 0900-1700.
Also provides tourist information.

Argentine Consulate in the UK
27 Three Kings Yard, London W1K 4DF, UK
Tel: (020) 7318 1340.
E-mail: fclond@mrecic.gov.ar
Opening hours: Mon-Fri 0930-1400
(general enquiries by telephone);
0930-1300 (visa applications in person).

Embassy of the Argentine Republic in the USA
1600 New Hampshire Avenue, NW, Washington, DC 20009, USA
Tel: (202) 238 6400 *or* 6460 (consular section).
Website: www.embajadaargentinaeeuu.org

Money

Currency: Peso (ARS; symbol AR$) = 100 centavos. Peso notes are in denominations of AR$100, 50, 20, 10, 5 and 2. Coins are in denominations of AR$1 and 50, 25, 10, 5 and 1 centavos.
Currency exchange: While the US Dollar is generally (though not officially) accepted as legal tender, foreign currencies can be exchanged in banks and authorised *cambios* (bureaux de change), which are available in all the major cities.
Credit & debit cards: Most major credit cards are widely accepted. Check with your credit or debit card company for details of merchant acceptability and other services which may be available. ATMs are available in most cities but it is still best to carry alternative forms of payment.
Traveller's cheques: It is often difficult to exchange these in the smaller towns. To avoid additional exchange rate charges, travellers are advised to take traveller's cheques in US Dollars.
Currency restrictions: The import and export of both local and foreign currency is limited to US$10,000. Gold must be declared.
Banking hours: Mon-Fri 1000-1500.

Exchange rate indicators:
Rate at time of publishing

£1.00=	AR$5.22
$1.00=	AR$2.88

Note: The Government has changed the Peso fixed rate to the US Dollar, devaluating the local currency which is now under free flotation.

Duty Free

The following goods may be imported into Argentina without incurring customs duty:
(a) Travellers over 18 years of age coming from Bolivia, Brazil, Chile, Paraguay or Uruguay, or residents returning to Argentina after less than one year's stay in these countries, may import the following goods to a value of US$100:
200 cigarettes and 25 cigars; *1l of alcohol*; *2kg of foodstuffs*.
(b) Travellers over 18 years of age coming from countries other than those listed above, or residents returning to Argentina after less than one year's stay in countries other than those above, may import the following goods to a value of US$300:
400 cigarettes and 50 cigars; *2l of alcohol*; *5kg of foodstuffs*.
Prohibited items: Animals and birds from Africa or Asia (except Japan) without prior authorisation, parrots and fresh foodstuffs, particularly meat, dairy products and fruit. Explosives, inflammable items, narcotics and pornographic material are also forbidden.
Note: All gold must be declared. It is wise to arrange customs clearance for expensive consumer items (cameras, computers, etc) to forestall any problems.

Public Holidays

Below are listed Public Holidays for the January 2006-June 2007 period.
2006: Jan 1 New Year's Day. **Apr 2** Veterans' Day (Malvinas). **Apr 14** Good Friday. **May 1** Labour Day. **May 25** Anniversary of the First Independent Argentine Government. **Jun 19** National Flag Day. **Jul 9** National Independence Day. **Aug 21** Anniversary of the Death of General José de San Martín. **Oct 16** Columbus Day. **Dec 8** Immaculate Conception Day. **Dec 25** Christmas Day.
2007: Jan 1 New Year's Day. **Apr 2** Veterans' Day (Malvinas). **Apr 6** Good Friday. **May 1** Labour Day. **May 25** National Day (Anniversary of the 1810 Revolution). **June 18** National Flag Day.

Health

	Special Precautions?	Certificate Required?
Yellow Fever	No	No
Cholera	Yes	2
Typhoid & Polio	3	N/A
Malaria	4	N/A

Note: *Regulations and requirements may be subject to change at short notice, and you are advised to contact your doctor well in advance of your intended date of departure. Any numbers in the chart refer to the footnotes below.*

1: Following WHO guidelines issued in 1973, a cholera vaccination certificate is not a condition of entry to Argentina. However, precautions are advised. Up-to-date advice should be sought before deciding whether these precautions should include vaccination as medical opinion is divided over its effectiveness; see the *Health* appendix for more information.
2: Typhoid fever is not common but a risk exists.
3: Malaria risk, exclusively in the benign *vivax* form is low and exists in pockets in the provinces of Salta, Jujuy, Misiones and Corrientes. Protection in the form of chloroquine chemoprophylaxis administered weekly is advised, plus general mosquito bite protection.
Food & drink: Tap water is considered safe to drink. Drinking water outside main cities and towns may be contaminated and sterilisation is advisable. Pasteurised milk and dairy products are safe for consumption. Avoid unpasteurised milk as *brucellosis* occurs. Local meat, poultry, seafood, fruit and vegetables are generally considered safe to eat.
Other risks: *Hepatitis A* and *intestinal parasitosis* are widespread. Both *cutaneous* and *mucocutaneous leishmaniasis* occur. There is some risk of *dengue fever* and *anthrax*. Asthma, sinus and bronchial problems may be aggravated by the polluted atmosphere of the major cities. *Rabies* is present. For those at high risk, vaccination before arrival should be considered. If bitten, seek medical advice without delay. For more information, consult the *Health* appendix.
Health care: Medical insurance is recommended as there are no reciprocal health agreements. Medical facilities are

generally of a high standard, though of varying quality outside Buenos Aires. Immediate cash payment is often expected by doctors.

Travel - International

AIR:

 The national airline is Aerolíneas Argentinas (AR) (website: www.aerolineas.com.ar). Many other airlines serve Argentina.

Approximate flight times: From Buenos Aires to *London* is 13 hours, to *Los Angeles* is 16 hours, to *New York* is 14 hours 15 minutes, to *Singapore* is 29 hours 30 minutes and to *Sydney* is 16 hours.

Main airports: *Ezeiza Ministro Pistarini International Airport (EZE)* (tel: (11) 5480 6111), is 37km (23 miles) from Buenos Aires. *To/from the airport:* There are bus services to the city operating between 0500-2000 (travel time – 40 minutes). Taxis are also available. There is also a coach connection to *Jorge Newbery* airport (locally called *Aeroparque*) for domestic flight connections. To reach the city by car, drive in the Teniente General Ricchieri freeway. *Facilities:* 24-hour bank, restaurants, tourist information kiosk, bureau de change, duty free shops and car hire.

Air passes: *The Mercosur Airpass* is valid within Argentina, Brazil, Chile (except Easter Island), Paraguay and Uruguay. Participating airlines include TAM Mercosur (PZ), Pluna (PU), TAM Linhas Aéreas (JJ) and VARIG (RG). The pass can only be purchased by passengers who live outside South America, who have a return ticket. Only eight flight coupons are allowed with a maximum of four coupons for each country and it is valid for seven to a maximum of 30 days. At least two countries must be visited and the flight route cannot be changed. A maximum of two stopovers is allowed per country.

The *Visit South America Pass* is valid within Argentina, Bolivia, Brazil, Colombia, Chile (except Easter Island), Ecuador, Paraguay, Peru, Uruguay and Venezuela. Participating airlines include *Aer Lingus (EI), American Airlines (AA), British Airways (BA), Cathay Pacific (CX), Finnair (AY), Iberia (IB), LAN (LA)* and *Qantas (QF)*. The pass must be bought outside South America in country of residence. It allows unlimited travel to 34 cities. A minimum of three flights must be booked, with no maximum; the maximum stay is 60 days, with no minimum, and prices depend on the amount of flight zones. For further details, contact one of the participating airlines.

Departure tax: Approximately US$18. For flights to Montevideo (Uruguay) and regional flights, the departure tax is US$8. Passengers in transit and children under two years of age are exempt. Visitors are advised to check with their airline or travel agent as the departure tax is subject to frequent changes. There is also an immigration tax of US$10 on all international flights.

SEA/RIVER:

 Main ports: *Buenos Aires, Quequén* and *Bahía Blanca*. Ferries and hydrofoils link Buenos Aires with Montevideo in Uruguay, and there are ferry connections down the Paraná River from Paraguay.

RAIL:

 The major direct international route is from Buenos Aires to Asunción in Paraguay. There are also direct rail links with Bolivia, Brazil, Chile and Paraguay. Services are often disrupted and delays can be expected.

ROAD:

 Argentina has a network of approximately 217,762km (136,101 miles) of roads, of which around 156,789km (97,993 miles) are paved. There are well-maintained road routes from Uruguay, Brazil, Paraguay, Bolivia and Chile. **Coach:** Direct daily services between Buenos Aires, Puerto Alegre, São Paulo and Rio de Janeiro.

Travel - Internal

AIR:

 Domestic flights from *Jorge Newbery (Aeroparque)* and *Córdoba (COR) (Pajas Blancas)* to destinations throughout Argentina are run by *Aerolíneas Argentinas (AR)*. Air travel is the most efficient way to get around, but the services are very busy and can be subject to delay. There is a 30-day *Visit Argentina Pass* available, with four to eight coupons for flights within the country, with many accompanying airlines. It is also possible to buy a 60-day air pass.

Domestic airports: *Buenos Aires Aeroparque Jorge Newbury (AEP)* is located on the bank of the Rio de la Plata, a few minutes away from the main financial and commercial district. *To/from the airport:* There are frequent bus and taxi services to all areas of the city as well as a coach connection to *Ezeiza Ministro Pistarini* international airport. *Facilities:* Bank/bureau de change, left luggage, car rental and a tourist information kiosk.

Departure tax: Between US$7.05 to US$8, and subject to frequent changes.

RAIL:

 Owing to severe underfunding of State railways and recent privatisation, many long haul services have been disrupted, although some suburban lines have been greatly improved. The domestic rail network extends over 43,000km (27,000 miles), which makes it one of the largest in the world. Children under three travel free and children aged three to 11 pay half fare. There are three classes: air conditioned, first class and second class. There are restaurant and sleeping facilities for first-class passengers. Second-class rail travel is good value. There are six main rail routes from Buenos Aires: Buenos Aires–Rosario (where one branch goes to Tucumán and Jujuy via Córdoba and the second branch goes to Tucumán and Jujuy via La Banda), Buenos Aires–Rojas, Buenos Aires–Santa Rosa, Buenos Aires–Mar del Plata, Buenos Aires–Las Flores–Quequén Necochea and Buenos Aires–Bahía Blanca (where a branch goes to San Carlos de Bariloche). Rail travellers are warned that once out of Buenos Aires, information is very hard to come by.

Special fares: The *Argempass* entitles visitors to unlimited first-class train travel, but is only sold in Argentina at railway booking offices. Passes are available for 30 days, 60 days and 90 days. A supplement is charged for sleeping car accommodation. The passes must be used within 30 days of purchase and are valid from the first day of use to the last day at 2400. Other discount tickets include: *Group Pass:* 10 to 25 per cent discount for a group of 10 to 25 people; *Family Pass:* 25 per cent discount for a parent and up to two children; *Youth Pass:* 25 per cent discount for people under 30 years of age; *Senior Pass:* 25 per cent discount for women aged 55 and over and men aged 60 and over; and *Student Pass:* 25 per cent discount for students.

ROAD:

 Major privatisation programmes have resulted in many trunk roads being upgraded, and roads are generally in good condition. Expect tolls on motorways. Rural roads, composed of packed dirt, become impassable after rain. Nonetheless, buses are considered to be a more reliable form of long-distance transport than trains. **Regulations:** Traffic drives on the right. Drivers must be at least 21 years of age (sometimes up to 25 years of age) in order to be valid for hiring a car. **Car hire:** There are a number of agencies in Buenos Aires. **Documentation:** An international Driving Permit is required and this must be stamped at the offices of the *Automóvil Club Argentino* (website: www.aca.org.ar). These documents must be carried at all times whilst driving: proof of ownership, proof of insurance and receipt for last tax payment. **Taxi:** Available in most cities and large towns and can either be hailed on the street or found at taxi ranks. They are usually recognisable by their yellow roofs. It is best to use hotel-recommended

URBAN:

 Buenos Aires is generally well served by public transport. The city's underground, the *Subte*, was the first to be constructed in Latin America. Recently privatised, its old glitzy stations (adorned with ceramic tiles portraying scenes of Argentine life) are now being renovated. There are five lines, labelled A to E. Services operate from early morning to late at night on a fixed-fare basis; tokens can be purchased at booking offices. **Bus:** Services are provided by *colectivo* buses operating 24 hours a day on an inexpensive flat fare; however, these are often crowded, particularly at rush hour, but are usually prompt. There are extensive bus services in other towns, including trolleybuses in Rosario. The main bus station is in Buenos Aires, at Av. Ramos Mejia 1680, close to Retiro Station. taxis.

Travel times: The following chart gives approximate travel times (in hours and minutes) from **Buenos Aires** to other major cities/towns in Argentina.

	Air	Road	Rail
Córdoba	1.10	9.00	12.00
Bariloche	2.10	22.00	36.00
Iguazú	1.40	20.00	-
Rosario	0.50	4.00	4.00

Travel Advice

Most visits to Argentina are trouble-free but you should be aware of the global risk of indiscriminate international terrorist attacks, which could be against civilian targets, including places frequented by foreigners.

In addition, Argentina has recovered strongly from the economic and political crisis of 2001/02, but there are still occasional outbreaks of social unrest. Travellers are advised to avoid public gatherings and demonstrations. Crime has increased since the crisis.

This advice is based on information provided by the Foreign and Commonwealth Office in the UK. It is correct at time of publishing. As the situation can change rapidly, visitors are advised to contact the following organisations for the latest travel advice:

British Foreign and Commonwealth Office
Tel: (0845) 850 2829.
Website: www.fco.gov.uk

US Department of State
Website: http://travel.state.gov/travel

Accommodation

HOTELS:

 Hotels range in standard from the most luxurious in Buenos Aires to the lowest class in the rural areas. Grading ranges from 5-star (highest) to 1-star (lowest). In Buenos Aires, the cheaper hotels can mostly be found around Avenida de Mayo. Generally, service is excellent. All hotels add approximately 3 per cent tourism tax, 24 per cent service charge for food and drink and 15 per cent room tax. Check correct charges when booking. Most are air-conditioned and have good restaurants. For further information, contact the *Secretaría de Turismo de la Nación*.

BED & BREAKFAST:

 Available in small family hotels in Buenos Aires and other cities. Maid service is generally included in the price, but laundry service often requires a small extra charge. Bed & breakfast hotels can also offer useful tourist advice.

SELF-CATERING:

 It is possible to rent cheap self-catering apartments and flats, with or without maid service, either by the day or week. Some can provide meals. Most apartments are in Buenos Aires.

CAMPING/CARAVANNING:

 Most resort cities welcome campers, and there are motels, campsites and caravan sites throughout Argentina. Campsites can be found in virtually every major region. Campervans can be hired.

YOUTH HOSTELS:

There are youth hostels throughout Argentina, from Tilcaru in the north to El Calafate and Ushaia in the south.

ACCOMMODATION INFORMATION

Hostelling International Argentina
Florida 835, C1005AAQ Buenos Aires, Argentina
Tel: (11) 4511 8712.
Website: www.hostels.org.ar

Top Things To See

- Step into the **Capital Federal District** - one of the world's largest metropolitan areas - which has, at its heart, **Buenos Aires**: gawp at the gigantic **Catedral Metropolitana** (Metropolitan Cathedral), which contains the remains of San Martín, Argentina's liberator; delight in the atmosphere of **San Telmo**, with its many cafes, antique shops, tango night spots and a Sunday flea market on **Plaza Dorrego**; and have a walk through the chic and upper-class **Recoleta** borough, famous for its **Cementerio de la Recoleta** (where many members of Argentina's elite are buried) and the renowned **Museo Nacional de Bellas Artes** (Museum of Fine Arts), which has works by Renoir, Rodin, Monet, Van Gogh and numerous Argentine artists.

- See the top spots of **The Pampas** and visit the scenic peaks of **Sierra de la Ventana**, located within the **Ernesto Tornquist Provincial Park**; note the traces of colonial past in **Santa Fe**; glimpse the pink granite rock formations (reaching up to 600m/1968ft) of **Lihue Calel National Park**, an area consisting mostly of desert, located some 226km (142 miles) southwest of the city of **Santa Rosa**.

- Go see that **Resistencia** is not called the 'city of sculptures' for nothing: there are over 200 of them in this capital of the **El Chaco Province**; and **Campo del Cielo** is a nearby area famous for its meteorite fragments dating back some 6000 years.

- Be dazzled by the sheer power of the **Iguazú Falls** (parts of which are located in neighbouring Brazil), within the UNESCO World Heritage-listed **Iguazú National Park**, whose subtropical rainforest provides a habitat for over 2000 identified plant species and 400 bird species: the Iguazú Falls are a majestic phenomenon that can be viewed from many channels, the most impressive of which is **Garganta del Diablo** (Devil's Throat), which can be approached via a system of catwalks. At their highest point, the falls have a vertical drop more than one and a half times the full length of Niagara Falls. Visitors can catch a good view of the falls from a tower near the visitor centre, which also organises free trips to the **Isla San Martín**, another good lookout point for an extensive and crowd-free view.

- Visit one of Argentina's oldest cities, **Corrientes**, and see the **Santísima Cruz de los Milagros**, among Corrientes' oldest churches, and the **Convento de San Francisco**: Corrientes is also the land of the *chamamé*, a characteristic type of rhythmic music derived from the polka.

- Gaze at the **Andes** mountain ranges whilst sipping a glass of wine in the **Mendoza Province**: near the border with Chile lies the famous **Mount Aconcagua** (6995m/22,944ft), the highest mountain in the Western hemisphere, located within the Aconcagua National Park, and **Uspallata**, located in a serene valley surrounded by mountains; the striking **Puente del Inca** is a natural stone bridge over the River Mendoza; and **Cristo Redentor** (Christ the Redeemer) is a famous monument in the high Andes, nearly 4000m (13,120ft) above sea level, offering magnificent views.
- Discover the mountains, canyons, gorges and red-earthed plains of the **La Rioja Province**, in which the **Talampaya Canyon** is one of the most famous natural attractions, owing mostly to its peculiar rock formations, and **La Puerta de Talampaya** is well known for its petroglyphs.
- See large herds of seals, sea lions, blue whales and thousands of penguins in the huge area known as **Patagonia**, the southernmost portion of South America, which is a vast region with numerous parks and nature reserves, including: the southern Lake District, **San Carlos de Bariloche**, surrounded by lakes, glaciers and forested mountains, which has both modern tourist amenities such as shopping areas and picnic sites; **Nahuel Huapi National Park**, which contains the massive **Nahuel Huapi Lake**, stretching over 100km (63 miles) to the border with Chile; **San Martín**, connected to Bariloche by a scenic road (also called 'the route of the seven lakes'), leading past spectacular lakes and through a landscape of snow-capped mountains, waterfalls and gigantic trees; the **Lanín National Park**, a fairly untouched area dominated by the extinct, snow-capped **Volcán Lanín** (3776m/12,386ft), and characterised by rare plant and animal species (including *raulí*, a type of beech, and *pehuén*, the monkey puzzle tree); the **Punta Tombo** reserve, known for its vast colonies of Magellanic penguins (around half a million of which use the reserve as a breeding ground from September to April); **los Alerces National Park**, which protects vast stretches of the tall and long-lived (400 years) alerce conifer trees; and the UNESCO World Heritage-listed **los Glaciares National Park**, an area of great natural beauty with rugged mountains and numerous glacial lakes, including **Lake Argentino** and, the centrepiece, **Moreno Glacier**, one of the earth's few advancing glaciers, where huge icebergs calve and topple into Lake Argentino at the so-called **Canal de los Témpanos** (Iceberg Channel) - there are nearby catwalks and platforms from which to observe this event.
- Although half of this remote southern province belongs to Chile, make the most of being in Argentina and venture into **Tierra del Fuego** and its **national park**, the gateway to the Antarctic: the **Museo del Fin del Mundo** (Museum of the End of the World) has exhibits dedicated to the Indians, nature, local history and the many shipwrecks that happened in the area at **Ushuaia**, the world's most southernmost city, located in a dramatic setting, with jagged glacial peaks rising from sea level to nearly 1500m (4920ft).
- Wander around the **Ischigualasto National Park**, a desert valley also referred to as 'the valley of the moon', owing to its distinctive rock formations and fossils dating back some 180 million years.

Top Things To Do

- **Trek** Argentina's vast landscapes, alpine parks, lakes and deserts; stunning scenery is guaranteed in locations such as the **Andean Lake District**, the **Sierras de Córdoba**, the **Sierra de la Ventana** (in Buenos Aires Province) and **Patagonia**.
- Be bold and **mountaineer** up some of Argentina's most dramatic peaks along the **Fitzroy Range** and at **Aconcagua** (near **Mendoza**), the **Sierra de la Ventana** (for experienced climbers only) and nearby **Cerro de la Ventana** (1136m/3408ft).
- **Ski** down the eastern slopes of the Andes: the season is generally from May to September and Bariloche is the oldest, most established and best-equipped ski resort, although the runs at **San Antonio**, **San Bernado**, **La Canaleta** and **Puente del Inca** offer exciting skiing too.
- Embrace a range of possible **watersports** on offer and truly make the most of Argentina's diverse landscape: the rivers descending from the Andean ranges attract **whitewater rafting** enthusiasts; **swimming** can be enjoyed in rivers, lakes and small resorts along the Atlantic coast; **water-skiing** is recommended along the **San Antonio River** in the **Tigre Delta Region**; **scuba diving** in Patagonia is memorable; **yachting** and **boating** are well-catered for along the **River Plate**; and **fishing** on the Atlantic coast off the piers is always a rewarding past-time.
- **Dine** at a *parrillada*, or grill room, where a large variety of barbecue-style dishes can be sampled in authentic Argentinean fashion.
- Get into the rhythm of the city and **tango dance** at various lively *milongas* (tango parties), throughout Buenos Aires - the old artists' quarter of **La Boca** is the definitive home of the tango - and, if you are lucky, you might even catch the **Buenos Aires Tango Festival** (usually February/March).
- **Shop** until you drop in Buenos Aires, with its well-earned reputation as a shopper's paradise: the elegant and cosmopolitan *microcentro* (north of Avenida de Mayo) includes the Florida and Lavalle pedestrian malls and the Plaza San Martín.
- Splash out on a night out at the famous **Teatro Colón**, the world's largest opera house (with a capacity of 2500 seats), which occupies an entire block on the massive Avenida 9 de Julio, the city's major thoroughfare.

TOURIST INFORMATION

Argentina Government Tourist Office in the USA
12 West 56th Street, New York, NY 10019, USA
Tel: (212) 603 0443.
Website: www.turismo.gov.ar

Entertainment

FOOD & DRINK: North American, Continental and Middle Eastern cuisine is generally available, whilst local food is largely a mixture of Basque, Spanish and Italian. Beef is of a particularly high quality and meat-eaters should not miss out on the chance to dine at a *parrillada*, or grill room, where a large variety of barbecue-style dishes can be sampled. In general, restaurants are good value. They are classified by a fork sign with three forks implying a good evening out. Hotel residents are usually asked to sign a charge slip. Argentine wines are very good and inexpensive. Local distilleries produce their own brands of most well-known spirits. Whiskies and gins are excellent, as are classic and local wines. Caribbean and South American rum adds flavour to cocktails. There are no licensing laws.

National specialities:

- *Carbonada stew*, made with beef, corn, pumpkin, tomatoes, potatoes and yams.
- *Puchero* (tasty mulligan stew).
- *Tartas*, a kind of vegetable pie.
- *Empanadas del horno* are puff pastry stuffed with different ingredients; commonly, minced meat.
- *Charrasco Argentino* is a large, juicy Gaucho steak - a must-eat for carnivores
- *Alfajores* (cookies) filled with *dulche de leche* (caramelised milk sauce) and coated in chocolate
- There is plenty of Italian food on offer, including pizza and Ñoquis (Gnocchi).
- *Panqueques* are delicious crepe deserts.
- Sweet squash in cream.
- *Locro* (pork and maize stew).

National drinks:

- *Yerba mate* (tea-like drink).
- *Quilmes* is the national brand of lager.

Legal drinking age: The legal age for drinking alcohol in a bar/cafe is 18.

Tipping: Tips are theoretically outlawed but some hotels or restaurants will add 25 per cent service charge, plus a 21 per cent tax charge. In these cases, a minimal tip is still expected. Otherwise, 10 per cent on top of the bill will suffice. The same applies in bars. Taxi drivers tend to expect tips from visitors.

NIGHTLIFE: Buenos Aires' nightlife is vibrant. There are many theatres and concert halls showcasing foreign artists. Nightclubs featuring jazz and tango are plentiful. Tango lessons and dancing can be enjoyed at lively *milongas* (tango parties), throughout Buenos Aires. There are also many intimate *boîtes* (clubs) and stage shows. There are casinos throughout Argentina.

SHOPPING: Buenos Aires has traditionally enjoyed a reputation as a shopper's paradise, possibly of even being the best shopping city in Latin America. Leather goods are a good buy, as are native crafts and souvenirs. **Shopping hours:** Mon-Fri 0900-2000, Sat 0900-1300. In the outskirts and provinces, they tend to close at midday.

Business

- **GDP:** US$537.2 billion (2005 estimate).
- **Main exports:** Food and live animals, mineral fuels, cereals and machinery.
- **Main imports:** Machinery and equipments, motor vehicles, chemicals, metal manufactures and plastics.
- **Main trade partners:** Brazil, EU, USA, Chile, China, Germany, Spain, Italy, France and Japan.

ECONOMY: Argentina is rich in natural resources and also has a large and profitable agricultural sector; the country is one of the world's major exporters of wheat and also produces maize, oilseeds, sorghum, soya beans and sugar. Beef is no longer the dominant trading commodity that it once was but animal products are still a valuable export earner. Agricultural goods aside, Argentina exports textiles and some metal and chemical products. These, along with oil refining and vehicle production, are also the main components of Argentina's manufacturing industry. Hydroelectricity and coal meet the bulk of the country's energy requirements. Brazil is the largest of Argentina's South American trading partners. There are also important trading relationships with the USA, which is the main source of manufactured products, and the countries of the former Soviet Union, which buy large quantities of grain. Elsewhere, trade with Japan and the EU – especially Germany and The Netherlands – has grown rapidly in recent years.

For all the potential of the Argentinean economy, it has been historically blighted by two major problems – high inflation and a massive foreign debt. The Menem government of the mid-1990s made a reasonable attempt to tackle these, using the orthodox market measures of dismantling the public sector, free competition, asset sales, and swingeing cuts in public spending. In addition, the value of the Argentinean Peso was fixed to that of the US dollar. The immediate results were reductions in the national debt and the inflation rate – as well as considerable hardship for the poorer sections of the population. However, the policy of Peso-Dollar parity had unintended side effects which led to a sharp fall in exports and in government tax revenues, as well as a large increase in government debt. With external debt topping US$130 billion in 2001, Argentina was on the point of defaulting on its overseas debts, potentially leading to a complete economic meltdown. At the end of the year, the government was forced to introduce draconian currency control measures – a substantial devaluation, along with a block on normal access to bank accounts – as it struggled to bring the situation under control. Since then, the Duhalde government, which took office at the end of 2001, effectively stabilised the economy, which is now undergoing something of a resurgence. In mid-2004, growth was 9 per cent. In March 2005, President Kirchner declared restructuring of the country's debt to be a success.

BUSINESS ETIQUETTE: Business cards are usually given and businesspeople expect to deal with someone of equal status. Punctuality is expected by visitors. Literature is in Spanish, although many Argentinean businesspeople speak English as a second language. **Office hours:** Mon-Fri 0900-1200 and 1400-1900.

COMMERCIAL INFORMATION

Cámara Argentina de Comercio (Chamber of Commerce)
Avenida Leandro N. Alem 36, C1003AAN Buenos Aires, Argentina
Tel: (11) 5300 9000.
Website: www.cac.com.ar

Armenia

Location: Caucasus, east of Turkey.

Time: GMT + 4 (GMT + 5 from last Sunday in March to last Sunday in October).

Overview

Armenia was the first country to adopt Christianity as its state religion in AD 301. To explore Armenia is to delve into history: from Erebuni, an archaeological site studded with over 200 ancient rock engravings; and Ughtasar, an ancient fortress perched on top of a mountainous plateau; to countless monasteries and churches embedded in dramatic landscape. Yerevan, the capital of Armenia, is one of the oldest cities in the world, founded nearly 2800 years ago during the time of ancient Babylon. Although most of the old town was demolished in the 1930s, it is now decked out in more modern Soviet design. Indeed, Yerevan represents the very crux of Armenia: withholding both its ancient origins, a turbulent passage through time and now the forging of new beginnings.

Despite the violence of its history, Armenia is beautiful. Lake Sevan is the largest lake in the Caucasus, much praised for its pure waters and stunning setting, whilst North Dilijan is a resort touted for its medicinal mineral waters. Touristic infrastructure is continually improving and there is greater opportunity to hike and horse ride every year. This greatness of the scenery complies with Armenia's past (albeit brief) status as a great power. Before it was incorporated into the Roman Empire in AD114, the Armenian Empire stretched from the Caspian Sea in the east to the Mediterranean in the west.

Since then, the country has been tragically dogged by lost territory, national persecution and mass emigration. Subsequent Armenian history has been comprised of foreign domination and dissent, most notably when, at the outbreak of World War I, Turkish government catalysed the first genocide of the 20th century, in which an estimated one-and-a-quarter million Armenians were massacred and hordes more fled or were forced into exile. Nature itself seized power in December 1988 when a massive earthquake destroyed much of the capital, Diaspora, killing several thousand people. Rather than wilt in collective gloom, the Armenian mood strengthened and the country eventually gained Independence. Even the murder of Premier Sarkisian and seven other leading politicians in 1999 temporarily paralysed the country's politics but did not halt progress. Armenians have not quieted their protests: in early 2004, thousands of opposition supporters marched against the allegedly corrupt President, Kocharian.

Armenian character is key: the towns and cities are relics of endurance. It is the character of the locals that leads them to proudly inform visitors that Winston Churchill always insisted on Armenian brandy in preference to French. We advise you to follow their advice and raise a glass to Armenia.

General Information

AREA: 29,743 sq km (11,484 sq miles).

POPULATION: 3.33 million (official estimate 2002).

POPULATION DENSITY: 111.9 per sq km.

CAPITAL: Yerevan. **Population:** 1.24 million (official estimate 1999).

GEOGRAPHY: Armenia lies on the southern slopes of the Armenian Mountains in the Lesser Caucasus and is bordered by Georgia, Turkey, Azerbaijan and Iran. Its highest peak is Mount Aragats, 4090m (13,415ft), and even its deepest valleys lie 450 to 700m (1200 to 1870ft) above sea level. Its biggest lake is Lake Sevan in the east.

GOVERNMENT: Republic. Gained independence from the Soviet Union in 1991. **Head of State:** President Robert Kocharyan since 1998. **Head of Government:** Prime Minister Andranik Markaryan since 2000. **Recent history:** At the most recent poll on March 2003, Robert Kocharyan faced a major challenge from Stepan Demirchian standing on an anti-corruption platform. He nevertheless comfortably won the first round. Kocharyan won further second-round elections, although Parliamentary elections fell short of international standards and a referendum rejected early constitutional amendments concerning the role of Parliament. In early 2004, thousands of opposition supporters marched against the President and allegations of corruption still persist.

A new constitution was adopted in 1995, allowing for a directly elected Legislature and Presidency. The former, the *Azgayin Zhogov*, has 131 members elected for a four-year term – 75 are chosen from single-seat constituencies; the remaining 56 by proportional representation. The executive President, who selects a Council of Ministers, subject to approval by the legislature, also serves a four-year term.

LANGUAGE: Armenian. Russian is usually understood, but rarely used; Kurdish is sometimes used in broadcasting as 56,000 Kurds inhabit Armenia.

RELIGION: 94 per cent Armenian Apostolic Church, with Catholic and Protestant communities and a Russian Orthodox minority. Armenia is the oldest Christian nation in the world, its conversion dating from the year AD 301. The Armenian Apostolic Church developed separately from both the Catholic and Orthodox branches of Christianity.

ELECTRICITY: 220 volts AC, 50Hz. European plugs with two round pins are used.

SOCIAL CONVENTIONS: Almost all entertaining takes place in private homes, and guests may find themselves subjected to overwhelming hospitality and generosity, as well as being expected to eat enormously and participate in endless toasts. Visitors invited to an Armenian's home should arrive bearing some kind of small gift, such as flowers and alcohol (preferably imported) or chocolates. Handshaking is the normal form of greeting. Business cards are invariably exchanged at any kind of official meeting and not infrequently on first meeting people socially as well. Conversation tends to be highly politicised, and guests may be well advised to avoid expressing strong opinions. Homosexuality is now decriminalised but is still an unacceptable lifestyle for many Armenians, and discretion should be exercised when in public. Women tend to be less retiring than in nearby Muslim countries, and can usually dress in normal western-style clothing (especially in the capital), although short skirts and shorts should be avoided.

Photography: Refrain from photographing sites such as military bases equipment and installations. Also be aware of cultural sensitivities when photographing churches and other religious sites.

Climate

Continental, mountain climate (over 90 per cent of the territory of the republic is over 900m/2286ft above sea level). During the summer, days can be hot and dry with temperatures falling sharply at night. Winters are extremely cold with heavy snow. May to June and September to October are good times to visit the country, as the weather is warm but mild.

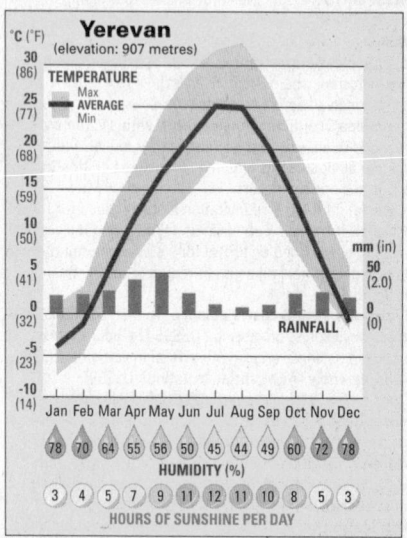

Communications

Telephone: IDD is available to Yerevan. Country code: 374. Outgoing calls to other CIS countries can be made by dialling with the appropriate codes, but only with difficulty. Outgoing international calls to other countries must be made through the operator. Some hotels and many businesses now have satellite links.

Mobile telephone: Roaming agreements exist with some international mobile phone companies. Coverage is limited to average, limited to Yerevan and the west of the country.

Internet: Available in large cities and resorts. There are many internet cafes in Yerevan. Some, such as the *Zeon Club* on 31 Tumanian Street, are open 24 hours.

Post: International postal services are available to most countries but may be slow and unreliable, although there have been significant improvements in recent years. The main post office is located at Republic Square, Yerevan. Post office hours: Mon-Fri 0900-1700.

MEDIA: Armenian government oversees national TV and radio. Libel and defamation are punishable by prison terms and journalists have been sentenced under these laws in the past. All print and broadcast media must register with the Justice Ministry. Self-censorship is common.

Press: The main newspapers are *Aravot*, *Azg* and *Yerkir*, all of which are published only in Armenian (Russian editions have been discontinued since the Russian minority in the republic dropped). *Golos Armenii* (The Voice of Armenia) and *Respublika Armenia* survive as the main Russian-language papers. *Noyan Tapan*, an English-language weekly circulated primarily among the foreign missions and small foreign business community, is published by an independent information agency based in Yerevan.

TV: *Public TV of Armenia* is a national, state-run station, whilst *Armenia TV* and *Prometheus TV* are commercial.

Radio: There are both private radio stations (the first of which was *Hai FM*) and national and state-run stations, such as *Public Radio of Armenia*.

Passport/Visa

	Passport Required?	Visa Required?	Return Ticket Required?
Full British	Yes	Yes	No
Australian	Yes	Yes	No
Canadian	Yes	Yes	No
USA	Yes	Yes	No
Other EU	Yes	Yes	No
Japanese	Yes	Yes	No

Note: *Regulations and requirements may be subject to change at short notice, and you are advised to contact the appropriate diplomatic or consular authority before finalising travel arrangements. Any numbers in the chart refer to the footnotes below.*

Credit: ©Armenian Tourism Development Agency

PASSPORTS: Passport valid for at least four months required by all.
VISAS: Required by all except:
(a) nationals of CIS countries (except Azerbaijan and Turkmenistan, who *do* require a visa);
(b) nationals of Serbia & Montenegro;
(c) nationals continuing their journey within 72 hours, provided remaining in the airport transit lounge and holding all documents required for the next destination and confirmed onward ticket
Note: (a) (b) A letter of invitation is still required for these nationals if travelling on business. (c) If leaving the airport, a visa may be issued on arrival for a stay of maximum three days, provided holding a visa (if required) for the final destination.
Types of visa and cost: *Ordinary/Tourist*: US$60, US$86 (three day express processing), US$95 (24-hour express processing). *Single-entry* (with official invitation): US$35. *Multiple-entry* (with official invitation): US$65. *Transit*: US$18 (single-entry); US$36 (double entry).
Note: There is no charge for diplomatic and official visas, or for those issued to persons under 18 years of age.
Validity: *Tourist/Ordinary*: 21 days. *Single-entry* and *Multiple-entry*: three months. *Transit*: three days. Visas must be used within 90 days of date of issue.
Application to: Embassy (or Consular Section at Embassy); see *Passport/Visa Information.*
Application requirements: (a) Completed application form. (b) One recent passport-size photo. (c) Passport valid for at least four months. (d) Fee, payable by money order or certified cheque. (e) Postal applications should be sent by registered mail or by courier. *Single-entry/Multiple-entry*: (a)-(e) and, (f) Official invitation letter, duly authorised in Armenia (for stays over 21 days).
Working days required: Seven. Urgent visas can be processed in one or three days for a higher fee (see above).
Temporary residence: For stays of longer than three months, a residency permit must be obtained from the Foreign Ministry in Yerevan.

PASSPORT/VISA INFORMATION

Embassy of the Republic of Armenia in the UK
25A Cheniston Gardens, London W8 6TG, UK
Tel: (020) 7938 5435.
E-mail: armemb@armenianembassyuk.com
Opening hours: Mon-Fri 1000-1200 and 1500-1700.

Embassy of the Republic of Armenia in the USA
2225 R Street, NW, Washington, DC 20008, USA
Tel: (202) 319 1976 or 2983 (Consular section).
Website: www.armeniaemb.org
Also deals with enquiries from Canada.

Money

Currency: Armenian Dram (AMD) = 100 luma. Dram notes are printed in denominations of AMD50,000, 20,000, 10,000, 5000, 1000, 500, 200, 100, 50, 25 and 10. Coins are in denominations of AMD500, 200, 100, 50, 20, 10 and 1, and 50 and 20 luma.
Note: The government is intending to phase out all banknotes less than AMD500.
Currency exchange: Foreign currencies can be exchanged at the airports, banks and most hotels and shops during normal opening hours. US Dollars are the most widely recognised foreign currency. Visitors using the national currency are advised to carry plenty of small change as some shops and, particularly markets, may be unable to accept large denominations.
Credit & debit cards: Major credit cards are accepted in most cities. ATMS are available in major cities.
Traveller's cheques: These are accepted in a few shops and hotels. To avoid additional exchange rate charges, travellers are advised to take traveller's cheques in US Dollars.
Currency restrictions: The import of local and foreign currency is unlimited, however cash amounts in excess of $10,000 or equivalent must be declared. The export of local and foreign currency is unlimited, however cash amounts in excess of US$10,000 or equivalent are prohibited and must be transferred via a bank.
Banking hours: Mon-Fri 0900-1500. Exchange Offices are open until midnight and also operate at weekends and on public holidays.
Exchange rate indicators:
Rate at time of publishing
£1.00= AMD811.32
$1.00= AMD450.00

Duty Free

The following goods may be imported into Armenia by persons over 18 years of age without incurring customs duty:
400 cigarettes; 2l or one bottle of alcoholic beverage; 5kg of perfume (or perfume to the value of US$500); other goods up to the amount of US$500, for personal use only.
Note: It is advisable to declare valuables on arrival.
Prohibited imports: Weapons and ammunition, narcotics, pornography, fruit and vegetables (without proper documents).
Prohibited exports: Weapons, ammunition, narcotics, pornography, fruit and vegetables (without proper documents), works of art and antiques (unless permission has been granted by the Ministry of Culture). An export tax of approximately US$10 is payable on each item. Contact the Embassy for further information (see *Passport/Visa Information*).

Public Holidays

Below are listed Public Holidays for the January 2006-June 2007 period.
2006: Jan 1-2 New Year. **Jan 6** Armenian Orthodox Christmas. **Mar 8** International Women's Day. **Apr 7** Motherhood and Beauty Day. **Apr 14** Good Friday. **Apr 24** Genocide Memorial Day. **May 9** Victory and Peace Day. **May 28** First Republic Day. **Jul 5** Constitution Day. **Sep 21** Independence Day. **Dec 7** Earthquake Memorial Day. **Dec 31** New Year's Eve.
2007: Jan 1-2 New Year. **Jan 6** Armenian Orthodox Christmas. **Mar 8** International Women's Day. **Apr 6** Good Friday. **Apr 7** Motherhood and Beauty Day. **Apr 24** Genocide Memorial Day. **May 9** Victory and Peace Day. **May 28** First Republic Day.

Health

	Special Precautions?	Certificate Required?
Yellow Fever	No	No
Cholera	No	No
Typhoid & Polio	1	N/A
Malaria	2	N/A

Note: *Regulations and requirements may be subject to change at short notice, and you are advised to contact your doctor well in advance of your intended date of departure. Any numbers in the chart refer to the footnotes below.*

1: Typhoid fever is common. *Poliomyelitis* eradication activities are underway but the disease should still be assumed to be a threat.
2: There is some risk of malaria from June to October in some villages in the Ararat Valley. No risk in main tourist areas.
Food & drink: All water should be regarded as being a potential health risk. Water used for drinking, brushing teeth or making ice should have first been boiled or otherwise sterilised. Only eat well-cooked meat and fish, preferably served hot. Pork, salad and mayonnaise may carry increased risk. Vegetables should be cooked and fruit peeled. Milk is pasteurised and dairy products should be safe for consumption, however, the incidence of communicable diseases among livestock is increasing because of a breakdown in vaccination programmes.
Other risks: *Diphtheria*, *hepatitis B* and *E*, *tick-borne encephalitis*, *brucellosis*, *echinococcosis* and *leishmaniasis* (cutaneous) may all occur. Visitors are advised to take precautions which may include vaccination.
There may be a risk of *rabies* although there has been no reported incidence in animals or humans since 1997. If you are bitten, seek medical advice without delay. For more information, consult the *Health* appendix.
Health care: A reciprocal agreement for urgent medical treatment exists with the UK, although proof of UK residence is required. Power shortages and disrupted medical supplies have undermined normal health services to such a degree that travellers would be well advised to consider a health insurance policy guaranteeing emergency evacuation in case of serious accident or illness, as medical insurance is not often valid within the country. Doctors and hospitals often expect immediate cash payment for health services and credit or debit cards will not be accepted; most will want treatment paid for in local currency. Travellers are also advised to take a supply of those medicines that they are likely to require (but check first that they may be legally imported) as there is a severe shortage of even the most basic medical supplies, such as disposable needles, anaesthetics and antibiotics. Elderly travellers and those with existing health problems may be at risk owing to inadequate medical facilities.

Travel - International

AIR:
Armenian Airlines (website: www.armenianairlines.com) is the national airline. For political reasons, there are no direct international transport links between Armenia and Azerbaijan; Georgia is sometimes used as a stopover point.
Main airports: *Zvartnots (EVN)* 10km (6 miles) from Yerevan. *To/from the airport*: Buses and taxis are available to the city centre. Buses run every 15 minutes between 0700-2100 (travel time - 30 minutes).
Departure tax: US$20 per person (usually payable in local currency). Although this is normally paid at the airport, visitors staying in the large hotels may sometimes pay at their hotel, and present the receipt at the airport check-in desk. Transit passengers and children under 12 years of age are exempt.
RAIL:
Armenia's rail links to Azerbaijan and Turkey have been closed indefinitely, but an international service still runs to Georgia (every other day) and to Iran. Passengers travelling to Georgia should be aware of the possibility of theft or robbery. The main station is Sasuntsi Davit on Tigran Mets Avenue.
ROAD:
A road link between Armenia and Iran, the Kajaran highway, has become the most important international road link. There are two highways linking Armenia to Georgia; these routes, especially the Yerevan-Tbilisi road, have a bad reputation for highway robbery, although efforts by the Georgian authorities to enforce law and order are reported to be paying off. The Azerbaijan and Turkey borders are both currently closed. It is possible to travel by road to the enclave of Nagorno Karabakh, however, it is essential to obtain a visa from the permanent representative of Nagorno Karabakh in Yerevan. Turkey and Azerbaijan have imposed a blockade against Armenia and closed borders with it. **Bus:** Kilikia Central Bus Station is where most buses depart. There is a weekly bus service to Istanbul and a daily (except Fridays) bus service to Tehran. There is also a weekly bus service to Moscow.

Travel - Internal

AIR:
Yerevan has a small domestic airport as well as an international airport, which offers some flights to other destinations in Armenia.
RAIL:
The main railway station is the Sasuntsi Davit Station on Tigran Mets Avenue. There are daily trains to most major towns. The trains are often overcrowded and poorly maintained. Belongings should be secured.
ROAD:
The road network comprises 7705km (4788 miles). Road surfaces can be very poor, even in the case of major highways, and care should be taken to avoid children and animals on the road. Supplies of petrol, diesel and oil are at present limited. It is common practice to flag down private cars as well as official taxis. Local drivers have a tendency to flout traffic regulations and ignore signals. Visitors should take care when driving or crossing the road. **Bus:** There are city minivans available (marshrutni or Marshrutka) which operate on 100 different routes and may be flagged down. **Coach:** Coaches run between the major centres of population. **Car hire:** There are plenty of care hire companies operating, including *Hertz*.
URBAN: There is a small underground system in Yerevan (0630-2300). Buses and trolleybuses run in the city. Taxis are available in the city centre or can be ordered by telephone. Chauffeur-driven cars are available but are expensive. It is advisable to obtain them through official channels, such as hotels or travel agencies in Yerevan.

Accommodation

HOTELS:
Hotels previously run by Intourist are now mostly being privatised - for instance, the Armenia Marriott Hotel. The Hotel Hrazdan, mainly occupied by foreign missions, also has its own generator, but is state owned and functions primarily as a guest house for official visitors. Private individuals may occasionally be allowed to stay there by special arrangement. There are now plenty of varying hotels for the traveller to pick.

BED & BREAKFAST:

Armenia has several B&Bs. Information on accommodation can be obtained from the Armenian Tourist Office (see *Top Things To See*). There are tourist information bureaux in the Armenia Hotel (Republic Square) and the newly refurbished Ani Plaza Hotel (19 Sayat Nova Avenue). Tours and other activities can be organised through these bureaux.

Top Things To See

• See the sites that emphasise Armenia's status as the first country to adopt Christianity as the official state religion (with the exception of the now vanished kingdom of King Abgar of Edessa), such as **Noah's Ark** - which is believed to be the origin of the settling after flood - and **Mount Ararat**.

• Go to **Echmiadzin**, the capital of Armenia from AD 180-340, which remains the site of the country's most important cathedral, and home of the church's *Supreme Catholicos*; the **Cathedral of St Gregory the Illuminator** is believed to stand on the site of a much older church, itself predated by a pagan shrine. The existing 17th-century cathedral is a fine example of Armenian ecclesiastical architecture, with a squat bell tower and elaborately carved dome. In addition to chalices, vestments and other religious artefacts, the cathedral's treasury contains a spearhead believed to have been used to pierce the side of the crucified Christ.

• Visit one of the oldest cities in the world, founded nearly 2800 years ago in the time of ancient Babylon: **Yerevan**. Sadly, little remains to remind the visitor of the city's ancient heritage. Most of the old town was demolished in the 1930s and has been rebuilt using the attractive pinkish-brown volcanic *tufa* stone seen throughout the republic in so-called 'Armenian national style' architecture – solid, sometimes imposing, and essentially Soviet in character. However, there is still much to occupy your time: go to the **National Gallery** (founded 1919); the **Yerevan library** of ancient manuscripts (*Materadaran*), which houses over 13,000 texts, many beautifully illuminated and some dating as far back as the ninth century; or the **Vernisaj flea market**, which takes place at weekends. Nearby sites of interest include the fortress of **Erebuni** (an archaeological site studded with over 200 ancient rock engravings [petroglyphs] and surrounded by a pristine lake) and **Ughtasar** (3km above sea level on a mountainous plateau in the mesmerising region of **Syunik**, an ancient fortress not to be missed).

• Climb up a steep, rocky valley to view one of Armenia's most dramatic sights, the **Geghard Monastery**: Geghard means 'spear' or 'lance' in Armenian, and harks back to Christ's crucifixion. The monks, who still inhabit the monastery, occasionally sacrifice sheep on an open-air stone altar. 'Wishing trees' by the road approaching the site are decorated with coloured scraps of cloth, tied on by pilgrims and travellers hoping their prayers will be answered. A monastery has occupied this site since the fourth century AD, and the existing churches, all magnificently carved, date from the 13th century. Leading from the vaulted chambers of the main church and adjoining *jamatoun*, or meeting room, are two chapels hewn into the rock of the mountain itself. One of these contains a holy spring, the other a burial vault decorated with an ornate coat of arms. Higher up the slope, a passage leads into the mountainside to the 13th-century tomb of Prince Papak and his wife Rouzakan, a structure noted for its extraordinary acoustics.

• On the road between Geghard and Yerevan, **Garni** is the site of a temple to the Roman god Mithras. In the first century AD, Nero sent money and slaves to build the temple as a tribute to the Armenian King Tiridates for his support in fighting off the Parthians. Repeated earthquakes have destroyed most of the original structure, but the temple's vertiginous position, dominating the valley from a plateau 300m (984ft) above the Azat River, is breathtakingly beautiful. A ruined ninth-century church stands near the restored temple, and a Roman bathhouse has recently been excavated, revealing a well-preserved mosaic floor. It stands, as it did two millennia earlier, adorned by two dozen ionic columns.

• Take in the panorama of **Lake Sevan**, situated 70km (43 miles) east of Yerevan and the largest lake in the Caucasus, much vaunted for its pure waters, stunning setting and delicious salmon trout.

• Go to what was a major cultural centre in medieval Armenia, and one of the very few perfectly preserved examples of the architecture of its period (10th to 13th centuries), the **Agartsin Monastery**, which is a few kilometres east of Dilijhan in a wooded gorge and has a particularly prized refectory building.

• Well worth visiting are the Monasteries of **Haghpat** and **Sanakin**, which are in close proximity to the banks of the Debed River, and are a UNESCO World Heritage Site: these were first built in the 10th century and have undergone many different constructions and expansions. It is believed that the great Armenian troubadour-poet, Sayat-Nova, was born in Sanakin, and became a monk at Haghpat.

Top Things To Do

• **Hike** through Armenia's spectacular countryside: specialist tour operators in Yerevan can organise tailor-made walking tours, and hotels will also often supply information.

• **Watch** for rare species' of **birds**, including eagles, which can be seen all over the country.

• **Horse ride** on **Mount Aragats** in the spring, when you can traverse over Armenia's tallest mountain.

• Dip into Lake Sevan with a **fishing** rod, and find Armenia's famous species of trout, the **Salmon trout** (*Ishkhan*), plus many more that swim in Armenia's other lakes and rivers.

• **Sample** some of Armenia's excellent **brandies**, which Winston Churchill always insisted on after first tasting it at the Yalta conference.

TOURIST INFORMATION

Armenian Tourist Office Representative in the UK
Sunvil House, 9 Upper Square, Old Isleworth,
Middlesex, TW7 7BJ, UK
Tel: (020) 8568 8899.
Website: www.sunvil.co.uk

Entertainment

FOOD & DRINK: A restaurant and cafe culture is starting to flourish again in Armenia, with street stalls and privately run establishments replacing the colourless state restaurants typical of the Soviet era. New cafes and restaurants open daily. Many of the cafes are in parks, and are very popular in summer with locals and tourists alike.

Things to know: Much Armenian cooking is based on lamb, either grilled and served as *shashlik* with flat bread, or prepared as soup (the most popular being *bozbash*, a dish which exists in infinite variations) or stew, often in combination with fruit or nuts. A meal usually starts with a large spread of hors d'oeuvres, which may include peppers and vine leaves stuffed with rice and meat, pickled and fresh vegetables, salty white sheep's cheese eaten with fresh green herbs and flat bread, and various kinds of cured meat (*basturma*).

During the season following the grape harvest, locals sell effervescent, mildly fermented grape juice from roadside stands. Armenia is also abundant in all kinds of sweet-tasting fruits, from figs to pomegranates to quince. Coffee is served Turkish-style – strong and black in tiny cups – although in view of national sensibilities, visitors would be ill-advised to refer to this cultural similarity.

National specialities:
• *Sharots* (*Sujukh*) is cooked with grape juice and a dark cherry-coloured syrup called *doshab*.
• *Lavash* is a think, paper-like bread.
• *Shampours* are skewers that are jam-packed with all kinds of marinated meat and vegetables
• Delectable walnut jam (*popok muraba*).
• *Tolma* (vegetables, grape leaves and lentils).
• *Ghapama* is pumpkin stew with rice, raisins, apples and cinnamon.
• *Khash* is a national institution rather than just a dish, with poems and songs throughout the centuries being composed in homage to it: in case you are wondering, *khash* is a delicious broth made from hamhocks and herbs and served with lots of garlic and bread.
• *K'rchik* is pickled cabbage cooked with wheat kernels.
• Among Armenia's many varieties of fresh fish available, try steamed *Ishkhan* (lake trout).
• Almost magical, health-giving properties are ascribed to dried apricots from the Caucasus.
• For dessert, eat a dish made from grape juice, dried into thin sheets of a deep, reddish brown colour, and then rolled up into long cylinders around walnuts or other nuts.

National drinks:
• Brandies are exceptional (*Dvin*).
• *Kotayk* and *Kihikia* are Armenian beers worth giving a go.
• Armenian wine is well worth tasting: the *Areni* red wine is particularly lauded and many are semi- sweet or dessert wines and are world-renowned.
Legal drinking age: There is no minimum.
Tipping: Expected by waiters and doormen in restaurants - sometimes in advance to ensure service. Taxi fares should always be negotiated before starting a journey, and visitors should be aware that rates proposed initially are likely to be unreasonably high, in the expectation that foreigners will have unlimited cash and little idea of how much they ought to be paying. It is therefore advisable to make enquiries about 'going rates' per kilometre of travel before entering into negotiations with taxi drivers. The same applies to market stall holders and so on.

NIGHTLIFE: There are restaurants and nightclubs featuring local music in Yerevan. There are several restaurants, clubs and discos. There are several casinos. Opera, theatre and ballet performances are of a high standard, and tickets are cheap (about the equivalent of US$5). Armenians love music, from the traditional, liturgical songs (*Sharakans*) with distinctive musical instruments, to contemporary jazz and pop. There will often be venues accommodating for this at night. There are often concerts at the Philharmonic, Chamber Music Hall and Opera & Ballet House in Yerevan.

SHOPPING: Although Armenia's economy is still relatively undeveloped, new shops are now opening. The *Vernisaj* flea market in Yerevan attracts sellers of all kinds of goods and is popular with tourists. **Shopping hours:** Mon-Fri 0900-1700. Shops stay open longer in the summer.

Business

• **GDP:** US$2.83 billion (2001).
• **Main exports:** Processed and unprocessed diamonds, machinery, metal products and foodstuffs.
• **Main imports:** Natural gas, petroleum, tobacco products, foodstuffs and diamonds.
• **Main trade partners:** Russia, Belgium, Iran, USA, Turkmenistan and Georgia.

ECONOMY: Armenia has recovered slowly from the massive economic crisis caused by the 1988 earthquake and the collapse of the Soviet Union but is still seriously affected by the results of the war with Azerbaijan, which include a partial economic blockade and border closures with Azerbaijan and Turkey. Other regional difficulties, such as upheavals in neighbouring Georgia, had a detrimental effect on the country's economy and Armenian foreign trade suffered badly as a result. Many people rely on subsistence agriculture. Mineral deposits including copper, zinc, gold, marble, bauxite and molybdenum have brought some foreign revenue and investment, although this sector is relatively undeveloped. The industrial sector comprises textile and chemical industries, aluminium production and some mechanical engineering. The government embarked on a reform programme in the mid-1990s, which included privatisation, a new fiscal structure and the introduction of a new currency, the Dram, to replace the Russian Rouble. The country remains dependent on foreign aid and remittances from *émigrés* but is steadily improving. The privatisation programme has since been extended to include major parts of the national infrastructure, such as the electricity grid. The volume of foreign investment is growing, despite concerns about widespread corruption and poor financial controls. The government has also signed important economic co-operation agreements with the Russian Federation and Iran. In the international arena, negotiations for Armenia to join the World Trade Organization are reaching their final stages.

BUSINESS ETIQUETTE: Business is generally conducted formally, and visitors should dress smartly; appointments are necessary. **Office hours:** Mon-Fri 0900-1800.

COMMERCIAL INFORMATION

Ministry of Trade and Economic Development
5 M. Mkrtchian, 375010, Yerevan, Armenia
Tel: (1) 560 274 or 560 505 (tourism department).
Website: www.minted.am

Ministry of Foreign Affairs
2 Republic Square, Yerevan 375010, Armenia
Tel: (1) 544 041.
Website: www.armeniaforeignministry.com

Chamber of Commerce and Industry
11 Khanjyan Street, Yerevan 375010, Armenia
Tel: (1) 560 184 or 587 871 or 524 730.
Website: www.armcci.am

Armenian Development Agency
17 Charents Street, Yerevan 375025, Armenia
Tel: (1) 570 170.
Website: www.businessarmenia.com

Aruba

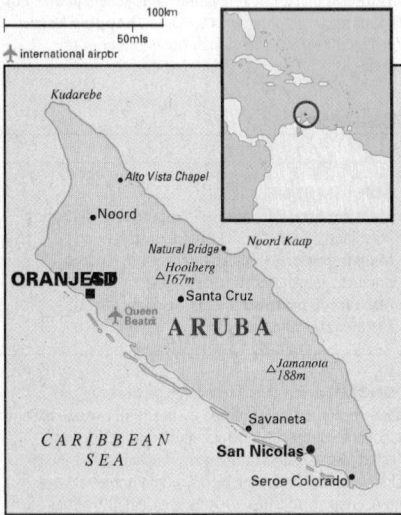

Location: South Caribbean.

Time: GMT - 4.

Aruba is a dependency of the Netherlands and represented abroad by Royal Netherlands Embassies – see *The Netherlands* section for Embassy contact details.

Overview

It does not take a wizard with words to realise that Aruba's capital, Oranjestad, is so-named because it is in some way connected to the colour orange. Disembarking from the nearby port or airport, it is difficult for any visitor to the town to not be dazzled by the row of orange facades that brightly array the architecture. The colour indicates Aruba's historical ties with The Netherlands: although seceded from The Netherlands in 1986, its Head of State is still the Dutch ruling Monarch. William I, Prince of Orange, was the main leader of the Dutch revolt against the Spanish that triggered the Eighty Year's War that led to Dutch independence. Indeed, Aruba's connection to The Netherlands has been a rare case of peaceful jurisdiction. Perhaps this is because Arubans are too busy enjoying their beautiful, balmy island. Nowhere else does the orange chrome seem more fitting than on an island where the dry climate guarantees hot days all-year-round, and everyone you meet seems of a sunny disposition.

Arubans know that they live on an island with the best that Caribbean sea and sand has to offer. Progressing on from Oranjestad, it is not just the main town that is colourful. The Chapel of Alto Vista is a vivid yellow. The sea is populated by creatures of all colours: parrotfish splashed in dazzling teal and gold are a popular sight in Aruba's waters. Indeed, Aruba's waters are popular full-stop: there is something for everyone, with certain beaches regarded best for activities such as snorkelling, surfing, windsurfing, diving and, even, lounging.

But Aruba does not just offer the option of beaches. Oranjestad has some of the best duty free shops in the Caribbean. There are flamingos to spot in the national park, desert flora to see, caves with ancient drawings to explore and natural phenomenon to gawp at.

The trademark windswept *divi-divi* trees in the Cunucu look like they are leaning back and relaxing, staring up at Aruba's light blue skies, rather than being blown into that position by northeasterly trade winds. It is not difficult to lean back and take it easy on an island such as Aruba. Its way of life is just the tonic for any frazzled visitor: like the aloe vera gel whose origin of plant is everywhere on the island, there is something here to soothe anyone's daily stresses and abrasions.

General Information

AREA: 193 sq km (74.5 sq miles).

POPULATION: 101,000 (UN official estimate 2000).

POPULATION DENSITY: 523.3 per sq km.

CAPITAL: Oranjestad. **Population:** 20,046 (1991).

GEOGRAPHY: Aruba is the smallest island in the Leeward group of the Dutch Caribbean islands, which also include Bonaire and Curaçao. They are popularly known as the ABCs. As the westernmost island of the group, Aruba is the final link in the long Antillean chain, lying 20km (12.5 miles) off the Venezuelan coast. The island is 30km (19.6 miles) long and 9km (6 miles) across at its widest and has a flat landscape dominated by Jamanota Mountain (188m/617ft). The west and southwest coast, known as Palm Beach, boasts 11km (7 miles) of palm-fringed powder-white sands while, in complete contrast, the east coast has a desolate, windswept shoreline of jagged rocks carved into peculiar shapes by the pounding surf.

GOVERNMENT: Dependency of the Netherlands. In 1986 Aruba separated from the rest of the Netherlands Antilles.

Head of State: Queen Beatrix of the Netherlands, represented locally by Governor-General Fredis Refunjol since 2004. **Head of Government:** Prime Minister Nelson Oduber since 2001. **Recent history:** *Movimiento Electoral di Pueblo* (MEP) won at the most recent poll in September 2001. Nelson Oduber took over as Premier. Aruba is a separate entity within the Kingdom of The Netherlands, with a Governor appointed by the Dutch monarch, a 21-member Parliament (or *Staten*), directly elected for a four-year term, and a Council of Ministers.

LANGUAGE: The official language is Dutch. English and Spanish are also spoken. The islanders also speak Papiemento, which is a combination of Dutch, Spanish, Portuguese, English and Indian languages.

RELIGION: 80 per cent of the population are Roman Catholic. There are also Protestant, Hindu, Muslim, Confucian and Jewish communities present.

ELECTRICITY: 110 volts AC, 60Hz.

SOCIAL CONVENTIONS: Much of the social activity takes place in hotels where the atmosphere will be informal, often American in feel. The islanders do not wear shorts in town though it is acceptable for visitors to do so. Bathing suits are strictly for beach or poolside. In the evenings people tend to dress up, especially when visiting the casinos. Jackets are not required for men, except for official Government functions.

Climate

With a mean temperature of 28°C (82°F), this dry and sunny island is made pleasantly cool throughout the year by constant trade winds. Showers of short duration occur during the months of October, November and December.

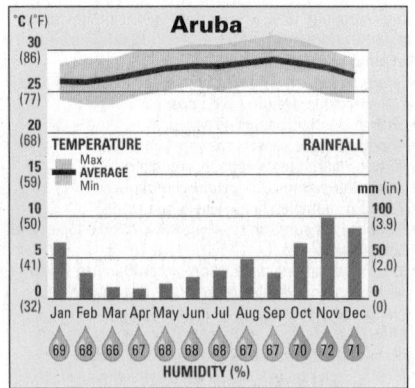

Communications

Telephone: IDD available. Country code: 297. Payphones, from which international calls can be made are located all over the island.

Mobile telephone: Roaming agreements exist with a few mobile phone companies. Coverage is average.

Internet: Available throughout Aruba, with Internet cafes throughout at around US$5 per hour. There are also WIFI hotspots.

Post: Post office hours: 0730-1200 and 1300-1630.

MEDIA:

Press: The oldest established newspaper (in Dutch) is *Amigoe di Aruba* and the English-language papers are *Aruba Today* and *The News*. *Diario Aruba* and *Bon Dia* are also popular.

TV: *ATV* and *Tele Aruba* are prime TV channels.

Radio: Radio stations include *Radio Kelkboom*, *Magic 96.5* and *Canal 90*.

Passport/Visa

	Passport Required?	Visa Required?	Return Ticket Required?
Full British	Yes	No	Yes
Australian	Yes	No	Yes
Canadian	1	No	Yes
USA	2	No	Yes
Other EU	3	No	Yes
Japanese	Yes	No	Yes

Note: *Regulations and requirements may be subject to change at short notice, and you are advised to contact the appropriate diplomatic or consular authority before finalising travel arrangements. Any numbers in the chart refer to the footnotes below.*

PASSPORTS: Passport valid for at least three months after intended return to home country required by all except:
(a) **1.** nationals of Canada holding a birth certificate, baptismal certificate, valid driver's license, proof of Canadian citizenship or certificate of naturalisation;
(b) **2.** nationals of the USA holding an official birth certificate with a raised seal accompanied by photo ID, a certificate of naturalisation or an alien registration card (green card);
(c) **3.** nationals of Belgium, Luxembourg and The Netherlands holding a National Identity Card.

VISAS: Required by all except the following:
(a) nationals of countries referred to in the chart above for up to three months;
(b) nationals of Andorra, Antigua & Barbuda, Argentina, The Bahamas, Barbados, Belize, Bolivia, Brazil, Brunei, Chile, Costa Rica, Dominica, Ecuador, El Salvador, Grenada, Guatemala, Guyana, Honduras, Hong Kong (SAR), Iceland, Israel, Korea (Rep), Liechtenstein, Macau (SAR), Malaysia, Mexico, Monaco, New Zealand, Nicaragua, Norway, Panama, Paraguay, St Kitts & Nevis, St Lucia, St Vincent & the Grenadines, San Marino, Singapore, Surinam, Switzerland, Trinidad & Tobago, Uruguay, Vatican City and Venezuela for stays of up to three months;
(c) nationals continuing to a third country within 24 hours by the same aircraft, holding tickets with reserved seats and all documents for onward journey;
(d) many nationals can visit for a period of 14 days, as tourists only, provided they have a return or onward ticket, proof of sufficient funds for the length of stay and the necessary documents for returning to their home country. The list is extensive, however, so it is advisable to check with your nearest relevant Consulate or Embassy prior to making travel arrangements.

Note: (a) For stays of over 14 days and less than 30 days, the traveller will be issued with a Temporary Certificate of Admission by the Immigration authorities on arrival in Aruba. (b) All visitors require a return or onward ticket.

Types of Visa and Cost: *Single-entry:* approximately £16, depending on the exchange rate.

Application to: Nearest Embassy of the Kingdom of the Netherlands *or* directly through the Department of Foreign Affairs, J E Irausquinplein 2A, Oranjestad, Aruba (tel: (58) 34705; fax: (58) 38108).

Application Requirements: (a) Passport valid for a minimum of three months after intended return to home country. (b) One fully completed application form. (c) Two recent, passport sized photos per person endorsed on passport, with daytime phone number and address written clearly on the back. (d) Fee; payable by postal order (to Royal Netherlands Embassy) or cash. Cheques are not accepted. (e) Proof of sufficient funds (three most recent bank statements) and return/onward tickets as well as any other necessary documents. (f) Letter of invitation. (g) Letter showing employment, salary, length of service and guarantee of employment upon return to country.

Note: (a) All visitors wishing to work in Aruba for a number of months must have a written permit from the Department of Immigration and Naturalisation. Further information and application forms for Written Permits can be obtained free of charge from the Department of Immigration and Naturalisation, Kaya Dek Cooper 11, Sint Nicolas (tel: (58) 43322; fax: (58) 43534). (b) Potential immigrants in Aruba are required to take an HIV test. (c) Visitors who are not nationals of the country of residence must submit a residency permit.

Working days required: Up to four weeks.

Money

Currency: Aruba Florin or Guilder (AFl) = 100 cents. Notes are in denominations of AFl500, 250, 100, 50, 25 and 10. Coins are in denominations of AFl5, 2.5 and 1, and 50, 25, 10 and 5 cents.

Note: The Aruba Florin is tied to the US Dollar.

Currency exchange: The US Dollar is widely accepted. Other currencies can be exchanged in banks. Currency can also be obtained from ATMs in Oranjestad.

Credit & debit cards: Major credit cards are widely

accepted by many shops and hotels. They can also be used in ATMs if the card bears CIRRUS or Plus System logos.
Traveller's cheques: To avoid additional exchange rate charges, travellers are advised to take traveller's cheques in US Dollars or Euros.
Currency restrictions: The import and export of local and foreign currency is unlimited. The import of Dutch currency and currency from Surinam is prohibited. The Aruba Florin cannot be exchanged outside Aruba.
Banking hours: Mon-Fri 0800-1200 and 1330-1600. Some remain open for lunch.
Exchange rate indicators:
Rate at time of publishing
£1.00= AFl3.22
$1.00= AFl1.79

Duty Free

The following items may be imported into Aruba without incurring customs duty:
200 cigarettes or 50 cigars; 1l of spirits or 2.25l of wine or 3l of beer; gifts to a value of AFl100.
Note: A duty free allowance is only available to persons over 16 years of age. The importation of leather goods and souvenirs from Haiti is not advisable. There are no restrictions on the import of perfume. Goods worth more than AFl500 must be declared.

Public Holidays

Below are listed Public Holidays for the January 2006-June 2007 period.
2006: Jan 1 New Year's Day. **Jan 25** GF Croe's Day. **Mar 18** National Anthem and Flag Day. **Apr 14-17** Easter. **Apr 30** Queen's Day. **May 1** Labour Day. **May 25** Ascension Day. **Dec 25-26** Christmas.
2007: Jan 1 New Year's Day. **Jan 25** GF Croe's Day. **Mar 18** National Anthem and Flag Day. **Apr 6-9** Easter. **Apr 30** Queen's Day. **May 1** Labour Day. **May 17** Ascension Day.

Health

	Special Precautions?	Certificate Required?
Yellow Fever	Yes	1
Cholera	No	No
Typhoid & Polio	No	N/A
Malaria	No	N/A

Note: *Regulations and requirements may be subject to change at short notice, and you are advised to contact your doctor well in advance of your intended date of departure. Any numbers in the chart refer to the footnotes below.*

1: A yellow fever vaccination certificate is required from travellers over six months of age arriving from infected areas.
Food & drink: Tap water is considered safe to drink. Milk is pasteurised and dairy products are safe for consumption. Local meat, poultry, seafood, fruit and vegetables are generally considered safe to eat.
Health care: There are excellent medical facilities and many hotels also have doctors on call. The main hospital is the Dr Horacio Oduber. There is also the Centro Medico. In rare circumstances, air evacuation to Curaçao may be necessary. Full medical insurance is advised. There is no reciprocal health agreement with the UK.

Travel - International

AIR:

Air Aruba is the national airline. Many other airlines serve Aruba but usually a stopover or connecting flight will be needed.
Approximate flight times: From Oranjestad to *London* is 11 hours 40 minutes (including a connection, normally in Amsterdam), to *Los Angeles* is 10 hours and to *New York* is four hours.
Main airports: *Queen Beatrix (AUA)* is 3.5km (2.5 miles) southeast of Oranjestad. *To/from the airport:* A taxi service is available between the airport and the town. Bus services run to the town centre. *Facilities:* Duty free shop, bank, restaurants and left-luggage facilities.
Departure tax: US$36.75 per person for all passengers travelling to the USA; US$33.50 for all other destinations. Children under two years of age and those in transit in Aruba for less than 24 hours are exempt. Departure tax is normally included in the ticket price.
SEA:

Aruba has extensive duty free shopping and many cruise ships call in on their Caribbean itineraries. **Main ports:** *Oranjestad:* Boats dock in the heart of town: only a five-minute walk to the centre. However, there are also taxis available on the dock itself, plus car rental companies at the port.

Travel - Internal

SEA:

Ferries depart daily to De Palm Island from the mainland. Crossings run every half an hour between 1000-1800.
ROAD:

The road system throughout the island is very good. Driving is on the right and international signs are used. There is free parking throughout the island and no right turns on red lights. **Bus:** *Arubus* operates an inexpensive and reliable public bus service between the towns and hotels on Eagle Beach and Palm Beach, San Nicolas and the main bus station in Oranjestad; check with the tourist office or hotels for schedule. **Taxi:** The main taxi office is at Pos Abou. Taxis are not metered. Rates are fixed and should be checked before getting into the cab. There is no need to tip drivers except for help with unusually heavy luggage. **Car hire:** There are plenty of cars available for hire and touring by car or by 4-wheel drive jeep is one of the most pleasant ways to explore the island. Most major companies have offices in Aruba; there are also many well-established local car hire firms. It is possible to hire scooters, motorcycles (*Harleys* can even be rented!) and cycles. Minimum age for hiring a car is 21 to 25 (maximum 65 to70), depending on the firm. Hotels can assist with bookings. **Documentation:** A valid foreign licence or an International Driving Permit, held for at least two years, are both acceptable. Insurance is recommended.

Travel Advice

Most visits to Aruba are trouble-free but you should be aware of the global risk of indiscriminate international terrorist attacks, which could be against civilian targets, including places frequented by foreigners.
This advice is based on information provided by the Foreign and Commonwealth Office in the UK. It is correct at time of publishing. As the situation can change rapidly, visitors are advised to contact the following organisations for the latest travel advice:

British Foreign and Commonwealth Office
Tel: (0845) 850 2829.
Website: www.fco.gov.uk

US Department of State
Website: http://travel.state.gov/travel

Accommodation

HOTELS:

The majority of hotels are in the Palm Beach and Eagle Beach resort area on the southwest coast, offering accommodation of a very high standard. Many of these luxury hotels have beach frontage and their own swimming pools, plus extensive sport, entertainment and shopping facilities. Rates are much lower in the summer, which is the island's low season. Some tour operators offer out-of-season accommodation packages. Rooms are subject to a 5 per cent government room tax and hotels also add a 16.6 per cent service charge. The Aruba Tourism Authority provides a 24-hour customer service hotline (tel: (58) 39000) which is available to visitors wishing to make complaints or favourable comments about hotels and other establishments.
GUEST HOUSES:

There is limited scope for this kind of accommodation. Many guest houses are in the Noord area not far from the main hotel area. Contact the Tourism Authority for details.
SELF-CATERING:

There are apartment complexes and a list is available through the Aruba Tourism Authority offices.

ACCOMMODATION INFORMATION

Aruba Hotel and Tourism Association (AHATA)
LG Smith Boulevard 174, PO Box 542, Oranjestad, Aruba
Tel: (58) 22607.
Website: www.ahata.com

Top Things To See

- See the **pastel-coloured** gabled **buildings** of **Oranjestad**, where the Dutch heritage of Aruba is obvious, most typically exemplified by the **windmill** that was constructed by Dutch materials, brought piece by piece, and has now been converted into a restaurant; also here is **Fort Zoutman**, the oldest building on Aruba (1796), with the **Willem III-Tower** having been added in 1868.
- Find paradise at **Bucuti Beach**, rated one of the top beaches in the Caribbean and one of the best 100 beaches in the world.

Credit: ©Aruba Tourism Authority

- See yellow at the **Chapel of Alto Vista** on the north coast, which boasts a 100-year-old hand-carved **oak altar** behind the bright yellow exterior.
- Find the local **iguana** community in **Seroe Colorado**, notable also for its fine beaches.
- Spot Aruba's unofficial trademark – the distinctive shape of the *divi-divi* trees (also known as *watapanas*), windblown and windswept, stretched out at alarming angles in a land of cactus in the **Cunucu**.
- See **cave drawings** amongst Aruba's several systems of caves: **Fontein** was once used by the Arawak Indians who were the original inhabitants of the island and on the walls of these caves are ancient drawings thought to be part of the Indian sacrificial rite; the caves at **Guadirikiri** are a haven for bats; **Huliba Cave** is nicknamed the 'tunnel of love'; and **Arikok**, which has been designated a national park, has by far the best-preserved Indian drawings of all.
- **Hooiberg** (**Mount Haystack**) looms out of the flat landscape of the interior to the northwest of **Santa Cruz**: walk up a series of several hundred steps to see across to Venezuela at the 165m (541ft) peak.
- North from Santa Cruz, turning back towards the coast, the road to **Casibari** and **Ayo** passes spectacular **boulders**, the result of an unexplained geological catastrophe.
- Spot one of Aruba's vivid **parrotfish** amidst the **coral** at **De Palm Island**.
- Stare at the eerie **salt pans** along the southern coast.
- Be surrounded by **flamingos** in **Arikok National Park**.

Top Things To Do

- Get an insight into local customs, music and cuisine, as well as a chance to get to know the islanders, at the **Bonbini Festival**, held every Tuesday 1830-2030 throughout the year in the courtyard of the **Historical Museum**.
- **Birdwatch** at the **Bubali Bird Sanctuary**.
- Get into **watersports**: windsurf at **Arashi Beach** (near **California Point** on Bachelor's Beach) and maybe even attend the **Hi-Winds Amateur World Challenge Windsurfing Tournament** every June; surf at **Rodger's Beach** (at **Seroe Colorado**), **Dos Playa Beach** and Andicouri Beach; explore the surrounding shallow water

Credit: ©Aruba Tourism Authority

with specially equipped **submarine vessels**; **dive** amongst the wreck of a German freighter from World War II, which is now the home of countless exotic fish, or any of Aruba's other 40 dive sites with good visibility (often up to 30m/100ft) and a rich marine life (manta rays, barracuda and the green moray), in which wall diving, coral reef diving and wreck diving are all available, with water temperatures averaging at around 28ºC (82ºF) - scuba diving qualifications can be taken on the island and further details are available from the Aruba Tourism Authority, who also publish a brochure, *Discover Scuba in Aruba*; **snorkel** along **Windjammer Beach**, on the right side of the island, or **Arashi**, **Boca Grandi**, **Baby Beach** and - most recommended of all – **Hadikurari** (snorkelling gear can be hired from watersports centres at hotels); **swim** on the southern coast, in beaches such as **Eagle Beach**, **Druif Beach**, **Baby Beach** and **Rodgers Bay**; go **parasailing** on **Palm Beach**.

- Go on one of Aruba's romantic moonlight, sunset, dinner or dancing **cruises**: there are a variety of **underwater tours** available in glass-bottomed boats or on the **Atlantis Submarine** (website: www.atlantisadventures.com).
- Get into **golf** and feel environmental whilst you do so, since Aruba **Tierra del Sol**'s par-71 championship 18-hole course was designed by the Robert Trent Jones II Group, renowned for protecting the natural ecology of sites; the course is located on the northwestern tip of the island, near the **California Lighthouse** and affords magnificent views.
- Go **horse riding** like the locals: there are riding trips in the **Cunucu** (countryside) and along the coast.
- Buy fresh fish straight from the boat at **Oranjestad**'s daily **market** in the **Paardenbaai** (**Schooner Harbour**).
- Cheer the parades at Aruba's annual colourful **Carnival** in January.
- Go **duty free shopping** along the main drag in Oranjestad's **Caya GF Betico Croes**, where many malls and unique and designer stores can be found.

Entertainment

FOOD & DRINK: Not much food is grown locally, but the variety in the local cuisine is extensive. There is a very wide range of international cuisine and several of the more famous fast-food chains have premises on the island.

National specialities:
- *Grouper sandwich*: this fish inhabits shallow to mid-range reefs and is a white, sweet, mild-tasting fish. Fried in a proper batter, grouper is the main ingredient of many a lunch sandwich.
- *Keshi Yena* has its roots in Aruba's Dutch influence: cooks take a wheel of Gouda cheese, pack the hollowed-out center with a spicy meat mixture of either chicken or beef, and then bake the whole concoction to be eaten year-round but particularly at Christmas.
- Lamb or goat stew (*stobà*).
- *Cala* (bean fritters).
- *Pastechi* are meat- or cheese-stuffed turnovers.
- Take a bite of *ayacas*, which are leaf-wrapped meat rolls.
- The delicious *sopi di pisca* (fish chowder) makes the most of the elements.

National drinks:
- There is no national drink as such but, as ever in the Caribbean, all alcoholic punches and cocktails will usually be given a 'kick' with a liberal dose of rum.

Legal drinking age: 18 but it should be considered that such age restrictions are not usually endorsed.

Tipping: Hotels add a 15 per cent service charge to any food or beverage bill. Restaurants may add 15 per cent service to the bill; if not, 10 to 15 per cent is normal. Taxi fares do not include tips, but there may be charges for luggage and tips are well appreciated.

NIGHTLIFE: There is one drive-in and one indoor cinema screening current American, European and Latin American films. The highlight of Aruba's nightlife, however, is the casinos, of which there are 11, open from 1100 until the early morning. It is possible to take a dinner cruise. There are several bars and discos in Oranjestad, as well as nightclubs offering revues and live music. Themed nights and limbo dancing are a local speciality.

SHOPPING: As a 'free zone', duty on most items in Aruba is so low that shopping here can have obvious advantages. Stores carry goods from all parts of the world and there are some excellent buys, including perfume, linens, jewellery, watches, cameras, crystal, china and other luxury items plus a range of locally made handicrafts. **Shopping hours:** Mon-Sat 0800-1800; some shops close for lunch between 1200-1400. Shops in malls and shopping centres may open 0930-1800 and may open Sundays when cruise ships are in port.

Business

- **GDP:** US$1.94 billion.
- **Main exports:** Oil products and animals.
- **Main imports:** Machinery and electrical equipment, crude oil for refining and re-export, chemicals and foodstuffs.
- **Trade partners:** The Netherlands, USA, Colombia and Venezuela.

ECONOMY: Between 1824 and 1916, the economy was based on gold mining. Subsequently, an oil refinery opened in the mid-1920s and, once among the largest in the world, was the most important commercial operation on the island until its closure in 1985. However, it was re-opened in 1990, under an agreement with an American operator to establish transhipment (mainly between Venezuela and the USA), storage and refining facilities. Oil has now reassumed its central position in the Aruban economy. In the meantime, a sizeable tourism sector grew up. More recently, Aruba has been joined by offshore service industries, including finance and data processing. The country's free-port status, ship bunkering and repair facilities are the island's other main sources of revenue. However, in June 2000, Aruba was identified by the Organization for Economic Cooperation and Development (OECD) – the world's 30 largest economies – as one of 35 'tax havens' whose financial laws are believed to encourage large-scale tax evasion and money laundering. The government has since addressed most of the OECD's concerns.

Light industry is limited to the production of some tobacco products, drinks and consumer goods. Agriculture is confined to small-scale activity, because of poor soil quality. Aruba is classed as an Associate Overseas Territory of the European Union.

BUSINESS ETIQUETTE: Office hours: Mon-Fri 0800-1700.

Australia

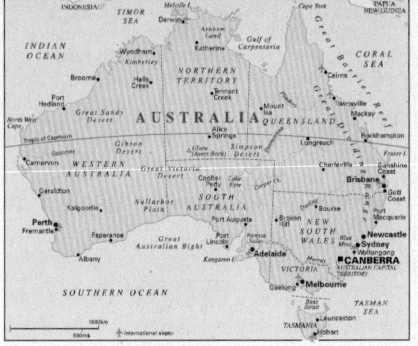

Location: Indian/Pacific Oceans.

Time: Australia spans three time zones:
Australian Western Time: GMT + 8.
Australian Central Time: GMT + 9.5 (GMT + 10.5 in South Australia from last Sunday in October to last Sunday in March).
Australian Eastern Time: GMT + 10 (GMT + 11 from first sunday in October to last Saturday in March, except in Queensland).

Overview

Australia has come a long way since the days when Captain Cook stumbled ashore to find an Aboriginal way of life that went back some 40,000 years. Indeed, Australia must really be divided into 'modern Australia' and 'indigenous Australia', since there is a wealth of disparate elements that constitute this compelling country.

The continent was first known to Europeans as *Terra Australis*. The first European settlements were initiated by the Dutch East India Company in 1606. By 1868, Britain had sent more than 160,000 convicts to Australia and several of modern Australia's biggest cities around the coast grew from the penal settlements. Eventually, the British crown claimed the entire continent. The colonisers unfortunately treated the Kooris, the indigenous population, with appalling brutality, which only worsened following the gold rush and the first wave of voluntary migration that spilled into the interior, where many Kooris had fled to.

The inaugural *National Sorry Day* was held in 1998 and has become an annual fixture on the Australian calendar. The day is a symbolic event that heralds modern Australia's willingness to face its inception. The didgeridoo and the boomerang have become modern Australian icons. Tourists flock to the breathtaking, epic monolith of Uluru (Ayers Rock) to watch the sun soak it in reds and oranges. This assimilation of Aboriginal culture has both negatives and positives, and the aim must be to harmonise rather than homogenise.

Many struggle to reconcile Aboriginal *Dreamtime* with the stereotype of carefree people in cork hats, swigging beer around a barbeque. But it is not difficult to 'take it easy' amidst miles of sun, sea and sand. You could even do the Aussie thing and ride some waves, with surfing schools on offer all over the country (website: www.surfingaustralia.com). Nevertheless, Australia may be an island, but it is also the world's largest one, and its size encompasses a range of stunning landscapes, from vast, barren deserts, where kangaroo and emu bound through the arid surroundings, to tropical rainforests and rugged mountains. Isolated from other continents, Australia has an abundance of unique plant and animal life.

Just as the surroundings surprise, so too may the people. Crocodile Dundee types have long been replaced by *fashionistas* browsing for bargains in Australia's world-renowned cities. Australia embraces its Pacific Rim location, with multicultural influence throughout, from Sydney's great harbour that welcomes worldwide visitors, to Melbourne's European ambience and lively Chinatown. Australia is a real hotchpotch of elements, catering for every kind of holidaymaker. This is the perfect time to discover the 'real' Australia, whatever you may find that to be.

General Information

AREA: 7,692,030 sq km (2,969,909 sq miles).

POPULATION: 20.09 million (estimate 2005).

POPULATION DENSITY: 2.54 per sq km.

CAPITAL: Canberra. **Population:** 309,900 (official estimate 1999).

GEOGRAPHY: Australia is bounded by the Arafura Sea and Timor Seas to the north, the Coral and Tasman Seas of the South Pacific to the east, the Southern Ocean to the south, and the Indian Ocean to the west. Its coastline covers 36,738km (22,814 miles). Most of the population has settled along the eastern and south-eastern coastal strip. Australia is the smallest continent (and the largest island) in the world. About 40 per cent of the continent is within the tropics and Australia is almost the same size as the mainland of the United States of America. The terrain is extremely varied, ranging from tortured red desert to lush green rainforest. Australia's beaches and surfing are world-renowned, while the country is also rich in reminders of its mysterious past. These range from prehistoric Aboriginal art to Victorian colonial architecture. The landscape consists mainly of a low plateau mottled with lakes and rivers and skirted with coastal mountain ranges, highest in the east with the Great Dividing Range. There are rainforests in the far northeast (Cape York Peninsula). The southeast is a huge fertile plain. Further to the north lies the enormous Great Barrier Reef, a 2000km (1200 mile) strip of coral that covers a total area of 345,000 sq km. Although Australia is the driest land on Earth, it nevertheless has enormous snowfields the size of Switzerland. There are vast mineral deposits. More detailed geographical descriptions of each State can be found in the individual State entries.

GOVERNMENT: Constitutional Monarchy. Gained independence from the UK in 1901. **Head of State:** HM Queen Elizabeth II, represented locally by Governor-General Michael Jefferey since 2003. **Head of Government:** Prime Minister John Winston Howard since 1996. All individual States and Territories have their own autonomous legislative, executive and judicial systems (though certain powers remain under the jurisdiction of the Federal Government). **Recent history:** In March 1996, tiring of Labour, the Australian public turned to the Liberal Party led by John Howard. Howard's centre-right coalition was returned to office for a third term at the 2004 general election. Aboriginal issues continue to affect Australian Governments. Since Howard's re-appointment, race riots have already occurred. The country's foreign policy is now geared to the strengthening of economic and political links with the countries of the Asian Pacific Rim and the affirmation of the existing links with the USA (exemplified by Australia's participation in the 2003 invasion of Iraq). Under the Howard Governments, migration has also come to dominate the Australian political agenda. The hard line which Howard set down has been rigorously pursued. The Government's hard line was reinforced by the October 2002 bomb in Bali, which killed 200 mostly Australian tourists. This brought Australia to the centre of the US-inspired global 'war against terrorism'.

The bicameral Federal Parliament holds legislative power. Both chambers are elected by universal adult suffrage. The 76-member Senate serves a six-year term, while the House of Representatives is voted in every three years. The Prime Minister is the leader of the largest party in the Lower House and wields executive power at the head of a Cabinet of Ministers. The Queen of England is formally Head of State, represented locally by a Governor General. Each of Australia's six states also has its own directly elected legislature, enjoying considerable autonomy in areas such as health, education and transport policy.

LANGUAGE: The official language is English. Many other languages are retained by minorities, including Italian, German, Greek, Vietnamese, Chinese dialects and Aboriginal languages.

RELIGION: 26 per cent Roman Catholic, 24 per cent Protestant and smaller minorities of all other major religions.

ELECTRICITY: 220/240 volts AC, 50Hz. Three-pin plugs are in use, however sockets are different from those found in most countries and an adaptor socket may be needed. Outlets for 110 volts for small appliances are found in most hotels.

SOCIAL CONVENTIONS: A largely informal atmosphere prevails; shaking hands is the customary greeting. Casual wear is worn everywhere except in the most exclusive restaurants, social gatherings and important business meetings. Most restaurants forbid smoking.

Climate

Australia is in the southern hemisphere and the seasons are opposite to those in Europe and North America. There are two climatic zones: the tropical zone (in the north above the Tropic of Capricorn) and the temperate zone. The tropical zone (consisting of 40 per cent of Australia) has two seasons, summer ('wet') and winter ('dry'), while the temperate zone has all four seasons.

November to March: (spring to summer): Warm or hot everywhere, tropical in the north, and warm to hot with mild nights in the south.

April to September: (autumn to winter): Northern and central Australia have clear warm days, cool nights; the south has cool days with occasional rain but still plenty of sun. Snow is totally confined to mountainous regions of the southeast.

Note: For further details, including climate statistics, see under individual State entries.

Required clothing: Lightweights during summer months with warmer clothes needed during the cooler winter period throughout most of the southern States. Lightweight cottons and linens all year in the central/northern States with warm clothes only for cooler winter evenings and early mornings. Sunglasses, sunhats and sunblock lotion are recommended year round in the north and during the summer months in the south.

Communications

Telephone: There are full facilities for national and international telecommunications. Full IDD is available. Country code: 61. Payphones are red, green, gold or blue. Only local calls can be made from red phones. Green, gold and blue phones also have International Direct Dialling (IDD) and Subscriber Trunk Dial (STD). Telstra Smart Phonecards are available at newsagents, supermarkets and chemists and can be used for local, STD or international calls. Creditphones, which take most major credit cards, can be found at airports, city-centre locations and many hotels.

Credit: ©David Bell and Juliet Sinclair

Credit: ©David Bell and Juliet Sinclair

Multimedia payphones are available in parts of Melbourne and Sydney. A touch screen allows visitors to gain access to information services, including tourist information which can be printed off for future reference. Phonecards for these telephones can be purchased from nearby shops.
Mobile telephone: Roaming agreements exist with most international mobile phone companies. Coverage is good, including in Tasmania; access in some of the more isolated, outback and rural areas is limited. US handsets are not compatible.
Internet: Available throughout Australia. Internet cafes are prevalent in all capital cities, including Tasmania, and individual hotels may also provide facilities.
Post: There are post offices in all the main towns of every State. Post office hours: Mon-Fri 0900-1700; some post office are also open Sat 0900-1200. Stamps are often available at hotel and motel reception areas and selected newsagents.
MEDIA: Australia's media scene is diverse and thriving. There is a long history of public broadcasting, but also many private TV and radio stations. Ownership of both print and broadcast media is highly concentrated. The Australian Broadcasting Corporation (ABC) operates national and local public radio and TV stations. The other main broadcaster is the Multicultural Special Broadcasting Service (SBS).
Press: The main daily newspapers are *The Australian* and *Australian Financial Review*. Newspapers generally have a high circulation throughout the continent.
TV: *ABC* and *SBS TV* are national public broadcasters. *Seven Network*, *Nine Network* and *Ten Network* are commercial broadcasters. Pay TV operator *Foxtel* is owned by News Corporation.
Radio: *ABC* is a public radio broadcaster that operates speech-cultural network *Radio National*, rolling news station *ABC NewsRadio*, youth-oriented *Triple J*, classical and contemporary music network, *ABC Classic FM* and local-regional services. *Radio Australia* is ABC's external service.

Passport/Visa

	Passport Required?	Visa Required?	Return Ticket Required?
Full British	Yes	Yes	No
Australian	N/A	N/A	N/A
Canadian	Yes	Yes	No
USA	Yes	Yes	No
Other EU	Yes	Yes	No
Japanese	Yes	Yes	No

Note: *Regulations and requirements may be subject to change at short notice, and you are advised to contact the appropriate diplomatic or consular authority before finalising travel arrangements. Any numbers in the chart refer to the footnotes below.*

PASSPORTS: Valid passport required by all.
VISAS: Required by all except the following:
(a) nationals of New Zealand;
(b) nationals of the following countries do not need to obtain a transit visa before travel if they are continuing their journey to a third country (and they hold confirmation of booking and documentation to enter country) within eight hours of arriving in Australia: Andorra, Argentina, Austria, Belgium, Brunei, Cyprus, Czech Republic, Canada, Denmark, Estonia, Fiji, Finland, France, Germany, Greece, Hungary, Hong Kong (SAR or BNO passport holders), Iceland, Indonesia, Ireland, Italy, Japan, Kiribati, Korea (Rep), Lativia, Liechtenstein, Lithuania, Luxembourg, Malaysia, Malta, Marshall Islands, Mexico, Micronesia (Federated States of), Monaco, Nauru, The Netherlands, New Zealand, Norway, Palau, Papua New Guinea, The Philippines, Poland, Portugal, Samoa (Western), San Marino, Singapore, Slovakia, Slovenia, Solomon Islands, South Africa, Spain, Sweden, Switzerland, Taiwan (if issued by the authorities in Taiwan), Thailand, Tonga, Tuvalu, UK (and its colonies), USA, Vanuatu, Vatican City and Zimbabwe.
All other nationals must obtain a transit visa before travel if intending to remain in Australia no longer than 72 hours and a 'stopover' is intended. Transit visas are free of charge.
Note: Not all airports remain open all night; travellers should check with the airline.
Electronic Travel Authority (ETA) visas: The ETA is an electronically stored authority for travel to Australia that allows people from certain countries (see below) to visit Australia for up to three months for tourism, short-term business or elective study purposes. An ETA is *invisible* and therefore will not show up in your passport.
ETAs (Visitor and Business - Short Validity ETAs only) may, for some nationals, be obtained online from the main Department of Immigration and Multicultural and Indigenous Affairs (DIMIA; website: www.eta.immi.gov.au) *or* from over 10,000 travel agents and airline offices throughout the UK.
Please note, the Australian High Commission in London does not offer an automatic ETA service.
Only nationals of the following countries are eligible for an ETA: Andorra, Austria, Belgium, British Overseas Territories, Brunei, Canada, Denmark, Finland, France, Germany, Greece, Hong Kong (SAR), Iceland, Ireland, Italy, Japan, Korea (Rep), Liechtenstein, Luxembourg, Malaysia, Malta, Monaco, The Netherlands, Norway, Portugal, San Marino, Singapore, Spain, Sweden, Switzerland, Taiwan (China), UK, USA and Vatican City.
Types of ETA and cost: *Tourist Visit/Business Visit (short-term)*: Free of charge.
Note: A service fee of A$20 is charged when applying for an ETA online through the DIMIA ETA website. Some travel agents and airlines issuing ETAs also charge a processing fee.
Validity of ETAs: *Tourist Visit* ETAs are valid for 12 months from date of issue (or until the passport expires, whichever comes first) and permit multiple entries into Australia for a stay of up to three months on each visit. *Short-term Business Visit* ETAs are valid for 12 months from date of issue (or until the passport expires, whichever comes first) for a single entry of up to three months. *Long-term Business Visit* ETAs are valid for 10 years (or the life of the passport) and permit multiple entries for a stay of up to three months for each visit.
Other types of visa and cost: Visitors not eligible for an ETA, or seeking a longer stay than an ETA offers, may apply for *Tourist Visit (Non ETA)* and *Temporary Business Short-stay* and *Temporary Business Long-stay (Non ETA)* visas. *Tourist Visit* and *Business Short-stay* visas cost £35; *Business Long-stay* visas cost £70. There are also student visas available, plus sponsored family visitor visas; please enquire at the Australian High Commission. Visa fees are generally adjusted on 1 January and 1 July each year.
Validity of non-ETA visas: For non-ETA visas, the validity varies according to the type of visa, the purpose of the trip and the validity of the passport. The validity will be stated on the visa label in your passport.
Application to: *ETA*: Authorised travel agents or airlines, by telephone or, in some cases, online through Australian Visas Ltd (see above). *Non-ETA*: Australian Embassies, High Commissions and Consulates; see *Passport/Visa Information*. There is a Tourist Short-Stay visa available online for passport holders of Bahrain, Cyprus, Czech Republic, Estonia, Hungary, Kuwait, Latvia, Lithuania, Oman, Poland, Qatar, Slovak Republic, Slovenia and the United Arab Emirates.
Application requirements: *ETA*: (a) Valid passport. (b) Fee (if applicable). (c) Completed application form giving details of passport number and expiry date, airline, names of travellers etc (if applying by post). *Tourist Visitor (Non ETA)*: (a) Completed application form. Application forms for tourist and business visitor visas can be downloaded from the Department of Immigration (website: www.immi.gov.au). (b) An A4 stamped, self-addressed, registered envelope for return of passport. (c) Valid passport with two unused visa pages. (d) Fee (payable by credit or debit card, American Express and Diners Card are not accepted). (e) One or more recent passport photos as required. (f) Evidence of sufficent funds.(g) Tourists over the age of 70 require a medical certificate. *Business Visitor (Non ETA)*: (a)-(f) and, (g) Applicant must provide proof of sponsorship and business interest. Business visa forms are also available from Australian Outlook, 3 Buckhurst Road, Bexhill on Sea, East Sussex TN40 1QF, UK. Transit: (a) Photo (signed on back), itinerary, onward booking, correct documentation to onward country and completed incoming passenger card.
Note: (a) Prior to lodging an application, visitors should confirm the current visa fees at www.immi.gov.au. (b) All travellers to Australia, except Australian citizens and permanent residents, must satisfy health and character requirements. (c) All travellers, including minors travelling on a parent's passport, require their own visa or ETA.
(d) Students must, before commencing study, pass a chest X-ray examination, carried out by a qualified radiologist.
Working days required: *ETA*: When issued through DIMIA's ETA website (website: www.eta.immi.gov.au), or through travel agents or airline offices, ETAs are usually processed and valid immediately or within three working days. *Non-ETA*: 10-15 working days.
Temporary residence: Applicants for temporary residence, working holidays and long-stay business visits to Australia should contact DIMIA online (website: www.immi.gov.au) *or* the High Commission online (website: www.australia.org.uk).

PASSPORT/VISA INFORMATION

Australian High Commission in the UK
Australia House, The Strand, London WC2B 4LA, UK
Tel: (020) 7379 4334 *or* (09065) 508 900 (24-hour immigration and citizenship enquiries; calls cost £1 per minute).
Website: www.australia.org.uk
Opening hours: Mon-Fri 0900-1700 (general); 0900-1100 (visa and immigration); 0930-1530 (passport and consular).

Embassy of the Commonwealth of Australia in the USA
1601 Massachusetts Avenue, NW, Washington, DC 20036, USA
Tel: (202) 797 3000 *or* (888) 990 8888 (visa information line; toll-free in the USA).
Website: www.austemb.org
All visa enquiries should be directed to the Embassy in Washington, DC or Consulate General in Los Angeles.

Department of Immigration
Website: www.immi.gov.au

Money

Currency: Australian Dollar (AUD; symbol A$) = 100 cents. Notes are in denominations of A$100, 50, 20, 10 and 5. Coins are in denominations of A$2 and 1, and 50, 20, 10 and 5 cents.
Currency exchange: Exchange facilities are available for all incoming and outgoing flights at all international airports in Australia. International-class hotels will exchange major currencies for guests. It is recommended that visitors change money at the airport or at city banks.
Credit & debit cards: Major credit cards are accepted. Use may be restricted in small towns and outback areas. Check with your credit or debit card company for details of merchant acceptability and other services which may be available.
Traveller's cheques: Widely accepted in major currencies at banks or large hotels. However, some banks may charge a fee for cashing traveller's cheques. To avoid additional exchange rate charges, travellers are advised to take traveller's cheques in a major currency.
Currency restrictions: Export and import of coins/notes in Australian or foreign currency above A$10,000 must be declared to customs at the port of entry or departure. Export of local currency above A$2000 must have reserve bank approval.
Banking hours: Mon-Thurs 0930-1600, Fri 0930-1700. These hours may vary slightly throughout the country.
Exchange rate indicators:
Rate at time of publishing
£1.00= A$2.81
$1.00= A$1.33

Duty Free

The following items may be imported into Australia by persons over 18 years of age without incurring customs duty:
250 cigarettes or 250g of tobacco or cigars; *2.25l of any alcoholic liquor*; *articles for personal hygiene and clothing, not including perfume or fur apparel*; *other goods to a value of A$900 (A$450 if under 18)*.
Prohibited items: There are very strict regulations against the import of non-prescribed drugs, weapons, firearms, wildlife, domestic animals and foodstuffs (including meat, poultry and dairy; plants or parts of plants [including fruit, nuts and seeds]; animal products [including wool, skins and eggs] and any equipment used with domestic animals) and other potential sources of disease and pestilence (such as vaccines or viruses). There are severe penalties for drug trafficking. For further details on customs regulations, contact the information centre of the Australian Customs Service (tel: (2) 6275 6666 (from outside Australia) *or* (1 300) 363 263 (from anywhere in Australia); website: www.customs.gov.au). Customs information booklets can be obtained from the Australian High Commission or Embassy.

Public Holidays

Below are listed Public Holidays for the January 2006-June 2007 period.
2006: Jan 1 New Year's Day. **Jan 26** Australia Day. **Apr 14-17** Easter. **Apr 25** ANZAC Day. **Dec 25-26** Christmas.
2007: Jan 1 New Year's Day. **Jan 26** Australia Day. **Apr 6-9** Easter. **Apr 25** ANZAC Day.
Note: Nationwide holidays only. If these dates fall on a Saturday or Sunday, a day may be given in lieu. There are numerous individual State holidays - see individual state sections for details.

Health

	Special Precautions?	Certificate Required?
Yellow Fever	No	1
Cholera	No	No
Typhoid & Polio	No	N/A
Malaria	No	N/A

Note: *Regulations and requirements may be subject to change at short notice, and you are advised to contact your doctor well in advance of your intended date of departure. Any numbers in the chart refer to the footnotes below.*

1: A yellow fever certificate is required from travellers over one year of age arriving within six days of leaving or transiting countries with infected areas.
Food & drink: Standards of hygiene in food preparation are very high. Milk is pasteurised and meat and vegetables are considered safe to eat. Care should be taken, however, when sampling 'bush tucker' in outback areas as some insects and fauna are highly poisonous unless properly cooked.
Other risks: Occasional outbreaks of *dengue fever* and *Ross River fever* have occurred in rural areas in northern Australia in recent years. There have been reports of *Murray Valley encephalitis* in the Northern Territory. Inland, there are suggestions that this risk extends from Western Australia to Queensland. Corals, jellyfish and fresh water crocodiles may prove a hazard to the bather, and heat is a hazard in the northern and central parts of Australia. Insectivorous and fruit-eating bats have been found to harbour a virus related to the *rabies* virus and should be avoided. Venomous snakes and spiders exist throughout Australia and can be extremely dangerous. Medical assistance should be sought immediately if bitten.
Note: There are strict customs and health controls on entering and leaving the country, and Australian law can inflict severe penalties on health infringements. Australia reserves the right to isolate any person who arrives without the required certificates. Carriers are responsible for expenses of isolation of all travellers arriving by air who are not in possession of the required vaccination certificates. All arriving aircraft are sprayed before disembarkation to prevent the spread of disease-carrying insects.
Health care: Doctors and dentists are highly trained and hospitals are well equipped. There is a reciprocal health agreement with the UK, in emergencies only, which allows residents from the UK free hospital treatment. Passport or proof of UK residence, such as an NHS medical card or a UK driving licence, must be shown. Prescribed medicines, ambulances and treatment at some doctors' surgeries must be paid for. Personal insurance for illness and accidents is highly recommended for all visitors. Those wishing to benefit from the agreement should enrol at a *Medicare* office; this can be done *after* treatment.

Travel - International

AIR:
The national airline is *Qantas (QF)* (website: www.qantas.com.au). About 25 international airlines fly to Australia.
Approximate flight times: From *London* to Adelaide is 24 hours 25 minutes, to Brisbane is 23 hours 25 minutes, to Cairns is 25 hours 45 minutes, to Darwin is 21 hours 25 minutes, to Melbourne is 23 hours, to Perth is 21 hours 50 minutes and to Sydney is 23 hours 30 minutes.
From *Los Angeles* to Sydney is 13 hours 30 minutes. From *New York* to Perth is 30 hours and to Sydney is 20 hours. From *Singapore* to Sydney is eight hours and to Perth is five hours.
Main airports:
Sydney Airport (SYD) (Kingsford Smith) (website: www.sydneyairport.com) is 8km (5 miles) south of the city (travel time - 30 minutes). *To/from the airport*: *Airport Link* connects the airport to Sydney Central Station (travel time - 13 minutes). Coaches meet all incoming international and domestic flights, departing every 20 to 30 minutes. There are many courtesy guest shuttles; enquire at hotel when booking is made. The international terminal is separate from the domestic terminal. Passengers may be set down at city airline terminals and some city hotels, motels and guest houses on request. There are also buses and taxis.
Adelaide Airport (ADL) (website: www.aal.com.au) is 6km (4 miles) west of the city (travel time - 30 minutes). A new terminal is currently under construction. *To/from the airport*: Coaches meet all international and domestic flights. Buses and taxis are available to the city and hotels.
Melbourne Airport (MEL) (Tullamarine) (website: www.melbourne-airport.com.au) is 22km (14 miles) northwest of the city (travel time - 30 minutes). *To/from the airport*: *Skybus Coach* (24 hours) or taxis are available to the city centre. There are also regional bus links from the airport.
Perth Airport (PER) (website: www.perthairport.com) is 12km (7 miles) northeast of the city (travel time - 25 minutes). There are separate international and domestic terminals. *To/from the airport*: Airport buses meet international and domestic flights. Taxis are available.
Brisbane Airport (BNE) (website: www.bne.com.au) is 13km (8 miles) northeast of the city (travel time - 35 minutes). *To/from the airport*: Coach services are available to the city, Gold Coast, Sunshine Coast and major hotels. Coaches meet all international flights. A rail link between the airport and the city was introduced in 2001. Taxis are also available.
Darwin Airport (DRW) (website: www.darwinairport.com.au) is 13km (8 miles) northeast of the city (travel time - 20 minutes). *To/from the airport*: Coaches and taxis meet all incoming international daytime flights.
Hobart Airport (HBA) (website: www.hobartairpt.com.au) is 16km (10 miles) east of the city (travel time - 25 minutes). *To/from the airport*: Coaches meet all incoming flights. Buses and taxis are available to the city.
Cairns Airport (CNS) is 8km (5 miles) north of the city (travel time - 10 minutes). *To/from the airport*: Coaches meet all incoming flights. There is also a shuttle taxi service, limousines, car hire and taxis.
Canberra Airport (CBR) (website: www.canberraairport.com.au) is 8km (5 miles) east of Canberra (travel time - 15 minutes). *To/from the airport*: Taxis and shuttle buses are available to the city centre.
Facilities: All airports have a duty free shop, bank/bureau de change, restaurant/bar, tourist information kiosk, car hire and taxi stand; these will almost always be available on arrival and departure of international flights.
Departure tax: None.
SEA:
Main ports: Cruise liners dock at Sydney (website: www.sydneyports.com.au), Melbourne(website: www.portofmelbourne.com), Hobart (website: www.hpc.com.au), Perth (Port of Fremantle) (website: www.fremantleports.com.au), Adelaide and Brisbane (website: www.portbris.com.au).

Travel - Internal

Note: Australia is a vast country and journeys should be planned, especially if travelling to remote areas. Health precautions should be taken when travelling in the Northern Territory and Queensland.
AIR:
Australians rely on aviation to get from place to place as inhabitants of smaller countries rely on trains and buses. The network of scheduled services extends to more than 150,000km (95,000 miles) and covers the whole continent. Both first-class and second-class service is available, with meals and hostess service on many routes. Recent deregulation of Australia's domestic airlines means that flight services are more competitively priced. Aircraft can be chartered by pilots who pass a written examination on Australian air regulations and have their licences validated for private operations within Australia.
The major domestic airlines are: *Jetstar Airways* (website: www.jetstar.com.au), *Qantas* (website: www.qantas.com.au) and *Virgin Blue* (website: www.virginblue.com.au), which serve the major resorts and cities throughout Australia. In addition, *Rex Regional Express* (website: www.rex.com.au) operate throughout New South Wales, South Australia, Tasmania and Victoria; *Air North* (website: www.airnorth.com.au) operate throughout the Northern Territory; *Macair Airlines* (website: www.macair.com.au) operate throughout Queensland; *Skywest* (website: www.skywest.com.au) operate throughout Western Australia and several small airlines operate to the islands off Tasmania (see *Tasmania* section).
Nearly all the domestic airlines operate special deals or air passes at greatly reduced prices.
Domestic airports: There are a great number of airports and landing strips throughout the country, including airports in all capital cities and regional centres such as *Alice Springs*, *Launceston* and *Uluru* (Ayers Rock). For further information contact Tourism Australia.
SEA/RIVER:
There are 36,738km (22,600 miles) of coastline and many lakes, inland waterways and inlets, all of which can be used for touring by boat. From paddle steamers along the Murray River to deep-sea fishing cruisers along the vast Barrier Reef, all are available for charter or passenger booking. Most tour operators also handle shipping cruises. The *Spirit of Tasmania* is an overnight car-ferry service linking Melbourne with Tasmania daily (website: www.spiritoftasmania.com.au).
RAIL:
Over 40,000km (24,850 miles) of track cover the country. Due to the vastness of the country, internal flights are a preferred option for travelling long distances, particularly as rail travel can be slow and relatively expensive. For further information on rail transport within the different States, see the individual State entries or contact Rail Australia (website: www.railaustralia.com.au).
Two services span the continent from coast to coast. The twice-weekly *Indian Pacific* travels 4350km (2704 miles) from Sydney on the east coast to Perth on the west coast, via Adelaide. The journey takes three days and three nights, crossing the Nullarbar Plain on the famous 478km (297 mile) stretch of straight track, the longest in the world. The *Ghan* travels 2979km (1891 miles) between Adelaide and Darwin, via Alice Springs. The service runs weekly in each direction and takes two nights. Both trains are fully air conditioned and soundproofed, with first- and second-class sleeping cars, a lounge car, bars and good restaurant facilities.
Other express service links (not always daily) from the state capitals are as follows:
The *Canberra Monaro Express* links Canberra with Sydney in four or five hours. The *XPT Express* runs from Melbourne to Brisbane via Canberra and Sydney. The *Sunlander* and the *Queenslander* link Brisbane with Cairns (31 hours). The *Prospector* links Perth with Kalgoorlie and this is one of Australia's fastest trains (six to seven hours). The *Spirit of the Outback* runs Brisbane to Longreach via Rockhampton.
There are also a number of scenic rail journeys available, including the *Kuranda Scenic Railway* that links Cairns with Kuranda via a 34km- (14 mile-) climb through tropical rainforest; the *Great South Pacific Express* service along the East Coast from Sydney to Cairns via Brisbane has been temporarily suspended.
Several routes have motor-rail facilities. Long-distance trains are air conditioned and have excellent catering facilities and showers. Reservations for seats and sleeping berths are essential on all long-distance trains and are accepted up to six months in advance. **Luggage allowance:** All interstate rail passengers are allowed 50kg (111lb). Medium-sized suitcases and hand luggage can be placed in the passengers' compartments. Large suitcases must be carried in the guard's van and checked in 30 minutes prior to departure. **Sleeping berths:** Single and twin apartments are available for a surcharge on most inter-capital overnight services. All 'Twinettes' have two sleeping berths and wash basin. Twinettes are available either first-class or holiday-class; the first also offer individual showers. 'Roomette' (single compartment) cars have showers at the end of each car. These are first-class only. **Cheap fares:** Unlimited travel, valid for 14, 21 and 30 days, with seven-day extensions available, is available with an *Austrailpass*, which must be purchased outside Australia, and can only be used by non-Australian passport holders. Only economy-class passes are available. Each State operator offers its own *Austrailpass* scheme. The *Austrail Flexi-Pass* is valid for eight, 15, 22 and 29 days within a six-month period, although it cannot be used on the *Ghan* or the *Indian Pacific*. The pass only offers economy-class accommodation. Both the *Austrailpass* and the *Austrail Flexi-Pass* must be purchased outside of Australia. The *East Coast Discovery Pass* offers six months' travel on the eastern coast. An *Austrailpass* does not include meal or sleeping berth charges. The passes must be used within 12 months of issue. There is also a *Backpacker Rail Pass* and a *Great Southern Railway Pass* available.
Representative in the UK: Rail Australia, c/o International Rail Limited, Chase House, Gilbert Street, Ropley, Hampshire SO24 0BY (tel: (0870) 751 5000; website: www.international-rail.com). Most major tourist attractions can be reached by train; tickets for multiple destinations can be purchased from travel agents outside Australia.
ROAD:
Traffic drives on the left. Road signs are international. The speed limit is 60kph (35mph) in cities and towns in most states but 50kph (31mph) in Victoria and Western Australia, 50kph/31mph in all suburban areas and 80-110kph (50-68mph) on country roads and highways unless signs indicate otherwise. Seat belts must be worn at all times and driving licences must be in the driver's possession when driving. Driving off major highways in the outback becomes more difficult between November and February because of summer rain, as many roads are little more than dirt tracks. Road travel is best between April and October. Distances between towns can be considerable, and apart from ensuring that all vehicles are in peak condition, it is advisable to carry spare water, petrol and equipment. Travellers are advised to check with local Automobile Associations before departure in order to obtain up-to-date information on road and weather conditions. Bicycle helmets must be worn by all cyclists.

A B C D E F G H I J K L M N O P Q R S T U V W X Y Z

Coach: Major cities are linked by an excellent national coach system, run by *Greyhound Pioneer* (website: www.greyhound.com.au). Tasmania also has its own coach service, *Tasmanian Redline Coaches* (website: www.redlinecoaches.com.au). There are numerous other companies operating State and Interstate services.

The main coach express routes are: Sydney to Adelaide, Melbourne (inland), Brisbane and Canberra; Canberra to Melbourne; Melbourne to Adelaide; Adelaide to Alice Springs, Perth and Brisbane; Darwin to Alice Springs, Cairns, Perth and Kakadu; Alice Springs to Ayers Rock; Cairns to Brisbane; Brisbane to Sydney (inland and coastal) and Melbourne.

Coach passes are available for travel on a variety of routes for between seven days and one year, such as the *All Australian*, the *Sunseeker*, the *Aussie Reef & Rock*, the *Coast to Coast* etc. The *Aussie Kilometre Pass* allows you to purchase your travel in kilometres and then travel in any direction on the national network to the distance purchased. It is advisable to purchase these passes before departure from country of origin.

Coaches are one of the cheapest ways to travel around Australia, as well as one of the most comfortable, with air conditioning, big adjustable seats and on-board bathrooms; some also have television and the latest videos.

Car Hire: Available at all major airports and major hotels to those over 21 years old. **Documentation:** An International Driving Permit is required by nationals of countries whose official language is not English. International, foreign or national driving permits are generally valid for three months. An International Driving Permit is only valid in conjunction with a valid national licence. Permits must be carried at all times while driving.

URBAN:

Comprehensive public transport systems are provided in all the main towns. The State capitals have suburban rail networks, those in Sydney and Melbourne being particularly extensive, and trams run in Melbourne and Adelaide. Meter-operated taxis can be found in all major cities and towns. There is a minimum 'flagfall charge' and then a charge for the distance travelled. Taxi drivers do not expect to be tipped. A small additional payment may be required for luggage and telephone bookings. Some taxis accept payment by credit card. For further details, see individual State entries.

Travel times: The following chart gives approximate travel times (in hours and minutes) from **Sydney** to other major cities in Australia.

	Air	Rail	Coach
Adelaide	**1.40**	**25.00**	**22.00**
Brisbane	**1.20**	**15.00**	**15.00**
Darwin	**5.00**	**-**	**92.50**
Melbourne	**1.10**	**10.00**	**14.00**
Perth	**4.00**	**65.00**	**56.00**

Travel Advice

Most visits to Australia are trouble-free but you should be aware of the global risk of indiscriminate international terrorist attacks, which could be against civilian targets, including places frequented by foreigners. On 2 November 2005, the Australian government said that it would introduce an urgent amendment to the country's counter-terrorism legislation, in response to an assessment by Australian intelligence agencies that a terrorist attack in Australia is feasible and could well occur.

This advice is based on information provided by the Foreign and Commonwealth Office in the UK. It is correct at time of publishing. As the situation can change rapidly, visitors are advised to contact the following organisations for the latest travel advice:

British Foreign and Commonwealth Office
Tel: (0845) 850 2829.
Website: www.fco.gov.uk

US Department of State
Website: http://travel.state.gov/travel

Accommodation

HOTELS/MOTELS:

Every State has a selection of hotels run by well-known and established international chains. More authentic accommodation can be found outside the cities. The highways out of the State cities are lined with good quality motels offering self-contained family units, and often an in-house restaurant service. Most hotels and motels provide rooms with telephones, private shower and/or bath, toilet, small fridge and tea- and coffee-making facilities.

The principal difference between a hotel and a motel in Australia is that a hotel must, by law, provide a public bar among its facilities. For this reason, there are many motels which are hotels in all but name, offering an excellent standard of comfort and service but preferring to reserve their bar exclusively for the use of their guests, rather than for the public at large. Hotels and motels in Australia are graded in a star rating system by the Australian Automobile Clubs. In most cases, different rooms will be offered at different rates depending on their size, aspect or facilities; this is particularly true of seafront hotels. In general, hotels in cities cost more than their rural counterparts. Grading definitions range from 5-star (highest) to 1-star (lowest). Some hotels are graded with an additional open or hollow star. This indicates a slightly higher grade of facilities than the normal facilities for its classification.

GUEST HOUSES/HOMESTAY/SELF-CATERING AND FARMSTAY HOLIDAYS:

Service apartments and self-contained flats are available at main tourist resorts, especially along the east coast. Many of the less accessible areas have accommodation on farmsteads, from guest houses on the huge sheep stations to basic staff quarters on smaller arable farms, giving an insight into an alternative aspect of Australian life. Bed & breakfast in private home accommodation is available throughout Australia, often at very low prices. Some companies offering budget bed & breakfast also offer tourist and general information services. Some hotels have self-catering apartments. Guest houses are not allowed to serve alcohol. Holiday units and apartments are classified according to a 5-star system, with criteria comparable to those for hotels and motels above.

COUNTRY PUB ACCOMMODATION:

These offer drinks, meals and simple but comfortable accommodation for travellers. Pubs tend to be easy to find and advance reservations are not always necessary. However, standards may vary according to the type of pub and its location.

CAMPUS ACCOMMODATION:

University colleges and halls of residence offer inexpensive accommodation for both students and non-students during the vacation periods (May, August and late November to late February).

CAMPING/CARAVANNING:

Camping tours cover most of the country, especially the wilder areas. Participants generally join a group under an experienced guide team and everyone helps with cooking, washing, etc. All equipment and transport is supplied; some also provide portable showers. More rugged tours with Land Rovers are available offering limited facilities, although company equipment is again provided with a driver/guide and cook. Campsite information is available from all major tourist centres. Camping is available in caravan parks, campsites, national parks and other areas. It is illegal to camp in undesignated areas.

With the constant threat of bushfire, a policy of 'no open fires' will sometimes be in force, especially during Fire Danger Season (Dec 1-Apr 30); check with local authorities for more information.

A number of companies can arrange **motor camper** rentals, with a range of fully-equipped vehicles. Full details can be obtained from the Tourism Australia (see *Top Things To See & Do*).

Caravan parks are classified according to a 5-star system with criteria similar to those for hotels and motels above. Accommodation is also available at many of Australia's sheep stations.

YOUTH HOSTELS:

Found throughout the country, but there are greater concentrations near cities and densely populated areas. Only YHA hostels meet Hostelling International standards.

ACCOMMODATION INFORMATION

Australian Hotels Association
National Press Club Building, Level 2, 16 National Circuit, Barton, ACT 2600, Australia
Tel: (2) 6273 4007.
Website: www.aha.org.au

Australian Hotels Association
Level 5, 8 Quay Street (Prince Centre), Sydney, NSW 2000, Australia
Tel: (2) 9281 6922.
Website: www.aha-nsw.asn.au

Australian Bed & Breakfast Council
Website: www.australianbedandbreakfast.com.au

Australian Youth Hostel Association
National Office, PO Box 314, Camperdown, NSW 1450, Australia
Tel: (2) 9565 1699.
Website: www.yha.com.au

VIP Backpacker Resorts of Australia
Website: www.backpackers.com

Nomads
Website: www.nomadsworld.com

Top Things To See & Do

Please refer to each individual State section.

TOURIST INFORMATION

Tourism Australia in the UK
Australia Centre, Australia House, 6th Floor, Melbourne Place, The Strand, London WC2B 4LG, UK
Tel: (020) 7438 4601 (trade enquiries only).
Website: www.australia.com
Opening hours: Mon-Fri 0900-1730.

Tourism Australia in the USA
6100 Center Drive, Suite 1150, Los Angeles, CA 90045, USA.
Tel: (310) 695 3200.
Website: www.australia.com

Entertainment

FOOD & DRINK: There are numerous Australian speciality dishes and foods. Australia also offers an enormous variety of cuisines, including Italian, French, Greek, Spanish, Chinese, Vietnamese, Malaysian, Thai, Japanese, Indian, African, Lebanese and Korean.

Things to know: Service is European-style and varies from waitress and waiter service to self-service. Bistros, cafes, family-style restaurants and 'pub' lunches at the counter offer good food at reasonable prices. Most restaurants and hotels are licensed to serve alcohol; private hotels and guest houses cannot be licensed by law. Some restaurants will allow guests to bring their own alcohol and are called 'BYO'. Licensing hours in public bars are 1000-2200 Mon-Sat, however most pubs are open until 2400; Sunday hours vary. Restaurants, clubs and hotel lounges have more flexible hours.

National specialities:

- Sydney rock oysters.
- *Barramundi* (freshwater fish).
- Tiger prawns.
- Macadamia nuts.
- *Yabbies.* (small freshwater lobsters).
- Beef is the most popular meat and lamb is also of a high quality.

National drinks:

- Australian wine.
- Australian beer.

The major vineyards (wineries) are outside Perth, Sydney, Melbourne, Hobart, Canberra and Adelaide. The largest single wine-growing region is in the Barossa Valley, South Australia, two hours' drive from Adelaide, where high-quality red and white wines are produced. Australian wines are good and inexpensive. Beer is served chilled (for further information, visit: www.australianwineand beer.com).

Legal drinking age: Drinking age is 18 years or over.

Tipping: Not as common as it is in Europe and America, nor is a service charge added to the bill in restaurants. 10 per cent for food and drink waiters is usual in top-quality restaurants, but is optional elsewhere. With taxis it is usual not to tip but round up the cost to the next dollar.

SHOPPING: Special purchases include excellent local wines; wool, clothing, leather and sheepskin products; opal and other precious or semi-precious stones; and modern art sculpture and paintings. Exhibitions of bark paintings, boomerangs and other tribal objects are on view and for sale in Darwin, Alice Springs and the State capitals; many depict stories from the Dreamtime. Many cities and towns have small shops devoted to the sale of 'Australiana', where Australian souvenirs, ranging from T-shirts to boomerangs, can be bought. **Shopping hours:** Opening hours for most stores in the cities are Mon-Fri 0900-1730, Sat 0900-1700. Late-night shopping is available Friday to 2100 in Melbourne, Adelaide, Brisbane, Hobart and Darwin. Late-night shopping is available Thursday at the same times in Sydney, Canberra and Perth. Major stores in some states are open 1000-1600 Sunday. Corner stores, restaurants and snack bars are open in most cities until well into the night. For further information on shopping and trading, contact the ACT Office of Fair Trading (tel: (2) 6207 0400; website: www.fairtrading.act.gov.au).

Business

- **GDP:** US$611.7 billion.
- **Main exports:** Ores and metals, wool, food and live animals, minerals, fuels, transport machinery and equipment.
- **Main imports:** Machinery and transport equipment, computers and office machines, telecommunication equipment and parts, crude oil and petroleum products.
- **Main trade partners:** USA, Japan, China, Germany and UK.

Credit: ©David Bell and Juliet Sinclair

ECONOMY: Australia has a very diverse economy and a high standard of living. The service sector accounts for almost three-quarters of GDP, although other sectors of the economy contribute significantly to Australian export earnings. Approximately one-third of export earnings is derived from agricultural products, although the main agricultural industry, sheep farming, now appears to be in long-term decline. The other major export industry is mining; Australia has vast reserves of coal (of which it is now the world's leading exporter), oil, natural gas, nickel, zircon, iron ore, bauxite and diamonds, as well as uranium (Australian ore fuels many of the Western nations' nuclear power plants). Most Australian manufacturing is concentrated in processing of mineral products and in the iron, steel and engineering industries.

The country's service industries, which now account for the major part of the economy, have continued to grow, despite some damage in the wake of the 1997 Asian financial crisis, which severely affected many of Australia's major trading partners. The most important development in the economy in recent years has been a shift in trading patterns away from Britain and Europe towards the Pacific Rim – 60 per cent of Australian exports are now sold in that region. Australia's single-largest trading partner is Japan, which takes approximately one-third of total exports, followed by the USA, South Korea, New Zealand, Singapore, Taiwan, China and then the EU nations (principally the UK and Germany). Japanese investment in Australia, particularly in property and tourist ventures, has reached the point where most of the eastern seaboard 'Gold Coast' is now Japanese owned.

The Australian economy has continued to perform steadily during the last few years; annual growth in early 2004 was just over 3 per cent. Inflation and unemployment are stable at 3 and 7 per cent respectively.

BUSINESS ETIQUETTE: Suits are usually worn in Sydney and Melbourne. Brisbane businesspeople may wear shirts, ties and shorts; visiting businesspeople should wear lightweight suits for the initial meeting. Prior appointments necessary. Punctuality is important. A great deal of business is conducted over drinks. Best months for business travel are March to November. Office hours: Mon-Fri 0900-1700.

COMMERCIAL INFORMATION

Australia Business
Dudley House, 34-35 Southampton Street, London
WC2E 7HE, UK
Tel: (0870) 890 0720.
Website: www.anzcc.org.uk

Australian Chamber of Commerce and Industry (ACCI)
Commerce House, Level 3,
24 Brisbane Avenue, Barton,
ACT 2600, Australia
Tel: (2) 6273 2311.
Website: www.acci.asn.au

International Chamber of Commerce
Level 3, 525 Collins Street, Melbourne, VIC 3000,
Australia
Tel: (3) 8608 2072 or 2547.

Association of Australian Convention Bureaux (AACB)
Level 2, 80 William Street, Sydney, NSW 2011,
Australia
Website: www.aacb.org.au

Australian Capital Territory

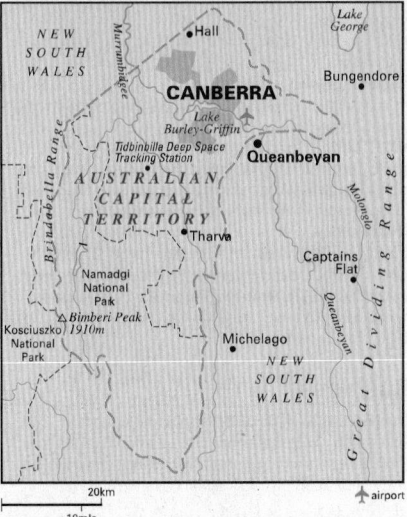

Location: Within New South Wales, southeast Australia.

Time: GMT + 10 (GMT + 11 from first Sunday in October to last Saturday in March).

Overview

Half of the Australian Capital Territory consists of nature reserves and Namadgi National Park. Yet this would be more impressive if we did not consider the Territory's miniscule size by comparison to other Australian States. The Australian Capital Territory is 50 miles (80km) from north to south and about 20 miles (30km) wide, carved out of pre-existing land because of a diplomatic compromise. Canberra was chosen as Australia's capital city in 1908, resolving a long-running debate between the main rivals of Sydney and Melbourne, and the Australian Capital Territory is the land that was placed around it.

Yet the beauty of the countryside suggests that size is not everything. There are parks and hills to roam, bushland to frolic in, wineries and wildlife parks. The Snowy Mountains, jutting out of nearby New South Wales, are a brilliant border to the Territory's picture-perfect scene.

Despite the world-famous cities of Melbourne and Sydney in relatively close proximity, Canberra retains its own distinct atmosphere. The city was designed by the American architect Walter Burley Griffin and is a deliberately spacious city, from its large areas of parkland to the 11km- (7 mile-) lake to the circular layout around the Parliamentary Centre. It is the fitting hub of a delightful State, all the better to explore because of its compact size.

General Information

AREA: 2400 sq km (1511 sq miles).
POPULATION: 320,000 (official estimate 2000).
POPULATION DENSITY: 131.7 per sq km.
CAPITAL: Canberra (also national capital). **Population:** 220,000 (official estimate 2000).
GEOGRAPHY: Canberra is located in the Australian Capital Territory on the western slopes of the Great Dividing Range, and was conceived in the early 1900s in order to create a capital city in a federal State separate from any of the

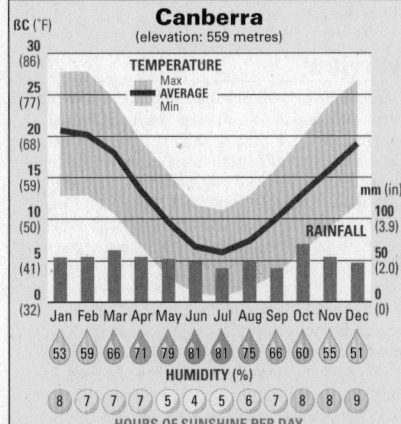

Canberra (elevation: 559 metres)

uniting States. Spectacular green countryside is ringed by mountains nearly 600m (2000ft) above sea level. Lake Burley-Griffin, a humanmade lake, is the centrepiece of this constantly expanding modern capital. Hills, trees and greenery remain prominent among the architecture of a city that is attractive, tidy, spacious and efficient as befits the national capital city.

Climate

Warm during the summer months with cool, crisp and clear winters. Rainfall occurs throughout the year. Canberra averages more hours of sunshine per year than any other capital city in Australia.
Required clothing: Lightweights during summer months with warmer mediumweight clothes necessary in winter. Waterproofing advisable throughout the year, especially in winter. A top coat is necessary during winter months.

Public Holidays

The Australian Capital Territory observes all the public holidays observed nationwide (see the main *Australia* section) and, in addition, the beneath Public Holidays listed for the January 2006-June 2007 period.
2006: Mar 20 Canberra Day. **Jun 12** Queen's Birthday Celebrations. **Oct 2** Labour Day.
2007: Mar 19 Canberra Day. **Jun 11** Queen's Birthday Celebrations.

Travel - International

AIR:
 Airlines serving Canberra include *Qantas* and *Virgin Blue. British Airways, Singapore Airlines* and *United Airlines* offer flights to Australia with connections through to Canberra.
Main airports: *Canberra International Airport (CBR)* (website: www.canberraairport.com.au) is not an international point of entry to Australia but is linked to Sydney, Melbourne and Brisbane by convenient connections. Overseas visitors can book through one of the carriers listed above, changing aircraft after arrival in Australia. The city centre is 8km (5 miles) from the airport. *To/from the airport:* Transport into the city is available by bus, taxi or rental car (travel time – 15 minutes).

RAIL:
 Through-trains run from Canberra to Sydney and Melbourne, with connections to other States. Economy *Australpass* tickets apply on both local and interstate systems, but must be purchased before travelling to Australia. For further information, contact *Countrylink* (tel: (2) 8202 2000; website: www.countrylink.com.au). Other discount tickets include the *East Coast Discovery Pass,* which permits six months' one-way economy-class travel between main cities in the New South Wales area with unlimited stopovers. Prices depend on the route taken; see online (website: www.railpage.org.au) for more information.

ROAD:
 Coach: Main road links, which are used by coach services, connect Canberra to Sydney (travel time – four hours 15 minutes) and to Melbourne (travel time – seven hours 30 minutes), thereby allowing access to all other parts of the country. *All Australian* and other tickets apply. *Greyhound Pioneer* (website: www.greyhound.com.au) and *Murray's* (website: www.murrays.com.au) operate regular daily services from Canberra to Sydney, Adelaide and Melbourne.

URBAN:
 Bus: An internal bus network operates for the city of Canberra. Pre-purchase day tickets and 10-journey multi-tickets are available. **Taxi:** Radio-controlled, metered taxis are available at all hours.

Accommodation

HOTEL/MOTEL:
 There is a wide range of hotels/motels in Canberra, from historic buildings and small boutique hotels to stylish hotel complexes.
BED & BREAKFAST:
 There are many Bed & Breakfasts in Canberra to suit all needs and budgets. Many are located near charming wineries or in the leafy suburbs of Canberra. For more details, contact Australian Capital Tourism (see *Top Things To Do*).
SELF-CATERING:
 A wide range of apartments are available, many of which are serviced. Many are located in the city centre or the inner city suburb of Kingston, close to shops and tourist sites.
CAMPING/CARAVANNING:
 A number of companies can arrange motor camper rentals, with a range of fully equipped vehicles. Full details can be obtained from Australian Capital Tourism.

ACCOMMODATION INFORMATION

Canberra Accommodation Association
Tel: (2) 6205 0044.
Website: www.canberraaccommodation.com.au

Canberra Getaways
Tel: (2) 6205 0444.

Top Things To See

- Observe where Parliament used to sit at the impressive **Old Parliament House** in **Canberra**'s elegant city of wide streets, gardens and parkland; learn more about the role and function of the Federal Parliament at the more modern **Parliament House**, a grand modern edifice completed in 1988, Australia's bicentennial year.
- See some of Australia's deadliest and most colourful reptiles at Canberra's **Australian Reptile Centre**.
- Peer down at the Australian Capital Territory on one of the many hills in the immediate area of Canberra; from the 195m- (650ft-) **Telstra Tower** to the 825m- (2750ft-) high **Black Mountain**.
- Explore a wealth of Australian fauna and wildlife in a natural bush setting at the **Tidbinbilla Nature Reserve** in **Tharwa**, just 40km (25 miles) southwest of the capital; a number of bushwalking trails are provided in which visitors can observe kangaroos, wallabies, koalas, platypus, bush birds and water birds in their natural habitat.
- Gaze at prehistoric sites with Aboriginal rock paintings, as well as a variety of rare sub-alpine species of flora and fauna, spectacular views and walking tracks, all to be found in the **Namadgi National Park**, which is part of the **Snowy Mountains**.
- Keep an eye on the skies at one of the most important bird habitats in the region, which becomes a refuge for large numbers of water birds from surrounding areas during drought in inland Australia: the **wetlands**.

Top Things To Do

- **Hot-air balloon** around Canberra or, for the less adventurous, glance up at a flurry of them at the **Balloon Fiesta** in Canberra every year (website: www.canberraballoonfiesta.com.au).
- Indulge in any of those stereotypically Australian activities at the **Glenloch Sheep Station**, located in Belconnen on the outskirts of Canberra: these include **sheep shearing**, **boomerang throwing** and **sheep-dog demonstrations**, and they are usually rounded off with a traditional Australian **barbecue** lunch.
- Round off a good **walk** or **horse ride** with a **picnic** in the scenic park area that is the **Murrumbidgee River Corridor**.
- Go **bushwalking**, **fishing** or **rock climbing** in one of the many parks and **natural reserves** in the Territory; the trails provided allow visitors to observe native animals and plants.
- Take a **whitewater rafting** trip (from one to four days) to the **Upper Murray**, **Murrumbidgee**, **Goodradigbee** and **Cotter** rivers.
- Make time for a round of **golf**, which the Territory is supremely well-catered for: the **Royal Canberra Golf Club**, located on the shores of **Lake Burley Griffin**, is ranked amongst the top-10 courses in Australia; the **Federal Golf Club** features views to the Brindabella mountain ranges; the 41-year-old **Yowani Country Club** has a tree-lined course with extensive fairways and greens; the **Gold Creek Country Club**, Canberra's most popular course, was designed by Bruce Devlin and hosts international championships; the **Gungahlin Lakes Course** is in a beautiful setting; the **Murrumbidgee Golf Club** offers a par 72 championship course in a country setting; and the **Woodhaven Green Golf Course**, a 27-hole public course, has been established for 20 years.
- Spend the annual **ANZAC Day** at the **Australian War Memorial** in Canberra, which is deservedly one of the city's most popular attractions, and the scene of the colourful annual **ANZAC Parade**; it contains archives, galleries displaying relics, photographs and art.

TOURIST INFORMATION

Australian Capital Tourism
Street address: 5/2 Brindabella Circuit, Brindabella Business Park, Canberra International Airport, Canberra ACT 2609, Australia
Postal address: Locked Bag 2001, Civic Square, Canberra ACT 2608, Australia
Tel: (2) 6205 0666.
Website: www.visitcanberra.com.au

Canberra and Region Visitors Centre
330 Northbourne Avenue, Dickson ACT, Australia
Tel: (2) 6205 0044.

Entertainment

FOOD & DRINK: The variety of cuisine available in Canberra is impressive, with over 300 restaurants offering food from all corners of the world, from Austria to Zanzibar.
Regional specialities:
- Trout from the streams and lakes of the Snowy Mountains.
- Beef and lamb come from the farmlands surrounding Canberra.

Regional drinks:
- Cool-climate wines and fine, full-flavoured *Chardonnays* and *Shiraz*.

NIGHTLIFE: Despite the daytime orderliness, nightlife is actively promoted by the large range of pubs, restaurants, nightclubs, acoustic venues and jazz, piano and wine bars. There are many film shows and a boutique casino.
SHOPPING: A wide range of goods, including Australian arts and crafts, is available from department stores and specialist shops. Galleries and museums are usually open seven days weekly. **Shopping hours:** Opening hours for most stores in the city are 0900-1700 Mon-Thurs, Fri 1000-1600 and Sat-Sun.

Business

CONFERENCES/CONVENTIONS: The National Convention Centre in Canberra has seating facilities for 2500. Other major convention centres include Australian Institute of Sport, Rydges Capital Hill and Parkroyal Canberra.

COMMERCIAL INFORMATION

ACT & Region Chamber of Commerce & Industry
12A Thesiger Court, Deakin, Canberra, ACT 2600, Australia
Tel: (2) 6283 5200.
Website: www.actchamber.com.au

Canberra Convention Bureau Inc
Suite 405, Level 4, Optus Centre, 10 Moore Street, Canberra, ACT 2600, Australia
Tel: (2) 6247 7500.
Website: www.canberraconvention.com.au

New South Wales

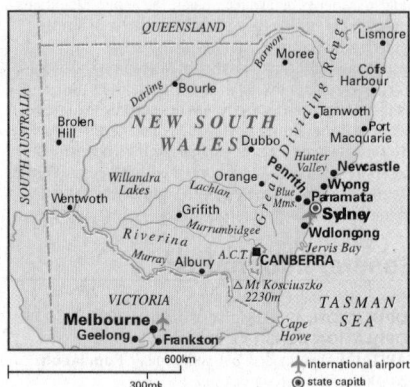

Location: Southeast Australia.

Time: GMT + 10 (GMT + 11 from first Sunday in October to last Saturday in March) except in the Broken Hill Area, which keeps GMT + 9.5.

Overview

New South Wales is the oldest and most populated State in Australia: it is also the most talked-about and walked-about. Perhaps this is because this one State manages to fulfil everything that a visitor might expect of the country as a whole: when people think of Australia, they will usually think of beaches (New South Wales has plenty, including the world-famous Bondi Beach), wild terrain (New South Wales teems with natural parks and reserves) and, of course, iconic symbols such as Sydney Harbour and its remarkable Opera House, whose architecture looks like sails full of wind, celebrating the city's nautical connections and also emphasising the sense of energy that permeates this city.
It is unlikely that Captain Cook could have foreseen Sydney's rapid ascent into a world-premier city when he first decked at what is now Sydney Harbour in 1770, claiming the State for the British and proclaiming it New

---

South Wales. But what existed before the growth of the settlements - and what continues to exist - is the serenity that can be found amidst the State's breathtaking natural scenery.
New South Wales is vast and varied and the variation never fails to startle: from snow-capped mountains with excellent skiing facilities to long, golden sandy beaches, and from the utter emptiness of the Outback to the cosmopolitan vitality of the State capital – New South Wales has it all.

General Information

AREA: 801,640 sq km (309,417 sq miles).
POPULATION: 6.68 million (official estimate 2003).
POPULATION DENSITY: 8 per sq km.
CAPITAL: Sydney. **Population:** 4.25 million (estimate 2003).
GEOGRAPHY: The landscape ranges from the subtropical north to the Snowy Mountains in the south, which contain Australia's highest point, Mount Kosciuszko. There are over 1300km (800 miles) of coastline with golden beaches and picturesque waterways and rivers, including the 1900km- (1200 mile-) Murray River.

Climate

Warm semi-tropical summers, particularly in lower central area. Mountain areas in the west are cooler, particularly in winter. Rainfall is heaviest from March to June.

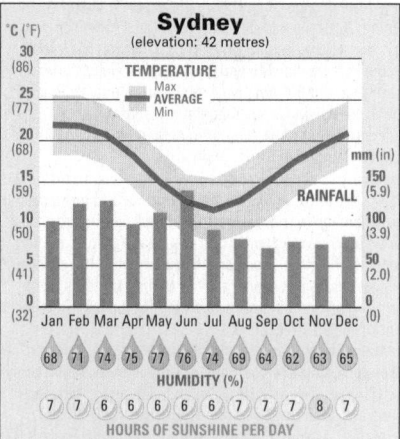

Public Holidays

New South Wales observes all the public holidays observed nationwide (see the main *Australia* section) and, in addition, the beneath Public Holidays listed for the January 2006-June 2007 period:
2006: Oct 2 Labour Day.
Note: The first Monday in August is also a public holiday in some parts of the state.

Travel - International

AIR:
Sydney is an international gateway to Australia, and international flights from Europe, New Zealand, Asia, Africa and the Americas all serve the city. The main domestic airlines operating in New South Wales are: *Aeropelican Air Services, Air Link, Eastern Australian, Jetstar, Qantas, Rex – Regional Express, Sunshine Express* and *Virgin Blue*.
Approximate flight times: From Sydney to *Bangkok* is nine hours 20 minutes, to *London* is 25 hours 15 minutes, to *Los Angeles* is 13 hours 30 minutes, to *New York* is 21 hours 30 minutes, to *Paris* is 23 hours five minutes and to *Singapore* is eight hours.
Main airports: *Sydney (SYD)* (website: www.sydneyairport.com.au) is Sydney's international airport; it is 8km (5 miles) from the city centre. *To/from the airport*: Ten minutes by rail link or 20 to 30 minutes by car. *Facilities*: Duty free shop, bank/bureau de change, restaurant/bar, tourist information kiosk, car hire and taxi stand.
SEA:
Main ports: *Sydney* is a major international port, and cruise lines call from Europe, the Far East and the USA. There are also many day- and half-day cruises from Sydney Harbour (Circular Quay), offering everything from sightseeing tours to nearby attractions such as wildlife and aboriginal communities, the Blue Mountains and the Hunter Valley wine region, to night-time cabaret showboats.

RAIL:

Sydney has through-trains to all other State capitals. The *Great South Pacific* connects Sydney to Brisbane and Cairns. An internal system of railways runs throughout the State, connecting all the most important towns, tourist resorts and running through to Canberra in the south. The two main rail operators are *Cityrail* (website: www.cityrail.nsw.gov.au) and *Countrylink* (website: www.countrylink.info). The main train interchanges are located at Central Station and Town Hall.

ROAD:

Sydney is the focal point of a network that connects every major city. Road distances from many places, however, are enormous, and a journey by even the fastest coach to Darwin, on the northern coast, takes over 92 hours. The State is well served with an excellent road system, as required by the most heavily populated region of the country. Main highways are the *Barrier Highway*, running west to Adelaide, the *Hume Highway* running south to Canberra and Melbourne, the *New England Highway* running north to Brisbane, the *Pacific Highway* running along the coast to Brisbane (one of Australia's most popular touring routes), the *Princess Highway* running south along the coast to Melbourne, and the *Mitchell Highway* running northeast to Charleville and connecting with the routes to Mount Isa and Darwin in the north. The State is well served by national coach operators and regional bus lines.

URBAN:

Sydney's extensive electrified suburban **rail** network includes a city-centre underground link, lightrail and a monorail link. The monorail runs in a loop, linking Darling Harbour and various tourist attractions. Lightrail services run from Sydney Central through Chinatown, Darling Harbour and other sights to Star City and Wentworth Park. There are also **bus** and **ferry** services (website: www.sydneybuses.nsw.gov.au). Weekly and other period passes are available, as are multi-journey tickets. The *Sydney Explorer Bus* stops at over 20 attractions on its route and visitors can join or leave it at any point.

Discount travel tickets: There is a wide variety of saver passes for transportation to a range of tourist attractions. A special *Sydney Pass*, valid for three, five or seven days, offers unlimited travel on Sydney's public transport including sightseeing tours, *Sydney Ferries'* harbour cruises, *Manly Ferry*, *JetCat* and *RiverCat* services, the *Sydney*, *Bondi* and *Bay Explorer* buses and return travel to the airport. Prices start at A$100 for an adult three-day pass. Other passes include *Sydney/Bondi Explorer Ticket*, *Sydney Bonus Ticket*, *See Sydney and Beyond Pass* and *Sydney YES ticket*. For more information, contact Tourism New South Wales (see *Top Things To Do*).

Meter-operated **taxis** service all major cities and towns. Taxi ranks can be found at transport terminals, major hotels and shopping centres or they can be hailed in the street.

Accommodation

HOTELS:

Sydney offers an excellent choice of hotels for all budgets and tastes. They range from 5-star international chains to smaller hotels and budget backpacker-style hostels. Further outside the city, visitors can stay on one of the sheep stations, to the west of the capital, amongst some of the best sheep country in the world. The State is well travelled by Australians themselves, and so offers an excellent network of accommodation outside the larger cities, mostly of motel or similar class.

CAMPING/CARAVANNING:

A number of companies can arrange motor camper rentals, with a range of fully-equipped vehicles.

Note: For further coverage of the range of accommodation available, see *Accommodation* in the general *Australia* section.

ACCOMMODATION INFORMATION

Caravan and Camping Industry Association (NSW)
PO Box H114, Harris Park, NSW 2150, Australia
Tel: (2) 9637 0599.
Website: www.caravanaustralia.com.au

Top Things To See

- No trip to New South Wales can be complete without seeing its State capital, **Sydney**. The iconic **Sydney Opera House** has a distinctive shape that echoes the sails of the boats in the equally famous **Sydney Harbour**. The city-centre skyline rivals that of Manhattan, with the added attraction that Sydney is far more likely to be seen under a clear blue sky. The city has a great number of concert halls, museums, art galleries and theatres. Another must-see is the awesome steel structure that is the **Harbour Bridge** (the third-longest single span bridge in the world). **The Rocks** area (the site of Australia's first European settlement) features cobbled streets, gas lamps, craft shops and small restaurants, and this district also contains one of Sydney's oldest buildings, **Cadman's Cottage** (1816), as well as the '**Lord Nelson**' and the '**Hero of Waterloo**', the city's oldest pubs. There are various quarters to explore, such as **Chinatown**, **Paddington** and **Kings Cross**, and **Darling Harbour** is one of Sydney's newest precincts, a five-minute monorail ride from the city centre, containing attractions that include the **Harbourside Shopping Centre**, **Gavala Aboriginal and Cultural Education Centre**, **Panasonic IMAX Theatre**, the **Chinese Garden**, **Cockle Bay Wharf** and the **Sydney Aquarium**. The city has many beautiful green spaces, and the stunning **Botanic Gardens** offer further views of the Bridge, Opera House and Harbour, for those who still have not taken enough photos.
- Gaze upon the World Heritage-listed **Blue Mountains** (a National Park) to the west of Sydney (Australian Heritage Council: tel: (02) 6274 1111; website: www.ahc.gov.au): the **Three Sisters** (so-named because of dreamtime legend), at **Echo Point** in the **Leura/Katoomba** region, rise 922, 918 and 906 metres (1,484, 1,447 and 1,458km) respectively, above the valley floor, and afford sensational views of this rugged wilderness.
- See the world's only source of black opal at **Lightning Ridge**.
- Have your breath taken away at the sight of Australia's highest peak, **Mount Kosciuszko**, in the **Snowy Mountains**.
- Get a taste of the original Australian wilderness at the uncommercialised and unpretentious **Broken Hill**, featuring ancient landscapes, aboriginal culture and unusual flora.
- Look at 370,000 hectares (913,000 acres) of semi-arid country in the **Willandra Lakes Region**, renowned as one of the world's earliest-known cremation sites - the archaeological discovery of skeletal remains and stone tools indicated that homo sapiens inhabited the area 40,000 years ago – and the region contains a system of Pleistocene lakes formed over the last two million years, most of which are fringed on the eastern shore by dunes.
- Take in as much countryside as you can cope with at New South Wales's many parks and nature reserves (NSW National Parks Centre; tel: (2) 9253 4600 or (1300) 361 967 (in Australia only); website: www.nationalparks.nsw.gov.au): the **Royal National Park** is the oldest park in Australia and the second-oldest in the world; **Ku-ring-gai Chase National Park** is noted for its Aboriginal rock carvings and extensive walking tracks, and the park also includes a koala sanctuary; the **Myall Lakes National Park** is the largest coastal lake system in the State and an important habitat for many species of waterbirds; the mountainous **Barrington Tops National Park** in the **Hunter** wine-making region is crossed by six rivers and is known for its dramatic altitude variations, allowing visitors to experience snow-capped mountains and subtropical rainforests in a day's walk; **Mount Warning National Park** offers a fantastic trek through rainforest communities, culminating in a challenging rock scramble, to reach the 1100m (3608ft) summit of the ancient volcano - views from the top take in the expanse of the bowl-shaped **Tweed Valley**; **Dorrigo National Park** and **Border Ranges National Park**, both in tropical New South Wales, contain large stretches of rainforest, and at **Border Ranges**, the rainforest grows on the rim of an extinct volcano; rock climbing and mountain walks attract visitors to **Warrumbungle National Park** whose 'Grand High Tops' track through the remnants of ancient volcanoes ranks high among Australia's many spectacular walks - the park is also noted for its bizarre rock outcrops; the **Kosciuszko National Park** and **Snowy Mountains National Park** feature some of Australia's highest mountains and greatest rivers; and **Mungo National Park** offers good opportunities for walks along the famous **Walls of China**, orange-and-white dunes, as well as many native species of birds and animals.

Top Things To Do

- Go **dolphin** and **whale watching** or even, for the especially adventurous, on a **shark encounter**: the best time to see dolphins and whales is from May to December, and **Port Stephens** and **Nelson Bay** are popular spots, whilst migrating whales can be spotted from **Cape Byron** between May and October.
- Be a real Aussie **surfer** at **beaches** such as **Bronte**, **Coogee**, **Collaroy**, **Palm** and **Byron Bay**. **Swim** in world-famous beaches such as **Bondi** and **Manly**, near to Sydney.
- Watch the annual **yacht race** from Sydney to Hobart in Tasmania, starting on 26 December each year and covering over 2000km (1250 miles) - maybe even indulge in a few maritime sports yourself around **Sydney Harbour**.
- Couple stunning scenery with nail-biting fun by **windsurfing**,

Credit: ©David Bell and Juliet Sinclair

kayaking and **whitewater rafting** in the **Great Lakes district**: its most popular resort is **Port Macquarie**.
- Celebrate all things Australian from bush heritage to the bustling city at the **Royal Easter Show**, a 14-day event held in Sydney every year that is Australia's largest event (website: www.eastershow.com.au).
- Top up that tan at Christmas and sing along to some **Carols by the Sea**, held at **Bondi Beach**.
- New South Wales is home to the **Great Dividing Range** and the **Snowy Mountains**, which are major destinations for **skiing**, **cross-country skiing** and **snowboarding**: the season generally runs from June to October.
- **Climb the Harbour Bridge** in **Sydney** via a network of archways, catwalks and ladders. The resulting view of the harbour is spectacular. The whole climb takes around three hours and is open to those aged over 12. Climbs require special clothing and are in small guided groups. Further information is available from Bridgeclimb (website: www.bridgeclimb.com).
- The new **Skywalk** atop **Sydney Tower** also enables the brave to literally 'walk across the city skyline', enjoying views as far afield as the Central Coast and the Blue Mountains. The Skywalk will take around 90 minutes to complete. However, for the more budget-minded (or those simply terrified of heights), the **Pylon Lookout** on Harbour Bridge is a considerably cheaper option and also gains great views across the city.
- Dine next to the lit-up spectacle of the beautiful **Sydney Opera House**.
- Drink some good **Australian wine** in the **Hunter Valley wine district**, famous for wine makers such as *Wyndham Estate*, *Rosemount* and *McGuigans*; the Hunter Valley has over 80 wineries and many restaurants.
- Coo at those furry Australian clichés: **Featherdale** has **wombats**, **kangaroos**, **wallabies**, **quokkas** and **koalas**.

TOURIST INFORMATION

Tourism New South Wales in the UK
Level 6, Australia Centre, Australia House, The Strand, London WC2B 4LG, UK
Tel: (0906) 863 3235 (brochure request line; calls cost 60p per minute) or (020) 7887 5003 (travel trade only).
Website: www.sydneyaustralia.com
Provides trade and media marketing information only.

Entertainment

FOOD & DRINK: Cooking in New South Wales, and Sydney in particular, reflects the State's multicultural makeup with Thai, Vietnamese, Japanese, Greek, Italian and Indian cuisine all represented. Gourmet food and wine trails exist throughout the State.

Things to know: General licensing hours for public bars are Mon-Sat 1000-2200 with varying hours on Sunday.

Regional specialities:
- Sydney rock lobsters are renowned and utterly delicious.
- Macadamia nuts are the perfect snack.
- Fruits are plentiful due to the pleasant climate: you can find avocados, guavas, passion fruit, *pepinos* (melon pears), pears and berries.
- Fish such as crayfish, red mullet, tuna, whitefish, shrimp and John Dory.

Regional drinks:
- Fine red and white wines from the Hunter Valley, and also light wines like *Chambourcin*.

NIGHTLIFE: Sydney is known for being a city that never

sleeps, and has a diverse selection of bars, pubs, nightclubs and music venues. Kings Cross in Sydney is an exciting nightlife area. There are also some night-time cruises offering dinner and dancing. For further information on Sydney's nightlife see online (website: www.spraci.com or www.citysearch.com.au).

SHOPPING: Best buys are Australian opals, precious and semi-precious stones, Aboriginal arts and crafts, woollen and sheepskin goods and fashion by top Australian designers. **Shopping hours:** In Sydney, shops open Mon-Fri 0900-1730, Sat 0900-1600 and Sun 1000-1600. Many shops also stay open until 2100 on Thursday.

Business

CONFERENCES/CONVENTIONS: Sydney has launched a major initiative to become an important convention and meeting destination. The Sydney Convention and Exhibition Centre at *Darling Harbour* has facilities for up to 5000 people. Other major convention centres include Centrepoint Exhibition and Convention Centre, University of NSW, RAS Exhibition Centre, Sydney Opera House, Powerhouse Museum, Sydney Town Hall, University of Sydney, YWCA, Queen Victoria Building, Bankstown Town Hall, Bondi Surf Bathers' Life Saving Club, Curzon Hall, Film Australia, Hills Centre, Taronga Centre and the NSW Harness Racing Club.

COMMERCIAL INFORMATION

State Chamber of Commerce (New South Wales)
Level 12, 83 Clarence Street, Sydney, NSW 2000, Australia
Tel: (1300) 137 153 (in Australia only).
Tel: (1300) 137 153 (in Australia only).
Website: www.thechamber.com.au

Department of State and Regional Development
Website: www.sydneyaustralia.com

Sydney Convention & Visitors Bureau
Level 13, 80 William Street, Sydney, NSW 2011, Australia
Tel: (2) 9331 4045.
Website: www.scvb.com.au

Sydney Convention & Visitors Bureau in the UK
c/o Axis Sales and Marketing, 421a Finchley Road, London NW3 6HJ, UK
Tel: (020) 7431 4045.
Website: www.scvb.com.au

Northern Territory

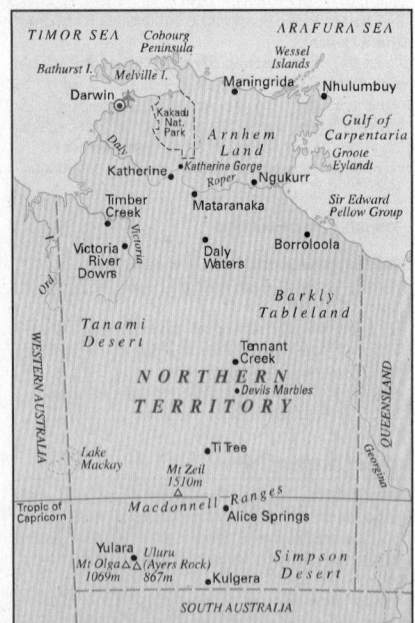

Location: Northern Australia.

Time: GMT + 9.5.

Overview

This colossal landscape, spanning land mass six times the size of the UK, sits more or less at the geographical heart of Australia and is also at the heart of its legacy.
The Northern Territory has immense historical significance to the Aborigines that inhabit the State, representing nearly one-fourth of its population. Much of the landscape was draped in dreamtime legend to ensure Aboriginal survival. There remains a raw mysticism to awesome set pieces such as Uluru (Ayers Rock) and Corroboree Rock. Kakadu National Park is still replete with Aboriginal relics. Aboriginal guides can take visitors bushwalking or bush tucker tasting. Although obviously no tourist attraction, the Aboriginal constituent grants visitors the opportunity to see an altogether different side to modern Australia.
The Northern Territory is as diverse as it is huge, comprising waterfalls and looming gorges, arid red desert and staggering outcroppings. Yet despite its enormity, the State is home to only one per cent of Australia's total population. Yet this never renders the Northern Territory sleepy. Although there is tranquility for those that seek it, there is also plenty of adventure, from crocodile boat tours to safaris and hot-air ballooning. The 'Outback' is 'Never Never' land, a title bestowed because of the book, *We of the Never Never* by Jeannie Gunn. Locals claim you either 'never never' want to stay or 'never never' want to leave. Just as the Territory is divided up into different terrain, the Territory also divides opinion.
To find out what your own is, this is somewhere you simply have to visit.

General Information

AREA: 1,349,130 sq km (520,902 sq miles).
POPULATION: 195,500 (official estimate 2000).
POPULATION DENSITY: 0.1 per sq km.
CAPITAL: Darwin. **Population:** 88,100 (official estimate 1999).
GEOGRAPHY: A wilderness stretching roughly 1670km (1038 miles) north to south and 1000km (620 miles) east to west, the Northern Territory comprises nearly one-sixth of Australia. The geography of the Northern Territory is the closest to the popular image of the Great Australian Outback.
The northern area, centred on the capital, Darwin, is tropical with rich vegetation and a varied coastline. Beyond Darwin, 251km (155 miles) east, is World Heritage-listed Kakadu National Park, which is part of the 12,600 sq km (4500 sq mile) area of Arnhem Land. It is an area of vast flood plains and rocky escarpments steeped in natural and cultural heritage. Aboriginal people have lived here for at least 40,000 years. Katherine township is 314km (195 miles) from Darwin and a further 30km (20 miles) northeast is Nitmiluk (Katherine Gorge) National Park with 13 gorges towering up to 60m (200ft) high.
The southern part of the Northern Territory is centred on the town of Alice Springs, which is almost at the geographical centre of Australia and the starting point of many of the Red Centre's unique and natural wonders, including Uluru (Ayers Rock) and the Uluru-Kata Tjuta National Park. Other notable features of the Red Centre are King's Canyon, Trephina, Ormiston and Glen Helen Gorge, the Olgas near Uluru (Ayers Rock) and the Devil's Marbles at Tennant Creek. There are also other parks and reserves with abundant bird and animal life.

Climate

Hot most of the year; the Top End has two seasons, dry and wet, whilst the Red Centre has the usual four: summer, autumn, winter and spring. Coastal areas have heavy monsoon rain from March to November.

Required clothing: Lightweight cottons and linens most of the year. Waterproofing is necessary in the northern areas during the rainy season. A warm sweater or jacket is advised for the centre during winter months, as evenings can be quite cool.

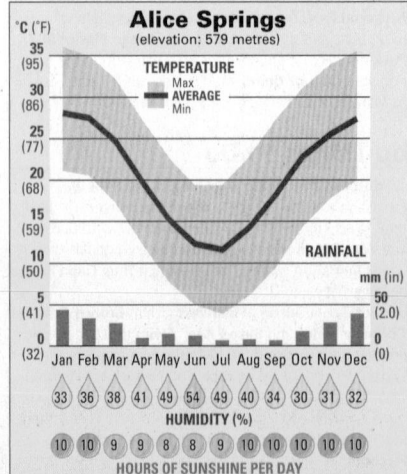

Public Holidays

The Northern Territory observes all the public holidays observed nationwide (see the main *Australia* section) and, in addition, the beneath Public Holidays listed for the January 2006-June 2007 period:
2006: May 1 May Day. **Jun 12** Queen's Official Birthday. **Aug 7** Picnic Day.
2007: May 7 May Day. **Jun 11** Queen's Official Birthday. **Aug 6** Picnic Day.

Travel - International

AIR:

The Northern Territory can be reached by international flights to Darwin from Bali, Bangkok, Brunei, East Timor, Europe, Singapore and the UK. At present, there are several international carriers operating to the Northern Territory, including *Australian Airlines, British Airways, Garuda Indonesia, Qantas* and *Royal Brunei*. Only the latter two airlines fly directly to Darwin; the others require connections.
There are several domestic airlines - including *Airnorth, Qantas* and *Virgin Blue* - that cover the Territory from all capital cities within Australia with connections from most other towns. Smaller commuter airlines connect some of the remoter areas within the Territory.
Approximate flight times: From Darwin to *London* is 16 hours 30 minutes, to *Singapore* four hours 30 minutes, to *Bangkok* five hours, to *Bali* 90 minutes, to *Brunei* four hours and to *Timor* two hours. Connections are available from most Asian airports.
Main airports: *Darwin Airport (DRW)* (website: www.darwinairport.com.au) is 13km (8 miles) from the city centre. The airport receives international flights. *To/from the airport:* Airport buses and taxis operate services to the city. For further information, see the main *Australia* section. *Alice Springs Airport (ASP)* is 15km (9 miles) from the city centre. *To/from the airport:* Airport buses and taxis operate services to the city. *Facilities:* Left luggage, bureau de change, bars and car hire.
Uluru/Ayers Rock Airport (AYQ) is 7km (4 miles) from the Uluru (Ayers Rock) resort. *To/from the airport:* All scheduled flights are met by a free shuttle service to the resort. Taxi services are also available. *Facilities:* Gift shop and small refreshment kiosk.
Katherine Airport (KTR) is 11km (7 miles) from Katherine.
SEA:

Main ports: *Darwin*, the Northern Territory's only large port.
RAIL:

The main rail service to the Territory is by the *Ghan* from Adelaide, which travels to Darwin via Alice Springs; see *Travel* in the main *Australia* section for more information. There is no internal network.
ROAD:

There are three main highways serving the Northern Territory: the *Stuart Highway*, south to Adelaide; the *Barkly Highway*, east to Mount Isa and Queensland; and the *Victoria Highway*, which runs west to join an unsealed road running across the top of the Western Desert which runs on to Perth. Off these roads there are many uncharted rough tracks often only suitable for 4-wheel drive vehicles, and often ending in impassable desert. The dangers of travelling off main roads in the Northern Territory without a qualified guide cannot be stressed too strongly. **Coach:** The national coach services are run by *Greyhound/Pioneer Bus Australia*, which serves the main townships within the Territory with direct services to all capital cities. Well-equipped coaches take over 92 hours to cover the distance from Darwin to Sydney; from Darwin, coaches depart daily to Kakadu National Park (travel time - four hours 50 minutes) and to Alice Springs (travel time - 19 hours).
URBAN:

There are local **bus** services in Darwin (running Monday to Saturday) from the coach terminal located 1km (0.5m) from the city centre and in Alice Springs. Darwin Harbour ferries operate Monday to Friday.

Accommodation

The *Northern Territory Holiday Directory 2005/2006*, published by the Northern Territory Tourist Commission, gives details of tours, holidays and accommodation in the Territory for the travel trade. In addition, there is a large selection of consumer brochures available from the Northern Territory Tourist Commission.
HOTELS:

International-standard hotels are found in Darwin, Alice Springs and Uluru (Ayers Rock), and a good standard of hotel and motel accommodation can be found in all the major tourist areas and centres of population.

LODGES/MOTELS:

Lodges and budget motels are available in some of the remote areas.

CAMPING/CARAVANNING:

The Northern Territory contains some of the most inhospitable country in the world. From Alice Springs, the nearest major town in any direction is Tenant Creek, 504km (313 miles) away, and consequently any car or caravan must be in prime mechanical condition. During the tropical summer from November to April, travel in the Outback is advisable only in suitable cross-country vehicles, as many conventional roads become impassable for ordinary cars. The Stuart Highway between Darwin and Alice Springs and through to Adelaide in South Australia is a fully sealed road accessible all year. A number of companies can arrange **motor camper** rentals, with a range of fully-equipped vehicles. Full details can be obtained from the Tourist Commission.

Note: For further coverage of the range of accommodation available, see *Accommodation* in the general *Australia* section.

Credit: ©David Bell and Juliet Sinclair

Top Things To See

- Visit the **Tiwi Islands**, comprising **Bathurst Island** and **Melville Island**, Aboriginal islands rich in history and culture.
- Take in the surprisingly modern charms of **Darwin**, the multicultural territorial capital, rebuilt and re-grown since the savaging by Cyclone Tracy on Christmas Eve 1974. The **Top End** is the area to see lush tropical vegetation, either in Darwin's Botanical Gardens or the **Crocodylus Park** just outside Darwin.
- **Alice Springs** is located in what is almost the geographical centre of the continent. A pleasant little town, set in red desert country, it is a popular tourist resort and a base for exploring the wonders of the Outback. In itself, there is enough to keep any visitor occupied, wandering around the **Dreamtime Gallery** or the **Aboriginal Arts & Culture Centre**. **Anzac Hill War Memorial** lies just behind Alice Springs and provides a panoramic view of the town and surrounding ranges.
- See colourful gorges, canyons, valley pools and awe-inspiring chasms: **Standley Chasm** is 57km (35 miles) west of Alice; **Glen Helen Gorge** is 140km (9 miles) west; **Ormiston Gorge** is 130km (80 miles) west; **Kings Canyon** is 330km (205 miles) southwest; and **N'Dhala Gorge** is 96km (59 miles) east, and notable for its ancient rock engravings. **Palm Valley** lies around one hour 30 minutes' drive to the southwest, and **Rainbow Valley** to the southeast on the edge of the **Simpson Desert**.
- See the Northern Territory's only vineyard, **Château Hornsby**, situated approximately 10km (6 miles) from the town centre and a venue for tastings, barbecues, and Aboriginal *corroborees*.
- No visit to the Northern Territory is complete without beholding the intense colours of **Uluru (Ayers Rock)**, approximately 460km (285 miles) or five hours' drive away. Uluru is the world's largest monolith and plays an important part in Aboriginal mythology, in which it is believed to have been created by ancestors of the Aborigines. Visitors may still climb the rock - although to do so is considered a gross sacrilege by the indigenous people - or explore some of the fascinating caves at its base. Sunset and sunrise may be seen as the sun's rays change the rock's colour from blazing orange to red and even deep purple, depending on the atmospheric conditions. The East and Western **MacDonnell Ranges** surround the area.
- For spectacular views, **Kings Canyon (Watarrka National Park)** is a must, and also enables visitors to discover the '**Lost City**' (a maze of eroded earth domes) and the '**Garden of Eden**' (a sheltered green waterhole) when walking around the canyon.
- Gaze at what the Aborigines believe are serpents' eggs at **The Devils Marbles**, an impressive formation of 7m (23ft) boulders.
- **Kakadu National Park** is bordered by the **Arnhem Land** escarpment, where the spectacular waterfalls of **Jim Jim** and **Twin Falls** cascade hundreds of feet into crystal-clear rock pools below. At **Ubirr (Obiri Rock)** and **Nourlangie Rock** are fascinating galleries of Aboriginal rock painting, many dating back over 20,000 years: be sure to make time to look upon paintings that show mythical and spiritual figures and an ancient lifestyle which still holds great significance for the Aboriginal people today.

Top Things To Do

- Take a **gold mine tour** at **Tennant Creek**.
- Enjoy excellent **fishing** in **Kakadu National Park**: numerous creeks, rivers and billabongs provide an ideal habitat for the much-prized *barramundi*, which is found in abundance. For those pretty confident of their fishing prowess, the Northern Territory is host to both

the **Barramundi Classic**, held in May, and the **Big Horse Creek Barra Classic**, held in April/May, annually (Department of Primary Industry and Fisheries, Fisheries Division, GPO Box 3000, Darwin, NT 0801; tel: (8) 8999 2146; website: http://kakadu.nt.gov.au).

- Go **bushwalking** through the **Stokes Range**, where you are unlikely to see another human being for miles. Indeed, the entire vast and beautiful landscape of the Northern Territory, with its many national parks and nature reserves, is ideal for walking (recommended destinations being the **Arnhem Land Plateau** (in Kakadu National Park) and the **West MacDonnell Ranges** along **Larapinta Trail**). Walkers are rewarded by regular sightings of **buffalo** and giant **crocodiles**.
- **Swim** in **natural hot springs** at the thermal 'bathtubs' at **Mataranka**: clear waters with a constant heat at body temperature, surrounded by palm forest, is a recipe for refreshment.
- Have an ice-cold beer at the famous **Daly Waters** Hotel, an historical pub (indeed, one of the oldest buildings in the Northern Territory, built in 1893) enriched by local history. In-between Darwin and Alice Springs, Daly Waters is considered the ideal stopover along the Stuart Highway. The pub itself is decorated with tokens of those who have stopped for its custom: flags, postcards, socks and shorts all adorn the walls and bar. Every night there is a steak and *barri* (barramundi) barbeque to welcome the weary traveller.
- Experience the true remoteness of central Australia: set up a **camp fire** and prepare for a night in the bush. Several camping safaris are in operation and for those well-equipped, settle down for a night by yourself, surrounded by the sounds of nature (a camping permit is required outside established camping areas: for further details, contact the Parks & Wildlife Commission of the NT, PO Box 496, Palmerston NT 0831; tel: (8) 8999 551; website: www.nt.gov.au/ipe/pwcnt).
- **Swim** in one of the Territory's many **waterfalls**: recommended are those at Litchfield National Park and in various water holes in both the **Top End** and **Red Centre**. Remember to check that the area is safe for swimming, as salt-water crocodiles are found throughout the region.
- Go on a **boat cruise** and explore the waterways along the **South Alligator River** or scenic **Yellow Water**, spotting **crocodiles** as you go. You may also catch a glimpse of the graceful **jabiru** (Australia's only stork) wading amongst the water lilies.
- Take a scenic **helicopter ride** above **Katherine Gorge**, one of Australia's great natural wonders. Around this region of Katherine Gorge and **Nitmiluk National Park**, spectacular gorges tower up to 60m (200ft) high. Each of the 13 gorges has its own glowing colours and fascinating outcrops. Steep canyon walls overlook cool, blue waters. There is also ample opportunity here for **canoeing**, **swimming** and **boat tours**.

TOURIST INFORMATION

Northern Territory Tourist Commission in the UK
Australia House, 6th Floor, Melbourne Place, The Strand, London WC2B 4LG, UK
Tel: (020) 8944 2992.
Website: www.travelnt.com

Northern Territory Tourist Commission in the USA
3601 Aviation Boulevard, Suite 2100, Manhattan Beach, CA 90266, USA
Tel: (310) 643 2636.
Website: www.outbacknt.com.au

Entertainment

FOOD & DRINK: Dining out has been made even more special by the addition of new restaurants at Cullen Bay Marina in Darwin, offering outdoor dining with beautiful ocean views. Cuisine from many countries, including Creole, Greek, Indian, Japanese, Malaysian, Mongolian and Thai, is available in the larger towns.

Regional specialities:
- The *ngarlkirdi*, or witchetty grub, is considered a delicacy. High in protein, eat it either raw or cooked, depending on how adventurous you feel!
- Spread your toast with some *Kakadu Plum Jam*.
- Grab a bite of the *quandongs*, a native peach with a delicate flavour, usually served stewed or in ice cream.
- *Damper* (bread) with honey is a popular snack.
- The Northern Territory is justly proud of their superb *barrumundi* (fish).
- For those who can stomach it, there is opportunity to eat kangaroos, emus and, even, crocodile.
- Macadamia nuts can be eaten raw or roasted.
- Roots and tubers are prevalent.

Regional drinks:
- The blue flowered herb, chicory, is a famous coffee substitute.
- Native plants such as *Leptospermum* provide the most commonly used bush tea, referred to as *tea tree*.
- Cappuccino is often seasoned with *wattle seed*.

NIGHTLIFE: There is plenty of exciting nightlife in Darwin, which also boasts the *SKYCITY Darwin*, built in an extraordinary modern architectural style. This A$30-million casino complex also encompasses luxury accommodation, restaurants, discos and sporting and convention facilities and is surrounded by lush gardens perched along the shores of Mindil Beach. Alice Springs also has a casino.

SHOPPING: Darwin specialities include Aboriginal artefacts and Outback clothing. Aboriginal items, bush clothing and opals are available in Alice Springs. Darwin's markets are great attractions.

Business

CONFERENCES/CONVENTIONS: Major convention centres in Darwin are The Beaufort Hotel, Darwin Performing Arts Centre, SKYCITY Darwin, Marrara International Indoor Sports Stadium and the Plaza Darwin. The Alice Springs Convention Centre boasts seven large function suites, that have a total capacity of 2000 persons, 140 hotel rooms and the latest conference facilities. Other major convention centres in Alice Springs are Aruluen Arts Centre and Plaza Hotel Alice Springs. There is also a number of resort convention facilities outside the cities, such as at Ayers Rock Resort.

COMMERCIAL INFORMATION

Northern Territory Department of Business, Industry and Resources Development
Second Floor, Development House, 76 The Esplanade, Darwin, NT 0800, Australia
Tel: (8) 8982 1700.
Website: www.dbird.nt.gov.au

Alice Springs Convention Centre
PO Box 2632, Alice Springs, NT 0871, Australia
Tel: (8) 8950 0200.
Website: www.alicespringsconventioncentre.com.au

Northern Territory Convention Bureau
PO Box 2531, Alice Springs, NT 0871, Australia
Tel: (8) 8951 8427.
Website: www.ntconventions.com.au

Queensland

Location: Northeast Australia.

Time: GMT + 10.

Overview

Queensland epitomises those Australian clichés: beaches, barbeques, *Castlemaine* beer. Hordes may flock to Uluru in or gawp at Sydney's Opera House, but it is the laid-back vibe and miles and miles of golden beach that any visitor to Australia seeks – and finds in Queensland.

Queensland is fringed with a spectacular coast and blessed with balmy weather, widely known as the 'Sunshine State'. Brisbane, Australia's third-largest city, may not have the cultural repute of Melbourne or the financial status of Sydney, but it exudes a sophisticated relaxation, and enjoys a wide range of attractions, including the ever-popular Lone Pine Koala Sanctuary, the world's oldest and largest sanctuary of its kind.

Yet you would be wrong to think that all those beaches and koala-hugs meant that Queensland was a calm and quiet State. Queensland is Australia's capital of adventure sports, and here you can sail, white-water raft, paraglide, and learn to dive and delve into the natural underwater wonder that is the Great Barrier Reef, awash with turquoise tints and sea-life. The Reef is a World Heritage-listed marine park that stretches for more than 1,250 miles (2,000km) along the Queensland coast, dotted with idyllic island resorts and containing one of the most diverse animal and plant ecosystems on earth.

Queenslands fulfils preconceptions of Australia, but also exceeds them. Besides beaches, Queensland is sated with ancient rainforests, parks and historic towns. There must be a reason why this is Australia's fastest-growing State: perhaps those who visit never leave. Certainly, the outlook of smug Queenslanders seems to be as 'sunny' as their State.

Credit: ©David Bell and Juliet Sinclair

General Information

AREA: 1,730,650 sq km (668,207 sq miles).
POPULATION: 3.88 million (official estimate 2004).
POPULATION DENSITY: 2.1 per sq km.
CAPITAL: Brisbane. **Population:** 1.77 million (official estimate 2004).
GEOGRAPHY: Two-and-a-half times the size of Texas or seven times the size of the United Kingdom, Queensland, more than half of which lies above the Tropic of Capricorn, is known as the 'Sunshine State'. Within its borders are the Great Barrier Reef, numerous resort islands, kilometres of golden sandy beaches, national park forests, vast plains, lush rainforests, forested mountains and extensive wilderness areas.

Climate

Queensland straddles the Tropic of Capricorn which accounts for the pleasant climate throughout most of the region. Exceptions are the far north and the arid western Outback. Brisbane enjoys an average of 7.1 hours of sunshine daily in the winter. The period between November to March is generally humid throughout the state, but sea breezes temper the humidity and make for perfect holiday conditions.

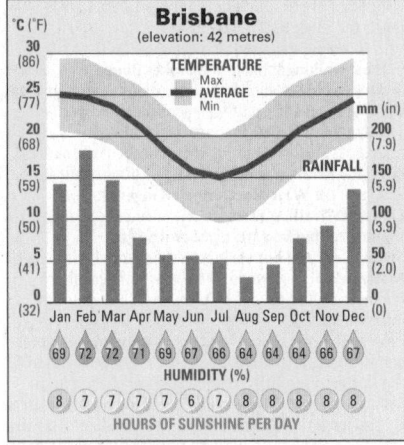

Public Holidays

Queensland observes all the public holidays observed nationwide (see the main Australia section) and, in addition, the beneath Public Holidays listed for the January 2006-June 2007 period.
2006: May 1 Labour Day. **Jun 12** Queen's Birthday. **Aug 16*** People's Day at the Brisbane Royal Show.
2007: May 1 Labour Day. **Jun 11** Queen's Birthday.
Note: *The Brisbane Royal Show is a holiday in Brisbane only.

Travel - International

AIR:
 There are several major air carriers serving Brisbane and Queensland, including *Air New Zealand*, *British Airways*, *Qantas*, *United Airlines* and *Virgin Atlantic*. For more flight details, see *Travel* in the general *Australia* section. Domestic carriers

include *Qantas* and *Virgin Blue*. Airlines such as *MacAir Airlines* offer charter flights and feeder services to Queensland's main towns and Barrier Reef island resorts. *Sunshine Express Airlines* also provide services from Brisbane to assorted towns throughout Queensland.
Aproximate flight times: Approximate flying time from Brisbane to *London* is 23 hours 30 minutes.
Main airports: *Brisbane International (BNE)* (website: www.bne.com.au) is 13km (8 miles) northeast of the city centre (travel time – approximately 35 minutes). Flights are available from Europe, Asia, the Far East, New Zealand, Canada and the USA. *To/from the airport:* Airport buses, taxis and trains operate services to the city. *Facilities:* Left luggage, first aid, banks, bureaux de change, bars, car hire, duty free shops, restaurants and tourist information.
Cairns (CNS) is 8km (5 miles) from the city. Cairns is an excellent gateway both to the Great Barrier Reef and the tropical north, and hosts flights from Europe, Asia, the Far East, New Zealand, Canada and the USA. *To/from the airport:* Airport shuttle buses (travel time – 30 minutes; costing anything from A$9 to A$40 per person, depending on company and distance being travelled) and taxis (costing approximately A$25 plus A$2 fee) operate services to the city. Trains also serve Brisbane City and the gold Coast seven days per week, running from 0500 to 2100.
The extensive internal airline system means that Queensland is connected with nearly all major Australian gateways. Brisbane is connected directly to Sydney, Melbourne, Adelaide, Alice Springs and Darwin, as well as having links with Cairns, Mount Isa, Townsville and other smaller airstrips within the state. Cairns and Townsville also offer easy connections to the rest of Australia.

RAIL:
 Queensland has its own railway system, run by QR (website: www.qr.com.au), the main routes being the *Sunlander* and the *Queenslander* which connect coastal towns from Brisbane to Cairns. In addition, other services, such as the *Inlander*, *Westlander* and *Spirit of Outback* (from Brisbane to Longreach) open up the Outback to travellers. The *Spirit of the Tropics* provides more coastal services. The main tourist services are the famous *Kuranda Scenic Rail* and the *Gulflander*. The *Great South Pacific Express* running from Brisbane to Sydney or Cairns is a luxury service operated by Orient Express Trains and Cruises. The *Tilt Train* provides a faster service from Rockhampton to Brisbane. The main train stations are Central and Roma Street.
The *Sunshine Railpass* allows unlimited travel on Queensland's rail routes. Passes are valid for 14, 21 and 30 days in first- or economy-class, offering excellent travel facilities for those intending extensive travel throughout the state. The *Sunshine Roadrail Pass*, for economy class only, offers 10 journeys over a 60-day period or 20 journeys over a 90-day period. For more information about rail travel and passes, visit QR online.

ROAD:
 There is a high standard of highways and road networks offering easy connections between towns and cities. The *Bruce Highway* runs down the whole east coast from Cairns to Brisbane and continues into New South Wales. An extensive **coach** network offers an easy and cheap way of getting around.
The inland areas can be explored with 4-wheel-drive vehicles, many of the interior roads being unsealed. The other main highways running into the interior are the *Capricorn Highway* (Rockhampton–Winton), the *Flinders Highway* (Townsville–Mount Isa, connecting with the network in the Northern Territory) and the *Warrego Highway* (Brisbane–Charleville). The *Mitchell* and *Landsborough Highways*, which in places have unsealed road surfaces, run roughly north–south, connecting the main east–west highways and terminating at Sydney. The *Newell Highway* runs inland between Brisbane and Melbourne. For more information about driving in Queensland, visit Queensland Transport online (website: www.queenslandholidays.com.au/transport/motor.cfm).

URBAN:
 Brisbane's electrified **rail** system is easy to use for suburban services, particularly cross-river. There are also cross-river **ferries**, and a comprehensive **bus** network with zonal fares and 10-journey pre-purchase fares obtainable through newsagents. Day and other period tickets are also available. The *City Sights Bus* stops at 18 places of interest around the city during a 90-minute tour for A$22 (adult) and A$16 (children). In Cairns, bus services operate Mon to Sat and there is a touring bus that follows a circular route, *Cairns Red Explorer* (which does operate on Sundays but only from May to October), that departs from the Transit Centre every hour. Day tickets are A$20 (adult) and A$10 (children). Taxis are also available.

Accommodation

HOTELS/MOTELS:

 International standard hotels are available in Brisbane, Cairns and the Gold Coast together with a high standard of hotel/motel accommodation throughout the state. Information regarding price and location of accommodation can be obtained through Tourism Queensland.
Motels are usually in - or on - the outskirts of towns and cities and normally offer self-contained rooms at reasonable rates.

SELF-CONTAINED APARTMENTS:

 These are available throughout the larger resort areas and offer a variety of facilities.

FARMSTAYS/HOMESTAYS:

 'Holiday Host' services operate throughout Australia, matching hosts with visitors, in stations, family homes and farm properties.

CAMPING/CARAVANNING:

 Parks are located in tourist areas around Queensland, and offer facilities of varying standards. Camping is permitted in parks, but permission must be sought. A number of companies can arrange **motor camper** rentals, with a range of fully-equipped vehicles. Full details can be obtained from Tourism Queensland.

YOUTH HOSTELS:

 Budget dormitory-style accommodation is available throughout Queensland.
Note: For further coverage of the range of accommodation available, see *Accommodation* in the general *Australia* section.

ACCOMMODATION INFORMATION

National Parks Association of Queensland Inc
36 Finchley St, Milton, QLD 4064, Australia
Tel: (7) 3367 0878.
Website: www.npaq.org.au

Top Things To See

- **Brisbane** may seem like it is just a stopover but there is plenty to see at Australia's fastest-growing city with its year-round warm subtropical climate. The **Lone Pine Koala Sanctuary** is extremely popular and can be reached via a river cruise. The **Botanic Gardens** is a splendid shady reserve at the south end of the city centre, accessible by a footbridge. **City Hall** in **King George Square** houses an art gallery, museum and clocktower observation deck. Other buildings of note include the **State Parliament House** with its glittering copper roof, **St John's Cathedral**, **The Mansions** and the **Old Windmill**, the city's oldest surviving building (built in 1828), and once a treadmill worked by convicts. The **Queensland Cultural Centre** at South Bank contains the **Queensland Art Gallery**, **Queensland Museum** and **Performing Arts Centre**. The **South Bank Parklands**, on the site of the *1988 World Expo*, boasts an interesting **Maritime Museum** and an enormous **artificial swimming beach**. The **Brisbane Powerhouse** is a lively alternative arts venue, and the looming art deco **Castlemaine Brewery** offers enjoyable daily tours with samples of its famous product.

- You have to see it to believe it: 42km (25 miles) of white surf beaches along the (arguably) best beach area in Australia, the **Gold Coast** region, with year-round sunshine and lively tourist facilities. The **Sunshine Coast** also competes with miles of untouched wilderness, lakes, mountains and beaches with surf. Other recommended beaches include **Mission Beach** with 14km (9 miles) of white sand, looking out to **Dunk Island**; the expanse of sand and sea around **Fraser Island**; **Hervey Bay**; and **Port Douglas**, with its charming old town.

- Lush green mountains, rainforests, walking trails and scenic villages are all to be found inland. Nature lovers will appreciate the **Lamington National Park** in the **McPherson Mountains** and the **Currumbin Bird Sanctuary**. Arts and crafts trails, nature walks and awe-inspiring views can be found in the hinterland, around the **Glasshouse Mountains**. There are rainforests to discover in the **Atherton Tableland**.

- Examine excellent examples of Aboriginal rock art at **Endeavour National Park**.

- Be gob-smacked by the beauty and size of the **Great Barrier Reef**, one of the world's great natural wonders. Stretching for 2000km (1200 miles) along the Queensland coast, its width varying from 25km (15 miles) to 50km (30 miles), it offers great views from both above and below, where unique plant and animal life can be found.

Credit: ©David Bell and Juliet Sinclair

Top Things To Do

- Be like the locals and get into watersports in one of the best possible places to do so: from **surfing** off the beaches in the south (the best surfing can be found at Surfers' Paradise, the **Sunshine Coast**, **Bribie**, **Moreton** and the **Stradbroke Islands**) to **deep-sea fishing** for black marlin to **sailing** round the islands and to **canoeing** and **sea-kayaking** around the Great Barrier Reef.

- **Bushwalk** around the cooler southern regions. **Lamington National Park** has a well-maintained, graded track system in the **McPherson Range** (on the border with New South Wales), which features tall rainforests, waterfalls and gorges; a three-day circuit is possible around Fraser Island, which has rainforest, huge sand dunes and beautiful lakes; a series of fairly demanding trails lead to the summit of the state's highest mountain, **Mount Bartle Frere**; popular day walks are available on the islands of **Dunk**, **Green** and **Hinchinbrook**. For more information, contact QLD Environmental Protection Agency, PO Box 15155, Ann Street, Brisbane QLD 4000; tel: (7) 3227 7111; website: www.epa.qld.gov.au).

- Seize the moment in the **adventure sports** capital of Australia: **paragliding** and **parasailing** can be practised all along the coast; **abseiling** is possible in the Lamington and **Carnarvon National Parks**; the **Sunshine Coast** and **Mount Tamborine** are the main destinations for **hang gliding**; the **Tully** and **Barron rivers** in the north are suitable for **whitewater rafting**; **speed boating** trips can be arranged in **Cairns**.

- Go to the **Wintermoon Festival**, a four-day music extravaganza held over the long weekend in April/May, which promises a unique experience in the foothills of **Eungella National Park**, watching a wonderful program of music, dancing, song and verse, and delicious food to sample.

- Queensland is full of fun (or tacky, depending on your disposition) **theme parks**. Unleash the inner child and try visiting one such as *Sea World*, *Movie World* or *Dreamworld*.

- Learn to **dive** and experience the subterranean splendour of the **Great Barrier Reef** (Queensland Dive Association; tel: (7) 4051 1510; e-mail: info@great-barrier-reef.net.au), with visibility often as deep as 60m (200ft). The following are some of the best dive spots/resorts to be found: **Heron** (reputed to support a record diversity of tropical fish) and **Lady Elliot Islands** are coral cays renowned as the best diving spots on the reef; **Thretford Reef**; the **Ribbon Reefs** (comprising a string of 10 coral ramparts covering a huge area, including the **Cod Hole**, **Pixie Pinnacle** and **Dynamite Pass**); **Magnetic Island**; the **Pompey Complex**; the **Swain Reefs** (near **Gladstone**); **Great Keppel Island**; **Bedarra** and **Orpheus Islands** are quiet, secluded and luxurious hideaways; **Long Island**, **Great Keppel Islands**, **South Molle**, **Hamilton** and **Lindeman Island** are all-year-round resorts with facilities for families; **Tropical Dunk Island** and **Brampton Island** are popular with honeymooners; and **Fitzroy** and **Hinchinbrook Islands** offer unspoilt beauty.

- **Party** hard on the yellow sand along the Gold Coast: **Surfers' Paradise** is a Miami-style high-rise strip overlooking a crowded beach.

TOURIST INFORMATION

Tourism Queensland in the UK
Sixth Floor, Australia Centre, Melbourne Place, The Strand, London WC2B 4LG, UK
Tel: (020) 7438 4601.
Website: www.queenslandholidays.co.uk *or* www.tq.com.au (corporate site).

Gold Coast Tourism Bureau
Level Two, 64 Ferny Avenue, Surfers' Paradise 4217, Australia
Tel: (7) 5592 2699.
Website: www.veryvg.com

Entertainment

FOOD & DRINK: The food of the area relies to a large extent on the sea and the subtropical climate for specialities in cuisine. In Fortitude Valley, just out of Brisbane city centre, there are a number of European, Asian and Chinese restaurants and trendy cafes.
Regional specialities:
- Delicacies such as mud crabs, king and tiger prawns, mackerel and fresh *barramundi*.
- Delicious range of fruits, such as avocados, mangoes, pawpaws, pineapples, strawberries and bananas.
- The recommended *macadamia nut*.
Regional drinks:
- Brisbane is supplied with local wines from vineyards at Stanthorpe to the southwest, producing both red and white wines, and from other Australian vineyards.
- All beers on sale are brewed locally.
- Queensland is the home of *Bundaberg Rum*, a sweet rum brewed with local sugar cane.
NIGHTLIFE: Although much of the tourist activity is centred on the beaches and the Barrier Reef, Brisbane offers a wide selection of entertainment. Most of the large hotels have dinner and dancing facilities and there are several nightclubs in the city, especially in Southbank Parklands where discos and restaurants abound. The Gold Coast has many nightclubs, as well as Jupiter's Casino. Townsville has the spectacular Sheraton Breakwater Casino on Sir Leslie Thiess Drive, offering a full range of gaming facilities and high-quality entertainment.
SHOPPING: Good buys include opals, Aboriginal art and handicrafts, woollen clothing, sheepskin coats and wood products. **Shopping hours:** Mon-Fri 0800-2100, Sat 0800-1700, although hours vary depending on the city. Shops in the Gold Coast, Brisbane City, Sunshine Coast and Cairns are open on Sundays.

Business

CONFERENCES/CONVENTIONS: Brisbane's major convention centres are Brisbane Convention & Exhibition Centre, Brisbane Entertainment Centre, Brisbane City Hall, Queensland Cultural Centre, RNA Exhibition Grounds, Sheraton Brisbane Hotel, Hilton International Hotel and the Carlton Crest International Hotel. Cairns' major convention centres are Cairns Convention Centre, Cairns International, Cairns Civic Centre, Cairns Show Grounds, the Botanical Gardens, Sheraton Mirage Resort and Cairns Hilton Hotel. The Gold Coast also has some excellent convention facilities, especially the Hotel Conrad and Jupiter's Casino with seating for 2300. Smaller centres can be found elsewhere along the Gold Coast at Royal Pines Resort and Sheraton Mirage Gold Coast.

COMMERCIAL INFORMATION

Queensland Chamber of Commerce and Industry
Industry House, 375 Wickham Terrace, Brisbane, QLD 4000, Australia
Tel: (7) 3842 2244.
Website: www.qcci.com.au

Brisbane Convention and Exhibition Centre
PO Box 3869, South Bank, Brisbane, QLD 4101, Australia
Tel: (7) 3308 3000.
Website: www.bcec.com.au

Cairns Convention Bureau (Tourism Tropical North Queensland)
PO Box 865, Cairns, QLD 4870, Australia
Tel: (7) 4031 7676 (ext 218).
Website: www.cairnsconventionbureau.com

A B C D E F G H I J K L M N O P Q R S T U V W X Y Z

South Australia

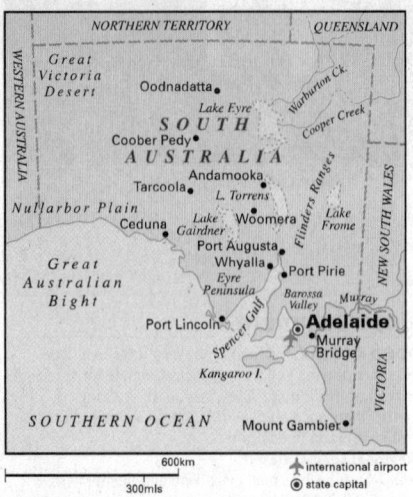

Location: Central Southern Australia.

Time: GMT + 9.5 (GMT + 10.5 from last Sunday in October to last Sunday in March).

Overview

South Australia deserves attention. Although no Sydney, Adelaide is an attractive State capital, and the State is filled with unique towns such as volcanic Mount Gambier and quaint Glenelg. There is no Uluru but there is Wilpena Pound, a huge natural amphitheatre with rocks protruding like gnarled fingers in Flinders Ranges National Park. There is no Sunshine Coast but there are great chunks of dramatic shoreline. Instead of reefs, South Australia is probably the best destination in Australia for seeing roaming native wildlife.

South Australia is the driest State in one of the driest Continents. As harsh as the scenery is, however, it encloses a distinct beauty. There are stunning National Parks to ramble, from the cerise dunes of Simpson Desert to Lake Eyre National Park and its enormous 'salt-sink' and wilderness, opening up giant skies. And even if the State occasionally gets thirsty, there is plenty to quench the thirst of the visitor. The Barossa Valley is just one prized wine-growing region in South Australia.

South Australia is the only State that was not colonised through convicts. Its early settlers were mostly religious non-conformists and South Australia has since paved the way in Australian reform: the first State to give women equal voting rights; first to appoint an Aboriginal and a female Governor; and the first in the British Commonwealth to employ policewomen.

South Australia still leads in innovation. It is host to some of the biggest worldwide challenges, from the World Solar Challenge to Tour Down Under. No wonder South Australia is called the 'Festival State'. There is always something to celebrate in such captivating land.

General Information

AREA: 983,480 sq km (379,723 sq miles).

POPULATION: 1.53 million (official estimate 2004).

POPULATION DENSITY: 1.6 per sq km.

CAPITAL: Adelaide. **Population:** 1.11 million (official estimate 2003).

GEOGRAPHY: Except for the State capital of Adelaide, South Australia is sparsely inhabited – it is four times the area of the UK. It is the country's driest State, a region of rocky plains and desert landscape broken by the fertile wine-growing areas, which include the Barossa Valley. South Australia stretches upwards to the Northern Territory, and eastwards to Queensland, New South Wales and Victoria and westwards to Western Australia. The countryside ranges from the beach resorts of the Adelaide suburbs to the vast expanses of isolated, semi-desert outback; from the craggy mountains of Flinders Ranges to the meandering Murray River. Offshore is the popular Kangaroo Island. Adelaide nestles in the foothills of Mount Lofty Ranges.

Climate

Adelaide boasts a Mediterranean climate, perfect for enjoying the great Australian outdoors. Warm and temperate with long hot summers, short mild winters and low rainfall. The average temperature ranges from 15°C (58°F) in July, to 29°C (84°F) in January. One of the hottest places in the area in summer is Coober Pedy, 863km (536 miles) northwest of Adelaide, reaching temperatures of up to 45°C (113°F).

Required clothing: Lightweight cottons and linens in summer, warmer mediumweights in winter. Waterproofing is advisable throughout most of the year, particularly in winter.

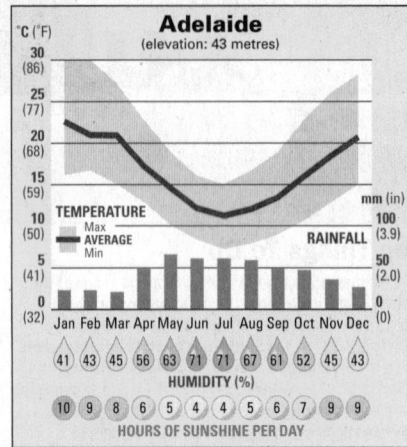

Public Holidays

South Australia observes all the public holidays observed nationwide (see the main *Australia* section) and, in addition, the beneath Public Holidays listed from the January 2006-June 2007 period

2006: Mar 13* Adelaide Cup Day. **Oct 2** Labour Day. **Dec 26** Proclamation Day.

2007: May 21* Adelaide Cup Day.

Note: * The Adelaide Cup is a holiday in Adelaide only.

Travel - International

AIR:

 International carriers operating to Adelaide include *Air Paradise*, *British Airways*, *Cathay Pacific*, *Garuda Airlines*, *Malaysia Airlines*, *Qantas* and *Singapore Airlines*. Approximate flying time from *London* is 22 hours. Flights from Europe stop off in the Far East, usually Singapore, Kuala Lumpur or Bali. Adelaide is also linked to every other Australian State capital city. For more flight details, see the main *Australia* section.

There is an excellent system of internal flights serving all regional towns, and the majority of flights are run by *Emu Air* (flights to Kangaroo Island), *O'Connor Airlines*, *Qantas*, *Regional Express* and *Virgin Blue*. There are nine Government and 20 private airfields in the region.

Main airports: *Adelaide Airport (ADL)* (website: www.aal.com.au), is 6km (4 miles) from the city centre. A new international terminal opened at the end of 2005. *To/from the airport*: A 15-minute drive. *Facilities*: Banks, bureaux de change, left luggage, restaurants, bars, shops and car hire.

SEA:

 Main ports: There are regular car-ferry services from *Cape Jervis* to *Kangaroo Island* (travel time – 45 minutes to one hour). *Adelaide* is an international port, with regular visits from several leading international cruise lines.

RAIL:

 Adelaide, where the popular *Ghan* train calls en route to Darwin (a scenic rail journey through a desert landscape), is a major terminal on the national rail network.

TransAdelaide (website: www.transadelaide.com.au) offers comprehensive suburban rail services across the state. The *Indian Pacific* from Sydney to Perth also stops in Adelaide, while *The Overland* travels between Melbourne and Adelaide. Other tourist services are the *Cockle Train*, a scenic trip on vintage steam locomotives between Goolwa and Victor Harbour on the Fleurieu Peninsula, and the *Pichi Richi Steam Train* which leaves Quorn in the Flinders Ranges on a two hours 30 minutes' round trip. Adelaide's rail terminal is located at Keswick, a few kilometres from the city centre.

ROAD:

 The southern states are fully connected to the national system of **coach** lines that crosses Australia from all the state capitals. Typical coach journey times are as follows: from Adelaide to *Melbourne* is eight hours, to *Alice Springs* is 17 hours, to *Sydney* is 20 hours 30 minutes, to *Brisbane* is 33 hours, and to *Perth* is 34 hours. People drive on the left-hand side of the road. The main highways north are the *Stuart Highway* to Darwin via Coober Pedy and Alice Springs, and the *Birdsville Track* to Queensland. The other main State highways are the *Eyre Highway* west to Perth, the *Prince's Highway* along the coast to Melbourne and the *Stuart Highway* east to Canberra and Sydney. **Car hire:** Services are available at all the main hotels, the railway station and the airport.

Documentation: Interstate visitors can drive on a current licence for up to three months, whilst those from overseas can drive on an International Driving Permit for up to 12 months.

URBAN:

 There is a fully integrated public transport system in Adelaide with **bus**, **tram** and local **rail** lines, plus the *O-Bahn* bus system. The system is divided into zones. Pre-purchase booklets of cash-fare tickets and weekly and other passes are all available. The so-called *Metrotickets* are available for single, daily and multiple (up to 10) journeys. There are two free bus services, the *BeeLine* and the *City Loop*.

Accommodation

HOTELS:

 South Australia has many hotels and guest houses, ranging from budget hostels to 5-star international hotels. Bed & breakfast, farmstay and cottage accommodation is available throughout the State. Further information is available from the South Australian Tourism Commission.

CAMPING/CARAVANNING:

 South Australia has approximately 200 caravan parks. They all offer sites with full amenities and power. A number of companies can arrange **motor camper** rentals, with a range of fully equipped vehicles. Full details can be obtained from the South Australian Tourism Commission. In addition, there is a wide variety of holiday flats and apartments for rent in the State. **Note:** For further coverage of the range of accommodation available in Australia, see *Accommodation* in the general *Australia* section.

Top Things To See

• **Adelaide**'s 30km- (18.6 mile-) stretch of attractive coastline with excellent white sandy beaches is worth a perusal: **Mount Lofty** offers the best view of Adelaide and the surrounding countryside. Adelaide itself is a spacious city surrounded by parkland, golf courses and the botanical and zoological gardens. The city has a European atmosphere, streets filled with cafes (especially in lively **Rundle Street**), European-style churches, art galleries and antique shops. Adelaide also has a vibrant nightlife along Rundle and **Gouger Street**. One of its key attractions is the **Festival Centre** complex in the parkland overlooking the **Torrens River**. It houses an excellent theatre company, and boasts a concert hall, two theatres, a restaurant and an amphitheatre. Another very popular attraction is the **Central Market** between Gouger and **Grote Street**.

• See the largest collection of Aboriginal artefacts in the world at the **South Australian Museum**, in Adelaide, which also has a huge exhibition of Melanesian art and New Guinean wildlife, plus one on the Antarctic Explorer, Sir Douglas Mawson. **Tandanya – National Aboriginal Cultural Institute** is worth a visit too for more insights into Australia's indigenous culture.

• Watch countless natural wildlife in their natural environment in Australia's third-largest island, in the **St Vincent Gulf**, **Kangaroo Island**. Any visitor here is rewarded with possible sightings of penguins, koalas, wallabies and kangaroos, as well as the large sea lion colony at **Seal Bay**.

• Step into the **Naracoorte Caves Conservation Park** near the southeast border with Victoria and see stalagmites, stalactites, bats and fossils.

• Set eyes on South Australia's best slice of the outback in the ancient Aboriginal heritage area of **Flinders Ranges**, a region of granite peaks and spectacular and colourful gorges, dotted with eucalyptus trees. Interesting sights include: the popular resort area of **Wilpena Pound** with a natural amphitheatre 16km (10 miles) long and 6km (3.7 miles) deep; weather-eroded **Remarkable Rocks** that jut out of the coastal surface; koalas hanging out of trees at **Rocky River**; and the opal town of **Coober Pedy**, which is so hot that 45 per cent of the inhabitants live underground - even the church is underground and, in fact, the name of the town means 'white man lives in a hole'.

• Watch penguins return from the ocean to feed their young every evening on **Granite Island**.

• Perceive the edge of a continent as you advance along the **Nullarbor Plain**, lying flat for hundreds of miles but then suddenly dropping 300ft (90 metres) to form the **Bunda Cliffs**, which tower above the Southern Ocean.

• Go to **Mount Gambier**, a town that has been built around a volcano, from the slopes to the caldera. But do not fret too much – the volcano is extinct! So with your mind at rest, you can better take in the town's many quirky and beautiful sights: sinkholes, limestone coastal area, and, of course, the **Blue Lake**, which boasts crystal-clear waters that change in colour with the seasons.

Top Things To Do

- Go on a **wine tasting tour** - where else is better to do so than in South Australia where over 70 per cent of Australia's wine exports come from? The **Barossa Valley**'s main townships are **Tanunda**, **Angaston** and **Nuriootpa**, all notable for Lutheran churches and their rolling vineyards. The other major wine regions in South Australia are the **Clare Valley**, **Riverland**, **McLaren Vale** and the **Coonawarra wine district** in the southeast.
- Enjoy some **bushwalking** around the remote **Flinders Ranges**, a vast area of plains, gorges and desert, which provides one of Australia's best gateways to the outback. The well-known **Heysen Trail**, the longest trail in Australia, begins at **Cape Jervis** and winds its way north through scenic coastal areas. Bushwalkers can also climb a one-day excursion to **St Mary's Peak**, a trek best tackled between May and October, when temperatures are milder and water more readily available (permits can be obtained from the ranger on site). More experienced walkers can embark on longer walks to the **Gammon Ranges National Park**, further north; the **Flinders Chase National Park** on **Kangaroo Island**; or the **Deep Creek Conservation Park** south of Adelaide. Further information can be obtained from the Department of Environment and Heritage, GPO Box 1047, Adelaide SA 5001 (tel: (8) 8204 9000; website: www.environment.sa.gov.au).
- Benefit from being near the third-largest river in the world, and get into **cruising**, **sailing** and **water-skiing** along **River Murray**, which winds its way through South Australia.
- **Dive** with **Great White Sharks**: good diving sites, in general, include **Port Lincoln**, **Kangaroo Island**, **Yorke Peninsula** and **Eyre Peninsula**.
- In March of even-numbered years, the world-renowned **Adelaide Bank Festival of Arts** is held, featuring everything from jazz to classical theatre and ballet, along with a diverse Edinburgh-style **Fringe Festival**.
- **Whale watch** on the **Fleurieu Peninsula** around **Victor Harbor** and on the **Nullarbor coast**, where large colonies of Southern Right whales breed from June to October.
- For **surfing** enthusiasts, South Australia offers uncrowded beaches and excellent waves, particularly at **Victor Harbor**, Kangaroo Island and the more remote **Yorke** and **Eyre peninsulas** (with Eyre's **Cactus Beach** attracting surfers from all over the world).
- Eat at the famous **Tasting Australia**, a popular biennial event that offers the best in both South Australian and Australian produce, plus wines, beers and hospitality.
- Cheer on participants at the **World Solar Challenge**, which excitingly combines ancient landscape and futuristic technology: the challengers have to traverse 3000km of Australian continent, from **Darwin** to **Adelaide**, in cars powered only by the sun, designed and built by some of the world's cleverest minds.
- Dig for the semi-precious stones at **Coober Pedy**, which produces 90 per cent of the world's supply of **opals**: all you have to do is obtain a miner's permit.
- Ride a historic **tram** through **Glenelg**, Adelaide's wonderfully charming seaside suburb.

Entertainment

FOOD & DRINK: Adelaide has a wide range of restaurants and cafes specialising in international cuisine, including US, Chinese, French, Greek, Italian, Indian, Indonesian, Japanese, Lebanese, Malaysian, Mexican, Mongolian and Vietnamese. Many of these offer alfresco dining. There are many excellent seafood restaurants.

There are many wine and food festivals throughout the region where local wines and beers can be tasted. One of these is the *Barossa Vintage Festival*, reminiscent in many ways of German beer festivals in Europe. There is also a brewery in Adelaide supplying stout and lagers, although whether in Adelaide itself, the hills or the outback, the pub experience should not be missed. South Australia contains

one of the most important valley regions producing wines; from the reds of Coonawarra to the Rieslings of the Eden Valley. Although specialising in table wines, the state is noted for its sparkling reds and whites.

Regional specialities:
- Snapper is a fish found in abundance.
- There are many German-style delicacies to be found, particularly in the Barossa region, which still bears the hallmarks of its German settlers: *mettwurst* (spicy cured sausage), *Bienenstich* (cream-filled yeast cake topped with a honey-nut layer) and pickles are popular.
- Seafood is excellent. Grab a bite of crabs, whiting, oysters, blue fin tuna and crayfish.
- Kangaroo steak is excellent and succulent.
- Other well-liked meats include emu, venison and fresh lamb.
- Pie carts are an institution in Adelaide, much-loved by rowdy night-time revellers. The *Pie Floater* is a particular specialty of South Australia - immersed in pea soup and with ketchup added, it may not be to everyone's taste!
- South Australia's climate yields a cornucopia of fruits and vegetables, such as citrus, grapes, stone fruits, melons, tomatoes, crops and *warrugul greens* (native spinach).
- Lemon myrtle (a fresh leaf) and *wattle seed* (a black variety of the acacia seed) are often added to dishes.

Regional drinks:
- Have a glug of what many consider to be the finest of Australian beers, the South Australian *Cooper's Ale*.
- South Australia is well known for its award winning wines such as *Penfold's Grange*. South Australian wines vary from region to region due to different climatic zones, soil type and wine maker influences. The most predominant red varieties used today include Shiraz, Cabernet Sauvignon, Grenache and Merlot. White varieties include Riesling, Chardonnay, Sauvignon Blanc and Semillon. Although most specialize in table wines, many are also noted for their sparklings, both red and white.
- *Two Dogs Lemonade* is a refreshing, naturally fermented alcoholic drink made from real lemons from the South Australian region.

NIGHTLIFE: Adelaide has an extraordinary nightlife scene. The Adelaide Casino, once a grand Victorian railway station, is now a haven for baccarat and roulette players amid its magnificent Corinthian columns. There is also a concentration of nightclubs and discos on Hindley Street in the heart of the city, opposite Rundle Mall. Large crowds also flock to the cosmopolitan atmosphere of the pubs and cafes in Rundle Street.

SHOPPING: Excellent quality wines are available from the Barossa Valley, which attracts 60 per cent of Australia's wine-tasting tourists. Adelaide is a city that concentrates on culture, and is full of antique shops, art galleries and stores that sell Australia's finest opals, handmade chocolates and stockman's hats. Opening hours are the same as for the rest of Australia. There are also some street markets in Adelaide, the Central market being located adjacent to Victoria Square. This market, made up of nearly 600 stalls, sells all kinds of produce, including fruit, vegetables, fish, cheese, meat, spices and other exotic delights.

Business

CONFERENCES/CONVENTIONS: Adelaide's major convention centres are the recently upgraded Adelaide Convention Centre and Exhibition Hall, Adelaide Festival Centre, Hilton International Adelaide, Royal Showground and Exhibition Centre.

Credit: ©David Bell and Juliet Sinclair

Tasmania

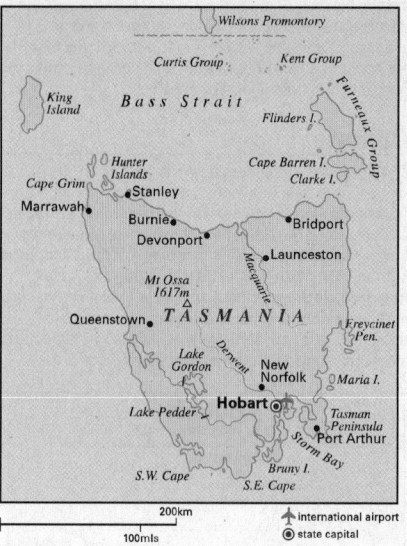

Location: South of mainland Australia.

Time: GMT + 10 (GMT + 11 from first Sunday in October to last Saturday in March).

Overview

Tasmania is Australia's only island-State. Long periods of isolation from the mainland meant that the Tasmanian Aborigines developed their own idiosyncracies, and Tasmania is full of remnants of their heritage. But those in pursuit of history will find gruesome details. When British colonisers sought a new penal colony, Tasmania's isolation rendered it favourite, triggering years of tragic violence against its Aborigines. Eeriness haunts the Victorian streets of Launceston and the penal colony, Port Arthur. Tasmania's preserved buildings are aesthetically wonderful and historically shocking.

Tasmania's relatively small size contradicts its ecological diversity. Being an island, it harbours distinct wildlife, many of which are endangered or extinct elsewhere: the infamous Tasmanian devil, the spotted-tail and the eastern quoll are the three biggest carnivorous marsupials on the planet. Additionally, its island-status has indirectly shaped its history. Tasmanian Aborigines displayed more resistance to invasion than mainland Aborigines because they had less land to escape to. War between colonisers and indigenous inhabitants meant that by 1876, the last full-blooded Tasmanian Aborigine had died, severing a link that had run roughly 60,000 years.

Tasmania has since sought to heal its historical scars by championing some of the most forward-thinking policies in Australia: outspokenly supportive of humane treatment for asylum seekers and keenly environmental. Indeed, Tasmania's countryside owes its conservation to decades of struggle - thankfully, considering some of the most beautiful spots in Australia are to be found here, from enchanting forests with the world's tallest and rarest trees, to 20 national parks with the world's last temperate-climate rainforest, to beautiful falls and soaring peaks. What could be more conducive to a tranquil trip?

General Information

AREA: 68,400 sq km (26,409 sq miles).
POPULATION: 480,000 (official estimate 2003).
POPULATION DENSITY: 7.0 per sq km.
CAPITAL: Hobart. **Population:** 199,886 (official estimate 2003).
GEOGRAPHY: A separate island located 240km (149 miles) south of Melbourne across Bass Strait. Roughly heart-shaped, Tasmania is 296km (184 miles) long, ranging from 315km (196 miles) wide in the north to 70km (44 miles) in the south. The island has a diverse landscape comprising rugged mountains (snow-capped in winter), dense bushland (including the Horizontal Forest, so-called because the tree trunks are bent over parallel to the ground), tranquil countryside and farmland. Approximately 40 per cent of Tasmania is protected in national parks and other reserves, over half of this being the World Heritage-listed temperate wilderness in the west of the island. Located midway between Victoria and the northwest of Tasmania in Bass Strait lies King Island. This rich and fertile island, famous for its beef and dairy products, is regularly serviced by air carriers and is a popular tourist destination. To the

northeast of Tasmania, also in Bass Strait, can be found Flinders Island, part of the Furneaux group of islands. Flinders Island is also popular with visitors and is particularly noted for its excellent coastal fishing and pristine beaches. Bruny Island, south of Hobart across the D'Entrecasteaux Channel, has superb beaches and an abundance of marine wildlife. The two parts of the island are joined by a narrow isthmus of sand dunes, the home of Fairy Penguins from August to April.

Climate

Similar climate to southern Australia, with warm, dry summers and cool, wet winters. However, climate in Tasmania is more variable and more changeable, with some areas (eg Hobart) receiving considerably less rainfall than others. Most of the rainfall is in the west of the island. There is often snow above 1000m (3280ft) in July and August. **Required clothing:** Cottons and linens in summer, warmer mediumweights in winter. Waterproofing is advisable throughout the year, particularly in highland areas. Jumpers are recommended for the evenings, all year round.

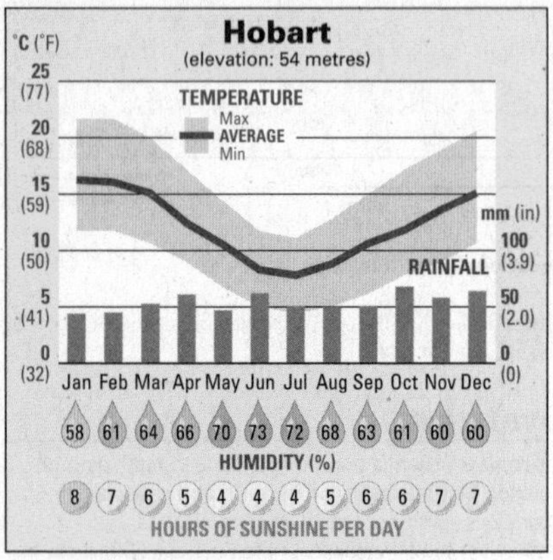

Public Holidays

Tasmania observes all the public holidays observed nationwide (see the main *Australia* section) and, in addition, the beneath Public Holidays listed from the January 2006-June 2007 period.

2006: Mar 13 Eight Hours Day. **Apr 18** Easter Tuesday. **Jun 12** Queen's Birthday Celebrations.

2007: Mar 12 Eight Hours Day. **Apr 10** Easter Tuesday. **Jun 11** Queen's Birthday Celebrations.

Travel - International

AIR:

Most flights come from the Australian mainland. Direct flights to Hobart arrive from Adelaide, Brisbane, Melbourne and Sydney, with quick connections available from Cairns, Canberra, Darwin and Perth. Launceston, Devonport and Burnie also receive flights from the mainland. Airlines serving Tasmania include *Jetstar, Qantas, Rex Regional Express* and *Virgin Blue*. The airport is 22km (14 miles) from Hobart city centre, a drive of about 35 minutes. *Island Airlines Tasmania* flies to Flinders Island. *King Island Airlines* and *TasAir* fly to King Island. Both islands are directly accessible from the Australian mainland, as well as from Tasmania.

Main airports: *Hobart (HBA)* lies 16km (10 miles) east of Hobart. *To/from the airport*: 15 to 20 minutes by taxi. *Facilities*: Banks/ATMs, bars and car hire.

SEA:

Main ports: *Devonport* on the northwest coast of the island.

RAIL:

There are no passenger services. However, the West Coast Wilderness Railway runs a tourist service between Queenstown and Strahan; it is a reconstruction of the original Abt railway that carried ore from the mines to the coast. The railway's steam locomotives use a rack-rail system to climb the steep gradients of the rainforest wilderness it passes through. It runs for 35km (22 miles), crossing around 40 rivers and passing through restored stations. In the northwest, the Don River Railway also runs regular excursions using both steam and diesel locomotives. For further information, contact Tourism Tasmania (see *Top Things To Do*).

ROAD:

All settlements on the island are linked by a road system running for 22,000km (13,670 miles), over which there are bus services connecting the main cities and towns. The main routes are: the *Lyell Highway* from Hobart to Queenstown; the *Huon Highway* from Hobart to Southport; the *Heritage Highway* from Hobart to Launceston; the *Tasman Highway* from Hobart along the east coast; and the *Bass Highway*, linking the ports of the north and northwest coast. There are 11 pre-planned touring routes to help discover the unique Tasmanian scenery and natural attractions. **Coach:** Tasmania has its own coach services: *Tasmanian Redline Coaches*, which offers a *Tassie Bus Pass* to out-of-state visitors; *Tasmania Wilderness Transport*, which serves the needs of bushwalkers; and *Tigerline Travel Tasmania* for travel around the state, plus day tours. **Bicycle:** Helmets must be worn at all times.

URBAN:

Local bus networks are operated in Hobart, Launceston and Burnie.

Accommodation

HOTELS, MOTELS AND GUEST HOUSES:

There are international hotels in Hobart and Launceston and a wide range of tourist hotels, motels and guest houses in all the major centres. Hotels tend to be slightly more expensive in Hobart and Launceston, and in the main tourist areas.

CAMPING/CARAVANNING:

A number of companies can arrange campervan or motorhome rentals, with a range of fully equipped vehicles. There are numerous camping and caravan sites in Tasmania. It should be noted that camping is not permitted in any roadside picnic or rest areas.

SELF-CATERING/FARM- AND HOMESTAYS:

These are also widely available. More detailed information on the range of accommodation available in Australia may be found by consulting *Accommodation* in the main *Australia* section.

HOSTELS:

There is an extensive network of backpacker hostels all over the island.

WILDERNESS LODGES:

These are located in wilderness areas, and are designed to blend in with their surroundings. Some offer a high standard of comfort, while others are more humble in style. They also organise activities such as kayaking, wildlife viewing and guided walks.

Note: For further coverage of the range of accommodation available, see *Accommodation* in the general *Australia* section.

ACCOMMODATION INFORMATION

Australian Hotels Association
11 Morrison Street, Hobart, Tasmania 7000
Tel: (3) 6224 7033.
Website: www.australianhotels.asn.au

Tourism Tasmania (official accommodation brochures can be downloaded online)
Website: www.discovertasmania.com

Top Things To See

- Tasmania's capital, **Hobart**, is Australia's second-oldest city after Sydney and is situated on the south side of the island. The city has strong links with the sea, typified by the wharves, jetties and warehouses - some dating back to the 19th century - which cluster around the waterfront. Hobart itself is an intriguing blend of heritage and lifestyle, scenery and culture. Examples of the island's history can be seen in the **Maritime Museum of Tasmania**, the convict-era buildings of **Battery Point** and the **Tasmanian Museum and Art Gallery**. **Salamanca Market** is a must-see, held every Saturday and a vibrant affair offering arts and crafts, local produce and environment. **Mount Wellington**, towering 1270m (4170ft) to the west of the city, provides the backdrop to Hobart. From the lookout at the top (about 20km/12 miles by road), the clear air offers a spectacular view of Hobart, its suburbs, the **Derwent Estuary** and **Storm Bay**. Apart from the view, the area has picnic facilities and walking trails. The **Royal Tasmanian Botanical Gardens** offer a long walk through beautiful scenery.
- Observe the **Blowhole** and **Tasmanian Arch** amongst spectacular coastal scenery on the **Tasmanian Peninsula**.
- See Australia's most significant convict site, the **Port Arthur Historic Site**, created with convict labour, impressive architecture and delightful gardens withhold chilling historical prison facilities.
- Walk along a rushing river and stare into the **Cataract Gorge**, which almost reaches into the middle of **Launceston**, and is surrounded by bushland.
- Study original Tasmanian and Aboriginal art at the **Queen Victoria Museum and Art Gallery** at **Inveresk**.
- Catch sight of the unique and fearsome little marsupial, the **Tasmanian Devil**.
- See Tasmania's dramatic mountain peak, situated in **Cradle Mountain/Lake St Clair National Park**, famous for the **Overland Track walk**, and also bursting with natural wonders such as rainforest, alpine heathlands, glacial lakes and ancient pines.
- View the autumnal colours of the only deciduous Australian tree - **nothofagus gunii**.
- Go to **Freycinet** on Tasmania's east coast and see **Wineglass Bay**, one of the world's top-10 beaches.
- See the 'picture-esque' town of **Sheffield**, where dozens of buildings have their walls colourfully decorated with murals.
- Watch the cascading of **Russell Falls**, a pretty display of nature in the **Mount Field National Park**, and contender for most-photographed waterfall in Australia.

Top Things To Do

- **Boat** or **sailing cruises** are popular ways to explore the port cities of Launceston and Hobart, as well as the outlying islands. **Tamar River Cruises** offer short morning, afternoon, lunch and evening tours on Tamar River in Launceston. Companies operating around Hobart include **Port Arthur Cruises** and **Hobart Cruises** to **Peppermint Bay**, and **Derwent River Cruises**. **Gordan River Cruises** operate out of **Strahan** on the west coast, where the World-Heritage-listed South-West Tasmanian coast can be explored.
- Take photos of **wildlife**, since Tasmania's 20 national parks are home to a rich variety of animals, many of them unique to the island. They include wombats, possums, platypus, wallabies, fairy penguins and the rare orange-bellied parrot. The Tasmanian Devil, a small, black, dog-like marsupial can be readily seen at night in the Narawntapu-, Mount William- and Cradle National Parks. Although it looks fierce, it is not usually harmful to humans. The hunt still continues for the so-called **Tasmanian Tiger** or **thylacine**, not sighted for 60 years and thought to be extinct. This creature, actually a marsupial wolf, is the state's official mascot.
- Walk the popular **Tahune AirWalk**, a one-and-a-half hour's drive from Hobart, offering a suspended 37m-high walkway above spectacular forest canopies. It is part of the Huon Trail which includes the Hastings thermal pool, caves and sheltered bays of the D'Entrecasteaux Channel.
- Go hit the pistes at **Ben Lomond**, Tasmania's main **ski** resort.
- Experience utter **wilderness** in **The Walls of Jerusalem National Park**: the perfect environment for lots of **hiking**, but be warned, the treks are not for novices.

TOURIST INFORMATION

Tourism Tasmania in the UK
12 Montpelier Place, London SW7 1HJ, UK
Tel: (020) 7584 6553.
Website: www.discovertasmania.com

Entertainment

FOOD & DRINK:

Regional specialities:

- Some of the best seafood in the world is available in Tasmania, including Angasi oysters, rock lobster, crayfish, scallops, Atlantic salmon, blue-lip mussels, rainbow trout, wild and farmed abalone and ocean trout.
- Tasmania is full of award-winning cheeses, such as those from the *King Island Cheese Company*.
- Goat, quail and venison are the area's speciality meats.
- Liqueur honey is delicious.
- Tasmania grows 60 per cent of Australia's apple exports.
- Other fruit and vegetables that are grown in Tasmania include asparagus, red tomatoes, apples, cherries, nectarines, berries and exotic mushrooms.
- *Périgord Truffles* are delicious black truffles.

Regional drinks:

- Tasmanian wine is favoured by Sydney's top restaurants and has won several international awards. Tasmania specialises in pinot noir. *Pirie* is the flagship sparkling wine produced by *Pipers Brook Vineyard*.
- Tasmania produces two popular beers: *Boags* and *Cascade*.

NIGHTLIFE: There are casinos in Hobart and Launceston. Hobart's waterfront area, Salamanca Place, is the home of many night-time haunts in its old stone warehouses. Small, traditional-style pubs, open all day and into the small hours of the morning, are a special feature here. Hobart boasts Australia's oldest theatre, the Theatre Royal, and the city's concert hall is the home of the Tasmanian Symphony Orchestra, generally considered to be one of Australia's best orchestras.

A B C D E F G H I J K L M N O P Q R S T U V W X Y Z

Business

CONFERENCES/CONVENTIONS: The major convention centres in Hobart are Wrest Point Federal Hotel, Casino and Convention Centre and Hotel Grand Chancellor Launceston. Launceston's major convention centres are Launceston Convention Centre/Albert Hall, Federal Launceston Country Club and Casino and Launceston International Hotel.

COMMERCIAL INFORMATION

Tasmanian Chamber of Commerce and Industry (TCCI)
Industry House, 30 Burnett Street, North Hobart, TAS 7000, Australia
Tel: (3) 6236 3600.
Website: www.tcci.com.au

Tasmanian Convention Bureau
Level 3, 18 Elizabeth Street, Hobart, TAS 7000, Australia
Tel: (3) 6224 6852.
Website: www.tasmaniaconventions.com

Victoria

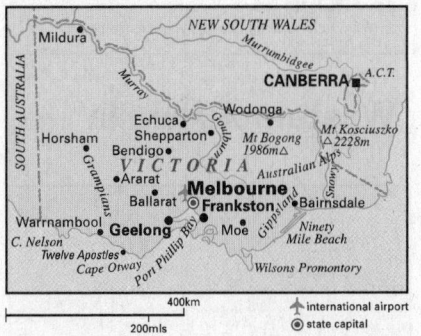

Location: Southeast Australia, south of New South Wales.

Time: GMT + 10 (GMT + 11 from first Sunday in October to last Saturday in March).

Overview

Victoria is the most densely populated of the mainland States in Australia, yet it is also the smallest. There are ample reasons for its popularity, despites its minor size. Victoria boasts everything from tranquil wine regions to multicultural cities.
Melbourne is thrilling. Its gastronomic selection is second-to-none, and its streets are strewn with museums, bars and art galleries. If you climb the Rialto Towers, you peer down at carefully planned grids that gainsay the vivacity that pulsates through the city. For those desperately seeking quietude, be assured that Victoria has plenty.
Affectionately referred to as the 'Garden State', its landscape is rippled by rolling hills and plunging valleys. Victoria's size means that most attractions are within easy reach of Melbourne. Victoria's hills also offer some of the best snow-sports in the country. And if its classic Australian beaches you want, look no further than Victoria's 1800km of coastline. The Great Ocean Road is considered one of the best scenic drives in Australia, with rock formations, such as the Twelve Apostles, obtruding from golden sand.
The sand, in fact, is as gold-tinged as Victoria's history. The State broke away from New South Wales in 1851. The celebrations continued when, only weeks later, it was announced that gold had been discovered in Victoria. The population grew quickly, as did Victoria's wealth. Towns such as Ballarat with its Sovereign Hill are now popular tourist sites, where visitors can still pan for gold, and historical houses from the gold-rush adorn the roads. Victoria is no longer Australia's most affluent state, but it still has a wealth of riches to tempt any visitor.

General Information

AREA: 227,600 sq km (141,000 sq miles).
POPULATION: 4.97 million (official estimate 2004).
POPULATION DENSITY: 22.0 per sq km.
CAPITAL: Melbourne. **Population:** 3.6 million (official estimate 2004).
GEOGRAPHY: Victoria is Australia's most diverse state and its major agricultural and industrial producer. Located in the southeast, bordered by South Australia and New South Wales, its landscape consists of mountains, rainforests,

Credit: ©David Bell and Juliet Sinclair

deserts, snowfields, beaches, vineyards, wheatlands and market gardens. The Australian Alps are only three hours away from Melbourne and the Great Ocean Road to South Australia is a day's drive. Victoria has 32 national parks, amounting to a third of Australia's total.

Climate

Hot summers and relatively cool winters. Rainfall is distributed throughout the year. Southern areas can have changeable weather even in summer, often with four seasons' weather in one day.

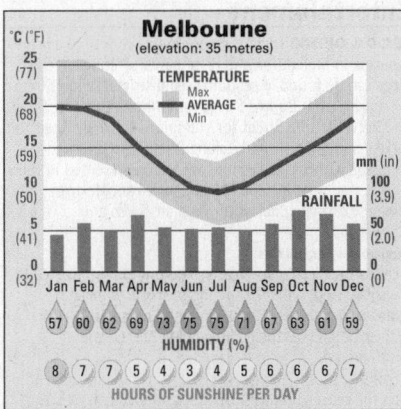

Public Holidays

Victoria observes all the public holidays observed nationwide (see the main *Australia* section) and, in addition, the beneath Public Holidays listed for the January 2006-June 2007 period.
2006: Mar 13 Labour Day. **Jun 12** Queen's Birthday Celebrations. **Nov 7*** Melbourne Cup Day.
2007: Mar 14 Labour Day. **Jun 11** Queen's Birthday Celebrations.
Note: *Melbourne metropolitan area only.

Travel - International

AIR:
 Main airports: *Melbourne (MEL) (Tullamarine)* (website: www.melbourne-airport.com.au) receives flights from the UK (approximate flight time from London – 20 hours), Europe, Asia and the USA. Major international airlines serving Melbourne include *British Airways, KLM, Malaysia Airlines, Qantas* and *United Airlines*. The airport is 22km (14 miles) from the city (travel time – 30 minutes). There are flights from Melbourne to all State capitals and many regional hubs. Domestic carriers include *Jetstar, Qantas* and *Virgin Blue. To/from the airport:* The *Skybus Super Shuttle* links Melbourne city with the airport. Taxis to the city centre cost around A\$40. For more flight details, see the main *Australia* section. *Facilities:* Restaurants, bars, foreign exchange centres, a children's playground and much, much more.
SEA:
 Main ports: An overnight passenger/vehicle ferry from Tasmania to *Melbourne* departs daily (website: www.spiritoftasmania.com.au). There are also ferry services from Melbourne to Williamstown across Port Phillip Bay; between Southgate, Princes Walk and the Melbourne Aquarium and Crown entertainment complex; and across the headlands of Port Phillip Bay between the beach towns of Queenscliff and Sorrento. Melbourne is an increasingly popular port for international cruise ships.

RAIL:
 V-Line (website: www.vlinepassenger.com.au) operates state rail services, with links from Melbourne to Ballarat, Bendigo, Echuca, Geelong, Sale, Seymour, Swan Hill, Traralgon and Wodonga. Overnight trains link Melbourne and Sydney (13 hours), and an overnight train – *The Overland* – runs to Adelaide (12 hours). Trains run to other main centres including Canberra (eight hours 30 minutes), Brisbane (48 hours) and Perth (72 hours).
ROAD:
 Victoria is connected to all States by coach services. To drive to *Adelaide* is nine hours, to *Sydney* is 10 hours, to *Brisbane* is 20 hours and to Perth is two days. There is a well-developed road system covering 156,700km (97,400 miles) on which local buses operate.
URBAN:
Melbourne has an extensive network of electric railways, linked in the city centre by an **underground** loop-line. There is also a **tram** network which has an integrated ticket structure with the **bus** and **rail** systems. Tickets should be purchased before boarding, or from onboard vending machines (trams only). Fares are zonal, with travel cards for daily or weekly travel and multi-journey tickets. The Melbourne *City Circle* tram, in distinct burgundy and gold colours, is free. Buses are relatively inexpensive and usually air-conditioned and equipped with video players. Buses from Adelaide take 11 hours; between Sydney and Melbourne, 12 hours. The *Melbourne City Explorer Bus* and the *City Wanderer Bus* leave hourly to major attractions in the city and the visitor may join or leave at any stopping point in the journey.

Accommodation

HOTELS:
 A variety of accommodation is available in Victoria, ranging from international-standard hotels in Melbourne to farm-stay, home-stay and self-catering holidays throughout the region. Numerous historic bed & breakfast establishments, some of them supported by the National Trust of Australia, are also on offer. There are some cutting-edge hotels now open in Victoria.
BED & BREAKFAST:
 These range from quiet lodges and cottages to farms and classic guest houses. **Farmstays** offer the opportunity to stay in a family homestead and participate in farm activities. Further information can be obtained from Tourism Victoria (see *Top Things To Do*).
CAMPING/CARAVANNING:
 A number of companies can arrange motor camper rentals, with a range of fully-equipped vehicles.

ACCOMMODATION INFORMATION

Australian Hotels Association Victoria
Tel: (3) 9654 7100.
Website: www.ahha.com.au

Parks Victoria
Level 10, 535 Bourke Street, Melbourne, VIC 3000, Australia
Tel: (3) 8627 4699.
Website: www.parkweb.vic.gov.au

Royal Automobile Club of Victoria (RACV)
(Produces a comprehensive guide to tourist park accommodation, available at RACV retail stores in Victoria and also online.)
Website: http://motoring.racv.com

Top Things To See

- **Melbourne** is frequently voted as one of the 'most liveable' cities in the world, and many-a-visitor falls under the spell of this hypnotic State capital, highly cosmopolitan, with sizeable Italian and Greek minorities. It also has its finger on Australia's cultural pulse. Located in **Carlton Gardens** on the northern edge of the city centre, the ultramodern **Melbourne Museum** is Australia's largest museum. The chilling **Old Melbourne Gaol** has Ned Kelly's armour on display (Victoria was the home of the outlaw Ned Kelly, often regarded as a national hero in Australia, and was the scene of the eventful days of bushranging during the gold rush of the 1850s and 1860s). The **National Gallery of Victoria: St Kilda Road** houses Australia's greatest collection of international fine art. **The NGV: Australian Art** is one of the attractions of **Federation Square**, a city block devoted to culture. Meanwhile, **Rialto Towers Observation Deck** offers panoramic views of the city and surrounds. Other places to visit include the **Royal Botanical Gardens**, **Parliament House**, the **Melbourne Cricket Ground** and the vibrant beach-side esplanade in **St Kilda** with its vibrant cafe culture and fun and creepy **Luna Park**, an old-fashioned funfair.
- The **Dandenong Ranges** provide excellent views of Melbourne over the peaks from the **Summit Lookout**. At **Mount Dandenong** itself is the sanctuary named after William Ricketts, one of the early champions of Aboriginal rights. His haunting carvings of Aboriginal faces still stare out over the forested landscape and are part of the **Galeena Beek Aboriginal Culture Centre**.
- **Sovereign Hill**, 120km (75 miles) northwest of Melbourne, is an old gold-rush town, now restored to its original condition. For towns of a similar era, a visitor has to also see **Ballarat** and **Bendigo** (laid over 35 acres and with huge granite, Victorian buildings).
- Stare up at the **Grampian Mountains**, famous for wild flowers and birdlife.
- See a huge variety of wildlife at places such as **Phillip Island Nature Reserve**, with birds, koalas, fairy penguins (which can be seen marching up the beach in the evenings), and fur seals (large colonies of which can be observed at the **Seal Rocks Sea Life Centre**). Another famous wildlife sanctuary is in the **Wilson's Promontory National Park**.
- Count the awesome rock formation along the **Great Ocean Road**, **The Twelve Apostles**, and discover there are only seven.
- Watch the fantastic surf at **Queenscliff**, a town which also has Victorian architecture and a historic railway, as well as horse and cart rides. There are some great handicraft and antique shops.

Top Things To Do

- **Bushwalk** across beloved destinations such as: **Bogong National Park** (with a possible six-day walk including the ascent of **Mount Bogong**, from October to April only); **Mount Feathertop** (a two-day circuit offering scenic mountain views, requiring walkers to be prepared for snowfalls at any time of the year); **Wilson's Promontory** (locally known as 'the Prom', a three-day circuit through beautiful stretches of coastline); and, best of all, the **Grampians** (a spectacular region of sandstone mountain ranges, forests, valleys and heaths, particularly famous for its displays of wildflowers between August to November). For further details, contact VIC Department of Sustainability and Environment, 240-50 Victoria Parade, East Melbourne VIC 3002 (tel: (3) 136 136 within Australia or 5332 5000 outside Australia; website: www.dse.vic.gov.au).
- Try some **wine tasting** at one of Victoria's 350 wineries: tasting tours are widely available. Outstanding wine-growing regions include the **Yarra Valley**; the **Mornington Peninsula**; and the **Rutherglen region** in the Grampians. The Victorian Wineries Tourism Council (website: www.visitvictoria.com/wineries) can provide further details.
- Be daring and try out some **downhill skiing** and **snowboarding** in some of Victoria's **High Country**: **Mount Buller**, **Falls Creek**, **Mount Hotham**, **Mount Buffalo** and **Mount Baw Baw** all have excellent facilities. The **Bogong High Plains**, **Lake Mountain**, **Mount St Gwinear** or **Mount Torbreck** are specifically designed for **cross-country skiing**.
- Attend the regular regatta, **Sail Melbourne**. Melbourne's **Port Philip Bay** is also one of the world's great **yachting** waterways.
- **Whale watch** at **Warrnambool**, where migrating whales can be observed between May and July.
- **Surfing** enthusiasts should head to **Bells Beach** and **Jan Juc** on the Great Ocean Road near **Torquay**, where the **Rip Curl Pro & Quit Classic**, a turtle-A world-rated international surfing contest, is held annually for a period of seven days over Easter. **Woolamai** in **Phillip Island** offers excellent surfing for the more experienced.

- Learn to play **Australian Rules Football**, or 'Aussie Rules', a mixture between football and rugby, which originated in Victoria. The climax of the season (starting in March) is the Australian Football League Grand Final, played in September at the famous **Melbourne Cricket Ground**, which also plays host to the highest standard of international and national cricket matches, and is ranked amongst cricket's most sacred pitches.
- Attend Victoria's biggest event of the season (they have even made it a public holiday): the 3.2km- (2 mile-long) **Melbourne Cup**, the highlight of Australia's **racing** year. This prestigious horse race offers the highest prizes in the southern hemisphere.
- You might strike lucky if you do your own **gold panning**. Northwest of Melbourne, **Sovereign Hill** is located within the country's most famous gold rush destination (Ballarat Tourism [website: www.ballarat.com]).
- Take a **drive** along the stunning **Great Ocean Road**. Make the most of Victoria's superb beaches, such as **Westernport Bay**, **Ninety Mile Beach** (in the **Gippsland Lakes** area) and along the **Bellarine Peninsula** near **Geelong**.

Entertainment

FOOD & DRINK: There is an enormous variety of cuisine available in Melbourne and restaurants offering specific types can be found in sectionalised districts: Lygon Street for Italian, Little Bourke Street for Chinese, Lonsdale Street for Greek, Victoria Street for Vietnamese, Sydney Road for Turkish and Spanish, and Acland Street for Central European. Other cuisines that are well represented in the city's restaurants include French, American, Mexican, Lebanese, African, Malaysian, Afghan, Swiss and Mongolian.

Regional specialities:
- Fish is excellent, particularly the signature Murray cod. Also try trout, chinook salmon and yellow perch.
- Meats such as venison, beef, lamb and game.
- Cheeses, such as the creamy goat cheese from Rutherglen.
- Fruits, such as cherries (sweet or sour morello, depending on the season, quinces, berries, stone fruit, apples and yabbies.
- The area is abound with treats of the countryside, including wild mushrooms, morel mushrooms and sweet chestnuts.

Regional drinks:
- Wine is popular, from a crisp Sauvignon blanc to a sturdy Cabernet Sauvignon.

NIGHTLIFE: Melbourne is home to a vibrant and varied entertainment culture that comes alive at night. There is everything from ballet, classical concerts and opera to plays in Melbourne's ornate theatres like the *Princess* and *Regent*, and street performers. There is an eclectic array of pubs, bars and nightclubs in and around Melbourne. Whatever your taste, there is something to suit everyone, whether it is a laid-back beer in an authentic Aussie pub, a comedy night, live bands playing jazz and blues music or upmarket dance clubs. The *Crown Casino Complex*, located on the bank of the Yarra River in Melbourne, is a complete amusement area that includes a casino, cinemas, restaurants, bowling alley and nightclubs.

SHOPPING: Food products such as honeys, jams, chutneys and the local wines of *Yarra Valley* are popular buys. Traditional sheepskins and the Australian's answer to the raincoat, the *drizabone*, can be found here. Melbourne is a major fashion centre, home to the world-famous surfing brand, *Quicksilver*, and shoppers looking for Australian and international designer wear should head for the city arcades or Howey Place. Unusual buys and bargains can be found at the Queen Victoria Market. **Shopping hours:** Mon-Wed 0900-1730; Thurs and Fri 0900-1730 but some will have a 'late-night shopping' policy and stay open until 1900 or even 2100; Sat and Sun 0900-1730 but some may not open until 1100 or 1200. All major supermarkets are open 24 hours.

Business

CONFERENCES/CONVENTIONS: Melbourne, Australia's second-largest city and gateway to the southern region, has convention facilities to match international standards – the Melbourne Exhibition and Convention Centre is the largest exhibition space in the southern hemisphere with 50 meeting rooms, 10,000sq m of exhibition space and

---

three state-of-the-art theatres. The World Congress Centre also has a large number of meeting rooms. A casino-leisure complex, Crown Towers, offers unsurpassed luxury with lavish guest rooms. Major convention facilities include Dallas Brooks Conference Centre, Melbourne Hilton on the Park, Hyatt on Collins, the Radisson President Hotel and Convention Centre, Regent of Melbourne, Royal Exhibition Building and Convention Centre, Southern Cross Hotel, Melbourne Park Tennis Centre and Victorian Arts Centre.

Western Australia

Location: Western part of Australia.

Time: GMT + 8.

Overview

Western Australia has a reputation for being bleak and vast. Its State Capital, Perth, is regarded as being 'the most isolated city on the planet' - one spot of civilisation amid a sprawling mix of outback, desert and wilderness.
It is true that Western Australia is the largest state in Australia, covering an area of around 2.5 million sq km (1 million sq miles), constituting one-third of the country. This one State could fit the Texan state *twice* into its perimeters. Such remoteness is somewhat a curse, with long distances between attractions.
However, the effort is truly worth it. Western Australia is vast but not solely bleak. Its diversity often astonishes, with extreme contrasts in climate from north to south. Although there is desert to the east, there is pristine coastline to the west. Although there is the desolate Kimberley region to the north, there are also emerald, rolling pastures to the south.
Lots of Western Australia's natural wonders are anything but barren: enormous lakes and gorges; spectacular waterfalls; the world's largest monocline, Mount Augustus; scores of colourful wildflowers that speckle the mid-west region; and the aptly named Shell Beach, one of only two in the world, and formed by the deposits of billions of tiny

white seashells. In this one State, you can go from hand-feeding friendly dolphins in Monkey Mia to riding camels at Cameleer Park.

With its wealth of natural resources, including gold (the largest open-cut gold mine is in Kalgoorlie), iron, ore, gas and minerals, the land of Western Australia is one blessed by ancient and astounding ecology.

General Information

AREA: 2,529,880 sq km (976,787 sq miles).
POPULATION: 2 million (official estimate 2004).
POPULATION DENSITY: 0.8 per sq km.
CAPITAL: Perth. **Population:** 1.5 million (official estimate 2003).
GEOGRAPHY: Western Australia covers one-third of Australia; it is larger than Western Europe, but has a population only one-sixth that of London. It is bordered in the east by South Australia and the Northern Territory and in the west by the Indian Ocean, with the Timor Sea to the north. The west coast is nearer to Bali and Indonesia than to Sydney, making Perth a viable stopover destination en route to the rest of Australia. To the south, the nearest land mass is Antarctica, 2600km (1600 miles) away. It has mineral wealth in iron, bauxite, nickel, natural gas, oil, diamonds and gold. There are vast wheatlands, forests and deserts, and several national parks. A popular resort is Rottnest Island; there are also many excellent mainland beaches, particularly around Perth. Kimberley, in the far north, is one of the oldest geological areas on earth, a region where time and weather have formed deep gorges and impressive mountains, arid red plains and coastal sandstone rich in fossils. In the northwest there are two notable features: Wolf Creek Crater, an immense hole left in the desert by a giant meteorite 50,000 years ago, and the Bungle Bungles, an ancient sandstone massif covering 3000 sq km (1160 sq miles). Southeast of Perth, near Hyden, is the 2700-million-year-old Wave Rock.

Climate

Hot summers (December to February), mild winters (June to August). North is tropical. South is subtropical to temperate. Rainfall varies from area to area.

Public Holidays

Western Australia recognises all the public holidays observed nationwide (see the main *Australia* section) and, in addition, the beneath Public Holidays listed for the January 2006-June 2007 period.
2006: Mar 6 Labour Day. **Jun 5** Foundation Day. **Oct 2** Queen's Birthday Celebrations.
2007: Mar 5 Labour Day. **Jun 4** Foundation Day.

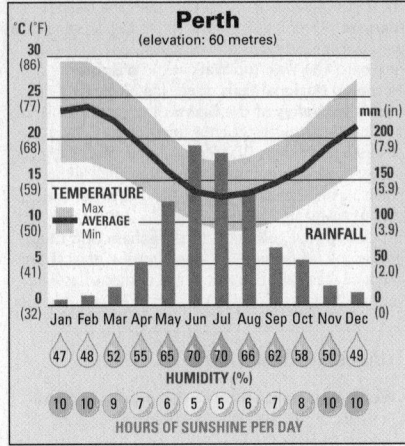

Perth
(elevation: 60 metres)

TEMPERATURE
Max
AVERAGE
Min

RAINFALL

HUMIDITY (%)
47 48 52 55 65 70 70 66 62 58 50 49

HOURS OF SUNSHINE PER DAY
10 10 9 7 6 5 5 6 7 8 10 10

Travel - International

AIR:

There are international flights to Perth from Europe and Asia. International airlines serving Perth include *Air Mauritius, Air New Zealand, British Airways, Cathay Pacific Airways, Garuda Indonesia, Malaysia Airlines, Qantas, Singapore Airlines, South Africa Airlines, Thai Airways International* and *United Airlines.* Flying time from *London* is 18 hours. There are internal flights from all state capitals. Domestic carriers include *Airnorth, Qantas, Skywest* (within Western Australia only) and *Virgin Blue.*
Main airports: *Perth International Airport (PER)* (website: www.perthairport.net.au) is 12km (7 miles) from the city (travel time – 25 minutes).

SEA:

Main ports: *Port of Fremantle* serves Perth. The port is 19km (11 miles) from Perth.

RAIL:

Western Australia is served by *Transwa* rail service (website: www.transwa.wa.gov.au). An electric tram runs between Perth and Fremantle. The *Indian Pacific* service runs from Perth to Sydney twice a week and is a three-day trip with beautiful scenery to admire as you travel.

ROAD:

The highway network of Western Australia is almost entirely concentrated in the coastal areas. The main exception is the *Great Northern Highway* which runs from Perth to Port Headland on the northwest coast. Along the south coast is the *Eyre Highway,* which runs into South Australia. The *Brand/Northwest Coastal Highway* runs from Perth

around the west coast to Kimberley. The journey between Perth and Sydney takes at least four days. Driving maps can be purchased via the Western Australian Tourism Commission (see *Top Things To Do* section). There is only one express **coach** route from Perth and it goes to Adelaide (travel time – 35 hours). *Integrity Coach Lines* and *South West Coachlines* run coach services throughout the southern part of Western Australia.
URBAN:

Transperth (website: www.transperth.wa.gov.au) offers a fully integrated service across all **bus**, **train** and **ferry** services within Perth. Local trains run from Perth to Armadale, Midland, Fremantle and Joondalup. A zonal fare structure covers all transport modes; tickets issued on one mode are valid for transfer to any of the others (bus, rail and ferry). A free *CAT Clipper Bus* service circles the city centres of Perth and Fremantle Monday to Saturday.

Accommodation

HOTELS:

There is a wide range of hotels and motels in Western Australia, including **5-star** (luxury), **4-star** (deluxe), **3-star** (standard) and **2-star** (economy).
HOLIDAY FLATS:

An extensive range of holiday flats is available, both in Perth and the rest of the State.

CAMPING/CARAVANNING:

There are many caravan parks and campsites in the State, most of which are located off the main highways. A number of companies also arrange **motor camper** rentals, with a range of vehicles.

Top Things To See

- Modern skyscrapers overshadow colonial buildings such as the **Town Hall** and **Perth Mint** in the perennially sunny **Perth**. The **Swan River** winds through this attractive State Capital. The **Swan Bells** is a futuristic tower resembling a giant swan that houses the old bells from St Martin-in-the-Fields, London. **Kings Park**, a beautiful park overlooking the town, the **Art Gallery of Western Australia** in James Street and the historic **His Majesty's Theatre** are also worth seeing. The most popular beach destinations are **Sorrento**, **Cottesloe**, **City**, **Scarborough** and the nude bathing beach at **Swanbourne**. AQWA **– The Aquarium of Western Australia** at **Hillary's Boat Harbour**, showcases over 4000 sea creatures in their natural environments, and **Adventure World** on **Bibra Lake** offers thrill rides, native animals, parkland and waterways in beautiful surroundings. **Fremantle**, 19km (12 miles) from the city, is a port full of historic houses and buildings such as the **Court House**, all of which have been superbly restored. The excellent **Western Australian Maritime Museum**

A B C D E F G H I J K L M N O P Q R S T U V W X Y Z

and **Fishing Boat Harbour**, with its many outdoor seafood restaurants, are its other attractions.

- Observe a 2700-million-year-old formation resembling a tidal wave about to crash onto prehistoric rock at **Wave Rock**.
- Glance at the peaks of the **Darling Ranges**, behind Perth, which are popular with visitors and contain several national parks. At **Mundaring**, you can step into the **Jewel Caves**, which feature the longest straw stalactite in any tourist cave. Other delights you can stumble across in some of the other caves in the Darling Ranges include the fossil of a Tasmanian tiger dating back about 25,000 years.
- Look at amazing limestone pillars in **Nanbung National Park**: **The Pinnacles** jut out of the sandy ground and provide the perfect snapshot; these calcified spires are around 30,000 years old.
- Stare out at **The Kimberley**, a wild semi-desert region steeped in Aboriginal legends.
- Watch for **whales** and spouting **blowholes** in the first European settlement in Western Australia - **Albany**, founded in 1827. The area includes a **Natural Bridge** which has been formed by ocean erosions and provides an impressive-looking arch.
- Glance at **Guildford**'s wonderful old buildings, original homes and quaint Antique shops. The town provides the perfect gateway to the wine-producing **Swan Valley**.
- Gawp at the imposing sight of the Bungle Bungle Range in **Purnululu National Park**, one of the most fascinating geological landmarks in Western Australia. From a helicopter, the Bungle Bungle Range is an especially imposing sight. Orange and black stripes streak across large, protruding mounds, encased in silica and algae. If you fly across this in helicopter, you are likely to be surprised by a beautiful, hidden world of gorges, pools and palms as you sweep further on.
- Be dazzled by Western Australia's assortment of **wildflowers**, which carpet the ground in Spring.

Top Things To Do

- Get cultural at the **Perth International Arts Festival** (usually held in February/March), which was founded in 1953 by The University of Western Australia and is the oldest international arts festival in Australia. Over 300,000 people each year attend its diverse program of theatre, dance, music, film, visual arts and literature events.
- Make the most of Western Australia's long stretches of unspoilt coastline along the Timor Sea in the north and the Indian Ocean in the southwest, by going **diving**. Major destinations include **Rottnest Island** (notably **Tortoise Bay**, **Jackson Rock** and **Transit Reef**); **Exmouth** (a good base for exploring the **Ningaloo Reef** and the **Muiron Islands**); the **Abroholos Islands** (three groups of islands rated amongst Australia's best dive sites); **Esperance** (the gateway to the **Recherche Archipelago**, which contains hundreds of islands); **Busselton** (good for jetty diving); and **Dunsborough** in the southwest (noted for its famous wreck dive to the *HMS Swan*). The best times for diving are from December to May (in the southern waters) and from March to August (in the northern waters).
- You are spoilt for choice if you want to get close to Western Australia's incredible range of sea-life: hand-feed and stroke wild but amazingly friendly **dolphins** at the well-known **Monkey Mia beach** in the **Gascoyne region** (whose nearby **Shark Bay** is also a World Heritage-listed area and a habitat for turtles, manta rays, whales and sharks); swim with **giant whale sharks**, the world's largest fish, which make frequent appearances between March and early June at **Ningaloo Reef**; and **whale watch** in the Cape to Cape region.
- Perth ranks as one of Australia's top **surfing** destinations and there are many surfing beaches close to the city, such as **City Beach**, **Cottesloe** and **Scarborough**. Other challenging surfing destinations include **Yallingup** and **Margaret River**, whose ominously named beaches, such as **Suicide** and **Grunters**, should attract hardcore surfers only.
- **Walk** in some of the most challenging but sensational land around: the **Bibbulmun Track** (963km/598 miles, from **Kalamunda** to **Albany**) has access to circuit walks through the southwestern *karri* forests as well as about 60 accommodation shelters along the route (website: www.bibbulmuntrack.org.au); the **Stirling Range** contains over 500 species of wild flowers; throughout the **Pilbara region**, the major attractions of which are the spectacular red-walled chasms, subterranean pools and waterfalls comprising **Karijini National Park**; and trek through the southwestern **Kimberley region**, Western Australia's main outback destination, which features a cliff-lined coast, rugged mountains and the spectacular **Purnululu (Bungle Bungle) National Park**, a 350-million-year old massif with distinctive beehive-like natural domes.
- Get tipsy on both the scenery and the **wine** in the **Margaret River Wine Region**. The 50 or so wineries in the region are open for cellar door sales and tastings. **Margaret River** is also popular for its surf, arts and crafts and caves, and is a much-loved tourist spot.
- Step onto **The Tree Top Walk at** the **Walpole-Nornalup National Park**, where imposing giant tingle trees in the **Valley of the Giants** offer the possibility of walking 38m (125ft) above the forest on specially designed floorboards. Granting awesome views (although not for those scared of heights!), many find it both humbling and exhilarating to be standing beside the peak of majestic giants.
- Sharpen up your **golf** skills at the **Denham Golf Club**, a unique golf course with "tees" and "greens" of black tar and sandy fairways. Carry a piece of artificial grass with you and then place your ball on it before you hit your shot!

TOURIST INFORMATION

Western Australian Tourism Commission in the UK
Australia Centre, 6th Floor, The Strand,
London WC2B 4LG, UK
Tel: (020) 7438 4647 or (08705) 022 000 (helpline).
Website: www.westernaustralia.com

Entertainment

FOOD & DRINK: A vibrant pavement coffee culture exists in Perth, and Fremantle's South Terrace is home to the aptly named *Cappuccino Strip*. There is also an abundance of international cuisine and interesting dining experiences; for example, eating fish and chips from a converted tram in Fremantle, sampling the excellent Asian food in Subiaco (Perth), enjoying a seafood barbecue in the bush or partaking of a culinary feast in a riverside restaurant along the Swan River.

Regional specialities:

- Excellent seafood comes from the coast around Perth, including king prawns, rock lobster (locals call this crayfish, dhufish, jewfish or barramundi), and special freshwater lobster called *marron*.
- Tropical fruits are abundant - especially banana, mango and papaya.
- Sardines in Fremantle are exceptional.
- Suckling veal, smoked meats and local sausages are all excellent meats.
- Try some *pearl meat*, a prized and costly delicacy that consists of the shell muscle of pearl oysters: the pearl industry is centred around Broome.

Regional drinks:

- There are excellent local wines in Western Australia and vineyards at Swan Valley, Mount Barker and Margaret River.
- *Redback* lager is infamous.

NIGHTLIFE: There are many nightclubs in the Northbridge area of Perth, which is located within easy walking distance from the bus and train stations. Here you can find club venues to cater for all music tastes, including mainstream, hardcore, gay and alternative beats. The large Burswood Resort and Casino complex is also only minutes from Perth city centre. In addition there are many cinemas in Leederville, Fremantle and Perth, as well as several theatres (see the *Independent Theatre Association* for information; website: www.theatre.asn.au).

SHOPPING: Best buys are Argyle diamonds, opals and Aboriginal art. Shops are open all day Saturday and some shops in the suburbs are also open 'late night' on Thursdays. Shops in Perth and Fremantle are open Friday and Sunday nights.

Business

CONFERENCES/CONVENTIONS: The major convention centres are the Hilton Hotel, Hyatt Regency Hotel, Observation City Resort Hotel, Perth International Hotel, Sheraton Hotel, the Superdrome and also Burswood Resort and Convention and Exhibition Centre, only 3km (2 miles) from the city centre, with seating available for 2000 for conventions or 21,000 for exhibitions.

COMMERCIAL INFORMATION

Chamber of Commerce and Industry of Western Australia (CCIWA)
PO Box 6209, East Perth, WA 6892, Australia
Tel: (8) 9365 7555.
Website: www.cciwa.com

Perth Convention Bureau
Level 7, 172 St Georges Terrace, Perth, WA 6000, Australia
Tel: (8) 9324 3355.
Website: www.pcb.com.au

Austria

Location: Central Europe.

Time: GMT + 1(GMT + 2 from last Sunday in March to last Sunday in October).

Overview

Austria is a country of startling contrasts, from the Austrian Alps in the west to the Danube Basin in the east. It is not only famous as one of the world's premier skiing regions, but also for its historical buildings, world-class museums and galleries, breathtaking scenery, magnificent mountains and established hiking trails. Visitors in search of culture and visitors in search of scenery are spoilt alike. In addition to natural wealth, the country contains numerous and glorious architectural riches, including frequent reminders of the once-powerful Hapsburgs, who dominated central Europe for seven centuries. It must be said that Austria bears the hallmarks of past Emperorship beautifully: the capital, Vienna, is magnificent with its ornate Opera House and the former imperial residence of the Hofburg; Austria's other cities are similarly infused with a historical magic, notably Salzburg, the birthplace of Mozart, with stunning Baroque churches set before a backdrop of snow-covered peaks; and Innsbruck, in the centre of the Austrian Alps. Many places in Austria are themselves worthy of artistic acclaim, so it is little wonder that Austria has produced and inspired a catalogue of cultural figures. During the 17th and 18th centuries, Austria – and, in particular, Vienna – became one of the major centres of the cultural renaissance associated with the terms Baroque and The Enlightenment; the musical achievements of this period are particularly notable and their note in cultural history still resounds. Remnants of Mozart's legacy are everywhere. However, Austria has also yielded people such as artists Klimt and Schiele, composers Mahler and Schubert, writers Rilke and Schnitzler, psychologists Freud and Rank, and philosophers such as Husserl and Wittgenstein. Nevertheless, Austria strives to cultivate its legacy of the future. The country is a hothouse of striking contemporary architecture, at the forefront of engineering, invention and design, and with a modern, efficient social system. Austria still has a justifiable reputation for music, literature and the arts, with Elfriede Jelinek recently winning the Nobel Prize for Literature in 2004. You are just as likely to find Alpine New Wave punk-rock as you are to find yodelling. In terms of gourmet culture, the legendary *Gemütlichkeit* – a relaxed enjoyment of life – is evident in the cafes where the art of coffee-drinking has been raised to a high art, and the many *Heurigen*, where the latest vintages are accompanied by vast quantities of food. Nightlife is versatile, offering laid-back taverns, beer gardens and excellent *après-ski*, as well as trendy clubs and dance venues packed to the small hours. It seems as if Austria is keen not to be regarded as simply a 'historical' country, but one that also proudly fosters the cultural and social present. Regardless, staring at classic Austrian landscape is a reminder that some things are timeless, destined to always be captivating.

General Information

AREA: 83,858 sq km (32,378 sq miles).
POPULATION: 8 million (UN estimate 2005).
POPULATION DENSITY: 97.4 per sq km.
CAPITAL: Vienna (Wien). **Population:** 1.6 million (official estimate 1999).
GEOGRAPHY: Austria is a landlocked country, bordered by Switzerland, Liechtenstein, Germany, the Czech Republic, the Slovak Republic, Hungary, Slovenia and Italy. It is a mountainous country, nearly half of which is covered with forests. Austria's nine Federal Provinces form a political entity,

Goldenes Kreuz
Privatklinik

Your well-being is close to our heart.

The GOLDENES KREUZ is a hospital that upholds both - tradition and progress - in the interest of the well-being of its patients.

Today, over ninety years after its foundation, this modern private hospital, with its famous maternity unit, maintains a comfortable, hotel-like atmosphere. The 100 beds are arranged in single/double rooms/apartments. All rooms are air-conditioned and equipped with bathrooms, telephone, cable TV, radio, safe and refrigerator. Patients and guests may enjoy the sunny roof terrace or the cafeteria in the winter garden.

Medical care is carried out by our own team of house physicians, who are available day and night, and have excellent practical and scientific training.

Additionally, the GOLDENES KREUZ offers patients the option of being treated by the physician of their choice, who assumes immediate medical responsibility, creating a relationship of trust between physician and patient.

Whenever necessary, specialist consultants of all branches of medicine are available. In the field of ophthalmology and ophthalmic surgery, the following operation can also be performed in the hospital under excellent conditions: special laser applications, cataract and glaucoma surgery, treatment of strabismus for children and adults, lid corrections, etc. Further, the GOLDENES KREUZ has expanded its dermatology and plastic surgical laser unit, incorporating the latest UltraPulse laser technology for precise layer-by-layer tissue removal. As part of the ongoing upgrading of the services – the GOLDENES KREUZ has a department of gynaecological endoscopic surgery and various interdisciplinary departments including one for gynaecological infections and sexually transmitted disease. Furthermore, there is a well equipt department specialized for treatment of diseases of the breast.

- Internal Medicine
- Surgery (including specific fields)
- Gynaecology and Obstetrics
- Neonatal Unit and Maternity Ward
- Anaesthesiology and Intensive Care
- Obstetric Anaesthesia and Chronic Pain Therapy
- Infertility Centre
- Institute for Physical Therapy
- X-ray Department
- Medical Laboratory

Goldenes Kreuz Privatklinik BetriebsGmbH
Lazarettgasse 16-18, A-1090 Wien, Austria
Tel. +43 (1) 40 111 - 0, Fax - 505
verwaltung@goldenes-kreuz.at
www.goldenes-kreuz.at

---

but reflect a diversity of landscapes falling into five sections: the Eastern Alps (62.8 per cent), the Alpine and Carpathian Foothills (11.3 per cent), the Pannonian Lowlands (11.3 per cent), the Vienna Basin (4.4 per cent) and the Granite and Gneiss Highlands or Bohemian Massif (10.1 per cent). Austria's highest mountain is Grossglockner (3798m/12,465ft). On its way from the Black Forest in southern Germany to the Black Sea, the River Danube flows approximately 360km (220 miles) through Austria. The vegetation changes according to the climate: the lower regions are densely wooded, with fir predominating above 1600ft and giving way to larch and stone-pine beyond 4000ft; the Alpine foothills consist predominantly of arable land and grassland (above 2000ft). The Pannonian region is characterised by scrub and heathland.
GOVERNMENT: Federal Republic. **Head of State:** President Heinz Fischer since 2004. **Head of Government:** Chancellor Wolfgang Schüssel since 2000. **Recent history:** Jorg Haider - an extreme right-wing populist - and his party entered Government in January 2000. After a furious initial reaction abroad, which included diplomatic sanctions, the rest of the EU came to terms with the new Government. Against expectations, the Government survived until the autumn of 2002, before an internal *Freiheitlichen* feud between party leader Haider and Riess-Passer spilled over into the administration as a whole and brought it down. The election that followed saw the collapse of the *Freiheitlichen* vote to just 10 per cent – a third of its 1999 level – but Haider's Chancellor Schüssel, who held on to his post, was unable to negotiate an alliance with either of the other two main parties – the SPÖ and the Greens – and was obliged to form a second 'black-and-blue' alliance with the *Freiheitlichen* (after their party colours). In early 2003, the People's Party agreed to form a Government with the Freedom Party, who then proceeded to disband in 2003 when Haider set up the Alliance for Austria's Future. In April 2004, Heinz Fischer was elected President. Austria still succeeds in generating issues of right-wing contention: recent figures in late 2003 indicated that Austria had the most restrictive asylum laws in Europe.
Austria is a federal Republic with bicameral legislature. The 183-member National Council is elected for four years; the 64 members of Federal Council do not have fixed terms. The President, elected for a six-year term, is Head of State. Executive power is held by the Chancellor, normally the leader of the largest party in Parliament, who leads a Cabinet of Ministers.

LANGUAGE: German is the official language. Regional dialects are pronounced and within the different regions of the country one will encounter marked variations from *Hochdeutsch*, ie 'standard' German. There are Croatian and Slovene-speaking minorities in the Burgenland and southern Carinthia respectively.
RELIGION: 78 per cent Roman Catholic, 5 per cent Protestant, 5 per cent Muslim, 12 per cent other religious sects.
ELECTRICITY: 220 volts AC, 50Hz. Round two-pin European plugs are standard.
SOCIAL CONVENTIONS: Austrians tend to be quite formal in both their social and business dealings. They do not use first names when being introduced, but after the initial meeting first names are often used. Handshaking is normal when saying hello and goodbye. It is considered impolite to enter a restaurant or shop without saying Guten Tag or, more usually, Grüss Gott; similarly, to leave without saying Auf Wiedersehen can cause offence. Social pleasantries and some exchange of small-talk is appreciated. If invited out to dinner, flowers should be brought for the hostess. The Church enjoys a high and respected position in Austrian society, which should be kept in mind by the visitor. It is customary to dress up for the opera or the theatre.

Climate

Austria enjoys a moderate continental climate: summers are warm and pleasant with cool nights, and winters are sunny, with snow levels high enough for widespread winter sports.
Required clothing: European clothes according to season. Alpine wear for mountain resorts.

Communications

Telephone: Full IDD facilities available. Country code: 43. Call boxes are grey and found in all areas. International calls can be made from payphones with four coin slots. Trunk calls within Austria and to 40 countries are cheaper Mon-Fri 1800-0800 and approximately 35 per cent cheaper at the weekend (from 1300 Saturday to 0800 Monday).
Mobile telephone: Roaming agreements exist with most international mobile phone companies. Coverage is good.
Internet: Available throughout Austria. There are many Internet cafes.

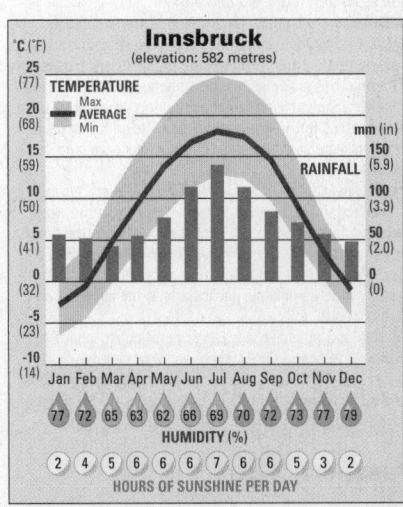

Innsbruck (elevation: 582 metres)

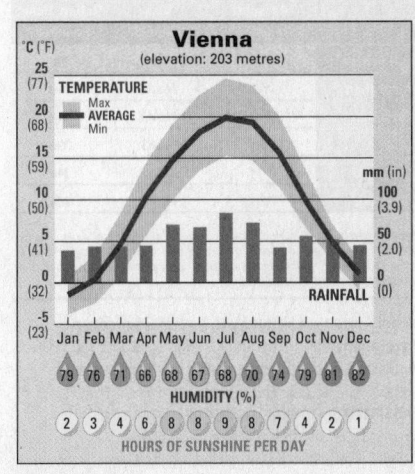

Vienna (elevation: 203 metres)

Credit: ©Austrian National Tourist Office

Post: Letters up to 20g and postcards within Europe are sent by airmail. Letters within Europe take two to four days, and to the USA four to six days. Postcards and letters within Austria and Europe cost €0.55 (€1 if non-priority); to all other countries the cost is €1.25. Post boxes are yellow or orange; red stripes mean that the box is also emptied weekends and bank holidays. Post office hours: generally Mon-Fri 0800-1200 and 1400-1800, and Sat various hours, but main post offices and those at major railway stations are open for 24 hours, seven days a week, including public holidays. Monetary transactions in all post offices permitted Mon to Fri until 1700, Sat 0800-1000.

MEDIA: Austria's public broadcaster, *Österreichischer Rundfunk*, has long-dominated the airwaves, but now faces growing competition from private broadcasters, particularly in Vienna. This is a relatively new phenomenon to Austria. Some German cable or satellite channels deliberately tailor their content for Austrian audiences. The print market is mainly privately owned and fiercely competitive and popular.

Press: Newspapers are in German. *The Wiener Zeitung*, established in 1703, is the oldest newspaper in the world. The national daily with the largest circulation is the *Neue Kronenzeitung*, followed by *Der Kurier*, *Der Standard* and *Die Presse*. English-language newspapers and magazines are also widely available, particularly in the big cities and tourist resorts.

TV: *ORF* is a public broadcaster, operating national TV channels *ORF1* and *ORF2*. There are also national commercial TV stations available terrestrially and via cable.

Radio: There are a number of both public and commercial radio stations.

Passport/Visa

	Passport Required?	Visa Required?	Return Ticket Required?
Full British	1	No	No
Australian	Yes	No/3	Yes
Canadian	Yes	No/3	Yes
USA	Yes	No/3	Yes
Other EU	1	No	No
Japanese	Yes	No/2	No

Note: *Regulations and requirements may be subject to change at short notice, and you are advised to contact the appropriate diplomatic or consular authority before finalising travel arrangements. Any numbers in the chart refer to the footnotes below.*

Note: Austria is a signatory to the 1995 **Schengen Agreement**. For further details about passport and visa regulations in the Schengen area, see the introductory section *How to Use This Guide*.

PASSPORTS: Passport valid for at least three months beyond length of stay required by all except:

1. EU/EEA nationals (EU + Iceland, Liechtenstein, Norway)

and Swiss nationals holding a valid national ID card.

Note: EU and EEA nationals are only required to produce evidence of their EU/EEA nationality and identity in order to be admitted to any EU/EEA Member state. This evidence can take the form of a valid national passport *or* national identity card. Either is acceptable. Possession of a return ticket, any length of validity on their document, sufficient funds for the length of their proposed visit should *not* be imposed.

(b) nationals of monaco.

VISAS: Required by all except the following:

(a) nationals of EU countries and nationals of Iceland, Liechtenstein, Norway and Switzerland for an unlimited period (nationals of Iceland and Norway cannot remain for an unlimited period);

(b) **2.** nationals of Japan for stays of up to 90 days;

(c) **3.** nationals of Andorra, Argentina, Australia, Bolivia, Brazil, Brunei, Bulgaria, Canada, Chile, Costa Rica, Croatia, East Timor, El Salvador, Guatemala, Honduras, Hong Kong (SAR), Israel, Korea (Rep), Macau (SAR), Malaysia, Mexico, Monaco, New Zealand, Nicaragua, Niue, Panama, Paraguay, Romania, San Marino, Singapore, Uruguay, USA, Vatican City and Venezuela for touristic stays of up to three months;

(d) transit passengers continuing their journey by the same or first connecting aircraft, provided holding valid onward or return documentation and not leaving the airport (only applicable if arriving from/departing to a non-Schengen country).

Note: Nationals of Afghanistan, Bangladesh, Congo (Dem Rep), Eritrea, Ethiopia, Ghana, Iran, Iraq, Liberia, Nigeria, Pakistan, Somalia and Sri Lanka passing through Austria *always* require a transit visa, even when not leaving the airport. Transit passengers are advised to check transit regulations with the relevant Embassy or Consulate before travelling.

Types of visa and cost: A uniform type of visa, the *Schengen* visa, is issued for all types of visit, costing £23.80. Spouses and children of EU nationals (providing spouse's passport and the original marriage certificate are produced) receive their visas free of charge; enquire at Embassy for details.

Validity: Validity according to documents presented. Visas cannot be extended; a new application must be made each time.

Application to: Consulate (or Consular section at Embassy); see *Passport/Visa Information*. Travellers visiting just one Schengen country should apply to the Consulate of that country; travellers visiting more than one Schengen country should apply to the Consulate of the country chosen as the main destination *or* the first country they will enter that requires them to have a visa (if they have no main destination).

Note: Visa applications can be sent by post or made in person. If using the latter method in the UK, an appointment will need to be arranged by telephone (tel: (020) 7344 3289) or online (e-mail: www.visa.london-ob@bmaa.gv.at).

Application requirements: *Transit/Airport Transit*: (a) Completed application form(s). (b) Passport valid for at least three months beyond the validity of the visa with at least one blank page. (c) Fee (cash or postal order only; postal order only for postal applications). (d) Two passport-size photos. (e) Proof of transport (airline tickets, vehicle papers, train reservation etc). (f) Visa for onward destination country, if applicable. (g) Proof of funds in the form of bank statements or traveller's cheques. A minimum of £30 per day, per person is required. (h) An all-risk medical insurance policy covering duration of visa (minimum coverage: £15,000 for entire period of stay). (i) Postal applicants should enclose a self-addressed, prepaid envelope (registered or recorded delivery) for the return of the passport. *Visitor*: (a)-(i) and, (j) Proof of occupation/student status. (k) Confirmed hotel or tour reservation or letter from business partner in Austria or letter of invitation from Austrian host.

Note: All documents must be submitted in both their original form, plus one duplicate.

Working days required: Five. Several weeks for nationals of Afghanistan, Algeria, Bangladesh, Burundi, Colombia, Congo (Dem Rep), Egypt, Ghana, Indonesia, Iran, Iraq, Jordan, Korea (Dem Rep), Kuwait, Lebanon, Libya, Nigeria, Pakistan, Palestine, The Philippines, Rwanda, Saudi Arabia, Somalia, Sudan, Surinam, Syrian Arab Republic, Togo and Yemen.

Temporary residence: Seek advice from the Austrian Embassy.

PASSPORT/VISA INFORMATION

Austrian Embassy in the UK
18 Belgrave Mews West, London SW1X 8HU, UK
Tel: (020) 7235 3731 *or* 7344 3289 *or* (09065) 508 961 (24-hour visa information).
Website: www.aussenministerium.at
Opening hours: Mon-Fri 0900-1200 (personal callers); 0900-1645 (telephone enquiries); 0900-1200 (visa section); 1400-1600 (telephone visa enquiries).

Embassy of the Republic of Austria in the USA
3524 International Court, NW,
Washington, DC 20008, USA
Tel: (202) 895 6700 *or* 895 6711 (consular section).
Website: www.austria.org

Money

Single European currency (Euro): The Euro is now the official currency of 12 EU member states (including Austria). The first Euro coins and notes were introduced in January 2002; the Austrian Schilling was in circulation until 28 February 2002, when it was completely replaced by the Euro. Euro (€) = 100 cents. Notes are in denominations of €500, 200, 100, 50, 20, 10 and 5. Coins are in denominations of €2, 1 and 50, 10, 5, 2 and 1 cents.

A B C D E F G H I J K L M N O P Q R S T U V W X Y Z

Currency exchange: Foreign currencies and traveller's cheques can be exchanged at all banks, savings banks and exchange counters at airports and railway stations at the official exchange rates.
Credit & debit cards: Major credit cards are accepted in large cities. However, some smaller hotels may require bills to be paid in cash.
Traveller's cheques: These are widely accepted. To avoid additional exchange rate charges, travellers are advised to take traveller's cheques in a major currency (Euros, US Dollars, Pounds Sterling).
Currency restrictions: No restrictions except for export of more than €7267.28, for which a permit is required.
Banking hours: Mon, Tues, Wed and Fri 0800-1230 and 1330-1500; Thurs 0800-1230 and 1330-1730. Different opening hours may be kept in the various Federal Provinces. The exchange counters at airports and at railway stations are generally open from the first to the last flight or train, which usually means 0800-2200 including weekends.
Exchange rate indicators:
Rate at time of publishing

£1=	€1.46
$1=	€0.82

Duty Free

The following goods may be imported into Austria by persons over 17 years of age arriving from non-EU countries without incurring customs duty:
200 cigarettes or 100 cigarillos or 50 cigars or 250g tobacco or a proportional mix of these products; 1l of spirits over 22 per cent or 2l of fortified wine or spirits up to 22 per cent or 2l of sparkling wine or liqueur and 2l of still wine; 500g of coffee or 200g of extracts, essences or concentrates of coffee, and 100g of tea or 40g of tea extracts; 50g of perfume or eau de toilette; medicinal products sufficient for the journey; goods up to a value of €175.
Abolition of duty free goods within the EU: On 30 June 1999, the sale of duty free alcohol and tobacco at airports and at sea was abolished in all of the original 15 EU member states. Of the 10 new member states that joined the EU on 1 May 2004, these rules already apply to Cyprus and Malta. There are transitional rules in place for visitors returning to one of the original 15 EU countries from one of the other new EU countries. But for the original 15, plus Cyprus and Malta, there are now no limits imposed on importing tobacco and alcohol products from one EU country to another (with the exceptions of Denmark, Finland and Sweden, where limits *are* imposed). Travellers should note that they may be required to prove at customs that the goods purchased are for personal use *only*.

Public Holidays

Below are listed Public Holidays for the January 2006-June 2007 period.
2006: Jan 1 New Year's Day. **Jan 6** Epiphany. **Apr 17** Easter Monday. **May 1** National Holiday. **May 25** Ascension Day. **Jun 5** Whit Monday. **Jun 15** Corpus Christi. **Aug 15** Assumption. **Oct 26** National Holiday. **Nov 1** All Saints' Day. **Dec 8** Immaculate Conception. **Dec 25-26** Christmas.
2007: Jan 1 New Year's Day. **Jan 6** Epiphany. **Apr 9** Easter Monday. **May 1** National Holiday. **May 17** Ascension Day. **May 28** Whit Monday. **Jun 7** Corpus Christi.

Health

	Special Precautions?	Certificate Required?
Yellow Fever	No	No
Cholera	No	No
Typhoid & Polio	No	N/A
Malaria	No	N/A

Note: *Regulations and requirements may be subject to change at short notice, and you are advised to contact your doctor well in advance of your intended date of departure. Any numbers in the chart refer to the footnotes below.*

Food & drink: Milk is pasteurised and dairy products are safe for consumption. Local meat, poultry, seafood, fruit and vegetables are generally safe to eat.
Other risks: Ticks often live in heavily forested areas during the summer months in some of the more easterly parts of Austria and can create discomfort and, in very rare cases, serious infection to people who are bitten. *Tick-borne encephalitis* is endemic and travellers likely to find themselves in wooded areas from spring to autumn should take a course of injections.
Rabies is present in Austria, although there have been no incidents reported in recent years. For those at high risk, vaccination before arrival should be considered. If you are bitten seek medical advice without delay. For more information, consult the *Health* appendix.

Health care:
European Economic Area (EEA) and Switzerland:
If you or any of your dependants are suddenly taken ill or have an accident during a visit to an EEA country or Switzerland, free or reduced-cost necessary treatment is available – in most cases on production of a valid European Health Insurance Card (EHIC). Each country has different rules about state medical provision. In some, treatment is free. In many countries you will have to pay part or all of the cost, and then claim a full or partial refund. The EHIC gives access to state-provided medical treatment only and the scheme gives no entitlement to medical repatriation costs, nor does it cover ongoing illnesses of a non-urgent nature, so comprehensive travel insurance is advised. Note that the EHIC replaces the Form E111, which will no longer be valid after 31 December 2005. Some restrictions apply, depending on your nationality.
The Regional Health Insurance Office (*Gebietskrankenkasse*) will give you a list of doctors working under the state scheme. If you use a private doctor you will be charged but may be entitled to a partial refund.
The following emergency numbers are used: Police: 133; Ambulance: 144. Fire: 122.
You can get prescribed drugs from any pharmacy but you will be charged a fixed amount.
You are covered for both out-patient and in-patient treatment in hospitals, but you need a doctor's referral. There is a non-refundable daily charge for the first 28 days in hospital. If you are treated privately, either at your own request or because of an emergency, you may be entitled to a refund from the Gebietskrankenkasse, which vary from hospital to hospital.
The Gebietskrankenkasse handles reimbursements. To claim money back, send original receipts with your claim. Keep copies of anything you send for your records.
More information can be obtained from the Gebietskrankenkasse responsible for the area where you are staying.

Travel - International

AIR:
Austria has three national airlines, all of which are part of the Austrian Airlines Group (website: www.aua.com): *Austrian Airlines (OS)*, *Austrian Arrows* (formerly Tyrolean Airways) *(VO)* and *Lauda Air (NG)*. Many European airlines serve Austria, as do some budget airlines.
Approximate flight times: From Innsbruck to *London* is two hours and from Salzburg is one hour 50 minutes. From Vienna to *London* is two hours 10 minutes, to *Los Angeles* is 15 hours, to *New York* is nine hours, to *Singapore* is 14 hours and to *Sydney* is 25 hours.
Main airports: *Vienna (VIE)* (Wien-Schwechat) (website: http://english.viennaairport.com) is 18km (11 miles) south-east of the city. *To/from the airport*: Airport buses run between the airport and the South Train and West Train Station for approximately €6 single fare (travel time – 30 minutes). Rail service is available at frequent intervals to and from stations. Local rail (*S-Bahn*) services also run to the city centre (travel time – 25 minutes). Return fare costs €8 (operates daily 0530-2400). The *City Airport Train* travels express from the City Airport Terminal located at Vienna Mitte (travel time - 16 minutes). Taxis are available to the city and can be found north of the Arrivals Hall, costing approximately €25-35. A chauffeur-driven car service is also available from the Arrivals Hall. *Facilities*: Duty free shops, banks, bureaux de change, post office, restaurants, cafes, left luggage, conference facilities, medical facilities, tourist information, car hire, car park and nursery.
Innsbruck (INN) (Kranebitten) (website: www.innsbruck-airport.com) is 5.5km (3.5 miles) west of the city. *To/from the airport*: Bus services are available every 10 minutes to the city centre (travel time – 15 minutes), costing approximately €1.80. Taxi services are also available and cost approximately €10. *Facilities*: Duty free shopping, currency exchange, restaurant, medical facilities and car hire.
Salzburg (SZG) (Maxglan) (website: www.salzburg-airport.com) is 4km (2.5 miles) west of the city. *To/from the airport*: Bus line 77 connects to the *Hauptbahnhof* (main railway station) in the city centre (travel time – 20 minutes) for €1.80. It is also possible to go by train (travel time - 15 to 20 minutes). Taxis are available from the front of the main building for approximately €12.50 (travel time – 15 minutes). Some hotels have courtesy coaches. *Facilities*: Duty free shopping, currency exchange, post office, restaurants and snack bars, bar, left luggage, conference rooms and car hire.
Klagenfurt (KLU) (Wörther See) (website: www.klagenfurt-airport.at) is 4km (2.5 miles) from the city. *To/from the airport*: Bus and taxi services are available. *Facilities*: Bar, duty free shop and car hire.
Linz (LNZ) (website: www.linz-airport.at) is 10km (6 miles)

Credit: ©Austrian National Tourist

from the city. *To/from the airport*: Taxi and bus services are available. *Facilities*: Bar, duty free shop, bank and car hire.
Graz (GRZ) (website: www.flughafen-graz.at) is 10km (6 miles) from the city. *To/from the airport*: Taxis are available to the city and cost €15. Buses operate (a single-way ticket costs €1.60 and there are hourly train services. *Facilities*: Bar, restaurant, bank and car hire.
Note: Airports have fixed charges for portering.
Departure tax: None.
RAIL:
Österreichische Bundesbahnen (ÖBB) (Austrian Federal Railways) operates a wide network of trains throughout and beyond Austria.
International connections from Vienna include trains to Germany (Berlin), to the Russian Federation (Moscow, via Warsaw/Kiev and Minsk), to Romania (Bucharest, via Budapest), to Greece (Athens) or Turkey (Istanbul, via Belgrade) and to Italy (Venice, Milan or Rome). The most common routes are from Brussels or Paris (Eurostar connection from London) to Vienna (see *Channel Tunnel*, below). For further details contact Österreichische Bundesbahnen, Elisabethstraße 9, A-1010 Wien (tel: (1) 930 000; website: www.oebb.at).
Rail passes: Several international rail passes permitting unlimited travel in a number of European countries are valid in Austria. The *Eurailpass* offers unlimited first-class train travel in 17 European countries. Tickets are valid for 15 days, 21 days, one month, two months or three months. The *Eurailpass Saver* ticket offers discounts for two or more people travelling together. The *Eurailpass Youth* ticket is available to those aged under 26 and offers unlimited second-class train travel. The *Eurailpass Flexi* allows either 10 or 15 travel days within a two-month period. The *Eurail Selectpass* is valid in three, four or five bordering countries and allows five, six, eight or 10 travel days (or 15 for five countries) in a two-month period. The *Eurail Regional Pass* allows four to 10 travel days in a two-month period in one of nine regions (usually two or more countries). Children receive a 50 per cent reduction. The passes cannot be sold to residents of Europe, Turkey, Morocco, Algeria, Tunisia or the Russian Federation. Available from *The Eurail Group* (website: www.eurail.com).
The *Inter-Rail* pass offers unlimited second-class train travel in up to 29 European countries (includes Morocco and Turkey) split into eight zones (A-H). Three different tickets are available: a ticket covering one zone (two to six countries, 16 days' validity), a ticket covering two zones (six to 10 countries, 22 days' validity) and an *All Zone Pass* (29 countries, one month's validity). Ferry services between Italy and Greece are included.
Passengers must be resident in Europe for at least six months before the pass is used. Travel is not allowed in the passenger's country of residence. Travellers under 26 years receive a reduction of about 30 per cent. Children's tickets are reduced by about 50 per cent. Supplements are required for some high-speed services, seat reservations and couchettes. Discounts are offered on *Eurostar* and some ferry routes. Available from *Inter Rail* (website: www.interrailnet.com).
The Channel Tunnel: *Eurostar* is a service provided by the railways of Belgium, the UK and France, operating direct high-speed trains from London (*Waterloo International*) to Paris (*Gare du Nord*) and to Brussels (*Midi/Zuid*). It takes two hours 40 minutes from London to Paris (via Lille) and two hours 20 minutes to Brussels. For further information and reservations, contact *Eurostar* (tel: (0870) 600 0792 (travel agents) or (08705) 186 186 (public; within

the UK) or +44 (1233) 617 575 (public; outside the UK); a £5 booking fee applies to all telephone bookings; website: www.eurostar.com); or *Rail Europe* (tel: (08705) 848 848; website: www.raileurope.co.uk). From Brussels, there is a morning and a night train to Vienna (travel time - approximately 13 hours); from Paris (*Gare de l'Est*), there are two trains to Vienna (travel time - 14 hours 45 minutes).

ROAD:

There are numerous and excellent road links with all neighbouring countries. For information on traffic regulations and required documentation, see the *Travel - Internal* section. **Coach:** Coaches run regularly to a large number of European destinations. There are numerous and excellent road links with all neighbouring countries. *Eurolines* (52 Grosvenor Gardens, London SW1W 0AU; tel: (08705) 143 219; website: www.eurolines.com) and *National Express* (Ensign Court, 4 Vicarage Road, Edgbaston, Birmingham B15 3ES; tel: 08705 808 080; website: www.nationalexpress.com) run regular coach services from the UK to Austria and other European cities. Passes: Travellers can either choose Mini-Pass breaks or book a 15-, 30- or 60-day pass. The six Mini-Passes give travellers the freedom to visit three cities, with prices starting from £55. Travellers can stay as long as they like in each city.

Some tour operators offer package holidays to Austria by coach from the UK. A full list is available from the Austrian National Tourist Office (see *Top Things To Do*).

The Channel Tunnel: *Eurotunnel* runs shuttle trains for cars, bicycles, motorcycles, coaches, minibuses, caravans, campervans and other vehicles over 1.85m (6.07ft) between Folkestone in Kent, with direct road access from the M20, and Calais, with links to the A16/A26 motorway (Exit 13). All road vehicles are carried through the tunnel in shuttle trains running between the two terminals. Terminals and shuttles are well-equipped for disabled passengers.

Passenger Terminal buildings contain a variety of shops, restaurants, bureaux de change and other amenities. The journey takes about 35 minutes from platform to platform and around one hour from motorway to motorway. There are up to four passenger shuttles per hour at peak times, 24 hours per day and services run every day of the year. Motorists pass through customs and immigration before they board, with no further checks on arrival. Fares are charged according to length of stay and time of year and whether or not you have a reservation. The price applies to the car, regardless of the number of passengers or size of the car. Promotional deals are frequently available, especially outside the peak holiday seasons. Tickets may be purchased in advance from travel agents, or from Eurotunnel Customer Services in France or the UK with a credit card. For further information, brochures and reservations, contact *Eurotunnel Customer Services UK*, Customer Relations Department, Saint Martin's Plain, Cheriton, Folkestone, Kent CT19 4QD (tel: (08705) 353 535; website: www.eurotunnel.com). For further information about departure times of shuttles at the French terminal, contact *Eurotunnel Customer Information* in Coquelles (tel: France +33 (3) 2100 6543).

Car ferry: There are regular ferry services across the English Channel. The quickest and most practical route from London to Vienna is via the Dover-Calais ferry (crossing time – one hour 30 minutes). The distance by road is approximately 1600km (1000 miles). It is one day's drive in summer, but can take longer in winter. Munich is four to five hours from Vienna; Milan and Zurich are a good day's drive.

RIVER:

DDSG-Blue Danube Schiffahrt operates a passenger service on the Danube from Germany (Passau) to Vienna. For information and reservations, contact them at Friedrichstrasse 7, A-1010 Vienna (tel: (1) 58880; website: www.ddsg-blue-danube.at). The German operator *Wurm und Köck* offers both passenger services and cruises to Linz. Overnight cruise packages from Passau to Linz include hotel accommodation for only slightly more than the regular one-way passenger fare. Evening and music cruises are available in the summer. For further information, contact *Wurm und Köck*, Untere Donaulände, 4020 Linz (tel: (732) 783 607; website: www.donauschiffahrt.at). *DDSG-Blue Danube Schiffahrt* also operates a hydrofoil service from the Praterlande hydrofoil dock in Vienna to Hungary (Budapest; travel time - six hours). *Brandner* concentrates its services between Melk and Krems. For further information, contact *Brandner* at Ufer 50, A-3313 Wallsee (tel: (7433) 259 021; website: www.ms-austria.at). A regular hydrofoil service also runs three times daily during the summer months from Vienna to the Slovak Republic (Bratislava; travel time – one hour 30 minutes). International rail tickets are valid on Danube river boats. More information on the above services, and connections to Serbia & Montenegro (Belgrade), Turkey (Istanbul) and Ukraine (Yalta), can be obtained from the Austrian National Tourist Office (see *Top Things To Do*).

Travel - Internal

AIR:

Vienna is connected to Graz, Klagenfurt, Linz and Salzburg by *Austrian Arrows* (formerly Tyrolean Airways) (VO). **Charter**: There are companies offering charter services for single- and twin-engined aircraft and executive jets.

RIVER/LAKE:

A number of operators run cruises along the Danube, and from Switzerland (Bregenz) across Lake Constance. On some cruises, a passport is needed; they last from one to eight days depending on the itinerary. These services run between spring and autumn. **Ferries:** There are regular passenger boat services from mid-May to mid-September along the Danube and on Austria's lakes. The Danube steamer services are run by *DDSG Blue Danube Schiffahrt* (tel: (1) 588 800) and private companies.

RAIL:

Österreichische Bundesbahnen (ÖBB) (Austrian Federal Railways) runs an efficient internal service, with 5700km network of tracks throughout Austria. There is a frequent intercity service from Vienna to Salzburg, Innsbruck, Graz and Klagenfurt, and regular motorrail services through the Tauern Tunnel. Information and booking can be obtained from railway stations *or* Austrian Federal Railways (see *Travel – International* for contact details). For bookings from the UK, contact *Deutsche Bahn* (German Rail) (tel: (020) 8339 4720; website: www.deutsche-bahn.co.uk); *or* Rail Europe (tel: (08708) 302 008). Tickets can be obtained from any station ticket office (*Reisebüro am Bahnhof*) or from most Austrian travel agents. For further information, consult the Austrian National Tourist Office (see *Top Things To Do*).

Discount fares: Throughout Austria, up to two children under six years who are accompanied or require no seat travel free and a third child qualifies for a 50 per cent discount. Children aged six to 15 pay half fare. **Rail tickets:** The *Vorteilscard* offers a 45 per cent discount on rail travel within a one-year period. This ID card can be purchased at all Austrian railway stations. Those under 26 years can purchase the *Vorteilscard* for approximately €19.90. Austria offers a number of discount rail passes. The *EuroDomino* pass enables holders anything from three to eight days' extensive travel within a one-month period on the entire rail network of their chosen country. It is valid in 28 European countries and North Africa, including the ferry service from Brindisi (Italy) to Igoumenitsa (Greece). To purchase a *EuroDomino* pass you must have been resident in Europe for at least six months and a passport number is required at time of booking. It is not permitted to purchase a pass for travel within your own country of residence.

To qualify for the youth rates, you must be under 26 years on the first date of validity of the pass. Children aged four-11 years inclusive pay half the adult fares rounded up to the nearest pound. Children under four years travel for free.

Seat reservations, couchette and sleeper charges are not included in the cost of the pass and are payable at the normal rate. Passholder fares are payable on some services. Reservation/Supplement charges are payable on all trains within Spain. Available from *Rail Europe* (website: www.raileurope.co.uk/railpasses/eurodomino.htm).

The *Austrian Rail Pass* is available to foreigners. Reductions are also available for groups of more than six people. For more information, contact *Austrian Federal Railways* (see *Travel – International* section) or enquire locally.

ROAD:

Austria has an excellent network of roads. Help is readily given by the Austrian Motoring Association (ÖAMTC); there is a fee for non-members. For emergency breakdowns, dial 120 *or* 123. **Regulations:** Tolls must be paid on all Austrian motorways and 'S' roads. Tourists can purchase either 10-day, two-month or one-year discs which are available at all major border crossings, newsagents, petrol stations, automobile clubs, ÖAMTC and ARBÖ, and at post offices. The 10-day disc costs approximately €7.60 for passenger cars and €4.30 for motorcycles. The two-monthly disc costs €21.80 for cars. Heavy vehicles pay higher tariffs and motorcycles pay less. Infringements will incur fines. All vehicles under 3.5 tonnes maximum permitted laden weight, using the motorways/expressways, require a small device called a Go-Box to be attached to their windscreens (including private vehicles, such as caravans). Drivers of vehicles close to the limit should carry their registration documents clearly stating this. This can be purchased for €5 at approximately 220 sales centres in Austria and neighbouring countries online (website: www.go-maut.at). Prohibitions may apply for vehicles over 7.5 tonnes laden weight, and visitors must check with their relevant Embassy. In addition to the disc to be attached to the vehicle's window, there are other charges for the following major roads: Arlberg-tunnel, Brenner Highway, Dachstein, Telbertauern, Gerlos Alpine, Großglockner-Alpine, Maltatal-Hochalm, Nockalm, Pyhrn Highway (Gleinalm Tunnel), Timmelsjoch, Villacher Alpine, Dobratsch, Sölden-Rettenbachferner-Tiefenbachferner, Tavern Highway, Pyhrn Highway (Bosruck Tunnel) and Silnretta. There are complex driving laws in Austria, especially for caravan and motorhome owners. With effect from 15 November 2005, it is compulsory that cars are driven with lights throughout the year. This regulation applies to all roads including city/towns. Seat belts must be worn and children under the age of 12 and under 150cm tall may not sit in the front seat unless a special child's seat has been fitted. All cars must have a first-aid kit and a warning triangle. All motorists must also carry high-visibility waistcoats complying with European standard EN471 and wear them whenever outside their vehicle on an Austrian roads (besides, obviously, when parked). Both driver and passenger on a motorcycle must wear helmets, and the vehicle must have lights on at all times. Speed limits are 50kph (31mph) in built-up areas (the speed limit in Graz is 30kph), 100kph (62mph) outside built-up areas and 130kph (81mph) on motorways. Traffic drives on the right. **Bus/coach:** Services are run by federal and local authorities, as well as private companies. There are over 1800 services in operation. Some 70 international coach services travel to or through Austria. For further information, contact *Central Bus Information* (tel: (1) 794 440; website: www.postbus.at). Coach excursions and sightseeing tours run from most major cities.

Car hire: There are car hire firms with offices in most cities, as well as at airports and major railway stations.

Documentation: National driving licences issued by EU countries, Norway, Iceland and Liechtenstein are accepted, and enable holders to drive in Austria for up to one year. UK licences without a photo must be accompanied by some form of photo ID such as a passport. The minimum legal age for driving is 18. Car registration papers issued in the UK are also valid in Austria. A Green Card is advised.

Credit: ©Austrian National Tourist Office

A B C D E F G H I J K L M N O P Q R S T U V W X Y Z

Credit: ©Austrian National Tourist Office

URBAN:

 Vienna has an extensive system of **metro**, **bus**, **light rail** and **tramway** services. Most routes have a flat fare, and there are pre-purchase multi-journey tickets and passes. The *Vienna Card* entitles visitors to 72 hours of unlimited travel by underground, bus and tram within four days. It also entitles the holder to reductions at several museums and other tourist attractions in the city, as well as shops, cafes and wine taverns. The card can be purchased at hotels or at Vienna Transport's ticket offices. Those trams marked *schaffnerlos* on the outside of the carriage do not have conductors, but tickets can be bought from machines on board. Tickets are available from newspaper shops or tobacconists called *Trafik*. It is excellent value at €16.90 and permits one child under 15 years to travel free with an adult cardholder. The classic way to travel round the capital is by **horse-drawn carriage** (*Fiaker*); fares should be agreed in advance. There are bus systems in all the other main towns, and also tramways in Linz, Innsbruck and Graz, and trolleybuses in Linz, Innsbruck and Salzburg.

Travel times: The following chart gives approximate travel times (in hours and minutes) from **Vienna** to other major cities/towns in Austria.

	Air	Road	Rail
Salzburg	0.45	3.00	3.18
Innsbruck	1.10	5.00	5.20
Klagenfurt	0.50	4.00	4.25
Graz	0.40	2.40	2.45

Travel Advice

Most visits to Austria are trouble-free but you should be aware of the global risk of indiscriminate international terrorist attacks, which could be against civilian targets, including places frequented by foreigners.

This advice is based on information provided by the Foreign and Commonwealth Office in the UK. It is correct at time of publishing. As the situation can change rapidly, visitors are advised to contact the following organisations for the latest travel advice:

British Foreign and Commonwealth Office
Tel: (0845) 850 2829.
Website: www.fco.gov.uk

US Department of State
Website: http://travel.state.gov/travel

Accommodation

HOTELS:

 87 per cent of 5-star hotels and 50 per cent of 4-star hotels in Austria belong to the Austrian Hotel Association. Classifications are according to the guidelines established by the International Hotel Association and relate to the facilities provided: 5-star for deluxe, 4-star for first class, 3-star for standard, 2-star for economy and 1-star for budget. Some hotels may still be under the old grades of A, B, C, etc.

SELF-CATERING:

 Holiday apartments, chalets, alpine huts and ski lodges are available for rent throughout Austria. For full details contact your local travel agent *or* the Austrian National Tourist Office.

FARM HOLIDAYS:

 There are approximately 29,000 farmhouses with a total of 300,000 beds providing accommodation. Lists of farmhouses taking paying guests for most provinces in Austria are available from the Austrian National Tourist Office. Listings include farms as well as pensions and inns with an attached farming operation.

CAMPING/CARAVANNING:

 There are approximately 500 campsites in Austria, all of which can be entered without any major formalities; approximately 160 sites are equipped for winter camping. Reductions for children are available, and for members of FICC, AIT and FIA. Fees are charged on the usual international scale for parking caravans, motorbikes and cars. The parking of caravans without traction vehicle on or beside the public highways (including motorway parking areas) is prohibited. One can park caravans with traction vehicle beside public highways, if the parking regulations are observed. Some mountain roads are closed to caravans. When camping in private grounds, permission from the landowner, police and municipal council is needed. For more details, contact the automobile clubs or Austrian National Tourist Office.

YOUTH HOSTELS:

Youth hostels can be found throughout Austria and are at the disposal of anyone carrying a membership card of the International Youth Hostel Association. It is advisable to book in advance, especially during peak periods.

DISABLED TRAVELLERS: There are hotels with special facilities for disabled persons in towns all over Austria. Hotel guides for disabled travellers (including a special guide for Vienna) are available from the Austrian National Tourist Office.

ACCOMMODATION INFORMATION

Austrian Hotel Association
Hofburg, Gottfried-von-Einem-Stiege,
A-1010 Vienna, Austria
Tel: (1) 5330 9520.
Website: www.oehv.at

**Österreichische Jugendherbergsverband
(Information on youth hostels)**
Schottenring 28, A-1010 Vienna, Austria
Tel: (1) 533 5353.
Website: www.oejhv.or.at

Camping & Caravanning Club
Schubertring 1-3, A-1010 Vienna, Austria
Tel: (1) 713 6151.
Website: www.campingclub.at

Top Things To See

- No visit to Austria is complete without seeing the capital city, **Vienna**, which oozes Baroque elegance. The *Ringstrasse* forms the boundary of the elegant First District (the *Innerstadt* or Inner City), with its fine architecture, shops and hotels, much of it pedestrianised. Every major architectural style from the Baroque onwards can be found, with especial importance given to the Art Nouveau (Secession) style, which had its roots here. The Hapsburgs, who ruled the country for six centuries, resided in the **Hofburg** where the **Kaiser-Appartements** (**Imperial Apartments**) are - the **Crown Jewels** are now open to the public. **Schloss Schönbrunn**, the sumptuous Imperial summer palace, can be compared with that at Versailles; its landscaped park is also home to the world's oldest zoo. For further culture, the **Akademie der bildenden Künste** (with works by Hieronymous Bosch) is internationally renowned, and there are scores of other galleries too. In addition, there are more than 50 museums open to the public, including the **Natural History Museum**, the **Museum of Modern Art** and the **Museumsquartier**. Immortalised in the film *The Third Man*, the **Ferris Wheel** (*Riesenrad*) in the Prater amusement park is also popular. Well worth a visit are **St Stephen's Cathedral**, the art collection at the **Belvedere Palace**, the **Chapel of the Hofburg**, the **Parliament**, and the **Votive church**. There are also **memorial sites** for Mozart, Haydn, Beethoven, Schubert, Strauss and Freud.

- A recent European Capital of Culture, **Graz** is also Capital of the **Styria region**. From the 15th century, it was a major bulwark against the Turks and, in the 17th century, adopted the Baroque before the rest of the Austrian empire. The city is compact and most important sights are within walking distance of the market square of the **Hauptplatz**. The **Landesmuseum Johanneum**, a large complex of museums, is one of the world's oldest, and includes the **Alte Galerie** with its superb Gothic paintings. The **Neue Galerie** in the **Herbenstrein Palace** displays 19th- and 20th-century paintings, including some works by Schiele and Klimt. There are also coffee houses galore. Other must-sees include the **Cathedral**; the **Mausoleum of Emperor Ferdinand II** (begun in 1614); the pedestrian zone of the old quarter; the **Schlossberg** (**Castle Hill**) with its **Uhrtrum** (clock tower); and the **Glockenturm** (bell tower).

- See the famous *Lipizzaner* **stallions** perform finely executed dressage manoeuvres to Viennese classical music in the **Hofburg** in Vienna, or at a **stud farm** in **Piber**, where they are looked after, trained and ridden.

- View multiple examples of Austria's mountainous landscape: the **Grossglockner** (3798m/12,457ft) in Carinthia is Austria's highest mountain; the **Karawanken Mountains** have a mild climate; the **Hohe Tauern National Park** is one of the last large undisturbed mountain environments in Europe; and the glaciers of the **Silvretta mountain ranges** drop dramatically to the shores of **Lake Constance** with its lush vegetation, plus those seeking Austrian eccentricity will find it in the

Credit: ©Austrian National Tourist Office

Vorarlbergers, who speak a dialect close to Swiss German and declared independence in 1918, requesting a union with Switzerland that was subsequently refused by the Allied Powers.

- Whilst you are at it, take in the awesome panorama of some of Austria's crystal-clear **lakes**: the province **Klagenfurt** lies on the western edge of the **Wörthersee**, the largest lake in the region; **Wolfgangsee**; **Traunsee**; **Hallstättersee**; the **Mondsee** is one of the warmest lakes in the **Salzkammergut**; **Carinthia**'s lakes famously reach temperatures of around 28°C (82°F) and have earned the European Environment Award for their superb water quality.
- Go visit a well-preserved medieval city, like **Retz**, which boasts subterranean wine-cellars, well-restored medieval city walls, windmills and a Dominican church.
- Go to the last protected area of **European rainforest** in the **Donau-Auen National Park**, a floodplain area of wilderness that nurtures a diversity of plants and animals.
- For an elegant and spacious baroque city, you cannot do better than **Salzburg**, watched by the snow-capped mountains of the **Hohe Tauern** to the south. The **Altstadt** (the old city) features the fortress, **Hohensalzburg**, and was granted World Heritage Status by UNESCO in 1996. Interesting sights include the **Peterskirche** (St Peter's Abbey, with cemetery and catacombs), the **Domkirche** (intended to rival St Peter's in Rome) and the **Alter Markt** (old market square). Salzburg's most famous son – although only after his death – is Wolfgang Amadeus Mozart. Mozart's birthplace (**Mozart Geburtshaus**) is in the **Getreidegasse**, also the city's main shopping street, while the family residence (**Mozart Wohnhaus**) is on the market square. Both are museums, with the residence offering a particularly detailed insight into his life and work.
- Be overwhelmed at the magical sight of the **Eisriesenwelt** in **Werfen**: ice caves, with wonderful ice sculptures all-year-round. These caverns are buried deep beneath the mountain wall that flanks the valley south of Salzburg.
- Situated in the heart of the Alpine region, **Tirol** is the most mountainous province, with forests, hamlets and alpine pastures, beautiful valleys and mountain lakes. Traditional Tirolean architecture is reflected in the villages, churches and castles. **Innsbruck** is the Tirolean capital, and twice home of the Winter Olympics. An 800-year-old university town, it has numerous fine buildings dating from Austria's cultural Renaissance in the 16th to 18th centuries, and a 12th-century castle. When Kaiser Maximilian based the imperial court here in the 1490s, the city became a European centre of culture and politics. For spectacular views over the town and southern Alps, take the funicular to **Hungerburg** and then the cable car to **Hafelekar** at 2334m (5928ft).

Top Things To Do

- Make the most of the stunning **Alps** that constitute approximately 60 per cent of the country's surface area, plus Austria's reputation as one of Europe's major destinations for wintersports: **skiing**; **snowboarding**; **tobogganing**; **sleigh rides**; **curling**; or **skating** are all available and with great facilities.
- Take an old 19th-century **steamtrain** and gaze at some picturesque Austrian scenery, including the famous and beautiful village of **St Wolfgang** in Salzkammergut.
- Once the snow has melted, **walk** and **hike** through the Alps' varied landscapes, ranging from forests and green slopes to glaciers and rocks; detailed walking maps can be obtained either from the Austrian National Tourist Office or from the local tourist offices, and guides can be hired locally. Footpaths are recognisable by red-white-red markings displayed on trees and rocks. Near Vienna, a network of city paths (**Stadtwanderwege**) lead through the Vienna woods or the nearby Danube wetlands. The **Vorarlberg**'s alpine pastures are well suited for gentle walks, while the **Hohe Tauern National Park** is popular for more demanding **trekking**.
- Go to the **Opera** in style; besides the many opera performances in Austria's major towns and cities, for one with a difference, journey to **Bregenz** and the **Upper City** with its **St Martinsturm** (St Martin's Tower), the world's largest floating stage for summer opera productions.
- **Climb** the peaks of the Alps; for the very adventurous, combine this with a spot of **hang-gliding**!
- Tour through one of Austria's **wine-growing regions**, such as **Lower Austria**, **Southern Styria** and the **Burgenland**; most wines, such as the well-known *Riesling* wine, are white, but there also some good red wines from **Baden** and **Burgenland**.
- Relax and watch the world go by as you submit to Austria's *Kaffeehaus* (coffee shop) culture: cakes and puddings (such as *Torte*, of which there are around 60 varieties) can be eaten guilt-free, knowing that it is all in the name of upholding a national institution.
- Dance the night away with elegance at a recreation of a traditional **Austrian ball**, at the annual **Johann Strauss Ball**, which takes place in a beautiful ballroom within the **Hofburg Palace** in Vienna.
- Admire traditional Austrian attire at the annual **Lederhosen Festival** in **Windischgarsten**, where the wearing of the aforementioned costume is optional, but drinking good beer and chuckling at the election of 'Miss Lederhose' is compulsory.
- Listen to classical music in the city that produced Mozart: the **Salzburg Festival** (website: www.salzburgfestival.at) provides a varied programme, from singers, actors, orchestras and opera, with a breathtaking baroque backdrop to boot.

Entertainment

FOOD & DRINK: Viennese cuisine is strongly influenced by southeast European cuisine, notably that of Hungary, Serbia, Romania and Dalmatia. Austrian desserts and cake are particularly renowned.

Things to know: The main meal of the day is lunch. All restaurants have waiter service. Generally the strict registration laws mean that the quality of the wine will be fully reflected in its price. Most bars or coffee houses have waiter service and bills are settled with the arrival of drinks.

National specialities:
- *Wiener Schnitzel* is a traditional dish of breadcrumbed and fried veal escalope.
- *Tafelspitz* is the most famous food, regarded as Austria's 'national dish' and consists simply of boiled beef.
- Calf's liver with herbs in butter (*Geröstete Leber*).
- *Goulash*, which is made of beef, pepper, paprika and onion.
- *Kaiserschmarrn* (dessert of shredded pancake and stewed fruit).
- *Palatschinken* (Austrian pancakes).
- *Powidl* is a plum stew.
- *Apfelstrudel*. the classic pudding.
- Cheese Danish, which is sweet and stuffed with raisins.
- Various types of smoked and cured pork.
- Dumplings (*Knödel*) with sauce.
- *Mehlspeisen* is the national term for cakes and puddings. There are around 60 varieties of *Torte*, which is often consumed with coffee.

National drinks:
- Local wines (often served in open carafes) are excellent and cheap: most of the wines are white and *Riesling* and *Veltliner* are particularly well-regarded.
- *Obstler* is a drink found in most German-speaking countries, and is made by distilling various fruits. It is usually very strong, and widely drunk as it is cheap and well flavoured.

Legal drinking age: 16 (for beer and wine); 18 (for spirits). There are no national licensing laws in Austria, but each region has local police closing hours.
Tipping: Widespread, but large amounts are not expected. On restaurant bills, a service charge of 10 to 15 per cent is included, but it is usual to leave a further 5 per cent. Attendants at theatres, cloakrooms or petrol pumps, expect to be tipped €0.15-0.25. Railway and airports have fixed charges for portering. Taxi drivers expect €0.25-0.50 for a short trip and 10 per cent for a longer one.
NIGHTLIFE: Viennese nightlife offers something for every taste: opera, theatre and cabaret as well as numerous discos, bars and nightclubs. There are cinemas of all types, some of them of architectural interest, showing films in different languages. A good way to spend a summer evening is in one of the beer gardens found all over Austria. The wine-growing area around Vienna features wine gardens (*Heurigen*) where visitors can sample local wines in an open-air setting.
SHOPPING: High-quality goods such as handbags, glassware, chinaware and winter sports equipment represent the cream of specialist items found in Austria. A 20 to 32 per cent value-added-tax (called MwSt) is included in the list price of items sold. **Shopping hours:** Shops and stores are generally open from Mon-Fri 0800-1800 (with a one- or two-hour lunch break in the smaller towns) and Sat 1200-1700. In tourist resorts, shops are usually open Mon-Fri until 2100 and Sat/Sun until 1800.

Business

- **GDP:** US$301 billion.
- **Main exports:** Machinery, metals, paper, textiles and food livestock.
- **Main imports:** Machinery and equipment, chemicals, metal goods, oil and oil products and foodstuffs.
- **Main trade partners:** EU, of which Germany is the main trade partner.

ECONOMY: Austria is one of the most prosperous countries in the world. Manufacturing, including mining, accounts for nearly 30 per cent of GDP. Since World War II, much of the country's industrial capacity has been in state hands and only recently has been removed from under the protective wing of the state holding company, OIAG. Iron and steel, chemicals, metalworking and engineering all fall into this category. Tourism is a hugely important part of the Austrian economy. Agriculture has proved equally successful, with domestic products meeting 90 per cent of the country's food needs. Crops include sugar beet, potatoes, grain, grapes, tobacco, flax, hemp and wine. Austria has moderate deposits of iron, lignite, magnesium, lead, copper, salt, zinc and silver. Although there are some oil reserves and an extensive hydroelectric programme, Austria must import the bulk of its energy requirements.
Austria was a member of the European Free Trade Association (EFTA) before it joined the EU in 1995; Germany is now Austria's largest trading partner by a considerable margin, followed by Italy, France, the UK and, outside the EU, Switzerland. Overall, the EU now accounts for approximately two thirds of total Austrian trade. In January 2006, Austria took over the six-month rotating presidency of the EU. The previously substantial trade with both the USA and the former USSR has fallen as a proportion of the total in recent years. After implementing austerity measures to cut government spending, Austria was able to meet the criteria for membership of the single European currency and joined it upon its inception at the beginning of 1999. Since then, in common with most of the EU, the economy has been sluggish. GDP growth was just over 2 per cent in 2004, but inflation was at 2.6 per cent in 2005, the highest in four years.
BUSINESS ETIQUETTE: Austrians are quite formal in their business dealings. A working knowledge of German will be very advantageous. Best times to visit are the spring and autumn months. **Office hours:** Mon-Fri 0800-1230 and 1330-1730.
CONFERENCES/CONVENTIONS: Austria has 31 conference venues, including over 20 in Vienna and a floating conference centre, the *MS Mozart*, on the river Danube. The provincial capitals of Salzburg, Innsbruck, Graz, Linz, Bregenz, Klagenfurt and Eisenstadt also offer convention venues, as do several health and spa resorts. Furthermore, there are approximately 70 hotels in Austria which specialise in the conference/convention field. For more detailed information, contact the Austrian National Tourist Office.

COMMERCIAL INFORMATION

Wirtschaftskammer Österreich (Austrian Federal Economic Chamber)
A-1010 Wien, Stubenring 8-10, Vienna, Austria
Tel: (1) 51450.
Website: http://wko.at/wein

Azerbaijan

Location: Caucasus, western Caspian Sea region.

Time: GMT + 4 (GMT + 5 from last Sunday in March to last Sunday in October).

Overview

There is a running joke among visitors to Azerbaijan - say that you are going to this country to the average Westerner and they will most likely respond with a 'where'? Yet the inability to pinpoint Azerbaijan on a map has proved inconsequential. The recently deceased President Heydar Aliyev succeeded in transforming the country from a relative backwater to a pivotal power in Central Asia. Azerbaijan's provision of airspace and intelligence to US forces after the September 2001 attacks greatly improved its standing in Washington and international affairs. Azerbaijan has expertly ridden the crest of the oil boom, and 5-star hotels have gradually emerged.
However, Azerbaijan has antithesis at its core: wealth mingles with poverty; Soviet blocks jostle with 10th century mosques. Azerbaijan's geographical status has made it a gateway between east and west, and the country was an important stop on the Silk Route. Over the centuries, Azerbaijan has been incorporated into most major regional empires. The process began with the Arabs establishing Islam in the seventh century. In the 11th century, the Seljuk Turks established a Turkish dialect as the main language. Iranians influenced the adherence to the *Shia* branch of Islam. Later, Azerbaijan would spend 40 years as a minor Soviet republic.
This mosaic of historical influence has arguably enriched Azerbaijan: Baku's oldest building, the Synyk Kalah Minaret, dates from 1093; the Shirvanshah's Palace and other fortresses are masterpieces of architecture from the 13th to 15th centuries; Gobustan's rock paintings are some 10,000 years old; and Sheki is one of the oldest settlements in the Caucasus, dating back 2500 years.
Azerbaijanis seem to adopt new cultural and social modes in their stride. Dishes that are Soviet leftovers are now permanent fixtures in traditional Azerbaijani weddings. There have, of course, been ongoing disputes with Armenia over the issue of Nagorno-Karabakh, an autonomous enclave inside Azeri territory with an overwhelming Armenian majority. Also, the current Government has overseen the murder of journalists, plus the use of force to prevent opposition rallies. But the everyday Azerbaijani overlooks such problems, preferring to lavish any visitor with pride of their country. The hospitality of the Azeris is legendary; as is their contentment at whiling away many an hour drinking tea in local restaurants and playing *nards* (backgammon).
Azerbaijan is charming because of its quirks. Some nationals still practice Zoroastrianism. Nature throws up a few surprises, such as the plenitude of mud volcanoes, or the endless burning of fire on the hills of Ramana. It is difficult to know whether it is true when Azerbaijanis claim that their country produces some of the world's longest-lived people. The country's climate, way of life and beauty suggest that it might be.

General Information

AREA: 86,600 sq km (33,400 sq miles).
POPULATION: 8.3 million (official estimate 2005).
POPULATION DENSITY: 95.8 per sq km.
CAPITAL: Baku. **Population:** 1.7 million (1999).
GEOGRAPHY: Azerbaijan is bordered by the Russian Federation, Georgia and Iran, and is divided by the Republic of Armenia into a smaller western part in the Lesser Caucasus and a larger eastern part, stretching from the Greater Caucasus to the Mugan, Mili and Shirvan Steppes and bordered by the Caspian Sea in the east. Its highest peaks are Mount Bazar-Dyuzi (4114m/13,497ft) and Sag-Dag (3886m/12,749ft).
GOVERNMENT: Democratic Republic. Gained independence from the Soviet Union in 1991. **Head of State:** President Ilham Aliyev since 2003. **Head of Government:** Prime Minister Artur Rasizada since 2003.
Recent history: In October 2003, when Heydar Aliyev won another landslide victory as President, many perceived the electoral process as a sham and corruption was suspected. Only two months later, Aliyev died - his death had long been seen as imminent - in hospital, aged 80, after heart and kidney problems. Ilham, his son, emerged as President in his wake.
Ilham Aliyev managed to unify and stabilise the country but at the price of routine corruption, chronic mismanagement and widespread human rights abuses. However, he also helped forge a greater international reputation for Azerbaijan, of which the discovery of potentially huge offshore oil and gas fields in the Azeri sector of the Caspian Sea was probably a major contributing factor.
In November 2005, the first Parliamentary elections were held in Azerbaijan since 2003. The ruling New Azerbaijan Party won 63 of the 125 seats, according to Azeri officials. However, the elections triggered some contention, with international observers complaining of irregularities in the Parliamentary vote and in vote-counting, and with the main opposition, Azadlyq Bloc, planning street protests in response to this result (they won just five seats). These street protests occurred a short time afterwards in November in the capital, Baku, when around 15,000 and then later 20,000 people, took to the streets, claiming that the elections had been rigged. The so-far peaceful demonstrations were calling for the resignation of President Aliyev. However, President Aliyev has asserted that he will permit no popular revolt, although he has ordered two re-runs and one recount in constituencies following the poll and has also promised to punish those responsible for fraud. It is uncertain whether President Aliyev's words will be matched by affirmative action.
Under its post-independence constitution, legislative power is vested in the 125-member *Milli Majlis* (National Assembly); 100 members are elected in single-seat constituencies and the remainder by proportional representation. Executive power is held by the President and a Council of Ministers, which the President appoints. Direct presidential and parliamentary elections are held every five years.
LANGUAGE: Azerbaijani. Russian is widely spoken; English may be spoken in Baku and other main centres.
RELIGION: Mostly Shia Muslim although there are Russian Orthodox and Jewish communities.
ELECTRICITY: 220 volts AC, 50Hz.
SOCIAL CONVENTIONS: Visitors to Azerbaijan may find themselves the recipients of an unexpected bounty in the form of gifts of flowers, food and souvenirs. It is therefore advisable to travel equipped with suitable items - consumables or souvenirs - with which to reciprocate. Local women, particularly in rural areas, tend to be extremely retiring. They will serve a meal, but seldom eat with foreign guests. Visitors may present women with flowers, but overenthusiastic attempts to engage them in conversation may cause offence and embarrassment. Foreign women are treated with elaborate courtesy which can develop into excessive attention. It is therefore advisable for women to dress modestly, especially in the rural areas, and cultivate a certain coolness of manner. Still, many local and foreign women dress in western-style clothes and this is seen as perfectly acceptable. Both men and women should, however, avoid wearing shorts as this will attract unwelcome attention. Although mostly Muslim in population, Azerbaijan is a largely secular society that views religion as a private matter. Handshaking is the normal form of greeting. Business cards are invariably exchanged at any kind of official meeting, and not infrequently on first meeting socially as well.

Climate

Generally very warm, but low temperatures can occur, particularly in the mountains and valleys. Most of the rain-fall is in the west. Please see climate chart on following page.

Communications

Telephone: IDD is available to anywhere in Azerbaijan. Country code: 994. International calls from Azerbaijan may be dialled directly from Baku; calls from other parts of the republic must be made through the operator.
Mobile telephone: Roaming agreements exist with a few

A B C D E F G H I J K L M N O P Q R S T U V W X Y Z

international mobile phone companies. Coverage is mostly limited to the capital and main towns.
Internet: Available in large cities and resorts.
Post: International postal services are sometimes disrupted. Delays occur, although letters should normally take 10 to 14 days to arrive. Parcels should be registered or sent by courier services to accelerate the process and ensure against loss.
MEDIA: There are a number of state-run and public media outlets that compete with private and opposition publications and private broadcasters.
Freedom of speech is guaranteed by the constitution and the media are theoretically free, although there are reported incidents of intimidation and violence against journalists and media outlets critical of the Government. A prominent opposition journalist, Elmar Huseynov, was murdered in 2005. Azerbaijan has made attempts to rectify these allegations by launching a public TV and radio service in 2005, intending to be free from Government control.
Press: Newspapers include *Azadliq*, *Ekho* and *Zerkalo* (in Russian and English). The government daily is *Azarbaycan*. The English-language newspaper is *Baku-Sun*.
TV: There is a newly launched state broadcaster with two national networks, *Azerbaijan TV*, plus *Public TV*. Private stations include *Private ANS TV*, *Space TV* and *Lider TV*.
Radio: There is a state broadcaster with two national networks, *Azerbaijan Radio*. There is also a state-run external service, *Voice of Azerbaijan*. Private-run FM stations include *ANS ChM*, *Radio Lider* and *Radio Azad Azerbaijan*.

Passport/Visa

	Passport Required?	Visa Required?	Return Ticket Required?
Full British	Yes	Yes	No
Australian	Yes	Yes	No
Canadian	Yes	Yes	No
USA	Yes	Yes	No
Other EU	Yes	Yes	No
Japanese	Yes	Yes	No

Note: *Regulations and requirements may be subject to change at short notice, and you are advised to contact the appropriate diplomatic or consular authority before finalising travel arrangements. Any numbers in the chart refer to the footnotes below.*

PASSPORTS: Passport valid for at least three months after date of return required by all.
VISAS: Required by all except nationals of CIS countries (except nationals of Armenia and Turkmenistan who *do* require visas).
Types of visa and cost: *Tourist*, *Private*, *Business* and *Transit*: £27 (single-entry); £54 (double-entry); £167 (multiple-entry). *Express visas*: £35 (single-entry); £70 (double-entry); £230 (multiple-entry).
Note: Multiple-entry visas are only available for *Business* or *Private* visits.
Validity: Contact the Consulate (or Consular section at Embassy) for details of visa validity.
Application to: Consulate (or Consular Section at Embassy); see *Passport/Visa Information*.
Application requirements: (a) Completed application form. (b) Two recent passport-size photos. (c) Valid passport. (d) Fee. *Tourist*: (a)-(d) and, (e) Letter of invitation from a travel agency in Azerbaijan or evidence of confirmed hotel reservation. *Private*: (a)-(d) and, (e) Letter of invitation from a person resident in Azerbaijan, processed through the Consular department of the Ministry of Foreign Affairs in Baku. *Business*: (a)-(d) and, (e) Letter of invitation from a company registered in Azerbaijan. *Transit*: (a)-(d) and, (e) Confirmed onward travel documentation. (f) Valid entry requirements for onward destination.
Note: Applications may be sent in by post, but must be collected from the Embassy either by the applicant or by a third party in possession of a letter of authorisation signed by the applicant.
Working days required: Three to four days for single-entry, five to seven days for multiple-entry and 48 hours for express visas. This does not count the day of lodging.

PASSPORT/VISA INFORMATION

Embassy of the Azerbaijan Republic in the UK
4 Kensington Court, London W8 5DL, UK
Tel: (020) 7938 3412 *or* 5482 (consular section).
E-mail: azembuk@btinternet.com
Opening hours: 0930-1800.
Consular opening hours (located on the lower ground floor of above address): Mon-Fri 1000-1300.

Embassy of Azerbaijan in the USA
2741 34th Street, NW, Washington DC 20008, USA
Tel: (202) 337 3500 *or* 5912 (consular section).
Website: www.azembassy.com

Money

Currency: Azeri Manat (AZM). Notes are in denominations of AZM50,000, 10,000, 1000, 500, 250, 100, 50, 10, 5 and 1.
Currency exchange: US Dollar, Pound Sterling and the Euro are the preferred currencies and can be exchanged at the airport, bureaux de change, all hotels, some restaurants and major banks. However, many local hotels, exchange bureaux and restaurants will not accept dollar bills dated before 1992 or those which are torn or in any way disfigured. Travellers are advised to take banknotes in small denominations and change small amounts of money as required. Rates offered by banks and bureaux de change are unlikely to vary significantly.
Credit & debit cards: Some major credit cards are accepted in Baku, at large hotels, restaurants and banks. However, generally, Azerbaijan is a cash-only economy. Credit cards can be used to purchase tickets at the airport.
Traveller's cheques: Not generally accepted.
Currency restrictions: The import and export of local currency is permitted for residents of Azerbaijan provided the amount is declared on the customs declaration. The import of foreign currency is unlimited although it must be declared on arrival. The export of foreign currency for non-residents is limited up to the amount declared on arrival. The export of foreign currency for residents is limited up to US$10,000 or equivalent; amounts in excess of US$1000 or equivalent are subject to 1 per cent tax.
Banking hours: Mon-Fri 0930-1730.
Exchange rate indicators:
Rate at time of publishing
£1.00= AZM8323.71
$1.00= AZM4618.00

Duty Free

The following goods may be imported into Azerbaijan by persons over 16 years of age without incurring customs duty:
1000 cigarettes or 1000g of tobacco products; *1.5l of spirits and 2l of wine*; *a reasonable quantity of perfume for personal use*; *goods up to a value of US$10,000*.
Note: On entering the country, tourists must complete a customs declaration form which must be retained until departure. This allows the import of articles intended for personal use, including currency and valuables which must be registered on the declaration form.
Prohibited imports: Weapons and ammunition, narcotics, live animals (subject to special permit), photographs and printed material directed against Azerbaijan, fruit and vegetables.
Prohibited exports: Weapons and ammunition, precious metals, works of art and antiques (unless permission has been granted by the Ministry of Culture) and furs.

Public Holidays

Below are listed Public Holidays for the January 2006-June 2007 period.
2006: Jan 1 New Year's Day. **Jan 20** Day of the Martyrs. **Mar 8** International Women's Day. **Mar 21** Novruz Bayramy. **May 9** Victory Day. **May 28** Republic Day. **Jun 15** Day of National Salvation. **Jun 26** Army and Navy Day. **Oct 18** Day of Independence. **Nov 12** Constitution Day. **Nov 17** Day of National Revival. **Dec 31** Day of Azeri Solidarity.
2007: Jan 1 New Year's Day. **Jan 20** Day of the Martyrs. **Mar 8** International Women's Day. **Mar 21** Novruz Bayramy. **Apr 6** Good Friday. **Apr 9** Easter Monday. **May 9** Victory Day. **May 28** Republic Day. **Jun 15** Day of National Salvation. **Jun 26** Army and Navy Day.
Note: Muslim festivals are timed according to local sightings of various phases of the moon and the dates given above are approximations. During the lunar month of Ramadan that precedes Ramazan Bayram, Muslims fast during the day and feast at night and normal business patterns may be interrupted. Some disruption may continue into Ramazan Bayram itself. Ramazan Bayram and Kurban Bayram may last up to several days, depending on the region. For more information, see the *World of Islam* appendix.

Health

	Special Precautions?	Certificate Required?
Yellow Fever	No	No
Cholera	Yes	No
Typhoid & Polio	1	N/A
Malaria	2	N/A

Note: *Regulations and requirements may be subject to change at short notice, and you are advised to contact your doctor well in advance of your intended date of departure. Any numbers in the chart refer to the footnotes below.*

1: Immunisation against typhoid is usually recommended and immunisation against poliomyelitis is sometimes advised.
2: Limited malaria risk, exclusively in the benign vivax form, exists from June through October in southern lowland areas, mainly in the area between the Kura and Arax rivers.
Food & drink: All water should be regarded as being a potential health risk. Water used for drinking, brushing teeth or making ice should have first been boiled or otherwise sterilised. Some parts of Baku have their own water supply from natural mineral springs. Milk is pasteurised and dairy products are safe for consumption. Only eat well-cooked meat and fish, preferably served hot. Salad and mayonnaise may carry increased risk. Vegetables should be cooked and fruit peeled.
Other risks: *Cholera* and *hepatitis A* and *B* do occur in some areas. Inoculation against *hepatitis A* and *B*, *diphtheria*, *tuberculosis* and *tetanus* is recommended before arrival. There may be some risk of *meningitis*, *tick-borne encephalitis* and *leishmaniasis* (cutaneous and visceral).
Rabies is present in some areas. For those at high risk, vaccination before arrival should be considered. If you are bitten, seek medical advice without delay.
Health care: The health service provides free medical treatment for all citizens. However, state-run services in Azerbaijan are limited. Private health care insurance covering emergency repatriation is recommended. Reciprocal health agreements exist between the UK and Azerbaijan, enabling travellers to receive free or low-cost emergency care. If a traveller becomes ill during an organised tour in Azerbaijan, emergency treatment is free, with small sums to be paid for medicines and hospital treatment. If a longer stay than originally planned becomes necessary because of illness, the visitor has to pay for all further treatment – travel insurance is therefore recommended. It is advisable to take a supply of those medicines that are likely to be required (but check first that they may be legally imported). Private chemists in Baku stock a range of the more basic medicines. Travellers are advised to take out an insurance policy which includes emergency repatriation in case of serious illness or accident.

Travel - International

AIR:
The national airline is *Azerbaijan Airlines (AZAL) (J2)*, which operates regular flights to Ankara, London (via Istanbul), Kiev, Dubai, Tehran and Tel Aviv. Some other airlines serve Azerbaijan, including *British Airways*, *Lufthansa*, *Turkish Airlines* and *United Airlines*. Flights into Baku from Moscow and St Petersburg are subject to frequent delays and cancellations.
Main airports: *Baku Bina (BAK)* is 25km (16 miles) east of Baku (travel time – 40 minutes). *To/from the airport*: Taxis and buses are available to the centre. Taxis usually cost AZM40,000 (€10). *Facilities*: Car hire, bank/bureau de change, left luggage facilities and a VIP lounge.
Departure tax: None.
SEA:
Winter storms may disrupt services in Azerbaijan. **Main ports:** *Baku* offers a range of shipping services across the Caspian Sea, including regular trips to Turkmenbashi in Turkmenistan, and to Bandar Anzali and Bandar Nowshar in Iran.
RAIL:
Azerbaijan is connected with Tbilisi in Georgia and Makhachkala in Dagestan (Russian Federation), as well as Moscow and other major cities in the CIS. There is a railway connecting the autonomous republic of Nakhichevan with Tabriz in Iran but there are not yet any connections to the main part of Azerbaijan. Rail travel is slow, and there have been reports of robbery by bandits on some routes.
ROAD:
There are routes from Azerbaijan to Iran, Georgia and the Russian Federation. It may be quicker to use public transport than to drive, owing to lengthy delays at the borders. **Bus:** There are regular services on the following routes: Baku–Tehran, Baku–Tbilisi and Baku–Derbent (Russian Federation).

Travel - Internal

ROAD:
Azerbaijan's road network totals around 57,770km (34,346 miles). Nowadays most roads are in better condition (but still pretty poor) and 4-wheel-drive vehicles are recommended for journeys into the mountains, eg west of Kuba. Roads are badly lit.
Regulations: Traffic drives on the right. Visitors should note that many local drivers do not adhere to traffic regulations and that cars are badly maintained. There is zero tolerance on alcohol consumption while driving. **Car hire:** Car hire facilities are available through *Avis* and *Hertz* in Baku. **Documentation:** An International Driving Permit is required or licence issued by an EU country.

Azerbaijan

URBAN: **Taxi** fares should always be negotiated before starting a journey, and visitors should be aware that rates proposed initially are likely to be unreasonably high. There is an **underground** system totalling 28km (17.5 miles) but most visitors use taxis or private cars. Baku Metro is poorly maintained and the system is often inadequately safe and overcrowded. **Buses** run from central Baku to the suburbs but they tend to be overcrowded.

Travel Advice

Travel to Nagorno-Karabakh, and to the militarily-occupied area around it, is advised against. For further advice, visitors should contact their local government travel advice department. Political rallies or a public gathering of a political nature should be avoided.
In addition, visitors should be aware of the global risk of indiscriminate international terrorist attacks, which could be against civilian targets, including places frequented by foreigners.
This advice is based on information provided by the Foreign and Commonwealth Office in the UK. It is correct at time of publishing. As the situation can change rapidly, visitors are advised to contact the following organisations for the latest travel advice:

British Foreign and Commonwealth Office
Tel: (0845) 850 2829.
Website: www.fco.gov.uk

US Department of State
Website: http://travel.state.gov/travel

Accommodation

HOTELS:
Most hotels are now private and standards of hygiene, service and catering have improved a great deal. Most hotels have satellite connection facilities, telephone and fax services. Many major hotel chains, including Hyatt Regency, Hyatt Park and Grand Hotel Europe, are now represented in Azerbaijan.

Top Things To See

- Immerse yourself in a distinctly Middle-Eastern and relaxed atmosphere within the medieval walled city of **Icheri Sheher** within **Baku**, with its tea-houses and busy street-life. Attractive, narrow streets and stone buildings spread up from the waterfront, where the 12th-century **Maiden's Tower** (*Gyz-Galasy*) looks out over the bay. The **Synyk Kalah Minaret** dates from 1093 and is the oldest building still standing in the city. Beyond the minaret is the 15th-century royal court complex, the **Palace of the Shirvanshahs**. Equally distinctive are the opulent houses and public buildings built during the Baku oil boom at the turn of the 20th century. Millionaire oil merchants indulged themselves with neo-gothic, mock oriental and pseudo-renaissance fantasies in stone, developing a local architectural confidence which spilled over into the Soviet period; the **Sabuchinsky railway station** for example, dating from 1926, is designed to resemble an enormous madrassah (Islamic religious academy).
- As long as you dress and behave respectfully, a visit to an Azerbaijani mosque can be an uplifting experience: there are a number of mosques located in the medieval city of Baku, such as the **Dzhuma Mosque**. The mosque of **Shamakha** outside of Baku is a 10th-century building, as interesting as it is old.
- Inspect glimpses of *Zoroastrianism*, one of the oldest religions in the world, founded by the prophet Zoroaster, and what paved the way for monotheistic acceptance. The **Surakhany Temple** was established by Parsee fire-worshippers living in Baku in the 18th century. The temple was predated by a much older Zoroastrian shrine on the same site. **Ramana**, on the Apsheron Peninsula, also features the remains of ancient oil fields where Zoroastrians still occasionally stage ritual dances, leaping over flames that rise from oil-soaked ground over natural gas vents.
- In the village of **Xinaliq**, outside **Quba**, you will find a unique ethnic group of 1000 *Tats*, who have preserved the original language, customs and traditions of this ancient and threatened Iranian ethnic group from the Caucasus.
- The **Apsheron Peninsula** stretches out into the Caspian Sea beyond Baku and has some stunning 14th-century fortresses built by the Shirvanshahs, fearing attack from the sea: the best-preserved of these are those at Ramana, **Nardaran** and **Mardakan**.
- Travel to the village of **Gobustan**, about 70km (43 miles) south of Baku, and see an unique array of rock paintings, some of them 10,000 years old and spread over 100 sq km (39 sq miles) of caves and rocky outcrops. The subject matter includes hunting scenes, ritual dances, religious ceremonies, ships, animals and constellations, and many of the rocks are further adorned with signatures and remarks added by visiting Roman soldiers in the first century AD, suggesting that the area has a long history as a tourist attraction.
- Visit what archaeological evidence suggests as one of the oldest settlements in the **Caucasus**, dating back 2500 years, at **Sheki**. Tourists can still visit the 18th-century frescoed summer palace and the fortress built by a local warlord who declared Sheki the capital of an independent *khanate*.

Top Things To Do

- Practise being Grand Master at several outdoor **chess**-playing areas (where Gary Kasparov reputedly practised as a boy) throughout Azerbaijan.
- Go to Shamakha, a modern **carpet-weaving** centre, where traditional techniques are demonstrated.
- Watch for **water buffaloes** near the village of Vandam.
- **Climb the multiple spiral staircase** inside Maiden's Tower, which overlooks the Caspian in the old city centre of Baku, and be privy to a stunning 360-degree view of the city.
- Go to the *caravanserai* in the old city centre of Baku, which was once a Silk Road route stopover, and bargain for any item amongst numerous splendid carpets, incense holders and other traditional Middle Eastern goods.
- Smell the fragrant scent of apple blossom in Quba, a gorgeous ancient town on the northeastern slopes of the Shahdag range, surrounded by verdant **apple orchards**.

TOURIST INFORMATION

Azerbaijan Republic Ministry of Youth, Sport & Tourism
370072 Olimpiya str. 4, Azerbaijan
Tel: (12) 906 442.
Website: www.mys.azeri.com

Entertainment

FOOD & DRINK: Azerbaijani food combines Turkish and central Asian elements. Rising pollution levels have given rise to alarm about falling fish stocks, but sturgeon is still widely available at a price. Baku has a reasonable selection of Western style restaurants which have opened recently. In the *chai khanas* (tea houses), men linger for hours drinking sweet black tea out of tiny glasses. A special place in the cuisine belongs to salads prepared from fresh vegetables. Salads are served together with main course. The national cuisine includes more than 30 kinds of soups.
Things to know: Although the majority of Azeris are nominally Shia Muslims, alcohol is widely available.
National specialties:
- The much celebrated *plov* is a delicious, spicy speciality made with pine nuts, vegetables and dried fruit, in addition to rice and mutton; certain types of *plov* use chicken instead of mutton and include chestnuts.
- Grilled kebabs of various kinds are popular, including *lyulya kebab* made from spiced, minced lamb pressed onto skewers.
- Meals often start with rich, heavy soups: *piti* is a mutton soup bulked out with chickpeas and slowly cooked in individual earthenware pots in the oven and served in the same pots; *dogva* is a sharp, yoghurt and spinach-based soup containing rice and meatballs.
- Sturgeon is served both smoked and fresh.
- Caviar has traditionally been fished from the Caspian Sea.
- *Kutab* pastries are stuffed with spinach or pumpkin and are similar to Turkish *birekas*.
- *Kutum Lavangy* is stuffed fish with cherries, walnuts and raisins.
- *Dolma* is minced mutton flesh with onions.
- *Badimjan Dolmasi* is mutton served with plenty of aubergine and tomatoes, basil, sour cream and butter.

National drinks:
- Wines and brandies are produced locally.
- *Sherbets* are popular soft drinks made of sugar, lemon, saffron, seeds of mint and basil and other fruit.
- Tea is often served accompanied by various jams such as quince, fig, apricot, white cherry and plum. Sometimes dried leaves or flowers of savory, clove, cardamom and other spices are added to tea. Tea made of cinnamon (*darchin*) and ginger is popular. Sometimes rose water is added.

Legal drinking age: No minimum age.
Tipping: Expected by waiters and doormen in restaurants – sometimes in advance to ensure service. It is advisable to make enquiries about 'going rates' before entering into negotiations with taxi drivers, market stallholders, etc. It is also customary to tip car park supervisors.
NIGHTLIFE: Several restaurants, late-night bars and nightclubs have opened in Baku in the last few years,

Credit: ©Azerbaijan Republic Ministry of Youth, Sport & Tourism

catering largely for the foreign business community and wealthy local business people. Popular bars include *Chaplin*, *Finnegan's* and *Lancaster Gate*. Concerts, theatre, opera and ballet are a source of local pride and very popular.
SHOPPING: If visitors are intent on acquiring an Azeri carpet, they are advised to visit the carpet-weaving centre at Nardaran. Locally produced silk, ceramics and other craftwork is also sold at the Sharg Bazary (a modern, covered market) in Baku. Prices here are likely to be negotiable. Any carpet or other artefact made before 1960 is subject to an export tax and must be certified for export by the Ministry of Culture. Items purchased at official art salons or tourist shops will already be duly certified. This is not true of goods sold at markets or by private individuals.
Shopping hours: Mon-Sat 0900-2000.

Business

- **GDP:** US$30.01 billion.
- **Main exports:** Oil and oil products.
- **Main imports:** Machinery and equipment, metals, chemicals and foodstuffs.
- **Main trade partners:** Italy, Israel, Georgia, Spain, Iceland, Russia and Turkey.

ECONOMY: Political upheaval – especially the war in Nagorno-Karabakh – and disruption of trading links within the former USSR resulted in a dramatic fall in production levels in Azerbaijan. Since the late 1990s, the economy has undergone a mild recovery. Agriculture is an important part of the economy, in terms of both employment and production. Cotton, grain, fruit and vegetables are the major products; livestock rearing is the other main contributor to the sector. Traditionally, heavy industry, in the form of chemicals, steel and metal products, dominated the industrial sector but there are now also important light industrial operations devoted to food processing and textiles. However, the oil and gas industry offers the greatest promise for Azerbaijan's future economic development. Most of the reserves are located in the Caspian Sea basin and the Azeri government has signed a number of major deals with a variety of consortia for the exploration and development of various offshore fields; the state oil corporation retains a partial share in all of these. In the last few years, the contribution of the service sector – especially transport, telecommunications and trade-related activities – has grown sharply and now accounts for a large part of the economy. Azerbaijan left the Rouble zone in 1993, introducing its own currency, the Manat, the following year. A major privatisation programme was also put into effect that transferred over three-quarters of productive activity into private ownership by 1998. As well as the IMF and the World Bank, which it joined in 1992, Azerbaijan has been accepted for membership of the Islamic Development Bank, the European Bank for Reconstruction and Development (as a 'country of operation') and a number of regional economic and trade organisations.

COMMERCIAL INFORMATION

US-Azerbaijan Chamber of Commerce
1212 Potomac Street, NW, Washington DC 20007, USA
Tel: (202) 333 8702.
Website: www.usacc.org

Chamber of Commerce and Industry
Istiglaliyat kucesi 31-33, 370001 Baku, Azerbaijan
Tel: (12) 928 912.
E-mail: expo@chamber.baku.az

A B C D E F G H I J K L M N O P Q R S T U V W X Y Z

The Bahamas

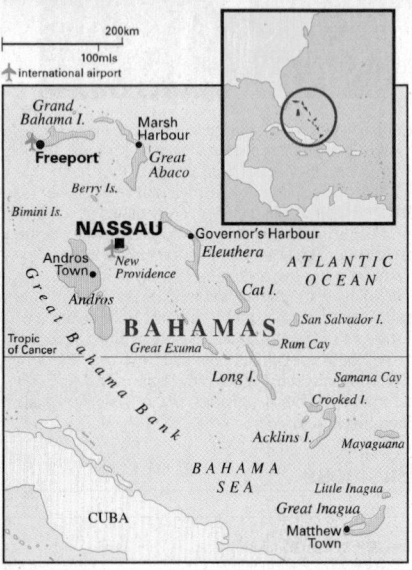

Location: Caribbean, southeast of Florida.

Time: GMT - 5 (GMT + 4 from first Sunday in April to last Sunday in October).

Overview

The 'Bahamas' gets its name from the Spanish, *baja mar*, meaning 'shallow sea'. The turquoise waters that lap this land are as calm and warm as its people. Throughout the 700-plus islands that constitute The Bahamas, residents tend to abide by 'island time', an affectionate term used to describe the Bahamians' laidback demeanour and their slow-moving way of life. It isn't too hard to fall into this habit: many of The Bahamas' islands are either uninhabited or sparsely populated, and from beaches strewn with beautiful seashells to homes painted in soft pastel shades, serenity is easy to find on The Bahamas.

Yet many forget that this mammoth archipelago is twice the size of Spain. For those who want a destination which offers something a bit more than just peaceful seclusion, they will find The Bahamas is large enough to accommodate everyone's tastes. From shopping in the bustling straw market, to golfing in world-class courses, to diving amidst shipwrecks and coral reefs, to windsurfing and parasailing, and then a bit of dancing the night away to the bubbly sounds of *goombay*, calypso and *Junkanoo* music, The Bahamas will not let you get bored if you do not want to be.

It is perhaps for these reasons that The Bahamas attracts fabulously wealthy people to its shores. The post of Governor, representing the British monarch, was once a remote but pleasant sinecure, sought after because of the association of The Bahamas with luxury. The Bahamas does, indeed, have its fair share of exclusive villas and hotel complexes, but The Bahamas was also once a haven for freed slaves and this accepting approach to people from all ways of life persists - you are still more likely to come across a clapboard house and that classic Bahamian hospitality than you are to stumble across a lavish resort. Although many attribute Bahamian 'island time' to its location and the Caribbean stereotypes of mellowness, The Bahamas is not actually classified as a Caribbean country, since it dwells in the Atlantic Ocean. This is just one of the many quirky 'facts' of The Bahamas, and underlines how geographically abstruse the country is. It is best to ignore such petty details, however, and instead contemplate exactly why it was The Bahamas where Ponce de León landed when in search of the legendary Fountain of Youth. Is it because nothing can be more salubrious than an orange sunset sliding into more sand and sea than you can cram into your vista?

General Information

AREA: 13,939 sq km (5382 sq miles).

POPULATION: 303,000 (official estimate 2000).

POPULATION DENSITY: 21.7 per sq km.

CAPITAL: Nassau. **Population:** 172,000 (1997).

GEOGRAPHY: The Bahamas consist of 700 low-lying islands, mostly islets (cays or keys) and rocks. The whole archipelago extends 970km (500 miles) southeastward from the coast of Florida, surrounded by clear, colourful waters. The soil is thin, but on the more developed islands, cultivation has produced exotic flowers. On other islands are large areas of pine forest, rocky and barren land, swamp and unspoilt beaches. The Bahamas are divided into two oceanic features, the Little Bahama Bank and the Great Bahama Bank.

GOVERNMENT: Constitutional monarchy. Gained independence in 1973. **Head of State:** HM Queen Elizabeth II, represented locally by Governor-General Dame Ivy Dumont since 2001. **Head of Government:** Prime Minister Perry Christie since 2002. **Recent history:** Former premier, Pindling, who dominated much of contemporary affairs in The Bahamas, retired from politics after his 1992 defeat and died in August 2000. Perry Christie is now Premier and a former colleague of Pindling. After Hurricane Frances caused extensive widespread damage in The Bahamas in late 2004, with Hurricane Jeanne following only weeks later, Christie is likely to set about devising plans to better detect such hurricanes, and better lessen their impact.

The bicameral Parliament – composed of a 16-member Senate, whose membership is appointed, and a 40-strong House of Assembly directly elected for a five-year term – has legislative powers. The British Monarch has formal executive powers, vested in a Governor General, although in practice the Governor General almost invariably acts upon the advice of a Cabinet of Ministers appointed from the House of Assembly.

LANGUAGE: The official and national language is English.

RELIGION: The three main Christian denominations are Baptist, Anglican and Roman Catholic.

ELECTRICITY: 110 volts AC, 60Hz. An adaptor is required for 220V appliances.

SOCIAL CONVENTIONS: The pace of life is generally leisurely. Informal wear is acceptable in the resorts with some degree of dressing up in the evenings, particularly for dining, dancing and casinos in Nassau or Freeport. Further from the main towns, dress is more casual, although there is still a tendency to dress up at night. Small outposts like Green Turtle Cay, for example, will not require more than a shirt and long trousers. It is not acceptable to wear beachwear in towns.

Climate

The Bahamas are slightly cooler than other Caribbean island groups owing to their proximity to the continental North American cold air systems. May to October is the rainy season. The hurricane season is from June to the end of November.

Required clothing: Lightweight or tropical, cottons all year round. Light raincoats are useful during the wet season.

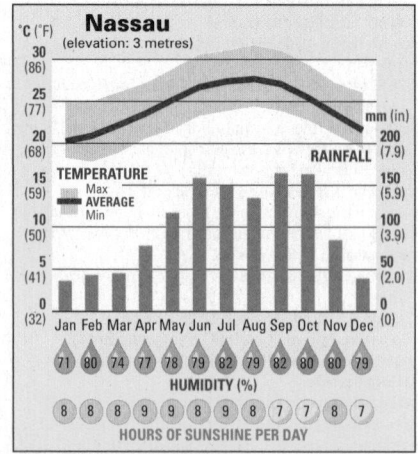

Communications

Telephone: IDD is available. Country code: 1 242. New Providence and all islands have automatic telephone systems. The state telephone company, *BaTelCo*, offers both manual- and automatic-dial mobile radio telephones, which allow callers to contact ships at sea. Phone cards can be purchased at discounted rates for international calls.

Mobile telephone: Roaming agreements exist with a few international mobile phone companies. Coverage is average. Handsets must be registered with *BaTelCo* (tel: 394 4000). Visitors will need to purchase a SIM card if their provider has no agreement with *BaTelCo*. Handsets can be hired locally.

Internet: Available in some towns. There are a few Internet cafes on Grand Bahama Island and Nassau Island open seven days a week. Laptop connections are available, as are webcams and facilities for scanning and copying.

Post: Postal service to Europe takes up to 10 days. Post office hours: Mon-Fri 0900-1700 and Sat 0900-1230.

MEDIA: The government operates a radio network and also the only television service on the island. There are, however, some private radio stations. The press is mostly privately owned and a wide variety of views is freely permitted, including criticism of the government.

Press: The four daily newspapers are the *The Bahamas Journal*, *Freeport News*, the *Nassau Guardian*, and *The Tribune*. *The Punch* is published twice a week. Both *Bahamas Tourist News* and *What's On Magazine* are printed once a month. International newspapers are available.

TV: *ZNS Bahamas* is government owned, commercially run by *Broadcasting Corporation of the Bahamas* (*BCB*).

Radio: Private and commercial stations include *Love 97 FM* and *100 Jamz*. *ZNS Bahamas*, government-owned, oversees *Inspiration 1240*, *Northern Service*, *Power 104.5* and *Radio Bahamas*.

Passport/Visa

	Passport Required?	Visa Required?	Return Ticket Required?
Full British	Yes	No/3	Yes
Australian	Yes	No/5	Yes
Canadian	1	No/5	Yes
USA	2	No/4	Yes
Other EU	Yes	No/3	Yes
Japanese	Yes	No/6	Yes

Note: *Regulations and requirements may be subject to change at short notice, and you are advised to contact the appropriate diplomatic or consular authority before finalising travel arrangements. Any numbers in the chart refer to the footnotes below.*

PASSPORTS: Passport valid for at least six months from date of departure from The Bahamas required by all except: (a) **1.** nationals of Canada, provided holding a birth certificate; (b) **2.** nationals of the USA.

However, conditions vary and nationals may wish to enquire what specific documents need to be submitted.

VISAS: Required by all except the following: (a) **3.** nationals of EU countries for stays of up to three months (eight months for nationals of Belgium, Denmark, Greece, Italy, Luxembourg, The Netherlands and the UK), except nationals of the Czech Republic, Estonia, Hungary, Latvia, Lithuania, Poland, the Slovak Republic and Slovenia who *do* need a visa; (b) **4.** nationals of Greenland, Iceland, Liechtenstein, Norway, San Marino, Switzerland, Turkey and the USA for stays of up to eight months; (c) **5.** nationals of Commonwealth countries for stays of up to eight months, except a) nationals of the Gambia who can stay for three months; b) nationals of Brunei, Cameroon, Ghana, India, Mozambique, Nigeria and Pakistan who *do* need a visa; (d) **6.** nationals of Chile, Israel, Japan, Korea (Rep), Martinique, Mexico, Norfolk Islands and Uruguay for stays of up to three months; (e) nationals of Argentina, Bolivia, Brazil, Costa Rica, Ecuador, El Salvador, Honduras, Nicaragua, Panama, Paraguay, Peru and Venezuela for stays of up to 14 days; (f) nationals of French, Dutch, Portuguese and Ecuadorean overseas territories, and of Bermuda, Cayman Islands, Cook Islands, Curaçao, Gibraltar, Hong Kong (SAR), Macau (Portuguese passport), Monaco, St Maarten, Tahiti, Turks & Caicos, Vatican City and Zimbabwe (who should contact the Consulate to find out the maximum length of visit without a visa); (g) transit passengers continuing their journey by the same or next connecting aircraft within three days, provided holding confirmed onward documentation and passport.

Note: Nationals of Haiti and the Dominican Republic *do* need a visa when in transit.

Types of visa and cost: *Single-entry:* £15; *Multiple-entry:* £20 (three to six months); £30 (six to 12 months). Payable by cash or cheque (with valid cheque guarantee card).

Validity: Usually three months. Applications for extension should be made to the Director of Immigration.

Application to: Consulate (or Consular Section at Embassy or High Commission); see *Passport/Visa Information*.

Application requirements: (a) Completed application form. (b) Valid passport. (c) Proof of sufficient funds to cover stay. (d) Two passport-size photos. (e) Itinerary of trip. (f) Return or onward ticket and documents to enter any other country to which travel is planned. (g) Stamped self-addressed envelope if applying by post. (h) Proof of employment or enrolment in University. (i) Proof of hotel booking or letter of invitation if staying at a private home.

Note: Only applications from the UK can be made via registered or recorded delivery.

Working days required: Dependent on nationality of applicant, a minimum of 48 hours, maximum of six weeks. Applications made by post and from some nationals may take longer to process. Applicants are advised to make their applications at least six weeks before their departure date to the Bahamas. Enquire at the Consulate or Embassy for further details.

Temporary residence: Apply to the Director of Immigration, PO Box N-831, Nassau, The Bahamas (tel: (242) 322 7531.

PASSPORT/VISA INFORMATION

Bahamas High Commission in the UK
10 Chesterfield Street, London W1J 5JL, UK
Tel: (020) 7408 4488 *or* 7659 0829 (visa enquiries).
Website: www.mfabahamas.org
Opening hours: Mon-Fri 0930-1730.

Embassy of the Commonwealth of The Bahamas in the USA
2220 Massachussetts Avenue, NW, Washington, DC 20008, USA
Tel: (202) 319 2660.
E-mail: bahemb@aol.com

Bahamas Consulate General in the USA
Bahamas House, 231 East 46th Street, New York, NY 10017, USA
Tel: (212) 421 6420.
Website: www.un.int/bahamas

Money

Currency: Bahamian Dollar (BSD; symbol B$) = 100 cents. Notes are in denominations of B$100, 50, 20, 10, 5, 3 and 1, and 50 cents. Coins are in denominations of 25, 15, 10, 5 and 1 cents. The Bahamian Dollar has parity with the US Dollar and the latter is also accepted as legal tender.

Note: The Bahamian Dollar is tied to the US Dollar.

Currency exchange: Available in banks and at exchange bureaux and hotels. ATMs are available on the major islands in airport terminals, at banks and casinos and at other convenient locations.

Credit & debit cards: American Express, Diners Club, MasterCard and Visa are widely accepted. Check with your credit or debit card company for details of merchant acceptability and other services which may be available.

Traveller's cheques: To avoid additional exchange rate charges, travellers are advised to take traveller's cheques in US Dollars.

Currency restrictions: Permission is required from the Central Bank of The Bahamas to import local currency, which may be exported up to a maximum of B$70. The import and export of foreign currency are unlimited.

Banking hours: Mon-Thurs 0930-1500, Fri 0930-1700.

Exchange rate indicators:
Rate at time of publishing
£1.00=   B$1.82
$1.00=   B$1.00

Duty Free

The following goods may be imported into The Bahamas by persons aged over 18 years of age without incurring customs duty:
200 cigarettes or 50 cigars or 454g of tobacco; 1.136l of spirits and 1.136l of wine; goods up to the value of US$100.

Note: Duty is payable on household items such as small electrical appliances (blenders, etc) which are taxed at 45 per cent of their cost. Laptop computers are considered to be personal effects and are therefore duty free.

Prohibited items: Firearms, ammunition, drugs and animals from countries with rabies.

Public Holidays

Below are listed Public Holidays for the January 2006-June 2007 period.

2006: Jan 1 New Year's Day. **Apr 14** Good Friday. **Apr 17** Easter Monday. **Jun 2** Labour Day. **Jun 5** Whit Monday. **Jul 10** Independence Day. **Aug 7** Emancipation Day. **Oct 12** National Heroes' Day. **Dec 25** Christmas Day. **Dec 26** Boxing Day.

2007: Jan 1 New Year's Day. **Apr 6** Good Friday. **Apr 9** Easter Monday. **May 28** Whit Monday. **Jun 1** Labour Day.

Health

	Special Precautions?	Certificate Required?
Yellow Fever	No	1
Cholera	No	No
Typhoid & Polio	2	N/A
Malaria	No	N/A

Note: *Regulations and requirements may be subject to change at short notice, and you are advised to contact your doctor well in advance of your intended date of departure. Any numbers in the chart refer to the footnotes below.*

1: A yellow fever vaccination certificate is required from travellers aged over one year travelling from an infected area.

2: Immunisation against typhoid is advised.

Food & drink: Tap water is safe to drink although it can often be salty in taste. Milk is pasteurised and dairy products are safe for consumption. Local meat, poultry, seafood, fruit and vegetables are generally considered safe to eat.

Other risks: *Diphtheria*, *tuberculosis* and *hepatitis B* vaccinations are sometimes recommended. *HIV/AIDS* is worryingly the leading cause of death among Bahamians aged 15-44. Appropriate precautions should be taken.

Health care: Medical facilities are on a par with the USA, but can be costly and, therefore, medical insurance is recommended. This should ideally cover the cost of air ambulance.

Travel - International

AIR:
The Bahamas' national airline is *Bahamasair (UP)* (website: www.bahamasair.com).

Approximate flight times: From Nassau to *Los Angeles* is eight hours, to *New York* is six hours, to *London* is nine hours and to *Singapore* is 26 hours.

Main airports: *Nassau International (NAS)* is 16km (10 miles) west of the city. *To/from the airport:* Taxi services are available. *Facilities:* Banking, car hire, post office, bars, restaurants and duty free shops.
Freeport International (FPO) is 5km (3 miles) from the city. *To/from the airport:* Taxis are available. *Facilities:* Banking, car hire, car parking, bar/restaurant and a duty free shop.
The international airport at Moss Town, *Exuma*, also offers a runway.
There are scheduled turbo-prop services between several airports in Florida and *Treasure Cay (TCB)* and *Marsh Harbour (MHH)*, Abaco Island; *Rock Sound (RSD)* and *Governor's Harbour (GHB)*, *Eleuthera*; and *Georgetown (GGT)*, Exuma.

Departure tax: US$18 (for all passengers leaving from Freeport). Children under six years of age are exempt.

SEA:
Main ports: A large number of international passenger ships from New York and Miami call at *Nassau*. Nassau has direct passenger–cargo connections with the USA, the UK, the West Indies and South America. In addition, a large number of cruise ships call there. Facilities for cruisers in Nassau and some

---

harbours of the Out Islands (*Eleuthera*, *Andros* and *Exuma*) are being improved. Contact the Bahamas Tourist Office for an up-to-date list of cruise operators to The Bahamas, with all relevant contact numbers.

Travel - Internal

AIR:
Charter services are available from *Airstream*, *Caribbean Aviation*, *Diving Safaris*, *Four Way Charter*, *Island Helicopters*, *LeAir Charter Ltd*, *Sky Unlimited*, *TAKEFLIGHT Air Charters* and *The Travel Club*.

Approximate flight times: From Nassau, New Providence Island to *Freeport* is 40 minutes, to *Marsh Harbour* or *Treasure Cay*, Abaco is 35 minutes, to *Governor's Harbour* is 30 minutes, and to *Georgetown* on Exuma is 40 minutes.

SEA:
The Out Islands are served by a leisurely mail boat which leaves Nassau several times a week carrying mail and provisions to the islands. Passengers share facilities with the crew. Arrangements should be made through boat captains at Potters Cay. Air-conditioned ferries operate twice-weekly between Nassau, Eleuthera and Harbour Island. For further details, contact *Bahamas Fast Ferries*, Dowdeswell Street, PO Box 3709 (tel: 323 2166; website: www.bahamasferries.com). There are also local ferries available.

ROAD:
Traffic drives on the left. **Bus:** The *jitney* (minibus) provides inexpensive touring and they operate in the hubs of Freeport and Nassau. Exact change is required. However, there is no public transport on any of the smaller islands. Paradise Island is served by a bus service which stops at every hotel. A horse-drawn ride, which takes three passengers, is available along the streets of Nassau. Care should be taken when using a bus service after dusk on routes away from the main tourist areas along Cable Beach and East and West Bay Streets.
Taxis are readily available and are the main form of transport on the smaller islands. Taxis in New Providence are metered and the rates are government controlled. For real Bahamian hospitality, keep an eye out for taxis with a Bahamahost sticker in the window. Surcharges often apply for more than two people and for extra luggage. **Car hire:** *Avis, Budget, Dollar* and *Hertz* are represented at the airports and in Nassau and Freeport. Motor **scooter** hire is also available. Helmets must be worn. Typical cost of hiring a scooter is B$25-35 per day. **Documentation:** International driver's licence. Drivers must be aged 25 or over. **Bicycles** can be rented by the day or by the week at popular tourist centres and hotels. **Documentation:** A national driving licence is valid for up to three months. Motorcycle riders and passengers are required to wear crash helmets.

Travel times: The following chart gives approximate travel times (in hours and minutes) from **Nassau** to other major centres.

	Air	Sea
Governor's Harbour, Eleuthera	0.30	2.00*
Freeport, Grand Bahama	0.30/0.45	12.00
Marsh Harbour, Abaco	0.45	11.00
George Town, Exuma	0.45	13.00

Travel times Note: * By Bahamas Fast Ferries; all other travel times are by mail boat.

Credit: ©Bahamas Tourist Office and Dave Saunders

Credit: ©Bahamas Tourist Office

Travel Advice

Most visits to The Bahamas are trouble-free but you should be aware of the global risk of indiscriminate international terrorist attacks, which could be against civilian targets, including places frequented by foreigners.

In addition, violent crime can be a problem in The Bahamas, mostly within the local community - although tourists have been subject to robbery, sometimes armed.

This advice is based on information provided by the Foreign and Commonwealth Office in the UK. It is correct at time of publishing. As the situation can change rapidly, visitors are advised to contact the following organisations for the latest travel advice:

British Foreign and Commonwealth Office
Tel: (0845) 850 2829.
Website: www.fco.gov.uk

US Department of State
Website: http://travel.state.gov/travel

Accommodation

Note: Currently, it is only the Royal Oasis Golf Resort & Casino that is still temporarily closed due to the effects of Hurricane Frances in 2004.

EDITOR'S CHOICE: COTTAGE COLONIES

Separate cottages or villas, with maid service, surrounding a main clubhouse with a bar and dining room – these are 'Cottage Colonies'. They are not equipped with kitchenette or facilities for the preparation of meals, although some have facilities for preparing beverages and light snacks. They offer the facilities of a hotel, such as a private beach/swimming pool, and are designed to offer maximum privacy.

HOTELS:

 Hotels vary in size and facilities. There are luxury hotels offering full porter, bell and room service, planned activities, sports, shops and beauty salons, swimming pools and entertainment; some have a private beach, golf course and tennis courts. The best known and most recognisable accommodation is probably the Atlantis on Paradise Island, a family vacation and gaming resort with two massive wings of rooms and suites, which can be seen from Nassau. Double and single rooms are often the same price. The small hotels are more informal and while activities are less extensive, they usually offer a dining room and bar. There are resorts situated on New Providence Island, which has sporting facilities and luxury accommodation. Some hotels include service charge on the bill. Many of the larger resorts offer accommodation on either a Modified American Plan (MAP), which consists of room, breakfast and dinner, or European Plan (EP), which consists of room only. Many hotels belong to The Bahamas Hotel Association (see *Accommodation Information*).

GUEST HOUSES:

 Often less expensive than hotels and located near downtown Nassau. Many offer European Plan only, but restaurants are plentiful. Rooms may be with or without a bath. The Out Islands' hotels are small with a casual atmosphere.

APARTMENT HOTELS:

 These consist of apartment units with complete kitchen and maid service. Other hotel facilities (ie swimming pool, sporting activities, restaurant and bar, etc) are normally available on the premises.

APARTMENT/COTTAGE UNITS:

 These have complete kitchen facilities and some have maid service. Generally, there are no restaurant facilities and tenants are required to prepare their own meals. A few are situated in landscaped but without the main clubhouse. Others offer inexpensive accommodation in less spacious but comfortable surroundings. Restaurant and bar facilities are not available.

CAMPING:

 Camping is not permitted on any of the islands of The Bahamas.

ACCOMMODATION INFORMATION

The Bahamas Hotel Association
SG Hambros Building, Goodman's Bay,
PO Box N-3318, Nassau, The Bahamas
Tel: 322 8381/2.
Website: www.bhahotels.com

Top Things To See

- The capital of The Bahamas, **Nassau**, stands on **New Providence Island**. The 18th-century **Fort Charlotte** on **West Bay Street** has a moat, open battlements, dungeons and a magnificent view of the harbour. The nearby **Ardastra Gardens** have tropical flowers and pink flamingos. Built in 1793, **Fort Fincastle** is in the shape of a ship's bow. The Water Tower is the highest point on the island, 85m (216ft) above sea level. An elevator takes visitors to an observation deck for panoramic views.
- Gaze out at golden sand: **Cable Beach** has 2.5 miles of it; **Paradise Island** boasts some beautiful beaches, a 14-acre aquarium, 34 acres of beautiful landscaped gardens, the Caribbean's largest casino and a multitude of resorts; **Eleuthera/Harbour Island** is characterised by colonial villages and pineapple plantations and boasts pink sandy beaches in an upscale part of the island that usually attracts newlyweds and couples in love seeking privacy, full of chic restaurants and good but not frenetic nightlife; there are also 8 acres of pristine white sand for the traveller to recline upon and observe the waters lapping against the versatile **Grand Bahama Island**; and enjoy total seclusion, surrounded by cerulean waters and pink sandy beaches, on **Cat Island**.
- On the perennially popular Grand Bahama Island, only 52 miles off the Florida coast, **Lucayan National Park** (there are 40 acres to sample here) and **Peterson Cay National Park** are both worth visiting. The main towns are **Freeport/Lucaya**, which has an airport, and **West End**. The **Garden of the Groves** has exotic flowers, waterfalls and colourful birds. A highlight of any trip here will be to watch the semi-wild dolphins gliding and soaring in **Sanctuary Bay**. Set eyes upon the world's third-longest **coral barrier reef** on **Andros**, amongst the **Out Islands**. Beyond the reef, the ocean floor drops away steeply to a depth of more than 1.5km (1 mile). **Captain Bill's Blue Hole** is 180ft deep, 440ft in diameter. In **Congo Town** is the world-famous **StarGate Blue Hole** where you can see Indian skulls discovered in the early 1990s. Overall, Andros is laced with creeks and densely forested inland, with a largely untouched and natural interior.
- On Eleuthera, a narrow island, 177km (110 miles) long but seldom more than 3km (2 miles) wide, see one of the oldest settlements in The Bahamas at **Dunmore Town**.
- On Cat Island, stare up at 60m (200ft) cliffs (a rare height for The Bahamas), then look around at dense natural forest and pre-Columbian Arawak Indian caves. On **Mount Alvernia** is the **Hermitage** built by Father Jerome.

- Enjoy close encounters with friendly bottle-nosed dolphins on **Blue Lagoon Island**.
- See **Dean's Blue Hole**, the deepest blue hole around, at 600 feet into the ocean floor, lying just offshore, on **Long Island**. Long Island certainly lives up to its name, being almost 100km (60 miles) long but rarely more than 5km (3 miles) wide. The landscape consists of rugged headlands dropping sharply down to the sea, fertile pastureland, rolling hills and sandy beaches washed by surf.
- See Columbus' first landing place in the New World near **Cockburn Town** on **San Salvador**.

Top Things To Do

- **Sail** around the **Exumas**: the waters surrounding this 160km- (100 mile-) long chain of islands have been described by yachtspeople as being the finest cruising region in the world. There are pristine cays and spectacular reefs, accessible by boat only. In short, it is an unforgettable 176-mile park of beauty, with outstanding marine life. For those who are particularly keen, **Nassau/Paradise Island** is the site of the popular **Christmas Sailing Regatta**.
- Plummet the azure waters of The Bahamas and **dive** around an underwater preserve where night dives can be arranged at **Pelican Cay National Park**, explore **Preacher's Cave** and the underwater caves at **Hatchet Bay**, admire the underwater rock formations and 5m (15ft) staghorn coral reefs off **Mamma Rhoda Rock** and explore over 30 shipwrecks at **Conception Island**. The temperature of the sea rarely drops below 21°C (70°F), even in midwinter. For those a little more wary of scuba-diving, and not even keen on snorkelling, the **South Shore** on **New Providence** is a particularly good location and offers **SUBs - personal underwater submarines**.
- Better your handicap in the **golf** capital of the world, offering one 9-hole and eight 18-hole golf courses, with the islands host to regular major tournaments. Grand Bahama Island has five world-class courses, two being at Lucaya Golf & Country Club. Treasure Cay also has an excellent golf course and Great Harbour Cay's is championship-standard.
- Play with bottle-nosed **dolphins** in waist-high water at **Blue Lagoon Island**.
- Enjoy **shopping** in **Nassau**'s bustling 'straw market', where local vendors create unique straw goods on the spot, or the more sophisticated shops in **Bay Street**.
- Go **fishing** in what are regarded as some of the best fishing centres worldwide. The island of **Bimini** lies between **Andros** and Florida, with the gulf stream running either side. Hemingway used to live in **Alice Town** in Blue Marlin Cottage, and mementos of his life can be seen in the local museum. There is an annual **Native Fishing Tournament** held here, usually in August. **Tongue of the Ocean**'s major attraction is its deep-water fishing. **The Berry Islands** are also popular because of their serene landscapes and white sand beaches - plus, the range of fish on offer is exceptional.
- Seek refreshment at Max's Conch Bar & Grill, which has become a tourist attraction in its own right, such is its notoriety. And remember - this is the land of that tasty tipple, the **Long Island Iced Tea**. You have been warned!

TOURIST INFORMATION

Bahamas Tourist Office in the UK
Bahamas House, 10 Chesterfield Street, London W1J 5JL, UK
Tel: (020) 7355 0800.
Website: www.bahamas.co.uk

Bahamas Tourist Office in the USA
150 East 52nd Street, 28th Floor North, New York, NY 10022, USA
Tel: (212) 758 2777.
Website: www.bahamas.com

Entertainment

FOOD & DRINK: There is a wide choice of restaurants and bars. Fresh fruit is available from the Out Islands, including sweet pineapple, mango, breadfruit and papaya. Local drinks are based on rum.

Things to know: Table service is usual in restaurants.

National specialities:

- Grouper cutlets, rock lobster, baked crab and red snapper fillets in anchovy sauce.
- Peas are used a lot, in the token *peas & rice*, and also in pea soup.
- There is another unique soup that is definitely worth tasting called *souse*, consisting purely of onions, water, lime juice, celery, peppers and meat.
- *Fish n' grits* is worth trying: fish cooked with salt pork, onions, and green peppers served with grits as a morning meal.

Credit: ©Bahamas Tourist Office

Bahrain

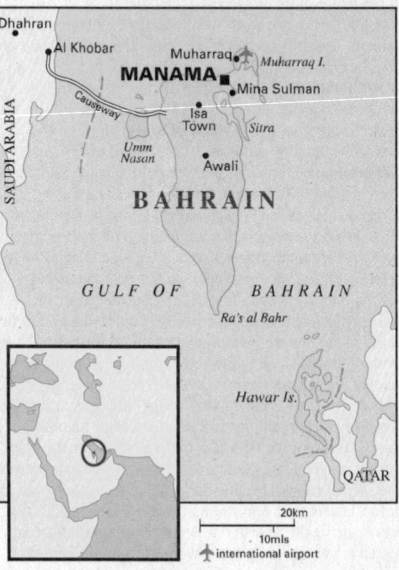

Location: Middle East, Gulf Coast.

Time: GMT + 3.

- Fresh fruit is available from the Out Islands, including pineapple, mango, breadfruit and papaya.
- Chicken and dough (dumplings).
- Conch is everywhere, and is popular in chowder, fritters, salad, scorched (raw and washed with seawater and lime juice, then rubbed with hot pepper, topped with fresh tomato and onion slices, served on a knife or skewer) and stew.
- *Johnnycake* is a mildly sweet bread served as a side-order.
- Curried mutton refers to either goat or sheep.
- Racoon stew.
- *Guava duff* is a dessert specialty of The Bahamas, made with sieved guava pulp, served with *hard sauce* (a blend of butter, confectioners' sugar, vanilla, and rum).

National drinks:
- The local liqueur is *Nassau Royal*, served alone or in coffee.
- A refreshing alcoholic drink is coconut water, sweet milk and gin.
- *Kalik* is the beer of The Bahamas.
- Besides rum punch, the three top tropical island cocktails are *Bahama Mama* (Vat 19, citrus juice, bitters, nutmeg, crème de cassis and grenadine), *Goombay Smash* (coconut rum, pineapple juice, lemon juice, triple sec, Vat 19 and syrup) and *Yellowbird* (crème de banana liqueur, Vat 19, orange and pineapple juice, apricot brandy and Galliano).

Legal drinking age: 18.

Tipping: 15 per cent is usual for most services including taxis. Some hotels and restaurants, however, include service charge on the bill. Bellboys and porters usually receive US$1 per bag.

NIGHTLIFE: Hotels have bars and nightclubs. Beach parties and discos are organised regularly. Live entertainment includes calypso, *goombay* music (traditional Bahamian sound) and limbo dancing. Nightclubs are found in Nassau and Freeport. On Paradise Island, *Dragons* and *Atlantis* offer nightclubs that serve up that classic Bahamian fusion of cultures: dance to club anthems interspersed with reggae and Bahamian classics. There are four casinos: one on Cable Beach, another on Paradise Island; on Grand Bahama, there is a casino in Freeport and one in Lucaya. All casinos feature restaurants and live entertainment.

SHOPPING: Special purchases include china, cutlery, leather, fabrics, spirits from Britain, Scandinavian glass and silver, Swiss watches, German and Japanese cameras and French perfume. Local products include all types of straw artefacts, seashell jewellery and woodcarvings. **Shopping hours:** Mon-Fri 0900-1700.

Business

- **GDP:** US$5.2 billion.
- **Main exports:** Pharmaceuticals, cement, rum, crawfish and refined petroleum products.
- **Main imports:** Foodstuffs, manufactured goods, crude oil vehicles and electronics.
- **Main trade partners:** USA, Canada, UK, other EU countries, Nigeria and Libya.

ECONOMY: One of the wealthiest countries in the Caribbean, The Bahamas depends heavily on its main industry of tourism. Other industries produce rum, oil, pharmaceuticals and salt. Transhipment through Freeport, which enjoys significant tax concessions as a free trade area, is another valuable source of revenue. The Bahamas also has a sizeable and growing offshore banking sector, although it has come under pressure as a result of competition from elsewhere and international efforts to tighten up on 'tax havens'. In June 2000, the Bahamas were identified by the Organisation for Economic Cooperation and Development (OECD) – the world's 30 wealthiest economies – as one of 35 countries whose financial laws were inadequate to prevent large-scale tax evasion and possible money laundering. The government has since taken measures to meet the OECD's requirements. Most foodstuffs and virtually all other products must be imported, mainly from the USA, although oil is purchased primarily from Indonesia and Saudi Arabia. Other than the USA, The Bahamas' major trading partners are the UK, the EU and Canada.

BUSINESS ETIQUETTE: Normal courtesies are observed, ie appointments are made and calling cards are exchanged. Office hours: Mon-Fri 0900-1700 and 0900-1730 (government offices).

CONFERENCES/CONVENTIONS: Conference venues can seat up to 2000 people. Information may be obtained from the Bahamas Tourist Office *or* the Bahamas Ministry of Tourism in Nassau.

COMMERCIAL INFORMATION

Bahamas Chamber of Commerce
PO Box 40808, Freeport, Grand Bahama, The Bahamas
Tel: 352 8329.
Website: www.thegrandbahamachamberofcommerce.com

Overview

Bahrain is an archipelago of 33 islands. The country was once named Dilmun by ancient Sumerians, considered an island paradise in which there was no disease, death or suffering, and where gods resided. Although modern Bahrain has not retained such mythical status, many still flock to frolic in its heavenly shoreline, and many still perceive the country as blissful respite from less lenient Islamic countries.

However, Bahrain is still imbued with Islamic tradition. Manama, the capital, is jam-packed with majestic mosques and minarets. Some females dress in western-style clothing but immodesty is still frowned upon. It is a symbolic bridge that connects the archipelago to Saudi Arabia's mainland.

Nevertheless, Bahrain is a wealthy country that has been unafraid to distinguish itself from other Islamic Gulf countries. Under Portuguese rule between 1521 and 1622, attacked by various tribes and groups for more than 100 years, and willingly becoming a British Protectorate between 1861 and 1971, Bahrain was ecstatic when it discovered oil in 1931. In just four decades, Bahrain's protectorate status was relinquished and Bahrain became one of the world's most affluent countries. Bahrain's first independent ruler, Sheikh Isa al-Khalifa, caused controversy by bolstering Bahrain's relationship with western countries: both British and US military forces were granted use of Bahraini ports and airfields, vital to the prosecution of the two Iraq wars and the 2002 Afghan war.

Despite the Islamic presence, about one-third of Bahrain's population are foreign expatriates who seek that ideal blend of stability and prosperity. Perhaps this influence has shaped modern Bahrain, now rapidly modernising, full of shopping malls and restaurants. Many argue, however, that the supposed liberal outlook of the country is a sham: alcohol and casinos cannot disguise that the country is an absolute monarchy in which dissent is barely tolerated. Regardless, visitors to Bahrain are more likely to want to revel in its antiquity, anyway. During construction of Bahrain's causeway, thousands of burial mounds were disinterred, dating back to the third millennium BC. Bahrain is now the proud owner of the largest ancient necropolis in the world, and its foundations still rest upon the ancient city of Dilmun and the ancient civilisation that resided there.

A B C D E F G H I J K L M N O P Q R S T U V W X Y Z

It is exactly this blend of eastern and western cultures, this commingling of mosque and skyscraper, which draws so many to Bahrain. Perhaps its famous Tree of Life – a verdant tree blooming out of arid desert – says it all: Bahrain is full of surprises and contradictions.

General Information

AREA: 710.9 sq km (274.5 sq miles).
POPULATION: 666,400 (official estimate 1999).
POPULATION DENSITY: 937.4 per sq km.
CAPITAL: Manama. **Population:** 140,401 (1992).
GEOGRAPHY: Bahrain is an archipelago of 33 islands in the Arabian Gulf, situated between Saudi Arabia's east coast and the Qatar peninsula. At the centre of the island is the highest point, Jebel Dukhan. The majority of Bahrain's oil wells are to be found in this area. The main island has the valuable asset of an adequate supply of fresh water, unique in the region, both on land and offshore. There are extensive date gardens to the north with irrigated vegetable and fruit gardens. The strategic 24km- (15 mile-) long King Fahad Causeway links Bahrain with Saudi Arabia.
GOVERNMENT: Constitutional monarchy. Gained full independence from the UK in 1971 (had been a British Protectorate from 1861). **Head of State:** King Sheikh Hamad bin Isa al-Khalifa since 1999. **Head of Government:** Prime Minister Sheikh Khalifa bin Salman al-Khalifa since 1971. **Recent history:** Sheikh Isa was succeeded by his son, Sheikh Hamad bin Isa al-Khalifa, in 1999. While the new Sheikh has retained ultimate control over the Bahraini political system, there undoubtedly have been significant moves to open up the political system. Among Sheikh Hamad's first actions was to declare an amnesty for political opponents. Then, in February 2002, he declared Bahrain a constitutional monarchy with himself as Head of State and announced that *majlis* elections would be held. These took place in October 2002. Women were allowed to stand as candidates for the first time, provoking complaints from traditionalist Islamists, while Islamist candidates were themselves allowed to stand for the first time. A small majority was secured by a bloc of independent and secular candidates. The first woman to be appointed to head a government ministry was Nada Haffadh in 2004, who was made Health Minister: a symbolic turn of events that hinted at genuine progress in women's rights in Bahrain.
In addition, a prominent opposition figure, Majid al-Alawi, recently returned from exile, and was appointed to a ministerial post in the new government. Early in 2003, there were further protests against the impending war against Iraq, and Bahrain's role in hosting American and British forces. In May 2003, thousands of victims of alleged torture petitioned the King to cancel the law that prevents them from suing suspected torturers. These protests instigated a general concern for security in Bahrain, and in 2004, the protests against fighting in Iraqi cities once again materialised. However, the King sacked his Interior Minister after police tried to prevent the protests. These kind of moves seem to render the country more stable and Sheikh Hamad appears to have succeeded in quelling the Shia opposition – at least for the time being.
Bahrain was a traditional Arab monarchy, ruled since 1782 by an Emir selected from the al-Khalifa dynasty through an appointed cabinet led by a Prime Minister. Constitutional changes introduced by the current Emir, Sheikh Hamad bin Isa al-Khalifa, in February 2002, establish him as Head of State of a constitutional monarchy. The Emir governs with the support of an appointed cabinet of Ministers. He is also advised by the *Majlis as-Shura* (People's Council), which was elected for the first time in October 2002. Its 40 members serve in single-seat constituencies for a four-year term.
LANGUAGE: The official language is Arabic. English is widely spoken.
RELIGION: Islam is practised by around 85 per cent of Bahraini society (of which 60 per cent is Shi'ite and 40 per cent Sunni). There are also other faiths, including Christianity, Hinduism, Judaism, Zoroastrianism and Buddhism.
ELECTRICITY: 230 volts AC, 50Hz (Awali, 110 volts AC, 60Hz). Lamp fittings are of both the bayonet and screw types. Plug fittings are normally of the 13-amp pin type.
SOCIAL CONVENTIONS: Traditional beliefs and customs are strong influences and people are generally more formal than Westerners. Attitudes to women are more liberal than in most Gulf States. Homosexuality, however, is illegal. Video cassettes will be withheld on arrival at the airport. It is illegal for Muslims to purchase alcohol from retail outlets. It is acceptable to sit cross-legged on cushions or sofas in people's homes but it is still insulting to display the soles of the feet or shoes or to accept food or anything else with the left hand. It is polite to drink two small cups of coffee or tea when offered. Guests will generally be expected to share a bedroom since guest bedrooms and privacy are almost unknown. Sports clothes may be worn in the street and short dresses are acceptable; however, revealing clothing should be avoided. Smoking is very common and cheap by European standards.

Climate

June to October, hot and humid (42°C), December to April, mild (10°-20°C). December through to March can be quite cool. Rainfall is slight and occurs mainly in winter. Spring and Autumn are the most pleasant months.
Required clothing: Lightweight cottons and linens from spring to autumn, mediumweight clothes from November to March. Warmer clothes are necessary in winter and on cool evenings.

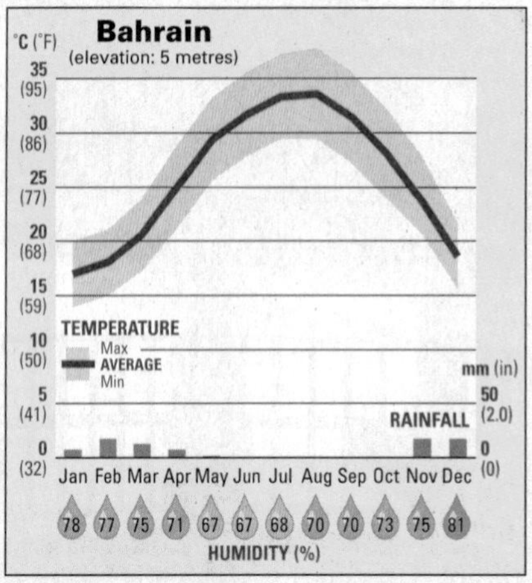
Bahrain
(elevation: 5 metres)
°C (°F)
35 (95)
30 (86)
25 (77)
20 (68)
15 (59)
10 (50)
5 (41)
0 (32)
TEMPERATURE
Max
AVERAGE
Min
mm (in)
50 (2.0)
RAINFALL
0 (0)
Jan Feb Mar Apr May Jun Jul Aug Sep Oct Nov Dec
78 77 75 71 67 67 68 70 70 73 75 81
HUMIDITY (%)

Communications

Telephone: Full IDD service is available to over 204 locations. Country code: 973. Blue phone booths are coin-operated, red booths are phonecard operated and silver booths are operated by both cards and coins. Facilities are provided for video conferencing, digital data networks, mobile links and satellite-linked skyphones for direct communication with airborne aircraft anywhere in the world.
Mobile telephone: Roaming agreements exist with some international mobile phone companies. Coverage is average.
Internet: Available in large cities and resorts.
Post: Airmail service to Europe takes three to four days. The main post office is near Bab al-Bahrain in Manama; opening hours Sat-Thurs 0700-1930. Efficient one-day international courier services operate out of Bahrain.
MEDIA: Bahrain's domestic radio and television stations are state-run. Some households have satellite TV. Bahrain is keen to promote itself as a regional media hub, and the London-based pan-Arab satellite broadcaster MBC chose Bahrain as the base for its *MBC-2* channel. Journalists have the legal right to operate independently and freely, but can be imprisoned for some offences, which include insulting the king. Self-censorship is practised.
Press: Private daily newspapers include *Al-Ayam* and *Al-Wasat*. Leading newspapers in English are *Bahrain Tribune* and the *Gulf Daily News*.
TV: *Bahrain Radio & Television Corporation* (*BRTC*) is state-run and operates five terrestrial TV networks.
Radio: *Bahrain Radio & Television Corporation* (*BRTC*) is state-run and operates *General Programme* in Arabic. *Second Programme* deals with cultural and local issues. Other stations include *Holy Koran Programme*, *Radio Bahrain*, which is an English-language service, and *Sports Service*.

Passport/Visa

	Passport Required?	Visa Required?	Return Ticket Required?
Full British	Yes	1	Yes
Australian	Yes	1	Yes
Canadian	Yes	1	Yes
USA	Yes	1	Yes
Other EU	Yes	1	Yes
Japanese	Yes	1	Yes

Note: *Regulations and requirements may be subject to change at short notice, and you are advised to contact the appropriate diplomatic or consular authority before finalising travel arrangements. Any numbers in the chart refer to the footnotes below.*

Restricted entry: Holders of Israeli passports.
PASSPORTS: Valid passport for at least six months from date of departure required by all except the following:
(a) nationals of Kuwait, Oman, Qatar, Saudi Arabia and the United Arab Emirates holding a valid national ID card.
VISAS: Required by all except the following:
(a) nationals of Kuwait, Oman, Qatar, Saudi Arabia and the United Arab Emirates;
(b) transit passengers continuing their journey by the first connecting flight, provided holding confirmed tickets and appropriate travel documents and remaining within the transit area.
Note: 1. Nationals of EU countries (except nationals of Cyprus, the Czech Republic, Estonia, Hungary, Latvia, Lithuania, Malta, Poland, the Slovak Republic and Slovenia), Andorra, Australia, Brunei, Canada, Hong Kong, Iceland, Japan, Liechtenstein, Malaysia, Monaco, New Zealand, Norway, San Marino, Singapore, Switzerland, USA and the Vatican City may obtain visas on arrival at Bahrain International Airport or King Fahad Causeway holding valid passports and possibly return/onward tickets for touristic or business stays of up to two weeks. The fee is approximately US$13. If working for a media company (eg a newspaper or TV company) a special invitation from the Bahrain authorities is required.
Types of visa and cost: *Tourist*: £20 (two-week, single-entry), renewable for two further weeks once in Bahrain, at the General Directorate of Immigration and Passports, Manama. *Business*: £40 (four-week, multiple-entry), only available to British, Canadian and US nationals.
Validity: Three months from date of issue (*Tourist*); five years (*Business*).
Application to: Consulate (or Consular Section at Embassy); see *Passport/Visa Information*.
Note: (a) No Objection Certificates are obtainable through various hotels, travel agencies and other companies licensed to carry out touristic activities in Bahrain. Organised groups are charged a fee of BHD5 per person (approximately US$13). Non-British students must obtain and validate an NOC from a Bahraini resident (relative, friend or hotel spokesperson) and also submit a letter from university detailing the student status to accompany it. Long-term business visas should be arranged by the employing company in Bahrain. (b) Some visitors can now apply for an electronic visa in Bahrain, through the website www.evisa.gov.bh. This has the added benefit of being 24-hour and enabling secure online credit payment and multiple applications, if necessary.
Application requirements: *Entry visa*: (a) Valid passport. (b) One passport-size photo. (c) One completed application form. (d) One registered, self-addressed envelope and cheque for £3 to cover return of passport if applying by post. (e) Fee, payable in cash or by company cheques only. (f) No Objection Certificate obtained by agent in Bahrain from the Ministry of Interior (only applies to certain nationals). *Tourist*: (a)-(e) and, (f) Letter stating the purpose and duration of the visit and the applicant's responsibility for all travel expenses. *Business*: (a)-(e) and, (f) Letter from the company stating the purpose and duration of the of the visit and the applicant's responsibility for all travel expenses.
Working days required: Two.

PASSPORT/VISA INFORMATION

Embassy of the Kingdom of Bahrain in the UK
30 Belgrave Square, London SW1X 8QB, UK
Tel: (020) 7201 9170.
Website: www.bahrainembassy.co.uk
Opening hours: Mon-Fri 0900-1600; 0900-1200 (visa section).

Embassy of the Kingdom of Bahrain in the USA
3502 International Drive, NW,
Washington, DC 20008, USA
Tel: (202) 342 1111.
Website: www.bahrainembassy.org

Money

Currency: Dinar (BHD) = 1000 fils. Notes appear in denominations of BHD20, 10, 5, and 1, and 500 fils. Coins are in denominations of 100, 50, 25 and 10 fils.
Currency exchange: Currency can be exchanged at the airport, at most hotels and in banks and bureaux de change. Rates are more preferential at the bureaux de change than at the airport or at hotels. ATMs are available in major cities.
Credit & debit cards: American Express, Diners Club, MasterCard and Visa are accepted in hotels, major stores and restaurants. Smaller shops may prefer to deal in cash. Check with your credit or debit card company for details of merchant acceptability and other services which may be available.
Traveller's cheques: To avoid additional exchange rate charges, travellers are advised to take traveller's cheques in US Dollars.
Currency restrictions: There are no restrictions on the import or export of either local or foreign currency.
Banking hours: Sat-Wed 0730-1200 and 1530-1730; Thurs 0730-1100. Government offices, businesses and most offices are closed on Friday, which is a weekly holiday.
Exchange rate indicators:
Rate at time of publishing

£1.00=	BHD0.68
$1.00=	BHD0.37

Duty Free

The following goods may be imported into Bahrain by persons over 18 years of age without incurring customs duty:
200 cigarettes and 50 cigars and 250g of tobacco in opened packets; 1l of alcoholic beverages and six cans of beer (non-Muslim passengers only); 8oz of perfume; and gifts up to the value of BHD250 (approximately US$600).
Prohibited items: Firearms, ammunition, drugs, methylated spirits and jewellery. There is also a temporary ban on all live poultry and birds from Cambodia, China (including Hong Kong [SAR]), Chinese Taipei, Indonesia, Korea (Rep), Pakistan, Thailand and Vietnam.

Public Holidays

Below are listed Public Holidays for the January 2006-June 2007 period.
2006: Jan 1 New Year's Day. **Jan 10** Eid al-Adha (Feast of the Sacrifice). **Jan 31** Al-Hijrah (Islamic New Year). **Feb 9** Ashura. **Apr 11** Mouloud (Birth of the Prophet). **Oct 22-24** Eid al-Fitr (End of Ramadan). **Dec 16** National Day. **Dec 31** Eid al-Adha (Feast of the Sacrifice).
2007: Jan 1 New Year's Day. **Jan 20** Al-Hijrah (Islamic New Year). **Jan 29** Ashura. **Mar 31** Mouloud (Birth of the Prophet).
Note: Muslim festivals are timed according to local sightings of various phases of the moon and the dates given above are approximations. During the lunar month of Ramadan that precedes Eid al-Fitr, Muslims fast during the day and feast at night and normal business patterns may be interrupted. Many restaurants are closed during the day and there are restrictions on smoking and drinking. Some disruption may continue into Eid al-Fitr itself. Eid al-Fitr and Eid al-Adha may last anything from two to 10 days, depending on the region. For more information, see the *World of Islam* appendix.

Health

	Special Precautions?	Certificate Required?
Yellow Fever	No	No
Cholera	No	No
Typhoid & Polio	No	N/A
Malaria	No	N/A

Note: Regulations and requirements may be subject to change at short notice, and you are advised to contact your doctor well in advance of your intended date of departure. Any numbers in the chart refer to the footnotes below.

Food & drink: Water is treated and considered safe by the Ministry of Health in Bahrain, although visitors may prefer to drink bottled water. All modern hotels have their own filtration plants. Visitors are advised to eat well-cooked meat and fish, preferably served hot.
Other risks: *Typhoid fever* and *hepatitis A* occur; *hepatitis B* is endemic.
Health care: There is a comprehensive medical service, with general and specialised hospitals in the main towns. An emergency health service is provided free of charge or at a nominal fee. Pharmacies are well-equipped with supplies.

Travel - International

AIR:
The national airline serving Bahrain is *Gulf Air (GF)*.
Approximate flight times: From Bahrain to *London* is approximately seven hours 15 minutes, to *Los Angeles* is 18 hours 15 minutes and to *New York* is 13 hours 30 minutes.
Main airports: *Bahrain International (BAH)* (Muharraq) (website: www.bahrainairport.com) is 6.5km (4 miles) northeast of Manama. *To/from the airport*: Bus and taxi services run across the causeway to the main island (travel time - 15 minutes). *Facilities*: Banks/bureaux de change, duty free shops, first aid, bars, snack bars, restaurants, nursery, prayer room, tourist information, post office, car hire (*Avis, Budget, Europcar* and *Hertz*) and car parking.
Departure tax: BHD3 (approximately US$8). Children under two years of age and transit passengers not leaving the airport are exempt.
SEA:
Main ports: *Mina Salman, Mina Manama* and *Mina Muharraq*. These ports offer a quick and efficient entry into the country from all parts of the world. Passenger ferries operate between Iran and Bahrain (travel time - 16 hours). A port tax of BHD3 may be payable.
ROAD:
A car drive to Dhahran (Eastern Province of Saudi Arabia) takes approximately one hour 30 minutes from Bahrain using the King Fahad Causeway. A toll fee of approximately BD2 is payable by persons driving out of Bahrain. Normal Saudi Arabian visa regulations apply.

Travel - Internal

AIR:
Several flights a week leave from Bahrain International Airport for other destinations within Bahrain. For further details, contact a local travel or tour operator.
SEA:
Transport between the smaller islands is by motorboat or *dhow*. For details, contact local travel agents.
ROAD:
Manama is served by an excellent road system. Traffic drives on the right. Road signs are written in English and Arabic. **Bus:** Routes now serve most of the towns and villages. **Taxi:** Metered taxis are readily available. They can be hired in the street or from stands outside hotels and at major tourist attractions. They are identifiable by their orange side-wings and yellow number plates. Taxis waiting outside hotels may charge more. Share-taxis which carry up to five passengers are also available. These are recognisable by a yellow circle with the licence number in black painted on the driver's door and by their white and orange number plates. There are several designated pick-up points. Meters are not used and fares should always be agreed beforehand. Radio cabs are also available. **Car hire:** Most of the major international car hire companies operate in Bahrain with representatives at the airport and at big hotels. **Traffic regulations:** Speed restrictions are in place: 100kph (60mph) on highways and between 50-80kph (30-50mph) on all other roads.
Documentation: An International Driving Permit is necessary (must be obtained prior to arrival) and must be endorsed by the Traffic and Licensing Directorate. Valid UK licence (if applicable) will be valid for three months only.

Travel Advice

Most visits to Bahrain are trouble-free but you should be aware of the global risk of indiscriminate international terrorist attacks, which could be against civilian targets, including places frequented by foreigners.
This advice is based on information provided by the Foreign and Commonwealth Office in the UK. It is correct at time of publishing. As the situation can change rapidly, visitors are advised to contact the following organisations for the latest travel advice:

British Foreign and Commonwealth Office
Tel: (0845) 850 2829.
Website: www.fco.gov.uk

US Department of State
Website: http://travel.state.gov/travel

Accommodation

HOTELS:
Bahrain offers an impressive choice of world-class hotels. Hotel accommodation ranges from 5-star comfort, to family-run hotels and 1-star budget establishments. The deluxe hotels are well represented by international chains with some providing a meet-and-greet service from the airport if sufficient notice is given.

Top Things To See

- **Manama**, Bahrain's capital, is modern, dominated by a Manhattan-style skyline. Much land, including the diplomatic area, has been reclaimed from the sea. The ancient city capital of **Bilad al-Qadim**, which dates from AD 900, is just outside the new city. The **souk** lies in the centre of the old town, near the archway of **Bab al-Bahrain** and, although much of the surrounding area is modern, the street layout and division of occupations still follow traditional lines: the **gold souk**, for example, is to be found to the southeast of the market area and is particularly impressive during the hours of darkness.
- To sample some of Bahrain's past, you must see the **A'ali Burial Mounds**. This is the site for probably the largest prehistoric cemetery in the world with approximately 170,000 burial mounds dating from between 3000 BC and AD 600.
- Look inside **The House of Beit al-Jasra**, which is the birthplace of the Amir, the ruler of Bahrain, and is a wonderful example of traditional Bahraini architecture (built in 1907), with exquisite external simplicity, constructed from local building materials such as coral stone.
- Stare at **ancient forts** such as those of **Arad**, **Bahrain** and **Riffa**.
- Go to the **National Museum**, which traces the archaeological development of Bahrain and see an **ancient burial mound** dating from 2800 BC.
- Look up at Bahrain's largest mosque, the **al-Fateh Grand Mosque**. In addition, the **Grand Masjid** is constructed of masses of fibreglass and is particularly awe-inspiring under floodlights at night.
- Examine the '**wind towers**' of ancient houses in the old town of Manama: constructed 5-6m (16-20ft) above the houses and open on all sides, they served as primitive air-conditioning units.
- Absorb the sight of long stretches of **sandy beach** and **coral reefs** in places such as **Al Jazair**, complete with beach huts, pavilions, and picnic areas.
- See endangered species such as **Arabian Onyx** at **al-Areen Wildlife Sanctuary**.
- Sit under the **Tree of Life**, which is a large green mesquite tree, astonishingly spouting from sterile desert ground. Hundreds of years old and the only tree for miles, it offers a welcome respite from the glaring heat.
- Look around the **Barbar Temples**, thought to have been built in worship of the God Enki and his wife. One Temple is built on a spring of water on which there is a basin of the sacred well, and the water was almost certainly considered holy. In their entirety, three Barbar Temples are built on top of one another, in degrees of antiquity, a general feature of Sumerian temples.
- **Bait al Quran** (**The House of the Qur'an**) is something resembling a museum of Holy Qur'ans and is definitely worth seeing for its rare collection of manuscripts revealing beautiful Islamic art and calligraphy, and for the architectural setting, which is serenely lovely.

Top Things To Do

- Go **swimming**, **scuba diving**, **snorkelling**, **water-skiing**, **windsurfing**, **parasailing** or **yachting** around Bahrain's sprinkling of islands.
- **Game fish** for grouper and barracuda.
- **Ride** a **camel** along a highway.
- Purchase an irreplaceable Bahraini souvenir and buy some authentic pottery by potters whose trade dates back hundreds of years at **A'ali Village Pottery**.
- **Haggle** for goods at local **souks**.

TOURIST INFORMATION

Bahrain Tourism Company
PO Box 5831, Manama, Bahrain
Tel: (17) 530 530 *or* 1122 *or* 534 321.
Website: www.alseyaha.com

Entertainment

FOOD & DRINK: There is a good selection of restaurants serving all kinds of food, including American, Arabic, Chinese, European, Indian, Japanese, Lebanese and Mexican. Arabic food is mainly spicy and strongly flavoured. Lamb is the principal meat with chicken, turkey and duck. Salad and dips are common. Strong Arabic coffee and tea is also widely available.
Things to know: The sale of alcohol is not encouraged, although it is available to non-Muslims in nightclubs, good restaurants and luxury hotels, except during Ramadan. Muslims in Bahrain are not allowed to drink alcohol at any age. Non-Muslims over the age of 18 are allowed to drink, but are not allowed to transport any alcohol and must drink their alcohol where they buy it. Even non-Muslim adults are forbidden to drink during Ramadan.
National specialities:
- *Machbous* is fish or meat served with rice.
- *Muchammar* is brown, sweet rice served with sugar or dates.
- *Baba ghanoush* is a delicious dinner of pureed garlic, aubergine, yoghurt and sesame paste, usually served with vegetables or pita bread.
- *Falafel* is widely eaten.
- *Shawarma* is lamb or chicken carved from a rotating spit and wrapped in flat bread.
- Small fried potatoes are a popular accompaniment.
- *Sambousan* are crisp pastry cases filled with meat, cheese, sugar or nuts.

National drinks:
- *Arak* (grape spirit flavoured with aniseed).
- Beer is commonly drunk.
- *Gahwa* (coffee) often has cardamom and saffron added to it.

Tipping: 10 per cent is expected by taxi drivers and waiters, particularly when service is not included, and is normal practice. Airport porters expect 100 fils for each piece of luggage.
NIGHTLIFE: Restaurants, nightclubs and cinemas showing English and Arabic films can be found in the main towns.
SHOPPING: There is a wide range of modern shopping complexes with imported luxury goods. Pearls are the main

local product. Famous red clay pottery is available from the village of A'ali. There are weavers at Bani Jamra village and basket-makers at Jasra village. **Shopping hours:** Sat-Thurs 0830-1230 and 1530-1930. Some shops are open for a few hours on Friday mornings in *souks*.

Business

- **GDP:** US$13.01 billion (2003 estimate).
- **Main exports:** Petroleum and petroleum products, aluminum and textiles.
- **Main imports:** Crude oil, machinery and chemicals.
- **Main trade partners:** USA, Korea (Rep), Saudi Arabia, Japan, UK and Germany.

ECONOMY: Oil dominates Bahrain's economy and, together with gas and petrochemicals, accounts for the bulk of exports and government revenue. That proportion is falling, however, as Bahrain seeks to diversify its economy and the reserves dwindle. Several successful industrial projects, including aluminium production, an iron-ore processing facility and an ammonia-methanol plant, have been set up. In the service sector, the financial services industry has expanded dramatically in recent years, as companies trading in the region have set up their regional centres in Bahrain, where the relatively relaxed environment is an important factor in a region where rigorous social mores are often the norm. In June 2000, Bahrain was identified by the Organisation for Economic Cooperation and Development (OECD) – the world's 30 wealthiest economies – as one of 35 countries whose financial laws are believed to encourage large-scale tax evasion and possible money laundering. The government has since taken measures to meet the OECD's demands, thereby avoiding the threat of future sanctions. In September 2004, a Free Trade Pact was signed with the US. However, Saudi Arabia condemned the move, saying it hindered regional economic integration.

BUSINESS ETIQUETTE: Businessmen are expected to wear suits and ties. Business must be done on a personal introduction basis. Normal social courtesies should be observed but introductions and greetings are important and polite conversation is expected before business discussions begin. Bargaining is common practice: Arabs regard their word as their bond and expect others to do the same. The best time to visit is October to April. **Office hours:** Usually Sat-Wed 0800-1300 and 1500-1730. Some offices work Sat-Thurs 0800-1530. **Government office hours:** Sat-Wed 0700-1415.

COMMERCIAL INFORMATION

Commercial Arbitration Centre
PO Box 16100, Adliya, Bahrain
Tel: (17) 825 540.
Website: www.gccarbitration.net

Bangladesh

100km
50mls
✈ international airport

Location: South Asia.

Time: GMT + 6.

Overview

Formerly known as East Pakistan, Bangladesh came into being only in 1971, when the two parts of Pakistan split after a bitter civil war which drew in neighbouring India. Bangladesh spent 15 years under military rule and, although democracy was restored in 1990, the political scene remains volatile. Most of the country is formed by the alluvial plain of the Ganges-Brahmaputra river system - the largest delta in the world; water flow is second only to that of the Amazon. To the east of the delta lie the Chittagong Hill Tracts. Flooding is normal and life has adapted to take account of this. Occasionally, excessive flooding, as in 1988, 1998 and 2004, causes widespread destruction and loss of life. On December 26th 2004, Bangladesh was affected by a tsunami that spread destruction across many parts of Asia, although the damage was far less severe in Bangladesh than in other countries, and travel, for the most part, has been unaffected. The landscape in Bangladesh is mainly flat with many bamboo-, mango- and palm-covered plains created by the effects of the great river systems of the Ganges and the Brahmaputra. The Sundarbans in southwest Bangladesh is one of the largest Mangrove forests in the world and the area supports a variety of wildlife, including the Royal Bengal Tiger, the national animal. Today, Bangladesh is one of the world's most densely populated countries and poverty is deep and widespread, although the population growth has reduced and the health and education systems have improved.

However, there have been political tensions in recent years and the country has been criticised for its human rights record. As a result, travellers are advised against all but essential travel to the Chittagong Hill Tracts (this does not include the city of Chittagong) because of the risk of being caught up in clashes between rival tribal groups, settlers and the military.

General Information

AREA: 147,570 sq km (56,977 sq miles).
POPULATION: 130 million (official estimate 2000).
POPULATION DENSITY: 882.3 per sq km.

CAPITAL: Dhaka. **Population:** 3,612,850 (1991).
GEOGRAPHY: The People's Republic of Bangladesh, formerly East Pakistan, is bordered to the west and northwest by West Bengal (India), to the north by Assam and Meghalaya (India), to the east by Assam and Tripura (India) and by Myanmar (Burma) to the southeast. The landscape is mainly flat with many bamboo, mango and palm-covered plains. A large part of Bangladesh is made up of alluvial plain, caused by the effects of the two great river systems of the Ganges (Padma) and the Brahmaputra (Jamuna) and their innumerable tributaries. In the northeast and east of the country, the landscape rises to form forested hills. To the southeast, along the Burmese and Indian borders, the land is hilly and wooded. About one-seventh of the country's area is under water and flooding occurs regularly.
GOVERNMENT: Republic. Gained independence from Pakistan in 1971. **Head of State:** President Iajuddin Ahmed since 2002. **Head of Government:** Prime Minister Khaleda Zia since 2001. **Recent history:** After 16 years of Presidential Government, punctuated by spells of martial law, Bangladesh reverted to its original Parliamentary system in August 1992, when constitutional amendments were approved by national referendum. The Prime Minister is the leader of the majority party in the *Jatiya Sangsad* (Parliament). Its members also elect the largely titular post of President, who is the Head of State. In October 2001, Khaleda Zia, the first female Prime Minister in Bangladesh, came to power following a landslide election victory of the four-party alliance led by her Bangladesh Nationalist Party. Her Government has pointed to successes in handling the economy and in tackling environmental issues. But it has struggled to deliver on its key election pledge of containing lawlessness and violence. Ms Zia has come under opposition pressure to call early elections, amid a background of general strikes and protests. There have been a spate of politically motivated violent incidents in Bangladesh in 2004/2005. In August 2004, 20 members of the Awami League were killed, including the Woman's Affairs Secretary, Ivy Rahman. In January 2005, former Finance Minister, Shah Kibria, was assassinated with four colleagues in another grenade attack at an Awami League rally in northern Bangladesh. Bangladesh has also ranked worst on Transparency International's Corruption Perception Index for the past four years.
LANGUAGE: The official language is Bengali (Bangla). English is widely spoken, especially in Government and commercial circles. Tribal dialects are also spoken.
RELIGION: 88 per cent Muslim, 10 per cent Hindus and 2 per cent Buddhist and Christian minorities. Religion is the main influence on attitudes and behaviour. Since 1988, Islam has been the official state religion.
ELECTRICITY: 220/240 volts AC, 50Hz. Plugs are of the British 5- and 15-amp, two- or three-pin (round) type.
SOCIAL CONVENTIONS: In someone's home it is acceptable to sit crossed-legged on cushions or the sofa. If a visitor wishes to bring a gift, money must not be given as it may cause offence. Religious customs should be respected by guests. There are severe penalties for possession and trafficking of illegal drugs. some drugs-related offences are punishable by death. For instance, women should not be specifically photographed unless it is certain that there will be no objection. Women should wear trousers or long skirts; revealing clothes should be avoided, particularly when visiting religious places. Dress is generally informal for men, though modesty must be maintained. Same-sex relations are illegal. **Photography:** In rural areas, people are becoming more used to tourists; however, permission should be requested before photographs are taken of individuals. Do not photograph military installations.

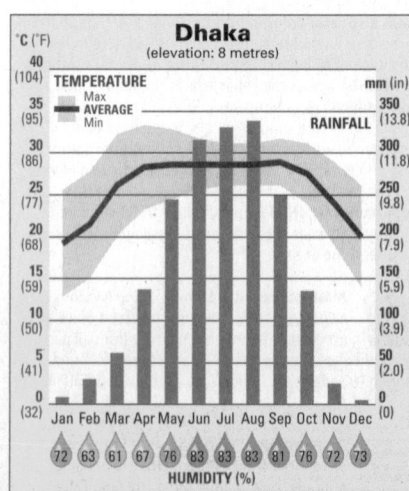

Climate

Very hot, tropical climate with a monsoon season from April to October when temperatures are highest; rainfall averages over 2540mm. The cool season is between November and March. The country is prone to widespread flooding and is also a high-risk earthquake zone.

Required clothing: Lightweight cottons and linens throughout the year. Warmer clothes are needed in the evenings during the cool season. Waterproofs are necessary during the monsoon season.

Communications

Telephone: Limited IDD available. Country code: 880. Public telephone booths are located at the principal marketplaces and in post offices in the main towns.
Mobile telephone: Coverage is limited to main towns.
Internet: Public Internet services exist in the main towns and there are also a few Internet cafes. Hotels in Dhaka and Chittagong offer Internet access (mainly to guests).
Post: Airmail takes three to four days to Europe; surface mail can take several months. Post boxes are blue for airmail and red for surface mail.
MEDIA: The main broadcast media in Bangladesh, *Radio Bangladesh* and *Bangladesh Television*, are state-owned and favourable to the Government. Little coverage is given to the political opposition, except in the run-up to general elections when a caretaker Government takes control. Although Bangladesh Television remains the country's sole terrestrial TV channel, private satellite-delivered TV stations have established a presence. The constitution guarantees press freedom, but journalists are subject to regular harassment from the police and political activists. Bangladeshi newspapers are diverse, outspoken and privately owned. English-language titles appeal mainly to the educated urban elite. The authorities sometimes withdraw foreign publications from circulation over articles or images considered malicious or offensive.
Press: There are some daily English-language papers, the most popular being the *Bangladesh Observer*, followed by the *Daily Star* and the *New Nation*. The main English-language weeklies include *Holiday*. The main Bengali dailies are *Dainik Ittefaq* and *Dainik Jugantor*. Almost all these newspapers are published in Dhaka and circulated throughout the country.
TV: Bangladesh Television (BTV) is Government-run. *ATN Bangla*, *Channel i* and *NTV* are private channels available via satellite and cable.
Radio: *Betar-Radio Bangladesh* is Government-run. *Radio Metrowave* is a commercial, music and news station aimed at younger listeners in Dhaka. The *BBC World Service* is available on FM in Dhaka.

Passport/Visa

	Passport Required?	Visa Required?	Return Ticket Required?
Full British	Yes	Yes	Yes
Australian	Yes	Yes	Yes
Canadian	Yes	Yes	Yes
USA	Yes	Yes	Yes
Other EU	Yes	Yes	Yes
Japanese	Yes	Yes	Yes

Note: *Regulations and requirements may be subject to change at short notice, and you are advised to contact the appropriate diplomatic or consular authority before finalising travel arrangements. Any numbers in the chart refer to the footnotes below.*

Restricted entry: The government of Bangladesh refuses admission and transit to nationals of Israel.
PASSPORTS: Passport valid for three months after departure required by all.
VISAS: Required by all except the following:
(a) nationals of Bangladesh or former Bangladeshi nationals holding British passports, provided they have the statement 'no visa required for travel to Bangladesh' stamped in their passport by the Bangladesh High Commission;
(b) nationals of Hong Kong (SAR) and Macau (SAR) for stays of up to 30 days;
(c) nationals of The Maldives (can obtain a visa on arrival);
(d) transit passengers continuing their journey by the same or first connecting aircraft, provided holding valid onward or return documentation and not leaving the airport.
Note: Some tourist and business travellers who do not have a mission for Bangladesh in their country of origin can obtain 30-day visas (for business and investment purposes) on arrival (provided holding letter of invitation from company based in Bangladesh, containing their Tax Identification Number and attestation from Chamber of Commerce or Bangladeshi Government ministries with corresponding passport name and passport number) and also 90-day visas at Chittagong, Dhaka and Zia international airports, provided holding return air tickets

and sufficient funds for stay and all documents for next destination. Citizens of countries where there is a Bangladesh Mission must obtain a visa before going to Bangladesh.
Types of visa and cost: *Tourist* and *Business*. Prices vary according to nationality; contact the Embassy for more details (see *Passport/Visa Information*). For UK passport holders: £40 (single-entry); £52 (double-entry); £75 (triple-entry); £104 (multiple-entry). Visas are issued free for nationals of India and Japan.
Validity: *Single-entry*: Three months; *Double-entry* and *Triple-entry*: Six months. *Multiple-entry*: Twelve months. Stays are for a maximum of 90 days each.
Application to: Consular Section at Embassy or High Commission; see *Passport/Visa Information*.
Application requirements: (a) Valid passport. (b) Completed application form. (c) Passport-size photos. (d) Fee, payable in cash (application in person) or postal order (postal application). (e) Letter from employer confirming applicant's identity and position in the company. (f) For postal applications, self-addressed, pre-paid registered envelope or pre-paid return courier. *Tourist*: (a)-(f) and, (g) Printed itinerary. (h) Hotel reservation letter, or invitation letter, which should be on official letterhead or, if it is from a private individual, have bank statement attached. *Business*: (a)-(f) and, (g) Invitation from a business organisation in Bangladesh. (h) Letter from the sponsoring organisation in the UK detailing their financial responsibility for the applicant.
Working days required: Three. At least seven days for postal applications. Application times are longer (two to three weeks) for non-British or Irish nationals and journalists.
Temporary residence: Enquire at Passport Control Office, Dhaka, Bangladesh.

PASSPORT/VISA INFORMATION

Bangladesh High Commission in the UK
28 Queen's Gate, London SW7 5JA, UK
Tel: (020) 7584 0081.
Website: www.bangladeshhighcommission.org.uk
Opening hours: Mon-Fri 1000-1730; Mon-Thurs 1030-1300 and 1500-1630, Fri 1030-1245; 1500-1630 (visa collection).

Bangladesh Embassy in the USA
3510 International Drive, NW, Washington, DC 20008, USA
Tel: (202) 244 0183.
Website: www.bangladoot.org

Money

Currency: Bangladesh Taka (BDT) = 100 paisa. Notes are in denominations of BDT500, 100, 50, 20, 10, 5, 2 and 1. Coins are in denominations of BDT5 and 1, and 50, 25, 10 and 5 paisa.
Currency exchange: All foreign currency exchanged must be entered on a currency declaration form. Hotel bills must be paid in a major convertible currency or with traveller's cheques. Many shops in the cities will offer better rates of exchange than the banks.
Credit & debit cards: Credit cards are not generally accepted outside the capital. Check with your credit or debit card company for details of merchant acceptability and other services which may be available. ATMs (Standard Chartered Bank) in Dhaka, Chittagong, Bogra, Sylhet, Narayanganj and Khulna. HSBC has ATMs in Dhaka and Chittagong. Both accept UK cashpoint cards.
Traveller's cheques: Can be exchanged on arrival at Dhaka Airport. To avoid additional exchange rate charges, travellers are advised to take traveller's cheques in US Dollars or Pounds Sterling.
Currency restrictions: The import and export of local currency is limited to BDT100. Reconversion of local currency is permitted up to BDT500 or 25 per cent of the amount exchanged on arrival. The import of foreign currency is allowed but amounts greater than US$150 must be declared on arrival. The export of foreign currency is limited to US$150 or the amount declared on arrival.
Banking hours: Sun-Wed 0900-1500, Thurs 0900-1300. Selected banks may open on Saturdays.
Exchange rate indicators:
Rate at time of publishing
£1.00=   BDT115.99
$1.00=   BDT65.73

Duty Free

The following goods may be imported into Bangladesh without incurring customs duty:
200 cigarettes or 50 cigars or 225g of tobacco; two bottles of alcoholic beverages or one bottle if not

travelling for touristic purposes (non-Muslims only); 250ml of perfume; gifts up to the value of BDT500.
Note: Duty free items may be bought at the duty free shop at Dhaka Airport on arrival:
Prohibited items: Firearms and some animals.

Public Holidays

Below are listed Public Holidays for the January 2006-June 2007 period.
2006: Jan 1 New Year's Day. **Jan 10** Eid ul-Adha (Feast of the Sacrifice). **Jan 31** Islamic New Year. **Feb 21** International Mother Language Day. **Mar 26** Independence Day. **Apr 11** Eid-e-Milad-un Nabi (Birth of the Prophet). **Apr 14** Bangla New Year. **May 1** Labour Day. **May 13** Buddha Purnima. **Sep 8** Shab-e Barat (Ascension of the Prophet). **Oct 2** Durga Puja (Dashami). **Oct 20** Shab e-Qadr (Evening of Destiny). **Oct 22-24** Eid al-Fitr (End of Ramadan). **Nov 7** National Revolution Day. **Dec 16** Victory Day (Bijoy Dibosh). **Dec 31** Eid ul-Adha (Feast of the Sacrifice).
2007: Jan 1 New Year's Day. **Jan 20** Islamic New Year. **Feb 21** International Mother Language Day. **Mar 26** Independence Day. **Mar 31** Eid-e-Milad-un Nabi. **Apr 14** Bangla New Year. **May 1** Labour Day. **May 2** Buddha Purnima.
Note: (a) Muslim festivals are timed according to local sightings of various phases of the moon and the dates given above are approximations. During the lunar month of Ramadan that precedes Eid al-Fitr, Muslims fast during the day and feast at night and normal business patterns may be interrupted. Many restaurants are closed during the day and there are restrictions on smoking and drinking. Some disruption may continue into Eid al-Fitr itself. Eid al-Fitr and Eid ul-Azha may last anything from two to 10 days, depending on the region. (b) Buddhist festivals are declared according to local astronomical observations and it is not possible to forecast the date of their occurrence exactly.

Health

	Special Precautions?	Certificate Required?
Yellow Fever	No	1
Cholera	2	No
Typhoid & Polio	3	N/A
Malaria	4	N/A

Note: *Regulations and requirements may be subject to change at short notice, and you are advised to contact your doctor well in advance of your intended date of departure. Any numbers in the chart refer to the footnotes below.*

1: A yellow fever certificate is required of all persons (including infants) arriving by air or sea within six days of departure from an infected area, or a country with infection in any part, or a country where the WHO judges yellow fever to be endemic or present; or has been in such an area in transit; or has come by an aircraft which has come from such an area and has not been properly diÂsinfected. Those arriving without a required certificate will be detained in quarantine for six days. For further information, see the *Health* appendix.
2: Following WHO guidelines issued in 1973, a cholera vaccination certificate is no longer a condition of entry to Bangladesh. However, cholera is a serious risk in this country and precautions are essential. Up-to-date advice should be sought before deciding whether these precautions should include vaccination as medical opinion is divided over its effectiveness; see the *Health* appendix.
3: Vaccination against typhoid is advised.
4: Malaria risk exists throughout the year in the whole country with the exception of Dhaka City. The malignant *falciparum* form is reported to be highly resistant to chloroquine and resistant to sulfadoxine-pyrimethamine. The recommended prophylaxis is likely to be mefloquine, doxycycline or atovaquone/proguanil: see advice before travel.
Food & drink: All water should be regarded as being potentially contaminated. Water used for drinking, brushing teeth or making ice should have first been boiled or otherwise sterilised. Milk is unpasteurised and should be boiled. Powdered or tinned milk is available and is advised, but make sure that it is reconstituted with pure water. Avoid all dairy products. Only eat well-cooked meat and fish, preferably served hot. Salad and mayonnaise may carry increased risk. Vegetables should be cooked and fruit peeled.
Other risks: *Dengue fever*, *visceral leishmaniasis*, *TB* and *hepatitis A, B* and *E* are present. *Japanese encephalitis* occurs. Humidity and pollution in downtown Dhaka, especially at certain times of the year, can cause problems. *Rabies* is present. For those at high risk, vaccination before arrival should be considered. If bitten abroad, seek medical advice without delay. For more information, consult the *Health* appendix.
Health care: There is no reciprocal health agreement with the UK and health insurance is essential. Visitors can also be treated at military hospitals.

Travel - International

AIR:

The national airline is *Biman Bangladesh Airlines (BG)*.
Approximate flight times: From Dhaka to *London* (direct) is nine hours, to *Los Angeles* is 21 hours and to *New York* is 23 hours.
Main airports: *Dhaka International (DAC) (Zia International)*. The airport is 20km (11 miles) north of the city (travel time – 45 minutes). *To/from the airport*: Biman Bangladesh coaches run every hour from 0800-2200. To return, pick up the coach from the Tejgaon old airport building, the Golden Gate or Zakaria hotels. Parjatan Coaches are also available. Bus and taxi services are available to the city. It is usual to give a 5 per cent tip to taxi drivers. It has been known for passengers to suffer harassment at International Airports, even by corrupt officials or unlicensed touts. It is best to arrange pickup in advance, preferably with the hotel or friends. The airport has, however, improved immeasurably in the last couple of years and improvement looks set to continue. Hopefully, these issues will eventually be resolved. *Facilities:* Restaurants, post office, banks, duty free shops and car hire. Other international airports include *Chittagong (CGP) (MA Hannan International Airport)* and *Sylhet (ZYL) (Osmani International Airport)*.
Departure tax: BDT300. Children under two years of age and passengers in immediate transit are exempt.

SEA:

The main seaport is *Chittagong*. Ferries from Myanmar and India run to the southern coastal ports. For details, contact the Embassy or High Commission of the People's Republic of Bangladesh (see *Passport/Visa Information*).

RAIL:

Rail connections (there are no through-trains) link Bangladesh with India (West Bengal and Assam). Cycle-rickshaw, bus or porter services provide the cross-border connections.

ROAD:

Overland crossings include the Benapol-Haridispur border (for Calcutta), the Chilihari-Haldibari border (for Darjeeling) and the Tamabil-Dawki border (for Shillong). The crossing at Benapol is the easiest and most used. It is advisable to check when the frontier posts will be open. Conditions are likely to be difficult during the monsoon season. All other frontier posts between the two countries are currently closed. Overland travel is not currently possible between Bangladesh and Myanmar. **Coach:** A direct daily service has recently been introduced between Dhaka and Calcutta via Benapol. For further details, contact Bangladesh Road Transport Corporation (tel: (2) 955 5553).

Travel - Internal

AIR:

Internal services are operated by *Aero Bengal Airlines, Air Parabat, Bengal Airlift LTD, Biman Bangladesh Airlines (BG)* and *GMG Airlines*.
Regular flights are run between Dhaka and several other main towns. These are cheap, and most routes are served at least two or three times a week. Airline buses connect with terminals.
Domestic airports: These include *Barisal, Cox's Bazar, Ishwdi, Jessore, Rajshahi* and *Saidpur*.
Departure tax: BDT25.

SEA/RIVER:

The country has about 8433km (5240 miles) of navigable waterways and water transport, if a little slow, is the least expensive method of getting around Bangladesh. Ferries operate between southern coastal ports and the Ganges River delta, where there are five **major river ports**: *Barisal, Chandpur, Dhaka, Khulna* and *Narayanganj*. Passages should be booked well in advance; for details, contact local port authorities. River services are operated by the Bangladesh Inland Waterway Transport Corporation (BIWTC), who run 'Rocket' ferries and launches on a number of routes. A ferry operates from Dhaka to Khulna four times a week (travel time – 28 hours). Ferries can often be dangerously overcrowded. The most recent incident was in February 2005 when 150 people drowned near Dhaka. In the past, these incidents have incurred greater casualties.

RAIL:

A slow but efficient network, operated by *Bangladesh Railway*, is limited by the geography of the country, but river ferries (see above) provide through links. Services are being upgraded. However, trains still occasionally derail and passengers have been injured. The main line is Dhaka–Chittagong, with several daily trains, some of which have air-conditioned cars. An inter-city express service is available between main towns. For details, contact the Embassy or High Commission for the People's Republic of Bangladesh (see *Passport/Visa Information*).

ROAD:

There are approximately 6240km (3877 miles) of roads, of which 3840km (2386 miles) are paved. Road safety is poor. Traffic is heavy and chaotic in urban areas. There are frequent and often lethal crashes caused by speeding, dangerous and aggressive overtaking, sudden manoeuvres, etc. Vehicles and roads are badly maintained and often unlit; drivers, if in lit vehicles, will often have the light full-beam. In addition to all this, banditry is a problem after dark. It is possible to reach virtually everywhere by road, but given the geography of the country, with frequent ferry crossings being a necessity, together with the poor quality of many of the roads, road travel can be very slow. Traffic drives on the left. **Bus:** The Bangladesh Road Transport Corporation (BRTC) provides a countrywide network of bus services. All major towns are served; fares are generally low. **Taxi:** Generally available at airports and major hotels. Fares should always be agreed upon before travelling. It is usual to give a 5 per cent to taxi drivers. **Car hire:** Cars may be hired at Dhaka airport, the Bangladesh Tourism Corporation Office or from the major hotels. However, in the major cities, it is relatively easy and inexpensive to hire chauffeur-driven cars. **Documentation:** International Driving Permit required.

URBAN:

There are **bus** services, which are usually very crowded and unreliable, in Dhaka, provided by the Bangladesh Road Transport Corporation. The Central Bus Station is on Station Road (Fulbaria); there are also several other terminals, which are, in general, for long-distance services. Buses and bus stations do not generally have signs in English. There are also an estimated 10,000 independent 'auto-rickshaw' 3-wheeler taxis (avoid night-time use). Conventional taxis are also available.
Travel times: The following chart gives approximate travel times (in hours and minutes) from **Dhaka** to other major cities/towns in Bangladesh.

	Air	Road	Rail
Chittagong	0.35	6.00	6.00
Sylhet	0.30	7.00	7.00
Rajshahi	0.45	12.00	13.00
Rangpur	-	11.30	11.30

Travel Advice

Travellers are advised against all but essential travel to the Chittagong Hill Tracts (this does not include the city of Chittagong) because of the risk of being caught up in clashes between rival tribal groups, settlers and the military. Travellers should be aware of the threat from terrorism in Bangladesh. Attacks using explosive devices continue to take place in locations throughout the country, including Dhaka and the Sylhet region, with increasing frequency. Such attacks are indiscriminate and are carried out in public places, including courts, markets, cinemas, shrines, cultural events and political gatherings. There is a risk that travellers might get caught up in such attacks.
Please also note that, on December 26th 2004, a massive earthquake registering 9.0 on the Richter scale struck off the west coast of Indonesia. The quake created a tsunami – a series of huge waves that spread destruction across many parts of Asia and reached as far as the east coast of Africa. The damage was far less severe in Bangladesh than in other countries and travel, for the most part, has been unaffected. This advice is based on information provided by the Foreign and Commonwealth Office in the UK. It is correct at time of publishing. As the situation can change rapidly, visitors are advised to contact the following organisations for the latest travel advice:

British Foreign and Commonwealth Office
Tel: (0845) 850 2829.
Website: www.fco.gov.uk

US Department of State
Website: http://travel.state.gov/travel

Accommodation

HOTELS:

There are a few 5-star hotels in Dhaka, Chittagong and Cox's Bazar. All rates are for European Plan. The Bangladesh Parjatan Corporation (see *Top Things To Do*) manages several modern hotels throughout the country. Bills are usually paid in hard currency or with traveller's cheques.

GUEST HOUSES:

Government-owned and private guest houses are available to hire throughout the country. Enquire at the Bangladesh Parjatan Corporation (see *Top Things To Do*).

Top Things To See

- In **Dhaka**, the historic city and capital of Bangladesh (north central), visit the old part of the city, to the south of the centre and on the banks of the river. Buildings of interest include the uncompleted 17th-century **Lalbagh Fort**, the stately **Ahsan Manzil Palace** and **Museum** (sometimes referred to as the **Pink Palace**), the **Chotta Katra** and a large number of mosques. To the north of this region is the European quarter (also known as British City), which contains the **Banga Bhavan**, the Presidential palace, several parks and the **Dhakeswari Temple**. It is worth noting the **Dharmarajika Buddhist Monastery** near Central Railway Station at **Kamalapur** (established in 1962), which enshrines the thousand-year-old **black stone Buddha**. The **Khan Mohammed Mirdha Mosque** and the **Mausoleum of Pari Bibi** are worth a visit, as are the **Baldha Gardens** with their collection of rare plants. There are dozens of mosques and bazaars to visit – the **Kashaitully Mosque** is especially beautiful.
- Immerse yourself in history in **Sonargaon**, about 30km (20 miles) east of Dhaka, the capital of the region between the 13th and early 17th centuries. The city retains a number of historical relics of interest, although many of these are now in ruins.
- More Hindu temples can be found in **Dhamrai**, northwest of Dhaka.
- Around 43km (27 miles) from Sylhet are the ruins of **Jaintiapur**, once the capital of an ancient kingdom.
- Although often ignored by tourists, the **Rajshahi Division**, in the northwest of the country, contains a large number of archaeological sites. The most important of these are at **Paharpur**, where the vast Buddhist monastery of **Somapuri Vihara** and the **Satyapir Vita** temple are located; there is also a museum.
- Other places of interest in the region include the ancient Hindu settlement of **Sherpur**, near Bogra; **Mahastanagar**, also near Bogra, which dates back to the third century BC; **Vasu Vihara**, 14km (9 miles) to the northwest, the site of an ancient but now ruined monastery; **Rajshahi**, on the Ganges, which has a museum displaying many of the archaeological relics of the area; and **Gaur**, very close to the border with the Indian state of West Bengal, which contains a number of old mosques.
- **Bogra** is a useful base for visiting the archaeological sites of **Paharpur**, **Mahastanagar** and **Sherpur**, although not intrinsically interesting itself. The Bangladesh Parjatan Corporation (NTO) offers package tours to these sites.
- In the southwest, places of interest include the mosque of **Sat Gumbad**, and the town of **Bagerhat** (home of Khan Jahan Ali, a well-known Sufi mystic).
- In **Kuakata** (southwest), see a 70ft-Buddhist statue.
- In the south, discover two pre-Moghul mosques: one, which boasts nine domes, is situated at the village of **Qasba Guarnadi**, and the other, built in 1464, is near **Patuakhali**.
- In **Chittagong** (southeast), the second-largest city in the country, the Old City retains many echoes of past European settlements, mainly by the Portuguese, as well as many mosques. These include the 17th-century **Shahi Jama-e-Masjid** – which closely resembles a fort – set astride a hilltop, and the earlier **Qadam Mubarek Mosque**. The **Chilla of Bada Shah** stands to the west of Bakshirhat in the old city. The **Dargah of Sah Amanat** is a holy shrine located in the heart of the town.
- Approximately 8km (5 miles) from Chittagong is the picturesque **Foy's Lake** in the railway township of **Pahartali**. The **Tomb of Sultan Bayazid Bostami**, a holy shrine situated on a hillock in **Nasirabad**, is situated 6km (4 miles) to the northwest of the town. At its base is a large **tank** with several hundred tortoises, supposedly the descendants of evil spirits.
- Be enchanted by beautiful panoramic scenery and waterfalls in **Madhabkunda**, north of Dhaka.
- Perched on the bank of the humanmade **Kaptai Lake**, northeast of Chittagong, **Rangamati** is also a place of scenic beauty and unspoiled tribal life.
- **Tamabil**, a border outpost on Sylhet–Shilong Road, also offers excellent views of the surrounding area, including some spectacular waterfalls across the Indian border. **Zaflong** is a scenic spot nearby, set amidst tea gardens and beautiful hills.

Top Things To Do

- In the capital city, **Dhaka**, spend some time at the **National Museum**, the **Zoo** or the **Botanical Gardens**.
- Go birdwatching in the **Rajendrapur National Park**, about 50km (30 miles) north of the capital, which is noted for its varied birdlife. The **Madhupur National Park and Game Sanctuary** is situated about 160km (99 miles) from Dhaka. Nature lovers will also like **Madubashah**, just 10km (6 miles) outside Barisal (south), which has a lake and a bird sanctuary.
- Spot **Royal Bengal Tigers**, the country's national animal, in the **Sundarbans National Park**, a supreme example of lush coastal vegetation and the variety of wildlife which it can support. Spotted deers, monkeys and a great variety of birds are also to be found here. Not surprising,

considering this area boasts the **largest mangrove forest in the world**. The park is located in the **Khulna Division**, which is principally marshland and jungle. Tours (usually for 10 people or more) are organised by the Bangladesh Parjatan Corporation during the winter; otherwise, boats can be hired from **Khulna** or **Mongla**, which is the main port for the Khulna region. Accommodation is available at **Heron Point**.

- Travellers in pursuit of **beaches** should head for **Kuakata**, a newly developed tourist resort. It is a scenic beauty spot on the southernmost tip of Bangladesh in the district of Patuakhali and has a wide sandy beach which is an ideal vantage point to watch the sun rise and set. Here, visitors can also observe the traditions and unique lifestyle of the Rakhane tribes.
- Step foot on the world's longest and broadest beach, **Inani Beach**, which can be found in **Cox's Bazar**, a thriving regional tourist centre and beach resort in the extreme south of Bangladesh, with a mixed population of Bengali and Burmese origin. The beach is 120km (75 miles) long and 55m (180ft) to 90m (300ft) broad (depending on the tide). The area has not, however, been fully developed for tourism. The town also has many thriving cottage industries for weaving and cigar making.
- The main tourist beach is **Patenga** (southeast), which is also broad and long.
- **Boating** enthusiasts may head to **Sunderbands National Park**, large parts of which are only accessible by rowing boat.
- Located in the Rangamati Hill District, **Kapati Lake** offers good opportunities for **sailing**, **swimming** and **fishing**.
- In February each year, join the annual 10-day **pilgrimage** in **Sitakund**, 37km from Chittagong (southeast), also famous for its temples, including Chandranath and Buddhist temples, a hot spring and the supposed footprint of Lord Buddha.
- Enjoy an excursion to **Sylhet**, North of Dhaka, known as 'the land of two leaves and a bud' because of its long tradition as a **tea-growing area**. **Srimongol** is the main centre of the Sylhet tea gardens.
- Enjoy a game of **cricket**, **hockey** or **football**. The Dhaka Metropolitan Soccer League season begins in April. Games are held in the city stadium and playgrounds.

TOURIST INFORMATION

Bangladesh Parjatan Corporation (National Tourism Organisation)
233 Airport Road, Tejgoan, Dhaka-1215, Bangladesh
Tel: (2) 811 7855-9.
Website: www.bangladeshtourism.org

Entertainment

FOOD & DRINK: There are plenty of good restaurants in Dhaka and main towns around the country. Western food can be found in most hotels and in some large restaurants.
Things to know: Alcoholic drink is expensive and strict Muslim customs severely limit availability and drinking times, although leading hotels have bars which will serve alcohol.
National specialities:
- Curries such as *korma*, *bhuna*, *masala gosht*, *kashmiri* and *tikka*.
- Dishes are usually served with rice, *naan* or *paratha* (griddle-fried flat breads).
- Seafood and fresh-water fish are in natural abundance and smoked *hilsa*, fresh *bhetki*, *chingri* and prawns are definitely worth trying.
- Desserts tend to be sweet and milky, such as *misti dhohi* (sweetened yoghurt), *zorda* (sweet rice with nuts) and *ros malai* (round sweets floating in thick milk).
National drinks:
- *Chai* (milky sweet tea).
- *Lassi* (yoghurt drink).
- Coconut water.
Tipping: Most services expect a tip in hotels; give 10 per cent for restaurant staff.

NIGHTLIFE: Leading hotels have bars, but Western-style nightclubs do not exist. Displays of local dance and music are occasionally to be seen, particularly during religious festivals. Traditional theatre can be seen in major cities and the Dhaka City Corporation has recently opened a modern theatre hall called *Dhaka Mohanagor Natya Mancha*.
SHOPPING: Bangladesh is famous for its pink pearl. Handloom fabrics, silks, printed saris, coconut masks, bamboo products, mother-of-pearl jewellery, leather crafts, wood and cane handicrafts and folk dolls are popular purchases. Duty free shops are available in Dhaka and international airports. **Shopping hours:** Generally Sat-Thurs 0900-2000, Fri 0900-1230 and 1400-2000 (shops in tourist districts often stay open later).

Business

- **GDP:** US$50.92 billion (2003).
- **Main exports:** Garments, jute and jute goods, leather, tea and seafood.
- **Main imports:** Machinery and equipment, chemicals, iron and steel, and foodstuffs.
- **Main trade partners:** Exports to: USA, Germany, UK and France; Imports from: India, China and Singapore.

ECONOMY: With few mineral resources, overcrowded Bangladesh depends mainly on subsistence agriculture, which suffers frequent and severe damage from cyclones and flooding. Tea and jute are the main cash crops – Bangladesh supplies about 90 per cent of the world's raw jute – production of both of which has dipped in recent years, again, largely owing to the weather. There are large reserves of natural gas and some deposits of low-grade coal, which meet the bulk of domestic energy requirements. Offshore gas production in the Bay of Bengal will improve the country's overall energy situation and provide a valuable source of export revenue. Most of the manufacturing workforce is based in jute-related industries; the remainder works in textiles, chemicals and sugar. However, Bangladesh will continue to rely heavily on foreign aid – at present, this derives from a variety of sources coordinated by the World-Bank-led 'Paris Club' of donors. The country's economic stability and consistent growth during the last decade has improved its international status. The major outstanding problem is corruption – measuring corruption is at best an inexact science but Bangladesh is widely recognised to be among the worst offenders. The informal 'hundi' banking system is especially vulnerable to illicit transfers and laundering. In May 2003, the Government established a national commission to tackle the problem. The USA is substantially the largest export market followed by Germany, Italy, the UK and France. India, China and Singapore are the country's main suppliers of imports, which are mostly manufactured goods. Bangladesh is a member of the seven-strong South Asian Association for Regional Co-operation – the main economic grouping in the region.
BUSINESS ETIQUETTE: Tropical-weight suits or shirt and tie are recommended. Suits are necessary when calling on Bengali officials. Cards are given and usual courtesies are observed. Visitors should not be misled by the high illiteracy rate and low educational level of most of the population. Given the opportunity, Bangladeshis prove to be good businesspeople and tough negotiators. The best time to visit is October to March. **Office hours:** Sun-Thurs 0900-1700 and 0800-1430 (Government offices).

COMMERCIAL INFORMATION

Federation of Bangladesh Chambers of Commerce and Industry
60 Motijheel Commercial Area, Dhaka-1000, Bangladesh
Tel: (2) 956 0102/3 *or* 0598.
Website: www.fbcci-bd.org

Barbados

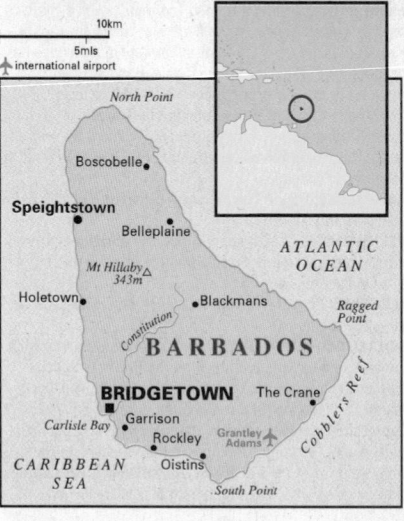

10km
5mls
↟ international airport

North Point
Boscobelle
Speightstown
Belleplaine
ATLANTIC OCEAN
Mt Hillaby △ 343m
Holetown
Blackmans
Ragged Point
BARBADOS
BRIDGETOWN The Crane
Cobblers Reef
Carlisle Bay Garrison
Rockley Grantley
Adams
CARIBBEAN SEA Oistins
South Point

Location: Caribbean, Windward Islands.

Time: GMT -4.

Overview

Little is known of the early history of Barbados – it was probably occupied by Arawak Indians from South America up until the arrival of the Spanish, in the region in the early-16th century. The earliest European arrivals were the Portuguese - also in the early-16th century - although the British established the first settlements in 1627. Barbados was declared a British colony in 1663. Slaves were brought to the island from Africa, to work on the sugar plantations until the abolition of slavery in the mid-19th century. Barbados joined the West Indies Federation in 1958 and was granted internal self-government three years later. Full independence within the British Commonwealth was achieved in 1966.
Today, this laid-back English colony combines pristine beaches, crystal clear water and vibrant flora with great music, a hopping night scene, delicious food and a strong sense of history and culture.
The handsome colonial buildings of the capital, Bridgetown, date mainly from the 18th century, while the later buildings of the suburbs sprawl inland. Many of the island's mixed race population are descendants of the African slaves, brought over to work the colonial sugar plantations.
The dramatic differences between the east and west coast must not be missed. The east (Atlantic side) is less developed and ruggedly beautiful. The west coast is the Caribbean side, where there is more hotel development, but the coastline remains elegant and attractive. The sea is calm and clear and this is the coast where watersports come into their own. Sailing, water-skiing, windsurfing, snorkelling and scuba-diving are just some of the watersports available. The warm Caribbean waters are teeming with colourful fish swimming in vibrant coral reefs. Hire a car, scooter, bicycle or *moke* (open-air jeep) to venture further afield, and visit underwater caves, lush tropical gardens, sugar-cane factories, rum distilleries or plantation houses. Barbados is also actively promoting ecotourism. The Barbados National Trust has implemented programmes to support this venture, owning and/or administering 10 sites that are open to the public.
The island has a lively nightlife with floorshows of limbo dancers and pulsing reggae music – a perfect accompaniment to the Bajan cuisine of spicy seafood, tropical fruits and vegetables, washed down with rum cocktails and fresh fruit juices.

General Information

AREA: 430 sq km (166 sq miles).
POPULATION: 272,000 (UN, 2005).
POPULATION DENSITY: 632.55 per sq km.
CAPITAL: Bridgetown. **Population:** 5928 (1990).
GEOGRAPHY: Barbados is the most easterly of the Caribbean chain of islands. It lies well to the east of the West Indies. To the west, beaches are made of fine white sand and there are natural coral reefs. Along the east coast there is a lively surf as the sea pounds the more rocky shoreline. Barbados is predominantly flat with only a few gently rolling hills to the north. The coral structure of the island acts as a natural filter and the waters of Barbados are amongst the purest in the world.
GOVERNMENT: Constitutional monarchy. Gained independence from the UK in 1966. **Head of State:** HM Queen Elizabeth II, represented locally by Governor-General Sir Clifford Husband since 1996. **Head of Government:** Prime Minister Owen Seymour Arthur since 1994. **Recent history:** Owen Arthur, a trained Economist, won a third term as Prime Minister in 2003 after his Barbados Labour Party (BLP) won 23 of 30 seats in Parliament. Barbados has been a stable democracy since it gained Independence. However, there is a strong lobby – backed by a recent Government Commission examining Barbados' constitutional future – for an elected President as Head of State. This would follow the example of Guyana, Trinidad & Tobago and Dominica.
LANGUAGE: The official language is English. Local Bajan dialect is also spoken.
RELIGION: Mainly Christian, with an Anglican majority, Roman Catholic minority, plus small Jewish, Hindu and Muslim communities.
ELECTRICITY: 110-115 volts AC, 50Hz. American-style two-pin plugs are in use.
SOCIAL CONVENTIONS: Social attitudes, like administration and architecture, tend to echo the British provincial market town. However, the optimistic attitude, laid-back manner and wonderful sense of humour of the Bajans is well appreciated by many tourists. Casual wear is acceptable in most places. Dressing for dinner in hotels and restaurants is suggested. Smoking is generally unrestricted. Topless bathing is frowned upon. Certain homosexual acts are illegal.

Climate

The balmy, tropical climate is cooled by constant sea breezes but is still sunnier and drier than the other islands. The dry season is from December to June; during the so-called wet season (July to November), some brief rain showers are likely. Average sunshine hours per day are eight to 10 from November to March and eight to nine from April to October. Tropical storms and hurricanes may occur between June and November.
Required clothing: Lightweight cottons are advised; beachwear is not worn in towns.

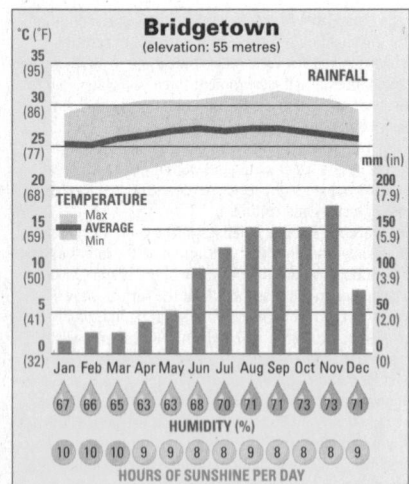

Communications

Telephone: Inward IDD service is available and outward IDD is available from most telephones. Country code: 1 246. Hotels have telephones available to both residents and non-residents. There are cardphones at the airport, the seaport, the university campus, in Bridgetown and at the offices of Barbados External Telecommunications (BET) in Wildey and Bridgetown. Payphones exist throughout the island, although it may be better to use cardphones for overseas calls. Overseas calls may also be made from the offices of BET at Wildey, St Michael. Local calls are free when calling from a residence. Collect overseas calls can be made from cardphones and payphones.

Credit: ©Frances Horder

Mobile telephone: Unregistered roaming is available – visitors with TDMA handsets can make calls without registering, provided they can give a credit card number.
Internet: There are about 20 Internet cafes throughout Barbados.
Post: Deliveries are made twice a day in Bridgetown and once a day in rural areas. Post boxes, which are red, are plentiful. Post office hours: Mon-Fri 0800-1700 at Bridgetown main office; other branches are open Mon 0730-1200 and 1300-1500, Tues-Fri 0800-1200 and 1300-1515.
MEDIA: Barbadians enjoy full freedom of expression. All newspapers are privately-owned, and there is a mix of private and public radio stations. Although the country's sole television station is run by the Government-owned Caribbean Broadcasting Corporation, it presents a wide range of political views.
Press: The main dailies are *The Barbados Advocate* and *The Nation*. Other publications include *Caribbean Week* (fortnightly), *Weekend Investigator* (weekly) and the *Broad Street Journal*, a business journal. Foreign newspapers are also available.
TV: Government-owned Caribbean Broadcasting Corporation (CBC) operates *CBC TV*.
Radio: Government-owned Caribbean Broadcasting Corporation (CBC) operates *CBC Radio 900 AM, Liberty 98.1 FM* and *Quality 100.7 FM* . Barbados Broadcasting Service operates commercial station *BBS FM*, and religious station *Faith 102 FM*. *HOTT 95.3 FM* is a commercial station run by Starcom Network. Starcom Network also operates commercial station *The Voice of Barbados, LOVE 104.1 FM and Gospel 790 AM*.

Passport/Visa

	Passport Required?	Visa Required?	Return Ticket Required?
Full British	Yes	No/1	Yes
Australian	Yes	No/2	Yes
Canadian	Yes	No/2	Yes
USA	Yes	No/3	Yes
Other EU	Yes	No/1	Yes
Japanese	Yes	No/4	Yes

Note: *Regulations and requirements may be subject to change at short notice, and you are advised to contact the appropriate diplomatic or consular authority before finalising travel arrangements. Any numbers in the chart refer to the footnotes below.*

PASSPORTS: Passport valid for duration of intended stay required by all.
VISAS: Tourist visas are required by all except the following:
(a) **1.** nationals of EU countries for stays of up to six months (nationals of the Czech Republic, Estonia, Hungary, Latvia, Lithuania, Poland, Portugal, Slovak Republic and Slovenia for stays of up to 28 days);
(b) **2.** nationals of Commonwealth countries for stays of up to six months (some nationals may be permitted visa-free for differing amounts - see other visa-exemption regulations below), except nationals of Cameroon, India, Mozambique, Namibia, Nauru, Pakistan and Papua New Guinea who *do* need a visa;

(c) **3.** nationals of Brazil, Iceland, Israel, Liechtenstein, Mali, Mauritania, Norway, San Marino, Switzerland, Tunisia, Turkey, Turks & Caicos Islands, USA and Zimbabwe for stays of up to six months;
(d) nationals of Turkey for stays of up to three months;
(e) **4.** nationals of Argentina, Chile, Colombia, Guyana, Japan, Korea (Rep) and Uruguay for stays of up to 90 days;
(f) nationals of Costa Rica for stays of up to 30 days;
(g) nationals of CIS countries for stays of up to 28 days;
(h) nationals of Albania, Bulgaria, Croatia, Cuba, Macedonia (Former Yugoslav Republic of), Mexico, Nicaragua, Panama, Peru, Romania, Surinam and Venezuela for stays of up to 28 days;
(i) transit passengers with valid passport and not leaving the airport but leaving by the same aircraft *or* transit passengers leaving for onward destination within 48 hours, provided holding confirmed tickets and other documents for the next destination.
Types of visa and cost: *Tourist*: £18 (single-entry); £22 (multiple-entry).
Validity: Three months from date of issue.
Application to: Consulate (or Consular Section at Embassy or High Commission); see *Passport/Visa Information*.
Application requirements: (a) One application form. (b) One passport-size photo. (c) Valid passport. (d) Evidence of return or onward flight. (e) Company letter where required. (f) Fee; payable by cash or postal order. (g) Valid visa, if required, to onward/returning country. (h) Special delivery, addressed envelope for postal applications.
Working days required: Two (in person and by post).
Temporary residence: Enquire at the Immigration Office in Barbados.

PASSPORT/VISA INFORMATION

Barbados High Commission in the UK
1 Great Russell Street, London WC1B 3ND, UK
Tel: (020) 7631 4975.
Website: www.foreign.gov.bb
Opening hours: Mon-Fri 0930-1730 (general enquiries); 1000-1600 (visa section).

Embassy of Barbados in the USA
2144 Wyoming Avenue, NW, Washington, DC 20008, USA
Tel: (202) 939 9200.
Website: www.barbados.org

Money

Currency: Barbados Dollar (BBD; symbol B$) = 100 cents. Notes are in denominations of B$100, 50, 20, 10, 5 and 2. Coins are in denominations of B$1, and 25, 10, 5 and 1 cents.
Note: The Barbados Dollar is tied to the US Dollar.
Currency exchange: The best exchange rates are available at commercial banks. The island is served by the Barbados National Bank and a range of at least six international banks, each with a main office in Bridgetown and further branches in Hastings, Holetown, Speightstown and Worthing. ATMs are available.

Credit & debit cards: American Express, Barclaycard, Carte Blanche, Diners Club, Eurocard, MasterCard and Visa are accepted in the resorts, but cash is preferred for customs duty payment. Discover Card may be used in certain places. Check with your credit or debit card company for details of merchant acceptability and other services which may be available.

Traveller's cheques: Accepted by all banks and most hotels. To avoid additional exchange rate charges, travellers are advised to take traveller's cheques in US Dollars or Pounds Sterling.

Currency restrictions: The import of local currency is unlimited, subject to declaration. The export of local currency is prohibited. The import and export of foreign currency is limited to the amount declared on arrival.

Banking hours: Generally Mon-Thurs 0800-1500, Fri 0800-1700.

Exchange rate indicators:
Rate at time of publishing
£1.00=   B$3.44
$1.00=   B$1.95

Duty Free

The following items may be imported into Barbados by persons over 18 years of age without incurring customs duty:

200 cigarettes or 250g of tobacco or other tobacco products; 750ml of spirits and 750ml of wine; 150ml of perfume and 300ml of all other scents; gifts up to a value of Bd$100.

Note: For certain items it is now possible, on presentation of airline tickets and travel documents, to obtain duty free goods any time from the day of arrival in the country. However, tobacco, alcohol and electronic goods must still be bought under the old system immediately prior to embarkation. A permit must be obtained from the Ministry of Agriculture and Consumer Affairs in order to import meat and meat products.

Prohibited items: Foreign rum and matches, fresh fruit and vegetables (only if grown in or conveyed through certain areas; contact the Ministry of Agriculture and Consumer Affairs for further information) and articles made of camouflage material.

Public Holidays

Below are listed Public Holidays for the January 2006-June 2007 period.

2006: Jan 1 New Year's Day. **Jan 21** Errol Barrow Day. **Apr 14** Good Friday. **Apr 17** Easter Monday. **Apr 28** National Heroes' Day. **May 1** Labour Day. **Jun 5** Whit Monday. **Aug 7** Emancipation Day; Kadooment Day. **Nov 30** Independence Day. **Dec 25-26** Christmas.
2007: Jan 1 New Year's Day. **Jan 21** Errol Barrow Day. **Apr 6** Good Friday. **Apr 9** Easter Monday. **Apr 28** National Heroes' Day. **May 1** Labour Day. **May 28** Whit Monday.

Health

	Special Precautions?	Certificate Required?
Yellow Fever	No	1
Cholera	No	No
Typhoid & Polio	2	N/A
Malaria	No	N/A

Note: *Regulations and requirements may be subject to change at short notice, and you are advised to contact your doctor well in advance of your intended date of departure. Any numbers in the chart refer to the footnotes below.*

1: A yellow fever vaccination certificate is required from travellers over one year of age coming from countries with infected areas.

2: A small risk of typhoid exists.

Food & drink: The water in Barbados is considered by some to be the purest in the world; it is filtered naturally by limestone and coral and pumped from underground rivers. Milk is pasteurised and dairy products are safe for consumption. Local meat, poultry, seafood, fruit and vegetables are generally considered safe to eat.

Other risks: Immunisation against *tetanus* and *hepatitis A* are usually recommended; *hepatitis B* may also be recommended for long-term travellers. A low risk of *dengue fever* exists. *Hay fever* and *asthma* can be exacerbated during the sugar cane harvesting season. *Leptospirosis* may occur during the rainy season (October/November). It is also important to note that there is a high prevalence of *HIV/AIDS*, particularly amongst the 20 to 45 age group, of which it is the second-biggest killer. All necessary precautions should be undertaken.

Health care: Excellent medical facilities are available in Barbados, with both private and general wards. Barbados has a reciprocal health agreement with the UK, which

entitles UK nationals to free hospital and polyclinic treatment, ambulance travel and prescribed medicines for children and elderly patients. However, prescribed medicines for those other than children or the elderly and all dental treatment must be paid for. To receive treatment, UK nationals must show their UK passport or NHS medical card, as well as their temporary entry permit. Medical insurance is recommended for all other nationals.

Travel - International

AIR:

Barbados does not have a national airline. Barbados is served by a number of international airlines including *Air Canada*, *Air Jamaica*, *American Airlines*, *British Airways*, *BWIA*, *Canadian Airlines* and *Virgin Atlantic*. *BWIA*, *Caribbean Star* and *LIAT* run flights to most of the neighbouring islands.

Approximate flight times: From Barbados to *Miami* is three hours 30 minutes, to *New York* is five hours, to *London* is seven hours 30 minutes and to *Los Angeles* is nine hours.

Main airports: *Barbados (BGI) (Grantley Adams International)* is 13km (8 miles) southeast of Bridgetown, in Christ Church. *To/from the airport:* There is a regular bus service to the city (travel time – 45 minutes) which departs every 10 minutes, and a 24-hour taxi service (travel time – 30 minutes). Please note that airport porters are ubiquitous and charge B$1 for transporting luggage between the luggage claim area and the street. *Facilities:* Bank, post office, bureaux de change, bar, shops and restaurant. The outgoing duty free shop carries a range of items including jewellery, perfumes, china, crystal, cameras, shoes and clothing. The official opening of the grand new arrivals terminal took place in October 2005. The expanded terminal is twice the size of its predecessor (over 70,000 sq ft of space. Four new jet boarding bridges, a new diplomatic lounge, an extension to the existing departure area have been given the green light by the Government. Other expansion plans include the construction of a multi-storey car park, a fully functional airport hotel and an aviation museum.

Departure tax: B$25 for all departures. Passengers in transit who will be remaining in Barbados for less than 24 hours and children aged under 12 are exempt.

SEA:

Main ports: Barbados, which has a deep-water harbour at *Bridgetown*, is a port of call for a number of British, European and US cruise lines (website: www.barbadosport.com). The Bridgetown Cruise Ship Terminal is a multi-purpose marketplace containing duty free shops, a local goods market, restaurant and bar, customs, immigration, health services and police facilities. Other services include a bureau de change, car hire, ATM and a communications centre with telephones, fax machines and mobile phone hire. There is a small departure tax.

Travel - Internal

AIR:

There are no internal services.

ROAD:

Barbados has a good network of roads which covers the entire island, but there are many potholes (except on the main highway) on the roads and care should be taken. In rural areas, roads are often narrow, unlit or lack sufficient grip. Driving time to the east coast from Bridgetown has been greatly reduced following the completion of the trans-insular highway. Traffic drives on the left. Speed limits are posted in kilometres per hour (40, 60 and 80 kph maximum) and are lower than in the UK. The road journey from Bridgetown to Speightstown takes about 30 minutes and to Holetown or Oistins about 20 minutes. **Bus:** Buses are frequent and provide comprehensive coverage of the island at a flat rate of approximately B$1.50 for all journeys. Although cheap, buses are crowded during the rush hours. All buses terminate at Speightstown. **Mini vans:** Licensed mini vans, identifiable by their 'ZR' licence plate, operate around the island and can be flagged down by tourists and locals. There are no fixed schedules, but service is frequent. Rates are the same as for buses, but mini-vans are usually quicker and not for the faint-hearted. **Taxi:** Taxis do not have meters but fares are regulated by the Government. Listings are available from the Tourist Office. It is advised to check the fare before travel. The fare can usually be paid in US dollars (fixed exchange rate: B$2 - US$1) as well as in Barbados dollars. **Car hire:** Anything from a mini-moke to a limousine may be hired at the airport, at offices in Bridgetown and at main hotels. Petrol is comparatively cheap. Cars may be hired by the hour, day or week. Cars can be booked by calling a car hire agency, which will then send a car over to the applicant's hotel. *Courtesy Car Rentals* is

the only car hire agency situated at the airport, and is located in the Arrivals Hall. **Documentation:** A Barbados driving permit is required. This can be obtained from car hire companies, the Ministry of Transport (Mon-Fri 0830-1430), the airport (every day 0800-2200) or police stations in Hastings, Worthing and Holetown. There is a registration fee of B$10. A valid national licence or an International Driving Permit should also be held.

URBAN:

Bridgetown has a local bus network and taxis are available.

Travel Advice

Most visits to Barbados are trouble-free but you should be aware of the global risk of indiscriminate international terrorist attacks, which could be against civilian targets, including places frequented by foreigners.

This advice is based on information provided by the Foreign and Commonwealth Office in the UK. It is correct at time of publishing. As the situation can change rapidly, visitors are advised to contact the following organisations for the latest travel advice:

British Foreign and Commonwealth Office
Tel: (0845) 850 2829.
Website: www.fco.gov.uk

US Department of State
Website: http://travel.state.gov/travel

Accommodation

HOTELS:

Accommodation includes uncompromising luxury and many first-class hotels. Hotel prices range to suit all budgets. Generally the luxury hotels are in the west, while the medium-priced ones can be found along the southwest coast. The east coast, owing to its exposure to the trade winds and wild Atlantic Ocean, has only a small number of hotels and guest houses. However, it is this area that is chosen by the Bajans for their own holidays. Hotel prices are higher in the winter than in the summer. The high season is from 16 December to 15 April, the low season runs for the remainder of the year. Rates are subject to a 7.5 per cent Government tax; a service charge of 10 per cent is also applicable at most hotels. Most hotels have air conditioning, many have swimming pools and housekeeping apartments. Most rates are for room only. There is a hotel inspection and grading system, as well as standard services, the main ones being European Plan (EP), which is room only, and Modified American Plan (MAP), where breakfast and dinner are included with the price of the room. In addition, the Barbados Tourism Authority (see *Top Things To Do*) gives full details on facilities.

GUEST HOUSES:

There are small guest houses throughout Barbados, particularly in Christchurch. Some offer self-catering facilities.

SELF-CATERING:

There are a large number of apartments, cottages and villas available for hire, and a number of modern complexes being built on the northwest coast. Older buildings, with a more local character, are available on the less popular east coast. There are also smaller, family-run apartment hotels and many apartment-style hotels which leave the visitor with a choice of self-catering or restaurant eating. Almost all provide a wide range of facilities. All rates are subject to a 7.5 per cent Government tax; a service charge of 10 per cent is also payable at most establishments.

CAMPING:

Camping is not generally permitted in Barbados except for organised trips by designated youth groups.

Top Things To See

• Discover **Bridgetown's** colonial history. Barbados was discovered by the Portuguese in 1536, but throughout its colonial history, which ended with the Declaration of Independence in 1966, it was under British sovereignty. This is strongly reflected in the old capital of Bridgetown which has a decidedly English character; so much so that there is even a **miniature of London's Trafalgar Square**, complete with a statue of Lord Nelson. The city is small and there are many excellent walking tours. Places worth a visit include the **Fairchild Market, St Michael's Cathedral** (built in 1789), **Belleville, Government House**, the **Barbados Museum**, the **Old Synagogue** and the **Garrison Savannah**. **Temple Yard** has a Rastafarian street market.
• Enjoy breathtaking views of the east coast from **St John's Parish Church**. The church's cemetery contains the grave

Credit: ©Hotel Spec

of Ferdinando Paleologus, a possible descendant of the Byzantine Emperors. Commanding view of the magnificent east coast beaches can also be had in the area near **Newcastle Coral Stone Gates.** Situated in St Joseph, these gates were erected by 20th Century Fox for the film *Island in the Sun.*

- Get confused in **Holetown** (**St James**). The monument in the town gives the date of the founding of Barbados' first settlement by the English as being 1605, although this event in fact took place in 1627. There are still a few structures dating from that time. **St James**, the first church, still retains a 17th-century font, and a bell inscribed 'God bless King William, 1696'.
- Visit the **Animal Flower Cave**, a cavern carved out by the sea with coral rock tinted almost every imaginable colour.
- Enjoy splendid views of **St George's Valley** at **Gun Hill Signal Station**, also notable for its lion carved out of a rock by a British soldier in the days when **Gun Hill** was an army look-out point.
- Discover a wonderful altarpiece at 18th-century **St George's Church**.

Top Things To Do

- Barbados is fringed by coral reefs which host a variety of marine life and offer excellent **scuba-diving** and **snorkelling**. Sea horses, frog fish, giant sand eels and the hawksbill turtle are among the creatures to be found around the island. Visiting the **barrier reefs** half a mile to two miles away from the shore is a must. Dive operators will provide equipment, advice and guided tours. **Carlisle Bay** near Bridgetown has 200 wrecks and is a good venue for beginners. **Folkstone Marine Park** features the popular wreck of the *Stavronikita*. The best conditions for **windsurfing**, **jet-skiing**, **parasailing** and **water-skiing** are on the south and west coasts. **Crane Beach** on the southeastern side is a pink-tinged stretch of sand that is ideal for bodysurfing but too rough for swimming. There is also good, regular **surfing** at the Soup Bowl, South Point and Rockley Beach. All watersports are easy to arrange. Lovers of watersports will also like **Bathsheba**, a small pastel-coloured houses cling to the chalky cliffs that rise above the Atlantic. On the **Platinum Coast**, also known as **Millionaires Row**, there are fine beaches of white sand and clear, turquoise waters.
- Charter a boat for game **fishing**, **spin fishing** and **inshore fishing**. Game fishing tournaments are held regularly, with the highlight of the deep-sea season being the **Mutual/ Mount Gay International Tournament** in April.
- Stables and horses are available and **horse riding** along the beach at sunset can be arranged. The Barbados National Trust organises regular guided **hikes**, as advertised in their 'Calendar of Hikes'. The hikes, which last for approximately three hours, begin at 0600, 1530 and 1730. Participants on evening (moonlight) walks need to bring a torch. For further details, contact the Tourist Board.
- Discover an array of exotic plants grown along terraced gardens in the **Andromeda Gardens**, one of the prettiest area of St Joseph. Alternatively, the **Welchman Hall Gully**, a botanic garden in St Thomas owned by the National Trust, is home to many rare fruit and spice trees. In the **Flower Forest**, a 50-acre botanical garden, travellers will find almost every plant that grows on Barbados. The grounds offer pleasant walks and spectacular views of **Chalky Mountain**, the Atlantic Ocean and **Mount Hillaby**.
- At the **Barbados Wildlife Reserve**, get close to Barbados wildlife, some indigenous and some introduced to the island, which roams free in a mahogany forest. Animals that visitors may expect to see during their visit include green monkeys, tortoises, deer, wallabies, pelicans and otters. There is also a screened aviary where peacocks, turkeys, toucans, macaws, lovebirds, parrots and an iguana may be viewed.
- Drive on the **East Coast Road,** one of the most exciting drives on the island, with the Atlantic crashing over treacherous reefs on to the rugged and beautiful coast.
- Visit some of Barbados' **plantations houses. Farley Hill**, although now in ruins, is still covered in hibiscus and poinsettias, while **St Nicholas Abbey** is graced with Persian arches and well-kept gardens.
- On the **Atlantic Coast**, the inland road takes you through sugar-cane country with little churches and tiny towns with pretty houses. See the dramatic view from **Crane Beach**.
- Visit **Speightstown**, a typical West Indian village, with attractive wooden houses, shops and old churches.
- Book an excursion to the eerie, luminous **Harrison's Cave (St Thomas)**. Completely lit, one can see every part from a special train which takes the visitor on a mile-long ride underground. Stalactites and stalagmites are in abundance among underground scenery boasting a crystal-clear waterfall and deep emerald lakes. It is open every day 0900-1600.
- Help Barbados promote **ecotourism**. The Barbados National Trust has implemented programmes to support this venture, owning and/or administering 10 sites that are open to the public. Various **hiking**, **cycling** and **walking** events are available and information can be obtained from the Barbados National Trust, Wildey House, Wildey, St Michael, Barbados (tel: 436 9033 *or* 426 2421; e-mail: natrust@sunbeach.net).
- Go bargain hunting in **Potteries**, a village is famous for its ceramic artworks.
- Book a night at **Sam Lord's Castle**, once an old plantation house, but now a hotel, beautifully decorated with furniture made from Barbados mahogany.
- Visit **Codrington College**, one of the oldest schools of theology in the Western hemisphere. The school was built in 1745 and situated near Consett Bay.
- Also in the east, visit **Morgan Lewis Mill**, a splendid example of a Dutch windmill from the days of the sugar cane planters. It has been completely restored and is open to the public.
- Taste **Mount Gay Rum**. There are 1000 rum bars in Barbados. The largest rum manufacturer of all is situated in the west coast. Taste tests are a standard component of any visit here. There is also a restaurant designed to soak up any excess alcohol.
- Enjoy a game of **cricket**, which is the national obsession. Test matches and the Inter-Caribbean Shield competition are played at the *Kensington Oval* in Bridgetown. Many of the great names of West Indian cricket are from Barbados, most notably Sir Garfield Sobers.
- Attend of the 20 **horse racing** meetings at the **Garrison Savannah** during the year's two main seasons (January to March and May to October), the highlight of which is the **Sandy Lane Gold Cup Race**, held on the first Saturday in March. **Polo** is played to a high level throughout the year.

TOURIST INFORMATION

Barbados Tourism Authority in the UK
263 Tottenham Court Road, London W1T 7LA, UK
Tel: (020) 7636 9448.
Website: www.barbados.org/uk
Opening hours: Mon-Fri 0930-1730.

Barbados Tourism Authority in the USA
800 Second Avenue, 2nd Floor, New York,
NY 10017, USA
Tel: (212) 986 6516 *or* (800) 221 9831
(toll-free in USA).
Website: www.barbados.org

Entertainment

FOOD & DRINK: There are many restaurants offering both international and traditional Bajan cuisine at a variety of prices.
Things to know: An exchange 'Dine Around' system is operated between some hotels of the same class and guests can eat at other hotels for no extra cost.
There are numerous bars which emulate the British pub and serve genuine British bitter and stout.
National specialities:
- Flying fish.
- Lobster.
- Crane chubb.
- The sea urchin (oursin or sea egg).
- Other specialities include sweet potatoes, plantains, breadfruit, yams and such fruits as avocados, pears, soursops, pawpaws, bananas, figs and coconuts.

National drinks:
- All types of rum-based cocktails, rum punch, planters punch, pina coladas and sangria.
- The two most famous rums are *Cockspur's Five Star* and, for the connoisseur, *Mount Gay* (the oldest rum blend on the island).
- The local beer is *Banks*.

Tipping: In restaurants or nightclubs, tips are usually 10 to 15 per cent. Porters' tips are at the customer's discretion.
NIGHTLIFE: Nightclubs, discos and bars provide entertainment including limbo dancing, fire-eaters, steel bands and dance bands. There is a small cover charge. As in all Caribbean countries, swinging nightspots tend to come and go with seasons. Coastal boat trips with live entertainment are very popular; most sail twice daily and run buffets, bars and live music. Calypso and reggae will always be in the air, ready to inject the night air with that lively West Indian ambience. Dinner shows are always well attended. The *Harbour Lights Extravaganza Dinner Show* offers a truly tropical evening of dancing, with a barbeque serving food and free drinks until 0300 (website: www.harbourlightsbarbados.com/beach_extravaganza.htm). The *Bajan Roots & Rhythms* at the Plantation Theatre is highly interactive with a party atmosphere but family-friendly, dishing up a traditional buffet for those who have exhausted themselves dancing (website: http://theplantation.bb/).
SHOPPING: Shopping is a delight and there is a wide range of goods with visitors being able to take some purchases home duty free on production of their passport and air ticket. Liquor and cigarettes are sent to the airport or port for collection on departure. Other items can be taken away at point of purchase. Prices tend to be on the high side, though for such things as jewellery, clothing and ceramics, the high quality often makes the expense worthwhile. Special purchases include rum, straw goods, coral and shell jewellery, prints (*batik*) and woodcraft. **Shopping hours:** Mon-Fri 0900-1700, Sat 0830-1600 (supermarkets are open longer on Saturdays).

Business

- **GDP:** US$4.56 billion (2004 estimate).
- **Main exports:** Cotton, flowers, plants, rum and oil.
- **Main imports:** Consumer goods, machinery, foodstuffs and construction materials.
- **Main trade partners:** Exports to: UK, USA, Trinidad and Tobago, Venezuela and Jamaica; Imports from: USA, Trinidad and Tobago, Japan, UK and Canada.

ECONOMY: The Bajan economy traditionally relied on sugar production but persistently low world market prices forced the Government to promote economic diversification. Most effort has concentrated on tourism, which is now the largest employer on the island and continues to show steady growth. Cotton, flowers and plants are being developed as export products. New light industrial projects, such as electronic components, have fared less well, mainly as a result of falling demand in the USA – the principal export market. The island's other important industry is oil. Two-thirds of offshore output is exported, with the remainder assigned for domestic consumption. Exploration activities have been intensified since the mid-1990s. In the service sector, Barbados has developed an 'offshore' financial industry that now accounts for 15 per cent of GDP. Barbados receives some overseas aid from British and US sources and is a member of the Caribbean economic community, CARICOM, which has boosted regional trade. The island has a good transport and communications infrastructure, which should assist future economic development. The main trading partners are the USA, UK and the other CARICOM nations.
BUSINESS ETIQUETTE: Lightweight tropical suits and shirt and tie are recommended. European courtesies should be observed. **Office hours:** Mon-Fri 0800-1600.
CONFERENCES/CONVENTIONS: For the business traveller, conference organiser or incentive group, there is a number of hotels with conference and meeting facilities. There is also a selection of conference centres, the newest being the Sherbourne Conference Centre. Located 3km (2 miles) from Bridgetown; it is adjacent to the main highway linking the south and west coast. The centre is fully air conditioned and equipped to handle seminars, meetings, international conferences, trade shows and exhibitions. Restaurants and cafe facilities are available to seat 120 and 300 persons respectively (see *Commercial Information*).

COMMERCIAL INFORMATION

Barbados Chamber of Commerce and Industry
1st Floor, Nemwil House, Collymore Rock, St Michael, W1, Barbados
Tel: 426 2056 or 0747.
Website: www.bdscham.com

Barbados Investment & Development Corporation
PO Box 1250, Pelican House, Princess Alice Highway, Bridgetown, Barbados
Tel: 427 5350.
Website: www.bidc.com

Barbados Conference Services Ltd
Sherbourne Conference Centre, Two Mile Hill, St Michael, Barbados
Tel: 467 8200.
Website: www.bcslbarbados.com

Belarus

Location: Eastern Europe.

Time: GMT + 2 (GMT + 3 from last Sunday in March to last Sunday in October).

Overview

Previously known by the name Belorussia (White Russia), the name Belarus was adopted when the country became Independent from the Soviet Union as the USSR disintegrated in 1991.

The post-Independence leadership was keen to maintain political and economic links with Moscow and was a leading proponent of the creation of the Commonwealth of Independent States – a loose alliance of ex-Soviet republics that came into being shortly afterwards and whose headquarters were in the Belarusian capital of Minsk. Belarus's close links with Russia has led the country into deeper international isolation. Today, the majority of all industry remains under the control of the state and is heavily regulated. Foreign investment has been limited due to an unfriendly business environment. Belarus's human rights record since President Lukashenko came to power in 1994 has been poor.

Despite this, Belarus does not deserve its reputation as a transit area on the way to or from Russia. Wide plains, picturesque villages, ancient castles and monasteries, deep forests, scenic landscapes, and thousands of lakes await nature-lovers, culture fans and sport enthusiasts. One-third of the Belarusian territory is covered with forests where birches, oaks, maple and pine trees dominate with a rich and diverse fauna: here one can find European bison, elk and deer, wild boar and wolf, bear and fox, beaver and lynx – not to mention myriad birds. Belarus also has a unique history and a rich cultural heritage, with hundreds of architectural monuments dating back to the 12th century. Time seems to have considerably slowed down in Belarus and the country's quiet charm at the heart of Europe should appeal to travellers willing to open their soul to this island of calmness.

General Information

AREA: 207,595 sq km (80,153 sq miles).
POPULATION: 9 million (UN, 2005).
POPULATION DENSITY: 42.1 per sq km.
CAPITAL: Minsk. **Population:** 1.7 million (2001).
GEOGRAPHY: Belarus is bordered by Latvia, Lithuania, Poland, Ukraine and the Russian Federation. It is covered largely by forests and lakes, which are rich in wildlife, and is crossed by major rivers such as the Dnieper.
GOVERNMENT: Republic since 1991. **Head of State:** President Aleksandr Lukashenko since 1994, reelected in 2006. **Head of Government:** Prime Minister Sergey Sidorsky since 2003. **Recent history:** The 1994

constitution, controversially amended in 1996, allows for legislative power to be held by a bicameral National Assembly (*Verchovny Soviet*). This comprises a 110-member House of Representatives directly elected for a four-year term and a 64-member Council of the Republic, of which eight members are Presidential appointees and the remainder elected by local authorities. The President, who is directly elected for a five-year term, exercises executive power, assisted by a Council of Ministers answerable to the National Assembly.

The current leader of Belarus, Alexander Lukashenka, originally came to power at the 1994 Presidential election. An important element of his platform was a promise to end corruption. Unfortunately, Lukashenka's rule became characterised by ever greater corruption, nepotism, censorship and arbitrary decision-making; it has since deteriorated further, with restrictions on religious and political assembly and, in the worst cases, the disappearance and death of prominent critics. In 1996, a dubious referendum had endorsed Lukashenka's intention to extend both his powers and his term of office to 2001.

The Lukashenka Government's conduct has completely undermined Belarus' relations with the West, which it had initially sought to develop. Lukashenka is now looking to Moscow and especially the integration project, under which the two countries will become united at political and economic levels, adding to an already extensive set of bilateral agreements. However, the issue of Government corruption still taints Belarus. In early 2005, Belarus was listed by the US as Europe's only remaining outpost of tyranny. The EU extended travel restrictions on senior officials and the USA imposed sanctions. Street protests throughout 2004 have highlighted that Belarusians wish to keep these complaints at the forefront of worldwide media. The official results of a referendum in October 2004 showed almost unanimous support for the removal of the two-term limit on Lukashenka's rule. At Parliamentary elections held at the same time, official results also showed that opposition parties failed to win a single seat. Foreign observers claim that there was widespread corruption involved with both votes, and protests on the streets followed the elections.

Alexander Lukashenka was reelected at the March 2006 Presidential elections with more than 82 per cent of the votes. Opposition leader Alexander Milinkevich said the result was a "fraud" and international observers commented that the ballot "did not meet the required international standards for free and fair elections".

LANGUAGE: The official languages are Belarusian and Russian.
RELIGION: Christian, mainly Eastern Orthodox and Roman Catholic with small Protestant, Jewish and Muslim communities.
ELECTRICITY: 220V, 50Hz. Adaptors are recommended.
SOCIAL CONVENTIONS: Handshaking is the usual form of greeting. Hospitality is part of the tradition and people are welcoming and friendly. Company or business gifts are well received. Smoking is acceptable unless stated otherwise.

Climate

Temperate continental climate.
Required clothing: Medium- to heavyweights in winter. Waterproofs are advisable throughout the year.

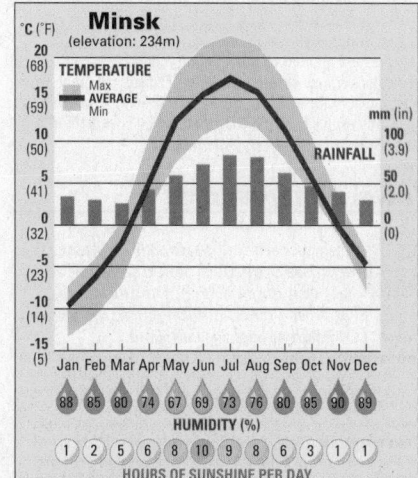

Communications

Telephone: IDD is available to all major cities, including Minsk (17) and Brest (162). Country code: 375. To make international calls it is necessary to dial 8, wait for a tone, then dial 10. Calls from Belarus to some countries must be

booked through the international operator. Public telephones take cards. Grey booths are for internal calls and blue ones for international calls.
Mobile telephone: Coverage is limited to main towns. Handsets can be hired at the airport (Belcel office) and in Minsk.
Internet: There are a few Internet cafes in Minsk. Access is also available at some post offices.
Post: Airmail to Western Europe takes a minimum of 10 days. The Central Post Office (Minsk, near the railway station; open 0800-2000) and the Yubileynaya and Planeta hotels in Minsk offer express mail services. DHL Worldwide Express and Federal Express also have branches in Minsk.
MEDIA: The Belarusian authorities have been heavily criticised by human rights and media organisations for suppressing freedom of speech, muzzling the independent press and denying the opposition access to state-owned media. The President's administration controls decisions on content and the appointment of senior editors of state media. Government-controlled newspapers enjoy considerable state subsidies and financial privileges, while many of the opposition print media have faced increased charges, been forced to close down, change name or publish abroad. But some leading privately-owned newspapers survive thanks to popular demand. The Belarusian National State Teleradio Company operates domestic radio and TV channels and an external radio service. Some radio stations target Belarusian listeners from outside the country.
Press: The English-language paper *Belarus Today* is published weekly. The principal dailies are *Narodnaya Hazeta* and *Respublika*, all printed in Belarusian and Russian. *Sovetskaya Beloroussiya* is printed in Russian. *Zvyazda* is printed in Belarusian. *Belorusskaya Delovaya Gazeta*, which temporarily closed in 2003, has since resumed publication and is the main private daily paper. *Belorusskaya Gazeta* is a weekly private publication.
TV: *Belarusian TV*, which is state-run, operates three channels, including satellite station *Belarus-TV*.
Radio: *Belarusian Radio*, which is state-run, operates three national networks and an external service. *Radio Baltic Waves* brodcasts from Lithuania while *Radio Ratsyya* is based in Poland.

Passport/Visa

	Passport Required?	Visa Required?	Return Ticket Required?
Full British	Yes	Yes	No
Australian	Yes	Yes	No
Canadian	Yes	Yes	No
USA	Yes	Yes	No
Other EU	Yes	Yes	No
Japanese	Yes	Yes	No

Note: *Regulations and requirements may be subject to change at short notice, and you are advised to contact the appropriate diplomatic or consular authority before finalising travel arrangements. Any numbers in the chart refer to the footnotes below.*

PASSPORTS: Passport valid for six months after departure required by all, except for nationals of Mongolia and Serbia & Montenegro with a National Identity Card.
VISAS: Required by all except the following:
(a) nationals of the CIS (except nationals of Turkmenistan, who *do* require visas);
(b) nationals of Cuba, Malaysia and Serbia & Montenegro, provided travelling for touristic purposes for up to 30 days;
(c) nationals of Bosnia & Herzegovina and Macedonia (Former Yugoslav Republic of), provided travelling for business purposes and holding an invitation letter;
(d) nationals of Mongolia, provided holding proof of touristic (return tickets), business or social (invitation to visit from Belize resident) visit;
(e) transit passengers continuing their journey to a third country provided holding valid onward or return documentation and not leaving the airport.
Note: All foreign nationals must hold medical insurance and register their passports at the local police station within three days of their arrival. If staying at a hotel, reception will do this automatically.
Types of visa and cost: *Visitor* and *Business*: £40 (single-entry); £72 (double-entry); £104 (triple-entry); £200 (multiple-entry). *Tourist*: £19 (individual); £10 per person (group). *Transit*: £15 (single-entry); £27 (double-entry); £39 (triple entry); £50 (multiple-entry); £10 per person (group). Express visas are available for a higher fee.
Note: (a) *Tourist* visas are only available to those booking through a travel agency in Belarus or from a travel agency in another country which has an agreement with Belarus state travel and can supply state travel vouchers. (b) Children travelling on their parents' passports do not need a visa but must be accounted for on parents' visa application form.
Validity: *Visitor* and *Business*: 90 days (single-, double-, and triple-entry); one year (multiple-entry). *Tourist*: 30 days. *Transit*: 48 hours.

Application to: Nearest Consulate (or Consular section at Embassy). Visas can be obtained at Minsk-2 International Airport in exceptional cases, such as illness or death of a Belarusian relative, only provided the traveller is met at the airport by their official sponsor with the original letter of invitation or tourist vouchers. In this case, the fee may be higher.
Application requirements: (a) Valid passport with at least one blank page. (b) One application form. (c) One recent passport-size photo. (d) Fee (postal order or cheque only). (e) Stamped, self-addressed envelope for return of passport if applying by post, sent by recorded delivery. *Tourist*: (a)-(e) and, (f) Copy of tourist voucher. (g) Copy of the confirmation from a Belarusian travel agency, including registration number. *Business*: (a)-(e) and, (f) Letter of invitation from a registered Belarusian company, written on headed paper, including registration number, date of issue, official's signature, corporate seal and expected duration of stay. *Visitor*: (a)-(e) and, (f) Invitation from Belarusian resident endorsed by a local Belarusian Visa and Registration office. *Transit*: (a)-(e) and, (f) Visa for destination country, or, if no visa is required, copy of the ticket or itinerary.
Note: Nationals of EU countries, Andorra, Argentina, Bahrain, Brazil, Bulgaria, Canada, Chile, Croatia, Iceland, Japan, Korea (Rep), Kuwait, Liechtenstein, Norway, Oman, Qatar, Saudi Arabia, South Africa, Switzerland, United Arab Emirates and Uruguay no longer need to submit formal letters of invitation to obtain *Visitor* and *Business* visas.
Working days required: Five, or 48 hours for express processing.

PASSPORT/VISA INFORMATION

Embassy of Belarus in the UK
6 Kensington Court, London W8 5DL, UK
Tel: (020) 7937 3288 *or* 7938 3677 (visa section).
Website: www.belembassy.org/uk
Opening hours: Mon-Fri 0900-1800; 0930-1230 (visa section).

Embassy of Belarus in the USA
1619 New Hampshire Avenue, NW, Washington, DC 20009, USA
Tel: (202) 986 1604 *or* 1606 (consular section).
Website: www.belarusembassy.org

Money

Currency: Belarusian Rouble (BYR). Notes are in denominations of BYR100,000, 50,000, 20,000, 10,000, 5000, 1000, 500, 100, 50, 20 and 10.
Currency exchange: Foreign currency should only be exchanged at banks, money-changing kiosks and official bureaux de change, and all transactions must be recorded on the currency declaration form which is issued on arrival. It is wise to retain all exchange receipts. It is best to change money in US dollars, Euros or Russian roubles since travellers may encounter difficulties with other currencies. Most aspects of a tour, including accommodation, transport and meals, are paid before departure (through *Belintourist* or a recognised tour operator), so large amounts of spending money are not necessary. The US dollar or Euros are the preferred foreign currencies. Some foreign currencies may be hard to exchange.
Credit & debit cards: Major European and international credit cards, including American Express, Cirrus, EC, Electron, EuroCard/MasterCard, Maestro and Visa are accepted in some larger hotels and at foreign currency shops and restaurants. Check with your credit or debit card company for details of merchant acceptability and other services which may be available. There are a number of ATMs in downtown Minsk.
Traveller's cheques: May be accepted at larger banks, but cash is easier to exchange. To avoid exchange rate charges, traveller's cheques should be taken in US dollars or Euros.
Currency restrictions: The import and export of local currency is prohibited. All remaining local currency must be reconverted at the point of departure. The import of foreign currency is unlimited, subject to declaration. The export of foreign currency is limited to the amount declared on arrival. Foreign banknotes and coins must be exported within two months of import.
Banking hours: Mon-Fri 0900-1700.
Exchange rate indicators:
Rate at time of publishing
£1.00= BYR3790.58
$1.00= BYR2148.32

Duty Free

The following goods may be imported into Belarus by persons over 18 years of age without incurring customs duty:
1000 cigarettes or 1000g of tobacco products; 1.5l of spirits and 2l of wine; a reasonable quantity of perfume for personal use; other goods up to a value of US$1000.

Note: On entering the country, tourists must complete a customs declaration form which must be retained until departure. This records the import of articles intended for personal use, including currency and valuables. Customs inspection can be long and detailed.
Prohibited imports: Weapons and ammunition, narcotics, photographs and printed matter directed against Belarus, and fruit and vegetables. Contact the Embassy for further details of import restrictions (see *Passport/Visa Information*).
Prohibited exports: Weapons and ammunition, precious metals, works of art and antiques (unless special permission has been granted by the Ministry of Culture) and furs.

Public Holidays

Below are listed Public Holidays for the January 2006-June 2007 period.
2006: Jan 1 New Year's Day. **Jan 7** Orthodox Christmas. **Mar 8** International Women's Day. **Mar 15** Constitution Day. **Apr 14-17** Catholic Easter. **Apr 21-24** Orthodox Easter. **May 1** Labour Day. **May 9** Victory Day. **Jul 3** Independence Day. **Nov 2** Dzyady. **Nov 7** Day of the October Revolution. **Dec 25** Christmas Day.
2007: Jan 1 New Year's Day. **Jan 7** Orthodox Christmas. **Mar 8** International Women's Day. **Mar 15** Constitution Day. **Apr 6-9** Orthodox Easter. **May 1** Labour Day. **May 9** Victory Day.

Health

	Special Precautions?	Certificate Required?
Yellow Fever	No	No
Cholera	No	No
Typhoid & Polio	1	N/A
Malaria	No	N/A

Note: *Regulations and requirements may be subject to change at short notice, and you are advised to contact your doctor well in advance of your intended date of departure. Any numbers in the chart refer to the footnotes below.*

1: Immunisation against poliomyelitis and typhoid is sometimes advised.
Other risks: Extensive epidemics of *diphtheria* were reported in the 1990s and immunisation may be recommended. There may be some risk of *tick-borne encephalitis*. Long-staying travellers should take precautions against *hepatitis A*. Certain foods should be avoided, especially dairy produce, mushrooms and fruits of the forest, as they may contain high levels of radiation as a long-term legacy of the Chernobyl disaster. Tap water should be filtered and boiled before drinking.
Rabies is present. For those at high risk, vaccination before arrival should be considered. If you are bitten, seek medical advice without delay. For more information, consult the *Health* appendix.
Health care: There is a reciprocal health agreement with the UK. Hospital treatment, some dental treatment and some other medical treatment is normally free. Visitors can expect to pay for prescribed medicines. A UK passport must be shown to receive medical treatment. It is advisable to take out adequate health insurance. Foreign visitors are usually required to pay medical insurance starting from €1 (up to 10 days) to €85 (up to one year). It is also advisable to carry an adequate supply of prescribed medicines which may be unobtainable in Belarus.
Travellers are advised to obtain comprehensive travel and medical insurance before travelling. Medical insurance cover is compulsory for a stay in Belarus. Travellers are advised to check any exclusions, and that their policy covers them for the activities they want to undertake.

Travel - International

AIR:
The national airline is *Belavia (B2)* (website: www.belavia.by). Other airlines serving Belarus include *Austrian Airlines*, *Baltic Air*, *Czech Airlines*, *El Al Israel Airlines*, *Estonian Airlines*, *Lithuanian Airlines*, *LOT Polish Airlines* and *Lufthansa*.
Approximate flight times: From Minsk to *London* is three hours, to *Frankfurt/M* or *Vienna* is two hours 25 minutes, to *Moscow* is one hour 30 minutes and to *Zurich* is three hours.
Main airports: *Minsk 2 (MSQ)* is 43km (27 miles) east of the city centre. *To/from the airport:* Buses and taxis are available to the city centre (travel time - 60 minutes). Taxis cost about €20 to get into town, according to official rates. *Facilities:* Banks and bureaux de change, bars, car hire (*Avis*), duty free shops, nursery, post office and restaurants. *Minsk 1* underwent a lengthy reconstruction but is back in use. It offers flights to destinations including Kiev and Stockholm, plus international flights to regional cities.
Departure tax: None.

RAIL:
All trains arrive and depart from Minsk Central Railway Station located in the centre of Minsk. There are several lines from Berlin via Warsaw and Brest with connections to Minsk. Another line runs from Vienna via Warsaw and Brest. Further direct trains are available from other cities, including Kaliningrad, Moscow, Odessa, Riga and Vilnius.
ROAD:
Visitors are advised to stay away from military establishments. Tourists may drive their own cars or may hire cars from some larger hotels. Those entering by car should have their visas registered at the hotel, motel or campsite where they stay for the first night and must insure their vehicle with a Belarusian insurance company at crossing points. On 1 January 2005, Belarus introduced a new system of fees for drivers of foreign vehicles wishing to use Belarus' highways. Payments are collected at border checkpoints and will vary according to the length of stay. Petrol stations accept cash and credit cards and are plentiful along the motorways and main roads. Contact the Embassy for information on the temporary documentation required to import a car. The following are approximate road distances from Minsk; Moscow: 690km (429 miles); St Petersburg: 900km (563 miles); Kiev: 650km (407 miles). **Documentation:** Valid International Driver's Licence. When travelling by private vehicle, travellers must be able to produce ownership documents or a letter of "power of attorney" at Custom's offices at border crossings. Only originals of these documents are accepted. Travellers must have third party car insurance or they may get an "on-the-spot" fine. Travellers can only buy this when entering Belarus. Motorists should enquire at Customs' border offices for information. The quality of driving in Belarus is erratic. Belarus' "A-class" highways are in average to good condition. The condition of "B-class" roads varies considerably and some are impassable for periods in winter. Drivers should note that road works and potholes are usually poorly marked. Pony and trap combinations are a specific hazard for drivers in rural unlit areas. Drivers should observe the speed limit at all times. The standard speed limit is 37 mph (60 kph) in built up areas; 55 mph (90 kph) outside built up areas; and 62 mph (100 kph) on motorways (Brest-Moscow). Visiting motorists who have held a driving licence for less than two years must not exceed 43 mph (70 kph). The authorities operate a nil-tolerance policy in respect of drink driving. Vehicles should have lights on at all times from 1 November to 31 March inclusive. Motorists should be aware that there may be long queues at the border, and that customs and immigration can be lengthy and bureaucratic. Drivers should ignore "private facilitators" who offer to help travellers pass through checkpoints and border crossings. There are also police checkpoints on all the main routes to and from Minsk. Drivers should stop at these when instructed, and have the vehicle documentation to hand, otherwise they risk a fine and delay. Motorists entering Belarus should ensure that they do not overstay the temporary import terms for their vehicles. Violation of the exit deadline may result in confiscation of the vehicle at the Belarusian border.
Coach: Coaches run from many points across Europe. There are three international bus stations in Minsk: Central Bus Station, Eastern (Vostochnaya) Bus Station and Moscow (Moskovskaya) Bus Station.

Travel - Internal

RAIL:
Services run regularly from Minsk to all other towns. For more information, contact Belarus Railways (website: www.rw.by). There have been instances of theft from travellers, especially on sleeper trains to Warsaw and Moscow.
ROAD:
Belarus has a road network of 51,547km (32,219 miles), most of which is hard-surfaced, although there are potholes and lighting is bad. Traffic drives on the right. **Regulations:** International traffic signs and regulations are in use. Driving under the influence of any alcohol is strictly forbidden. Speed limits are 60kph (37mph) in towns and cities and 90kph (55mph) on country lanes. There are frequent radar traps. **Documentation:** International Driving Permit required. Also needed are a driving license and a latter of attorney if not the owner of the car being driven (see *Travel International* section).
URBAN:
Public transport is cheap and efficient. The city of Minsk has an underground system with two lines that cover central Minsk (16 stations). It is in the process of being expanded. Trains run between 0530-0100, buses, trams and trolleybuses between 0535-0030. Tickets for buses, trams and trolleybuses can be purchased at news-stands or kiosks and are to be punched onboard. Entry to the underground is by tokens which are obtainable from stations. Taxis are available and carry a maximum of four passengers; fares can vary greatly.

Travel Advice

Visitors should be aware of the potential for pickpockets and muggers and take necessary precautions. However, the majority of visits to Belarus are trouble-free. Please note that Belarus is governed by a strong Presidential system with security forces loyal to it. Historically, the authorities have shown little tolerance for their opposition counterparts. This has often been reflected in the heavy-handed use of security forces to disperse or intimidate opposition events. Any demonstrations or rallies should be avoided.

This advice is based on information provided by the Foreign and Commonwealth Office in the UK. It is correct at time of publishing. As the situation can change rapidly, visitors are advised to contact the following organisations for the latest travel advice:

British Foreign and Commonwealth Office
Tel: (0845) 850 2829.
Website: www.fco.gov.uk

US Department of State
Website: http://travel.state.gov/travel

Accommodation

EDITOR'S CHOICE: DACHAS

Why not try a *dacha*, near the lakeshore of the Braslav Lake District, for instance? Since the 1960s a majority of Muscovites have come to own some type of dacha. These 'people's dachas' consist of a small cabin, sitting on the smallest possible plot of land in the countryside. In the Soviet time, one of the most important duties of trade unions was to obtain the land for the dachas and distribute it among the members of the union. Since everyone then was a member of one or another trade union, everyone had a chance to get the land - although there were very special dachas for party functionaries. The regular dacha was where people could escape cities and grow their own food. Dachas were formed as cooperatives supervised by trade unions making dachas owners devoted 'weekend farmers'. The typical size of land given by the state to a family varied from 4 to 12 *sotok*, 6 and 8 being the most common (a land area of 6 sotok is equal to 0.16 acres). However, dachas were much more than just a shack for most people. This is the place to escape from the rush and the problems of a big city.

HOTELS:

There are 2- and 3-star hotels in Brest, Gomel, Grodno, Mogilev and Pinsk. Minsk and Vitebsk have 2-, 3- and 4-star hotels. Two 5-star hotels are due to be built soon. There are also hotels in practically all small towns in Belarus. Belintourist can provide more information on accommodation.

CAMPING:

There are limited facilities for camping in Belarus, though several camping sites will be organised soon according to the National Program of Tourism Development. However, camping is permitted outside towns anywhere in the countryside, provided consideration is shown for other countryside users.

Top Things To See

- **Minsk**, the capital of Belarus, situated 340km (213 miles) northeast of Warsaw and 120km (75 miles) southeast of Vilnius, was first mentioned in 1067, but little of the old city now survives except a few 17th-century buildings. The city grew to be an important axis of communication and suffered badly during World War II. Modern Minsk is symmetrically designed with wide embankments flanking the **Svisloch River**.
- The suburb of **Troitskoye Predmestye** should not be missed; it gives an insight into the way Minsk once looked – 19th-century houses with colourful facades line the streets. There are also excellent examples of Baroque architecture, such as the **Cathedral of the Holy Spirit** (1642), the **Cathedral of St Peter and Paul** (1613) and the **Maryinsky Cathedral**, which has been rebuilt to its original shape.
- Belarus in the 13th century was the nucleus of the great principality of Lithuania and its capital was **Novogrudok**, featuring a 14th-century castle, **Lida**, where Adam Mitskevich, the great Belarusian poet, was born.
- Not far from Raubichi (10km/6 miles) is the idyllic **Minsk Lake**, dotted with numerous islets and surrounded by dense pines.
- The onion-shaped domes of Russian Orthodox churches dominate the landscape throughout the country, but especially around **Logoysk** (40km/25 miles from Minsk), **Krasnoe** (60km/38 miles from Minsk) and **Molodechno** (80km/50 miles from Minsk).
- The memorial at **Khatyn** commemorates its destruction by the German army during World War II.
- The village of **Zhirovitsa**, 190km (119 miles) from Minsk, is renowned for the beautiful 15th-century **Monastery of the Assumption**. Part of the monastery complex is a convent and a theological seminary (17th to 18th century).
- 120km (75 miles) from Minsk is the small town of **Mir** where one can see the **Jewish Cemetery** and the 15th-century **Mir Castle** (a UNESCO-listed World Heritage Site). Nearby, historic **Nesvizh** still retains its old buildings. The former residence of the Radzivill family is one of the most attractive palaces in the country. It is surrounded by a large park with numerous lakes and elaborate gardens. Only a short walk away is the imposing Catholic Church designed by the 16th-century Italian architect, Bernardoni.
- The centre of Christianity during the time of Rus (the first Russian state) lay in the Slavic town of **Polotsk**. Polotsk is the oldest of the Belarusian cities, founded in 862. An excellent example of architecture of the period is the 11th-century **Church of St Sophia**. Worth a visit are the two castles nearby. There is also a 12th-century convent, **St Ephrosinia of Polotsk**, and a 16th- to 17th-century **Epiphany Monastery**.
- **Pinsk** is 300km south of Minsk and is the second-largest city in the Brest region. It has an abundance of historical, architectural and cultural monuments. The city and its environs are also renowned for both their natural beauty and as the centre of the Belarusian **Polesye**, a low-lying land of waters and mists.
- In **Grodno**, the fifth-largest city of Belarus, major sites are the Old Town centre, the **Kalozh-Church** and the **Old Castle** (both from the 11th century).

Top Things To Do

- The cultural scene in **Minsk** is very diverse with the **Belarusian Ballet** and good museums such as the **National Museum of Belarusian History and Culture**, the **National Arts Museum**, the **Museum of History of the Great Patriotic War** and the **Museum of Old Belarusian Culture**. Other interesting museums deal with the major Belarusian writers, Kolas, Kupala, Bogdanovich and Brovka. Icons form a large part of the **National Gallery**. Museums generally open Tues-Sun 1000-1900.
- About 22km (14 miles) from the capital is the picturesque village of **Raubichi**, with an interesting **ethnographic museum** housed in a disused church.
- The **Museum of Folk Architecture** is situated in **Ozerto** (15km/ 10 miles southwest of Minsk), and features original pieces of century-old buildings from different regions in Belarus.
- The **Dudutki Museum of Material Culture** is to be found 40km/25 miles from the capital city and is the only private museum in Belarus showing traditional crafts and ways of life.
- **Vitebsk**, situated 270km (169 miles) from Minsk is the birthplace of the painter Marc Chagall. There is a cultural centre named after him, and his family house has been turned into a museum.
- Sports enthusiasts will enjoy excellent **cross-country skiing** in the **Raubichy Olympic Sports Complex**, 22km from Minsk, while for lovers of **mountain skiing**, there are now two modern resorts (**Logoysk and Silichy**) situated 30km from Minsk. **Skating** is also popular.
- The **Braslav Lake District** situated in the north and northeast of the country, near the borders of Lithuania and Latvia, is ideal for **boating** holidays. Several of the 30 lakes, situated in an atmospheric forest, are connected by canals. Special attention is currently being paid by the Government to the development of water tourism. Accommodation in the area is usually in small dachas along the lakeshore.
- **Belavezha Wood** is one of the last sites where rare animals such as bisons, bears and wolves can still be seen living in their natural habitat. Long scenic **hiking trails** are scattered throughout the **Nature Reserve of Berezinsky**, stretching from the source of the Berezina to **Palik Lake**. Primeval forests, marshland, deep rivers and a rich fauna and flora dominate this unique region, hence its UNESCO listing as a protected biosphere. This reserve historically provided a great trade route known as the way 'from the Varangians to the Greeks', connecting the Baltic and the Black Sea countries.
- **Vitebsk**, situated 270km (169 miles) from Minsk is the birthplace of the painter Marc Chagall. There is a cultural centre named after him, and his family house has been turned into a museum.
- One of the highlights of **Brest** is a tour of the **Fortress**, which was used to repel the German forces during World War II. Inside the Fortress is a museum which chronicles its history back to the 13th century. This history is further illustrated by a fascinating selection of exhibits in the **Museum of History and Archaeology**. In the surrounding countryside, time appears to have stood still for centuries; 500-year-old trees can be found in the state national park, **Belovezhskaya Pushcha**. Wild European (Belovezhskaya) bison roam the area - the symbol of Belarus. Here, there are 87.6 hectares of total area to explore and discover the 60 types of animal and 900 types of plants that it contains. For tourists seeking political history, it is here, in the village of Viskouli, that leaders of Belarus, Russia and the Ukraine signed the famous agreement stipulating the final disintegration of the USSR. Brest has a famous puppet theatre that is worth seeing and visitors should not miss out on the elegant design of the **Belaya Vezha** (White Tower), also known as the famous **Kamenets Tower**, that was built in the 13th century.

TOURIST INFORMATION

Belintourist (National Tour Operator)
19 Masherov Avenue, 220004 Minsk, Belarus
Tel: (17) 226 9840 *or* 9056.
Website: www.belintourist.by

Entertainment

FOOD & DRINK: In addition to Belarusian dishes, there is also a good selection of international and Russian specialities available.

Things to know: Beer and vodka can be bought round the clock from all-night kiosks and food shops. Coffee is generally available with meals and in cafes, although standards vary. Some bars are open until the early hours of the morning, while some close around 2100.

National specialities:
- Belarusian *borshch*, a soup made with beetroot, is served hot with sour cream.
- Other excellent specialities are *filet à la Minsk* and Minsk cutlet.
- Regional cooking is often based on potatoes with mushrooms and berries as favourite side dishes.
- Local dishes well worth trying are *dracheny*, a tasty potato dish with mushrooms, and *draniki* which is served with pickled berries.
- *Mochanka* is a thick soup mixed with lard accompanied by hot pancakes.

National drinks:
- *Beloveszhskaya Bitters* are made from over 100 different herbs and have an interesting flavour.
- A favourite drink is *chai* (black tea).

Tipping: 10 per cent is usual. In some hotels in Minsk and other cities a 10 to 15 per cent service charge is added to the bill. Porters expect a tip of US$1-2.

NIGHTLIFE: A thriving cultural scene with opera, ballet, theatre, circus and puppet theatre can be found in Minsk. Brest also has a renowned puppet theatre. Tickets can be bought in advance at underground stations or at the Central Theatre Ticket Office (Skoriny 13; opening hours: Mon-Sat 0930-2000, Sun 1100-1700). Same-day tickets are only available at the venue in question. Minsk now has a reasonable selection of restaurants, some of which offer live music. There are also discos, music venues and bars in the city. Many clubs are open all night.

SHOPPING: Wooden caskets, trinket boxes, straw items, decorative plates and other handicraft items are good buys. Typical Russian souvenirs like the wooden *matreshka* dolls and original *samovars* are also available. Scarina Avenue is the main street with antique shops and two department stores. Only Belarusian Roubles are accepted. However, nearly every shop has a currency exchange counter. Some shops are closed on Sunday, but tourist shops are usually open every day. Antiquities, valuables, works of art and manuscripts other than those offered for sale in souvenir shops require an export licence. **Shopping hours:** Mon-Sat 0900-2000. In big cities shops are open daily and many open 24 hours a day.

Business

- **GDP:** US$14.3 billion (2003).
- **Main exports:** Machinery and equipment, mineral products, chemicals and textiles.
- **Main imports:** Energy, mineral products and foodstuffs.
- **Main trade partners:** Russian Federation, Latvia, Ukraine, Lithuania, Poland, Germany, UK, The Netherlands and Italy.

ECONOMY: Despite a paucity of natural resources, Belarus enjoyed a relatively high level of prosperity during the Soviet era compared to other ex-Soviet republics. However,

A
B
C
D
E
F
G
H
I
J
K
L
M
N
O
P
Q
R
S
T
U
V
W
X
Y
Z

the last 12 years have brought continuous decline. The main agriculture crops are sugar beet, grain and potatoes; livestock breeding is also substantial. The manufacturing industry is focused on the production of agricultural machinery vehicles and chemicals, most of which have been exported in the past. Apart from a few oil and gas deposits, Belarus has no energy reserves and relies on imports, most of which come from the Russian Federation. Like other Soviet republics, Belarus suffered a sharp decline in output and a variety of other problems following the dissolution of the Soviet Union; this was then followed by a period of stabilisation, which took hold during the mid-1990s as the Government and people adjusted to new economic circumstances. A new currency, the Belarusian Rouble, was introduced at the beginning of 1995. The economy recorded GDP growth of 6.8 per cent in 2004; however, it still suffers from high inflation of about 28 per cent. Reluctance to implement measures recommended by the IMF, World Bank and the EBRD (which Belarus joined in 1992) has limited access to these sources of finance. The Government has since been engaged in a tentative programme of privatisation. In 2002, 200 state-owned enterprises in the Minsk area were privatised; the Government has (under Russian pressure) committed itself to selling major national enterprises.

Imminent membership of the World Trade Organization is another welcome development for the Government. Belarus' trade is largely conducted with the countries of the former Soviet Union. In 2002, these accounted for two-thirds of Belarusian trade (nearly 80 per cent of that was with Russia). Most of the remaining trade was with the EU, USA and Japan. Belarus has been trying to develop its trade links with the Arab world, especially Iraq and the Syrian Arab Republic, with limited results.

BUSINESS ETIQUETTE: For business meetings, visitors should dress smartly. English is widely used in management circles and knowledge of German might also be useful. Appointments should be made well in advance and should be confirmed nearer the time. Cards should have a Russian translation on the back. Business transactions are likely to take quite a long time. **Office hours:** Mon-Fri 0900-1800.
CONFERENCES/CONVENTIONS: The 3-star Hotel Yubileynaya offers conference facilities for up to 250 persons, including simultaneous translation services. This facility is operated by Belintourist (see *Top Things To Do*).

COMMERCIAL INFORMATION

Belarusian Chamber of Commerce and Industry
ul. Ya. Kolasa 65, 220113 Minsk, Belarus
Tel: (17) 226 0473.
Website: www.cci.by

Ministry of Foreign Affairs (Information on Conferences/Conventions)
ul Lenina 19, 220030 Minsk, Belarus
Tel: (17) 227 2922.
Website: www.mfa.gov.by

Belgium

Location: Western Europe.

Time: GMT + 1 (GMT + 2 from last Sunday in March to last Sunday in October).

Overview

Belgium epitomises a stable, cautiously progressive Western European liberal democracy. The alliance with The Netherlands and Luxembourg became the Benelux Union in 1958, which, in turn, became one of the foundation stones of the European Community. Brussels is the headquarters of both NATO and the EU. Today, the anachronistic images of 'boring Belgium' have been well and truly banished over the last decade as the country promotes its key destinations, along with a string of new attractions. Easy to travel around, this pocket-sized country is divided by the Flemish north (Flemish-speaking) and the Walloon south (French-speaking). Brussels, the capital, is the heart of the country and the European Union. Belgium always had a lot more going for it than the faceless political and bureaucratic buildings that litter its capital with a string of engaging cities in Bruges, Ghent, Liège - and Brussels itself - that offer impressive architecture, lively nightlife, first-rate cuisine and numerous other attractions for visitors. Then there is reinvented Antwerp, now a hotbed of fashion and modern design, and the more bucolic charms of the beauty of the mountainous Ardennes region to the east, as well as the sweeping sand of the coastline resorts of the western seaboard. Belgium is also a land whose specialities include ubiquitous beers, delicate chocolates, moules-frites and Belgian waffles. The principal domestic problem is the continuing tension between the Flemish-speaking north and the French-speaking south of the country, known as Wallonia, not forgetting the capital Brussels. However, throughout the years, Belgium has evolved towards an efficient federal system. Five reforms have been necessary to achieve this (in 1970, 1980, 1988-89, 1993 and 2001). In 2005, Belgium celebrated 25 years of federalism and for the first time ever, article one of the Belgian Constitution stated that: "Belgium is a federal state made out of communities and regions".

General Information

AREA: 30,528 sq km (11,787 sq miles).
POPULATION: 10 million (UN, 2005).
POPULATION DENSITY: 341 per sq km.
CAPITAL: Brussels (Bruxelles, Brussel). **Population:** 970,000.

GEOGRAPHY: Belgium is situated in Europe and bordered by France, Germany, Luxembourg and The Netherlands. The landscape is varied, the rivers and gorges of the Ardennes contrasting sharply with the rolling plains which make up much of the countryside. Notable features are the great forest of Ardennes near the frontier with Germany and Luxembourg and the wide, sandy beaches of the northern coast, which run for over 60km (37 miles). The countryside is rich in historic cities, castles and churches.
GOVERNMENT: Constitutional monarchy. The Kingdom of Belgium was established in 1830. In 1993, Belgium became a federal state comprising three autonomous regions. **Head of State:** King Albert II since 1993. **Head of Government:** Prime Minister Guy Verhofstadt since 1999. **Recent history:** The country is a hereditary constitutional monarchy with a bicameral Parliament comprising the 150-member directly elected Chamber of Representatives and the 71-member Senate. Both chambers are elected for a four-year term.

The political landscape in Belgium is complicated by the fact that each of the main political parties is split into two with one section representing the Dutch-speaking Flemish community and the other the French-speaking Walloons. A successful coalition must successfully balance the interests of both.

In May 2005, the Government survived a confidence vote, enabling it to shelve a dispute over the voting rights of French-speakers in Dutch-speaking areas around Brussels. Months of negotiations over the issue had failed, sparking a political crisis. The far-right *Vlaams Blok*, which wanted Flemish Independence and campaigned on an anti-immigration platform, increased its share of the vote substantially in regional and European elections in 2004. However, the High Court later ruled that the party was racist and stripped it of the right to state funding and access to television. The party was subsequently reconstituted under a new name, *Vlaams Belang*, Flemish Interest.

Throughout the years, Belgium has evolved towards an efficient federal system. Five reforms have been necessary to achieve this (in 1970, 1980, 1988-89, 1993 and 2001). In 2005, Belgium celebrated 25 years of federalism and for the first time ever, article one of the Belgian Constitution states that: "Belgium is a federal state made out of communities and regions".
LANGUAGE: The official languages are Dutch, French and German. Dutch is slightly more widely spoken than French, and German is spoken the least.
RELIGION: Mainly Roman Catholic, with small Protestant and Jewish communities.
ELECTRICITY: 220 volts AC, 50Hz. Plugs are of the round two-pin type.
SOCIAL CONVENTIONS: Belgians will often prefer to answer visitors in English rather than French, even if the visitor's French is good. It is customary to bring flowers or a small present for the hostess, especially if invited for a meal. Dress is similar to other Western nations, depending on the formality of the occasion. If black tie/evening dress is to be worn, this is always mentioned on the invitation. Smoking is generally unrestricted.

Climate

Seasonal and similar to neighbouring countries, with warm weather from May to September and snow likely during winter months.
Required clothing: Waterproofs are advisable at all times of the year.

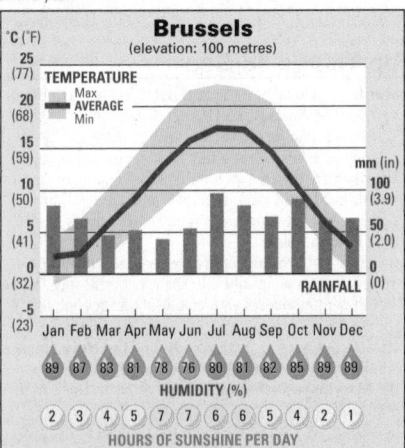

Communications

Telephone: Fully automatic IDD. For operator services, dial 1324. Country code: 32. There are call boxes in all major towns and country districts. Some coinless cardphones and credit card phones are also available. Telecards are available from newsagents, railway stations and post offices.

Mobile telephone: Roaming agreements exist with most international mobile phone companies. Coverage is excellent.

Internet: Internet cafes are widely available throughout the country.

Post: Airmail takes two to three days to other West European destinations. Post office hours: Mon-Fri 0900-1700 (post office hours vary) (website: www.post.be).

MEDIA: Belgian broadcasting mirrors the unique political and linguistic nature of the country. The cultural communities, rather than the federal authorities, are responsible for regulating radio and TV. As a result, Belgium has two separate public broadcasting organisations, with their own regulations, running their own radio, TV and external broadcasting. Some 95 per cent of Belgians receive cable TV, one of the highest take-up rates in the world. The cable services offer dozens of domestic and foreign channels, including Dutch and French TV stations. The Belgian press is self-regulated by the Federation of Editors - to which all editors of major newspapers belong. A small number of media groups own the main newspaper titles.

Press: Principal daily newspapers are *La Lanterne*, *La Libre Belgique*, *La Meuse*, *Le Soir* (French) and *De Morgen*, *De Gentenaar*, *De Standaard*, *Het Laatste Nieuws*, *Het Nieuwsblad*, *De Financieel Economische Tijd*, a business publication (Dutch) and *Grenz-Echo* (German). There is an English-language magazine, *The Bulletin*, printed in Belgium.

TV: RTBF, the French-language public broadcaster, operates *RTBF 1*, *RTBF 2* and international satellite channels. VRT, the Flemish public broadcaster, offers services such as *Een* (one). *VTM* and *VT4* are Flemish commercial broadcasters. *RTL* is a French-language commercial broadcaster.

Radio: The network operated by RTBF, the French-language public broadcaster, includes stations such as *La Premiere*, *Radio 21*, and external service *RTBF International*. The network operated by VRT, the Flemish public broadcaster, includes *Radio 1*, *Studio Brussel* and external service *Radio Vlaanderen International (RVI)*. *Belgischer Rundfunk (BRF)* broadcasts in German.

Passport/Visa

	Passport Required?	Visa Required?	Return Ticket Required?
Full British	1	No	No
Australian	Yes	No	Yes
Canadian	Yes	No	Yes
USA	Yes	No	Yes
Other EU	1	No	No
Japanese	Yes	No	Yes

Note: *Regulations and requirements may be subject to change at short notice, and you are advised to contact the appropriate diplomatic or consular authority before finalising travel arrangements. Any numbers in the chart refer to the footnotes below.*

Note: Belgium is a signatory to the 1995 **Schengen Agreement**. For further details about passport/visa regulations within the Schengen area, see the introductory section, *How to Use this Guide*.

PASSPORTS: Passport valid for at least three months beyond length of stay required by all except:

1. EU/EEA nationals (EU + Iceland, Liechtenstein, Norway) and Swiss nationals holding a valid national ID card.

Note: EU and EEA nationals are only required to produce evidence of their EU/EEA nationality and identity in order to be admitted to any EU/EEA Member state. This evidence can take the form of a valid national passport *or* national identity card. Either is acceptable. Possession of a return ticket, any length of validity on their document, sufficient funds for the length of their proposed visit should *not* be imposed.

(b) nationals of Andorra, Monaco and San Marino holding a valid national ID card;

VISAS: Required by all except the following for stays of no more than three months within a six-month period:

(a) nationals referred to in the chart and under passport exemptions above;

(b) nationals of Argentina, Bolivia, Brazil, holders of BNO (British National Overseas) passports and 'look-alike' passport holders of British Overseas Territories (except Gribraltar), plus British Indian Ocean Territory, Henderson Islands, Pitcairn, Ducie & Oeno and the St Helen Islands and dependencies, Brunei, Bulgaria, Chile, Costa Rica, Croatia, El Salvador, Guatemala, Honduras, Hong Kong (SAR), Iceland, Israel, Korea (Rep), Macau (SAR), Malaysia, Mexico, New Zealand, Nicaragua, Norway, Panama, Paraguay, Romania, Singapore, Uruguay, Vatican City and Venezuela;

(c) nationals remaining within the airport on transit, except for the following nationals, who *always* require an Airport Transit visa: Afghanistan, Angola, Congo (Dem Rep), Eritrea, Ethiopia, Gambia, Ghana, Guinea, Iran, Iraq, Nigeria, Pakistan, Sierra Leone, Somalia, Sri Lanka, Sudan

Credit: ©M van Hulst

and Syrian Arab Republic, if not possessing a valid residence permit for the EU member states or Andorra, Canada, Iceland, Japan, Liechtenstein, Monaco, Norway, San Marino, Switzerland or the USA.

Types of visa and cost: A uniform type of visa, the *Schengen* visa, is issued for tourist, business and private visits. All visas cost either £25.90 (short stay; up to 90 days) or £37 (long stay).

Note: Spouses and children (under 18 years) of EU nationals receive their visas free of charge (enquire at Embassy for details). The original marriage certificate, the spouse's passport and the birth certificate(s) for the child(ren) must be produced. Additional documents may also be required.

Validity: *Short-stay* (single- and multiple-entry): usually valid for six months from date of issue for stays of a maximum 30 or 90 days per entry. *Transit* (single- and multiple-entry): valid for a maximum of five days per entry, including the day of arrival. Visas cannot be extended and a new application must be made each time. *Schengen* collective visas are also available for group visits, subject to rules and regulations.

Application to: Consulate (or Consular Section at Embassy); see *Passport/Visa Information*. The consulate operates an appointment system and all applicants must make an appointment before attending the visa section (tel: (09065) 540 777; for those who reside in the London area. For those not leaving in the London area, applications can be made by post and a self-addressed special delivery envelope for return of passport must be enclosed with the application). Travellers visiting just one *Schengen* country should apply to the Consulate of that country; travellers

visiting more than one *Schengen* country should apply to the Consulate of the country in which their longest stay is situated. The Belgian Embassy will only issue a visa if the longest stay of the visit is to Belgium.

Application requirements: (a) Passport or official travel documents valid for at least three months after proposed stay with blank pages to affix visa stamp. (b) Completed and signed application form. (c) One passport-size photo. (d) Proof of sufficient funds to cover stay and to cover return to country of origin/transit to onwards country, plus funds to cover any possible medical expenses. This includes access to at least €38 per day if residing with an individual in Belgium, or €50 per day if residing in a hotel. If applying with a guarantor, the guarantor must have a minimum net income (enquire at Embassy for further details). (e) Valid travel insurance, with a minimum cover of €30,000. (f) Proof of purpose of stay such as a letter of invitation from a host in Belgium, a return ticket or hotel booking. (g) Letter from employer or from solicitor or bank manager if self-employed. If a student, letter from school or college confirming attendance. (h) Stamped, self-addressed registered envelope for postal applications. If visiting friends or family in Belgium, sponsorship from person in Belgium must be submitted along with business letter (with proof that national is a paid employee), providing evidence of sponsor's income, and certified at the Town Hall at which sponsor is registered. (i) Fee payable by postal order only, or cash if in person. (j) Return ticket(s) to country of residence for some nationalities. (k) Documents substantiating the purpose and circumstances of the proposed visit. *Business*: (a)-(k) and, (l) Invitation letter from overseas business associate.

Note: Nationals may identify a Belgian national or alien residing or established legally, and for a long period, in Belgium, as guarantor for subsistence and medical/travel costs incurred, if national cannot guarantee their own ability to do so. The person acting as guarantor does not necessarily have to be the person who invites the national. If the national chooses to be covered by an undertaking of responsibility, the national must, within six months of the undertaking being legalised, report to the Belgian diplomat or Consular authorities. This rule also applies to nationals exempt from a visa requirement but wishing to gain access to the *Schengen* states on the basis of an undertaking of responsibility. Consult the nearest Consular section for the list of documents to be submitted that are necessary to legalise any undertaking of responsibility.
Working days required: 48 hours to eight weeks, depending on nationality and resident status, and whether applying by post or in person. Certain nationals must apply in person (contact Consulate or Consular section at Embassy for further details). Visa processing can, on some occasions, take up to three months.
Temporary residence: Persons wishing to take up temporary residence (more than three months) should make a special application to the Belgian Embassy.

PASSPORT/VISA INFORMATION

Embassy of Belgium in the UK
103-105 Eaton Square, London SW1W 9AB, UK
Tel: (020) 7470 3734/35 (general enquiries) *or* (09065) 508 963 (recorded visa information; calls cost £1 per minute) *or* 540 777 (automated telephone appointments bookings service; calls cost £1.50 per minute).
Website: www.diplobel.org/uk
Opening hours: Mon-Fri 0900-1300 and 1400-1700.

Embassy of Belgium in the USA
3330 Garfield Street, NW, Washington, DC 20008, USA
Tel: (202) 333 6900.
Website: www.diplobel.us

Money

Single European currency (Euro): The Euro is now the official currency of 12 EU member states (including Belgium). Ten member states joined the EU on1 May 2004 but have yet to fulfil all the conditions that had to be met by the 'old' member states before adopting the euro. The first Euro coins and notes were introduced in January 2002; the Belgian Franc was still in circulation until 28 February 2002, when it was completely replaced by the Euro. Euro (€) = 100 cents. Notes are in denominations of €500, 200, 100, 50, 20, 10 and 5. Coins are in denominations of €2, 1 and 50, 20, 10, 5, 2 and 1 cents.
Credit & debit cards: American Express, Diners Club, MasterCard and Visa are widely accepted as well as Eurocheque cards. Check with your credit or debit card company for details of merchant acceptability and other services which may be available. ATMs are widespread.
Traveller's cheques: Widely accepted. To avoid additional exchange rate charges, travellers are advised to take traveller's cheques in Euros, Pounds Sterling or US Dollars.
Currency restrictions: There are no restrictions on the import and export of either local or foreign currency.
Banking hours: Mon-Fri 0900-1600.
Exchange rate indicators:
Rate at time of publishing
£1.00= €1.46
$1.00= €0.82

Duty Free

The following goods may be imported into Belgium by persons over 17 years of age arriving from non-EU countries without incurring customs duty:
200 cigarettes or 100 cigarillos or 50 cigars or 250g of tobacco; 2l of wine, 1l of spirits or 2l of sparkling wine or 2l of non-sparkling wine or 2l of fortified wine; 50g of perfume and 250ml of eau de toilette; other goods up to €64.45 or €24.79 for nationals under 15 years (subject to change – contact the Embassy for up-to-date information); 500g of coffee or 200g of coffee extract; 100g of tea or 40g of tea extract.
Prohibited items: Unpreserved meat products. Other unpreserved foodstuffs must be declared.
Abolition of duty free goods within the EU: On June 30 1999, the sale of duty free alcohol and tobacco at airports and at sea was abolished in all of the original 15 EU member states. Of the 10 new member states that joined the EU on May 1 2004, these rules already apply to Cyprus and Malta. There are transitional rules in place for visitors returning to one of the original 15 EU countries from one of the other new EU countries. But for the original 15, plus Cyprus and Malta, there are now no limits imposed on importing tobacco and alcohol products from one EU country to another (with the exceptions of Denmark, Finland and Sweden, where limits *are* imposed). Travellers should note that they may be required to prove at customs that the goods purchased are for personal use *only*.

Public Holidays

Below are listed Public Holidays for the January 2006-June 2007 period.
2006: Jan 1 New Year's Day. **Apr 17** Easter Monday. **May 1** Labour Day. **May 25** Ascension Day. **Jun 4** Whit Sunday. **Jun 5** Whit Monday. **Jun 11*** Flemish Community Holiday. **Jul 21** Independence Day. **Aug 15** Assumption of the Blessed Virgin Mary. **Sep 27*** French Community Holiday. **Nov 1** All Saints' Day. **Nov 11** Armistice Day. **Nov 15** Dynasty Day. **Dec 25** Christmas Day. **Dec 26** Boxing Day.
2007: Jan 1 New Year's Day. **Apr 9** Easter Monday. **May 1** Labour Day. **May 17** Ascension Day. **May 28** Whit Monday. **Jun 11*** Flemish Community Holiday.
Note: * Observed by the respective communities.

Health

	Special Precautions?	Certificate Required?
Yellow Fever	No	No
Cholera	No	No
Typhoid & Polio	No	N/A
Malaria	No	N/A

Note: Regulations and requirements may be subject to change at short notice, and you are advised to contact your doctor well in advance of your intended date of departure. Any numbers in the chart refer to the footnotes below.

Other risks: *Rabies* is present in a small number of animals. If you are bitten, seek medical advice without delay. For those at high risk, vaccination before arrival should be considered. For more information, consult the *Health* appendix.
Health care: European Economic Area (EEA) and Switzerland: If you or any of your dependants are suddenly taken ill or have an accident during a visit to an EEA country or Switzerland, free or reduced-cost necessary treatment is available – in most cases on production of a valid European Health Insurance Card (EHIC). The card gives access to state-provided medical treatment only and the scheme gives no entitlement to medical repatriation costs, nor does it cover ongoing illnesses of a non-urgent nature, so comprehensive travel insurance is advised. Note that the EHIC replaces the Form E111, which will no longer be valid after 31 December 2005. Some restrictions apply, depending on your nationality.
You will be charged for seeing a doctor or dentist and for prescribed drugs but you can claim back 75 per cent of these costs on provision of receipts. You will have to pay part of the costs of hospital treatment. Ambulance travel is not covered. Sickness Funds Offices (*Mutualité/Ziekenfonds*) handle reimbursements.

Travel - International

AIR:
Following the bankruptcy of Belgium's international carrier, *Sabena*, in 2001, Belgium's regional airline, *DAT* (*Delta Air Transport*), has launched its new European airline *SN Brussels Airlines (SN)*. Fifty-eight European destinations are served as well as others worldwide. For further information, check online (website: www.flysn.com). Several other international airlines operate to Belgium.
Approximate flight times: From Brussels to *London* is 50 minutes and from Antwerp is 50 minutes. From Brussels to *Los Angeles* is 16 hours and to *New York* is seven hours.
Main airports: *Brussels Zaventem (BRU)* (website: www.brusselsairport.be) is 12km (8 miles) northeast of the city (travel time – 35 minutes). *To/from the airport:* The *Airport City Express* train connects all three main railway stations (Brussels North, Central and South) with the airport, running every 15 minutes, 0600-0000 (travel time – 15 to 20 minutes). The airport station is located on level one below the terminal. Other trains also depart frequently for the city and for destinations all over Belgium. Coaches depart from the airport bus station on ground level for major cities in Belgium, France and The Netherlands. Buses run regularly to and from the city and the bus station is located below the Arrivals Hall. Taxis to the city cost approximately €30, and are only available from outside the Arrivals Hall; all licensed taxis are recognisable by their yellow and blue licence emblems. A tip is generally included in taxi fares. Hotel courtesy coaches go to Holiday Inn, Novotel and Sofitel. *Facilities:* Car parking (website: www.carparkhotel.com *or* www.worldairportguide.co.uk), car hire, post office, banks, bureaux de change, bars, restaurants, incoming and outgoing duty free shops, medical facilities, computer and fax facilities and conference and business facilities.
Brussels South Charleroi CRL)
(website: www.charleroi-airport.com) is 5km (3 miles) from Charleroi and 46km (29 miles) from Brussels. Airlines serving the airports include *Ryanair*, which operates cheap flights to several European destinations from Charleroi. *To/from the airport:* Buses depart every 30 minutes to Charleroi (travel time – 10 minutes). There are regular coaches and trains to Brussels (travel time – 45 minutes). *Facilities:* Automatic money changer, car hire, cafe, business lounge and duty free shop.
Antwerp (ANR) (Deurne) (website: www.antwerpairport.be) is 2km (1.2 miles) east of the city. *To/from the airport:* There is a regular bus service (no. 16) to Central Station. Taxis are available. *Facilities:* Outgoing duty free shop, car hire, bank and bar/restaurant. The airport offers three lounges, the Jero Business Centre. There is also an auditorium.
Ostend (OST) (website: www.ost.aero), 5km (3 miles) from the city. *Facilities:* Car parking, car hire, bureau de change, restaurant, bar and duty free shop.
Liège (LGG) (website: www.liegeairport.com). *To/from the airport:* There are taxis and a regular bus service to the centre, 5km (3 miles) away.
Departure tax: Brussels Zaventem: €20.93. Brussels South Charleroi: €13.49. Antwerp: €10. Ostend: €10. Liège: €7.
SEA:
Main ports: *Ostend*, Belgium's largest passenger and car-ferry port (website: www.portofoostende.be/info/index.htm), and *Zeebrugge* (www.portofzeebrugge.be).
RAIL:
The Belgium national railway, *Société Nationale des Chemins de Fer Belges (SNCB)* (website: www.b-rail.be), operates frequent day and night trains to destinations in Andorra, Austria, Czech Republic, Denmark, France, Germany, Hungary, Italy, Luxembourg, The Netherlands, Poland, Portugal, Switzerland and the UK.
High-speed trains – *Trains à Grande Vitesse* or *TGV* – operate between Belgium and France, connecting Brussels with destinations in Brittany, on the French Atlantic coast, the Côte d'Azur and the French Alps. Cities that can be reached from Brussels by TGV include Bordeaux, Cannes, Chambéry, Lyon, Marseille, Nice, Perpignan, Rennes and Valence. TGV trains depart from Brussels and need to be booked in advance. Further high-speed trains are operated by *Thalys* (website: www.thalys.com), a service jointly run by the the Belgium, French, German and Dutch national railways. The main international Thalys trains link Brussels to Amsterdam (The Netherlands), Cologne (Germany) and Paris (France).
Rail passes: International rail passes include the *Eurodomino* card permitting three to eight days' unlimited travel within a period of 30 days in any European country. Several *Eurodomino* cards can be purchased by people wishing to travel in more than one country. It is available to people who have resided for at least six months in a European country, a European CIS country, Algeria, Morocco or Tunisia. The *InterRail* pass permits unlimited travel for 16 days, 22 days or 30 days on 28 European networks, the Moroccan network and the Turkish network to people who have resided for at least six months in a European country, Algeria, Morocco or Tunisia. The *Benelux Tourrail ticket* offers five days of unlimited travel within a period of 30 days by rail in Belgium, Luxembourg and The Netherlands. The European travelcard *Railplus* entitles the buyer to a 25 per cent reduction on all international conventional trains, on condition that the journey crosses at least one frontier. There are different *Railplus* cards available: for young people aged 12 to 25 years, for adults aged 26 to 60 years, and for seniors over 60. For further information, contact *Rail Europe* (tel: (08708) 302 008; website: www.raileurope.co.uk) *or International Rail Ltd* (tel: (0870) 751 5000; website: www.international-rail.com).
Eurostar: *Eurostar*, a service provided by the railways of Belgium, France and the UK, operates direct high-speed trains from London (*Waterloo International*) via the Channel Tunnel to Brussels (*Midi/Zuid*). The travel time from London to Brussels is two hours 20 minutes. For further information and reservations, contact *Eurostar* (tel: (0870) 160 0052 (travel agents) *or* (0870) 518 6186 (public; within the UK) *or* (+44 1233) 617 575 (public; outside the UK); a £5 booking fee applies to all telephone bookings; website: www.eurostar.com); *or Rail Europe* (tel: (08708) 302 008). Complaints and comments may be sent to Eurostar Customer Relations Travel Centre, 1-1-G Eurostar House, Waterloo Station, London SE1 8SE, UK; (tel: (01777) 777 879; e-mail: new.comments@eurostar.co.uk).
ROAD:
There are good road links from most of the European countries. *Eurolines*, departing from Victoria Coach Station in London, serves

destinations in Belgium. For further information, contact *Eurolines* (52 Grosvenor Gardens, London SW1; tel: (08705) 143 219; website: www.eurolines.com *or* www.nationalexpress.com).
Channel Tunnel: *Eurotunnel* runs shuttle trains for cars, bicycles, motorcycles, coaches, minibuses, caravans, campervans and other vehicles over 1.85m (6.07ft) between Folkestone in Kent, with direct road access from the M20, and Calais with links to the A16/A26 motorway (Exit 13). All road vehicles are carried through the tunnel in shuttle trains running between the two terminals. Terminals and shuttles are well-equipped for disabled passengers. Passenger Terminal buildings contain a variety of shops, restaurants, bureaux de change and other amenities. The journey takes about 35 minutes from platform to platform and around one hour from motorway to motorway. There are up to four passenger shuttles per hour at peak times, 24 hours per day and services run every day of the year. Motorists pass through customs and immigration before they board, with no further checks on arrival. Fares are charged according to length of stay and time of year and whether or not you have a reservation. The price applies to the car, regardless of the number of passengers or size of the car. Promotional deals are frequently available, especially outside the peak holiday seasons. Tickets may be purchased in advance from travel agents, or from Eurotunnel Customer Services in France or the UK with a credit card. For further information, brochures and reservations, contact *Eurotunnel Customer Services*, Customer Relations Department, Saint Martin's Plain, Cheriton, Folkestone, Kent CT19 4QD, UK (tel: (08705) 353 535; website: www.eurotunnel.co.uk). For further information about departure times of shuttles at the French terminal, contact *Eurotunnel Customer Information* in Coquelle (tel: France (3) 2100 6543).

Travel - Internal

AIR:

As Belgium is such a small country, there are no internal flights. Bus services operate between Brussels airport to Antwerp, Ghent and Liège; see *Travel – International* section.

RAIL:

SNCB operates a dense railway network with regular trains on most lines. On the main lines there are more frequent trains. For more information contact *Belgian Railways* (tel: (2) 528 2828; website: www.b-rail.be) *or Rail Europe* (tel: (08708) 302 008; website: www.raileurope.co.uk). **Fares:** First- and second-class, single and return tickets are available. However, a return ticket is double the single fare and is only valid on the day of issue. Children under 12 travel for free in second class (restrictions apply). **Discount travel:** Weekend return fares are available from Friday (after 1900) to Sunday for the outward journey and on Saturday and Sunday for the return journey (on long holiday weekends, these periods are extended). A 50 per cent reduction card is also for sale. It entitles the holder to buy an unlimited number of half-price single tickets. *Go Pass* offers preferential tariffs for 10 second-class trips within one year to people aged under 26. The *Rail Pass* offers preferential tariffs for 10 second-class trips within one year to people over 26. People aged 65 and over benefit from special tariffs.

ROAD:

There are many different brands of petrol available, and prices vary. Traffic drives on the right. Main towns are connected by toll-free motorways. It is compulsory for seatbelts to be worn in the front and back of vehicles. Children under 12 are not permitted to travel in the front seat of a car. A warning triangle must be displayed at the scene of a breakdown or accident. It is compulsory to carry a fire extinguisher or first aid kit in all vehicles. The speed limit on motorways and dual carriageways is 120kph (75mph) with a minimum speed of 70kph (45 mph), on single carriageways outside built-up areas is 90kph (55mph), and in built-up areas is 50kph (31mph). Trams always have priority on roads. **Bus:** Extensive regional bus services are operated by the bus companies which publish regional timetables. There are long-distance stopping services between towns. **Taxi:** Plentiful in all towns. The tip is included in the final meter price. If there are no taxi stands, taxi companies may be telephoned for an extra charge of about €2.50. **Car hire:** Both self-drive and chauffeur-driven cars are available. The minimum age is 23 and the person must possess a valid full licence with at least one year of validity (and which will be required upon collection of the car). **Documentation:** A national driving licence is acceptable. EU nationals taking their own cars to Belgium must obtain a Green Card. The Green Card tops insurance cover up to the level of cover provided by the car owner's domestic policy.

URBAN:

There is a good public transport system in all the major towns and cities, with underground, tram and bus services in Antwerp and Brussels, bus and tramways in Charleroi, Ghent and Ostend and bus systems elsewhere. There is a standard flat-fare system, with discounts for 5- and 10-journey multi-ride tickets. One-day tickets and multi-mode tourist travelcards are also available.
Travel times: The following chart gives approximate travel times from **Brussels** (in hours and minutes) to other major cities and towns in Belgium.

	Air	Road	Rail
Antwerp	-	**0.40**	**0.41**
Bruges	-	**1.00**	**0.53**
Ghent	-	**0.50**	**0.28**
Liège	-	**1.10**	**1.22**

Travel Advice

Most visits to Belgium are trouble-free but you should be aware of the global risk of indiscriminate international terrorist attacks, which could be against civilian targets, including places frequented by foreigners.
This advice is based on information provided by the Foreign and Commonwealth Office in the UK. It is correct at time of publishing. As the situation can change rapidly, visitors are advised to contact the following organisations for the latest travel advice:

British Foreign and Commonwealth Office
Tel: (0845) 850 2829.
Website: www.fco.gov.uk

US Department of State
Website: http://travel.state.gov/travel

Accommodation

HOTELS:

Belgium has a large range of hotels from luxury to small family pensions and inns. The best international-class hotels are found in the cities. The Belgian Tourist Office issues a shield to all approved hotels by which they can be recognised. Hotels which display this sign conform to the official standards set by Belgian law which protects the tourist and guarantees certain standards of quality. Some hotels are also graded according to the Benelux system in which standard is indicated by a row of 3-pointed stars, from the highest (**5-star**) to the minimum (**1-star**). However, membership of this scheme is voluntary, and there may be first-class hotels which are not classified in this way. If an establishment providing accommodation facilities is classified under category H (plain hotel with moderate standards of comfort) or above (1, 2, 3, 4 or 5 stars), it may call itself hotel, hostelry, inn, guest house, motel or other similar names.

FARM HOLIDAYS:

In some regions of the country, farm holidays are now available. In the Polders and the Ardennes visitors can (for a small cost) participate in the daily work of the farm.

SELF-CATERING:

There are ample opportunities to rent furnished villas, flats, rooms, or bungalows for a holiday period. There is a particularly wide choice in the Ardennes and on the coast. These holiday houses and flats are comfortable and well-equipped. Rentals are determined by the number of bedrooms, the amenities, the location and the season. On the coast, many apartments, studios, villas and bungalows are classified into five categories according to the standard of comfort they offer. Estate agents will supply full details. For the Ardennes region, enquiries should be made to the local tourist office or to Belsud (for contact details, see above under *Farm Holidays*). Addresses of local tourist offices and lists of coastal estate agents can be obtained from Tourism Brussels-Wallonia/Tourism Flanders-Brussels.

YOUTH HOSTELS:

There are two youth hostel associations: the Vlaamse Jeugdherbergcentrale (VJHC) (website: www.vjh.be), which operates in Flanders, and the Centrale Wallonne (CWAJ) (website: www.laj.be), operating in the French-speaking area. The hostels of the former are large, highly organised and much frequented by schools and youth groups; the hostels of the CWAJ are smaller and more informal, similar in some ways to those in France. A complete list of youth hostels and other holiday homes for young people can be obtained from Belgian Tourist Office – Brussels & Wallonia *or* Tourism Flanders-Brussels (see *Top Things To Do*).

CAMPING/CARAVANNING:

The majority of campsites are in the Ardennes and on the coast; many of these are excellent. A list of addresses, rates and other information can be obtained from the Belgian Tourist Office – Brussels & Wallonia or Tourism Flanders-Brussels (see *Top Things To Do*). The local *Verblijftaks* or *Taxe de Séjour* is a tax usually included in the rates charged. On the coast during the summer season, a supplement of about 25 per cent is charged on the majority of tariffs. Camping out in places other than the recognised sites is permitted, provided the agreement of the landowner or tenant has been obtained.

ACCOMMODATION INFORMATION

Horeca Brussels Office (Hotel Association)
BP 4, Anspachlaan 111, B-1000 Brussels, Belgium
Tel: (2) 513 7814.
Website: www.horecabrussel.be

Horeca Wallonia Office
Avenue Gouverneur Bovesse 35, B-5100 Jambes, Belgium
Tel: (81) 721 888.
Website: www.horecawallonie.be

Horeca Flanders Office
Website: www.fedhorecavlaanderen.be

Flemish Federation for Farm and Country Tourism
Minderbroederstraat 8, B-3000 Leuven, Belgium
Tel: (16) 242 158.
Website: www.hoevetoerisme.be

Belsud (Information on Bed & Breakfast, Self-Catering Accommodation and Farm Holidays)
61 rue du Marché-aux-Herbes, B-1000 Brussels, Belgium
Tel: (2) 504 0280.
Website: www.wallonia-tourism.net

Top Things To See

- The highlight of **Brussels**, the capital, is most certainly the gothic **Grand Place**. Pose for a photograph in front of the famous **Manneken-Pis** and his less heralded sister the **Janneken Pis;** both statues hint at the exuberance and irreverence of the 'Bruxellois'. Other key sights in Brussels include **St Michael and St Gudule's Cathedral** and the **Mont des Arts** park, which links the upper and lower parts of the city. Then there is the elegant **Place Royale**, built between 1774 and 1780 in the style of Louis XVI. Among other areas worth exploring are the **Îlot Sacré**, the picturesque area of narrow streets to the northeast of the Grand-Place; the fashionable **boulevard de Waterloo**; the administrative quarter, a completely symmetrical park area commanding a splendid view of the surrounding streets; the **Grand Sablon**, the area containing both the flamboyant Gothic structure of the **Church of Our Lady of Sablon** and the Sunday antique market and, lastly, the **Petit Sablon**, a square surrounded by Gothic columns, which support 48 small bronze statues commemorating medieval Brussels guilds. A more modern attraction is the bizarre **Atomium**, a futuristic, atom-shaped aluminium tower built for the 1958 World Fair. **Note:** The *Brussels Card* now gives the visitor free access to 30-plus museums and also the use of public transport throughout the Brussels-Capital region, within a 72-hour period. This 'culture pass' is available at all participating museums - at the six sales offices of the Brussels Public Transport Company (STIB), at certain hotels and at the Brussels International Tourism Office, costing just €30.
- One important out-of-town attraction is the **Battle of Waterloo site**, 18km (11 miles) to the south of Brussels, commemorating the battle that shaped the future of both Belgium and modern Europe, of which Brussels is now such a crucial hub.
- Beyond modern **Antwerp**, the more traditional attractions complement the new, with the impressive **Grote Markt** containing the **Town Hall** and the **Brabo Fountain**, which commemorates the legend of the city's origin and also the 18th-century **Groenplaats**, with its Rubens statue.
- **Bruges** offers a variety of attractions such as the **Lake of Love**, which in the Middle Ages was the city's internal port; the 14th-century **Town Hall** featuring a façade decorated with bas-reliefs and statues of a Biblical nature; the **Cathedral of the Holy Saviour**, a fine example of 13th-century Gothic architecture and home to many treasures; and the **Grote Markt**, which was formerly the commercial hub of the city.
- The medieval heart of **Ghent** boasts many historic buildings, including three abbeys. Key attractions include **St Bavo's Cathedral**, place of Charles V's baptism and home to **The Adoration of the Mystical Lamb**, the Van Eyck brothers' masterpiece; the **Town Hall**, where the Treaty of Ghent was signed in 1576; the **Castle of the Counts**, a medieval castle surrounded by the **Lieve canal**; the 15th-century **Cloth Hall** and the **medieval town centre** with its guild houses.
- Explore the Belgian coastline, a largely sandy affair that stretches for 67km (42 miles) from **Knokke** near the Dutch border to **De Panne** on the French border, with over a dozen resorts. Bathing in the sea is free on all

A B C D E F G H I J K L M N O P Q R S T U V W X Y Z

Credit: ©Office de Promotion du Tourisme Bruxelles et Wallonie

beaches and there are facilities for sailing, sand yachting, riding, fishing, rowing, golf and tennis. Some of the best resorts are **Bredene**, **De Haan**, **De Panne**, **Lombardsijde**, **Nieuwpoort**, **Wenduine**, **Westende** and the town of **Ostend**, where Queen Victoria once took to the waters. **Knokke**, **Middelkerke** and **Ostend** are the liveliest resorts.

- **Liège**, a major city of Wallonia, the French-speaking portion of Belgium, is a popular tourist destination, situated on the banks of the **Meuse**. The view from the **Citadel** covers the old town, the most impressive part of the city. Liège's most notable buildings are the **Church of St James**, an old abbey church of mixed architecture, including an example of the Meuse Romanesque style, with fine Renaissance stained glass and the 18th-century **Town Hall**.
- In **Tournai**, the second-oldest city in Belgium, admire the oldest **Belfry** in Belgium at the **Cathedral of Our Lady** (12th century).
- Located in the **Ardennes** region, the town of **Dinant**, in the Meuse valley, boasts a medieval castle, while its most famous landmark is the Gothic church of **Notre-Dame**. **Annevoie** has a castle and some beautiful water gardens. The old university town of **Namur**, with cobbled streets in its centre, has a cathedral and a castle. The **River Semois** passes through **Arlon** and **Florenville**; nearby are the ruins of **Orval Abbey**, **Bouillon** and its castle, **Botassart**, **Rochehaut** and **Bohan**.

Top Things To Do

- The capital Brussels boasts many museums such as the **Museum of Ancient Art**, the **Museum of Modern Art**, the **Comic Strip Museum**, the **Museum of the City of Brussels - Maison du Roi** (for more information, visit: www.brusselsmuseums.be/en/musees/index.php). Discover the exuberance and irreverence of the 'Bruxellois', a spirit that reaches its zenith in the city's numerous bars which, along with the **1000 types of Belgian beer**, are not to be missed. This energy also surfaces in the trendy bars and hip nightclubs that have now joined the more traditional charms of the beer and gin bars that still pull in the more reserved drinkers in Antwerp, Europe's second-largest port.
- The work of local artistic luminary Peter Paul Rubens surfaces all over **Antwerp**, most notably at the **Royal Museum of Fine Arts**, home to what is arguably the world's finest collection of his work. The **Rubens' House**, the magnificent 17th-century house where the painter lived and worked, contains works by the painter and his associates as do many other museums and churches. Discover Antwerp's maritime heritage by joining **a tour of the port** or visit the **Steen**, a 12th-century fortress now housing the **National Maritime Museum**, that overlooks the buzzing new city of today. Be at the cutting edge of fashion and design with countless boutiques and shopping outlets across **Antwerp**.
- The perfectly preserved 'medieval heart' of **Bruges** can be explored from the comfort of a **canal boat ride**, which takes tourists around the myriad of waterways that lead to the city often being referred to as the 'Venice of the North'. Bruges boasts several good museums, including the **Groeninge Museum** which houses a comprehensive and fascinating collection of six centuries of Flemish paintings, from Jan van Eyck to Marcel Broodthaers. The **Memling Museum**, housed in the medieval **Saint John's Hospital**, is dedicated to the painter Hans Memling. The city is close to some excellent beaches and the fertile Polder region, dotted with abbeys and parks.

- Visit the **Museum of Fine Arts**, and the **Museum of Industrial Archaeology** in **Ghent**, which was once the largest medieval city in Europe after Paris.
- **Liège**, in Wallonia, boasts many fine museums with the highlights being **The Museum of Wallonian Life**, showcasing the unique culture of Wallonia; the **Museum of Wallonian Art**; the **Museum of Modern Art**, displaying the works of Corot, Monet, Picasso, Gauguin and Chagall, to name but a few, and the **Curtius Museum**, housing a large collection of coins, Liège furniture and porcelain.
- Tournai boasts the **Museum of Fine Arts**, one of the finest in Belgium, with works by Rubens and Bruegel, and the **Natural History Museum**.
- Explore the Ardennes, a mountainous area famous for its cuisine, forests, lakes, streams and grottoes. **Yvoir**, **Godinne** and **Profondeville** are well known for **watersports**. **Namur** has many museums. **Houyet** offers **kayaking** and other assorted outdoor activities. The **Amblève Valley** is one of the wildest in the Ardennes and the grottoes in the **Fond de Quarreux** are one of the great attractions of the region. Among these is the **Merveilleuse grotto** at **Dinant** and the cavern at **Remouchamps**. There are **prehistoric caverns** at **Spy**, **Rochefort**, **Hotton** and **Han-sur-Lesse**.
- Visiting the **World War I battlefields** is an increasingly popular activity, with a number of sites open with varying degrees of facilities. The killing fields of **Ypres** are the most accessible with a war museum, monuments, military cemeteries and the battlefields themselves all located around the town. In Ypres at 2000 each day, the Last Post is sounded under the Menin Gate. A number of commemorative events are organised by the regional tourist boards.
- Discover Belgium's hundreds of varieties of beer by taking part in a **brewery tour**. There are beers of all colours and types, brewed using different methods and ingredients – wheat beers, fruit beers, red beers, amber ales and 'spontaneously fermented beers', to mention but a few. Each beer has its own distinctive glass and label. Six kinds of trappist beer, brewed by monks to ancient recipes, are made in Belgium. Some breweries are open to the public. Trappist breweries open to the public include the **Bières de Chimay brewery** at **Bailleux** and the **Rochefortoise brewery** at **Eprave**. Visits to the Rochefortoise brewery must be booked by fax and confirmed two days in advance. These beers can all be sampled in Belgium's many cafes, pubs and restaurants.
- Enjoy Belgian **gastronomy**. The country has the highest number of Michelin stars per head of the population, and is the only country in the world where US fast food chains have been consistently losing money. The visitor has an array of fine restaurants, sophisticated cafes, and pubs to choose from. Specialist tour operators offer gastronomy trips where visitors can learn how to cook Flemish dishes using local produce and beers.
- Treat yourself to a visit to a **chocolate factory**. Belgian chocolate has an excellent reputation. Some chocolate factories are open to the public, though it is often necessary to book in advance. The **Chocolate and Cocoa Museum** on the Grand-Place in Brussels is open from Tuesday to Sunday (every day in July and August). The **Chocolaterie Jacques' museum** in Eupen near Liège is open to the public from Monday to Friday. Groups of more than 10 people need to book in advance (website: www.chocolatjacques.be).
- Take part in one of Belgium's dozens of yearly **carnivals**, including those in Binche and Stavelot in which local

people dress in various traditional costumes and parade through the streets, and the **CAT Festival** in Leper.

TOURIST INFORMATION

Office de Promotion du Tourisme Bruxelles et Wallonie in the UK (Belgian Tourist Office – Brussels and Wallonia)
217 Marsh Wall, London E14 9FJ, UK
Tel: (0906) 302 0245 (calls cost 60p per minute) *or* (0800) 954 5245 (free brochure request line; toll-free in UK) *or* (020) 7531 0391.
Website: www.belgiumtheplaceto.be

Toerisme Vlaanderen in the UK (Tourism Flanders - Brussels)
Flanders House, 1a Cavendish Square, London W1G 0LD, UK
Tel: (020) 7307 7730 (travel trade and press only) *or* (0800) 954 5245 (brochure request line; toll-free in UK) *or* (09063) 020 245 (live operator; calls cost 60p per minute).
Website: www.visitflanders.co.uk

Belgian Tourist Office in the USA (Headquarters for USA and Canada)
220 East 42nd Street, Suite 3402, New York, NY 10017, USA
Tel: (212) 758 8130.
Website: www.visitbelgium.com

Entertainment

FOOD & DRINK: Belgian cuisine is similar to French, based on game and seafood. Each region in Belgium has its own special dish. Butter, cream, beer and wine are generously used in cooking.

Things to know:
Most restaurants have waiter service, although self-service cafes are becoming quite numerous. Restaurant bills always include drinks, unless they have been taken at the bar separately. In the latter case, this is settled over the counter. Under a new law, the majority of cafes now have licences to serve spirits. Beers and wines are freely obtainable everywhere and there are no licensing hours.

National specialities:
- Mussels and chips.
- *Endives* with *Bechamel* sauce.
- Ardennes sausages and ham are also renowned.
- Belgian chocolate.
- Waffles.

National drinks:
There are over 400 beers brewed in Belgium, ranging from lagers and pilsners through to *Lambic*, made from wheat and barley, *white* and *fruit* beers, to *Trappist* monastery beers. Fruit beers, such as *Kriek* cherry beer, are a speciality. Famous names include *Stella Artois*, *Leffe*, *Hoegaarden*, *Duvel* and *Chimay*.

Tipping: A service charge of 16 per cent is usually included in hotel or restaurant bills, although an additional tip may be left at the discretion of the individual. Cloakroom attendants and porters may expect a tip per item of luggage.

NIGHTLIFE: As well as being one of the best cities in the world for eating out (both for its high quality and range), Brussels has a very active and varied nightlife. It has 10 theatres producing plays in both Dutch and French. These include the *Théâtre National de la Communauté Française* and the *Théâtre des Galeries*. The more avant-garde theatres include the *Théâtre Cinq-Quarante* and the *Théâtre de Poche*. Brussels' dozens of cinemas, numerous discos and many night-time cafes are centred on two main areas: the uptown Porte Louise area and the downtown area between Place Roger and Place de la Bourse. Nightclubs include *Le Fuse*, *Les Jeux d'Hiver* and *Le You*; jazz clubs include *The New York Cafe Jazz Club*, *The Sounds Jazz Club* and *The Music Village* (visit: www.brusselslife.be and www.trabel.com/brussel/brussels-nightlife.htm). Programmes and weekly listings of events can be found in the *BBB Agenda* on sale at tourist offices. This also covers information on the many festivals that take place in Brussels itself. Tourism Brussels-Ardennes/Tourism Flanders-Brussels should be consulted about folk music or drama festivals elsewhere in Belgium – the most famous of which is the *Festival of Flanders* for classical music concerts. The other large cities of Belgium, such as Antwerp, Ghent, Kortrijk, Leuven, Liège, Mons and Namur, all have similar (though less extensive) nightlife facilities.

SHOPPING: Special purchases include ceramics and hand-beaten copperware from Dinant; Belgian chocolates; crystals from Val Saint Lambert; diamonds; jewellery from Antwerp; lace from Bruges, Brussels and Mechelen (Malines); woodcarvings from Spa and *bandes dessinées* (comic-strip books) by a number of talented Belgian cartoon artists from Brussels. Main shopping centres are located in Antwerp, Bruges, Brussels, Ghent, Liège, Mechelen, Mons, Namur and Ostend. **Shopping hours:** Mon-Sat 1000-1800/1900. Department stores often remain open longer, up to 2100 on Friday. Outside main areas, some shops may close at lunchtime.

Business

- **GDP:** US$316.9 billion (2003).
- **Main exports:** Manufactured goods chemicals, diamonds, metals and metal products, foodstuffs and machinery.
- **Main imports:** Fuel products, machinery and equipment, chemicals, pharmaceuticals, foodstuffs, and transportation equipment.
- **Main trade partners:** Germany, The Netherlands, France and UK.

ECONOMY: The economies of Belgium and Luxembourg have been unified since 1921, when the two Governments signed a Convention of Economic Union; this is distinct from the Benelux Union (which includes The Netherlands) and the EU (Belgium being a founder member of both). The country's traditional industries of steel, motor vehicles and textiles suffered from the recession of the 1980s. While important, these no longer play the central economic role of the past. Coal mining ceased when the last mine was closed in 1992. Nuclear power accounts for almost two-thirds of Belgium's energy consumption; the remainder is generated from imported fuel products. Manufactured goods and machinery are the largest export sectors, with the major markets inside the EU – including France, Germany, The Netherlands and the UK. These are also Belgium's main source of imported goods. Belgium relies particularly heavily on export earnings – 70 per cent of GDP is exported, one of the highest proportions in the world. Successive Belgian Governments have been keen proponents of the process of European integration, including the introduction of a single European currency, which Belgium adopted upon its inception in 1999. The Verhofstadt Government has managed to reduce Belgium's high unemployment level to around 7 per cent, while keeping inflation below 2 per cent. Growth is sluggish at present, at just over 1 per cent.

BUSINESS ETIQUETTE: Suits should always be worn and business is conducted on a formal basis, with punctuality valued and business cards exchanged. Transactions are usually made in French or English. **Office hours:** Mon-Fri 0830-1730.

CONFERENCES/CONVENTIONS: There is an extensive range of meeting venues throughout the country. In 1994, Belgium was the seventh most popular conference destination, whilst Brussels was the third most popular city.

COMMERCIAL INFORMATION

Belgian-Luxembourg Chamber of Commerce in Great Britain
Riverside House, 27-29 Vauxhall Grove, London SW8 1SY, UK
Tel: (0870) 246 1610.
Website: www.blcc.co.uk

Chambre de Commerce et d'Industrie de Bruxelles
500 avenue Louise, B-1050 Brussels, Belgium
Tel: (2) 648 5002.
Website: www.500.be

Voka - Chamber of Commerce Antwerp-Waasland
Markgravestraat 12, B-2000 Antwerp, Belgium
Tel: (3) 232 2219.
Website: www.kvkaw.voka.be

Belgian Foreign Trade
Rue Montoyer 3, B-1000 Brussels, Belgium
Tel: (2) 206 3511.
Website: www.abh-ace.org

The Flanders Foreign Investment Office (FFIO) - Headquarters
Gaucheretstraat 90, B-1030 Brussels, Belgium
Tel: (2) 504 8871.
Website: www.ffio.com

Flanders-Brussels Convention Bureau
Grasmarkt 61, 1000 Brussels, Belgium
Tel: (2) 504 0355.
Website: www.meetingpoint.be

Belize

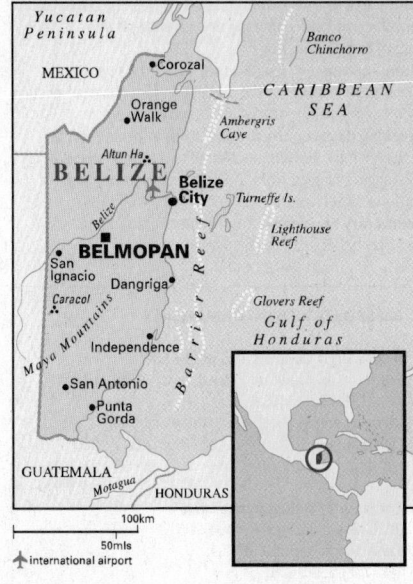

Location: Central America, Caribbean coast.

Time: GMT - 6.

Overview

For the outdoor enthusiast, Belize, formerly known as British Honduras, presents unlimited opportunities. The country, a constitutional monarchy in which the British Monarch is Head of State, has a lot more in common with the Caribbean island-states - its style of architecture, for example, than its Central American neighbours. Every destination in Belize has its share of archaeological and national parks, marine and nature reserves and wildlife sanctuaries. Mayan temples tower above rainforest canopies while an incredibly colourful array of marine wildlife finds protection in Belize's Barrier Reef.

Belize is a country of various culture, language and ethnic groups. Approximately 200,000 people in Belize consist of Creole, Garifuna, Mestizo, Spanish, Maya, English, Mennonite, Lebanese, Chinese and East Indian heritage. Due to racial harmony, religious tolerance and a relatively non-violent political culture, all of these different elements have mixed and blended successfully, to give Belize a widespread reputation for its friendly peoples.

General Information

AREA: 22,965 sq km (8867 sq miles).
POPULATION: 282,600 (2004).
POPULATION DENSITY: 31.9 per sq km.
CAPITAL: Belmopan City. **Population:** 12,300 (2004). Belize City (the former capital) has a population of 59,400.
GEOGRAPHY: Belize is situated at the base of the Yucatan Peninsula in Central America and borders Mexico and Guatemala, with the Caribbean Sea to the east. The country's area includes numerous small islands (Cayes) off the coast. The coastal strip is low and swampy, particularly in the north, with mangroves, many salt and freshwater lagoons and some sandy beaches crossed by a number of rivers. To the south and west rises the heavily forested Maya mountain range, with the Cockscomb range to the east and the Mountain Pine Ridge in the west. More than 65 per cent of the area of the country is forested. The land to the west along the borders with Guatemala is open and relatively scenic compared to much of the interior. The shallow offshore Cayes straddle a coral reef second only in size to the Great Barrier Reef of Australia.

GOVERNMENT: Constitutional monarchy. Gained independence from the UK in 1981. **Head of State:** HM Queen Elizabeth II represented locally by Governor-General Sir Colville Young since 1993. **Head of Government:** Prime Minister Said Musa since 1998. **Recent history:** The bicameral National Assembly is the legislature and consists of a nine-member Senate (appointed by the Governor General for a five-year term) and a 29-member House of Representatives (directly elected for a maximum five-year term). Executive power is in the hands of the Governor General, advised by the Cabinet. Said Musa was re-elected in 2003 with his People's United Party (PUP) winning 22 Assembly seats. Following a difficult start to their second term, with allegations of corruption and poor macro-economic management continuing against the government, Said Musa carried out a Cabinet reshuffle in January 2004. In August 2004, seven Ministers resigned expressing their disquiet over the Government's macro-economic performance - especially the growth of external debt and the use of government funds to support private sector ventures. A change to portfolios led to the return of the Ministers but three of them were then removed from the Cabinet in December 2004. Since January 2005, civil disturbances have taken place culminating in a riot in Belize City in April. Today, the Government's financial problems continue, the budget deficit has not been bridged and the country's credit ratings have decreased.
LANGUAGE: English is the official language, but Spanish is spoken to some extent by over half the population. Garifuna (Carib), Maya and Creole are also spoken as well as a German dialect (by the Mennonites).
RELIGION: The people of Belize are mainly Roman Catholic (approximately 60 per cent of the population). Other small groups practice Islam, Buddhism, Hinduism, and Bahai, as well as other Christian denominations.
ELECTRICITY: 110 volts AC, 60Hz. American-style two-pin plugs.
SOCIAL CONVENTIONS: British influence can still be seen in many social situations. Flowers or confectionary are acceptable gifts to give to hosts if invited to their home for a meal. Dress is casual, although beachwear should not be worn in towns. It may be inadvisable to discuss politics, particularly if of a partisan nature.

Climate

Subtropical with a brisk prevailing wind from the Caribbean Sea. High annual temperatures and humidity. Dry and hot climate from January to April, with rainy season from June. The hurricane season is from June to the end of November.

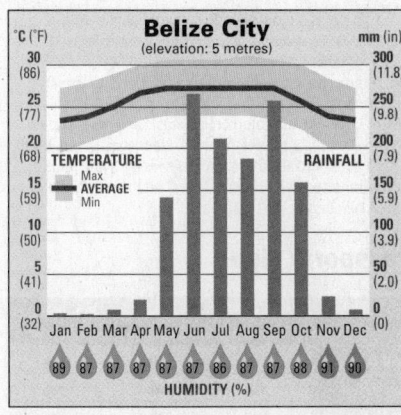

Communications

Telephone: IDD is available. Country code: 501.
Mobile telephone: Roaming agreements exist with most international mobile phone companies. Coverage is available in all six districts (check with *Belize Telecommunications Ltd*, website: www.digicell.bz). Handsets can be hired from *Belize Telecommunications Ltd* at US$5 per day, plus a deposit of US$150.
Internet: There is an e-mail service centre in the BTL office (website: www.btl.net) in central Belize City and Internet cafes in urban centres and popular tourist centres.
Post: Mail to Europe takes up to five days.
MEDIA: The constitution guarantees media freedom, but provides exceptions in the interest of national security, public order and morality. Belize has no daily newspapers; some of the privately owned weeklies are subsidised by political parties. State-run radio was privatised in 1998 and listeners now rely on a range of private commercial stations, most of them networked across the country. A number of private television stations are on the air and cable TV is available in the towns.
Press: The major weeklies include *Amandala*, *The Belize Times*, *The Reporter* and *The San Pedro Sun*, a community paper, published on the island of Ambergris Caye.

Credit: ©Demian Solano Photography

Belize Today is a monthly official paper published in English. *The Guardian* is a United Democratic Party-affiliated paper.
TV: Commercial channels include *Channel 5, Channel 7* and *Channel 9*.
Radio: *Love FM* is a commercial, music and news station. *Estereo Amor* is a private, Spanish-language station. *Krem FM* is a commercial station. *More FM* is a private, music station targeted at younger listeners and *Wave Radio* is United Democratic Party-affiliated.

Passport/Visa

	Passport Required?	Visa Required?	Return Ticket Required?
Full British	Yes	No	Yes
Australian	Yes	No	Yes
Canadian	Yes	No	Yes
USA	Yes	No	Yes
Other EU	Yes	No	Yes
Japanese	Yes	Yes/1	Yes

Note: *Regulations and requirements may be subject to change at short notice, and you are advised to contact the appropriate diplomatic or consular authority before finalising travel arrangements. Any numbers in the chart refer to the footnotes below.*

PASSPORTS: Passport valid for six months beyond the intended length of stay required by all.
VISAS: Required by all except the following for stays of up to 30 days:
(a) nationals indicated in the chart above and nationals of their overseas territories (except **1.** nationals of Japan who *do* need a visa);
(b) nationals of Commonwealth countries and nationals of their overseas territories (except nationals of Bangladesh, Cameroon, Chad, The Gambia, Ghana, India, Mozambique, Nauru, Nigeria, Pakistan, Sierra Leone and Sri Lanka who *do* need a visa);
(c) nationals of Caribbean Community Member States (CARICOM), except nationals of Haiti who *do* need a visa;
(d) nationals of Chile, Costa Rica, Guatemala, Iceland, Mexico, Norway, Tunisia and Uruguay.

Note: (a) All travellers are required to show evidence of sufficient funds (minimum £50 per day) and proof of return or onward ticket at the point of entry. (b) Each individual traveller regardless of age must make a separate visa application.
Types of visa and cost: *Tourist* and *Business. Single-entry:* £20. *Multiple-entry:* £30.
Validity: *Single-entry:* Three or six months. *Multiple-entry:* Three months, six months or one year.
Application to: Consulate (or Consular Section at Embassy or High Commission); see *Passport/Visa Information.*
Application requirements: (a) Application form. (b) One recent passport-size photo. (c) Valid passport. (d) Copies of tickets or a confirmed travel itinerary. (e) Copies of confirmed hotel reservations or full contact details of family or friends in Belize. (f) Copies of most recent bank statements. (g) Fee, payable by bank draft or postal order; personal cheques and credit cards are not accepted (you may pay in cash if the application is made in person). (h) £5 to cover postal applications, where applicable. *Business:* (a)-(h) and, (i) Letter from financial officer. (j) Letter of introduction from company or organisation and supporting documents.
Note: The visa recipient is advised to carry all evidence submitted in support of the application for possible inspection by the immigration official upon entry into Belize.
Working days required: Visas issued in person will be ready for the following day. Allow two to four weeks if clearance is needed from the Belize Immigration and Nationality Services.
Temporary residence: Apply to Immigration and Nationality Department, Belmopan.

PASSPORT/VISA INFORMATION

Belize High Commission in the UK
3rd Floor, 45 Crawford Place, London W1H 4LP, UK
Tel: (020) 7723 3603.
Website: www.belizehighcommission.com
Opening hours: Mon-Fri 1000-1800; 1000-1300 (consular section).

Embassy of Belize in the USA
2535 Massachusetts Avenue, NW, Washington, DC 20008, USA
Tel: (202) 332 9636.
Website: www.embassyofbelize.org

Money

Currency: Belize Dollar (BZD; symbol Bz$) = 100 cents. Notes are in denominations of Bz$100, 50, 20, 10, 5 and 2. Coins are in denominations of Bz$1, and 100, 50, 25, 10, 5 and 1 cents.
Note: The Belize Dollar is tied to the US Dollar at US$1 = Bz$2.
Currency exchange: Currency can be exchanged at most banks, hotels and travel agencies. Some businesses will even accept dollars. ATMs in Belize generally do not accept foreign cards.
Credit & debit cards: American Express, MasterCard (limited) and Visa are accepted. Check with your credit or debit card company for details of merchant acceptability and other services which may be available. Most establishments will add a 5 per cent service charge to the bills of customers using credit cards.
Traveller's cheques: These can be exchanged; commission will usually be charged.
Currency restrictions: The import and export of local currency is limited to Bz$100. The import of foreign currency is unlimited, provided declared on arrival. The export of foreign currency is limited to the equivalent of Bz$400 for residents, and up to the amount imported and declared for non-residents. Visitors are advised to carry a minimum of Bz$75 for each day they intend to stay.
Banking hours: Mon-Thurs 0800-1300, Fri 0800-1630. Times may vary according to destination.
Exchange rate indicators:
Rate at time of publishing
£1.00= Bz$3.47
$1.00= Bz$1.97

Duty Free

The following goods may be imported into Belize without incurring customs duty:
200 cigarettes or 50 cigars or 250g of tobacco; 568ml of alcoholic beverages; one bottle of perfume for personal use.
Prohibited items: The following items may not be exported from Belize: pre-Columbian articles, marine products, unprocessed coral or turtle shells.

Public Holidays

Below are listed Public Holidays for the January 2006-June 2007 period.
2006: Jan 1 New Year's Day. **Mar 9** Baron Bliss Day. **Apr 14-17** Easter. **May 1** Labour Day. **May 21** Commonwealth Day. **Sep 10** St George's Caye Day. **Sep 21** Independence Day. **Oct 12** Columbus Day. **Nov 19** Garifuna Settlement Day. **Dec 25-26** Christmas.
2007: Jan 1 New Year's Day. **Mar 9** Baron Bliss Day. **Apr 6-9** Easter. **May 1** Labour Day. **May 21** Commonwealth Day.

Health

	Special Precautions?	Certificate Required?
Yellow Fever	No	1
Cholera	2	No
Typhoid & Polio	3	N/A
Malaria	4	N/A

Note: *Regulations and requirements may be subject to change at short notice, and you are advised to contact your doctor well in advance of your intended date of departure. Any numbers in the chart refer to the footnotes below.*

1: A yellow fever vaccination certificate is required from all travellers coming from infected areas. Pregnant women and children under nine months should not normally be vaccinated.
2: Following WHO guidelines issued in 1973, a cholera vaccination certificate is no longer a condition of entry into Belize. However, imported cases of cholera were reported in 1996 and precautions are essential. Up-to-date advice should be sought before deciding whether these precautions should include vaccination as medical opinion is divided over its effectiveness. Cholera has been found in Mopan and Roaring Creek rivers in the Congo district.
3: Typhoid fever is a risk and immunisation is advised.
4: Malaria risk exists throughout the year, excluding Belize district and urban areas, predominantly in the benign *vivax* form. The risk is highest in the western and southern regions. A weekly dose of 300mg of chloroquine is the recommended prophylaxis.
Food & drink: While tap water is generally regarded as safe for consumption, purified water is readily available and is advised for the first few weeks of stay. Milk is unpasteurised and should be boiled. Powdered or tinned milk is available and is advised, but make sure that it is reconstituted with pure water. Avoid all dairy products. Only eat well-cooked meat and fish, preferably served hot. Pork, salad and mayonnaise may carry increased risk. Vegetables should be cooked and fruit peeled.
Other risks: *Amoebic* and *bacillary dysenteries* and other *diarrhoeal* diseases are very common. *Hepatitis A, B* and *C* occur. *Dengue fever* may also be present, and several cases recently occurred (in 2005). *Cutaneous* and *mucocutaneous leishmaniasis* occur. Snakes may be a hazard. Care should be taken swimming in the local rivers. *Rabies* is present. For those at high risk, vaccination before arrival should be considered. If you are bitten, seek medical advice without delay. For more information, consult the *Health* appendix.
Note: Visitors applying for residency will require an AIDS test (foreign tests may not be acceptable).
Health care: There are seven government hospitals – one in Belmopan, one in Belize City and one in each of the other five main district towns, but, generally, medical facilities are limited. Medical services in rural areas are provided by rural health care centres, and mobile clinics operate in remote areas. International travellers are strongly advised to take out medical insurance before departing for Belize.

Travel - International

AIR:

International services, mainly of a regional nature, are provided by *American Airlines, Caribbean Holidays (Tikal Jets), Continental, Delta Airlines, Grupo TACA, Maya Island Air, Tropic Air* and *US Airways*. There are flights from the USA, Guatemala and other Central American countries.
Approximate flight times: To Belize from *London* (via Miami) is 11 hours; from *Los Angeles* is eight hours; from *Miami* is two hours; from *Guatemala City* is two hours; from *Cancun* is one hour 30 minutes, and from *New York* is five hours.
Main airports: The *Philip S W Goldson International Airport (BZE)* is 16km (10 miles) northwest of Belize City. *To/from the airport:* Taxis are available to the city (travel time – 15 minutes); prices should be agreed with the driver beforehand. Taxi drivers are not tipped. There is an airport bus to the city centre (travel time – 30 minutes). *Facilities:* Duty free shops, bank, shops, restaurant and bar.
Note: Belmopan, the capital, is 84km (52 miles) from Belize City by road.
Departure tax: US$35 is levied on all passengers, apart

from transit passengers travelling on within 48 hours and children under 12 years of age, who must pay US$32.50.

SEA:

Main ports: *Belize City, Corozal, Dangriga, Punta Gorda* and *San Pedro*. Belize City is the primary port of call for most cruise ship lines. Regular scheduled boats carry passengers to shore to taste a bit of Belize at the newly constructed Belize Tourism Village. There are regular water taxi services between Punta Gorda and Puerto Barrios Guatemala and a direct twice-wekly service from Livingston.

ROAD:

There are road links with Chetumal on the Mexican border and Melchor de Mencos in Guatemala. Regular scheduled bus services serve these routes, leaving between every half hour or hour for Belize City. Border crossing fees may apply for a temporary importation permit, valid for one month. Documents may need to be produced. It is easy to enter Belize by **bus** from US border cities via Cancun, Mexico City and Chetumal.

Travel - Internal

AIR:

Local services link the main towns. *Maya Island* and *Tropic Air* fly 12 times daily from the municipal airstrip at Belize City to Ambergris Caye. Inner-Belize travel by plane is provided by *Caribee Air Service, Javier's Flying Service, Maya Island Air* and *Tropic Air*. There are scheduled flights daily to each of the main towns, and charter rates are offered to all local airstrips, of which there are 25. Several companies have charters from Belize City to the outlying districts.

SEA:

The sugar industry runs motorboat links along the coast. There is a scheduled boat service from Belize City to Ambergris Caye, Caye Chapel and Caye Caulker. Small boats irregularly ply between the small Cayes off the coast. This transport used to be the only means of travel to the interior, along the Belize, Hondo and New rivers, but services have dwindled since the advent of all-weather roads.

ROAD:

Approximately 1600km (1000 miles) of all-weather roads link the eight towns in the country, though torrential rain seasonally severs these links, particularly at ferry points. Belize has a less developed network of roads than the rest of Central America but it is steadily being improved, especially in the north, as is the Belize stretch of the road to Mexico, while the Belize–Belmopan road is in generally good condition. However, road traffic accidents are still a common occurrence and local driving standards are poor. Traffic drives on the right. **Bus:** There are good and inexpensive daily bus services to all the large towns, and to both the Mexican and Guatemalan borders. Many of the buses are modern and air conditioned. See the tourist board website for details of schedules (see *Top Things To Do*). **Car hire:** *Auto Rental, Budget, Euphrates, Hertz, Jabiru, National, Pancho's, Thrifty* and *Vista Auto Rental* operate in Belize City and there are many other companies in Ladyville, Dangriga and San Ignacio. 4-wheel-drive vehicles are recommended for excursions south of Belize City. **Documentation:** A national driving licence is acceptable for three months, after which an International Driving Permit is required.

Travel times: The following chart gives approximate travel times (in hours and minutes) from **Belize City** to other major cities/towns in the country.

	Air	Road
Northern Border	**2.20**	**-**
Corozal Town	**-**	**2.00**
Orange Walk Town	**1.15**	**-**
Punta Gorda	**0.45**	**4.00**

Travel Advice

There have recently been a series of protests, mainly in Belize City, against alleged mismanagement of the economy by the Government. In April 2005, there was a riot in the city and looting took place. Telecommunications may be disrupted. There have also been occasional violent incidents against visitors in Belize City. However, most visits are trouble-free. This advice is based on information provided by the Foreign and Commonwealth Office in the UK. It is correct at time of publishing. As the situation can change rapidly, visitors are advised to contact the following organisations for the latest travel advice:

British Foreign and Commonwealth Office
Tel: (0845) 850 2829.
Website: www.fco.gov.uk

US Department of State
Website: http://travel.state.gov/travel

Accommodation

HOTELS:

Belize has few first-class hotels, but smaller establishments give good value. There are mountain lodges in the interior and resort hotels on the Caribbean coast. Most accommodation establishments are listed by the Belize Tourism Industry Association (see *Top Things To Do*). The BTIA represents more than 50 per cent of all establishments. **Grading:** Hotels have been divided into three categories according to price and standard. Rates are subject to change without notice. It is advisable to confirm reservations and rates in advance. Classes of hotels are as follows: **Expensive:** All hotels provide a private bath/shower and have a restaurant and bar. There is air conditioning in all rooms. Some rooms also have a phone and TV. **Moderate:** All hotels provide a private bath/shower and full or partial air conditioning. **Budget:** Nearly all provide a private bath/shower, though sometimes baths/showers are shared. On the Barrier Reef Cayes there are numerous resort hotels of roughly the same standard as those given above.

APARTMENTS:

Long-stay visitors can rent apartments on a monthly basis.

CAMPING/CARAVANNING:

There are budget campsite facilities in Belize, Cayo and Corazal districts and a slightly more expensive campsite in the Toledo district. There is a caravan site in Corozal Town, and also outside San Ignacio. Camping on the beach is forbidden. Camping on private beach yards in Caye Caulker and in Tobacco Caye is available.

Top Things To See

- In **Belize City,** the country's biggest city, which serves as the main commercial area and seaport, witness a mixture of colonial architecture, functional wooden buildings and historic cathedrals. Sights include the oldest Anglican cathedral in Latin America, **St John's**, and **Government House**, the Belize City residence of the British Governor, built in 1814.
- In mainland Belize, visit **Belmopan**, the country's new capital city, carved out of the tropical jungle in the geographic centre of Belize, near the foothills of the **Maya Mountains**. The most imposing building is the **National Assembly** on **Independence Hill**, patterned in an ancient Mayan motif.
- Follow 'La Ruta Maya' ('the pathways into Mayan culture') and find some unspoilt and rarely visited Mayan ruins in and around Belize. Day cruises of the **New River**, south of Orange Walk, are available with stops at the spectacular Mayan citadel ruin of **Lamanai** (Submerged Crocodile). Lamanai is one of the largest Mayan centres and, as an archaeological reserve, also contains a museum, the remains of two 16th-century Spanish churches and a 19th-century sugar mill. The site is situated on the banks of the New River Lagoon in the North of Belize and accommodation is available in local guest houses and jungle lodges.
- At the **Temple of the Masks**, visitors can see the tremendous head of the sun god, Kinich Ahau, carved into the limestone.
- One of the most famous Mayan ruins in Belize is **Altun Ha** (Water of the Rock), located 50km (31 miles) north of Belize City on the Northern Highway. The site was a major ceremonial centre and trading centre in the Classic period (AD 250-900), and an extraordinary head of the sun god, ornately carved in jade, was found here and is now a national symbol of Belize. Several tour operators run trips to the site, which is inaccessible by public transport.
- Just outside Corozal, at the centre of Belize's thriving sugar industry, are two interesting Mayan ruins: **Santa Rita**, just 1 mile north of Corozal with a view of the town and its waterfront; and **Cerros**, once a coastal trading centre which can be reached by a 20-minute boat ride across Corozal Bay. Cerros lies on a peninsula overlooking Corozal Bay and consists of three large acropolises dominated by pyramid structures.
- Not far from **San Ignacio** in the Cayo district are several Mayan sites, including **El Pilar** and the magnificent **Xunantunich** (Stone Woman) with its 1500-year-old 43m- (130 ft-) high **El Castillo** (The Castle), the second-tallest building in Belize. The Xunantunich ruins also include six plazas and 25 temples and palaces. To access the site requires taking a bus 12.8km (8 miles) west of San Ignacio town and a ferry over the Mopan River, before walking a further 1.6km (1 mile) to the grounds. It is advisable to book the trip through a travel operator or company. For further details, contact the Belize Tourist Board (see *Top Things To Do*).
- Situated in the Chiquibul Rain Forest of the Cayo District, **Caracol** (Snail) is home to the tallest human-made structure in Belize; Canaa (Sky Place) Pyramid rises 43m (140ft) high. Although hard to get to during the rainy season, trips and the necessary entry permits can be organised with travel agents in Belize. This site has been claimed to rival such other famous sites as Tikal in neighbouring Guatemala.
- Also in Cayo are the waters of **Rio on Pools** in the Mountain Pine Ridge Forest Reserve.
- Discover the famous perfectly carved crystal skull found in a temple vault on the Mayan site of **Lubaantum,** near the town of San Antonio, located in the Toledo District inland from Punta Gorda.
- See the tallest carved stele in Belize at the Mayan ruin of **Nim Li Punit,** 40km (25 miles) north of the fishing villlage of **Punta Gorda,** the southernmost outpost of Belize.
- Enjoy fine views and secluded streams in the **Mountain Pine Ridge Forest Reserve,** located south of the Western Highway about 115km (70 miles) from Belize City. The area contains the **Hidden Valley Falls**, which plunge 500m (1600ft) into the valley.

Top Things To Do

- Belize ranks among the best **scuba-diving** and **snorkelling** destinations in the western Caribbean. At a length of 296km (185 miles), Belize's **Barrier Reef** is the longest in the Western hemisphere and offers divers a nearly continuous wall of coral (stretching almost 224km (140 miles) from Mexico to the Sapodilla Cayes). The best developed sections of the reef are south of **Columbus Reef**. Some of the best dive sites include **Lighthouse Reef**, where divers can explore walls with spectacular drops of thousands of feet, and the **Blue Hole.** Boats to both sites can be hired. Visitors can either arrange diving trips with an offshore resort, sign on with one of the many live-aboard boats or hire a charter boat from one of the dive resorts along the coast. Visitors should also be aware of the restrictions on the removal of coral, orchids and turtles, and on spearfishing in certain areas. Wrecks and treasures are also Government-protected. For further information and a list of dive operators, contact the Belize Tourist Board (see *Tourist Information*). Travellers can also enjoy diving while observing southern stingray and nurse sharks in shark ray alley at **Hoi Chan Marine Reserve**. Situated 58km (36 miles) north of Belize City, it is accessible by daily scheduled air flights and boat transfers.
- The Belize **Cayes** (pronounced 'keys') are islands and/or mangroves located between the mainland and the barrier reef, on the barrier reef, and on or within the barrier reef perimeters of the offshore atolls. Although the mangrove cayes are normally uninhabitable for humans, they do provide an ideal habitat for birds and marine life. The island cayes, which are distinguishable by their palm trees, have provided the foundation for the development of many fine resorts to serve watersports enthusiasts and marine naturalists. **Ambergris Caye**, with its many beaches and the fishing village of **San Pedro**, is the most popular tourist destination. Along with the other Cayes, it is a paradise for divers with access to one of the most unspoilt coral reefs in the world. **Caye Caulker** has an extensive underwater cave system which has made it popular with divers, whilst those who wish to explore the reef without getting wet can see photographs of reef fish at the museum. There are many other Cayes with facilities for those interested in fishing, diving and seeing wildlife.
- **Windsurfing** is also a perfect activity for the Cayes. The water is so clear beneath, it may be possible to spot fish, stingrays and even dolphins as you sail. The windy season is usually from February to April.
- **Cerros** is located on the fringe of a beautiful expanse of blue-green water which is ideal for **watersports**. Across the bay is an archaeological site. **Dangriga (Stann Creek)** provides a good base for excursions to the offshore islands and nearby forests. Natural waterfalls can be seen at the **Cockscomb Basin Wildlife Sanctuary** situated at the foothills of the Mayan Mountains. Close by lies the diving and snorkelling haven, **Southwater Caye**.
- **Fishing, swimming** and **sunbathing** can also be enjoyed in the protected lagoon of **Placencia,** a village situated at the tip of the 20km- (12 mile-) long Placencia peninsula.
- Visit one of Belize's **national parks**. Belize has a rich natural geography, from jungle forests, karst terrain and swampy mangroves to tropical beaches. Consequently, the country is eager to promote ecotourism and there exists a number of protected areas, including marine reserves and national parks. 19.3km (12 miles) southeast of Belmopan, the **Blue Hole National Park** pays tribute to the curious **Blue Hole**, a collapsed water sinkhole, 7.6m (25 feet) deep, of intense colour. The park is a natural forest reserve that is home to an abundance of birds, animals, flora and **St Herman's Cave**, an ancient Mayan cave. **Five Blues Lake National Park** is situated at the foot of the spectacular Mayan Mountains and covers over 1619 hectares (4000 acres) of tropical forest. The eponymous lake is a collapsed cave system, known as a cenote or blue hole, and appears in an array of aqua hues. There is an amazing wealth of wildlife and fauna to be seen here. At the junction to the Cayo District from the Hummingbird

and Western highways, lies **Guanacaste National Park**, taking its name from the giant Guanacaste trees at the edge of the reserve. With over a hundred species of bird and highlighted trails with information on the trees and plants within the forest, the park is popular as an introduction to the diverse environment of Belize. **Laughing Bird Caye National Park** is a shelf atoll, ideal for diving, but is also a habitat for the unusual laughing gulls. The Caye is situated 21km (13 miles) southeast of Placencia Village in the **Stann Creek District**. **The Rio Bravo Conservation and Management Area** contains 81,745 hectares (202,000 acres) of preserved forests and marshlands, which provides a home for a rich array of birds and endangered species, including jaguars, pumas, black howler monkeys, margays, ocellated turkeys and brocket deers. Over 40 Mayan ruins have also been discovered here. The conservation park is located near the **Orange Walk** district of Belize.

- Observe hundreds of different bird species, particularly in the national parks - notably, the **Cockscomb Basin Wildlife Sanctuary**, **Crooked Tree Wildlife Sanctuary** (where the jabiru stork, the largest bird in the western hemisphere can be seen, along with howler monkeys, crocodiles and many indigenous birds), **Silk Grass Greek Road** and the **Mountain Pine Ridge**. On **Half Moon Caye** at Lighthouse Reef is the **Red-Footed Booby Bird Sanctuary**, founded in 1982 to protect the booby and other birds and animals. Inland from Belize City on the Belize River is the **Community Baboon Sanctuary** with one of the few robust black howler monkey populations in Central America. The **Belize Zoo** on the Western Highway, around 32km (20 miles) south of Belize, has more than 100 species of indigenous animals, including monkeys, jaguars and tapirs.

TOURIST INFORMATION

Belize Tourism Board
Street address: New Central Bank Building, Level 2, Gabourel Lane, Belize City, Belize
Postal address: PO Box 325, Belize City, Belize
Tel: (22) 31913 *or* 1800 624 0686 (toll-free within CA).
Website: www.travelbelize.org

Belize Tourism Industry Association (BTIA)
Street address: 10 North Park Street
Belize City, Belize
Postal address: PO Box 62, Belize City, Belize
Tel: (22) 75717 *or* 71144.
Website: www.btia.org

Carribean Tourism Organisation in the UK
22 The Quadrant, Richmond, Surrey TW9 1BP, UK
Tel: (020) 8948 0057.
Website: www.onecaribbean.org *or* www.doitcaribbean.com

Carribean Tourism Organisation in the USA
80 Broad Street, 32nd Floor, New York, NY 10004, USA
Tel: (212) 635 9530.
Website: www.doitcaribbean.com

Entertainment

FOOD & DRINK: There is a selection of restaurants which serve international, Chinese, Creole and Latin American food. Service and quality vary but the food is generally cheap.

National specialities:
- Tacos, corn or flour tortillas, with shredded chicken, onions, cabbage and cilantro.
- Hot meat pies.
- Travellers will find it hard to spend a holiday in Belize without eating rice-and-beans. It is the national staple and some people eat it every single day. For a change of pace, switch to beans-and-rice. It is important to be clear when ordering in a restaurant because beans-and-rice is where the beans are cooked separately and spooned with their own gravy over white rice.
- Another favourite is split peas and pigtail over rice.
- A lot of items are stewed: stewed fish, oxtail, beef, chicken or pork. There is even stewed lobster, when the season is open.
- Game meats include deer, hicatee, iguana or gibnut.
- Fried to a sweet golden brown, plantains make a tasty side addition to any meal.

National drinks:
- Bars are plentiful and local drinks include coconut rum mixed with pineapple juice.
- The local *Belikin* beer is worth sampling.
- Travellers will also be able to order fresh orange, lime, watermelon or cantaloupe juice.

Tipping: Few places add service charges, and 15 per cent is normal.

NIGHTLIFE: There is live dancing late in the evenings at Bellevue Hotel and quiet music at Fort George Bar overlooking the harbour. In addition, there are popular nightclubs throughout Belize that feature local bands at weekends.

SHOPPING: Handicrafts, woodcarvings and straw items are on sale. Jewellery in pink and black coral, and tortoiseshell (not to be imported to the USA) used to be good buys, but now there are severe restrictions on the export of these and some other goods in the interests of wildlife conservation. 'In-Bond' stores carry watches, perfumes and other duty free purchases, but Belize is not comparable in size to other free ports in the Caribbean. **Shopping hours:** Mon-Sat 0800-1200, 1300-1630 and 1900-2100.

Business

- **GDP:** US$1.77 billion (2004 estimate).
- **Main exports:** Sugar, citrus and banana.
- **Main imports:** Foodstuffs, machinery and transport equipment.
- **Main trade partners:** USA, UK, Thailand and Mexico.

ECONOMY: Agriculture is the most important economic sector – the main products are citrus fruit, bananas and sugar cane. Timber is also important, especially mahogany and other tropical hardwoods. Fishing and livestock are being developed. The fastest-growing area of the Belize economy has been the service sector, particularly 'offshore' activities, including the lightly regulated banking sector and a 'flag of convenience' shipping register. However, these have started to cause political difficulties for the Belizean government. In June 2000, Belize was identified by the Organisation for Economic Cooperation and Development (OECD) – the world's 30 wealthiest economies – as one of 35 'tax havens' whose financial laws are believed to encourage large-scale tax evasion and money laundering. The government has since taken measures to meet the OECD's demands. Tourism, fuelled by foreign investment, has also expanded in recent years, although not at the rate the government had originally hoped – net tourist expenditure in Belize is approximately US$100 million annually. Industry is dominated by the processing of agricultural products (for example, the production of rum from sugar) and light industries such as textiles. The country has no natural energy resources, although the search for oil reserves continues both on- and offshore and hydroelectric projects are underway. The USA is the largest single trading partner, providing half of all imports and taking about 60 per cent of Belizean exports. Belize is a member of CARICOM, the Caribbean economic community, and provides some transit facilities for trade to and from other countries in the region. Belize is a significant recipient of overseas aid from Britain, the EU and North America. Recently, things have been looking up for the Belize economy. The unemployment rate dropped to 11.6 per cent in 2004. GDP growth in 2004/2005 was estimated at 4.2 per cent. Tourism is proving strong for Belize, plus there have been pleasing performances in agricultural and construction sectors. However, due to borrowing funds from other counties (predominantly the USA) on less-than-favourable terms, the crucial fixed exchange rate (BZ$2 to US$1) looks increasingly under pressure.

BUSINESS ETIQUETTE: Lightweight, tropical suits are often worn. Appointments should be made and calling cards are acceptable. October to March are the best months for visits. **Office hours:** Mon-Fri 0800-1200 and 1300-1700. Some businesses are open Saturdays.

COMMERCIAL INFORMATION

Belize Chamber of Commerce and Industry
PO Box 291, 63 Regent Street, Belize City, Belize
Tel: (22) 73148 *or* 70668.
Website: www.belize.org

Belize Trade & Investment Development Service (BELTRAIDE)
14 Orchid Garden Street, Belmopan City, Cayo, Belize
Tel: (8) 222 832.
Website: www.belizeinvest.org.bz

Ministry of Tourism, Investment and Culture (Information on Conferences/Conventions)
14 Constitution Drive, Belmopan, Belize
Tel: (8) 223 393/4.
E-mail: tourismdpt@btl.net

Benin

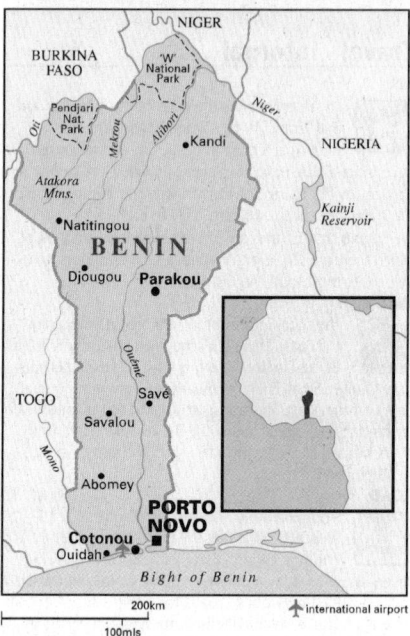

Location: West Africa.

Time: GMT + 1.

Overview

Benin, formerly known as Dahomey, was one of the first countries in the 1990s to successfully effect the transition from dictatorship to a pluralistic political system. Today, it is one of the most stable countries in Africa.

In the 15th century, the O*bas* - single rulers - brought great prosperity and a highly organised state to Benin. They also established good relations and an extensive trade (which included slaves) with the Portuguese and Dutch, who arrived from the 15th century onwards.

The decline of the Obas began in the 18th century, when a series of internal power struggles began, which lasted into the 19th century, paving the way for the French takeover and colonisation of the country in 1872. In 1904, the territory was incorporated into French West Africa as Dahomey. On 4 December 1958, it became the République du Dahomey, self-governing within the French community, and gained full independence from France on August 1 1960. Between 1960 and 1972, a succession of military coups brought about many changes of Government; the last of these brought to power Major Mathieu Kérékou. The new ruler, who was at the head of a regime professing strict Marxist-Leninist principles, remained in power until the beginning of the 1990s, when, with French encouragement, the Kérékou Government introduced a new democratic constitution and held presidential and legislative elections. Although defeated in the 1991 elections, Mr Kérékou made a comeback in 1996.

Although Benin has seen economic growth over the past few years and has a high standing with the international community, it remains among the world's poorest countries. Within West Africa, Benin enjoys stable relations with Nigeria, the main regional power. The only significant problem has been a long-running border dispute with Benin's northern neighbour, Niger, over ownership of islands in the Niger River. This was finally resolved in July 2005 by the International Court of Justice, which awarded 16 islands to Niger and 9 to Benin. Both countries accepted the ruling. Although no security issues exist in Benin, there are occasional incidents of mugging and personal assault in

Cotonou and some armed robberies have been reported in other areas, notably the border area with Nigeria. Travellers are advised to be vigilant. Medical facilities are also poor in Benin, particularly in rural areas and travellers are advised to have comprehensive travel and medical insurance, which covers a provision for medical evacuation.

General Information

AREA: 112,622 sq km (43,484 sq miles).
POPULATION: 7.1 million (UN, 2005).
POPULATION DENSITY: 63.4 per sq km.
CAPITAL: Porto Novo (administrative). **Population:** 200,000 (1994). (Cotonou is the economic capital with an estimated population of 750,000 in 1994.)
GEOGRAPHY: Benin is situated in West Africa and is bordered to the east by Nigeria, to the north by Niger and Burkina Faso, and to the west by Togo. Benin stretches 700km (435 miles) from the Bight of Benin to the Niger River. The coastal strip is sandy with coconut palms. Beyond the lagoons of Porto Novo, Nokoue, Ouidah and Grand Popo is a plateau rising gradually to the heights of the Atakora Mountains. From the highlands run two tributaries of the Niger, while southwards the Ouémé flows down to Nokoue lagoon. Mono River flows into the sea at Grand Popo and forms a frontier with Togo.
GOVERNMENT: Republic. Gained independence from France in 1960. **Head of State and Government:** President Yayi Boni since 2006. **Recent history:** Political newcomer Yayi Boni won the second round of Presidential elections in March 2006, gaining more than 74 per cent of the vote. His rival was the former parliamentary speaker, Adrien Houngbedji. Mathieu Kérékou, his predecessor, was barred by the constitution from running for a third term as he was over the age limit of 70. Benin's President heads the Government, the state and the military and appoints members of the Cabinet.
LANGUAGE: The official language is French. However, many ethnic groups have their own languages: Bariba and Fulani are spoken in the north, Fon and Yoruba in the south. Some English is also spoken.
RELIGION: 35 per cent animist/traditional, 35 per cent Christian (mainly Roman Catholic) and the majority of the rest are Muslim.
ELECTRICITY: 220 volts AC, 50Hz.
SOCIAL CONVENTIONS: Normal courtesies are appreciated; it is customary to shake hands on arrival and departure. However, religious beliefs play a large part in society and these should be respected. Voodoo is perhaps the most striking and best-known practice, and has acquired considerable social and political power. Only priests can communicate with voodoos and spirits of the dead. If travelling, it is advisable to clear itineraries with district or provincial authorities. Casual wear is acceptable in most places.

Climate

The south has an equatorial climate with four seasons. It is hot and dry from January to April and during August, with rainy seasons through May to July and September to December. The north has more extreme temperatures, hot and dry between November and June, cooler and very wet between July and October.
Required clothing: Lightweight cottons and linens. A light raincoat or an umbrella is necessary in rainy seasons and warmer clothes are advised for cool evenings.

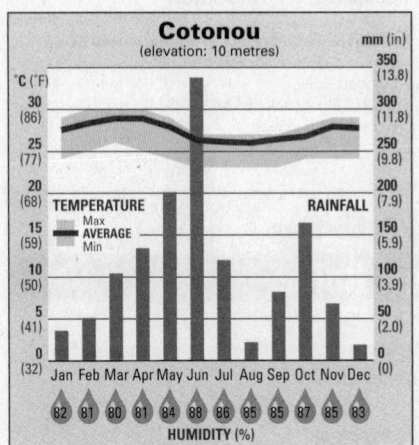

Communications

Telephone: IDD is available. Country code: 229. There is an additional charge for calls made from a coin box.
Mobile telephone: Some roaming agreements exist. Coverage is limited. Handsets can be hired locally. Further

information can be obtained from the *Office des Postes et Télécommunications du Bénin* (website: www.opt.bj).
Internet: Public access is available in Cotonou.
Post: Airmail takes three to five days to reach Europe. Surface mail letters or parcels take from six to eight weeks. Post office hours: Mon-Sat 0800-1400.
MEDIA: The constitution guarantees media freedom although harsh libel laws have been used against journalists. Benin has more than 50 newspapers and periodicals, one state TV channel, a handful of commercial TV channels and more than 30 state, commercial and local radio stations. In 2003, the authorities paved the way for a further expansion of the private media scene, allocating frequencies for five private TV stations and 10 commercial radio stations. The BBC World Service and Radio France Internationale are available on FM in Cotonou.
Press: *La Nation* is the daily official newspaper. Other private dailies include *Le Matinal*, *Fraternité*, *Le Républicain*, *L'Aurore* and *L'Evènement du Jour*.
Television: *Télévision Nationale* is state-run; *Golfe TV* and *LC2* are commercial channels.
Radio: *Radio Benin* is a national, state-run station; *Golfe FM* is a commercial station; *Radio Immaculée Conception* is a catholic radio station.

Passport/Visa

	Passport Required?	Visa Required?	Return Ticket Required?
Full British	Yes	Yes	No
Australian	Yes	Yes	No
Canadian	Yes	Yes	No
USA	Yes	Yes	No
Other EU	Yes	Yes	No
Japanese	Yes	Yes	No

Note: *Regulations and requirements may be subject to change at short notice, and you are advised to contact the appropriate diplomatic or consular authority before finalising travel arrangements. Any numbers in the chart refer to the footnotes below.*

Restricted entry: All visitors over one year of age are required to produce a yellow fever certificate on entry to Benin.
PASSPORTS: Valid passport required by all except nationals of the following countries in possession of a national identity card: Burkina Faso, Cameroon, Central African Republic, Chad, Congo, (Rep of), Côte d'Ivoire, Gabon, Ghana, Madagascar, Mali, Mauritania, Niger, Rwanda, Senegal and Togo.
VISAS: Required by all except the following:
(a) nationals of ECOWAS member countries;
(b) those in transit continuing their onward journey within 24 hours, provided holding confirmed tickets and not leaving the airport.
Note: All children of nationals who require a visa, issued with their own passport, *do* require a visa.
Types of visa and cost: *Tourist* and *Business*. Visas cost £45 for 15 days; £55 for 30 days; £65 for 90 days.
Validity: Visas are valid for a 15-, 30- or 90-day period within three months of date of issue.
Application to: Consulate (or Consular Section at Embassy); see *Passport/Visa Information*.
Application requirements: (a) Valid passport. (b) Application form completed in duplicate. (c) Two passport-size photos. (d) Pre-paid registered envelope large enough to fit passport, if applying by post. (e) Fee. (f) For a Business visa, a letter from the applicant's company.
Working days required: Callers at the Consulate are usually able to obtain visas on the same day.
Temporary residence: Enquire at Consulate (or Consular Section at Embassy).

PASSPORT/VISA INFORMATION

Honorary Consulate of Benin in the UK
Millennium House, Humber Road, Nr Staples Corner, London NWZ 6DW, UK
Tel: (020) 7435 0665.
E-mail: l.landau@btinternet.com
Opening hours: Mon, Wed and Fri: 1000-1630.

Embassy of the Republic of Benin in France
87 avenue Victor Hugo, 75116 Paris, France
Tel: (1) 4500 9882 *or* 4222 3191 (consular section).
Website: www.ambassade-benin.org

Embassy of the Republic of Benin in the USA
2124 Kalorama Road, NW,
Washington, DC 20008, USA
Tel: (202) 232 6656.
Website: www.beninembassyus.org

Money

Currency: CFA (*Communauté Financiaire Africaine*) Franc (XOF) = 100 centimes. Notes are in denominations of XOF10,000, 5000, 2000 and 1000. Coins are in denominations of XOF500, 200, 100, 50, 25, 10, 5 and 1. Benin is part of the French Monetary Area. Only currency issued by the *Banque des Etats de l'Afrique de l'Ouest* (Bank of West African States) is valid; currency issued by the *Banque des Etats de l'Afrique Centrale* (Bank of Central African States) is not. The CFA Franc is tied to the Euro.
Currency exchange: Currency can be exchanged at banks and in major hotels.
Credit & debit cards: American Express, Diners Club, MasterCard and Visa are accepted on a limited basis. Check with your credit or debit card company for details of merchant acceptability and other services which may be available. Some banks may advance cash or visa cards.
Traveller's cheques: To avoid additional exchange rate charges, travellers are advised to take traveller's cheques in Euros or Pounds Sterling.
Currency restrictions: The import of local currency is unlimited, subject to declaration. The export of local currency is unlimited for EU residents; other nationalities must declare currency that is to be exported (proof of origin might be demanded). The import of foreign currency is unlimited, subject to declaration. The export of foreign currency is limited to the equivalent of XOF100,000.
Banking hours: Mon-Fri 0800-1100 and 1500-1700. Some banks may open on Saturday.
Exchange rate indicators:
Rate at time of publishing
£1.00=   XOF968.31
$1.00=   XOF548.37

Duty Free

The following items may be imported into Benin by persons over 15 years of age without incurring customs duty:
200 cigarettes or 100 cigarillos or 25 cigars or 250g of tobacco; one bottle of wine and one bottle of spirits; 500ml of eau de toilette and 250ml of perfume.

Public Holidays

Below are listed Public Holidays for the January 2006-June 2007 period.
2006: Jan 1 New Year's Day. **Jan 10** Traditional Day/Tabaski (Feast of the Sacrifice). **Apr 10** Prophet's Birthday. **Apr 17** Easter Monday. **May 1** Labour Day. **May 25** Ascension Day. **Jun 5** Whit Monday. **Aug 1** Independence Day. **Aug 15** Assumption. **Oct 26** Armed Forces Day. **Nov 1** All Saints' Day. **Oct 23** Eid al-Fitr (End of Ramadan). **Nov 30** National Day. **Dec 25** Christmas Day. **Dec 31** Tabaski (Feast of the Sacrifice).
2007: Jan 1 New Year's Day. **Jan 10** Traditional Day. **Mar 31** Prophet's Birthday. **Apr 9** Easter Monday. **May 1** Labour Day. **May 17** Ascension Day. **May 28** Whit Monday.
Note: Muslim festivals are timed according to local sightings of various phases of the moon and the dates given above are approximations. For further details, see the *World of Islam* appendix.

Health

	Special Precautions?	Certificate Required?
Yellow Fever	Yes	1
Cholera	Yes	2
Typhoid & Polio	3	N/A
Malaria	4	N/A

Note: *Regulations and requirements may be subject to change at short notice, and you are advised to contact your doctor well in advance of your intended date of departure. Any numbers in the chart refer to the footnotes below.*

1: A yellow fever vaccination certificate is required by all travellers over one year of age. Risk occurs in all rural areas, but especially in Atakora and Borgou.
2: Following WHO guidelines issued in 1973, a cholera vaccination certificate is no longer a condition of entry to Benin. However, cholera is a serious risk in this country and precautions are essential. Up-to-date advice should be sought before deciding whether these precautions should include vaccination as medical opinion is divided over its effectiveness; see the *Health* appendix.
3: Vaccination against typhoid is advised.
4: Malaria is a risk all year throughout the country. It occurs predominantly in the malignant *falciparum* form. Resistance to chloroquine is common and resistance to sulfadoxine-pyrimethamine has been reported. A weekly dose of 250mg of mefloquine is recommended.
Food & drink: All water should be regarded as being potentially contaminated. Water used for drinking, brushing

teeth or making ice should have first been boiled or otherwise sterilised. Milk is unpasteurised and should be boiled. Powdered or tinned milk is available and is advised, but make sure that it is reconstituted with pure water. Avoid all dairy products. Only eat well-cooked meat and fish, preferably served hot. Pork, salad and mayonnaise may carry increased risk. Vegetables should be cooked and fruit peeled.

Other risks: *Hepatitis A* and *E* are widespread. *Hepatitis B* is hyperendemic. *Hepatitis C* occurs. *Meningococcal meningitis* is a risk, depending on the area and the time of year. Immunisation against *hepatitis B*, *diphtheria* and *meningococcal A* and *C* is sometimes recommended. *Bilharzia* (schistosomiasis) is present. Avoid swimming and paddling in fresh water; swimming pools which are well chlorinated and maintained are safe. *Onchocerciasis* (river blindness) exists and precautions are recommended. *TB* occurs. *Haemorrhagic fevers* can be a risk in rural areas; rat-contaminated food should be avoided. The hot, dusty, windy environmental conditions in November and December may exacerbate respiratory problems. *HIV/AIDS* is prevalent. *Rabies* is present. For those at high risk, vaccination before arrival should be considered. If you are bitten, seek medical advice without delay. For more information, consult the *Health* appendix.

Health care: Medical facilities are limited, especially outside the major towns, and not all medicines are available. Doctors and hospitals often expect immediate cash payment for health services. Medical insurance is strongly recommended.

Travel - International

AIR: The main airline is *Air Burkina* (website: www.air-burkina.com).
Main airports: *Cotonou Cadjehoun (COO)* is 5km (3 miles) west of the city. *To/from the airport:* Taxis and limousines are available to the city (travel time – 15 to 20 minutes). *Facilities:* Duty free shop, restaurant, bar, post office, business centre, 24-hour medical facilities, bank and car hire.
Departure tax: None.

SEA: **Main port:** *Porto Novo*. Several shipping lines run regular cargo services from Marseille to Cotonou. Local shipping from Lagos arrives in Porto Novo.

RAIL: The railway line from Parakou (via Gaya) to Niamey in Niger, currently under construction, will provide the first rail link into Niger.

ROAD: There are at least three good main roads: one connecting Cotonou with Niamey in Niger; another connecting Lagos with Porto Novo, Cotonou, Lomé and Accra; and a third connecting Parakou with Kara in Togo. Buses and taxis are available.

Travel - Internal

AIR: Government aeroplanes run services between Cotonou, Parakou, Natitingou, Djougou and Kandi. It is also possible to charter two-seater aeroplanes.

RAIL: Benin has about 600km (400 miles) of rail track. Trains run from Cotonou to Pobé, Ouidah and Parakou. Food is available on some services. Upholstered seats are available only in first-class cars and these exist only on the route to Parakou. Children aged under four travel free and children aged four to nine pay half fare. Approximate travel times from Cotonou to *Parakou* is 12 to 14 hours, to *Segboroué* is two hours 30 minutes and to *Pobé* is four hours.

ROAD: There is no totally reliable public transportation in Cotonou. The roads are, however, in reasonably good condition (although some are poorly lit) and many of those which run from Cotonou to Dassa, and Parakou to Malanville, are paved. There are also continual efforts to improve the roads. A new carriageway from the new bridge in Cotonou to the start of the Lome road has recently been finished. Tracks are passable during the dry season but often impassable during the rainy season. Traffic drives on the right. Minibus and bush taxi services run along major road routes. Minibuses are cheaper but slower. **Car hire:** A number of local firms are available in Cotonou.
Documentation: An International Driving Permit is required.

URBAN: Taxis are widely available in the main towns. Taxi fares should be agreed in advance.

Travel Advice

Most visits to Benin are trouble-free but you should be aware of the global risk of indiscriminate international terrorist attacks, which could be against civilian targets, including places frequented by foreigners.
This advice is based on information provided by the Foreign and Commonwealth Office in the UK. It is correct at time of publishing. As the situation can change rapidly, visitors are advised to contact the following organisations for the latest travel advice:

British Foreign and Commonwealth Office
Tel: (0845) 850 2829.
Website: www.fco.gov.uk

US Department of State
Website: http://travel.state.gov/travel

Accommodation

Main towns and urban areas have a variety of hotels. Top-end hotels are, however, mainly found in and around the capital. There are also some campsites in and around Cotonou. There are a few establishments (*campements*) for game viewing at Porga near Pendjari National Park.

Top Things To See & Do

- Visit the **museum** in **Abomey**, situated about 100km (60 miles) northeast of the capital **Porto Novo**. The museum covers the history of the Abomey kingdoms and contains a throne made of human skulls. You can also pay a visit to the **Fetish Temple** and the nearby **Centre Artisanal** where local craft products are sold at reasonable prices.
- In **Cotonou**, go to the market, the **Dan Tokpa**, which is normally open every four days. The museum here is well worth a visit too.
- Another market worth a visit is the weekly market at **Boukombe** in the northwest of the country, where tourists can buy the goods made by the Somba people, who live in this region.
- The lake village of **Ganvie**, 18km (11miles) northwest of Cotonou, has houses built on stilts and a water-market.
- The town of **Ouidah** is notable for its old **Portuguese fort** and the **Temple of the Sacred Python**.
- In **Porto Novo**, the capital and the administrative centre of the country, you can see many examples of colonial and pre-colonial art and architecture. The **Ethnological Museum** is probably the most notable place of interest for a visitor.
- See a wide range of **wildlife** including cheetahs, hippos and crocodiles at Benin's two national parks. **Pendjari** is normally only open between December and June. Accommodation is available. The **'W' National Park** straddles the frontier region between Niger, Benin and Burkina Faso and is less developed.
- Although facilities for **watersports** on the coast are limited, there are good beaches at **Grand Popo** and **Ouidah** but visitors should note that tides and currents can render the sea very dangerous and only the strongest swimmers should venture in at certain places.
- Sail at the Yacht Club in **Cotonou**, or hire a dug-out **canoe** or **motorboat** on **Nakoue Lagoon**.

TOURIST INFORMATION

Direction de la Documentation et de l'Administration du Réseau Internet du Gouvernement (DDARIG)
01 BP 120, Cotonou, Benin
Tel: 306 835.
Website: www.gouv.bj

Entertainment

FOOD & DRINK: There is a selection of restaurants and hotels in Cotonou, serving French food with table service, although some also serve local African specialities, particularly seafood. **Tipping:** It is normal to tip 10 per cent of the bill in hotels and restaurants.
NIGHTLIFE: Cotonou offers several nightclubs, but elsewhere there is little nightlife except during festivals.
SHOPPING: In Cotonou, along the marina, there are many stalls selling handicrafts and souvenirs. The Dan Tokpa market borders the Cotonou Lagoon and is stocked with many goods from Nigeria and elsewhere, as well as traditional medicines and artefacts. Crafts and local goods can be purchased in many towns and villages elsewhere, particularly in markets. Good buys include ritual masks, tapestries, elongated statues and pottery. **Shopping hours:** Mon-Sat 0900-1300 and 1600-1900.

Business

- **GDP:** US$3.7 billion (2003).
- **Main exports:** Cotton, peanuts, coffee and palm oil.
- **Main imports:** Energy.
- **Main trade partners:** Nigeria, France, China and India.

ECONOMY: Since the transition to democratic government in 1991, Benin has undergone a remarkable economic recovery. A large injection of external investment from both private and public sources has alleviated the economic difficulties of the early 1990s, caused by global recession and persistently low commodity prices (although the latter continues to affect the economy). Benin, poor in natural resources, is traditionally a trading nation and its economy is heavily dependent on the success of its much larger neighbour, Nigeria. Benin is hugely dependent on its import/export trade with the latter. A large part of the economy is based on the re-export of goods to Nigeria. Benin's economy is principally agricultural – it is self-sufficient in basic foodstuffs, the main export commodities being cotton, peanuts, coffee and palm oil. The manufacturing sector is confined to some light industry, mainly involved in processing primary products and the production of consumer goods. A planned joint hydroelectric project with neighbouring Togo is intended to reduce Benin's dependence on imported energy (mostly from Ghana), which currently accounts for a significant proportion of the country's imports. The service sector has grown quickly, stimulated by economic liberalisation and fiscal reform. Membership of the CFA Franc Zone offers reasonable currency stability, as well as access to French economic support. Benin is also a member of the West African economic community ECOWAS. The economy remains fragile and largely dependent on international aid.
BUSINESS ETIQUETTE: It is essential to be able to conduct conversations in French. Normal courtesies should be observed and punctuality is especially important. Lightweight tropical suits should be worn. **Office hours:** Mon-Fri 0800-1230 and 1500-1830.

COMMERCIAL INFORMATION

Chambre de Commerce et d'Industrie du Bénin
Avenue du Général de Gaulle, 01 BP 31, Cotonou, Benin
Tel: 312 081 *or* 314 386 *or* 311 238.
Website: www.ccib.bj

Bermuda

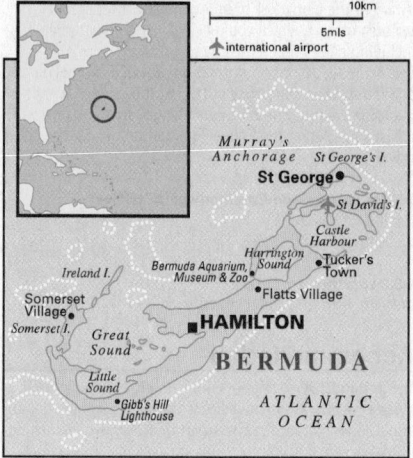

Location: Western Atlantic Ocean.

Time: GMT - 4 (GMT - 3 from first Sunday in April to last Sunday in October).
Bermuda is a British Dependent Territory, and is represented abroad by British Embassies – see *United Kingdom* section.

Overview

Bermuda consists of a chain of some 180 coral islands and islets lying 1046km (650 miles) off the coast of Cape Hatteras, North Carolina, in the Atlantic Ocean. Its coastlines are characterised by small bays with beaches of fine pale pink coral sand and surrounding vivid blue-green waters. Inland is an abundance of subtropical plants and flowers.

Bermuda was first discovered by Juan de Bermudez, a Spanish sailor, in 1505. It was claimed in England's name by Sir George Somers, in July 1609. After colonisation, the island prospered and has continued to do so almost continuously ever since. The tourist industry, catering particularly for the American market, began in Victorian times. Today, there are still elements of British culture and customs in almost every aspect of life on the islands.
In 1968, the island was granted internal self-government – formally a British Dependent Territory – while Britain retained control of defence and foreign policy. The issue of independence currently dominates in Bermuda with the present pro-independence Government. In December 2004, the Premier W Alex Scott announced the formation of the Bermuda Independence Commission to explore the subject of independence for Bermuda. A referendum on independence was last held in 1995 but a low turnout produced a majority against independence. In June 2005, opinion polls showed 20.1 per cent supported self-governance, with 65 per cent opposed.

General Information

AREA: 53.74 sq km (20.75 sq miles).
POPULATION: 65,000 (official estimate 2005).
POPULATION DENSITY: 1209 per sq km.
CAPITAL: Hamilton. **Population:** 1100 (1991).
GEOGRAPHY: Bermuda consists of a chain of some 180 coral islands and islets lying 1046km (650 miles) off the coast of Cape Hatteras. The seven largest of the islands are linked by bridges and one causeway to form the principal mainland. There are no rivers or streams and the islands are entirely dependent on rainfall for fresh water.
GOVERNMENT: British Crown Colony since 1684. Gained internal autonomy in 1968. **Head of State:** HM Queen Elizabeth II, represented locally by Governor Sir John Vereker since 2002. **Head of Government:** Premier W Alex Scott since 2003. **Recent history:** Bermuda is a British Dependent Territory. Its bicameral legislature – the Senate with 11 appointed members and the 40-member House of

Assembly, elected by universal adult suffrage for a five-year term – is responsible for most internal affairs, although foreign policy and security matters are decided by the Governor (John Vereker, since 2002) who is appointed by and represents the British Monarch. He in turn appoints the majority leader in the House of Assembly as Premier; the latter appoints the Cabinet. Alex Scott, the Prime Minister, took office in July 2003. He succeeded the Progressive Labour Party's Jennifer Smith following a revolt by party members who refused to serve under her. Mr Scott's PLP supports independence from Britain, and the Premier has called for a national debate on the issue.
LANGUAGE: English is the official language. There is a small Portuguese population. Other languages are spoken by Bermuda's residents originating from around the world.
RELIGION: Anglican, Roman Catholic, AME and Seventh Day Adventist and other Christian denominations.
ELECTRICITY: 110 volts AC, 60Hz. American (flat) two-pin plugs are standard.
SOCIAL CONVENTIONS: Many of Bermuda's social conventions are British influenced, and there is a very English 'feel' to the islands. It is quite customary to politely greet people on the street, even if they are strangers. Casual wear is acceptable in most places during the day, but beachwear (including short tops and 'short' shorts) should be confined to the beach. Almost all hotels and restaurants require a smart casual dress in the evenings; check dress requirements in advance. Non-smoking areas will be marked. Drinking alcohol in public outside of a licensed premise is prohibited.

Climate

Sub-tropical, with no wet season. The Gulf Stream which flows between Bermuda and the North American continent keeps the climate temperate. Change of seasons comes during mid-November to mid-December and from late March through to April when spring or summer weather may occur and visitors should be prepared for both. Showers may be heavy at times but the skies usually clear quickly. Summer temperatures prevail from May to mid-November with the warmest weather in July, August and September – this period is occasionally followed by high winds. Visitors should note that such high winds between June 1 and November 30 can (albeit rarely) turn into hurricanes and tropical storms. Since Bermuda is a small target, most storms brush by and only bring elevated surf. There are exceptions, however - the most recent being 'Fabian', a direct hit on September 5 2003.
Required clothing: Lightweight cottons and linens. Light waterproofs or umbrellas are advisable and warmer clothes for cooler months.

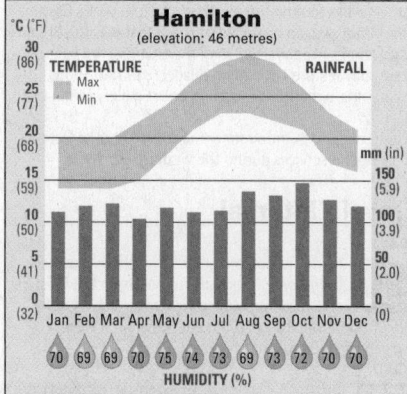

Communications

Telephone: IDD is available. Country code: 1 441. The internal telephone system is operated by Bermuda Telephone Limited. Bermuda numbers dialled from within Bermuda should be prefixed with the last two digits of the country code (29 or 23) but there are no conventional area codes.
Mobile telephone: Coverage is good.
Internet: There are Internet cafes in the Royal Naval Dockyard, City of Hamilton and Town of St George.
Post: Most letters will automatically travel airmail even if surface rates are paid, although paid-for airmail will be given priority. Airmail letters to Europe take five to seven days. Post office hours: Mon-Fri 0830-1700. In addition, the General Post Office in Hamilton is open on Saturday mornings until 1200.
MEDIA: The islands' broadcasting scene is dominated by two players, the Bermuda Broadcasting Company and VSB. As well as home-grown broadcast media, most homes and hotel rooms have access to the multichannel, international offerings of cable and satellite TV services.
Press: The main newspapers are *The Mid-Ocean News* (weekly), *The Royal Gazette* (daily) and *The Bermuda Sun* (twice-weekly).

Credit: ©Bermuda Department of Tourism

TV: Bermuda Broadcasting Company (BBC) operates *ZFB TV* (Channel 7) and *ZBM TV* (Channel 9); VSB operates *VSB TV* (Channel 11).
Radio: Bermuda Broadcasting Company (BBC) operates *ZBM AM*, *ZFB AM*, *ZBM FM 89* and *Power 95*; VSB operates *Mix 106*, *1450 Gold*, *VSB 2* and *VSB 3*.

Passport/Visa

	Passport Required?	Visa Required?	Return Ticket Required?
Full British	Yes	No	Yes
Australian	Yes	No	Yes
Canadian	1	No	Yes
USA	1	No	Yes
Other EU	Yes	No/1	Yes
Japanese	Yes	No	Yes

Note: *Regulations and requirements may be subject to change at short notice, and you are advised to contact the appropriate diplomatic or consular authority before finalising travel arrangements. Any numbers in the chart refer to the footnotes below.*

Note: Before entering Bermuda, it is essential to be in possession of either a return or onward ticket to a country to which one has a legal right of entry. Anyone arriving in Bermuda and intending to return to their own country via another one which requires a visa *must* obtain such a visa before arrival in Bermuda. Visitors are advised to check details with the British Overseas Territories Visa Section (see *Passport/Visa Information*).
Restricted entry: Admission will be refused to travellers intending to immigrate from Bermuda to the USA. Those who intend to visit the USA must possess an onward ticket to a country beyond the USA and the necessary documents to enter that country.
PASSPORTS: Passport valid for six months after date of entry into Bermuda required by all except:
1. nationals of Canada and the USA with an original birth certificate and official photo ID.
VISAS: Required by all except the following:
(a) nationals of countries referred to in the chart above, and of their overseas territories, except nationals of the Slovak Republic and Slovenia, who *do* need a visa;
(b) citizens of Commonwealth countries (except nationals of Ghana, Jamaica, Nigeria, Pakistan and Sri Lanka who *do* need a visa);
(c) nationals of Andorra, Angola, Argentina, Benin, Bhutan, Bolivia, Brazil, Burkina Faso, Burundi, Cape Verde, Central African Republic, Chad, Chile, Colombia, Comoro Islands, Congo (Dem Rep), Congo (Rep), Costa Rica, Cote d'Ivoire, Dominican Republic, East Timor, Ecuador, El Salvador, Equatorial Guinea, Eritrea, Ethiopia, Gabon, Guatemala, Guinea, Guinea-Bissau, Honduras, Iceland, Indonesia, Israel, Korea (Rep), Laos, Libya, Liechtenstein, Madagascar, Mali, Mexico, Micronesia (Federated States of), Monaco, Mynamar, Nepal, Nicaragua, Niger, Norway, Panama, Paraguay, Peru, The Phillippines, Puerto Rico, Rwanda, San Marino, São Tomé e Principe, Senegal, Sudan, Surinam, Switzerland, Taiwan (China), Thailand, Togo, Turkey, Uruguay, Vatican City, Venezuela and Zimbabwe.
Note: (a) Visa-controlled nationals who have the right to reside in the United States (Permanent Resident), Canada (Permanent Resident) or the United Kingdom (no limit on stay in the United Kingdom), and are in possession of proof of such status and a valid passport, do *not* require Bermuda entry visas. (b) Transit passengers from countries mentioned above must continue to a third country within five hours by the same aircraft, hold confirmed onward tickets and documentation and not leave the airport.
Types of visa and cost: *Tourist:* £28.
Validity: The permitted length of stay is initially three months. For extensions, permission should be sought from

the immigration authorities in Bermuda (see address below).

Application to: Visa Section at UK Passport Office; see *Passport/Visa Information*.

Application requirements: (a) Valid passport with two blank pages. (b) One application form. (c) Proof of onward or return ticket. (d) Fee payable in cash.

Working days required: Four weeks. Processing by post may take longer.

Temporary residence: Persons intending to take up residence and/or employment will require prior authorisation from the Department of Immigration, Government Administration Building, 30 Parliament Street, Hamilton HM 12, Bermuda (tel: 295 5151 *and/or* ext 1378; fax: 295 4115).

PASSPORT/VISA INFORMATION

Bermuda is a British Dependent Territory, and is represented abroad by British Embassies – see United Kingdom section.

The UK Passport Service
London Passport Office, Globe House, 89 Ecclestone Square, London SW1V 1PN, UK
Tel: (0870) 521 0410 (24-hour national advice line) or (020) 7901 2150 (visa enquiries for British Overseas Territories).
Website: www.passport.gov.uk or www.ukpa.gov.uk
Opening hours: Mon-Fri 0730-1900; Sat 0900-1600. Personal callers for visas should go to the agency window in the collection room of the London office.

Money

Currency: Bermuda Dollar (BMD; symbol BD$) = 100 cents. Notes are in denominations of BD$100, 50, 20, 10, 5 and 2. Coins are in denominations of BD$1, and 25, 10, 5 and 1 cents.

Note: The Bermuda Dollar is at par with the US Dollar.

Currency exchange: US Dollars are generally accepted at parity. It is illegal to exchange money other than at authorised banks or bureaux de change.

Credit & debit cards: American Express, MasterCard and Visa are accepted at most large hotels, shops and restaurants. Check with your credit or debit card company for details of merchant acceptability and other services that may be available.

Traveller's cheques: US Dollar cheques are widely accepted. To avoid additional exchange rate charges, travellers are advised to take traveller's cheques in US Dollars.

Currency restrictions: There is no limit to the import of local or foreign currency, provided declared on arrival. Unless especially authorised, the export of local currency is limited to BD$250. There is no limit to the export of foreign currency. A police officer may seize and detain any cash which is being imported into or exported from Bermuda if the officer has reasonable grounds for suspecting that it directly or indirectly represents any person's proceeds of criminal conduct or is intended by any person for use in any criminal conduct.

Banking hours: This ranges between Mon-Fri 0900-1630, with one bank having additional hours of Sat 1000-1500.

Exchange rate indicators:
Rate at time of publishing
£1.00=   BD$1.76
$1.00=   BD$1.00

Duty Free

The following goods may be imported into Bermuda by persons over 18 years of age without incurring customs duty:

200 cigarettes and 50 cigars and 5kg of tobacco; 1 litre of spirits and 1 litre of wine.

Prohibited items: Spear guns for fishing. All visitors should declare any prescribed drugs on arrival as regulations are strictly observed. Clearance of merchandise and sales materials for use at trade conventions must be arranged in advance with the hotel concerned.

Public Holidays

Below are listed Public Holidays for the January 2006-June 2007 period.

2006: Jan 1 New Year's Day. **Jan 2** New Year's Day (forwarded to Monday). **Apr 14** Good Friday. **May 24** Bermuda Day. **Jun 12** Queen's Birthday Celebrations. **Aug 3** Emancipation Day. **Aug 4** Somer's Day. **Sep 4** Labour Day. **Nov 11** Remembrance Day. **Nov 13** Remembrance Day (forwarded to Monday). **Dec 25** Christmas Day. **Dec 26** Boxing Day.
2007: Jan 1 New Year's Day. **Apr 6** Good Friday. **May 24** Bermuda Day. **Jun 11** Queen's Birthday Celebrations.

Health

	Special Precautions?	Certificate Required?
Yellow Fever	No	No
Cholera	No	No
Typhoid & Polio	No	N/A
Malaria	No	N/A

Note: *Regulations and requirements may be subject to change at short notice, and you are advised to contact your doctor well in advance of your intended date of departure. Any numbers in the chart refer to the footnotes below.*

Health care: Health insurance is essential as medical costs are very high. The King Edward VII Memorial Hospital, located in Paget Parish (near the city of Hamilton), is a 327-bed, acute and long-term care facility that provides comprehensive medical care to the population of Bermuda and overseas visitors.

Travel - International

AIR:
 Bermuda has no national airline, but *British Airways* operates regular weekly flights to and from London Gatwick and Bermuda. Other airlines serving Bermuda include *Air Canada, American Airlines, Continental Airlines, Delta, Iberia, United* and *US Airways.*

Approximate flight times: To Bermuda from *London* is seven hours 45 minutes and from *New York* is one hour 45 minutes.

Main airports: *Bermuda International (BDA)* (website: www.bermudaairport.com), is 15km (9 miles) from Hamilton (travel time – 25 minutes). *To/from the airport:* Pre-arranged transportation is available by Bee-Line Transportation and Bermuda Hosts (buses) meet all arrivals. Taxis are also available. *Facilities:* Duty free shops, cafes, bar and bureaux de change. Duty free goods may also be purchased in town shops for collection at the airport on departure.

Departure tax: A tax of BD$25 is included in air tickets. Children under two years and passengers in immediate transit are exempt.

SEA:
 Main ports: The traditional port is the *City of Hamilton*, the capital and the most commercial area on the Island. Many ships tie up in the *Town of St George*, where you walk off the vessel into a charming town of 17th-century buildings, narrow lanes, and small boutiques. The *West End*, Bermuda's third port of call, is fast becoming the preferred place to be. Its Royal Naval Dockyard, an erstwhile shipyard that was the British Royal Navy's headquarters until March 1995, has been beautifully restored as a mini-village. *Facilities:* Shops, restaurants, a maritime museum, an art gallery, and a crafts market.

Cruises operate in the summer months of April to October and suspend services during the winter.

Travel - Internal

SEA:
 Ferries run on a regular daily schedule across Hamilton Harbour and to points on the West End and East, and May to November between the City of Hamilton, RN Dockyard and Town of St George (website: www.seaexpress.bm).

ROAD:
 The main island has an extensive road network, but foreign visitors may not drive cars in Bermuda. Motorcycles and scooters may be hired (see below). Caution should be taken as many roads are narrow and winding. Outside main urban areas, there is also little street lighting. The speed limit is 35kph (20mph) and traffic drives on the left. **Bus:** Buses are modern, frequent and punctual. Bermuda's state-run buses (painted pink and blue) are a pleasant and inexpensive way to visit points of interest. The trip from the city of Hamilton to the town of St George, the northeastern tip of Bermuda, takes about 30 minutes, with the ride from the city of Hamilton to the Royal Naval Dockyard, Bermuda's southernmost point, taking about 45 minutes. It is essential to have the correct fare in coins. A route and schedule map is available free, and books of tickets are available at sub-post offices with transportation passes available for one, three, four and seven days' unlimited use on both buses and ferries. **Taxi:** All taxis are metered with Government-set rates, with a surcharge after midnight; there is a maximum of four passengers per taxi. Blue Flag taxi drivers are qualified guides approved by the Bermuda Department of Tourism. A 25 per cent surcharge operates between midnight and 0600. **Carriages:** Horse-drawn carriages are available in the city of Hamilton and the town of St George.

Motorcycle/bicycle hire: Lightweight motor-assisted bicycles ('livery cycles') may be hired throughout the island; a driver's licence is not required for this. Crash helmets must be worn. Third party insurance is compulsory. Bicycles can also be hired from some liveries.

Travel times: The following chart gives approximate travel times from **Hamilton** (in hours and minutes) to other major towns and the airport on Bermuda.

	Road	Sea
Airport	0.30	-
Town of St George	0.30	-
Somerset	0.35	0.20
Naval Dockyard	0.45	0.25

Travel Advice

Most visits to Bermuda are trouble-free but you should be aware of the global risk of indiscriminate international terrorist attacks, which could be against civilian targets, including places frequented by foreigners.

This advice is based on information provided by the Foreign and Commonwealth Office in the UK. It is correct at time of publishing. As the situation can change rapidly, visitors are advised to contact the following organisations for the latest travel advice:

British Foreign and Commonwealth Office
Tel: (0845) 850 2829.
Website: www.fco.gov.uk

US Department of State
Website: http://travel.state.gov/travel

Accommodation

The Bermuda Department of Tourism provides a pictorial *Where to Stay* listing of all licensed tourist accommodation, and also a separate *Accommodation Rates*, which includes rates, packages, taxes, etc: both are available in brochure form and also online (website: www.bermudatourism.com). Reduced rates are available during the Golf and Spa, or 'low' season, which runs from November to March, and there are many special package tours for special interest holidays. A Government tax, called Hotel Occupancy Tax, of 7.25 per cent is added to hotel bills on check-out, and a service charge - or gratuity charge - of between 10 and 15 per cent is also added to the final bill.

EDITOR'S CHOICE: COTTAGE COLONIES

These feature a main clubhouse with dining room, lounge and bar. The cottage units are spread throughout landscaped grounds and offer privacy and luxury. Though most have kitchenettes for beverages or light snacks, they are not self-catering units. All have their own beach and/or pool.

HOTELS:
 Resort hotels and smaller hotels are both of a high standard. The resort hotels offer a range of facilities including shops, restaurants, organised entertainment, beauty salon, spa and taxi rank. They usually have their own beach or beach club and pool(s). Several have their own golf course. **Grading:** There is no formal grading system in Bermuda. There is only a meal plan structure: MAP, AP, BP, CP and EP. MAP is Modified American Plan; breakfast and dinner included with the price of the room, plus, in some places, British-style afternoon tea. AP is American Plan; room, breakfast, lunch and dinner. BP is Bermuda Plan; room and full breakfast only. CP is Continental Plan; room and light breakfast. EP is European Plan; room only. Resort hotels with many facilities make up about 7 per cent of accommodation in Bermuda. Smaller hotels (around 16 per cent) have fewer than 150 rooms. Normally less expensive than the self-contained resorts, they have smaller-scale on-site facilities for shopping and entertainment and are less formal.

BED & BREAKFAST AND INNS:
 Most of these properties are historical Bermuda homes in lush garden settings modernised into comfortable guest rooms. Bed & Breakfast, a small guest house concept, offers an intimate and traditional setting. Inns, usually larger and more spacious, also include a lounge and provide the feeling of a guest house on a more formal and grand scale. A few have their own waterfront and/or pool. **Grading:** Most Bed & Breakfast establishments and inns offer BP or CP plans. All offer relaxed living. Some have kitchenette units while others provide shared kitchen facilities for preparation of snacks. The bed & breakfast establishments and inns constitute 50 per cent of accommodation in Bermuda.

CLUB RESORTS (PRIVATE): These are noted for privacy and luxury and are for members or by introduction only. There are two club resorts on the main island.

SELF-CATERING AND APARTMENTS: This is self-catering accommodation, otherwise known as housekeeping cottages. The large category consists of properties situated in landscaped estates with their own beach and pool, much like cottage colonies, but without a main club-house. The smaller category is less expensive with fewer amenities. All units of both categories have full kitchen or kitchenette facilities and offer mostly the EP plan; the BP and CP plan is available at only some. All of the accommodation in this category are nonetheless comfortable. Some have a pool and all have minimal daily maid service.

CAMPING/CARAVANNING: There are no camping facilities for visitors in Bermuda.

ACCOMMODATION INFORMATION

Bermuda Hotel Association
61 King Street, Hamilton HM 19, Bermuda
Tel: 295 2127.
Website: www.bermudahotels.com

Top Things To See

- Explore **Hamilton**, Bermuda's capital city, situated at the end of Hamilton Harbour on the inner curve of the 'fish hook'. Here, between Parliament Street and Court Street, is **The Cabinet Building** where the Senate – the Upper House of Bermuda's Parliament – meets. The Lower Chamber of Parliament, housed in the **Sessions House (House of Assembly)**, also located between Parliament and Court Streets, is open to the public. **Front Street** is Hamilton's main street which runs west to east along the water's edge from **Albuoy's Point**, site of the **Ferry terminal** and the **Royal Bermuda Yacht Club**, to King Street in the east. The restored 19th-century **Fort Hamilton** welcomes visitors to its formidable ramparts, cannon, underground web of limestone tunnels and spectacular view of Hamilton.
- In **Somerset**, on the western end of the island, you will find the smallest drawbridge in the world, **Somerset Bridge**.
- **Fort Scaur** is a good place to picnic, swim and enjoy the panoramic view of the picturesque **Great Sound**.
- At the far eastern end of the chain of islands is the 17th-century **Town of St George**, Bermuda's first capital, founded in 1612, which was recognised as a UNESCO World Heritage Site in December 2000. The Town has been the focus of considerable recent restoration; today, its narrow winding lanes and historic landmarks appear much as they did more than three centuries ago. At the corner of Duke of Kent Street and Featherbed Alley is a working model of a 17th-century printing press in the **St George's Historical Society Museum**. Also to be seen is the **Bermuda National Trust Museum** in the **Globe Hotel**, once an office for Confederate officers during America's Civil War; the **Stocks & Pillory**; and the replica of the **Deliverance**, one of Bermuda's first ships. **St Peter's Church** on Duke of York Street is also worth a visit. St George also has many excellent pubs, restaurants and shops.
- A comfortable walk from the Town is **Gates Fort**, which dates back to the 1620, and is built on a promontory overlooking **Town Cut** and the sea, offering a spectacular view of the ocean and harbour.
- Nearby is **Fort St Catherine**, built in 1614, the largest and one of the most fascinating of the island's fortifications.
- At the very opposite tip of Bermuda, on the western side, is the **Royal Naval Dockyard** on **Ireland Island North**. Here you will find the 6-acre **Keep**, the island's largest fort and home of the **Bermuda Maritime Museum**.
- Discover the best view of the island from **Gibbs' Hill Lighthouse**, in Southampton parish.

Top Things To Do

- In **Hamilton Parish** are the **Bermuda Underwater Exploration Institute**, an oceanic discovery centre, **Museum** and **Zoo**, which is located in **Flatts Village**, and the **Crystal Caves of Bermuda**, featuring two of the best-known **caves**, **Crystal** and **Fantasy**, made up of sprawling underground systems and crystalline tidal pools. They are open daily all year.
- Enjoy a **ferry trip** round **Hamilton Harbour**, or a longer cruise through the Great Sound to the west stopping at Somerset Bridge, the rural village of Somerset, and the Royal Naval Dockyard.
- According to oriental legend, honeymooners should make a wish while walking through **Moongates**, circles of stone brought to Bermuda in the 19th century by a sea captain who had seen them on a voyage to China.
- Bermuda's most famous **beaches** lie along the island's southern edge. Some of the most beautiful are at **Chaplin**, **Horseshoe Bay**, **Stonehole** and **Warwick Long Bay**. A vast range of water activities is available such as **snorkelling** and **scuba-diving**. Visibility underwater is often as much as 61m (200ft). Experienced scuba-divers can go below for a historic 'tour' of old wrecks, cannons and other remnants of past disasters on the reefs. All necessary equipment is easy to hire – visitors should note, however, that spear guns are not allowed. For **sailing** enthusiasts, the **Blue Water Cruising Race** – from Marion, Massachusetts, to Bermuda – takes place in June bi-annually, in odd-numbered years. The **Newport to Bermuda Ocean Yacht Race** is also held bi-annually, in even-numbered years; this world-famous June Blue Water Classic (fondly referred to as the 'Thrash to the Onion Patch') attracts scores of the finest racing craft afloat. The week-long festivities, which follow the arrival of the boats, are held at the **Royal Bermuda Yacht Club**. In August, the **Non-Mariners Race** is held. Sailboats and skippers are available for hire from 'Sail Yourself' charter agencies.
- Bermuda is one of the world's finest **fishing** centres, especially for light-tackle fishing. Equipment may be rented for shore fishing and there are charter boats for reef and deep-sea fishing. For deep-sea aficionados, wahoo, amberjack, marlin and tuna abound. On the reefs, there are amberjack, great barracuda, grey snapper and yellowtail. Shore fishermen can test their skills on bonefish and pompano. The best fishing is from May to November, when trophies are awarded.
- There are eight golf courses on the island: seven 18-hole courses, including the **Mid-Ocean Club,** which is world-renowned for its challenge and beauty, and **Port Royal**, situated in oceanside terrain; and one 9-hole layout, Ocean View. For information on Amateur, Professional and Pro-Am tournaments, write to the Bermuda Golf Association, PO Box 433, Hamilton, Bermuda (tel: 238 1367; website: www.bermudagolf.org).
- Enjoy a game of **tennis**. There are almost 100 courts on the island, with a variety of surfaces. Most of the larger Bermuda hotels have their own courts, many of them floodlit for night play. Tournaments are held all year round and several are open to visitors. The **Cup Match**, an island-wide, two-day public holiday (played since 1902 in July/August), is held once a year, when the St George's and Somerset Cricket clubs vie for the Championship Cup.

TOURIST INFORMATION

Bermuda Tourism UK/Europe
Tulip House, Suite 9, 70 Borough High Street,
London SE1 1XF, UK
Tel: (020) 7864 9924,
Website: www.bermudatourism.co.uk

Bermuda Department of Tourism in the USA
675 Third Avenue, 20th Floor,
New York, NY 10017, USA
Tel: (212) 818 9800.
Website: www.bermudatourism.com

Entertainment

FOOD & DRINK: There is a vast variety of restaurants, cafes, bars and taverns to suit all pockets. Service will vary although generally table service can be expected. Hotel cooking is usually international with some Bermudan specialities.

National specialities:

- Bermuda lobster (in season from September to mid-April).
- Mussel pie.
- Conch stew.
- Cassava pie.
- *Wahoo* steak.
- *Hoppin' John* (black-eyed peas and rice).
- Fish chowder laced with sherry, peppers, rum and shark.
- Other seafoods include rockfish, red snapper, *guinea chick* (shiny lobster) and yellowtail.
- Peculiar to Bermuda is the Bermuda onion. Other fine home-grown products include pawpaw and strawberries in January and February, and a variety of local citrus fruit.
- Traditional Sunday breakfast is codfish and potatoes, which are served with red sauce, avocado and banana, while desserts include sweet potato pudding, bay grape jelly and loquat jam.

National drinks:

- National drinks and cocktails have *Golsing's Bermuda Black Seal* rum as a base, and have colourful names such as *Dark and Stormy* (traditional local drink) and the famous *Rum Swizzle*.
- British, European and US beer is available.

Tipping: When not included in the bill, 15 per cent generally for most services. Hotels and guest houses add a

Credit: ©Bermuda Department of Tourism

set amount per person in lieu of tips to the bill.

NIGHTLIFE: Most hotels offer a variety of entertainment. Dancing, barbecues, nightclubs and discos are all available. There are also island cruises such as the *Hawkins Island Don't Stop the Carnival Party*, which enables exclusive access to Hawkins Island (it is accessible only by boat) for entertainment - even the locals attend. Local music is a mixture of Calypso and Latin American, and steel band music is very popular. All the latest listings can be found in *Preview Bermuda* and *This Week in Bermuda*.

SHOPPING: The best buys are imported merchandise such as French perfumes, English bone china, Swiss watches, Danish silver, American costume jewellery, German cameras, Scottish tweeds, and various spirits and liqueurs. Bermuda-made articles include handicrafts, pottery, cedar ware, fashions, rum, honey, Bermuda Rum cakes, Sherry Peppers condiments, records and paintings by local artists. Antique shops may have the odd good bargain and shops in the countryside offer many souvenirs. Bathing suits, sports clothes, straw hats and, of course, Bermuda shorts, are other good buys. There is no sales tax or VAT. **Shopping hours:** Mon-Sat 0900-1700, with some closing early on Thursday. Shops at the Royal Naval Dockyard are open on Sun 1000-1700.

Business

- **GDP:** US$4 billion (2003).
- **Main exports:** Pharmaceuticals.
- **Main imports:** Oil, machinery, manufactured goods and food.
- **Main trade partners:** USA, Japan, Germany and UK.

ECONOMY: Bermuda's economy is dominated by two industries – tourism and international business, financial, insurance and re-insurance services – which together account for approximately 90 per cent of GDP. Offshore banking and related services have been the mainstay of the financial sector, although in recent years, insurance has grown to the point where Bermuda is now the world's third-largest insurance market. Tax receipts from several thousand offshore companies registered in Bermuda, plus customs duties, go some way to offsetting the island's large annual visible trade deficit of around US$500 million. The small light-manufacturing base in Bermuda is engaged in boat building, ship repair and perfume and pharmaceutical production. There is some agriculture, concentrated in the growing of fruit and vegetables, although most of Bermuda's food is imported along with all its oil, machinery and most manufactured goods. Bermuda has recently established an important diamond market.

BUSINESS ETIQUETTE: Lightweight suits or shirt and tie are acceptable, as are Bermuda shorts, when worn in the appropriate manner. Visiting cards and, occasionally, letters of introduction are used. Codes of practice are similar to those in the UK. **Office hours:** Mon-Fri 0900-1700.

COMMERCIAL INFORMATION

Bermuda Chamber of Commerce
PO Box HM 655, Hamilton HMCX, Bermuda
Tel: 295 4201.
Website: www.bermudacommerce.com

Bermuda International Business Association (BIBA)
Century House, 16 Par-La-Ville Road,
Hamilton HM 08, Bermuda
Tel: 292 0632.
Website: www.biba.org

Bhutan

Location: South Asia (between Assam in northeast India and China).

Time: GMT + 6.

Overview

The Bhutanese name for Bhutan, *Druk Yul*, means 'Land of the Thunder Dragon'. Existing archives trace Bhutanese history back to AD450, although many of the intervening events remain a mystery. Guru Rinpoche is believed to have brought Mahayana Buddhism to Bhutan from Tibet in the eighth century. Bhutan, which first became a coherent political entity around the 17th century, has never been conquered or ruled by another foreign power.

Trade agreements with India, essential to sustain the Bhutanese economy, have been the subject of regular rounds of negotiation since the 1940s. Yet despite its close relations with Delhi, Bhutan has occasionally switched its support to its other great neighbour, China. Over the years, relations with China have been dominated by the issue of Tibet – thousands of refugees entered Bhutan after the Chinese occupation of Tibet in 1959; the country has since become a centre for Tibetan exile politics. The refugee issue also dominates relations with Bhutan's other neighbour, Nepal, which hosts an estimated 100,000 Bhutanese refugees housed in camps in the east of the country. Most are ethnic Nepalis whose citizenship is in dispute. (The Bhutanese population is divided between two main ethnic groups – the Nepalis and the Drupka.) The Nepali government wants them to return to Bhutan; the Bhutanese refuse to take them.

The Kingdom of Bhutan has adopted a very cautious approach to tourism in an effort to avoid the negative impact of tourism on the country's culture and environment. All tourists must travel on a pre-planned, pre-paid, guided package tour through one of the 120 registered tour operators in Bhutan or their counterparts abroad. The rate is fixed and controlled by the Government. There are still plenty of takers wanting to explore the breathtaking terrain of this astonishing country: the world's last Buddhist kingdom. The Royal Government of Bhutan adheres strongly to a policy of low-impact/volume, high-value tourism. The tourism industry in Bhutan is founded on the principle of sustainability, meaning that tourism must be environmentally and ecologically friendly, socially and culturally acceptable and economically viable. The number of tourists visiting Bhutan is also regulated to a manageable level because of the lack of infrastructure.

General Information

AREA: 38,364 sq km (14,812 sq miles).

POPULATION: 2.2 million (official estimate 2005). It should be noted that population estimates vary hugely for Bhutan - some are as low as around 700,000.

POPULATION DENSITY: 57.3 per sq km.

CAPITAL: Thimphu. **Population:** 716,200 (official estimate 2002).

GEOGRAPHY: Bhutan is located in the eastern Himalayas, bordered to the north by China and to the south, east and west by India. The altitude varies from 300m (1000ft) in the narrow lowland region to 7000m (22,000ft) in the Himalayan plateau in the north, and there are three distinct climatic regions. The foothills are tropical and home to deer, lion, leopards and the rare golden monkey as well as much tropical vegetation, including many species of wild orchids. The Inner Himalaya region is temperate; wildlife includes bear, boar and sambar, and the area is rich in deciduous forests. The High Himalaya region is very thinly populated, but the steep mountain slopes are the home of many species of animals, including snow leopards and musk deer.

GOVERNMENT: Constitutional Monarchy. **Head of State and Government:** Druk Gyalpo ('Dragon King') Jigme Singye Wangchuk since 1972. **Recent history:** Bhutan is a Buddhist Kingdom and there are close links between the Monarchy and the priesthood. Since the 1950s Bhutan has established some representative political institutions, including an indirectly elected 150-member National Assembly (*Tshogdu Chhenmo*) and elected village herdsmen, but there are no political parties. In 1998, the King gave up some of the Monarch's absolute powers and the Assembly elected a Cabinet for the first time. Ministers have a five year term, after which they face a vote of confidence. Elections for the National Assembly were last held on 28 June 2003. All six Cabinet Ministers retained their positions. A draft constitution is now with the King and his Ministers, and will soon be debated by the members of the National Assembly. The preservation of the environment and distinctive social, cultural and religious ways of life of the *Drukpas* is likely to continue to dominate policy formulation in Bhutan.

LANGUAGE: Dzongkha is the official language. A large number of dialects are spoken, owing to the physical isolation of many villages. Sharchop Kha, from eastern Bhutan, is the most widely spoken. Nepali is common in the south of the country. English has been the language of educational instruction since 1964 and is widely spoken.

RELIGION: The Tantric form of Mahayana Buddhism (*Drukpa Kagyu*) is the state religion; the majority of Bhutanese people follow the Drukpa school of the Kagyupa sect. Those living in the south are mainly Hindu.

ELECTRICITY: 220 volts AC, 50Hz.

SOCIAL CONVENTIONS: The lifestyle, manners and customs of the Bhutanese are in many respects unique to the area. The strongest influence on social conventions is the country's state religion, and everywhere one can see the reminders of Buddhism and the original religion of Tibet, Bonism. There are no rigid clan systems and equal rights exist between men and women. The majority of the Bhutanese live an agrarian lifestyle. In 1989, it was made compulsory for citizens to wear national dress in public; the men wear a *gho*, a robe resembling a dressing gown with upturned white silk cuffs and knee-high socks, whilst the women wear a *kira*, a sari-like garment that is furnished with ornate brooches and worn over a wraparound skirt. Bhutan has also now outlawed the sale of tobacco products, and also banned smoking in public places. The political leaders of the country have also been religious leaders historically. For years the country has deliberately isolated itself from visitors, and has only recently opened up to the outside world, a policy which is now to some extent being reversed. But Bhutan continues to bear the hallmarks of seemingly peculiar customs borne from legacy and legend. Giant phalluses can often be seen painted onto walls, etc, in order to ward off evil spirits. Dogs are regarded as being the highest animal lifeform, with the best chance of being reborn as humans. They are treated with reverence and often run freely and noisily through villages.

Climate

There are four distinct seasons similar in their divisions to those of Western Europe. The Monsoon occurs between June and August when the temperature is normally between 8° and 21°C (46°-70°F). Temperatures drop dramatically with increases in altitude. Days are usually very pleasant (average about 10°C/50°F) with clear skies and sunshine. Nights are cold and require heavy woollen clothing, particularly in winter. Generally, October, November and April to mid-June are the best times to visit – rainfall is at a minimum and temperatures are conducive to active days of sightseeing. The foothills are also very pleasant during the winter.

Required clothing: Lightweight cottons in the foothills, also linens and waterproof gear, light sweaters and jackets for the evenings. Upland areas: woollens for evenings, particularly during the winter months.

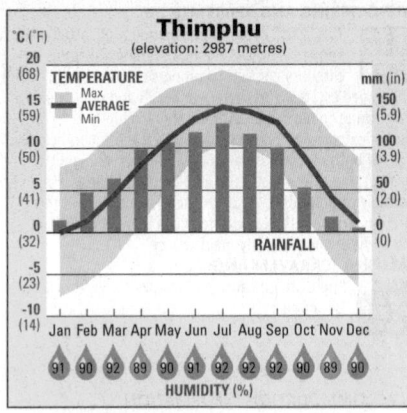

Communications

Telephone: Country code: 975. Services are restricted to the main centres. All other calls must go through the international operator.

Mobile telephone: Some roaming agreements exist. Coverage is limited to main cities.

Internet: Limited access. There are Internet cafes in Thimphu.

Post: Airmail letters to Bhutan can take up to two weeks. Mail from Bhutan is liable to disruption, although this is due not to the inefficiency of the service but rather to the highly prized nature of Bhutanese stamps which often results in them being steamed off the envelopes en route.

MEDIA: Television was only introduced in 1999 because for years Bhutan had a deliberate policy of isolation, fearing that outside influences would undermine its absolute Monarchy, freedom and culture. The state-run *Bhutan Broadcasting Service (BBS)* launched the first TV service as part of celebrations surrounding King Jigme Singye Wangchuk's silver jubilee. The launch marked the end of a general ban on television. Radio broadcasting began in 1973 and the first Internet service was introduced in 1999. Media freedom is restricted by the Government. There are no private broadcasters, but cable television is said to be thriving with rival operators offering around 25 channels.

Press: *Kuensel* is the autonomous weekly and only regular newspaper.

Television: *Bhutan Broadcasting Service (BBS)* is state-owned; *Cable Sat Club* and *Tshela Cable* are commercial channels.

Radio: *Bhutan Broadcasting Service (BBS)* is a state-owned radio station.

Passport/Visa

	Passport Required?	Visa Required?	Return Ticket Required?
Full British	Yes	Yes	Yes
Australian	Yes	Yes	Yes
Canadian	Yes	Yes	Yes
USA	Yes	Yes	Yes
Other EU	Yes	Yes	Yes
Japanese	Yes	Yes	Yes

Note: *Regulations and requirements may be subject to change at short notice, and you are advised to contact the appropriate diplomatic or consular authority before finalising travel arrangements. Any numbers in the chart refer to the footnotes below.*

Restricted entry: Tourists to Bhutan are obliged to use *Druk Air* (the only airline serving Bhutan) either on entering or leaving the country. The Government may refuse entry to those wishing to visit for mountaineering, publicity and other research activities.

PASSPORTS: Valid passport required by all.

VISAS: Required by all except nationals of India.

Note: (a) There are two ways of entering Bhutan: by air to Paro Airport or by road to the Bhutanese border town of Phuentsholing. All travellers entering the country by road must ensure that they have the necessary documentation for transiting through that part of India to Phuentsholing. Consult the *Passport/Visa* section for *India*. Visitors are also advised to contact the Government of India Tourist Office (see *India* section) to check exactly what special permits or other documents may be necessary as these regulations are subject to change at short notice. (b) Visitors are required to book with a registered tour operator in Bhutan, which can be done directly through an affiliated travel agent abroad. (c) A yellow fever certificate is required by all if arriving within six days from an infected area.

Types of visa and cost: *Tourist*: US$20 (payable in hard currency).

Validity: Visas are initially granted for stays of up to 14 days. The Bhutan Tourism Corporation Limited (BTCL) can apply for an extension of tourist visas for an additional fee per person.

Application to: Visa applications for all tourists processed by the travel/tour agent through the Tourism Authority of Bhutan (TAB). Only once the visa has been cleared can visitors travel to Bhutan. Visas are issued (stamped in passport) on arrival at Paro Airport or at Phuentsholing check post.

Application requirements: (a) Application forms, which may be obtained from the BTCL, who should be contacted directly (see *Passport/Visa Information*). (b) Faxed details of passport to the BTCL prior to arrival. (c) All necessary documents for transiting India (see *Note* above). (d) Confirmed onward or return ticket. (e) Sufficient funds for length of stay (Mar-May, Sep-Nov: US$200 per day; Jun-Aug, Dec-Feb: US$165 per day). (f) Fee. (g) Two passport-size photos.

Working days required: Visa clearance takes at least 10 days to process and should be applied for at least 60 days prior to arrival in Bhutan.

PASSPORT/VISA INFORMATION

Royal Bhutanese Embassy in India
Chandragupta Marg, Chanakyapuri,
New Delhi 110 021, India
Tel: (11) 2688 9230 or 9806/7.

Bhutan Tourism Corporation Limited (BTCL)
PO Box 159, Thimphu, Bhutan
Tel: (2) 324 045 *or* 322 647.
Website: www.kingdomofbhutan.com

Bhutan Tourism Corporation Limited (BTCL) in the USA
c/o Far Fung Places, 1914 Fell Street,
San Francisco, CA 94117, USA
Tel: (415) 386 8306.
Website: www.farfungplaces.com *or* www.kingdomofbhutan.com

Money

Currency: 1 Ngultrum (BTN) = 100 chetrum (Ch). The Ngultrum is pegged to the Indian Rupee (which is also acccepted as legal tender). Notes are in denominations of BTN500, 100, 50, 20, 10, 5, 2 and 1. Coins are in denominations of BTN1, and 100, 50, 25, 10 and 5 chetrum. US Dollars are also widely accepted throughout the kingdom.

Currency exchange: Leading foreign currencies are accepted but traveller's cheques are preferred and receive a better exchange rate. Major hotels in Thimphu and Phuentsholing, and the Olathang Hotel in Paro, will also exchange foreign currency.

Credit & debit cards: American Express and Diners Club have very limited acceptability. Check with your credit or debit card company for details of merchant acceptability and other services which may be available.

Traveller's cheques: These can be exchanged in any branch of the Bank of Bhutan or at all BTCL hotels. Travellers are advised to take traveller's cheques in US Dollars.

Currency restrictions: None, but foreign currency must be declared on arrival.

Banking hours: Mon-Fri 1000-1300. Some smaller branches may be open Saturday or Sunday for currency exchange.

Exchange rate indicators:
Rate at time of publishing
£1.00= BTN78.13
$1.00=. BTN44.26

Duty Free

The following goods may be imported into Bhutan by persons over 17 years of age or over without incurring customs duty:
400 cigarettes and 150g of pipe tobacco; 2l of spirits; personal effects for daily use, instruments or appliances for professional use and electronic equipment for personal use.

Prohibited items: Firearms, narcotics, plants. The export of antiques, religious objects, manuscripts, images and anthropological materials is strictly prohibited (regarded as those 100 years or older) and closely monitored by the Bhutanese authorities.

Note: Cameras, videos, mobile telephones and all other electronic equipment for personal use must be registered with the authorities on arrival and will be checked by customs on departure. All visitors must fill out a customs' form upon arrival to be immediately submitted to the customs authorities. Import of plants/soil is subject to quarantine.

Public Holidays

Below are listed Public Holidays for the January 2006-June 2007 period.
2006: Aug 8 Independence Day. **Nov 11, 12, 13** Birthday of HM Jigme Singye Wangchuck. **Dec 17** National Day of Bhutan.

Note: The traditional Buddhist holidays are observed, including Winter Solstice, Day of Offerings, Losar (New Year), Shabdung Kuchoey, Birthday of Drukgyal Sumpa, Lord Buddha's Parinirvana, Coronation Day, Birthday of Guru Rinpoche, First Sermon of Lord Buddha, Thimphu Tsechu and Thimphu Tsechu Domchoe, Blessed Rainy Day, Dashain and the Descending Days of Lord Buddha, The Meeting of Nine Evils and the National Day. Also to be noted is the Birth Anniversary, Coronation and Death Anniversary of Third King HM Jigme Dorje Wangchuck. Buddhist festivals are declared according to local astronomical observations and it is not possible to forecast the date of their occurrence.

Health

	Special Precautions?	Certificate Required?
Yellow Fever	Yes	1
Cholera	Yes	2
Typhoid & Polio	3	N/A
Malaria	4	N/A

Note: Regulations and requirements may be subject to change at short notice, and you are advised to contact your doctor well in advance of your intended date of departure. Any numbers in the chart refer to the footnotes below.

1: A yellow fever vaccination certificate is required by all travellers if coming from an infected area.

2: Following WHO guidelines issued in 1973, a cholera vaccination certificate is no longer a condition of entry to Bhutan. However, cholera is a serious risk in this country and precautions are essential. Up-to-date advice should be sought before deciding whether these precautions should include vaccination as medical opinion is divided over its effectiveness; see the *Health* appendix.

3: Typhoid fever is common. Polio eradication has begun and is reducing the risk, although it must still be assumed to be a risk.

4: Malaria risk exists throughout the year in the southern belt of the following five districts: Chhukha, Geylegphug, Samchi, Samdrup Jongkhar and Shemgang. Resistance to chloroquine and sulfadoxine/ pyrimethamine has been reported in the malignant *falciparum* form of the disease. Mefloquine, doxycycline or atovaquone/proguanil is the recommended prophylaxis.

Food & drink: All water should be regarded as being potentially contaminated. Water used for drinking, brushing teeth or making ice should have first been boiled or otherwise sterilised. Milk is unpasteurised and should be boiled. Powdered or tinned milk is available and is advised, but make sure that it is reconstituted with pure water. Avoid all dairy products. Only eat well-cooked meat and fish, preferably served hot. Pork, salad and mayonnaise may carry increased risk. Vegetables should be cooked and fruit peeled.

Other risks: *Hepatitis A* and *E* occur; *hepatitis B* is endemic. *Giardiasis* is common. *Meningitis* is a sporadic risk and vaccination is advised. *TB* exists. *Visceral leishmaniasis* is prevalent and a small risk of *Japanese encephalitis* exists in southern lowland areas. *Altitude sickness* may be a problem.
Rabies is present. For those at high risk, vaccination should be considered. If you are bitten, seek medical advice without delay. For more information, consult the *Health* appendix.

Health care: There is no reciprocal health agreement with the UK. Full medical insurance is strongly advised. Medical facilities are good but scarce.

Travel - International

AIR:

Druk Air (KB) (website: www.drukair.com.bt), the national airline of Bhutan, is the only airline serving Bhutan and has two 72-seater planes, plus a new fleet of two 114-seater Airbus 319 planes. It is compulsory for all visitors to Bhutan to travel at least one-way by *Druk Air*. Owing to the changeable Himalayan weather, travellers may experience delays.

Druk Air operates flights from New Delhi and Kolkata (India), Dhaka (Bangladesh), Bangkok (Thailand) and Khathmandu (Nepal). The airline flies two to five times a week to each of the above destinations. Additional flights are offered during the high seasons (from March to April and from September to October).

Main airports: *Paro (PBH)*, Bhutan's only airport, is located in a deep valley, some 2190m (7300ft) above sea level, surrounded by hills and high mountains. Operating conditions are fairly difficult and the approach into Paro airport is entirely by visual flight rules. *To/from the airport:* Buses and taxis are available to the city centre (travel time – 90 minutes).
Departure tax: BTN300.

RAIL:

The nearest railhead is Siliguri (India).

ROAD:

The road from Bagdogra (West Bengal) enters Bhutan at the border town of Phuentsholing, which is 179km (111 miles) from Thimphu, and borders West Bengal, India. The border crossing at Samdrup Jongkhar in eastern Bhutan has recently opened, allowing tour operators to take travellers across Bhutan on a single-lane road which crosses into Assam, India.

Travel - Internal

AIR:

Druk Air operates an hour-long scenic mountain flight – the so-called 'Kingdom of the Sky' – which offers visitors spectacular views of the mountains, lakes and waterfalls that are part of Bhutan's beautiful scenery. The plane's seating capacity is 72, with 32 window seats. However, there are no domestic airline routes within Bhutan.

ROAD:

Traffic drives on the left. The country has a fairly good internal road network with 3100km (1926 miles) of surfaced road. The average speed is less than 40 kph (25 mph). The main routes run north from Phuentsholing to the western and central regions of Paro and Thimphu, and east-west, across the Pele La Pass linking the valleys of the eastern region. The northern regions of the High Himalayas have no roads. **Bus:** Those services which were formerly Government-owned are now privately run, though yaks, ponies and mules are the chief forms of transportation. The main routes are from Phuentsholing to Thimphu, Thimphu to Bumthang, Bumthang to Tashigang, Tashigang to Samdrup Jongkar and from Tongsa to Gaylegphug. **Documentation:** An International Driving Permit is required.

Travel times: The following chart gives approximate travel times (in hours and minutes) from **Thimphu** to other major towns in the country.

	Road
Paro	1.30
P'sholing	6.00
Punakha	2.30
Bumthang	8.45

Travel Advice

Travellers must arrange any visit to Bhutan through an authorised travel agent. Those travelling independently are not permitted to enter Bhutan. Most visits are trouble-free. This advice is based on information provided by the Foreign and Commonwealth Office in the UK. It is correct at time of publishing. As the situation can change rapidly, visitors are advised to contact the following organisations for the latest travel advice:

British Foreign and Commonwealth Office
Tel: (0845) 850 2829.
Website: www.fco.gov.uk

US Department of State
Website: http://travel.state.gov/travel

Accommodation

HOTELS/COTTAGES/GUEST HOUSES:

There are comfortable hotels, cottages and guest houses (many constructed to accommodate foreign guests during the coronation of the present King in 1974). Hotels have hot and cold running water, electricity and room telephones. All hotels run by the Bhutan Tourism Corporation Limited are decorated in traditional Bhutanese style and are now equipped with international direct dial telephones and fax machines, and with clean bathrooms decked in a western style. Two new luxury hotels have also recently opened up for business. The *Uma Paro Resort* is situated high on a hill above Paro Valley in West Bhutan. Guests can indulge in yoga and relaxing treatments during their stay in one of the 29 lavish bedrooms on offer. It is serene accommodation for an elite market, with a vaguely monastic and meditative ambience. Also now open is the *Amankova Resort*, part of the Aman chain, which has a plain exterior that belies a sumptuous interior, where guests pay up to US$900 per night to luxuriate. For further information, contact the BTCL (see *Top Things To Do*).

Top Things To See

- Visit **Thimphu**, the capital of Bhutan, which lies at a height of over 2400m (8000ft) in the fertile valley traversed by the **Wangchhu River**. In many ways it resembles a large, widely dispersed village rather than a capital.
- The **Tashichhodzong** is the main administrative and religious centre of the country; it was rebuilt in 1961 after being damaged by fire and earthquake. Its hundred-odd spacious rooms house all the Government departments and ministries, the **National Assembly Hall**, the **Throne Room of the King** and the country's **largest monastery**, the summer headquarters **of the Je Khempo** and 2000 of his monks.
- Monasteries and temples are plentiful in Bhutan. **Simtokha**, 8km (5 miles) from Thimphu, has Bhutan's most ancient *Dzong* (fortified monastery). The small town of **Phuentsholing** is a commercial and industrial centre, as well as the gateway to Bhutan. A short walk from the hotel is the **Kharbandi Monastery**. **Punakha** is the former capital of the country; situated at a lower altitude, it enjoys a comparatively benign climate. The valley contains many sacred temples, including **Machin Lhakhag** where the remains of Ngawang Namgyal, the unifier of Bhutan, are entombed. **Tongsa** is the ancestral home of the Royal family. The Dzong at Tongsa commands a superb view of the river valley and contains a magnificent collection of rhino horn sculptures. **Tashigang**, a silk-spinning district, also has an interesting Dzong.
- A visit to the **Paro Valley**, where the **Taktsang (Tiger's Nest) Goemba** clings dizzily to the face of a 900m (2952ft) precipice, is highly recommended. Legend has it that it was here that Guru Rinpoche flew into Bhutan on the back of a tiger and meditated in a cave for three months. Other attractions in the area include the **Drukgyul Dzong**, further up the Paro Valley (now in ruins after the earthquake in 1954), which once protected Bhutan against numerous Tibetan invasions. The temperate **Punakha Valley** houses many sacred temples, including the **Machin Lhakhag** in the **Punakha Dzong**.
- The district of **Wangdiphodrang** is known for its slate carving and bamboo weaving.
- Make your way to the 3100m- (10,170ft-) high **Dochu La Pass,** which commands a breathtaking view of the eastern Himalayan chain. You may even spot Bhutan's national animal, the *takin* - a peculiar-looking beast.

Top Things To Do

- Witness one of the Bhutan's numerous **Buddhist festivals**. Festivals are full of masks, dancing and ritual, generally centre on *Dzongs* (fortified monasteries) in cobbled courtyards, the most famous of which is at Paro. More than 40 religious or folk dances are performed by the monks recounting tales of Buddhist history and myth. Formal dress is required for all festivals. For a complete list of special events, contact the Tourism Corporation of Bhutan (see *Tourist Information*). At the **Thimphu Festival**, held every September, in the courtyard directly in front of the National Assembly Hall, hundreds of monks in *Trashi Chhoe Dzong* watch the Dance of the Stag and the Hounds - which represents the conversion of the hunter Gonpo Dorji to Buddhism by the saint Milarepa.
- Visit the **Handicraft Emporium**, which displays a wide assortment of unique souvenirs such as beautifully handwoven and crafted products. Shopping is otherwise limited as **Phuentsholing** has the first and only department store of Bhutan.
- Bhutan is well known for its stamps, and the best place to buy them is in Phuentsholing, where the **Philatelic Office of Bhutan** has its headquarters.
- Visit the **National Museum of Bhutan**, located in the **Paro Watchtower** in the Paro Valley.
- Much of the pleasure of visiting Bhutan is enjoying the breathtaking scenery by **trekking** around the valleys and the mountain gorges. From **Bumthang**, travellers can start four- and seven-day cultural tours through the rural villages, including **Mongar**. Climbing some of the Himalayan peaks is banned, however, due to the belief that the mountains are the repository of the gods. Similarly, swimming, or even throwing stones into rivers, is forbidden: it is thought to disturb the souls of deities. However, **mountain biking** along **Paro Valley** is an exhilarating and recommended experience. The country boasts over 320 varieties of **birds**, including the rare black-necked crane. The **Manas Game Sanctuary** has a wide variety of **wildlife** (a special permit is necessary).
- Appreciate the skills of the Bhutanese in **archery** (*datse*), Bhutan's national sport. Competitions are held frequently. These events usually prove fun and raucous, with alcohol consumed freely. The male-only archers shout lewd and disparaging comments at the opponents, often concerning their sexual prowess, whilst female 'cheerleaders' rally support for their husbands and/or male members of their family.

Entertainment

FOOD & DRINK: Restaurants are relatively scarce and most tourists eat in their hotels.
National specialities:
- Meals are often buffet-style and mostly vegetarian.
- Cheese is a very popular ingredient in dishes and the most popular cheeses are *datse* (cow's milk cheese), sometimes served in a dish with red chillies (*emadatse*), and yak cheese.
- The country is replete with apple orchards, rice paddies and asparagus, which grows freely in the countryside.
National drinks:
- The most popular drink is *souza* (Bhutanese tea).
Tipping: Not widely practised.
SHOPPING: Markets are held regularly, generally on Saturday and Sunday, and are a rich source of local clothing and jewellery, as well as foodstuffs. The handicraft emporium on the main street in the capital is open daily except Sunday and offers a magnificent assortment of handwoven and handcrafted goods. Silversmiths and goldsmiths in the Thimphu Valley are able to make handcrafted articles to order. **Shopping hours:** Mon-Sun 0900-2000 (closed Tue).

Business

ECONOMY: Almost all the working population is involved in agriculture, forestry or fishing. The economy is therefore mainly one of subsistence and dependent on clement climatic conditions. The main products are cereals and timber – about 60 per cent of the land area is forested. Over 90 per cent of the population are subsistence farmers, living a life unchanged over generations. There is some small-scale industry – contributing no more than 5 per cent of GDP – producing textiles, soap, matches, candles and carpets. Recent economic policy has concentrated on export industries, of which electric power generation and transmission is the major earner. Tourism and stamps are major sources of foreign exchange. But this is a country where Gross National Happiness is an official part of the constitution, which measures the population's physical, emotional and spiritual well-being when assessing the country's 'wealth'. Bhutan is a member of the South Asian Association for Regional Cooperation.
BUSINESS ETIQUETTE: Lightweight or tropical suit or a shirt and tie for the south. In the capital, a full business suit and tie are recommended. The best time to visit for business is October and November.

Bolivia

Location: South America.

Time: GMT - 4.

Overview

Bolivia is named after Simon Bolivar, who led the country to independence in 1825. Throughout the country's colonial history, Bolivia was known as 'Upper Peru'. The country's name therefore instigates great national pride, but such pride is marred by past turmoil – a past that has been dogged by the succession of *caudillos* (military dictators) who tried, with mixed success, to integrate the country's three disparate regions – the central region, the eastern Andes and the Altiplano – into a national entity in the early years of independence.

Since then, 'liberation' retains a dual meaning in Bolivia. Bolivia is a country of great expanse, extensive lakes and salt plains, which induce an elated sense of freedom for any traveller. But there is little of such freedom for Bolivians, many of whom descend from indigenous tribes and many of whom count for some of the poorest people in South America. Although, domestically, Bolivia has entered an unprecedented era of political stability, such stability has ended a record of military coups and recurrent internal strife that has been little short of ludicrous – there were 192 coups in the 156 years from independence to 1981: an average of one every 10 months.

The fight to keep their land and preserve their landscape mirrors the Bolivians' fight to preserve their traditions. One such example is the significance of the *Pachamama*, otherwise known as 'Mother Earth'. Shrines to Her are everywhere. Talismans of Her can be bought. These archaic customs belie a deep regard for the environment, presumably because it has on countless occasions been so physically harsh and so politically precarious. Such traditions are also easier to uphold in a country still so steeped in antiquity, from the remnants of the ancient Aymará civilization who lived on Lake Titicaca around 1500 BC, to the Incas in the Bolivian highlands, to the people who forged great ruins of rock at Tiahuanaco.

'Mother Earth' is kind in return: Bolivia is beautiful and striking. There are currently 10 national parks and eight protected areas in Bolivia, as well as many other areas being re-evaluated for park or protected area status. Although it once held claim to the Atacama coastal strip (lost in the 1928 Wars against Paraguay), Bolivia is now landlocked but never feels claustrophobic, blessed with breathtaking lakes and lofty mountains. It is difficult to know what is more stunning: the Bolivian's gentle struggle to survive amidst a legacy of poverty and unrest, or the struggle of the Altiplano to ascend ever higher. Standing as tall as the mountains, the pride that the Bolivians have for their homeland is always evident – and always justified.

General Information

AREA: 1,098,581 sq km (424,164 sq miles).
POPULATION: 9 million (UN estimate 2005).
POPULATION DENSITY: 7.6 per sq km.
CAPITAL: Legal: Sucre. **Population:** 223,436 (official estimate 2000). **Administrative:** La Paz. **Population:** 1 million (official estimate 2000).
GEOGRAPHY: Bolivia is a landlocked country bordered by Peru to the northwest, Brazil to the north and east, Paraguay to the southeast, Argentina to the south and Chile to the west. There are three main areas: the first is a high plateau known as the 'Altiplano', a largely barren region lying approximately 4000m (13,000ft) above sea level. It comprises 10 per cent of the country's area and contains 70 per cent of the population, nearly one-third of whom are urban dwellers. The second area is a fertile valley situated 1800m (5900ft) to 2700m (8850ft) above sea level. The third area comprises the lowland tropics which stretch down to the frontiers with Brazil, Argentina and Paraguay, taking up some 70 per cent of the land area. Rainfall in this region is high, and the climate is hot.
GOVERNMENT: Republic. Gained independence from Spain in 1825. **Head of State and Government:** President Evo Morales since January 2006. **Recent history:** The 2002 presidential election returned the Movimiento Nacional Revolucionario's Gonzalo Sanchez de Lozada as president, his party dominating both houses of Congress. However, a police revolt stemming from multiple fractious factors, such as economic recession and longstanding ethnic tensions, nearly toppled the government of President Lozada, who eventually resigned - following further bloody demonstrations - in 2003. Carlos Mesa assumed presidency and, for a while, seemed the man for the job of quieting this turbulent country. However, he resigned in June 2005 after a surge of protests swept the country. The protests were triggered in May when Congress approved an increase in taxes on foreign gas companies. Demonstrators, drawn mainly from Bolivia's indigenous majority and left-wing groups, claimed that these rises were not enough and were asking for nationalisation of Bolivia's primary - one might say only - source of wealth: energy reserves, namely, oil. There were also cries for constitution re-writes so that more power was distributed to the indigenous peoples. La Paz was at a virtual standstill with road blockades catalysing exhausts in fuel supplies and rising prices. Matters subsided somewhat following Mesa's resignation (although protests weren't really specifically aimed at Mesa), and the appointment of interim President, Eduardo Rodriguez. Presidential elections took place in December 2005. The frontrunners were Evo Morales, a leftist candidate from Bolivia's indigenous peoples, and former President Jorge Quiroga. Morales won a decisive victory and was inaugurated as president in January 2006. Irrespective of the complexion of the government, the most important domestic issue for the government for the last decade has been the US-sponsored 'war on drugs' – coca and its products, in the case of Bolivia – which is widely unpopular in a country where coca is considered to be both a traditional product and a valuable cash crop. The government had originally announced that all coca plantations would be eradicated by the end of 2002. This was always highly unlikely and the government eventually conceded 12,000 hectares (approximately 50 sq miles) of plantation for 'traditional' purposes. However, since the economic crisis in Argentina and Brazil, which has affected Bolivia badly, impoverished farming communities are making strong demands to be allowed to grow coca once again. The government faces a difficult balancing act between two determined parties; the American administration (which controls most of the purse strings) and an increasingly restless population. Other important foreign policy issues for Bolivia are the development of regional cooperation, principally concerned with trade and economic harmonisation and – on a bilateral level – Bolivia's persistently problematic relations with Chile.
The bicameral congress is the legislature. This is made up of the 27-member Senate and 130-member Chamber of Deputies. Both the Congress and the president, who is Head of State and wields executive power with a Cabinet of Ministers, are directly elected for terms of four years.
LANGUAGE: The official languages are Spanish, Quechua, Aymará and Tupi Guaraní. English is also spoken by a small number of officials and businesspeople in commercial centres.
RELIGION: Roman Catholic with a Protestant minority.
SOCIAL CONVENTIONS: Normal social courtesies in most Bolivian families and respect for traditions should be observed. Remember to refer to rural Bolivians as *campesinos* rather than Indians, which is considered an insult. Western dress and diet are gradually being adopted by the *campesinos* (although great poverty remains further to the north); a suit and tie for men and dress for women should be worn for smart social occasions. Casual wear is otherwise suitable. Smoking is accepted except where indicated.

Climate

Bolivia has a temperate climate but with wide differences between day and night. The wettest period is November to March, which, in extreme circumstances, may induce landslides in mountainous areas, and cause certain roads to become impassable. The northeast slopes of the Andes are semi-tropical. Visitors often find La Paz uncomfortable because of the thin air due to high altitude. The mountain areas can become very cold at night.
Required clothing: Lightweight linens with a raincoat. A light overcoat is necessary at night, particularly in the Altiplano and the Puna.

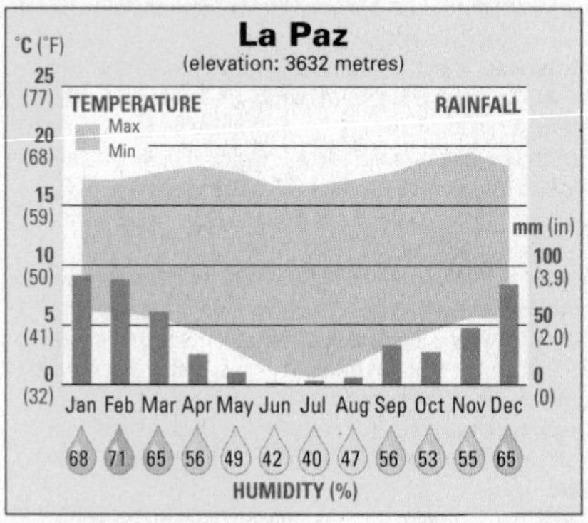

Communications

Telephone: IDD is available. Country code: 591.
Mobile telephone: Roaming agreements exist with some international mobile phone companies. Coverage is average.
Internet: Available in large cities and resorts. There are Internet cafes in main towns.
Post: Airmail to Europe takes three to four days.
MEDIA: Media ownership is highly concentrated. Bolivia's media are dominated by privately run press and broadcasting outlets. There are serious concerns over Bolivia's previous treatment of journalists who covered social unrest or were involved in defamation or slander. As a result, self-censorship is usually exercised.Low literacy levels impede upon newspaper readership. Radio tends to have precedence.
Press: The main papers published in La Paz are *El Diario* and *La Razón*. Santa Cruz dailies include *El Deber* and *El Mundo*.
TV: *Televisión Boliviana* (Canal 7) is the government-run, commercial station. Private stations in Santa Cruz are *Bolivisión* (Canal 4) and *Unitel* (Canal 9). Private stations in La Paz are *ATB Red Nacional* (Canal 9), *Red Uno* (Canal 11) and *TV Universitaria* (Canal 13). *Red PAT* is a national private TV station.
Radio: Radio stations dealing with news and talk include *Radio Fides* (Catholic-based), *Radio Metropolitana* and *Radio Panamericana*. *Radio Cadena Nacional* (RCN) is the major national radio station. *Radio Illimani* is a popular state-run station.

Passport/Visa

	Passport Required?	Visa Required?	Return Ticket Required?
Full British	Yes	1	Yes
Australian	Yes	1	Yes
Canadian	Yes	1	Yes
USA	Yes	1	Yes
Other EU	Yes	1	Yes
Japanese	Yes	1	Yes

Note: *Regulations and requirements may be subject to change at short notice, and you are advised to contact the appropriate diplomatic or consular authority before finalising travel arrangements. Any numbers in the chart refer to the footnotes below.*

PASSPORTS: Passport valid for at least one year beyond the intended length of stay required by all except holders of an identity card issued to nationals of Argentina, Paraguay, Peru and Uruguay.
VISAS: Required by all except the following, provided travelling for touristic purposes:
(a) **1.** nationals of countries mentioned in the chart above (except nationals of Malta who *do* require a visa);
(b) nationals of Andorra, Argentina, Brazil, Chile, Colombia, Costa Rica, Ecuador, Holy See, Iceland, Liechtenstein, Mexico, Monaco, New Zealand, Netherlands Antilles, Norway, Panama, Paraguay, Peru, The Philippines, Serbia & Montenegro, Switzerland, Turkey, Uruguay and Venezuela;
(c) transit passengers (except nationals of China (PR)) continuing their journey by the same or first connecting aircraft within 24 hours, provided holding valid onward or return documentation and not leaving the airport.

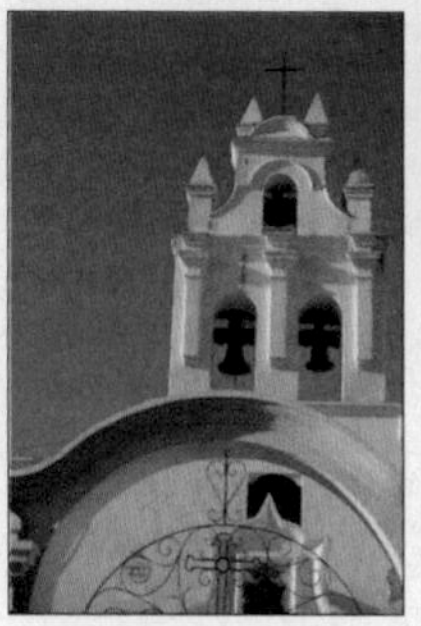
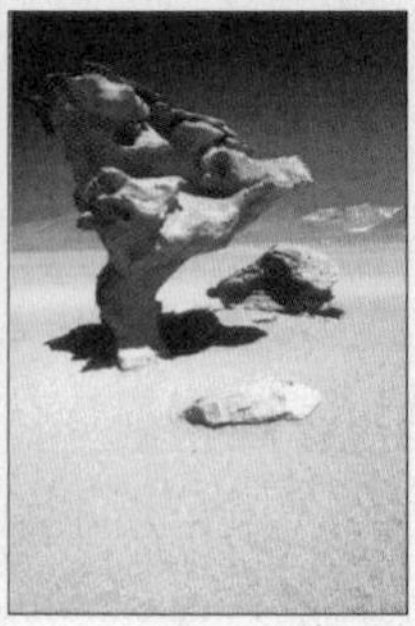
Credit: ©Viceministerio de Turismo, Bolivia

Note: (a) All nationals travelling on business *do* need a Specific Purpose visa. (b) Nationals not requiring a tourist visa are usually allowed to stay for a period of 30 to 90 days; check with the Embassy (or Consular section at Embassy). (c) In addition to a visa, nationals of the following countries also require special authorisation: Afghanistan, Cambodia, Congo (Dem Rep), Korea (Dem Rep), Iran, Iraq, Laos, Libya, Nigeria, Pakistan, Sudan and the Syrian Arab Republic.
Types of visa and cost: *Tourist/Transit*: Cost depends on nationality; enquire at the Embassy (or Consular section at Embassy). *Specific Purpose*: £61.50. *Student*: £31.
Validity: Tourist visas are valid for 30 days but can be extended for up to 90 days (depending on nationality) from the date of entry. Specific Purpose visas are valid for 30 days and can be renewed for 60 or 90 additional days at the immigration office in Bolivia. Student visas are valid for 60 days. Transit visas are valid for 15 days.
Application to: Consulate (or Consular section at Embassy); see *Passport/Visa Information*.
Application requirements: (a) One passport-size photo. (b) Completed application form. (c) Passport with remaining validity of at least one year. (d) Fee, payable by cash or cheque. (e) Return airline ticket or travel itinerary as proof of onward travel. (f) A yellow fever vaccination certificate may be required (see *Health* section). (g) For Specific Purpose visas, a letter of introduction from the relevant company or institution as proof of business intentions and the dates of travel. (h) Sufficient funds. *Student*: (a)-(h) and, (i) Medical certificate proving that applicant possesses no contagious diseases.
Working days required: One to two for nationals requiring tourist visas without special authorisation. Approximately six weeks for all other nationals requiring tourist visas and special authorisation from the Bolivian Ministry of Foreign Affairs.
Temporary residence: Enquire at Bolivian Consulate.

PASSPORT/VISA INFORMATION

Embassy and Consulate of the Republic of Bolivia in the UK
106 Eaton Square, London SW1W 9AD, UK
Tel: (020) 7235 4248 *or* 2257.
Website: www.embassyofbolivia.co.uk
Opening hours: Mon-Fri 0930-1730 (general enquiries); 1000-1230 (consular and visa enquiries).

Embassy of the Republic of Bolivia in the USA
3014 Massachusetts Avenue, NW,
Washington, DC 20008, USA
Tel: (202) 483 4410 *or* 232 4828 (consular section).
Website: www.bolivia-usa.org

Money

Currency: 1 Boliviano (BOB: symbol B$) = 100 centavos. Notes are in denominations of B$200, 100, 50, 20 and 10. Coins are in denominations of B$2 and 1, and 50 and 20 centavos.
Note: The Boliviano is tied to the US Dollar.
Currency exchange: Money can be changed in hotels and *casas de cambio*.
Credit & debit cards: American Express, Diners Club, MasterCard and Visa have limited acceptance. Check with your credit or debit card company for details of merchant acceptability and other services which may be available.
Traveller's cheques: US Dollar traveller's cheques are probably the best form of currency to take. Sterling cheques can sometimes be exchanged, but only with difficulty.
Currency restrictions: There are no restrictions on the import or the export of either local or foreign currency, subject to declaration.

A B C D E F G H I J K L M N O P Q R S T U V W X Y Z

Banking hours: Mon-Fri 0830-1200 and 1430-1800. Some banks open Sat 0830-1200.
Exchange rate indicators: The following figures are included as a guide to the movements of the Boliviano against Sterling and the US Dollar:
Rate at time of publishing
£1.00= B$14.50
$1.00= B$8.03

Duty Free

The following goods may be imported into Bolivia by persons over 18 years of age without incurring customs duty:
400 cigarettes and 50 cigars or 500g of tobacco; 3l of alcoholic beverages; new articles up to US$1000; photographic camera, non-professional camcorder and accessories, personal stereo, electronic memo book, mobile phone and portable computer for personal use; sporting gear.

Public Holidays

Below are listed Public Holidays for the January 2006-June 2007 period:
2006: Jan 1 New Year's Day. **Feb 27** Carnival. **Apr 14** Good Friday. **May 1** Labour Day. **Jun 15** Corpus Christi/Labour Day. **Aug 6** Independence Day. **Nov 1** All Saints' Day. **Dec 25** Christmas Day.
2007: Jan 1 New Year's Day. **Feb** Carnival. **Apr 6** Good Friday. **May 1** Labour Day. **Jun 7** Corpus Christi.
Note: There are other additional holidays celebrated in individual provinces and towns. For further details, contact the Embassy *or* the Viceministerio de Turismo.

Health

	Special Precautions?	Certificate Required?
Yellow Fever	Yes	1
Cholera	2	No
Typhoid & Polio	3	N/A
Malaria	4	N/A

Note: *Regulations and requirements may be subject to change at short notice, and you are advised to contact your doctor well in advance of your intended date of departure. Any numbers in the chart refer to the footnotes below.*

1: A yellow fever vaccination certificate is required from travellers arriving from infected countries. Vaccination is recommended for incoming travellers from non-infected zones visiting risk areas such as the Departments of Beni, Cochabamba, Santa Cruz and the subtropical part of the La Paz Department.
2: Following WHO guidelines issued in 1973, a cholera vaccination certificate is no longer a condition of entry to Bolivia. However, cases of cholera were reported in 1996 and precautions are essential. Up-to-date advice should be sought before deciding whether these precautions should include vaccination as medical opinion is divided over its effectiveness; see the *Health* appendix for more information.
3: A moderate to high risk of typhoid exists, especially outside main cities and tourist areas.
4: Malaria risk exists throughout the year below 2500m, in the Departments of Beni, Pando, Santa Cruz and Tarija, and provinces of Lacareja, Rurenabaque, and North and South Yungas in the La Paz Department. Resistance to chloroquine and sulfadoxine-pyrimethamine has been reported. The recommended prophylaxis is general mosquito bite prevention plus chloroquine chemoprophylaxis, except on the northern affected parts of Bolivia - mefloquine, doxycycline or atovaquone. The disease occurs predominantly in the benign *vivax* form but *falciparum* malaria occurs in Beni and Pando, especially within the localities of Guayaramerín, Puerto Rico and Riberalta. There is lower-risk malaria in Cochabamba and Chuquisaca.
Food & drink: Water used for drinking, brushing teeth or making ice should be boiled or otherwise sterilised. Milk is unpasteurised and should be boiled. Pouwdered or tinned milk is available and is advised, but make sure that it is reconstituted with pure water. Avoid all dairy products which are likely to have been made from unboiled milk. Only eat well-cooked meat and fish, preferably served hot. Pork, salad and mayonnaise may carry increased risk. Vegetables should be cooked and fruit peeled.
Other risks: *Diarrhoeal* diseases and *hepatitis A* are common. *American trypanosomiasis* (*Chagas disease*) and cutaneous and mucocutaneous leishmaniasis occur. *Hepatitis B* and *C*, *Japanese encephalitis* and *TB* are a risk. Epidemics of *viral encephalitis* and *dengue fever* may occur. *Plague* has been reported in natural foci.
Rabies is present. For those at high risk, vaccination before arrival should be considered. If you are bitten, seek medical advice without delay. For more information, consult the *Health* appendix.
Health care: There is no reciprocal health agreement with the UK. Medical insurance is strongly recommended. All travellers, but especially those with heart conditions, should allow time to acclimatise to the high altitude of La Paz. In case of a medical emergency, La Paz has a good US clinic.

Travel - International

AIR:
The national airline is *Lloyd Aéreo Boliviano (LB)*.
Approximate flight times: From La Paz to *London* is 14 hours 30 minutes and from Santa Cruz is 14 hours 40 minutes.
Main airports: *La Paz (LPB)* (El Alto) is 14km (8.5 miles) southwest of La Paz. *To/from the airport*: Coach services to the city depart whenever there are scheduled flight arrivals (travel time - 20 minutes). Services from the city to the airport depart from Plaza Isabel La Católica. Minibus and taxis are also available.
Santa Cruz (VVI) (Viru-Viru) is 16km (10 miles) from the centre of Santa Cruz. *Facilities*: Restaurant and duty free facilities are available.
Air passes: The *Visit South America Pass* is valid within Argentina, Bolivia, Brazil, Colombia, Chile (except Easter Island), Ecuador, Paraguay, Peru, Uruguay and Venezuela. Participating airlines include *Aer Lingus* (EI), *American Airlines* (AA), *British Airways* (BA), *Cathay Pacific* (CX), *Finnair* (AY), *Iberia* (IB), *LAN* (LA) and *Qantas* (QF). The pass must be bought outside South America in country of residence. It allows unlimited travel to 34 cities. A minimum of three flights must be booked, with no maximum; the maximum stay is 60 days, with no minimum, and prices depend on the amount of flight zones. For further details, contact one of the participating airlines.
Departure tax: US$25. Payable in US Dollars for all non-residents. For visitors staying longer than 90 days: US$50.
SEA:
Although it is a member of the International Maritime Organisation, Bolivia is wholly landlocked. However, it is possible to reach ports in Argentina, Brazil, Chile, Paraguay and Peru by ship and, from there, there are rail connections to La Paz or Santa Cruz. The nearest seaport is Arica in the extreme north of Chile. There are also crossings at Port Heath on the Madre de Dios river (Peru), the Bermejo or Pilcomayo rivers (Argentina) and from Brasilia to Cobija across to the Acre river and from Guayaramerin across the Heinez river (both in Brazil).
LAKE:
Steamers cross Lake Titicaca to the Peruvian port of Puno from Guaqui, the most important port on the lake. Situated 90km (56 miles) from La Paz, it is accessible both by road and rail, though services are generally slow.
RAIL:
There is a connection from La Paz to La Quiaca and Pocitos (Argentina), and a connection to Arica (Chile), as well as to Coroba (Brazil). There is also a train to Calama (Chile) with bus connections to Antofagasta.
ROAD:
The Pan-American Highway which links the Argentine Republic with Peru crosses Bolivian territory from the south to the northwest. Driving in the rainy season may be hazardous. During recent years, much attention has been given to new roads, and the principal highways are now well-maintained.

Travel - Internal

Note: Visitors should heed the dangers of altitude sickness, especially in the Highlands.
AIR:
Airlines operating internal flights are *AeroXpress*, *LAB* and *TAM* (the military airline). Because of the country's topography and tropical regions, air travel is the best method of transport, although delays, cancellations and general unreliability is highly possible. *La Paz* (El Alto) - which is the highest airport in the world - and *Santa Cruz* (Viru-Viru) are the chief internal airports.
Departure Tax: Usually B$15, but variable depending on airport and destination. It is advisable to check locally.
RIVER/LAKE:
Double-decker passenger boats operate between the various small islands on Lake Titicaca and traverse the many rivers of the Amazon basin (the main thoroughfares being Ichilo, Mamoré, Beni, Madre de Dios and Guaporé rivers); most of them leave from Copacabana.
RAIL:
Bolivia has 3697km (2297 miles) of track, which goes to make up separate and unconnected networks in the eastern and western parts of the country. Since privatisation, the railway services have been reduced and services are, by and large, slow and disorganised. The Eastern network is particularly inefficient. Some trains have restaurant cars, but there are no sleeping-car services. The railways have recently renewed their rolling stock with Fiat railway carriages from Argentina. There are joint plans with the Brazilians to link Santa Cruz and Cochabamba.
ROAD:
The internal road system covers 50,419km (31,330 miles). Work is in progress to improve the condition of major highways, since the overall road network is rather poor, due to the lack of paved roads. Traffic drives on the right. **Bus:** Long bus trips off the main routes can be erratic. Most long-distance bus trips are overnight. **Taxi:** All have fixed rates and sharing taxis is a common practice. Tipping is not necessary. **Car hire:** *Hertz* and local companies exist in La Paz.
Documentation: An International Driving Permit is required. This can be issued by Federación Inter-Americana de Touring y Automóvil on production of a national licence, but it is wiser to obtain the International Permit before departure.
URBAN:
Bus services in La Paz are operated by a confederation of owner-operators. There are also some fixed route taxi 'Trufi' and 'Trufibus' systems which show coloured flags for particular routes. Fares are regulated. In some cases, catching a 'truck' can prove a better means of transport, being half the price of a bus and usually more reliable - although transportation is less comfortable.
Travel times: The following chart gives approximate travel times from **La Paz** (in hours and minutes) to other major cities/towns in Bolivia.

	Air	Road	Rail
Cochabamba	0.25	6.00	-
Santa Cruz	0.50	24.00	-
Tarija	1.00	18.00	-
Sucre	0.35	11.00	13.00
Potosí	0.40	12.00	12.00
Beni	0.35	-	-

Travel Advice

Most visits to Bolivia are trouble-free but you should be aware of the global risk of indiscriminate international terrorist attacks, which could be against civilian targets, including places frequented by foreigners.
In addition, unpredictable bouts of social unrest can affect main tourist areas and internal travel. It is best to avoid demonstrations and respect roadblocks.
This advice is based on information provided by the Foreign & Commonwealth Office in the UK. It is correct at time of publishing. As the situation can change rapidly, visitors are advised to contact the following organisations for the latest travel advice:

British Foreign and Commonwealth Office
Tel: (0845) 850 2829.
Website: www.fco.gov.uk

US Department of State
Website: http://travel.state.gov/travel

Accommodation

HOTELS:
Bolivia has several deluxe and first-class hotels. Service charges and taxes amounting to 25-27 per cent are added to bills. Rates are for room only, except where otherwise indicated. There is an assortment of middle-range hotel accommodation available, generally of good value.
GUEST HOUSES:
Several pensions in La Paz, Cochabamba and Santa Cruz provide visitors with reasonable comfort at a reasonable price.
CAMPING/CARAVANNING:
There are few camping areas anywhere in South America. However, adventurous travellers may often find adequate lodging for the small fee usually charged at most US or European campsites. Despite no formal organisation or marked zones, camping is possible in Bolivia. Mallasa, Valencia and Palca in the river gorge below the suburb of La Florida are recommended, also Chinguihue, 10km (6 miles) from the city.

ACCOMMODATION INFORMATION

Cámara Departamental de Hotelería
(Bolivian Chamber of Hotel Management)
Calle Panamá, esquina Plaza Uyuni, edificio Shopping Miraflores, 3°, oficina 303, La Paz, Bolivia
Tel: (2) 222 2618/6290.

Top Things To See

- See the world's highest capital city: **La Paz** is situated 3632m (11,910ft) above sea level and is overlooked by **Mount Illimani**.
- Survey **Lake Titicaca**, the highest commercially navigable lake in the world. Located in the Andes, the enormous freshwater lake is a beautiful sight. For those wishing to venture onto land, there are nine artificial islands made of floating reeds to explore.
- Behold exceptional rock formations in the **Moon Valley**. Travel around the salt plains and come across **Laguna Colorado**. Its fiery red waters illuminate wandering **flamingoes** that criss-cross the terrain, framed by copper mountains.
- Discover the garden city, **Cochabamba**, 2558m (8390ft) above sea level and boasting a long tradition of local culture and folklore.
- See what was once the most important and populous city on the continent: **Potosí** is known as the imperial city and is situated at the foot of **Rich Mountain**,famed for its mineral wealth. A tour around the mines of Potosí comes highly recommended. Potosí is one of the continent's greatest historical memorials. The **House of Coins** is just one example of this.
- Ponder the mysteries that surround **Tiahuanaco**, within the Bolivian Andes, full of great stone markers and temples that dominate the landscape. It is believed that Tiahuanaco was the capital of the Pre-Inca civilisation and was built by the Aymara, Native South Americans who inhabited the Lake Titicaca basin. Regardless, many believe Tiahuanaco to be the oldest city in the world, dating from around 700 BC. And no-one doubts the enigmas that such precise, expert and heavy masonry evokes. There have even been suggestions that the constructions were built by aliens or giants!
- Stare into what looks like the biggest mirror in the world. Scores of cracks in the majestic **Salt Lakes** and their plains appear like sparkling crystals. This enormous expanse of eerie but beautiful terrain covers almost 7000 sq miles.

Top Things To Do

- Go **trekking** through Bolivia's large range of geographical regions and climates: ancient Inca routes through the Cordillera Real end up in the Yungas - an area of deep valleys that separates the high Andes from the Amazon basin – near La Paz; the La Cumbre to Coroico trail (three days); the Taquesi route through the Cordillera Real (two days), also known as the Inca Trail; and the El Camino de Oro route (six days), starting at Sorata and ending at the Río Tipuani gold fields.
- Venture into the Amazon jungle – a good start is from Rurrenabaque (235km/145 miles northeast of La Paz). Typical **jungle trips** include a motorised canoe trip up the rivers Beni and Tuichi, with rainforest walks and camping en route. Most tours are led by local guides who have an intimate knowledge of the indigenous plants and wildlife (which includes hundreds of species of tropical birds). Further popular itineraries for treks in the Amazon region include expeditions to the pampas (good for wildlife viewing); the remote Parque Nacional Noel Kempff; and river trips along the Río Mamoré.
- **Climb** the Cordillera Real, which has several peaks above 5000m (14,500ft). Climbing excursions (complete with mules, porters and guides) can also be booked in Sorata, which is set in a beautiful valley with an abundance of trees and flowers.
- **Ski** in what is reputedly the world's highest ski resort: Mount Chacaltaya, at an altitude of 5486m (18,000ft). The best time to attempt skiing there is from April to June.
- Attend one of the most extraordinary and faithful expressions of folklore in South America. The famous Carnival, held every year in February/March, is at its most loved in Oruro, at the Diablada. With parades and dances and night-long celebrations, it is often viewed as one of the world's last 'authentic' cultural celebrations.
- Purchase a Pachamama, a talisman that represents Mother Earth, and is thought to guarantee safety.
- Take a **drive** through some of Bolivia's spectacular mountain scenery and glide over the clouds themselves.

Entertainment

FOOD & DRINK: Bolivian food is distinctive and is generally good. Dishes are dominated by meat. International- and local-style restaurants are available in La Paz and other main towns. Mineral water and bottled drinks are available.
Things to know: Local bars are increasing in number and are unrestricted with no licensing hours.
National specialities:
- Empanada salteña (a mixture of diced meat, chicken, chives, raisins, diced potatoes, hot sauce and pepper baked in dough).
- Lomo montado (fried tender loin steak with two fried eggs on top, rice and fried banana).
- Picante de pollo (southern fried chicken, fried potatoes, rice, tossed salad with hot peppers).

Credit: ©Viceministerio de Turismo, Bolivia

- Cuño (naturally freeze-dried potato used in soup called chairo).
- Lechón al horno (roast suckling pig served with sweet potato and fried plantains).
- lajhua (a hot sauce consisting of tomatoes and pepper pods) will often be used to add spice and flavour to dishes.
National drinks:
- Bolivian beer, especially paceña, is some of the best on the continent.
- Chicha, made from fermented cereals and corn, is very strong.
Tipping: It is customary to add 10 per cent as a tip to the 13 per cent service charge added to hotel and restaurant bills. Porters also expect tips for each piece of luggage.
NIGHTLIFE: La Paz has many nightclubs, which generally open around midnight. There are also numerous whiskerias, local bars. On Fridays and Saturdays there are folk music and dancing shows, which start late in the evening. Cochabamba and Santa Cruz have several discos.
SHOPPING: Special purchases include woodcarvings, jewellery, llama and alpaca blankets, Indian handicrafts and gold and silver costume jewellery. **Shopping hours:** Mon-Fri 0930-1230 and 1500-1930; Sat 1000-1500.

Business

- **GDP:** US$8.1 billion (2004).
- **Main imports:** Petroleum products, plastics, paper, aircraft and aircraft parts, prepared foods, automobiles, insecticides and soybeans.
- **Main exports:** Natural gas, soybeans and soy products, crude petroleum, zinc ore and tin.
- **Main trade partners:** Brazil, Argentina and Peru.

ECONOMY: Bolivia has the second-lowest per capita income in Latin America. Economic growth of 4.5 per cent was forecast in 2005. Agriculture employs nearly half the working population, although it suffers from relatively low productivity. The main cash crops are soya, sugar and coffee, while beef and hides from the extensive livestock-rearing industry are valuable export earners. The other key primary product is timber. Bolivia has developed a unique system of sustainable development, which allows for commercial exploitation of high-quality tropical hardwoods without over-depleting the forests. There is also a substantial unregistered and illegal trade in coca, the plant source for cocaine, which provides a livelihood for many peasants – its economic value is thought to be approximately US$1 billion annually. This is a major political issue in the country.
Bolivia has large mineral deposits, especially of tin – of which it is one of the world's leading producers – and also natural gas, petroleum, lead, antimony, tungsten, gold and silver. Oil and gas deposits serve to meet much of the country's energy needs and are increasingly valuable export commodities. Reliance on primary products has made Bolivia vulnerable to fluctuations in world commodity prices. Having accepted international demands during the 1990s to liberalise its economy and open it up to foreign competition, the Bolivians have been frustrated by a perceived lack of 'reciprocity' – in other words, access to foreign markets for Bolivian products. Bolivia is a member of the Latin American Integration Association, the River Plate Basin Alliance and, most importantly, of the Andean Pact.
BUSINESS ETIQUETTE: Suit or a shirt and tie should be worn. Appointments should be made in advance. **Office hours:** Mon-Fri 0830-1200 and 1430-1830; Sat 0900-1200 (some offices).

COMMERCIAL INFORMATION

Cámara Nacional de Industrias
Edificio Cámara Nacional de Comercio, Piso 14, Avenida Mariscal, Santa Cruz 1392, La Paz, Bolivia
Tel: (2) 237 4477.
Website: www.bolivia-industry.com

Cámara Nacional de Comercio de La Paz
Avenida Mariscal, Santa Cruz 1392,
Edificio Cámara Nacional de Comercio,
Pisos 1 and 2, La Paz, Bolivia
Tel: (2) 237 8606.
Website: www.boliviacomercio.org.bo

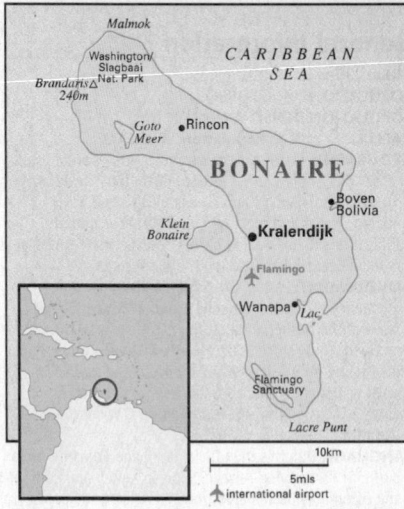

Location: Caribbean, 80km (50 miles) north of Venezuela.

Time: GMT - 4.

Bonaire is part of the Netherlands Antilles represented abroad by Royal Netherlands Embassies – see The Netherlands section.

Overview

Bonaire literally translates as "good air". This might give you some indication as to just how salubrious Bonaire is. The second-largest island in the Dutch Antilles teems with contrasts, its desert-like terrain offset by its inviting turquoise waters. On parts of the island, giant salt lakes loom on the horizon. Beneath the water's surface, rainbow-hued fish drift in between coral.
Indeed, Bonaire is paradise for watersports lovers. The translucency of the sea beckons you in to go diving and snorkelling. Some argue it is the best to be found in the Caribbean, since Bonaire's relative lack of tourism has meant that much of its coral has gone undisturbed. For those seeking sailing or windsurfing, those characteristic divi divi trees, with their windswept postures, convey that Bonaire's climate – warm, dry and breezy – is ideal. Scattered amidst such delights are eerie remnants of Bonaire's connection to the slave trade, such as its glaring white slave huts. When the Dutch had settled in Bonaire in 1634 and later consolidated their position as colonial rulers, the Dutch West Indies Company introduced economic development schemes for which they imported hundreds of slave workers. The abolition of slavery and the end of the plantations which depended on slave labour heralded a long period of economic depression, but as an indigenous economy began to emerge in the 1950s, Bonaire entered its current phase of comparative prosperity. Bonaire is justly proud of its leap out of depression, but there is a noticeable keenness on the island to not buffer its economic situation by expanding tourism to the island.
In fact, Bonaire is the least developed of all the ABC Islands (together with Aruba and Curacao). Instead, the island is highly eco-friendly and keen not to impair the fragile infrastructure of the coral, nor unsettle Bonaire's serenity with heavy development and glitzy nightlife. The Marine Park set up by Bonaire in 1979 enforces a strict maintenance policy for these very reasons. Consequently, Bonaire's beautiful beaches and safe waters have remained intact. Flamingos still wander the landscape of multi-hued salt plains; some even say that they outnumber Bonaire's human population. Multitudes of birds seek sanctuary in Bonaire, and any visitor to the island should be as alert to

Credit: ©Dutch Caribbean Travel Center

the sky as to the sea.

Don't come to Bonaire if you are seeking razzmatazz and revelry – but if you want to celebrate a bit of nature at its loveliest, then this is the place to come.

General Information

AREA: 290 sq km (112 sq miles).

POPULATION: 14,200 (1996).

POPULATION DENSITY: 49 per sq km.

CAPITAL: Kralendijk. **Population:** 1800 (2002).

GEOGRAPHY: Bonaire is the second-largest island in the Netherlands Antilles and is located 80km (50 miles) north of Venezuela and 48km (30 miles) east of Curaçao. The landscape is flat and rocky and, owing to low annual rainfall, Bonaire has a fairly barren desert climate. The island has small beautiful beaches and safe waters.

GOVERNMENT: Part of the Netherlands Antilles; dependency of The Netherlands. **Head of State:** Queen Beatrix of the Netherlands, represented locally by Governor Frits Goedgedrag since 2002. **Head of Government:** Prime Minister Etienne Ys since 2002. The Netherlands Antilles consist of Bonaire, Curaçao, Saba, St Eustatius and St Maarten. The capital of the island group is Willemstad, Curaçao.

LANGUAGE: Dutch is the official language. Papiamento (a mixture of Portuguese, African, Spanish, Dutch and English) is the commonly used *lingua franca*. English and Spanish are also widely spoken.

RELIGION: Predominantly Roman Catholic with a Protestant minority. There are many evangelical churches of different denominations, and a new mosque has also been erected on the island.

ELECTRICITY: 127 volts AC, 50Hz.

SOCIAL CONVENTIONS: Dutch customs are still prevalent throughout the islands, although they are increasingly subject to US influence. Dress is casual and lightweight cottons are advised. Bathing suits should be confined to beach and poolside areas only. Nudity is prohibited on beaches except at Sorobon Beach Resort, a privately owned nudist resort.

Climate

Hot throughout the year, but tempered by cooling trade winds. The average temperature is 28°C (82°F) and the average rainfall is 50cm (20 inches) per year.

Required clothing: Lightweights with warmer top layers for evenings; showerproof clothing is advisable throughout the year.

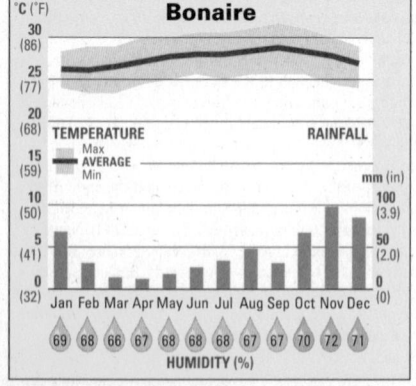

Communications

Telephone: IDD is available. Country code: 599. It is cheaper to make international calls from phone booths in the Telbo building than from resorts.

Mobile telephone: Roaming agreements exist with some international mobile phone companies. Coverage is average.

Internet: ISPs include *Bonairelive* (website: www.bonaire live.net), which operates an Internet Access Center. There

are Internet cafes in Kralendijk and a coin-operated Internet kiosk at the Harborside Mall and also in Kralendijk.

Post: Airmail to and from Europe takes four to six days. Surface mail takes up to six weeks.

MEDIA: Press: *The Bonaire Reporter* is a popular weekly newspaper.

TV: There is a Government-run TV station broadcast from Curaçao.

Radio: *Voz di Bonaire* is popular. There are several other radio stations broadcast from the rest of the Netherlands Antilles.

Passport/Visa

	Passport Required?	Visa Required?	Return Ticket Required?
Full British	Yes	1	Yes
Australian	Yes	3	Yes
Canadian	Yes	3	Yes
USA	Yes	1	Yes
Other EU	Yes	1/2/3	Yes
Japanese	Yes	3	Yes

Note: *Regulations and requirements may be subject to change at short notice, and you are advised to contact the appropriate diplomatic or consular authority before finalising travel arrangements. Any numbers in the chart refer to the footnotes below.*

PASSPORTS: Passport valid for at least three months after intended return to home country required by all (although these are exceptions and certain nationals may be able to enter with valid national identity cards, etc - it is best to contact the nearest Consulate prior to departure).

VISAS: Required by all except the following:
(a) **1.** nationals of Belgium, Bolivia, Chile, Costa Rica, Ecuador, France, Germany, Hong Kong (SAR), Israel, Jamaica*, Korea (Rep), Luxembourg, The Netherlands, San Marino, Surinam*, the UK and USA for touristic stays of up to three months;
(b) **2.** nationals of Czech Republic, Hungary, Poland, Slovak Republic and Spain for stays of up to 14 days but also with the highly likely chance of having this extended to up to three months upon arrival;
(c) **3.** other nationals for touristic stays of up to 14 days, although there still many who *always* require a visa; contact the nearest Embassy or Consulate directly regarding this;
(d) most nationals continuing to a third country within 24 hours by the same means of transportation and not leaving the airport and holding tickets with reserved seats and documents for their onward journey.

Note: * These nationals must still withold proof of sufficient means of support and onward/return documents, even when travelling visa-free.

Note: All stays can be extended locally by the same period that they are valid for.

Types of visa and cost: All visas, regardless of duration of stay or number of entries permitted on visa, cost £15.

Validity: Visas are generally issued for as long as duration of stay, up until a maximum 90 days from date of issue.

Application requirements: (a) Valid passport with at least one blank page. If passport is new, the old passport must also be submitted. (b) One fully completed application form. (c) One recent passport-size photo per person endorsed on passport. (d) Fee, payable by postal order (to Royal Netherlands Embassy) or cash. Cheques are not accepted. (e) Evidence of sufficient funds amounting to a minimum of US$150 for each day of stay (cash not accepted), eg original bank statements, credit card with credit limit statement, traveller's cheques. (f) It may be necessary to submit a recent and original letter from employer, stating commencement date, with last payslip. If self-employed, submit letter from solicitor, accountant or company house. If unemployed, submit social benefit booklet. If in education, submit a recent and original letter from school/college/university, confirming attendance. (g) Valid medical or travel insurance. *Tourist:* (a)–(g) and, (h) Invitation from family or proof of hotel booking. (i) Return or onward ticket. *Business:* (a)–(g) and, (h) Invitation from Dutch company confirming duration and purpose of stay.

Note: All individuals (including residents) travelling within the Netherlands Antilles must hold proof of identity (including photo) if aged 14 years and above.

Application to: Nearest Embassy of the Kingdom of The Netherlands. All further information about visa requirements may be obtained from The Royal Netherlands Embassies, which formally represent the Netherlands Antilles; see *Passport/Visa Information* in *The Netherlands* section.

Working days required: Applications should be lodged at least one month prior to departure.

Temporary residence: Enquire at the office of the Lieutenant Governor of the Island Territory of Bonaire, Plaza Reina Wilhelmina 1, Kralendijk, Bonaire. In certain cases, Dutch Europeans may be permitted to reside in the

Netherlands Antilles without having to apply for a residence permit. However, it is best to consult the nearest Dutch Embassy/Consulate in advance to ascertain whether this is applicable taking into consideration the individual circumstances of the traveller.

> **PASSPORT/VISA INFORMATION**
>
> **Office of the Minister Plenipotentiary of the Netherlands Antilles**
> Antillenhuis, Badhuisweg 173-175, PO Box 90706, Badhuisweg 173-175, 2597 JP The Hague, The Netherlands
> Tel: (70) 306 6111.
>
> See also *Passport/Visa Information* in *The Netherlands* section.

Money

Currency: Netherlands Antilles Guilder or Florin (ANG) = 100 cents. Notes are in denominations of ANG250, 100, 50, 25, 10 and 5. Coins are in denominations of ANG5, 2.5, 1, 0.5, 0.25, 0.1, 0.05 and 0.01 cents. The US Dollar is accepted everywhere although change is given in Guilders. Notes in denominations greater than US$20 will only be accepted in banks.

Note: The Netherlands Antilles Guilder is tied to the US Dollar.

Currency exchange: Most major currencies, including US Dollars, Pounds Sterling and Euros, are easily exchanged. ATMs are located around the island.

Credit & debit cards: American Express, Diners Club, MasterCard and Visa are widely accepted. Check with your credit or debit card company for details of merchant acceptability and other services which may be available.

Traveller's cheques: To avoid additional exchange rate charges, travellers are advised to take traveller's cheques in US Dollars.

Currency restrictions: There are no restrictions on the import or export of local or foreign currency. The import of Dutch or Surinam silver coins is forbidden.

Banking hours: Mon-Fri 0900-1200 and 1400-1600.

Exchange rate indicators:

Rate at time of publishing

£1.00=	ANG1.78
$1.00=	ANG3.21

Duty Free

The following items may be imported into Bonaire by persons over 15 years of age without incurring customs duty:

200 cigarettes or 100 cigarillos (or of 3g each) or 50 cigars or 250g of tobacco; 2l of alcoholic beverages or 2l of wine; an unlimited quantity of perfume; gifts up to a value of ANG100.

Note: If the total value of goods per passenger exceeds ANG500, a declaration should be made on a customs form and cleared at the freight department. It should also be noted that the import of leather articles from Haiti is not advisable.

Public Holidays

Below are listed Public Holidays for the January 2006-June 2007 period.

2006: Jan 1 New Year's Day. **Jan 19** Carnival Rest Day. **Apr 14-17** Easter. **Apr 30** Queen's Birthday Celebrations and Rincon's Day. **May 1** Labour Day. **May 25** Ascension Day. **Sep 6** Bonaire Day. **Dec 25-26** Christmas.

2007: Jan 1 New Year's Day. **Jan 19** Carnival Rest Day. **Apr 6-9** Easter. **Apr 30** Queen's Birthday Celebrations and Rincon's Day. **May 1** Labour Day. **May 17** Ascension Day.

Health

	Special Precautions?	Certificate Required?
Yellow Fever	No	1
Cholera	No	No
Typhoid & Polio	2	N/A
Malaria	No	N/A

Note: *Regulations and requirements may be subject to change at short notice, and you are advised to contact your doctor well in advance of your intended date of departure. Any numbers in the chart refer to the footnotes below.*

1: A yellow fever certificate is required from all travellers over six months of age coming from infected areas.

2: Polio and typhoid are not endemic in Bonaire; however, precautions are advised as a few areas of risk exist within the general region of the Caribbean.

Food & drink: All mains water on the islands is distilled from seawater and is thus safe to drink. Bottled mineral water is widely available. Milk is pasteurised and dairy products are safe for consumption. Local meat, poultry, seafood, fruit and vegetables are generally considered safe to eat.
Other risks: *Hepatitis A* is present. Outbreaks of *dengue fever* occur in the area.
Health care: The San Francisco Hospital is equipped to deal with emergencies and has a decompression chamber and an ambulance aircraft.

Travel - International

AIR:
KLM offers direct flights twice a day from Europe and South America to Bonaire. *American Eagle* has daily flights between Puerto Rico and Bonaire. *Air Jamaica* operates from Montego Bay on Saturdays. *American Airlines* operates direct flights to Curaçao from many US cities, and *Delta* flies from Atlanta to Curaçao, with connections to Bonaire. *Divi Divi* also flies to/from Curaçao. *BonairExcel* operates several daily flights to Curaçao with additional flights to Aruba, although connections with *KLM* sometimes occur. *Continental Airlines* flies between Houston and Bonaire.
Approximate flight times: From Bonaire to *London* is 11 hours, to *Amsterdam* is nine hours 30 minutes, to *Los Angeles* is 10 hours and to *New York* is four hours. Times vary considerably depending on connections.
Main airports: *Flamingo Airport (BON)* is 4km (2.5 miles) from Kralendijk. *To/from the airport*: Taxis are available into Kralendijk and cost about US$8 daytime and US$10 at night.
Departure tax: US$5.75 to destinations within the Netherlands Antilles and US$20 for international flights.
SEA:
There are no international boat connections to Bonaire. However, Bonaire is regularly visited by cruise ships during high season (December to April).

Travel - Internal

ROAD:
Roads are reasonably good, although jeeps may be needed for extensive touring of the island. A good **taxi** service exists on the island. Rates are Government controlled. There are numerous car hire firms located at hotels, the airport and Kralendijk. Reservations should be made in advance to get the best rates. Pick-ups and mini-vans are available for shore divers.
Car hire tax is US$4 per day, plus 5 per cent on the rental fee. Bikes, scooters and motorbikes can also be hired without any difficulty.
Regulations: Traffic drives on the right.
Documentation: A national driving licence is acceptable if held for at least two years, although drivers must be at least 21 years of age (minimum age varies according to hire company and type of car). Drivers under a certain age may also be restricted as to what type of car they may hire, and most cars are manual/standard transmission.

Travel Advice

The threat from terrorism is low, but you should be aware of the global risk of indiscriminate terrorist attacks which could be against civilian targets, including places frequented by foreigners.
Travellers should be aware that the Netherlands Antilles are used as a drug passageway from South America to Europe and North America and should never leave bags unattended nor agree to carry a package for anyone.
Petty theft and street crime is on the increase, but most visits to Bonaire are trouble-free.
This advice is based on information provided by the Foreign and Commonwealth Office in the UK. It is correct at time of publishing. As the situation can change rapidly, visitors are advised to contact the following organisations for the latest travel advice:

British Foreign and Commonwealth Office
Tel: (0845) 850 2829.
Website: www.fco.gov.uk

US Department of State
Website: http://travel.state.gov/travel

Accommodation

Note: Rates for accommodation will be approximately 20 to 40 per cent cheaper in the off-peak season (15 April-15 December). A room tax of around US$5.50-6.50 per person per night is added to the bill. An additional service charge of 10 to 15 per cent may also be levied.

HOTELS:
There are excellent hotels and resorts on the island with good facilities for the holidaymaker, particularly in the provision of watersports equipment, etc. Advance booking is essential.
GUEST HOUSES:
The visitor can opt for accommodation in beach villas or private apartments. Various property companies can be contacted – details are available from BONHATA (see address below).

ACCOMMODATION INFORMATION

Bonaire Hotel and Tourism Association (BONHATA)
PO Box 358, Kaya Gob Debrot 67, Kralendijk, Bonaire
Tel: (717) 5134.
Website: www.bonhata.com

Top Things To See

- Enjoy Bonaire's **Marine Park**, centred on a spectacular coral reef, which is maintained and protected throughout the year by marine experts.
- See the salt flats change colour according to fluctuations in the resident algae population, from breathtaking fuchsia to a subtle pink.
- Contemplate the bright white stucco huts that were once inhabited by the salt workers until the abolition of slavery in 1863. The eerily small holes on their frontage served as doors, which the slaves would crawl through at night.
- Watch flocks of flamingos wander around the beautiful lagoon of **Goto Meer**.
- Look out over Bonaire's highest point: **Mount Brandaris**, situated in **Washington/Slagbaai National Park**.

Top Things To Do

- The waters around the island are clear, safe and teeming with fish of every size and hue. In short, Bonaire is a diver's paradise and you'd be a fool to forgo the **scuba-diving** and **snorkelling** on offer. The popularity of these waters is underlined by the amount of festivals that take place in Bonaire, such as *Dive into Earth Week* in April and the *Annual Dive Festival* in June.
- **Sailing** charters comes highly recommended: half- or full-day cruises can be arranged round the bay or to Klein Bonaire, the island's tiny uninhabited sister isle. Every second week of October there is a *Sailing Regatta*, during which there is a carnival atmosphere on the island. The focus of the regatta is the marina, just a few minutes out of Kralendijk: berthing facilities for various types of vessel, a shipyard, and a drydock make Bonaire a pleasure boater's retreat.
- **Windsurfing** is a breeze with Bonaire's climate: whilst you're at it, why not attend some of the competitions hosted by Bonaire, such as the *Dutch Antilles Windsurfing Challenge* or the *Annual King of the Caribbean Freestyle Windsurfing Competition*?
- Attend one of Bonaire's many fun-loving festivals, from the colourful *Carnival* and its finale of the *Burning of King Momo* and its spectacular fireworks, to the *Simadan (Harvest) Festival* in Rincon with its songs and dances, and *Rincon Day*, celebrating the traditions and culture of Bonaire in the island's oldest village.

TOURIST INFORMATION

Tourism Corporation Bonaire in Europe
Basis Communicatie BV, Wagenweg 252, PO Box 472, NL 2000, Al-Haarlem, The Netherlands
Tel: (23) 543 0705.
Website: www.infobonaire.com

Caribbean Tourism Organisation in the UK
22 The Quadrant, Richmond, Surrey, TW9 1BP, UK
Tel: (020) 8948 0057.
Website: www.doitcaribbean.com *or* www.onecaribbean.org

Tourism Corporation Bonaire in the USA
Adams Unlimited Public Relations & Marketing, 10 Rockefeller Plaza, Suite 900, New York, NY 10020, USA
Tel: (212) 956 5912 *or* (800) 266 2473 (toll-free in USA and Canada).
Website: www.infobonaire.com

Credit ©Dutch Caribbean Travel Center

Entertainment

FOOD & DRINK: The restaurants serve predominantly Creole cooking, particularly seafood dishes, including conch shell meat, grilled spicy fish and lobster. A variety of Chinese, French, Indonesian, Italian and international cooking can also be found. There are several hotels, restaurants and bars in Kralendijk to choose from.
Things to know: Restaurants and bars are usually closed by midnight.
National specialities:
- Iguana soup.
- *Kabrito stoba* (goat stew).
- Conch and cactus may be on the menu, as will be plenty of plantains and ochra.
- Salted meat is prevalent.
- *Pika Siboyo* is a popular sauce made with onions marinated in vinegar and hot peppers.
- *Pastechis* are plump pastries filled with spicy meat, shrimp or fish, and are a favoured snack.
- *Sopi di Binja* is wine soup made with wine, naturally, but also prunes, cinnamon and cornstarch.
- *Cocada* is an ideal treat - sweet cocunut candy never tasted so good.

Legal drinking age: 18.
Tipping: There is normally a 10 per cent service charge in restaurants and a 6 per cent tax. Tipping is not widely practised but porters are usually given 50 cents-US$1 per bag; taxi drivers are generally given 10 per cent of the fare.
NIGHTLIFE: This is centred on both the main hotels and restaurants. Having eaten, evening entertainment includes dancing or listening to reggae groups or calypso steel bands at the many oceanside bars and cafes. The island has two discos and two casinos.
SHOPPING: The reductions on duty free imports make the purchase of some perfume, jewellery or alcohol worthwhile. Bonaire prides itself on its unique, specialist stores. Watches, Dutch cheese, fine China and Cuban cigars are usually sold.
Shopping hours: Mon-Sat 0800/0900-1200 and 1400-1800. Larger supermarkets are open Mon-Sat 0730/0800-1900, with some open Sun 1100-1400. Hours generally vary widely and those stated above must be treated simply as guidelines.

Business

- **GDP:** US$2.45 billion.
- **Main exports:** Petroleum products.
- **Main imports:** Crude petroleum, food and manufactured goods.
- **Main trade partners:** Venezuela, Mexico, USA, Brazil and Gabon.

ECONOMY: During the 1950s, Bonaire began a gradual climb out of chronic economic depression, aided by investment in tourism and the revival of a long-dormant salt industry. The economy gained a further boost in the mid-1970s, when the Bonaire Petroleum Corporation (Bopec) set up an oil transfer depot with a deep-water port, with facilities for transferring oil from ocean-going to coastal tankers. However, plans to build a refinery in Bonaire have been indefinitely shelved. Other economic activities on Bonaire include rice processing and shipping. There is also some agriculture – Bonaire grows a variety of fruit and vegetables; in particular, it is a major producer and exporter of aloes. Bonaire has benefited from the offshore financial industry, which has built up among the island group, although most of the companies engaged in the sector are located on Curaçao and St Maarten. As part of the Kingdom of the Netherlands, Bonaire is an overseas territory in association with the EU; it also holds observer status at the regional CARICOM trading bloc.
BUSINESS ETIQUETTE: General business practices prevail.
Office hours: Mon-Fri 0730-1200 and 1330-1630.

COMMERCIAL INFORMATION

Bonaire Chamber of Commerce and Industry
PO Box 52, Princess Marie-Straat, Kralendijk, Bonaire
Tel: (717) 5595.

Bosnia & Herzegovina

Location: Southeastern Europe.

Time: GMT + 1 (GMT + 2 from last Sunday in March to last Sunday in October).

Overview

When thinking of Bosnia & Herzegovina, it is difficult not to focus on the Yugoslav wars that blighted the Balkan region for much of the 1990s. At a loss of hundreds of thousands of lives, huge landmass was shredded into civil combat. Much of Bosnia & Herzegovina's landscape is still riddled with mines, and ramshackle buildings loll across its towns and villages. However, the country remains beautiful, and its winding aqua rivers have lost none of their lustre.

Modern-day Bosnia formed when the territory expanded southwards to absorb the province of Hum (now Herzegovina). As a province of the Ottoman Empire, much of the population converted to Islam but, as a frontier province, the country was the first line of defence against incursions and consequently suffered recurring invasions. Then, under expulsion of the Turks in 1876, Bosnia was assigned to the Austro-Hungarian Empire and an influx of non-Muslims from the north brought Bosnia close to its present-day ethnic mix. Vienna's decision to fully annex Bosnia in 1908 produced a destabilising chain of events that triggered the First Balkan war and World War I. Serbia eventually annexed Bosnia as part of the new 'Kingdom of Serbs, Croats and Slovenes', renamed 'Yugoslavia' in 1929. After Yugoslavia's dismemberment during World War II, the area was incorporated into a so-called 'Independent State of Croatia', ruled by the fascist Ustasa movement. This resulted in genocide against the local Serbs. Concomitantly, the area was the major battleground of the Yugoslav civil war proper between royalist Chetnik forces and Partisans, led by Tito. Following Communist take-over in 1945, Bosnia & Herzegovina became a constituent republic of the new Yugoslav federation.

Communist rule largely suppressed ethnic rivalries. However, they resurfaced once the Yugoslav federation began to unravel circa 1990. With a population split almost equally between Serbs, Croats and Muslims, Bosnia was always likely to be the centrepiece of the struggle for influence. Serbia's initial dominance floundered when the UN imposed sanctions on Serbia because of racial atrocities, and, in 1995, NATO aided the Croat and Muslim armies in retaking much of Bosnia's Serb-occupied territory. Robust American diplomacy split Bosnia between Serbs and Muslim-Croats. Since the end of war, the Dayton Accord has been reasonably successful in returning Bosnia to normality. Although economic stagnation and international isolation is

yet to be overcome, there is non-negative history in abundance, from stunning old mosques to amphitheatres and Catholic shrines. Countryside varies from woodland to mountains to rolling hills. Perhaps most wonderful is the rebuilt bridge in Mostar - what used to be a pre-war ancient overpass. Now re-opened to the public, it is hard not to walk across it and hope it symbolic of new beginnings.

General Information

AREA: 51,129 sq km (19,741 sq miles).

POPULATION: 4 million (estimate 2005).

POPULATION DENSITY: 78.2 per sq km.

CAPITAL: Sarajevo. **Population:** 420,000 (estimate 2005).

GEOGRAPHY: Roughly triangular in shape, and the geopolitical centre of the former Yugoslav Federation, Bosnia & Herzegovina shares borders with Serbia & Montenegro in the east and southeast, and Croatia to the north and west, with a short Adriatic coastline of 20km (12 miles) in the southeast, but no ports.

GOVERNMENT: Parliamentary Democracy. Under the terms of the 1995 Dayton Peace agreement, Bosnia & Herzegovina consists of two entities: *Federacija Bosne i Hercegovine* (the Federation of Bosnia & Herzegovina) and *Republika Srpska* (the Serbian Republic). Each has its own president, although there is also a three-member rotating presidency, elected every four years. The presidency then appoints a Chairman of the Council of Ministers. A central government, based in Sarajevo, is responsible for national functions including foreign, external trade and finance policies. Two thirds of the seats in the National Assembly are reserved for Federation candidates and one third for Serbs. In addition, *Republika Srpska* elects its own President and National Assembly, while the Federation elects a National Assembly. **Heads of State:** The presidency of Bosnia & Herzegovina consists of two Members and one Chairperson: one Bosniak, one Serb and one Croat. Current Members and Chairman are: Ivo Miro Jovic (since 2005), Sulejman Tihic (since 2002) and Borislav Paravac (since 2003). The chair rotates every eight months. **Head of Government:** Prime Minister Adnan Terzic (since 2003).

Recent history: The first set of post-war elections under the terms of the Dayton Accord took place in October 1996. These brought victories for the main nationalist parties representing each of the three communities – the Party of Democratic Action (KCD) for the Muslims, the Croat Democratic Party (HDZ) and the Serb Democratic Party (SDS). These have since remained the dominant political forces in their respective territories, despite none-too-subtle efforts by the international community to promote more moderate political forces, which it is hoped will eventually guide the country towards reunification and ultimately NATO and EU membership. At the 2000 polls, effective opposition parties did emerge for the first time on both sides – *Sloga* on the Serb side mounted a serious challenge to the SDS, while in the Muslim-Croat Federation, the Croat Social Democratic Party did likewise to the Croat HDZ. The KCD remained pre-eminent as the main representative party of the Muslim population. However, the most recent polls, in October 2002, reaffirmed the dominant position of the three main nationalist parties – the SDS governs *Republika Srpska* while the KCD is the largest single party in the Muslim-Croat Federation. There has been some friction within the Federation but so far it has held together as a political entity. The 2002 elections were also notable for the fact that they were the first to have been organised domestically; previous polls had been administered and supervised by the international community. There was evidence of possible corruption from the Croat member of presidency, Covic, but he was promptly sacked by High Representative Paddy Ashdown in 2005 and replaced by Ivo Miro Jovic.

LANGUAGE: The official languages are Bosnian, Serbian and Croatian. The Croats and Bosniaks use the Latin alphabet, whereas the Serbs use the Cyrillic.

RELIGION: 40 per cent Muslim, 31 per cent Orthodox, 15 per cent Roman Catholic, 4 per cent Protestant and 10 per cent other denominations and religions.

ELECTRICITY: 220 volts AC, 50Hz. Two-pin plugs are in use.

SOCIAL CONVENTIONS: Bosnia & Herzegovina is charaterised by its ethnic and religious diversity and visitors should respect the customs and traditions of the various ethnic and religious groups. The main ethnic groups are the Bosniaks (48 per cent, also sometimes referred to as Bosnian Muslims), the Serbs (37.1 per cent) and the Croats (14.3 per cent). As a sign of acknowledgement of the three main religious communities (Islamic, Orthodox and Roman Catholic), the Government of Bosnia & Herzegovina allows its citizens to take off two working days per year for religious purposes. Visitors should be aware that drinking alcohol in public may be considered offensive by Muslims. Visitors should avoid expressing opinions about the war or other sensitive issues.

Climate

Dominated by mountainous and hilly terrain, and drained by major rivers to the north (Sava) and east (Drina), Bosnia & Herzegovina has a climate that is as variable as the rest of the former Yugoslav federation, with moderate continental climatic conditions generally the norm (very cold winters and hot summers).

Required clothing: In winter, heavyweight clothing and overcoat. In summer, lightweight clothing and raincoat required, with mediumweight clothing at times in the colder and wetter north, and at higher altitudes elsewhere.

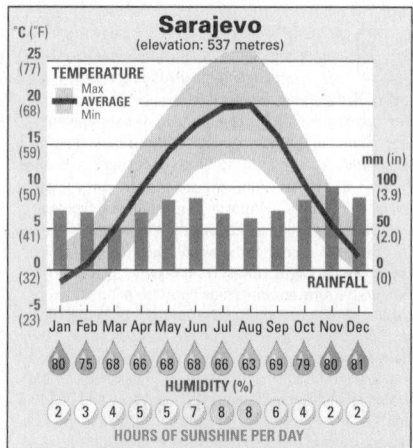

Communications

Telephone: Country code: 387. The national network of telecommunications is operated by *BH telecom* (website: www.telecom.ba).

Mobile telephone: Roaming agreements exist with some international mobile phone companies. Coverage is average.

Internet: Available in some towns. There are few Internet cafes; however, hotels might provide facilities.

Post: Post office hours: Generally Monday to Friday 1000-1700. Normal post takes approximately one week to reach its destination, while heavier packages could take up to 10 days. Coins, bank notes, precious metals and stones, narcotics, alcohol, firearms and ammunition are not permitted to be sent by mail.

MEDIA: Since the war in Bosnia & Herzegovina, the media is no longer steeped in propaganda, but it is still only partially free, with journalists under pressure from state bodies and political parties to somewhat censor their content. This is thanks to the 1995 Dayton Peace Accord efforts, although this has had limited success.

The most influential broadcasters are the public radio and TV stations operated by the Bosnian Muslim-Croat and Serb entities. A national public broadcasting service is now in development.

Press: The main newspaper for the Federation of Bosnia & Herzegovina, *Dnevni avaz*, is published in Sarajevo. Serbian newspapers include *Nezavisne novine*, published in Banja Luka. *Dnevni list* and the weekly *Hratska rijec* are Croatian-language papers, published in Banja Luka and Sarajevo, respectively.

TV: *Public Broadcasting Service of Bosnia Herzegovina* is a state-wide public broadcaster. *Mezra* and *Open Broadcast Network* are commercial broadcasters with near-national coverage. *Federation TV* operates two public networks within a Bosnia Muslim-Croat entity. *Serf Republic Radio-TV* is a public TV broadcaster of Bosnian Serb entity.

Radio: *Public Broadcasting Service of Bosnia Herzegovina* is a state-wide public broadcaster, operating *BH Radio 1*. *Radio FBiH* is a public radio service of Bosnian Muslim-Croat entity. *Serf Republic Radio TV* operates a public radio service of Bosnian Serb entity. *Bosanska Radio Mreza* is a private network, as are *BM Radio* (Zenica-based) and *Radio Stari Grad* (Sarajevo-based).

Passport/Visa

	Passport Required?	Visa Required?	Return Ticket Required?
Full British	Yes	No	Yes
Australian	Yes	No	Yes
Canadian	Yes	No	Yes
USA	Yes	No	Yes
Other EU	Yes	No	Yes
Japanese	Yes	No	Yes

Note: *Regulations and requirements may be subject to change at short notice, and you are advised to contact the appropriate diplomatic or consular authority before finalising travel arrangements. Any numbers in the chart refer to the footnotes below.*

PASSPORTS: Valid passport required by all except:
(a) holders of valid National Identity Cards issued to nationals of Austria, Belgium, Finland, France, Germany, Greece, Italy, Luxembourg, The Netherlands, Norway, Portugal, Spain and Sweden;
(b) nationals of Germany holding valid identity cards issued for minors called a *Kinderausweis*, with photo.
Restrictions: Bosnia & Herzegovina does not recognise passports issued by the Former Yugoslav Federation Republic (Serbia & Montenegro), which has a red cover.
VISAS: Required by all except the following for a stay of up to 90 days:
(a) nationals of countries referred to in the chart above;
(b) nationals of Andorra, Brunei, Croatia, Iceland, Korea (Rep), Kuwait, Liechtenstein, (Former Yugoslav Republic of) Macedonia, Malaysia, Monaco, New Zealand, Norway, Qatar, Russian Federation, San Marino, Serbia & Montenegro (not applicable for UNMIK passport holders), Switzerland, Turkey and Vatican City;
(c) nationals continuing their journey to a third country by the same or first connecting aircraft, holding onward tickets, onward documents and not leaving the airport.
Types of visa and cost: *Tourist*, *Business* and *Private*: £20 (single-entry); £36 (multiple-entry for up to 90 days); £45 (multiple-entry for more than 90 days).
Application to: Consulate (or Consular Section at Embassy); see *Passport/Visa Information*.
Application requirements: (a) Passport or official travel document valid for at least three months beyond the expiry date of the visa. (b) One completed application form. (c) Two passport-size photos. (d) Return/onward ticket. (e) Sufficient funds for duration of stay. *Tourist*: (a)-(e) and, (f) Copy of the invoice from tour operator. *Private*: (a)-(e) and, (f) Invitation letter from host, endorsed by the authorities. *Business*: (a)-(e) and, (f) Invitation letter from the host company in Bosnia & Herzegovina, endorsed by the Chamber of Commerce.
Note: Applicants from certain countries might have to submit evidence of cash assets (such as a recent bank statement), as well as evidence of a negative HIV test.
Working days required: Approximately three weeks, as all applications are now sent to Bosnia & Herzegovina for approval.
Temporary residence: Enquire at the Ministry of Interior in Bosnia & Herzegovina.

PASSPORT/VISA INFORMATION

Embassy of Bosnia & Herzegovina in the UK
5-7 Lexham Gardens, London W8 5JJ, UK
Tel: (020) 7373 0867.
Opening hours: Mon-Fri 0900-1700; Mon-Fri 1000-1300 (consular section, personal callers).

Embassy of Bosnia & Herzegovina in the USA
2109 E Street, NW, Washington, DC 20037, USA
Tel: (202) 337 1500 or 6473/6479 (consular section).
Website: www.bhembassy.org

Money

Currency: Bosnia and Herzegovina Konvertibilna Marka (BAM) = 100 pfeninga. Notes are in denominations of BAM200, 100, 50, 20, 10, 5 and 1 and 50 pfenings. Coins are available in denominations of BAM2 and 1, and 50, 20 and 10 pfenings. Some Euro notes - but not coins - are widely accepted.
Currency exchange: The Euro and US Dollar are the preferred foreign currencies. The Pound Sterling is of relatively little value in the republic and rarely used. Included in the Dayton Peace Agreement, signed in 1995, were provisions for a Central Bank of Bosnia and Herzegovina. This bank acts as a currency board and is the sole authority for the issue of the Bosnia and Herzegovina Konvertibilna Marka.
Credit & debit cards: Credit cards are not generally accepted. Check with your credit or debit card company for details of merchant acceptability. ATMs are available in some cities (in Sarajevo and Mostar, for example), and their quantity is continually increasing. Cash is still generally advised.
Traveller's cheques: Bosnia and Herzegovina is generally a cash-only economy and traveller's cheques are exchanged only at select banks.
Currency restrictions: The import and export of local currency are limited to BAM200,000. There are no restrictions on the import and export of foreign currencies.
Banking hours: Mon-Fri 0800-1900.
Exchange rate indicators:
Rate at time of publishing
£1.00= KM2.89
$1.00= KM1.60

Duty Free

The following goods may be imported into Bosnia & Herzegovina without incurring customs duty:
200 cigarettes or 20 cigars or 200g of tobacco; 1l of wine or spirits; one bottle of perfume; gifts to the value of €76.70.
Prohibited items: Works of art.

Public Holidays

Below are listed Public Holidays for the January 2006-June 2007 period.
2006: Jan 1 New Year's Day. **Jan 6-7** Orthodox Christmas. **Jan 14-15** Orthodox New Year. **Jan 27** St Sava's Day. **Feb 2** Kurban Bajram. **Mar 1** Independence Day. **Apr 14-17** Easter. **May 1** Labour Day. **Aug 15** Velika gospa (Western Christian Assumption). **Nov 1** All Saints' Day. **Nov 25** National Statehood Day. **Dec 25** Christmas.
2007: Jan 1 New Year's Day. **Jan 6-7** Orthodox Christmas. **Jan 14-15** Orthodox New Year. **Jan 27** St Sava's Day. **Feb 2** Kurban Bajram. **Mar 1** Independence Day. **Apr 6-9** Easter.
Note: In addition to the above dates, the Government of Bosnia & Herzegovina has decided to allow its citizens two working days per year to fulfil their religious needs. These days are not considered official holidays and the measure has been introduced to respect the religious and ethnic diversity of the country.

Health

	Special Precautions?	Certificate Required?
Yellow Fever	No	No
Cholera	No	No
Typhoid & Polio	1	No
Malaria	No	N/A

Note: *Regulations and requirements may be subject to change at short notice, and you are advised to contact your doctor well in advance of your intended date of departure. Any numbers in the chart refer to the footnotes below.*

1: Immunisation or tablets against typhoid and polio are recommended; immunisation against typhoid may be less important for short stays in first-class conditions.
Food & drink: Water is generally considered safe to drink, although bottled water is recommended. Local meat, poultry, seafood, fruit and vegetables are generally considered safe to eat, although it is advisable to peel vegetables and fruit and only eat cooked meat and fish, preferably served hot. Unpasteurised milk must be boiled. Avoid dairy products that are likely to have been made from unboiled milk.
Other risks: *Hepatitis A* occurs and vaccination is usually advised. Immunisation against *hepatitis B*, *diphtheria*, *tuberculosis* and *tick-borne encephalitis* is recommended. *Rabies* is present. For those at high risk, vaccination before arrival should be considered. If you are bitten, seek medical advice without delay. For more information, consult the *Health* appendix.
Health care: Facilities are limited, especially outside Sarajevo and other major towns. There is no reciprocal healthcare agreement for British nationals. All medical and dental care must be paid for in cash at the point of treatment. Tourists are strongly advised to take out full travel and medical insurance before travelling to Bosnia & Herzegovina.

Travel - International

AIR:
The national airline is *B&H Airlines (JA)*, which operates flights from Cologne/Bonn and Stuttgart (Germany), Istanbul and Izmir (Turkey), and Zurich (Switzerland) to Banja Luka, Mostar and Sarajevo.
Main airports: *Sarajevo (SJJ)* is the main international airport. *Banja Luka (BNX)* and *Mostar (OMO)* also receive a small number of international flights.
Departure tax: US$12. Transit passengers not leaving the airport transit area are exempt.
RAIL:
The railway system was badly damaged during the civil war but restoration is underway. Rail services link Sarajevo, Mostar, Doboj and Banja Luka to Zagreb, Belgrade, Ljubljana and Ploce. However, services are slow; the Sarajevo-Zagreb journey takes around nine hours.
ROAD:
Bosnia & Herzegovina's road network is still in the process of being reconstructed, following massive damage during the 1992-1995 civil war. It is possible to enter the country by car from Croatia. Green Cards are compulsory There are frequent bus services from Sarajevo to many Eastern and Central European cities, including London (website: www.eurolines.com).
Note: The border crossing from Croatia at Bosanski Brod is now open.

Travel - Internal

RAIL:
Rail links between Bosnia & Herzegovina and Republika Srpska have been restored. In addition, a few local services are operating.
ROAD:
Travel by road is the usual means of transport in Bosnia & Herzegovina. During winter and spring, block ice and landslides can make driving difficult. Road conditions are still poor, but many roads are now being restored. The safety and condition of urban roads is generally fair, although rural road maintenance is seriously lacking. The risk of landmines has decreased in the last few years, as most mines remaining from the war are now clearly marked. However, visitors are still advised to exercise caution when travelling outside main cities and towns. Caution should also be taken when driving at night or during winter. Drivers should keep to the main roads. The emergency number for roadside assistance is 987. The capital, Sarajevo, is the nodal point for all Bosnia & Herzegovina's main communications routes, which go west to Banja Luka, and then to Zagreb, capital of Croatia; north to Doboj, and then to Osijek in Croatia; east to Zvornik, and then to Belgrade in Serbia & Montenegro; south to Mostar, and then the Adriatic Sea; and southeast to Foca, and then to Podgorica (formerly Titograd). **Documentation:** An International Driving Permit is required. All Green Cards, etc, should include cover for the 20km-strip of coastline at Neum on the Dalmatian Coast highway.

Travel Advice

Unexploded landmines remain a real danger and travellers should be careful not to stray from roads and paved areas. All public demonstrations or gatherings must be eschewed. Visitors should also be aware of the global risk of indiscriminate international terrorist attacks, which could be against civilian targets, including places frequented by foreigners.
This advice is based on information provided by the Foreign and Commonwealth Office in the UK. It is correct at time of publishing. As the situation can change rapidly, visitors are advised to contact the following organisations for the latest travel advice:

British Foreign and Commonwealth Office
Tel: (0845) 850 2829.
Website: www.fco.gov.uk

US Department of State
Website: http://travel.state.gov/travel

Accommodation

HOTELS:
There are a number of national and international hotels, particularly in Sarajevo and the major cities.
BED & BREAKFAST/GUEST HOUSES:
These are also available.

Top Things To See

- The reconstruction of **Mostar**, once a prime tourist destination, is an ongoing process, but the town is still worth seeing. Although most of the town's monuments were destroyed in the war, including all the 16th- and 17th-century mosques and the famous Turkish bridge, a few medieval buildings and cobbled streets survived the war completely. Also, there is something moving about watching restoration in progress: the ancient bridge was recently rebuilt and opened in mid-2004 to the public. Stone roofs huddle together in Mostar, and the ambience is one of calm resolve.
- See the most western Muslim settlement in Europe in the **Bihac** pocket in northwestern Bosnia & Herzegovina, close to Croatia. For further Muslim beauty, view the **Fethija Mosque** in central Bihac, one of the very few old mosques not to have been destroyed during the war, dating back to the 13th century, and with its church-origins exposed by the building's gothic-esque traces.
- For a bit of sea, head to the short stretch of coast that belongs to Bosnia & Herzegovina, in which **Neum** is a functional spot, with gorgeous waters.
- Enter into the **Ostrozac Castle**, partly still in ruins, but offering lovely gardens, welcome privacy and a wonderful view out over the Una river valley.
- Gaze at one of the most important shrines in Catholicism:

A B C D E F G H I J K L M N O P Q R S T U V W X Y Z

the **Medjugorje** is in the southeast of Bosnia &
Herzegovina, and it is here where many claim to have
seen apparitions of the Virgin Mary.
- Look at one of the most beautiful rivers in the country,
the **river Una**, which cascades into the town of **Jajce**.
- Regard how 500 years of Turkish rule have left their trace
on Bosnia & Herzegovina's capital, **Sarajevo**. The Turkish
quarter and the town centre have been largely rebuilt and
the city, although scarred by war, is coming back to life.
The colourful **bazaars** are testament to the city's
Ottoman heritage and present-day energy.
- See what is is alleged to contain hairs from Muhammad's
beard: the **many-coloured mosque** near the base of **ul
Hendek**.
- Go to **Banja Luka**, the capital of the Republika Srpska,
and behold its **16th-century fort** and **amphitheatre**.

Top Things To Do

- Listen to the sad and beautiful strains of Bosnian folk
songs, **sevdah**.
- Although some are still not open to skiing, there is plenty
of sumptuous scenery and pampering on offer in
mountain health **spa resorts** such as Bjelasnica, Igman
and Jahorina. There are also several spas in the Republika
Srpska area, most of which are operating again. Dubica,
Laktasi, Srebrenica, Telic and Visegrad all have natural
mineral springs and medical facilities.
- **Fishing** is unrestricted on the coast. For rivers and lakes, a
special permit (which can be issued by hotels and regional
authorities) is needed, with regulations differing in
individual regions.
- Attend the **Winter Festival** in Sarajevo (usually held in
February/March), which is an arts festival established long
before the war in the 1980s and, indeed, was
determinedly held every year during the siege (the festival
is usually bi-annual). The festival is a two-month
celebration of worldwide talent and is a symbol and
celebration of creativity and freedom within diverse
cultures (website: www.sarajevskazima.ba).
- Take a **road trip** through Bosnia's spectacular mountain
scenery, enhanced by algae-brightened rivers, waterfalls
and canyons.
- In some regions around Bihac, it is possible to go **rafting**
and **kayaking**: the River Una in particular is renowned for
its clear, blue waters.
- The **Sarajevo Film Festival** (website: www.sff.ba) is the
most popular of all of Sarajevo's festivals. The festival
showcases films from mostly neighbouring countries,
often neglected in terms of press, but who consistently
produce films of an excellent artistic standard. Any visitor
in Sarajevo in August would be a fool to miss it.

TOURIST INFORMATION

Ministry of Foreign Affairs
Musala 2, Sarajevo, Bosnia & Herzegovina
Tel: (33) 281 100.
Website: www.mvp.gov.ba
There is limited tourist information available.

Entertainment

FOOD & DRINK: The traditional cuisine of the region
includes obvious Turkish influences, with lots of meat
dishes.
National specialities:
- *Bosanski lonac* (Bosnian meat and vegetable stew).
- *Lokum* (Turkish delight).
- *Halva* (crushed sesame seeds in honey).
- *Cevapcici* are sausages that are popular, as are
hamburger-like patties called *pleskavica*, served with pita
bread.
- *Burek* (filled pastries).
- *Baklava* is a popular dessert – sweet nuts and honey in
pastry.

National drinks:
- Brandy is very popular, especially the homemade plum
brandy called *rakija*.
- Turkish-style coffee and yogurt drinks are prevalent.
Legal drinking age: 18.
Tipping: Tipping is customary for taxis, as well as in hotels
and restaurants; the bill is often rounded up.
NIGHTLIFE: Bosnia & Herzegovina's nightlife, particularly
in Sarajevo, is widely reputed to be excellent. In the capital,
the cosmopolitan atmosphere is tangible. The city apparently
has more cafes per capita than any other European city and a
relaxed cafe culture is prominent. There are many opportunities
for nightlife activities, from cinemas and clubs to opera and
theatre performance. There are also frequent festivals,
showcasing such popular pastimes as jazz and film.
SHOPPING: Traditional purchases include woodcarvings,
brass coffee-pots, ceramics, handmade carpets, woollen
goods, wines, folk-art, tapestries, embroidery and leather
boxes. **Shopping hours:** 0800-2000.

Business

- **GDP:** US$7 billion.
- **Main exports:** Wood and paper and metal products.
- **Main imports:** Machinery and equipment,
chemicals, fuels and foodstuffs.
- **Main trade partners:** Croatia, Germany, Italy,
Austria, Slovenia and Hungary.

ECONOMY: The collapse of the internal Yugoslav market
at the beginning of the 1990s placed the Bosnian economy
in serious difficulty, especially as it relied heavily on the sale
of its agricultural produce and mineral ores to the rest of
the Yugoslav federation. The main agricultural products are
tobacco and fruit; livestock rearing is also important. There
are extensive mineral resources, particularly of copper, lead,
zinc and gold, plus iron ore and lignite coal. The civil war
that broke out in 1992 then brought the economy to a
virtual standstill. Reconstruction was backed by
international aid of US$5 billion. Although the division of
the economy between two jurisdictions has made economic
policy-making difficult, the Bosnian economy as a whole
recorded exceptional growth during the 1990s (at some
stages, exceeding 30 per cent annually). A central bank has
been set up and a common currency, Konvertibilna Marka
(fixed in value to the Euro), successfully introduced.
Initially, most of the post-war international aid was directed
to the Muslim-Croat region. The *Republika Srpska* managed
to get much of its industrial sector working again but relied
heavily on the support of Yugoslavia. The war between
NATO and Yugoslavia in the late 1990s thus set the Bosnian
Serb economy back once again. Since then, the central
Government has received a series of loans, totalling
approximately US$250 million, from the IMF. Bosnia has
begun a slow transformation to a market economy. The
Government is hoping that opening up the economy will
attract both inward investment and, equally important, the
return of the country's skilled and professional workforce –
most of whom have been living in exile since the war.

COMMERCIAL INFORMATION

Foreign Trade Chamber of Bosnia & Herzegovina
Branislava Djurdjeva 10, Sarajevo,
Bosnia & Herzegovina
Tel: (33) 663 631
Website: www.komorabih.com

Central Bank of Bosnia & Herzegovina
Marsala Tita 25, 71000 Sarajevo,
Bosnia & Herzegovina
Tel: (33) 278 100.
Website: www.cbbh.gov.ba

Botswana

Location: Central southern Africa.

Time: GMT + 2.

Overview

Botswana is a vast land, highly prized for its safaris and
game. If what you are seeking is big expanse dappled with
roaming wildlife, then this is the destination of your
dreams.
Indeed, Botswana is a country that you feel is keen to
conserve what makes it beautiful and utilise its assets.
Astonishingly, around 17 per cent of the country is
designated national park, and when Botswana's huge
private concessions are also toted up, the figure swells to a
proud 40 per cent. This is one of the largest percentage
bestowed to wildlife worldwide, and explains why – in some
parts – there are nearly as many tourists craning their necks
out of jeeps as there is roving game. Furthermore, Botswana
has ensured that its spectacular Delta region has been well-
developed touristically, with its impressive lagoons
crammed with hovering birdlife, and elephants, giraffes and
other exotic animals that happily amble through its vast
grass flats. Incidentally, this is the largest inland delta in the
world, which explains its wealth of wildlife. It is almost
enough to make you forget that most of Botswana is given
over to desert.
Botswana was also once an economic wasteland. The
country gained independence in 1966, having been a British
Protectorate, and at this time it was amongst the poorest
nations in the world. Nature was then kind to Botswana,
when once again natural assets became apparent, ready to
be exploited. The Government discovered diamonds and
Botswana has enjoyed a growth rate that still continues to
soar, especially when put into a context with much of the
rest of Africa.
Despite this success story, Botswana is afflicted by
controversy. There have been claims that parts of the
Kalahari Desert Region have been closed at the expense of
the world's last few remaining Ancient people, the
Bushmen, who roam this area. The Bushmen's previously
nomadic lifestyle has mostly been quashed and they now
reside in settlements. There is also the HIV/AIDS pandemic
to contend with – Botswana's infection rate is amongst the
world's highest, with 20 per cent of the country's
population being estimated to have contracted the virus.
Nevertheless, these are issues that do not seem to worry

Botswana's wildlife. For them, the struggle to survive beneath a great span of star-stuffed sky carries on, regardless. Having a sundowner, unwinding in the glare of a sunset and hearing the sounds of singing birds and roaming game, it is easy to forget global troubles. Botswana is both a country to relax in and a country to have adventure in. When you are riding on the back of an elephant, game walking or sailing in a hot-air balloon, you will feel as wild as the game you are seeking.

General Information

AREA: 581,730 sq km (224,607 sq miles).
POPULATION: 1.64 million (estimate 2005).
POPULATION DENSITY: 2.9 per sq km.
CAPITAL: Gaborone. **Population:** 208,411 (estimate 2005).
GEOGRAPHY: Botswana is bordered to the south and east by South Africa, to the northeast by Zimbabwe, to the north and west by Namibia and touches Zambia just west of the Victoria Falls. The tableland of the Kalahari Desert covers most of Botswana. National parks cover 17 per cent of the country, with 38 per cent of the country dedicated to wildlife areas. To the northwest is the Okavango Delta, the largest inland delta in the world. The Moremi Game Reserve occupies two-thirds of the delta's area. The Chobe National Park in the north includes the Savute and Linyanti regions. To the far southwest is the Kgalagadi Transfrontier National Park, which ranges across the borders of Botswana, South Africa and Namibia, but is managed as a single entity. The majority of the population lives in the southeast around Gaborone, Serowe and Kanye along the South African border. The vast arid sandveld of the Kalahari occupies much of north, central and western Botswana. The seasonal rains bring a considerable difference to the vegetation, especially in the Makgadikgadi Pans and the Okavango Delta in the north. The latter, after the winter floods, provides one of the wildest and most beautiful nature reserves in Africa.
GOVERNMENT: Republic since 1966. **Head of State and Government:** President Festus Gontebanye Mogae since 1998. **Recent history:** The Botswana Democratic Party (BDP) has dominated the country's politics since independence, having won all six sets of national elections since then. The latest of these was in October 2004 at which Festus Mogae won the BDP a new five-year term by a landslide majority. The main opposition party, the Botswana National Front (BNF), has made substantial progress against the BDP at local level – especially in urban areas – but the BDP's overwhelming support in rural areas ensures its continuing rule. The government's main domestic priority is to tackle the HIV/AIDS pandemic. Botswana's infection rate, estimated at 20 per cent of the total population, is among the world's highest. Abroad, Botswana has benefited both politically and economically from the advent of democratic government in Pretoria. Relations with its other neighbours are normally cordial, although Botswana is beginning to feel the effects of the disintegration of neighbouring Zimbabwe, mainly in the form of thousands of migrants who have turned to Botswana to escape food shortages and political repression.
The National Assembly is the country's legislature and serves a five-year term. Forty of the 47 members are popularly elected; four others are co-opted by the elected members; two others serve ex-officio; the Speaker makes up the full complement. The Assembly appoints a President, who holds executive power and appoints a Cabinet. The House of Chiefs also serves as an important advisory body to the president.
LANGUAGE: English is the official language. Setswana is the national language, with minorities speaking Kalanga and Sekgalagadi.
RELIGION: A significant proportion of the population holds animistic beliefs, although the 2001 census showed that 71 per cent claimed to be Christians. There are small Muslim communities and the Bahá'í Faith is also represented.
ELECTRICITY: 220-240 volts AC, 50Hz. 15- and 13-amp plug sockets are in use.
SOCIAL CONVENTIONS: As most people in Botswana follow their traditional pattern of life, visitors should be sensitive to customs which will inevitably be unfamiliar to them. Outside urban areas, people may well not be used to visitors. Casual clothing is acceptable and, in urban centres, normal courtesies should be observed.
Photography: Airports, official residences and defence establishments should not be photographed. Permission should be obtained to photograph local people.

Climate

Mainly temperate climate. Summer, between October and April, is very hot and combined with the rainy season. Dry and cooler weather exists between May and September with an average temperature of 25ºC (77º). Early mornings and evenings may be cold and frosty in winter. Annual rainfall decreases westwards and southwards.

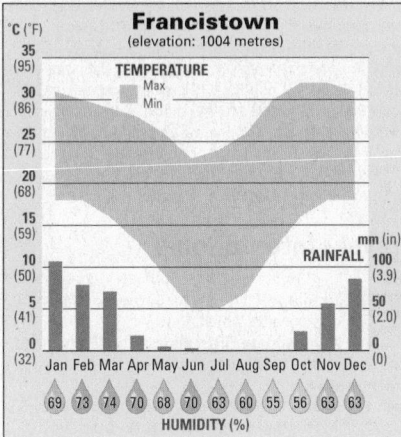

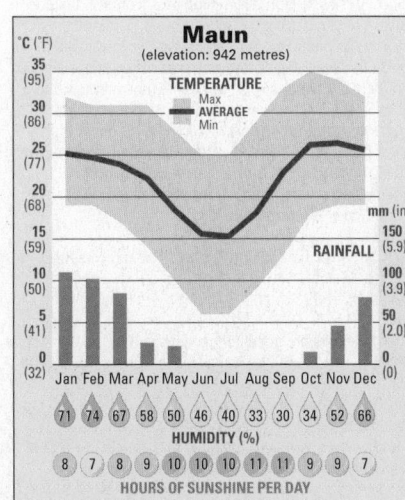

Communications

Telephone: IDD is available to over 80 countries. Country code: 267. There are very few public phone boxes.
Mobile telephone: Roaming agreements exist with a few international mobile phone companies. Coverage is average.
Internet: Available in large cities and resorts.
Post: There are post offices in all towns and the larger villages. Post office hours: Weekdays 0815-1245 and 1400-1600; Sat 0800-1100. Services are slow but cheap. Airmail service to Europe takes from one to three weeks. There are post offices in all the main towns, although there are no deliveries and post must be collected from boxes.
MEDIA: There are claims that there are government limits on ability to broadcast freely on the radio but, overall, Botswana welcomes public debate and freedom of expression, as its constitution dictates. State-run television did not appear until 2000 but radio tends to have more dominance as a medium. Printed media are mostly limited to major cities and towns.
Press: The daily newspaper is the *Dikgang tsa Gompieno* (*Botswana Daily News*), published in Setswana and English. Other English-language newspapers include *The Botswana Gazette*, *The Botswana Guardian* (Sundays only), *The Midweek Sun* and *Mmegi* (*The Reporter*), all published weekly.
TV: Botswana TV emerged in 2000 and is a state-run broadcaster. *Gaborone Television* is a privately run broadcaster.
Radio: *Radio Botswana* is state-run and broadcasts in both English and Setswana. *Gabz FM* and *Ya Rona FM* are both privately run. *Radio Botswana 2* is commercial-run but limited to Gaborone.

Passport/Visa

	Passport Required?	Visa Required?	Return Ticket Required?
Full British	Yes	No	Yes
Australian	Yes	No	Yes
Canadian	Yes	No	Yes
USA	Yes	No	Yes
Other EU	Yes	1	Yes
Japanese	Yes	No	Yes

Note: *Regulations and requirements may be subject to change at short notice, and you are advised to contact the appropriate diplomatic or consular authority before finalising travel arrangements. Any numbers in the chart refer to the footnotes below.*

PASSPORTS: Passports valid for at least six months required by all.
VISAS: Required by all except the following for stays of up to 90 days:
(a) nationals referred to in the chart above (except **1.** nationals of Czech Republic, Estonia, Hungary, Latvia, Lithuania, Poland, Slovak Republic and Slovenia, who *do* need a visa);
(b) nationals of Commonwealth countries (except nationals of Antigua & Barbuda, Bangladesh, Brunei, Cameroon, Dominica, Ghana, India, Kiribati, The Maldives, Nigeria, Pakistan, St Kitts & Nevis, St Lucia, St Vincent & the Grenadines, Sri Lanka, Tuvalu and Vanuatu who *do* need a visa);
(c) nationals of Hong Kong (SAR), Iceland, Liechtenstein, Norway, San Marino, Serbia & Montenegro, Switzerland and Uruguay and Zimbabwe;
(d) transit passengers provided continuing their journey by the same or first connecting aircraft and not leaving the airport.
Types of visa and cost: *General Entry*: £60 (single- or multiple-entry).
Validity: Maximum of 90 days from the date of issue.
Application to: Consulate (or Consular Section at Embassy or High Commission); see *Passport/Visa Information*.
Application requirements: (a) Two completed application forms. (b) Two recent colour passport-size photos. (c) Passport valid for at least six months, with at least one blank page. (d) Fee (cash or postal order only). (e) Tourists must be able to produce evidence of their itinerary in Botswana. (f) Letter of invitation or letter of offer of employment if travelling on business.
Working days required: One to three.
Temporary residence: Anyone wishing to stay for more than 90 days should contact the Immigration and Passport Control Officer, PO Box 942, Gaborone.

PASSPORT/VISA INFORMATION

Botswana High Commission in the UK
6 Stratford Place, London W1C 1AY, UK
Tel: (020) 7499 0031 *or* 7647 1000 *or* (09065) 508 954 (recorded visa information; calls cost £1 per minute). Opening hours: Mon-Fri 0900-1300 and 1400-1700.

Embassy of the Republic of Botswana in the USA
1531-33 New Hampshire Avenue, NW, Washington, DC 20036, USA
Tel: (202) 244 4990.
Website: www.botswanaembassy.org

Money

Currency: Pula (P) = 100 thebe. Notes are in denominations of P100, 50, 20 and 10. Coins are in denominations of P5, 2 and 1, and 50, 25, 10 and 5 thebe. Various gold and silver coins were issued to mark the country's 10th anniversary of independence, and are still legal tender.

Currency exchange: Money should be exchanged in banks at market rates. There are four main commercial banks in the country (Barclays Bank of Botswana, First National Bank, Stanbic Bank Botswana and Standard Charted Bank) with branches in major towns and villages. Owing to limited facilities in small villages, it is advisable to change money at the airport or in major towns, where credit card cash advances may also be available. There are also Exchange Bureaux at major border posts.

Credit & debit cards: American Express, Diners Club, MasterCard and Visa are widely accepted. Check with your credit or debit card company for details of merchant acceptability and other services which may be available.

Traveller's cheques: To avoid additional exchange rate charges, travellers are advised to take traveller's cheques in US Dollars or Pounds Sterling. Traveller's cheques are accepted in large cities but with a high surcharge.

Currency restrictions: There are no restrictions on the import of local or foreign currencies, provided declared on arrival. Export of local currency is limited to P50 and foreign currencies up to amount declared on arrival.

Banking hours: Mon-Fri 0900-1530; Sat 0815-1045. Most banks work these core hours with occasional regional differences.

Exchange rate indicators:
Rate at time of publishing
£1.00=   P9.78
$1.00=   P5.39

Duty Free

The following goods may be imported into Botswana without incurring customs duty:
400 cigarettes and 50 cigars and 250g of tobacco; 2l of wine and 1l of spirits; 50ml of perfume and 250ml of eau de toilette; goods up to the value of P500.

Public Holidays

Below are listed Public Holidays for the January 2006-June 2007 period.
2006: Jan 1 New Year. **Apr 14-17** Easter. **May 1** Labour Day. **May 25** Ascension Day. **Jul 1** Sir Seretse Khama Day. **Jul 15-16** President's Day. **Sep 30** Botswana Day. **Dec 25-26** Christmas.
2007: Jan 1 New Year. **Apr 6-9** Easter. **May 1** Labour Day. **May 17** Ascension Day.

Health

	Special Precautions?	Certificate Required?
Yellow Fever	No	3
Cholera	No	No
Typhoid & Polio	1	N/A
Malaria	2	N/A

Note: *Regulations and requirements may be subject to change at short notice, and you are advised to contact your doctor well in advance of your intended date of departure. Any numbers in the chart refer to the footnotes below.*

1: Risk of *typhoid* fever exists throughout the region, especially if travelling outside cities. Botswana is practically free of *poliomyelitis*.
2: *Malaria* risk exists from November to May/June in the northern part of the country (Boteti, Chobe, Ngamiland, Okavango and Tutume districts/subdistricts), predominantly in the malignant *falciparum* form. Some of the *falciparum*-related cases have been reported as chloroquine-resistant; in which case, the recommended prophylaxis in risk areas is mefloquine.
3: A *yellow fever* vaccination certificate is required from all travellers over one year of age travelling from infected areas.
Food & drink: Tap water is considered safe to drink, although drinking water outside main cities and towns may be contaminated and sterilisation is advisable. Mineral water is available in most tourist centres. Milk is pasteurised and dairy products are safe for consumption. Local meat, poultry, seafood, fruit and vegetables are generally considered safe to eat.
Other risks: *Hepatitis A, C* and *TB* occur. *Hepatitis B* is hyperendemic. *Bilharzia (schistosomiasis)* is endemic. Avoid swimming and paddling in fresh water; swimming pools which are well chlorinated and maintained are safe. *Trypanosomiasis* (sleeping sickness) is transmitted by tsetse flies in the Moremi Wildlife Reserve, Ngamiland and western parts of the Chobe National Park. Protective

clothing and insect repellent are recommended. *Tick-bite fever* can be a problem when walking in the bush. It is advisable to wear loose-fitting clothes and to search the body for ticks. The disease may be treated with tetracycline, though pregnant women and children under eight years of age should not take this medicine. Natural foci of *plague* have been reported. In recent years, there has been a high prevalence of *HIV/AIDS* cases detected. Visitors should therefore take necessary precautions.
Rabies is present in animals. For those at high risk, vaccination before arrival should be considered. If you are bitten, seek medical advice without delay. For more information, consult the *Health* appendix.
Health care: The dust and heat may cause problems for asthmatics and people with allergies to dust. Those with sensitive skin should take precautions. Botswana's altitude, 1000m (3300ft) above sea level, reduces the filtering effect of the atmosphere. Hats and sunscreen are advised. The public health system is made up of 23 district health teams, three referral hospitals (Francistown, Gaborone and Lobatse), 12 district hopsitals, 17 primary hospitals, 222 clinics, 330 health posts and 740 mobile stops. All main towns have chemists, and pharmaceutical supplies are readily available. Health insurance is essential. There is a government medical scheme and medicines supplied by government hospitals are free.

Travel - International

AIR:

The national airline is *Air Botswana (BP)* which only operates within Africa.
Approximate flight times: From Gaborone to *London* is 15 hours (including stopovers).
Departure tax: None.
Main airports: *Sir Seretse Khama International (GBE)* is 15km (9 miles) northwest of Gaborone. *To/from the airport:* There are no regular bus services to and from the airport but several hotels run minibuses (combis). Taxis are available to the city centre (travel time – 15 minutes). *Facilities:* Left luggage, bank (*Barclays Bank* available for all flights), bar, snack bar, restaurant, post office, shops and car hire. There is a major airport at Kasane (north Botswana) and at Selebi-Phikwe, which take international flights. *Maun International Airport (MUB)* receives direct flights from Johannesburg, Windhoek and Gaborone. This gateway to the Okavango Delta is served by *Air Botswana, Air Namibia* and several charters. For information on charters, see the *Travel – Internal* section.

RIVER:

A car ferry operates across the Zambezi River to Zambia.

RAIL:

There are good connections between South Africa and Botswana (Johannesburg–Mafikeng–Ramatlhabama–Gaborone) and Botswana and Zimbabwe (Gaborone–Francistown–Bulawayo–Harare). From Gaborone to Bulawayo takes 20 hours; passengers are advised to take their own food and drink as the buffet has a limited range. There are three classes, and sleeping compartments are available. First-class cars have comfortable reclining seats. Complicated formalities may be necessary for crossing the border from Zimbabwe and to or from South Africa, where the South African Customs Union agreement is in operation. Botswana has assisted in the construction of the Limpopo line from Zimbabwe to Mozambique, an act which will speed up the availability of alternative routes into Botswana. Other plans include extending the network into Namibia.

ROAD:

There are reasonable roads running roughly along the same routes as the railway, linking Botswana with South Africa and Zimbabwe. There is also road access from Namibia. **Bus:** Services are available from Namibia and Zimbabwe. Frequent services also operate between Gaborone and Johannesburg.

Travel - Internal

AIR:

Major areas of the country are linked by air. There are airports in Francistown, Ghanzi, Jwaneny, Kasane, Maun, Pont Drift and Selebi-Phikwe. Many visitors use charter companies based in Maun to fly to the various lodges in Botswana. These include *Delta Air, Mack Air, Moremi Air Services, Northern Air, Sefofane* and *Wildlife Helicopters. Kalahari Air Services* offers charters within Botswana and to Lesotho, Namibia, South Africa, Swaziland, Zambia and Zimbabwe.

RAIL:

The main railway line runs between Ramatlhabama and Francistown. Work on upgrading and extending the rail network continues. In Botswana, children under seven travel free and children aged seven to 11 pay half fare.

ROAD:

Botswana has good tarmac roads on the following routes: running from south to north from Lobatse to Francistown up to Ramokgwebana and from Lobatse to Jwaneng; running from Francistown to Kazungula via Nata. There are over 2500km (1500 miles) of bitumised roads in the country. Others are either gravel or sand tracks. Visitors should be careful as many drivers ignore safety rules. There are plans to construct a road network with more major highways. Reserve fuel and at least 20l of water, plus emergency supplies, should always be carried on journeys into more remote areas, and visitors are advised to make careful enquiries before setting out. Wildlife and stray livestock may occasionally pose a hazard, especially in more remote areas. **Bus:** There are bus services between Gaborone and Francistown, and from Francistown to Nata and Maun. Buses from Francistown to Maun run every day. The journey takes about six hours. Timetables can be obtained from bus operators. **Taxi:** There is a taxi service in all major towns, and it is generally safe. Prices should, however, be agreed before embarking on a journey. **Car hire:** Services are available in Gaborone, Francistown or Maun. 4-wheel-drive vehicles are necessary in many areas. *Toyota Double Cabs* are particularly recommended. **Regulations:** Traffic drives on the left and seat belts must be worn. It is advisable to keep the petrol tank at least half full as distances between towns can be long. There is a speed limit of 120kph (75mph) outside built-up areas, and about 60kph (37mph) in built-up areas. Speed limits are strongly enforced with high fines.
Documentation: An International Driving Permit is not legally required, but is recommended for stays of up to six months, but a European licence valid for six months after arrival will also usually suffice; thereafter, a Botswana driving licence must be obtained, which will be issued without a test if a valid British licence is produced.

URBAN:

Public transport within towns consists of share-taxis or minibus services operating at controlled flat fares. Exclusive use of taxis is sometimes available at a higher charge although fares should always be agreed before setting off.
Travel times: The following chart gives approximate travel times from **Gaborone** (in hours and minutes) to other major cities and towns in Botswana.

	Air	Road	Rail
Francistown	0.50	5.00	6.35
Lobatse	0.20	0.45	1.50
Kasane	2.50	13.30	-
Tshabong	2.00	15.00	-
Ghanzi	1.25	11.00	-

Travel Advice

Most visits to Botswana are trouble-free but you should be aware of the global risk of indiscriminate international terrorist attacks, which could be against civilian targets, including places frequented by foreigners.
This advice is based on information provided by the Foreign and Commonwealth Office in the UK. It is correct at time of publishing. As the situation can change rapidly, visitors are advised to contact the following organisations for the latest travel advice:

British Foreign and Commonwealth Office
Tel: (0845) 850 2829.
Website: www.fco.gov.uk

US Department of State
Website: http://travel.state.gov/travel

Accommodation

EDITOR'S CHOICE: SAFARI LODGES & CAMPS

The majority of the safari lodges are found in the Chobe National Park, Moremi Game Reserve and Okavango Delta and there are a few lodges and camps in the Makgadikgadi Pans and Tuli Block. Standards are generally high, with luxury and comfort being the order of the day. Some lodges are permanent structures but the majority are tented. The tents are luxurious and spacious with ensuite facilities. Most lodges only accommodate between 10 and 28 people so the emphasis is on personalised service. Along the banks of the Chobe river near Kasane, there are also luxury hotels and lodges. It is recommended to spend at least two nights at each lodge and do a circuit of the various tourist regions in the country. Charter flights on six-seater planes are the standard means of transfer. Visitors can also do a mobile safari, camping in a variety of different regions. Standards vary from simple to luxurious.

HOTELS:
Although there is no grading system, all hotels generally maintain a reasonable standard, particularly those in main centres in the east of the country. The largest number of hotels and motels are in or near Gaborone, Francistown, Kasane and Maun, some with air conditioning, swimming pools and facilities for films, bands and entertainment. Many other hotels have fairly basic amenities. A booklet entitled *Where To Stay In Botswana*, giving details of prices and facilities, may be obtained from the Department of Tourism (see *Top Things To Do*).

CAMPING:
There are campsites at Chobe National Park, Makgadikgadi Pans National Park, Moremi Game Reserve and Nxai Pan National Park. These campsites need to be pre-booked with the Department of Wildlife and National Parks. Permission should be sought before camping on private land. Grass fires should not be started, and all litter should be buried or removed. The presence of lions and other dangerous animals in all the National Parks and Game Reserves as well as in some of the more remote areas makes it advisable to exercise extreme care, such as keeping tents zipped up and not walking around at night. It is not permitted to leave your vehicle in a national park or game reserve unless in a designated camping or picnic area.

ACCOMMODATION INFORMATION

The Hotel and Tourism Association of Botswana (HATAB)
Private Bag 00423, Gaborone, Bostwana
Tel: 395 7144 *or* 6498.
E-mail: hatab@info.bw

Top Things To See

- See the many **craftworks** on offer in the capital, **Gaborone**, situated in the southeast of the country. There are markets galore from which to hunt down pottery, basketwork, leatherwork and handwoven objects. There is also an excellent National Museum with natural history and ethnological exhibitions. See scores of grass-lurking animals: antelopes at the 600-hectare **Gaborone Game Reserve**, the 3000-hectare **Mokolodi Nature Reserve** and the **Okavango Delta**; zebras within the sands of the **Makgadikgadi Pans** and Okavango Delta; and giraffes in the Okavango Delta and **Khutse Game Reserve**. Cautiously watch lions laze (in the **Moremi** and Khutse Game Reserve) and leopards stalk (in the Khutse Game Reserve). Steer clear of charging buffalo in Moremi Game Reserve and **Chobe National Park**; the rare brown hyena in Khutse Game Reserve and the **Kgalagadi Transfrontier National Park**; and small numbers of white rhino at the Mokolodi Nature Reserve, plus all of Botswana's rhino collection, gathered to protect them from poachers, at the **Khama Rhino Sanctuary** in **Serowe**.
- Gaze at the delights that occupy Botswana's low-lying rivers and deltas. Hippos are strewn along the **Chobe River**, in the Moremi Game Reserve and in the Okavango Delta - be wary of crocodiles in the Okavango Delta, too! And the sands of the **Makgadikgadi Pans** gleam white with salt in the dry season and transform into a shimmering lake in the rainy season, which heralds the must-see sight of thousands of brilliant pink flamingos paddling in the brine.
- Watch **baboons** playing in scattered rocky kopjes in the **Savuti** area, which marks the northern shore of what was once the giant superlake that covered most of Botswana.
- Espy **Bushmen** (*San* or *Basarwa*), one of the last Stone Age races on earth, said to have populated these parts for roughly 20,000 years. Their nomadic lifestyle of past has seemingly dwindled and now the Bushmen tend to live in settlements. In the **Tsodilo Hills**, four granite ridged hills (Male, Female and Child Hills, plus a fourth, unnamed and said to be the first discarded wife) are considered to be a sacred site by the Bushmen, who regard them as the final resting place of the dead and the home of the gods. Known to have been inhabited for at least 100,000 years, they have been decorated with around 4000 rock paintings, mostly portraying animal life; the eldest of the paintings is believed to date back more than 4000 years. In the Khutse Game Reserve, some Bushmen even serve as guides and teach visitors about the environment. The **Central Kalahari Game Reserve** is also a remote and virtually unexplored reserve specifically set up as a refuge both for animals and the country's few remaining Bushmen, although the removal of Bushmen by Botswana's Government is dogged by constant controversy. The terrain is very varied here, with open plains, salt pans, sand dunes, mopane scrub, bushveld and woodland.
- Look out for a dazzling array of rare and wonderful birds in the **Okavango Delta** and in the **Tuli Block**.
- Pay your respects at the **Khama III Memorial Museum** at the base of **Serowe Hill**, the birthplace of Botswana's charismatic first President, Sir Seretse Khama, who is buried in the local graveyard. On Khama III's grave (Sir Seretse's grandfather) is a bronze duiker sculpted by the famous South African artist Anton van Wouw.
- Gaze at the pot pourri of rocks, varying in age from 2700 million to 3700 million years old, that make up the incredible scenery of the Tuli Block. It has a patchwork of private game ranches and is quite different to anywhere else in Botswana, with ruggedly beautiful countryside and giant, shallow salt lakes in the **Nxai Pan National Park** that break the flatness of the countryside.
- For the chance of watching a large, beautiful elephant waddling towards you, go to the **Chobe National Park**, which boasts the highest elephant population in the world, with an estimated 45,000 to 90,000 elephants. Elephants can move in their thousands along the well-worn paths of the Chobe River every afternoon to drink. The tourists, like the elephants, all tend to congregate in a narrow, 20km (12 mile) strip in the north of the park, doing game drives from the lodges in Kasane. These elephants have the distinction of being the largest in body size of all living elephants.
- See the greatest inland **delta system** in the world in the **Kgalagadi** (or **Kalahari**) **Desert**, an extremely beautiful region covering an area of about 15,000 sq km (5600 sq miles) and composed of vast grass flats, low tree-covered ridges and a widespread network of narrow waterways opening into lagoons. The thick reeds and grasses that thrive in these waters make much of the delta section impenetrable except by dug-out canoe (*mokoro*), which is the local people's traditional form of transport. Most of the land in the delta is carved up into giant private concessions, scattered by luxury lodges and camps. Bizarrely, with the channels and lagoons shifting every season, these lodges, as the only permanent landmarks, have become an integral part of mapping and navigating in the Delta.
- Glance at beautiful stalactites in the **Gcwihaba Caverns**, about 240km (150 miles) from **Tsau**.
- See for yourself what is to be the first of a number of '**peace parks**' planned to cross national boundaries and re-open ancient animal migration routes, at the Kgalagadi Transfrontier National Park, which straddles the border with South Africa. The park has deep fossil river beds and high sand dunes, and the area is also known for its salt pans which reflect amazing colour changes during the day.

Top Things To Do

- Have a *sundowner*: sip a cool drink, be entertained by your lodge (if applicable) and watch a beautiful sun set into a large, flat expanse.
- Go on a **game walk** - though beware, this is not for the faint-hearted. Guides will ensure you do not get too close to the more dangerous animals, but there is nothing like the shadows of reeds and bushes to convince you that you have spotted a bloodthirsty buffalo! Once you have swallowed your fears, a game walk is an exhilarating experience, getting closer to game that you would normally do so.
- **Climb on the back of an elephant** for a safari trek to remember: see semi-habituated herb absorbed in their daily foraging.
- Float along on a ***mokoro***, a traditional vessel of the Okavango Delta, which is a dugout canoe, ideal for mastering those shallow waterways, and expertly poled by the person who stands in the stern.
- Fly over parts of Botswana in a **hot-air balloon**, and experience the thrill of landing in an open floodplain.

TOURIST INFORMATION

Department of Tourism in the UK
c/o Southern Skies Marketing, Old Boundary House, London Road, Sunningdale, Berkshire SL5 0DJ, UK.
Tel: (01344) 298 980.
Website: www.botswanatourism.org.uk

Entertainment

FOOD & DRINK: Restaurants and bars can be found in main towns, often within hotels. Millet and sorghum porridge constitutes much of the cuisine. Beef and goat are very popular meats. Most lodges and safari camps also have restaurants and licensed bars, although food is generally basic outside major hotels and restaurants. The standard of food in lodges and camps is generally very good. There is local beer and no real restrictions on alcohol.

National specialities:
- *Morama* (an underground tuber).
- The *Kalahari* truffle.
- The *Mopane* worm (boiled, cooked or deep-fried).
- Beans such as cow peas, *ditloo* and *letlhodi*, dried bean leaves, plus nuts like peanuts and groundnuts.
- Wild spinach, *morogo* is very tasty.
- Plenty of watermelons, plus other varieties of melon.
- *Seswaa* or *Chotlho* is a popular traditional meat dish cooked with only salt and water and served with pap, a soft maize meal.
- Variations upon bread meals, such as dumplings (*matemekwane*), flat cakes (*diphaphatha*) and fat cakes (*magwinya*).

National drinks:
- Palm wine (which is extremely strong) and *Kgadi* (made from distilled sugar or fungus).
- Traditional beer such as *khadi* or *bojalwa*, which tastes a bit like apple cider.
- Homemade ginger beer is popular.
- Bush tea - or *Rooibos* - is a reddish caffeine-free tea that is soothing and delicious, although something of an acquired taste.

Tipping: A discretionary 5 to 10 per cent. In many places, a service charge is automatically added. It is customary to tip the game guide and lodge staff while on safari.

NIGHTLIFE: Most people get up early in the morning, and nightlife is not very extensive. However, there are some bars and restaurants in Gaborone. The city also has a cinema. Maun has a handful of restaurants and a small cinema.

SHOPPING: Woodcarvings, handcrafted jewellery, woven goods and attractive basketry (particularly at Etsha, Shakawe and Shorobe) are recommended. Modern Bushman art can be seen, and perhaps purchased, at D'Kar, 25 miles north of Ghanzi. There also occasional exhibitions at the National Museum in Gaborone. **Shopping hours:** Mon-Fri 0800-1800; Sat 0830-1300.

Business

- **GDP:** US$13.9 billion (2003).
- **Main imports:** Foodstuffs, machinery, electrical goods, transport equipment, textiles, fuel and petroleum products, wood and paper products, metal and metal products.
- **Main exports:** Diamonds, copper, nickel, soda ash, meat and textiles.
- **Main trade partners:** European Free Trade Association (EFTA), the Southern African Customs Union (SACU) and Zimbabwe.

ECONOMY: As a key foreign exchange earner, livestock farming is the most important part of Botswana's agricultural sector. In addition, there is substantial subsistence agriculture, cultivating maize, sorghum and millet. The country's other main export industry is mining, extracting diamonds (of which Botswana is the world's largest producer by value), nickel, gold, cobalt, copper, salt and coal (the principal source of energy) and soda ash. The small manufacturing sector is largely devoted to the production of food products and textiles. Botswana is economically closely connected to South Africa and is a member of the Southern African Customs Union (SACU). It also hosts the Southern African Development Conference, which is the principal mechanism for economic co-operation.
The bulk of the country's imports come from within SACU, other African countries and Korea. Europe is the key export market. Prudent management and the successful development of new mineral resources have afforded Botswana healthy economic growth of around 5 per cent since the late 1990s. But the vulnerability of the agricultural sector to bad weather and commodity price fluctuations has led the government to seek to develop a service sector, with tourism and financial services being the best prospects. However, the HIV/AIDS epidemic, which is extremely serious in Botswana and mainly afflicts the productive, young and middle-aged population, is starting to have a negative effect on the country's economy.

BUSINESS ETIQUETTE: Lightweight or tropical suits should be worn. **Office hours:** Mon-Fri 0800-1700 April-October; 0730-1630 October-April. **Government office hours:** 0730-1630 all year round.

COMMERCIAL INFORMATION

Botswana Export Development & Investment Authority (BEDIA)
Plot 28, Matsitama Road, The Main Mall, Gaborone, Botswana
Tel: 318 1931.
Website: www.bedia.co.bw

Brazil

Location: South America.

Time: Brazil spans several time zones:
Eastern Standard Time: GMT - 3 (GMT - 2 from third Sunday in October to third Saturday in February in Distrio Federal, Espito Santo, Goias, Minas Gerais, Parana, Rio de Janeiro, Rio Grande do Sul, Santa Caterina and Sao Paulo).
Western Standard Time: GMT - 4 (GMT - 3 from third Sunday in October to third Saturday in February in Matto Grosso and Matto do Sul).
Acre State: GMT - 5.
Fernando de Noronha Archipelago: GMT - 2.

Overview

Brazil is South America's biggest and most influential country and takes up almost half the continent. It is one of the world's economic giants and is revered for its football prowess, coffee production and distinctive music such as samba and bossa nova. Two-thirds of Brazil's population lives near the coast, meaning that life is a beach for locals and tourists alike. People are the essence of the country, and while Brazil is home to a multitude of ethnic groups of varying economic status, there are some characteristics that everyone shares – energy and passion. It is not all reserved for football either; Brazilians enjoy a good party whatever the circumstances. Rio is the hottest of destinations, particularly around Carnival time. Dancers gyrate, the music beats and the summer temperature rises. Almost anything goes. Bodies of all ages, colours and sizes don the very minimum in beachwear and idle away the days on the sun-kissed Copacabana and Ipanema beaches. Volleyball, swimming and people-watching are but a few of the activities in which you can indulge. Brazil's landscape is as diverse as the people who inhabit it. Few tourists venture far from Brazil's spectacular beaches but a trip into the interior reveals a different Brazil, one with a great deal to offer the visitor. Brazil includes much of the world's biggest rain forest around the Amazon, whose exploitation has become a major environmental worry. Almost entirely covered with dense rainforest, Brazil's northern interior is split into the vast regions of Amazonas, Pará, Acre and Rondônia. These massive federal states easily outstrip the land resources of many European countries and, combined, cover over 3,400,000 sq km (1,300,000 sq miles) of endless jungle home to lush vegetation and countless species of life. Brazil's massive assortment of people and places renders it ripe for choice.

General Information

AREA: 8,547,404 sq km (3,300,170.9 sq miles).
POPULATION: 186 million (official estimate 2005).

POPULATION DENSITY: 22 per sq km.
CAPITAL: Brasília. **Population:** 2 million (2000).
GEOGRAPHY: Brazil covers almost half of the South American continent and it is bordered to the north, west and south by all South American countries except Chile and Ecuador; to the east is the Atlantic. The country is topographically quite flat and at no point do the highlands exceed 3000m (10,000ft). Over 60 per cent of the country is a plateau; the remainder consists of plains. The River Plate Basin (the confluence of the Paraná and Uruguay rivers, both of which have their sources in Brazil) in the far south is more varied, higher and less heavily forested. North of the Amazon are the Guiana Highlands, partly forested, partly stony desert. The Brazilian Highlands of the interior, between the Amazon and the rivers of the south, form a vast tableland, the Mato Grosso, from which rise mountains in the southwest that form a steep protective barrier from the coast called the Great Escarpment, breached by deeply cut river beds. The population is concentrated in the southeastern states of Minas Gerais, Rio de Janeiro and São Paulo. The city of São Paulo has a population of over 10 million, while over 5.5 million people live in the city of Rio de Janeiro.
GOVERNMENT: Federal Republic. **Head of State and Government:** President Luiz Inácio Lula da Silva since 2002.
Recent history: Luiz Inácio Lula da Silva, a former shoeshine boy and metal worker, became Brazil's first left-wing President in four decades when he beat his Government-backed rival by a wide margin in the October 2002 elections. The Lula Government faces a difficult balancing act. It has committed itself to a major programme of social and economic reform but a reminder of the power of international capital came shortly before the election when, amid fears of a Lula victory, market activity brought the Brazilian economy to the brink of collapse. Lula has managed to keep both popular sentiment and the international markets more or less on track. He has implemented pension reforms as well as bringing about an increase in the minimum wage. In 2005, however, his party faced claims of corruption and he was forced to apologise on television, saying he knew nothing of the supposed corruption.
LANGUAGE: The official language is Portuguese, with different regional accents characterising each State. Spanish, English, Italian, French and German are also spoken, particularly in tourist areas. Four linguistic roots survive in the indigenous areas: Gê, Tupi-guarani, Aruak and Karib.
RELIGION: There is no official religion, but approximately 70 per cent of the population adhere to Roman Catholicism. A number of diverse evangelical cults are also represented, as are animist beliefs (particularly spiritism, *umbanda* and *candomblé*).
ELECTRICITY: Brasilia and Recife, 220 volts AC; Rio de Janeiro and São Paulo, 127 volts AC or 220 volts in larger hotels. Plugs are of the two-pin type. Most hotels provide 110-volt and 220-volt outlets, transformers and adaptors.
SOCIAL CONVENTIONS: Handshaking is customary on meeting and taking one's leave, and normal European courtesies are observed. Frequent offers of coffee and tea are customary. Flowers are acceptable as a gift on arrival or following a visit for a meal. A souvenir from the visitor's home country will be well received as a gift of appreciation. Casual wear is normal, particularly during hot weather. In nightclubs, smart-casual (eg blazer, no tie) is acceptable. For more formal occasions the mode of dress will be indicated on invitations. Smoking is acceptable unless notified otherwise. The Catholic Church is highly respected in the community, something which should be kept in mind by the visitor.

Climate

Varies from arid scrubland in the interior to the impassable tropical rainforests of the northerly Amazon jungle and the tropical eastern coastal beaches. The south is more temperate. Rainy seasons occur from January to April in the

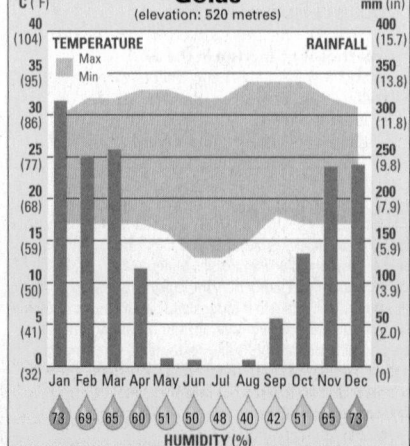

north, April to July in the northeast and November to March in the Rio/São Paulo area.

Required clothing: Lightweight cottons and linens with waterproofing for the rainy season. Warm clothing is needed in the south during winter (June to July). Specialist clothing is needed for the Amazon region. Warm clothing is advised if visiting the southern regions in winter time. The sunlight is extremely bright and sunglasses are recommended.

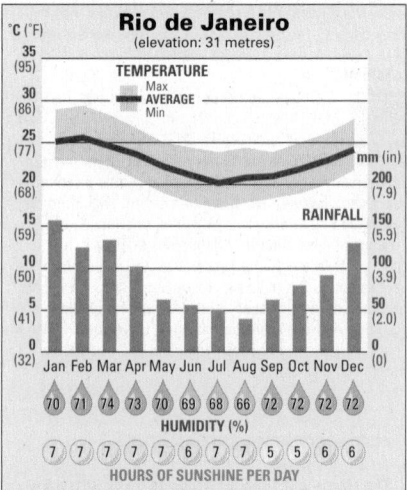

Communications

Telephone: Country code: 55. Full IDD services are available for the whole country and abroad. Rio's airport provides 24-hour telecommunication services. Public telephones accept telephone cards (*cartões telefónicos*), most of which cost R$20. Some older telephones may require metal discs (*fichas*), which can be obtained from cash desks or newspaper kiosks. International calls from Brazil are expensive: to the UK, the rate is approximately US$3 per minute, to the USA and Canada, it is approximately US$2.50 per minute. 25 per cent cheaper calls can be made daily from 2000-0500.
Mobile telephone: US-style analogue and digital networks exist. Roaming agreements exist with most international mobile phone companies, but travellers should check with their service providers. Coverage and cost vary from state to state. It is possible to rent mobile phones, which can be collected at the airport or delivered to a hotel.
Internet: Hotels generally provide Internet access to guests. Internet cafes can be found in main towns and cities, and there are often Internet booths at airports. In smaller towns, public access is sometimes available at post offices.
Post: Services are reasonably reliable. Sending mail registered or franked will eliminate the risk of having the stamps steamed off. Airmail service to Europe takes four to six days. Surface mail takes at least four weeks. Post office hours: Mon-Fri 0800-1800, Sat 0800-1200.
MEDIA: Brazil's constitution guarantees a free press. There are thousands of radio stations and hundreds of TV channels in Brazil, South America's largest media market. Media ownership is highly concentrated and home-grown conglomerates such as *Globo*, Brazil's most successful broadcaster, dominate the market, operating TV and radio networks, newspapers and pay-TV. Brazilian dramas and soaps are exported around the world. Game shows and reality TV are hugely popular.
Press: In Rio de Janeiro, there is an English-language publication, the *Rio Visitor*, which gives tourist information. *Brazil Post* is a global news service providing information on the latest stories and current affairs in Brazil (website: www.brazilpost.com). Daily newspapers include *O Dia*, *O Correio Braziliense* and *O Globo*. International magazines and newspapers are also available throughout the country.
TV: Major commercial networks include *Sistema Brasileiro de Televisao (SBT)*, *TV Record* and *Rede Globo*; NBR is operated by state-run *Radiobras*; *TV Cultura* is a public network offering cultural programming.
Radio: Radiobras operates *Radio Nacional*; Globo runs commercial station *Radio Globo*; *Radio Cultura* offers cultural programming.

Passport/Visa

Restricted entry: Passports issued by Bhutan, Central African Republic and Chinese Taipei are not recognised by the Brazilian Government. Holders of such passports should hold a Laissez-Passer issued by the Brazilian authorities. For further details, check with the nearest Consulate or Consular section of Embassy.
PASSPORTS: Passports valid for at least six months from date of entry required by all except nationals of Argentina, Chile, Paraguay and Uruguay arriving in Brazil directly from

their own countries and holding a national identity card.
Note: Persons under 18 years of age, when not accompanied by both parents, must have a birth certificate (an original or authenticated photocopy). This must be in English, French, Portuguese or Spanish, otherwise an official translation must be presented as well. When travelling alone or with one parent, a declaration from the absent parent(s) must be presented authorising the journey and giving the name and address of the person in Brazil who will be responsible for the minor. In the case of divorced or deceased parents, papers attesting to full custody must be presented.

	Passport Required?	Visa Required?	Return Ticket Required?
Full British	Yes	1	Yes
Australian	Yes	Yes	Yes
Canadian	Yes	Yes	Yes
USA	Yes	Yes	Yes
Other EU	Yes	1	Yes
Japanese	Yes	Yes	Yes

Note: *Regulations and requirements may be subject to change at short notice, and you are advised to contact the appropriate diplomatic or consular authority before finalising travel arrangements. Any numbers in the chart refer to the footnotes below.*

VISAS: Required by all except the following:
(a) nationals mentioned under passport exemptions above;
(b) **1.** nationals of EU countries (except nationals of Cyprus, Czech Republic, Estonia, Latvia, Lithuania, Malta and Slovak Republic who *do* require a visa) for touristic and business stays of up to 90 days;
(c) nationals of Andorra, Argentina, The Bahamas, Barbados, Bolivia, Chile, Colombia, Costa Rica, Ecuador, Iceland, Israel, Korea (Rep), Liechtenstein, Malaysia, Mexico, Monaco, Morocco, Namibia, New Zealand, Norway, Panama, Paraguay, Peru, The Philippines, San Marino, South Africa, Sovereign Order of Malta, Surinam, Switzerland, Thailand, Trinidad & Tobago, Tunisia, Turkey, Uruguay, Vatican City and Venezuela for touristic and business stays of up to 90 days (except nationals of Andorra, The Bahamas, Barbados, Bolivia, Liechtenstein, Malaysia, Namibia, Panama, Trinidad & Tobago and Venezuela who must *always* obtain a visa if travelling to Brazil for business purposes);
(d) transit passengers continuing their journey to a third country by the same or first connecting flight, provided holding onward documentation and not leaving the airport.
Note: All travellers must be in possession of onward or return tickets and sufficient funds to cover their stay.
Types of visa and cost: *Tourist*: cost varies according to nationality. Generally, it is around £16. Other prices, based on reciprocity, are £28 (for nationals of Australia); £32 (for nationals of Canada and Nigeria); free, but £80 processing fee (for nationals of the USA); £44 processing fee for nationals of the United Arab Emirates; £40 (for nationals of Japan and the Russian Federation). *Business*: £48 (£12 processing fee for nationals of the United Arab Emirates; £80 processing fee for nationals of the USA). *Transit*: contact the Consulate for details of cost. Postal applications, and those via courier or travel agent, cost an additional £8. Some countries must pay an extra £20.
Validity: 90 days from date of issue. Tourist visas can be used for multiple entry within the period of validity. For an extension of the (up to three months) tourist visa, apply in Brazil, although this is always at the discretion of the Brazilian Immigration Authorities.
Application to: Consulate (or Consular section at the Embassy); see *Passport/Visa Information*.
Application requirements: *Tourist/Transit*: (a) Valid passport for at least six months. (b) Application form. (c) Proof of sufficient funds to cover duration of stay or return or onward tickets (photocopy, or letter from carrier giving flight details). (d) One passport-size photo. (e) Certificate of vaccination, if necessary; enquire at Embassy/Consulate. (f) Fee (paid at any post office in the UK with a Giro slip obtainable from the Consulate). (g) If participating in conferences, seminars, an artistic or sports event, a letter from the organisers is required. *Business*: (a)-(g) and, (h) Letter from applicant's company stating the purpose and duration of the visit and contacts to be maintained by the applicant.
Note: For postal applications, travellers should also submit a special delivery or guaranteed delivery, self-addressed, pre-paid envelope and a written request stating nationality, status and length of residence in the UK (where applicable) and validity of the British visa (where applicable).
Working days required: Depends on nationality. A minimum of three working days in person, 10 by post, 15 for those who require consultation.
Temporary residence: Apply to Consulate (or Consular section at Embassy).

Money

Currency: Real/Reais (R$) = 100 centavos. Notes are in denominations of R$100, 50, 10, 5 and 1. Coins are in denominations of R$1, and 50, 25, 10, 5, 2 and 1 centavos.
Currency exchange: All banks, *cambios*, travel agencies and authorised hotels exchange recognised traveller's cheques and foreign currency. There is an extensive network of ATMs around the country. The US Dollar is the most widely accepted foreign currency.
Credit & debit cards: Most major international credit cards are accepted, though not universally. Check with your credit or debit card company for details of merchant acceptability and other services which may be available.
Traveller's cheques: Exchangeable at hotels, banks and tourist agencies. Tourists cannot exchange US traveller's cheques for US banknotes but they may, however, benefit

from a 15 per cent discount when paying hotel or restaurant bills in foreign currency or traveller's cheques. To avoid additional exchange rate charges, travellers are advised to take traveller's cheques in US Dollars.

Currency restrictions: The import and export of local currency is unlimited, provided amounts over R$10,000 are declared.

Banking hours: Mon-Fri 1000-1600.

Exchange rate indicators:

Rate at time of publishing

£1.00= R$3.95

$1.00= R$2.26

Duty Free

The following goods may be imported into Brazil by persons over 18 years of age without incurring customs duty: *clothes and other articles for personal use; books and periodicals; 400 cigarettes or 25 cigars; maximum 24 units of alcohol; up to US$500 worth of goods bought duty free in Brazilian airports; any other articles with total value not exceeding US$500 or equivalent in other currency*.

Note: Tourists/visitors may also bring, in addition to duty free mentioned above, a tape recorder, typewriter, camera, portable video, pair of binoculars, movie camera, provided used and for personal use only.

Prohibited imports: Meat and dairy products; fruit and vegetables; and plants or parts of plants.

Public Holidays

Below are listed Public Holidays for the January 2006-June 2007 period.

2006: Jan 1 New Year's Day. **Jan 20*** Founding of Rio de Janeiro. **Jan 25*** Founding of São Paulo. **Feb 25-Mar 1** Carnival. **Apr 14** Good Friday. **Apr 21** Tiradentes. **May 1** Labour Day. **Jun 15** Corpus Christi. **Sep 7** Independence Day. **Oct 12** Our Lady Aparecida, Patron St of Brazil. **Nov 2** All Soul's Day. **Nov 15** Republic Day. **Dec 24** Christmas Eve (half day). **Dec 25** Christmas Day. **Dec 31** New Year's Eve (half day). **2007: Jan 1** New Year's Day. **Jan 20*** Founding of Rio de Janeiro. **Jan 25*** Founding of São Paulo. **Feb 17-21** Carnival. **Apr 6** Good Friday. **Apr 21** Tiradentes. **May 1** Labour Day. **Jun 7** Corpus Christi.

Note: *Regional observances only.

Health

	Special Precautions?	Certificate Required?
Yellow Fever	Yes	1
Cholera	Yes	2
Typhoid & Polio	3	No
Malaria	4	N/A

Note: *Regulations and requirements may be subject to change at short notice, and you are advised to contact your doctor well in advance of your intended date of departure. Any numbers in the chart refer to the footnotes below.*

1: A *yellow fever* vaccination certificate is required from all travellers over nine months old arriving within from infected regions. Vaccination is strongly recommended for those intending to visit rural areas in the states of Acre, Amapá, Amazonas, Goiás, Maranhão, Mato Grosso, Mato Grosso do Sul, Pará, Rondônia, Roraima, Tocantins, and certain areas of Minas Gerais, and specific areas of Espirito Santo, Piani, Bahia, São Paulo, Paraná, Santa Catarin and Rio Grande do Sul. If in any doubt, please contact the Brazilian Consulate General (see *Passport/Visa Information*).
2: Following WHO guidelines issued in 1973, a *cholera* vaccination certificate is no longer a condition of entry to Brazil. However, cases of *cholera* are still reported, especially in the northeast, and precautions are essential. Up-to-date advice should be sought before deciding whether these precautions should include vaccination as medical opinion is divided over its effectiveness; see the *Health* appendix for more information.
3: Immunisation against *typhoid* is recommended. A *polio* vaccination certificate is required for children aged between three months and six years old.
4: *Malaria* risk exists throughout the year (78 per cent *vivax* form and 22 per cent *falciparum* form) below 900m (2953ft) in Acre, Amapá, Amazonas, Maranhão (western part), Mato Grosso (northern part), Pará (except Belém City), Rondônia, Roraima and Tocantins states, as well as some larger cities, such as on the periphery of Pôrto Velho, Boa Vista, Macapá, Manaus, Santerém, Rio Branco and Maraba. The malignant *falciparum* form of the disease is reportedly highly resistant to both chloroquine and sulfadoxine-pyrimethamine. Mefloquine, doxycycline or atovaquone/proguanil is the recommended prophylaxis.

Food & drink: All water should be regarded as being potentially contaminated. Water used for drinking, brushing teeth or making ice should have first been boiled or otherwise sterilised. Even filtered water in more remote areas should be avoided and

bottled mineral water should be drunk instead. Pasteurised milk and cheese is available in towns and is generally considered safe to consume. Milk outside of urban areas is unpasteurised and should be boiled; powdered or tinned milk is available and is advised in rural areas, but make sure that it is reconstituted with pure water. Avoid dairy products which are likely to have been made from unboiled milk. Only eat well-cooked meat and fish, preferably freshly prepared and served hot. Pork, salad and mayonnaise may carry increased risk. Vegetables should be cooked and fruit peeled.

Other risks: *Bilharzia* (*schistosomiasis*) is present. Snakes and leeches may be a hazard. Avoid swimming and paddling in fresh water; swimming pools that are well-chlorinated and maintained are safe. Other infectious diseases prevalent in Brazil include *trypanosomiasis* (*Chagas disease*) and *mucocutaneous leishmaniasis* (on the increase). The former is widespread in rural and poor areas of Brazil and is spread by either insect bites or ingestion of byproducts in contaminated foods/drinks of the vector insect. *Dengue fever* is on the increase, especially after rain in densely populated areas. *Visceral leishmaniasis* is endemic (especially in the northeast). *Onchocerciasis* (especially northern Brazil) and *Bancroftian filariasis* are also present. *Hepatitis A, B* and *D, Brazilian purpuric fever, amoebiasis, shigella infection, leptospirosis icterohaemorrhagica* and *brucellosis* all occur. There are epidemics of *meningococcal meningitis* in and around the Rio area. Air pollution, especially in São Paulo City, may aggravate chest complaints.

Rabies is present. For those at high risk, vaccination before arrival should be considered. If you are bitten, seek medical advice without delay. For more information, consult the *Health* appendix.

Health care: There is no reciprocal health agreement with the UK or USA. Full insurance is strongly recommended as medical costs are high. English-speaking medical staff are found mainly in São Paulo and Rio de Janeiro. The main hospital in São Paulo is the Hospital das Clinicas.

Travel - International

AIR:

 The national airlines are *TAM (KK)* (website: www.tam.com.br) and *Varig (RG)* (website: www.varig.com.br).

Approximate flight times: From *London* to São Paulo and to Rio de Janeiro is approximately 11 hours. From *Los Angeles* to Rio de Janeiro is 14 hours. From *New York* to Rio de Janeiro is 10 hours. From *Sydney* to Rio de Janeiro is 20 hours.

Main airports: *Brasilia International (BSB)* is 11km (7 miles) south of the city. *To/from the airport:* Buses run regularly to the city centre (travel time - 30 minutes). Taxis are also available (travel time - 15 minutes). *Facilities:* Left luggage, first aid, snack bar, post office, banks/bureaux de change, bar, restaurant, shops and car hire. *Rio de Janeiro (GIG)* (Galeão) is 20km (13 miles) north of the city. *To/from the airport:* Public buses operate 0530-2330 to the city (travel time - 40 minutes). There is an airport shuttle bus which stops at all major resorts and hotels, running every hour. Taxis are also available. *Facilities:* Left luggage and lockers, banks, bureaux de change, duty-free shops, a pharmacy and a small 24-hour hospital, restaurant, snack bar, car parking, tourist information, post office and car hire companies.

São Paulo (GRU) (Guarulhos) is 25km (16 miles) northeast of the city. *To/from the airport:* An airport bus runs every 30 minutes (travel time - 30 minutes). Taxis are also available. *Facilities:* Left luggage and lockers, duty-free shops, banks, bureaux de change, pharmacies, restaurants, snack bar, post office and car hire.

Further information on Brazilian airports can be found on the following website (www.infraero.gov.br).

Air passes: The *Mercosur Airpass* is valid within Argentina, Brazil, Chile (except Easter Island), Paraguay and Uruguay. Participating airlines include *TAM Mercosur* (PZ), *Pluna* (PU), *TAM Linhas Aéreas* (JJ) and *VARIG* (RG). The pass can only be purchased by passengers who live outside South America, who have a return ticket. Only eight flight coupons are allowed with a maximum of four coupons for each country and it is valid for seven to a maximum of 30 days. At least two countries must be visited and the flight route cannot be changed. A maximum of two stopovers is allowed per country.

The *Visit South America* pass is valid within Argentina, Bolivia, Brazil, Colombia, Chile (except Easter Island), Ecuador, Paraguay, Peru, Uruguay and Venezuela. Participating airlines include *Aer Lingus (*EI), *American Airlines* (AA), *British Airways* (BA), *Cathay Pacific* (CX), *Finnair* (AY), *Iberia* (IB), *LAN* (LA) and *Qantas* (QF). The pass must be bought outside South America in the country of residence. It allows unlimited travel to 34 cities. A minimum of three flights must be booked, with no maximum; the maximum stay is 60 days, with no minimum, and prices depend on the amount of flight zones. For further details, contact one of the participating airlines.

Departure tax: None.

SEA:

 The main port is *Rio de Janeiro*, which is used by many international cruise ships. Other popular ports include *Manaus, Fortaleza, Recife, Salvador* and *Vitória*. Passenger services are limited although *Grimaldi Freighter* do offer sailings from Europe. Most major international cruiselines sail to Brazilian ports.

RAIL:

 Limited rail services link Brazil with Argentina, Bolivia and Chile, although travelling by train is not a popular option. The main international routes include Rio de Janeiro-Buenos Aires, Rio de Janeiro-Santiago, Rio de Janeiro-São Paulo-Montevideo, São Paulo-Bauru- Corumba-Santa Cruz-La Paz, São Paulo-Antofagasta.

ROAD:

 It is possible to drive or take a bus to Brazil from the USA, but it is wise to check any changes in political status or requirements in Central America before travelling. It is also possible to travel from Rio de Janeiro to other Latin American countries. The journeys tend to be long; for example, from Rio de Janeiro to Buenos Aires (Argentina) is 44 hours.

Travel - Internal

AIR:

 There is a shuttle service between São Paulo and Rio de Janeiro, a regular service from São Paulo to Brasília, and a shuttle service from Brasília to Belo Horizonte. There are air services between all Brazilian cities, Brazil having one of the largest internal air networks in the world. At weekends it is advisable to book seats as the services are much used. The monthly magazine *Panrotas* (website: www.panrotas.com.br) gives all timetables and fares for internal air travel. No-frills airlines include *GOL Linhas* (website: www.voegol.com.br) and *OceanAir* (website: www.oceanair.com.br). Air taxis are available between all major centres.

Domestic airports: São Paulo (VCP) (Viracopos), 96km (60 miles) southwest of the city. *Facilities:* Banking, a duty free shop and a restaurant.

São Paulo (CGH) (Congonhas), 14km (8 miles) from the city. *Manaus* (Internacional Eduardo Gomes) *(MAO)*, 14km (9 miles) from the city. *To/from the airport:* There are coach services into the city and to other destinations.

Salvador (SSA) (Dois de Julho), 36km (22 miles) from the city. *To/from the airport:* 24-hour taxi facilities are available. *Facilities:* A bank, duty free shop and restaurant.

The Brazil Airpass: *The Brazil Airpass* is available through *VARIG* and can be purchased only outside of Brazil. Any IATA international carrier may be used. The pass costs US$560 for one to five coupons. Extra coupons cost US$100 each, up to a maximum of nine coupons; validity is for 21 days from first day of travel. The same route cannot be travelled twice. The similar *Star Alliance VARIG Brazil Airpass* must be used in conjunction with a *Star Alliance* or *Pluna* international carrier ticket. The pass costs US$399 for one to four coupons; extra coupons cost US$100. The *Star Alliance Northeast Airpass* is valid in the northeastern region of Brazil only and costs US$299 for one to four coupons. It is also possible to buy an airpass with *TAM*, using any international carrier.

Departure tax: None.

SEA/RIVER:

 Ferries serve all coastal ports. River transport is the most efficient method of travel in the Amazon Delta. The government-owned *Empresa de Navegação de Amazônia* (ENASA) has now virtually suspended its passenger-boat services, but private companies have stepped in and provide constantly improving services on rivers throughout the country. Boat trips from the mainland to the popular and beautiful islands of Ilha Grande, Ilhabela and Ilha de Santa Catarina are also possible.

RAIL:

 Limited rail connections exist to most major cities and towns, but there has been a substantial decline in the provision of long-distance services from the 18 major regional networks. Most (95 per cent) of Brazil's 22,000km (13,640 miles) of rail lines are located within 480km (300 miles) of its Atlantic coastline. Because of the great distances and the climate, some of these journeys can be uncomfortable. Daytime and overnight trains with restaurant and sleeping-cars link São Paulo and Rio de Janeiro. Brazil's most scenic rail routes are from Curitiba to Paranagua (originating in São Paulo) and from São Paulo to Santos. Other major rail routes include Belo Horizonte- Itabira-Vitoria (with buffet car), Campo Grande-Ponte Pora (with restaurant car), Porto Santana-Serra do Navio (second-class only), Santos Ana Costa-Juquia (second-class only), São Luis A Guarda-Parauapebas (with buffet car), Curitiba-Foz do Iguacu, São Paulo-Panorama (second-class only), São Paulo-Presidente Prudente (first-class, air conditioned, buffet and sleeping cars available), Araguari- Campinas (restaurant or buffet car) and Santa Maria-Pôrto Alegre (with restaurant car). Children under three travel free. Children from three to nine pay half fare.

ROAD:

General: Brazil has 1.94 million km (1.20 million miles) of roads. Traffic drives on the right. **Regulations:** The minimum driving age is 18. The speed limit is 110 kph (70 mph) on most national highways and 80 kph (mph) in cities. Passing on the right is forbidden. Road conditions vary. **Documentation:** International Driving Permit required.

Car hire: Available in all major centres but rates are expensive and the whole procedure very bureaucratic. Parking in cities is very difficult and it is best to avoid driving through the often congested urban areas if at all possible.

Bus: Inter-urban transport is very much road-based (accounting for 97 per cent of travel), compared with air (2.2 per cent) and rail (less than 1 per cent). High-quality coaches have been increasingly introduced on the main routes, which are well served. Services connect all inhabited parts of the country. Standards and timetables vary, and the visitor must be prepared for overnight stops and long waits between connecting stages.

URBAN:

There are extensive bus services in all the main centres, often with air-conditioned express executive coaches running at premium fares. Rio and São Paulo both have two-line metros and local rail lines, and there are trolleybuses in São Paulo and a number of other cities. Trolleybuses are increasingly being introduced as an energy-saving measure. Fares are generally regulated with interchange possible between some bus and metro/rail lines; for instance, on the feeder bus linking the Rio metro with Copacabana. **Taxi:** In most cities these are identified by red number plates. Fares are inexpensive, costing a little more with the 'special' taxis with air conditioning and better comfort. Willingness to accept a taxi driver's advice on where to go or where to stay should be tempered by the knowledge that places to which he takes a visitor are more than likely to give him a commission – and the highest commissions will usually come from the most expensive places. Taxis are metered and passengers should insist that the meter is turned on. Tipping taxi drivers is not normal practice.

Travel times: The following chart gives approximate travel times (in hours and minutes) from **Rio de Janeiro** to other major cities/towns in Brazil.

	Air
Brasília	**1.30**
Manaus	**5.00**
Recife	**2.45**
Salvador	**2.00**
São Paulo	**0.55**

Travel Advice

Most visits to Brazil are trouble-free. However, levels of crime and violence are high, especially in major cities. Travellers should be vigilant, especially when going out after dark. Travellers should be aware of the global risk of indiscriminate terrorist attacks which could be against civilian targets, including places frequented by foreigners. Drug trafficking and use is a growing problem, with severe penalties in Brazil.

This advice is based on information provided by the Foreign and Commonwealth Office in the UK. It is correct at time of publishing. As the situation can change rapidly, visitors are advised to contact the following organisations for the latest travel advice:

British Foreign and Commonwealth Office
Tel: (0845) 850 2829.
Website: www.fco.gov.uk

US Department of State
Website: http://travel.state.gov/travel

Accommodation

HOTELS:

Accommodation varies according to region. First-class accommodation is, by and large, restricted to the cities of the south and is generally expensive. There are also a number of *pousadas*, small, privately run hotels that are less expensive than the major hotels.

Rio de Janeiro/São Paulo: Many modern hotels, ranging from the very expensive deluxe hotels to moderately priced hotels. It is vital to book well in advance for the Carnival (which takes place annually in February/March).

Brasília: Small number of good hotels. Most tourists visit Brasilia by air from Rio or São Paulo for a day trip, or make a single-night stopover.

Bahia (Salvador): Small number of good hotels, some moderately priced hotels, several demi-pensions. The Bahia carnival takes place after Christmas (from December to March).

Amazon Basin: This region is being developed in part as a tourist attraction and has numerous lodges. Visitors are reminded that hotel tariffs are subject to alteration at any time, and are liable to fluctuate according to changes in the exchange rate.

Note: The best guide to hotels in Brazil is the 'Guia do Brasil Quatro Rodas', which includes maps available from the Brazilian Tourist Board (EMBRATUR) and from any news-stand in Brazil. **Grading:** The Brazilian Tourist Board has a star-rating system, but the classification is not the standard used in Europe and North America. Grading ranges from 5-star to 1-star.

CAMPING/CARAVANNING:

Cars may be hired, and camping arranged on safari tours or group 'exploration' trips in the Amazon region. The road network in Brazil is good and is being expanded, but since many parts are wild, or semi-explored, it is wise to drive on main roads, to camp with organised groups under supervision and with official permits, or otherwise to stay in recognised hotels. The country is peaceful, but because it is so large there is a real danger of getting lost, or being injured or killed by natural accident or lack of local survival skills.

The Camping Clube do Brasil has 52 sites in 14 states. Those with an 'international camper's card' pay only half the rate of a non-member (about US$4 per person). For those on a low budget, service stations can be used as campsites. These are equipped with shower facilities and can supply food.

YOUTH HOSTELS:

There are over 80 youth hostels (*albergues de juventude*).

OTHER TYPES OF ACCOMMODATION:

Eco-Hotels: Owing to a recent government initiative to invest in ecotourism, there are now a relatively small number of 'eco-hotels' available, located mostly in or near the Amazonian rainforest. Some provide visitors with luxury accommodation built on treetops and also arrange informative tours to the surrounding area; prices tend to be very high. **Budget:** *Dormitórios*, which have several beds to a room, cost as little as US$5 per night, though standards are correspondingly basic (with shared bathroom facilities); a *pousada* (small guest house) costs approximately US$10 per night. Rooms with bathrooms are called *apartamentos*, those without a bathroom are called *quartos*.

ACCOMMODATION INFORMATION

Associacão Brasileira da Industria de Hoteis (Information on Hotels)
sala 213, Avenida das Americas, 3.120 Bl.1, Rio de Janeiro, Brazil
Tel: (21) 3410 5131.
Website: www.riodejaneirohotel.com.br

Camping Clube do Brasil (Information on Camps)
Divisao de Campings, Rua Senador Dantas 75, 29 andar, 20037 Rio de Janeiro, Brazil
Tel: (21) 210 3171.
Website: www.campingclube.com.br.

Federação Brasileira dos Albergues da Juventude (Information on Youth Hostels)
Rua General Dionisio 63, Botafogo, 22271-050 Rio de Janeiro, Brazil
Tel: (21) 2286 0303.
Website: www.hostel.org.br

Top Things To See

- Enjoy one of the most beautiful settings in the world in **Rio de Janeiro**, the *cidade maravilhosa* (the marvellous city). The city's spectacular harbour is dominated by the famous rocky outcrop, **Pão de Açúcar (Sugar Loaf)**, and, further up, the **Corcovado (Hunchback)** peak, rising 709m (2326ft) above the **Baía de Guanabara** and providing the focal point for the classic Rio skyline. Do not miss the **Cristo Redentor (Christ the Redeemer) statue** which stands on top of the **Corcovado peak** 396m (1300ft) above Rio and the Baía de Guanabara. The Corcovado peak is located within the **Parque Nacional da Tijuca**.
- Rio has many interesting museums, including the **Museu Histórico Nacional**, located in the **São Tiago Fortress**. The **Museu de Arte Moderna do Rio de Janeiro** contains Brazil's most important collection of modern art. The **Museu de Arte Contemporânea de Niterói**, designed by famous architect Oscar Niemeyer and overlooking Boa Viagem beach, showcases contemporary Brazilian art. The **Museu do Folclore Edison Carneiro** displays folk art and art naif. The **Museu do Índio** contains some 14,000 objects made by Brazilian Indians and is one of the nation's most important Indian heritage museums. The **Museu da República** is set in the well-restored **Palácio do Catete** and reveals a fascinating insight into Brazilian history.
- Discover South America's largest city (over 10 million inhabitants) and Brazil's financial, commercial and industrial heartland from the top of **São Paulo's** tallest building, the **Edificio Italiano**. Famed throughout the continent for its abundant nightlife and shopping, São Paulo's rapidly growing population resides in a sprawling urban maze characterised by perpetual traffic jams and a chronic lack of space. While São Paulo's concrete jungle is a far cry from the colour and charm of other Brazilian cities, there are some cultural attractions on offer, notably the **MASP – Museu de Arte de São Paulo** with an internationally renowned collection of impressionist paintings (with works by Van Gogh and Degas amongst many others).
- In the Northeast of Brazil, head for the state capital, **Salvador da Bahia. Cidade Alta**, the heart of the old city, is perched at the top of a 50m-high cliff, linked to **Cidade Baixa** by steep streets, a funicular railway and the marvellous **Art-Deco Elevador Lacerdo**. The majority of Salvador's museums, palaces and churches are concentrated within **Cidade Alta** and thus the city is ideal for exploring on foot. This UNESCO World Heritage Site boasts a staggering number of churches, including the impressive **Church of São Francisco** and the fascinating **Church of Bonfim**. However, religion in Bahia is not limited to the established church. The state's African legacy extends to *candomble*, a fusion of African and Catholic religions. *Candomble* followers dress in white and honour hundreds of native deities in *terreiros* (or cult houses) all over the city; it is possible to witness ceremonies as some *terreiros* accept visitors as long as they dress accordingly and are respectful. Salvador also has some of the best museums in Brazil and next to the opulent **Catedral Basilica** is the **Museu Afro-Brasileiro**, a fascinating insight into afro-Brazilian culture, with sections on *candomble*, *capoeira* and *Carnaval*. Other interesting museums include the **Casa de Jorge Amado**, Bahia's best-known novelist, the **Museu da Cidade** and the **Museu de Arte Sacra**, the latter housed in a 17th-century convent.
- Also in Bahia state, the **Diamantina National Park** is well worth a visit; it contains several underground lakes (such as **Lago Azul**) and spectacular waterfalls (such as **Veu da Noiva**).
- In the **Piauí** State, the UNESCO World Heritage site of the **Serra da Capivara National Park** contains ancient cave paintings estimated to be over 25,000 years old.
- **Pernambuco** state capital, **Recife**, has been the beneficiary of sizeable investment to promote tourism. However despite being one of the most visited cities in the Brazilian Northeast, it still suffers from a poor infrastructure and the influx of rich, foreign tourists has made begging and street crime a real problem in the city. A world away is the nearby historical town of **Olinda**, infamous for its *Carnaval* celebrations and one of Brazil's eight UNESCO World Heritage Sites.
- **Ceará**'s capital, **Fortaleza**, sprawls lazily along a spectacular coastline. Blessed with excellent restaurants and an abundance of attractions for the visitor, the city is also a great place to organise a trip to **Jericocoara**. Just four hours by car, this heavenly village is nestled between a dazzling white sand-dune desert and a balmy turquoise sea.
- As its name suggests, **Minas Gerais** was so called after the abundant gold and diamond mines that transformed the state into a treasure trove of gold and also of baroque art. During the 18th century, the stream of riches from this region was so relentless that the Portuguese lacked sufficient ships to transport it to Europe. Almost all the gold that gilded altars in cathedrals and churches from as far north as **Olinda** came from Minas. In towns such as **Ouro Preto**, **Tiradentes**, **Sabará** and **Mariana**, this tidal wave of wealth resulted in the construction of hundreds of churches and civic buildings in lavish baroque style. All of the *cidades históricas* are immaculately preserved examples of Brazil's colonial heritage and are accessible by road from the state capital **Belo Horizonte**. This region's highlight for art-lovers is Aleijadinho's interpretation of 'The Passion' at the **Basilica de Bom Jesus de Matosinhos**. Set in gardens that gently slope towards **Matosinhos** town, the work is positioned in six small domed chapels filled with life-size statues that dramatise the scenes. All of the figures, including the 12 magnificent soapstone statues of prophets from the Old Testament, are more poignant for being sculpted by an artist almost completely disabled by the advanced stages of leprosy and who, therefore, knew it to be his final work.
- Learn about Brazil's future in **Brasília**, the country's capital, built on land originally covered by *cerrado* (sub-tropical forest). Although it attracts far fewer visitors than the huge cities of Rio and São Paulo or the tropical paradise of the Northeast, as it has little to offer the visitor interested in Brazilian history and culture, Brasilia is renowned for its futuristic architecture, most notable in the **Praça dos Três Poderes**, **Palácio do Planalto** and the **National Congress**.
- In the rich southern state of **Rio Grande do Sul**, **Porto Alegre** has excellent museums, art galleries and restaurants to entertain the visitor, as well as delightful surrounding countryside. To the west, travellers can visit

the ruins of the 300-year-old **Jesuit missions**, abandoned when the Jesuits were expelled from Spain. One of the most fascinating is **Saõ Miguel das Missões**, yet another UNESCO World Heritage Site, located 58km (36 miles) from the town of **Santo Angelo** (a good starting point for visiting the missions).

- **Blumenau** and **Joinville** are both living testaments to the last century's massive influx of German immigration with both towns constructed in predominantly German architecture. Germanic culture is still vibrant in small towns like **Pomerode** (near Blumenau) where German remains the *lingua franca* with Portuguese only used in government offices. Blumenau's annual three-week **Oktoberfest** is not to be missed..
- **Paraná** is a prime coffee-producing state with a bright modern capital, **Curitiba**, whose public transport system could be the envy of European capitals like London or Paris. Curitiba is famous for its parks, two of which are worth seeking out; visitors will be fascinated by the riot of vivid plumage in the aviaries of the **Passeio Público**, where several species of local birds are kept. A fascinating insight into frontier life and the endeavours of countless European immigrants, who moved here during the last 150 years, is the **Museu de Imigração Polenesa** in the centre of **Bosque João Paulo**. The museum's best exhibits are the log cabins, built by Polish immigrants in the 1880s and relocated here over 100 years later.
- The train journey between **Curitiba** and **Paranaguá** is a spectacular journey through dense jungle, its route strewn with memorials for the many workers who perished from tropical diseases as they constructed the tracks. Accessible by road or air from Curitiba are the world-famous **Iguazu Falls**, a spectacular set of 70m waterfalls with 275 cataracts, including the impressive **Garganta del Diablo** (Devil's Throat). The deafening roar of 5000 cubic metres of water cascading down each second accompanies a perpetual mist that envelopes visitors. Boat trips to the falls from Rio are available and take two days. Good aerial views can be enjoyed from a **helicopter tour** of the falls that can be booked on location. The area encompasses two national parks, each boasting hundreds of species of plant and animal life, and spans the borders of two countries, Argentina and Brazil, divided by the **River Paraná**. For a good view of the entire set of falls, visit the Brazilian side of the Park in **Foz de Iguazu**. To get close enough to stare into the watery abyss, visit the Argentine side. Unfortunately, there is no access to Brazil from the Argentine Park or vice versa, so visitors wishing to see both parks must travel overland to the border crossing, about 10km south. Due to Foz de Iguazu's proximity to both the Argentine and Paraguayan borders, it is possible to visit both countries in a day trip from Foz.
- In the **Northern Interior** and the **Amazon, Rondônia and Acre,** created in 1991, has suffered extensive deforestation. There are still natural wonders hidden away such as the stunning **Teotonio** and **Santo Antônio Falls**, accessible from capital **Porto Velho**. Other attractions include river trips to the **Forte Principe de Beira** or to Bolivia, where air taxis operate to La Paz from Guayaramerin. Territorially annexed from Bolivia in the early 20th century, Acre is a state of contrasts with a funky capital in **Rio Branco**, a thriving market and university town on the river. Because of its student population, Rio Branco has good nightlife and its geographical position as a trading post has made the town an important handicrafts centre.
- In **Amazonas,** the state capital, **Manaus,** was transformed by the 19th-century rubber boom and nowhere is this more evident than in the **Teatro Amazonas**, built in 1896 in the elaborate style of the Italian Renaissance. In front of the theatre, a marble square is designed to reflect the four continents represented by four great ships. Along **Avenida Sete de Setembro** are numerous museums worth a visit; the **Museo de Indio**, **Museo de Amazonas** and the marvellous colonial mansion that houses the **Centro Cultural de Palacio Rio Negro**, an extensive archive of naturalist Alexandre Ferreira. The city is easy to navigate and offers the visitor both fine restaurants and tax-free bargains in the free trade zone. As a major port for river-traffic with arrivals and departures to Colombia, Peru and Venezuela, Manaus is an excellent starting point for **river trips** and guided tours into the **rainforest.**
- The Eastern Amazon region is split between the states of **Para** and **Amapa**. Para's state capital **Belem** was founded in 1616. Situated at the Atlantic end of the Amazon estuary at the mouth of the **Rio Tocantins**, Belem is a thriving port city with an exquisite historical centre, dotted with splendid churches and elegant parks.

The Goeldi Museum boasts the largest collection of tropical plants in the world. The docks are the location of the early-morning **Ver O Peso** (**See the Weight**) market, which was originally a slave market but still exists these days although the stalls now mostly sell fruit and produce.

Top Things To Do

- Enjoy the greatest party in the world at the **Rio de Janeiro's Carnival.** Brazilians themselves remark that the **Recife** and **Olinda** celebrations are the most distinctive but it is cities like Rio or Salvador that receive the most foreign visitors. Celebrations can last from four days in the South to two weeks in northern cities such as Salvador and Recife. However in every town and village in Brazil, Carnival is a time to celebrate and the visitor will see processions in every region during Carnival time. Accommodation is traditionally prepaid in four- or five-day blocks and overland travel during Carnival is notoriously difficult, although always entertaining!
- Sample the **samba, bossa nova** or **lambada.** The major cities, particularly Rio de Janeiro, are full of cafes with live music and dancing. Salvador is also renowned for being the hub of Brazilian music and Salvador's central district of **Pelourinho** is home to numerous bars and clubs showcasing live music and *afoxé* (Salvador's carnival bands). **Gefieiras** are samba parlours where visitors can either watch or join in. In Rio, many gefieiras are located on the south side. The **Copacabana beach**, where parties are staged nearly 24 hours a day, is also a good location for sampling some Latin American entertainment. An exciting way to experience the genuine samba is by attending a rehearsal at the **escolas de samba** (samba schools), which open their doors to visitors a couple of months before the beginning of Rio de Janeiro's *Carneval*. *Bandas*, the non-professional equivalent of the samba schools, are also a good place to practice. Tickets for the carnival go on sale two weeks before the beginning. The best costumes and most spectacular samba parades can be seen at the **Sambódromo** (Sambadrome), a stadium on Rua Marquês de Sapucaí, where 14 samba schools parade on Carnival Sunday and Monday. It is possible for visitors to take part in a parade. One week of preparation should be allowed and hotels can often make all the necessary arrangements.
- Avid shoppers should head for **Salvador's Mercado Modelo** for a wide variety of goods including many examples of local handicrafts. The local cuisine (*comida bahiana*) is among the best in Brazil, focusing on rich African flavours. **Natal** also has several large markets and is famous for its cotton and leather handicrafts.
- Explore the **jungle.** The Amazon rainforest is the world's largest biological reserve. It contains one-third of all living species on the earth and is crossed by 10 of the world's 20 largest rivers, including the River Amazon (the largest river in the world). The usual base for trips to the Amazon is the city of Manaus, where numerous tour operators can arrange anything from standard day trips to month-long expeditions to more remote areas. It is best to hire a local guide (trips without guides are only allowed on certain trails). During the rainy season (February to April), the flooded rainforest can be explored by boat or canoe. Several jungle lodges and hotels offer **ecotourism** packages, though many of these tend to be expensive. River cruises to the so-called 'wedding of the waters', where the clear waters of the Rio Negro meet the muddy Amazon, are popular. In the southern state of **Rio Grande do Sul,** the region's **Gramado** and **Canela Mountains** provide ample opportunities for **walking** and **trekking**.
- Discover Brazil's **wildlife. Mato Grosso** is the gateway to the **Pantanal**, a vast area of wetlands approximately half the size of France and Brazil's largest ecological reserve. Flooded by the **Rio Paraguai** during the wet season (October to March), this region is the best place in Brazil to see wildlife. However, the region is sparsely populated, with few towns or villages and only one major road (the '*Transpantaneira*'). Therefore, in order to get the most out of the area, wildlife enthusiasts should choose an organised tour with experienced guides.
- **Hiking** and **climbing** are best done from April to October. Rio de Janeiro is the centre of Brazilian rock climbing: over 300 climbs can be reached within 40 minutes from the city centre. There are many great hiking trails in the national parks and along the coastline.
- Brazil is one of the world's top **surfing** destinations. The best places to surf in Brazil include **Joaquina Beach** (near Florianópolis in Santa Catarina state, which hosts the annual Brazilian surfing championships); **Saquarema** (in Rio state); **Búzios** (a chic resort area on the Cabio Frio Peninsula); and **Itacoatiara.** Rio has numerous beaches, most notably the infamous **Copacabana** and **Ipanema**. Beach life is a ritual In Brazil and different beach sections reflect different ways of life and fashions. **The Girl from Ipanema** beach is particularly popular with young people and is located at Posto Nine in Ipanema. Owing to strong waves and undertows, swimming off Ipanema can be dangerous. Rio's other main beaches include **Arpoador**, **Barra da Tijuca**, **Botafogo**, **Flamengo**, **Leblon**, **Leme**, **Pepino** and **Vidigal**. There are hundreds of beaches along the coastline suitable for many types of watersports, some of the best being at **Buzios; Angra** (on the Costa Verde, which is fairly uncrowded, with access to hundreds of offshore islands); **Fortaleza; Niteroi** (near Rio, with three good beaches); and **Itamaraca Island** (north of Recife). **Alagoas** state capital, **Maceiô**, is deservedly proud of its fantastic beaches, reputedly the finest in all of Brazil.
- **Diving** can be practised in **Fernando de Noronha** (a small archipelago off Brazil's north eastern coast in Pernambuco state, where a strict environmental protection programme allows a maximum of 420 visitors at a time); **Angra dos Reis** (a seaside village in Rio de Janeiro state, part of Ilha Grande Bay, with possible diving trips to 300 surrounding islands); **Bonito** (located in the fairly untouched and undeveloped Panatal region); **Recife** (the 'birthplace' of Brazil, offering excellent diving in the vicinity); and **Parcel Manoel Luís**. Diving clubs are located all along the coastline. For further information, contact the Brazilian Tourist Board – EMBRATUR (see *Tourist Information*).
- Watch a game of **football** in the Brazilian **Maracana Stadium**, the largest in the world.

TOURIST INFORMATION

Brazilian Tourist Office in the UK
32 Green Street, London W1K 7AT, UK
Tel: (020) 7629 6909.
Website: www.brazil.org.uk

Brazilian Tourism Office in the USA
@ Brazil Information Center, 2141 Wisconsin Avenue NW, Suite E-2, Washington, D.C. 20008, USA
Tel: (800) 727 2945 *or* (800) 7BRAZIL.
www.braziltourism.org

Entertainment

FOOD & DRINK: Many regional variations are very different from North American and European food. One example is Bahian cookery, derived from days when slaves had to cook scraps and anything that could be caught locally, together with coconut milk and palm oil. Types of establishment vary. If resident in a hotel, drinks and meals can often be charged to an account.

National specialities:
- *Vatapá* (shrimps, fish oil, coconut milk, bread and rice).
- *Sarapatel* (liver, heart, tomatoes, peppers, onion and gravy).
- *Caruru* (shrimps, okra, onions and peppers).

From Rio Grande do Sul comes:
- *Churrasco* (barbecued beef, tomato and onion sauce).
- *Galleto al primo canto* (pieces of cockerel cooked on the spit with white wine and oil).

From Amazonas comes:
- *Pato no tucupi* (duck in rich wild green herb sauce).
- *Tacacá* (thick yellow soup with shrimps and garlic).
- In the northeast, dried salted meat and beans are the staple diet.
- In Rio de Janeiro, a favourite dish is *feijoada* (thick stew of black beans, chunks of beef, pork, sausage, chops, pigs' ears and tails on white rice, boiled green vegetables and orange slices).

National drinks:
All kinds of alcoholic drinks are manufactured and available and there are no licensing hours or restrictions on drinking. Some bars have waiters and table service.
- Beer is particularly good and draught beer is called *chopp*.
- The local liqueur is *cachaça*, a type of rum popular with locals, but not so much with visitors.
- This phenomenally strong spirit is often mixed with sugar, crushed ice and limes to make *caipirinha*, a refreshing if intoxicating cocktail, and the Brazilian national drink.
- Southern Brazilian wine is of a high quality.
- Brazilian coffee is served in espresso-sized cups and is extremely popular.

Tipping: 10 to 15 per cent is usual for most services not included on the bill.

NIGHTLIFE: The best entertainment occurs in Rio de Janeiro and São Paulo. In Rio, the major clubs do not present their main acts until after midnight, and the daily paper gives current information; small clubs (*boites*) provide nightly entertainment throughout the city. São Paulo nightlife is more sophisticated, with greater choice; the shows tend to start earlier.

SHOPPING: In Rio and São Paulo, major shops and markets stay open quite late in the evening. Rio and Bahia specialise in antiques and jewellery. Special purchases include gems (particularly emeralds), jewellery (particularly silver), souvenirs and permissible antiques, leather or snakeskin goods. Fashions and antiques, crystal and pottery are a speciality of São Paulo. Belém, the city of the Amazon valley, specialises in jungle items, but be careful that you are not purchasing objects that have been plundered from the jungle, contributing to the general destruction. Check for restrictions on import to your home country of goods made from skins of protected species. **Shopping hours:** Mon-Sat 0900-1900. Supermarkets are open Mon-Sat 0800-2200.

Major shopping centres also open on Sundays 1500-2200. All the above times are subject to local variations and many shops open until late in the evenings, especially in December.

Business

- **GDP:** US$604 billion (2004).
- **Exports:** Transport equipment, iron ore, soya, footwear, coffee, orange juice and cars.
- **Imports:** Machinery, electrical and transport equipment, chemical products and oil.
- **Main trade partners:** Exports to: USA, Argentina and China; Imports from: USA, Argentina and Germany.

ECONOMY: Brazil has the world's 14th-largest economy. Agriculture remains the largest sector in terms of employment and Brazil is the world's second-largest exporter of agricultural products, principally coffee, sugar, soya beans, orange juice, beef, poultry and cocoa. Sisal, tobacco, maize and cotton are also produced. Orange juice and coffee are key export earners. There is also a substantial industrial sector, concentrated in machinery, electrical goods, construction materials, rubber and chemicals, and vehicle production. The country also possesses large mineral reserves including iron ore – of which Brazil is the world's largest exporter – bauxite, gold, titanium, manganese, copper and tin. Plans to develop Brazil's potentially vast oil and gas resources will serve to reduce the country's large current energy import bill but face opposition both at home and abroad on environmental grounds.

After difficulties throughout the 1980s, as the economy adjusted to new liberal economic policies, Brazil recorded a fairly strong economic performance during most of the 1990s. Industrial efficiency and financial management were improved while the government bolstered its coffers through a programme of privatisation. However, little of this money was directed towards investment and Brazil has suffered the consequences of years of under-investment in infrastructure and public services. In 1994, the Government introduced a new currency, the Real, to replace the Cruzeiro. Despite several bouts of serious speculative attack – the 1997 Asian financial crisis, the 1999 Mexico financial crisis and in the run-up to the 2002 election – the Real has survived with the support of several bail-outs from the IMF and World Bank, which have, as ever, demanded austerity measures in return. The Lula government, which took office with a series of radical social programmes at the beginning of 2003, was soon forced to make budget cuts. Its main target has been the country's costly pension system, which is now being overhauled.

The economy recorded slow growth – below 2 per cent – in 2001-2003, but experienced improved growth in 2004 (5.2 per cent), while inflation dropped to 7.6 per cent (2004 estimate). Brazil's principal trading partners are the USA, Argentina, China and Germany, as well as its fellow members of the southern Latin American trading bloc, MERCOSUR. Brazil also has important trading links with a number of Arab countries, notably Saudi Arabia.

BUSINESS ETIQUETTE: Business suits are worn when meeting senior officials and local heads of business, for semi-formal social functions and in exclusive restaurants and clubs. Exchange of business cards is usual. **Office hours:** Mon-Fri 0900-1800.

COMMERCIAL INFORMATION

International Chamber of Commerce
Avenida General Justo 307, 8 Andar, 20021-130
Rio de Janeiro, Brazil
Tel: (21) 2532 6015.
Website: www.iccwbo.org

Brazilian-American Chamber of Commerce (BACC) in the USA
509 Madison Avenue, Suite 304, New York,
NY 10022, USA
Tel: (212) 751 4691.
Website: www.brazilcham.com

American Chamber of Commerce for Brazil
Rua da Paz, 1431 CEP 04713-001 São Paulo, Brazil
Tel: (11) 5180 3804.
Website: www.amcham.com.br

Alternatively, contact the trade and commercial sections of Brazilian Embassies (for contact numbers, see *Passport/Visa Information*).

British Overseas Territories

Overview

British Overseas Territories: From 1998, what were once known as British Dependent Territories became British Overseas Territories, enjoying the same rights as nationals of Gibraltar and the Falklands Islands, with full British citizenship and residence within the UK. All territories are required to adhere to EU standards, particularly regarding financial regulations and human rights. The territory is under the sovereignty and formal control of the UK but is not an actual part of the UK. Most Overseas Territories are self-governing but rely on the UK in crucial matters of foreign policy etc. Since they are separate jurisdictions, there is no Overseas Territories' representation in the British Parliament. The UK exerts its formal control through a Governor of each Territory, appointed by the British Monarch.
British Crown Dependencies: These include the Isle of Man and the Channel Islands, which are dependencies of the British Crown whilst exercising considerable self-government in domestic affairs. The British Government is solely responsible for defence and international representation. Many British aspects are apparent in the Crown Dependencies, such as the UK telephone numbering plan or a BBC presence, although this is not always the case. Acts of the British Parliament rarely – but occasionally – apply to the Crown Dependencies.
Information on the **Isle of Man** and the **Channel Islands** has been placed at the end of the *United Kingdom* section.

The following countries all have their own sections in the *World Travel Guide*: **Anguilla, Bermuda, British Virgin Islands, Cayman Islands, Falkland Islands, Gibraltar, Montserrat, Turks & Caicos Islands.**

Ascension Island

Overview: A dependency of St Helena, the island was first occupied in 1815 and remained under British Admiralty control until 1922. Its airfield was built by US forces during World War II. The main importance of the island is as a communications centre and a military base, but attempts are being made to attract tourists to what was once a closed island. The island's administrative costs are borne collectively by the user organisations. The Royal Air Force has a facility supporting its garrison in the Falklands and there is a small US Air Force base on the island. Public services are provided by Ascension Island Services. The island is famous for green turtles and is also a breeding ground for Wideawakes (Sooty Tern).
Time: GMT.
Administrator's Office
Georgetown, Ascension Island,
South Atlantic Ocean, ASCN 1ZZ
Tel: 6311 (office).
Website: www.ascension-island.gov.ac
Location: South Atlantic. **Area:** 88 sq km (34 sq miles).
Population: 1100 (2003). **Population density:** 12.5 per sq

km. **Geography:** Ascension Island lies 1207km (750 miles) northwest of St Helena and is of purely volcanic origin.
Religion: Anglican and Roman Catholic.
COMMUNICATIONS: Telephone: Country code: 247. The *BBC World Service* and their contractors *Merlin Communications* operate their Atlantic Relay Station on the island. *Cable & Wireless* (website: www.cw.com/ascension) operates telecommunications services and the *European Space Agency* has a monitoring station. **Post:** There is a Royal Mail ship with a monthly shipping service to the UK available. **MEDIA: Press:** *The Islander* is published weekly. **Money:** The St Helena/Ascension Island Pound is equivalent to the UK Pound Sterling.

British Antarctic Territory

Overview: The British Antarctic Territory is the oldest territorial claim to a part of the continent. It includes all the lands and islands in a wedge extending from the South Pole to 60° S latitude between longitudes 20° W and 80° W. There is no indigenous population but the British Antarctic Survey has three research stations and the Royal Navy maintains an ice patrol vessel during the austral summer. The Territory has its own legal and postal system. The Territory is financially self sufficient. Despite the UK claiming sovereignty over the region, there are also overlapping claims by Argentina and Chile. Under the terms of the Antarctic Treaty, all territorial claims remain frozen to ensure that the continent is used peacefully in the pursuit of scientific endeavour. The Territory is replete with historical sites that featured in previous expeditions. There is also a great wealth of marine life, such as colonies of penguins and seals. The landscape is wide and varied, including mountains, islands and ice caps.
British Foreign and Commonwealth Office
See *Passport/Visa and Tourist Information*.
Location: Within the Antarctic Treaty area (between 20° west and 80° west of longitude). **Area:** Approximately 1,709,400 sq km (660,003 sq miles) of land. **Population:** There are no permanent inhabitants, and the territory is used only for scientific purposes. The population is about 50 in the winter, rising to about 400 in summer. The region is administered by the Overseas Territories Department at the British Foreign and Commonwealth Office; see also the *Antarctica* section. **Geography:** The territory also includes the South Shetlands and the South Orkneys.

British Indian Ocean Territory

Overview: Established as a territory of the UK in 1965, a number of the British Indian Ocean Territory (BIOT) islands were transferred to the Seychelles when it attained independence in 1976. The largest and most southerly of the islands, Diego Garcia, is jointly used by the UK and USA for military purposes. Diego Garcia is a 17-sq-mile atoll of sand and coral in the middle of the Indian Ocean has proven useful for Cold War activity and during both Gulf Wars. It also proved instrumental in the US War against Afghanistan, when bomb attacks were launched from the island to suspected Taliban strongholds. In its history, it has also been a dependency of Mauritius, although it was first explored by the Portuguese. All other islands are uninhabited. Those previously resident in Diego Garcia were controversially moved to Mauritius and the Seychelles between 1967 and 1973. Although a British High Court ruling invalidated the local immigration order that had excluded them from the archipelago in 2000, the special military status of Diego Garcia was retained. An 'Order of Council' was issued to prohibit the islanders from ever returning to Diego Garcia.
Time: GMT + 6.
British Foreign and Commonwealth Office
See *Passport/Visa and Tourist Information*
Location: The Territory consists of the Chagos Archipelago, 1930km (1199 miles) northeast of Mauritius, and includes the coral atoll of Diego Garcia. **Area:** 60 sq km (23

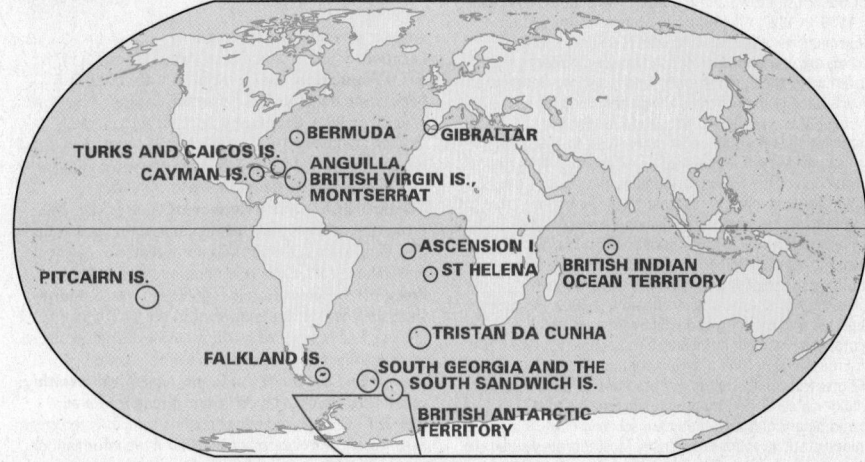

sq miles) of land and over 54,400 sq km (21,100 sq miles) of sea. **Population:** In September 2003, there were approximately 3000 people stationed in the Territory, consisting of US and British military personnel and their supporting workforce. **Money:** UK Pound Sterling; the US Dollar is also accepted.

Pitcairn Islands

Overview: If you call at Pitcairn, you will see a unique community of Anglo-Tahitian descent which turned a naval mutiny into a celebrated romance.

Pitcairn officially became a British settlement in 1887. Since 1989, Henderson has been included in the UNESCO World Heritage List as a bird sanctuary. An exclusive economic zone (EEZ) was declared in 1992 including 370km (200 nautical miles) of the islands' waters. The islanders live in and around Adamstown, the original home of the mutineers.

Pitcairn is actually a group of islands but it is Pitcairn Island, the largest island of these, which has a history that continues to fascinate. Originally the home of ex-sailors with Polynesian families, it has a community formed from the mutiny of the armed ship Bounty, which led to the founding of the Pitcairn community.

Pitcairn's history is one afflicted by murder, necessary emigration and claims of underage rape by male islanders, including the mayor – but also happier times of peace and pride. Most people who left Pitcairn originally, for areas such as Norfolk Island, soon returned to Pitcairn in a bout of homesickness.

However, population growth is currently a problem. Following a peak of around 200 in the 1930s, population now hovers around the 40 mark, with many having emigrated to New Zealand. There are also concerns over Pitcairn's increasing isolation. Although plans were approved for further development on the islands, designed to attract and accommodate more travellers, there is still no airfield, and the number of ships stopping at Pitcairn is decreasing. Ironically, Pitcairn Island was more visited in the 19th century, in the era of whaling.

Time: GMT - 8.5.

Office of the Governor of Pitcairn, Henderson, Ducie and Oeno Islands in New Zealand
c/o British High Commission, 44 Hill Street, Thorndon, PO Box 1812, Wellington, New Zealand
Tel: (4) 924 2888.
E-mail: PPA.Mailbox@fco.gov.uk

Pitcairn Islands Administration in New Zealand
Private Box 105696, Auckland, New Zealand
Tel: (9) 366 0186.
Website: www.government.pn

Location: Central South Pacific. **Area:** 35.5 sq km (13.7 sq miles). **Population:** 45 in Pitcairn (2003). **Population density:** 10.3 per sq km (2003). **Geography:** Equidistant from Panama and New Zealand. The group includes the uninhabited islands of Oeno, Henderson and Ducie.
Language: English and Pitcairn; the latter is a mixture of English and Tahitian, and became an official language in 1997. **Religion:** Seventh Day Adventist.
COMMUNICATIONS: Telephone: No direct dialling. Telephone calls must be booked via the international operator. **MEDIA: Press:** The *Pitcairn Miscellany* is a monthly four-page mimeographed news sheet. **Money:** New Zealand money is used on the island. This is on a par with the Pitcairn dollar. There are no banking facilities, but personal and traveller's cheques may be cashed at the Island Secretary's office. **Health:** A yellow fever vaccination certificate is required of all travellers over one year of age coming from infected areas; see the *Health* appendix for more information.

South Georgia and The South Sandwich Islands

Overview: In 1775, Captain Cook claimed South Georgia for the British Crown and the island was annexed by Britain in 1908. In 1927, Argentina laid claim to South Georgia. Dependencies of the Falkland Islands up until 1985, the islands are now a distinct British Overseas Territory governed by the Commissioner, who is also the Governor of the Falkland Islands. There is a local administrator who is Harbour Master, Fishery Officer and Customs and Immigration Officer (amongst other titles). In 1993, the British government announced an extension of its territorial jurisdiction of the waters surrounding the islands from 12 to 200 nautical miles, in response to the Argentine government's decision to sell fishing licences for the region's waters. The British Antarctic Survey carries out scientific research on behalf of the Government of the Territory; the small British garrison, stationed there following a brief Argentine occupation in 1982, has now departed. The economy is driven by fisheries and ecotourism. Attractions include a museum at Grytviken and Sir Ernest Shackleton's grave. In addition, South Georgia has the greatest concentration of Antarctic and sub-Antarctic wildlife on earth, and this, set against the island's extraordinary, glaciated mountain scenery, makes it a unique destination for ecotourism. Most tourists visiting the islands do so as part of a cruise. For details of cruises to Antarctica, contact the International Association of Antarctic Tour Operators based in the USA (tel: (970) 704 1047; website: www.iaato.org).

Time: GMT - 2.

The Commissioner for South Georgia and the South Sandwich Islands
Government House, Stanley, Falkland Islands,
South Atlantic, via United Kingdom
Tel: (+500) 27433.
Website: www.sgisland.org

Location: South Atlantic. **Area: South Georgia:** 3592 sq km (1387 sq miles); **South Sandwich Islands:** 311 sq km (120 sq miles). **Population:** There are no permanent inhabitants. **Geography:** South Georgia lies about 1309km (864 miles) southeast of the Falkland Islands, and the South Sandwich Islands lie about 640km (400 miles) southeast of South Georgia, of which 50 per cent is comprised of permanent ice. The South Sandwich Islands consist of a chain of 11 volcanic islands some 350km long. Parts of the islands are protected areas or Sites of Special Scientific Interest, with wildlife including four species of seal; four species of penguin, giant and other petrels; and four species of albatross and Antarctic tern. **COMMUNICATIONS:** All telephone, fax and e-mail communications are through international satellite systems. Public telephone and fax facilities are not available. **Post:** Mail can be posted using South Georgia stamps, but the postal service may take up to two months. **Money:** The South Georgia and South Sandwich Islands Pound is the official currency but the UK Pound Sterling and US Dollars are also in use on the island. MasterCard and Visa are accepted at the museum shop. **Health:** The islands have no hospital facilities or rescue services. Sunburn may be a particular problem and visitors should take sufficient precautions. Former whaling stations (at Grytviken, Husvik, Leith Harbour, Prince Olav Harbour and Stromness) are still emitting wind-blown debris that contains asbestos dust. It is therefore prohibited to enter or approach these stations within 200 metres. **Travel:** There are no road or air links; sole passage to the islands is by sea. However, the South Sandwich Islands' Antarctic climate means that in winter, the islands may be surrounded by pack ice, which combined with westerly storms and lack of sheltered anchorages, may make landing very difficult. All visitors must apply to the Commissioner, in advance of travel, for permission to land, and landing on South Georgia will require a fee of £55. On arrival, all visitors must report to the Marine Officer at King Edward Point, Cumberland, Bay East.

St Helena

Overview: St Helena was discovered on May 21 1502 by the Portuguese navigator Joan da Nova. In 1658, Richard, Lord Protector, authorised the British East India Company to colonise and fortify the island. Later, Napoleon Bonaparte was exiled here in 1815 until his death in 1821. In 1834, the island became a crown colony. St Helena depends on aid from the UK, although fishing, livestock, handicrafts and timber are important to the economy.

The island also has two museums: Longwood House, Napoleon's home during the last years of his life; and the island's own museum, managed by the St Helena National Trust, situated in Jamestown, overlooking the harbour where the East India Company's ships used to anchor for rest periods. In addition, there are two National Parks: one is abound with rare flora; the second is full of geological structures which expose St Helena's volcanic origins.

Time: GMT.

Office of the Governor
The Castle, Jamestown, St Helena, South Atlantic Ocean
Tel: 2555 *or* 2525.
E-mail: OCS@helanta.sh

Tourist Office
Main Street, Jamestown, St Helena STHL 1ZZ,
South Atlantic Ocean
Tel: 2158.
Website: www.sthelenatourism.com

Location: South Atlantic Ocean. **Area**: 122 sq km (47 sq miles). **Population:** 4647 (official estimate 2000).
Population density: 59.9 per sq km. **Capital:** Jamestown (population 884). **Geography:** Located approximately 1930km (1200 miles) west of the Angolan coast. The island has a rare flora and fauna with some 40 species that are unique to St Helena. **Religion:** Mostly Anglican.
COMMUNICATIONS: Telephone: Country Code: 290. Credit card calls are permitted to Canada, the UK and the USA. Euro, MasterCard and Visa are accepted as payment of telephone calls. Cable & Wireless operates. **MEDIA: Press:** The *St Helena Herald* is published weekly. **Money:** The St Helena Pound is equivalent to the UK Pound Sterling. Visa is accepted by some businesses and shops. Traveller's cheques can be cashed at the Finance Department Cash Office, The Castle, Jamestown. **Health:** A yellow fever vaccination certificate is required for all travellers over one year of age coming from infected areas in Africa; see the *Health* appendix for more information. There is no National Health Service but there is a reciprocal health agreement with the UK, which entitles all those with proof of UK residence (ie NHS medical card) to hospital treatment in out-patient clinics during normal clinic times at local rates. **Travel:** There are no railways or airfields, but the *RMS St Helena* visits the island 25 times a year (15 visits from Ascension Island, including 4 from Cardiff and 10 visits from Cape Town). All effort is currently concentrating on constructing an airport on St Helena (on Prosperous Bay Plain) by 2008. In October 1999, the UK and the USA announced that Wideawake Airfield on Ascension Island should be opened on a limited basis to civilian aircraft. Negotiations to bring this into effect are ongoing. Roads on St Helena are nearly all single lanes. Driving is on the left-hand side of the road, with strict drink-driving regulations applied, plus a closely observed etiquette that all drivers coming down must make way for up-coming traffic.

Tristan da Cunha

Overview: Tristan da Cunha is composed of six islands: Gough, Inaccessible, Middle, Nightingale, Stoltenhoff and also Tristan da Cunha itself.

Tristan da Cunha was discovered in 1506 by the Portuguese navigator, Tristao da Cunha, and garrisoned in 1816 to prevent its possible use as a rescue base for Napoleon Bonaparte.

The first island settlers were mostly whalers and sealers from the USA, seeking a temporary base. Islanders survived by bartering for fresh vegetables and water, relying on passing ships for provisions. Because of the trade winds by Tristan da Cunha, these ships were in fairly frequent supply and helped to supplement the island's subsistence economy. The British connection was forged due to Tristan da Cunha's reputation for helping survivors of shipwrecks, and this also ensured the island a certain protection. By the mid-19th century, there were close to 100 inhabitants. However, the decline of whaling reduced numbers, forcing many inhabitants to emigrate elsewhere.

Later, shipwrecked Italian sailors and Irish women met in war boosted Tristan da Cunha's population, although a volcanic eruption in 1961 once again forced emigration, this time to the UK. Nevertheless, as soon as it was deemed safe to return to the island – two years later – the islanders did so. Tristan da Cunha's economy is now based on fishing and fish processing (mainly rock lobster), handicrafts and stamps. The Government and the lobster fishing industry are the only employers.

Time: GMT.

Administrator's Office
Settlement of Edinburgh of the Seven Seas,
Tristan da Cunha, South Atlantic Ocean
Tel: +870 (682) 087 155.
E-mail: hmg@cunha.demon.co.uk

Location: South Atlantic. **Area:** 98 sq km (38 sq miles).
Population: 290 (2000). **Population density:** 2.96 per sq km. **Geography:** Tristan da Cunha lies 2778km (1726 miles) west of Cape Town, South Africa. It is the most remote uninhabited island in the world. The group also includes Inaccessible Island, the three Nightingale Islands and Gough Island. **Religion:** Anglican with a small Roman Catholic minority. **COMMUNICATIONS:** Calls have to be placed through the international operator, unless made via satellite links. There is a public satellite telephone. **Money:** Pound Sterling is used for currency. **Travel:** There is no airport. All passengers must arrive by boat, if weather conditions permit.

PASSPORT/VISA AND TOURIST INFORMATION

The UK Passport Service
London Passport Office, Globe House, 89 Eccleston Square, London SW1V 1PN, UK
Tel: (0870) 521 0410 (national advice line) *or* (020) 7901 2150 (visa enquiries for British Overseas Territories).
Website: www.passport.gov.uk *or* www.ukpa.gov.uk
Opening hours: Mon-Fri 0730-1900, Sat 0900-1600 (appointments only).
Regional offices in: Belfast, Durham, Glasgow, Liverpool, Newport and Peterborough.
Personal callers for visas should go to the agency window in the collection room of the London office.

Royal Commonwealth Society in the UK
18 Northumberland Avenue, London WC2N 5BJ, UK
Tel: (020) 7930 6733.
Website: www.rcsint.org

British Foreign and Commonwealth Office in the UK
Overseas Territories Department, Room WH3/417, King Charles Street, London SW1A 2AH, UK
Tel: (020) 7008 2749.
Website: www.fco.gov.uk

British Virgin Islands

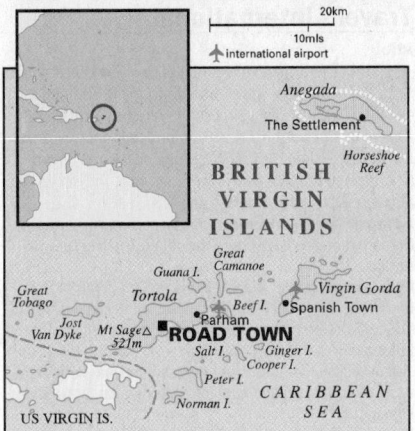

Location: Caribbean, Leeward Islands.

Time: GMT - 4.

The British Virgin Islands are a British Overseas Territory represented abroad by British Embassies – see *United Kingdom* section.

Overview

Some may be aware that Norman Island, one of 36 idyllic islands that constitute the archipelago of the British Virgin Islands, was supposedly the location that Robert Louis Stevenson based *Treasure Island* on. Today, you might not stumble across swashbuckling pirates or half-concealed troves of treasure, but what you will find – throughout the British Virgin Islands – is a highly prized booty of soft sand and gentle, teal waters.

The British Virgin Islands comprise sloping hills of green and the impressive Mount Sage National Park, but are really renowned for the nautical thrills on offer. Year-round winds provide exceptional conditions for sailing, and the British Virgin Islands happily celebrate this asset by staging frequent regattas and fairs. In addition, extensive coral reefs and famous shipwrecks are enough to entice anyone into the waters for a dive, and novices will be pleased to know that there is tuition here for those that seek it. Even if you just want to watch the sea rather than get into it, there is the breathtaking chance of spotting dolphins and whales criss-crossing the surface.

If you had time amongst all the maritime marvels to contemplate why this archipelago was called the British Virgin Islands, then you would be interested to know that the islands were annexed by the British in 1672. Two hundred years later, they were incorporated into the British colony of the Leeward Islands. The Governor of the Leewards continued to run the Virgin Islands until 1960, at which point direct responsibility was assumed by an administrator (later restyled Governor) appointed from London. The 1967 constitution then gave the islands internal self-government. Since then, the British Virgin Islands have been quite successful at tackling drug trafficking and drug use, forming a party for the 1995 election called the Concerned Citizens' Movement. It seems as if islanders are keen to preserve their home as a 'paradise'. Nevertheless, for those that seek a little legal fun, Jost Van Dyke is the party island, where holidaymakers and locals can shake their bodies to calypso and gulp at tasty cocktails.

'Paradise' does come at a cost. Overall, the British Virgin Islands are quite an expensive destination. But, for some, this is the necessary price of saving a Caribbean gem from over-commercialisation.

General Information

AREA: 153 sq km (59 sq miles).
POPULATION: 21,000 (2002).
POPULATION DENSITY: 137.3 per sq km.
CAPITAL: Road Town, Tortola. **Population:** 13,568 (1991).

Credit: ©British Virgin Islands Tourist Board

GEOGRAPHY: The 60-plus islands, rocks and cays of the British Virgin Islands, only 16 of which are inhabited, make up the larger part of an archipelago forming the northern extremity of the Leeward Islands in the eastern Caribbean. They are situated approximately 100km (62 miles) east of Puerto Rico, adjoining the US Virgin Islands. The islands are volcanic in origin, with the exception of Anegada, which is formed of coral and limestone and is the lowest lying. The topography is otherwise mountainous, the highest point being Tortola's Sage Mountain, which rises to 550m (1800ft). There are remnants of a primeval rainforest on Tortola.

GOVERNMENT: British Overseas Territory since 1672.
Head of State: HM Queen Elizabeth II, represented locally by Governor Tom Macan since 2002. **Head of Government:** Chief Minister Orlando Smith since 2003.
Recent history: In May 1999, the islands' politics fragmented further with the formation of the National Democratic Party (NDP). The party performed spectacularly well, although it fell narrowly short of the 38 per cent vote attracted by the Virgin Islands Party (VIP), under the leadership of Ralph O'Neal. Nonetheless, by winning five seats on the Legislative council, the NDP eclipsed both the Concerned Citizens' Movement (with just one seat) and the United Party (which won no seats at all), to become the main opposition to the VIP. These gains were eventually transformed into a win, when Orlando Smith of the NDP won the most recent general elections in 2003, and succeeded in bringing closure to VIP rule since 1986. Under the 1977 constitution, the British Monarch appoints a Governor to take responsibility for defence, foreign affairs and internal security. The Governor also chairs the Executive Council, which has five other members. The Legislative Council has 13 directly elected members, one ex-officio member and a speaker.

LANGUAGE: English.
RELIGION: Mainly Christian, including Methodist (45 per cent), Anglican (21 per cent) and Roman Catholic (6 per cent).
ELECTRICITY: 110/60 volts AC, 60Hz. American two-pin plugs are used.
SOCIAL CONVENTIONS: The British Virgin Islands remain linked to the British Commonwealth, and the islanders reflect many British traditions and customs. The development of tourism proceeds with great caution; hence the unspoilt charm of these islands and cays remains the chief attraction. The pace of life is very easygoing and visitors can expect old-fashioned British courtesies. Shaking hands is the customary form of greeting. Dress is informal for most occasions apart from the formal requirements of some hotels. Beachwear should be confined to the beach or poolside.

Climate

The climate is subtropical and tempered by trade winds. There is little variation between summer and winter. Rainfall is low, varying slightly from island to island. Night-time temperatures drop to a comfortable level. Visitors should note that the British Virgin Islands are susceptible to hurricanes and earthquakes, although these are by no means a frequent occurrence. The primary hurricane season is from June to November.
Required clothing: Tropical lightweights. Dress is generally informal but beachwear is confined to beaches.

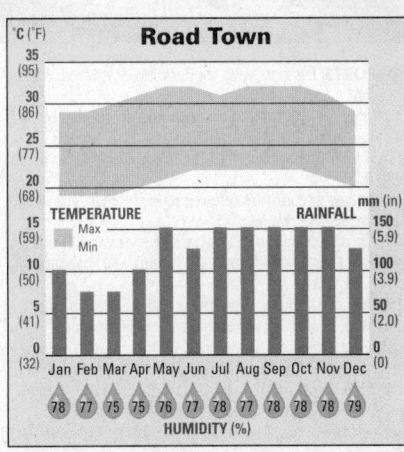

Communications

Telephone: IDD is available. Country code: 1 284 49. There are no area codes.
Mobile telephone: Roaming agreements exist with a few international mobile phone companies. Handsets can be hired.
Internet: Internet is available in some hotels. There are a few Internet cafes.
Post: Airmail to Europe takes up to a week.
MEDIA: There are no public broadcasters based in the British Virgin Islands and all TV and radio stations are operated by private investors. Multichannel and international TV services are widely available via cable and satellite. There is freedom in the British Virgin Islands' press to criticise the Government.
Press: The *BVI Beacon*, *The BVI StandPoint* and the *Island Sun* are published weekly. The tourist board publishes *The Welcome* every two months.
TV: *Virgin Islands TV Network* is the private TV broadcaster.
Radio: *ZBVI* is a private AM station; *ZBVI*, *Z-Gold*, *Z-Hit* and *ZROD* are private FM stations.

Passport/Visa

	Passport Required?	Visa Required?	Return Ticket Required?
Full British	Yes	No	Yes
Australian	Yes	No	Yes
Canadian	1	No	Yes
USA	1	No	Yes
Other EU	Yes	No	Yes
Japanese	Yes	No	Yes

Note: *Regulations and requirements may be subject to change at short notice, and you are advised to contact the appropriate diplomatic or consular authority before finalising travel arrangements. Any numbers in the chart refer to the footnotes below.*

Credit: ©British Virgin Islands Tourist Board

PASSPORTS: Passport valid for duration of stay required by all except:
1. nationals of Canada and the USA with an original birth certificate and official photo ID.
VISAS: Required by all except the following for stays of up to 30 days:
(a) nationals of countries referred to in the chart above and their overseas territories;
(b) citizens of Commonwealth countries (except nationals of Cameroon, Guyana, Mozambique, Nigeria and Pakistan, who *do* require visas);
(c) nationals of Andorra, Argentina, Bolivia, Brazil, Chile, Costa Rica, Croatia, East Timor, Ecuador, El Salvador, Guatemala, Honduras, Hong Kong (SAR), Iceland, Korea (Rep), Liechtenstein, Marshall Islands, Mexico, Micronesia (Federated States of), Monaco, Nicaragua, Norway, Panama, Paraguay, Romania, San Marino, Serbia & Montenegro, Switzerland, Tunisia, Turkey, Uruguay, Vatican City and Venezuela.
Types of visa and cost: *Tourist, Business, Transit:* £28.
Validity: All visitors are initially allowed for a stay of up to 30 days, but extensions to a maximum of six months can be granted by the British Virgin Islands Immigration Department, Road Town, Tortola, British Virgin Islands (tel: 43471).
Application to: UK Passport Agency (see *Passport/Visa Information*) or the nearest British Consulate or Embassy.
Application requirements: (a) Valid passport. (b) One application form. (c) Proof of onward or return ticket. (d) Fee payable in cash.
Working days required: Generally four weeks.
Temporary residence: Work permit and residence permit required. For further details, contact the Immigration authorities in the British Virgin Islands.

PASSPORT/VISA INFORMATION

The UK Passport Service
London Passport Office, Globe House, 89 Eccleston Square, London SW1V 1PN, UK
Tel: (0870) 521 0410 (national advice line) or (020) 7901 2150 (visa enquiries for British Overseas Territories).
Website: www.passport.gov.uk or www.ukpa.gov.uk
Opening hours: Mon-Fri 0730-1900, Sat 0900-1600 (appointments only).
Personal callers for visas should go to the agency window in the collection room of the London office.

Money

Currency: US Dollar (USD; symbol US$) = 100 cents. Notes are in denominations of US$100, 50, 20, 10, 5, 2 and 1. Coins are in denominations of US$1 and 50, 25, 10, 5 and 1 cents.
Credit & debit cards: Major credit cards are accepted in some establishments. Check with your credit or debit card company for details of merchant acceptability and other services which may be available.
Traveller's cheques: Accepted in most places, particularly US Dollar cheques. All cheques are liable to a 10c stamp duty.
Currency restrictions: The import of local and foreign currency is unlimited, subject to declaration. The export of local and foreign currency is restricted to the amount declared on import.
Banking hours: Mon-Fri 0900-1400. Barclays Bank opens until 1500 and Chase Manhattan until 1600.
Exchange rate indicators:
Rate at time of publishing
£1.00=   US$1.75

Duty Free

The following goods may be imported by persons over 18 years of age without incurring customs duty:
200 cigarettes or 50 cigars or 230g of tobacco; 0.94l of wine or spirits.
Note: (a) Import licences are required for a small number of goods, mostly foodstuffs. (b) Heavy fines and long jail sentences are imposed for the possession, sale or use of narcotics.

Public Holidays

Below are listed Public Holidays for the January 2006-June 2007 period.
2006: Jan 1 New Year's Day. **Mar 6** H Lavity Stoutt's Birthday. **Mar 13** Commonwealth Day. **Apr 14-17** Easter. **Jun 5** Whit Monday. **Jun 12** Sovereign's Birthday. **Jul 1** Territory Day. **Aug 7-9** Festival Days. **Oct 21** St Ursula's Day. **Dec 25-26** Christmas.
2007: Jan 1 New Year's Day. **Mar 5** H Lavity Stoutt's Birthday. **Mar 12** Commonwealth Day. **Apr 6-9** Easter. **May 28** Whit Monday. **Jun 11** Sovereign's Birthday.

Health

	Special Precautions?	Certificate Required?
Yellow Fever	No	No
Cholera	No	No
Typhoid & Polio	1	N/A
Malaria	No	N/A

Note: *Regulations and requirements may be subject to change at short notice, and you are advised to contact your doctor well in advance of your intended date of departure. Any numbers in the chart refer to the footnotes below.*

1: A small risk of typhoid exists in some rural areas.
Food & drink: Mains water is normally chlorinated and, whilst relatively safe, may cause mild abdominal upsets. Bottled water is available and is advised for the first few weeks of stay. Milk is pasteurised and dairy products are safe for consumption. Local meat, poultry, seafood, fruit and vegetables are generally considered safe to eat.
Other risks: Outbreaks of *dengue fever* and *dengue haemorrhagic fever* can occur, and *bacillary* and *amoebic dysentery* are common in the Caribbean. *Hepatitis A* has been reported in the northern Caribbean.
Rabies is present, particularly in the mongoose. If you are bitten, seek immediate medical advice. Anyone at high risk should consider vaccination before departure.
Health care: There is only one hospital on the British Virgin Islands, as well as Government Community Clinics. Since medical facilities are limited, certain medical cases may be transferred to hospitals in the US Virgin Islands, Puerto Rico or mainland USA. There is a reciprocal health agreement with the UK. Hospital and other medical treatment for persons aged 70 or over and school-age children is normally free on presentation of proof of UK residence. Other visitors are charged for all services at rates applicable to residents and are advised to take out medical insurance before departure.

Travel - International

AIR:

There are no direct flights from the USA, Canada, Europe or South America to the British Virgin Islands' main airport, the Terrence B Lettsome, located on Beef Island. British Virgin Islands are served from the UK via Antigua. *British West Indies Airways, Virgin Atlantic* and *British Airways* fly to Antigua. The islands are also accessible via St Maarten and Miami.
Approximate flight times: From Beef Island or Virgin Gorda to *London* is 10 hours, including stopover time in Antigua.
Main airports: *Beef Island (EIS)* is 14.5km (9 miles) from Road Town on Tortola; the islands are connected via a road bridge. *To/from the airport:* An airport bus departs three times a day to the city (travel time – 20 minutes). Taxis are also available. *Facilities:* Light refreshments/bar, restaurant, tourist information and hotel reservations, car hire and left luggage.
Virgin Gorda (VIJ) is 3.5km (2 miles) from Spanish Town on Virgin Gorda. There is also an unpaved airport on the island of Anegada. *To/from the airport:* Taxis are available.
Departure tax: US$10. Children under five years are exempt.
SEA:

The British Virgin Islands' main ports are *West End, Beef Island* and *Road Town* on *Tortola*, as well as *Spanish Town* and the *Yacht Harbour* on *Virgin Gorda*. Regular services operate from Road Town, Jost Van Dyke and Virgin Gorda to the US Virgin Islands (St Thomas and St John).
Departure tax: US$5 for all international departures, US$7 for cruise ship passengers.

Travel - Internal

AIR:

Clair Aero Services operates between Tortola and Anegada (travel time – 15 minutes). *Fly BVI* operates between Tortola and Virgin Gorda, with occasional flights to Anegada.
SEA:

Yacht charter is one of the major industries, and bareboats can be hired for all cruises. A permit is required for all charter boat passengers. Local boats can be hired for special tours. The high season is from December to April. For current prices and a full list of boats for charter and hire, contact the British Virgin Islands Tourist Board (see *Top Things To See & Do*). **Ferries:** The main routes are from Tortola to Marina Cay, Jost Van Dyke, Peter Island and Virgin Gorda (Bitter End and Spanish Town).
ROAD:

There is a good network, although due to steep and narrow mountain roads, plus poor driving standards, conditions may be precarious. Driving is on the left and there is a maximum speed limit of 64kph (40mph) throughout all the islands. **Taxi:** The *BVI Taxi Association* operates a wide selection of vehicles on a range of standard journeys at fixed rates. All drivers are capable tour guides. Taxis can also be hired on an hourly or daily basis. **Car hire:** There are many car hire companies in the British Virgin Islands, including the best-known companies. **Documentation:** A temporary British Virgin Islands licence is required; this will be issued on production of a current foreign licence for a fee of US$10. Otherwise, a temporary driving permit may suffice. Insurance and British Virgin Islands licences are available from car hire companies.
Travel times: The following chart gives approximate travel times (in hours and minutes) from **Beef Island, Tortola** to other major destinations in the British Virgin Islands and the surrounding area:

	Air	Sea
Virgin Gorda	0.05	0.30
Peter Is.	-	0.30
Guana Is.	-	0.20
Jost van Dyke	-	0.40

A B C D E F G H I J K L M N O P Q R S T U V W X Y Z

Travel Advice

Most visits to the British Virgin Islands are trouble-free but you should be aware of the global risk of indiscriminate international terrorist attacks, which could be against civilian targets, including places frequented by foreigners. The British Virgin Islands are susceptible to hurricanes, floodings and earthquakes.

This advice is based on information provided by the Foreign and Commonwealth Office in the UK. It is correct at time of publishing. As the situation can change rapidly, visitors are advised to contact the following organisations for the latest travel advice:

British Foreign and Commonwealth Office
Tel: (0845) 850 2829.
Website: www.fco.gov.uk

US Department of State
Website: http://travel.state.gov/travel

Accommodation

HOTELS:

A wide range of hotel accommodation is available; a full list can be obtained from the British Virgin Islands Tourist Board (see *Top Things To See & Do*). There is a 7 per cent hotel accommodation tax added to all hotel bills. Although there is no grading structure, many hotels in the Caribbean offer accommodation according to one of a number of plans. FAP is Full American Plan; room with all meals (including afternoon tea, supper, etc). AP is American Plan; room with three meals. MAP is Modified American Plan; breakfast and dinner included in the price of the room and, in some places, British-style afternoon tea. CP is Continental Plan; room and breakfast only. EP is European Plan; room only.

SELF-CATERING:

Villas, houses and cottages can be hired on a weekly or longer basis. Information on properties is available from the Tourist Board.

CAMPING:

Only permitted on authorised sites. Details of sites and facilities are available from the Tourist Board. Backpacking is actively discouraged.

ACCOMMODATION INFORMATION

British Virgin Islands Chamber of Commerce and Hotel Association
PO Box 376, Wickham's Cay, Road Town, Tortola, British Virgin Islands
Tel: 43514.
Website: www.bvihotels.org

Top Things To See & Do

• Delight in West Indian-style houses and a colourful market in **Road Town**, the capital of the British Virgin Islands, on the south coast of Tortola.
• Gain excellent views of the island and its coast from **Sage Mountain**, 550m (1800ft) above sea level, in the gorgeous **Mount Sage National Park**.
• Sink into sand and gaze upon shimmering aquamarine waters in beaches such as **Smugglers' Cove**, **Long Bay**, **Brewer's Bay** and **Marina Cay**.
• Look upon **Salt Island**, where salt is harvested each year and a bag sent to the British Monarch, Queen Elizabeth II.
• Enter a world of sea-shanties and tales of treasure in **Norman Island**, the legendary setting for *Treasure Island*.
• Step into the famous **Baths** in **Virgin Gorda**, a unique rock formation of dimly lit **grottoes** and **caves**, most of which can only be reached by foot or boat, but all of which provide magical, intimate scenes.
• Unsurprisingly, one thing you should do in somewhere with water like the British Virgin Islands is **dive** straight in. The clear waters and unspoilt reefs are ideal, and qualified instructors are widely available. There are over 60 dive sites, many of which are within the **Underwater National Park** System. Night diving can be especially spectacular. Vertical walls, underwater pinnacles, coral reefs, caverns and wrecks, notably the **RMS Rhone**, which sank in 1867 off Salt Island, can all be visited. The marine life includes most Caribbean and Atlantic species of **tropical fish** and marine invertebrates. Humpback **whales**, **dolphins**, **turtles** and **manta rays** also make occasional appearances. Certification is necessary for equipment rental and air fills. When diving or **swimming**, it is important not to over-exert, especially if unused to swimming in sea conditions, if unfit, or if having consumed alcohol. There is, however, a Virgin Islands Search & Rescue (VISAR) to respond to emergencies. Coral reefs are very fragile and divers should take great care not to touch the reefs or remove anything, dead or alive, from the

Credit: ©British Virgin Islands Tourist Board

ecosystem. For further details on how to protect the marine environment, contact the British Virgin Islands Association of Reef Keepers (tel: 53237; website: www.arkbvi.org).
• **Sailing** is extremely popular and there are numerous modern marinas. The Yacht Club in Road Town, **Tortola**, organises races and regattas and offers instruction in sailing and navigation. Yacht charter and one-day sailing trips are available. Day trips are also offered on the **Gli Gli**, an authentic replica of a traditional Carib Indian dugout canoe. The highlight of the sail racing season in the British Virgin Islands is the **BVI Spring Regatta**, the largest regatta in the prestigious Caribbean Ocean Racing Triangle (CORT) series. The race and its shore-side activities and entertainment attract large crowds of spectators and party-goers. For entry forms and further information, contact the Royal BVI Yacht Club (tel: 43286; website: www.rbviyc.net).

TOURIST INFORMATION

British Virgin Islands Tourist Board in the UK
15 Upper Grosvenor Street, London W1K 7PJ, UK
Tel: (020) 7355 9585.
Website: www.bvitourism.com
No personal callers.

British Virgin Islands Tourist Board in the USA
1270 Broadway, New York, NY 10001, USA
Tel: (212) 696 0400 *or* (800) 835 8530 (toll-free in USA and Canada).
Website: www.bvitourism.com

Entertainment

FOOD & DRINK: There is no shortage of excellent restaurants and inns serving local and international dishes. Most food is imported but local island specialities are often available. In addition to the hotels, eateries can be found on Tortola, Virgin Gorda and Jost van Dyke.
National specialities:
• Lobster (the Anegada lobster is reputedly the best in the Caribbean), fish chowder, snapper, whelks, mussel pie, conch stew, shark and other fish delicacies.
• *Roti* is a flavourful East Indian flat bread, filled with meat or vegetables.
• *Paté* is a dish baked or grilled, containing spiced meat, seafood or vegetables, stuffed into pita bread.
• *Fungi* is not actually related to the mushroom but instead refers to a delicious mixture of cornmeal and okra, usually served with seafood and probably closest to the Italian polenta in flavour and consistency.
• Delicious local fruits such as soursop, papaya, mango, pineapple, guava, sugar apple, passion fruit and tamarind.
National drinks:
• All kinds of rum punch and cocktails.
• Local spirits include *Pusser's Rum* (originally produced for the Royal Navy's pursers).
Legal drinking age: 18 years and older.
Tipping: All hotels add a 10 to 12 per cent service charge.
NIGHTLIFE: Many hotels have special nights with live music or dancing. There are several bars offering live music

and/or DJs on both Virgin Gorda and Tortola. A full moon party takes place on the beach at Apple Bay, Tortola every month. There is one cinema (on Tortola). The British Virgin Islands Tourist Board publishes details of all forthcoming events in its publication, *The Welcome*, which appears every two months.
SHOPPING: Special purchases include carved wooden items, straw-work, jewellery made from conch (pronounced 'konk') shell, seeds and the attractive *batik* material, designed and made locally.

Business

• **GDP:** US$287 million (1999).
• **Main exports:** Rum, fresh fish, fruit, animals, gravel and sand.
• **Main imports:** Building materials, automobiles, foodstuffs and machinery.
• **Main trade partners:** US Virgin Islands, Puerto Rico and USA.

ECONOMY: Tourism and financial services are the islands' main economic activities. Agricultural production is limited by poor soils, and relies mainly on livestock rearing, but some fruit and vegetables are produced for export, along with fish, livestock, gravel and sand. Rum is an important export commodity, and its distilling is the principal industrial activity. There is also a small mining industry, producing salt and materials for the construction industry. Tourism employs one-third of the working population directly or indirectly. The hotel and restaurant sector is particularly strong, with many customers arriving on day-trips as well as extended stays. The majority of visitors come from the USA – 350,000 annually – but the Government is looking to attract custom from elsewhere, as well as trying to dampen the islands' reputation as a resort for the wealthy.
The offshore financial sector, which has been operating since the mid-1980s, has been a spectacular success, by virtue of the British connection, benign legislation and political uncertainty in rival centres (notably Hong Kong and Panama). However, in the last three years, the Government has been forced to respond to international pressure to tighten its regulatory regime in order to prevent money-laundering.
BUSINESS ETIQUETTE: A shirt and tie are required for the summer months, with lightweight suits being acceptable at all other times. Best time to visit is December to April.
Office hours: Mon-Fri 0900-1700. **Government office hours:** Mon-Fri 0830-1630.

COMMERCIAL INFORMATION

Development Bank of the Virgin Islands
PO Box 275, 1 Wickham's Cay, Road Town, Tortola, British Virgin Islands
Tel: 43737.
E-mail: devbankbvi@surfbvi.com

Brunei

Location: South-East Asia, island of Borneo.

Time: GMT + 8

Overview

Although a tiny state with a small population on the northern coast of Borneo in South-East Asia, Brunei has one of the highest standards of living in the world thanks to sizeable deposits of oil and gas.

The country only gained independence in 1984, but has the world's oldest reigning monarchy and centuries of royal heritage. At the helm of the only remaining Malay Islamic Monarchy in the world, the Sultan of Brunei comes from a family line that dates back over 600 years. The first Sultan ascended the throne in 1405, founding a dynasty of which the current Sultan, His Majesty Sultan Haji Hassanal Bolkiah, is the 29th ruler. In 1984, the Sultan declared Negara Brunei Darussalam ("Brunei, The Abode of Peace") as a sovereign, democratic and independent Malay Muslim Monarchy (*Melayu Islam Beraja*) which would be administered according to the teachings of Islam. Sultan Hassanal Bolkiah has been on the throne for 38 years and is one of the world's richest individuals.

Brunei is a heavily forested state, and most human activity is restricted either to coastal areas or estuaries. Visitors will encounter the grandeur of Islamic architecture and royal tradition in Brunei and cannot miss architectural treasures such as the Sultan Omar Ali Saifuddien Mosque, with its gleaming gold dome.

General Information

AREA: 5765 sq km (2226 sq miles).
POPULATION: 374,000 (UN, 2005).
POPULATION DENSITY: 59 per sq km.
CAPITAL: Bandar Seri Begawan. **Population:** 27,285 (2001).
GEOGRAPHY: Brunei is a small coastal state just 443km (277 miles) north of the equator in the northwest corner of Borneo, bordered on all landward sides by Sarawak (Malaysia), which splits Brunei into two parts. The landscape is mainly equatorial jungle cut by rivers. Most settlements are situated at estuaries. The state is made up of four districts: Brunei-Muara (the capital district), Tutong and Belait (Brunei's centre of oil and gas exploitation, in the west of the country); and Temburong, the eastern district, which has large areas of virgin rainforest. The islands in Brunei Bay fall within the Brunei-Muara or Temburong districts.
GOVERNMENT: Traditional Islamic monarchy. Gained full independence from the UK in 1984. **Head of State and Government:** Sultan Haji Hassanal Bolkiah since 1967.
Recent history: Brunei is a traditional Islamic monarchy, with supreme political power vested in the Sultan. He is advised by the Privy Council, the Religious Council, the Council of Cabinet Ministers and the Council of Succession. His Majesty Paduka Seri Baginda Sultan Haji Hassanal Bolkiah Mu'izzaddin Waddaulah is 29th in the dynasty. He took over in 1967, following the abdication of his father, Sultan Omar. Political activity in his realm is kept on a very short leash. After toying with orthodox politics, the government invoked the concept of *Melayu Islam Beraja* (Malay Islamic Monarchy) as a state ideology at the end of the 1980s; Islam consequently has become a steadily stronger influence in the life of the country. Electoral politics have generally been an anathema to the Sultan. Political parties were allowed to operate openly for a brief period in the 1980s and again in the mid-1990s, although were ultimately suppressed. The Sultan's intention to maintain the leading role of the dynasty was reflected by an official announcement in August 1998, stating that his eldest son, Prince al-Muhtadee Billah, will succeed him as Sultan upon his death or retirement. In 2004, the Sultan reopened Parliament 20 years after it was suspended; this has been seen as a step towards giving some political power to the country's citizens.

LANGUAGE: Malay is the official language. English is widely used and Chinese dialects are also spoken.
RELIGION: Most of the Malay population are Sunni Muslims. There are also significant Buddhist, Confucianist, Daoist and Christian minorities. Large numbers of the indigenous groups practise traditional animist forms of religion.
ELECTRICITY: 220/240 volts AC 50Hz. Plugs are either round or square three-pin.
SOCIAL CONVENTIONS: Shoes should be removed when entering Muslim homes and institutions and visitors should not pass in front of a person at prayer or touch the Koran, the Muslim holy book. Traditionally, a Bruneian shakes hands lightly, bringing his hands to his chest. However, any physical contact between members of opposite sexes is avoided. Non-Muslims should not be found in the company of a Muslim member of the opposite sex in private: sexual contact, or even compromising behaviour, between non-Muslims and Muslims is punishable by deportation. There are many honorific titles in Brunei: *Awang* (abbreviated to Awg), for instance, is equivalent to 'Ms' or 'Mrs'. *Adat* (customary law) governs many occasions and ceremonies. Food may be served without cutlery: eat using the right hand only. Avoid giving or receiving with the left hand or pointing the soles of one's feet towards companions. Gifts (particularly food) should only be passed with the right hand, although it is acceptable to use the left hand under the right wrist for support. It is also considered impolite to point with the index finger (the right thumb should be used instead) or to beckon someone with your fingers (the whole hand should be waved instead, with the palm facing downwards). The right fist should never be smacked into the left palm, and children (or adults) should not be patted on the head. It is widely regarded as discourteous to refuse refreshment when it is offered by a host, or to eat or drink in public places, especially during Ramadan when Muslims are fasting. Visitors should note that there are severe penalties for all drug offences, and that the legal system in Brunei is partly based on Shariah law and can, occasionally, apply to non-Muslims, including visitors. Dress is informal except for special occasions. Women should ensure that their head, knees and arms are covered.

Climate

Very hot, humid tropical climate most of the year. Heavy rainfall in the monsoon season, November to December. Average temperature is 28°C (82°F).
Required clothing: Lightweight cottons and linens. Waterproofing is advisable all year.

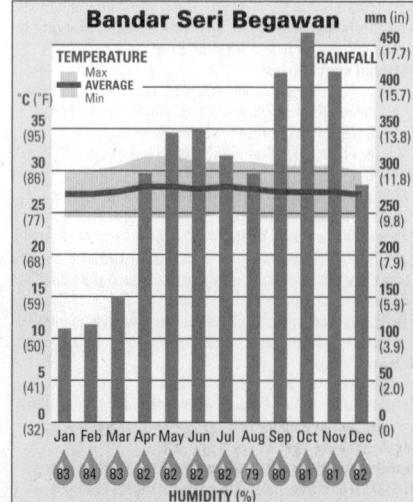

Communications

Telephone: Full IDD is available. Country code: 673. Public telephones are available in most post office branches and main shopping areas and there is a private internal service. There are both coin and card operated public telephones in Brunei. Telephone cards can be obtained at post offices or at the Telecom office.
Mobile telephone: Roaming agreements exist with some international mobile phone companies. There is good coverage around main cities and business areas, particularly in the northwest.
Internet: Internet cafes are available in Bandar Seri Begawan. A wireless network supporting ISDN lines is being launched, initially in the Rimba-Gadong area.
Post: Airmail letters to Europe take two to five days. Registered, recorded and express postal services ('Speedpost') are all available. Post office opening hours: Mon-Thurs 0745-1630.
MEDIA: Brunei's media are neither diverse nor free. The privately-owned press is either owned or controlled by the sultan's family, or exercises self-censorship on political and religious matters. A press law provides prison terms of up to three years for reporting "false news". The only local broadcast media are operated by the government-controlled *Radio Television Brunei*. Foreign TV stations are available via a cable network. Access to the Internet is said to be unrestricted.
Press: The only independent English-language newspaper is the daily *Borneo Bulletin*; *Media Permata* is a Malay-language newspaper.
TV: State-controlled *Radio Television Brunei* broadcasts in Malay and English.
Radio: State-controlled *Radio Television Brunei* broadcasts in Malay, English, Mandarin Chinese and Gurkhali.

Passport/Visa

	Passport Required?	Visa Required?	Return Ticket Required?
Full British	Yes	1	Yes
Australian	Yes	2	Yes
Canadian	Yes	3	Yes
USA	Yes	4	Yes
Other EU	Yes	1	Yes
Japanese	Yes	3	Yes

Note: *Regulations and requirements may be subject to change at short notice, and you are advised to contact the appropriate diplomatic or consular authority before finalising travel arrangements. Any numbers in the chart refer to the footnotes below.*

Restricted entry: Nationals of Israel may not be granted entry to Brunei.
PASSPORTS: Passport valid for at least six months from date of departure required by all. Travellers must be entitled to return to home country.
VISAS: Required by all except the following:
(a) **1.** nationals of the United Kingdom holding full British passports, and nationals of Germany, Ireland (tourist purposes only) and The Netherlands (tourist purposes only) for up to 30 days. Nationals of Belgium, Denmark, France, Hungary (tourist purposes only), Italy, Luxembourg, Poland (tourist purposes only), Slovak Republic (tourist purposes only), Spain and Sweden for up to 14 days (nationals of other EU countries *do* require a visa);
(b) **2.** nationals of Australia are advised to obtain visas before arrival although it is possible to obtain one at Brunei International Airport for a stay of up to 14 days (a visa is required in advance for longer stays);
(c) **3.** nationals of Canada, Indonesia, Japan, Korea (Rep), Liechtenstein, Maldives, Norway, Peru (tourist purposes only), The Philippines, Switzerland, Thailand and Vietnam for up to 14 days.;
(d) **4.** nationals of the USA for up to 90 days for social and business visits;
(e) nationals of Malaysia, New Zealand, Oman, Singapore and United Arab Emirates for touristic stays of up to 30 days.
Note: A return ticket is necessary for visa-free trips. All visitors must possess sufficient funds to support themselves whilst in the country and a yellow fever vaccination certificate is required from travellers aged one year and over who have visited infected or endemic areas within the previous six days.
Types of visa and cost: *Short Visit:* £10 (single-entry); £15 (multiple-entry). Cost changes frequently and depends on prevailing exchange rate.
Validity: Single-entry: three months. The validity of multiple-entry visas is at the discretion of the Consulate.
Application to: Consulate (or Consular section at Embassy or High Commission); see *Passport/Visa Information*.
Application requirements: (a) Passport valid for six months from date of departure with at least four blank pages. (b) One passport-size photo. (c) Application form.

(d) Fee, payable by cash, bank draft or postal order, payable to the High Commission of Brunei Darussalam. Personal cheques are not accepted. (e) A letter from employer and invitation letter from business counterpart in Brunei Darussalam, both stating purpose of visit if on *business.* (f) For *social* visits: if staying with Bruneian friends or relatives who work for the Brunei Government, an invitation letter is required. (g) For *students* in the UK, a letter from school or university confirming status and duration of course. (h) Proof of hotel booking. (i) Evidence of sufficient funds for the duration of stay, eg recent bank statement or traveller's cheques. (j) Stamped, self-addressed envelope for postal applications. (k) Confirmed onward or return tickets (copies of flight itinerary or travel agent's booking confirmation).
Working days required: Three. Applications which need to be referred to Brunei can take up to two months for processing.

PASSPORT/VISA INFORMATION

High Commission of Brunei Darussalam in the UK
19-20 Belgrave Square, London SW1X 8PG, UK
Tel: (020) 7581 0521 (ext 111/137 for consular section).
E-mail: bhcl@brunei-high-commission.co.uk
Opening hours: Mon-Fri 0930-1300 and 1400-1630.
Also provides tourist information.

Embassy of Brunei Darussalam in the USA
3520 International Court, NW,
Washington, DC 20008, USA
Tel: (202) 237 1838.
Website: www.bruneiembassy.org

Money

Currency: Brunei Dollar (BND; symbol Br$) = 100 cents. Notes are in the denominations Br$10,000, 1000, 500, 100, 50, 25, 10, 5 and 1. Coins are in the denominations 50, 20, 10, 5 and 1 cents. The Brunei Dollar is officially on a par with the Singapore Dollar.
Currency exchange: Foreign currencies and travellers cheques can be exchanged at any bank.
Credit & debit cards: American Express, Diners Club, MasterCard and Visa are generally accepted by hotels, department stores and major establishments. Check with your credit or debit card company for details of merchant acceptability and other services that may be available.
Traveller's cheques: To avoid additional exchange rate charges, travellers are advised to take traveller's cheques in US Dollars or Pounds Sterling. Hotels and many department stores will also cash traveller's cheques.
Currency restrictions: The import of local currency is unlimited. The export of local currency is limited to Br$1000 in notes. The Singapore Dollar may be imported and exported up to the equivalent of Br$1000. Indian banknotes may not be imported. Free import of other foreign currencies, subject to declaration. Export of foreign currencies for foreigners is unlimited up to amount imported and declared.
Banking hours: Mon-Fri 0900-1500; Sat 0900-1100.
Exchange rate indicators:
Rate at time of publishing
£1.00= Br$2.98
$1.00= Br$1.69

Duty Free

The following goods may be imported into Brunei by travellers aged over 17 years without incurring customs duty:
200 cigarettes or 250g tobacco products; 2 1l bottles of liquor plus 12 cans of beer (by non-Muslims for personal consumption only, provided declared at customs upon arrival); 60ml of perfume and 250ml of eau de toilette.

Public Holidays

Below are listed Public Holidays for the January 2006-June 2007 period.
2006: Jan 1 New Year's Day. **Jan 10** Hari Raya Aidiladha (Feast of the Sacrifice). **Jan 30** Chinese New Year. **Jan 31** Hijriah (Islamic New Year). **Feb 23** National Day. **Apr 11** Maulud (Birth of the Prophet). **May 31** Anniversary of Royal Brunei Malay Regiment. **Jul 15** Sultan's Birthday. **Aug 21** Israk Mikraj (Ascension of the Prophet). **Sep 25** Start of Ramadan. **Oct 10** Anniversary of the revelation of the Quran. **Oct 22-24** Hari Raya Aidilfitri (End of Ramadan). **Dec 25** Christmas. **Dec 31** Hari Raya Aidiladha (Feast of the Sacrifice).
2007: Jan 1 New Year's Day. **Jan 20** Hijriah (Islamic New Year). **Feb 18** Chinese New Year. **Feb 23** National Day. **Mar 31** Maulud (Birth of the Prophet). **May 31** Anniversary of Royal Brunei Malay Regiment. .
Note: Muslim festivals are timed according to local sightings of various phases of the moon and the dates given above are approximations. During the lunar month of Ramadan that precedes Hari Raya Puasa, Muslims fast during the day and feast at night and normal business patterns may be interrupted. Restaurants are closed during the day and Muslims are prohibited from smoking and drinking. Some disruption may continue into Hari Raya Puasa itself. Hari Raya Puasa and Hari Raya Haji may last anything from two to 10 days.

Health

	Special Precautions?	Certificate Required?
Yellow Fever	No	1
Cholera	Yes	2
Typhoid & Polio	3	N/A
Malaria	No	N/A

Note: Regulations and requirements may be subject to change at short notice, and you are advised to contact your doctor well in advance of your intended date of departure. Any numbers in the chart refer to the footnotes below.

1: A yellow fever vaccination certificate is required from travellers aged one year and over who have visited infected or endemic areas within the previous six days.
2: Following WHO guidelines issued in 1973, a cholera vaccination certificate is no longer a condition of entry to Brunei. However, precautions are still advisable. Up-to-date information should be sought before deciding whether these precautions should include vaccination as medical opinion is divided over its effectiveness; see the *Health* appendix.
3: Typhoid fever occurs.
Food & drink: All water should be regarded as being potentially contaminated. Water used for drinking, brushing teeth or making ice should have first been boiled or sterilised. Milk is unpasteurised and should be boiled. Powdered or tinned milk is available and advised, but should be reconstituted with pure water. Avoid all dairy products. Only eat well-cooked meat and fish, preferably served hot. Pork, salad and mayonnaise may carry increased risk. Vegetables should be cooked and fruit peeled.
Other risks: *Amoebic* and *bacillary dysentery* and *hepatitis A* and *E* may occur. *Hepatitis B* is highly endemic in the region. *Dengue fever* and *Japanese encephalitis* occur occasionally.
There have been no reported cases of *Avian influenza* (bird flu) in Brunei, however there have been over 80 deaths reported in Asia since 2004. Visitors to Asia should be mindful of prolonged exposure to poultry or the consumption of poultry that has not been cooked to a high internal temperature.
There have been outbreaks of *Hand, Foot* and *Mouth Disease (HFMD)* across Brunei. HFMD is a communicable disease, whcih affects all age groups, but children are particularly vulnerable.
Health care: Medical insurance is advised. Medical facilities are of a high standard. The health administration of Brunei reserves the right to vaccinate arrivals not in possession of required certificates and to take any other action deemed necessary to ensure arrivals present no health risk.

Travel - International

Note: All involvement with drugs of any kind must be avoided: possession of even very small quantities can lead to imprisonment or the death penalty.
AIR:
The national airline is *Royal Brunei Airlines (BI)*; it flies to Dubai, Kota Kinabalu, Kuala Lumpur, London and Singapore (daily), Jakarta and Manila (5 times a week), Bankok, Frankfurt/M and Hong Kong (4 times a week), Brisbane, Darwin, Perth and Surabaya (3 times a week), Bali and Jeddah (twice a week).
Approximate flight times: From Brunei to *London* is 17 hours, to *Los Angeles* is 18 hours 30 minutes including stopover in Hong Kong, to *New York* is 23 hours 20 minutes including stopover in Hong Kong, to *Singapore* is two hours and to *Sydney* is 12 hours 40 minutes including stopover in Perth.
Main airports: *Bandar Seri Begawan (BWN)* is 11km (7 miles) south of the city. *To/from the airport:* Taxi services are available to the city with surcharges after 2200. Lower rates are charged by taxis leaving from the airport car park. *Facilities:* Bank, bureaux de change, car hire, duty free shops, post office, restaurants and shops.
Departure tax: Br$5 for flights to Kota Kinabalu and Kuching; Br$12 (just over £4) for all other destinations. This is payable in local currency in cash, at the airport check-in desk.
SEA:
Ports at *Muara* and *Kuala Belait* are the entry points for sea cargo. There are passenger services between Singapore and Muara port. Ships and water taxis run a service between Bandar Seri Begawan and the Malay city of Luaban (Sabah).
ROAD:
There are access roads into Brunei from Sarawak at various locations, although some are unpaved.

Travel - Internal

Note: It is easy to get lost in the rainforest and visitors are advised to use well-known and recognised guides, and to also stay on the designated footpaths.
AIR:
There are no internal air services.
SEA/RIVER:
There are water taxi services to Kampong Ayer, with stations at Jalan Kianggeh and Jalan McArthur. Water taxis are the most common form of transport in Kampong Ayer, Brunei's renowned water village. Fares are negotiable. Regular water taxi and boat services also ply between Bandar Seri Begawan and Bangar (in Temburong) between 0745 and 1600, and also service Limbang (in Sarawak), Labuan and some towns in the Malaysian state of Sabah.
ROAD:
There are approximately 2525km (1570miles) of roads in the country; the best-developed road network is in the Brunei-Muara district, including a coastal highway which runs from Muara to Jerudong and then on to Tutong. Traffic drives on the left.
Bus: Services operate to Seria (91km; 57 miles) from Bandar Seri Begawan, Kuala Belait (16km; 10 miles) from Seria, Tutong (48km; 30 miles) from Bandar Seri Begawan and Muara (27km; 17 miles) from Bandar Seri Begawan. There is a bus station located at the multi-storey car park on Jalan Cator in the town centre. The city bus system is well maintained and inexpensive. There are six bus routes in Bandar Seri Begawan, operating from 0630 until 1800. **Car hire:** Self-drive or chauffeur-driven cars are available at the airport and major hotels. It is important to specify whether an air-conditioned car is required. **Documentation:** An International Driving Permit is required to hire a car. A temporary licence to drive in Brunei is available on presentation of a valid driving licence from the visitor's country of origin.
URBAN:
Taxis are available in Bandar Seri Begawan, in the multi-storey car park at Jalan Cator. There are also airport taxis and taxis in most hotels and shopping centres. Fares are usually metered; if not, they should be agreed before the journey. There is a 50 per cent surcharge after 2300 for airport taxi services. Tipping is not necessary.

Travel Advice

Most visits to Brunei are trouble-free but you should be aware of the global risk of indiscriminate international terrorist attacks, which could be against civilian targets, including places frequented by foreigners.
Travellers should not become involved with drugs of any kind: possession of even very small quantities can lead to imprisonment or the death penalty.
This advice is based on information provided by the Foreign and Commonwealth Office in the UK. It is correct at time of publishing. As the situation can change rapidly, visitors are advised to contact the following organisations for the latest travel advice:

British Foreign and Commonwealth Office
Tel: (0845) 850 2829.
Website: www.fco.gov.uk

US Department of State
Website: http://travel.state.gov/travel

Accommodation

Accommodation outside the main towns is not readily available. Hotel accommodation in Bandar Seri Begawan ranges from those of 7-star luxury standard to budget accommodation. Visitors should, however, note that budget accommodation is scarce and mid-range accommodation may be a better option. Serviced apartments combining home comforts with hotel luxury are also growing in popularity. Contact the High Commission of Brunei Darussalam (Consular and Tourist Information Section) for further information (see *Passport/Visa Information*).

Top Things To See & Do

- In **Bandar Seri Gegawan**, the capital, discover a fine view over the town and stilt village from the minaret crowning the golden-domed **Sultan Omar Ali Saifuddien Mosque**, which stands in the middle of its own artificial lagoon. A glittering example of Brunei's majestic royal heritage, **Istana Nurul Iman** is the Sultan's lavish home in the capital; situated on the top of a hill overlooking the city, the palace is an enigmatic symbol of Brunei's enduring monarchy and seat of the nation's government. Other sites include the ancient **Tomb of Sultan Bolkiah**, the fifth sultan, known as the 'singing admiral' for his love of both music and conquest; the **Royal Regalia Building** in the heart of the capital, home to a collection of ceremonial objects, including the royal chariot and the jewel encrusted crown worn by the Sultan during his coronation; the **Brunei Museum**; and the **Malay Technology Museum** showing traditional crafts.

- Walk around the wooden walkways between the houses, which combine traditional architecture with modern facilities such as Internet connections, in **Kampong Ayer**, a water village on the outskirts of the capital, reputed to be the largest collection of **stilt habitations** in the world.
- Outside the capital within the Brunei-Muara district, **Jerudong Theme Park**, best reached by road, offers free modern amusements and rides next to a beach.
- Other beaches can be found at **Muara**, **Serasa**, **Kuala Belait** and **Lumut Beach** near Tutong, where **watersports** are popular. Many traditional sporting activities are also available such as **gasing**, a game involving highly polished giant tops, and **kite flying**. Most hotels will have details of activities on offer.
- Local travel agents offer half-day boat tours to **Pulau Selirong**, a mangrove island 45 minutes from Muara by boat, where wildlife includes proboscis monkeys, macaques, kingfishers and eagles.
- **Tasek Merimbun**, Brunei's largest lake, is in a hill resort in the Tutong District just over an hour's drive from Bandar Seri Begawan; enjoy peaceful **picnicking**, **birdwatching** facilities and **jungle trails**. Many unspoiled jungle areas in other districts are accessible only by boat.
- There are splendid traditional longhouses in the Temburong district, which contains large tracts of virgin rainforest. Travel agents offer day or overnight tours to the **Ulu Temburong National Park** with forest canopy trails on wooden walkways; trips can include **rafting** and **swimming**. In the Belait district near **Kampong Labi**, there are more traditional longhouses including **Rampayoh**. River safaris up the **Belait River** offer opportunities to visit remote forest communities, longhouses, hot springs and waterfalls.
- Recreational parks in the Belait district include **Luagan Lalak**, where there is a picnic area and a wooden walkway across the lake.
- The **Billionth Barrel Monument** near **Kuala Belait** is a testament to the continuing importance of oil to Brunei's economy.
- Play **golf** in style at the 18-hole Jack Nicklaus-designed championship golf course with views over the South China Sea at the Empire Hotel & Country Club; Brunei's only beach resort. An architectural masterpiece, set in a 180-hectare (445-acre) tropical garden estate, the hotel is located at the doorstep of one of the oldest rainforests in South-East Asia (website: www.empire.com.bn/main.htm).

TOURIST INFORMATION

Brunei Tourism
Jalan Menteri Besar, Bandar Seri Begawan
BB3910, Brunei
Tel: (2) 382 825 or 830 or 831.
Website: www.tourismbrunei.com

Entertainment

FOOD & DRINK: European food is served in hotel restaurants, along with Malaysian, Chinese and Indian dishes. Local food is similar to Malay cuisine with fresh fish and rice, often quite spicy.
National specialities:
- *Daging Masak Lada Hitam*, spicy beef with potato beans.
- *Udang Sambal Serai Bersantan*, prawns with chilli and coconut milk.
- *Serondeng Pandag*, chicken fried with garlic wrapped in pandan leaves.

Things to know: Alcohol is prohibited, although it may be imported in certain quantities if reported to Customs. Most restaurants are open until 2100 or 2200 although this varies at the weekend.

Tipping: Most hotels and restaurants add 10 per cent to the bill.
SHOPPING: Special purchases include handworked silverware, brassware and bronzeware such as jugs, trays, gongs, boxes, napkin rings, spoons and bracelets; resplendent gold and silver threaded material known as Jona Sarat, fine handwoven baskets and mats of pandan leaves. Shopping centres at Bandar Seri Begawan, Seria and Kuala Belait offer local products and imported items. The 'Tamu' Night Market in Bandar Seri Begawan is open from early morning to late at night and sells many fruits, spices, poultry and vegetables, as well as antiques. Food is available there at the lowest prices in town. **Shopping hours:** Mon-Sat 0800-2100.

Business

- **GDP:** US$4.8 billion (2003).
- **Main exports:** Crude oil, natural gas and petroleum products.
- **Main imports:** Chemicals, food, machinery and transport equipment and manufactured goods.
- **Main trade partners:** Australia, Japan, Korea, Malaysia, Singapore, Thailand, UK and USA.

ECONOMY: Brunei's economy depends on its oil and natural gas deposits, which are mostly offshore, and its investments. Although these are not extensive by world standards, Brunei's small population enjoys a very high standard of living. The economy has grown slowly in recent years due to temporarily lower oil and gas production as production facilities were repaired and upgraded. Risk also stems from volatility in oil prices. Dependence on oil and gas are being reduced to ensure current standards of living can continue. In January 2003, Brunei unveiled plans aimed at attracting US$4.5 billion in foreign investment by 2008. Efforts are being made to move away from hydrocarbons towards areas such as, communications technology, financial services, rubber, rice farming, halal (Muslim dietary law) food, and forestry services, plus energy-intensive industries like petrochemicals, oil refining, and aluminum smelting. The education system aims to improve training in line with the country's requirements. Brunei belongs to the Association of South East Asian Nations (ASEAN) and subscribes to its major projects, including the plan to establish a free-trade zone among member states in around 2010/2015. In 1995, Brunei joined the IMF and World Bank, making available technical and consultative advice from those institutions (it hardly needs their financial support). The Asian financial crisis in 1997 had little effect on Brunei, because of the country's lack of indebtedness. However, it has since become apparent that a substantial proportion of the country's financial resources, which are under the exclusive control of the royal family, have been dissipated through individual profligacy.

Suits are recommended. Business visits are best made outside the monsoon season (between November and December). The services of a translator will not normally be required as English is widely spoken. **Office hours:** Mon-Thurs 0800-1700, Sat 0800-1200. **Government office hours:** Mon-Thurs and Sat 0745-1215 and 1330-1630. Shortened office hours operate during the fasting month of Ramadan.

COMMERCIAL INFORMATION

Brunei Darussalam International Chamber of Commerce and Industry
PO Box 2285, Bandar Seri Begawan, Brunei
Tel: (2) 226 000.

National Chamber of Commerce and Industry of Brunei Darussalam
PO Box 115, Bandar Seri Begawan, BS8670, Brunei
Tel: (2) 243 321.

Bulgaria

Location: Southeastern Europe.

Time: GMT + 2 (GMT + 3 from last Sunday in March to last Sunday in October).

Overview

Despite a turbulent history, Bulgaria is the oldest surviving state in Europe to have kept its original name (since AD681) and most of the population are descendants of the Bulgar invasion of the south Danube around that time.
Part of the Ottoman empire for around 500 years and a former satellite of the Soviet Union for nearly half a century, Bulgaria succeeded in integrating into western alliances when it became a NATO member in March 2004. The 10 November 1989 marked the beginning of the democratic changes in Bulgaria. In 1990 Zhelyu Zhelev became the first democratically elected President of Bulgaria. A new constitution was adopted (1991), the political parties were restored, and privatisation and restitution of the land started. After joining NATO, the key priority in Bulgaria's foreign policy is to join the European Union. Depending on the pace of reforms, it should be on course for membership in 2007.
A Balkan country with spectacular mountains and a coastline on the Black Sea, Bulgaria has a lot to offer visitors. With mountains occupying half the country's territory, Bulgaria is emerging as a new bargain ski destination. Visitors can stay in towns and villages that have aimed to preserve the authentic Bulgarian spirit and hospitality. Bulgaria is especially proud of its rich folklore traditions. Folk dances, music, national costumes and traditional rituals play an important part in the life of Bulgarians. In addition, the Black Sea Coast has over 370km (232 miles) of coastlines with sandy beaches and numerous attractive resorts which are ideal for both traditional seaside family holidays or more active stays.

General Information

AREA: 110,994 sq km (42,855 sq miles).
POPULATION: 7.8 million (official estimate 2005).
POPULATION DENSITY: 70.7 per sq km.
CAPITAL: Sofia. **Population:** 1.2 million (2005).
GEOGRAPHY: Bulgaria is situated in Eastern Europe and bordered to the north by the River Danube and Romania, to the east by the Black Sea, to the south by Turkey and Greece and to the west by Serbia & Montenegro and the Former Yugoslav Republic of Macedonia. The Balkan Mountains

cross the country reaching to the edge of the Black Sea and its golden beaches. The land is heavily cultivated, covered with forests and crossed by rivers. Although Bulgaria lies in the very southeast corner of Europe, the climate is never extreme in summer, even on the red-earthed plains of Southern Thrace. The Black Sea resorts have some of the largest beaches in Europe and offer sunbathing from May until October, while in winter heavy falls of snow are virtually guaranteed in the mountain skiing resorts.

GOVERNMENT: Democratic Republic since 1990. **Head of State:** President Georgi Purvanov. **Head of Government:** Prime Minister Sergei Stanishev since 2005. **Recent history:** Legislative power is held by the 240-seat National Assembly, whose members are directly elected for maximum four-year terms by proportional representation. The Assembly elects a Council of Ministers, headed by the Prime Minister. The Council of Ministers assists the President of the Republic, who as head of state wields supreme executive power and who is directly elected for a five-year term. Presidential elections are due in 2006. The Socialist Party, led by Sergei Stanishev, won the latest election in summer 2005, but did not win enough seats to form a government on its own. The liberal Movement for Simeon II (NMS), which led the former coalition, came second and the mostly ethnic Turkish Movement for Rights and Freedoms (MRF) third. Mr Stanishev has said that EU membership is his government's top priority. He has also promised to intensify the campaign against corruption and organised crime.

LANGUAGE: Bulgarian is the official language and the Cyrillic alphabet is used. Turkish and Macedonian are amongst the minority languages. English, German, French and Russian are spoken in major tourist resorts and hotels.

RELIGION: The majority of the population are Christian, the main denomination being Bulgarian Orthodox Church with a membership of 83 per cent of the population. Eastern Orthodox Chrisitianity is considered to be the traditional religion in Bulgaria. There is also a significant Muslim minority (13 per cent) and a small Jewish community.

ELECTRICITY: 220 volts AC, 50Hz. Plugs are two-pin.

SOCIAL CONVENTIONS: Normal courtesies should be observed and handshaking is the normal form of greeting. Dress should be conservative but casual. If invited to the home, a small souvenir from one's homeland is an acceptable gift. Do not give money. Remember that a nod of the head means 'No' and a shake means 'Yes'. Smoking: Since 1 January 2005, Bulgarian restaurants, cafes, nightclubs etc have zones for smokers and non-smokers. There is no smoking in public places.

Climate

Varies according to altitude. Summers are warmest with some rainfall, with the south feeling the influence of the Mediterranean. Winters are cold with snow. It rains frequently during spring and autumn.

Required clothing: Mediumweights most of the year; warmer outdoor wear necessary in winter.

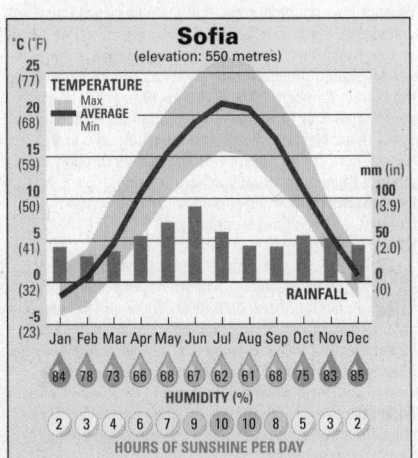

Communications

Telephone: Telephone: IDD is available to main cities. Country code: 359. Calls from some parts of the country must be placed through the international operator. There are many public telephones in the main towns.

Mobile telephone: Roaming agreements exist with most international mobile phone companies. Coverage is good to patchy in most of the country.

Internet: There are Internet cafes and centres in Sofia and Plovdiv.

Post: Airmail to Western Europe takes from four days to two weeks. The General Post Office in Sofia, at 4 Gurko Street, is open 24 hours. Post office hours: usually Mon-Fri 0830-1730.

MEDIA: Bulgaria passed a broadcasting law in 1996, one of the last European countries to do so. National radio and TV

were given the status of public services and granted independence. bTV, Bulgaria's first national commercial channel, was launched in May 2000 by Balkan News Corporation (part of Rupert Murdoch's News Corporation). Nova TV won the bid for a second national commercial TV licence in 2003. Several privately-owned regional television stations are also on the air.

Press: The weekly newspaper, Sofia Echo, is available in English, as is the daily business publication Pari (Money). Both of these are available in print or online versions. The most popular dailies include 24 Chasa (24 Hours) and Trud (Labour) .

TV: BNT (Bulgarian National Television) is publicly owned and operates Kanal 1 and satellite channel TV Bulgaria; bTV and Nova TV are national, commercial networks; 7 Dni is private.

Radio: Publicly owned BNR (Bulgarian National Radio) operates Horizont, cultural network Hristo Botev and external service Radio Bulgaria. Darik Radio is a national, commercial station.

Passport/Visa

	Passport Required?	Visa Required?	Return Ticket Required?
Full British	Yes	No/1	No
Australian	Yes	No/2	No
Canadian	Yes	No/2	No
USA	Yes	No/2	No
Other EU	Yes	No/1	No
Japanese	Yes	No/1	No

Note: *Regulations and requirements may be subject to change at short notice, and you are advised to contact the appropriate diplomatic or consular authority before finalising travel arrangements. Any numbers in the chart refer to the footnotes below.*

PASSPORTS: Passport with at least one blank page valid for at least three months beyond departure required by all.

VISAS: Required by all except the following:
(a) **1.** nationals of EU countries for stays of up to 90 days within each six-month period (except nationals of Ireland and the UK, who may stay for up to 30 days within a six-month period);
Note: UK nationals living overseas *do* need a visa.
(b) nationals of Croatia, Chile, Japan, Korea (Rep), Liechtenstein, Malaysia, Norway, San Marino and Switzerland for stays of up to 90 days within a six-month period;
(c) **2.** nationals of Andorra, Australia, Canada, Israel, Macedonia (Former Yugoslav Republic of), Monaco, New Zealand, Romania, Serbia and Montenegro, USA and Vatican City for stays of up to 30 days within each six-month period;
(d) nationals of Tunisia and Yugoslavia, provided they hold a valid passport.

Types of visa and cost: *Single-entry*: £34. *Multiple-entry*: £41 (three months); £61 (six months); £81 (12 months). *Urgent single-entry*: £44. *Transit*: £28 (single-entry); £41 (double-entry); from £54 (multiple entry).
Note: Nationals of Afghanistan, Angola, Bangladesh, Congo (Dem Rep), Eritrea, Ethiopia, Ghana, Iran, Iraq, Liberia, Nigeria, Pakistan, Somalia, Sri Lanka and Sudan must apply for an airport transit visa and may not leave the airport transit lounge. They need to present a valid flight reservation to get the visa.

Validity: Single-entry visas for tourist visits are normally valid for three months from date of issue for a maximum stay of 30 days. Multiple-entry visas are for business visits and are normally valid for three months from date of issue. *Transit:* Up to 24 hours. Enquire at the Embassy for further details.

Application to: Consulate (or Consular section at Embassy); see *Passport/Visa Information*. Applications should be made in person or by courier, not by post.

Application requirements: (a) Valid passport. (b) Application form. (c) One passport-size photo. (d) Return ticket or documentation for next destination. (e) Fee, payable in cash or by postal order only. (f) UK Resident visa (if applicable). (g) Prepaid tourist vouchers from the travel agency. (h) Proof of sufficient funds (at least €50 for each entry). *Transit:* (a)-(h) and, (i) Visa issued by country of final destination. (j) Proof of paid fare for onward destination. (k) For motor vehicle transit, proof of an extra €200 for each entry. (l) Proof of a secured return trip. *Business:* (a)-(h) and, (i) Letters from the applicant's company and from the Bulgarian business partner, endorsed by the Bulgarian Chamber of Commerce. *Private:* (a)-(h) and, (i) A letter of invitation by a Bulgarian citizen endorsed by the local authorities.

Working days required: Visas take up to 10 days to be processed (with the exception of long-term visas which take up to 30 days) and should be applied for in person if resident in the UK.

Temporary residence: Enquire at the Bulgarian Embassy (see *Passport/Visa Information*).

Credit: ©Bulgarian Tourism Authority

PASSPORT/VISA INFORMATION

Embassy of the Republic of Bulgaria in the UK
186-188 Queen's Gate, London SW7 5HL, UK
Tel: (0870) 060 2350 or 2351 or (09065) 508 950 (visa section; recorded information; calls cost £1 per minute) or (020) 7589 3763 (visa section; individual enquiries; from Mon-Fri 1300-1500 only).
Website: www.bulgarianembassy.org.uk
Opening hours: Mon-Fri 0900-1800 (general enquiries) or 0930-1150 (visa applications; closed Wed and weekends).

Embassy of the Republic of Bulgaria in the USA
1621 22nd Street, NW, Washington, DC 20008, USA
Tel: (202) 387 0174 or 387 7969 (consular office).
Website: www.bulgaria-embassy.org

Bulgarian Consulate General in the USA
121 East 62 Street, New York, NY 10021, USA
Tel: (212) 935 4646.
Website: www.bulgaria-embassy.org

Money

Currency: Lev (BGN) = 100 stotinki. Notes are in denominations of BGN50, 20, 10, 5, 2 and 1. Coins are in denominations of 50, 20, 10, 5, 2 and 1 stotinki.
Note: (a) The Lev is tied to the Euro at a fixed rate; €1 = BGN1.955. (b) Notes dated 1997 and earlier are now out of circulation.

Currency exchange: A *bordereaux* receipt indicating the amount of currency exchanged will be given, and must be kept until departure. Visitors are advised to exchange money at banks and at large hotels. Travellers should not change currency on the black market , and they should exercise caution when exchanging money in bureaux de change since some have been known to dupe customers with misleading rates of exchange. No store, bank or change bureau will accept mutilated, torn or excessively dirty foreign currency. ATMs are widespread, although it is best to check with the relevant bank/card provider prior to travel.

Credit & debit cards: American Express, Diners Club, MasterCard and Visa are accepted in large cities, in larger hotels and car hire offices, and in some restaurants and shops, mainly in Sofia. Check with your credit or debit card company for details of merchant acceptability and other services that may be available. However, Bulgaria is still a country that operates mainly on cash, rather than credit cards.

Traveller's cheques: Accepted in major hotels and restaurants. To avoid additional exchange rate charges, travellers are advised to take traveller's cheques in US Dollars or Pounds Sterling.

Currency restrictions: The import and export of local currency is prohibited. The import of foreign currency is unlimited, provided declared on arrival. The export of foreign currency is limited to the amount declared on arrival. Local currency can be exchanged at the airport on production of a *bordereaux*.
Note: Travellers should check the currency regulations just prior to departure, as they may change.

Banking hours: Mon-Fri 0900-1600.

Exchange rate indicators:
Rate at time of publishing
£1.00=	BGN2.86
$1.00=	BGN1.63

Duty Free

The following goods may be taken into Bulgaria by all persons irrespective of age without incurring customs duty: *200 cigarettes or 50 cigars or 250g of tobacco; 1l of spirits and 2l of wine; 50g of perfume and 100g eau de toilette; reasonable amount of gifts.*
Prohibited items: Any foodstuffs for personal consumption originating from cloven-footed animals, due to the outbreak of Foot & Mouth disease in the UK in 2001.

Public Holidays

Below are listed Public Holidays for the January 2006-June 2007 period.
2006: Jan 1 New Year's Day. **Mar 3** National Day (Day of Liberation). **Apr 16-17** Easter. **May 1** Labour Day. **May 6** St George's Day (Day of Bulgarian Army). **May 24** St Cyril and Methodius Day (Day of Culture and Literacy). **Sep 6** The Unification of Bulgaria. **Sep 22** Independence Day. **Nov 1** Day of the Bulgarian Revival Leaders. **Dec 24-26** Christmas. **Dec 31** New Year's Eve.
2007: Jan 1 New Year's Day. **Mar 3** National Day (Day of Liberation). **Apr 8-9** Easter. **May 1** Labour Day. **May 6** St George's Day (Day of Bulgarian Army). **May 24** St Cyril and Methodius Day (Day of Culture and Literacy).

Health

	Special Precautions?	Certificate Required?
Yellow Fever	No	No
Cholera	No	No
Typhoid & Polio	1	N/A
Malaria	No	N/A

Note: *Regulations and requirements may be subject to change at short notice, and you are advised to contact your doctor well in advance of your intended date of departure. Any numbers in the chart refer to the footnotes below.*

1: It is sometimes advised to get immunisation against typhoid and poliomyelitis.
Food & drink: Mains water is normally chlorinated and, whilst relatively safe, can cause mild abdominal upsets. Some travellers may prefer to drink bottled water for the first few weeks of their stay. Milk is pasteurised and dairy products are safe for consumption. It is sometimes recommended to avoid local fruit and vegetables unless they have been peeled and cooked. Some types of fish (including barracuda, red snapper, grouper, amber jack and sea bass) may contain poisonous biotoxins even when cooked.
Other risks: *Hepatitis B* is endemic. *Hepatitis C* may occur. *Tick-borne encephalitis* exists. Immunisation against *hepatitis A* is recommended for all travellers. Immunisation against *diphtheria* and *tuberculosis* is also sometimes recommended. Up-to-date immunisations of *tetanus* and *measels-mumps-rubella* are advised. *Bacillary dysentery* and *typhoid fever* are common, especially in summer and *influenza* is especially common from November until April. *Rabies* is present. For those at high risk, vaccination before arrival should be considered. If you are bitten, seek medical advice without delay. For further information, consult the *Health* appendix.
Health care: There is a reciprocal health agreement with the UK. On production of a UK passport and an NHS medical card, hospital and other medical and dental care will normally be provided free of charge; prescribed medicines must be paid for and can be supplied by public pharmacies. Basic medical supplies are widely available but specialised treatments may not be.

Travel - International

AIR:

The national airline is *Bulgaria Air* (website: www.air.bg).

Approximate flight times: From Sofia to *London* is three hours and to *New York* is 14 hours.
Main airports: *Sofia (SOF)* (website: www.sofia-airport.bg) is 10km (6 miles) east of the city (travel time – 20 minutes). *To/from the airport:* Buses run approximately every 10 minutes to the city centre during the day and every 20 minutes between 2100-0030. The bus station is located close to the Arrivals terminal and services operate 0500-2300. A single ticket costs BGN0.50 and a single ticket must also be bought for large luggage. Coaches are available by arrangement through tour operators. Taxis are also available, although taxi drivers may not use their meters and travellers are advised to agree on the fare beforehand. The airport itself only advises its passengers to use the taxi company *OK Supertrains* (tel: (2) 973 2121; website: www.oktaxi.net). *Facilities:* Banks and currency exchange (24 hours), post office, duty free shop, nursery,

restaurant, bar and car hire is located in the public area of the Arrivals Hall.
Varna (VAR) (website: www.varna-airport.bg) is 9km (5.5 miles) from the city. *To/from the airport:* A bus service to Varna city centre departs every 20 minutes. A coach service is available by arrangement with various tour operators. A taxi service is also available. *Facilities:* Outgoing duty free shop, banking and currency exchange (24 hours), a restaurant, bar and car hire by prior arrangement with travel agents.
Bourgas (BOJ) is 13km (8 miles) from the city. *To/from the airport:* A bus service departs every 20 minutes to the city centre. A coach service is available by prior arrangement with tour operators. A taxi service is also available. *Facilities:* Outgoing duty-free shop, banking and currency exchange (24 hours), a restaurant, bar and car hire (by prior arrangement).
Departure tax: None except for US nationals who will be charged US$20.

SEA:

Main ports: *Bourgas* (website: www.port-bourgas.com) and *Varna* (website: www.port-varna.bg) on the Black sea.

RIVER:

The official crossing points into Romania are by ferry from Vidin to Calafat and by road bridge from Ruse to Giurgiu.

RAIL:

There are frequent services between Sofia and Budapest, Belgrade, Bucharest, Thessaloniki and Istanbul. Sofia is also directly connected with Paris, Vienna, Munich and Berlin. Dining car facilities are available on all routes. For details contact the Railway Ticket Agency (RILA) (website: www.bdz-rila.com).
Rail passes: The *Inter-Rail* pass offers unlimited second-class train travel in up to 29 European countries (includes Morocco and Turkey) split into eight zones (A-H). Three different tickets are available: a ticket covering one zone (two to six countries, 16 days' validity), a ticket covering two zones (six to 10 countries, 22 days' validity) and an *All Zone Pass* (29 countries, one month's validity). Ferry services between Italy and Greece are included. Passengers must be resident in Europe for at least six months before the pass is used. Travel is not allowed in the passenger's country of residence. Travellers under 26 years receive a reduction of about 30 per cent. Children's tickets are reduced by about 50 per cent. Supplements are required for some high-speed services, seat reservations and couchettes. Discounts are offered on *Eurostar* and some ferry routes. Available from *Inter Rail* (website: www.interrailnet.com).

ROAD:

Main entry points include Koulata and Novo Selo (from Greece); Ruse, Kardom, Durankulak and Silistra (from Romania); Svilengrad and Kapitan Andrikeevo (from Turkey); Kalotina, Zlatarevo and Vrashkachuka (from Serbia & Montenegro) and Guyeshevo (from the Former Yugoslav Republic of Macedonia). Foreign citizens entering Bulgaria in a motor vehicle must have documentation to prove their ownership of the vehicle and evidence that their motor insurance is valid for Bulgaria. They must also state their proposed border crossing and pay suitable road tax. **Bus:** There are daily bus connections from other cities, including Istanbul, Athens and Thessaloniki to Sofia. *Eurolines* (52 Grosvenor Gardens, London SW1W 0AU; tel: (08705) 143 219; website: www.eurolines.com) and *National Express* (Ensign Court, 4 Vicarage Road, Edgbaston, Birmingham B15 3ES; tel: 08705 808 080; website: www.nationalexpress.com) run regular coach services from the UK to Bulgaria and other European cities.
Passes: Travellers can either choose Mini-Pass breaks or book a 15-, 30- or 60-day pass. The six Mini-Passes give travellers the freedom to visit three cities, with prices starting from £55. Travellers can stay as long as they like in each city.

Travel - Internal

AIR:

The national airline, *Bulgaria Air* (tel: (2) 8659 557 *or* 517 (flight information and reservations); website: www.air.bg), and the national airline *Hemus Air* (tel: (2) 981 8330 (reservations); website: www.hemusair.bg) operate domestic services connecting Sofia with the coast and main towns. The journeys from Sofia to Bourgas and Varna can be made in about one hour. Air travel is comparatively cheap, and is only slightly more expensive than rail travel.

RIVER:

Regular boat and hydrofoil services along the Bulgarian bank of the Danube link many centres, including Vidin, Lom, Kozloduj, Orjahovo, Nikopol, Svishtov, Tutrakan and Silistra.

RAIL:

There are over 4200km (2625 miles) of railways in the country. Bulgarian State Railways connects Sofia with main towns. Reservations are essential and first-class travel is advised. For details, contact the State Railway Office (3 Ivan Vasov St, Sofia, 1080; tel: (2) 932 5560; website: www.bdz.bg).
Rail passes: The *EuroDomino* pass enables holders anything from three to eight days' extensive travel within a one-month period on the entire rail network of their chosen country. It is valid in 28 European countries and North Africa, including the ferry service from Brindisi (Italy) to Igoumenitsa (Greece). To purchase a *EuroDomino* pass you must have been resident in Europe for at least six months and a passport number is required at time of booking. It is not permitted to purchase a pass for travel within your own country of residence. To qualify for the youth rates, you must be under 26 years on the first date of validity of the pass. Children aged four to 11 years inclusive pay half the adult fares rounded up to the nearest pound. Children under four years travel free. Seat reservations, couchette and sleeper charges are not included in the cost of the pass and are payable at the normal rate. Passholder fares are payable on some services. Reservation/Supplement charges are payable on all trains within Spain. Available from *Rail Europe* (website: www.raileurope.co.uk/railpasses/eurodomino.htm).

ROAD:

There are over 13,000km (8000 miles) of roads linking the major centres; their quality is variable and some main roads have major potholes, plus driving standards are generally poor. Traffic drives on the right. International road signs are used, although roadworks are often not signposted. Night driving can be dangerous owing to poor lighting. Tolls are charged on motorways and main roads out of town. Prices are €5 for a one-week vignette and €12 for one month. Vignettes can be purchased at ports, border points, post offices and DZI bank offices. Additionally, if the vehicle is stolen in Bulgaria, import duty and related taxes must be paid: insurance may be taken to cover this. Speed limits are strictly adhered to: 50kph (30mph) in built-up areas, 90kph (55mph) outside built-up areas and 120kph (75mph) on motorways. In addition, the driver may be banned from driving in Bulgaria for up to three years. The nationwide alcohol limit is 0.05 per cent; on-the-spot fines of BGN50-150 are imposed for offences. Spare parts are easily available and 24-hour road assistance is available (tel: (2) 980 3308). There are numerous petrol stations. It should also be observed that car-theft is on the increase in Bulgaria, and all cars should ideally be fitted with alarms and other visible security measures. Car-jacking is also becoming more frequent, usually occurring at night, and with some criminals even impersonating traffic policemen in the process. It is best to drive in daylight. **Bus:** There is a good network of buses that are cheap and convenient but with erratic timetabling. **Taxi:** Available in all towns and also for intercity journeys. Vehicles may not be in top condition. Vehicles are metered, unless they are privately owned. Taxi meters may be rigged so that foreign passengers can be overcharged; foreign visitors should therefore take great caution in determining the correct fare before travel. A 5 to 10 per cent tip is appreciated. **Car hire:** Available through hotel reception desks. Available car hire companies include *Avis* and *Hertz*. There are no fly-drive arrangements through the airlines. Payment is usually in hard currency.
Documentation: An International Driving Permit is required. A Green Card is compulsory.

URBAN:
Bus, tramway and trolleybus services operate in Sofia; in addition, a metro has been built in the the city, operating 0530-0000. Trains arrive every six minutes during peak periods and every eight minutes at all other times. Flat fares are charged on all transport and tickets must be pre-purchased. Buses and taxis operate in all the main towns. There are also trolleybuses in Plovdiv and Varna.
Travel times: The following chart gives approximate travel times from *Sofia* (in hours and minutes) to other major cities/towns in Bulgaria.

	Air	Road	Rail
Varna	1.00	6:30	8.00
Bourgas	1.00	5:30	7.00
Plovdiv	0.40	2.00	2.00
Pamporovo	-	3.00	-

Travel Advice

Most visits to Bulgaria are trouble-free but you should be aware of the global risk of indiscriminate international terrorist attacks, which could be against civilian targets, including placed frequented by foreigners.
This advice is based on information provided by the Foreign and Commonwealth Office in the UK. It is correct at time of publishing. As the situation can change rapidly, visitors are advised to contact the following organisations for the latest travel advice:

British Foreign and Commonwealth Office
Tel: (0845) 850 2829.
Website: www.fco.gov.uk

US Department of State
Website: http://travel.state.gov/travel

Accommodation

HOTELS:

Advance booking is advisable. **Grading:** Hotels are classified according to the European star-grading system, but standards are comparatively low. Special care has been taken in some hotels to conform to international standards.

GUEST HOUSES:

Accommodation is available in small villas with private rooms, particularly near the coast, but also in guest houses in a lot of small towns and villages inland.

CAMPING/CARAVANNING:

Campsites are classified from I to III, and the top two categories have hot and cold water, showers, electricity, grocery stores, restaurants, telephones and sports grounds. The camping areas are located in main tourist areas.

YOUTH HOSTELS:

These are situated in over 30 main towns.

ACCOMMODATION INFORMATION

Bulgarian Hotel and Restaurant Association
Triaditsa 5b, 1000 Sofia, Bulgaria
Tel: (2) 987 6586.
Website: www.bhra-bg.org

USIT Colours (Affiliated to the International Youth Hostel Federation)
35 Vassil Levski Boulevard, 1000 Sofia, Bulgaria
Tel: (2) 981 1900.
Website: www.usitcolours.bg

Top Things To See

- Dating back to the fourth century BC, the ancient capital of **Sofia** has a wealth of different architectural styles including Greek, Roman, Byzantine, Bulgarian and Turkish. The city boasts many theatres and museums (including those of archaeology and ethnography), opera houses and art galleries (including the **National Art Gallery** housed in the former Royal Palace), as well as universities, open-air markets, parks (over 300 of them, including the **Borisova Park**) and sports stadiums. Visitors should see the extraordinary **Alexander Nevski Memorial Church** (which dominates the city with its gold-leaf dome), built to celebrate Bulgaria's liberation from the Turks in the Russo-Turkish war at the end of the last century. The crypt hosts an exhibition of beautiful icons and the choir is excellent and well worth hearing. Other churches in Sofia include **St Sophia**, which is Byzantine and dates from the sixth century; **St George**, which dates back to the fifth century and contains 14th-century frescoes; **St Petka Samardziiska**, which is 14th-century, and **St Nedelya**. There is an archaeological museum housed in the nine cupolas of the **Bouyouk Mosque** (the largest in Sofia). The **Banya Bashi Mosque** is also worth a visit. An example of modern architecture is the **Alexander Batenberg Square**, which contains the **Government Buildings** and some Roman remains nearby, together with a reconstruction of the city as it was in Roman times. Other attractions include the Turkish baths and the markets at **Hali** (covered market), **Georgi Kirkov** and **Kristal Square** (flea market and antique shops).
- Be fascinated by the vast collection of murals, woodcarvings, old weapons, coins, manuals and bibles written on parchment at **Rila Monastery**, 121km (75 miles) from Sofia. Fire has destroyed most of the early 10th-century architecture and the present buildings date from the 19th century, with the exception of the 14th-century **Khrelio's Tower**. There is good accommodation in the monastery and a nearby hotel.
- In **Blagoevgrad**, South of Sofia, watch the **Pirin State Ensemble**, a world-renowned folkloric group.
- Further south still, travellers can visit two of Bulgaria's museum towns: **Melnik** is known for its wine cellars, 18th- to 19th-century architecture and its proximity to **Rozhen Monastery** with its beautifully carved altar, stained-glass windows, murals and icons; and the museum town of **Bansko**, at the foot of Pirin Mountain, contains the **Holy Trinity Church** with its carved ceilings and murals, and its monastery-like houses with high stone walls.
- Founded in 432 BC and the country's second-largest city,

Credit: ©Bruce Logan

the museum town of **Plovdiv** is divided by the Maritsa River and contains both an old quarter and a new commercial section. The old part contains many buildings dating from the 18th and 19th centuries (and earlier) in typical National Revival style. It is possible to wander along the narrow cobbled streets and see Roman ruins (including an amphitheatre), picturesque medieval houses and 17th-century buildings with their upper sections hanging out into the street and almost touching those opposite. The **Archaeological Museum** has collections of gold Thracian artefacts, including cooking utensils, and the **Ethnographic Museum** is also worth seeing, as are the churches of **St Marina** and **St Constantine & Helen**.
- 8 km (5 miles) from Plovdiv is **Batchkovo Monastery**, founded in the 11th century, with some rare frescoes, icons, manuscripts and coins. Batchkovo lies within the area known in ancient times as Thrace (partly occupied by the **Rhodopi Mountains**) and many items of archaeological interest have been discovered, including wonderful gold Thracian objects.
- For centuries Bulgarians have planted roses, picked their flowers and extracted their heavenly essence – *attar* of roses. The **Rose Valley** is magically transformed with breathtaking blooms in May and early June each year when The **Festival of Roses** is celebrated in many towns of the region. Rose picking rituals and folklore displays are presented. Visit the **Museum of Rose Production** in Kazanluk. The valley of Kazanluk itself has countless archaeological and historic treasures – Greek, Roman, Thracian and Ottoman.
- **Veliko Turnovo**, ancient capital of the Second Bulgarian Empire (1187-1393), is another museum town, situated on three hills circled by the River Yantra. It contains extraordinary collections of historic works of art, including church relics.
- **Turnova** has many fine examples of houses built in the National Revival style (18th to 19th century), many of which were designed by master builder Kolyo Phicheto and typically seem to grow out of the steep slopes flanking the river. The **Preobrazhenski Monastery** is quite close, as is the open-air folk museum at **Etar**, near the town of **Gobrovo**.
- The picturesque village of **Arbanassi**, a museum town located 4km (2.5 miles) from Veliko, is noted for its unique stone-built houses, its two monasteries, **St Nikola** and **Holy** Virgin, and in particular, the beautiful murals of the **St Elija Chapel**.
- 8 km (5 miles) northwest of Plovdiv, the museum town of **Koprivshtitsa** is one of Bulgaria's best-preserved towns, with primary coloured **examples** of National Revival architecture apparent everywhere. The town is perhaps best known for its **Great Koprivshtitsa Folklore Festival**, held every four years.
- Further museum towns to the east of Plovdiv include **Tryavna,** again with many examples of houses in the National Revival style; **Kotel**, which is located in a small valley in the Balkan mountain range, and is famous as a centre for carpet making; and the village of **Zheravna**, in the Eastern Balkan range, containing beautiful 17th-century wooden houses.
- Discover rare flora and fauna in Bulgaria's **national parks**. Guided tours or private visits are possible; for some areas, a permit is required. For details, contact the Ministry of Economy (website: www.mi.government.bg). The **Pirin National Park** is situated on the highest part of the Pirin mountain range. The landscape varies from the ancient Baikusheva pine forests to crystalline lakes

and limestone rocks. Many rare plant species, such as the near extinct Edelweiss, are preserved within the park, which also contains nearly 180 glacier lakes. In the southwest, the **Rila National Park** covers nearly half of the Rila mountain range and is renowned for its seven lakes and its 10th-century monastery. **Vitosha National Park**, just outside Sofia, is home to many species of butterflies and offers shelter to wolves, bears and wild cats. The **Vratchansky Balkan National Park**, in the northwest, has spectacular rock formations, waterfalls and ancient caves. It incorporates the **Vratchansky Karst Nature Reserve**, whose caves provide a habitat for many species of bats. The **Central Balkan National Park**, located to the northeast of Sofia and reached via the Troyan Pass, is noted for the **Raiskoto Praskalo waterfall** – the highest in Bulgaria - and its 50 protected plant species, many of them native to these mountains. The small **Sinite Kamani National Park** has spectacular rock formations and is home to the royal eagle, long-legged buzzard and the peregrine falcon. The **Strandzha National Park** in the southeast is Bulgaria's largest. Other national parks include the **Shoumen Plateau National Park** near the town of Shoumen, the **Roussenski Lom National Park** close to the town of Rousse and the **Ropotamo Reserve** on the banks of the River Ropotamo.
- Discover Bulgaria's nine **UNESCO-listed World Heritage Sites**. The **Thracian Kazanluk Tomb**, located in the Valley of Roses near the town of Kazanluk, has perfectly preserved murals dating from the fourth century BC. The **Sveshtari Tomb** is situated in an archaeological reserve near the town of Razgrad; it was built 2300 years ago for a Thracian king. The **Madara Horseman**, an image carved into a rock of a horseman piercing a lion with his spear dates from the early Middle Ages (eighth century); it is located on the Madara Plateau in the Danube plain. The 13th-century **Boyana Church** is located at the foot of the Vitosha mountain in the Sofia suburb of Boyana and is famous for its murals, which include replicas of icons from Constantinople. The **Ivanovo Rock Monasteries** near the city of Rousse stretch for more than 5km (3.1 miles) and consist of cells, churches and chapels dug into the rocks by hermit monks who settled there between the 11th and 14th centuries. Close to Sunny Beach is the seventh-century fishing village of **Old Nessebur** with its wooden fishermen's houses and its famed four dozen Byzantine churches. The 11th-century **Rila Monastery** is set on Rila Mountain, 121km (75 miles) from Sofia. The **Sreburna Lake** nature reserve is located near the Danube river, 16km (10 miles) west of the town of Silistra. It stretches over an area of 600 hectares (1482 acres) and is listed for its unique fauna and wildlife, including the rare Dalmatian pelican, the cormorant and the ibis. The **Pirin National Park** (for details, see National Parks section above) is a protected area of 27,400 hectares (67,678 acres).

Top Things To Do

- **Swim** in the **Black Sea**, which has half the salt content of the Mediterranean. The Black Sea coast has over 370km (232 miles) of coastline with sandy beaches and there are dozens of attractive resorts on the Black Sea Riviera. **St Constantine and Elena Resort** is Bulgaria's oldest Black Sea spa, centred on the Grand Hotel Varna, the largest and one of the most luxurious hotels on the Riviera. **Albena**, named after a famous local beauty, is situated on the edge of a lovely forest, and is a showcase and vivid monument to contemporary Bulgarian design, with good food and lively nightlife. Golden Sands is the largest resort on the Northern Black Sea coast. It has good facilities and probably the best nightlife on the Black Sea Riviera. **Sunny Day** offers a wide range of beauty and health treatments in two of its four hotels. In a forested setting overlooking the sea, it is only 10km (6 miles) from **Varna**, the Black Sea capital founded in the sixth century BC, which contains many Roman and Byzantine remains. **Sunny Beach** is a large purpose-built family resort with beautiful and safe beaches. The Black Sea port town of **Burgas** has a maritime park and an extensive beach.

- **Ski** at **Borovets**, a World Cup venue, in operation from November until April. It is only 72km (45 miles) from Sofia, at 1350m (4300ft) in the Rila Mountains, and is the oldest and largest mountain resort in Bulgaria. The 2400m (8000ft) *Yastrebets* (Hawk's Nest) is a steep, twisting red trail for the advanced skier. Seven comfortable, friendly and well-run hotels provide most of the accommodation and there is a village of timber-framed houses (each sleeping six) nearby. In Bulgarian resorts, hotels usually provide most of the nightlife. There is a disco, a wine bar and some folk taverns (mehana); sleigh rides through the snow are also available.

- At **Pamporovo**, in the Rhodopi Mountains, 85km (53 miles) from Plovdiv, there is one of the finest **ski schools** in Europe. Pamporovo is also the most southerly ski resort in Europe. The major ski runs start from the top of the 1926m (6318ft) **Snejanka Peak**. **Vitosha**, 1800m (6000ft) high and home of the National Ski School based on the FIS methods, overlooks Sofia. All the resorts have been purpose-built to blend in with the magnificent natural scenery of mountains and forest. The most recent resort is **Bansko**, a small town in southwest Bulgaria at the foothills of the Pirin Mountain. There are slalom and giant slalom runs available, as well as a 5km (3.1-mile) cross-country track.

- **Hike** along Bulgaria's 35,000km (21,749 miles) of waymarked paths. One- or two-week trips through the wild mountains can be arranged. Guides are provided and accommodation is usually in mountain chalets, guest houses or camps.

- Organised **mountaineering** and **climbing** trips can be arranged by specialised companies in the areas of **Vratsa, Veliko Tarnovo, Trojan, Maliovitza** and **Roussenski Lom**. The steep rocks of the **Pirin, Rhodope, Rila** and **Stara Planina** are popular with expert climbers. Bulgaria has twice hosted the orienteering World Championships and a national orienteering cup takes place annually on the Shoumensko Plateau. Many companies also offer organised **caving** trips to the country's numerous caves and spectacular subterranean rock formations (many of which have ancient cave paintings).

- **Horse riding** has traditionally been popular in Bulgaria and there is a choice of one- or two-week tours available; possible itineraries include the **Danube Valley, the Balkan, Rila and Stara Planina mountains** and the **Valley of Roses**. It is also possible to travel the country by horse and cart.

- For **mountain biking** enthusiasts, the **Rhodope mountains** provide excellent trails, while cycling along the Black Sea coast is a popular family activity.

- **Cruise** along the **Danube**, sailing through seven countries (website: www.bluedanubeholidays.com/european_cruises_new.htm).

- Relax in Bulgaria's many mineral water **spas**. The curative properties of the Bulgarian mineral waters have been known and used for centuries. Ancient mineral complexes were built near the mineral springs: **Hisaria** – ancient Augusta; **Kyustendil** – ancient Pautalia, **Bourgas mineral baths** – Aque Kalite, later Thermopiles; **Sapareva Banya** – Germaneia; **The Sliven Baths** – Tanzos and **Sofia** – Ulpia Serdika.

TOURIST INFORMATION

National Tourist Information Centre
1 Svete Nedelia Square, 1040 Sofia, Bulgaria
Tel: (2) 987 9778.
Website: www.bulgariatravel.org

Entertainment

FOOD & DRINK: The main meal is eaten in the middle of the day. Dinner is a social occasion, with dancing in many restaurants. Food is spicy, hearty and good. A lot of meals include meat, potatoes and cheese. Fruit is particularly good and cheap throughout the year. There is a wide variety of national dishes, as well as Western European standard dishes, which can be chosen on the spot at any restaurant. All good hotels have restaurants and there are many

attractive folk-style restaurants and cafes throughout the country.
National specialities:
- *Tarator* (cold soup made from cucumber, walnuts and yoghurt.).
- *Kavarma* (individual casseroles of pork or veal, onions and mushrooms).
- *Shishkebab* (stuffed vine or cabbage leaves and moussaka).
- *Kebapcheta* (small, strongly spiced, minced meat rolls).
- *Banitsa* (pastry stuffed with fruit or cheese).
National drinks:
- Coffee, heavily sweetened, is particularly popular.
- Drinks made from infusions of mountain herbs and dried leaves, particularly lime.
- White wines include *Evksinograde, Karlouski Misket* and *Tamianka*.
- Heavy red wines include *Mavroud* and *Trakia*.
- Liquors include *mastika* and *rakia*.
Tipping: Until recently not applicable but some restaurants now include a 10 to 12 per cent service charge.
NIGHTLIFE: Some restaurants have folk dancing and music. Opera is performed at the State Opera House in Sofia; other classical concerts include the National Folk Ensemble. There are nightclubs with floor shows and dancing in Sofia and in Bourgas, Plovdiv, Stara Zagora and Varna, etc; other classical concerts include the National Folk Ensemble. There are nightclubs with floor shows and dancing in Sofia, as well as in most major towns and all the resorts.
SHOPPING: The main shopping area of Sofia is the Vitosha Boulevard. Bulgarian products, handicrafts, wines, spirits and confectionery can all be purchased. **Shopping hours:** Shops and stores are generally open Mon-Fri 1000-2000, Sat 1000-1400.

Business

- **GDP:** US$23.74 billion (2004).
- **Main exports:** Food stuffs, tobacco, wine, *attar* (oil) of roses, metals, chemicals, petrochemicals, electronics and machinery.
- **Main imports:** Foodstuffs, fuel products, chemicals, machinery and textiles.
- **Main trade partners:** Russian Federation, Germany, Italy and Greece.

ECONOMY: In general, Bulgaria has suffered the usual problems experienced by centrally planned economies adjusting to market conditions. Successive governments have followed the path taken by other former Communist governments, under which most of industry and agriculture was privatised, trade liberalised and reforms of the fiscal and banking systems instituted. However, some key privatisations (tobacco, telecoms, banking) have already - or are - experiencing difficulties, possibly threatening the stability of the government. The value of the Bulgarian Lev was fixed to the Deutschmark by the currency control board created in 1997; it is now linked to the Euro. The economy grew at a healthy 4.3 per cent in 2004; inflation has been brought down to single figures. In 1990, Bulgaria joined the IMF, which has had a major influence on the country's economic policy, along with the World Bank and the European Bank for Reconstruction and Development. Bulgaria has applied to become a full member of the EU and expects to join in 2007.
BUSINESS ETIQUETTE: Suits and prior appointments are necessary. Interpreters can be organised through tourist agencies. If arranged in advance through foreign trading organisations, services are free. It is common for the visiting business person to offer hospitality to the contact in Bulgaria. **Office hours:** Mon-Fri 0900-1730.

COMMERCIAL INFORMATION

Bulgarian Chamber of Commerce and Industry
42 Parchevich Street, 1058 Sofia, Bulgaria
Tel: (2) 987 2631.
Website: www.bcci.bg

British-Bulgarian Chamber of Commerce in the UK
P.O Box 123, Bromley, BR1 4ZX, UK
Tel: (020) 8464 5007.

North American-Bulgarian Chamber of Commerce in the USA
851 Irwin Street, Suite 200, San Rafael, CA 94901, USA
Tel: (415) 454 8001.
Website: www.nabcc.org

Burkina Faso

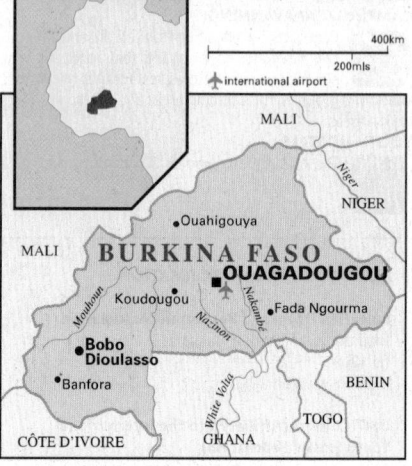

400km
200mls
✈ international airport

Location: West Africa.

Time: GMT

Overview

Burkina Faso was once part of the Great Mossi Empire, one of the strongest of ancient African kingdoms. The Mossi kingdom was established by invaders from the south, who displaced the Bobo, Lobi and Gurunsi tribes that occupied the region at the time. The region itself is in the path of several historic migrations of population. The Mossi Empire was still in place when the whole region was annexed by the French in 1896. After a period as part of the colony of Upper Senegal-Niger, the territory was reorganised as the separate colony of Upper Volta in 1919. It was then carved up between Côte d'Ivoire, Niger and 'French Sudan' in 1932, only to be reconstituted as an independent entity in 1947, as an 'Overseas Territory' of France.
Internal self-government was granted in 1957, with full independence (as Upper Volta) following three years later. The early years of independence were largely dominated by the military, notably the regime of General Sangoul J Lamizana, who ousted the civilian government of Maurice Yameogo in 1966 and ruled until 1980.
In 1984, the country changed its name to Burkina Faso (roughly 'Land of Dignity'). Under pressure from abroad, principally France, a pluralist system of government was adopted with the new 1991 constitution (endorsed by popular referendum).In general, Burkina Faso has enjoyed a fairly stable political environment since then, with just a single failed coup organised by members of the security service in 1996. Its current President, Captain Blaise Compaoré, was elected for a third term in 2005.
The landlocked state of Burkina Faso remains poor even by West African standards. However, the Government is investing in tourism and measures have been taken to increase the accommodation available in the country and to make tourist destinations more attractive. Wildlife is a key element of this objective in the eastern part of the country while the central part around Ouagadougou concentrates on business tourism. The west focuses on cultural tourism, the north on the discovery of nomadic populations and traditions.

General Information

AREA: 274,200 sq km (105,870 sq miles).
POPULATION: 13.9 million (UN, estimate 2005).
POPULATION DENSITY: 48 per sq km.
CAPITAL: Ouagadougou. **Population:** 962,100 (2005).
GEOGRAPHY: Burkina Faso is situated in West Africa and bordered to the north and west by Mali, to the east by Niger, to the southeast by Benin and to the south by Togo, Ghana and Côte d'Ivoire. The southern part of the country,

less arid than the north, is wooded savannah, gradually drying out into sand and desert in the north. The Sahara desert is relentlessly moving south, however, stripping the savannah lands of trees and slowly turning the thin layer of cultivatable soil into sun-blackened rock-hard *lakenite*. Three great rivers, the Mouhoun, Nazinon and Nakambé (Black, Red and White Volta), water the great plains. The population does not live in the valleys along the river banks due to the diseases prevalent there.

GOVERNMENT: Republic. Gained independence from France in 1960. Changed its name from Upper Volta to Burkina Faso (Land of Dignity) in 1984. **Head of State:** President Blaise Compaoré since 1987. **Head of Government:** Prime Minister Paramanga Ernest Yonli since 2000. **Recent history:** Elections in 1998 and 2000 returned Blaise Compaoré and his party with substantial majorities but their integrity was undermined by opposition boycotts amid allegations of fraud of malpractice. By contrast, the 2002 national assembly poll was a relatively transparent affair; the Compaoré political vehicle, now named the Congrès pour la Démocratie et le Progrès, won a narrow victory after its representation was cut in half from its previous level. In 2005, despite an amendment to the constitution in 2000 limiting each head of state to two terms of office, the Constitutional Court allowed Compaoré to run in the November presidential elections. He was re-elected with a significant majority, though the opposition feared the vote would be rigged and there was criticism of the amount of money he spent on the campaign.

LANGUAGE: The official language is French. Several other languages such as Mossi, Mooré, Dioula, Peul, Fulfuldé and Gourmantché are also spoken.

RELIGION: More than 40 per cent follow animist beliefs; 50 per cent are Muslim and 10 per cent Christian (mostly Roman Catholic).

ELECTRICITY: 220 volts AC, 50Hz. Two-pin plugs are standard.

SOCIAL CONVENTIONS: Women are always expected to dress modestly since this is a Muslim country. Within the urban areas, many French customs prevail. Dress should be casual and appropriate for hot weather (yet short skirts and shorts are best avoided). Lounge suits for men and formal wear for women are required for evening entertainment. Burkina Faso is a fascinating country because of its diversity: over 60 ethnic groups dwell in this country, proud to be Burkinabé, and yet keen to preserve their own social and cultural idiosyncrasies. Outside the cities, little has changed for centuries and visitors should respect local customs and traditions.

Climate

Tropical. The dry season lasts from November to March and the rainy season from June to October. The best months are November to February when the *Harmattan* wind blows from the east producing dry and cool weather. However if you have allergies avoid December to February as the *Harmattan* turns Burkina Faso into a dust bowl. Rainfall is highest in the southwest and lowest in the northeast. Aviod travelling in late March to May as the climate is too hot and dry to bear even for the locals.

Required clothing: Lightweights and rainwear for the rainy season. Plenty of scarves and handkerchiefs are recommended during the months when the *Harmattan* blows.

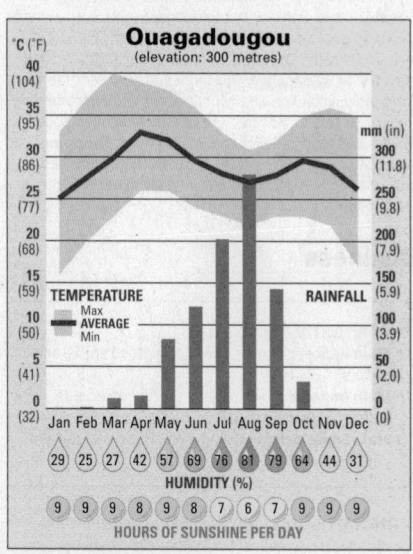

Ouagadougou (elevation: 300 metres)

Communications

Telephone: IDD is available. Country code: 226.
Mobile telephone: Roaming agreements exist with some international mobile phone companies. Coverage is

available in the five main towns. Handsets can be hired (against a large deposit).

Internet: Available in some hotels and Internet cafes. There are three Internet cafes in Ouagadougou and one in Bobo Dioulassou. Power cuts can hamper Internet use.

Post: There are few post offices, but stamps can often be bought at hotels. There is no local delivery, and all other mail must be addressed to a box number. Airmail to Europe takes up to two weeks. Post office opening hours: Mon-Fri 0730-1230 and 1500-1730. The main post office in the capital is open Mon-Sat 0830-1200 and 1500-1830.

MEDIA: The Ministry of Communication and Culture regulates the media. Despite practising self-censorship many media outlets, particularly private ones, are often critical of the government. Some journalists are reported to have been threatened or arrested. There are about a dozen private radio stations, a private television channel and many private publications.

Press: French-language only. The main daily newspapers are *L'Observateur Paalga*, *Le Pays* and *Sidwaya Quotidien*.
TV: *Television Nationale du Burkina* is state-run.
Radio: *Radio Burkina* is state-run; *Pulsar Radio* and *Radio Horizon FM* are private stations. The *BBC World Service*, *Voice of America* and *Radio France Internationale* are available via local relays in Ouagadougou.

Passport/Visa

	Passport Required?	Visa Required?	Return Ticket Required?
Full British	Yes	Yes	Yes
Australian	Yes	Yes	Yes
Canadian	Yes	Yes	Yes
USA	Yes	Yes	Yes
Other EU	Yes	Yes	Yes
Japanese	Yes	Yes	Yes

Note: *Regulations and requirements may be subject to change at short notice, and you are advised to contact the appropriate diplomatic or consular authority before finalising travel arrangements. Any numbers in the chart refer to the footnotes below.*

PASSPORTS: Valid passport required (minimum six month validity) by all except nationals of ECOWAS countries, when holding national identity cards.

VISAS: Required by all except:
(a) those mentioned under passport exemptions above, for up to 90 days;
(b) those persons continuing their journey within 24 hours to another country, provided holding onward tickets and the appropriate travel documents and not leaving the airport.

Types of visa and cost: *Tourist*, *Business* and *Transit*: €61 (three months); €82 (six months). Visa costs vary with the exchange rate. Visitors should contact the nearest Embassy for up-to-date details.

Validity: Visas are valid for three, six and 12 months from the date of entry and permit multiple entry.

Application to: Nearest Consulate (or Consular Section at Embassy); see *Passport/Visa Information*.

Application requirements: (a) Valid passport. (b) Three application forms. (c) Three passport-size photos. (d) Fee, payable in cash or by postal order only. (e) For postal applications, arrangements must be made for the passport to be returned by a courier service. (f) Company letter if on business.

(These requirements are subject to change depending on country of application.)

Working days required: Visas can be granted within one day at an additional cost if papers are in order. Normal waiting time is seven to 10 days.

Temporary residence: Application to be made to the Central Government of Burkina Faso. Enquire at Consulate or Embassy for further information.

PASSPORT/VISA INFORMATION

Ambassade du Burkina Faso in Belgium
16 Place Guy d'Arezzo, 1180 Brussels, Belgium
Tel: (2) 345 9912.
Website: www.ambassadeduburkina.be

British Honorary Consulate in the UK
St Nicholas Road, Sutton, Surrey, SM1 1EL, UK
Tel: (020) 8710 6290.

Embassy of Burkina Faso in the USA
2340 Massachusetts Avenue, NW,
Washington, DC 20008, USA
Tel: (202) 332 5577.
Website: www.burkinaembassy-usa.org

Money

Currency: CFA (*Communauté Financiaire Africaine*) Franc (XOF) = 100 centimes. Notes are in denominations of XOF10,000, 5000, 2500, 1000 and 500. Coins are in denominations of XOF250, 100, 50, 25, 10, 5 and 1. Burkina Faso is part of the French Monetary Area. Only currency issued by the *Banque des Etats de l'Afrique de l'Ouest* (Bank of West African States) is valid; currency issued by the *Banque des Etats de l'Afrique Centrale* (Bank of Central African States) is not. The CFA Franc is tied to the Euro.

Currency exchange: Can be exchanged in banks and major hotels.

Credit & debit cards: Diners Club and MasterCard have limited acceptance. Check with your credit or debit card company for details of merchant acceptability and other services which may be available. No ATMs available.

Traveller's cheques: To avoid additional exchange rate charges, travellers are advised to take traveller's cheques in Euros or US Dollars. Banks often require proof of purchase, so all receipts should be kept as a precautionary measure. It is advised to take at least some Euros in cash.

Currency restrictions: No restrictions on import of local or foreign currency, provided declared on arrival. The export of local and foreign currency is allowed up to the amount imported and declared for non-residents.

Banking hours: Mon-Thurs 0730-1130 and 1500-1600. Friday 0730-1130 and 1530-1700.

Exchange rate indicators:
Rate at time of publishing
£1.00=   XOF1035
$1.00=   XOF534

Duty Free

The following items may be imported into Burkina Faso by persons over 15 years of age without incurring customs duty:
200 cigarettes or 25 cigars or 100 cigarillos or 250g of tobacco; 0.75l of spirits and 0.75l of wine; 500ml of eau de toilette and 250ml of perfume.
Note: Permission from the Ministry of Administration is required for the use of photo-, film- or video cameras.

Public Holidays

Below are the listed Public Holidays for the January 2006-June 2007 period.
2006: Jan 1 New Year's Day. Jan 3 Anniversary of the 1966 Coup d'État. Jan 10 Aid El Kébir (Feast of the Sacrifice). Jan 31 El am Hejir (New Year). Mar 8 Women's Day. Apr 11 Mouloud (Birth of the Prophet). Apr 17 Easter Monday. May 1 Labour Day. May 25 Ascension. Aug 4 Revolution Day. Aug 5 Independence Day. Aug 15 Assumption. Oct 15 Anniversary of the 1987 Coup d'État. Oct 22-24 Aid El Segheir (End of Ramadan). Nov 1 All Saints' Day. Dec 11 Proclamation of the Republic. Dec 25 Christmas. Dec 31 Aid El Kébir (Feast of the Sacrifice).
2007: Jan 1 New Year's Day. Jan 3 Anniversary of the 1966 Coup d'État. Jan 20 El am Hejir (New Year). Mar 8 Women's Day. Mar 31 Mouloud (Birth of the Prophet). Apr 9 Easter Monday. May 1 Labour Day. May 17 Ascension.
Note: Muslim festivals are timed according to local sightings of various phases of the moon and the dates given above are approximations. During the lunar month of Ramadan that precedes Aid El Segheir, Muslims fast during the day and feast at night, and normal business patterns may be interrupted. Many restaurants are closed during the day and there may be restrictions on smoking and drinking. Some disruption may continue into Aid El Segheir itself. Aid El Segheir and Aid El Kébir may last anything from two to 10 days, depending on the region. For more information, refer to the *World of Islam* appendix.

Health

	Special Precautions?	Certificate Required?
Yellow Fever	Yes	1
Cholera	Yes	2
Typhoid & Polio	3	N/A
Malaria	4	N/A

Note: *Regulations and requirements may be subject to change at short notice, and you are advised to contact your doctor well in advance of your intended date of departure. Any numbers in the chart refer to the footnotes below.*

1: A yellow fever vaccination certificate is required from all travellers over one year of age. High-risk areas are rural areas, particularly the Poni province. Vaccinations against the A, C and W135 strains are highly recommended. There has been an outbreak of yellow fever in the Batie, Gaoua and Banfora districts of south-east Burkina Faso.
2: Following WHO guidelines issued in 1973, a cholera

A B C D E F G H I J K L M N O P Q R S T U V W X Y Z

vaccination certificate is no longer a condition of entry to Burkina Faso. However, cholera is a serious risk in this country and precautions are essential. Up-to-date advice should be sought before deciding whether these precautions should include vaccination as medical opinion is divided over its effectiveness; see the *Health* appendix.
3: Typhoid immunisation or boosters are recommended. Poliomyelitis is endemic.
4: Malaria risk exists all year throughout the country, predominantly in the malignant *falciparum* form. Resistance to chloroquine has been reported. A weekly dose of 250mg of mefloquine is the recommended prophylaxis.
Food & drink: Water is scarce and all found water should be regarded as being potentially contaminated. Drinking water outside main cities and towns is likely to be contaminated and sterilisation is considered essential. Milk is unpasteurised and should be boiled. Powdered or tinned milk is available and is advised, but make sure that it is reconstituted with pure water. Avoid all dairy products made from unboiled milk. Only eat well-cooked meat and fish, preferably served hot. Pork, salad and mayonnaise may carry increased risk. Vegetables should be cooked and fruit peeled.
Other risks: *Bilharzia* (schistosomiasis) is present. Avoid swimming and paddling in fresh water; swimming pools that are well chlorinated and maintained are safe. *Onchoerciasis* (river blindness) and *trypanosomiasis* (sleeping sickness) occur. Vaccination against *meningococcal meningitis, tetanus* and *hepatitis A* is recommended. There was an outbreak of meningitis across West Africa in September 2005. *Hepatitis B* is hyperendemic. *Hepatitis E, TB* and *dengue fever* occur. *HIV/Aids* is prevalent. The hot, dusty environment can exacerbate breathing problems.
Rabies is present. For those at high risk, vaccination before arrival should be considered. If you are bitten, seek medical advice without delay. For more information, consult the *Health* appendix.
Health care: Health insurance is strongly recommended.

Travel - International

AIR:

The national airline is *Air Burkina (2J)* (website: www.air.burkina.co). Other airlines serving Burkina Faso include *Air Algérie, Air France* and *Air Ivoire*. There are regular flights from Paris and Brussels to Ouagadougou.
Approximate flight times: There are no direct flights from the UK or the USA. To Ouagadougou from *London* (via Paris) is 8 hours 15 minutes; from *New York* (via Paris) is 12 hours 20 minutes.
Main airports: *Ouagadougou (OUA)* is 8km (5 miles) from the city. *To /from the airport:* Taxi and bus services are available to the city. *Facilities:* Banks, post office, shops, restaurants and car hire. *Borgo,* 16km (10 miles) from Bobo Dioulasso, handles mainly domestic flights (see *Travel – Internal*).
Departure tax: US$13.

RAIL:

The only route is the international line from Abidjan, Côte d'Ivoire, running through to Ouagadougou. There are around three trains a week between the two capitals. The line has recently been taken over by a French company. Work is underway to extend the line from Ouagadougou to Tambao on the Mali border, but this project may have to be cancelled to meet foreign debt requirements.

ROAD:

Routes are from Benin, Côte d'Ivoire, Ghana, Mali, Niger and Togo, although these are often barely adequate. Regular bus services run during the dry season, from Bobo to Bamako in Mali, and from Ouagadougou to Niamey in Niger and to Abidjan in Côte d'Ivoire. The road from Ghana is being improved. Bush taxis also serve most routes.

Travel - Internal

AIR:

Borgo, 16km (10 miles) from Bobo Dioulasso, is the principal domestic airport. Flights run to Bamako, Bouake and Tambao on *Air Burkina.* Air taxis are available. Passenger and postal flights are also operated by *Air Inter-Burkina.*

RAIL:

There is a limited daily service from Ouagadougou and Bobo Dioulasso. Two classes are available, but can become overcrowded.

ROAD:

In general, roads are impassable during the rainy season (July to October). Police checkpoints are a common cause of delays. Traffic drives on the right. It is inadvisable to drive at night, as there are few street lights and some vehicles do not have headlights. Visitors should be aware that there have been recent incidents involving armed groups stopping vehicles to rob them in the north of the country (including the Gorom-Gorom to Djibo road in February 2004). **Bus:** Buses and vans are called *cars* in Burkina Faso. Regular bus services are operated in the dry season to all major towns and it is necessary to book at least 48 hours in advance. These buses are also cheap and plentiful. **Taxi:** Shared taxis are available in major centres; fares are negotiable. **Car hire:** Available from hotels in Ouagadougou. Car hire is still a recent phenomenon in Burkina Faso, and vehicles may be in poor condition. Visitors are therefore advised to lease cars for a day or two before committing themselves to a longer contract. Chauffeur-driven cars are also available.
Documentation: A temporary licence to drive is available from local authorities on presentation of a valid national driving licence, but an International Driving Permit is recommended.

Travel Advice

Most visits to Burkina Faso are trouble-free but you should be aware of the global risk of indiscriminate international terrorist attacks, which could be against civilian targets, including places frequented by foreigners.
This advice is based on information provided by the Foreign and Commonwealth Office in the UK. It is correct at time of publishing. As the situation can change rapidly, visitors are advised to contact the following organisations for the latest travel advice:

British Foreign and Commonwealth Office
Tel: (0845) 850 2829.
Website: www.fco.gov.uk

US Department of State
Website: http://travel.state.gov/travel

Accommodation

HOTELS:

There are hotels in Ouagadougou, Bobo Dioulasso, Gorom Gorom and Gaoua with some air-conditioned rooms and additional facilities. Elsewhere there are small lodges. There is also a group of tourist-class bungalows at Arly National Park. **Grading:** Hotels are rated by the Government in stars.
CAMPING AND CARAVANING:

May be allowed in certain areas. Usually only part of group excursions.

YOUTH HOSTELS:

There are some available in Ouagadougou, but beds are limited.

ACCOMMODATION INFORMATION

Direction du Tourisme et de l'Hôtellerie
BP 624, Ouagadougou 01, Burkina Faso
Tel: 5030 6396.

Top Things To See & Do

- In the capital, **Ouagadougou**, visit the **Ethnography Museum**, which contains a substantial collection of Mossi artefacts, the town being the centre of one of the many ancient Mossi kingdoms.
  Other museums include the **National Museum** in the Lycée Bogodogo and the **Snake Museum** in the Collège de la Salle. There is also a tourist office in the town. Witness the **Moro-Naba ceremony**, with traditional costumes and drums, which takes place outside the **Moro-Naba Palace** every Friday morning around 0600.
- At around 0600 on Fridays, Nabayius Gou ('the Emperor goes to war') is a traditional 'drama' performed at the **Moro-Naba Palace** in Ouagadougou depicting the magnificently bedecked emperor being restrained by his wife and subjects as he sets off to make war with his brother. Traditional music and dancing can also be seen on festivals and holidays, especially in the southwest region which is rich in folklore.
- In October-November, go bargain hunting at the **International Arts and Crafts Fair** in Ouagadougou.
- Discover the attractive streets and the bustling market, the **Grand Marché**, of **Bobo Dioulasso**, the largest town inhabited by the Bobo people. Other city attractions are the **Musée Provincial du Houët** with regional relics, arts and crafts, and the **Grande Mosquée** in the Kibidwé district. Excursions outside the city include the scenic sacred fish pond of **La Mare aux Poissons Sacrés de Dafra**, 8km (5 miles) southeast of the city; the excellent bathing pond of **La Guinguette**, located in **La Fôret de Kou**, 18km (11 miles) from the city; and the **Mare aux Hippopotames**, 66km (41 miles) northeast of the city, where visitors may be taken out in a **pirogue** to view the hippos for a small fee.
- Southwest of Bobo Dioulasso is the town of **Banfora**, from where the impressive **Karfiguéla Waterfalls** can be seen, located 12km (3 miles) northwest of the town. Approximately 50km (31 miles) west of Banfora is the town of **Sindou**, the area where the extraordinary **Sindou Rock Formations** can be seen.
- From Ouagadougou, excursions include a wildlife-viewing trip to a small artificial lake 18km (11 miles) to the north. **Pabre**, an ancient Mossi village, is a short distance from another large reservoir north of the city. At **Sabou**, crocodiles can be seen at close quarters. The national parks and reserves are the best places to view **wildlife**. Tour operators in Ouagadougou can organise trips of varying duration. Entrance fees are payable to all reserves. The three national parks – at Kabore Tembi, at 'W' near the Benin and Niger border, and at Arli – are the most important. South of Ougadougou, near Po, the **Ranch de Nazinga** is a game reserve with a large population of elephants, antelopes, monkeys, baboons and warthogs.
- The best areas for **hiking** are in the southwest of the country near **Banfora**. Excellent views of the whole region can be had from the top of the **Banfora Escarpment**. The **Sénoufo** region west of Banfora is also very pleasant, as is the **Lobi** region around Gaoua, southeast of Bobo Dioulasso. **Mountain bike** trips can be arranged in the areas around **Bobo Dioulasso** and Banfora, in the Lobi region and in the Nazinga Ranch south of Ouagadougou.

TOURIST INFORMATION

Direction du Tourisme et de l'Hôtellerie
BP 624, Ouagadougou 01, Burkina Faso
Tel: 5030 6396.

Entertainment

FOOD & DRINK: Outside hotels, there are few restaurants in Ouagadougou and in Bobo Dioulasso. Staple foods include sorghum, millet, rice, maize, nuts, potatoes and yams.
National specialities:
- Rice with sauce.
- Beef and aubergine with sauce.
- Local vegetables and strawberries are available in season.
- *Brochettes* (meat cooked on a skewer).
- Chicken dishes.
National drinks:
- Beer is the drink of choice and is fairly cheap.
Tipping: Service is generally included in the bill (about 10 to 15 per cent) although it is customary to tip taxi drivers, porters and hotel staff. Tipping is more expected in the better-class restaurants.
NIGHTLIFE: Nightlife is particularly good in Ouagadougou and Bobo Dioulasso. There are several nightclubs in Ouagadougou, some with live music, and several cinemas, both open-air and air conditioned. The Wassa Club and Les Bambous are popular venues. Bobo Dioulasso has a lively street-cafe scene, good open-air bars and restaurants and a number of open-air and air-conditioned discos.
SHOPPING: Good markets exist in Bobo Dioulasso, Dori, Gorom-Gorom, Oahigouya and Ouagadougou. Bargaining in the traditional marketplace is recommended. Purchases include wooden statuettes, bronze models, masks, worked skins from the tannery in Ouagadougou, jewellery, fabrics, hand-woven blankets and leather goods and crafts ranging from chess sets to ashtrays. The Grande Marché in Bobo Dioulasso is much smaller and less cramped. **Shopping hours:** Mon-Sat 0800-1200 and 1500-1800. Some shops may be open Sunday and there are daily markets in the main towns.

Business

- **GDP:** US$120.7 billion (2005).
- **Main exports:** Cotton, shea butter, food stuffs, and textiles.
- **Main imports:** Machinery, electrical goods and agricultural products.
- **Main trade partners:** Singapore, France, China, and Côte d'Ivoire.

ECONOMY: Burkina Faso's economy is predominantly agricultural, employing 90 per cent of the population and contributing to approximately half the total output. During years unaffected by drought – a frequent and recurring problem – it maintains subsistence agriculture (sorghum, millet, maize and rice), plus cash crops of cotton, groundnuts, sesame and shea-nuts, red onions, and shea butter, which accounts for 60 per cent of external revenue.

Mineral deposits, including gold and manganese, have been located, although comparatively little has been exploited – in August 1999, the country's largest gold mine was closed as being unviable. Burkina Faso has a small manufacturing sector producing textiles, sugar and flour. New hydroelectric schemes should reduce the country's dependence on imported fuels. Economic policy has been dominated by the liberalisation measures implemented by the Compaoré government since the late 1990s, with particular stress on the reduction of the state sector, trade liberalisation and attraction of foreign investment. The economy has been growing at approximately 6 per cent annually since 2000, although it is still very poor, with an average annual per capita income of US$300 and depends heavily on overseas aid, particularly from France and the EU. Burkina Faso belongs to the CFA Franc Zone, which fixes the value of the local currency to that of the Euro (formerly the French Franc). Imports outweigh exports in value by a factor of five. Over one-third of exports are bought by France, which provides a similar quantity of Burkina Faso's imports.

BUSINESS ETIQUETTE: Suits should be worn for government and official business, otherwise a shirt and tie should suffice. Most officials prefer to wear national dress. French is the main language spoken in business circles and if the visitor does not have a command of French, interpreter services should be sought from the British Embassy. **Office hours:** Mon-Fri 0700-1230 and 1500-1730.

COMMERCIAL INFORMATION

Chambre de Commerce, d'Industrie et d'Artisanat du Burkina Faso
01 BP 502, Ouagadougou 01, Burkina Faso
Tel: 5030 6114 *or* 6115.
Website: www.ccia.bf

Burundi

Location: Central Africa.

Time: GMT + 2.

Overview

Burundi is geographically at the heart of Africa but, sadly, has also been at the heart of African horrors in recent years. Here is a country of wonderful landscapes, from mountaintops to forests, huge lakes to tropical plateau. Yet this topographical patchwork mirrors Burundi's cultural patchwork, one which has interwoven both Hutu and Tutsi tribal strands, often with violent consequences.

The agricultural Hutu and pastoralist Tutsi have occupied Burundi for many centuries. The society was never highly centralised and proved unable to withstand the advances of the Germans during the scramble for Africa in the 19th century. The country subsequently became part of German East Africa. Shuffled around yet again after 1919, Burundi and neighbouring Rwanda were administered by the Belgians. During this time, the Belgians unfortunately demarcated the Hutu and Tutsi tribes further, believing the Tutsis to be superior to the Hutus and bestowing on the Tutsis better jobs and status. When both Burundi and Rwanda gained independence in 1962, Burundi's chronic instability worsened, sporadically flaring up into mass violence and the massacre of tens of thousands, especially in 1972 and 1988 (although it has never reached the scale of neighbouring Rwanda, where the same ethnic split prevails).

Politically, Burundi has also been split by several coups; three occurred between 1966 and 1987. President Buyoya seemed to herald positive progression in 1992, with a change of constitution and the introduction of multiparty elections for a National Assembly. Against widespread expectation, the incumbent President Buyoya – representing the main Tutsi party (UPRONA) - was peacefully displaced by Melchior Ndadaye, a Hutu banker who headed the Front for Democracy in Burundi (FRODEBU). In October 1993, another military coup was unsuccessful but claimed the life of President Ndadaye. In January 1994, another Hutu, Cyprien Ntaryamira, took over but had an equally short tenure; returning from an overseas trip with Rwandan President Juvénal Habyarimana, he was killed in a plane crash (see Rwanda). This was the incident that set off the genocide in Rwanda. Burundi narrowly avoided the same fate, although tensions between Tutsi and Hutu sharply increased and the civil war that followed

claimed 300,000 lives – in Nelson Mandela's words: 'a slow-burning genocide.'

Burundi's situation is improving. President Nkurunziza, democratically elected in 2005, is engaged in peace talks and has announced applauded measures, such as that of introducing free education. However, there is still a danger of indiscriminate attacks from rebel groups in Burundi. Until these incidents are fully quashed, many will miss out on seeing the beauty of Burundi for themselves. Amongst the debris of human nature at its most vicious, nature itself in Burundi remains gorgeous and tranquil.

General Information

AREA: 27,816 sq km (10,740 sq miles).
POPULATION: 7.3 million (2005).
POPULATION DENSITY: 262.4 per sq km.
CAPITAL: Bujumbura. **Population:** 200,000 (2005).
GEOGRAPHY: Burundi is a land-locked country in the heart of Africa, a little south of the equator, on the eastern shore of Lake Tanganyika. It is bordered by Rwanda to the north, by the Democratic Republic of Congo to the west and by Tanzania to the south and east. The interior is a broken plateau sloping east to Tanzania and the valley of the River Malagarasi. The southern tributary of the Nile system rises in the south of the country. The landscape is characterised by hills and valleys covered with eucalyptus trees, banana groves, cultivated fields and pasture. In the east, the fertile area gives way to savannah grassland, and tea and coffee are now grown on mountainsides.
GOVERNMENT: Republic. Gained independence from Belgium in 1966. **Head of State and Government:** President Pierre Nkurunziza since 2005. **Recent history:** In the final years of the 1990s, the guerrilla war between Hutu rebels and the Tutsi-dominated army intensified. However, mediation efforts by the Tanzanians and, crucially, Nelson Mandela, drew most of the parties into a draft accord in March 2000, with a final settlement in November 2001. The largest Hutu rebel group, the Forces for the Defence of Democracy (FDD), signed the accord, although dissident FDD elements, along with the other main rebel group, the National Liberation Front (which has not signed) continued their guerrilla war against the Government. Nonetheless, the accord has worked out reasonably well and been implemented on schedule. A transitional Government jointly led by Buyoya and FRODEBU leader Domitien Ndayizeye, held power until April 2003, when Buyoya stood down and Ndayizeye became the country's sole leader. A South African-led African Union peacekeeping force has been brought in to try and control the country – a formidable task by any standards. Former rebel leader Pierre Nkurunziza was elected as President in August 2005 in the final step of a deal to end 12 years of war between Hutu rebels and the Tutsi army. Although he was the only candidate, he is the first President chosen through democratic means since the start of the civil war in 1993. Under the new terms of the deal agreed between the Government and Hutu rebels, democracy will be balanced with guarantees for the Tutsi minority.

Under the 1998 constitution, modified from the 1992 constitution, executive power rests with an elected President. Two Vice-Presidential posts, assigned to the two main ethnic groups, were also created. Legislative power is held by the National Transitional Assembly, comprising the 81 elected members of the former National Assembly elected under the old 1992 constitution, plus 40 additional members appointed from political parties and 'civil society'.
LANGUAGE: The official languages are French and Kirundi, a Bantu language. Swahili and English are also spoken.
RELIGION: 77 per cent of the population are Christian, the majority of which are Roman Catholic; there are Anglican and Pentecostal minorities. 22 per cent adhere to animist beliefs. There is also a small (1 per cent) Muslim community.
ELECTRICITY: 220 volts AC, 50Hz.
SOCIAL CONVENTIONS: Normal social courtesies apply. However, outside the cities people may not be used to visitors, and care and tact must be used in respect of local customs. Inhabitants of major towns generally have a more modern way of life. Dress should be reasonably conservative.

Climate

A hot equatorial climate is found near Lake Tanganyika and in the Ruzizi River plain. It is often windy on the lake. The rest of the country is mild and pleasant. Burundi has two rainy seasons – the major one from February to May, with a minor rainy season between September and November, and two dry seasons: the long dry season from June to August and the shorter dry season between December and January.
Required clothing: Lightweight cottons and linens with waterproofs for the rainy season. Warm clothes are recommended for the evening.

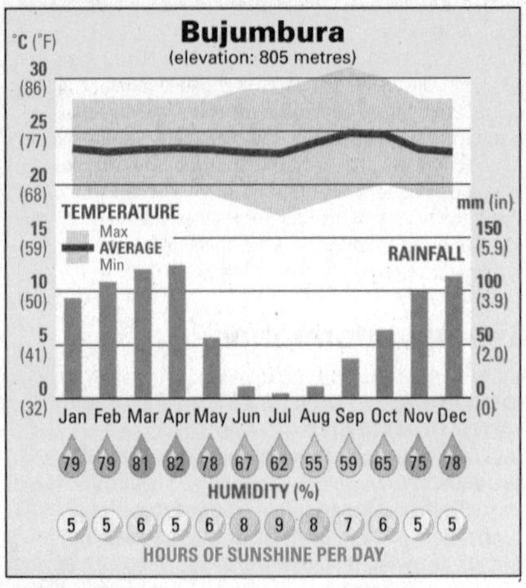
Bujumbura
(elevation: 805 metres)
°C (°F)
30 (86)
25 (77)
20 (68)
15 (59)
10 (50)
5 (41)
0 (32)
TEMPERATURE
Max
AVERAGE
Min
mm (in)
150 (5.9)
100 (3.9)
50 (2.0)
0 (0)
RAINFALL
Jan Feb Mar Apr May Jun Jul Aug Sep Oct Nov Dec
79 79 81 82 78 67 62 55 59 65 75 78
HUMIDITY (%)
5 5 6 5 6 8 9 8 7 6 5 5
HOURS OF SUNSHINE PER DAY

Communications

Telephone: IDD is available. Country code: 257.
Mobile telephone: Coverage mainly in the west of the country.
Internet: Available in some areas. There are a few Internet cafes in Bujumbura.
Post: The main post office in Bujumbura is open Mon-Fri 0730-1200 and 1400-1730, Sat 0830-1200.
MEDIA: Burundi's media are self-censored and also receive occasional Government censorship. Nevertheless, a range of political views are sometimes aired. There is a high turnover rate for newspapers. The sale of newspapers is quite low due to small print runs and low levels of literacy. The main source of information for many Burundians is therefore the radio. The only radio station with national coverage is Government-owned, as is Burundi's only TV station.
Press: No English-language newspapers are published. Most publications are in French (such as *Le Renouveau du Burundi*) or local languages (such as *Ubumwe* in Kirundi). The two main newspapers are Government-controlled.
TV: *RTNB* is Government-controlled and broadcasts in English, French, Kirundi and Swahili.
Radio: *Radio Burundi* is Government-controlled (by RTNB), and also operates an educational network. *Radio Isanganiro* and *Radio Publique Africaine* are private (although the latter receives some UN and overseas funding). *Radio CCIB+* is operated by the Burundi Chamber of Commerce. Other radio broadcasters in operation with the aid of funding include *Bonesha FM* (funded by international organisations with the intention of promoting reconciliation) and *Radio Culture* (partly funded by the health ministry).

Passport/Visa

	Passport Required?	Visa Required?	Return Ticket Required?
Full British	Yes	Yes	Yes
Australian	Yes	Yes	Yes
Canadian	Yes	Yes	Yes
USA	Yes	Yes	Yes
Other EU	Yes	Yes	Yes
Japanese	Yes	Yes	Yes

Note: Regulations and requirements may be subject to change at short notice, and you are advised to contact the appropriate diplomatic or consular authority before finalising travel arrangements. Any numbers in the chart refer to the footnotes below.

PASSPORTS: Valid passport for at least six months required by all.
VISAS: Required by all except nationals of Rwanda and Uganda. Passengers arriving at Bujumbura airport from countries where Burundi does not have diplomatic representation can obtain visas on arrival, providing they have previously informed their travel agency of their passport number, identity and flight details. Those who are continuing onto a third country within 72 hours may also obtain a visa upon arrival. It is better to obtain a visa in advance from the nearest Burundi embassy.
Types of visa and cost: *Tourist* or *Business* (valid for up to 30 days): US$80 or US$40 (non-US citizens); single- or multiple-entry. Visas cost US$160 for stays exceeding 30 days. The validity of the visa is at the discretion of the Immigration Department. A transit visa is not required for passengers continuing their journey to a third country if staying up to 24 hours, provided holding valid onward documentation and not leaving the airport. If staying up to 72 hours, a fee of US$10 is required. A Re-entry Permit is required for all alien residents.
Application to: Consulate (or Consular section at Embassy); see *Passport/Visa Information*.
Application requirements: (a) Valid passport. (b) Three application forms (requests for application forms should be accompanied by a stamped, self-addressed envelope). (c) Three passport-size photos. (d) Return ticket or copy of flight itinerary, plus proof of accommodation. (e) Fee, payable in cash, postal order or company cheque. (f) Stamped, self-addressed envelope for recorded delivery. (g) Yellow fever vaccination certificate. *Business*: (a)-(g) and, (h) Letter from the applicant's employer and the sponsoring company in Burundi. Letter must state the nature of business, name and address of referee to be visited, guarantee of return transport, sufficient funds for duration of stay and must be signed by the officer of company. *Visitor*: (a)-(g) and, (h) Invitation letter from family members or friends.
Working days required: Two. Applications should be made as far as possible in advance of the intended date of departure. A rush fee of US$25 is available.

PASSPORT/VISA INFORMATION

Embassy of the Republic of Burundi in Belgium
46 square Marie-Louise, 1000 Brussels, Belgium
Tel: (2) 230 4535.

Embassy of the Republic of Burundi in the USA
Suite 212, 2233 Wisconsin Avenue, NW,
Washington, DC 20007, USA
Tel: (202) 342 2574.
Website: www.burundiembassy-usa.org

Money

Currency: Burundi Franc (BIF) = 100 centimes. Notes are in denominations of BIF5000, 1000, 500, 100, 50, 20 and 10. Coins are in denominations of BIF10, 5 and 1.
Currency exchange: All exchange transactions must be conducted through one of the main banks in Bujumbura or Gitega.
Credit & debit cards: Major credit cards are not generally accepted; there is limited use in some major hotels.
Traveller's cheques: To avoid additional exchange rate charges, travellers are advised to take traveller's cheques in US Dollars or Euros. Commission rates are usually high.
Currency restrictions: The import and export of local currency is limited to BIF2000. The import and export of foreign currency is unlimited, subject to declaration.
Banking hours: Mon-Fri, mornings only.
Exchange rate indicators:
Rate at time of publishing
£1.00= BIF1828.24
$1.00= BIF1035.79

Duty Free

The following goods may be imported into Burundi without incurring customs duty:
1000 cigarettes or 1kg of tobacco; 1l of alcoholic beverages; a reasonable amount of perfume.
Note: A deposit may be required for items such as cameras, recorders and laptop computers.
Currency and cameras should be declared upon arrival.

Public Holidays

Below are listed Public Holidays for the January 2006-June 2007 period.
2006: Jan 1 New Year's Day. **Feb 5** Unity Day. **Mar 12** Labour Day. **May 25** Ascension. **Jul 1** Independence Day. **Aug 15** Assumption. **Oct 13** Anniversary of Rwagasore's Assassination. **Oct 21** Anniversary of President Ndadaye's Assassination. **Nov 1** All Saints' Day. **Dec 25** Christmas Day.
2007: Jan 1 New Year's Day. **Feb 5** Unity Day. **Mar 12** Labour Day. **May 17** Ascension.

Health

	Special Precautions?	Certificate Required?
Yellow Fever	Yes	1
Cholera	Yes	2
Typhoid & Polio	3	N/A
Malaria	4	N/A

Note: Regulations and requirements may be subject to change at short notice, and you are advised to contact your doctor well in advance of your intended date of departure. Any numbers in the chart refer to the footnotes below.

1: A yellow fever vaccination certificate is required from travellers over one year of age arriving from infected areas. The country is officially considered endemic for yellow fever. Travellers arriving from non-endemic zones should note that vaccination is strongly recommended for travel outside the urban areas, even if an outbreak of the disease has not been reported and they would normally not require a vaccination certificate to enter the country.
2: Despite WHO guidelines issued in 1973, a cholera vaccination certificate may still be a condition of entry to Burundi. Cholera is a serious risk in this country and precautions are essential; there was a serious outbreak in the Rumonage District in 1999, and there were several clusters of cholera cases in 2004. Up-to-date advice should be sought before deciding whether these precautions should include vaccination as medical opinion is divided over its effectiveness; see the *Health* appendix.
3: Vaccines against poliomyelitis and typhoid are advised.
4: Malaria risk exists throughout the year, predominantly in the malignant *falciparum* form, in the whole country. Resistance to chloroquine has been reported. The recommended prophylaxis is mefloquine.
Food & drink: All water should be regarded as being potentially contaminated. Water used for drinking, brushing teeth or making ice should have first been boiled or otherwise sterilised. Milk is unpasteurised and should be boiled. Powdered or tinned milk is available and is advised, but make sure that it is reconstituted with pure water. Avoid dairy products that are likely to have been made from unboiled milk. Only eat well-cooked meat and fish, preferably served hot. Avoid food from street vendors. Pork, salad and mayonnaise may carry increased risk. Vegetables should be cooked and fruit peeled.
Note: Visitors may be asked to show proof of vaccination against meningococcal meningitis. The following vaccinations should be up-to-date: tetanus (for those over 10 years); flu (for those over 50 years); hepatitis B; mumps, measles and rubella; and chickenpox.
Other risks: *Hepatitis A* and *E*, *dysentery* and *typhoid fever* are widespread. *Hepatitis B* is hyperendemic. *Meningitis* is present all year (see note above). *Bilharzia* (schistosomiasis) is present; avoid swimming and paddling in fresh water. Swimming pools that are well chlorinated and maintained are safe. It is advised not to go barefoot, even on beaches. *Onchocerciasis* (river blindness) is present, as is *human trypanosomiasis* (sleeping sickness) in certain areas. *HIV/Aids* is prevalent.
Rabies is present. For those at high risk, vaccination before arrival should be considered. If you are bitten, seek medical advice without delay. For more information, consult the *Health* appendix.
Health care: Full medical insurance, including repatriation, is essential. Medical supplies are limited. In the event of a serious accident, evacuation by air ambulance may be required.

Travel - International

AIR:
The national airline is *Air Burundi (8Y)*. However, this airline is not approved by the International Air Transport Association. Other airlines serving Burundi include *Ethiopian Airlines*, *Kenya Airways* and *KLM*.
Main airports: *Bujumbura International (BJM)* is 11km (7 miles) north of the city. *To/from the airport*: Taxis are available to and from the city. *Facilities*: Banks/bureaux de change, bars, duty free shops, post office, tourist information, light refreshments and car hire.
Departure tax: US$20.
LAKE: Cargo/passenger ferries ply Lake Tanganyika between Kigoma (Tanzania) and Mpulungu (Zambia) calling at various ports including Bujumbura, when political conditions permit. There are normally some ferries to Kalemi (Congo, Dem Rep) and to Kigoma (Tanzania). The MV Mwongozo ferry sails along Lake Tanganyika between Bujumbura and Kigoma. There are three classes. Ferries can often be delayed depending on the cargo being loaded or unloaded.
ROAD:
It is normally possible to drive into Burundi from Congo (Dem Rep), either from the north or south. Roads from Rwanda are reasonable, but from Tanzania, poor. Visitors are advised against using the Bujumbura to Butare (Rwanda) road unless travelling as part of a UN convoy, due to the likelihood of ambushes. However the viability of crossing these borders depends on prevailing political conditions, and border areas can be very dangerous. Burundi's border with Congo (Democratic Republic) is liable to close at short notice.

Travel - Internal

AIR:
There are no scheduled internal flights at present.

ROAD:

Most roads are sealed. There are main roads east from Bujumbura to Muramvya (once the royal city of Burundi) and south to Gitega. Both journeys can be completed without too much strain during the dry season, but any road travel can be difficult in the rainy season. Traffic drives on the right. Travellers should exercise extreme caution when travelling on roads to Bujumbura. Roads can be subject to ambushes and are often closed during military operations; major roads are closed after 1600. All roads outside of Bujumbura City are unsafe to travel. **Bus:** There are services around Bujumbura and main towns only. Japanese-style minibuses operate between towns and are normally cheaper and less crowded than share-taxis; departures (when the vehicle is full) are normally from bus stations. The destination of the minibus is usually displayed in the front window. **Taxi:** *Tanus-tanus* (truck taxis) are usually available but they are often crowded. **Car hire:** It may be possible to arrange some form of car hire via a local garage. **Documentation:** Driving licences issued by the UK are acceptable.

Travel Advice

All but essential travel to Bujumbura is advised against due to the high threat from indiscriminate attacks by rebel groups, and all travel to other parts of Burundi, unless with an organised UN Mission, particularly in the Bujumbura Rural Province. In Bujumbura, there is a high risk of street crime and muggings at gun point. Travellers are advised not to walk in the streets after dark, especially since there is a curfew throughout the country (from 2300-0600), nor to carry large amounts of money. Attacks on public transport in the Provinces are reported on most days, and the risk of being a victim of indiscriminate violence is high, with foreigners being occasional targets. Public transport outside Bujumbura is reported to be dangerous.

In addition, you should be aware of the global risk of indiscriminate international terrorist attacks, which could be against civilian targets, including places frequented by foreigners.

This advice is based on information provided by the Foreign and Commonwealth Office in the UK. It is correct at time of publishing. As the situation can change rapidly, visitors are advised to contact the following organisations for the latest travel advice:

British Foreign and Commonwealth Office
Tel: (0845) 850 2829.
Website: www.fco.gov.uk

US Department of State
Website: http://travel.state.gov/travel

Accommodation

HOTELS:

Almost all the hotels in the country are situated in the capital, Bujumbura, although there are a few in Gitega, Kirundo, Muyinga and Ngozi. Elsewhere in the country there is virtually no accommodation for visitors.

CAMPING:

Currently very dangerous. Generally frowned upon, particularly near towns. Permission should always be obtained from the local authorities.

ACCOMMODATION INFORMATION

NITRA
BP 1402, 7 place de l'Indépendence,
Bujumbura, Burundi
Tel: 222 321.
E-mail: nitra@usan-bu.net

Top Things To See & Do

- Go to the capital port-city of **Bujumbura**, a bustling town with a population of some 200,000 inhabitants. The area was colonised by Germany at the end of the 19th century, and there is still architecture dating from that period of Burundi's history, including the **Postmaster's House**. Other attractions include three museums (including the **musée vivant**, a reconstructed open-air village displaying Burundian culture) and the **Islamic Cultural Centre** There is also an excellent **market**.
- Around 10km (6.2 miles) south of Bujumbura is a stone that marks the **historic meeting-place of Stanley and Livingstone** in 1871.
- Gaze upon the **monument** near **Rutovu**, in **Bururi Province**, which marks Burundi's claim to the source of the Nile.
- Stare at a beautiful vista of central plains and the expanse of the former royal city, **Gitega**, from the mountaintops that constitute the peak Congo Nile. Gitega has an exquisite charm of its own, from the **Chutes de la Kagera** waterfall to its recently renovated **National Museum**.
- Study the **arts and crafts** of the Burundians: leather, ceramics, ivory and wood-carvings in the **Craftwares Village** at **Giheta**, plus sculptures, wickerware and paintings in the town's **Art School**.
- Behold the country's diverse **flora and fauna**, from savannah to steppers, mountain forests to blooming fields.
- Be seduced by the scenic and fun pleasures of **Lake Tanganyika**, where (in normal circumstances) cafes and restaurants line the lake. Here, there are some opportunities for **watersports**, including sailing, water-skiing and fishing.
- Compete in the ancient game of *urubugu* (also know as *mancala*). It is played with pebbles or seashells on hollows scooped out on the ground, or with seeds on expensive, elaborately carved wooden boards.
- In **Kirundo**, in the far north of Burundi and with its three lakes of **Cohoha**, **Rweru** and **Rwihinda**, settle down for some **bird-watching**: the third lake, Rwihinda, is even nicknamed 'Birds Lake' because of the sheer quantity of birds (around 20 different species) that settle there . A large amount of birds can also be viewed in **Kibira Natonal Park**.

TOURIST INFORMATION

Office National du Tourisme
2 avenue des Euphorbes, BP 902, Bujumbura, Burundi
Tel: 222 023 or 229 390.
E-mail: ontbur@cbinf.com

Entertainment

FOOD & DRINK: The choice is limited. Most food is boiled, stewed or roasted over wood fire. Meals in Bujumbura's hotels are reasonable, but expensive and of fairly average quality. The French, Greek and Asian restaurants in the town are good. There are few restaurants outside the capital and Gitega.

National specialities:
- All beans are in plentiful supply, particularly red kidney beans.
- Rice is served with nearly everything.
- Other staple ingredients include plantains, sweet potatoes, cassava, peas and maize.
- Fish is more common than meats.
- People snack on fruit, cane sugar and groundnuts.
- Spicy carrots are a side dish of carrots mixed with mustard seeds and chilli peppers.

National drinks:
- *Urwarwa* is a homemade banana wine drunk during celebrations.

- *Primus* beer is produced in Burundi, as is *impeke*, a home-brewed beer made from sorghum, and often drunk through straws.

Tipping: As a rule, no service charge is levied automatically; 10 per cent is the recommended tip for good service.
NIGHTLIFE: There are several nightclubs, restaurants and bars in Bujumbura.
SHOPPING: Local crafts, particularly basketwork, make excellent buys. **Shopping hours:** Mon-Fri 0800-1200 and 1500; Sat 0830-1230.

Business

- **GDP:** US$600 million (2005).
- **Main exports:** Coffee, tea, sugar, cotton and hides.
- **Main imports:** Capital goods, petroleum products and foodstuffs.
- **Main trade partners:** Switzerland, Germany, Belgium, Thailand, USA, Italy, Japan, Kenya, Tanzania, Uganda, France, Rwanda and Zambia.

ECONOMY: Subsistence agriculture employs 90 per cent of the workforce and accounts for approximately half of the total economic output. Cassava and sweet potatoes are the main subsistence crops, while coffee (the country's leading export), tea and cotton are the main cash crops. Hides and skins also produce valuable income. The country's small mining industry produces gold, tin, tungsten and tantalum. Deposits of vanadium, uranium and nickel – perhaps 5 per cent of known global reserves – have also been located and are due to be exploited in the near future. Oil deposits are believed to be present, although the quantities are unknown. Manufacturing is confined to small textile concerns. Burundi has economic cooperation agreements with Rwanda and the Democratic Republic of Congo through the Economic Community of the Great Lakes Countries and is a member of the Common Market for Eastern and Southern Africa (COMESA) and of the International Coffee Organisation. Burundi is also a member of the African Union (AU) and the World Tourism Organisation. As one of the poorest countries in the world, with an annual per capita income of just US$100, Burundi remains heavily dependent on foreign aid, principally from France, Germany, Belgium (these three are also its major sources of imports), the EU and the World Bank. It appeared, in 2001, that Burundi's future prospects had been improved by the largely successful implementation of the Mandela peace accord. However, sustainable peace between the Tutsi minority, who dominates Government, and the Hutu majority, has looked increasingly doubtful, and has hampered Burundi's economic development - GDP plummeted to -1 per cent in 2004. Burundi's major export markets are the countries of the CFA Franc zone, which take approximately one-third of the total.
BUSINESS ETIQUETTE: Lightweight suits are necessary. April to October and December to January are the best times to visit. **Office hours:** Mon-Fri 0730-1200 and 1400-1730.

COMMERCIAL INFORMATION

Chambre de Commerce et de l'Industrie du Burundi
BP 313, Bujumbura, Burundi
Tel: 222 280.

Intercontact (Information on Conferences and Conventions)
BP 982, 19 rue de l'Industrie, Bujumbura, Burundi
Tel: 226 618 or 666.
Website: www.intercontactservices.com

Cambodia

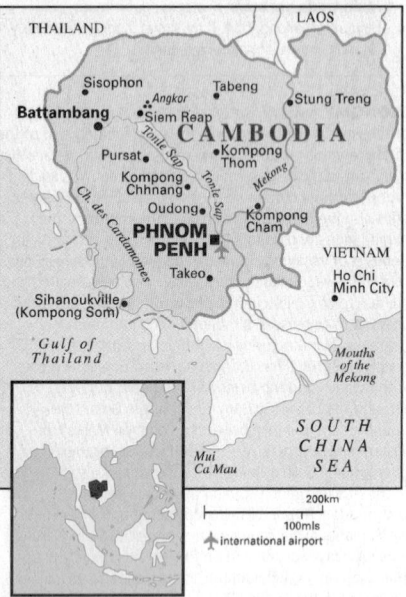

Location: South-East Asia.

Time: GMT + 7.

Overview

Little is known of the early history of Cambodia, although there is evidence of habitation in parts of the country as far back as 4000BC. Much of Cambodia is strewn with staggering artefacts of the dynasty that ruled throughout the 12th and early 13th centuries, based at the famous temple complex of Angkor Wat. These temples are regarded as some of the most astounding architectural creations worldwide. Large and intricate balustrades, pillars and causeways loom out of surrounding jungle. Yet these monuments are also a wistful chronicle of Cambodia's comparable fall into ruin: by the end of the 15th century, Angkor had been abandoned.

Likewise, the magnificence of Cambodia is now marred by unexploded landmines and dangerous roads, largely abandoned by tourists until quite recently. Khmer Rouge Communist guerrillas took control of Cambodia in 1975 with Prime Minister Pol Pot at the helm. Pol Pot manufactured a unique ideology based on elements of Maoist thought and Medieval quasi-mysticism, rooted in the history of the Angkor state. 'Year Zero' was established in 1975, under which Cambodia was to be converted into a pure Communist state centred on basic agricultural production. Currency was abolished, intellectuals purged, churches and temples destroyed and thousands of urban dwellers driven into the countryside for 're-education' and primitive labour. The outcome was a regime of horrific brutality, which was responsible for another of the 20th century's genocides – it is estimated that one third of the population died during the four years of Khmer Rouge rule. Following the overthrow of the Khmers by the Vietnamese army, Phnom Penh, a ghost city under the Khmer Rouge, was re-populated by 1982. Although Cambodia drifted in and out of penury and semi-chaos during the 1980s, in 1998 Cambodia finally complied with the international community and was reinstated as a member of ASEAN. Pol Pot died of natural causes in the same year and his death seemed to symbolise a collective 'moving on'. Tourists are now beginning to return. Cambodians have regained pride in their country, which is as beautiful as it ever was: for the traveller who seeks it, there is sprawling jungle, verdant fields, snaking rivers and golden beaches. Cambodia remains afflicted by poverty and authoritarian regimes that hide behind the veneer of democratic practice but for those who dare believe in it, there is also hope.

General Information

AREA: 181,035 sq km (69,900 sq miles).

POPULATION: 14.8 million (UN estimate, 2005).

POPULATION DENSITY: 81.7 per sq km.

CAPITAL: Phnom Penh. **Population:** 1,17 million (2005).

GEOGRAPHY: Cambodia shares borders in the north with Laos and Thailand, in the east with Vietnam and in the southwest with the Gulf of Thailand. The landscape comprises tropical rainforest and fertile cultivated land traversed by many rivers. In the northeast area rise highlands. The capital is located at the junction of the Mekong and Tonle Sap rivers. The latter flows from a large inland lake, also called Tonle Sap, situated in the centre of the country. There are numerous offshore islands along the southwest coast.

GOVERNMENT: Constitutional monarchy since 1993.

Head of State: King Norodom Sihamoni since 2004. **Head of Government:** Prime Minister Hun Sen since 1998.

Recent history: The authoritarian, extreme-left KPK (Kanakpak Pracheachon Kâmpuchéa -Cambodian People's Party) remained in Government following the 2003 elections, suggesting that Cambodia was, to some extent, still dominated by an authoritarian regime hiding behind the veneer of democratic practice. Further symptoms of turbulence include the recent abdication of King Norodom Sihanouk in late 2004, who abdicated due to old age and frail health, but also, he claimed, because of the worry of more violence in a land still traumatised by Pol Pot's brutal rule in the 1970s, without a clear succession. This event diagnosed the nation's widespread and continuing fears and frictions. Last-minute legislation had to be administered since the constitution did not permit abdication and, eventually, the nine-member throne council appointed his son, Norodom Sihamoni, as the new King. King Norodom Sihamoni has vowed to remain politically neutral and open to ideas from all Cambodians. Only time will tell if the succession marks a new, more optimistic, era for Cambodia. Legislative power belongs to the 120-member National Assembly, which is popularly elected for a term of five years. Executive power is vested in the Cabinet of Ministers headed by the Prime Minister. The King holds the post of Head of State.

LANGUAGE: Khmer is the official language and spoken by 95 per cent of the population. Chinese and Vietnamese are also spoken. French was widely spoken until the arrival of the Pol Pot regime and is still taught in schools, but English is now a more popular language to learn among the younger generation.

RELIGION: 90 per cent Buddhist (Theravada), the remainder Muslim and Christian. Buddhism was reinstated as the national religion in 1989 after a ban on religious activity in 1975.

ELECTRICITY: 220 volts AC, 50Hz and two-pin plugs are in use. Power cuts are frequent. Outside Phnom Penh, electrical power is available only in the evenings from around 1830-2130.

SOCIAL CONVENTIONS: Sensitivity to politically-related subjects in conversation is advisable. Avoid pointing your foot at a person or touching someone on the head. Women should wear long clothing that covers the body.

Photography: Permitted, with certain restrictions, such as the photographing of military installations, airports and railway stations. It is polite to ask permission before photographing Cambodian people, especially monks.

Climate

Tropical monsoon climate. Monsoon season is from May to November. The most pleasant season is the dry season, from November/December to April. In the north, winters can be colder, while throughout most of the country temperatures remain fairly constant. There is often seasonal flooding in Phnom Penh and the rest of Cambodia in late-July and early-August; travel may be disrupted.

Required clothing: Lightweight clothing and cottons are worn all year. Rainwear is essential during the rainy season.

Communications

Telephone: IDD is available to Cambodia. At present, outgoing international calls cannot be made. Country code: 855. Phnom Penh code: 23. Prepaid telephone cards are available in post offices, hotels and supermarkets for public phones around Phnom Penh and Siem Reap.

Mobile telephone: Roaming agreements exist with a few international mobile phone companies. Coverage is good in Phnom Penh and patchy elsewhere.

Internet: Available in some areas. Internet cafes are available in Phnom Penh and Siem Reap.

Post: Airmail to Europe takes four to five days, and seven to 10 days to the USA. The Post & Telephone Office (PTT) in Phnom Penh is located across from the Hotel Monorom at the corner of Achar Mean Boulevard and 126 Street and is open 0700-1200 and 1300-2300. The main post office in Phnom Penh is located on the western side of 13 Street between 98 Street and 102 Street, open 0630-2100. General post office hours: Mon-Fri 0730-1200 and 1430-1700.

MEDIA: Much of Cambodia's media depends on support from political parties. Press freedom is not guaranteed but Prime Minister Hun Sen has declared his public support for press freedom. There are no restrictions on satellite dish ownership and neighbouring foreign radio broadcasts are easily received. **Press:** The *Cambodia Daily*, *Cambodia Times* (weekly) and *Phnom Penh Post* (fortnightly) are printed in English. There are also a few pro-Government dailies.

TV: *Television National Television of Cambodia (TVK)* is a state broadcaster; *Aspara TV* and *TV3* are commercial stations; *CTN*, *CTV9* and *TV5* are private broadcasters.

Radio: The *National Radio of Cambodia* is a state broadcaster; *FM 95* (operated by Bayon Radio and TV News Agency, Agence Kampuchea Presse (AKP)), *Radio FM 97* (operated by Aspara Radio and TV Radio) and *Radio FM 103* are commercial broadcasters.

Passport/Visa

	Passport Required?	Visa Required?	Return Ticket Required?
Full British	Yes	Yes	No
Australian	Yes	Yes	No
Canadian	Yes	Yes	No
USA	Yes	Yes	No
Other EU	Yes	Yes	No
Japanese	Yes	Yes	No

Note: *Regulations and requirements may be subject to change at short notice, and you are advised to contact the appropriate diplomatic or consular authority before finalising travel arrangements. Any numbers in the chart refer to the footnotes below.*

PASSPORTS: Passport valid for at least six months at time of entry required by all.

VISAS: Required by all except nationals of Malaysia, The Philippines and Singapore for between 21-30 days.

Note: Visitors arriving by air can obtain a visa for stays of up to 30 days on arrival at *Phnom Penh International Airport*, Phnom Penh or *Siem Reap International Airport*, Angkor. Visas are also available from Immigration at the border posts of Bavet, Poi Pet and Koh Kong. Visitors are advised to check current situation before travelling.

Types of visa and cost: *Tourist* (single-entry): £15 (£30 for express); *Business* (single-entry): £25 (£40 for express). *Express* visas are issued within 24 hours.

Validity: All visas are valid for a one month period, and visas issued by the Embassy must be used within three months of date of issue. Extensions of up to one extra month for *Tourist* visas or six or 12 months for *Business* visas (which can be multiple) may be granted by the Ministry of the Interior at the Immigration Office in Phnom Penh.

Application to: Consulate (or Consular section of Embassy); see *Passport/Visa Information*. Tourists on package tours will normally have their visas arranged by the tour operator.

Note: Applications by post will only be accepted through a recognised visa courier. For further details, contact the nearest Consulate (or Consular section of Embassy).

Application requirements: (a) One completed application form. (b) Two passport-size photos. (c) Valid passport. Children need a passport and visa also. (d) Fee in cash only. (e) Self-addressed prepaid envelope if applying by post.

Note: (a) Children travelling on their parent's passport must submit an extra photo. (b) Nationals of Afghanistan, Algeria, Bangladesh, Iran, Iraq, Pakistan, Saudi Arabia, Sri Lanka and

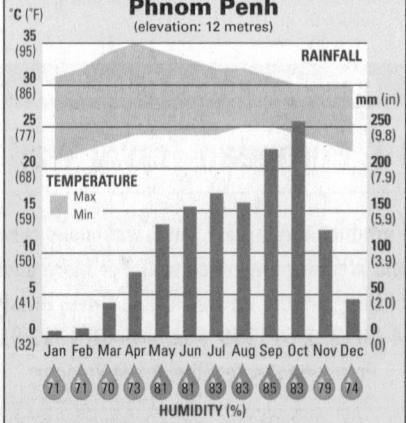

Sudan also need a return ticket. They will also require a routine check-up. For *Tourist* visas, a letter of guarantee from the travel agent, and for *Business* visas, a business letter.
Working days required: Five from day of receipt of application form. Express visas are issued within 24 hours.

PASSPORT/VISA INFORMATION

Royal Embassy of Cambodia in the UK
Wellington Building, 28-32 Wellington Road,
St John's Wood, London NW8 9SP, UK
Tel: (020) 7483 9063 *or* 9064 (consular section).
Website: www.cambodianembassy.org.uk

Royal Embassy of Cambodia in the USA
4530 16th Street, NW, Washington, DC 20011, USA
Tel: (202) 726 7742.
Website: www.embassy.org/cambodia

Money

Currency: Riel (KHR). Notes are in denominations of KHR100,000, 50,000, 20,000, 10,000, 5000, 2000, 1000, 500, 200 and 100.
Currency exchange: US Dollars and Thai Baht are widely accepted and exchanged, but other currencies are generally not recognised.
Credit & debit cards: Credit cards are not generally accepted, but can be used in upmarket hotels and restaurants catering to visitors. There are no ATMs in Cambodia. It is always best to carry cash (US dollars if necessary) in small denominations.
Traveller's cheques: Limited acceptance. Traveller's cheques are generally not recommended. Traveller's cheques in US dollars can be changed at the official rate at the Foreign Trade Bank in Phnom Penh, and other larger banks and hotels.
Currency restrictions: Import and export of local currency is prohibited. Foreign currency may be exported up to the limit declared at customs on arrival. Amounts over US$10,000 have to be declared.
Banking hours: Mon-Fri 0800-1500. Some banks are open on Saturdays.
Exchange rate indicators:
Rate at time of publishing
£1.00 KHR7225.30
$1.00 KHR4094.35

Duty Free

The following goods may be imported into Cambodia without incurring customs duty:
200 cigarettes or equivalent in tobacco; one opened bottle of perfume for personal use.
Note: Currency must be declared.

Public Holidays

Below are listed Public Holidays for the January 2006-June 2007 period.
2006: Jan 1 New Year's Day. **Jan 7** Victory Day. **Feb 13** Meak Bochea Day. **Mar 8** Women's Day. **Apr 14-16** Cambodian New Year. **May 1** Labour Day. **May 13** Visaka Buja Day (Birth of Buddha). **May 13-15** King Sihamoni's Birthday. **May 16** Royal Ploughing Day Ceremony. **Jun 1** International Children's Day. **Jun 18** Queen's Birthday. **Sep 21-23** Pchum Ben Day. **Sep 24** Constitution and Coronation Day. **Oct 23** Paris Peace Agreement. **Oct 30-Nov 1** King Sihanouk's Birthday. **Nov 4-6** Water Festival. **Nov 9** Independence Day. **Dec 10** Human Rights Day
2007: Jan 1 New Year's Day. **Jan 7** Victory Day. **Feb** Meak Bochea Day. **Mar 8** Women's Day. **Apr** Cambodian New Year. **May 1** Labour Day. **May 2** Visaka Buja Day (Birth of Buddha). **May 13-15** King Sihamoni's Birthday. **May** Royal Ploughing Day Ceremony. **Jun 1** International Children's Day. **Jun 18** Queen's Birthday.
Note: The religious festivals are determined by the Buddhist lunar calendar and are therefore variable. Public holidays falling on a Saturday or Sunday are carried forward to the following working day.

Health

	Special Precautions?	Certificate Required?
Yellow Fever	No	1
Cholera	Yes	2
Typhoid & Polio	3	N/A
Malaria	4	N/A

Note: *Regulations and requirements may be subject to change at short notice, and you are advised to contact your doctor well in advance of your intended date of departure. Any numbers in the chart refer to the footnotes below.*

1: A yellow fever vaccination certificate is required by travellers arriving from infected areas.
2: Following WHO guidelines issued in 1973, a cholera vaccination certificate is no longer a condition of entry to Cambodia. However, cholera is a serious risk in this country and precautions are essential. Up-to-date advice should be sought before deciding whether these precautions should include vaccination as medical opinion is divided over its effectiveness; see the *Health* appendix for further information.
3: Immunisation against typhoid is recommended. Polio vaccination should be up-to-date.
4: Malaria risk exists all year outside the capital and close around Tonle Sap. Malaria does occur in the tourist areas of Angkor Wat. The malignant *falciparum* strain predominates and is reported to be highly resistant to chloroquine and sulfadoxine-pyrimethamine. Resistance to mefloquine has been reported from the western provinces. The recommended prophylaxis is mefloquine (including within the Angkor Wat area) but doxycycline in the western provinces.
Food & drink: All water should be regarded as being potentially contaminated. Water for drinking, brushing teeth or making ice should first be boiled or otherwise sterilised. Milk is unpasteurised and should be boiled. Powdered or tinned milk is available and is advised, but make sure that it is reconstituted with pure water. Avoid dairy products which are likely to have been made from unboiled milk. Only eat well-cooked meat and fish, preferably served hot. Pork, salad and mayonnaise may carry increased risk. Vegetables should be cooked and fruit peeled.
Other risks: *Bilharzia* (schistosomiasis) is present. Avoid swimming and paddling in fresh water; swimming pools which are well chlorinated and maintained are safe. *Giardiasis, dysentery, typhoid fever* and *dengue fever* are common throughout Cambodia. *Hepatitis A* occurs, *hepatitis B* is hyperendemic. *Japanese encephalitis* occurs in rural areas from May to October and is relatively common in the highlands.
Epidemics of *avian influenza* (bird flu) were reported in Asia in 2004 and again in 2005, and some human cases were confirmed. Visitors should avoid bird farms or markets, where contact with poultry might occur.
Rabies is present. For those at high risk, vaccination before arrival should be considered. If you are bitten, seek medical advice without delay. For more information, consult the *Health* appendix.
Health care: Health insurance, including emergency evacuation, is absolutely essential. Doctors and hospitals expect cash payments for any medical treatment. The cost of medical evacuation is high. The hospital in Phnom Penh is reliable. It is suggested that any visitors bring adequate supplies of any essential personal medication, since that medication may not be available in Cambodia.

Travel - International

AIR:
Bangkok Airways and *Thai International* fly to Phnom Penh from Bangkok. *Malaysia Airlines* flies from Kuala Lumpur, *Vietnam Airlines* from Hanoi, *Aeroflot* from Moscow, *Silkair* from Singapore and *Lao International Aviation* from Vientiane.
Approximate flight times: From *London* to Phnom Penh is 12 hours 30 minutes (with a stopover in Bangkok).
Main airports: *Pochentong (PNH)* is 8km (5 miles) from Phnom Penh. *To/from the airport*: A bus service (travel time – 15 minutes) and taxis (travel time – 10 minutes) to the city are available. Taxi fares are approximately US$8 and motorbikes are US$1. For pre-arranged tours a pick-up service is available. *Facilities:* Left luggage, banks/bureaux de change, bars, shops, post office and light refreshments.
Departure tax: US$25 levied on international departures at Phnom Penh and Siem Reap International Airports; US$20 elsewhere; US$15 for holders of Cambodian passports. Children less than four years of age are exempt.
SEA:
Main ports: *Phnom Penh* and *Sihanoukville* can be reached via the Mekong delta through Vietnam. This route is served by regular passenger ferry crossings.
RAIL/ROAD:
The Thai border is open for overland access. The main highway links the capital with the Vietnam border. Border checkpoints include Poipet, Cham Yeam (Thailand), Bavet, Kaam Samhar (Vietnam) and Stung Treng (Laos).

Travel - Internal

Note: In terms of the risk of armed robbery (particularly in Phnom Penh and Sihanoukville) after dark, the greatest danger faces those travelling on motorcycles, especially regarding bag-snatching. There have also been violent incidents around popular tourist spots such as Street 154/174 of Phnom Penh.

AIR:
Internal flights operate between Phnom Penh and Siem Reap for Angkor (travel time – 45 minutes), Battambang, Koh Kong, Sihanoukville and Stung Treng. **Domestic airports:** The upgraded *Siem Reap Airport*, the main gateway for visitors going to see the ancient temples at Angkor, is a seven to 10-minute taxi ride from the city. Taxi fares are approximately US$5. Other airports include *Bottambang, Mondulkiri, Phnom Penh, Rattanakhiri* and *Stung Treng*.
Departure tax: US$20 for foreign nationals.
SEA:
Government-run ferries depart from the *Psar Cha Ministry of Transport Ferry Landing* between 102 and 104 Streets and go to Kompong Cham, Kratie, Stung Treng, Kompong Chhnang and Phnom Krom. Boats are also available from Phnom Penh to Siem Reap, a route popular with travellers. Due to the present rise in crime, inter-city boat travel should be restricted to the fast boats to Kompong Cham and Kratie. Some boats have been reported as poorly maintained and over-crowded; some are reported to not contain life-jackets. Care should be taken to ensure the best and most safety-conscious boat travel available is selected.
RAIL:
Some rail services operate; they are cheap but take much longer than the buses. There are plans to restore the international service to Bangkok, but a great deal of repair work is needed. If possible, other modes of transport with better maintained infrastructure should be taken.
In the meantime, a train leaves Phnom Penh every second day (on even-numbered days) in the early morning and travels to Pursat (travel time: six hours) and Battambang (travel time: 14 hours).
ROAD:
Traffic drives on the right. Most roads are in very poor condition, although the highway to Vietnam is open. It is possible to drive from Phnom Penh to Ho Chi Minh City in a day but there are formalities involved regarding the use of the same vehicle all the way. Right-hand drive vehicles (quite common in Cambodia) are not allowed entry to Vietnam. Both Cambodian and Vietnamese visas must be obtained in advance and the Vietnamese visa must mention 'Moc Bai' (the border point on the Vietnamese side) as a point of entry/exit, otherwise travellers run the risk of being turned back. Care should be taken while driving as Cambodian drivers are prone to recklessness and accidents are relatively frequent. The safety of road travel outside urban areas varies greatly from region to region. If travel is undertaken in vehicle convoy during daylight hours only, potential risks can be reduced. Other vehicles cannot always be relied on to use headlights. Given the predominant use of motorcycles for urban public transportation, travellers should ensure that any insurance policies provide coverage for riding as a driver or passenger. Cattle often stray onto the roads. In Siem Reap, the local police have banned rental outlets from hiring motorcycles to tourists. Reliable information about security should be obtained before considering extensive road journeys. **Bus**: Buses to Phnom Penh suburbs are available from 182 Street and the bus station is open 0530-1730. **Taxi**: Taxis can be hired in main cities. However, *cyclos* (tricycles) or *motodops* (motorcycles) are a slow but inexpensive way to see the city and some of the drivers, especially those found outside main hotels, speak a little French or English. **Car hire**: Official visitors can arrange to hire a Government car and driver. Enquiries about car hire should be addressed to the Ministry of Tourism (see *Top Things To Do* section).
Documentation: An International Driving Permit is not recognised in Cambodia, but car hire is generally not recommended. Visitors are advised to hire a car with a driver instead which is only slightly more expensive than car hire.

Travel Advice

You should be aware of the global risk of indiscriminate terrorist attacks, which could be against civilian targets, including places frequented by foreigners. Public order is fragile; however, most visits to Cambodia are trouble-free. The greatest risks to travellers are from road traffic accidents, armed robbery after dark, landmines and unexploded ordnance in rural areas.
There has been a renewed outbreak of avian influenza (bird flu) amongst poultry in Cambodia. Visitors to Cambodia are unlikely to be affected, but should avoid visiting live animal markets, poultry farms and other places where they may come into close contact with wild or caged birds; and ensure poultry dishes are thoroughly cooked.
This advice is based on information provided by the Foreign & Commonwealth Office in the UK. It is correct at time of publishing. As the situation can change rapidly, visitors are advised to contact the following organisations for the latest travel advice:

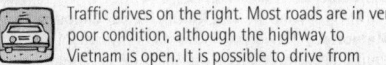

Cambodia

British Foreign and Commonwealth Office
Tel: (0845) 850 2829.
Website: www.fco.gov.uk

US Department of State
Website: http://travel.state.gov/travel

Accommodation

HOTELS/GUEST HOUSES: There is now a variety of good hotels available. The capital Phnom Penh and Siem Reap have numerous luxury hotels offering high standards and a range of recreational facilities. Hotels and guest houses are also available throughout the country, but standards generally tend to be basic.

CAMPING/CARAVANNING: This is available but advice should be sought prior to travel.

YOUTH HOSTELS: This is available in Siem Reap.

SELF-CATERING: Cottages and villas are available to rent in the larger towns.

Top Things To See

- Delight in Cambodia's **Buddhist temples**, such as **Preah Vihear**, close to the border with Thailand in the **Dongrek mountains**, which is the site of various celebrations, especially during the **Cambodian New Year**.
- The interrogation centre of the Pol Pot regime in **Phnom Penh** is now the chilling **Toul Sleng Museum of Genocide**, also called **S-21** (security office 21). Here, you can also contemplate **The Killing Fields/Cheoung Ek Memorial**. Although obviously no tourist attraction, and courting controversy as a 'Top Thing To See', these remnants of mass murder nevertheless disclose deplorable facts of history that may be necessary to grasp to ensure they are never repeated.
- Phnom Penh's **Royal Palace** has a stunning and famous **Silver Pagoda**. Be sure to pay extra attention to the floor – it contains 5000 silver tiles.
- The **French Embassy** re-opened in a new building in 1996 and is well worth a visit for clearly being Phnom Penh's outstanding landmark of contemporary architecture. The Embassy has a flat roof and white facade, and is set in magnificent grounds on the same site of the former Embassy.
- Many would believe that the greatest monuments to Hinduism would reside in India, but they do not: for glimpses of what veneration to the gods can inspire, a trip to the famous and magnificent temples at **Angkor**, in the country's northwest, is compulsory. These breathtaking temples are unfortunately hard and dangerous to reach by road but may be reached by regular flights from Phnom Penh, Ho Chi Minh City, Singapore, Kuala Lumpur and Bangkok. This ancient temple complex is what remains of the capital of the once mighty Khmer civilisation. **Angkor Wat** itself, built AD 879–1191 to honour the Hindu god Vishnu, is often hailed as one of the most extraordinary architectural creations ever built, with its intricate bas reliefs, strange acoustics and magnificent soaring towers.
- **Oudong**, 30km (19 miles) from Phnom Penh, is located on a hill overlooking vast plains and is famous for the **burial** chedis of the Khmer kings.
- Step into the fairytale world of **Ta Phrom**, near **Tonle Bati**. This ancient temple in the middle of the Cambodian jungle spawns wild undergrowth and has huge tree roots draped over its edifice, possessing a truly unique and unruly beauty.

Top Things To Do

- Attend the re-established and famed **National Ballet**, which has been assembled of surviving dancers from the Pol Pot regime.
- Look out at one of the world's major rivers, the **Mekong River**. You may just spot some of Cambodia's famous freshwater **dolphins**. If not, try taking a **river cruise** down to the **Tonle Sap**, the most significant inland wetland in South-East Asia.
- Go for an **elephant ride** in **Ratanakiri** and **Mondulkiri**; remember to grab yourself a tour guide! Meanwhile, Sam Bo is **Phnom Penh**'s resident elephant. Enjoy this regal mode of transport on Cambodia's famed elephant and be sure to win Sam Bo over with offerings of banana and bread.
- Be a part of the extravagant **Water Festival** (October or November) – sometimes known as the **Festival of the Reversing Current**. The festival is seen as a thanksgiving to the rivers. It is also around this time of year that the Tonle Sap changes direction in flow, leaving behind an abundance of fish. Over three days, multitudes mingle on the banks of the Tonle Sap and Mekong Rivers in Phnom Penh to watch hundreds of brightly coloured boats and their paddlers battle it out for top honours, originally to prove the strength of the powerful Khmer marine forces during the Khmer empire. The days' events are usually closed with a brilliant firework display.
- Watch a **traditional Cambodian dance**, often involving fish traps! **Siem Reap** is probably the best place to watch a dance display, although you can occasionally catch a spontaneous one in the villages.

> **TOURIST INFORMATION**
>
> **Ministry of Tourism**
> 3 Monivong Boulevard, Phnom Penh 12258, Cambodia
> Tel: (23) 211 593 or 222 409.
> Website: www.mot.gov.kh
>
> **Diethelm Travel (Cambodia) LTD**
> No 65, Street 240, PO Box 99, Phnom Penh, Cambodia
> Tel: (23) 219 151.
> Website: www.diethelm-travel.com

Entertainment

FOOD & DRINK: Restaurants and other businesses abound in Phnom Penh, although the city remains poor. Food stalls are also common in Phnom Penh and can usually be found in and around the Central Market, O Ressei Market and Tuol Tom Pong Market. Khmer cuisine is very similar to Thai, but with fewer spices involved.

National specialities:
- Popular dishes include soup and salad, almost always incorporating Cambodia's favourite flavours of coriander, lemongrass and mint.
- There is a plethora of sweet dishes, such as sticky rice cakes and pudding.
- Succulent fruits include banana, coconut, the *durian* fruit (known for its distinctive odour), jackfruit, *longan* fruit, lychee, pineapple and *Rambutan* (which has translucent white flesh) fruit, to name just a few.
- Grilled fish, or fish cut up, rolled in lettuce or spinach and dipped into fish sauce.
- Khmer cuisine is unique in its use of *prahok*, a fermented fish paste.
- Showing its French influence, also expect plenty of roasted turtle and frog legs.
- Rice noodles.
- The most common skewer or brochette is *golden sapek*: small pieces of pork tenderloin alternated with strips of pork fat and rounds of Chinese sausage, cooked on a grill over hot coals.

National drinks:
- Palm wine.
- Tea.
- *Choum* (a rice-based spirit).
- The local beer is called *Angkor*.
- The most popular Khmer drink is soda water with a squeeze of lemon.

Legal drinking age: There are no age-restrictions.
Tipping: Tips are appreciated in hotels and restaurants where no service charge has been added, and by tour guides.
NIGHTLIFE: The major hotels offer entertainment, and weekly Apsara dance performances are often held from November to March in some hotel gardens. The *Holiday International Hotel* is a popular nightclub which also offers a karaoke bar and casino. For further information, contact Diethelm Travel (see *Top Things To Do*).
SHOPPING: Antiques, woodcarvings, *papier mâché* masks, brass figurines, *kramas* (checked scarves), material for *sarongs* and *hols*, and items and jewellery made of gold, silver and precious stones are Cambodia's best buys. Visitors are advised that there are strict controls on the export of antiques - and stone carvings in particular. The Central Market, Tuol Tom Pong Market and the Old Market are among the best places for buying jewellery and the Fine Arts School sells many of the above goods in its shop. Clothing and materials are available at the Central Market.
Shopping hours: Mon-Sun 0800-2000.

Business

> - **GDP:** US$4.2 billion.
> - **Main exports:** Dried fish, pepper, rice, rubber, tobacco, clothing, wood and vegetables.
> - **Main imports:** Petroleum products, gold, construction materials, cigarettes, machinery, motor vehicles and pharmaceutical products.
> - **Main trade partners:** Vietnam, USA, Germany, UK, Thailand, Hong Kong (SAR), Singapore, China, Taiwan and Korea (Rep).

ECONOMY: The Cambodian economy was all but destroyed by the war in South-East Asia, following the rule of the Khmer Rouge between 1975 and 1979. Since the ousting of the Khmer Rouge from power by the Vietnamese in 1979, Cambodia has undergone a slow process of recovery. Restoration of agriculture – the foundation of the Cambodian economy and the main source of employment – has been slow but steady. Rice is the staple; other products include maize, sugar cane, cassava and bananas. The timber industry has also grown quickly on the back of heavy foreign investment and meets both domestic fuel demands and export markets - but at the expense of worrying deforestation. Timber is, along with rubber, the source of most of Cambodia's export earnings. Other mineral resources, which include phosphates, iron ore, bauxite, silicon and manganese, are limited. There is a small but fast-growing industrial sector concentrated in the production of consumer goods, processed foods and light manufacturing. This has largely relied on foreign investment, most of which has come from elsewhere in East Asia (especially Thailand), as more developed economies seek to take advantage of Cambodia's lower labour costs. GDP growth has reached 6 per cent annually since 2000, with construction activity particularly extensive, especially in the capital. The effects of the 1997 currency crisis on the economy were transitory, given the relatively undeveloped state of the Cambodian economy. Cambodia aspires to the status of an Asian 'tiger' economy and has joined, along with its neighbour Vietnam, the Association of South-East Asian Nations (ASEAN), now the principal regional economic co-operation body.
BUSINESS ETIQUETTE: Shirt and tie should be worn. Some knowledge of French would be useful. **Business hours:** Mon-Fri 0800-1200 and 1400-1700.

Cameroon

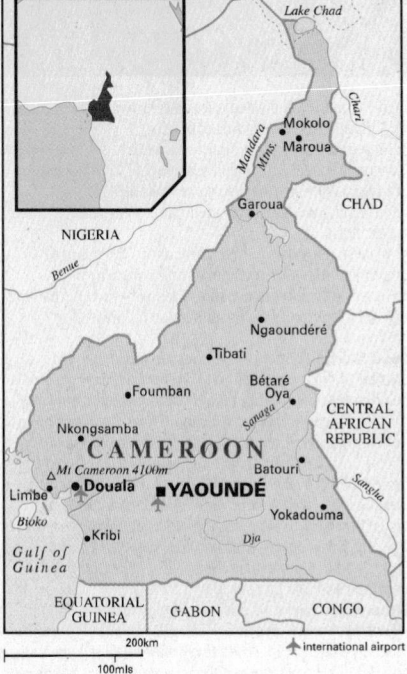

Location: Central Africa.

Time: GMT + 1

Credit: ©Tourism Ministry of Cameroon

Overview

It is now a cliche to say that Cameroon is Africa in miniature but, as with cliches sometimes, there is an element of truth in the statement: everything you would expect from the African continent seems to be consolidated in Cameroon. The South has tropical rainforests and deserted golden beaches, whilst the northern parts have great expanses of desert, vast lakes and savannah, and volcanic mountains inbetween. Wildlife is scattered throughout the country, with ample opportunity to view elephants, lions and other creatures large and small. With such diversity and the possibility of game-viewing, it comes as a surprise to many that Cameroon is not a more frequently visited tourist destination. Yet poverty continues to blight the country and much of Cameroon's infrastructure is underdeveloped, from transport to accommodation. The unemployment rate is high and those who are employed perform mostly agricultural tasks. Cameroon is also a divided country. It became a German protectorate in the 1880s but after Germany's defeat in World War I, the country was divided between Britain and France under a League of Nations (and later a United Nations) mandate. French Cameroon achieved independence in 1957 and a plebiscite was soon held to decide the future of British Cameroon – the northern provinces voted to become part of Nigeria, while the south opted for union with French Cameroon. The major spoken languages are still French and English but a multitude of more than 200 ethnic languages are also in circulation, with various tribes populating the country. In recent years, divisions have once again been accentuated, particularly on account of opposition to President Biya from Muslim communities in the north and Anglophone regions that fear discrimination at the hands of the predominately francophone regime. Relations with Nigeria, Cameroon's powerful neighbour, are also awkward as the result of several outstanding border disputes (linked in part to

control of the oil-rich Niger delta); the main one, involving an area known as the Bakassi peninsula, has seen occasional small-scale military clashes between the two sides. For those who brave these aforementioned troubles, Cameroon has a wealth of activities and beautiful destinations to keep any traveller enthralled. Go, before it becomes 'discovered'.

General Information

AREA: 475,442 sq km (183,569 sq miles).

POPULATION: 16 million (2003).

POPULATION DENSITY: 33.7 per sq km (2003).

CAPITAL: Yaoundé (constitutional). **Population:** 649,000 (1987). Douala (economic). **Population:** 810,000 (1987).

GEOGRAPHY: Situated on the west coast of Africa, Cameroon is bordered to the west by the Gulf of Guinea, to the northwest by Nigeria, to the northeast by Chad (with Lake Chad at its northern tip), to the east by the Central African Republic and to the south by Congo, Gabon and Equatorial Guinea. The far north of the country is a semi-desert broadening into the vast Maroua Plain, with game reserves and mineral deposits. This is bordered to the west by the lush Mandara Mountains. The Benue River rises here and flows westwards into the Niger. The country to the northwest is very beautiful; volcanic peaks covered by bamboo forest rise to over 2000m (6500ft), with waterfalls and villages scattered over the lower slopes. Further to the south and west are savannah uplands, while dense forest covers the east and south. The coastal strip is tropical and cultivated. Cameroon derives its name from the 15th-century Portuguese sailor Fernando Po's description of the River Wouri: *Rio dos Cameroes* ('river of shrimps').

GOVERNMENT: Republic. Gained independence in 1961.

Head of State: President Paul Biya since 1982; won a new seven-year term in 2004. **Head of Government:** Prime Minister Ephraim Inoni since 2004. **Recent history:** At the most recent Presidential poll in October 2004, Biya secured another seven-year term in office, winning 70 per cent of the votes. International observers claim that the poll was fair and transparent but opposition parties made allegations of widespread fraud. Cameroon joined the UN Security Council in 2002, as one of three African representatives (with Angola and Guinea) and as a result found itself subject to serious pressure over the Iraq issue during early 2003. The President and the 180-seat *Assemblée Nationale* (National Assembly) hold executive and legislative power respectively. Both are elected for five-year terms. Further revisions to the existing 1972 constitution allow for the introduction of a second National Assembly chamber at a later date.

LANGUAGE: The official languages are French and English. They are given equal importance in the Constitution but French is the more commonly spoken. Spanish is spoken in some urban centres. There are 24 major African language groups. Pidgin English is also spoken.

RELIGION: 53 per cent Christian (mainly Roman Catholic), 25 per cent traditional animist beliefs, 22 per cent Muslim.

ELECTRICITY: 110/220 volts AC, 50Hz. Plugs are round two-pin; bayonet light-fittings are used.

SOCIAL CONVENTIONS: Handshaking is the customary form of greeting. In the north, where the population is largely Muslim, Islamic traditions should be respected. Visitors should never step inside a Muslim prayer circle of rocks. In other rural areas, where traditional beliefs predominate, it is essential to use tact. **Photography:** Cameras should be used with discretion, particularly in rural areas. Always ask permission before taking a photograph. Do not photograph airports, military establishments, official buildings, or military personnel in uniform.

Climate

The south is hot and dry between November and February. The main rainy season is from July to October. Temperatures in the north vary. On the Adamaoua Plateau, temperatures drop sharply at night; the rainy season is from May to October. Grassland areas inland are much cooler than the coast with regular rainfall.

Required clothing: Lightweight cotton clothes, canvas or light leather shoes or sandals. Rainwear is necessary for coastal areas.

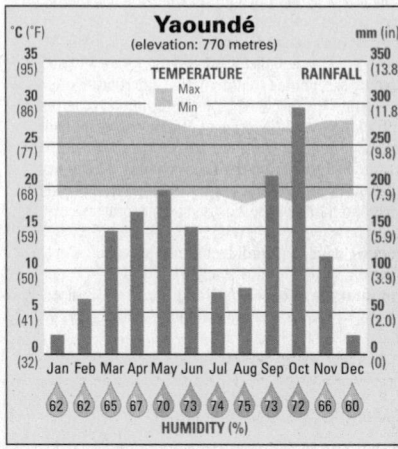

Communications

Telephone: Telephone: IDD is available to and from Cameroon. Country code: 237. International calls can be made from *CAMTEL* offices. Telephones can usually be found in post offices and restaurants, and there are telephone booths in the towns. Phonecards are available. The main towns in Cameroon are linked by automatic dialling, although this service is often unreliable.

Mobile telephone: Roaming agreements exist with a few international mobile phone companies. Coverage is average.

Internet: Available in main towns, which will have Internet cafes. Charges are significantly higher outside Yaoundé and Douala.

Post: Stamps can only be obtained from post offices. Mail takes about a week to reach addresses in Europe. Post office hours: Mon-Fri 0730-1530.

MEDIA: Media is highly Government-controlled. However, Cameroon's first private TV station was launched in 2001. This followed a general liberalisation of media in 2000, and a spate of private stations also emerged around this time. Nevertheless, libel laws inhibit journalists and some have even been jailed in the past. This is regarded as a genuine problem by the international community, who believe that Cameroon is becoming one of the most repressive countries worldwide in regards to freedom of expression.

Press: The main newspaper is the (Government-controlled) *Cameroon Tribune*, published daily in French and English. Other English-language newspapers include the *Cameroon Post* (weekly), *Cameroon Times* (weekly) and *The Herald* (three times a week).

TV: *Cameroon Radio Television* is the state-run broadcaster, whilst *TV Max* is a relatively new private broadcaster on the scene.

Radio: *Cameroon Radio Television* also operates state-run radio stations. *Radio Reine*, however, is a Catholic-owned station, whilst *Radio Siantou* is a private broadcaster.

Credit: ©Tourism Ministry of Cameroon

Passport/Visa

	Passport Required?	Visa Required?	Return Ticket Required?
Full British	Yes	Yes	Yes
Australian	Yes	Yes	Yes
Canadian	Yes	Yes	Yes
USA	Yes	Yes	Yes
Other EU	Yes	Yes	Yes
Japanese	Yes	Yes	Yes

Note: *Regulations and requirements may be subject to change at short notice, and you are advised to contact the appropriate diplomatic or consular authority before finalising travel arrangements. Any numbers in the chart refer to the footnotes below.*

Restricted entry: A yellow fever vaccination certificate must be presented on arrival by all travellers.

PASSPORTS: Passport valid for a minimum of six months required by all.

VISAS: Required by all except the following:
(a) nationals of Central African Republic, Chad, Congo (Rep), Mali and Nigeria for stays not exceeding 90 days;
(b) those in transit continuing their journey on the first or same aircraft within 24 hours provided holding onward tickets and not leaving the airport.

Types of visa and cost: *Tourist* and *Short-stay*: £33.25 (three months). *Business*: £33.25 (three months); £66.50 (six months). *Transit*: £33.25 (five days). All visas are for multiple-entries.

Validity: *Tourist* and *Short-stay* visas are valid for up to three months; *Business* visas for up to six months. *Transit* visas are valid for up to five days.

Application to: Consulate (or Consular section at Embassy); see *Passport/Visa Information*. Visas are also available on arrival for countries where Cameroon has no diplomatic representation.

Application requirements: (a) Passport valid for six months. (b) Two completed application forms. (c) Two passport-size photos. (d) International Certificate of Vaccination for Yellow Fever; (e) Return ticket or letter of confirmation from travel agent. (f) Copy of recent bank statement or letter from the bank verifying that applicant has sufficient funds. (g) For a business visa, a letter from applicant's company and a letter from business partners in Cameroon that must be legalised by the local police. (h) Appropriate fee.

Working days required: Two if the application is delivered in person; several for postal applications.

Temporary residence: Applicants must have Residence and Work Permits. Apply to immigration authorities in Cameroon.

PASSPORT/VISA INFORMATION

Cameroon High Commission in the UK
84 Holland Park, London W11 3SB, UK
Tel: (020) 7727 0771.
Opening hours: Mon-Fri 0930-1600; 0930-1230 (visa applications).

Embassy of the Republic of Cameroon in the USA
2349 Massachusetts Avenue, NW,
Washington, DC 20008, USA
Tel: (202) 265 8790.
Website: www.ambacam-usa.org

Credit: ©Tourism Ministry of Cameroon

Money

Currency: CFA (*Franc de la Communauté Financière Africaine*) Franc (XAF) = 100 centimes. Notes are in denom-inations of XAF10,000, 5000, 2000, 1000 and 500. Coins are in denominations of XAF250, 100, 50, 25, 10, 5 and 1. Cameroon is part of the French Monetary Area. Only currency issued by the *Banque des États de l'Afrique Centrale* (Bank of Central African States) is valid; currency issued by the *Banque des États de l'Afrique de l'Ouest* (Bank of West African States) is not. The CFA Franc is tied to the Euro.

Currency exchange: Euros are the easiest currency to exchange. US Dollars are the next most acceptable. Travellers should bring cash in preference to travellers cheques.

Credit & debit cards: Major credit cards are accepted on a very limited basis (some airline offices and hotels will take them). Cards cannot be used in banks to obtain cash advances.

Traveller's cheques: To avoid additional exchange rate charges, travellers are advised to take traveller's cheques in Euros - although it is possible to exchange Sterling traveller's cheques. Commission rates tend to be high.

Currency restrictions: Import of local currency is limited to XAF20,000. Import of foreign currency is unlimited. Export of local currency is limited to XAF20,000 if travelling for touristic purposes, or XAF450,000 if travelling for business purposes. There is no limit on the export of foreign currency.

Banking hours: Mon-Fri 0730-1530.

Exchange rate indicators:
Rate at time of publishing
£1.00=   XAF968.02
$1.00=   XAF548.56

Duty Free

The following goods may be imported into Cameroon without incurring customs duty:
400 cigarettes or 50 cigars or five packets of tobacco; one bottle of alcoholic beverage; five bottles of perfume.
Note: Sporting guns require a licence.

Public Holidays

Below are listed Public Holidays for the January 2006-June 2007 period.
2006: Jan 1 New Year's Day. **Jan 10** Eid Al Adha (Festival of Sacrifice). **Feb 11** Youth Day. **Apr 11** Eid Milad Nabi (Prophet's Anniversary). **Apr 14-17** Easter. **May 1** Labour Day. **May 20** National Day. **May 21** Sheep Festival. **May 25** Ascension. **Aug 15** Assumption. **Oct 1** Unification Day. **Oct 22-24** Djoulde Soumae (End of Ramadan). **Dec 25** Christmas. **Dec 31** Eid Al Adha (Festival of Sacrifice).
2007: Jan 1 New Year's Day. **Feb 11** Youth Day. **Mar 31** Eid Milad Nabi (Prophet's Anniversary). **Apr 6-9** Easter. **May 1** Labour Day. **May 17** Ascension. **May 20** National Day. **May 21** Sheep Festival.
Note: Muslim festivals are timed according to local sightings of various phases of the moon and the dates given above are approximations. During the lunar month of Ramadan that precedes Djoulde Soumae (Eid al-Fitr), Muslims fast during the day and feast at night and normal business patterns may be interrupted. Many restaurants are closed during the day and there may be restrictions on smoking and drinking. Some disruption may continue into Djoulde Soumae itself. Djoulde Soumae may last anything from two to 10 days, depending on the region.

Health

	Special Precautions?	Certificate Required?
Yellow Fever	Yes	1
Cholera	Yes	2
Typhoid & Polio	3	N/A
Malaria	4	N/A

Note: *Regulations and requirements may be subject to change at short notice, and you are advised to contact your doctor well in advance of your intended date of departure. Any numbers in the chart refer to the footnotes below.*

1: A yellow fever vaccination certificate is required of all travellers over one year of age.
2: Following WHO guidelines issued in 1973, a cholera vaccination certificate is no longer a condition of entry to Cameroon. However, cholera is a serious risk in this country and precautions are essential. In June 2004, 2924 cases of cholera were confirmed in littoral to West Regions areas, since January of the same year. Although this has since abated, visitors should continue to monitor the situation. Up-to-date advice should be sought before deciding whether these precautions should include vaccination as

medical opinion is divided over its effectiveness. For more information, see the *Health* appendix.
3: Immunisation against diphtheria, hepatitis A and typhoid is recommended. Poliomyelitis is endemic and inoculation is advised. Vaccines are also sometimes advised for hepatitis B, meningococcal meningitis, rabies and tuberculosis.
4: Malaria risk exists all year throughout the country, predominantly in the malignant *falciparum* form. Resistance to chloroquine and sulfadoxine-pyrimethamine has been reported. The recommended prophylaxis is mefloquine.

Food & drink: Water precautions are recommended outside of main hotels but all water should be regarded as being potentially contaminated. Water used for drinking, brushing teeth or making ice should have first been boiled or otherwise sterilised. Bottled water is readily available. Milk is unpasteurised and should be boiled. Powdered or tinned milk is available and is advised, but make sure that it is reconstituted with pure water. Avoid dairy products which are likely to have been made from unboiled milk. Only eat well-cooked meat and fish, preferably served hot. Pork, salad and mayonnaise may carry increased risk. Vegetables should be cooked and fruit peeled.

Other risks: *Hepatitis B* is hyperendemic in the region. *Hepatitis A* and *E*, *dysentery*, *dengue fever* and *typhoid fever* are widespread. *Lassa fever* may be spread via rat populations in rural areas. *Onchocerciasis* (river blindness) exists and *cutaneous* and *visceral leishmaniasis* may be found in drier areas. *Human trypanosomiasis* (sleeping sickness) is reported in certain locations. *Bilharzia* (schistosomiasis) is present. Avoid swimming and paddling in fresh water; swimming pools which are well chlorinated and maintained are safe. *Meningococcal meningitis* risk exists during the dry season (December to June) in northern areas. *Paragonimiasis* (oriental lung fluke) has been reported. *HIV/Aids* is prevalent.
Rabies is present. For those at high risk, vaccination before arrival should be considered. If you are bitten, seek medical advice without delay. For more information, consult the *Health* appendix.

Health care: There are roughly 250 hospitals in Cameroon, although health facilities are not recommended to foreign travellers. Sanitation levels are low, even in the best hospitals and clinics. Facilities outside Yaoundé and Douala are extremely limited. International travellers are strongly advised to take out full medical insurance before departure.

Travel - International

AIR:

The national airline is *Cameroon Airlines (UY)*. The first direct commercial flight from the UK to Douala for more than five years was recently launched: *Arkh-View African Airlines* (website: www.avairlines.com).

Approximate flight times: From Douala to *Paris* is six hours 40 minutes; from Yaounde to *Paris* is eight hours 35 minutes; from Douala to *London* is nine hours 15 minutes.

Main airports: *Aeroports de Cameroon SA (ADC)* oversees the seven airports, including *Douala International*, *Garoua International* and *Yaoude Nsimalen International*. *Douala (DLA)* is situated 10km (6 miles) southeast of the city. *To/from the airport*: Taxis to the city are available at a cost of approximately XAF3000. *Facilities*: Duty free shop, bar, post office, bank, shops and buffet/restaurant.
Yaounde Nsimalen International (NSI) airport is situated 25km (15.5 miles) from the city. *To/from the airport*: Taxis to the city are available at a cost of approximately XAF3000 (travel time – 20 minutes).

Departure tax: Around US$15.

SEA:

Main ports: Cargo boats from *Douala* to Malabo (Equatorial Guinea) sometimes accept passengers. Speedboats and cargo boats ply the coastal route between Idendao (northern Cameroon) and Oron (Nigeria). However, these services are not regulated.

RIVER:

There are ferry services across the Ntem River, on the border with Gabon. Pirogues also operate across this river to Equatorial Guinea.

RAIL:

There is a rail route running from Douala to Nkongsamba, with a branch line leading off from Mbanga to Kumba. The Trans-Cameroon railway runs from Douala to Ngaoudere, with a branch line from Ngoumen to Mbalmayo. There are plans to extend the rail network from Mbalmayo to Bangui in the Central African Republic.

ROAD:

There are road connections to Chad, the Central African Republic, Equatorial Guinea, Gabon and Nigeria. Travel on these routes is rough, and should not be attempted in the rainy season. 4-wheel drive vehicles are recommended. Drivers should avoid travelling at night. Problems might be experienced at the borders with Gabon and the Central African Republic. Armed robberies have been reported in the three provinces of Adamaoua, the north and the far north (bordering Chad). Gendarmerie detachments are posted along the road between Maroua and Chad. The Trans-Africa Highway from Kenya to Nigeria is still under construction; the border area with Nigeria, neighbouring the Bakassi peninsula, should be avoided. The border with the Republic of Congo has been closed. **Bus**: Minibuses and bush taxis run from Yaoundé and Douala to all neighbouring countries (except where borders are closed). It may be necessary to change at the border.

Travel - Internal

Note: Petty theft is common on trains, coaches and bush-taxis, and visitors to Cameroon who rely on its transport are urged to remain vigilant.

AIR:

This is the most efficient means of national transport. There are daily flights between Douala and Yaoundé; less regular flights to other interior towns, served by *Unitair*.

Departure tax: XAF500.

RAIL:

Cameroon Railways (CAMRAIL) is the national service provider. Services are good, if relatively slow, and it is much quicker to go by train than by bus. There are daily services from Yaoundé to Ngaoundéré on the 'Gazelle du Nord', that runs from Douala to Ngaoundéré via Yaoundé and Belabo. Daily trains also run from Yaoundé to Douala, with onward connections to Nkongsamba. Couchettes are available, as are first- and second-class seats. Trains usually have a restaurant car. Tickets must be booked on the day of travel.

ROAD:

There are paved roads from Douala to Yaoundé, Limbé, Buéa, Bafoussam and Bamenda and between main centres. Other roads are generally poorly maintained and become almost impassable during the rainy season. Many vehicles are poorly lit and badly driven. Traffic drives on the right. Night driving is not recommended. Car hijackings and violent muggings are increasingly common, particularly in the three provinces of Adamaoua, the North and the far North, so sensible precautions should be taken. Driving on the Yaoundé/Douala trunk road should be avoided, since accidents are common there. Roadside assistance is non-existent. Travellers should consult official government advice services for further information about security while driving. **Bus**: Modern coach services are available between Yaoundé and Douala, Bafoussam and Bamenda, Foumban and Dschanga. Bus services also exist between other main centres and more rural areas but tend to be unreliable and are often suspended during the rainy season. Bus services also have a reputation for being dangerous, as road safety is not a priority for Cameroon drivers and accidents are common. **Car hire**: This is limited and expensive and is available in Douala, Yaoundé and Limbé, with or without a driver. **Documentation**: An International Driving Permit is not a legal requirement but recommended, especially for those hiring a car. By law, a driving licence must be carried when driving; a Cameroonian licence can be obtained within 24 hours for a small fee.

URBAN:

Taxis and share-taxis are available at reasonable fixed rates (none are metered). A 10 per cent tip is optional. City taxis do not generally comply with basic security norms and seatbelts are often absent. Violent assaults on taxi passengers are not uncommon, so the choice of taxi must be considered carefully. However, they are cheap and fast.

Credit: ©Tourism Ministry of Cameroon

Travel times: The following gives approximate travel times (in hours and minutes) from **Yaoundé**.

	Air	Road	Rail
Douala	**0.30**	**3.00**	**4.00**
Garoua	**2.30**	**18.00**	**-**
Kribi	**0.45**	**-**	**-**
Maroua	**3.45**	**24.00**	**-**
Ngaoundéré	**2.40**	**12.00**	**10.00**

Travel Advice

All travel to the border area with Nigeria is advised against (in the region of Bakassi Peninsula), since this area is still subject to a territorial dispute between the two countries and tensions are rife, with localised violent incidents often occurring with little warning. All non-essential travel to the border area with the Central African Republic is advised against. The border area with Congo (Rep) is closed. In addition, there is a danger of mugging and banditry in Cameroon, including car-hijacking and robbery, often armed and violent, particularly in Douala, Yaoundé, Kribi and Maroua. Jewellery and valuables should not be worn or carried in more isolated, poor regions of Cameroon (notably Yaoundé, la Briquetterie and Mokolo).

In addition, you should be aware of the global risk of indiscriminate international terrorist attacks, which could be against civilian targets, including places frequented by foreigners.

This advice is based on information provided by the Foreign and Commonwealth Office in the UK. It is correct at time of publishing. As the situation can change rapidly, visitors are advised to contact the following organisations for the latest travel advice:

British Foreign and Commonwealth Office
Tel: (0845) 850 2829.
Website: www.fco.gov.uk

US Department of State
Website: http://travel.state.gov/travel

Accommodation

HOTELS:

Good accommodation of international standard is available in Bamenda, Douala, Garoua, Maroua and Yaoundé. The good hotels (Government-rated 2-star and above) have air conditioning, sports facilities and swimming pools; most rooms have showers. Some large hotels will accept major credit cards. Rates are for the room only. Cheaper accommodation is also available. *Campement* accommodation, with two pavilions and individual rooms comprised of straw huts, is available just outside Waza National Park, north of Maroua in the far north of the country. Hotel facilities are in heavy demand; it is advisable to book in advance and obtain written confirmation of your booking. For more information on hotels in Cameroon, contact the Ministry of Tourism (see *Top Things to Do*).

CAMPING:

Permitted in Boubandjidah National Park, on the banks of Mayo Lidi River, and near the entrance of Waza National Park. Elsewhere, camping is considered unsafe due to the possibility of robberies.

Top Things To See

- See Cameroon's capital city, **Yaoundé**, standing on seven hills. Museums include the **Benedictine Monastery**'s **Musée d'Art Cameroonais,** a collection of traditional arts and crafts on **Mont Fébé**, and the newer National **Museum of Yaoundé**. To the northwest, jungle-clad mountains rise to an altitude of 1000m (3280ft).
- Be dazzled by beautiful white sandy beaches not far from **Limbé** (formerly Victoria), a pleasant port with a botanical garden and 'jungle village'. The tourist season runs between November and February. There is also a beautiful beach resort at **Londji Beach** in **Kribi**.
- Discover many traditional buildings dating from Cameroon's period of German colonisation in **Foumban**, northeast of Dschang, whose **Bafut Fon's Palace** includes a craft centre. There is also the **Musée du Palais**, whose collection includes bejewelled thrones, armaments, musical instruments and dancing masks, the **Musée des Arts et des Traditions Bamoun**, and a market.
- The village of **Rhumsiki** features a maze of paths linking the small farms known as the Kapsiki; the Kirdi live here, whose customs and folklore have changed little for centuries. The village is surrounded by the jutting Kapsiki range, framed by their soaring beauty.
- Cameroon has a plethora of national parks to explore. **Waza National Park** covers 170,000 hectares (420,079 acres) and is open from mid-November to mid-June. There is a forest area and a vast expanse of grassy and wet plains, called Yaeres. Elephants, giraffes, antelopes, hartebeest, cobs, lions, cheetahs and warthogs are numerous. There is also a rich variety of birds, including eagles, crested cranes, maribous, pelicans, ducks, geese and numerous guinea-fowl. Accommodation and other facilities are available in the nearby **Waza** village. A vehicle and a guide are required for entrance to the park. **Bénoué National Park** covers 180,000 hectares (444,790 acres) and has buffalo, hippopotamuses, crocodiles, hyena, giraffes, panthers, lions and a variety of primates, and can be visited all year round. **Korup National Park** is home to Africa's oldest and most biologically diverse rainforest. Accessible by bush taxi, it is located in the westernmost corner of the country, along the Nigerian border near the town of **Mundemba**, which is about 150km (93miles) northwest of Douala. A wide variety of primates, birds, trees and other plants, including dozens of recently discovered species are there. Travellers should dress to cope with the 100 per cent humidity and the fording of waist-high pools. **Bouba Ndjidah National Park** is situated on the banks of **Mayo Lidi River** in the far north of the country; bordering Chad. Its wildlife includes elan and buffalo, black rhinoceroses, elephants and lions. There are several other parks and reserves which are not open to the public. Dinosaur fossils have been discovered here. It is also a convenient starting point for tours to local villages and the **Campo Game Reserve** region. Buffaloes, lions and elephants roam the virgin forests inland. **Kalamaloué Reserve** is small but offers opportunities for viewing several species of antelopes, monkeys and warthogs; some elephants cross the reserve.

Top Things To Do

- Go on a **photo safari**: a seven- to 10-day tour of northern Cameroon sets out from Ngaoundéré and includes sports activities at **Ngaoundaba Ranch**, safari photography at **Bénoué** and **Waza National Parks**, visits to **Garoua**, the volcanic landscapes of **Rhumsiki**, the traditional village of **Oudjila**, the **Maga Dam** and a crafts workshop at **Maroua**, before returning to Garoua; an organised tour of western Cameroon and the **Bamileke** region sets out from **Douala** and includes visits to **Nkongsamba** coffee plantations, **Batié** and **Dschang** mountain towns, and **Foumban** with its museums of arts, crafts and culture, before returning to Douala.
- Watch horses race through the streets of **Kumbo** in western Cameroon during **Nso Cultural Week**.

Credit: ©Tourism Ministry of Cameroon

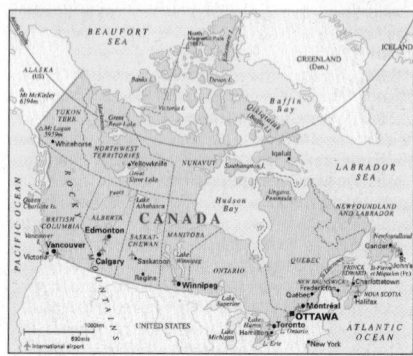

- **Mount Cameroon**, the highest mountain in West Africa and Africa's highest active volcano and highest peak, is a popular mountaineering destination. **Bueau** still has red postboxes and is a pretty colonial town from which to base yourself when attempting to climb this mountain-volcano. No special equipment is required but permits and guides are compulsory. The climb to the summit takes approximately three to four days; huts are available en route for accommodation. The best time to attempt the climb is in the dry season, between November and May. In **Mindif**, a park south of the northern town of Maroua, there is a huge rock known as **Le Dent de Mindif**, which is highly regarded for rock climbing. For those favouring really strenuous exercise, an **international marathon** is held annually at the mountain. Favourite **hiking** areas include the northern region near **Mora** (not far from the Nigerian border) and the highland area around **Bamenda** in the southwest. The **Mandara Mountains** west of Maroua are a good area for trekking. A permit is not required, but it is advisable to take a guide. A variety of **trails**, featuring coastal terrain, a focus on biodiversity, adventure or riverside terrain, are offered by **Jungle Village** in **Limbe Botanic Gardens**.
- Attend the **Cameroon National Festival**, the country's biggest non-religious festival and a lively spectacle of parades and happy celebration.
- **Drive** down the road southwards to **Nkongsamba** and Douala, which passes through some splendid scenery – spectacular valleys and waterfalls.

TOURIST INFORMATION

Ministère du Tourisme
BP 266, Yaoundé, Cameroon
Tel: 224 4411.
Website: www.mintour.gov.cm

Entertainment

FOOD & DRINK: Local food is excellent; French or Lebanese cuisine is also available. Luxury items can be extremely expensive. There are many restaurants in big towns and cities, with good service. Most international hotels have bars.
National specialities:
- Manioc leaves (*feuille*).
- West african peanut soup.
- Banana bread.
- *Zom* (spinach with meat).
- Fried sweet potatoes or plantains.
- Beef with pineapple or coconut.
- The country abounds in avocado pears, citrus fruits, pineapples and mangoes.
- Prawns are in plentiful supply in the south.
- Many dishes are served with rice, couscous or mashed potato.
Legal drinking age: 18 years.
Tipping: The average tip for porters and hotel staff should be about 10 per cent, otherwise service charges are usually inclusive.

NIGHTLIFE: In Douala and Yaoundé particularly, nightclubs and casinos can be found independently or within most good hotels. There are also some cinemas. There are no licensing hours, and hotel bars stay open as long as there is custom.
SHOPPING: Local handicrafts include highly decorated pots, drinking horns, jugs, bottles and cups, great earthenware bowls and delicate pottery, dishes and trays, mats and rugs woven from grass, raffia, jewellery and camel hair or cotton and beadwork garments. **Shopping hours**: Mon-Sat 0730-1800.

Business

- **GDP:** US$13.6 billion.
- **Main exports:** Crude oil and petroleum products, timber, cocoa, aluminium, coffee and cotton.
- **Main imports:** Machinery, electrical equipment, transport equipment and food products.
- **Main trade partners:** France, Italy, Nigeria, Belgium, Spain, The Netherlands, Germany and the USA.

ECONOMY: Cameroon has enjoyed broad economic success since independence, by virtue of consistent agricultural performance and the rapid growth of its oil industry, although it has suffered some reverses through persistently low world commodity prices. The main agricultural products are cocoa (of which Cameroon is one of the world's largest producers), coffee, bananas, cotton, palm oil, wood and rubber. There are sizeable but largely unexploited deposits of iron ore, bauxite, copper, chromium, uranium and other metals. Hydro-electric projects meet almost all the country's energy needs, so that oil and gas are largely treated as export products. There are some offshore oil deposits, although the largest are located near the disputed Bakassi peninsula. The manufacturing industry is concentrated on processing of primary products – most of these are indigenous, although imported raw materials (such as Guinean bauxite, which feeds the aluminium industry) also play an important role. Wood and timber products, oil and coal, and food and drinks are the main sectors. During the 1990s, the government opened up much of the economy to competition. The economy has been growing steadily at an annual rate of approximately 5 per cent since 2000. The IMF agreed a structural adjustment programme with Cameroon in 1995; this was extended beyond the normal three-year term and continues to set the ground rules for the country's economic policy. The capital, Douala, now hosts one of sub-Saharan Africa's few stock exchanges, which was opened in 2002.
BUSINESS ETIQUETTE: Office hours: Mon-Fri 0730-1700. **Government office hours**: Mon-Fri 0730-1530.

COMMERCIAL INFORMATION

Chambre de Commerce
BP 36, Yaoundé, Cameroon
Tel: 222 4776.

Location: North America.

Time: Canada spans six time zones. Information on which time zone applies where may be found in the regional entries following this general introduction. The time zones are:

Pacific Standard Time: GMT - 8 (GMT - 7 from first Sunday in April to last Sunday in October).
Mountain Standard Time: GMT - 7 (GMT - 6 from first Sunday in April to last Sunday in October).
Central Standard Time: GMT - 6 (GMT - 5 from first Sunday in April to last Sunday in October. Most of Saskatchewan does not observe DST).
Eastern Standard Time: GMT - 5 (GMT - 4 from first Sunday in April to last Sunday in October).
Atlantic Standard Time: GMT - 4 (GMT - 3 from first Sunday in April to last Sunday in October).
Newfoundland Standard Time: GMT - 3.5 (GMT - 2.5 from first Sunday in April to last Sunday in October).

Overview

Few countries in the world offer as many choices to the traveller as Canada. Whether your passion is skiing, sailing, museum-combing or indulging in exceptional cuisine, Canada has it all. Western Canada is renowned for its stunningly beautiful countryside; Eastern Canada mixes the flavour and charm of Europe with the bustle of trendy New York; wildlife viewing is at its best in Northern Canada; and, everywhere, you will be surprised by how much more there is to this country than just maple syrup and Mounties. However, Canada also has its fair share of unsavoury history. Traces of up to a dozen distinct groups of Inuit (Eskimos – Canada's indigenous peoples) have been discovered across Canada's far northern regions. The Inuit maintain that traditional lands were taken from them by force or subterfuge by previous governments, bearing some resemblance to the plight of the Aborigines in Australia. However, there have been some small measures to tackle their remonstrations: in 1991, a 350,000 sq km (135,135 sq miles) area of the Northwest Territories was relinquished to the Inuit as the semi-autonomous Nunavut territory; and additional lands and measures of self-government were granted to the territory in 1999. There is certainly room in Canada to accommodate for these peoples: despite Canada's gigantic size, the country is sparsely populated. Most people congregate around urban centres, and venturing into more remote rural areas, you may well have only the country's stunning scenery as your companion. Indeed, Canada is so beautifully diverse that it makes it that little bit easier to comprehend why so many people fought for possession of it. During the 17th century, the Anglo-French war over Canada ended with the capitulation of the French Canadian capital, Québec, to the besieging forces of the English General Wolfe. The Americans made a number of efforts to seize control of Britain's Canadian territories after British defeat in the American War of Independence, but failed, and the two countries thereafter evolved along different historical paths. In 1791, Canada was divided between regions occupied by the English-speaking and the longer-established French-speaking community, but the arrangement did not work and was replaced by a unified system.

A B C D E F G H I J K L M N O P Q R S T U V W X Y Z

Canada now promotes itself as a country of peace, most notably in recent times in its opposition to the US-led war against Iraq. Canada happily governs itself independently but still has the British Monarch as its Head of State, with relatively little dissent. These factors are typical of a country that somehow succeeds in unifying incredible range: whatever your passion, Canada has a place for it. After all, this country spans six time zones and borders three of the world's four oceans.

General Information

AREA: 9,984,670 sq km (3,855,101 sq miles).
POPULATION: 32 million (2005, UN).
POPULATION DENSITY: 3.2 per sq km.
CAPITAL: Ottawa. **Population:** 1.14 million (2004, including Gatineau).
GEOGRAPHY: Canada is bordered to the west by the Pacific Ocean and Alaska, to the east by the Atlantic Ocean, to the northeast by Greenland, and to the south by the 'Lower 48' of the USA. The polar ice cap lies to the north. The landscape is diverse, ranging from the Arctic tundra of the north to the great prairies of the central area. Westward are the Rocky Mountains, and in the southeast are the Great Lakes, the St Lawrence River and Niagara Falls. The country is divided into 10 provinces and three territories. A more detailed description of each province can be found under the separate provincial entries.
GOVERNMENT: Constitutional Monarchy. **Head of State:** HM Queen Elizabeth II, represented by Governor-General Michaëlle Jean since 2005. **Head of Government:** Prime Minister Paul Martin since 2003, re-elected in June 2004.
Recent history: Long-serving Jean Chrétien stepped down as Prime Minister in late 2003, replaced by Paul Martin. It seemed as if restoring relations with the USA was a primary concern of Martin's since the USA had barely concealed their frustrations with their neighbour for the refusal to support the 2003 war against Iraq. However, soon after being sworn in, Martin's Liberal Government became embroiled in a scandal concerning the misappropriation of millions of dollars of public money, with the Liberal Party supposedly receiving kickbacks from advertising contracts awarded in Québec in the late 1990s. Martin barely survived a confidence motion in Parliament in May 2005: just one vote saved him. However, in November 2005, his Government lost a confidence vote, Parliament was dissolved and an election was called for January 2006. After 12 years of Liberal rule, Canada swung to the right in the 2006 general election with conservative Stephen Harper succeeding Paul Martin as Prime Minister. Conservative leader Stephen Harper has pledged to cut taxes and tackle violent crime and corruption.
Executive power is vested in the British Monarch, the Head of State, who is responsible for appointing the Governor General, currently Michaëlle Jean. The Prime Minister, elected Cabinet Ministers, a 104-member Senate and a House of Commons make up the Federal Parliament. Members of the House of Commons are directly elected, while members of the Senate are appointed by the Prime Minister. The ten provinces of Canada each has a Lieutenant Governor and a local legislature, in power for up to 5 years. There are also three territories (Yukon, the Northwest Territories and Nunavut) constituted by Acts of Parliament. Several recent attempts to amend the Constitution have been rejected by popular referendum.
LANGUAGE: Bilingual: English and French. The use of the two languages reflects the mixed colonial history – Canada has been under both British and French rule.
RELIGION: 75 per cent of the population belong to the Christian faith: Anglican, Roman Catholic and United Church of Canada. There are numerous other active denominations and religions.
ELECTRICITY: 110-120 volts AC, 60Hz. American-style (flat) two-pin plugs are standard.
SOCIAL CONVENTIONS: Handshaking predominates as the normal mode of greeting. Close friends often exchange kisses on the cheeks, particularly in French areas. Codes of practice for visiting homes are the same as in other Western countries: flowers, chocolates or a bottle of wine are common gifts for hosts and dress is generally informal and practical according to climate. It is common for black tie and other required dress to be indicated on invitations. Exclusive clubs and restaurants often require more formal dress. **Smoking** has been banned in most public areas. Most restaurants, theatres and cinemas, if they permit smoking, have large 'no smoking' areas.

Climate

Climate graphs for the various provinces and territories may be found in the relevant entries below.
Note: Summer thunderstorms are common throughout Canada. Occasionally, these may become 'severe'. Tornados also occur throughout Canada, with May to September being prime months. The peak season is June and early July in southern Ontario, Alberta, southeastern Québec, and a band stretching from southern Saskatchewan and

Credit: ©Tourisme Québec – Linda Turgeon

Manitoba, through to Thunder Bay. The interior of British Columbia and western New Brunswick are also tornado zones. Earth tremors occur in the western mountains. Forest fires can occur at any time, regardless of the season, particularly in the grasslands and forests of western Canada.
Required clothing: *March:* Moderate temperatures. Winter clothing with some mediumweight clothing.
April: Milder days but the evenings are cool. Mediumweight clothing including a topcoat is recommended.
May: Warm days but cool at night. Mediumweight and summer clothing recommended.
June: Warm, summer clothing with some mediumweight clothing for cool evenings. The weather in June is ideal for travel and all outdoor activities.
July/August: These are the warmest months of the year. Lightweight summer clothing is recommended.
September: Warm days and cool evenings. Light- to mediumweight clothing recommended.
October: Cool, with the first frost in the air.
November: Cool to frosty. Medium- to heavyweight clothing is recommended. First signs of snow. Motorists should have cars prepared for winter and snow tyres are recommended. *December/January/February:* Winter temperatures. Winter clothing is necessary (eg overcoat, hat, boots and gloves). Heavy snowfall in most provinces.

Communications

Telephone: Most public telephones operate using 25-cent coins. There is a reduced rate Mon-Fri 1800-0900, Sat 1200 to Mon 0900. For long-distance calls, telephone cards are available. Credit card telephones are to be found in larger centres. Full IDD is available. Country code: 1.
Mobile telephone: Roaming agreements exist with most international mobile phone companies. Coverage is good.
Internet: Available throughout Canada, as are Internet cafes.
Post: All mail from Canada to outside North America is by air. Stamps are available in hotels, some pharmacies and local stores, or in vending machines outside post offices and shopping centres. Post office hours: generally Mon-Fri 0930-1700, Sat 0900-1200, but times vary according to province and location; city offices will have longer hours.
MEDIA: Canada has a long history of public broadcasting. The Canadian Broadcasting Corporation (CBC) was set up in the 1930s in response to the growing influence of American radio. Broadcasting is in both French and English. The corporation also operates two national TV channels, TV and radio services for indigenous peoples in the north, plus the international broadcaster, Radio Canada International. There is freedom of speech in media throughout Canadian media. The broadcasting regulator rules that quotas of Canadian material - usually 30 or 35% - must be carried by TV and radio stations.
Press: The main national daily newspaper is *The Globe and Mail. The National Post* also has national distribution. Daily newspapers published in the larger population centres have a wide local and regional circulation. French-language dailies are published in seven cities, including Montréal, Ottawa and Québec. In Alberta, the main English-language newspapers are the *Calgary Herald, The Calgary Sun, The Edmonton Journal* and *The Edmonton Sun;* in British Columbia, the *Vancouver Sun;* in Manitoba, the *Winnipeg Free Press* and *The Winnipeg Sun;* in New Brunswick, the *Daily Gleaner* and *The Times and Transcript;* in Newfoundland & Labrador, the *Telegram* and *The Western Star;* in Nova Scotia, *The Chronicle-Herald* and *The Daily News;* in Ontario, *The Ottawa Citizen, Ottawa Sun, The Toronto Star* and the *The Toronto Sun;* in Prince Edward Island, the *Guardian* and the *Journal Pioneer;* in Québec,

The Gazette (daily); in Saskatchewan, the *Daily Herald, Leader Post, Star-Phoenix* and the *Times-Herald* ; and in Yukon, *The Whitehorse Daily Star.*
TV: CBC owns the English-language cable news channel *CBC Newsworld.* Société Radio-Canada is another public broadcaster that operates the French-language network and cable news channel *RDI. CTV* is a major commercial network, whilst *TVA* is a major French-language commercial network. CPAC is the parliamentary and political channel.
Radio: CBC operates English-language *Radio One* and cultural network *Radio Two;* Société Radio-Canada operates French-language *Première Chaîne* and *Espace Musique;* and CBC runs the external service, *Radio Canada International.*

Passport/Visa

	Passport Required?	Visa Required?	Return Ticket Required?
Full British	Yes	No/4	Yes
Australian	Yes	No	Yes
Canadian	1	N/A	N/A
USA	2	No	No
Other EU	3	5	Yes
Japanese	Yes	No	Yes

Note: *Regulations and requirements may be subject to change at short notice, and you are advised to contact the appropriate diplomatic or consular authority before finalising travel arrangements. Any numbers in the chart refer to the footnotes below.*

Restricted entry and transit: The Government of Canada refuses admission to: (a) holders of passports, identity or travel documents issued by Bophuthatswana, Ciskei, Transkei, Venda or the All Palestinian Government; (b) holders of passports issued by the UK Government entitled "British Temporary Resident's Passport"; (c) holders of passports purported issued by the government of Somalia.
Note: Visitors to Canada must satisfy an examining officer at the Port of Entry that they are genuine visitors, in good health, with no criminal convictions, and have sufficient funds to maintain themselves during their stay in Canada and to return to their country of origin, as well as evidence of confirmed onward reservations out of Canada. Persons under 18 years of age who are unaccompanied by an adult should bring with them a letter from a parent or guardian giving them permission to travel to Canada.
PASSPORTS: Passport valid for at least one day beyond the intended departure date from Canada required by all except the following:
(a) **1.** Canadian citizens holding a Canadian Certificate of Identity, Canadian birth certificate or a certificate of Canadian citizenship;
(b) permanent residents of Canada with proof of status, ie Permanent Resident Card, Record of Landing, Returning Resident Permit or a Refugee Travel Document issued by the Government of Canada to refugees who have been resettled in Canada;
(c) **2.** citizens of the USA holding proof of citizenship (eg US birth certificate or US naturalisation papers);
(d) persons entering from St Pierre & Miquelon or the USA who are legal permanent residents of the USA and hold a US alien registration card (Green Card);
(e) **3.** citizens of France who are residents of and entering from St Pierre & Miquelon;
(f) nationals who are residents of and entering from Greenland.

Note: Identity/travel documents issued to non-national residents of the country of issue, refugees or stateless persons are recognised for travel to Canada.

VISAS: Required by all (visitor or transit) except the following for stays of up to six months:
(a) nationals of countries indicated in the chart above, including **4.** citizens of British dependent territories (except holders of passports endorsed 'British Subjects' and 'British Protected Persons', who *do* require a visa);
(b) **5.** nationals of EU countries (except Czech Republic, Estonia, Hungary, Latvia, Lithuania, Poland and Slovak Republic, who *do* require a visa);
(c) nationals of Andorra, Antigua & Barbuda, Bahamas, Barbados, Botswana, Brunei, French Overseas Possessions and Territories, Greenland, Guernsey, Hong Kong (SAR), Iceland, Israel (National passport holders only), Jersey, Korea (Rep), Liechtenstein, Mexico, Monaco, Namibia, New Zealand, Norway, Papua New Guinea, St Kitts & Nevis, St Lucia, St Vincent & the Grenadines, Samoa, San Marino, Singapore, Solomon Islands, Swaziland, Switzerland and the Vatican City.
(d) those visiting Canada who, during that visit, also visit the USA or St Pierre & Miquelon (a French Overseas Territory) and return directly to Canada as visitors within the period authorised on their initial entry (or any extension thereto).

Types of visa and cost: *Visitor*: C$75 (single-entry); C$150 (multiple-entry). *Family*: C$400 (for families of six or more persons). *Transit*: gratis. Transit visas are necessary for all nationals who require a visitor visa. Although transit visas are not required by British citizens, they may be required by foreign nationals with British passports; check with the Embassy or High Commission for details. *Employment*: C$150 (individual); C$450 (group of three or more). *Student*: C$125. Fees to be paid in the form of a Canadian Dollar bank draft made payable to 'Receiver General for Canada.' Bank drafts must be no older than two months with name and address of applicant printed on the back. For further information, contact the High Commission. Prices are subject to frequent change.

Validity: Up to six months depending on circumstances of individual applicant. The determination regarding length of stay in Canada can only be decided by the examining officer at the port of entry, but visas cannot exceed the validity of the passport and cannot be longer than five years. If no actual departure date is indicated within the visitor's passport, then the visitor will be required to depart within three months from the date of entry. Visitors must effect their departure from Canada on or before the date authorised by the examining officer on arrival. If an extension of stay is desired, an application must be made in writing to the nearest Canada Immigration Centre at least three weeks before the expiry of the visitor visa. Multiple-entry visas cannot be valid longer than passport. Transit visas are only allocated if a national's flight/onward journey is continuing within 24 hours. Single-entry visas can be used multiple times by nationals of St Pierre & Miquelon and the USA.

Note: (a) A single-entry visa is still valid if used to visit the USA. (b) Persons wishing to attend a course of six months duration or less, at any level, do not require a study permit. However, if there is the possibility that you will extend your period of study in Canada, or if you are a full time student and wish to work on campus, you may apply for a study permit.

Application to: Consulate (or consular section at Embassy or High Commission); see *Passport/Visa Information*.

Application requirements: (a) Valid passport. (b) Proof of immigration status in country of residence. (c) Application form. (d) Two recent passport-size photos. (e) Proof of sufficient funds for length of stay (this may entail providing a letter from one's employer, mortgage statements or bank statements or letter of invitation from a Canadian resident). (f) Evidence of employment (in some cases). (g) Details of travel plans. (h) Visa processing fee payable in bankers draft only. (i) For those applying by post, an 8" x 6", registered, self-addressed envelope with 50p (C$1) stamp. *Transit*: (a)-(i) and, (j) Onward/return tickets.

Note: (a) Children under 18 years must have information with them on the people responsible for their welfare, if travelling alone; this includes a letter of permission to travel from guardian(s), and also a letter from the custodian in Canada. (b) Depending on circumstance and nationality, certain applicants may need to undergo a medical examination in order to receive their visas; this must be carried out by a physician on Canada's list of Designated Medical Practitioners.

Temporary residence: A work permit is required for temporary residence in Canada. Persons who wish to proceed to Canada for the purposes of study or temporary employment should contact the nearest Canadian High Commission, Embassy or Consulate, as authorisation is normally required prior to arrival. Those taking up temporary employment will require an Employment Authorization, for which a fee is charged. Persons going for study purposes must obtain a Student Authorization; a charge is made for this service.

Working days required: 10 days are required from receiving applications, but applications should be made at least one month prior to the intended date of departure; eight weeks if applying by post. Certain nationals are subject to longer processing times. For urgent applications it is advised to apply in person.

PASSPORT/VISA INFORMATION

Canadian High Commission in the UK
Immigration division: 38 Grosvenor Street, London W1K 4AA, UK
Tel: (020) 7258 6600 *or* (020) 7258 6699 (recorded visa information).
Website: www.canada.org.uk *or* www.cic.gc.ca
Opening hours: Mon-Fri 0800-1100 excluding public holidays (personal callers only).
Consular section: Canada House, 5 Pall Mall East, Trafalgar Square, London SW1Y 5BJ, UK
Tel: (020) 7258 6600.
Website: www.international.gc.ca/canadaeuropa/united_kingdom

Canadian Embassy in the USA
501 Pennsylvania Avenue, NW, Washington, DC 20001, USA
Tel: (202) 682 1740.
Website: www.canadianembassy.org

Canadian Consulate General in the USA
1251 Avenue of the Americas, New York, NY 10020-1175, USA
Tel: (212) 596 1628.
Website: www.dfait-maeci.gc.ca/can-am/new_york

Money

Currency: Canadian Dollar (CAD; symbol C$) = 100 cents. Notes are in denominations of C$100, 50, 20, 10 and 5. Coins are in denominations of C$2 and 1, and 25, 10, 5 and 1 cents.

Credit & debit cards: Major credit cards are widely accepted.

Traveller's cheques: To avoid additional exchange rate charges, travellers are advised to take traveller's cheques in Canadian Dollars; these are widely negotiable.

Currency restrictions: There are no restrictions on the import or export of either local or foreign currency. The export of silver coins over C$5 is prohibited. Amounts equal to or greater than C$10,000 must be declared on entry and exit.

Banking hours: Mon-Fri 0930-1600/1700 with extended hours in some locations. Business accounts can only be set up on presentation of a letter of credit from a home bank.

Exchange rate indicators:

Rate at time of publishing
£1.00 = C$2.09
$1.00 = C$1.17

Duty Free

The following goods may be imported into Canada by non-residents without incurring customs duty:
200 cigarettes and 50 cigars or cigarillos and 200g of loose tobacco and 200 tobacco sticks per person over 18 years of age; 1.5l bottle of wine or 1.14l bottle of liquor or 24 bottles or cans (355ml) of beer or ale per person over 18 years of age if entering Alberta, Manitoba and Québec, and over 19 years if entering British Columbia, New Brunswick, Newfoundland & Labrador, Northwest Territories, Nova Scotia, Ontario, Prince Edward Island, Saskatchewan and Yukon; gifts to the value of C$60 per gift (excluding advertising matter, tobacco or alcoholic beverages).

Prohibited items: The import of firearms, explosives, endangered species of animals and plants, animal products, meat, dairy, food and plant material is subject to certain restrictions and formalities. The import of soft shell turtles from any country and articles from Haiti made of animal skins (eg drums) is prohibited. The plant Qhat (Kat), although legal in the UK and various other locations, is illegal in Canada. Enquire at the Canadian High Commission or Embassy for further details.

Note: There are three different forms of sales tax throughout Canada, these are added onto the price of goods at the till. A **Goods and Services Tax** (GST) of 7 per cent is added on to the sale of all goods and services (in Québec, GST is known as TPS). A **Provincial Sales Tax** (PST) is payable on most items purchased in shops, on food in dining establishments and, in some cases, on hotel and motel rooms in British Columbia, Saskatchewan, Manitoba, Ontario, Québec and Prince Edward Island. The level of PST will vary from province to province. A **Harmonised Sales Tax** (HST) of 15 per cent has replaced GST and PST in Newfoundland and Labrador, Nova Scotia and New Brunswick.
Visitors may reclaim GST or HST on accommodation and any goods purchased and taken out of the country. The goods must be available for inspection on leaving the country. The total amount on each receipt for eligible exported goods must be at least C$50 and the total purchase amount (before taxes) must be at least C$200. However, GST is not reclaimable on food, drink, tobacco or any form of transport. To claim a rebate, a form must be completed, with all original receipts and aircraft boarding pass attached, and posted to the address on the form. Forms are available in hotels and tourist offices. In Québec, the provincial sales tax can be reclaimed at the same time as GST on the GST form (see Shopping in the *Social Profile* section for further information on provincial sales tax). GST forms should be sent to Visitor Rebate Program, Summerside Tax Centre, Canada Revenue Agency, 275 Pope Rd, Suite 104, Summerside, Prince Edward Island, C1N 6C6 Canada. Or a form can be downloaded from the website: www.cra-arc.gc.ca.
For cameras, radios, personal computers etc, a deposit may be requested at the port of entry; this will be refunded to the owner upon submission of proof of export.
Canada Customs require nationals to declare whether they intend to visit a farm within 14 days. UK nationals were subject to particular questioning, following their Foot and Mouth epidemic in 2001.

Public Holidays

Below are listed Public Holidays for the January 2006-June 2007 period.

2006: Jan 1 New Year's Day. **Jan 2** New Year's Day (forwarded to Monday.) **Apr 14** Good Friday. **Apr 17** Easter Monday. **May 22** Victoria Day. **July 1** Canada Day. **Sept 4** Labour Day. **Oct 9** Thanksgiving Day. **Nov 11** Remembrance Day. **Dec 25** Christmas Day. **Dec 26** Boxing Day.

2007: Jan 1 New Year's Day. **Apr 6** Good Friday. **Apr 9** Easter Monday. **May 17** Victoria Day.

Health

	Special Precautions?	Certificate Required?
Yellow Fever	No	No
Cholera	No	No
Typhoid & Polio	No	N/A
Malaria	No	N/A

Note: *Regulations and requirements may be subject to change at short notice, and you are advised to contact your doctor well in advance of your intended date of departure. Any numbers in the chart refer to the footnotes below.*

Other risks: In the summer months, extremely high temperatures can be reached, so visitors at this time may wish to guard against the problems of heat and sunstroke. *Rabies* is present in animals. For those at high risk, vaccination before arrival should be considered. If you are bitten, seek medical advice without delay. For more information, consult the *Health* appendix.

Health care: There is no reciprocal health agreement with the UK, but doctors will continue medication for prescriptions issued in Europe. Private health insurance of up to C$50,000 is absolutely essential as hospital charges are very high (from US$1000-2000 a day, often with 30 per cent surcharge for non-residents imposed in some provinces). Health facilities are excellent (similar to the USA). Personal first-aid kits should be carried by travellers to more remote northern areas. Dial 911 for emergencies.

Note: Visitors intending to stay in Canada for more than 6 months - either as tourists, students or employees - may be required to take a medical examination. Visitors working in an occupation in which protection of public health is essential may be required to undergo a medical examination even if employment is only temporary. Check with the Canadian Consulate or High Commission for further information.

Travel - International

AIR:

Canada's principal national airline is *Air Canada* (AC) (website: www.aircanada.ca).

Approximate flight times: From *London* to Calgary is 9 hours 10 minutes, to Halifax is 7 hours 5 minutes, to Montréal is 7 hours 20 minutes, to Toronto is 7 hours 55 minutes and to Vancouver is 9 hours 45 minutes.
From *Los Angeles* to Montréal is 6 hours 5 minutes, to Toronto is 5 hours 15 minutes and to Vancouver is 2 hours 50 minutes.
From *New York* to Montréal is 1 hour 15 minutes, to Toronto is 1 hour 30 minutes and to Vancouver is 5 hours.
From *Singapore* to Montréal is 23 hours 45 minutes, to Toronto is 21 hours 35 minutes and to Vancouver is 27 hours 50 minutes.
From *Sydney* to Montréal is 24 hours 30 minutes, to

Canada

Toronto is 20 hours 30 minutes and to Vancouver is 19 hours 50 minutes.

Main airports: Canada has 13 international airports. All have full banking and catering facilities, duty free shops and car hire. Airport-to-city bus and taxi services and, in some cases, rail links, are available.

Calgary (YYC) (website: www.calgaryairport.com) is 20km (12.5 miles) from the city (travel time - 45 minutes).

Montréal (YUL) (Dorval) (website: www.admtl.com) is 25km (16 miles) from the city (travel time - 25 minutes).

Ottawa (YOW) (Macdonald-Cartier) (website: www.ottawa-airport.ca) is 15km (8 miles) from the city (travel time - 20 to 45 minutes).

Toronto (YYZ) (Lester B Pearson) (website: www.gtaa.com) is 27km (17 miles) from the city (travel time - 30 minutes).

Vancouver (YVR) (website: www.yvr.ca) is 13km (8 miles) from the city (travel time - 20 to 45 minutes).

Departure tax: An Airport Improvement Fee (AIF) has been implemented at all major airports, the cost is per person and is added to the price of the air ticket. Vancouver charges C$5 for flights within British Columbia and Yukon and C$15 for all other flights. Calgary's AIF is C$15. Toronto has a departure tax of C$8 for connecting flights and C$15 for all others. Ottawa and Montréal levy an AIF of C$15.

Note: An Air Travellers Security Charge (ATSC) was introduced in 2002, which helps to pay for the additional security following 11 September 2001. This charge is levied on all passengers departing from any Canadian airport for domestic, national and international flights. The charge is currently C$17 per person for national and international departures and C$5-17 per person per flight for all domestic services.

SEA:

Main ports: Canada has many ports which are all served by international shipping lines. *Montréal* (www.port-montreal.com) is the only port for passenger liners from Europe.

Toronto's port (www.torontoport.com) is on the northwestern shore of Lake Ontario.

Halifax, Nova Scotia, (www.portofhalifax.ca), *St John*, New Brunswick (www.sjpa.com) and *St John's*, Newfoundland (www.sjport.com) are the principal ports on the Atlantic Ocean.

The port of *Vancouver* (www.vancouverport.com) is on the west coast.

RAIL:

The Canadian rail system connects to the USA at several points. Major routes are: New York–Montréal, New York–Buffalo–Niagara Falls–Toronto, Chicago–Sarnia–London–Toronto, Cleveland–Buffalo–Niagara Falls–Toronto and Detroit–Windsor–Toronto. *VIA Rail Canada*, the country's main rail operator, issues a discount pass for rail travel within Canada and the USA: The *North American Rail Pass* (available to anyone) is valid for 30 days and allows 12 days unlimited travel within that 30-day period on VIA trains in Canada and practically any *Amtrak* train in the USA, with direct access to over 900 Canadian and US cities and towns. For details of ticket prices and reservations, contact VIA Rail in Canada (tel: (1 888) 842 7245 (toll-free in Canada); website: www.viarail.ca) *or* their UK representative *1st Rail* (tel: (0845) 644 3552/3; website: www.1strail.com).

ROAD:

The only road access to Canada is through the southern border with the USA or from the west through Alaska. Apart from private motoring, the most popular way of travelling by road is by bus. The biggest coach company in the world is the *Greyhound Bus Company* (see the Coach section in *Travel – Internal*) and this is one of the most common routes to Canada from the USA. There are many crossing points from the USA to Canada, but some of the most common are: New York to Montréal/Ottawa; Detroit to Toronto/Hamilton; Minneapolis to Winnipeg; Seattle to Vancouver/Edmonton/Calgary.

Travel - Internal

AIR:

Air Canada has a low-cost airline called *Tango* that offers reduced flights from most Canadian provinces and Fort Lauderdale, Orlando and Tampa in Florida, USA to a number of internal destinations. For further information about *Tango* services contact Air Canada, PO Box 64239, Thorncliffe Outlet, 5512 Fourth Street, NW, Calgary, Alberta, T2K 6J0 (tel: (800) 315 1390 (toll-free in Canada); website: www.flytango.com).

There are also around 75 airlines operating local services, the principal ones being: *Air Nova* (for eastern Canada) (website: www.airnova.ca), *Air Alliance*, *Air Ontario* and *WestJet* (website: www.westjet.com) (for central Canada). Reductions are available for those aged 13 to 21, with substantial reductions for those under 12.

Departure tax: From C$5 to C$28, depending on the airport of departure and the destination.

Note: An Air Travellers Security Charge (ATSC) was introduced in 2002, which helps to pay for the additional security following 11 September 2001. This charge is levied on all passengers departing from any Canadian airport for domestic, national and international flights. The charge is currently C$17 per person for national and international departures and C$5 per person per flight for all domestic services to a maximum of C$17 per person per ticket.

SEA/RIVER/LAKE/CANAL:

Canada has many thousands of miles of navigable rivers and canals, a vast number of lakes and an extensive coastline. The whole country is well served by all manner of boats and ships, particularly the east and west coasts, where the ferries are fast, frequent and good value. The St Lawrence Seaway provides passage from the Atlantic Ocean to the Great Lakes. For further details, see individual regional entries *or* contact the Visit Canada Centre (see *Top Things To See & Do*).

RAIL:

VIA Rail Canada operates extensive services across Canada. The regional railways are *Algoma Central*, *British Columbia Railway*, *Great Canadian Railtour Company*, *Ontario Northland*, *Québec North Shore & Labrador*, *Toronto Hamilton & Buffalo Railway* and *White Pass & Yukon Route*. Children under two years of age not occupying a separate seat may travel free (one per adult) and children two to 11 years of age pay half fare. Persons over 60 years of age and students carrying an International Student Card (ISIC), will receive a 10 to 50 per cent discount (depending on the type of ticket); student discount fares also apply to young people aged 12 to 17.

VIA Rail operates a Western transcontinental service (*the Canadian*) between Toronto (Ontario) and Vancouver (British Columbia), running three times weekly east and west, transiting Winnipeg, Saskatoon, Edmonton and Jasper. Passengers are drawn to this route by the spectacular scenery of the three mountain ranges which are passed en route – the Rockies, the Selkirks and the Coastal. The route also features views of ancient glaciers, large lakes and waterfalls. The journey takes three days and all trains operating on this route include showers in the sleeping cars. The transcontinental service can be accessed by regular services from the Atlantic provinces and from Québec City and Montréal. Rapid intercity services are available between Québec, Montréal, Halifax, Toronto, Windsor and Ottawa. On these journeys, the fare price includes a meal, snacks and drinks. *VIA Rail* also operates an overnight Eastern transcontinental service (*the Ocean*) between Montréal (Québec) and Halifax (Nova Scotia). Long-distance trains are extremely comfortable, with full restaurant services, air conditioning and spacious reclining seats.

The Rocky Mountaineer service (website: www.rockymountaineer.com) runs from April to October and offers the opportunity to travel between Calgary, Banff, Jasper and Vancouver during daylight hours, enabling passengers to view the extraordinary passing scenery. Customers can purchase either a one-way or round-trip fare. A one-way trip takes two days and covers approximately 442km (275 miles) each day. Included in the price is a one-night stopover in Kamloops, bus transfer from train to Kamloops hotel, two continental breakfasts, two light lunches and complimentary beverages (coffee, tea, fruit juices and soft drinks). Alcoholic beverages, films and souvenirs are available on board at an additional cost.

For visitors seeking a route into the Canadian wilderness, the *Polar Bear Express* (www.polarbearexpress.ca), Toronto–North Bay–Cochrane– Moosonee, runs daily (except Monday) from late June to early September. Passengers are advised to make hotel reservations in Moosonee in advance. Particularly scenic routes include Sault Ste. Marie–Eton–Hearst (with superb views of the Montréal River and hundreds of lakes), Winnipeg–Hudson Bay–Churchill, Jasper–Prince George–Prince Rupert (with exceptional scenery between Burns Lake and Prince Rupert), Victoria–Courtenay (along sheer cliffs to Malahat Summit with good views of Vancouver Island) and Vancouver–Whistler (along the fjord-like coast of Howe Sound, then the craggy cliffs and rushing white-water streams in the heavily forested Cheakamus Canyon to Alta Lake) (website: www.whistlermountaineer.com).

VIA Rail also offers tailor-made adventure rail trips (*VIA Adventures*) to far-flung destinations, some of which are inaccessible by road, offering drop-off and pick-up services and special facilities for carrying bulky items such as canoes and bicycles.

Discount Rail Passes: The *Canrailpass* must be purchased outside Canada and a valid passport presented at time of purchase; it allows unlimited journeys on the Canadian railway system (except for the Bras d'Or tourist train) for 12 days (up to three extra days can be added to the pass at any time) within a 30-day period, and is only valid on *VIA Rail* trains. There is also a *Student Canrailpass* available to holders of International Student Cards (ISIC) and a *Senior Canrailpass* available to persons aged 60 and over. There is a reduced fare for children. The *Alaska Pass* (website: www.alaskapass.com) offers eight-, 12-, 15- and 21-day travel within Alaska and British Columbia, including travel on *Alaska Ferry*, *Alaska Railroad*, *Holland America Motorcoaches* and *White Pass & Yukon Railroad*.

Credit: ©Tourisme Québec - Robin Edgar

For more information on rail itineraries, timetables, fares and special discounts, contact *VIA Rail* in Canada (tel: (416) 366 8411; website: www.viarail.ca); *or* the Visit Canada Centre (see *Top Things To See & Do*).

ROAD:

The Canadian road network covers vast distances as the country is over 7600km (4800 miles) from west to east and 4800km (3000 miles) from north to south. The longest road is the Trans-Canada Highway (website: www.transcanadahighway.com), running west to east for 8000km (5000 miles) from Victoria, British Columbia to St John's, Newfoundland. On country roads, visitors should be mindful of wild animals that may be roaming, such as deer or moose. Petrol and oil are sold by the litre, and costs per litre should be obtained at time of travel. The *Canadian Automobile Association* (tel: (613) 247 0117; website: www.caa.ca) is affiliated to most European organisations, giving full use of facilities to members. Road signs are international. Right turns on red lights are not permitted in some parts of Québec. Traffic drives on the right. Road speeds (per hour) and distances are in kilometres, and speeds are: 100kph (60mph) on motorways, 80kph (55mph) on rural highways and 50kph (30mph) in cities. Many road signs throughout the country are bilingual (English and French). Seatbelts are compulsory for all passengers. Radar detection devices are strictly prohibited in many states and may not be carried in automobiles. Studded tyres are illegal in Ontario, but are permitted, without seasonal limitations, in the Northwest Territories, Saskatchewan and Yukon, and are allowed only in winter in other provinces. Many provinces require drivers to keep headlights on during the day. International Driving Permits are recommended - car hire companies may want to see one as well as a passport and air tickets.

Note: The official date on which winter begins, for this and other purposes, will vary from province to province.

Coach: One of the cheapest and most convenient ways of travelling the country apart from private motoring is by coach. Each region is well served by a large network of coach lines, the most extensive being the *Greyhound Bus Company*, which covers more than 193,000km (120,000 miles) of North America. *Greyhound's International Discovery Pass* system offers a variety of options to travellers from outside Canada and the USA. The ticket must be purchased outside of North America and entitles the holder to unlimited travel in the region specified on the pass. The *International Canada Pass* offers travel over periods of seven, 10, 15, 21, 30, 45 and 60 days in Canada. The *International North America CanAm Pass* offers travel over periods of 15, 21, 30, 45 and 60 days in Canada and the USA. The *International Eastern CanAm Pass* offers 10 or 21 days in Ontario, Quebec, New Brunswick, Nova Scotia, Prince Edward Island and the eastern coast of the USA. The *International West Coast CanAm pass* offers 10 or 21 days travel in British Columbia, Whitehorse, Yukon, Alberta and the western coast of the USA. The *Greyhound Discovery Passes* include all scheduled routes on *Greyhound* plus *Greyhound Lines Inc*: Montréal to New York and Vancouver to Seattle; *Voyageur Colonial*: Toronto to Montréal/Ottawa and North Bay to Montréal; *Brewster Transportation*: Banff to Jasper; *Adirondack Trailways*: New York to Buffalo to Toronto; *Canada Coach Services*: Toronto to Niagara Falls and Buffalo and Toronto to Detroit; *Grey Goose Bus Lines*: routes between Manitoba and Ontario; *Laidlaw Coach Lines*: services on Vancouver Island; *Saskatchewan Transportation Co*: Alaska to Saskatoon; and *VIA Rail*: Toronto to Ottawa to Montréal. For further information, contact *Greyhound Canada* (tel: (403) 265 9111 *or* (800) 661 8747 (toll-free in USA and Canada); website: www.greyhound.ca).

Gray Line is another bus company that offers excursions to major Canadian resorts (website: www.grayline.ca).

Canada also has regional bus services, the most important of which are:

Atlantic Canada: Acadian Lines, CN Roadcruiser, SMT Eastern and Terra Nova Transport.

Central Canada: Canada Coach Lines, Grey Goose Bus Lines Limited, Orleans Express, Saskatchewan Transportation, Voyageur and Voyageur Colonial.

West Canada: Brewster Transport and Vancouver Island Coach Lines.

Other coach companies operating in Canada include: *Gray Coach*: Toronto to Niagara Falls and Buffalo; *Arctic Frontier Carriers*: Hay River to Yellowknife. Discounts are available

A B C D E F G H I J K L M N O P Q R S T U V W X Y Z

for children under 16, persons over 62 years and students. The *Moose Travel Network* (website: www.moosetravelnetwork.com) offers a 'jump on, jump off' service for backpackers and independent travellers. Besides long-distance travel, all these companies operate a range of services, such as regional tours and escorted sightseeing for groups. *RoutPass* (www.routpass.com) runs between May and December. It offers 14-, 15-, 16- and 20-day passes for unlimited bus travel in Ontario and Québec. Children are not charged if under five years old; half the adult fare is charged for children aged five to 11 years old. Contact individual operators for details.

Bus: Metropolitan buses operate on a flat-fare system (standard fares, irrespective of distance travelled). Fares must be paid exactly, which means that drivers do not carry change or issue tickets. Transfers should be requested when boarding a bus.

Car Hire: Available in all cities and from airports to full licence holders over 21 years of age. For some rental companies drivers may need to be at least 25 years old. Major companies from which cars can be booked in the UK for use in Canada are *Alamo*, *Avis*, *Budget*, *Dollar*, *Hertz*, *Holiday Autos*, *Pelican Car Hire* and *Thrifty*.

Documentation: It is advised to apply for an International Driving Permit. Visitors may drive on their national driving licences for up to three months in all provinces, with the following exceptions: Yukon – one month; Prince Edward Island – four months; British Columbia, New Brunswick and Québec – six months.

Travel times: The following chart gives approximate travel times from **Ottawa** (in hours and minutes) to other major cities/towns in Canada.

	Air	Road	Rail
Toronto	1.00	5.00	4.00
Montréal	0.30	2.00	2.00
Winnipeg	2.30	32.00	32.00
Vancouver	5.00	62.00	75.00

Travel Advice

Most visits to Canada are trouble-free but you should be aware of the global risk of indiscriminate international terrorist attacks, which could be against civilian targets, including places frequented by foreigners.

This advice is based on information provided by the Foreign and Commonwealth Office in the UK. It is correct at time of publishing. As the situation can change rapidly, visitors are advised to contact the following organisations for the latest travel advice:

British Foreign and Commonwealth Office
Tel: (0845) 850 2829.
Website: www.fco.gov.uk

US Department of State
Website: http://travel.state.gov/travel

Accommodation

HOTELS/GUEST HOUSES/BED & BREAKFAST/SELF-CATERING:
 International hotel chains are represented in major cities, but advance booking is essential. Guest houses, bed & breakfast establishments and self-catering lodges are available throughout the country. There is no national system of accommodation grading. Some provinces operate their own voluntary grading programmes; see the individual Provinces/Territories sections for details.

CAMPING/CARAVANNING:
 Camping facilities in the National Parks are generally only open from mid May until the end of September. Mobile trailers and caravans are extremely popular ways of traversing the enormous expanse of the Canadian landscape. There are two different types of vehicle available: a 'motorhome' is a vehicle that combines driving cab and living space equipped for up to five adults. A 'camper' is a vehicle with a separate driving cab, more like a truck with a caravan on the back, equipped for up to three adults. There are different models according to the size of the accommodation and facilities required, but most have a fridge, cooker, sink, heater, fitted WC and showers. All vehicles are fitted with power steering. Petrol consumption is about 24km (15 miles) per imperial gallon (but petrol costs half as much as it does in Europe). Hiring is available to those who hold full licences and are aged over 25. The cost of hire can vary according to the season. High season runs from June to the end of September, and low season runs for the rest of the year. Full details can be obtained from the Visit Canada Centre (see *Top Things To See & Do*).

YOUTH HOSTELS:
 There are youth hostels in major cities and national parks across the country.

LODGES:
 Remote hunting lodges are available to rent. This accommodation is ideal for fishing, hunting and hiking enthusiasts. They are fully furnished and equipped with spacious living areas and some have spa facilities. They are a popular way to sample life in the wilderness.

OTHER ACCOMMODATION: Most universities offer budget-price accommodation during the summer vacation.

ACCOMMODATION INFORMATION

Hotel Association of Canada
Suite 1206, 130 Albert Street, Ottawa, Ontario K1P 5G4, Canada
Tel: (613) 237 7149.
Website: www.hotelassociation.ca

Canadream Campers
2510-27 St NE, Calagry, Alberta T1Y 7G1, Canada
Tel: (403) 291 1000
Website: www.canadream.com

Hostelling International Canada
205 Catherine Street, Ottawa, Ontario K2P 1CS. Canada
Tel: (613) 237 7884.
Website: www.hihostels.ca

Top Things To See & Do

For a detailed description of the historic sites and natural attractions of each region, see *Top Things To See* and *Top Things To Do* in the individual Provinces/Territories sections.

TOURIST INFORMATION

Visit Canada Centre in the UK
PO Box 170, Ashford, Kent, TN24 0ZX, UK
Tel: (0906) 871 5000 (Mon-Fri 0900-1730, recorded information line; calls cost 60p per minute).
Website: www.travelcanada.ca
Deals with consumer enquiries.

Canadian Tourism Commission in the UK
62-65 Trafalgar Square, London WC2N 5DY, UK
Tel: (0870) 161 5151 (travel trade only).
Website: www.travelcanada.ca

Canadian Tourism Commission deals with marketing and trade enquiries only. Consumer enquiries should be directed to the Visit Canada Centre.

Entertainment

FOOD & DRINK: Canadian cuisine is as varied as the country. The colonial influence is still strong, with European menus available in all major cities. The French influence in Québec is easily discernible in the many restaurants which specialise in French cuisine. Waiter service in restaurants is common. Dress requirements and billing procedures vary. A selection of European/US wines and spirits are imported.

Regional specialities:
- The hundreds of miles of coastline offer varied seafood.
- The central plains provide first-class beef and agricultural produce.
- Some more unusual produce might include elk, bison and caribou.

Regional drinks:
- Canadians also enjoy their own *rye whisky*.

Things to know: Spirits may only be purchased from specially-licensed liquor stores or restaurants displaying the sign 'Licensed Premises'. Many allow customers to bring their own beer or wine. A wide variety of alcohol is sold in most hotels, restaurants and bars. Bars may have table or counter service and payment is generally made after each drink. Opening hours vary from province to province.

Legal drinking age: The minimum drinking age is either 18 or 19, depending on the province/territory. See *Social Profile* in the individual Provinces/ Territories sections. Nunavut is an exception because alcohol is prohibited in some communities.

Tipping: Normal practice is usually 15 per cent of the bill, more if service is exceptional. Waiters, barbers, hairdressers and taxi drivers should be tipped this amount. Porters at airports and railway stations, cloakroom attendants, bellhops, doormen and hotel porters generally expect C$1 per item of luggage. Tipping your server is standard practice in bars and nightclubs.

NIGHTLIFE: Every major provincial capital in the more populated areas has nightclubs, and hotel dinner/dancing. Montréal, Ottawa, Toronto, Vancouver and Winnipeg are centres for ballet, opera and classical music, with visits from leading orchestras and internationally renowned performers. Entertainment in the more remote towns is scarce.

SHOPPING: Fine examples of Canadian craftware are available, such as art woodcarvings, pottery, cottons and native artefacts. Some countries have restrictions against the import of endangered animal species products, such as polar bear, seal, walrus etc, so visitors should check entry regulations in their home country before departure. A 7 per cent goods and service tax (GST) is levied on most goods and services in Canada. In addition, most provinces (except Alberta, Northwest Territories and Yukon) levy a provincial service tax (PST) of 5 to 7 per cent in shops, restaurants and short-term accommodation. In the provinces of Newfoundland, Nova Scotia and New Brunswick, a 15 per cent harmonised sales tax (HST) has replaced the GST and PST. Visitors to Canada are entitled to claim a rebate of GST and HST (except on food, drink, tobacco and transport). The province of Quebec also allows visitors to apply for a rebate of its provincial sales tax (TVQ). For further information, see the special note under the *Duty-Free* section or contact Canada Border Services Agency (CBSA) (website: www.cbsa-asfc.gc.ca). **Shopping hours**: Mon-Sat 0900-1800, with late-night shopping in some stores Thur-Fri, up to 2100. Some shops and stores are also open on Sunday, and some are open 24 hours a day.

Business

- **GDP:** US$991 billion (2004).
- **Main exports:** Motor vehicles and parts, wood pulp, timber, crude petroleum, machinery, natural gas, aluminum, telecommunications equipment, aircraft, plastics and electricity.
- **Main imports:** Machinery and equipment, crude oil, chemicals, motor vehicles and parts, durable consumer goods and electricity.
- **Main trade partners:** China, France, Japan, Mexico, Taiwan, UK and USA.

ECONOMY: Canada is the seventh-largest trading nation and a member of the G8 group of major industrial economies. The country has immense natural resources and a high standard of living. Agriculture and fisheries are particularly important; Canada exports more than half of its agricultural produce – principally grain and oil seeds – and is the world's leading exporter of fish. Timber is another important sector, given that more than 40 per cent of the land area is forest. As a mineral producer, Canada exports crude oil and natural gas, copper, nickel, zinc, iron ore, asbestos, cement, coal and potash. Energy requirements are met by a mixture of hydroelectric (two-thirds), nuclear and oil-fired generating stations. Manufacturing covers a wide range of industries from heavy engineering and chemicals to vehicle production and agro-business to office automation and commercial printing.

After running a substantial trade deficit throughout much of the 1990s, Canada now enjoys a net trade surplus, currently estimated at US$40 billion for the year 2000-2001. Slightly more than 75 per cent of the country's trade is with the USA, making this the world's largest single bilateral trade route. In common with most OECD countries, GDP growth slowed during 2002 to just over one per cent although the outlook for the next few years is rather better. The 1989 free trade agreement signed with the USA formed the basis for the North American Free Trade Agreement (NAFTA); Mexico has joined as the third signatory and other Latin American countries may sign up in due course.

BUSINESS ETIQUETTE: Usual courtesies observed, including exchange of business cards and making appointments. **Office hours:** Mon-Fri 0900-1700.

CONFERENCES/CONVENTIONS: All the major business centres, such as: Calgary, Edmonton, Montréal, Ottawa, Toronto and Vancouver, offer extensive convention and conference facilities. For general information on conferences and conventions in Canada, contact the Meetings and Incentive Officer at the Canadian High Commission, in London. Consult the individual Provinces/Territories sections for more information.

COMMERCIAL INFORMATION

Canada–United Kingdom Chamber of Commerce
38 Grosvenor Street, London W1K 4DP, UK
Tel: (020) 7258 6576 *or* 6578 (trade information service; enquiries cost £10 plus VAT for non-members).
Website: www.canada-uk.org

Canadian Chamber of Commerce
Head Office, Delta Office Tower, 350 Sparks Street, Suite 501, Ottawa, Ontario K1R 7S8, Canada
Tel: (613) 238 4000.
Website: www.chamber.ca

Alberta

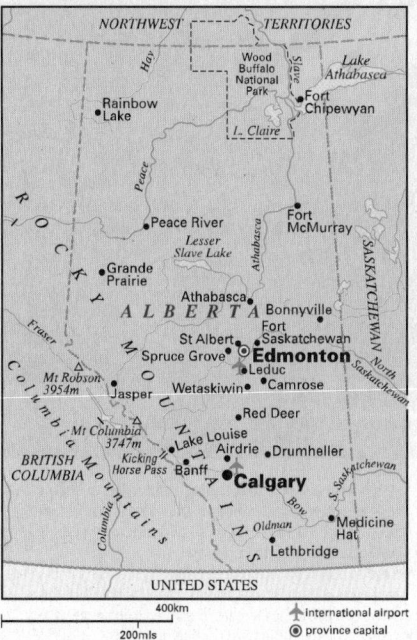

NORTHWEST TERRITORIES

Wood Buffalo National Park

Rainbow Lake

Lake Athabasca

Fort Chipewyan

Peace River

Fort McMurray

Lesser Slave Lake

Grande Prairie

Athabasca

Bonnyville

St Albert · Fort Saskatchewan

Spruce Grove · Edmonton

Mt Robson 3954m

Jasper · Wetaskiwin · Leduc · Camrose

Red Deer

Mt Columbia 3747m

Lake Louise · Airdrie · Drumheller

Kicking Horse Pass · Banff · Calgary

BRITISH COLUMBIA

ALBERTA

SASKATCHEWAN

Oldman

Medicine Hat

Lethbridge

UNITED STATES

400km · 200mls

✈ International airport
◉ province capital

Location: Western Canada.

Time: GMT - 7 (GMT - 6 in summer).
Summer officially lasts from the first Sunday in April to the Saturday before the last Sunday in October.

Overview

Alberta is a nature-lover's paradise: enriched by wide open spaces and sweeping, red sunsets. In terms of nature, what the Province is most renowned for are the sensational peaks of the Rocky Mountains.
Alberta also has huge level plains; parkland that almost begs to be explored. Although very pretty, any traveller to the more mountainous regions, such as the Rockies, will find their jaw continually dropping as awesome alpine views sweep into focus. Whether you are driving along the Icefields Parkway or hiking in a National Park, you will constantly be

Credit: ©Travel Alberta

gawping at a wilderness of woodland, mountains and lakes. If anything exemplifies 'picture-postcard', it is this.
Even in Alberta's cities, there is a large amount of green space, including Canada's largest historical park, Fort Edmonton Park. Also in Edmonton (and other towns) is the lingering of traditional prairie attitudes. This may be because the people of Alberta love to hark back to the Klondike Gold Rush of 1897. The discovery of oil in the Edmonton area in 1947 assured the city of its future, making it one of the fastest-growing metropolitan areas in Canada. This love affair with the past reaches its apogee in the annual 'Klondike Days' extravaganza, held each July, when Edmontonians relive the days of the Gold Rush. What most people consider to be Alberta's true 'gold', however, is the scenery. And that makes Alberta one very rich Province indeed.

General Information

AREA: 638,233 sq km (246,422 sq miles).
POPULATION: 3.25 million (2005).
POPULATION DENSITY: 5.1 per sq km.
CAPITAL: Edmonton. **Population**: 1 million (2005 estimate).
GEOGRAPHY: Alberta is the most westerly of the 'prairie and plains' provinces, bordered to the west by British Columbia and the Rockies, to the southeast by the badlands and prairie, while in the north, along the border with the Northwest Territories, there is a wilderness of forests, lakes and rivers. Mount Columbia on the western Rocky Mountain border is the highest point rising to 3747m (12,293ft). Alberta also has permanent icefields covering 340 sq km (122 sq miles) and releases meltwaters which supply the Mackenzie River flowing into the Arctic Ocean, and the Saskatchewan River flowing into Hudson Bay.
LANGUAGE: Although Canada is officially bilingual (English and French), English is more commonly spoken in Alberta.

Climate

Summer, between May and September, is warm, while winters are cold, with particularly heavy snowfalls in the Rockies. Spring and summer evening temperatures can be cool.
Required clothing: Light- to mediumweights during warmer months. Heavyweights are worn in winter, with alpine wear in mountains. Waterproof wear is advisable throughout the year.

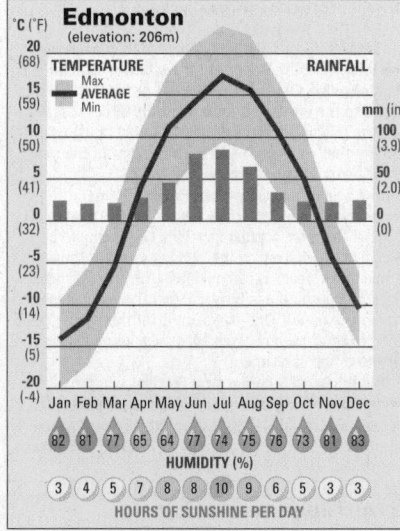

Edmonton (elevation: 206m)

°C (°F)

TEMPERATURE — Max — AVERAGE — Min

RAINFALL — mm (in)

Jan Feb Mar Apr May Jun Jul Aug Sep Oct Nov Dec

HUMIDITY (%)
82 81 77 65 64 77 74 75 76 73 81 83

3 4 5 7 8 8 10 9 6 5 3 3
HOURS OF SUNSHINE PER DAY

Public Holidays

Alberta observes all the public holidays observed nationwide (see the general *Canada* section) and, in addition, the beneath Public Holidays listed for the January 2006-June 2007 period.
2006: Feb 20 Alberta Family Day. **Aug 1** Heritage Day.
2007: Feb 19 Alberta Family Day.

Travel - International

AIR:

The province is served by *Air Canada (AC)*. Many other airlines also serve the province from worldwide destinations.
Approximate flight times: From Edmonton/Calgary to *London* is 8 hours 30 minutes, to *Los Angeles* is 3 hours, to *New York* is 5 hours and to *Sydney* is 15 hours.
Main airports: Edmonton (YEG) (tel: (780) 890 8900; website: www.edmontonairports.com) is 28km (17 miles) from the city. *To/from the airport*: A bus service to the city operates every 20 minutes (travel time – 40 minutes).
Calgary (YYC) (tel: (403) 735 1200; website:

www.calgaryairport.com) is 20km (12.5 miles) from the city.
To/from the airport: A bus service to the city operates every 30 minutes (travel time – 20 minutes).
Facilities: Both *Edmonton* and *Calgary* also receive domestic services and both have duty free shops, banks, restaurants and car parking.

RAIL:

VIA Rail (tel: (888) 842 7245 (toll-free in the USA and Canada); website: www.viarail.ca) serves Edmonton and Jasper three times a week. The Western transcontinental train (*The Canadian*), crosses the province thrice weekly originating from Toronto, Ontario in the east through Edmonton and Jasper, to Vancouver in the west and vice versa. This train connects with the *Skeena* service at Jasper with a thrice-weekly service to Prince Rupert, British Columbia. The seasonal *Rocky Mountain Railtours* (website: www.rkymtnrail.com) is the only other rail service operating into the province. This is a two-day, all-daylight tour from either Calgary, Banff or Jasper to and from Vancouver, running between mid-April and mid-October (tel: (604) 606 7245; toll-free in Canada and USA only).

ROAD:

The Yellowhead Highway (Winnipeg-Edmonton-Prince Rupert-Vancouver) and Highway 2 (USA-Calgary-Red Deer-Edmonton-North Alberta) are the two main roads serving Alberta. Most of the roads in Edmonton are constructed into a grid system, making it easier to navigate.
Coach: Greyhound Canada (tel: (800) 661 8747) runs coach services into Alberta, thereby connecting Edmonton with all other major capitals. The main *Greyhound* terminals are at Banff, Calgary, Edmonton, Fort McMurray, Grand Prairie, Lethbridge and Red Deer. Coaches are also operated in Alberta by *Brewster Transportation and Tours* (Banff) (website: www.brewster.ca) and *Gray Line Sightseeing Tours* (Calgary), which organise coach tours in the area. A coach is operated between the two city centres of Calgary and Edmonton by *Red Arrow* (on behalf of VIA Rail) six times a day (tel: (800) 232 1958; website: www.redarrow.pwt.ca). **Car hire** is available in all large towns and at Edmonton and Calgary airports. National driving licences are accepted in Alberta.
Note: When visiting in late autumn, winter or spring, travellers are advised to either ensure that their vehicle has snow tyres or to carry chains. It is also advisable to have an adequate supply of anti-freeze when crossing through mountain passes.

URBAN:

Buses and the light rail system in Calgary are operated on a flat-fare system. Exact fares are required if tickets are purchased upon boarding; pre-purchased single- and multi-journey tickets are available. Edmonton, where there is a similar fares system, has buses, trolleybuses and a light rail route. Local buses operate in all other major towns.
Travel times: The following chart gives approximate travel times from **Edmonton** (in hours and minutes) to other major cities/towns in Alberta.

	Air	Road	Rail
Calgary	0.45	3.00	-
Banff	-	5.00	-
Jasper	-	4.30	5.20

Accommodation

HOTELS/HOSTELS/BED & BREAKFAST/LODGES:

Travel Alberta can provide a comprehensive guide to the province's accommodation (see *Top Things To Do*). Accommodation ranges from top-quality hotels to motorway motels, lodge estates and hostels. Banff National Park is famous for its two baronial-quality hotels, offering approximately 2000 rooms. Many lodges offer various levels of self-catering, often in conjunction with fishing and hiking trips. Several agencies offer bed & breakfast and ranch vacations throughout Alberta. *Canada Select* star ratings (blue stars) and *Access Canada* (showing as A1, A2, A3 and A4 in the amenity symbols; for those who are senior or disabled), are both optional programmes that accommodations can participate from. However, much of Alberta's accommodation is, at present, already supervised by the provincial government under a voluntary scheme to ensure high standards of cleanliness, comfort, construction and maintenance of furnishings and facilities. Look for the 'Approved Accommodation' sign which means that the establishment conforms to these standards.

CAMPING/CARAVANNING:
The northern area of Alberta contains hundreds of lakes and forests, with abundant game such as deer, moose, bears and the rare trumpeter swan. There are numerous campsites in the National Parks. *Camping Select* have given campsites star ratings but the permanent facilities tend to be more basic in the north and some campsites have a fire ban. A number of companies can arrange **motor camper** rentals, with a range of fully-equipped vehicles. Full details can be obtained from Travel Alberta (see *Top Things To Do*); see also Camping/Caravanning in the general *Canada* section.

A B C D E F G H I J K L M N O P Q R S T U V W X Y Z

ACCOMMODATION INFORMATION

Alberta Hotel & Lodging Association
Suite 401, Centre 104, 5241 Calgary Trail, Edmonton,
Alberta T6H 5G8, Canada
Tel: (780) 436 6112.
Website: www.ahla.ca

Alberta Bed & Breakfast Association
Website: www.bbalberta.com

Alberta Resort and Campground Association
Suite 216, 17008 90th Avenue, Edmonton,
Alberta T4T 1L6, Canada
Website: www.explorealberta.com

**Bed & Breakfast Association of Greater Edmonton
(BBAGE)**
Tel: (780) 432 7116.
Website: www.bbedmonton.com

Top Things To See

- See some of the sights that put Alberta into the record books: the world's largest mall, the **West Edmonton Mall**, boasts theatres, restaurants, nightclubs, amusement areas (including a miniature golf course, ice rink, swimming pool, waterpark and amusement park), aviaries, aquariums and museums; there is also the world's largest indoor amusement park, **Fantasyland**; and Canada's largest planetarium, the **Space & Science Center**.
- Explore Alberta's oldest surviving structure, the historic **log cabin of Father Lacombe**, in the town of **St Albert**, 30km (19 miles) northwest from downtown **Edmonton**. At one time it was the centre of a thriving French-speaking Métis settlement (native peoples of mixed heritage).
- View an abundance of wildlife at **Elk Island National Park**. Originally established in 1906 as an elk preserve, this completely fenced park is now home to over 44 different kinds of animals (including elk, moose, coyote, bear and beaver), as well as massive herds of plains bison. At **Wood Buffalo National Park** (Canada's largest national park and bigger than Switzerland), granted World Heritage status by UNESCO in 1983, vast expanses of boreal plains provide a perfect habitat for many rare species of wildlife, including the world's largest free-roaming bison herd.
- Glimpse at a heritage of ranching at **Cochrane Ranche**, established in 1881, sitting 30km (19 miles) west of Calgary. Country-and-western-themed shops are speckled around the downtown area and genuine cowboys still live and work in this area. Pop into a saloon and savour the unique atmosphere of a historic landmark, which was 'the largest ranch in the Dominion' by 1888.
- Be gobsmacked by those characteristic Canadian views: stunning lake scenery in **Waterton Lakes National Park**, joined to **Glacier National Park** in Montana to form the **Waterton-Glacier International Peace Park**; and **Banff National Park** in the heart of the Canadian Rockies, the first of the country's national parks and a UNESCO World Heritage Site, offering spectacular wilderness with mountain, river and lake scenery – notably **Lake Louise**.
- Study the remains of dinosaurs first discovered in 1874 in the banks of the **Red Deer River**, on the 48km (30 mile) **Dinosaur Trail** near **Drumheller**. A few minutes from the downtown area is the **Royal Tyrrell Museum of Palaeontology**, with hands-on exhibitions, ongoing site work and one of the world's largest collections of dinosaur remains. Southwest of Drumheller, the **Dinosaur Provincial Park** continues this theme with reconstructed skeletons of duck-billed dinosaurs.
- Ignore the horrific-sounding name and take in an unparalleled view of the surrounding prairie at **Head-Smashed-In Buffalo Jump**, 50km (36 miles) south of **Lethbridge**. This cliff-top is among the largest and best-preserved jump sites in the world; it was used by the native people for more than 10,000 years to drive thousands of buffalo to their deaths, thus providing them with food, shelter and clothing.
- Look up at (or look down from, depending on how brave you are!) the city of **Calgary**'s most recognisable feature. Officially opened in 1968, the **Calgary Tower**'s 191m (626ft) height offers panoramic views of Calgary, local towns and the **Rocky Mountains**. For those who especially love the view, why not eat in the rotating dining room at the top, providing an ever-changing vista whilst you eat?

Top Things To Do

- The southern part of the Rockies (**Banff**, **Jasper**, **Kootenay** and **Yoho**) are an obvious starting point for visitors in search of the great outdoors. Make the most of such wonderful mountain scenery and engage in a plethora of winter sports. **Skiing**, both **cross-country** and **downhill**, is a major pastime in the Rockies in the winter.

Credit: ©Travel Alberta

Snowboarding is also very popular. Other snow-based activities include **dog sledding** (trekking along mountain trails with teams of huskies under the supervision of experienced guides), **ski-joring** (being pulled along on skis by teams of huskies), **wildlife tracking**, **igloo building** and **snowshoeing**. Longer treks allow the visitor to penetrate deeper into the pristine wilderness. Accommodation is usually in log cabins or winter camps. Visitors should note that certain regulations apply to national parks and that some activities are not allowed (snowmobiles are prohibited for example). Provincial parks, such as **Kananaskis** or **Mount Robson** may offer the visitor more freedom in this respect.
- The **Calgary Stampede**, one of Canada's biggest rodeos, is held in July each year (website: http://calgarystampede.com) and attracts many competitors and spectators. Lasting for 10 days, it includes stage shows, parades, concerts, rodeo and agricultural exhibits, and offers one of the largest prizes in North America.
- Drive the **Icefields Parkway** (Highway 93), running the length of the two parks and affording magnificent views of the lakes, forests and the glaciers of the **Columbia Icefield**, which incorporates the **McKinley Glacier** and the **Columbia Glacier**. The Parkway provides the best access to the wilderness trails in the area. For those who want to remain seated, 230km (143 miles) of highway ensures that your vehicle travels past some of the most beautiful mountain scenery in the world.
- For the bold of heart, try **alpine scuba-diving**! **Horseshoe Lake**, **Patricia Lake** and **Lake Annette** are three of the more popular locations. Divers should be experienced and employ the 'buddy' system as the water is cold and visibility is often limited. The local Rangers Station opposite the railway station can supply maps and other information. One-day permits for these parks cost C$5 per adult, with children aged six years and under admitted free of charge.
- Attend the **Banff Summer Arts Festival**, which is Alberta's biggest showcase of the arts (with dance, theatre, film, lectures and art) and takes place over three months annually: all amidst the stunning backdrop of the **Rocky Mountains**.

TOURIST INFORMATION

Travel Alberta in the UK
24a Friday Street, Warnham, West Sussex RH12 3QX
Tel: (01403) 754 424 *or* (01403) 257 200 (brochure requests).
Website: www.explorealberta.com or www.travelalberta.com

Travel Alberta
PO Box 2500, Edmonton, Alberta, T5J 2Z4, Canada
Tel: (800) 252 3782 *or* (780) 427 4321 *or* (403) 297 2700 (travel trade).
Website: www.travelalberta.com

Entertainment

FOOD & DRINK: Alberta's prairie is ideal for cattle rearing and its Western beef is world famous. Apart from traditional foods, Alberta's towns and cities offer an excellent range of international cuisine. Alcohol is sold in 'liquor stores', although beer may be obtained in the majority of hotels.
Regional specialities:
- Beef is barbecued, braised, grilled, minced and skewered with different complements such as onions, mushrooms,

green peppers, rice, sauces and beans: Alberta beef is renowned worldwide and is extraordinarily succulent.
- Stew (combination of diced steak, garden vegetables and biscuits cooked in rich gravy).
- *Beef mincemeat* (combines chopped suet, fruits and spices) is used in pies and tarts and as a traditional Christmas dish served with ice-cream, cream or rum sauce.
- Wild berries and nuts are used in desserts.
- During the season, try the blueberry muffins from local bakeries.
- Honey is made from alfalfa and clover nectar and is a widely used sweetener and breakfast food.
Legal drinking age: 18 years.
NIGHTLIFE: Both Edmonton and Calgary have a rich variety of night time entertainment. Nightclubs, cabarets, taverns, lounges and that infamous Alberta watering hole, the beer parlour, combine to provide constant local and international entertainment. Calgary and Edmonton boast full-scale orchestras.
SHOPPING: Alberta is the only province (apart from the Northwest Territories and Yukon) that does not apply an extra sales tax on all purchases over and above the general sales tax of seven per cent. Artwork available in the province includes pottery, ceramics, sculptures and paintings. There are numerous malls in Edmonton, including Heritage Mall and the huge West Edmonton Mall. Speciality shops can be found in the Old Strathcona district, from boutiques to a farmer's market. The Kensington district – Calgary's village in the city – has over 140 excellent shops and restaurants. **Shopping hours:** Mon-Fri 1000-1700; Sat 1000-2100 (malls are generally open until 2100).

Business

CONFERENCES/CONVENTIONS: Banff, Calgary, Edmonton and Jasper offer conference and convention venues. Information can be obtained from the Visit Canada Centre (see general *Canada* section) *or* Travel Alberta (see *Top Things To Do*).

COMMERCIAL INFORMATION

Alberta Chambers of Commerce
1808 Merrill Lynch Tower, 10025-102A Avenue,
Edmonton City Centre, Alberta T5J 2Z2, Canada
Tel: (780) 425 4180.
Website: www.abchamber.ca

Calgary Convention & Visitors Bureau (Information on Conferences/Conventions)
Suite 200, 238 11th Avenue SE, Calgary,
Alberta T2G 0X8, Canada
Tel: (403) 263 8510.
Website: www.tourismcalgary.com

Banff/Lake Louise Tourism Bureau (Information on Conferences/Conventions)
PO Box 1298, Banff, Alberta T1L 1B3, Canada
Tel: (403) 762 8421.
Website: www.banfflakelouise.com

Jasper Tourism and Commerce (Information on Conferences/Conventions)
PO Box 98, 409 Patricia Street, Jasper,
Alberta T0E 1E0, Canada
Tel: (780) 852 3858.
Website: www.jaspercanadianrockies.com

British Columbia

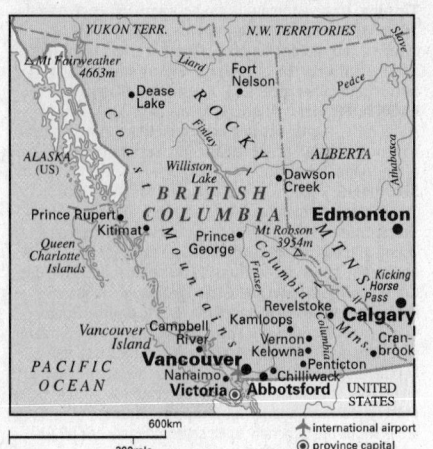

Location: Western Canada.

Time: GMT - 8. Small areas of the province near the Alberta border are GMT - 7.

Overview

Canada's most westerly Province, British Columbia is huge and diverse. If you love the great outdoors, you will never be bored in a Province that is so beautiful, with such variation, and with so many opportunities for hiking, rafting, sailing and skiing, to name just a few.
British Columbia is mostly studded with mountains that puncture vast, blue skies. Such scenery is overwhelmingly beautiful, but it is not all that British Columbia offers. You will also find long stretches of rugged coastline, sandy beaches, wineries, forests and algae-fed lakes that glisten with an intense, aqua hue. There is even Canada's only desert: the Okanagan is home to rattlesnakes, scorpions and prickly pear cacti. If you are seeking unspoiled wilderness, then British Columbia is the perfect Province to be delightfully alone in. If you happen to get lonely, there are plenty of modern and lively cities and towns in British Columbia. Vancouver has scores of galleries, museums and bars. But even in Vancouver you are never too removed from nature: the city contains Canada's largest city park, Stanley Park.
This may be because, with nine national parks and plenty of provincial parks, British Columbia is first and foremost a destination renowned for its natural settings rather than its urban ones. From kayaking with whales off the Province's islands to driving down a highway that is flanked by mountains, British Columbia will enchant you.

General Information

AREA: 892,677 sq km (344,662 sq miles).
POPULATION: 4,254,500 (2005).
POPULATION DENSITY: 4.76 per sq km.
CAPITAL: Victoria. **Population:** 330,000 (2005 estimate).
GEOGRAPHY: British Columbia is Canada's most westerly province, bordered to the south by the USA (Washington, Idaho and Montana states), to the east by Alberta, to the north by the Northwest Territories and the Yukon, and to the west by the Pacific Ocean and the 'Alaskan Panhandle'. It is mainly covered by virgin forests and encompasses the towering Rocky Mountains (rising to 3954m/12,972ft), vast expanses of semi-arid sagebrush, lush pastures on Vancouver Island's east coast, farmland in the Fraser River delta, and fruitland in the Okanagan Valley. The highest mountain is Fairweather at 4663m (15,298ft). Between the eastern and coastal mountains is a lower central range. The coastal range sinks into the Pacific, with larger peaks emerging at Vancouver and Queen Charlotte islands. The Columbia River flows from the Rockies into Washington State and out into the Pacific Ocean.
LANGUAGE: Although Canada is officially bilingual (English and French), English is more commonly spoken in British Columbia.

Climate

The southern coast is one of the mildest regions in Canada, with very warm summers and relatively mild winters. Heavy snowfalls in the Rockies.
Required clothing: Lightweights for most of the summer, with warmer clothes sometimes necessary in the evenings. Mediumweights are worn during winter, with Alpine wear in the mountains. Waterproof clothing is advisable throughout the year.

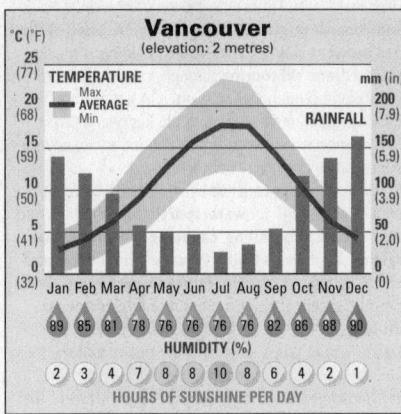

Vancouver (elevation: 2 metres)

Public Holidays

British Columbia observes all the Public Holidays observed nationwide (see the general *Canada* section) and, in addition, the beneath Public Holidays listed for the January 2006-June 2007 period.
2006: Aug 7 British Columbia Day.

Travel - International

AIR:
Air Canada serves British Columbia, and many other airlines from worldwide destinations also serve the Province.
Main airports: *Vancouver (YVR)* (website: www.yvr.ca) is 15km (9 miles) southwest of the city. It is served by airlines from the USA, Europe and the Far East. *To/from the airport:* The journey to the city centre takes about 25 minutes. *Facilities:* Banks and ATMs, a post office, business centre, restaurant, car parking, garage, car rental, nursery and duty free shop.
Victoria (YYJ) (website: www.cyyj.ca) is 22km (14 miles) north of Victoria. *To/from the airport:* The journey into the city centre takes about 30 minutes. Transit bus services, an airport shuttle and taxis are available. *Facilities:* ATM, foreign exchange, shops, restaurants and cafes.
Abbotsford (YXX) (website: www.abbotsfordairport.ca) is 68km (42 miles) east of Vancouver. *To/from the airport:* The journey into Vancouver takes about one hour.
Kelowna (YLW) (website: www.kelownaairport.com) is north of Kelowna. *To/from the airport:* The journey into Kelowna takes about 20 minutes. Shuttle services are available. *Facilities:* Duty free shopping, restaurant, gift shop, ATMs, car rental and a cappucino bar.
SEA:
Main ports: *Vancouver* is an international passenger port, with regular sailings to the Far East and ports on the USA's northwestern coast. Ferry services to and from all coastal ports in British Columbia are available. Ferry services link three points on Vancouver Island with Vancouver city's north (Horseshoe Bay) and south (Tsawwassen) terminals on the mainland. Foot passengers can take coaches which travel from Vancouver city centre to Victoria city centre. BC Ferries operates a total of 25 routes between 46 ports of call in coastal British Columbia, including a scenic, luxury, 15-hour, one-way, daylight voyage from Port Hardy on the northern tip of Vancouver Island along the Inside Passage to Prince Rupert, a crossing from Prince Rupert to the Queen Charlotte Islands (see *Top Things to Do* section), and the Discovery Coast Passage, a summer route between Port Hardy and Bella Coola on the mid-coast mainland that runs either direct in a day or with stops at various inlets. There is also a high-speed catamaran from Victoria to Seattle (USA), the *Victoria Clipper*, leaving twice a day. The crossing takes two hours 30 minutes (website: www.victoriaclipper.com). For further information on ferries, contact *BC Ferries* (tel: (250) 386 3431 *or* (888) 223 3779 (toll-free in British Columbia); website: www.bcferries.com) *or* consult *The Ferry Traveller*, a website with general ferry information (tel: (800) 686 0446; website: www.ferrytravel.com).
RAIL:
VIA Rail (website: www.viarail.ca) train routes to and within British Columbia are: Edmonton to Prince Rupert via Jasper (Alberta); Victoria to Courtenay; Vancouver to Edmonton via Kamloops and Jasper, and on to Toronto three times a week (*Western Transcontinental*).
ROAD:
The Trans-Canada Highway (Highway 1) reaches British Columbia via Calgary, Alberta and continues through the south of the province to Vancouver, over to Nanaimo, and onto Victoria. The other main highways are numbers 3, 5, 16, 37, 95 and 97.

Highway 99 runs from the US/Canadian border into Vancouver. Apart from Highway 97 and the remote scenic Highway 37, which run northwards to the Yukon, the province's road network is concentrated in the south. Road signs are international. There are good roads south to Seattle in the USA. **Bus:** *Translink* supplies buses to the Greater Vancouver area as part of an integrated public transport service. For timetable details, contact *Translink* (tel: (604) 953 3333; website: www.translink.bc.ca). *BC Transit* provides a network of buses to many communities within British Columbia, including the capital, Victoria, and the resort town of Whistler. Timetable details are available (tel: (250) 385 2551; website: www.bctransit.com). *Malaspina Coachlines* provides services from Vancouver International airport to Vancouver and the Sunshine Coast (tel: (877) 227 8287; website: www.malaspinacoach.com). *Pacific Coachlines* provides services from various Vancouver locations to Victoria and Namaimo (tel: (800) 661 1725 (toll-free in Canada) *or* (604) 662 7575; website: www.pacificcoach.com). *Island Coach lines* with *Gray Line West* provide services on Vancouver Island including sightseeing routes (tel: (800) 667 0882 (toll-free in Canada) *or* (250) 388 6539; website: www.victoriatours.com).
URBAN:
Most of Vancouver's public transport network is operated by *Translink* (tel: (604) 453 4500; website: www.translink.bc.ca), including buses, commuter rail services between Vancouver and Mission, *SkyTrain* between Vancouver and Surrey, and *SeaBuses* between Vancouver and North Vancouver. Ferries between the mainland and Vancouver Island are provided by *BC Ferries*. Buses in Victoria are run by *BC Transit*.
TRAVEL TIMES: The following chart gives approximate travel times from **Vancouver** (in hours and minutes) to other major cities/towns in British Columbia.

	Air	Road	Rail
Victoria	0.25	3.30	-
Kamloops	0.55	4.00	9.00
Whistler	0.30	2.00	-
Prince George	1.00	10.00	-

Accommodation

HOTELS/COTTAGES/CABINS/BED & BREAKFAST:
Accommodation ranges from top-class hotels in Victoria and Vancouver and motels beside the main southern highways to simple cabins high up in the Rockies. Cottages and cabins are widely available on Vancouver Island. 'Ranch Holidays' are popular in the Cariboo Chilcotin Coast tourism region of central British Columbia. Standards are overseen by Tourism British Columbia and approved hotels display a white 'Approved Accommo-dation' sign to indicate that Tourism BC's standards of courtesy, comfort and cleanliness have been met.
CAMPING/CARAVANNING:
There are nearly 10,000 campsites situated in over 150 parks and recreation areas. Several of the parks are designated as 'Nature Conservancy Areas', where all motor vehicles are banned and transport must be on foot. The type of parkland available varies from sandy beaches with vehicle access, to lakes and glaciers reached only by aircraft or boat. A number of companies can arrange **motor camper** rentals, with a range of fully-equipped vehicles.

ACCOMMODATION INFORMATION

British Columbia & Yukon Hotels' Association
2nd Floor, 948 Howe Street, Vancouver, British Columbia V6Z 1N9, Canada
Tel: (604) 681 7164.
Website: www.bcyha.com

Old English B & B Registry
1226 Silverwood Crescent, North Vancouver, British Columbia V7P 1J3, Canada
Tel: (604) 986 5069.
Website: www.oldenglishbandb.bc.ca

Western Canada Bed & Breakfast Innkeepers Association
PO Box 74534, 2803 West 4th Avenue, Vancouver, British Columbia V6K 4P4, Canada
Website: www.wcbbia.com

British Columbia Lodging and Campgrounds Association
Suite 209, 3003 St John's Street, Port Moody, British Columbia V3H 2C4, Canada
Tel: (604) 945 7676.
Website: www.bclca.com

Discover Camping
Website: www.discovercamping.ca

Top Things To See

- **Vancouver** is Canada's third-largest city and a major port, overlooking the **Burrard Inlet** on the Pacific Ocean, backed by the **Coastal Mountain Range**. Downtown Vancouver has one of the largest Chinese quarters in North America, and large German and Ukrainian populations. **Gastown**, the reconstructed old centre of Vancouver, is a pleasant array of cobblestone streets, cafes and shops. Of the several museums and galleries, most notable are the **Police Centennial Museum**, University of British Columbia's **Museum of Anthropology** (housing excellent examples of northwest First Nations art and artefacts), **Science World** (including four galleries of hands-on exhibits) and the **Maritime Museum**. More points of interest are **Stanley Park**, one of North America's largest civic parks, and the **Grouse Mountain Skyride** on the North Shore. The latter offers views of the city and the fjords of the Pacific coast. Nearby, **Burnaby Mountain Park** affords a breathtaking view of the city and Gulf Islands on Vancouver's west coast.
- See the towns dotted along the historic **Cariboo Gold Rush route**. **Mayne Island**'s **Miners Bay** is so-named because of gold-seekers who took advantage of the island's halfway position between **Vancouver Island** and the mouth of the **Fraser River**. Near **William's Lake, 100 Mile House** is an historic marker of the Cariboo Gold Rush days, when pioneers measured journeys by the distance of a day's horse ride and the relative distance from the Gold Rush town of **Lillooet**, otherwise known as **'Mile 0'**.
- Known as BC's 'playground', the azure blue waters of **Lake Okanagan** and the stunning vistas of the surrounding vineyards are only two of the major draws to this area. The northern tip of Mexico's Sonora Desert actually ends here – in the rich, lush countryside of British Columbia's interior. The Okanagan's fall wine tours attract visitors from across Europe and North America. At the northern tip of the **Okanagan Valley**, **Shuswap Lake** offers resort-like summer weather and excellent boating opportunities. Those seeking close proximity to nature can observe black bears meander and munch on berries in their natural environment; prime viewing areas include **Wells Gray Provincial Park**, as well as rural roads nears **Kamloops** and **Merritt**.
- Survey vast tracts of untamed lakeland, forest and wilderness in the **Cariboo**. The arid, desert-like terrain is best known for its guest ranch accommodations and winter lodge facilities.
- See more than 400 glaciers continue to sculpt the dramatic Columbia Mountains and to feed the crystal-clear rivers in the spectacular **Glacier National Park**.
- Located near Terrace is the **Nisga'a Memorial Lava Bed**, a sacred Aboriginal site. The park offers visitors a chance to explore the unique volcanic landscape, whilst also learning about the culture and legends of the Nisga'a people. The **Queen Charlotte Islands** are also inhabited by several Aboriginal communities, accessible only by boat or floatplane.
- Inspect fossils dating back more than 10 million years at **Driftwood Canyon Provincial Park**.
- Combine seeing more than one million seabirds and animals with standing in one of Canada's many UNESCO World Heritage Sites at the **Gwaii Haanas National Park Reserve**.

Top Things To Do

- Practically every type of **walking** activity is available in British Columbia. In **Vancouver**, **EcoWalk tours** of **Stanley Park** provide interesting information on Canada's unique West coast ecology as well as on the aboriginal First Nations' culture and legends of the park (website: www.ecowalkbc.com). Long-distance hiking trails include the beautiful **West Coast Trail** in the **Pacific Rim National Park** (**Vancouver Island**), so much in demand that a quota system is in place; and the **Juan de Fuca Marine Trail**, also on Vancouver Island. Giant trees may be seen in the old coastal rainforests on the Island and the Pacific coast. The delicate sub-alpine terrain of **Bulkley valley** and the **Babine Mountains Recreational Area** offer 32,400ha (80,060 acres) of hiking, biking and horseback trails. Ample camping and other facilities exist in the national parks.
- Take advantage of the excellent facilities for **skiing** and other snow-based activities in the **Rocky and Coast Mountains**. Canada's best-known ski resort is **Whistler Blackcomb**, which has over 200 marked runs; this and some other resorts (including **Cypress Mountain** and **Hemlock Valley**) lie conveniently close to Vancouver. Other well-known centres include **Mount Washington** on **Vancouver Island**, **Red Mountain** in **Rossland** (home to Canada's Olympic ski medallists), the **Kimberley Alpine Resort** and **Big White Ski Resort** in the Okanagan Valley. Other activities on offer include **snowboarding**, **glacier skiing** (in summer), **heli-skiing** and **snowcat skiing**. **Cross-country skiing** is widely practised, and **ski touring** through snow-covered forests is popular; accommodation is often in simple huts. The hundreds of watersheds among the Rocky and Coast Mountains have provided British Columbia with countless rivers and lakes in every park area.
- British Columbia is enriched by swathes of water – giving ample opportunity for **watersports**. Large lakeland and rivers are ideal for **sailing**, **canoeing** and **whitewater rafting**. The famous **Inside Passage** from the southern end of Vancouver Island to **Prince Rupert** in the north provides excellent opportunities for protected **ocean cruising**, which can be done by charter yacht, ocean kayak, ferry or cruise ship. For independent **sailors**, there are many anchorages and marinas providing facilities for safe moorage and other services. Beautiful views of the fjord-indented coastline and the snow-capped **Coast Mountains** beyond are one of the attractions of sailing here.
- British Columbia is famous for its **fishing**. Salmon is especially plentiful around **Vancouver Island** and the **Kootenay Rockies** offer the best bass fishing in the province. Other fish in the waters include halibut, cod, trout, whitefish and burbot. The **Kamloops** region has more than 200 lakes within an hour of the city and is especially popular amongst sporting fishermen. Appropriate licences are required.
- **Whale-watching** cruises provide the chance to view orca (killer), humpback, grey and minke whales. In March, the **Pacific Rim Whale Festival** celebrates the yearly migration of Pacific grey whales from Baja California, Mexico to Vancouver Island. Watch for whales in the remote towns of **Tofino** and **Ucluelet**, near the popular ecological attraction of the **Pacific Rim National Park** on the west coast which is full of sandy beaches and wilderness.
- Take a **winery tour** along the **Okanagan Wine Route** in the vineyards of the **Thompson Okanagan Valley,** the oldest wine producing region in British Columbia. There are 60 wineries along the route and the valley holds a **Orkanagan Wine Festival** each season of the wine producing year.
- Take the **Silvery Slocan Circle Driving Tour** past numerous historic landmarks, such as the historic logging town of **Kaslo**, which populates the hills and shoreline of **Kootenay Lake** and the city of **Nelson**, home to 350 heritage buildings.

TOURIST INFORMATION

Tourism British Columbia in the UK
3rd Floor, British Columbia House, 3 Regent Street, London SW1Y 4NS, UK
Tel: (0906) 871 5000 (Visit Canada Centre; calls cost 60p per minute) *or* (020) 7930 6857 (trade and media enquiries).
Website: www.hellobc.com

Tourism British Columbia
12th Floor, 510 Burrard Street, Vancouver, British Columbia V6C 3A8, Canada
Tel: (604) 660 2861 *or* (800) 435 5622
Website: www.hellobc.com

Entertainment

FOOD & DRINK: The cuisine of the province is enhanced by English traditions.
Things to know: Spirits, beer and wine can be served in licensed restaurants, dining rooms, pubs and bars. Taverns (pubs) are open until 0100, bars and cabarets until 0200.
Regional specialities:
- The Pacific Ocean yields a great variety of seafood, including king crab, oysters, shrimp and other shellfish, as well as cod, haddock and salmon (*coho*, *spring*, *chum*, *sockeye* and *pink*) which are smoked, pan-fried, breaded, baked, canned or barbecued, and complemented by local vegetables.
- Fruits grown in the province include apples, peaches, pears, plums, apricots, strawberries, blackberries, the famous *Bing* cherries, cranberries and loganberries.
- *Victoria creams*, a famous chocolate delicacy derived from a recipe dating back to 1885, are exported worldwide from British Columbia. The original confectioners shop is situated in Victoria on Vancouver Island.

Regional drinks:
- Sparkling wines are produced in the Okanagan Valley and all the usual alcoholic beverages are widely available.

Legal drinking age: 19 years.
Tipping: It is customary to tip between 15 per cent and 20 per cent at bars and restaurants in BC. Tips are also given to tour guides, and for taxi service, spa treatments and haircuts. Porters at airports, railway stations and hotels generally expect C$1-2 per item of luggage.
NIGHTLIFE: Major cities and towns have top-class restaurants, nightclubs and bars, sometimes in pub style. Vancouver has an active theatre life. Better nightspots are often found in hotels.
SHOPPING: Vancouver is a shopper's paradise. *Robson Street* offers fashion boutiques, souvenir and speciality shops. *Yaletown* is the shopping ground of Vancouver's young and aspirational, with designer fashions, art galleries and trendy home decor shops. Other popular areas include *Chinatown*, *Gastown* and *Granville Island*. Indoor shopping downtown includes the *Pacific Centre*, *Royal Centre* and the *Sinclair Centre*, while *Metrotown* is a large suburban mall (with over 500 shops and food outlets). Popular handicrafts include Pacific Northwest and Inuit arts and crafts: soapstone sculptures, carved masks, totem poles, pottery, jewellery and prints. **Shopping hours**: In the larger areas shops are generally open seven days a week 0930-1800 (Thurs-Fri until 2100).

Business

CONFERENCES/CONVENTIONS: There are conference/convention centres in Penticton, Vancouver, Victoria and Whistler as well as over 200 hotels throughout the province which can offer meeting facilities.

COMMERCIAL INFORMATION

Ministry of Small Business & Economic Development
Marketing, Investment & Trade, Ste 730 999 Canada Place, Vancouver BC V6C 3E1, Canada
Tel: (604) 844 1900.

The Greater Victoria Chamber of Commerce
850 Courtney Street, Victoria, V8W 1CA, Canada
Tel: (250) 383 7191.
Website: www.victoriachamber.ca

The Greater Vancouver Convention and Visitors Bureau
Suite 210-200 Burrard Street, Vancouver V6C 3L6, Canada
Tel: (604) 682 2222.
Website: www.tourismvancouver.com

Manitoba

Location: Central Canada.

Time: GMT - 6 (GMT - 5 in summer).
Summer officially lasts from the first Sunday in April to the Saturday before the last Sunday in October.

Overview

Manitoba is a huge Province with comparably few residents. Instead of hordes of people, you will instead find immense countryside that is as diverse as its population: Manitoba is the centre of the cultural festival *Folklarama*, a celebration of Canada's ethnic communities; Manitoba chosen because of its vibrant international mix, which includes Icelandic, Japanese and Italian.

In Manitoba, utter peace and quiet is apparent as you amble around a landscape that is carved up into sprawling rivers, desert dunes and forest. You can travel from arctic coastline to fields that bloom with a startling patchwork of red, yellow and purple. When the sun sets into the flat, open land, the sky can often turn a similar, sumptuous colour.

This abundance of nature is a haven for wildlife, which is why Manitoba is home to hundreds of species of birds, who flock to the Province's countless lakes and marshes. Additionally, you can expect to see wolves, bears, elk, moose, beavers, polar bears or whales, depending on your location in the Province. Although it gets cold in Manitoba and it is sometimes referred to as the 'Great White North', Manitoba is supposedly Canada's sunniest Province.

It is guaranteed that you will have a sunny smile on your face by the time you've fully explored this wide-ranging wonderland.

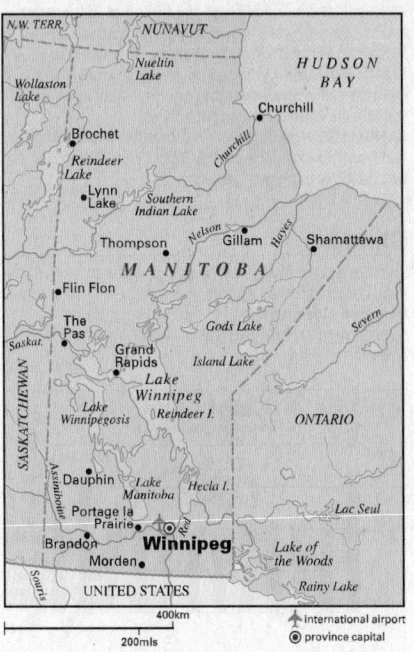

General Information

AREA: 547,704 sq km (211,468 sq miles).

POPULATION: 1.17 million (2005 estimate).

POPULATION DENSITY: 2.15 per sq km.

CAPITAL: Winnipeg. **Population:** 702,400 (2004).

GEOGRAPHY: Manitoba is bordered by the US states of North Dakota and Minnesota to the south, Saskatchewan to the west, Ontario to the east, and the Northwest Territories and Nunavut to the north. The province is also known as Heartland Canada. The landscape is diverse, ranging from rolling farmland to sandy beaches on the shores of Lake Winnipeg, and from the desert landscape of the south to northern parkland covered by lakes, forests and sub-Arctic tundra.

LANGUAGE: Although Canada is officially bilingual (English and French), English is commonly spoken in Manitoba.

SOCIAL CONVENTIONS: Smoking is prohibited in Manitoba in all public places including restaurants, drinking establishments, shopping malls and sporting events.

Climate

Summers are warm and sunny. Winters are cold, particularly in the north. Rainfall is highest in May.

Required clothing: Light- to mediumweights during warmer months, heavyweights in winter. Waterproofing is advisable throughout the year.

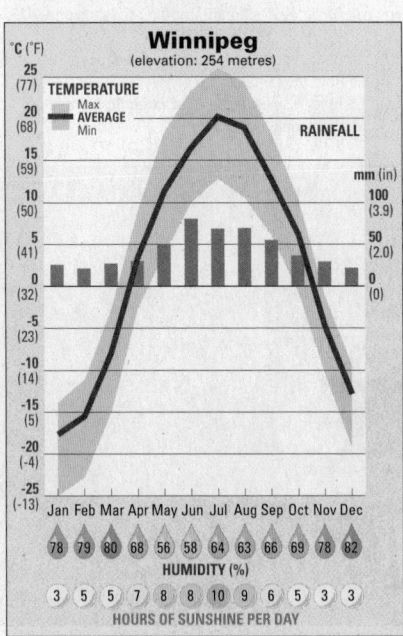

Public Holidays

Manitoba observes all the Public Holidays observed nationwide (see the general *Canada* section).

Travel - International

AIR:

Air Canada (AC) runs inter-provincial and international (US) flights. Other airlines also provide such a service to Manitoba.

Main airports: *Winnipeg International Airport (YWG)* (website: www.waa.ca) is 10km (6 miles) northwest of the city centre. *To/from the airport:* There is a regular bus service every 20 minutes (travel time – 20 minutes). *Facilities:* Duty free shop, post office, shops, hotel, restaurant, banks, car rental and car parking.

SEA:

Main ports: The only major coastal port is *Churchill* on Hudson Bay, which is frozen from November to early June. In summer, there are services to Nunavut and Ontario.

RAIL:

Winnipeg is the most central hub of *VIA Rail's* Canadian network. *The Canadian* train connects Vancouver in the west to Toronto in the east, passing through Winnipeg three times a week in each direction. A thrice weekly train (*The Hudson Bay*) runs northwards within Manitoba from Winnipeg to The Pas (the interchange station for services to Lynn Lake), Thompson and Churchill. For timetables and fares, contact a local *VIA Rail* office.

ROAD:

Excellent road services connect Manitoba with Ontario (through Kenora), Saskatchewan (Regina) and the USA (Grand Forks and Bismarck, North Dakota). The road system within Manitoba is also excellent and covers over 19,794km (12,300 miles). **Bus:** Services are run by local authorities, and inter-state services are run by *Beaver, Grey Goose Bus Lines* and *Greyhound.* For timetables and fares, contact local offices. **Taxi:** Available in all larger towns. Taxi drivers expect a 15 per cent tip. **Documentation:** National driving licences are accepted.

URBAN:

There are comprehensive bus services in Winnipeg where a flat fare is charged. There are also good bus services in other towns.

Accommodation

HOTELS/GUEST HOUSES/FARM HOLIDAYS/BED & BREAKFAST:

Manitoba has a wide selection of accommodation, ranging from first-class hotels in Winnipeg to guest houses and farm holiday camps. Farm vacations are controlled by their own association, ensuring high standards. Bed & breakfast accommodation is available at a reasonable price.

CAMPING/CARAVANNING:

The parklands and the enormous spread of lakes and forests in northern Manitoba are major attractions. Camping facilities are widespread. A number of companies can arrange **motor camper** rentals, with a range of fully-equipped vehicles. Full details can be obtained from Travel Manitoba (see *Top Things To Do*).

ACCOMMODATION INFORMATION

Manitoba Hotel Association
Canada Select Suite 1505, 155 Carlton Street, Winnipeg, Manitoba R3C 3H8, Canada
Tel: (204) 942 0671.
Website: www.canadaselect.mb.ca

Manitoba Association of Campgrounds and Parks
Box 129, Arnes, Manitoba, R0C 0C0, Canada
Tel: (204) 642 5671.
Website: www.macap.mb.ca

Manitoba Government (Information on Provincial Parks)
Tel: (204) 945 3744 *or* (866) 626 4862 (toll-free in USA and Canada) *or* (800) 665 0040 (tourist information).
Website: www.gov.mb.ca

Top Things To See

- See one of Canada's most culturally and racially diverse cities: **Winnipeg.** The city has a well-known ballet troupe and symphony orchestra. Places of note include the **Legislative Building** with Manitoba's symbol, the **Golden Boy**, balancing triumphantly on its dome; the **Manitoba Museum** which recreates past and present life on the prairies; and The **Forks National Historic Site**, a 13.6 acre park with river walks, historic port,

market, theatrical tours, restaurants and concerts. **St Boniface Cathedral Basilica** is in the French Quarter of Winnipeg, **St Boniface.** In the suburbs, the **Royal Canadian Mint**, with its high-tech building, and **Lower Fort Garry**, an old fur-trading post, are both worth visiting. Paddlesteamers offer excursions through Winnipeg's urban and residential areas on the **Red** and **Assiniboine rivers.** The famous *Winnie the Pooh* was named after Winnipeg. A statue commemorates the bear in **Assiniboine Park** along with the only known oil painting of the cub in the **Pavilion Gallery.**

- Any trip to Manitoba must slot in a glimpse of the large **Lake Winnipeg** on the eastern edge of the **Interlake Region.** The lake has good sandy beaches and boats for hire. The western shore of the lake was once New Iceland, a self-governing area settled by thousands of Icelanders fleeing volcanic eruptions in their homeland.
- Get a close-up view of early Mennonite life in the German-speaking Mennonite town of **Steinbach.**
- Travel to the **Western Region** and see moose and wood bison in densely wooded parklands, plus the **Spirit Sands**, a 5 sq km tract of blowing sand dunes towering over 30m, in the **Spruce Wood Provincial Park.** Also situated in the Western region is the flourishing tourist centre of **Minedosa** with shopping areas, a beach, restaurants and nature trails.
- Watch for beluga whales that congregate at the mouth of the **Churchill River** in the summertime. Churchill, a sub-Arctic seaport in the far northeast, is best reached by air across the vast flatlands running into **Hudson Bay.** It is known for its bird-watching opportunities.
- Look up at the skies and hope to view the *aurora borealis* (northern lights): **Churchill** is a good spot in which to do so in winter.
- **Wapusk National Park** is a remote area with a severe sub-Arctic climate and home to one of the world's largest known polar bear den sites, in addition to hundreds of thousands of waterfowl and shorebirds.
- Soak up the flat, moss-wrapped terrain of **Whiteshell Provincial Park**, with its gorgeous lakes and forests.

Top Things To Do

- Go to the summer **Icelandic Festival of Manitoba** (Islendingadagurinn) in Gimli (website: www.icelandicfestival.com). This is the largest Icelandic gathering outside Iceland itself and occurs because of the Province's historical connections to the country, with many there having Icelandic ancestral links. It is an unbeatable and surreal experience eating Icelandic food and watching people dressed in Icelandic garb whilst in typical Canadian land!
- The easternmost of the three 'prairie provinces', Manitoba is dominated in the south by its two huge lakes, **Lake Winnipeg** and **Lake Manitoba.** Altogether, the province has over 100,000 lakes. There are ample opportunities for all types of **watersports** on the lakes and rivers. Rivers offering particularly good **canoeing** include **Bloodvein River** in **Atikaki Provincial Wilderness Park**, which flows through wild rice marshes into Lake Winnipeg; and **Seal River** in the north, one of the most challenging canoe routes in Canada. **Fishing** for trout, northern pike, walleye, channel catfish and Arctic grayling is especially popular. Several of the northern lakes are only accessible by air, and remote fly-in lodges are the answer for an angler's wilderness dream. There are some excellent beaches around the lakes, the best known being **Grand Beach** on Lake Winnipeg, one of North America's top 10 beaches. Backed by high, grass-topped sand dunes, the beach is a favourite **swimming** spot amongst local people, owing to its shallow water and easy access from Winnipeg. **Sailboarding, windsurfing** and **sailing** are also available here.
- **Folklorama** in **Winnipeg** (website: www.folklorama.ca) is Canada's primary cultural celebration. Go and be entertained and educated by a rich and diverse spread of food, music, dance and history from around the world – in particular, Canada's ethnic communities.
- Walk across the **River Souris** on Canada's **longest free suspension foot bridge.** It is over 100 years old and is a massive 177m (582ft) long.
- Use Manitoba's national parks, such as the vast recreational area of **Riding Mountain National Park**, to be active surrounded by stunning scenery: **wildlife viewing, biking, backpacking** and **horseback riding** are all available.

TOURIST INFORMATION

Travel Manitoba
7th Floor, 155 Carlton Street, Winnipeg, Manitoba R3C 3H8, Canada
Tel: (204) 945 3777 *or* (800) 665 0040 (toll-free USA and Canada)
Website: www.travelmanitoba.com

A B C D E F G H I J K L M N O P Q R S T U V W X Y Z

Entertainment

FOOD & DRINK: Winnipeg offers opportunities to experience the cuisine of the many and diverse cultures that typify the city in restaurants or at numerous festivals showcasing the food and culture of the region, such as the *Folklorama 'A Taste of Winnipeg'* Icelandic festival. Rural Manitoba also offers a wide choice of restaurants, from the very expensive to the moderately priced with good home cooking.

Things to know: It is customary to tip waiters 15 per cent of the bill. Off-licence alcohol is available only from Government outlets. Opening hours are generally 1100-2100.

Regional specialities:
- Traditional First Nations foods, such as bison, game, fish and wild fruits and grains.
- *Bannock*, a flat bread cooked over an open fire, to which dried fruit or berries are sometimes added.
- Smoked fish and meats - try some delicious smoked Lake Winnipeg *goldeye*.
- Due to strong multicultural ties, you are likely to find Japanese *sushi* or Ukrainian *borscht* on the menu, to name just a few culinary imports.
- French-Canadian dishes, such as pea soup, *tourtière* and sugar pie.
- Local ingredients such as pickerel, wild rice or blueberries.
- Local beef or pork.
- A delectable dessert from Iceland: the *vinarterta*, consisting of thin cake layers sandwiched together with a cardamom-scented prune filling.

Regional drinks:
- Whisky, vodka and rum are all extremely popular.

Legal drinking age: 18 years, but those under 18 can drink with a meal if it is purchased by a parent or guardian.

NIGHTLIFE: Winnipeg's nightlife is vibrant. Many cinemas, theatres, clubs, restaurants and bars also provide entertainment. Winnipeg is home to a mixture of performing arts: the Royal Winnipeg Ballet, the Winnipeg Symphony Orchestra, Manitoba Opera and several theatre, dance and music companies. The city also offers dining and moonlit dancing cruises aboard riverboats on its scenic Red and Assiniboine rivers. The main stages at Club Regent and McPhillips Street Station casinos also feature entertainment.

SHOPPING: There are several nationally known department stores in Winnipeg, with branches throughout Manitoba. Winnipeg also has a number of shopping districts such as *Academy Road, Craydon Avenue* and *The Exchange District. The Forks Market* sells many fresh and speciality foods and has over 50 shops all housed in an old horse stable. There are also shopping malls: *Garden City,* 20 minutes drive from the centre, *Grant Park Shopping Centre* and *Polo Park Shopping Centre* with 200 shops, a cinema and a bowling alley. North of The Pas is a Native American handicraft shop where visitors can watch Native American women making moccasins, mukluks, jackets and jewellery. At the Rock Shop in Souris, costume jewellery made from rock from a local quarry can be bought, and the visitor may obtain a permit to collect his own rock.

Shopping hours: Mon-Fri 0930-2130, Sat 0930-1800, Sun 1200-1800.

Business

COMMERCIAL INFORMATION

Manitoba Chamber of Commerce
227 Portage Avenue, Winnipeg, Manitoba R3B 2A6, Canada
Tel: (204) 948 0100.
Website: www.mbchamber.mb.ca

Destination Winnipeg (Information on Conferences/Conventions)
Tourism Division, 259 Portage Avenue, Winnipeg, Manitoba R3B 2A9, Canada
Tel: (204) 943 1970 *or* (800) 665 0204 (toll-free in USA and Canada).
Website: www.destinationwinnipeg.ca

New Brunswick

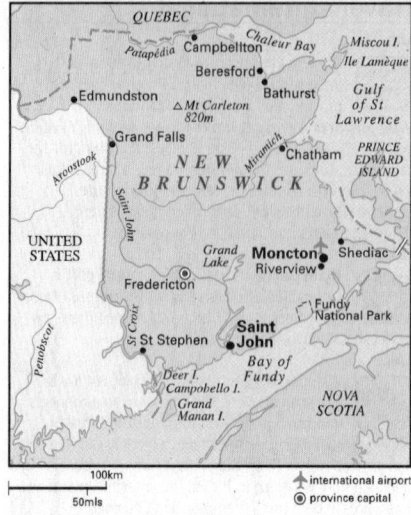

Location: East coast of Canada.

Time: GMT - 4 (GMT - 3 in summer).
Daylight saving officially lasts from the first Sunday in April to the Saturday before the last Sunday in October.

Overview

New Brunswick is a maritime province with three coastlines – on Chaleur Bay, the Northumberland Strait and the Bay of Fundy. Routes along these coasts can provide an interesting introduction to the area, opening up a vista of dramatic rocks, such as Hopewell Cape, and sea dotted with islands that boast astonishing glimpses of unusual fauna, birds and wildlife. Millions of flowers dot the land as far as the eye can see, carpeting the Province in colour.
New Brunswick is the most heavily forested of all Canada's Provinces (indeed, arguably, the most forested in North America!) and this, therefore, stretches its nautical associations further. Criss-crossed as it is with lakes, rivers and streams, escapes into the New Brunswick's wilderness are likely to be based around activities such as canoeing, kayaking or swimming.
Consequently, the produce from New Brunswick's waters is exceptional. Shediac is reputed to be the lobster capital of the world, such is the quantity and quality of the town's cooked crustacean. In addition, the salmon is succulent, the scallops are plump and juicy and year-round blue mussels are moistly flavoursome.
From staring out at the 50-foot tides of the Bay of Fundy to staring out at the vast Washademoak Lake, there is much in New Brunswick to whet the appetite.

General Information

AREA: 71,569 sq km (27,632 sq miles).
POPULATION: 752,000 (2005 estimate).
POPULATION DENSITY: 10.5 per sq km.
CAPITAL: Fredericton. **Population:** 124,172 (2005).
GEOGRAPHY: New Brunswick, which is below the Gaspé Peninsula, shares its western border with Maine and has

2250km (1400 miles) of coast on the Gulf of St Lawrence and the Bay of Fundy. Its landscape comprises of forested hills with rivers cutting through them. The main feature is St John River Valley in the south. Northern and eastern coastal regions give way to the extensive drainage basin of the Miramichi River in the central area.
LANGUAGE: New Brunswick is officially bilingual (English and French) with approximately 33 per cent of the population being French speaking.

Climate

Summer is warm with cooler evenings. Autumn is relatively mild. Winters are cold with heavy snows.
Required clothing: Light- to mediumweights during summer months, heavyweights in winter. Waterproofing is advisable all year.

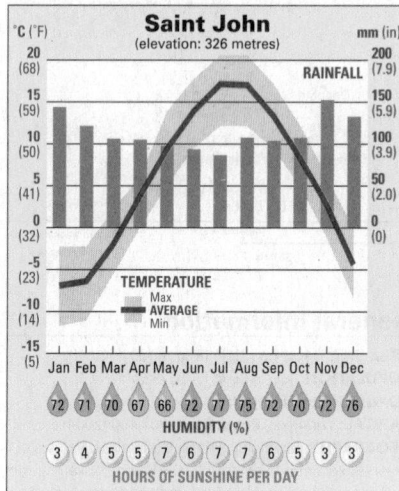

Public Holidays

New Brunswick observes all the Public Holidays observed nationwide (see the general *Canada* section) and, in addition, the beneath Public Holidays listed for the January 2006-June 2007 period.
2006: Aug 7 New Brunswick Day.

Travel - International

AIR:
 The national airline is *Air Canada. Air Canada Jazz* offers inter-provincial flights to Montréal, Halifax, Toronto and Bathurst (more limited service) from Fredericton, Saint John and Moncton. *Corsair* flies to Paris from Moncton and other international connections can often be made via Halifax, Nova Scotia.
Main airports: *Greater Moncton Airport (YQM)* (website: www.gma.ca). *To/from the airport:* Car hire is available. *Facilities:* Foodcourt, ATM and seafood shop.
Fredericton (YFC) (website: www.frederictonairport.ca). *To/from the airport:* Taxis and are available from the terminal. *Facilities:* Restaurant, car hire, gift shop and ATMs.
Saint John Airport (YSJ) (website: www.saintjohnairport.com). *To/from the airport:* Taxis are available from the terminal. A journey into St John costs about C$30 for a single person. *Facilities:* Restaurant, car hire and car parking.

Credit: ©New Brunswick Tourism & Parks

SEA:

Ferries run from Nova Scotia to Saint John, from Maine to the Fundy Islands and from Québec to Dalhousie near Campbellton. The Confederation Bridge connects Cape Jourimain, New Brunswick with Borden-Carleton, Prince Edward Island. It is 13km (8 miles) long, takes approximately 10 to 12 minutes to cross and is open 24 hours a day. A toll is payable on return over the bridge only (C$39.50 per car in 2005) (tel: (888) 437 6565). Ferry services no longer operate on this route. There is a full coastal ferry service between all ports in New Brunswick. For timetables, contact the local tourist information office.

RAIL:

VIA Rail runs six times a week from Montréal to Halifax, three times via Mont Joli and via Saint John.

ROAD:

The Trans-Canada Highway (Highway 1) follows the St John River Valley from Edmundston in the north to Moncton in the east, with the majority of the highways branching off it. There are over 16,000km (10,000 miles) of roads in the province.

Accommodation

HOTELS/GUEST HOUSES/BED & BREAKFAST/YOUTH HOSTELS:

There are around 200 hotels/motels, 250 bed & breakfast inns and 15 condo cottages available to rent. The main centres of population are on the coast and in the river valleys, and these generally offer the best choice of hotel or motel accommodation. There are also numerous guest houses, bed & breakfast establishments and youth hostels. For information on accommodation, contact Tourism New Brunswick (see *Top Things To Do*). Accommodation is graded by the New Brunswick Grading Authority according to the *Atlantic Canada Accommodations Grading Program*, from **5-star** (deluxe) to **1-star** (basic).

CAMPING/CARAVANNING:

New Brunswick has 11 provincial parks which have extensive camping facilities. More than 100 privately owned campsites operate in the area. A number of companies can arrange **motor camper** rentals, with a range of fully-equipped vehicles.

Top Things To See

- Travel to the **Bay Of Fundy Coastal Drive Region** and see the **Reversing Falls**, a natural phenomenon caused by the powerful tidal waters of the Bay of Fundy finding an upstream outlet into the rocky river gorge. The coastline is battered by the tempestuous 14m (46ft) tides of the **Bay of Fundy**, resulting in dramatic scenery such as the **Hopewell Cape**'s sandstone '**flowerpots**' – enormous rock formations that have been likened to flowerpots because of their shape and peculiar sprouts of green foliage. Visitors should stay alert to the powerful incoming tide, however, which can rise as much as 14m (46ft). **St Andrews** has some well-preserved 18th-century houses as well as **The Blockhouse**, built in 1812 to defend the town from US incursions.
- See beautiful rare flora and fauna in the little-known and unspoilt **Fundy Islands**, of which **Grand Manan** is the largest and is a birdwatching paradise, once the favourite haunt of the famous ornithologist, James Audubon. Whales and dolphins can often be spotted from the shoreline of these islands. Indeed, whale-watching is extremely popular due to the Bay of Fundy's boast of more whale species. More often than anywhere else in the world, the waters of the Bay of Fundy are home to over 15 species, including the rare right whale. Whale-watching tours depart from different regions around the province, including **Campobello Island**, **Deer Island**, **Grand Manan** and **St Andrews**.
- Watch open-mouthed as your car is pulled uphill by an invisible source! This is just one of the attractions on offer at **Moncton**, the Province's second-largest city. Other family entertainments are provided at the **Magic Mountain Water Theme Park** and **Crystal Palace Amusement Park**. And, if you're curious, your car is being pulled uphill not by magnetism, as the name **Magnetic Hill** implies, but because of an optical illusion.
- Study some fine neo-classical and Victorian architecture in **Fredericton** - the Province's capital and its legislative and academic centre - like the **Legislative Building**, **Christ Church Cathedral** and **Government House**. The **Beaverbrook Art Gallery** is one of the finest in Canada with an extensive collection of Canadian, British and Renaissance paintings. Salvador Dali's painting *St James the Great* forms the centrepiece of the collection.
- Look around the aboriginal town of **Metepenagiag** (**Red Bank First Nation**), just outside of the town of **Miramichi**, and New Brunswick's oldest town with archaeological finds that date back more than 3000 years.
- The eastern shoreline, once a French stronghold, has a

Credit: ©New Brunswick Tourism & Parks

temperate climate and some excellent beaches that are well-worth seeing, particularly near **Kouchibouguac National Park** where a network of boardwalks protect the fragile sand dune ecology: The park is the home of more than 223 species of birds, and ocean canoe trips are offered to view nearby seal colonies. **La Dune de Bouctouche**, one of the world's last surviving white sand dunes, has an award-winning eco-visitor centre. Nearby, **Parlee Beach** is the largest and best beach in the province.

Top Things To Do

- Enjoy New Brunswick's vast network of **walking**, **hiking** and **biking** trails: the **International Appalachian Trail**, a network of paths linking to the Appalachian Trail in the US at Mount Katahdin; **Le Petit Temis**, a cycling and hiking trail stretching from Edmundston to Riviere-du-Loup in Québec; the **Fundy Trail Parkway**, 27km (17 miles) of hiking and cycling trails along the **Bay of Fundy**; and the **Acadian Coastal Trail**, a network of walking and biking routes beginning at **Dalhousie**.
- New Brunswick's beaches are renowned for their warm water and there are 42 so-called 'ocean hot spots' which are particularly good for **swimming**, notably **Parlee Beach** and **Kelly's Beach** (in **Kouchibouguac National Park**).
- There are plenty of opportunities for fishing in New Brunswick's 3814km (19,884 miles) of rivers and streams. The **Mirimachi River**, in particular, is famous for **salmon fishing**. **Deep-sea fishing** boats are open for charter. The booklet *Fish New Brunswick*, which gives details on fish species, seasons and regulations, is available free of charge from the Department of Natural Resources and Energy, Fish and Wildlife Branch, PO Box 6000, Fredericton NB, E3B 5H1 (tel: (506) 453 3826).
- **Kayak** in the Bay of Fundy, interweaving between the gravity-defying rocks of **Hopewell Cape**. For those who wish to engage in some **canoeing**, New Brunswick's many rivers are an ideal location to do so.
- Have lunch in one of New Brunswick's many picturesque lighthouses, which have safeguarded the maritime province for decades. Some particularly lovely ones to have a **picnic** beside include **Cocagne Lighthouse**, **Cape Enrage Lightstation**, **Quaco Head Lighthouse** and **Richibucto Head Lighthouse**.
- See some of New Brunswick's numerous pretty and quirky, historic **covered bridges**. A particular bridge of note is **Salmon Bridge**, complete with original iron braces and the longest covered bridge in the world, the peculiar claim to fame of the small town of **Hartford**.

TOURIST INFORMATION

Tourism New Brunswick
Street address: 670 Centennial Building, 5th Floor, Fredericton, New Brunswick E3B 1G1, Canada
Postal address: PO Box 6000, Fredericton, New Brunswick E3B 5H1, Canada
Information centre:
Street address: 26 Roseberry Street, Campbellton, New Brunswick E3N 2G4, Canada
Postal address: PO Box 12345, Campbellton, New Brunswick E3N 3T6, Canada
Tel: (800) 561 0123 (toll-free in USA and Canada).
Website: www.tourismnewbrunswick.ca

Entertainment

FOOD & DRINK: The province is famous for seafood. Fredericton, Saint John and Moncton offer international cuisine.

Regional specialities:

- Atlantic salmon with its delicate flavour, served with butter, new potatoes and *fiddleheads* (young fronds of ostrich fern served with butter and seasoned or used cold in salads).
- Apples, blueberries and cranberries are common dessert ingredients.
- Home-made baked beans and steamed brown bread are served as traditional Saturday-night supper.

- *Rapée pie*, made with chicken, is an Acadian speciality for Sundays or festivals.
- Shediac is reputed to be the lobster capital of the world.
- New Brunswick *dulse*, an edible seaweed, is a local speciality.

Legal drinking age: 19 years.

NIGHTLIFE: Music is very much a part of the lives of New Brunswick citizens. Many bars and clubs throughout the province, especially in Fredericton, Saint John and Moncton, feature live music, much of it with a French, Scottish and Irish flavour. The area has recently acquired a reputation for jazz and blues.

SHOPPING: Special purchases include local and provincial handicrafts which are especially worthwhile in New Brunswick. The best markets in Saint John are between Charlotte and Germain streets, forming the *Old City Market*. This is open all week, with farmers taking over on Friday and Saturday. Moncton has three large shopping areas: Champlain Place, Moncton Mall and Highfield Square. **Shopping hours:** Mon-Sat 0900-1730; 1000-2200 in malls.

Credit: ©New Brunswick Tourism & Parks

Business

COMMERCIAL INFORMATION

Atlantic Provinces Chamber of Commerce
Suite 21, 236 St George Street, Moncton, New Brunswick E1C 1W1, Canada
Tel: (506) 857 3980.
Website: www.apcc.ca

Greater Moncton Chamber of Commerce
Suite 100, 910 Main Street, Moncton, New Brunswick E1C 1G6, Canada
Tel: (506) 857 2883;
website: www.gmcc.nb.ca

Business New Brunswick (Information on Conferences/Conventions)
Postal address: PO Box 6000, Centennial Building, Fredericton, New Brunswick E3B 5H1, Canada
Street address: Centennial Building, 670 King Street, Fredericton, New Brunswick E3B 1G1, Canada
Tel: (506) 444 5228.
Website: www.gnb.ca

City of Fredericton Tourism Division (Information on Conferences/Conventions)
Postal address: PO Box 130, Fredericton, New Brunswick E3B 4Y7, Canada
Street address: 11 Carleton Street, Fredericton, New Brunswick E3B 3T1, Canada
Tel: (506) 460 2041 *or* (888) 888 4768 (toll-free in USA and Canada).
Website: www.city.fredericton.nb.ca

Tourism Saint John (Information on Conferences/Conventions)
PO Box 1971, 11th Floor, City Hall, Saint John, New Brunswick E2L 4L1, Canada
Tel: (506) 658 2990.
Website: www.tourismsaintjohn.com

Tourism Moncton (Information on Conferences/Conventions)
City Hall, 655 Main Street, Moncton, New Brunswick, E1C 1EB
Tel: (506) 853 3590 *or* (800) 363 4558 (toll-free in USA and Canada).
Website: www.gomoncton.com

A B C D E F G H I J K L M N O P Q R S T U V W X Y Z

A
B
C
D
E
F
G
H
I
J
K
L
M
N
O
P
Q
R
S
T
U
V
W
X
Y
Z

Newfoundland and Labrador

Location: Eastern Canada.

Time: Newfoundland: GMT - 3.5 (GMT - 2.5 in summer).
Labrador: GMT - 4 (GMT - 3 in summer).
Summer officially lasts from the first Sunday in April to the Saturday before the last Sunday in October.

Overview

Newfoundland and Labrador is more than 400,000 square kilometres, larger than New Brunswick, Nova Scotia, and Prince Edward Island combined, and bordered by 17,000 kilometres of craggy coastline.

It is a Province that signals the beginning of the 'New World' and its links to European settlers. Water Street on St John's is the oldest street in North America. And it is strange to think that you are actually closer here to Ireland's Cape Clear than to Ontario's Thunder Bay. The Province is filled with historical towns and landmarks documenting its beginnings as Canadian land, and its much-lauded maritime connections. In addition, many of its indigenous peoples (the First Nations, Métis and the Innu) still reside here; although in isolated communities, they are more than willing to integrate and provide a wonderful opportunity to dispel any pre-existing misconceptions and gain insight into how their own history has shaped the Province's present.

Nature throws up its own surprises in Newfoundland & Labrador. From grazing moose and caribou to amazing sightings of whales, and from scores of soaring seabirds to glimpses of black bears, this Province is bursting with wildlife; wildlife that wanders around ancient landscape, such as the unique and beautiful geological features of the UNESCO World Heritage-listed Gros Morne National Park, or the colossal mountain ranges of the Torngat, Kaumajet or Kiglapait and their primeval exposed rock.

General Information

AREA: 405,720 sq km (156,648 sq miles).
POPULATION: 516,000 (2005 estimate).
POPULATION DENSITY: 1.27 per sq km.
CAPITAL: St John's. **Population:** 180,631 (2005).
GEOGRAPHY: Newfoundland and Labrador is the most easterly Canadian province. It consists of the Island of Newfoundland and the mainland plateau region of Labrador which borders the province of Québec. The province stretches approximately 1700km (1063 miles) north to south, and has approximately 17,000km (10,625 miles) of coastline, much of it rugged and heavily indented with bays and fjords. The interior of Newfoundland is a combination of forest, heath, lakes and rivers spread over a terrain that ranges from mountainous in the west to rolling hills in the centre and east. Labrador is also mountainous in the west, although its rivers are larger and wilder.
LANGUAGE: Although English is officially bilingual (English and French), 95 per cent of this province speaks English as a first language.

SOCIAL CONVENTIONS: Newfoundland society shows the dominant influence of northern European – especially English and Irish, but also French – settlers in its dialects, folk music and dance. Aboriginal peoples with distinct cultures and traditions include the Mi'kmaq on Newfoundland and the Inuit, Innu and Métis in Labrador. Geographical isolation nurtured a fiercely independent spirit in the province, which joined the Canadian Union as late as 1949.

Climate

Very cold winters and mild summers.
Required clothing: Light- to mediumweights in warmer months, heavyweights in winter. Waterproofing is advisable throughout the year.

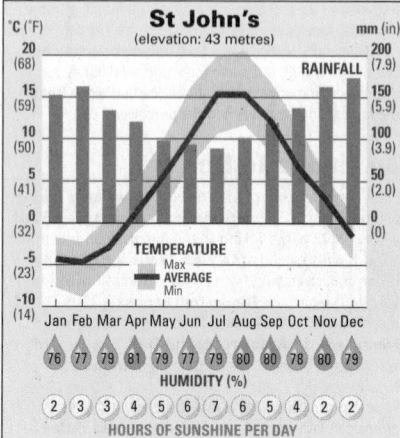

Public Holidays

Newfoundland & Labrador observes all the Public Holidays observed nationwide (see the general *Canada* section) and, in addition, the beneath Public Holidays listed for the January 2006–June 2007 period.
2006: Jun 24 Discovery Day.

Travel - International

AIR:

*Air Canada (AC)*operates regular services to Newfoundland and Labrador. Other airlines also serve the Province.
Main airports: *Gander (YQX)* (www.ganderairport.com) is 3km (2 miles) from the city centre. *To/from the airport*: A 24-hour taxi service is available from the domestic arrivals area and *DRL Coachlines Ltd* operates a daily scheduled passenger coach service across Newfoundland (tel: (888) 263 1852; website: www.drlgroup.com). *Facilities:* Car parking, restaurant, duty free shop and banks.
St John's (YYT) (www.stjohnsairport.com) is 8km (5 miles) from the city centre (travel time – 15 minutes). *To/from the airport*: A taxi service is available. *Facilities:* Gift shop, duty free shop, restaurant and pub.
Other major airports are at *Deer Lake (YDF)*, *St Anthony (YAY)*, and *Wabush (YWK)*.
SEA:

A year-round daily passenger and vehicle ferry service runs between North Sydney, Nova Scotia and Port aux Basques on Newfoundland's southwest coast (crossing time – six hours). Summer services run three times a week between North Sydney and Argentia on Newfoundland's Avalon Peninsula, mid-June to mid-September (crossing time – 14 hours). Reservations can be made with *Marine Atlantic* (tel: (709) 695 4200; website: www.marine-atlantic.ca). There is also a summer ferry to the French islands of St Pierre & Miquelon from Fortune on Newfoundland's Burin Peninsula (crossing time – 90 minutes) (tel: (800) 563 2006 (toll-free in USA and Canada) *or* (709) 832 0429; website: www.spmexpress.net). Intra-provincial ferries connect island communities with larger towns. A seasonal once- or twice-daily ferry (tel: (866) 535 2567 for reservations) connects Blanc Sablon in southern Labrador and St Barbe on Newfoundland's Great Northern Peninsula with an 80-minute crossing from April to January. Remote communities on the Labrador coast and Newfoundland's south coast are also served by coastal boats. All intra-provincial ferry services can be checked online (website: www.gov.nl.ca/ferryservices). Also available on this website are details of a summer car ferry service between Lewisporte on Newfoundland's northwest coast and Happy Valley-Goose Bay on Lake Melville in Labrador.

RAIL:

A passenger service provided by *The Québec North Shore & Labrador Railway* operates between Sept Isles in Québec and Labrador City in western Labrador (tel: (709) 944 8205).
ROAD:

A modern paved highway (Route 1, the Trans-Canada Highway) crosses Newfoundland from Port aux Basques in the southwest to the capital of St John's in the east. The distance is 905km (565 miles). Paved secondary roads connect most communities to the main highway. Visitors can reach western Labrador along a partially paved highway from Baie Comeau, Québec. Route 500, dubbed the 'Freedom Road' by residents, crosses Labrador from Happy Valley Goose Bay to Wabush and connects at the Québec-Labrador boundary with Québec Route 389. There are limited services along this road.
Coach: *DRL Coachlines* (website: www.drlgroup.com) operates a daily scheduled bus service between St John's and Port aux Basques (Route 1). Stops along the route include Gander, Grand Falls-Windsor and Corner Brook (journey time - 14 hours). Route 510 connects communities along Labrador's southeast coast between Red Bay and Cartwright with Class A gravel, but is usually closed for a couple of months after the Christmas period due to snow conditions. The road is paved for the first 85km to Red Bay and is Class A gravel from there to Charlottetown (160km). From L'Anse au Claire to Cartwright is 400km. **Car rental** is also available.

Accommodation

HOTELS/BED & BREAKFAST:
There are around 550 establishments in the province with a total of about 7300 rooms. Many towns offer hotel or bed & breakfast accommodation, although this is often seasonal. Most of the settlements in the province are on the coast rather than the wild interior (where some cabins and lodges are, however, available). As St John's is now an 'oil boom town', accommodation there can be hard to come by, and advance reservations are recommended. For information on hotels and bed & breakfast accommodation, contact the Department of Tourism, Culture and Recreation (see *Top Things To Do*). Accommodation is graded according to the *Canada Select Accommodations Grading Program* from **5-star** (deluxe) to **1-star** (basic).
CAMPING/CARAVANNING:
The wildness of the province offers superb camping facilities, both for motorhomes and tents. Both national parks (Gros Morne in western Newfoundland and Terra Nova in eastern Newfoundland), as well as 13 provincial and 56 private campgrounds, provide camping services. Facilities on campsites are basic rather than luxurious, the emphasis being on seclusion and privacy. Full details can be obtained from the Department of Tourism, Culture and Recreation (see *Top Things To Do*).

Top Things To See

• See the Province's many remnants of history: home to the majority of Newfoundland's population, the **Avalon Peninsula** is full of historic settlements dating back to the 17th century; **Trinity** records the history of European explorers' first encounter with the ancient Beothuk people. The town of **Placentia**, like many of the older towns of this region, was established by Basque fishermen almost 500 years ago and later became the French capital of **Newfoundland** in the 17th and 18th centuries. **Water Street** on **St John's** is one of the oldest shopping streets in North America and still bustles with activity; **The Cathedral of St John the Baptist** is on **Church Hill**; **Signal Hill**, the reception point for Guglielmo Marconi's first transatlantic radio transmission from England in 1901, is Canada's second-largest national historic site and offers a good view of the town and harbour to the west; **Newfoundland Museum** is on the harbour front; a national historic site at nearby **Port au Choix** pays homage to the Maritime Archaic People, whose local history dates back more than 5000 years; and the 16th-century Basque whaling station of **Red Bay** on Labrador's southern coast is the oldest industrial complex in the New World.

• **Terra Nova National Park** is an area of scenic rugged coastline adjoining **Bonavista Bay**. The **Burin Peninsula** in the south has some beautiful coastal villages. Icebergs can be seen from the sandy shores of **Cape Freels**.

• Newfoundland & Labrador is a fascinating Province because it comprises a huge range of ethnicity and indigenous peoples. Coming into contact with these peoples helps any visitor to gain an insight into a fascinating way of life. An interpretive centre and excavation site at **Boyd's Cove** on the **Kittiwake Coast** recounts the history of Newfoundland's mysterious Beothuk people, who once populated much of

Newfoundland's shores. Labrador has two Innu communities, at **Sheshatshiu** and **Natuashish**. The Métis Aboriginal community subsists in Labrador, mainly around **Lake Melville**.

- The **Point Amour lighthouse** is the tallest lighthouse in Atlantic Canada and is definitely worth getting a glimpse of. Built from 1854 to 1857, it is still an automated working lighthouse and the residential part of it is used to display a series of exhibits that portray the maritime history of the **Labrador Straits**.
- Watch enormous herds of Caribou roaming along the **Trans-Labrador Highway**.
- Look out from the **Long Range Mountains**, along which runs a 715km (444 mile) coastal road affording good views of fjords, mountains and beaches.
- The **Great Northern Peninsula** is a wilderness area of outstanding scenic beauty. It is best seen from **Gros Morne National Park**, a blend of rugged mountains, deep fjords and bays on the **Gulf of St Lawrence**. Its 600m **Tablelands** are spectacular ancient rock exposed from the earth's interior. There are regularly scheduled boat tours. At the northernmost tip of the peninsula at **L'Anse aux Meadows** (a UNESCO World Heritage Site) lie the restored remains of the earliest European settlement in the New World, a group of six sod houses built by Norsemen around the year AD 1000.
- Do not just visit Newfoundland - be sure to make time to explore Labrador, also, with its largely undisturbed wilderness, populated by only 27,000 people. Labrador can be reached by air or by ferry from the port of **St Barbe** on Newfoundland's northern coast. Close by, the **Labrador Straits Museum** has displays on the Maritime Archaic Indians who built a burial mound nearby at **L'Anse-Amour** around 5500 BC. Much of Labrador is undeveloped and uninhabited. There are two principal road systems in Labrador and a coastal highway that extends along the eastern coastline and links most of the region's Atlantic fishing villages. Both provide opportunities for short day tours. Longer trips to the Labrador interior can be arranged through the many tour operators and outfitters that service the Labrador region. There's also a summer car ferry service between **Lewisporte** on Newfoundland's northeast coast and **Happy Valley-Goose Bay** on Lake Melville in Labrador. It sails from Lewisporte once a week. Visitors should remember that winters can be bitterly cold.
- If you're lucky, you might get to see the **northern lights** (*aurora borealis*), which sometimes charge up the skies here, particularly in Labrador. This luminous meteoric phenomenon produces spectacular astral fireworks that are truly humbling.
- Newfoundland's coastline offers a rich concentration of marine life. The province is famous for its 60 major seabird colonies that are the summer nesting sites of millions of puffins, gannets, kittiwakes, murres and petrels. Many birds and whales can be seen in the **Witless Bay Ecological Reserve**, which visitors can travel through by boat or **kayak**. Caribou and black bears can be found in the **Avalon Wilderness Reserve**, while **Cape St Mary's Ecological Reserve** is best known for its golden-headed gannets. Illustrated talks, guided walks and nature hikes with experienced naturalists can be booked at the visitor centre. **Whale watching** is very popular around the waters of **Bay Bulls and Witless Bay**, which are home to a large population of humpback whales as well as smaller pods of fin and minke whales.

Top Things To Do

- Eastern **Newfoundland**, a region of sheltered coves and sandy beaches, is a popular destination for sailing and swimming.
- The **Gros Morne National Park** offers **hiking, trekking** and **climbing** and over 100km (65 miles) of hiking trails. The **T'Railway Park** comprises over 900km (565 miles) of hiking trails between **Port aux Basques** and **St John's**, through widely varied landscapes.
- Do not shy away from the cold – why not make the most of the Province's winter weather by indulging in some fun **wintersports**? **Skiing** is popular at the Island of Newfoundland's **Marble Mountain**, 8km (5 miles) east of **Corner Brook**, the Province's second city. In Feburary, the **Corner Brook Winter Carnival** is held in the area. **Labrador** ski resorts include **Smokey Mountain** (near Labrador City), and **White Hills** in eastern Newfoundland. The best **cross-country skiing** trails can be found in Labrador.
- Be entertained by the sweet, plaintive tones of Newfoundland's (and particularly St John's') famous **folk music**; there are plenty of bars in the Provincial capital where visitors can see live performances by local bands. The **Newfoundland and Labrador Folk Festival** takes place annually in **Bannerman Park** during the first weekend in August.
- In the interior, **salmon fishing** is particularly good in the **Exploits** and **Gander rivers**. The salmon fishing season runs from 24 May to 15 September. Near Route 91, visitors can be guided around a man-made salmon ladder

on the **Rocky River Falls** and learn about salmon enhancing in the area. A qualified guide is required for visitors intending to fish in licensed rivers in Newfoundland and in all waters in Labrador.

TOURIST INFORMATION

Department of Tourism, Culture & Recreation
PO Box 8700, St John's, Newfoundland A1B 4J6, Canada
Tel: (709) 729 2831 *or* (800) 563 6353 (toll-free in USA and Canada).
Website: www.newfoundlandandlabradortourism.com

Entertainment

FOOD & DRINK: The Province boasts a hearty cuisine.
Regional specialities:
- Dishes make full use of fat pork, molasses, salt fish, salt meat, boiled vegetables and soups.
- Fish is a staple food, predominantly cod made into stews and fish cakes, or it can be eaten fried, salted, dried or fresh. Salmon, trout and halibut are also available.
- *Brewis* is a hard water biscuit that needs soaking in water to soften, then gentle cooking.
- Often salt or fresh cod is served with *scrunchions*, which are bits of fat pork, fried and crunchy.
- *Damper dog* (a type of fried bread dough).
- *Cod sound pie* (made from tough meat near the cod's backbone).
- *Crubeens* (Irish pickled pigs' feet).
- *Fat back and molasses dip* (rich mixture of pork fat and molasses for dipping bread).
- Pies, jams, jellies and puddings are made from wild berries.
- *Jigg's dinner* (a mixture of salt beef, potatoes, carrots, cabbage and turnips) with *Peas Pudding*, a traditional family meal.

Regional drinks:
- Available brews include *Kyle*, *Killick*, *Raspberry Wheat Ale*, *Hemp Ale*, *Black Horse*, *Jockey Club* and *Dominion Ale*.
- *Screech* is Jamaican-style rum that is the historic result of trade between Newfoundland and Jamaica (Jamaica got salt cod in return).
- Tea and Carnation milk.

Legal drinking age: 19 years.

NIGHTLIFE: A St John's pub crawl is a real cultural experience, with a particularly strong English and Irish influence. Water Street and Duckworth Street offer fine restaurants and nightclubs. Newfoundland also has its own music, mostly English and Irish, which can be found everywhere in local festivals, nightclubs, bars, taverns and concerts. George Street in St John's has become a club and restaurant zone and holds a variety of seasonal festivals. However, on the whole, night entertainment in many regions is scarce.

SHOPPING: Water Street and Duckworth Street in downtown St John's are a must for any shopper – Water Street is one of the oldest shopping streets in North America, and European merchants, sailors and privateers have bartered here since the 16th century. Handicrafts, Grenfell parkas and Labradorite jewellery are the best known products of the Newfoundland and Labrador area.
Shopping hours: Mon-Wed 1000-1700, Thurs-Fri 1000-2200, Sat 1000-1800, Sun 1200-1700. (Malls generally open Mon-Sat 1000-2200.) Malls and downtown stores may or may not open on Sundays, according to individual preferences of the owners.

Business

COMMERCIAL INFORMATION

Atlantic Provinces Chamber of Commerce
Suite 21, 236 St George Street, Moncton, New Brunswick E1C 1W1, Canada
Tel: (506) 857 3980.
Website: www.apcc.ca

St John's Board of Trade
PO Box 5127, St John's, Newfoundland A1C 5V5, Canada
Tel: (709) 726 2961.
Website: www.bot.nf.ca

Department of Innovation, Trade and Rural Development
Head Office, Confederation Building, PO Box 8700, St John's, Newfoundland A1B 4J6, Canada
Tel: (709) 729 7000.
Website: www.intrd.gov.nl.ca

Meetings and Conventions Co-ordinator
Department of Tourism, Culture and Recreation, PO Box 8700, St John's, Newfoundland A1B 4J6, Canada
Tel: (709) 729 0862.

Northwest Territories

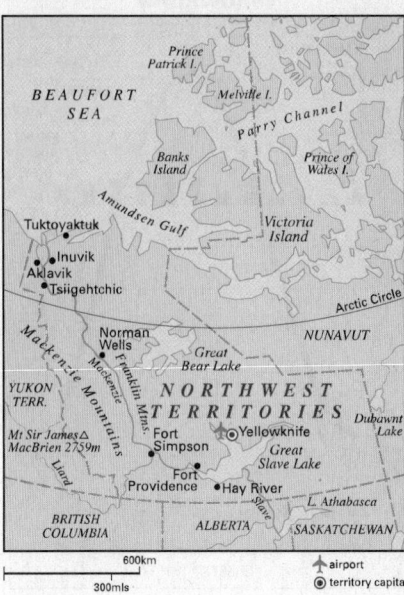

Location: Northern Canada.

Time: West of 102°W: GMT - 8 (GMT - 7 in summer). Summer officially lasts from the last Sunday in April to the Saturday before the last Sunday in October.

On 1 April 1999 the former Northwest Territories was divided, creating two new territories: Nunavut (which means 'our land' in Inuktitut) in the east, and the Northwest Territories in the west.

Overview

The Northwest Territories are part of Canada's vast, remote north. Most of the Territory's population and commercial activity is based in Yellowknife and around the Great Slave Lake. The Territories consist largely of wilderness, punctuated in places by human settlements, mainly of native peoples but also intrepid adventurers. The Inuit and Dene communities comprise almost 50 per cent of the Territories' population and have existed for hundreds or thousands of years. In terms of topography, the Territories are not as barren as one might anticipate. Thick evergreen forests and verdant mountains are a recurrent feature of the landscape. Sparsely populated, you are more likely to spot a herd of bison or come across a grizzly bear than you are to encounter a human. The sheer sum of wildlife in the Northwest Territories is superb. Venturing further north, it is easy to forget that the Territories extend far above the Arctic Circle – something you might remember when you spot some polar bears! Don't forget to look up at the skies too: the Northwest Territories' skies contain some of the rarest species of birds worldwide.
The Northwest Territories are, admittedly, stark in places, but it is an austerity that is tinged with beauty. Surrounded by wildlife, pretty flowers on rolling tundra and the sound of running water through a crystal-clear river, it would be understandable to think that you had stepped back in time.

General Information

AREA: 1,004,471 sq km (387,826 sq miles).
POPULATION: 43,000 (2005 estimate).
POPULATION DENSITY: 0.04 per sq km.
CAPITAL: Yellowknife. **Population**: 19,000 (2005 estimate).
GEOGRAPHY: The Northwest Territories stretch from the Mackenzie Mountains on the Yukon border to the open barrenlands to the east, from the shores and islands of the Arctic Ocean to the woodlands in the south. Canada's longest river, the Mackenzie, flows 1800km (1125 miles) from Great Slave Lake to its delta on the Beaufort Sea.
LANGUAGE: Although Canada is officially bilingual (English and French), English is more commonly spoken in the Northwest Territories.

Climate

The region experiences a diverse climate. The north has Arctic and sub-Arctic winters whereas the south is more temperate with mild summers and cold winters.
Required clothing: Winter weather requires down-filled and other polar-temperature gear. Special clothing is

required for adventure expeditions. Good-quality windproof and waterproof clothes, warm jerseys, gloves and moulded-sole shoes are needed at all times of the year. In the summer, thinner clothes are required.

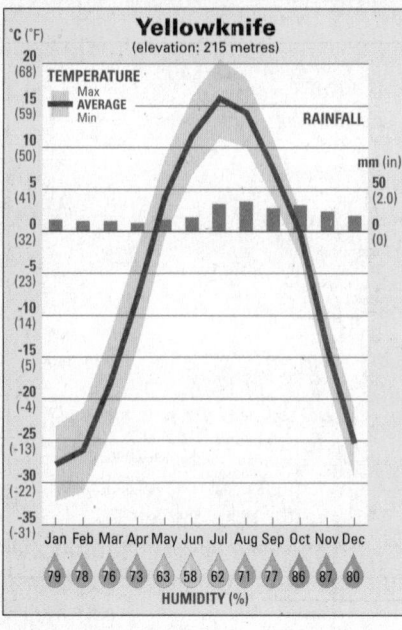

Yellowknife
(elevation: 215 metres)

TEMPERATURE
Max
AVERAGE
Min

RAINFALL

HUMIDITY (%)
79 78 76 73 63 58 62 71 77 86 87 80

Public Holidays

The Northwest Territories observe all the Public Holidays observed nationwide (see the general *Canada* section) and, in addition, the beneath Public Holidays listed for the January 2006–June 2007 period.
2006: Aug 7 Civic Holiday.

Travel - International

AIR:

The best way to reach the more remote areas within the Territory is by air. Float planes are commonly used to reach the northern lakes. The largest operators into the region are *Air Canada* and *First Air* (website: www.firstair.ca). Numerous regional airlines offer scheduled and charter services to communities within the Northwest Territories.

Airports: *Yellowknife Airport (YZF)* is less than 1km (0.6 miles) from the town centre (travel time – 10 minutes). International visitors will need to fly to Calgary, Edmonton (in Alberta) or Winnipeg (in Manitoba) and board a domestic flight to Yellowknife or Inuvik.

SEA/LAKE/RIVER:

Ferry crossings for road travellers are provided free during the summer months by the territorial government for the Mackenzie River at Fort Providence, for the Mackenzie and Arctic Red Rivers at Tsiigehtchic, for the Liard River at Fort Simpson and for the Peel River at Fort McPherson. During winter, ice bridges are provided at these crossings, but no crossing is available for some weeks in spring and autumn each year during the break-up and freeze-up of the ice (tel: (800) 661 0750 for day-to-day information). Cruises are available on Great Slave Lake and from Yellowknife to Inuvik on the Mackenzie River during the summer. Speedboat tours, guided canoe trips and river rafting trips are offered on Great Slave Lake, the Mackenzie Delta, the Nahanni River and other more remote rivers. Sail boats are available on Great Slave Lake for charter or package tours.

ROAD:

The major routes are along the Dempster Highway from the Yukon to Inuvik, the Mackenzie Highway from Edmonton, Alberta to the Great Slave Lake region and the Liard Highway from British Columbia to the junction of the Liard and Mackenzie Rivers, near Fort Simpson. During the winter months, ice roads providing supply routes to remote communities almost double the size of the highway network. Headlights and seatbelts are required at all times whilst driving in the Northwest Territories. The road quality varies. The Mackenzie Highway is paved; however, the other highways are hard-packed gravel. **Documentation:** International driver's licences are accepted in the Northwest Territories. Drivers should ensure that their insurance is valid and take advice on precautions for driving in cold weather conditions. Ice roads require special vehicles. **Coach:** There are two bus companies running scheduled services in the region: *Frontier Coachlines* (tel: (867) 874 2566) serves Yellowknife, Fort Smith and Fort Simpson from Hay River. *Greyhound Canada* (tel: (800) 661 8747; toll-free in USA

and Canada) runs services from Edmonton, Alberta to Hay River and Yellowknife. Companies offering charter and organised bus tours for groups include *Arctic Nature Tours*, Box 1530, Inuvik, Northwest Territories, X0E 0T0 (tel: (867) 777 3300; website: www.arcticnaturetours.com) and the *Arctic Tour Company*, Box 325, Tuktoyaktuk, Northwest Territories X0E 1C0 (tel: (867) 977 2230), whose tours include a five-day Dempster Highway tour, Beluga whale watching and viewing of the Aurora Borealis (Northern Lights).

Accommodation

HOTELS/BED & BREAKFAST:

Although most of the towns have hotels and bed & breakfast establishments open all year, accommodation can be scarce and often quite basic. There can be long distances between settlements of any size, especially in the Arctic zone. 'Lodges' designed for outdoor activity holidays can be found in many settlements and many can only be reached by air. For details, contact Northwest Territories Tourism for an *Explorers' Guide* (see *Top Things To Do*).

CAMPING/CARAVANNING:

Campsites are generally open from mid-May to mid-September and are run by both government and private organisations. Some outfitters have established 'outposts' (semi-permanent camps), with tents, beds and meals usually offered as part of organised trips. Camping is on a 'leave no trace' basis. A number of companies can arrange **motor camper** rentals, with a range of fully-equipped vehicles. Full details can be obtained from Northwest Territories Tourism (see *Top Things To Do*).

Top Things To See

- **Yellowknife**, the Territories' capital and the diamond capital of North America, is situated on the north shore of the **Great Slave Lake**. **The Prince of Wales Northern Heritage Centre** details aboriginal history in the area. Nearby are the *Dene* (aboriginal) settlements of **Dettah**, **Rae-Edzo, N'dilo** and **Wekweti**, or **Rock Lake** (formally known as Snare Lake), where a largely traditional way of life is still maintained and is fascinating to see.
- **Nahanni National Park** is a wonderful UNESCO World Heritage Site in the **Mackenzie Mountains**. Access to the park itself is by air from Fort Simpson, Fort Liard (BC) or Watson Lake (Yukon) as there are no roads in the wilderness area. Several operators offer boat and raft tours on the river taking in the magnificent 100m high (312ft) **Virginia Falls**, which are twice the height of Niagara.
- **Wood Buffalo National Park**, south of the **Great Slave Lake**, is one of the largest parks on earth. It is a noted centre for naturalists and birdwatchers, hosting Canada's largest herd of free-roaming bison. The cliffs and valleys of **Tuktut Nogait**, the Territories' newest National Park, harbour birds of prey and offer lush habitat for caribou and musk oxen. Over 700,000 barren-ground caribou migrate across the Northwest Territories and special tours can be arranged to their calving grounds along the shore of the **Beaufort Sea**. Moose live in the boreal forests, grizzly bears roam freely and Dall's sheep graze in the mountains. Beluga whales, polar bears, birds and sea mammals can be observed near the coast. All in all, the Northwest Territories are a great place in which to view a variety of wildlife.
- The **Waterfalls Route**, a 325km (203 mile) driving route beginning at the NWT/Alberta border on Highway 1, links the traveller with more than seven unusual territorial parks and waterfalls. **Twin Falls Territorial Park**, just north of **Enterprise**, has two waterfalls, **Louise Falls** and **Alexandra Falls** are linked together by a 3km (1.9-mile) hiking trail along the spectacular **Hay River Canyon**.
- See an Arctic coastline with a spectacular landscape and a fascinating history. **Inuvik**, in the far northwest, sits on the majestic **Mackenzie River Delta** and is accessible by road from Dawson City in the Yukon (at limited times of the year). Cruises on the *Delta* and the *Inuvialuit* and Dene settlements such as **Aklavik** are the main attractions. Aulavik, on **Banks Island**, includes archaeological sites dating back more than 3000 years. Much of this rough and forbidding terrain is best visited as part of a package tour or with other experts, but should definitely not be bypassed.
- Look as the landscape takes on a surreal quality during the midsummer when light lasts all night.

Top Things To Do

- **Canoeing** and **whitewater rafting** are extremely popular. Tours and trips can be arranged to suit all levels of ability, although the area is most attractive to advanced canoeists. A favourite destination is the **Nahanni River** in the southern **Mackenzie Mountains**, featuring rapids, rapids and torrents flowing through a highland wilderness. A trip along its entire length would take 10 to 20 days. The Mackenzie River itself offers good

canoeing, as do other rivers in the area. Those in the west are more popular, while in the east the rivers are less often tackled. River reports are available on a daily basis and novice canoeists are advised to go with a guide.
- **Fishing** on the thousands of clear, unpolluted lakes is highly recommended. Chief catches are trout, great northern pike and grayling.
- Take a camera with a macro lens and get a beautiful photograph of the hosts of tiny **wild flowers** that cover the tundra area during its brief Spring.
- Five national parks provide trails for **hiking** and other facilities. Sandy hills known as *eskers* offer easy hiking with good viewpoints. More challenging hiking can be found on the **Canol Heritage Trail**, through mountains and valleys to the Yukon.
- **Boats** can be hired for trips on the Mackenzie River and the **Great Slave** and **Great Bear** Lakes. These tours often follow old trapping and fur-trading routes. An experienced guide is essential.

TOURIST INFORMATION

Northwest Territories Tourism
PO Box 610, Yellowknife, Northwest Territories
X1A 2N5, Canada
Tel: (867) 873 7200 *or* (800) 661 0788 (toll-free in Canada and USA).
Website: www.explorenwt.com

Entertainment

FOOD & DRINK: Most alcohol is imported and supplies vary from town to town. Hotels and restaurants in main towns normally have a good selection, including Canadian whiskies.
Regional specialities:
- Arctic char, grayling, musk ox and caribou.
SHOPPING: There are over 40 co-operatives in the Territories specialising in handicrafts, furs, fisheries, print shops and retailing. First Nations handicrafts and footwear are made locally for sale. The often higher cost of goods (an increase of up to 20 per cent on the rest of Canada) is due to the supply and distribution charges caused by the large distances involved.

Business

COMMERCIAL INFORMATION

Yellowknife Chamber of Commerce
4807 49th Street, Yellowknife, Northwest Territories X1A 3T5, Canada
Tel: (867) 920 4944.
Website: www.ykchamber.com

Nova Scotia

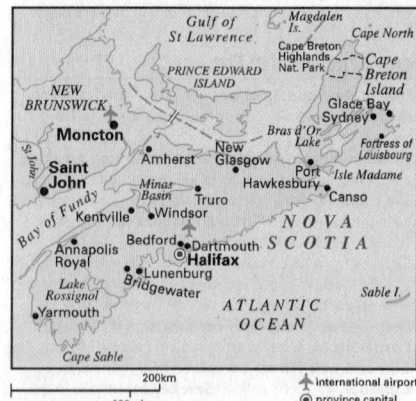

Location: East coast of Canada.

Time: GMT - 4 (GMT - 3 in summer).
Summer officially lasts from the first Sunday in April to the Saturday before the last Sunday in October.

Overview

The Scots were, arguably, the first settlers on this Province, hence the proud Latin name, Nova Scotia, translating to 'New Scotland'. Nova Scotia is also awash with French and English settlers but it is perhaps the Scottish influence that really sticks into your mind as you wander over conifer-covered highland and stumble across a kilt-clad man playing the bagpipes.

Nova Scotia seems to precariously hang off the mainland by a narrow isthmus. It is therefore understandably celebrated for its watery wonders. The residents of Nova Scotia are justly proud of their miles upon miles of beautiful, sandy coast and many lakes and rivers. Sampling some of the delicious sea-produce is a must, from the ubiquitous lobster (Nova Scotia is the world's largest lobster exporter) or fresh scallops from Digby. If you prefer to watch marine life rather than eat it, what can be more relaxing than espying whales darting in and out of the sea? If you want to actually get in the water, Nova Scotia is hugely popular when it comes to canoeing and kayaking.

In what is a mostly rural Province, visitors are always spoiled, whether by the coastal fringe or simply inland. Valleys and highlands dominate the landscape, and bears and coyote happily traverse it.

General Information

AREA: 52,841 sq km (20,402 sq miles).
POPULATION: 937,900 (2005 estimate).
POPULATION DENSITY: 17.74 per sq km.
CAPITAL: Halifax. **Population**: 379,800 (2005 estimate).
GEOGRAPHY: Nova Scotia comprises the peninsula of Nova Scotia, connected to the mainland by a narrow isthmus, and Cape Breton Island in the northern part of the province, linked by the world's deepest causeway, which is 1.6km (1 mile) long. The Atlantic batters the eastern shore. The Bay of Fundy separates the southern part of the peninsula from the mainland, with the Gulf of St Lawrence to the north. The northeast is rural and rocky, while the south and southwest are lush and fertile. The Fundy region's red soil was originally part of the present North African continent. Much of the province is covered by rivers. The land rises to 540m (1770ft) on the northeast islands.
LANGUAGE: Although Canada is officially bilingual (English and French), English is the main language spoken in Nova Scotia, but services are often in French as well.

Climate

Moderately cold winters, warm summers and long, mild autumns. Nova Scotia has a mild overall climate due to ocean currents.
Required clothing: Light- to mediumweights in summer months. Heavyweights in winter. Waterproofing is advisable all year.

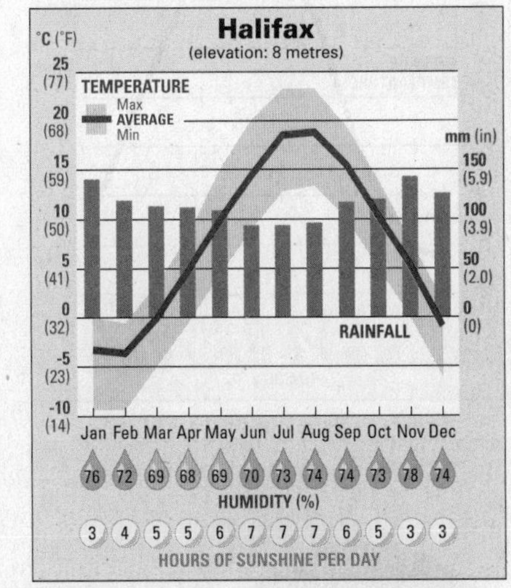
Halifax
(elevation: 8 metres)
°C (°F)
TEMPERATURE
Max
AVERAGE
Min
mm (in)
RAINFALL
25 (77)
20 (68)
15 (59)
10 (50)
5 (41)
0 (32)
-5 (23)
-10 (14)
150 (5.9)
100 (3.9)
50 (2.0)
0 (0)
Jan Feb Mar Apr May Jun Jul Aug Sep Oct Nov Dec
76 72 69 68 69 70 73 74 74 73 78 74
HUMIDITY (%)
3 4 5 5 6 7 7 7 6 5 3 3
HOURS OF SUNSHINE PER DAY

Public Holidays

Nova Scotia observes all the Public Holidays observed nationwide (see the general *Canada* section) and, in addition, the beneath Public Holidays listed for the January 2006-June 2007 period.
2006: Dec 24 Christmas Eve (half-day).
Note: Observed on the last Friday before this date.
Note: An additional holiday is given where there is a recognised Provincial or Civil holiday in a specific area. If there is no recognised holiday, this falls on the first Monday in August.

Travel - International

AIR:
Air Canada (AC) offers direct flights from London and other major centres.
Main airports: *Halifax (YHZ)* (website: www.hiaa.ca), 42km (26 miles) from the city. *To/from the airport:* Taxis and limousines are available. The *Airporter* bus services various Halifax hotels. Shuttle buses operate to other destinations in the province, as well as to Prince Edward Island. *Facilities*: Duty free shops, car hire, currency exchange, ATMs and restaurants.

SEA:
There are regular sailings to Nova Scotia from Portland and Bar Harbor, Maine (USA), New Brunswick, Prince Edward Island and Newfoundland. North America's fastest ship *The Cat* (website: www.catferry.com) operates between Yarmouth and Bar Harbor in the USA (travel time – two hours 45 minutes). Several ferries and shipping lines offer local services in and around the province. Enquire locally for further details. A growing number of cruise lines also visit Halifax as part of the New Atlantic Frontier itinerary. Ferry and cruise operators include *Bay Ferries* and *Northumberland Ferries* (website: www.nfl-bay.com), *Marine Atlantic* (website: www.marine-atlantic.ca) and *Scotia Prince Cruises* (website: www.scotiaprince.com).

RAIL:
VIA Rail trains run from Montréal to Halifax (the *Ocean* line) six times a week with bus connections to the rest of Nova Scotia (website: www.viarail.ca).

ROAD:
The Trans-Canada Highway enters the province from New Brunswick and ends at North Sydney on the northeast coast. Smaller provincial highways branch off it and circumnavigate the coastline. The scenic travelways include Sunrise Trail, Lighthouse Route and Glooscap Trail. Ferry services or causeways connect most islands with the mainland. There are two toll bridges which operate in Nova Scotia: The A Murray Mackay and The Angus L MacDonald. The cost of a one-way journey is C$0.75 (2005 price). The maximum speed on highways in Nova Scotia is 100km/h; in urban areas it is 50km/h. **Bus**: *Acadian Lines* provides services throughout the province (website: www.smtbus.com). There are connections with *SMT Eastern* from New Brunswick, *Voyageur* from Quebec and Ontario, and *Greyhound* from the USA. **Car hire**: There are agencies at Halifax and Sydney airports and throughout the province.

URBAN:
Comprehensive bus services are provided in the Halifax-Dartmouth area by *Metro Transit*, which operates a zonal fare system. There are connections with the harbour ferry on both sides.

Accommodation

Nova Scotia offers a wide range of accommodation and campsites. Advance reservations are recommended, especially during the summer. All establishments are inspected and recommended by Tourism Nova Scotia. Farmhouse holidays are possible and many Nova Scotians provide bed & breakfast for visitors in the tourist season (late April to November). Some accommodation is graded on a voluntary basis according to the *Canada Select Accommodations Grading Program* from **5-star** (deluxe) to **1-star** (basic).

CAMPING/CARAVANNING:
Much of Nova Scotia is luxuriant parkland, and one of the best ways to see the province is by motorhome or camper; a number of companies can arrange rentals, with a range of fully-equipped vehicles. Full details can be obtained from Tourism Nova Scotia (see *Top Things To Do*), which also publishes a comprehensive guide to the province.

ACCOMMODATION INFORMATION

Nova Scotia's 'Check-in and Reservation Service'
Tel: (800) 565 0000 (toll-free in USA and Canada) *or* (902) 425 5781.
Website: www.checkinnovascotia.com *or* www.novascotia.com

Top Things To See

- The Provincial capital, **Halifax**, is the commercial, administrative and maritime centre for the whole of Atlantic Canada. Situated at the mouth of the **Bedford Basin**, it claims to be the second-largest natural harbour in the world (after Sydney in Australia) and has a long and distinguished history as a naval and military base. Harbour tours and deep-sea fishing charters are available. Despite the city's boom over the past 15 years, the historic **Waterfront Area**, comprising of important 18th- and 19th-century buildings, has been kept intact. Excellent shopping, nightlife and restaurants are to be found in both the old and new sections of the city. Worth seeing are **Province House**, the birthplace of Canadian democracy in 1819; **St Paul's**, the oldest Protestant church in Canada; the **Museum of Natural History**; the **Maritime Museum of the Atlantic** (featuring Titanic exhibits) and the 17-acre **Victorian Halifax Public Gardens**. The 1km- (0.6 mile-) long Boardwalk is also worth a visit. Halifax itself is dominated by the Citadel, a star-shaped granite fortress built in 1749 and one of Canada's most visited National Historic Sites. It is known for its kilted regiment and changing of the guard display. A good view of the city and harbour can be had from its ramparts.
- Go to **Peggy's Cove** and see Canada's most photographed lighthouse, in an area known for its rugged and beautiful coastal scenery.
- Travel to **Lunenburg**, a German settlement established in 1753, and what is now a listed UNESCO World Heritage Site. This town's beautiful waterfront speaks of a rich history of fishing, shipbuilding and other maritime activities.
- See for yourself Nova Scotia's close ties with Scotland: street signs in **Pugwash** are in English and Gaelic and highland games are held annually in **Antigonish**.
- **Cape Breton Island** attracts many nature lovers. Some of the island's most spectacular scenery can be found at the **Cape Breton Highlands National Park**. There is superb inland sailing in the **Bras d'Or Lakes**. **Sydney**, a centre of shipping and industry, is the island's main city. Southeast of this is the **Fortress of Louisbourg**, North America's largest historical restoration. **Baddeck** on Cape Breton Island is home to the **Alexander Graham Bell Museum**. Bell (1847-1922) made Baddeck his home in the latter part of his life and his final resting place.
- The **Provincial Wildlife Park** at **Shubenacadie** is home to the province's most characteristic **wildlife**, which includes moose, bear, cougar, coyote, the horse and the bald eagle (of which it has a particularly high population).

Top Things To Do

- The **Cabot Trail**, voted North America's most spectacular **ocean drive** by the American Bus Association, is a ribbon of road around the northern highlands of the province which passes through **Cape Breton Highlands National Park**. The **Lighthouse Route** travels the southern shore where seafaring traditions are especially strong. The **Evangeline Trail** is a rural road that goes through the beautiful **Annapolis Valley**, known for its orchards, forts and Victorian mansions. The **Sunrise Trail** follows the **Northumberland Strait** which features 35 sandy beaches and the warmest waters north of the Carolinas.
- Amongst the wide range of possible outdoor activities, watersports predominate. The **Kejimkujik National Park** offers good **canoeing** facilities. **Sailing**, **kayaking** and canoeing are good along the coast or on the myriad inland kayaking routes; swimming on **Melmerby Beach** in the Northumberland Strait and **deep-sea fishing** are popular. Anglers intending to fish in Nova Scotia's 9000 freshwater lakes require a valid fishing licence, which is obtainable from any Department of Natural Resources office in the province. Tidal bore rafting is available on the **Minas Basin**, located in the **Bay of Fundy**, which has one of the highest tides in the world.
- Catch a glimpse of some **dolphins** and **whales**: tours leave from a string of ports along the coast – those from **Digby Neck** (two daily trips from June to early October) and **Westport** are among the best.
- Scavenge for amethyst, agate, quartz and jasper around **Parrsboro**. **Fossil hunting**-enthusiasts can also sign up for a cliff tour at **Joggins**.
- The **Halifax Highland Games and Scottish Festival** is a popular and fun event that celebrates Nova Scotia's Celtic influences, and is held every summer in **Citadel Hill**. For another taste of the island's Old World heritage, try the **Celtic Colours International Festival**.

TOURIST INFORMATION

Tourism Nova Scotia
6th Floor, World Trade and Convention Centre,
PO Box 456, 1800 Argyle Street, Halifax, Nova Scotia
B3J 2R5, Canada
Tel: (902) 425 5781 *or* (800) 565 0000 (toll-free in USA and Canada).
Website: www.novascotia.com

Entertainment

FOOD & DRINK: Seafood features strongly on most menus. The Pub District in Halifax is said to be one of the best in North America, with over 55 establishments.
Things to know: Beer and alcoholic beverages are sold by the glass in licensed restaurants (food must also be ordered) and in licensed lounges (opening hours generally 1100-1400). Beer by the bottle and draught beer is sold by the glass in taverns, pubs and beverage rooms, which offer great snacks and light meals; opening hours are normally from 1000 until early morning the next day.
Regional specialities:

- Scallops, fried, baked or grilled, are usually served with tartar sauce.
- Fish and clam chowders and lobster and salmon.
- *Solomon gundy* (a herring dish).
- *Lunenburg sausage* exemplifies the German influence, as do *hugger in buff, fish and scrunchions, Dutch mess* and *house bunkin* - all names for tasty combinations of fish and potatoes covered in cream sauce with onions and salt pork.
- Desserts make use of plentiful fruit and berries and include a stewed fruit and dumplings dish called *grunt*, and baked apple dumplings wrapped in pastry and served with cream, sugar or lemon sauce.

Regional drinks:

- *Nova Scotia beer warmer* is a glass of beer with a dash of hot pepper sauce to get the blood circulating again. Provincial beers include *Alexander Keith's* and *Propeller*.
- Nova Scotia has recently become a popular wine producing area, especially in the Annapolis Valley. A number of good vintages have been produced there.

Legal drinking age: 19 years.

NIGHTLIFE: Nightclubs are mostly centred in Halifax. Scottish bagpipe music and Gaelic songs can be heard all over the territory in concerts, bars, hotels and restaurants. Professional and amateur theatre is very popular; details of forthcoming attractions are available from Tourism Nova Scotia.

Shopping: Large shops such as supermarkets and most department stores remain closed on Sundays. However, some convenience stores are generally open and some small shops may also open.

Business

CONFERENCES/CONVENTIONS: Nova Scotia has a wide range of conference and convention venues. The Halifax Metro Centre arena in downtown Halifax has facilities for 10,000 people. Connected to this is the World Trade & Convention Centre, a striking landmark building made of brick and glass with a sumptuous interior. It has three convention floors, all with excellent catering and audio-visual facilities, and enough room for 2600 people at a stand-up reception, or 1700 for a banquet. A number of hotels in Halifax and Dartmouth offer good meeting facilities. The Dartmouth Sportsplex arena is another excellent large group facility. The city of Sydney offers Centre 200, an arena and convention complex built in celebration of Sydney's bicentennial in 1985, with various flexible meeting rooms for trade shows, receptions and banquets for up to 800. There are also some meeting facilities in more rural settings: The Pines Resort, overlooking the Annapolis Basin and the Bay of Fundy; Dundee Resort, overlooking the Bras D'Or Lakes; Keltic Lodge, overlooking Cape Smoky and the Atlantic Ocean; Liscombe Lodge, tucked into the evergreens where the Liscomb River meets the sea; and Lansdowne Lodge, east of Truro along the Glooscap Trail and near the beautiful Upper Stewiacke Valley.

COMMERCIAL INFORMATION

Atlantic Provinces Chamber of Commerce
Suite 21, 236 St George Street, Moncton, New Brunswick E1C 1W1, Canada
Tel: (506) 857 3980.
Website: www.apcc.ca

Destination Halifax
Suite 802, 1800 Argyle Street, Halifax B3J 3N8, Nova Scotia, Canada
Tel: (902) 422 9334 *or* (877) 422 9334 (toll-free in USA and Canada).
Website: www.destinationhalifax.com

Nunavut Territory

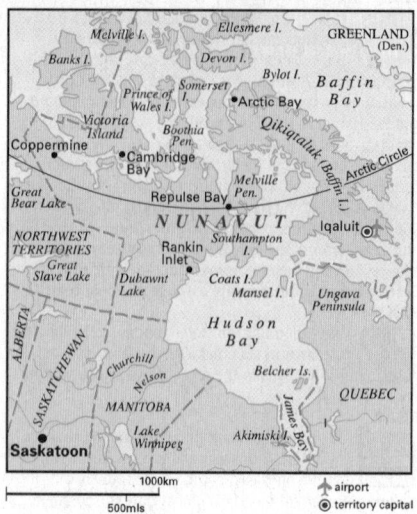

Location: Northern Canada.

Time:
Eastern Standard Time GMT - 6 (GMT - 5 in summer).
Central Standard Time GMT - 7 (GMT - 6 in summer).
Mountain Standard Time GMT - 8 (GMT - 7 in summer).
Daylight Saving Time (summer) officially lasts from the first Sunday in April to the Saturday before the last Sunday in October.

Overview

Nunavut became Canada's largest and newest Territory in 1999, when it was separated from the Northwest Territories. It emerged from around 20 years of negotiations by the Inuit communities that constitute about 80 per cent of this Arctic Territory. Nunavut means 'our land' in the language of the Inuit people, Inuktitut, and it is a land that is both Canadian and uniquely distinct from the country's other Provinces and Territories.

In Nunavut is a wilderness that forms one-fifth of Canada. Polar bears and whales pepper the landscape, and it is possible to do all those things that visitors may associate with the Arctic, from enjoying a dog sled to exploring an igloo to watching the Northern Lights (*aurora borealis*) illumine the dense darkness. There are also less traditional but equally adventurous activities to get your teeth into, such as mountain and rock climbing or challenging hikes across breathtaking National Parks. The landscape is one of ice and snow but also spectacular flora and fauna, all the more startling and beautiful for their sparseness and their contrast to the barren scene that they have managed to wriggle out of and flourish in.

Any visitor to Nunavut will most likely also flourish, in an area with plenty of indigenous history and plenty of stunning tundra, mountains and deep fjords.

General Information

AREA: 2,241,919 sq km (865,605 sq miles).
POPULATION: 30,000 (2005 estimate).
POPULATION DENSITY: 0.013 per sq km.
CAPITAL: Iqaluit. **Population:** 6,000 (2005 estimate).
GEOGRAPHY: The Nunavut Territory covers one-fifth of Canada, stretching from Ellesmere Island off Greenland's north coast to a border that runs north from the Saskatchewan/Manitoba border and then angles west to the arctic coast near Amundsen Gulf. The mainland portion of the territory is an untouched wilderness, where the stark northern tundra changes into cliffs and plateaux along the Northwest Passage. To the north and east, the Arctic Islands are surrounded by pack ice for most of the year and the region extends to the glaciers, jagged mountains and fjords of the eastern shores of Baffin and Ellesmere Islands.
LANGUAGE: Although Canada is officially bilingual (English and French), Inuktitut is an official language in Nunavut. English is commonly spoken throughout.

Climate

Owing to the vast size of the territory, there are great variations in the weather. Winters can be severe – the northernmost community of Grise Fiord has a mean January temperature of -35ºC (-31ºF) and a mean July temperature of 10ºC (50ºF). Summers are milder, but the temperature can drop suddenly.

Note: Conditions in all parts of the territory can become hazardous when there is a combination of a low temperature and a strong wind. Local advice concerning weather conditions should be followed very carefully. Nevertheless, the summer months are suitable for a wide range of activities.

Required clothing: Winter weather requires down-filled and other polar-temperature gear. Special clothing is required for adventure expeditions. Good-quality windproof and waterproof clothes, warm jerseys, gloves and moulded sole shoes are needed at all times of the year. In the summer, thinner clothes are required. Sunglasses and protective lotion are strongly advised. Mosquitoes are a significant irritant in some areas during July and August. A mosquito net and repellent are essential.

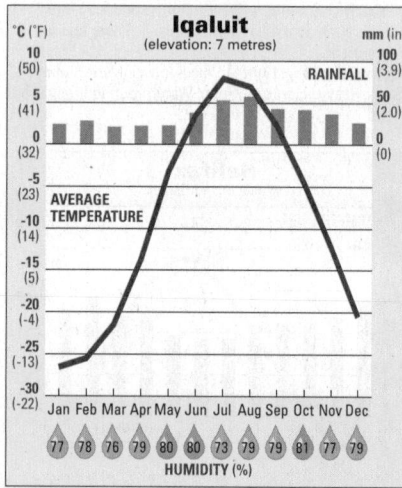

Credit: ©Nunavut Tourism

Public Holidays

Nunavut observes all the Public Holidays observed nationwide (see the general *Canada* section).

Travel - International

AIR:

The usual way to reach the communities within the Territory is by air. Most communities are served daily by at least one regional airline, with smaller communities being served less frequently. However, an increasing number of expedition cruise ships are sailing into Nunavut each summer. Float planes are rarely used owing to tidal areas, but do provide access to some northern lakes. The three airlines providing scheduled flights into the region are *Calm Air* (website: www.calmair.com), *Canadian North (CP)* (website: www.cdn-north.com) and *First Air* (website: www.firstair.ca). Other carriers provide scheduled or charter flights within Nunavut which are generally timed to meet inbound flights.

Main Airports: *Iqaluit Airport (YFB)* is less than 1km (0.6 miles) from the town centre (travel time – five minutes). International visitors will need to fly to Ottawa (Ontario), Montréal (Québec), Edmonton (Alberta) or Winnipeg (Manitoba) to board domestic flights to the Nunavut entry airports – Iqaluit, Cambridge Bay or Rankin Inlet.

SEA/LAKE/RIVER:

There is no water access to Nunavut for visitors except on cruises during the open water season – July to September. A number of tour operators offer Northwest Passage, Hudson Bay and High Arctic cruises each year.

ROAD:

There are no roads to Nunavut and only one road in Nunavut, between the communities of Nanisivik and Arctic Bay – 21km (13 miles) in length.

Travel Advice

Nunavut's sparsely populated and untouched Arctic wilderness is best visited as part of a package tour or in the company of an experienced guide. Individual travellers should note that they are likely to be exposed to a number of hazards, including severe cold, reduced hours of daylight and potentially aggressive wildlife, including bears. Before setting out on individual trips, travellers should contact Nunavut Tourism for advice (see *Tourist Information*).

Accommodation

HOTELS:

All communities have accommodation facilities, hotels, hostels and/or bed & breakfast establishments open all year. Space is limited so the accommodation and facilities may be shared, and are often quite basic. There are, however, full service hotels in the larger centres that also have meeting and conference facilities. Hotels can be very expensive. Iqaluit, the capital, now hosts approximately 260 rooms, including hotels and bed & breakfast establishments. 'Lodges' designed for outdoor activity holidays or naturalist trips can be found in some areas. For the more adventurous travellers, staying with an Inuit family is an option. Families are very hospitable but the accommodation is not regulated. Nunavut Tourism publishes an annual vacation planner detailing accommodation and other tourism services in Nunavut (see *Top Things To See & Do*).

CAMPING:

Backpacking and tent camping is a popular summer activity. Ellesmere Island National Park, Auyuittuq National Park and Katannilik Territorial Park are particularly popular with hikers.

Top Things To See & Do

- Take a trip across the frozen tundra by **dog sled** with an Inuit guide in Iqaluit.
- Stay a night in an **igloo**.
- **Wildlife viewing** plays an important part in most tours and wildlife is particularly abundant in the summer at the so-called 'floe edge', where the land ice meets the open sea and the blooming plankton attract large schools of shrimp and fish as well as seals, whales and polar bears. **Pond Inlet** and **Arctic Bay** are good locations for spotting arctic life. Musk ox or tundra swans can be seen in their natural environment on the **Northwest Passage** and the herd of 40,000 caribou in Nunavut is the largest in the world. Visitors can take a boat trip to **Coats Island** in **Hudson Bay** where there are herds of giant walrus and polar bears. In the **Thelon Game Sanctuary** in the Kivalliq interior many species roam freely across the tundra.
- Learn about Nunavut's fauna, flora, culture and history by going on one of the Territory's **nature** and **cultural tours**.

Credit: ©Nunavut Tourism

- The seasonal variations in light and temperature, and the dramatic scenery, provide rewarding conditions for **photography** enthusiasts. One of the best times for taking photographs is during the sunlit hours (between 2000 and 0300 in spring and summer), when shadows are long and colours and textures are particularly well defined. Photography tours are organised.
- Go on an **Inuit art tour**, which offer visitors an opportunity to learn about native carving, tool-fashioning, jewellery-making and hat-making (out of *Quivviuq* wool collected from the land).
- Immerse yourself in utter wilderness and **hike** over staggering destinations such as the mountains of **Auyuittuq National Park**, the willow forest of **Katannilik Park**, **North Ellesmere National Park** (which has particularly rich wildlife), the **Sirmilik National Park** (surrounding the scenic community of Pond Inlet) or the trail from **Kugluktuk** (**Coppermine**) to the **Bloody Falls**.
- Enjoy some **fishing**: catch of the day includes Arctic char and lake trout. Enthusiasts should note that catch-and-release is practised in all areas and that possession limits are based on regular and seasonal evaluation of stock.
- Test your endurance to the limit in July's annual **Nunavut Midnight Sun Marathon** (website: www.nunavutrun.com), held in Arctic Bay. Here is the chance to run, hike and explore terrain of outstanding beauty in a period when the sun bewilderingly does not set in the course of 24 hours.

TOURIST INFORMATION

Nunavut Tourism
PO Box 1450, Iqaluit, Nunavut Territory X0A 0H0, Canada
Tel: (867) 979 6551 *or* (866) 686 2888 (toll-free in USA and Canada) *or* (800) 491 7910 (visitor information).
Website: www.nunavuttourism.com
Publishes 'The Nunavut Travel Planner' brochure, which contains a directory of tour operators and outfitters, plus a brief description of their offerings.

The Nunavut Handbook
Website: www.arctic-travel.com

Entertainment

FOOD & DRINK: Known as 'country food', the cuisine of Nunavut is mostly based around subsistence living and produce that comes from hunting and fishing.

Things to know: In group meals, elders are usually served first. Alcohol is controlled in Nunavut and in some communities is prohibited. Hotels and restaurants in Iqaluit are licensed.

Regional specialities:
- Arctic char (with a taste somewhere between salmon and trout), mussels, scallops (especially from Cumberland Sound), clams, turbot (especially from the Baffin region) and Greenland shrimp.
- Musk ox and caribou.
- Local *bannock* (a mixture of flour and water blended into a dough and cooked slowly in a frying pan) dates from the old prospecting rations which kept for weeks in an easily transportable form.
- *Muktuk* (skin of the whale).

Regional drinks:
- Melting glacier ice is collected and provides water in many communities. Bottled water is available.

SHOPPING: There are general retail stores in almost all communities in Nunavut; some specialise in handicrafts, furs, fisheries and Inuit Art. The high cost of goods (an increase of up to 50 per cent on the rest of Canada) is due to the supply and distribution costs caused by the large distances that goods must be transported by air or sea. **Shopping hours**: Mon-Fri 1000-2000, Sat 1000-1800 (although these may vary regionally).

Business

COMMERCIAL INFORMATION

Baffin Regional Chamber of Commerce
PO Box 59, Iqaluit, Nunavut Territory X0A 0H0, Canada
Tel: (867) 979 4653.
Website: www.nunanet.com/~brcc/

A B C D E F G H I J K L M N O P Q R S T U V W X Y Z

Ontario

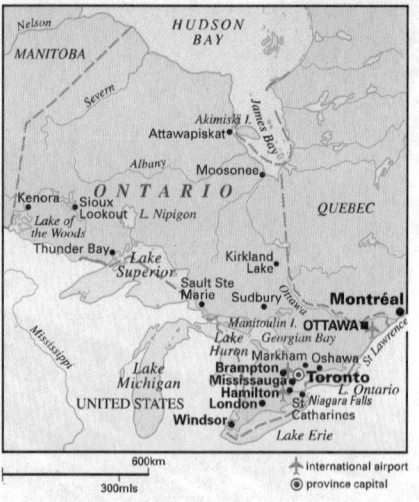

Location: Eastern central Canada.

Time: East of 90°W: GMT - 5 (GMT - 4 in summer).
West of 90°W: GMT - 5.
Summer officially lasts from the first Sunday in April to the Saturday before the last Sunday in October.

Overview

Ontario is Canada's most populous Province, and denotes this through the sheer size and energy of its two cities (one the Federal capital, the other the Provincial capital), Ottawa and Toronto. Toronto, in particular, is widely regarded as one of the most vibrant and cosmopolitan cities on the continent, in part due to its huge influx of immigrants. The city heaves with galleries, museums and shops, all against the backdrop of both heritage buildings (such as the Old City Hall, built in 1899) and innovative modern architecture (such as the CN Tower, arguably the world's tallest building). Yet away from the cities, due to the enormity of the Province, there are always plenty of places where you can savour some silence. The far north and west of Ontario is a largely uninhabited wilderness of lakes, swamps and forests. Throughout Ontario are six national parks and 260 provincial parks. And, surreal as it may seem when compared to the Province's urban centres, there are parts of this Province where you can see more polar bears than humans.
Ontario is also a Province of water, containing four of the five 'Great Lakes' of North America. There is also Niagara Falls for those who crave their watery landscapes a little more dramatic; partly lodged in Ontario (and partly in New York State, USA), the Falls provide a snapshot of Nature at its most phenomenal.

General Information

AREA: 916,734 sq km (353,951 sq miles).
POPULATION: 12.54 million (2005).
POPULATION DENSITY: 13.68 per sq km.
CAPITAL: Toronto (provincial). **Population:** 5,203,600 (2004). Ottawa (federal). **Population:** 1.14 million (2004; statistic combined with Gatineau).

GEOGRAPHY: Ontario is an eastern-central province bordered by Manitoba and Québec, with a northern coastline on James Bay and Hudson Bay; it also shares the shores of the Great Lakes with the USA. The two main populated areas, around Toronto and Ottawa, are in the southern spur, and the north remains a landscape of forests and lakes. The province contains the Niagara Falls, one of the most spectacular sights in the world.
LANGUAGE: Although Canada is officially bilingual (English and French), English is more commonly spoken in Ontario.

Climate

Summers can be very warm, while spring and autumn are cooler. Winters are cold with snowfall.
Required clothing: Light- to mediumweights during warmer months, heavyweights in winter. Waterproofing is advisable throughout the year.

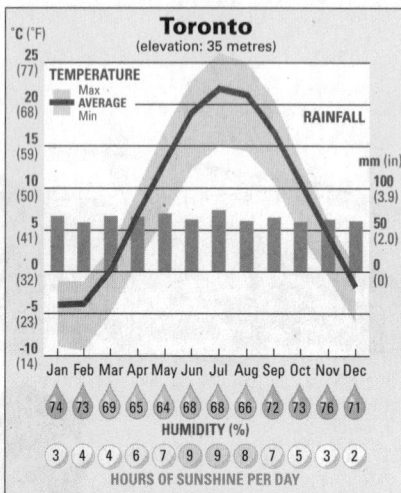

Public Holidays

Ontario observes all the Public Holidays observed nationwide (see the general *Canada* section) and, in addition, the beneath Public Holidays listed for the January 2006–June 2007 period.
2006: Aug 7 Simcoe Day.

Travel - International

AIR:

International air services are available through *Air Canada (AC)*. Many other international airlines offer direct services into Toronto. Charter airlines often offer an economical alternative to the scheduled airlines. Local air services are operated by a number of operators.
Main airports: *Ottawa (YOW)* (Macdonald-Cartier) (website: www.ottawa-airport.ca) is 10km (6 miles) south of the city. *To/from the airport*: A regular bus service departs every 30 minutes (travel time – 45 minutes). Taxis are also available (travel time – 20 minutes). *Facilities:* Bar, restaurants, cafes, duty free shops, currency exchange and ATMs.
Toronto (YYZ) (Lester B Pearson) (website: www.gtaa.com) is 27km (17 miles) northwest of the city. *To/from the airport*: A regular bus service departs every 20 to 30 minutes (travel

time – 20 to 30 minutes). Taxis are also available. *Facilities:* Duty free shops, cafes, restaurants and bar.
SEA:

Main ports: The only port on James Bay with rail links to the south is *Moosonee*, which is also the base for a limited local air service. The principal ports receiving sailings from the USA are *Windsor* (to Detroit/Lake St Clair); *Sarnia* (to Port Huron/St Clair River); *Leamington* (to Sandusky/Lake Eire); *Kingston*, *Brockville*, *Cornwall* and *Ogdensburg* (to the USA across the St Lawrence Seaway); and *Wolfe Island* to New York.
RAIL:

VIA Rail (website: www.viarail.com) connects Toronto to western Canada. Several corridor services connect Toronto, Windsor and Ottawa with Montréal and Québec City in Québec. Links to the USA are with *Amtrak* (website: www.amtrak.com) and *VIA Rail*. Services run from Toronto to New York via Niagara Falls, and to Chicago via Windsor and Sarnia. *VIA Rail* also serves all the major cities of the province, concentrating in the southern region, which holds most of the population. *Ontario Northland Rail* (website: www.ontc.on.ca) runs services from Toronto to Timmins, with a connection at Porquis for Cochrane and Kapuskasing. From Cochrane, services run northeast to Moosonee and west to Hearst. For details, contact local offices.
ROAD:

There are several bridges connecting Canadian and US territories, notably at Cornwall, Fort Erie, Fort Frances, Niagara Falls, Rainy River, Sarnia, Sault Ste Marie and Windsor. A tunnel also connects Windsor to Detroit. The domestic highway network is excellent around the Great Lakes, but does not extend to the north of the province. Good trunk roads run throughout. **Bus:** Services linking most towns are operated by *Go-Transit, Greyhound Canada, Ontario Northland, PMCL, Trentway-Wagar Bus Lines* and *Voyageur Colonial*. **Car hire:** Facilities are available from all hotels, at Ottawa and Toronto airports, and at main railway stations (including *Avis, Budget, Discount, Hertz, National* and *Thrifty*). Drivers must be over 21 years old and the wearing of seatbelts is strictly enforced.
URBAN:

Bus, trolleybus, metro, tramway services and "red rocket" street cars are provided by the *Toronto Transit Commission* (website: www.ttc.ca). Flat fares are charged and there are free transfers. Pre-purchase tokens and multi-tickets may be obtained. Services are integrated with those of the regional *Go-Transit* bus and rail system. Bus services in Ottawa, Carleton and surrounding areas are provided by *OC Transpo*. A flat fare operates with a premium on express routes. There are free transfers, and pre-purchase multi-journey tickets and passes are sold. An unlimited one-day pass (cost: C$8) is available for use on all forms of transport within the Toronto Metropolitan area. **Taxis:** Metered with standard fares. Drivers expect a 10-15 per cent tip. **Bus:** Drivers do not give change. Exact amount required. **Parking:** In Ottawa, parking is prohibited on the streets Nov-Apr 0100-0700. The prohibition is not signed and is enforced only when seven or more centimetres of snow is forecast. To be safe, park off-street overnight if you can.
TRAVEL TIMES: The following chart gives approximate travel times from **Toronto** (in hours and minutes) to other major cities/towns and tourist destinations in the surrounding area.

	Air	Road	Rail
Niagara Falls	–	1.50	2.00
Ottawa	1.00	4.50	4.00
Sudbury	1.05	5.00	8.00
Thunder Bay	1.45	15.00	–

Accommodation

Most of the accommodation is in the southern spur of the province where the majority of the population is located.
HOTELS:

Hotel costs vary according to class. Both Ottawa and Toronto have international-standard hotels. Accommodation is graded on an entirely voluntary basis by Tourism Ontario, a private non-profitmaking federation of food service, accommodation, recreation and travel associations and businesses. There are over 1000 participating members (there are also several other associations of a less general nature). Tourism Ontario grades hotels in Ontario according to a 5-star system, ranging from **5-star** (deluxe) to **1-star** (basic). Just over 75 per cent of participating hotels are in the 3- or 4-star category.
BED & BREAKFAST:
For help with bed & breakfast accommodation, contact the Federation of Ontario Bed & Breakfast Accommodation (FOBBA) (see *Accommodation Information* below).

Credit: ©Tourism Toronto

SELF-CATERING:

Furnished cottages are available throughout the region.

CAMPING/CARAVANNING:

The best way to explore the wilderness of the north with its lakes and forestry is to hire a **motorhome** or **camper**. A number of companies can arrange rentals of fully-equipped vehicles.

ACCOMMODATION INFORMATION

Ontario Accommodation Association
347 Pido Road, Unit 2, RR6 Peterborough, Ontario K9J 6X7, Canada
Tel: (705) 745 4982 *or* (800) 461 1972 (toll-free in the USA, the UK and Canada).
Website: www.ontarioaccommodation.com

Northern Ontario Tourist Outfitters Association (NOTO) (information on lodges)
386 Algonquin Avenue, North Bay, Ontario P1B 4W3, Canada
Tel: (705) 472 5552.
Website: www.noto.net

Federation of Ontario Bed & Breakfast Accommodation (FOBBA)
95 King Street West, Gananoque, Ontario K7G 2G2, Canada
Website: www.fobba.com

Ontario Private Campground Association
RR5 Owen Sound, Ontario N4K 5N7, Canada
Tel: (519) 371 3393.
Website: www.campgrounds.org

Resorts Ontario
29 Albert Street North, Orillia, Ontario L3V 5J9, Canada
Tel: (705) 325 9115 *or* (800) 363 7227 (toll-free in USA and Canada).
Website: www.resorts-ontario.com

Top Things To See

- **Ottawa** is situated on the south bank of the Ottawa River facing the French-speaking city of Hull in Québec. The imposing Gothic-style **Parliament Buildings** overlook the confluence of the rivers **Ottawa**, **Rideau** and **Gatineau** and are surmounted by the 92m (302ft) **Peace Tower**, affording a panoramic view of the city and its surroundings. **Confederation Square**, site of the **National War Memorial**, is the focal point of central Ottawa. The **National Arts Center**, a hexagonal complex on the banks of the **Rideau Canal**, houses an opera company, theatres, studios and restaurants. The Rideau Canal and the **Rideau-Trent-Severn Waterway** are part of a complex of recreational lakes and canals linking Ottawa to **Lake Ontario** and **Georgian Bay**. Outstanding among the city's many museums and galleries are the **National Gallery of Canada**, the **Canada Science and Technology Museum**, the **Canadian Museum of Nature**, the **Canadian War Museum** and the **Museum of Civilisation** (over the bridge in nearby Hull).
- **Toronto** is the Provincial capital and Canada's largest city. The city is laid out on a rectangular grid broken only by the **Don River** and **Humber River**, the banks of which provide a host of recreational amenities. The **CN Tower**, the world's tallest free-standing structure, has glass-fronted elevators rising 553m (1815ft) to indoor and outdoor observation decks that afford a 120km (75-mile) panoramic view on a clear day. The twin gold towers of the **Royal Plaza** make it the most eye-catching of the many avant-garde commercial buildings in the city. Toronto's latest attraction, **SkyDome**, at the foot of the CN Tower, is a multi-purpose entertainment complex and sports stadium and was the world's first to have a retractable roof – baseball's *World Series* has been played here more than once. Together with modern developments, the city has seen the renovation of old neighbourhoods, particularly the tree-lined streets of Victorian houses characteristic of the city. **Yorkville**, the hip part of town in the 1960s, now caters to the tastes of the city's upwardly mobile, but is a good spot to go window shopping or enjoy a cup of coffee. **Queen Street**, further south towards the lake, attracts a younger, more style-conscious crowd. In the eastern suburbs, the spectacular **Ontario Science Centre** and the **Metro Toronto Zoo** are both worth seeing.
- **Niagara Falls** is a must-see; a legacy of the Ice Age that gushes out half a million gallons of water every second. Situated in the storybook town of **Niagara-on-the-Lake**, the north shore of **Lake Erie** is dotted with resorts and good beaches; **St Thomas** and **Port Stanley** are particularly popular.

Credit: ©Ottawa Tourism

- See and explore the protected wilderness of **Algonquin Park**, Ontario's oldest Provincial park; 7600 sq km (2934 sq miles) of forest and lakeland provide the perfect environment for outdoor recreation.
- **Lake Superior Provincial Park**'s many beautiful ravines, lakes and waterfalls. In particular, its **Agawa Rock Pictographs** are highly famed. These are the largest collections of Indian rock art in Ontario; anything from human figures to animals and mythical beasts are depicted on the rock-face in a paint presumed to be a mixture of grounded haematite rock and animal fat. The pictographs remain one of Superior's most sacred spots.
- See the beautiful and unique (to Ontario) **monarch butterflies** which stop off at **Point Pelee** on **Lake Erie** in September during their annual migration. These colourful insects cover the trees, providing an amazing spectacle.

Top Things To Do

- **Ontario** is particularly well known for **canoeing**, and has more canoe routes than any other region in the world – more than 1496km (930 miles) of routes in northern Ontario alone. Good locations for canoeing include **Kilarney** and **Algonquin Provincial Parks** in the south of Ontario near **Lake Huron**, the latter being within three hours' drive of Toronto.
- Go **hiking** on the **Bruce Peninsula** where the views are spectacular.
- Go to **Warkworth** and attend the annual **Maple Syrup Festival**. Amongst the many demonstrations, races and contests is also the chance to sample lots of this sweet and sticky liberally poured onto anything from pancakes to sausages. The maple trees and their sap are unique to eastern North America and Ontario is very proud of its culinary links to the syrup.
- **Midland** commands a spectacular view of the **Georgian Bay Lake District** and is a popular resort, mainly because of the various minor **ski** resorts located around Georgian Bay, mostly on the **Niagara Escarpment**.
- Hurtle up to the top of the **CN Tower** in **Toronto** (website: www.cntower.ca): Canada's national tower is also the world's tallest building (if you count those without habitable space) and with its **Sky Pod**, possesses the world's tallest public observation desk.

TOURIST INFORMATION

Tourism Toronto
PO Box 126, 207 Queens Quay West, Suite 590, Toronto, Ontario M5J 1A7, Canada
Tel: (416) 203 2600.
Website: www.torontotourism.com

Ontario Tourism Marketing Partnership
10th Floor, Hearst Block, 900 Say Street, Toronto, Ontario, M7A 2E1, Canada
Tel: (800) 668 2746.
Website: www.ontariotravel.net

Ontario Tourism in the UK
4 Vencourt Place, Hammersmith, London W6 9NU, UK
Tel: (020) 8237 7998 *or* (01622) 832 288 (brochure request line).
Website: www.ontariotravel.net

Entertainment

FOOD & DRINK: International cuisine can be enjoyed in all major towns. Toronto is rated as one of the best cities for dining out on the continent. Bars and restaurants offer an international selection of alcohol. Each autumn, the *Niagara Grape and Wine Festival* is held in Niagara-on-the-Lake. Alcohol is sold in Provincial Liquor Control Board outlets. Domestic beer is available at Brewer's Retail.

Domestic wines are also sold through company stores.
Things to know: Liquor and beer stores are run and operated by the Government. Licensing hours are daily 1100-0200. Beer and liquor stores are open on Sundays. It is illegal to consume alcohol unless you are in a residence or a licensed establishment.
Regional specialities:
- Maple syrup can accompany everything, from waffles, toast, pancakes and even baked beans!
- Try Haliburton pheasant or one of the dazzling varieties of fish from the countless lakes and rivers.

Regional drinks:
- *Icewine*: a sweet nectar with a tantalising complexity of flavours.
- Ontario has extensive vineyards providing much of Canada's wine.

Legal drinking age: 19 years.
Tipping: It is customary to tip between 15 per cent and 20 per cent at bars and restaurants in Ontario. Tips are also given to tour guides, and for taxi service, spa treatments and haircuts. Porters at airports, railway stations and hotels generally expect $1-2 (CDN) per item of luggage.
NIGHTLIFE: Both main cities have establishments offering all forms of entertainment, from quiet clubs featuring a lone pianist, through Latin American combos to dance and rock bands and big-name international entertainers. Toronto is recognised as the third most important theatre centre after London and New York, and cabaret/dinner theatres are also especially popular in Toronto. Toronto is also known as a good jazz and blues town. Both Toronto and Ottawa host jazz festivals in the summer. Theatres with classical entertainment are also found in Ottawa.
SHOPPING: Toronto offers everything from antiques to luxury lingerie, if the visitor has the money and time to spend. There are large suburban shopping centres and the *Eaton Centre*, a glass-domed galleria in the heart of the city, is linked to 4.8km (3 miles) of interconnecting underground shopping malls with 1000 retail outlets. Toronto's villages are full of colourful streets of renovated Victoriana, with garment shops, art galleries, antique stores and open-air cafes in summer. The run-down Queen Street Strip has been taken over by collector's comic-book shops, punk day-glo leather emporia, sci-fi bookstores, junk and antique shops. Ottawa also has a wide choice of shops and handicraft centres. *Sparks Street Mall* offers a variety of shops including those selling excellent authentic native work. Byward Market is a popular area of craft shops, farmers' market stalls and cafes. *Vaughan Mills* is the newest mega-mall in Ontario including 200 shops. **Shopping hours:** Shops stay open until 1800 in most parts of Ontario. Many city and suburban shops are open until 2100.

Business

CONFERENCES/CONVENTIONS: Ontario offers a wide range of conference venues. Ottawa usually hosts between 35 and 40 major international conferences per year.

COMMERCIAL INFORMATION

Ontario Chamber of Commerce
180 Dundas Street West, Suite 505, Toronto, Ontario M5G 1Z8, Canada
Tel: (416) 482 5222.
Website: www.occ.on.ca

Toronto Convention & Visitor Association
PO Box 126, Suite 590, 207 Queen's Quay West, Toronto, Ontario M5J 1A7, Canada
Tel: (416) 203 2600.
Website: www.torontotourism.com

Niagara Falls Tourism (Information on Conferences/Conventions in Niagara Falls)
Marketing Department, 5515 Stanley Avenue, Niagara Falls, Ontario L2G 3X4, Canada
Tel: (905) 356 6061 *or* (800) 563 2557 (toll-free in USA and Canada).
Website: www.niagarafallstourism.com

The New City of Hamilton (Information on Conferences/Conventions in Hamilton)
Economic Development Department, 8th Floor, 1 James Street South, Hamilton, Ontario L8P 4R5, Canada
Tel: (905) 546 2424 x4222 *or* (800) 868 1329 (toll-free in USA and Canada).
Website: www.myhamilton.ca

Ottawa Tourism and Convention Authority
Suite 1800, 130 Albert Street, Ottawa, Ontario K1P 5G4, Canada
Tel: (613) 237 5150 *or* (800) 363 4465 (toll-free in USA and Canada).
Website: www.ottawatourism.ca

Prince Edward Island

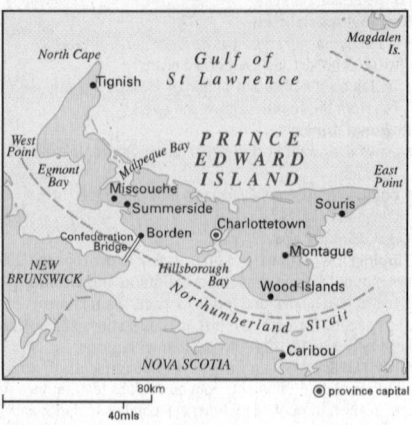

Location: East coast of Canada.

Time: GMT - 4 (GMT - 3 in summer).
Summer officially lasts from the first Sunday in April to the Saturday before the last Sunday in October.

Overview

Even entering Prince Edward Island is elating. Confederation Bridge, the longest bridge in Canada and the longest bridge over ice-covered waters worldwide, connects this island Province with Canada's mainland, dramatically stretching far into the distance over shimmering blue waters.
Once you enter Prince Edward Island, the countryside proves as memorable as this overpass. The entire island seems plunged in red: red soil, red sand and, in Autumn, an incredible menagerie of reds transform the island's foliage. Since this Province is an island, it is also surrounded by wonderful sandy beaches and terrific, lofty cliffs; from the rugged North Cape to the pretty bays around Prince Edward National Park. Prince Edward Island is Canada's smallest province, nestled in the North Atlantic between the warm waters of the Northumberland Strait and the St. Lawrence Seaway. It has a suitably small population, but one that is proud of its land. There is even a local saying that to be a true Prince Edward Islander you will have to have been born here. Yet Prince Edward Islanders enthusiastically welcome visitors, happy to share with them some of their delicious homegrown produce, such as the famed Prince Edward Island's new potatoes or the abundance of tasty lobster. Life on Prince Edward Island is a way of life most people could get used to.

Climate

Temperate climate with cold winters (mean January/February daytime high of -3°C/26°F) and warm summers (mean July/August daytime high of 23°C/73°F).
Required clothing: Light- to mediumweights in warmer months, heavyweights in winter. Waterproof wear is advisable all year.

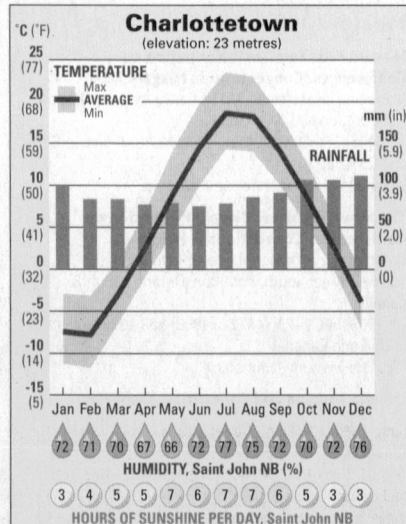

General Information

AREA: 5660 sq km (2185 sq miles).
POPULATION: 138,100 (2005).
POPULATION DENSITY: 24.39 per sq km.
CAPITAL: Charlottetown. **Population:** 38,114 (2001).
GEOGRAPHY: Prince Edward Island is a crescent-shaped island in the Gulf of St Lawrence comprising red farm fields, northern evergreen forests and white sand beaches. It is 224km (139 miles) long and between 6km (4 miles) and 65km (40 miles) wide.
LANGUAGE: English and some French are spoken.

Public Holidays

Prince Edward Island observes all the Public Holidays observed nationwide (see the general *Canada* section).

Travel - International

AIR:

Air Canada is the national airline which operates daily flights from Toronto to Charlottetown. *Air Canada Jazz* has four daily flights from Nova Scotia and Montreal (with more over the summer months). In 2005, *Westjet* began flights from Toronto and *Northwest Airlines* began flights from Detroit.
Main airport: *Charlottetown (YYG)* (website: www.flypei.com) airport is 3km (2 miles) from the city.
SEA:

Northumberland Ferries (website: www.nfl-bay.com) sail from Wood Islands on the southeast coast to Caribou in Nova Scotia from May to mid-December (travel time - 75 minutes). Advance reservations are not accepted. *CTMA Ferry* (website: www.ctma.ca) sails to Souris on the east coast from the Magdalen Islands in Québec from early April to the end of January (travel time - five hours). Advance reservations are recommended during the summer schedule from mid-June to early September (tel: (888) 986 3278).
RAIL:

There are no passenger services on the island.

ROAD:

The Confederation Bridge connects Borden-Carleton, Prince Edward Island with Cape Jourimain, New Brunswick. The bridge, which is 13km (8 miles) long, takes approximately 10 to 12 minutes to cross and is open 24 hours a day. A toll is payable on return over the bridge only (C$39.50 per car in 2005) (tel: (888) 437 6565). Ferry services no longer operate on this route. There are three scenic drives following the coast of the Island: Lady Slipper Drive (west), Blue Heron Drive (central) and King's Byway (east). Seatbelts for adults and children are mandatory on Prince Edward Island.

Accommodation

HOTELS:

Prince Edward Island offers a wide range of quality accommodation, from conventional hotels to lodges and family farms. Most of the towns have excellent hotels and one is never far from the sea.
BED & BREAKFAST:

Standards for Bed & Breakfast and Country Inn accommodation are overseen by the Bed & Breakfast and Country Inns Association. Owners of accommodation in Prince Edward Island are invited to participate in the Canada Select Rating Program. Participation in the grading system is voluntary. The star ratings are based on the extent of facilities, quality of facilities, extent of services and amenities, ranging from **5-star** (exceptional) to **1-star** (basic).
CAMPING/CARAVANNING:
There are over 65 travel parks for camping near sandy beaches or in the interior. Camping fees vary, depending on the facilities offered. Most private sites accept reservations. A number of companies can arrange **motor camper** rentals, with a range of fully-equipped vehicles. Full details can be obtained from Tourism Prince Edward Island (see *Top Things To Do*).

ACCOMMODATION INFORMATION

Canada Select Rating Program
Quality Tourism Services, 375 University Avenue, Unit 1B, Charlottetown, Prince Edward Island C1A 4N4, Canada
Tel: (902) 566 3501.
Website: www.canadaselect.com

Department of Tourism
Parks Division, PO Box 2000, Charlottetown, Prince Edward Island C1A 7N8, Canada
Tel: (902) 368 5540 *or* (888) 734 7529.
Website: www.gov.pe.ca

Top Things To See

- **Charlottetown**, the provincial capital, is a well-designed colonial seaport with tree-lined streets and rows of woodframe houses. Main places of interest are **Province House**, a fine Georgian building of Nova Scotia sandstone, the site of the 1864 discussions that led to the Canadian Confederation, and the **Confederation Centre of the Arts**, which houses art galleries, theatres, a restaurant and a museum. **Founders' Hall**, located on Charlottetown waterfront, is a newly opened attraction which tells the story of Canada from the 1864 **Charlottetown Conference** to the present day.
- Gaze upon 45km (25 miles) of fine white sand beaches and Prince Edward Island's trademark red sandstone capes in **Prince Edward Island National Park**.
- In Cavendish in **Prince Edward Island National Park** is **Green Gables**, the farmhouse immortalised in the book *Anne of Green Gables* by Lucy Maud Montgomery, and now an extremely popular museum. Further along the route, through **Stanley Bridge** where there is a large marine aquarium, is **New London**, where the author was born and wrote; there is also a museum in the house where she lived.
- Enjoy **seal-watching** in the **King's Byway** region.
- **Point Prim**, located on a long promontory to the southeast, has the oldest lighthouse on the Island, built in 1846 and still in use.
- Watch for bison and white-tailed deer in **Buffaloland Provincial Park**.
- Gaze at a 13km-long engineering marvel: **Confederation Bridge** connects the island to the mainland. Tolls are collected on departure. However, crossing is a price worth paying because you are not just paying for the convenience of getting to the island, you are also crossing the world's largest bridge over ice-covered waters – and the longest bridge in Canada. Gazing across at the waters that loom into the distance as you journey across this two-lane overpass is a truly exhilarating experience.
- The warm waters of the **Gulf of St Lawrence** and the **Northumberland Strait** have a moderating influence on the island's climate and help to create one of the longest **autumn foliage viewing** periods in northeastern North America. The best time to go on these scenic forest walks is from mid-September until late October.

Top Things To Do

- The park's northern shore (situated in **Queen's County**), where the beaches are protected by cliffs and sand dunes, is particularly well suited for **swimming**, and attracts thousands of visitors during the summer.
- Try some **deep-sea fishing**, a popular sport, with chartered boats widely available from July to September. Although the most common type of charters are for cod, mackerel and flounder, the waters around Prince Edward Island are particularly renowned for giant bluefin tuna. The tuna season begins in mid-August, and many tuna charters are available. Fishing equipment and bait are provided by the captain, but anglers are reminded that if they catch large fish such as tuna, the catch belongs to the captain. Those bringing in tuna may be offered a free charter for one day.
- There are plenty of recommended **cycling** routes around Prince Edward Island, including the 275 km (170 mile) **Confederation Trail**. This runs from **Tignish** in the west to **Souris** in the east, with several interconnecting lines branching off to virtually every corner of the province.
- There are excellent facilities for **skiing** and **cross-country skiing** at **Brookvale Provincial Ski Park**, which hosted the 1991 Canada Winter Games. Prince Edward Island has over 1000km (625 miles) of **snowmobiling** trails.
- Sample some of Prince Edward Island's sumptuous **seafood**: the **International Shellfish Festival** in September (website: www.peishellfish.com) offers a fantastic chance to munch on lobster and chowder from some of Canada and the world's top gourmet chefs and celebrity cooks.
- Take one of many scenic **drives** around Prince Edward Island: a tourist route known as the **Blue Heron Drive** heads westwards from **Charlottetown** to **Port-la-Joye-Fort Amherst**, the original French settlement on the Island, and on to **Prince Edward Island National Park**; the **Lady Slipper Drive** circles **Prince County**, home to most of the province's French-speaking residents, passing through **Miscouche**, which has an **Acadian Museum**, and **Mont Carmel**, which has an **Acadian Pioneer Village**; and the **King's Byway** traverses the hilly farming region of the eastern interior, passing through Souris, where ferries depart regularly for the Québecois Magdalen Islands, and North Lake, where boats can be chartered for what is claimed to be some of the best tuna fishing in the world.

TOURIST INFORMATION

Prince Edward Island Tourism
PO Box 2000, Charlottetown, Prince Edward Island C1A
7N8, Canada
Tel: (902) 368 4444 *or* (888) 734 7529.
Website: www.gov.pe.ca

Entertainment

FOOD & DRINK: The island offers plenty of plain,
wholesome, home-cooked food in restaurants. Service is
informal and friendly. There are also many seafood outlets
where fresh fish and shellfish can be bought in season and
taken away for cooking on barbecues or camp fires.
Things to know: Waiters expect a 10 to 15 per cent tip.
Most dining rooms are licensed to sell alcohol. Licensed
premises are open until 0200. Off-licences (liquor stores)
are open six days a week from 1000-2200 during the
summer months. Hours of operation vary in winter.
Regional specialities:

- Shellfish – lobster, in particular – is a mainstay of the
dinner table. Lobsters are steamed or boiled and included
in casseroles and salads. Lobster suppers are a tradition
on Prince Edward Island and they are often held in
church basements or community halls where fresh
lobster is served, along with home-made chowder, rolls,
cakes and pies. 'Seconds' are available of everything
except lobster.
- Oysters are popular; they may be served with tangy
sauce, deep-fried, in pies, scalloped, in soufflés, soups
and stews.
- Prince Edward Island is famous for its new potatoes –
small, round potatoes – and a favourite with locals are
new potatoes boiled with their skins, then mashed and
served with lots of butter, salt and pepper.
- Fish cakes made with salt cod and potatoes.

Legal drinking age: 19 years.
NIGHTLIFE: Lounges on the Island usually have some live
entertainment for all or part of the week. Theatres, located
mainly in Charlottetown, Victoria, Georgetown, Mont
Carmel and Summerside, offer cultural, musical or light
entertainment.
SHOPPING: The Island's crafts include highly original
pottery, weaving, leatherwork, woodwork, quilting, hand-
painted silk and jewellery. Various guilds preserve the
standards of production. There are also several antique
dealers, second-hand stores, auctions, yard sales and flea
markets. There are downtown malls and shopping outlets
in the main shopping centres: Charlottetown,
Summerside, Montague and Cavendish. **Shopping hours:**
Mon-Thurs and Sat 0900-1700, Fri 0900-2100 (although
these may vary depending on the area and the time of
year).

Business

COMMERCIAL INFORMATION

Atlantic Provinces Chamber of Commerce
Suite 21, 236 St George Street, Moncton, New
Brunswick E1C 1W1, Canada
Tel: (506) 857 3980.
Website: www.apcc.ca

Meetings Prince Edward Island
(Information on Conferences/Conventions)
129 Queen Street, Charlottetown, Prince Edward Island
C1A 4B3, Canada
Tel: (902) 368 3688 *or* (877) 633 8734 (toll-free in the
USA and Canada).
Website: www.meetingspei.com

Québec

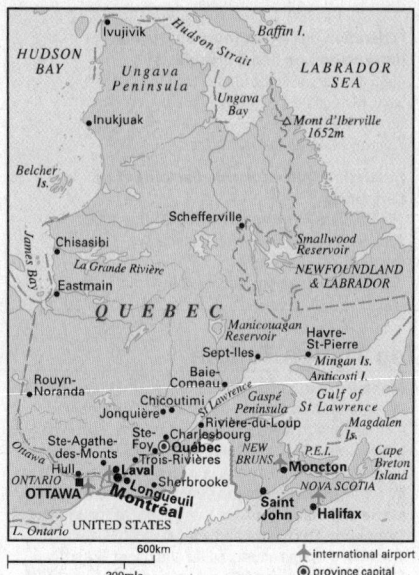

Location: Eastern Canada.

Time: GMT - 5 (GMT - 4 in summer).
Summer officially lasts from the first Sunday in April to the
Saturday before the last Sunday in October.

Overview

Québec is Canada's largest Province and consists of hilly
agricultural land along the banks of the St Lawrence and
vast tracts of barren mountains in the north: a breathtaking
panorama of towering rock faces, 6000km (3750 miles) of
coastline, looming canyons and craggy fjords. The Province's
22 natural parks and 14 wildlife reserves provide
opportunities for all types of outdoor activities. More than
100,000 lakes provide excellent fishing (chiefly for trout and
salmon), whilst in the northern tundra of Québec's Far
North (Nouveau-Québec), caribou and other game roam the
land.
What mainly distinguishes Québec from other Canadian
Provinces is its French heritage, which has been sustained
over around 200 years, despite repeated attempts
throughout history by English-speaking nations to capture
it. Québec's official language is French and both of its two
main cities, Québec City (the Provincial capital) and
Montréal (the Province's largest city) are filled with
Chateaux and cobblestoned streets.
Indeed, there is debate over whether Québec deliberately
isolates itself from the rest of (the predominantly English-
speaking) Canada. Nevertheless, two referendums issued
last century to determine the fate of the Province returned
a 'no' to the issue of separation – although the verdict was
extremely close both times.
Regardless of the political situation, Québec offers a friendly
welcome to all who visit, and such a welcome precedes a
host of delights: the greatest gastronomy in Canada;
cosmopolitan shopping; wide, sandy beaches; and excellent
facilities for adventures ranging from wintersports,
watersports and to hiking.

General Information

AREA: 1,357,812 sq km (524,252 sq miles).
POPULATION: 7.59 million (2005 estimate).
POPULATION DENSITY: 5.59 per sq km.
CAPITAL: Québec City. **Population:** 710,700 (estimate,
2004).
GEOGRAPHY: The Province of Québec is in the east of
Canada, with coasts on the North Atlantic and Hudson and
James Bays; the St Lawrence Seaway, the major shipping
channel of the Canadian east coast, cuts through the
populous south; the cities of Québec and Montréal
(Canada's second-largest city) stand beside it. In the north,
the Laurentians resort area has snow-covered mountains in
winter and scenic lakes. The far north is a spread of forest
and lakes forming one of the largest areas of wilderness in
Canada.
LANGUAGE: French is the official language and 82 per
cent of the population speak it as a first language; 35 per
cent of the population speak English either as a first
language or in addition to French.

Credit: ©Tourisme Québec – Linda Turgeon

Climate

Summer months (Jun to Aug) are hot with cooler evenings.
Autumn and spring are cooler and winters are very cold and
snowy.

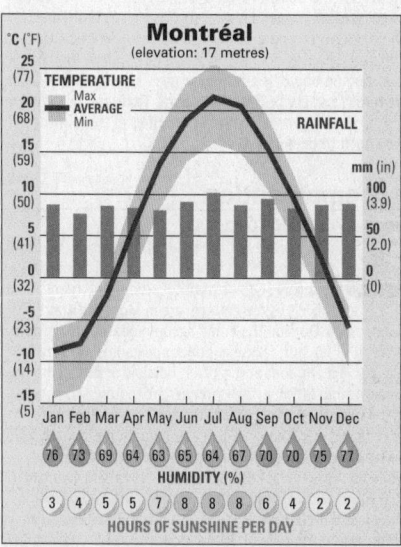

Montréal
(elevation: 17 metres)

Public Holidays

Québec observes all the Public Holidays observed
nationwide (see the general *Canada* section) and, in
addition, the beneath Public Holidays listed for the January
2006-June 2007 period.
2006: Jan 2 New Year. **Jun 24** Quebec National Day or St
Jean Baptiste Day.
2007: Jan 1 New Year. **Jun 24** Quebec National Day or St
Jean Baptiste Day.

Canada: Québec

A B C D E F G H I J K L M N O P Q R S T U V W X Y Z

Travel - International

AIR:

Air Canada (AC) and other international carriers fly into Montréal. Commuter services between Montréal and Toronto, Québec City and New York also exist. Local air services operate between the cities in the south and float planes serve the lakes and parkland of the north.

Main airports: Montréal has two international airports, *Trudeau (YUL)*, 25km (16 miles) west of Montréal, and *Mirabel (YMX)*, 53km (33 miles) northwest of Montréal (website for both airports: www.admtl.com). All international scheduled flights are from Montréal-Trudeau. Charter flights are from Montréal-Mirabel. Several daily trans-border US services also operate from Montréal-Trudeau. *To/from the airports*: A regular shuttle service connects the two airports. Buses leave *Trudeau* every 30 minutes (0700-0100) and *Mirabel* every 90 minutes (0100-2330 and until 2200 Thurs) for Montréal and its major hotels. Taxi and limousine services are also available for a fixed flat fee.

SEA:

Main ports: *Québec City* and *Montréal* are the most important Canadian ports on the St Lawrence Seaway, which links the Atlantic Ocean with the Great Lakes and the industrial heartland of Canada and the USA. Several international passenger carriers sail to both ports; European carriers dock only at Montréal. Most of the province's lakes and rivers (notably the Ouatouais, the Richelieu and the Saguenay) are served by local ferries, some of which are able to take heavy lorries. For schedules and fares, enquire locally.

RAIL:

VIA Rail connects Montréal and Québec City to Toronto with fast, regular services. It also offers services to Halifax from Montréal and Québec City. Links to the USA are with *Amtrak* and *VIA Rail*. *VIA Rail* connects all major provincial towns, and *Amtrak* operates two daily trains to the USA. *VIA Rail* services also connect the major cities in the south of the province, with thrice-daily mainline services from Montréal to Québec.

ROAD:

The best way of travelling into and around Québec by road is by long-distance coach, especially *Orléans Express* (website: www.orleansexpress.com). The services in the southern region are especially frequent. Motorhomes and campers are best for seeing the northern parklands, and the area is connected to the south by several good highways, although the most extensive network is around the populous areas in the south.

URBAN:

Montréal's bus and metro services are fully integrated, fast, clean and operate on a flat-fare system. Tickets for single journeys are not usually issued unless a transfer is required. For transfers from metro to bus, transfer-tickets should be obtained from machines before leaving the underground. If transferring from bus to metro, ask the bus driver for a ticket. Passes for one day, three days and seven days are sold as well as multi-ticket books. Metro fares are the lowest in North America. Québec City's bus services operate on a flat-fare system. No change is carried on board. Pre-purchase passes are available. There are good bus services in other towns. **Taxis** can be hailed on the street in Montréal, but in other cities in the province they need to be ordered.

Accommodation

HOTELS/LAKESIDE LODGES:

The majority of the population lives in the south of the province, where all the large cities offer an extensive choice of hotel accommodation. Some of the best hotels in the country are in Montréal and Québec City. Outside the cities, accommodation takes on a more rural flavour; lakeside lodges and cabins are very popular. Accommodation is often possible in private homes. All accommodation establishments are required to have a classification certificate from the Minister of Regional Development & Tourism. All accommodation is awarded **1** to **6 stars** according to their facilities and level of comfort, while bed & breakfast establishments (*gîtes*) are awarded 1 to 6 suns for their atmosphere, architecture and welcome. The precise definition of the star allocation system varies according to the type of accommodation.

BED & BREAKFAST:

There are numerous organisations in Québec that provide information regarding bed & breakfast accommodation, including Réseau des Gîtes Classifiés (see *Accommodation Information*, below).

CAMPING/CARAVANNING:

Northern Québec is a vast area of forest and lakes and one of the best areas for wilderness camping in Canada. A number of companies can arrange motor camper rentals with a range of fully-equipped vehicles.

ACCOMMODATION INFORMATION

Réseau des Gites Classifiés
10 Rue de la Chapelle, La Malbaie G5A 3A3, Canada
Tel: (418) 665 2323.
Website: www.gites-classifies.qc.ca

Fédération des Agricotours du Québec (Information on Bed & Breakfast)
4545 avenue Pierre de Coubertin, PO Box 1000, Succ. M, Montréal H1V 3R2, Canada
Tel: (514) 252 3138.
Website: www.agricotours.qc.ca

Fédération Québécoise de Camping et de Caravaning
4545 avenue Pierre de Coubertin, PO Box 1000, Succ. M. Montréal H1V 3R2, Canada
Tel: (514) 252 3003.
Website: www.campingquebec.com

Top Things To See

- **Montréal** is Canada's second-largest city, on a 48km- (30 mile-) long island, and a sophisticated cosmopolitan metropolis with a 65 per cent francophone population in what is a spacious and beautiful modern city. A series of underground shopping and recreation complexes, linked by walkways and the metro, is centred on **Place Ville-Marie**. The **Place des Arts** is the home of the **Montréal Symphony Orchestra** and several theatres offering year-round drama, music, ballet and opera. Both the **Montréal Museum of Fine Arts** and the **Museum of Contemporary Arts** have good collections. **Vieux-Montréal**, the historic waterfront section, has been carefully restored. Main places of note here are: **Place Jacques-Cartier**, the former French governor's residence; **Château Ramezay**; the city's oldest church, **Notre-Dame-de-Bonsecour**; and **Pointe-à-Callière**, the **Montréal Museum of Archaeology and History**. **Mont-Royal Park** is the city's highest point, offering an excellent vista from the centre of Montréal. The park is also home to the world's tallest leaning building, the **Botanical Gardens** and the **Biodôme**. The area around **St-Denis** is renowned for its many jazz cafes and small restaurants.
- See the old city walls and characteristic green copper roofs and fortified **Citadel** of **Québec City**; the Provincial capital is one of the most European cities in North America; it was declared a World Heritage Site by UNESCO in 1985. It is the cradle of French culture in Canada with a 95 per cent French-speaking population. The city is split into two levels, connected by stone stairways and a municipal lift. Surrounded by the old city walls is the 'Upper Town' with some fine 18th- and 19th-century architecture, notably the **Place D'Armes** and the **Château Frontenac** (a first-class hotel). In front of the Château Frontenac is a wide promenade with 310 wooden steps leading up to the Citadel which affords incredible views across the **St Lawrence River**. Small street cafes, cobblestoned streets and shaded squares emphasise the European air of the 'Upper Town'. In the 'Lower Town', a network of 17th-century streets are centred on **Place Royale**. For art lovers, the **Notre-Dame de Québec Basilica** houses a unique collection.
- See the **Rocher Percé** ('the pierced rock': a massive, arched sandstone rock rising from the Atlantic). in the **Gaspé Provincial Park**, a park which protects herds of caribou in a beautiful landscape of woods, lakes and streams.
- The **Duplessis Peninsula** is the site of some of the earliest landfalls in the New World. Remains left by these Viking sailors can be seen in the museum at **Sept-Îles**, the largest city in the area. The bizarre geological formations of the nearby **Mingan Archipelago** are best explored by boat.
- Discover miles of white sandy beaches and a host of unspoilt fishing villages in the **Magdalen Islands**, 215km (134 miles) east of the Gaspé peninsula in the **Gulf of St Lawrence**.

Top Things To Do

- A variety of **watersports** can be practised, from **whitewater rafting** to gentle **boating**, and **canoes**, **kayaks**, **sailboards** and other equipment can be hired in the parks. Detailed maps of canoe-camping itineraries are available at information centres. Excellent watersports facilities exist on the **St Lawrence River**, especially for **sailing**, **swimming** and **water-skiing**. The **Rivière Rouge** is especially popular for whitewater rafting.
- Go **cycling**: the cycling network, **La Route Verte** (the 'Green Circuit'), so far boasts more than 3000km (1865 miles) of marked paths and designated roadways. The **St Lawrence River Valley** is good for moderate cycling, while the terrain in the **Laurentides** region is more challenging. **Mountain bike** enthusiasts will find plenty of trails in the parks and nature reserves, especially **Parc de la Jacques-Cartier** and **Mont-Sainte-Anne** near **Québec City**.
- **Wintersports** facilities are outstanding. There are around 200 ski centres in the province. The season is long and there is plenty of snow. The three main skiing regions in the province are **The Laurentians, The Eastern Townships** and the **Greater Quebec/Charlevoix area**. International downhill skiing competitions are held to the north of **Montréal** at **Mont-Tremblant** and at **Mont-Sainte-Anne** near Québec City. Another popular ski resort near Québec City is **Stoneham. Cross-country skiing** is very popular, and trails are extensive. **La Traversée de Charlevoix** is the most challenging trail east of the Rocky Mountains. There are ample opportunities for **snowmobiling** on some of these trails. Other winter activities include **snowshoe trekking**, **dog sledding**, **ice fishing** and **ice climbing**. Various activities are available in the far north of the province, including **wildlife viewing** and **air safaris**.
- From May to October **humpback whales** can be seen in the **St Lawrence** as they migrate for a plentiful supply of fish. **Whale-watching tours** are available. In late February, thousands of **harp seals** give birth on the ice floes of the **Magdalen Islands**. Visitors can take a helicopter ride to the ice fields in March.
- Why not indulge your taste buds? Québec people take their food very seriously, and there are many opportunities to partake in the delights of the local cuisine. Several food and drink festivals take place each year. One of the highlights of the culinary year is the **maple harvest** which takes place from March until the end of May. Québec produces some 80 per cent of Canada's maple syrup total. *Érablières* (maple farms) and **cabanes à sucre** (sugar shacks) are situated all over the province and most are open to the public in the season. Visitors can watch the harvest and sample maple toffee (made by pouring molten syrup onto fresh snow). Barn dance parties are held and meals featuring local specialities are served. These celebrations are popular with locals and visitors alike
- Go to the **Québec City's Winter Carnival**, usually held in January/February and with the aim of raising the spirits during what is often a long, harsh winter in this region. It is the third-largest Lenten festival in the world and is a thrilling spectacle of parties, ice baths, dog sled races, ice palaces, sculptures, snowmobile races and Viennese-style dance balls.

TOURIST INFORMATION

Destination Québec in the UK
Suites 11-16, 35-37 Grosvenor Gardens House, Grosvenor Gardens, London SW1W 0BS, UK
Tel: (020) 7233 8011.
Website: www.quebec4u.co.uk
Deals with trade enquiries only. Members of the public should contact the Destination Québec brochure service by telephone or e-mail.

Destination Québec Brochure Service
PO Box 1939, Maidenhead, Berks SL6 1AJ, UK
Tel: (08705) 561 705 (24-hour brochure hotline).
E-mail: brochures@quebectourism.co.uk

Tourism Québec
Street address: 1255 Peel Street, Office 100, Montréal, Québec H3B 4V4, Canada
Postal address: PO Box 979, Montréal, Québec H3C 2W3, Canada
Tel: (514) 873 2015 *or* (877) 266 5687 (toll-free in USA and Canada).
Website: www.bonjourquebec.com

Entertainment

FOOD & DRINK: Québec proudly reflects a tradition of French culture, never more so than in the restaurants and cuisine of the province. French food here is as excellent as anywhere in Europe. Immigrants from many countries provide a vast selection. English, Greek, Italian, Japanese and Spanish cuisine are all available in Montréal and Québec. International menus are found at all the larger hotels, but the best food is found by wandering around the backstreets of the cities and sampling the small but excellent restaurants scattered throughout both cities. The Île d'Orléans is an island northeast of Québec City that provides abundant fruit and vegetables for the city. Québec follows French tradition in having excellent standards of wine and spirits to complement the high standards of cuisine. Some spirits and rarer wines are imported from Europe.

Credit: ©Tourisme Québec - Heiko Wittenborn

Things to know: Taverns and brasseries serve alcoholic beverages from 1200-0300 every day. Cocktail lounges and cabarets stay open until 0200 and 0300, respectively, in Québec and Montréal.

Regional dishes:
- *Ragoût de boulettes* (pork meatballs with seasoning).
- *Cretons du Québec* (chilled minced pork).
- *Tourtière* (a meat pie).
- Beans and pork baked in maple syrup.
- *Tarte au sucre* (maple sugar pie).
- As in France, there is an abundance of cheeses to sample.
- Game, such wild boar, venison, and even caribou and wapiti (deer).
- *Queues de Castor* translates as 'beaver tails' but are actually a fast-food delight of deep-fried pastry, either sweet with cinnamon and sugar or raspberry jam, or savoury, such as with garlic butter or cheese.

Regional drinks:
- Wines and spirits based on maple sap are a speciality of the region, among them maple cider and maple whiskey.
- Local mead is said to be good.

Legal drinking age: 18 years.

Tipping: It is customary to tip between 10 and 15 per cent at bars and restaurants in Quebec.

NIGHTLIFE: Québec City and Montréal offer some of the best nightclubs and cabarets to be found anywhere in Canada. In Montréal, the action seldom begins before 2200 and usually continues until 0300 the next morning. Nightlife is concentrated in the western part of the downtown area along Crescent and Bishop Streets and around Ste-Catherine Street, where there are many bars, restaurants and clubs of all kinds. For a particularly French flavour, try the many clubs, bars, restaurants, cafes and bistros further east around Saint-Denis and Saint-Laurent.

SHOPPING: Québec City and Montréal have excellent shopping facilities, both in large department stores and small street markets. Specialities include furs, Native American crafts, haute couture, antiques, specialist fashion boutiques and discount retail outlets. **Shopping hours**: Mon-Wed 0900-1800, Thurs-Fri 0900-2100, Sat 0900-1700. Most shops are open on Sunday.

Business

CONFERENCES/CONVENTIONS: Montréal is a major meeting and convention centre.

COMMERCIAL INFORMATION

Board of Trade of Metropolitan Montréal
380 St Antoine Street West, Suite 6000, Montréal, Québec H2Y 3X7, Canada
Tel: (514) 871 4000.
Website: www.ccmm.qc.ca

Tourisme Montréal (Information on Conferences/Conventions in Montréal)
CP 979, Montréal, Québec H3L 2W2, Canada
Tel: (514) 873 2015.
Website: www.tourisme-montreal.org

Greater Québec Area Tourism & Convention Bureau
2nd Floor, 399 St-Joseph Street East, Québec City, Québec G1K 8E2, Canada
Tel: (418) 641 6654.
Website: www.quebecregion.com

Saskatchewan

Location: Central Canada.

Time: East of 106°W: GMT - 6.
Most of Saskatchewan does not observe Daylight Saving Time.

Overview

Saskatchewan is named after the Native American word for river systems (Kis-is-ska-tche-wan), probably because the Province has close to 100,000 lakes and rivers. Although Saskatchewan is commonly thought of as consisting mainly of vast prairies, the landscape is quite varied. The wide, treeless plains in the south are broken up by river valleys and ranges of low-lying hills, and there are large forests in the north of the province and Saskatchewan's two national parks, Prince Albert National Park of Canada in the north and Grasslands National Park in the southwest, cover nearly 5,000,000 acres (2,000,000 hectares) between them. However, it is true that the south and centre do enjoy a more mellow landscape, encompassing prairie and grasslands, badlands and river valleys.

Indeed, Saskatchewan is not a Province to escape to for a slice of urban lifestyle: there are few permanent settlements and many regions are accessible only by air. This is, instead, a laidback Province with a pleasant remoteness. Although there is definitely adventure and rodeo for those who seek it, perhaps you are best off savouring Saskatchewan's nature and wildlife: wolves, moose and caribou inhabit the northern forests, while elk and deer can be found further south

General Information

AREA: 570,113 sq km (220,121 sq miles).
POPULATION: 994,100 (2005 estimate).
POPULATION DENSITY: 1.74 per sq km.
CAPITAL: Regina. **Population**: 198,600 (2005 estimate).
GEOGRAPHY: Saskatchewan is bordered by Manitoba to the east, the Northwest Territories to the north, Alberta to the west and the US States of North Dakota and Montana to the south. Its landscape is mainly prairie, parkland, forests and lakes. Prince Albert National Park of Canada is the gateway to Saskatchewan's wilderness. The highest elevation is the Cypress Hills in the southwest, 1392m (4566ft) above sea level.
LANGUAGE: Although Canada is officially bilingual (English and French), English is more commonly spoken in Saskatchewan.

Climate

Temperate in the south with cold winters in the north. The highest rainfall occurs between April and June. Summers are hot and dry with long hours of sunshine, but winter temperatures are generally cold and snowy until early March, but sunny.
Required clothing: Light- to mediumweights during warmer months. Heavyweights are worn in winter. Waterproof wear is advisable throughout the year.

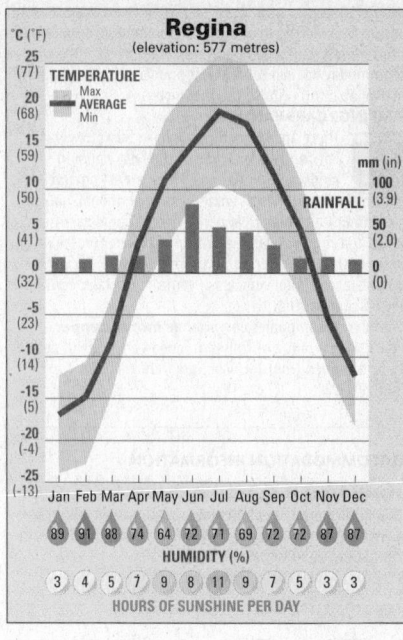

Public Holidays

Saskatchewan observes all the Public Holidays observed nationwide (see the general *Canada* section) and, in addition, the beneath Public Holidays listed for the January 2006-June 2007 period.
2006: Aug 7 Saskatchewan Day.

Travel - International

AIR:
 Air Canada (AC) provides a daily scheduled service connecting Saskatoon and Regina to the rest of the world. *Northwest Airlines* (www.nwa.com) and *Westjet Airlines* (www.westjet.ca) also serve the area.
Main airports: *Saskatoon (YXE)* (website: www.yxe.ca) is 7km (4.5 miles) from the city centre (travel time - 15 minutes). *Facilities:* Car hire, car parking, restaurant and gift shop.
Regina International Airport (YQR) (website: www.yqr.ca) is 5km (3 miles) from the city centre. *Facilities*: Car rental, restaurants and gift shops.

RIVER:
 Ferry services operate from various locations connecting communities within the province. Houseboats may also be chartered in certain areas.

RAIL:
 VIA Rail, Canada's national passenger train service, operates the Winnipeg-Saskatoon-Edmonton link (*The Canadian*).

ROAD:
 Saskatchewan has six travel corridors, namely the Northern Woods and Water Route (9 and 55) east-west, Yellowhead Highway (16) east-west, the Trans-Canada Highway (1) east-west, Red Coat Trail (13) east-west, CanAm International Highway north-south and the Saskota International Highway (9) north-south. Saskatchewan has more road surface than any other province in Canada - a total of 250,000km (150,000 miles). **Bus:** A scheduled motorcoach service is provided by *Greyhound Bus Lines*, *Moose Mountain Bus Lines* and *Saskatchewan Transportation Company* (website: www.stcbus.com). Charter motorcoach services are also available from a number of cities and operators. **Car hire**: Hire cars are available in most cities. Saskatchewan law requires that anyone driving or riding in a motor vehicle must wear available seatbelts at all times.

Accommodation

The majority of accommodation suitable for travellers is found in the south and central portion of the province, especially in Regina, Saskatoon, Moose Jaw, Prince Albert, Swift Current, Weyburn, Melfort, Yorkton, Estevan and the Battlefords. Saskatchewan Tourism's annual guide describes accommodation as **Mod** (modern); **Smod** (semi-modern), **Nmod** (non-modern) and **Lhk** (light housekeeping unit).

EDITOR'S CHOICE - HOUSEBOATS

'Houseboat charters' on the lakes are a special feature of Saskatchewan. These are available on Lac La Range.

Saskatchewan Accommodation Guide is available through Tourism Saskatchewan and is a comprehensive directory of hotels/motels, parks, campgrounds, lakeside accommodation, bed & breakfast and vacation farms that are available throughout the province.

CAMPING/CARAVANNING:

 There are 460 campgounds in Saskatchewan. Parklands offer some of the best camping landscapes in Canada. There are 34 provincial parks in the categories of wilderness, recreational, natural environment and historical parks, two national parks, as well as 101 regional parks, all offering different rates of service with some offering accommodation for those without recreational vehicles or tents. For details, contact the local park authorities.

A number of companies can arrange **motor camper** rentals, with a range of fully-equipped vehicles. Full details can be obtained from Tourism Saskatchewan (see *Top Things To Do*).

ACCOMMODATION INFORMATION

Hotels Association of Saskatchewan
302 20AD Broad Street, Regina, Saskatchewan S4P 1Y3, Canada
Tel: (306) 522 1664.
Website: www.hotelsofsask.com

Top Things To See

- Cast your eyes on some dashing 'Mounties': **Regina**, the Provincial capital, is the home of Canada's only training academy for **Royal Canadian Mounted Police** and the **RCMP Centennial Museum**. Regina was once called 'Pile of Bones' but was renamed in honour of Queen Victoria. Its centrepiece is the **Wascana Centre**, a huge urban park (one of the largest in North America) containing the **McKenzie Art Gallery** and **Saskatchewan Centre of the Arts**. The park also provides an impressive setting for the **Legislative Building**, the **Royal Saskatchewan Museum** and the **Kramer/IMAX Theatre**.
- Check out **Moose Jaw**, once a quiet trading post, which achieved notoriety during Prohibition in the 1920s when it played host to gangsters, including Al 'Scarface' Capone, and played a pivotal role in the distilling, bootlegging and rum running business. The **Tunnels of Moose Jaw** tours provide an excellent account of the town's turbulent and exciting history. Another popular Moose Jaw attraction is the **Temple Gardens Mineral Spa and Resort**. Visitors can take the waters (drawn from porous rock formations more than 1350m (4500ft) below ground) in the hot indoor and outdoor mineral pools. The **Highway** follows the cavernous **Qu'Appelle Valley**, a sunken garden studded with lakes that runs two thirds of the way across the province.
- At **Fort Qu'Appelle**, gaze out at the shimmering and serene lakeside recreation parks, **Katepwa Point** and **Echo Valley**. The **Good Spirit Lake Provincial Parks** are also very pretty.
- Venture upon the highest point of land between Labrador and the Rocky Mountains and look upon the afforested oasis of **Cypress Hills Park**.
- Find the Ukrainian influences upon Saskatchewan: the **Yellowhead Highway**, running eastwards from **Saskatoon** to **Yorkton**, near the border with Manitoba, is a good way to tour the grain belt, once settled by Ukrainians. This is evident through the area's many silver-domed Orthodox churches, such as that at **Veregin**.
- There are two national parks in Saskatchewan. **Prince Albert National Park of Canada** is a hilly, forested area with hundreds of lakes, ponds and rivers, consisting of nearly 30 per cent water. Animal species that can be seen in the park include bison (in the southwest corner), white pelicans (**Lavallée Lake**), lynx, timber wolf, elk, moose and black bear. Its most developed area is at **Waskesiu Lake**, which has lodge and cottage accommodation and good facilities for camping, recreation and watersports, including water-skiing, sailing, canoeing and kayaking. Further off to the northwest is **Meadow Lake**, which has

---

good accommodation and facilities for hunting and winter sports. The **Grasslands National Park of Canada** is in the southwest of the province.

Top Things To Do

- The south of the province is particularly good for **birdwatching**. The **Network Reserve** sites of **Chaplin Lake** and **Quill Lakes** are home to over 300 species including rare ferruginous hawks, peregrine falcons and Hudsonian godwits.
- The **fishing** season is from May to March, and ice fishing is popular in the winter. There are over 68 species of fish found in Saskatchewan, and 100,000 lakes, rivers and streams. Especially excellent fishing opportunities are available on **Lac la Ronge** and on the **Churchill River**.
- Try some **wintersports**: **skiing**, **skating** and **ice hockey** are all provided for. There are at least 13 downhill and over 25 cross-country skiing areas. **Curling** is also popular and was named the official sport of Saskatchewan in 2001.
- Enjoy some traditional parades and **rodeo**. **Buffalo Days** in the capital, **Regina**, is a festival lasting several days at the beginning of August. On the west side of the Province, **Swift Current** also hosts an annual **Frontier Days Festival**.
- **Manitou Beach** has the **Manitou Springs Mineral Spa**, where visitors may relax and float effortlessly in the very salty, warm, mineral-rich waters which are pumped from **Little Manitou Lake** into pools in the spa and are believed to provide relief from a variety of ailments.

TOURIST INFORMATION

Tourism Saskatchewan
1922 Park Street, Regina, Saskatchewan S4N 7M4, Canada
Tel: (306) 787 9600 *or* (877) 237 2273 (toll-free in USA and Canada).
Website: www.sasktourism.com

Entertainment

FOOD & DRINK: A good selection of restaurants can be found in all the province's cities and major towns catering to all tastes and budgets. Alcohol is sold only in licensed stores, licensed restaurants, cocktail lounges, dining and beverage rooms. Retail outlets operate throughout the province.

Regional specialities:
- Whitefish and pickerel are marketed by Native American co-operatives.
- Wild rice harvested by Native Americans is an excellent accompaniment to the abundant wild fowl which includes partridge, prairie chicken, wild duck and goose.
- *Saskatoon berries*, similar to blueberries, are used for jams, jellies and *saskatoon pie*, eaten with fresh country cream. Other wild berries include pinchberries and cranberries which make a tart and tangy jelly, ideal with wild fowl meals.

Legal drinking age: 19 years.

NIGHTLIFE: There are several nightclubs in the major cities; bars and restaurants in most main towns have live entertainment as well as music and dancing. The best times for nightlife are during the annual summer fairs held regularly in all the major towns. The days of the settlers and cowboys are recreated with people dressing in costumes and eating traditional foods. The emphasis changes in each town and according to the time of year. An example can be found in the capital, Regina, with a festival lasting several days – *Buffalo Days* (see *Top Things To Do*).

SHOPPING: There are many small craft stores that offer pottery, stained glass, silkscreens, rock jewellery, potash clocks, embroidered leather, beadwork, woodwork and denim. All the major chains are well represented in Saskatchewan

Business

COMMERCIAL INFORMATION

Saskatchewan Chamber of Commerce
1920 Broad Street, Regina, Saskatchewan S4P 3V2, Canada
Tel: (306) 352 2671.
Website: www.actionsask.com

Saskatchewan Industry and Resources
2103 - 11th Avenue, Regina, Saskatchewan S4P 3V7, Canada
Tel: (306) 787 4765 (head office) *or* (866) 727 5427.
Website: www.ir.gov.sk.ca

Yukon

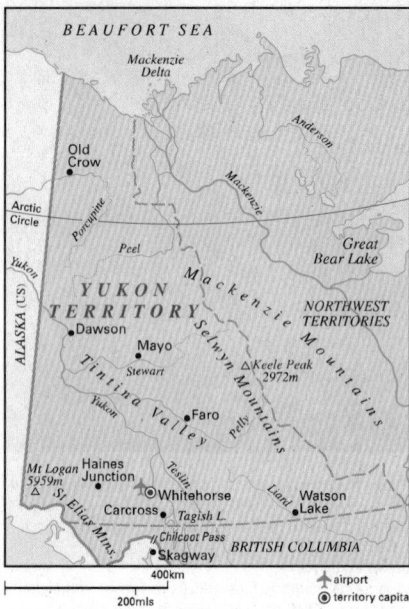

Location: Northwest Canada.

Time: GMT - 8 (GMT - 7 in summer).
Summer officially lasts from the first Sunday in April to the Saturday before the last Sunday in October.

Overview

The Yukon Territory, in Canada's far northwest, is perhaps best known as the site of the Klondike Gold Rush. Towns such as Dawson City still offer a snapshot of the spirit of those times of boom and discovery at the turn of the last century. Even the food across the Territory recalls the meals of prospectors, such as sourdough bread and pancakes. You can still enter certain bars in the Yukon and sip at tipples such as the 'Gold Rush' cocktail, a blend of gold foil and whisky - two of the Territory's most important exports.

However, what might intrigue adventure- or nature lovers more than its human history is its landscape of endless skies, gigantic lakes and sharp, clean air. The Yukon Territory consists mainly of mountain ranges cut by the mighty Yukon River and its tributaries. Indeed, Canada's highest mountain, Mount Logan, is situated in the Yukon. Another popular draw to the Territory is its high recordings of the Northern Lights (*aurora borealis*), ribbons of colour that illuminate the vast night skies. This unspoilt wilderness is relatively well served by roads left over from the days of the gold rush and from an attempt to exploit oil reserves. The Yukon Territory therefore combines the best of scenes with the best of facilities and accessibility.

Whether you seek solitude or escapade, everything is catered for here – and by nature itself.

General Information

AREA: 531,844 sq km (205,345 sq miles).
POPULATION: 31,000 (2005 estimate).
POPULATION DENSITY: 0.06 per sq km.
CAPITAL: Whitehorse. **Population:** 16,843 (2001).
GEOGRAPHY: The Yukon Territory, Canada's 'last frontier', is a largely mountainous and forested wilderness located in the northwest of the country. It borders the US State of Alaska to the west, Canada's Northwest Territories to the east and British Columbia to the south. The Yukon Territory is bisected by the valley of the Yukon River, which passes to the west of the Mackenzie Mountains. Mount Logan, in the St Elias Range on the border with Alaska, is the second-highest peak in North America at 5959m (19,550ft).
LANGUAGE: Although Canada is officially bilingual (English and French), English is more commonly spoken in the territory.

Climate

Summers are warm with almost continuous daylight during June. Winters are bitterly cold.

Required clothing: *Summer* – days can be hot, but sweaters and light jackets are advised for the evenings. *Spring and Autumn* – coats and gloves are required for outdoor activities. *Winter* – thermal underwear, wool sweaters, parkas, wool gloves or mittens and mukluks or felt-lined boots are advised for the winter.

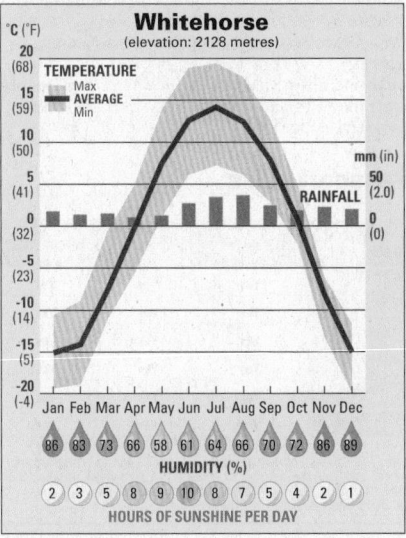

Public Holidays

Yukon Territory observes all the Public Holidays observed nationwide (see the general *Canada* section) and, in addition, the beneath Public Holidays listed for the January 2006-June 2007 period.
2006: Feb 24 Heritage Day. Aug 15 Discovery Day.
2007: Feb 23 Heritage Day.

Travel - International

AIR:

 The main international services are run by *Air Canada (AC)*, who operate regular flights from Whitehorse to Vancouver. *Air North* provides flights from Calgary, Edmonton and Vancouver to Whitehorse and *First Air* flies from Whitehorse to Fort Simpson and Yellowknife, Northwest Territories.
Main airport: *Whitehorse International Airport (YXY).*
SEA:

 Cruise ships and passenger and vehicle ferries operate from Bellingham in Washington (USA) and Vancouver and Prince Rupert in British Columbia, arriving at Skagway in Alaska and connecting with Whitehorse by motorcoach, or train/motorcoach combination. Whitehorse is approximately 180km (113 miles) from Skagway. Ferry information can be obtained by phone (tel: (800) 642 0066; toll-free in USA and Canada).
ROAD:

 The major road in the region is the Alaska Highway, running from Alaska to British Columbia through Whitehorse. The Dempster Highway connects Dawson City with Inuvik in the north. The Klondike Highway connects Skagway, Alaska to Dawson City, Yukon. **Bus/Coach:** Scheduled bus services are available between most Yukon communities. *Greyhound Canada* operates services six times a week from Edmonton, Alberta and Vancouver, British Columbia to Whitehorse during the summer. Direct coach transfers run daily from May to September between Stagway and Whitehorse or combination *White Pass and Yukon Route* rail and coach transfers are available.

Accommodation

HOTELS:

 There are 86 hotel/motels with approximately 2500 rooms in the Yukon Territory. Because of the heavy tourist flow through the region in summer, reservations should be considered. The majority of hotels and motels are located in the larger centres, but facilities are available along the highways and in the smaller communities. Some hotels are closed for the winter. Whilst not mandatory, some Yukon Territory accommodation have opted to be graded through the Canada Select Program. For further information, contact Tourism Yukon.

BED & BREAKFAST:

 There are many bed & breakfast properties in the Yukon Territory.

CAMPING/CARAVANNING:

 Camping is advised only in summer and allowed only on government or private campsites. A number of companies can arrange **motor camper** rentals, with a range of fully-equipped vehicles. Full details can be obtained from Tourism Yukon.

ACCOMMODATION INFORMATION

Bed & Breakfast Association of Yukon
PO Box 31518, Whitehorse, Yukon Y1A 6K8, Canada
Website: www.yukonbandb.com

Top Things To See

- Yukon's capital since 1953, **Whitehorse**, lies on the west bank of the **Yukon River**, the water route taken by thousands of eager prospectors during the **Klondike Gold Rush** of 1898. The majority of the Territory's population is concentrated here. The **McBride Museum** houses many of the artefacts of the gold rush era, including **Sam McGee's Cabin**. On the river itself, the **SS Klondike**, a restored sternwheeler vessel, is open for viewing. The **MV Schwatka** offers a two-hour cruise of the **Miles Canyon**.
- **Carcross**, an hour's drive south of Whitehorse, lies between the **Nares** and **Bennett Lakes** at the foot of **Nares Mountain**; the **Caribou**, Yukon's oldest hotel, can be found here. Carcross connects to Skagway in Alaska via the **Klondike Highway**.
- Stare up at **Mount Logan**, which is the highest mountain in Canada at 5959m (19,545ft), in **Kluane National Park and Reserve**. The park is also host to the largest non-polar icefields in the world. Special flightseeing tours of this park can be arranged from Whitehorse and a variety of other Yukon Territory communities.
- In the north of the Territory are two further national parks, **Ivvavik** and **Vuntut**. Ivvavik has a non-glaciated landscape with abundant wildlife, significant archaeological sites and the **Firth River**. The recently established **Vuntut National Park** currently has no facilities or visitor information centre. Owing to the lack of a tourist infrastructure, most visitors might prefer to undertake expeditions to the wild backcountry of the Yukon Territory in the company of a licensed outfitter or guide.
- Look up at the skies and you may just see the **Northern Lights** (*aurora borealis*) flashing against the darkness. The magical ambience of Yukon winter with its crisp air and snowy scene is perfect for watching this dynamic display. The **Northern Lights Space and Science Centre** is situated on **Watson Lake**.

Top Things To Do

- **Canoeing** is particularly popular. In summer, the tributaries of the *Yukon River* (including the **Teslin**, the **Big Salmon** and the **Pelly**) offer fast-flowing, flat water. Most trips are easy to arrange because starting and ending points have roadside access. There is also the advantage of being able to re-supply from communities located along the riverbank. Trips ranging from a few hours to several weeks can be organised. There is no shortage of white water for more experienced canoeists. While wild rivers such as the **Bonnet Plume** and the **Firth** must be reached by bush plane, other spectacular rivers, such as the **Tatchenshini** and the **South Macmillan** are accessible by road. Simple riverside campsites provide accommodation. River travellers are advised to leave details of their itineraries with the authorities before setting out.
- **Mount Logan**, in the **St Elias Range** in **Kluane National Park**, is the second-highest peak in North America at 5959m (19,550ft). **Cross-country skiing** is possible in winter.
- Near Skagway (Alaska) is **Dyea**, the starting point of the famous 50km **Chilkoot Trail**, where **hikers** can retrace the footsteps of the gold rush stampeders. **Dawson City**, at the heart of the **Klondike**, can be reached by road or by the Yukon River. Many areas of the city have now been designated national historic sites, with buildings such as the **Commissioner's Residence** and the **Palace Grand Theatre** bearing witness to its former glories. Each summer the latter produces an authentic 1898 vaudeville show – the **Gaslight Follies**. **Tours** on the Yukon River on the miniature sternwheeler Yukon Lou visit the **Sternwheelers Graveyard**

and **Pleasure Island**. Visitors can **pan gold** at Guggieville or Claim 33 on Bonanza Creek, the site of the original claim which sparked off the 1898 **Gold Rush**.

- Set up **camp** in **Tombstone**, with its spectacular views: you'll have mountains and lakes at every angle. You will most likely need a permit to camp and you will only be able to camp in designated areas, but you should not miss out on the chance to set up tent beneath the stars in pristine wilderness. You'll also have your head in the clouds – both literally and figuratively!
- Go **mountain biking** on Yukon's impressive mountain ranges, through flourishes of colour, from the turquoise skies to the purple fireweed flowers that speckle the highland. The Yukon Territory is a mosaic of historical trails. Arduous climbs and rapid descents are compensated by the chance to race through stunning scenery. If you fancy a challenge, why not enter Yukon's annual **Kluane/Chilkat International Bike Relay**, which sees contenders cycling through a UNESCO World Heritage Site?

TOURIST INFORMATION

Tourism Yukon
Street address: 1st Floor, 100 Hanson Street, Whitehorse, Yukon Y1A 2C6, Canada
Postal address: PO Box 2703, Whitehorse, Yukon Y1A 2C6, Canada
Tel: (867) 667 5340 *or* (800) 661 0494 (toll-free) *or* (800) 789 8566 (brochure request).
Website: www.touryukon.com

Yukon First Nations Tourism Association
Street address: One 1109 First Avenue, Whitehorse, Yukon Y1A 5G4, Canada
Postal address: PO Box 4518, Whitehorse, Yukon Y1A 2R8, Canada
Tel: (867) 667 7698.
Website: www.yfnta.org

Entertainment

FOOD & DRINK: Some of Yukon's food is very distinctive but difficult to produce commercially. There are restaurants throughout the area, but the best selection is in Whitehorse, Dawson City and Watson Lake. Most alcohol is imported from other areas of Canada and the USA.
Regional specialities:
- Moose meat is cooked in several ways from steaming to smoking or pot roasting, and accompanied by *sourdough* and vegetables.
- Dall sheep, mountain goat, caribou and porcupine are also eaten, often in burgers.
- Wild fish feature on most menus.
- Lots of seafood, including Arctic grayling, trout, Kokanee salmon, Alaska King Crab and halibut.
- Yukon's gold mining past is reflected in some specialities served there, such as buffalo burgers, musk ox chops and Alaskan salmon.
Regional drinks:
- A local speciality is *hooch* (a blend of imported and Canadian rum); it is only available in the Yukon Territory.
- Whitehorse is home to the *Chilkoot Brewing Company*, which produces unique beers and ales.
NIGHTLIFE: Nightlife is best during the historical festivals and carnivals reflecting the pioneer spirit that explored the region. However, Dawson City has legalised gambling, live vaudeville theatre and a floor show at *Gertie's* featuring Cancan girls and honky-tonk piano.
SHOPPING: Special items include First Nation moccasins, jewellery, art and carvings. Check with Revenue Canada or the Visitor Reception Centres to determine qualification for the Goods and Services Tax rebate. **Shopping hours**: Mon-Wed and Sat 1000-1800, Thurs-Fri 1000-2100.

Business

COMMERCIAL INFORMATION

Yukon Chamber of Commerce
Suite 101, 307 Jarvis Street, Whitehorse, Yukon Territory Y1A 2H3, Canada
Tel: (867) 667 2000 *or* (800) 661 0543.
Website: www.yukonchamber.com

Yukon Convention Bureau
Suite 205, 4133 Fourth Avenue, Whitehorse, Yukon Territory Y1A 1H8, Canada
Tel: (867) 668 3555.
Website: www.ycb.ca

A B C D E F G H I J K L M N O P Q R S T U V W X Y Z

Cape Verde

100km
50mls
✈ international airport

Santo Antão
Porto Novo
São Vicente
Mindelo
Santa Luzia
Branco
Raso
Vila da
Ribeira Brava
São Nicolau
Sal
Santa
Maria

Vila de
Sal Rei
Boa
Vista

CAPE
VERDE

ATLANTIC
OCEAN

Sotavento

Santiago
Maio
Pico do Cano
Fogo 2829m
Brava
São Filipe
Porto Inglês
PRAIA

Location: Atlantic Ocean, off coast of West Africa.

Time: GMT - 1.

Overview

The Portuguese discovered Cape Verde in the 15th century; its islands were uninhabited and there was no evidence of previous settlement. By the late 15th century, settlement had begun. Situated in the Atlantic Ocean, 600km (450 miles) west-northwest of Senegal, Cape Verde comprises 10 volcanic islands and five islets in two groups: the Balavento (Windwards) and the Sotavento (Leewards). The Cape Verde islands count as Africa's most westerly point.

Evidently, the islands are no longer as verdant as they were when the Portuguese named them, but they offer much to interest the traveller: spectacular mountain scenery and beautiful deserted beaches. Indeed, every island on Cape Verde seems to have its own distinct character, from the lush and lively Santiago to the sandy and salty Sal, and from the volcanic Sao Nicolau to the diving paradise of Boa Vista. There are also good markets on some of the islands, and some are livelier than others. São Vicente's is renowned for its exuberant Carnival, whilst the Baia das Gatas Festival is a more traditional affair but one that still has people boogying until the early hours to Cape-Verdean rhythms. In all the islands, however, is a fascinating admixture of African and European custom and conduct. This is best reflected in the foods on offer, with Portuguese foods (such as fish- and seafood-based dishes, olive oil, garlic, lemon and sausage) and African foods (stews, beans, maize and tropical crops) comfortably combined on most menus.

Many of the towns on the islands have retained their Portuguese architecture and worth a visit just to see these. Cape Verde's Government is now trying to develop the tourist industry, and the infrastructure is being expanded to accommodate the increasing number of visitors attracted to this unusual but attractive destination. As Cape Verde comprises islands, it will come as no great surprise to learn that, in the midst of a vibrant Creole culture, are very good conditions for watersports, such as windsurfing, diving (with shipwrecks dating back to the 16th century) and sailing. However, many might argue that Cape Verde's isolation is a blessing, leaving these islands unspoiled and comparatively undiscovered. Since achieving independence in 1975, Cape Verde has struggled somewhat economically (it has few natural

resources and frequently suffers from very low rainfall). However, the Government is sure to succeed in attracting visitors to Cape Verde when it offers so much natural beauty, which will surely bolster the islands' fiscal situation.

General Information

AREA: 4033 sq km (1557 sq miles).

POPULATION: 482,000 (2005).

POPULATION DENSITY: 112.5 per sq km.

CAPITAL: Cidade de Praia. **Population:** 106,757 (2005).

GEOGRAPHY: Cape Verde is situated in the Atlantic Ocean, 600km (450 miles) west-northwest of Senegal and comprises 10 volcanic islands and five islets in two groups: *Balavento* (Windwards) and *Sotavento* (Leewards). In the former group are the islands of São Vicente, Santo Antão, São Nicolau, Santa Luzia, Sal and Boa Vista, along with the smaller islands of Branco and Raso; the Sotavento group comprises the islands of Santiago, Maio, Fogo and Brava, along with the smaller islands of Rei and Rombo. Most have mountain peaks; the highest being Pico do Cano, an active volcano, which is on Fogo. The islands are generally rocky and eroded, and have never been able to support more than subsistence agriculture (maize, bananas, sugar cane and coffee are the main crops); low rainfall over the last 10 years has crippled food production and forced the islands to depend on international aid.

GOVERNMENT: Republic. Gained independence from Portugal in 1975. **Head of State:** President Pedro Pires since 2001. **Head of Government:** Prime Minister José Maria Neves since 2001. **Recent history:** The MPD held onto both Presidency and National Assembly in 1995 but lost both to the PAICV at the most recent elections in early 2001. The extremely close Presidential race was won by the PAICV's Pedro Rodrigues Pires with a margin of just 17 votes over the MPD's Carlos de Carvalho. Cape Verde has pursued a determinedly non-aligned foreign policy, reflected in its being chosen as mediator in the settlement of a variety of international disputes, including Angola. More recently, in 1998, it hosted talks to reach a settlement of the conflict in Guinea Bissau. Cape Verde maintains close relations with Portugal, Brazil and other Portuguese-speaking African countries in the PALOP group (Angola, Guinea-Bissau, Mozambique and São Tomé).

A new constitution introduced in 1992 allows for the election of an *Assembleia Nacional* (national assembly) with 79 deputies and a President who serves as Head of State, both elected by adult suffrage for five-year terms.

LANGUAGE: The official language is Portuguese. Creole is spoken by most of the inhabitants. Some English, French, German and Spanish are widely spoken.

RELIGION: 92.8 per cent of the population are Roman Catholic with a Protestant minority of one per cent.

ELECTRICITY: 220 volts AC, 50Hz.

SOCIAL CONVENTIONS: The usual European social courtesies should be observed.

Climate

Generally temperate, but rainfall is very low. The rainy season is August to October when rainfall is unpredictable.

Required clothing: Lightweight throughout the year, tropical for midsummer.

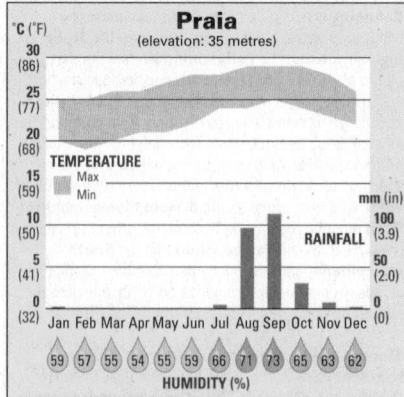

Praia
(elevation: 35 metres)

°C (°F)
30 (86)
25 (77)
20 (68)
15 (59)
10 (50)
5 (41)
0 (32)

TEMPERATURE
Max
Min

mm (in)
100 (3.9)
RAINFALL
50 (2.0)
0 (0)

Jan Feb Mar Apr May Jun Jul Aug Sep Oct Nov Dec

59 57 55 54 55 59 66 71 73 65 63 62
HUMIDITY (%)

Communications

Telephone: Country code: 238. IDD is possible to main cities. Improvements to rural areas are in progress.

Mobile telephone: Roaming agreements exist with some international mobile phone companies, but travellers should check with their service provider. Coverage is variable, but generally good in towns.

Internet: Major hotels offer laptop connections. Public access is available at the offices of *Cabo Verde Telecom*. Privately-run business centres in the main towns offer e-mail, Internet and fax facilities.

Post: Postal facilities can be slow with deliveries to Europe, normally taking over a week.

MEDIA: A free press is guaranteed by law, but most media are state-controlled. There are a few private radio stations. Portuguese and French radio are available via FM relays.

Press: Newspapers are in Portuguese. There are no daily newspapers. The weekly newspapers with the highest circulation figures are *Horizonte* and the independent *A Semana*.

TV: *Televisao Nacional De Cabo Verde* is a state-run channel.

Radio: Stations include state-run *Radio Nacional De Cabo Verde*, as well as *Radio Nova* in Sao Vicente and *Radio Comercial* in Praia.

Passport/Visa

	Passport Required?	Visa Required?	Return Ticket Required?
Full British	Yes	Yes	Yes
Australian	Yes	Yes	Yes
Canadian	Yes	Yes	Yes
USA	Yes	Yes	Yes
Other EU	Yes	Yes	Yes
Japanese	Yes	Yes	Yes

Note: *Regulations and requirements may be subject to change at short notice, and you are advised to contact the appropriate diplomatic or consular authority before finalising travel arrangements. Any numbers in the chart refer to the footnotes below.*

PASSPORTS: Passport valid for at least six months required by all.

VISAS: Required by all except the following:
(a) nationals of ECOWAS countries, Angola and South Africa;
(b) former nationals of Cape Verde, their spouses and children, provided holding proof of origin;
(c) those continuing their journey to a third destination provided holding onward documentation and not leaving the airport.

Types of visa and cost: *Transit, Tourist, Business:* €38 (single entry); €72 (multiple-entry, for *Business* visas only); paid by cheque or postal order. Prices may fluctuate - enquire at nearest Embassy or Consulate for details.

Validity: Valid for six months from date of issue for visits of up to 90 days, multiple-entry visas are valid for up to one year.

Note: US nationals can obtain visas valid for five years.

Application to: Consulate (or Consular Section at Embassy); see *Passport/Visa Information.*

Application requirements: (a) Two passport-size photos. (b) One application form. (c) Valid passport. (d) Fee. (e) Return/onward ticket. (f) A stamped addressed envelope if applying by mail.

Working days required: Where there are no complications, visas may be issued immediately; however, it is advisable to anticipate up to two days' delay.

PASSPORT/VISA INFORMATION

Embassy of the Republic of Cape Verde in the USA
3415 Massachusetts Avenue, NW, Washington, DC 20007, USA
Tel: (202) 965 6820.
Website: www.virtualcapeverde.net

Embassy of the Republic of Cape Verde in the UK
18-20 Stanley Street, Liverpool L1 6AF, UK
Tel: (0151) 236 0206.

Money

Currency: Cape Verde Escudo (CVE) = 100 centavos. Notes are in denominations of CVE5000, 2000, 1000 and 500. Coins are in denominations of CVE200, 100, 50, 20, 10, 5 and 1.

Currency exchange: Available at the airport and in local banks. Currency cannot be reconverted, except in Portugal. There are ATMs found in Sal, Praia and São Vincent.

Credit & debit cards: Credit cards are rarely used. A few major hotels accept Visa. Currency can be obtained in banks from credit cards but charges are very high.

Traveller's cheques: Accepted in main towns and tourist areas. To avoid additional exchange rate charges, travellers are advised to take traveller's cheques in Pounds Sterling or US Dollars.

Currency restrictions: The import and export of local currency is prohibited. The import of foreign currency is unlimited, subject to declaration on arrival and on departure. The export of foreign currency is limited to the equivalent of CVE1,000,000 or the amount declared on arrival, whichever is the larger.

Banking hours: Mon-Fri 0800-1400.
Exchange rate indicators:
Rate at time of publishing
£1.00= CVE163.94
$1.00= CVE92.88.

Duty Free

The following goods may be imported into Cape Verde without incurring customs duty:
200 cigarettes; one litre of liquor; a reasonable amount of perfume, lotion and eau de cologne in opened bottles.
Currency must be declared on arrival.
Note: There is, in principle, no free import of tobacco products and alcoholic beverages.

Public Holidays

Below are listed Public Holidays for the January 2006-June 2007 period.
2006: Jan 1 New Year's Day. **Jan 20** Heroes' Day. **Feb 27** Carnival. **May 1** Labour Day. **Jul 5** Independence Day. **Aug 15** Assumption (Day of Our Lady of Grace). **Sep 12** National Day. **Nov 1** All Saints' Day. **Dec 25** Christmas Day.
2007: Jan 1 New Year's Day. **Jan 20** Heroes' Day. **Feb 27** Carnival. **May 1** Labour Day.

Health

	Special Precautions?	Certificate Required?
Yellow Fever	2	2
Cholera	No	1
Typhoid & Polio	3	3
Malaria	4	N/A

Note: *Regulations and requirements may be subject to change at short notice, and you are advised to contact your doctor well in advance of your intended date of departure. Any numbers in the chart refer to the footnotes below.*

1: Following WHO guidelines issued in 1973, a cholera vaccination certificate is not a condition of entry to Cape Verde. However, cholera is a risk in this country and precautions could be considered. Up-to-date advice should be sought before deciding whether these precautions should include vaccination as medical opinion is divided over its effectiveness. For more information, see the *Health* appendix.
2: Yellow Fever is endemic. A certificate of vaccination is required if travelling from other countries in the endemic zone.
3: Typhoid fever is widespread and vaccination may be necessary. Polio vaccination may also be advised.
4: There is a limited risk of malaria from September to November on São Tiago Island.
Food & drink: All water should be regarded as being potentially contaminated. All drinking water should be bottled, boiled or carbonated. Water used for brushing teeth or making ice should have first been boiled or otherwise sterilised. Milk is unpasteurised and should be boiled. Powdered or tinned milk is available and is advised, but make sure that it is reconstituted with pure water. Avoid all dairy products and food from street vendors. Only eat well-cooked meat and fish, preferably served hot. Pork, salad and mayonnaise may carry increased risk. Vegetables should be cooked and fruit peeled.
Other risks: *Hepatitis A* and *E* are highly endemic in sub-saharan Africa, but have very low occurrence in Cape Verde, but precautions are still advisable. *Hepatitis B* is hyperendemic in the region. Vaccination against *tetanus* is advised. *Giardia* occurs.
Health care: Health insurance, including emergency repatriation cover, is advised, although in-patient treatment is free in general wards on presentation of a passport. Treatment is private and expensive on the smaller islands.

Travel - International

AIR:
The national airline is *TACV* (website: www.tacv.cv) which offers flights to several European cities, including Amsterdam, Lisbon, Madrid, Milan, Paris and Porto, as well as to Las Palmas (Canary Islands). Information on international and internal flights, and flight tickets may be obtained from Cape Verde Travel, TACV's agent in the UK (tel: (01964) 536 191; website: www.capeverdetravel.com).
Approximate flight times: From *London* to Lisbon (Portugal) is 2 hours and from *Lisbon* to Sal is 4 hours; from *Boston* to Sal is 7 hours; from *Paris* to Sal is 6 hours. Note that the stopover in Lisbon will sometimes be overnight if flying by *TAP Air Portugal*. The most convenient routes from *London* are via Paris and Amsterdam, where there are direct connections with no stopover time.
Main airports: *Amílcar Cabral (SID)* on Sal, 2km (1 mile) south of Espargos is the only airport with a runway long enough to take jets; there are six others throughout the islands. *To/from the airport:* Taxis are available to the city centre and to resort areas. *Facilities:* Several banks, duty free shops, refreshments, tourist information, car hire and left luggage facilities.
Praia International Airport, Santiago, opened at the end of 2005, taking flights from Paris, Amsterdam and Lisbon. International airports are under construction on the islands of St Vincent and Boa Vista, due to open 2007-2008.
Departure tax: None.
SEA:
Main ports: *Mindelo* and *Praia* are the principal ports. *São Vicente* is served by passenger and cargo ships, but sea services are not frequent and may be costly.

Travel - Internal

AIR:
TACV – Cabo Verde Airlines (website: www.tacv.cv) is the main domestic carrier. There are internal flights available to all inhabited islands except Brava and San Antao.
Passes: The *Cape Verde Airpass*, available from TACV to passengers booking their long-distance tickets through the airline or their agents, offers discounted flights within Cape Verde. A minimum of two internal flights must be booked and the pass is valid for 21 days. These must be purchased with transatlantic tickets. Private charters are available from the *Cape Verde Express* (website: www.capeverdeexpress.com) air-taxi service.
SEA:
There is a daily ferry service operating between the port of Mindelo, São Vincente and Santo Antao. Cargo ships may also accept passengers and regular services connect Santiago, Fogo and Brava; however, these are primaily for cargo supply and demand and so are inconsistent. Sea conditions around Cape Verde are sometimes treacherous, due to many submerged rocks. Travel by sea to the southern islands of Brava and Fogo can be particularly disrupted.
ROAD:
There are over 2250km (1400 miles) of roads on the islands, of which one-third are cobbled. There is a road improvement programme underway to convert cobblestone roads into asphalt. Road conditions and driving standards are generally of a reasonable quality, although paved roads are mostly narrow and winding. Traffic drives on the right and seat belts must be worn at all times. Children under 12 years old should sit in the back seat. Local transport is usually provided by an *Aluguer* (minibus or pick-up truck); they are used by locals and visitors. Taxi fares should be agreed in advance, although some prefer to use the taximeter. Drivers can be hired to see the main sights on the islands. Buses are satisfactory. **Car hire**: Available on the main islands, book in advance when possible. **Documentation**: An International Driving Permit is legally required and proof of insurance should be displayed on the car windscreen.
TRAVEL TIMES: The following chart gives the approximate travel times (in hours and minutes) from **Cidade de Praia** to other major cities/towns in Cape Verde:

	Air	Sea
Saõ Vicente	**0.45**	**-**
Sal	**0.45**	**-**
Boa Vista	**0.30**	**-**
Brava	**-**	**12.00**

Travel Advice

Most visits to Cape Verde are trouble-free but you should be aware of the global risk of indiscriminate international terrorist attacks, which could be against civillian targets, including places frequented by foreigners.
This advice is based on information provided by the Foreign and Commonwealth Office in the UK. It is correct at time of publishing. As the situation can change rapidly, visitors are advised to contact the following organisations for the latest travel advice:

British Foreign and Commonwealth Office
Tel: (0845) 850 2829.
Website: www.fco.gov.uk

US Department of State
Website: http://travel.state.gov/travel

Accommodation

HOTELS/PENSIONS:
The range of accommodation is increasing rapidly. There are international hotels on the main islands. Otherwise, there are small hotels on the smaller islands. There are also *pensions*. For further information, contact CI - Carbo Verde Investimentos *or* Cape Verde Travel (see *Top Things To Do*).

Top Things To See & Do

- **Santiago**, the largest and most populated of Cape Verde's nine populated islands, has a mountainous, lush interior fringed by small sandy beaches. The island's capital, **Praia**, is a lively, pleasant town with a good nightlife. Other attractions include **Cidade Velha**, the first Portuguese settlement on Cape Verde. There are ruins and old buildings and, on the hill above, the **Fort Real de San Felipe**, an old Portuguese fort. The attractive fishing village of **Tarrafal** features one of the island's best beaches and contains the old colonial prison where the Portuguese dictator, Salazar, held dissidents from all over his empire in the first two-thirds of the 20th century. This is currently being restored.
- Make sure you check out Cape Verde's fantastic **beaches**: in particular, go see the fine white sand beaches of **Sal** and the black sand beaches of **Sao Nicolau**. The ever-present sea provides great **sailing**. **Surfing** and **windsurfing** are available on Sal, although the surfing is not generally suitable for beginners. **Diving** is gaining in popularity, mainly on the islands of Sal and **Boa Vista**, which offer qualified personnel and equipment. These islands also offer good wreck sites. Water temperatures are good all year round, though the seas can be rough.
- Find the famous **salt pits** of Sal, after which the island is named, which produced salt for much of the former Portuguese empire.
- Listen to some **live music** on the island where Cape Verde's most famous daughter, Cesaria Evora (an internationally-known singer who performs in the traditional style), hails: **São Vicente**. Music is an integral part of daily life in islands such as this one. The deep-water port of **Mindelo** is a lively town with old colonial buildings and a thriving local music scene. São Vicente's **Carnival** is the liveliest in Cape Verde, while the traditional **Baia das Gatas Festival**, which usually falls in August, has become internationally renowned for the standard of its music.
- Unveil an abundance of unique **plant life** on **Brava**, a lush island with more rainfall than most, offering beautiful views of the coast from its plateau.
- **Walk** or **climb** the spectacular scenery and rugged coastline of **Santo Antão**. It is one of Cape Verde's greener islands and its interior contains forested hills. Many of the deep flat-bottomed valleys are the craters of extinct volcanoes, long overgrown by trees and tropical vegetation. Its **Ribeira Grande Mountain** takes a day to climb but is well worth the effort. It is advisable to take a guide. The mountainous island of **Fogo** is also great for hikes with excellent views, and it also has an active volcano in its midst.
- Sample **Cape Verdean rum** or **grog**, produced on Santo Antão.

TOURIST INFORMATION

Agência Cabo-verdiana de Promoção do Investimentos (CI)
Rotundo do Cruz do Papa, Achada Santo António, PO Box 89C, Praia, Santiago, Cape Verde
Tel: 260 4111/0 *or* 262 1488 *or* 2689.
Website: www.virtualcapeverde.net

Cape Verde Travel in the UK
14 Market Place, Hornseam, East Yorkshire HU18 1AW, UK
Tel: (01964) 536 191.
Website: www.capeverdetravel.co.uk

Entertainment

FOOD & DRINK: There is an increasing number of restaurants and cafes on the islands.
National specialities:
• *Pastel com diablo dentro* ('pastry with the devil inside') - a mix of tuna, onions, tomatoes and pastry, made from boiled potatoes and corn flour.
• *Cachupa*, a mess of maize and beans.
• Fruits include mangoes, bananas, papayas, *goiabas* (guavas), *zimbrão*, *tambarinas*, *marmelos*, *azedinhas*, *tamaras* and *cocos*.
National drinks:
• *Aguardiente* (sugar cane rum).
• A San Antao liquor made from coffee, cinnamon, fig leaf, peppermint, orange or lime.
• *Manecome* (local wine from Fogo).
Tipping: It is normal to give 10 per cent for good service.
NIGHTLIFE: Some hotels provide evening entertainment. Small villages will have a lively taverna. Most nightlife is on the main islands: there are 21 nightclubs in Cape Verde - eight on Santiago, seven on Sal, five on São Vicente and one on Fogo. Praia has a cultural centre at which local Cape Verdean artists and instrumentalists perform.

SHOPPING: There are daily markets. The Santa Catarina market is held Wednesday and Saturday. Coconut shells are carved by local craftspeople; there is also pottery, lacework and basketry. **Shopping hours:** Mon-Sat 0800-1200 and 1500-1900.

Business

- **GDP:** US$825 million.
- **Main exports:** Shoes, clothes, fish, bananas, hides, salt and *pozzolana* (volcanic rock used in making cement).
- **Main imports:** Petroleum, foodstuffs, consumer goods and machinery.
- **Main trade partners:** Portugal, Japan, Netherlands and USA.

ECONOMY: About one-quarter of the working population is engaged in agriculture. Maize and beans are the main crops; a variety of fruit and vegetables are also grown. The agricultural sector is especially vulnerable to the periodic droughts that afflict the islands, often lasting for several years. Meanwhile, throughout the 1990s, the fishing industry has received substantial international aid, reflected in the result that the islands' catches now contribute almost half of the total export earnings. Cape Verde joined the International Whaling Commission in 2002 and, with the incentive of an aid package from Japan, has supported the resumption of commercial whaling. The small industrial sector is dominated by fish processing and canning factories, to which electrical and other machinery, chemicals and textiles have recently been added. Mining is confined to salt and pozzolana. Future economic development is being focused on tourism, transhipment facilities and 'offshore' financial services. A further vital source of national income are the remittances provided by émigré communities – some 700,000 Cape Verdeans live abroad, mainly in the USA. Cape Verde is a member of the West African Economic Community (ECOWAS).

BUSINESS ETIQUETTE: All correspondence should be in English or French. Most business links are with Portugal. **Office hours:** Mon-Fri 0800-1230 and 1430-1800.

CONFERENCES/CONVENTIONS: The larger hotels on the main islands can provide conference facilities.

COMMERCIAL INFORMATION

Câmara de Comercio Industria, Agricultura e Serviços de Barlavento
Rua de Luz 31, CP 728, Mindelo, São Vicente, Cape Verde
Tel: 328 495.
Website: www.cciasb.com

Câmara de Comercio Industria e Servícos de Sotavento
Av. Andrade Corvo, Edificio Shopping Moeda, Praia, Santiago, Cape Verde
Tel: 615 352.

Ministry for Education, Science, Youth and Sport (Information on Conferences/Conventions)
Palácio do Governo, Santiago, Praia, Cape Verde
Tel: 610 507.

Cayman Islands

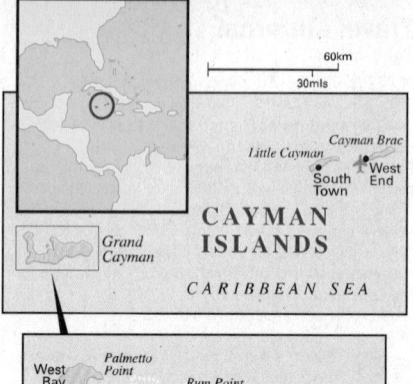

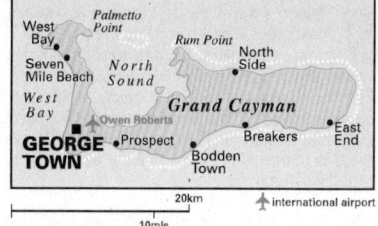

Location: Caribbean, south of Cuba, 770km (480 miles) southwest of Miami.

Time: GMT - 5.

Overview

There are three islands in this British Overseas Territory: Grand Cayman, Little Cayman and Cayman Brac. The latter two are the smaller of the Cayman islands and were discovered by Columbus in 1503. Sir Francis Drake explored the area in 1586, but it was 1670 before the islands came under full British rule. Grand Cayman was settled from Jamaica by 1672; Little Cayman and Cayman Brac were settled some time later and maintained a separate administration until 1877. The Governor of Jamaica held administrative responsibility for the islands until 1962, when Jamaica itself became independent. Since then the islands have had their own Governor appointed by the British Crown (see *Government* in *General Information* section).

It is unlikely that the British, or anybody else for that matter, would have desired the Cayman Islands quite so much when they were first discovered. Columbus originally named the islands 'Las Tortugas' (The Turtles) because they were utterly covered in them. More worryingly, the word 'Cayman' probably derives from the Carib word, 'Caymanas', meaning 'marine crocodile', suggesting that the islands were also the favoured home of scores of lizards. In addition to this, the Cayman Islands have long been associated with the history of buccaneers and pirates, who once established hideouts here. All of this is easy to forget as you luxuriate on wide, sandy beaches with crystal-clear waters that teem with coral reefs and marine creatures. The Seven Mile Beach on Grand Cayman is particularly popular and deservedly so. Rather than combating pirate invasion, the closest you will probably get to exertion is diving in shipwrecks, walking through rainforest, and letting velvety stingray brush against your legs.

The Cayman Islands are indeed a stress-free haven, framed by deep blue skies, twinkling sea and golden sand.

General Information

AREA: 260 sq km (100 sq miles).

POPULATION: 44,270 (official estimate 2005).

POPULATION DENSITY: 168 per sq km (2005).

CAPITAL: George Town. **Population**: 29,000 (2005).

GEOGRAPHY: The Cayman Islands are situated in the Caribbean, 290km (180 miles) northwest of Jamaica, 240km (150 miles) south of Cuba and 770km (480 miles) south of Miami. The island country comprises Grand Cayman, the largest and most populous of the islands, and the sister islands of Little Cayman and Cayman Brac, which lie approximately 143km (89 miles) northeast of Grand Cayman and are separated from each other by a channel about 12km (8 miles) wide. The islands are peaks of a subterranean mountain range extending from Cuba towards the Gulf of Honduras. The beaches are said to be the best in the Caribbean, the most notable being Seven Mile Beach on Grand Cayman. Tall pines line many of the beaches; those located on the east and west coasts are equally well protected offshore by the Barrier Reef.

GOVERNMENT: British Crown Colony since 1670. **Head of**

Credit: ©Cayman Islands Department of Tourism

State: HM Queen Elizabeth II, represented locally by Governor Bruce Dinwiddy since 2002. **Recent history:** McKeeva Bush was defeated in the May 2005 general elections by the *People's Progressive Movement*, led by Kurt Tibbetts.

Following a change of policy, the British Government has announced that it is prepared, in principle, to grant full British citizenship to the inhabitants of the Cayman Islands. As a British Overseas Territory, the Caymans have a Governor who is appointed by the British Monarch. The Governor is responsible for external affairs, security and defence. He is also Chairman of the Executive Council comprising three members appointed by the Governor and four members from the Legislative Assembly, elected by that body itself. The Legislative Assembly comprises the above three members of the Executive Council appointed by the Governor and 15 members elected by universal adult suffrage every four years.

LANGUAGE: English is the official language, with a distinctive 'brogue' reflecting heritage of Welsh, Scottish and English ancestors still distinguishing the speech of the Caymanian people. The number of Jamaican residents in the workforce means the Jamaican *patois* and accompanying heavier accent is also common. Spanish, particularly regional dialects of Central America and Cuba, is also widely spoken.

RELIGION: Mainly Presbyterian with Anglican, Roman Catholic, Seventh Day Adventists, Pilgrims, Pilgrim Holiness Church of God, Jehovah's Witnesses and Bahai minorities on Grand Cayman; Baptists on Cayman Brac.

ELECTRICITY: 120 volts AC, 60Hz. American-style (flat) two-pin plugs are standard.

SOCIAL CONVENTIONS: The mode of life on the Cayman Islands is a blend of local traditions and of US and British patterns of behaviour. Handshaking is the usual greeting. Because of the large number of people with a similar surname (such as Ebanks and Bodden), a person may be introduced by his christian name (such as Mr Tom or Mr Jim). Flowers are acceptable as a gift on arrival or following a visit for a meal. Dinner jackets are seldom worn. Short or long dresses are appropriate for women in the evenings. Casual wear is acceptable in most places, but beachwear is best confined to the beach to avoid offence. Topless bathing is prohibited.

Climate

Very warm, tropical climate throughout the year. High temperatures are moderated by trade winds. The rainy season is from May to October but showers are generally of short duration. The hurricane season is from June to November and, since the islands are low-lying, there is a high risk of flooding if a storm hits them.

Required clothing: Lightweight cottons and linens and a light raincoat or umbrella for the rainy season. Warmer clothes may be needed on cooler evenings.

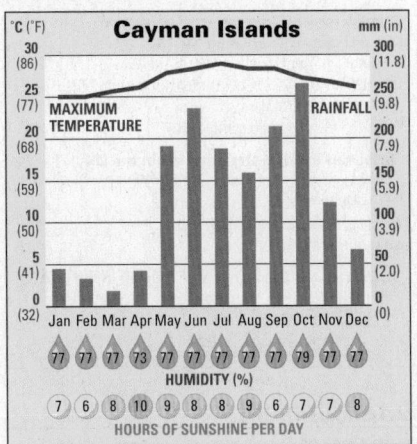

Communications

Telephone: Country code: 1 345. A modern telephone system links the Cayman Islands to the world by submarine cable and satellite. Full IDD is available. A Cardphone service is available at select locations on all three islands. Pre-paid phonecards in values of CI$10, CI$15 and CI$30 can be purchased at the *Cable & Wireless* main office in Anderson Square in George Town and at the *Cayman Brac* post office and petrol stations.

Mobile telephone: Roaming agreements exist with a few international mobile phone companies. There is a TDMA network. Unregistered roaming is available – visitors with TDMA handsets can make calls without registering, provided they can give a credit card number.

Internet: There are many Internet cafes throughout the Cayman Islands and many hotels also offer Internet access.

Post: Mail is not delivered to private addresses in the Cayman Islands, but collected from numbered PO boxes. Post office hours: Mon-Fri 0830-1530, Sat 0830-1200.

MEDIA: Press: *The Cayman Net News* and *The Caymanian Compass* are published weekdays.

TV: There are four TV stations and two of these are run by religious organisations. The *CITN Cayman 27* is a popular private TV station. Cable and satellite offer a variety of US and international stations.

Radio: Private FM radio stations (including the popular *Z-99*) operate alongside Government-owned *Radio Cayman*.

Passport/Visa

	Passport Required?	Visa Required?	Return Ticket Required?
Full British	1	No	Yes
Australian	Yes	No	Yes
Canadian	1	No	Yes
USA	1	No	Yes
Other EU	Yes	No	Yes
Japanese	Yes	No	Yes

Note: *Regulations and requirements may be subject to change at short notice, and you are advised to contact the appropriate diplomatic or consular authority before finalising travel arrangements. Any numbers in the chart refer to the footnotes below.*

PASSPORTS: 1. Passport valid for period of stay required by all except nationals of Canada, the USA and the UK, provided holding proof of nationality (such as a birth certificate or a notarised affidavit of citizenship) and provided return or onward ticket shows that the visitor will leave the Cayman Islands within one month. Photo identification is also required, such as a driving licence.

VISAS: Any person resident in the USA or Canada who arrives in the Cayman Islands directly from the USA or Canada and who, on landing, can produce a valid US Alien Registration Card may be permitted to enter and remain without a visa for up to 90 days. A visa is required by all except the following for a period of up to 90 days:
(a) nationals of countries mentioned in the chart above;
(b) nationals of Commonwealth countries (except nationals of Bangladesh, Cameroon, The Gambia, Ghana, India, Nigeria, Pakistan, Sierra Leone, Sri Lanka, and Uganda who *do* require a visa);
(c) nationals of Andorra, Argentina, Brazil, Chile, Costa Rica, Dominican Republic, El Salvador, Guatemala, Iceland, Israel, Liechtenstein, Mexico, Monaco, Norway, Panama, San Marino, Switzerland and Venezuela;
(d) transit passengers continuing their journey by the same or first connecting aircraft provided holding onward or return documentation and not leaving the airport.

Note: (a) Cruise ship passengers do not require visas to enter the Cayman Islands. (b) Visitors are prohibited from engaging in any form of employment unless holding a Work Permit. A short-term Work Permit can usually be obtained within one to two weeks.

Types of visa and cost: *Tourist*, *Transit* and *Business*. All visas cost £56 (US$100), which is a non-refundable fee.

Validity: Three months, though this may vary. Visitors may remain in the Cayman Islands for up to one month, although an extension of up to six months may then be applied for, provided return tickets and proof of financial means/funding is submitted on arrival or at the immigration department.

Application to: Nearest Embassy.

Application requirements: (a) Two application forms. (b) Valid passport. (c) Sufficient funds to cover duration of stay.

Working days required: Dependent upon nature of application. Allow three to four weeks.

PASSPORT/VISA INFORMATION

The UK Passport Service
London Passport Office, Globe House, 89 Eccleston Square, London SW1V 1PN, UK
Tel: (0870) 521 0410 (national advice line) *or* (020) 7901 2150/1.
Website: www.passport.gov.uk
Opening hours: Mon-Fri 0745-1900, Sat 0915-1515 (passport office); Mon-Fri 0900-1600 (visa section). *Personal callers for visas should go to the agency window in the collection room of the London office.*

Money

Currency: Cayman Islands Dollar (KYD; symbol CI$) = 100 cents. Notes are in denominations of CI$100, 50, 25, 10, 5 and 1. Coins are in denominations of 25, 10, 5 and 1 cents.

Note: The Cayman Islands Dollar is tied to the US Dollar at a fixed rate of CI$1 = US$1.25 although bank charges for currency exchange may result in minor fluctuations.

Currency exchange: US Dollars circulate freely and are the best currency to exchange. ATMs accepting Visa and MasterCard with Cirrus affiliation are located at Cayman National Bank (and other banks) and at Owen Roberts International Airport.

Credit & debit cards: Major credit cards are widely accepted. Check with your credit or debit card company for details of merchant acceptability and other services which may be available.

Traveller's cheques: Readily accepted. To avoid additional exchange rate charges, travellers are advised to take traveller's cheques in US Dollars.

Currency restrictions: No restriction on import or export of foreign or local currency apart from import of Jamaican dollars, which is restricted to CI$20.

Banking hours: Mon-Thurs 0900-1600, Fri 0830/0900-1530/1630. Some banks are open on Saturday mornings.

Exchange rate indicators:
Rate at time of publishing
£1.00= CI$1.56
$1.00= CI$0.82

Duty Free

The following goods may be imported into the Cayman Islands by persons over 18 years of age without incurring customs duty:
200 cigarettes or 50 cigars or 250g of tobacco; 1l of alcoholic beverages (including wines).

Prohibited items: Base or counterfeit coins, instruments and appliances for gambling, narcotics and utensils. Other goods include life plants and plant cuttings, beef, and raw fruit and vegetables.

Note: A permit from the commissioner of police/district commissioner is required for the import of firearms, ammunition and explosives (besides gun powder and blasting powder).

Visitors should be aware that products made from farmed green sea turtles available in limited selections at the *Cayman Turtle Farm* are offered for local consumption. The importation of genuine sea turtle products is strictly prohibited by any countries that have signed the *Convention on International Trade in Endangered Species (1978)*, including the USA, Canada and the UK.

The export of lobster, conch or conch meat is prohibited (unless in transit). There are also a number of marine and animal specimens that may not be taken from the Islands; it is best to check prior to travel.

Public Holidays

Below are listed Public Holidays for the January 2006-June 2007 period.

2006: Jan 1 New Year's Day. **Jan 23** National Heroes Day. **Mar 1** Ash Wednesday. **Apr 14** Good Friday. **Apr 17** Easter Monday. **May 15** Discovery Day. **Jun 12** Queen's Birthday. **Jul 4** Constitution Day. **Nov 11** Remembrance Day. **Dec 25** Christmas Day. **Dec 26** Boxing Day.

2007: Jan 1 New Year's Day. **Jan 26** National Heroes Day. **Feb 9** Ash Wednesday. **Apr 6** Good Friday. **Apr 9** Easter Monday. **May 17** Discovery Day. **Jun 14** Queen's Birthday.

Health

	Special Precautions?	Certificate Required?
Yellow Fever	No	No
Cholera	No	No
Typhoid & Polio	1	N/A
Malaria	No	N/A

Note: *Regulations and requirements may be subject to change at short notice, and you are advised to contact your doctor well in advance of your intended date of departure. Any numbers in the chart refer to the footnotes below.*

1: Immunisation against typhoid is advised.

Other risks: Outbreaks of *dengue fever* and *dengue haemorrhagic fever* can occur. *Hepatitis A* has been reported in the northern Caribbean. Immunisations against *TB*, *diphtheria* and *hepatitis B* and *C* are sometimes advised.

Health care: Modern medical facilities are available, particularly on Grand Cayman and Cayman Brac, including Government-operated hospitals on both islands. There is also an island-wide, 24-hour 911 (or 555) emergency service. Serious cases may be transferred to Miami. Health costs are similar to the UK. Private insurance is recommended. Insect repellent is useful to counter mosquitoes and sandflies.

Note: Divers should note that the George Town Hospital also has a two-man, double-lock decompression chamber staffed by trained operators supervised by a physician experienced in treating diving-related accidents.

Travel - International

AIR:

The Cayman Islands' national airline is *Cayman Airways (KX)* (Website: www.caymanairways.com).

Approximate flight times: From *London* to Grand Cayman is nine hours 55 minutes and from *Miami* to Grand Cayman is one hour five minutes. From *Miami* to Cayman Brac is one hour 35 minutes.

Main airports: *Grand Cayman (GCM) (Owen Roberts International Airport)* is 2km (1 mile) east of the city. *To/from the airport*: Taxis are available to the centre (travel time - 10 minutes), operating from 0600 to 2300, for a fare of about US$10. There is also an airport bus available that must be pre-booked. *Facilities*: Outgoing duty free shop for all international departures, banks/bureaux de change, post office, car hire and a bar/restaurant (open for all arrivals and departures).

Cayman Brac (CYB) (Gerard Smith Airport) is 8km (5 miles) from the town. *To/from the airport*: Taxis meet all flights (travel time - 10 minutes).

Departure tax: CI$20 or US$25. Travellers under 12 years of age and transit passengers continuing their journey within 24 hours are exempt.

SEA:

Main ports: *Grand Cayman* is one of the most popular Caribbean ports and a busy port of call for leading international cruise lines operating from North America, Mexico and Europe. The Cayman Islands are legally supposed to limit the number of cruise passengers to 6000 (three to four ships) per day. There is no cruise ship dock and passengers are ferried ashore by tenders to the North or South dock terminals in George Town. A wide range of cruise lines serve the Cayman Islands.

Travel - Internal

AIR:

The main island of Grand Cayman is connected to Cayman Brac and to Little Cayman by internal flights run by *Cayman Airways* and *Island Air* and to Little Cayman by *Island Air* , plus a service between Cayman Brac and Little Cayman.

ROAD:

A good road network connects the coastal towns of all three main islands. **Bus**: Public minibuses operate from George Town to West Bay (every 15 minutes), to Bodden Town (every 30 minutes) and to East End and North Side (every hour). Fares are CI$1.50 to CI$2 each way. The bus terminal is located opposite the public library on Edward Street in central George Town. Services are normally from 0600-2400 (until midnight at weekends for most routes). There are circa 40 minibuses operated by licensed operators. Routes are colour coded (with colours marked on the front and rear of the buses). Public buses have blue licence plates and standard fares are displayed inside. **Mopeds and scooters**: Available for hire on Grand Cayman and Cayman Brac. Riders are required by law to wear a helmet at all times. The average fee is US$27.50 per day, which includes helmet and personal insurance. **Bicycles**: Available for hire on all three islands. On Cayman Brac and Little Cayman, most hotels have bicycles available for complimentary guest use. **Taxi**: There are large fleets of taxis operating from all resorts, the cruise dock at George Town and the international airports. **Car hire**: Most major car hire companies are represented in George Town. 4-wheel-drive vehicles are also available. Private limousine services are available on Grand Cayman for special events and airport transfers. Driving is on the left and drivers must be over 21 years of age. Speed limits are strictly enforced and seat belts must be worn at all times. Full insurance is required and must be arranged with the car hire company; some companies will not insure drivers under 25.

Documentation: A temporary local driving licence is required, which will be issued at a nominal charge on presentation of a valid licence from the traveller's country of origin.

Travel times: The following chart gives approximate travel times (in hours and minutes) from **George Town**, Grand Cayman, to other major centres in the islands.

	Air	Road	Sea
Cayman Brac	0.30	-	-
Little Cayman	0.45	-	-
Rum Point	-	0.45	1.15
Cayman Kai	-	0.45	-

Note: Cayman Brac to Little Cayman is 10 minutes by air.

Travel Advice

Most visits to the Cayman Islands are trouble-free but you should be aware of the global risk of indiscriminate international terrorist attacks, which could be against civilian targets, including places frequented by foreigners. The hurricane season runs from 1 June to 30 November. This advice is based on information provided by the Foreign and Commonwealth Office in the UK. It is correct at time of publishing. As the situation can change rapidly, visitors are advised to contact the following organisations for the latest travel advice:

British Foreign and Commonwealth Office
Tel: (0845) 850 2829.
Website: www.fco.gov.uk

US Department of State
Website: http://travel.state.gov/travel

Accommodation

HOTELS/CONDOMINIUMS/LODGES:

There is a wide variety of accommodation, ranging from luxury hotels and self-catering condominiums to more economical hotels and dive lodges. Most of Grand Cayman's condominiums are superbly situated on beaches and coastal areas and guests can walk out of the apartments onto beautiful beaches with crystal clear water. Many condominiums have been built in the last few years and are equipped with the latest fittings and furnishings, as well as central facilities such as swimming pools and tennis courts. The leading hotels are located on the coast. Some of the best known overlook Grand Cayman's renowned Seven Mile Beach, a dazzling stretch of fine powdery sand said to be one of the world's most beautiful beaches. There is also a fine selection of diving resort hotels. Hotels providing accommodation with 100 rooms are considered large in the Cayman Islands and are generally only found on Grand Cayman. Prices are seasonal, being higher in the winter than in the summer (when some hotels offer free accommodation for children under 12). The high season begins on 15 December and usually runs through to 15 April. During that time, visitors should expect to pay up to 50 per cent more for a room. A 10 per cent government accommodation tax is payable to the hotel on departure. Most also add a service charge (about 10 per cent). For more information, contact the Cayman Islands Department of Tourism (see *Top Things To Do*). A Government board of control monitors standards in various hotels and establishments. Hotels vary in standard from **luxury** (very comfortable, with some outstanding features) to **tourist** class (budget hotel).

SELF-CATERING:

There is a wide variety of apartments and villas available, from the most luxurious to the relatively austere. The Department of Tourism can give full details of these, and also of beach cottages for families, and dive lodges.

CAMPING AND CARAVANNING:

No camping or caravanning allowed.

Top Things To See

- See the Cayman Islands' very own 'Great Wall of China', a 6km- (4 mile-) stone wall at **Bodden Town** on **Grand Cayman**: it was built to protect residents from pirate attacks.
- **Seven Mile Beach** on Grand Cayman is the main tourist centre, a huge sandy beach flanked by tranquil, turquoise ocean. Although highly developed, it retains its charm.
- Go to **Hell** and back - literally. This area of Grand Cayman, Hell, is named because of its peculiar rock formation, evolved from skeletons of shells and corals solidified by salt and lime deposits. A close examination reveals petrified forms of sea life supposedly up to 20 million years old.
- The capital of Grand Cayman is **George Town**. Along the harbour front are traditional Caymanian gingerbread-style buildings and, close by, modern banks and finance houses. **The Cayman Islands National Museum**, based in the centre of George Town, offers a complete history of the islands. The **Pedro St James** historic site on Grand Cayman features a historically accurate restoration of the early 19th-century Pedro St James great house and grounds in Savannah. The site has a visitor centre and a multimedia theatre, and also organises historic tours.
- A 45-minute drive from George Town is the popular **Queen Elizabeth II Botanic Park** with a 2-acre heritage garden, visitor's information centre, 2-acre lake, and 2.5-acre floral garden with a vivid array of cacti, shrubs and native flowers. The park has become an important habitat for the endangered Cayman blue iguana. Other wildlife that can be spotted are tri-coloured herons, black-necked stilts, cattle egrets and rare West Indian whistling ducks. **Little Cayman**, home to approximately 170 people, has many more wild birds and iguanas.

Top Things To Do

- There are over 40 professional dive operators in the Cayman Islands, and few other island groups offer as many easily accessible dive sites. On **Seven Mile Beach**, **diving** begins 183m (200 yards) from the shore. Diving shops and boats can be found at most hotels. Some diving resorts offer an underwater photography service, including camera rentals, training and repairs, along with overnight processing of slides. Dive sites in the Cayman Islands range from shallow dives near offshore reefs to the celebrated **North Wall** off Grand Cayman - a sheer drop to the bed of the ocean. The famous **Stingray City** offers divers and snorkellers the opportunity to come into close contact with the friendly southern stingray. Various locations also offer wreck diving, particularly **Cayman Brac**, where a Russian warship (renamed **MV Captain Keith Tibbets**) was intentionally sunk. The abundance of fish, marine and coral life around the islands is protected by strict conservation measures. Those not wishing to dive can enjoy the reefs from the **Atlantis Submarine**, which offers hour-long underwater trips for up to 46 passengers.
- The deep waters around **Grand Cayman** are a migratory path for numerous species of large fish, including marlin, tuna, dolphin, swordfish and wahoo. **Fishing** is possible all year round. The best fishing is between Grand Cayman's west coast and the banks, 7.5km (12 miles) offshore; the **Trench**, 6 to 13km (4 to 8 miles) off the west coast, is particularly good. The inshore lakes of **Little Cayman**, the smallest of the three islands which make up the Cayman Islands, are known for tarpon and bonefish. The Million Dollar Month fishing festival, which established the Cayman Islands as a leading game-fishing destination, has now been replaced by an **annual international fishing tournament**.
- The **Family Recreation and Motorsports Park** at Breakers offers a 12 hectare- (30 acre-) **racetrack** which claims to be the best in the Caribbean, with family recreation areas and a nature reserve; no alcohol is permitted in the park. The **Lakeview Raceway** in George Town features stock car racing on the first Sunday of every month.
- Enjoy the Cayman Islands' connections to nautical adventure at the **Pirates Week Festival** (website: www.piratesweekfestival.com), October/November, where events range from music, street dances, sports events, fireworks to - the highlight - the mock 'pirate invasion' in **George Town Harbour**.
- On the **North Side** of the Cayman Islands, linking **Frank Sound** to **Old Man Bay**, walk the **Mastic Trail**, which dates back to the 19th century and is surrounded by stunning scenery and local wildlife, and takes hikers into one of the Caribbean's last remaining **rainforests**.

TOURIST INFORMATION

Cayman Islands Government Office and Department of Tourism in the UK
6 Arlington Street, London SW1A 1RE, UK
Tel: (020) 7491 7772 (Government office) *or* 7771 (Department of Tourism).
Website: www.caymanislands.co.uk

Caribbean Tourism Organisation in the UK
22 The Quadrant, Richmond, Surrey TW9 1BP, UK
Tel: (020) 8948 0057.
Website: www.doitcaribbean.com *or* www.onecaribbean.org

Cayman Islands Department of Tourism in the USA
3 Park Avenue, 39th Floor, New York, NY 10016, USA
Tel: (212) 889 9009.
Website: www.caymanislands.ky

Entertainment

FOOD & DRINK: There is a strong Jamaican influence. There are various standards of restaurants with good service, most of which accept credit cards. Bars and restaurants are well stocked with all beverages normally consumed in America and Europe. Draught beer is available in a few bars.

National specialities:
- Jerk curry, rice and peas and plantain.
- Turtle steaks.
- Conch chowder.
- Red snapper.
- Sea bass.
- Lobster.

National drinks:
- Beer.
- Cocktails.

Tipping: For most services, five to 10 per cent is normal. Hotels and apartments state the specific amount. Restaurant bills usually include a 10 to 15 per cent charge in lieu of tipping.

NIGHTLIFE: Grand Cayman has a lively nightlife with comedy clubs, bars and nightclubs. Music is varied and clubs offer everything from live DJs to salsa, reggae, calypso and disco. Concerts are held at the Lions Centre in Red Bay and theatre productions are shown at either the Harquail Theatre on West Bay Road or the Prospect Playhouse in Red Bay. Dinner cruises onboard a replica pirate ship and 19th-century tall ship can be booked through local watersports operators. For further information about entertainment on the Islands, visitors should consult the free local *What's Hot* magazine or the *What's Happening* column in the Friday issue of the *Caymanian Compass* newspaper.

SHOPPING: As a shopping centre, George Town, with its fascinating boutiques and duty-free shops, is now one of the leading centres in the Caribbean region. Delicious local foods can be bought or sampled at the Farmers Market Cooperative on Thomas Russell way or Frankie's Fresh Fruits and Juices on Red Bay Road. Half a dozen modern and sophisticated shopping centres have recently been established, offering a choice of North American and European fashion brands, furnishings and household goods. Local products include the Tortuga Rum company speciality rum and rum cake, shell jewellery, Caymanite (the island's semi-precious stone), tropical fruit and woodcarvings. Special purchases include china, crystal, silver, French perfume and local crafts of black coral, sculptures, tortoise and turtle shell jewellery (turtles are bred at Cayman Turtle Farm, which also undertakes conservation measures). Travellers should note that turtle products cannot be imported, even by persons in transit, into any country which has signed the Convention on International Trade in Endangered Species – this includes the USA, Canada and the UK. Many luxury goods and essential foodstuffs are duty free but duty of up to 20 per cent is charged on other items. **Shopping hours:** Mon-Sat 0900-1700 (on weekends some shops will stay open untill midnight).

Business

- **GDP:** US$1.391 billion (2005).
- **Main exports:** Fish and cut flowers.
- **Main imports:** Machinery, food stuffs, fuel and chemicals.
- **Main trade partners:** USA, UK, Japan and the Netherlands Antilles.

ECONOMY: The Cayman Islands have no direct taxation and have become important as an offshore financial centre and a tax haven. The finance industry has grown rapidly since the late 1980s when many companies relocated to the islands from Panama, which was racked by political instability. Good communications and infrastructure helped to sustain its growth, to the point where the islands are now the world's fifth-largest banking centre. A key agreement on information exchange signed with the US Government in 1990 – extended in 2001 – has spared the Cayman Islands many of the problems (money laundering and large-scale tax avoidance) that have bedevilled other aspirant offshore financial centres. Nor has it been subject to the critical scrutiny of the OECD which has been leading the global assault on cross-border financial malpractice. Tourism is the islands' other main source of revenue. There is little agriculture, and most of the foodstuffs for the islands are imported. Industry is confined to construction and food-processing. The standard of living on the islands is generally high, and the per capita income is the highest in the region. The healthy state of the economy has attracted migrant workers from Jamaica, Europe and North America who now make up 30 per cent of the working population. The Cayman Islands have observer status at the Caribbean Common Market, CARICOM, and associate membership of the European Union.

BUSINESS ETIQUETTE: Business suits are recommended when calling on senior officials and local heads of business and also for semi-formal or formal functions. Exchange of calling cards is usual and letters of introduction are sometimes used. It is generally easy to gain access to offices of senior Government officials, politicians and business executives. Civil servants are precluded from accepting gifts except for diaries or calendars at Christmas. Monetary gifts or expensive presents are not encouraged in the private sector. **Office hours:** Mon-Fri 0900-1700.

CONFERENCES/CONVENTIONS: Many hotels have conference facilities. Contact the Cayman Islands Department of Tourism for details (see *Top Things To Do*).

COMMERCIAL INFORMATION

Cayman Islands Chamber of Commerce
PO Box 1000 GT, Grand Cayman, Cayman Islands
Tel: 949 8090.
Website: www.caymanchamber.ky.

Central African Republic

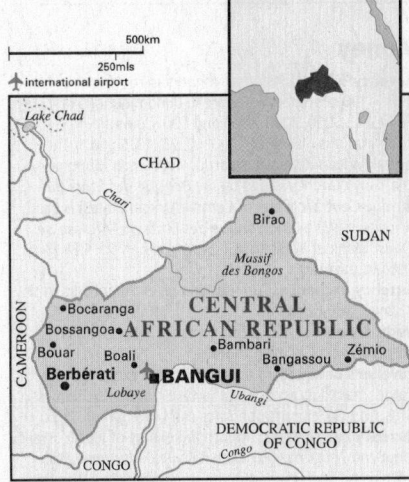

Location: Central Africa.

Time: GMT + 1.

Overview

The public face of the Central African Republic is one that is both politically brutal and environmentally savage, troubled by recurrent *Harmattan* winds. Yet the private face of this country is one with an attractive countenance of forests, waterfalls and magnificent national parks that teem with wildlife. Despite the dangers that lurk in a city such as Bangui, the country's capital is friendly, with a strong emphasis on arts and crafts.

However, the Central African Republic's history has impacted on everything. In 1910, the area known as Ubangi-Chari became incorporated into French Equatorial Africa and turned over to a number of concessionaires who ran separate fiefdoms as commercial operations with little or no regard for the indigenous people. Numerous unsuccessful revolts were launched until, immediately after World War II, the territory was granted its own assembly and representation in the French National Assembly. Internal self-government followed - the most notorious Prime Minister being Bokassa.

The self-styled 'Emperor' Bokassa's rule was a particularly profligate one, with his 1977 'coronation' alone estimated to have used up over a quarter of the country's annual income. The country was renamed the 'Central African Empire' in a flourish of self-regard. Bokassa was bafflingly tolerated by the French until he appeared to have been personally involved in the massacre of 100 schoolchildren; French paratroops then helped depose the 'Emperor'.

The country reverted to its original title but there was little improvement in its fortunes. Instead, the Central African Republic was subjected to further coups. Positive changes finally looked likely for the Central African Republic in the early 1990s as protests for democracy forced the introduction of a multi-party system. In the first election held under this new democratic constitution in 1993, Patassé was announced President, only to be ousted by a coup in 2003: Bozizé was now President. Since this farcical stream of coups, order has mostly been restored in the capital (although street-crime is still

common) but outside of Bangui, the situation remains potentially dangerous. Bozizé was eventually democratically elected in the May 2005 elections. He has pledged to bring security to the country. The world waits with bated breath to see what results from this pledge, since many believe the Central African Republic to be a beautiful country that has been made ugly by discord for too long.

General Information

AREA: 622,984 sq km (240,535 sq miles).
POPULATION: 3.9 million (UN, 2005).
POPULATION DENSITY: 6.2 per sq km.
CAPITAL: Bangui. **Population:** 690,000.
GEOGRAPHY: The Central African Republic is bordered to the north by Chad, to the east by Sudan, to the south by the Democratic Republic of Congo and the Republic of Congo, and to the west by Cameroon. It is a large, landlocked territory of mostly uninhabited forest, bush and game reserves. The Chari River cuts through the centre from east to north; towards the Cameroon border the landscape rises to 2000m (6560ft) west of Bocaranga in the northwest corner, while the southwest has dense tropical rainforest. Most of the country is rolling or flat plateau covered with dry deciduous forest, except where it has been reduced to grass savannah or destroyed by bush fire. The northeast becomes desert scrubland and mountainous in parts.
GOVERNMENT: Republic. **Head of State:** President François Bozizé since 2003. **Head of Government:** Prime Minister Elie Doté since June 2005. **Recent history:** The two dominant figures in the country's recent history have been André Kolingba, a former army commander who took over in 1981's military coup, and Ange-Félix Patassé, who later emerged as Kolingba's principal opponent. During the 1980s, Kolingba consolidated his rule as leader of the country's sole legal political party, *Rassemblement Démocratique Centrafricain* (RDC). In the early 1990s, as democracy swept through Francophone Africa, violent domestic protests and heavy French pressure forced Kolingba to concede the introduction of a multi-party system.
Patassé won the first election held under the new democratic constitution in 1993, defeating both Kolingba and Dacko. In December 1998, elections to the National Assembly returned the MLPC as the largest party but short of an absolute majority. In September the following year, Patassé and Kolingba once again competed for the Presidency, and again Patassé won a comfortable victory. The last few years have seen a series of attempted coups by Kolingba and his principal supporter, army chief Francois Bozizé: first in May 2001, then in October 2002, and finally in March 2003. On the third occasion, Patassé was out of the country and, despite the intervention of French troops, the coup was successful and Bozizé proclaimed himself President.
Following a transitional period which led to presidential and parliamentary elections in May 2005, François Bozizé was elected as President. He chose Elie Doté as Prime Minister. The Government is a Republic comprised of a strong executive branch (President, Vice President, Prime Minister and Council of Ministers) and weak legislative and judicial branches. The National Assembly is made up of 109 members elected by popular vote to serve five-year terms.
LANGUAGE: The national language is Sango, but French is the official administrative language and is essential for business. Another 68 languages and dialects have been identified in addition to these.
RELIGION: 25 per cent of the population is Protestant. 25 per cent is Roman Catholic. There is a small Islamic minority of 15 per cent and 35 per cent of the population have indigenous beliefs.
ELECTRICITY: 220 volts AC, 50Hz.
SOCIAL CONVENTIONS: Dress is informal. Care should be taken to dress modestly in Muslim areas, and Muslim customs should be respected and observed; visitors should not, for instance, show the soles of their feet when sitting. Shorts are also generally frowned upon, and women are expected to dress modestly. It is customary to shake hands. Women are strictly segregated, especially in towns. In Muslim areas, visitors should not smoke or drink in public during Ramadan. **Photography:** Film is expensive and should be sent abroad for developing. Show caution and discretion when photographing local people; ask for permission. Do not photograph military installations or government buildings.

Climate

Hot all year with a defined dry season. Especially hot in the north, with greater humidity in the south. The rainy season is mainly from May to October. Heavy rainfall is typical in the southwestern forest areas.
Required clothing: Linens and tropical waterproof clothing.

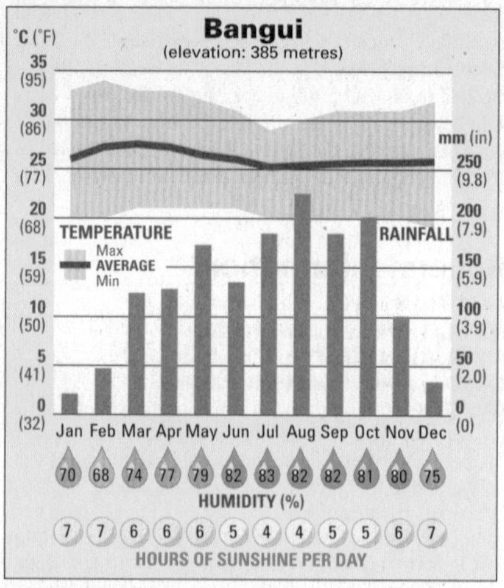
Bangui
(elevation: 385 metres)
°C (°F)
35 (95)
30 (86)
25 (77)
20 (68)
15 (59)
10 (50)
5 (41)
0 (32)
mm (in)
250 (9.8)
200 (7.9)
150 (5.9)
100 (3.9)
50 (2.0)
0 (0)
TEMPERATURE
Max
AVERAGE
Min
RAINFALL
Jan Feb Mar Apr May Jun Jul Aug Sep Oct Nov Dec
70 68 74 77 79 82 83 82 82 81 80 75
HUMIDITY (%)
7 7 6 6 6 5 4 4 5 5 6 7
HOURS OF SUNSHINE PER DAY

Communications

Telephone: IDD is available, although some calls are still directed through the operator. Country code: 236.
Mobile telephone: Roaming agreements exist with a few international mobile phone companies. Coverage is limited to the capital, Bangui.
Internet: Available in some towns.
Post: There is a post office in each prefecture. Local postal services are unreliable. Both postal and telecommunications services are in the course of development. Airmail services to Europe take approximately one week, although it is often much longer; surface mail can take up to three months. Post office hours: Mon-Fri 0730-1130 and 1430-1630; Sat 1430-1830; Sun 0800-1100, open for stamps and telegrams only.
MEDIA: There is journalistic freedom in the Central African Republic to the extent that private newspapers criticise Government policies and allegations of corruption, but these are likely permitted because most of the populace both cannot afford them and cannot read them (there is a high rate of illiteracy in the country). Those radio and TV stations that are are state-run provide little to no coverage of the political opposition. It was only until recently, in 2004, that prison terms for press offences were abolished.
Press: There are several daily newspapers, including *Le Citoyen* (an independent publication), *Le Confident* (an independent publication) and *L'Hirondelle* (an independent publication). The weekly publications have limited distribution and are in French. *Centrafrique-Presse* is a state-owned bi-monthly publication.
TV: *Television Centrafricaine* is state-run.
Radio: The national state-run broadcaster is *Radio Centrafrique*. *Radio Notre Dame* is a Roman Catholic broadcaster based in Bangui. The UN-sponsored *Radio Ndeke Luka* can be relied upon for a balanced viewpoint. It also often re-broadcasts international news programmes. *Radio Nostalgie* is privately run.

Passport/Visa

	Passport Required?	Visa Required?	Return Ticket Required?
Full British	Yes	Yes	Yes
Australian	Yes	Yes	Yes
Canadian	Yes	Yes	Yes
USA	Yes	Yes	Yes
Other EU	Yes	Yes	Yes
Japanese	Yes	Yes	Yes

Note: *Regulations and requirements may be subject to change at short notice, and you are advised to contact the appropriate diplomatic or consular authority before finalising travel arrangements. Any numbers in the chart refer to the footnotes below.*

PASSPORTS: Passport valid for six months after entry into the Central African Republic required by all.
VISAS: Required by all except the following:
(a) nationals of Benin, Burkina Faso, Cameroon, Chad, Congo (Democratic Republic of), Congo (Rep), Côte d'Ivoire, Equatorial Guinea, Gabon, Israel, Liberia, Liechtenstein, Mauritius, Monaco, Niger, Rwanda, Senegal, Sudan, Switzerland and Togo provided travelling from their own countries;
(b) transit passengers continuing their journey by the same or first connecting aircraft provided holding valid onward or return documentation and not leaving the airport.
Note: Nationals of Lebanon are visa-exempt if in possession of written proof of their status as businessperson, banker or technician.
Types of visa and cost: *Tourist/Business* and *Transit*: €50 (for stays of up to 30 days); €152 (for stays of up to three months). Fees paid in other currencies depend on exchange rates.
Validity: *Tourist* and *Business* visas are valid for stays of maximum three months. For transit through the Central African Republic, enquire at the Consulate (or Consular sections at Embassy).
Application to: Consulate (or Consular section at Embassy); see *Passport/Visa Information* .
Application requirements: (a) Two application forms. (b) Fee. (c) Two passport-size photos. (d) Return/onward ticket. (e) Letter from company stating that applicant will resume work on returning. (f) Yellow fever vaccination certificate. (g) Stamped, self-addressed envelope.
Working days required: Normally two unless application is referred to the authorities in the Central African Republic.

PASSPORT/VISA INFORMATION

Embassy of the Central African Republic in France
30 rue des Perchamps, 75016 Paris, France
Tel: (1) 4224 4256.

Embassy of the Central African Republic in the USA
1618 22nd Street, NW, Washington DC 2008, USA
Tel: (202) 483 7800.

Money

Currency: CFA (*Communauté Financiaire Africaine*) Franc (XAF) = 100 centimes. Notes are in denominations of XAF10,000, 5000, 2000, 1000 and 500. Coins are in denominations of XAF500, 100, 50, 25, 10, 5 and 1. The Central African Republic is part of the French Monetary Area. Only currency issued by the *Banque des Etats de l'Afrique Centrale* (Bank of Central African States) is valid; currency issued by the *Banque des Etats de l'Afrique de l'Ouest* (Bank of West African States) is not. The CFA Franc is tied to the Euro.
Currency exchange: Currency can be exchanged at banks in Bangui and Berbérati.
Credit & debit cards: Credit cards are not generally accepted, except in major hotels.
Traveller's cheques: To avoid additional exchange rate charges, travellers are advised to take traveller's cheques in Euros. Even so, commission rates can be very high.
Currency restrictions: Import and export of local currency from Benin, Burkina Faso, Côte d'Ivoire, Mauritania, Niger, Senegal and Togo is unlimited; for all other countries the import and export of local currency is limited to CFAfr75,000. The import of foreign currency is unlimited provided it is declared. The export of foreign currency is limited to the amount imported and declared.
Banking hours: Mon-Fri 0700-1230.
Exchange rate indicators:
Rate at time of publishing
£1.00= XAF964.71
$1.00= XAF546.42

Duty Free

The following goods may be imported by visitors over 18 years of age into the Central African Republic without incurring customs duty:
1000 cigarettes or cigarillos or 250 cigars or 2kg of tobacco (for women, cigarettes only); five bottles of alcoholic beverages; five bottles of perfume.
Note: Firearms must be declared before entering. When leaving the Central African Republic, any animal skins and diamonds must be declared. Dogs and cats must be accompanied by a veterinary certificate.

Public Holidays

Below are listed Public Holidays for the January 2006-June 2007 period.
2006: Jan 1 New Year's Day. **Mar 29** Anniversary of the Death of Barthélemy Boganda. **Apr 17** Easter Monday. **Aug 13** Independence Day. **Aug 15** Assumption. **Nov 1** All Saint's Day. **Dec 1** National Day. **Dec 25** Christmas.
2007: Jan 1 New Year's Day. **Mar 29** Anniversary of the Death of Barthélemy Boganda. **Apr 9** Easter Monday.

Health

	Special Precautions?	Certificate Required?
Yellow Fever	Yes	1
Cholera	Yes	2
Typhoid & Polio	3	N/A
Malaria	4	N/A

Note: *Regulations and requirements may be subject to change at short notice, and you are advised to contact your doctor well in advance of your intended date of departure. Any numbers in the chart refer to the footnotes below.*

1: A yellow fever vaccination certificate is required from travellers over one year of age.
2: Following WHO guidelines issued in 1973, a cholera vaccination certificate is not a condition of entry to the Central African Republic. However, cholera is a serious risk in this country and precautions are essential. Up-to-date advice should be sought before deciding whether these precautions should include vaccination as medical opinion is divided over its effectiveness. See the *Health* appendix for more information.
3: Immunisation against typhoid is usually recommended.
4: Risk of malaria (and of other insect-borne diseases) exists all year throughout the country. The malignant *falciparum* form is prevalent. Resistance to chloroquine and sulfadoxine-pyrimethamine has been reported. The recommended prophylaxis is mefloquine.
Food & drink: All water should be regarded as being potentially contaminated. Water used for drinking, brushing teeth or making ice should have first been boiled or otherwise sterilised. Milk is unpasteurised and should be boiled. Powdered or tinned milk is available and is advised, but make sure that it is reconstituted with pure water. Avoid dairy products which are likely to have been made from unboiled milk. Only eat well-cooked meat and fish, preferably served hot. Pork, salad and mayonnaise may carry increased risk. Vegetables should be cooked and fruit peeled.
Other risks: *Hepatitis A* and *E* are present and *hepatitis B* is hyperendemic. *Diarrhoeal* illnesses are common. *Cutaneous* and *visceral leishmaniasis* occur during the dry season. *Bilharzia* (schistosomiasis) is present. Avoid swimming and paddling in fresh water; swimming pools which are well-chlorinated and maintained are safe. *Onchocerciasis* (river blindness) and *African trypanosomiasis* (sleeping sickness) are also prevalent. *Meningococcal meningitis* is particularly prevalent during the dry season in December, especially in the north of the country. In March 2004, two districts (Nana Bongila with 39 cases/five deaths and Zere with four cases/two deaths) had attack rates above the epidemic threshold. Vaccination is strongly recommended. There is also a high incidence of HIV/AIDS; sensible precautions should be taken. *Rabies* is present. For those at high risk, vaccination before arrival should be considered. If you are bitten, seek medical advice without delay. For more information, consult the *Health* appendix.
Health care: Full health insurance is essential, and should include air evacuation to Europe in case of serious accident or illness. Medical facilities are severely limited outside the major centres and visitors should travel with their own supply of remedies for simple ailments such as stomach upsets: pharmaceutical supplies are usually very difficult to obtain.

Travel - International

AIR:
The main airlines serving the Central African Republic are *Air France (AF)*, *Benin Golf Air*, Cameroon Airlines and Sudan Airways. There are regular flights from Bangui to various African cities, including Libreville and N'Djaména.
Approximate flight times: From *London* to Bangui is 10 hours 50 minutes (including approximately one hour stopover in Paris). There are also connections between Bangui and Douala (Cameroon), Lagos (Nigeria), and other West African destinations.
Main airports: *Bangui M'Poko (BGF)* is 7km (4 miles) southeast of Bangui of the city (travel time - 30 minutes).
To/from the airport: Taxis are available to the city (travel time - 15 minutes), during flight hours for a fare of about CFAfr2500. A bus service to the city meets all flights.
Facilities: Restaurant, post office, bar and car hire/parking.
Departure tax: XAF10,000 is levied on all passengers.
RIVER:
The route by ferry along the Ubangi to Bangui from the Congo (Rep) or the Congo (Dem Rep) is run by ACCF (Tel: 610 967) and SOCATRAF (Tel: 614 315). However, it is not operating at present, owing to rebel activity in the northern part of the Democratic Republic of Congo. A car/passenger ferry normally operates across the Ubangi between the Central African Republic and the Democratic Republic of Congo, Bangui–Zongo and Bangassou–Ndu. Fares are very low, although the service breaks down frequently and may be disrupted by political instability. It is sometimes possible to hire a boat, although this is expensive. Visitors may not cross the river to the Congo (Dem Rep) on Saturday or Sunday, as the customs posts in that country do not operate at the weekend.
ROAD:
Road access is from the Congo (Dem Rep), Chad and Cameroon. There are reasonable all-weather roads from Yaoundé (Cameroon) and N'Djaména (Chad). The border with Cameroon may be closed; it is necessary to check locally near the time of travel. Theoretically, all borders are open; however, non-residents can experience difficulty obtaining permission to cross them.

Travel - Internal

Note: Identification (eg residence permit or certified copy of passport) must be carried on persons at all times. Failure to do so can result in detention by police. Incidents of theft and robbery occur regularly, and armed gangs are known to operate in the outlying areas of Bangui.

AIR:
Scheduled flights sometimes operate to Berbérati. However, most domestic flying is limited to chartered planes. Contact *Minair* (Tel: 611 963 *or* 612 236) *or BADICA* (Tel: 613 726/7) for details.

RIVER:
Ferries sail from Bangui to several towns further up the Ubangi.

ROAD:
Good roads connect the few main towns (although few are paved), but the majority are often impassable during the rainy season and travellers should expect delays. Most roads will require a 4-wheel-drive to render them passable. Outside the urban areas, motor vehicles are rare and spare parts virtually impossible to find. Traffic drives on the right. Travellers must carry as large a petrol supply as possible, since deliveries to stations outside the towns are infrequent and petrol shortages are common. **Bus:** Local services run between towns; they are a cheap but sometimes gruelling way to travel. It is also possible to pay for a lift on the numerous goods trucks which drive between the main towns. **Car hire:** Self-drive or chauffeur-driven cars are available. **Documentation**: International Driving Permit required.

URBAN:
Limited bus services run in Bangui on a two-zone tariff. Taxis are only available in the urban areas; they do not have meters and fares must be negotiated.

Travel Advice

All but essential travel to the Central African Republic is advised against. Following a coup d'etat in March 2003 order has yet to be restored to much of the country outside Bangui. Travellers who must travel outside Bangui are strongly recommended to check on the situation in the areas through which they are travelling with their local contacts, the local authorities and diplomatic missions before proceeding.

The threat from terrorism is low but you should be aware of the global risk of indiscriminate terrorist attacks, which could be against civilian targets, including places frequented by foreigners.

This advice is based on information provided by the Foreign and Commonwealth Office in the UK. It is correct at time of publishing. As the situation can change rapidly, visitors are advised to contact the following organisations for the latest travel advice:

British Foreign and Commonwealth Office
Tel: (0845) 850 2829.
Website: www.fco.gov.uk

US Department of State
Website: http://travel.state.gov/travel

Accommodation

HOTELS:
There are good hotels in Bangui, some of which are very exclusive and expensive. The better hotels have air conditioning and swimming pools. Pre-booking is essential - ideally several weeks in advance. Outside Bangui, accommodation of any standard may be difficult to find, although guest houses exist in smaller towns, principally Bangassou, Boali, Bambari and Bossangoa.

CAMPING AND CARAVANNING:
Most of the country is unpopulated or traversed by nomadic herdsmen, and there are few organised facilities for camping and caravanning. Sufficient provisions should be carried with vehicles at all times.

Top Things To See & Do

• Discover the present-day capital, **Bangui**, which rests beside the **River Ubangi**. Built on a rock, Bangui is shaded by tropical greenery and features many modern buildings. Places of interest include the colourful **Central Market** (renowned for its malachite necklaces), the **Boganda Museum**, the **Arts and Crafts School**, the cathedral and the **Saint Paul Mission**, whose small brick church overlooks the river, and the **Hausa quarter**. The **Grande Corniche** leads to the banks of the Ubangi and provides a picturesque view of the fishermen's round huts and canoes.
• See **indigenous forest tribes** living in encampments of small, low huts made of lianas and roofed with leaves in

the **Lobaye Region**, 100km (60 miles) from the capital. There are coffee plantations on the fringe of the forest.
• Watch the flow of the **Boali Waterfalls**, near the charming and picturesque village of **Boali**. They are 250m (820ft) wide and 50m (165ft) high, with a stunning view from the restaurant at the top. The nearby hydroelectric power plant can also be visited.
• At **Bouar**, in the east of the country, see **burial mounds** thought to be thousands of years old, studded with upright megaliths (*tanjunu*).
• In **Bangassou**, near the **Ubangi River** on the border with the Democratic Republic of Congo, any venture to the extraordinary **Kembe Falls** on the **River Kotto** is definitely worth it.
• In the dry season, take a **4-wheel-drive vehicle** and try and spot some **wildlife** in the Central African Republic's national parks. The three most important parks are **Manovo-Gounda St Floris**, known for its high concentration of hippos; **Bamingui-Bangoran** in the north; and **Dzanga-Sangha** in the southwest. The game population of these National Parks is impressive, although the activities of poachers have led to a considerable decrease in recent years - elephants and rhinos being the worst affected species. It is also possible to view gorillas in **Bayanga**. Please note that there is no accommodation available: all supplies, including bedding, must be taken.
• Try shooting some hoops: **Basketball** is Africa's most popular sport and a good way to forge connections with the people of the Central African Republic.
• See some rare examples of beautifully forged **wooden houses** in the town of **Zinga** on the **Oubangui river**.

Entertainment

FOOD & DRINK: Western food is only available in the capital, Bangui. Most of the top-class hotels have good restaurants. The standard of these restaurants is high, but they do tend to be expensive. Otherwise travellers must call at local villages and barter for provisions. Local food is basic. Many dishes contain okra (*gombo*), although other popular ingredients include rice, bananas and cassava.
Bars are numerous in Bangui with both table and counter service. Drinking and smoking are not encouraged in Muslim society; in Muslim areas, drinking is best done in private. Elsewhere, there are numerous beer halls offering beverages of a high standard.

National specialities:
• *Muamba de Galinha* is chicken with palm oil and okra.
• Chicken and cumin stew.
• Palm butter soup.
• Shrimps eaten with boiled yams or sweet potatoes.
• Spinach stew, which might also include tomato, peppers, chiles, onions and peanut butter.
• Banana leaves stuffed with beef, onions and peanuts.
• *Dongo-Dongo*, which is halfway between a soup and a sauce, and is always served with okra and sometimes fish or meat too.

National drinks:
• Two of the most popular brews are palm wine and banana wine.

Tipping: 10 per cent is appropriate in expensive hotels and restaurants. Bargaining is normal.

NIGHTLIFE: The few hotels in Bangui have expensive clubs catering for tourists and businessmen; local nightlife is centred on the district known as 'Kilomètre Cinq'.

SHOPPING: Bangui has reasonable shopping facilities, notably for ebony, gold jewellery, butterfly collections and objets d'art made from butterfly wings. However, one of the best methods of finding bargain souvenirs is by bartering with villagers outside the urban areas for their handmade goods. **Shopping hours:** Mon-Sat 0800-1200 and 1600-1900. Some shops close on Monday. The market in Bangui is open 0730-dusk.

Business

ECONOMY: Agriculture, upon which most of the population depends, is concentrated on subsistence crops plus coffee, cotton and wood as cash crops for export. Livestock and tobacco are also exported. The main cash earner is timber, which has been heavily exploited with little government restriction. The country's mining industry is largely devoted to diamonds; a small quantity of gold is also produced. Other deposits, including uranium, copper, manganese and iron ore, are yet to be exploited. The small manufacturing sector is devoted to the processing of primary products to produce food and drinks, wood products and textiles. The overall economic development of the Central African Republic has been limited by an adverse climate, poor infrastructure and low world commodity prices. With a per capita annual income of just US$260, the Central African Republic is one of Africa's poorest countries; the GDP real growth rate was 0.5 per cent in 2004 (CIA est.) and the annual growth rate a modest 1.1 per cent. The Central African Republic is a member of the Central African Economic and Monetary Union (CEMAC), the main regional trading organisation. France provides extensive economic and financial aid and is the country's main trading partner. Belgium and Luxembourg are both important export markets.

BUSINESS ETIQUETTE: A knowledge of French is essential. Interpreter and translation services may be available at large hotels. Business cards should be in French and English. Formal wear is expected (suits and ties for men). The best months for business visits are between November and May. **Office hours**: Mon-Fri 0730-1530.

Chad

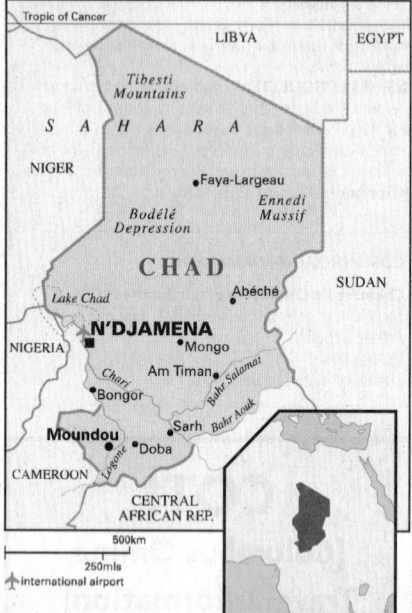

Location: Central Africa.

Time: GMT + 1.

Overview

Indications of population around the shores of Lake Chad date back to Neolithic times. The shores were an important junction for several major trans-Saharan caravan routes for centuries. From the 11th to the 15th century, the state of Kanem was the dominant force in the region, occupying much of the area that makes up present-day Chad. In the 15th and 16th centuries, the state of Borno, which had its centre on the other side of Lake Chad (in present-day Nigeria), exercised a major influence. A gradual process of Islamisation took place in the region from this time, especially during the 16th and 17th centuries during the kingdoms of the Bagirmi and Ouaddai. The slave trade was a key component of their economies and as this declined from the early 19th century onwards, so did the kingdoms. In the 1880s, riven by internecine feuding, they were conquered by the Sudanese warlord Rabih al-Zubair. The Europeans arrived a few decades later, in the latter stages of their carve-up of the African continent.

Chad was first defined as a national territory in 1910, as one of the four making up French Equatorial Africa. Chad achieved independence in 1960 with François Tombalbaye, leader of the *Parti Progressiste Tchadien* (PPT), as Prime Minister. Its history since then has been characterised by political instability and tensions, largely due to religious and cultural divisions between the Muslim north and Christian/animist south – a pattern that may be found in many other African countries, including Nigeria and Sudan. However, there is still much to recommend in Chad. Its capital, N'Djamena, is a friendly and laidback city with a wonderful Central Market, where the whole experience of haggling for African produce is exceptionally good fun. Lake Chad, once one of the largest freshwater lakes in the world, is still a serene sight to behold, despite its gradual shrinkage due to climate change and increased demands. It is still of huge economic importance, providing water to millions of people in surrounding countries. Indeed, Chad itself, although one of the poorest of Africa's nations, is still geographically staggering, ranging from desert in the north to fertile farmland in the south, all under the canopy of a blue, blisteringly hot sky.

General Information

AREA: 1,284,000 sq km (495,800 sq miles).

POPULATION: 8.6 million (2003).

POPULATION DENSITY: 6.7 per sq km.

CAPITAL: N'Djaména. **Population:** 700,000.

GEOGRAPHY: Chad is situated in central Africa, bordered by Libya to the north, Niger, Nigeria and Cameroon to the west, the Central African Republic to the south, and Sudan to the east. The topography ranges from equatorial forests to the driest of deserts. In the northeast lies Ennedi, and to the north the volcanic Tibesti range - largely sheer cliffs, ravines and canyons set among Saharan sand dunes.

GOVERNMENT: Republic. Gained independence from France in 1960. **Head of State**: President Idriss Déby since 1990. **Head of Government**: Prime Minister Moussa Faki since 2003. **Recent history:** Since former army commander, Idriss Déby, took power, he has managed to stabilise the political situation to some extent and install a working democratic constitution. Déby's political vehicle, the *Mouvement Patriotique du Salut* (*MPS*), controls the National Assembly, with a sizeable opposition party in the form of the *Union pour le Renouveau et la Démocratie* (*URD*) led by Wadal Abdelkader Kamougue. The main extra-Parliamentary opposition is the *Mouvement pour la Démocratie and la Justice au Tchad* (MDJT), led by Déby's ex-Defence Minister, Youssouf Toigimi, which launched an armed rebellion in the northern Tibesti region in October 1998, although its potency has diminished following serious injuries to Toigimi suffered in August 2002.

In 2003 and 2004, unrest in neighbouring Sudan's Dafur region spilled across the border, along with thousands of refugees. Of additional importance has been the discovery of large oil deposits in the southern Doba region of the country (see *Business* section), which has provided the Government with an opportunity to develop the economy. It has also heightened interest in Chad – a relative international backwater – from outside, and has led to some improvement to previously rocky relations with France, the USA, and international institutions such as the World Bank.

Under the terms of the constitution adopted by national referendum in March 1996, the President is directly elected for a five-year term and holds executive power, assisted by an appointed Prime Minister and Cabinet. Legislative power is vested in a bicameral legislature, comprising the 125-strong National Assembly, which is directly elected for a four-year term in a mixture of single-member and multi-member constituencies; and the Senate, which is elected for a six-year term (one-third of which is renewed every two years). Voters backed a change in constitution which will allow Mr Déby to stand for a third term in 2006. The opposition cried foul over the referendum.

LANGUAGE: The official languages are French and Arabic. Other widely spoken African languages include Sara (in the south). The territory's boundaries enclose a small but highly diverse population.

RELIGION: 50 per cent Muslim, 35 per cent Christian, 15 per cent animist and other.

ELECTRICITY: 220 volts AC, 50Hz. Round two-pin plug.

SOCIAL CONVENTIONS: Chadians are a relaxed and friendly people, but respect for traditional beliefs and customs is expected. Dress is informal but conservative in respect of Muslim laws. There is strict segregation of women in the Muslim areas. It is customary to shake hands. The left hand should never be used for offering or accepting

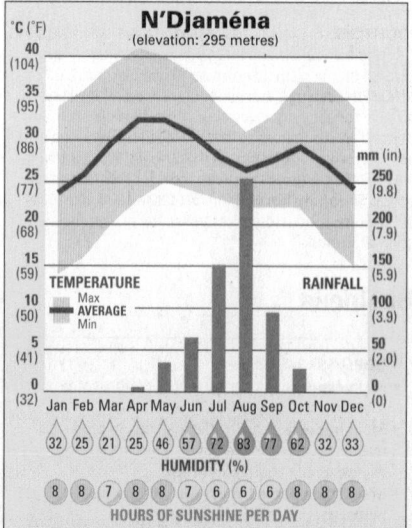

food, nor should the sole of the foot be exposed in the presence of a Muslim. Identification should be carried at all times; failure to do so may result in detention by police.

Photography: It is necessary to obtain a permit from the Ministry of Information in order to take photographs. Photographing military sites, airports and official buildings is prohibited. Other photography requires a Government permit.

Climate

Hot, tropical climate, though temperatures vary in different areas. The southern rainy season lasts from May to October and the central rains from June to September. The north has little rain all year. The dry season is often windy and cooler during the evenings.

Required clothing: Linens and tropical waterproof clothing.

Communications

Telephone: Country code: 235. It may be necessary to go through the operator.

Mobile telephone: Roaming agreements exist with some international mobile phone companies, but travellers should check with their service provider. Coverage is good to variable around N'Djaména and the southwest and patchy to non-existent elsewhere.

Internet: Limited access; available in N'Djaména but speeds are very slow and connection is difficult to establish.

Post: Airmail takes about one week. Post office hours: Mon-Fri 0700-1130 and 1530-1830, Sat 0730-1100.

MEDIA: The broadcast media are state-controlled, with coverage generally favouring the Government. Radio is the main means of mass communication. There are about a dozen private radio stations on the air, despite high licensing fees. These are subject to close official scrutiny. Some are run by non-profit groups. Private newspapers, critical of the Government, circulate freely in N'Djaména but have little impact among the largely rural and illiterate population.

Press: Newspapers are printed in French and generally have a low circulation. *Le Progres* is a daily newspaper; *Le Temps* is a weekly publication.

TV: State-owned *Teletchad* is the only channel.

Radio: *Radiodiffusion Nationale Tchadienne* is the national state-owned channel. *Dja FM* was Chad's first private station, *FM Liberté* is owned by a group of human rights organisations and *La Voix du Paysan* is owned by the Catholic Church.

Passport/Visa

	Passport Required?	Visa Required?	Return Ticket Required?
Full British	Yes	Yes	Yes
Australian	Yes	Yes	Yes
Canadian	Yes	Yes	Yes
USA	Yes	Yes	Yes
Other EU	Yes	Yes	Yes
Japanese	Yes	Yes	Yes

Note: *Regulations and requirements may be subject to change at short notice, and you are advised to contact the appropriate diplomatic or consular authority before finalising travel arrangements. Any numbers in the chart refer to the footnotes below.*

PASSPORTS: Passport valid for at least six months required by all.

VISAS: Required by all except those continuing their journey within 48 hours by the same or first connecting aircraft provided holding tickets with reserved seats and valid travel documents. All visitors must register at the *Sûreté* (immigration department) within 72 hours of arrival; two passport photographs are also required.

Types of visa and cost: *Ordinary visa* (includes visas issued for business or touristic purposes): €17 (single-entry); €100 (multiple-entry).

Validity: One month.

Note: Single parents or adults travelling alone with children should be aware that documentary evidence of parental responsibility may be requested.

Application to: Consulate (or consular section at Embassy); see *Passport/Visa Information* for details. In countries with no Chadian representation, French consulates may deal with applications.

Application requirements: (a) Valid passport. (b) Two passport-size photos. (c) Two application forms. (d) Letters of recommendation from employer (for business visits). (e) Valid return ticket. (f) Fee. (g) Yellow fever vaccination certificate, provided upon arrival. Failure to do so may result in a further vaccination being administered, for which a charge will be made.

Working days required: Three.

PASSPORT/VISA INFORMATION

Embassy of Chad in France
65 rue des Belles Feuilles, 75116 Paris, France
Tel: (1) 4553 3675.

Embassy of Chad in the USA
2002 R Street, NW, Washington, DC 20009, USA
Tel: (202) 462 4009.
Website: www.chadembassy.org

Money

Currency: CFA (*Communauté Financiaire Africaine*) Franc (XAF) = 100 centimes. Notes are in denominations of XAF10,000, 5000, 2000, 1000 and 500. Coins are in denominations of XAF250, 100, 50, 25, 10, 5 and 1. Chad is part of the French Monetary Area. Only currency issued by the *Banque des Etats de l'Afrique Centrale* (Bank of Central African States) is valid; currency issued by the *Banque des Etats de l'Afrique de l'Ouest* (Bank of West African States) is not. The CFA Franc is tied to the Euro.
Currency exchange: It is advisable to bring US Dollars or Euros rather than Sterling into the country. CFA Francs can be difficult to exchange outside the French Monetary Area.
Credit & debit cards: Diners Club, MasterCard and Visa are accepted at two hotels in N'Djaména. It may not be possible to obtain cash advances at banks on credit cards.
Traveller's cheques: May be exchanged at one or two banks in N'Djaména. To avoid additional exchange rate charges, travellers are advised to take traveller's cheques in Euros.
Currency restrictions: If importing or exporting local currency from other countries in the French monetary area, there are no restrictions; the import or export of local currency from any other country is limited to XAF10,000. Import of foreign currency is unrestricted, provided declared upon arrival. Export of foreign currency is limited to the amount imported and declared.
Banking hours: Mon-Sat 0700-1300, Fri 0700-1030.
Exchange rate indicators:
Rate at time of publishing
£1.00 = XAF967.90
$1.00 = XAF548.44

Duty Free

The following goods may be imported into Chad by persons over 18 years of age without incurring customs duty:
400 cigarettes (or cigarillos) or 125 cigars or 500g of tobacco (women are permitted to import cigarettes only); three bottles of wine and one bottle of spirits.
Note: There is free export of 1000 cigarettes or 250 cigars or 1kg of tobacco.

Public Holidays

Below are listed Public Holidays for the January 2006-June 2007 period.
2006: Jan 1 New Year's Day. **Jan 10** Eid al-Adha (Feast of the Sacrifice). **Apr 13** National Day. **Apr 17** Easter Monday. **May 1** Labour Day. **May 25** Liberation of Africa (anniversary of the OAU's foundation). **Aug 11** Independence Day. **Nov 1** All Saints' Day. **Oct 22-24** Eid al-Fitr (End of Ramadan). **Nov 28** Proclamation of the Republic. **Dec 1** Day of Liberty and Democracy. **Dec 25** Christmas Day. **Dec 31** Eid al-Adha (Feast of the Sacrifice).
2007: Jan 1 New Year's Day. **Apr 9** Easter Monday. **Apr 13** National Day. **May 1** Labour Day. **May 25** Liberation of Africa (anniversary of the OAU's foundation).
Note: Muslim festivals are timed according to local sightings of various phases of the moon and the dates given above are approximations. During the lunar month of Ramadan that precedes Eid al-Fitr, Muslims fast during the day and feast at night and normal business patterns may be interrupted. Many restaurants are closed during the day and there may be restrictions on smoking and drinking. Some disruption may continue into Eid al-Fitr itself. Eid al-Fitr and Eid al-Adha may last anything from two to 10 days, depending on the region. For more information, see the *World of Islam* appendix.

Health

	Special Precautions?	Certificate Required?
Yellow Fever	Yes	1
Cholera	Yes	2
Typhoid & Polio	3	N/A
Malaria	4	N/A

Note: *Regulations and requirements may be subject to change at short notice, and you are advised to contact your doctor well in advance of your intended date of departure. Any numbers in the chart refer to the footnotes below.*

1: A *yellow fever* certificate is required from travellers over one year of age.
2: Following WHO guidelines issued in 1973, a *cholera* vaccination certificate is no longer a condition of entry to Chad. However, cholera is a serious risk in this country and precautions are essential. Up-to-date advice should be sought before deciding whether these precautions should include vaccination as medical opinion is divided over its effectiveness. See the *Health* appendix for more information.
3: Immunisations or boosters for *typhoid* and *polio* are recommended.
4: Risk of *malaria* (and of other insect-borne diseases) exists all year throughout the country. The malignant *falciparum* form is prevalent. Resistance to chloroquine is reported. The recommended prophylaxis is mefloquine.
Food & Drink: All water should be regarded as being potentially contaminated. Water used for drinking, brushing teeth or making ice should have first been boiled or otherwise sterilised. Milk is unpasteurised and should be boiled. Powdered or tinned milk is available and is advised, but make sure that it is reconstituted with pure water. Avoid all dairy products. Only eat well-cooked meat and fish, preferably served hot. Pork, salad and mayonnaise may carry increased risk. Vegetables should be cooked and fruit peeled.
Other risks: *Bilharzia* (*schistosomiasis*) is present, but only in the south and southeast of the country. Avoid swimming and paddling in fresh water; swimming pools which are well chlorinated and maintained are safe. *River blindness* (*onchocerciasis*) and *sleeping sickness* (*trypanosomiasis*) are also prevalent. *Meningococcal meningitis* occurs, particularly in the savannah areas during the dry season (November to May). Immunisation against *diphtheria* and *hepatitis B* should be considered for longer visits. *Hepatitis A* and *E* are widespread in the region (especially in the north and east of Chad). Between June and August 2004 there were 672 cases/21 deaths of *acute jaundice syndrome* (AJS) in Coz Amer, where lies a camp of Sudanese refugees - and the *hepatitis E* virus has been confirmed. There has also been an outbreak of measles in N'Djaména and the surrounding southern provinces. *HIV/AIDS* is prevalent.
Rabies is present. For those at high risk, vaccination before arrival should be considered. If you are bitten, seek medical advice without delay. For more information, consult the *Health* appendix.
Health care: Medical facilities are poor, particularly in the north, and health insurance (to include emergency repatriation) is essential.

Travel - International

AIR:
There are at least two flights a week from Paris to Chad and several times a week from Congo, Ethiopia and the Central African Republic. Airlines serving Chad include *Air France*, *Cameroon Airlines* and *Ethiopian Airlines*.
Approximate flight times: From N'Djaména *to Paris* is five hours 30 minutes. There are no direct flights or good connections for those travelling from London. Overnight transit costs may be covered by some airlines.
Main airports: *N'Djaména (NDJ)* is 4km (2.5 miles) northwest of the city. *To/from the airport*: Taxis are available, operating 24 hours, for a fare of about XAF5000. *Facilities*: Post office, car hire, refreshments and bar, as well as restaurants.
Departure tax: XAF5000 (tourist tax) and XAF3000 (security tax). Students and transit passengers continuing their journey within 24 hours are exempt.
RAIL:
There is no railway network in Chad. There have been long-standing plans for a rail link with Cameroon but construction is not yet underway.
ROAD:
There are routes from Cameroon, Central African Republic, Niger and Nigeria. The border between Cameroon and Chad is the River Logone, which flows into Lake Chad. Boats ply across the river (there is no bridge). Access from Nigeria is via a sliver of northern Cameroon. There is a road from N'Djaména via Sarh to the Central African Republic. The road from N'Djaména to Maidguri in Niger is paved. Roads can be inaccessible during the rainy season and the best time to travel by road is between November and May. It is not possible, or advisable, to cross the border from Sudan. Care should be taken when travelling in the area around the border with Cameroon as there have been reports of armed bandits. **Bus:** Minibuses and bush taxis operate between N'Djaména and Kousséri in Cameroon. Rudimentary public transport is available to the Central African Republic, Niger and Nigeria, although it may be necessary to change vehicles at the border.

Travel - Internal

AIR:
At present, there is a poor domestic service by *Air Tchad* connecting N'Djaména to Maundou, Sarh and Mao. Enquire at the Direction de la Promotion Touristique for further details; see *Top Things To See & Do*.
ROAD:
Travel by road outside N'Djaména is possible by 4-wheel-drive vehicle and permits are usually needed. In rural areas drivers should watch out for livestock. There are also no emergency services so drivers should exercise extreme caution. Road service is limited to Good Samaritans. Buses run fairly regularly to Sarh during the dry season. Security conditions and a lack of housing, food, petrol and vehicle repair facilities have resulted in the Government restricting travel, especially in the central and northern areas of the country. Petrol is expensive and petrol stations are not widely available. Many roads urgently need repair, and are impassable during the rainy season, especially in the south. It is advised to travel in convoy, keep doors locked, carry spare fuel and supplies, and not travel after dark, due to the potential for highway bandits. Traffic drives on the right. For travel to all areas outside N'Djaména, authorisation from the Ministry of the Interior is required, which is usually granted without difficulty after a few days. **Documentation**: International Driving Permit required for car hire (which is expensive) as well as an official *autorisation de circuler*.
URBAN:
The city of N'Djaména has an adequate road system and there are limited self-drive and chauffeured car hire facilities. Minibuses and taxis operate in N'Djaména, with a flat fare charged. A 10 per cent tip is expected by taxi drivers.

Travel Advice

Travellers are advised against all travel to the area of Chad bordering the Darfur region of Sudan where, due to rebel activity and the conflict in Darfur, the security situation is extremely unstable.
Travellers are advised against all travel to the Borkou-Ennedi-Tibesti provinces *in* the north of the country, to the area bordering the Central African Republic (CAR) and to the area south of Goz Beida. The Sudan and Libyan borders are subject to closure.
When travelling in Northern Chad, tourists must be accompanied by a local guide provided by the local authorities or *sous-préfet*.
The tri-border area where Chad, Sudan and CAR meet should be avoided.
Terrorists are active in countries neighbouring Chad, including Algeria.
This advice is based on information provided by the Foreign and Commonwealth Office in the UK. It is correct at time of publishing. As the situation can change rapidly, visitors are advised to contact the following organisations for the latest travel advice:

British Foreign and Commonwealth Office
Tel: (0845) 850 2829.
Website: www.fco.gov.uk

US Department of State
Website: http://travel.state.gov/travel

Accommodation

HOTELS:
There are several good hotels in N'Djaména, but accommodation elsewhere is very limited. There are some small hotels at Sarh, a modern hotel complex in Zakouma National Park, and various small hunting hotels in the southwest. It is advisable to book in advance and prospective travellers should contact the Embassy of Chad in France for the latest information (see *Passport/Visa Information*).

Top Things To See & Do

- **N'Djamena**, Chad's capital, is slowly regaining its pre-war reputation as one of Central Africa's liveliest cities. Bullet holes in buildings serve as a reminder of troubled times, but the atmosphere here is increasingly upbeat. The historic quarter, with its colourful daily **market**, is fascinating and a good place to pick up colourful Chadian rugs and jewellery. The **National Museum** has collections of the Sarh culture dating back to the ninth century. There is a distinctive difference between the Arab section of town (very quiet at night) and the area where the southerners live (lively and full of bars).
- **Zakouma National Park** is located on an immense plain, across which the Bahr Salamat and its tributaries flow from north to south. The Government and the EU have restocked and refurbished the park since it was ravaged by civil war and poachers. Visitors can now see huge flocks of elephants, giraffes and lions.
- **Lake Chad** must be seen, not only since it was once the centre of Africa's lucrative salt trade, and one of the largest freshwater lakes in the world, but also because you may be running out of time to see it: Lake Chad is

shrinking. The lake is best seen during the August to December period, when the water level is highest and the occasional hippo or crocodile can be seen drifting by.
- Take a glug of Moundou's beer from the **Gala Brewery**, some of the best in the country.
- Visit **Abéché**, a former capital of the powerful Ouadaï sultanate and surrounded by desert; the town has retained much of its oriental charm with interesting mosques, cobbled narrow streets and old markets.
- Try and catch a glimpse of some of the best **camel racing** in the world in the **Tibesti Mountains**, home of the fierce Toubou tribe. The inhabitants are distantly related to the Tuareg of the Western Sahara, and were made famous by Herodotus as the 'Troglodytes' – stocky but immensely agile cave-dwellers. This astonishing region of chasms and crags has seldom been seen by non-Muslims and remains closed to travellers, so is best watched from afar. It will not be difficult to look out for, since it contains **Emi Koussi**, a high peak, 3414m (11,200ft) above sea level.

TOURIST INFORMATION

Direction du Tourisme
BP 86, N'Djaména, Chad
Tel: 522 303.

Entertainment

FOOD & DRINK: N'Djaména offers a fair selection of restaurants serving mainly French and African food. Standard European-style service is normal. Outside the capital, restaurants tend to be cheap and cheerful and there is an acute shortage of some foodstuffs. Visitors should exercise caution with street market food.
National specialities:
- Peanut sauce over rice, often eaten in Southern Chad.
National drinks:
- Chad's excellent beer, *Gala*, is brewed in Moundou and is widely available in the non-Muslim parts of the capital.
- *Karkanji*, a drink made from Hibiscus flowers.
Tipping: 10 per cent is normal for most services (US Dollars are the preferred currency).
NIGHTLIFE: Lively dancing and music is to be found in the capital, where there is an increasing number of nightclubs. *Pari-matches* take place on most Saturdays and Sundays in N'Djaména (non-Muslim areas): groups of women hire bars and sell drinks all day. Outside N'Djaména, nightlife is limited, although bars and open-air dancing can generally be found.
SHOPPING: Chad has an excellent crafts industry. Items include camel-hair carpets, all kinds of leatherware, embroidered cotton cloths, decorated *calabashes*, knives, weapons, pottery and brass animals.

Shopping hours: Tues-Sat 0900-1200 and 1600-1930. Food shops open Sunday morning. The market in the capital is open from 0730 until dusk.

Business

- **GDP:** US$1.9 billion (2002 estimate).
- **Main exports:** Cotton, cattle and Gum Arabic.
- **Main imports:** Machinery and transportation equipment, industrial goods, petroleum products, foodstuffs and textiles.
- **Main trade partners:** France, USA, China, Cameroon, Portugal and Germany.

ECONOMY: Chad is one of the world's poorest countries, with a per capita annual income of just US$200. Civil war, poor infrastructure, few natural resources and droughts have hampered any development of the economy during the last few decades. Subsistence level farming occupies 80 per cent of the population, producing mainly sorghum, millet and groundnuts. Cotton is the main cash crop. Nonetheless, there are chronic food shortages which can, in many areas, only be met by international food aid. Agro-industrial operations, most of which are based in the south of the country, dominate the small industrial sector. Mineral deposits including tungsten, tin, bauxite, gold and iron ore have been located: only natron (hydrated sodium carbonate) is mined in commercial quantities. However, the country now has a unique opportunity to transform its economic fortunes following the discovery of large oil deposits in the Doba Basin in the southwest. A 1000km pipeline linking the fields to the Cameroonian port of Kribi (Chad is landlocked) opened in 2003. Chad is expected to earn around US$3 billion over 25 years, which will increase national income by around 50 per cent. To avoid the corruption that oil has given rise to in other African countries, a law requires that 80 per cent of oil revenue is spent on development projects. Chad is a member of the Central African Economic and Customs Union (CEEAC).
BUSINESS ETIQUETTE: A knowledge of French is essential as there are no professional translators available. Best months for business visits are between November and May.
Office hours: Mon-Sat 0700-1400, Fri 0700-1200.

COMMERCIAL INFORMATION

Chambre de Commerce, d'Industrie, d'Agriculture, des Mines et d'Artisanat
13 avenue du Colonel Moll, BP 458, N'Djaména, Chad
Tel: 525 264.

Chile

1000km / 500mls — ✈ International airport

Location: West coast of South America.

Time: Mainland and Juan Fernández Islands: GMT - 4 (GMT - 3 from second Sunday in October to second Saturday in March).
Easter Island: GMT - 6 (GMT - 5 from second Sunday in October to second Saturday in March).

Overview

Chile is situated in South America, bounded by Peru, Bolivia, Argentina, the Antarctic and the Pacific Ocean. Home of the Andes mountain range, it is a thin ribbon of land, 4200km (2610 miles) long and nowhere more than 180km (115 miles) wide.
The Araucanian Indians were the original inhabitants of Chile. The Spanish conquered the country in the 16th century and ruled until the country's independence in 1818. As a result of the War of the Pacific (1879-1883), Chile gained Tarapacá, Tacna and Arica from Bolivia, and took control of the Atacama. Border disputes between Chile and Bolivia have been a recurrent element in Chile's history ever since.
Elections in 1970 brought *Unidad Popular*, led by the Marxist Dr Salvador Allende, to power. A military coup followed, during which Allende committed suicide rather than surrender to his attackers. General Augusto Pinochet Ugarte was declared Supreme Chief of State and President, and remained in power despite considerable opposition from many sectors of society. The ruling military junta assumed wide-ranging powers, its main aim being to eliminate the Communist Party and other leftist opposition. During the 'state of siege', political opponents were imprisoned (and many of them 'disappeared'), censorship was systematic and all non-Government political activity banned.
These powers were gradually relaxed during the 1980s. Patricio Aylwin, leader of the *Concertación de los Partidos de la Democracia* (*CPD*), a 17-party coalition in which the Christian Democrats (PCD, usually classified as centre-left, in contrast with European practice) were the largest component, stood against the General and won in the Presidential elections of December 1989. In 1998, Pinochet

Chile

officially retired and Chile has begun to come to terms with his legacy. His arrest and subsequent detention in London in October 1998 following an extradition request from Spain polarised Chilean society. It also broke a taboo, culminating in court decisions which stripped him of his immunity from prosecution although the former ruler has not been prosecuted yet.
Because of its unusual geography, Chile has a hugely varied climate ranging from the world's driest desert in the north, through a Mediterranean climate in the centre, to a snow-prone Alpine climate in the south. Travellers will enjoy the country's abundant fauna and flora and spectacular scenery consisting of huge glaciers, fjords, waterfalls, blue lakes and numerous national parks where trekking is a very popular activity amongst tourists.

General Information

AREA: 756,096 sq km (291,930 sq miles).
POPULATION: 15.82 million (2004 estimate).
POPULATION DENSITY: 20.9 per sq km.
CAPITAL: Santiago (de Chile). **Population**: 6 million.
GEOGRAPHY: Chile is situated in South America, bordered to the north by Peru, to the east by Bolivia and Argentina, to the west by the Pacific and to the south by the Antarctic. The country exercises sovereignty over a number of islands off the coast, including the Juan Fernández Islands and Easter Island. Chile is one of the most remarkably shaped countries in the world; a ribbon of land, 4200km (2610 miles) long and nowhere more than 180km (115 miles) wide. The Andes and a coastal highland range take up one-third or half of the width in parts, and run parallel with each other from north to south. The coastal range forms high, sloped cliffs into the sea from the northern to the central area. Between the ranges runs a fertile valley, except in the north where transverse ranges join the two major ones, and in the far south where the sea has broken through the coastal range to form an assortment of archipelagos and channels. The country contains wide variations of soil and vast differences of climate. This is reflected in the distribution of the population, and in the wide range of occupations from area to area. The northern part of the country consists mainly of the Atacama Desert, the driest in the world. It is also the main mining area. The central zone is predominantly agricultural. The south is forested and contains some agriculture; further south, the forests on the Atlantic side give way to rolling grassland on which sheep and cattle are raised.
GOVERNMENT: Republic. Gained independence from Spain in 1810. **Head of State and Government**: President Michelle Bachelet since 2006. **Recent history:** President Ricardo Lagos Escobar was elected for a six year term and took office in March 2000. He stepped down in early 2006. His successor, socialist Michelle Bachelet, beat conservative billionaire and former Senator Sebastian Pinera in the January 2006 Presidential election. She is the first woman President.
On 16 August 2005, a bill embodying 58 constitutional reforms was approved by Congress, and endorsed by President Lagos. The reforms came into effect on 11 March 2006. The key features of the reforms include: the reduction of the Presidential terms from six to four years; the end of designated senators and 'senators for life' (previously awarded to former Presidents) - the remaining 38 senators will be elected by popular vote; responsibility removed from the armed forces as 'institutional guarantors'; the change in functions of the National Security Council (*Cosena*); and the restoration of power to the President to remove the commanders-in-chief of the armed forces and the forces of order. The reform is a milestone for Chile's continuing transition to democracy as it eliminates the so-called 'authoritarian enclaves' (military Government appointees who had occupied seats in the Senate and who have traditionally been a block to reforms proposed by the governing left-wing coalition). Although President Escobar did not succeed in gaining the support of all the political forces in order to change the binominal electoral system (another Pinochet legacy which gives disproportionate representation to the right), he, at least, succeeded in opening up the debate. Michelle Bachelet has already committed to reforming the electoral system during her Presidential term.
LANGUAGE: The official language is Spanish, but English is widely spoken.
RELIGION: Predominantly Christian, of which 72 per cent are Roman Catholic.
ELECTRICITY: 220 volts AC, 50Hz. Three-pin plugs and screw-type bulbs are used.
SOCIAL CONVENTIONS: Handshaking is the customary form of greeting. Most Chileans use a double surname and only the first part should be used in addressing them. Normal courtesies should be observed when visiting local people. It is very common to entertain at home and it is acceptable for invitees to give small presents as a token of thanks. Informal, conservative clothes are acceptable in most places but women should not wear shorts outside resort areas.

Climate

Ranges from hot and arid in the north to very cold in the far south. The central areas have a mild Mediterranean climate with a wet season (May to August). Beyond Puerto Montt in the south is one of the wettest and stormiest areas in the world.
Required clothing: Lightweight cottons and linens in northern and central areas. Rainwear is advised during rainy seasons. Mediumweights and waterproofing are needed in the south.

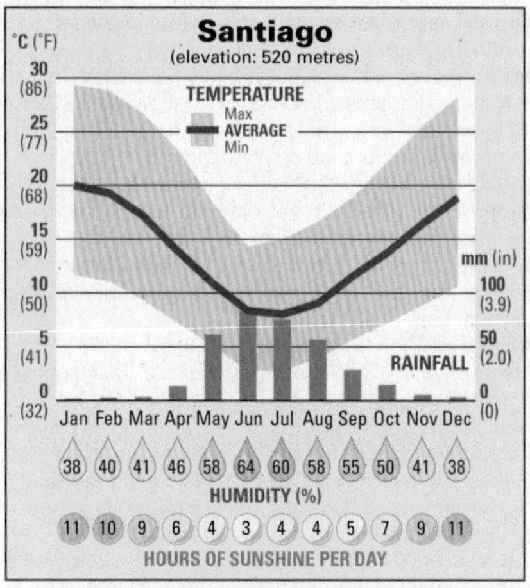

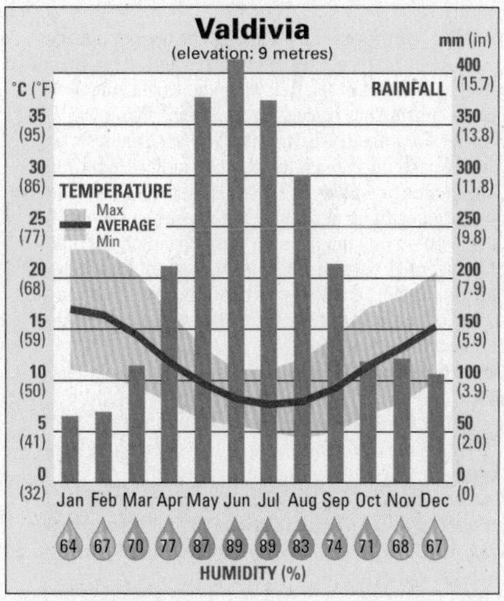

Communications

Telephone: Full IDD available. Country code: 56. *Compañia de Teléfonos de Chile* provides most services, though there are a few independent companies. Cheap rate is applicable Mon-Fri 1800-0500 and all day Saturday, Sunday and public holidays.
Mobile telephone: Roaming agreements exist. Quality of coverage can be variable.
Internet: There are some Internet cafes in the main towns.
Post: Daily airmail services to Europe take approximately three to four days. Post office hours in Santiago: Mon-Fri 0900-1800; Sat 0900-1300. The Central Post Office in Santiago is located at Agustinas 1137, Plaza de Armas.
MEDIA: Chile's national and local TV channels operate alongside extensive cable TV networks, which carry many US and international stations. The constitution provides for freedom of speech and of the media, and this is generally respected by the authorities. A 2001 Press Freedom Act supressed many of the Pinochet-era restrictions on the media.
Press: Spanish dailies include *El Mercurio*, *La Tercera*, conservative evening newspaper *La Segunda*, business newspaper *El Diari* and *La Nacion* which is Government-owned. Foreign newspapers are available. The *Santiago Times* is published in English.
TV: Although state-owned, *National Television of Chile* is not under direct Government control; *TV Universidad Catolica de Chile (TVUC)* and *Universidad Catolica de Valparaiso* are owned by Catholic universities; *Chilevision* is owned by Venezuela's Cisneros Group; *Megavision* is a private network; *Red TV* is a commercial channel.
Radio: Radio stations include *Radio Nacional de Chile;* news-based national commercial network *Radio Cooperativa*; commercial networks, *Pudahuel FM*; *Bio Bio La Radio* and *El Conquistador*; *FM and* music-based FM network, *Radio Horizonte*.

Passport/Visa

	Passport Required?	Visa Required?	Return Ticket Required?
Full British	Yes	No/1	Yes
Australian	Yes	1/2	Yes
Canadian	Yes	1/2	Yes
USA	Yes	1/2	Yes
Other EU	Yes	1	Yes
Japanese	Yes	No/1	Yes

Note: *Regulations and requirements may be subject to change at short notice, and you are advised to contact the appropriate diplomatic or consular authority before finalising travel arrangements. Any numbers in the chart refer to the footnotes below.*

PASSPORTS: Valid passport required by all except:
(a) nationals of Argentina, Brazil, Colombia, Paraguay and Uruguay, provided not entering under commercial contract or as students or as immigrants, can enter with a special identity card (*Cédula de Identitad*) for short-term visits (except foreign residents of these countries who *do* need a passport); (b) Chinese residents of Taiwan (China) and nationals of Taiwan, Mexico and Peru who have an official travel document issued by the Organisation of American States. Documents have to remain valid for six months after departure.
Note: Passports issued to children must contain a photo and state the nationality.
VISAS: A visa is not required by the following:
(a) **1.** nationals of countries mentioned in the chart above for a touristic stay of up to 90 days (except nationals of Greece, who can stay up to 60 days, and nationals of Latvia, who *do* need a visa);
(b) nationals of Andorra, Antigua & Barbuda, The Bahamas, Barbados, Bolivia, Bulgaria, Croatia, Dominican Republic, Ecuador, El Salvador, Grenada, Guatemala, Honduras, Iceland, Israel, Jamaica, Korea (Rep), Liechtenstein, Mauritius, Mexico, Monaco, New Zealand, Nicaragua, Norway, Panama, St Kitts & Nevis, St Lucia, San Marino, Serbia & Montenegro, South Africa, Surinam, Switzerland, Tonga, Turkey and Venezuela for stays of up to 90 days;
(c) nationals of Indonesia and Peru for stays of up to 60 days;
(d) nationals of Belize, Costa Rica, Malaysia and Singapore for touristic stays of up to 30 days;
(e) transit passengers continuing their journey on the same or first connecting aircraft provided holding required travel documents for onward destination and not leaving the airport transit lounge.
Note: 2. Nationals of Australia, Canada, Mexico and the USA entering Chile for touristic purposes will be charged a processing fee payable on arrival and in cash only. For nationals of the USA, the fee is US$100; for nationals of Canada, the fee is US$55; for nationals of Australia, the fee is US$34; and for nationals of Mexico, the fee is US$15.
Types of visa and cost: *Tourist*, *Visitor* (visa required for nationals of countries with no diplomatic relations with Chile), *Residence* (visa required if intending to carry out paid employment or study in Chile). Cost varies according to nationality of applicant. Enquire at Consulate or consular section of the Embassy for further information.
Validity: Tourist and Visitor (up to 90 days depending on nationality); Residence (enquire at Embassy).
Application to: Consulate (or consular section at Embassy); see *Passport/Visa Information*.
Application requirements: (a) Valid passport. (b) Evidence of sufficient funds to cover stay. (c) Return or onward ticket. (d) Fee.
Working days required: Up to 15 depending on nationality and whether application has to be referred to the relevant authorities.
Temporary residence: Not readily granted. Enquire at the Consulate or consular section of the Embassy (see *Passport/Visa Information*).

PASSPORT/VISA INFORMATION

Embassy and Consulate of the Republic of Chile in the UK
12 Devonshire Street, London W1G 7DS, UK
Tel: (020) 7580 6392 (embassy) *or* 1023 (consular section).
Website: www.echileuk.demon.co.uk
Working hours: Mon-Thurs 0900-1730, Fri: 0900-1430; Open to public: Mon-Fri 0900-1330.

Embassy of the Republic of Chile in the USA
1732 Massachussets Avenue, NW, Washington, DC 20036, USA
Tel: (202) 785 1746.
Website: www.chile-usa.org

Chilean Consulate General in the USA
Suite 601, 6th Floor, 866 United Nations Plaza, New York, NY 10017, USA
Tel: (212) 980 3366.
Website: www.chileny.com

A B C D E F G H I J K L M N O P Q R S T U V W X Y Z

Money

Currency: Chilean Peso (CLP; symbol CH$) = 100 centavos. Notes are in denominations of CH$20,000, 10,000, 5000, 2000, 1000 and 500. Coins are in denominations of CH$500, 100, 50, 10, 5 and 1.

Currency exchange: Foreign exchange transactions can be conducted through commercial banks, *casas de cambio*, or authorised shops, restaurants, hotels and clubs. Visitors should not be tempted by the premiums of 10 to 15 per cent over the official rate offered by black marketeers. *Casas de cambio* are open daily 0900-1900.

Credit & debit cards: American Express, Diners Club, MasterCard and Visa are accepted. Check with your credit or debit card company for details of merchant acceptability and other services which may be available.

Traveller's cheques: Must be changed before 1200 except in *casas de cambio* (which in any case tend to offer better rates than banks). There may be some difficulty exchanging traveller's cheques outside major towns. To avoid additional exchange rate charges, traveller's are advised to take traveller's cheques in US Dollars.

Currency restrictions: There are no restrictions on the import and export of either local or foreign currency.

Banking hours: Mon-Fri 0900-1400.

Exchange rate indicators:
Rate at time of publishing
£1.00=   CH$935.74
$1.00=   CH$530.25

Duty Free

The following goods may be imported into Chile without incurring customs duty:
400 cigarettes and 500g of tobacco and 50 large cigars or 50 small cigars; 2.5l of alcohol (only for visitors over 18 years of age); a reasonable quantity of perfume for personal use.

Note: Edible products of animal origin, flowers, fruits and vegetables are only permitted with a certificate (Fitosanitario) issued by the Department of Agriculture in the country of origin.

Prohibited items: Parrots.

Public Holidays

Below are listed Public Holidays for the January 2006-June 2007 period.
2006: Jan 1 New Year's Day. **Apr 14** Good Friday. **Apr 15** Holy Saturday. **May 1** Labour Day. **May 21** Navy Day. **Jun 12*** Corpus Christi. **Jun 29*** St Peter and St Paul. **Aug 15** Assumption. **Sep 11** Reconciliation Day. **Sep 18** Independence Day. **Sep 19** Army Day. **Oct 12*** Dia de la Raza (Columbus Day). **Nov 1** All Saints' Day. **Dec 8** Immaculate Conception. **Dec 25** Christmas Day.
2007: Jan 1 New Year's Day. **Apr 6** Good Friday. **Apr 7** Holy Saturday. **May 1** Labour Day. **May 21** Navy Day. **Jun 7*** Corpus Christi. **Jun 26*** St Peter and St Paul.
Note: *If Corpus Christi, St Peter and St Paul and Dia de la Raza (Columbus Day) fall on a day other than Saturday, Sunday or Monday, the holiday is usually held on the nearest Monday.

Health

	Special Precautions?	Certificate Required?
Yellow Fever	1	No
Cholera	No	No
Typhoid & Polio	2	N/A
Malaria	No	N/A

Note: *Regulations and requirements may be subject to change at short notice, and you are advised to contact your doctor well in advance of your intended date of departure. Any numbers in the chart refer to the footnotes below.*

1: Immunisation against Yellow Fever is required if going to Easter Island within six days of visiting infected countries.
2: Immunisation against typhoid and Polio are sometimes advised.

Food & drink: All water should be regarded as being potentially contaminated. Water used for drinking, brushing teeth or making ice should have first been boiled or otherwise sterilised. Milk is pasteurised and is safe to drink without boiling, except in very remote areas of the countryside. Only eat well-cooked meat and fish, preferably served hot. Pork, salad and mayonnaise may carry increased risk. Vegetables should be cooked and fruit peeled.

Other risks: Immunisation against *tetanus* and *hepatitis A* is advised. Epidemic outbreaks of *meningococcal meningitis* occur. *Chagas' disease* has been reported in rural areas but other insect-borne diseases are largely absent. *Rabies* is present in animals. For those at high risk,

vaccination before arrival should be considered. If you are bitten, seek medical advice without delay. For more information, consult the *Health* appendix.

Health care: Health insurance is essential.

Travel - International

AIR:
Chile has one privately owned national airline: *LAN-Chile (LA)* (website: www.lan.com), which deals with international flights. Its subsidiary, *Lanexpress (LU)* deals with domestic flights.

Approximate flight times: From Santiago to *London* is 16 hours 50 minutes.

Main airports: *Santiago (SCL) (Arturo Merino Benitez)* (website: www.aeropuertosantiago.cl). The airport is 21km (11 miles) northwest of Santiago (travel time – 30 minutes). *To/from the airport:* Bus services to the city centre operate from 0530 to 2400 every day. Underground services operate to Los Héroes, Central, Universidad de Santiago, Las Rejas and Pajaritos stations. Taxis to the city are also available. Official taxis are blue with official documentation. *Facilities:* Bar, bureaux de change, restaurants, car hire, post office and tourist office.

Air passes: *The Mercosur Airpass:* The pass is valid within Argentina, Brazil, Chile (except Easter Island), Paraguay and Uruguay. Participating airlines include *Pluna (PU), TAM Mercosur (TAM), TAM Linhas Aéreas (JJ)* and *VARIG (RG)*. The pass can only be purchased by passengers who live outside South America and who have a return ticket. Only eight flight coupons are allowed with a maximum of four coupons for each country and is valid for seven to a maximum of 30 days. At least two countries must be visited (to a maximum of five) and the flight route cannot be changed. A maximum of two stopovers is allowed per country.

The Visit South America Pass: Must be bought outside South America in country of residence and allows unlimited travel to 34 cities in the following countries: Argentina, Bolivia, Brazil, Chile (except Easter Island), Colombia, Ecuador, Paraguay, Peru, Uruguay and Venezuela. To be eligible, passengers must fly with *Lan* airlines (*LanChile, LanEcuador* or *LanPeru*). A minimum of three flights must be booked, with no maximum; the maximum stay is 60 days, with no minimum, and prices depend on the amount of flight zones covered. There is no discount for children, although infants travelling without need of a seat may do so free of charge. For further details, contact one of the participating airlines.

Departure tax: US$18.

SEA:
Main ports: *Empremar* (website: www.portvalparaiso.cl) in Valparaíso to/from where many shipping lines operate such as *Compañia Chilena de Navegación Interoceánica (CCNI)* (website: www.ccni.cl) and *Compañia Sud Americana de Vapores (CSAV)* (from New York and European ports) (website: www.csav.cl).

RAIL:
Some rail connections with neighbouring countries use buses for part of the journey. There are trains running between Arica and Tacna in Peru and La Paz in Bolivia.

ROAD:
The Pan American Highway enters Chile through Arica. TEPSA buses come to Chile from as far north as Ecuador. There are also services from Argentina and Brazil to Santiago.

Travel - Internal

AIR:
There are frequent services to main towns. The southern part of the country relies heavily on air links. Reservations are essential. Internal passenger air services are operated by the domestic subsidary of *LAN-Chile, Lanexpress (LU)* and *Sky Airline* (website: www.skyairline.cl), as well as by a number of air taxi companies. Services connecting the main towns are frequent during weekdays, and are fairly regular. There are one-month 'Visit Chile' tickets available from *Lanexpress* and *LAN-Chile* covering the north and the south of the country. Air passes sold in conjunction with *LAN* transatlantic flights cost US$250 for the first three coupons and US$60 per additional coupon (up to a maximum of six). A coupon is worth one sector of a flight. When travelling long haul with another airline, the costs are US$350 and US$80 per additional coupon. Passes must be obtained abroad and it is advisable to make reservations well in advance. Once purchased, reservations can be changed at no additional cost; but for re-routing, a charge of US$30 is made for each change. There are regular flights by *Lanexpress* from Santiago to Easter Island, which stop at the island en route to Tahiti. The flights are twice-weekly from November to February,

once-weekly at other times; it is essential to book in advance throughout the year. The flight takes 5 hours. Discounted flights to Easter Island can only be purchased in conjunction with *LAN* long-haul flights. An air taxi runs a daily service during the summer months to the Juan Fernández Islands from Valparaíso and Santiago.

Departure tax: CH$4521 or 3444. For distances under 270km, the departure tax is CH$1781.

SEA:
Coastal passenger shipping lines are unreliable and infrequent. Boat services run from Valparaíso to Easter Island and Robinson Crusoe Island (part of the Juan Fernández Islands) once a month. Contact local travel agents on arrival for details.

RAIL:
The state railway (run by the *State Railway Company*, website: www.efe.cl) runs between Santiago and Temuco. Services are limited by the geography of the country, but there is one daily train each way at 2000, with sleeping and restaurant cars, and some air conditioned accommodation. Principal trains also carry vehicles. Children under 1.20m in height travel free. Train fares are from £10-53. For details, contact *SERNATUR* (see *Top Things To Do*).

ROAD:
Chile has about 80,000km (49,460 miles) of good roads. The Pan American Highway crosses the country from north to south (a total of 3455km or 2147 miles) from the Peruvian border to Puerto Montt. It is advisable in remoter areas to carry spare petrol and an additional spare tyre. Tyres should be hard-wearing. Traffic drives on the right. You may consider a four wheel drive for driving in the countryside. **Bus:** Intercity buses are cheap and reliable. There is a luxury north-south service running most of the length of the country. Most long-distance coaches have toilets and serve food and drink. Sometimes a lower fare can be negotiated. For details, contact *SERNATUR* (see *Top Things To Do*). **Taxi:** Most have meters, but for long journeys fares should be agreed beforehand. A surcharge of 50 per cent applies on Sundays after 2100. Taxis in Santiago are black and yellow. Tipping is not expected. **Car hire:** Self-drive cars are available at the airport and in major city centres. They are hired on a daily basis, plus a mileage charge and 20 per cent tax. A large guarantee deposit is often required. Road maps are available from the Automóvil Club de Chile, Andrés Bello 1863, Santiago, Chile (tel: (2) 431 1000; website: www.cmet.net/acchi).

Documentation: An international, inter-American driving permit or a new European format driving licence bearing a photograph is necessary .

URBAN:
Santiago has three metro lines, as well as bus, minibus and shared 'Taxibus' services. A fourth and fifth metro line is under construction. Fares on the metro depend on the time of day in which travel occurs. 10-journey tickets (*carnets*) are available. Taxis are plentiful, the number approaching 1 per 100 inhabitants, an extremely high figure. They can be flagged down in the streets. The different tariffs are displayed in the taxis. Taxi drivers do not expect tips. The buses and minibuses have flat fares. There is a higher rate for shared taxis. There are bus and taxi services in most towns.

Travel times: The following chart gives approximate travel times from **Santiago** (in hours and minutes) to other major cities/towns in Chile.

	Air	Road	Rail
Arica	3.30	28.00	-
Concepción	1.00	9.00	7.00
Punta Arenas	4.20	120.00	-
Easter Island	5.00	-	-

Travel Advice

Most visits to Chile are trouble-free but you should be aware of the global risk of indiscriminate international terrorist attacks, which could be against civilian targets, including places frequented by foreigners.

Pickpocketing, other thefts and muggings are increasingly common.

Minefields are located in regions I, II and XII. Travellers are advised to contact the local authorities before travelling to the border areas of these regions.

This advice is based on information provided by the Foreign and Commonwealth Office in the UK. It is correct at time of publishing. As the situation can change rapidly, visitors are advised to contact the following organisations for the latest travel advice:

British Foreign and Commonwealth Office
Tel: (0845) 850 2829.
Website: www.fco.gov.uk

US Department of State
Website: http://travel.state.gov/travel

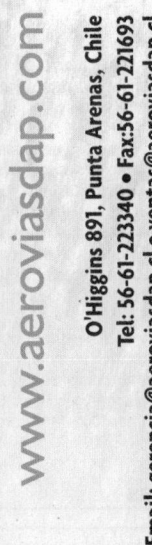

FULL DAY PROGRAM AND TWO DAYS ONE NIGHT PROGRAM

ACTIVITIES AT KING GEORGE ISLAND
(Full day + Two days one night)

- Visit Villa Las Estrellas, (first site to be inhabited by civilians)

- Visit the Sea Lion colony in the Drake Sea

- Walk to the Chinese Station to observe Marine Birds, Penguins and Weddell Seals.

- Cross over to Ardley Island, where Papua Penguin colonies live.

- Return to Punta Arenas (Chile)

ONLY TWO DAYS ONE NIGHT PROGRAM:

- On the following day we visit different Antarctic Research Stations and will be able to speak to researchers about their work.

- If time permits, we can visit additional areas of attraction before returning to Punta Arenas (Chile).

HELICOPTER IN ATARCTICA
Once on King George Island you can catch our Bo –105 Helicopter that will fly you to nearby glaciers, where you can enjoy a wonderful sight of millenary ice fields in Antarctica.

SHIP IN ANTARTICA
Dap Mares has recently incorporated an Oceanographic Ship mainly oriented to support scientific expeditions to Antarctica and to provide logistic for different Antarctic Bases.

For General Conditions and pricing, please visit our web site at www.aeroviasdap.com

Accommodation

HOTELS:

 Chile offers excellent accommodation. Several new luxury hotels have recently opened in Santiago and throughout the country. In all regions of Chile, whatever hotels lack in facilities is made up for by a comfortable, homely atmosphere; Chile's famous hospitality is very apparent in provinces where it is common to see the owner or manager sit down to dinner with guests. Advance bookings are essential in resort areas during the high season. The cost of accommodation in Santiago is higher than in the provinces. Rates in Valparaíso, Viña del Mar and other holiday resorts may be increased during the summer holiday from January to March. Members of foreign motoring organisations can obtain discounts at hotels by joining the Automóvil Club de Chile (see address in *Travel – Internal* section). **Grading**: Hotels in Chile are graded from 5 (luxurious rooms) to 2 stars (basic commodities - only 30 per cent of rooms with private bathroom).

Government tax: VAT of 19 per cent is levied on all hotel bills, except those paid in foreign currencies by foreign visitors for which an export bill is required.

CAMPING/CARAVANNING:

 Camping facilities exist throughout Chile. A list of campsites may be obtained from the Tourist Office. Official sites are expensive.

YOUTH HOSTELS:

 There are 13 hostels in Chile. Membership of the **Asociación Chilena de Albergues Turísticos Juveniles** (*see Accommodation Information*) is required; many hostels are extremely crowded and it is advised to book in advance where possible.

ACCOMMODATION INFORMATION

Chilean National Hotel Association (HOTELGA)
Nueva Tajamar 481, Oficina 806, North Tower,
Las Condes, Santiago, Chile
Tel: (2) 203 6625.
E-mail: hotelga@cebri.cl

Asociación Chilena de Albergues Turísticos Juveniles (Youth Hostels)
Av. Hernando de Aguirre 201, of. 602, Providencia, Chile
Tel: (2) 233 3220.
Website: www.hostelling.cl

Top Things To See

- **Arica**, near the northern border with Peru, is an excellent tourist centre. It has good beaches and the famous **San Marcos Cathedral**. The unique landscape of **Altiplano**, near Arica, where vast volcanoes, salt marshes and lakes exist together upon a 12,000ft plateau, is home to the indigenous Aymara Indians. Llamas and alpacas can be seen here. Travelling south through the **Atacama Desert**, excursions can be made to the hot springs of **Mamina** and to the oasis of the **Pica Valley**. The port of **Antofagasta** is the stopping point for air services and for most shipping lines. From here, a visit can be made to **Chuquicamata**, the world's largest opencast copper mine, and also to the archaeological oasis town of **San Pedro de Atacama** and to the geysers at **El Tatio**.
- Further south is **Coquimbo**, situated in one of the best harbours on the coast. Nearby is the beautiful bathing resort of **Los Vilos**. Nine miles north of Coquimbo is **La Serena**, the provincial capital. This charming and well laid-out town is graced with fine buildings and streets, and good reproductions of the attractive Spanish colonial style of architecture. The town is at the mouth of the **Elqui River** and excursions can be made from here to the rich fruit-growing region of the **Elqui Valley**, which is also full of reminiscences of the Chilean Nobel Prize Winner, Gabriela Mistral. Tours can also be arranged to the **Tololo Observatory**, the largest in the southern hemisphere.
- **The Central Region** and the **Islands** are the most temperate and pastoral regions of the country, where the snow-capped peaks of the **Andes** provide a backdrop for rolling green fields, vineyards and orange groves. **Valparaíso**, the principal port, has many attractions.
- From Valparaíso there are excellent road and rail services to **Santiago**, where visitors will find all the conveniences of a modern capital city, including good hotels to suit all tastes. The **Virgin Mary** guards the city from the peak of the 860m (2822ft) **Cerro San Cristóbal** (**Saint Christopher's Hill**), in the northeast of the city, where a zoo, gardens, restaurants and fine views of the city can be found.
- Immediately south of Santiago, in the heartland of Chile, one can visit many **vineyards** where much excellent Chilean wine is produced. Travelling south through the heartland of Chile, one reaches **Talca** with its fine parks and museums.

- 650km (403 miles) west of Valparaíso are the **Juan Fernández Islands**, which can be reached either by plane or boat from the Chilean mainland. Alexander Selkirk was shipwrecked here in the early 18th century, and Defoe based his novel *Robinson Crusoe* on Selkirk's adventures.
- **Easter Island** is another Pacific Chilean possession, situated 3800km (2361 miles) west of the mainland. It is most famous for the **Moai**, gigantic stone figures up to 9m (30ft) tall which are found all over the island. Other sites include the crater of the volcano **Rano Kao**, the rock carvings at **Oronco**, and the museum in the main town of **Hanga Roa**. The best method of travel to the island is by air. Tour guides and guest house keepers tend to meet every plane, so although it is possible to book good hotel accommodation from Santiago or Valparaíso, it is not essential. Many of the hotels specialise in catering for groups and will arrange tours if asked. Tours can also be arranged with a tour guide. Jeeps, trucks, motorbikes and horses can all be hired.
- In the **Southern Region**, a visit to the impressive waterfalls at **Laguna de Laja** is recommended.
- **Temuco** marks the beginning of the **Lake District**, where **Lake Villarica** and the **Trancura** and **Cincira** rivers combine to create beautiful scenery, and an angler's paradise. **Lake Todos los Santos** is also well worth a visit.
- At the southernmost end of the railway line and the Pan American Highway, there is the picturesque town of **Puerto Montt** and, nearby, the colourful small fishing port of **Angelmo**.

Top Things To Do

- Only 8km (5 miles) to the north of Valparaíso is **Viña del Mar**, Chile's principal and most fashionable seaside resort with casinos, clubs and modern hotels. The **Valparaíso Sporting Club** offers a **race course**, **polo grounds** and **playing fields**.
- One of Chile's most popular regions for **trekking** is the **Lake District**, which lies some 900km (560 miles) south of Santiago, and where several of the country's national parks can be visited. Here, naturalists wishing to follow in the footsteps of Charles Darwin (who wrote extensively about Chile's fauna and flora) will also discover Chile's incredible vegetation and animals. The **Lago Verde Trail** in the **Parque Nacional Huerquehue** leads through beech forests, past waterfalls and offers good views of the **Volcán Villarica**. The fairly remote **Parque Nacional Queulat** (characterised by glaciers, fjords and volcanic peaks) is a popular destination for adventure travel package tours. Guided hikes, ecology tours and boat trips are available at **Parque Nacional Conguillio**. Inveterate travellers should not miss the UNESCO Biosphere Reserve of **Torres del Paine National Park** (located in Chilean Patagonia), which is simply one of the most beautiful, unspoiled and remote places on the planet. It offers abundant wildlife and spectacular scenery consisting of huge glaciers, fjords, waterfalls and blue lakes dotted with icebergs; the park has a well-developed network of trails complemented by trekking huts. Guanacos (or *llama guanicoe*) roam freely in the park, which is also a good place to observe giant condors. In many cases, visitors intending to trek through Chile individually must register with local rangers or at the nearest CONAF (*Corporación Nacional Forestal*) office. At the Parque Nacional Torres del Paine, solo treks are not allowed. The whole area of **Magallanes** and **Tierra del Fuego** is worth exploring during the summer season. Naturalists may also head to the **Juan Fernández Islands** (located in the Pacific, some 965km/600 miles west of Santiago) which contain numerous indigenous plants and animals, most notably the Juan Fernández fur seal and the Juan Fernández hummingbird.
- The UNESCO World Biosphere Reserve, the **Parque Nacional Lauca** (155km/95 miles from Arica) is filled with flamingos, rheas (an ostrich-like bird) and llamas.
- Magellanic penguins can be seen at **Chiloé Island** (485km/300 miles from Santiago), a region of evergreen forests and fjords. The abundant coastal wildlife of Patagonia and Tierra del Fuego includes large colonies of sea elephants, sea lions and penguins.
- The Lake District's **Volcán Villarrica** and **Volcán Osorno** are the most popular destinations for **climbing**. Various companies offer guided ascents, but ice gear is required. Guides are compulsory.
- **Fishing** is particularly good in the **Lake District** and in **Patagonia**, South America's southernmost region. The lakes near **Puerto Montt**, a port city whose economy is mainly based on fishing, offer excellent **trout fishing**. In **Arica**, near the northern border with Peru, conditions in the area are ideal for **deep-sea fishing**.
- The **Maipo, Claro, Trancura** and **Bio-Bio rivers** are the main destinations for **whitewater rafting**. Specialist operators can organise week-long trips. The scenery around the Bio-Bio includes hot springs and waterfalls, but the construction of several dams along the river will

change conditions. Chile's coastline is indented by many bays and fjords where various types of other watersports, including **swimming**, **diving**, **water-skiing** and **boating** can be enjoyed.
- **Portillo** (150km/95 miles northeast of Santiago) is a world-famous ski resort offering both downhill and cross-country **skiing** and **ice skating** (on the spectacular **Laguna del Inca**). Other ski slopes in the area can be found at **Farellones-El Colorado, La Parva** and **Valle Nevado**. The best time to ski is August (with the season running from June to September).
- Departing from **Puerto Montt**, **glacier cruises** follow a spectacular route through Chile's Inside Passage, the **Beagle Channel** and around **Cape Horn**, passing through glacial valleys (notably at **Laguna San Rafael**), fjords and past huge icebergs. Passengers can disembark at various points en route, notably at **Puerto Natales** and on the Argentinian portion of Tierra del Fuego.
- Chile's southernmost city, **Punta Arenas** (located 2170km/1350 miles south of Santiago), is one of the most widely used departure points for **trips to Antarctica**.

TOURIST INFORMATION

Servicio Nacional de Turismo (SERNATUR) (Tourist Office)
Avenida Providencia 1550, PO Box 7500548, Santiago, Chile
Tel: (2) 731 8419.
Website: www.sernatur.cl

Entertainment

FOOD & DRINK: Santiago has many international restaurants; waiter service is usual. The evening will often include floor shows and dancing.
National specialities:
- *Empanada* is a combination of meat, chicken or fish, with onions, eggs, raisins and olives inside a flour pastry.
- *Humitas* is a seasoned corn paste, wrapped in corn husks and boiled.
- *Cazuela de ave* is a soup with rice, vegetables, chicken and herbs.
- *Bife a lo pobre* is a steak with french fries, onions and eggs.
- *Parrillada* is selection of meat grilled over hot coals, often including delicacies such as intestines, udders and blood sausages.
- Seafood is good. Best known are the huge lobsters from Juan Fernández Islands. Abalone, sea urchins, clams, prawns and giant *choros* (mussels) are also common.
National drinks:
- Chile is famous for its wine.
- *Pisco* is a powerful liqueur distilled from grapes after wine pressing.
- Grapes are also used to make the sweet brown *chicha* as well as *aguardiente*, similar to brandy.
- Beer is drunk throughout the country.
Tipping: Restaurants and bars add 10 per cent to the bill. However, waiters will expect a 10 per cent cash tip in addition.

NIGHTLIFE: While many restaurants and hotels offer entertainment, there are also a number of independent discos and nightclubs. **Casinos:** The Municipal Casino in Viña del Mar offers large gambling salons, full cabaret and boîte with Chile's best dance bands. A casino operates in Gran Hotel in Puerto Varas between September and March. Arica also has a casino operating throughout the year with baccarat, roulette, black jack, a restaurant and late-night cabaret.

SHOPPING: Special purchases include textiles such as colourful handwoven ponchos, vicuna rugs and copper work. Chilean stones such as lapis lazuli, jade, amethyst, agate and onyx are all good buys. **Shopping hours**: Mon-Fri 1000-2000, Sat 1000-1400. Large shopping malls are open daily 1000-2100.

Business

- **GDP:** US$73.8 billion (2004).
- **Main exports:** Copper, fruit and fish products.
- **Main imports:** Petroleum and petroleum products, chemicals, electrical and telecommunications equipment.
- **Main trade partners:** Exports to: Asia, NAFTA (North America Free Trade Agreement), EU and Mercosur; Imports from: Mercosur, NAFTA, EU and Asia.

ECONOMY: With well-developed industrial and service sectors, Chile has one of Latin America's strongest economies. However, it still depends on export of primary commodities – metals and ores, fruit, fish and wood – for a large proportion of its export earnings. Chile has a large surplus of fruit and vegetables available for export to North America and Europe but is not entirely self-sufficient in agricultural produce. The industrial base has grown substantially over the last 30 years and now includes steel manufacturing, oil production, ship building, and the production of cement and consumer goods. The mainstay of the export economy for the time being is metals and ores: Chile is the world's leading exporter of copper and also produces zinc, iron ore, molybdenum, manganese, iodine and lithium. Imported oil and natural gas provide most of Chile's energy requirements, but coal and hydro-electricity also make an important contribution. The service sector has developed rapidly in recent years, especially financial services, following the government's introduction in the mid-1990s of a unique comprehensive pension scheme. Chile's economic performance has been strong since 2000 with annual growth around 6 per cent and low inflation; unemployment hovers just below 10 per cent. Chile is a member of the Latin American Integration Association (ALADI), the southern free trade zone (Mercosur), and the Rio Group. This latter organisation, established in 1987, comprises a dozen Latin American countries with common interests in promoting free trade, suppressing corruption and drug trafficking, and other matters. The country was also admitted in 1994 to the Asia-Pacific Economic Cooperation Forum and may be the first South American country to join the North American Free Trade Area (NAFTA, presently comprising the USA, Canada and Mexico). Chile has an extensive network of bilateral and multilateral free trade agreements (FTAS), including with the EU, the US, South Korea, Mexico and Canada and is in the process of negotiating FTAS with China and India.

BUSINESS ETIQUETTE: Businesspeople should wear formal clothes in dark colours for official functions, dinners, smart restaurants and hotels. Dress is usually stipulated on invitations. There is a tendency to formality with many Old World courtesies. Best months for business visits are April to December. **Business hours:** Mon-Fri 0900-1800.

COMMERCIAL INFORMATION

Cámara de Comercio de Santiago de Chile AG
Monjitaf 392, Santiago, Chile
Tel: (2) 360 7000.
Website: www.ccs.cl

Cámara Nacional de Comercio de Chile
Merced 230, Santiago, Chile
Tel: (2) 365 4391 or 4114 (in English).
Website: www.cnc.cl

Santiago Convention Bureau (Information on Conferences/Conventions)
Officina 64, Avenida El Bosque Norte 0140, Las Condes, Santiago, Chile
Tel: (2) 333 8085 or 333 7977.
Website: www.scb.cl.

China

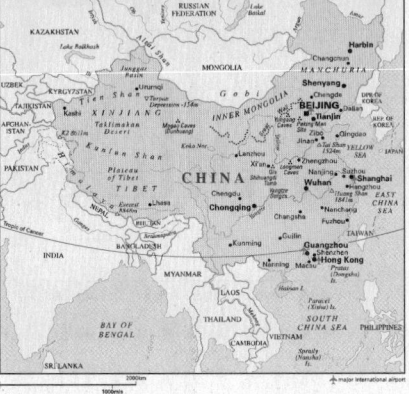

Location: East Asia.

Time: GMT + 8.
Despite the vast size of the country, Beijing time is standard throughout China.

Overview

China is the cultural treasure-house of East Asia: its social riches and 5000 years of tumultuous history place it, without doubt, among the world's greatest travel destinations. China has one of the world's oldest continuous civilisations. The Great Wall, X'ian's Terracotta Army, the Forbidden Palace and Tiananmen Square: the very names reverberate with history and legend.
China's paradoxes are many: Shanghai's skyscrapers contrast with Beijing's historical treasures, while in rural provinces, mechanisation is slow. This is not simply due to its sheer enormity and population of over one billion. China's history is one characterised by the collapse of a dynasty or the accession of a weak ruler that would fragment the country into smaller kingdoms until reunited.
What has defined China most in recent times is the outcome of the civil war in 1945. Defeated Nationalists fled to Taiwan, while victorious Communists founded the People's Republic of China. Internally, the China of the 1960s was dominated by the convulsions of the Cultural Revolution. But in 1976, the two towering figures of post-revolutionary China, Premier Zhou Enlai and Communist Party Chairman Mao Zedong, both died.
China's contentious policies, however, did not end there. A major reform programme allowing little political 'liberalisation', despite economic change, prompted widespread protest; in 1989, thousands occupied

Tiananmen Square in Beijing, only for the army to clear the Square with great loss of life and the Government to reassert political control. US support for Taiwan is a constant irritant. Within East Asia, China is involved in an intractable territorial dispute concerning the status of the Spratly Islands, claimed by no less than six nations and thought to sit above substantial oil fields. In the continuing tension between India and Pakistan, China has provided military support to Pakistan, considering India a political rival. When the Japanese imperial army invaded China in 1937, eight years of brutal occupation followed, which sours relations between the two countries to this day.
Such complex history and politics are worrying, but, for some, infuse the landscape with greater allure. And what a landscape it has – this is the land of the Yangtze River, the Silk Route and the bamboo forests of the panda, bringing the vistas of rivers and misty peaks in traditional ink paintings to life. China justifiably holds 23 UNESCO World Heritage Sites within its borders. Even Chinese food ranks among the world's great cuisines. From acrobatics to martial arts, calligraphy to Chinese opera, the vibrant, distinctive culture of this great land is everywhere to be seen.
Tibet (Xihang) is known as 'the Roof of the World' and even the mere mention of the word evokes dreamy images of a mystical and dramatic territory. Tibet has only been open to tourists since 1980, so if you get the chance to go there, you should not turn it down. The Cultural Revolution, driven by Han Chinese, inflicted serious damage on Tibet's cultural identity, but despite this, it has preserved its own way of life and religious traditions, helped in some cases by apologetic Chinese attempts at restoration. What any potential visitor should bear in mind is that the Chinese authorities react strongly to overseas visitors becoming involved with any political activity for Tibetan independence, including taking photographs or videotaping demonstrations, or taking Tibetan nationals' correspondence or parcels out of the country. What makes up for this political quagmire is the spectacular scenery and uniquely fascinating Tibetan culture: its tradition of esoteric Buddhism is followed across Asia and is of great historical importance.
China's rapid economic growth, with predictions that it may become the world's major economic power within decades, has generated controversy surrounding global warming and insufficient oil supplies. However, it has also spurred on China's rapidly improving tourist infrastructure. Beijing is a perfect example. The city is currently undergoing great investment in both tourism infrastructure and historical renovation due to the 2008 Beijing Olympic Games.
Flexibility and patience are still required to travel around China but, in return, China rewards visitors with memories to be treasured for a lifetime.

General Information

AREA: 9,572,900 sq km (3,696,100 sq miles).
POPULATION: 1.3 billion (2005). Roughly a quarter of the world's population lives in China.
POPULATION DENSITY: 135.4 per sq km.
CAPITAL: Beijing (Peking). **Population:** 13.8 million. The largest city in the country, Shanghai, has a population of over 18 million and, as of 2004, 11 other cities had a population of over two million and 23 cities had a population of one to two million.
GEOGRAPHY: China is bordered to the north by Russia and Mongolia; to the east by Korea (Dem Rep), the Yellow Sea and the South China Sea; to the south by Vietnam, Laos, Myanmar, India, Bhutan and Nepal; and to the west by India, Pakistan, Afghanistan, Tajikistan, Kyrgyzstan and Kazakhstan. China has a varied terrain ranging from high plateaux in the west to flatlands in the east; mountains take up almost one-third of the land. The most notable high

Credit: ©Juliet Sinclair

mountain ranges are the Himalayas, the Altai Mountains, the Tian Shan Mountains and the Kunlun Mountains. On the border with Nepal is the 8848m-(29,198ft-) high Mount Qomolangma (Mount Everest). In the west is the Qinghai/Tibet Plateau, with an average elevation of 4000m (13,200ft), known as 'the Roof of the World'. At the base of the Tian Shan Mountains is the Turpan Depression or Basin, China's lowest area, 154m (508ft) below sea level at the lowest point. China has many great river systems, notably the Yellow (Huang He) and Yangtze Kiang (Chang Jiang). Only 10 per cent of all China is suitable for agriculture.

GOVERNMENT: People's Republic. China comprises 23 Provinces, five Autonomous Regions, two Special Administrative Regions and four Municipalities directly under Central Government. **Head of State**: President Hu Jintao since 2003. **Head of Government**: Premier Wen Jiabao since 2003. Jiang Zemin, the previous Premier who had retained much of his influence, stood down from the very powerful position of Central Military Commissioner in 2004. **Recent history:** The National People's Congress (NPC) is the most powerful organ of state and elects all those with the principal executive functions – the President and Vice-President of the People's Republic, the Premier and Vice-Premier of the State Council (after nomination by the President), other members of the State Council and the heads of individual ministries. The State Council reports to the NPC or, when the Congress is not sitting, to its Standing Committee. The NPC is held every five years and attended by some 3000 delegates drawn from the provincial administrations, the military and various state organs. The NPC membership and all major appointments are ultimately under the control of the Chinese Communist Party, whose 22-member Politburo is effectively the country's governing body. Hu Jintao became the Presidential heir-apparent at the 16th Communist Party Congress in 2002, when he succeeded Jiang Zemin as Head of the party. Hu Jintao has made the fight against corruption a priority. However, he has rejected Western-style political reforms.

LANGUAGE: The official language is Mandarin Chinese. Among the enormous number of local dialects, large groups speak Cantonese, Shanghaiese, Fuzhou, Hokkien-Taiwanese, Xiang, Gan and Hakka dialects in the south. Mongolia, Tibet and Xinjiang, which are autonomous regions, have their own languages. Translation and interpreter services are good. English is spoken by many guides.

RELIGION: China is officially Atheistic, but the stated religions and philosophies are Buddhism, Daoism and Confucianism. There are 100 million Buddhists and approximately 60 million Muslims, five million Protestants (including large numbers of Evangelicals) and four million Roman Catholics, largely independent of Vatican control.

ELECTRICITY: 220 volts AC, 50Hz. Two-pin sockets and some three-pin sockets are in use. However, most 4-5 star hotels are wired for the use of 110 volt appliances.

SOCIAL CONVENTIONS: Cultural differences may create misunderstandings between local people and visitors. The Chinese do not usually volunteer information and the visitor is advised to ask questions. Hotels, train dining cars and restaurants often ask for criticisms and suggestions, which are considered seriously. Do not be offended by being followed by crowds, this is merely an open interest in visitors who are rare in the remoter provinces. The Chinese are generally reserved in manner, courtesy rather than familiarity being preferred. The full title of the country is 'The People's Republic of China', and this should be used in all formal communications. 'China' can be used informally, but there should never be any implication that another China exists. Although handshaking may be sufficient, a visitor will frequently be greeted by applause as a sign of welcome. The customary response is to applaud back. Anger, if felt, is expected to be concealed and arguments in public may attract hostile attention. In China, the family name is always mentioned first. It is customary to arrive a little early if invited out socially. When dining wait until your seat is allocated by a nod or subtle indication. You should not begin eating until indicated to do so, and if using chopsticks do not position them upright in your rice bowl as the gesture symbolises death. Toasting at a meal is very common, as is the custom of taking a treat when visiting someone's home, such as fruit, confectionery or a souvenir from a home country. If it is the home of friends or relatives, money may be left for the children. If visiting a school or a factory, a gift from the visitor's home country, particularly something which would be unavailable in China (a text book if visiting a school, for example), would be much appreciated. Stamps are also very popular as gifts, as stamp-collecting is a popular hobby in China. A good gift for an official guide is a Western reference book on China. Conservative casual wear is generally acceptable everywhere and revealing clothes should be avoided since they may cause offence. Visitors should avoid expressing political or religious opinions. **Photography**: Not allowed in airports. Places of historic and scenic interest may be photographed, but permission should be sought before photographing military installations, government buildings or other possibly sensitive subjects.

Climate

China has a great diversity of climates. The northeast experiences hot and dry summers and bitterly cold winters. The north and central region has almost continual rainfall, hot summers and cold winters. The southeast region has substantial rainfall, with semi-tropical summers and cool winters. Central, southern and western China are also susceptible to flooding, China is also periodically subject to seismic activity.

Required clothing: *North* – heavyweight clothing with boots for the harsh northern winters. Lightweight clothing for summer. *South* – mediumweight clothing for winter and lightweight for summer.

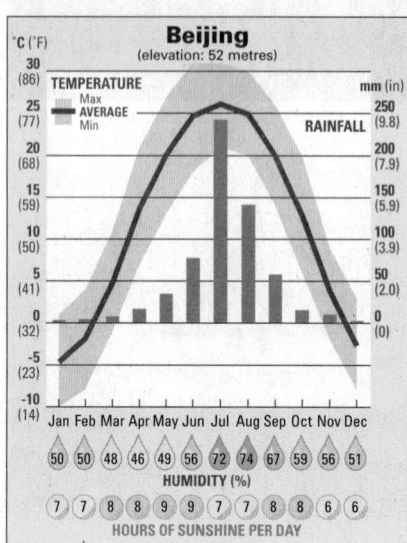

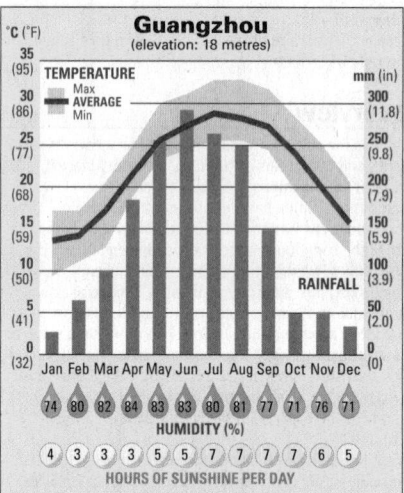

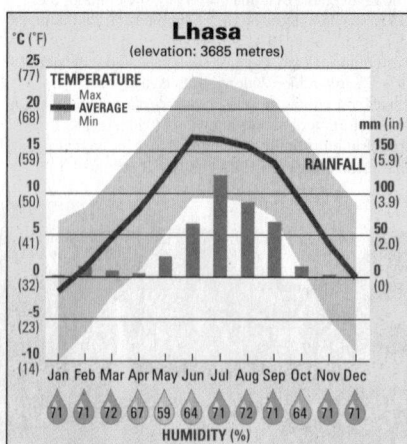

Communications

Telephone: IDD is available. Country code: 86. Antiquated internal service with public telephones in post offices, hotels and shops displaying a telephone unit sign. Domestic calls are cheaper to make between 2100 and 0700; it is also easier to get a connection during this time. It is often easier to make international phone calls from China than it is to make calls internally. There is a three-minute minimum charge for international calls.

Mobile telephone: Roaming agreements exist with some international mobile phone companies. There is coverage in most major urban areas in the southeastern and eastern regions, including Chengdu and Chongqing. There is also coverage in Xi'an, Lhasa, Ürümqi. Elsewhere is sporadic coverage.

Internet: Internet is available in many areas of China; there are Internet cafes in Beijing and other main towns. The number of Internet users passed the 100 million mark in 2005. Beijing routinely blocks access to sites run by the banned spiritual movement Falun Gong, rights groups and some foreign news organisations. Postings by 'bloggers' are now being actively curbed.

Post: Service to Europe takes from between two days and one week. Tourist hotels usually have their own post offices. All postal communications to China should be addressed 'People's Republic of China'. Post office hours: 0800-19.00.

MEDIA: China's media are tightly controlled by the country's leadership. The industry has been opened up in the areas of distribution and advertising but not in editorial content. Access to foreign news providers is limited and re-broadcasting and the use of satellite receivers is restricted; shortwave radio broadcasts are jammed and websites are blocked. In general, the press report on corruption and inefficiency among officials, but the media avoid criticism of the Communist Party's monopoly on power. Hong Kong so far has retained its editorially free media. Each city has its own newspaper, usually published by the local Government, as well as a local Communist Party daily. Agreements are in place which allow selected channels - including stations run by AOL Time Warner, News Corp and the Hong Kong-based Phoenix TV - to transmit via cable in Guangdong province. In exchange, Chinese Central TV's English-language network is made available to satellite TV viewers in the US and UK. Beijing says it will only allow relays of foreign broadcasts which do not threaten 'national security' or 'political stability'. All foreign-made TV programmes will be subject to approval before broadcast.

Press: The main English-language daily is the *China Daily*. There is also the weekly news magazine *Beijing Review*, with editions in English, French, German, Japanese and Spanish. National newspapers include *The People's Daily* and *The Worker's Daily*, with many provinces having their own local dailies as well. News agencies include the state-run Xinhua and Zhongguo Xinwen She (aimed mainly at overseas Chinese nationals).

TV: *Chinese Central TV* (*CCTV*) is a state-run national broadcaster, with networks that include English-language *CCTV-9*.

Radio: China National Radio is state-run; China Radio International is a state-run external broadcaster with programmes in more than 40 languages.

Passport/Visa

	Passport Required?	Visa Required?	Return Ticket Required?
Full British	Yes	Yes	Yes
Australian	Yes	Yes	Yes
Canadian	Yes	Yes	Yes
USA	Yes	Yes	Yes
Other EU	Yes	Yes	Yes
Japanese	Yes	1	Yes

Note: *Regulations and requirements may be subject to change at short notice, and you are advised to contact the appropriate diplomatic or consular authority before finalising travel arrangements. Any numbers in the chart refer to the footnotes below.*

Note: (a) China does not recognise dual nationality (eg US-Chinese, Canadian-Chinese). (b) Travellers are required to complete a health declaration certificate on arrival in China. HIV-positive travellers are not permitted to enter the country.

PASSPORTS: Required by all. Passport must be valid for at least six months for a single or double entry within three months of the date of visa issue; at least nine months for multiple entries within six months.

VISAS: Required by all except:
(a) **1.** nationals of Brunei, Japan and Singapore for stays of up to 15 days;
(b) transit passengers (except nationals of the USA, who *always* require a visa) continuing their journey by the same or first connecting plane to another country within 24 hours who hold valid onward documentation and do not leave the airport.

Types of visa and cost: *Tourist/Business/Transit* (UK nationals): £30 (single-entry); £45 (double-entry); £60 (multiple-entry for business visas only; six months); £90 (multiple entry for business visas only; 12 months and two to five years). *Group* (at least five people): £24 per person. Visa charges for other nationals vary; check with Embassy for further information.

Validity: *Tourist*, *Business* and *Group* visas are normally valid for three months from the date of issue (single and double-entry). Multiple-entry visas are normally valid for six months, 12 months or two to five years. The validity of *Business* visas varies. *Transit* visas are generally valid for up to seven days.

Application to: Consulate (or consular section at Embassy); see *Passport/Visa Information*. Visas should be applied for in person at least one month before departure. Group visas will usually be obtained by the tour operator or travel agent.

Application requirements: (a) Completed application form. (b) One recent passport-size photo. (c) Valid passport with at least one blank page. (d) Fee (payable in cash or by postal order only). *Tourist*: (a)-(d) and, (e) Return airline ticket or travel information about itinerary and confirmation of hotel reservation in China. *Business*: (a)-(d) and, (e) Official invitation (letter/fax) from a Chinese Government department or a Government-approved company indicating duration of stay and purpose of visit (original copies must be submitted for multiple-entry visas). *Student*: (a)-(d) and, (e) JW-201 or JW-202 form issued by the Ministry of Education of China, and letter of admission from Chinese university/college. *Group* (six people or more): (a)-(d) and, (e) Confirmation letter or fax from an authorised Chinese travel company. A list of all group members should be presented in triplicate. Photocopies of all group passports with the visa form number for each member. The serial number given to group members should be listed in order on the group visa form. There should be a front page covering information about the group. *Transit*: (a)-(d) and, (e) Visa for the next country of destination and letter from employer (if applicable).

Working days required: Three (72 hours). Two weeks for Group visas. Applications should be made at least one month in advance. A same-day service may be available at an extra cost of £20 per person, or a 48-hour service at £15 per person. Visas, however, cannot be issued on the same day unless the same-day airline ticket or itinerary is presented.

Note: (a) The majority of visits to China tend to be organised through the official state travel agency *CITS* (China International Travel Service). This liaison with *CITS* is generally handled by the tour operator organising the inclusive holiday chosen by the visitor, though it is possible for individuals to organise their own itinerary. Once the tour itinerary details have been confirmed to the visitor or visiting group, finances to cover accommodation and the cost of the tour must be deposited with *CITS* through a home bank. Once again, for package trips, all the necessary formalities for a visit to China can be handled by the tour operator concerned. (b) Those wishing to visit Tibet are strongly advised to join a travel group. Individual travellers need a special permit and should obtain permission to visit Tibet or Xinjiang from the following organisation before applying: Tibet Tourism Office (see *Passport/Visa Information*). Applicants will need to supply their Chinese Visa validity dates.

Temporary residence: Enquiries should be addressed to the Chinese Embassy.

PASSPORT/VISA INFORMATION

Embassy of the People's Republic of China in the UK
49-51 Portland Place, London W1B 1JL, UK
Tel: (020) 7299 8426.
Website: www.chinese-embassy.org.uk
Opening hours: Mon-Fri 0900-1230 and 1330-1700.
Consular and visa section: 31 Portland Place, London W1B 1QD, UK
Tel: (020) 7631 1430 (telephone enquiries: 1400-1600 only) *or* (09001) 880 808 (recorded visa and general information; calls cost 60p per minute).
Opening hours: Mon-Fri 0900-1200.

Embassy of the People's Republic of China in the USA
2300 Connecticut Avenue, NW, Washington, DC 20008, USA
Tel: (202) 328 2500.
Website: www.china-embassy.org
Visa section: Room 110, 2201 Wisconsin Avenue, NW, Washington, DC 20007, USA
Tel: (202) 338 6688.

Tibet Tourism Office
Room 3423 Poly Plaza, 14 Dongzhimen Nandajie, Beijing 100027, People's Republic of China
Tel: (10) 6500 1188 (ext 3423) *or* 6593 6538.
Website: www.tibettour.net.cn/en

Money

Currency: 1 Renminbi Yuan (CNY) = 10 chiao/jiao or 100 fen. Notes are in denominations of CNY100, 50, 20, 10, 5, 2 and 1, and 5, 2 and 1 chiao/jiao. Coins are in denominations of CNY1, 5 and 1 chiao/jiao and 5, 2 and 1 fen.
Currency exchange: CNY is not traded outside China.

Credit: ©Juliet Sinclair

Foreign banknotes and traveller's cheques can be exchanged at branches of The Bank of China. In hotels and *Friendship Stores* for tourists, imported luxury items such as spirits may be bought with Western currency. Scottish and Northern Irish banknotes cannot be exchanged.
Credit & debit cards: American Express, Diners Club, Eurocard/MasterCard and Visa are widely accepted in major provincial cities in designated establishments. However, the availability of ATMs is often limited, and the acceptance of credit cards often unlikely away from the major cities.
Traveller's cheques: To avoid additional exchange rate charges, travellers are advised to take traveller's cheques in US Dollars.
Currency restrictions: Import and export of local currency is limited to CNY20000. Import of foreign currency is up to US$1000 (US$5000 for non-residents). Higher amounts should be declared upon arrival. Export of foreign currency is limited to the amount imported and declared.
Banking hours: Mon-Fri 0900-1200, 1400-1700.
Exchange rate indicators:
Rate at time of publishing
£1.00= CNY14.27
$1.00= CNY8.09

Duty Free

The following items may be imported into China by passengers staying less than six months without incurring customs duty:
400 cigarettes (600 cigarettes for stays of over six months); two bottles (up to 75cl each) of alcoholic beverages (four bottles for stays of over six months); a reasonable amount of perfume for personal use.
Prohibited items: Arms and ammunition (prior approval may be obtained courtesy of the travel agency used), imitation arms, pornography (photographs in mainstream Western magazines may be regarded as pornographic), radio transmitters/receivers, exposed but undeveloped film, loaded recording tapes and video, storage media for computers, fruit and certain vegetables (tomatoes, aubergines and red peppers), political and religious pamphlets (a moderate quantity of religious material for personal use is acceptable). Any printed matter directed against the public order and the morality of China. Only one of the following electrical appliances per person: camera, portable tape recorder, portable video camera, portable cine camera and portable computer.
Note: Customs officials may seize audio and videotapes, books, records and CDs to check for pornographic, political or religious material. Baggage declaration forms must be completed upon arrival noting all valuables (such as cameras, watches and jewellery); this may be checked on departure. Receipts for items such as jewellery, jade, handicrafts, paintings, calligraphy or other similar items should be kept in order to obtain an export certificate from the authorities on leaving. Without this documentation, such items cannot be taken out of the country.

Public Holidays

Below are listed the Public Holidays for the January 2006-June 2007 period.
2006: Jan 1 New Year. **Jan 29-31** Spring Festival, Chinese New Year. **May 1** Labour Day. **Oct 1-3** National Day.

2007: Jan 1 New Year. **Feb 18-20** Spring Festival, Chinese New Year. **May 1** Labour Day.
Note: In addition to the above, other holidays may be observed locally and certain groups have official Public Holidays on the following dates: **Mar 8** International Women's Day. **May 4** National Youth Day. **May 23** Tibet Liberation Day. **Jun 1** International Children's Day. **Aug 1** Army Day.

Health

	Special Precautions?	Certificate Required?
Yellow Fever	Yes	1
Cholera	Yes	2
Typhoid & Polio	3	N/A
Malaria	4	N/A

Note: *Regulations and requirements may be subject to change at short notice, and you are advised to contact your doctor well in advance of your intended date of departure. Any numbers in the chart refer to the footnotes below.*

1: A yellow fever vaccination certificate is required from all travellers arriving within six days of leaving an infected area.
2: Following WHO guidelines issued in 1973, a cholera vaccination certificate is not a condition of entry to China. However, cholera is a slight risk in this country and precautions could be considered. Up-to-date advice should be sought before deciding whether these precautions should include vaccination as medical opinion is divided over its effectiveness. For more information, see the *Health* appendix. A strain of *Bengal cholera* has been reported in western areas.
3: *Poliovirus* transmission has been shown by reliable data to have been completely interrupted since 1999 through eradication programmes.
4: Malaria risk exists throughout the country below 1500m except in Beijing, Gansu, Heilongjiang, Inner Mongolia, Jilin, Ningxia, Qinghai, Shanxi, Tibet (Xizang, except in the Zangbo River Valley in the extreme southeast) and Xinjiang (except in the Yili River Valley). North of 33°N, the risk lasts from July to November, between 33°N and 25°N from May to December, and south of 25°N throughout the year. The disease occurs primarily in the benign *vivax* form but the malignant *falciparum* form is also present and has been reported to be multidrug-resistant. The recommended prophylaxis in risk areas is atovaquone, doxycycline, or mefloquine in Hainan and Yunnan.
Food & drink: Outside main centres, all water used for drinking, brushing teeth or freezing should have first been boiled or otherwise sterilised. Only eat well-cooked meat and fish, preferably served hot. Pork, salad and mayonnaise may carry increased risk. Vegetables should be cooked and fruit peeled.
Other risks: Bilharzia (*schistosomiasis*) is endemic in the central Yangtze river basin. Avoid swimming and paddling in fresh water; swimming pools that are well chlorinated and maintained are safe. There is some risk of *plague*. *Hepatitis E* is prevalent in northeastern and northwestern China and *hepatitis A* is common across the country.

Hepatitis B is highly endemic. *Tuberculosis* is common in indigenous populations. *Oriental liver fluke* (*clonorchiasis*), *oriental lung fluke* (*paragonimiasis*) and *giant intestinal fluke* (*fasciolopsiasis*) are reported, and *brucellosis* also occurs. *Bancroftian* and *brugian filariasis* are still reported in southern China, *visceral leishmaniasis* is increasingly common throughout, and *cutaneous leishmaniasis* has been reported from Xinjiang. *Haemorrhagic fever with renal syndrome* is endemic; the most recent epidemic was in September 2005 in the Jilin Province. There was a *meningitis C* epidemic in February 2005. Precautions should be taken against *Japanese encephalitis*, particularly in rural areas. *Mite-borne* or *scrub typhus* may be found in scrub areas of southern China. *Altitude sickness* can be a problem in parts of Gansu, Qinghai, Sichuan, Tibet, Xinjiang and Yannan. There have been occurrences of *avian influenza* (bird flu) amongst poultry (see *Travel Advice*) and the *SARS* virus. There were reported outbreaks of *meningitis C* in 2005.

Rabies is present, although the Government policy that bans dogs and cats from main cities makes this less of a risk in these areas. For those at high risk, vaccination before arrival should be considered. If you are bitten, seek medical advice without delay. For more information, consult the *Health* appendix.

Health care: Medical costs are low. Many medicines common to Western countries are unavailable in China. Medical facilities in international hospitals are excellent. There are many traditional forms of medicine used in China, the most notable being acupuncture. Medical insurance is strongly advised.

Travel - International

AIR:

The national airline is *Air China* (CA) (website: www.airchina.com.cn/en). Airlines serving China include: *British Airways*, *KLM*, *Lufthansa*, *Singapore Airlines* and many others.

Note: Travellers should ensure that they re-confirm their return flight reservations, as overbooking by airlines has led to people being stranded in China.

Approximate flight times: From Beijing to *London* is approximately 10 hours, to *New York* is 22 hours, to *Los Angeles* is 12 hours, and to *Sydney* is 12 hours.

Main airports: *Beijing/Peking (BJS/PEK)* airport (Capital International Central) is 28km (18 miles) northeast of the city. *To/from the airport*: Buses and taxis. Travel time - 40 minutes.

Guangzhou Baiyun International airport opened in 2004 and is 12km (7 miles) north of Guangzhou (travel time - 25 minutes).

Shanghai Hongqiao (SHA) airport is 13km (8 miles) southwest of the city (travel time - 25 to 40 minutes).

Shanghai Pudong (PVG) airport, in the eastern financial district, is 30km (19 miles) from the city centre. *To/from the airport*: Buses and taxis. Travel time - 50 minutes. Pudong is a major international airport with a magnetic levitation train and an underground link.

Facilities: All the above airports have duty free shops, banks/bureaux de change, post offices, business facilities, internet access, bars and restaurants.

There are also airports at other major cities.

Departure tax: CNY90. Paid in Chinese currency only. Children under 12 and transit passengers (proceeding within 24 hours) are exempt.

SEA:

Main ports: *Fuzhou* (*Foochow*), *Guangzhou* (*Canton*), *Hong Kong/Kowloon*, *Qingdao* (*Tsingtao*) and *Shanghai*. *Pearl Cruises* operates over 20 cruises a year to China. Other cruise lines include *Holland America*, *Princess*, *Seabourn* and *Silversea*. There are regular ferry services linking most Chinese ports with Kobe in Japan and the west coast of Korea (Dem Rep). There are regular ferries between Shanghai and Osaka in Japan. Regular ferry services operate between Weihai, Qingdao, Tianjin and Shanghai in China to Incheon in Korea (Dem Rep). There are daily hovercraft services between Hong Kong and Guangzhou, which also serves Shekou, Shenzhen and Zhuhai.

RAIL:

International services run from Beijing to Moscow (Russian Federation), on both the Trans-Mongolian Railway (via Ulaanbaatar in Mongolia) and the Trans-Manchurian Railway (via Zabaikalsk in northern China). The Trans-Siberian Express operates two weekly services, a train to Russia servicing Moscow and Beijing via Harbin and a China train via Ulaanbaatar and Nanning in Guangxi province, linked to Hanoi, Vietnam. A second cross boarder service runs from Kunming via Lao Cai, to Hanoi. There are also services from Beijing to Pyongyang (Korea, Dem Rep). Owing to demand, it may be necessary to book up to two months in advance. A regular train service runs from Hong Kong to Guangzhou (Canton), and is of a higher standard than internal trains in China. There are several trains daily. Kowloon-Canton Railway Corporation (KCRC) has express trains servicing Kowloon to Guangzhou and an indirect Kowloon to Lowu service. The services between Shanghai-Kowloon/Hong Kong (travel time - 29 hours) and Beijing-Kowloon/Hong Kong (travel time - 30 hours) both run on alternate days. There are twice-weekly trains from Almaty in Kazakhstan to Urumqi. There are three types of fare: hard sleeper, soft sleeper and deluxe soft sleeper.

Note: Travellers on the Trans-Mongolian or Trans-Manchurian Railways are strongly advised to search their compartments and lock the doors before departure, owing to an increase in smuggling via this route.

ROAD:

The principal road routes into China follow the historical trade routes through Myanmar, India, the former Soviet republics and Mongolia. It is also possible to travel from Pakistan to Xinjiang on the Karakoran highway. Motorways exist between Guangzhou and Shenzhen and Guangzhou and Zhuhai. These roads link the cities of Dongguan, Zhongshan, Foshan, Jiangmen, Huizhou and Shunda to Hong Kong and Macau. Motorway links to major cities in neighbouring countries are few.

Travel - Internal

AIR:

Most long-distance internal travel is by air. The *Civil Aviation Administration of China (CAAC)* operates along routes linking Beijing to over 80 other cities by 14 regional airlines, covering all major cities and some sites. CAAC controls several other private carriers including *China Eastern*, *China Northern*, *China Southern*, *Great Wall* and *Yunnan Airlines*. Tickets will normally be purchased by guides and the price will be included in any tour costs. Independent travellers can also book through the local Chinese International Travel Service (CITS), which charges a small commission, or alternatively buy tickets in booking offices or at some hotel travel desks. It is advisable to purchase internal air tickets well in advance if travelling during May, September or October. The tourist price for a ticket is 70 per cent on a train ticket and 100 per cent on an air ticket. There are many connections to Hong Kong from Beijing/Guangzhou (Peking/Canton) as well as other cities. Tickets are always overbooked so seats must be confirmed before travel. Inevitable delays in services must be taken into account. Airport announcements are not multilingual. Safety records are variable.

Note: Where possible, travellers are advised to fly in UK or North American aircrafts which are used by larger airlines.

Departure tax: CNY50. Payable in Chinese currency only.

SEA/RIVER:

All major rivers are served by river ferries, especially the Yangzi. Coastal ferries operate between Dalian, Tianjin (Tientsin), Qingdao (Tsingtao) and Shanghai. There are regular ferry services between mainland China and Hong Kong, conditions on which vary.

RAIL:

Railways provide the principal means of transport for goods and people throughout China. The routes are generally cheap, safe and well maintained. Routes operate between major cities; services include Beijing to Guangzhou, Shanghai, Harbin, Chengdu and Urumqi. There are three types of train, of which Express is the best. There are four types of fare: hard seat, soft seat (only on short-distance trains such as the Hong Kong to Guangzhou (Canton) line), hard sleeper and soft sleeper. Children under 1m (3ft) tall travel free and those under 1.3m (4ft) pay a quarter of the fare. Generally rail travel is comfortable but time-consuming due to vast distances between destinations.

The 1142km (710 miles) Qinghai to Tibet railway from Golmud in Qinghai to Lhasa in Tibet will be put into trial operation by July 2006. It is the most elevated rail route in the world, reaching an altitude of up to 5072m (16,640 feet).

ROAD:

It is possible to reach 80 per cent of settlements by road. Roads are not always of the highest quality. Distances should not be underestimated and vehicles should be in prime mechanical condition as China is still very much an agricultural nation without the mechanical expertise or services found in the West. From Beijing to Shanghai is 1461km (908 miles), and from Beijing to Nanjing (Nanking) is 1139km (718 miles). A superhighway links Beijing and Tianjin, and a 138 km (86 miles) four-lane toll highway links Hangzhou and the port of Ningbo in the Zhejiang province. Traffic drives on the right.

Bus: Reasonable services are operated between the main cities. Buses are normally crowded, but reach parts of the country that trains do not. There are some more expensive luxury buses. **Car hire**: Available, but most rental companies' policy of retaining the driver's passport makes self-drive car hire impossible in practice for visitors. Cars with a driver can be hired on a daily or weekly basis. Driving standards are erratic.

URBAN:

There is a metro system in Shanghai and limited metro services in Beijing and Tianjin, and tramways and trolleybuses in a number of other cities. New lines are under construction in Beijing. Guides who accompany every visitor or group will ensure that internal travel within the cities is as trouble-free as possible. Most cities have public transit systems, usually bus.

Taxi: Taxis are available in large cities from most hotels and shopping districts, and are permitted to stop at the passenger's signal. It is best to check if the taxi is metered. If not, then it is important to agree a fare beforehand, especially at railway stations where it is best to bargain before getting into the taxi. Visitors should write down their destination before starting any journey as most drivers do not speak English. Taxis can be hired by the day. Most people travel by bicycle or public transport. In most cities, bicycles or other types of rickshaws are available for short rides.

Travel times: The following chart gives approximate travel times (in hours and minutes) from **Beijing** to other major cities/towns in China.

	Air	Rail
Shanghai	**1.50**	**20.00**
Chengdu	**2.25**	**60.00**
Kunming	**3.20**	**80.00**
Guangzhou	**3.00**	**37.00**

Travel Advice

Most visits to China are trouble-free but you should be aware of the global risk of indiscriminate international terrorist attacks, which could be against civilian targets, including places frequented by foreigners.

There have been outbreaks of Avian Influenza (Bird Flu) amongst poultry in China. Since November 2005, there have been a small number of human cases in Liaoning, Guangxi, Anhui and Hunan provinces, some of which have been fatal. The individuals affected are thought to have come into contact with infected poultry before becoming sick. No evidence of human-to-human transmission is reported. The World Health Organisation continues to monitor the situation.

This advice is based on information provided by the Foreign and Commonwealth Office in the UK. It is correct at time of publishing. As the situation can change rapidly, visitors are advised to contact the following organisations for the latest travel advice:

British Foreign and Commonwealth Office
Tel: (0845) 850 2829.
Website: www.fco.gov.uk

US Department of State
Website: http://travel.state.gov/travel

Accommodation

HOTELS:

China has no shortage of accommodation even in peak season, with around 4500 tourist hotels. Main hotels in major cities are of a reasonable standard and there is a good range from budget to luxury. There are international-standard hotels in Tianjin, Hainan, Xiamen, Fujian, Hangzhou and Shenzhen. Most of these hotels are comfortable and are considered good value for money. Many have facilities including restaurants, coffee shops, bars, swimming pools and massage rooms. Some even include shopping and business malls, banks and post offices.

DORMITORIES: These are found in most tourist centres and provide cheaper accommodation for budget travellers. Standards range from poor to adequate.

YOUTH HOSTELS:

Good progress has been made in the construction of a network of hostels, covering, in particular, Beijing, Guangdong, Guangxi, Shanghai and Yunnan; good progress is being made.

ACCOMMODATION INFORMATION

China Tourism Hotel Association
9A Jianguomennei Avenue, Beijing 100740, People's Republic of China
Tel: (10) 6520 1114 *or* 6512 2905

China Hotel and Buyers' Guide
Website: www.hotelschina.com

IYHF (Youth Hostels)
Tel: (20) 8668 1851 *or* 8734 5080.
Website: www.yhachina.com

Top Things To See

- The entire area of **Beijing** within the city limits is - in many ways - one great historic museum. The innermost rectangle is the **Forbidden City**, now a museum and public park, but formerly the residence of the Ming and Qing emperors. The second rectangle forms the boundaries of the **Imperial City**, enclosing residences and parks for the former senior Government officials. The outer rectangle forms the outer city with its markets and old residential districts. The **Imperial Palace**, lying inside the Forbidden City and surrounded by a high wall and broad moat, is probably China's greatest surviving historical site. Dating from the 15th century, the Palace was home to a total of 24 emperors and, today, its fabulous halls, palaces and gardens house a huge collection of priceless relics from various dynasties. The surviving **city walls** are impressive monuments, as are the traditional *hutongs*, enclosed neighbourhoods of alleys and courtyards. Other points of interest are the **Coal Hill** (**Mei Shan**), a beautiful elevated park with breathtaking views; **Beihai Park**, the loveliest in Beijing; **Tiananmen Square**, the largest public square in the world, surrounded by museums, parks, the zoo and Beijing University; the **Temple of Heaven**, an excellent example of 15th-century Chinese architecture; the **Summer Palace**, the former court resort for the emperors of the Qing Dynasty reconstructed in traditional style in the early 1900s after Western attacks, looking out over the **Kunming Lake**; and the **Ming Tombs**, where 13 out of the 16 Ming emperors chose to be buried.
- They say that the **Great Wall**, built up in stages over 2000 years, is the only humanmade structure visible from the moon; but why not save yourself the bother of shuttling into space and see this spectacular sight in its stunning, mountainous location? Stretching for a distance of 5400km (3375 miles), it starts at the **Shanhaiguan Pass** in the east and ends at the **Jiayuguan Pass** in the west. The section at **Badaling**, built in stone and brick and dating back to the Ming Dynasty, is roughly 8m (26ft) high and 6m (20ft) wide.
- Be dazzled by China's great monuments to Buddhism. **The Yungang Caves** near **Datong**, west of Beijing, have awe-inspiring monumental Buddhist effigies carved into them. In **Luoyang**, Xi'an's historical twin capital, the fifth-century **Longmen Buddhist Caves** are among some of China's finest, lined with carved effigies and monuments. **Lanzhou**, the capital of Gansu Province, is chiefly noteworthy as a centre to visit the 34 early Buddhist caves at **Bingling Lamasery**. **Dunhuang** is famous for the **Mogao Caves**, some of the oldest Buddhist shrines in China and a UNESCO World Heritage Site. **Chengdu** is a base for visiting **Emei Shan**, a famous mountain to which Buddhist pilgrims flock every year, and the holy mountains of **Gongga** and **Siguniang**. There is also the spectacular **Grand Buddha** of **Leshan**, a 70.7m- (225ft-) high coloured sculpture carved out of a cliff, so enormous that 100 people can fit on its instep, with the **Grand Buddha Temple** and **Lingbao Pagoda** beside it.
- China brims over with staggering documents of history. The **Yingxian Pagoda** is China's oldest surviving wooden pagoda. **Kaifeng**, a Northern Song Dynasty capital, has an **Iron Pagoda** from AD 1049, and a **Fan Bo Pagoda** (c. AD 977), plus other relics of ancient courts and poets. Jinan's **Square Four Gate Pagoda** is the oldest stone pagoda in China. **Guangzhou** (**Canton**) contains the **Huaisheng Mosque** built by Arab merchants in AD 650, and the **Tomb of the King of Southern Yue**, a 2000-year-old relic of one of the region's short-lived splinter kingdoms. In **Qufu**, close to Qingdao, the **Mansion of Confucius** was home to the sage's descendants, and the enormous **Temple of Confucius**, with its many pavilions, was a centre for his worshippers. **Confucius's tomb** is in a cemetery just north of Qufu. The **North Imperial Tomb**, about 20km (13 miles) from **Shenyang**, is the burial place of the founding father of the Qing (Ch'ing) Dynasty. **Hohhot** (meaning 'green city' in Mongolian) is the capital of the Inner Mongolia Autonomous Region, and one of the most colourful cities in China, with unique local architecture including the **Five-Pagoda Temple**. **Nanjing** possesses the **Xiaoling Tomb** of the Ming Emperor Zhu Yuanzhang, founding father of the Ming Dynasty and the only Ming emperor to be buried outside Beijing. The **Sun Yat-sen Mausoleum** of China's first President, Dr Sun Yat-sen, is also here.
- Whilst you are absorbing such history, pay a visit to **Xi'an**, the capital of **Shaanxi Province** in the north and often regarded as the true historical capital of China. For 13 dynasties, from the 11th century BC, the city was also the capital of China and is now, after Beijing, the most popular tourist attraction in China. The city is most famous for the **Tomb of Emperor Qin Shi Huang Di**, who first united China under the Qin Dynasty in 200 BC, and its terracotta figures - over 6000 life-sized **Terracotta Warriors** and horses buried along with the emperor. Despite damage inflicted during the Cultural Revolution, there are still numerous tombs, pavilions, museums and pagodas to be seen, such as the **Big Wild Goose Pagoda** with its spiral staircase, and the **Small Wild Goose Pagoda**.
- In the **Eastern Provinces**, **Shanghai** is one of the world's largest cities and one of China's most famous - more like New York or Paris than Beijing. Lying on the estuary of the Chang Jiang (Yangtze) River, it is the centre of China's trade and industry. European-style architecture, traditional Chinese buildings and sleek modern developments all co-exist in this cosmopolitan metropolis. The **Yuyuan Gardens** date back over 400 years: although relatively small, they are impressive thanks to their intricate design, with pavilions, rockeries, ponds and a complete traditional theatre woven together in an ornate maze. The gardens are reached via the **Town God Temple Bazaar**, a touristy but impressive warren of lanes and stalls. The **French Concession** area has quiet, characterful colonial parks and neighbourhoods, while the **Bund** (a waterfront promenade) along the **Huangpu River** has the celebrated strip of Art Deco towers. From here, the dynamic Pudong Development Area and the **Oriental Pearl Tower** can be viewed across the water.
- Discover **Hangzhou**, one of China's seven ancient capital cities. Known as 'Paradise on Earth', Hangzhou was also described by Marco Polo as 'the most beautiful and magnificent city in the world'. The city is also famous for its excellent silk and tea products. Today's city is a beauty spot still visited by Chinese and foreign tourists in great numbers. By far the most attractive excursion is to the **West Lake** area, dotted with weeping willows and peach trees, stone bridges, rockeries and painted pavilions. Here can be found the **Pagoda of Six Harmonies**, various tombs and sacred hills, monasteries and temples, not least the **Linyin Temple**.
- See China's version of Venice, **Suzhou**, dating back some 2500 years. An old proverb says that 'in Heaven there is Paradise; on earth, Suzhou'. Its riverside streets many famous water gardens are guaranteed to delight. There are over 400 historical sites and relics under the protection of the Government, such as the **Blue-Waves Pavilion Garden** on the outskirts, the **Lion-Grove Garden** which has rockeries resembling lions, the **Humble Administrator's Garden** and the **Garden of the Master of the Nets**. The **Grand Canal** and **Tiger Hill** are also worth a visit. There are numerous silk mills producing exquisite fabrics, and the local embroidery is an unparalleled art form.
- Spot some unique wildlife: **Chengdu**'s ancient parks and bamboo forests are the last stronghold of the **giant panda**. In the **Jiuzhaigou Ravine** in northern Sichuan Province, there is a vast nature reserve where giant pandas can be seen in their natural habitat.
- **Tibet**'s main town, **Lhasa**, is known as the 'city of the gods', standing at an altitude of 3700m (12,000ft). Its wonderful light and clear skies are peculiar to its high mountainous terrain.The main highlights for tourists lie in the **Potala** or **Red Palace**, home to successive Dalai Lamas, which dominates Lhasa and the valley. This seventh-century edifice, built on a far more ancient site, is now a unique museum whose exhibits include labyrinths of dungeons beneath the Palace, gigantic bejewelled Buddhas and vast treasure hoards, numerous chapels with human skull and thigh-bone wall decorations and wonderful Buddhist frescoes, with influences from India and Nepal. The Potala Palace is a UNESCO World Heritage Site. Other buildings of interest include the **Norbulingka** (**Summer Palace**) and the **Jokhang Temple** with its golden Buddhas.
- Journey the **Silk Road** and explore this ancient trading route, opened up by the Han Dynasty power from 138 BC, when Emperor Han Wudi sent a mission into Central Asia and launched westwards extensions of the Great Wall into the Gobi Desert. Used by silk merchants from the second century AD until its decline in the 16th century, the Silk Road is open in parts to tourists eager to explore its heritage. This long string of caravan trails, oases, roads and mountain passes, stretched from northern China, through bleak and foreboding desert and mountainous terrain to the ports on either the Caspian Sea or Mediterranean Sea, and was the conduit for goods and ideas passing between ancient China and the West. The Mongols later used the Silk Road to bind their vast empire, as Marco Polo found when he travelled it in the 13th century. The two main routes are split into the north route and the south route: the north starting in China at Xi'an, running through the **Gansu Corridor**, **Dunhuang**, **Jade Gate Pass** to the neck of the Gobi desert, following the **Tianshan mountains** round the fringes of the **Taklimakan desert** to **Kashgar** (**Xinjiang Province**), across the **Pamirs** to **Samarkand** or Tashkent (Uzbekistan) onto the Caspian Sea. The south route runs with the north until the Jade Gate Pass and then stretches round the southern edges of the Taklimakan desert to Kashgar and then over the Karakorum mountain range (see Karakorum Highway in the *Pakistan* section) into India. The Silk Road was a major highway for the spread of Buddhism into East Asia, and later for the growth of Islam. Within China, the main sights are found in Xinjiang Province, including the Buddhist grottos at Dunhuang and ancient relics at the architecturally distinct **Turpan** (it has retained its Islamic character and is also the hottest place in China, lying in the **Turpan Depression**, the second-lowest point on Earth next only to the Dead Sea), such as the ruins of the city of **Jiaohe**, the lively Sunday market at **Kashgar** and the **Flaming Mountains**, which glow brightly at sunset. **Tianchi** (**Heavenly**) **Lake** is a clear turquoise-coloured lake set in the midst of the **Tian Shan** range of mountains.

Credit: ©Juliet Sinclair

Top Things To Do

- An estimated 300 million Chinese people use the bicycle as a means of transport and, not surprisingly, bicycle hire shops can be found everywhere, even in smaller towns. China offers ideal and diverse terrain for **cycling**.
- China's main natural attractions are its scenic mountains, waterfalls, caverns and great rivers and lakes. No permit is required for **hiking**, although a **trekking** permit is compulsory (and fairly expensive) for visiting more remote areas. The **Qinghai-Tibet Plateau** (also known as 'the roof of the world') is one of the world's most famous **mountaineering** destinations. Some of the world's highest mountains define the southern border of Tibet, including **Mount Everest** (or **Qoomolangma**), 8848m (29,021ft), **Namcha Barwa**, 7756m (25,445ft), around which the **Brahmaputra River** carves a fantastic gorge to enter India, and **Gurla Mandhata**, 7728m (25,355ft). Among the 14 peaks on earth above 8000m, five are located in Tibet. The Tibetan approach to Mount Everest provides far better views than the Nepal side. Some 27,000 sq km around Everest's Tibetan face have been designated as the **Qoomolangma Nature Reserve**. For foreign travellers, the Everest Base Camp has become the most popular trekking destination in Tibet. The two access points are **Shegar** and **Tingri**, along the **Friendship Highway** to Nepal. 4-wheel-drive vehicles can also take visitors all the way to base camp along the Shegar track.
- The capital of Shandong Province, Jinan's **Mount Taishan**'s 72 peaks make up a mountain park with ancient pine and cypress trees, spectacular waterfalls, 1800 stone sculptures and a kilometre-long mountain stairway known as the '**Ladder to Heaven**'. **Laoshan** is a fine mountain region. Near Yangzhou, **Huangshan Mountain** has trees that cling to its breathtaking rocky precipices amongst seas of cloud and clear natural springs and lakes. A UNESCO World Heritage Site for its natural beauty and wildlife, the mountain has a cablecar linking the summit and base. The six official 'scenic spots' among the snowy peaks of the **Sichuan Province** include **Shuzheng**, with waterfalls and 40 lakes of different colours where **swimming** and **boating** are allowed. Further north, the concentration of mineral salts in the water at **Huanglong** (**Yellow Dragon**) nature reserve has created beautifully coloured natural talpatate ponds and rock formations. **Chongqing** is perched magnificently above the **Chang Jiang** (**Yangtze**) River and is a natural starting point for excursions to the **Yangtze Gorges**, whose most popular stretches are further east with poetic names like **Witches Gorge** and **Shadowplay Gorge**. These natural wonders are due to be completely submerged by 2009 after the completion of the Three Gorges Dam, so should be seen with much haste as

A B C D E F G H I J K L M N O P Q R S T U V W X Y Z

possible. Near Fuzhou, **Mount Wuyi** is an outstanding area of natural beauty and the cradle of neo-Confucianism. **Lushan Mountain** is a well-known scenic area and summer resort with tranquil scenery and a comfortable climate. The mountain has been a haven for poets and hermits for centuries, and more recently for Chiang Kaishek, Mao Zedong, Harry Truman and other dignitaries. At its centre is **Guling Town**, at an altitude of 1167m. In **Guilin** is a spectacular landscape of bizarre limestone formations. Steep monolithic mountains rise dramatically from a flat landscape of meandering rivers and paddy fields. Visitors can climb the hills, take river trips and visit the parks, lakes and caves. Further north is the **Wulingyuan** basin, centred on the town of **Zhangjiajie**. The **Zhangjiajie National Forest Park** contains dense primeval forest and several thousand steep mountain peaks, as well as **Yellow Dragon Cave**, Asia's largest, with gnarled stalactites. Outside of **Kunming** are the major attractions of **Xi Shan**, the holy mountain, and the petrified limestone forest called **Shilin**.

- You might not associate China with beaches but **Hainan Island** off the south coast of **Guangdong Province** has just that. This tropical island has some fine sea and sand, palm groves, fresh seafood and coconuts. In 1989, Hainan Island became a separate province in its own right, and is now one of several Special Economic Zones. It is still not yet the 'Hawaii of China' it aspires to be, but it is certainly China's 'latest' holiday area.
- Try the ancient 'shadow art' of **Tai Chi**, a series of linked movements performed in a slow relaxed manner using the entire body whilst focusing the mind. Traditionally practised in towns throughout China, particularly in the early morning hours, visitors wishing to learn or participate are welcome.
- Attend the **Spring Festival**, the most important festival in the year for the Chinese, when families get together and share a sumptuous meal on the eve of the Chinese New Year. Homes are festooned with banners and pictures to bring good fortune. Other activities associated with the festival include the lion dance, the dragon-lantern dance and stilt walking.
- **Chinese New Year** festivities have to be seen to be believed: an extravaganza of colour and custom, there are guaranteed to be parades, lantern shows, singing and dancing.

TOURIST INFORMATION

China National Tourist Office (CNTO) in the UK
71 Warwick Road, London SW5 9HB, UK
Tel: (020) 7373 0888 *or* (09001) 600 188 (brochure request and general information; calls cost 60p per minute).
Website: www.cnta.gov.cn

China National Tourist Office (CNTO) in the USA
Suite 6413, 350 Fifth Avenue, Empire State Building, New York, NY 10118, USA
Tel: (888) 760 8218 (information and trade enquiries).
Website: www.discoverchinaforever.com

Tibet Tourism Administration
18 Yuanlin Road, Lhasa, Tibet 850001, People's Republic of China
Tel: (891) 633 5472.

Tibet Tourism Office in Beijing
Room 4284 Oriental Kenzo Plaza, Dongzhimen, Beijing 100027, People's Republic of China
Tel: (10) 8447 7899 *or* 6703 *or* 6503.
Website: www.tibettour.net.cn/en

Entertainment

FOOD & DRINK: Chinese cuisine has a very long history and is renowned all over the world. Cantonese (the style the majority of Westerners are most familiar with) is only one regional style of Chinese cooking. There are eight major schools of Chinese cuisine, named after the places where they were conceived: Anhui, Fujian, Guangdong, Hunan, Jiangsu, Shandong, Sichuan and Zhejian. For a brief appreciation of the cuisine, it is possible to break it down into four major regional categories:

Northern cuisine: Beijing food has developed from the Shandong school of cuisine.

Specialities:
- *Peking Duck*, which is roasted in a special way, and eaten in a thin pancake with cucumber and a sweet plum sauce.
- *Mongolian Hotpot*, a Chinese version of fondue. It is eaten in a communal style and consists of a central simmering soup in a special large round pot into which is dipped a variety of uncooked meats and vegetables, which are cooked on the spot.
- A cheap and delicious local dish is *shuijiao*, which is pasta-like dough wrapped round pork meat, chives and onions, similar in idea to Italian ravioli. These can be bought by the *jin* (pound) in street markets and small eating houses, and are a good filler if you are out all day and do not feel like a large restaurant dinner. It should, however, be noted that in the interest of hygiene, it is best to take your own chopsticks.

Southern cuisine: Guangdong (Cantonese) food is famous for being the most exotic in China. The food markets in Guangzhou are a testimony to this, and the Western visitor is often shocked by the enormous variety of rare and exotic animals that are used in the cuisine, including snake, dog, turtle and wildcat.

Specialities:
- *Dim sum* served at lunch.
- Shrimp wonton noodle soup.

Eastern cuisine: Shanghai and Zhejiang cooking is rich and sweet, often pickled. Noted for seafood, hot and sour soup, noodles and vegetables.

Specialities:
- *La Mian* (pulled noodles) served with curry beef soup.
- *Xiao Long Bao* (small steamer bun), pan fried pork buns eaten dipped in vinegar.

Western cuisine: Sichuan and Hunan food is spicy, often sour and peppery, with specialities such as diced chicken stirred with soy sauce and peanuts, and spicy *doufu* (beancurd).

Specialities:
- Sweet and sour chicken.
- Orange beef.

National drinks:
- One of the best-known national drinks is *maotai*, a fiery spirit distilled from rice wine.
- Local beers are of good quality, notably *Qingdao*, which is similar to German lager.
- There are now some decent wines, which are produced mainly for tourists and export, such as *Qingdao* white wine.

NIGHTLIFE: Visitors can follow itineraries drawn up in advance, when sampling the nightlife of the larger cities, including a selection of prearranged restaurant meals and visits to Chinese opera, Chinese state circus, ballet and theatre. Local Chinese will tend to only drink socially with a formal meal so bars and nightclubs will generally only be found in the more cosmopolitan cities and major towns. Karaoke (written *OK+* on Chinese signs) is a popular form of evening entertainment.

SHOPPING: All consumer prices are set by the Government, and there is no price bargaining in shops and department stores, although it is possible to bargain fiercely in small outdoor markets (of which there are many) for items such as jade, antique ceramics and also silk garments. All antiques over 100 years old are marked with a red wax seal by the authorities, and require an export customs certificate. The antique market in Changqing opens everyday. Access to normal shops is available, offering inexpensive souvenirs, work clothes, posters and books; this will prove much easier if accompanied by an interpreter, although it is possible to point or get the help of a nearby English-speaker. Items are sometimes in short supply, but prices will not vary much from place to place. In large cities such as Beijing and Shanghai, there are big department stores with four or five floors, selling a wide range of products. The best shopping is in local factories, shops and hotels specialising in the sale of handicrafts. Arts and crafts department stores offer local handicrafts. Special purchases include jade jewellery, embroidery, calligraphy, paintings and carvings in wood, stone and bamboo. Shop personnel often pack and arrange shipping for bulky items. It is advisable to keep receipts, as visitors may be asked to produce them at Customs prior to departure. **Shopping hours**: Mon-Sun 0900-1900.

Business

- **GDP:** US$4.5 trillion.
- **Main exports:** Machinery and equipment, plastics, optical and medical equipment, iron and steel.
- **Main imports:** Machinery and equipment, oil, mineral fuels, plastics, organic chemicals, optical and medical equipment, iron and steel.
- **Main trade partners:** USA, Japan, Hong Kong (SAR), Korea (Rep) and Germany.

ECONOMY: The vast Chinese economy has developed in fits and starts since the founding of the People's Republic in 1949. Its basic structure is mostly that of a developing country, with the majority of the population employed on the land. However, there is a significant industrial base and expanding pockets of advanced manufacturing and technological enterprises, concentrated on the eastern coast and the Special Administrative/Economic Zones (including Hong Kong and Macau).

The economy has undergone rapid and consistent growth of approximately 8 to 9 per cent annually since the introduction of economic reforms in the late 1980s. However, the new wealth has not been evenly distributed and there are now major disparities between what are sometimes known as the 'blue China' – the coastal cities and Special Zones – and the inland 'brown China' of low-grade agriculture, antiquated industrial operations and

Credit: ©Juliet Sinclair

widespread social and economic deprivation. Although modernisation of the agricultural sector is underway, there has been a major shift of population from the countryside to the cities. And the Government is still prepared to undertake massive engineering projects such as the Three Gorges Dam hydro-electric project, which may displace anything up to one million people.

China is the world's largest producer of rice and a major producer of cereals and grain. Large mineral deposits, particularly coal and iron ore, provide the raw material for an extensive steel industry. China is self-sufficient in oil and is developing a petrochemicals industry. Other important minerals include tungsten, molybdenum, tin, lead, bauxite (aluminium), phosphates and manganese. In the last 10 years, central Government policy has switched the emphasis in development from heavy to light industry and promoted the evolution of a service sector. Chemicals and high technology industries have grown particularly quickly. The fundamental changes that have taken place in the Chinese economy were introduced under what was described as the 'socialist market economy', under which market mechanisms were introduced to attract foreign investment and improved trade terms. Foreign companies were encouraged both to sell products in China and to establish joint ventures – under certain conditions – with Chinese commercial organisations. Such problems as emerged were put into perspective by the 1997 Asian economic crisis. China, because of its vast domestic market and highly regulated banking system, did not suffer nearly as badly as many of the region's smaller economies. Government targets for production and growth continued to be met and still are. In 2003, the economy accelerated to reach 10 per cent growth, the trade balance showed a healthy surplus, and price inflation was negligible. The economy has already begun to show the benefits of China's recently acquired membership of the World Trade Organization in 2001. (This was a major foreign policy objective for the Jiang Government.) However, Chinese markets will now face competition from abroad. In 2005, China's central bank announced that it will stop pegging its currency to the US dollar; this could have potentially far-reaching effects on the global economy and US consumers.

BUSINESS ETIQUETTE: Weights and measures are mainly metric, but several old Chinese weights and measures are still used. Liquids and eggs are often sold by weight. The Chinese foot is 1.0936 of an English Foot (0.33m). Suits should be worn for business visits. Appointments should be made in advance and punctuality is expected. Visiting cards should be printed with a Chinese translation on the reverse. Business visitors are usually entertained in restaurants where it is customary to arrive a little early and the host will toast the visitor. It is customary to invite the host or hostess to a return dinner. Business travellers in particular should bear in mind that the Government of the United Kingdom recognises the Government of the People's Republic of China as being the only Government of China, as do the United Nations. Best months for business visits are April to June and September to October. **Office hours**: Mon-Fri 0800-1700, midday break of one to two hours.

COMMERCIAL INFORMATION

China Council for the Promotion of International Trade (CCPIT)
London office: 40-41 Pall Mall, London SW1Y 5JQ, UK
Tel: (020) 7321 2044.
Website: www.ccpit.com
Beijing office: 1 Fu Xing Men Wai Jie, Beijing 100860, People's Republic of China
Tel: (10) 6801 3344.
Website: www.ccpit.com

China – Hong Kong

Location: East Asia.

Time: GMT + 8.

Overview

On 1 July 1997, Hong Kong became a Special Administrative Region of China in an arrangement that will last for 50 years. Operating under a 'one country, two systems policy', Hong Kong maintains its own political, social and economic systems. English remains an official language and Hong Kong's border with China still exists.

Now reunited with the mainland, visually stunning Hong Kong offers a warp-speed 'shop till you drop' lifestyle combined with enclaves of tradition.

Hong Kong was part of the Chinese empire before coming under British administration as a direct result of the 19th-century Opium Wars. When peace terms were drawn up in 1841, the Emperor of China agreed that Hong Kong Island should be ceded to Britain and five other ports licensed for foreign trade. The British controlled Hong Kong from then – apart from a four-year period during World War II when the territory was occupied by the Japanese – until 1997, when it was returned to China. The terms were settled and signed in 1984 and contained guarantees that the territory would enjoy a high degree of autonomy, especially in the economic field.

Hong Kong is a popular tourist destination as well as being one of the world's major business centres. It has over 260 outlying islands but only a few are inhabited. This means that Hong Kong offers a great range of contrasts, with numerous islands that provide a tranquil alternative to its frenetic energy elsewhere. Hong Kong Island is an eclectic mix of modern skyscrapers, colonial buildings and traditional temples.

Much has changed since 1841 when Lord Palmerston - who was then foreign secretary - wrote that Hong Kong was 'nothing but a barren island without a house upon it'.

General Information

AREA: 1098 sq km (424 sq miles).
POPULATION: 7.2 million (UN estimate, 2005).
POPULATION DENSITY: 6557.4 per sq km.
GEOGRAPHY: Hong Kong is located in East Asia, just south of the Tropic of Cancer. Hong Kong Island is 32km (20 miles) east of the mouth of Pearl River and 135km (84 miles) southeast of Canton. It is separated from the mainland by a good natural harbour. Hong Kong Island was ceded to Britain in 1842 by the Treaty of Nanking; and the Kowloon Peninsula (south of Boundary Street and Stonecutters

Island) in 1860 by the Convention of Peking. The area of Boundary Street to Shenzhen River and a group of 260 islands, now known as the New Territories, were leased to Britain in 1898 for a period of 99 years. The New Territories (plus the 260 islands) comprise 891 sq km (380 sq miles). Shortage of land suitable for development has led to reclamation from the sea, principally from the seafronts of Hong Kong Island and Kowloon.
GOVERNMENT: Special Administrative Region of the People's Republic of China since 1997. **Head of Government**: Chief Executive Donald Tsang. **Recent history:** Beijing selected the shipping tycoon Tung Chee Hwa to fill the new post of Chief Executive with powers comparable to those of the former Governor. A pro-Beijing political party created shortly before the handover, the Democratic Party for the Betterment of Hong Kong (DAB), took control of the LegCo after the first election held under Chinese rule in May 1998. The result has been more or less repeated in subsequent polls. The limited powers of the LegCo and the restricted nature of the electoral franchise mean that no serious opposition can be mounted to the policies of the administration. In June 2002, Tung Chee Hwa was confirmed in a second term of office as Chief Executive. The timing for the new regime was unfortunate in as much as the Asian financial crisis hit the region just months after the territory had changed hands. Initially, it seemed that Hong Kong would come through largely unscathed: in fact, the economy has been depressed for most of the last five years (see *Economy* section). This has given rise to some political discontent and the self-confidence that previously characterised Hong Kong is now waning severely. Since 2003, there have been protests calling for a more democratic and representative system of Government. On 10 March 2005, Tung Chee-Hwa announced he had resigned as Chief Executive for reasons of ill heath. In accordance with basic law, the Chief Secretary Donald Tsang, became Acting Chief Executive. He was appointed by the Central People's Government in Beijing for a two-year term on 21 June 2005. China is pushing the administration to introduce an anti-subversion law, principally to combat the Falun Gong Christian religious sect.

Hong Kong is now a Special Administrative Region of the People's Republic of China (PRC). Under the Basic Law which is the governing instrument of the region, executive power is held by a Chief Executive, who is appointed by an 'Election Committee' composed of 800 'representatives of the community'. The Chief Executive is answerable to the State Council of the PRC (see *China (People's Republic of)* section) and serves a five-year term. The Chief Executive appoints a 15-member Executive Council to assist in the administration of the Region. Hong Kong's legislature is the 60-member Legislative Council; 24 members are directly elected in geographical constituencies, 30 members are selected from 'functional constituencies' (mostly professional bodies and business interests) and the remaining six by the 'Election Committee'.
LANGUAGE: Chinese and English are the official languages, with Cantonese most widely spoken. English is spoken by many, particularly in business circles.
RELIGION: Buddhist, Confucian and Taoist, with Christian and Muslim minorities, but there are also places of worship for most other religious groups.
ELECTRICITY: 220 volts AC, 50Hz.
SOCIAL CONVENTIONS: Handshaking is the common form of greeting. In Hong Kong, the family name comes first, so Wong Man Ying would be addressed as Mr Wong. Most entertaining takes place in restaurants rather than in private homes. Normal courtesies should be observed when visiting someone's home. During a meal, a toast is often drunk saying *Yum Sing* at each course. There may be up to 12 courses served in a meal, and although it is not considered an insult to eat sparingly, a good appetite is always appreciated and it is considered cordial to taste every dish. It is customary to invite the host to a return dinner. Informal wear is acceptable. Some restaurants and social functions often warrant formal attire. Smoking is widely acceptable and only prohibited where specified. Police who speak English have a red shoulder badge.

Climate

Hong Kong experiences four distinct seasons, with the climate influenced in winter by the north-northeast monsoon and in summer by the south-southwest monsoon. Summers are very hot, with the rainy season running from June to August. Spring and autumn are warm with occasional rain and cooler evenings. Winter can be cold, but most days are mild. There is a risk of typhoons and tropical storms from April to October, although direct hits are rare.
Required clothing: Lightweight cottons and linens are worn during warmer months, with warmer clothes for spring and autumn evenings. It should be noted that even during the hottest weather, a jacket or pullover will be required for the sometimes fierce air conditioning indoors. Warm mediumweights are best during winter. Waterproofing is advisable during summer rains.

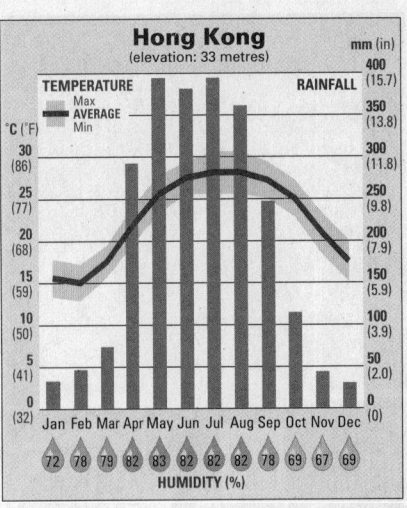

Communications

Telephone: Directory enquiries services are computerised. For directory enquiries, dial 1081 (English) *or* 1083 (Chinese). Full IDD is available. Country code: 852. Local public telephone calls can be made either with phonecards or coins. Local calls are free from private phones.
Mobile telephone: Roaming agreements exist with most international mobile phone companies. Mobile telephones also function all over the underground network, thanks to transmitters installed in the tunnels. It is possible to rent a mobile phone during your stay at the international airport.
Internet: Internet facilities are available at libraries and Internet cafes and are plentiful nationwide.
Post: Regular postal services are available. Airmail to Europe takes three to five days. Post office hours: Mon-Fri 0800-1800; Sat 0800-1400.
MEDIA: Hong Kong has one of the world's largest film industries and is a major centre for broadcasting and publishing. Hong Kong's media is a lot more editorially free than the rest of China. However, there is still reported self-censorship and pressure on editorial policies. Many international and pan-Asian broadcasters are based in the territory. Hong Kong's terrestrial commercial TV networks, TVB and ATV, can also be received in neighbouring Guangdong Province. Public broadcaster Radio-TV Hong Kong (RTHK) operates several radio and TV networks. There are scores of Chinese-language newspapers and a handful of English-language dailies.
Press: *Renmin Ribao* (*People's Daily*) is the communist party daily newspaper. English-language dailies include *Asian Wall Street Journal*, *International Herald Tribune* and *South China Morning Post*.
TV: *Radio-TV Hong Kong* (RTHK) is Government-funded; *Asia TV* (ATV) and *Television Broadcasts* (TVB) are private, terrestrial broadcasters.
Radio: *Radio-TV Hong Kong* (RTHK) operates seven networks in English, Cantonese and Mandarin. Commercial Radio operates *CR1, CR2* networks in Cantonese and mediumwave (AM) station *AM 864*. *Metro Broadcast* operates *Metro Showbiz*, *Metro Finance* and the English-language *Metro Plus*.

Passport/Visa

	Passport Required?	Visa Required?	Return Ticket Required?
Full British	Yes	No/1	Yes
Australian	Yes	No/2	Yes
Canadian	Yes	No/2	Yes
USA	Yes	No/4	Yes
Other EU	Yes	No/3	Yes
Japanese	Yes	No/4	Yes

Note: *Regulations and requirements may be subject to change at short notice, and you are advised to contact the appropriate diplomatic or consular authority before finalising travel arrangements. Any numbers in the chart refer to the footnotes below.*

Entry restrictions: All visitors must show evidence of sufficient funds to support themselves during their stay.
PASSPORTS: Passport valid for at least six months after the period of intended visit required by all.
VISAS: Required by all except the following:
(a) **1**. British Citizens for stays of up to 180 days (British Overseas Citizens, British Subjects, British Protected Persons and nationals of British Dependent Territories may stay for up to 90 days);
(b) **2**. nationals of Commonwealth countries for stays of up to 90 days (except nationals of Samoa, South Africa and

Credit: ©Hong Kong Tourism Board

Validity: Three months. Extensions are possible for about HK$135. Enquire at the Immigration Department in Hong Kong or at the nearest Chinese Embassy (or consular section).

Application to: Chinese Consulate (or consular section at the Embassy), Hong Kong Economic Office or the Hong Kong Immigration Department.

Application requirements: (a) Passport valid for at least six months with photocopies of the relevant pages of information. (b) Completed application form. (c) Valid travel documents (onward or return tickets, unless on transit to China (PR) or Macau (SAR), and accommodation bookings). (d) Sufficient funds to cover duration of stay. (e) Two passport-size photos. (f) Evidence of employment (employment certificate, company letter etc). (g) Fee. (h) For business visas, a letter of invitation from a ministry, firm or an official Hong Kong organisation is required, accompanied by a copy of the sponsor's Hong Kong identity card.

Working days required: Five (if the application is processed by a Chinese Consulate or Embassy); four to six weeks if the application needs to be considered by the Hong Kong Immigration Department. Note that there is no refund if the application is turned down.

PASSPORT/VISA INFORMATION

Hong Kong Economic and Trade Office in the UK
6 Grafton Street, London W1S 4EQ, UK
Tel: (020) 7499 9821.
Website: www.hketolondon.gov.hk

The Embassy of the People's Republic of China in the USA deals with enquiries relating to Hong Kong (See *China (People's Republic)* section).

Hong Kong Immigration Department
2nd Floor, Immigration Tower, 7 Gloucester Road, Wan Chai, Hong Kong
Tel: 2824 6111.
Website: www.immd.gov.hk

Money

Currency: Hong Kong Dollar (HKD; symbol HK$) = 100 cents. Notes are in denominations of HKD1000, 500, 100, 50, 20 and 10. Coins are in denominations of HKD10, 5, 2 and 1, and 50, 20 and 10 cents.

Currency exchange: Foreign currency can be changed in banks, hotels and bureaux de change. Banks usually offer the best rate of exchange. There are also plenty of ATMs.

Credit & debit cards: American Express, Diners Club, MasterCard and Visa are widely accepted. Check with your credit or debit card company for details of merchant acceptability and other services which may be available.

Traveller's cheques: Accepted almost everywhere. To avoid additional exchange rate charges, travellers are advised to take traveller's cheques in Pounds Sterling, US Dollars or Euros.

Currency restrictions: There are no restrictions on the import or export of either local or foreign currency.

Banking hours: Mon-Fri 0900-1630, Sat 0900-1230. Some banks and branches are open slightly longer hours.

Exchange rate indicators:

Date	At time of publishing
£1.00=	HK$13.61
$1.00=	HK$7.76

Duty Free

The following goods may be imported into Hong Kong by persons over 18 years of age without incurring customs duty:

Non-residents: *200 cigarettes or 50 cigars or 250g of tobacco; 1l of wine or spirits; reasonable quantity of other items for personal use.*

Residents: *60 cigarettes or 15 cigars or 75g of tobacco; 750ml of still wine; reasonable quantity of other items for personal use.*

Note: (a) Antibiotic drugs are prohibited unless confirmed by a medical note. (b) The import of animals is strictly controlled.

Prohibited items: Firearms, narcotics, psychotropic drugs, counterfeit items, ammunition, copyright-infringed goods, plants, endangered species (dead or alive) and products deriving from them, game, poultry and fireworks and other explosives. Import/export of these items require a valid licence or permit issued in advance.

Public Holidays

Below are listed Public Holidays for the January 2006-June 2007 period.
2006: Jan 1 New Year's Day. **Jan 29-31** Chinese New Year.
Apr 5 Ching Ming Festival. **Apr 14-15** Easter. **May 1** Labour Day. **May 5** Lord Buddha's Birthday. **May 31** Tuen Ng

(Dragon Boat) Festival. **Jul 1** Hong Kong Special Administrative Region Establishment Day. **Oct 1** National Day. **Oct 6** Chinese Mid-Autumn Festival. **Oct 30** Chung Yeung Festival. **Dec 25** Christmas Day. **Dec 26** Boxing Day.
2007: Jan 1 New Year's Day. **Feb 18-20** Chinese New Year. **Apr 5** Ching Ming Festival. **Apr 6** Good Friday. **Apr 9** Easter Monday. **May 1** Labour Day. **May 24** Lord Buddha's Birthday. **Jun 15** Tuen Ng (Dragon Boat) Festival.

Note: Religious festivals are timed according to the lunar calendar and variations may occur. The above represent all holidays on which banks, schools, public offices and Government departments close. There are also statutory holidays on which all employees receive a day's holiday. For further details of these dates, contact the Hong Kong Tourism Board.

Health

	Special Precautions?	Certificate Required?
Yellow Fever	No	No
Cholera	No	No
Typhoid & Polio	1	N/A
Malaria	2	N/A

Note: *Regulations and requirements may be subject to change at short notice, and you are advised to contact your doctor well in advance of your intended date of departure. Any numbers in the chart refer to the footnotes below.*

1: Vaccination against typhoid and polio is advised.
2: There may be a slight risk of malaria in the rural areas although prophylaxis is not considered necessary.

Food & drink: All water direct from Government mains in Hong Kong exceeds the United Nations WHO standards and is fit for drinking. However, all hotels also provide bottled water in guest rooms. Milk is pasteurised and dairy products are safe for consumption. Local meat, poultry, seafood, fruit and vegetables are generally considered safe to eat.

Other risks: *Japanese encephalitis* may occur in the New Territories between April and October. Immunisation against *hepatitis A, B, diphtheria* and *TB* is sometimes recommended. *Dengue fever* is increasing. Outbreaks of *Severe Acute Respiratory Syndrome, SARS,* occurred in 2003.

Health care: Upon arrival at immigration all passengers pass through body heat scanners. Charges are made for all services and treatment; visitors are required to pay HK$570 if using Accident and Emergency in public hospitals. All visitors are advised to take out private health insurance. Hotels have a list of Government-accredited doctors. First-class Western medicine is practised. Excellent dental care is available. For emergency medical services, dial 999.

Travel - International

AIR:

The major international airline is *Cathay Pacific (CX)* (website: www.cathaypacific.com), which flies to Hong Kong thrice-daily from London Heathrow and Los Angeles, twice-daily from New York (John F Kennedy Airport) and Vancouver, and once a day from Toronto. Other airlines operating to Hong Kong include *Air Canada, British Airways, China Airlines, Japan Airlines, KLM, Lufthansa, Qantas, Singapore Airlines, SWISS, United Airlines* and *Virgin Atlantic.*

Approximate flight times: From Hong Kong to *London* is 12 hours 50 minutes, to *Los Angeles* is 14 hours 15 minutes, to *New York* is 17 hours, to *Singapore* is three hours 40 minutes, to *Sydney* is nine hours, and to *Tokyo* is four hours 20 minutes.

Main airports: *Hong Kong International Airport (HKG)* (Chek Lap Kok) (website: www.hongkongairport.com) is located on Lantau Island, 34 km (21 miles) from central Hong Kong. It is one of 10 Airport Core Programme (ACP) projects, one of the largest infrastructural projects ever undertaken in the world. It includes the 2.2km- (1.4 mile-) Tsing Ma Bridge, the world's largest road and rail suspension Bridge, linking Lantau Island to the mainland New Territories. About three-quarters of the 12,480 sq km (7800 sq miles) airport site was constructed from land reclaimed from the sea, with the rest formed from the excavation of the existing islands of Chek Lap Kok and Lam Chau. The airport terminal building, designed by the British architect Sir Norman Foster, is Hong Kong's largest single building and its wing-like roof and glass walls have been hailed as a landmark in modern architecture.

To/from the airport: Rail, bus and taxi links from *Hong Kong International Airport* to central Hong Kong leave from the Transportation Centre adjacent to the passenger terminal and cross the Tsing Ma bridge to the mainland New Territories. The easiest connection is via the *Airport Express Line (AEL)*, an all-seater business class high-speed train. The AEL leaves the airport every 12 minutes, operating from 0550-0115 (last train from Hong Kong

---

Uganda for stays of up to 30 days, and nationals of Bangladesh, Ghana, India, Lesotho and Mozambique for stays up to 14 days); nationals of Cameroon, Côte d'Ivoire, Ethiopia, Grenada, Nigeria, Pakistan, Sierra Leone, the Solomon Islands and Sri Lanka *do* require a visa;

(c) **3**. nationals of EU countries for stays of up to 90 days (except **1**. British citizens for stays of up to 180 days);

(d) **4**. nationals of Argentina, Andorra, Anguilla, Bermuda, Brazil, British Antarctic Territory, British Indian Ocean Territory, British Virgin Islands, Bulgaria, Cayman Islands, Chile, Colombia, Ecuador, Egypt, Falkland Islands and Dependencies, Faroe Islands, Gibraltar, Greenland, Iceland, Israel, Japan, Korea (Rep), Liechtenstein, Mexico, Monaco, Montserrat, Norway, Pitcairn Henderson Ducie and Oeno Islands, Romania, St Helena and Dependencies, St Kitts & Nevis, San Marino, Switzerland, the South Georgia and South Sandwich Islands, the Sovereign Base Areas of Akrotiri and Dhekelia, Turkey, Turks & Caicos Islands, Uruguay (except holders of passports issued under decree 289/90, who *do* require a visa), USA, Venezuela and Zimbabwe for stays of up to 90 days;

(e) nationals of Bolivia, Cape Verde, Costa Rica (except holders of a provisional passport and holders of 'Documento de Identidad Y Viaje' issued by the Costa Rican Government, who *do* require a visa), Dominican Republic, El Salvador, Guatemala, Honduras, Indonesia, Morocco, Paraguay, Peru (except for holders of Peruvian special resident's passports, who *do* require a visa), Thailand, Tunisia, United Arab Emirates and Yemen for stays of up to 30 days;

(f) nationals of Algeria, Bahrain, Benin, Bhutan, Bosnia & Herzegovina, Burkina Faso, Central African Republic, Chad, Comoro Islands, Congo (Rep), Croatia, Djibouti, Equatorial Guinea, Gabon, Guinea, Guinea-Bissau, Haiti, Jordan, Kuwait, Macedonia (Former Yugoslav Republic of), Madagascar, Mali, Marshall Islands, Mauritania, (Federated States of) Micronesia, Mongolia, Niger, Oman, Palau, The Philippines, Qatar, Rwanda, São Tomé e Príncipe, Saudi Arabia, Surinam, Togo, US Territory of Pacific Islands and Vatican City for stays of up to 14 days;

(g) People in transit not leaving the airport transit area except for nationals of Eritrea, Iraq, Liberia, Pakistan (except holders of Diplomatic and Official passports) and Sierra Leone who *do* require a transit visa;

(h) all other nationals for stays of up to seven days (except for nationals of Eritrea, Iraq, Liberia, Pakistan (except holders of Diplomatic and Official passports) and Sierra Leone who *do* require a visa at all times).

Types of visa and cost: *Tourist; Business* (single- and multiple-entry); visas generally cost HK$135, but this varies according to nationality and nature of visit. Enquire at the Chinese Consulate (or consular section at the Embassy) or the Hong Kong Immigration Department for details.
Transit: HK$70.

station is 0048). It is a 24-minute journey to Hong Kong station, also stopping at Kowloon and Tsing Yi, with free shuttle buses running from Hong Kong and Kowloon station for airport express passengers to various hotels (a single ticket to Hong Kong station from the airport costs HK$100). Many bus routes operate between the airport and Hong Kong and Kowloon, including nine Airbus services. Fares range between HK$20–45. High-speed ferries run between Tung Chung's new development pier at Chek Lap Kok and Tuen Mun, with a shuttle bus from the pier to the airport. Ferries operate from Tuen Mun between 0540-2300, and from Tung Chung's new development pier 0600-2320 and cost HK$15. The bus from the airside of the airport runs to the Skypier for the connection to cities Dangguan, Macau, Shekou and Shenzen. There are also 18 pick-up bays for coaches providing group and organised tour hotel transfers, and a car park for more than 3000 vehicles. Taxis to Hong Kong are readily available. *China Travel Service* and a number of other coach companies offer a variety of travel services for journeys to mainland China or Macau. *Facilities*: Tourist information desks and computer kiosks, several currency exchange counters, banks and ATMs, food and drink outlets, a post office, duty free shops and medical centre, good physical accessibility for passengers with disabilities and a large Hong Kong Sky Mall shopping centre with duty free shopping available. *Hong Kong International* is also one of only a few airports to have an Automated People Mover (APM), a driverless train at basement level that transports passengers between terminals.

Departure tax: All passengers aged 12 and above departing from Hong Kong International Airport must pay HK$120 (normally included in the ticket price). However, passengers who arrive and depart the same day are exempt.

SEA:

Main ports: A large number of cruise ships visit *Hong Kong* port. The following is a list of those that are UK-based; *Cunard, P&O, Radisson Seven Seas, Seabourn* and *Silversea*. Hovercraft services operate four times a day to and from Guangzhou and several times daily to and from Zhuhai. Departures are from the Hong Kong ferry terminal in Kowloon to Shenzhen or Guangzhou. Enquire locally for details. There are frequent daily services to and from Macau by jetfoil – 60 minutes; by hovercraft- 75 minutes; Jet cat - 75 minutes; and high-speed ferry - 90 minutes. (See also the *Macau* section.)

RAIL:

The *Kowloon–Canton Railway Corporation (KCRC)* operates a service from Kowloon to Guangzhou (formerly Canton), several times a day. There are also services from Hong Kong to Foshan and Changping. Restaurant cars are only available if travelling first class. Local KCRC trains run regularly (every five to 10 minutes) to Lo Wu, the last stop before the Chinese border. It is then possible to cross the border to Shenzhen, a special economic zone, in China over the border. To go as far as Lo Wu, travellers must hold a visa for China, otherwise it is only possible to get to Sheung Shui. Children under three years old travel free. Children aged three to nine years pay half fare. For more information, contact the KCRC information line (tel: 2929 3399; website: www.kcrc.com).

Travel - Internal

SEA:

Cross-harbour passenger services (shortest route seven to 10 minutes) are operated by *Star Ferries* between Hong Kong Island and Kowloon (sailing every six to 12 minutes) from 0630-2330. Fares are HK$1.70 for the lower deck and HK$2.20 for the upper deck. There are frequent passenger and vehicle services on other cross-harbour routes. Ferries and hydrofoils service the outlying islands, Peng Chau, Cheung Chau, Lamma Island and Lantau Island, including Discovery Bay. Ferry services are run by New World First Ferry Services (website: www.nwff.com.hk), the Hong Kong Kowloon Ferry (website: www.hkkf.com.hk) and Discovery bay Transportation Services Ltd (website: www.hkri.com). *Wallah wallahs* (small motorboats) provide 24-hour service. However, the opening of the Cross Harbour Tunnel means that *wallah wallahs* are decreasing in popularity. Tours of the harbour and to Aberdeen and Yaumatei typhoon shelters are available by *watertours* junks, and visits to outlying islands are possible by public ferry. Weekdays are the best time to go, since ferries tend to be very crowded at weekends. During the typhoon season (May to November), all ferry services may be suspended during bad weather.

RAIL/METRO:

Mass Transit Railway (MTR) has six lines: Kwun Tong, Tsuen Wan, Island, Tung Chung, Tseung Kwan O and Disneyland resort, which provides a cross-harbour line. It is more expensive than the ferry, but quicker, particularly for those travelling further into Kowloon than Tsimshatsui or to Lantau Island. Trains run between 0600-0100. A single ticket costs HK$4-26. For visitors staying for a week or more it is worth getting an *Octopus Card*, an electronic ticket from which the cost of the journey is automatically deducted when it is placed on

a sensor. The card costs HK$50, and value can be added to the card at machines in any MTR station. Any other credit remaining is also refunded when the card is handed in. At present, the card may be used on MTR services, as well as on the Kowloon-Canton Railway, major bus routes, trams, minibuses and some ferries. The *Airport Express Tourist Octopus Card* is valid for three days, entitling passengers to two single Airport Express journey and three days of unlimited travel by MTR. Cards cost HK$300 (or HK$220 if only one single Airport Express journey is required). A deposit of HK$50 is required but is refunded along with any unused credit when the card is returned. For further details, contact the MTR information line (tel: 2881 8888; website: www.mtr.com.hk). The Kowloon–Canton Railway Corporation (KCR) has 13 stations within Hong Kong. Trains run between 0530-0025 from Hung Hom (Kowloon) to Shenzhen in China; see *Travel – International* section for more information. KCRC also run the Light Rail (LR) which connects the north west new territories Tuen Mun and Yuen Long. For further information, contact Light Rail (tel: 2468 7788).

ROAD:

The road network is extensive and of high quality but often congested in central areas. Traffic drives on the left. **Bus**: The *Octopus Card* (see above) can be used on buses. Routes run throughout the territory, with cross-harbour routes via the tunnels. These, however, are often very crowded. Exact change is required. Air-conditioned coaches operate along certain Hong Kong and Kowloon routes. Final destinations are marked clearly in Chinese and English. **Minibus**: These carry up to 16 passengers and can pick up and stop on request except at regular bus stops and other restricted areas. *Octopus Cards* are accepted. **Trams**: The *Octopus Card* (see above) can be used on trams. They are only available on Hong Kong Island, running from Kennedy Town to Shau Kei Wan (via Happy Valley racecourse). Double-decker trams are also available and provide magnificent views. All trams run from 0600-0100 and fares are HK$2 in exact change. *Peak Tram* on the Island has operated since 1888 and is a cable tramway to the upper terminus on Victoria Peak. *Octopus Cards* accepted. **Taxi**: These are plentiful in Hong Kong and Kowloon. There is an extra charge (HK$10) for the Cross Harbour Tunnel. Red taxis serve Hong Kong Island except Tung Chung Road and the south side of Lantau Island, green ones the rural areas of the New Territories, and blue ones Lantau Island. All taxis operate to and from Hong Kong International Airport. Maxicabs, however, operate on fixed routes without fixed stops. Many drivers speak a little English, but it is wise to get your destination written in Chinese characters. **Rickshaws**: These are gradually disappearing and are now purely a tourist attraction. It is advisable to agree the fare in advance. **Car hire**: A wide selection of self-drive and chauffeur-driven cars are available, although car hire is not that popular in Hong Kong. **Documentation**: An International Driving Permit is recommended, although it is not legally required. A valid national licence is accepted for up to 12 months. Minimum age is 18 years. Third Party insurance is compulsory. **Travel times:** The following chart gives approximate travel times (in hours and minutes) from **Hong Kong Island** to main tourist districts and outlying islands.

	Road	Metro	Sea
Kai Tak	0.35	-	-
Kowloon	0.20	0.04	0.10
Aberdeen	0.20	-	-
Lantau Is.	-	-	1.00

Accommodation

HOTELS:

Hong Kong offers a wide range of luxury hotels with all the major international chains represented. Smaller hotels specialising in 'family style' hospitality can be a cheaper alternative. There are also a number of fairly new hotels in the New Territories, providing a range of recreational facilities. Guest house accommodation, with good standards and facilities, is also available. In spite of the large number of hotel rooms available in Hong Kong, visitors are strongly advised to make an advance booking, especially during the peak season (May until November). There is a Hotel Reservation Centre at Hong Kong International Airport on Chek Lap Kok Island (open daily from 0600-0100) which can offer assistance. A 10 per cent service charge and 5 per cent Government tax are added to the bill. 80 member hotels belong to the Hong Kong Hotels Association. Though there is no grading structure as such, hotel members of the HKTA fall into one of four categories: High Tariff A Hotels, High Tariff B Hotels, Medium Tariff Hotels and Hostels/Guest houses.

SELF-CATERING:

Resort houses on the outlying islands can be hired.

CAMPING/CARAVANNING:

Permitted in the countryside, though permission is required within the Country Park protection area. There are also campsites in rural areas.

YOUTH HOSTELS:

There are several main YMCA/YWCAs in Hong Kong.

ACCOMMODATION INFORMATION

Hong Kong Hotels Association
508-511 Silvercord Tower II, 30 Canton Road,
Tsimshatsui, Kowloon, Hong Kong (SAR)
Tel: 2375 3838.
Website: www.hkha.org

YMCA
41 Salisbury Road, Tsimshatsui, Kowloon,
Hong Kong (SAR)
Tel: 2268 7000.
Website: www.ymcahk.org.hk

Hong Kong Youth Hostels Association Ltd
Room 225, Block 19, Shek Kip Mei Estate, Shek Kip Mei,
Kowloon, Hong Kong (SAR)
Tel: 2788 1638.
Website: www.yha.org.hk

Top Things To See

- See the country's oldest Chinese temple, **Man Mo Temple** on **Hong Kong Island**, which honours the gods of literature (Man) and war (Mo).

- View the incredible density and scale of the city from **Victoria Peak**. The view here has been further enhanced by the **Peak Tower**, a seven-storey, futuristic-looking building, incorporating a viewing area, restaurant and entertainment centre. Reached by the **Peak Tram**, that rises 386m (1266ft) up the mountainside within eight minutes, the summit offers an exceptional panorama, whether by day or night. In the **New Territories**, the **Waterfront Park** in **Tai Po** has a futuristic **Lookout Tower** that provides breathtaking views across **Tolo Harbour**.

- Observe glimpses of Hong Kong's colonial past, such as **Government House**, the residence of 25 British Governors from 1855 until Hong Kong's handover to China in 1997. Other vestiges are seen in **St John's Cathedral**, thought to be the oldest Christian church in the Far East.

- Go to the **Flagstaff House Museum of Tea Ware**, located in **Hong Kong Park**; the museum is an imposing colonial-style building housing ancient Chinese artefacts used in tea-making.

- See Hong Kong's tallest building, the impressive 78-storey **Central Plaza**. Visitors can view the city from the **Sky Lobby** on its 46th floor. After 1800 each day, neon lights upon the building's rooftop change colour every hour to denote the time of evening.

- Visit the pristine beach of **Repulse Bay**, overlooked by the **Tin Hau Temple**. **Lantau Island** has the white sandy beach, **Cheung Sha**, and the amazing **Shek Pik Reservoir Dam**. Day trips to Lantau and tours can be arranged from **Hong Kong Island**.

- In **Kowloon**, look at the time at the old **Clock Tower** near to the star ferry pier, the remaining piece from the Kowloon-Canton railway station that was re-located to Hung Hom in 1975.

- For a more spiritual retreat, visit either the **Chi Lin Nunnery**, a spectacular Tang Dynasty-style complex, or **Wong Tai Sin Temple**, built in honour of a shepherd who earned immortality. Many fortune-tellers congregate here.

- Mingle with the crowds at **Mong Kok**, thought to be the world's most densely populated urban area, which heaves with selling and buying. Exotic fish and amphibians are sold at the **Goldfish Market**, and near the **Yuen Po Street Bird Garden**, intricate bamboo birdcages and songbirds can be purchased.

- Venture up to the **Ten Thousand Buddhas Monastery** in the New Territories, situated in the hills above **Sha Tin**, which actually houses around 13,000 small Buddha statues, and is well worth visiting.

- Whilst in the New Territories, amble around a beautifully designed complex, located in **Tuen Mun**, which features pavilions, bonsai trees, lotus ponds and a Taoist temple that contains lanterns from Beijing's Imperial Palace.

- See Hong Kong's only historic pagoda, the **Tsui Shing Lau Pagoda** built in 1486 in the **Yuen Lang** district.

- On the border with China is the fantastic **Fung Ying Seen Koon Temple**, built in the traditional Taoist style with a double-tiered roof of orange tiles.

- On the Outlying Islands, **Lantau Island** is famed for its **Giant Buddha** that sits upon **Ngong Ping Plateau** at the **Po Lin Monastery**. At 26m high and weighing in at 202 tonnes of bronze, it is the world's largest seated outdoor Buddha. **Ngong Ping 360** (opened in early 2006) is a 5.7km (3.5-mile) cable car ride to the Giant Buddha.

A B C D E F G H I J K L M N O P Q R S T U V W X Y Z

Top Things To Do

- Watch the **Tuen Ng (Dragon Boat) Festival**, usually held in June. This lively, vibrant spectacle is underscored by the beating of heavy drums.
- Go to **Central**, the financial and commercial hub of Hong Kong Island, and catch the famous **Star Ferry** to the **Kowloon Peninsula**.
- A unique way to experience the buzz of city life is by riding the 800m-long **central-mid-levels escalator** (the world's longest covered outdoor escalator) which transports tens of thousands of people each day and has created its own escalator culture of cafes and restaurants.
- **MacLehose Trail**, the longest trail, at 100km (62 miles), crosses the **New Territories**, taking in Hong Kong's highest peak, **Tai Mo Shan** (985m/3231ft). It can be joined at 10 different points, all of them accessible by public transport, and is recommended for experienced hikers. The 70km- (43 mile-) **Lantau Trail** runs around **Lantau Island**, via **Lantau Peak** (934m/3064ft) and **Po Lin Monastery**, home to the world's tallest seated Buddha. The **Hong Kong Trail** runs through five country parks on Hong Kong Island, and the **Wilson Trail** runs for 78km from the south of **Hong Kong Island** to the north of the New Territories, necessitating a ferry ride across the harbour. A popular walk is the **Dragon's Back** on Hong Kong Island, which follows a ridge, giving spectacular views. This can be concluded with dinner in one of the restaurants in **Shek-O Village**.
- Hear the **Noon Day Gun** that has fired at midday since the 1840s.
- On the south of Hong Kong Island, dine at the famous neon-lit **Jumbo Floating Restaurant** (one of the largest in the world).
- Go **shopping** down **Nathan Road** in **Kowloon**, a smart and fashionable shopping street, considered the equivalent of Fifth Avenue or the Champs Elysées. Alternatively, try and grab a bargain at **Mong Kok's** and **Yau Ma Tei's** unique bustling **markets**. In **Yau Ma Tei**, **Temple Street** is a normal commercial road until 1400 when makeshift stalls and carts appear for the **Night Market**, selling everything from electrical goods to incense sticks.
- **Cyclists** will enjoy the **Tolo Harbour Cycling Track**, running from **Sha Tin** to **Tai Po**, an easy ride through scenic countryside. Bikes are available for rental near KCR stations. Most of the outlying islands do not allow cars and are therefore very peaceful. They are best visited in the week because they attract many visitors at weekends.
- There are over 30 highly-acclaimed **beaches** throughout the territory. Excellent **skindiving**, **water-skiing**, **sailing**, **kayaking**, **windsurfing**, and **fishing** (from a boat or at a reservoir) are available. Watersports equipment can be hired from beaches and hotels in **Stanley** and **Sai Kung**, and from other centres. One-day **island hopping** tickets allow unlimited ferry trips between islands.
- People may be surprised that less than an hour away from the built-up urban areas of Hong Kong is a plethora of **nature** and **wildlife**. Excellent **country parks** can be found at **Sai Kung East** and **West**. There is a wide variety of vegetation, including native and imported species of trees. It is possible to spot macaque monkeys, wild boar, civet cats, barking deer and the Chinese pangolin, a scaly mammal which resembles an armadillo. Hong Kong's prime **birdwatching** site is at the **Mai Po** marshes near **Yuen Long** in the east of the New Territories. Black-headed gulls, Saunders gull, osprey, Dalmatian pelicans and Chinese pond herons all visit the site to feed on the fish in the mud flats and mangroves there, and many other species can also be seen. Hong Kong's waters are home to the Chinese **pink dolphin**, which can be observed near Lantau Island.
- **Horse racing** is the most popular sport among local people. Try and attend a race meeting, at which vast sums of money change hands, which are held from September to June, Saturday or Sunday afternoon, and Wednesday evening. The two main **racecourses** are at **Happy Valley** (**Hong Kong Island**) and **Shatin** (New Territories).
- **Disneyland Hong Kong** is Disney's latest theme park, located in the lush setting of **Lantau Island**. The 310-acre park incorporates four lands (Main Street USA, Fantasyland, Adventureland and Tomorrowland) and two hotels. Visitors can meet characters old and new, from Mickey Mouse to Buzz Lightyear, and can tour the park aboard the Hong Kong Disneyland Railroad. Attractions range from the adventurous Jungle River Cruise to the magical Sleeping Beauty Castle to the dizzying heights of Orbitron, where guests can pilot their own rocket. Live entertainment includes the Festival of the Lion King, inspired by the Disney film, while cuisine caters for Western and Asian tastes. The park can be reached via the new MTR Disneyland Resort Station (tel: 183 0830; website: www.hongkongdisneyland.com).
- **Cheung Chau** and **Peng Chau** are still traditional fishing islands with simple temples and unspoilt beaches. Cheung Chau holds an annual **Bun Festival** in celebration of Pak Tai (a god that influences good sailing and fishing). Bamboo towers covered in steamed buns are constructed as an offering to the god.

TOURIST INFORMATION

Hong Kong Tourism Board in the UK
6 Grafton Street, London W1S 4EQ, UK
Tel: (020) 7533 7100.
Website: www.discoverhongkong.com

Hong Kong Tourism Board in the USA
115 East 54th Street, Second Floor, New York, NY 10022-4512, USA
Tel: (212) 421 3382.
Website: www.discoverhongkong.com

Entertainment

FOOD & DRINK: Hong Kong is one of the great centres for international cooking. Apart from Chinese food, which is superb, there are also many Indian, Vietnamese, Filipino, Singapore/Malaysian and Thai restaurants. It is the home of authentic Chinese food from all the regions of China, which may be sampled on a sampan in Causeway Bay, on a floating restaurant at Aberdeen, in a Kowloon restaurant, in a street market or at a deluxe hotel. Hotels serve European and Chinese food but there are also restaurants serving every type of local cuisine.
Chinese regional variations on food include Cantonese, Northern (Peking), Chiu Chow (Swatow), Shanghai, Sichuan and Hakka.
Things to know: The Chinese do not usually order a drink before dinner.
Regional specialities:

- Cantonese is based on parboiling, steaming and quick stir-frying to retain natural juices and flavours. The food is not salty or greasy and seafoods are prepared especially well, usually served with steamed rice. Specialities include *Dim sum* (savoury snacks, usually steamed and served in bamboo baskets on trolleys). These include *Cha siu bao* (barbecue pork bun), *Har gau* (steamed shrimp dumplings) and *Shiu mai* (steamed and minced pork with shrimp).
- The emphasis in Northern food is on bread and noodles, deep-frying and spicy sauces. Specialities include *Peking duck* and hotpot dishes.
- Shanghainese food is diced or shredded, stewed in soya or fried in sesame oil with pots of peppers and garlic.
- *Chiu chow* is served with rich sauces.
- Hakka food is generally simple in style with baked chicken in salt among the best dishes.
- Sichuan food is hot and spicy with plenty of chillies. A speciality is barbecued meat.

Regional drinks:

- *Zhian jing* (a rice wine served hot like sake).
- *Liang hua pei* (potent plum brandy)
- *Kaolian* (a whisky) and *Mao toi*.
- Popular beers are the locally brewed *San Miguel* and *Tsingtao* (from China), with imported beverages widely available.
- *Yeun yeung* is an even mixture of tea and coffee.

Tea culture:
Yum Cha (drinking tea), is an integral part of Hong Kong's culinary culture and is the perfect compliment to most dishes. There are many tea houses in Hong Kong where tea can be drunk accompanied by *Bow law yau*, a steaming hot bun stuffed with melted butter, or *Yau char gwai*, a deep fried dough. In tea houses, you are expected to pay at the counter; a tip is not required.
Tipping: Most hotels and restaurants add a 10 per cent service charge and an additional 5 per cent gratuity is also expected. Small tips are expected by taxi drivers, doormen and washroom attendants.
NIGHTLIFE: There are many nightclubs, discos, hostess clubs, theatres and cinemas. Cultural concerts, plays and exhibitions can be seen at Hong Kong's City Hall which also has a dining room, ballroom and cocktail lounge. The Hong Kong Cultural Centre, including a 2100-seat Concert Hall, 1750-seat Grand Theatre, a studio theatre with 300 to 500 seats and restaurants, bars and other facilities, has become the major venue for cultural concerts, plays and operas. Hong Kong Art Centre in Wan Chai supplements the City Hall's entertainment with culture in the form of Chinese opera, puppet shows, recitals and concerts. American, Chinese, European and Japanese films with subtitles are shown at a number of good air-conditioned cinemas. Two daily papers, the *Hong Kong Standard* and the *South China Morning Post*, contain details of entertainment. An unusual event to watch is night horseracing held Wednesday nights from September to May. Night cruises are operated by Star Ferries and is an excellent way to see Hong Kong by night. Most pubs and clubs are in east Tsim Sha Tsui and Lan Kwai Fong.
SHOPPING: Whether one is shopping in modern air-conditioned arcades or more traditional street markets, the range of goods available in Hong Kong is vast. Many famous-name shops have opened in Hong Kong, bringing the latest styles in great variety. Places that display the QTS sign (Quality Tourism Services) are the best guarantee of satisfaction. Bargaining is practised in the smaller shops and side stalls only. There are excellent markets in Stanley on Hong Kong Island, which is in a beautiful setting in a small village on the coast, open everyday 0900-1800, and Yuen Po Street bird garden, in Kowloon, is a market popular with the songbird owners in Hong Kong, selling many interesting creature comforts, including intricately crafted cages, open 0700-2000. Tailoring is first class. Except for a few items, such as liquor and perfume, Hong Kong is a duty-free port. **Shopping hours**: Hong Kong Island (Central & Western): 1000-1900 (1000-2000 along Queen's Road). Hong Kong Island (Causeway Bay & Wan Chai): 1000-2130. Kowloon (Tsimshatsui & Yau Ma Tei and Mong Kok): 1000-2100. Many shops are open Sunday. Shopping hours may vary greatly.

Business

- **GDP:** US$164.4 billion (2004).
- **Main exports:** Electrical machinery and appliances, textiles, apparel, footwear, watches and clocks, toys, plastics, precious stones and printed material.
- **Main imports:** Raw materials and semi-manufactures, consumer goods, capital goods, foodstuffs and fuel (most is re-exported).
- **Main trade partners:** China (People's Republic of), Japan, USA, Taiwan, Singapore and Korea (Rep).

ECONOMY: Hong Kong's economy has moved away from manufacturing and is now service-based. The region is a major corporate and banking centre as well as a conduit for China's burgeoning exports. Manufacturing is concentrated in textiles, consumer electronics and other consumer goods (Hong Kong is the world's largest producer of children's toys). The shipping industry is assisted by Hong Kong's natural deep-water harbour, probably the best in the region. Much regional trade is still conducted through Hong Kong. Within months of the handover of the territory to China in July 1997, a financial crisis which affected the whole region started to take hold. With a more mature and stable banking system than most of the rest of the region, Hong Kong showed few immediate ill effects. However, the severe impact on many of the territory's major trading partners and the depression of the regional economy was sure to cause some damage, and did so in the form of a 7 per cent drop in output during 1999. There was some recovery during 2000, but unexpectedly this did not last and by mid-2002, the economy was contracting at an annual rate of 1.5 per cent. Unemployment, meanwhile, peaked at 8 per cent. The economy is now seeing a steady rebound, unemployment is falling and the property market has picked up. Tourism and trade are now the key drivers of growth.
BUSINESS ETIQUETTE: Businesspeople are generally expected to dress smartly. Local businesspeople are usually extremely hospitable and speak English. Appointments should be made in advance and punctuality is appreciated. Business cards are widely used with a Chinese translation on the reverse. Most top hotels provide business centres for visiting businesspeople, with typing, duplication, translation and other services. **Office hours**: Mon-Fri 0900-1300 and 1400-1700, Sat 0900-1300. Some Chinese offices open earlier than 0900 and close later than 1700.
CONFERENCES/CONVENTIONS: The Hong Kong Convention and Incentive Travel Bureau is a division of the Hong Kong Tourist Association, which specialises in promoting Hong Kong as a leading venue with a special East/West position; it publishes lavish and detailed brochures showcasing the region for conference and incentive planners, together with a glossy catalogue of promotional material and a directory of associations and societies in Hong Kong. There are venues with seating for up to 12,500 persons.

COMMERCIAL INFORMATION

Hong Kong Trade Development Council
16 Upper Grosvenor Street, London W1K 7PL, UK
Tel: (020) 7616 9500.
Website: www.tdctrade.com

Hong Kong Trade Development Council
38th Floor, Office Tower, Convention Plaza, 1 Harbour Road, Wan Chai, Hong Kong (SAR)
Tel: 183 0668.

Hong Kong General Chamber of Commerce
22nd Floor, United Centre, 95 Queensway, Hong Kong (SAR)
Tel: 529 9229.
Website: www.chamber.org.hk

Hong Kong Convention and Exhibition Centre
1 Expo Drive, Wanchai, Hong Kong (SAR)
Tel: 2582 8888.
Website: www.hkcec.com.hk

China – Macau

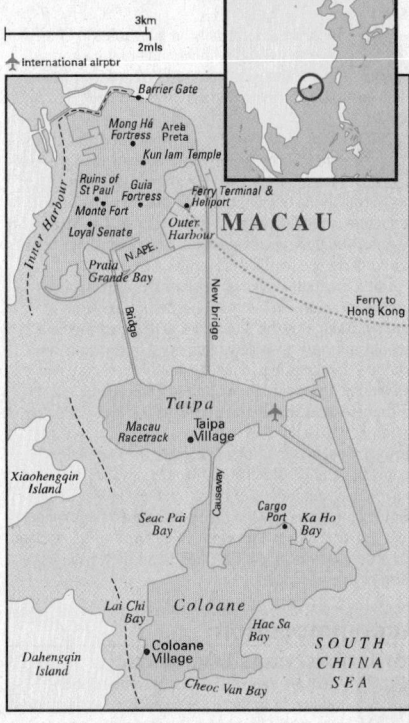

Location: South China coast.

Time: GMT + 8.

Overview

Macau was added to the UNESCO World Cultural Heritage Site list in 2005, apparently to retain Macau's 'uniqueness'. And Macau's centre is certainly that – its admixture of colonial Portuguese architecture sits beautifully alongside its East-Asian flair.

Macau was officially founded in 1557 during the great era of Portuguese overseas exploration. Macau soon became the major entrepôt between the Far East and Europe; several other colonial powers made repeated attempts to conquer the Province. Eventually, in 1670, Macau was confirmed as a Portuguese possession by the Chinese. Macau went into decline as a regional trading centre from the early 19th century, when the British, the most recent colonial power in the region, began to settle along the Chinese coast and occupied Hong Kong. Macau continued to be held under firm Portuguese control until the leftist military coup in 1974. The new Portuguese regime immediately determined that all remaining territories undergo a rapid transition to full independence. Macau demanded more delicate handling because of the Chinese interest. In 1999, Macau, like Hong Kong, became a 'Special Administrative Region' within China. Operating under a 'one country, two systems' policy, Macau will maintain its own political, social and economic systems in an arrangement that will last for 50 years. Portuguese and Chinese will both remain the official languages.

Parts of Macau offer serenely traditional countryside, such as beach resorts, ancestral Chinese villages and pine-forested hills. A lot of 'old' Macau is preserved on its islands, including fishing boat-building yards, colonial mansions, Chinese temples and floating fisherfolk communities. Yet Macau also entices visitors because of its glitzy casinos and highly regarded motor-racing fixtures. It is these inconsistencies, and its juxtaposition of style and influence, that make it such an interesting destination.

General Information

AREA: 26.80 sq km (10.35 sq miles).

POPULATION: 469,800 (2005 estimate). 95 per cent of the population is Chinese and 5 per cent is Portuguese, European and from other regions.

POPULATION DENSITY: 17,530 per sq km.

CAPITAL: Macau.

GEOGRAPHY: Macau is situated on a tiny peninsula at the mouth of the Pearl River. Two bridges of 2.5km (1.5 miles) and 4.5km (2.8 miles) respectively link it to its nearest island, Taipa, which in turn is joined to the island of Côloane by a 2.2 km- (1.3 mile-) long causeway. At the extreme northern end of the peninsula, on a narrow isthmus, is the imposing gateway (*Portas do Cerco*, or Border Gate), which leads to the Zhuhai and Zhongshan areas of the People's Republic of China. Some 60km (37.5 miles) to the east-northeast, across the mouth of the river, is Hong Kong.

GOVERNMENT: Special Administrative Region of the People's Republic of China since 1999. **Head of State**: Hu Jintao. **Head of Government**: Chief Executive Edmund Ho Hau-Wah. **Recent history:** Previously a Special Territory of Portugal, Macau became a Special Administrative Region of the Republic of China on 20 December 1999. The SAR Government comprises a 10-member executive Council, headed by the chief executive, and a 27-member Legislative Council. The Legislative Council comprises 10 members who are directly elected; the remainder are indirectly elected (by a 300-strong Election Committee representing corporate and organisational interests) and/or directly appointed by the Chief Executive. In December 1999, Edmund Ho Hau-Wah was appointed to the post of Chief Executive. An equally important figure in the territory is the tycoon Stanley Ho, whose company was the only one licensed to operate casinos and gambling parlours. In early 2002, the Government decided to break the monopoly by licensing three casino operators (the new licences have been taken up by American interests).

The first elections for the Legislative Assembly were held in September 2001. The complexion of the new Council was much the same as its predecessor, with the exception of two candidates from the New Democratic Macau Association which polled unexpectedly well. The third elections for the Legislative Assembly were held in September 2005. Turnout was a record high with 58.4 per cent of the eligible population registering its vote. A total of 125 candidates ran for the 12 seats in the direct elections. The 10 candidates for the 10 functional constituency seats were returned unopposed.

LANGUAGE: The official languages are Chinese (Cantonese) and Portuguese. English is widely spoken by those engaged in trade, tourism and commerce. Hokkien and Mandarin are also spoken.

RELIGION: The main religions are Buddhism, Roman Catholicism, Protestantism and Taoism. The majority are Buddhists.

ELECTRICITY: Usually 220 volts AC, 50Hz.

SOCIAL CONVENTIONS: Entertaining generally takes place in restaurants and public places. It is rare to be invited to a private home, unless the person is wealthy. Spirits are standard gifts in return for hospitality. Apart from the most formal occasions in restaurants and nightclubs, casual wear is acceptable.

Climate

Subtropical climate with very hot summers and a rainy period during the summer months. Most rain occurs in the afternoon. Winds can reach gale force and typhoons are not unknown. The best season is autumn (October to December), when days are sunny and warm and the humidity low.

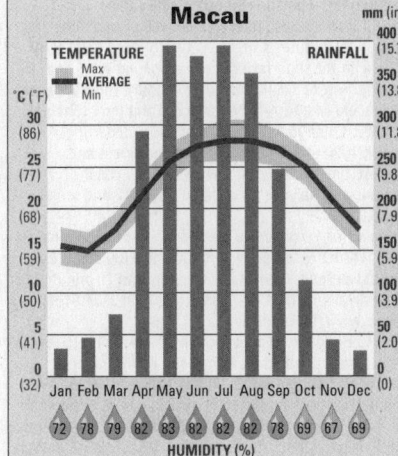

Macau

Credit: ©Macau Government Tourist Office

Communications

Telephone: IDD service is available. Country code: 853. International facilities are available at the General Post Office at Leal Senado Square, Macau City, the Central Post Offices in Taipa and Côloane, as well as all phone booths.

Mobile telephone: Roaming agreements exist with some international mobile phone companies and coverage is good; dual band GSM network covers the whole territory.

Internet: Internet facilities are available at the UNESCO centre and the central library at Macau and its branches. There are also many Internet cafes in the city.

Post: Airmail to Europe takes five to seven days. Automatic vending machines are available at various locations for stamps.

MEDIA: Press: Newspapers are in Portuguese or Chinese, including Portuguese dailies *Hoje Macau* and *Jornal Tribuna de Macau*, and Chinese dailies *Macau Daily News* and *Va Kio Daily*. There are English-language papers from Hong Kong.

TV: *Teledifusao Macau* operates Chinese and and Portuguese-language networks.

Radio: *Radio Macau* operates Chinese and Portuguese-language networks.

Passport/Visa

	Passport Required?	Visa Required?	Return Ticket Required?
Full British	Yes	No/1	No
Australian	Yes	No/2	No
Canadian	Yes	No/2	No
USA	Yes	No/2	No
Other EU	Yes	No/1	No
Japanese	Yes	No/1	No

Note: *Regulations and requirements may be subject to change at short notice, and you are advised to contact the appropriate diplomatic or consular authority before finalising travel arrangements. Any numbers in the chart refer to the footnotes below.*

PASSPORTS: Passport valid for at least one month required by all, except nationals of China who have a China Identity Card or travel permit and nationals of Hong Kong (SAR) who have a Hong Kong Identity Card (HKIC).

VISAS: Required by all except the following:

(a) **1**. nationals of all EU countries (UK nationals for stays of up to six months), Andorra, Cape Verde, Croatia, Egypt, Iceland, Israel, Japan, Korea (Rep), Lebanon, Mali, Mongolia, Norway, Romania and Tanzania for stays of up to 90 days;

(b) **2**. nationals of Australia, Brazil, Canada, Chile, India, Indonesia, Kiribati, Liechtenstein, Malaysia, Mexico, Monaco, Namibia, New Zealand, The Philippines, Samoa, Seychelles, Singapore, South Africa, Switzerland, Thailand, Turkey, Uruguay and the USA for stays of up to 30 days;

(c) nationals of China (PR) with valid Macau entry/departure documents, including residents of mainland China, Hong Kong (SAR), Taiwan (China) and overseas Chinese for stays of up to 30 days;

(d) holders of a Hong Kong Identity Card (HKIC) or Hong Kong Permanent Identity Card or those with a Hong Kong Re-entry Permit for stays of up to one year;

(e) holders of a laissez passer issued by the UN;

(f) holders of Consular documents issued by Macau (SAR) or Hong Kong (SAR).

Types of visa and cost: *Individual*: MOP100 (MOP50 for children under 12). *Family*: MOP200 (must be husband

travelling with wife and/ or children under 12 of the same surname or with proof of relationship. *Group*: MOP50 per person for bona fide groups of 10 people or more and children of 12 years of age or less. All are for single stays.
Validity: 30 days. Can be extended on application to the immigration office.
Application to: Individual visitors requiring a visa may obtain it upon arrival in Macau at the Immigration Police counter, for a fee of MOP100. Visas can also be obtained from Consulates or Embassies of China (People's Republic of); see *China* section.

Money

Currency: Pataca (MOP) = 100 avos. Notes are in denominations of MOP1000, 500, 100, 50, 20 and 10. Coins are in denominations of MOP10, 5, 2 and 1, and 50, 20 and 10 avos. Hong Kong dollars are widely accepted.
Note: The Pataca is loosely pegged to the Hong Kong Dollar.
Currency exchange: Foreign currency may be exchanged at hotels, banks and licensed bureaux de change. There are 24-hour exchange counters at Macau International Airport (Taipa Island), and the Lisboa Hotel (Macau). Numerous ATMs are available for cash withdrawal by credit card.
Credit & debit cards: MasterCard and Visa are accepted. Check with your credit or debit card company for details of merchant acceptability and other services which may be available.
Traveller's cheques: These may be exchanged at banks, bureaux de change and at many hotels. To avoid additional exchange rate charges, travellers are advised to take traveller's cheques in US Dollars, Pounds Sterling or Euros.
Currency restrictions: There are no restrictions on the import or export of either local or foreign currency.
Banking hours: Mon-Fri 0900-1700, Sat 0900-1200.
Exchange rate indicators:
Rate at time of publishing:

£1.00=	MOP14.65
$1.00=	MOP8.28

Duty Free

The following goods may be imported into Macau without incurring customs duty:
200 cigarettes, 50 cigars, 100 cigarillos or 250g of tobacco products; 1l of wine and 1l of spirits (each not exceeding 30 per cent volume); other goods up to a value of MOP5000; other items are not restricted as long as carried in reasonable quantities, and are not commodities subject to prior authorisation or quarantine.
Restricted imports: Pharmaceutical products, chemical products, stupefactant and psychotropic substances, dutiable commodities, equipment and raw materials for production of optical disks, transceivers, arms and ammunitions, endangered species of wild fauna and flora, all require an import permit.
Prohibited items: Drug trafficking is punishable by law.
Note: There are no export duties, but as travel is almost invariably via Hong Kong, the relevant Hong Kong import/export regulations must be observed (see *Hong Kong* within the *China (People's Republic of)* section).

Public Holidays

Below are listed Public Holidays for the January 2006-June 2007 period.
2006: Jan 1 New Year's Day. **Jan 29-31** Chinese New Year. **Apr 5** Ching Ming Festival. **Apr 14-15** Easter Holidays. **May 1** Labour Day. **May 5** Feast of Buddha (Feast of the Bathing of Lord Buddha). **May 31** Dragon Boat Festival (Tun Ng). **Oct 1-2** National Day of the People's Republic of China. **Oct 6** Mid-Autumn Festival. **Oct 30** Chung Yeung Festival. **Nov 1** All Souls' Day. **Dec 8** Feast of the Immaculate Conception. **Dec 20** Macau Special Administrative Region Establishment Day. **Dec 22** Winter Solstice. **Dec 24-25** Christmas.
2007: Jan 1 New Year's Day. **Feb 18-20** Chinese New Year. **Apr 5** Ching Ming Festival. **Apr 6** Good Friday. **Apr 9** Easter Monday. **May 1** Labour Day. **May 24** Feast of Buddha (Feast of the Bathing of Lord Buddha). **Jun 15** Dragon Boat Festival (Tuen Ng).

Health

	Special Precautions?	Certificate Required?
Yellow Fever	No	No
Cholera	No	No
Typhoid & Polio	1	N/A
Malaria	No	N/A

Note: *Regulations and requirements may be subject to change at short notice, and you are advised to contact your doctor well in advance of your intended date of departure. Any numbers in the chart refer to the footnotes below.*

1: Vaccination against *Typhoid* and *Polio* are recommended, but not essential.
Food & drink: Tap water is generally regarded as safe, but bottled water may be advisable for the first few days. Milk is pasteurised, but avoid dairy products which are likely to have been made from unboiled milk. Vegetables should be cooked and fruit peeled.
Health care: Health insurance is recommended. There are good medical facilities, and religious orders or hotels will also give assistance.
Other risks: *Japanese encephalitis* may occur in the New Territories between April and October. *Diarrhoeal diseases, hepatitis A* and *B* and *Oriental lung fluke* (*paragonimiasis*) may occur in this area. Immunisation against *hepatitis A, B, diphtheria* and *tuberculosis* is sometimes recommended. *Rabies* is present. There is some incidence of *dengue fever*.

Travel - International

AIR:

The territory has its own airline, *Air Macau (NX)* (website: www.airmacau.com.mo), which operates regional flights. Other airlines serving Macau include *Air Asia* and *TransAsia Airways*. A variety of charter airlines operate from Japan.
Approximate flight times: Flights from Europe and North America are usually via Hong Kong. From Hong Kong to *London* is 14 hours; for other flight times, see *Hong Kong (SAR)* in the *China (People's Republic of)* section.
Main airports: *Macau International Airport (MFM)* (website: www.macau-airport.gov.mo) is 7km (5 miles) southeast of the city. *To/from the airport*: Buses run to the city and Macau-Hong Kong ferry terminal via major hotels (travel time - 45 minutes). Bus fares cost MOP4-6. Taxis to the city centre are also available for approximately MOP40 (travel time - 15 minutes); each piece of luggage carried is paid for separately. *Facilities*: Banks and bureaux de change, car hire, duty free shops and restaurants.
An *ExpressLink* service is also available, allowing fast, trouble-free transfer between Macau and Hong Kong airports. Ferries depart approximately every 15 minutes (travel time - 55 minutes). On arrival at Macau Ferry Terminal, passengers travel by a special shuttle bus to the enclave's airport. Travellers should allow approximately one hour between ferry arrival time in Macau and departure time from Macau International Airport.
Departure tax: Passengers departing for destinations in Mainland China must pay a Passenger Tax of MOP90 per person (MOP50 per child aged two to 12). Travellers to other destinations pay MOP130 (MOP80 per child aged two to 12). Passengers in transit departing Macau within 48 hours pay MOP40. Children under two, and those in direct transit, are free. Payment *must* be made in local currency, and credit cards are not accepted.
Helicopter: *East Asia Airlines* and *Helicopters Hong Kong Limited* (website: www.helihongkong.com) operate daily flights (every 30 minutes; 0930-2259) between Hong Kong and Macau, (0900-2230, Macau to Hong Kong). Travel time is 16 minutes. Cost before tax: HK$1500 (non-peak day) or HK$1600 (peak day) one way. Helicopters depart from the Macau Maritime and Heliport Terminal, situated in the Outer Harbour.
SEA:

Main ports: A wide variety of vessels sail the 60km (37 mile) distance between *Macau* and Hong Kong: jetfoils, ferries and catamarans are run by *Turbo JET* or *First Ferry*. There are more than 100 scheduled sailings each way throughout the day, while jetfoils operate round the clock. Passengers are advised to be at the terminals at least 30 minutes before the scheduled departure time in order to complete immigration formalities; there is always a standby queue for a prior boat for passengers who arrive unexpectedly early.
TurboJET is the fastest, travelling between Hong Kong and Macau in 55 minutes. Trips are between Hong Kong ferry terminal (in the shun Tak centre and Sheung Wan) and Macau ferry terminal (in the outer habour). There are also Turbojet and First Ferry services to Fu Yong ferry terminal in Shenzhen, China (travel time - one hour), departing between 1030 and 1845 daily. (For ticket prices and departure times, see website: www.turbojet.com.hk. Discounts are available for children under 12 and senior citizens.)
There is a First Ferry service from Tsim Sha Tsui in China to Macau which departs between 0700 and 2100 and is 24 hours at weekends; the service takes around 70 minutes. For further details, contact First Ferry (tel: (852) 2131 8181; website: www.nwff.com.hk).
Tickets to Hong Kong can be bought in Macau up to seven days in advance. For travel from Hong Kong to Macau, tickets can be bought up to 28 days before travel. A computerised booking system is available from Hong Kong MTR Travel Service Centres in the MTR stations of Admiralty, Central, Tsim Shat Sui, Causeway Bay, Mongkok, Tseun Wan and Kowloon Bay.
Telephone bookings for jetfoil services can be made by holders of various credit cards. The baggage allowance is 10kg per person for hand luggage on high-speed ferries and, in general, is limited to hand-carried items. Tour operators can arrange luggage-handling where required. Porters are available for heavy luggage.
ROAD:

The crossing point into China is via the Barrier Gate (Portas de Cerco) (open 0730-0000 daily) or the COTAI Frontier post (open 0900-2000 daily). Buses run frequently to and from this point from 0800-1830 (travel time - two hours 30 minutes). Starting in September 2005, passenger traffic trough Lotus bridge/the COTAI checkpoint will be closed for maintenance for one year.
The Kee Kwan Motor Road Company runs a service between Macau and Guangzhou between 0715 and 2130 (website: www.keekwan.com).

Travel - Internal

SEA:

There are several daily harbour tours in Chinese junks between the inner and outer harbours (travel time - 30 minutes). Tours depart from Pier 1 and cost MOP10 (children under 12 travel free).
ROAD:

Traffic drives on the left. There are two bridges: one to Taipa Island, and a bridge carrying a four-lane highway from the international airport to the Macau-China border at Zhuhai. **Bus**: Services operate frequently around Macau and to the islands. **Car hire**: Available through several agencies. Drivers must be over 21. Passports may be required, as well as a credit card for a deposit. Chauffeur-driven limousines are also available.
Documentation: An International Driving Permit is required. **Taxi**: Most taxis are black with a cream-coloured top, but some are all-yellow radio taxis. To eliminate any misunderstandings regarding destination, most taxis have a destination guide written in Chinese, English and Portuguese. **Rickshaws** and **pedicabs** (bicycles with a two-seater section at the back) are also available for hire. The ferry terminal and the Hotel Lisboa are the two main pick-up locations. Prices should be agreed in advance. It is worth remembering that many of the attractions in Macau are located on hilltops, beyond the reach of even the strongest-legged pedicab driver. **Bicycles** can be hired on Taipa Island and cost approximately MOP20 per hour. They may not be taken to the mainland.

Accommodation

HOTELS/INNS/VILLAS/APARTMENTS:

There are various types of accommodation, ranging from first-class to economy-class hotels, plus inns, villa-apartments housed in new buildings, and older colonial hotels. At weekends, the hotels, villas and inns are usually full, so it is wise to make a reservation. There are currently about 9000 hotel rooms in Macau. Most hotels are air conditioned and rooms have private baths. Weekend rates are generally 20 per cent higher than weekdays and rates are subject to a 10 per cent service charge, plus a 5 per cent Government tax.

ACCOMMODATION INFORMATION

Macau Hotels Association
Rua Luis Gonzaga Gomes S/N, BLIV, R/C Centro
Actividades Turisticas, Room B, Macau (SAR)
Tel: (853) 703 416.
Website: www.macauhotel.org

Top Things To See & Do

- **Racing** takes place at the **Canidrome** on **Avenida General Castelo Branco** on Monday, Thursday, weekends and some public holidays. The Canidrome is the only greyhound racing stadium in Asia and its excellent facilities include two grandstands, several private boxes and a VIP lounge. Over 300 dogs take part in races on each racing day. The **Macau Jockey Club** organises flat **horse races** at its track on the island of Taipa. **Riding lessons** are also provided for all levels of ability. The Far East's gala **motorcycle** and Formula III car racing event, the **Macau Grand Prix**, is held during the third week in November. Near the Grand Prix circuit is the **Macau Grand Prix Museum**.
- For the majority of travellers, **gambling** is Macau's great attraction. There are nine official **casinos**, all operated under Government franchise and all open 24 hours a day. Both familiar western games and popular eastern games are on offer, and an assortment of slot machines are available - these are called 'hungry tigers' by the locals. Compared to western casinos, the atmosphere is unglamorous, with the emphasis on serious betting.

- The most famous sight in Macau is probably the ruins of the **Church of St Paul's**, originally built in 1602 and rebuilt in 1835 after a disastrous typhoon.
- See the oldest lighthouse on the China coast: the 17th-century **Guia Fortress**.
- Standing at 130ft high over the Praia Grande Bay, the **Gate of Understanding** (designed by Charters Almeida) is a symbolic structure which represents the goodwill between China and Portugal.
- The complex of temples known as **Kun Iam Tong** is the biggest and wealthiest of Macau's temples and dates from the time of the Ming Dynasty, about 400 years ago, and contains, amongst other works of art, a small statue of Marco Polo.
- The **Macau Museum** seeks to embody the life of Macau and its people from the first settlement to the present day. The museum contains a vast collection of historic and social memorabilia. It is possible to buy a Museum
- The finest expression of Portuguese architecture is probably the **Largo do Senado square**, making the heart of the city a pedestrian paradise.
- **São Domingo's Church**, built in the 17th century, is one of the most beautiful religious buildings in Macau. It has recently reopened after a large-scale renovation programme. A new **Museum of Sacred Art** has opened on three floors of the renovated belfry, and is home to 300 works of sacred art that illustrate the history of the Roman Catholic church in Asia.
- The **Macau Tower** is an entertainment and convention centre situated on the waterfront on the **Nam Van Lakes**. The 338m tower is the 10th tallest in the world and provides panoramic views of the region.
- Go and visit **Taipa**, a busy, colourful place with interesting shops and colonial Portuguese offices in narrow streets and alleys, where many traditional crafts are still followed. **Pou Tai Un Temple** is one of the best endowed and picturesque temples in Macau and has a very good vegetarian restaurant.
- **Colôane** has several beaches, as well as **Seac Pai Van Park**, which has nature trails threading among the hills, and a walk-in aviary with rare and beautiful species. The best beach is the black-sanded **Hác Sá**. **A-Ma Statue** has recently been unveiled on the highest point on the island, from which there are spectacular views. Colôane Village has interesting Chinese temples, the **Chapel of St Francis Xavier** (a classic, Portuguese-style chapel built in 1928) and good restaurants.

Credit: ©Macau Government Tourist Office

TOURIST INFORMATION

Macau Government Tourist Office in the UK
c/o Representation Plus, 11 Blades Court, 121 Deodar Road, London SW15 2NU, UK
Tel: (020) 8877 4504/1.
Website: www.macautourism.gov.mo

Macau Government Tourist Office in the USA
3601 Aviation Boulevard, Suite 2100, Manhattan Beach, Los Angeles, CA 90266, USA
Tel: (310) 643 2630 or (866) 656 2228 (toll-free in USA and Canada).
Website: www.macautourism.gov.mo

Entertainment

FOOD & DRINK: Hotels, inns and restaurants offer a wide variety of food. Some specialise in Portuguese dishes, while others offer cuisine from China, Japan, Korea and Indonesia. Local Macau food is spicy, a unique combination of Chinese and Portuguese cooking methods with influences of Indian and African spices. All restaurants offer a variety of Portuguese red and white wines and sparkling *vinho verde*, as well as port and brandy, all at low prices.
Things to know: Most restaurants have table service. Alcohol is easily obtainable. There are no licensing laws.
Regional specialities:
- *Bacalhau* (cod served baked, grilled, stewed or boiled).
- *Caldo verde* and *sopa a alentejana* (rich soups with vegetables, meat and olive oil).
- 'African chicken' (grilled with hot spices).
- *Galinha a portuguesa* (chicken baked with potatoes, onions, eggs and saffron – the appearance of curry without the spice).
- *Minche* (minced meat with fried potato and onion).
- Macau sole (fried fish usually served with salad).
- *Feijoados* (from Brazil, stews of kidney beans, pork, potatoes, cabbage and spicy sausage).
- The speciality of *dim sum* (Chinese savoury snacks steamed and served in bamboo baskets on trolleys) includes *cha siu bao* (steamed pork dumplings), *har gau* (steamed shrimp dumplings) and *shui mai* (steamed and minced pork with shrimp).
Tipping: A 10 per cent service charge will be added to most hotel and restaurant bills, but a small tip should also be left.
NIGHTLIFE: Most of the nightlife is centred on the hotels, many of which have nightclubs with cabaret, Portuguese

folk dancing, lively dance bands, discos, international menus and bars. In summer, there are several open-air *esplanadas* serving soft drinks. Many locals, however, tend to relax in the evening in some of the many lively restaurants. Gambling is a big attraction for visitors to Macau and the casinos are open 24 hours, providing famous entertainers, baccarat, blackjack, roulette and Chinese games like *fantan* and *dai-siu* (big and small).
For the most popular discos in town head for *Avenida do Infante D. Henrique* and *NAPE*. Here, the music is modern with some local touches, international pop sung in Cantonese, Mandarin, Thai and Japanese.
At *Cineteatro*, international and Chinese films can be seen.
SHOPPING: Macau's most popular buys are jewellery (particularly gold and jade), Chinese antiques, porcelain, pottery, electronic gadgetry, cameras, watches and beading work. They are available at duty free prices because Macau is a free port and no sales tax is charged. Bargaining is expected on many items although most shops will have the same minimum price. Other popular buys are Chinese herbs and medicines, dried seafood (such as sharks' fins), abalone, Chinese and Macau pastries, and locally-made knitwear sold at stalls. When purchasing antiques, gold and jewellery, it is advisable to patronise shops recommended by the Goldsmiths' and Jewellers' Association and the Macau Government Tourist Office. A warranty and a receipt should be asked for when buying jewellery, gold, cameras, watches and electrical goods. The main shopping area is located along the Avenida do Infante D Henrique and Avenida Almeida Ribeiro, São Domingos Market, Rua de Palha, Rua do Campo and Rua Pedro Nolasco da Silva. Antiques and unique gifts may be found in Macau's flea market in the lanes around Rua das Estalagens (near St Paul's Ruins). There is an Artisan's Fair every Saturday evening in *Santo Agostinho Square*. Excursions can be made across the Chinese border to Zhuhai, where the first floor of the Gongbei market is well known for antiques, ceramics and fabrics. Software is also a good buy in Zhuhai. **Shopping hours:** Generally Mon-Sun 1000-1900. Some shops may close on the first day of every month.

Business

- **GDP:** US$10 billion (2004).
- **Main exports:** Clothing, textiles, footwear, toys, electronics, machinery and parts.
- **Main imports:** Raw materials and semi-manufactured goods, consumer goods (foodstuffs, beverages and tobacco), capital goods, mineral fuels and oil.
- **Main trade partners:** USA, China, Hong Kong, Japan, Germany, Taiwan and Singapore.

ECONOMY: Macau has long been an important distribution outlet for Chinese products and, in this respect, is similar to Hong Kong. Agriculture is negligible

and there are very few natural resources (Macau relies almost entirely on imported oil to meet its energy needs.) The territory has an active manufacturing and export sector. Macau has recovered well since the 1998 Asian financial crisis; during 2004 Macau registered a year-on-year GDP increase of 20 per cent. Macau is also well known in the region for its extensive gambling facilities: the associated tourism has become a major source of income. Development of new infrastructure and facilities for the 2005 East Asian Games bolstered the construction sector. Trade between Macau and the neighbouring Chinese Special Economic Zone of Zhuhai has grown rapidly and contributed substantially to Macau's present trade surplus. The closer economic partnership agreement (CEPA) between Macau and mainland China came into effect in January 2004 and offers many Macau-made products tariff-free access to the mainland. The range of products covered by CEPA was increased in January 2005. Sino-Portuguese agreement, under which Macau reverted to Chinese rule in December 1999, guarantees the continuation of Macau's economic status for a minimum of 50 years. Macau's currency, the Pataca, has been retained indefinitely.
BUSINESS ETIQUETTE: Businesspeople are expected to dress smartly. Calling cards are essential, appointments should be made in advance and punctuality is appreciated. The World Trade Centre (16th Floor, 918 Edificio World Trade Centre, 918 Avenida da Amizade (tel: 727 666; e-mail: wtcmc@macau.ctm.net) offers assistance and various facilities for businesses, including a VIP Club restaurant.
Office hours: Mon-Fri 0900-1300 and 1500-1730 and Sat 0900-1230.
CONFERENCES/CONVENTIONS: Macau's major meetings venues include the Conference Centre at the University of Macau (with seating for up to 764), the Forum (a multipurpose complex with seating for up to 4035), the Tourist Activities and Conference Centre (with seating for up to 600) and Macau Landmark (featuring a unique 'skyroof'). The majority of hotels also have facilities, and support services can be provided by the World Trade Centre. A new cultural centre (website: www.ccm.gov.mo) was inaugurated in March 1999 on the Outer Harbour waterfront. It includes two auditoria, one seating 1200 people and the other 400 people. The territory's newest convention venue is the conference centre in the Macau Tower, the world's 10th tallest building (website: www.macautower.com.mo). The tower also features a revolving restaurant, an entertainment area and shopping facilities. For further information, contact the Macau Government Tourist Office.

COMMERCIAL INFORMATION

Associação Comercial de Macau
Edificio ACM, 5th Floor, Rua de Xangai, Macau (SAR)
Tel: 576 833.

Colombia

Location: Northwest South America.

Time: GMT - 5.

Overview

The Republic of Colombia was formally established in 1855. Over the next 100 years, Colombian politics were dominated by the Conservative-Liberal feud, which often broke out into warfare. Periods of democratic Government alternated with dictatorships. There were occasions, however, when the two parties were able to unite to see off a common threat. The 1970 election was a turning point in Colombia's recent history. Disaffected members of ANAPO (*Alianza Nacional Popular*) formed a guerrilla movement known as Movimiento 19 de Abril (M-19), which initiated a 15-year-long guerrilla campaign against the Government and acquired other left-wing groups.

Meanwhile, a third potent force emerged during the 1980s, in the form of organised drug traffickers (known as cartels). Large sums of money began to be turned into political power and leading politicians increasingly became tainted by connections with drug money. By 1998, the country was in the grip of the struggle between the Government, traffickers, right-wing paramilitaries and left-wing guerrillas. Leftist guerrillas created 'liberated areas', within which Government forces were unable or unwilling to operate. The US administration became infuriated and, in 2000, the US Clinton administration unveiled 'Plan Colombia', a massive military support programme for the Colombian armed forces. Although portrayed as the latest phase of the 'war on drugs', it is clear that the programme is essentially political and strategic – the objective is to destroy FARC (Revolutionary Armed Forces of Colombia) and its allies. The Bush administration inherited 'Plan Colombia' after victory at the US November 2000 poll and endorsed the plan with some modifications. Its first effects became apparent the following year, when military forces retook part of the former 'liberated zone'. The new hard line adopted by the Government was confirmed in May 2002, when the right-winger Alvaro Uribe, who favours all-out war against the left-wing guerrillas, won a comfortable

victory at the Presidential election. Uribe immediately declared a partial state of emergency, allowing him to impose security measures by decree. In early 2003, American special forces troops became directly engaged for the first time in the eastern province of Arauca.

Yet what has endured in the midst of such ever-changing, violent proceedings is a calm and beautiful landscape that has much to offer, from nature (much is covered by the Amazon Basin; large lakes are surrounded by mountains; a Caribbean coastline twinkles with azure water) to manmade wonders (archaeological digs unearth historical wealth; colonial houses adorn the towns; the Guajira Peninsula is home to more than 100,000 nomadic Indians). There must be hope that the political climate becomes just as clement very soon.

General Information

AREA: 1.14 sq km (440,831 sq miles).

POPULATION: 45.6 million (2005).

POPULATION DENSITY: 39 per sq km.

CAPITAL: Santa Fe de Bogotá. **Population:** 6.9 million (2005).

GEOGRAPHY: Colombia is situated in South America, bordered to the north by the Caribbean, to the northwest by Panama, to the west by the Pacific Ocean, to the southwest by Ecuador and the south by Peru, to the northeast by Venezuela and to the southeast by Brazil. The Andes Mountains extend into the country in three ranges running south to north, dipping finally into the lowlands of the Caribbean coast. Along the southern part of the Pacific coast run wide, marshy lowlands rising to a relatively low but rugged mountain chain. East of this range, the southwestern coastal lowlands extend in a low trough running from the port of Buenaventura on the Pacific coast to the Caribbean. East of this rise the slopes of the Western Cordillera which, with the Central Cordillera range, runs north to the Caribbean lowlands from Ecuador, separated by a valley, filled in the south by volcanic ash to a height of 2500m (8202ft). Further north lies the fertile Cauca Valley, which extends to Cartago where it becomes a deep gorge running between the Cordilleras to the Caribbean lowlands. The Eastern Cordillera, the longest range, rises north of the Ecuadorean border and runs north then northeast towards Venezuela. Flat grassy prairies in the east along with the jungles and towering rainforests of the Amazon make up over half the country's area. There are also two small islands, San Andrés and Providencia, located 700km (430 miles) north of the Colombian coast, that have belonged to Colombia since 1822.

GOVERNMENT: Republic. Colombia declared its independence from Spain in 1810; however, it was proclaimed the Republic of Gran Colombia in 1819. **Head of State and Government**: President Álvaro Uribe since 2002.

LANGUAGE: Spanish is the official language. Local Indian dialects and some English, French, German and Italian are also spoken.

RELIGION: Christianity, with 95 per cent Roman Catholic; small Protestant and Jewish minorities.

ELECTRICITY: Mostly 110 volts AC, 60Hz. American-style two-pin plugs.

SOCIAL CONVENTIONS: Normal courtesies should be observed. It is customary to offer guests black Colombian coffee, well sugared, called *tinto*. Spanish style and culture can still be seen in parts of the country, although in Bogotá, North American attitudes and clothes are becoming prevalent. Casual clothes can be worn in most places; formal attire will be necessary for exclusive dining rooms and social functions. Smoking is allowed except where indicated. The visitor is advised that many of the main cities in Colombia are notorious for street crime, particularly at night. Drug-related crimes are a serious problem throughout the country and the visitor should be wary of the unsolicited attention of strangers.

Climate

The climate is very warm and tropical on the coast and in the north, with a rainy season from May to November. This varies according to altitude. It is cooler in the upland areas and cold in the mountains. Bogotá is always spring-like, with cool days and crisp nights.

Required clothing: Lightweight cottons and linens with waterproofing during rainy season in coastal and northern areas. Medium- to heavyweights are needed in upland and mountainous areas.

Communications

Telephone: IDD service to most areas; calls to smaller centres must be made through the international operator. Country code: 57. Many public telephones now work only with phone cards produced by *Empresa de Teléfonos de Bogotá (ETB)*, which can be bought in many shops and kiosks.

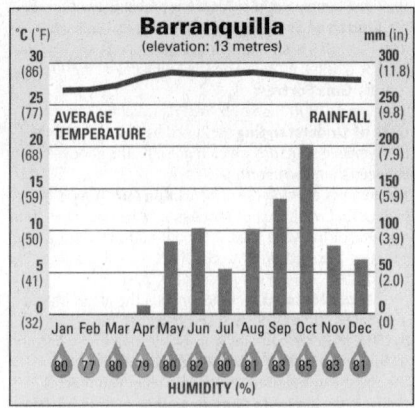

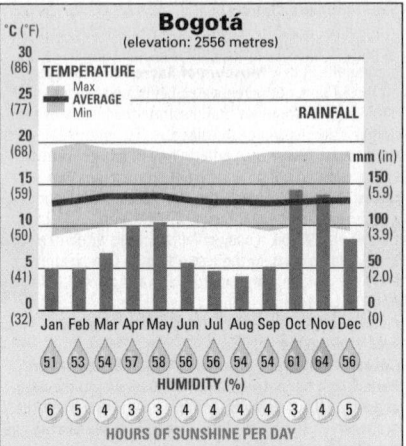

Mobile telephone: Roaming agreements exist with a few international mobile phone companies. Coverage is variable.

Internet: Internet cafes exist in the main cities.

Post: Post offices are marked *Correos*. Post office opening hours: Mon-Sat 0800-1200. There are two types of service: urban post (green letter boxes) and inter-urban and international (yellow boxes). Letters and packets sent by airmail normally take five to seven days to reach their destination.

MEDIA: Colombia is a very dangerous place for journalists who face intimidation by drug traffickers, guerrillas and paramilitary groups. More than 120 Colombian journalists were killed in the 1990s, many for reporting on drug trafficking and corruption.

Press: Spanish dailies include *El Tiempo*, *El Espacio*, *El Nuevo Siglo* and *Vanguardia Liberal*.

TV: *Senal Colombia* is state-run; *Caracol TV* is a private commercial network. Other channels include *Cadena Uno*, *Telecaribe* and *RCN TV*.

Radio: There are hundreds of stations. The main networks are state run Radio Nacional de Colombia, Cadena Super including *Radio Super* and *Super Stereo FM*, Caracol, which runs flagship station *Caracol Colombia* and Radio Cadena Nacional (*RCN Radio*) which is a mediumwave (AM) network with many affiliates.

Passport/Visa

	Passport Required?	Visa Required?	Return Ticket Required?
Full British	Yes	No	Yes
Australian	Yes	No	Yes
Canadian	Yes	No	Yes
USA	Yes	No	Yes
Other EU	Yes	No/1	Yes
Japanese	Yes	No	Yes

Note: *Regulations and requirements may be subject to change at short notice, and you are advised to contact the appropriate diplomatic or consular authority before finalising travel arrangements. Any numbers in the chart refer to the footnotes below.*

PASSPORTS: Passport valid for at least six months required by all.

VISAS: Required by all except the following for up to 180 days:

a) **1**. nationals listed in the table above (except for nationals of the Czech Republic, Estonia, Hungary, Republic of Ireland, Latvia, Poland and Slovenia);

b) nationals of Andorra, Antigua & Barbuda, Argentina, The Bahamas, Barbados, Belize, Bolivia, Brazil, Chile, Costa Rica,

Cyprus, Dominica, Ecuador, El Salvador, Grenada, Guatemala, Guyana, Honduras, Iceland, Indonesia, Israel, Jamaica, Korea (Rep), Liechtenstein, Malaysia, Mexico, Monaco, New Zealand, Norway, Panama, Paraguay, Peru, The Philippines, Romania, San Marino, St Kitts & Nevis, St Lucia, St Vincent & the Grenadines, Singapore, Switzerland, Trinidad & Tobago, Turkey, Uruguay and Venezuela.
Types of visa and cost: *Tourist*: £25 (depends on nationality). *Temporary visitor*: £60. *Business*: £95. *Student*: £25. Fees have to be paid in the form of bank deposit. For other types and costs contact the Consulate or consular section at Embassy.
Validity: *Tourist* and *Temporary Visitor*: Valid six months (multiple entry). *Business*: Valid four years for multiple entries with maximum stays of six months each. *Student*: Valid five years with multiple entry.
Application to: Consulate (or consular section at Embassy); see *Passport/Visa Information*.
Application requirements: (a) Valid passport with at least one blank page to affix the visa (two pages for business visas). (b) Three recent passport-size photos. (c) Two copies of application form. (d) Onward or return tickets. (e) Most recent bank statement as proof of sufficient funds to cover stay. (f) Fee, payable by bank deposit only. (g) Must call in person for interview. *Tourist*: (a)-(g) and, (h) Letter of Invitation from a Colombian national or resident, or proof of hotel accommodation. *Temporary Visitor*: (a)-(g) and, (h) Letter of invitation from a sponsoring organisation or a Colombian national or resident. *Business*: (a)-(g) and, (h) Letter form company stating applicant's position, purpose and duration of visit, and taking responsibility for travel expenses, if self-employed, letter must also include purpose of trip, bank references and names of commercial contacts in Colombia. (i) Company's UK registration certificate.
Note: Photocopies of all the above documentation are required All documents will need to be translated into Spanish, and some of them will need to be legalised by the Consulate. Nationals will be required to undergo an interview prior to being issued with a visa. Contact the nearest Colombian Consulate or consular section at Embassy for further details
Working days required: Depends on the visa issued. Five for Tourist and Business visas; one week for Temporary Visitors Visas. It is generally advised to allow plenty of time for applications.
Temporary residence: Enquire at Consulate or consular section of Embassy for further details; see *Passport/Visa Information*.

PASSPORT/VISA INFORMATION

Embassy of the Republic of Colombia in the UK
Flat 3A, 3 Hans Crescent, London SW1X 0LN, UK
Tel: (020) 7589 9177.
Consular Section: Tel: (020) 7495 4233.
Website: www.colombianembassy.co.uk
Opening hours: Mon-Fri 0900-1800.

Colombian Consulate in the UK
West Cott House, 3rd Floor, 35 Portland Place, London W1B 1AE, UK
Tel: (020) 7637 9893.
Website: www.colombianconsulate.co.uk
Opening hours: Mon-Fri 0900-1330 (personal callers); 1500-1700 (telephone enquiries).

Embassy of the Republic of Colombia in the USA
2118 Leroy Place, NW, Washington, DC 20008, USA
Tel: (202) 387 8338.
Website: www.colombiaemb.org

Colombian Consulate in the USA
10E 46th Street, New York, NY 10017-2499, USA
Tel. (212) 370 0004.

Money

Currency: Colombian Peso (COP) = 100 centavos. Notes are in denominations of COP50,000, 20,000, 10,000 and 5000. Coins are in denominations of COP1000, 500, 200, 100 and 50.
Currency exchange: The exchange rate tends to be lower on the Caribbean coast than in Bogotá, Medellín and Cali. The US Dollar is the easiest currency to exchange at hotels, banks, shops and travel agencies, but all establishments charge an exchange fee. Travellers are advised to only use reputable exchange houses.
Credit & debit cards: All major cards are accepted, but check with your credit or debit card company for details of merchant acceptability and other services which may be available.
Traveller's cheques: These are not always easy to change in the smaller towns, except at branches of the Banco de la República. To avoid additional exchange rate charges, travellers are advised to take traveller's cheques in US Dollars which can be exchanged at banks, foreign exchange and large hotels.
Currency restrictions: The import and export of local currency is unlimited. The import of foreign currency is unlimited subject to declaration on arrival. The export of foreign currency is limited to US$25,000.
Banking hours: Bogota: Mon-Fri 0900-1500. In other cities: Mon-Fri, 0800-1130 and 1400-1630. On the last business day of every month, banks close at 1200.
Exchange rate indicators:
Rate at time of publishing
£1.00= COP4038.45
$1.00= COP2288.50

Duty Free

The following goods may be taken into Colombia by people up to 18 years of age without incurring customs duty:
200 cigarettes and 50 cigars and up to 500g of tobacco; two bottles of alcoholic beverage; a reasonable quantity of perfume; one ordinary camera and one video camera.
Note: Emeralds and items made from gold or platinum need a receipt from the place of purchase that must be presented to customs on departure.
Prohibited items: Ammunition and firearms, unless prior authorisation has been obtained, and item(s) are declared on arrival. Vegetables, plants or plant material; meat and food products of animal origin.

Public Holidays

Below are listed Public Holidays for the January 2006-June 2007 period.
2006: Jan 1 New Year's Day. **Jan 6** Epiphany. **Mar 20** St Joseph's Day. **Apr 13** Maundy Thursday. **Apr 14** Good Friday. **May 1** Labour Day. **May 25** Ascension. **Jun 15** Corpus Christi. **Jun 26** Sagrado Corazon (Sacred Heart). **Jul 3** Saint Peter and Saint Paul. **Aug 7** Battle of Boyacá. **Jul 20** Independence Day. **Aug 15** Assumption. **Nov 11** Independence of Cartagena City. **Dec 8** Immaculate Conception. **Dec 25** Christmas Day.
2007: Jan 1 New Year's Day. **Jan 6** Epiphany. **Mar 19** St Joseph's Day. **Apr 5** Maundy Thursday. **Apr 6** Good Friday. **May 1** Labour Day. **May 17** Ascension. **Jun 6** Corpus Christi. **Jun 18** Sagrado Corazon (Sacred Heart).

Health

	Special Precautions?	Certificate Required?
Yellow Fever	1	1
Cholera	2	No
Typhoid & Polio	3	N/A
Malaria	4	N/A

Note: *Regulations and requirements may be subject to change at short notice, and you are advised to contact your doctor well in advance of your intended date of departure. Any numbers in the chart refer to the footnotes below.*

1: Vaccination is recommended for travellers who visit the following areas considered to be endemic for *yellow fever*: middle valley of the Magdalena River, eastern and western foothills of the Cordillera Oriental from the frontier with Ecuador to that with Venezuela, Urabá, the foothills of the Sierra Nevada, eastern plains (Orinoquia) and Amazonia. All travellers intending to visit Magdalena, Cesar, La Guajira, Atlantico, Santander, Norte de Santander and Amazona areas should possess yellow fever inoculations and carry vaccination certificates. Colombian Immigration officials may insist upon seeing such proof.
2: Following WHO guidelines issued in 1973, a *cholera* vaccination certificate is not a condition of entry to Colombia. However, there may be a risk of cholera in this country; autochthonous cases were reported in 1996, and precautions should be considered. Up-to-date advice should be sought before deciding whether these precautions should include vaccination as medical opinion is divided over its effectiveness. See the *Health* appendix.
3: *Typhoid* immunisation or boosters are recommended.
4: *Malaria* risk exists throughout the year in rural and jungle areas below 800m. There is high risk in the following municipalities: Urabá-Bajo Cauca, Amazonia, Orinoquia and Pacífico. The highest risk is in the following departments: Amazonia, Chocó, Córdoba, Guainía, Guaviare, Putumayo and Vichada. The malignant *falciparum* form of the disease is reported to be highly resistant to chloroquine in Amazonia, Pacífico and Urabá-Bajo Cauca. The recommended prophylaxis is chloroquine plus proguanil in Amazonia and Pacífico, and in Urabá-Bajo Cauca, mefloquine.
Food & drink: All water should be regarded as being potentially contaminated outside major cities. Water used for drinking, brushing teeth or making ice should have first been boiled or otherwise sterilised. Milk may be unpasteurised in places and should be boiled. Powdered or tinned milk is available and is advised, but make sure that it is reconstituted with pure water. Avoid dairy products which are likely to have been made from unboiled milk. Only eat well cooked meat and fish, preferably served hot. Pork, salad and mayonnaise may carry increased risk. Vegetables should be cooked and fruit peeled.
Other risks: *American trypanosomiasis* (Chagas disease), as well as *cutaneous* and *mucocutaneous leishmaniasis* occur in Colombia. *Hepatitis A, B* and *C* occur. *Dengue fever* and *TB* are also found. Booster vaccinations for *tetanus* and *measles* are recommended. For further details, see the *Health* appendix.
Rabies is present. For those at risk, vaccination before arrival should be considered. If you are bitten, seek medical advice without delay.
Health care: Health facilities in the main cities are good. In rural areas, services can be very limited. Travellers are strongly advised to take out full medical insurance. There are nine firms in Colombia offering prepaid medical care and medical insurance which may be purchased from travel agents, a list of which is available from the Embassy.

Travel - International

AIR:
The national airline is *Avianca (AV)* (website: www.avianca.com.co). *Avianca* and *British Airways* each operate flights daily to Bogotá. Other airlines flying to Colombia include *Air France, American Airlines, British Airways, Continental Airlines, Delta Airlines, Iberia* and *Spanair*, but, as with *Avianca*, some may not fly directly there but with other airlines as part of a Code Share agreement.
Approximate flight times: From *London* to Bogotá is 11 hours 45 minutes, from *Los Angeles* is 10 hours 30 minutes, from *New York* is six hours 30 minutes, and from *Sydney* is 29 hours.
Main airports: *Bogotá* (El Dorado) *(BOG)* is situated 12km (8 miles) east of the city. *To/from the airport*: Buses to the city depart every 20 minutes from 0600-2200 (travel time – 30 minutes). Taxis are also available. *Facilities*: Bank, duty free shop, bar, restaurant, tourist information, post office, chemist/pharmacist and car hire.
Barranquilla (Ernesto Cortissoz) *(BAQ)* is 10km (6 miles) from the city. *Facilities*: Car hire is available.
Cali (Palmaseca) *(CLO)* is 19km (10 miles) from the city.
Cartagena (Crespo) *(CTG)* is 2km (1 mile) from the city.
Departure tax: Either collected upon ticket issuance or levied upon embarkation. Transit passengers continuing their journey on the same day are exempt. The price will be £28 or possibly more - payable by cash only.
The Visit South America Pass: This must be bought outside South America in country of residence and allows unlimited travel to 34 cities in the following countries: Argentina, Bolivia, Brazil, Colombia, Chile (except Easter Island), Ecuador, Paraguay, Peru, Uruguay and Venezuela. Participating airlines include *Aer Lingus (EI), American Airlines (AA), British Airways (BA), Cathay Pacific (CX), Finnair (AY), IBERIA (IB), LAN-Chile (LA)* and *Qantas (QF)*. A minimum of three flights must be booked, with no maximum; the maximum stay is 60 days, with no minimum, and prices depend on the amount of flight zones covered. Children under 12 years of age are entitled to a 33 per cent discount and infants (under two years old) only pay 10 per cent of the adult fare. For further details, contact one of the participating airlines. For more information visit www.oneworld.com.
Note: All air tickets purchased in Colombia for destinations outside the country are liable to a total tax of 15 per cent on one-way tickets and 7.5 per cent on return tickets.
SEA:
Major ports on the Caribbean coast include *Cartagena, Baranquilla, Santa Marta* and *Turnaco. Buenaventura* is the main port on the Pacific coast. Many ships and cruise lines visit these ports from the USA, Mexico, Venezuela, Central America and the Caribbean Islands. *Leticia* is the upper Amazonian port.
RAIL:
There are no international rail connections.
ROAD:
Colombia can be reached from Panama via the Darien Gap, but the route is not advised as it can be long, arduous and dangerous. Vehicles can also be freighted from Panama to one of Colombia's Caribbean or Pacific ports. There are also road links with Ecuador and Venezuela, although travellers should check with the local embassy about safety of roads before crossing the border to Venezuela. **Coach/bus:** *TEPSA* buses connect with Venezuela. Coaches are comfortable and services good. There are second-class buses from Maracaibo to Santa Marta and Cartagena, but this method of travelling can be uncomfortable.

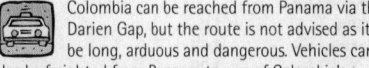

A B C D E F G H I J K L M N O P Q R S T U V W X Y Z

Travel - Internal

AIR:

There is an excellent internal air network connecting major cities, including those in the Caribbean coastal area. There are also local helicopter flights. There are flights between the mainland and the islands of San Andrés and Providencia operating from most major Colombian cities. Services are offered by *Avianca*, *SAM* and *Aires*. San Andrés is a regular stop for *Avianca*, *Lacsa* and *Sahsa* airlines.

Avianca-Colombia Airpass: This must be bought with an international air ticket and includes travel to all Colombian domestic points served by *Avianca*, *SAM* and *Aires*. It excludes travel to Leticia and San Andres Pass. Air passes are valid for a maximum of 30 days if longhaul flight is with Avianca and 21 days if longhaul flight with any other carrier.

Departure tax: COP6800-8500, usually included in the ticket price.

SEA:

There is a ferry service between the mainland and the islands of San Andrés and Providencia, leaving from the Muelle de los Pegasos. The journey is long (72 hours) but cheap. Information about other sailings to San Andrés can be obtained from the Maritima San Andrés office.

RIVER:

The Magdalena River is the main artery of Colombia. Some cargo boats take passengers, though this is a slow way to travel. It is possible to hire boats for particular trips. Paddle steamers no longer run services up and down the river and hiring can be expensive. From Leticia, on the Peruvian border, a number of operators run sightseeing tours and jungle expeditions up the Amazon. It is necessary to make enquiries in situ, and wise to shop around before booking on any one trip.

RAIL:

Although trains still carry freight, inter-city passenger services are virtually non-existent. Services have been frequently suspended during recent years owing to operators' financial difficulties. The main route is between Bogotá and Santa Marta on the Caribbean coast, east of Barranquilla. Because of the distances, it is easier to take a plane if speed is important.

ROAD:

A good highway links Santa Marta in the east with Cartagena, and passes Barranquilla en route. The Trans-Caribbean Highway has placed Barranquilla only five hours away from Venezuela. Northeast of Santa Marta, in the Guajira Peninsula, roads are usually passable except during rainy periods. There is highway transportation between the coastal cities and the capital and other cities of the interior, but much of the highway is rutted. Travellers are advised against driving in rural areas as guerilla and paramilitary groups have a strong presence. **Bus**: The long distances make air travel advisable. However, the best bus lines are said to be the *Flota Magdalena*, Expreso *Bolivariano* and, especially, the *Expreso Palmira*. Approximately 40 companies with modern buses and minibuses provide transportation between coastal towns and cities. There are also *collectivos* (taxi-buses) for shorter distances which can often be a cheaper alternative. **Car hire**: Major car hire companies have offices, but driving in cities is not recommended. Traffic drives on the right. Seat belts in the front two seats are mandatory; however, car seats for children are not compulsory. Children under ten years of age cannot sit in the front seat. The urban speed limit is 45-60kph (28-37mph) and the rural speed limit is 80kph (50mph). **Documentation**: An International Driving Permit is required.

URBAN:

Bogotá has extensive trolleybus, bus and minibus services, and a funicular railway; flat fares are charged. There are also shared taxis (*buseta*) which are not expensive and stop on demand. Drivers are authorised to add a supplement for out-of-town trips and to airports. At hotels, the green-and-cream coloured taxis are available for tourists. They are more expensive than the others, but some of the drivers may have a working knowledge of English. Passengers should insist that meters are used. For those without a meter the fare should be agreed before starting a journey.

Travel times: The following chart gives approximate travel times from **Bogotá** (in hours and minutes) to other major towns/cities in Colombia.

	Air
Barranquilla	**1.15**
Medellin	**1.15**
Manizales	**1.00**
Cali	**1.00**
Leticia	**2.00**

Travel Advice

Travellers are strongly advised against all travel to Putumayo, Meta, Arauca, Narino, Caqueta and Norte de Santander departments, and to rural areas of Sucre, Bolivar, Choco, Antioquia, Valle de Cauca and Cauca departments. There is a high risk to personal safety in these areas and a serious risk of kidnapping and crime.

The threat from terrorism, especially Colombian domestic groups, is high. Travellers should be extremely vigilant, particularly in public places used by foreigners, such as hotels, bars, restaurants, nightclubs and shopping malls. The Colombian authorities have increased security around Government buildings and public transport.

This advice is based on information provided by the Foreign and Commonwealth Office in the UK. It is correct at time of publishing. As the situation can change rapidly, visitors are advised to contact the following organisations for the latest travel advice:

British Foreign and Commonwealth Office
Tel: (0845) 850 2829.
Website: www.fco.gov.uk

US Department of State
Website: http://travel.state.gov/travel

Accommodation

HOTELS:

It is advisable to choose hotels recommended by the official Colombian Hotel Organisation, COTELCO, Carrera 7, no. 60-92, Bogotá (tel: (1) 310 3640; website: www.cotelco.org). Two tariffs are levied: 'European tariff' from May to November, and 'American tariff' from December to April, which is much higher. It is advisable to make reservations well in advance. There are several hotels and *residencias* on the island of San Andrés, and one on Providencia. Prices rise on average 10 per cent a year; visitors are advised to check current prices when making reservations. A five per cent tax is added to all hotel bills throughout the country. There is a star grading system similar to that operating in Europe.

CAMPING/CARAVANNING:

Camping is possible in Colombia, although there are very few official camping areas. Two of the better campsites in the country are *Camping del Sol* and *Camping de Covenas*.

Top Things To See

- **Bogotá**, the capital, founded in 1538, is the largest city and situated almost in the centre of the country at an altitude of 2600m (8600ft). Bogotá reflects a blend of Colombian tradition and Spanish colonial influences. Many historical landmarks have been preserved, such as the **Capitol Municipal Palace** and the cathedral, the **Capilla del Sangrario**, on the main square, the **Plaza Bolivar**. Bogotá also contains the **Gold Museum**, with its unique collection of over 100,000 pre-Colombian artworks.
- Travel to **Zipaquirá**, an area well-known for its many salt mines, and see the famous **Salt Cathedral** (capable of accommodating 8400 people), an underground church built within a salt mine, in the body of a mountain. Stalactites and specks of salt jostle with crosses and chapels, all bathed in subdued lighting.
- **Guatavita** is best known for its **Laguna de Guatavita**, the ritual centre and sacred lake of the Muisca Indians. Flanked by undulating hills, it is a calm and beautiful lake that is definitely worth a visit.
- Amble around the colourful **market** on the side channel of the **Magdalena** in **Barranquilla**.
- Enjoy the peaceful vista of Colombia's many **beaches**. The main tourist resorts on Colombia's 1600km- (1000 mile-) long Caribbean coast lie near **Santa Marta**, one of the first major cities founded by the Spanish in South America. Its modern hotels, white beaches and proximity to fashionable beach resorts now make it a popular base for visitors wishing to explore the coast.
- Go to the **Tayrona National Park**, some 35km (22 miles) south of Santa Marta, to see one of the country's most popular parks. Its major attraction is its deep bays, shaded with coconut trees, beautiful beaches and several coral reefs.
- **Cartagena**, an ancient walled fortress city on the north coast, is also worth a visit, particularly for its fascinating **Old Town**. Tourist facilities have been considerably developed in recent years, particularly at **El Laguita**, an L-shaped pensinsula, now packed with hotels and expensive restaurants.
- Some 35km (22 miles) west lie the **Islas del Rosario**, an archipelago of about 25 small coral islands now declared a national park. Cruises and tours are widely available and can be booked in Cartagena.
- Easily reached from Cartagena, by plane or boat, are the islands of **San Andrés** and **Providencia**, nearly 500km (300 miles) north of the Colombian coast. San Andrés was once the headquarters of the English pirate, Captain Henry Morgan, the scourge of the Caribbean. The islands are duty free, and consequently often crowded, but there are still several less spoilt parts. Popular excursions include visits by boat to **Johnny Cay** and the **Aquarium**.

Top Things To Do

- **Water-skiing**, **boating**, **sailing** and **skindiving** can all be practised on the coast (check with authorities before diving, as sharks and barracudas have caused fatalities). **Providencia** with its paradisacal waters, is ideal for **scuba diving**.
- **Mountain climbing** begins 48km (30 miles) east of **Santa Marta**, with peaks of up to nearly 6000m (19,000ft).
- Watch the major **cycle race**, the **Tour of Colombia**, which takes place every March and April.
- Good **skiing** can be found on the slopes of **Nevado del Ruiz** (5400m/ 17,700ft), 48km (30 miles) from **Manizales**.
- Try swinging your hips at the world's capital of **salsa**: **Cali**.
- Take a **jungle tour** into the **Amazon basin**, which covers almost one-third of Colombia's territory, an area of thick tropical forest in the southeast, with no roads and inhabited mostly by Indians. The most popular base for tourists wishing to explore the area is **Leticia**, a small town with well-developed tourist facilities, located on the banks of the **Amazon River** and close to the border with Brazil and Peru. The jungle trips to the nearby **Amacayu National Park** are widely available and highly recommended, often including visits to Indian tribes.
- For those interested in **archaeology**, why not dig for or examine the great number of relics and massive stone statues in **San Augustín Archaeological Park**? For architectural history, the traditional city of **Popayan** is the birthplace of many of Colombia's most illustrious statesmen, and contains many fine colonial houses and churches, as well as hosting a fantastic **Holy Week procession**. **Tierradentro**, in the southwest of the country, has beautiful manmade burial **caves** painted with pre-Colombian geometric patterns.

TOURIST INFORMATION

Ministerio de Comercio, Industria y Turismo
Calle 28, 13A-15, Bogotá, DC, Colombia
Tel: (1) 606 7676.
Website: www.mincomercio.gov.co

Fondo de Promoción Turística de Colombia
Carrera 16A No.78-55 Oficina. 604, Bogotá, Colombia
Tel: (1) 611 4330.
Website: www.turismocolombia.com

Entertainment

FOOD & DRINK: Restaurants offering international cuisine and table service is the norm. Local dishes are varied and tasty, with a touch of Spanish influence. It is safest to drink bottled water. Colombians rarely drink alcohol with meals. *Gaseosa* is the name given to non-alcoholic, carbonated drinks.

Colombian wines are generally of poor quality. Chilean and Argentinian wines are available in restaurants at reasonable prices. There are no licensing hours.

National specialities:

- *Ajiaco* (chicken stew with potatoes, served with cream, corn on the cob and capers).
- *Arepas* (corn pancakes made without salt, eaten in place of bread).
- *Bandeja paisa* (meat dish accompanied by cassava, rice, fried plantain and red beans), served in the area of Medellín.
- Seafood (*mariscos*) is plentiful on the Caribbean coast - lobsters in particular are renowned for their flavour.

National drinks:

- *Tinto* (small black coffee) - but this term is also used to describe red wine or *vino tinto*.
- *Canelazo* (rum-based cocktail taken hot or cold).

Tipping: Taxi drivers expect 10 per cent tips. Porters at airports and hotels are usually given c. pesos500 per item. Many restaurants, bars and cafes add 10 per cent service charge to the bill or suggest a 10 per cent tip, although a 15 per cent tip is becoming increasingly common. Maids and clerks in hotels are also tipped. Bogotá's shoeshine boys live on their tips and expect about COP1000.

NIGHTLIFE: Bogotá's *Colon Theatre* presents ballet, opera, drama and music, with international and local groups. There are many nightclubs and discos in the major towns of Colombia.

SHOPPING: Special purchases include local handicrafts, cotton, wood and leather goods, woollen blankets, *ruana* shawls, and travelling bags. Hotel shops carry excellent gold reproductions of ancient Colombian jewellery. Colombia produces first-grade stones, and the emeralds are among the most perfect in the world. **Shopping hours**: Mon-Sat 0900-2000

Business

- **GDP:** US$81.3 billion.
- **Main imports:** Industrial equipment, transportation eqipment, consumer goods, chemicals, paper products, fuels and electricity.
- **Main exports:** Oil, coal, coffee, textiles, software, sugar, bananas, cut flowers, cotton products, emeralds and gold.
- **Main trade partners:** USA, Venezuela, Brazil, Japan, Germany, Mexico and China.

ECONOMY: Agriculture is extensive and varied; it accounts for 75 per cent of export earnings. Coffee has traditionally been the principal crop (Colombia is the world's second-largest producer) but as production has declined and prices fallen. Illegal farming of cocoa is also widespread in the more remote parts of the country. The country is self-sufficient in consumer goods and exports of manufactured goods – textiles, leather goods, metal products, chemicals, pharmaceuticals and cement – have been steadily increasing. Colombia has sizeable oil reserves, which are now on stream. Coal deposits are the largest in Latin America, although development of these has been slow. Recent economic performance has been moderate, with annual growth of just over 1 per cent during 2002. In the same year, inflation was 7 per cent, although official unemployment is still close to 20 per cent (the true figure is probably rather higher). The ongoing internal conflict, which shows little sign of resolution at present, is a huge millstone around the country's neck, as far as prospects for economic development go. Colombia is a member of the Andean Pact and of the *Asociación Latinoamericana de Integración* (ALADI), which is seeking to regularise tariffs throughout South America. In addition, Colombia is establishing a three-country free trade zone with Venezuela and Mexico.

BUSINESS ETIQUETTE: Businesspeople are expected to dress smartly. English is widely understood in many business circles; the Colombian Ministry of Foreign Affairs has an official translation service, and there are a number of commercial interpreter services. A command of Spanish is always appreciated. Business visitors will sometimes be invited out to dinner, which may be preceded by a long cocktail party, with a meal starting around 2300. The best months for business visits are March to November. The business community generally takes holidays from September to February, the driest months. **Office hours:** Mon-Fri 0900-1800.

COMMERCIAL INFORMATION

Confederación Colombiana de Cámaras de Comercio (CONFECAMARAS) (National Chamber of Commerce)
Apdo Aéreo 29750, Carrera 13, 27-47, Oficina 502, Santa Fe de Bogotá, Colombia
Tel: (1) 346 7055.
Website: www.confecamaras.org.co

Proexport Colombia
Edificio Bancafe, Calle 28, 13A-15, Piso 37, Santa Fe de Bogotá, Colombia
Tel: (1) 341 2066.
Website: www.proexport.com.co

Colombian Government Trade Bureau in the USA
1901 L Street, Suite 700, NW, Washington DC, 20036, USA
Tel: (202) 887 9000.
Website: www.coltrade.org

CORFERIAS (National Centre of Trade Fairs)
Carrera 40, 22C-67, Santa Fe de Bogotá, Colombia
Tel: (1) 381 0000.
Website: www.corferias.com

Comoros Islands

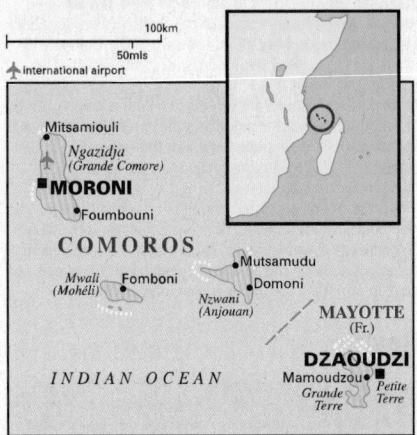

Location: Indian Ocean, between the East African coast and Madagascar.

Time: GMT + 3.

Overview

A previous French Overseas Territory, the Comoros Islands only became fully independent in 1975, despite consistent pressure on the French from the islands' Government. The main reason was the position of Mayotte, one of the original Comoros island group, which insisted upon retaining its links with France. With Mayotte going its own way, the Comoros Islands joined the United Nations as the Federal Islamic Republic of the Comoros, comprising three islands: Ngazidja (formerly Grande Comore), Nzwani (formerly Anjouan) and Mwali (formerly Mohéli). Mahoré (Mayotte) is administered by France but is claimed by the Federal Islamic Republic of the Comoros.
Since independence, instability has characterised post-independence politics on the islands with several coup attempts.
The islands' vegetation is rich and varied: 65 per cent of the world's perfume essence comes from the Comoros Islands, being processed from the blossoms of ylang-ylang, jasmine and orange. Spices, including nutmeg, cloves, pepper, basil and vanilla, are another mainstay of the economy. The islands are of volcanic origin and are surrounded by coral reefs and the more energetic travellers will be eager to climb to the top of Mount Karthala, an active volcano on Ngazidja, or enjoy a vast range of watersports.

General Information

AREA: 1862 sq km (719 sq miles).
POPULATION: 812,000 (UN, 2005).
POPULATION DENSITY: 436 per sq km.
CAPITAL: Moroni. **Population:** 60,200 (2003).
GEOGRAPHY: The Comoro archipelago is situated in the Indian Ocean north of Madagascar and consists of four main islands of volcanic origin, surrounded by coral reefs: Ngazidja (formerly Grande Comore), Nzwani (formerly Anjouan), Mwali (formerly Mohéli) and Mahoré (Mayotte). The latter is administered by France but is claimed by the Federal Islamic Republic of the Comoros. Land can only support subsistence agriculture but the surrounding seas are rich in marine life.
GOVERNMENT: Federal Islamic Republic. **Head of State:** President Azali Assoumani, since the military coup of April 1999. **Recent history:** Following the military coup of May 1999, the existing 1996 constitution and the Federal Assembly were suspended. A new constitution

---

allowing for greater autonomy and individual elected administrations on each of the islands was introduced in 2002. Executive power is in the hands of the President, who is elected for a six-year term. Colonel Azzali Assoumani was declared President of the newly entitled Union of Comoros – which includes Anjouan and Moheli – after a disputed election in May 2002. Under the new constitutional arrangements, each island Governor may appoint eight Ministers to deal with local affairs, whilst the Union authorities will control foreign affairs, finance, defence, justice and religious matters. However, there remained areas where the division of authority was unclear, resulting in the signature of an agreement in 2003 to resolve the crisis. As a result, Parliamentary elections were held in 2004. The majority of seats were won by island rather than state candidates.
LANGUAGE: The official languages are French, Arabic and Comorian, a blend of Arabic and Swahili.
RELIGION: Muslim (mostly Sunni) with Roman Catholic minority.
ELECTRICITY: 220 volts AC, 50Hz. Electricity shortages occur.
SOCIAL CONVENTIONS: Religious customs associated with Islam should be respected. Although Comorans are tolerant towards other cultures (for instance, alcohol is not banned and is available in hotels and restaurants), they expect moderate behaviour from non Muslim visitors, such as no consumption of alcohol in public places and modest dress in public. Homosexuality is not illegal in the Comoros Islands. Sex with minors is. Anyone found guilty of drug smuggling or possession will be imprisoned for four to five years. On release, the person will be fined (in proportion to the quantity of drugs seized) and then deported.

Climate

The climate is tropical and very warm. Coastal areas are hot and very humid, interspaced with rains and seasonal cyclones (January to April). The upland areas are cooler, particularly at night, and have higher rainfall. The rainy season is from November to April.
Required clothing: Lightweight cottons and linens with waterproofing during the rainy season. Warmer garments and rainwear are needed for the mountains.

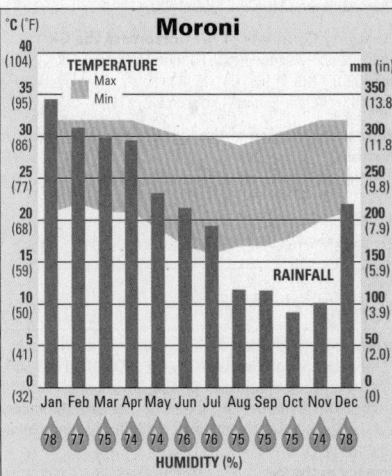

Communications

Telephone: Outgoing international calls must be made through the international operator. Country code: 269.
Mobile telephone: Limited coverage.
Internet: A few hotels have Internet access.
Post: Mail to Western Europe takes at least one week.
MEDIA: There is no single national newspaper. Although several private newspapers criticise the Government, self-censorship is reportedly common. Local radio and TV stations operate without overt Government interference.
Press: The main (weekly) papers are *Al Watwan* (state-owned) published on Grand Comore, *Kuesi* published on the French island of Mayotte and *La Gazette des Comores* (independent). *L'Archipel* (independent) is published monthly. There are no English-language newspapers.
TV/Radio: There is a national radio station, *Radio Comoros*, and a national TV service. *RFO Mayotte*, run by French public radio and TV, broadcasts French and locally-produced radio and TV programmes from the French island of Mayotte and can be received in parts of the archipelago. Other radio stations include: *Radio Dziyalandze Mutsamudu (RDM)*, an FM station on Anjouan, which relays *Radio France Internationale* and *Radio Ngazidja*, the official station on Grand Comore.

Passport/Visa

	Passport Required?	Visa Required?	Return Ticket Required?
Full British	Yes	Yes	Yes
Australian	Yes	Yes	Yes
Canadian	Yes	Yes	Yes
USA	Yes	Yes	Yes
Other EU	Yes	Yes	Yes
Japanese	Yes	Yes	Yes

Note: Regulations and requirements may be subject to change at short notice, and you are advised to contact the appropriate diplomatic or consular authority before finalising travel arrangements. Any numbers in the chart refer to the footnotes below.

PASSPORTS: Passport valid for at least six months required by all.
VISAS: Required by all except those continuing their journey by the same or first connecting aircraft without leaving the airport and holding documents certifying onward/return travel.
Types of visa and cost: *Ordinary*: US$10.
Validity: Two weeks.
Application to: Visas are issued on arrival in the Comoros Islands or by some of their diplomatic representations, such as Antananarivo, Cairo, Paris and London (the Honorary Consulate in London can issue a tourist visa valid for 90 days for £10).
Application requirements: (a) Application form (provided at airport). (b) Valid passport with at least three months' remaining validity. (c) Two passport-sized photos for visas issued outside the country. (d) Fee (payable in Comoros Francs, Euros or US Dollars only). (e) Return/onward tickets.
Note: Single parents or other adults travelling alone with children should be aware that some countries require evidence of parental responsibility before allowing them to enter the country. For further information, contact the Comoran Embassy in Paris (see *Passport/Visa Information*).

PASSPORT/VISA INFORMATION

Embassy of the Federal Islamic Republic of the Comoros in France
20 rue Marbeau, 75016 Paris, France
Tel: (1) 4067 9054. Fax: (1) 4845 1365.
Opening hours: Mon-Fri 1000-1600.

Honorary Consulate of the Comoros in the UK
Flat 6, 24-26 Avenue Road, London NW8 6DU, UK
Tel: (020) 7722 1146.
E-mail: kchehabi@blueyonder.co.uk

Permanent Mission of the Comoros to the United Nations
866 United Nations Plaza, Suite 418, New York, NY 10017, USA
Tel: (212) 750 1637.
Website: www.un.int/comoros

Money

Currency: Comoros Franc (KMF) = 100 centimes. Notes are in denominations of KMF10,000, 5000, 2500, 1000 and 500. Coins are in denominations of KMF20, 10, 5, 2 and 1, and 20 centimes. The Comoros Franc is part of the French Monetary Area and Euros are also commonly used. The Comoros Franc is tied to the Euro.
Currency exchange: Foreign currency may be exchanged in banks in the towns. Banque Nationale des Comores is the only established bank on Grande Comore. Banking facilities are very limited on the other islands.
Credit & debit cards: There is limited acceptance of most international credit cards (mainly in upmarket hotels), but check with your credit or debit card company for details of merchant acceptability and other services which may be available. Some hotels and restaurants will accept foreign currencies, mostly Euros and US dollars. Change may be given in local currency.
Traveller's cheques: The Banque Internationale des Comores (BIC) is the only bank that will change travellers cheques. To avoid additional exchange rate charges, travellers are advised to take travellers cheques in Euros.
Currency restrictions: There are no restrictions on the import and export of either local or foreign currency.
Banking hours: Mon-Thurs 0730-1300; Fri 0730-1100.
Exchange rate indicators:
Rate at time of publishing:
£1.00= KMF730.92
$1.00= KMF399.99

Duty Free

The following goods may be imported into the Comoros Islands by persons 18 years of age and over without incurring customs duty:
400 cigarettes or 100 cigars or 500g of tobacco; one bottle of alcoholic beverage; one bottle of perfume.
Prohibited items: Plants or soil, except on presentation of an import permit issued from the Comoros Islands' Agriculture Department, together with a phytosanitary certificate of the place of origin.

Public Holidays

Below are listed Public Holidays for the January 2006-June 2007 period.
2006: Jan 10 Eid al-Adha (Feast of the Sacrifice). **Jan 31** Muharram (Islamic New Year). **Feb 9** Ashoura. **Mar 18** Anniversary of the Death of President Said Mohamed Cheikh. **May 25** Anniversary of the Organisation of African Unity. **May 29** Anniversary of the Death of President Ali Soilih. **Jul 6** Independence Day. **Oct 22-24** Eid al-Fitr (End of Ramadan). **Nov 26** Anniversary of the Death of President Ahmed Abdallah. **Dec 25** Christmas Day. **Dec 31** Eid al-Adha (Feast of the Sacrifice).
2007: Jan 20 Muharram (Islamic New Year). **Jan 30** Ashoura. **Mar 18** Anniversary of the Death of President Said Mohamed Cheikh. **May 25** Anniversary of the Organisation of African Unity. **May 29** Anniversary of the Death of President Ali Soilih.
Note: Muslim festivals are timed according to local sightings of various phases of the moon and the dates given above are approximations. During the lunar month of Ramadan that precedes Eid al-Fitr, Muslims fast during the day and feast at night and normal business patterns may be interrupted. Many restaurants are closed during the day and there may be restrictions on smoking and drinking. Some disruption may continue into Eid al-Fitr itself. Eid al-Fitr and Eid al-Adha may last anything from 2 to 10 days, depending on the region. For more information, see the *World of Islam* section.

Health

	Special Precautions?	Certificate Required?
Yellow Fever	No	1
Cholera	Yes	2
Typhoid & Polio	3	N/A
Malaria	4	N/A

Note: Regulations and requirements may be subject to change at short notice, and you are advised to contact your doctor well in advance of your intended date of departure. Any numbers in the chart refer to the footnotes below.

1: Some travellers from areas infected with *yellow fever* have been asked to provide vaccination certificates, but this is not an official policy.
2: Following WHO guidelines issued in 1973, a *cholera* vaccination certificate is not an official condition of entry to the Comoros Islands. However, outbreaks of cholera still occur periodically. Up-to-date advice should be sought before deciding whether precautions should include vaccination, as medical opinion is divided over its effectiveness; see the *Health* appendix.
3: *Typhoid* fevers are present.
4: *Malaria* risk exists all year throughout the whole country, predominantly in the malignant *falciparum* form. Resistance to chloroquine has been reported. The recommended prophylaxis is mefloquine. There have been cases of *Dengue fever* reported on Grande Comore. Travellers should take strict prevention measures against mosquito bites, by using repellents and by wearing sleeved shirts and long trousers.
Food & drink: All water should be regarded as being potentially contaminated. Water used for drinking, brushing teeth or making ice should have first been boiled or otherwise sterilised. Milk is unpasteurised and should be boiled. Powdered or tinned milk is available and is advised, but make sure that it is reconstituted with pure water. Avoid dairy products which are likely to have been made from unboiled milk. Only eat well-cooked meat and fish, preferably served hot. Pork, salad and mayonnaise may carry increased risk. Vegetables should be cooked and fruit peeled.
Other risks: *Hepatitis A* and *E* are widespread. *Hepatitis B* is hyperendemic. Both *cutaneous* and *visceral leishmaniasis* may be found. Outbreaks of *yellow fever* occur periodically.
Health care: There is no reciprocal health agreement with the UK. Medical facilities are basic and most are private. In order to secure even basic medical care, visitors are strongly advised to take out comprehensive health insurance.

Travel - International

AIR:
Airlines operating to the Comoros Islands include *Air Austral, Air Madagascar, Air Tanzania Corporation, Sudan Airlines* and *Yemenia Yemen Airways. Air France* operates regularly from Paris via Réunion.
Approximate flight times: To Moroni from *London* takes a minimum of 20 hours; this includes stopovers (usually in Paris and Réunion).
Main airports: *Moroni International Prince Said Ibrahim (HAH)*, 25km (16 miles) north of the city. *To/from the airport:* Taxis are available to the town (travel time - 30 minutes). Taxis do not have meters but prices are fixed. Make sure you know the price before boarding the taxi. *Facilities:* Bars and light refreshments, left luggage and a post office are available for international flights. There are no money-changing facilities at the airport.
Departure tax: None.
SEA:
There are irregular sailings from East Africa (Mombasa, Kenya), Madagascar, Mauritius, Réunion or Zanzibar to Moroni or Mutsamudu. These are mostly cargo ships which might carry passengers.

Travel - Internal

AIR:
Each island has an airfield and there are services between the islands in the region.
SEA:
The islands are linked by regular ferry services. Travellers can hire motorboats, sailing craft and canoes in port villages and towns. A boat can be especially useful for Mwali (Mohéli) where the road system is rudimentary.
ROAD:
Bush taxis (*taxis-brousses*), hired vehicles or private cars are the only forms of transport on the islands. Traffic drives on the right. All the islands have tarred roads. 4-wheel-drive vehicles are advisable for the outlying islands and in the interior, especially in the rainy season. Roads are narrow and domestic animals often roam free, so visitors should drive slowly. Share-taxis provide transport in and around towns.
Car hire: Available on Ngazidja (Grande Comore).
Documentation: An International Driving Permit is valid for up to three months.

Travel Advice

Most visits to the Comoros Islands are trouble-free but travellers should be aware of the global risk of indiscriminate international terrorist attacks, which could be against civilian targets, including places frequented by foreigners.
The Comoros Islands are generally crime-free, but travellers are advised not to walk around town centres unaccompanied at night and to take sensible precautions against pickpocketing and mugging. Travellers should keep a copy of their passport with them, and if possible keep the original in a safe place (such as a hotel safe or deposit box). The Union of the Comoros is predominantly Muslim, and it is important for visitors to respect the customs associated with Islam.
This advice is based on information provided by the Foreign and Commonwealth Office in the UK. It is correct at time of publishing. As the situation can change rapidly, visitors are advised to contact the following organisations for the latest travel advice:

British Foreign and Commonwealth Office
Tel: (0845) 850 2829.
Website: www.fco.gov.uk

US Department of State
Website: http://travel.state.gov/travel

Accommodation

Although accommodation on the Comoros Islands is being upgraded, there are only a few hotels and pensions, located mostly in Moroni and Mutsamudu, which handle the needs of travelling businesspeople, government officials and other visitors. Room sharing is quite common. There are simple shelters (*gîtes*) on the slopes of Karthala (an active volcano).

Top Things To See & Do

- The capital **Moroni** on **Ngazidja** (**Grande Comore**) is a charming, peaceful town containing a few broad squares and modern Government buildings, as well as old, narrow, winding streets and a market place. There are numerous fine mosques including the **Vendredi Mosque**, from the top of which there is an attractive view.
- The more energetic may climb to the top of **Mount Karthala** and then descend into the crater of this active volcano. The crater is claimed to be the largest still active anywhere in the world. It is usual to make one overnight stop at the shelter provided. The Karthala volcano erupted in 2003 and it may be worth checking the situation between travelling to this part of the island. Fit hikers may

also travel to **Dziani Boundouni**, a sulphurous crater lake at the centre of the sparsely populated island of Mwali (Mohéli), which can be reached on day-walks from its capital, Fomboni. Owing to political instability, visitors are advised to check the latest travel advice from an official organisation (such as an Embassy) before contemplating a trip to Mohéli.

• **Itsandra**, a fishing village 6km (4 miles) from Moroni, has a fine beach and there are opportunities to see dances performed by the local men. The town was once the ancient capital of the island, complete with royal tombs and a fortress. **Mitsamiouli**, a town in the north of the island, is known both for its good diving facilities and for having the best Comoran dancers. There are many bats and spiders on the island, the former often appearing in broad daylight.

• There are hot sulphur springs at **Lac Salé** and a 14th-century village at **Iconi**.

• On **Mwali (Mohéli)**, the smallest of the main islands, travellers will be able to see *dhows* (Arab sail boats) being built on the beach at **Fomboni**.

• There is a fine waterfall at **Miringoni**.

• Discover the local wildlife. The Comoros Islands' distinctive (and now protected) **green turtle** can be seen in the marine reserve off Mohéli's southern coast. Trips by motorised *pirogues* (canoes) can be arranged with local fishermen from Niumashuwa. Giant turtles may be seen at **Niumashuwa Bay**.

• **Nzwani (Anjouan)** is notable for its waterfalls and abundant vegetation. The main town of **Mutsamudu** is built in Swahili-Shirazi style, complete with 17th-century houses with carved doors, twisting alleyways, mosques and a citadel. The ancient capital of **Domoni** is also worth a visit. The best beaches are in the **Bimbini** area. There are perfume distilleries at **Bambao**.

• **Mahore (Mayotte)**, the French-administered island, is surrounded by a coral reef and has good beaches and excellent scuba-diving facilities. Tourists may explore the **lagoon** (claimed to be the largest in the world) by dugout canoe. The town of **Dzaoudzi** contains some old fortifications worthy of a visit. **Pamanzi** is a forested islet, 5km (3 miles) offshore, fragrant with a wealth of vegetation. At **Sulu**, a waterfall plunges straight into the sea. There are the remains of an old mosque at **Tsingoni**. Elsewhere, there are 19th-century **sugar refineries**. For further information, see the French Overseas Possessions section.

Note: Travel to Mayotte from the Comoros Islands may be problematic owing to the fact that this is disputed territory.

• There is excellent **diving** in the archipelago. The **Trou du Prophète** in Misamiouli on Ngazidja, **Niumashuwa Bay** on Mwali and **Pamanzi** islet off Mahore are particularly fine. There are many excellent beaches on all the islands and **Galawa Beach** on Grande Comore has a diving school. Other good beaches include **Bouni, Chomoni** (near a sheltered bay), **Itsandra** and the palm-fringed **Planet Plage**. **Pirogue** (canoe) **races** are occasionally staged in the lagoon that surrounds Mahore. Sailing boats and canoes are available for hire in many ports.

TOURIST INFORMATION

Société Comorienne de Tourisme et Hôtellerie (COMOTEL)
Itsandra Hotel, BP 1027, Njazidja, Comoros Islands
Tel: 732 365.

Entertainment

FOOD & DRINK: Restaurants serve good food with spiced sauces and rice-based dishes.
Things to know: There may be restrictions on drink within Muslim circles.
National specialities:
• Cassava.
• Plantain.
• Couscous.
• Barbecued goat meat.
• Seafood.
• Tropical fruits.
Tipping: Normally 10 per cent.
SHOPPING: Comoran products can be purchased at Moroni on Ngazidja (Grande Comore). These include gold, pearl and shell jewellery, woven cloth, embroidered skull-caps (*koffia*) and slippers, carved chests, panels and *portes-croix* (lecterns), pottery and basketry. Most items can be bought in the villages where they are made. **Shopping hours**: Mon-Sat 0830-1200 and 1500-1830 (often shops remain open until later).

Business

• **GDP:** US$441 million (2002 estimate).
• **Main exports:** Vanilla, cloves, ylang-ylang (perfume oil) and copra.
• **Main imports:** Rice and petroleum products.
• **Main trade partners:** Exports to: France, USA, Singapore and Germany; Imports from: France, South Africa, Japan, Thailand, Indonesia, Singapore and China.

ECONOMY: The bulk of the working population is employed in agriculture, which produces vanilla and cloves (the main exports), basil, ylang-ylang (an essence extracted from trees) and copra. There is a small fishing industry and a minimal industrial base devoted mainly to processing vanilla. The tourism industry has grown rapidly during the last 10 years to the extent that the service sector as a whole now accounts for almost 60 per cent of total domestic output: chronic political instability on the islands has however, prevented the industry from reaching its full potential. Moreover, the agricultural economy is vulnerable to low world commodity prices. Substantial French aid remains essential. France is also the country's major trading partner, providing almost half of the Comoros' imports and taking two-thirds of its exports. China, Kenya, Tanzania and Madagascar are the other major importers into the islands. Per capita income is estimated at US$450 (World Bank, 2003). The economy grew slowly at 2.5 per cent (est. 2002).
BUSINESS ETIQUETTE: Lightweight suit or shirt and tie required. Business is conducted in French or Arabic; English is seldom spoken. **Office hours**: Mon-Thurs 0730-1430, Fri 0730-1130, Sat 0730-1200.

COMMERCIAL INFORMATION

Chambre de Commerce, d'Industrie et d'Agriculture
BP 763, Moroni, Comoros Islands
Tel: 730 958.
E-mail: pride@snpt.km

Columbus Travel Publishing

World City Guide

The perfect companion for visiting or researching 150 of the most exciting cities around the world.
Whether for business or leisure travel, the World City Guide covers all you need to know.
For more information contact
Columbus Travel Publishing, Media House, Azalea Drive, Swanley, Kent BR8 8HU
Tel: +44 (0) 1322 616344 • Fax: +44 (0) 1322 616323
Email: booksales@nexusmedia.com

Congo, Democratic Republic of

Location: Central Africa.

Time: Kinshasa and Mbandaka: GMT + 1. Haut-Zaïre, Kasai, Kivu and Shaba: GMT + 2.

Overview

Congo (Dem Rep) has many beautiful landscapes, with lakes and forests, waterfalls and wildlife. However, this is a vast country, with an almost non-existent transport infrastructure. It is mired in current conflict and a long and intricate history. The Belgian Congo was created in 1885 as the personal property of the Belgian Monarch, King Leopold II. The Belgians provided nothing other than the minimum infrastructure necessary to support the extraction of the country's vast mineral wealth, setting a pattern which has dominated this benighted country ever since. The Belgian Congo was eventually granted independence, with minimal preparation, in 1960.

The first post-independence Government included an African leader whose radical politics and close relations with the Soviet Union raised serious concerns among Western Governments. With the support of the Americans and Belgians, and exploiting the country's myriad factional, tribal and regional disputes, that Government was deposed in an army coup led by Colonel Joseph Mobutu, who later established the regime which ruled Zaire – as the country had been renamed – for the next three decades. Under its self-styled philosophy of 'Mobutuisme', Zaire became a byword for gargantuan corruption, nepotism and state-sponsored larceny. Zaire was reduced to penury, barely functioning as a nation state. After the end of the Cold War, the political settlement in South Africa brought the regime to an end.

The military campaign which finally brought down the Mobutu regime was triggered by genocide in neighbouring Rwanda. Once genocide ended, Rwanda's Hutu militia fled into northeastern Zaire. Laurent Kabila then seized control, renaming the country the Democratic Republic of Congo. (Mobutu left for Morocco, where he died shortly afterwards.) Kabila proved incapable either of handling the multifarious elements in his coalition or tackling the country's huge problems.

By mid-1998, full-scale fighting had broken out between disenchanted former allies and forces loyal to Kabila. The war disintegrated into a complex set of distinct and savage conflicts, with participants as concerned with securing access to the country's copious mineral and other resources as with stabilising the country. The civilian population suffered, with thousands of refugees desperately searching for food and shelter. The ruined economy, compounded by a lack of medical care and a high rate of *HIV/AIDS*, contributed to a humanitarian disaster whose scale, by the most conservative estimates, includes at least two million deaths. Laurent Kabila was assassinated in 2001 and his son took over the Presidency. There have been a number of attempts by the UN and the South Africans since then to broker a settlement, most recently in 2003, although fighting has repeatedly resumed. The next election is scheduled for 2006 but sustained peace is, unfortunately, improbable, and it will likely be several decades before the Democratic Republic of Congo is able to function properly.

General Information

AREA: 2.35 million sq km (905,563 sq miles).
POPULATION: 60.09 million (UN estimate 2005).
POPULATION DENSITY: 26 per sq km.
CAPITAL: Kinshasa. **Population**: 6.54 million (UN estimate 2005).
GEOGRAPHY: The Democratic Republic of Congo is the third-largest country in Africa and is bordered to the north by the Central African Republic and Sudan, to the east by Uganda, Rwanda, Burundi and Tanzania, to the south by Zambia and Angola, and to the west by the Republic of Congo and the Angolan enclave, Cabinda. The country has a coastline of only 27km (17 miles), at the outlet of the Congo River, which flows into the Atlantic. The country straddles the Equator and has widely differing geographical features, including mountain ranges in the north and west, a vast central plain through which the Congo River flows, and the volcanoes and lakes of the Kivu region. The river has given rise to extensive tropical rainforests on the western border with the Republic of Congo.
GOVERNMENT: Republic. Gained independence from Belgium in 1960. **Head of State**: President Joseph Kabila since 2001. Kabila took over following the assassination of his father, Laurent-Désiré Kabila. **Recent history:** Laurent Kabila, then a little-known Zairian opposition figure who had been based in Uganda for several decades, was adopted as leader of this newly-formed anti-Mobutu coalition. By the autumn of 1996, this disparate formation, operating as the *Alliance des Forces Démocratiques pour la Liberation du Congo-Zaire* (AFDL), had completed their takeover of the entire country. However, once in power, Kabila proved incapable either of handling the multifarious elements in his coalition or tackling the huge problems which faced the country, which was renamed the Democratic Republic of Congo. By the middle of 1998, full-scale fighting had broken out in the northeast of the country between disenchanted former allies and forces loyal to Kabila, who appealed for support from other African countries: Angola, Namibia and Zimbabwe came in on Kabila's side; Uganda and Rwanda against him. As ever, it is the civilian population who have suffered the most. Laurent Kabila was assassinated in 2001 by one of his bodyguards; his son Joseph took over the Presidency. There have been a number of attempts by the UN and the South Africans to broker a settlement. The most recent one, signed in April 2003, brought a European-led peace-keeping force into the north-eastern region where much of the fighting has taken place.
A constitutional decree issued in May 1997 placed all executive and legislative powers in the hands of the President. A referendum on a new constitution was held in December 2005. If approved, this would pave the way for the country's first democratic election in 2006. It would also limit the power of the President, give more influence to the regions, and strengthen the judicial system.
LANGUAGE: The official language is French. There are many local languages, the most widely spoken being Lingala, Swahili, Tshiluba and Kikongo.
RELIGION: Roman Catholic 50 per cent, Islam 10 per cent, Protestant 20 per cent, indigenous beliefs 10 per cent and Kimbanguist 10 per cent.
ELECTRICITY: 220 volts AC, 50Hz.
SOCIAL CONVENTIONS: Casual clothes are widely suitable although scanty beachwear should be confined to the beach or poolside. **Photography**: A permit is required. Even then, local authorities are likely to be sensitive. Avoid official areas, airports and riverbanks.

Climate

Varies according to distance from the Equator, which lies across the north of the country. The dry season in the north is from December to February, and in the south, April to October. The temperature is warm year round and humidity is high.
Required clothing: Lightweight clothes are recommended all year, with rainwear during the rainy season.

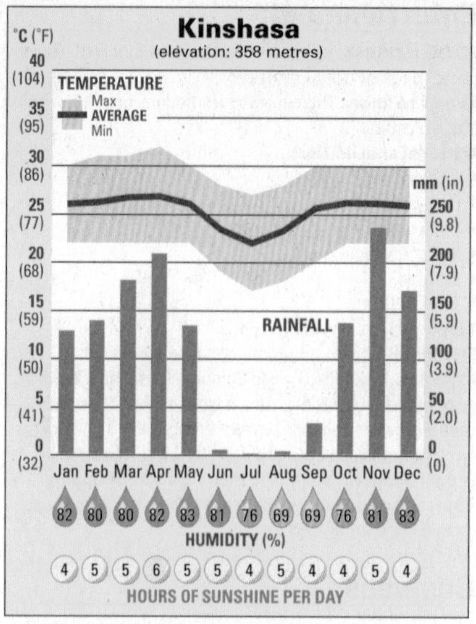
Kinshasa
(elevation: 358 metres)
°C (°F)
TEMPERATURE
Max
AVERAGE
Min
mm (in)
RAINFALL
Jan Feb Mar Apr May Jun Jul Aug Sep Oct Nov Dec
82 80 80 82 83 81 76 69 69 76 81 83
HUMIDITY (%)
4 5 5 6 5 5 4 5 4 4 5 4
HOURS OF SUNSHINE PER DAY

Communications

Telephone: IDD is available. Country code: 243. Internal telephone service is often unreliable and exists only in major towns. Satellite or cellular telephones are often used by international organisations.
Mobile telephone: Roaming agreements exist with a few international mobile phone companies. Using a handset in public can attract unwanted attention and make the user a target for robbery.
Internet: Available, though power shortages may cause difficulties. There are Internet cafes in Kinshasa.
Post: Post office hours: Mon-Sat 0800-1700. The country is included in the Universal Postal Union and the African Postal Union. Airmail to Europe officially takes four to 18 days but in practice can take much longer.
MEDIA: The Congolese media operate against a backdrop of political power struggles and sometimes violent unrest. The press has been able to criticise the Government bodies in certain publications but the media still do so at the risk of threats and possible violence. There are several daily newspapers; many more publications appear sporadically. There are many privately run TV and radio stations. Church radio networks are growing, but the state-controlled broadcasting network reaches the largest numbers of citizens.
Press: The daily newspapers are in various African languages. The main newspapers are *L'Analyste, Boyoma* and *Mjumbe.*
TV: *Radio-Television Nationale Congolaise* (RTNC) operates state-controlled terrestrial and satellite TV. *Television Congolaise* is a Government commercial station run by RTNC. *Canal Kin* and *Raga TV* are private stations. *Antenne E* is a private, commercial station. *Canal Z* is a commercial station.
Radio: *Radio Okapi* is UN-backed and aims to become the only media outlet with national coverage and to enable dialogue across the political divides; available on FM and shortwave. *La Voix du Congo* is state-controlled and operated by RTNC, broadcasting in French, Swahili, Lingala, Tshiluba and Kikongo. The *BBC* and *Voice of America* can be heard in Kinshasa via *Raga FM*. Kinshasa listeners can hear *Radio France Internationale* broadcasts from neighbouring Brazzaville.

Passport/Visa

	Passport Required?	Visa Required?	Return Ticket Required?
Full British	Yes	Yes	Yes
Australian	Yes	Yes	Yes
Canadian	Yes	Yes	Yes
USA	Yes	Yes	Yes
Other EU	Yes	Yes	Yes
Japanese	Yes	Yes	Yes

Note: *Regulations and requirements may be subject to change at short notice, and you are advised to contact the appropriate diplomatic or consular authority before finalising travel arrangements. Any numbers in the chart refer to the footnotes below.*

PASSPORTS: Passport valid for at least six months required by all, plus proof of sufficient funds and a return ticket.
VISAS: Required by all except transit passengers continuing their journey by the same or first connecting aircraft within 48 hours, provided holding valid onward or return documentation and not leaving the airport. French nationals are also exempt.
Types of visa and cost: *Tourist* and *Business. Single-entry*: £40 (one month); £73 (two months); £105 (three months); £145 (six months). *Multiple-entry*: £65 (one month); £97 (two months); £121 (three months); £194 (six months). *Transit*: £24 (seven days).
Validity: Three month from date of issue, although multiples are available.
Application to: Consulate (or consular section at Embassy); see *Passport/Visa information.*
Application requirements: (a) Passport valid for at least six months. (b) One application form. (c) One passport-size photo. (d) Yellow fever vaccination certificate. (e) Stamped, self-addressed envelope (or cost of return postage) for postal applications. (f) Fee (payable on submission of documents for application of visa; cash or postal orders only). (g) Return or onward travel documentation or itinerary from travel agent. *Tourist*: (a)-(g) and, (h) Letter from employer/university giving proof of status. (i) Letter from bank/building society giving proof of sufficient funds. *Business*: (a)-(g) and, (h) Official letter of invitation endorsed by the Congolese authorities (only if a private company). (i) Letter from company in the UK. *Visits to friends and relatives*: (a)-(g) and, (h) Letter from friends/relatives endorsed by the Congolese authorities.
Working days required: Two weeks in person or by post.

PASSPORT/VISA INFORMATION

Embassy of the Democratic Republic of Congo in the UK
281 Gray's Inn Road, London WC1 X8QF, UK
Tel: (020) 7278 9825.
Opening hours: Mon-Fri 0930-1400.

Embassy of the Democratic Republic of Congo in the USA
1726 M Street, Suite 601, NW, Washington, DC 20036, USA
Tel: (202) 234 7690/1.

Money

Currency: Franc Congolais (CDF) = 100 centimes. Owing to the precarious nature of the economy, the denominations of the currency are subject to rapid change.
Currency exchange: Because of the parlous state of the economy, the only true repository of value is the US Dollar. Free circulation of foreign currencies is now allowed within the country. Note that purchase of airline tickets within the country can be made only with money exchanged officially.
Credit & debit cards: The use of MasterCard and Visa is limited to Kinshasa's major hotels. Credit cards cannot be used to obtain cash advances at banks.
Traveller's cheques: Not recommended. Commission fees are very high, and traveller's cheques are not accepted outside Kinshasa.
Currency restrictions: The import and export of local currency is prohibited. The import of foreign currency is limited to US$10,000. The export of foreign currency is unlimited.
Banking hours: Mon-Fri 0800-1130.
Exchange rate indicators:
Rate at time of publishing
£1.00= CDF811.90
$1.00= CDF460.00

Duty Free

The following items may be imported into Congo (Dem Rep) by persons over 18 years of age without incurring customs duty:
200 cigarettes or 50 cigars or 227g of tobacco; one bottle of alcoholic beverage; a reasonable amount of perfume for personal use; cameras if temporarily imported by tourists.
Note: Radios, tape recorders, record players and gifts are subject to duty. An import licence is required for arms and ammunition.

Public Holidays

Below are listed Public Holidays for the January 2006-June 2007 period.
2006: Jan 1 New Year's Day. **Jan 4** Commemoration of the Martyrs of Independence. **Jan 17** National Heroes' Day. **May 1** Labour Day. **May 17** National Liberation Day. **Jun 30** Independence Day. **Aug 1** Parents Day. **Oct 14** Youth Day. **Nov 17** Army Day. **Dec 25** Christmas.
2007: Jan 1 New Year's Day. **Jan 4** Commemoration of the Martyrs of Independence. **Jan 17** National Heroes' Day. **May 1** Labour Day. **May 17** National Liberation Day. **Jun 30** Independence Day.

Health

	Special Precautions?	Certificate Required?
Yellow Fever	Yes	1
Cholera	2	No
Typhoid & Polio	3	N/A
Malaria	4	N/A

Note: *Regulations and requirements may be subject to change at short notice, and you are advised to contact your doctor well in advance of your intended date of departure. Any numbers in the chart refer to the footnotes below.*

1: A *yellow fever* vaccination certificate is required by travellers over one year of age.
2: Following WHO guidelines issued in 1973, a *cholera* vaccination certificate is not an official condition of entry to Congo (Dem Rep). However, *cholera* is a serious risk in this country and precautions are essential. Up-to-date advice should be sought before deciding whether these precautions should include vaccination as medical opinion is divided over its effectiveness. See the *Health* appendix.
3: Immunisation or boosters for *typhoid* are recommended and vaccination against *poliomyelitis* is sometimes advised.
4: *Malaria* risk, predominantly in the malignant *falciparum* form, exists throughout the year in the whole country. The malignant form is reported to be highly resistant to chloroquine and sulfadoxine-pyrimethamine. Mefloquine is the recommended prophylaxis.
Food & Drink: All water should be regarded as being a potential health risk. Water used for drinking, brushing teeth or making ice should have first been boiled or otherwise sterilised. Milk is unpasteurised and should be boiled. Powdered or tinned milk is available and is advised, but make sure that it is reconstituted with pure water. Avoid dairy products that are likely to have been made from unboiled milk. Only eat well-cooked meat and fish, preferably served hot. Pork, salad and mayonnaise may carry increased risk. Vegetables should be cooked and fruit peeled.
Other risks: *Bilharzia* (*schistosomiasis*) is present. Avoid swimming and paddling in fresh water; swimming pools which are well chlorinated and maintained are safe.
Hepatitis A, B and *E* are present and *meningococcal meningitis* may occur. *Plague* is present in natural foci. Further information should be sought from the Department of Health. There is a very high risk of *diarrhoeal diseases*, the *dysenteries* and various *parasitic worm infections*; observe strict food and drink caution. *Leishmaniasis* and human *trypanosomiasis* (sleeping sickness) are present. *Ebola* outbreaks have occurred. The Government has, as of October 2005, imposed a quarantine zone on the Congo (Dem Rep)-Angola border in response to the outbreak of the Marburg fever in the Uige Province, northern Angola. Avoid tick bites which spread *African tick typhus*. Wear shoes to avoid soil-borne parasites.
Rabies is present. For those at high risk, vaccination before arrival should be considered. If you are bitten, seek medical advice without delay. For more information, consult the *Health* appendix.
Health care: Government expenditure on health is low and the quality of hospitals is poor. It is advisable to take specific personal medicines as well as supplies such as syringes and drip needles, as medical facilities are available only in larger centres. Doctors and hospitals expect cash payment in full for health services. Health insurance is *essential* and it is advisable to include cover for emergency air evacuation.

Travel - International

AIR:
Airlines serving Congo (Dem Rep) include *Air France, Air Gabon, Cameroon Airlines, Ethiopian Airlines, Kenya Airways, KLM* and *South African Airways*.
Approximate flight times: From Kinshasa to *London* is 10 hours 30 minutes including stopover in Brussels.
Main airports: *Kinshasa (N'Djili) (FIH)* is 25km (15 miles) east of the city. *To/from the airport*: Buses run to and from the city. Taxis are available. *Facilities*: 24-hour bank/bureau de change, post office, restaurant and car hire, but all services are erratic and unreliable.
Departure tax: CDF500.
SEA/RIVER:
The international port is *Matadi* on the Congo River. There are no passenger services to or from Matadi at present. *To/from the port*: Ferries usually operate across the Congo River from Brazzaville to Kinshasa, although services are sporadic at present. In peacetime, there are ferries along the Oubangui River to the Central African Republic.
RAIL:
In peacetime, there are rail services to Dar es Salaam in Tanzania and Lobito in Angola; and connections to Zambia, Zimbabwe, Mozambique and South Africa.
ROAD:
Most of Congo's (Dem Rep) borders are closed or very dangerous. Even in peacetime, the roads are mostly in bad condition and impassable in the rainy season. There are connecting roads to surrounding countries, the major routes being through Sudan, Uganda and Zambia.

Travel - Internal

AIR:
There are connections from *N'Djili Airport* (Kinshasa) to over 40 internal airports and 150 landing strips. Small planes may be available for charter.
RIVER:
Over 1600km (1000 miles) of the Congo River are navigable and, in normal circumstances, there are services from Kinshasa to the upriver ports of Kisangani and Ilébo. Services at present, however, are unreliable owing to political instability and fuel shortages.
RAIL:
The main internal railway runs from Lubumbashi to Ilébo, with a branch to Kalemie and Kindu, and from Kinshasa to the port of Matadi. Rail services are generally subject to disruption. There is no air conditioning, but there are couchettes and dining cars on the principal trains.
ROAD:
Traffic drives on the right. Owing to poor maintenance, the roads are among the worst in Africa and only achieve a fair standard around the main towns. It is wise to check that bridges are safe before crossing. Vehicle thefts, including hijackings at gunpoint, occur. **Bus**: Services run between the main towns but are crowded and unreliable. **Taxi**: Available in Kinshasa but unreliable. **Car hire**: Available on a limited basis at the airport. **Documentation**: International Driving Permit required.
URBAN:
Conventional bus services in Kinshasa can be severely overcrowded. Minibuses and converted truck-buses also offer public transport, and are known as *fula fulas*. Pick-up trucks are known as 'taxibuses'. A better standard of transport is provided by shared taxis, which are widely available. There is little or no public transport in most other large centres.

Travel Advice

Travellers are advised against all travel to eastern and northeastern Congo (Democratic Republic of), which remains insecure. This includes entering Congo (Dem Rep) from Uganda or Rwanda.
There are indefinite restrictions on tourist travel within or across the country. A permit from the Ministry of the Interior is required for all travel outside the capital. Government curfews are in force in Kinshasa. There are safety concerns about all public transport, including Congolese aircraft.
The threat from terrorism is low but there remains recurrent demonstrations and clashes. Political demonstrations in Kinshasa and elsewhere on 30 June 2005 were dispersed but with some casualties and arrests. There has also been an increase in street robbery of foreigners in Kinshasa by individuals posing as plain-clothes police.
The Government has, as of October 2005, imposed a quarantine zone on the Congo (Dem Rep)-Angola border in response to the outbreak of the Marburg fever in the Uige Province, northern Angola.
This advice is based on information provided by the Foreign and Commonwealth Office in the UK. It is correct at time of publishing. As the situation can change rapidly, visitors are advised to contact the following organisations for the latest travel advice:

British Foreign and Commonwealth Office
Tel: (0845) 850 2829.
Website: www.fco.gov.uk

US Department of State
Website: http://travel.state.gov/travel

Accommodation

The difficult terrain has resulted in relatively few settlements except along river banks. Accommodation is essentially restricted to the main cities, and is virtually non-existent in the interior. For further details, contact the Embassy. The few hotels that cater for visitors are expensive and generally booked up well in advance. The majority of hotels are in Kinshasa, with others in Boma, Bukavu, Kerning, Kisangani, Kolwezi, Lubumbashi, Matadi, Mbandaka, Mbanzangunu and Muanda.

Top Things To See & Do

Note: See *Travel Advice* before travelling to Congo (Dem Rep).

- **Kinshasa**, the capital does not have many sights of historic interest, but the visitor interested in the past should not miss the prehistoric and ethnological museums at **Kinshasa University**, an ensemble of light, rectangular, well laid-out buildings standing on a hillside. A brightly coloured chapel crowns the top of the hill. Nearby is a corner of the equatorial forest surrounding a beautiful lake called **Ma Vallée** with a tavern on its banks. Other attractions include the **fishing** port of **Kinkole**, the **Gardens of the Presidential Farm of Nsele** made of pagodas, and the extensive pools where angling and swimming may be enjoyed. In both the markets and the suburbs of Kinshasa, there are craftspeople who produce wood and metal items. The **National Museum** includes some unique pieces of national art.
- In the southwest, the **Inkisi Falls** (60m/197ft high) at **Zongo**, and the caves in the region of **Mbanza-Ngungu**, may be visited in one day, but it is preferable to stay for two or three days, for Mbanza-Ngungu is a pleasant resort with a good climate.
- While in the Mbanza-Ngungu area, stop at **Kisantu** to visit the **Frère Gillet Botanic Gardens** with their world-famous rare **orchids**.
- The woods, caves and waterfalls of **Boma** and equatorial **Mayumbe** and the **Tombs of Tshela** can be visited on the way to the ocean beach of **Moanda**.
- **Upemba National Park** straddles the **River Lualaba**, northeast of **Bukama**, and includes several lakes inhabited by hippos, crocodiles and numerous aquatic birds. Here too are fishermen, cattle farmers and peasants, as well as a number of mining communities. In the north is the **Garamba National Park**, covering 400,000 hectares and featuring lions, leopards, elephants, rhinos and giraffes. Virunga National Park comprises two jagged mountain ranges and **game** that includes lions, elephants, warthogs, buffaloes, hippos and antelopes. Best of all, this park is also renowned for its **mountain gorillas**.
- Enjoy the Democratic Republic of Congo's areas of watery beauty: **Kalemie** and the banks of **Lake Tanganyika** are reminiscent of the French Riviera; the whole of the south is dotted with freshwater lakes such as **Munkamba**, **Fwa** and **Kasai**, with **Lake Albert** containing more fish than any other lake in Africa and **Lake Edward** being home to birds of all sizes and colours; and there are numerous impressive waterfalls, such as **Kiobo**, on the **River Lufira**, and **Lofol**, 384m (1259ft) high, north of **Lubumbashi**.
- **Bunia** is the point of departure for numerous excursions into the forests and mountains, native villages, the **Caves of Mount Hoyo** and the **Escaliers de Venus Falls**.
- See the highest peak in the **Ruwenzori range**, the **Pic Marguerite**, at an altitude of 5119m (15,795ft). The snowline is at 533m (1776ft). This region is also inhabited by gorillas and by the extremely rare okapi. The **mountain** scenery between **Goma** and **Beni** was regarded as some

of the most spectacular in Africa, although the volcanic eruption of **Nyiragongo**, 3470m (11,385ft) in January 2002, damaged the surrounding area to some extent.

TOURIST INFORMATION

Office National du Tourisme in Congo
2 A/B Avenue des Oranges, BP 9502, Kinshasa-Gombe, Congo (Dem Rep)
Tel: (12) 30070.

Entertainment

FOOD & DRINK: There are a number of good restaurants in Kinshasa and Lubumbashi, but prices are high. Hotels and restaurants which cater for tourists are generally expensive and serve international and national dishes. Small restaurants and snack bars offer Chinese, French and Belgium food.
National specialities:
• *Moambe* chicken with rice and spinach.
• Fried yams.
• Corn and beans.
National drinks:
• *Paupau paradise.*
• *Pineapple bugada.*
• *White elephant* (coconut, rum and milk).
Tipping: 10 per cent service charge is added to hotel and restaurant bills. Extra tipping is unnecessary.
NIGHTLIFE: Kinshasa is the best place for nightlife, especially in the sprawling township of the *Cité*, where most of the population live. In spite of recent political turmoil, the local music scene is thriving. There are hundreds of dance clubs in Kinshasa. Congolese music is popular throughout Africa as well as in Europe and the USA.
SHOPPING: Local craftware includes bracelets, ebony carvings and paintings. The large towns all have markets and shopping centres, selling everything from fresh ginger to baskets and African carvings. **Shopping hours:** Mon-Sat 0800-1200 and 1500-1800.

Business

• **GDP:** US$42.74 billion.
• **Main exports:** Diamonds, crude oil, coffee, copper and cobalt.
• **Main imports:** Food stuff, fuels, machinery and transport equipment.
• **Main trade partners:** France, Belgium, South Africa and Finland.

ECONOMY: With rich agricultural land and extensive mineral and energy deposits, the Democratic Republic of Congo is potentially one of the richest countries on the African continent. However, decades of chronic neglect at the hands of the corrupt Mobutu left it as one of the poorest, with a per capita annual income of just US$150. Such plans as the Kabila governments may have had for development have been undermined by the civil war. Moreover, no significant development aid – essential to rebuild the country's infrastructure – can be expected until the conflict has ended. At least two-thirds of the population are engaged in subsistence farming: farmers produce palm oil, coffee, tea, cocoa, rubber, cotton, tropical woods, fruit, vegetables and rice. Industry runs well below capacity due to a lack of spare parts and foreign exchange with which to buy them. The country could be one of the world's largest producers of copper and cobalt, but production is far short of its potential; what is produced is sold by the warring party in control of the mine to finance continued fighting. (In some cases, mining concessions have been handed over to a government ally in exchange for military support: Zimbabwe, which controls several copper mines in the south is the most notable example.) The mining sector can also produce manganese, zinc, uranium and tin. There are also some oil deposits located off the short Atlantic coastline. Manufacturing for domestic consumption dominates the industrial sector, producing textiles, cement, food and beverages, wood products and plastics. Businesspeople should wear lightweight suits. Interpreter and translation services are available as business is mainly conducted in French. The best time to visit is in the cool season (which varies from one part of the country to another). **Office hours:** Mon-Fri 0730-1500, Sat 0730-1200.

COMMERCIAL INFORMATION

Chambre de Commerce, d'Industrie et d'Agriculture de la République Démocratique du Congo
BP 7247, 10 avenue des Aviateurs, Kinshasa, Congo (Dem Rep)
Tel: (12) 22286.

Congo, Republic of

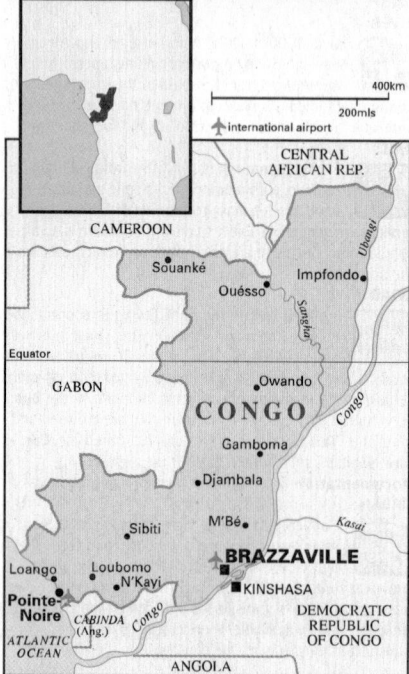

Location: West coast of Central Africa.

Time: GMT + 1.

Overview

In 1960, the country now known as the Republic of Congo was granted full independence. Abbé Fulbert Youlou, a Catholic priest, was elected President and guided the Congo into a single-party state, in accordance with the trend throughout Africa. Since independence, the country has been plagued by civil wars and militia conflicts. The former French colony experienced the first of two destructive bouts of fighting when disputed Parliamentary elections in 1993 led to bloody, ethnically-based fighting between pro-Government forces and the opposition and in 1997, ethnic and political tensions exploded into a full-scale civil war, fuelled in part by the prize of the country's offshore oil wealth, which motivated many of the warlords. By the end of 1999, the rebels had lost all their key positions to the Government forces, who were backed by Angolan troops. Although a peace accord was signed with southern rebels in 2003, remnants of the civil war militias, known as Ninjas, are still active in the southern Pool region. Such in-fighting and poverty contrast strongly with the Republic of Congo's rich landscape of falls, swamps and rapids, with the northern country distinguished by huge tracts of virgin forest and an abundance of wildlife. The forest is also home to several indigenous tribes who have maintained their traditional way of life. The narrow sandy coastal plain is broken by lagoons, behind which rise the Mayombe Mountains. The capital, Brazzaville, has a host of fascinating sights to see and places to explore, and local musicians enliven the atmosphere at night.

General Information

AREA: 342,000 sq km (132,046 sq miles).
POPULATION: 3 million (UN estimate 2005).
POPULATION DENSITY: 11 per sq km.
CAPITAL: Brazzaville. **Population:** 600,000 (2005).
GEOGRAPHY: Congo is situated in Africa, bordered to the north by Cameroon and the Central African Republic, to the south and east by the Democratic Republic of Congo, to the

---

southwest by the Atlantic, and to the west by Gabon. The Cabinda Enclave, belonging to Angola, lies to the southwest, on the Atlantic coast. Vast areas are swamps, grassland or thick forests with rivers being virtually the only means of internal travel. The vast River Congo and its major tributaries form most of the country's border with the Democratic Republic of Congo, drawing much of its water from the swamplands in the north of the country. The narrow sandy coastal plain is broken by lagoons, behind which rise the Mayombe Mountains. Most of the population lives in the south of the country.
GOVERNMENT: Republic. Gained independence from France in 1960. **Head of State and Government:** President Denis Sassou-Nguesso since 1997. **Recent history:** In the summer of 1992, the *Union Panafricaine pour la Démocratie Sociale* (UPADS) was brought to power as the major party in both the National Assembly and the Senate, while its leader, Pascal Lissouba, won the Presidential poll. Over the next few years, there were occasional outbreaks of fighting between the army and militias loyal to Sassou-Nguesso. These intensified from 1997 onwards when, with some support from allies in Angola, Sassou-Nguesso launched a full-scale military campaign against the Lissouba Government. In October 1997, Sassou-Nguesso's troops took the capital and installed their leader as President. A National Transitional Council was established in January 1998 to plot a course towards national elections and a return to civilian rule. However, over the next four years, the military Government came under sustained military assault, first from supporters of Lissouba and then from ex-Government troops loyal to ex-premier Bernard Kolelas who had been dismissed by Sassou-Nguesso. Repeated attempts at mediation by outside parties failed until, in April 2001, a formula devised by President Omar Bongo of Gabon and backed by the Organisation of African Unity secured the agreement of both sides. Under the banner of United Democratic Forces, Sassou-Ngessou stood at the March 2002 presidential election, defeating four other token candidates and securing 90 per cent of the vote. Kignomba Mbougou, standing for UPADS (Lissouba's party) gained just three per cent. By mid-2003, the country was largely at peace, although there has been fighting in the Pool region, adjacent to the capital, Brazzaville, between the army and a rebel group known as the Ninjas: although this has been sporadic, it has caused a serious refugee problem with an estimated 150,000 displaced as a result.
LANGUAGE: The official language is French. Other major languages are Lingala, Munukutuba and Kikongo. English is spoken very little.
RELIGION: The majority follow Christian beliefs (mainly Roman Catholic: 50 per cent), with most of the remainder following animist belief systems (48 per cent). There are small Protestant and Muslim minorities.
ELECTRICITY: 220/230 volts AC, 50Hz.
SOCIAL CONVENTIONS: Normal courtesies should be observed when visiting people's homes. Gifts are acceptable as a token of thanks, especially if invited for a meal. Dress should be casual, and informal wear is acceptable in most places. Mini-skirts and shorts should not be worn in most public places. Artistic carving, both traditional and modern dance, as well as folk songs, play an important part in Congolese culture, which is strongly based on tradition. Do not smoke or drink alcohol in public places during Ramadan.
Photography: It is forbidden to photograph public buildings.

Climate

Equatorial climate with short rains from October to December and long rains between mid-January and mid-May. The main dry season is from June to October.
Required clothing: Practical lightweight cottons and linens with a light raincoat or umbrella in the rainy season.

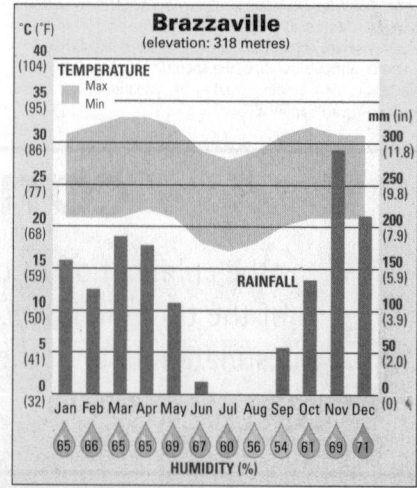

Communications

Telephone: IDD service is available in major cities only. Country code: 242. Links with Western Europe are generally poor.
Mobile telephone: Roaming agreements exist with a few international mobile phone companies. Coverage is mainly limited to Brazzaville and Pointe Noire.
Internet: Limited acces. Facilities are available at some hotels.
Post: There is an unreliable internal service. Post office hours: Mon-Fri 0730/0800-1200 and 1430-1730; and (for stamps and telegrams) Mon-Sat 0800-2000; Sun and public holidays 0800-1200. Post takes four to 18 days to arrive in Europe.
MEDIA: Broadcasts on state-run radio and television stations generally reflect Government views. Broadcasts from neighbouring Congo (Dem Rep) can be received, and rebroadcasts of *Radio France Internationale*, the *BBC* and *Voice of America* are available in Brazzaville. There are now no prison terms for libel and insult but incitement to violence and racism remains punishable. All newspapers in Brazzaville are all privately-owned and some may include criticism of the Government.
Press: Daily papers, which are all published in French, include *ACI Actualité*, *Aujourd'hui* and *Mweti Journal de Brazzaville*.
TV: *TV Congo* is operated by state-run Radiodiffusion Television Congolaise.
Radio: *Radio Brazzaville* and *Radio Congo* are state-run (the former is limited to the capital area only). *Radio Liberte* is a privately-run station.

Passport/Visa

	Passport Required?	Visa Required?	Return Ticket Required?
Full British	Yes	Yes	Yes
Australian	Yes	Yes	Yes
Canadian	Yes	Yes	Yes
USA	Yes	Yes	Yes
Other EU	Yes	Yes	Yes
Japanese	Yes	Yes	Yes

Note: *Regulations and requirements may be subject to change at short notice, and you are advised to contact the appropriate diplomatic or consular authority before finalising travel arrangements. Any numbers in the chart refer to the footnotes below.*

PASSPORTS: Passport valid for at least six months required by all.
VISAS: Required by all.
Note: Nationals of Congo possessing dual nationality *do* require visas if travelling on their other passport.
Types of visa and cost: *Tourist* and *Business*: £40 for 15 days; £60 for one month; £100 for three months. All visas are multiple entry.
Validity: Dependent on length of visa.
Application to: Consulate (or consular section at Embassy); see *Passport/Visa Information*.
Application requirements: (a) Valid passport. (b) One completed application form. (c) One passport-size photo in colour. (d) Return or onward ticket. (e) Fee, payable in cash or by postal order. (f) Yellow fever vaccination certificate for travellers aged over one year. (g) Stamped, self-addressed envelope (or cost of return postage) for postal applications. *Tourist*: (a)-(g) and, (h) Authorised lodging certificate, provided by a resident or national of the Republic of Congo or a hotel reservation. (i) Proof of sufficient funds (credit card, pay slips, proof of employment). *Business*: (a)-(g) and, (h) Letter from employer verifying the applicant's identity, purpose of travel and length of stay, giving the name and address of a contact in the Republic of Congo and taking responsibility for the applicant.
Note: (a) Applications made by post must be accompanied by a postal order (cheques not accepted) for £5 to cover postal charges (UK and Republic of Ireland only).
(b) A stamped, self addresssed envelope. (c) Vaccination certificates for cholera and tetanus may also be required. (d) All journalists, photographers and researchers must obtain written permission to carry out filming or research *before* entering the country.
Working days required: Visas issued immediately for applications made in person or 24 hours after date of receipt for postal applications.

PASSPORT/VISA INFORMATION

Honorary Consulate of the Republic of Congo in the UK
Arena, 24 Southwark Bridge Road, London SE1 9HF, UK
Tel: (020) 7922 0695.
Opening hours: Mon-Fri 1030-1530.

Embassy of the Republic of Congo and Tourist Office in France
37 bis rue Paul Valéry, 75116 Paris, France
Tel: (1) 4500 6057.

Embassy of the Republic of Congo in the USA
4891 Colorado Avenue NW, Washington DC 20011, USA
Tel: (202) 726 0825 or 5500.

Money

Currency: CFA Franc (XAF) = 100 centimes. Notes are in denominations of XAF10,000, 5000, 2000, 1000 and 500. Coins are in denominations of XAF250, 100, 50, 25, 10, 5 and 1. Congo is part of the French Monetary Area. Only currency issued by the *Banque des États de l'Afrique Centrale* (Bank of Central African States) is valid; currency issued by the *Banque des États de l'Afrique de l'Ouest* (Bank of West African States) is not. The CFA Franc is tied to the Euro. However, US dollars are the prefered currency.
Credit & debit cards: Diners Club and MasterCard all have limited use. Check with your credit or debit card company for details of merchant acceptability and other services which may be available. Hotels in Brazzaville and Point Noire accept major credit or debit cards, although prefer cash. One bank in Brazzaville has an ATM.
Traveller's cheques: To avoid additional exchange rate charges, travellers are advised to take traveller's cheques in Euros or Pounds Sterling. These are accepted only in the larger cities.
Currency restrictions: The import and export of local currency is prohibited, except between countries of the Central African group. The import of foreign currency is unrestricted, although amounts over £234/US$335 must be declared upon arrival. Export of foreign currency is restricted to the amount imported. Exchanging money is illegal.
Banking hours: 0630-1300 Monday to Friday (counters close at 1130).
Exchange rate indicators:
Rate at time of publishing:

£1.00=	XAF952.73
$1.00=	XAF541.38

Duty Free

The following items may be imported into Congo by visitors over 18 years of age without incurring customs duty:
200 cigarettes or one box of cigars or tobacco (women are permitted to import cigarettes only); one bottle of spirits and one bottle of wine; a reasonable quantity of perfume in opened bottles.
Note: If importing expensive items such as watches and cameras, it is advisable to present the receipt.

Public Holidays

Below are listed Public Holidays for the January 2006-June 2007 period.
2006: Jan 1 New Year's Day. **Mar 8** Congolese Women's Day. **May 1** Labour Day. **Jun 10** Commemoration of the National Sovereign Conference. **Aug 15** National Day. **Dec 25** Christmas.
2007: Jan 1 New Year's Day. **Mar 8** Congolese Women's Day. **May 1** Labour Day. **Jun 10** Commemoration of the National Sovereign Conference.

Health

	Special Precautions?	Certificate Required?
Yellow Fever	Yes	1
Cholera	Yes	2
Typhoid & Polio	3	N/A
Malaria	4	N/A

Note: *Regulations and requirements may be subject to change at short notice, and you are advised to contact your doctor well in advance of your intended date of departure. Any numbers in the chart refer to footnotes below.*

1: A *yellow fever* vaccination certificate is required for all travellers over one year of age.
2: Following WHO guidelines issued in 1973, a cholera vaccination certificate is no longer a condition of entry to Congo. However, cholera is a serious risk in this country and precautions are essential. Up-to-date advice should be sought before deciding whether these precautions should include vaccination as medical opinion is divided over its effectiveness; see the *Health* appendix.
3: Immunisations or boosters for *typhoid* and *poliomyelitis* are advised.
4: Malaria risk exists all year throughout the country, predominantly in the malignant *falciparum* form. Resistance to chloroquine and sulfadoxine-pyrimethamine has been reported. A weekly dose of 250mg of mefloquine is the recommended prophylaxis.
Food & Drink: All water should be regarded as being potentially contaminated. Water used for drinking, brushing teeth or making ice should have first been boiled or otherwise sterilised. Milk is unpasteurised and should be boiled. Powdered or tinned milk is available and is advised, but make sure that it is reconstituted with pure water. Avoid dairy products which are likely to have been made from unboiled milk. Only eat well cooked meat and fish, preferably served hot. Pork, salad and mayonnaise may carry increased risk. Vegetables should be cooked and fruit peeled.
Other risks: *Bilharzia (schistosomiasis)* is present. Avoid swimming and paddling in fresh water; swimming pools which are well chlorinated and maintained are safe. *River blindness (onchocerciasis)* and *sleeping sickness (trypanosomiasis)* are also prevalent. *Hepatitis A* is widespread and *hepatitis B* is hyperendemic. *Meningococcal A* and *C* have been reported and immunisation is recommended. As of May 2005, there has been an outbreak of the deadly virus, *ebola haemorrhagic fever*, in the northeastern town of Etoumbi and in Mbomo. The former town was placed in quarantine and the virus was contained. It is thought that the virus was spread by consuming infected monkey meat. Nationals and all visitors are warned not to eat bush meat whilst the containment continues. Visitors may wish to be extra prudent and bypass the Cuvette West region.
Rabies is present. For those at high risk, vaccination before arrival should be considered. If you are bitten, seek medical advice without delay. For more information, consult the *Health* appendix.
Health care: Medical and dental facilities are generally very limited outside Brazzaville. Health insurance is essential. Medicines are in short supply and it is advised that, if needs dictate, visitors bring their own medicine, with official labels, into the country.

Travel - International

AIR:
Aero Benin, *Air France*, *Air Service Gabon* and *Cameroon Airlines* operate international services to Congo (Rep of).
Approximate flight times: From *London* to Brazzaville is approximately 11 hours (including up to three hours for stopover in Paris).
Main airports: *Brazzaville (BZV)* (Maya Maya) is 4km (2 miles) northwest of the city. *To/from the airport*: Buses and taxis are available to the city. *Facilities*: A restaurant and car hire.
Pointe-Noire (PNR) is 5.5km (3.5 miles) from the city. *To/from the airport*: Taxis are available to the city.
Departure tax: XAF500.
SEA/RIVER:
Cargo ships dock at *Pointe-Noire*. An hourly car ferry operates between Kinshasa (Democratic Republic of Congo) and *Brazzaville* across the Congo River (travel time – 20 minutes). Ferries operate to and from the Central African Republic on the Ubangi.
ROAD:
There is a road connection from Lambaréné in Gabon to Loubomo and Brazzaville. The road from Cameroon is usable only during the dry season. There is a good road between Pointe-Noire and Cabinda (Angola). Entry can also be made via the Democratic Republic of Congo. **Documentation**: A *carnet de passage en douane* is needed to cross land borders between Congo and the neighbouring countries. Further information can be obtained from national motoring organisations.

Travel - Internal

AIR:
The national airline, *Lina Congo (GC)*, operates regular services from Brazzaville to Pointe-Noire, with stops in Loubomo and Ouesso. Private charters are available.
Departure tax: XAF 3400.

A B C D E F G H I J K L M N O P Q R S T U V W X Y Z

RIVER:
Inland steamers ply from Brazzaville up the Congo and Ubangi. Rivers are vital to internal transport.
RAIL:
Congo-Océan railway company operates services between Brazzaville and Pointe-Noire (travel time – up to three days). Known as the 'Peace Train', this service endured a long suspension due to civil war, and still incurs occasional disruptions. Services between Mbinda and Pointe-Noire are also due to resume soon. Advance booking is recommended. Children under five years travel free. Half-fare is charged for children aged five to nine.
ROAD:
Roads are mostly earth tracks, sandy in dry season and impassable in the wet, suitable for 4-wheel drive vehicles only. There are 1207km (750 miles) of paved roads. Traffic drives on the right. Poorly marked army checkpoints, often manned by undisciplined soldiers, exist throughout the country. Travel at night on unfamiliar roads can be dangerous and should be avoided. **Car hire**: There are several car hire firms represented in Brazzaville, lists of which can be obtained from main hotels.
Documentation: An International Driving Permit is required.
URBAN:
Brazzaville has a minibus and taxi service. Taxis are also available in Pointe-Noire and Loubomo. Taxi fares have a flat rate and fares should be agreed beforehand.

Travel Advice

The threat from terrorism is low.
Travellers are advised against all but essential travel outside the main cities of Brazzaville and Pointe Noire as there is some instability and risk of rebel activity in the countryside. There were armed clashes in the Bacongo area of Brazzaville in 2006, which reportedly left seven civilians dead.
There was an outbreak of the Ebola-virus in the Mbomo and Etoumbi regions in May 2005.
This advice is based on information provided by the Foreign and Commonwealth Office in the UK. It is correct at time of publishing. As the situation can change rapidly, visitors are advised to contact the following organisations for the latest travel advice:

British Foreign and Commonwealth Office
Tel: (0845) 850 2829.
Website: www.fco.gov.uk

US Department of State
Website: http://travel.state.gov/travel

Accommodation

HOTELS:
There are five good hotels in Brazzaville, three in Loubomo and four in Pointe-Noire. Prices and advance bookings can be obtained via *Air France*. Outside the towns mentioned above, accommodation for visitors is limited.
CAMPING/CARAVANNING:
Available at Cargo-Point, southeast of Moruya. Be sure to hire a guide and take essentials such as water and food.
SELF-CATERING:
Available in Point-Noire and Brazzaville. Be expected to pay high prices.

Top Things To See & Do

- The capital city of **Brazzaville** is situated on the west side of **Malebo Pool** on the **River Congo**. Sights to see include the beautiful **Basilique Sainte Anne**, the colourful suburb of **Poto Poto**, the **Temple Mosque**, the markets at **Oluendze** and **Moungali**, the **National Museum**, the **Municipal Gardens** and the house constructed for de Gaulle when Brazzaville was the capital of Free France.
- Play **golf** at the golf course in Brazzaville, the **Cité du Djoué**.
- The first church in Congo was built in 1882 by a French priest and is located in **Linzolo**, 30km (19 miles) from the capital. The city is also home to the regional seat of the **World Health Organization** and a very good **market**.
- The historic village of **M'Bé** is the capital of **King Makoko**.
- Some good **fishing** is available at **Lac Bleu**.
- Visit the **Valley of Butterflies**.
- Venture onto the **Congo Rapids**. **Waterskiing** on the Congo and **Kouillou rivers** is a popular sporting activity in peacetime.
- Find a panoramic view of the surrounding countryside at the **Loufoulakari Falls** (held to be the most impressive falls in the region) and the **Trou de Dieu**.
- The main town on the coast is **Pointe-Noire** (with its lively evening **market**), and there are several good beaches close by in the region known as the **Côte Sauvage**. Around 20km (12 miles) from the city are the villages of **Loango** and **Diosso**. Loango was the main embarkation port for slaves and it is estimated that more than 2 million people were transported from here. The **Gorges of Diosso**, spectacular cliffs formed by the erosion of the sea and the wind, are worth visiting.

TOURIST INFORMATION

Direction Générale du Tourisme et des Loisirs
BP 456, Brazzaville, Congo (Rep)
Tel: 830 953.

Entertainment

FOOD & DRINK: The main hotels in Brazzaville have good restaurants serving French cuisine, and there are also restaurants specialising in Italian, Lebanese and Vietnamese dishes. Some restaurants, such as those at Nanga Lake and Grand Hotel in Loubomo, specialise in African dishes. Pointe-Noire and Loubomo also have restaurants and bars, usually in hotels, with table service. Some bars also have counter service.
National specialities:
- Fish (giant oysters and shrimps).
- *Piri piri chicken* (with chili pepper).
- *Mouamba* (chicken in palm oil).
- *Saka saka* (ground cassava leaves cooked with palm oil and peanut paste).
- *Maboke* (freshwater fish cooked in large *marantacee* leaves).

National drinks:
- Beer.
- Fruit juice (pineapple, and mango are the favourites).

Tipping: Normally 10 per cent in hotels and restaurants. Porters and taxi drivers do not expect tips.
NIGHTLIFE: Local groups are popular in the main towns. Brazzaville and Pointe-Noire have several nightclubs.
SHOPPING: In Brazzaville, there are shops and colourful markets. An arts and crafts centre at Poto Poto sells, amongst other things, local paintings and carved wooden masks and figures. The two main markets are Moungali and Ouenze. Avenue Foch is crowded with street vendors. Basketwork can be bought at the villages of Makana and M'Pila (3km/2 miles from Brazzaville), with pottery and an open-air market. **Shopping hours**: Mon-Sat 0800-1200 and 1500-1800. Some shops close on Monday afternoon and a few open on Sunday morning.

Business

- **GDP:** US$42.74 billion.
- **Main exports:** Petroleum, sawn timber, diamonds, cocoa and sugar.
- **Main imports:** Machinery, steel, foodstuffs and iron.
- **Main trading partners:** France, Germany, China, Italy, USA and Belgium.

ECONOMY: About 60 per cent of the country is covered by tropical forest, roughly half of which can be exploited economically. Forestry is thus an important part of the economy and, along with agriculture, employs about two-thirds of the working population. Both subsistence crops (cassava, plantains) and cash crops (sugar, palm oil, coffee, cocoa) are grown; even so, Congo continues to depend on a large quantity of imported food. A further 20 per cent of the workforce is employed in various industries, of which the most important is oil. The first field came on stream in 1960 and the industry now accounts for 90 per cent of Congo's export earnings; it also allows the country a trade surplus under normal circumstances, even though the oil sector's contribution to GNP has dropped from 40 per cent in 1985 to its current level of about 20 per cent. Strengthening of the non-oil economy remains the main long-term objective. Unfortunately, the Government's economic planning and reforms have been undermined by political instability, erratic implementation, and fractious relations with the IMF and World Bank (which have underwritten it). The USA is the largest oil purchaser, followed by France and Spain. France provides two-thirds of Congo's imports, consisting largely of machinery, transport equipment, chemicals, iron and steel as well as foodstuffs. Annual per capita income, at US$800, is relatively high by regional standards. Congo is a member of the CFA Franc Zone and of the Central African Economic and Customs Union (CEEAC).
BUSINESS ETIQUETTE: Jackets and ties are not usually worn by men on business visits but are expected when visiting Government officials. A knowledge of French is essential as there are no professional translators available. Normal courtesies should be observed and the best months for business visits are January to March and June to September.
Office hours: Usually Mon-Fri 0700-1400, Sat 0700-1200.

Cook Islands

Location: South Pacific, Polynesia.

Time: GMT - 10.

The Cook Islands are self governing 'in free association' with New Zealand and are represented abroad in countries where they have no Consular offices by New Zealand Embassies and High Commissions (see *New Zealand* section).

Overview

The Cook Islands are situated 3500km (2200 miles) northeast of New Zealand and 1000km (600 miles) southwest of Tahiti in the South Pacific, forming part of Polynesia. The islands fall into two groups: the scattered Northern Group are all coral atolls while the Southern Group is of volcanic origin. Most of the larger islands include lagoons surrounded by small areas of fertile land above which rise volcanic hills. Unsurprisingly, given their beauty, the Cook Islands have been used as the setting for several films, the best known being *Merry Christmas Mr Lawrence*.
The islands were named after Captain James Cook, who became the first European to sight them in 1733. However, credit for the first discovery of these islands must go to the Polynesians who discovered them during their great migratory journeys across the Pacific in the seventh and eighth centuries. The main island, Rarotonga, was rediscovered by the Bounty Mutineers in 1789. In 1888 they became a British protectorate, and in 1901 became part of New Zealand. But in 1965, the islands achieved self-government as a New Zealand Dependency.
People come to the Cook Islands for the beaches – and unspoiled ones, at that. The Cook Islands, despite covering a vast area, have a very small population, and the islands do not possess any of the large tourist resorts that some might expect from a lush holiday destination. Yet others might delight in the pristine, powdery beaches and the utter tranquillity. There are, of course, more developed resorts on certain islands than others, such as those on Rarotonga (where the airport is situated) and Aitutaki, which cater for various activities. For those simply wanting to swim, the best beaches of all are at Muri Lagoon and Titikaveka. But it won't take much to entice you to dive beneath those clear, turquoise waters, which are teeming with colourful fish and swaying coral reefs. Rarotonga also offers a variation in scenery, should you – unlikely though it is – grow tired of tropical paradise, since it is a mountainous island with plenty of verdant scenery. The older volcanic island of Kauai offers comparable aural treasures.
For those who also grow weary of soaking up the sun under palm trees, the Cook Islands may not be overly-developed, but there is certainly plenty to do here, whether you are canoeing, kayaking or snorkelling, attending one of the islands' many festivals or clapping along as dance groups bop at various hotels: there is always something to entertain and engage.

General Information

AREA: 237 sq km (91.5 sq miles).
POPULATION: 21,388 (2005).
POPULATION DENSITY: 90.2 per sq km.
CAPITAL: Avarua (on Rarotonga). **Population:** 9000.
GEOGRAPHY: The Cook Islands are situated 3500km (2200 miles) northeast of New Zealand and 1000km (600 miles) southwest of Tahiti in the South Pacific, forming part of Polynesia. The islands fall into two groups: the scattered Northern Group are all coral atolls while the Southern Group is of volcanic origin. Rarotonga is the largest and highest island with a rugged volcanic interior, its highest peak being Te Manga, at 652m (2140ft). Coral reef surrounds the island and the population lives between reef and hills where rich soil supports both tropical and subtropical vegetation. Most of the island is covered by thick evergreen bush. Most of the larger islands include lagoons surrounded by small areas of fertile land, above which rise volcanic hills. The best beaches found on Aitutaki are also part of the eight-island Southern Group. The Northern Group comprises seven islands, the largest being Penrhyn, Manihiki and Pukapuka.
GOVERNMENT: Self-governing state in 'free association' with New Zealand. (New Zealand retains responsibility for external affairs.) Gained self-governing status in 1965.
Head of State: HM Queen Elizabeth II, represented locally by Frederick Goodwin. New Zealand is represented locally by High Commissioner Rob Moore-Jones since 1998. **Head of Government:** Prime Minister Jim Marurai was elected in December 2004. **Recent history:** Jim Marurai, of the Demo Tumu party was sworn in as Prime Minister in December 2004 after winnig the backing of MPs. His predecessor Robert Woonton stood down after a recount of the September 2004 general election votes revealed a tie for the seat between Mr Woonton and his challenger. Executive power is formally held by the New Zealand High Commissioner (High Commissioner Rob Moore-Jones since 1998) but effectively devolved to the Cabinet. This, in turn, is responsible to the 25-member Parliament, directly elected every five years. 24 of the members each represent districts of the Cook Islands and one represents Cook Islanders who live overseas. The House of Ariki, which is composed of all the paramount chiefs of the Cook Islands, serves as an advisory body. Advice is given on legislation concerning customs and traditions, though the House of Ariki has no powers of legislation itself. New Zealand is responsible for defence and foreign affairs. In 2005 the Cook Islands celebrated 40 years of self governance.
LANGUAGE: The official languages are English and Cook Islands Maori.
RELIGION: Mainly Cook Islands Christian Church (58 per cent); also Roman Catholic, Latter Day Saints, Seventh Day Adventists and Assembly of God.
ELECTRICITY: 220 volts DC, 50Hz.
SOCIAL CONVENTIONS: Dress code is informal, though modest attire should be worn when visiting towns or villages. Women are expected to wear dresses for church services and social functions.

Climate

Weather can be quite changeable from day to day and varies throughout the islands. It is generally hot throughout the year, although the trade winds provide some moderating influence. Rainfall is heaviest in Rarotonga, while the northern atolls tend to be drier. The coolest months are June to August, while November to March marks the warmer season, which also has the highest rainfall.
Required clothing: Lightweight cottons and linens throughout the year. Warmer clothes are advised for the evenings.

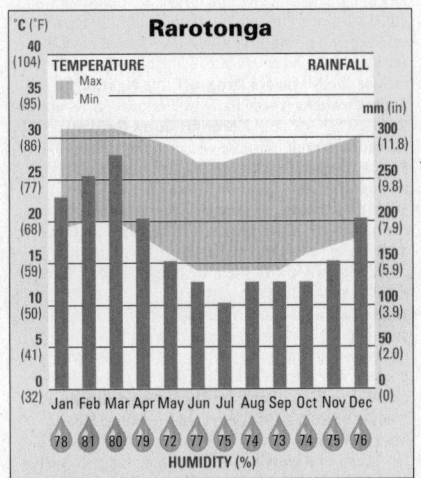

Communications

Telephone: IDD is available. Country code: 682. International telephone is available 24 hours from the telecommunications office (Telecom Cook Islands).
Mobile telephone: Roaming agreements exist with international mobile phone companies. Travellers arriving from New Zealand, Australia and Samoa can arrange roaming with their own network providers. Those from other destinations must purchase a Cook Islands' sim card for NZ$25.00 and top-up cards. Mobile coverage is available in Rarotonga and Aitutaki.
Internet: There are Internet facilities in Avarua at the Telecom Cook Islands office (open 24 hours a day), at the post office, at Internet cafes and at computer stores.
Post: Post office hours: Mon-Fri 0800-1600.
MEDIA: The main radio and TV stations are operated by the privately-owned Elijah Communications, which also publishes weekly newspapers. There are plans in progress for a public radio service.
Press: The independent daily, *Cook Islands News*, is published in Maori and English. *The Cook Islands Herald* and *Cook Islands Independent* are private weekly publications, owned by Elijah Communications.
TV: *Cook Islands Television* (CITV) is private, operated by Elijah Communications.
Radio: *Radio Cook Islands* is a private mediumwave (AM) station, operated by Elijah Communications. *Radio Ikurangi* is a private FM station.

Passport/Visa

	Passport Required?	Visa Required?	Return Ticket Required?
Full British	Yes	1/2	Yes
Australian	Yes	1/2	Yes
Canadian	Yes	1/2	Yes
USA	Yes	1/2	Yes
Other EU	Yes	1/2	Yes
Japanese	Yes	1/2	Yes

Note: *Regulations and requirements may be subject to change at short notice, and you are advised to contact the appropriate diplomatic or consular authority before finalising travel arrangements. Any numbers in the chart refer to the footnotes below.*

PASSPORTS: Valid passport required by all, including nationals of New Zealand. Passports should be valid for six months after the initial 31-day stay in the Cook Islands.
VISAS: 1. Issued on arrival to visitors for tourist stays of up to 31 daysl. Confirmed onward/return tickets and documentation are required, as are accommodation arrangements and proof of adequate finances for duration of stay.
2. Nationals arriving in the Cook Islands on business *do not* require a work visa; however business must be completed within a 31-day period.
Validity: Visitors can extend length of stay on a monthly basis up to an additional five months, providing they have sufficient funds, use licensed accommodation and are not taking up employment. A fee is payable with each application within 14 days before the expiry of the permit. Three-month extensions cost NZ$70 and five-month extensions may be obtained for a fee of NZ$120. For visitors wanting to stay longer than six months, a visa must

be applied for from their country of residence. There is no fee for applicants aged under 15 years but they must report to immigration for official paperwork to be completed.
Application to: Cook Islands Representative *or* the Principal Immigration Officer (see *Passport/Visa Information*).
Application requirements: A return ticket and proof of sufficient funds are required for those wishing to extend their stay in the Cook Islands.
Temporary residence: Applicants should refer to the Principal Immigration Officer (see *Passport/Visa Information*).

PASSPORT/VISA INFORMATION

Cook Islands Commission in New Zealand
PO Box 12, 242-56 Mulgrave Street, Thorndon, Wellington, New Zealand
Tel: (4) 472 5126/7.
E-mail: cooks@cookhicom.org.nz

Principle Immigration Officer
PO Box 105, Rarotonga, Cook Islands
Tel: 29347.
Website: www.mfai.gov.ck

Money

Currency: New Zealand Dollar (NZD; symbol NZ$) = 100 cents, supplemented by notes and coins minted for local use which are not negotiable outside the Cook Islands. Notes are in denominations of NZ$100, 50, 20, 10 and 5. Coins are in denominations of NZ$2 and 1, and 50, 20, 10 and 5 cents.
Currency exchange: Exchange facilities are available at the airport, banks and in some larger stores and hotels. EFTPOS and ATM machines are available at both *ANZ* and *Westpac* banks on Rarotonga and Aitutaki, and also major stores and restaurants.
Credit & debit cards: American Express, Diners Club, MasterCard and Visa are all accepted. Check with your credit or debit card company for details of merchant acceptability and other services which may be available.
Traveller's cheques: Accepted in hotels and some shops.
Currency restrictions: There are no restrictions on the import of either local or foreign currency. Local currency can be exported up to NZ$250. Foreign currency can be exported up to the amount imported and declared subject to bank authorisation.
Banking hours: Mon-Thur 0900-1500; Fri 0900-1600. Some banks are open Sat 0900-1100.
Exchange rate indicators:
Rate at time of publishing
£1.00= NZ$2.53
$1.00= NZ$1.43

Duty Free

The following goods may be imported into the Cook Islands by persons over 18 years of age without incurring customs duty:
200 cigarettes or 50 cigars or 1kg of tobacco; 2l of spirits or wine or 4.5l of beer; goods up to the value of NZ$250.
Prohibited items: Fruit, plants, meat and livestock (unless arriving from New Zealand); firearms, gunpowder,

Credit: © Tipani

Rarotonga chart

°C (°F)
40 (104)
35 (95)
30 (86)
25 (77)
20 (68)
15 (59)
10 (50)
5 (41)
0 (32)

TEMPERATURE — Max, Min
RAINFALL
mm (in)
300 (11.8)
250 (9.8)
200 (7.9)
150 (5.9)
100 (3.9)
50 (2.0)
0 (0)

Jan Feb Mar Apr May Jun Jul Aug Sep Oct Nov Dec

78 81 80 79 72 77 75 74 73 74 75 76
HUMIDITY (%)

A B C D E F G H I J K L M N O P Q R S T U V W X Y Z

Credit: © Tipani Tours

ammunition, cartridges and cartridge cases, unless prior permission is obtained from the Minister of Police; and fireworks.

Frozen, canned or vacuum-packed foods are permitted but must be declared on arrival.

Public Holidays

Below are listed Public Holidays for the January 2006-June 2007 period.
2006: Jan 1-2 New Year. **Apr 14** Good Friday. **Apr 17** Easter Monday. **Apr 25** ANZAC Day. **Jun 5** Queen's Birthday. **Jul 25** Gospel Day (Rarotonga). **Oct 26** Constitution Day. **Oct 27** Flag Raising Day. **Dec 25** Christmas Day. **Dec 26** Boxing Day. **2007: Jan 1-2** New Year. **Apr 6** Good Friday. **Apr 9** Easter Monday. **Apr 25** ANZAC Day. **Jun 5** Queen's Birthday.

Health

	Special Precautions?	Certificate Required?
Yellow Fever	No	No
Cholera	No	No
Typhoid & Polio	1	N/A
Malaria	No	N/A

Note: *Regulations and requirements may be subject to change at short notice, and you are advised to contact your doctor well in advance of your intended date of departure. Any numbers in the chart refer to the footnotes below.*

1: *Typhoid* immunisations should be up-to-date.
Food & drink: Tap water is relatively safe but may cause mild abdominal upsets. Bottled water is available and is advised for the first few weeks of the stay. Milk is pasteurised and dairy products are safe for consumption. Local meat, poultry, seafood, fruit and vegetables are generally considered safe to eat.
Other risks: *Hepatitis A* occurs in the region and *hepatitis B* is endemic. Inoculation against *tetanus* is recommended. Bathers should be aware of the possible hazard caused by sharp coral reefs.
Health care: There is no direct reciprocal health agreement with the UK, but such an agreement exists with New Zealand which may, in some circumstances, also apply to the Cook Islands; enquire at the Cook Islands Representative (see *Passport/Visa Information*). Comprehensive travel insurance is recommended. There is one Government hospital (on Rarotonga).

Travel - International

AIR:
 The Cook Islands are served by *Air New Zealand (NZ)* (website: www.airnz.co.nz), which offers regular flights from New Zealand, Tahiti and Fiji. There are also frequent connections from Australia, North America and Europe. For details, contact the Cook Islands Tourist Bureau (see *Top Things To See & Do*).
Air passes: The *Visit the South Pacific Pass* is valid for many airlines operating in the South Pacific, including most of the larger ones, such as *Air Caledonie International* (website: www.aircalin.nc), *Air Marshall Islands*, *Air Nauru*, *Air Niugini*, *Air Pacific*, *Air Vanuatu*, *Polynesian Airlines*, *Qantas*, *Royal Tongan Airlines* and *Solomon Airlines*. Offering reductions of up to 40 per cent on normal airfares,

this sector-based pass allows for flexible island-hopping between the destinations of the Cook Islands, Fiji, Nauru, New Caledonia, Samoa, Tahiti, Tonga, Vanuatu and the more remote Melanesian and Micronesian islands, together with major cities in Australia (Brisbane, Melbourne and Sydney) and New Zealand (Auckland, Christchurch and Wellington). It is only available for people resident outside of the South Pacific. The journey must be started outside the South Pacific and only one stopover in Australia is allowed. A minimum of two sectors must be bought before departure (extra sectors can be purchased en route up to a maximum of eight in total). There is a maximum of one pass per person, and passes must be used within six months of the first day of travel. Children pay 67 per cent of the adult fare and infants under two years of age pay 10 per cent of the adult fare. For details and conditions, contact the South Pacific Tourist Organisation (website: www.spto.org).
Approximate flight times: From Rarotonga to *London* is 24 hours (*Air New Zealand* flies via Los Angeles and Auckland).
Main airports: *Rarotonga (RAR)* is 3km (2 miles) west of Avarua. *To/from the airport:* (Travel time – 10 minutes.). Hotel coaches meet each flight. Taxis and buses are also available. *Facilities:* Open according to flight arrivals and departures and include 24 hour luggage storage facilities, duty free shops, bank/bureau de change, bars, shops and car rental.
Departure tax: NZ$30 for passengers over 12 years of age; NZ$15 for passengers aged two to 12 years.
SEA:
 Main ports: It is possible to moor yachts at *Avatiu Harbour*; for maritime matters, contact the Harbour Master, Ports Authority, PO Box 84, Rarotonga, Cook Islands (tel: 28814).
Cargo lines operating to the Cook Islands are run by *Express Cook Islands Line Shipping Ltd* and *Hawaii-Pacific Maritime Ltd*.

Travel - Internal

AIR:
 Air Rarotonga (GZ) (website: www.airraro.com) runs regular inter-island services to Aitutaki, Atiu, Mangaia, Mauke, Manihiki, Mitiaro and Penrhyn. Services do not operate on Sundays.
Inter-island flight times: From Rarotonga to *Aitutaki* is 50 minutes, to *Atiu* is 45 minutes, and to *Mauke* and *Mitiaro* is 50 minutes. The *Discover Cook Islands Pass* offers discount travel around the islands. For more information, contact the Cook Islands Tourist Bureau (see *Top Things To See & Do*).
ROAD:
 Traffic drives on the left. There are two main roads that circle the island; the Ara Tapu sealed road that runs through villages and past beaches, and the older inland road which winds through local farmlands. **Bus:** The 'Round the Island Bus' operates regular services around Rarotonga from Monday to Saturday. The buses will pick up and drop off anywhere on request. **Taxi:** Available on Rarotonga. **Car hire:** Several companies offer cars for hire from a number of shops and hotels. Motor scooter and bicycle hire is also popular. **Documentation:** Drivers of all vehicles are required to have a current Cook Islands driver's licence, which costs NZ$10 and is obtainable from the Police Station in Avarua on presentation of an international or Commonwealth licence.

Travel Advice

Most visits to the Cook Islands are trouble-free but you should be aware of the global risk of indiscriminate international terrorist attacks, which could be against civilian targets, including places frequented by foreigners. This advice is based on information provided by the Foreign and Commonwealth Office in the UK. It is correct at time of publishing. As the situation can change rapidly, visitors are advised to contact the following organisations for the latest travel advice:

British Foreign and Commonwealth Office
Tel: (0845) 850 2829.
Website: www.fco.gov.uk

US Department of State
Website: http://travel.state.gov/travel

Accommodation

HOTELS:
 Accommodation of a high standard is increasing yearly. There are several resorts, hotels and a number of villas, motels, bungalows and self-catering apartments. Most are situated close to, if not on, a beach. Advance booking is essential, and it is probably wiser to book via an inclusive tour operator specialising in Pacific destinations. For more information on hotels, contact the Cook Islands Tourist Bureau (see *Top Things To See & Do*).
CAMPING:
 This is not permitted.

Top Things To See & Do

- The best **swimming** beaches are at **Muri Lagoon** and **Titikaveka**.
- A variety of **tours** are available, including inland **trekking**, historical tours, guided walking trips, sightseeing by air, and **horse-drawn** and **motorised drives** around the islands. **Kayaking** tours in the lagoon are also available, as are **lagoon cruises** to the coral reefs in glass-bottomed boats or in a semi-submersible vessel. The three-hour 'cultural village tour' offers the opportunity to enjoy demonstrations in weaving, coconut husking, fire making, carving and other Cook Islands' traditions.
- A scenic **drive** into the **Takuvaine/Avatiu Valleys** offers a panorama of lush tropical scenery.
- **Papua (Wigmore's) Waterfall**, the only waterfall on the island, is located at **Vaimaanga**. There are even **pony treks** to the waterfall, an opportunity not to be missed, although advance booking is recommended.
- During the year, various **festivals** take place. These are generally celebrated with singing and dancing, often with a strange mixture of traditional ritual grafted on to the somewhat later Christian music and ceremony. The choirs of the Cook Islands are renowned.
- Places of **historical interest** include: the **Takamoa Mission House**, built in 1842, and believed to be the second-oldest building in the South Pacific; the old **Palace of Makea** at **Taputapuatea**; **Pa's Palace** in **Takitumu**, which is built of coral and lime; and **Arai-Te-Tonga** (*Marae*), consisting of stone structures which, in the islands' pre-European history, formed a *koutu*, or royal court, where the investiture of chiefs took place. This spot is still regarded as sacred.
- **Scuba-diving** and **snorkelling** are excellent in the clear waters of the islands' many lagoons. Visibility is seldom less than 30m (100ft) and the scenery is quite varied, with canyons, caves, 73 types of live coral and a rich marine life. A maximum of 10 persons can dive at any one site at any one time. There are four dive companies operating in Rarotonga and Aitutaki, usually offering two diving trips a day. Divers must have a recognised diving certificate. Some of the best dive sites include the **Matavera Drop-off**; the **Ngatangiia Swimthroughs** (particularly well-known for its unusual and rare fish species); **Koromiri Coral Garden**; **Mataora Wreck** (purposely sunk in December 1990); **Papua Canyon** (known for its eagle ray population); and **Sand River**.
- **Whale watching** can be practised in the Cook Islands: the humpback whale season is from July to October. In addition to observing the whales from a boat, it is possible to swim with them wearing a snorkel; for details, contact local operators.
- **Game fishing** excursions (usually five-hour trips) are available. Visitors can also watch flying fish being netted at night in outrigger canoes equipped with bright lights. Aitutaki's magnificent 50 sq km- (19 sq mile-) lagoon is suitable for **fly** and **bait fishing**. It holds the world all-tackle record for **Hump Head Maori Wrasse**.
- The island of **Rarotonga** offers a wide range of **walks** for all ages and fitness levels. There are 13 marked

trails, and guides should be hired for all routes leading into the inland area of Rarotonga. Details are available from hotels and other tourist establishments. The most popular trails include the **Cross Island Trek** (a four-and-a-half-hour trek through the centre of the island on trails known to be ancestral war paths); **Pa's Mountain Walk** (a four- to five-hour walk through the lush interior); **Te Kou Trek** (a five-hour trek with steep ascents and good views); and the **Ikurangi Trek** (a four-hour trek for experienced hikers only, also providing the opportunity for rock climbing around the top of the mountain). The **Takitumu Conservation Area Walk** also offers **birdwatching**. Guided **lagoon reef walks** are possible at low tide along Rarotonga's coral fringe.

TOURIST INFORMATION

Cook Islands Tourist Bureau in the UK
c/o Hills Balfour, 36 Southwark Bridge Road, London
SE1 9EU, UK
Tel: (020) 7202 6365 (consumer line) *or* 6380 (trade enquiries).
Website: www.cook-islands.com

Entertainment

FOOD & DRINK: There are restaurants in hotels, and a variety of independent eating places as well, as a result of the increasing tourist trade. Local produce includes a wide variety of citrus and tropical fruits, island chestnuts and garden vegetables. Seafood features on many restaurant menus and so does coconut as the coconut palms produce an abundant supply of fruit all year round. Local meat and poultry are available.

National specialities:
- At larger resorts you can try the traditional Polynesian feast known as the *'Umukai'*, which involves baking food in an underground oven and is usually accompanied with traditional entertainment by local people.
- *Matu rori* (sea cucumber), served with lemon and cooked green banana. This dish is likened to spaghetti from the sea.

National Drinks:
- *Tumunu*, traditionally brewed alcohol made from fermented oranges.

Tipping: Tradition says that all gifts require something in return and tipping is therefore not practised.

NIGHTLIFE: Island feast and dance groups feature at major hotels and details are available from local tourist information offices or hotel receptionists.

SHOPPING: Best buys are woodcarvings, pearls, shell craft, woven products, pottery, hats and baskets made out of coconut fibre. Coins and stamps are considered to be valuable collectors' items. Another popular buy is a brightly coloured, all-purpose wrap-around cloth garment worn by both men and women called a *Pareu*, and ideal for casual wear in the hot climate. *Island Craft* (website: www.islandcraft.com) has factories in Avarua where hand-carved items can be purchased. The art of carving may be observed in Punanganui Market Place. There is also a wide range of duty-free items. **Shopping hours:** Mon-Fri 0800-1600, Sat 0800-1200. Some stores in tourist areas remain open for longer.

Business

- **GDP:** US$105 million (2001).
- **Main exports:** Copra, papaya, fresh fruit and canned citrus fruit, coffee, fish, pearls, pearl shells and clothing.
- **Main imports:** Foodstuffs, textiles, fuels, timber and capital goods.
- **Main trade partners:** Australia, New Zealand, Japan, Fiji and USA.

ECONOMY: Tourism and agriculture is the principal industry. The islands are economically underdeveloped and depend on extensive aid from New Zealand. The Government is seeking to build up the islands' infrastructure as a precursor to further development.
BUSINESS ETIQUETTE: Tropical or lightweight suits are advised. **Office hours:** Mon-Fri 0800-1600.

COMMERCIAL INFORMATION

Chamber of Commerce
PO Box 242, Rarotonga, Cook Islands
Tel: 20925.

Costa Rica

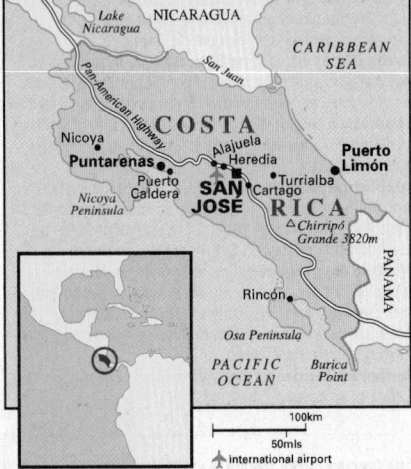

Location: Central America.

Time: GMT - 6.

Overview

Columbus landed in what is now Costa Rica in 1501. Under the rule of General Tomas Guardia between 1870 and 1882, Costa Rica developed many of its principal modern characteristics, notably the minimal role of the Catholic Church in secular matters and a relatively isolationist foreign policy. Throughout the 20th century, Costa Rica has enjoyed peace and a steady growth in prosperity, with the notable exception of a civil war in 1948 which followed a disputed Presidential election. In recent times, one of the most prominent political figures has been President Oscar Arias Sanchez of the *Partido de Liberacion Nacional* (PLN) who was awarded the Nobel Peace Prize in 1987 for his efforts in bringing warring parties elsewhere in Central America to the negotiating table.

Costa Rica has a surprising diversity of terrain. In the cities and towns, the country's Spanish heritage provides the main features of interest. Elsewhere, Costa Rica's national parks are its greatest glory. Partly in order to continue to encourage ecotourism, the Costa Rican authorities have set aside a large proportion of the country (around 26 per cent of the total land area) as national parks and protected areas, which are well-kept and well-guarded. The country has a stunning variety of landscapes, micro-climates, flora and fauna, and nature lovers will not be disappointed.

General Information

AREA: 51,100 sq km (19,730 sq miles).
POPULATION: 4.25 million (2004).
POPULATION DENSITY: 83.1 per sq km.
CAPITAL: San José. **Population:** 328,293 (official estimate 2002) (Province of San San José: 1.1 million).
GEOGRAPHY: Costa Rica, lying between Nicaragua and Panama, is a complete coast-to-coast segment of the Central American isthmus. Its width ranges from 119km to 282km (74 to 176 miles). A low thin line of hills, that rises between Lake Nicaragua and the Pacific Ocean in Nicaragua, broadens and rises as it enters northern Costa Rica, eventually forming the high, rugged, mountains of volcanic origin in the centre and south. The highest peak is Chirripó Grande, which reaches 3820m (12,530ft). More than half the population live on the Meseta Central, a plateau with an equitable climate. It is rimmed to the southwest by the Cordillera range, and provides the setting for the country's capital, San José. There are lowlands on both coastlines, mainly swampy on the Caribbean coast, with grassland savannah on the Pacific side merging into mangrove towards the south. Rivers cut through the mountains, flowing down to both the Caribbean and the Pacific.
GOVERNMENT: Republic. Gained independence from Spain in 1821. **Head of State and Government:** President Oscar Arias since 2006. **Recent history:** Nobel Peace Prize winner Oscar Arias won the Presidential elections held in February 2006. The election on 5 February became Costa Rica's hardest-fought vote in the last four decades. Otton Solis, his rival only gave up after losing a manual recount and a series of legal challenges. Mr Arias is committed to taking Costa Rica into a controversial free trade pact with the United States.
LANGUAGE: Spanish is the official language. English is widely spoken. French, German and Italian are also spoken.
RELIGION: Almost entirely Christian, with Roman Catholic majority.
ELECTRICITY: 110 volts AC, 60Hz. Two-pin plugs are standard.
SOCIAL CONVENTIONS: Handshaking is common and forms of address are important. Christian names are preceded by *Don* for a man and *Doña* for a woman. Normal courtesies should be observed when visiting someone's home and gifts are appreciated as a token of thanks, especially if invited for a meal. For most occasions casual wear is acceptable, but beachwear should be confined to the beach.

Climate

In the Central Valley, where the main centres of population are located, the average temperature is 22°C (72°F). In the coastal areas, the temperature is much hotter. The rainy season starts in May and finishes in November. The 'warm' dry season is December to May, though temperature differences between summer and winter are slight.
Required clothing: Lightweight cottons and linens most of the year, warmer clothes for cooler evenings. Waterproofing is necessary during the rainy season.

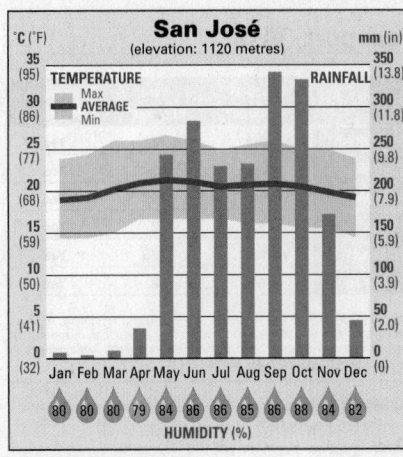

Communications

Telephone: IDD is available. Country code: 506. Telephone booths are available all over the country.
Mobile telephone: Roaming agreements exist with some countries. Handsets can be hired, although this can be difficult and time-consuming (website: http://www.ice.go.cr).
Internet: There are Internet cafes and some hotels also provide facilities.
Post: Airmail letters to Western Europe usually take between six and 10 days.
MEDIA: Costa Rica has nine major newspapers, several private and public TV stations and a busy FM radio scene. Cable TV is widely available.
Press: Daily newspapers printed in Spanish include *Al Dia*, *Diario Extra*, *El Heraldo*, *La Nacion*, *La Prensa Libre* and *La República*. The *Tico Times* is a weekly newspaper published in English.
TV: The public channel is *Rede Nacional* (channel 13). Private channels include: *Teletica* (channel 7), *Repretel* (channels 4, 6, 11) and *Conexion* (channel 2).
Radio: *Radio Reloj* is a popular national radio; *Radio Columbia* and *Radio Monumental* are news and talk stations; *Radio Eco* is a news station; *Radio Faro del Caribe* is a religious station. *Radio Uno* and *Radio Dos* are commercial stations.

Credit: ©Costa Rica Tourist Board

Passport/Visa

	Passport Required?	Visa Required?	Return Ticket Required?
Full British	Yes	1	Yes
Australian	Yes	3	Yes
Canadian	Yes	2	Yes
USA	Yes	2	Yes
Other EU	Yes	2/3	Yes
Japanese	Yes	2	Yes

Note: *Regulations and requirements may be subject to change at short notice, and you are advised to contact the appropriate diplomatic or consular authority before finalising travel arrangements. Any numbers in the chart refer to the footnotes below.*

PASSPORTS: Passport valid for at least six months at date of entry required by all.

VISAS: Required by all except the following:
(a) **1.** nationals of the UK and its dependencies for stays of up to 90 days;
(b) **2.** nationals of Andorra, Argentina, Austria, Belgium, Brazil, Canada, Cyprus, Czech Republic, Denmark, Finland, France, Germany, Greece, Hong Kong (British passport holders only), Hungary, Israel, Italy, Japan, Korea (Rep), Latvia, Liechtenstein, Lithuania, Luxembourg, Malta, Monaco, The Netherlands, Norway, Panama, Paraguay, Poland, Portugal, Puerto Rico, Romania, Slovenia, Spain, Sweden, Switzerland, Trinidad & Tobago, Uruguay and USA for stays of up to 90 days;
(c) **3.** nationals of Antigua & Barbuda, Australia, The Bahamas, Barbados, Belize, Bolivia, Bulgaria, Chile, Dominica, El Salvador, Estonia, Grenada, Guatemala, Guyana, Honduras, Iceland, Ireland, Jamaica, Mexico, New Zealand, The Philippines, Russian Federation, St Kitts & Nevis, St Lucia, St Vincent & The Grenadines, San Marino, Singapore, Slovak Republic, South Africa*, Surinam, Taiwan (China), Turkey, Vatican City and Venezuela for stays of up to 30 days;
(d) transit passengers continuing their journey to a third country by the same or first connecting flight within 12 hours, provided holding confirmed onward tickets and not leaving the airport (except nationals of China (PR) who *do* need a transit visa authorised by the Immigration Department in San José). ·

Note: (a) * Persons holding passports issued by the former homelands of Transkei and Venda *do* need a visa authorised

by the Immigration Department in San José. (b) Nationals of countries listed above must obtain an exit visa from the Immigration Department in San José at least three weeks before leaving Costa Rica. Those who stay for less than 30 days are exempt if in possession of a disembarkation card. (c) Nationals of the following countries may enter Costa Rica with a *consular visa* for stays of up to 30 days: Belarus, Colombia, Ecuador, Dominican Republic, Egypt, Malaysia, Nicaragua, Peru, Thailand and Zimbabwe; nationals of these countries will have to apply for a consular visa in their country of origin or if they are permanent residents in a country of group (b) 2. in the country where they have permanent residency. (d) All other nationals require a visa. In some cases, an authorisation from the Immigration Department in San José is also necessary and visitors should consult the Consulate for an up-to-date list. Temporary visitors must hold return or onward tickets, except those holding a visa showing an exit ticket is not required.

Types of visa and cost: *Tourist.* Visas cost approximately £12 ($20). All passengers requiring a visa must hold documents required for the next destination.

Validity: Visas are valid for 30 or 90 days, depending on nationality. Contact the Immigration Department in Costa Rica for renewal or information on the extension procedure.

Application to: Consulate (or consular section of Embassy; see *Passport/Visa Information*). Applications should be made in person.

Application requirements: (a) Completed application form. (b) Two passport-size photos. (c) Passport valid for six months at time of entry. (d) Proof of sufficient funds to cover duration of stay. (e) Return or onward ticket.

Working days required: One to two, depending on nationality of applicant. Some visas need the authorisation of the Immigration Department in Costa Rica (ask the Consulate or Consular section of Embassy for details) and may take up to three weeks.

Temporary residence: Apply to the Consulate or consular section of Embassy.

PASSPORT/VISA INFORMATION

Embassy and Consulate of the Republic of Costa Rica in the UK
Flat 1, 14 Lancaster Gate, London W2 3LH, UK
Tel: (020) 7706 8844.
Website: http://costarica.embassyhomepage.com
Opening hours: Mon-Fri 1000-1500 (embassy); 1000-1300 (consulate).

Embassy of the Republic of Costa Rica in the USA
2114 S Street, NW, Washington, DC 20008, USA
Tel: (202) 234 2945 *or* 328 6628 (consular enquiries).
Website: www.costarica-embassy.org

Money

Currency: Costa Rican Colón (CRC) = 100 céntimos. Notes are in denominations of CRC10,000, 5000, 2000, 1000 and 500. Coins are in denominations of CRC100, 50, 25, 20, 10 and 5. US Dollars are also widely accepted.

Currency exchange: Visitors should consult their banks for the current rate of exchange (there is no direct local quotation for sterling; the cross rate with the US Dollar is used). ATMs are available throughout the country.

Credit & debit cards: Diners Club, MasterCard and Visa are all accepted; American Express slightly less so, but check with your credit or debit card company for details of merchant acceptability and other services which may be available.

Traveller's cheques: To avoid additional exchange rate charges, travellers are advised to take traveller's cheques in US Dollars.

Currency restrictions: Up to US$10,000 can be brought to Costa Rica without any restrictions. Amounts above that figure must be declared to customs upon arrival.

Banking hours: Mon-Fri 0800/0900-1500/1800.

Exchange rate indicators:
Rate at time of publishing
£1.00=   CRC886.70
$1.00=   CRC485.78

Duty Free

The following goods may be imported into Costa Rica without incurring customs duty:
400 cigarettes or 50 cigars or 500g tobacco; 3l of alcoholic beverages (people aged over 18 only); a reasonable quantity of perfume for personal use.

Public Holidays

Below are listed Public Holidays for the January 2006-June 2007 period.
2006: Jan 1 New Year's Day. **Apr 11** Juan Santamaría's Day.

Apr 14-17 Easter. **May 1** Labour Day. **Jul 25** Guanacaste Annexation. **Aug 2** Virgin of Los Angeles, Feast of Patroness of Costa Rica*. **Aug 15** Mothers' Day and Assumption. **Sep 15** Independence Day. **Oct 12** Dia de la Raza (Columbus Day)*. **Dec 25** Christmas Day.
2007: Jan 1 New Year's Day. **Apr 6-9** Easter. **Apr 11** Juan Santamaría's Day. **May 1** Labour Day.
* not legally binding.
Note: Most businesses close for the whole of Holy Week and between Christmas and New Year.

Health

	Special Precautions?	Certificate Required?
Yellow Fever	No	No
Cholera	1	No
Typhoid & Polio	No	N/A
Malaria	3	N/A

Note: *Regulations and requirements may be subject to change at short notice, and you are advised to contact your doctor well in advance of your intended date of departure. Any numbers in the chart refer to the footnotes below.*

1: Following WHO guidelines issued in 1973, a *cholera* vaccination certificate is no longer a condition of entry into Costa Rica. However, cases of cholera were reported in 1996 and precautions should be considered. Up-to-date advice should be sought before deciding whether these precautions should include vaccination as medical opinion is divided over its effectiveness; consult the *Health* appendix for further information.

2: *Malaria* risk exists throughout the year, mostly in the benign *vivax* form, in the rural areas below 700m, especially in the cantons of Matina, Los Chiles (Alajuela province) and Talamanca (Limón province). Lower transmission risk exists in 20 cantons in the provinces of Guanacaste, Alajuela and Heredia. There is negligible or no risk of malaria in the other cantons of the country. There have been many confirmed cases of *dengue fever* in the areas of Puntarenas and Guanacaste on the Pacific Coast, and Limón on the Atlantic Coast. Cases have also been reported in the Central Valley around the capital, San José. Deaths from secondary infections have occurred. Travellers should take strict prevention measures against mosquito bites, by using repellents and by wearing long sleeved shirts and long trousers.

Food & drink: Mains water is normally heavily chlorinated and, whilst relatively safe, may cause mild abdominal upsets. Drinking water outside main cities and towns may be contaminated and sterilisation is advisable. Bottled water is available and is advised for the first few weeks of the stay. Milk is pasteurised and dairy products are safe for consumption. Local meat, poultry, seafood, fruit and vegetables are generally considered safe to eat.

Other risks: *Hepatitis A, B* and *C* occur. *Paragonimiasis* (oriental lung fluke) and *lymphatic* and *bancroftian filariasis* have been reported in Costa Rica. *Cutaneous* and *mucocutaneous leishmaniasis* have also been reported. *Rabies* is widespread throughout Central America. For those at high risk, vaccination before arrival should be considered. If you are bitten, seek medical advice without delay. For more information, consult the *Health* appendix.

Health care: Health insurance is recommended. Reliable medical services are available in Costa Rica. Standards of health and hygiene are among the best in Latin America.

Travel - International

AIR:

The national airline is *Taca International Airlines (TA)* (website: www.taca.com), an amalgamation of the airlines *Aviateca, Lacsa, Nica* and *Taca*. *Taca International* flies direct to Costa Rica from nine major cities in the United States - including Miami, New Orleans, Los Angeles, New York, Toronto, plus Mexico and other destinations in Central and South America. It has the only scheduled flight between Cuba and North America. The *Visit Central America Pass* is available from *Grupo Taca* and is an economical way to travel to Costa Rica from the USA and from Costa Rica to other Central American countries.

Approximate flight times: From San José to *London* is 12 hours (including stopover time), to *Los Angeles* is six hours and to *New York* is seven hours.

Main airports: *Juan Santamaría (SJO)* is 23km (14 miles) northwest of the city. To/from the airport: Coaches depart every 20 minutes (0500-2400); return pickups stop at various hotels. Buses depart to the city every 15 minutes (travel time - 20 minutes). Some hotels have shuttle services to the airport; these are 24 hours and free of charge. Taxis are also available to the city (travel time - 15 minutes). The airport in Liberia has been upgraded and may be used for some international flights.

Departure tax: US$26 (or the equivalent in Costa Rican Colon), payable if staying more than 24 hours.

SEA:

Main ports: *Puntarenas* and *Caldera* are the two main ports in the Costa Rican Pacific coast. Since December 2004, Puerto Limón has been redeveloped to receive two cruise ships at once.

ROAD:

The Inter-American Highway runs through Costa Rica from La Cruz on the Nicaraguan border through San José to Progreso on the Panamanian border.

Travel - Internal

AIR:

SANSA (website: www.flysansa.com), the national airline, operates services between San José and provincial towns and villages. A bus is provided from the airline offices in San José to the airport. A number of smaller airlines also provide internal flights, such as *Nature Air* (website: www.natureair.net).

RAIL:

There is a train from San José to Caldera. For more information and reservations, call 233 3300.

ROAD:

The standard of the roads is generally very good. There are 35,583km (22,110 miles) of all-weather highways including 663km (412 miles) of the Inter-American Highway and highways linking San José with the other principal towns. Traffic drives on the right. **Bus**: Regular and inexpensive services to most towns, but buses are often crowded so pre-booking is advisable. Costa Rica offers a wide variety of sightseeing tours. Most tour companies feature bilingual guides and round-trip transportation from hotels. For full details, contact the Instituto Costarricense de Turismo (see *Top Things To Do*). **Taxi**: Numerous and inexpensive in San José. The taxis are coloured red (except those serving the Juan Santamaría International Airport, which are orange). Taxis are usually metered. **Car hire**: Major car hire companies as well as local firms have offices in San José. Distances are measured in kilometres. A speed limit of 88kph (55mph) is enforced on most highways. **Documentation**: Drivers must have a national licence or International Driving Permit.

URBAN:

San José has privately run bus services, charging fares on a two-zone system.

Travel times: The following chart gives approximate travel times (in hours and minutes) from **San José** to other major cities/towns.

	Air	Road
Alajuela	-	0.30
Cartago	-	0.30
Puntarenas	-	2.00
Puerto Limón	0.25	3.00

Travel Advice

Most visits to Costa Rica are trouble-free but you should be aware of the global risk of indiscriminate international terrorist attacks, which could be against civilian targets, including places frequented by foreigners.

Incidents of violent crime, some targeted at tourists, are on the increase.

This advice is based on information provided by the Foreign and Commonwealth Office in the UK. It is correct at time of publishing. As the situation can change rapidly, visitors are advised to contact the following organisations for the latest travel advice:

British Foreign and Commonwealth Office
Tel: (0845) 850 2829.
Website: www.fco.gov.uk

US Department of State
Website: http://travel.state.gov/travel

Accommodation

HOTELS:

There is a good range of reasonably priced hotel accommodation. Most proprietors speak English. San José has many hotels, from the extravagant to the smaller, family-run hotels in the less fashionable districts. There are several good hotels out of town near the airport. Larger hotels have swimming pools and other leisure facilities. The majority have their own restaurants which are generally good and reasonably priced. Hotel tariffs are likely to alter at any time. A 16.39 per cent government tax and tourism tax is added to hotel prices. Outside the capital, accommodation ranges from mountain lodges, luxury resorts to family owned cabins. **Grading**: Hotels are graded from **A** to **D** according to price range. The A-grade category accounts for 20 per cent of all hotels and costs from the equivalent of US$100. About 20 per cent of hotels are in the B-range and cost US$50-70. C-grade hotels cost US$30-50 and D-range hotels, about 30 per cent, cost US$10-30. Some hotels feature a leaf and a number to show that they strive to uphold the ICT's tourism guidelines established in the *Certification for Sustainable Tourism (CST)* program. For further information check with the Costa Rica Chamber of Hotels online (website: www.costaricanhotels.com).

CAMPING/CARAVANNING:

Facilities exist at San Antonio de Belén, 8km (5 miles) from San José. There is also a camping and caravan site close to Alajuela. Most, but not all, national parks allow camping at designated sites.

Top Things To See

- Discover a mixture of traditional and modern Spanish architecture in the capital **San José**. Places of interest include the **Teatro Nacional**, the **Legislative Assembly building**, and the **Parque Central**, east of which is the Cathedral. The **National Museum** and the **Museum of Gold** are also worth a visit.
- San José is a good centre for excursions into the beautiful **Meseta Central** region. The nearby town of **Cartago** was founded in 1563, but there are no old buildings as earthquakes destroyed the town in 1841 and 1910. However, some of the reconstruction was in the colonial style. Excursions can be made from here to the crater of **Irazú** and to the beautiful valley of **Orosi**, with its colonial church.
- Some of the country's great attractions are its eight **active volcanoes**. The sight of **Arenal,** in the Sierra Volcánica Guanacaste in the northwest, erupting at night is truly spectacular.
- There are numerous beaches, ports and towns worth visiting on the **Caribbean Coast**. The biggest is **Puerto Limón**; others include **Guapiles**, **Tortuguero**, **Barra del Colorado**, **Cahuita** and **Puerto Viejo**. On the Pacific Coast, head for the towns of **Quepos**, **Nicoya**, **Liberia** and **Samara**.

Top Things To Do

- Relax in **San José**'s numerous parks, including the **Parque Nacional**, the **Parque Bolivar** and the **Parque Morazán**.
- Partly in order to continue to encourage **ecotourism**, the Costa Rican authorities have set aside a large proportion of the country (around 26 per cent of the total land area) as national parks and protected areas. There is good road access to most of these areas, and public transport is available. **Braulio Carrillo National Park** is located in the central region of the country just 23km (14 miles) north of San José. It has five kinds of forest, some with characteristic rainforest vegetation. Orchids and ferns, jaguars, ocelots and the Baird tapir may be seen here. There are trails through the park and many lookouts. **Poás Volcano National Park** contains the smouldering **Poás Volcano** and has the only dwarf cloudforest in Costa Rica. The crater of the volcano is 1.5km (1 mile) wide and contains a hot-water lake which changes colour from turquoise to green to grey. Access is possible by road. **Tortuguero National Park** protects the Atlantic green turtle egg-laying grounds; it is in an area of great ecological diversity. Its network of canals and lagoons serves as waterways for transportation and exploration. There are camping facilities and lodges. **Santa Rosa National Park** has the last large strand of tropical dry forest in Central America. There are 10 habitats including extensive savannahs and deciduous and non-deciduous forests. In addition to its abundant wildlife, recreational facilities are provided on some of the beaches. The virgin rainforest in **Corcovado National Park** contains many endangered species. It has the largest tree in Costa Rica, a *ceibo* which is 70m (230ft) high. **Cano Island Biological Reserve** has a bird sanctuary. **Cahuita National Park** protects the only coral reef on Costa Rica's Carribbean coastline. Its other attractions include howler and white-faced monkeys, racoons and 500 species of fish. Costa Rica's highest mountain, **Chirripó** (12,533ft/3828m) is in **Chirripó National Park**. The upper slopes of the mountains are often covered by **cloudforest**, characterised by the algae, mosses and lichens on the permanently wet surfaces. Numerous orchids and ferns grow here, but the forests' most notable inhabitant is the **Resplendent Quetzal** (said to be Latin America's most beautiful bird). Lower down is the **rainforest**. Best visited in the company of an experienced guide (in part, because it is so easy to get lost), these forests are filled with elusive wildlife. Among the creatures they harbour are monkeys, armadillos, sloths, crocodiles, and birds such as toucans, parrots and macaws. **Manuel Antonio National Park** and the **Barra del Colorado National Wildlife Refuge** are also worth a visit, and many of the tiny islands in the **Gulf of Nicoya**, near Puntarenas, are 'biological protection areas'.

Credit: ©Costa Rica Tourist Board

- **Mountain biking** can be done on the trails in the forests and national parks. Hotels have equipment for hire and some specialist operators organise trips. **Horseriding** is also easily arranged. Because a different type of saddle and stirrups are used, even experienced riders may need to take some time to get used to their mounts. Beginners should arrange to have tuition beforehand, as working ranch horses are often used on rides. **Canopy touring** is becoming popular as well; it entails being attached to a harness and 'flying' through the jungle canopy via a series of cables. **Bungee jumping** and **ballooning** are also available.
- In the foothills of **Rincón de la Vieja**, the mud pools bubble permanently and it is possible to bathe in the hot springs in this area. The Central Highlands are the most accessible for the visitor, and feature **Poás,** whose crater contains a boiling sulphurous lake, and **Irazú**, its desolate landscape resembling the surface of the moon.
- The most popular adventure sport is **white water rafting**. Outfitters and guides can arrange trips. The **Reventazón River** (class III) is suitable for beginners, while more experienced rafters can tackle the **Pacuare** (class IV) and the **Pascua** (class V) rivers. The best times to go are from May to November. **Lake Arenal** is one of the world's top **windsurfing** spots. Situated at 5580ft (1700m) above sea level, the lake offers its best windsurfing between April and December. **Puerto Soley** on the northern Pacific coast offers good **ocean windsurfing**. **Surfing** is possible at many beaches, being especially popular at **Pavones** on the Pacific coast and at **Playa Naranjo** in the northwest. This part of the country also offers excellent **diving** and **snorkelling**, with more than 20 local dive sites. Tuition and equipment hire are widely available. **Cocos Island**, praised by Jacques Cousteau, and **Caño Island**, off the southwest coast, are also good diving areas.
- On the **Pacific Coast,** the beaches around **Puntarenas** are rather poor, although **San Lucas Island**, just off the port, has magnificent beaches. There are beautiful beaches in the **Guanacaste** area, near **Quepos** in the Central Pacific and near **Golfito** in the South. **Puerto Caldera**, a few miles south of Puntarenas, is a popular port of call for cruise liners.
- The Pacific coast, from the **Gulf of Papagayo** to **Golfito** offers excellent **sport fishing**. Sailfish, marlin, tuna and wahoo are among the catches. The **Tortuguero Canals** and the area around **Barra del Colorado** offer good freshwater game fishing, while trout can be caught in the country's mountain streams.

TOURIST INFORMATION

Instituto Costarricense de Turismo (ICT)
Street address: Costado Este del Puente Juan Pablo II, Sobre Autopista General Cañas, San José, Costa Rica
Postal address: Apartado 777, 1000 San José, Costa Rica
Tel: 299 5800.
Website: www.visitcostarica.com

Cámara Nacional de Turismo (CANATUR)
Apartado 828, 1000 San José, Costa Rica
Tel: 234 6222.
Website: www.costarica.tourism.co.cr

Fundación de Parques Nacionales
300 Metros Norte, 175 Metros Este, Iglesia Santa Teresita, San José, Costa Rica
Tel: 257 2239.
Website: www.fpncostarica.org

Entertainment

FOOD & DRINK: Restaurants in towns and cities serve a variety of foods including Chinese, French, Italian, Mexican and North American. Food is satisfactory, from the most

A B C D E F G H I J K L M N O P Q R S T U V W X Y Z

expensive to the cheapest eating places (which are generally found west of the city centre). Food *sodas* (small restaurants) serve local food.

National specialities:
- *Casado* (rice, beans, stewed beef, fried plantain, salad and cabbage).
- *Olla de carne* (soup of beef, plantain, corn, yuca, nampi and chayote).
- *Sopa negra* (black beans with a poached egg).
- *Picadillo* (meat and vegetable stew).
- *Gallos* (filled tortillas).
- *Tortas* (containing meat and vegetables).

National drinks:
There are many types of cold drinks made from fresh fruit, milk or cereal flour, for example:
- *Cebada* (barley flour).
- *Pinolillo* (roasted corn).
- *Horchata* (corn meal with cinnamon).

Imported alcoholic and soft drinks are widely available. Coffee is good value and has an excellent flavour.

Tipping: Tipping is not necessary but is acceptable if the service was particularly outstanding. Restaurants add a 23 per cent service charge to the bill.

NIGHTLIFE: San José especially has many nightclubs, venues with folk music and dance, theatres and cinemas.

SHOPPING: Special purchases include wood and leather rocking chairs (which dismantle for export), as well as a range of local crafts available in major cities and towns. Local markets are also well worth visiting. Prices are slightly higher than in other Latin American countries. Best buys are wooden items, ceramics, jewellery and leather handicrafts.

Shopping hours: Mon-Sat 0900-1800/1900. There may be variations between areas.

Business

- **GDP:** US$18.4 billion (2004).
- **Main exports:** Electronic components, fruits and vegetables.
- **Main imports:** Petroleum products, chemical products and alcoholic beverages.
- **Main trade partners:** USA, Central America and EU.

ECONOMY: Electronics represent 27 per cent of Costa Rica's export revenues while 22 per cent of export earnings are derived from agriculture (melons, pineapple, coffee, bananas, meat, sugar and cocoa). Staple crops are also grown for domestic consumption. Manufacturing industry consists of food processing, textiles, chemicals and plastics and is steadily expanding with Government encouragement. New industries include aluminium production, following the discovery of a large bauxite deposit. Oil and hydroelectricity meet the bulk of the country's energy needs. Tourism dominates the service sector and is the most important source of foreign exchange earnings. The economy is nearly static at present with annual growth under one per cent. Costa Rica receives some international aid through international bodies such as the IMF, the Inter-American Development Bank and from the USA, which is Costa Rica's main trade partner. Costa Rica is also a member of the Central American Common Market.

BUSINESS ETIQUETTE: Customs tend to be conservative. Advance appointments, courtesy and punctuality are appreciated. It is preferable to have some knowledge of Spanish, although many locals speak English. Best months for business visits are November and December; avoid the last week of September, which is the end of the financial year.

Government office hours: Mon-Fri 0800-1600.

COMMERCIAL INFORMATION

Cámara de Comercio de Costa Rica (Chamber of Commerce)
Apartado 1114-1000, 1000 San José, Costa Rica
Tel: 221 0005.
Website: www.camara-comercio.com

Cámara de Industrias de Costa Rica (Chamber of Industries)
350 metros sur de la Fuente de la Hispanidad, San Pedro de Montes de Oca, Apartado 10003, San José, Costa Rica
Tel: 281 0006.
Website: www.cicr.com

Costa Rican-American Chamber of Commerce
Apartado 4946-1000, San José, Costa Rica
Tel: 220 2200.
Website: www.amcham.co.cr

Promotora del Comercio Exterior de Costa Rica (PROCOMER)
Apartado 1278-1007, San José, Costa Rica
Tel: 299 4700.
Website: www.procomer.com

Côte d'Ivoire

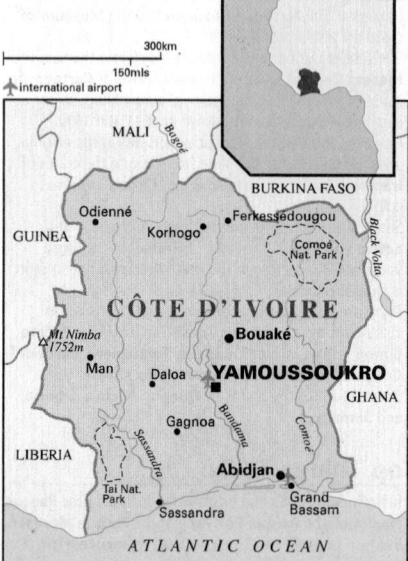

Location: West African coast.

Time: GMT

Overview

During Medieval times, the region that is now Côte d'Ivoire was at the centre of several major African trade routes, linking the empires which then existed in Ghana and Mali. European traders had been present in the region since the 15th century, but it was not until the 19th that the French undertook a determined penetration of the region.

The territory was later incorporated into French West Africa until it was granted independence in August 1960. The leadership of the country was taken over by Félix Houphouët-Boigny, a quirkily effective politician who dominated the country's political life for the next 30 years. Houphouët-Boigny retained close links with the West – especially France, but also apartheid South Africa. During his time in office, Côte d'Ivoire was renowned as the most prosperous and most stable country in the West African region. It also hosted the largest French community in francophone Africa. His rule was shaken by economic recession in the 1980s, when commodity prices of the main exports, cocoa and coffee, plunged. Domestic pressure for democratisation produced further stresses.

The first multi-party elections since independence were held in 1990 which Houphouët-Boigny easily won against veteran opposition leader Laurent Gbagbo. Houphouët-Boigny died in December 1993 and was replaced by the former speaker of the National Assembly, Henri Konan Bédié. The careful ethnic and regional balance which Houphouët-Boigny had nurtured, together with his welcoming of immigrant workers, was soon compromised. Bedie introduced the concept of 'Ivoirite' (Ivorian nationalism) into the political discourse, which quickly acquired xenophobic connotations. This began a sequence of events which was to deprive the country of its long record of stability and prosperity.

An armed rebellion in 2002 split the nation in two, and the main players in the conflict have so far failed to find a political solution. Although the fighting has stopped, the country remains divided and peacekeepers patrol the buffer zone between the rebel-held north and the Government-controlled south.

General Information

AREA: 322,462 sq km (124,503 sq miles).

POPULATION: 17.1 million (2005).

POPULATION DENSITY: 53 per sq km.

CAPITAL: Yamoussoukro (administrative and political capital since 1983). **Population**: 110,000 (2005). Abidjan (economic capital). **Population**: 3 million (2005).

GEOGRAPHY: Côte d'Ivoire shares borders with Liberia, Guinea, Mali, Burkina Faso and Ghana. There are 600km (370 miles) of coast on the Gulf of Guinea (Atlantic Ocean). The southern and western parts of the country are forested, with undulating countryside rising to meet the savannah plains of the north and the mountainous western border. Three rivers, the Sassandra, the Bandama and the Comoé, run directly north–south and, on their approach to the coast, flow into a series of lagoons. Birdlife is plentiful throughout the country, but particularly so near the coast.

GOVERNMENT: Republic. Gained independence from France in 1960. In 1999, the army took power and installed a National Council for Public Salvation. **Head of State**: President Laurent Gbagbo since 2000. **Head of Government**: Interim Prime Minister Charles Konan Banny since December 2005. **Recent history:** Political tensions are on the rise following the postponement of Presidential elections scheduled for 30 October 2005. Mr Gbagbo has invoked a law to stay in office even though his five-year term was set to end in October. The African Union recommended that Mr Gbagbo should stay in power for a further 12 months, but urged him to appoint a prime minister - acceptable to all parties - with executive powers. A historian by profession, Laurent Gbagbo is a former trade union activist who, since the 1980s, has taken a strongly nationalist stance, espousing the concept of pure Ivorian parentage. There have been an increasing number of rallies in Côte D'Ivoire calling for an end to Gbagbo's mandate. Elections are now scheduled within the next 12 months. In December 2005, the South African and Nigerian Presidents - entrusted by the UN to try to solve the Côte d'Ivoire crisis - chose Charles Konan Banny as interim Prime Minister for the transition period, which will end in October 2006. This followed wide consultations with Ivorian political parties.

LANGUAGE: The official language is French. The main African languages are Yacouba, Senoufo, Baoulé, Betie, Attie, Agni and Dioula (the market language).

RELIGION: 34 per cent Christian, 27 per cent Muslim, 15 per cent traditional beliefs. It is important to note, however, that these percentages are based on census results in 1998, of which some Muslim foreign workers may have been excluded - therefore, the Muslim percentage may be higher than is indicated here.

ELECTRICITY: 220 volts AC, 50Hz. Round two-pin plugs are standard.

SOCIAL CONVENTIONS

One of the most striking features of Côte d'Ivoire, distinguishing it from many other African countries, is the extreme ethnic and linguistic variety. The size of each of the 60 groups – which include the Akar, Kron, Nzima, Hone, Voltaic and Malinke peoples – varies widely and the area they occupy may cover a whole region. With very few exceptions every Ivoirian has a mother tongue which is that of the village, along with traditions, family and social relations within their ethnic group. French has become the official language of schools, cities and government and therefore has an influence on lifestyle even at a modest level. Handshaking is normal. Tropical lightweight clothes are essential, a light raincoat in the rainy season and a hat for the sun. Casual wear is widely acceptable but beachwear should be confined to the beach or poolside. Dress tends to err on conservative - men wearing long trousers and women wearing knee-length or longer skirts, dresses and trousers. Ties need only be worn for formal occasions. Small tokens of appreciation, a souvenir from home or a business gift with the company logo are always welcome. Normal courtesies should be observed and it is considered polite to arrive punctually for social occasions. There are no restrictions on smoking. Snakes are regarded as sacred by some ethnic groups.

Climate

Dry from December to April, long rains from May to July, a short dry season from August to September, short rains in October and November. In the north the climate is more extreme – rains (May to October) and dry (November to April).

Required clothing: Tropical lightweights; warmer clothing for evenings.

Communications

Telephone: International telecommunications are available in major towns and centres. IDD is available. Country code: 225.

Mobile telephone: Roaming agreements exist with international mobile phone operators.

Internet: Public access is available at Internet cafes in Abidjan.

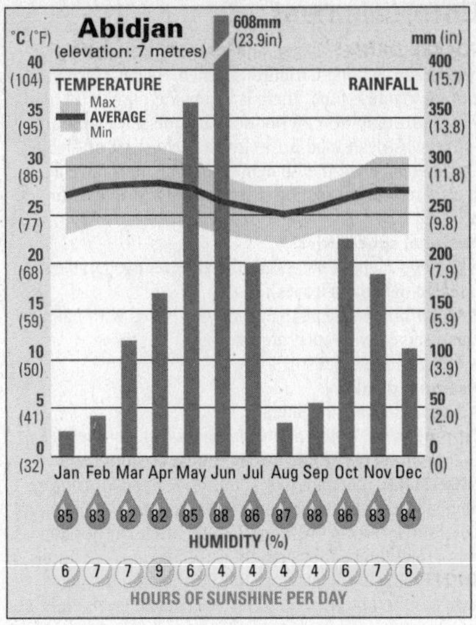
Abidjan
(elevation: 7 metres)
608mm (23.9in)
°C (°F)
mm (in)
TEMPERATURE
RAINFALL
Max
AVERAGE
Min
40 (104)
35 (95)
30 (86)
25 (77)
20 (68)
15 (59)
10 (50)
5 (41)
0 (32)
400 (15.7)
350 (13.8)
300 (11.8)
250 (9.8)
200 (7.9)
150 (5.9)
100 (3.9)
50 (2.0)
0 (0)
Jan Feb Mar Apr May Jun Jul Aug Sep Oct Nov Dec
85 83 82 82 85 88 86 87 88 86 83 84
HUMIDITY (%)
6 7 7 9 6 4 4 4 4 6 7 6
HOURS OF SUNSHINE PER DAY

Post: Airmail to Europe takes up to two weeks. Post office opening hours: Mon-Fri 0730-1200 and 1430-1800.

MEDIA:

The Government has used the media under its control, particularly the state broadcaster Radiodiffusion Télévision Ivoirienne (RTI), as a powerful tool in the country's ongoing crisis. As Ivorian forces launched attacks on rebels in the north in late 2004, state media fell into propaganda while opposition and independent newspapers based in Abidjan were raided and ceased publication. FM relays of foreign stations in the city such as the *BBC*, *Radio France Internationale* and *Africa No1* were disrupted. Radio is Ivory Coast's most-popular medium. There are approximately 30 low-power, non-commercial community radio stations, including some run by the Catholic Church. There are no private terrestrial TV stations, although pay-TV services are provided by Canal Satellite Horizons. Rebels in the centre of the country use state radio and TV facilities in Bouake for their own broadcasts. In August 2004, UN peacekeepers launched their own radio station, *ONUCI FM*. The station is now available in Abidjan and rebel-held towns in the north.

Press: All newspapers are in French. The main dailies include state-owned newspaper *Fraternité Matin*, *Notre Voie*, which is owned by the ruling party, opposition newspaper *Le Patriote; Soir Info, Le Jour, Le Front, L'Inter* and *24 Heures* are all privately owned.

TV: State-run Radiodiffusion Télévision Ivoirienne (RTI) operates *La Première* and *TV2*.

Radio: State-run Radiodiffusion Télévision Ivoirienne (RTI) operates *La Chaîne Nationale* and *Fréquence 2; Radio Nostalgie* is a private, Abidjan FM station; *Africa No1* is a relay of a Gabon-based pan-African station, with some local programming; *Radio Espoir* is an Abidjan Catholic station; *Radio Paix Sanwi* is an Aboisso Catholic station.

Passport/Visa

	Passport Required?	Visa Required?	Return Ticket Required?
Full British	Yes	Yes	Yes
Australian	Yes	Yes	Yes
Canadian	Yes	Yes	Yes
USA	Yes	Yes	Yes
Other EU	Yes	Yes	Yes
Japanese	Yes	Yes	Yes

Note: *Regulations and requirements may be subject to change at short notice, and you are advised to contact the appropriate diplomatic or consular authority before finalising travel arrangements. Any numbers in the chart refer to the footnotes below.*

PASSPORTS: Passports valid for three months after intended length of stay required by all except nationals of Benin, Burkina Faso, Mali, Mauritania, Niger, Senegal and Togo holding national ID cards.

VISAS: Required by all except the following:

(a) nationals of other ECOWAS countries for stays of up to three months;

(b) **1.** nationals of Andorra, Chad, Monaco, Morocco, Seychelles, Tunisia and the Vatican City for stays of up to three months;

(c) transit passengers leaving on the same or first connecting flight within 12 hours, provided holding onward or return documentation and not leaving the airport.

Types of visa and cost: Prices vary according to nationality. Prices given are for UK nationals. *Tourist*, *Business* and *Transit*: £35 (single-entry); £45 (multiple-entry).

Validity: Three months.

Application to: Consulate (or Consular section at Embassy); see *Passport/Visa Information*.

Application requirements: *Tourism*: (a) Valid passport. (b) One application form. (c) One passport-size photo. (d) Evidence of hotel booking or faxed letter of invitation from a Côte d'Ivoire resident. (e) Return ticket or travel itinerary. (f) Stamped, self-addressed, registered envelope for return of passport (if applying by post). (g) Fee. *Business*: (a)-(g) and, (h) Fax from home company confirming financial responsibility for the applicant and an invitation letter faxed from Côte d'Ivoire.

Visa Note: Along with a valid visa, the following nationals require an authorisation from the Ministry of Security well in advance: Afghanistan, Albania, Algeria, Angola, Bangladesh, Bolivia, Cambodia, Chile, China (PR), Colombia, Cuba, Egypt, Iran, Iraq, Indonesia, Jordan, Korea (Dem Rep), Laos, Lebanon, Libya, Myanmar, Nicaragua, Pakistan, Phillippines, Singapore, Sudan, Sri Lanka, Syrian Arab Republic, Thailand, Vietnam and Yemen.

Note: A yellow fever vaccination certificate is required for all travellers over one year of age.

Working days required: Two to three days, although it may take longer, depending on nationality.

PASSPORT/VISA INFORMATION

Embassy of the Republic of Côte d'Ivoire in the UK
2 Upper Belgrave St, London SW1X 8BJ, UK
Tel: (020) 7201 9601.
Opening hours: Mon-Fri 1000-1300; 1400-1700 (visa application); 1400-1730 (visa collection).

Embassy of the Republic of Côte d'Ivoire in the USA
2424 Massachusetts Avenue NW, Washington DC 20008, USA
Tel: (202) 797 0300.
Also deals with tourism enquiries.

Money

Currency: CFA (*Communauté Financiaire Africaine*) Franc (XOF) = 100 centimes. Notes are in denominations of XOF10,000, 5000, 2000, 1000 and 500. Coins are in denominations of XOF250, 100, 50, 25, 10, 5 and 1. Côte d'Ivoire is part of the French Monetary Area. Only currency issued by the *Banque des États de l'Afrique de l'Ouest* (Bank of West African States) is valid; currency issued by the *Banque des États de l'Afrique Centrale* (Bank of Central African States) is not. The CFA Franc is tied to the Euro.

Currency exchange: Currency can be exchanged at the airport as well as at main banks and hotels.

Credit & debit cards: American Express and MasterCard are widely accepted; Diners Club and Visa have more limited use. Check with your credit or debit card company for details of merchant acceptability and other facilities which may be available.

Traveller's cheques: These are accepted in hotels, restaurants and some shops.

Currency restrictions: The import of local currency is unlimited. The export of local currency is limited to amounts up to the value of XOF10,000. The import of all foreign currency other than Euros must be declared. The export of foreign currency is limited to amounts up to the equivalent of XOF25,000 or the amount imported and declared on arrival. There is no restriction on the re-export of unused travellers cheques and letters of credit.

Banking hours: Mon-Fri 0930-1300 and 1400-1730.

Exchange rate indicators:

Rate at time of publishing

£1.00=	XOF967.54
$1.00=	XOF548.32

Duty Free

The following goods may be imported into Côte d'Ivoire by passengers over 15 years of age without incurring customs duty:

200 cigarettes or 25 cigars or 250g of tobacco or 100 cigarillos; one bottle of wine; one bottle of spirits; 0.5l of toilet water and 0.25l of perfume.

Restricted items: Duty must be paid on video cameras, which may be imported for personal use only. A deposit must be paid on entry and is refundable on departure. Sporting guns can be imported under licence. Limits are placed on certain other personal effects; contact the Consulate prior to departure.

Public Holidays

Below are listed Public Holidays for the January 2006-June 2007 period.

2006: Jan 1 New Year's Day. **Jan 10** Eid al-Adha (Feast of the Sacrifice). **Apr 10** Mouloud (Birth of the Prophet). **Apr 17** Easter Monday. **May 1** Labour Day. **May 25** Ascension. **June 5** Whit Monday. **Aug 7** Independence Day. **Aug 15** Assumption. **Sep 1** Lailat al-Miraj (Ascent of the Prophet). **Nov 1** All Saints' Day. **Oct 22-24** Eid al-Fitr (End of Ramadan). **Nov 9** Day of Mourning. **Nov 15** Peace Day. **Dec 7** Félix Houphouët-Boigny Remembrance Day. **Dec 25** Christmas. **Dec 31** Eid al-Adha (Feast of the Sacrifice).

2007: Jan 1 New Year's Day. **Apr 9** Easter Monday. **Mar 31** Mouloud (Birth of the Prophet). **May 1** Labour Day. **May 17** Ascension. **May 28** Whit Monday.

Note: (a) Holidays that fall on a Sunday are often observed on the following day. (b) Muslim festivals are timed according to local sightings of various phases of the moon and the dates given above are approximations. During the lunar month of Ramadan that precedes Eid al-Fitr, Muslims fast during the day and feast at night and normal business patterns may be interrupted. Some disruption may continue into Eid al-Fitr itself. Eid al-Fitr and Eid al-Adha may last anything from two to 10 days, depending on the region. For more information, see the *World of Islam* appendix.

Health

	Special Precautions?	Certificate Required?
Yellow Fever	Yes	1
Cholera	Yes	2
Typhoid & Polio	3	N/A
Malaria	4	N/A

Note: *Regulations and requirements may be subject to change at short notice, and you are advised to contact your doctor well in advance of your intended date of departure. Any numbers in the chart refer to the footnotes below.*

1: A yellow fever vaccination certificate is required from travellers over one year of age coming from all countries.

2: Following WHO guidelines issued in 1973, a cholera vaccination certificate is no longer a condition of entry to Côte d'Ivoire. However, cholera is a serious risk in this country and precautions are essential. Up-to-date advice should be sought before deciding whether these precautions should include vaccination, as medical opinion is divided over its effectiveness; see the *Health* appendix for more information.

3: Immunisation against typhoid is usually advised.

4: Malaria risk (and risk of other insect-borne diseases) exists throughout the year in the whole country, including urban areas. The malignant *falciparum* form is prevalent. Resistance to chloroquine and sulfadoxine-pyrimethamine has been reported. A weekly dose of mefloquine is the recommended prophylaxis.

Food & drink: All water should be regarded as being potentially contaminated. Water used for drinking, brushing teeth or making ice should have first been boiled or otherwise sterilised. Milk is unpasteurised and should be boiled. Powdered or tinned milk is available and is advised, but make sure that it is reconstituted with pure water. Avoid dairy products which are likely to have been made from unboiled milk. Only eat well cooked meat and fish, preferably served hot. Pork, salad and mayonnaise may carry increased risk. Vegetables should be cooked and fruit peeled.

Other risks: *Bilharzia* (schistosomiasis) is present. Avoid swimming and paddling in fresh water; swimming pools which are well chlorinated and maintained are safe. *Hepatitis B* is hyperendemic and *hepatitis A* and *E* are widespread. *Meningitis* risk is present depending on area visited and time of year. *Sleeping sickness* (trypanosomiasis) is reported. There have been recent cases of *ebola*. There is a high incidence of *HIV/AIDS*.

Rabies is present. For those at high risk, vaccination before arrival should be considered. If you are bitten, seek medical advice without delay. For more information, consult the *Health* appendix.

Health care: Health care facilities in the main towns are up to international standards but expensive; medical insurance is essential.

Travel - International

AIR:

Airlines serving Côte d'Ivoire include *Air Burkina*, *Air France, British Airways, Egyptair, Kenya Airways, SN Brussels, South African Airways, Trans African Airlines* and *VLM*. Côte d'Ivoire has a shareholding in *Air Afrique*, although the future of this airline, due to financial difficulties, is still under negotiation. It is recommended that visitors re-confirm returns flights 72 hours in advance.

Approximate flight times: From Abidjan to *London* is 6 hours, to *New York* is 12 hours.

Main airports: *Abidjan (ABJ)* (Félix Houphouët-Boigny) (website: www.aeria.ci) is 16km (10 miles) southeast of Abidjan (travel time – 25 minutes). *To/from the airport:* Buses and taxis are available to the city (travel time - 25

A B C D E F G H I J K L M N O P Q R S T U V W X Y Z

minutes). *Facilities:* Duty free shop, restaurant, shops, banks/bureaux de change, post office, pharmacy and car hire. *Yamoussoukro (ASK) (San Pedro)* has been upgraded to international standard.
Departure tax: XOF3000 for African destinations and XOF5000 for all other departures (from Abidjan airport - prices differ according to airport flown from).

SEA:
Main ports: *Abidjan* is the main port in Cote d'Ivoire; however, there are no regular passenger sailings. Cargo liners provide limited accommodation for passengers travelling from Europe.

RAIL:
The Abidjan-Niger Railway extends to Burkino Faso. There are two through-trains with sleeping and restaurant cars from Abidjan to Ouagadougou (Burkina Faso) daily (travel time - 25 to 27 hours). Those intending to travel should be aware that the Burkina Faso rail network is under constant threat of closure because of financial difficulties: check with the appropriate authorities before finalising arrangements.

ROAD:
There are road links of varying quality from Kumasi (Ghana) and from Burkina Faso, Guinea and Liberia and Mali. Borders close at night. **Bus**: Frequent services operate to Accra (Ghana) and Ouagadougou (Burkina Faso). There is a service approximately once a week to Bamako (Mali); the journey can be very long (36 to 96 hours). Bush **taxis** also operate on these routes.

Travel - Internal

AIR:
Air Ivoire (VU) (website: www.airivoire.com) no longer runs domestic flights. Check with travel agent for new options.
Departure tax: XOF800.

RAIL:
The Abidjan–Ouagadougou railway is one of the most efficient in Africa and runs trains daily from Abidjan to Bouaké and Ferkessédougou. Children under four years of age travel free. Children aged between four and 9 pay half fare.

ROAD:
Côte d'Ivoire has a good road system by West African standards, with 68,000km (42,250 miles) of roads, 5600km (3480 miles) of which are surfaced. However, drivers should be extra aware of potholes and poorly lit vehicles. Petrol stations are frequent except in the north. Traffic drives on the right. **Bus**: Small private buses and bush taxis operate throughout the country; they are efficient, although often extremely overcrowded. There are also larger coaches for the longer journeys. **Taxi**: These are available in main cities, although often of unsound mechanical condition. **Car hire**: Cars may be hired in Abidjan, main towns and at the airport. **Documentation**: Insurance is compulsory for the driver. The driver requires a UK or most other (applicable) national driving licences, accompanied by attestation from the Embassy of the issuing country that it is genuine.

URBAN:
Extensive bus and boat services are operated in Abidjan by *SOTRA* on a two-tiered fare structure. Taxis are usually red and metered; rates are doubled from 0000-0600.

Travel times: The following chart gives approximate travel times (in hours and minutes) from **Abidjan** to other major towns in the Côte d'Ivoire.

	Air	Rail
Bondoukou	**1.20**	-
Man	**0.50**	-
Odienne	**2.20**	-
San Pedro	**1.00**	-

Travel Advice

All travel is advised against to Côte d'Ivoire. If travellers do decide to travel to Côte d'Ivoire, they should take strong security precautions.
Following the postponement of Presidential elections scheduled for 30 October 2005, an increase in political tension remains high. Events can move fast and violence could erupt at short notice.
Travellers should take particular care in public places and avoid all crowds and demonstrations.
The threat from terrorism in Côte d'Ivoire is low.
This advice is based on information provided by the Foreign and Commonwealth Office in the UK. It is correct at time of publishing. As the situation can change rapidly, visitors are advised to contact the following organisations for the latest travel advice:

British Foreign and Commonwealth Office
Tel: (0845) 850 2829.
Website: www.fco.gov.uk

US Department of State
Website: http://travel.state.gov/travel

Accommodation

Hotels and restaurants are expensive in the larger towns. There are several hotels of international standard in Abidjan. In general, there is a choice between luxury, medium-range and cheaper accommodation in the larger towns. In all cases it is advisable to book in advance. For further information, contact the Office Ivoirien du Tourisme et de l'Hôtellerie (see *Accommodation Information*). **Grading**: Hotels are graded from **1** to **5 stars**.

ACCOMMODATION INFORMATION

Office Ivoirien du Tourisme et de l'Hôtellerie
2nd Floor, ex-EECI Building, place de la République,
Abidjan 01 BP 8538, Côte d'Ivoire
Tel: 2025 1600.
Website: www.tourismeci.org

Top Things To See & Do

- **Yamoussoukro** the new administrative and political capital since 1983, is about 230km (143 miles) north of Abidjan. Discover the town's lively market, the **Palace and Plantations of the President** and the **Mosque**. Also of architectural interest but, above all, of statistical interest, is the **Cathédrale Notre-Dame-de-la-Paix**. Fractionally smaller than St Peter's in Rome, it incorporates a greater area of stained glass than the total area of stained glass in France. Roman Catholicism is a minority religion in Côte d'Ivoire (some say that the Cathedral could accommodate every Roman Catholic in the country several times over). Yamoussoukro was the birthplace of Félix Houphouët-Boigny, who was Côte d'Ivoire's President for 33 years. The cathedral was paid for almost entirely out of his own pocket.
- The former capital and largest city, **Abidjan** is dominated by the **Plateau**, the central commercial district. The older, more traditional heart of the city is **Treichville**, home of many bars, restaurants and nightclubs as well as the colourful central market. There is a very good museum, the **Ifon Museum** as well as the **National Museum** containing historic artifacts, statues and ivory. Suburbs have grown up along the banks of the lagoon; these include **Cocody**, **Marcory** and **Adjamé**.
- About 100km (60 miles) east of the former capital is the beach resort of **Assouinde**; other places being developed as tourist attractions include **Tiagba**, a stilt town; **Grand Bassam**, whose sandy beaches make the place a favourite weekend retreat for the inhabitants of Abidjan; and **Bondoukou**, one of the oldest settlements in the country. Please note that in Abidjan and the surrounding coastal resorts, there is a dangerous deep current and swimmers should stay near the shore. Local advice should be taken.
- There is also good coastal and river **fishing**. Red carp, barracuda, mullet and sole can all be caught from the shores of the lagoons. Sea trips can be organised through travel agencies to catch shark, swordfish, bonito and marlin. Boats and instructors are available in Abidjan, where **water-skiing** facilities are also available.
- In the west of the country, visit the attractive town of **Man**, situated in a region of thickly forested mountains and plateaux. The nearby **waterfalls** are a popular attraction, as are **climbs** to the peak of **Mount Tonkoui** and visits to the villages of **Biankouma** and **Gouessesso**, 55km (34 miles) away.
- Other towns of interest include **Korhogo**, the main city of the north and centre of a good fishing and hunting district; the former capital of **Bingerville**; and the town of **Bouaké** in the centre of the country.
- Discover **African wildlife.** The national parks are largely inaccessible for visitors without their own vehicles. Local guides are necessary and easily available. The largest and oldest national park is **Comoë National Park** in the northeast, where lions, waterbucks, hippopotami and other animals can be observed. A landing strip nearby facilitates access. The **Abokouamekro Game Reserve is** about an hour outside Yamoussoukro.
- Although much of Côte d'Ivoire has been deforested, there is good **hiking** in the west near **Man** (nicknamed the 'city of 18 mountains'). A guide is necessary for longer walks.

TOURIST INFORMATION

Office Ivoirien du Tourisme et de l'Hotellerie
2nd Floor, ex-EECI Building, place de la République,
Abidjan 01 BP 8538, Côte d'Ivoire
Tel: 2025 1600.
Website: www.tourismeci.org

Entertainment

FOOD & DRINK: Abidjan and other centres have restaurants serving Caribbean, French, Italian, Lebanese and Vietnamese food. There is a growing number of African restaurants catering for foreigners. The best area for spicy African food is the Treichville district of Abidjan. The blue pages of the Abidjan telephone book have a special restaurant section. There are no restrictions on drinking.

National specialities:
- *Kedjenou* (chicken cooked with different vegetables and sealed in banana leaves).
- *N'voufou* (mashed bananas or yam mixed with palm oil and served with aubergine sauce).
- *Attieké* (cassava dish).

National drinks:
- *Bangui* (local palm wine).

Tipping: Most hotels and restaurants include a service charge in the bill; if not, 15 per cent is acceptable.
NIGHTLIFE: There are nightclubs in most major centres. Abidjan is the most lively area with its hotels and lagoon-side tourist resorts. There are also theatres, casinos and bars. Traditional entertainment is offered in some hotels.
SHOPPING: In the markets, hard bargaining is often necessary to get prices down to reasonable levels. Special purchases include wax prints, Ghanaian *kente* cloth, indigo fabric and woven cloth, wooden statuettes and masks, bead necklaces, pottery and basketware. **Shopping hours**: Mon-Fri 0800-1200 and 1430-1830, Sat 0800-1200 and 1500-1900.

Business

- **GDP:** US$24.8 billion.
- **Main imports:** Consumer goods, foodstuff and capital goods.
- **Main exports:** Cocoa, coffee, timber, rubber, cotton, palm oil, pineapples and bananas.
- **Main trade partners:** USA, France, Germany, The Netherlands, Nigeria and Italy.

ECONOMY: The timber industry in Côte d'Ivoire has declined from previous levels due to excessive exploitation, although the Government has now limited production in order to protect the remaining forests. A light industrial sector has grown up processing primary agricultural products and produces textiles, chemicals and sugar – again, these are aimed towards export markets. Newly discovered offshore oil and gas deposits will boost the country's industrial sector as well as meeting future energy needs. Côte d'Ivoire already has an established oil refining operation which, along with cigarette manufacture, forms the main components of the country's industrial economy. It will also reduce Côte d'Ivoire's reliance on imported fuel to supplement the hydroelectric installations that are its main source of power. A service sector is gradually developing, centred on tourism, financial services (exploiting the dominant role of the Abidjan stock exchange in the region) and telecommunications. Côte d'Ivoire is one of the more prosperous economies in West Africa, although its recent progress has been undermined by severe political instability and the difficulty in meeting the standards of international donors; the economy contracted by 1.9 per cent in 2004. The country is a member of all the main regional economic organisations, including the Economic Community of West African States (ECOWAS) and the various bodies associated with the CFA Franc zone.
BUSINESS ETIQUETTE: French is predominantly used in business circles, although executives in larger businesses may speak English. Translators are generally available. Punctuality is expected, although the host may be late. Visiting cards are essential and given to each person met. It is usual for business visitors to be entertained by local hosts in a hotel or restaurant. Businessmen need only wear cotton safari suits. **Office hours**: Mon-Fri 0730-1200 and 1430-1800, Sat 0800-1200.
CONFERENCES/CONVENTIONS: In Abidjan, the *Palais des Congrès* which is part of the *Inter-Continental Hotel* can host conferences for more than 3000 persons. The political capital Yamoussoukro has a capacity for over 5000. For details, contact the Office Ivoirien du Tourisme et de l'Hôtellerie (see *Top Things To See & Do*).

COMMERCIAL INFORMATION

Chambre de Commerce et d'Industrie de Côte d'Ivoire
01 BP 1399, 6 avenue Joseph Anoma,
Abidjan 01, Côte d'Ivoire
Tel: 2033 1600.
Website: www.ccici.org

Croatia

Location: Southeastern Europe.

Time: GMT + 1 (GMT + 2 from last Saturday in March to Saturday before last Sunday in October).

Overview

Converted to Roman Catholicism in the seventh century, the Croats established an independent kingdom during the 10th century, while the Serbs opted for the Eastern Orthodoxy of the Byzantine Empire, culminating in the Great Schism of 1054. In 1529, following the defeat of the Hungarians by the Ottoman Turks, the Habsburg and Ottoman Empires divided Hungary's territories, thereby creating a militarised border in Croatia between the Islamic and Christian worlds, running roughly along the present border between Croatia and Bosnia & Herzegovina. Serbs settled in areas of Croatia known as *Krajina* (border lands), the source of much Croat-Serb conflict thereafter.

Following the Communist takeover of 1945, Croatia became a constituent republic of the new Yugoslav federation led by Josip Broz Tito who, although himself an ethnic Croat, opposed any expression of Croatian nationalism. However, Croatian nationalism grew following Tito's death in 1980.

The disintegration of Yugoslavia began in 1990, after multi-party elections in Slovenia and Croatia. The fighting in Croatia, between the Yugoslav National Army (JNA) and Serb militia on one side and hastily assembled Croat defence forces on the other, was ended by a UN-brokered ceasefire in January 1992.

Although having emerged into the new millennium from a decade in which it experienced a bitter war, and from several years of authoritarian nationalism under the late President, Franjo Tudjman, by early 2003 Croatia had made sufficient progress to apply for EU membership. With 1778km (1111 miles) of mainland coast, emerald-blue waters, secluded pebble beaches and countless unspoilt islands, Croatia is an ideal destination for lovers of sea and sunshine who want to avoid the crowds. While the vast majority of tourists head straight for the Adriatic coast, inland Croatia also holds several places of interest, notably the capital, Zagreb, while Dubrovnik is considered the jewel of the Adriatic.

General Information

AREA: 56,542 sq km (21,831 sq miles).
POPULATION: 4.43 million (official estimate 2004).
POPULATION DENSITY: 78.4 per sq km.
CAPITAL: Zagreb. **Population**: 779,145 (official estimate 2004).
GEOGRAPHY: Croatia stretches along the Adriatic coast, narrowing north-south; the major ports being Rijeka, Pula, Zadar, Sibenik, Split and Dubrovnik. with a larger inland area running west-east from Zagreb to the border with Serbia & Montenegro. The northern two-thirds of this border are formed by the River Danube. The country borders Slovenia and Hungary to the north, Serbia & Montenegro to the east and Bosnia & Herzegovina (southeast from Zagreb; northeast from the Adriatic coastline).
GOVERNMENT: Republic. Independence from the Federal Republic of Yugoslavia proclaimed in 1991. **Head of State**: President Stjepan Mesic since 2000. **Head of Government**: Prime Minister Ivo Sanader since 2003. **Recent history:** The Croatian Parliament is vested with the legislative power. After the first democratic elections in 1990, the first multiparty Parliament (*Sabor*) consisted of two chambers: the Chamber of Representatives (*Zastupnicki Dom*) and the Chamber of Districts (*Zupanijski Dom*). In 2000, the constitution was changed and the semi-Presidential system became a Parliamentary system. After the elimination of the Chamber of Districts under the constitutional amendment enacted in 2001, the Croatian Parliament became unicameral. Currently, it has 152 members who were elected in 2003. Executive power is held by the President, elected for five years, who appoints a Cabinet of Ministers.

The death of President Franjo Tudjman in December 1999 ushered in a new era of Croatian politics. The following month, the *Hrvatska Demokratska* (HDZ) was ousted from control of the Sabor, by a five-party centre-left alliance led by the Social Democratic Party. Then, in February 2000, the Presidential election was won by Stipe Mesic, representing the *Hrvatska Narodna Stranka* (HNS), a member of the governing coalition. Along with a new Prime Minister, social democrat Ivica Racan, Croatia has since adopted a more conciliatory approach both at home and abroad. Treating with the Hague tribunal remains a delicate issue: even limited cooperation has sparked ministerial resignations. The military officers concerned are considered war heroes at home and the issue always has the potential to destabilise the coalition Government. Nonetheless, the broad approach

Croatia

of the Mesic/Racan Government has paid dividends, including membership of the World Trade Organisation and membership of post-NATO security organisation 'Partnership for Peace'. Croatia also has a place on the fast track to EU membership. A formal application was submitted and accepted in February 2003. Croatia may therefore be able to join with the batch of candidate countries scheduled for entry around 2007/8, which includes Bulgaria and Romania: Croatia's economy is in better condition than either of these, but the Hague tribunal problem has to be resolved once and for all. Within the Balkans, steady progress has been made in improving relations with both Bosnia and Serbia & Montenegro.

LANGUAGE: Croatian, Serbian, Italian, Slovene, Slovak and German.

RELIGION: Roman Catholic Croats (76.5 per cent of the total population) and Eastern Orthodox Serbs (11 per cent), as well as small communities of Protestants, Jews and Muslims.

ELECTRICITY: 220 volts AC, 50Hz.

SOCIAL CONVENTIONS: People normally shake hands upon meeting and leaving. Smoking is generally acceptable but there are restrictions in public buildings and on public transport. **Photography**: Certain restrictions exist.

Climate

Croatia has a varied climate, with continental climate conditions in the north and Mediterranean ones on the Adriatic coast.

Required clothing: Lightweights with rainwear for summer. Mediumweights for winter with heavier clothing for inland areas.

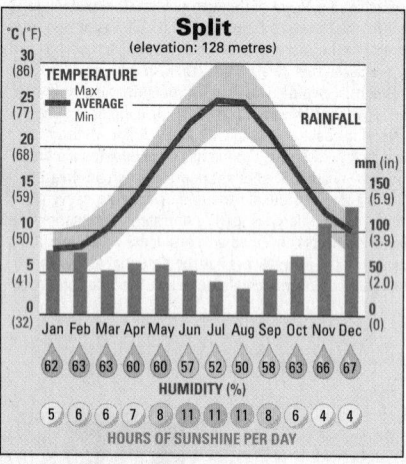

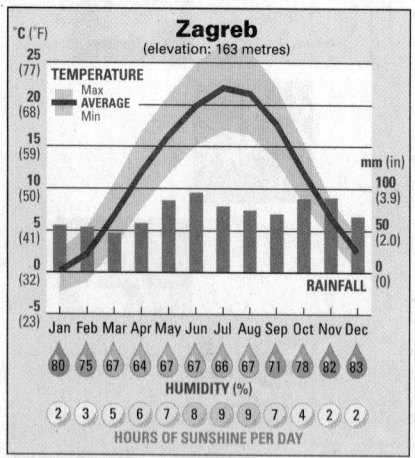

Communications

Telephone: IDD is available. Country code: 385. Telephone booths are operated by phonecards available at post offices, news stands and in some tourist shops.

Mobile telephone: Roaming agreements exist with most international mobile phone companies. Coverage is good.

Internet: Internet cafes can be found in Zagreb and other main towns.

Post: Post offices hours: Mon-Fri 0700-1900 and Sat 0700-1300. Some may be open until 2200 in larger cities. Stamps are available in post offices and from news stands.

MEDIA: Croatia's media operate in a climate of relative freedom following the restrictions of President Tudjman's era. The constitution bans censorship and guarantees press freedom. Croatian Radio-Television, *HRT*, is a national state-owned public broadcaster and is financed by a mixture of

advertising and licence-fee revenues. The frequencies of HRT's third national TV network were allocated to a private bidder in September 2003. Public TV is the main source of news and information. National commercial networks and dozens of private local TV stations compete for viewers.

Press: There are no English-language newspapers at present. The main daily local newspapers are *Novi List* (Rijeka), *Slobodna Dalmacija* (Split) and *Vecernji List* (Zagreb). The weekly press includes *Feral Tribune* and *Nacional*.

TV: *Croatian TV* is public and operates national networks; *RTL Televizije* and *Nova TV* are national, private channels.

Radio: *Croatian Radio* is public and operates three national networks; *Radio 101*, *Otvoreni Radio* and *Narodni Radio* are commercial stations.

Passport/Visa

	Passport Required?	Visa Required?	Return Ticket Required?
Full British	Yes	No	Yes
Australian	Yes	No	Yes
Canadian	Yes	No	Yes
USA	Yes	No	Yes
Other EU	No/1	No	Yes
Japanese	Yes	No	Yes

Note: *Regulations and requirements may be subject to change at short notice, and you are advised to contact the appropriate diplomatic or consular authority before finalising travel arrangements. Any numbers in the chart refer to the footnotes below.*

Restricted entry and transit: Croatia does not recognise passports issued by Chinese Taipei, Palestine and the Turkish Republic of Cyprus.

PASSPORTS: Passport valid for at least the length of stay required by all, except:

1. nationals of EU countries, and nationals of Andorra, Iceland, Liechtenstein, Monaco, Norway, San Marino, Switzerland and Vatican City, with valid national photo ID cards.

VISAS: Required by all except the following for stays of up to 90 days:

(a) nationals listed in the chart above (including the Sovereign Military Order of Malta, although such passport holders may not enter Croatia with national ID cards);

(b) nationals of Andorra, Argentina, Bolivia, Bosnia & Herzegovina, Brazil, Brunei, Bulgaria, Chile, Costa Rica, Ecuador, El Salvador, Guatemala, Honduras, Hong Kong (SAR), Iceland, Israel, Korea (Rep), Liechtenstein, Macau (SAR), Macedonia (Former Yugoslav Republic of), Malaysia, Mexico, Monaco, New Zealand, Nicaragua, Norway, Panama, Paraguay, Romania, San Marino, Serbia & Montenegro, Singapore, Switzerland, Turkey, Uruguay, the Vatican City and Venezuela;

(c) nationals of Russian Federation, if they have a letter of invitation from a Croatian resident or a valid tourist voucher;

(d) transit passengers continuing their journey by the same or first connecting aircraft within 24 hours, provided holding confirmed onward and return documentation and not leaving the airport. **Note:** nationals of Afghanistan, Bangladesh, Congo (Dem Rep), Eritrea, Ethiopia, Ghana, Iraq, Iran, Nigeria, Pakistan, Somalia and Sri Lanka *do* require airport transit visas unless they have a permit for staying in the EU, Andorra, Iceland, Liechtenstein, Monaco, Norway, San Marino, Switzerland or the USA.

Types of visa and cost: *Travel/Transit:* £15 (single-entry); £19 (double-entry); £30 (multiple-entry).

Validity: *Travel:* Valid for a one-year period, with continuous stay or the overall duration of repeated entries not exceeding 90 days, during a six-month period starting from day of entry. *Business:* Valid for one year; can be issued to members of a foreign company provided it is registered in Croatia. For further information on company registration, contact the Croatian Chamber of Economy (see *Business Profile* section). *Transit:* Valid for a six-month period for up to five days maximum; can sometimes be multiple-entry. *Airport Transit:* One or more transit through the Airport International Transit area over a period not exceeding 24 hours. *Group:* Five to 50 persons based on submission of group travel documents, for one entry or transit not exceeding a 30-day period.

Application to: Consulate (or consular section at Embassy); see *Passport/Visa Information*.

Application requirements: (a) Valid passport. (b) Completed application form. (c) Passport-size photo (30 x 35mm and in colour). (d) Proof of sufficient funds to cover duration of stay (minimum of €100 per day). (e) Proof of accommodation within Croatia or documentation regarding the purpose and means of travel (such as business/invitation letter, return or onward ticket, holiday arrangements).

Working days required: Five days to four weeks, depending on nationality and type of visa required.

Multiple-entry visas: Four to six weeks.

PASSPORT/VISA INFORMATION

Embassy of the Republic of Croatia in the UK
21 Conway Street, London W1T 6BN, UK
Tel: (020) 7387 2022 *or* 1144 (consular section).
Website: http://uk.mvp.hr
Opening hours: Mon-Fri 0900-1700; Mon-Thurs 1100-1400, Fri 1000-1200 (visa section).

Embassy of the Republic of Croatia in the USA
2343 Massachusetts Avenue, NW,
Washington, DC 20008, USA
Tel: (202) 588 5899.
Website: www.croatiaemb.org

Money

Currency: Kuna (HRK) = 100 Lipa. Notes are in denominations of HRK1000, 500, 200, 100, 50, 20, 10 and 5. Coins are in denominations of HRK25, 5, 2 and 1, and 50, 20, 10, 5, 2 and 1 lipa.

Currency exchange: Foreign currency can be exchanged in banks, by authorised dealers and post offices. ATMs are widespread.

Credit & debit cards: American Express, Diners Club, MasterCard and Visa are widely accepted. Check with your credit or debit card company for details of merchant acceptability and other facilities which may be available.

Traveller's cheques: To avoid additional exchange rate charges, travellers are advised to take traveller's cheques in US Dollars, Pounds Sterling or Euros.

Currency restrictions: The import and export of local currency is limited to HRK15,000 (in banknotes up to HRK500). The import and export of foreign currency is unlimited but it is compulsory to declare in writing the amounts that exceed the value equivalent to HRK40,000.

Banking hours: Mon-Fri 0700-1900, Sat 0700-1300. Some banks may open on Sundays in larger cities.

Exchange rate indicator:
Rate at time of publishing
£1.00=   HRK10.91
$1.00=   HRK6.18

Duty Free

Travellers are exempt from customs duty for goods of a non-commercial nature which they carry in their personal luggage up to the value of HRK300. In addition, the following goods may be taken into Croatia without incurring customs duty:

200 cigarettes or 50 cigars or 100 cigarillos or 250g of tobacco; 2l of wine and 1l of spirits and 2l of liqueur; 250ml of eau de cologne and perfume up to 50g.

Note: (a) Articles of archaeological, historical, ethnographic, artistic and other scientific or cultural value require an export licence issued by the Croatian authorities. (b) When crossing the state border, travellers must report to the police weapons and ammunition they are bringing in.

Public Holidays

Below are listed Public Holidays for the January 2006-June 2007 period.

2006: Jan 1 New Year's Day. **Jan 6** Epiphany. **Apr 14-17** Easter. **May 1** Labour Day. **Jun 15** Corpus Christi. **Jun 22** Anti-Fascist Resistance Day. **Jun 25** Croatian National Day. **Aug 5** Victory Day and National Thanksgiving Day. **Aug 15** Assumption. **Oct 8** Independence Day. **Nov 1** All Saints' Day. **Oct 22-24*** End of Ramadan. **Dec 25-26** Christmas. **2007: Jan 1** New Year's Day. **Jan 6** Epiphany. **Apr 6-9** Easter. **May 1** Labour Day. **Jun 7** Corpus Christi. **Jun 22** Anti-Fascist Resistance Day. **Jun 25** Croatian National Day.

Note: *The end of Ramadan, while not an official public holiday, is celebrated as such by the Muslim community, and some shops and businesses may be closed on this day.

Health

	Special Precautions?	Certificate Required?
Yellow Fever	No	No
Cholera	No	No
Typhoid & Polio	1	N/A
Malaria	No	N/A

Note: *Regulations and requirements may be subject to change at short notice, and you are advised to contact your doctor well in advance of your intended date of departure. Any numbers in the chart refer to the footnotes below.*

1: Immunisation against both diseases is advisable unless staying solely in first-class accommodation.

Food & drink: Mains water is normally chlorinated, and whilst relatively safe, may cause mild abdominal upsets.

Credit: © Croatian Tourist Board - Ivo Pervan

Built in 1967 Hotel Vicko is a 3-star hotel consisting of 23 rooms, a large air-conditioned restaurant, coffee shop, exchange office, souvenir shop, supermarket, watched parking and a children's playroom. The hotel offer is based on active vacationing: visit to the 6 national parks, rafting, hiking, mountaineering, cave visiting, mountain bike tours, Velebit Canal boat cruising, team-building, paintball, picnics, promotions and professional counselling, seminars and congresses combined with healthy food based on Velebit medical herbs and prepared according to the old recipes of this Velebit region.

In 2004 the new Villa Vicko was built, with a 4 star rating, is situated next to the sea, with 14 rooms and 2 apartments luxuriously furnished and equipped.

**JOSE DOKOZE 20 HR – 23244 STARIGRAD-PAKLENICA
TEL/FAX: +/385/23/369-304   M.B. 3490661
WEB: http:// www.hotel-vicko.hr
e-mail: hotel-vicko@zd.htnet.hr**

Bottled water is available and is advised for the first few weeks of the stay. Milk is pasteurised and dairy products are safe for consumption. Local meat, poultry, seafood, fruit and vegetables are generally considered safe to eat.
Other risks: *Hepatitis A* occurs. Precautions should be taken against tick bites. Immunisation against *tick-borne encephalitis* is advised.
Rabies is present. For those at high risk, vaccination before arrival should be considered. If you are bitten, seek medical advice without delay. For more information, consult the *Health* appendix.
Health care: For UK nationals, hospital and other medical treatment as well as some dental treatment is normally free on presentation of a UK passport. UK residents who are not nationals, should obtain a certificate of insurance from the Inland Revenue Centre for Non-Residents to get medical treatment. Prescribed medicines must be paid for. All other international travellers are advised to take out full medical insurance.

Travel - International

AIR:

The national airline is *Croatia Airlines (OU)* (website: www.croatiaairlines.hr).
Approximate flight times: From Zagreb to *London* is two hours 30 minutes, to *New York* is 10 hours 35 minutes.
Main airports: *Zagreb (ZAG)* (Pleso International) (website: www.zagreb-airport.hr) is 17km (10 miles) southeast of the city. *To/from the airport:* An airport bus runs 0700-2000 to the city centre (travel time – 25 minutes); taxis are also available (travel time – 20 minutes). *Facilities:* Left luggage, banks/bureaux de change, restaurants, snack bars, bars, business lounge, duty free shops, post office, tourist information, first aid and car hire.
Dubrovnik (DBV) (website: www.airport-dubrovnik.hr) is 18km (11 miles) southeast of the city. *To/from the airport:* An airport bus runs to the city (travel time – 20 minutes). *Facilities:* Banks/bureaux de change, post office, bars, duty free shop, shops and car hire.
Split (SPU) (website: www.split-airport.hr) is 25km (16 miles) northwest of the city. *To/from the airport:* An airport bus runs to the city (travel time – 40 minutes). *Facilities:* Banks/bureau de change, post office, car hire, duty free shops and bar/restaurant.

Pula (PUY) (website: www.airport-pula.com) is 8km (5 miles) northwest of the city. *To/from the airport:* An airport bus runs to the city (travel time – 15 minutes). *Facilities:* Bureau de change, car hire, duty free shop and snack bar/restaurant.
Departure tax: None.
SEA:

Main ports: *Dubrovnik.* Passenger and car ferry services run to Italy. The main routes are: Split–Ancona, Zadar–Ancona, Split–Pescara and Dubrovnik–Bari. Fast hydrofoil services operate on some routes.
RAIL:

Direct trains run from Austria, Bosnia & Herzegovina, France, Germany, Hungary, Italy, Serbia, Slovakia, Slovenia and Switzerland.
Express services run from Zagreb to major cities including Berlin, Budapest, Munich, Venice and Vienna.
ROAD:

There are routes from all neighbouring countries. The National Autoclub of the Republic of Croatia (website: www.hak.hr) can provide information.
Bus: There are regular international buses connecting Croatia with Austria, Bosnia & Herzegovina, Germany, Hungary, Italy and the Slovak Republic. *Eurolines* (52 Grosvenor Gardens, London SW1W 0AU; tel: (08705) 143 219; website: www.eurolines.com) and *National Express* (Ensign Court, 4 Vicarage Road, Edgbaston, Birmingham B15 3ES; tel: 08705 808 080; website: www.nationalexpress.com) run regular coach services from the UK to Croatia and other European cities.
Passes: Travellers can either choose Mini-Pass breaks or book a 15-, 30- or 60-day pass. The six Mini-Passes give travellers the freedom to visit three cities, with prices starting from £55. Travellers can stay as long as they like in each city.

Travel - Internal

AIR:

The main domestic airports are located at *Rijeka (RJK)*, 27km from the Island of Krk (travel time – 35 minutes by bus), and at *Split (SPU)*, *Pula (PUY)* and *Dubrovnik (DBV)*, which also receive international flights.
SEA:

There are regular connections between the main ports and the offshore islands. Rijeka, Zadar, Split and Dubrovnik are linked by passenger and car ferries.
RAIL:

The network connects all major cities except Dubrovnik. However, it is often quicker to travel by bus.
ROAD:
In 1996, there were 27,247km of roads in Croatia, including 495km of motorways. A 10-year road-building programme was announced in that year. Unexploded ordinance may remain in Eastern Slavonia and the former Krajina; motorists should avoid these areas. A toll is payable on motorways. Unleaded petrol is available. **Regulations:** Traffic drives on the right. Speed limits are 130kph (81mph) on motorways, 100kph (62mph) on dual carriageways, 50kph (31mph) in built-up areas and 80kph (50mph) outside built-up areas. Heavy fines are imposed for speeding. **Documentation:** National or International Driving Permit. All motorists should also carry a valid passport as proof of identity at all times. A Green Card should be carried by visitors (except EU nationals) taking their own car into Croatia. Without it, insurance cover is limited to the minimum legal cover; the Green Card augments this to the level of cover provided by the car owner's domestic policy. National registration in country of origin is required for all foreign vehicles. **Bus:** There are regular services to destinations all over Croatia. Timetable information is available from Zagreb Central Bus Station (website: www.akz.hr; see links from tourist board website: www.croatia.hr).

Travel Advice

Most visits to Croatia are trouble-free but you should be aware of the global risk of indiscriminate international terrorist attacks, which could be against civilian targets, including places frequented by foreigners.
Unexploded land mines are still a danger. Highly populated areas and major routes are now clear of mines and are safe to visit. However, isolated areas in the mountains and countryside have not all been cleared. Travellers should therefore be careful not to stray from roads and paved areas without an experienced guide.
This advice is based on information provided by the Foreign

Credit: © Croatian Tourist Board – Ivo Pervan

and Commonwealth Office in the UK. It is correct at time of publishing. As the situation can change rapidly, visitors are advised to contact the following organisations for the latest travel advice:

British Foreign and Commonwealth Office
Tel: (0845) 850 2829.
Website: www.fco.gov.uk

US Department of State
Website: http://travel.state.gov/travel

Accommodation

HOTELS:
Croatia has the best of its hotels on its Adriatic coast. Elsewhere, deluxe hotels are only to be found in Zagreb, plus the Plitvice Lakes tourist area on the border with Bosnia & Herzegovina near Bihac, although the situation is rapidly changing. **Grading**: Hotels in Croatia are now officially graded by the Ministry of Tourism into five categories according to the standard of accommodation: **5-star**: Luxury. **4-star**: Deluxe. **3-star**: First class. **2-star**: Moderate. **1-star**: Basic and budget.
Many hotels are still in the process of upgrading their facilities to match EU standards. For a list of classified hotels, contact the Croatian National Tourist Board (see *Top Things To Do*).

CAMPING AND CARAVANNING:
There are over 148 campsites in Croatia, including some naturist camps.

PRIVATE ACCOMMODATION: Private accommodation is increasingly available in Croatia. It is even possible to stay in some lighthouses.

ACCOMMODATION INFORMATION

Croatian Association of Hoteliers
Vladimira Nazora 3, Opatija, Croatia
Tel: (51) 711 415 *or* 567.
Website: www.huh.hr

Top Things To See

- **Zagreb**, Croatia's economic, cultural and administrative heart, sits on the north bank of the river **Sava**. Its historic nuclei, **Gradec** and **Kaptol**, in **Gornji Grad** (Upper Town), were founded in the Middle Ages. Here, a labyrinth of peaceful cobbled streets links the city's oldest and finest monuments: the **Cathedral**, **St Mark's Church** (noted for its red, white and blue tiled roof) and the **Sabor** (seat of the Croatian Parliament). At the foot of the Upper Town lies **Trg Bana Jelacic**, the main square, and **Dolac**, the colourful open-air market. The main square links the Upper Town to **Donji Grad** (Lower Town), the commercial centre of modern-day Zagreb, with theatres, shops, cinemas, museums and cafes. A number of important 19th-century public buildings are located here, including **Glavni Kolodvor** (the main train station), the imposing neo-Baroque **Croatian National Theatre** and the **Academy of Arts and Sciences**. The city boasts one of Europe's first planned parks: **Maksimir**, a magnificent feat of landscaping, with lakes, pavilions and sculptures, dating back to 1794.
- North of Zagreb lies **Zagorje**, a rural area of undulating hills and vineyards with several castles open to the public, the most visited being **Veliki Tabor** and **Trakošcan**.
- Unanimously considered the jewel of Croatia, **Dubrovnik** in the southernmost region of Croatia is best known for its well-preserved **historic centre** contained within 13th-century city walls, its **terracotta rooftops**, and a stunning location overlooking the Adriatic. Today a UNESCO World Heritage Site, the city was a wealthy independent republic up until 1808. The finest monuments date back to those golden years: the 16th-century **Rector's Palace**, the **Franciscan Monastery** (home to Europe's oldest pharmacy) and a number of delightful baroque churches, including the **Cathedral**, **St Blaise's Church** and the **Jesuit Church**.
- Croatia's second-largest city, **Split** is also the economic and cultural capital of Central Dalmatia. The city was founded in the third century AD by the Roman Emperor Diocletian. Today, the traffic-free historic centre lies within the imposing walls of **Diocletian's Palace**, now a UNESCO World Heritage Site. A vibrant cafe scene focuses on the Roman **Peristil**, presided over by the majestic **Cathedral** with its 13th-century Romanesque bell tower. On the hill above town, **Marjan**, an extensive nature reserve planted with pine woods and fragrant Mediterranean shrubs, affords stunning views over the Adriatic.
- Nearby, the tiny medieval city of **Trogir**, founded by the Greeks in the third century BC, is a UNESCO World Heritage Site noted for its beautiful Venetian Gothic stone buildings.
- **Istria** is the largest peninsula on the Croatian coast and, thanks to its easy transport links with nearby Italy and Austria, has also become the country's major tourist destination. The region's administrative centre and chief port, **Pula**, was founded by the Romans in the fifth century BC. Several interesting buildings remain from this period, notably the **Arena**, a well-preserved amphitheatre, which hosts summer concerts and the annual film festival. The city is a good starting point for excursions to **Brijuni National Park**, an archipelago of 14 unspoilt islands. It is possible to stay overnight on the largest island, **Veli Brijun**, where a range of tourist facilities is available.
- On the west coast of Istria lies Croatia's most visited resort, **Porec**. Fortunately, the large hotel complexes of **Plava Laguna** and **Zelena Laguna** are situated out of town, a little way along the coast, leaving the historic centre intact. Built on a small peninsular, Porec dates back to Roman times, and its star attraction is the UNESCO World Heritage-listed **Euphrasius Basilica**, decorated with stunning sixth-century Byzantine mosaics.
- Inland Istria, with romantic hill towns such as **Motovun** and **Groznjan**, makes an ideal day trip from the coast.
- The economic and administrative centre of **Kvarner**, a popular and busy island region, is **Rijeka**, Croatia's largest port. Other than **Trsat Castle**, built on a hilltop commanding splendid views out to sea, Rijeka has little architectural interest, its main claim to fame being the exuberant celebrations it puts on each year in February for **Carnival**.
- In **Northern Dalmatia,** the chief city and port is **Zadar**, the historic centre of which is made up of narrow cobbled streets, some Roman remains and several interesting churches, notably the 12th-century Romanesque **Cathedral**.
- The region's second city is **Sibenik**, worth seeing for its 15th-century UNESCO-listed **Cathedral**, and a good base for visiting **Krka National Park**. Here, the river **Krka** has sculpted a picturesque canyon, famed for its spectacular **Skradinski buk** (Skradin Waterfalls) and the islet of **Visovac**, home to a **Franciscan Monastery**, which can be visited by boat.

Top Things To Do

- In **Zagreb**, visit the **Museum of Arts and Crafts,** which traces Croatian craftsmanship from the Renaissance up until the present day, while the **Mimara Museum** presents a rich collection of painting, sculpture and ceramics from abroad. Also worth visiting are the **Museum of Zagreb**, the **Archaeological Museum** and the **Gallery of Naïve Art**.
- Learn about **Dubrovnik**'s former importance as a world naval power at the city's **Maritime Museum**.
- In Split, the **Museum of Croatian Archaeological Monuments** displays early Croatian religious art, while the **Meštrovic Gallery** celebrates the country's best-known 20th-century sculptor.
- Enjoy the **Dubrovnik Summer Festival**, which takes place each summer, from mid-July to late August, featuring various cultural events plus open-air evening performances of theatre, jazz and classical music. Zagreb and Split also have Summer Festivals.
- **Istria**'s second most popular resort, **Rovinj**, was originally built on a small island, though the narrow strait that separated it from the mainland was filled in during the 18th century. Just out of town lies **Zlatni Rt**, a blissful park affording access to several secluded coves for bathing. Also by the sea, midway between Porec and Rovinj, lies **Vrsar**, home to **Koversada**, Europe's largest nudist resort.
- The main touristic centres of the **Kvarner** region are **Opatija**, **Crikvenica** and **Novi Vinodolski** (sometimes referred to as the 'three rivieras'), all of which have extensive pebble beaches complemented by good accommodation and recreational facilities. Opatija, Croatia's oldest tourist resort, was popular with the Austro-Hungarian nobility and some of its former *fin-de-siècle* elegance remains. Of the many islands scattered throughout the Kvarner Bay, **Krk**, connected to the mainland by a road bridge, is the most developed as well as the largest, with clean beaches and extensive tourist facilities. Further out lies **Rab**, home to the delightful medieval **Rab Town** with a number of elegant Romanesque bell towers; **Cres**, which contains the **Vransko Lake** and is popular with nature lovers; and **Lošinj**, which has pine woods and numerous bays with beaches. Inland from Rijeka, the **Risnjak National Park** is located in the mountains of **Gorski Kotar** and rises to 1528m (510ft) above sea level, making it a popular destination for hiking and climbing.
- In **Northern Dalmatia,** the main attraction is the **Kornati National Park**, an archipelago consisting of over 90 islands scattered over an area of 300 sq km (116 sq miles). Virtually uninhabited, the islands display a harsh, rocky landscape practically devoid of vegetation. Most visitors arrive on organised day trips by boat, though several renovated stone cottages provide 'Robinson Crusoe'-type holiday accommodation. Inland from Zadar, on the southern slopes of the **Velebit Massif**, lies **Paklenica National Park**, also a popular destination for hiking and climbing.
- In Northern Dalamatia, the resorts of the **Makarska Riviera**, centred around the pretty town of **Makarska**, boast long stretches of pebble beaches and are able to accommodate large numbers of holidaymakers. However, the highlight of Central Dalmatia has to be its islands, which are less exploited than those in the north of the country. Taking Split as a base, the closest island, **Brac**, is best known for its magnificent beach, **Zlatni Rat** (Golden Cape), close to the well-equipped but unspoilt resort of **Bol**. **Hvar**, possibly Dalmatia's most beautiful island, is renowned for its rugged coastline, excellent wines and lavender fields. The largest settlement, **Hvar Town**, is built around a picturesque harbour presided over by a hilltop fortress. Chic cafes and restaurants focus on the main square, lined with elegant 15th-century 'palaces' and the much-photographed Renaissance **Cathedral**. Hvar Town claims to have more hours of sunshine than any other resort on the Adriatic, and hotels offer free accommodation in the unlikely event of a snowfall. Slightly less sophisticated, but equally well equipped with hotels and bathing areas, is the friendly town of **Jelsa**. **Vis**, Croatia's most remote inhabited island, is wild and unspoilt. Due to its former status as a Yugoslav military base, it was closed to foreigners until 1989 and has very limited tourist facilities.
- In the southernmost region of Croatia near Dubrovnik, a group of tiny traffic-free islands, known as the **Elaphites**, offer secluded beaches and basic tourist amenities. Further up the coast, the island of **Korcula** is reigned over by the beautifully preserved **Korcula Town**, a marvel of medieval urban planning which has charmed foreign visitors since the first tourists arrived in the 1920s. During summer, regular performances of the colourful *More¯ska* sword dance are staged here. Nearby, the village of **Lumbarda** is home to one of Croatia's few sand beaches. On the island of **Mljet**, the green and unspoilt **Mljet National Park** boasts dense indigenous forests and two interconnected saltwater lakes – **Veliko Jezero** and **Malo Jezero**. In the centre of the larger lake sits the exquisite **St Mary's Island**, crowned by a **Benedictine Monastery**. A series of paths, perfect for mountain biking or hiking, runs round the lakes and through the woods. Back on the mainland, south of Dubrovnik, **Cavtat** is a pretty holiday resort with numerous hotels and pebble beaches. South from here lies the border with **Montenegro**.
- East of Zagreb lies the flat fertile region of Slavonia, the major city of which, **Osijek**, makes an ideal base for visiting **Kopacki Rit Nature Park**, a vast expanse of wetland popular with birdwatchers. South of Zagreb, on the edge of the Dalmatian hinterland, lies one of Croatia's biggest tourist attractions, the UNESCO-listed **Plitvice Lakes National Park**. Situated in a densely forested valley, the park features 16 beautiful blue-green lakes joined together by a succession of spectacular waterfalls. There are numerous hotels, motels and campsites in the area, although tourism development has thankfully been combined with strict environmental preservation policies.

TOURIST INFORMATION

Croatian National Tourist Office in the UK
2 The Lanchesters, 162-164 Fulham Palace Road,
London W6 9ER, UK
Tel: (020) 8563 7979.
Website: www.croatia.hr

Croatian National Tourist Office in the USA
350 Fifth Avenue, Suite 4003, New York, NY 10118, USA
Tel: (212) 279 8672 *or* (800) 829 4416 (toll-free).
Website: www.croatia.hr

Entertainment

FOOD & DRINK:

National specialities:
- Much Croatian food contains cheese and oil, often mixed with other ingredients in pies or 'donuts'.
- The Adriatic coast is renowned for its variety of seafood dishes, including scampi, *prstaci* (shellfish) and *brodet* (mixed fish stewed with rice), all cooked in olive oil and served with vegetables.
- In the interior, visitors should sample *manistra od bobica* (beans and fresh maize soup).

National drinks:
- The regional wines are good.
- Italian espresso is popular and cheap.

Tipping: 10 per cent is expected in hotels, restaurants and taxis.

SHOPPING: Traditional handicrafts like embroidery, woodcarvings and ceramics make good souvenirs. Tourists can reclaim VAT on expenditure of more than HRK500. Visitors should ensure that all receipts are retained after any purchase is made, as financial police have the power to fine visitors without relevant documents. This is to prevent VAT evasion by shopkeepers. **Shopping hours:** Mon-Fri 0800-2000, Sat 0800-1400/1500. Some shops in cities may now open on Sundays.

Business

- **GDP:** US$34.2 billion.
- **Main exports:** Capital goods, chemicals and manufactures.
- **Main imports:** Food, fuel and energy and capital goods.
- **Main trade partners:** EU and Bosnia & Herzegovina.

ECONOMY: After Slovenia, Croatia was the most developed republic of the former Yugoslavia. With substantial support and investment from abroad, the Croatian economy recovered well after the break up of Yugoslavia and several years of civil war. Industry is the most important sector in the economy, producing textiles, chemicals, processed foods, finished metal goods and construction materials. Agriculture, which produces maize, wheat and sugar beet, is important for domestic purposes but has never contributed significantly to the export economy. Mineral deposits of exploitable size include oil, coal and natural gas. Croatia also has an important tourism industry, based on the Dalmatian coast: after being all but wiped out by the civil war, it has recovered and prospered; it now accounts for about 15 per cent of GDP and has been largely responsible for Croatia's recent economic progress. Annual GDP growth is around 4 per cent. After independence, the Government introduced a programme of privatisation and other market reforms in line with those adopted throughout eastern Europe. Croatia joined the IMF in January 1993, the European Bank for Reconstruction and Development and the World Trade Organisation. In May 1994, the Government introduced a new currency, the Kuna: low inflation has allowed the government to keep its value reasonably stable.

BUSINESS ETIQUETTE: In many ways one of the more conservative areas of the former Yugoslav Federation, Croatia tends towards formal business protocol, but this image of Western-style efficiency is often belied by the fact that things go very slowly on account of the cumbersome bureaucracy. Communication, however, is no problem as English and German are widely used as second languages. Business cards including professional or academic titles should be exchanged just after formal introductions. There is also a large number of local agents, advisers, consultants and, to a lesser extent, lawyers, willing to act for foreign companies, but none should be engaged before being thoroughly checked in advance. Croatia has created a more liberal framework for foreign investments so that foreign investors are guaranteed special rights and incentives for investing in Croatia. **Office hours:** Mon-Fri 0800-1600.

COMMERCIAL INFORMATION

Croatian Chamber of Economy
Trg Rooseveltov 2, 10000 Zagreb, Croatia
Tel: (1) 456 1555.
Website: www.hgk.hr

Zagreb Convention Bureau (Information on Conferences/Conventions)
Koptol 4, 10000 Zagreb, Croatia
Tel: (1) 489 8555.
Website: www.zagreb-convention.hr

The Croatian National Tourist Office can also offer advice through their Convention Bureau (see *Top Things To Do*).

Cuba

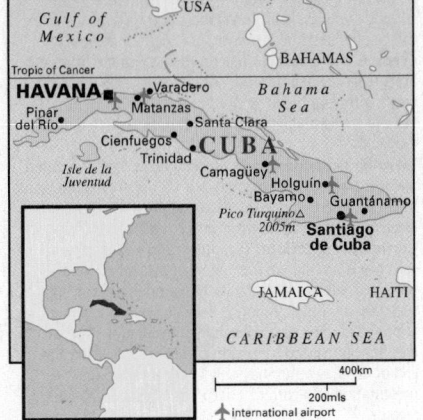

Location: Northwest Caribbean.

Time: GMT - 5 (GMT - 4 from the first Sunday in March to the last Sunday in October.)

Overview

Cuba is an island that assaults the senses. Surprisingly for one of the last remaining communist countries, the visitor is greeted with strains of exotic rhythms – the salsa or rhumba – emanating from every corner.

Cuba has undergone a transformation since it first opened its doors to global tourism after almost three decades of isolation. Most noteworthy has been the rapid growth in private accommodation, the extensive network of *casas particulares* (private home stays) allowing the independent traveller the opportunity, not only to experience life as it is lived by the average Cubano, but also to explore corners of the country that had previously been inaccessible or off-limits. Good news for the tourist is the growing choice of resorts and the number of new or refurbished hotels that are opening in towns across the country. In addition, an ever-increasing range of flights and hotels are opening up previously inaccessible corners.

Once faded and crumbling houses, with ornate wrought iron balconies, and central courtyards are now being lovingly restored, while weathered *campesinos* sucking on titanic cigars watch contentedly as visitors discover this intoxicating island.

While ecotourism is still in its infancy and much of the island's extraordinary natural beauty remains to be discovered, the government is already making strides in the right direction. An aquamarine sea laps the white, palm-fringed beaches of Varadero and offshore Cayos Largo and Coco. Here you can try your hand at blue marlin or barracuda fishing, just as Hemingway depicted in his novel *The Old Man and the Sea*, or dive to the coral reef and search for shipwrecks. The little visited Zapata Peninsula or the Bahia de Naranjo Nature Park offer the chance to swim with dolphins. Inland, only the roar of 1950s US cars disturbs deserted roads. The tobacco-growing area of Viñales with its intriguing limestone *mogotes* (outcrops), contrasts dramatically with the rugged tree-covered mountains of the Sierra Maestra. Cuba's rich history as a Spanish colony is evident in the wealth of colonial architecture in major towns such as Havana and Santiago de Cuba.

Travellers should not forget that the country prides itself in its sporting achievements and participates in many sports in the Olympic Games. Baseball is the national sport; soccer and a variety of ball games are also played. There are many stadiums, and both playing and watching sport is one of the national pastimes.

General Information

AREA: 110,860 sq km (42,803 sq miles).

POPULATION: 11.3 million (official estimate 2005).

POPULATION DENSITY: 102 per sq km.

CAPITAL: Havana. **Population:** 2.2 million (2005).

GEOGRAPHY: Cuba is the largest Caribbean island, about the size of England, and the most westerly of the Greater Antilles group, lying 145km (90 miles) south of Florida. A quarter of the country is fairly mountainous. West of Havana is the narrow Sierra de los Organos, rising to 750m (2461ft) and containing the Guaniguanicos hills in the west. South of the Sierra is a narrow strip of 2320 sq km (860 sq miles) where the finest Cuban tobacco is grown. The Trinidad Mountains, starting in the centre, rise to 1100m (3609ft) in the east. Encircling the port of Santiago are the rugged mountains of the Sierra Maestra. A quarter of the island is covered with mountain forests of pine and mahogany.

GOVERNMENT: Socialist Republic. Gained independence from Spain in 1898. **Head of State and Government:** President Fidel Castro Ruz since 1959. **Recent history:** Under the terms of the 1976 constitution, all legislative power in the Republic of Cuba is vested in a 499-member National Assembly of People's Power, which is elected every 5 years by municipal deputies. A 31-member Council of State is elected by the Assembly from the Assembly. The Council's President is both Head of State and Head of Government. Executive and administrative power is vested in a Council of Ministers, appointed by the Assembly, on the Head of State's recommendation. The constitution, mostly recently amended in 2002, also guarantees that the Communist Party (PCC) should remain not only the sole legal party in Cuba but also 'the leading force of society and state'. As Castro now approaches 80, speculation is growing about his likely successor and whether the system which he and the Communist Party have created will survive his departure.

LANGUAGE: The official language is Spanish.

RELIGION: Roman Catholic majority. There are also minority Afro-Cuban religions.

ELECTRICITY: 110/230 volts AC, 60Hz. American-style flat two-pin plugs are generally used, except in certain large hotels where the European round two-pin plug is standard.

SOCIAL CONVENTIONS: A handshake is the normal form of greeting. Cubans generally address each other as *compañero*, but visitors should use *señor* or *señora*. Some Cubans have two surnames after their Christian name and the first surname is the correct one to use. Normal courtesies should be observed when visiting someone's home and a small gift may be given if invited for a meal. Formal wear is not often needed and hats are rarely worn. Men should not wear shorts except on or near the beach. Women wear light cotton dresses or trousers during the day and cocktail dresses for formal evenings.

Climate

Hot, sub-tropical climate all year. Most rain falls between May and October and hurricanes can occur in autumn (August to November). Humidity varies between 75 per cent and 95 per cent. Cooler months are January to April when the least rain falls.

Required clothing: Lightweight cottons and linens most of the year; the high humidity makes it unwise to wear synthetics close to the skin. Light waterproofs are advisable all year round.

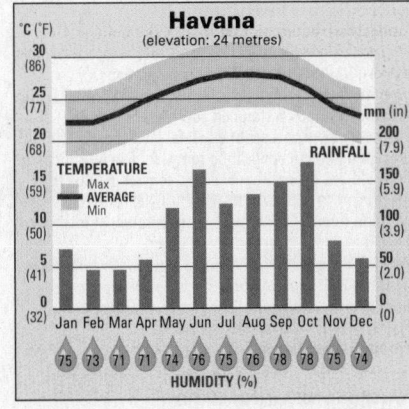

Communications

Telephone: IDD to Havana only. Country code: 53. Phonecards for both internal and external calls are readily available from shops and kiosks. Some calls must be made through the international operator, and may be subject to delays.

Mobile telephone: Roaming agreements exist with Canada and some European and Latin American countries. For further details, check online (website: www.cubacel.com). Coverage is limited.

Internet: Available at hotels and some Internet cafes.

Post: Letters to Western Europe can take several weeks. It is advisable to use the airmail service.

MEDIA: The Cuban media are tightly controlled by the Government. Journalists must operate within the confines

A B C D E F G H I J K L M N O P Q R S T U V W X Y Z

of laws against anti-Government propaganda. Private ownership of electronic media is prohibited by the constitution, and foreign news agencies must hire local journalists only through Government offices.
Press: Papers are in Spanish, although the Communist Party daily newspaper, *Granma*, publishes a weekly edition, called *Granma International*, in English, German, Portuguese and French. There is also a fortnightly international newspaper, *Prisma*, published in Spanish and English.
TV: Channels include *Cubavision*, *Tele-Rebelde* and *CHTV*, a subsidiary of *Tele-Rebelde*.
Radio: Radio stations include news, music and sport station *Radio Rebelde*, *Radio Reloj* and *Radio Habana Cuba*, an external broadcaster broadcasting in Spanish, English, French and Portuguese.

Passport/Visa

	Passport Required?	Visa Required?	Return Ticket Required?
Full British	Yes	Yes	Yes
Australian	Yes	Yes	Yes
Canadian	Yes	Yes	Yes
USA	Yes	Yes	Yes
Other EU	Yes	Yes	Yes
Japanese	Yes	Yes	Yes

Note: *Regulations and requirements may be subject to change at short notice, and you are advised to contact the appropriate diplomatic or consular authority before finalising travel arrangements. Any numbers in the chart refer to the footnotes below.*

PASSPORTS: Passports valid for at least six months after the departure date from Cuba required by all nationals without diplomatic representation in Cuba.
Note: Persons of Cuban origin who are nationals of other countries must travel with a Cuban passport if they left Cuba after 1970.
VISAS: Required by all except:
a) those nationals whose countries have signed visa-exemption agreements with Cuba (contact the Consulate for further information);
b) transit passengers continuing their journey to a third country within 72 hours, provided they hold confirmed onward tickets and US$50 per day.
Note: Neither visa exemptions nor Tourist Visa Card facilities are applicable to foreign passport holders born in Cuba, unless holding a document proving withdrawal of Cuban citizenship.
Exit permits: Required by those whose stay in Cuba exceeds 90 days.
Types of visa and cost: *Tourist Visa Card:* £15. *All other visas:* £32 (plus a £15 processing fee.)
Validity: *Tourist visa card*: 30 day stay, within 180 days of issue; further 30 day extension available in Cuba. *Business*: 30 days.
Application to: Consulate (or consular section at Embassy); see *Passport/Visa Information*. Application forms for tourist visa cards can be obtained from certain tour operators and travel agents.
Application requirements: *Tourist Visa Card*: (a) One completed (signed) application form. (b) Photocopy of valid passport. (c) Proof of travel arrangements and accommodation. (d) Fee (payable in cash and postal). (e) For postal applications, a stamped addresses or recorded delivery envelope. *All other visas*: (a) Valid passport. (b) Two completed (signed) application forms. (c) Two passport-size photos. (d) Invitation from business contact in Cuba or information on the purpose of the trip. (e) Letter of invitation from Cuban company, organisation or institution. (f) Fee (payable in cash and postal order).
Working days required: *Tourist visa card*: One day (seven days for postal applications). *Tourist visa*: 48 hours. *Business and Family visa*: 72 hours (two weeks for postal applications). *Journalist visa:* six weeks.
Temporary residence: Enquire at Embassy.

PASSPORT/VISA INFORMATION

Embassy of the Republic of Cuba in the UK
167 High Holborn, London WC1V 6PA, UK
Tel: (020) 7240 2488.
Website: www.cubaldn.com
Opening hours: Mon-Fri 0900-1700.

Cuban Consulate in the UK
167 High Holborn, WC1V 6PA London, UK
Tel: (0870) 240 3675 (recorded information line; calls cost 60p per minute).
Opening hours: Mon-Fri 0930-1230.

Cuban Interests Section in the USA
2639 16th Street, NW, Washington DC 20009, USA
Tel: (202) 797 8518-20.

Money

Currency: Cuban Peso (CUP) = 100 centavos. Notes are in denominations of CUP100, 50, 20, 10 and 5. Coins are in denominations of CUP1, and 20, 5, 2 and 1 centavos. The US Dollar was also introduced as legal tender in 1993 forming a vital part of the economy. But as of 8 November 2004, Cuba has banned the use of US Dollars in commercial transactions - a response to the US's tighter embargoes, which put caps on the remittances Cubans living in the US were able to send back to the island. Dollars must now be exchanged for Convertible pesos (CUC) where a 10 per cent commission will be charged. In some tourist and large urban areas, the Euro is also accepted. Hard currency must be used in most transactions.
Currency exchange: Money should be exchanged at official foreign exchange bureaux, banks or international air- and seaports, which issue receipts for transactions. ATMs are currently only available in Varadero and Havana, but cash can be obtained in banks with Visa credit or debit cards.
Credit & debit cards: MasterCard and Visa are increasingly accepted, provided they are not issued by a US bank, but check with your credit or debit card company for details of merchant acceptability and other services which may be available.
Traveller's cheques: US Dollar, Pound Sterling and other major currencies are accepted, but US Dollar cheques issued by US banks are not accepted. The white exchange paper received upon encashment must be retained.
Currency restrictions: The import and export of local currency is prohibited. The import of foreign currency is unlimited, subject to declaration of amounts exceeding US$5000 on arrival; export is allowed up to the amount imported and declared. Generally, a maximum of pesos10 may be reconverted to foreign currency for re-export at the end of the stay but it may only be reconverted on presentation of a correctly filled out official exchange record.
Banking hours: Mon-Fri 0830-1200 and 1330-1500, Sat 0830-1030. Hours may vary and banks may be open all day in larger cities.
Exchange rate indicators:
Rate at time of publishing
£1.00= CUP1.75
$1.00= CUP1.00

Duty Free

The following goods may be taken into Cuba by persons aged 18 years and over without incurring customs duty:
200 cigarettes or 50 cigars or 250g of tobacco; three bottles of alcoholic beverages; gifts up to a value of US$50 (articles up to US$200 will be subject to customs duty payments); 10kg of medicines.
Prohibited items: Natural fruits, seeds, beans or vegetables; meat and dairy products; weapons and ammunition; video cassettes and household appliances; all pornographic material and drugs.
Note: Electrical items with heavy power consumption may be confiscated and returned upon departure.

Public Holidays

Below are listed Public Holidays for the January 2006-June 2007 period.
2006: Jan 1 Liberation Day. **Jan 2** Victory of Armed Forces. **May 1** Labour Day. **May 20** Independence Day. **Jul 25-27** Days of Rebelliousness. **Oct 10** Anniversary of the beginning of the War of Independence in 1868. **Dec 25** Christmas Day.
2007: Jan 1 Liberation Day. **Jan 2** Victory of Armed Forces. **May 1** Labour Day. **May 20** Independence Day.

Health

	Special Precautions?	Certificate Required?
Yellow Fever	No	No
Cholera	No	No
Typhoid & Polio	1	N/A
Malaria	No	N/A

Note: *Regulations and requirements may be subject to change at short notice, and you are advised to contact your doctor well in advance of your intended date of departure. Any numbers in the chart refer to the footnotes below.*

1: Typhoid may be a risk in remote rural areas.
Food & drink: Mains water is chlorinated and, whilst relatively safe, may cause mild abdominal upsets. Bottled water is available and is advised for the first few weeks of stay. Milk is pasteurised and dairy products are safe for consumption. Local meat, poultry, seafoods and fruit are generally considered safe to eat.
Other risks: *Hepatitis A* has been reported in the northern Caribbean Islands, and immunoglobin is not always readily available. *Human fascioliasis* is endemic. *Dengue fever* may occur in the area as well as outbreaks of *dengue haemorrhagic fever* and *meningitis*, particularly in urban areas such as Havana. Rabies is present. For those at high risk, vaccination should be considered. If you are bitten, seek medical advice without delay. For more information, consult the *Health* appendix.
Health care: Cuba's medical services are very good and some emergency treatment may be available to visitors at no cost. However, health insurance is necessary, as foreigners must pay most of their own health care costs. Some hospitals may ask for proof of ability to pay for treatment prior to receiving sufficient medical attention.

Travel - International

AIR:
Cuba's national airline is *Cubana (CU)* (website: www.cubana.cu).
Approximate flight times: From Cuba to *London* is eight hours, to *Los Angeles* is nine hours and to *New York* is three hours.
Main airports: *Havana (HVA)* (José Martí International) is 15km (9 miles) southwest of the city. *To/from the airport:* Bus and taxi services to the city are available (travel time: bus - 1 hour; taxi - 20 to 30 minutes). *Facilities*: Duty free shops, bank and bureau de change, tourist information/hotel reservation, restaurants and bars, and car hire.
There are also international airports at *Camagüey, Cayo Coco, Cayo Largo, Ciego de Avila, Cienfuegos, Holguin, Manzanillo, Santiago de Cuba* and *Varadero*.
Departure tax: 25 Convertible Pesos (around £15) per person. Transit passengers departing within the same day and not leaving the transit area, plus children under two years, are exempt. US dollars are not accepted.
SEA:
Due to the US blockade, there are no scheduled passenger ships and only some cruise ships call at Cuba (*Riviera Holiday Cruises, Sunquest Vacations* and *West Indies Cruises*). It is possible, however, to call in on a private yacht, although the authorities must be contacted prior to arrival.

Travel - Internal

AIR:
Cubana operates scheduled services between most main towns but advance booking is essential as flights are limited. It is advised that, where possible, internal flights are undertaken with internationally recognised tour operators.
RAIL:
The principal rail route is from Havana to Santiago de Cuba, with four daily trains. Some trains on this route have air conditioning and refreshments. There are also through trains from Havana to other towns. Previously, the rail network connected the vast majority of the country but has been badly affected by natural disasters and now only certain parts of the country are accessible by rail.
ROAD:
Sightseeing can be pre-arranged, although internal travel arrangements may be made through any of the several ground handlers. Roads are signposted and adequate, although often poorly lit. Traffic drives on the right. In view of serious accidents that have involved tourists, travellers should not use mopeds or three-wheel Coco-Taxis for travel around Cuba.
Bus: Most tours will include travel by air-conditioned buses. Cuba's national bus service *Astro* (*Asociaciones de Transportes por Omnibus*) connects all the main towns and suburbs at least once or twice a day; fares are low and services are reliable, but the buses can be very crowded, especially during the rush hour. Four seats are saved for tourists or foreign visitors on each bus. Increasingly popular, however, are the state-operated, air-conditioned *Viazul* 'tourist buses' (website: www.viazul.cu), which connect most major cities and tourist destinations daily. These top-range coaches have air conditioning, toilets, and must be paid for in US dollars (larger offices should accept payment by credit/debit card).
Taxi: Taxis and chauffeur-driven cars can work out to be as cheap as the bus or train. An influx of comfortable, modern cars makes this a viable form of transport. It is usual to order them through the hotel. All official taxis have meters but, in private taxis, fares should be pre-arranged. Especially in and around the airports, and old Havana, many bogus tour agents/taxi companies operate, so visitors should ensure any taxis used are officially recognised.
Car hire: There are several good and inexpensive car hire companies with representatives at most hotels, and due to Cuba's well-maintained road system, this is often regarded as one of the best forms of getting around the island. Bicycles can be hired.
Documentation: Valid national driving licence required. Drivers must be aged 21 or over.

URBAN:

Buses, minibuses and plentiful shared taxis operate in Havana at low flat fares. Buses are frequent but often very crowded, and foreigners may have difficulty paying the fare in pesos.

Travel Times: The following chart gives approximate travel times (in hours and minutes) from **Havana** to other major towns in Cuba.

	Air	Road
Varadero	**0.15**	**2.00**
Trinidad	**0.20**	**5.00**
Santiago de Cuba	**1.15**	**17.00**
Pinar del Rio	**0.15**	**2.00**

Travel Advice

In view of serious accidents that have involved tourists, travellers should not use mopeds or three-wheel Coco-Taxis for travel around Cuba.

Most visits to Cuba are trouble-free but you should be aware of the global risk of indiscriminate international terrorist attacks, which could be against civilian targets, including places frequented by foreigners.

Travellers are warned that crime is on the increase.

This advice is based on information provided by the Foreign and Commonwealth Office in the UK. It is correct at time of publishing. As the situation can change rapidly, visitors are advised to contact the following organisations for the latest travel advice:

British Foreign and Commonwealth Office
Tel: (0845) 850 2829.
Website: www.fco.gov.uk

US Department of State
Website: http://travel.state.gov/travel

Accommodation

HOTELS:

The best hotels are in Havana, Trinidad, Cayo Coco or at Varadero Beach. Since many visitors to Cuba go as part of a package holiday, the hotel will have been selected in advance. The hotels are clean, functional and adequate. Contact the Cuba Tourist Board for further information (see *Top Things To Do*).

CASAS PARTICULARES:

Literally private houses, these are - as the name suggests - similar to bed & breakfast. In certain towns only (most notably not in Varadero), it is possible for Cubans to rent out rooms to visitors. The rooms normally have a private bathroom and the deal often includes breakfast. It may also be possible to have other meals there as well. Legal *casas particulares* are recognised by a blue triangle on a white background on the front door.

Top Things To See

- Enjoy the vibrant life of **Havana (La Habana),** one of the largest cities in the Caribbean. **Havana** boasts an old town which features on UNESCO's World Heritage List. The surrounding 19th-century district of densely packed, crumbling houses and narrow streets has its own appeal, as does the high-rise city centre (**Vedado**), developed during the 1940s and 1950s when US influence was strongest. The most famous of the hotels here is the **Nacional**, still patronised by Hollywood film stars. Dating from the same period is **Miramar**, the leafy embassy district reminiscent of Miami. Havana is closely associated with the US writer, Ernest Hemmingway. One of his favourite haunts was the bar, **La Bodeguita del Medio**, only a stone's throw from the city's magnificent 18th-century cathedral. Enjoy wonderful rooftop views of the city from the **Museo de la Ciudad** on **Plaza de Armas** and the recently opened **Palacio del Segundo Cabo**, former residence of the Captains General. As an alternative, enjoy a relaxing drink on one of the **Habana Vieja hotel rooftops** to enjoy the views. The splendidly refurbished rooms of the **Museo de Arte Colonial** are also worth a visit. The **Castillo de la Real Fuerza** is the oldest of Havana's three forts. The **Capitolio**, modelled on the Capitol in Washington DC, was once home to the Cuban government and is sumptuously decorated. The huge **Museo de la Revolución** occupies the former presidential palace. Outside under a glass case is the **Granma**, the yacht which brought Castro and the leading rebels back to Cuba in 1956.
- Head for **Pinar del Río**. The countryside is amazingly diverse, but the outstanding feature must be the *mogotes* (oddly rounded limestone mountains, covered in lush vegetation). The caves here, notably the **Cueva del Indio**, are well worth a visit, with stalactites and stalagmites and underground rivers. The town of **Pinar del Río** should be explored in its own right, and is home to several cigar factories that are open to the public. The tobacco plantations at **Vuelta Abajo**, a short distance southwest of Pinar del Río can also be visited during the growing season from December to April. The road from **Viñales** to the coast makes a scenic drive.
- Pop in **Cienfuegos**, a prosperous modern city built around a fine harbour at the foot of the **Escambray Mountains**. Its 19th-century core was built with the help of French settlers from Louisiana, which explains why many of the town's finest buildings are reminiscent of New Orleans. The main sights around **Parque José Martí** include the cathedral and the late 19th-century **Teatro Tomás Terry**, worth exploring for its florid interior. Closer to the harbour are the castle, **Castillo de Jagua** and the **Palacio de Valle**. Built in an appealing mixture of architectural styles, with Moorish influences to the fore, it is now a restaurant with a roof-top terrace that affords splendid views of the bay and surrounding countryside.
- Enjoy the atmosphere of an old colonial town in **Trinidad**. The presence of many beautiful buildings dating from the 17th to 19th centuries accounts for its place on UNESCO's World Heritage List. The main attractions include the elegant **Parque Martí** and several museums in the colonial mansions, the best of which, the **Museo Romántico**, having been beautifully refurbished in period style. The **Taller Alfarero**, a ceramics workshop where traditional techniques are still used, is also worth visiting. Mention should also be made of the **Torre de Manaca Iznaga** (50m/165ft), a lookout tower offering great views of the **Valley of the Sugar Mills** (**Valle de los Ingenios**) and the **Escambray Mountains**.
- Don't miss **Santa Clara,** a bustling city closely associated with the revolutionary hero Ernesto 'Ché' Guevara who captured the town for the Cuban revolution days before the resignation of the dictator, General Batista. The government is also investing in the area's other potential attractions, which include **Remedios** and the beaches around **Cayo Las Brujas**.
- Take it easy in **Sancti Spíritus** which has a laid-back feel and a good range of state and private accommodation. The bridge over the **Yayabo River** is made of stone - the oldest one on the island. Strolling through the sleepy streets while admiring the colonial architecture is the main attraction. The best example of the style is the **Colonial Art Museum**.
- **Camagüey** is one of the more heavily promoted towns of the eastern part of the island. Its attractions include a number of churches and museums and a thriving (and very photogenic) **peso market**. Camagüey lies in the centre of a fertile plain, exploited for sugar.
- Delight yourself in **Bayamo**, a charming little town with one of the few pedestrianised centres on the island. Bayamo was the birthplace of the 19th-century revolutionary, Manuel de Céspedes, who launched Cuba's struggle for independence here in 1868-9. From here it is possible to explore the nature trails of the **Parque Nacional del Granma** around the fishing hamlet of **Cabo Cruz**.
- **Holguín** is familiar to most tourists for its airstrip, but the old colonial town is worth a couple of hours at least for its attractive squares and streets.
- Soak up **Santiago de Cuba**'s heady atmosphere. The city, 780km (485 miles) from Havana, was the island's first capital. It owed this distinction to a superb deepwater harbour, the majestic **Sierra Maestra Mountains** forming a dramatic backdrop. Despite losing its primacy early in the day, Santiago was never eclipsed by Havana thanks to the French plantation owners and their slaves who arrived in the 18th century, turning the region over to coffee and sugar production. Santiago consequently acquired a cosmopolitan flavour that accounts for its cultural importance, especially in music - the **Son** originated here. In July, the town hosts one of the most spectacular carnivals in the country, which has even spawned its own museum. Highlights of Santiago's old quarter (around the square, **Parque Céspedes**) are the cathedral, the **Casa de Diego Velázquez**, one of Cuba's oldest colonial mansions, and the **Museo Emilio Bacardí**, which contains the rum magnate's collection of antiques and fine art. Adjacent to the square is the **Casa Granda Hotel**, located adjacent to the square in the area, a favourite haunt of the British author Graham Greene. The **Moncada Barracks**, where Fidel Castro and his revolutionary insurgents launched an abortive uprising in 1953, is the most visited sight outside the town centre.
- Venture into Santiago de Cuba's surrounding countryside. Excursions on offer include the **Castillo del Morro**, once an important fortress and now a museum of piracy with superb vistas of the surrounding countryside. The shrine to the Virgin of **Cobre** is housed in a magnificent basilica. This important centre of pilgrimage was the focus of Pope John Paul II's visit to Cuba in 1998.
- In **Baracoa**, witness where Christopher Columbus planted a wooden cross after coming ashore in 1492. It was later transferred to the **Church of Our Lady of the Assumption** where it is still on view. Baracoa lies between two bays on Cuba's eastern tip and is one of the island's most beautiful towns. Until the 1960s, when a road connecting it to the mainland was constructed, Cuba's oldest European settlement was accessible only by boat. The town's role as a former Spanish outpost is evidenced by its three forts, the **Fuerte Matachín** (now housing the municipal museum), the **Castillo de Seboruco** (now a hotel), and the **Fuerte de la Punta** (which now also houses a restaurant).

Top Things To Do

- In **Havana,** the capital, stroll the sea wall, known as the **Malecón** - which extends for 8km (5 miles), with the locals.
- Try rolling your own cigars at one of Cuba's **tobacco factories** such as at **Fábrica de Tabacos Partagás** in **Havana**. The town of **Pinar del Río** is also home to several cigar factories that are open to the public. Do not leave Cuba without your supply of cigars.
- Relax on Cuba's numerous beaches. Havana's best beaches, the **Playas del Este**, are about 20km from the centre. **Isla de la Juventud** (Isle of Youth), a large island to the south of Cuba, is the largest of the 350 islands making up the **Canarreos archipelago**. Once known as 'Parrot Island', the Isle of Youth was a hideout for pirates, including the notorious Englishman, Captain Henry Morgan. It is also supposed to have inspired Robert Louis Stevenson's *Treasure Island*. The island offers excellent **reef diving**. Wildlife, including turtles and iguanas, can be observed on the coral keys to the east. In the same archipelago is **Cayo Largo**, another of Cuba's well-known tourist resorts, considered to have some of the best beaches in the Caribbean. **Varadero**, a sheltered peninsula on Cuba's north coast, is the island's best-known beach resort. The 21 km- (13 mile-) long **Varadero Beach**, offers good **diving** and **snorkelling**. For those not wanting to venture underwater, **boat tours** to the reef are available. Near Trinidad, many tourists stay at the beach resort of **Playa Ancón**. The unspoilt **Camagüey archipelago** is also known as **Jardines del Rey**. Within the natural park are some 20km (12.5 miles) of landscaped white-sand beaches, the best known of which are **Cayo Coco** and **Cayo Guillermo**, the latter a favourite haunt of Ernest Hemmingway who came to fish here. There is also very good diving from resorts in the **Pinar del Río** province in the northwest of the island, an area characterised by clear water and long white-sand beaches. Beautiful corals can be seen off the coast.
- Learn more about Amero-Indian culture at **Guama**, in the south of **Matanzas Province**, a reconstruction of an Amero-Indian village, which is a Government showpiece built on a series of islands linked by wooden bridges. There are boat trips along the **Treasure Lake** (**Laguna del Tesoro**), while most visitors will also enjoy the **crocodile nursery**. This part of Mantanzas is also famous for **bird life** and the attractive **beaches** of **Playa Girón** and **Playa Larga**, location for the disastrous Bay of Pigs invasion in 1961.
- **Pico Turquino,** Cuba's highest mountain, is in the **Sierra Maestra** range, offering good **hikes** and **treks**. The **Sierra de Cubitas** range near Camagüey is characterised by river gorges and cliffs, while the **Escambray Mountains** near Trinidad contain dense rainforest. **Guama**, on the Zapata peninsula is an extensive marshy area, which hosts many interesting varieties of birds, including parrots.
- The **Cordillera de Guaniguanico** in the north of the island features spectacular scenery with rivers and limestone mountains and caves.
- Enjoy the **Havana Carnival**, which takes place in July-August.

TOURIST INFORMATION

Cuba Tourist Board in the UK
154 Shaftesbury Avenue, London WC2H 8JT, UK
Tel: (020) 7240 6655 *or* (09001) 600 295 (24-hour brochure request line; calls cost 60p per minute).
Website: www.cubatravel.cu

Entertainment

FOOD & DRINK: Restaurants (both table- and self-service) are generally inexpensive. Cuisine is continental or Cuban with a strong emphasis on seafood. Cuban food uses more garlic and less chilli than elsewhere in the Caribbean. Bars generally have waiter and counter service.

National specialities:

- Omelettes, often stuffed with meat and/or cheese.
- Maize fritters.
- Soup made of chicken or black beans.
- Roast suckling pig.
- Chicken and rice.
- Plantains baked or fried.
- Cuban ice cream.

National drinks:
- Cuban coffee (strong) and Cuban beer (tasty, yet weak).
- Rum (used in cocktails such as *daiquiris* and *mojitos* pronounced 'moh-hee-tos').

Tipping: Moderate tipping is expected. However, as more foreigners pass through Cuba, many people who would not normally merit them have begun to demand tips.

NIGHTLIFE: Nightlife is concentrated in Havana, Varadero Beach and in the major tourist resorts. Cuba is renowned for its salsa dancing and visitors can attend dance classes or swing their hips with the locals at the *Tropicana* and *Varadero Mambo* nightclubs. Look for *Casa de la Musica* in Havana and other cities where live bands perform. Even medium-sized bars usually have a house band playing Cuban classics. There is a choice of floor show entertainments, nightclubs and theatres. The *Tropicana* nightclub stages spectacular open-air shows. Theatre, opera and ballet are staged all year round in Havana and seats are very cheap.

SHOPPING: Special purchases include cigars, rum, coffee and local handicrafts. The main hotels have a few luxury shops. There are duty free shops at the airport and in the centre of Havana. **Shopping hours**: Mon-Sat 0900-1700, Sun 0900-1200.

Business

- **GDP:** US$33.92 billion (2005).
- **Main exports:** Sugar, nickel, tobacco, fish, citrus and coffee.
- **Main imports:** Foodstuffs, petroleum, chemicals, machinery and equipment.
- **Main trade partners:** Spain, Germany, China, Canada, Italy and Mexico.

ECONOMY: The agricultural component of Cuba's economy is dominated by sugar, of which it is one of the world's largest exporters. However, due to persistently low world prices throughout the 1980s and 1990s, the Government has attempted to diversify into other crops. Tobacco (Cuban cigars are renowned throughout the world) and citrus fruits are the most successful of these. Cuban industry is largely devoted to the processing of agricultural products but also produces cement, fertilisers, textiles, prefabricated buildings, agricultural machinery and domestic consumer goods. Tourism, the only significant service industry, has proved to be a growth industry and a vital source of foreign exchange; the Government has invested heavily in developing infrastructure for that purpose. Development of the Cuban economy has long been hampered by the blockade imposed by successive American Governments, even though bilateral US-Cuban trade is estimated at US$300 million annually, mostly in telecommunications traffic and various financial instruments, such as credit cards. While the Soviet Union was able to provide aid and markets, especially for Cuba's sugar output, this was not an insurmountable hurdle. However, during the last decade, since the demise of the USSR, Cuba has faced increasing economic difficulties. In June 2001, the lack of markets and low world price forced the Government to close down half the country's sugar mills. Nevertheless, domestic reforms of the previously rigid state-controlled structure – opening up to foreign investment and creating export-processing zones – have allowed erratic growth to take place. A substantial informal dollar economy also grew up during the 1990s. As with the political structure in Cuba, most observers are awaiting what form of Government emerges after Castro to determine which direction the economy will take.

BUSINESS ETIQUETTE: Courtesy is expected and hospitality should not be lavish, being offered to groups rather than individuals. Best months for business visits are November to April. **Office hours**: Mon-Fri 0830-1230 and 1330-1630, some offices also open on alternate Saturdays from 0800-1700.

CONFERENCES/CONVENTIONS: Modern facilities are available at Havana International Conference Center, Pabexpo, ExpoCuba and the Varadero Plaza America.

COMMERCIAL INFORMATION

Cámara de Comercio de la República de Cuba
Calle 21, No 661, esq. Calle A, Vedado, Havana, Cuba
Tel: (7) 551 321/2/4 or 551 654 or 551 452 or 551 746.
Website: www.camaracuba.cubaweb.cu

Cubanacan UK Ltd (Information on Conferences/Conventions)
Unit 49, Skylines, Limeharbour, London E14 9TS, UK
Tel: (020) 7537 7909 or 536 8173.
Website: www.cubanacan.cu

Buró de Convenciones de Cuba, COCAL (Information on Conferences/Conventions)
Edificio Focsa, Calle M entre la 17 y 19, Vedado, Havana, Cuba
Tel: (7) 552 923 or 662 629.
Website: www.cubameeting.org

Curaçao

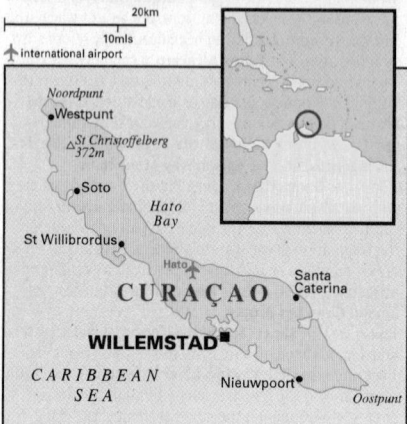

Location: Caribbean, 56km (35 miles) north of Venezuela.

Time: GMT - 4.

Overview

The Netherlands Antilles group, of which Curaçao is the largest and most prosperous, was first discovered by Europeans in 1499, when Alonso de Ojmeda – one of Columbus' lieutenants – reached the island. It was settled by the Spanish, in the early 1500s, who retained possession until the Dutch East India Company seized it in 1634. Thousands of slaves were then imported to provide labour for the island group's plantation agricultural schemes. In the early 19th century, persistent attacks by the British and French destabilised the island for a while. By 1816, the Dutch had reasserted control and introduced further plantations.

The abolition of slavery in 1863 set off a long period of economic decline, relieved in 1916, by the opening of an oil refinery. This and other oil-related industries became the mainstay of a booming economy until the 1980s. On the back of this, Curaçao became the most prosperous of the Netherlands Antilles, a position that caused some resentment among the other islands in the group, particularly Aruba. Nonetheless, constitutional referenda held in 1994 on the three smaller islands (St Eustatius, St Maarten and Saba) produced majorities in favour of remaining with the Antilles group.

What at first seems to be a monotonous desert landscape turns out to be a scenery teeming with life. Tourists are able to choose between intimate rocky coves surrounded by massive cliffs or long sandy beaches, either secluded by nature or bustling with activities. With average temperature of about 27° C (mid-80s F) and cooling trade winds blowing constantly from the east, the one thing they all share is crystal-clear turquoise water and perfect weather. Although the island is a mix of nationalities, African descendents make up the majority. African influence can be seen in the language of *Papiamentu*, a language once used to bridge the gap between the slaves and owners, but now the keystone of Curaçao communication, and *Tambú*, the 'Curaçao Blues' which the African descendents used to express their outrage and sorrow at slavery through song, music and dance, food, religion and spirituality.

General Information

AREA: 444 sq km (171 sq miles).
POPULATION: 224,000 (UN 2005).
POPULATION DENSITY: 504 per sq km.
CAPITAL: Willemstad. **Population:** 125,000 (UN estimate 2001, including the suburbs).
GEOGRAPHY: Curaçao, the largest island in the Netherlands Antilles, is geographically part of the Dutch

Leeward Islands. It is flat, rocky and fairly barren owing to its low rainfall. There are many excellent beaches.

GOVERNMENT: Part of the Netherlands Antilles; dependency of The Netherlands. The Netherlands Antilles consist of Bonaire, Curaçao, Saba, St Eustatius and St Maarten. The capital of the island group is Willemstad, Curaçao. The Netherlands Antilles, Aruba and The Netherlands each have equal status within the Kingdom of the Netherlands, as regions autonomous in internal affairs. The Dutch Monarch is locally represented by a Governor, while the Netherlands Antilles are represented in the Government of the Kingdom by a Minister Plenipotentiary. Foreign policy and defence matters are decided by a Council of Ministers of the Kingdom, including the Plenipotentiary, and executed under the authority of the Governor. The internal affairs of the islands are administered by the Central Government of the Netherlands Antilles, which is based in Willemstad, Curaçao, and responsible to the Staten, or Legislative Assembly. Curaçao may elect by non-compulsory adult suffrage 14 out of 22 members to the Staten. Routine local affairs on each island group (Bonaire, Curaçao and the Windward Islands) are managed by an elected Island Council presided over by a Lieutenant Governor. **Head of State:** HM Queen Beatrix of The Netherlands, represented locally by Governor Frits Goedgedrag since 2002. **Head of Government:** Prime Minister Etienne Ys since 2002. **Recent history:** Island rivalries are at least as important as ideological ones in Netherlands Antilles politics. The most recent election in January 2002 returned no party with more than five seats (out of 22) in the *Staten*. The present Government is a six-party coalition led by the FOL under the premiership of Mirna Louisa-Godett. Of the main parties, only the PAR, still led by the veteran politician and former Premier Miguel Fournier, is excluded. In the referendum held in April 2005 on Curaçao, the citizens of the island expressed themselves in favour of an autonomous status for Curaçao in the Dutch Kingdom. The Island Council of the Island Territory of Curaçao formally ratified the results of the referendum a week later. Efforts will be made to realise the status of an autonomous state for Curaçao by July 2007.

LANGUAGE: Dutch is the official language. Papiamentu (a mixture of Dutch, Spanish, Portuguese, English, Arawak Indian and several African languages) is the *lingua franca*; English and Spanish are also widely spoken. There are 55 different nationalities.

RELIGION: The majority of the population is Roman Catholic, with Protestant minorities, both evangelical and other low-church denominations. There is also a Baha'i temple and a synagogue.

ELECTRICITY: 110/130 volts AC, 50Hz.

SOCIAL CONVENTIONS: The social influences are predominantly Dutch, combined with Indian and African traditions. Dress for men should include tropical lightweight suits for business appointments and formal wear for evening engagements. Similarly, women should take some evening wear, but dress for daytime is casual. Swimwear should be confined to the beach and poolside.

Climate

Hot throughout the year, but tempered by cooling trade winds. The main rainy season is from October to December. The annual mean temperature is 27.5°C (81.5°F), rainfall is 515mm (20 inches) and humidity is 75.9 per cent. The island lies outside the Caribbean hurricane belt.

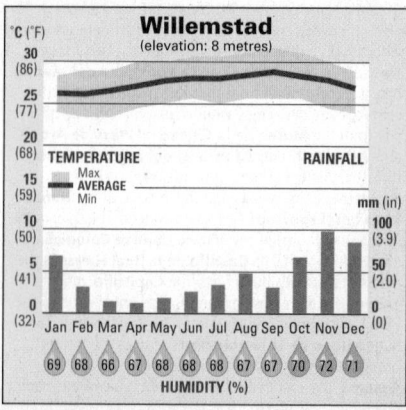

Communications

Telephone: Good IDD service to Europe. Country code: 599.
Mobile telephone: Roaming agreements exist with international mobile phone companies. Handsets can be hired at the airport post office. There is a 5 per cent tax.
Internet: There is an Internet cafe in Willemstad.
Post: Airmail to Western Europe takes four to six days.
MEDIA: Press: Newspapers include *La Prensa* (daily) and

Credit: © Dutch Caribbean Travel Center

Amigoe (daily in Dutch). English-language newspapers include the *Bonaire Reporter* (weekly), *Business Curaçao* and *The Daily Herald (*Sint Maarten) .
TV: *TeleCuraçao* is Government-run.
Radio: Radio stations include *Radio Hoyer, Easy FM* and *Dolfijn FM.*

Passport/Visa

	Passport Required?	Visa Required?	Return Ticket Required?
Full British	Yes	1	Yes
Australian	Yes	2	Yes
Canadian	Yes	2	Yes
USA	Yes	2	Yes
Other EU	Yes	1/2	Yes
Japanese	Yes	2	Yes

Note: *Regulations and requirements may be subject to change at short notice, and you are advised to contact the appropriate diplomatic or consular authority before finalising travel arrangements. Any numbers in the chart refer to the footnotes below.*

PASSPORTS: Passport or official travel documents valid for at least three months after intended return to home country required by all.
VISAS: Required by all except the following:
(a) **1.** nationals of Belgium, Bolivia, Burkina Faso, Chile, Costa Rica, Czech Republic, Ecuador, Germany, Hungary, Israel, Jamaica, Korea (Rep), Luxembourg, Malawi, Mauritius, The Netherlands, Niger, The Philippines, Poland, San Marino, Slovak Republic, Spain, Swaziland, Togo and the UK for touristic stays of up to three months;
(b) **2.** all other nationals for touristic stays of up to 14 days, except nationals of Albania, Bosnia & Herzegovina, Bulgaria, Cambodia, China (PR) (except Hong Kong SAR), CIS, Colombia, Cote d'Ivoire, Croatia, Cuba, Dominican Republic, Estonia, Ghana, Guinea-Bissau, Haiti, Kenya, Korea (Dem Rep), Latvia, Libya, Lithuania, Macedonia (Former Yugoslav Republic of), Mali, Nigeria, Romania, Serbia & Montenegro and Vietnam who *always* need a visa;
(c) most nationals continuing to a third country within 24 hours by the same means of transportation and not leaving the airport and holding tickets with reserved seats and documents for their onward journey.
Note: All stays can be extended locally by the same period that they are valid for.
Types of visa and cost: All visas, regardless of duration of stay or number of entries permitted on visa, cost £15.
Validity: Visas are generally issued for as long as duration

of stay, up until a maximum 90 days from date of issue.
Application to: Nearest Embassy of the Kingdom of The Netherlands. All further information about visa requirements may be obtained from The Royal Netherlands Embassies, which formally represent the Netherlands Antilles; see *Passport/Visa Information* in *The Netherlands* section.
Application requirements: (a) Valid passport with at least one blank page. If passport is new, the old passport must also be submitted. (b) One fully completed application form. (c) One recent passport-size photo per person endorsed on passport. (d) Fee, payable by postal order (to Royal Netherlands Embassy) or cash. Cheques are not accepted. (e) Evidence of sufficient funds amounting to a minimum of £30 for each day of stay (cash not accepted), eg original bank statements, credit card with credit limit statement, traveller's cheques. (f) A recent and original letter from employer, stating commencement date, with last payslip. If self-employed, submit letter from solicitor, accountant or company house. If unemployed, submit social benefit booklet. If in education, submit a recent and original letter from school/college/university, confirming attendance. (g) Valid medical or travel insurance. *Tourist*: (a)-(g) and, (h) Invitation from family or proof of hotel booking. (i) Return or onward ticket. *Business*: (a)-(g) and, (h) Invitation from Dutch company confirming duration and purpose of stay.
Working days required: Applications should be lodged at least one month prior to departure.
Temporary residence: Enquire at the office of the Lieutenant Governor of the Island Territory of Curaçao, Concordiastraat 24, Willemstad, Curaçao. In certain cases, Dutch Europeans may be permitted to reside in the Netherlands Antilles without having to apply for a residence permit. However, it is best to consult the nearest Dutch Embassy/Consulate in advance to ascertain whether this is applicable based on the individual circumstances of the traveller.

PASSPORT/VISA INFORMATION

Curaçao is part of the Netherlands Antilles, represented abroad by Royal Netherlands Embassies (see *The Netherlands* section).

Office of the Minister Plenipotentiary of the Netherlands Antilles
PO Box 90706, Badhuisweg 173-175, 2597 JP The Hague, The Netherlands
Tel: (70) 306 6111.
E-mail: serphos@kymna.nl

Money

Currency: Netherlands Antilles Guilder or Florin (NAG) = 100 cents. Notes are in denominations of NAG250, 100, 50, 25, 10 and 5. Coins are in denominations of 100, 50, 25, 10, 5, 2.5 and 1 cents. US Dollars are accepted everywhere. However, it is best to take notes in small denominations; US$50 and US$100 notes are not always easy to change.
Note: The Netherlands Antilles Guilder or Florin is tied to the US Dollar.
Currency exchange: Available in banks and bureaux de change. There are some ATMs.
Credit & debit cards: Major credit cards are widely accepted. Check with your credit or debit card company for details of merchant acceptability and other services which may be available. Debit cards are accepted in large shops and supermarkets.
Traveller's cheques: Widely accepted. To avoid additional exchange rate charges, travellers are advised to take traveller's cheques in US Dollars.
Currency restrictions: The import and export of local and foreign currency is unlimited. The import of Dutch or Surinam silver coins is forbidden.
Banking hours: Mon-Fri 0800-1530.
Exchange rate indicators:
Rate at time of publishing
£1.00=   NAG3.14
$1.00=   NAG1.78

Duty Free

The following items may be imported into Curaçao by persons over 15 years of age without incurring customs: *200 cigarettes or 100 cigarillos (of 3g each) or 50 cigars or 250g of tobacco; 2l of alcoholic beverages or 2l of wine; an unlimited amount of perfume; gifts up to the value of NAG100.*
Note: If the total value of the goods per passenger exceeds NAG500, a declaration should be made on customs' forms and cleared at the freight department.
Prohibited: Dogs and cats from Central and South America, except from Surinam; monkeys from the South American continent.

Public Holidays

Below are listed Public Holidays for the January 2006-June 2007 period.
2006: Jan 1 New Year's Day. **Jan 26** Indian Republic Day. **Feb 27** Carnival Monday. **Apr 14** Good Friday. **Apr 16** Easter Sunday. **Apr 30** Queen's Birthday. **May 1** Labour Day. **May 25** Ascension. **Jul 2** Curaçao Flag Day. **Oct 21** Antillean Day. **Dec 24-26** Christmas. **Dec 31** New Year's Eve.
2007: Jan 1 New Year's Day. **Jan 26** Indian Republic Day. **Feb 19** Carnival Monday. **Apr 6** Good Friday. **Apr 8** Easter Sunday. **Apr 30** Queen's Birthday. **May 1** Labour Day. **May 17** Ascension.

Health

	Special Precautions?	Certificate Required?
Yellow Fever	No	1
Cholera	No	No
Typhoid & Polio	2	N/A
Malaria	No	N/A

Note: *Regulations and requirements may be subject to change at short notice, and you are advised to contact your doctor well in advance of your intended date of departure. Any numbers in the chart refer to the footnotes below.*

1: A yellow fever certificate is required from travellers over six months of age coming from infected areas.
2: Immunisation against typhoid is sometimes advised.
Food & drink: All mains water on the island is distilled from sea water and is thus safe to drink. Bottled mineral water is widely available. Milk is pasteurised and dairy products are safe for consumption. Local meat, poultry, seafood, fruit and vegetables are generally considered safe to eat.
Other risks: *Hepatitis A* and B occur and immunisation is sometimes recommended. *Dengue fever* may occur. There are potential risks from sea urchins, jellyfish and coral whilst swimming.
Health care: There are three hospitals on Curaçao as well as some medical centres. The largest, St Elizabeth, is well equipped. Health insurance is recommended.

Travel - International

AIR:
 Dutch Caribbean Airlines, the national airline of the Netherlands Antilles, ceased operations in October 2004. *KLM* operates daily flights to

Curaçao from Amsterdam. Other airlines serving Curaçao include *Air Jamaica*, *American Airlines* and *Avianca Airlines*.

Approximate flight times: From Curaçao to *London* is 11 hours (depending on connection time), to *Los Angeles* is 10 hours 30 minutes, to *Miami* two hours 30 minutes and to *New York* is seven hours.

Main airports: *Curaçao (CUR)* (Hato) is 12km (7 miles) from Willemstad. *To/from the airport:* Buses to the city centre operate daily 0600-2300 (travel time – 45 minutes). Taxis are also available (travel time – 30 minutes). *Facilities:* Duty free shop, bar, restaurant, light refreshments, banks/bureaux de change, ATMs, post office, hotel reservation facilities and car hire.

Departure tax: NAG36 (US$20) per person.

SEA:

Main ports: The *Port of Willemstad* is deep, wide and naturally sheltered (website: www.curports.com). Many international cruise lines call at Curaçao.

Travel - Internal

AIR:

Windward Islands Air International (WM) (website: www.fly-winair.com) operates to Saba, St Eustatius and St Maarten.

Departure tax: NAG10 (US$7) to other islands in the Netherlands Antilles; children under two years of age and passengers transiting within 24 hours are exempt.

ROAD:

Traffic drives on the right. A good public **bus** service runs throughout the island and many of the main hotels provide their own **minibus** services to Willemstad.

Taxi: These are plentiful as are **car hire** firms (both international and local), which are located at the airport and in the main hotels, as well as in the capital. Taxis are easily recognisable by their signs and also the letters TX on registration plates. Taxis have no meters but fares are standard and are based on one to four people with a 25 per cent surcharge for a fifth passenger and/or after 2300. Prices should be agreed in advance. Tipping, while not obligatory, is usually about 10 per cent of the fare.

Documentation: An International Driving Permit is required.

Travel Advice

Most visits to Curaçao are trouble-free but you should be aware of the global risk of indiscriminate international terrorist attacks, which could be against civilian targets, including places frequented by foreigners.

Travellers should be aware that the Netherlands Antilles are used as a drug passageway from South America to Europe and North America. Never leave bags unattended nor agree to carry a package for anyone.

Petty theft and street crime is on the increase.

This advice is based on information provided by the Foreign and Commonwealth Office in the UK. It is correct at time of publishing. As the situation can change rapidly, visitors are advised to contact the following organisations for the latest travel advice:

British Foreign and Commonwealth Office
Tel: (0845) 850 2829.
Website: www.fco.gov.uk

US Department of State
Website: http://travel.state.gov/travel

Accommodation

HOTELS:

There are a few luxury hotels on Curaçao, all offering air conditioning, restaurants, swimming pools and/or beach access, and a choice between European Plan (room only) and Modified American Plan (half-board). Most also offer some sort of in-house entertainment, a baby-sitting service and cable TV. Some have their own casinos. Out-of-town hotels provide their guests with free transport to and from Willemstad. A 7 per cent Government tax and 12 per cent service charge are normally levied on all hotel bills.

GUEST HOUSES:

For details of more modest accommodation – guest houses, commercial hotels and self-catering – contact the Curaçao Tourism Development Bureau (see *Top Things To Do*).

CAMPING AND CARAVANNING:

There are a few campsites. However, these sometimes only take larger groups that have been organised in advance.

Top Things To See

- **Willemstad,** the capital, is noted for its brightly coloured, Dutch-style houses and a range of other interesting and complementary architectural styles, including *cunucu* houses (based on African-style mud and wattle huts), thatched cottages and country houses. It has been declared a **UNESCO World Heritage Site** and is one of the finest shopping centres in the Caribbean.

- Monuments of interest in Willemstad include the **Statue of Manuel Piar**, a famous freedom fighter, and two statues associated with World War II: one given by the Dutch royal family to the people of Curaçao (in recognition of their support), and one in commemoration of those who lost their lives.

- The mustard-coloured **Fort Amsterdam**, now the seat of government of the Netherlands Antilles, stands at the centre of **historic Willemstad**, which from 1648 to 1861 was a fortified town of some strategic importance. The **fort's church**, still standing, doubled as a storehouse for provisions saved in case of siege. Other specially designed storerooms for food, sails and other essentials may still be seen. A cannonball is still embedded in the church's southwest wall. Nearby is the present **Governor's Residence**, dating back to the Dutch colonial days.

- Also worth seeing in Willemstad are the **Queen Emma Pontoon Bridge** and the **Queen Juliana Bridge**. The latter spans the harbour at a height of 490m (1600ft). The harbour itself has a **floating market** where colourful barges full of agricultural produce can be seen. Nearby is the **new market building**, the design of which is very striking. The market comes to life after 0600 on a Saturday morning.

- Take in the architecture of the **Scharloo** area in Willemstad, reached by crossing the **Wilhelmina Drawbridge**, dating from 1700. The **Mikvé Israel Synagogue** is the oldest in the Americas and, like the Jewish **Beth Heim Cemetery**, is worth a visit. Its courtyard **museum** has a fine collection of historical artefacts.

- Just outside Willemstad is the modern site of the **Netherlands Antilles University** and, further along the western road, is the **Landhuis Papaya** (a country house), the **Ceru Grandis** (a three-storey plantation house) and the driftwood beach of **Boca San Pedro**.

- Discover **Boca Tabla**, the thundering underwater cave of the north coast and the picturesque fishing village of **Westpoint**.

- Explore **St Christoffel National Park**, occupying the most northwestern part of the island, a nature reserve dominated by the **St Christoffel Mountain**. There are several caves decorated with **Arawak Indian paintings**, some unusual rock formations and many fine views across the countryside; the ruins of the **Zorguliet Plantation** and the privately owned **Savonet Plantation** and the **Savonet Museum** may be seen at the base of the mountain. The latter dates back to the 18th century and is still in use today. The indigenous flora includes orchids and some interesting evergreens. Exotic birdlife, iguanas and the shy Curaçao deer may also be observed at the park.

- Pay a visit to the interesting **Caves of Hato**. Magnificent stalactite formations, wall paintings and underground streams with cascading waterfalls can be seen within the 4900m (16,076ft) labyrinth.

Top Things To Do

- **Watersports** are widely promoted and facilities on Curaçao are well developed. There are excellent beaches for **swimming** along the sheltered **southwestern coast** (some charge an entrance fee). **Windsurfing**, **sailing** and **water-skiing** are popular on the island and the hotels and watersports centres are well equipped. **Snorkelling**, **scuba-diving** and **deep-sea fishing** are also popular and there are plenty of opportunities to participate in these sports. The waters are teeming with underwater life. Tuition is available.

- Celebrate with the locals at the **Curaçao Carnival**. The ancient Carnival began as a Catholic rite to represent the Christian practice of 'Carne Levale' or giving up meat for Lent. Today, the event is one of the largest and longest lasting Carnival spectacles of the Caribbean – starting in early January and ending late February/March. The main marches, the product of weeks of enthusiastic preparation, take place in February and March. They feature hordes of fantastic floats, costumes and characters, plus Carnival 'royalty' elected during full-scale beauty contests.

Entertainment

FOOD & DRINK: Restaurant styles vary from informal bistro to the very expensive.

National specialities:
- Traditional Dutch food (particularly using fresh seafood and cheeses) is popular.
- Creole food (*criollo*) makes good use of the great variety of fresh fish.
- French, Italian and other international cuisines are also on offer.

National drinks:
- A wide variety of alcohol is available. Curaçao liqueur, which is made from the sun-dried peel of a bitter orange and a mixture of spices, is a popular local drink.

Tipping: Hotels add a 5 to 10 per cent Government tax and a 12 per cent service charge. Bar staff, waiters, porters and doormen expect a 10 per cent tip.

NIGHTLIFE: There are several discos run by hotels on the island and some hotels have a casino. Performances of drama and music can be found at the *Centro Pro Arte*.

SHOPPING: Curaçao (and other Netherlands Antilles islands) is a thriving centre for duty free shopping. An enormous range of imported goods are on sale at considerably reduced prices. Locally made curios are available for the tourist. A particularly popular souvenir is the Curaçao liqueur (see *Food & Drink* section). **Shopping hours**: Mon-Sat 0800-1200 and 1400-1800. Hours may vary.

Business

- **GDP:** US$2.45 billion (Netherlands Antilles, 2003 estimate).
- **Main exports:** Petroleum products.
- **Main imports:** Crude petroleum, food and manufactured goods.
- **Main trade partners:** Venezuela, USA and The Netherlands.

ECONOMY: Curaçao is the most prosperous of the Netherlands Antilles island group. The economy is based on tourism, telecommunications and transport, the financial services sector and trade and industry. The capital, Willemstad, is at the centre of a network of offshore banking facilities and other financial services. Curaçao also houses one of the largest dry docks in the western Caribbean. Oil refining and transhipment are the other key economic activities. Import substitution has also been successfully pursued and a wide range of consumer goods are now produced locally. Venezuela, which supplies most of the crude oil for the refineries, and the USA are the island's principal trading partners.

BUSINESS ETIQUETTE: Suits should be worn and punctuality is essential. **Office hours**: Mon-Fri 0730-1200 and 1330-1630.

CONFERENCES/CONVENTIONS: There are facilities at the World Trade Centre, Conference Centre Kura Hulanda and Tres Tan Conference Centre.

Cyprus

Location: Europe, eastern Mediterranean.

Time: GMT + 2 (GMT + 3 from last Sunday in March to last Sunday in October).

Overview

The turbulent history of the island can be traced back over 10,000 years. Like many Mediterranean islands, Cyprus has long been seen as an important strategic base and has suffered a variety of occupations. From 1571, the Ottoman Turks ruled Cyprus for over three centuries, before ceding it to Britain in 1878.

Independence was achieved in August 1960. The island's new constitution was an elaborate compromise between the British and the rival Greek and Turkish communities, between whom considerable distrust remained.

In July 1974, President Makarios was deposed by a military coup (allegedly backed by the military regime then in power in Greece). Within days, Turkish troops arrived on the northern coast of Cyprus, having been 'invited' by the Turkish Cypriot leader, Rauf Denktash, to intervene in order to protect the Turkish community on the island. After the Turkish army had taken control of the northern third of the island, a ceasefire was arranged under UN auspices. The island has remained partitioned ever since and UN peacekeeping forces maintain a truce between the two sides.

In November 1983, the Turkish part of the island proclaimed itself independent. However, formal recognition of the self-styled country only has been granted by Turkey and various other statelets (for example, the Azeri enclave of Nakhichevan). For the vast majority of the international community, the legitimate Government of Republic of Cyprus (Kipriaki Demokratia) is the Greek-Cypriot administration in Nicosia. Today, the principal issue for the Greek-Cypriot Government remains the same; how to normalise relations with the northern occupied part of the island and reunify the island.

Despite its political problems, Cyprus is a modern country that effortlessly marries European culture with ancient enchantment. Here, visitors will discover a compact world of alluring beaches and fragrant mountain peaks, vineyards studded with olive trees and ancient ruins that stir the imagination, citrus groves and old stone villages where sweet wine flows as freely as conversations at the local café.

General Information

AREA: 9251 sq km (3572 sq miles, including Turkish-occupied territory).
POPULATION: 793,100 (2001, including Turkish-occupied region).

POPULATION DENSITY: 119.3 per sq km
CAPITAL: Nicosia (Lefkosia). **Population:** 205,633 (2001, excluding Turkish-occupied portion).
GEOGRAPHY: Cyprus is an island in the eastern Mediterranean. The landscape varies between rugged coastlines, sandy beaches, rocky hills and forest-covered mountains. The Troodos Mountains in the centre of the island rise to almost 1952m (6400ft) and provide skiing during the winter. Between these and the range of hills which run eastward along the north coast and the 'panhandle' is the fertile Messaoria Plain. The Morphou Basin runs around the coast of Morphou Bay in the west.
GOVERNMENT: Republic since 1960. **Head of State and Government**: President Tassos Papadopoulos since 2003.
Recent history: The majority of the international community recognises the Greek-Cypriot administration in Nicosia as the legitimate Government of the Republic of Cyprus (Kipriaki Demokratia). Until February 2003, this had been led for a decade by President Glafkos Clerides. That month, he was deposed at the most recent presidential election by Tassos Papadopoulos, candidate of the centre-right Komma Dimokratiko (Democratic Party). The present Government is a coalition of DIKO, AKEL – the Communist Party which has long been the single largest force in Greek-Cypriot politics – and the smaller KISOS party.
The northern occupied part of the island was run by Rauf Denktash, who was the dominant political figure in the enclave for almost 30 years. However, in 2005, Mehmet Ali Talet was elected leader of the Turkish Cypriot community. President Papadopoulos oversaw the Republic of Cyprus' entry, along with nine others, into the European Union in May 2004 despite the absence of a political settlement between the two parts of the island. (This had previously been a precondition of Cypriot entry).
The principal issue for the Greek-Cypriot Government remains the same; how to normalise relations with the northern occupied part of the island and reunify the island.
LANGUAGE: The majority (approximately 80 per cent) speak Greek and approximately 20 per cent speak Turkish. The Greek Cypriot dialect is different from mainland Greek. Turkish is spoken by Turkish Cypriots. English, German and French are also spoken in tourist centres.
RELIGION: Greek Orthodox, with Muslim minority.
ELECTRICITY: 240 volts AC, 50Hz. Square 13-amp three-pin plugs (UK-type) are used.
SOCIAL CONVENTIONS: Respect should be shown for religious beliefs. It is customary to shake hands and other normal courtesies should be observed. It is viewed as impolite to refuse an offer of Greek coffee or a cold drink. It is acceptable to bring a small gift of wine or confectionery, particularly when invited for a meal. For most occasions, casual attire is acceptable. Beachwear should be confined to the beach or poolside. More formal wear is required for business and in more exclusive dining rooms, social functions, etc. **Photography**: Photography is forbidden near military camps or installations. A licence from the appropriate authorities is required to photograph museum artefacts - this can sometimes be purchased from the museum's ticket desk. No flash photography is allowed in churches with murals or icons.

Climate

Warm Mediterranean climate. Hot, dry summers with mild winters during which rainfall is most likely.
Required clothing: Lightweight cottons and linens during summer months; warmer mediumweights and rainwear during the winter.

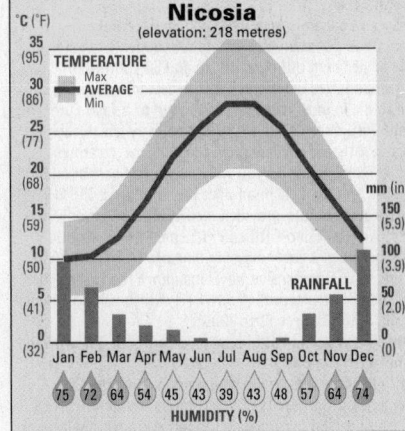

Communications

Telephone: Full IDD is available. Country code: 357. Telecard (C£3, 5 or 10 denominations) or coin-operated public telephones are installed at various central locations in towns and villages. Call Direct (cheaper than ordinary collect calls) is available to most EU countries, as well as Australia, USA and Canada.
Mobile telephone: Roaming agreements exist with most international mobile phone companies. Coverage is good.
Internet: Public access is available in Internet cafes located in the cities, for instance, Nicosia, Larnaca, Limassol, Pafos and Ayia Napa.
Post: There are daily airmail services to all developed countries. Service within Europe takes three to four days. District Post office opening hours: Mon-Fri 0730-1330 and 1500-1800 except Wednesday, Saturday 0830-1030 during the winter period (1 Sep to 30 Jun); Mon-Fri 0730-1330 and 1600-1900 except Wednesday, Sat 0830-1030 during the summer period (1 Jul to 31 Aug). Other post office opening hours: Mon-Fri 0730-1330, Thurs 1500-1800 at other times.
MEDIA: The Cypriot media reflects the island's political divide, with the Turkish-controlled zone in the north operating its own press and broadcasters. State-run services compete with a large number of private TV and radio stations. Relays of Greek and Turkish stations are available across the island. Newspapers on both sides of the divide are frequently critical of the authorities.
Press: Newspapers published in English include the *Cyprus Financial Mirror*, *Cyprus Mail* (daily), *Cyprus Today* (Turkish Cypriot) and *Cyprus Weekly*. *Simirini* is in Greek, while *Kibris Gazette* is in Turkish. Most English papers are available.
TV: The public *Cyprus Broadcasting Corporation (CyBC)* operates channels *RIK 1* and *RIK 2*. In northern Cyprus, *Bayrak Radio-TV* operates channels *BRT 1* and *BRT 2*.
Radio: *Radio 1* (in Greek), *Radio 2* (in English, Turkish and Armenian), *Radio 3* (in Greek) and *Love Radio* are operated by CyBC. Commercial stations include *Radio Proto* and *Astra 92.8*. Bayrak Radio-TV operates *Bayrak Radio 1* (in Turkish), *Bayrak International* (in English), *Bayrak FM* and *Bayrak Klasik*. In addition, the CTO sponsors programmes for tourists Mon-Sat on 603kHz (498m) and FM94.8. The times are as follows: German 0800; English 0830; French 0900; Swedish 0930; Arabic 1000.

Passport/Visa

	Passport Required?	Visa Required?	Return Ticket Required?
Full British	1	No	Yes
Australian	Yes	No	Yes
Canadian	Yes	No	Yes
USA	Yes	No	Yes
Other EU	1	No	Yes
Japanese	Yes	No	Yes

Note: *Regulations and requirements may be subject to change at short notice, and you are advised to contact the appropriate diplomatic or consular authority before finalising travel arrangements. Any numbers in the chart refer to the footnotes below.*

Restricted Entry: (a) Holders of Former Yugoslav Republic passports bearing the stamp 'Macedonia'. (b) Holders of passports issued illegally by the 'Turkish Republic of Northern Cyprus'. Other nationalities having stamps or visas of the 'Turkish Republic of Northern Cyprus' in their passports are only allowed to enter Cyprus after the visas/stamps are cancelled by the Immigration Authorities of the Republic of Cyprus.
PASSPORTS: Passport valid for at least three months beyond the period of intended stay required by all except: (a) 1. EU/EEA nationals (EU+ Iceland, Liechtenstein, Norway) and Swiss nationals holding a valid national ID card.
Note: EU and EEA nationals are only required to produce evidence of their EU/EEA nationality and identity in order to be admitted to any EU/EEA Member State. This evidence can take the form of a valid national passport *or* national identity card. Either is acceptable. Possession of a return ticket, any length of validity on their document, sufficient funds for the length of their proposed visit should *not* be imposed.
VISAS: Required by all except the following for stays of up to 90 days:
(a) nationals of countries referred to in the chart above;
(b) nationals of Andorra, Argentina, Bolivia, Brazil, Brunei, Bulgaria, Chile, Costa Rica, Croatia, El Salvador, Guatemala, Honduras, Hong Kong (SAR), Iceland, Israel, Korea (Rep), Liechtenstein, Macau (SAR), Malaysia, Mexico, Monaco, New Zealand, Nicaragua, Norway, Panama, Paraguay, Romania, San Marino, Singapore, Switzerland, Uruguay, Vatican City and Venezuela;
(c) transit passengers continuing their onward journey by the same or first connecting aircraft within 24 hours, provided holding valid onward or return documentation and not leaving the airport, except nationals of Afghanistan, Bangladesh, Congo (Dem Rep), Eritrea, Ethiopia, Ghana, Iran, Iraq, Nigeria, Somalia, Sri Lanka and Turkey, who require an *Airport Transit* visa.
Types of visa and cost: *Tourist/Business*: C£6 (free of charge to nationals of Egypt, Russian Federation, Syrian

A B C D E F G H I J K L M N O P Q R S T U V W X Y Z

Arab Republic and Ukraine, provided holding onward or return tickets and sufficient funds to cover the duration of their stay). Multiple-entry visas are only issued to those who require it for business purposes and cost C£20. *Transit*: C£6. *Airport Transit*: C£6.
Validity: *Tourist/Business*: Three months. *Transit*: Five days.
Application to: In person to the Consulate (or consular section at Embassy or High Commission).
Application requirements: (a) Passport valid at least six months after returning from Cyprus. (b) One completed application form. (c) One passport-size photo. (d) Proof of sufficient funds to cover duration of stay. (e) Provisional booking or itinerary of travel arrangements and evidence of hotel reservation or letter of invitation from resident of Cyprus. (f) Fee (payable by cash or postal order only, subject to rate of exchange). (g) Application must be submitted in person; however, those who reside more than 200miles (300km) from the Consulate may apply by post and send a registered self-addressed special delivery envelope. *Business*: (a)-(g) and, (h) Introductory letter from the applicant's company, giving details of salary. (i) Official letter of invitation from a company in Cyprus.
Working days required: In most cases personal applications will be processed on the same day or within 24 hours after an interview, but it may take up to a minimum of 10 days if application needs to be referred to Cyprus (depending on nationality, eg Turkey).
Temporary residence: Nationals of any country coming to Cyprus for employment or studies must secure an employment or student's permit through the Migration Officer, Nicosia prior to arrival. Applications should be submitted by the prospective employers or the directors of the schools.

PASSPORT/VISA INFORMATION

High Commisson of the Republic of Cyprus in the UK
93 Park Street, London W1K 7ET, UK
Tel: (020) 7499 8272 *or* 7491 2955 *or* 7629 6288 (Cyprus Trade Centre) *or* 5350 (consular section).
Website: www.cyprus.gov.cy
Opening hours: Mon-Fri 0930-1700; 0930-1300 (consular section).

Embassy of the Republic of Cyprus in the USA
2211 R Street NW, Washington DC 20008-4082, USA
Tel: (202) 462 5772 *or* 462 0873.
Website: www.cyprusembassy.net

Consulate of the Republic of Cyprus in the USA
13 East 40th Street, New York, NY 10016, USA
Tel: (212) 686 6016/7.

Money

Currency: Cyprus Pound (CYP; symbol C£) = 100 cents. Notes are in denominations of C£20, 10, 5 and 1. Coins are in denominations of 50, 20, 10, 5, 2 and 1 cents.
Currency exchange: Visitors wishing to obtain non-Cypriot currency at Cypriot banks for business purposes are advised that this is only possible by prior arrangement. There are ATMs in main towns and tourist areas.
Credit & debit cards: All major credit cards are accepted at most places. Check with your credit or debit card company for details of merchant acceptability and other services which may be available.
Traveller's cheques: May be cashed in all banks. To avoid additional exchange rate charges, travellers are advised to take traveller's cheques in Pounds Sterling or Cyprus Pounds.
Currency restrictions: The import of local currency is unrestricted, subject to declaration; foreign currency for amounts over US$1000 (or the equivalent in other currency) must be declared. The export of local and foreign currency is limited to the amount declared on arrival. Local currency withdrawn from Cypriot banks may be exported provided a holding certificate is obtained by the bank.
Banking hours: Generally Mon-Fri 0830-1230 in June, July and August; Mon-Fri 0815-1230 and Mon 1515-1645 rest of year. Certain central banks may also open Tues-Fri in the afternoon. Banks in Larnaca and at Pafos International Airport are open all day.
Exchange rate indicators:
Rate at time of publishing

£1.00=	C£0.83
$1.00=	C£0.47

Duty Free

The following goods may be imported into Cyprus without incurring customs duty:
200 cigarettes or 50 cigars or 250g of tobacco; 1l of spirits (over 22 per cent volume) or 2l of fortified wine or sparkling wine, 2l of still wine; 50g of perfume and 250ml of eau de toilette; goods (excluding jewellery) up to €175 The limit is reduced to £90 for travellers under 15 years of age to all EU countries except Denmark, Germany, the Netherlands and the UK.
Prohibited imports: Agricultural products and propagating stock, such as natural fruit, flowers, seeds etc. without the approval of the relevant authorities; the importation of a number of other articles such as uncooked meat, fish and dairy products, animals, fire arms and explosives, pirated or counterfeit goods, obscene publications is also prohibited or restricted.
Abolition of duty free goods within the EU: On 30 June 1999, the sale of duty free alcohol and tobacco at airports and at sea was abolished in all of the original 15 EU member states. Of the 10 new member states that joined the EU on 1 May 2004, these rules already apply to Cyprus and Malta. There are transitional rules in place for visitors returning to one of the original 15 EU countries from one of the other new EU countries. But for the original 15, plus Cyprus and Malta, there are now no limits imposed on importing tobacco and alcohol products from one EU country to another (with the exceptions of Denmark, Finland and Sweden, where limits *are* imposed). Travellers should note that they may be required to prove at customs that the goods purchased are for personal use *only*.
Note: Goods are considered to be for your own use if you have no more than: *800 cigarettes or 200 cigars or 1kg of tobacco; 10l of spirits, 20l of fortified wine, 90l wine, 110l beer.*

Public Holidays

Below are listed Public Holidays for the January 2006 - June 2007 period.
2006: Jan 1 New Year's Day. **Jan 6** Epiphany. **Mar 6** Green Monday. **Mar 25** Greek National Day. **Apr 1** Greek Cypriot National Day. **Apr 21** Greek Orthodox Good Friday. **Apr 24** Greek Orthodox Easter Monday. **May 1** Labour Day. **June 12** Pentecost (Kataklysmos). **Aug 15** Assumption. **Oct 1** Cyprus Independence Day. **Oct 28** Greek National Day (Ochi Day). **Dec 24-26** Christmas.
2007: Jan 1 New Year's Day. **Jan 6** Epiphany. **Mar 6** Green Monday. **Mar 25** Greek National Day. **Apr 1** Greek Cypriot National Day. **Apr 6** Greek Orthodox Good Friday. **Apr 9** Greek Orthodox Easter Monday. **May 1** Labour Day.

Health

	Special Precautions?	Certificate Required?
Yellow Fever	No	No
Cholera	No	No
Typhoid & Polio	No	No
Malaria	No	No

Note: *Regulations and requirements may be subject to change at short notice, and you are advised to contact your doctor well in advance of your intended date of departure. Any numbers in the chart refer to the footnotes below.*

Food & drink: Milk is pasteurised and tap water is generally safe to drink. Powdered and tinned milk are available. Only eat well-cooked meat and fish, preferably served hot. Pork, salad and mayonnaise may carry increased risk. Vegetables should be cooked and fruit peeled.
Other risks: Immunisation against *hepatitis A* is sometimes recommended.
Health care:
European Economic Area (EEA) and Switzerland:
If you or any of your dependants are suddenly taken ill or have an accident during a visit to an EEA country or Switzerland, free or reduced-cost necessary treatment is available - in most cases on production of a valid European Health Insurance Card (EHIC). Each country has different rules about state medical provision. In some, treatment is free. In many countries you will have to pay part or all of the cost, and then claim a full or partial refund. The EHIC gives access to state-provided medical treatment only and the scheme gives no entitlement to medical repatriation costs, nor does it cover ongoing illnesses of a non-urgent nature, so comprehensive travel insurance is advised. Note that the EHIC replaces the Form E111, which will no longer be valid after 31 December 2005.
Note: A European Health Insurance Card (EHIC) is not valid in the north (Turkish) part of Cyprus.
Health facilities are generally of a good standard. The emergency departments of all hospitals are manned with English-speaking personnel, although it is advisable to seek the assistance of an interpreter for more complex medical matters.
Travellers can get treatment from doctors or dentists practising in state health centres. They will be charged a patient contribution of CYP1.00 for each visit to a doctor or dentist and CYP40.00 for each denture. These charges are not refundable. Prescriptions issued by a state doctor are free. However, they must be presented to a state pharmacy. If you do not have your EHIC, you will have to get them from a private pharmacy and you will be charged. You can only get in-patient treatment if a state doctor refers you to hospital, or if you are admitted through the accident and emergency department of a state hospital. More information can be obtained from the Ministry of Health (website: www.moh.gov.cy).

Travel - International

Note: Since October 1974, the Cyprus government has declared the ports of Famagusta (Ammochostos) and Kyrenia, and the airport of Ercan, all in the northern part of the island, as illegal ports of entry to Cyprus.
AIR:
Over 40 airlines, including the national airline *Cyprus Airways (CY)* (website: www.cyprusairways.com), operate scheduled flights within, to and from Cyprus.
Approximate flight times: From Pafos and Larnaca to *London* is four hours 30 minutes, to *Paris* is three hours 30 minutes, to *Zurich* is three hours, to *Frankfurt* is three hours 30 minutes, to *Athens* is one hour 40 minutes and to *Stockholm* is five hours.
Main airports: *Larnaca (LCA)* is 5km (3 miles) south of Larnaka and 50km (31 miles) from Nicosia. *To/from the airport*: Taxis are available outside the airport terminal. *Facilities:* Duty free shop, tourist information, bank/bureau de change, bars and restaurants, Cyprus Hotel Information and Reservation Office, first aid, facilities for disabled travellers, car hire and post office.
Pafos (PFO) is 15km (9 miles) east of the city (travel time - 25 minutes). *Facilities:* Tourist information, duty free, Cyprus Hotel Information, cafeteria, special facilities for disabled travellers and car hire facilities.
Departure tax: None.
SEA:
Main ports: Passenger ships from the ports of *Limassol* and *Larnaca* connect Cyprus with various Greek and Middle Eastern ports, including Piraeus, Rhodes, Heraklion, Haifa, Port Said, Jounieh and many Greek islands. Services are reduced during the winter months. For detailed information on ferry boats and shipping lines, contact the Cyprus Tourism Organisation (see *Top Things To Do*). One-day cruises are organised from May to October, weather permitting. Several cruise lines call at Cyprus, including *Classical Cruises, Costa, Cunard Line, Euro Cruises, Norwegian Cruise Lines, Princess* and *Swan Hellenic Cruises. Louis Cruise Lines* sail to Egypt and the Holy Land (tel: (25) 570 000 *or* (0800) 018 3883 toll-free UK; website: www.louiscruises.com). *Paradise Cruises* also operates to Egypt, Greece and Lebanon (tel: (25) 357 604; website: www.paradise.com.cy).

Travel - Internal

ROAD:
Bus: Services connect all towns and villages on the island every day except Sunday and public holidays. Service is efficient and cheap. **Urban buses:** They operate frequently during the daytime and, in some areas during the summer, timetables extend until midnight. **Rural buses:** Limited to one or two services each day and can be slow; however, they are a good way of seeing the more remote villages. **Taxi:** These run 24-hours between all the main towns on the island. Fares are regulated by the Government and all taxis have meters. Rural taxis can only be hired from the base station and do not have a meter installed. *Transurban Service Taxis* offers an excellent, cheap service using seven-seat taxis running fixed routes between main points. Taxis run to a timetable. Services operate every 30 minutes (Mon-Fri, 0600-1800; Sat and Sun, 0600-1700) and can be booked by phone. Fares under this system are often one-tenth of the usual rate. **Car hire:** Cars are one of the best ways to explore the island. They may be hired at airports and commercial centres, but should be reserved well in advance during the summer season. Road signs are in both Greek and English. Traffic drives on the left. Although most roads are of a good standard, driving standards are not. It should also be noted that there are strict repercussions for those not wearing seatbelts or a crash helmet, or using a mobile telephone/under the influence of alcohol whilst driving.Visitors wishing to bring their car to Cyprus can do so for up to three months provided the car has a valid registration licence for its country of origin. **Motorcycles:** Riders and pillion passengers must wear crash helmets if the motorcycle is over 50cc. **Documentation:** An International Driving Permit or national driving licence is valid for one year.
URBAN:
Nicosia has its own privately run bus company operating efficient services at flat fares, which offers a comprehensive service covering the urban area of Limassol and linking the port with the tourist area. For more details, contact the *Limassol Urban Bus Company (E.A.L.) Limited*, PO Box 51117 (tel: (25) 354 050.

Taxis are widely available: a 15 per cent surcharge is in operation from 2300-0600. Tipping is expected.
Travel times: The following chart gives approximate travel times (in hours and minutes) from **Nicosia** to other main towns and tourist centres in Cyprus.

	Road
Limassol	1.00
Pafos	2.15
Larnaca	0.50
Ayia Napa	1.10

Travel Advice

Most visits to Cyprus are trouble-free but you should be aware of the global risk of indiscriminate international terrorist attacks, which could be against civilian targets, including places frequented by foreigners.
This advice is based on information provided by the Foreign and Commonwealth Office in the UK. It is correct at time of publishing. As the situation can change rapidly, visitors are advised to contact the following organisations for the latest travel advice:

British Foreign and Commonwealth Office
Tel: (0845) 850 2829.
Website: www.fco.gov.uk

US Department of State
Website: http://travel.state.gov/travel

Accommodation

HOTELS:

There are over 500 hotels and hotel apartments scattered throughout the island. There are also simple hotels that are ungraded. A VAT charge of 15 per cent is added to bills. Most hotels and hotel apartments offer discounts during the low season, which for seaside resorts is from 6 November to 15 March (excluding the period 20 December to 6 January) and for hill resorts from 1 October to 30 June. There are discounts for children occupying the same room as their parents: *under one year*, by private arrangement; *one to six years*, 50 per cent discount; *six to 10 years*, 25 per cent discount. Some hotels may only charge 80 per cent of the daily room rate for single occupancy of a double room. Visitors should check discounts with their hotel prior to arrival. **Grading:** Hotels range from deluxe **5-star** to **1-star**. Hotel apartments are classified A, B or C.

GUEST HOUSES:

Located mainly in Nicosia, Limassol, Pafos and Larnaca. The Cyprus Agrotourism Company (See *Accommodation Information*) offers traditional countryside accommodation.

CAMPING/CARAVANNING:

There are seven organised camping sites, at Polis (open March to October), Kalymnos Beach (open all year round), Forest Beach (open June to October), Feggari (open all year round), Geroskipou Zenon Gardens (open April to October) and Ayia Napa (open April to October). Facilities available in camping sites include showers, toilets, washing facilities, mini-market, and usually a snackbar or restaurant. Rates for camping sites range between C£1-C£2 per day for a tent space, plus C£1-C£1.50 per person daily for service and taxes.

YOUTH HOSTELS:

There are youth hostels in Nicosia, Larnaca, Pafos and Troodos Mountains (April to October, weather permitting) open to members of the International Youth Hostels Association. Non-members are also accepted, but on arrival at the hostel they will be provided with a guest card.

ACCOMMODATION INFORMATION

Cyprus Hotel Association
PO Box 2772, 1303 Nicosia, Cyprus
Tel: 22 152 820.
The Hotel Association also has an office at Larnaca International Airport (tel: 24 643 186).

Cyprus Youth Hostel Association
34 Theodotu Street, PO Box 24040, 1700 Nicosia, Cyprus
Tel: 2267 0027 *or* 2267 5574.

The Cyprus Agrotourism Company
Tel: 22 340 071.
Website: www.agrotourism.com.cy

Top Things To See

- The capital of Cyprus since the 12th century, **Nicosia** stands at the heart of the **Mesaoria Plain**. It is currently divided by the 'Green Line', a UN buffer zone that separates the Turkish-occupied north of the island and

Credit: ©Cyprus Tourism Organisation

the Government-controlled south. The Old City, which is being renovated in part, is defined by 16th-century walls built by the Venetians. Among attractions and points of interest are: the **Cyprus Museum**, a storehouse of the island's archaeological treasures; the **Folk Art Museum**; the new **Archbishop's Palace**; **St John's Cathedral**; Byzantine churches; the **Byzantine Museum/Makarios Cultural Centre**; and the **Ömeriye Mosque**.
- From Nicosia, go on an excursion to the **Royal Tombs** and **Agios Irakleidios Monastery** at **Tamassos**; the five-dome church and the mosque in **Peristerona**; the **Panagia Chrysospiliotissa Church**, in a cliff-side cave near **Deftera**. Further into the rugged **Pitsylia Region**, in the hills southwest of Nicosia, is **Machairas Monastery**, close to the restored and protected traditional villages of **Fikardou**, **Gourri** and **Lazanias**.
- In the resort town of **Larnaka**, stroll on the seafront promenade which is fringed with palm trees, cafes and tavernas. Places of interest include: the **Agios Lazaros Church** and its associated **Byzantine Museum**; **Larnaka Fort**; the **District Archaeological Museum**; the **Pierides Museum** (a private archaeological museum); the **Natural History Museum**; the **Tornaritis-Pierides Palaeontology Museum**; and the scant ruins of ancient **Kition**.
- Near Larnaca's airport is the **Hala Sultan Tekkesi**, a historic mosque standing in beautiful gardens on the edge of **Larnaka Salt Lake** (dry in summer), a winter home of migratory flamingoes. Nearby, in Kiti, **Panagia Angeloktisti Church** contains a superb sixth-century Byzantine mosaic of the Virgin and Child.
- In the hills to the west is the village of **Lefkara**, famous for its handmade lace, and the **Convent of Agios Minas**. Off the Limassol–Nicosia road are the hilltop **Stavrovouni Monastery**, and the Crusader-era **Chapelle Royal** near Pyrga. Further west, on a hillside at **Choirokoitia**, are the remains of a neolithic village from 5800 BC, one of the earliest settlements in Cyprus.
- Head for **Limassol Castle** which stands guard over the old harbour and houses the **Cyprus Medieval Museum**. There is also a **Folk Art Museum**, the **Limassol District Archaeological Museum** and, in the **Municipal Gardens**, a small zoo.
- In **Amathus**, now in ruins and partly covered by the sea, discover the **Acropolis**, the **Necropolis** and the remains of an early **Christian basilica**. Further east lies **Agios Georgios Alamanos Convent** and the black sands of **Governor's Beach**. **Kolossi Castle** is the headquarters of the Crusader Knights of St John of Jerusalem.
- In the ancient city of **Kourion**, on a steep hillside near **Episkopi**, discover a superbly sited **Graeco-Roman theatre** where concerts and Shakespearean plays are performed in summer. Kourion contains other interesting sites, including the House of **Eustolios**, which has beautiful mosaics; the **Acropolis**; the ruins of the Roman-era forum; the **Christian Basilica**; and public buildings.

- Beyond Kourion to the west are the city's stadium and the **Sanctuary of Apollo Ylatis**. All of these sites lie within the **Akrotiri-Episkopi** British Sovereign Base Area.
- Do not miss **Pafos**, the booming main town and year-round resort in the west, which consists of **Upper Pafos**, built on a rocky escarpment that commands a superb view of the coastline, and **Lower Pafos**, with a taverna-fringed harbour and a long seafront lined with hotels. Pafos is rich in ancient sites, in particular a cluster of excavated Roman villas near the harbour, among them the **House of Dionysos** and the **Villa of Theseus**, that contain superb mosaic floors, and the **Tombs of the Kings**. Other attractions include: the **Pafos District Museum**; the **Byzantine Museum**; **Pafos Fort** commanding the harbour; the remains of the Byzantine castle of **Saranda Kolones**; and **Panagia Chrysopolitissa Church**, the largest early Christian basilica on the island. **Pafos Aquarium** is of more recent origin.
- To the east and northeast of Pafos, the land rises through vineyards and the **Pafos Forest** to Cedar Valley, part of the **Tripylos Nature Reserve**, centred on the **Stavros tis Psokas Forest Station**. Wild mountain sheep (moufflon) are being protected here. The **Panagia Chrysorrogiatissa Monastery** is situated in scenic surroundings and is an interesting stop on the way.
- At the edge of the **Akamas Peninsula**, witness where, according to legend, the Greek goddess of love bathed at the **Baths of Aphrodite**, a grotto containing a freshwater pool.
- Going east from Polis, the fishing harbour at **Agios Georgios** is overlooked by cliffs into which ancient tombs are cut; at the top is an excavated early **Christian basilica**.
- At **Lara Bay**, beyond the rugged **Avakas Gorge**, a reserve has been established to protect the dwindling number of loggerhead turtles that nest here.
- At **Kouklia** visit the ruins of ancient **Palaia Pafos** and the **Temple of Aphrodite**. At the coast are **Petra tou Romiou (Rock of Aphrodite)**.
- The scenery in the forested – or, more accurately, reafforested – **Troodos Mountains** is spectacular. **Platres**, 1200m (3937ft) above sea level on the southern slopes, is the ideal base for excursions. It lies on the approaches to **Mount Olympus**, at 1952m (6404ft), the highest peak in Cyprus, with a summit that is invariably snow-covered in winter and has skiing slopes and facilities.
- **Omodos**, a restored conservation village, has the **Stavros Monastery** and a small **Folk Art Museum**. **Foini** is a centre of local craft pottery.
- See a golden icon of the Virgin Mary at the **Kykkos Monastery; Throni tis Panagias**, uphill from the monastery, the tomb of the late Archbishop Makarios III, the first President of Cyprus, occupies a setting that commands a magnificent view; discover the small but prettily situated **Kaledonia Falls** and the monasteries of

Credit: ©Cyprus Tourism Organisation

Mesa Potamos and **Trooditissa**.

• Visit the nine Byzantine churches in the Troodos mountains listed by UNESCO as World Heritage Sites for their magnificently frescoed interiors. These are **Panagia tis Asinou** near **Nikitari**, one of the finest examples of Byzantine art in the Levant; **Stavros tou Agiasmati** near **Platanistasa**; **Agios Ioannis Lampadistis** in **Kalopanagiotis**; **Panagia tou Araka** near **Lagoudera**; **Agios Nikolaos tis Stegis** southwest of **Kakopetria**; **Panagia tis Podythou** outside **Galata**; **Archangelos Michail** at **Pedoulas**; **Panagia tou Moutoulla** in Moutoullas; and **Timiou Stavrou** in **Pelendri**. Please note these are not open to visitors at all times.

Top Things To Do

• Celebrate the **feast of Kataklysmos** (the Greek Orthodox Whitsun); although celebrated throughout Cyprus, there is special enthusiasm in **Larnaka**, where crowds throng the shore for watersports, singing, dancing, eating and drinking.

• The many unspoilt areas in Cyprus make the land ideal for **hiking** and **trekking**. Recommended Nature Trails include **Atalante**, **Kaledonia** and **Persephone** in the Troodos area and **Aphrodite** and **Adonis** in the Akamas area, with other trails in the forests of **Machairas** and **Limassol**.

• Cyprus is also becoming established as a destination for **winter sports** with some hoteliers and tour operators, offering off-peak incentives. Both **Platres** and **Kakopetria** are conveniently placed for the skiing season on **Mount Olympus**, which usually lasts from January to mid-March, but **Troodos** is actually the nearest resort to the skiing area; it has hotels and cafes. There are four ski-lifts on Mount Olympus. The *Ski-Club*, which is based in Troodos, has its own shelter and accepts tourists as temporary members. Ski equipment can be hired there, PO Box 22185, CY 1518, Lefkosia, Cyprus (tel: (22) 675 340; website: www.cyprusski.com).

• Opportunities abound for **windsurfing, paragliding** and **swimming**. Recommended beaches include **Geroskipou, Dasoudi,Larnaca, Dassoudi Beach** and **Germasogeia** (latter two at Limassol). South of Limassol, on the **Akrotiri Peninsula** (and also inside the British military base), **Lady's Mile Beach** is a long stretch of excellent sand. On the coast north of Pafos, **Coral Bay** is a fast-growing resort around a small but good beach. On the north coast, **Polis** is a small town that until recently was virtually undeveloped and is now a bustling resort, though it retains traces of its former 'alternative' character. There is a busy small resort at **Pissouri Bay**. On the coast south of Famagusta lie busy resorts, speckled with golden sand beaches, that are ideal for children, like those at **Fig Tree Bay** and **Flamingo Bay**. **Agia Napa** has an increasingly boisterous reputation as a major **clubbing resort**. It also attracts families to its beaches, Waterworld leisure centre

and Go-Karts track. Boat tours leave from the harbour. Family-oriented **Protaras** and **Pernera** resorts have good beaches, with cafes and beach bars. Other attractions in the area include **rock climbing**. Around **Cape Gkreko**, the coastline becomes indented with rocky coves and small sandy beaches, ideal for **snorkelling** and **scuba-diving** (both for experienced practitioners), explorations by boat and picnics. The **Potamos Creek** fishing harbour presents a scene of colourful fishing boats. Inland, the small town of **Paralimni** provides entertainment in its restaurants, dance clubs and cafes. The *Cyprus Federation of Underwater Activities*, PO Box 21503, 1510 Nicosia (tel: (22) 754 647) and *Cydive* (tel: (26) 934 271; website: www.cydive.com) can provide information on diving facilities.

• Practise **fishing**; Note that a licence needs to obtained from the *Department of Fisheries*, Aiolou 13, CY, Nicosia (tel: (22) 807 861). Licences cost C£3 for each reservoir or C£10 for all reservoirs. Those who do not fish can still taste freshly caught fish in one of the tavernas around the harbour at the fishing port and resort of **Latchi (Lakki)**.

• In September, enjoy free wine during the Limassol's **wine festival**. During the **pre-Lenten Carnival**, Limassol also bursts into celebration, with bands, gaily decorated floats and dancing. West of Limassol, at **Fassouri**, are extensive citrus orchards and the **Water Mania** leisure park.

• Southeast of Pafos, try some Greek Delight (like Turkish Delight) at **Geroskipou** village, which also has a small **Folk Museum**.

• Eat the island's best apples in **Prodromos**, the highest village on Cyprus, 1530m (5019ft) above sea level. **Pedoulas** in the fertile **Marathasa Valley** is famous for cherries (and in spring for cherry blossom) and other fruits. **Kalopanagiotis** also has orchards. **Moutoullas** is a source of mineral water bottled and sold locally as well as exported to the Middle East. **Agros** produces rose water, mineral water and wine. The **Commandaria Region**, midway down the southern slopes, where the grapes for the Commandaria sweet red dessert wine are grown, has attractive villages like **Zoopigi**, where almond and walnut trees grow.

TOURIST INFORMATION

Cyprus Tourism Organisation in the UK
17 Hanover Street, London W1S 1YP, UK
Tel: (020) 7569 8800.
Website: www.visitcyprus.org.cy

Cyprus Tourism Organisation in the USA
13 East 40th Street, New York, NY 10016, USA
Tel: (212) 683 5280.
Website: www.visitcyprus.org.cy
Also deals with enquiries from Canada.

Entertainment

FOOD & DRINK: Major resorts have bars and restaurants of every category. At larger hotels, the cuisine tends to international although authentic local dishes may also be available. All over the island there are restaurants offering genuine Cypriot food. One of the best ways of enjoying Cypriot food is by ordering *mezze* (snacks), a large selection of a number of different local dishes. However, the cuisine varies according to whether the visitor eats in the North or the Republic of Cyprus. Waiter service is normal and counter service is common in bars. There are no licensing hours. The highlight of the wine year is the annual wine festival in Limassol, usually held in September, when free wine flows and local food is on offer.

National specialities:
• *Tava* (a tasty stew of meat, herbs and onions).
• *Dolmades* (vine leaves stuffed with minced meat and rice).
• *Kebabs* (pieces of lamb or other meat skewered and roasted over a charcoal fire).
• *Stifado* (a stew of beef or hare cooked with wine, vinegar, onion and spices).
• Fresh seafood: *Tsipoura* (seabream), *Lavraki* (seabass) and *Garides* (prawns).
• *Loukoumades*, Cyprus doughnuts with honey syrup.

National drinks:
• Coffee is Greek-style (short, strong and unfiltered)
• Cyprus produces excellent wines, spirits and beer which can only be bought in the south.

Tipping: A service charge is added to all bills, but tipping is still acceptable and remains at the discretion of the individual.

SHOPPING: Cypriot purchases include handmade lace, woven curtains and tablecloths, silks, basketwork, pottery, silverware and leather goods. Jewellery is an art which has been practised on the island since the Mycenean period; craftspeople working in contemporary and traditional styles produce some very fine pieces. Silver spoons and forks are a traditional symbol of Cypriot hospitality. Lefkara lace is famous throughout the world as one of the products most closely associated with Cypriot workmanship; the name originates from the village Lefkara, situated on a hill on the Nicosia–Limassol road. The local wines and brandy also make good purchases. Imported goods sell at competitive prices, including cameras, perfume, porcelain and crystal.

Shopping hours: Shops are closed Wednesday after 1400 as well as all day Sunday. Otherwise opening hours are 0800-1300 and 1600-1930 (summer, or until 1900 spring and autumn); 0800-1300 and 1430-1800 (winter). On Fridays, shops are generally open until 2000/2030.

Business

• **GDP:** US$15.4 billion.
• **Main imports:** Citrus, grapes, wine, potatoes, pharmaceuticals, clothing and footwear.
• **Main exports:** Consumer goods, raw materials, petroleum and lubricants, food and feed grains.
• **Main trade partners:** EU (especially UK, Greece, Italy and Germany), Lebanon, Egypt, Gulf States, Libya and Russia.

Tourism is the main component of the southern service economy but, in recent years, financial services – including 'offshore' enterprises – have also assumed an important role. The UK's sovereign military bases on the southern coast and near the partition boundary are a major source of revenue for the south. Economic development of the northern occupied part of Cyprus has been severely limited by lack of diplomatic recognition and it continues to rely heavily on economic support from Turkey. The profile of the northern occupied part of Cyprus's agricultural sector is similar to that of the south; manufacturing is relatively insignificant; tourism relies heavily on visitors from the Turkish mainland. Both parts of the island rely on imported raw fuels for their energy supplies. The decision of the north to allow visits across the partition may presage the development of a cross-border economy, but this may take some time. This concession on the part of the north was driven mainly by the acceptance of the south into the European Union in 2004. Turkey, which ultimately controls the fate of the northern part of Cyprus, is an aspirant member of the EU, and a solution to the present division of the island is an essential precursor to their own accession.

CONFERENCES/CONVENTIONS: Many quality hotels have first class conference facilities; Nicosia is a popular destination for budget-priced conferences and has a number of modern facilities. Advice can be obtained from the Cyprus Tourism Organisation.

COMMERCIAL INFORMATION

Cyprus Chamber of Commerce and Industry
38 Grivas Digenis Avenue, Chamber Building,
PO Box 21455, 1509 Nicosia
Tel: (22) 889 800.
Website: www.ccci.org.cy

Czech Republic

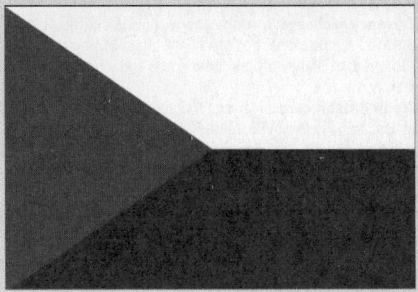

200km
100mls
✈ international airport

Location: Central Europe.

Time: GMT + 1 (GMT + 2 from last Sunday in March to last Sunday in October).

Overview

Part of Czechoslovakia until the 'Velvet Divorce' in January 1993, the Czech Republic has a rich cultural heritage represented by classical composers such as Dvorak and writers like Kafka. Tourism in the Czech Republic really dates from the 1989 'Velvet Revolution' when the communists were ousted out and a democratic government was installed with Vaclav Havel as President.

Tourism has largely focused on Prague, with its great museums, galleries, concerts and other attractions. Many day trips are possible from Prague, including the great western spa towns of Karlovy Vary and Mariánské Lázni, early settlements like Kutná Hora and castles like Karltejn. However, the rest of the country has much to offer the independent traveller. Although prices have risen over the past decade, the country still represents very good value for money.

Šumava Mountains of south Bohemia offer excellent rambles and a range of sports, and well-preserved medieval towns like Cesky Krumlov. Northeastern Bohemia's mountains, like the Cesky Ráj, offer superb hiking amidst unusual scenery. In Moravia, the eastern half of the country, life is even less hectic; Brno provides an excellent base for exploring important historic towns like Olomouc and Kromížíž.

The country possesses an immense number of fascinating castles, churches and other architectural gems. It has always been known for its musicians, and there are an enormous number of all types of concerts and festivals to choose from.

General Information

AREA: 78,866 sq km (30,450 sq miles).

POPULATION: 10.2 million (UN, 2005).

POPULATION DENSITY: 129.4 per sq km.

CAPITAL: Prague. **Population:** 1.25 million.

GEOGRAPHY: The Czech Republic is situated in central Europe, sharing frontiers with Germany, Poland, the Slovak Republic and Austria. Only about one-quarter of the size of the British Isles, the republic is hilly and picturesque, with historic castles, romantic valleys and lakes, as well as excellent facilities to take the waters at one of the famous spas or to ski and hike in the mountains. Among the most beautiful areas are the river valleys of the Vltava (Moldau) and Labe (Elbe), the hilly landscape and rocky mountains. Bohemia, to the west, is one of two main regions. Besides Prague, tourists are drawn to the spa towns of Karlovy Vary and Mariánské Lázne, and to the very beautiful region of south Bohemia. The Elbe flows through eastern Bohemia from the Krkonoçse/Giant mountains, one of the most

popular skiing regions. The eastern part, the rich agricultural area of Moravia offers a variety of wooded highlands, vineyards, folk art and castles. There are many historic towns such as Olomouc, Kromeríz and Telc. Brno is Moravia's administrative and cultural centre.

GOVERNMENT: Republic since 1993. **Head of State:** President Václav Klaus since 2003. |**Head of Government:** Prime Minister Jiri Paroubek since April 2005. **Recent history:** Jiri Paroubek, deputy leader of the centre-left Social-Democratic Party, became Prime Minister in April 2005 after weeks of crisis ended with the resignation of party leader Stanislav Gross amid a scandal over the financing of a luxury apartment. Mr Paroubek is the country's third Prime Minister since July 2004 when disastrous results in European Parliament elections prompted the resignation of Vladimir Spidla. Like both his predecessors, Mr Paroubek governs in coalition with the Christian Democrats and the Freedom Union. His Government's objective will be to continue with reforms aimed at reducing public spending in preparation for membership of the Eurozone. General elections will take place in June 2006.

LANGUAGE: The official language is Czech. English and German are also spoken.

RELIGION: Mostly Roman Catholic and some Protestant, including churches such as the Reformed, Lutheran, Methodist, Unity of Czech Brothers and Baptist. There is a small community of Jews, mainly in Prague. According to the March 2001 national census, 60 per cent of the population profess no religious beliefs.

ELECTRICITY: Generally 220 volts AC, 50Hz. Most major hotels have standard international two-pin razor plugs.

SOCIAL CONVENTIONS: Dress should be casual, but conservative, except at formal dinners and at quality hotels or restaurants.

Credit: ©Czech Tourism Archives

Climate

The weather is quite unsettled, with generally cold winters and mild summers. Spring and summer have the highest rainfall.

Required clothing: Mediumweights, heavy topcoat and overshoes for winter; lightweights for summer.

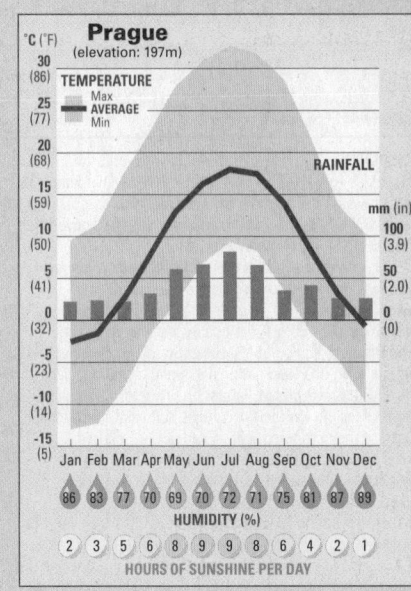

Czech Republic

A B C D E F G H I J K L M N O P Q R S T U V W X Y Z

Credit: ©Czech Tourism Archives

Communications

Telephone: Full IDD is available. Country code: 420. There are public telephone booths, including special kiosks for international calls. Surcharges can be quite high on long-distance calls from hotels. Most of the public telephone boxes take phonecards, which can be purchased at all Telecom points of sale and at newsagent and tobacconist shops.
Mobile telephone: Roaming agreements exist with most international mobile phone companies. Coverage is good.
Internet: There are Internet cafes in Prague and other cities.
Post: Main post office in Prague: 14 Jindrisská Street, Prague 1. 24-hour service: Hybernska 15, Prague 1. Post office hours: Mon-Fri 0800-1800.
MEDIA: Private media in the Czech Republic mushroomed in the 1990s, and private radio and TV stations provide stiff competition for public broadcasters. Public TV broadcaster Ceska Televize (CT) operates two networks and a 24-hour news channel. Czech public radio, Cesky Rozhlas (CRo), operates three national networks as well as local services. Two major private television channels broadcast nationally and there are more than 70 private radio stations. Though press freedom is protected by a charter of basic rights, the media are not always considered editorially independent. An angry dispute over the control of Czech public television at the end of 2000 showed that efforts to rid state media of political interference were ongoing.
Press: The *Prague Post* and *Prague Tribune* (both weekly) are published in English. The main Czech dailies include *Mladá Fronta Dnes*, *Právo* and *Lidove Noviny*.
TV: *Ceska Televize* is public and operates mainstream channel *CT1* and cultural channel *CT2;* CT 24 is a public news channel; *TV Nova* and *Prima* are commercial channels.
Radio: Public broadcaster *Czech Radio* operates national and regional networks; *Radio Prague* has programmes in a number of languages including English; *Frekvence 1* and *Radio Impuls* are private national stations.

Passport/Visa

	Passport Required?	Visa Required?	Return Ticket Required?
Full British	1	No/1	No
Australian	Yes	No	No
Canadian	Yes	No	No
USA	Yes	No	No
Other EU	1	No/2	No
Japanese	Yes	No	No

Note: *Regulations and requirements may be subject to change at short notice, and you are advised to contact the appropriate diplomatic or consular authority before finalising travel arrangements. Any numbers in the chart refer to the footnotes below.*

PASSPORTS: Passport valid for 90 days beyond the expected length of stay for visas up to 90 days; at least 455 days for visas over 90 days. For nationals who do not require a visa, passport must be valid for 90 days beyond the expected length of stay except for:
1. EU/EEA nationals (EU+ Iceland, Liechtenstein, Norway) and Swiss nationals holding a valid national ID card.
Note: EU and EEA nationals are only required to produce evidence of their EU/EEA nationality and identity in order to be admitted to any EU/EEA Member State. This evidence can take the form of a valid national passport *or* national identity card. Either is acceptable. Possession of a return ticket, any length of validity on their document, sufficient funds for the length of their proposed visit should *not* be imposed.
Note: Minors are allowed to travel on their parents' passports up until aged 15 years.
VISAS: Required by all except the following:
(a) **1.** British nationals with a passport valid for the duration of their stay;
(b) **2.** nationals listed in the chart above and nationals of Andorra, Argentina, Bolivia, Brazil, Brunei, Chile, Costa Rica, Croatia, El Salvador, Guatemala, Honduras, Hong Kong (SAR), Israel, Korea (Rep), Macau (SAR), Malaysia, Mexico, Monaco, New Zealand, Nicaragua, Panama, Paraguay, San Marino, Sovereign Military Order of Malta, Switzerland, Uruguay, Vatican City and Venezuela for up to 90 days;
(c) nationals of Bulgaria, Romania and Singapore for up to 30 days;
(d) transit passengers continuing their journey within 24 hours and not leaving the airport, providing holding onward tickets and relevant travel documentation. *Airport transit/transit visas are, however, *always* required for nationals of Afghanistan, Bangladesh, Congo (Dem Rep), Eritrea, Ethiopia, Ghana, Iran, Iraq, Lebanon, Nigeria, Pakistan, Somalia, Sri Lanka and the Syrian Arab Republic (this does not apply if the above national holds a valid residence visa or permit of any EU country, Iceland, Liechtenstein or Norway, or holds a permanent or long-term residence permit in Andorra, Canada, Japan, Monaco, San Marino, Switzerland or the USA);
(e) holders of a UN laissez-passer for as long as is necessary.
Note: (a) EU and EEA nationals, and those who do not require visas, whose stay will exceed 30 days, must register with the Alien and Border Police within 30 days of arrival. All other nationals must register with the Alien and Border Police within three days of arrival, regardless of intended length of stay. Generally, accommodation providers will arrange this for their guests. (b) British Overseas Citizens require visas as do holders of British Travel Documents (blue) under the 1951 Geneva Convention, and holders of British Travel Documents (brown) for tourism and business trips, and must apply in person.
Types of visa and cost: *Single-entry, Multiple-entry, Single-transit, Double-transit, Multiple-transit* and *Airport-transit*. Prices vary according to the nationality of the applicant and according to currency rates. For UK nationals, single-entry visas cost £18, multiple-entry visas cost £69, for stays not exceeding 90 days. *Single-transit/double-transit*: £18. There are no visa fees for nationals of Albania, Ecuador, Japan, Seychelles, South Africa and Turkey, or for children under 15 years of age.
Validity: *Single-* and *multiple-entry*: Six months from date of issue for a visit of a specified period not exceeding 90 days. *Transit* (single, double and multiple-transit): Six months from date of issue for a visit of a specified period not exceeding five days.
Application to: Consulate (or consular section at the Embassy); see *Passport/Visa Information* for details. Please note that some nationals must apply in person for a visa and submit slightly different application requirements (see below). Check with the Embassy for further details.
Application requirements: (a) One original application form. (b) One recent passport-size photo (attach with glue; do not staple). (c) Passport valid for at least 90 days beyond the requested length of visa, with at least one blank page and a photocopy of the data page. Children included on their parents' passports are permitted to travel with their parents up to the age of 15, from when they will require a separate passport. (d) Fee (payable in cash, by banker's draft or by postal order). (e) Proof of sufficient funds (eg recent bank statement or letter from host or sponsor). (f) Postal applications should be accompanied by a self-addressed envelope pre-paid for special delivery. (g) Valid travel insurance policy covering emergency hospital treatment and repatriation. *Business*: (a)-(g) and, (h) Letter from employer or invitation letter from company in the Czech Republic. *Student*: (a)-(g) and, (h) Letter from school or college confirming that you are a student and confirmation of available accommodation.
Note: All documents must be submitted in both original form, plus one photocopy.
Working days required: Seven (in person); 14 (by post); maximum 30.
TEMPORARY RESIDENCE: EU citizens may apply if intending to stay longer than three months, for a temporary or permanent resident permit with the Alien and Border Police in the Czech Republic. The process will take about 60 days. Alternatively, applications may be filed with diplomatic missions abroad (processing time: up to 180 days). The issue of the permit is not a condition for the stay.

PASSPORT/VISA INFORMATION

Embassy of the Czech Republic in the UK
26-30 Kensington Palace Gardens, London W8 4QY, UK
Tel: (020) 7243 1115 *or* (09069) 101 060 (24-hour recorded visa information; calls cost £1 per minute).
Website: www.mzv.cz/london
Opening hours: Mon-Thurs 0830-1715; Fri 0830-1600; Mon-Fri 0900-1100 (visa application); 1315-1500 (visa collection).

Embassy of the Czech Republic in the USA
3900 Spring of Freedom Street, NW,
Washington, DC 20008, USA
Tel: (202) 274 9100 (general) *or* 9123 (consular).
Website: www.mzv.cz/washington

Money

Currency: Koruna (CZK) or Crown = 100 haler. Notes are in denominations of CZK5000, 2000, 1000, 500, 200, 100, 50 and 20. Coins are in denominations of CZK50, 20, 10, 5, 2 and 1, and 50, 20 and 10 haler.
Currency exchange: Foreign currency (including travellers cheques) can be exchanged at all bank branches and at authorised exchange offices, main hotels and road border crossings.
Credit & debit cards: Major cards such as American Express, Diners Club, Discover, Visa, MasterCard and others may be used to exchange currency and are also accepted in some hotels, restaurants and shops. Check with your credit or debit card company for details of merchant acceptability and other services which may be available.
Traveller's cheques: These are widely accepted. To avoid additional exchange rate charges, travellers are advised to take traveller's cheques in US Dollars, Euros or Pounds Sterling.
Currency restrictions: The import and export of local currency is limited to CZK200,000 or 10 golden coins. The import and export of foreign currency is unlimited.
Banking hours: Generally Mon-Fri 0800-1800. Some banks close early on Fridays.

Exchange rate indicators:
Rate at time of publishing
£1.00= CZK43.67
$1.00= CZK24.74

Duty Free

The following goods may be imported into the Czech Republic without incurring customs duty:
200 cigarettes or 100 cigarillos or 50 cigars or 250g tobacco (if over 16 years of age); 1l of spirits and 2l of wine (if over 18 years of age); 50g of perfume or 250ml of eau de toilette; gifts up to a value of €175 (if over 15 years of age) or €90 (if under 15 years of age); foods, fruits, flowers and medication for personal use.
Note: The export of cultural heritage pieces is only possible with prior approval by the Czech Ministry of Culture.
Abolition of duty free goods within the EU: On 30 June 1999, the sale of duty-free alcohol and tobacco at airports and at sea was abolished in all of the original 15 EU member states. Of the 10 new member states that joined the EU on 1 May 2004, these rules already apply to Cyprus and Malta. There are transitional rules in place for visitors returning to one of the original 15 EU countries from one of the other new EU countries. But for the original 15, plus Cyprus and Malta, there are now no limits imposed on importing tobacco and alcohol products from one EU country to another (with the exceptions of Denmark, Finland and Sweden, where limits *are* imposed). Travellers should note that they may be required to prove at customs that the goods purchased are for personal use only.

Public Holidays

Below are listed Public Holidays for the January 2006-June 2007 period.
2006: Jan 1 New Year's Day. **Apr 17** Easter Monday. **May 1** May Day. **May 8** Liberation Day. **Jul 5** Day of the Apostles St Cyril and St Methodius. **Jul 6** Anniversary of the Martyrdom of Jan Hus. **Sep 28** Czech Statehood Day. **Oct 28** Independence Day. **Nov 17** Freedom and Democracy Day. **Dec 24-26** Christmas.
2007: Jan 1 New Year's Day. **Apr 9** Easter Monday. **May 1** May Day. **May 8** Liberation Day.

Health

	Special Precautions?	Certificate Required?
Yellow Fever	No	No
Cholera	No	No
Typhoid & Polio	No	No
Malaria	No	No

Note: *Regulations and requirements may be subject to change at short notice, and you are advised to contact your doctor well in advance of your intended date of departure. Any numbers in the chart refer to the footnotes below.*

Food & drink: Mains water is normally chlorinated and, whilst relatively safe, may cause mild abdominal upsets. Bottled water is available and advised. Milk is pasteurised and dairy products are safe for consumption. Local meat, poultry, seafood, fruit and vegetables are generally considered safe to eat.
Other risks: *Tick-borne encephalitis* exists in rural forested areas during summer months. Immunisation against *hepatitis A* and *B* is sometimes advised.
Rabies is present. For those at high risk, vaccination before arrival should be considered. If you are bitten, seek medical advice without delay. For further information, consult the *Health* appendix.

Credit: ©Czech Tourism Archives

Health care:
European Economic Area (EEA) and Switzerland:
If you or any of your dependants are suddenly taken ill or have an accident during a visit to an EEA country or Switzerland, free or reduced-cost necessary treatment is available – in most cases on production of a valid European Health Insurance Card (EHIC). Each country has different rules about state medical provision. In some, treatment is free. In many countries you will have to pay part or all of the cost, and then claim a full or partial refund. The EHIC gives access to state-provided medical treatment only and the scheme gives no entitlement to medical repatriation costs, nor does it cover ongoing illnesses of a non-urgent nature, so comprehensive travel insurance is advised. Note that the EHIC replaces the Form E111, which is no longer valid. Some restrictions apply, depending on your nationality.
All treatment that a doctor or dentist considers necessary is free of charge. However, travellers must make sure they are contracted to the public health service (the Health Insurance Fund). Prescriptions are issued through doctors and dispensed by pharmacies. Travellers will be asked to pay a share of the costs, which are not refundable. More information can be obtained from the *Centrum mezistátních úhrad* (Centre for International Reimbursements) (website: www.cmu.cz/languages/en.htm).

Travel - International

AIR:

The national airline is *Czech Airlines (OK)* (website: www.csa.cz). Other airlines include *British Airways* and *easyJet*. *Ryanair* also offers a connection between London and Brno.
Approximate flight times: From Prague to *London* is two hours 15 minutes; to *New York* is eight hours 10 minutes.
Main airports: *Prague (PRG)* (Ruzyne) is 20km (12 miles) northwest of the city. *To/from the airport:* Airport bus (*Cedaz*) every 30 minutes from 0600-2100 (travel time – 30 minutes); bus 119 runs approximately every 20-40 minutes, from 0430-2330 (travel time – 30 minutes) between the north terminal and the nearest metro station, Dejvická (there are also night-buses in operation); low floor bus 100 goes from Zlicin metro terminus to Ruzyne airport and back in 15 minutes (every 15 minutes on working days, 30 minutes at week ends); it is necessary to buy a ticket from a vending machines or newsagents before boarding the bus; minibuses are available between the airport and the city centre; taxis are also available to the city centre (24-hour service, surcharge at night); big hotels operate shuttle-bus services during the summer months to the major hotels in the city. *Facilities:* Duty free shops, post office, banks/bureaux de change, restaurant and bar, car parking and car hire.
Departure tax: Prague (Ruzyne): CZK700
RAIL:

The Czech Republic forms part of the European InterCity network. The most convenient routes to the Czech Republic from Western Europe are via Berlin, Cologne, Frankfurt, Nuremburg, Munich, Vienna, Würzburg or Zurich to Prague. The *Vindobona Express* is a once-daily through train that travels from Vienna to Prague (main station) and on to Berlin. Rail travel information is available from Czech Railways (tel: 412 503 113; website: www.cdrail.cz).
ROAD:

The Czech Republic can be entered via Germany, Poland, the Slovak Republic or Austria.

Bus: There is an international bus network covering most European cities. There are connections to Amsterdam,

Frankfurt, London, Munich, Vienna and other main cities from the Florenc and Zelivskeho Bus Terminals (Metro stations). *Kingscourt Express* runs services Monday to Saturday between London Victoria to Prague and Brno (tel: (2) 6671 3032; website: www.eurobus.cz). *Eurolines* (52 Grosvenor Gardens, London SW1W 0AU; tel: (08705) 143 219; website: www.eurolines.com) and *National Express* (Ensign Court, 4 Vicarage Road, Edgbaston, Birmingham B15 3ES; tel: 08705 808 080; website: www.nationalexpress.com) run regular coach services from the UK to the Czech Republic and other European cities. Passes: Travellers can either choose Mini-Pass breaks or book a 15-, 30- or 60-day pass. The six Mini-Passes give travellers the freedom to visit three cities, with prices starting from £55. Travellers can stay as long as they like in each city.

Travel - Internal

AIR:

Czech Airlines (OK) operates an extensive domestic service. There are regular domestic flights from Prague to Ostrava, Brno and Karlovy Vary.
RIVER:

Navigable waterways can be found in the country and the main river ports are located at Prague, Ústí nad Labem and Decin.

RAIL:

The rail network is operated by *Czech Railways* (*České Drahy*, see above). There are several daily express trains between Prague and main cities and resorts. Reservations should be made in advance on major routes. Fares are low, but supplements are payable for travel by express trains.
ROAD:

Traffic drives on the right. Speed limits are 31mph (50kph) in built-up areas, 55mph (90kph) outside built-up areas and 80mph (130kph) on motorways. Motorways run from Prague to Plzen, Podebrady to Bratislava (Slovak Republic) via Brno. Users of the Czech motorways have to buy a *vignette* (season ticket), which costs approximately CZK800 for each year. A 10-day *vignette* costs approximately CZK100. Many petrol stations open 24 hours. There is a road emergency breakdown service available by calling 1230 or 1240. **Car hire:** Self-drive cars may be hired through *Avis*, *Hertz* and other companies.
Regulations: Seat belts are compulsory and drinking is absolutely prohibited. In Winter (October to May), lights must be switched on. Since January 2005, all private cars, including those of foreign visitors, must carry: one fluorescent green high visibility safety jacket, one first aid kit, one spare pair of prescription glasses (if necessary) kept in the glove compartment, one warning triangle and one complete set of spare bulbs. **Documentation**: A valid national driving licence. If this has no photocard, an International Driving Permit is also required. **Bus:** The extensive bus network mostly covers areas not accessible by rail and is efficient and comfortable. Buses are mostly run by the State Bus Company; see online for timetables (website: www.vlak-bus.cz).
URBAN:

Public transport is excellent. See online (website: www.dp-praha.cz) for timetables and other information on transport in Prague. There is a **metro** service in Prague that runs from 0500-0000. Three flat fares are charged. There are also **tram** and **bus** services (for which tickets must be purchased in advance from tobacconist shops, newsagents, metro stations, information centres or travel agents). Night trams and buses run from 0000-0430 in Prague. Buses, trolleybuses and trams also exist in Brno, Ostrava, Plzen and several other towns. Most services run from 0430-0000. All the cities operate flat-fare systems and tourist passes can be purchased in advance that are valid for a number of journeys. Tickets should be validated in the appropriate machine on entering the tram or bus. A separate ticket is required when changing routes. There is a fine for fare evasion. Blue badges on tram and bus stops indicate an all-night service. Taxis are available in all the main towns and are metered, higher fares are charged at night. For further information about public transport in Prague, contact the Czech Tourist Authority (Prague Information Line); see *Top Things To Do*.
Travel times: The following chart gives approximate travel times (in hours and minutes) from **Prague** to other major towns/cities in the Czech Republic.

	Air	Road	Rail
Brno	2.45	2.15	2.15
Karlovy Vary	0.30	2.00	2.10
Ostrava	1.00	6.45	4.30

Travel Advice
Most visits to the Czech Republic are trouble-free but you should be aware of the global risk of indiscriminate international terrorist attacks, which could be against civilian targets, including places frequented by foreigners.

This advice is based on information provided by the Foreign and Commonwealth Office in the UK. It is correct at time of publishing. As the situation can change rapidly, visitors are advised to contact the following organisations for the latest travel advice:

British Foreign and Commonwealth Office
Tel: (0845) 850 2829.
Website: www.fco.gov.uk

US Department of State
Website: http://travel.state.gov/travel

Accommodation
The Czech Republic is able to offer a full range of accommodation to suit every pocket. There is a wide range of hotels, graded from **1 to 5 stars**, boarding hostels and private apartments. Many campsites are also open during the summer. For further information on the range of accommodation available, contact the Czech Tourist Authority (see *Top Things To Do*) or visit www.travelguide.cz or www.discoverczech.com.
YOUTH HOSTELS:
There are 35 youth hostels in the Czech Republic, with several in Prague. Contact the International Youth Hostel Federation in the Czech Republic, check online for more information (website: www.iyhf.cz/iyhf).

Top Things To See

• Picturesquely sited on the banks of the **Vltava (Moldau) River**, **Prague** is noted for magnificent Gothic, Baroque, Romanesque, Belle Epoque/Art Nouveau and Cubist architecture, as well as its cultural scene. Since the fall of Communism, Prague has rapidly regained its cafe culture and is again very much the 'Paris of the East'. The city's historical centre, never bombed in World War II, is a UNESCO World Heritage Site. Key places to visit are the **Hradcany** complex of **Prazsky hrad (Prague Castle)**, including Palace rooms like the **Vladislavsky sál (Vladislav Hall)** which was once used by Bohemian knights for jousting, the **Katedrála sv Víta (St Vitus Cathedral)** and the **Basilica sv Jirí (St George Basilica)**.

Credit: ©Czech Tourism Archives

A
B
C
D
E
F
G
H
I
J
K
L
M
N
O
P
Q
R
S
T
U
V
W
X
Y
Z

Credit: ©Czech Tourism Archives

Views over the Vltava, spanned by many bridges, including the famous medieval **Karluv most (Charles Bridge)**, contribute to Prague's reputation as a 'fairytale city'. The **Lesser Town (Mala Strana)** beneath the castle is a quarter of winding, narrow streets with palaces from the 17th and 18th centuries and small artisan houses. The **Old Town (Stare Mesto)** across the Charles Bridge includes important tourist sites like the **Old Town Hall (Staromestska radnice)** with its astronomical clock, the Gothic **Tyn Church** behind the square and the **Jewish Town** with its old cemetery and six synagogues. The area around **Vaclavske namesti (Wenceslas Square)** is the principal shopping area of the city. To the south is **Vysehrad** with its **Slavin Cemetery** (honouring intellectuals and artists), and its Cubist villas.

- Near to Prague is a grim reminder of the horrors of World War II – the 'show' concentration camp at **Terezin** is now a museum.
- Also in the area are the castles of **Karlstejn**, **Krivoklat** and **Konopiste**. Near **Karlstejn** is the **Cesky kras (Bohemian Karst)**, a region of limestone caves, of which **Konepruské jeskyne** is open to the public.
- Discover the historic silver mining town of **Kutna Hora** with the dominating Gothic cathedral of **sv Barbora (St Barbara)**, which is another UNESCO World Heritage Site.
- North of Prague, at the confluence of the **Vltava** and the **Labe rivers**, is **Melnik**, with its **Zamek (Castle)**, built by the Lobkowitz family; this area is now returning to its former role as an important **wine-making region**.
- Heavy industrialisation in **Northern Bohemia** has taken its toll and many of the forests suffer greatly from the effects of acid rain. However, the north remains a popular destination with Czech and German tourists. Much of the area's interest lies in the sandstone **'rock-cities'** (spectacular mini-canyons and steep bluffs of volcanic rocks in a densely forested area) of the **Cesky Svycarsko (Bohemian Switzerland)** especially around Tisa, the **Cesky raj (Bohemian paradise)** between **Turnov** and **Jicin** and the area around **Broumov**.
- Southwest of Prague, **Plzen** is the second-largest city in Bohemia. It boasts eclectic architecture from the Gothic to Art Nouveau, interesting museums and galleries, like the **Brewery Museum** and the **Západoceské Galérie** (one of the best art galleries outside Prague), and the world-famous *Pilsner* beer to which the town has given its name; beer had been brewed since the town's foundation in 1295 but it was only in 1842 that the Pilsner style was established. Guided tours of the **Plzensky Prazdroj brewery** are available.
- **Southern Bohemia**, with its lakes and woods, has for a long time been a favourite holiday place for families, since it has many recreational facilities and points of historic interest. The country is also famed for its **caves**: the rock formation of the mountain ranges form underground rivers and chambers with stalactites and stalagmites.
- **Ceske Budejovice (Budweis)**, whose wealth was founded on silver mines, and the salt route from Linz to Prague boasts one of Europe's largest **town squares**. However, it is the local beer, *Budvar (Budweiser)* which is the town's main claim to fame.
- The medieval town of **Cesky Krumlov** (a UNESCO World Heritage Site) has its enormous castle perched on a ridge

above the young **River Vltava**, and the region to the border is full of castles, monasteries and churches.

- **Brno**, the capital of **Moravia**, dates from the 13th century and has the fine **Moravian Museum**; an important **Augustinian Monastery** where the great geneticist, Mendel, was Abbot; the **Capuchin Church** with its mummies; and the Gothic **Spilberk Castle**.
- To the northeast of Brno is the **Moravsky krás**, the area of great limestone caves around **Blansko**. To the northwest, the Gothic castle of **Pernstejn** is probably closest to most people's idea of what a medieval castle should look like; the hour-long train journey to it up the **Svratka Valley** is an attractive trip.
- Southwest of Brno, three towns in particular stand out as tourist locations: **Moravsky Krumlov** with its **Mucha**

Gallery, including great pictures, such as *Slovanska epopej* (The Slav Epic); **Slavkov** (Austerlitz), near the Napoleonic battlefield; and **Bucovice**, whose castle features the remarkable **Zajeci sal (The Hall of Hares)**.

- In the **Vysocina (Bohemian-Moravian Uplands)** to the east, the towns of **Telc** (a UNESCO Cultural Heritage Site) and **Slavonice** are two of the most perfect examples of Renaissance towns in Europe. **Telc**, including the **Zamec (Castle)**, was completely rebuilt after the fire of 1530; medieval arcades surround the town square with its gabled and pedimented houses.
- In **Zdar nad Sazavou**, about 40km (25 miles) northeast of **Jihlava**, the Cistercian monastery and pilgrimage church dedicated to sv Jan Nepomucky (St John of Nepomuk) was designed by Prague-born Giovanni Santini, one of the greatest artists of the Czech Counter-Reformation, who married Gothic and Baroque forms, often with a humour lacking in other architects. Nearby in **Ostrov nad Oslavou**, he designed a *hostinec* (pub) shaped like the letter 'W' to honour a fellow architect, and the village church at **Obyctov**, shaped like a turtle, one of the Virgin Mary's more obscure symbols.
- The area between the small wine-making towns of **Lednice** and **Valtice** was once a possession of the Grand Dukes of Liechtenstein. Several impressive castles, landscaped parks and structural follies are dotted over an area of 250 sq km (96 sq miles), broken up by numerous ponds and forests.
- Northeast of Brno, **Kromeriz** (accessible as a day trip from Prague) is a beautifully preserved Baroque town; its great Bishop's Palace includes an important art collection (including paintings from the auction which followed the execution of the English King Charles I), and superb water gardens which run down to the banks of the **Morava** river.
- Despite many ecological disaster zones and the great – and unpleasant – industrial centre of **Ostrava**, **northern Moravia** has much to offer the independent traveller. **Olomouc**, now happily recovered from its era as a Soviet garrison, is once again an attractive university town noted for its parks, its Baroque churches, sculptures and fountains. The surrounding **Haná** region is strongly agricultural, with many villages having attractive harvest festivals in late September.
- The excellent open-air *skansen* (Folk Museum) at **Roznov pod Radhostem**, begun in 1925, is the largest in the country; another good *skansen* is at **Velke Karlovice**. *Valchs* architecture can be found to the south in the villages in the **Vsetinska Becva valley**, including **Bzove**, **Jezerne** and **Ratkov**.

Credit: ©Czech Tourism Archives

A B C D E F G H I J K L M N O P Q R S T U V W X Y Z

Top Things To Do

- The Czech nation is one of the most musical in Central Europe. Throughout the year there are many occasions to enjoy **music** in concert halls, theatres, stately homes and churches. Most towns have their own folk festivals, with dancing, local costumes and food. These tend to be in the summer months leading up to the harvest festivals in September.
- Treat yourself to a **spa**. The many thermal springs and mineral baths in **Bohemia** and **Moravia** have been frequented for centuries by patients seeking cures for various ailments. Beethoven, Wagner, Edward VII and Goethe all admired the resort of **Marianske Lazne (Marienbad)**, whilst the town of **Karlovy Vary (Karlsbad)**, the king of the spas, has attracted the crowned heads of Europe to bathe in its sulphurous waters. **Frantiskovy Lazne**, however, is the most typical spa town, laid out in perfect symmetry with delightful parks and 24 springs used to cure heart disease and infertility. There is also a nature reserve near the town. There are world-famous radioactive springs in **Jáchymov**, which specialises in the treatment of disorders of the nervous system, while **Janské Lazne** in the Krkonoše is also a very popular resort. In northern Moravia, the most significant spas are at **Jesenik** and **Luhacovice**, where Vincenc Priessnitz, a local doctor, developed methods of treatment which are still followed today. All the spa resorts are located in beautiful surroundings. **Trebon** in South Bohemia is a perfect medieval spa town. The enormous **Zamek (Castle)** was built by Peter Vok, the last Rozmberk heir; its large 'English park' now provides walks for the spa patients.
  For further information on spa stays, contact the Czech Tourist Authority (see *Tourist Information*).
- The **Sumava/Bohemian Forest** towards the German border is the country's largest National Park, and with the **Bavarian Forest** across the border forms the largest forest complex in Europe. The park includes glacial lakes, many areas of virgin forest and important historic monuments. Good **wintersports** centres include **Zelezna Ruda, Spicak, Zadov, Churanov** and **Kramolin**. The northern shore of **Lake Lipno** has many small popular summer resorts.
- The area between **Znojmo** and **Vranov** on the **River Dyji (Thaya** in German) is an area of untouched river valley, now a joint National Park on both sides of the Austrian border.
- **Skiing** is a very popular activity, and there are many well-established resorts. The most frequented areas for downhill skiing are in the **Krkonošoe** (Giant Mountains) **National Park** in northern Bohemia, where **Pec pod Snezkou, Spindlorov Mlyn** and **Harachov** are the main resorts. The **Krkonoše** are the Czech Republic's highest mountain range, with the country's highest peak, **Snezka** (1602m/5255ft). Facilities are also to be found in the **Jeseniky** and **Besniky** ranges, and in the **Orlické Hory** (Eagle Mountains). **Spindleruv Mlyn**, on the banks of **River Labe**, is the most visited mountain town in the park. To the east of Ostrava, the hilly **Beskydy** region (which extends through Poland into the Ukraine) is the area of the *Vlachs* (Wallachs), whose culture still survives in folklore and architecture. This area is also excellent for **hiking** and **winter sports**.
- **Cross-country skiing** is also a widespread sport, and facilities and tracks are to be found not only in the **Krkonoše**, but also in the **Šumava** (Bohemian Forest) in southern Bohemia. In summer, these areas become havens for **hikers**, and contain well-marked trails. Less strenuous walks can be pursued in other natural areas, such as the **Beskidy** range. **Rock climbers** should go to the sandstone rock formations in the north (**Cesky raj, Adršpach Rocks** and **Ceskosaské švycarsko**).
- **Cavers** should go to the **Moravsky Kras** (Moravian karst) near Brno, where there are interesting caves.
- There are many lakes, both natural and artificial, and a variety of **watersports** can be pursued there. **South Bohemia** and **Lednice-Valtice** (south Moravia) contain extensive **fishing** lakes. For more information on fishing, contact the Czech Angling Federation (tel: (2) 7481 1751; fax: (2) 7481 1754). **Canoeing** is done on rivers such as the Luznice, upper Vltava and Sazava. **Windsurfing** and **sailing** equipment can be hired at various locations.

TOURIST INFORMATION

Czech Tourist Authority in the UK
13 Harley Street, London W1G 9QG, UK
Tel: (020) 7631 0427 *or* (09063) 640 641 (24-hour enquiry line; calls cost 60p per minute). Website: www.czechtourism.com

Czech Tourist Authority in the USA
1109 Madison Avenue, New York, NY 10028, USA
Tel: (212) 288 0830.
Website: www.czechtourism.com

Entertainment

FOOD & DRINK: Food is often based on Austro-Hungarian dishes. Western-style fresh vegetables are often missing in lower-class restaurants. There is a wide selection of restaurants, beer taverns and wine cellars.
National specialities:
- *(Wiener) Schnitzel* and pork are very popular.
- *Bramborak*, a potato pancake delicacy filled with garlic and herbs.
- Prague ham.
- Meat dishes are mostly served with *knedliky*, a type of large dough dumpling, and *zeli* (sauerkraut).

National drinks:
- Popular beverages include beers (lager, dark ales, *pilsner*); red, white and sparkling wines from Bohemia and Moravia; fruit juices and liqueurs.
- Particular specialities include *becherovka* (herb brandy) and two Moravian favourites, *slivovice* (plum brandy) and *merunkovice* (apricot brandy).

There are no rigid licensing hours.
Tipping: A 5 to 10 per cent tip is usual.
NIGHTLIFE: Theatre and opera are of a good standard. Nightclubs, bars and casinos are to be found in major cities.
SHOPPING: Souvenirs include Bohemian glass and crystal, pottery, porcelain, wooden folk carvings, hand-embroidered clothing, and food items. There are a number of excellent shops specialising in glass and crystal, while various associations of regional artists and craftspeople run their own retail outlets (pay in local currency). Other special purchases include pottery (particularly from Kolovec and Straznice); china ornaments and geyserstone carvings from Karlovy Vary; delicate lace and needle embroidery from many Moravian towns; and blood-red garnets and semi-precious stones from Bohemia. **Shopping hours**: Mon-Fri 0900-1800, Sat 0900-1200. Supermarkets and food shops in large towns and cities are open from 0700 and often stay open until late. The number of shops also open on Sunday is constantly increasing.

Business

- **GDP:** US$123 billion (2004).
- **Main exports:** Machinery and transport equipment, chemicals, raw materials and fuel.
- **Main imports:** Machinery and transport equipment, raw materials, fuels and chemicals.
- **Main trade partners:** Germany, Slovakia, Austria, France and UK.

ECONOMY: Under Soviet control, the former Czechoslovak economy was subject to a particularly high level of state control, lacking even the small-scale private enterprise that existed to some extent in all other Eastern European economies. In the aftermath of the 'Prague Spring', especially, economic development was concentrated for political reasons on heavy industry at the expense of traditional strengths in light and craft-based industries. In the immediate post-Soviet era at the beginning of the 1990s, these inefficient and, in some cases, redundant industrial monoliths appeared to be a considerable impediment to the growth of the economy. The other problem was a dearth of natural resources – the country relied heavily on the former Soviet Union for most of its raw materials, particularly oil.

After a period of political and economic crisis, which ended with the separation of the Czech and Slovak Republics in 1993 and a dispute with the Soviets over oil supplies, the Czech Government pushed ahead with a rapid programme of market reforms, including a programme of mass privatisation, and a major overhaul of the country's financial system. The Government identified priority industries for development. These included: aircraft and vehicles, electronics, nuclear energy, gasification of coal, transport and communications, as well as traditionally strong light industries such as textiles, leather, ceramics and glass, and a variety of agricultural and service industries. Although more than three-quarters of economic output is now in private hands, the State retains a major influence through minority shareholdings and state-owned banks (which in turn own parts of major corporations). The results have been fairly good, with the exception of a mild recession during 1997-98. The Czech Republic has recorded steady growth within, on the whole, a sound fiscal and monetary environment. Annual growth is now slowly climbing, at 4.3 per cent (final quarter of 2004). The country joined, along with nine other countries, the European Union in May 2004. Trade links with Austria and Germany in particular, and with the EU generally, have grown substantially (70 per cent of trade). The Czech Republic has already acquired membership of the IMF, World Bank and the European Bank for Reconstruction and Development.
BUSINESS ETIQUETTE: Businessmen wear suits. A knowledge of German is useful as English is not widely spoken among the older generation. Long business lunches are usual. Avoid visits during July and August as many businesses close for holidays. **Office hours**: Mon-Fri 0800-1700.
CONFERENCES/CONVENTIONS: The Prague International Congress Centre can seat up to 15,000 people. There are also facilities in many hotels throughout the country. Trade fairs are held in Brno. For more information, see *Commercial Information*.

COMMERCIAL INFORMATION

Hospodárská Komora Ceské Republiky
(Economic Chamber of the Czech Republic)
Freyova 27, 190 00 Prague 9, Czech Republic
Tel: (2) 9664 6111.
Website: www.hkcr.cz *or* www.komora.cz

Brno Trade Fairs and Exhibitions
(Information on Conferences/Conventions)
ýstaviste 1, 647 00 Brno, Czech Republic
Tel: (5) 4115 1111
Website: www.bvv.cz

Prague Convention Bureau
Rytírská 26, 110 00 Prague 1, Czech Republic
Tel: (2) 2423 5159.
Website: www.pragueconvention.cz

Credit: ©Czech Tourism Archives

A B C D E F G H I J K L M N O P Q R S T U V W X Y Z

Denmark

Location: Western Europe.

Time: Mainland: GMT + 1 (GMT + 2 from last Sunday in March to last Sunday in October).
Faroe Islands and Torshavn: GMT (GMT + 1 from last Sunday in March to last Sunday on October.)

Overview

The Jutland peninsula and its 400 surrounding islands form one of Europe's smallest countries: Denmark. Denmark has an abundance of picturesque villages and towns, historic castles and monuments, and a coastline which varies delightfully from broad sandy beaches to small coves and gentle fjords. Throughout the country, rolling hills and gentle valleys provide a constant succession of attractive views; there are cool and shady forests of beech trees, extensive areas of heathland, a beautiful lake district, sand dunes and white cliffs resembling those of Dover; nor should one forget the Danish islands, each of which has its own unique attractions. The Danes have taken strong measures to keep their coastline clean and tidy, keen for visitors to sample the many unspoilt beaches. Inland from the 4800km (3000 miles) of white-sand beaches and unspoiled islands, you'll find a landscape eminently suitable for cycling. Sleepy villages clustered around whitewashed churches occupy a landscape of heather moors, rolling hills and rich farmland dotted with windmills and thatched farmhouses. Ferries ply between the mainland and the islands, competing with awesome bridges like the 16km (10 miles) Øresund link to Sweden.
Amidst such tranquillity, it now almost seems surreal to consider that this country once spawned a seafaring race of people, the Viking Warriors, feared throughout northwestern Europe. Today, visitors to Denmark find a country that is peaceful, introspective, neutral and egalitarian. Its hallmarks are good taste, world-class design and uniformly high standards that apply equally to its accommodation and transport. Cuisine is excellent, especially in the realm of dairy products and scrumptious pastries. Add to this a people both amiable and helpful, with a facility for languages, and the result is an overwhelming sense of welcome.
Denmark, in addition to its modernity, retains some of its long-lived associations with fairytales, probably consolidated by the fact that this nation produced the great story-teller, Hans Christian Andersen. Enchanting moated castles and historical rickety buildings are still frequent sights throughout Denmark. Copenhagen is a wonderful

cobbled city with many quaint medieval streets and buildings, but there is more to Denmark than its capital, and any visitor to the country is strongly advised to explore elsewhere, too.
From the spirited nightlife and lively cafe and music scene of Copenhagen to a countryside that abounds in Renaissance churches, medieval castles and 18th-century fishing villages, Denmark is a synergy of harmonious relationships.

General Information

AREA: 43,098 sq km (16,640 sq miles).
POPULATION: 5.43 million (UN estimate, 2005).
POPULATION DENSITY: 125 per sq km.
CAPITAL: Copenhagen. **Population:** 1.17 million (2005).
GEOGRAPHY: Denmark is the smallest Scandinavian country, consisting of the Jutland peninsula, north of Germany, and over 400 islands of various sizes, some inhabited and linked to the mainland by ferry or bridge. The landscape consists mainly of low-lying, fertile countryside broken by beech woods, small lakes and fjords. Greenland and the Faroe Islands are also under the sovereignty of the Kingdom of Denmark, although both have home rule. The Faroe Islands are a group of 18 islands in the North Atlantic inhabited by a population of 46,962 (2005), whose history dates back to the Viking period. Fishing and sheep farming are the two most important occupations. Tórshavn (population 19,282 (2004), the capital of the Faroes, is served by direct flights from Copenhagen. During the summer months, there are direct flights from Aberdeen and Glasgow.
GOVERNMENT: Constitutional monarchy. **Head of State:** Queen Margrethe II since 1972. **Head of Government:** Prime Minister Anders Fogh Rasmussen since 2001. **Recent history:** The dominant issue in Danish politics during the 1990s was relations with the European Union, which Denmark joined in 1973. Along with the UK, Denmark is the most 'Eurosceptic' nation, as became apparent when a 1992 referendum rejected Danish acceptance of the Maastricht Treaty on the future development of the EU. (A repeat plebiscite the following year secured a narrow victory.) Since then, Denmark has decided to stay out of the first wave of countries joining the single European currency. The Government, which generally favours membership, made another attempt to persuade the public prior to a referendum held in September 2000. Once again, however, they failed.
Despite that critical defeat, the Social Democrat Government continued to enjoy broad popular support on most issues. In November 2001, it decided – unwisely, as it transpired – to try and exploit this by calling a snap election. After a closely fought campaign, which was dominated by the issue of immigration policy, the eight-year-old Social Democrat Government was supplanted by a Liberal/Conservative coalition led by Anders Fogh Rasmussen. Immigration has become a major political factor in Europe in the last few years and this has fuelled the growing popularity of extreme right-wing parties throughout the continent. Denmark is no exception. Despite lacking a seat in Government, the right-wing anti-immigration Danish People's Party and its leader, Pia Kjaersgaard, have already exercised considerable influence over Government policy during the last two years. Parliamentary elections held in February 2005 returned the Liberal/Conservative coalition for another term of up to four years.
Denmark is a constitutional monarchy. The constitutional charter of 1953 gives the hereditary monarch and the unicameral Parliament (*Folketing*) legislative power. The monarch has no personal political power. Members are elected to the parliament by proportional representation.
LANGUAGE: The official language is Danish. Many Danes also speak English, German and French.
RELIGION: Predominantly Evangelical Lutheran with a small Roman Catholic and Muslim minority.
ELECTRICITY: 230 volts AC, 50Hz. Continental two-pin plugs are standard. On many campsites, 110-volt power plugs are also available.
SOCIAL CONVENTIONS: Normal courtesies should be observed. Guests should refrain from drinking until the host toasts his or her health. Casual dress is suitable for most places but formal wear is required at more exclusive dining rooms and social functions. Smoking is restricted on public transport and in some public buildings.

Climate

Summer extends from June to August. Winter is from December to March, wet with long periods of frost. February is the coldest month. Spring and autumn are generally mild.
The *Faroe Islands* are under the influence of the warm current of the Gulf Stream, and they enjoy a very mild climate for the latitude. Winters are warm, but the islands are cloudy, windy and wet throughout the year. Summers are cool, but with little sunshine.

Required clothing: Lightweight for summer and heavyweight for winter snows.

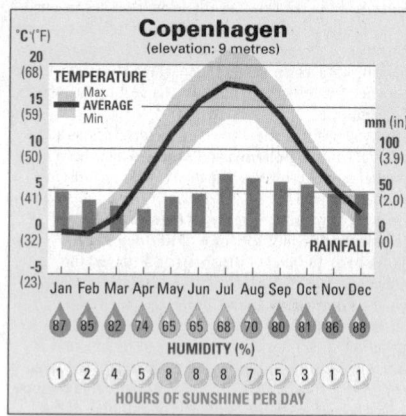

Communications

Telephone: Full IDD is available. Country code: 45. There are no area codes.
Mobile telephone: Roaming agreements exist with most international mobile phone companies. Coverage is excellent.
Internet: Internet cafes are available in most urban areas.
Post: All telephone and postal rates are printed at the post offices. Post office hours: Mon-Fri 0900-1730; some are open Sat 0900-1200.
MEDIA: A free press operates under Danish law and the media, which cover a broad range of political views, are frequently critical of government policy. *Danmarks Radio (DR)*, funded by a licence fee, is Denmark's main public broadcaster, operating two TV networks as well as national and regional radio stations. *TV2*, a national public-service TV station, is partly state funded. Private satellite and cable TV stations also exist. There are some 250 local commercial and community radio stations on the air. Two commercial networks, one national and one semi-national, were launched in 2003 and quickly became popular.
Press: Newspapers are largely regional: the main papers in the capital include *Berlingske Tidende*, *Dagbladet Information*, *Ekstra Bladet* and *Politiken*. English-language newspapers and magazines are also available.
TV: *DR1* and *DR2* are publicly-owned. *TV2* is a part-public, part-commercial channel. *TV Danmark* operates a terrestrial network of local commercial channels.
Radio: *Danmarks Radio* operates publicly-owned *P1*, *P2*, *P3* and *P4* national networks. Commercial stations include *Sky Radio*, *Radio 100 FM* and *Radio 2*.

Passport/Visa

	Passport Required?	Visa Required?	Return Ticket Required?
Full British	1/2	No/3	No
Australian	Yes	No	Yes
Canadian	Yes	No	Yes
USA	2	No	Yes
Other EU	1/2	No	No
Japanese	Yes	No	Yes

Note: *Regulations and requirements may be subject to change at short notice, and you are advised to contact the appropriate diplomatic or consular authority before finalising travel arrangements. Any numbers in the chart refer to the footnotes below.*

Note: Denmark is a signatory to the 1995 **Schengen Agreement**. For further details about passport/visa regulations within the Schengen area, see the introductory section, *How to Use this Guide*.
PASSPORTS: Passport valid for three months after the last day of stay required by all except the following:
(a) **1.** EU/EEA nationals (EU+ Iceland, Liechtenstein, Norway) and Swiss nationals holding a valid national ID card.
Note: EU and EEA nationals are only required to produce evidence of their EU/EEA nationality and identity in order to be admitted to any EU/EEA Member State. This evidence can take the form of a valid national passport *or* national identity card. Either is acceptable. Possession of a return ticket, any length of validity on their document, sufficient funds for the length of their proposed visit should *not* be imposed.
(b) **2.** holders of a Gibraltar Identity Card issued to British Citizens or British Dependent Citizens for tourist visits of up to three months.
VISAS: Required by all except the following for stays of up to three months (no paid or self-employed work allowed):
(a) nationals of countries referred to in the chart above;

Credit: ©VisitDenmark/Ted Fahn

(b) nationals of Andorra, Argentina, Bermuda (provided holding a British Dependent Territories passport), BNO (British Nationals Overseas), Bolivia, Brazil, Brunei, Bulgaria, Chile, Costa Rica, Croatia, El Salvador, Guatemala, Honduras, Hong Kong (SAR), Iceland, Israel, Korea (Rep), Liechtenstein, Macau (SAR), Malaysia, Mexico, Monaco, New Zealand, Nicaragua, Norway, Panama, Paraguay, Romania, San Marino, Singapore, Switzerland, Uruguay, Vatican City and Venezuela;
(c) holders of a UN *laissez-passer*.
Note: 3. (a) Holders of the following also *do not* require a visa: 'British Citizen' passports, including those from the Channel Islands and Isle of Man, with the endorsement 'Holder has the right of re-admission' *or* 'Holder is entitled to re-admission to the United Kingdom' *or* 'Holder has the right of abode in the United Kingdom', provided holders of such passports have not stayed outside the UK for more than two years (including the expected stay in Denmark); 'British Dependent Territories Citizens' passports (BDTC) issued to persons with the right of abode in Gibraltar with the endorsement 'Holder is defined as a UK national for Community purposes'; British National Overseas passports (BNO) with permanent residence in Hong Kong are visa exempt for up to three months. (b) Holders of the following *do* require a visa: 'British Protected Persons' passports endorsed 'Holder is subject to control under the Immigration Act 1971'.
Airport transit: Passengers continuing their journey by the same or first connecting aircraft within the international zone of the *Schengen* airport, without gaining access to the national territory of the *Schengen* member state, may not require a transit visa, provided they are holding valid onward or return documentation.
Nationals of the following countries *always* need a visa to transit through a Danish airport: Afghanistan, Bangladesh, Congo (Dem Rep), Eritrea, Ethiopia, Ghana, India (not required for Indian nationals in possession of a valid visa to an EU or EEA country, USA or Canada), Iran, Iraq, Nigeria, Pakistan, Somalia and Sri Lanka (the above list is subject to changes; please check with the Embassy or Consular section at Embassy). However, if any of these nationals are residents in an EU member state, an EEA country, the USA or Canada, and hold permission to return a minimum of three months after transiting Denmark, a visa is not required.
Types of visa and cost: *Tourist*, *Business*, *Transit*, *Airport Transit*: £23. An additional fee of £11 is payable for applications lodged at Honorary Consulates.
Note: (a) Spouses and children of EU and EEA nationals (providing spouse's passport and the original marriage certificate/proof of joint household are produced), and nationals of some other countries, if related in direct line of ascent or descent to such nationals or their spouses, receive their visas free of charge.
Validity: Validity depends on type of visa, nationality and purpose of visit. For further information, contact the Consulate (or Consular section at Embassy); see *Passport/Visa Information*.
Application to: Consulate (or consular section at Embassy); see *Passport/Visa Information*. Applications should be made in person. Travellers visiting just one Schengen country should apply to the Consulate of that country; travellers visiting more than one *Schengen* country should apply to the Consulate of the country chosen as the main destination *or* the country they will enter first (if they have no main destination).
Application requirements: (a) Passport valid for a minimum of three months after expiry of visa, or official travel document valid for at least six months, both with a blank page for the visa sticker. (b) One signed and completed application form, containing parental consent for minors (if applicable). (c) One passport-size colour photograph on light background. (d) Fee, payable in cash or cheque with a cheque guarantee card. (e) Proof of purpose of visit and accomodation, eg a letter from relatives or a hotel reservation (e-mails not accepted). (f) Evidence of occupation, eg letter from employer or university or, if unemployed, benefit booklet. (g) Evidence of sufficient funds for duration of stay, eg original, recent bank statement, travellers cheques, credit card statement with credit limit. (h) A prepaid and self-addressed envelope (special delivery) if the visa is to be returned by post. (i) Valid health insurance. (j) Residents of the UK who are returning to the UK after a visit to Denmark are required to hold a residence work permit valid for at least three months beyond the validity of the visa (at least six months for holders of travel documents). *Business*: (a)-(j) and, (k) The original invitation from the business contact in Denmark.
Note: Some further documents and guarantees might be required for the processing of visas. All applications must initially be made in person at the Embassy/Consulate and by first arranging an appointment through the appointment booking system (for UK, tel: (09065) 540 755).
Working days required: Applications can take several weeks to be processed (applicants may apply up to 12 weeks before the start of their trip).
Temporary residence: Persons wishing to stay in Denmark for more than three months should make their application *in their home country* well in advance of their intended date of departure.

Money

Currency: Danish Krone (DKK) = 100 øre. Notes are in denominations of DKK1000, 500, 200, 100 and 50. Coins are in denominations of DKK20, 10, 5, 2 and 1, and 50 and 25 øre.
Currency exchange: There are plenty of ATMs. Personal cheques cannot be used by visitors to Denmark. Some banks may refuse to exchange large foreign bank notes.
Credit & debit cards: American Express, Diners Club, MasterCard and Visa are widely accepted, as well as Eurocheque cards. Check with your credit or debit card company for details of merchant acceptability and other services which may be available.
Traveller's cheques: Can be cashed by banks and hotels, and can be used at most restaurants and shops. To avoid additional exchange rate charges, travellers are advised to take traveller's cheques in Euros, Pounds Sterling or US Dollars.
Currency restrictions: No limitations on the import or export of either local or foreign currencies, although declarations should be made for amounts exceeding €15,000 (approximately DKK112,000). The form (12.021) can be obtained from the tax authorities (*ToldSkat*) at the border or from the website, www.toldskat.dk. There is no limit on the export of foreign currency, apart from gold coins.
Banking hours: Mon to Wed and Fri 0930-1700; Thurs 0930-1800. Some banks in Copenhagen are open Mon-Fri 0930-1700. Some bureaux de change are open until midnight.
Exchange rate indicators:

Rate at time of publishing	
£1.00=	DKK10.86
$1.00=	DKK6.20

Duty Free

The following goods may be imported into Denmark without incurring customs duty:
(a) Non-Danish residents arriving from an EU country with duty-paid goods purchased in an EU country:
10l of spirits or 20l of fortified wine (maximum 22 per cent); 90l of table wine; 800 cigarettes or 400 cigarillos or 200 cigars or 1kg of tobacco; 110l beer; other commodities: no limit.
(b) Residents of non-EU countries entering from outside the EU (excluding Greenland) with goods purchased in non-EU countries:
1l of spirits or 2l of sparkling fortified wine (maximum 22 per cent); 2l of table wine; 200 cigarettes or 100 cigarillos or 50 cigars or 250g of tobacco; 500g of coffee or 200g of coffee extracts; 100g of tea or 40g of tea extracts; 50g of perfume; 250ml of eau de toilette; other articles, including beer: up to DKK1350.
Note: Alcohol and tobacco allowances are for those aged 17 or over only, coffee and coffee extracts allowances are for those aged 15 or over. It is forbidden to import fresh foods into Denmark unless vacuum packed. Special rules apply to tobacco products when travelling to Denmark from Hungary, Latvia, Lithuania, Poland, Slovakia and Slovenia. Travellers are only allowed to import certain quantities without paying excise duty. More information is available from the website, www.toldskat.dk.
Abolition of duty free goods within the EU: On 30 June 1999, the sale of duty free alcohol and tobacco at airports and at sea was abolished in all of the original 15 EU member states. Of the 10 new member states that joined the EU on May 1 2004, these rules already apply to Cyprus and Malta. There are transitional rules in place for visitors returning to one of the original 15 EU countries from one of the other new EU countries. But for the original 15, plus Cyprus and Malta, there are now no limits imposed on importing tobacco and alcohol products from one EU country to another (with the exceptions of Denmark, Finland and Sweden, where limits *are* imposed). Travellers should note that they may be required to prove at customs that the goods purchased are for personal use *only*.

Public Holidays

Below are listed Public Holidays for the January 2006-June 2007 period.
2006: Jan 1 New Year's Day. **Apr 13** Maundy Thursday. **Apr 14** Good Friday. **Apr 17** Easter Monday. **Apr 26** Common Prayer Day. **May 25** Ascension. **May 16** Whit Monday. **Jun 5** Constitution Day. **Dec 24-26** Christmas. **Dec 31** New Year's Eve.
2007: Jan 1 New Year's Day. **Apr 5** Maundy Thursday. **Apr 6** Good Friday. **Apr 9** Easter Monday. **Apr 26** Common Prayer Day. **Apr 28** Whit Monday. **May 17** Ascension. **Jun 5** Constitution Day.

Health

	Special Precautions?	Certificate Required?
Yellow Fever	No	No
Cholera	No	No
Typhoid & Polio	No	No
Malaria	No	No

Note: Regulations and requirements may be subject to change at short notice, and you are advised to contact your doctor well in advance of your intended date of departure. Any numbers in the chart refer to the footnotes below.

Health care: European Economic Area (EEA) and Switzerland:
If you or any of your dependants are suddenly taken ill or have an accident during a visit to an EEA country or Switzerland, free or reduced-cost necessary treatment is available – in most cases on production of a valid European Health Insurance Card (EHIC). Each country has different rules about state medical provision. In some, treatment is free. In many countries you will have to pay part or all of the cost, and then claim a full or partial refund. The EHIC gives access to state-provided medical treatment only and the scheme gives no entitlement to medical repatriation costs, nor does it cover ongoing illnesses of a non-urgent nature, so comprehensive travel insurance is advised. Note that the EHIC replaces the Form E111, which will no longer be valid after 31 December 2005. Some restrictions apply, depending on your nationality. Please note that Swiss nationals and people who do not have UK, EU or EEA nationality are not covered by the EHIC in Denmark.
Medical facilities in Denmark are excellent. The telephone number for emergencies is 112. Local tourist offices will tell visitors where to contact a doctor or dentist. Copenhagen has an emergency dental service outside office hours; fees are paid in cash. Consultations are covered. Ask if they are registered with the Danish Public Health Service. Travellers will be charged, but can claim back the full amount of the doctor's consultation and part of their dental costs.
Only medicine prescribed by Danish or other Scandinavian doctors can be dispensed at a chemist (*Apotek*). Many medicines that can be bought over the counter in the UK can only be obtained with prescriptions in Denmark. Travellers will be charged for their prescriptions. Refund rates for approved medicines vary. There are no refunds of expenditure under DKK520 for persons over 18 (for children, 50 per cent is refunded).
In addition to the free emergency treatment at hospitals and casualty departments allowed to all foreign visitors, free hospital treatment can normally be arranged by a doctor, but if you can't see one, show your European Health Insurance Card (EHIC) to the hospital authorities and ask them to arrange free treatment for you.
The local council (*Kommunens Social og Sundhedsforvaltning*) handles reimbursements. Travellers who show their EHIC will be given a special card to register their prescription purchases on their first visit to a pharmacy. If not, travellers should keep all their prescriptions and original receipts and apply for a refund to the local council before leaving Denmark.

Credit: ©VisitDenmark/Ole Malling

Travel - International

AIR:

The national airlines are *SAS (SK)* (website: www.flysas.com) and *Sterling Airlines (SA)* (formerly *Maersk Air*) (website: www.sterlingticket.com). The major carriers are *British Airways* and *SAS*.

Approximate flight times: From Copenhagen to *London* is one hour 50 minutes (from Århus to *London* is one hour 40 minutes), to *Los Angeles* is 11 hours 15 minutes, to *New York* is seven hours 40 minutes, to *Singapore* is 15 hours five minutes and to *Sydney* is 22 hours 50 minutes.

Main airports: *Copenhagen (CPH)* (Kastrup) (website: www.cph.dk) is 8km (5 miles) southeast of the city (travel time - 15 to 30 minutes). *To/from airport*: A rail link connects the airport and main railway station in Copenhagen (travel time - 12 minutes). There are also high-speed Intercity trains to Funen (travel time - 1 hour) and Jutland (travel time - 2 hours) with additional connections to Malmø (Sweden) on a 30-minute journey via the Øresund link. There are also regular bus services from the airport departing every 10 to 20 minutes (travel time - 20 minutes). *Facilities*: An outgoing duty free shop, a wide range of car hire firms, bank/bureau de change, and several restaurants and bars.

Århus (AAR) (Tirstrup) (website: www.aar.dk) is 44km (27 miles) from the city. *To/from the airport*: Buses connect with flight arrivals; taxis are also available. *Facilities*: Duty free shop, a wide range of car hire firms, bank/bureau de change, a post office and a restaurant.

Billund Airport (BLL) (Billund) (website: www.billund-airport.dk) is approximately 2km (1.3 miles) from Legoland.

Departure tax: None.

SEA:

Main ports: *Copenhagen* (website: www.cmport.com), *Esbjerg* (website: www.port-of-esbjerg.dk), *Frederikshavn* (website: www.frederikshavn.dk), *Hanstholm* (website: www.hanstholmshavn.dk) and *Hirtshals*. There are regular ferries to and from the Faroe Islands, Germany, Iceland, Norway, Poland, Sweden and the UK. *DFDS Seaways* (website: www.dfdsseaways.co.uk) is one of the main operators. North Jutland is connected to the Faroes, Iceland, Norway and Scotland during the summer by ferries. There are no departure taxes when leaving Denmark by sea. Several major cruise lines call at Copenhagen.

RAIL:

Copenhagen is connected by rail to all other major European cities, and typical express journey times from Copenhagen are: to *London* 24 hours; to *Hamburg* four hours 30 minutes; to *Berlin* 11 hours 25 minutes. All international trains connect with ferries where applicable.

ROAD:

All the major road networks of Europe connect with ferry services to Copenhagen; it is advisable to book ferries in advance. The completion of the 18km- (11 mile-) long toll Great Belt bridge and tunnel, linking Copenhagen (which is situated on the island of Sjælland) with the island of Funen, now provides the first seamless surface connection from the European continent to Copenhagen. It includes the world's second-longest suspension bridge at 6.5km (4 miles) long. A second bridge and tunnel, the Øresund connection, links Copenhagen with Malmø in Sweden. This consists of an 8km (5 mile) bridge and an 8km (5 mile) tunnel linked by an artificial island. Tolls are applicable for both bridges. *Eurolines*, departing from Victoria Coach Station in London, serves destinations in Denmark. For further information, contact Eurolines, 4 Cardiff Road, Luton, Bedfordshire LU1 1PP, UK (tel: (08705) 143 219; website: www.eurolines.com *or* www.nationalexpress.com).

See *Travel – Internal* for information on **documentation** and traffic regulations.

Travel - Internal

AIR:

The network of scheduled services radiates from *Copenhagen* (Kastrup). Other airports well served by domestic airlines include Ålborg, Århus, Billund, Esbjerg, Karup, Rønne, Skrydstrup, Sønderborg and Thisted. Domestic airports are generally situated between two or more cities which are within easy reach of each other. Domestic flights are usually of no more than 30 minutes' duration. Limousines are often available. Discounts are available on certain tickets bought inside Denmark. Family, children and young person's discounts are also available.

SEA:

There are frequent ferry sailings from Kalundborg to Århus, Ebeltoft to Sjællands Odde and Rønne to Copenhagen. The larger ferries usually have restaurants or cafes and may have TV, video and cinema lounges, shops, play areas for children and sleeping rooms. Local car ferries link most islands to the road network.

RAIL:

The main cities on all islands are connected to the rail network: Ålborg, Copenhagen, Esbjerg, Herning, Horsens, Odense and Randers. *Danish State Railways (DSB)* (tel: 7013 1418; website: www.dsb.dk) operates a number of express trains called *Lyntogs* which provide long-distance, non-stop travel; it is often possible to purchase newspapers, magazines and snacks onboard these trains. Payphones are also available. Intercity *IC3* trains are faster and more direct. Seat reservations are compulsory. Children under 10 years old travel free. There are also price reductions for persons over 65 and groups of eight people or more. The *Englænderen* boat-train runs between Esbjerg and Copenhagen and connects with ferries from the UK. DSB passenger fares are based on a zonal system. The cost depends on the distance travelled; the cost per kilometre is reduced the longer the journey. The *Scanrail Pass* allows unlimited travel within Denmark, Finland, Norway and Sweden. Standard-class prices for adults are approximately £266 for 21 days and £171 for five days in two months. As elsewhere in Europe, *Inter-Rail* passes are valid in Denmark. Bus and ferry and, of course, rail tickets may be purchased at all railway stations.

ROAD:

The road system in the Danish archipelago makes frequent use of ferries. Country buses operate where there are no railways, but there are few private long-distance coaches. Motorways are not subject to toll duty. Emergency telephones are available on motorways and there is a national breakdown network called *Falck*, which can be called out 24 hours a day. There are petrol stations on motorways, generally with other services such as restaurants. Many petrol stations are automatic. A maximum of 10 litres of petrol is allowed to be kept as a reserve in suitably safe containers. The Danish Motoring Organisation is *Forenede Danske Motorejere (FDM)*, Firskovvej 32, PO Box 500, 2800 Kgs. Lyngby (tel: 7013 3040; website: www.fdm.dk). Speed limits are 110kph (68mph) on motorways, 80kph (50mph) on other roads and 50kph (30mph) in built-up areas (signified by white plates with town silhouettes). Speed laws are strictly enforced, and heavy fines are levied on the spot; the car is impounded if payment is not made. **Cycling:** There are cycle lanes along many roads and, in the countryside, many miles of scenic cycle track. Bikes can easily be taken on ferries, trains, buses and domestic air services. **Car hire:** Available to drivers over the age of 20, and can be reserved through travel agents or airlines. However, many car rental firms will only hire vehicles out to drivers over 25 years of age. **Regulations:** The minimum driving age is 18. Traffic drives on the right. The wearing of seat belts is compulsory. Motorcyclists must wear helmets and drive with dipped headlights at all times. Headlamps on all vehicles should be adjusted for right-hand driving. All driving signs are international. Children under 12 years old need to travel in the rear of the car. **Documentation:** A national driving licence is acceptable. EU nationals taking their own cars to Denmark are strongly advised to obtain a Green Card. Without it, insurance cover is limited to the minimum legal cover in Denmark; the Green Card tops this up to the level of cover provided by the car owner's domestic policy.

URBAN:

Car repair is often available at petrol stations; costs include 25 per cent VAT on labour and materials, which is not refunded when you leave the country. **Parking:** Parking in cities is largely governed by parking discs, available from petrol stations, post offices, tourist offices, banks and some police stations. These allow up to three hours parking in car parks (one hour in Copenhagen). Kerbside parking is allowed for one hour Mon-Fri 0900-1700, Sat 0900-1300 unless stated otherwise. The hand of the disc should point to the quarter hour following time of arrival. The disc is to be placed on the side of the screen nearest the kerb. Where discs do not apply, parking meters regulate parking. Parking on a metered space is limited to three hours Mon-Fri 0900-1800, Sat 0900-1300. Meter charges differ according to the area of the city.

Travel Times: The following chart gives approximate travel times from **Copenhagen** (in hours and minutes) to other major cities/towns in Denmark.

	Air	Road	Rail
Ålborg	0.45	6.00	4.30
Århus	0.30	4.30	3.08
Esberg	1.00	5.00	3.12
Sønderborg	0.30	5.30	3.45

Travel Advice

Most visits to Denmark are trouble-free but you should be aware of the global risk of indiscriminate international terrorist attacks, which could be against civilian targets, including places frequented by foreigners.

This advice is based on information provided by the Foreign and Commonwealth Office in the UK. It is correct at time of publishing. As the situation can change rapidly, visitors are advised to contact the following organisations for the latest travel advice:

British Foreign and Commonwealth Office
Tel: (0845) 850 2829.
Website: www.fco.gov.uk

US Department of State
Website: http://travel.state.gov/travel

Accommodation

Contact VisitDenmark (see *Top Things To Do*) for information on booking hotels and for details of the savings from the use of a *Scandinavian Bonus Pass* (which must be applied for in advance) or *Inn Cheques*.

HOTELS:

Travellers without reservations can book at one of the provincial tourist offices. Denmark's fine beaches attract many visitors, and there are hotels and pensions in all major seaside resorts. Hotels are graded **1** to **5 stars**. Approximately 470 hotels and holiday centres (some 85 per cent of Denmark's total hotel capacity) are part of the grading scheme. VisitDenmark publishes an annual list of about 1000 establishments, describing facilities and tariffs; quoted prices are inclusive of *MOMS* (VAT). A number of hotels and hostels in Denmark are also participating in a grading scheme based on environmental concerns. To receive an eco-friendly certificate (a so-called '**Green Key**'), participating establishments have to fulfil 55 strict ecological criteria.

INNS: Excellent inns are to be found all over the country. Some are small and only cater for local custom, but others are tailored for the tourist and have established high culinary reputations for both international dishes and local specialities. For further details, contact VisitDenmark (see *Top Things To Do*).

BED AND BREAKFAST:

There are private rooms to let, usually for one night, all over Denmark. Signs along the highway with *Zimmer frei* or *Vårelse* on them indicate availability of accommodation. In Copenhagen, rooms can be booked in person through the Tourist Information Department for a small fee. Local tourist offices may be contacted, either by writing or in person.

SELF-CATERING:

Chalets are available in various parts of the country.

CAMPING/CARAVANNING:

Campers must purchase a camping *carnet*, available at campsites. Over 500 campsites are officially recognised and graded for facilities and shelter. Prices vary greatly; it is half price for children under four years. Grading is from **1** (lowest) to **5 stars** (highest), controlled by the Danish Camping Board; approved sites carry the sign of a pyramid-shaped tent. For more information and a list of campsites, contact VisitDenmark (see *Top Things To Do*).

YOUTH AND FAMILY HOSTELS:

There are 100 Youth and Family Hostels scattered around the country, all of which take members of affiliated organisations. A membership card from the National Youth Hostel Association is required. Hostels are classified from **1 to 5 stars**.

FARMHOUSE HOLIDAYS:

Rooms are often available for rent in farmhouses. Visitors stay as paying guests of the family and, although it is not expected, are welcome to help with the daily chores of the farm. Alternatively, in some cases, separate apartments are available close to the main farmhouse. Many farms have their own fishing streams. All holiday homes and farmhouses are inspected and approved by the local tourist office.

HOME EXCHANGE: Introductions between families interested in home exchange for short periods can be arranged. The major expense for participants is travel, plus a fee of DKK500. The best period (because of school holidays) is from late June to early August.

ACCOMMODATION INFORMATION

HORESTA
(Association of the Danish Hotel, Restaurant and Tourism Industry)
Vodroffsvej 46, DK-1900 Frederiksberg C, Denmark
Tel: 3524 8080.
Website: www.danishhotels.dk or www.horesta.dk

The Green Key
(See HORESTA address above.)
Website: www.dengroennenoegle.dk

Danhostel
(Information on Family and Youth Hostels)
Vesterbrogade 39, DK-1620 Copenhagen V, Denmark
Tel: 3331 3612.
Website: www.danhostel.dk

HomeLink Denmark
(Information on Home Exchange)
Dansk Bolig Bytte, PO Box 53, Bernstorffsvej 71A, DK-2900 Hellerup, Denmark
Tel: 3961 0405.
Website: www.bbdk.dk

Top Things To See

- The largest urban centre in Scandinavia, **Copenhagen** has many old buildings, fountains, statues and squares, as well as the attraction of the **Little Mermaid** at the harbour entrance. Organised tours include the Vikingland tour to the **Viking Ship Museum**; a Royal tour to the **Christianborg Palace** (the seat of Parliament), **Rosenborg Castle** and **Amalienborg Palace**; a coach tour to old-world **Bondebyen** and its open-air museum; and a brewery tour, which takes in the famous **Carlsberg** brewery, including an exhibition on the history of brewing and on this particular brewery. **Tivoli**, Copenhagen's world-famous amusement park, is open from late April to mid-September.

- **Jutland**'s west coast has superb sandy **beaches** but bathing there is often unsafe, due to the changing winds and tides. Nevertheless, it is a beautiful coastline to gaze out at, especially when watching many ferries and ships embark and disembark from **Esbjerg** the major port of Jutland. Main towns and resorts include Aalborg, Århus, **Esbjerg, Frederikshavn, Holstebro, Kolding, Randers, Silkeborg, Vejle** and **Viborg**. Around **Fynn**, there are also a number of beautiful beaches, particularly on the southern islands of **Langeland, Tåsinge** and **Ærø**. Excellent beaches can be found in **Sjælland**, particularly in the north of the island.

- **Aalborg** contains the largest Viking burial ground, as well as a cathedral, monastery and castle. The biggest Renaissance buildings in Denmark are in Aalborg. **Århus** has a collection of more than 60 17th- and 18th-century buildings – houses, shops, workshops and so on – from all over the country, re-erected on a spacious landscaped site; as well as **Marselisborg Castle** and a museum of prehistory. **Esbjerg** and **Fanø** are also historically interesting. **Rosenholm, Clausholm** and **Vœrgard** castles are all worth a visit. Known as the 'Garden of Denmark', **Fyn** (**Funen**), connected to Jutland by bridges,

also has some of Denmark's most picturesque and historic castles and manor houses, set in age-old parks and gardens. **Egeskov Castle** is a superb moated Renaissance castle, which is fairytale in every detail. Other castles in the area include **Nyborg** (seat of the former National Assembly) and **Valdemar**, which houses a naval museum. On **Lolland, Bornholm** contains **Hammershus,** Denmark's largest castle ruin (built in 1260), as well as many fine churches. The small town of **Svaneke** was awarded the European Gold Medal in Architectural Heritage Year (1975). On **Sjaelland, Frederiksborg Castle** is to be seen at **Hillerød**, which houses the **National History Museum**. The 12th-century cathedral at **Roskilde** and the **Viking Museum** are both also worth a visit.

- Go and see the birthplace of the great fairytale writer **Hans Christian Andersen** (1805-1875) in **Odense** in Fyn. Odense has a **festival** every July and August celebrating the life and works of Andersen. Visitors can also have a look around the **Hans Christian Andersen Museum** and his childhood home.

- Gaze at around 500 species of trees, flowers and plants at **Knuthenborg Park** on Lolland, Denmark's largest; it also contains a **safari park**.

- Behold the setting for Shakespeare's *Hamlet* at the old fortress of **Kronborg**, famed as the most imposing edifice in Scandinavia, which can be found at **Helsingør (Elsinore)** on the island of Sjaelland.

- **Legoland (Billund)** provides good entertainment for children.

Top Things To Do

- Because **Lolland** is generally flat, it is perfect for **cycling** across. **Bornholm** is set 150km (90 miles) apart from the Danish mainland and is made up of fertile farmland, white beaches and rocky coastlines. It is criss-crossed with more then 200km (125 miles) of **bicycle routes**. Many local tourist offices offer all-inclusive cycling trips, (bicycle rental, detailed route descriptions, maps, ferry tickets and accommodation) arranged in advance. Prices are lower for those bringing their own bicycles. The routes are laid out by local experts. For independent cyclists, a wide range of detailed cycling maps is available. Bicycles can be hired from local tourist offices or bicycle shops. Bicycles are allowed on all Danish ferries and several small passenger boats (in most cases, against payment); most trains (*InterCity* trains require prior reservation and reservations are not possible on Interregional trains); buses (which have room for up to four bicycles, although prams have priority) and aeroplanes (special packing requirements apply). For details, contact the Danish Cyclists' Association (*Dansk Cyklist Forbund*), Rømersgade 5-7, DK-1362 Copenhagen K (tel: 3332 3121; website: www.dcf.dk).

- Go **horse riding**: this is easily arranged in Denmark, which has horses to hire from riding schools and centres almost everywhere. Many riding schools offer riding holidays with half or full board.

- Spoil yourself with a relaxing treatment from a **health resort**, which are widespread throughout Denmark. Some offer medical and physiotherapeutic treatment, others simply offer recreation in beautiful, quiet surroundings.

- Denmark has excellent facilities for both **freshwater** and **saltwater fishing**. Sea fishing tours can be arranged with local fishermen at many Danish harbours (for instance in **Copenhagen**, Elsinore or **Frederikshavn**); large groups may charter a boat for themselves. Fishing off the shores of Denmark's 7500km- (5000 mile-) long coastline is widely available. Anglers must not take up position within 50m (164ft) of a dwelling place. Fishing rights in lakes and streams are usually privately owned but are often let

to local societies which issue day or week cards. A fishing licence is required in all cases (except for under 18s and over 65s, who are free) and can be obtained from Danish post offices, local tourist offices and angling shops. Special licences for tourists (valid from one day to one week) are available. Anglers are obliged to inform themselves about fishing restrictions and closed seasons. For further information and addresses of angling societies, contact the Danish Sports Fishing Association (*Danmarks Sportsfiskerforbund*), Worsåesgade 1, DK-7100 Vejle (tel: 7582 0699; website: www.sportsfiskeren.dk).

- Be daring, and go **nude bathing**. This is quite common at Danish seaside resorts. At beaches where nude bathing is not officially permitted, bathers are requested to show consideration and follow the directions of the local lifeguards. The only beaches where it is actually prohibited are **Henne Strand** and **Holmsland Klit** (both on Jutland's western coast). At **Bellevue Beach** in the metropolitan area, walking in the nude is prohibited while bathing or sunbathing in the nude is not. See online for more information (website: www.strandguide.dk).

- The long inlets and protected shores on the Danish coast offer easy conditions for **windsurfing** (and are thus particularly suitable for beginners). Facilities for **sailing** are excellent: over 500 yachting harbours can be found along the coast and anchorage is allowed at a further 500 islands. Boat hire facilities are widespread. Detailed handbooks and marine charts are available from the Danish Yachting Association (*Dansk Sejlunion*) (tel/fax: 4326 2182; website: www.sejlsport.dk) or the National Survey and Cadastre (*Kort & Matrikelstyrelsen*) (tel: 3587 5050; website: www.kms.dk); charts are available for direct download from the KMS Internet site. All **jetski** traffic is under general prohibition within the Danish sea territory.

TOURIST INFORMATION

VisitDenmark (Danish Tourist Board) in the UK
55 Sloane Street, London SW1X 9SY, UK
Tel: (020) 7259 5959 (Mon, Wed and Fri 1000-1300) *or* (09001) 600 109 (24-hour brochure request line; calls cost 60p per minute).
Website: www.visitdenmark.com

VisitDenmark (Danish Tourist Board) in the USA
PO Box 4649, Grand Central Station, New York, NY 10063, USA
Tel: (212) 885 9700.
Website: www.goscandinavia.com *or* www.visitdenmark.com
Also deals with enquiries from Canada. Not open to public.

Entertainment

FOOD & DRINK: Danes do not mix the various dishes on their plates but have them in strict order. Given its geographical position, it is not surprising that shellfish forms an important part of Danish cuisine. Apart from traditional dishes, French or international cuisine is the order of the day. In Copenhagen, superb gourmet restaurants can be found, whilst Ålborg is noted for its number of restaurants. Most towns have fast food outlets and the sausage stalls on most street corners, selling hot sausages, hamburgers, soft drinks and beer, are popular. There are no licensing hours.

National specialities:

- *Smørrebrød* is a highly popular traditional Danish dish that is often eaten for lunch. It consists of a slice of dark bread with butter, topped with slices of meat, fish or

Credit: ©Klaus Bentzen

cheese and generously garnished. It needs to be eaten sitting down with a knife and fork.

- Buffet-style lunch (the *koldt bord*) is also popular with a variety of fish, meats, hot dishes, cheese and sweets, usually on a self-service basis.
- A normal Danish breakfast, or *morgen-complet* , consists of an assortment of breads, rolls, jam and cheese, often also sliced meats, boiled eggs and warm Danish pastries.

National drinks:
- Danish coffee is delicious.
- Denmark also has many varieties of beer, famous breweries being Carlsberg and Tuborg. Most popular is *pilsner* (lager) but there are also darker beers.
- *Akvavit*, popularly known as *snaps*, is meant to be drunk with cold food, preferably with a beer chaser. It is served ice cold..

Tipping: Hotels and restaurants quote fully inclusive prices and tipping is not necessary. Taxi fares include tips. Railway porters and washroom attendants expect to receive tips.
Note: The Danish Hotel and Restaurant Association displays signs indicating restaurants where the needs of **diabetics** are given special attention. It consists of the words *'Diabetes mad – sund mad for alle'* ('Food for Diabetics – healthy food for everyone') encircling a chef's head.
NIGHTLIFE: There is a wide selection of nightlife, particularly in Copenhagen, where the first morning restaurants open to coincide with closing time at 0500. Jazz and dance clubs in the capital city are top quality and world-famous performers appear regularly. There are numerous beer gardens.
SHOPPING: Copenhagen has excellent shopping facilities. Special purchases include Bing & Grøndal and Royal Copenhagen porcelain, Holmegård glass, Bornholm ceramics, handmade woollens from the Faroe Islands and Lego toys. Visitors from outside the EU can often claim back some of the *MOMS* (VAT) on goods purchased that are sent straight to their home country from the shop in Denmark.
Shopping hours: Mon-Fri 0900/1000-1730/1800; Sat 0900-1700. Supermarkets are often open Mon-Fri 0900-2000. Opening hours vary from town to town. At some holiday resorts, bakers, florists, and souvenir shops are open Sunday and public holidays.

Business

- **GDP:** US$174.4 billion.
- **Main exports:** Machinery, foodstuffs, chemicals, windmills and ships.
- **Main imports:** Consumer goods, chemicals, foodstuffs, petroleum and raw materials.
- **Main trade partners:** UK, USA, Sweden, Norway and Germany.

ECONOMY: The standard of living is generally high, with annual GDP per capita of US$32,200. Compared to most industrialised countries, Denmark retains a large and important agricultural sector, two-thirds of whose produce is exported. Danish manufacturing depends on imports of raw materials and components. Iron, steel and the production of other metals are the most important industries, followed by electronics, chemicals and biotechnology, paper and printing, textiles, furniture and cement. Food processing and drinks also make a significant contribution. Since the discovery of offshore oil and gas reserves in the 1980s, production has gradually increased to the point where the country can meet all its domestic energy needs. Most of Denmark's trade is conducted within the EU, of which it is a member, although it has proved reluctant to adopt measures which are perceived as threatening to its sovereignty. It has thus so far refused to join the single European currency zone. Recent economic performance has been steady: inflation (2 per cent) and unemployment (6 per cent) are near the EU average; in 2004, annual growth remained at 0 per cent. Denmark is a member of the Nordic Union. Its links with Scandinavia have been further enhanced by the road and rail bridge linking it to Sweden across the Øresund Strait which opened in 2000.
BUSINESS ETIQUETTE: English is widely used for all aspects of business. Local businesspeople expect visitors to be punctual and the approach to business is often direct and straightforward. Avoid business visits from mid-June to mid-August, which are prime holiday periods. **Office hours:** Mon-Fri 0900-1600/ 1730 (some offices close earlier Fri).

COMMERCIAL INFORMATION
Handelskskammeret (Danish Chamber of Commerce)
Børsen, DK-1217 Copenhagen K, Denmark
Tel: 7013 1200.
Website: www.hts.dk

Djibouti

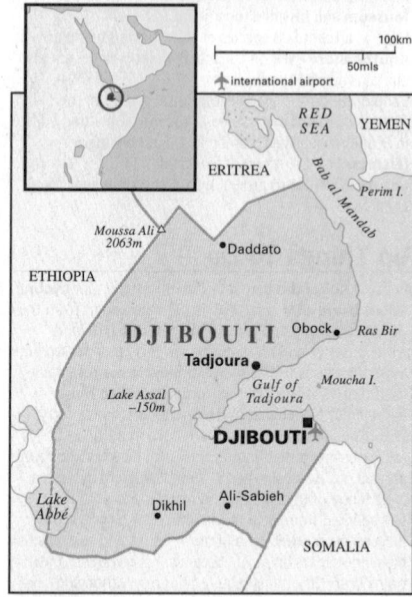

100km

50mls

✈ international airport

Location: Northeast Africa, Gulf of Aden.

Time: GMT + 3.

Overview

Djibouti was originally inhabited by nomadic tribes, the main ones being the Afars and the Issas, who are strongly linked to Ethiopia and Somalia respectively. In 1862, the French signed a treaty with the Afar leaders, giving them land on the north coast. During the rest of the 19th century, Djibouti gradually became more firmly associated with France. In 1945, French Somaliland (as the area was called) was declared an 'overseas territory' and in 1967, it became the French territory of the 'Afars and Issas'. In 1977, the French agreed to withdraw, and the country achieved independence.
Controlling access to the Red Sea, Djibouti is of major strategic importance. During the Gulf War it was the base of operations for the French military, who continue to maintain a significant presence, contributing directly and indirectly to more than half the country's income.

General Information

AREA: 23,200 sq km (8958 sq miles).
POPULATION: 721,000 (UN, 2005).
POPULATION DENSITY: 31.1 per sq km
CAPITAL: Djibouti. **Population:** 575,100 (2005).
GEOGRAPHY: Djibouti is part of the African continent, bordered to the northeast and east by the Red Sea, the southeast by Somalia, the southwest by Ethiopia and to the north by Eritrea. The country is a barren strip of land around the Gulf of Tadjoura, varying in width from 20km (12 miles) to 90km (56 miles), with a coastline of 300km (188 miles), much of it white sandy beaches. Inland is semi-desert and desert, with thorn bushes, steppes and volcanic mountain ranges.
LANGUAGE: The official languages are Arabic and French. Afar and Somali are spoken locally. English is spoken by hoteliers, taxi drivers and traders.
GOVERNMENT: Republic. Gained independence from France in 1977. **Head of State:** President Ismail Omar Guelleh since 1999 (re-elected in 2005). **Head of Government:** Prime Minister Dileita Mohamed Dileita since 2001. **Recent history:** Ismail Omar Guelleh succeeded his uncle, Hasan Gouled Aptidon, in April 1999. He won the Presidential elections as the RPP candidate with 74 per cent of the vote. The RPP joined with FRUD to form a new ruling coalition, l'*Union pour la Majorité Présidentielle* (UMP). The

---

UMP took 62.7 per cent of the votes but won all 65 seats in the Chamber of Deputies due to Djibouti's unusual first-past-the-post list system in the Parliamentary elections in January 2003. Presidential elections were held on 8 April 2005. Guelleh claimed 96.85 per cent of the vote. The opposition l'*Union pour l'Alternative Démocratique (UAD)* disputed the high turnout figure of 78.9 per cent and called for a boycott of the polls. Guelleh is now serving his second six-year term and will not be eligible to stand again.
RELIGION: Predominantly Muslim (94 per cent) with Roman Catholic, Protestant and Greek Orthodox minorities.
ELECTRICITY: 220 volts AC, 50Hz.
SOCIAL CONVENTIONS: Casual wear is widely acceptable, but visitors are reminded that Djibouti is a Muslim country and certain codes of behaviour should be observed.

Climate

Extremely hot and particulary arid between June and August when the dusty *Khamsin* blows from the desert. Between October and April it is slightly cooler with occasional light rain; however, there is generally less than 150mm of rainfall annually.

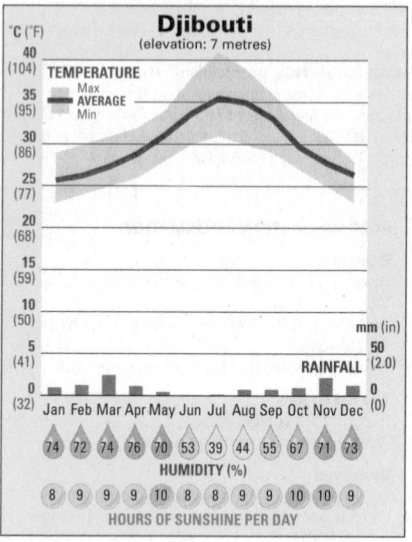

Communications

Telephone: IDD available. Country code: 253.
Mobile telephone: Roaming agreements exist with most international mobile phone companies. Coverage is good in and around the capital and parts of the coast, and poor to non-existent elsewhere.
Internet: Services are accessible in the main post office and some hotels. There is at least one Internet cafe in Djibouti.
Post: Letters and parcels to western Europe can take about one week by airmail or up to three weeks by surface mail
MEDIA: The main newspaper, *La Nation*, is owned by the government, as is *Radiodiffusion-Television de Djibouti (RTD)*, which operates the national radio and TV. There are no private broadcasters. All electronic media is closely controlled by the government. Private newspapers and other publications are generally allowed to circulate freely, but journalists exercise self-censorship. The official media does not criticise the government. US-sponsored Arabic-language *Radio Sawa* broadcasts programmes to East Africa and Arabia from a transmitter in Djibouti.
Press: Djibouti has no daily papers. A weekly newspaper, *La Nation*, is government-owned and published in French. There is at least one Arabic newspaper. Other weekly newspapers published in French include *Le Renouveau*, *La Republique* (both owned by the opposition party), *Le Progrès*, and *Le Temps*.
TV: *Djibouti Television* is government-owned.
Radio: *Radio Djibouti* is government-owned and broadcast in Afar, Arabic and Somali.

Passport/Visa

	Passport Required?	Visa Required?	Return Ticket Required?
Full British	Yes	Yes	No
Australian	Yes	Yes	No
Canadian	Yes	Yes	No
USA	Yes	Yes	No
Other EU	Yes	Yes	No
Japanese	Yes	Yes	No

Note: *Regulations and requirements may be subject to change at short notice, and you are advised to contact the appropriate diplomatic or consular authority before finalising travel arrangements. Any numbers in the chart refer to the footnotes below.*

PASSPORTS: Passport valid for six months beyond date of departure required by all.
VISAS: Required by all except transit passengers not disembarking and continuing their journey by the same aircraft or ship.
Types of visa and cost: Entry (visa de séjour); Tourist (visa de tourisme); Business (visa d'affaires); Transit (visa de transit). All visas cost €50.
Validity: From one day to three months. An extension may be granted in Djibouti on request to the Headquarters of the Police Nationale.
Application to: The Embassy in Paris (see Passport/Visa Information). 10-day transit visas can be issued at the point of entry to visitors holding confirmed return air tickets. A fee will be charged. This facility is only available to nationals from countries where Djibouti has no diplomatic representation. Contact the Embassy in Paris for further information.
Application requirements: (a) Valid passport. (b) Two application forms completed in French. (c) Two passport-size photos. (d) Fee of €50 plus €5 to cover postage within France or €6 to cover postage from abroad; the amount should be sent in the form of a postal or money order, not a cheque. (e) Return or onward ticket. Business: (a)-(e) and, (f) Letter from the employer or a letter of invitation from the company in Djibouti.
Working days required: Three working days.

PASSPORT/VISA INFORMATION

Embassy of the Republic of Djibouti in France
26 rue Emile Menier, 75116 Paris, France
Tel: (1) 4727 4922.
Opening hours: Mon-Fri 0900-1600.

Embassy of the Republic of Djibouti in the USA
1156 15th Street, Suite 515, NW, Washington DC 20005, USA

Money

Currency: Djibouti Franc (Djf) = 100 centimes. Notes are in denominations of Djf10,000, 5000, 2000, 1000 and 500. Coins are in denominations of Djf500, 100, 50, 20 and 10.
Currency exchange: Currency can be exchanged at major banks and hotels, or at authorised bureaux de change in the capital. The bureaux de change are open all day, while the banks have limited opening hours.
Credit & debit cards: These are only accepted by airlines and some of the larger hotels.
Traveller's cheques: To avoid additional exchange rate charges, travellers are advised to take traveller's cheques in US Dollars or Euros. Euro and Sterling cheques are not accepted unless marked as 'External Account' or 'Pour Compte Etranger'. The majority of banks are in the place du 27 juin area.
Currency restrictions: There are no restrictions on the import or export of either foreign or local currency. Currency must be declared on arrival.
Banking hours: Sat-Thurs 0715-1145.
Exchange rate indicators:
Rate at time of publishing
£1.00= Djf319.45
$1.00= Djf182.39

Duty Free

As for France (see France section). Currency must be declared on arrival. Firearms must be declared on entry and exit.

Public Holidays

Below area listed Public Holidays for the January 2006-June 2007 period.
2006: Jan 1 New Year's Day. **Jan 10** Eid al-Adha (Feast of the Sacrifice). **Jan 31** El-am-Hejir (Islamic New Year). **Apr 10** Mouloud (Birth of the Prophet). **May 1** Labour Day. **Jun 27** Independence Day. **Oct 23** Eid al-Fitr (End of Ramadan). **Dec 25** Christmas Day. **Dec 31** Eid al-Adha (Feast of the Sacrifice).
2007: Jan 1 New Year's Day. **Jan 20** El-am-Hejir (Islamic New Year). **May 1** Labour Day. **Mar 31** Mouloud (Birth of the Prophet). **Jun 27** Independence Day.
Note: Muslim festivals are timed according to local sightings of various phases of the moon and the dates given above are approximations. During the lunar month of Ramadan that precedes Eid al-Fitr, Muslims fast during the day and feast at night and normal business patterns may be interrupted. Many restaurants are closed during the day and there may be restrictions on smoking and drinking. Some disruption may continue into Eid al-Fitr itself. Eid al-Fitr and Eid al-Adha may last anything from two to 10 days, depending on the region. For more information, see the appendix World of Islam section.

Health

	Special Precautions?	Certificate Required?
Yellow Fever	Yes	1
Cholera	Yes	2
Typhoid & Polio	3	N/A
Malaria	4	N/A

Note: Regulations and requirements may be subject to change at short notice, and you are advised to contact your doctor well in advance of your intended date of departure. Any numbers in the chart refer to the footnotes below.

1: A yellow fever vaccination certificate is required from travellers over one year of age coming from infected areas.
2: Following WHO guidelines issued in 1973, a cholera vaccination certificate is no longer a condition of entry to Djibouti. However, cholera is a serious risk in this country and precautions are essential. Up-to-date advice should be sought before deciding if these precautions should include vaccination as medical opinion is divided over its effectiveness. For more information, consult the Health appendix.
3: Immunisation against typhoid is usually advised.
4: Malaria risk, predominantly in the malignant falciparum form, exists throughout the year in the whole country. Resistance to chloroquine has been reported. Mefloquine, doxycycline or atovaquone/proguanil are recommended.
Food & drink: Mains water is normally heavily chlorinated and, whilst relatively safe, may cause mild abdominal upsets. Bottled water is available and is advised for the first few weeks of the stay. Drinking water outside main cities and towns is likely to be contaminated and sterilisation is considered essential. Milk is unpasteurised and should be boiled. Powdered or tinned milk is available and is advised, but make sure that it is reconstituted with pure water. Avoid dairy products which are likely to have been made from unboiled milk. Only eat well-cooked meat and fish, preferably served hot. Pork, salad and mayonnaise may carry increased risk. It is advised not to buy food from street vendors. Vegetables should be cooked and fruit peeled.
Other risks: Diarrhoeal disease, giardiasis, dysentery and typhoid fever are widespread throughout the country. Onchocerciasis (river blindness) exists and cutaneous and visceral leishmaniasis may be found in drier areas. Human trypanosomiasis (sleeping sickness) is reported in certain locations. Bilharzia (schistosomiasis) is present. Travellers are advised to avoid swimming and paddling in fresh water; swimming pools which are well chlorinated and maintained are safe. It is recommended to avoid walking bare foot, even on beaches. Hepatitis A, B and E occur and precautions should be taken. Visitors should also consider immunisation against diphtheria. Meningococcal meningitis risk exists, depending on area and time of year.
Rabies is present. For those at high risk, vaccination before arrival should be considered. If you are bitten, seek medical advice without delay. For more information, consult the Health appendix.
Health care: Health insurance is advisable. Doctors and hospitals may expect immediate cash payment for any form of medical treatment.

Travel - International

AIR:

Djibouti-based Daallo Airlines (D3) (website: www.daallo.com) operates flights to Paris and services to Ethiopia, Kenya, Saudi Arabia and Somalia.
Approximate flight times: From Djibouti to London is 10 hours (including stopovers).
Main airports: Djibouti (JIB) is 5km (3 miles) south of the city. To/from the airport: Taxis are available. Facilities: Duty free shops, restaurants, left luggage, tourist information, car hire (Maril), bureau de change and a craft shop.
Departure tax: $US20 is levied on all passengers.
RAIL:

The Djibouti–Ethiopian Railway operates regular trains between Addis Ababa and Dire Dawa with one train daily connecting with Djibouti; in theory, tourists and businesspeople can use this service (for which they should book first-class tickets only), but it is not recommended as trains are old, fairly unreliable and the volatile security situation in Ethiopia is causing considerable risks to all travellers.
ROAD:

There are roads from Djibouti to Assab (Eritrea) and going west into Ethiopia via Dikhil. Travellers using them should be aware that road conditions are generally poor (the roads are more often dirt tracks than asphalted) and personal security might be at risk when travelling – particularly to Ethiopia (see Travel – Internal section for information on documentation required). Visitors are also advised to check transit regulations as

political conditions in Ethiopia and Eritrea are changeable. Currently, there are no problems with travelling to Eritrea and no formal border posts. Travel to neighbouring Somalia (which has bus links with Djibouti) is not recommended due to the highly unstable political situation.

Travel - Internal

AIR:

Private charters may be available.

SEA:

Ferry services sail daily from L'Escale (Djibouti) to Tadjoura and Obock (on the northeast coast of the Gulf of Tadjoura). The journey takes 3 hours.
RAIL:
The only service is provided by daily train to the border with Ethiopia (see Travel – International section).
ROAD:
Four-wheel-drive vehicles are recommended for the interior. There is a new highway from Djibouti to Tadjoura. Traffic drives on the right.
Bus: Buses operate from Djibouti to most towns and villages throughout the country. Buses leave when they are full. **Car hire:** Available in Djibouti and at the airport. It is advisable to carry water and petrol on any expedition off main routes. **Documentation:** An International Driving Permit is recommended, although not legally required. A temporary licence to drive is available from local authorities on presentation of a valid British or Northern Ireland driving licence. Insurance is not required.
URBAN:
A minibus service operates in Djibouti, stopping on demand. A flat-fare system is used. **Taxi:** These are available in Djibouti and from the airport to the town; also in Ali-Sabieh, Dikhil, Dorale and Arta. Fares increase by 50 per cent after dark.

Travel Advice

Djibouti shares with the rest of the region a high threat from terrorism. Travellers are at risk from terrorist attacks in areas frequented by Westerners.
Travellers should be aware of the risk of banditry if travelling outside the capital city.
This advice is based on information provided by the Foreign and Commonwealth Office in the UK. It is correct at time of publishing. As the situation can change rapidly, visitors are advised to contact the following organisations for the latest travel advice:

British Foreign and Commonwealth Office
Tel: (0845) 850 2829.
Website: www.fco.gov.uk

US Department of State
Website: http://travel.state.gov/travel

Accommodation

Hotels in Djibouti tend to be expensive and the few cheap hotels are somewhat rundown. There is a small number of first-class hotels.
Outside Djibouti, accommodation is limited, although attention is being given to upgrading and adding to the accommodation available in the hinterland. The Rest Shelter at Ali-Sabieh, a provincial town in the hills, has a large shaded terrace and simple cooking facilities. There are also hotels or pensions in Dikhil, Obock and Tadjara; however, much remains to be done. The Government would like to establish a network of rest houses similar to the one at Ali-Sabieh throughout the country. In addition, it hopes to build several beach shelters.

Top Things To See & Do

- In **Djibouti**, a late 19th-century city with a distinctly Arabic feel, visit the lively **Central Market** (Le Marché Central) near the Mosque.
- Also worth seeing in Djibouti is the **Tropical Aquarium** with underwater exhibits from the Red Sea (open daily 1600-1830), and the **Presidential Palace**.
- Just outside Djibouti, stroll in the **Ambouli** palm grove during the cooler parts of the day.
- The beaches at **Doralé** and **Khor-Ambado**, which are both about 15km (10 miles) from Djibouti, offer safe **swimming**. Another good beach can be found at **Ghoubet al Kharab**, which is about an hour's drive from Lake Assal, and where black-lava cliffs border the beach.
- The **Gulf of Tadjoura** (especially **Obock**) contains many species of fish and coral and is ideal for **diving**, **snorkelling** and **underwater photography**; in many places, the coral reefs in the Red Sea are easily accessible from the beaches. The best time for these activities is

from September to May when the waters of the Red Sea are clear. **Waterskiing** and **windsurfing** can also be arranged.

- **Geology** and **wildlife** enthusiasts may head to the wilderness around **Lake Abbé** (accessible by 4-wheel-drive vehicles only), a gathering place for flamingos and pelicans and the location of strange natural steaming chimneys.
- Djibouti lies within a geological feature known as the **Afar Triangle**, one of the hottest and most desolate places on Earth. Part of the **Great Rift Valley** system, it is a wedge of flat desert pushing into the Ethiopian Massif. Much of it is below sea level.
- Surrounded by dormant volcanoes and lava fields, **Lake Assal**, 100km (60 miles) to the southwest of Djibouti city, is one of the lowest surface areas anywhere on the planet (150m (570 ft) below sea level); and is reachable only by 4-wheel-drive vehicle. It is possible to **windsurf on wheels** in the desert areas.

Note: Hunting is forbidden throughout the country.

TOURIST INFORMATION

Office National du Tourisme de Djibouti (ONTD) (Djibouti National Tourist Office)
place du 27 juin, BP 1938, Djibouti, Djibouti
Tel: 352 800 *or* 353 790.
Website: www.office-tourisme.dj
Opening hours: Sat-Wed 0730-1230 and 1630-1830, Thurs 0730-1230.

Entertainment

FOOD & DRINK: Restaurants serve Arab, Chinese, French and Vietnamese local specialities.
National specialities:
- Lentils, fried meat and unleavened bread are all popular.
- Fish from the Red Sea.

National drinks:
- Drinking is not a social activity and so alcohol is not widely available.

Tipping: A 10 per cent service charge is usually added to bills. Tipping is rare and never requested. Not usual for taxi drivers. A tariff is normally set but visitors will be charged at a higher rate.
SHOPPING: Lively and colourful local markets selling local crafts and artefacts are well worth visiting.
Shopping hours: Sat-Thurs 0730-1200 and 1600-1900.
NOTE: Friday is a holiday for offices and government institutions. Djibouti observes all Islamic feasts and holidays.

Business

- **GDP:** US$596.6 million.
- **Main imports:** Foodstuffs, beverages, transport equipment, chemicals and petroleum products.
- **Main exports:** Re-exports, hides and skins and coffee.
- **Main trade partners:** Somalia, Yemen, Ethiopia, Saudi Arabia, India, China, USA and France.

Djibouti's economic output fell by one-third during the 1990s, largely due to the chaos which afflicted the Horn of Africa. Little of the mainly desert land will support crops and agriculture, and is therefore concentrated in rearing livestock; this is mostly conducted by nomadic tribes. There is a small industrial sector devoted to light manufacturing of locally consumed products. Djibouti's economic potential lies in the development of its service sector; in particular, transport facilities and banking. The deep-water port on the Bab-El-Mandeb Straits, which has developed as a major refuelling and transhipment facility, is vitally important to the country, as it is on the major oil route between the Gulf of Aden and the Red Sea. In addition, the Government hopes to develop Djibouti as a general trading centre between Africa and the Middle East and as an important telecommunications hub for the region. However, at present, the country remains dependent on foreign aid, the bulk of which comes from France and Saudi Arabia. Djibouti is a member of Common Market of Eastern and South Africa (COMESA), the League of Arab States, the United Nations (UN) and African Union (AU). Unemployment, which affects perhaps half the workforce, is a particular problem.
BUSINESS ETIQUETTE: Suits should be worn. French and Arabic are the main languages used in business. As there are few, if any, interpreter services of note, a knowledge of either of these languages is essential. Business entertainment takes place in hotels or restaurants. **Office hours:** Sat-Thurs 0620-1330.

COMMERCIAL INFORMATION

Chambre de Commerce et d'Industrie de Djibouti
BP 84, Djibouti
Tel: 351 070 *or* 350 826.

The Chambre de Commerce et d'Industrie de Djibouti can also provide information on Conferences/Conventions.

Dominica

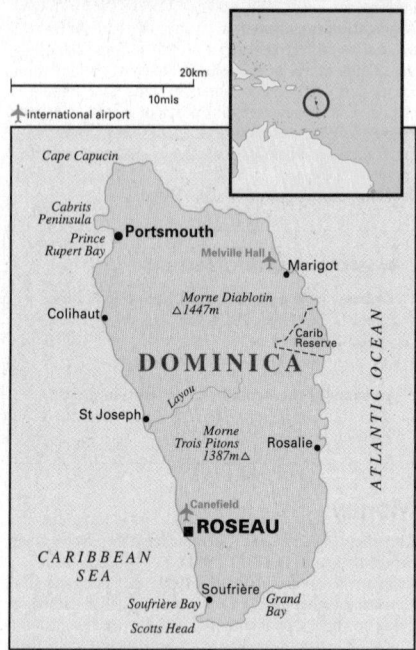

Location: Caribbean, Leeward Islands.

Time: GMT - 4.

Overview

The island, which was originally occupied by Carib Indians (some of whose descendants remain), was discovered by Columbus in 1493 and colonised by the French in the 1600s. In 1805, the island became a British possession and remained under British rule until 1967, when internal self-Government was granted, followed by full independence in 1978. Post-independence politics have been somewhat stormy, with two coup attempts by leftist members of the island's Defence Force, during the early 1980s.
The largest and most mountainous of the Windward Islands, with volcanic peaks, mountain streams and rivers, beaches of both black (volcanic) and golden sands, dense forests, quiet lakes, waterfalls, geysers and boiling volcanic pools, Dominica is potentially a major tourist destination. It has a relatively low crime rate for the Caribbean and although it is among the poorest countries in the region, disparities in wealth are not as marked as in the larger Caribbean islands. However, poor infrastructure and the absence of a large airport has impeded the growth of tourism. Proposals to build an airport capable of taking large jet aircraft have yet to materialise as there is concern that an increase in tourist arrivals, even with the promotion of eco-tourism, would damage the island's finely balanced environment.

General Information

AREA: 754 sq km (290 sq miles).
POPULATION: 69,029 (2005).
POPULATION DENSITY: 91.5 per sq km.
CAPITAL: Roseau. **Population:** 14,500 (UN estimate 2005).
GEOGRAPHY: Dominica is a large and mountainous island, geographically part of the Leeward Islands, though historically for administrative purposes it has been grouped with the Windward Islands. It boasts volcanic peaks, mountain streams and rivers, dense forests, quiet lakes, waterfalls, geysers and boiling volcanic pools. There are beaches of both black (volcanic) and golden sands, while orchids and untamed subtropical vegetation grow in the valleys. Guadeloupe lies to the north and Martinique to the south.
GOVERNMENT: Republic. Gained independence from the UK in 1978. **Head of State:** Nicholas Liverpool since 2003. **Head of Government:** Prime Minister Roosevelt Skerrit

since 2004. **Recent history:** Roosevelt Skerrit, who was 31 when he took office, was sworn in as Dominica's youngest Prime Minister two days after the sudden death of his predecessor, Pierre Charles, in January 2004. Mr Skerrit pledged to boost Dominica's sluggish economy, which relies heavily on tourism and the export of bananas. In 2004, Mr Skerrit's Government cut diplomatic relations with Taiwan in favour of ties with mainland China, which had agreed to give more than US$100 million in aid to Dominica.
LANGUAGE: The official language is English, but Creole French, the national language, is spoken by most of the population.
RELIGION: Almost entirely Christian, with Roman Catholic majority.
ELECTRICITY: 220/240 volts AC, 50Hz. Three-pin European-style plugs are usual.
SOCIAL CONVENTIONS: Casual dress is normal. Evening clothes are informal but conservative. The Catholic Church is one of the most dominant social influences. **Photography:** Visitors should ask before taking photographs of local people.

Climate

Hot, subtropical climate throughout the year. The main rainy season is between June and October, when it is hottest.
Required clothing: Lightweight cottons and linens. Waterproofing is advisable throughout most of the year.

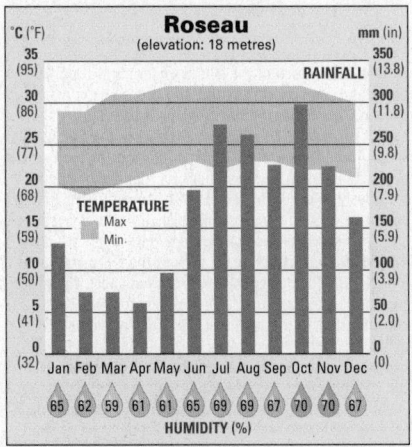

Roseau (elevation: 18 metres)

Communications

Telephone: IDD available. Country code: 1 767.
Mobile telephone: TDMA network. Unregistered roaming is available – visitors with TDMA handsets can make calls without registering, provided they can give a credit card number. Handsets can be hired.
Internet: Access is available at the offices of *Cable & Wireless* in Roseau, at an Internet cafe and in some hotels.
Post: There are no *Poste Restante* facilities. Post office hours: Mon-Fri 0800-1600; smaller branches: 1500-1700. The main post office is located at Bayfront, Roseau. Mail takes one to three weeks to arrive in Europe and the USA.
MEDIA: There are no daily newspapers in Dominica. There is no national television service, but a private cable TV network covers part of the island. There is a mix of public and private radio stations. All media are free from Government interference.
Press: Newspapers are in English. These include *The Chronicle*, *The Sun* and the *The Tropical Star*.
TV: *Marpin Telecom and Broadcasting* is a cable TV provider.
Radio: *DBS Radio* is operated by state broadcaster Dominica Broadcasting Corporation; *Q95 FM* is a commercial station; *Kairi FM* is operated by Island Communication Corporation; *Voice of Life Radio-ZGBC* is a religious station.

Passport/Visa

	Passport Required?	Visa Required?	Return Ticket Required?
Full British	Yes	No/3	Yes
Australian	Yes	No/4	Yes
Canadian	1	No/4	Yes
USA	1	No/5	Yes
Other EU	Yes/2	No/3	Yes
Japanese	Yes	No/5	Yes

Note: *Regulations and requirements may be subject to change at short notice, and we are advised to contact the appropriate diplomatic or consular authority before finalising travel arrangements. Any numbers in the chart refer to the footnotes below.*

PASSPORTS: Passport valid for at least six months required

by all except the following:
(a) **1.** nationals of Canada and the USA holding proof of citizenship bearing a photograph and return or onward tickets;
(b) **2.** nationals of France holding National Identity Cards (*Carte d'Identité*) for stays of up to two weeks.
VISAS: Required by all except the following:
(a) **3.** nationals of EU countries for stays of up to six months (except Austria, Czech Republic, Estonia, Finland, Hungary, Latvia, Lithuania, Poland, Slovak Republic and Slovenia for stays of up to 21 days);
(b) **4.** nationals of Commonwealth countries for stays of up to six months;
(c) **5.** nationals of Argentina, China (PR), Costa Rica, Israel, Japan, Korea (Rep), Malta, Mexico, Norway, Surinam, Taiwan (China), USA and Venezuela for stays of up to six months;
(d) nationals of *all other countries* for tourist stays of up to 21 days, provided they have a return ticket and satisfy the immigration officer that they do not wish to stay for longer. For an extension, visitors should apply to the Immigration Department at the Police Headquarters in Roseau, Dominica.
Types of visa and cost: *Single-entry:* £25.
Application to: Consular section at High Commission or Embassy (see *Passport/Visa Information*).
Application requirements: (a) Valid passport. (b) Two passport-size photos. (c) Return ticket or receipt from travel agent. (d) Fee (plus extra £5 if require return of passport by registered mail). (e) Letter explaining the length of stay required. (f) Sufficient funds for travellers stay.
Temporary residence: Those applying for temporary residence must obtain a work permit.

PASSPORT/VISA INFORMATION

Office of the High Commission for the Commonwealth of Dominica in the UK
1 Collingham Gardens, London SW5 0HW, UK
Tel: (020) 7370 5194/5.
Website: www.dominica.co.uk
Opening hours: Mon-Fri 0930-1730.

Embassy of the Commonwealth of Dominica in the USA
3216 New Mexico Avenue, NW, Washington, DC 20016, USA
Tel: (202) 364 6781.

Money

Currency: East Caribbean Dollar (XCD; symbol EC$) = 100 cents. Notes are in denominations of EC$100, 50, 20, 10 and 5. Coins are in denominations of EC$1, and 50, 25, 10, 5, 2 and 1 cents. US Dollars and Pounds Sterling are also legal tender.
Note: The Eastern Caribbean Dollar is tied at a fixed rate to the US Dollar.
Currency exchange: Foreign currencies can be exchanged at banks and bureaux de change.
Credit & debit cards: American Express, MasterCard (limited) and Visa are accepted. Check with your credit or debit card company for details of merchant acceptability and other services which may be available. ATMs are located around the island.
Traveller's cheques: Accepted by most hotels. To avoid additional exchange rate charges, travellers are advised to take travellers cheques in US Dollars.
Currency restrictions: The import of local and foreign currency is unlimited, subject to declaration on arrival. The export of local and foreign currency is limited to the amount declared on arrival. If holding a credit card, export is limited to EC$2500 and any currency in excess of this will require proof of conversion.
Banking hours: Mon-Thurs 0800-1500, Fri 0800-1700.
Exchange rate indicators:
Rate at time of publishing
£1.00=	EC$4.66
$1.00=	EC$2.70

Duty Free

The following goods may be imported into Dominica without incurring customs duty by passengers aged 18 and above:
200 cigarettes, one box of cigars or equivalent of tobacco products; 2l of alcoholic beverages; tools for professional use; two bottles of perfume for personal use.
Prohibited items: Various plants including bananas, coconuts, coffee, avocados, animal products, paints, varnishes and chemicals. A licence is needed to import firearms.
Note: There is no allowance on gifts.

Public Holidays

Below are listed Public Holidays for the January 2006-June 2007 period.
2006: Jan 1-2 New Year. **Feb 27** Carnival. **Apr 14** Good Friday. **Apr 17** Easter Monday. **May 1** Bank Holiday. **Jun 5** Whit Monday. **Aug 7** August Monday. **Nov 3** Independence Day. **Nov 4** Community Service Day. **Dec 25** Christmas Day. **Dec 26** Boxing Day.
2007: Jan 1-2 New Year. **Feb 19** Carnival. **Apr 6** Good Friday. **Apr 9** Easter Monday. **May 7** Bank Holiday. **May 28** Whit Monday.

Health

	Special Precautions?	Certificate Required?
Yellow Fever	No	1
Cholera	No	No
Typhoid & Polio	2	N/A
Malaria	No	N/A

Note: *Regulations and requirements may be subject to change at short notice, and you are advised to contact your doctor well in advance of your intended date of departure. Any numbers in the chart refer to the footnotes below.*

1: A *yellow fever* vaccination certificate is required from travellers over one year of age coming from infected areas.
2: *Typhoid* may be a risk in rural areas.
Food & drink: Mains water is normally chlorinated, and whilst relatively safe, may cause mild abdominal upsets. Bottled water is available and is advised for the first few weeks of the stay. Drinking water outside main towns may be contaminated and sterilisation is advisable. Milk is pasteurised and dairy products are safe for consumption. Local meat, poultry, seafood, fruit and vegetables are generally considered safe to eat.
Other risks: *Hepatitis A* is common, as are *bacillary* and *amoebic dysentries*. Outbreaks of *dengue fever* occur in the area, as well as *dengue haemorrhagic fever*.
Health care: As visitors are required to pay up front for treatment, international travellers are strongly advised to take out full medical insurance. There are four main hospitals across the island; Also some private clinics, but with high charges.

Travel - International

AIR:

The main airline to serve Dominica is *LIAT (LI)* (website: www.liatairline.com.) Other airlines serving Dominica include *American Eagle* (website: www.aa.com), and *Caribbean Star* (website: www.flycaribbeanstar.com). There are currently no direct, non-stop flights from Europe or the USA, mostly because the two airports are too small for jets. Popular routes from Europe are via Antigua, Barbados, Guadeloupe, Martinique or Puerto Rico, then a local flight to Dominica.
Approximate flight times: From Roseau to *London* via Antigua is approximately 10 hours (depending on length of stopover), to *Los Angeles* is 10 hours and to *New York* is seven hours.
Main airports: (turbo-prop only): Melville Hall (DOM), the older of the two airports, is approximately 64km (40 miles) northeast of Roseau.
Canefield (DCF) is approximately 5km (3 miles) north of Roseau. *Facilities:* Snack bars, tourist information office, shops, left luggage and car hire (*Avis* and *Budget.*) *To/from the airport:* Taxis are widely available, but look for the uniformed taxi drivers who are trained and authorised. Buses are available from Roseau, and travel to all the major towns.
Departure tax: US$17 for Dominican residents and US$21 for non-residents. Transit passengers continuing their journey on the same day and children under 12 years of age are exempt.
SEA:

Main ports: *Woodbridge Bay, Roseau* and *Prince Rupert Bay, Portsmouth. Geest* and several other island-hopping freight lines stop in Dominica. Generally, passenger accommodation is comfortable but numbers are limited, so book well in advance. *L'Express des Îles*, a scheduled ferry service, connects Dominica with Guadeloupe, St Lucia and Martinique on a 300-seat catamaran. *Caribbean Ferries* also operate regular services between Dominica, Guadeloupe and Martinique. There is an EC$20 departure tax. Cruise liners stop at Woodbridge Bay, 5km (3 miles) outside Roseau. There is a cruise ship jetty at Prince Rupert Bay, Portsmouth.

A B C D E F G H I J K L M N O P Q R S T U V W X Y Z

Travel - Internal

ROAD:

There are more than 700km (450 miles) of well-maintained roads on the island and there is little traffic outside Roseau. Traffic drives on the left. There is a 32kmph (20mph) speed limit in towns and villages. **Bus:** Services connect all towns and villages. **Taxis** are efficient. **Car hire:** Available (see *Travel – International* section) but some roads can be difficult. Visiting drivers must be between 25 and 65 years old and have had at least two years' driving experience in order to apply for a local driver's permit; permits cost US$12 or EC$30 for three months. Jeep and minibus tours operated by local firms offer the best means of sightseeing; all vehicles chartered for this purpose must be hired for at least three hours; Reservation is advisable for better rates; Speed limits are 20mph on most roads. **Documentation:** International Driving Permit recommended. A valid foreign licence can be used to get a Temporary Visitor's Permit.
Travel Times: The following chart gives approximate travel times (in hours and minutes) from **Roseau** to other places in Dominica.

	Road
Canefield Airport	0.15
Melville Hall Airport	1.15

Travel Advice

Most visits to Dominica are trouble-free but you should be aware of the global risk of indiscriminate international terrorist attacks, which could be against civilian targets, including places frequented by foreigners.
Cases of robbery and crime do occur.
This advice is based on information provided by the Foreign and Commonwealth Office in the UK. It is correct at time of publishing. As the situation can change rapidly, visitors are advised to contact the following organisations for the latest travel advice:

British Foreign and Commonwealth Office
Tel: (0845) 850 2829.
Website: www.fco.gov.uk

US Department of State
Website: http://travel.state.gov/travel

Accommodation

HOTELS:

The number of hotels has expanded in recent years; most are small- to medium-sized, and well equipped; the largest has 170 rooms. There are three hotels at the fringe of an area designated as a National Park. Information can be obtained from the Dominica Hotel and Tourism Association (website: www.dhta.org). There is a 10 per cent Government room tax added to hotel bills. **Grading:** Many of the hotels offer accommodation according to one of a number of 'Plans' widely used in the Caribbean; these include Modified American Plan (MAP), which consists of room, breakfast and dinner, and European Plan (EP), which consists of room only.

APARTMENTS/COTTAGES:

These offer self-catering, full service and maid service facilities and are scattered around the island.

GUEST HOUSES:

There is a variety of guest houses and inns around the island which offer a comfortable and very friendly atmosphere. There is a 5 per cent government tax and 10 per cent service charge on rooms.

CAMPING/CARAVANNING:

Facilities are available. Overnight safari tours are run by local operators.

YOUTH HOSTELS:

Facilities are available at Calibishie, Portsmouth and Rosaline. Prices vary.

Top Things To See & Do

- In February, enjoy the **Carnival** (*Mas Dominik*). This entails two weeks of celebrations, culminating in parades.
- Arrange a **jeep safari tour** to the hinterland of the country from **Roseau**, the main centre for visitors on the southwest coast.
- Dominica is characterised by a lush, green landscape and a mountainous interior covered in dense tropical forests. Some of the best **hiking** trails can be found in the **Morne Trois Pitons National Park**, which covers 7000 hectares (17,000 acres) in the south-central part of Dominica. Places of interest in the park include the (volcanic) **Boiling Lake**, the second-largest actively boiling lake in the world, which can be reached after a strenuous four-hour walk, and the **Emerald Pool**, **Middleham Falls**, **Sari Sari Falls**, **Trafalgar Falls**, **Freshwater Lake**, **Boeri**

Lake and the **Valley of Desolation**. The Dominican authorities adhere to strict nature conservation policies and a number of brochures, including special hiking guides, are recommended.

- **Cabrits Historical Park** was designated a park in 1987. Attractions include the **Cabrits Peninsula**, which contains the historical ruins of **Fort Shirley** and **Fort George**, 18th- and early 19th-century forts, and a museum at Fort Shirley.
- Discover the **Carib Indian Territory**, home to the only remaining Carib Indians in the Caribbean.
- Other places of interest include the **Sulphur Springs**, the **Central Forest Reserve**, **Botanical Gardens**, **Titou Gorge**, **L'Escalier Tête Chien**, several areas of rainforest and a variety of fauna and flora.
- There are good opportunities for **scuba-diving** and **snorkelling**, the latter being very popular in the **Soufrière** area, south of the capital Roseau, where volcanic cliffs drop into the sea. Visibility is usually up to 80m (263ft). Special diving excursions take visitors to the best spots. Divers need to have a certified diving qualification or be engaged in a training course conducted by one of the island's dive authorities. Spear fishing is prohibited and divers should also refrain from taking any living organism from the seabed or removing any artefacts from sunken wrecks. In some places you can reach good snorkelling sights by **kayaking** along the coast. Equipment may be hired through hotels and local tour operators.
- **Whale** and **dolphin watching** is on offer.
- The beaches are mainly black volcanic sand, but there are a few white-sand beaches on the northeast of the island. **Swimming** is possible in the sea or in the island's secluded rock pools, notably at **Trafalgar Falls**, **Emerald Pool** and **Titou Gorge**, where two hot springs filter into a rock pool fed by a river.
- There are facilities for **parasailing**, **windsurfing** and **water skiing** at coastal hotels. 15-minute parasailing flights are available for parties of four or more. Windsurfing boards may be hired. Speedboats can be hired for water skiing. **Motor boats** and **sailing boats** can also be chartered along the coast and **fishing charters** can be arranged for larger groups.

Entertainment

FOOD & DRINK: In general, it is wise to order the speciality of the house or of the day to ensure freshness. Island cooking includes Creole, Continental and American dishes. Food prices on Dominica are usually reasonable. Restaurants close at about midnight weekdays but are open later at weekends. Root vegetables, such as yams and turnips, are often referred to as 'provisions' on a menu. Local spirits, rum especially, are inexpensive. Wines (mainly French and Californian) are expensive. There is a wide choice of beers. There are no licensing hours.
National specialities:
- *Tee-tee-ree* (tiny freshly spawned fish).
- *Lambi* (conch).
- *Agouti* (a rodent).
- *Manicou* (small opossum).
- *Crab backs* (seasoned crab meat).
- *Bello Hot Pepper Sauce* is made locally and served everywhere with almost everything.
National drinks:
- Island fruit juices are excellent.
- Rum punches, particularly coconut rum punch (made from fresh coconut milk, sugar, rum, bitters, vanilla and grenadine).
- *Sea Moss* is a non-alcoholic beverage made from sea moss or seaweed, with a slightly minty taste.
Tipping: A 10 per cent service charge is added by most hotels and some restaurants. Other less touristic places do not add service to the bill and therefore tipping is discretionary; 10 to 15 per cent of the bill is acceptable. Taxi rates are set by law and taxi drivers do not expect tips.

NIGHTLIFE: Some hotel lounges stay open until 2300 and there is music at weekends at several hotels. A favourite haunt in Roseau, *La Robe Creole*, has dance music nightly with live bands at weekends. Popular local discos include *The Warehouse*, *Scorpio* and *Doubles International*. There are often folklore evenings with authentic costumes and music. Hotel staff will generally be able to advise visitors as to the best places.

SHOPPING: There is no duty free shopping, but there are some excellent buys to be found among local handicrafts including hats, bags and rugs made from vetiver grass joined with wild banana strands. The *Carib Reserve Crafts Centre* produces bags made from two layers of reeds that are buried in the ground to achieve a three-colour effect and covered with a layer of broad banana-type leaf to make them waterproof. **Shopping hours:** Mon-Fri 0800-1300 and 1400-1600, Sat 0800-1300.

Business

- **GDP**: US$282 million.
- **Main exports**: Bananas, soap, coconuts, grapefruit and galvanized sheets.
- **Main imports**: Foodstuffs, live animals, machinery, transport and mineral fuels.
- **Main trade partners**: UK, USA, Canada, Japan, Barbados and Guadeloupe.

ECONOMY: Much of the land is under cultivation, with bananas, coconuts, citrus fruits and cocoa as the main produce. The banana industry, which is the country's main export earner, has been under serious pressure following a World Trade Organization ruling outlawing the preferential access to its main European markets that Dominica had previously enjoyed. This, and the -1 per cent GDP rate have added urgency to the Government's efforts to diversify the country's economic base and improve the country's inadequate infrastructure. At present there is a little light industry producing vegetable oil, canned juices, cigarettes, soap and other consumer goods largely for domestic consumption. In the service sector, tourism initially developed rather more slowly in Dominica than elsewhere in the Caribbean but it has become a vital component of the economy. The government has lately sought to promote Dominica as an ecotourism hotspot. In recent years, the Government has also been trying to promote an offshore financial services industry; in a highly competitive market, it has enjoyed limited success. Dominica is a member of the Caribbean economic bloc CARICOM and of the Organisation of East Caribbean States.
BUSINESS ETIQUETTE: Businesspeople should usually dress smartly and dealings will be formal, initially at least.
Government office hours: Mon 0800-1300 and 1400-1700, Tue-Fri 0800-1300 and 1400-1600.

COMMERCIAL INFORMATION

Dominica Association of Industry and Commerce (DAIC)
PO Box 85, 6 Cross Lane, Roseau, Dominica (Commonwealth of)
E-mail: daic@marpin.dm

Dominican Republic

Location: Caribbean, island of Hispaniola, east of Cuba.

Time: GMT - 4.

Overview

Columbus discovered the island of Hispaniola (which he called La Espaniola) in 1492 and established it as his main base for the further exploration of the region. In 1697, the western part of the island came under French control, with the east remaining under Spanish control. In 1795, the city of Santo Domingo – the oldest city in the Americas, founded in 1496 by Columbus' brother, – was ceded to the French, followed by the rest of the island of Hispaniola later the same year. The battle of Palohincado, in 1808, in which Dominican General Ramirez inflicted an important defeat on the French, heralded the collapse of French rule in the eastern part of the island. The colony reverted to Spanish sovereignty in 1809, and in 1821, the colonial treasurer, José Nunez de Caceres, proclaimed Santo Domingo's independence. This independence was short-lived – in 1822, the Haitians invaded the colony and occupied it for 22 years, until, on 27 February 1844, the territory of Santo Domingo recovered its sovereignty and declared independence once again, this time permanently, as the Dominican Republic. Today, the Dominican Republic shares the island of Hispaniola with Haiti, a former French colony. Most tourists who come to the island are initially attracted by the magnificent golden sand beaches along its 1400 km (870-mile) coast line. The island's northern, Atlantic side contains the majority of tourist attractions, hotels and resorts, particularly in the 40-mile zone between Puerto Plata and Cabarete. Santo Domingo, in the south features the very first monuments of the American continent: the first cathedral, the first hospital, the first chapel and the first university. In the centre of the country, the three main mountain ranges run roughly parallel to each other in an easterly/westerly direction. The Cordillera Central is the highest mountain range on the island. It includes Pico Duarte, the highest mountain in the Caribbean at a height of 3,175m (over 10,000ft).

Western influence can be seen in the numerous colonial buildings of the capital Santo Domingo while the African heritage, when the Spanish brought African slaves to the island, is reflected in its music. The popular song and dance, the merengue, blends both heritages and is celebrated in several festivals which draw large numbers of national and international musicians.

General Information

AREA: 48,072 sq km (18,696 sq miles).

POPULATION: 9 million (UN estimate, 2005).

POPULATION DENSITY: 187.2 per sq km.

CAPITAL: Santo Domingo. **Population:** Approx 3 million.

GEOGRAPHY: The Dominican Republic is in the Caribbean, sharing the island of Hispaniola with Haiti and constituting the eastern two-thirds of land. The landscape is forested and mountainous, with valleys, plains and plateaux. The soil is fertile with excellent beaches on the north, southeast and east coasts, rising up to the mountains.

GOVERNMENT: Republic. Gained independence in 1865, after successive attempts. **Head of State and Government:** President Leonel Fernandez since 2004.

Recent history: The bicameral National Congress comprises the legislature. Members of both the 150-seat *Camara de Diputados* (Chamber of Deputies) and the 32-seat *Senado* (Senate) are popularly elected. So is the President, who wields executive power. All are elected for four-year terms. In the most recent elections, in 2004, Leonel Fernandez became President again after promising to reduce inflation, stabilise the exchange rate and restore investor confidence. He had already served as President in 1996.

LANGUAGE: Spanish is the official language. Some English and French are spoken.

RELIGION: Almost all Christian, with 95 per cent Roman Catholic; there are small Protestant and Jewish minorities.

ELECTRICITY: 110 volts AC, 60Hz. American-style two-pin plugs are in use.

SOCIAL CONVENTIONS: The Dominican lifestyle is more American than Latin, with short siestas without long, late lunches. The non-Latin ambience is reflected by the fact that, though the culture is rich in Roman Catholic and Spanish influences, 72-hour divorces may be obtained. Daytime dress is generally casual but beachwear and shorts are only acceptable in resorts and at pools; it is considered offensive to enter a church wearing shorts and a t-shirt. Evenings tend to be smarter, with jackets recommended for men at better restaurants, hotels and for social functions.

Climate

Hot with tropical temperatures all year with coastal areas being warmer than central regions. There are two rainy seasons; the first is from May to August and is the heaviest, whilst the second from November to December is the lightest. Hurricanes may sometimes occur during these periods.

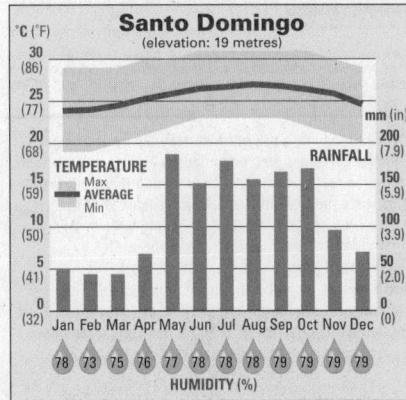

Communications

Telephone: Full IDD available. Country code: 1 809. CODETEL, Dominican Republic's telecommunications company, has produced the *Comunicard*, which enables tourists visiting the country to phone anywhere abroad from any touchtone phone. For further information, contact CODETEL, Av Tiradentes 1169, Santo Domingo (tel: 220 5168; website: www.codetel.net.do).

Mobile telephone: Roaming agreements exist with some international mobile phone companies.

Internet: There are Internet cafes in larger cities.

Post: Airmail takes about 10 days to reach western Europe. It is advisable to post all mail at the Central Post Office in Santo Domingo to ensure rapid handling.

MEDIA: Ownership of TV channels, radio stations and newspapers is concentrated in a few economically or politically powerful hands. There are several terrestrial TV channels and some 30 multichannel cable TV operators. There are more than 200 radio stations, most of them commercial. There are two government owned stations. The media are regulated by the government and are considered to be only partially free. Although the government rarely interferes with programmes, some subjects, such as the Catholic Church and the army, are generally avoided.

Press: All daily papers are in Spanish and include *El Caribe*, *Hoy*, *Listin Diario* and *El Nacional*. The English-language *Santo Domingo News* is published weekly on Wednesday and may be obtained in hotels. *Dominicana News*, a monthly Tourism Promotion Council publication, has the main Dominicana tourism industry items.

TV: *Radio Television Dominicana* (Canal 4) and *Rahintel* (Canal 7) are state-owned channels. Other channels include: *Color Vision* (Canal 9), *Canal 6*, *Telesistema* (Canal 11), *Teleantillas* (Canal 2) and *Cadena de Noticias (CDN)*, a news-based channel.

Radio: *Cadena de Noticias (CDN) Radio* is a news station; *Radio Television Dominicana* is Government-owned; *Rumba FM* is one of Santo Domingo's many merengue and salsa music stations.

Passport/Visa

	Passport Required?	Visa Required?	Return Ticket Required?
Full British	Yes	3	Yes
Australian	Yes	3	Yes
Canadian	Yes	3	Yes
USA	Yes	3	Yes
Other EU	Yes	3	Yes
Japanese	Yes	4	Yes

Note: *Regulations and requirements may be subject to change at short notice, and you are advised to contact the appropriate diplomatic or consular authority before finalising travel arrangements. Any numbers in the chart refer to the footnotes below.*

PASSPORTS: Passports valid for twice as long as the person will remain in the Dominican Republic required by all.

Note: These nationals will also require *Tourist Cards*, which may be purchased on arrival.

Tourist Cards: Issued to travellers visiting the Dominican Republic for touristic purposes for stays of up to two weeks. Tourist Cards can be applied for in advance at a cost of £8, or can be issued on arrival at a cost of US$10, though this can be a lengthy process. Extensions of up to three months are possible by visiting the Immigration Department in Santo Domingo; failure to do so will result in a surcharge at the airport upon departure.

Nationals of the following countries are eligible for a Tourist Card:

(a) **3.** nationals of the countries mentioned in the chart above (except nationals of Cyprus, Estonia, Latvia, Malta and Slovak Republic, who *do* need a visa);

(b) nationals of Andorra, Antigua & Barbuda, Aruba, The Bahamas, Barbados, Bolivia, Brazil, Costa Rica, Croatia, Curaçao, Dominica, El Salvador, French Guiana, Guadeloupe, Guatemala, Guyana, Honduras, Jamaica, Macedonia (Former Yugoslav Rep), Martinique, Mexico, Monaco, Norway, Paraguay, Puerto Rico, Reunion, St Kitts & Nevis, St Lucia,

A B C D E F G H I J K L M N O P Q R S T U V W X Y Z

St Maarten, St Vincent & the Grenadines, San Marino, Serbia & Montenegro, Surinam, Switzerland, Trinidad and Tobago, Turks & Caicos Islands, US Virgin Islands and Venezuela.
(c) Nationals of Ukraine and Russia for a limited time
Validity: 30 days.
Application to: Consulate (or Consular section at Embassy); see *Passport/visa information*.
Application requirements: (a) Photocopy of the photo page of the passport, containing personal details of the applicant. (b) Fee, payable by postal order or bank draft. Applicant's name and address must be written on the back. (c) Stamped, self-addressed A5 envelope for postal applications.
Note: Some foreign nationals with permanent legal residency in countries such as the UK need to get a note from the Embassy of the Dominican Republic, and may then be able to travel visa-free.
Working days required: Seven if application made via the post.
VISAS: Required by all except:
(a) holders of a Tourist Card;
(b) **4.** nationals of Argentina, Chile, Japan, Korea (Rep), Liechtenstein, Peru and Uruguay may enter the Dominican Republic without a visa or Tourist Card.
Note: In addition to a valid visa, nationals of China (PR) require an authorisation from the Director of the Migration/Immigration Department.
Types of visa and cost: *Tourist* (single entry): £100. *Business* (single entry): £170. There is no charge for visas for nationals of Italy, Mexico, Norway, Panama, Spain and the USA. *Student*: £60. (£30 (non-refundable) for each application form and the remainder is payable when the visa is approved.)
Validity: Tourist visas and single-entry business visas are valid for 60 days. Multiple-entry business visas are valid for up to one year.
Application to: Consulate (or Consular section at Embassy); see *Passport/Visa information*. Multiple entry visas can only be applied for once in the Dominican Republic.
Application requirements: (a) Passport, valid for at least four months from the date of application. (b) Completed application form. (c) Four passport-size photos. (d) Fee (payable by cash or postal order). (e) Three months of bank account statements, plus any other proof of sufficient funds. (f) Stamped, registered self-addressed envelope for postal applications. (g) Employer's or school's reference letter. *Tourist*: (a)-(g) and, (h) Flight itinerary and reservation. *Business*: (a)-(g) and, (h) Reference letter or letter of invitation from a company in the Dominican Republic. *Student*: (a)-(g) and, (h) Letter of request stating applicant's name, nationality and place of residence. (i) Acceptance letter from the university of centre of learning. (j) Certificate of good conduct or equivalent, issued no more than 30 days before application. (k) Certificate from the health authority of the applicant's country of residence.
Working days required: Two weeks. Approximately four weeks for visas which have to be referred to the authorities in the Dominican Republic, unless requested by fax (the cost of which must be paid by the applicant). In cases of emergency, documents may be processed in one working day. There is a £100 fee for this service.
Temporary residence: Consult the Consulate or consular section at the Embassy; see *Passport/Visa Information*.

PASSPORT/VISA INFORMATION

Embassy of the Dominican Republic in the UK
139 Inverness Terrace, Bayswater, London, W2 6JF, UK
Tel: (020) 7727 6285.
Website: www.dominicanembassy.org.uk
Opening hours: Mon-Fri 1000-1400.

Honorary Consulate of the Dominican Republic in the UK
539 Martin's Building, 4 Water Street, Liverpool, L2 3SX, UK
Tel: (0151) 236 0722.
Opening hours: Tues-Fri 0930-1230.

Embassy and Consulate of the Dominican Republic in the USA
1715 22nd Street, NW, Washington, DC 20008, USA
Tel: (202) 332 6280.
Website: www.domrep.org

Money

Currency: Dominican Republic Peso (DOP) = 100 centavos. Notes are in denominations of peso2000, 1000, 500, 100, 50, 20, 10 and 5. Coins are in denominations of peso1, and 50, 25, 10, 5 and 1 centavos.
Currency exchange: The peso is not available outside the Dominican Republic. Currencies of Canada, France, Germany, The Netherlands, Spain, Switzerland, UK and USA may be converted into local currency. On departure, up to 30 per cent of the exchanged currency can be reconverted into US Dollars at any bank, provided original receipts are shown. All exchange must be done through official dealers such as banks and hotels approved by the Central Bank. Some street vendors in touristic areas accept US dollars as legal tender.
Credit & debit cards: American Express, Diners Club, MasterCard and Visa are all accepted. Check with your credit or debit card company for details of merchant acceptability and other services which may be available.
Traveller's cheques: Traveller's cheques are accepted by some banks. To avoid additional exchange rate charges, travellers are advised to take traveller's cheques in US Dollars.
Currency restrictions: The import and export of local currency is limited to DOP20,000 in notes and DOP100 in coins; the import of foreign banknotes is allowed provided they are declared on arrival if they are over US$10,000 or the equivalent and reexport is intended. The import and export of traveller's cheques is unlimited.
Banking hours: Mon-Fri 0830-1700.
Exchange rate indicators:
Rate at time of publishing

£1.00=	DOP57.09
$1.00=	DOP32.50

Duty Free

The following goods may be imported into the Dominican Republic without incurring customs duty by travellers over 16 years of age:
200 cigarettes or one box of cigars; one litre of liquor; two bottles of perfume (opened) for personal use; gifts of up to US$100.
All baggage must be declared on arrival and departure.
Prohibited items: All animal products, agricultural and horticultural products and drugs.

Public Holidays

Below are listed Public Holidays for the January 2006-June 2007 period.
2006: Jan 1 New Year's Day. **Jan 6** Epiphany. **Jan 21** Our Lady of Altagracia. **Jan 26** Duarte's Birthday. **Feb 27** Independence Day. **Apr 14** Good Friday. **May 1** Labour Day. **Jun 15** Corpus Christi. **Aug 16** Restoration Day. **Sep 24** Our Lady of las Mercedes. **Nov 6** Constitution Day. **Dec 25** Christmas Day.
2007: Jan 1 New Year's Day. **Jan 6** Epiphany. **Jan 21** Our Lady of Altagracia. **Jan 26** Duarte's Birthday. **Feb 27** Independence Day. **Apr 6** Good Friday. **May 1** Labour Day. **Jun 7** Corpus Christi.

Health

	Special Precautions?	Certificate Required?
Yellow Fever	No	No
Cholera	No	No
Typhoid & Polio	1	N/A
Malaria	2	N/A

Note: *Regulations and requirements may be subject to change at short notice, and you are advised to contact your doctor well in advance of your intended date of departure. Any numbers in the chart refer to the footnotes below.*

1: *Typhoid* may be a risk in rural areas. Vaccination against typhoid and polio is recommended.
2: *Malaria* risk, exclusively in the malignant *falciparum* form, exists throughout the year in rural areas of the western provinces of Castañuelas, Hondo Valle and Pepillo Salcedo, which border Haiti. Chloroquine is the recommended prophylaxis.
Food & drink: All water should be regarded as being potentially contaminated and sterilisation should be considered essential. Water used for drinking, brushing teeth or making ice should have first been boiled or otherwise sterilised. Milk is pasteurised. Powdered or tinned milk is available. Only eat well-cooked meat and fish, preferably served hot. Pork, salad and mayonnaise may carry increased risk. Vegetables should be cooked and fruit peeled.
Other risks: *Bilharzia* (*schistosomiasis*) is endemic. Avoid swimming and paddling in fresh water; swimming pools which are well chlorinated and maintained are safe. *Diffuse cutaneous leishmaniasis* has been reported. *Hepatitis A* and *B* may occur. Outbreaks of *dengue fever* occur in the area. Longer-term travellers may contract *lymphatic filariasis*. *Rabies* may be present. For those at high risk, vaccination before arrival should be considered. If you are bitten, seek medical advice without delay. For more information, consult the *Health* appendix.
Health care: Health insurance (to include emergency repatriation) is strongly recommended. Medical care is limited and variable in quality. An emergency service is available in Santo Domingo.

Travel - International

AIR:
The Dominican Republic's national airline is *Air Santo Domingo (EX)*. *American Airlines* offers daily flights from London via Miami. Direct flights from the USA are operated by *American Airlines* (from New York) and *Continental Airlines* (from New Jersey). *Iberia* operates every day to Santo Domingo via Madrid. Other airlines operating flights from Europe are *Air Canada, Air France, Air Martinique, British Airways, BMI, Condor, Martinair, Spanair* and *Virgin Atlantic*.
Approximate flight times: From *London* to Santo Domingo is 11 hours (including stopover).
Main airports: *Santo Domingo (SDQ) (Internacional de las Americas)*, 18km (11 miles) east of the city (travel time - 30 minutes). *To/from the airport:* Taxi services are available to Santo Domingo. *Facilities:* Outgoing duty free shop, post office, bank/bureau de change, restaurants, bars and car hire.
Puerto Plata International Airport (POP) (Internacional General Gregorio Luperón). *Facilities:* Outgoing duty free shop, banking and exchange facilities, gift shop, post office, restaurant, bar and car hire.
Punta Cana International Airport (PUJ) is 10 to 30 minutes' travel time from the Punta Cana and Bávaro resorts. *Facilities:* Gift shops, duty free shop and taxi.
Departure tax: US$20 for a stay of up to two weeks and US$25 for more than two weeks. Passengers in direct transit and children under two years of age are exempt. A 'stay tax' is also levied on all passengers staying longer than three months: DOP60.48 (three to nine months); DOP100.80 (nine to 12 months) or DOP160.16 - DOP600.32 (one year or more).
Note: When buying an international air ticket in the Dominican Republic a tax of approximately 12 per cent is levied on the carrier by the Government. This expense is passed on directly to the customer on the price of the ticket. If the ticket is bought outside the Dominican Republic, there is no tax.
SEA:
Cruise lines calling at the Dominican Republic include *Holland America, Seabourn* and *Windjammer*.
ROAD:
There are three routes from Haiti: on the road from Port-au-Prince to Santo Domingo at Jimaní/Malpasse; on the road from Cap-Haitian to Santiago at Dajabón/Ouanaminthe; and a third route near the centre of the island at Elías Piñá/Belladere. The borders are open from 0800-1600.

Travel - Internal

AIR:
There are regular flights between Santo Domingo, Santiago, Samaná, Punta Cana and Puerto Plata by *Air Santo Domingo*. Planes may also be chartered. For more information, contact the airline directly.
ROAD:
Traffic drives on the right. There is a reasonable network of roads, including the *Sanchez Highway* running westwards from Santo Domingo to Elias Pina on the Haitian frontier; the *Mella Highway* extending eastwards from Santo Domingo to Higuey in the southeast and the *Duarte Highway* running north and west from Santo Domingo to Santiago and to Monte Cristi on the northwest coast. Not all roads in the Dominican Republic are all-weather and 4-wheel-drive vehicles are recommended for wet weather. Checkpoints near military installations are ubiquitous, though no serious difficulties have been reported (those near the Haitian border are most likely to be sensitive). The speed limit is up to 60kph (37.5mph) in cities and 80-100kph (50-62.5mph) on motorways. Driving at night is not recommended because of poor lighting and and signage. Keep doors and windows locked at all times and seatbelts are required to be worn. **Bus:** Cheap and efficient air-conditioned bus and coach services run from the capital to other major towns. **Taxi:** Travellers are recommended to hire tourist taxis or radio taxis that can be arranged in advance. Avoid unmarked taxis. **Car hire:** There are several car hire companies in Santo Domingo. Minimum age for car hire is 25. A credit card is required for car hire transactions. Insurance is compulsory. **Documentation:** A national or International Driving Permit is accepted, but is only valid for 90 days.
URBAN:
Santo Domingo has flat-fare bus and minibus services, and an estimated 7000 share-taxis called *Carro de Conchos*. These operate a 24-hour service in Santo Domingo, Santiago and Puerto Plata. Hotel taxis are also available. In old Santo Domingo, the streets are narrow with blind corners, so care should be

taken, particularly as Dominican drivers have a tendency to use their horns rather than their brakes. Horse-drawn carriages are available for rent in tourist areas for tours around parks and plazas.

Travel times: The following chart gives approximate travel times (in hours and minutes) from **Santo Domingo** to other major cities and towns in the Dominican Republic.

	Air	Road
Puerto Plata	0.45	3.15
Samaná	0.35	3.30
La Romana	0.25	3.30
Barahona	-	3.30

Credit: ©The Dominican Republic Tourist Board

Travel Advice

Most visits to the Dominican Republic are trouble-free but there has been an increase in violent crime.

Travellers should also should be aware of the global risk of indiscriminate international terrorist attacks, which could be against civilian targets, including places frequented by foreigners.

This advice is based on information provided by the Foreign and Commonwealth Office in the UK. It is correct at time of publishing. As the situation can change rapidly, visitors are advised to contact the following organisations for the latest travel advice:

British Foreign and Commonwealth Office
Tel: (0845) 850 2829.
Website: www.fco.gov.uk

US Department of State
Website: http://travel.state.gov/travel

Accommodation

HOTELS:

Following a period of intensive development, the Dominican Republic now boasts over 55,000 hotel rooms, making it the largest room supply in the entire Caribbean. The southeast coast is noted for its modern hotels and beautiful beaches. In the capital the choice ranges from clean and cheap to plush, with rates remaining the same all year because of steady business traffic. At resort hotels winter prices are higher and, in summer, prices drop by up to 10 per cent. Hotels outside Santo Domingo and La Romana are considerably less expensive, whatever the season. A service charge of 10 per cent and a 12 per cent sales tax will be added to all bills.
Grading: There is a **5-star** grading system, but visitors should note that even the highest grade is somewhat lower in standard than is general in the Caribbean.

GUEST HOUSES:

Guest houses are very economical, and best found after arrival in the country

SELF-CATERING:

Self-catering establishments are available in Puerto Plata at very reasonable rates.

CAMPING:

There are no official sites. Camping is only possible in rural areas with permission from the landowner. National Parks are also available for camping with the permission of the National Parks Office.

ACCOMMODATION INFORMATION

Asociación Nacional de Hoteles y Restaurantes (ASONAHORES)
Calle President Gonzalez esq, Avenida Tiradentes, Edificio la Cumbre, Santo Domingo, Dominican Republic
Tel: 540 4676.
Website: www.drhotels.com

Top Things To See

- Appreciate the charm of colonial **Santo Domingo**, which is home to the first university, cathedral and hospital built in the New World. The modern city of Santo Domingo, by contrast, is a thriving port city, equipped with discos, gambling casinos, shops and the **Cultural Plaza**, which houses the **Gallery of Modern Art** and the **National Theatre**.
- Just a few miles east of the city is a remarkable cave complex, **Los Tres Ojos de Agua (The Three Eyes of Water)**, so-called because it contains three turquoise lagoons on three different levels, each fed by an underground river and surrounded by countless stalactites, stalagmites and lush tropical vegetation.
- To the west of Santo Domingo is **San Cristóbal**, where the first constitution was signed on 6 November 1844. It features **historical sites** linked to the life of **Trujillo**, the dictator who governed the country with an iron fist from 1930-61.
- Stop at the ruins of the colonial city in **Pueblo Viejo**.

- The **Amber Coast** (northern coast), is so-named because some of the most beautiful amber in the world is mined here. The **Amber Museum** houses a good display of amber pieces found in this area.
- Pay a visit to **Fort San Felipe,** built in the 1600s by the Spanish to protect the settlement from pirates.
- Discover colonial architecture in **Puerto Plata** (the **Silver Port**) founded in 1504.
- See beathtaking views of the Atlantic and the port of Puerto Plata from **Mount Isabel de Torres** where a cable car climbs over 760m (2500ft) above sea level. ten sq km (4 sq miles) of botanical gardens can also be explored here.

Top Things To Do

- Join the locals in celebrating the patron saint's day with drums and dance rituals in the church and **Caves of Santa Maria**.
- Near **Punta Cana**, visit the **Manatí Park**, a theme park which includes a zoo, gardens, a recreated **Taino village** and a variety of exotic animals; visitors have the opportunity to swim with dolphins.
- Alternatively, go to **Cabritos Island**, a national park in the centre of **Lake Enriquillo**, which is the greatest preserve of the wild American Crocodile, has large populations of flamingos and two species of iguana.
- The Atlantic coast of the country is renowned for its miles of unspoilt beaches that surround **Puerto Plata**, the most popular being **Sosúa. Windsurfing** and **diving** are particularly good here. **Boat trips** to the marine caves of the **Gri Gri Lagoon** near Sosúa are a popular tourist attraction. Just 3km (2 miles) from Sosua is the **Playa Dorada** resort complex. Just outside, in Puerto Plata, is the **Costambar Beach Resort**, with 5km (3 miles) of beach. **Río San Juan** is a lovely resort town, which has not yet been reached by mass tourism. Discover **Playa Grande** (with a few resorts under construction) and the beautiful **Playa El Caletón**.
- You can also dive in **Cabrera** (freshwater cave diving with an underground lake) and **Las Terrenas**; **Punta Rucia** (good for coral diving); **La Caleta National Underwater Park** (accessible by boat from Boca Chica); **Catalina** and **Saona islands** (accessible by boat from La Romana); and **Barahona** (an area currently being developed for ecotourism). Experienced divers can also join the North Caribbean Research Group and participate in a government-funded project to recover and remove artefacts from sunken ships, some dating back to the 16th century. Snorkelling and diving equipment can be borrowed or hired from dive operators and resort hotels.
- The **Samaná Peninsula** is located on the northern portion of the island. **Samaná**, with its transparent blue waters, miles of unspoilt beaches, and dozens of caves, is a romantic paradise. Other resorts include **The Gran Bahía Beach Resort**, **Cayo Levantado** and **El Portillo Beach Club**.
- Go **offshore fishing** for marlin, sailfish, dorado, bonito and other game fish. Hotels can organise charter boats for visitors. **River fishing** in flat-bottomed boats with guides can be arranged at **Boca de Yuma** and on the north coast.
- Enjoy the understated elegance and graceful charm of the 28 sq km (7000-acre) **Casa de Campo** resort, designed by Oscar de la Renta in the city of **La Romana**. Nestled within the resort is **Altos de Chavón**, a reconstructed 15th-century Mediterranean-style village of culture and art which is perched high on a cliff overlooking the tropical Chavón River and the Caribbean Sea. Here, you can attend an event in a 5000-seat **Greek amphitheatre**, built in the traditional design of Epidaurus.
- **Whitewater rafting** is available on the **Río Yaque del Norte** in Jarabacoa. The best places for **tubing**, in which participants individually float down the rapids in oversized rubber tubes, are on the **Río Jamao del Norte**, the **Río Yaque del Norte** and the **Río Isabela** in Santo Domingo.

- **Cascading** involves climbing up to the top of a waterfall and rapelling down the cascade tied to a rope; the best places to do this are **Cascada del Limón**, **Cascada Ojo de Agua**, **El Salto de Baiguate** and **El Salto de Jimenoa**.
- **Hiking** and **climbing** enthusiasts may join the locals' annual pilgrimage to the Caribbean's highest mountain, the **Pico Duarte** (3210m/10,700ft), which they can conquer either on foot or by riding a mule. Similar tours can also be made at **El Mogote**, **Mount Isabel de Torres**, **Pico Yaque** and, in the southwest, the **Sierra de Bahoruco**.
- Watch a game of **baseball**, which is not only the national sport, but also a national obsession, and even the smallest communities have floodlit stadiums. The centre of the country's baseball is the industrial seaport of **San Pedro de Macoris**. The professional winter season runs from October to January. Visitors should ask local people or look in the local paper for schedules and the nearest game.
- Following on from the *42nd Caribbean Golf Championships*, which were held in the Dominican Republic in 1998, the country continues to actively promote itself as a major international golf destination. Some of the best courses can be found at **Casa de Campo, Dientes de Perro (Teeth of the Dog), Gran Diablo Links, Playa Dorada** (designed by Robert Trent Jones), **La Romana Country Club**, and **Santo Domingo Country Club**. For more information, contact the Federation of Dominican Golf (FEDOGOLF), Aut. Duarte KM 201, Santo Domingo (tel: 231 4719 *or* 4720; website: www.golfdominicano.com).

TOURIST INFORMATION

Secretaría de Estado de Turismo (Ministry of Tourism)
Street address: Avenida México esq, 30 de Marzo, Oficinas Gubernanentales Bloque B, Santo Domingo, Dominican Republic
Postal address: Apdo 497, Santo Domingo, Dominican Republic
Tel: 221 4660.
Website: www.dominicana.com.do

Dominican Republic Tourist Board in the UK
18-21 Hand Court, High Holborn, London WC1V 6JF, UK
Tel: (020) 7242 7778.
Website: www.dominicanrepublic.com

Caribbean Tourism Organisation in the UK
22 The Quadrant, Richmond, Surrey, TW9 1BP, UK
Tel: (020) 8948 0057.
Website: www.caribbean.co.uk

Dominican Republic Tourist Board in the USA
136 East 57th Street, Suite 803, New York, NY 10022, USA
Tel: (212) 588 1012.
Website: www.dominicanrepublic.com

Entertainment

FOOD & DRINK: Native Dominican cooking combines Spanish influences with local produce. Beef is expensive (Dominicans raise fine cattle, but most is exported) and local favourites are pork and goat meat. Locally produced beer and rums are cheaper than imported alcohol which tends to be expensive. There is plenty of fresh fish and seafood, island-grown tomatoes, lettuce, papaya, mangoes and passion fruit and all citrus fruits are delicious.

National specialities:
- *La bandera* (meaning 'the flag', comprising white rice, red beans, stewed meat, salad and fried plaintain).
- *Chicharrones* (crisp pork rind).
- *Chicharrones de pollo* (small pieces of fried chicken).
- *Casava* (fried yucca).

- *Moro de habichuelas* (rice and beans).
- *Sopa criolla dominicana* (native soup of meat and vegetables).
- *Pastelón* (baked vegetable cake).
- *Sancocho* (stew with anything up to 18 ingredients).

National drinks:

- *Presidente* (Dominican beer) is very good
- Rum drinks such as the local *Brugal* or *Bermudez*.
- *Rum añejo* (old, dark rum) with ice makes a good after-dinner drink. Native coffee is excellent and very strong.

Tipping: Hotel and restaurant bills automatically include a 10 per cent service charge (on top of a 12 per cent charge for tax purposes) but an additional tip may be given as an appreciation of good service. Taxi drivers on the fixed routes do not expect tips.

NIGHTLIFE: Choice varies from a Las Vegas-style revue, discos and casinos to a quiet cafe by the sea in Santo Domingo. Hotels offer more traditional shows, including folk music and dancing. Popular dances are the *merengue*, played very loudly almost everywhere; *bachata*, which is becoming very popular in tourist hotspots; *perico ripiao*; and the *salsa. The Malecón*, Santo Domingo's seaside boulevard is known fo its nightlife. Concerts and other cultural events are often held at the *Casa de Francia* and *Plaza de la Cultura* in Santo Domingo, among other venues.

SHOPPING: Best buys are products made on the island including amber jewellery and decorative pieces. These are a national speciality, some pieces encasing insects, leaves or dew drops within ancient petrified pine resin. Larimar or Dominican turquoise is another popular stone. Milky blue and polished pink pieces of conch shell are also made into jewellery. Rocking chairs, woodcarvings, macramé, pottery, Taino artefacts, Creole dolls, baskets, limestone carvings and CDs of salsa and merengue also make good buys. Bargaining is recommended. **Shopping hours:** Mon-Sat 0800-1200 and 1430-1830.

Business

- **GDP:** US$55.68 billion.
- **Main imports:** Food, petroleum, cotton and fabric, chemicals and pharmaceuticals.
- **Main exports:** Ferronickel, sugar, gold, silver, coffee, cocoa, tobacco, meats and consumer goods.
- **Main trade partners:** Canada, Colombia, Japan, Mexico, Korea (Rep), Netherlands, USA and Venezuela.

ECONOMY: Sugar, coffee and cocoa are the main agricultural cash crops. The mining industry produces ferro nickel, gold and silver. These primary products are the basis of the Dominican Republic's economy and its main export commodities. Exploration of other potential deposits has been underway since the early 1990s but, although some gold and silver has been located, the expected oil deposits have failed to materialise. Industry is mainly concentrated in production of food and drinks, chemicals and refining of imported oil. In the service sector, tourism has had a major impact on the Dominican Republic's economy during the last 20 years and now contributes one-sixth of total output. The economy grew slowly but steadily during most of this period, but has recently experienced some problems. Growth turned negative in 2004 and unemployment rose to 16.5 per cent, while the Dominican peso has lost a third of its value against the dollar. (A major cause is the collapse of the international sugar market.) The country relies on substantial foreign aid, principally from the USA and the Inter-American Development Bank. The Dominican Republic is a member of CARICOM, the major regional reading bloc.

BUSINESS ETIQUETTE: It is usual for businesspeople to dress smartly and to deal formally with each other at first, although the general atmosphere is informal. Some formal events may require wearing a tuxedo or a white suit. Spanish is the main business language and a knowledge of it will be of assistance. Enquire at your hotel for interpreter services. **Office hours:** Mon-Sat 0800-1200 and 1400-1800. **Government office hours:** Mon-Fri 0800-1500.

COMMERCIAL INFORMATION

Cámara de Comercio y Producción de Santo Domingo
Apartado Postal 815, Arz. Nouel 206, Santo Domingo, Dominican Republic
Tel: 682 2688.
Website: www.ccpsd.org.do

East Timor

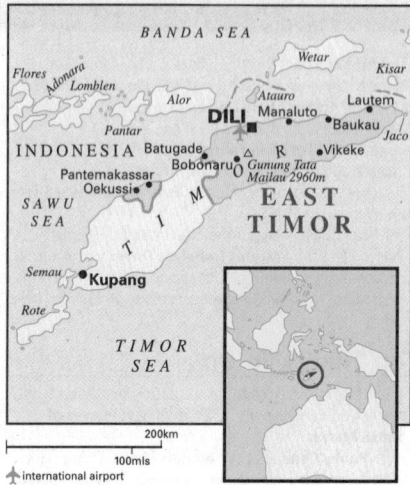

Location: South-East Asia.

OFFICIAL NAME OF COUNTRY: The Democratic Republic of Timor-Leste.

Time: GMT + 9.

Due to the fact that East Timor only became fully independent on 20 May 2002 and the fact that the UN is still playing a significant role in the running of the country, some information and details, including diplomatic representation, may be unclear or impossible to obtain at the time of writing.

Overview

In May 2002, after 450 years of continuous foreign occupation, East Timor became the world's newest independent state. However, East Timor's road to independence was long and traumatic.

The Portuguese first arrived on the island in the early 16th century and by the 1550s had occupied the eastern part. The Dutch took control of the western part, which became part of the Dutch East Indies and, after independence, Indonesia.

In 1975, the new left-wing Portuguese Government relinquished all of its colonies. East Timor then enjoyed just a few days of independence, before the Indonesians annexed it as their 27th province. There was little local resistance and the international community largely acquiesced. The main Timorese independence movement, FRETILIN (Frente Revolucionario de Este Timor Independente), which was originally formed to fight the Portuguese, now had to gear up again to combat a new and even more brutal occupier. In the savage counter-insurgency campaign that followed, the Indonesian army killed over 100,000 East Timorese. It was not until the 1997 Asian economic crisis and the subsequent removal of veteran Indonesian President Suharto (see *Indonesia* section) that the growing international criticism of the Indonesian campaign began to have some effect. In June 1999, President Habibie of Indonesia announced that a referendum would be held in East Timor, offering independence or autonomy within Indonesia. The referendum was held in August 1999 and 80 per cent opted for independence. By way of revenge, the Indonesian army, along with local militias that they had armed and financed, indulged in an orgy of destruction and killing that displaced hundreds of thousands of people and destroyed the territory's already fragile economic base.

In October 1999, a UN transitional administration (UNTAET) was set up in East Timor, pending the conduct of national elections. The new country faced a massive reconstruction task and the government has found it difficult to deliver on many of its initial promises.

Colonial architecture, Portuguese fortresses and other remains from the 100-year-long Portuguese occupation can be found all over the country. However, many towns and villages were destroyed during the Indonesian occupation and the fighting in 1999, and these are only slowly being rebuilt. Many houses are still built on stilts in the traditional way, using materials such as grass, bamboo and tree trunks.

General Information

AREA: 14,609 sq km (5735 sq miles). Disputes over land boundaries have yet to be resolved so this figure may change.

POPULATION: 857,000 (UN, 2005).

POPULATION DENSITY: 58.66 per sq km.

CAPITAL: Dili. **Population:** 167,777 (2004).

GEOGRAPHY: East Timor makes up the eastern half of the island of Timor (the western half belongs to Indonesia) which is situated off the northern coast of Western Australia. Also included within East Timor is the Oekussi Ambeno enclave on the northwest coast of the island, as well as the islands of Ataúro (Pulo Cambing) and Jaco (Pulo Jako). East Timor is mountainous in the interior.

GOVERNMENT: Republic. Declared full independence 20 May 2002 after the UN Transitional Authority in East Timor (UNTAET) had run the country for nearly three years during its transition to independence. Prior to UNTAET, the country had been under Indonesian control since 1975. **President:** Xanana Gusmao since May 2002. **Prime Minister:** Mari Alkatiri since May 2002. **Recent history:** East Timor is governed according to a constitution agreed between UNTAET and the provisional East Timorese government in March 2002. This allows for an 88-member Parliament, the *Assembleia Constituinte*, which holds legislative authority and is elected to serve a five-year term – 75 members are elected by proportional representation, the other 13 in single-seat constituencies. Executive power is vested in the President, who is also elected for a five-year term.

The United Nations Mission of Support in East Timor (UNMISET) was established by UN Security Council Resolution 1410, initially until May 2002 but later extended to May 2003, to assist the East Timorese government with core administrative functions, and to provide interim internal and external security. The United Nations Security Council (UNSC) agreed in May 2004 to further extend the mandate of UNMISET for a period of six months, with a view to subsequently extending the mandate for a further and final period of six months, until May 2005. In May 2005, the UN Security Council passed resolution 1599 establishing a UN Office in Timor Leste (UNOTIL) with a mandate until 20 May 2006.

LANGUAGE: Tetum is the main dialect and is the official language along with Portuguese; English is often used for administrative purposes (due to the high numbers of English-speaking relief and UN workers still working in East Timor). More than 30 other languages are also used in East Timor.

RELIGION: Christian majority with 86 per cent Catholic. Islam and animist beliefs are also practised.

ELECTRICITY: 220 V, 50 Hz. Electricity supplies may be erratic with many power cuts.

SOCIAL CONVENTIONS: Most social courtesies are fairly formal. Many conventions will be similar to those of Indonesia (despite their political and religious differences) and many old East Timorese conventions will doubtless come to the fore in the coming years.

Climate

Tropical monsoon climate. It is very hot and dry from July to November with the western monsoon bringing the rains from December to March. It is cooler and more humid in the mountain region.

Required clothing: Lightweights with rainwear throughout the year. Warmer clothes are needed for cool evenings and mountain areas.

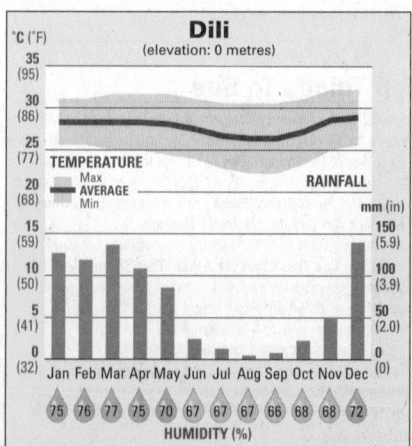

Communications

Telephone: International calls can be made from and to Dili. The code for Dili is 390.

Mobile telephone: Coverage provided by *Timor Telecom International* in and around Dili and other main urban areas. International roaming agreements are stilll being set up but cannot be relied upon as yet. In some parts of the country, however, telephone communication may still only be possible with satellite telephones.

Internet: Facilities are not generally available to the public at the present time but VPM Internet Services (www.vpm.com) does operate in the country.

Post: A limited postal service does exist.

MEDIA: East Timor's national public radio and TV services began broadcasting in May 2002 when the country gained independence, replacing the interim broadcasting services operated by the UN. Public radio services are said to reach some 90% of the population; public TV has a smaller coverage. Community radio stations have played a key role in the process of national reconstruction. Many of the stations receive funding, training and equipment from international agencies and organisations.

Press: East Timor has two daily newspapers, *Suara Timor Lorosae* and the *Timor Post*, and a number of weekly titles including *Jornal Nacional Semanario*.

TV: *Televisao de Timor Leste (TVTL)* is public.

Radio: *Radio Nacional de Timor Leste (RTL)* is public; *Radio Falintil/Voz da Esperanca* is a community station which began life as a clandestine station operated by East Timor rebels; *Radio Timor Kmanek (RTK)* is a Catholic Church radio. *BBC World Service* programmes in English and Portuguese are available in Dili on FM frequencies.

Passport/Visa

	Passport Required?	Visa Required?	Return Ticket Required?
Full British	Yes	1	Yes
Australian	Yes	1	Yes
Canadian	Yes	1	Yes
USA	Yes	1	Yes
Other EU	Yes	1	Yes
Japanese	Yes	1	Yes

Note: *Regulations and requirements may be subject to change at short notice, and you are advised to contact the appropriate diplomatic or consular authority before finalising travel arrangements. Any numbers in the chart refer to the footnotes below.*

Note: Potential travellers are advised against all non-essential travel to East Timor and to monitor the situation regularly. The following visa information was obtained from the UK Foreign and Commonwealth website.

PASSPORTS: Passports must be valid for at least six months beyond the intended date of departure from East Timor.

VISAS: 1. Visas are currently not necessary as long as travellers have a valid passport. Upon arrival, an entry permit valid for 30 days will be issued. If the traveller can prove that he/she has valid grounds for staying in East Timor, they can then obtain an extension.

Types of visa and cost: From 19 April 2003, East Timor began to charge a fee for visas issued on arrival. They cost US$30 for stays of 30 days and less; extensions cost US$30 for each subsequent period of 30 days. Fines of US$50 apply to each 30-day period if advance payment and extension of visas have not been sought and approved. There is a US$10 fee for airport tax, paid at the airport on the day of departure.

> **PASSPORT/VISA INFORMATION**
>
> **Embassy of East Timor in Belgium**
> Avenue de Cortenbergh, Cortenberghlaan 12, 1040 Brussels, Belgium
> Tel: (2) 280 0096.
>
> **Embassy of East Timor in the USA**
> 3415 Massachusetts Avenue, NW, Washington, DC 20007, USA
> Tel: (202) 965 1515.

Money

Currency: The US Dollar (US$) is the official currency. For local transactions, the Indonesian Rupiah (IDR) may be accepted in border areas, but this should not be relied on.

Currency exchange: Travellers should take plenty of cash. Both the Australian ANZ bank and the Portuguese Banco Nacional Ultramarino have branches in Dili. Cirrus/Maestro credit cards can be used to withdraw US Dollars from an ATM. Banks will not exchange Pounds Sterling.

Credit & debit cards: These can only currently be used in the very few expensive hotels in East Timor. Check with your credit or debit card company for further details of merchant acceptability and other services which may be available.

Traveller's cheques: Travellers cheques are not widely exchangeable. Only some top-of-the-range hotels may be able to exchange them.

Currency restrictions: Import is allowed, although amounts of US$5000 and above must be declared.

Banking hours: Mon-Fri 0930-1530.

Exchange rate indicators:

Rate at time of publishing

£1.00= US$1.76

Duty Free

Information not available at the time of writing.

Public Holidays

Below are listed Public Holidays for the January 2006-June 2007 period.

2006: Jan 1 New Year's Day. **Apr 14** Good Friday. **May 20** Independence Day. **Aug 15** Assumption. **Aug 30** Consultation Day. **Sep 20** Liberation Day. **Nov 1** All Saints' Day. **Nov 12** Santa Cruz Day (memorial day for the 1991 massacre in the cemetery of the Santa Cruz church). **Dec 8** Immaculate Conception. **Dec 25** Christmas Day.
2007: Jan 1 New Year's Day. **Apr 6** Good Friday. **May 20** Independence Day.

Health

	Special Precautions?	Certificate Required?
Yellow Fever	No	1
Cholera	Yes	2
Typhoid & Polio	3	N/A
Malaria	4	N/A

Note: *Regulations and requirements may be subject to change at short notice, and you are advised to contact your doctor well in advance of your intended date of departure. Any numbers in the chart refer to the footnotes below.*

1: A *yellow fever* vaccination certificate is advisable for travellers coming from infected areas. The countries and areas included in the yellow fever endemic zones are considered by East Timor as infected areas. For a map of yellow fever endemic zones, see the *Health* appendix.

2: Following WHO guidelines issued in 1973, a *cholera* vaccination certificate is no longer a condition of entry to East Timor. However, cholera is a serious risk in this country and precautions are essential. Up-to-date advice should be sought before deciding whether these precautions should include vaccination as medical opinion is divided over its effectiveness; see the *Health* appendix.

3: *Poliomyelitis* is endemic. *Typhoid* occurs frequently.

4: *Malaria* risk exists throughout the year. Some resistance to chloroquine has been reported.

Other risks: *Dengue fever* (there was a particularly large outbreak of this in 2005) and *Japanese encephalitis* occur. *Tuberculosis* and *hepatitis A* are prevalent and *rabies* may also be present.

Food & drink: All water should be regarded as a potential health risk. Water used for drinking, brushing teeth or making ice should have first been boiled or otherwise sterilised. Milk is unpasteurised and should be boiled. Powdered or tinned milk is available and is advised, but make sure that it is reconstituted with pure water. Avoid dairy products that are likely to have been made from unboiled milk. Only eat well-cooked meat and fish, preferably served hot. Salad and mayonnaise may carry increased risk. Vegetables should be cooked and fruit peeled.

Health care: Medical services in East Timor are extemely limited. There are currently no optical or dental services. It is essential to take out comprehensive medical and travel insurance which includes emergency repatriation cover.

Travel - International

AIR:

Airnorth (4N) (website: www.airnorth.com.au) flies daily from Darwin, Australia to Dili.
Approximate flight times: From *Darwin* to Dili is one hour 45 minutes.

Main airports: *Comoro Airport (DIL)*, Dili. Some international flights use *Baucau Airport (BCH)* in the province of Baucau.

Departure tax: US$10.

ROAD:

The border crossings at Batugede and Oesilo, into Indonesian West Timor, are open. Roads and driving conditions are very poor (including in Dili) and drivers must take extreme caution. Travellers need a valid driver's licence or permit either from their country or issued in East Timor, and detailing which class of vehicle they are entitled to drive. Third-party motor vehicle insurance is not available.

Travel - Internal

SEA:

There is one weekly barge between Oekusi and Dili, carrying both freight and passengers.

ROAD:

Most of the buses that existed prior to 1999 were destroyed in the fighting; the few that survived are in very bad technical shape and chronically overcrowded. The roads are generally in very bad condition and driving can be very hazardous. Car hire is available in Dili. Mountain bikes may be a viable form of transport outside of the capital. *Mikrolets* are the main transport in East Timor as they are extremely cheap. These are mini-vans converted into people carriers.

TAXI: Taxis are available in Dili. Be sure to negotiate a price before travelling.

Travel Advice

East Timor shares with other countries in South East Asia a threat from terrorism. Attacks could be indiscriminate and against civilian targets. Travellers should avoid demonstrations and large crowds should be avoided. Travellers should consult their local embassy before travelling to border areas, as there remains the potential for trouble there.

This advice is based on information provided by the Foreign and Commonwealth Office in the UK. It is correct at time of publishing. As the situation can change rapidly, visitors are advised to contact the following organisations for the latest travel advice:

British Foreign and Commonwealth Office
Tel: (0845) 850 2829.
Website: www.fco.gov.uk

US Department of State
Website: http://travel.state.gov/travel

Accommodation

HOTELS AND MOTELS:

Hotel rooms and other accommodation are still very limited and very expensive, especially for independent travellers. A Government tax of 12 per cent is added to all bills.

APARTMENTS AND SELF CATERING:

Available in Dili only. Expect to pay high prices.

YOUTH HOSTELS:

Youth hostels are popular in East Timor and are widely available.

CAMPING AND CARAVANNING:

Camping/Caravanning are unavailable at present.

Top Things To See & Do

- Along with a **Portuguese castle** dating from 1627, discover abundant colonial architecture in **Dili,** the capital of Portuguese East Timor, and today the administrative capital of the new country. Another attraction is the **State Museum of East Timor**, founded in 1995, with one-tenth of its collection still surviving. The collection includes religious woodcarvings, wood figures, traditional crafts, musical instruments and paintings. Most of the city was destroyed in 1999, with any surviving buildings bearing considerable war wounds. UNTAET led restoration works by rebuilding the most important government and official buildings. There are many **catholic churches** in Dili and a famous, large statue of Christ on a hilltop near **Cape Fatucama**.

- Despite the devastation it has incurred, visitors will enjoy the charm of **Baucau**, the second-largest city in East Timor. The city boasts Portuguese colonial architecture and caves used by the Japanese during the occupation in World War II.

- Relax on the beach. Outside Dili, there are numerous beautiful beaches, the most popular being **Areia Branca** ('white sand'). Due to its location, Baucau is always comfortably cool and the **beaches** 5km (3 miles) from the city are breathtaking. The four-hour journey between Dili and Baucau is well worth taking, offering some of the finest coastal views.

- **Oecussi province** belongs to East Timor politically, yet is a part of Indonesian West Timor culturally and geographically; it was 95 per cent destroyed during the fighting and the remaining inhabitants mostly live in small hamlets and villages. Its capital, **Pantemakassar**, was the first Portuguese settlement and, as such, has special meaning for the East Timorese. A sleepy little town, it lies between the coast and the mountains. Coral reefs off the nearby coast offer the opportunity for **diving** and **snorkelling**. **Mountain biking** and **hiking** are possible in the interior or in the mountains.

- Head for **Com**, a beautiful **fishing village**, popular for weekend getaways. The main activities are fishing and snorkelling. The 20 sublime rooms of the Com Beach Resort, are a sign of things to come, with talk of a real five-star resort being developed in the future.
- **Fatsuba** is a notable reminder of the Portuguese period, with an old garrison that overlooks the town of Pantemakassar from a hill. In front of the mountain, in a courtyard, is a little coral grotto which houses a statue of the Virgin Mary.
- In **Maubara,** visit the 17th century **fort**. The fort once a prison, has a substantial coastal wall that faces the sea with cannons pointing out.

TOURIST INFORMATION

Turismo de Timor-Leste (East Timor Government Tourism Office)
Ministry of Development, Apartado 194, Dili, East Timor
Tel: (3) 310 371 *or* 339 178.
Website: www.turismotimorleste.com

Entertainment

FOOD & DRINK: The staple diet for most East Timorese is similar to that of Indonesians – rice and spices – although, there may well be difficulty in obtaining a variety of foods outside main urban areas due to the unstable political situation, the financial situation of many of the people and internal logistical difficulties. In Dili, there are a number of restaurants and cafes serving western cuisine, catering to the foreigners living and working there.

National specialities:
- Fish (preferably fried, with delicacsies being prawns).
- Curries (chicken is a favourite).
- Authentic Chinese, Japanese and Portuguese dishes.

National drinks:
- Coffee (East Timor coffee is very high in caffeine, organically grown and renowned for its sharp flavour).
- Beer.

Tipping: There is no service charge added to bills, but if the service calls for it, a 10 per cent tip is sufficient.

NIGHTLIFE: There are numerous bars and nightclubs in Dili, with many on the beachfront. All are open late, and serve food as well as drinks. Try the *Poy Cholor* for food service until 0500, a live band and a DJ. If you are looking for something more adventurous then the *Caz* bar hires kayaks for late night fun, while a barbecue cooks fried fish.

SHOPPING: Batik and embroidered fabrics in traditional patterns and colours are a good souvenir; woodcarvings and silverwork.

Business

- **GDP:** US$370 million.
- **Main exports:** Coffee, sandlewood and timber.
- **Main imports:** Petroleum, foodstuffs, and construction material.
- **Main trade partners:** Indonesia and Australia.

ECONOMY: Subsistence agriculture, forestry and fishing sustain most of the population. The sole export products are coffee beans, timber and sandalwood. The economy as a whole was chronically underdeveloped as a result of centuries of neglect by the Portuguese. The Indonesians built some basic infrastructure (roads, power, telecommunications), but most of that was destroyed or removed by the Indonesians themselves and their client militias in the aftermath of the August 1999 vote for independence. Since then, East Timor's principal source of income has been international aid. However, the country's originally poor economic prospects have been transformed by the discovery of large oil and gas fields in the Timor Sea, which lies between Timor itself and the north coast of Australia. Under the terms of a deal negotiated between East Timor and the Australian government, the East Timorese will receive a fixed income of around US$180 million from 2006. (Additional oil and gas deposits have also been discovered in the same area.) There are some doubts about the integrity of the deal. In any event, until then, East Timor will remain one of the region's poorest nations, with a per capita annual income of US$550 (2005 estimate).

COMMERCIAL INFORMATION

Limited information and advice is available from the **Department for Economic Affairs and Planning**
Website: www.gov.east-timor.org

Ecuador

Location: South America.

Time: Mainland: GMT – 5.
Galapagos Islands: GMT – 6.

Overview

Ecuador – including the ancient Kingdom of Quito, established by the Shiris – was populated by several mutually antagonistic tribes at the time of the Inca conquest in the mid-15th century. When the Spanish arrived from Peru in the 1530s, they found that while many of the inhabitants were hostile, others hailed them as liberators from Inca repression. Spanish rule lasted until the early 19th century – after suppressing several rebellions, the Spaniards were finally overthrown in 1822, by a force backed by Simon Bolivar, fresh from victory in Colombia. Soon afterwards, in 1828, the country declared war on Peru, whose armies had invaded Gran Colombia. A year later, a peace treaty was signed and Ecuador's boundaries were permanently established. However, relations between Ecuador and Peru have been tense ever since. Today, Ecuador remains a multiethnic and multicultural nation, where more than 14 indigenous groups maintain their own traditions and ways of life, to the delight of visitors.

The discovery of oil and the sharp increase in world oil prices in the late and mid 70s should have transformed Ecuador's economic fortunes. However, the windfall was largely squandered and Ecuador has suffered persistent economic difficulties ever since.

The Minister of Tourism, Maria Isabel Salvador, has put as

Credit: ©Ministry of Tourism, Ecuador

goal for the short and medium term, to turn Ecuador in one of the five best destinations of the American continent. To make tourism a tool that enables the country to surpass poverty, she considers that there must be ample cooperation between the authorities, the public sector and citizens in general.

The country's varied and beautiful landscape should make this goal feasible. Straddling the equator in western South America, Ecuador has territories in both the Northern and the Southern hemispheres. The country is geographically divided into the Amazon, the Highlands, the Coast, and the Galapagos Islands.

Ecuador's coastal region (the western lowlands) is made up of fertile plains, rolling hills, and sedimentary basins traversed by a plethora of rivers that rush from the heights of the Andes to the Pacific Ocean. All five coastal provinces, encompassing 640 kilometres of coastline between them, have attractive beaches and plenty of hotels and resorts for tourists.

The Andes Mountain Range crosses the country from north to south.

The Amazon Region can be geographically divided into two sub regions: the High Amazon and the Amazon Lowlands. The Highlands is comprised of the Andean foothills which slowly descend towards the Amazon River Basin. The Napo, Galeras, Cutucú, and Cóndor ranges are located here. The most impressive elevated regions of this area are in the north and include Volcano Sumaco. The Lowlands, found further to east, are home to some of the nation's most beautiful and important rivers: the Putumayo, the Napo, and the Pastaza.

The Archipelago of Colón (commonly known as the Galapagos Islands) is made up of 13 main islands, 17 islets, and dozens of ancient rock formation. Apart from its beautiful beaches and unique and varied ecosystems, the Galapagos Islands are home to towering active volcanoes.

General Information

AREA: 272,045 sq km (105,037 sq miles).
POPULATION: 13.4 million (2005, UN).
POPULATION DENSITY: 49.2 per sq km.
CAPITAL: Quito. **Population:** 1.8 million (2005).
GEOGRAPHY: Ecuador is bordered to the north by Colombia, to the east and south by Peru, and to the west by the Pacific Ocean. There are three distinct zones: the *Sierra* or uplands of the Andes, running from the Colombian border in the north to Peru in the south (of this there are two main ranges - the Eastern and Western Cordilleras, which are divided by a long valley); the *Costa*, a coastal plain between the Andes and the Pacific with plantations of bananas, cacao, coffee and sugar; and the *Oriente*, the upper Amazon basin to the east, consisting of tropical jungles threaded by rivers. The latter, although comprising 36 per cent of Ecuador's land area, contains only 3 per cent of the population. Colonisation is, however, increasing in the wake of the oil boom.

GOVERNMENT: Democratic republic since 1978. **Head of State and Government:** President Alfredo Palacio González since April 2005. **Recent history:** Alfredo Gutierrez was ousted out by Congress in April 2005 amid violent protests against his ruling. Upon his appointment to President, Palacio ordered the arrest of his predecessor but, instead, Gutierrez took political asylum in Colombia. The new President has vowed to reform Ecuador's political system, increase spending on health and education and revise contracts with foreign oil companies.

The constitution was approved by national referendum in 1978, taking effect in 1979. The President, elected for a term of four years, holds executive power. He is assisted by the Vice-President and a Cabinet, which includes 12 Ministers and a Secretary General. Legislative power is unicameral and resides in the House of Representatives, with 69 members; there are 12 national representatives and the remainder represent the Provinces.

LANGUAGE: Spanish is the official language but Quechua and other indigenous languages are common. Some English is spoken.

RELIGION: More than 90 per cent are nominally Roman Catholic.

ELECTRICITY: 110/120 volts AC, 60Hz.

SOCIAL CONVENTIONS: Casual wear is widely acceptable, but businesspeople are expected to dress smartly. It is important to be punctual when arriving for meetings. Smart clothes are often required when visiting hotel dining rooms and better restaurants. Beachwear should only be worn on the beach and revealing clothes should not be worn in towns. Smoking is widely accepted. **Photography:** A tip may be requested if you wish to take someone's photograph and it is better to seek permission first.

Climate

Warm and subtropical. Weather varies within the country due to changes in the Andes mountain range and coastal changes. Andean regions are cooler and it is especially cold at nights in the mountains. Rainfall is high in coastal and jungle areas. In the Galápagos the weather is dry and mild.

Required clothing: Lightweight cottons and linens, and rainwear in subtropical areas. Warmer clothes are needed in upland areas.

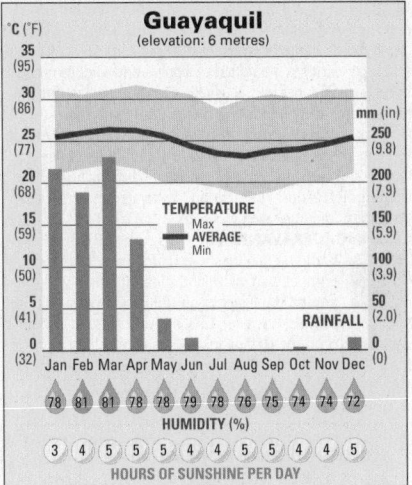

Guayaquil
(elevation: 6 metres)

TEMPERATURE — Max, AVERAGE, Min

RAINFALL

| Jan | Feb | Mar | Apr | May | Jun | Jul | Aug | Sep | Oct | Nov | Dec |

HUMIDITY (%): 78 81 81 78 78 79 78 76 75 74 74 72

HOURS OF SUNSHINE PER DAY: 3 4 5 5 5 4 4 5 5 4 4 5

Communications

Telephone: Country code: 593.
Mobile telephone: Roaming agreements exist with one international mobile phone company, since a GSM 850 network was set up in 2003. Coverage is variable.
Internet: Limited access.
Post: Airmail to western Europe and the USA takes up to one week, but incoming deliveries are less certain.
MEDIA: Under the Ecuadorian Constitution, journalists are given freedom of speech; however, there is some censorship, especially regarding political and military matters. Defamation in Ecuador is punishable by prison sentences of up to three years. By law, the Government is given free space or air-time on radio and TV.
Press: Dailies are in Spanish and include *El Comercio* (website: www.elcomercio.com); *El Tiempo* (website: www.eltiempo.com.ec); *La Hora*, a daily with regional editions (website: www.lahora.com.ec); *Hoy* (website: www.hoy.net), published in Quito; and *El Telégrafo* (website: www.telegrafo.com.ec) and *El Universo* (website: www.eluniverso.com), published in Guayaquil. There are two English-language newspapers, *Inside Ecuador* and *Q*, though both are published irregularly. International newspapers and magazines are available at international airports, main post offices and in some bookshops.
TV: *TC Television* is the national, commercial station. Other stations include *Ecuavisa* and *Teleamazonas*.
Radio: *Cadena Radial Ecuatoriana (CRE)* is a Guayaquil-based commercial network and *Radio Nacional del Ecuador* is Government-owned. *Radio Centro* is privately owned.

Passport/Visa

	Passport Required?	Visa Required?	Return Ticket Required?
Full British	Yes	1	Yes
Australian	Yes	1	Yes
Canadian	Yes	1	Yes
USA	Yes	1	Yes
Other EU	Yes	1	Yes
Japanese	Yes	1	Yes

Note: *Regulations and requirements may be subject to change at short notice, and you are advised to contact the appropriate diplomatic or consular authority before finalising travel arrangements. Any numbers in the chart refer to the footnotes below.*

PASSPORTS: Passport valid for at least six months required by all, except holders of nationals identification cards issued by Bolivia, Chile, Colombia and Peru.
Note: Passports must be carried at all times.
VISAS: Required *only* by:
(a) nationals of Algeria, Bangladesh, China (PR), Costa Rica, Cuba, Guatemala, Honduras, India, Iran, Iraq, Jordan, Korea (Dem Rep), Korea (Rep), Lebanon, Libya, Nigeria, Pakistan, Palestinian Authority Area, Sri Lanka, Sudan, Syrian Arab Republic, Taiwan (China), Tunisia, Vietnam and Yemen;
(b) **1.** all nationals wishing to remain in Ecuador for more than three months.
Note: (a) Nationals listed above also require a visa even when in transit, unless continuing their journey to a third country by the same or first connecting flight or within 48 hours, provided holding confirmed onward tickets and not

leaving the airport. As this list may change at short notice, visitors to Ecuador are advised to check with the nearest Consulate *before* travelling. (b) Those with visas must register with the Ministry of Government and the Director General of Migration in Ecuador within 30 days of their entry.
Types of visa and cost: Visas are issued free of charge to nationals of Colombia, Germany, Spain, Paraguay and the USA. Cultural exchange visas are issued free of charge. *Tourist:* £30. *Business:* £153.
Validity: *Tourist, transit* and *business* visas are valid for up to six months; *Student* and *cultural exchange* visas are valid for one year (a student visa is renewable).
Application to: Consulate (or consular section at Embassy); see *Passport/Visa Information.*
Application requirements: (a) Completed application form. (b) Two passport-size photos. (c) Valid passport. (d) Fee. (e) Return ticket. (f) Proof of economic solvency; for instance, the applicant's last three bank statements. *Tourist:* (a)-(f) and, (g) Letter of invitation from an Ecuadorian resident or proof of hotel reservation. *Business:* (a)-(f) and, (g) Letter from applicant's firm and sponsoring company. *Student:* (a)-(e) and, (f) Certificate of the course registration in Ecuador. (g) Certificate of financial solvency (eg a bank deposit with a letter stating the intention of the bank to pay the student 10 per cent of that amount per month) *or* a document signed by a relative stating that the student is supported by a family member. *Cultural Exchange:* (a)-(e), and (f) Application from the Ecuadorian authority sponsoring the student/teacher with a copy of the agreement under which the programme is carried out and, for teachers, a signed document stating that they will not receive any Ecuadorian funds for their work.
Note: A measles vaccination certificate is required by all nationals travelling from Colombia, Germany, Italy and Venezuela and must be shown on arrival.
Working days required: Applications must be made in person (an appointment is necessary) and a visa is usually issued on the same day.
Temporary residence: Persons wishing to stay longer than six months should apply to the Consulate for details.

PASSPORT/VISA INFORMATION

Embassy of the Republic of Ecuador in the UK
Flat 3B, Hans Crescent, London SW1X 0LS, UK
Tel: (020) 7584 2648.
Website: www.ecuador.embassyhomepage.com
Opening hours: Mon-Fri 0930-1300

Embassy of the Republic of Ecuador in the USA
2535 15th Street, NW, Washington, DC 20009, USA
Tel: (202) 234 7200 *or* 7166 (Consulate).
Website: www.ecuador.org

Money

Currency: US Dollar (USD; symbol US$) = 100 cents. Notes are in denominations of US$100, 50, 20, 10, 5, 2 and 1. Coins are in denominations of US$1 and 50, 25, 10, 5 and 1 cents.
Currency exchange: Foreign currencies can be exchanged at banks and at exchange houses (*casas de cambio*), the latter being generally the best option. It may be difficult to exchange money in the Oriente. The rate of commission varies between 1 per cent and 4 per cent, so it is worth shopping around. ATMs are available in large urban areas.
Credit & debit cards: American Express, Diners Club, MasterCard and Visa are accepted in most cities. Check with your credit or debit card company for details of merchant acceptability and other services which may be available.
Traveller's cheques: Traveller's cheques are generally accepted in the larger cities and can be exchanged into currency at most banks.
Currency restrictions: There are no restrictions on the import and export of either local or foreign currency.
Banking hours: Mon-Fri 0900-1330 and 1430-1800; Sat 0900-1800.
Exchange rate indicators:
Rate at time of publishing
£1.00= US$1.77

Duty Free

The following goods may be imported into Ecuador without incurring customs duty:
300 cigarettes or 50 cigars or 500g of tobacco; 1l of alcohol; a reasonable amount of perfume; gifts and personal effects up to US$200 (for stays of up to seven days) or US$500 (for stays of two years onwards).
Note: Prior permission is required for the import of firearms, ammunition, fresh or dry meat and meat products, plants and vegetables.
The export of gold bars/antiques is prohibited.

Public Holidays

Below are listed Public Holidays for the January 2006-June 2007 period.
Jan 1 2006 New Year's Day. **Feb 12** Amazon and Galapagos Day. **Feb 27** Civicism and National Unity Day. **Apr 14** Good Friday. **May 1** Labour Day. **May 24** Battle of Pichincha. **Aug 10** Independence Day. **Oct 9** Guayaquil Independence Day **Nov 2** All Souls' Day. **Nov 3** Cuenca Independence Day **Dec 25** Christmas Day. **Dec 31** New Year's Eve.
Jan 1 2007 New Year's Day. **Feb 12** Amazon and Galapagos Day. **Feb 27** Civicism and National Unity Day. **Apr 6** Good Friday. **May 1** Labour Day **May 24** Battle of Pichincha.
Note: Ecuador's Carnival (in March/April), the Foundation of Guayaquil (usually in October), the Foundation of Cuenca (usually in November) and the Foundation of Quito (usually in December) are not official public holidays, but are widely observed. Other holidays, in addition to the above, may be marked locally.

Health

	Special Precautions?	Certificate Required?
Yellow Fever	Yes	1
Cholera	2	No
Typhoid & Polio	3	N/A
Malaria	4	N/A

Note: *Regulations and requirements may be subject to change at short notice, and you are advised to contact your doctor well in advance of your intended date of departure. Any numbers in the chart refer to the footnotes below.*

1: A yellow fever vaccination certificate is required from all travellers over one year of age arriving from infected areas. Travellers arriving from non-endemic zones should note that vaccination is strongly recommended for travel outside the urban areas, even if an outbreak of the disease has not been reported and they would normally not require a vaccination certificate to enter the country.
2: Following WHO guidelines issued in 1973, a cholera vaccination certificate is no longer a condition of entry to Ecuador. However, cholera is a serious risk in this country and precautions are essential. Up-to-date advice should be sought before deciding whether these precautions should include vaccination as medical opinion is divided over its effectiveness; see the *Health* appendix for further information.
3: Typhoid poses some risk in rural areas.
4: Malaria risk, predominantly in the benign *vivax* form, is high throughout the year below 1500m (4920ft) in 148 cantons in 19 provinces. A high proportion of *falciparum* cases in Esmeraldas Province are reportedly resistant to chloroquine. There is no risk in Guayaquil or Quito.
Notes: A measels vaccination certificate is required by all nationals travelling from Colombia, Germany, Italy and Venezuela and must be shown upon arrival.
Food & drink: All water should be regarded as being potentially contaminated. Water used for drinking, brushing teeth or making ice should have first been boiled or otherwise sterilised. Bottled water is available. Milk is unpasteurised and should be boiled. Powdered or tinned milk is available and is advised, but make sure that it is reconstituted with pure water. Avoid dairy products which are likely to have been made from unboiled milk. Only eat well-cooked meat and fish, preferably served hot. Pork, salad and mayonnaise may carry increased risk. Vegetables should be cooked and fruit peeled.
Other risks: *Endemic onchocerciasis* occurs in rural areas. *Hepatitis A* and *B* are hyperendemic and inoculation with gamma globulin is highly recommended. *Hepatitis D* is endemic in the Amazon Basin. *Dengue fever, filariasis, leishmaniasis, onchocerciasis* and *American trypanosomiasis* are diseases carried by insects and might occur. *Brucellosis* may be contracted by eating or drinking contaminated dairy products. *Altitude sickness* is a risk flying directly into Quito (2800m/9186ft).
Rabies is present. For those at high risk, vaccination before

arrival should be considered. If you are bitten, seek medical advice without delay. For more information, consult the *Health* appendix.
Health care: Medical facilities outside the major towns are extremely limited. Acute surgical and cardiac services are not available on the Galápagos Islands; therefore, for more serious illnesses, patients may be evacuated to the USA. Health insurance (to include emergency repatriation) is strongly recommended.

Travel - International

AIR:
Ecuador's national airlines are *TAME (EQ)* (website: www.tame.com.ec) and *LAN Airlines* (website: www.lanecuador.net). *American Airlines, bmi, British Airways* and *Continental Airlines* offer services from London to Quito (with at least one stop). *American Airlines, Continental Airlines* and *Virgin Atlantic* offer indirect services from London to Guayaquil.
Approximate flight times: From Quito to *London* is 17 hours, to *Los Angeles* is nine hours and to *New York* is nine hours 30 minutes.
Main airports: *Quito (UIO)* (Mariscal Sucre) (website: www.quitoairport.com) is 8km (5 miles) from the city centre. *To/from the airport*: A bus service operates frequently, 1100-0300 (travel time 20 to 30 minutes). Return is from Avenida 10 de Agosto. Taxis are also available. *Facilities*: Medical department, bars, car hire, duty free shops, post office and restaurants.
Guayaquil (GYE) (Simón Bolívar) is 5km (3 miles) from the city. *To/from the airport*: There are bus and taxi services into the city.
Departure tax: US$25.
The Visit South America Pass: This must be bought outside South America in country of residence and allows unlimited travel to 36 cities in the following countries: Argentina, Bolivia, Brazil, Colombia, Chile (except Easter Island), Ecuador, Paraguay, Peru, Uruguay and Venezuela. Participating airlines include *Aer Lingus (EI), American Airlines (AA), British Airways (BA), Cathay Pacific (CX), Finnair (AY), Iberia (IB), LAN-Chile (LA)* and *Qantas (QF)*. A minimum of three flights must be booked, with no maximum; the maximum stay is 60 days, with no minimum, and prices depend on the amount of flight zones covered. Children under 12 years of age are entitled to a 33 per cent discount and infants (under two years old) only pay 10 per cent of the adult fare. For further details, contact one of the participating airlines. For more information, visit online (website: www.oneworld.com).
SEA:
There are regular passenger/cargo services from Europe, including *Hamburg-South American, Johnson Lines, Knutsen* and *Royal Netherlands* which take 20 to 22 days from Rotterdam and Le Havre. Others sail from Antwerp, Genoa and Liverpool, and the US West Coast (*Delta Line Cruises*). *Guayaquil* is the main port in Ecuador for both passengers and freight(website: www.puertodeguayaquil.com) However, it is becoming increasingly difficult to secure this kind of passage.
ROAD:
The Pan-American Highway bisects the country. It begins at the Colombian border in the Carchi province and runs south on to Quito, Riobamba, Cuenca, Loja and ending at Macará near the border with Peru. Part of the highway is toll-administered and the condition of the road is mostly quite good but it mainly goes through mountains which make it fairly dangerous to drive on. **Bus:** *Panamericana Internacional* operates direct services to Caracas, Venezuela (tel: (2) 250 1585). *Rutas de América* operates direct services to Colombia, Peru and Venezuela with connections to Argentina, Bolivia, Brazil, Chile, Paraguay and Uruguay (tel: (2) 254 8142). Visitors should remember to carry their passports at all times as there may be frequent checks, both within Ecuador and at border crossings.

Travel - Internal

AIR:
The national airline, *TAME*, flies frequently between Guayaquil, Quito and other destinations throughout the country. A number of small airlines serve the coast and eastern part of the country. Flying is the usual mode of transport for intercity travel. Other airports include *Coca, Cuenca, Esmeraldas, Lago Agrio* and *Manta*.
Departure tax: 12 per cent of the ticket price, paid with the ticket.
Galapágos Islands: There are daily flights to the Galápagos Islands on national airlines from both Quito and Guayaquil; note that non-Ecuadorians have to pay more for their tickets on this route (US$100 for adults and US$50 for children is charged for visiting any national park). The main airports in the Galápagos are *Baltra* and *Caráquez*.
SEA/RIVER:
Ecuador's rocky coastline makes coast-hopping an inefficient and even dangerous means of transport for visitors. Several navigable rivers flow eastwards into the Amazon basin. Dugout canoes, which carry up to about 25 people, are widely used as a means of transport in roadless areas, particularly in the Oriente jungles and in the northwest coastal regions. There are few passenger services between the mainland and the Galápagos Islands; once there, however, tourist boats, local mail steamers and hired yachts may be used to travel between islands.
RAIL:
The journey from Guayaquil to Quito offers spectacular views, as the train climbs to 3238m (10,623ft) in 80km (50 miles), reaching its highest point at Urbina (3609m/11,841ft). Railway enthusiasts will also enjoy the particularly scenic parts on the Alausi-Duran and Ibarra-San Lorenzo sections. Landslides caused by heavy rain frequently disrupt train services. Always check for further details on arrival in the country.
ROAD:
Traffic drives on the right. An extensive network of roads spreads out from the main north-south axis of the Pan-American Highway. The Government and *PetroEcuador* are developing highways into the Oriente. In general, road improvements are being put into effect rapidly but, due to the effect of earthquakes and flooding (in the south) during the last 10 years, conditions remain variable; potholes and cracks in the road are sometimes sizeable. The roads between Quito and Guayaquil and between Quito, Latacunga, Ambato and Riobamba are completely paved. A road connects Quito, Otavalo, Ibarra and Tulcán, the frontier with Colombia.
Bus: Long-distance buses leave from central bus stations (*terminal terrestre*) but timetables can be unreliable. Tickets should be bought in advance to secure a seat. *Busetas* are 22-seater small buses which travel long distances quickly, larger *autobuses* are slower. In general, buses tend to be crowded and fairly uncomfortable. Travellers are advised to keep their passports with them at all times when travelling on buses as transit police checks are common. **Taxis:** These are widely available, particularly in larger cities and towns. Fares tend to be low but should be negotiated in advance. Taxis are metered in Quito, but rarely elsewhere. Taxis may be hired for a whole day. **Car hire**: *Avis, Budget* and *Hertz* car hire companies all operate in Ecuador. **Documentation:** An International Driving Permit is not required.
URBAN:
Guayaquil and Quito have bus and minibus services operating at flat fares.
Travel Times: The following chart gives approximate travel times (in hours and minutes) from **Quito** to other major cities and towns in Ecuador.

	Air	Road	Rail
Guayaquil	0.50	7.00	-
Cuenca	1.30	9.30	-
Esmeraldas	-	-	-
Puerto Ayora	2.30	-	-

Travel Advice

Travellers are advised against travel to the northern border area, including the Provinces of Sucumbios and Orellana. Armed groups are active in these areas and there is a risk of kidnapping and crime.
Before visiting the town of Baños and the surrounding area, travellers should ensure they are aware of the current levels of alert for the Tunguraha volcano, areas of highest risk in the event of an eruption and evacuation plans. For further information, contact the National Ecuadorian Geophysics Institute (website: www.igepn.edu.ec).
Travellers should be aware of the risks of crime in all areas and take sensible precautions at all times. Travellers should be particularly vigilant in poorer urban areas, after dark and on public transport. It is not recommended to travel alone.
The threat from terrorism is low, but you should be aware of the global risk of indiscriminate terrorist attacks which could be against civilian targets, including places frequented by foreigners.
This advice is based on information provided by the Foreign and Commonwealth Office in the UK. It is correct at time of publishing. As the situation can change rapidly, visitors are advised to contact the following organisations for the latest travel advice:

British Foreign and Commonwealth Office
Tel: (0845) 850 2829.
Website: www.fco.gov.uk

US Department of State
Website: http://travel.state.gov/travel

Accommodation

HOTELS:
Hotel rooms should be booked at least one week in advance. Outside the main towns, a more or less standard price is charged per person for one night in a *provision residencia*, or a hotel. There is, however, a minimum charge per person. A 10 per cent service charge and 5 per cent tax are added to upper- and middle-range hotel bills. Cheaper hotels usually charge 5 per cent at the most. Hotel accommodation is very limited on the Galápagos Islands. Hotels in Ecuador have been graded into three main categories according to standard and price bracket. All categories provide at least basic facilities. Booking hotels during fiestas and festivals can be difficult. Visitors should book well in advance.
CAMPING/CARAVANNING:
Camping facilities in Ecuador are run by US or European agencies and these are mainly found around the beaches on the Pacific coast or in the Andean highlands; however, they are very limited. Camping is prohibited on the Galápagos Islands except in one of the three designated campsites. A permit is required and can be obtained from the park offices.

ACCOMMODATION INFORMATION

Federación Hotelera del Ecuador (AHOTEC)
Avenida América 5378 y Diguja, Edificio San Francisco, Piso 2, Quito, Ecuador
Tel: (2) 244 3425.
E-mail: ahotec@interactive.net.ec

Top Things To See

- **Quito**, Ecuador's capital (and second-largest) city, has a setting of great natural beauty, overshadowed by the volcano **Pichincha** , with its twin peaks of **Ruco** and **Guagua**. Located at 2850m (9348ft) above sea level and only 22km (14 miles) from the Equator, Quito used to be a major Inca city that was destroyed shortly before the arrival of the Spanish conquistadors. Although no Inca traces remain, the city has preserved much of its Spanish colonial character, the cathedral in the **Plaza de la Independencia** (the oldest church in South America) and the many old churches and monasteries being among the most notable instances. Also in the plaza is the **Municipal Palace**, the **Archbishop's Palace** and the **Palacio Presidencial**. Many of the city's famous churches and monasteries contain priceless examples of Spanish art and sculpture, particularly the **Monasterio de San Francisco** (located in the beautiful plaza of the same name) and the **Jesuit church of La Compañía**. Most of Quito's colonial churches are located in the **Old Town**, parts of which have been listed by UNESCO as a World Heritage Site. Perhaps the best preserved colonial street is the historic alley of **la Ronda**. As the cultural and political capital, Quito has a number of museums of colonial and modern art. The **Museo del Banco Central**, located in the **Casa de la Cultura**, has a vast archaeological repertory as well as displays of colonial furniture and religious art. Also of interest is the **Museo Guayasamín**, home to many fine works of Ecuador's renowned modern artist, Oswaldo Guayasamín.
- Be fearless and approach **volanoes**. The region of **Latacunga** and **Ambato** has much fine scenery, marked by an avenue of volcanoes. The greenish-blue alkaline waters of the volcanic **Laguna Quilotoa** are eye-catchingly beautiful and provide a well-earned photo opportunity. Two active volcanoes are located within the **Parque Nacional Sangay**, a national park of outstanding beauty which has been listed by UNESCO as a World Heritage Site. The park is characterised by a variety of landscapes, ranging from rainforests to glaciers, as well as numerous indigenous animal species, such as the mountain tapir and the Andean condor. Also within the park, the **Tunguraha** volcano (5016m/16,453ft) is popular with tourists, especially at night, since it became active again in 1999. West of Latacunga, the **Parque Nacional Cotopaxi** is Ecuador's most visited national park. It includes the active **Cotopaxi volcano** which, at 5895m (19,345ft), is the world's highest active volcano.
- See the granite monument that marks the **Equator**, as you approach Quito.
- The city of **Cuenca** was founded in 1577 and still contains many examples of Spanish colonial architecture. Contrasting with this, a vast cathedral has recently been built. The nearby ancient Inca settlement at **Ingapirca**, 50km (32 miles) north of Cuenca, is worth visiting.
- Ecuador's biggest city, **Guayaquil** is also the chief port and commercial centre. A good starting point for sightseeing is the **Rotonda**, the city's most historic landmark, which faces the beautiful garden promenade of **Paseo de las Colonias**. Across the **Malecón Simón**

Bolivar are the **Government Palace** and city hall while, at the northern end, one can find the ancient fortress of **la Planchada**. Other places of interest include the **Church of Santo Domingo**, the old residential section of **Las Penas** and the **Municipal Museum**.

- Travel to the **Litoral**, a narrow coastal belt, 560km (350 miles) in length. The chief ports provide visitors with some of the best resorts for deep-sea fishing on the west coast. Particularly attractive are the towns of **Playas Posoria** and **Salinas**, while **Esmeraldas**, one of the country's most important ports, is also known for its beautiful beaches. The relaxing island of **Muisne** is fast becoming a popular destination. Journey into the **Machalilla National Park**, located on the central coast, which contains stunning dense mangrove forests, and contains a wonderful stretch of beach - **Los Frailes**, virtually deserted, with golden sand and pretty seashells.
- Observe ancient traditional customs, such as those in the region of **Santo Domingo de los Colorados**, situated some 90km (55 miles) west of Quito, which remains the domain of the **Colorados Indians**. Indeed, the **El Oriente** is the term used by Ecuadorians to refer to the Amazon basin in eastern Ecuador, and is still a primeval world of virgin forests and exotic flora and fauna, mainly inhabited by Indians. In January 1999, the Ecuadorian President issued a decree blocking future oil exploration, mining and colonisation by oil companies of the **Cuyabeno-Imuya** and **Yasuni** national parks. These parks are home to thousands of **indigenous people**, including the **Huaorani**, the **Tagaeri**, the **Taromenare**, the **Secoyas** and the **Sionas**. In recent years, the region has experienced ongoing conflicts between oil companies seeking to develop the area and indigenous communities afraid that development will lead to the destruction of their ancestral homeland and loss of their traditional way of life. The principal towns of the area are **El Puyo**, **Lago Agrio**, **Macas**, **Sucúa**, **Tena** and **Zamora**. Tourist excursions are available along the rivers, which provide the principal method of transport. One of the main rivers in this region is the **Napo** which, like most of the rivers in the Oriente, is a tributary of the Amazon (which lies further east in Peru). **Baños** is worth visiting, taking its name from the numerous springs and pools of hot and cold mineral waters. It is also the gateway to the Amazon region, passing through the spectacular gorge of the **River Pastaza**.
- Lay eyes on what inspired the theories of Charles Darwin by paying a visit to the **Galápagos Islands**, situated about 1000km (625 miles) west off the Ecuadorian mainland. The islands (13 main islands and six smaller islands) are bleak, barren and rocky. Made famous by Darwin's scientific voyage in the '*Beagle*' during the 19th century, the islands' unique wildlife – which includes giant tortoises, lizards and iguanas – fascinates the modern-day visitor. Some 50 per cent of the islands' species are found nowhere else in the world. The islands have been turned into a national park in an attempt to preserve their natural state, and, in 1978, UNESCO declared the Galápagos to be 'the universal natural heritage of humanity'. In 1998, the Government enacted a law for the 'Special Regime for the Conservation and Sustainable Development of the Galápagos Province', which states that the protection of the area is a state responsibility. Accommodation and travel can generally be arranged either inclusively from the visitor's home country or through local tour operators once in Ecuador. It is advisable to shop around and take advice before booking as the quality of service and reliability can vary greatly. For further information, contact the International Tour Operators Association (website: www.igtoa.org).

Top Things To Do

- Travellers wishing to explore the **rainforest** of the **lower Amazon basin** and its abundant plant and animal life should head to the **Oriente region**. It is probably best to do this as part of an organised **tour**, which can be booked with a number of local operators providing tailor-made itineraries and experienced guides. The presence of hundreds of waterways, many of which are tributaries of the great **River Amazon**, means that such tours invariably involve travelling by **boat**. Usually, these are large motorised **canoes** travelling up the main rivers (such as the **Aguarico** or the **Napo**), although trips on non-motorised boats along the smaller waterways are also available, which is a far better way to observe the wildlife. Several indigenous communities living in the region have preserved their traditional lifestyles and are actively engaged in resisting the ongoing attempts by oil companies to develop and exploit the Ecuadorian rainforest.
- Go **hiking** along trails in **Cotopaxi National Park**, one of them following the shores of **Lago Limpiopungo**, located at an altitude of 3800m (12,465ft). The **Parque Nacional Podocarpus** is a popular destination for **walking**.
- **Baños** is Ecuador's tourist mecca for **adventure sports** and trips to the rainforest, offering **climbing** expeditions to the nearby volcanoes. Experienced climbers may head to the **Cotopaxi volcano** which, at 5985m (19,345ft), is one of the world's highest and is best reached from **Quito**.
- Ecuador's rich **wildlife** is best represented in the **Galápagos Islands**, whose most famous inhabitants are the giant Galápagos tortoises (weighing up to 272kg/600lb). Adventure tours around the islands are available, either in large cruise ships or in smaller ships and yachts (advance booking is essential). The amount of time visitors are allowed to stay on the islands is regulated by the Government.
- There are 2800km (1750 miles) of coastline along the mainland, with **beach** resorts offering various types of **watersports**. Good **snorkelling** is available via chartered boat trips around the **Isla de la Plata** (located in the **Parque Nacional Machalilla**, Ecuador's only coastal national park).
- Take a **scenic train journey** along several of Ecuador's railway routes, particularly those in the **Andes**, which pass through spectacular mountain scenery, often at dramatic altitudes. The Ecuadorian custom of riding on the roof of the train makes the views even more breathtaking. One of the most famous routes, whose climax is the precipitous **'Devil's Nose' passage**, is from **Riobamba** down to the Pacific coast. Train schedules are fairly erratic and visitors should check locally prior to travelling.
- Go to a lively traditional **street market**, such as **Chota**'s **Indian market** (particularly good for traditional art and weavings), renowned throughout Ecuador.

TOURIST INFORMATION

Ministerio de Turismo (Ministry of Tourism)
Avenida Eloy Alfaro N32-300 y Carlos Tobar, Quito, Ecuador
Tel: (2) 222 8304.
Website: www.vivecuador.com

Camara Provincial de Turismo (CAPTUR)
Av. Amazonas y Patrica (esq.), Edifico Cofiec, Piso 3, Quito, Ecuador
Tel: (2) 223 1198.
Website: www.captur.com

Entertainment

FOOD & DRINK: Ecuador has some of the best beer in South America; the most popular brand is *Pilsner*. Good Chilean wine is available, alongside expensive international drinks. Restaurants have waiter service and there are cafe-style bars.

Things to know: Alcohol cannot be sold after 0200.

National specialities:

- *Llapingachos* (pancakes stuffed with mashed potato and cheese).
- The best of the jungle fruits include *chirimoya*, with a delicious custard-like inside; *mamey*, which has a red, sweet, squash-like meat; and *pepinos*, a sweet white and purple striped cucumber-like fruit.
- Shrimp or lobster *ceviche*. This is traditionally accompanied by popcorn and *chifles* (thinly sliced and fried green bananas).
- *Locro* (stew of potatoes and cheese).
- *Humitas* (flavoured sweetcorn *tamales*).
- Roasted guinea pig.
- *Patacones* (squashed fried green bananas).
- *Empanadas* (hot crispy meat- or cheese-filled pastries).

National drinks:

- *Naranjilla* (fruit juice with a taste somewhere between citrus and peach).
- *Canelazo*, made from sugar cane, alcohol, lemon, sugar and cinnamon.
- *Pisco*, the local brandy.

Tipping: 10 per cent service charge is usually added to the bill in hotels and restaurants. Taxi drivers do not expect tips.

NIGHTLIFE: There is little nightlife except in Quito and Guayaquil where there are excellent restaurants and other attractions. In smaller towns, social life takes place in the home and in private clubs. The cinema is the most popular form of entertainment.

SHOPPING: Bargaining is acceptable in small shops and in markets, but prices are usually fixed in 'tourist stores'. A few stores around the major hotels have fixed prices. In the Province of Azuay, the cities of Cuenca and Gualaceo offer a wide variety of handicrafts at *ferias* or special market days. The top attractions are the *ferias* of Otavalo, Ambato, Latacunga, Saquisili and Riobamba, most held once a week. They offer the visitor excellent bargains for Indian crafts and silver. Principal silver stores are in Quito. Special purchases include native woodcarvings, varnished and painted ornaments made of bread dough, Indian tiles, woollen and orlon rugs, blankets, baskets, leather goods,

Credit: ©Ministry of Tourism, Ecuador

shigras (shoulder bags) and hand-loomed textiles, indigenous art and native weapons. **Shopping hours:** Mon-Fri 1000-2000, Sat 0800-2100 (times are for shopping malls; local stores may have shorter opening hours). Some shops open Sunday.

Business

- **GDP:** US$32 billion.
- **Main imports:** Vehicles, medicinal products, telecommunications equipment and electricity.
- **Main exports:** Petroleum, bananas, cut flowers and shrimp.
- **Main trade partners:** Brazil, Chile, Colombia, China, Italy, Japan, Mexico, Panama, Peru, USA and Venezuela.

ECONOMY: Ecuador's economy rests on the twin pillars of oil and agriculture. Some commentators believe that the potential fluctuation in oil prices leaves the country susceptible to market crashes. It is the world's largest exporter of bananas and also grows coffee, cocoa, palm oil and sugar in significant quantities. The timber industry yields valuable hardwoods and the country is also a leading producer of balsa wood. Fishing is another important sector: seafood exports have expanded rapidly to the point where Ecuador is now the world's second-largest producer of shrimps. The mining sector produces gold, silver, copper and other metals, but it is the discovery of substantial new oil reserves in the mid-1990s that could transform Ecuador's economy. In August 1997, work began to expand the trans-Ecuadorian pipeline. The other main components of the industrial sector are food processing, chemicals and textiles. Ecuador pursued an isolationist foreign and trade policy for many years until a programme of economic reform was begun during the 1990s. In November 1992, Ecuador withdrew from OPEC and, in August 1995, joined the World Trade Organization. Since then, the country's increasing oil revenues have largely been devoted to paying off the country's substantial foreign debt. In addition, after a period of poor relations with the IMF, Ecuador has sold many former state assets as part of a deal with the IMF in 2002 to secure future funding. Ecuador is a member of the main regional integration bodies: the Andean Union and ALADI (*Asociación Latinoamericana de Integración*).

COMMERCIAL INFORMATION

Federación Nacional de Cámaras de Comercio del Ecuador.
(This chamber usually swaps location, between Quito and Guayaquil, every two years. It has been in Quito since March 2004.)
Amazonas y República, Edificio las Cámaras, Apartado 17-01-202, Quito, Ecuador
Tel: (2) 244 3787.
Website: www.pequenaindustria.com
Note: In 2006, it is in Guayaquil:
Francisco de Orellana y Miguel Alciras, Ciudadela Kennedy Norte, Edificio Las Cámaras, Guayaquil, Ecuador
Tel: (4) 268 2771.

Centro de Exposiciones Quito de la Federación Ecuatoriana de la Pequeña Industria de Pichincha (Information on Conferences/Conventions)
Avenidas Amazonas y Atahualpa no 34-332, Centro de Exposiciones, Quito, Ecuador
Tel: (2) 244 3388.
Website: www.capeipi.com

Egypt

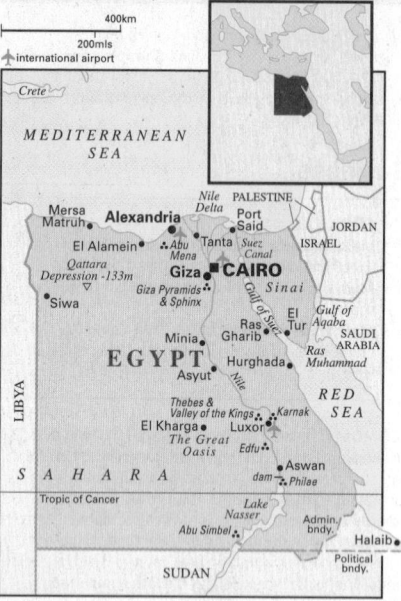

Location: Middle East, North Africa.

Time: GMT + 2 (GMT + 3 from last Friday in April to last Thursday in September).

Overview

Travellers have marvelled at Egypt's archaeological wonders for centuries, ever since the Ancient Greeks visited the pyramids. Today, the ancient wonders attract millions of tourists each year to the pyramids, temples, mosques and great monuments of the Nile Valley, as well as the stunning diving resorts of the Red Sea.

In 430 BC, when Herodotos exclaimed in awe over the magnificent monuments in Egypt, many of them were already 2500 years old. Most, from the pyramids of Giza to the astonishingly beautiful temples of Karnak or Philae, or the painted tombs in the Valley of the Kings, can still be visited today. The sheer age of this great civilisation is mind-blowing.

The life-giving Nile pours across the map, feeding an emerald ribbon of irrigated fields adjacent to villages shaded by date palms. Whether on a cruise ship or traditional *felucca*, life on the water is a constant visual feast, while the few huge, dusty cities – Cairo, Alexandria, Aswan and Luxor – are a babble of exotic sounds and smells. Hurghada and Sharm el-Sheik, on the Red Sea coast, are doors to a magical underwater world of technicolour fish and coral favoured by divers, while other adventurous travellers head inland. Here, you can discover monasteries amid the arid mountains of Sinai or the distant desert oases, homes of the hardy nomads whose camel trains still wander the Saharan sands.

While best known for its pyramids and ancient civilisations, Egypt is at the centre of the Arab world and has played a central role in the political situation within the region in modern times. After three wars in 1948, 1967 and 1973, peace was achieved with Israel in 1979 leading to Egypt's expulsion from the Arab League. Following the assassination of Anwar Al-Sadat in 1981 by Islamic extremists, Hosni Mubarak was elected President and oversaw the return of Egypt to the Arab League in 1991. During this time, Egypt joined the international coalition which drove Iraqi occupation forces out of Kuwait and since then, Egypt has played a vital role in the Middle East Peace Process.

General Information

AREA: 1 million sq km (386,874 sq miles).

POPULATION: 74.9 million (UN, 2005).

POPULATION DENSITY: 74.8 per sq km.

CAPITAL: Cairo (El Qahira). **Population:** 16.7 million (2005 estimate).

GEOGRAPHY: Egypt is bordered to the north by the Mediterranean, to the south by Sudan, to the west by Libya, and to the east by the Red Sea and Israel. The River Nile divides the country unevenly in two, while the Suez Canal provides a third division with the Sinai Peninsula. Beyond the highly cultivated Nile Valley and Delta, a lush green tadpole of land that holds more than 90 per cent of the population, the landscape is mainly flat desert, devoid of vegetation apart from the few oases that have persisted in the once fertile depressions of the Western Desert. Narrow strips are inhabited on the Mediterranean coast and on the African Red Sea coast. The coast south of Suez has fine beaches and the coral reefs just offshore attract many divers. The High Dam at Aswan now controls the annual floods that once put much of the Nile Valley under water; it also provides electricity.

GOVERNMENT: Republic. **Head of State:** President Muhammad Hosni Mubarak since 1981. **Head of Government:** Ahmed Nazif since 2004. **Recent history:** Hosni Mubarak is Egypt's longest-serving ruler since Muhammad Ali in the early 19th century and one of the longest-serving leaders in the Arab world. President Mubarak was re-elected on 7 September 2005 for his fifth successive term. On 25 May 2005, a constitutional amendment was passed to allow for free and direct Presidential elections to be contested by multiple candidates following pressure form the US and domestic political groups. In previous elections, Egyptians voted yes or no for a single candidate appointed by Parliament. The only opposition organisation which has broad public support, the Muslim Brotherhood, is outlawed and could not field a candidate. Mr Mubarak succeeded Anwar Sadat, who was assassinated in 1981. He is a great survivor, having escaped no fewer than six assassination attempts. The President appoints the Prime Minister. Ahmed Nazif has occupied this post since July 2004. Elections to the 454-member *Majlis al-Sha'ab* are held every five years. The first stage of a three-stage election took place on 9 November 2005.

LANGUAGE: Arabic is the official language. English and French are widely spoken.

RELIGION: According to the 1986 census, over 94 per cent of the population follows Islam; the majority of the rest is Christian. All types of Christianity are represented, especially the Coptic Christian Church. There is also a small Jewish minority.

ELECTRICITY: Most areas 220 volts AC, 50Hz. Certain rural parts still use 110 to 380 volts AC.

SOCIAL CONVENTIONS: Islam is the dominant influence and many traditional customs and beliefs are tied up with religion. The people are generally courteous and hospitable and expect similar respect from visitors. Shaking hands will suffice as a greeting. Because Egypt is a Muslim country, dress should be conservative and women should not wear revealing clothes, particularly when in religious buildings and in towns (although the Western style of dress is accepted in modern nightclubs, restaurants, hotels and bars in Cairo, Alexandria and other tourist destinations). Official or social functions and smart restaurants usually require more formal wear. Smoking is very common. **Photography:** Tourists will have to pay a fee to take photographs inside pyramids, tombs and museums.

Climate

Hot, dry summers with mild, dry winters and cold nights. Rainfall is negligible except on the coast. In April, the hot, dusty *Khamsin* wind blows from the Sahara.

Required clothing: Lightweight cottons and linens during summer, with warmer clothes for winter and cooler evenings.

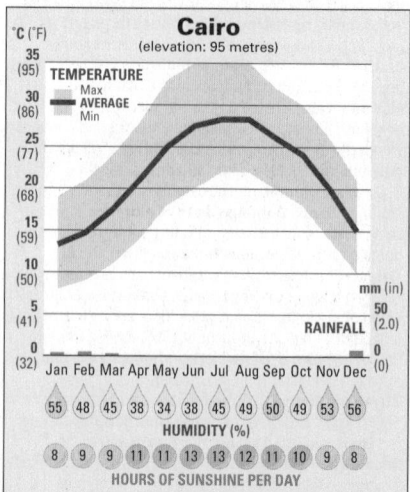

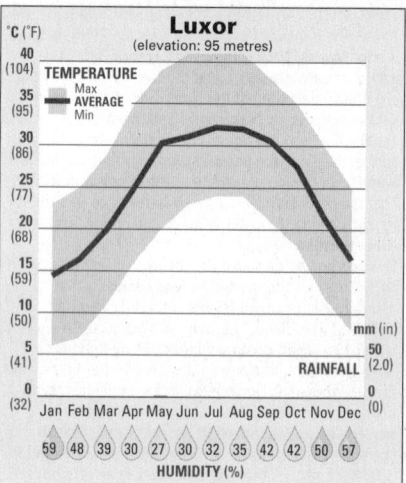

Communications

Telephone: Full IDD is available. Country code: 20.

Mobile telephone: Roaming exist with many international mobile phone companies. Coverage is limited to Cairo, Alexandria and along the north coast line of the Red Sea from Suez to Sharm el-Sheikh and the major towns along the Nile.

Internet: There are Internet cafes in the main cities, including Cairo, Alexandria, Dahab and Luxor. Tourists can also access the Internet in hotels.

Post: The postal system is efficient for international mail. Airmail takes about five days to western Europe, and eight to 10 days to the USA. All post offices are open daily 0830-1500 except Friday, and the Central Post Office in Cairo is open 24 hours.

MEDIA: The Egyptian press is one of the most influential and widely-read in the region, while Egyptian TV and film industry supplies much of the Arab-speaking world with shows from its Media Production City, an enterprise launched with a view to creating the "Hollywood of the East". Press laws which allow prison sentences for libel and "insults" and an ongoing state of emergency have encouraged self-censorship on sensitive issues. Egypt has two state-run national TV channels and six regional

channels. It is a key player in satellite TV; the Egyptian Space Channels are widely watched across the Arab-speaking world. The channels enjoy the support of the country's huge programme-making industry and have access to a large archive of Egyptian films and TV programmes. Egypt was the first Arab nation to have its own satellite, Nilesat 101. The country's first private TV stations came on air in 2001, broadcasting via satellite. The state monopoly on radio broadcasting was broken with the arrival of private, commercial music stations in 2003.

Press: The most influential Egyptian daily is *Al-Ahram,* the oldest newspaper in the Arab world; others include *Al-Akhbar* and several weekly and periodical publications. *Al-Ahahi* and *Al-Wafd* are opposition publications. The *Middle East Observer* is the main weekly English-language business paper. *Al-Ahram Weekly* is also published in English.

TV: State-run Egypt Radio Television Union (ERTU) operates domestic networks; It also operates satellite networks such as *Nile TV International,* which broadcasts some programmes in English and Hebrew; Dream TV, a privately-owned satellite network, operates *Dream 1* targeting young viewers and *Dream 2,* an entertainment channel.

Radio: Egypt Radio Television Union (ERTU) operates eight national networks and external services *Radio Cairo* and *Voice of the Arabs; Nile FM* and *Nogoum FM* are private stations. *Nile FM* broadcasts Western pop while *Nogoum FM* broadcasts Arabic pop.

Passport/Visa

	Passport Required?	Visa Required?	Return Ticket Required?
Full British	Yes	Yes	No
Australian	Yes	Yes	No
Canadian	Yes	Yes	No
USA	Yes	Yes	No
Other EU	Yes	Yes	No
Japanese	Yes	Yes	No

Note: *Regulations and requirements may be subject to change at short notice, and you are advised to contact the appropriate diplomatic or consular authority before finalising travel arrangements. Any numbers in the chart refer to the footnotes below.*

PASSPORTS: Passport valid for at least six months required by all.

VISAS: Required by all except the following:
(a) nationals of Kuwait, who are allocated a six months' residence permit upon arrival;
(b) Palestinians holding an Egyptian residence card, provided the stay outside Egypt does not exceed six months;
(c) nationals of Bahrain, Djibouti, Guinea, Jordan (only with a passport with at least five years' validity), Libya, Oman, Saudi Arabia, the United Arab Emirates and Yemen Republic for stays of up to three months;
(d) nationals of Malaysia for stays of up to 15 days;
(e) those continuing their journey to a third country within 24 hours, provided holding confirmed tickets.
(f) cruise ship passengers entering Egypt, at any port, for a maximum of three days.

Note: (a) The amount of stay permitted in Egypt in which visa exemptions apply to such nationals varies. It is advised to contact the nearest Embassy/Consulate prior to travel to confirm the details. (b) Those in possession of a residence permit to Egypt are not required to obtain an entry visa if they leave Egypt and return within the validity of their residence permit or within six months, whichever period is less. (c) Nationals of Afghanistan, Iran, Lebanon, The Philippines and holders of Palestinian documents must not leave the airport transit lounge if travelling en route to onward destination (and must do so by the same or first connecting aircraft). All other nationals must remain within the airport.

Types of visa and cost: *Tourist* and *Business* (single- and multiple-entry). Cost varies according to nationality. For UK nationals: *Tourist:* £15 (single-entry); £18 (multiple-entry); see *Passport/Visa Information* section. *Business:* £53 (single-entry); £91 (multiple-entry). For US nationals: All visas £12. Processing fees for other nationals vary considerably; check with the appropriate Consulate (or Consular section of Embassy) for details; see *Passport/Visa Information.*

Validity: Varies, but are usually valid for six months from the date of issue for stays of up to three months. Visas cannot be post-dated. Visas can be extended one week before the end of the permitted stay in Egypt at Immigration.

Application to: Consulate (or consular section at Embassy); see *Passport/Visa Information* section.

Note: It is, however, possible for most tourists and visitors to obtain an entry visa at any of the major ports of entry. Visitors should check with their nearest Egyptian Consular mission for more details concerning visa regulations applying to their citizenship.

Application requirements: (a) Passport valid for at least

Credit: ©Photo Hutter

six months with at least one blank page. (b) Application form, completed and signed. (c) One recent passport-size photo. (d) Postal applicants must enclose a registered- or recorded-delivery and self-addressed envelope. (e) Fee, payable by cash or postal order. (f) Business letter for Business visa.

Working days required: Same day for personal applications; seven days or more from day of receipt for postal applications. Processing may take longer (estimated six to eight weeks) for the following nationals, who require pre-approval from the relevant authorities in Cairo: Algeria, Bangladesh, China (PR), Eritrea, Ethiopia, Iran, Iraq, Lebanon, Morocco, Somalia, Sudan and Tunisia.

Note: Visitors from all countries except the EU and the USA must register with the police within one week of arrival in Egypt, although this service is usually undertaken by the hotel.

PASSPORT/VISA INFORMATION

Embassy of the Arab Republic of Egypt in the UK
26 South Street, London W1Y 6DD, UK
Tel: (020) 7499 3304.
Opening hours: Mon-Fri 0930-1630 (1000-1500 during Ramadan).

Egyptian Consulate in the UK
2 Lowndes Street, London SW1X 9ET, UK
Tel: (020) 7235 9777
Website: www.egyptianconsulate.co.uk
Opening hours: Mon-Fri 0930-1230 (lodging applications); 1430-1600 (visa collection).

Embassy of the Arab Republic of Egypt in the USA
3521 International Court, NW, Washington, DC 20008 USA
Tel: (202) 895 5400.
Website: www.egyptembassy.us

Money

Currency: Egyptian Pound (EGP; symbol E£) = 100 piastres. Notes are in denominations of E£100, 50, 20, 10, 5, 1, 50 piastres and 25 piastres. Coins are in denominations of 20, 10 and 5 piastres.

Currency exchange: Available at banks, official bureaux de change and most hotels. Banks often have better exchange rates than bureaux de change or hotels. All common international currencies are accepted.

Credit & debit cards: American Express, Diners Club, MasterCard and Visa are accepted, but only bigger hotels or restaurants in Cairo and restaurants in tourist areas will accept credit cards as payment. Check with your credit or debit card company for details of merchant acceptability and other services which may be available.

Traveller's cheques: To avoid additional exchange rate

charges, travellers are advised to take traveller's cheques in US Dollars, Euros or Pounds Sterling.

Currency restrictions: The import and export of foreign currency is unlimited. The import of local currency is unlimited. The export of local currency is prohibited.

Banking hours: Sun-Thurs 0830-1400.

Exchange rate indicators:
Rate at time of publishing
£1.00= E£10.20
$1.00= E£5.81

Duty Free

The following goods may be imported into Egypt without incurring customs duty:
200 cigarettes or 25 cigars or 200g of tobacco; 1l of alcoholic beverages; 1l of perfume or eau de cologne; gifts up to the value of E£500.

Note: Persons travelling with valuable electronic equipment such as cameras, video cameras or computers may be required to list these in their passports to ensure that they will be exported on departure.
All cash, travellers cheques and gold over E£500 should be declared on arrival.

Prohibited items: Narcotics, firearms, cotton, gold and silver purchased locally unless for personal use only and in small quantities; for a full list, contact the Egyptian Commercial Office, 23 South Street, London W1L 2XD (tel: (020) 7499 3002).

Public Holidays

Below are listed Public Holidays for the January 2006-June 2007 period.
2006: Jan 7* Coptic Christmas Day. Jan 10 Grand Feast. **Jan 31** Islamic New Year. Apr 23 Sham el-Nassim (Coptic Easter). **Apr 25** Sinai Liberation Day (Sinai only). **May 1** Labour Day. Jun 18 Liberation Day. **Jul 23** Revolution Day. **Aug 15** Wafa'a el Nil (Flooding of the Nile). **Sept 11*** Coptic New Year. **Oct 6** Armed Forces Day. **Oct 22** Bairam Feast (end of Ramadan). **Oct 24** suez Victory Day. **Dec 23** Victory Day. **Dec 31** Grand Feast.
2007: Jan 7* Coptic Christmas Day. Jan 20 Islamic New Year. Apr 8 Sham el-Nassim (Coptic Easter). **Apr 25** Sinai Liberation Day (Sinai only). **May 1** Labour Day. Jun 18 Liberation Day.

Note: (a)*These holidays are not official, although Coptic Christians may observe them. (b) Muslim festivals are timed according to local sightings of various phases of the moon and the dates given above are approximations. During the lunar month of Ramadan that precedes the Bairam Feast, Muslims fast during the day and feast at night and normal business patterns may be interrupted. Some restaurants are closed during the day but most tourist attractions and hotels are not affected. Some disruption may continue into the three-day Grand Feast itself. For more information, see the *World of Islam* appendix.

Health

	Special Precautions?	Certificate Required?
Yellow Fever	No	1
Cholera	Yes	2
Typhoid & Polio	3	N/A
Malaria	4	N/A

Note: *Regulations and requirements may be subject to change at short notice, and you are advised to contact your doctor well in advance of your intended date of departure. Any numbers in the chart refer to the footnotes below.*

1: A yellow fever vaccination certificate is required from travellers over one year of age coming from infected areas (see below). Those arriving in transit from such areas without a certificate will be detained at the airport until their onward flight departs. The following countries and areas are regarded by the Egyptian health authorities as being infected with yellow fever: all countries in mainland Africa south of the Sahara with the exception of Lesotho, Mauritania, Mozambique, Namibia, South Africa, Swaziland and Zimbabwe (and including Chad, Mali and Niger); Sudan south of 15°N (location certificate issued by a Sudanese official is required in order to be exempt from vaccination certificate); São Tomé e Principe. *Also* in the endemic zone are Belize, Bolivia, Brazil, Colombia, Costa Rica, Ecuador, French Guiana, Guyana, Panama, Peru, Surinam, Trinidad & Tobago and Venezuela.
2: Following WHO guidelines issued in 1973, a cholera vaccination certificate is no longer a condition of entry to Egypt and the country is currently not listed as infected. However, sporadic cases of cholera have been reported and precautions could be considered. Up-to-date advice should be sought before deciding whether these precautions should include vaccination as medical opinion is divided over its effectiveness; see the *Health* appendix for further information.
3: Vaccination against typhoid and polio is advised.
4: Limited malaria risk, in the malignant *falciparum* and benign *vivax* forms, may exist from June to October in the El Faiyoum area. There is no risk in Cairo or Alexandria at any time.
Food & drink: Mains water is normally chlorinated and, whilst relatively safe, may cause mild abdominal upsets. Bottled water is available and is advised for the first few weeks of the stay. Milk is unpasteurised and should be boiled. Powdered or tinned milk is available and is advised, but make sure that it is reconstituted with pure water. Avoid dairy products which are likely to have been made from unboiled milk. Only eat well-cooked meat and fish, preferably served hot. Pork, salad and mayonnaise may carry increased risk. Vegetables should be cooked and fruit peeled. Drinking water outside main cities and towns carries a greater risk and should always be sterilised.
Other risks: Precautions against *hepatitis A* and *E* and *diphtheria* should be considered. Immunisation against *hepatitis B* is sometimes advised. *Dengue fever* occurs in epidemics. *Onchocerciasis* (river blindness) and *leishmaniasis* occur. *Bilharzia* (schistosomiasis) is present in the Nile Delta and the Nile Valley. Avoid swimming and paddling in fresh water; swimming pools which are well chlorinated and maintained are safe. *Filariasis* may occur in the Nile Delta. There may be a danger of snakes and scorpions in certain areas. Sandstorms are also a risk in some parts.
Rabies is present. For those at high risk, vaccination before arrival should be considered. If you are bitten, seek medical advice without delay. For more information, consult the *Health* appendix.
Health care: Public hospitals and chemists are open to tourists. Health insurance is strongly advised.

Travel - International

AIR:
The national airline is *EgyptAir (MS)* (website: www.egyptair.com.eg).
Approximate flight times: From Cairo to *London* is four hours 45 minutes (from Luxor to *London* is five hours 35 minutes), from Cairo to *Los Angeles* is 16 hours 40 minutes, to *New York* is 14 hours 25 minutes, to *Singapore* is 12 hours 35 minutes, and to *Sydney* is 20 hours.
Main airports: *Cairo International (CAI)*, 24km (15 miles) northeast of the city at Heliopolis (travel time - 1 hour). *To/from the airport:* There are bus services every 30 minutes, and taxis are available. Special limousines are offered by local and international operators. Hotel cars may also be available. *Facilities:* Incoming and outgoing duty free shops selling a wide range of goods, several car hire firms, post office, bank/bureau de change, restaurants and bar, hotel reservation service, souvenir shops, bookshop and travel insurance services.
Borg El Arab (HBE), has replaced El Nouzha airport as the main international airport for Alexandria. It lies 60 km (37 miles) southwest of Alexandria. *Facilities:* Duty free shop, bank and exchange services, VIP lounge, post office and restaurant.
Luxor Airport (LXR) is 5.5km (3.5 miles) from Luxor. *To/from the airport:* There is a regular bus service to the city centre (travel time - 15 minutes). Special limousine and local taxi services are available. *Facilities:* Car hire, bank and exchange services, and a bar and restaurant. Improvement works have taken place and are expected to continue to meet the increasing flow of tourists.
Departure tax: None.
SEA:
The main coastal ports are *Alexandria, Nuweiba, Port Said* and *Suez*. The Saudi Sea Transport Company runs a regular car ferry service between Suez and Jeddah. A ferry service usually travels twice per week up the Nile between Wadi Halfa (Sudan) and Egypt High Dam; it departs from High Dam on Saturday and Wadi Halfa on Tuesday. However, it is occasionally suspended. For further information, contact the Nile Valley Association (tel: (2) 578 9256). There is also a ferry service that operates twice-daily between South Sinai and Aqaba (Jordan). There are special rates for children under 12 and under three years of age. For more information, contact the Cairo Navigation Agency (tel: (2) 574 5755 *or* 575 5568). Many cruise ships stop over in Egypt as part of their African itinerary.
RAIL:
There are no international rail links to any of Egypt's northwestern neighbours. The railheads at Aswan and Wadi Halfa, Sudan are connected by a ferry across Lake Nasser.
ROAD:
The road border between Libya and Egypt is open. There are two border crossings between Israel and Egypt: one runs from Cairo via El Arish to Rafiah on the north Sinai coast; and the other from Cairo via Suez and Taba to Eilat. Daily coaches leave early in the morning from Tel Aviv and Jerusalem in Israel for travel via El Arish/Rafiah to Cairo and vice versa. There are no direct buses from Eilat to Cairo; it is necessary to change in Taba. The crossing from Taba to Eilat is now open 24 hours a day. Passengers in taxis and rented cars are not permitted to cross the borders between Israel and Egypt. Privately owned vehicles may be taken across other borders, provided the appropriate documentation is obtained. All private vehicles entering Egypt must have a three-month *triptyche* or *Carnet de passage en douane* from an automobile club in the country of registration. The driver must hold an international drivers' licence. Visas should normally be obtained in advance; however, travellers entering Egypt via Taba may be able to obtain visas at the border. Contact the Tourist Office for further details of entry restrictions (see *Top Things To Do*).

Travel - Internal

AIR:
EgyptAir operates daily flights between Cairo, Alexandria, Luxor, Aswan, Abu Simbel, and Hurghada. For information on schedules, contact local offices *or* see online (website: www.egyptair.com.eg). *Air Sinai* operates services from Cairo to Eilat, El Arish, Hurghada, Luxor, Ras El Nakab, St Catherine, Sharm el-Sheikh and Taba.
SEA/RIVER:
There are slow and fast ferry services linking Hurghada with Sharm el-Sheikh in Sinai. Slow ferries operate from Sharm el-Sheikh to Hurghada on Mon, Wed, Fri; and from Hurghada to Sharm el-Sheikh on Tues, Thurs, Sun (travel time - six hours). Fast ferries operate in both directions on Mon, Thurs and Sat (travel time - one hour 30 minutes). The traditional Nile sailing boats, *feluccas*, can be hired by the hour for relaxed sailing on the Nile. Regular Nile cruises operate between Luxor and Aswan, and sometimes between Cairo and Aswan, usually for the following periods: four nights, five days (standard tour); six nights, seven days (extended tour), and 14 nights, 15 days (full Nile cruise). There are over 160 individually owned boats of all categories operating on the Nile.
RAIL:
A comprehensive rail network run by Egyptian State Railways (tel: (02) 574 9474 *or* 575 3555) offering a high standard of service is operated along an east-west axis from Sallom on the Libyan border to Alexandria and Cairo, and along the Nile to Luxor and Aswan. There are also links to Port Said and Suez. There are frequent trains from Cairo to Alexandria, and also several luxury air-conditioned day and night trains with sleeping and restaurant cars from Cairo to Luxor and Aswan for the Nile Valley tourist trade. For the overnight train, bookings should be made one week in advance through a travel agent or through Abela Egypt, Ramses Station, Ramses Square, Cairo (tel: (2) 574 9274 *or* 574 9474; website: www.sleepingtrains.com). On Egyptian state railways, children under four years travel free. Children aged four to nine years pay half fare. Holders of Youth Hostel cards can get reductions. For details of other possible reductions, contact the Tourist Office.
ROAD:
Traffic drives on the right. Besides the Nile Valley and Delta, which hold an extensive road network, there are paved roads along the Mediterranean and African Red Sea coasts. The road looping through the Western Desert oases from Asyut to Giza is fully paved. The speed limit is usually 90kph (56mph) on motorways and 100kph (62mph) on the desert motorway from Cairo to Alexandria (there are substantial fines for speeding). Private motoring in the desert regions is not recommended without suitable vehicles and a guide. For more details, contact the Egyptian Automobile Club in Cairo. **Bus:** The national bus system serves the Nile Valley and the coastal road. Main routes are from Cairo to St Catherine, Sharm el-Sheikh, Dahab, Ras Sudr, El-Tour, Taba and Rafah; from Suez to El-Tour and Sharm el-Sheikh; and from Sharm el-Sheikh to Taba, Neweiba, El-Tour, Dahab and St Catherine. Coach services operate between Cairo and Agami, Marakia-Mrabila, Marina-Aidda Sidi Abd El Rahman, Matrouh, Ma'amoura Beach and Hurghada. **Taxi:** These are available in all the larger cities and are metered (see also *Urban* below). Long-distance group taxis for all destinations are cheap. Fares should be agreed in advance. In Cairo, taxis are white and black, in Alexandria they are orange and black. Taxis which are Peugeot 504s are 'service' taxis. They are larger but more expensive. **Car hire:** This is available through international and local companies. The driver must be at least 25 years of age. Travel through the desert wilderness is available through local tour operators. It should be borne in mind that desert travel is extremely hazardous without an experienced guide, ample supplies of water and a vehicle in good mechanical condition.
Documentation: Visitor's own insurance and an International Driving Permit are required to drive any motor vehicle. *Carnet de Passage* or a suitable deposit is necessary for the temporary import of visitor's own vehicle. All vehicles (including motorcycles) are required by law to carry a fire extinguisher and a red hazard triangle.
URBAN:
The government-owned *Cairo Transport Authority* runs buses and tram services in Cairo and also operates cross-Nile ferries. There is a central area flat fare. In addition, there are other buses and fixed-route shared taxi and minibus services run by private operators. Vehicles normally wait at city terminals to obtain a full load, but there are frequent departures. Fares are three to four times higher than on the buses. Cairo's suburban railways have been upgraded to provide a rapid transit network, including Africa's first underground railway. Alexandria also has buses and tramways, with first- and second-class seats and distance-regulated fares.
Travel times: The following chart gives approximate travel times (in hours and minutes) from **Cairo** to other major cities/towns in Egypt.

	Air	Road	Rail
Alexandria	0.30	-	2.30
Aswan	-	-	-
Marsa Matr'h	1.30	-	-
Suez	-	-	-

Travel Advice

Most visits to Egypt are trouble-free. However, there is a high threat from terrorism and the Egyptian security services have tightened security throughout Egypt.
This advice is based on information provided by the Foreign and Commonwealth Office in the UK. It is correct at time of publishing. As the situation can change rapidly, visitors are advised to contact the following organisations for the latest travel advice:

British Foreign and Commonwealth Office
Tel: (0845) 850 2829.
Website: www.fco.gov.uk

US Department of State
Website: http://travel.state.gov/travel

Accommodation

Tourism is one of Egypt's main industries and accommodation is available around all the major attractions and the larger cities. Egypt has all types of accommodation on offer, from deluxe hotels to youth hostels, at prices to suit all budgets.
HOTELS:
The main cities have moderately priced quality hotels, which *must* be booked well in advance, especially during the winter months. Smaller hotels are very good value. Hotel bills are subject to a tax and service charge of 12 per cent.

CAMPING/CARAVANNING:

There are only a few official campsites in the country. Tourists are advised to contact the local tourist offices on arrival for further details.

YOUTH HOSTELS:

There are 16 youth hostels altogether, which are located mainly in large towns, on the coast and in popular tourist regions.

ACCOMMODATION INFORMATION

Egyptian Hotel Association
8 El Sad El Ali Street, Dokki, Giza, Cairo, Egypt
Tel: (2) 761 1400.
Website: www.egypttourism.org
Contact the Association to obtain a copy of the 'Egyptian Hotel Guide'.

Egyptian Youth Hostels Associaton
1 El-Ibrahimy Street, Garden City, Cairo, Egypt
Tel: (2) 794 0527 *or* 796 1448.
Website: www.egypttourism.org.

Top Things To See

- In **Islamic (Medieval) Cairo**, wander around narrow congested streets filled with donkey carts, spice traders and imposing mosques. A central landmark is **Midan Hussein**, a large open square with tea houses around the perimeter, and dominated by the sacred **Mosque of Sayyidna Al-Hussein**. The **Al-Azhar Mosque** contains the oldest university in the world (AD 970). The pre-Ottoman **Madrassa and Mausoleum of Al-Ghouri**, has Sufi dancing, and opposite is **Wakala of Al-Ghouri**, an attractively preserved cultural centre. Exhibits in the **Museum of Islamic Art** bring Islamic Cairo to life, with arts, ceramics, mosaics and calligraphy. The **Citadel** was home to Egypt's rulers for 700 years; an imposing medieval fortress offering sweeping views of the city. Within is the **Midan Salah al-Din** with the unmissable **Sultan Hassan** and **Rifai Mosques**. The **Mohammad Ali Mosque** has classic Ottoman minarets and interior. Other attractions within the Citadel include the **Military National Museum, Al-Gawhara Palace and Museum** and the **National Police Museum**. **City of the Dead (Northern Cemetery)** is a Mamluk necropolis with hundreds of thousands of tombs dating from the 12th century. In **Sharia Talat Harb** street and **Midan Tahrir (Liberation Square)** spend time at one of the country's greatest attractions; the **Museum of Egyptian Antiquities** housing over 130,000 exhibits, including Pharaonic and Byzantine art and sculpture, the **Mummy Room** and the celebrated **Tutankhamun** exhibition. In the south of Cairo, home to the Coptic Orthodox Christians, visit the **Coptic Museum** which has the world's greatest collection of Coptic art. The **Hanging Church, Monastery of St George** and the churches of **St Sergius** and **St Barbara** are all in the same area. The **Ben Ezra Synagogue** is one of the oldest in Egypt, and represents what remains of the Jewish community.
- The small island of **Gezira** is a more upmarket area with the **Opera House** (a US$30 million arts complex) containing the **Museum of Modern Art**, and the **Cairo Tower** with great city views.
- Cairo is most famous for the **Great Pyramids**, Egypt's most visited monuments. Of the three main pyramids (**Cheops, Chephren** and **Mycerinus**), the largest is 137m (449ft) high and contains some three million blocks of stone. Exploring the interiors is possible via labyrinthine tunnels and staircases.
- Adjacent is the bewitching **Sphinx**, as named by the ancient Greeks, with the head of a woman and body of a lion. In the evenings there are *son et lumière* performances - extravagant sound and light shows telling the story of ancient Egypt. Camels, horses and donkeys can be hired to explore the site.
- See the remains of the Old Kingdom's capital **Memphis**; at **Saqqara**, visit the necropolis and the **Step Pyramid** - the latter is older than those at Giza, with well-preserved wall reliefs and royal tombs. **Dahshur** has only been open to foreigners since 1996, and is famous for its **Bent Pyramid** and a huge field of royal tombs.
- In **Luxor**, once the ancient city of **Thebes**, the highlight is the **Karnak Temple**, covering an immense 100 acres (40.5 hectares). The whole site has colossal statues, reliefs, obelisks and halls and the **Avenue of the Sphinxes**. There are nightly *son et lumière* shows. Along the riverbank, **Luxor Temple** is guarded by a huge statue of **Ramses II**. A pleasant walk north along the corniche brings you to the **Luxor Museum** where a small, interesting collection of relics from the Theban Temples and Necropolis can be viewed. The **Mummification Museum** has exhibits of human, reptile and bird mummies, as well as explanations of how they are made.

- On the **West Bank** of the Nile is the vast **Theban Necropolis**, containing some of the world's finest tombs: the **Valley of the Kings, Valley of the Queens** and **Tombs of the Nobles**. Highlights include the **Tomb of Tutankhamun, Ramses II** and the **Tomb of Nefertari**, reputed to be the country's finest.
- A beautiful winter resort, relaxing **Aswan** is the gateway to Africa, and steeped in Nubian culture. The corniche provides attractive riverside walks, and a stop-off for many cruise ships. In the evenings, floating restaurants provide a lively gathering place, and a folkloric dance troupe performs nightly during winter months at the **Cultural Centre**. The **Old Cataract Hotel** is famous as the location of the film *Death on the Nile*.
- **Elephantine Island** is easily accessible by river taxi from Aswan. Formerly Egypt's frontier town, recent excavations of this ancient site have revealed **temples** and a **fortress**. **Aswan Museum** contains exhibits found in Nubia and Aswan.
- Head south to the the tiny **Island of Plants**, presented to Lord Horatio Kitchener in the 1890s in recognition of his military services. Importing exotic flowers and plants from India and Malaysia, he created a beautiful botanical garden, attracting a wide variety of birds.
- On the **West Bank** of the Nile lies the **Monastery of St Simeon**, which resembles a fortress. Nearby is the domed granite and sandstone **Mausoleum of Aga Khan**.
- Be impressed by the sheer size of the **Aswan Dam**, built by the British at the beginning of the century. It is 11,811 feet (364m) high and provides electricity and irrigation for the whole of Egypt.
- Also near Aswan is the **Temple of Philae**, on the **Island of Philae**. The Temple is one of Egypt's most famous attractions, and after being under threat from flooding from the High Dam, UNESCO moved it stone by stone to a higher point on the island.
- Do not miss **Abu Simbel**, the magnificent **Sun Temple of Ramses II**, also rescued from flooding by UNESCO. Ramses had four gigantic statues of himself built in order to intimidate travellers entering Egypt from Africa, especially the Nubians.
- **Kom Ombo** ('The city of gold'), 30km (18 miles) north of Aswan, is a largely Nubian settlement, known for its **Temple of Haroeris and Sobek**.
- **Edfu** is famed for the largest and best preserved Pharaoronic Temple in Egypt, the **Temple of Horus**. It is a favoured end point for *felucca* trips to and from Luxor.
- In **Alexandria**, Egypt's second city, see relics from the third century BC in the **Graeco-Roman Museum**. There is a recently excavated **Roman Amphitheatre**. **Fort Quait Bey** is a 15th-century fort built on the foundations of the long-gone **Pharos Lighthouse**, one of the Seven Wonders of the World. The modern **Mosque of Abu al-Abbas Mursi** dominates the main square on **Sharia Tatwig**, and other places of interest include the **Museum of Fine Arts**, and **Montazah Palace** with attractive gardens, often the summer venue of theatre performances.
- The ancient city of **Rosetta**, 65km (39 miles) away from Alexandria, is famed for being where the Rosetta Stone was discovered (now housed in the British Museum) and has attractive Ottoman, 'Delta Style' architecture.
- **El Alamein** is a small coastal village 100km (60 miles) west of Alexandria and an easy day trip. Famous as the scene of a decisive Allied victory, which determined the

fate of Egypt and Britain's Empire, there is a **War Museum, Cemetery** and **Memorial** to the soldiers who died in battle.
- A great example of modern engineering, the **Suez Canal** links the Red Sea with the Mediterranean. Completed in 1869, it has repeatedly been the cause of dispute, most recently when blocked during the 1967 war with Israel. **Port Said** is the main city. Anyone travelling to Sinai by road would cross the Suez on a small shuttle boat, or under the tunnel.

Top Things To Do

- Try your skills at bargaining at Cairo's famous **Khan-el Khalili**, one of the world's largest bazaars, pulsing with commerce and crammed with spices, coppersmiths, perfume and trinkets. Here, **Fishawi's tea house** has been in business for over 200 years, and is still a great people-watching venue. For an even more exotic touch, go to the **Camel Market (Souq al-Gamaal)**, held every morning at **Birqash**, around 35km (21 miles) from Cairo, located on the edge of the Western Desert. Hundreds of camels are sold daily, most having been brought from Sudan. A livestock market is held every Tuesday morning at **El-Hebel**, a village 4km (2.4 miles) from Luxor.
- Escape the city in Egypt's six oases. All have accommodation and can be accessed by public transport. The largest and most developed oasis is **Kharga**, with a Berber community, temples and museums. **Dhakla Oasis** has hot springs, and camel rides over the sand dunes. The nearby village of **Bashandi** sells handicrafts made by local girls. The smallest is **Farafra**, an ancient fort town; **Bahariyya** is made up of several small villages, famed for its olives and dates. **Al-Faiyum Oasis** is 100km (60 miles) southwest of Cairo, and the area contains small pyramids, the old city of **Karanis**, and temples. **Siwa** is the furthest west and remote, but the most picturesque and idyllic. The community is traditional and Berber-speaking.
- Go on a **Nile cruise**, usually between **Luxor** and **Aswan**, and generally lasting around five days. Also see *Top Things To See*. Along the Nile, *felucca* owners tout for custom; from Luxor, it is possible to hire one for a brief sunset cruise to **Banana Island**, or even to organise a trip upriver to Aswan. **Hot-air balloon trips** are also available, offering the best views of Luxor.
- **Alexandria**, 'The Pearl of the Mediterranean' still attracts wealthy Cairenes as a summer retreat. Swimming and diving are popular, although beaches tend to be overcrowded in summer. **Ma'amoura** is a more liberal and Westernised beach, and further out of the city **Agami** and **Hannoville** are cleaner and less crowded. Diving is possible on **Montazah** beach. Further west from El Alamein is the coastal resort of **Mersa Matruh**.
- The **Red Sea Coast** sits strategically between Africa and Asia, rich in mineral wealth and revered as the place of miracles and prophets in Judaism, Islam and Christianity. God is said to have appeared to Moses here, and delivered the Israelites from the Egyptian army by parting the Red Sea. These days, the region is revered for its spectacular **diving resorts, beaches, stunning coastline** and **vast deserts**. This area has some of the best diving and snorkelling in the world, and has a more liberal atmosphere than the rest of Egypt. The coastline attracts tourists ranging from top-class package holidaymakers, to backpackers in campsites: **Sharm el-Sheikh** is a large

Credit: ©Photo Hutter

Credit: ©Photo Hutter

resort, and is best for diving. **Na'ama Bay** is much better developed and upmarket, with private beaches. A few kilometres north is **Shark Bay**, a quieter resort camp. The beaches at **Dahab** are spectacularly framed by jagged mountains. Holiday villages within a Bedouin settlement are close by. **Nuweiba** is a port city, with a plethora of resorts. Local Bedouins offer jeep safaris into the interior. Between here and **Taba**, there are many small, quiet resorts that are under threat of being overshadowed by a huge new tourist development, **Taba Heights**. On the west of the Red Sea Coast, the biggest diving resort is **Hurghada**, once a fishing village and now a major commercial tourist centre. **Ras Muhammed** is the southernmost point on the peninsula, fringed with lagoons and reefs, and is now a **National Park**.

- Little is accessible in **Sinai**'s interior, a barren area with rocks and sands, and the best way to explore this is by **treks** or **safari** by camel or jeep. One of the highlights is **St Catherine's Monastery**, now home to Greek Orthodox monks. It has been a place of pilgrimage since the 4th century. Within the monastery is the 'burning bush' from which God is said to have appeared to speak to Moses. **Mount Sinai**, revered as the site of God's revelation of the Ten Commandments, is a craggy and sheer-faced mount of grey and red, dramatic and steep. Care should be taken when ascending.

TOURIST INFORMATION

Egyptian State Tourist Office in the UK
Egyptian House, 3rd Floor, 170 Piccadilly, London W1V 9EJ, UK
Tel: (020) 7493 5283 *or* (09001) 600 299 (24-hour brochure service; calls cost 60p per minute).
Website: www.egypttreasures.gov.eg

Egyptian Tourist Authority in the USA
630 Fifth Avenue, Suite 2305, New York, NY 10111, USA
Tel: (212) 332 2570.
Website: www.egypttourism.org

Entertainment

FOOD & DRINK: Egyptian cuisine is excellent, combining many of the best traditions of Middle Eastern cooking, and there are both large hotel restaurants and smaller specialist ones throughout the main towns. Some of the larger hotels in Cairo and its environs have top quality kitchens serving cosmopolitan dishes. In the centre of Cairo, American-style snack bars are also spreading. Restaurants have waiter service. Although Egypt is a Muslim country, alcohol is available in cafe-style bars and good restaurants. The legal drinking age is 21.

National specialities:
- *Foul* (bean dishes).
- Stuffed vine leaves.
- Roast pigeon.
- Grilled aubergines.
- Kebabs.
- *Humus* (chickpeas).

National drinks:
- *Kahwa* (thick, strong coffee).
- *Shay bil na'na'* (mint tea).
- *Karkaday* (clear, bright red drink made from hibiscus flowers).
- *Aswanli* (dark beer made in Aswan).
- *Zibib* (alcoholic aniseed flavoured drink).

Tipping: 10 to 12 per cent is added to hotel and restaurant bills but an extra tip of 5 per cent is normal. Taxi drivers generally expect 10 per cent.

NIGHTLIFE: Sophisticated nightclubs, discos, casinos and good restaurants can be found in Cairo, Alexandria and most large towns. The nightlife in Luxor and Aswan often includes barbecues along the Nile.

SHOPPING: The most interesting shopping area for tourists in Cairo is the old bazaar, *Khan-el-Khalili*, specialising in reproductions of antiquities. Jewellery, spices, copper utensils and Coptic cloth are some of the many special items. There are also modern shopping centres available, particularly near Tehrir Square. Haggling is expected, and sometimes encouraged, as a way of communication and human contact. **Shopping hours:** *Winter:* Tues, Wed, Fri and Sat 0900-1900, Mon and Thurs 0900-2000. During Ramadan, hours vary, with shops often closing on Sunday. *Summer:* Tues, Wed, Fri-Sun 0900-1230 and 1600-2000.

Business

- **GDP:** US$316.3 billion.
- **Main imports:** Machinery and equipment, foodstuffs, chemicals, wood products and fuels.
- **Main exports:** Crude oil, petroleum products, cotton, textiles, metal products and chemicals.
- **Main trade partners:** China, France, Germany, Italy, Saudi Arabia, Syria, Spain, UK and USA.

ECONOMY: On taking power in 1952, President Nasser quickly instituted a Soviet-style command economy that was closed to Western investment. After Nasser's death, his successor, Anwar Sadat, gradually dismantled the existing system in favour of a policy of *infitah* (openness) towards investment. Egypt's economy underwent rapid growth during the 1970s with the swift expansion of the oil industry, tourism and the Suez Canal. During the 1990s, stern fiscal policies, agreed with the IMF and World Bank, and further market-oriented measures brought the Egyptian economy to its current condition. As of mid-2004, annual growth had fallen to 3 per cent, inflation was about 14 per cent, while official unemployment was 10 per cent (although there is considerable under-employment). Egypt's major industries are textiles, fertilisers, rubber products and cement. There are also steel production works and several vehicle assembly plants. The main crops are cotton, rice, wheat, sugar, maize and a range of fruit and vegetables. Expansion of the tourist sector has been hampered by the terrorist activities of Islamic fundamentalists. Agriculture, which relies on irrigation from the Nile, employs one-third of the working population. Foreign aid, especially from the USA, is an important source of government funds.

CONFERENCES/CONVENTIONS: Cairo has many hotels and three large meeting halls (seating up to 2000 people), which are equipped for use as conference centres. The Cairo International Conference Centre, 12km (7 miles) east of Cairo International Airport, has seating for 2500 people, with an exhibition hall, banquet hall and comprehensive facilities. There is also a convention centre at Alexandria University, which has a main hall with seating for 2400.

COMMERCIAL INFORMATION

Egyptian-British Chamber of Commerce in the UK
PO Box 4EG, 4th Floor, 299 Oxford Street, London W1A 4EG, UK
Tel: (020) 7499 3100.
Website: www.theebcc.com

Federation of Egyptian Chambers of Commerce
4 Midan el-Falaky Square, Cairo, Egypt
Tel: (2) 795 1136.

Cairo Chamber of Commerce
(address as for the Federation)
Tel: (2) 354 2943.

Cairo International Conference and Exhibition Centre
Nasr Road, Nasr City, Cairo, Egypt
Tel: (2) 263 4631 *or* 263 4632.
Website: www.cicc.egnet.net

Egyptian General Company for Tourism and Hotels (Information on Conferences/Conventions)
6th floor, 4 Latin America Street, Garden City, Cairo, Egypt
Tel: (2) 795 7867 *or* 795 0603.

The Egyptian State Tourist Office in the UK can also provide information on conferences and conventions (see Top Things To Do).

El Salvador

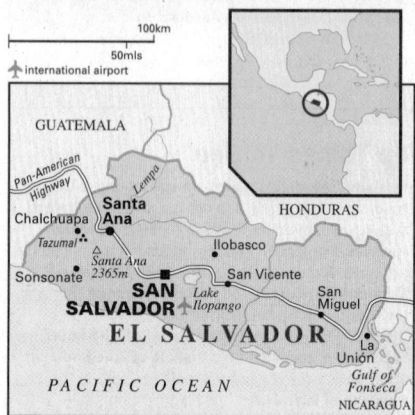

Location: Central America.

Time: GMT - 6.

Overview

Most of El Salvador ("the saviour" in Spanish) is volcanic. The country has been wracked by civil war and a succession of natural disasters which have left it physically devastated and psychologically traumatised.

In the 1920s, the military entered the political arena – by virtue of successfully putting down a farm workers' revolt led by Augustin Farabundo Marti – and has retained a central role ever since. The economic problems grew throughout the 1950s, 60s and 70s. The 1980 assassination of Archbishop Romero – a leading critic of civil rights abuses – by right-wing elements, accelerated the country's plunge into civil war.

As the war spread throughout the country during the 1980s, the Government received huge amounts of US military and civil aid. A formal ceasefire, under UN auspices and supervised by a joint forum of the two sides, entitled the National Commission for the Consolidation of Peace (COPAZ), came into force at the beginning of 1992. Political differences were temporarily set aside in January 2001, when the country was struck by a massive earthquake, which killed several thousand and left tens of thousands homeless. The reconstruction period has been overshadowed once again by the legacy of the civil war. There have been repeated clashes over compensation, between ex-fighters and security forces, while in 2002, several former generals in exile in the USA have been convicted in US courts of human rights abuses. Despite the scars left by civil war, poverty and natural disasters, visitors will appreciate the resilience and optimism such tragedy seems to have inspired in El Salvadorans. Poor communities such as Ilobasco and La Palma have become renowned for their handicrafts and folk art. Even though crime is still a problem for those visiting the country, the National Civilian Police (PNC), created in the wake of war, is working on improving safety.

The country's major attractions include volcanoes, mountains (especially those in Cerro Verde National Park), beaches, tropical nature preserves and archaeological sites from the Maya civilisation.

General Information

AREA: 21,040 sq km (8124 sq miles).
POPULATION: 6.7 million (official estimate 2005).
POPULATION DENSITY: 318.67 per sq km.
CAPITAL: San Salvador. **Population:** 504,700 (city); 1.78 million (metropolitan area) (official estimate 2005).
GEOGRAPHY: El Salvador is located in Central America and is bordered north and west by Guatemala, north and east by Honduras and south and west by the Pacific Ocean. Most of the country is volcanic uplands, along which run

Credit: ©Corsatur

two almost parallel rows of volcanoes. The highest are Santa Ana at 2365m (7759ft), San Vicente at 2182m (7159ft) and San Salvador at 1943m (6375ft). Volcanic activity has resulted in a thick layer of ash and lava on the highlands, ideal for coffee planting. Lowlands lie to the north and south of the high backbone.

GOVERNMENT: Republic. **Head of State and Government:** Elias Antonio Saca since 2004.

LANGUAGE: The official language is Spanish. English is widely spoken.

RELIGION: 83 per cent Roman Catholic; there are also some other Christian denominations. There is a growing population of evangelical Protestants.

ELECTRICITY: 115 volts AC, 60Hz. El Salvador accepts five types of plugs; flat blade plugs, three round pins arranged in a triangle, two parallel flat pins with ground pin, v-shaped flat prongs and two round pins.

SOCIAL CONVENTIONS: Visitors should not point their finger or their foot at anyone. First names should not be used to address someone unless invited to do so. Conservative casual wear is acceptable. **Photography:** Sensitive (eg military) areas should not be photographed. A handshake is always offered as a greeting. Men and women who already know each other greet with a kiss on the cheek. Siesta is still a tradition from around 1200-1400.

Climate

Hot, subtropical climate affected by altitude. Dry season or summer runs between November and April. Coastal areas are particularly hot, with a rainy season between May and October. Upland areas have a cooler, more temperate climate.

Required clothing: Lightweight cottons and rainwear during the wet season in coastal areas. Waterproof clothing is advisable all year round. Warm clothing should be taken for higher altitudes.

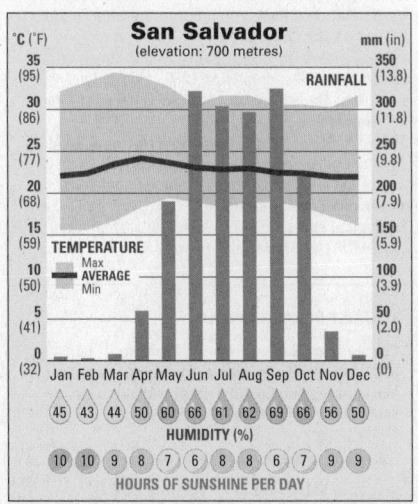

Communications

Telephone: Country code: 503. IDD is available to Europe, the USA and certain international ports.

Mobile telephone: Roaming agreements exist with some international mobile phone companies.

Internet: Internet access is readily available throughout El Salvador.

Post: Airmail to Europe takes up to two weeks. Post office

hours: Mon-Fri 0830-1600. The main branch is in Centro de Gobierno.

MEDIA: Press freedom is guaranteed under El Salvador's constitution. El Salvadoran broadcasting is dominated by private operators, with a handful of national TV networks. There are some 70 radio stations in the capital alone. Cable TV is available across much of the country and carries a wide range of international channels.

Press: Six daily newspapers are published in San Salvador, including *El Diario de Hoy*, *El Mundo* and *La Prensa Gráfica*. There are several provincial papers.

TV: Commercial channels include *Teledos*, *Canal Seis* and *TV Doce*.

Radio: *Radio El Salvador* is state-run. *Radio YSKL*, *FM Globo*, *Femenina 102.5* and *Radio Cadena Central* are commercial stations.

Passport/Visa

	Passport Required?	Visa Required?	Return Ticket Required?
Full British	Yes	No	Yes
Australian	Yes	No	Yes
Canadian	Yes	No	Yes
USA	Yes	No	Yes
Other EU	Yes	No	Yes
Japanese	Yes	No	Yes

Note: *Regulations and requirements may be subject to change at short notice, and you are advised to contact the appropriate diplomatic or consular authority before finalising travel arrangements. Any numbers in the chart refer to the footnotes below.*

PASSPORTS: Passport valid for at least six months after day of departure required by all.

VISAS: Required by all except the following for stays of up to 90 days:
(a) nationals of countries mentioned in the table above;
(b) nationals of all British, French and Dutch overseas territories, and nationals of Hong Kong (when the passport is marked 'Nationality: British Citizen' *only*);
(c) nationals of Andorra, Antigua & Barbuda, Argentina, The Bahamas, Bahrain, Barbados, Belize, Brazil, Brunei, Bulgaria, Chile, Costa Rica, Croatia, El Salvador, Guam, Guatemala, Honduras, Iceland, Israel, Kuwait, Liechtenstein, Macedonia, Madagascar, Malaysia, Marshall Islands, Mexico, Monaco, New Zealand, Nicaragua, Norway, Panama, Paraguay, Qatar, Romania, St Kitts & Nevis, St Lucia, St Vincent & the Grenadines, San Marino, Sao Tomé e Príncipe, Singapore, Solomon Islands, South Africa, Switzerland, Taiwan (China), Trinidad & Tobago, Turkey, Tuvalu, Uruguay, Vanuatu and Vatican City;
(c) transit passengers continuing their journey within 12 hours by the same or first connecting aircraft provided holding valid onward or return documentation and not leaving the airport.

Note: Nationals of Afghanistan, Albania, Algeria, Armenia, Angola, Bangladesh, Bolivia, Bosnia & Herzegovina, Botswana, China (PR), Colombia, Congo, Congo (Rep), Cuba, East Timor, Ecuador, Eritrea, Ethiopia, Ghana, Haiti, India, Indonesia, Iran, Iraq, Jordan, Korea (Dem Rep), Laos, Lebanon, Liberia, Libya, Mali, Mongolia, Mozambique, Nepal, Nigeria, Oman, Pakistan, Palestinian Authority, Peru, Sierra Leone, Somalia, Sri Lanka, Sudan, Syrian Arab Republic, Venezuela, Vietnam and Yemen need authorisation from the immigration authorities in El Salvador and their visa processing time can therefore take up to three weeks. Applicants should apply in plenty of time.

Types of visa and cost: *Tourist* and *Business*: US$30 (single entry); US$45 (multiple-entry, valid six months); US$60 (multiple-entry, valid 12 months).

Validity: *Tourist* and *Business*: single entry, valid up to 30 days; multiple-entry, valid either six or 12 months. Visas can be renewed at the Immigration Office in El Salvador.

Application to: Consulate (or consular section at Embassy); see *Passport/Visa Information*.

Application requirements: (a) Completed application form. (b) One passport-size photo. (c) Valid passport. (d) For tourist visas, a photocopy of the return ticket is necessary or, if the tickets have not yet been purchased, an original letter from the travel agency stating that the tickets are being purchased, or a travel itinerary. (e) Fee, payable in cash (US$ *only*) or by cheque (in US dollars, made payable to 'Direccion General de Tesoreria'). Visa fees are non-refundable. *Business:* (a)-(e) and, if from a country listed above as requiring authorisation from El Salvador, (f) Letter of invitation from the company being visited in El Salvador and a letter from the company the applicant is representing, both translated into Spanish.

Working days required: Tourist and business visas are normally issued within 24 hours. If authorisation from the Immigration Department in El Salvador is needed, processing time is approximately 21 days.

Temporary residence: Apply to Ministry of Interior in San Salvador.

PASSPORT/VISA INFORMATION

Embassy of El Salvador in the UK
Mayfair House, 39 Great Portland Street, London W1W 7JZ, UK
Tel: (020) 7436 8282.
Opening hours: Mon-Fri 0900-1600.

Embassy of El Salvador in the USA
2308 California St, NW, Washington, DC 20008, USA
Tel: (202) 265 9671/2 (ext 248/244 - tourism section).
Website: www.elsalvador.org

Money

Currency: Colón (SVC) = 100 centavos. Notes are in denominations of ¢200, 100, 50, 25, 10 and 5. Coins are in denominations of SVC1, and 50, 25, 10, 5 and 1 centavos. Due to the introduction of the US Dollar into the country, dollars have been accepted as dual currency since January 2001 and are now widely used and will eventually completely replace the Colón.

Note: Visitors should reconvert all unspent Colóns before leaving the country, as they are neither exchanged nor accepted in these countries.

Note: Most banks are closed for balancing the books on 29-30 June and 30-31 Dec. These dates may vary for individual banks.

Currency exchange: Visitors are advised to change currency only at banks and official bureaux de change.

Credit & debit cards: American Express, MasterCard and Visa are widely accepted, whilst Diners Club has more limited use. Check with your credit or debit card company for details of merchant acceptability and other services which may be available. There are a small number of ATM machines around the country.

Travellers cheques: These may be cashed at any bank or hotel on production of a passport.

Currency restrictions: No restrictions on import and export of local currency. Import of foreign currency is unlimited, but declaration is advised. Export of foreign currency is unlimited but limited to the amount declared on import for larger amounts.

Banking hours: Generally Mon-Fri 0900-1300 and 1345-1700; Sat 0900-1300 (limited service).

Exchange rate indicators:
Rate at time of publishing
£1.00=   SVC18.95
$1.00=   SVC10.83

Duty Free

The following goods may be imported into El Salvador without incurring customs duty:
200 cigarettes or 50 cigars; 2l of alcoholic beverages; up to six units of perfume; gifts to the value of US$500.

Note: There are restrictions on import and export of fruit, vegetables, plants and animals; meat products: ham and sausage are only allowed if sterilised by heat, boneless and hermetically canned.

Public Holidays

Below are listed Public Holidays for the January 2006-June 2007 period.

2006: Jan 1 New Year's Day. **Apr 12-16** Holy Week. **May 1** Labour Day. **Aug 4** Transfiguration Bank Holiday. **Aug 5-6** Festival El Salvador Mundo **Sep 15** Independence Day. **Oct 9** Columbus Day. **Nov 2** All Souls' Day. **Nov 5** Cry of Independence Day. **Dec 24** Christmas Eve. **Dec 25** Christmas Day. **Dec 31** New Year's Eve.

2007: Jan 1 New Year's Day. **April 6-9** Holy Week. **May 1** Labour Day.

Health

	Special Precautions?	Certificate Required?
Yellow Fever	No	1
Cholera	2	No
Typhoid & Polio	3	N/A
Malaria	4	N/A

Note: *Regulations and requirements may be subject to change at short notice, and you are advised to contact your doctor well in advance of your intended date of departure. Any numbers in the chart refer to footnotes below.*

1: A yellow fever vaccination certificate is required from travellers over six months of age coming from infected areas.
2: Following WHO guidelines issued in 1973, a cholera vaccination certificate is no longer a condition of entry into El Salvador. However, cases of cholera were reported in 1996 and precautions are essential. Up-to-date advice

should be sought before deciding whether these precautions should include vaccination, as medical opinion is divided over its effectiveness.

3: Typhoid is common and vaccination against typhoid and polio is advised.

4: Very low malaria risk, predominantly in the benign *vivax* form, exists all year in Santa Ana Province and in rural areas of migratory influence.

Food & drink: All water should be regarded as being potentially contaminated. Water used for drinking, brushing teeth or making ice should have first been boiled or otherwise sterilised. Milk is unpasteurised and should be boiled. Powdered or tinned milk is available and is recommended, but make sure that it is reconstituted with pure water. Avoid dairy products that are likely to have been made from unboiled milk. Only eat well-cooked meat and fish, preferably served hot. Pork, salad and mayonnaise may carry increased risk. Vegetables should be cooked and fruit peeled.

Other risks: *Dengue fever* (including *dengue haemorrhagic fever*) is reported to be on the increase. Travellers should ask their doctor for advice before travelling. *Visceral leishmaniasis* occurs in this country, as well as *cutaneous* and *mucocutaneous leishmanisis*.
Hepatitis A occurs and precautions should be taken; see the *Health* appendix for further information.
Rabies is widespread, particularly in dogs and bats. If you are bitten, seek medical advice without delay. For persons at high risk of exposure on a continuing basis, it may be advisable to have a course of rabies vaccine. Persons taking animals to El Salvador should be certain that the animals are immunised against rabies.

Health care: There are about 50 state-run hospitals with a total of more than 7000 beds. Medical facilities are limited and doctors and hospitals expect immediate cash payment. Health insurance is essential as there is no reciprocal health agreement with the UK. Most hospitals accept credit cards for hospital charges, but not for doctor's fees.

Travel - International

AIR:

The national airline is *Taca International Airlines (TA)* (website: www.taca.com). **Approximate flight times:** From San Salvador to *London*, excluding stopover time in USA (usually overnight), is 10 hours 20 minutes.
Main airports: *San Salvador (SAL)* (El Salvador International) is 62km (38 miles) from the city. *To/from the airport:* Coaches to the city operate every 30 minutes (travel time – 40 minutes). Taxis to the city are also available. **Facilities:** Restaurant, duty free shops, car hire, disabled facilities, pharmacy, bank/bureau de change, tourist information and left luggage.
Departure tax: US$27.15 (including a US$2.65 Immigration Tax), payable in US Dollars or Colones. Children under two years are exempt, but *do* need to pay the Immigration Tax.

SEA:

The principal ports are *Acajutla*, *La Unión* and *La Libertad* on the Pacific coast.

RAIL:

There are currently no rail links to Guatemala. Contact the Embassy for passage details.

ROAD:

There are frequent buses from San Salvador to Guatemala City and Tegucigalpa (Honduras). If arriving at the border during off-duty hours (from Mon-Fri 1200-1400, 1800-0800 and Saturday from 1200 to Monday 0800), a duty must be paid.

Travel - Internal

AIR:

Services are available from San Salvador to San Miguel, La Unión and Usulután.

RAIL:

There are over 600km (372 miles) of railways, linking San Salvador with Acajutla, Cutuco, San Jerónimo and Angiuatu.

ROAD:
Traffic drives on the right. There are more than 12,000km (7440 miles) of roads around the country; a third of this network is either paved or improved to allow all-weather use. Car hijacking and burglaries are frequent in El Salvador (especially in the cities) and drivers are advised to travel only by day and with the doors locked at all times. New cars, particularly with foreign licence plates, are frequent targets. There are petrol stations in every town and at motorway junctions. **Bus:** A good service exists between major towns, although there can be delays if the weather is bad. Buses can be hailed. Buses travel to Costa Rica,

Nicaragua and Panama. **Car hire:** Available in San Salvador and from the airport. **Documentation:** A national or International Driving Permit is required. A vehicle may remain in the country for 30 days, and for a further 60 days on application to the Customs and Transport authorities.

URBAN:

Bus: City buses offer a good service, but are often crowded. **Taxi:** Plentiful but not metered, so it is advisable to agree the fare beforehand. Taxis are yellow and can usually be found cruising the streets looking for pick ups. Alternatively, head to the town square (or similar), where taxis usually congregate between fares. Many large hotels have their own taxi services.
Travel times: The following chart gives approximate travel times (in hours and minutes) from **San Salvador** to other major cities/towns in El Salvador.

	Road
Costa del Sol	1.30
Santa Ana	1.15
San Miguel	3.00

Travel Advice

There are very high crime rates in El Salvador. Travellers should take great care if travelling alone or at night. The threat from terrorism is low, but you should be aware of the global risk of indiscriminate terrorist attacks, which could be against civilian targets, including places frequented by foreigners.
This advice is based on information provided by the Foreign and Commonwealth Office in the UK. It is correct at time of publishing. As the situation can change rapidly, visitors are advised to contact the following organisations for the latest travel advice:

British Foreign and Commonwealth Office
Tel: (0845) 850 2829.
Website: www.fco.gov.uk

US Department of State
Website: http://travel.state.gov/travel

Accommodation

The main hotels are in the capital, and accommodation should be booked in advance. Due to a high crime rate, foreign visitors should seek advice from the Embassy before stepping outside. Lake Coatepeque is a popular resort in Western El Salvador, which has good hotels, restaurants and lodging houses. **Grading:** Hotels can be classified into three groups: deluxe, first-class and budget hotels.

YOUTH HOSTELS:

Are available in San Salvador, Juagua and El Imposible. Expect to pay US$15-20 per night.

APARTMENTS AND SELF CATERING:

Available in San Salvador, San Luis, Talpa, Playa Costa and Costa Del Sol. Cottages, flats, houses, villas, and mansions are available at variable costs.

CAMPING AND CARAVANNING:

Advisable only as part of tours to the countryside. Tour guides will be on hand for safety precautions.

ACCOMMODATION INFORMATION

El Salvador Hotel Association
Website: www.elsalhoteles.com

Top Things To See

- Founded by the Spaniard Pedro de Alvarado in 1525, the capital, **San Salvador** is a blend of modern buildings and colonial architecture, broad plazas and monuments, parks and shopping centres. The most important public buildings are downtown. Standing within a short distance of each other are the **Catedral Metropolitana** (metropolitan cathedral), the **Palacio Nacional** (national palace), the **National Treasury** and the **Teatro Nacional** (national theatre). Among the many beautiful colonial churches to be seen are **St Ignatius Loyola** (once the shrine of the Virgin of Guadalupe) with a traditional Spanish colonial facade, the **Juayua** and the **Suchitoto**. The amusement park on **San Jacinto Mountain** can be reached by cable car and gives a panoramic view of the city.
- Enjoy a bird's-eye view of San Salvador from the 1200m (3900ft) rock formation, the **Puerta del Diablo** (Devil's Doorway), just south of the **Balboa Park**, 11km (7 miles) from the capital.
- From San Salvador, excursions can be made by road to

Panchimalco, 15km (9 miles) south of the capital, around which live the Pancho Indians (pure-blooded descendants of the original Pipil tribes), who retain many of their old traditions and dress. The village of **San Sebastián**, approximately one hour by car from San Salvador, is known for its beautiful woven materials. The village is situated near **Lake Ilopango**, the largest of El Salvador's lakes, surrounded by volcanoes and mountains, and is a popular destination for outdoor and watersports enthusiasts. The mountain village of **Ilobasco**, northeast of the capital, is renowned for its beauty and its craftwork.

- Book an organised **cultural tour** to El Salvador's archaeological sites from the Maya civilisation, some dating back to the third century BC. The Mayan village of **Joya de Cerén** was buried under volcanic ash 1400 years ago and is now a UNESCO World Heritage Site. Also close to the capital is the **San Andrés** region, where fertile soil once housed Mayan settlements and where the architectural jewel, the **acropolis**, is a highlight. El Salvador's earliest people lived between 300 BC and AD 1200 at **Chalchuapa** in the Tazumal region, 78km (46 miles) from San Salvador. During this period, five important ceremonial centres were built: **Pampe**, **El Trapiche**, **Las Victorias**, **Casablanca** and the beautiful ruins at **Tazumal**, which boasts structures over 30m (90ft) high and a ball court where the Maya practised unusual sporting rites. Other interesting sites include the pre-Columbian **Tehuacán** site near **San Vicente**; the monumental **Santa Leticia** sculptures near the town of **San Miguel**; and the pre-Columbian village of **Quelepa**, also in San Miguel.

Top Things To Do

- El Salvador has a 320km- (200 mile-) Pacific Coast line with resort hotels, unspoiled beaches, fishing villages and pine forests. Beaches include **La Barra de Santiago**, **El Cuco**, **El Sunzal** and **El Tamarindo**. The best resorts tend to be found along the **Costa del Sol**, easily accessible via a modern highway.
- **Surfing** is popular, with the biggest waves rolling in at **Punta Roca** and **Los Cóbanos**.
- **Boat excursions** on the Gulf of Fonseca, a large stretch of water shared by El Salvador, Honduras and Nicaragua, are also possible, including stopovers at the many volcanic islands dotting the Gulf.
- For an inland resort, the western region of **Lake Coatepeque** at the foot of the Santa Ana volcano is recommended and offers a range of **watersports**. It also has several good hotels, restaurants and lodging houses.
- **Canoeing** and **whitewater rafting** are possible on some of the rivers, notably the **Tórtola.** Visitors can also practise **fishing** and **sailing**.
- Go on a **hiking** or **trekking** expedition to the volcanoes, lakes and parks. There are more than 25 volcanoes in El Salvador, three of which – the **Izalco**, **San Miguel** and **Santa Ana** (the largest) – are still considered active. The extinct **San Salvador** volcano is within close proximity of the capital. Another extinct volcano, the easily accessible **Cerro Verde** in the west, is located within the **Cerro Verde National Park**, also home to the popular and beautiful **Lake Coatepeque**, which sits on top of a volcanic crater. The nearby **Santa Ana** volcano, which is still active and last erupted in 1966, is located near the town of Santa Ana, whose cathedral is the most famous in El Salvador.
- Also within the area is **El Imposible National Park**, the country's most important ecological reserve, where varied vegetation and fauna offer a refuge for numerous bird and wildlife species, including the rare Black Hawk Eagle. **Ecological tours** are available. For details, contact CORSATUR (see *Tourist Information*).

TOURIST INFORMATION

Corporacion Salvadoreña de Turismo (CORSATUR) (Salvadorian Tourism Corporation)
Avenida el Espino 68, Urbanización Madre Selva, Santa Elena, Antigua Cuzlatan, El Salvador
Tel: 243 7835.
Website: www.elsalvadorturismo.gob.sv

Instituto Salvadoreño de Turismo (ISTU) (Salvadorian Institute of Tourism)
Calle Rubén Darío 619, San Salvador, El Salvador
Tel: 222 8000 (ext 131/151).
Website: www.istu.gob.sv

Entertainment

FOOD & DRINK: There are numerous Chinese, Mexican, Italian, French and local restaurants, plus several fast-food chains.

National specialities:
- Rice, beans, meat and salad is a popular meal.
- Seafood.
- Corn tortillas.
- Iguana.
- Armadillo.
- *Pupusa* (a fried sandwich made of tortillas and filled with pork, cheese and sausage).

National drinks:
- Coffee.
- Frescos (natural fruit drinks).
- Beer (*Pilsner* and *Suprema*).
- *Tic tac* and *Torito* (alcoholic beverages made from distilled sugar cane).

Tipping: 10 per cent in hotels and restaurants; 15 per cent is appropriate for smaller bills. Taxi drivers do not expect tips, except when the taxi has been hired for the day. Airport porters are usually tipped $1 per bag.

NIGHTLIFE: San Salvador has a few nightclubs and cocktail lounges with dinner and dancing, some of which require membership. There are many cinemas, some showing English-language films with subtitles; there are also some 'jukebox' dance-halls and theatres. The Teatro Cafe in the national theartre building, features a guitarist during the week and a variety of cultural events such as poetry and literature readings. If you like traditional Mexican style Mariachi music, head for the Boulevard de Los Heroes. Mariachi groups gather there nightly waiting for hired parties or other special occasions. Inexpensive restaurants fill this area and several Mariachis groups work the streets.

SHOPPING: Various goods can be bought at the Mercado Cuartel crafts market, including towels in Maya designs. Other shopping centres can be found at Basilea, Galerias Escalón, Metrocentro, Metrosor and Villas Españolas.

Shopping hours: Mon-Sat 0800-1200 and 1400-1800. Some shops, especially those that sell food and drink, open till late.

Business

- **GDP:** US$32.28 billion.
- **Main exports:** Coffee, corn, cotton, sugar and foodstuff.
- **Main imports:** Consumer goods, raw materials, fuels, petroleum and foodstuff.
- **Main trade partners:** USA, Germany, Japan and Guatemala.

ECONOMY: The long-running civil war caused a significant decline in El Salvador's mainly agricultural economy. Although there has been a steady recovery since the political settlement took hold, El Salvador remains one of the poorest economies in the region. The economy is also still vulnerable to the vagaries of the regional climate – hurricanes, floods and drought. There is a sizeable manufacturing sector – the largest in Central America – producing footwear, textiles, leather goods and pharmaceuticals. Hydroelectricity and imported oil are the main sources of energy. Tourism is the main service industry. Remittances from Salvadorans working abroad are a vital source of income for many families. The Flores Government adopted a number of radical measures in an effort to kick-start the economy, including fixing the Colón (the Salvadoran currency) to the US dollar. It has also made substantial investments in national infrastructure and the education system, but these will take some time to show results. In 2004, GDP growth was 1.4 per cent. El Salvador still relies heavily on aid from the US and the EU, as well as loans from the International Monetary Fund. El Salvador is a member of the Central American Common Market.

BUSINESS ETIQUETTE: Businesspeople are expected to wear suits. Although some local businesspeople speak English, a good knowledge of Spanish is important. Visiting cards are essential. The best months for business visits are September to March, avoiding the Christmas period. **Office hours:** Mon-Fri 0800-1200 and 1400-1600 or 1700, Sat 0800-1200.

COMMERCIAL INFORMATION

Cámara de Comercio e Industria de El Salvador
Avd. Hermanos Bon 79 12003, Castelloni, El Salvador
Tel: 356 500.
Website: www.camaracs.es

Banco Central de Reserva de El Salvador, CENTREX
Alameda Juan Pablo Segundo, Entre 15 y 17 Avenida Norte, San Salvador, El Salvador
Tel: 281 8000.
Website: www.bcr.gob.sv

Equatorial Guinea

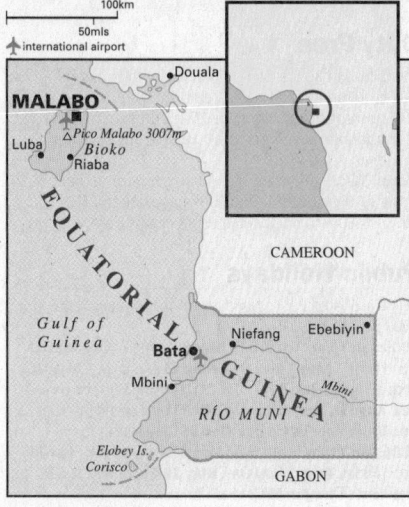

Location: West Coast of Central Africa, Gulf of Guinea.

Time: GMT + 1.

Overview

Belying its troubled political past, Equatorial Guinea is a country of luscious vegetation and beautiful scenery, including tropical forests and snow-capped volcanoes. The capital, Malabo, is a rather rundown but attractive town, with pleasant Spanish colonial architecture, a striking volcanic setting and a lively market. The white-sand beaches around the islands are stunning. No wonder the country was first of all named 'Formosa', meaning 'beautiful', by the Portuguese who first colonised it. The area now occupied by Equatorial Guinea and the island of Bioko was first colonised by the Portuguese in the late 15th century and developed as a major slave market. In 1788 the territory was handed over to the Spanish who ran it as a protectorate of Spanish Guinea until 1959. At this point the colony was granted internal self-Government and full independence followed in 1968. The first decade was blighted by the brutal and incompetent rule of President Macias Nguema. He was overthrown in a military coup led by his nephew, Lieutenant Colonel Teodoro Obiang, in 1979. Initially, conditions improved somewhat, as Equatorial Guinea gained international recognition and aid; it also joined the CFA Franc Zone. Relations with Spain, the former colonial power, remained touchy, as its bilateral aid was made dependent on progress in democratising the political system. Throughout the 1980s, Obiang maintained his opposition to the establishment of a multi-party system while shoring up his position at home through systematic repression. A democratic constitution was finally conceded in 1991 and the first multi-party legislative elections were held in November 1993. However, the Government's conduct of the election was such that the main opposition movement boycotted the poll, alleging systematic intimidation. This pattern of malpractice has continued more or less unabated at every election – for both the Presidency and the national assembly – which has been held since then. Despite being a mainly 'undiscovered' country with a history of human rights' abuses, Equatorial Guinea's financial fortunes appear to be looking up of late, following the discovery of oil and gas deposits in the Gulf of Guinea. Although this find has not alleviated the problem of a corrupt, inept and abusive Government, it might hopefully put the country back on the global map and ensure that more are aware of both this country's plight and its splendour.

General Information

AREA: 28,051 sq km (10,831 sq miles).
POPULATION: 521,000 (UN, 2005).
POPULATION DENSITY: 18.57 per sq km.
CAPITAL: Malabo. **Population:** 38,000 (2001).
GEOGRAPHY: Equatorial Guinea is bordered to the south and east by Gabon, to the north by Cameroon and to the west by the Gulf of Guinea. The country also comprises the island of Bioko, formerly Fernando Po, 34km (21 miles) off the coast of Cameroon, and the small offshore islands of Corisco, Great Elobey, Small Elobey and Annobón (formerly Pagalu). The mainland province, Rió Muni, is mainly forest, with plantations on the coastal plain and some mountains. Bioko rises steeply to two main peaks in the north and south. The southern area is rugged and inaccessible. Cultivation and settlements exist on the other slopes; above the farming land, the forest is thick. The beaches around the islands are extremely beautiful.
GOVERNMENT: Republic. Declared independence from Spain in 1968. **Head of State:** President Teodoro Obiang Nguema Mbasogo since 1979. **Head of Government:** Miguel Abia Biteo Boriko since 2004. **Recent history:** Miguel Abia Biteo Borico became the new Prime Minister in June 2004.
As an impoverished African backwater, Equatorial Guinea attracted little international attention, and the EU – the country's principal source of aid in recent years – had all but given up on it. This has since changed, along with Equatorial Guinea's economic fortunes, following the discovery of oil and gas deposits in the Gulf of Guinea. This windfall has had two other important consequences. Firstly, the resolution of a long-standing territorial dispute with Nigeria in September 2000, since when the two countries have begun joint explorations. Secondly, the revival of independence aspirations on the island of Bioko (formerly Fernando Po), which is part of Equatorial Guinean territory and hosts most of the new oil and gas facilities.
The constitution, allows for the introduction of multi-party politics and an elected Presidency and legislature. The President is elected for a seven-year term, while the 80-seat *Cámara de Representantes del Pueblo* (House of People's Representatives) is elected in multi-member constituencies for a five-year term.
LANGUAGE: Spanish and French are the official languages. The main African dialects spoken are Fang and Bubi (which is common on Bioko).
RELIGION: No official religion, but around 90 per cent are Roman Catholic, with an animist minority.
ELECTRICITY: 220/240 volts AC.
SOCIAL CONVENTIONS: Foreign visitors (especially Europeans) are a comparative rarity in Equatorial Guinea and are liable to be met with curiosity and, possibly, suspicion. Foreign cigarettes are appreciated as gifts. A knowledge of Spanish is useful. **Photography:** A permit is required from the Ministry of Information and Tourism. Care should be taken when choosing subjects. Photographing the presidential palace, airports, ports, military bases and other sensitive areas could lead to imprisonment.

Climate

Tropical climate all year round. Rainfall is heavy for most of the year, decreasing slightly in most areas between December and February.
Required clothing: Lightweight cottons and linens. Waterproofing is necessary.

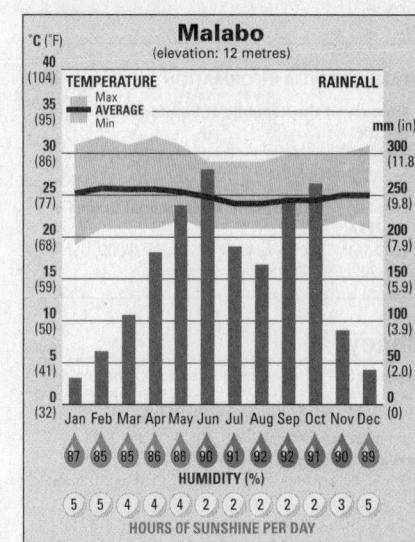

Communications

Telephone: IDD is available. Country code: 240. Operator assistance may be required when making international calls from the country.
Mobile telephone: Roaming agreements exist with a few international mobile phone companies. Coverage is limited to Malabo and a few other inhabited areas.
Internet: Internet is available in limited areas; coverage is variable.
Post: Service to Western Europe takes up to two weeks.
MEDIA: The main broadcasters are state-controlled. There are a few private newspapers and underground pamphlets that publish irregularly. Mild criticism of public institutions is allowed but criticism of the leadership is not tolerated and self-censorship is widespread.
Press: Spanish language weekly publications include *Hoja Parroquial* and *El Sol*, produced in Equatorial Guinea. There is also the state-owned *Ebano* and the privately-owned *La Nación* and *La Opinión*.
TV: *La Nación* and *La Opinión* are private stations. Ebano is a state-owned station.
Radio: *Radio France Internationale* is available on FM in Malabo. *Radio Nacional de Guinea Ecuatorial* is a state-run station and *Radio Asonga* is privately owned by the son of the country's President.

Passport/Visa

	Passport Required?	Visa Required?	Return Ticket Required?
Full British	Yes	Yes	Yes
Australian	Yes	Yes	Yes
Canadian	Yes	Yes	Yes
USA	Yes	No	Yes
Other EU	Yes	Yes	Yes
Japanese	Yes	Yes	Yes

Note: *Regulations and requirements may be subject to change at short notice, and you are advised to contact the appropriate diplomatic or consular authority before finalising travel arrangements. Any numbers in the chart refer to the footnotes below.*

PASSPORTS: Passport valid for a minimum of six months required by all.
Note: Carry copies of appropriate documentation at all times.
VISAS: Required by all except nationals of the USA.
Types of visas and cost: *Tourist, Business* and *Transit*: £100.
Validity: Enquire at Embassy (or Consular section at Embassy); see *Passport/Visa Information*.
Application to: Consulate (or consular section at Embassy); see *Passport/Visa Information*.
Application requirements: (a) Passport valid for at least six months after return date (and photocopy). (b) One completed application form. (c) Two passport-size colour photos. (d) Original copy of return ticket or proof of confirmed airline reservation. (e) Yellow fever vaccination certificate. (f) Fee, payable in cash, money order or company cheque. (g) Self-addressed, stamped envelope for postal applications. *Tourist*: (a)-(g) and, (h) Proof of hotel booking. *Business*: (a)-(g) and, (h) Letter of invitation from the company in Equatorial Guinea declaring responsibility for the applicant. *Private*: (a)-(g) and, (h) Letter of invitation, stamped by the Director General of Security in Marabo. *Transit*: (a)-(g) and, (h) Valid visa for the destination country.
Working days required: 48 hours (shorter if application is urgent; longer in exceptional circumstances or if applying by post).

PASSPORT/VISA INFORMATION

Embassy of the Republic of Equatorial Guinea in the UK
13 Park Place, St James's, London SW1A 1LP, UK
Tel: (020) 7499 6867.

Embassy of the Republic of Equatorial Guinea in the USA
2020 16th Street, NW, Washington, DC 20009, USA
Tel: (202) 518 5700.

Money

Currency: CFA (*Communauté Financiaire Africaine*) Franc (CFAfr or XAF) = 100 centimes. Notes are in denominations of XAF10,000, 5000, 1000 and 500. Coins are in denominations of XAF500, 100, 50, 25, 10 and 5.
Currency exchange: Equatorial Guinea is part of the French Monetary Area. Only currency issued by the *Banque des Etats de l'Afrique Centrale* (Bank of Central African States) is valid; currency issued by the *Banque des Etats de l'Afrique de l'Ouest* (Bank of West African States) is not. The

CFA Franc is tied to the Euro. Foreign currencies are best exchanged at banks, of which, however, there are few. Receipts for currency exchange should be retained.
Credit & debit cards: Equatorial Guinea has a strictly cash-only economy. Credit cards and cheques are not accepted. ATMs are not available.
Traveller's cheques: Most businesses do not accept traveller's cheques.
Currency restrictions: The import of local and foreign currency is unrestricted provided declared on arrival. The export of local currency is limited to XAF50,000. The export of foreign currency is limited to the amount declared on arrival. It is worth remembering that XAF Franc notes cannot easily be exchanged outside the XAF Franc area.
Banking hours: Mon-Sat 0800-1200.
Exchange rate indicators:
Rate at time of publishing
£1.00= XAF960.64
$1.00= XAF548.72

Duty Free

The following goods may be imported into Equatorial Guinea without incurring customs duty:
200 cigarettes or 50 cigars or 250g of tobacco; 1l of wine; 1l of alcoholic beverages; a reasonable amount of perfume.
Note: Visitors for business and tourism must declare any currency in excess of XAF50,000 (approximately £50) on arrival. Failure to do so could result in a fine on departure.

Public Holidays

Below are listed Public Holidays for the January 2005-June 2006 period.
2005: Jan 1 New Year's Day. **Mar 8** Women's Day. **Mar 25** Good Friday. **May 1** May Day. **May 25** Africa Day. **May 26** Corpus Christi. **Jun 5** President's Day. **Aug 3** Armed Forces Day. **Aug 15** Constitution Day. **Oct 12** Independence Day. **Dec 10** Human Rights Day. **Dec 25** Christmas.
2006: Jan 1 New Year's Day. **Mar 8** Women's Day. **Apr 14** Good Friday. **May 1** May Day. **May 25** Africa Day. **Jun 5** President's Day. **Jun 15** Corpus Christi.

Health

	Special Precautions?	Certificate Required?
Yellow Fever	Yes	1
Cholera	2	No
Typhoid & Polio	3	N/A
Malaria	4	N/A

Note: *Regulations and requirements may be subject to change at short notice, and you are advised to contact your doctor well in advance of your intended date of departure. Any numbers in the chart refer to the footnotes below.*

1: Equatorial Guinea is listed as one of the countries in the endemic zone and a yellow fever vaccination should be considered. You should also note that most countries require a yellow fever vaccination certificate from travellers one year of age and older coming from infected areas.
2: Following WHO guidelines issued in 1973, a cholera vaccination certificate is no longer a condition of entry to Equatorial Guinea. However, cholera is a serious risk in this country and precautions are essential. Up-to-date advice should be sought before deciding whether these precautions should include vaccination as medical opinion is divided over its effectiveness; see the *Health* appendix for further information.
3: Immunisation against typhoid and poliomyelitis is advised.
4: Malaria risk, predominantly in the malignant *falciparum* form, exists all year throughout the country. Resistance to chloroquine has been reported.
Food & drink: All water should be regarded as being potentially contaminated. Water used for drinking, brushing teeth or making ice should have first been boiled or otherwise sterilised. Milk is unpasteurised and should be boiled. Powdered or tinned milk is available and is advised, but make sure that it is reconstituted with pure water. Avoid dairy products which are likely to have been made from unboiled milk. Only eat well-cooked meat and fish, preferably served hot. Pork, salad and mayonnaise may carry increased risk. Vegetables should be cooked and fruit peeled. Avoid eating produce from street vendors.
Other risks: *Diarrhoeal* diseases, including *giardiasis*, as well as *typhoid fevers* , are common. *Hepatitis A, B* and *E* occur. *Dengue fever, leishmaniasis, filariasis* and *bilharzia* (*schistosomiasis*) are contracted by mosquitoes or parasites and are present in Equatorial Guinea. Avoid swimming and paddling in fresh water; swimming pools which are well-chlorinated and maintained are safe. *Onchocerciasis* (river blindness) is present. *Trypanosomiasis* (sleeping sickness)

has recently been reported. *Meningococcal meningitis* may occur, especially during the dry season.
Rabies is present. For those at high risk, vaccination before arrival should be considered. If you are bitten, seek medical advice without delay. For more information, consult the *Health* appendix.
Health care: Comprehensive medical insurance, including emergency repatriation, is strongly advised.

Travel - International

AIR:
 Iberia (IB) (website: www.iberia.com) operates direct flights from Madrid to Malabo five times a week. *Cameroon Airlines (UY)* operates regular flights to Malabo from London, Paris and Rome. Other airlines serving Equatorial Guinea include *Air France, British Airways, KLM, SN Brussels, Swiss* and *Spanair*.
Approximate flight times: From Malabo to *Madrid* is five hours 40 minutes.
Main airports: There are international airports at *Malabo (SSG/FGSL)* (Santa Isabel) 7km (4 miles) from the city centre and *Bata (BSG)*, 6km (3.7 miles) from the city centre. *Facilities*: Both airports have basic facilities, including car hire (*Avis*).
Departure tax: None.
SEA:
 Main ports: *Malabo* and *Bata*. Passenger services operate to Douala (Cameroon).

ROAD:
 Roads link Equatorial Guinea with Cameroon and Gabon (bush taxis are available), although road surfaces are not always good. Most travellers enter from Douala in Cameroon. Borders are often closed without any notice, so travellers are recommended to check before travelling (see *Travel Warnings* for latest travel advice).

Travel - Internal

AIR:
 The country's national airline operates flights between Malabo and Bata every day except Sunday, and it is advisable to book in advance.
Note: It is reported that maintenance procedures used on internal flights are not always properly observed.
SEA:
 There is a ferry between Malabo, Bata and Douala. The trip takes about 12 hours. There are four classes of fare.
ROAD:
 Not all roads are paved, although the majority are. On Bioko, the north is generally better served with tarred roads. During the rainy season some roads are only passable in a 4-wheel-drive vehicle. Police and military roadblocks are common; travellers may need to show their passport, driving license and/or vehicle registration and explain their reason for travelling. New roads are under construction and repair in Malabo, Bata and a few outlying areas. **Minibuses** run from Bata to Mbini and Acalayong on the coastal road. **Bush taxis** connect Malabo with the island's two other main towns, Luba and Riaba, and also run from Bata to Mongomo and Ebebiyin; they can be hired hourly or daily. There are some **car hire** facilities (*Avis*).

Travel Advice

Travellers wishing to travel outside Malabo on the island of Bioko, or outside Bata on the mainland, will need to inform the Protocol Division of the Ministry of Foreign Affairs, Cooperation and Francophonie in advance.
The threat from terrorism is low, but you should be aware of the global risk of indiscriminate terrorist attacks, which could be against civilian targets, including places frequented by foreigners.
This advice is based on information provided by the Foreign and Commonwealth Office in the UK. It is correct at time of publishing. As the situation can change rapidly, visitors are advised to contact the following organisations for the latest travel advice:

British Foreign and Commonwealth Office
Tel: (0845) 850 2829.
Website: www.fco.gov.uk

US Department of State
Website: http://travel.state.gov/travel

Accommodation

HOTELS:
 Malabo, Bata, Luba and Ebebiyan offer several hotels of variable standards. In Malabo, there are also a few hostels offering basic cheap

accommodation with shared bathroom facilities (two of which are located in Avenida de las Naciónes). For more information, contact the Embassy for the Republic of Equatorial Guinea (see *Passport/Visa Information*).

Top Things To See & Do

- On **Bioko Island**, the capital, **Malabo**, is located on the north coast and overlooked by the striking **Pico Malabo** volcano, which provides a number of secluded **hiking** trails and opportunities for **mountain climbing**. As this is a military area, a Government permit is required and travellers should always check with the authorities before undertaking an expedition to the volcano. Malabo is a small but attractive town, with pleasant Spanish colonial architecture, open plazas and a lively market. Frederick Forsyth wrote his novel *The Dogs of War* in Malabo. The **Spanish Cultural Centre**, **Malabo Catherdral** and **Malabo Court** are worth a visit.
- Climbing up the 3000m- (9843ft-) **Pico Basile** provides a panoramic view of the island and, on a clear day, **Mount Cameroon** can be seen. There is a road up to the top but a special permit must be obtained from the Government before venturing up there.
- **Arena Blanca,** situated on the west coast, is the only white beach on Bioko Island. There is a 1km (0.6-mile) trail down to the beach from the road and, during the dry season, thousands of butterflies can be seen. **Luba** also has some lovely deserted, white-sand beaches and breathtaking *vistas*. **Bata** is the principle town in the region of **Río Muni** on the mainland. It is a lively town with a few restaurants, bars, hotels and markets. It is also close to some beautiful beaches, notably those at **Mbini**, 50km (32miles) south of Bata.
- The town of **Moca** is situated in the **Moca valley** in the southern highlands. The area supports a range of natural attractions with cultural significance and is also a spiritual centre for the Bubi people, the earliest inhabitants of Bioko Island.
- The **Cascades of Moca, Lake Biao** and **Lake Loreta** are popular visitor destinations which are inhabited by several species of monkey. The small village of **Ureca** is on the south coast of the island. During the dry season, turtles come ashore to lay their eggs. An hour's hike from the village are the **Rio Eola** waterfalls with clear, cool pools beneath, perfect for **swimming**.
- The **Monte Alen National Park** is an area spanning 1400 sq km (540 sq miles). It is accessible via a series of trails through the jungle and inhabited by elephants, leopards and several species of bird.

Business

- **GDP:** US$5.5 billion.
- **Main imports:** Petroleum sector equipment and other equipment.
- **Main exports:** Petroleum, methanol, timber, coffee, cocoa, bananas and spices.
- **Main trade partners:** Cameroon, Canada, China, Côte d'Ivoire, France, Italy, Spain, Taiwan (China), UK and USA.

ECONOMY: During the 1990s, the long overdue development of the country's oil and gas reserves – which now account for about a quarter of GDP – produced spectacular economic growth (up to 20 per cent annually) and such growth has persisted at a steady rate. Equatorial Guinea also has confirmed deposits of gold, uranium, iron ore, tantalum and manganese. Intervention by the IMF in the mid-1990s has led to restructuring of the public and financial sectors. A long legacy of maladministration, corruption (the country's largest companies are still largely owned by members of the ruling family) and the lack of even the most basic services has hampered development. Nonetheless, Equatorial Guinea has made considerable economic strides in the last decade and, on the basis of its oil, will continue to make progress for some time yet. Equatorial Guinea is a member of the Central African Customs and Economic Union (CEEAC) and the CFA Franc Zone, and receives large injections of foreign aid from a variety of sources.
BUSINESS: Business tends to be conducted in Spanish; few speak English or French.

COMMERCIAL INFORMATION
Cámara de Comercio
Agrícola y Forestal de Malabo, Avenida de la Independencia 43, Apartado Postal 51, Bioko, Equatorial Guinea
Tel: (9) 2343.

Eritrea

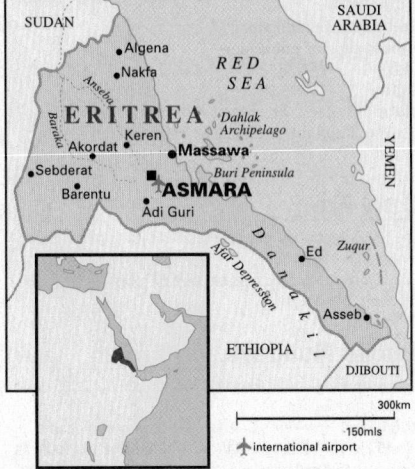

Location: Northeast Africa, on the Red Sea coast.

Time: GMT + 3.

Overview

Eritrea stretches along the Red Sea and is a low-lying coastal area with a mountainous interior. The Turkish and Egyptian colonial periods left their legacy in the form of numerous interesting buildings and sites, and the cuisine reflects the period of italian rule.

Eritrea was largely an independent country until coming under Ottoman rule in the 16th century. Over the next 300 years, control of the territory was disputed between the Ottomans, Ethiopia, Egypt and Italy. In 1889, a treaty between Italy and King Menilek of Ethiopia recognised Italian possessions on the Red Sea coast, which were formally adopted as Italian colonies the following year. Eritrea then became one of the six provinces of Italian East Africa, until the Italians were expelled by the British in 1941. After the departure of the British, Eritrea was merged into Ethiopia in a federal arrangement brokered by the UN in 1952 and incorporated fully into Ethiopia 10 years later. After a decade of changing fortunes for both the Government and the Eritrean People's Liberation Front (EPLF), fighting against the Communist Government within Ethiopia, the guerrillas finally expelled Government forces from Eritrea in early 1991. In 1992, the EPLF-controlled Provisional Government of Eritrea announced a referendum over the future status of the area. With 99.8 per cent support registered in favour of independence at an UN-supervised referendum in April 1993, full nationhood was declared the following month.

Despite its many vicissitudes, Eritrea boasts an abundance of natural attractions, including a vast array of wildlife. Native to the country are elephants, lions, baboons, gazelles, leopards, ostriches and turtles. Off any of Eritrea's stunning beaches, it is not uncommon to see angelfish, barracudas, butterfly fish and several varieties of crabs, sea cucumbers and jellyfish beneath the azure ocean waters.

General Information

AREA: 121,144 sq km (46,774 sq miles).
POPULATION: 4.4 million (UN, 2005).
POPULATION DENSITY: 36.3 per sq km.
CAPITAL: Asmara. **Population:** 435,000 (2005).
GEOGRAPHY: Eritrea stretches along the Red Sea for almost 1000km (625 miles). To the south and west it borders Ethiopia, to the southeast Djibouti and to the northwest Sudan. The low-lying coastal area is very humid. The mountainous interior is largely cultivated.
GOVERNMENT: Independent State since 1993. **Head of State and Government:** President Isaias Afewerki since 1993. **Recent history:** In the 1990s, Eritrea entered into costly wars with both Yemen and Djibouti. But by far the

most serious threat to long-term stability was the unexpected and catastrophic breakdown in relations with neighbouring Ethiopia. Initially, relations were good – but fighting broke out between the two countries in May 1998, ostensibly over minor land disputes and border incursions. Ethiopia was also unhappy with Eritrea's introduction of its own currency (the Nakfa) in 1997. Eritrea, for its part, voiced fears that its hard-won independence might be infringed upon by an expansionist Ethiopia. Finally, after a two-month spell of heavy fighting, the UN managed to broker a settlement in June 2000. A 4000-strong peacekeeping force UNMEE (UN Mission in Eritrea and Ethiopia) was installed while a permanent solution was sought. This remains elusive. Whilst war has not yet returned, the Government responded drastically to domestic opposition following the war, which alienated many of the new Government's most important foreign backers, especially in Europe. Within Eritrea, an alliance of a dozen opposition groups has now formed a military wing to pursue their campaign against the Afewerki regime. The new constitution, adopted in May 1997, allows for political pluralism under a presidential system of Government. However, no elections have yet been held and the People's Front for Democracy and Justice (PFDJ), the political arm of the Eritrean People's Liberation Front, is the only authorised political party. At present, President Afewerki holds executive power while legislative authority is vested in the 104-member *Hagerawi Baito* (National Assembly), comprising 60 appointed members and 44 representatives of the PFDJ.
LANGUAGE: Tigrinya, Tigre, Arabic and English are spoken. English is rapidly becoming the language of business and education.
RELIGION: Roughly half Ethiopian Orthodox Christians and half Muslim, but some have traditional beliefs.
ELECTRICITY: 110/220 volts AC; there are occasional power surges.
SOCIAL CONVENTIONS: Shaking hands is the normal form of greeting. Casual tourist wear is suitable for most places, but visitors should dress modestly. For business, a suit is most appropriate. Coffee is a delicacy in Eritrea and to be asked to take coffee is a symbol of hospitality and the way that Eritreans honour their guests. It takes up to an hour for the coffee to be prepared in a coffee ceremony and it is standard practice that you must have three cups and compliment the taste before leaving. Smoking is not popular with traditional or elderly Eritreans. Shoes should be taken off in churches and, particularly, in mosques. Homosexual behaviour is illegal. **Photography:** It is not permitted to photograph Government or military buildings.

Climate

Summer months (April to August) can be hot with temperatures reaching up to 40°C (100 °F) on the western plateau. Although temperatures rarely drop below 18°C (64 °F) along the coast, winters in the central and western plateau regions (December to February) can be freezing with dramatic temperature differences between day and night. The short rainy season is usually between March to April and a longer one from late June to the beginning of September.
Required clothing: Lightweight and mediumweight clothing is recommended but warm clothes may be needed because the temperature drops at night. An umbrella and a raincoat are recommended during the rainy season.

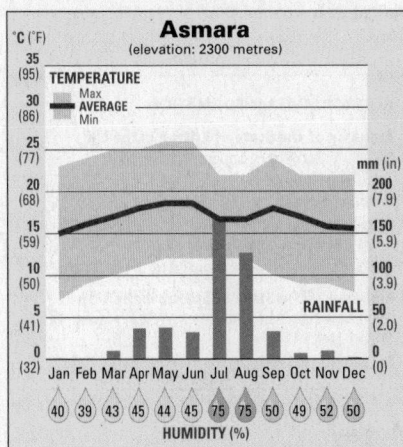

Communications

Telephone: IDD is available to Asmara, Massawa and Assab. Country code: 291. Operator assistance may be required. All larger cities are connected via the internal system.
Mobile telephone: Roaming agreements exist with mobile phone companies.

A B C D E F G H I J K L M N O P Q R S T U V W X Y Z

A B C D E F G H I J K L M N O P Q R S T U V W X Y Z

Internet: There is Internet access in the main towns, and coverage is variable.
Post: International post services have not been resumed with all countries. Delays are likely. Post office hours (for the main post office in Asmara): Mon to Sat 0800 - 1200, 1400-1900; Sun 1900-1200.
MEDIA: Eritrea is the only African country to have no privately-owned news media. It also has no private radio or TV stations. No criticism of the Government is tolerated. The Government closed the private press in 2001 on the premise that it endangered national security.
Press: The *Eritrea Profile* is published weekly in English. *Hadas Eritrea* is published three times a week in English, Arabic and Tigrinya. A pro-government youth paper called *Tirigta* is published once a week.
TV: *Eri TV* is a state-run broadcaster.
Radio: *Voice of the Broad Masses of Eritrea* (*Dimtsi Hafash*) is state-run and operates two networks with programmes in 11 languages; *Radio Zara* has a state-run, FM network.

Passport/Visa

	Passport Required?	Visa Required?	Return Ticket Required?
Full British	Yes	Yes	Yes
Australian	Yes	Yes	Yes
Canadian	Yes	Yes	Yes
USA	Yes	Yes	Yes
Other EU	Yes	Yes	Yes
Japanese	Yes	Yes	Yes

Note: *Regulations and requirements may be subject to change at short notice, and you are advised to contact the appropriate diplomatic or consular authority before finalising travel arrangements. Any numbers in the chart refer to the footnotes below.*

PASSPORTS: Passport valid for a minimum of three months beyond intended departure date required by all.
VISAS: Required by all except the following:
(a) nationals of Kenya and Uganda;
(b) transit passengers continuing their journey to a third country within six hours, provided holding valid onward or return documentation and not leaving the airport transit lounge.
Types of visas and cost: *Tourist*: £25 (single-entry only). *Business*: £40 (single-entry); £55 (multiple-entry for up to three months); £80 (multiple-entry for up to six months). *Transit*: £10. An additional fee of £5 is payable for Express Service visas.
Validity: *Single-entry business visas*: up to one month. Extensions are possible. Apply to the Foreign Ministry in Asmara. Apply on arrival in Eritrea. *Transit visas*: 24 hours.
Application to: Consulate (or Consular section at Embassy); see *Passport/Visa Information*.
Application requirements: (a) Application form. (b) Valid passport. (c) One passport-size photo. (d) Fee. (e) Yellow fever certificate, if arriving within six days of visiting an infected area (except for passengers in transit and not leaving the airport). (f) Stamped, self-addressed registered envelope for postal applications. *Tourist*: (a)-(f) and, (g) A valid onward ticket and travel documents. (h) Proof of traveller's cheques of minimum US$40 per day, or bank statement. *Business*: (a)-(f) and, (g) Company letter stating the purpose of the visit.
Working days required: One. Five hours for Express Service.

PASSPORT/VISA INFORMATION

Embassy of the State of Eritrea in the UK
96 White Lion Street, London N1 9PF, UK
Tel: (020) 7713 0096.
Email: eriemba@freeuk.com
Opening hours: Mon-Fri 0930-1300 (visa application); 1400-1600 (visa collection).
The Eritrean Consulate is based at the Embassy.

Embassy of the State of Eritrea in the USA
1708 New Hampshire Avenue, NW, Washington, DC 20009, USA
Tel: (202) 319 1991.

Money

Currency: Nakfa (ERN) = 100 cents. Notes are in denominations of ERN100, 50, 10, 5 and 1. Coins are in denominations of ERN100, 50, 25, 10, 5 and 1.
Note: The IMF and the World Bank have recognised the circulation of Nakfa in both coin and paper note denominations.
Currency exchange: US Dollar bills are the most convenient form of exchange. Foreign currencies can be exchanged at the Commercial Bank of Eritrea in Asmara (which provides the best exchange rate), private currency exchange offices and major hotels.
Credit & debit cards: Credit cards are accepted in major hotels, airlines and major travel agencies. However, a commission of up to five per cent may be charged. Check with your credit or debit card company for details of merchant acceptability.
Traveller's cheques: Major banks in Asmara and Massawa accept traveller's cheques as well as major hotels. US Dollar traveller's cheques are recommended; however, getting them changed at the bank can be a lengthy process.
Currency restrictions: Import and export of local or foreign currency is unrestricted.
Banking hours: Mon-Fri 0800-1200 and 1400-1700, Sat 0800-1200.
Exchange rate indicators:
Rate at time of publishing
£1.00= ERN26.13
$1.00= ERN15.00
Note: * Values are given against the Euro rather than Sterling as accurate exchange rate against Sterling is not available.

Duty Free

The following goods may be imported into Eritrea without incurring customs duty:
200 cigarettes or 50 cigars or 250g of tobacco; 1l of alcoholic beverages.

Public Holidays

Below are listed Public Holidays for the January 2006-June 2007 period.
2006: Jan 1 New Year's Day. **Jan 6** Orthodox Ephiphany. **Jan 10** Eid-Ul-Adha. **Mar 8** Women's Day. **Apr 10** Prophet's Anniversary. **Apr 17** Easter Monday. **May 24** Independence Day. **Jun 20** Martyrs' Day. **Sep 1** Anniversary of the Start of the Armed Struggles. **Oct 22-24** End of Ramadan. **Dec 25** Christmas Day. **Dec 31** Eid-Ul-Adha.
2007: Jan 1 New Year's Day. **Jan 6** Orthodox Ephiphany. **Mar 8** Women's Day. **Mar 31** Prophet's Anniversary. **Apr 9** Easter Monday. **May 24** Independence Day. **Jun 20** Martyrs' Day.

Health

	Special Precautions?	Certificate Required?
Yellow Fever	Yes	1
Cholera	2	No
Typhoid & Polio	3	N/A
Malaria	4	N/A

Note: *Regulations and requirements may be subject to change at short notice, and you are advised to contact your doctor well in advance of your intended date of departure. Any numbers in the chart refer to the footnotes below.*

1: A yellow fever vaccination certificate is required from travellers arriving within six days from infected areas. Travellers arriving from non-endemic zones should note that vaccination is strongly recommended for travel outside the urban areas, even if an outbreak of the disease has not been reported and they would normally not require a vaccination certificate to enter the country.
2: Following WHO guidelines issued in 1973, a cholera vaccination certificate is no longer a condition of entry to Eritrea. However, cholera is a serious risk in this country and precautions are essential. Up-to-date advice should be sought before deciding whether these precautions should include vaccination, as medical opinion is divided over its effectiveness; see the *Health* appendix for further information.
3: Typhoid is widespread, especially in rural areas and poliomyelitis is endemic. Vaccination against both is advised.
4: Malaria risk, predominantly in the malignant *falciparum* form, exists throughout the year in all areas below 2000m (682ft). Highly chloroquine-resistant *falciparum* has been reported. There is no malaria risk in Asmara.
Food & drink: All water should be regarded as being potentially contaminated. Water used for drinking, brushing teeth or making ice should have first been boiled or otherwise sterilised. Milk is unpasteurised and should be boiled. Powdered or tinned milk is available and is advised, but make sure that it is reconstituted with pure water. Avoid dairy products which are likely to have been made from unboiled milk. Only eat well-cooked meat and fish, preferably served hot. Pork, salad and mayonnaise may carry increased risk. Vegetables should be cooked and fruit peeled. Avoid buying food from street vendors.
Other risks: *Bilharzia* (schistosomiasis) is present. Avoid swimming and paddling in fresh water; swimming pools which are well-chlorinated and maintained are safe. *Dengue, filariasis, leishmaniasis, Rift Valley fever* and *African trypanosomiasis* (sleeping sickness) are present. *Hepatitis A* and *E* are widespread and *hepatitis B* is hyperendemic. Vaccinations against *hepatitis B, measles* and *tetanus* are recommended. *Meningococcal meningitis* is a risk, particularly in savannah areas and during the dry season. Endemic foci of *onchocerciasis* (river blindness) exist. *Rabies* is present. For those at high risk, vaccination before arrival should be considered. If you are bitten, seek medical advice without delay. For more information, consult the *Health* appendix.
Health care: Time is needed to acclimatise to the high altitude and low oxygen level. Those who suffer from heart ailments or high blood pressure should consult a doctor before travelling. Medical services are limited throughout the country: modern facilities are not always available and supplies can be irregular. Visitors should bring a supply of any necessary drugs and prescriptions. Chemists can be found in larger towns. The country has an extensive network of health workers. Regional and district clinics and the central hospital in Asmara deal with emergencies. Comprehensive health insurance is strongly advised.

Travel - International

AIR:
The national airline is *Eritrean Airlines*. Other airlines operating to Eritrea include *Alitalia Airlines* (from London), *KLM* (from London), *Lufthansa* (from Frankfurt), *Saudi Arabian Airlines* (from Jeddah) and *Yemenia* (from Sanaa). Flights from Europe and the USA can be booked through Ericommerce International Ltd, Robin House, 2A Iverson Road, London NW6 2HE, UK (tel: (020) 7372 7242; website: www.ericommerce.com).
Approximate flight times: From Asmara to *London* is seven hours.
Main airports: *Asmara (ASM)* is 6km (4 miles) from the city. *To/from the airport*: Buses and taxis are available to the city centre. *Facilities*: Left luggage, bank/bureau de change, post office, bars, duty free shop and restaurants.
Departure tax: US$20.
SEA:
Massawa port in Eritrea is the largest deep-water port in the Red Sea. The other main port in Eritrea is *Assab*. However, there are very limited scheduled passenger services. There is a weekly ferry service from Massawa to Jeddah.
ROAD:
Currently, borders with Sudan and Ethiopia are closed. The border with Djibouti remains open. Travellers are advised to check with the relevant authorities beforehand as this situation could alter.

Travel - Internal

Note: A permit is required by the Ministry of Tourism in Eritrea to travel to all areas except Keren, Dekemhare, Mendeferra and Massawa. They are usually granted on the day an application is submitted.
AIR:
Internal flights operate between Asmara and Assab but are limited. *Assab (ASA)* is 15 km (9 miles) from Assab. Buses and taxis travel to the town (travel time - 15 to 30 minutes).
Departure tax: Domestic: ERN15. International: ERN100 (nationals). US$20 for all others.
RAIL:
Work was completed on the Asmara-Massawa railway in 2003. There are eight locomotives operating on the line. There are no timetables and services are not regular.
ROAD:
The infrastructure suffered badly during the protracted fighting. Repairs and a modernisation programme are currently underway. Roads between major cites are paved and in relatively good condition, others are not paved and can be of very poor quality. Bad weather can make them worse. 4-wheel-drive vehicles are recommended on all other roads and tracks. Traffic drives on the right. **Bus:** Services connect all larger towns and cities. There are usually two buses per day to larger towns and one bus per day to smaller towns. They leave a destination when full. **Taxi:** These can be found in the capital and at the airport. They usually carry multiple passengers and there is a tendency not to wear a seatbelt. For a higher fee travellers can hire a taxi for themselves. Fares are higher at night (usually double) and should be negotiated in advance as taxis are not metered. **Car hire:** Cars can be booked through the Eritrean Tour Service (see *Top Things to Do*). **Documentation:** An International Driving Permit is required.

Travel Advice

Travellers are advised against all travel to the border areas with Ethiopia and Sudan. This advice includes Tesseney, near the Sudan border. Travellers are also advised against travel in the area north of Afabet in the Sahel region and along the single road in the west of the country.

Travellers should be aware that there is a continuing threat to Western targets from terrorism in Eritrea as there is in other countries in East Africa and the Horn.

Travellers should be aware that travel options to and from Asmara are limited following the cancellation of scheduled flights between Asmara and Nairobi.

This advice is based on information provided by the Foreign and Commonwealth Office in the UK. It is correct at time of publishing. As the situation can change rapidly, visitors are advised to contact the following organisations for the latest travel advice:

British Foreign and Commonwealth Office
Tel: (0845) 850 2829.
Website: www.fco.gov.uk

US Department of State
Website: http://travel.state.gov/travel

Accommodation

HOTELS/GUEST HOUSES:

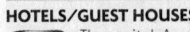
The capital, Asmara, has several good hotels which can sometimes offer seminar rooms and small exhibition spaces. Similar standard hotels can be found in Massawa and Assab. It is advisable to book in advance. Meals are available in all hotels. There are also hotels and guest houses in smaller towns; prices are, in general, slightly lower than those in the main centres. When making reservations, check for service charges and sales taxes. Hotel bills must be paid in hard currency. For further information, contact the Eritrean Tour Service (see *Top Things To See & Do*).

Top Things To See & Do

- Eritrea's capital, **Asmara**, was a cluster of four villages at the beginning of the 19th century; the literal translation of the town's name is 'the four are united'. In 1897, the Italian colonial government moved the administration there from Massawa. Today, it is under Eritrean control (since 1991) yet Italian architecture prevails in the city. The magnificent **Cathedral** (1922), built in the Lombardian style, is not far from a bustling market. Fruit and vegetables, bric-a-brac, spices, used furniture, ceramics, handicrafts and clothes are sold on the stalls. There are a number of churches and mosques which can be visited. Marble from the Italian **Carrara quarry** was used to build the largest mosque, **Al Khulafa Al Rashiudin**. Gold and silver jewellery is on offer at the nearby market. Palms and colourful bougainvillaea line the main avenues. The **National Avenue** is the major thoroughfare of the city; an ideal place to meet people and enjoy the numerous cafes and bars. The Avenue is also the address for the **Government Administrative Centre**, the **Asmara Theatre** (built 1918), the **Nda Mariam Catholic Cathedral** and the **Town Hall**. The former residence of the colonial rulers, the *Ghibi* or palace, is used today as the **National Museum**. The **University** and the **Mai Jahjah Fountain** are also interesting.
- **Massawa** was an important centre in ancient times and remains the largest natural deep-water port on the Red Sea. If Asmara is an Italianate city, Massawa is Turko-Egyptian style, reflecting the periods of Ottoman and Egyptian rule from the 16th century to the late 19th century. The city is made up of three parts: two islands (**Batse** and **Tualud**) and the mainland part of Massawa. Two causeways connect the separate areas but the majority of the population live on the mainland. The port and old town of Batse were damaged during the civil war but are still impressive. The **Iman Hanbeli Mosque** escaped damage. **Batse Island** is a good area for restaurants, cafes and bars; visitors can take a small boat to **Sheikh Said Island** (also known as **Isola Verde**), a favourite picnic spot. Tualud has fine examples of Italian architecture, including **St Mariam's Cathedral**. There is also a badly damaged *Ghibi*, or palace. It was originally built in the 15th century, but has been much altered and restored since then. It was badly damaged in the civil war and is again in need of restoration. The **Port Club** has a restaurant, a museum, a small library and sporting facilities.
- **Emberemi** is famous for the mausoleums of **Sheikh el Amin** and **Muhammad Ibn Ali**. It is an important pilgrimage site.
- Visit the religious sites of the **Tomb of Said Abu Bakr el Mirgani** and the **Mariam de Arit**. **Debre Sina**, near **Elabered** on the **Asmara–Keren road**, is also a noteworthy monastery.

- Go to the **beach**: the modern city of **Asseb** in the southeasterly **Province of Denkalia** has many pleasant beaches. Wide sandy beaches and calm seas along the **Red Sea coast**, such as **Gugussum**, **Buri Peninsula**, **Zula Bay**, **Mersa Gulbub**, **Mersa Ibrahim** and **Ras Kuba**, are ideal locations for **swimming** and **sunbathing**. The **Dahlak Archipelago** has recently been given National Park status and consists of more than 200 islands with flat reef gardens and a variety of fish offering abundant opportunities for **snorkelling** and **scuba diving**. However, travellers cannot go alone or without permission.
- The Turkish and Egyptian colonial periods left numerous interesting buildings and sites in **Akordat** (Barka Province), including the tomb of **Said Mustafa wad Hasan**. **Qohaito**, **Metera** and **Rora Habab** are also important archaeological sites.
- Although **cycling** is one of the country's popular sports, it is unusual for bicycles to be rented out to tourists. However, each year Eritrea hosts one of the toughest races along the Asmara-Keren road. Regular meetings are organised by the Cycling Federation (PO Box 1500, Asmara, Eritrea; tel: (1) 117 280, or 120 933).
- Journey the spectacular road from Asmara to Massawa, 105km (65 miles). It descends from 2438m (8000ft) to sea level, with hairpin bends on the escarpment, and magnificent views over the coastal desert strip. It passes the famous Orthodox **Monastery of Debre Bizen**.

TOURIST INFORMATION

Ministry of Tourism
PO Box 1010, Asmara, Eritrea
Tel: (1) 126 997.
Website: www.shaebia.org/mot.html

Eritrean Tour Service (ETS)
Street address: 61 Hartnet Avenue, Asmara, Eritrea
Postal address: PO Box 889, Asmara, Eritrea
Tel: (1) 124 999.

Entertainment

FOOD & DRINK: Italian cuisine dominates in the restaurants of the larger cities. Massawa is renowned for its excellent seafood, especially prawns and lobster.

National specialities:
- *Kitcha* (a thin bread made from wheat).
- *Injera* (a spongy pancake).
- *Tsebhi* (meat sauté of either lamb or beef with fresh tomatoes and hot peppers).
- *Alicha birsen* (lentil curry).

National drinks:
- *Bun* (coffee) and *shahi* (plain tea). Tea and espresso are drunk black with a lot of sugar. In some regions, coffee is served with ginger or black pepper and sugar.
- *Swa* (beer brewed from a local grain).
- Fruit juices (banana, mango and papaya) are usually available.

Tipping: Hotels and restaurants add a service charge, usually around 10 per cent. Tipping is fairly common, in small amounts. Taxi drivers are not usually tipped.

SHOPPING: Good buys are gold and silver jewellery (sold by weight), woodcarvings, leather items, spears, drums, carpets and wicker goods. A certain amount of bargaining is expected in marketplaces but prices at shops in towns are usually fixed. **Shopping hours:** Mon-Sat 0830-1300, 1430-2030 (regional variations occur).

Business

- **GDP:** US$667 million.
- **Main imports:** Machinery, petroleum products, food and manufactured goods.
- **Main exports:** Sorghum, textiles, livestock, food and small manufactures.
- **Main trade partners:** China, France, Germany, Ireland, Italy, Japan, Malaysia, Poland, Turkey, UK and USA.

ECONOMY: The long-running Ethiopian civil war left Eritrea, which was, until 1991, the northernmost province of Ethiopia, with its economy in a parlous condition. Since the split from Ethiopia in 1993, Eritrea has been engaged in a series of military campaigns which have stunted its economic development. The most recent border war with Ethiopia cost Eritrea several hundred million dollars. Agriculture sustains the bulk of the population with indigenous grains, maize, wheat and sorghum as the main crops. However, reconstruction has been hampered by the legacy of war (damage to land, mines, lack of equipment) and poor rainfall, and the country still needs substantial food aid. The small industrial economy produces glass, cement and textiles. The Government has been developing fishing and mineral industries, particularly as there are thought to be significant oil and gas deposits within Eritrea's territorial waters (which may in part explain its border disputes). Exploration rights have been granted by the Government to several major multinational oil companies to conduct surveys of the area. With an average annual per capita income of just US$160, Eritrea is one of the world's poorest countries. But, albeit from a low base, the economy has been expanding rapidly since the end of the Ethiopian war. However, erratic rainfall and below-average cereal production has stumped growth somewhat. Growth rate was 2 per cent in 2004. Eritrea has been granted admission to the ACP group of Third World countries, which receive preferential access to certain European Union markets, and it is now a member of the International Monetary Fund. In 1997, Eritrea introduced its own currency, the Nakfa, in place of the Ethiopian Birr.
BUSINESS ETIQUETTE: Local businesspeople tend to speak English or Italian. A knowledge of French can also be useful. May to October is best for business visits. **Office hours:** In Asmara, Mon-Thurs 0700-1200, 1400-1800, Fri 0700-1130, 1400-1800. In other towns, hours may vary slightly.

COMMERCIAL INFORMATION

Eritrean National Chamber of Commerce
PO Box 856, Abiot Av 46, Asmara, Eritrea
Tel: (1) 121 589 *or* 388 *or* 122 456.

Estonia

Location: Northern Europe.

Time: GMT + 2. (GMT + 3 from the last Sunday in March to the last Sunday in October).

Overview

Estonia, bordered by the Baltic Sea, the Russian Federation and Latvia, and the most northerly of the three former Soviet Baltic republics, is a country of great scenic beauty with many forests, lakes and islands.

The history of Estonia – and indeed of the other Baltic States – has been one of constant struggle to maintain independence and national integrity against the predatory instincts of larger neighbours.

The Russians who were determined to secure a 'window onto the Baltic' for economic as well as strategic reasons acquired Estonia from Sweden, at the Treaty of Nystadt, in 1721.

Following the German invasion of the Soviet Union during World War Two, Estonia became one of the 15 Soviet Socialist Republics. Four decades passed before the advent of Mikhail Gorbachev offered the prospect of change for the Baltic States.

In March 1990, the Estonian Communist Party voted in favour of full independence from the Soviet Union. Rapid international recognition of Estonia as a sovereign state, followed by admission to the United Nations, completed the transition to full nationhood. Estonia joined the European Union in 2004.

Credit: ©Estonian Tourist

Estonia is an unspoilt, sparsely populated country, nearly half of which is covered with forests. Wetlands, together with primeval forests, represent preserved communities which have for the most part been destroyed in Europe. More than 1000 lakes dot the countryside, which is relatively flat – almost two thirds of the territory lies less than 50m (164ft) above sea level. While seven thousand rivers and streams carry rainwater to the sea, bogs and wooded swamplands of different types cover over one fifth of the country – a world index topped only by the northern neighbour, Finland.

General Information

AREA: 45,226 sq km (17,462 sq miles).

POPULATION: 1.33 million (UN, 2005).

POPULATION DENSITY: 29 per sq km.

CAPITAL: Tallinn. **Population:** 401,694 (official estimate 2005).

GEOGRAPHY: Estonia is the most northerly of the three Baltic Republics and is bordered to the north and west by the Baltic Sea, to the east by the Russian Federation and to the south by Latvia. The country is one of great scenic beauty with many forests, more than 1400 lakes and 1500 islands..

GOVERNMENT: Republic since 1918. Regained independence in 1991. **Head of State:** President Arnold Rüütel since 2001. **Head of Government:** Prime Minister Andrus Ansip since 2005. **Recent history:** Former Economy Minister in the previous coalition government of Juhan Parts, Andrus Ansip became Prime Minister in April 2005. He is leader of the centre-right Reform Party. Mr Parts resigned after two years in office when Parliament passed a vote of no confidence in his Justice Minister over proposed anti-corruption measures. It is Estonia's eighth administration in 12 years. Mr Ansip's main objective is to steer Estonia towards Euro membership in 2007.

LANGUAGE: Estonian is the official language. Most people also speak Russian, which is the mother tongue of around 30 per cent of the population. However, since independence, the indiscriminate use of Russian could on occasion cause offence. In addition to Russian, the most common foreign languages are English, Finnish and German.

RELIGION: Predominantly Protestant (Lutheran).

ELECTRICITY: 220 volts AC, 50Hz. European-style two-pin plugs are in use.

SOCIAL CONVENTIONS: A handshake is the customary greeting. Normal courtesies should be observed. The Estonians are proud of their culture and their national heritage, and visitors should take care to respect this.

Climate

Temperate climate, but with considerable temperature variations. Summer is warm with relatively mild weather in spring and autumn. Winter, which lasts from November to mid-March, can be very cold. Rainfall is distributed throughout the year with the heaviest rainfall in August. Heavy snowfalls are common in the winter months.

Required clothing: Light- to mediumweights are worn during the summer months. Medium- to heavyweights are needed during winter. Rainwear is advisable all year.

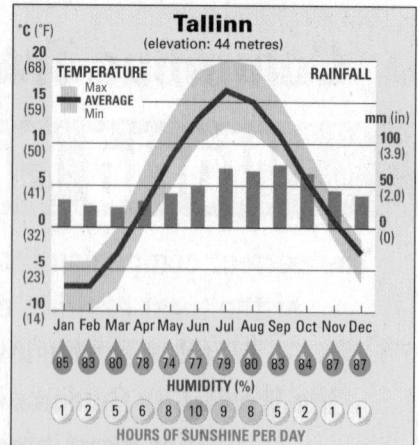

Communications

Telephone: IDD service is available. Country code: 372. Public telephones, which are plentiful, are operated by phonecards, available from kiosks.

Mobile telephone: Roaming agreements exist with most international mobile phone companies. Good coverage.

Internet: Public access is available at Internet cafes and libraries in main towns and cities. There is free Internet access at Tallinn Airport.

Post: Post to Western Europe takes up to six days. Post office hours: Mon-Fri 0900-1800, Sat 0930-1500 (central post office: Mon-Fri 0800-1900, Sat 0900-1700).

MEDIA: Newspapers proliferated in the post-independence years of the early 1990s but smaller publications then struggled to survive. Broadcasting witnessed spectacular growth after 1991, attracting a number of foreign players; the two main commercial TV stations are owned by Swedish and Norwegian concerns. Public radio and TV services are run by Eesti Televisioon (ETV) and Eesti Raadio (ER). Take-up of cable TV is extensive. The service offers channels in Finnish, Swedish, Russian and Latvian.

Press: Newspapers are published in Estonian, the most popular being *Eesti Ekspress*, *Postimees* and *SL Õhtuleht*. *Estoniya* is published in Russian. The English-language newspaper *The Baltic Times* is published in Latvia and available weekly.

TV: *Eesti Televisioon* is public; *TV3* and *Kanal 2* are privately-owned.

Radio: Public station *Eesti Raadio* operates four networks including flagship station *Vikerraadio*; *Raadio Elmar* is a private, music-based station; *Kuku Radio* was Estonia's first privately-owned station.

Passport/Visa

	Passport Required?	Visa Required?	Return Ticket Required?
Full British	1	No	No
Australian	Yes	No/2	No
Canadian	Yes	No/2	No
USA	Yes	No/2	No
Other EU	1	No	No
Japanese	Yes	No/2	No

Note: *Regulations and requirements may be subject to change at short notice, and you are advised to contact the appropriate diplomatic or consular authority before finalising travel arrangements. Any numbers in the chart refer to the footnotes below.*

PASSPORT: Passport valid for three months beyond intended period of stay except:

1. 1. EU/EEA nationals (EU+ Iceland, Liechtenstein, Norway) and Swiss nationals holding a valid national ID card.

Note: EU and EEA nationals are only required to produce evidence of their EU/EEA nationality and identity in order to be admitted to any EU/EEA Member State. This evidence can take the form of a valid national passport *or* national identity card. Either is acceptable. Possession of a return ticket, any length of validity on their document, sufficient funds for the length of their proposed visit should *not* be imposed.

VISA: Required by all except the following:

(a) nationals of the EU and Iceland, Liechtenstein, Norway and Switzerland with valid passport or personal ID card;

(b) **2.** nationals of Andorra, Argentina, Australia, Bolivia, Brazil, Brunei, Bulgaria, Canada, Chile, Costa Rica, Croatia, El Salvador, Guatemala, Honduras, Hong Kong (SAR), Israel, Korea (Rep), Japan, Macau (SAR), Malaysia, Mexico, Monaco, New Zealand, Nicaragua, Panama, Paraguay, Romania, San Marino, Singapore, Uruguay, USA, Vatican City and Venezuela for stays of up to three months in a six month period;

(c) nationals of South Africa when holding a visa for Latvia or Lithuania.

Note: Visitors arriving on cruise ships to Estonian ports from 1 May to 31 October will be able to enter Estonia for a period of 12 hours without a visa. The cruise ship must be stopping at an Estonian harbour for no more than 72 hours and the visitors must have a valid travel document recognised by Estonia. Tourists can disembark only if their name is on a list guaranteed by the ship's Captain and previously presented to the Border Guard.

Types of visa and cost: *Short-term:* Single-entry: £14 (up to 30 days); £24 (up to 90 days); Multiple-entry: £17 (up to 30 days); £24 (up to 90 days); £34 (up to one year). *Transit:* £17. *Airport transit:* £14; *Long term visa:* £55 (one year).

Validity: *Transit:* Up to 48 hours. *Single-entry:* Up to six months. *Multiple-entry:* Up to five years. *Long term:* Up to one year. In the case of South Africans, visas for Estonia are also valid for Latvia and Lithuania and vice versa.

Applications to: Consulate (or consular section at Embassy); see *Passport/Visa Information*. Applications must be made in person.

Application requirements: (a) One completed application form. (b) Passport valid for at least three months after expiry of visa, and with at least two blank pages. (c) One colour passport-size photo. (d) Fee. (e) Health insurance (with coverage of at least EEK160,000) valid for entire duration of stay. (f) Documents confirming purpose of visit (visa invitation, letter of invitation, travel vouchers, documents confirming employment or similar). (g) Proof of sufficient funds (equal to one-fifth of the minimum monthly wage [currently €33] for every day of planned stay in Estonia). (h) Documents confirming accommodation. (i) A

receipt proving the payment of state fees.
Note: All documents must be original. Children 15 years and over must possess their own travel documents with a recent photo.
Working days required: Up to 30. Postal applications are possible if there is no Estonian Embassy in country of residence.

PASSPORT/VISA INFORMATION

Embassy of the Republic of Estonia in the UK
16 Hyde Park Gate, London SW7 5DG, UK
Tel: (020) 7589 3428.
Website: www.estonia.gov.uk
Opening hours: Mon-Fri 0900-1700 (embassy); Mon and Fri 1000-1300, Tue and Thurs 1300-1600 (consular section).

Embassy of the Republic of Estonia in the USA
2131 Massachusetts Avenue, NW, Washington, DC 20008, USA
Tel: (202) 588 0101.
Website: www.estemb.org

Consulate of the Republic of Estonia in the USA
600 Third Avenue, 26th Floor, New York, NY 10016, USA
Tel: (212) 883 0636.
Website: www.nyc.estemb.org

Money

Currency: 1 Kroon (EEK) = 100 sents. Notes are in denominations of EEK500, 100, 50, 25, 10, 5, 2 and 1. Coins are in denominations of EEK1 and 5, and 50, 20, 10 and 5 sents.
Currency exchange: All major currencies can be exchanged at banks and bureaux de change. The value of the Kroon has been tied to the Euro. There are ATMs in most towns.
Credit & debit cards: Credit cards are widely accepted. Check with your credit or debit card company for details of merchant acceptability and other services which may be available. Most banks will give cash advances on credit cards with a passport.
Traveller's cheques: Traveller's cheques can be changed in banks in most larger towns. To avoid additional exchange rate charges, travellers are advised to take traveller's cheques in US Dollars, Pounds Sterling or Euros. The most widely accepted traveller's cheques are Amex, Thomas Cook and Eurocheque.
Banking hours: Mon-Fri 0900-1600, Sat 0900-1500; hours may vary. Most banks are usually closed, however currency exchange offices are open on Sat 0900-1500 and some on Sundays. The main banks in Estonia who serve tourists are Hansapank, Sampo-Pank and Uhispank.
Currency restrictions: There are no restrictions on the import or export of either local or foreign currency.
Exchange rate indicators:
Rate at time of publishing
£1.00=   EEK23.15
$1.00=   EEK13.10

Duty Free

The following goods may be imported into Estonia without incurring customs duty, by persons aged 18 or over:
200 cigarettes or 50 cigars or 250g tobacco; 1l of alcohol over 22 per cent or 2l of alcohol up to 22 per cent and 2l of wine; 10kg of foodstuffs.
Note: Restrictions apply to certain items, including plants and vegetable products, meat, milk, firearms, diamonds and antiques. Contact the authorities for further information (tel: (6) 967 436; website: www.customs.ee).
Abolition of duty free goods within the EU: On June 30 1999, the sale of duty free alcohol and tobacco at airports and at sea was abolished in all of the original 15 EU member states. Of the 10 new member states that joined the EU on May 1 2004, these rules already apply to Cyprus and Malta. There are transitional rules in place for visitors returning to one of the original 15 EU countries from one of the other new EU countries. But for the original 15, plus Cyprus and Malta, there are now no limits imposed on importing tobacco and alcohol products from one EU country to another (with the exceptions of Denmark, Finland and Sweden, where limits *are* imposed). Travellers should note that they may be required to prove at customs that the goods purchased are for personal use *only*.

Public Holidays

Below are listed Public Holidays for the period January 2006-June 2007.
2006: Jan 1 New Year's Day. **Feb 24** Independence Day. **Apr 14** Good Friday. **May 1** May Day. **Jun 23** Victory Day. **Jun 24**

Midsummer's Day. **Aug 20** Restoration of Independence Day. **Dec 25-26** Christmas.
2007: Jan 1 New Year's Day. **Feb 24** Independence Day. **Apr 6** Good Friday. **May 1** May Day. **Jun 23** Victory Day (Anniversary of the Battle of Võnnu).
Jun 24 Midsummer's Day.

Health

	Special Precautions?	Certificate Required?
Yellow Fever	No	No
Cholera	No	No
Typhoid & Polio	No	N/A
Malaria	No	N/A

Note: *Regulations and requirements may be subject to change at short notice, and you are advised to contact your doctor well in advance of your intended date of departure. Any numbers in the chart refer to the footnotes below.*

Other risks: *Hepatitis A* occurs. Cases of *diphtheria* have been reported. Vaccination against *tick-borne encephalitis* is advisable if visiting forested areas. Precautions should be taken against *tuberculosis*, as cases of this disease have increased. *HIV* testing is required for foreigners requesting work permits or residency.
Rabies is present. For those at high risk, vaccination before arrival should be considered. If you are bitten, seek medical advice without delay. For more information, consult the *Health* appendix.
Health care: European Economic Area (EEA) and Switzerland:
If you or any of your dependants are suddenly taken ill or have an accident during a visit to an EEA country or Switzerland, free or reduced-cost necessary treatment is available – in most cases on production of a valid European Health Insurance Card (EHIC). Each country has different rules about state medical provision. In some, treatment is free. In many countries you will have to pay part or all of the cost, and then claim a full or partial refund. The EHIC gives access to state-provided medical treatment only and the scheme gives no entitlement to medical repatriation costs, nor does it cover ongoing illnesses of a non-urgent nature, so comprehensive travel insurance is advised. Note that the EHIC replaces the Form E111, which will no longer be valid after 31 December 2005.
You will have to pay part of the cost of any treatment you receive from doctors and dentists, including home visits from a doctor. The charges are not refundable. Children under 19 can get free dental treatment, and adults do not have to pay for teeth to be removed or abscesses lanced. You will be charged a standard fee for prescriptions. Sometimes, you will also have to pay a percentage of the costs above the standard fee. If the medicine is not on the national list of medicinal products, you will have to pay the full costs. This is not refundable.
Hospital treatment: if you are admitted as an in-patient, you will have to pay a fee of up to EEK25 per day for up to 10 days per hospitalisation. There is no in-patient fee for children below the age of 19, cases related to pregnancy and childbirth, and intensive care. Ambulance travel is free in an emergency. Over the counter medicines are available at pharmacies in every town. Pharmacies are open from Mon-Fri 1000-1900 and one stays open all night in Pärnu. It is suggested travellers bring their own supply with proof in the form of a prescription or a doctor's note. However, customs will only allow five medicines per traveller in their original packaging. More information can be obtained from the Estonian Health Insurance Fund (*Eesti Haigekassa*) (website: http://www.haigekassa.ee/eng).

Travel - International

AIR:

The national airline is *Estonian Air (OV)* (website: www.estonian-air.ee), which operates six direct flights a week (everyday except Saturday) between Gatwick and Tallinn. For more information, contact the *Estonian Air* office in the UK (tel: (020) 7333 0196).
Approximate flight times: From Tallinn to *London* is approximately three hours, to *Frankfurt/M* is approximately two hours 30 minutes, to *Los Angeles* is approximately 22 hours (via Helsinki), and to *New York* is approximately 13 hours 30 minutes (via Helsinki).
Main airports: *Tallinn (TLL)* (website: www.tallinn-airport.ee) is located 5km (3 miles) northwest of the city.
To/from the airport: Buses run between the city and the airport (travel time – 15 minutes). A shuttle bus to the main hotels and the city centre meets all flights. Taxis are also available. *Facilities:* Banks/bureaux de change, duty-free shops, shops, post office, restaurants, two business lounges, tourist information and car hire. *Kärdla (KDL)* (website: www.hiiumaa.ee) is located 5km (3 miles) east of the city.
To/from the airport: Taxis run from central Kärdla to the

airport (travel time - 20 minutes). *Facilities:* Banks/bureaux de change, post office, tourist information, car hire, travel agent, parking, a hotel and restaurants/bars.
Departure tax: None.
SEA:

Main ports: *Tallinn* (website: www.portoftallinn.com). Ferries operate between Tallinn and *Helsinki* (Finland) (travel time – 3 hours 45 minutes), *Stockholm* (Sweden) (travel time – 11 hours) and *Rostock* (Germany) in high season (travel time – 21 hours). Express services run between Tallinn and Helsinki in the high season.
RAIL:

Estonian Railways (Eesti Raudtee) (website: www.evr.ee) is underdeveloped, although there is a route on the EVR Express between St Petersburg (Russian Federation) and Tallinn. There is no longer a train route between Estonia and Latvia. Travel is slower than bus. Children up to seven years may travel free if accompanied by an adult and not taking a separate seat.
ROAD:

There are direct routes along the Baltic coast into Latvia, Lithuania and Kaliningrad, and also east into the Russian Federation. Routes into the Baltic states are via Poland and Belarus or Poland and Lithuania; border points: Terespol (Poland) – Brest (Belarus) and Ogrodniki (Poland) – Lazdijai (Lithuania). **Bus:** Long-distance services run regularly to Riga, Vilnius, Kaliningrad and St Petersburg. There are numerous excellent road links with all neighbouring countries. *Eurolines* (52 Grosvenor Gardens, London SW1W 0AU; tel: (08705) 143 219; website: www.eurolines.com) and *National Express* (Ensign Court, 4 Vicarage Road, Edgbaston, Birmingham B15 3ES; tel: 08705 808 080; website: www.nationalexpress.com) run regular coach services from the UK to Estonia and other European cities. **Passes:** Travellers can either choose Mini-Pass breaks or book a 15-, 30- or 60-day pass. The six Mini-Passes give travellers the freedom to visit three cities, with prices starting from £55. Travellers can stay as long as they like in each city.

Travel - Internal

AIR:

There are domestic flights from Tallinn to the islands of Saaremaa and Hiiumaa (this service does not operate during the winter). Charter flights operate between Tartu and Tallinn and the daily Baltic Ekspress runs between Tallinn and Warsaw. The Baltic Aeroservice links Tallinn with Kärdla and Kuressaare. Prices vary, though these services are expensive.
SEA/RIVER:

Frequent ferry services connect the mainland with the larger islands, and boats operate on Lake Peipsi and the Emajõgi River.
RAIL:

The rail system is underdeveloped but most major cities are connected to the network. Rail services to Tartu take about three hours (express trains 2 hours 30 minutes) from Tallinn.
ROAD:
Estonia has a high density of roads although there are few major highways. Signs are not illuminated and fairly small, so driving at night is best avoided. Car headlights must be used 24 hours a day. Lead-free and 4-star petrol are widely available and a good network of petrol stations (many of them open 24 hours) has been developed. Payment is in local currency or by credit card. Traffic drives on the right. The minimum driving age is 18. **Bus:** There is a wide network covering most of the country, including express services. Prices are very low and buses are still the most important means of transport. The buses to and from Tallinn are generally quite fast and there are more of them compared to the other cities. There are seven buses a day travelling to Pärnu. Tickets bought from the driver are more expensive (EEK15) then if bought on a newsstand (EEK10). Travellers can also buy a 10 ticket package for EEK80. Travellers can buy anything from a one hour-ticket to a three-day ticket. Buses tend to be overcrowded. Tickets for minivans have to be paid for on board. Buses, trolleys and trams run daily from 0600-2300.
Taxi: Private taxis must display the name of the company and their number on the roof. Fares should be agreed upon beforehand. *Marshrut-taxis* are minibuses which operate on fixed routes stopping on request. They can take up to 10 people. **Car hire:** Can be arranged at the airport or in Tallinn. Available from Avis, Europcar, Hertz, National and Sixt. **Parking:** Parking on streets in the city, the old town and the Pirita area must be paid for. The first 15 minutes is for free. Travellers can purchase a parking ticket from a roadside machine. In some areas tickets are sold by parking wardens. Prices vary from EEK3 for 15 minutes to EEK2500 for a month pass. **Regulations:** Speed limits are 120kph (74mph) on some roads, 90kph (55mph) outside built-up areas and 50kph (31mph) in built-up areas. The consumption of alcohol while driving is strictly forbidden.

Documentation: EU nationals should be in possession of an EU or national driving licence and insurance.

URBAN:

Taxis in Tallinn are inexpensive. All parts of the city are served by bus, trolley-bus and tram. Tickets can be bought at stalls in the main shopping areas.

Travel Advice

Most visits to Estonia are trouble-free but you should be aware of the global risk of indiscriminate international terrorist attacks, which could be against civilian targets, including places frequented by foreigners.

In recent years, there have been several bomb attacks on buildings or vehicles in Estonia. While these were connected with organised crime, and not targeted at foreigners, travellers are advised to remain alert for suspect packages. This advice is based on information provided by the Foreign and Commonwealth Office in the UK. It is correct at time of publishing. As the situation can change rapidly, visitors are advised to contact the following organisations for the latest travel advice:

British Foreign and Commonwealth Office
Tel: (0845) 850 2829.
Website: www.fco.gov.uk

US Department of State
Website: http://travel.state.gov/travel

Accommodation

HOTELS:

Since independence there has been a scramble from Western and Estonian firms to turn the old state-run hotels into modern Western-standard enterprises. Many more joint ventures with firms from all over Western Europe and the United States will ensure that the standard of accommodation in Estonia rapidly reaches Western European levels. Outside Tallinn, which for the time being is the main location of the current expansion, Estonia enjoys an adequate range of acceptable accommodation, left over from the pre-independence days or built by Estonian entrepreneurs, including large hotels and smaller pension-type establishments.

CAMPING:

There are over 80 campsites in Estonia. The most popular include: Camping & Motel Peoleo, 12km (7.5 miles) south of Tallinn; Camping Valgerand in Pärnu; and Camping Malvaste on Hiiumaa Island. Standards are improving, though are not yet as high as in Western European countries. Many campsites are open throughout the year.

RURAL ACCOMMODATION:

The Estonian Rural Tourism Association provides accommodation in the countryside across Estonia, from farm-stays to local bed & breakfasts.

YOUTH HOSTELS:

The majority of youth hostels have saunas and seminar facilities.

APARTMENTS AND SELF CATERING:

Villas, apartments, cottages and houses are available in Tallinn. Prices vary according to specification.

ACCOMMODATION INFORMATION

Estonian Hotel and Restaurant Association
Kirku 6, 10130, Tallinn, Estonia
Tel: (6) 411 428.
Website: www.ehrl.ee

Estonian Rural Tourism Association
Vilmsi 53b, 10147 Tallinn, Estonia
Tel: (6) 009 999.
Website: www.maaturism.ee

Estonian Youth Hostels Association
Natva mnt., 10120 Tallinn, Estonia
Tel: (6) 461 455.
Website: www.baltichostels.net/eyha.html

Top Things To See

- **Tallinn**, the capital of Estonia, is an ancient Hanseatic city. Discover its wealth of historical and architectural monuments, particularly in the old town centre which is dominated by the soaring steeple of the medieval **Town Hall** (14th to 15th centuries), the oldest in northern Europe. More than two-thirds of the original **City Wall** still stands and a superb view of the narrow streets, the gabled roofs and the towers and spires of old Tallinn is afforded from **Toompea Castle**, situated on a cliff top. A favourite recreation spot is **Kadriorg Park**, which contains the palace built for Peter the Great. The **Open Air Museum** offers visitors a glimpse into the way of rural life in the 18th and 19th centuries.
- Drive to **Pärnu**, about two hours' from Tallinn, a small town situated on the banks of the **Pärnu River** where it emerges into the Gulf of Riga. Established in the 13th century, the town is a seaport and a health resort. Among its attractions are its **theatre** and its 3km- (2 mile-) long sandy **beach**.
- **Tartu** is Estonia's second-largest city, about 176km (110 miles) from Tallinn on the **Emajõgi River**. Visit the city's **old university**. Other sights include the **Vyshgorod Cathedral** (13th to 15th centuries), the **Town Hall** (18th century) and the university's **Botanical Garden**.
- Head for **Narva,** one of the oldest towns in Estonia, situated on the western banks of the **River Narva.** The **Herman Castle** is the oldest architectural monument and the city museum, which is situated in the castle, is well worth seeing.
- See old windmills, stone churches, fishing villages and a restored Episcopal castle dating back to the 13th century on **Saaremaa,** the largest island in Estonia. **Hiiumaa** (Estonia's second-largest island) is also worth a visit.
- Visit **Mustvee**, situated on the shores of the beautiful vast **Lake Peipsi**, and **Kuremäe**, the site of the only functioning **convent** in Estonia.

Top Things To Do

- Relax in **Haapsalu,** a small town on the western coast which has been a well-known resort since the 19th century. It is the ideal place to get away from it all with its romantic wooden houses and tree-lined avenues.
- Explore the countryside and see unspoiled forest and swamps, picturesque old fishing villages and historic manor houses in one of Estonia's three national parks. Situated on the northern coast, **Lahema National Park** (70km/44 miles from Tallinn), the country's largest national park, contains limestone cliffs, waterfalls, lakes and forests. **Bog walks** can be undertaken in this area. Walkways on wooden boards give visitors the opportunity to observe the special flora and fauna of the deep peat bogs. In the **Soomaa National Park**, near Pärnu, the ancient bogs (said to be inhabited by witches) can be explored in traditional canoes. The third park is the **Vilandsi National Park**. Estonian **wildlife** includes large mammals such as lynx, bears, wolves and elk. Birdlife is abundant, and **birdwatchers** are well catered for in reserves such as the **Käina Bay Bird Reserve** and **Matsalu Nature Reserve**. Eagles, storks and a variety of wetland birds are among the species to be seen. Butterflies are also numerous in parts of Estonia.
- **Trainspotting:** Owing to the wide-gauge track, unusual trains can be spotted, an activity popular amongst local people. The **National Railway Museum** in **Haapsalu** is a source of information for trainspotters. Behind the museum, a 'train graveyard' contains vehicles of special interest.
- **Swimming** is popular all over Estonia. The beaches are often long and wide with white sand; pools and lakes abound in the interior of the country. In the north of the country, it is possible to find small coves used for **nude bathing**, though there are no designated areas for this.
- **Fishing** and **boating** are very popular.
- **Hike** or **cycle** on unspoiled **Saaremaa Island**.
- **Otepää** in the southeast, with its lakes and forests, is a good location to practice **outdoor activities** and for **skiing** in the winter. **Canoeing** can be arranged with specialist companies.

Credit: ©Estonian Tourist Board

TOURIST INFORMATION

Estonian Tourist Board
1315 Liivalaia Street, 10118 Tallinn, Estonia
Tel: (6) 279 770.
Website: www.visitestonia.com

Entertainment

FOOD & DRINK: Hors d'oeuvres are very good and often the best part of the meal.

National specialities:
- *Sült* (jellied veal).
- *Täidetud vasikarind* (roast stuffed shoulder of veal).
- *Rosolje* (vinaigrette with herring and beets).
- Braised goose stuffed with apples and plums.
- Solid rye bread.
- Estonian wild mushroom soup.

National drinks:
- Saare beer (dark and heavy yet tasty).
- Mulled wine.

Legal drinking age: The legal drinking age is 21.

Tipping: Taxi fares and restaurant bills include a tip.

NIGHTLIFE: Tallinn is used to entertaining daytrippers from Finland and has a wide range of restaurants, cafes and bars. There is also an opera and ballet theatre.

SHOPPING: Amber and local folk art are good buys. Craft markets sell traditional handmade thick wool jumpers.

Shopping hours: Mon-Fri 0900-1800. Many shops are also open at the weekend. In larger towns, shops have longer opening hours.

Business

- **GDP:** US$19.23 billion.
- **Main exports:** Machinery equipment, foodstuffs, furniture, wood/paper and textiles.
- **Main imports:** Transportation equipment, textiles and foodstuff.
- **Main trade partners:** China, Finland, Germany, Japan, Scandanavia and Sweden.

ECONOMY: Economic autonomy was a key demand from Estonia during the negotiations that led to its independence. The Baltic states were the most prosperous areas of the former Soviet Union and they were keen to develop economic links with their Western neighbours outside the straitjacket of central planning. Other than oil-shale, which is present in significant quantities and provides the basis of the country's power generation, Estonia has few raw materials of its own and relies mostly on imported commodities to produce finished goods. Light machinery, electrical and electronic equipment and consumer goods are the main products. Fishing, forestry and dairy farming dominate the agricultural sector. Estonia's infrastructure, particularly the road network, is well-developed by regional standards. Post-Soviet economic policy has followed a customary pattern of deregulation and privatisation. In June 1992, Estonia became the first former Soviet Republic to introduce its own currency, the Kroon, which is the legal tender and is now fixed in value to the Euro. Estonia's service sector was the most developed in the former USSR, and has since expanded further with increased tourism and Western investment. There is a thriving financial services industry and the country is also famous for its high-tech business sector. Overall, trade with the West has increased dramatically with important trading partners (as above). Despite this, Estonia still has fundamental economic links with the Russian Federation, and the 1998 Russian economic crisis led to a recession in Estonia the following year. Growth in 2004, however, was around 5 per cent.

In 1999, Estonia joined the World Trade Organisation, adding to its previous membership of the IMF, World Bank and the European Bank for Reconstruction and Development. In May 2004, Estonia, along with its Baltic neighbours and seven other countries, achieved a long-cherished ambition when it joined the European Union.

BUSINESS ETIQUETTE: Prior appointments are necessary. Business is conducted formally. Business cards are exchanged after introduction. **Office hours:** Mon-Fri 0800-1800.

COMMERCIAL INFORMATION

Estonian Chamber of Commerce and Industry
Toom Kooli 17, 10130 Tallinn, Estonia
Tel: (6) 460 244.
Website: www.koda.ee

Ethiopia

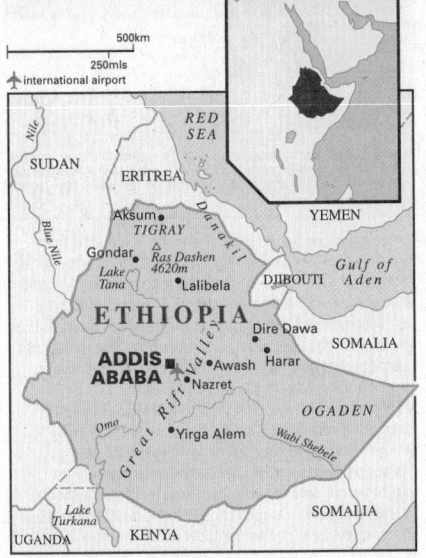

Location: Northeast Africa.

Time: GMT + 3

Overview

Ethiopia is the only country in Africa never to be fully colonised, despite the efforts of Italy, who suffered a series of devastating defeats at the hands of the Ethiopians in the late 19th centur.

The 20th-century history of Ethiopia is dominated by the figure of Haile Selassie, who became emperor in 1930 and ruled until the military coup of 1974. The country was occupied by the Italians between 1936 and 1941.

In 1977, a further coup brought Lieutenant Colonel Mengistu to power. Agricultural backwardness was the country's most urgent problem; all attempts at land reform were resisted. The government itself was perhaps too preoccupied with fighting secessionist movements in Tigray and Eritrea, and with occasional border clashes with Somalia (one of which escalated into full-scale war during 1977). This, along with severe drought, economic mismanagement and the mutual mistrust between the government and Western aid agencies contributed to the widespread and heavily-publicised 1983 famine in Ethiopia. The civil war continued until May 1991, when President Mengistu fled the country for Zimbabwe.

In June 2001, after 10 separate attempts, the UN finally managed to broker a settlement between Ethiopia and Eritrea. A 4,000-strong peacekeeping force, UNMEE, holds the line between the two sides, but a final resolution of the conflict seems as distant as ever. This was a war that neither side could afford. Ethiopia has been in need of food aid for some years and distribution to the most needy and remote areas was disrupted by the fighting. Large imports of emergency aid were needed during the summer of 2003 to prevent a famine which might otherwise have affected up to 15 million people. In 2005, contested general elections led to more social unrest.

Although Ethiopia can claim some of the highest and most stunning places on the African continent, such as the jaggedly carved Simien Mountains, and some of the lowest, such as the Danakil Depression, with its sulphur fumaroles and lunar-like landscape, visitors are advised to only go to Ethiopia for essential travel until the situation settles.

General Information

AREA: 1.13 million sq km (437,600 sq miles).
POPULATION: 74.2 million (UN, 2005).
POPULATION DENSITY: 65.5 per sq km.
CAPITAL: Addis Ababa. **Population:** 2.4 million (1994 Census).

Credit: ©Bruce Logan

GEOGRAPHY: Ethiopia is situated in northeast Africa, bordered by Eritrea, Sudan, Kenya, Somalia and Djibouti. It is about twice the size of France. The central area is a vast highland region of volcanic rock forming a watered, temperate zone surrounded by hot, arid, inhospitable desert. The Great Rift Valley, which starts in Palestine, runs down the Red Sea and diagonally southwest through Ethiopia, Kenya and Malawi. The escarpments on either side of the country are steepest in the north where the terrain is very rugged. To the south, the landscape is generally flatter and more suited to agriculture.

GOVERNMENT: Federal Republic. **Head of State:** President Woldegiorgis Girma since 2001. **Head of Government:** Prime Minister Meles Zenawi since 1995. With the exception of a five-year occupation by Mussolini's Italy, Ethiopia is the only African country never to have been colonised by Europeans. **Recent history:** The Ethiopian People's Revolutionary Democratic Front (EPRDF) of incumbent Premier Meles Zenawi won bitterly contested elections in May 2005, his third five-year mandate as Prime Minister, despite a sharp increase in public support for opposition parties. A large number of electoral complaints were made and the EPRDF and the main opposition both claimed victory as the initial results were announced. Around 36 people were killed and hundreds were arrested in protests sparked by opposition allegations of electoral fraud by the ruling party. The final results, announced in September 2005, gave the EPRDF and its affiliates control of the 547-seat Parliament.

LANGUAGE: Amharic is the official language, although about 80 other native tongues are spoken including Aromo and Tigrinya. English is widely used and some Arabic, Italian and French is spoken.

RELIGION: Ethiopian Orthodox (*Tewahido*) and Coptic Church, mainly in the north, 40 per cent; Islam, mainly in the east and south, 40 per cent. There are also significant Evangelical, Protestant and Roman Catholic communities.

ELECTRICITY: 220 volts AC, 50Hz.

SOCIAL CONVENTIONS: Casual wear is suitable for most places, but Ethiopians tend to be fairly formal and conservative in their dress. Private informal entertaining is very common. Most religious houses are not open to women. **Photography:** In the smaller towns the locals may expect a small payment in return for being photographed. Video photography in famous tourist attractions occasionally carries a small charge. Photography may be prohibited in airports and near military camps.

Climate

Hot and humid in the lowlands, warm in the hill country and cool in the uplands. Most rainfall is from June to September.

Required clothing: The lightest possible clothing in lowland areas; medium- or lightweight in the hill country. Warm clothing may be needed at night to cope with the dramatic temperature change.

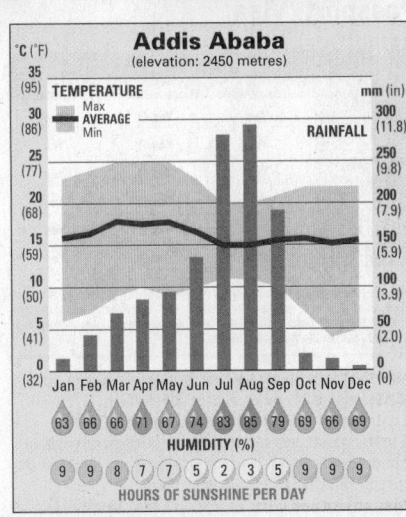

Addis Ababa
(elevation: 2450 metres)

TEMPERATURE — Max — AVERAGE — Min

RAINFALL

HUMIDITY (%)
63 66 66 71 67 74 83 85 79 69 66 69

HOURS OF SUNSHINE PER DAY
9 9 8 7 5 2 2 5 9 9 9

Communications

Telephone: IDD is available. Country code: 251.
Mobile telephone: Ethio-Mobile covers Addis Ababa and the surrounding areas (Ethiopian Telecommunications Corporation; website: www.telecom.net.et/ethiomobile). Ethio-Mobile have roaming agreements with many international mobile phone companies.
Internet: There are Internet cafes in Addis Ababa. Some top-end hotels may also offer services, although connections may be difficult.
Post: Service to and from Europe takes up to two weeks. Post office hours: Mon-Fri 0800-1600.
MEDIA: Although the state controls radio and television, the print and broadcast media have seen dramatic changes after the overthrow of the dictator Mengistu. Deregulation has been on the cards for some years. Licence application forms were given to would-be private radio broadcasters in 2004. Some opposition groups beam radio broadcasts to Ethiopia using shortwave transmitters overseas. The number of privately-owned newspapers has grown. The Walta website also hosts a few pro-government English-language newspapers. The relationship between the press and the authorities has sometimes been difficult, especially after the violent protests that followed the 2005 elections.
Press: Amharic newspapers published in the capital include state-owned *Addis Zemen*. The English-language state-owned daily in Ethiopia is *The Ethiopian Herald*. A number of other weeklies are also available such as *Menelik*, *Addis Admas* and *Tobya*. *The Sun* and the *Addis Tribune* are private English-language weekly publications.
TV: *Ethiopian Television (ETV)* is state-owned.

Credit: ©Bruce Logan

Radio: State-owned Radio Ethiopia operates *National Service* and *External Service*. *Voice of Tigray Revolution* is Tigray Regional State government's radio. *Radio Fana* was founded in 1994 by the ruling party.

Passport/Visa

	Passport Required?	Visa Required?	Return Ticket Required?
Full British	Yes	Yes/1	Yes
Australian	Yes	Yes/1	Yes
Canadian	Yes	Yes/1	Yes
USA	Yes	Yes/1	Yes
Other EU	Yes	Yes/1	Yes
Japanese	Yes	Yes/1	Yes

Note: *Regulations and requirements may be subject to change at short notice, and you are advised to contact the appropriate diplomatic or consular authority before finalising travel arrangements. Any numbers in the chart refer to the footnotes below.*

PASSPORTS: Passport valid for six months required by all.
VISAS: Required by all except the following:
(a) nationals of Kenya for stays of up to three months;
(b) transit passengers continuing to a third country within 12 hours, provided not leaving the airport and holding valid travel documents for onward destination.
Types of visa and cost: *Tourist:* £12 (single-entry); £18 (multiple-entry, three months); £24 (multiple-entry, six months). *Business:* £12 (single-entry); £18 (multiple-entry, three months); £30 (multiple-entry, six months); £60 (multiple-entry, one year). *Transit:* £12 (single-entry); £18 (double-entry).
Note: The above prices do not apply to US citizens. By special arrangement with the US goverment, citizens receive a two-year multiple entry visa for both business and tourism for £42.
Validity: *Tourist* and *Business:* Single-entry visas are valid for 30 days, multiple-entry visas are valid for three or six months and business visas also up to twelve months. Applications for extensions should be made to the Immigration Department in Ethiopia. *Transit:* Seven days.
Application to: Consulate (or Consular section at Embassy); see *Passport/Visa Information*, in person, by post or on arrival (see below).
VISA APPLICATION ON ARRIVAL:
1. Some tourist visas can be issued on arrival at Addis Ababa Bole International Airport. Tourist visas can be issued on arrival to:
(a) Foreign nationals coming from countries where there is no Ethiopian mission.
(b) Foreign nationals coming from and who are permanent residents in any of the following internationally recognised tourist generating countries: Argentina, Australia, Austria, Belgium, Brazil, Canada, China, Greece, Ireland, Israel, Italy, Japan, Korea, Kuwait, Luxembourg, Mexico, The Netherlands, New Zealand, Norway, Poland, Portugal, Russian Federation, South Africa, Spain, Sweden, Switzerland, UK and USA.
If applying for a tourist visa on arrival, visitors will require two passport photographs and US$100. Application can take up to two hours.

Application requirements: (a) Completed application form. (b) Passport valid for at least six months (containing residence permit, if applicable). (c) One passport-size photo. (d) Fee (payable by cash, banker's draft or postal order) made payable to The Ethiopian Embassy. (e) Proof of sufficient funds to cover stay i.e a bank statement. (f) Return or onward ticket. (g) For postal applications, a self-addressed special-delivery envelope. *Business:* (a)-(g) and, (h) Letter from sponsor on headed paper, accepting financial responsibility for applicant, or if self employed a letter from solicitor or Company House. *Student:* (a)-(g) and, (h) Letter from educational institution, or invitation from Ethiopian reference.
Note: A yellow fever vaccination, whilst advisable, is not compulsory. Consult the embassy for up-to-date advice on whether applications will be accepted without the certificate.
Working days required: Two to three days, longer if application is by post. Applications should be made well in advance.
Exit permit: Required by all nationals of Ethiopia and visitors staying more than 30 days.

PASSPORT/VISA INFORMATION

Embassy of the Federal Democratic Republic of Ethiopia in the UK
17 Princes Gate, London SW7 1PZ, UK
Tel: (020) 7838 3888.
Website: www.ethiopianembassy.org.uk
Opening hours: Mon-Fri 0900-1700 (general); Mon-Fri 0900-1600 (visa applications and collections).

Embassy of the Federal Democratic Republic of Ethiopia in the USA
3506 International Drive, NW, Washington, DC 20008, USA
Tel: (202) 364 1200.
Website: www.ethiopianembassy.org

Money

Currency: Ethiopian Birr (ETB) = 100 cents. Notes are in denominations of ETB100, 50, 10, 5 and 1. Coins are in denominations of 50, 25, 10, 5 and 1 cents.
Currency exchange: US Dollar bills are the most convenient currency to exchange.
Credit & debit cards: Diners Club and MasterCard are accepted on a very limited basis (only the Hilton Hotel is certain to accept them). Check with your credit or debit card company for details of merchant acceptability and other services which may be available.
Travellers cheques: To avoid additional exchange rate charges, travellers are advised to take travellers cheques in US Dollars or Pounds Sterling.
Currency restrictions: The import of local currency is limited to ETB100. The export of local currency up to ETB100 is permitted, provided the traveller holds a re-entry permit. The import and export of foreign currency is unlimited, subject to declaration on arrival.
Banking hours: Mon-Thur 0800-1500, Fri 0800-1100 and 1330-1500, Sat 0830-1100.
Exchange rate indicators:
Rate at time of publishing
£1.00=   ETB15.80
$1.00=   ETB8.78

Duty Free

The following goods may be imported into Ethiopia without incurring customs duty:
200 cigarettes or 50 cigars or 227g of tobacco; 1l of alcoholic beverages; two bottles or 500ml of perfume; gifts up to the value of ETB500.
Note: Export certificates are required for skins, hides and antiques.

Public Holidays

Below are listed Public Holidays for the January 2006- June 2007 period.
2006: **Jan 7*** Ethiopian Christmas. **Jan 10** Eid-al Adha (Arafat). **Jan 19*** Timket (Epiphany). **Mar 2** Victory of Adowa. **Apr 10** Mawlid al-Nabi (Birth of the Prophet). **Apr 21*** Ethiopian Good Friday. **Apr 23*** Ethiopian Easter. **May 28** Downfall of the Dergue. **Sep 11*** Ethiopian New Year (Entutatash). **Sep 26** * Finding of the True Cross (Meskel). **Oct 22-24** Eid al-Fitr (End of Ramadan). **Dec 31** Eid-al Adha (Arafat).
2007: Jan 7* Ethiopian Christmas. **Jan 19*** Timket (Epiphany). **Mar 2** Victory of Adowa. **Mar 31** Mawlid al-Nabi (Birth of the Prophet). **Apr 6*** Ethiopian Good Friday. **Apr 8*** Ethiopian Easter. **May 28** Downfall of the Dergue.
Note: (a) *Indicates Coptic holidays. (b) Ethiopia still uses the Julian calendar, which is divided into 12 months of 30

days each, and a 13th month of five or six days at the end of the year; hence the date for Christmas. The Ethiopian year commences on 11 September. The Ethiopian calendar is seven years and eight months behind our own. (c) Muslim festivals are timed according to local sightings of various phases of the moon and the dates given above are approximations. During the lunar month of Ramadan that precedes Eid al-Fitr, Muslims fast during the day and feast at night and normal business patterns may be interrupted. Some disruption may continue into Eid al-Fitr itself. Eid al-Fitr and Eid al-Adha may last anything from two to 10 days, depending on the region. For more information, see the *World of Islam* appendix.

Health

	Special Precautions?	Certificate Required?
Yellow Fever	Yes	1
Cholera	2	No
Typhoid & Polio	3	N/A
Malaria	4	N/A

Note: *Regulations and requirements may be subject to change at short notice, and you are advised to contact your doctor well in advance of your intended date of departure. Any numbers in the chart refer to the footnotes below.*

1: A yellow fever vaccination certificate is required from travellers over one year of age coming from infected areas. Ethiopia is listed in the endemic zone for yellow fever and travellers arriving from non-endemic zones should note that vaccination is strongly recommended for travel outside the urban areas, even if an outbreak of the disease has not been reported and they would normally not require a vaccination certificate to enter the country.
2: Following WHO guidelines issued in 1973, a Cholera vaccination certificate is no longer a condition of entry to Ethiopia. Cholera is a serious risk in this country and precautions are essential. Up-to-date advice should be sought before deciding whether these precautions should include vaccination as medical opinion is divided over its effectiveness; see the *Health* appendix for more information.
3: Typhoid is widespread. Poliomyelitis is endemic. Vaccination against both is advised.
4: Malaria risk, predominantly in the malignant *falciparum* form, exists throughout the year in all areas below 2000m (6562ft). Highly chloroquine-resistant *falciparum* is reported. No malaria risk exists in Addis Ababa.
Food & drink: All water should be regarded as being potentially contaminated. Water used for drinking, brushing teeth or making ice should have first been boiled or otherwise sterilised. Milk is unpasteurised and should be boiled. Powdered or tinned milk is available and is advised, but make sure that it is reconstituted with pure water. Avoid dairy products which are likely to have been made from unboiled milk. Only eat well-cooked meat and fish, preferably served hot. Pork, salad and mayonnaise may carry increased risk. Vegetables should be cooked and fruit peeled.
Other risks: *Diarrhoeal* diseases, including giardiasis, and *typhoid fevers* are common. *Bilharzia* (schistosomiasis) is present. Avoid swimming and paddling in fresh water; swimming pools which are well-chlorinated and maintained are safe. *Onchocerciasis* (river blindness) occurs. Cases of *Trypanosomiasis* (sleeping sickness) have increased in recent years in tourists visiting national parks. *Hepatitis A* and *E* are widespread; *hepatitis B* is hyperendemic. *Meningococcal meningitis* risk is present, particularly in dry areas and during the dry season. *Visceral leishmaniasis* may be found in the drier areas. *Trachoma* is widespread. Immunisation against *diphtheria and measles* is also recommended. *Tetanus* vaccinations should be up to date. *Rabies* is present. For those at high risk, vaccination before arrival should be considered. If you are bitten, seek medical advice without delay. For more information, consult the *Health* appendix.
Health care: Health facilities are extremely limited in Addis Ababa and inadequate outside the city. Travellers should bring their own prescription drugs accompanied by a doctor's note. The high altitude and low oxygen level of much of Ethiopia need time to be acclimatised to. Anyone who suffers from heart ailments or high blood pressure should consult a doctor before travelling. Health insurance is strongly advised; see the *Health* appendix.

Travel - International

AIR:

The national airline is *Ethiopian Airlines (ET)* (website: www.flyethiopian.com), which operates three flights a week from London, with a stopover either in Frankfurt/M or in Cairo, and three times a week from Washington.
Approximate flight times: From Addis Ababa to *London* is 10 hours.

Main airports: *Addis Ababa (ADD) (Bole International)* is 8km (5 miles) southeast of the city (travel time – 25 minutes). *To/from the airport:* A coach service departs regularly to the city. Taxis are also available. *Facilities:* Duty free, car hire, banks, bureaux de change, left luggage, post office, first aid facilities, restaurant and bar.

Departure tax: US$20, payable in US Dollars only. Exact amount only. Transit passengers not leaving the airport and children under two are exempt.

RAIL:

 A 784km- (487 mile-) rail service between Djibouti and Addis Ababa is run jointly by the two governments.

ROAD:

 The main route is via Kenya. There is an all-weather road from Moyale on the border via Yabelo, Dila and Yirga to Addis Ababa. The following border points are also open: Dewale/Galafi (from Djibouti) and Humera/Metema (from Sudan). The road linking Nairobi and Addis Ababa forms part of the Trans-East African Highway.

Travel - Internal

AIR:

 Ethiopian Airlines runs internal flights to over 40 towns, although services may be infrequent. Airports throughout Ethiopia are currently being upgraded in a step to encourage tourism. *Ethiopian Airlines* also operates an *Historic Route Service* for tourists taking in the most famous historic sites.

Departure tax: ETB10.

RAIL:

 The only working line runs between Addis Ababa and Djibouti, via Dire Dawa and Harar. Travellers should be prepared for occasional delays.

ROAD:

 A good network of all-weather roads (4,100km/2,562 miles of asphalt) services most business and tourist centres. Otherwise, 4-wheel-drive vehicles are recommended (19,000km/11,875 miles) of gravel and dirt roads). Frequent fuel shortages can make travel outside Addis Ababa very difficult. Vehicle travel after dark outside Addis Ababa is risky. Traffic drives on the right.

Bus: Services throughout the country are run by the Government as well as private companies. The bus terminus can provide schedules and tickets. Bus trips can be slow as there is often a lengthy wait to assemble a convoy (necessary in more dangerous areas). **Taxi:** Available in Addis Ababa and other major towns. These include blue and white mini buses; they sometimes offer service on a shared basis and are inexpensive. Fares are not usually metered and should be negotiated before travelling. Personalised and specific trips should be negotiated with the driver in advance of travel. In Addis Ababa, the National Tour Operation (NTO) operates luxury taxis. They are stationed outside major hotels and at the airport. There are also yellow taxis at the airport. Neither have meters. **Car hire:** This is available from *Avis* and *Hertz* in Addis Ababa.

Documentation: Full valid international or Ethiopian licence is required. Licence from country of origin must be endorsed locally.

Travel Advice

Following serious disturbances in November 2005, the situation remains volatile. Visitors are advised not to travel to the Gambella Region at any time, where continuing unrest and sporadic violence has led to many deaths since December 2003. In October 2005, a further outbreak of violence resulted in the death of police officers and civilians. The situation remains tense.

Visitors are also advised against all travel within 20 kms (12,5 miles) of the Eritrean border in the Tigray and Afar regions at any time, which remain predominantly military zones. The Ethiopia/Eritrea border remains closed.

Visitors are advised against crossing the Ethiopia/Somalia border by road at any time, and against all but essential travel in the area east of the Harar to Gode line. A number of explosions occurred in Jijiga on 24 July 2005. There is a high threat from terrorism in Ethiopia. This advice is based on information provided by the Foreign and Commonwealth Office in the UK. It is correct at time of publishing. As the situation can change rapidly, visitors are advised to contact the following organisations for the latest travel advice:

British Foreign and Commonwealth Office
Tel: (0845) 850 2829.
Website: www.fco.gov.uk

US Department of State
Website: http://travel.state.gov/travel

Accommodation

Good hotels can be found in Addis Ababa and other main centres, although they tend to be better in the north than in the south. Some offer facilities for small exhibitions and conferences. There are hotels in the other larger towns; prices are, in general, slightly lower than those in the main centres. There is a 5 to 10 per cent service charge. Camping is allowed in most areas but local advice must be sought. There is no camping equipment hire. For more information, contact the Ethiopian Commission for Tourism (see *Top Things To Do*).

Top Things To See

- Go to **Addis Ababa**, Ethiopia's capital, located at an altitude of 2440m (8000ft) in the central highlands. To the east is the government and education sector. Places worth visiting include the **University**, the **National Museum**, the **Menelik School**, the **Berhan Ena Selam** printing press, the **old Menelik Palace**, the **Jubilee Palace**,the **Meskal (Revolution) Square**, St George's **Cathedral**, the **Ethnology Museum**, the **Menelik Mausoleum**, the **Trinity Church** and the **Old Ghibi Palace**. In the central sector, largely devoted to commerce, visit the **National Theatre**. The western sector is famous for its **mercato**, one of the largest markets in Africa.
- **Aksum**, the ancient royal capital of the earliest Ethiopian kingdom, in the north of the country, is renowned for its multi-storeyed ancient carved granite **obelisks**, its **archaeological remains** and its **church**, which claims to house the **Lost Ark of the Covenant**.
- Do not miss the **Blue Nile Falls** (also called **Tissisat**), one of the most spectacular waterfalls in Northern Africa. They are situated about 35km (22 miles) from Bahar Dar.
- **Gondar** was the capital of Ethiopia from 1632 to 1855 and is the site of many **ruined castles**.
- **Lalibela** is famous for its 12th-century, rock-hewn **churches**.
- **Harar** is a famous Muslim walled city and the centre for the coffee trade.

Top Things To Do

- Go on a **wildlife safari**. There are 14 major wildlife reserves in Ethiopia: the **Simien Mountain National Park** (in the northern mountain massif); the **Awash National Park** (east of the capital); the **Omo** and **Mago National Parks** (southwest of the capital); the **Shalla-Abijatta Lakes National Park** (south of the capital), famous for its birdlife; the **Nechisar National Park** (Gambo region); **Yangudi-Rassa National Park** (Harerge region); and the **Bale Mountains National Park**, on high southern moorland country, which has its own unique flora and fauna. Safaris are usually in 4-wheel-drive vehicles, but walking safaris (with a guide only) or travelling by mule are also possible.

Credit: ©Bruce Logan

- The wild terrain and beautiful landscapes offer good **trekking** and **hiking** opportunities. The best areas for these activities include: **Simien Mountains National Park**, which has spectacular views and a large variety of wildlife; the moorlands of the **Bale Plateau**; the countryside around **Lalibela**; the wilderness of the **Awash River**. Trips last between four and 11 days, and English-speaking guides can be hired locally.
- The **Simien Mountains**, the **Bale Plateau** and many other areas are perfect for **mountain climbing**. Equipment is rarely available and should be brought along by the traveller. **Caving** is also available near **Dire Dawa** where there is evidence of prehistoric habitation. Local guides are essential.
- Horses and mules still play an important part in the transportation of people and goods, and horseriding can be practised in most parts of Ethiopia. **Pony treks** in the **Simien Mountains** allow visitors to reach remote areas not accessible by car.
- There is excellent **swimming** in the lakes of the Rift Valley, especially **Lake Langano**, which has a resort with well-developed facilities offering **windsurfing** and **waterskiing**. Natural springs in the **Awash National** Park and at **Sodere Filwoha** create pools suitable for swimming and are highly valued for their therapeutic purposes, though at present they are not fully utilised.
- The rivers and streams of the **Bale Mountains**, in the southeast, and the many lakes in the **Rift Valley** provide excellent **fishing**, particularly for trout. Local fishermen offer trips in their own boats. Dugout canoes or traditional papyrus boats can also be hired.
- **Sailing** and organised **boat trips** are available on the spectacular **Lake Tana**, Ethiopia's largest lake which contains 37 islands, many of which also have monasteries that can be visited. **Whitewater rafting** is possible on parts of the **Omo River** and the **Blue Nile**.

TOURIST INFORMATION

Ethiopian Tourist Commission
PO Box 2183, Addis Ababa, Ethiopia
Tel: (1) 517 470.
Website: www.tourismethiopia.org

Entertainment

FOOD & DRINK: Menus in the best hotels offer international food and Addis Ababa also has a number of good Chinese, Italian and Indian restaurants. Traditional restaurants in larger cities serve food in a grand manner around a brightly coloured basket-weave table called a *masob*. Before beginning the meal, guests will be given soap, water and a clean towel, and the right hand (never the left) is used to break off pieces of bread with which the rest of the meal is gathered up. Cutlery is not used.

National specialities:

- Ethiopian food is based on dishes called *we't* (meat, chicken or vegetables, cooked in a hot pepper sauce), served with or on *injera* (a flat spongy bread).
- Dishes include *shivro* and *misir* (chickpeas and lentils, Ethiopian-style) and *tibs* (crispy fried steak).

Credit: ©Bruce Logan

• There is a wide choice of fish including sole, Red Sea snapper, lake fish, trout and prawns.

National drinks:
• Ethiopian coffee from the province of Kaffa, with a little rue added for extra aroma, is called 'health of Adam'.
• Local red and dry white wines are worth trying.
• *Talla* (Ethiopian beer).
• *Kaitaka* (a pure grain alcohol), cognac (a local brandy) and *tej* (an alcoholic drink based on fermented honey).

Tipping: In most hotels and restaurants, a 10 per cent service charge is added to the bill. Tipping is a usual, but amounts are small.

SHOPPING: Special purchases include local jewellery (sold by the weight of gold or silver), woodcarvings, illuminated manuscripts and prayer scrolls, wood and metal crosses, leather shields, spears, drums and carpets. In marketplaces, bargaining is expected, but prices at shops in towns are fixed. **Shopping hours:** Mon-Fri 0800-1300, 1400-2000; Sat 0900-1300, 1500-1900 (local variations).

Business

• **GDP:** US$6.7 billion (2003, World Bank).
• **Main exports:** Coffee, qat, gold, leather products, live animals and oilseeds.
• **Main imports:** Food and live animals, petroleum and petroleum products, chemicals, machinery, motor vehicles, cereals and textiles.
• **Main trade partners:** Saudi Arabia, Djibouti, USA, Germany, China, Japan, Italy and UK.

ECONOMY: Ethiopia is one of the world's least developed countries, with an average annual per capita income of US$91, minimal infrastructure and a serious shortage of skilled labour. The value of Ethiopia's exports per capita is the lowest in the world. Economic development has also been hampered by the effects of the long-running civil war and, more recently, a series of military clashes with both neighbours (notably Eritrea) and internal opposition. The Eritrean war (1998-2000) is estimated to have cost Ethiopia around US$3 billion – half the country's entire annual economic output. To this litany of ill-fortune can be added severe drought and flooding, which have hampered post-war reconstruction work. The economy is largely dependent on subsistence agriculture, which employs almost 85 per cent of the workforce, and accounts for half the country's GDP. Growth has been seriously affected by the fall in agriculture production due to the droughts in 2002 and 2003. However, sound macroeconomic policies and HIPC (Heavily Indebted Poor Country) debt relief, coupled with improved rains and harvest in 2004 should result in a rebound in agricultural production and economic growth. Coffee is the main export earner, and the collapse of world coffee prices hit Ethiopia hard. After the end of the civil war, the government set about dismantling the command economy established by the Mengistu regime, not least in an attempt to tackle the country's huge debt burden. Not surprisingly, Ethiopia relies on substantial quantities of food aid. The Ethiopian Goverment published its poverty reduction strategy in 2002. The manufacturing and service sectors are both small. However, there is one bright prospect in the form of a large natural gas field, which promises substantial future revenues.

BUSINESS ETIQUETTE: Businesspeople should wear suits and ties for business visits. English is widely used for trade purposes but Italian and French are also useful. Nonetheless, knowledge of a few words of Amharic will be appreciated. Normal courtesies should be observed and business cards can be used. Best months for business visits are October to May. **Office hours:** Mon-Thu 0830-1230, 1330-1730 and Fri 0830-1130, 1330-1730.

COMMERCIAL INFORMATION

Commercial Bank of Ethiopia
PO Box 255, Unity Square, Addis Ababa, Ethiopia
Tel: (11) 5515 004.
Website: www.combanketh.com

Addis Ababa Chamber of Commerce
PO Box 2458, Mexico Square, Addis Ababa, Ethiopia
Tel: (11) 5515 055.
Website: www.addischamber.com

Ethiopian Trade Promotions Section in the UK
17 Princes Gate, London SW7 1PZ, UK
Tel: (020) 7589 7217.
Website: www.ethioembassy.org.uk

United Nations Conference Centre (Information on Conferences/Conventions)
PO Box 3001, Addis Ababa, Ethiopia
Tel: (11) 5514 874 or 5514 945.
Website: www.un.org

Falkland Islands

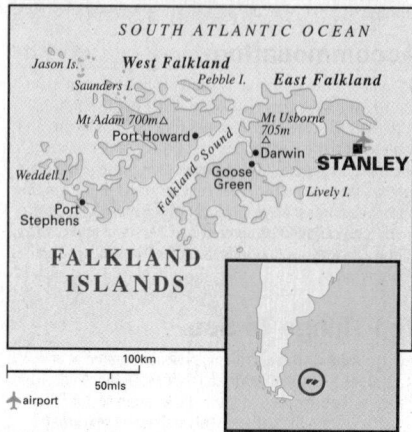

Location: South Atlantic.

Time: GMT - 3. (GMT - 4 from third Sunday in April to first Saturday in September.)

The Falkland Islands is a British Overseas Territory represented abroad by British Embassies – see *United Kingdom* section.

Overview

Until the war of 1982, the rainy, windswept Falkland Islands were a forgotten remnant of the old British Empire. First occupied by the French in 1764, the islands were quickly ceded to Spain, which then ruled the adjacent territory in Latin America. However, the Spanish only established themselves on West Falkland and, in 1765, the British took control of the eastern island. By 1816, both powers had removed their respective garrisons and the Falkland Islands had no permanent inhabitants. A vessel from newly independent Argentina was sent in 1820 to establish a permanent settlement but was driven out by a British expedition in 1832. The British declared full sovereignty over the Falkland Islands the following year. Argentina refused to recognise British sovereignty and has maintained a consistent claim to sovereignty ever since. This claim was pursued periodically through diplomatic channels until 1982, when an Argentine force overran the British garrison and established a military base on 'Islas Malvinas', a name derived from the original French settlers, who named the islands after their home port of St Malo. After various attempts at negotiation and mediation had failed, a British task force, which had been dispatched at the start of the crisis, was ordered to continue its journey and engage the Argentines. Argentina formally surrendered on 14 June, 10 weeks after the invasion. In the subsequent contact between the two Governments, it has become apparent that the issue of sovereignty is a stumbling block and that the Falkland Islands' issue will remain a key aspect of Argentine foreign policy in the foreseeable future.
The Falkland Islands are home to a plethora of marine life, from five different species of penguins to the whales and sea birds that hover around Stanley Harbour. 19th-century shipwrecks await exploration, while battlefields in the 1982 conflict such as Goose Green and Pebble Island have become tourist attractions.

General Information

AREA: 12,173 sq km (4700 sq miles).
POPULATION: 2379 (official estimate 2001).
POPULATION DENSITY: 0.2 per sq km.
CAPITAL: Stanley. **Population:** 2200 (Commonwealth Secretariat, 2004).
GEOGRAPHY: The Falkland Islands are located 560km (350 miles) off the east coast of South America and consist of two main islands and hundreds of small outlying islands, amounting to approximately 3 million acres (1.2 million hectares). Generally, the main islands are mountainous, with low-lying and undulating terrain in the south of East Falkland. The highest mountain is Mount Usborne at 712m (2312ft).

GOVERNMENT: British Overseas Territory since 1833. Not recognised by Argentina, which considers the Falkland Islands to be part of Argentina. Existing Constitution adopted in 1985. **Head of State:** Queen Elizabeth II, represented locally by Governor Howard Pearce since 2002. The Governor presides over the Executive Council, the country's ruling body. The Executive Council consists of two official members and three elected members. Elections are held every four years. The Legislative Council has two ex-officio members and eight members elected by universal suffrage. There is no party-political activity on the Islands.

Recent history: Negotiations were opened between Argentina and the UK under UN auspices during 1988. The UK adamantly refused to discuss sovereignty and has not moved from this position ever since – the wishes of the islanders, who are determined to stay British, remain paramount. The islanders have also been granted full British citizenship. Some practical progress has been made on economic issues such as fisheries control and other trade matters, but the Falklands' leadership has still refused to move on other issues such as aircraft landing rights. Despite the political inertia, the Falkland Islands has made substantial economic progress in the two decades since the war (see *Economy* section). The seabeds surrounding the Islands are thought to contain substantial oil reserves which have yet to be located and exploited.

LANGUAGE: English.
RELIGION: Christian, with Catholic, Anglican and United Reformed Church of Stanley denominations.
ELECTRICITY: 240 volts AC, 50Hz.
SOCIAL CONVENTIONS: The lifestyle in the Falkland Islands resembles that of a small English or Scottish village/town and communities on the Falkland Islands are highly self-contained. The influx of the British Forces has obviously had an effect on the Islands. More people now visit for a variety of reasons. The islanders themselves have benefited from the additional amenities offered by the Forces.

Climate

The climate is temperate and largely conditioned by the surrounding sea being cooled by the Antarctic Current.
Required clothing: A windproof jacket is essential, as is a stout pair of walking boots when crossing the rugged terrain. Because the air is so clear and unpolluted, suntan lotion is advisable.

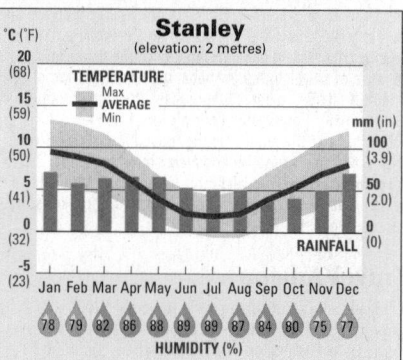

Communications

Telephone: IDD available. Country code: 500. Good satellite telephone links to the Islands. The *Cable & Wireless* office is open Mon-Thurs 0815-1200 and 1315-1630 (on Friday closes at 1615) and sells phone cards for use in the international telephone service booths situated in the office.
Mobile telephone: Cable & Wireless launched a mobile phone service in December 2005. Coverage is in Stanley and Mount Pleasant with fairly good coverage along the MPA road and more limited coverage between MPA and Goose Green. No roaming agreements have been declared.
Internet: There is an Internet cafe in Stanley.
Post: Airmail to Europe takes four to seven days.
MEDIA: Coverage of local affairs is provided by a radio station and by the territory's sole newspaper. Satellite television channels are widely available.
Press: There are no daily local papers, but *Penguin News* (weekly) is published in Stanley and all British national newspapers are also available. The *Falkland Islands Gazette* is a Government publication. The *Falkland Islands News Network* relays news daily via fax and e-mail.
TV: *KTV* is a multi-channel provider.
Radio: *BFBS Radio Falklands* provides radio coverage for British forces. The *Falkland Islands Broadcasting Station* (*FIBS*) operates on both AM and FM.

Passport/Visa

	Passport Required?	Visa Required?	Return Ticket Required?
Full British	Yes	No	Yes
Australian	Yes	No	Yes
Canadian	Yes	No	Yes
USA	Yes	No	Yes
Other EU	Yes	No	Yes
Japanese	Yes	No	Yes

Note: *Regulations and requirements may be subject to change at short notice, and you are advised to contact the appropriate diplomatic or consular authority before finalising travel arrangements. Any numbers in the chart refer to the footnotes below.*

PASSPORTS: Passport valid for a minimum of three months beyond departure required by all.

VISAS: Required by all except the following for stays of up to four months:
(a) nationals of countries mentioned in the chart above;
(b) nationals of Andorra, Argentina, Bolivia, Brazil, Chile, Hong Kong (SAR), Iceland, Israel, Korea (Rep), Liechtenstein, New Zealand, Norway, Paraguay, San Marino, South Africa, Switzerland, Uruguay and Vatican City.

Note: (a) An Overseas Territory of a country is deemed to be part of that country when negotiating visa exemption.
(b) All nationals (including non-visa nationals) must obtain a visitors permit, normally valid for four weeks. An extension of up to 12 months may be granted by applying to the Immigration Office on arrival and providing proof of sufficient funds and accommodation during stay. A visitors permit is issued after completing a visitors form and requires proof of return tickets, sufficient funds and accommodation. Visitors permits can be obtained from the Falkland Islands Government Office in London (see *Passport/Visa Information*), the nearest British Consulate (or Consular section at the Embassy) *or*, on arrival, at the Falkland Islands Immigration Office (see *Passport/Visa Information*).

Types of visa and cost: One type of visa is issued for all types of travel. The cost is £20.

Note: All persons leaving the Falkland Islands by air are charged an Embarkation Tax of £20.

Validity: Valid for the time the applicant wishes to stay in the country. Three years is the maximum.

Application to: Falkland Islands Government Office (see *Passport/Visa Information*), the nearest British Consulate (or consular section at the Embassy) *or* the Falkland Islands Immigration Office.

Application requirements: (a) Application form. (b) Passport valid beyond the expiry of the visa. (c) Two passport-size photographs. (d) Proof of sufficient funds for the duration of stay, accommodation booking and onward/return tickets. (e) Fee.

Working days required: Five working days. Two to four weeks for applicants applying by post. It is advisable, however, to apply in plenty of time.

PASSPORT/VISA INFORMATION

Falkland Islands Immigration Office
3 H Jones Road, Stanley, FIQQ 1ZZ, Falkland Islands
Tel: 27340.
Website: www.falklands.gov.fk

Falkland Islands Government Office
(Incorporating the Falkland Islands Development Corporation and the Falkland Islands Tourist Board)
Falkland House, 14 Broadway, London SW1H 0BH, UK
Tel: (020) 7222 2542.
Website: www.falklandislands.com
Opening hours: Mon-Fri 0900-1730.
The Falkland Islands Government Office issues visas and visitor forms, helps to promote trade and investment in the Islands, offers RAF flight bookings to the Islands, assists immigrants and promotes the Falkland Islands' interests in all respects.

Money

Currency: Falkland Islands Pound (FKP) and the British Pound Sterling (GBP; symbol £) = 100 pence. Notes are in denominations of £50, 20, 10 and 5. Coins are in denominations of £1 and 2, and 50, 20, 10, 5, 2 and 1 pence.

Currency exchange: Exchange facilities are available in Stanley and the Standard Chartered Bank. British Pound Sterling cheques up to £50 from Barclays, Lloyds and Natwest banks can be cashed on production of a valid cheque card, but a fee will be charged. The Falklands' currency cannot be exchanged anywhere outside the Islands. There are no ATMs. English Sterling banknotes and US dollars

Credit: ©Connie Stevens/Falkland Islands Tourist Board

are accepted by most businesses. Travellers are advised to carry some currency in US dollars in case flights are diverted.

Credit & debit cards: MasterCard and Visa are accepted in most hotels shops in Stanley but few shops outside the main town will accept credit cards. American Express and Diners Card are accept by some businesses.

Traveller's cheques: May be changed at the Standard Chartered Bank and at some commercial outlets. To avoid additional exchange rate charges, travellers are advised to take traveller's cheques in Pounds Sterling.

Currency restrictions: No restrictions on the import and export of local and foreign currency.
For a guide to the movement of the US Dollar against the Falkland Islands Pound, see the *United Kingdom* section.

Banking hours: Mon-Fri 0830-1500.
For exchange rates see UK section.

Duty Free

The following items may be imported into the Falkland Islands without incurring customs duty:
200 cigarettes or 50 cigars or 100 cigarillos or 250g tobacco; 1l of alcoholic beverage over 38.8 per cent or 2l up to 22 per cent proof and 2l of sparkling or still table wine, 10l of beer or cider.

Restricted items: Import licences are required from Department of Agriculture for plants, meat, poultry and dairy produce. An import licence is required from the Falkland Islands' Policy Authority for firearms and ammunition.

Prohibited items: Drugs, pornography and counterfeit goods.

Public Holidays

Below are listed the Public Holidays for the January 2006-June 2007 period.
2006: Jan 1 New Year's Day. **Apr 14** Good Friday. **Apr 21** Queen's Birthday. **Jun 14** Liberation Day. **Oct 2** Spring Holiday. **Dec 8** Battle Day. **Dec 25-28** Christmas.
2007: Jan 1 New Year's Day. **Apr 6** Good Friday. **Apr 21** Queen's Birthday. **Jun 14** Liberation Day.

Health

	Special Precautions?	Certificate Required?
Yellow Fever	1	No
Cholera	No	No
Typhoid & Polio	No	N/A
Malaria	No	N/A

Note: *Regulations and requirements may be subject to change at short notice, and you are advised to contact your doctor well in advance of your intended date of departure. Any numbers in the chart refer to the footnotes below.*

1: Although not an official requirement, the Ministry of Defence recommends inoculation against yellow fever in case flights are diverted to a risk area.

Other risks: *Hepatitis A* occurs; *viral hepatitis* occurs but is rare.

Health care: Hospital, dental and other medical treatments are free, as are prescribed medicines and ambulance travel to visitors whose country has a reciprocal NHS agreement. Otherwise, medical insurance is recommended. Proof of residence in the UK (eg medical card or UK driving licence) or an EHIC form for other nationals are required to benefit from free treatments.

Travel - International

AIR:

Travel to and from *The Falkland Island International Airport* at Mount Pleasant (MPN) is courtesy of the UK Ministry of Defence. There are six direct flights in any four-week period by Tristar from RAF *Brize Norton*, Oxfordshire, in the UK. Tour operators and travel agents will make the necessary arrangements if the trip is booked through them; independent travellers need to contact a travel coordinator at the Falkland Islands Government Office (see *Passport/Visa Information*). Return flights from the UK are via Ascension Island. The other option is to fly *British Airways* from London Gatwick to Santiago (Chile) and connect with a *LanChile* flight (once a week only, on Saturdays) to Punta Arenas and Puerto Montt in southern Chile and then on to Stanley. Return flights leave the Islands on Saturdays and connecting flights to London leave Santiago on Sundays. Bookings for this flight can be made through *British Airways* (website: www.ba.com), *LanChile* (website: www.lan.com) or agents. The Falkland Islands Tourist Board can provide up-to-date information on changes to the normal schedule.

Approximate flight times: From *Brize Norton* to Mount Pleasant is 18 hours (including a refuelling stop at Ascension Island); from Mount Pleasant to *Punta Arenas* (Chile) is five hours.

Main airports: *Mount Pleasant Airport (MPN)* is approximately 56km (35 miles) from Stanley. *To/from the airport*: Buses connect the airport and Stanley. *Facilities*: Limited duty free shopping.

Departure tax: £20. Children under two years of age are exempt.

SEA:

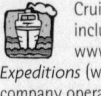

Cruise companies operating to the Falklands include *Wildlife Worldwide* (website: www.wildlifeworldwide.com) and *Zegrahm Expeditions* (website: www.zeco.com). The main shipping company operating to and from the UK is *Darwin Shipping*, The Falkland Islands Company, Crozier Place, Stanley, F1QQ 1ZZ, Falkland Islands (tel: 27600; website: www.the-falkland-islands-co.com).

Travel - Internal

AIR:

Most of the settlements and offshore islands in the Falklands can be reached by light aircraft. This service is run by the *Falkland Islands Government Air Service (FIGAS)* (tel: 27219). There are no fixed schedules but daily flights operate to all parts of the Islands, subject to demand. Capacity for flights is eight passengers and the luggage limit is 14kg per person.

Credit: ©Connie Stevens/Falkland Islands Tourist Board

SEA:

Boats may be chartered for day trips from Stanley and elsewhere in the Islands. Some settlements may be able to offer the use of landing vessels or other craft to reach the outlying Islands. There are plenty of tour operators and guides to choose from in Stanley. Contact the Falkland Islands Tourist Board for further information (see *Top Things To See & Do*).

ROAD:

Outside the capital, overland travel is difficult and vehicles can frequently get bogged down. However, there is one asphalt road linking Stanley, the Mount Pleasant airport complex and Goose Green, and an all-weather graded track linking Mount Pleasant with Goose Green and Stanley with Port Louis, Estancia, Salvador and various settlements in the north of East Falkland as far as Port San Carlos. A similar track on West Falkland links Port Howard, Chartres, Fox Bay, Hill Cove and Roy Cove. Four-wheel-drive vehicles are the best form of transport in this terrain. But road networks are continually improving. Falkland Island Tours and Travel Service offer a service from Mount Pleasant to the airport for £13 per person, (website: www.falklandislandtravel.com). **Coach:** There are routes to and from the airport and trips can be organised to particular destinations. **Taxi:** Taxi services are available in Stanley and the Airport. **Car hire:** 4-wheel-drive and other vehicles can be hired from the Falkland Islands Company Ltd (tel: 27678).

Travel times: The following chart gives approximate travel times in hours and minutes from Stanley to other islands in the surrounding area.

	Air	Road
Mount Pleasant	0.15	0.50
Pebble Island	0.40	-
Port Howard	0.40	-
Sea Lion Island	0.30	-

Travel Advice

Most visits to the Falkland Islands are trouble-free but you should be aware of the global risk of indiscriminate international terrorist attacks, which could be against civilian targets, including places frequented by foreigners. This advice is based on information provided by the Foreign and Commonwealth Office in the UK. It is correct at time of publishing. As the situation can change rapidly, visitors are advised to contact the following organisations for the latest travel advice:

British Foreign and Commonwealth Office
Tel: (0845) 850 2829.
Website: www.fco.gov.uk

US Department of State
Website: http://travel.state.gov/travel

Accommodation

HOTELS/GUEST HOUSES/BOARDING HOUSES/ FARM HOLIDAYS/BED & BREAKFAST:

Accommodation is limited and should be booked in advance. There are hotels, lodges and boarding houses in the Falkland Islands, as well as full-board accommodation on a farm. There are two hotels, three guest houses and a growing number of bed and breakfasts in Stanley. There are also lodges at Pebble Island, Port Howard, San Carlos and Sea Lion Island. Self-catering accommodation is also available throughout the Islands. All ground arrangements can be made through Stanley Services Limited, Stanley (tel: 22622; website: www.stanley-services.co.fk). The Falkland Islands Tourist Board can help with finding available accommodation. A new grading system is now in use. Contact the Falkland Islands Tourist Board for full details (see *Top Things to See & Do*).

Top Things To See & Do

- **Stanley**'s history is closely associated with the days when great **sailing** ships and early steam vessels called into port on their journeys around Cape Horn. A self-guided *Maritime History Trail* has been set up in the capital. A half-day **trail** leads from Stanley to Cape Pembroke, offering an interesting introduction to the Falkland Islands' **birdlife**. The capital has pubs, snack bars and restaurants, as well as a golf course and racecourse. **Government House**, **Stanley Museum** and the **Cathedral** are all worth visiting.
- Take a trip to some of the **Battlefield Sites** associated with the 1982 conflict (including *Wireless Ridge*, *Mount Tumbledown* and *Sapper Hill*). There are also **military cemeteries**, **memorials** and **museums** dealing with the conflict.
- Migratory species, such as **penguins**, arrive to breed in September and depart late March/early April. Be sure to catch a glimpse of some of these delightful creatures. There are five species of penguins on the Falkland Islands. In terms of other **wildlife**, how about some sheep or Southern sea lions at **Pebble Island**? One of the most ecologically balanced islands is **Sea Lion Island** which has a resident population of four and amazing wildlife, including elephant seals, sea lions and King penguins, as well as Killer whales offshore. It is the most southerly inhabited island, and all areas are accessible by four-wheel drive or on foot from the **Sea Lion Lodge**.
- Take a **tour** around **Stanley Harbour** in an inflatable craft. A number of lodges have **motor boats** for taking guests to view wildlife and places of interest. Tours around **Kidney Island** and **Sparrow Cove** can be arranged. Contact *South Atlantic Marine Services Ltd* (tel: 21145; website: www.falklands-underwater.com).
- The **fishing** season runs from September to the end of April, but September to October and mid-March to mid-April are best for good runs of sea trout. Falklands Mullet is available throughout the period. A licence is required for some areas. It is obtainable from the **Stanley Post Office** and a log book is issued with it which needs to be returned to the Fisheries Department before departure. Visitors are advised that a catch and return policy applies, that barbless hooks are used and that 12 is the maximum number of fish allowed to be taken. The best locations in West Falkland are **Warrah** and **Little Chartres**, while in East Falkland, **San Carlos** and **Murrel** are good. Port Howard and **Hill Cove** also allow fishing.
- Go **horse riding**, which is available in Port Howard. There is also the opportunity to learn about the traditional horse equipment used in the Falkland Islands.
- Stanley used to be a safe anchorage for whalers and merchant vessels travelling around the Horn, but not all made it. *South Atlantic Marine Services Ltd* in Stanley can arrange **wreck and kelp reef diving expeditions**. Nineteenth-century sailing ships and iron vessels can be seen at Stanley and **Darwin**. The views in winter are spectacular due to the 'grey beards', but winter waves can reach a height of 4.5m (15ft).
- Buy some **knitwear** from **Port Howard**.

TOURIST INFORMATION

Falkland Islands Government Office (Incorporating the Falkland Islands Development Corporation and the Falkland Islands Tourist Board)
Falkland House, 14 Broadway, London SW1H 0BH, UK
Tel: (020) 7222 2542.
Website: www.falklandislands.com
Opening hours: Mon-Fri 0900-1730.
The Falkland Islands Government Office issues visas and visitor forms, helps to promote trade and investment in the Islands, offers RAF flight bookings to the Islands, assists immigrants and promotes the Falkland Islands' interests in all respects.

Entertainment

FOOD & DRINK: Almost everything is home-cooked and many traditional recipes, generally British in character, have been handed down through several generations.
National specialities:
- Lamb, mutton, beef, sea trout, mullet and home-grown vegetables.

National Drinks:
- *Smoko*; tea or coffee with homemade cakes.

Tipping: If no service charge has been added to the bill, 10 per cent is appropriate. Taxi drivers expect a tip.
NIGHTLIFE: There is a variety of clubs and societies which welcome visitors. There are several pubs in Stanley, as well as restaurants and cafes.
SHOPPING: Costs tend to be slightly higher than in the UK, as much has to be imported, though smaller luxury goods may be cheaper. There is a good range of shops in Stanley selling the same type of goods found in a small town in Britain and a variety of souvenirs. Sweaters made from pure Falkland Wool and local art, jewellery made from Falkland Islands' pebbles, coins, stamps and books are also sold. Fresh vegetables are available all year round but many Islanders are virtually self-sufficient. Print film is available but it is advisable to bring a supply. **Shopping hours:** Shopping hours vary, but shops are generally open Mon-Sat 0800-1800; some shops may stay open until 2100 in some areas. Earlier closing times on Sundays.

Business

- **GDP:** £70million (2001).
- **Main exports:** Wool, hides and meat.
- **Main imports:** Fuel, food and drink, building materials and clothing.
- **Main trade partners:** UK, Spain, Chile and France.

ECONOMY: The economy is dominated by fishing and sheep-farming. The poor quality of the land precludes large scale crop-growing. Productivity in sheep-farming has increased sharply since the mid-1980s with improved working practices. However, it is the fishing sector that now accounts for the islands' much improved economic performance. The industry has grown substantially since 1982, assisted by the introduction of a licensing system in Falklands territorial waters. The presence of large quantities of squid, a very popular dish in several parts of the world, has fuelled an economic boom and the emergence of a 'squidocracy' – a group of individuals living on the islands who have become extremely wealthy as a result. There are some concerns about stock depletion, and controls have now been introduced. Other plans for the Falklands' economic development have proved less successful. Restrictions on Antarctic development have undermined the islands' hope of deriving benefit from being an en route staging post. The search for oil and gas reserves began in earnest in 1995 after the signing of an agreement between the UK and Argentina; test drilling started in 1998 but no viable deposits have yet been located. However, as long as the squid last, the Falklands economic outlook remains bright. Tourism, especially eco-tourism, is increasing rapidly with about 30,000 visitors in 2001. Another significant source of income is interest paid on money that the Government has in the bank. The British military presence also provides a sizable economic boost. Despite the improvement in relations with Argentina, trade between the islands and the mainland is small and most trade is still conducted with Britain. The Government introduced 'The Islands Plan, 2002/2005' which laid out plans to take the Islands forward over that period in sectors such as financial management, sustainable economy, quality of life and communications. Part of the plan was also to focus on relationships with Latin America, including co-operation with Argentina on matters of common interest such as oil exploration and fisheries.
BUSINESS ETIQUETTE: Punctuality for meetings is expected. **Office hours:** 0800-1200, 1300-1630 (Government); 0800-1200, 1300-1700 (Private).

COMMERCIAL INFORMATION

Falkland Islands Development Corporation (FIDC)
Shackleton House, Stanley, FIQQ 1ZZ, Falkland Islands.
Tel: 27211.

Falkland Islands Chamber of Commerce
Website: www.falklandislandschamberofcommerce.com

Location: South Pacific, Melanesia.

Time: GMT + 12.

Overview

Comprised of more than 300 volcanic and coral islands, the Fiji archipelago is at the cross roads of the South Pacific. In the days of sailing ships, it was known as The Cannibal Isles and carefully avoided by mariners because of its fierce warriors and treacherous waters. More then anything else, Fiji is an exotic destination. More recently, Fiji's tropical climate and location on Pacific air routes have made it a prime spot for tourists.

However, a coup by indigenous Fijians in 1987, followed by a further coup in 2000, caused immense harm to the tourism industry and to its international reputation. Rancour over the 2000 coup persists, with bitter divisions over a proposed bill that would give amnesties to those involved in it. Although the islands now enjoy reasonable stability, nothing has been done to address the underlying causes of Fiji's political problems.

Fiji's population, which resides mostly on the two main islands of Viti Levu and Vanua Levu, is divided almost equally between indigenous Fijians and Indo-Fijians, the descendents of indentured labourers brought from India. Mixing between the two groups is minimal, and informal segregation runs deep at almost every level of society. Despite the troubled past of the archipelago, Fijians are known as some of the friendliest people in the world. They are not judgmental of other people and will rarely express a negative opinion. Customs still prevail in the more traditional villages, especially those distant from towns and urban centres. And of course, Fiji is where the Cloud Breaker, the incredible six-metre wave was found offshore at Tavarua, a place which still draws surfers from around the world.

General Information

AREA: 18,376 sq km (7056 sq miles).
POPULATION: 854,000 (UN, 2005).
POPULATION DENSITY: 46 per sq km.
CAPITAL: Suva. **Population:** 167,000 (2005).
GEOGRAPHY: Fiji is located in the South Pacific, 3000km (1875 miles) east of Australia and approximately 1930km (1200 miles) south of the Equator. It comprises 322 islands, 105 of which are uninhabited (some are little more than rugged limestone islets or tiny coral atolls). The three largest are Viti Levu (Great Fiji), Vanua Levu (Great Land of the People), both of which are extinct volcanoes rising abruptly from the sea, and Taveuni. There are thousands of streams and small rivers in Fiji, the largest being the Rewa River on Viti Levu, which is navigable for 128km (80 miles).

Mount Victoria, also on Viti Levu, is the country's highest peak, at 1322m (4430ft).
GOVERNMENT: Republic since 1987. **Head of State:** President Ratu Josefa Ilolio since 2000. The President is appointed for a five-year term by the Great Council of Chiefs (Bosu Levu Vakaturaga), a traditional body with roughly 70 members, consisting of every hereditary Fijian chief (or *ratu*). **Head of Government:** Prime Minister Laisenia Qarase since 2000. **Recent history:** The 1987 general election, the poll brought to power a coalition between the main ethnic Indian party, the National Federation Party, led by Marendra Chaudhry and the newly-formed Labour Party. The new Government had a majority of Indian ministers, which proved too much for many nationalist native Fijians (referred to as *Taukei*). This was the trigger for an army coup d'état, headed by Colonel Sitiveni Rabuka. Colonel Rabuka declared himself head of an interim military Government and introduced a new constitution, under which blocs of seats in a new assembly were allocated to specific ethnic groups, thereby guaranteeing a *Taukei* majority. Under this format, the 1992 elections brought to power a coalition dominated by the principal ethnic Fijian party. Rabuka assumed the premiership. By the time the revised constitution came into effect in 1998, Fiji's poor economic performance had undermined the Rabuka Government's popularity. The Fijian Labour Party was now able to secure an absolute majority in the *Vela* and an Indian Prime Minister, Mahendra Chaudhry, took office. In May 2000, George Speight organised a coup, holding Chaudhry and other ministers as hostages while he issued a series of demands. The stand-off lasted two months. After initially conceding to most of the rebel demands (including the dismissal of Chaudhry), the military, led by Commodore Frank Bainanarama, took control at the beginning of July. A few weeks later, the military moved against Speight and his followers, who were arrested. An interim Government under the veteran *Taukei* politician, Ratu Josefa Iloilo, was installed with Laisenia Qarase as Premier. Following the elections in August 2001, a coalition Government was formed between the the Fiji United Party and the smaller Conservative Alliance Party (*Matanitu Vanua*) and, despite the fact that most votes were won by the Labour Party, Laisenia Qarase remained as Prime Minister. The islands have since enjoyed reasonable stability, although nothing has been done to address the underlying causes of Fiji's political problems.
LANGUAGE: The principal languages are Fijian and Hindustani, but English is widely spoken and is also taught in schools. Chinese and Urdu are heard in the markets.
RELIGION: Methodist and Hindu with Roman Catholic and Muslim minorities. A strictly fundamentalist Methodist version of Christianity is enshrined in, and informs, the Fijian Constitution.
ELECTRICITY: 240 volts AC, 50Hz. Larger hotels also have 110-volt razor sockets.
SOCIAL CONVENTIONS: Fijians are a very welcoming, hospitable people and visitors should not be afraid to accept hospitality. The ethnic variety of Fiji society can be seen mainly in the towns. There are powerfully built Fijians dressed in wrap-around *sulus*, numerous Indians, men in Western clothes, women wearing colourful *saris* and a scattering of European, Chinese and other Pacific Islanders. One celebrated tradition is the practice of fire-walking; the Indian variant is performed for religious reasons. Tourists can pay to see these ceremonies but the ritual remains a religious penance and not merely a tourist attraction. Informal casual wear is generally acceptable. Smoking is only restricted where specified. **Tips about visiting villages:** Before visiting, it is customary to purchase a bundle of unpounded *yaqona* (kava) – the traditional *sevusevu* (gift); half a kilo, which is an appropriate amount for a gift, costs approximately $20. When approaching the village, visitors should not enter immediately but wait until someone comes to greet them and ask the purpose of their visit. They will then be taken to the Chief or *Turaga Ni Koro* (Headman), to whom the kava should be offered. Visitors who are accepted by the Chief will be assigned a guide and host. Once inside the village, please also note the following: visitors should dress modestly and not wear shorts or hats and women should not have their shoulders bare; shoes should always be taken off when entering someone's house or any other village building; visitors should speak softly and not raise their voices too much as this may be interpreted as expressing anger; visitors should show respect but be cautious about praise as Fijians will feel obliged to make a gift of an object if visitors show too much liking for it; Fijians will always, out of custom, ask visitors to stay or eat with them, but if one has already been invited, new invitations should be politely declined and possibly arranged for a later date; visitors who spend a night in the village should reward their host with a useful gift of similar value for each member of the party; it is not recommended to give money.

Climate

Tropical. Southeast trade winds from March to November bring dry weather. The rainy season is from December to April. On average there are 15 cyclones per decade, effecting some part of Fiji and two to four actually cause severe damage. They occur from November to April with greatest frequency in January and February. There is more risk in the outlying north-west island groups.
Required clothing: Lightweight for summer, rainwear for the wet season.

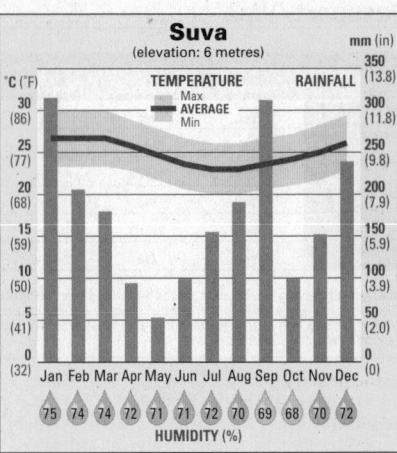

Communications

Telephone: IDD is available. Country code: 679. International calls can be made from hotels via an operator, or from the Fiji International Telecommunications (*FINTEL*) office at 158 Victoria Parade, Suva.
Mobile telephone: Roaming agreements exist with many international mobile phone companies. Phone rentals are available from the airport.
Internet: The main Internet cafe is Connect Internet Cafe, on Victoria Parade in the General Post office building in Suva. Opening hours: Mon-Fri 0800-2000; Sat: 0800-2200; Sun: 1000-1800. Access time costs on average US$3 per hour. There are also Internet cafes in Nadi and Lautoka.
Post: Airmail to Europe takes up to 10 days. Post office hours: Mon-Fri 0800-1630, Sat 0800-1300. The main Post office is the General Post Office on Victoria Parade, Suva. Opening hours: Mon-Fri 0800-1630; Sat: 0900-1200.
MEDIA: Fiji's private press includes English-language dailies and Fijian- and Hindi-language weeklies. The Government has a stake in several publications. Radio is a key source of information, particularly on the outer islands. There are both publicly and privately-owned stations.
Press: The main English-language daily is the *Fiji Times*, which claims to be 'the first newspaper published in the world today' – a reference to Suva's position just to the west of the International Date Line; the other main English language paper is the *Fiji Daily Post*. The *Fiji Sun* is privately

Credit: ©Fiji Visitors Bureau

owned. *Sartaj* and *Shanti Dut* are weekly publications in Hindi. *Fiji Calling* is the bi-annual tourist newspaper, which may be of interest to visitors.

TV: *Fiji 1* is a national free-to-air channel; *Sky Fiji* is a pay-TV channel; both are operated by Fiji Television Ltd.

Radio: State-owned commercial company Fiji Broadcasting Corporation operates Fijian-language *Radio Fiji One*, Hindi-language *Radio Fiji Two*, music-based *Bula 100 FM*, Hindi entertainment station *Bula 98 FM* and music-based *Bula 102 FM*. The *BBC World Service* and *Radio Australia* are available on FM.

Passport/Visa

	Passport Required?	Visa Required?	Return Ticket Required?
Full British	Yes	No	Yes
Australian	Yes	No/2	Yes
Canadian	Yes	No/2	Yes
USA	Yes	No	Yes
Other EU	Yes	No/1	Yes
Japanese	Yes	No	Yes

Note: *Regulations and requirements may be subject to change at short notice, and you are advised to contact the appropriate diplomatic or consular authority before finalising travel arrangements. Any numbers in the chart refer to the footnotes below.*

Restricted entry: Entry will be denied to persons who have been deported or removed from another country.

PASSPORTS: Passport valid for at least six months beyond intended period of stay required by all except nationals of Fiji when holding a Certificate of Identity including a photograph of the bearer. Holders of the certificate must obtain approval from the Fiji Immigration Department before arrival.

VISAS: Required by all except the following who are issued a visitor's permit valid for one month (extendable to four months) on arrival:

(a) nationals of countries shown in the chart above, except **1.** nationals of Lithuania who *do* need a visa;

(b) **2.** nationals of Commonwealth countries (except nationals of Cameroon, Mozambique, Namibia and Sri Lanka who *do* need a visa);

(c) nationals of Argentina, Brazil, Bulgaria, Chile, Colombia, Iceland, Indonesia, Israel, Kenya, Korea (Rep), Liechtenstein, Marshall Islands, Mexico, Micronesia (Federated States), Moldova, Monaco, Norway, Paraguay, Peru, The Philippines, Romania, Russian Federation, Switzerland, Taiwan (China), Thailand, Tunisia, Turkey, Ukraine, Uruguay, Venezuela, Vatican City and Zimbabwe;

(d) transit passengers continuing their journey to a third country within three hours, provided holding valid onward or return documentation and not leaving the airport.

Note: All visitors must hold onward or return tickets and sufficient funds to cover stay.

Types of visa and cost: *Single-entry*: £45. *Multiple-entry*: £80.

Validity: Visas are valid for stays of up to three months, but can be extended on application to: Immigration Dept, Level 3, Suvavou House, Victoria Parade, Suva (*street address*); or PO Box 2224, Government Buildings, Suva, Fiji (*postal address*) (tel: 331 2622).

Application to: Consular section of High Commission or

Embassy; see *Passport/Visa Information.*

Application requirements: (a) Valid passport. (b) Completed application form. (c) Three passport-size photos. (d) Onward/return air ticket. (e) Copy of travel ticket/itinerary. (f) Fee payable by banker's draft, bank cheque or by cash (if application is made in person). (g) Police clearance report (proof of no criminal record) from local police station (must be in English). (h) Sufficient funds for duration of stay.

Note: Applicants must make their own arrangements for collection/return of passport.

Working days required: Seven to 21.

Temporary residence: Enquiries should be directed to the High Commission or Embassy of Fiji.

PASSPORT/VISA INFORMATION

Fiji High Commission in the UK
34 Hyde Park Gate, London SW7 5DN, UK
Tel: (020) 7584 3661.
Website: www.fijihighcommission.org.uk
Opening hours: Mon–Thurs 0930-1300, 1400-1700, Fri 0930-1300, 1400-1600; Mon-Fri 0930-1230 (consular section).

Embassy of the Republic of Fiji in the USA
Suite 240, 2233 Wisconsin Avenue, NW, Washington, DC 20007, USA
Tel: (202) 337 8320.
Website: www.fijiembassy.org

Money

Currency: Fijian Dollar (FJD; symbol F$) = 100 cents. Notes are in denominations of F$50, 20, 10, 5 and 2. Coins are in denominations of F$1, and 50, 20, 10, 5, 2 and 1 cents.

Currency exchange: Exchange facilities are available at the airport, at trading banks and at most hotels. ATMs may not accept foreign credit cards.

Credit & debit cards: American Express, Diners Club, MasterCard and Visa are accepted at a number of establishments. Check with your credit or debit card company for details of merchant acceptability and other services which may be available. American Express, Diners Club, Visa, JCB International and MasterCard have representatives in Suva. American Express and Visa can replace lost and stolen credit cards and traveller's cheques.

Traveller's cheques: To avoid additional exchange rate charges, travellers are advised to take traveller's cheques in Australian Dollars or Pounds Sterling.

Currency restrictions: There are no restrictions on the import of foreign or local currency, provided declared on arrival. Unspent local currency can be re-exchanged on departure up to the amount of foreign currency imported. The export of local currency is limited to F$500. The export of foreign currency as cash is limited to the equivalent of F$500.

Banking hours: Mon–Thurs 0930-1500, Fri 0930-1600. Restricted Foreign Exchange Dealers (authorised to issue foreign currency and traveller's cheques for travel-related purposes only): Mon-Fri 0830-1700, Sat 0830-1200.

Exchange rate indicators:
Rate at time of publishing
£1.00=   F$3.07
$1.00=   F$1.71

Duty Free

The following items may be imported by persons 17 years of age and over into Fiji without incurring customs duty:
500 cigarettes or 500g of tobacco goods; 2l of spirits or 4l of wine or 4l of beer; 114ml of perfume for personal use; goods to the value of F$400.

Note: There has been an increase in the Value Added Tax (VAT) on most items in the Fiji Islands to 12.5 per cent.

Prohibited items: All categories of firearms, ammunition and all narcotics. The import of vegetables, seeds, meat and dairy products requires a special permit from the Ministry of Agriculture, Fisheries and Forests. The import of meat and dairy products from Tasmania is not permitted. Earth, rock, soil, mineral samples, equipment used with horses or other animals, biological specimens or tissues (human or animal) are also prohibited.

Public Holidays

Below are listed Public Holidays for the January 2006-June 2007 period.
2006: Jan 1 New Year's Day. **Apr 10** Birth of the Prophet Muhammad. **Apr 14** Good Friday. **Apr 15** Easter Saturday. **Apr 17** Easter Monday. **May 5** National Youth Day. **May 29** Ratu Sir Lala Sukuna Day. **Jun 12** Queen's Birthday. **Oct 9** Fiji Day. **Oct 21** Diwali. **Dec 25-26** Christmas.
2007: Jan 1 New Year's Day. **Mar 31** Birth of the Prophet Muhammad. **Apr 6** Good Friday. **Apr 7** Easter Saturday. **Apr**

9 Easter Monday. **May 4** National Youth Day. **May 28** Ratu Sir Lala Sukuna Day. **Jun 11** Queen's Birthday.
Note: (a) Muslim and Hindu festivals are timed according to local sightings of various phases of the moon and therefore dates can only be approximations. (b) Some holidays are annually set by the Government, or moved to either Friday or Monday, if the normal day of observance falls on a weekend.

Health

	Special Precautions?	Certificate Required?
Yellow Fever	No	1
Cholera	No	2
Typhoid & Polio	3	N/A
Malaria	No	N/A

Note: *Regulations and requirements may be subject to change at short notice, and you are advised to contact your doctor well in advance of your intended date of departure. Any numbers in the chart refer to the footnotes below.*

1: A yellow fever vaccination certificate is required from travellers over one year of age arriving within 10 days of leaving infected areas.
2: Following WHO guidelines issued in 1973, a cholera vaccination certificate is not a condition of entry to Fiji. However, cholera is a serious risk in this country and precautions are essential. Up-to-date advice should be sought before deciding whether these precautions should include vaccination, as medical opinion is divided over its effectiveness; see the *Health* appendix for more information.
3: Vaccination against typhoid and polio is advised.
Food & drink: Mains water is normally heavily chlorinated and, whilst relatively safe, may cause mild abdominal upsets. Bottled water is available and is advised for the first few weeks of the stay. Milk is pasteurised and dairy products are safe for consumption. Local meat, poultry, seafood, fruit and vegetables are generally considered safe to eat.
Other risks: *Diarrhoeal diseases* are common. *Hepatitis A* occurs. *Hepatitis B* is endemic. *Dengue fever* may occur. Mosquitoes may transmit *dengue fever* and pandemic outbreaks occur. Personal protective measures are important. Marine hazards include corals, jellyfish, sharks, sea urchins and sea snakes. Only bathe in marked and patrolled beaches.
Health care: The main hospitals are located in Ba, Labasa, Lautoka, Levuka, Savusavu, Sigatoka, Suva and Taveuni, with clinics and medical representations elsewhere throughout the islands. Medical insurance is recommended. There is a private hospital in Suva that provides western style medical care and maintains the Fiji Decompression Chamber for the benefit of scuba divers. Medical emergencies may be referred to Australia, New Zealand or the USA. Doctors and hospitals expect immediate cash payment for health services.

Travel - International

AIR:

The national airline is *Air Pacific (FJ)* (website: www.airpacific.com), which operates to the Pacific Island nations as well as to Australia, New Zealand and the USA.

Approximate flight times: From Nadi to *London* is 27 hours 45 minutes (plus connection/stopover time), to *Los Angeles* is 10 hours and to *Sydney* is three hours 50 minutes.

Main airports: *Nadi (NAN)* is 8km (5 miles) north of Nadi town on Viti Levu island (website: www.afl.com.fj). *To/from the airport:* A bus to the city operates 0700-1830 (travel time – 20 mintues). Taxis are also available. *Facilities:* 24-hour bank/bureaux de change, duty free shops, 24-hour bar, restaurants, 24-hour left luggage office, tourist information, parents room, porter service, post office and car hire.

Suva (SUV) is at Nausori, 16km (10 miles) from Suva. Travel time: 30 minutes. *To/from the airport:* Taxis and car rental. *Facilities:* Parking, a small duty free shop, a snack bar, and car hire.

Nadi is where most international flights arrive, while Suva is the internal hub.

Air passes: The *Visit the South Pacific Pass* is valid for airlines operating in the South Pacific, including most of the larger ones, such as *Air Caledonie, Air Marshall Islands, Air Nauru, Air Niugini, Air Pacific, Air Vanuatu, Polynesian Airlines, Qantas, Royal Tongan Airlines and Solomon Airlines.* Offering reductions of up to 40 per cent on normal airfares, this sector-based pass allows for flexible island-hopping between the destinations of the Cook Islands, Fiji, Nauru, New Caledonia, Samoa, Tahiti, Tonga, Vanuatu and the more remote Melanesian and Micronesian islands, together with major cities in Australia (Brisbane, Melbourne and Sydney) and New Zealand (Auckland, Christchurch and Wellington). It is only available for people resident outside of the South Pacific. The journey must be started outside the South Pacific and only one stopover in Australia is allowed. A minimum of two sectors must be bought before departure (extra sectors can be purchased en route). There is a maximum of one pass per person, and passes must be used within six months of the first day of travel. Children under 12 years of age pay 75 per cent of the adult fare. For details and conditions, contact the South Pacific Tourist Organisation (see Top Things To See & Do).

Departure tax: F$30. Children under 12 years of age and transit passengers leaving within 12 hours are exempt.

SEA:

Main ports: *Suva* (website: www.portofsuva.com/) and *Lautoka* (Viti Levu). Passenger lines serving Fiji include *Crystal*, *Cunard*, *Peter Deilmann*, *Princess Cruises*, *Seabourn* and *Society*. Several cargo lines stop at Fiji including *Bank Line* and *Pacific Forum Line*. There are regular sailings to Kiribati, Nauru, Samoa and Tuvalu.

Travel - Internal

AIR:

Fiji's domestic airlines, *Air Fiji*, *Air Pacific* and *Sun Air*, operate shuttle services around the islands, particularly between Nadi and Suva (Nausori) with additional regular flights to Vanua Levu, Kadavu and Taveuni. The flight time from Nadi to Suva is approximately 30 minutes. *Air Fiji* also operates from Suva to Ovalau, Koro, Cicia in the Lau group and Gau, and from Nadi to Labasa. A *Discover Fiji* ticket is available which gives virtually unlimited flights (Rotuma and Funafuti in Tuvalu not included) for 30 days. Contact *Air Fiji*, PO Box 1259, Suva (tel: 331 3666 or 331 5055; website: www.airfiji.com.fj). *Sun Air* operates daily flights to Malololailtai (for Musket Cove and Plantation Village), Kadavu, Labasa, Taveuni and Savusavu from Nadi (tel: 723 016; website: www.fiji.to). *Pacific Crown Aviation LTD* operates a helicopter service out of Suva which is available for charter. *Turtle Airways* (website: www.turtleairways.com) flies to Turtle Island from Nadi. The flight time is approximately 30 minutes; flight prices are high as the island is privately owned; Only 14 couples are allowed on the island at one time.

SEA:

Government and local shipping companies operate freight and passenger services linking the outer islands. Cruises to offshore islands leave Nadi/Lautoka and Suva. A ferry goes back and forth regularly from Suva to Labasa, and to Ovalau and Koro Island. Yachts and cabin cruisers are available for charter. Inter-island trips can take anything from a few hours to a few weeks, and are usually very inexpensive. In general, timetables are not posted. Persons wishing to travel about the islands in this way should enquire at the offices of one of the local shipping agents, being sure to confirm all arrangements with the captain once the vessel is in port. A number of ferries now operate between the major islands, greatly reducing travel times. These boats can take between 300 and 500 passengers and have a full range of facilities, including bar, TV lounge and snack bar. A F$2.5 million catamaran called *Lagilagi*, launched by Beachcomber island resort, provides two cruises from Fiji, servicing Lautoka, Nadi, Nanu-i-ra, Savusavu and Wananvu. It leaves Port Denarau every Saturday morning at various times.

ROAD:

Traffic drives on the left. There are about 5000km (3100 miles) of roads, 1500km (930 miles) of which are paved and useable all year round. The speed limit in built-up areas is 50km/h (30mph) and highways are 80km/h (50mph). Beware of livestock on the roads as they wander freely during the night, although it is best to avoid driving during the night altogether. When driving past villages, slow down as locals use the roads as footpaths. Front seat passengers must wear their seat belt at all times. The approximate driving time from Nadi to Suva is three hours (on a sealed road). The main roads on Viti Levu follow the coast, linking the main centres. **Bus:** Local open-windowed buses operate across Viti Levu and the other main islands between all towns and on suburban routes. Express air-conditioned buses operate between Suva and Nadi and between Suva and Lautoka. **Taxi:** These are metered in towns. A fare table for long distances is required. **Car hire:** Car hire is available. Limousines and chauffeurs are available. Contact Fiji Visitors Bureau (see *Top Things To Do*)

Documentation: International Driving Permit required if driving a locally registered vehicle. Overseas and international permits are valid for six months.

Travel Advice

Penalties for possession of any amount of marijuana carry a mandatory prison sentence.

There has been an increase in robbery, theft and assault. Travellers should take appropriate precautions.

The threat from terrorism in Fiji is low, but you should be aware of the global risk of indiscriminate terrorist attacks, which could be against civilian targets, including places frequented by foreigners.

Cyclones are mostly confined to the period from November to April with greatest frequency in January and February. On average there are 15 cyclones per decade, effecting some part of Fiji and two to four actually cause severe damage. There is more risk in the outlying north-west island groups.

This advice is based on information provided by the Foreign and Commonwealth Office in the UK. It is correct at time of publishing. As the situation can change rapidly, visitors are advised to contact the following organisations for the latest travel advice:

British Foreign and Commonwealth Office
Tel: (0845) 850 2829.
Website: www.fco.gov.uk

US Department of State
Website: http://travel.state.gov/travel

Accommodation

HOTELS:

There are a good number of luxury hotels, the majority of which are located in Douba, Lautoka, Nadi, Raki Raki, Sigatoka, Suva and Tavua and off Viti Levu at Ovalau and Savusavu. There are also many small inexpensive hotels throughout the islands. Increasing numbers of establishments are offering dormitory accommodation at cheap rates. Small resort islands include Beachcomber Island, Castaway Island, Mana Island, Plantation Island and Treasure Island. A 5 per cent hotel tax is levied on all hotel services charged to guests' accounts, including meals in hotel restaurants. For information, contact the Fiji Visitors Bureau (see *Top Things To See & Do*), which can supply listings of hotels, their cost and facilities; *or* the Fiji Hotel Association. **Grading:** A star system is used to indicate the price range, as follows: 3-star (deluxe), 2-star (medium) and 1-star (budget).

GUEST HOUSES:

These are known as *Budgetels*. They are clean, comfortable and most have a licensed bar, pool and restaurant; some are air conditioned with kitchens. There is also a youth hostel in Suva.

APARTMENTS AND SELF CATERING:

Bungalows are available in Viti Levu, Mamancas and Yaswas. Bungalows come with a standard room and bathroom (some have shared bathrooms). Meals are often prepared by your host and served in the main house. This is an ideal form of getting away from the mainstream tourism and spending a few days as a guest of a village. Prices range from F$55 per person a night for a standard bungalow to F$220 for a deluxe. Some resorts, such as the Beachcomber, have overwater, beachfront bungalows with a separate living room and air conditioning. Many larger resorts also have a spa where massages and facials are available.

YOUTH HOSTELS:

Backpacker hostels are available at Viti Levu, Yasawas and Mamancas. Prices vary.

ACCOMMODATION INFORMATION

Fiji Hotel Association
PO Box 13560, 42 Gorrie Street,
Suva, Fiji
Tel: 330 2980/2975.
Website: www.fha.com.fj

Top Things To See

- In the capital **Suva**, places of historic interest include the **National Museum**, situated in the lush surrounds of **Thurston Gardens** next to **Government House**, and the old **Parliament Buildings**. Visitors can buy various artefacts and handicrafts in the city's many old shops and markets.
- Discover the **Sri Siva Subramaniya Temple**, the largest Hindu temple in the southern hemisphere.
- Explore the **Naihere Sacred Caves** deep in the Sigatoka valley.
- Discover Fiji's copra, ginger, sugar cane and cocoa **plantations**.
- See beautiful murals at the **Church of Saint Francis Xavier**, high on the hill overlooking the dusty Kings Road on the north western side of Viti Levu. While the church looks traditionally European from the outside, the use of mats instead of pews for parishioners (around 2000 Catholics from the surrounding province) gives it a Fijian village flavour.

Top Things To Do

- Visit the **Cultural Centre** at **Orchid Island,** a natural river formation, which has been cultivated into a microcosm of Fiji.
- Arrange a **cruise** by schooner or yacht to the different islands, or a **coach tour** around the main islands.
- The mangrove-lined tidal corridors can be explored on **jet-boat** trips, which depart every 15 minutes from **Port Denauru**, 7km (4 miles) from Nadi Town.
- **Bamboo rafting** (referred to locally as a *bilibili* ride) is available along the streams and rivers.
- **Hiking** in the mountains with dramatic views of the islands is another option.
- Particularly well known for their soft coral reefs, Fiji's islands offer excellent **scuba diving** and **snorkelling**. On Viti Levu, the best dive sites are found on the Coral Coast and Pacific Harbour (both on the western side), where the well-known **Beqa Lagoon**, the crater of an extinct volcano that measures 16km (10 miles) across, is often frequented by groups. About 12km (7 miles) off the Viti Levu coast, **Vatulele** is known for its red prawns, regarded as sacred by local people. Northwest of Viti Levu, divers head to the **Yasawa** and **Mamanuca** island groups; to the south lies **Kadavua**, where the **Astrolabe, Namalata, Solo** and **Tavuki** reefs are located. **Vanua Levua** and **Taveuni** are particularly good for land-based diving, and ecologically-minded operators have buoyed dozens of sites to prevent damage from anchors. The best sites around these islands include the **Somosomo Straits** (home to the **Great White Wall**, one of Fiji's most famous dive sites) and the **Rainbow Reef** (where over 20 dive sites can be found). Live-aboard dive tours are available to the more remote islands, such as **Ngau**, which has no resorts and where the local chief has to grant permission to dive in the waters.
- Many hotels and resorts also offer opportunities to go **sailing**, **windsurfing**, **waterskiing**, **canoeing**, **kayaking**, **parasailing** and **game fishing**.
- **Surfing** is a popular activity with a huge choice of locations. The famous 'Cloud Breaker' (6m/18ft-wave) was found offshore at **Tavarua**, attracting surfers from around the world. Fiji's waves typically break on coral reefs. Most of the well-known spots are off **Viti Levu** and can often only be reached by boat. There are several surf camps, notably on **Beqa** and **Yanuca** islands. Visitors should note that there are dangerous rip tides along the reefs.
- Explore Fiji's network of marked **nature trails**, either individually or on organised guided walks. Activities such as **birdwatching** (as for example in the **Colo-i-Suva Forest Park** just 11km (7 miles) from Suva), **ecotourism** (in the **Taveuni Island Reserve**) and **swimming** at the waterfalls are often combined with hiking tours. Visitors are reminded to respect local customs when passing through villages (see *Social Conventions* in the *General Information* section). The **Lavena Coastal Walk** starts at Lavena and follows the southeastern coastline of Taveuni, ending at the **Wainabau Waterfalls**; the **Vidawa Forest Walk** is a guided trip through the **Bouma Forest Park**. Marked trails (including wooden walkways and bridges) also exist in the **Kula Eco Park**, an area of coastal rainforest rich in wildlife (including fruit bats, parrots and marine turtles).
- Other natural attractions include the acres of orchids and flowering plants in the **Garden of the Sleeping Giant**, at the foot of the **Sabeto Mountains**, and the **Sigatoka Sand Dunes** off the main Queens Highway on Viti Levu.
- Watch and participate in a **Meke**, the performance of the Fijian dancing involving locals dressed entirely in national costume of flower leis, grass skirts and tapa cloth - beaten from the bark of the Paper Mulberry tree and handpainted using brown paints made from mangroves, bark and nuts. The men perform warrior dances while the women sing.

TOURIST INFORMATION

Fiji Visitors Bureau in the UK
Albany House, Albany Crescent, Claygate,
Surrey, KT10 0PF, UK
Tel: (01372) 469 818
Website: www.bulafiji.com

Fiji Visitors Bureau in the USA
5777 West Century Boulevard,
Los Angeles 90045, USA
Tel: (310) 568 1616 *or* (800) 932 3454 (toll-free).
Website: www.bulafiji.com *or* www.bulafijiislands.com

South Pacific Tourism Organisation
PO Box 13119, Suva, Fiji
Tel: 330 4177.
Website: www.spto.org

Entertainment

FOOD & DRINK: International cuisine is available, but the local cooking is Fijian and Indian. Table service is normal, although some establishments offer buffet-style food at lunchtime. Hotels often serve meals to non-residents. Bars and cocktail lounges have table and/or counter service. Only licensed restaurants, clubs and hotel bars can serve alcohol.
National specialities:
- *Kakoda* (a marinated local fish steamed in coconut cream and lime).
- *Rourou* (a taro leaf dish).
- *Kassaua* (tapioca, often boiled, baked or grated and cooked in coconut cream with sugar and mashed bananas).
- *Duruka* (an unusual asparagus-like vegetable in season during April and May).
- Breadfruit.
- *Iovo* (feast of meat, fish, vegetables and fruit cooked in covered pits).

National drinks:
- A wide range of drinks is available including the traditional *kava*. Traditionally, the drink was prepared by virgins, who chewed the root into a soft pulpy mass before adding water. It is made from the root of the pepper plant and the *yaqona* drinking ceremony is still important in the Fijian tradition, although it has also become a social drink.
- *Carlton* (a local beer brewed in Suva).
- Fiji Bitter (brewed in Lautoka).
- *Meridan Moselle* and *Suvanna Moselle* (local wines).
- *Booth's Gin, Bounty Fiji Golden Rum, Cossack Vodka* and *Old Club Whisky* (produced by South Pacific Distilleries).

Tipping: Give small tips only for special services..
NIGHTLIFE: Major hotels and resorts have live bands and dancing. There are also nightclubs with entertainment, especially in Suva. Cinemas show English-language and Indian films. Most social activity, however, is in private clubs and visitors can obtain temporary membership through hotels. Hotels offer Fijian entertainment (*meke*). Suva has many bars, nightclubs and restaurants. Just off Victoria Parade travellers will find various places to wile the night away. There is a jazz and blues bar, a pizzeria and even an Irish-themed pub. The many nightclubs include *Signals, The Planet* and *Purple Haze* playing an electric mix of music.
SHOPPING: Favourite buys are filigree jewellery, woodcarvings (such as *kava* bowls), polished coconut shells, seashells, woven work (such as mats, coasters, hats, fans and trays), *tapa* cloth and pearls. Bargaining is not the norm in shops. Some shopkeepers will give a discount with large purchases. Duty free items are available and include cameras, televisions, watches, binoculars, clocks, lighters, hi-fi equipment, pewter, crystal and porcelain. **Shopping hours:** Mon-Fri 0800-1900, Sat 0800-1300 (some shops have half-day closing on Wednesday and are open later on Friday).

Business

- **GDP:** US$5.17 billion.
- **Main exports:** Sugar, garments, gold, timber, fish, molasses and cocoa oil.
- **Main imports:** Manufactured goods, machinery and transport equipment, petroleum, foodstuff and chemicals.
- **Main trade partners:** Australia, Singapore, New Zealand, USA, UK, Samoa and Japan.

ECONOMY: The Fijian economy has a sizeable subsistence agricultural economy as well as producing cash crops, of which sugar is the most important. In 2002, the Government began a wholesale reorganisation of the state-owned sugar monopoly, which was close to collapse through years of inefficiency and the state of the world sugar market. Fish and timber, especially mahogany (of which Fiji is the world's second-largest producer) are also vital export earners. The industrial sector exploits low-grade copper deposits. There are also a number of light industrial enterprises producing goods such as cement, paint, cigarettes, biscuits, flour, nails, barbed wire, furniture, matches and footwear, mainly for domestic consumption. Tourism is the main service industry, and was severely affected by recent political upheavals, although visitors are gradually returning. Foreign trade and investment have both declined, while many ethnic Indian members of the business community have left the country. GDP growth in 2002 was 4.8 per cent. More recently, closer economic relations have been forged with other Asian countries, including China, Korea (Rep) and Taiwan.
BUSINESS ETIQUETTE: Lightweight or tropical suits are acceptable. **Office hours:** Mon-Fri 0830-1630/1700 (some offices close one hour earlier on Fridays).

COMMERCIAL INFORMATION

Suva Chamber of Commerce
PO Box 337, Suva, Fiji
Tel: 338 0975.

Finland

Location: Scandinavia, Europe.

Time: GMT + 2 (GMT + 3 from last Sunday in March to last Sunday in October).

Overview

Visiting Finland has been likened to stepping into a refreshing shower on a hot day. Even in the cultured capital, Helsinki, the air is clean, and the countryside has a cool beauty. The western coast is fringed with countless islands, while the southern Saimaa district is drenched by myriad sapphire lakes. Here you can sail, fish, or take a relaxing sauna – followed, of course, by a dip in the lake. In Kuusamo, there are ancient forests where bears and wolves roam, and where lichens glisten on the trees lining the waymarked walking trails. And in Lapland, far to the north, the indigenous Sami people still tend their reindeer herds – when they're not surfing the Internet: Finland is one of the most technologically switched-on countries in the world. It is also renowned for its design and architecture, in particular those of Alvar Aalto, whose humanist approach to modernism extended into fields such as glassware, furniture and major buildings.
Indeed, besides such innovation, Finland's rich and sometimes turbulent history is also revealed in its buildings: onion-domed Orthodox churches speak of the days when it was part of Russia, while fortresses like Suomenlinna Castle recall centuries of Swedish rule. During the first millennium BC, various peoples settled in Finland, including the nomadic Saami, who inhabited the north of the country, and the Tavastians from central Europe. Competition for influence in the area was fierce, with a tug-of-war between Sweden and Russia continuing for hundreds of years. In 1917, Finland was an autonomous region within the Russian Empire but, in the aftermath of the Bolshevik Revolution, Finland declared independence, which the new Soviet Government accepted after brief efforts to re-assert control. Further fighting between the two took place on the fringes of World War II, between 1939 and 1941. Under a formal peace treaty signed in 1947, the Finns agreed to cede territory to the Soviet Union and pay reparation.
Finland's scenery and climate has marked seasonal variations , particularly in the north; in Lapland, with its austere winter and midnight sun. Autumn is also worth seeing for, in September, the first frosts produce the vivid colours of 'Ruska'. In southern Finland, spring comes earlier and summer is longer. Such variation ensures that Finland contains whatever a visitor is seeking.

General Information

AREA: 338,145 sq km (130,559 sq miles).
POPULATION: 5.2 million (UN, 2002).
POPULATION DENSITY: 15.37 per sq km.
CAPITAL: Helsinki. **Population:** 560,000 (FCO).
GEOGRAPHY: Finland is situated in the far north of Europe, bordered to the west by Sweden and the Gulf of Bothnia, to the north by Norway, to the east by the Russian Federation and to the south by the Gulf of Finland. There are about 30,000 islands off the Finnish coast, mainly in the south and southwest, and inland lakes containing a further 98,000 islands. The Saimaa lake area is the largest inland water system in Europe. Of the total land area, 10 per cent is under water, and 65 per cent is forest; Finland is situated almost entirely in the northern coniferous zone. In the south and southwest, the forest is mainly pine, fir and birch. In Lapland, in the far north, trees become more sparse and are mainly dwarf birch. Eight per cent of the land is cultivated.
GOVERNMENT: Republic. **Head of State:** President Tarja Halonen since 2000. **Head of Government:** Prime Minister Matti Vanhanen since 2003. **Recent history:** The main change in the political landscape has been caused by the emergence of the right-wing National Coalition Party (Kokoomus, referred to as 'Kok'). Finland's long-serving President, Mauno Koivisto, the architect of the delicate balancing act between East and West, stood down in 1993, after two terms. He was replaced by the SDP candidate, former senior UN official Martti Ahtisaari. He was succeeded in turn by another Social Democrat, Tarja Halonen – the first woman to hold the post – at the beginning of 2000. The SDP has also dominated successive coalition Governments. Paavo Lipponen, the leader of the SDP, assumed the post of Prime Minister following the General Election of March 1995. Lipponen survived the 1999 General Election, and finally ceded office following the most recent poll in March 2003. This was won by the Centre Party, whose leader Anneli Jaatteenmaki took over as Premier, although the Social Democrats were brought into the new coalition Government along with the Swedish People's party, which represents Finland's ethnic Swedish population. Jaatteenmaki's tenure was short-lived. Brought down by a political scandal, she was replaced in June 2003 by Martti Vanhanen. Left-leaning President Tarja Halonen won the first round of the Presidential election in January 2006, but did not obtain the 50 per cent she needed to avoid a secound round.
The constitution allows for a President, who is Head of State, and a single-chamber Assembly, the *Eduskunta*. The President is elected by direct popular vote for a term of six years, while the 200-strong Parliament is elected (by proportional representation) every four years.
LANGUAGE: There are two official languages: Finnish, spoken by 93.4 per cent of the population, and Swedish, spoken by 5.9 per cent of the population. There are small Lapp and Russian speaking minorities. English is taught as the first foreign language.
RELIGION: 86 per cent Evangelical Lutheran, one per cent Finnish Orthodox; there are also Baptists, Methodists, Free Church, Roman Catholic, Jews and Muslims.
ELECTRICITY: 220 (230) volts AC, 50Hz. Continental two-pin plugs are standard.
SOCIAL CONVENTIONS: Shaking hands is customary. It is customary for the guest to refrain from drinking until the host or hostess toasts their health with a 'kippis' or a 'skol'. Casual dress is acceptable. Finns appear sometimes to be rather reserved and visitors should not feel alarmed if there is a lack of small talk during the first half hour or so. Shoes are usually removed when entering someone's home.

Climate

Temperate climate, but with considerable temperature variations (see below). Summer is warm with relatively mild weather in spring and autumn. Winter, which lasts from November to mid-March, is very cold. In the north (see the chart for Sodankyla), the snow cover lasts from mid-October until mid-May, but, in the brief Arctic summer, there may be up to 16 hours of sunshine a day. Rainfall is distributed throughout the year with snow in winter, but the low humidity often has the effect of making it seem warmer than the temperature would indicate (even in Lapland, the temperature can rise to over 30°C). During warm weather, gnats and mosquitos can be a hazard, particularly in the north of the country. Bring a good supply of insect repellant. The *Twilight* season lasts for two months in the north during winter.
Required clothing: Light- to mediumweights in warmer months. Medium- to heavyweights in winter, with particularly warm clothing needed for the Arctic north. Waterproofing is essential throughout the year.

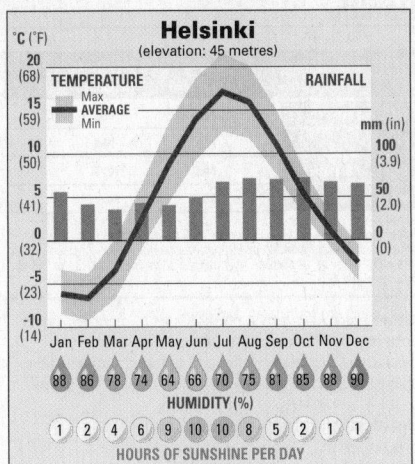

Helsinki
(elevation: 45 metres)

TEMPERATURE — Max / AVERAGE / Min

RAINFALL

Jan	Feb	Mar	Apr	May	Jun	Jul	Aug	Sep	Oct	Nov	Dec

HUMIDITY (%)

| 88 | 86 | 78 | 74 | 64 | 66 | 70 | 75 | 81 | 85 | 88 | 90 |

HOURS OF SUNSHINE PER DAY

| 1 | 2 | 4 | 6 | 9 | 10 | 10 | 8 | 5 | 2 | 1 | 1 |

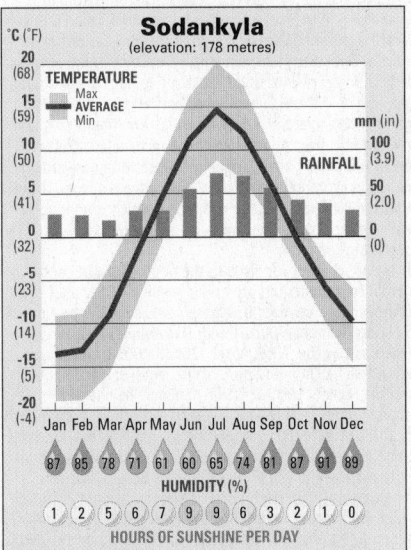

Sodankyla
(elevation: 178 metres)

TEMPERATURE — Max / AVERAGE / Min

RAINFALL

Jan	Feb	Mar	Apr	May	Jun	Jul	Aug	Sep	Oct	Nov	Dec

HUMIDITY (%)

| 87 | 85 | 78 | 71 | 61 | 60 | 65 | 74 | 81 | 87 | 91 | 89 |

HOURS OF SUNSHINE PER DAY

| 1 | 2 | 5 | 7 | 9 | 9 | 9 | 6 | 3 | 2 | 1 | 0 |

Communications

Telephone: Full IDD is available. Country code: 358. Local and international calls can be made from booths, hotels and post offices. Many public telephones operate using a pre-paid card purchased from R-kiosks, Sonera shops and some post offices.

Mobile telephone: Roaming agreements exist with some international mobile phone companies. Coverage is intermittently good.

Internet: Public access is available in Internet cafes. There are also many Internet booths in Helsinki.

Post: Letters and postcards sent by airmail usually take about three days to reach destinations within the rest of Europe. Stamps are available from post offices, bookshops and newspaper shops, stations and hotels. The Central Post Office at Mannerheimintie 11, 00100 Helsinki, is open Mon-Fri 0800-2100, Sat 0900-1800, Sun 1100-2100. General post offices hours: Mon-Fri 0900-1800; closed Saturday, with regional variations.

Media: Finland has embarked on a comprehensive digitisation programme. Analogue TV transmissions are expected to cease in 2007. Public service *YLE* provides national radio and TV programming. Newspapers are privately owned and reflect a broad spectrum of political views.

Press: There are over 200 daily newspapers, with the most popular including: *Aamulehti*, *Helsingin Sanomat* (contains English-language pages), *Ilta-Sanomat* and *Iltalehti*. *Apu* and *Seura* are weekly illustrated news magazines. *Kauppalehti* is one of the leading daily business newspapers. There are no English-language newspapers published in Finland, but most UK and US daily newspapers are available, as well as international papers in many different languages.

TV: *Yleisradio Oy* (YLE) is a public service broadcaster that operates several channels in Finnish and Swedish. *MTV3* and *Nelonen* (Channel 4) are private stations.

Radio: *Yleisradio Oy* (YLE) is a public service that operates radio channels in Finnish, Swedish and Sa'mi (Lappish). *Radio Finland* is another public, external broadcaster. Commercial stations include *Kiss FM*, *Classic FM* and *Radio Nova*.

Credit: ©Finnish Tourist Board

Passport/Visa

	Passport Required?	Visa Required?	Return Ticket Required?
Full British	1	No	No
Australian	Yes	No	No
Canadian	Yes	No	No
USA	Yes/6	No	No
Other EU	1	No	
Japanese	Yes/6	No	No

Note: *Regulations and requirements may be subject to change at short notice, and you are advised to contact the appropriate diplomatic or consular authority before finalising travel arrangements. Any numbers in the chart refer to the footnotes below.*

Note: Finland is a signatory to the 1995 **Schengen Agreement**. For further details about passport/visa regulations within the Schengen area, see the introductory section, *How to Use this Guide*.

PASSPORTS: Passport valid for at least three to six months required by all except the following provided they hold a valid national ID card:
(a) **1.** EU/EEA nationals (EU+ Iceland, Liechtenstein, Norway) and Swiss nationals holding a valid national ID card.
Note: EU and EEA nationals are only required to produce evidence of their EU/EEA nationality and identity in order to be admitted to any EU/EEA Member State. This evidence can take the form of a valid national passport *or* national identity card. Either is acceptable. Possession of a return ticket, any length of validity on their document, sufficient funds for the length of their proposed visit should *not* be imposed.

VISAS: Required by all except the following for a period of up to 90 days:
(a) EU nationals and all nationals listed in the chart and under passport exemptions (with national ID cards) above;
(b) nationals of Andorra, Argentina, Bolivia, Brazil, Brunei, Bulgaria, Chile, Costa Rica, Croatia, El Salvador, Guatemala, Honduras, Hong Kong (SAR), Israel, Korea (Rep), Macau (SAR), Malaysia, Mexico, Monaco, New Zealand, Nicaragua, Panama, Paraguay, Romania, Singapore, Uruguay, Vatican City and Venezuela. Visas are required for stays exceeding 90 days and by all who wish to work during their stay except nationals of Denmark, Iceland, Norway and Sweden;
(c) holders of a UN or EU laissez-passer.

Types of visa and cost: The *Schengen* visa, is issued for tourist, business and private visits. All visas are £24 (35), regardless of duration of stay or whether single-, double- or multiple-entry. Visa fees may vary with the rate of exchange. The transfer of a visa costs £14.
Note: Spouses and children of EU nationals (providing spouse's passport and the original marriage certificate/children's full birth certificate is produced), and nationals of some other countries, receive their visas free of charge (enquire at Embassy for details).
Validity: Transit visas are valid for up to five days. Single-entry and double-entry visas are valid for up to 90 days within a six-month period. Multiple-entry visas are valid for up to one year. Applications for renewal or extension should be made to the Embassy or Authorities in Finland.
Application to: Consulate (or consular section at Embassy); see *Passport/Visa Information*. Visas must be applied for in person at Embassy of *Schengen* country visited. If visiting more than one *Schengen* country, apply to the Embassy of the main destination *or* to the Embassy of the country entered first (if there is no main destination).
Note: Nationals must apply in person at the London Embassy if they are applying for a visa in the UK and reside in the vicinity of London.

Application requirements: (a) One completed, signed application form. (b) One passport-size photo. (c) Passport valid for at least three months from the date of return. An alien's spouse and children under 16 years may travel with passport holder if their names and dates of birth are in the passport, plus photo of spouse and photos of any children under seven years. (d) Re-entry permit into the UK valid for at least 90 days (for applicants applying at the Finnish Embassy in London). (e) Valid travel insurance other than EHIC. (f) Hotel reservation or original invitation from either a family or company in Finland. (g) Reservation of travel tickets (possibly original return tickets also) and proof of funds. (h) Fee (non-refundable; payable in advance in cash or by postal order only). (i) For minors under 18 years, letter from college/university and written permission from both parents, plus copy of parents' passports. (j) Proof of funds (eg bank statement, credit card). *Business*: (a)-(j) and, (k) Letter of invitation from the Finnish company confirming length and purpose of stay and a letter from current employer. If *Student*, letter from educational institution.
Note: All documents should be submitted both in their original form and with photocopy attached.
Working days required: Up to two weeks, although sometimes longer.
Temporary residence and work: Apply to Finnish Embassy. Work permits and Residence permits should be arranged well in advance. EU nationals and nationals of Iceland, Liechtenstein, Norway and Switzerland are allowed to live and work in Finland without visas or permits for up to 90 days; for periods exceeding 90 days, they can obtain a residence permit (a work permit is not required) from the local police station. Contact the Directorate of Immigration for more information (website: www.uvi.fi).
Note: Those wishing to visit the CIS from Finland are advised to obtain their visa in their country of origin; applications made in Helsinki take at least eight working days.

PASSPORT/VISA INFORMATION

Embassy of Finland in the UK
38 Chesham Place, London SW1X 8HW, UK
Tel: (020) 7838 6200.
Website: www.finemb.org.uk
Opening hours: Mon-Fri 0830-1230, 1330-1630;
0900-1200 (consular affairs in person), 1400-1600
(consular telephone enquiries).

Embassy of Finland in the USA
3301 Massachusetts Avenue, NW,
Washington, DC 20008, USA
Tel: (202) 298 5800.
Website: www.finland.org

Money

Single European currency (Euro): The Euro is now the official currency of 12 EU member states (including Finland). The first Euro coins and notes were introduced in January 2002; the Finnish Markka was still in circulation until 28

Credit: ©Helsinki Tourist & Convention Bureau/ Juhani Seppovaara

February 2002, when it was completely replaced by the Euro. Euro (€) = 100 cents. Notes are in denominations of €500, 200, 100, 50, 20, 10 and 5. Coins are in denominations of €2 and 1, and 50, 20, 10, 5, 2 and 1 cents.

Currency exchange: Foreign currency and traveller's cheques can be exchanged in banks and at bureaux de change at ports, stations and airports.

Credit & debit cards: American Express, Diners Club, MasterCard and Visa are widely accepted, as are Eurocheque cards. Check with your credit or debit card company for details of merchant acceptability and other services which may be available. Up-to-date information is available in Helsinki from American Express (tel: (9) 6132 0400) *or* Diners Club (tel: (9) 693 991).

Traveller's cheques: Traveller's cheques are also accepted in banks and some shops. To avoid additional exchange rate charges, travellers are advised to take traveller's cheques in Euros, Pounds Sterling or US Dollars.

Currency restrictions: Unrestricted export and import of local and foreign currency.

Banking hours: Mon-Fri 0915-1615 (regional variations may occur).

Exchange rate indicators:
Rate at time of publishing
£1.00=   €1.46
$1.00=   €0.82

Duty Free

The following items may be imported into Finland from non-EU countries without incurring customs duty:
200 cigarettes or 50 cigars or 250g of tobacco or 100 cigarillos; 2l of alcoholic beverages of less than 22 per cent by volume or 1l of alcoholic beverages of more than 22 per cent by volume, 2l of sparkling wine and 16l of beer; 50g of perfume and 250ml of eau de toilette; 100g of tea or 40g of tea extract and essence and 500g of coffee or 200g of coffee extract or essence.
Except for fuel, a passenger from another EU state is allowed an unrestricted amount of products that are acquired for own use. The tax-free importation of tobacco from countries which acceded to the EU as of May 2004 is

restricted during a transitional period:
Czech Republic: 200 cigarettes or 100 cigarillos or 50 cigars or 250g tobacco; Hungary, Latvia, Lithuania, Poland, Slovak Republic and Slovenia: *200 cigarettes;* Estonia: *200 cigarettes or 250g of tobacco.*
Note: The import of alcoholic beverages over 22 per cent is only allowed by persons aged 20 years or over; alcoholic beverages up to 22 per cent may be imported by persons aged 18 years or over.

Restricted items: The import and export of certain foods, plants, medicines (must be accompanied by a doctor's note), firearms and works of art are subject to certain restrictions and formalities. The import of drinks containing more than 60 per cent alcohol by volume is prohibited. Contact the Finnish Tourist Board for further details (see *Top Things To Do*).

Abolition of duty free goods within the EU: On 30 June 1999, the sale of duty free alcohol and tobacco at airports and at sea was abolished in all of the original 15 EU member states. Of the 10 new member states that joined the EU on 1 May 2004, these rules already apply to Cyprus and Malta. There are transitional rules in place for visitors returning to one of the original 15 EU countries from one of the other new EU countries. But for the original 15, plus Cyprus and Malta, there are now no limits imposed on importing tobacco and alcohol products from one EU country to another (with the exceptions of Denmark, Finland and Sweden, where limits *are* imposed). Travellers should note that they may be required to prove at customs that the goods purchased are for personal use *only*.

Public Holidays

Below are listed Public Holidays for the January 2006-June 2007 period.
2006: Jan 1 New Year's Day. **Jan 6** Epiphany. **Apr 14-17** Easter. **May 1** May Day. **May 25** Ascension. **Jun 4** Whit Sunday. **Jun 23** Midsummer's Eve. **Jun 24** Midsummer's Day. **Nov 1** All Saints' Day. **Dec 6** Independence Day. **Dec 24-26** Christmas
2007: Jan 1 New Year's Day. **Jan 6** Epiphany. **Apr 6-9** Easter. **May 1** May Day. **May 17** Ascension. **May 27** Whit Sunday. **Jun 24** Midsummer's Eve. **Jun 25** Midsummer's Day. .

Health

	Special Precautions?	Certificate Required?
Yellow Fever	No	No
Cholera	No	No
Typhoid & Polio	No	N/A
Malaria	No	N/A

Note: *Regulations and requirements may be subject to change at short notice, and you are advised to contact your doctor well in advance of your intended date of departure. Any numbers in the chart refer to the footnotes below.*

Other risks: *Hepatitis A* occurs. Cases of *diphtheria* have been reported. Campers and trekkers should take precautions against tick bites and consider immunisation against *tick-borne encephalitis.* Most cases occur in visitors to the Åland Islands.

Health care: European Economic Area (EEA) and Switzerland:
If you or any of your dependants are suddenly taken ill or have an accident during a visit to an EEA country or Switzerland, free or reduced-cost necessary treatment is available – in most cases on production of a valid European Health Insurance Card (EHIC). Each country has different rules about state medical provision. In some, treatment is free. In many countries you will have to pay part or all of the cost, and then claim a full or partial refund. The EHIC gives access to state-provided medical treatment only and the scheme gives no entitlement to medical repatriation costs, nor does it cover ongoing illnesses of a non-urgent nature, so comprehensive travel insurance is advised. Note that the EHIC replaces the Form E111, which is no longer valid. Some restrictions may apply depending on your nationality.
There are charges for visits to the doctor, hospital and dental treatment, and prescribed medicines. Some of these charges may, however, be partially refunded by the Finnish Sickness Insurance Department (*Kansaneläkelaitoksen Paikallistoimisto – KELA*; tel: (20) 434 5058; website: www.kela.fi). On production of the required documents, visitors seeking treatment will generally be charged approximately €11-22 for a visit to a doctor at a municipal health centre (outside regular hours, patients may be liable to an additional €15 charge), €22 for a visit to a hospital outpatient clinic and €26 per day for hospitalisation (charges may vary depending on the municipality). Those receiving private treatment should keep the receipt and submit it to the local KELA office as they may be entitled to a partial refund. For emergency dental treatment, visitors should contact the dentist on duty at the municipal health centre. A standard fee will be charged. Prescribed drugs may be obtained from any pharmacy and are charged at the full amount, though costs may be partially claimed back from the local KELA. For most prescribed medicines, a 50 per cent refund is available on amounts exceeding around €8. For emergencies, dial 112. The pharmacy at Mannerheimintie 96, Helsinki (tel: 0203 20200) is open 24 hours.

Travel - International

AIR:

The national airline of Finland is *Finnair (AY)* (website: www.finnair.com). Finland is served by many international airlines, including *Air Canada, Air France, American Airlines, British Airways, Cathay Pacific Airways, KLM, Lufthansa, Qantas, SWISS* and *United Airlines.*

Approximate flight times: From Helsinki to *London* is two hours 55 minutes, to *New York* is eight hours, to *San Francisco* is 10 hours 10 minutes, to *Singapore* is 14 hours, to *Toronto* is eight hours 45 minutes and to *Zurich* is two hours 55 minutes.

Main airports: *Helsinki (HEL)* (Helsinki-Vantaa) (website: www.ilmailulaitos.com) is Finland's principal international airport, 19km (12 miles) north of the city (travel time – 25 minutes). *To/from the airport*: Finnair City Bus and the airport bus operate to the city regularly (travel time – 35 minutes). Taxi services are available. Some Helsinki hotels run courtesy coaches. *Facilities*: Banks/bureaux de change, duty free shops, hair salon, car hire, hotel reservation service, VIP lounge, a multimedia centre, conference rooms, restaurants, cafes and bars.
The other international airports are *Turku (TKU)*, 7km (4 miles) north of the city; *Tampere (TMP)*, 15km (9 miles) from the city; and *Rovaniemi (RVN)*, 10km (6 miles) from the city.

Departure tax: None.

SEA:

Main ports: *Naantali , Turku* and *Vaasa.* Car ferries sail daily from Stockholm and other Swedish ports. There are also ferry services to Finland from Rostock, Grisslehamn, Kapellskär and Travemünde (Germany) and Tallinn (Estonia). *DFDS*

Seaways Ferries sail from the UK to Scandinavia: from Newcastle to Gothenberg and Sweden; Norwich to Esbjerg, Denmark, Grisslehamn and Kapellskär. Cruise lines with ships docking in Finnish ports include *Cunard* (website: www.cunard.com), *Eckerö Line* (website: www.eckeroline.fi), *Fred Olsen* (website: www.fredolsencruises.com), *P&O* (website: www.cruiseline.co.uk), *Princess* (website: www.princess.com), *Radisson*, *Seabourn* and *Silversea* (website: www.silversea.com).

RAIL:

Rail-sea links exist from Hamburg, Copenhagen and Stockholm to Helsinki or Turku. There is a rail connection between Haparanda/Tornio in the north from Sweden, and daily trains to Moscow and St Petersburg.

Rail Passes: The *Inter-Rail pass* offers unlimited second-class train travel in up to 29 European countries (includes Morocco and Turkey) and is split into eight zones (A-H). Three different tickets are available: a ticket covering one zone (two to six countries, 16 days' validity), a ticket covering two zones (six to 10 countries, 22 days' validity) and an *All Zone Pass (29 countries, one month's validity).* Ferry services between Italy and Greece are included. Passengers must be resident in Europe for at least six months before the pass is used. Travel is not allowed in the passenger's country of residence. Travellers under 26 years receive a reduction of about 30 per cent. Children's tickets are reduced by about 50 per cent. Supplements are required for some high-speed services, seat reservations and *couchettes*. Discounts are offered on *Eurostar* and some ferry routes. Available from *Inter Rail* (website: www.interrailnet.com).

The *Eurailpass* offers unlimited first-class train travel in 17 European countries. Tickets are valid for 15 days, 21 days, one month, two months or three months. The Eurailpass Saver ticket offers discounts for two or more people travelling together. The *Eurailpass Youth* ticket is available to those aged under 26 and offers unlimited second-class train travel. The *Eurailpass Flexi* allows either 10 or 15 travel days within a two-month period. The *Eurail Selectpass* is valid in three, four or five bordering countries and allows five, six, eight or 10 travel days (15 for five countries) in a two-month period. The Eurail Regional Pass allows four to 10 travel days in a two-month period in one of nine regions (usually two or more countries). Children receive a 50 per cent reduction. The passes cannot be sold to residents of Europe, Turkey, Morocco, Algeria, Tunisia or the Russian Federation. Available from The Eurail Group (website: www.eurail.com).

The *ScanRail pass* can be used five or 10 days in two months or 21 consecutive days across Denmark, Finland, Norway and Sweden. Payment of a supplement is required on some trains. Seat reservations, *couchette*, sleeper or cabin charges are not included in the cost of the pass and are payable at the normal rate. The ScanRail pass also entitles holders to free travel on some ferry and bus routes as well as up to 50 per cent discount on ferries, buses and private railways throughout Scandinavia, free or discounted admission (up to 50 per cent off) to railway museums in Denmark, Finland, Norway and Sweden and reduced room rates at 160 hotels throughout Scandinavia. Available from Rail Europe (website: www.raileurope.co.uk/railpasses/scanrail.htm).

ROAD:

There are eight official border crossing places between Finland and the Russian Federation, six between Finland and Norway and 10 between Finland and Sweden. The most frequented borders are at Vaalimaa (from the Russian Federation), Karigasniemi (from Norway) and Tornio (from Sweden). Approaching from Denmark will give the opportunity to experiance the magnificent bridge between Denmark and Sweden. This route through Sweden to the north end of the Gulf of Bothnia avoids the need to cross the Baltic by ship. Most direct road routes include sea ferry links from Sweden or Germany, though there is a northern land link via northern Norway or Sweden to Finnish Lapland, which involves travel within the Arctic Circle. **Coach:** There are coach services from many European cities, including direct services from London to Stockholm (Sweden) or Tallinn (Estonia). From both cities there are frequent crossings to Finland. There are also routes from Norway and the Russian Federation.

Travel - Internal

AIR:

There are 22 domestic airports in Finland. *Finnair* runs an excellent network of domestic services. For further information, contact their UK Head Office, 14 Clifford Street, London W1S 4BX, UK (tel: (0870) 241 4411; website: www.finnair.com). Other domestic airlines include *Blue 1* (website: www.blue1.com) and *Golden Air* (website: www.goldenair.se).

Cheap fares: There are some money-saving offers available. These include: *Group discounts* which vary depending on the size of the group; *Senior Citizens' fares* giving special rates (with some restrictions) for persons over 65; *Junior fares* giving special rates for children aged 12 to 16; and *Youth fares* giving special rates (with some restrictions) for persons aged 17 to 25. There are special 'Midnight Sun' packages to Rovaniemi (Lapland) in June and July. For further information, contact Norvista, 31-35 Kirby Street, London EC1N 8TE, UK (tel: (0870) 744 7315; website: www.norvista.co.uk); *or* the Finnish Tourist Board (see *Top Things To Do*).

RIVER/LAKE: Traffic on the inland waterways is serviced by regular waterbuses and ferries. There is a wide choice of routes and distances and trips can last for a few hours or one or two days. Popular routes are the *Silver Line* (website: www.finnishsilverline.com*)* between Hämeenlinna and Tampere and the *Poet's Way* between Tampere and Virrat. *Saimaa Ferries* (website: www.saimaaferries.fi) operate lake routes from Lieksa, Nurmes, Koli and Joensuu. *Lake Päijänne Cruises* run services from Lahti, Heinola and Jyväskylä and *Roll Cruises* operate from Kuopio and Savonlinna. On Lake Pielinen, there are regular services, also by car ferry. Overnight accommodation in small cabins plus meals and refreshments are available on lake cruises. For more detailed information on schedules and routes, contact the Finnish Tourist Board (see *Top Things To Do*).

RAIL:

There are 6000km (3700 miles) of rail network with modern rolling stock. Finnish trains are spaceous, comfortable and clean. *VR Ltd* (website: www.vr.fi) operates an extensive rail service around Finland. The *Pendolino* fast train runs at a maximum speed of 220km/h (132mph) and is designed to operate on all main routes by the end of 2006. Current lines include Helsinki-Turku, Helsinki-Tampere-Jyväskylä, Jyväskylä-Kuopio Helsinki-Kouvola-Issalmi and Helsinki-Seinäjoki-Oulu. The cheapest option by train are the express trains (for which seats must be booked in advance); on some lines these are being replaced by new rail cars. They have already been replaced on the Pieksämäki-Joensuu line. There are also night trains and car-carrier trains, regional trains and InterCity trains (InterCity2 trains have double-decker cars). Rail travel is cheap and efficient. Children under six years of age travel free of charge and children aged six to 16 pay half price.

Cheap fares: Special tickets offering discounts are available, including: *Group tickets* (minimum of three people), giving 20 per cent discount, valid for one month; *Family tickets* allow six to 16 year olds to travel free when travelling with one adult from the same household; *Finnrail pass* gives unlimited travel for three, five or 10 days within a period of one month; first- or second-class tickets are available for €120-€330 (six to 16 year olds pay 50 per cent); *Finnish Senior Citizens Rail Card* for persons over 65 years of age, entitle the holder to a 50 per cent discount (passport has to be shown); *Student Rail Discounts*, entitle the student to 50 per cent discounts with a valid student card.

For further details and reservations, contact the Finnish Tourist Board (see *Top Things To Do) or Finnish Railways*, PO Box 488, FI 00101 Helsinki (tel: 319 2902 from abroad *or* 060 041 902 internally; website: www.vr.fi).

The *EuroDomino pass* enables holders three to eight days' travel within a one-month period on the entire rail network of their chosen country. It is valid in 28 European countries and North Africa, including the ferry service from Brindisi (Italy) to Igoumenitsa (Greece). To purchase a EuroDomino pass you must have been resident in Europe for at least six months and a passport number is required at time of booking. It is not permitted to purchase a pass for travel within your own country of residence. To qualify for the youth rates, you must be under 26 on the first date of validity of the pass. Children aged four-11 inclusive pay half the adult fares rounded up. Children under four travel free. Seat reservations, *couchette* and sleeper charges are not included in the cost of the pass and are payable at the normal rate. Passholder fares are payable on some services. Reservation/supplement charges are payable on all trains within Spain. Available from *Rail Europe* (website: www.raileurope.co.uk/railpasses/eurodomino.htm).

ROAD:

There are 77,000km (47,000 miles) of road. The main roads are passable at all times and are surfaced with asphalt or oil and sand. There are weight restrictions on traffic from April to May in southern Finland, and from May to early June in northern Finland, but this does not usually affect private cars. Traffic drives on the right. Horn-blowing is frowned upon. In some areas, warnings of elk, deer and reindeer crossing will be posted. Drivers involved in an elk or reindeer collision should report the event to the Police immediately. Many petrol stations are unmanned so credit cards are essential. **Bus:** This is an excellent means of transport, the coach network is one of the most comprehensive in Europe and covers more than 90 per cent of the public road network. There are over 40,000 daily bus departures and timetables are adapted to fit rail, air and ship services. Coach services are run by *ExpressBus* (a consortium of 30 bus companies; website: www.expressbus.com) with over 300 services daily from Helsinki. Connections can be made to the most remote and isolated parts of the country. The state post office also runs a bus service with routes that serve the rural areas. In Lapland, buses are the major means of surface travel. Bus stations have restaurants and shops. Baggage left at one station is dispatched to its destination, even when bus transfers and different bus companies are involved. Two children under four are carried free if accompanied by a passenger over 12 years of age (children aged four to 11 years pay half fare). Seats for coaches can be reserved in advance by paying the full fare and reservation fee. For coach information and timetables contact Oy Matkahuolto Abs Coach station, authorised agents and travel agencies throughout Finland (website: www.matkahuolto.fi). **Cheap fares:** Group tickets are sold for groups travelling at least 80km (50 miles) and including at least three persons (at least one of whom is aged over 12 years). There is a 50 per cent discount for students, and a 30 per cent discount on one-way tickets for passengers between 12 and 16 or over 65 years of age when travelling a minimum of 80km. **Taxi:** Available in every city and from airports or major hotels. Taxi drivers are not tipped. Taxis have a yellow *taksi* sign which is lit when the taxi is vacant. They can be booked at taxi ranks, signalled from the street or by calling locally (tel: 0100 0700). Fares are more expensive at nights (Sun-Fri 2000-0600, Sat 1600-0600). **Car hire:** Cars can be rented in Helsinki and other places. The minimum age varies from 20 to 25 years of age depending on the company; all drivers must have a minimum of one year's driving experience. A few caravans are for hire. **Regulations:** Seat belts must be worn by the driver and all passengers (front and back seat). Car headlights must be kept on at all times. Cars towing caravans may not exceed 80kph (50mph). Cars and caravans must have the same tyres. Studded tyres are allowed from 1 November until the first Sunday after Easter or when weather conditions are appropriate. From 1 December until 31 March, snow tyres are a legal requirement for vehicles under 3.5 tonnes. It is possible to hire snow tyres. Further information can be obtained from *Autoliitto* (Automobile and Touring Club of Finland), Hämeentie 105A, 4th Floor, 00550 Helsinki (tel: (9) 7258 4400; website: www.autoliitto.fi). If involved in an accident, immediately contact the Finnish Motor Insurer's Bureau (*Liikennevakuutuskeskus*), Bulevardi 28, 00120 Helsinki (tel: (9) 680 401; website: www.vakes.fi). **Documentation:** National driving licence or International Driving Permit and insurance required.

URBAN:

Efficient and integrated bus, metro and tramway services, suburban rail lines and ferry services to Suomenlinna Islands are operated in Helsinki. A common fares system applies to all the modes (including the ferries) with a zonal flat fare and free transfer between services. Multi-trip tickets are sold in advance, as are various passes. Tickets can be purchased from the driver, ticket machine or via mobile phone text message (Finnish service providers only). The peninsular location of the city has led to an emphasis on public transport. *Tramline 3T* runs past most of the main tourist attractions – a free brochure in English is available for those who wish to take the trip. **Helsinki Card:** This is available for one, two or three days. Once purchased, it gives free travel on public transport (including the Suomenlinna ferry) and free entry to about 50 museums and other sights in the city. The card comes with a guidebook giving details of the museums, sights and other discounts on offer. For every Adult Helsinki card purchased, one child Helsinki card is given for free. Enquire at Helsinki City Transport (website: www.hel.fi) *or* the Finland Tourist Board (see *Top Things To Do*) for prices and further details. Other cities in Finland offer similar transport cards.

Travel times: The following chart gives approximate travel times (in hours and minutes) from **Helsinki** to other major cities/towns in Finland.

	Air	Road	Rail
Tampere	0.35	2.50	1.50
Turku	0.30	2.40	1.50
Rovaniemi	1.15	13.30	9.10

Travel Advice

Most visits to Finland are trouble-free but you should be aware of the global risk of indiscriminate international terrorist attacks, which could be against civilian targets, including places frequented by foreigners.

This advice is based on information provided by the Foreign and Commonwealth Office in the UK. It is correct at time of publishing. As the situation can change rapidly, visitors are advised to contact the following organisations for the latest travel advice:

British Foreign and Commonwealth Office
Tel: (0845) 850 2829.
Website: www.fco.gov.uk

US Department of State
Website: http://travel.state.gov/travel

Credit: ©Finnish Tourist Board

easy reach of main roads and towns. Camping outside official campsites is allowed providing no damage is caused to crops or other items, and the camp is at least 150m (492ft) from human habitations. Permission must be given by the landowner. The camping season starts in late May or early June and ends in late August or early September. In southern Finland, it is possible to sleep under canvas for about three months and in the north for about two months. Most campsites have indoor accommodation, camping cottages and holiday cottages suitable for family accommodation. *Camping Card Scandinavia* is valid in Finland; the cost is €6, holders receive discounts on campsite fees, cottage accommodation and programme services. If a camper has an international camping card (FICC), a national camping card is not required. Sites are classified into five grades. Further details can be obtained from the Finnish Tourist Board (see *Top Things To Do*) or from Camping in Finland.

ACCOMMODATION INFORMATION

Finnish Hotel and Restaurant Association
Merimiehenkatu 29, 00150 Helsinki, Finland
Tel: (9) 622 0200.
Website: www.shr.fi

Lomarengas Finnish Country Holidays
Eteläesplanadi 22 C, 3rd floor,
FI-00130 Helsinki, Finland
Tel: (9) 5766 3300.
Website: www.lomarengas.fi

Hostelling International Finland (also provides information on summer hotels)
Yrjönkatu 38B-15, 00100 Helsinki, Finland
Tel: (9) 565 7150.
Website: www.srmnet.org

Camping in Finland
Website: www.camping.fi

Top Things To See

- **Helsinki**, the capital, is surrounded by parks, forests, shoreline and lakes. It is also endowed with historical sights as well as buildings by the best-known Finnish architects; **Dipoli Hall**, at the **Helsinki University of Technology** in **Otaniemi**, is an internationally acclaimed 20th-century masterpiece. **Senate Square** in Helsinki, with its cathedral, is perhaps Finland's most photographed building. The **Suomenlinna Maritime Fortress** is the world's largest maritime fortress and is a UNESCO World Heritage Site. Helsinki has numerous museums, a rich musical life and a wide variety of exhibitions and events.

- Along Finland's coastline, in the Eastern areas of the archipelago, are the islands of **Kimito** (with its islets) and **Särkisalo**. **Bengtskär Lighthouse** is the tallest lighthouse in the Nordic countries. It has been refurbished and houses a museum, chapel, cafe and hotel.

- See Finland's oldest city: **Turku**. The country's former capital city boasts a magnificent medieval castle, a fine cathedral and several stylish restaurants and intriguing museums. Enjoy the wonderful craftwork in the **Luostarinmaki Handicrafts Museum**.

- Go to southwest Finland and the **Åland Islands**, the warmest part of the country and where more deciduous trees grow here than anywhere else in the country. For historical reasons, a large proportion of the Swedish-speaking population of Finland lives in this region and the region must be seen if only for the fact it is often spoken of as the cradle of Finnish civilisation: the area has a larger concentration of granite churches and manors than elsewhere.

- Gaze at any of Finland's 180,000 lakes; most are situated between the coastal area and the eastern frontier, covering an area some 100km (60 miles) wide. The country's **Lakeland** is a veritable maze with its profusion of bays, headlands and islands. Sometimes they open out into broader stretches. They are linked to each other by rivers, straits and canals forming waterways which in former times were a principal means of communication. Nowadays, they are attractive routes for the tourist. As the lakes are usually shallow and the surrounding land is not high, the water soon becomes warm in summer. The interconnected lakes of the eastern regions is dominated by **Lake Saimaa**, a vast expanse of water. Dotted over the surface is a network of waterways that joins the lively Savo towns. The Western Lakeland comprises two major waterways, the oldest of which, the **Finnish Silverline**, runs between **Hämeenlinna**, birthplace of Sibelius, and **Tampere**, through fertile agricultural lands which are fairly densely populated.

- Venture into **Savonlinna**, an enchanting town that boasts the best preserved medieval castle in Scandinavia, the **Olavinlinna Castle**.

Accommodation

Further details on accommodation and grades of accommodation are given in the publications available from the Finnish Tourist Board.

HOTELS:

 There is usually a sauna and often a swimming pool in Finnish hotels and motels. The price level varies from district to district, being higher in Helsinki and some areas of Lapland. Many hotels and motels include breakfast in their rates. Advance reservations are advisable in the summer months. Details of hotels are listed in the brochures available from Finnish Tourist Board offices. Accommodation at reduced rates is often possible, especially for groups and during weekends. Reductions are also possible for guests participating in special schemes run by hotel chains throughout Scandinavia. Information can be obtained from the Finnish Hotel and Restaurant Association.

Summer hotels: During summer (June 1 to August 31), when the universities are closed, student accommodation becomes available to tourists. Rooms are modern and clean and cheaper than regular hotels. They are located around the country in major cities..

BED & BREAKFAST:

There are approximately 100 bed & breakfast host families in Finland. Children aged under 12 years are free of charge. A list of bed & breakfast outlets can be supplied by the Finnish Tourist Board (see *Top Things To Do*) and the brochure *Finland Country Holidays – Bed & Breakfast*, published by Lomarengas, who can also take bookings. The brochure also includes information on farm holidays.

FARMHOUSE HOLIDAYS:

Hundreds of farmhouses take guests on a bed & breakfast and full- or half-board basis. They are in rural settings and almost always close to water. The guest rooms may be without modern conveniences but are clean. Some farms also have individual cottages for full-board guests, or self-catering apartments with kitchen, fridge and electric stove. Guests can tipically join the host family for meals, take a sauna, row, fish, walk in the forests or join in the work of the farm. Full-board rates include two hot meals, coffee twice a day

and a sauna twice a week (children receive a discount). The majority of farms are in central and eastern Finland, some on the coast and in the Åland Islands. Farmhouses are graded on a scale from **1** to **5 stars.**

SELF-CATERING COTTAGE HOLIDAYS:

 There are plenty of Holiday Villages in Finland, many in the luxury class with all modern conveniences. These villages consist of self-contained first-class bungalows by a lake and offer varied leisure activities, such as fishing, rowing, hiking and swimming. All cottages have a sauna as standard. The best villages are open all year round and can be used as a base for winter holidays and skiing. Minimum hire is one week during the peak seasons. Some of the villages also have hotels and restaurants.. There are also thousands of individually owned holiday cottages for hire, ranging from the humblest fishing hut on the coast to the luxury villas of the inland lakes. They are all furnished and have cooking utensils, crockery and bed linen as well as fuel for heating, cooking and lighting and, in some cases, a boat. Most inland cottages are near a farm where food can be bought. Reductions are available out of season. Enquire at tourist offices for details. Classification is from **1** to **5 stars**.

YOUTH HOSTELS:

 There are about 100 youth hostels in Finland. Many of them are only open from June to August. Some of the hostels are in empty educational establishments, with accommodation and fairly large rooms, but a lot of them also offer family rooms.. The hostels do not usually provide food, but coffee and refreshments are available at most and some have self-catering kitchens. There are no age restrictions. Sheets can be hired. For more information, contact Hostelling International Finland. Youth hostels are classified into four categories according to their facilities.

CAMPING/CARAVANNING:

There are about 200 campsites in Finland that have been fully inspected and graded by the Finnish Camping Site Association. Sites are classified into five grades. The majority have cooking facilities, kiosks and canteens where groceries can be bought. Campsites are generally along waterways, within

- The west coast area of **Ostrobothnia**, with its long sandy beaches and the dunes of **Kalajoki**, is an agricultural region with a sunny and drier climate than elsewhere. The **Sanifani Spa** is located in **Kalajoki**.
- Discover the interesting fauna of **Hailuoto Island**, which can be reached by ferry from **Oulu**, the area's chief commercial and university centre. Picturesque old wooden houses are still a feature of the coastal towns.
- Go the Finnish **Lapland** region and search for a sight of the rare golden **cloudberry**.
- Watch some 200,000 reindeer roam freely on the fells around the Finnish Lapland. They are the property of different owners. There are reindeer round-ups from September to January and special **reindeer-driving competitions** take place in March with participants from all over Lapland.
- Go to **Haltia Fell**, the highest range in Finland, at 1300m (4265ft), and **Saana Fell**, 1029m (3376ft), which lie on the border between Finland, Norway and Sweden.

Top Things To Do

- Go **cross-country skiing** on Finland's marked and often illuminated tracks all over the country. There are over 100 **downhill skiing** resorts, offering instruction, equipment hire and extensive *après-ski* facilities. Many resorts have halfpipes and 'snowboard streets' for **snowboarding** enthusiasts. **Off-piste skiing** (for experienced skiers only) is available through private companies. The skiing season is from December to mid-April (southern and central Finland) and November to early May (northern Finland). The major ski resorts include: **Pallastunturi**, **Saariselkä**, **Pallas**, **Levi**, **Ylläs** and **Luosto/Pyhä** (in the North); **Rovaniemi**, **Ruka**, **Iso-Syöte**, **Vuokatti**, **Koli** and **Tahko** (in central Finland); and **Himos** and **Lahti** (in the south).
- Keep an eye on the skies: northernmost Finland is above the Arctic Circle and enjoys a spell of **polar night** (*kaamos*) between November and May, when the sun barely rises above the horizon, and it is at this time that the **Northern Lights** or **Aurora Borealis**, can be seen; the **Midnight Sun** period is also extremely popular.
- Take a **walk** through Finland's countryside in early autumn, when trees and vegetation take on the beautiful hues and colours of the *ruska* season, especially beautiful in Lapland.
- Try some **reindeer-watching**, notably in **Salla Safari/ Reindeer Park** (website: www.sallareindeerpark.fi).
- **Canoe**, particularly in areas such as **Saimaa**, **Lake Oulujärvi** and **Lake Inari**. Owing to strong currents, guides are recommended for trips to remote areas. City tourist offices can supply ready-planned canoeing routes. Further information can be obtained from the Finnish Canoe Federation, Olympiastadion, Eteläkaarre, 00250 Helsinki (tel: (9) 494 965; website: www.kanoottiliitto.fi). The **Kukkolankoski rapids** provide the biggest unharnessed rapids in the world; **white-water rafting** is organised here. In **Oulanka National Park**, rivers with rapids run through gorge-like valleys.
- Take a **horse trek** along the **forest trails** of **Munio** (website: www.harriniva.fi). There are around 150 **riding** schools in Finland, most of them located outside the towns and cities. **Kuuma Farm** in South Finland is one of the leading riding centres in Finland.
- Release those stress-created toxins at a **sauna**, one of the best-known Finnish traditions. The country has an estimated 1.6 million saunas – nearly one for every three inhabitants. Most hotels, holiday villages, campsites and even log cabins come equipped with a sauna, usually built close to the water. The **Ounasvaara Spa Complex**, **Santasport**, near **Rovaniemi**, is the ideal location to try a traditional Finnish smoke sauna or **peat bath**. During winter it is not uncommon to cut a hole (*avanto*) into the ice through which seasoned sauna fans may take a dip. **Sauna tours**, notably to the sauna village of **Muurame**, are possible. Health-conscious travellers can also go on a spa tour, taking in some of Finland's **spas** at, for instance, **Naantali** or **Haikko**.
- For cutting-edge design, embark on an **architecture tour**, which puts particular emphasis on buildings and designs by the internationally acclaimed Alvar Aalto, one of Finland's most famous architects. There are also **design tours** available that focus on glassware, jewellery and household items, as well as fireplaces and log houses, and which often includes a visit to Helsinki's **Iittala Glass Museum** or **Glassworks**.
- Attend a traditional **lumberjack competition** at **Porttikoski** and **Simo**, held every summer.
- Spend a night at the **Mammut Snow Hotel** (website: www.snowcastle.net), located in **Kemi**, where visitors can stay in rooms at temperatures of 5 degrees celsius (warm sleeping bags are provided).
- Air-guitar to your heart's content at the downright silly, utterly surreal but immensely good-fun **Air Guitar World Championships** (website: www.airguitarworldchampionships.com), held in **Oulu** in late August.

TOURIST INFORMATION

Finnish Tourist Board in the UK
PO Box 33213, London W6 8JX, UK
Tel: (020) 7365 2512 (information and brochures) *or* 8600 5680 (press and trade section).
Website: www.visitfinland.com/uk

Finnish Tourist Board in the USA
PO Box 4649, Grand Central Station, New York, NY 10163-4649, USA
Tel: (212) 885 9700.
Website: www.gofinland.org *or* www.goscandinavia.com.

Entertainment

FOOD & DRINK: Potatoes, meat, fish, milk, butter and rye bread are the traditional mainstays of the Finnish diet, but food in Finland has been greatly influenced both by Western (French and Swedish) and Eastern (Russian) cooking. Tourists can expect excellent fresh fish such as pike, trout, perch, whitefish, salmon and Baltic herring. All are in abundance most of the year. Each region has its own traditional dishes. In restaurants (*ravintola*), the menu is continental with several Finnish specialities. Inexpensive lunches are served at places called *kahvila* and *baari* (the latter is not necessarily a licensed bar).

Things to know:
Restaurants are divided into two classes: those serving all kinds of alcohol and those serving only beers and wines. Waiter service is common although there are many self-service snack bars. Bars and cafes may have table and/or counter service and all internationally known beverages are available. In restaurants, beer is served from 0900 and other liquor from 1100. All alcohol is served until half an hour before the restaurant closes. Nightclubs are open to serve drinks until 0200 or 0400. Service begins at 1100 and continues until the restaurant closes. The age limit for drinking is 18 years, but consumers must be 20 before they can buy the stronger alcoholic beverages. There are strict laws against drinking and driving.

National specialities:
- The province of Åland has *Skärgårdssmak*, or 'Island flavours', and features mainly local fish.
- *Karelia à la carte* focuses on the Karelian buffet traditions and wholesome stews and casseroles.
- *Lapland à la carte* features reindeer meat, smoked or in other forms, fish and Lapp *puikula* potatoes, with *cloudberries* for desert, often served with hot toffee sauce.
- *Kalakukko*, a kind of fish and pork pie, baked in a rye flour crust, and *karjalan piirakat*, a pastry of rye flour stuffed with rice pudding or potato and eaten with egg butter.
- Various kinds of thick soups are also popular.
- Crayfish is available from July to August.

National drinks:
- *Koskenkorva* or Finlandia vodka schnapps, traditionally drunk with lamprey, Baltic herring or other cold fish.
- The Finnish berry liqueurs, *mesimarja* (arctic bramble), *lakka* (cloudberry) and *polar* (cranberry).
- Finnish vodka, usually served ice-cold with meals.
- Finnish beer is of a high quality and mild beers are served in most coffee bars.

Tipping: Tipping, once non-existent in Finland, is becoming common. A 15 per cent service charge is included in the bill in hotels. Restaurants and bars have a 14 per cent service charge weekdays and 15 per cent on weekends and holidays. The obligatory cloakroom or doorman fee is usually clearly indicated. Taxi drivers are not normally tipped.

Restaurant classification: Prices for alcohol vary according to the restaurant's classification.
E: Elite price category.
G: General price category.
S: Self-service price category.
A: Fully licensed.
B: Licensed for beer and wine.

SHOPPING: Finnish handicrafts, jewellery, handwoven *ryijy* rugs, furniture, glassware, porcelain, ceramics, furs and textiles are amongst the many Finnish specialities. Excellent supermarkets and self-service shops can be found all over the country. Helsinki railway station has the first underground shopping centre in the country, where the shops are open 0800-2200 (Sun and public holidays 1200-2200). *Itäkeskus* is the largest enclosed shopping centre in the Nordic countries. *Kiseleff Bazaar* is great for handicrafts and souvenirs. At the *Katajanokka boat harbour*, there is a shop selling glass, china, wooden articles and textiles. **Duty free:** Anyone permanently resident outside the EU can claim back purchase tax at the time of departure. Repayment can be made (on presentation of a special cheque provided by the retailer) at the following gateways: Helsinki, Turku, Tampere, Mariehamn, Vaasa and Rovaniemi airports; onboard ferries and ships operated by *Polferries*, *Silja Line*, *Vaasaferries* and *Viking Line*; and at the main checkpoints on the land borders with Sweden, Norway and the Russian Federation. **Shopping hours:** Mon-Fri 0900-1800, Sat 0900-1400. Shops are generally open on Sunday from June to August. Many departments stores are also open 0900-2100 during the week and Sat 0900-1800.

Business

- **GDP:** US$133.5 billion (2003).
- **Main exports:** Machinery and equipment, chemicals, metals, timber, paper and pulp.
- **Main imports:** Foodstuffs, petroleum and petroleum products, chemicals, transport equipment, iron and steel, machinery, textiles yarn and fabrics and grains.
- **Main trade partners:** The EU (mainly Germany, Sweden and UK), the Russian Federation and USA.

ECONOMY: Finland is a highly industrialised country, producing a wide range of industrial and consumer goods. Timber and related industries are a key component of the economy, accounting for 40 per cent of all Finnish exports, but the country is consequently vulnerable to fluctuations in world market prices and demand levels for timber, paper and finished products such as furniture. Per capita annual income is currently just under US$26,000. Agriculture is relatively important by the standards of most European industrialised economies and, despite its climatic and geographical conditions (which only allow a very short growing season), Finland enjoys virtual self-sufficiency in basic foodstuffs such as grain, dairy products and root crops. The largest industrial sector is engineering, where traditional 'metal bashing' industries are also relatively important by the standards of most industrialised countries. Mining is relatively small, although exportable quantities of gold are produced and diamond deposits were discovered in 1994. Industry is heavily dependent on imported components. The service sector is notable for the spectacular growth of mobile communications to which Finns are now among the world's highest per capita subscribers. A number of Finnish companies are also prominent in parts of the global telecommunications equipment market. After a sharp decline in GDP growth in 2001 from six per cent to under one per cent, caused by a collapse in exports, Finland has undergone a gradual recovery. Estimated annual growth as of 2004 was 1.9 per cent. Unemployment rates remain stubbornly high at nine per cent: efforts to reduce it now form a centrepiece of government economic policy. Through its geographical position and political neutrality, Finland has developed unique trading links with East and West. Its principal partners are now Germany, Sweden and the UK. Finland joined the EU along with Sweden and Austria in January 1995. Since then, after meeting the required fiscal and budgetary targets, Finland has joined the European Monetary Union and adopted the Euro at its inception in 2001. Finland is also a member of the Nordic Council and the Organisation for Economic Co-operation and Development.

BUSINESS ETIQUETTE: Businesspeople are expected to dress smartly. Most Finnish businesspeople speak English and/or German. Finnish is a complex language related to Hungarian and Estonian; details of available courses may be obtained from the Council for the Instruction of Finnish for Foreigners, Pohjoisranta 4 A 4, 00171 Helsinki, Finland (tel: (9) 134 171). Local tourist boards and travel agents will be able to assist in finding translation services. Punctuality is essential for business and social occasions. Calling cards are common. Best months for business visits are February to May and October to December. **Office hours:** Mon-Fri 0800-1615.

CONFERENCES/CONVENTIONS: Finland is among the world's top-20 conference destinations. There are a wide selection of meeting facilities from state-of-the-art conference centres to ice castles. Information may also be obtained from the Finnish Tourist Board, which produces a brochure entitled *Meeting Planner's Guide to Finland*.

COMMERCIAL INFORMATION

FINPRO
Finland Trade Centre, Embassy of Finland, 177-179 Hammersmith Road, London W6 8BS, UK
Tel: (020) 8600 7260.
Website: www.finpro.fi/uk

Keskuskauppakamari (Central Chamber of Commerce of Finland)
PO Box 1000, 00101 Helsinki, Finland
Tel: (9) 696 969.
Website: www.kauppakamari.fi

Finland Convention Bureau (Information on Conferences/Conventions)
Fabianinkatu 4 B 11, 00130 Helsinki, Finland
Tel: (9) 668 9540.
Website: www.finlandconventionbureau.fi

Location: Western Europe.

Time: GMT + 1 (GMT + 2 from last Sunday in March to last Sunday in October).

For information on French Overseas Departments, Overseas Territories and Overseas *Collectivités Territoriales*, consult the *French Overseas Possessions* section. See also the individual sections on *French Guiana, Guadeloupe, Martinique, New Caledonia, Réunion* and *Tahiti and her Islands*.

Credit: ©Angus Henderson

Overview

It is hard to generalise about France. As Charles de Gaulle, the war time leader of the anti-Nazi government in exile once remarked, 'how could one describe a country which has 365 kinds of cheese?' Yet there is something about this magnificent land which draws millions of francophiles back year after year for a taste of *la vie française*.

Could it be the chic boulevards of Paris, the sparkling ski slopes of the Alps, sunlit vineyards and sun-baked beaches, a dusty game of boules, or coffee and croissants in an undiscovered village? Or perhaps it is a tour of the majestic châteaux of the Loire that appeals, the glamorous jet-set lifestyle of the Mediterranean, or a relaxing picnic in Provence, where the air is fragrant with wild herbs and lavender? Consider also the delights of other lesser-known regions such as Franche-Comté, Gascony or Berry, deep in the green heart of France – regions firmly rooted to the land, whose sleepy villages offer visitors a chance to sample the true *douceur de vivre* of provincial France and the unspoilt and rugged atmosphere of the island of Corsica, described as 'a mountain in the sea'.

France's fight for the 'equality of the individual before the law' during its 1789 revolution is still engraved in the French spirit. The revolutionary motto 'Liberty, Equality, Fraternity' is included in the constitution and the French national heritage and the storming of the Bastille on 14 July is still celebrated each year with a mixure of solemn military parade and celebratory dancing and fireworks. Eager to avoid the destruction caused by the two World Wars ever again, France was a founding member of the European Union. It continues to be a driving force behind the EU's progress towards economic and political harmonisation and has been a keen proponent of EU expansion. Beyond that, France is still active in almost every other part of the world. This arises from a combination of historical reasons (its colonies and self-image as a nuclear and world power), coupled with a desire to confront a perceived Anglo-American pursuit of global hegemony.

General Information

AREA: 545,630 sq km (339,054 sq miles) (not including overseas territories).
POPULATION: 60.65 million (official estimate 2005).
POPULATION DENSITY: 111 per sq km.
CAPITAL: Paris. **Population:** 12.2 million (2.15 million in the city; 10.5 million in the suburbs) (2005).
GEOGRAPHY: France, the largest country in Europe, is bordered to the north by the English Channel (*La Manche*), the northeast by Belgium and Luxembourg, the east by Germany, Switzerland and Italy, the south by the Mediterranean (with Monaco as a coastal enclave between Nice and the Italian frontier), the southwest by Spain and Andorra, and the west by the Atlantic Ocean. The island of Corsica, southeast of Nice, is made up of two *départements*. The country offers a spectacular variety of scenery, from the mountain ranges of the Alps and Pyrénées to the attractive river valleys of the Loire, Rhône and Dordogne and the flatter countryside in Normandy and on the Atlantic coast. The country has some 2900km (1800 miles) of coastline.
GOVERNMENT: Republic since 1792. **Head of State:** President Jacques Chirac since 1995. **Head of Government:** Prime Minister Dominique de Villepin since May 2005. **Recent history:** Jacques Chirac is now in his ninth year as President after winning the most recent presidential election in 2002, which will keep him in office until 2009. This latter poll was notable for the strong performance of the neo-fascist *Front National* (FN) leader Jean-Marie le Pen, who came second in the first round of voting (although he lost the second decisively when all other parties, including the left, united to support Chirac). 2002 also saw the centre-right, operating under the umbrella banner of the *Union for a Presidential Majority*, regain control of the National Assembly, bringing to an end five years of 'co-habitation' – the situation where the presidency and the national assembly are in the hands of different parties. President Chirac, who had thrown his weight firmly behind the proposed European Union constitution, suffered a major setback in May 2005 when voters rejected it in a referendum. He acknowledged that the outcome was to some degree a reflection of voter dissatisfaction with the policies of his Government. The vote precipitated profound changes in the Government line-up, including the appointment of a new Prime Minister.
In November 2005, the accidental death of two youths in the Paris suburb of Clichy sous Bois, which has large African and Arab communities, led to violent clashes between the police and thousands of rioters in several French cities. These three weeks of violence led the Government to impose a state of emergency which was only lifted in January 2006. In early 2006, large demonstrations against the Government's proposed youth employment law, also took place in Paris and other cities throughout France.
LANGUAGE: French is the official language, but there are many regional dialects. Basque is spoken as a first language

by some people in the southwest, and Breton by some in Brittany. Many people, particularly those connected with tourism in the major areas, speak at least some English.
RELIGION: Approximately 83 per cent Roman Catholic; Protestant two per cent; Muslim five per cent; Jewish one per cent; unaffiliated nine per cent .
ELECTRICITY: 220 volts AC, 50Hz. Two-pin plugs are widely used; adaptors recommended.
SOCIAL CONVENTIONS: Shaking hands and, more familiarly, kissing both cheeks, are the usual forms of greeting. The form of personal address is simply *Monsieur* or *Madame* without a surname and it may take time to get on first-name terms. At more formal dinners, it is the most important guest or host who gives the signal to start eating. Mealtimes are often a long, leisurely experience. Casual wear is common. Social functions, some clubs, casinos and exclusive restaurants warrant more formal attire. Evening wear is normally specified where required. Topless sunbathing is tolerated on most beaches but naturism is restricted to certain beaches – local tourist offices will advise where these are. Smoking is prohibited on public transport and in cinemas and theatres. Tobacconists (*tabacs*) display a red sign in the form of a double cone.

Climate

A temperate climate in the north; northeastern areas have a more continental climate with warm summers and colder winters. Rainfall is distributed throughout the year with some snow likely in winter. The Jura Mountains have an alpine climate. Lorraine, sheltered by bordering hills, has a relatively mild climate.
Mediterranean climate in the south; mountains are cooler with heavy snow in winter.
The Atlantic influences the climate of the western coastal areas from the Loire to the Basque region, where the weather is temperate and relatively mild with rainfall throughout the year. Summers can be very hot and sunny. Inland areas are mild and the French slopes of the Pyrénées are renowned for their sunshine record. A Mediterranean climate exists on the Riviera, and in Provence and Roussillon. Weather in the French Alps is variable. Continental weather is present in Auvergne, Burgundy and the Rhône Valley. Very strong winds (such as the *Mistral*) can occur throughout the entire region.
Required clothing: European, according to season.

Communications

Telephone: Full IDD is available. Country code: 33. International calls are cheaper between Mon-Fri 1900-0800 and all day Sat-Sun.
Mobile telephone: Roaming agreements exist with most international mobile phone companies. Coverage is excellent. The use of mobile telephones is prohibited at petrol stations.
Internet: Public access is available at Internet cafes in most cities.
Post: Stamps can be purchased at post offices and *tabacs*. Post normally takes a couple of days to reach its destination within Europe. Post office hours: Mon-Fri 0900-1900, Sat 0900-1200. In smaller towns and villages, post offices may close earlier and for lunch, while in Paris the main office is open 24 hours, but only to send mail in the evenings. The main office is the PTT, 52 Rue du Louvre, Paris.
MEDIA: France enjoys a free press and has more than 100 daily newspapers. Most newspapers are in private hands and are not linked to political parties. State-run *Radio France* runs services for the domestic audience, French overseas territories and foreign audiences. France's international broadcasters have a significant audience abroad.
Press: Daily newspapers include *Le Monde, Libération, France-Soir* and *Le Figaro*. The main English-language daily is the *International Herald Tribune*. Outside the Ile-de-France, however, these newspapers are not as popular as the provincial press. International newspapers and magazines are widely available, particularly in the larger cities.
TV: *France 2, France 3, France 5* are national, public channels; *TF1* and *M6* are national, commercial channels; *Arte* is a cultural channel originally launched by French and German public channels; *La Chaine Info* is a rolling news channel; *TV5* is an international French-language channel and *Canal Plus* is a national, subscription channel. International cable and satellite channels are available.
Radio: *Radio France Internationale (RFI)* is an international broadcaster, available via shortwave and numerous FM relays worldwide; *Europe 1* is a major commercial, news and entertainment station and *RTL* is a major commercial station, with a mix of speech and music programmes.

Passport/Visa

	Passport Required?	Visa Required?	Return Ticket Required?
Full British	1	No	No
Australian	Yes	No	Yes
Canadian	Yes	No	Yes
USA	Yes	No	Yes
Other EU	1	No	Yes
Japanese	Yes	No	Yes

Note: *Regulations and requirements may be subject to change at short notice, and you are advised to contact the appropriate diplomatic or consular authority before finalising travel arrangements. Any numbers in the chart refer to the footnotes below.*

Note: France is a signatory to the 1995 **Schengen Agreement**. For further details about passport/visa regulations within the Schengen area, see the introductory section, *How to Use this Guide*.

PASSPORTS: Passport valid for at least three months beyond length of stay required by all except:
(a) **1.** EU/EEA nationals (EU+ Iceland, Liechtenstein, Norway) and Swiss nationals holding a valid national ID card.

Note: EU and EEA nationals are only required to produce evidence of their EU/EEA nationality and identity in order to be admitted to any EU/EEA Member State. This evidence can take the form of a valid national passport *or* national identity card. Either is acceptable. Possession of a return ticket, any length of validity on their document, sufficient funds for the length of their proposed visit should *not* be imposed.
(b) nationals of Andorra, Monaco and San Marino, holding a valid national ID card.

VISAS: Required by all except the following for a period not exceeding three months:
(a) nationals of countries referred to in the chart and under passport exemptions above;
(b) nationals of Argentina, Bermuda, Bolivia, Brazil, Brunei, Bulgaria, Chile, Costa Rica, Croatia, El Salvador, Guatemala, Honduras, Hong Kong (SAR; blue passport holders only), Iceland, Israel, Korea (Dem Rep), Macau, Malaysia, Mexico, New Zealand, Nicaragua, Norway, Panama, Paraguay, Romania, Singapore, Uruguay, Vatican City and Venezuela;
(c) transit passengers continuing their journey by the same or first connecting aircraft, provided holding valid onward or return documentation and not leaving the airport. The following nationals *always* require an airport transit visa when not leaving the airport, unless they are permanent residents in the UK, or Indian nationals with a visa for the UK: Afghanistan, Albania, Angola, Bangladesh, Congo (Rep), Eritrea, Ethiopia, Ghana, Guinea, Haiti, Iran, Iraq, Liberia, Libya, Nigeria, Pakistan, Sierra Leone, Somalia, Sri Lanka, Sudan, Syrian Arab Republic and holders of Palestinian refugee travel documents issued by the Egyptian, Lebanese or Syrian authorities.

Note: (a) Pupils travelling on a school trip may also be exempt from visa regulations if their names are entered on a 'List of Travellers' obtainable from the British Council (tel: (0161) 957 7755), for those resident in the UK. (b) Nationals of Bermuda, although visa-exempt when entering France, may still require visas to enter other Schengen countries. (c) Visa-exempt nationals may still be required to produce proofs of financial means of support, hotel bookings or a return ticket to country of residence, either at borders of entry or within the Schengen area.

Types of visa and cost: A uniform *Schengen* visa, is issued for *Short-stay* visits (tourist, business and students), *Airport Transit*, *Transit* and *Long-validity* (circulation) visits. A circulation visa allows the holder to freely travel within the Schengen visa area for one to three years. The visa will be given to those who can prove their frequent trips are for family or business purposes. Visa application fees must be paid at the time of application. No visa application fee can be refunded, whatever the result of the application. A *Long-Stay* visa is available for those who wish to reside (more than 90 days), retire, work or study in France, Andorra, Monaco or a *DOM/TOM* (French Overseas Territory) .

Schengen visa applications are charged at a fixed rate of €35, irrespective of the duration of stay requested (except for long-stay visas: stays over 90 days). The fee remains payable in Pounds Sterling only, approximately £22-26; Long-Stay visas are approximately £66-£70; Student fee is £35 to £40.

Note: (a) Prices change with the prevalent exchange rate, so visitors are advised to check the exact price before travelling. Payment is by cash or by credit/debit card (excluding American Express and Diners), and in Pounds Sterling only. (b) Spouses and children of EU nationals can obtain a visa free of charge on presentation of relevant documentation.

Validity: Short-stay visas are valid for a maximum of six months from date of issue for single or multiple entries of maximum 90 days in total. Transit visas are valid for single or double entries of maximum five days per entry, including the day of arrival. Visas cannot be extended; a new application must be made each time. Circulation visas are valid for one to three years from date of issue, for single or multiple entries for a maximum of 90 days over a six month period.

Application to: All persons wishing to apply must make an appointment by telephone or on the Internet before attending and submitting their documents in person at the consulate. An automated telephone appointment booking service is available; see *Passport/Visa Information*. It is also possible to arrange a meeting by post although this is much slower. Travellers visiting just one Schengen country should apply to the Consulate of that country; travellers visiting more than one Schengen country should apply to the Consulate of the country chosen as the main destination *or* the country they will enter first (if they have no main destination).

Application requirements: (a) Passport valid for at least three months longer than validity of the visa with blank pages to affix visa stamp. If British, the British Residence Permit must exceed the validity of the requested visa by more than three months. An exception will be made (one month) for those returning permanently to their country on presentation of travel tickets. (b) One completed application form. (c) Two passport-size photos. (d) Evidence of sufficient funds for stay (eg a recent bank statement less than one month old or traveller's cheques; a minimum of £40 per day spent in France is required). (e) Proof of occupation with letter from employer, accountant, school or university (less than three months old) and last three payslips. If self-employed, submit up-to-date letter from solicitor/accountant/bank manager/local Chamber of Commerce; if student, submit up-to-date letter from educational institution (less than three months old), stating course, type of studies and attendance record; if inactive and married, submit letter from spouse's employer and marriage certificate. (f) Return ticket to country of residence, and visa for next destination if required, or confirmed booking from travel agent. (g) Evidence of hotel reservations, a certificate of board and lodging to be obtained by your French host from the local town hall, means of support or proof of official invitation from host or company. (h) Evidence of medical insurance (including repatriation and covering the duration of the requested

A B C D E F G H I J K L M N O P Q R S T U V W X Y Z

France

Credit: © Nathalie Peyre

visa). (i) Fee; payable by cash or credit/debit card. If applying by post, fee must be paid by credit card or postal order only. (j) For business travellers: a letter of invitation from a French company. (k) For student trips: a letter from school stating dates of trip, address in France and name of persons responsible for student. (l) A self-addressed, pre-paid special delivery envelope for the safe return of documents. (m) Minors: Birth certificate of the child with an official translation in French or English, certified by the consular representation of the country of the applicant; passports of both parents or certified copies; minors who apply for a visa without their parents, or with one parent, must provide a letter from their parents or legal representative authorising them to reside in France. This authorisation must be certified by a lawyer or the consular representation of the country of the applicant. A copy of the parents' passport must be sent with the form.

Note: (a) Postal applications are only acceptable for certain nationals; consult the Consulate (or website: www.ambafrance-uk.org) for further information. (b) Each document must be presented with one photocopy. (c) Minors under 18 must present original full birth certificate, stating both parents' names with official translation if not in French or English, plus parents' original passports or certified copies if the parents are residing abroad. If travelling alone or with only one parent, nationals will need to submit a completed and signed application form granting parental authorisation, and appointing the person responsible for the minor's welfare. This letter must be duly authenticated by a solicitor or Commissioner of Oaths, or by a Consular Officer of the applicant's nationality. In cases of adoption/fostering, contact the Embassy for further advice. (d) For Long-Stay visas the application requirements depend on the individuals circumstances; Contact the consulate general for information (see *Passport/Visa Information*).

Working days required: From a few hours to several weeks depending on nationality and if applying by post.

Temporary residence: A Work Permit may have to be obtained in France. For full details, contact the long stay visa section of the Consulate General; see *Passport/Visa Information*.

PASSPORT/VISA INFORMATION

Embassy of the French Republic in the UK
58 Knightsbridge, London SW1X 7JT, UK
Tel: (020) 7073 1000.
Website: www.ambafrance-uk.org

French Consulate General in the UK
21 Cromwell Road, London SW7 2EN, UK
Tel: (020) 7073 1200 (consular section) or 508 940 (visa information service; calls cost £1 per minute) or (09065) 540 700 (automated telephone appointment booking) or (020) 7073 1295 (visa applications in progress; Mon-Thurs 1500-1700 only) or (09065) 266 654 (24-hour visa application form request service; calls cost £1.50 per minute).

Visa section: 6A Cromwell Place,
London SW7 2EW, UK
Opening hours: Mon-Wed 0845-1500, Thurs-Fri 0845-1200 (general enquiries); Mon-Fri 0845-1130 (visa applications).
Website: www.consulfrance-londres.org

Embassy of the French Republic in the USA
4101 Reservoir Road, NW,
Washington, DC 20007, USA
Tel: (202) 944 6195.
Website: www.ambafrance-us.org or www.consulfrance-washington.org (consular section).

Money

Single European currency (Euro): The Euro is now the official currency of 12 EU member states (including France). The first Euro coins and notes were introduced in January 2002; the French Franc was still in circulation until 17 February 2002, when it was completely replaced by the Euro. Euro (€) = 100 cents. Notes are in denominations of €500, 200, 100, 50, 20, 10 and 5. Coins are in denominations of €2 and 1, and 50, 20, 10, 5, 2 and 1 cents.

Currency exchange: Some first-class hotels are authorised to exchange foreign currency. Shops and hotels are prohibited from accepting foreign currency by law. Travellers should check with their banks for details and current rates.

Credit & debit cards: American Express, Diners Club, MasterCard, Visa and Eurocard are widely accepted. Check with your credit or debit card company for details of merchant acceptability and other services which may be available.

Traveller's cheques: Traveller's cheques are accepted nearly everywhere.

Currency restrictions: The import and export of local and foreign currency is unrestricted. Amounts over €7600 must be declared.

Banking hours: Mon-Sat 0900-1200 and 1400-1700. Some banks close Monday and some are open Saturday. Banks close early (1200) on the day before a bank holiday; in rare cases, they may also close for all or part of the day after.

Exchange rate indicators:
Rate at time of publishing
£1.00= €1.46
$1.00= €0.82

Duty Free

The following goods may be imported into France without incurring customs duty by passengers 17 years of age or older arriving from non-EU countries:
200 cigarettes or 50 cigars or 100 cigarillos or 250g of tobacco; 1l of spirits over 22 per cent or 2l of alcoholic beverage up to 22 per cent; 2l of wine; 50g of perfume and 250ml of eau de toilette; 500g of coffee or 200g of coffee extract; 100g of tea or 40g of tea extract; medication: quantities corresponding to the needs of the patient; other goods up to the value of €175 (€90 per person under 15 years of age);

Restricted items: (a) Plants and plant products. (b) Meat and meat products from Africa. (c) Pharmaceutical products (except those needed for personal use). (d) Works of art. (e) Collectors' items and antiques. (f) Gold jewellery: other than personal jewellery below 500g in weight must be declared.

Abolition of duty free goods within the EU: On 30 June 1999, the sale of duty-free alcohol and tobacco at airports and at sea was abolished in all of the original 15 EU member states. Of the 10 new member states that joined the EU on 1 May 2004, these rules already apply to Cyprus and Malta. There are transitional rules in place for visitors returning to one of the original 15 EU countries from one of the other new EU countries. But for the original 15, plus Cyprus and Malta, there are now no limits imposed on importing tobacco and alcohol products from one EU country to another (with the exceptions of Denmark, Finland and Sweden, where limits *are* imposed). Travellers should note that they may be required to prove at customs that the goods purchased are for personal use *only*.

Public Holidays

Below are listed Public Holidays for the January 2006-June 2007 period.
2006: Jan 1 New Year's Day. **Apr 17** Easter Monday. **May 1** Labour Day. **May 8** 1945 Victory Day. **May 25** Ascension. **Jun 5** Whit Monday. **Jul 14** Bastille Day. **Aug 15** Assumption. **Nov 1** All Saints' Day. **Nov 11** Remembrance Day. **Dec 25** Christmas Day.

2007: Jan 1 New Year's Day. **Apr 9** Easter Monday. **May 1** Labour Day. **May 8** 1945 Victory Day. **May 17** Ascension. **May 28** Whit Monday.
Note: In France, the months of July and August are traditionally when the French take their holidays. For this reason, the less touristic parts of France are quiet during these months, while coastal resorts, especially in the south, are very crowded.

Health

	Special Precautions?	Certificate Required?
Yellow Fever	No	1
Cholera	No	No
Typhoid & Polio	No	N/A
Malaria	No	N/A

Note: *Regulations and requirements may be subject to change at short notice, and you are advised to contact your doctor well in advance of your intended date of departure. Any numbers in the chart refer to the footnotes below.*

1: A yellow fever certificate is required for travellers coming from South American and African countries.
Other risks: Visitors to forested areas should consider vaccination for *tick-borne encephalitis*.
Rabies is present. For those at high risk, vaccination before arrival should be considered. If you are bitten, seek medical advice without delay. For more information, consult the *Health* appendix.

Health care:
European Economic Area (EEA) and Switzerland:
If you or any of your dependants are suddenly taken ill or have an accident during a visit to an EEA country or Switzerland, free or reduced-cost necessary treatment is available – in most cases on production of a valid European Health Insurance Card (EHIC). Each country has different rules about state medical provision. In some, treatment is free. In many countries you will have to pay part or all of the cost, and then claim a full or partial refund. The EHIC gives access to state-provided medical treatment only and the scheme gives no entitlement to medical repatriation costs, nor does it cover ongoing illnesses of a non-urgent nature, so comprehensive travel insurance is advised. Note that the EHIC replaces the Form E111, which will no longer be valid after 31 December 2005.
Doctors, dentists and prescriptions: Travellers should make sure the doctor or dentist they consult is *conventionné* - ie they work within the French health system. After treatment, obtain a signed statement of the treatment given (a *feuille de soins*) as you cannot claim a refund without it. You will be charged for the treatment you receive, as well as for any prescribed medicines, and the amount(s) should be shown on the *feuille de soins*. Around 75 per cent of standard doctors' and dentists' fees are refunded, and between 35 and 65 per cent of the cost of most prescribed medicines. The cost of common remedies and items such as bandages are refunded at the lower rate. The cost of medicines marked with a /\ vignette or NR is not recoverable.
Hospital treatment: Travellers must pay for out-patient treatment and then claim a partial refund from the local Sickness Insurance Office (*Caisse Primaire d'Assurance-Maladie or CPAM*). If you are treated as an in-patient in an approved hospital and show your European Health Insurance Card (EHIC), the office will pay 75 per cent or more of the cost direct to the hospital. You pay the balance. You must also pay a fixed daily hospital charge (*forfait journalier*). The 25 per cent balance and the *forfait journalier* are non-refundable.
Local Sickness Insurance Offices handle reimbursements. Travellers should send their application for a refund (the *feuille de soins* and any prescriptions) to the nearest Sickness Insurance Office while still in France. The refund will be sent to their home address later, but it may be subject to a bank charge. Before sending the money order, the French authorities will send an itemised statement of the amount to be refunded. This refund process normally takes around two months. When you are obtaining prescribed medicines, the pharmacist will hand you back your prescription and you should attach it to the *feuille de soins* in order to claim a refund. Medicine containers also carry detachable labels (*vignettes*), showing the name and price of the contents. Stick these in the appropriate place on the *feuille de soins*, and sign and date the form at the end. There are a wide network of pharmacies in most towns. Hours of business are usually the same as for ordinary stores. The standard of medical facilities and practitioners in France is very high but so are the fees, and health insurance is recommended. More information can be obtained from the Centre de Liaisons Européennes et Internationales de Sécurité Sociale (CLEISS), 11 rue de la Tour des Dames, 75436, Paris Cedex 09, France (Tel: (1) 4526 3341).

Travel - International

AIR:

The national airline is *Air France (AF)* (website: www.airfrance.com). Many airlines operate to France, including an increasing number of low-cost airlines from the UK including Easyjet (www.easyjet.com) and Ryanair (www.ryanair.com).

Approximate flight times: From Paris to *London* is one hour five minutes; from Nice and Marseille is two hours. From Paris to *Los Angeles* is 15 hours five minutes; to *New York* is eight hours; to *Singapore* is 15 hours five minutes; and to *Sydney* is 25 hours five minutes.

Main airports: *Paris-Charles de Gaulle (CDG)*, also known as *Roissy-Charles de Gaulle*, (website: www.adp.fr) is 23km (14 miles) northeast of the city (travel time - 40 minutes). *To/from the airport:* Coaches to the city run at least every 20 minutes. Taxis are readily available and journeys to the centre cost around €38. An airport limousine service can also be hired for approximately €90. *Roissybus* services operate from the airport to Place de l'Opéra between 0545-2300 every 15 minutes. Fare is approximately €8 and takes approximately 60 minutes. *Air France* coaches run from Étoile via Porte Maillot, from Montparnasse via Gare de Lyon and from Orly Airport to Roissy-Charles de Gaulle. Services run every 12 to 20 minutes and take 40 to 50 minutes. Fares are approximately €11. The airport is also easily accessible by train on the RER B line or SNCF with connecting ADP shuttle bus. A new €145 million inter-terminal train service will be launched in the autumn of 2006 called CDGVAL. The airport claims the train will link passengers with all the terminals within eight minutes rather then the usual 25 minutes. The train will run 24 hours a day, seven days a week, with a train every four minutes.

Paris-Orly (ORY) (website: www.adp.fr) is 14km (9 miles) south of the city. *To/from the airport:* Coaches and buses run to the city every 12 minutes (travel time - 25 minutes) from outside Orly Ouest. Taxis are available. RER B and C line trains run every 15 minutes via Saint-Michel (travel time - 30 minutes).

Bordeaux (BOD) (Merignac) (website: www.bordeaux.aeroport.fr) is 12km (8 miles) west of the city. *To/from the airport*: There are coaches, buses and taxis to the city.

Lyon (LYS) (Lyon-Saint-Exupéry) (website: www.lyon.aeroport.fr) is 25km (15 miles) east of the city. *To/from the airport:* Coaches or taxis are available to the city.

Marseille (MRS) (Marseille-Marignane) (website: www.marseille-provence.aeroport.fr) is 30km (19 miles) northwest of the city. *To/from the airport:* A coach service departs to the city and taxis are available.

Nice (NCE) (Nice-Côte d'Azur) (website: www.nice.aeroport.fr) is 6km (4 miles) west of the city. *To/from the airport:* Buses depart every 20 minutes. Taxis to the city are available.

Toulouse (TLS) (Blagnac) (website: www.toulouse.aeroport.fr) is 10km (6 miles) northwest of the city. *To/from the airport:* Buses to the city depart every 20 minutes. Taxis and trams are available to the city.

Facilities: The airports listed above are all of a high international standard and include banks/bureaux de change, duty free shops, restaurants, bars and car hire.

For information about other airports, contact Union des Chambres de Commerce et Etablissements Gestionnaires d'Aéroports (UCCEGA) (website: www.aeroport.fr).

Departure tax: None.

SEA:

Numerous services (scheduled passenger crossings, leisure boating and cruises) are available to the French islands, to European and other international destinations.

Main ports: Atlantic: *La Rochelle* (website: www.portla rochelle.com): leisure boating.

North Sea: *Boulogne* (website: www.portboulogne.com): leisure boating and cross channel services; *Calais* (website: www.calais-port.com): cross-channel services; *Le Havre* (website: www.havre-port.net): scheduled services and cruise lines to national and international destinations.

Mediterranean: *Marseille* (www.marseille-port.fr): cruises and scheduled services to Corsica, Sardinia, Algeria and Tunisia; *Nice*: leisure boating and ferries to Corsica (website: http://www.ccinice-cote-azur.com/port_nice.html).

For information on other ports, contact the French Transport and Sea Ministry (website: www.mer.equipement.gouv.fr)

RAIL:

International trains run from the channel ports and Paris to destinations throughout Europe. For up-to-date routes and timetables, contact *French Railways (SNCF)* (tel: (08) 2588 8088; website: www.sncf.com) *or* in the UK, *Rail Europe* (tel: (08705) 848 848; website: www.raileurope.co.uk). **Eurostar:** *Eurostar* is a service provided by the railways of Belgium, the UK and France, operating direct high-speed trains from London (*Waterloo International*) to Paris (*Gare du Nord*) and to

Credit: © Annie Launois

Brussels (*Midi/Zuid*). It takes two hours 40 minutes from London to Paris (via Lille) and two hours 20 minutes to Brussels. For further information and reservations, contact *Eurostar* (tel: (0870) 600 0792 (travel agents) or (08705) 186 186 (public; within the UK) or +44 (1233) 617 575 (public; outside the UK); a £5 booking fee applies to all telephone bookings; website: www.eurostar.com); or *Rail Europe* (tel: (08705) 848 848; website: www.raileurope.co.uk).

Rail passes: The *Inter-Rail* pass offers unlimited second-class train travel in up to 29 European countries (includes Morocco and Turkey) split into eight zones (A-H). Three different tickets are available: a ticket covering one zone (two to six countries, 16 days' validity), a ticket covering two zones (six to 10 countries, 22 days' validity) and an All Zone Pass (29 countries, one month's validity). Ferry services between Italy and Greece are included. Passengers must be resident in Europe for at least six months before the pass is used. Travel is not allowed in the passenger's country of residence. Travellers under 26 years receive a reduction of about 30 per cent. Children's tickets are reduced by about 50 per cent. Supplements are required for some high-speed services, seat reservations and *couchettes*. Discounts are offered on *Eurostar* and some ferry routes. Available from *Inter Rail* (website: www.interrailnet.com).

The *Eurailpass* offers unlimited first-class train travel in 17 European countries. Tickets are valid for 15 days, 21 days, one month, two months or three months. *The Eurailpass Saver* ticket offers discounts for two or more people travelling together. The *Eurailpass Youth* ticket is available to those aged under 26 and offers unlimited second-class train travel. The *Eurailpass Flexi* allows either 10 or 15 travel days within a two-month period. The *Eurail Selectpass* is valid in three, four or five bordering countries and allows five, six, eight or 10 travel days (or 15 for five countries) in a two-month period. The *Eurail Regional Pass* allows four to 10 travel days in a two-month period in one of nine regions (usually two or more countries). Children receive a 50 per cent reduction. The passes cannot be sold to residents of Europe, Turkey, Morocco, Algeria, Tunisia or the Russian Federation. Available from *The Eurail Group* (website: www.eurail.com).

ROAD:

There are numerous and excellent road links with all neighbouring countries. *Eurolines* (52 Grosvenor Gardens, London SW1W 0AU; tel: (08705) 143 219; website: www.eurolines.com) and *National Express* (Ensign Court, 4 Vicarage Road, Edgbaston, Birmingham B15 3ES; tel: 08705 808 080; website: www.nationalexpress.com) run regular coach services from the UK to France. **Passes:** Travellers can either choose Mini-Pass breaks or book a 15-, 30- or 60-day pass. The six Mini-Passes give travellers the freedom to visit three cities, with prices starting from £55. Travellers can stay as long as they like in each city.

For **documentation** and **traffic regulations**, see the *Travel - Internal* section.

The Channel Tunnel: *Eurotunnel* runs shuttle trains for cars, bicycles, motorcycles, coaches, minibuses, caravans, campervans and other vehicles over 1.85m (6.07ft) between Folkestone in Kent, with direct road access from the M20, and Calais, with links to the A16/A26 motorway (Exit 13). All road vehicles are carried through the tunnel in shuttle trains running between the two terminals. Terminals and shuttles are well-equipped for disabled passengers. Passenger Terminal buildings contain a variety of shops, restaurants, bureaux de change and other amenities. The journey takes about 35 minutes from platform to platform and around one hour from motorway to motorway. There are up to four passenger shuttles per hour at peak times, 24 hours per day and services run every day of the year. Motorists pass through customs and immigration before they board, with no further checks on arrival. Fares are charged according to length of stay and time of year and whether or not you have a reservation. The price applies to the car, regardless of the number of passengers or size of the car. Promotional deals are frequently available, especially outside the peak holiday seasons. Tickets may be purchased in advance from travel agents, or from *Eurotunnel Customer Services* in France or the UK with a credit card. For further information, brochures and reservations, contact *Eurotunnel Customer Services UK*, Customer Relations Department, Saint Martin's Plain, Cheriton, Folkestone, Kent CT19 4QD (tel: (08705) 353 535; website: www.eurotunnel.com). For further information about departure times of shuttles at the French terminal, contact Eurotunnel *Customer Information* in Coquelles (tel: France +33 (3) 2100 6543).

Travel - Internal

AIR:

Air France flies between Paris (from both Orly and Charles de Gaulle airports) and around 45 cities and towns. It also connects regional airports. For information, contact *Air France* (tel: (08) 2082 0820 (omit the 0 when dialling from abroad) or (0845) 359 1000 (within the UK only); website: www.airfrance.com). Details of independent airlines may be obtained from the French Government Tourist Office (see *Top Things To Do*).

RAIL:

French Railways (SNCF) operate a nationwide network with 34,200km (21,250 miles) of line, over 12,000km (7500 miles) of which has been electrified. The *TGV (Train à grande vitesse)* runs from Paris to Brittany and southwest France at 300kph (186mph) and to Lyon and the southeast at 270kph (168mph).

The *SNCF* is divided into five systems (East, North, West, Southeast and Southwest). The transport in and around Paris is the responsibility of a separate body, the *RATP*, at 54 quai de la Rapée, 75599 Paris (tel: (08) 9268 7714; website: www.ratp.fr). This organisation provides a fully integrated bus, rail and *métro* network for the capital.

Rail tickets: There are various kinds of tickets (including Family and Young Person's Tickets) offering reductions which can usually be bought in France. In general, the fares charged will depend on what day of the week and what time of the day one is travelling; timetables giving further details are available from *SNCF* offices. It is essential to validate (*composter*) tickets bought in France by using the orange automatic date-stamping machine at the platform entrance. There is a range of special tickets on offer to foreign visitors; they usually have to be bought before entering France and some are only available in North America; others are unique to Australia and New Zealand. There are also special European *Rail and Drive* packages. For more information, contact your local French Government Tourist Office (see *Top Things To Do*).

Credit: ©Angus Henderson

Motorail (car sleeper): Services are operated from Boulogne, Calais, Dieppe and Paris to all main holiday areas in both summer and winter. Motorail information and booking is available from *Rail Europe* (tel: (0870) 830 2000; website: www.raileurope.co.uk); see *Travel - International* section.

ROAD:

Traffic drives on the right. France has over 9000km (5600 miles) of motorways (*autoroutes*), some of which are free whilst others are toll-roads (*autoroutes à péage*). Prices vary depending on the route, and caravans are extra. There are more than 28,500km (17,700 miles) of national roads (*routes nationales*). Motorways bear the prefix 'A' and national roads 'N'. Minor roads (marked in yellow on the Michelin road maps) are maintained by the *départements* rather than by the Government and are classed as 'D' roads. It is a good idea to avoid travelling any distance by road on the last few days of July/first few days of August and the last few days of August/first few days of September as during this time, the bulk of the holiday travel takes place and the roads can be jammed for miles. A sign bearing the words *Sans Plomb* on a petrol pump shows that it dispenses unleaded petrol. The *Bison Futé* map provides practical information and is available from the French Government Tourist Office. **Bus:** Information on services may be obtained from local tourist offices. Local services outside the towns and cities are generally adequate. **Car hire:** Available from international companies. A list of other agencies can be obtained at local tourist offices (*Syndicats d'Initiative* or *Offices de Tourisme*). Fly-drive arrangements are available through all major airlines. *French Railways (SNCF)* also offer reduced train/car hire rates. **Caravans:** These may be imported for stays of up to six months. There are special requirements for cars towing caravans which must be observed; eg cars towing caravans are prohibited from driving within the boundaries of the *périphérique* (the Paris ring road). Contact the French Government Tourist Office for details. **Regulations:** The minimum age to drive a car in France is 18 and 15 for a motorcycle under 125cc. The minimum age for hiring a car in France ranges from 21 to 25 depending on the company; some companies may also include additional charges for drivers under 25. The maximum age limit is generally 70. Speed limits are 50kph (31mph) in built-up areas, 90kph (56mph) outside built-up areas, 110kph (68mph) on dual carriageways separated by a central reservation, and 130kph (81mph) on motorways. Visitors who have held a driving licence for less than two years may *not* travel faster than 80kph (56mph) on normal roads, 100kph (62mph) on dual carriageways and 110kph (68mph) on motorways. The police fine motorists on the spot for driving offences such as speeding. Radar traps are frequent; drivers caught travelling at more then 25km/h above the limit can have their license confiscated on the spot. Random breath tests for drinking and driving are common. Seat belts must be worn by all front- and rear-seat passengers. Under-10s may not travel in the front seat. *Priorité à droite*: particularly in built-up areas, the driver must give way to anyone coming out of a side-turning on the right. The *priorité* rule does not apply at most roundabouts - the driver should give way to cars which are already on the roundabout with the signs *vous n'avez pas la priorité* or *cédez le passage*; but watch for signs and exercise great caution. All roads of any significance outside built-up areas have right of way, known as *Passage Protégé*, and will normally be marked by signs consisting either of an 'X' on a triangular background with the words 'Passage Protégé' underneath, or a broad arrow, or a yellow diamond. A red warning triangle must be carried for use in the event of a breakdown. All headlamp beams must be adjusted for rightside driving by use of beam deflectors or (on some cars) by tilting the headlamp bulbholder. For further details on driving in France, a brochure called The *Traveller in France* is available from French Government Tourist Offices and must be ordered by telephone (see *Top Things To Do*). It contains a section on motoring. **Documentation:** A national driving licence is acceptable. An international sign, distinguishing your country of origin (eg GB sticker or plate), should be positioned clearly on the vehicle. EU nationals taking their own cars to France are *strongly advised* to obtain a Green Card. Without it, insurance cover is limited to the minimum legal cover in France; the Green Card tops this up to the level of cover provided by the car owner's domestic policy. The car's registration document must also be carried. UK registered vehicles displaying Euro-plates (circle of 12 stars above the national identifier on a blue background) no longer need a GB sticker when driving in EU countries.

URBAN:

Urban public transport is excellent. There are comprehensive bus systems in all the larger towns. There are also tramways, trolleybuses and an underground in Marseille; trolleybuses, an underground and a funicular in Lyon; and a tramway and automated driverless trains in Lille. There are tramway services in St Etienne and Nantes and trolleybuses in Grenoble, Limoges and Nancy. The systems are easy to use, with pre-purchase tickets and passes. Good publicity material and maps are usually available.

Paris: The RATP (*Régie Autonome des Transports Parisiens*) controls the underground (*métro*), rail (RER) and bus services in and around Paris. The public transport network is split into several different fare zones and a single ticket will allow travel on any of the systems within that zone (although interchange is only permitted on the métro and RER, and not on buses). Other useful transport links provided by the RATP include: *Orlybus* and *Roissybus* (special airport buses), *Orlyval* (rail service linking RER stations of Antony and Orly airport) and *Montmartre funicular* (special railway connecting the foot of Montmartre to the top, near the Sacré-Coeur church). For the *Orlybus* and *Roissybus* travellers need a special ticket which is on sale on buses and airport terminals. **Métro:** This was built during the Paris Exhibition in 1900. Its dense network of 14 lines in the central area makes the *métro* the ideal way to get about in Paris. Trains run from approximately 0530-0115. **Rail:** *RER* (fast suburban services) operate five main lines connecting most areas of the capital. There is also an extensive network of conventional suburban services run by French Railways (SNCF), with fare structure and ticketing integrated with the other modes of public transport. **Bus:** A comprehensive network operates within the city. Services include *PC* buses that run around the outskirts of Paris; *Noctambus* services which run through the night; *Balabus* services which run between La Défense and the Gare du Lyon, navigating around La Seine and major tourist attractions; *Montmartrobus* services that run from Pigalle to Mairie du XVIII Jules Joffrin via Montmartre; sightseeing tourist buses, *l'Opentour* (tel: (33) 0142 1200; website: www.paris-opentour.com) and *Paris Trip* (tel: (01) 4266 5656; website: www.paris-trip.com). *Eurolines* offers a long-distance bus service covering multiple destinations to 87 French cities and towns. Buses are comfortable and fitted with ABS, air conditioning, televisions and lavatories. **Special tickets:** *Disneyland Passeport* offers a combined ticket price of RER travel and entrance fee to the theme park at a reduced rate. *Paris Visite Pass* offers superb value for money with a choice of unlimited travel on the entire RATP network (métro, RER, bus etc) for a period of one to five days. A variety of discounts are available with the pass such as reduced prices at over 70 museums, monuments, cinemas, restaurants and shops in Paris and Ile de France. Paris transport tickets can be bought in the UK from *Allo France* (tel: (08702) 405 903; website: www.allofrance.co.uk). All other tickets can be purchased from the RATP Tourist Office at 54 quai de la Rapée, 75599 Paris (tel: (1) 4468 2020 *or* (08) 9268 7714 (within France only); website: www.ratp.fr) or from 50 of the *métro* stations, all mainline railway stations and certain banks. Children under four years of age travel free on buses and underground, while children between four and 11 years travel half price. **Taxi:** Day and night rates are shown inside each cab. There are extra charges on journeys to and from racecourses, stations and airports and for luggage. **Private car:** Parking is now prohibited in many areas of the centre. Otherwise there are parking meters or parking time is restricted to usually 15 minutes in waiting bays, although the driver must remain in the vehicle (*zone bleue*). Car parks charging a fee are plentiful all over Paris and on the outskirts. Limousines are available from various companies. Fines are given for illegal parking.

Note: Travellers must always carry a valid identification document with them as they can be checked at any time; when walking down a street or driving.

EDITOR'S CHOICE: NAVIGABLE WATERWAYS

There are almost 9000km (5600 miles) of navigable waterways in France, and all of these present excellent opportunities for holidays. The main canal areas are the north (north and northeast of Paris) where most of the navigable rivers are connected with canals; the Seine (from Auxerre to Le Havre, but sharing space with commercial traffic); the east, where the Rhine and Moselle and their tributaries are connected by canals; in Burgundy, where the Saône and many old and picturesque canals crisscross the region; the Rhône (a pilot is recommended below Avignon); the Midi (including the Canal du Midi, connecting the Atlantic with the Mediterranean); and Brittany and the Loire on the rivers Vilaine, Loire, Mayenne and Sarthe, and the connecting canals.

Each of these waterways offers a magnificent variety of scenery, a means of visiting many historic towns, villages and sites and an opportunity to see rural France at a very leisurely pace.

Cruising boats may be chartered with or without crews, ranging in size from the smallest cabin cruiser up to converted commercial barges (*péniches*), which can accommodate up to 24 people and require a crew of eight. Hotel boats, large converted barges with accommodation and restaurant, are also available in some areas, with a wide choice of price and comfort. For further information, contact the national or regional tourist board.

State-run car ferries known as '*BACs*' connect the larger islands on the Atlantic coast with the mainland; they also sail regularly across the mouth of the Gironde. The island of Corsica is served by ferries operated by the *Société Nationale Maritime Corse-Mediterranée (SNCM)*, BP 90, 13472 Marseille Cedex 2 (tel: (0825) 888 088; website: www.sncm.fr). Services run from Marseille, Toulon and Nice to Ajaccio, Propriano, Porto Vecchio and Bastia on the island.

Travel Advice

Most visits to France are trouble-free but you should be aware of the global risk of indiscriminate international terrorist attacks, which could be against civilian targets, including places frequented by foreigners.

This advice is based on information provided by the Foreign and Commonwealth Office in the UK. It is correct at time of publishing. As the situation can change rapidly, visitors are advised to contact the following organisations for the latest travel advice:

British Foreign and Commonwealth Office
Tel: (0845) 850 2829.
Website: www.fco.gov.uk

US Department of State
Website: http://travel.state.gov/travel

Credit: ©Angus Henderson

Accommodation

HOTELS:

Room and all meals, ie full-board or pension terms, are usually offered for a stay of three days or longer. Half-board or *demi-pension* (room, breakfast and one meal) terms are usually available outside the peak holiday period. Hotels charge around 30 per cent extra for a third bed in a double room. For children under 12, many chains will provide another bed in the room of the parents for free. *Logis de France* are small- or medium-sized, inexpensive and often family-run hotels which provide good, clean, basic and comfortable accommodation with a restaurant attached. **Hotels in Paris:** Hotel bookings can be made in person through tourist offices at stations or at the Paris Tourist Office. **Guides:** Regional lists of hotels are available, as well as the *Logis de France* guide and various chain/association guides from the French Government Tourist Office (see *Top Things To Do*) and bookshops. The Tourist Office publishes guides to hotels in Paris and the Ile-de-France, available free of charge. **Grading:** *Hôtels de Tourisme* are officially graded into five categories according to the quality of the accommodation, which are fixed by government regulation and checked by the *Préfecture of the Départements*: **4-star:** Deluxe. **3-star:** First class. **2-star:** Standard. **1-star:** Budget. *Logis de France* are subject to a specific code usually above basic requirements for their grade and are inspected regularly to ensure that they conform to the standards laid down.

SELF CATERING:

Gîtes de France are holiday homes (often old farmhouses) in the country, all of which conform to standards regulated by the non-profitmaking National Federation. *Villas, Houses and Apartments Rental*: Villas and houses can be rented on the spot. Local *Syndicats d'Initiative* can supply a complete list of addresses of local rental agencies. Tourists staying in France for over one month may prefer to live in an apartment, rather than in a hotel.

CAMPING/CARAVANNING:

There are 7000 campsites throughout France. A few have tents and caravans for hire. Prices vary according to location, season and facilities. All graded campsites will provide water, toilet and washing facilities. Touring caravans may be imported for stays of up to six consecutive months. There are 100 British companies offering camping holidays in France. The French Government Tourist Office has a full list of tour operators who run all types of tours, including camping and special interest holidays.

YOUTH HOSTELS:

There are hundreds of these in France, offering very simple accommodation at very low prices. There are hostels in all major towns. Stays are usually limited to three or four nights, or a week in Paris.

Hostels are open to all members of the National Youth Hostel Association upon presentation of a membership card. Lists are available from national youth hostel organisations. **Note:** Visitors are usually asked to pay a tourism tax (variable or flat-rate) which is fixed by the local authority and values from €0.15 to €1.07 per person per day, according to the quality and standard of the accommodation. Where the tourism tax is a variable percentage, children under four years are exempt and children under 10 are charged half the rate. This tax is collected by the owner of the accommodation and will be included in the hotel bill or rent.

Top Things To See

As the world's most popular tourist destination, France manages to be all things to all people. Any list of French attractions is, by virtue of the country's rich and eclectic nature, bound to be incomplete.

- Fall under the romantic charm of **Paris** famous for its **Eiffel Tower** (website: www.tour-eiffel.fr), the **Notre Dame Cathedral** on **Ile de la Cité** (website: www.cathedraledeparis.com/), the **Panthéon**, the **Arc de Triomphe** (website: www.monum.fr) leading to **Champs Elysées**, famous for its cafés, commercial art galleries and sumptuous shops, the **Sacré Coeur** in the heart of **Montmartre** and the **Louvres Pyramid**, the most controversial addition to the **Palais du Louvre**. For a more modern feel, head for the business quarter of **La Défense** and enjoy wonderful views from its **Grande Arche**.
- Go back in time at the **Château de Versailles** and enjoy magnificent fireworks in the summer months.
- Visit one of the numerous **Loire valley châteaux** (castles) including **Blois, Chambord, Chenonceaux, Azay le Rideau** and **Chinon.**
- Mind the tide when visiting **Mont St Michel** in Brittany (website: www.mont-saint-michel.net).
- Enjoy the rugged and unspoilt atmosphere of **Corsica**, a French island, made up of two French departments, with the picturesque towns of **Bastia** and **Ajaccio**, famous for its Napoleonic memorabilia.
- Discover the recently built **Millau bridge**, over the **Tarn Gorges**, designed by British Architect, Norman Foster (website: www.viaducdemillau.com).
- The 2000-year-old **Pont de Gard** is one of humanity's greatest architectural accomplishments and merits a special trip.
- Head south and discover magnificent Roman (and some Gallic) ruins in the Languedoc-Roussillon region; the **Maison Carré**, **Diana's Temple** and the **Roman Arena** in **Nimes** (the Rome of the Gauls) are among the finest examples of Greco-Roman architecture to be found today.
- See traces of the Greek and Roman domination in **Provence** where many monuments from that period are still scattered across the countryside. They include walled hill towns, triumphal arches, theatres, colosseums, arenas, bridges and aqueducts. Christianity brought the **Palace of the Popes** in Avignon, many churches and hundreds of roadside shrines or 'oratories' which have given the name *oradour* to many communities along the Rhône. Near Avignon is **Orange** with its stunning **Roman ampitheatre** and Roman ruins.
- In **Marseille**, France's most important commercial port on the Mediterranean, there are many sites of interest – the old port, the hilltop church of **Notre-Dame-de-la-Garde**, several museums, **Le Corbusier's Unité d'Habitation**, the **Hospice de la Vieille Charité** and the **Château d'If**, one of the most notorious of France's historic island fortresses.
- Visit France's numerous **cathedrals**, including **Rheims** (where Clovis, the first French King was baptised), **Chartres** and **Tours**.

Top Things To Do

- Among Paris' 80 museums and 200 art galleries, visit the **Orsay Museum**, located in a beautifully restored railway station, the **Palais du Louvre**, the **Hôtel des Invalides** (containing Napoleon's tomb), the **Georges Pompidou Centre of Modern Art**, also know as **Beaubourg**, or **Musée Rodin**.
- Relax in the **Jardins du Luxembourg** in Paris, close to the **Latin Quarter** (Boulevards St Michel and St Germain), which is the focus of most student activity (the **Sorbonne University** is here).
- Discover the future at the **City of Science and Technology** in la Villette or at the **Futuroscope** in Poitiers.
- Visit Mickey Mouse at the **EuroDisney** theme park in Marne la Vallée (website: www.disneylandparis.com)
- Enjoy a wide range of **watersports** activities at France's 3000km of coastline (ranging from the English Channel, the Atlantic coast in the north and west to the sunny shores of the French Riviera, also known as Côte d'Azur). Famous resorts include: **St Enogat** and **St Jacut** on the **Emerald coast** in Northern Brittanny, **Etables** in the bay of **St Brieuc, Perros-Guirec, Trégastel** and **Trébeurden** on the coast from **Paimpol, La Grande Motte, Port Leucate** and **Port Bacarès** in Languedoc-Roussillon, **Cannes, Nice, St Tropez, Golfe Juan, Juan Les Pins, Antibes** and **Menton**, also famous for its lemon festival, on Côte d'Azur.
- Enjoy the jetsetting lifestyle of the **Côte d'Azur**, stroll on the **Promenade des Anglais in Nice**, famous for its **Flower Carnival** in January, mingle with celebrities at the **Cannes Film Festival** held in January-February or visit the perfumeries of **Grasse**.
- Sail from/to **La Rochelle**, a popular sailing port in the Charente Maritime region. Close by, the islands of **Oléron** and **Ré** are connected to the mailand by bridges.
- Enjoy a wide range of **winter sports** in the **French Alps** or the **Pyrenees**.
- Be pampered at a spa in **Biarritz, Contréxeville** or **Vittel**.
- Go on a pilgrimage to **Lourdes**, in the south west, famous since the visions of Bernadette Soubirous in the mid-19th century.
- See a bull fight at the **Arènes d'Arles** in the south west.
- Hit the jackpot at the **casino of Monaco** or the **casino of Deauville**, also famous for its golf course and race track.

Credit: ©Angus Henderson

- Have a go at a traditional **game of boules** (also called pétanque), played in public squares, especially in the south of France. The game requires as much social skill as manual dexterity and visitors wishing to join in may find it easier if they speak French.
- Enjoy a **wine tour** or take part in **harvesting the grapes**: There are 10 principal wine regions including Alsace, Burgundy, Champagne, Rhône Valley, each with its own identity based on grape varieties and *terroir* (soil). Highlights on the wine calendar include the annual appearance of *Beaujolais Nouveau* (released fresh from the cellars on the third Thursday of November); the *Vendanges* (grape harvest) festivals in Burgundy during autumn; and champagne tasting in Champagne (with many producers in Rheims and Epernay offering free samples). In various regions, the most famous wine routes (*routes du vin*), as well as special sales and auctions, are signposted. Wine tours are frequently combined with **cheese tasting**. In **Roquefort**, you can visit the windy caves that store the famous ewe's milk cheese. For further information, see Food & Drink in the Social Profile section. An illustrated map with details of cheeses, wines and regional dishes is available from the French National Tourist Office (website: www.franceguide.com).
- Follow the **Tour de France** cycling race in the summer (website: http://france.br.com/tour-de-france-official-site.html); attend the **French Open** at **Roland Garros** near Paris, one of the four Grand Slam tennis tournaments; go to the **24-hour motor race at Le Mans** or the **Monaco Grand Prix**; place your bets on a horse race at the **Prix de l'Arc de Triomphe**, which takes place in Longchamp close to the Bois de Boulogne, held on the first Sunday in October each year.
- West of the Rhône, discover the colourful and mysterious nature of the volcanic highlands of the **Massif Central**, historically known as **Auvergne**. The **National Park** here offers magnificent **walking** country – a land of lakes, rivers, forests, mountains, plains and extinct volcanoes (the Cantal crater may once have been 30km/20 miles wide). There are 10 spa resorts within its boundaries, as well as many lakes, rivers and forests.
- On the far side of the Rhône is the wild, marshy area known as the **Camargue**, long used for the breeding of beef cattle and horses, for the evaporation of sea water to make salt and, more recently, for growing rice. Nature lovers will be delighted to see vast flocks of waterbirds nesting here in a **national bird reserve**, among them pink flamingos and snow-white egrets.

Entertainment

FOOD & DRINK: With the exception of China, France has a more varied and developed cuisine than any other country. The simple, delicious cooking for which France is famous is found in the old-fashioned bistro and restaurant. There are two distinct styles of eating in France. One is, of course, 'gastronomy' (*haute cuisine*), widely known and honoured as a cult with rituals, rules and taboos. It is rarely practised in daily life, partly because of the cost and the time which must be devoted to it. The other is family-style cooking, often just as delicious as its celebrated counterpart.

Things to know: Almost all restaurants offer two types of meal: *à la carte* (extensive choice for each course and more expensive) and *le menu* (a set meal at a fixed price with dishes selected from the full *à la carte* menu). At simple restaurants, the same cutlery will be used for all courses. The bill (*l'addition*) will not be presented until it is asked for, even if clients sit and talk for half an hour after they have finished eating. Many restaurants close for a month during the summer, and one day a week throughout the rest of the year. It is always wise to check that a restaurant is open, particularly on Sunday. Generally speaking, mealtimes in France are strictly observed. Lunch is served from 1200 to 1330, dinner usually from 2000-2130, but the larger the city, the later the dining hour.

National specialities:
- *Ratatouille niçoise* (stew of courgettes, tomatoes and aubergines, braised with garlic in olive oil).
- In the north of France (Nord/Pas de Calais and Picardy), fish and shellfish are the star features in menus – oysters, *moules* (mussels), *coques* (cockles) and *crevettes* (shrimps) are extremely popular.
- In Picardy, duck pâtés and *ficelle picarde* (ham and mushroom pancake) are popular.
- Alsace and Lorraine are the lands of *choucroute* (sauerkraut) and *kugelhof* (a special cake), *quiche lorraine* and *tarte flambée* (onion tart).
- Spicy and distinctive sauces are the hallmark of Breton food, and shellfish is a speciality of the region, particularly *homard à l'armoricaine* (lobster with cream sauce). Brittany is also famous for producing some of the finest butter in the world.
- Lyon, the main city of the Rhône Valley, is the heartland of French cuisine, though the food is often more rich than elaborate. A speciality of this area is *quenelles de brochet* (pounded pike formed into sausage shapes and usually served with a rich crayfish sauce).
- Aquitaine cuisine (in the south-west of France) is based on goosefat. A reference to 'Périgord' will indicate a dish containing truffles.
- In the Pyrénées, especially around Toulouse, visitors will find salmon and *cassoulet*, a hearty dish with beans and preserved meat.
- Desserts include: *soufflé grand-marnier; oeufs à la neige* (meringues floating on custard); *mille feuilles* (layers of flaky pastry and custard cream); *Paris-Brest* (a large puff-pastry with hazelnut cream); *ganache* (chocolate cream biscuit); and fruit tarts and flans.

National drinks:
- Wine is by far the most popular alcoholic drink in France, and the choice will vary according to region. Cheap wine (*vin ordinaire*) can either be very palatable or undrinkable, but there is no certain way of establishing which this is likely to be before drinking.

Wines are classified into AC (*Appellation Contrôlée*), VDQS (*Vin Délimité de Qualité Supérieure*), *Vin de Pays* and *Vin de Table*. There are several wine-producing regions in the country; some of the more notable are Bordeaux, Burgundy, Loire, Rhône and Champagne. The popular wine *Muscadet* comes from the extreme southern point of Britanny. Brittanny is also famous for its cider. The waiter will usually be glad to advise an appropriate choice. In expensive restaurants, this will be handled by a *sommelier* or wine steward. If in doubt, try the house wine; this will usually be less expensive.
- There is also a huge variety of *apéritifs* available. Typically French apéritifs are *Pastis, Ricard* or *Pernod*.
- The region of Nord Pas de Calais and Picardy does not produce wine, but brews beer and cider. Alsace is said to brew the best beer in France but fruity white wines, such as Riesling, Straminer and Sylvaner, and fine fruit liqueurs, such as Kirsch and *Framboise (raspberry)*, are also produced in this area.
- Coffee is always served after the meal, and will always be black, in small cups, unless a *café au lait* (or *café crème*) is requested.
- Brandies such as Armagnac and Cognac and liqueurs such as *Chartreuse* and *Genepi* (an unusual liqueur made from an aromatic plant) are available. Many of these liqueurs, such as *eau de vie* and Calvados (apple brandy) are very strong and should be treated with respect, particularly after a few glasses of wine. A good rule of thumb is to look around and see what the locals are drinking. Spirit measures are usually doubles unless a baby is specifically asked for.

Legal drinking age: The legal age for drinking alcohol in a bar/café is 18. Minors are allowed to go into bars if accompanied by an adult but they will not be served alcohol. Hours of opening depend on the proprietor but, generally, bars in major towns and resorts are open throughout the day; some may still be open at 0200. Smaller towns tend to shut earlier. There are also all-night bars and cafes in larger towns.

Tipping: A 12 to 15 per cent service charge is normally added to the bill in hotels, restaurants and bars, but it is customary to leave small change with the payment; more if the service has been exceptional. Other services such as washroom attendants, beauticians, hairdressers and cinema ushers expect tips. Taxi drivers expect 10 to 15 per cent of the meter fare.

NIGHTLIFE: In major cities such as Paris, Lyon or Marseille, there are lively nightclubs that sometimes charge no entry fee, although drinks are likely to be more expensive. Alternatively, the entrance price sometimes includes a *consommation* of one drink. Nightclubs are everywhere and in even the remotest corners of France. Their style and music vary widely from one place to another. Nightclubs have a fixed closing time of 0500. As an alternative to a nightclub, there are many late-night bars and cafes. In Paris and the regions, theatres offer a wide variety of shows from great classics to light comedy, from one-man shows to cabaret. Tourist offices publish an annual and monthly diary of events available free of charge. Several guides are also available which give information about entertainments and sightseeing in the capital. Guides for events in Paris are sold at newspaper kiosks (*Pariscope, L'official des Spectacles* and *Zurban*). They list all cinema programmes, museums, exhibitions and all other types of shows. Kiosks on the forecourt of

Credit: © Annie Launois

the Montparnasse railway station and at Place de la Madeleine offer same day theatre tickets at reduced rates. Travellers can also buy tickets for concerts from FNAC and Virgin sales outlets or from the venue themselves. In the provinces, the French generally spend the night eating and drinking, although in the more popular tourist areas, there will be discos and dances. All weekend festivals in summer in the rural areas are a good form of evening entertainment. There are over 130 public casinos in the country.

SHOPPING: Special purchases include lace, crystal glass, cheeses, coffee and, of course, wines, spirits and liqueurs. Arques, the home of Crystal D'Arques, is situated between St Omer and Calais. Lille, the main town of French Flanders, is known for its textiles, particularly fine lace. Most towns have fruit and vegetable markets on Saturday. Hypermarkets, enormous supermarkets which sell everything from foodstuffs and clothes to hi-fi equipment and furniture, are widespread in France. They tend to be situated just outside of town and all have parking facilities. For bargain hunters, bric-a-brac or *brocante* is found in a number of flea markets (*marché aux puces*) on the outskirts of town, most notably at the Porte de Clignancourt, in Paris. There are several antique centres (**Louvre des Antiquaires**, **Village Suisse**, etc) where genuine antique furniture and other objects are on sale. Amongst the larger department stores in Paris are the **Printemps** and the **Galeries Lafayette** near the Opéra, the **Bazar Hôtel de Ville (BHV)** and the **Samaritaine** on the Right Bank; and the **Bon Marché** on the Left Bank. Paris has many varied markets, including the flower market on the Ile de la Cité and bird, organic and food markets in every quarter. Another Parisian speciality is book markets. Travellers will find booksellers' stalls along the banks of the Seine, around the Saint Michel quarte, crammed with all kinds of books plus comics and postcards. In the regions, the town centre often has a number of clothes shops which are just as good as those in Paris. Some have good second hand shops.

Shopping hours: Department stores are open Mon-Sat 0900-1830. Some shops close 1200-1430. Food shops open 0700-1830/1930. Some food shops (particularly bakers) open Sunday mornings, in which case they will probably close Monday. Many shops close all day or Monday afternoon. Hypermarkets are normally open until 2100 or 2200.

Business

- **GDP:** US$1.7 trillion.
- **Main exports:** Machinery, equipment, aircraft, plastics, chemicals, iron, steel and beverages.
- **Main imports:** Vehicles, crude oil, aircraft, plastics and chemicals.
- **Main trade partners:** Germany, Belgium, Italy, Spain, UK, USA and The Netherlands.

ECONOMY: France has the fourth-largest economy in the world, after the USA, Japan and Germany, and has an annual per capita income of US$23,000. It has a wide industrial and commercial base, covering everything from agriculture to heavy and light industrial concerns, advanced technology and a burgeoning service sector. France is also Western Europe's leading agricultural nation with over half of its land area devoted to farming. Wheat is the most important crop; maize, sugar beet and barley are also produced in large quantities. The country is self-sufficient in these (which are produced in sufficient surplus for major exports) and the majority of other common crops. The livestock industry is also expanding rapidly. France is famously one of the world's leading wine producers. Despite the widespread belief in some quarters (not least the UK) that French agriculture is inefficient, the sector has regularly turned in good profit margins and a sound export performance. French companies are prominent in many industries, particularly steel, motor vehicles, aircraft, mechanical and electrical engineering, textiles, chemicals and food processing. In advanced industrial sectors, France has one of the world's largest nuclear power industries, which meets nearly three-quarters of the country's energy requirements (coal mining, once important, is in terminal decline), and is a world leader in computing and telecommunications. The service sector is dominated by tourism, which has long been a major foreign currency earner, although financial services have grown rapidly since the early 1990s.
Recent economic policy has been characterised by a gradual relinquishing of state holdings in 'strategic' industries and a steady reduction in government spending. Economic growth was 2.3 per cent in 2003, and is still below one per cent. France suffers from a relatively high unemployment rate of 10 per cent, which

Credit: © Annie Launois

is climbing again after several years of decline. France was a founder member of the European Community and has benefited greatly from its participation. It was also a founder member of the European Monetary Union and adopted the Euro upon its inception.

BUSINESS ETIQUETTE: Businesspeople should wear conservative clothes. Prior appointments are expected and the use of calling cards is usual. While a knowledge of French is a distinct advantage in business dealings, it is considered impolite to start a conversation in French and then have to revert to English. Business meetings tend to be formal and business decisions are taken only after lengthy discussion, with many facts and figures to back up sales presentations. Business entertaining is usually in restaurants. Avoid the holiday period of mid-July to mid-September for business visits. **Office hours:** Generally Mon-Fri 0900-1200, 1400-1800.

CONFERENCES/CONVENTIONS: Paris is the world's leading conference city, with the total amount of seating available (over 100,000 seats) exceeding that of any rival city. Also in demand are the Riviera towns of Nice and Cannes (the Acropolis Centre in Nice being the largest single venue in Europe); other centres are Lyon, Strasbourg and Marseille. The Business Travel Club (CFTAR) is a government-sponsored association of cities, departments, hotels, convention centres and other organisations interested in providing meeting facilities and incentives; it has over 80 members. Enquiries should be made through the French Government Tourist Office, which has a special department for business travel in several cities; these include London, Frankfurt, Düsseldorf, Milan, Madrid and Chicago.

COMMERCIAL INFORMATION

Chambre de Commerce et d'Industrie de Paris
27 Avenue de Friedland 75382 Paris, Cedex 08, France
Tel: (1) 5565 5565.
Website: www.ccip.fr

Centre de Renseignements des Douanes
84 rue d'Hauteville, 75498 Paris, France
Tel: (0825) 308 263.
Website: www.douane.gouv.fr

Assemblée des Chambres Françaises de Commerce et d'Industrie
45 Avenue d'Iena, 75116 Paris, Cedex 16, France
Tel: (1) 4069 3700.
Website: www.acfci.cci.fr

Maison de la France in the UK, Conference and Incentive Department
178 Piccadilly, London W1J 9AL, UK
Tel: (020) 7399 3521.
Website: www.franceguide.com

French Guiana

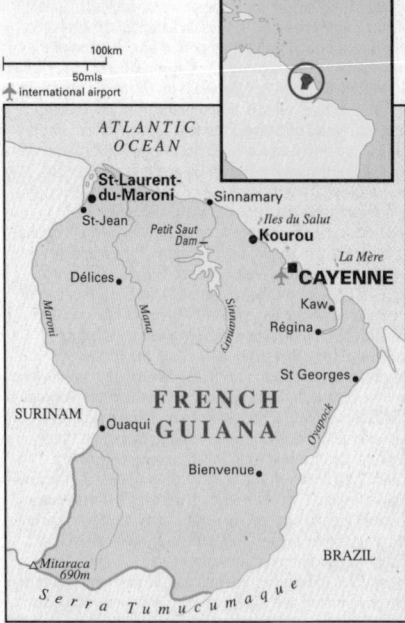

100km
50mls
✈ international airport

ATLANTIC OCEAN

St-Laurent-du-Maroni
St-Jean
Sinnamary
Iles du Salut
Kourou
Petit Saut Dam
La Mère
CAYENNE
Délices
Maroni
Mana
Sinnamary
Kaw
Régina
St Georges
SURINAM
Ouaqui
FRENCH GUIANA
Oyapock
Bienvenue
△ *Mitaraca 690m*
BRAZIL
Serra Tumucumaque

Location: South America, northeast coast.

Time: GMT - 3.

French Guiana is an Overseas Department of the Republic of France, and is represented abroad by French Embassies – see *France* section.

Overview

French Guiana was discovered by the Spanish in 1496, who established a few settlements in 1503 and 1504. The French first moved in a century later. Numerous changes in control followed over the next 200 years, alternating between France, Britain, the Netherlands and Portugal, until the territory was finally confirmed as French in 1817. The colony enjoyed a brief period of prosperity in the 1850s when gold was discovered, but afterwards went into a decline from which it has never fully recovered.
French Guiana was finally given French Overseas Department status in 1946, under which the territory effectively became an integral part of the French nation. However, the territory was largely neglected by Paris and continued to deteriorate until civil unrest broke out in the 1970s. After a security crackdown, the central government promised various improvements. These failed to materialise until the Mitterrand presidency, under which a series of reforms were introduced in 1982-83. Some decentralisation also took place: local affairs are now dealt with by the Regional Council.
French Guiana has the benefit of an ideal geographical situation, set between the Caribbean and the Amazon. Little wonder, then, that its environment is so rich. Visitors may have the privilege of observing a great many protected species in carefully preserved areas.
French Guiana is also home to a colourful blend of different cultural backgrounds. A native land, a land of exploration and a land of enslavement, the extraordinary history of French Guiana has left its traces in every sector of today's society and can still be sensed in a number of almost mythical places: Iles du Salut, which include the infamous Devil's Island where political prisoners were held, Mount Favard, the Saint-Laurent du Maroni transportation camp and the Iracoubo Church.
French Guiana is also a land of social progress and a symbol of modernity as is demonstrated in Kourou, the main French Space Centre.

From encounters with authentic cultures, to watching the birth of the leatherback turtles, from life as a convict in a penal colony to travelling by canoe down majestic rivers, from panning for gold to watching toucans fly or following the vapour trail of Ariane, French Guiana has a lot to offer.

General Information

AREA: 83,534 sq km (32,253 sq miles).

POPULATION: 178,000 (2005 estimate).

POPULATION DENSITY: 2.1 per sq km.

CAPITAL: Cayenne. **Population:** 50,594 (1999).

GEOGRAPHY: French Guiana is situated on the northeast coast of South America and is bordered by Brazil to the south and the east and by Surinam to the west. The southern Serra Tumucumaque Mountains are part of the eastern frontier, whilst the rest is formed by the River Oyapock. Surinam is to the west along the rivers Maroni-Itani and to the north is the Atlantic coastline. Along the coast runs a belt of flat marshy land behind which the land rises to higher slopes and plains or savannah. The interior is comprised of equatorial jungle. Off the rugged coast lie the Iles du Salut and Devil's Island. Cayenne, the capital and chief port, is on the island of the same name at the mouth of the Cayenne River.

GOVERNMENT: French Guiana is an Overseas Department of France and, as such, is an integral part of the French Republic. **Head of State:** President Jacques Chirac since 1995, represented locally by Prefect Ange Mancini since 2002. **Recent history:** French Guiana has held French Overseas Department Status since 1946. Since a series of reforms introduced under the Mitterand government in 1982-83, local affairs have been dealt with by the Regional Council. Antoine Karam, the President of the Regional Council since March 1992, is French Guiana's single representative in the French Senate. Karam is a member of the *Parti Socialiste Guyanais* (PSG), which has long been the strongest political party and is allied to its French namesake. The other major parties are the *Forces Démocratiques Guyanaises* (FDG), allied with the Walwaries, and the centre-right *Union pour un Mouvement Populaire* (UMP), incorporating the old *Rassemblement pour la République* (RPR). The PSG is the largest party on the Regional Council following the most recent election in March 2004 in which it gained 17 of the 31 seats. (The FDG-Walwaries and UMP won seven seats each.). The domestic political agenda has been generally dominated by repeated complaints over the territory's relatively poor social and economic conditions compared to those in France. The alternatives to being an integral part of the French state are self-government and independence. However, enthusiasm for either is lacking and the small independence movement has made little headway in recent years. Paris has also made it clear that it will not countenance any change in French Guiana's status for the time being.

LANGUAGE: The official language is French, though most of the population speak a Creole *patois*. English is also widely spoken.

RELIGION: Roman Catholic majority, although there are other Christian churches.

ELECTRICITY: 220/127 volts AC, 50Hz.

SOCIAL CONVENTIONS: Conservative casual wear is suitable almost everywhere. On beaches, modest beachwear is preferred.

Climate

Tropical. Dry season is August to December; rainy season is December and January and April to July. Hot all year round, with cooler nights. Average temperature is 27°C (85°F).

Required clothing: Tropical lightweights and rainwear.

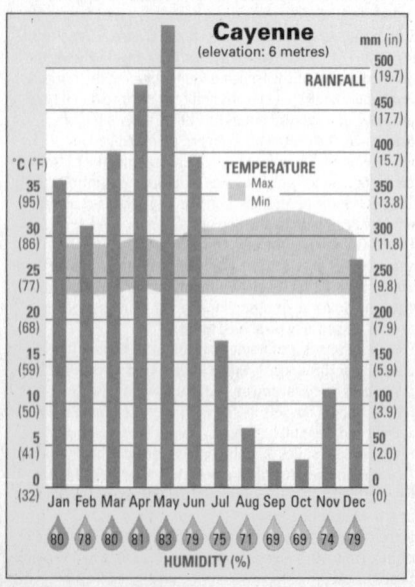

Cayenne (elevation: 6 metres)

Communications

Telephone: Country code: 594. IDD available.

Mobile telephone: Roaming agreements exist with most international mobile phone operators. Coverage is limited to main towns. Handsets can be hired locally.

Internet: There are Internet cafes in Cayenne, Kourou, Saint Laurent. Libraries also provide access.

Post: Postal services are reliable in Cayenne (where the central post office is located on route Baduel); post takes around seven days to reach western Europe. Post office hours in Cayenne: Mon-Fri 0700-1800.

MEDIA: Press: The daily newspapers include *France-Guyane* and *La Presse de Guyane*. There are no English-language newspapers.

TV: The public channel *Télé Guyane* is operated by Réseau France Outre-mer. Other channels include the commercial *Antenne Créole Guyane* and pay-TV *Canal+ Guyane*.

Radio: *Radio Guyane* is operated by Réseau France Outre-mer. *Radio Caraïbes International* is a commercial station.

Passport/Visa

	Passport Required?	Visa Required?	Return Ticket Required?
Full British	Yes	No	Yes
Australian	Yes	No	Yes
Canadian	Yes	No/2	Yes
USA	Yes	No/2/3	Yes
Other EU	Yes/1	No/2	Yes
Japanese	Yes	No/2	Yes

Note: *Regulations and requirements may be subject to change at short notice, and you are advised to contact the appropriate diplomatic or consular authority before finalising travel arrangements. Any numbers in the chart refer to the footnotes below.*

PASSPORTS: Passport valid for at least three months beyond applicant's last day of stay required by all except the following:

1. nationals of EU, EEA, Monaco and Switzerland who are holders of national identity cards.

VISAS: Required by all except the following:

(a) nationals of countries referred to in the chart above for stays of up to three months;

(b) nationals of Andorra, Argentina, Bermuda, Brunei, Chile, Costa Rica, Croatia, El Salvador, Ecuador, Guatemala, Honduras, Iceland, Korea (Rep), Liechtenstein, Malaysia, Mexico, Monaco, New Zealand, Nicaragua, Norway, Panama, Paraguay, San Marino, Singapore, Switzerland, Uruguay and Vatican City for stays of up to three months;

(c) Holders of French residence permits.

Note: (a) Nationals of the EU and EEA, and Monaco do not need a a long-stay visa (trips exceeding three months). (b) **2.** Nationals of Canada, Cyprus, Japan, Korea (Rep), Malaysia, Malta, Mexico, Singapore, USA and Venezuela should apply for a visa if they are to receive a salary, even if their trip is a short stay. (c) **3.** US nationals need a visa if they are crew members, or journalists on assignments, or students enrolled at schools and universities in any of the French Overseas Departments.

Types of visa and cost: All visas, for stays or up to 90 days, regardless of the number of entries permitted, cost €35. For visas valid for more than 90 days the cost is €99. Visas must be paid for in local currency. In most circumstances, no fee applies to students, recipients of government fellowships and citizens of the EU and their family members.

Validity: *Short-stay* (up to 30 days). *Short-stay* (31 to 90 days and single- or multiple-entry): valid for six months, one year *or* two to five years from date of issue. *Long-stay* (90 days plus). *Transit:* valid for single- or multiple-entries of maximum five days per entry, including the day of arrival. *Transit Visa:* Allows transit through the airport.

Application to: French Consulate General (for personal visas), or Consular section at Embassy (for diplomatic or service visas); see *Passport/Visa Information* for France. All applications must be made in person.

Application requirements: (a) Valid passport with blank page to affix the visa. Minors travelling alone must submit notarised parental authorisation, signed by both parents, plus one copy. (b) Up to two completed application forms. (c) One passport-size photo on each form. (d) Fee, to be paid in cash or by credit card. (e) Evidence of sufficient funds for stay (two last bank statements, plus copy, or other proof of funds equivalent to US$100 for each day of trip). (f) Letter from employer, or proof of stay in country of residence. (g) Proof of address. (h) Medical insurance. (i) Return ticket and travel documents for remaining journey. (j) Proof of accommodation during stay. (k) Detailed itinerary, including reservations and round-trip airline tickets (only required when visa is issued), plus one copy. (l) Proof of employment (eg last payslip or letter from employer). (m) Proof of valid health/travel insurance with worldwide coverage, plus copy. *Business:* (a)-(m) and, (n) Business invitation guaranteeing

payment of travel expenses, plus one copy.

Working days required: One day to three weeks, depending on nationality.

Temporary residence: If intending to work or stay for longer than 90 days, nationals should contact the long stay visa section of the Consulate General or Embassy (see *Passport/Visa Information*).

PASSPORT/VISA INFORMATION

Embassy of the French Republic in the UK
58 Knightsbridge, London SW1X 7JT, UK
Tel: (020) 7073 1000.
Website: www.ambafrance-uk.org

French Consulate General in the UK
21 Cromwell Road, London SW7 2EN, UK
Tel: (020) 7073 1200 (consular section) *or* 508 940 (visa information service; calls cost £1 per minute) *or* (09065) 540 700 (automated telephone appointment booking) *or* (020) 7073 1295 (visa applications in progress; Mon-Thurs 1500-1700 only) *or* (09065) 266 654 (24-hour visa application form request service; calls cost £1.50 per minute).

Visa section: 6A Cromwell Place, London SW7 2EW, UK
Opening hours: Mon-Wed 0845-1500, Thurs-Fri 0845-1200 (general enquiries); Mon-Fri 0845-1130 (visa applications).
Website: www.tourisme-guyane.com *or* www.consulfrance-londres.org

Embassy of the French Republic in the USA
4101 Reservoir Road, NW,
Washington, DC 20007, USA
Tel: (202) 944 6195.
Website: www.ambafrance-us.org *or* www.consulfrance-washington.org (consular section).

Money

Currency: Since 1 January 1999, the Euro, which was introduced in January 2002, has been the official currency for the French Overseas Departments (*Départements d'Outre-Mer*) French Guiana, Guadeloupe, Martinique and Réunion. For further details, exchange rates and currency restrictions, see *France* section.

Currency exchange: There are bureaux de change at Rochambeau airport and in Cayenne. They will exchange money every day except Saturday.

Credit & debit cards: American Express, *Carte Bleue*, Diners Club, MasterCard and Visa are accepted. Check with your credit or debit card company for details of merchant acceptability and other services which may be available. ATMs can be found in Cayenne, Ile de Cayenne, Kourou and Saint Laurent du Maroni.

Traveller's cheques: These are accepted in a few places in Cayenne and Kourou. To avoid additional exchange rate charges, travellers are advised to take traveller's cheques in Euros, US Dollars or Pounds Sterling.

Currency restrictions: For details of currency restrictions, see *France* section.

Banking hours: Mon-Fri 0730-1200, 1430-1730.

Duty Free

See *France* section.

Public Holidays

Below are listed Public holidays for the January 2006-June 2007 period:

2006: Jan 1 New Year's Day. **Feb 28** Mardi Gras. **Mar 1** Ash Wednesday. **Mar 23** Mi Carême (mid Lent). **Apr 17** Easter Monday. **May 1** Labour Day. **May 8** VE Day. **May 25** Ascension. **Jun 5** Whit Monday. **Jun 10** Abolition of Slavery. **Jul 14** Bastille Day. **Aug 15** Assumption. **Oct 15** Cayenne Festival. **Nov 1** All Saints' Day. **Nov 2** All Souls' Day. **Nov 11** Remembrance Day. **Dec 25** Christmas Day.
2007: Jan 1 New Year's Day. **Feb 20** Mardi Gras. **Feb 21** Ash Wednesday. **Mar 15** Mi Carême (mid Lent). **Apr 9** Easter Monday. **May 1** Labour Day. **May 8** VE Day. **May 17** Ascension. **May 28** Whit Monday. **Jun 10** Abolition of Slavery.

Health

	Special Precautions?	Certificate Required?
Yellow Fever	Yes	1
Cholera	No	No
Typhoid & Polio	2	N/A
Malaria	3	N/A

Note: *Regulations and requirements may be subject to change at short notice, and you are advised to contact your doctor well in advance of your intended date of departure. Any numbers in the chart refer to the footnotes below.*

1: A yellow fever vaccination certificate is required from travellers over one year of age coming from all countries, except for transit passengers remaining in the airport.
2: Immunisation against typhoid and polio is sometimes advised.
3: Malaria risk, predominantly in the malignant *falciparum* form, is high throughout the year in the nine municipalities of French Guiana bordering Brazil (Oyapock river valley) and Surinam (Maroni river valley). In the other 13 municipalities, the transmission risk is low or negligible. High level of multi-resistant *falciparum* reported in areas influenced by Brazilian migration. Atovaquane/proguanil, doxycycline, mefloquine or primaquine (in special cases) are recommended.
Food & drink: Mains water is normally heavily chlorinated and, whilst relatively safe, may cause mild abdominal upsets. Bottled water is available and is advised for the first few weeks of the stay. Drinking water outside main cities and towns is likely to be contaminated and sterilisation is considered essential. Milk is unpasteurised and should be boiled. Powdered or tinned milk is available and is advised, but make sure that it is reconstituted with pure water. Avoid dairy products which are likely to have been made from unboiled milk. Local meat, poultry, seafood, fruit and vegetables are generally considered safe to eat.
Other risks: *Hepatitis A* is common. *Hepatitis B* and *D* are highly endemic. *American trypanosomiasis* (*Chagas disease*) and *cutaneous* and *mucocutaneous leishmaniasis* occcur. *Brucellosis* is common.
There is a slight risk of *rabies* if in contact with wild animals. For those at high risk, vaccination before arrival should be considered. If you are bitten, seek medical advice without delay. Mosquitos in the area can transmit *dengue fever*. For more information, consult the *Health* appendix.
Health care: There are medical facilities in Cayenne, Kourou and St Laurent du Maroni but very few elsewhere. Medical insurance is advisable.

Travel - International

AIR:
The national airline is *Air Guyane (GG)* (website: www.airguyane.com) but it only offers internal services. *Air France* (website: www.airfrance.com) operates six flights a week to Cayenne from Paris. Other airlines serving the country include *Air Canada* (website: www.aircanada.com) and *Surinam Airways*.
Approximate flight times: From Cayenne to *London* (via Paris) is 11 hours 30 minutes.
Main airports: *Cayenne (CAY)* (Rochambeau) is 15km (9 miles) southwest of the city. *To/from the airport*: Taxis are available to the city or hotel (travel time – 25 minutes). *Facilities*: Air conditioning, bars, banks/bureaux de change, a newsagents and car hire.
Departure tax: None.
SEA AND RIVER:
Main ports: *Cayenne*, *Kourou* and *St Laurent du Maroni*. There are ferries across the Maroni River from St Laurent du Moroni to Albina (Surinam), from where there is a road to Paramaribo. Services also operate from St Georges to Oiapoque (Brazil) across the Oyapock River.
ROAD:
A road runs along the coast from Guyana through Surinam to French Guiana. There is an all-weather road connecting Cayenne with St Laurent, but it may be impassable in the rainy season. It is possible to drive from Cayenne to Paramaribo (Surinam), but it is safer to leave the car at St Laurent and take public transport (minibus) to Paramaribo. The Cayenne district is served by a good road system.

Travel - Internal

AIR:
Air Guyane serves the interior of the country from Cayenne, including Maripasoula, St Georges de l'Oyapock and Saül et Régina. **Helicopters** are available from *Héli Inter Guyane* (tel: 356 231) and *Héli Union Guyane* at Cayenne airport.
SEA/RIVER:
There are numerous coastal and river transport services. Contact local authorities for information.
ROAD:
There is a road along the coast from Cayenne to Kourou and beyond. Traffic drives on the right. **Bus:** The city of Cayenne and its suburbs have a regular network of regular buses run by *SMTC* (tel: 302 100). There is a daily service from Cayenne to St Laurent du Maroni. Faster minibuses follow the same route. Bus services also operate along the coast. There are no bus services on Sundays. **Taxi:** Available in Cayenne. Pick-up is from the Laussat Canal and the airport. **Car hire:** Available at the airport or in Cayenne, Kourou and St Laurent. International rental agencies include *Hertz* (website: www.hertz.com) and *Europcar* (website: www.europcar.com). **Documentation:** An International Driving Permit is recommended, although it is not legally required. An International Driving Permit will be required at car rental agencies from holders of driving licences with characters that are not readable.

Travel Advice

Most visits to French Guiana are trouble-free but you should be aware of the global risk of indiscriminate international terrorist attacks, which could be against civilian targets, including places frequented by foreigners. Please note that travellers must produce a yellow fever certificate on arrival.
This advice is based on information provided by the Foreign and Commonwealth Office in the UK. It is correct at time of publishing. As the situation can change rapidly, visitors are advised to contact the following organisations for the latest travel advice:

British Foreign and Commonwealth Office
Tel: (0845) 850 2829.
Website: www.fco.gov.uk

US Department of State
Website: http://travel.state.gov/travel

Accommodation

HOTELS:
Since French Guiana was chosen as a site for the European Space Agency, a number of well-appointed air-conditioned hotels have been built. International chains are found mainly along the coast. Prices are the highest on the continent. Cayenne, Kourou, Sinnamary and St Laurent du Maroni all offer excellent accommodation. Most have a ranking with a level of service up to three stars. For further details, contact the *Comité du Tourisme de la Guyane* (see *Top Things To Do*).
GITES AND SELF-CATERING:
Gîtes de France (website: www.gites-de-france.fr) promotes environmentally-friendly tourism and has forest-located self-catering properties. *Gîtes d'Amazonie* are inspired by traditional Amerindian homes, located in a well-preserved natural environment, usually near a river. Gîtes which display the *Gîtes Panda Tropicales* sign have signed a charter of good environmental practice with the *WWF*.
APARTMENTS:
Clévacances network offer apartments for rental with or without bed and breakfast. These are mainly in Cayenne, Kourou and occasionally in more rural areas. The number of keys indicates the level of comfort. For further information contact the *Comité du Tourisme de la Guyane* (see *Top Things To Do*).
CAMPING/CARAVANNING:
Carbets d'Hôtes (a jungle version of a shack), provide bed (in a hammock) and breakfast in a natural setting. The host will introduce lodgers to local specialities. It is also possible to hire a camping-car. For further information contact the *Comité du Tourisme de la Guyane* (see *Top Things To Do*).

Top Things To See

- In **Cayenne**, French Guiana's atmospheric capital and chief port, points of interest include the Jesuit-built residence of the Prefect in the **Place de Grenoble**, the **Canal Laussat** (built in 1777) and the **Botanical Gardens**. In the centre of town, the **Musée Départemental Franconie** and the **Musée des Cultures Guyanaises** feature good exhibits on indigenous peoples and the notorious penal settlements on Devil's Island. Lively cafes and market stalls are to be found in the **Place des Palmistes**.
- **Kourou,** the main **French Space Centre,** is something of a European enclave. Ultra-modern buildings now dominate the city and there are several restaurants and two good hotels. A tour of the **Space Centre** is a must.
- **Iles du Salut** include the infamous **Devil's Island** where political prisoners were held. Do not miss the **Iracoubo Church** painted entirely by hand by the famous convict Huguet. There is a hotel (an ex-mess hall for the prison warders) on **Ile Royale**.
- Visit the Amerindian villages in **Haut-Maroni** and **Haut-Oyapoc.** Visits are restricted and a permission must be obtained from the *Préfecture* in Cayenne before arrival in the country.

Top Things To Do

- **Swim, water-ski** or **sail** at **Ile de Cayenne**, **Kourou** and **Montjoly**, all patrolled by life guards.
- **Montjoly**, Cayenne's best beach, is a short drive away from the city. Watch **leatherback turtles** lay their eggs here from April to July.
- **Sea fishing** is popular and can be undertaken from rocks, as well as from boats. Fishing for sharks and other big fish can be done in the open sea. **Devil's Island** is popular with swimmers and fishermen alike. **Freshwater fishing** and **fly fishing** are also popular.
- Organise a trip in a **dugout canoe.** Trips range from an hour and a half to full day adventures and take place throughout the country including the **Kourou, Iracabo, Counamana** and the lower **Sinnamary**. The rivers are a mixture of calm water and rapids such as those at **Hermina.**
- Organise a picnic at the **Fourgassé Falls,** located about an hour from Kourou.
- Discover nature and wildlife at the **Mouragues Nature Reserve**, which stretches from Roura to Régina and is renowned for its diverse scenery and flora. The **Kaw Swamps**, near Rora, are host to many species of birds, such as the Toco toucan and the flamingo.
- **Trek** into the interior; jungle shelters are available for overnight stops. A special permit is necessary from the *Préfecture* in Cayenne.
- **Microlighting** can be organised, and **mountain bikes** can be hired in Cayenne, Saül, Montsinery-Tonnegrade, St Laurent and St Georges, for trips through the primary forest.
- Enjoy yourself at the **carnival**. 'King Carnival' starts after Epiphany and goes on until Ash Wednesday. Every Sunday for over two months, carnival groups delight the thronging crowds with their multicolored costumes and the frenetic rhythm of their music. On Mardi Gras, the towns are almost literally painted red for the parade of the red devils. Ash Wednesday sees the crowd dressed in black and white and ready to witness the final moments of the life of King Carnival, soon to be burnt at the stake amid a seemingly incessant hullabaloo.

TOURIST INFORMATION

Comité du Tourisme de la Guyane (Guiana Tourism Committee)
Street address: 12 rue Lallouette, 97338 Cayenne Cédex, French Guiana
Postal address: BP 801, Cayenne, French Guiana
Tel: (594) 296 500.
Website: www.tourisme-guyane.com

Comité du Tourisme de la Guyane (Guiana Tourism Committee) in France
1 rue Clapeyron, 75008 Paris, France
Tel: (331) 4294 1516.
Website: www.tourisme-guyane.com

Entertainment

FOOD & DRINK: There is a fairly good selection of restaurants and hotel dining rooms offering a number of different cuisines. The majority of them are in Cayenne, although French, Continental, Vietnamese, Chinese, Creole and Indonesian restaurants can be found elsewhere.
National specialities:
- A local speciality is the *bouillon d'aoura*, a dish of smoked fish, crab, prawns, vegetables and chicken, served with aoura, the fruit of Savana trees.
- The forest also provides a rich supply of game such as, collard peccary, paca and tapir. These are usually eaten as a fricassee and are accompanied by rice and kidney beans.

National drinks:
- *Ti' Punch*, a traditional aperitif of lime, sugar cane syrup and rum, accompanied by cod rolls and black pudding.

NIGHTLIFE: There are nightclubs in Cayenne, Kourou and St Laurent du Maroni. Cayenne also has one cinema featuring French-language films. Cinemas can also be found in Kourou and St Laurent.
SHOPPING: Within the past few years, a great many new boutiques have opened offering a wide range of merchandise. Good buys are basketry, embroidery, hammocks, pottery, wood sculpture and gold jewellery.
Shopping hours: Mon-Sat 0800-1300, 1600-1830, Sun 0900-1230. **Tipping:** In hotels and restaurants, a 10 per cent tip is usual.

Business

- **GDP:** US$1.5 billion.
- **Main imports:** Food (grains and processed meats), machinery and transport equipment, fuel and chemicals.
- **Main exports:** Shrimp, timber, gold, rum, rosewood essence and clothing.
- **Main trade partners:** France, USA, Trinidad and Tobago, Italy and Switzerland.

ECONOMY: French Guiana's economy is heavily dependent on that of France. Thanks to the French social security system and subsidies from Paris, the population enjoys one of the highest standards of living on the South American continent. Besides the French Space Centre at Kourou, fishing and forestry are the most important economic activities, occupying most of the workforce. Vegetables and rice are the principal crops, most of which are consumed domestically. Exploitation of French Guiana's mineral resources, which, in addition to timber from the country's extensive forests, include gold, bauxite and kaolin, is steadily growing. Gold production continues to flourish, with actual production levels and sales suspected to be far higher than official estimates. Exploration expanded in the mid-1990s, following the construction of a major new road allowing access to the interior. Development of the service sector, particularly tourism (and the promising field of ecotourism), had previously been hampered by poor infrastructure. The country's other notable economic asset, acquired by virtue of its position close to the equator, is the European Space Agency's satellite launch facility at Kourou. The French Space Centre accounts for a quarter of GDP. French Guiana runs a huge trade deficit, with exports less than 10 per cent of imports. In common with most French Overseas Territories, French Guiana has a high unemployment level, of about 22 per cent.

BUSINESS ETIQUETTE: Lightweight suits are required. English will be understood by practically everyone, although a working knowledge of French may be of assistance. The best time to visit is August to November. **Office hours:** Mon-Fri 0730-1230, 1500-1800. Hours are shorter on Wednesdays and Fridays.

COMMERCIAL INFORMATION
Chambre de Commerce et d'Industrie de la Guyane
BP 49, Hôtel Consulaire, place de l'Esplanade, 97321 Cayenne, French Guiana
Tel: 299 600.
Website: www.guyane.cci.f

French Overseas Possessions

Overview

Scattered throughout the world are several French *Départements d'Outre-Mer* (DOM, overseas departments), *Territoires d'Outre-Mer* (TOM, overseas territories), *Collectivités Territoriales* and one overseas country (New Caledonia). The following DOM-TOM all have their own sections in the *World Travel Guide*: **French Guiana, Guadeloupe, Martinique, New Caledonia, Réunion** and **Tahiti**. Basic information is given here on the others. Further information on all of the French Overseas Possessions can be obtained from French embassies; see *France* section.

French Overseas Departments:
There are four *Départements d'Outre-Mer*, each one an integral part of the French Republic. **Guadeloupe** (also including the islands of St Martin and St Barthélemy) and **Martinique** are in the Caribbean. **French Guiana** is on the northwest coast of South America. **Réunion** is in the Indian Ocean. Despite the greater autonomy achieved with the formation of their own individual Regional Councils in 1974, each French Overseas Department still returns elected representatives to the Senate and National Assembly in Paris, as well as to the European Parliament in Strasbourg.

French Overseas Territories:
Like the French Overseas Departments, the three *Territoires d'Outre-Mer* are integral parts of the French Republic. **Tahiti (French Polynesia)** is in the central South Pacific and, although it has been a French territory since 1946, it received autonomous status in 1996. **French Southern and Antarctic Territories** are located in the Southern Indian Ocean and the **Wallis and Futuna Islands** are located in the southwest Pacific. However, each one is administered by an appointed representative of the French Government, and the level of autonomy is restricted.

Overseas Collectivités Territoriales:
There are two Overseas Collectivités Territoriales that have a status in between that of an Overseas Department and an Overseas Territory. **Mayotte** is located off the northwest coast of Madagascar and **St-Pierre et Miquelon** are found near Newfoundland, Canada. They are integral parts of the French Republic and are administered by a Prefect appointed by the French Government.

French Overseas Country:
New Caledonia, located in the South Pacific, east of Australia and formerly an Overseas Territory, became the only Overseas Country in 1999 following the Nouméa Accord in 1998. The French Government is represented in New Caledonia by the High Commissioner and two deputies are also elected to the National Assembly in Paris.

French Southern and Antarctic Territories (TAAF)

OVERVIEW:
The territories consist of a thin slice of Antarctic mainland and a few small islands located in the Southern Indian Ocean. A French territory since 1955, the TAAF consists of the islands of St Paul, Amsterdam, the Crozet Islands, the Kerguelen Islands and Terre Adélie; the total area is 439,822 sq km (161,815 sq miles). All are rugged volcanic islands. Indeed, Ile Amsterdam and Ile Saint-Paul are extinct volcanoes. Much research of worldwide importance is being carried out there on the atmosphere, meteorology, pollution, the environment, the Earth's interior and surface, biology and oceanography. One particular staffed research station of note is at Base Dumont d'Urville. There are no indigenous inhabitants except those who operate the research stations, usually from Summer (July) to Winter (January), and who usually top the 150-mark in

numbers. The economy of the islands is based on fishing (seaweed, krill and salmon). The fish catches landed on Iles Kerguelen by foreign ships are exported to France and Réunion.

Wallis and Futuna Islands

OVERVIEW:
Although discovered by the Dutch and the British in the 17th and 18th centuries, it was the French who declared a protectorate over the islands in 1842 and, in 1959, the inhabitants of the islands voted to become a French overseas territory. If preparing to travel to this slice of Polynesian paradise, it is worth noting that such French heritage is deeply rooted in Wallis and Futuna; so much so that, along with the enjoyably surreal experience of drinking bubbly and munching on croissants in the Pacific, is the harsh reality of a population that speak little or no English. Any visitor should grasp at least the fundamentals of the French language prior to travel. But Wallis and Futuna is certainly worth such efforts. The islands teem with sensational crater lakes, such as Lake Lalolalo, and lagoons. Gloriously colourful churches often spring out of verdant background. And many of the islands are surrounded by a barrier reef, full of coral treasures. Whether you view undeveloped touristic infrastructure as a negative or a positive, you are bound to be delighted by the profusion of cultures and traditions, and the sheer friendliness of the Polynesian people.

GENERAL INFORMATION:
Location: Southwest Pacific between Fiji, Samoa and Tonga.
Time: GMT + 12. **Area:** 274 sq km (170 sq miles).
Population: 16,025 (2005 estimate). **Population density:** 58.49 per sq km. **Capital:** Mata-Utu (Wallis Island).
Population: 1137 (1996). **Government:** There are three kingdoms, one on Wallis and two on Small Futuna island. The kings still have a seat in the Territory Assembly, which is unique in Republican France. The Assembly consists of 20 members, and a deputy and senator to the French national Parliament. The three traditional Polynesian kings help to decide internal policy matters. **Religion:** Roman Catholic.

COMMUNICATIONS:
Telephone: Main lines exist. **Mobile telephone:** Currently, no roaming agreements with international mobile phone companies are in operation. **Internet:** There are no Internet hosts but Internet is available, with limitations. **Media: TV:** There are two broadcast stations. **Radio:** There are three broadcast stations: on AM, FM and shortwave.

PASSPORT & VISA:
The passport and visa requirements for persons visiting the Wallis and Futuna Islands are the same as for New Caledonia. For further details, see the *New Caledonia* section.

HEALTH:
Vaccinations against *typhoid* and *tetanus* are advised. Precautions should also be taken against *hepatitis A*, *hepatitis B*, *diphtheria* and *measles*. There are two hospitals, one on Wallis and one on Futuna, and three dispensaries. Mains water is suitable for drinking on Wallis but not on Futuna.

TRAVEL:
Air:
 Main airports: *Hihifo (WLS)* on Wallis Island, 5km (3 miles) from Mata-Utu. Approximate flight time from *London* is 25 hours. There is also an airport in *Alo* in the southeastern part of Futuna Island. *Air Calédonie* is the main airline serving the Islands under *AirCalin* (website: www.aircalin.nc). There are also plans currently underway to upgrade the small domestic airport on Futuna and turn it into a major international point of entry, as well as introduce the Islands' first international airline, *Air Wallis*. **Sea:** Boat services no longer operate from New Caledonia; however, a fast ferry service is being planned between Wallis and Futuna. **Road:** There are 120km of road on the islands; minibus services operate on Futuna and car hire is available. However, only 16km of the roads are surfaced and these are on Wallis Island.

ACCOMMODATION:
Hotels:
 There are a small number of hotels on the islands; for details of booking accommodation and other information, contact the French Government Tourist Office.

BUSINESS:
Main exports: Copra, chemicals and construction materials.
Main imports: Chemicals, machinery, passenger ships and consumer goods. **Main trade partners:** Italy, Croatia, the USA, Denmark, France, Australia and New Zealand.
Economy: There has been steady emigration from Wallis & Futuna to New Caledonia in recent years. The economy is limited to traditional subsistence agriculture, livestock and fishing. About 4 per cent of the population is employed in

COMMUNICATIONS:

Telephone: Country dialling code: 508. Telephone services are adequate. **Mobile telephone:** Roaming agreements exist with one international mobile phone company. **Media: TV:** There are no broadcast stations but there are, however, two stations that rebroadcast programmes/repeats from France, Canada and the USA. **Radio:** There are two stations, one on AM and one on FM.

PASSPORT & VISA: Nationals of the EU require a valid passport (also necessary for transit into Canada); nationals of other countries require a valid passport and may need a visa (depending on nationality). Requirements are the same as for French Guiana, Guadeloupe, Martinique and Réunion. For further details, see any of these separate sections.

HEALTH: No special precautions are required. There are no reciprocal agreements with the UK or USA but visitors have the right to be treated and charges are made. Medical insurance is recommended.

TRAVEL:

Air:

Main airport: *St-Pierre*, which has international flights from Paris via Montréal, Halifax or St John's; and from London via Paris and St John's (stopovers are generally not permitted). Domestic services operate between St-Pierre and Miquelon. St-Pierre is served by *Air Saint Pierre (PJ)*.

Sea:

Boat services operate between St-Pierre, Miquelon and Langlade and there is an international ferry service from Fortune in Newfoundland (travel time – one hour). Buses, taxis and hire cars are available.

ACCOMMODATION:

Hotels/Guest Houses: Available on the island. For more information, contact: Hotels and Restaurants Association, BP 4207, 97500, St Pierre.

CLIMATE: The dry season is from May to October, and the hot season is from November to April. Monsoons may occur from December to March.

Government. The French Government provides subsidies, and fishing rights are also licensed to Japan and Korea (Rep), providing revenue.

Mayotte

OVERVIEW:

Mayotte was ceded to France along with the other islands of the Comoros group in 1843. It was the only island in the archipelago that voted in 1974 to retain its link with France and forego independence. It is a land that gently undulates, riven with deep ravines and ancient volcanic peaks. It is also a territory that is host to one of the biggest – and most spectacular – lagoons on the planet, with a surface nearly a thousand kilometres long, and a barrier reef that is over 150 kilometres long. If you reach the top of Mont Chungi, the highest spot on Mayotte, you will be rewarded with lavish views of unspoiled ocean waters and fine, golden sand. Dolphins have been known to frolic in such waters, and giant turtles are a welcome feature of the land. Meanwhile, territorial disputes remain: the Comoros have claimed Mayotte as their own territory. On 2 July 2000, the population voted again for a closer integration with France and the process of becoming an overseas department will be completed in 2010.

GENERAL INFORMATION:

Location: Part of the Comoro archipelago off the northwest corner of Madagascar. **Time:** GMT + 3. **Area:** 374 sq km (144 sq miles). **Population:** 160,265 (2002). **Population density:** 428.5 per sq km. **Capital:** Dzaoudzi. **Population:** 12,308 (2002). Country dialling code: 269.

PASSPORT & VISA:

French nationals require an identity card or passport that has been issued in the last 10 years; nationals of other EU countries require current valid passport; nationals of all other countries require a visa which is valid for three months.

DUTY FREE:

200 cigarettes, 100 cigars; 2l of wine, one bottle of liquor and two bottles of whisky.

HEALTH:

Vaccinations against *tuberculosis, diphtheria, tetanus, polio, rubella, measles* and *hepatitis B* are compulsory before entering Mayotte. Vaccinations against *hepatitis A* and *typhoid* and precautions against *malaria* are advised. Although mains water is chlorinated, bottled water should be drunk for the first few weeks of the stay. Medical services are available free of charge. The island is divided into six sections, each of which has a medical professional. Full medical insurance is advised.

TRAVEL:

Air:

The easiest way to get to Mayotte is to fly to Réunion and catch a connecting flight to Mayotte. *Air Austral* (www.air-austral.com) operates flights from Réunion to Mayotte daily (journey time - two hours). *Air Madagascar* (www.airmadagascar.mg) also offers flights on a weekly basis from Majunga to Mayotte. **Main airports:** *Pamandzi* on the island of Petite Terre; services are available from Paris (via Réunion), the Comoros Islands, Madagascar, the Seychelles and Kenya.

Sea:

There is a regular boat service to Grande Terre. **Road:** There are approximately 90km (55 miles) of roads on the island. Car hire is available.

ACCOMMODATION:

Hotels:

There is a small number of hotels on the islands; contact the French Government Tourist Office for details of booking accommodation.

CLIMATE: The island has an annual average temperature of 25 degrees Celsius. The year is divided into two seasons: a dry temperate season from May to October and a hot season from November to April with monsoons from the northwest from December to March.

St Pierre et Miquelon

OVERVIEW:

Previously enjoying Departmental status, the islands have, since 1955, been a part of the *collectivités territoriales*, partly as a result of a dispute with Canada over fishing and mineral rights in the area. This conflict in 'status' pinpoints the enticing convergence of French and North American influence in St-Pierre et Miquelon. In between is much pristine wilderness, great food and wine, wildlife, and hundreds of years of history. Indeed, St-Pierre et Miquelon is one last remaining vestige of France's once-large possessions on this continent. Today, both Saint-Pierre and Miquelon combine the best of both modern and quaint. The territory retains its reputation for fishing, its clear waters containing an abundance of catch. The skies are filled with birds, drawing bird watchers year after year. There are plenty of other beautiful, untouched ecosystems to explore as well. In short, St-Pierre et Miquelon is the ideal destination for quietly unwinding amidst nature.

GENERAL INFORMATION:

Location: This small group of small islands lies off the southern coast of Newfoundland, Canada. **Time:** GMT - 3 (GMT - 2 from first Sunday in April to Saturday before last Sunday in October). **Area:** 242 sq km (93.4 sq miles). **Population:** 6316 (1999). **Population density:** 26.1 per sq km. **Capital:** St Pierre. **Population:** 5683 (1990); almost all of the population live in the capital or elsewhere on the small island of the same name.

Gabon

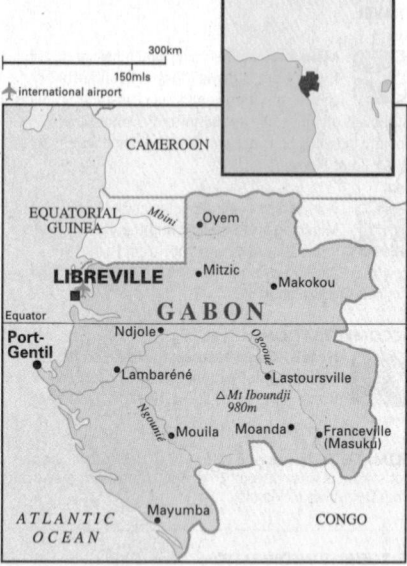

Location: West Coast of Central Africa.

Time: GMT + 1.

Overview

Gabon is bordered by the Atlantic Ocean, Equatorial Guinea, Cameroon and the Congo. The 800km- (500 mile-) long sandy coastal strip is a series of palm-fringed bays, lagoons and estuaries. The lush tropical vegetation (which covers much of the interior) gives way in parts to the savannah. There are many rivers along which settlements have grown. Many of the Bantu people are concentrated in coastal areas and villages along the banks of the many rivers. The main cities are Libreville, Port Gentil, Lambaréné, Moanda, Oyem, Mouila and Franceville.

Many of the cities hint at Gabon's history but, unfortunately, little is known about Gabonese prehistory. The earliest of the present inhabitants are the Pygmies; from AD 1100 onwards, various Bantu tribes began migrating into the area. It was in 1472, during this period of migration - which continued for several centuries - that the Portuguese discovered Gabon. Thereafter, Gabon was primarily of interest to the Dutch, French and British, who negotiated with the coastal tribes for slaves and ivory from the interior. Between the 16th and 18th centuries, the region was part of the Loango empire, during which time the main inhabitants were the Omiéné and Fang tribes. The slave trade ceased in the middle of the 19th century, but not before it had destroyed the social inter-relationships of the tribes it affected. Land on either side of the Gabon River was annexed peacefully by the French during the mid-19th century as a province of French Equatorial Africa.

The Republic of Gabon moved peacefully into independence in 1960 after a three-year period of internal self-government. A French-style constitution was adopted the following year and Léon M'Ba became Gabon's first President. After seven years of stormy pluralism, the ruling *Parti Démocratique Gabonais* (PDG) declared Gabon a one-party state, but retained broadly pro-Western policies. President Omar Bongo, who succeeded M'Ba on the latter's death in 1967 and is now one of Africa's longest serving heads of state, has maintained them ever since. In 2003, a change of constitution meant that Bongo could run for office as many times as he wanted and Bongo, now in his 70s, is likely to remain as president for life. Gabon's only problem in the region concerns the island of Mbagne which lies in the Corisco Bay, potentially the site of large oil and gas deposits: occupied by Gabon in 1970, it is also claimed by Equatorial Guinea.

But touristic natural resources are likely to centre around features such as stunning white beaches, an abundance of wildlife, including gorillas, panthers, parrots and elephants, and verdant forests.

General Information

AREA: 267,667 sq km (103,347 sq miles).

POPULATION: 1.4 million (2005, UN).

POPULATION DENSITY: 5.23 per sq km.

CAPITAL: Libreville. **Population:** 673,995 (2005).

GEOGRAPHY: Gabon is bordered to the west by the Atlantic Ocean, to the north by Equatorial Guinea and Cameroon, and to the east and south by the Congo. The 800km- (500 mile-) long sandy coastal strip is a series of palm-fringed bays, lagoons and estuaries. The lush tropical vegetation (which covers about 82 per cent of the interior) gives way in parts to the savannah. There are many rivers and they remain the main communication routes along which settlements have grown. Of the 40 or so Bantu tribes, the largest are the Fang, Eshira, Mbele and Okande. Only a small percentage of native Gabonese live in the towns, as the population is concentrated in the coastal areas and villages along the banks of the many rivers, following a more traditional rural style of life.

GOVERNMENT: Republic. Gained independence from France in 1960. **Head of State:** President Omar Albert Bernard Bongo since 1967. **Head of Government:** Prime Minister Jean François Ntoutoume-Emane since 1999.

Recent history: From 1990, in common with much of the rest of Africa, President Omar Bongo and his Government effected the transformation from a one-party state to a pluralistic political system. The 120-seat elected National Assembly has acquired genuine political power although it remains dominated by the *Parti Démocratique Gabonais* (PDG), which at the last poll in December 2001 captured almost three-quarters of the seats. The remainder were largely shared between the two principal opposition parties, the *Parti Gabonais de Progrès* and the *Rassemblement National des Bûcherons* (National Woodcutters' Party). A prominent PDG figure and close ally of Bongo, Jean-Francois Ntoutoume-Emane, retained the premiership to which he had first been appointed in 1999. Despite its overwhelming majority, widespread discontent with the social and political situation prompted Bongo to invite the Woodcutters into Government. Following heavy lobbying by its leader, Father Paul Mba Abessolle (who is also mayor of the capital, Libreville), the party agreed to join a 'Government of collective management' – the first time that any party other than the PDG has been represented in Government.

A new constitution, adopted in March 1991 and amended in 1997, allows for an executive President and bicameral legislature. The President, elected for a seven-year term, appoints a Council of Ministers headed by a Prime Minister. The legislature comprises the 120-seat Assemblée Nationale and the 91-member Sénate, both of which are directly elected for five-year and six-year terms respectively. In 2003, the constitution was amended once again, allowing the president to serve any number of terms (it had previously been limited to two). This enabled Bongo to run again in the November 2005 presidential election, in which he won 79 per cent of the vote, giving him a further seven years in power.

LANGUAGE: The official language is French. The principal African language is Fang. Eshira is spoken by a tenth of the population. Bantu dialects spoken include Bapounou, Miene and Bateke.

RELIGION: About 60 per cent Christian (mainly Roman Catholic), the remainder follow Muslim and animist beliefs.

ELECTRICITY: 220 volts AC, 50Hz.

SOCIAL CONVENTIONS: Dance, song, poetry and myths remain an important part of traditional Gabonese life.

Photography: It is absolutely forbidden to photograph military installations. In general, permission to photograph anything should be requested first, to prevent misunderstandings.

Climate

Equatorial with up to 80 per cent humidity. The dry season is from June to August, and the main rainy season is from October to May. Average temperatures are 25 degrees celcius.

Required clothing: Lightweight tropical, with raincoats advised during the rainy season.

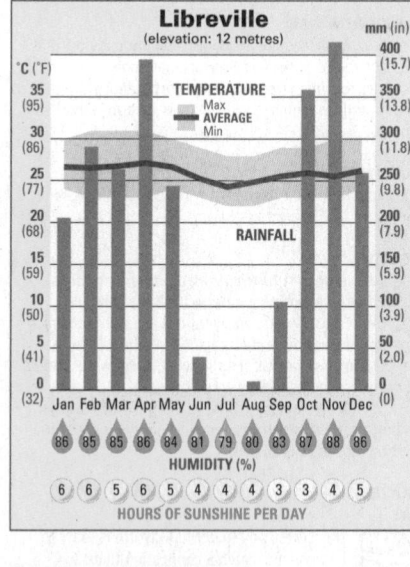

Communications

Telephone: IDD is available. Country code: 241. No area codes required.

Mobile telephone: Roaming agreements exist with some international mobile phone companies. Coverage is variable.

Internet: Internet is increasingly available; there are a growing number of Internet cafes in Libreville.

Post: Airmail from Gabon takes at least one week to Western Europe. Urgent letters should be sent by special delivery to ensure their safe arrival. Post office hours: 0800-1200 and Mon-Fri 1430-1800.

MEDIA: Mostly, Gabon's media is Government-controlled

Credit: ©Gabontour

and journalistic pressure is subtle but ever-present.
Press: The two daily newspapers are *Gabon Matin* and
L'Union, published in French. There are several private
weeklies, published mainly on the topics of the Government
and the economy. Official bulletins are published in French
and have a limited circulation.
TV: Gabon's national state broadcaster (*Radiodiffusion-
Television Gabonaise*) operates two TV stations. *TeleAfrica*
is a private station and *TV Say* is a pay-TV operator.
Radio: There is a French-language radio network and a
network of provincial stations. *Africa No 1* is a Pan-African
broadcaster based in Gabon, heard across Africa on
shortwave and on FM relays in many cities. French concerns
have a financial stake *Radio France Internationale* is
available via an FM relay.

Passport/Visa

	Passport Required?	Visa Required?	Return Ticket Required?
Full British	Yes	Yes	Yes
Australian	Yes	Yes	Yes
Canadian	Yes	Yes	Yes
USA	Yes	Yes	Yes
Other EU	Yes	Yes	Yes
Japanese	Yes	Yes	Yes

Note: *Regulations and requirements may be subject to change at short
notice, and you are advised to contact the appropriate diplomatic or
consular authority before finalising travel arrangements. Any numbers in
the chart refer to the footnotes below.*

PASSPORTS: Passport valid for more than six months
required by all.
VISAS: Required by all.
Types of visa and cost: *Single-entry:* £50 (Tourist or
Transit); £70 (Business). *Double-entry:* £100 (Tourist or
Transit); £140 (Business). *Multiple-entry:* £280 (Tourist,
Transit or Business).
Validity: *Single-entry:* Three months from date of issue.
Application to: Consulate (or consular section at
Embassy); see *Passport/Visa Information*.
Application requirements: (a) One passport-size photo.
(b) One application form. (c) Fee, payable in cash or by
cheque only. (d) Valid passport valid for six months, with
one blank page. (e) Registered stamped, self-addressed
special delivery envelope for postal applications. *Tourist:*
(a)-(e) and, (f) Hotel reservation, or invitation from resident
of Gabon legalised in the town hall. *Business:* (a)-(e) and, (f)
Letter from the company stating the date of departure and
the reasons for the visit.
Note: (a) While possession of references is not an official
requirement when applying for a tourist visa, they may help
speed up the application process. (b) Both yellow fever,
tropical disease and cholera vaccination certificates may be
required to enter Gabon but are not necessary when
applying for a visa. However, it is best to check with the
Embassy prior to travel.
Working days required: Minimum of four days.

Money

Currency: CFA (*Communauté Financiaire Africaine*) Franc
(CFAfr *or* XAF) = 100 centimes. Notes are in denominations
of XAF10,000, 5000, 2000, 1000 and 500. Coins are in
denominations of XAF500, 100, 50, 25, 10, 5 and 1. Only
currency issued by the *Banque des États de l'Afrique
Centrale* (Bank of Central African States) is valid; currency
issued by the *Banque des États de l'Afrique de l'Ouest*
(Bank of West African States) is not. The CFA Franc is tied to
the Euro.
Note: Libreville is one of the most expensive cities in the
world.
Currency exchange: Gabon is part of the French Monetary
Area.
Credit & debit cards: American Express, MasterCard and
Visa are not widely accepted. Check with your credit or
debit card company for merchant acceptability and other
facilities which may be available.

Credit: ©Gabontour

Traveller's cheques: To avoid additional exchange rate
charges, travellers are advised to take traveller's cheques in
Euros.
Currency restrictions: The import of local and foreign
currency is unlimited, subject to declaration. The export of
local and foreign currency is limited to XAF200,000.
Banking hours: Mon-Fri 0730-1130, 1430-1630.
Exchange rate indicators:
Rate at time of publishing
£1.00=   XAF996.47
$1.00=   AXF543.94

Duty Free

The following goods may be imported into Gabon by
persons over 17 years of age without incurring customs
duty:
*400 cigarettes/cigarillos or 125 cigars or 500g of tobacco
(women – cigarettes only); 1l bottles of wine (up to three),
1l of liquor; 50g of perfume; two cameras; 10 rolls of film
per camera; gifts up to XAF5000.*
Restricted items: Guns and ammunition require a licence
from the Ministry of Home Affairs in Libreville.

Public Holidays

Below are listed Public Holidays for the January 2006-June
2007 period.
2006: Jan 1 New Year's Day. **Jan 10** Eid al-Adha (Feast of the
Sacrifice). **Mar 12** Renovation Day. **Apr 17** Easter Monday.
May 1 Labour Day. **May 6** Martyrs' Day. **Jun 5** Whit Monday.
Aug 15 Assumption. **Aug 17** Independence Day. **Oct 22-24**
Eid al-Fitr (End of Ramadan). **Nov 1** All Saints' Day. **Dec 25**
Christmas Day. **Dec 31** Eid al-Adha (Feast of the Sacrifice).
2007: Jan 1 New Year's Day. **Mar 12** Renovation Day. **Apr 9**
Easter Monday. **May 1** Labour Day. **May 6** Martyrs' Day.
May 28 Whit Monday.
Note: Muslim festivals are timed according to local
sightings of various phases of the moon and the dates
given above are approximations. During the lunar month
of Ramadan that precedes Eid al-Fitr, Muslims fast
during the day and feast at night and normal business
patterns may be interrupted. Some disruption may
continue into Eid al-Fitr itself. Eid al-Fitr and Eid al-Adha
may last anything from two to 10 days, depending on
the region. For more information see the *World of Islam*
appendix.

Health

	Special Precautions?	Certificate Required?
Yellow Fever	Yes	1
Cholera	Yes	2
Typhoid & Polio	3	N/A
Malaria	4	N/A

Note: *Regulations and requirements may be subject to change at short
notice, and you are advised to contact your doctor well in advance of your
intended date of departure. Any numbers in the chart refer to the
footnotes below.*

1: A *yellow fever* vaccination certificate is required from all
travellers over one year of age. Yellow fever risk is
particularly high in Ogooue-Ivindo province.
2: Following WHO guidelines issued in 1973, a *cholera*
vaccination certificate is not a condition of entry to Gabon.
However, cholera is a serious risk in this country and
precautions are essential. Up-to-date advice should be
sought before deciding whether these precautions should
include vaccination as medical opinion is divided over its
effectiveness; see the *Health* appendix for more
information.
3: Immunisation against *typhoid* and *poliomyelitis* is often
recommended.
4: Malaria risk, predominantly in the malignant *falciparum*
form, exists all year throughout the country. Resistance to
chloroquine has been reported.
Food & drink: All water should be regarded as potentially
contaminated. Water used for drinking, brushing teeth or
making ice should have first been boiled or otherwise
sterilised. Milk is unpasteurised and should be boiled.
Powdered or tinned milk is available and is advised, but
make sure that it is reconstituted with pure water. Avoid
dairy products which are likely to have been made from
unboiled milk. Only eat well-cooked meat and fish,
preferably served hot. Pork, salad and mayonnaise may carry
increased risk. Vegetables should be cooked and fruit peeled.
Avoid eating food from street vendors.
Other risks: *Diarrhoeal diseases*, including *giardiasis*, and
typhoid fevers are common. *Hepatitis A* and *E* are
widespread. *Hepatitis B* is hyperendemic. *Bilharzia*
(schistosomiasis) is present. Avoid swimming and paddling
in fresh water; swimming pools which are well-chlorinated
and maintained are safe. *Onchocerciasis* (river blindness)
and *trypanosomiasis* (sleeping sickness) are present.
Leishmaniasis and *dengue fever* can be transmitted by
worms and insects. Epidemics of *meningococcal disease*
may occur, particularly in the savannah areas and during
the dry season. Immunisation against *diphtheria* is
sometimes recommended. *Oriental lung fluke* has been
reported. Travellers are advised to update vaccinations for
tetanus-diptheria, MMR (measles-mumps-rubella) and
Varicella (chickenpox).
Rabies is present. For those at high risk, vaccination before
arrival should be considered. If you are bitten, seek medical
advice without delay. For more information, consult the
Health appendix.
Health care: Travellers in rural areas should take a first-aid
kit with anti-tetanus and anti-venom serums. Medical
facilities are limited. Comprehensive medical insurance is
essential.

Travel - International

AIR:
 The national airline is *Air Gabon (GN)*, which
operates direct flights from Paris and London to
Libreville. *Air France* operates daily flights from
London to Gabon, with a stopover in Paris. Other airlines
also serve Gabon.
Approximate flight times: From Libreville to *London* is
approximately 8 hours (excluding stopovers).
Main airports: Libreville (LBV) is 12km (7 miles) north of

Credit: ©Gabontour

the city. *To/from the airport*: Taxis are available to the city (travel time – 10 minutes). *Facilities*: Bureaux de change, shops, tourist information, left luggage, car hire, hotel reservation desk and duty free shops.

Departure tax: None.

SEA:

Main ports: *Owenda*, 10km (6miles) from Libreville. Ferries depart quite regularly to São Tomé. Freight ships to Cameroon may take passengers; enquire locally for details.

ROAD:

There are roads to Bitam and Ambam (Cameroon), Bata via Cocobeach (Equatorial Guinea) and the Congo.

Travel - Internal

AIR:

Air Gabon (GN) operates regular flights from Lambaréné, Libreville, Mitzic, Oyem and other cities. Gabon has a total of nearly 200 airstrips. There are local airports at *Franceville (MVB)* and *Port Gentil (POG)*.

SEA:

Ferries run regularly along the coast from Libreville to Port Gentil (travel time – four hours).

RIVER:

Riverboats ply the Ogoué River between Port Gentil and Lambaréné (travel time – 10 to 24 hours). Some boats continue on to Ndjolé.

RAIL:

The *Trans-Gabon Railway* is the only railway line in Gabon; it is 410km- (254 miles-) long and connects Libreville (Owendo station, 10km (6 miles) from the city centre) with Franceville. Stops along the way include Ndjole and Moanda. Plans proposing an extension of the railway to Brazzaville in the Republic of Congo regularly surface. Children under four years travel free. Children aged from four to 11 years pay half fare.

ROAD:

Traffic drives on the right. There are nearly 7518km (4672 miles) of road, but only 614km (382 miles) are tarred. Most of the country consists of impenetrable rainforest and the roads are generally of a poor standard. Road travel in the rainy season (October to mid-December and mid-February to May) is inadvisable. There is no road connection between the second-largest city of Port Gentil or any other part of the country. Check points are common in Gabon and drivers will be asked to show passports, driving licence or vehicle registration documents. **Bus:** Inter-urban travel is mainly by minibus or pick-up truck. Daily minibus services run from Libreville to Lambaréné, Mouila, Oyem and Bitam (the last two usually involving night stops). Seats for these and other less frequent routes can be obtained in Libreville. However, this is not normally necessary for the main routes as seats will be readily available in the 'bus station' near the central market (0600-0800). There are also conventional buses on the Mouila route and other services out of Mouila. **Car hire:** Cars may be hired from main hotels and airports, although they tend to be expensive. **Documentation:** International Driving Permit and international insurance are required.

URBAN:

There are extensive share-taxis. There are bus services in Port Gentil and Masuku (Franceville), and share-taxis in other centres. Taxi rates vary.

Travel Advice

The threat from terrorism is low, but you should be aware of the global risk of indiscriminate terrorist attacks, which could be against civilian targets, including places frequented by foreigners.

Crime is increasing, particularly in Libreville and Port-Gentil, including incidents of robbery and armed attacks.

Following a number of carjackings within Libreville it is recommended that travellers keep their car windows closed and car doors locked if they are travelling at night.

Public demonstrations in Port Gentil have on occasion turned violent. Travellers should avoid demonstrations, rallies and large public gatherings.

This advice is based on information provided by the Foreign and Commonwealth Office in the UK. It is correct at time of publishing. As the situation can change rapidly, visitors are advised to contact the following organisations for the latest travel advice:

British Foreign and Commonwealth Office
Tel: (0845) 850 2829.
Website: www.fco.gov.uk

US Department of State
Website: http://travel.state.gov/travel

Accommodation

HOTELS:

There are private hotels and hotel chains in Libreville and other major cities and towns but, like most of the accommodation in Gabon, they are expensive. Tourist facilities, including tourist camps, are being expanded throughout the country, especially along the coast and in towns close to the National Parks.

CAMPING:

Free but limited. Caution should be used as to where camp is made.

Top Things To See & Do

- Take a stroll around Gabon's lively, charming and cosmopolitan oceanside capital, **Libreville**. Its white buildings contrast with the green of the nearby **equatorial forest**.
- Visit the **National Museum** in Libreville, which contains some of the most beautiful **woodcarvings** in Africa, especially the indigenous Fang style of carving which influenced Picasso's figures and busts.
- Gawp at the sheer expenditure that is behind the construction of the **Presidential Palace** in Libreville; it was built in the 1970s costing US$800 million, and has Italian and Greek marble columns.
- The **Cathedral of St Michael** in Libreville is famous because of its 31 unusual wooden columns which were carved by a blind Gabonese craftsman; each of the columns depicts a Biblical scene.
- Do not miss the hustle and bustle of the **Mount Bouet Market** in Libreville.
- **Walk** the winding route from Libreville to the beach of **Cap Estérias**, where the rocks abound with sea urchins, oysters and lobsters: on the way, you will pass through a forest of giant trees. This is a good place to **swim**.
- Visit **Lambaréné**, the town made famous by Doctor Albert Schweitzer, the tropical disease specialist and musician. Now in its 70th year, **Schweitzer Hospital** is open to visitors as part of it has been made into a museum. A **tour** on **Evaro Lake** can be organised.
- The villages of **M'Bigou** and **Eteke** are famous for their local **crafts** and **gold mines** and are well worth a visit.
- For **wildlife**, enter the region of **Bateke Plateau** , which comprises **savannah** and forest galleries and tumultuous rivers spanned by **liana bridges**, such as the one at Poubara. Creatures include forest elephants, buffaloes, sitatunga, river hogs, gorillas, panthers, crocodiles, monkeys and parrots. Gabon's National Parks are all rich in wildlife. The largest National Park in Gabon is the **Lopé-Okanda Reserve**, near **La Lopé** in the centre of the country, and its landscape, containing a mixture of savannah and dense forest, encloses gorillas, chimpanzees and elephants, as well as a variety of other primates, large mammals and around 350 species of bird. Alternatively, traverse the enchanting **Mayumba** , a thin strip of land set between sea and lake, and try to spot some of the many creatures that lurk here; you can even go whale watching. **Whale watching** is popular all along the south coast from July to September each year, when up to 3000 humpback whales can be seen.
- Bathe in some of the **beaches** on the Atlantic coast. For peace and quiet, the deserted beaches of **Pointe Denis** and **Ekwata beach** are in the north, **Mayumba** and **Sette Cama** are in the south. **Port Gentil** at the mouth of the **River Ogooué** and Libreville have beaches with facilities for **water-skiing** and other watersports. **Mayumba** in the south and **Cap Estérias**, 35km (22 miles) from Libreville, are popular watersports centres at weekends. **Perroquet** and Pointe Denis both offer good **skindiving**. **Kayaking** is also a popular sport among visitors.
- Go **fishing**: popular among European visitors, many of the rivers offer excellent catches. Equipment can be hired at Port Gentil. Fish abound in Gabonese rivers and lakes, but the local fishermen can find the largest variety along the coast and in the numerous lagoons located at the mouth of the **Ogooué**.

TOURIST INFORMATION

Centre Gabonais de Promotion Touristique (GABONTOUR)
Street address: 622 Avenue du Colonel Parant, Centre Ville, Libreville, Gabon
Postal address: BP 2085, Libreville, Gabon
Tel: 728 504 *or* 723 949.
Website: www.gabontour.ga

Entertainment

FOOD & DRINK: Most hotels and restaurants serve French and continental-style food and are expensive. Gabonese food is distinctive and delicious, but not always readily available, as most restaurants serve Senegalese, Cameroonian and Congolese food. European food is also served.

Gabon is the world's 20th-largest consumer of French champagne. Licensing hours are similar to those in France.

National specialities:

- Braised fish (bass and red fish).
- *Nyembwé*.
- Manioc leaves.
- *Bouillon de poisson* (fish stew).

Tipping: 10 to 15 per cent unless service is included in the bill.

NIGHTLIFE: There are nightclubs in Libreville with music and bars. Food is often served, although this can be expensive. The African quarter of Libreville is full of fairly cheap places to eat and drink. There are also casinos at several hotels.

SHOPPING: In Libreville, there are two bustling markets at Akebe-Plaine, Nkembo and Mon-Bouet. Stone carvings can be bought on the outskirts of both, fashioned by a group of carvers who have adapted traditional skills for the tourist market. Crafts from local villages can also be bought from stalls in the streets or from the villagers themselves. African (Fang) mask carvings, figurines, clay pots and traditional musical instruments can also be bought. **Shopping hours:** Mon-Sat 0800-1200 and 1500-1900. Some shops close Monday.

Business

- **GDP:** US$4.8 billion.
- **Main imports:** Machines and equipment, foodstuff, chemicals and construction materials.
- **Main exports:** Crude oil, timber, manganese and uranium.
- **Main trade partners:** China, France, Germany, Japan, The Netherlands, UK and USA.

ECONOMY: Oil reserves and mineral deposits have allowed Gabon to develop into one of Africa's more successful economies. At US$3200, Gabon has one of the highest per capita incomes on the African continent. One-third of GDP comes from the oil industry; there are also significant mining operations producing manganese and uranium. There are confirmed deposits of iron ore (which are substantial) and also a number of rare metal ores. There is a small manufacturing base engaged in oil refining and the production of plywood, paints, varnishes and detergents, dry batteries, cement, cigarettes and textiles. Future industrial growth in this sector is likely to be limited by a shortage of skilled labour, high costs and inadequate infrastructure. Meanwhile, agriculture remains important, as it still employs two-thirds of the working population. Gabon produces coffee, sugar cane, rubber and some other cash crops – also cassava and maize for domestic consumption. Both the timber and fishing industries, while making strong contributions to the national economy, may be the subject of future expansion as export earners, although timber production is likely to be limited by environmental concerns. Like all primary producers, Gabon remains vulnerable to fluctuations in commodity prices.

Gabon is a member of the Central African Customs and Economic Union (CEEAC) and of the CFA Franc Zone. In June 1996, Gabon announced its withdrawal from OPEC, after 23 years' membership.

BUSINESS ETIQUETTE: Tropical suits are required. French is the principal language used in business circles. Translators and interpreters are available through the Embassy. Strong business ties remain with France despite competition from the USA and Japan. **Office hours:** Mon-Fri 0730-1200 and 1430-1800.

CONFERENCES/CONVENTIONS: Further information can be obtained from the Chambre de Commerce, d'Agriculture, d'Industrie et des Mines du Gabon (see *Commercial Information*).

COMMERCIAL INFORMATION

Chambre de Commerce, d'Agriculture, d'Industrie et des Mines du Gabon
PO box 2234, Libreville, Gabon
Tel: 722 064.

The Gambia

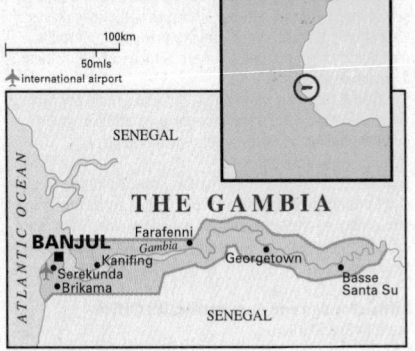

100km
50km
✈ international airport

SENEGAL

THE GAMBIA

ATLANTIC OCEAN

BANJUL
Farafenni
Gambia
Kanifing
Serekunda Georgetown
Brikama Basse
Santa Su

SENEGAL

Location: West Africa.

Time: GMT.

Overview

The River Gambia was known to the Carthaginians in the fifth century BC, and subsequently the area became part of several successive African empires. During the colonial period, several European powers contested for ownership of the river and the rich trade which it carried. Britain eventually gained control of the mouth and lower reaches of the river, thereby establishing an enclave in the surrounding French territories of Senegal and a useful base from which to launch attacks on French trading settlements. The Gambia was Britain's first and last colony, being officially colonised in 1765 (although until 1843 it was united with Sierra Leone) and gaining independence 200 years later in February 1965.

Since it became independent, the country has enjoyed long spells of stability, which unfortunately has not translated into prosperity for its inhabitants. Tourism is an important source of foreign exchange and is considered as a priority sector for investment.

Although The Gambia is Africa's smallest nation, it offers landscapes and attractions of great diversity, ranging from broad, sandy beaches on the Atlantic to lush tropical forests, swamps, marshes and large areas of wooded savannah. The River Gambia is one of Africa's great waterways and dominates the country. It provides opportunities for fishing, boating and sailing and there are many camps and lodges along its banks.

The Gambia is a thin strip of land of mainly low-lying plateaus that runs inland and is packed with exotic sights and sounds for the visitor. Particularly well worth visiting is the Abuko Nature Reserve, which has crocodiles, monkeys, birds and antelopes, and Makasutu for its incredible wildlife. The Gambia is a birdwatcher's paradise, with over 540 different species of bird. In fact, the country has one of the largest concentrations of bird species per square mile in the world.

General Information

AREA: 11,295 sq km (4361 sq miles).
POPULATION: 1.5 million (UN estimate 2005).
POPULATION DENSITY: 132.8 per sq km.
CAPITAL: Banjul. **Population:** 38,828 (2003).
GEOGRAPHY: The Gambia is situated on the Atlantic coast at the bulge of Africa. The country consists of a thin ribbon of land, at no point wider than 50km (30 miles), running east-west on both banks of the River Gambia. The Gambia is bordered to the west by the Atlantic Ocean and on all other sides by Senegal. It is also the smallest and westernmost African nation. The country mainly consists of a low plateau, which decreases in height as it nears the Atlantic coast. The plain is broken in a few places by low

flat-topped hills and by the river and its tributaries. The area extending from MacCarthy Island, where Georgetown is located, to the eastern end of the country, is enclosed by low rocky hills. The coast and river banks are backed mainly by mangrove swamps, while the lower part of the river has steep red ironstone banks which are covered with tropical forest and bamboo. Away from the river, the landscape consists of wooded, park-like savannah, with large areas covered by a variety of trees such as mahogany, rosewood, oil palm and rubber. On the coast, the river meets the Atlantic with impressive sand cliffs and 50km (30 miles) of broad, unspoiled beaches, palm-fringed and strewn with shells.

GOVERNMENT: Republic. Gained independence from the UK in 1965. **Head of State and Government:** President Yahya Jammeh since 1996. **Recent history:** The most recent Presidential and legislative polls in October 2001 and January 2002 repeated the results of five years earlier, leaving Yahya Jammeh and his Armed Forces Provisional Ruling Council (APRC) firmly in control of The Gambia. Many of the international economic and political links damaged by the 1994 coup have since gradually been restored. However, Jammeh has dropped Jawara's rigid pro-Western stance and has looked further afield for new donors and trading partners: these now include Libya and Taiwan, as well as Cuba, Iran and Nigeria. New agreements were also signed with neighbouring Senegal.

LANGUAGE: The official language is English. Local languages are Creole, Fula, Jola, Mandinka, Manjango, Serahule, Serere and Wolof.

RELIGION: Over 85 per cent Muslim, with the remainder holding either Christian or animist beliefs.

ELECTRICITY: 230 volts AC, 50Hz. Plugs are either round three-pin or square three-pin (15 or 13 amps).

SOCIAL CONVENTIONS: Handshaking is a common form of greeting; *Nanga def* ('How are you?') is the traditional greeting. Gambians are extremely friendly and welcoming and visitors should not be afraid to accept their hospitality. Many Gambians are Muslim and their religious customs and beliefs should be respected by guests; however, most understand the English customs and language. Visitors should remember that the right hand must be used for the giving or receiving of food or objects. Casual wear is suitable, although beachwear should only be worn on the beach or at the poolside. Only the most exclusive dining rooms encourage guests to dress for dinner. Despite the effects of tourism, traditional culture in music, dancing and craftsmanship still flourishes in the many villages on both banks of the River Gambia. Travellers are advised not to photograph Banjul airport or military bases and to ask the permission of any locals if wishing to photograph them and their village.

Climate

The Gambia is generally recognised to have the most agreeable climate in West Africa. The weather is subtropical with distinct dry and rainy seasons. From mid-November to mid-May, coastal areas are dry, while the rainy season lasts from June to October. Inland the cool season is shorter and daytime temperatures are very high between March and June. Sunny periods occur on most days even during the rainy season.

Required clothing: Lightweight or tropical for most of the year with rainwear for the rainy season.

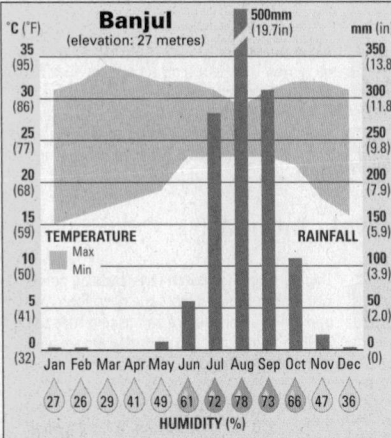

Banjul (elevation: 27 metres)

TEMPERATURE Max Min   RAINFALL

°C (°F) / mm (in)

Jan Feb Mar Apr May Jun Jul Aug Sep Oct Nov Dec
27 26 29 41 49 61 72 78 73 66 47 36
HUMIDITY (%)

Communications

Telephone: Country code: 220. The country has an automatic telephone system. IDD is available.
Mobile telephone: Roaming agreements exist with most international mobile phone companies. Coverage is good around Banjul and patchy to non-existent elsewhere.
Internet: E-mail can be accessed in Internet cafes in major towns.

Post: The postal service can be slow and unreliable. The main Post office is on Wellington Street, Banjul. Travellers can buy a rich array of postcards and stamps. Post office hours: Mon-Fri 0800-1300 and 1400-1700, Sat 0800-1100.
MEDIA: State-run Gambia Television and Radio Gambia broadcast tightly-controlled news. Private media are severely restricted, with radio stations and newspapers having to pay large licence fees. A media bill passed in March 2002 was considered as a threat to press freedom. The law set up a commission whose powers range from issuing licences to jailing journalists. In 2004, further legislation was introduced allowing for jail terms for journalists found guilty of libel or sedition.
Press: *The Observer* is a daily newspaper in English. Other publications include *The Independent, Foroyaa (bi-weekly)* and *The Point (thrice-weekly).*
TV: The government operates the only national television station, *Gambia Television; Premium TV Network* is a private satellite channel.
Radio: State-run national broadcaster *Radio Gambia* transmits programmes in English and local languages. Private stations include *Radio 1 FM* (music), *West Coast Radio* and *Sud FM. Radio France Internationale* is available via an FM relay.

Passport/Visa

	Passport Required?	Visa Required?	Return Ticket Required?
Full British	Yes	No	Yes
Australian	Yes	No	Yes
Canadian	Yes	No	Yes
USA	Yes	Yes/1	Yes
Other EU	Yes	Yes/1	Yes
Japanese	Yes	Yes/1	Yes

Note: *Regulations and requirements may be subject to change at short notice, and you are advised to contact the appropriate diplomatic or consular authority before finalising travel arrangements. Any numbers in the chart refer to the footnotes below.*

PASSPORTS: Passport valid for at least three months after date of return required by all.
VISAS: Required by all except the following for a maximum stay of three months:
(a) nationals of countries referred to in the chart above, except **1.** nationals of Austria, Czech Republic, Estonia, France, Hungary, Japan, Latvia, Lithuania, Poland, Portugal, Slovak Republic, Slovenia, Spain and the USA who *do* need a visa;
(b) nationals of ECOWAS countries;
(c) nationals of The Bahamas, Botswana, Iceland, India, Jamaica, Kenya, Malawi, New Zealand, Norway, San Marino, Tanzania, Uganda, Zambia and Zimbabwe;
(d) transit passengers continuing their journey by the same or first connecting aircraft within two hours provided holding valid onward or return documentation and not leaving the airport.
Note: (a)* These nationals may not always require a visa, but *do* require clearance from the Embassy/High Commission. (b) Nationals of some countries always require a transit visa; enquire with airline for details. (c) All visitors must hold return or onward tickets, all documents for their next destination and sufficient funds for their stay.
Types of visa and cost: *Tourist* and *Business*: £20 (single-entry); £40 (multiple-entry).
Validity: Single-entry visas are valid for six months. Multiple-entry visas are valid for 12 months. Extensions are possible and should be applied for at the Immigration Office in The Gambia.
Application to: Consulate (or consular section at Embassy); see *Passport & Visa Information.*
Application requirements: (a) Valid passport. (b) One application form. (c) One passport-size photo. (d) Fee, payable in cash, cheque or postal order only. (e) Stamped, self-addressed envelope (by registered post).
Working days required: 48 hours in person. At least one week by post.
Temporary residence: Enquiries should be referred to The Gambian Embassy, High Commission or Consulate (see *Passport/Visa Information*).

PASSPORT/VISA INFORMATION

High Commision of the Republic of The Gambia in the UK
57 Kensington Court, London W8 5DG, UK
Tel: (020) 7937 6316.
Email: gambia@gamhighcom.fsnet.co.uk
Opening hours: Mon-Thurs 1000-1600, Fri 1000-1200.

Embassy of the Republic of The Gambia in the USA
Suite 905, 1156 15th Street, NW, Washington, DC 20005, USA
Tel: (202) 785 1399 *or* 1425.
Email: gambiaembassy1@aol.com

Money

Currency: Gambian Dalasi (GMD) = 100 bututs. Notes are in denominations of GMD100, 50, 25, 10 and 5. Coins are in denominations of GMD1, and 50, 25, 10, 5 and 1 bututs.
Currency exchange: There is a bank/bureau de change (Meridien Bank) at the airport operating during scheduled flights. The capital, Banjul, also has a number of banks where foreign currencies can be exchanged. Some hotels and tourist resorts also offer foreign exchange facilities, but tend to charge high commissions. ATMs are available in large urban areas, but are not always reliable. As The Gambia is a cash economy travellers are advised to carry sufficient currency to cover expenses of a planned visit.
Credit & debit cards: American Express, MasterCard and Visa are accepted in most hotels if arranged at the beginning of the stay. Check with your credit or debit card company for details of merchant acceptability and other services which may be available. Due to credit card and bank fraud, caution is advised when using credit cards and ATMs.
Traveller's cheques: To avoid additional exchange rate charges, travellers are advised to take traveller's cheques in Pounds Sterling or US Dollars.
Currency restrictions: The thriving black market for hard currency is officially discouraged, and visitors must complete a currency declaration form on arrival. Currency from Algeria, Ghana, Guinea, Mali, Morocco, Nigeria, Sierra Leone and Tunisia is neither accepted nor exchanged. There are no restrictions on the import of local or other foreign currencies. Export of local or other foreign currencies is up to the amount imported. CFA Francs are accepted. Local currency may be difficult to exchange outside the country but there are no restrictions on its import and export.
Banking hours: Mon-Thurs 0800-1330, Fri 0800-1100 (banks in Banjul); Mon-Fri 0800-1200 and 1600-1800, Sat 0800-1300 (banks elsewhere).
Exchange rate indicators:
Rate at time of publishing
£1.00=   GMD49.26
$1.00=   GMD28.30

Duty Free

The following goods may be imported into The Gambia without incurring customs duty:
200 cigarettes or 50 cigars or 250g of tobacco (or mixed to the same total weight); *1l of spirits; 1l of wine or beer; goods up to a value of GMD1000 (members of families travelling together may aggregate their individual allowances provided no single article exceeds GMD1000 in value).*

Public Holidays

Below are listed Public Holidays for the January 2006-June 2007 period.
2006: Jan 1 New Year's Day. **Jan 10** Tabaski (Feast of the Sacrifice). **Feb 18** Independence Day. **Apr 10** Milad al-Nabi (Birth of the Prophet). **Apr 14** Good Friday. **Apr 17** Easter Monday. **May 1** Labour Day. **Jul 22** Revolution Day. **Aug 15** Assumption. **Oct 22** Koriteh (End of Ramadan). **Dec 25** Christmas. **Dec 31** Tabaski (Feast of the Sacrifice).
2007: Jan 1 New Year's Day. **Feb 18** Independence Day. **Mar 31** Milad al-Nabi (Birth of the Prophet). **Apr 6** Good Friday. **Apr 9** Easter Monday. **May 1** Labour Day.
Note: Muslim festivals are timed according to local sightings of various phases of the moon and the dates given above are approximations. During the lunar month of Ramadan that precedes Koriteh, Muslims fast during the day and feast at night and normal business patterns may be interrupted in a few instances. For more information, see the *World of Islam* appendix.

Health

	Special Precautions?	Certificate Required?
Yellow Fever	Yes	1
Cholera	Yes	2
Typhoid & Polio	3	N/A
Malaria	4	N/A

Note: *Regulations and requirements may be subject to change at short notice, and you are advised to contact your doctor well in advance of your intended date of departure. Any numbers in the chart refer to the footnotes below.*

1: A *yellow fever* vaccination certificate is required from all travellers over one year of age arriving from endemic or infected areas. Travellers arriving from non-endemic zones should note that vaccination is strongly recommended for travel outside the urban areas, even if an outbreak of the disease has not been reported and they would not normally require a vaccination certificate to enter the country.
2: Following WHO guidelines issued in 1973, a *cholera* vaccination certificate is no longer a condition of entry to The Gambia. However, cholera is a risk in this country and

precautions are necessary. Up-to-date advice should be sought before deciding whether these precautions should include vaccination as medical opinion is divided over its effectiveness; see the Health appendix for more information.
3: Immunisation against *typhoid* and *poliomyelitis* is often advised.
4: *Malaria* risk, predominantly in the malignant *falciparum* form, exists all year throughout the country. Chloroquine and sulfadoxine-pyrimethamine resistance has been reported.
Food & drink: All water should be regarded as being potentially contaminated. Water used for drinking, brushing teeth or making ice should have first been boiled or otherwise sterilised. Milk is unpasteurised and should be boiled. Powdered or tinned milk is available and is advised, but make sure that it is reconstituted with pure water. Avoid dairy products that are likely to have been made from unboiled milk. Only eat well-cooked meat and fish, preferably served hot. Pork, salad and mayonnaise may carry increased risk. Vegetables should be cooked and fruit peeled.
Other risks: *Diarrhoeal diseases*, including *giardiasis*, and *typhoid fevers* are common. *Bilharzia* (schistosomiasis) is present. Avoid swimming and paddling in fresh water; swimming pools that are well chlorinated and maintained are safe. *Hepatitis A* and *E* are widespread. *Hepatitis B* is endemic. Epidemics of *meningococcal disease* may occur throughout tropical Africa, particularly in the savannah areas and during the dry season. Immunisation against *diphtheria* is sometimes recommended.
Rabies is present. For those at high risk, vaccination before arrival should be considered. If you are bitten, seek medical advice without delay. For more information, consult the *Health* appendix.
Health care: Visitors are advised to bring good supplies of sunscreen, insect repellent and indigestion/diarrhoea medicines; all of these may be needed and they can prove expensive or, in some cases, impossible to buy in The Gambia. The Government provides both therapeutic and preventative medical and health services, and plays a dominant role in health services. Health insurance is strongly advised. Travellers in possession of prescriptive drugs should carry proof of their prescriptions preferably in labelled containers. Police have on occasion arrested travellers carrying unlabelled containers.

Travel - International

AIR:

The main airlines to serve The Gambia are *Air Senegal* (www.air-senegal-international.com), *Gambia International Airlines* (www.gia.gm) and *Ghana Airways*. There are also many charter services.
Approximate flight times: From Banjul to *London* is approximately 5 hours 30 minutes (direct).
Main airports: *Banjul (BJL)* (Yundum International)(website: www.gambia.gm/gcaa) is 20km (11 miles) southwest of the city. *To/from the airport:* Taxis are available to the city (travel time – approximately 30 minutes). During 1989, NASA built new airport facilities to enable it to serve as an emergency space-shuttle landing site. *Facilities:* Banks/bureaux de change, internet cafe, bars, restaurants, tourist information, duty-free shops, post office and car hire.
Departure tax: None.
Tourist tax: A tourist tax applies for all tourists arriving at Banjul International Airport, no matter from which country. Travellers can pay in Euros (10), Sterling (£5) or US Dollars (US$10).
RIVER:

Main ports: *Banjul Port* is the official port for all ferries. There is a ferry service between Banjul and Dakar in Senegal.
ROAD:

Taxis can be hired between Dakar (Senegal) and Barra. Buses also travel between Senegal and The Gambia.

Travel - Internal

RIVER:

There are nearly a dozen ferry crossing points where travellers can cross the river. Tour operators run adventure and fishing trips using converted yachts or pirogues, as well as day cruises along the river with lunch or dinner and a live band.
ROAD:

Traffic drives on the right. There are more than 3000km (1875 miles) of roads in the country, about 450km (280 miles) of which are paved. Roads in and around Banjul are mostly bituminised, but unsealed roads often become impassable in the rainy season. Extensive road improvements are underway; the latest additions are the Kombo coastal roads which have improved access to the airport and other popular sights and attractions. **Bus:** Local buses operate between Banjul and a number of towns and villages throughout the country. The services are fairly reliable, but tend to be overcrowded. **Taxis:** There are three types of taxis: *Tourist Taxis* are usually

painted green and are licensed by the Gambian Tourist Authority. They operate a queue system outside hotels and resort areas and have a published tariff for set distances inside the taxi; *General Purpose Taxis* are usually painted yellow with green stripes - these are usually shared and used for short distances; *Collective 'Bush' Taxis* are usually seven-seater vans and go anywhere in the country, stopping wherever passengers want to get off, and picking up new passengers when there is room. It is advisable to settle taxi fares in advance. **Car hire:** *AB* and *Hertz* operate in the Gambia; check with the car hire company for details before travelling. Driving in The Gambia can be difficult at times due to poor road conditions, particularly during the rainy season (June to October). **Documentation:** An International Driving Permit will be accepted for a period of three months. A temporary licence is available from the local authorities on presentation of a valid UK licence. **Bicycle hire:** Bikes are available to rent at many hotels and resorts.

Travel Advice

Crime against tourists is rare, but travellers should take sensible precautions and remain vigilant in public places. Care should be taken when driving or walking on roads, particularly at night, due to unpredictable driving standards and lack of street lighting.
The threat from terrorism is low, but you should be aware of the global risk of indiscriminate terrorist attacks, which could be against civilian targets, including places frequented by foreigners.
This advice is based on information provided by the Foreign and Commonwealth Office in the UK. It is correct at time of publishing. As the situation can change rapidly, visitors are advised to contact the following organisations for the latest travel advice:

British Foreign and Commonwealth Office
Tel: (0845) 850 2829.
Website: www.fco.gov.uk

US Department of State
Website: http://travel.state.gov/travel

Accommodation

EDITOR'S CHOICE: AFRICAN BUNGALOWS

Community-run Tumani Tenda offers bungalows in traditional African surroundings. All the profits from a traveller's stay are kept in the village and are used to pay for development projects. The village houses 300 people and is set in beautiful surroundings. Travellers can stay in one of five traditional African style houses, each individually designed by a family in the village.

HOTELS:

By African standards, The Gambia has a fairly developed tourist industry, with many hotels geared primarily to package tours. During the tourist season (November to May), accommodation is often booked up and confirmation of advance booking is advised. Most of the hotels are self-contained complexes offering a wealth of tourist facilities, including swimming pools, bars, restaurants, shops, sporting facilities and spacious gardens. Bedrooms will not always be air conditioned. The number of hotels has increased greatly in recent years and this is expected to continue; today there are over 30 hotels with more than 6000 beds, both in Banjul and along the coast. Around 75 per cent of establishments belong to The Gambia Hotel Association, which can be contacted c/o PO Box 2637, The Bungalow Beach Hotel, Serrekunda, Kotu (tel: 446 5288; email: bbhotel@qanet.gm). There are about a dozen camps, lodges and motels in rural areas which provide basic but comfortable accommodation and meals. The most luxurious of these is Sindola Safari Lodge located at Kanilai, the home of the President of The Gambia. There are others along the Atlantic coast line and they are a great place for boat rides and birdwatching trips - a boon for ecotourists. For further information on different types of accommodation, contact The Gambia Tourism Authority (see *Top Things To See & Do*).
CAMPING/CARAVANNING:

Camping is available on MacCarthy Island. Safari tents with fans and lighting are already set up for travellers, overlooking the river. There is a small area set aside for travellers with their own tents or it is possible to hire a two-man dome tent including bedding. Those who have travelled through the Sahara are welcome to park their caravans here too.
APARTMENTS/SELF CATERING:

Self-catering apartments and bungalows are available in the main resorts.

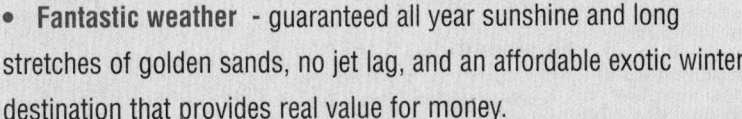

Top Things To See & Do

- In the only sizeable town in the country, **Banjul,** visit the **National Museum**.
- Discover Banjul's colonial atmosphere in the area around **MacCarthy Square**, with pleasant 19th-century architecture. Nearby is the **craft market**. Souvenirs and local handicrafts can also be bought at various *bengdulala* (meaning a 'meeting place' in the Mandinka language); shopping areas consisting of African-style stalls, usually built near hotels. In the heart of the capital is lively **Albert market** where travellers can buy clothes, shoes, fruit and vegetables, household goods and local handicraft.
- Enjoy excellent views from **Arch 22**, Gambia's tallest building, built to commemorate the military takeover led by the now President Yahya Jammeh.
- The Atlantic coast to the south of Banjul boasts some of the finest beaches in all of Africa with no less than 15 hotels in the **Banjul**, **Kombo** and **St Mary** area. The estuary of the **River Gambia** provides miles of magnificent beaches with warm seas throughout the year for **swimming**. Due to strong currents, caution is necessary when swimming, but the beach at **Cape St Mary** is safe for both children and adults.
- **Sailing** is possible at The Gambia Sailing Club at Banjul, which welcomes visitors. A notable event is the race to **Dog Island**. The River Gambia is the dominant feature of the country and it is possible to take boat trips up the river. The whole river and the numerous creeks (known locally as *bolongs*) which join it, are fascinating to both the bird lover and the student of nature.
- **Fort Bullen** at **Barra Point** was built by the British 200 years ago to cover the approaches to Banjul and the river, succeeding **James Island Fortress** (destroyed by the French) as the main point of defence in the colony. It can be reached by direct ferry from the capital. **Oyster Creek** is the centre of an area of creeks and waterways which can be visited from Banjul.
- Both sea and river **fishing** is good all year round, particularly line-fishing from the beaches. Several sport-fishing boats are available for sea-angling trips.
- Walk through the jungle of the **Abuko Nature Reserve**, which has crocodiles, monkeys, birds and antelopes. Details of cruises can be found on hotel noticeboards. The **Kiang West National Park** also has a rich birdlife as well as other animal species. The **Niokolo-Koba National Park** in the Upper Casamance regions is a World Heritage site of outstanding beauty.
- Upriver from Banjul, go to **Albreda,** which was the main French trading post before they withdrew from The Gambia. Nearby is the village of **Juffure**, the alleged home of the ancestors of black American writer Alex Haley, author of *Roots*.
- Visitors who want to see more of the countryside may cross by ferry from Banjul to Barra and travel by road to Juffure and Albreda (the journey lasts about 50 minutes), and then by canoe to **James Island** in the calm waters of the River Gambia.
- The popular tourist destination of **Tendaba** is 160km (100 miles) from Banjul by river or road.
- Further upriver, catch sight of the fascinating circles of standing stones around **Wassau**, which have been identified as burial grounds more than 1200 years old.
- **Janjangbureh** (formerly **Georgetown**) was the 'second city' of colonial days, and is still the administrative and trading centre of the region.
- **Basse Santa Su** is the major trading centre for the upper reaches of the Gambia River. Stroll along handsome trading houses built at the turn of the century.
- Watch **bouts** (a traditional sport) which can be seen on most weekends in Banjul and its suburbs, Serrekunda and Bakau.

Entertainment

FOOD & DRINK: Western food is available at most tourist hotels and restaurants, as is traditional Gambian delicacies.
National specialities:
- *Benachin* (also called 'Jollof Rice', a mixture of spiced meat and rice with tomato puree and vegetables).
- *Base nyebe* (rich stew of chicken or beef with green beans and other vegetables).
- *Chere* (steamed millet flour balls).
- *Domodah* (meat stewed in groundnut puree and served with rice).

- *Plasas* (meat and smoked fish cooked in palm oil with green vegetables) served with *fu-fu* or mashed *cassava chura-gertek* (a sweet porridge consisting of pounded groundnuts, rice and milk).
- Mangoes, bananas, grapefruit, papayas and oranges.
National drinks:
- Spirits, beers and wines.
- *Jul Brew* is the local speciality beer.
- Fresh fruit juice.
Tipping: 10 per cent service charge is sometimes included in hotel and restaurant bills. Although if the service calls for it a further tip can be given.
NIGHTLIFE: In general the nightlife is subdued, although there are nightclubs and bars in Bakau, Banjul, Farjara and Serrekunda. There are organised performances of Gambian ballet, drumming and dancing, and also fire-eating displays.
SHOPPING: Souvenirs can be bought in Banjul at the craft market across from MacCarthy Square and at *bengdulalu* (see *Top Things To See & Do*). One of the most popular purchases is the Gambishirt, made of printed and embroidered cotton cloth, mostly in bright colours. Some of the souvenirs are gaudy, others exceedingly attractive. Woodcarvings, beaded belts, silver and gold jewellery and ladies' handbags are also popular items. Other West African handicrafts made of straw, beads, leather, cloth or metal can be purchased here. **Shopping hours:** Mon-Thurs 0900-1200 and 1430-1800, Fri-Sat 0900-1300. Some shops may stay open until 2200.

Business

- **GDP:** US$2.8 billion (2004 estimate).
- **Main exports:** Peanut products, fish, cotton, lint, palm kernals, palm oil, palm wood and beeswax.
- **Main imports:** Foodstuff, fuel, machinery and transport equipment.
- **Main trade partners:** Iran, Libya, Taiwan, Cuba and Nigeria.

ECONOMY: The economy of The Gambia is basically agricultural, with groundnuts (in the form of nuts, oil and cattle cake) accounting for 50 per cent of total exports. Cotton and citrus fruits are also cultivated for export. Forestry and fishing are also important. Rice, millet and maize are the main staples, but The Gambia must import large quantities of rice along with various other foodstuffs and petroleum products. There are no viable mineral deposits although surveys have located some oil deposits. The small industrial sector is dominated by agro-industrial activities; drinks and construction materials are produced for the domestic market. After a disastrous spell following the 1994 coup, tourism is once again a viable generator of foreign exchange, and has performed relatively well since then. Principal markets for exports are Belgium, Luxembourg, Japan and Guinea. Government economic strategy aims to position The Gambia as a regional hub for trade, based on an important re-export trade (mostly of Senegalese goods) as well as finance and telecommunications: the strategy has had mixed success in the last few years. Overall, the economy has performed fairly well, achieving annual growth since 2000, averaging annual growth of 3 per cent in 2004. Substantial infrastructural progress has been made (such as the construction of schools and hospitals, a new airport terminal and modernised port facilities). In 1998, the government, unusually, renationalised the groundnut industry, which had been privatised four years earlier but performed poorly under private ownership. International aid remains essential to the health of The Gambia's economy.
BUSINESS ETIQUETTE: Businessmen wear jackets and ties for business meetings. A personal approach is important in Gambian business circles. Punctuality is appreciated and it is advisable to take business cards, although their use is not widespread. **Office hours**: Mon-Thurs 0800-1600, Fri 0800-1230.

Georgia

Location: Caucasus, north of Turkey.

Time: GMT + 4.

Overview

Throughout the centuries Georgia has been a victim of the aggression of powerful neighbours. The nation's history has been a constant struggle for survival, interspersed with brief interludes of peace.

At the end of the 18th century, King Erekle II, a descendant of the Bagratids who ruled Georgia in the 12th century, forged a vital alliance with Catherine the Great of Russia, who was then presiding over the southward expansion of her empire. The Bagratid line was deposed by the Russians in 1801 after which the whole region was steadily absorbed into the Russian Empire.

A strong Georgian nationalist movement grew up from around this time, the precursor of the irrepressible Georgian nationalism which has shaped the republic's history during the Soviet and post-Soviet periods. Although Stalin was himself a Georgian – his real name was Djugashvili – the republic suffered terribly during the purges of the 1930s and 40s. Nonetheless, many Georgians continue to this day to idolise their most notorious son.

Stalin's repressive policies failed to stamp out Georgian nationalism. In a referendum held in April 1991, an overwhelming majority voted in favour of independence from the Soviet Union and a formal declaration of independence was made in May.

Apart from the dire state of the Georgian economy, the country's main problems have been the secessionist revolts in the outlying Georgian provinces of Abkhazia on the Black Sea coast (where Gamsakhurdia was located) and South Ossetia in the north. In 1994, after two years of sporadic fighting, South Ossetia was brought back into the fold, but the Abkhazia problem has proved quite intractable. The only existing mediation effort, on the part of the UN, is at a standstill and Abkhazia is now effectively isolated from the rest of Georgia. The government also faces problems in the Pankisi Gorge region, which is reputed to be a haven for Islamic militants.

Formerly the holiday haunt of the privileged elite of the Soviet Union, Georgia is blessed with stunning scenery, a balmy climate and a rich variety of flora and fauna. Enclosed high valleys, wide basins, health spas with famous mineral waters, caves and waterfalls combine in this land of varied landscapes and striking beauty. With its stone houses built around vine-draped courtyards, and winding streets, the capital, Tbilisi, has a lively, Mediterranean atmosphere. Sukhumi, the capital of Abkhazia in the far northwest of Georgia, was until civil unrest began a relaxed, sunny port/resort, renowned for its beaches fringed with palms and eucalyptus trees, lively open-air cafes and cosmopolitan population.

General Information

AREA: 69,700 sq km (26,911 sq miles).
POPULATION: 5 million (UN, 2005).
POPULATION DENSITY: 71.7 per sq km.
CAPITAL: Tbilisi. **Population:** 1.5 million.
GEOGRAPHY: Georgia is a mountainous country bordered by the Russian Federation in the north, Turkey in the southeast, Armenia in the south, Azerbaijan in the east and by the Black Sea in the west, which forms a 330km- (206 mile-) long coastline. It includes the two autonomous republics Abkhazia and Ajaria. The state is crossed by the ranges of the Greater Caucasus (highest peak: Mt Kazbek, 5047m/16,554ft). Enclosed high valleys, wide basins, health spas with famous mineral waters, caves and waterfalls combine in this land of varied landscapes and striking beauty.
GOVERNMENT: Republic. Gained independence from the Soviet Union in 1991. **Head of State and Government:** President Mickheil Saakashvili was elected in 2004. **Recent history:** The Parliamentary elections which took place in November 2003 were criticised by international organisations as being flawed. Peaceful demonstrations led to the resignation of President Shevardnadze and the Speaker of Parliament, Nino Burjanadze, was appointed Acting President until presidential elections were held in January 2004. Mickheil Saakashvili, leader of the National Movement, who was the main figure behind the November demonstrations, was elected by a landslide victory. Mr Saakashvili's party and coalition partners won the parliamentary elections held in February 2005.
Following Saakashvili's election as President, tensions between the semi-autonomous region of Ajara and its autocratic leader Abashidze grew. Abashidze stepped down. Georgia's Parliament introduced a new Ajaran Constitution and fresh Ajaran legislative elections were held. They were won by a local offshoot of President Saakashvili's National Movement party.
LANGUAGE: The official language is Georgian, the only language in the Ibera Caucasian family written in ancient script, with its own unique alphabet. Russian, Armenian, Azeri, Ossetian and Abkhazian are also spoken.
RELIGION: Christian majority, mainly Georgian Orthodox church. Also Eastern Orthodox, Muslim, Jewish and other Christian denomination minorities.
ELECTRICITY: 220 volts AC, 50 Hz. European-type, two-pin plugs are used. The supply of electricity can be intermittent between November and March, and visitors are advised to bring a torch with them.
SOCIAL CONVENTIONS: Georgians pride themselves on their reputation for gregariousness and hospitality. Visitors sitting in restaurants are likely to be offered drinks by complete strangers. They will then be invited to raise (and empty) their glasses in response to an endless string of elaborate toasts, preferably interpolating a few suitably enthusiastic toasts of their own into the sequence. Smoking is widespread. Visitors may also be entertained in private homes. On such occasions, gifts such as chocolates, flowers or alcohol are well received. On social occasions foreign women will find themselves the object of immense flattery. Those finding such attentions oppressive should avoid giving any hint of encouragement. Appropriate clothing should be worn when entering a church; visitors should ensure they are not wearing shorts and women should cover their heads. Visitors should also be aware that street crime is far from uncommon. Anyone travelling in the republic should be cautious when venturing out after dark, carry as few valuables as possible, and beware of the risk of being robbed and possibly attacked.

Climate

Hot summers with mild winters, particularly in the southwest. Low temperatures are common in alpine areas. Heaviest rainfall exists in the subtropical southwest.

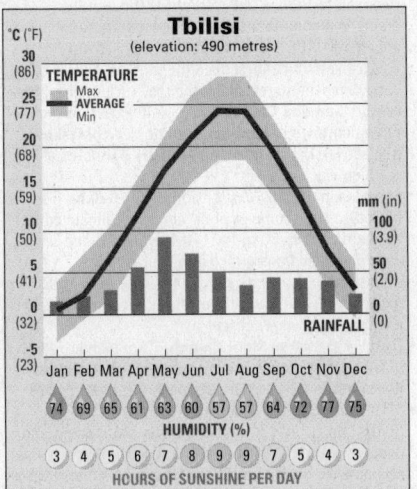

Tbilisi (elevation: 490 metres)

Communications

Telephone: IDD is, in theory, available. Country code: 995. Some outgoing calls from Georgia, except to other parts of the CIS, must be made through the operator and long waits can occur. It is possible for visitors to set up an account with the local telecom company that enables them to make direct long-distance calls without the operator's assistance. Many businesspeople and journalists now use satellite links to overcome the considerable problems of ordinary telephone communication. The Metekhi Palace Hotel is equipped with its own satellite phones.
Mobile telephone: *Geocell Ltd* (website: www.geocell.com.ge) and *Magti Com* (website: www.magtigsm.com) have roaming agreements with international mobile phone companies. It is possible to rent mobile hand-sets from Geocell Ltd. Coverage is good throughout the country, but there is limited coverage in the north west.
Internet: There are some internet cafes in Tbilisi.
Post: International postal services can be severely disrupted. Long delays may occur and parcels should be registered or delivered through courier services such as *Air Express* and *DHL*, based locally. It is advisable to post letters in central post offices rather than using the post boxes in the street.
MEDIA: Much of the Georgian media are considered to be free but there have been reports of journalists investigating corruption being harassed, and sometimes physically attacked. The outspoken private TV station *Rustavi-2* has regularly angered the police and officials. The authorities operate the national state TV and radio networks.
Press: The daily press includes *Sakartvelos Respublika* (Republic of Georgia), which is state-owned and *Rezonansi* (Resonance), which is private; *Akhali Versia* (New Version) is a weekly publication. *Svobodnaya Gruzia* (Free Georgia) is published in Russian. *Georgian Times* and *Georgia Today* are English-language weeklies. There are 200 privately owned newspapers. Other foreign newspapers are available.
TV: Georgian State TV is state-run. *Rustavi-2, Imedi TV* and *Ajara TV* (Batumi-based) are private channels.
Radio: Stations include *Georgian State Radio* and private Tbilisi-based FM stations *Fortuna* and *Radio 105*.

Passport/Visa

	Passport Required?	Visa Required?	Return Ticket Required?
Full British	Yes	No/1	No
Australian	Yes	Yes	No
Canadian	Yes	No/2	No
USA	Yes	No/2	No
Other EU	Yes	No/1	No
Japanese	Yes	No/2	No

Note: *Regulations and requirements may be subject to change at short notice, and you are advised to contact the appropriate diplomatic or consular authority before finalising travel arrangements. Any numbers in the chart refer to the footnotes below.*

PASSPORTS: Passport valid for at least six months required by all.
VISAS: Required by all except:
(a) nationals of CIS (except nationals of Russian Federation and Turkmenistan who *do* require a visa). (b) **1.** Nationals of EU countries. (c) **2.** Nationals of Canada, Israel, Japan, Switzerland and USA.
Note: (a) All visitors must register with the police within three days of arrival.
Types of visa and cost: *Ordinary:* £8 (one month); £23 (three months); £4 (transit). *Double-entry:* £12 (one month); £35 (three months); £8 (transit visa). *Multiple-entry:* £77 (one year). For all other types of visa, contact the Embassy directly.
Visa Note: Passengers on cruise ships which stay on a Georgian port for less than 72 hours do not require a visa.
Validity: Tourist visas are valid from one to three months from date of issue. Multiple-entry visas are valid for 12 months from date of issue for stays of up to three months each. Transit visas are normally valid for a maximum of three days (provided transit passengers are also holding valid onward or return documentation).
Application to: *Individual* travellers should apply to the Embassy (or consular section at Embassy) or send their application by post; see *Passport/Visa Information*. Nationals of countries where there is no Georgian diplomatic representation may obtain visas for US$10 at Tbilisi international airport, where a 24-hour service is provided by the Visa Branch of the Consular Department of the Ministry of Foreign Affairs (tel: (32) 284 698; website: www.mfa.gov.ge). Visitors should note that this service is only applicable for short-stay visits (maximum 30 days or 15 days for nationals of Turkey). Visa Consular services are also available at Batumi and Kutaisi airports and the ports

of Batumi and Poti. It is also recommended that the Consular Department of the Ministry of Foreign Affairs be informed in advance of the visitor's planned visit by the inviting party.
Tourist travellers must submit all documentation to the tour operator making the travel arrangements.
Application requirements: (a) Completed application form. (b) One recent colour passport-size photo. (c) Passport, valid for at least six months from the date of application. (d) Fee (cheques and postal orders are accepted, payable to Embassy of Georgia). (e) Stamped, self-addressed envelope for postal applications. *Business:* (a)-(e) and, (f) Letter of invitation from the inviting company. (g) Letter of introduction from the employer. *Transit:* (a)-(e), and (f) Visa for country of destination (if applicable). (g) Photocopy of confirmed return air ticket to and from Georgia (if applicable). (h) An official letter from an employer may also be required for the processing of transit visas (if applicable).
Working days required: Two to 10 for personal applications; two weeks to one month for multiple-entry visas; postal applicants must allow at least three to four working days for the return of passport and visa. If urgent, single- and double-entry visas can be processed the next working day during opening hours. Multiple-entry visas can also be processed, if urgent, within two weeks. An additional fee is required to process visas urgently. Note: Applications should be made no later than three working days and not earlier than three months from the date of departure.

PASSPORT/VISA INFORMATION

Embassy of Georgia in the UK
4 Russell Gardens, London W14 8EZ, UK
Tel: (020) 7603 7799.
Website: www.geoemb.org.uk
Opening hours: Mon-Fri 1000-1800; 1000-1300 (visa lodging and collection), except Wednesdays (closed for consular information but not general enquiries).

Embassy of the Georgian Republic in the USA
1101 15th Street, Suite 602, NW, Washington DC 20005, USA
Tel: (202) 387 9150 *or* 393 6060 (consular section).
Website: www.georgiaemb.org
Opening hours: Mon-Fri 1000-1230.

Money

Currency: Lari (GEL) = 100 tetri. Notes are in denominations of GEL100, 50, 20, 10, 5, 2 and 1. Coins are in denominations of 50, 20, 10 and 5 tetri.
Currency exchange: Euros, Roubles or US Dollars can be exchanged at special exchange shops, found throughout the city, while other currencies must be exchanged in banks. Cash is the preferred method of payment, and visitors are advised to carry notes in small denominations. Visitors are also advised to carry US$ in cash. Euros and Russian Roubles are also in use. There is unlikely to be a substantial difference between rates offered by banks or bureaux de change.
Credit & debit cards: Credit cards are accepted in certain hotels, restaurants and shops in Tbilisi. Check with your credit or debit card company for details of merchant acceptability and other services which may be available.
Traveller's cheques: Euros or US Dollars are recommended.
Currency restrictions: The import and export of local currency is unrestricted. The import of foreign currency is permitted. The export of foreign currency is limited to US$500 or equivalent.
Banking hours: Mon-Fri 1000-1800.
Exchange rate indicators:
Rate at time of publishing
£1.00=   GEL3.12
$1.00=   GEL1.79

Duty Free

The following goods may be imported into Georgia without incurring customs duty:
200 cigarettes; 3l of wine or 10l of beer; personal goods up to the weight of 100kg.
Note: If importing more than 20kg of a good, the good will be taxed at GEL1 per kilo. On entering the country, tourists are advised to complete a customs declaration form, which they should retain until departure. This allows for the import of articles intended for personal use, including currency and valuables (such as jewellery, cameras and computers) which must be registered on the declaration form. Customs inspections are detailed.
Prohibited imports: Military weapons and ammunition, narcotics and drug paraphernalia, pornography, loose pearls and anything owned by a third party that is to be carried in for that third party.

Prohibited exports: Works of art and antiques (unless permission has been granted by the Ministry of Culture). In this case, the passenger should also hold a photo of the work of art or antique.

Public Holidays

Below are listed Public Holidays for the January 2006-June 2007 period.
2006: Jan 1 New Year's Day. **Jan 7** Orthodox Christmas. **Jan 19** Orthodox Epiphany/Baptism. **Mar 3** Mothers' Day. **Mar 8** Women's Day. **Apr 9** National Day. **Apr 23** Orthodox Easter. **Apr 24** Orthodox Easter Monday. **May 9** National Holiday. **May 12** National Holiday. **May 26** Independence Day. **Aug 28** Mariamoba (Assumption). **Oct 14** Svetitskhovloba (Georgian Orthodox Festival). **Nov 23** Giorgoba (St George's Day). **2007: Jan 1** New Year's Day. **Jan 7** Orthodox Christmas. **Jan 19** Orthodox Epiphany/Baptism. **Mar 3** Mothers' Day. **Mar 8** Women's Day. **Apr 8** Orthodox Easter. **Apr 9** National Day/ Orthodox Easter Monday. **May 12** National Holiday. **May 26** Independence Day.

Health

	Special Precautions?	Certificate Required?
Yellow Fever	No	No
Cholera	No	No
Typhoid & Polio	1	N/A
Malaria	2	N/A

Note: *Regulations and requirements may be subject to change at short notice, and you are advised to contact your doctor well in advance of your intended date of departure. Any numbers in the chart refer to the footnotes below.*

1: Immunisation against *poliomyelitis* and *typhoid* is sometimes recommended.
2: *Malaria* risk in the benign *vivax* form exists from July to October in some villages in the southeastern part of the country.
Food & drink: All water should be regarded as being a potential health risk. Boiled water is readily available and should be used. Milk is pasteurised and dairy products are safe for consumption. Only eat well-cooked meat and fish, preferably served hot. Pork, salad and mayonnaise may carry increased risk. Vegetables should be cooked and fruit peeled.
Other risks: *Hepatitis A* occurs. Immunisation against *hepatitis B* should be considered. Outbreaks of *diphtheria* and *anthrax* have been reported.
Rabies is present. For those at high risk, vaccination before arrival should be considered. If you are bitten, seek medical advice without delay. For more information, consult the *Health* appendix. Travellers staying for more than one month must present a medical certificate proving they are HIV-negative. If not holding the required documentation, they will be subject to a compulsory *AIDS* test on arrival.
Health care: The health system is undergoing dramatic change, medical facilities are available but owing to the present state of medical services, emergency evacuation travel insurance is recommended for all travellers. It is also advisable to take a supply of those medicines that are likely to be required (but check first that they may be legally imported) as medicines can prove very difficult to get hold of.

Travel - International

AIR:

Airzena Georgian Airlines (A9) (website: www.airzena.com), the national airline, operates regular flights from Athens, Frankfurt/M, Kiev, Moscow, Paris, Prague, Tel Aviv and Vienna.
Approximate flight times: From Tbilisi to *London* is 6 hours 45 minutes; to *New York* is 15 hours (both times include stopovers); and to *Paris* is 4 hours 45 minutes.
Main airports: *Tbilisi (TBS)* is 18km (11 miles) east of Tbilisi city centre. *To/from the airport:* Mini-buses and taxis are available to the city centre (travel time – 30 minutes), state buses run from 0800-2200 (website: www.airport-transfer.ge). *Facilities:* Bureaux de change, bars, restaurants, duty free shops. In winter, power failures may affect the airport.
Departure tax: None.
SEA:

Main ports: *Batumi* and *Poti.* Batumi and Poti provide international connections with sea ports in Bulgaria, Ukraine and Russia.
RAIL:
The *Transcaucasian railway* operates overnight services between Baku (Azerbaijan) and Yerevan (Armenia). The main line runs towards the Russian Federation through Georgia along the Black Sea coast. The *Silk Road Express* also runs a service from Baku to Tbilisi. War in the breakaway region of Abkhazia has

adversely affected Georgia's rail link with Russia, and it is currently not available.
ROAD:

Access is from Turkey, Armenia and Azerbaijan via the Dariali Gorge. The Russia-Georgia checkpoint at Kazbegi (the Georgian Military Highway), Tskhinvali (the Roki Tunnel) and routes across the Georgian-Abkhaz boarder are currently closed.

Travel - Internal

AIR:

Domestic flights operated by *Airzena Georgian Airlines* (website: www.airzena.com) run between Tbilisi and Butani, Kutaisi and Senaki.
RAIL:

In total, Georgia has almost 1600km (987 miles) of railway. The Government has now restored order on the railway, which had suffered from fuel shortages, armed attacks on trains, sabotage of track and bridges, and there is now a fundamentally sound infrastructure. However, rail travel through the Russian border in the north and west is not possible owing to the conflict in Abkhazia and visitors are advised not to undertake long-distance rail travel. Rail passengers are advised to store their valuables in the compartment under the seat/bed and not to leave the compartment unattended. It is also a good idea to ensure the compartment door is secure from the inside by tying it closed with wire or strong cord. Reservations are required for all trains. There are two classes of trains, primarily distinguished by the comfort of the seats. Children under five years of age travel free and children from five to nine years of age pay half fare.
ROAD:

Traffic drives on the right. Georgia has approximately 20,000km (12,428 miles) of asphalted roads, and there is an ambitious project to construct a motorway connecting the Black Sea ports to the border with Azerbaijan, passing through Tbilisi. Travellers attempting to drive around Georgia independently should be aware that it is difficult to buy fuel without highly specialised local knowledge and that an adequate supply of fuel should be obtained in Tbilisi beforehand. Also, reliable road maps or signposts do not exist. **Buses** are in poor condition and timetables change often and can not be relied upon. **Documentation:** It is possible for holders of an EU licence to drive in Georgia but an International Driving Permit is required to hire a vehicle.
URBAN:

Tbilisi is served by buses, trolleybuses, cable cars and a small underground system. The underground system has three lines and 16 stations. Tickets cost 20 Tetri. Regular big buses and trolleybuses cost 10-25 Tetri and minibuses cost 30-50 Tetri. It is common practice to flag down official taxis, but fares should always be negotiated in advance, bearing in mind the likelihood that rates set for foreigners will be unreasonably high. In view of the rising crime rate, foreigners should take precautions before getting into a car, and it is generally safer to use officially marked red taxis which should not be shared with strangers. It is inadvisable to take a ride if there is already more than one person in the car.

Travel Advice

All travel to the breakaway regions of South Ossetia, Abkhazia, the Pankisi gorge beyond Akhmeta and the Svaneti region (northwest Georgia) should be avoided because of the heightened military and police tensions in these regions. Travel to Ajara is possible since tensions have eased.
Entering or leaving Georgia via land borders with the Russian Federation should not be attempted under any circumstances.
Attacks on foreigners have risen particularly in urban areas of Tbilisi. Travelling alone in Georgia should be avoided and all precautions against the high levels of crime, including kidnapping and car hijacking should be undertaken.
This advice is based on information provided by the Foreign and Commonwealth Office in the UK. It is correct at time of publishing. As the situation can change rapidly, visitors are advised to contact the following organisations for the latest travel advice:

British Foreign and Commonwealth Office
Tel: (0845) 850 2829.
Website: www.fco.gov.uk

US Department of State
Website: http://travel.state.gov/travel

Accommodation

Under the former Soviet Government, hotels in Georgia were mainly state-owned. Much has changed recently, with many hotels now privatised and standards of tourist

facilities far higher than in previous years. Tbilisi has luxury hotels with correspondingly high prices, one of which also houses the British Embassy (for further information on staying in Tbilisi visit the website: www.info-tbilisi.com). There are also a number of good hotels in Batumi and Kutaisi. Some of the large public hotels now provide temporary accommodation for refugees from Abkhazia and do not serve tourists. Most of the accommodation facilities currently available in Georgia are bed & breakfast-type smaller hotels and guest houses typically serving eight to 16 guests, often with shared bathroom facilities. In rural areas, visitors can stay as guests in private houses.

Top Things To See

- Enjoy the Mediterranean atmosphere of **Tbilisi**, the capital of Georgia, which stands on the banks of the **River Mtkvari**, in a valley surrounded by hills. The name for the city derives from the word *tbili* (warm). It is best seen from the top of **Mount Mtatsminda**.
- The old city in Tbilisi, spreading out from the south bank of the river, has numerous frescoed churches (the most noteworthy being the fifth century **Sioni Cathedral**), 19th-century houses with arcaded open galleries on the upper floors, a castle and a surprising number of cafes and enticing tourist shops selling locally produced arts and crafts.
- **Prospekt Rustaveli**, Tbilisi's main thoroughfare, features an assortment of stylish public buildings testifying to the city's prosperity at the turn of the century.
- Spend some time at the **Georgian State Museum** on Prospekt Rustaveli in Tbilisi, which houses a collection of icons, frescoes and porcelain, as well as an outstanding display of jewellery discovered in pre-Christian Georgian tombs. The **Georgian Museum of Arts**, in the centre of town, includes many works by the much-loved 19th-century 'primitive' artist, Niko Pirosmani. The open-air **Museum of Ethnography**, located in a western suburb, has interesting examples of rural buildings and artefacts.
- Enjoy nice views of the old part of Tbilisi from the **Narikala Fortress**, first established by the Persians in the fourth century AD and most recently rebuilt in the 17th century.
- Head for **Mtskheta**, today a UNESCO World Heritage Site, which remained the centre of Georgian Christianity until the 12th century. The 15th-century **Svetitskhoveli Cathedral** (Pillar of Life), standing at the confluence of the **Mtkvari** and **Aragvi** rivers, was the holiest place in old Georgia. According to legend, the church is built on the spot where Christ's crucifixion robe was dropped to the ground in AD 328, having been brought from Jerusalem by a local Jew, and fragments of the robe are said to be kept inside the cathedral. The existing church has some impressive royal tombs, a fine icon stand and distinctive carved decoration, including bulls' heads and semi-pagan fertility symbols.
- Also of interest in Mtskheta are the **Samtavro Monastery** (still functioning although founded in the 11th century, it is famous as the burial place for the first Christian king, Mirian and his wife Nana) and the sixth-century **Jvari Cathedral**, the design of which became a prototype for Georgian ecclesiastical architecture.
- The remote village of **Shatili** is an outstanding monument of Georgian construction art, located on the main Caucasus ridge; towers are clustered together to create a single fortress.
- Follow the **Georgian Military Highway.** Leading 220km (137 miles) from Tbilisi to **Vladikavkaz** (formerly Ordzhonikidze) in North Ossetia (now part of the Russian Federation), this route was built by the Russians in the 19th century to help them control their conquered Georgian territories. The road winds through the dramatic mountain scenery of the high Caucasus, apparently little changed since the 19th-century novelist Lermontov described the route in *A Hero of our Time*. Sites of interest along the road include the 14th-century **Sameba Church** (Holy Trinity), overlooking the mountain town of **Kazbegi**, and the city of **Mtskheta** (see above). The ski resort of **Gudauri** is situated along the highway.
- Some 10km (6 miles) east of Gori is **Uplistsikhe** (Fortress of God), a large complex of natural caves. Inhabited from the sixth century BC to the 14th century AD, the caves were gradually transformed into increasingly sophisticated dwellings, shops and public buildings, including the most ancient theatre in Georgia, dungeons and enormous wine cellars.
- Discover the **Ateni Sioni Church**, 10km (6 miles) south of Gori, which stands in a beautiful setting and is highly prized for its 11th-century stonecarvings and frescoes.
- 10km (6 miles) from Bakuriani, heading towards Bordzhomi, is the 12th-century **Daba Monastery**, and nearby a 60m (197ft) waterfall. During the summer it is also possible to visit **Lake Tabatskuri**, sunk into a hollow high in the mountains.

- Of Georgia's many spectacular cultural monuments, the following were declared UNESCO World Heritage sites: in 1994, the old Georgian capital of **Mtskheta**, including **Jvari Monastery**, **Svetiskhoveli Cathedral** and the **Samtavro Monastery Complex**; the same year, the **Gelati Monastery** and **Bagrati Cathedral** in Kutaisi and in 1996, the architecturally unique **Svanetian village of Ushguli**, an exceptional example of mountain scenery with medieval houses and stone defence towers.
- Discover the Turkish character of **Batumi**, the capital of the Ajarian Autonomous Republic. The **mosque**, 19th-century **bath house**, **Ajarian Museum** (with its superb national costume collection), **circus**, **park**, **Botanical Garden** and the **theatre** are well worth visiting.

Top Things To Do

- Go to a concert. Davit Aghmashenebeli Prospekt in Tibili is the base for the **Georgian State Philharmonic Orchestra** and the internationally known **Georgian National Dance Troupe**.
- In October, commemorate the founding of Tbilisi during the **Tbilisoba**, the largest annual celebration in Georgia. For commemorations in other cities, consult the Embassy of Georgia (see Passport/Visa Information).
- Experiment with health-giving **sulphur baths** in a domed, oriental-style 19th-century bath house just north of the Metekhi Bridge in Tbilisi. Popular with visitors today, Georgian sulphur baths were also frequented by writers such as Pushkin and Tolstoy.
- The spa town of **Borjomi**, 150km (93 miles) west of Tbilisi in the Tori region, developed by Tsar Nicholas in the 19th century as a spa town, produces much acclaimed mineral water. It is possible to **hike** in the surrounding hills.
- Set inside the Lesser Caucasus around the Borjami-Kharagauli National Park, the former health resorts of **Abastumani**, **Saime**, **Badgadi** and **Nunisiare** are returning to life.
- A seaside resort and port in the southwest of the republic on the **Black Sea Coast**, **Batumi** is the capital of the Ajarian Autonomous Republic. Close to the Turkish border (20km/12.5 miles), the town has a decidedly Turkish character. Its charm lies less in any particular sights than in its lush, subtropical setting, among citrus groves and tea plantations, with mountains rising up from the edge of the sea.
- Other sea resorts include **Sarpi**, **Kueriati**, **Gonia**, **Kobuleh**, **Grigoleti** and **Ureki**.
- 40 per cent of the country remains covered by forests. There are five national parks open to visitors to enjoy the country's unique beauty. **Trekking** and **mountain activities** are popular in the **Tusheti National Park** which is a mountainous landscape reaching up to 4800m. Many of the endemic species can be seen here, the Caspian sea wolf, Caucasian Lynx and many bird species. Tourists can explore the park by foot, horse or vehicle. The **Tusheti Villages** are protected as historical sites, and are situated here.
- **Vashlovani National Park and Nature Reserve** is located in the innermost part of Georgia, where hyena, brown bear, wolf, lynx, griffin vulture and Egyptian vulture can be seen. This park can also be explored by foot or horse, but is open to scientific and educational tourism only.
- **Lagodechi National Park and Nature Reserve** gives tourists the opportunity to trek through the untouched natural ecosystems, beautiful lakes and waterfalls.
- Other national parks are **Borjomi-Kharogauti** and **Kolcheti National Parks**.
- **Note:** For visits to national parks and organised treks visit Georgia's Protected Areas Development Project (tel: 3225 1566; website: www.gpadc.org) or contact the Georgia Tourist Board (see *Tourist Information*). It should be noted that political unrest makes certain areas inaccessible and dangerous, notably the breakaway regions of Abkhazia (in the far northwest) and South Ossetia. Areas bordering these regions are also best avoided. The country's infrastructure can also present problems to those attempting to reach remote areas without their own transport. For these reasons, it is best to arrange trips through a specialist operator. A guide is usually necessary for visits to the mountains, and porters may be hired.
- The mountain regions of the Caucasus, which extend from the Black Sea to the Caspian Sea, offer numerous opportunities for **hiking**, **skiing**, **ski touring**, **heli-skiing** and **snowboarding**. Mount Shkora is the highest summit at 5068m and **Mount Kazbegi** or **Mkinvartsveri**, meaning 'ice top', (5033m) is the most attractive to mountain-climbers. Accommodation is available in two meteorological stations along the way, and special equipment is necessary to attempt the summit. **Gudauri and Bakuriani** used to be the Soviet Union's most popular ski resort. Both resorts are suitable for skiiers of all abilities. Snow cover is guaranteed from December to April.

- The **Roshka Valley** with its glaciers and the **Chaukhi Mountains** also offer strenuous wilderness treks and stark mountain scenery. Lowland walks are possible in both the north and the south of the country.
- The area around the ski resort of **Gudauri** (120km/75 miles north of Tbilisi) makes a good starting point for **summer walks** through mountain meadows full of flowers. Even in the lowland areas, eagles soar overhead and spectacular views can be had. The mountains in the south and east can offer more gentle walks.
- These regions are also suitable for **horse riding** and **mountain biking**, and there are numerous mountain roads and tracks. Special Caucasian horses bred for their endurance and beauty, such as the Kabardo and the Tusheti, are the traditional means of transport in this area. Trips can be started at the mountain resort of **Bakuriani**. Gentler rides can be done along the Black Sea coast. From horseriding to village stays, to camping in the Tushetian mountains to river rafting and multi-day sports activities, trips can be organised from one day to three weeks in length.
- **Bird watching** is another of Georgia's attractions. Approximately 360 species can be found, depending on the season, and the number of birds increases considerably during the spring and autumn migrations. Raptors including the bearded vulture, the long-legged buzzard and the white-tailed eagle can be seen in the Caucasus in summer. In the autumn, the wetlands and mountain steppes in the south near the Armenian border harbour white pelicans, white storks, cranes and Caspian snowcocks.
- Go **wine tasting** in the **Kakheti** province in the far east of the country, Georgia's wine-growing region. Apart from being an ancient tradition, drinking wine is also a social skill, with the traditional toast (or *Tamada*) being the prerogative of the most powerful male at the table. Other age-old rituals surround the harvesting, preparation and consumption of wine, which is usually of high quality.

TOURIST INFORMATION

State Department of Tourism and Resorts
80 Chavchavadze Avenue, 0162 Tbilisi, Georgia
Tel: (32) 226 125.
Website: www.tourism.gov.ge *or* www.parliament.ge

Entertainment

FOOD & DRINK: According to Georgian legend, when God was distributing land among the peoples of the world, the Georgians were so busy eating and drinking that they lost their place in the queue and there was no land left for them. But when they invited God to join the party, he enjoyed himself so immensely he gave them all the choicest bits of land he had been saving for himself. Georgians pride themselves, with some justification, on being the *bons viveurs* of the former Soviet Union, and their culinary tradition has survived better than most the dead hand of Soviet mass-catering. The cuisine makes extensive use of walnuts, which are used to thicken soups and sauces (anything including the word *satsivi* will be served in a rich sauce flavoured with herbs, garlic, walnuts and egg). Cafes, restaurants and street-food traditions are all better established in Georgia than in many of the other former Soviet republics, and the markets are full of locally grown fruit and vegetables. Privately run restaurants, cafes and bars, which began to thrive during the Gorbachev period, were badly hit by the post-independence breakdown of civil order, but in recent times have begun to bounce back. The future looks bright.

Things to know: Over 500 original varieties of grape are grown here, more than any other country. Both red and white wine is produced in Georgia.

National specialities:
- Meals usually start with an array of hot and cold dishes which may include spicy grilled liver and other offal.
- Walnuts feature in sauces and soups. They are also used in desserts, coated in caramelised sugar, *gozinaki*, or in *churchkhela*, when they are threaded on string then dipped in thickened, sweetened grape juice which is subsequently dried into chewy, flavoursome 'candles'.
- There is less emphasis on lamb to the exclusion of other kinds of meat than in other parts of the Caucasus. Roast suckling pig is often served, and beef and chicken are grilled or casseroled in various sauces, one of the commonest forms being *chakhokhbili*, a stew involving herbs, tomatoes and paprika.
- *Lobio*, a bean and walnut salad.
- Marinated aubergines, *pkhali*, made from young spinach leaves pounded together with spices.
- *Khachapuri*, consisting of layers of flat bread alternated with melting cheese.
- *Basturma*, cured meat and assorted fresh and pickled vegetables.

National drinks:
- *Kindzmareuli*, a fruity, red wine, is reputed to have been Stalin's favourite tipple.
- *Akhasheni* and *Teliani* are two of the commoner red wines, fruity and dry respectively.
- *Tsinandali* is a dry white wine, as is *Gurdzhaani*.

Tipping: For service in restaurants, cafes or taxis, the bill is usually rounded up

NIGHTLIFE: Nightlife in the republic is to be found primarily in international hotels although there are some bars and restaurants in Tbilisi. The *Georgian State Dancers* are highly praised but only occasionally to be glimpsed in Tbilisi, being almost constantly on tour. The *Rustaveli Georgian Drama Theatre* also has a good reputation and is particularly renowned for its Shakespeare productions. The Georgian folk theatre *Nabadi* holds performances depicting the history of the country in modern and traditional forms.

SHOPPING: Georgian ceramics, embroidery and jewellery are all distinctive, and may be bought in art salons or special tourist shops. Visitors may also develop a liking for locally produced wines and brandies. Antiques such as rugs and icons attract a heavy export duty and must be licensed for export by the Ministry of Culture. Goods acquired in markets or from private individuals will not come with an export licence, whereas official tourist shops usually take responsibility for certification. Most shops are open Mon-Sat 1000-1800, some open on Sundays. The main shopping streets are *Rustaveli* and *Chavchavadze Avenue*.

Business

- **GDP:** US$4 billion (2003).
- **Main exports:** Scrap metal, machinery, chemicals, fuel re-exports, citrus fruits, tea and wine.
- **Main imports:** Fuel, machinery and parts, transport equipment, grain and other food stuffs and pharmaceuticals.
- **Main trade partners:** Russia, UK, Turkey, other EU, Azerbaijan, Ukraine and Armenia.

ECONOMY: Georgia has experienced considerable economic difficulties during the last decade and is one of the poorest of the former Soviet republics with an annual per capita income of US$600. Disruption of the centrally organised Soviet trade and supply networks, plus civil war and political instability produced hyper-inflation and a slump in production. Major structural reforms, centring on the transfer of almost all small-scale enterprises to private ownership and a parallel reduction in the economic role of the state, were instituted. The measures have since contributed to strong annual growth for most of the post-Soviet period (it is currently 5 per cent) and a manageable rate of inflation. Unemployment, however, remains high, as does widespread poverty. A new national currency, the Lari, was introduced in 1995.

The agricultural sector, which accounts for about one-third of total output, produces fruit, tobacco, grain and sugar beet; sheep and goats are widely farmed. There is some heavy industry, notably shipbuilding, but most of Georgia's industry is light and engaged in food processing and production of fertiliser. Coal and manganese are mined in commercial quantities. The Government aims to establish the main ports of Poti and Batumi as regional transport and re-export hubs, which will also be able to handle oil refining and transhipment. (Part of this plan involves the laying of a set of pipelines running east-west across the entire country, linking the oil and gas fields of central Asia to the Turkish Mediterranean port of Ceyhan). Further reforms, including the privatisation of major industries such as energy, are planned but the government has so far moved cautiously. In 1992, Georgia joined the IMF, which has been centrally involved in the economic reform programme, the World Bank and the European Bank for Reconstruction and Development as a 'Country of Operation'. It has also acquired membership of the World Trade Organization. Turkey is now Georgia's principal trading partner, followed by Russia, Turkmenistan and Azerbaijan.

Office hours: Government office opening hours are usually 1000-1800. Private sector offices are usually open on Saturdays.

COMMERCIAL INFORMATION

Chamber of Commerce and Industry of Georgia
Prospekt Chavchavadze 11, 380079 Tbilisi, Georgia
Tel: (32) 230 045.

Germany

Location: Western/Central Europe.

Time: GMT + 1 (GMT + 2 from last Sunday in March to last Sunday in October).

Overview

Germany is an intoxicating brew (a bit like its wonderful beer) of fast cars and fairytale castles. The German people enjoy a reputation for accuracy, precision and efficiency –

although an equally enduring image is of *lederhosen*-clad Bavarians hoisting beer steins at Munich's famous *Oktoberfest*. Neither of these stereotypes reflects the diversity of Germany's towns and cities, from romantic Heidelberg, the medieval Nuremberg, to the cosmopolitan decadence of Berlin. The country boasts 30 UNESCO World Heritage Sites throughout 16 Federal States, each awash with a torrent of enchanting sites to explore, plus thrilling activities to pursue. Every area has its distinct regional foods and offers a huge choice of local wines and beers. Such diversity might be explained by Germany's history, which is suitably rich and complex. Germany fragmented into five large duchies (Saxony, Bavaria, Franconia, Lorraine and Swabia) in the 10th century, whose dukes managed to establish a *de facto* hereditary tenure over each of their respective fiefdoms. Various Houses and Dynasties then grew in power and influence. By the late 13th century, the country was seething with civil war and the House of Habsburg was later to emerge, who ruled the empire, with only a brief interruption, until 1806. By this time Germany had dissolved into a patchwork of over 300 states. After 1815, the German Confederation was established with 39 states. German unification continued apace throughout the century until a revolt in Serbia precipitated a chain of events which led to World War I and Germany adopting the democratic constitution; and this coupled with serious domestic political instability compounded by the Great Depression of the 1920s and 30s, paved the way for the rise of Adolf Hitler's Nationalist Socialists. Hitler sought to reverse the perceived humiliation imposed by the 1919 Treaty of Versailles and set about creating the Third Reich. When Hitler threatened Poland, the UK and France drew the line: from there, it was a short route to World War II. After six years of global warfare, at an estimated cost of 60 million lives, the German army was defeated in 1945 by the allied armies of the USA, the USSR, the UK and others. This produced the post-war division of Europe into Western and Soviet spheres of influence: the eastern, Soviet-controlled portion became the German Democratic Republic (GDR), the western part emerged to become the Federal Republic of Germany. Then, a dramatic process of events culminated in the fall of the Berlin Wall at the end of 1989, and the collapse of the East German state. Unified Germany, with nearly 80 million people and twice the GNP of the EU's next largest member, dominated the Union economically. Germany is still the largest economy in Europe and maintains great global influence. The shadow of modern-day warfare is lifting and people can finally see that the great beauty of the country remains undiminished.

General Information

AREA: 357,027 sq km (137,849 sq miles).

POPULATION: 82.5 million (UN, 2005).

POPULATION DENSITY: 231 per sq km.

CAPITAL: Berlin. **Population:** 3.4 million (2005 estimate).

GEOGRAPHY: The Federal Republic of Germany shares frontiers with Austria, Belgium, Czech Republic, Denmark, France, Luxembourg, The Netherlands, Poland and Switzerland. The northwest of the country has a coastline on the North Sea with islands known for their health resorts, while the Baltic coastline in the northeast stretches from the Danish to the Polish border. The country is divided into 16 states (*Bundesländer*), including the formerly divided city of Berlin. The landscape is exceedingly varied,

with the Rhine, Bavaria and the Black Forest being probably the three most famous features of western Germany. In eastern Germany, the country is lake-studded with undulating lowlands which give way to the hills and mountains of the Lausitzer Bergland, the Saxon Hills in the Elbe Valley and the Erzgebirge, whilst the once divided areas of the Thuringian and Harz ranges in the central part of the country are now whole regions again. River basins extend over a large percentage of the eastern part of Germany, the most important being the Elbe, Saale, Havel, Spree and Oder. Northern Germany includes the states of Lower Saxony (Niedersachsen), Schleswig-Holstein, Mecklenburg-West Pomerania and the city states of Bremen and Hamburg. The western area of the country consists of the Rhineland, the industrial sprawl of the Ruhr, Westphalia (Westfalen), Hesse (Hessen), the Rhineland-Palatinate (Rheinland-Pfalz) and the Saarland. In the southern area of the country are the two largest states, Baden-Württemberg and Bavaria (Bayern), which contain the Black Forest (Schwarzwald), Lake Constance (Bodensee) and the Bavarian Alps. Munich (München), Stuttgart and Nuremberg (Nürnberg) are the major cities. The eastern part of the country is made up of the states of Thuringia, Saxony, Brandenburg, Saxony-Anhalt and Berlin. The major cities in eastern Germany are Dresden, Leipzig, Erfurt, Halle, Magdeburg, Potsdam, Schwerin and Rostock. Apart from Leipzig and Rostock, these are also all recently reconstituted state capitals.

GOVERNMENT: Federal Republic. **Head of State:** President Horst Köhler since 2004. **Head of Government:** Chancellor Angela Merkel since 2005. **Recent history:** From 1995 onwards, a new leadership under would-be Chancellor Gerhard Schröder emerged to challenge a Helmut Kohl Government (leader of the right-wing Christian Democrats (CDU)), now entering a stale twilight period. The Social Democratic (SPD) party duly won the 1998 general election and, after 17 years as Chancellor and 25 years as party leader, Kohl stood down. With a cleverly worked campaign which drew in part on widespread popular concern about a future Middle East war, Schröder out-manoeuvred the Christian Democrats and held on to power in the September 2002 general election. Schröder then sought to continue Helmut Kohl's aim of a more activist German foreign policy. Along with French president Jacques Chirac, Schröder opposed much Anglo-American policy in the Middle East. However, Schröder's reign came to an end amidst stultifying confusion in the national elections held on 18 September 2005. Angela Merkel's Christian Democrats won Germany's election by just three seats, falling far short of a majority. As both Mrs Merkel and Mr Schröder claimed they had a mandate to be Chancellor, Germany faced weeks of uncertainty, which only resulted in a deal between the CDU and the SPD on 10 October. Angela Merkel was declared Germany's first woman Chancellor and sworn in in late November. She is also the first Chancellor to have grown up in the former Communist, eastern part of the country. Merkel's foreign stance is more pro-US than her predecessor and she has pledged to overhaul the German economy. Therefore it remains to be seen whether Schröder's stance on foreign policy is challenged. However, Merkel has been sworn in as part of a CDU-SPD 'grand coalition', under which the SPD will take eight ministerial posts, against six for the CDU and their CSU allies. This may mute the power of Merkel somewhat. For now, the same major political issues remain in Germany: Germany hosts the largest number of immigrants of any EU nation, and the debate has coincided with the growth of violent neo-Nazism.

The present constitution dates from May 1949, the Federal Republic of Germany being formally established four months later. The country is a parliamentary democracy with a bicameral legislature (*Bundesrat* and *Bundestag*, with 68 and 663 members respectively). Executive authority lies with the Federal Government, led by the Federal Chancellor. The Federal President is the constitutional head of state. Each of the states has its own legislature with power to pass laws on all matters not expressly reserved for the competence of the Federal Government. The former German Democratic Republic has been absorbed into this system, adding five new states to the total.

LANGUAGE: German. English is widely spoken and French is also spoken, particularly in the Saarland. In the north of Schleswig-Holstein, Danish is spoken by the Danish minority and taught in schools. In Brandenburg and Saxony, Sorbic is spoken by the ethnic minority called the Sorbs and is also taught in about 50 schools. Regional dialects often differ markedly from standard German.

RELIGION: Approximately 34 per cent Protestant, 34 per cent Roman Catholic, with Jewish, Muslim and other non-Christian minorities.

ELECTRICITY: 230 volts AC, 50Hz. European-style round two-pin plugs are in use. Lamp fittings are screw type.

SOCIAL CONVENTIONS: Handshaking is customary. Normal courtesies should be observed and it is common to be offered food and refreshments when visiting someone's home. Before eating, it is normal to say *Guten Appetit* to

A B C D E F G H I J K L M N O P Q R S T U V W X Y Z

PUBLICIS

"I AM A SAXIST."

More and more people are openly declaring their Saxism. No wonder because what Saxony offers ignites passion: the fascinating combination of culture & nature, cities & landscapes far from the beaten track. *For further information visit* www.saxonytourism.com *or call (503) 227-1750*

When will you become a Saxist?

SUCH
AN
EXPERIENCE
OF GERMA**NY**

A B C D E F **G** H I J K L M N O P Q R S T U V W X Y Z

the other people at the table to which the correct reply is *Ebenfalls*. It is customary to present the hostess with unwrapped flowers (according to tradition, one should always give an uneven number and it is worth noting that red roses are exclusively a lover's gift). Courtesy dictates that when entering a shop, restaurant or similar venue, visitors should utter a greeting such as *Guten Tag* (or *Grüss Gott* in Bavaria) before saying what it is that they want; to leave without saying *Auf Wiedersehen* can also cause offence. Similarly, when making a telephone call, asking for the person you want to speak to without stating first who you are is considered rude. Casual wear is widely acceptable, but more formal dress is required for some restaurants, the opera, theatre, casinos and important social functions. Evening wear is worn when requested. Smoking is prohibited where notified and on public transport and in some public buildings. Visitors should be prepared for an early start to the day with businesses, schools, etc opening at 0800 or earlier. It is very common practice to take a mid-afternoon stroll on Sunday; town and city centres at this time are often very animated places, in stark comparison with Saturday afternoons when, owing to the early closing of shops, town centres can seem almost deserted.

Climate

Temperate throughout the country with warm summers and cold winters, but prolonged periods of frost or snow are rare. Rain falls throughout the year.

Required clothing: European clothes with light- to mediumweights in summer, medium- to heavyweights in winter. Waterproofs are needed throughout the year.

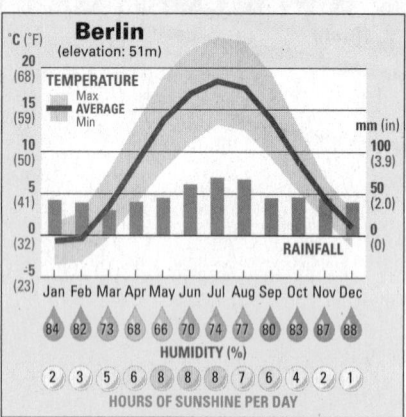

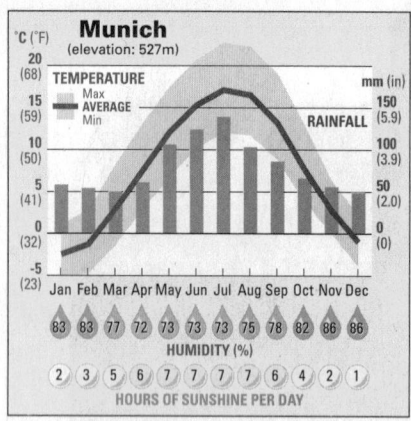

Communications

Telephone: Full IDD is available. Country code: 49. National and international calls can be made from coin- or card-operated telephone booths. Calls can be made from post offices. Cheap rate applies Mon-Fri 1800-0800 and all day Saturday and Sunday. Discount phonecards from private companies can be bought from shops and kiosks.
Mobile telephone: Roaming agreements exist with many international mobile phone companies. Coverage is good. It is illegal to use a hand-held mobile telephone while driving.
Internet: Internet is readily available; there are many Internet cafes all over the country. Large Internet access centres exist in most main cities. Hotels also provide facilities.
Post: Stamps are available from hotels, slot machines and post offices. A five-figure postal code is used on all internal addresses. Post office hours: Mon-Fri 0900-1800, Sat 0900-1200. Smaller branches may close for lunch.
MEDIA: Germany's competitive TV market is the largest in Europe. Each of the country's 16 regions regulates its own private and public broadcasting, and operates public TV and radio services. Around 90 per cent of German households have

Credit: ©GNTB/DZT/BSB

cable or satellite TV. Germany is home to some of the world's largest media conglomerates, such as Bertelsmann. While the press and broadcasters are free and independent, the display of swastikas and statements endorsing Nazism are illegal.
Press: The most influential dailies include the *Die Welt*, *Frankfurter Allgemeine Zeitung* and the *Süddeutsche Zeitung*. The most widely read of the weekly publications are *Der Spiegel* and *Die Zeit*. Some new or revamped newspapers, such as *Berliner Kurier*, have emerged out of eastern Germany and are competing well with western German papers. Most major English newspapers and international magazines are also available in Germany.
TV: Premiere is a pay-TV operator. *ARD* is the organisation of regional public broadcasters and operates *Das Erste*, the main public TV channel. Other commercial broadcasters include *N24* (rolling news), *RTL* (entertainment channels) and *ZDF* (operates the second public national TV channel). *Deutsche Welle TV* is the international TV service, and operates in English and Spanish, as well as German.
Radio: *Deutsche Welle TV* broadcasts radio in many languages. *Deutschlandradio* operates national public radio stations, *Deutschlandfunk* and *Deutschlandradio Kultur* (broadcasting news/current affairs and cultural programmes). *ARD* is an umbrella organisation of many public radio services, including regional stations.

Passport/Visa

	Passport Required?	Visa Required?	Return Ticket Required?
Full British	1	No	No
Australian	Yes	No	No
Canadian	Yes	No	No
USA	Yes	No	No
Other EU	1	No	No
Japanese	Yes	No	No

Note: *Regulations and requirements may be subject to change at short notice, and you are advised to contact the appropriate diplomatic or consular authority before finalising travel arrangements. Any numbers in the chart refer to the footnotes below.*

Note: Germany is a signatory to the 1995 **Schengen Agreement**. For further details about passport/visa regulations within the Schengen area, see the introductory section, *How to Use this Guide*.
PASSPORTS: Passport valid for at least three months beyond length of stay required by all except:
1. EU/EEA nationals (EU+ Iceland, Liechtenstein, Norway) and Swiss nationals holding a valid national ID card.
Note: EU and EEA nationals are only required to produce evidence of their EU/EEA nationality and identity in order to be admitted to any EU/EEA Member State. This evidence can take the form of a valid national passport *or* national

identity card. Either is acceptable. Possession of a return ticket, any length of validity on their document, sufficient funds for the length of their proposed visit should *not* be imposed.
VISAS: Required by all except the following for periods not exceeding three months and for non-business (paid work) purposes:
(a) nationals referred to in the chart and under passport exemptions above;
(b) nationals of Andorra, Argentina, Bolivia, Brazil, Bulgaria, Chile, Costa Rica, Croatia, El Salvador, Guatemala, Honduras, Hong Kong (SAR), Israel, Korea (Rep), Macau (SAR), Malaysia, Mexico, Monaco, New Zealand, Nicaragua, Niue, Panama, Paraguay, Romania, San Marino, Singapore, Switzerland, Uruguay, Vatican City and Venezuela;
(c) passengers continuing their journey by the same or first connecting aircraft, provided holding confirmed onward tickets and travel documents. However, the following nationals always need a visa even if transiting by the same aircraft*: Afghanistan, Angola, Bangladesh, Congo (Dem Rep), Eritrea, Ethiopia, The Gambia, Ghana, India, Iran, Iraq, Jordan, Lebanon, Nigeria, Pakistan, Somalia, Sri Lanka, Sudan, Syrian Arab Republic and Turkey. Visitors should check with the Embassy (or Consular section at Embassy).
Note: *A transit visa is not required by some of these nationals if in possession of a residence permit or visa for the UK, or they possess a "Leave to remain in the UK for an indefinite period" or a "Certificate of entitlement to the right of abode"; contact nearest German Embassy or Consulate for more information, since there are some other exceptions.
Types of visa and cost: All types of visa cost €35 (€17.50 for minors under 18 years). The price is fixed in Euros but payable in Pounds Sterling. This is about £24 (£13 for minors under 18 years). Fees are payable in cash only.
Note: Spouses and children of EU nationals (providing spouse's passport and the original marriage certificate is produced with copy, plus valid travel health insurance by Form E111; visitors are advised that E111 forms issued before 1 June 2004 are no longer valid) and nationals of some other countries receive their visas free of charge (enquire at Embassy for details; see *Passport/Visa Information*).
Validity: Depends on nationality and individual circumstance.
Application to: Consulate or Consular section at Embassy (see *Passport/Visa Information*). Travellers visiting just one Schengen country should apply to the Consulate of that country; travellers visiting more than one Schengen country should apply to the Consulate of the country chosen as the main destination *or* the country they will enter first (if they have no main destination). All applicants must book an appointment (tel: (09065) 540 740) in order to process a visa.
Application requirements: (a) Passport with at least three months' validity beyond period of visa, with at least one blank page. Each child endorsed in a passport and travelling

also requires a separate application form with photo and birth certificate. (b) Application form(s). (c) Colour passport-size photo(s). (d) A self-addressed, special delivery envelope if applicants would like their documents returned. (e) Proof of health insurance, covering at least £20 per day, and valid for all *Schengen* states. (f) Fee (payable in cash only). *Visitors*: (a)-(e) and, (f) Formal obligation from host in Germany. *Tourist*: (a)-(f) and, (g) Proof of purpose of visit and/or a hotel reservation. (h) Proof of adequate means of support during stay (eg bank statement or traveller's cheques). (i) Evidence of occupation or student status. *Business*: (a)-(f) and, (g) A letter from employer, or official invitation by fax, from overseas business associate explaining nature and duration of stay, plus guarantee of payment of costs incurred during stay. If self-employed, a letter from a solicitor, accountant, bank manager or local Chamber of Commerce.

Note: (a) Applicants under 18 years of age must also submit a letter from their parents/guardian authorising the visit and appointing the person who will be responsible for them. (b) If individual has obtained a German *Schengen* visa from the USA within the 12 months previous to the visa application, the individual may apply for a German Schengen visa this time by post. A self-addressed 'Special Delivery' envelope must be supplied and the visa paid for by postal order. (c) Nationals of Afghanistan, Algeria, Bahrain, Colombia, Congo (Dem Rep), Egypt, Indonesia, Iran, Iraq, Jordan, Korea (Dem Rep), Kuwait, Lebanon, Libya, Oman, Pakistan, The Philippines, Qatar, Saudi Arabia, Somalia, Sudan, Surinam, Syrian Arab Republic, United Arab Emirates and Yemen, must, in addition to the required visa documents, supply an extra application form and passport-size photo, a copy of their passport data page and provide the full address (including postcode) of a reference in Germany. (d) Minors under 18 must produce a declaration from both parents authorising their travel and stay in a Schengen country, and appointing the person responsible for the minor's welfare in their absence.

Working days required: For UK residents applying in the UK, visas will normally be issued within two days; however, applications from some nationals can take up to 14 days to process. If the stay is likely to be for more than three months, applications should be made up to 10 weeks in advance of the intended date of departure. Visa applications by non-residents have to be referred to the German Embassy in the applicant's home country, and may take several days or weeks to be issued. Applications by post take up to eight days, although the process may take longer on occasion.

Temporary residence: Nationals of EU and nationals of Australia, Canada, Iceland, Israel, Japan, Korea (Rep), Liechtenstein, New Zealand, Norway and the USA may apply for a permit from the local immigration office in Germany, no later than three months after entry. For further details on temporary residence in Germany, enquire at the Consulate (or Consular section at Embassy).

Work permits: EU nationals do not need a visa or work permit to work in Germany. A residence permit must, however, be obtained for stays of over three months (see above). Non-EU nationals must obtain a visa/residence permit before entering Germany; permits take up to 10 weeks to process. An information sheet, *Working and Living in Germany*, is obtainable from the German Embassy (see *Passport/Visa Information*).

Credit: ©GNTB/Jim McDonald

Money

Single European currency (Euro): The Euro is now the official currency of 12 EU member states (including Germany). The first Euro coins and notes were introduced in January 2002 and completely replaced the Deutschmark on 28 February 2002. Euro (€) = 100 cents. Notes are in denominations of €500, 200, 100, 50, 20, 10 and 5. Coins are in denominations of €2 and 1, and 50, 20, 10, 5, 2 and 1 cents.

Note: Eurocheques are no longer guaranteed and can no longer be accepted for encashments. However, they may still be used for payments without the guarantee in certain places.

Currency exchange: Foreign currencies and traveller's cheques can be exchanged at banks, bureaux de change, post offices, airports, railway stations, ports and major hotels at the official exchange rates.

Credit & debit cards: These are accepted in approximately 60 per cent of all shops, petrol stations, restaurants and hotels. Nationals of other Western European countries, Canada and the USA, will find less credit card availability than they are used to in their own countries and it is advisable to carry cash or a Eurocheque card as well. All major credit cards are accepted. Check with your credit or debit card company for details of merchant acceptability and other services which may be available.

Traveller's cheques: Generally provide the best rate of exchange. To avoid additional exchange rate charges, travellers are advised to take traveller's cheques in Euros, Pounds Sterling or US Dollars. Visitors are advised to have their traveller's cheques exchanged at bureaux de change as banks often refuse to change them and they are not accepted as payment in general stores.

Currency restrictions: There are no restrictions on the import or export of either local or foreign currency.

Banking hours: Generally Mon-Fri 0830-1300 and 1400-1600, Thurs 0830-1300 and 1430-1730 in main cities. Main branches do not close for lunch. Bureaux de change in airports and main railway stations are open 0600-2200.

Exchange rate indicators:
Rate at time of publishing
£1.00=   €1.46
$1.00=   €0.82

Duty Free

The following goods may be imported into the Federal Republic of Germany without incurring customs duty by visitors arriving from countries outside the EU:

200 cigarettes or 100 cigarillos or 50 cigars or 250g of tobacco; 1l of spirits with an alcohol content exceeding 22 per cent by volume or 2l of spirits or liqueurs with an alcohol content not exceeding 22 per cent by volume or 2l of sparkling or liqueur wine; 2l of any other wine; 50g of perfume or 250ml of eau de toilette; 500g of coffee or 200g of coffee extracts; personal goods to the value of €175.

Note: (a) The tobacco and alcohol allowances are granted only to those over 17 years of age. (b) Wine in excess of the above allowances imported for personal consumption and valued at less than €128 will be taxed at an overall rate of 16 per cent.

Abolition of duty free goods within the EU: On 30 June 1999, the sale of duty-free alcohol and tobacco at airports and at sea was abolished in all of the original 15 EU member states. Of the 10 new member states that joined the EU on May 1 2004, these rules already apply to Cyprus and Malta. There are transitional rules in place for visitors returning to one of the original 15 EU countries from one of the other new EU countries. But for the original 15, plus Cyprus and Malta, there are now no limits imposed on importing tobacco and alcohol products from one EU country to another (with the exceptions of Denmark, Finland and Sweden, where limits *are* imposed). Travellers should note that they may be required to prove at customs that the goods purchased are for personal use *only*.

Public Holidays

Below are listed Public Holidays for the January 2006-June 2007 period.
2006: Jan 1 New Year's Day. **Jan 6*** Epiphany. **Apr 14** Good Friday. **Apr 17** Easter Monday. **May 1** Labour Day. **May 25** Ascension. **Jun 5** Whit Monday. **Jun 15*** Corpus Christi. **Aug 15*** Assumption Day. **Oct 31** Reformation Day. **Nov 1** All Saints' Day. **Nov 20** day of Prayer and Repentence. **Dec 25-26** Christmas.
2007: Jan 1 New Year's Day. **Jan 6*** Epiphany. **Apr 6** Good Friday. **Apr 9** Easter Monday. **May 1** Labour Day. **May 17** Ascension. **May 28** Whit Monday. **Jun 7*** Corpus Christi.
Note: *Epiphany, Corpus Christi, Assumption, Day of Reformation, All Saints' Day and Day of Prayer and Repentance are not observed in all areas. Consult the German National Tourist Office for details (see *Top Things To Do*).

Health

	Special Precautions?	Certificate Required?
Yellow Fever	No	No
Cholera	No	No
Typhoid & Polio	No	N/A
Malaria	No	N/A

Note: *Regulations and requirements may be subject to change at short notice, and you are advised to contact your doctor well in advance of your intended date of departure. Any numbers in the chart refer to the footnotes below.*

Other risks: *Tick-borne encephalitis* is present in forested areas of southern Germany. Vaccination is advisable. HIV testing is required for foreigners staying more than 180 days in Bavaria. Foreign tests are not accepted.
Rabies is present; look out for 'Tollwut' signs. For those at high risk, vaccination before arrival should be considered. If you are bitten, seek medical advice without delay. For more information, consult the *Health* appendix.
Health care: European Economic Area (EEA) and Switzerland:
If you or any of your dependants are suddenly taken ill or have an accident during a visit to an EEA country or Switzerland, free or reduced-cost necessary treatment is available – in most cases on production of a valid European Health Insurance Card (EHIC). Each country has different rules about state medical provision. In some, treatment is free. In many countries you will have to pay part or all of the cost, and then claim a full or partial refund. The EHIC gives access to state-provided medical treatment only and the scheme gives no entitlement to medical repatriation costs, nor does it cover ongoing illnesses of a non-urgent nature, so comprehensive travel insurance is advised. Note that the EHIC replaces the Form E111, which will no longer be valid after 31 December 2005. Some restrictions apply depending on your nationality.

Doctors and dentists: The emergency telephone number is 112. The insurance fund you contact will have a list of doctors and dentists who treat patients under the state scheme (including hospitals). Travellers will need to pay a fixed charge to see a doctor or dentist, which is not refundable.
Medicines prescribed by the doctor can be obtained from any pharmacy in exchange for the prescription. You will be liable for a percentage of the prescription charge. These costs are non-refundable. For 'minor' drugs and medicines, such as painkillers and cough mixtures, you may be charged the full amount. Chemists are open Mon-Fri 0900-1800, Sat 0900-1200.
Travellers can be referred to a hospital by a doctor. In an emergency, you can go directly to a contracted hospital. The hospital will then contact the insurance fund so that they can confirm that your treatment costs will be met. For the first 14 days of hospital in-patient treatment, you will have to pay a fixed daily hospital charge, which will not be reimbursed. Patients up to the age of 18 do not have to pay this charge.
The local Health Insurance Fund (*Allgemeine Ortskrankenkasse* or *AOK*) handles reimbursements. Private insurance is recommended for specialist medical treatment outside the German National Health Service, which can be very expensive.

Travel - International

AIR:

The national airline is *Lufthansa (LH)* (website: www.lufthansa.com).
Approximate flight times: From Bremen to *London* is one hour 15 minutes; from Hamburg to *London* is one hour 40 minutes; Hannover to *London* is one hour 20 minutes; from Cologne/ Bonn to *London* is one hour 25 minutes; from Frankfurt/M to *London* is one hour 40 minutes; from Nuremberg to *London* is one hours 35 minutes; and from Munich to *London* is two hours 35 minutes (with one stop). From Frankfurt/M to *Los Angeles* is 11 hours 20 minutes, to *New York* is eight hours 20 minutes, to *Singapore* is 13 hours and to *Sydney* is 23 hours.
Main airports: *Berlin-Tegel (TXL)* (Otto Lilienthal) (website: www.berlin-airport.de) is located 8km (5 miles) northwest of the city (travel time – 20 minutes). *To/from the airport*: Bus nos 109, 128 and X9 go to the city every five to 10 minutes from 0500-2400; return is from Bahnhof Zoo, Budapester Strasse, Charlottenburg station or Kurfürstendamm underground station. *Facilities:* Duty free shop, banks/bureaux de change, left luggage, 24-hour medical facilities, post office, restaurant, bars, tourist information, conference rooms and car hire.
Düsseldorf (DUS) (Rhein-Ruhr) (website: www.duesseldorf-international.de) is 8km (5 miles) north of the city. *To/from the airport*: Trains depart to the city every 20 minutes (the airport station is under the arrival hall). Return is from Hauptbahnhof (main railway station) every 30 minutes. An S-Bahn connection (S7) every 20 to 30 minutes and bus services are also available. Taxis run a 24-hour service to Düsseldorf. *Facilities:* Duty free shop, bank, medical facilities, post office, restaurant, bars, tourist information, car hire and conference rooms.
Frankfurt/M (FRA) (Rhein/Main) (website: www.airportcity-frankfurt.de) is 13km (8 miles) southwest of the city. *To/from the airport*: Travel to and from the city is by buses no. 61 and 62 every 20 minutes, returning from Hauptbahnhof (main railway station). Lines S8 and S9 go to the city (the station is underneath the arrival hall). S-Bahn S8 also goes directly to Mainz and Wiesbaden (travel time – 40 minutes). There is a 24-hour taxi service to Frankfurt. The airport has its own InterCity railway station which also offers international services (Austria, Hungary and Switzerland). The *Lufthansa Courtesy Airport Bus* connects with Mannheim (travel time – one hour) and Heidelberg (travel time – one hour 30 minutes). Long-distance bus services from the airport include the T271 to Ostrava in the Czech Republic (travel time – four hours) and the *Lufthansa Airport Bus* to Strasbourg in France (travel time – three hours). *Facilities:* Left luggage, medical facilities, duty free shops, banks, restaurants, bars, 28 conference rooms, post office, tourist information and car hire.
Hannover (HAJ) (Langenhagen) (website: www.hannover-airport.de) is 11km (7 miles) north of the city (travel time – 30 minutes). *To/from the airport*: S-Bahn S5 runs between the airport and the main railway station every 30 minutes (travel time - 12 minutes). A 24-hour taxi service runs to Hannover. *Facilities:* Duty free shop, luggage lockers, medical facilities, banks/bureau de change, bars, post office, restaurants, tourist information and car hire.
Munich (MUC) (Franz Joseph Strauss) (website: www.munich-airport.de) is 28.5km (18 miles) northeast of the city (travel time – 38 minutes). *To/from the airport*: Direct links with the S-Bahn S8 and S1 run every 10 minutes from Hauptbahnhof (main railway station) (0313-0042; return 0355-0115). The Airport City Bus runs every 20 minutes from 0650-1930 to the Hauptbahnhof and every 30 minutes from 0755-2055; further bus services are available. Coach Oberbayern runs every 10 minutes to the city centre. *Facilities:* Duty free shop, left luggage, 24-hour medical facilities, snack bar, restaurants, post office, banks, conference centre, car hire and bars. The airport also has a Visitors' Park, an aircraft simulator, cinema, a play area and restaurant.
Stuttgart (STR) (Echterdingen) (website: www.stuttgart-airport.de) is 14km (9 miles) south of the city (travel time – 35 minutes). *To/from the airport*: An S-Bahn link (lines S2 and S3) is available with trains running at 10-minute intervals. There is a 24-hour taxi service to Stuttgart. *Facilities:* Duty free shops, luggage lockers, conference centre, 24-hour medical facilities, bank/bureau de change, bars, post office, restaurant and car hire.
Departure Tax: None.
SEA:

Main ports: *Bremen* (website: www.bremen-ports.de), *Bremerhaven* (website: www.bremen-ports.de), *Emden* (website: www.emden-port.de), *Hamburg* (website: www.hafen-hamburg.de), *Nordenham*, *Rostock* (website: www.rostock-port.de), and *Wilhelmshaven* (website: www.wilhelmshaven-port.de).
The following shipping lines serve routes to Germany from the UK:
DFDS Seaways (website: www.dfds.co.uk): Harwich-Cuxhaven; Newcastle-Amsterdam.
Stena Line (website: www.stenaline.com): Harwich–Hook of Holland.
P&O Ferries (website: www.poferries.com): Dover-Calais; Hull-Rotterdam; Hull-Zeebrugge.
SeaFrance (website: www.seafrance.com): Dover-Calais.
Norfolkline (website: www.norfolkline.com): Dover-Dunkerque.
Superfast Ferries (website: www.superfast.com): Rosyth-Zeebrugge.
Ferry connections also exist from Germany to Denmark, Finland, Latvia, Lithuania, The Netherlands, Norway, the Russian Federation and Sweden.

Credit: ©GNTB/Stuttgart Marketing GmbH

Credit: ©GNTB/Jochen Keute

RAIL:

Eurostar: *Eurostar* is a service provided by the railways of Belgium, the UK and France, operating direct high-speed trains from London (*Waterloo International*) to Paris (*Gare du Nord*) and to Brussels (*Midi/Zuid*). It takes two hours 40 minutes from London to Paris (via Lille) and two hours 20 minutes to Brussels. For further information and reservations, contact *Eurostar* (tel: (0870) 600 0792 (travel agents) *or* (08705) 186 186 (public; within the UK) *or* +44 (1233) 617 575 (public; outside the UK); a £5 booking fee applies to all telephone bookings; website: www.eurostar.com); *or Rail Europe* (tel: (08705) 848 848; website: www.raileurope.co.uk). There are connections from Brussels or Paris to Munich.

There are excellent connections between the Federal Republic of Germany and other main European cities. In 1998, *Deutsche Bahn* extended their international network eastwards and it now connects with 13 European countries, including Croatia, Hungary and Slovenia. For more information, contact *Deutsche Bahn* in the UK at Passenger Services, UK Booking Centre, PO Box 687A, Surbiton, Surrey KT6 6UB, UK (tel: (0870) 243 5363; website: www.bahn.de). A number of scenic rail journeys begin in Germany and go to Austria or Switzerland, such as the routes through the Black Forest: Frankfurt/M-Offenburg-Singen- Schaffhausen and Würzburg-Zürich.

Rail passes: The *Inter-Rail* pass offers unlimited second-class train travel in up to 29 European countries (includes Morocco and Turkey) split into eight zones (A-H). Three different tickets are available: a ticket covering one zone (two to six countries, 16 days' validity), a ticket covering two zones (six to 10 countries, 22 days' validity) and an *All Zone Pass* (29 countries, one month's validity). Ferry services between Italy and Greece are included. Passengers must be resident in Europe for at least six months before the pass is used. Travel is not allowed in the passenger's country of residence. Travellers under 26 years receive a reduction of about 30 per cent. Children's tickets are reduced by about 50 per cent. Supplements are required for some high-speed services, seat reservations and couchettes. Discounts are offered on *Eurostar* and some ferry routes. Available from *Inter Rail* (website: www.interrailnet.com). The *Eurailpass* offers unlimited first-class train travel in 17 European countries. Tickets are valid for 15 days, 21 days, one month, two months or three months. The *Eurailpass Saver* ticket offers discounts for two or more people travelling together. The *Eurailpass Youth* ticket is available to those aged under 26 and offers unlimited second-class train travel. The *Eurailpass Flexi* allows either 10 or 15 travel days within a two-month period. The *Eurail Selectpass* is valid in three, four or five bordering countries and allows five, six, eight or 10 travel days (or 15 for five countries) in a two-month period. The *Eurail Regional Pass* allows four to 10 travel days in a two-month period in one of nine regions (usually two or more countries). Children receive a 50 per cent reduction. The passes cannot be sold to residents of Europe, Turkey, Morocco, Algeria, Tunisia or the Russian Federation. Available from *The Eurail Group* (website: www.eurail.com).

ROAD:

Germany is connected to all surrounding countries by a first-class network of motorways and trunk roads. In every major city, there are *Mitfahrzentralen* (car-sharing agencies) which offer shared car travelling to all European cities on the basis of shared costs; an agency fee is charged. See *Travel - Internal*

section for information on documentation and traffic regulations. **The Channel Tunnel:** *Eurotunnel* runs shuttle trains for cars, bicycles, motorcycles, coaches, minibuses, caravans, campervans and other vehicles over 1.85m (6.07ft) between Folkestone in Kent, with direct road access from the M20, and Calais, with links to the A16/A26 motorway (Exit 13). All road vehicles are carried through the tunnel in shuttle trains running between the two terminals. Terminals and shuttles are well-equipped for disabled passengers. Passenger Terminal buildings contain a variety of shops, restaurants, bureaux de change and other amenities. The journey takes about 35 minutes from platform to platform and around one hour from motorway to motorway. There are up to four passenger shuttles per hour at peak times, 24 hours per day and services run every day of the year. Motorists pass through customs and immigration before they board, with no further checks on arrival. Fares are charged according to length of stay and time of year and whether or not you have a reservation. The price applies to the car, regardless of the number of passengers or size of the car. Promotional deals are frequently available, especially outside the peak holiday seasons. Tickets may be purchased in advance from travel agents, or from Eurotunnel Customer Services in France or the UK with a credit card. For further information, brochures and reservations, contact *Eurotunnel Customer Services UK*, Customer Relations Department, Saint Martin's Plain, Cheriton, Folkestone, Kent CT19 4QD (tel: (08705) 353 535; website: www.eurotunnel.com). For further information about departure times of shuttles at the French terminal, contact *Eurotunnel Customer Information* in Coquelles (tel: France +33 (3) 2100 6543). **Coach:** There are numerous and excellent road links with all neighbouring countries. *Eurolines* (52 Grosvenor Gardens, London SW1W 0AU; tel: (08705) 143 219; website: www.eurolines.com) and *National Express* (Ensign Court, 4 Vicarage Road, Edgbaston, Birmingham B15 3ES; tel: 08705 808 080; website: www.nationalexpress.com) run regular coach services from the UK to Germany and other European cities.

Passes: Travellers can either choose Mini-Pass breaks or book a 15-, 30- or 60-day pass. The six Mini-Passes give travellers the freedom to visit three cities, with prices starting from £55. Travellers can stay as long as they like in each city.

Travel - Internal

AIR:

Internal services are operated by *Deutsche BA*, *Lufthansa* and several other regional airlines. Frankfurt/M is the focal point of internal air services and all airports in the Federal Republic of Germany can be reached by an average of 50 minutes' flying time. There are several airports in the country apart from those listed above which offer internal air services. *Helgoland (HGL), Sylt (GWT)* and some other Friesian Islands are served by seasonal services operated by regional airlines or air taxi services. Connections by air are run daily from Berlin, Bremen, Cologne/Bonn, Düsseldorf, Frankfurt/M, Hamburg, Hannover, Munich, Nuremberg, Stuttgart and Westerland/Sylt (summer only). The majority of western airports offer daily flights to Leipzig and several flights a week to Dresden. For further information on internal flights contact Lufthansa (tel: (08457) 737 747; website: www.lufthansa.com).

SEA/RIVER:

Regular scheduled boat services operate on most rivers, lakes and coastal waters, including the Danube, Main, Moselle, Neckar, Rhine and the Weser, and also on Ammer See, Chiemsee, Königssee and Lake Constance. Ferry services are operated on Kiel Fjord and from Cuxhaven to Helgoland and to the East and North Friesian Islands as well as to Scandinavian destinations. Besides these scheduled services, special excursions are available on all navigable waters. The *KD German Rhine Line* (website: www.k-d.de) covers the Rhine and Moselle rivers, and has comfortable ships which operate daily from April to late October. In conjunction with the '*White Fleet*' *Dresden*, the KD also organises cabin cruises on the Elbe between Dresden and Hamburg. Further routes include the rivers Saale and Elbe, several lakes and the Mecklenburger Lake District. *Hapag-Lloyd* (website: www.hlag.de) operates cruises of one to 21 days from Warnemünde, Hamburg and Kiel in summer. Lake Constance (Europe's third-largest inland lake) is served by regular steamers, pleasure boats and car ferries between the German, Swiss and Austrian shores. The *Lake Constance Adventure Pass* (Bodensee-Erlebniskarte) gives free travel on many rides listed in the *Bodensee Adventure Planner*, throughout the Lake Constance area. This includes scheduled ferry services offered by the German, Swiss and Austrian railways as well as some bus, local train and mountain railway routes. The pass is valid for either three, seven or 14 days. Children up to six years of age travel free. In addition to the pass, there is a Family Ticket which is available free of charge and allows children between six and 16 years of age free travel; unmarried young persons between 16 and 26 years of age pay half price. In both cases they have to be accompanied by a parent. The Family Ticket is only valid on boats together with the Bodensee Adventure Pass.

RAIL:

Several InterCity and ICE connections are on offer running every one or two hours to 32 destinations (mainly in Germany but trains also run to Austria, Belgium, The Netherlands and Switzerland). Within Germany, trains also operate on the following routes: Berlin-Frankfurt/M-Karlsruhe, Berlin-Cologne-Basel, Munich-Frankfurt/M-Berlin and Hamburg-Berlin-Dresden with direct links to Prague. The *ICE-Business-Sprinter* runs non-stop on the following routes: Frankfurt/M-Hannover, Wiesbaden-Hannover, Frankfurt/M-Hamburg, Wiesbaden- Hamburg, Mannheim-Hamburg, Karlsruhe-Hamburg and Frankfurt/M-Munich. Seats on these services have to be booked in advance; yearly ticket holders can use the Sprinters without surcharge. Generally, reservations are advised on all services. Children under six years of age travel free of charge; those aged six to 11 pay half fare; young people aged 12 to 26 pay 75 per cent of the standard fare. For latest information leaflets, contact German Rail in the UK (see below).

German National Railways (*Deutsche Bahn*) operates tens of thousands of passenger trains each day. Work on the 3200km- (2000 mile-) fast-train network has already started and should be completed by 2010. The network does not radiate around the capital as the federal structure provides an integrated system to serve the many regional centres. More than 50 cities, including Berlin, Erfurt, Dresden and Leipzig, are served hourly by *InterCity* trains – and increasingly by *InterCity Express* trains; regional centres are connected every two hours (west Germany), or every two to four hours in the eastern part of the country,

Credit: ©GNTB/Ostbayern, Tourismusverband

through the *InterRegio* system. Details of up-to-date prices, and where tickets can be bought, are available from *German Rail* (tel: (08702) 435 363; website: www.bahn.co.uk) *or* the Tourist Office.

Deutsche Bahn and Lufthansa have introduced an innovative project aimed at replacing internal German flights with more environmentally friendly rail transport. For travellers using Frankfurt airport wanting to transfer to or from Stuttgart or Cologne, train and flight timetables will be coordinated; one ticket will cover the whole journey and check in/check out will take place at Stuttgart Station. Boarding the train with just hand luggage, the travellers can pick up their luggage at the flight destination or Stuttgart Station. This offer is currently available for every airport Lufthansa flies to from Frankfurt (except Tel Aviv). The following section gives brief descriptions of the major special fares and tickets which are currently on offer. Some of these can only be obtained in Germany. Other new schemes, or modifications to existing ones, may be introduced in the future.

The introduction of the high-speed *InterCity Express*, travelling at 300kph (187mph), reduced travel times between the major centres immensely. The service is operating hourly only on some connections at the moment, but this number is increasing; a supplement is payable. The extensive *InterCity* network (300 trains per day) connects the major centres at hourly intervals, and ensures swift interchange between trains. A supplement is charged for first- or second-class on *EuroCity* and *InterCity* trains. Smaller towns are linked by the 26 *InterRegio* lines at two-hour intervals. Supplementing the system of these longer-distance trains are several commuter networks in larger cities.

Facilities and services: Buffet cars with some seating for light refreshments and drinks are provided on *InterRegio* (IR) trains. Most *EuroCity* and *InterCity* trains carry a 48-seat restaurant, offering a menu and drinks throughout the journey. The newer generation *InterCity Express* trains combine both of the above-mentioned facilities, offering a selection of snacks and menus in their restaurant cars. First-class passengers are provided with 'at-your-seat' service. The *InterCity Express* also provides a service car with conference compartment, card telephones and fully equipped office (photocopier, fax, etc). **Sleeping cars:** Many have showers, and air conditioning is provided on most long-distance overnight trains. Beds can be booked in advance. Some trains provide couchettes instead. Sleeping-car attendants serve refreshments. Seat reservations should be made for all long-distance trains well in advance. When reserving a seat on *EuroCity*, *InterCity* and *InterCity*

Express trains, specify *Grossraumwagen*, which is a carriage with adjustable seats and without compartments, or *Abteilwagen*, which is made up of compartments. **Bicycles:** At a vast number of stations in areas suited for cycle tours, the DB operates a bicycle hire service. It is also possible to carry your bike on the train but you may need to pre-book a space for it so check prior to travel (some rush hour services may be excluded). For a list of all the stations operating this service, contact the German National Tourist Office (See *Top Things To Do*). **Mountain railways:** Cable cars, chairlifts or cogwheel railways serve all popular mountain sites.

Rail passes: The following is a selection of rail passes available on German railways. Details may change and travellers are advised to check with Deutsche Bahn. Because of the large range of promotions available at any one time, it is not possible to list them all, so visit www.bahn.co.uk for the latest information and offers. Some passes can only be purchased outside Germany (see **Note** below).

Saverticket: Available for a return journey on one weekend or within one month.

Supersaverticket: Available for a return journey on a Saturday or within one month (not valid Friday, Sunday and during peak days).

Twenticket: Available for second-class single or return journeys for regional and long-distance travel between the ages of 12 and 25. Valid for up to two months, the ticket gives up to 20 per cent discount on the regular fare.

Welcome cards: Many cities in Germany offer *Welcome Cards* or *City Passes*. They allow unlimited transport throughout the city for the whole day. Some also include reductions into museums and attractions. Bonn, Bremen, Cologne, Dresden, Dusseldorf, Erfurt, Frankfurt, Hanover, Hamburg, Lubeck, Munich, Rostock, Stuttgart, Trier and Würtzburg all offer the card. Regional Welcome Cards are also available.

Regional Lander tickets: These tickets offer unlimited travel for up to five people of the whole day and are priced at €32 (£22). Valid on all local trains, second-class only.

Happy Weekend Ticket: Available for up to five persons travelling together at a weekend, from Sat to Mon (0300). Valid on all local trains, second-class only.

Euro Domino: The *EuroDomino* pass enables holders anything from three to eight days' extensive travel within a one-month period on the entire rail network of their chosen country. It is valid in 28 European countries and North Africa, including the ferry service from Brindisi (Italy) to Igoumenitsa (Greece). To purchase a *EuroDomino* pass you must have been resident in Europe for at least six months and a passport number is required at time of booking. It is

not permitted to purchase a pass for travel within your own country of residence.

To qualify for the youth rates, you must be under 26 years on the first date of validity of the pass. Children aged four to 11 years inclusive pay half the adult fares rounded up to the nearest pound. Children under four years travel free. Seat reservations, couchette and sleeper charges are not included in the cost of the pass and are payable at the normal rate. Passholder fares are payable on some services. Reservation/Supplement charges are payable on all trains within Spain.

Available from *Rail Europe* (website: www.raileurope.co.uk/railpasses/eurodomino.htm).

The German variety of the ED-ticket is valid on the complete network of the *Deutsche Bahn*; all *InterCity* trains, including the *InterCity Express*, can be used without paying a supplement. *Motorail* is exempt. Where seat reservation is required, a reduced fee is charged; the usual rates apply for couchette and sleeping-cars.

BahnCard: The BahnCard ticket offers half-price rail travel with a choice of first- or second-class travel and is valid for one year. In addition, there are reduced versions for married couples, families, senior citizens, young people and children.

Good Evening Ticket: This ticket is only available in Germany. It offers travel on nearly all routes within Germany for a flat fare between 1900-0300 daily except Christmas, Easter and other major travelling dates. The ticket has to be bought at the station of departure.

Motorail: The German Railway has a fully integrated motorail network, connecting with the rest of the European motorail network. Trains run mostly during the summer and at other holiday periods; most have sleeper, couchette and restaurant/buffet cars; for details see online (website: www.dbautozug.de).

Note: Conditions may apply to some of these tickets. There are certain discount rail passes that can only be purchased outside Germany. The following rail passes can only be purchased through German Rail offices and travel agencies outside Europe: *German Railpass* (valid for four to 10 days for either first- or second-class travel); *German Rail Youthpass* (second-class travel for travellers aged 12 to 25 years old); and the *German Rail Twinpass* (for two persons travelling together, first- or second-class, for four to 10 days). The pass includes travel on rail as well as some ship tours. Travellers aged six to 11 years get a 50 per cent reduction.

ROAD:

Traffic drives on the right. Germany is covered by a modern network of motorways (*Autobahnen*). Use of the network is free at present, but the introduction of a road toll is being discussed and charges have been levied on some sightseeing roads in Bavaria. Lead-free petrol is obtainable everywhere. The breakdown service of the *German Automobile Association* (ADAC) is available throughout the country, though in the eastern part of the country, the *Auto Club Europa* (ACE) and the *Allgemeiner Deutscher Motorsportverband* (ADMV) also provide a service. Help is given free of charge to members of affiliated motoring organisations, such as the *AA*, and only parts have to be paid for. Breakdown services, including a helicopter rescue service, are operated by the ADAC. In the event of a breakdown, use emergency telephones located along the motorway and ask for road service assistance (*strassenwachthilfe*). In almost all cases, the number to dial for emergency services is 110; if in doubt, dial the fire brigade, 112. Although motorways in eastern Germany are of a reasonable standard, many secondary roads are still being improved to match western Germany's standards.

Bus: Buses serve villages and small towns, especially those without railway stations. There are few long-distance services. *Europabus/Deutsche Touring* runs services on special scenic routes such as the *Romantic Road* (Wiesbaden/Frankfurt to Munich/Füssen) and the *Castle Road* (between Mannheim/Heidelberg to Rothenburg and Nuremberg).

Taxi: These are available everywhere. Visitors should watch out for waiting-period charges and surcharges. All taxis are metered at approximately €1.30 per km with a €2.50 minimum charge.

Car hire: Self-drive cars are available at most towns and at over 40 railway stations. Chauffeur-driven cars are available in all large towns. Some firms offer weekly rates including unlimited mileage. VAT at 16 per cent is payable on all rental charges. Several airlines, including *Lufthansa*, offer 'Fly-drive'. Contact the German National Tourist Office for details (see *Top Things to Do*).

Motoring organisations: The *Allgemeiner Deutscher Automobil Club* (ADAC) (website: www.adac.de) based in Munich and the *Automobilclub von Deutschland* (AvD) (website: www.avd.de) based in Frankfurt/M have offices at all major frontier crossings and in the larger towns. They will be able to assist foreign motorists, particularly those belonging to affiliated motoring organisations. They also publish maps and guidebooks, which are available at their offices. German Automobile Association (ADAC) operates an emergency service to relay radio messages to motorists.

In both winter and summer, there are constant radio reports on road conditions and traffic.

Regulations: Traffic signs are international. Speed limits in western Germany are 50kph (31mph) in built-up areas and 100kph (62mph) on all roads outside built-up areas. Motorways (*Autobahnen*) and dual carriageways have a recommended speed limit of 130kph (81mph). Speed limits in eastern Germany vary according to the condition of the road. Although officially the same as in western Germany, some motorways and dual carriageways carry varying speed limits and are signposted. Children under 12 must travel in a special child seat in the back. Seat belts must be worn in the front and back. All visitors' cars must display vehicle nationality plates. The warning triangle and a first-aid box are compulsory. The nationwide alcohol limit is 0.5 per cent. Disabled drivers should be warned that, although Germany is well-organised for disabled travellers, an orange badge as used in the UK will not entitle the disabled motorist to park freely in Germany. From November to March drivers are advised to buy or hire snow chains for their vehicle wheels, especially for travelling in areas of medium to high altitude; failure to do so could result in a fine.

Documentation: If you are driving, your car insurance will provide the minimum cover for EU countries, which is liability to third parties. Travellers may want to ask their insurer to extend their cover. Travellers are unlikely to be covered for breakdown. Insurance is legally required. EU nationals taking their own cars are strongly advised to obtain a Green Card. Without it, insurance cover is limited to the minimum legal cover; the Green Card tops this up to the level of cover provided by the car owner's domestic policy. Foreign travellers may drive their cars for up to one year if in possession of a national licence or International Driving Permit and car registration papers. Members of the EU, the USA and Australia do not need an international driving licence to drive in Germany.

URBAN:

All urban areas have highly efficient and well-established bus services. These are supplemented in a number of larger cities by underground and suburban railway trains. In many larger cities, tickets for a local transport journey have to be purchased from ticket machines before boarding the suburban train (*S-Bahn*), underground (*U-Bahn*), bus or tram. Ticket inspections are frequent and passengers without valid tickets will be fined on the spot. Timetables and brochures are available at stations.

Berlin: The city's excellent public transport includes an extensive network of buses, underground and *S-Bahn* in three travel zones. In the eastern part of the city, tram services and the ferries of the *Berliner Verkehrs-Betriebe*, *BVG* (Berlin Public Transport; website: www.bvg.de), in conjunction with east Berlin's '*White Fleet*', provide further services. The underground lines 1 and 9 run a 24-hour service Friday night to Saturday and Saturday night to Sunday. The Berlin-Ticket is valid for 24 hours for unlimited travel on bus, underground, S-Bahn and the BVG ferries. The special BVG-excursion coaches are exempt. Holders of the Combined Day-Ticket enjoy unlimited travel with bus, underground and S-Bahn, as well as on the complete ferry network of either organisation. A special Weekly Ticket with a validity of seven days can only be obtained at *Zoo* station. Further details are available from BVG (see above).

Note: Pedestrians should be aware that it is an offence to cross a road when the pedestrian crossing lights are red, even if there is no traffic on the road. On-the-spot fines for offenders are common.

Travel times:

(1): The following chart gives approximate travel times (in hours and minutes) from **Berlin** to other major cities and towns in the Federal Republic of Germany.

	Air	Road	Rail
Hamburg	0.45	4.00	2.25
Frankfurt	1.10	6.30	4.00
Munich	1.20	7.00	6.20
Dresden	-	2.30	2.00

(2): The following chart gives approximate travel times (in hours and minutes) from **Bonn** to other major cities and towns in the Federal Republic of Germany.

	Air	Road	Rail	River
Hamburg	0.55	4.00	4.00	-
Cologne	-	0.20	0.15	0.40
Munich	1.00	7.00	5.30	-
Berlin	1.05	8.00	5.00	-

[a]: There is a hydrofoil service (not daily) between Cologne and Mainz via Koblenz and Bonn which takes about three hours 30 minutes.

Note: All the above times are average times by the fastest and most direct route, by motorways in the case of road journeys, and by the quickest hydrofoil service for the time by river. The slow boat from Bonn to Cologne, for instance, takes three hours.

Travel Advice

Most visits to Germany are trouble-free but you should be aware of the global risk of indiscriminate international terrorist attacks, which could be against civilian targets, including places frequented by foreigners.

This advice is based on information provided by the Foreign and Commonwealth Office in the UK. It is correct at time of publishing. As the situation can change rapidly, visitors are advised to contact the following organisations for the latest travel advice:

British Foreign and Commonwealth Office
Tel: (0845) 850 2829.
Website: www.fco.gov.uk

US Department of State
Website: http://travel.state.gov/travel

Accommodation

HOTELS:

There is a good selection of hotels in the Federal Republic of Germany and comprehensive guides can be found at the German National Tourist Office. They can also provide the *German Hotel Association Guide*, published by the Deutscher Hotel- und Gaststättenverband (DEHOGA), Am Weidendamm 1A, 10873 Berlin (tel: (30) 726 252/0; website: www.dehoga.de). Approximately 50 per cent of establishments offering accommodation in the Federal Republic of Germany belong to the association, which can supply further information on accommodation. A special accommodation guide for the disabled, *Hilfe für Behinderte*, is available through Bundesverband Selbsthilfe Körperbehinderter e.V (BSK), Altkrautheimer Strasse 20, 74238 Krautheim (tel: (6294) 42810; website: www.bsk-ev.de). Some hotels are situated in old castles, palaces and monasteries. Alongside these are modern, comfortable hotels on well-planned and purpose-built premises. Examples of accommodation for a family on holiday is a country inn offering bed, breakfast and meals. More demanding visitors are also well catered for with medium to luxury hotels. The German hotel trade is extremely well equipped with facilities from swimming pools and saunas to exercise gyms. When touring the country with no fixed itinerary, it is obviously often difficult to make reservations in advance. Watch out for *Zimmer frei* (vacancies) notices by the roadside, or go to the local Tourist Office (usually called *Verkehrsamt*). Visitors should try to get to the town where they want to stay the night by 1600, particularly in summer. DEHOGA (website: www.hotelsterne.de) introduced a hotel grading system, which follows the usual grading of **1** to **5 stars**.

Gasthof: A 'Gasthof' (inn) must provide the same facilities as a hotel except for the common rooms such as a lounge, etc. 30 per cent of establishments fall into this category.

Pension: A 'Pension' must provide accommodation and food only for guests. It does not have to provide a restaurant for non-residents, nor common rooms. 16 per cent of establishments fall into this category.

Hotel Garni: Provides accommodation and breakfast only for guests. 27 per cent of establishments fall into this category.

HISTORIC HOLIDAYS:

Information about holidays in castles, stately mansions and historic hostelries may be obtained by contacting the German National Tourist Office.

SELF-CATERING:

All-in self-catering deals are available that include sea travel to a German or other Channel port, and accommodation at the resort. The latter might be in anything from a farmhouse to a castle. Details are available from the German National Tourist Office (see *Top Things To Do*).

FARMHOUSES:

The booklet *Urlaub auf dem Bauernhof* (*Holidays on the Farm*) is published in conjunction with the German Agricultural Society and can be obtained from *DLG*-Agrartour GmbH. Regional guides on most tourist regions can also be obtained from the GermVerlag; *Agrartour GmbH* offers agricultural studies. For more information, contact the German National Tourist Office. All aforementioned booklets are published in German only. A basic knowledge of German will be required for such a holiday. A catalogue with addresses for the whole of the country can be ordered from Landschriften-Verlag GmbH.

YOUTH HOSTELS:

There are over 600 youth hostels throughout both eastern and western Germany. They are open to members of any Youth Hostel Association affiliated to the International Youth Hostel Association. Membership can be obtained from the YHA or *Deutsches Jugendherbergswerk* (German Youth Hostel Organisation).

CAMPING/CARAVANNING:

There are many campsites in Germany. They are generally open from April to October, but some sites, mostly in wintersports areas, stay open in the winter and have all necessary facilities. Campsites in the

Credit: ©GNTB/Hessen Touristik Service e.V.

A B C D E F **G** H I J K L M N O P Q R S T U V W X Y Z

Credit: ©GNTB/Hessen Touristik Service e. V.

eastern part of the country are of a very basic standard. The permission of the proprietor and/or the local police must always be sought before camp is pitched anywhere other than a recognised campsite. It is not normally possible to make advance reservations on campsites. A free map/folder giving details of several hundred selected campsites throughout the country is available from the German National Tourist Office. The German Camping Club publishes a camping guide of the best sites in Germany. The *AA Guide to Camping and Caravanning on the Continent* lists nearly 2000 European campsites, including a large section on Germany.

ACCOMMODATION INFORMATION

Deutscher Hotel- und Gaststättenverband (DEHOGA) (publishes the German Hotel Association Guide)
Am Weidendamm 1A, 10873 Berlin, Germany
Tel: (30) 726 252/0.
Website: www.dehoga.de

DLG-Agrartour GmbH (publishes the booklet Urlaub auf dem Bauernhof (Holidays on the Farm))
Eschborner Landstrasse 122,
60489 Frankfurt/M, Germany
Tel: (69) 2478 8305.
Website: www.dlg-verlag.de

GermVerlag (provides regional tourist guides)
Eschborner Landstrasse 122,
60489 Frankfurt/M, Germany
Tel: (69) 2478 8451.
Website: www.dlg-verlag.de or
www.landtourismus.de

Landschriften-Verlag GmbH (provides addresses for further information on farm holidays)
Landferien Tourist Center, Zentrale für den
Landurlaub, Heerstrasse 73, 53111 Bonn, Germany
Tel: (228) 963 020.
Website: www.bauernhofurlaub.com

Deutsches Jugendherbergswerk (German Youth Hostel Organisation)
Bismarckstrasse 8, 32756 Detmold, Germany
Tel: (5231) 74010.
Website: www.djh.de

Deutscher Camping-Club (DCC)
Mandlstrasse 28, 80802 Munich, Germany
Tel: (89) 380 1420.
Website: www.camping-club.de

Top Things To See

- Venture into **Berlin**, the largest city in Germany, the country's capital, and the seat of Government. The **German Parliament (Reichstag)**, designed by British architect Norman Foster, testifies to the construction boom in the German capital. Since November 1989 when the Wall came down, nearly 100 streets have been reconnected, disused 'ghost' railway stations have sprung back to life and the watchtowers, dogs and barbed wire that divided the city, the country and indeed the continent for 28 years have virtually disappeared. Nevertheless, there is often stark contrast between the two parts of the city, partly due to economic contrasts between East and West, but also because they have never been of a uniform character.

- Explore the **eastern side of Berlin** to help conceive what life might have been like when the Wall still stood. The east contains the densely populated working-class quarters of **Mitte**, **Pankow**, **Prenzlauer Berg** and **Friedrichshain**, which inspired the theatre of Erwin Piscator and Bertolt Brecht. After the city was occupied by the four post-war victorious powers, the two halves diverged even more as West Berliners broke away from their past and embraced the idea of a new, intensely western, Americanised city. At the same time, eastern counterparts chose to retain what remained of the old Berlin instead. This is why the eastern half of the city probably gives a more accurate image of what Berlin was like in the 1920s and 30s. To find areas retaining the pre-war atmosphere, visitors must move away from the city centre. The **People's Park Friederichshain** in the eastern part of the city is the largest and oldest park in east Berlin. The **Deutsche Staatsoper (German State Opera)** stages performances in a classical setting. **Alexanderplatz** was one of the main centres of 1920s Berlin as well as of post-war East Berlin. It is an important focal point in the city. Relentless modernisation, however, has changed the character of the Alexanderplatz, which is now a bustling if faceless area of cafes, hotels and the 368m- (1207ft-) high **Television Tower (Fernsehturm)**, which dominates the skyline of the city. It is also home to the **World Time Clock** and **The Fountain of International Friendship**.

- Stand next to the site of the **Berlin Wall**. **Unter den Linden** was what Frederick the Great saw as the centrepiece of his royal capital and which changed from one of the premier thoroughfares of the old unified city to the showpiece of the German Democratic Republic. Restored monumental buildings and diplomatic missions to the former GDR capital now line it. However, for nearly 30 years it was a dead-end, cut off by the Wall. At its western end, the **Brandenburg Gate (Brandenburger Tor)** has been the supreme symbol of the city of Berlin since it was built in 1791. The Wall once partly obscured the view of the Gate from the West, so it became a potent symbol of European division. Now it is again accessible from both East and West. The Berlin Wall has all but gone and walkers and cyclists now roam along what was once nicknamed '**Todesstreifen**' - or Death Strip. Quite a few tourists bought their 'own' piece of the Wall – museums also display pieces.

- Germany is awash with cultural highlights preserved in museums and galleries. Berlin houses three opera houses, over 150 theatres and playhouses and no fewer than 170 museums and galleries. Included in this is the **Berlin Wall Museum** situated at the former **Checkpoint Charlie** in Friedrichstrasse. The **Ägyptisches Museum (Egyptian Museum)** in **Charlottenburg** contains the world-famous bust of Queen Nefertiti. The **Berlin Museum** is in the old **Supreme Court Building** in **Kreuzberg**. East Berlin has a rich array of museums, five of which can be found on **Museumsinsel (Museum Island)** in a fork of the **River Spree**. The most famous is the **Pergamon Museum** which houses works of classical antiquity such as the **Pergamon Altar** and art of the Near East, Islam and the Orient. The Bavarian capital, **Munich (München)**, the third-largest German city and 800 years old, contains numerous museums and galleries. The **Alte Pinakothek** is home to the largest collection of Rubens paintings in the world. Two other galleries of note are **Pinakothek der Moderne**, and the **Museum der Fantasie**. The **Glyptothek** on the **Königsplatz** houses Greek and Roman sculptures. **Bonn** was administrative capital of Germany until 2000 and is still host to a number of museums on the **Museum Mile**, including **Kunstmuseum Bonn (Bonn Art Museum), Kunst und Ausstellungshalle der Bundersrepublik Deutchland** (art and exhibition Hall) and the **Museum Alexander Koening** (zoological centre).

- You must see one of Germany's exquisite castles and, to be truthful, you are downright spoiled. The country has many of them and their quality matches their quantity. **Coburg Castle** (13th to 16th centuries) is one of the largest fortified sites in Germany, and towers over the former ducal capital (and one-time refuge of Martin Luther) of **Coburg**, in Bavaria. In the **Baden-Württemberg region**, the **Neckar Valley** - a major wine-growing region - is located around castles such as **Gutenberg**, **Hornberg** and **Hirschhorn**, each of which offers splendid views of the surrounding landscape. Traces of Frederick the Great are evident at **Rheinsberg**, immortalised by Kurt Tucholsky's tale of the same name, whose interior of the beautifully situated castle is still undergoing restoration, but visits are possible, and one of the towers houses a **Tucholsky Memorial**. **Schwerin Castle**, on the lake of the same name, surrounded by a terraced garden crossed by a canal and the state capital of **Mecklenburg-Western Pomerania**, was for many decades the residence of the Dukes of Mecklenburg and is one of the finest examples of German Gothic architecture. **Rüdesheim**, famous for its **Drosselgasse**, a narrow lane with many little wine bars and pubs, some serving the delicious *Rüdesheimer Kaffee* (locally produced brandy with coffee), has a cable car which takes visitors up to the beautiful **Niederwald Castle**, a starting point for walks in the **Taunus** hills. Perhaps the most famous castle of all is within the **Upper Bavaria region**. A spectacular feat of architecture, and epitomising the fairytale landscape of Bavaria, **Neuschwanstein Castle**, built by Ludwig II, is constructed on the ridge of a mountain valley surrounded by snow-capped peaks. It is a vision from fairyland during the day, and indeed inspired Disney's portrayal of the beautiful castle in *Sleeping Beauty*, while at night it changes into the perfect sinister home for Count Dracula.

- Pay a visit to one of Germany's host of romantic university towns: **Freiburg** is the gateway to the **Black Forest** and an Archepiscopal see and old university town, with its architectural masterpiece, the Gothic **Cathedral** (12th to 15th centuries) with magnificent tower (116m/380ft), the historic red **Kaufhaus** on the Cathedral Square (1550), Germany's oldest inn, **Zum Roten Bären**, and many excellent wine taverns; **Heidelberg** is the most famous place on the **Neckar River** and Germany's oldest university town, dominated by the ruins of its famous 14th-century castle; **Tübingen**, south of **Stuttgart**, is a world-famous romantic university town also on the **River Neckar**, with an unspoilt old town centre complete with the **Castle of the Count Palatine** (1078), a late Gothic **Collegiate Church** (1470) with royal burial place and former student dungeons (1514); and **Mainz**, state capital of **Rhineland-Palatinate**, is a university town and Episcopal see dating back 2000 years, situated on the rivers **Rhine** and **Main**, with an 1000-year-old **Cathedral**.

- Go to **Constance (Konstanz)**, a German university and cathedral town, and stare across at the enormity and beauty of the **Bodensee (Lake Constance)**, which has shores in Austria, Switzerland and Germany. Constance is a frontier anomaly, a German town on the Swiss side of the lake, completely surrounded by Swiss territory except for a strip on the waterfront. Attractions include the

Konzilsgebäude (14th century); Renaissance **Town Hall** (16th century); historic old **Insel Hotel** (14th century); **Barbarossa-Haus** (12th century); **Hus-Haus** (15th century); and the old town fortifications **Rheintorturm**, **Pulverturm** and **Schnetztor**. The town has theatres, concert halls, a casino and hosts an international music festival as well as the **Seenachtfest**, a lake festival. As an area, Lake Constance is the focal point of a delightful holiday district, rich in art treasures and facilities for outdoor activities.

- Germany also has some spectacular countryside, from its well-known Black Forest to vineyards such as those which nestle inbetween Bavarian towns and are famous for their **Bocksbeutel** (specially formed bottle). The picturesque **Schorfheide** area of forest, north of Berlin, contains beavers, otters and eagles, and in the centre of this landscape of birches and pines lies the **Werbellin Lake**. **East Friesland**, on the North Sea coast of Lower Saxony, consists of a wide plain interspersed by ranges of tree-covered hills known for their health resorts and modern spa facilities, as well as their fine sandy beaches. The traffic-free **East Friesian Islands** also offer relaxing health-oriented holidays. Sea air and scenery along the coast guarantee a happy and restful holiday atmosphere. In contrast is the large nature reserve between the rivers **Elbe** and **Aller** further inland. The countryside comprises moorland with wide expanses of heather, grazing sheep, clumps of green birch trees and junipers. In **Rhineland** are the vast plains of the **Lower Rhine farmlands**, the strange volcanic crater lakes of the **Eifel Hills**, the **Bergische Land** with its lakes and **Altenberg Cathedral** and the **Siebengebirge**. Rhineland and the **Moselle Valley** attract visitors not only for their beauty and romanticism, but also for the convivial atmosphere engendered by wine and song. Like most of its tributaries, vineyards line the Rhine wherever the slopes face the sun. Alternating with the vineyards are extensive orchards, which are heavy with blossom in spring. The **Ahr Valley** in the Eifel region is particularly renowned for its lush scenery and its red wine.

- In **Hessen**, follow the **German Fairy Tale Road**. **Schwalmstadt** was the home of *Little Red Riding Hood*, a town where people still wear traditional costumes to church on Sunday and at folk festivals. In the **Reinhardswald**, **Sababurg** - now a castle-hotel - inspired the Brothers Grimm to write *Sleeping Beauty*. The romantic scenery of the rolling hill country of the **Odenwald** is one rich in legend and folklore. **Kassel** is home of the **Grimm Brothers Museum**. Away from the Fairy Tale Road, but still worth a visit, is the town of **Hameln** (**Hamlyn**), famed for the tale of the *Pied Piper*, found in the **Weser Valley** near **Hannover**. A play about the infamous piper is re-enacted during the summer months every Sunday at noon.

- Explore the medieval **Hanseatic League**, whose main members were the towns of **Hamburg**, **Lübeck**, **Bremen** and **Rostock**. The Hanseatic League was an alliance of these four trading cities who established and maintained a trade monopoly over the Baltic Sea and most of northern Europe between the 13th and 17th centuries. Their greatness and wealth through such trade is evident in the long-lasting delights of these towns. Hamburg is the second-largest city in Germany with a population of 1.8 million people and its attractions include the Baroque **Church of St Michael** (*der Michel*), the **Town Hall** with its distinctive green roof, the elegant **Hanseviertel** and the **Alster Lake**, the biggest lake inside a European city. In the city's heart is the **Planten und Blomen** park near the **Congress Centrum Hamburg**, with its spectacular fountain displays during the summer evenings. **Lübeck** is a picturesque oval-shaped old town, ringed by water, which still has many reminders of the city's medieval golden age and is a UNESCO World Heritage Site. It justly claims to be the most beautiful town in northern Germany. The **Holsten Gate**, the **Rathaus** and the many examples of northern red brick town houses are part of the historic heritage. Thomas Mann set his famous novel, *Buddenbrooks*, here, and **Buddenbrook House** (**Buddenbrookhaus**) contains the Heinrich and Thomas Mann Centre, giving information on the life and works of both authors. Bremen is the oldest German maritime city, having been a market town since AD 965, but for all its history, also boasts two of the country's most modern high-tech visitor attractions: the interactive **Universum Science Centre** and the **Space Travel Visitor Centre**. Historic Bremen clusters around the marketplace, featuring the **Gothic Town Hall** (1405-1410), in front of which stands the **Roland**, the statue of a medieval knight and symbol of the city. The extensive pedestrian zone includes a sculpture of the **Bremer Stadtmusikanten** (Musicians of Bremen), made famous in the fairy tale by Grimm. Also part of this zone is the **Schnoorviertel**, a district full of medieval charm, with narrow cobbled streets now housing art galleries and exclusive shops. Lastly, Rostock has a **University** founded in 1419, the first in Northern Europe, and its attractions include the

Credit: ©GNTB/Düsseldorf Marketing & Tourismus GmbH

elegant burghers' houses in **Thälmann Square**, the 15th-century **Town Hall**, the late-Gothic **St Marien Church** with its 15th-century astronomical clock and Baroque organ, and the district of **Warnemünde** with its fishing harbour and seaside resort.

- Almost midway between **Rüdesheim** and **Koblenz**, see the symbol of the Rhine, **Lorelei Rock** - which has provided the inspiration for many songs about its legendary siren for centuries.

- **Leipzig** has a fascinating history. Lenin printed the first issues of his Marxist newspaper here. Lessing, Jean-Paul Sartre and Goethe all studied at the university. Music and books are important - there are no fewer than 38 publishers in the city, and it is Wagner's birthplace. The **German Museum of Books** claims to be the world's oldest of its kind. Mendelssohn was director of music, and Bach was choirmaster, at the now completely restored **St Thomas' Church**, between 1723 and 1750. There are museums dedicated to both composers in the city. Bach's church choir still exists and is of an excellent standard, as is the city's **Gewandhaus Orchestra**, and visitors can go to **Mendelssohn's House** where he lived and died. The old **University** (1407), the famous **Auerbach's Kellar** and the **Coffe Baum**, the most famous of the city's cafes, are further attractions in the city. Today, Leipzig stages major international trade fairs.

- One of the most famous **Reformation towns** is where Martin Luther nailed his '95 Theses Against Indulgences' to the door of the castle church in 1517. Numerous magnificent buildings from the 16th century – **Luther's House**, the **Melanchton House**, the **Castle Church** and the buildings of the former **University** – bear witness to the town's historical significance. Martin Luther is an extremely important figure in German history, having effected the standardisation of the German language. His theology also paved the way for modern religion, and therefore **Wartburg Castle**, where Martin Luther sought refuge and translated the New Testament into German, is a UNESCO World Heritage Site and dominates the town of **Eisenach**. The cultural centre of **Thuringia** contains an **Augustinian Abbey** where Martin Luther lived as a monk.

- See the southern 1000-year-old town of **Weimar**, home to many great men, including Luther, Bach, Liszt, Wagner and Schiller. An important cultural centre of the past, the city experienced its golden age in the 18th and 19th centuries. Johann Wolfgang von Goethe lived here for 50 years and was a major influence as a civil servant, theatre director and poet. His house is now the **Goethe National Museum**. Literature enthusiasts should not miss the **Goethe and Schiller Archive**. Bach was Court Organist and Court Concertmaster, Liszt and Richard Strauss were both directors of music. There is documentation of their private and public lives kept in hotels and museums in the town. Weimar was also the original home of the Bauhaus architectural school before it moved to **Dessau**.

Top Things To Do

- The **Harz Mountains**, Black Forest (**Schwarzwald**) and the **Bavarian Forest** are some of the best areas for **walking**. The network of marked **trails** amounts to some 132,000km (82,500 miles). The **District of Templin** in the **March of Brandenburg** provides 480km (300 miles) of paths. The **Black Forest**'s fine mountain scenery and beautifully situated lakeside resorts like **Titisee-Neustadt** and **Schluchsee** are sure-fire winners with walkers in summer and skiers in winter. The vast Bavarian Forest in the east, bordering the Czech Republic, contains the first German national park which was founded in 1970; it is also Europe's largest protected closed woodland area. This unspoiled and peaceful region is ideal for walking. **Saxony** (**Sachsen**) has a mountainous wooded landscape that is ideal for walkers in the summer and skiers in the winter. **Sächsische Schweiz (Saxon Switzerland)** is a national park, its sandstone mountains attracting many visitors. **Thuringia (Thüringen)** lies between Saxony and **Hesse**, and is the most westerly of the old 'East' German states. Major centres include **Erfurt**, **Jena** and **Weimar**. The wooded heights and slate mountains of the **Thuringian Forest** contain the well-known hiking route, the **Rennsteig**, which stretches for over 168km (105 miles). The towering scenery of the **Harz Mountains** is most popular of all: a region ideal for walking and wintersports holidays, dotted with villages with attractive carved timber-fronted houses, the Harz is also one of the most beautiful **hiking** areas in Germany, with its celebrated **Brocken** (highest point of the Harz).

- **Football** is loved by Germans, and their record in competition proves their skill at it: the national men's team were world champions in 1990, a title they previously won in 1954 and 1974, as well as having been runners-up in 1966, 1982, 1986 and 2002, and quarter finalists in 1998. More recently, the women's national football team won the world cup in 2003. With the **FIFA World Cup Championships 2006** set to be held in Germany, thrilled anticipation is brewing once again. Germany has extensive facilities for football throughout the country. If you just want to watch, league matches take place between Friday and Sunday when up to 300,000 fans a week go and see their teams play and millions more watch from home.

- Try having a go at some **wintersports**: there are lots of resorts in the **Suhl** area, in the south of the country. The main resort, **Oberhof**, offers excellent **ski-jumping** and **tobogganing**. **Ice hockey** and **skating** are both popular. In **Bavaria**, skiing is available at resorts such as **Berchtesgaden**, **Garmisch-Partenkirchen**, **Inzell**, **Oberstdorf**, **Reit im Winkl**, as well as in the southern mountains. Other areas are the Bavarian Forest, the Black Forest and the Harz Mountains. **Todtnauberg** in the Upper Black Forest is the highest resort in the Black Forest (1006m/3300ft) and a perfect observation point is the

Credit: ©GNTB/Andrew Cowin

Belchen summit nearby. The highest mountain is the **Feldberg**, with its popular winter skiing slopes. The season runs from November to April.

• Have a delectable glass of Germany **wine**, fresh from one of its many **vineyards**. These vineyards welcome visitors and are situated around the rivers **Rhine**, **Moselle** and **Neckar** in the west of the country and, further east, near the **Saale**, **Unstrut** and **Elbe** rivers. For motorists, there is a signposted '**wine road**' (Weinstrasse) running through each area. The **50-Mile Wine Tasting Route** travels from **Bockenheim** to **Schweigen-Rechterbach**, in South-West Germany. **Trier**, the oldest German town close to the Luxembourg border, stands on the **The Rhine Valley** between **Cologne** and **Mainz** and is also world famous for its wines and **wine festivals** during the autumn. The majority of German wines are white and light, with such varieties as Riesling and Silvaner. Wines are officially classified by the Government as either *Tafelwein/Landwein* (table wine/country wine) or *Qualitätswein* (higher-quality wine from a specified area). *Qualitätswein mit Prädikat* is the highest category. Within this last category, the wine is classed according to ripeness and quality: *Kabinett* for example is a light, low-alcohol wine made from fully ripened grapes, while *Trockenbeerenauslese* is a sweet wine made from grapes which have shrivelled almost to raisins. For a list of private vineyards open to the public, contact the German Wine Institute, PO Box 1660, 55116 Mainz (tel: (6131) 28290; website: www.deutscheweine.de).

• Germany has over 300 **spas** and **health resorts** that offer a wide range of traditional and modern treatments, and you are strongly advised to pay at least one of these a visit. All are strictly regulated by the Government, and promise beneficial results for such conditions as rheumatism, respiratory problems, nervous disorders or stress. Spa stays are very popular with Germans, not only because they are a national tradition, but because they offer holistic treatment combined with relaxation. Under medical supervision, visitors can take the waters or undergo treatments involving mud and peat. Many spas are situated on the North Sea and Baltic coasts. The Romans first recognised the therapeutic powers of the Black Forest's springs. The region's best-known spa town, **Baden-Baden**, was the summer capital of Europe during the last century. Travellers still flock to this delightful town to 'take the waters', which may be inhaled as a vapour, bathed in or simply drunk. Fortified by the water's therapeutic powers, one can take advantage of the town's many sporting facilities. There are many other charming villages and resorts in the surrounding area, principally

Freudenstadt, which claims to have more hours of sunshine than any other German town. The climatic spa of **Triberg** has 162m- (531ft-) high waterfalls and a swimming pool surrounded by evergreens. The beautiful spa town of **Aachen** (**Aix-la-Chapelle**) was capital of the empire of Charlemagne and stands 50km (30 miles) west of Cologne on the borders of three countries – Germany, Belgium and The Netherlands – and nearby is a point where a person can stand in all three at once. These are just some of 350 officially recognised medical spas and watering places with modern equipment providing therapeutic treatment and recreational facilities for visitors seeking rest and relaxation. A list of the spas and health resorts and various treatments can be ordered from the German National Tourist Office *or* directly from Deutscher Heilbäderverband e.V. (German Spas Association), Schumannstrasse 111, 53113 Bonn (tel: (228) 201 200; website: www.deutscher-heilbaederverband.de).

• **Drive** down the **Romantic Road**, which connects the northern area of Bavaria with the south, and is the most famous of all the German scenic roads. The towns along the way give visitors an excellent insight into the region's history, art and culture. It travels from **Würzburg** to **Fuessen**. Places of particular interest are **Würzburg**; medieval **Rothenburg**, **Dinkelsbühl** and **Nördlingen**; **Augsburg**, founded in 15BC by the Romans; the pilgrimage church **Wieskirche** in the meadows; **Steingaden Abbey**; and, the most popular site of all, **Neuschwanstein Castle** near the village of **Schwangau**.

• Gulp down lip-smackingly good beer with the best of them at **Oktoberfest**. **Munich** hosts this best-known of all German events, the **beer festival** that has its origins in 1810 when Crown Prince Ludwig of Bavaria married Princess Therese von Sachsen-Hildburghausen. The people liked the festival so much that it became a regular feature and now takes place annually for two weeks – the first Sunday in October is always the last day of the festival. Munich's nine breweries all have their own beer tents at the festival, but the city has many famous permanent beer cellars, including the **Hofbräuhaus**.

• Visit **Bayreuth** and witness the famous **Wagner Opera Festival**, which takes place every year from late July to August. Other attractions, many of which are connected with the life and works of the composer, include the **Festival Theatre** (1872-1876); **Villa Wahnfried** (Wagner's home, now a museum); **Wagner Memorial** ('Chiming Museum'); and **Freemasons' Museum**, Wagner's grave in the **Court Gardens**.

• Germany is a fantastic country for setting the scene at Christmas, and if you are lucky enough to be around in

December, head towards a **Christmas Fair**, like the one in **Nuremberg** (**Nürnberg**), whose international toy fair and famous *Christkindlmarkt* attract streams of visitors. Nuremberg has even been nicknamed 'Christmas City' by some, mesmerised by its aroma of cinnamon, mulled wine and roasted almonds.

TOURIST INFORMATION

German National Tourist Office in the UK
PO Box 2695, London W1A 3TN, UK
Tel: (020) 7317 0908 *or* (09001) 600 100 (recorded information and brochure request line; calls cost 60p per minute).
Website: www.germany-tourism.co.uk

German National Tourist Office in the USA
20th Floor, 122 East 42nd Street,
New York, NY 10168-0072, USA
Tel: (212) 661 7200 *or* (800) 651 7010 (toll free).
Website: www.cometogermany.com

Entertainment

FOOD & DRINK: The main meal of the day in Germany tends to be lunch with a light snack eaten at about seven in the evening. Breakfast served in homes and hotels usually consists of a boiled egg, bread rolls with jam, honey, cold cuts and cheese slices. Available from snack bars, butcher shops, bakers and cafes are grilled, fried or boiled sausages (*wurst*) with a crusty bread roll or potato salad. There are also bread rolls filled with all kinds of sausage slices, hot meat filling (such as *leberkäse*), pickled herring, gherkins and onion rings or cheese. In bakeries, *strudel* with the traditional apple filling, a variety of fruits and *fromage frais* is available. There is also an astonishingly wide variety of breads. A set menu meal in a simple *gasthof* or cafe usually includes three courses: soup is the most popular starter. The main meal consists of vegetables or a salad, potatoes, meat and gravy. For pudding, there is often a sweet such as a *blancmange*, fruit or ice cream. Restaurants often serve either beer or wine. Cakes and pastries are normally reserved for the afternoon with kaffee und kuchen ('coffee and cakes') taken at home or in a cafe. Cafes serving *kaffee und kuchen* are not only to be found in cities, towns and villages but also at or near popular excursion and tourist spots. International speciality restaurants, such as Chinese, Greek, Turkish and others, can be found everywhere in the western part of the country. Waiter or waitress service is normal although self-service restaurants are available. Bakeries and dairy shops specialise in lighter meals if preferred.

Things to know: Bars can either have table service and/or counter service, although customers will often find that the drinks bought are simply marked down on a beer mat to be paid for on leaving. The legal age for drinking alcohol in a bar or cafe is 18. Minors are allowed to go into a bar if accompanied by an adult but they will not be served alcohol. Opening hours depend on the proprietor but generally bars in major towns and resorts are open all day and close around midnight or later. Exceptions are Berlin and Hamburg where every pub can open for 24 hours.

National specialities:

Frankfurt and Hesse:
• *Rippchen mit sauerkraut* (spare ribs).
• *Frankfurter* sausages.

Westphalia and Northern Rhineland:
• Westphalia is famous for its smoked ham, sausages and bread such as *pumpernickel*.
• *Rheinischer sauerbraten* (beef marinaded in onions, sultanas, pimento, etc.).

Stuttgart and Baden:
• *Schlachtplatte* (sauerkraut, liver sausage and boiled pork).
• *Schwarzwälder kirschtorte* (Black Forest gateau).

Munich and Bavaria:
• *Leberkäs* (pork and beef loaf).
• *Weisswurst* (white sausage).

Hamburg and Northern Germany:
• *Hamburger aalsuppe* (eel/lobster/crayfish soup).
• *Rumtopf* (fruit marinated in rum).

Bremen:
• *Hannoversches blindhuhn* (hotpot with bacon, potatoes, vegetables and fruit).
• *Kohn und pinkel* (kale and sausages).

Berlin:
• *Eisbein mit sauerkraut* (leg of pork) and mashed potatoes.
• *Eierpfannkuchen* (pancakes).

March of Brandenburg:
• *Mohnprielen* and *mohnstriezel* (pastries with poppy seeds).
• *Schwarzsauer mit backpflaumen und klößen* (black pudding with prunes and dumplings).

Saxony:
• *Dresdner stollen* (German christmas cake).

- *Speckkuchen* (bacon flan).

Saxony-Anhalt:
- *Lehm und stroh* (sauerkraut with mushy peas).
- *Baumkuchen* (literally tree cake, the thin layers of pastry are like the rings of trees).

Thuringia:
- *Thüringer rostbratwürste* (grilled sausages).
- *Hefeplinsen* (pancakes with raisins).

Mecklenburg-West Pomerania:
- *Plum'n un klüt* (plums and dumplings).
- *Spickbost* (smoked goose breast).

Tipping: It is customary to tip taxi drivers, hairdressers, cloakroom attendants, bar and restaurant staff; a 10 per cent tip in standard.

National drinks:

Munich and Bavaria:
- *Weizenbier*.

Hannover:
- *Mumme* (bittersweet beer without hops).

Frankfurt and Hesse:
- *Appelwoi* (cider).

Stuttgart and Baden:
- *Cannstatter* (white wine).
- *Kirschwasser* (cherry schnapps).

Wurtzburg:
- *Wurtzburger* (dry white wine).

NIGHTLIFE: In all larger towns and cities in western Germany and also in the major eastern cities, visitors will have the choice between theatre, opera (*Deutsche Oper Berlin*, *Hamburgische Staatsoper* and the *National Theatre* in Munich are some of the most famous names), nightclubs, bars with live music and discos catering for all tastes. Berlin, in particular, is famous for its large selection of after-hours venues. Traditional folk music is found mostly in rural areas. There are *Bierkellers* in the south and wine is drunk in small wine cellars in the Rhineland Palatinate, Franconia and Baden region.

SHOPPING: Special purchases include precision optical equipment such as binoculars and cameras, porcelain, handmade crystal, silver, steelware, Solingen knives, leatherwear, sports equipment, toys from Nuremberg and Bavarian *Loden* cloth. Special purchases in eastern Germany include musical instruments, wooden carved toys from the Erzgebirge Mountains, and Meissen china (the workshops in Meissen are open to the public). **Shopping hours:** Most shops are open Mon-Fri 0900-1830, and 0900-1400 on Saturday. All shops, except a few bakeries, are closed on Sunday. New laws mean shops can now open until 2000 during the week and until 1600 on Saturday. Smaller shops may close 1300-1500 for lunch.

Business

- **GDP:** US$2.7billion.
- **Main imports:** Food, petroleum products, manufactured goods, electrical products, motor vehicles and clothing.
- **Main exports:** Chemicals, motor vehicles, iron and steel products, manufactured goods and electrical products.
- **Main trade partners:** France, The Netherlands, UK and USA.

Credit: ©GNTB/Brandenburg TMB

ECONOMY: From the ruins of the Third Reich, both halves of divided post-war Germany emerged over the next two decades as the economic powerhouses of their respective European blocs. The unified German economy is now the fifth-largest in the world. The bulk of its production is in the West (the pre-unification Federal Republic). The Western economy has large chemical and car manufacturing plants, mechanical, electrical and electronic engineering, and rapidly growing advanced technology and service sectors in computing, biotechnology, information processing and media. The East's (former Democratic Republic's) economy never dominated COMECON, the Soviet bloc Council for Mutual Economic Assistance, in the way that the West's did the EU, but it consistently recorded the highest growth and per capita income within the bloc.

Reunification illustrated starkly how far the East had fallen behind the West. After initial difficulties, and much pessimistic forecasting, the Eastern economy was absorbed fairly painlessly into the West albeit at considerable financial cost. Among the benefits was a head start for German companies entering the new markets of Eastern Europe. Nonetheless, Germany's most important trading partners are its fellow members of the EU. Trade with China is on a similar scale to that with several Eastern European nations. The huge expenditure incurred as a result of unification – estimated at US$100 billion – had a knock-on effect on the speed of the German pursuit of economic and political union in Europe as the Government needed to ensure that Germany met the economic criteria (budget deficit, total debt) for entry into European Monetary Union (EMU) and the introduction of the single currency. The high cost of unification and long-term structural problems in the economy (especially the stagnation of key industrial sectors) have put the German economy under pressure since the late 1990s. Entry into EMU has demanded further fiscal discipline. In 2004, annual growth was 1.6 per cent while unemployment remained close to 0.1 per cent.

BUSINESS ETIQUETTE: Businesspeople are expected to dress smartly. English is spoken by many local businesspeople, but it is an advantage to have a working knowledge of German, or an interpreter. Appointments should be made well in advance, particularly in the summer. Appointments may be suggested slightly earlier in the day than is often the custom in the UK. Once made, appointment times should be strictly adhered to. Some firms may close early Friday afternoon. Always use titles such as *Herr Doktor* or *Frau Doktor* when addressing business contacts. Punctuality is essential for business visits. **Office hours:** Mon-Fri 0900-1700 (many close earlier on Fridays).

COMMERCIAL INFORMATION

Deutscher Industrie und Handelstag (Association of German Chambers of Industry and Commerce)
Breite Strasse 29, 10178 Berlin, Germany
Tel: (30) 203 080.
Website: www.diht.de.
The organisation is affiliated with 83 Chambers of Industry and Commerce. There are also Chambers of Industry and Commerce in all major German towns and a regional Chamber of Commerce for each of the states.

German-British Chamber of Industry and Commerce
Mecklenburg House, 16 Buckingham Gate, London SW1E 6LB, UK
Tel: (020) 7976 4100.
Website: www.ahk-london.co.uk *or* www.germanbritishchamber.co.uk.
This organisation also has branch offices in most major Western European capitals.

German American Chamber of Commerce
24th Floor, 12 East 49th Street, New York, NY10017, USA
Tel: (212) 974 8830.
Website: www.gaccny.com
This organisation has other branches throughout the USA.

German Convention Bureau (Deutsches Kongressbüro)
Website: www.gcb.de
This organisation has branches in Frankfurt/M and USA.
Frankfurt/M:
Münchner Strasse 48, 60329 Frankfurt/M, Germany
Tel: (69) 242 9300.
New York:
122 East 42nd Street, 52nd Floor, New York, NY 10168-0072, USA
Tel: (212) 661 4582.
Founded in 1973, the Bureau is a non-profit-making organisation sponsored by Germany's major convention cities, hotels, travel agents and carriers, as well as the country's leading travel and tourist associations, including German National Tourist Board, Lufthansa and German Railways.

Credit: ©GNTB/Brandenburg TMB

Ghana

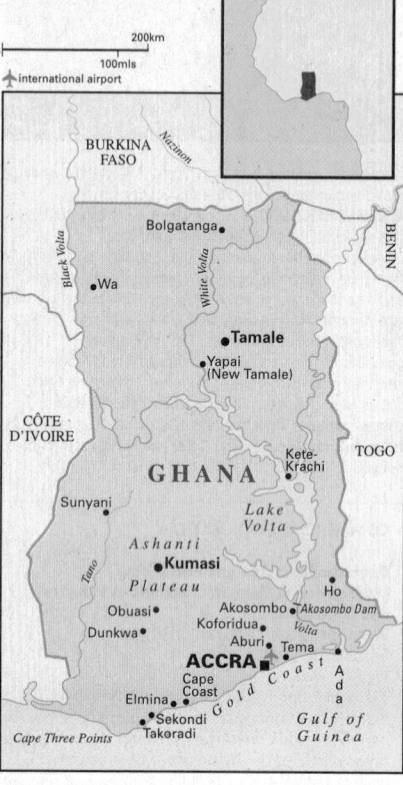

200km
100mls
▲ international airport

Location: West Africa.

Time: GMT.

Overview

Until independence from British colonial rule on 6 March 1957, Ghana was known as the Gold Coast. The Portuguese were the first Europeans to arrive in the late 15th century. During the next 300 years, the Gold Coast became a major trading centre, mainly in gold and slaves. From the beginning of the 19th century, an increasingly assertive Ashanti kingdom drove out many of the European colonists. The important exception was the British who took control of the whole of the Gold Coast in 1874. The colony's lands were supplemented in 1917 by parts of neighbouring Togoland. Together, these formed what in 1957 became the independent state of Ghana – the first British territory in Africa to be decolonised.

Credit: ©Ghana Ministry of Tourism

Under Dr Nkrumah, Ghana made rapid and remarkable progress in education, industrial and infrastructure development and in the provision of social services. At the same time, the country played a leading role in the struggle for the liberation of other African countries. However, Nkrumah's growing dictatorial tendencies at home disaffected many, especially in the armed forces, leading to a coup in 1966. A pattern of fledgling civilian governments aborted by the intervention of the armed forces has dogged Ghana for much of the time since then.

There remain many traces of the country's rich history. Ghana still boasts 42 European forts and castles including Elmina and Cape Coast Castles which are all recognised by UNESCO as World I Heritage Monuments as well as sites of wars between the British and the indigenous population. Colourful traditional festivals full of pomp and pageantry with Chiefs and Queen Mothers riding on lushly gilded palanquins can still be seen throughout the country while traditional open markets provide the sounds and sights of the African bazaar.

The country's natural heritage is also very rich. A narrow grassy plain stretches inland from the coast, widening in the east, while the south and west are covered by dense rainforests which are being developed into nature parks for the ecology-minded tourists such as the new National Park at Kakum. Although Ghana's national parks and game reserves are relatively small compared to other African countries, species of antelope, monkeys, lions and elephants can be seen here. Birds and butterflies are particularly numerous in Ghana's forests. Ghana's coastline is dotted with sandy palm-fringed beaches and lagoons where watersports can be practised.

General Information

AREA: 238,537 sq km (92,100 sq miles).

POPULATION: 21.8 million (UN, 2005).

POPULATION DENSITY: 91.39 per sq km.

CAPITAL: Accra. **Population:** 2.2 million (World Bank estimate).

GEOGRAPHY: Ghana is situated in West Africa and is a rectangular-shaped country bordered to the north by Burkina Faso, the east by Togo, the south by the Atlantic Ocean and the west by Côte d'Ivoire. A narrow grassy plain stretches inland from the coast, widening in the east, while the south and west are covered by dense rainforest. To the north are forested hills, beyond which is dry savannah and open woodland. In the far north is a plateau averaging 500m (1600ft) in height. In the east the Akuapim Togo hills run inland from the coast along the Togo border. The Black and White Volta rivers enter Ghana from Burkina Faso, merging into the largest manmade lake in the world, Lake Volta. Ghana's coastline is dotted with sandy palm-fringed beaches and lagoons.

GOVERNMENT: Republic. Gained independence from the UK in 1957. **Head of State:** President John Agyekum Kufour. **Recent history:** Mr Kufour won a closely-fought election in December 2000 against John Atta Mills, former deputy of long-time leader Jerry John Rawlings. Kufour's party, the New Patriotic Party, also replaced Rawlings' National Democratic Congress as the largest party in the Ghanaian Parliament. With most of the senior echelons of the government and security forces occupied by long-term Rawlings loyalists, Kufour was obliged to move cautiously at first. But, growing in confidence, he has since set up a 'reconciliation commission' to investigate human rights abuses during military rule. The Kufour government has also had to deal with inter-communal violence and land disputes in the north of the country. The greatest controversy, however, has concerned its decision to sell the country's largest and most important company, Ashanti Goldfields (see *Business*). Since coming to power, economic growth has been Kufour's priority. The country has seen drops in inflation and borrowing costs. Kufour was re-elected in 2004.

LANGUAGE: The official language is English. Local Ghanaian languages are widely spoken, including Akan, Ewe, Fante, Ga, Dagomba and Twi.

RELIGION: Christian (69 per cent), Muslim and traditional beliefs. All forms of religion have a strong influence on Ghanaian life.

ELECTRICITY: 220 volts AC, 50Hz; usually three-pin plugs. Single phase three-pin plugs are used in larger buildings. Older buildings have two-pin plugs. Light bulbs are of the bayonet type.

SOCIAL CONVENTIONS: Ghanaians should always be addressed by their formal titles unless they specifically request otherwise. Handshaking is the usual form of greeting. It is customary in much of West Africa not to use the left hand for touching food. **Photography:** Permission should be sought before photographing military installations, government buildings or airports.

Climate

A tropical climate, hot and humid in the north and in the forest land of Ashanti and southwest plains. There are two rainy seasons in Ghana: from March to July and from September to October.

Required clothing: Tropical lightweight clothing. Sunglasses are advisable.

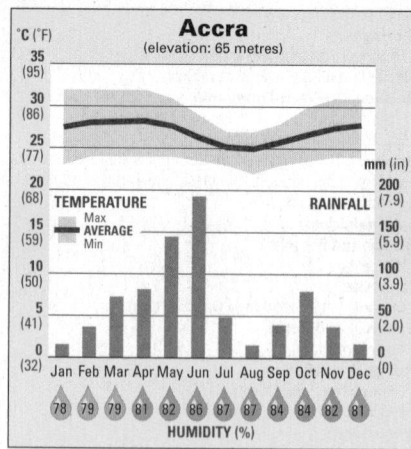

Accra (elevation: 65 metres)

Communications

Telephone: Country code: 233. IDD service is available in most parts of the country. Payphones can be found in main towns.

Mobile telephone: Coverage is good around main towns and patchy to non-existent elsewhere.

Internet: Internet facilities can be found throughout the country in most towns but connection is usually very slow (56K). Hotels have faster access.

Post: Airmail letters to Europe may take two weeks or more to arrive.

MEDIA: A free press operates in Ghana. There are no major restrictions on private press and broadcasters, who are regularly critical of government policy. Lively radio phone-in programmes are common and popular. Numerous private radio stations compete for limited advertising revenue in Accra and elsewhere. The state-run Ghana Broadcasting Corporation (CBC) runs national TV and radio networks.

Press: Daily and weekly newspapers are available in English and include *Daily Graphic*, *The Ghanaian Times* (both daily) and *The Mirror* (weekly).

TV: *Ghana TV* (GTV) is run by the GBC. *Metro TV* is part public, part private. Other channels include *TV3* (privately owned) and cable operator *Multichoice*.

Radio: GBC operates *Radio 1* (programmes in English and local languages), *Radio 2* and local Accra station *Unique FM*. Among the plethora of private stations are *Adom FM*, *Happy FM*, *Space FM* and *Vibe FM*. *BBC World Service* and *Radio France Internationale* are available on FM in Accra.

Passport/Visa

	Passport Required?	Visa Required?	Return Ticket Required?
Full British	Yes	Yes	Yes
Australian	Yes	Yes	Yes
Canadian	Yes	Yes	Yes
USA	Yes	Yes	Yes
Other EU	Yes	Yes	Yes
Japanese	Yes	Yes	Yes

Note: *Regulations and requirements may be subject to change at short notice, and you are advised to contact the appropriate diplomatic or consular authority before finalising travel arrangements. Any numbers in the chart refer to the footnotes below.*

PASSPORTS: Passport valid for six months required by all except nationals of ECOWAS countries who will be allowed entry with a valid travel certificate.

VISAS: Required by all except the following for stays of up to three months:

(a) nationals of ECOWAS countries;

(b) nationals of Egypt, Hong Kong (SAR), Kenya, Mauritius and Singapore;

(c) those in transit to a third country travelling within 24 hours, as long as they hold onward tickets with reserved seats and do not leave the airport.

Note: The following nationals may obtain visas upon arrival at the port of entry: Botswana, Lesotho, Malawi, Swaziland, Tanzania, Uganda and Zambia.

Types of visa and cost: *Tourist/Business:* £30 (single-entry); £40 (multiple-entry; six months); £60 (multiple-entry; one year); £70 (multiple-entry; two years); *Transit:* £10.

Validity: Valid for three months from the date of issue.

Credit: ©Ghana Ministry of Tourism

However, length of stay is at the discretion of airport officials and only one month is guaranteed. Visas may be extended when in Ghana. Visas for one year may be granted for specific purposes.
Application to: Consulate (or Consular section at Embassy or High Commission); postal applications are accepted; see *Passport/Visa Information* for details. A visa can be issued on arrival to nationals of countries without a Ghanaian Mission or Consulate, but only if prior notice is given to the Director of Immigration by the traveller or their sponsor prior to arrival; see *Passport/Visa Information*.
Application requirements: (a) Valid passport. (b) Completed entry permit application form (two copies, or four if making a postal application). (c) Two passport-size photos, or four if making a postal application. (d) For postal applications, registered or recorded self-addressed envelope. (e) Fee (payable by cash, postal order or bankers' draft made payable to the High Commission; cash is not valid for postal applications). (f) Evidence of onward/return ticket. (g) Evidence of sufficient funds. (h) If travelling at invitation of host in Ghana, a letter of invitation should be submitted. (i) Valid certificate of inoculation against Yellow Fever, if applicable. *Business*: (a)-(i) and, (j) Letter of guarantee from a company in support of the application (the letter should explain the nature of business the applicant will be conducting in Ghana).
Working days required: Four for personal, a minimum of 10 for postal applications.
Temporary residence: Application with sufficient notice to be made to High Commission or Embassy.
Note: Single parents or other adults travelling alone with children should note that some countries require documentary evidence of parental responsibility before allowing lone parents to enter the country or in some cases before permitting the children to leave the country. For exact requirements contact the Ghana High Commision or Embassy (see *Passport/Visa Information*).

PASSPORT/VISA INFORMATION

Ghana High Commission (Education, Visas and Trade) in the UK
104 Highgate Hill, London N6 5HE, UK
Tel: (020) 8342 7500 *or* 7580; (020) 8342 7580 *or* 7558 *or* 7501 (Visa section).
Website: www.ghana-com.co.uk
Consulate opening hours: Mon-Fri 0930-1300 (visa collection).

Embassy of the Republic of Ghana in the USA
3512 International Drive, NW, Washington, DC, USA
Tel: (202) 686 4520.
Website: www.ghanaembassy.org

Money

Currency: Cedi (GHC) = 100 pesewas. Notes are in denominations of GHC20,000, 10,000, 5000, 2000 and 1000. Coins are in denominations of 500, 200, 100 and 50 pesewas. The Cedi is pegged to the US$ at an adjustable rate.
Currency exchange: The exchange rate system has been liberalised and foreign currency is freely available through authorised dealers including banks and foreign exchange bureaux. Cash is exchanged at a more preferential rate than traveller's cheques.
Credit & debit cards: Credit cards (mainly American Express, Diners Club and Visa) are accepted by leading hotels, restaurants, banks, businesses and some shops. Check with your credit or debit card company for details of merchant acceptability and other services which may be available. Some banks may give cash advances against leading cards. However, those using credit cards should be aware that credit card fraud is common. In large urban areas such as Accra and Kumasi ATMs are commonplace.
Traveller's cheques: To avoid additional exchange rate charges, travellers are advised to take traveller's cheques in US Dollars or Pounds Sterling. Traveller's cheques can be exchanged in large hotels, banks and foreign exchange bureaux.
Currency restrictions: The import of local currency is limited to amounts which have previously been permitted to be taken out of the country and this must be noted in the passport/travel documents; it must also be declared. Unused local currency can be re-exchanged on proof of authorised exchange, and visitors are advised to retain all currency exchange receipts. The export of local currency is limited to GHC5000. The import of foreign currency is unlimited, subject to declaration (on exchange control form T5 which must be retained to record transactions). The export of foreign currency is limited to US$5000.
Banking hours: Mon-Fri 0830-1500.
Exchange rate indicators:
Rate at time of publishing
£1.00= GHC15,904.00
$1.00= GHC9135.00
Note: The Cedi is pegged to the US Dollar at an adjustable rate.

Duty Free

The following goods may be imported into Ghana by persons aged 16 and over without incurring customs duty:
400 cigarettes or 100 cigars or 454g of tobacco; 1.1l of spirits or 1.1l of wine; 284ml of perfume.
Note: Duty must be paid on gifts. Those wishing to export handicrafts and antiques not exempt, must obtain a certificate from the Museums and Monuments Board, these are available from the main craft centre or the National Museum.
Restricted items: Animals, firearms, ammunition and explosives.

Public Holidays

Below are listed Public Holidays for the January 2006-June 2007 period.
2006: Jan 1 New Year's Day. **Jan 10** Eid al-Adha (Feast of the Sacrifice). **Mar 6** Independence Day. **Apr 14** Good Friday. **Apr 17** Easter Monday. **May 1** Labour Day. **May 25** Africa Day. **Jun 4** Anniversary of the 1979 Coup. **Jul 1** Republic Day. **Oct 22-24** Eid al-Fitr (End of Ramadan). **Dec 1** National Farmers' Day. **Dec 25-26** Christmas. **Dec 31** Revolution Day; Eid al-Adha (Feast of the Sacrifice).
2005: Jan 1 New Year's Day. **Mar 6** Independence Day. **Apr 6** Good Friday. **Apr 9** Easter Monday. **May 1** Labour Day. **May 25** Africa Day. **Jun 4** Anniversary of the 1979 Coup.
Note: Muslim festivals are timed according to local sightings of various phases of the moon and the dates given above are approximations. During the lunar month of Ramadan that precedes Eid al-Fitr, Muslims fast during the day and feast at night and normal business patterns may be interrupted. Many restaurants are closed during the day and there may be restrictions on smoking and drinking. Some disruption may continue into Eid al-Fitr itself. Eid al-Fitr and Eid al-Adha may last anything from two to 10 days, depending on the region. For more information, see the *World of Islam* appendix.

Health

	Special Precautions?	Certificate Required?
Yellow Fever	Yes	1
Cholera	Yes	2
Typhoid & Polio	3	N/A
Malaria	4	N/A

Note: *Regulations and requirements may be subject to change at short notice, and you are advised to contact your doctor well in advance of your intended date of departure. Any numbers in the chart refer to the footnotes below.*

1: A yellow fever vaccination certificate is required by all nationals entering the country.
2: Following WHO guidelines issued in 1973, a cholera vaccination certificate is no longer a condition of entry to Ghana. However, cholera is a serious risk in this country and precautions are essential. During the rainy seasons (May to Jul and Sep to Oct) there are seasonal outbreaks of cholera. Recent outbreaks have occurred in parts of Accra and Kumasi. Up-to-date advice should be sought before deciding whether these precautions should include vaccination as medical opinion is divided over its effectiveness; see the *Health* appendix.
3: Immunisation against typhoid is usually advised. An outbreak of poliomyelitis occured in 2003.
4: Malaria risk, predominantly in the malignant *falciparum* form, exists all year throughout the country.
Food & drink: According to the Ghanaian High Commission in London, tap water in cities is safe to drink. Other water sources should be regarded as being potentially contaminated, and water used for drinking, brushing teeth or making ice should have first been boiled or otherwise sterilised. Milk is unpasteurised and should be boiled. Powdered or tinned milk is available and is advised, but make sure that it is reconstituted with pure water. Avoid dairy products which are likely to have been made from unboiled milk. Only eat well-cooked meat and fish, preferably served hot. Pork, salad and mayonnaise may carry increased risk. Vegetables should be cooked and fruit peeled.
Other risks: *Diarrhoeal diseases*, including *giardiasis*, and *typhoid fevers* are common. *Bilharzia* (*schistosomiasis*) is present. Avoid swimming and paddling in fresh water; swimming pools that are well chlorinated and maintained are safe. *Hepatitis A* and *E* are widespread. *Hepatitis B* is endemic. *Hepatitis C* occurs, as do *dengue fever* and *TB*. Epidemics of *meningitis* and *meningococcal disease* may occur throughout tropical Africa, particularly in the savannah areas and during the dry season. Immunisation against *diphtheria* is sometimes recommended.
Those visiting beaches should be aware that swimming can be dangerous due to riptides.
Rabies is present. For those at high risk, vaccination before arrival should be considered. If you are bitten, seek medical advice without delay. For more information, consult the *Health* appendix.
Health care: Health insurance is essential, preferably with cover for emergency evacuation. Medical facilities exist in all the regional capitals as well as in most towns and villages. Emergency medical facilities are extremely limited.

Travel - International

AIR:
The national airline is *Ghana International Airlines* (website: www.fly-ghana.com). Commercial operations began in October 2005, flying from London to Accra daily.
Approximate flight times: From *London* to Accra is six hours 30 minutes (direct) or eight hours 25 minutes (with stopover in Kano). From *New York* is nine hours 30 minutes (direct).
Main airports: *Accra (ACC)* (Kotoka) is 10km (6 miles) north of Accra (travel time – 20 minutes). *To/from the airport*: Taxis to the city are available. *Facilities*: Banks/bureaux de change, car hire, duty free shops, restaurants and tourist information.
Departure Tax: GHC22,000 for international departures and GHC500 for domestic departures. Rates are subject to change without warning.
SEA:
Main ports: *Takoradi* and *Tema*. Ships run between Tema and Nigeria, Côte d'Ivoire, Cameroon and South Africa.
ROAD:
A coast road links Lagos (Nigeria), Cotonou (Benin) and Lomé (Togo) to Accra. The best internal road from Abidjan (Côte d'Ivoire) runs inland through Kumasi. The main north-south route is also in good condition. Buses and taxis run between Burkina Faso, Côte d'Ivoire, Togo and Ghana. The road from Burkina Faso crosses the border at Navrongo. Long-distance taxis operate between Ghana and neighbouring countries. See *Travel – Internal* for information on documentation.

Travel - Internal

AIR:
There are domestic services between Accra, Kumasi and Tamale.
Departure tax: GHC500.
LAKE:
The Yapei Queen, a lake steamer, runs twice weekly across Lake Volta between Akosombo and Yeji. Ferries connect at Yeji for Buipe and Makongo, both from which it is possible to arrange onward transportation to Tamale. Booking is advised and can be organised from the Ministry of Tourism (see *Top Things To Do*).
RAIL:
The rail network is limited to a 1000km- (600 mile-) loop by the coast connecting the cities of Accra, Takoradi and Kumasi and several intervening towns. There is also a rail link between the two main ports of Tema and Takoradi. Trains run at least twice a day on all three legs of this single-track triangle. There are two classes of ticket. Passenger cars are not air conditioned. Children under three years of age travel free; half-fare is charged for children aged three to 11.

ROAD:

There are 38,940km (24,196 miles) of roads, generally in good condition, but roads outside of the towns are in poor condition. Traffic drives on the right. **Car hire:** Available but extremely expensive, with or without driver. **Coach:** State-run and private coach services connect all major towns. The most popular national coach line is the *Intercity STC*. *Vansef STC* and *Neoplans Buses* shuttle hourly between Kumasi and Accra. Other regional capitals and major towns can be reached by bus or by *tro tros* from Kumasr. **Documentation:** An International Driving Permit is required. A British driving licence is valid for 90 days.

URBAN:

Roads in the major towns have undergone massive renovation to improve traffic flow. Accra has extensive **bus** and **taxi** services operated by the private sector. There is an abundance of taxis in the towns. Prices are reasonable. Drivers do not generally expect tips. Other ways of getting around, for the more adventurous traveller, are *tro-tros* (minibuses) and *mammy wagons* (converted pick-up trucks).

Travel Advice

The Government of Ghana lifted the state of emergency in the Tamale municipality and Yendi District of the Northern Region of Ghana in July 2004, which had been in effect for two and a half years following an outbreak of inter-ethnic fighting at Yendi. However, travellers considering travelling to the Northern Region should remain alert to the potential for new outbreaks of fighting. It is recommended you keep in touch with daily developments through the local media. Violent crime can occur at any time. While most visits to Ghana are trouble-free, travellers are advised to exercise a high level of vigilance in public areas, and when travelling by road.

You should be aware of the global risk of indiscriminate terrorist attacks, which could be against civilian targets, including places frequented by foreigners.

This advice is based on information provided by the Foreign and Commonwealth Office in the UK. It is correct at time of publishing. As the situation can change rapidly, visitors are advised to contact the following organisations for the latest travel advice:

British Foreign and Commonwealth Office
Tel: (0845) 850 2829.
Website: www.fco.gov.uk

US Department of State
Website: http://travel.state.gov/travel

Accommodation

HOTELS:

There are a few international chain hotels in Ghana, all located in the capital. In addition to these there are international-standard hotels, hostels, park lodges and guest houses throughout the country, although they are mainly concentrated in the urban centres. Budget accommodation is available at university campuses in Accra, Cape Coast and Kumasi during the student holidays (Christmas, Easter and summer; June to September). **Grading:** Hotels, hostels and guest houses are star-graded and licensed by the Ministry of Tourism.

CAMPING:

Camping in national parks is possible, but only for the very adventurous, as it can be dangerous. In game reserves, visitors must be accompanied by an armed guide. Camping is also available on the beach in many of the fishing villages but permission must be granted first from the local authorities.

BEACH HUTS:

Ghana offers some basic beach hut accommodation, made from local materials, in popular beach resorts. For a list of such accommodation, contact the Ministry of Tourism (see *Top Things To Do*) or Ghanaweb (website: www.ghanaweb.com).

Top Things To See

- See a large collection of Ghanaian art in **Accra**'s **National Museum**. The **Kwame Nkrumah Mausoleum** on the High Street is a magnificent monument to the first President of Ghana. **Independence Square**, dominated by the **Independence Arch** and the **Memorial of the Unknown Soldier**, is the venue for many national celebrations.
- Funerals are an important occasion when Ashantis celebrate life and bid farewell to the dead. Just outside Accra at **Nungua** are the carpentry workshops of the world famous **Fantasy Coffins** of Paa Joe and Paa Willie. Among the Ga people it is fashionable to be laid to rest in a coffin that bears a relationship to what the deceased did in life. The coffins come in all shapes from vegetables to animals and birds. On the western coast, the historic towns of **Duakwa** and **Mensa Krom** are home to some of the region's best woodcarvers.
- The central region of Ghana borders the Gulf of Guinea and is home to ancient castles and forts that were often used during the slave trade as holding areas for human cargo. Go to the **Cape Coast Castle**, built in the 16th century and later reconstructed and enlarged, which served as the seat of British administration in the then Gold Coast until 1877 (when administration moved to Christiansborg Castle in Accra). Head further west to the **Castle of Elmina** ('the mine'). Elmina was the first Portuguese settlement in Ghana. This huge 15th-century fort, that largely remains intact, is the location of one of the first Catholic churches in sub-Saharan Africa. **Fort St Jago** was primarily used as a military base and stands on a hill commanding fabulous views of both Elmina and the Atlantic Ocean. Cultural shows are often performed at the castles and guided tours are available. All Ghana's castles and forts have been declared World Heritage Monuments by UNESCO.
- In **Kumasi,** the historic capital of the Ashanti civilisation, examine the ruins of the **Manhyia Palace** and the **Royal Mausoleum** burnt down by Lord Baden-Powell. The **Cultural Centre** is a complex comprising a museum, library and outdoor auditorium largely devoted to the Ashanti. There is also a **'Living Museum'**, a farm and reconstituted village, where craftspeople such as potters, goldsmiths and sculptors can be seen at work using traditional methods. Of particular interest are weavers making the vividly coloured *kente* cloth, the ceremonial dress of the region.
- In the north, the **Larabanga Mosque,** situated 8km (5 miles) north of Mole National Park, is well worth visiting. Built in the style of former Western Sudanese Empires, it houses a holy Koran and is believed by locals to be a 'God-built mosque'.
- Pay a visit to the **Witches' settlements,** located at Ngani in the Yendi district, Gamaga in the east Mamprusi district and Kpatinga in the Fushegu district. These are santuaries for people, mostly women, accused of witchcraft.

Top Things To Do

- In Accra, purchase crafts, *kente* and other traditional cloths at the **Centre for National Culture,** which is an arts centre and crafts market. Alternatively, go to the **Makola Market**, which is amongst the most famous markets of Accra, a large and busy open-air market located on Kojo Thompson Road. Traders from surrounding villages bring their wares every day. There is also the **Osu Night Market**, where hundreds of lanterns and candles illuminate the stalls.
- Watch a musical show, play or dance at Accra's **National Theatre** , which is a Chinese showpiece.
- Attend a **Ghanaian festival** and enjoy drumming, dancing and feasting. Every part of the country has its own annual festivals for the affirmation of tribal values, the remembrance of ancestors and past leaders, and the purification of the state in preparation for another year (for example, the *Kente Festival*, Bonwire, Ejisu Juaben district in January, which commemorates the origin of the *kente* cloth, or the *Kobine Festival* in September).
- Arrange a surface visit to the pleasant gold-mining city of **Obuasi** in the Ashanti region.
- Located 38km (24 miles) to the north of Accra, **Aburi** is in the **Akwapim Hills**. The **Sanatorium** (now a rest house), built there in the 19th century, is indicative of the refreshing climate. Walk through the **Botanical Gardens**, planted by British naturalists in colonial days, which have a comprehensive array of subtropical plants and trees.
- View wildlife in Ghana's national parks. The country's newest national park is the **Kakum Nature Reserve,** a protected conservation area 20km (12 miles) from Cape Coast which has monkeys, antelopes and water buffalo. Visitors can view wildlife at tree canopy level from the 333m (1093 feet) tree-top walkway and it is possible to stay in the **Kakum Conservation Area Tree House**, 12m (40 feet) above the forest floor; contact the Ministry of Tourism for details (see *Tourist Information*). **Safaris** are available in all of Ghana's game reserves, including the **Owabi Wildlife Sanctuary, the Bia National Park, the Bui National Park, the Mole Game Reserve** and **Kakum Nature Reserve** all of which are also good options for **hiking** and exploring the savannah and rainforest. Visitors can also explore the **Shai Hills Game Reserve,** on horseback.
- West of the northern region's main town, **Tamale,** lies **Mole National Park**, which is the largest and one of the best-equipped nature reserves in Ghana. Visitors can go either on foot or hire a 4-wheel drive vehicle, but must always be accompanied by a guide. Routes are planned to take in species of antelope, monkeys, buffalo, warthog and - more rarely - lions and elephants which have been introduced into the region. Visitors are allowed to camp and explore the area at will rather than being confined to a car on a set route. Tourist facilities exist at the entrance to the park; these include a motel which overlooks an elephant bath, with restaurant. There is also a small landing strip for light aircraft.
- Bird enthusiasts should go to the **Owabi Forest Reserve and Bird Sanctuary,** located to the west, close to Kumasi. Further to the northeast is the **Bomfobiri Wildlife Sanctuary**, containing the spectacular **Bomfibiri Falls**.
- Relax on the beaches of the Atlantic coast. **Labadi Pleasure beach** and **Kokrobite beach** are just 25km west of Accra. The new **Coco Beach Resort** located at Teshie-Nungua, east of Accra has excellent accommodation and a serene atmosphere. Although Ghana's coast offers miles of sandy beaches, strong currents and tides can make bathing quite dangerous.
- There are many popular beach resorts along the western coast. At **Dixcove,** there is a fish market and the 17th-century British **Fort Metal Cross**. Nearby **Busua** is a tropical beach with palms and spectacular Atlantic breakers. In this area, there are small rocky inlets that are safe for swimming.
- A popular resort at the mouth of the Volta, **Ada** is where Ghanaians and tourists go for **watersports**. Swimming is safe in the river mouth, but it is not advisable to swim upstream. Anglers have the opportunity to catch barracuda and Nile perch. Nearby are the salt marshes of the **Songow Lagoon**, famous for their birdlife.
- The Volta region is dominated by **Volta Lake**, the largest manmade lake on earth. The waterway stretches for two-thirds of the length of the country. Enjoy a round trip on the car ferry to **Kete-Krachi** which takes one day; alternatively, take the three-day trip to the northern capital of **New Tamale** at the head of the lake. There are facilities for **sailing, water-skiing** and **other watersports**. Ferry links across the lake now make the region more accessible (see *Travel – Internal*). **Lake Bosomtwi** is also great for diving, swimming and mountaineering. Canoe trips through the mangrove jungle of the **Ankobra River** lasting eight days are organised by *Continental Africa Tours*. Contact the Ministry of Tourism for further details (see *Tourist Information*).
- Another exhilarating experience is to be taken out over the surf in a local **fishing** boat. Sport fishing for barracuda is popular. The best spots for **surfing** are at **Fete, Dixcove** (both west of Accra) and **Kokrobite** (16km/10 miles from Accra).
- Akosombo, centre to the important **Akosombo irrigation dam**, is developing as a holiday resort, particularly for **watersports**. Visitors can take part in several traditions such as funerals and naming **ceremonies**. Funerals are normally held on Saturdays and members of the public are expected to participate. Mourners adorn themselves in black and red 'Adinkra' cloths. *Village Exchange Ghana* offers internships and **volunteer opportunities** in the area, and also runs excursions in this region (website: www.villageexchangeinternational.org).
- **Aduklu Mountain hike tours** are available through the Ministry of Tourism, and **Afadjato Mountain** in the Volta region attracts climbers of all ages. **Mount Afadjato** and **Togbo Falls** at Liati Wote are excellent for hiking.

TOURIST INFORMATION

Ministry of Tourism
PO Box 4386, Accra, Ghana
Tel: (21) 666 701.
Website: www.ghanatourism.gov.gh

Consulate General of Ghana (Visas and Tourist Information) in the USA
19 East 47th Street, New York, NY 10017, USA
Tel: (212) 832 1300.
Website: www.ghanaweb.com

Entertainment

FOOD & DRINK: International food is available in most large hotels and many restaurants serve a range of local traditional foods. In Accra there are also restaurants serving Middle Eastern, Chinese, French and other European cuisine.

National specialities:

- *Kenkey* (hot peppers and fried fish, eaten mostly in the Accra region).
- On the coast, prawns and other seafood are popular.
- *Akyeke* (cassava couscous served with avocado).
- *Fufu* (pounded cassava beans, yam, plantain or rice, usually accompanying traditional soups (palmnut, groundnut), *kontomere* and *okro* (stews)).
- *Fante fante* (a palm oil stew with small fish, popular in the central region).

A B C D E F G H I J K L M N O P Q R S T U V W X Y Z

- *Akrantee* (bushmeat).
- *Green green* snails.
- *Nkontomire* (yam leaf soup).

National drinks:
- *Pito* is a beer brewed in the Northern region made from millet.
- *Zom koom* (toasted millet flour in water).
- Palm wine.
- Coconut juice.

Tipping: Tipping is permitted, it is not usually included in the bill.

NIGHTLIFE: In Accra and other major centres, there are nightclubs with Western popular music and Afro beat. Concerts can be seen at the national theatre in Accra. The School of Performing Arts, University of Ghana, Legon often hosts drama, poetry and cultural dancing shows. Foreign and Ghanaian films can be seen at the Ghana Film Theatre and Executive Film House in Accra.

SHOPPING: Almost all commodities, including luxury items, can be found in the shops and markets. Artefacts from the Ashanti region and northern Ghana can be bought along with attractive handmade gold and silver jewellery. Modern and old African art is also available (although prices are high), in particular, Ashanti stools and brass weights formerly used to measure gold. In all the northern markets, earthenware pots, leatherwork, locally woven shirts and *Bolgatanga* baskets woven from multi-coloured raffia are sold. Ghana is home to the traditional Kente cloth. Shopping day trips are organised by the Ministry of Tourism (see *Top Things To Do*). **Shopping hours:** Mon-Tue, Thurs-Fri 0800-1200 and 1400-1730, Wed and Sat 0800-1300.

Business

- **GDP:** US$7.5 billion (2003).
- **Main exports:** Gold, cocoa, timber, tuna, bauxite, aluminium, manganese ore and diamonds.
- **Main imports:** Capital equipment, petroleum and foodstuffs.
- **Main trade partners:** Mexico, Nigeria, China, UK, USA, France and the Netherlands.

ECONOMY: Agriculture occupies most of the working population, producing both subsistence and cash crops. The most important of the latter is cocoa, of which Ghana is one of the world's major producers. Coffee and various fruit are the other main crops. Fishing has grown in importance since the acquisition of modern vessels. The country's main industry is mining, particularly for diamonds and gold (produced at the famous Ashanti gold field), and this is both a major employer and an important foreign currency earner. Although recent mineral exploration failed to discover anticipated oil and gas deposits, new bauxite and manganese deposits have been identified. Manufacturing is concentrated in food processing, textiles, vehicles and chemicals. The country's energy needs are met by hydroelectric projects; these produce a surplus which Ghana sells to its neighbours. As a primary commodity producer, Ghana has suffered from consistently low-world prices for its main products throughout much of the last 20 years. Since the late 1980s, Ghana has been something of a laboratory for a new regime for less developed countries devised by the International Monetary Fund and known as a Structural Adjustment programme. Customised for each state, the IMF, in conjunction with the World Bank, offers steady financial support to the national exchequer in exchange for government undertakings to implement agreed economic policies. The latter are based on liberalisation of the economy, the removal of trade barriers, privatisation of state-owned assets and firm budgetary control (leading invariably to cuts in social and welfare spending). The Government is now aiming to improve social services to its citizens. Despite the notable lack of tangible benefits to the population as a whole, the Ghana programme has been judged a qualified success and the country has since been regularly cited as role models for the developing world. Receipts from the Gold sector helped sustain GDP growth in 2004, however inflation remains a major internal problem. Ghana is a member of the Economic Community of West African States (ECOWAS).

BUSINESS ETIQUETTE: Appointments are customary and visitors should always be punctual for meetings. Best time for business visits is from September to April. **Office hours:** Mon-Fri 0800-1200 and 1400-1700, Sat 0830-1200.

COMMERCIAL INFORMATION

Ghana National Chamber of Commerce
PO Box 2325, Accra, Ghana
Tel: (21) 662 427.
Website: www.g77tin.org/gncchp.html

Gibraltar

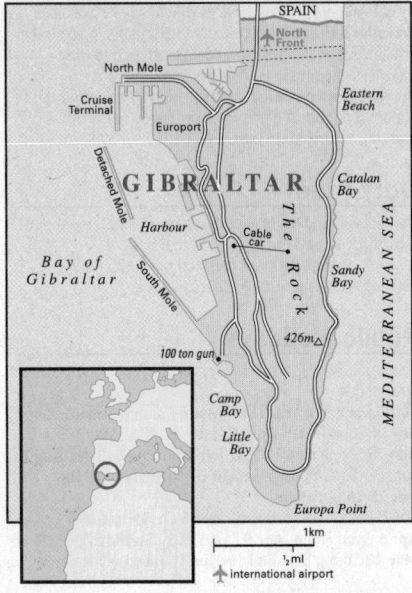

Location: Western entrance to the Mediterranean, southern tip of Europe.

Time: GMT + 1 (GMT + 2 from last Sunday in March to last Sunday in October).

Gibraltar is a British Crown Colony, and is represented abroad by British Embassies – see *United Kingdom* section.

Overview

Gibraltar derives from Gibel Tariq – Tariq's Mountain – which is named after Tariq Ibn Zeyad who led the eighth-century conquest of Spain by a combined force of Arabs and Berbers crossing from Africa. Gibraltar's unusual status was not acquired until almost 1000 years later, long after the Islamic invaders had been driven out by the Spanish, as a consequence of the 1713 Treaty of Utrecht which brought to an end the War of the Spanish Succession and gave the territory to Britain. The British interpretation of the treaty moreover holds that the territory was ceded to them indefinitely. The presence of a foreign-owned mini-state on the Spanish mainland has been an irritant to Anglo-Spanish relations ever since.

The current Spanish position was first outlined by Felipe González, Spain's Socialist Premier during the 1980s, when he suggested joint Anglo-Spanish sovereignty. Successive Spanish Governments, including the present Zapatero administration, have since refined the proposals, allowing for possible EU or NATO involvement. The British have no major objection, in principle, to the Spanish recovering full sovereignty over the territory – provided they are guaranteed continued access to its military base facilities. The problem is that the Gibraltarians are having none of it. In response to the latest round of talks between London and Madrid which began in 2001 and explored in detail possible joint sovereignty models, the Gibraltar Government led by Peter Caruana organised a referendum in November 2002 to assess the popular mood. As expected, it returned a huge majority in favour of the status quo.

Known as the the 'Rock', Gibraltar contains 143 caves, over 48km (30 miles) of road and miles of tunnels. From rock touring, to sailing, diving, fishing and bird watching, visitors will be pleasantly surprised with the diverse range of attractions on offer in Gibraltar. Located at the southernmost tip of the Iberian Peninsula, where Europe meets Africa, visitors are also assured of breathtaking scenery, wildlife and architecture, that captures the unique flavour of this Mediterranean city. As a VAT-free jurisdiction, Gibraltar's popularity with visitors is further enhanced by its value added shopping experience in famed Main Street.

General Information

AREA: 6.5 sq km (2.5 sq miles).

POPULATION: 28,231 (2001).

POPULATION DENSITY: 4343.23 per sq km.

CAPITAL: Gibraltar.

GEOGRAPHY: Gibraltar is a large promontory of jurassic limestone, situated in the western entrance to the Mediterranean. The rock is 5km (3 miles) long and the highest point is 426m (1400ft) above sea level. An internal self-governing British Crown Colony, Gibraltar has given its name to the Bay and the Straits, which it overlooks. Spain is to the north and west, and Morocco is 26km (16 miles) to the south.

GOVERNMENT: British Crown Colony since 1713. **Head of State:** HM Queen Elizabeth II, represented locally by Governor Sir Francis Richards since 2003. **Head of Government:** Chief Minister Peter Caruana QC since 1996, re-elected in 2003. **Recent history:** Gibraltar is a British Crown Colony, where the British monarch is represented by a Governor, currently Sir Francis Richards who assumed the post in 2003. The Chief Minister, currently Peter Caruana, presides over the Council of Ministers which administers domestic affairs. The 17-member House of Assembly, which represents the population's local interests, comprises 15 elected members. The ex-officio members are the Attorney General and the Financial and Development Secretary. Britain is responsible for defence and foreign affairs. Peter Caruana, the leader of the Gibraltar Social Democrats, won a third term in office in elections in November 2003. Mr Caruana strongly opposes the idea of shared sovereignty with Spain and oversaw a 2002 referendum that roundly rejected the concept.

LANGUAGE: English is the official language. Most Gibraltarians are bilingual in English and Spanish.

RELIGION: Roman Catholic majority, also Church of England, Church of Scotland, Jewish, Hindu and other minorities.

ELECTRICITY: 220/240 volts AC, 50Hz. UK-style three-pin plugs are in use.

SOCIAL CONVENTIONS: Gibraltar is a strongly traditional society with an attractive blend of British and Mediterranean customs.

Climate

Warm throughout the year, with hot summers and mild winters. Summer (May to September) can be very hot and humid.

Required clothing: Lightweights for summer and mediumweights for winter months.

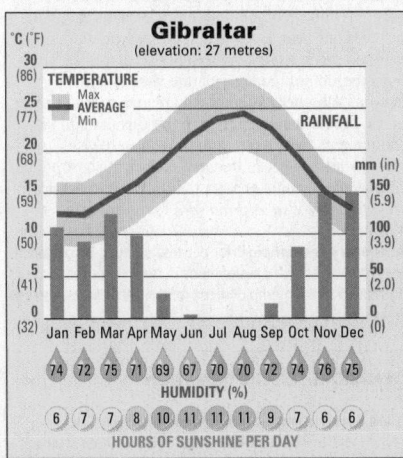

Communications

Telephone: IDD is available. Country code: 350.

Mobile telephone: Coverage spans the whole of Gibraltar and a large part of the sea around. Handsets can be hired from Gibtel, at 25 South Barracks Road.

Internet: There is at least one Internet cafe – *Cyber World*, *Ocean Heights Gallery*, Queensway.

Post: Airmail within Europe takes one to five days. Airmail flights are usually daily. Post office hours: Mon-Fri 0900-1630 (0900-1415 in summer), Sat 1000-1300.

MEDIA: Television and radio services are operated by the Gibraltar Broadcasting Corporation (GBC). The broadcaster's services are partly funded by TV licence fee revenues. Radio and TV stations based in Spain, and broadcasts for British forces in the territory, can be received.

Press: Newspapers are in English; some have Spanish sections. The *New People*, *Panorama* (website: www.panorama.gi) and *Vox* are published weekly. The *Gibraltar Chronicle* (established 1801) is the only daily (website: www.chronicle.gi).

TV: *GBC TV* is provided by the Gibraltar Broadcasting Corporation.
Radio: The local radio station is *Radio Gibraltar*. *BFBS Radio Gibraltar* is for British forces.

Passport/Visa

	Passport Required?	Visa Required?	Return Ticket Required?
Full British	Yes	No	No
Australian	Yes	No	No
Canadian	Yes	No	No
USA	Yes	No	No
Other EU	1	No	No
Japanese	Yes	No	No

Note: *Regulations and requirements may be subject to change at short notice, and you are advised to contact the appropriate diplomatic or consular authority before finalising travel arrangements. Any numbers in the chart refer to the footnotes below.*

PASSPORTS: Required by all except: **1.** EU nationals in possession of a valid national identity card.
VISAS: Required by all except the following:
(a) nationals of countries referred to in the chart above;
(b) nationals of Commonwealth countries (except nationals of Bangladesh, Cameroon, Fiji, Gambia, Guyana, India, Jamaica, Kenya, Mozambique, Nigeria, Pakistan, Sierra Leone, Sri Lanka, Tanzania, Uganda and Zambia who *do* need a visa to enter Gibraltar);
(c) nationals of Andorra, Argentina, Bolivia, Chile, Costa Rica, East Timor, El Salvador, Federated States of Micronesia, Guatemala, Honduras, Iceland, Israel, Korea (Rep), Liechtenstein, Marshall Islands, Mexico, Monaco, Nicaragua, Norway, Panama, Paraguay, San Marino, Switzerland, Uruguay and Venezuela.
Note: Transit visas are not required by passengers continuing their journey by the same or first connecting aircraft, provided holding valid onward or return documentation and not leaving the airport.
Types of visa and cost: *Tourist*, *Business* and *Transit*. All visas cost £28.
Application to: Any British visa-issuing post abroad or in the UK, or the visa section of the UK Passport Service in London (see *Passport/Visa Information* section).
Application requirements: (a) One application form. (b) Valid passport with two clear pages. (c) Proof of hotel reservation. (d) Fee. (e) Return ticket.
Working days required: Applications are referred to Gibraltar and are normally processed within 20 days.
Note: (a) Holders of multiple-entry UK visas valid for a period of one year or more, and persons with indefinite leave to remain who do not require separate UK entry clearance, do not require separate visas to enter Gibraltar. All other nationals who require a visa to enter the UK need a separate visa to enter Gibraltar. (b) Visa requirements for other nationals wishing to visit Gibraltar are subject to frequent change at short notice and travellers should contact the UK Passport Service (see *Passport/Visa Information*) for up-to-date information.
Temporary residence: Prior permission must be obtained from the Ministry of Employment in New Harbours, Gibraltar if seeking employment (nationals of EU countries are exempt).

PASSPORT/VISA INFORMATION

UK Foreign and Commonwealth Office
Overseas Territories Department, King Charles Street, London SW1A 2AH, UK
Tel: (020) 7008 1500 (general enquiries) *or* 8438 (visa enquiries) *or* 0117 (services for Britons overseas) *or* (0870) 606 0290 (travel advice).
Website: www.fco.gov.uk
Handles Gibraltar's foreign affairs. All other enquiries should be made to the Gibraltar Tourist Board.

The UK Passport Service
London Passport Office, Globe House, 89 Eccleston Square, London SW1V 1PN, UK
Tel: (0870) 521 0410 (24-hour national advice line) *or* (020) 7901 2150 (visa enquiries for British Overseas Territories).
Website: www.passport.gov.uk *or* www.ukpa.gov.uk
Opening hours: Mon-Fri 0730-1900; Sat 0900-1600.
Regional offices in: Belfast, Durham, Glasgow, Liverpool, Newport and Peterborough.
Personal callers for visas should go to the agency window in the collection room of the London office.

Money

Currency: Gibraltar Pound (GIP; symbol £) = 100 new pence. The Gibraltar government issues banknotes of Gib£50, 20, 10 and 5 for local use only. Coinage is the UK coinage with a different reverse design. The Gibraltar government also issues its own coins in denominations of Gib£5, 2 and 1, and 50, 20, 10, 5, 2 and 1 pence. All UK notes are accepted. For exchange rates, see *United Kingdom* section. Most establishments accept Euros and some accept US Dollars.
Currency exchange: Tourists from the UK are strongly advised to change their unspent Gibraltar pounds into UK currency at parity in Gibraltar before departure as UK banks charge for exchanging the Gibraltar Pound.
Credit & debit cards: All major cards accepted. Check with your credit or debit card company for details of merchant acceptability and other services which may be available.
Traveller's cheques: Widely accepted. To avoid additional exchange rate charges, travellers are advised to take traveller's cheques in Pounds Sterling.
Currency restrictions: There are no restrictions on the import or export of either local or foreign currency.
Banking hours: Mon-Thurs 0900-1530, Fri 0900-1630.

Duty Free

The following goods may be taken into Gibraltar without incurring customs duty:
A reasonable quantity of tobacco products, alcoholic beverages and perfume for personal use.

Public Holidays

Below are listed Public Holidays for the January 2006-June 2007 period.
2006: Jan 1 New Year's Day. **Mar 8** Commonwealth Day. **Apr 14** Good Friday. **Apr 17** Easter Monday. **May 1** May Day. **May 29** Spring Bank Holiday. **Jun 12** Queen's Birthday. **Aug 28** Summer Bank Holiday. **Sep 10** Gibraltar National Day. **Dec 25-26** Christmas.
2007: Jan 1 New Year's Day. **Mar 8** Commonwealth Day. **Apr 6** Good Friday. **Apr 9** Easter Monday. **May 7** May Day. **May 28** Spring Bank Holiday. **Jun 11** Queen's Birthday.

Health

	Special Precautions?	Certificate Required?
Yellow Fever	No	No
Cholera	No	No
Typhoid & Polio	No	N/A
Malaria	No	N/A

Note: *Regulations and requirements may be subject to change at short notice, and you are advised to contact your doctor well in advance of your intended date of departure. Any numbers in the chart refer to the footnotes below.*

Food & drink: Mains water is normally chlorinated. Bottled water is available and is advised for the first few weeks of the stay. Milk is pasteurised and dairy products are safe for consumption. Local meat, poultry, seafood, fruit and vegetables are generally considered safe to eat.
Other risks: Visitors to forested areas should consider vaccination for *tick-borne encephalitis*.
Health care: European Economic Area (EEA) and Switzerland:
If you or any of your dependants are suddenly taken ill or have an accident during a visit to an EEA country or Switzerland, free or reduced-cost necessary treatment is available – in most cases on production of a valid European Health Insurance Card (EHIC). Each country has different rules about state medical provision. In some, treatment is free. In many countries you will have to pay part or all of the cost, and then claim a full or partial refund. The EHIC gives access to state-provided medical treatment only and the scheme gives no entitlement to medical repatriation costs, nor does it cover ongoing illnesses of a non-urgent nature, so comprehensive travel insurance is advised. Note that the EHIC replaces the Form E111, which will no longer be valid after 31 December 2005.
Gibraltar is a British Crown Colony; therefore, UK citizens are entitled to free treatment in public wards at St Bernard's Hospital and at Casemates Health Centre on presentation of a UK passport during stays of up to 30 days in the colony. Other EEA nationals are similarly entitled on presentation of a European Health Insurance Card. Under the Group Medical Scheme, treatment is free and available at the Primary Care Centre, a small charge is payable for each medicine prescribed. The scheme applies to emergency cases but not dental treatment. Dental treatment must also be paid for but extractions are undertaken for a nominal charge at St Bernard's Hospital during normal weekday working hours. Visitors are only eligible for treatment if their illness or condition arises during a short visit to Gibraltar.
Note: Passengers travelling from Gibraltar to Spain or Morocco are advised to refer to the *Health* sections for those countries.

Travel - International

AIR:
British Airways (BA) (website: www.britishairways.com), operated by the independent carrier GB Airways Ltd and *Monarch Airlines (ZB)* (website: www.flymonarch.com) operate daily direct services from the UK.
Approximate flight times: From Gibraltar to *London* is two hours 30 minutes.
Main airports: *Gibraltar (GIB)* (North Front) is 1km (0.6 miles) north of the town centre. *To/from the* airport: A bus to the centre departs every 15 minutes from 0800-2030. Return is from the Market Place bus stop. Bus no. 3, which runs every 30 minutes, also goes to the airport. Taxis and courtesy coaches are available. The airport is only a 10 minute walk from the city centre. *Facilities*: Restaurants, banks/bureaux de change, tourist information, duty free shops and car hire.
SEA:
Main port:
The port of *Gibraltar* (website: www.gibraltarport.com). Many international cruise ships stop in Gibraltar. There is a regular ferry service to Tangier, Morocco as well as a catamaran service running from the new ferry terminal to Tangier (travel time – 75 minutes).
ROAD:
The only international land access is the frontier with Spain at La Linea.
RAIL:
No railway systems operate in Gibraltar; however, the neighbouring towns of San Roque and Algeciras, in Spain, are only a few minutes drive away and are both serviced by the national rail network of Spain, RENFE (website: www.renfe.es).

Travel - Internal

ROAD:
Traffic drives on the right. The speed limit is 50kph (31mph), except where otherwise indicated. Seatbelts are compulsory and it is compulsory to drive with dipped headlights at night. **Bus:** There are good local bus services operating at frequent intervals. **Taxi:** There are plenty of taxis and the driver is required by law to carry and produce on demand a copy of the taxi fares. **Car hire:** Both self-drive and chauffeur-driven cars are available. Touring outside Gibraltar can also be arranged. **Documentation:** Third Party insurance is compulsory. Valid national driving licences are accepted. A certificate of registration is required. Vehicles must have a national number plate.
Travel times: The following chart gives approximate travel times (in hours and minutes) from **Gibraltar** to major foreign cities.

	Air	Road	Rail	Sea
London	2.30	-	-	-
Tangier	0.20	-	-	2.00
Malaga	-	2.00	-	-
Madrid	-	12.00	10.00	-

Travel Advice

Most visits to Gibraltar are trouble-free but you should be aware of the global risk of indiscriminate international terrorist attacks, which could be against civilian targets, including places frequented by foreigners.

Credit: ©Gibraltar Tourist Board

312 World Travel Guide 2006-2007

- *Akrantee* (bushmeat).
- *Green green* snails.
- *Nkontomire* (yam leaf soup).

National drinks:
- *Pito* is a beer brewed in the Northern region made from millet.
- *Zom koom* (toasted millet flour in water).
- Palm wine.
- Coconut juice.

Tipping: Tipping is permitted, it is not usually included in the bill.

NIGHTLIFE: In Accra and other major centres, there are nightclubs with Western popular music and Afro beat. Concerts can be seen at the national theatre in Accra. The School of Performing Arts, University of Ghana, Legon often hosts drama, poetry and cultural dancing shows. Foreign and Ghanaian films can be seen at the Ghana Film Theatre and Executive Film House in Accra.

SHOPPING: Almost all commodities, including luxury items, can be found in the shops and markets. Artefacts from the Ashanti region and northern Ghana can be bought along with attractive handmade gold and silver jewellery. Modern and old African art is also available (although prices are high), in particular, Ashanti stools and brass weights formerly used to measure gold. In all the northern markets, earthenware pots, leatherwork, locally woven shirts and *Bolgatanga* baskets woven from multi-coloured raffia are sold. Ghana is home to the traditional Kente cloth. Shopping day trips are organised by the Ministry of Tourism (see *Top Things To Do*). **Shopping hours:** Mon-Tue, Thurs-Fri 0800-1200 and 1400-1730, Wed and Sat 0800-1300.

Business

- **GDP:** US$7.5 billion (2003).
- **Main exports:** Gold, cocoa, timber, tuna, bauxite, aluminium, manganese ore and diamonds.
- **Main imports:** Capital equipment, petroleum and foodstuffs.
- **Main trade partners:** Mexico, Nigeria, China, UK, USA, France and the Netherlands.

ECONOMY: Agriculture occupies most of the working population, producing both subsistence and cash crops. The most important of the latter is cocoa, of which Ghana is one of the world's major producers. Coffee and various fruit are the other main crops. Fishing has grown in importance since the acquisition of modern vessels. The country's main industry is mining, particularly for diamonds and gold (produced at the famous Ashanti gold field), and this is both a major employer and an important foreign currency earner. Although recent mineral exploration failed to discover anticipated oil and gas deposits, new bauxite and manganese deposits have been identified. Manufacturing is concentrated in food processing, textiles, vehicles and chemicals. The country's energy needs are met by hydroelectric projects; these produce a surplus which Ghana sells to its neighbours. As a primary commodity producer, Ghana has suffered from consistently low-world prices for its main products throughout much of the last 20 years. Since the late 1980s, Ghana has been something of a laboratory for a new regime for less developed countries devised by the International Monetary Fund and known as a Structural Adjustment programme. Customised for each state, the IMF, in conjunction with the World Bank, offers steady financial support to the national exchequer in exchange for government undertakings to implement agreed economic policies. The latter are based on liberalisation of the economy, the removal of trade barriers, privatisation of state-owned assets and firm budgetary control (leading invariably to cuts in social and welfare spending). The Government is now aiming to improve social services to its citizens. Despite the notable lack of tangible benefits to the population as a whole, the Ghana programme has always be punctual for meetings. Best time since been regularly cited as role models for the developing world. Receipts from the Gold sector helped sustain GDP growth in 2004, however inflation remains a major internal problem. Ghana is a member of the Economic Community of West African States (ECOWAS).

BUSINESS ETIQUETTE: Appointments are customary and visitors should always be punctual for meetings. Best time for business visits is from September to April. **Office hours:** Mon-Fri 0800-1200 and 1400-1700, Sat 0830-1200.

COMMERCIAL INFORMATION

Ghana National Chamber of Commerce
PO Box 2325, Accra, Ghana
Tel: (21) 662 427.
Website: www.g77tin.org/gncchp.html

Gibraltar

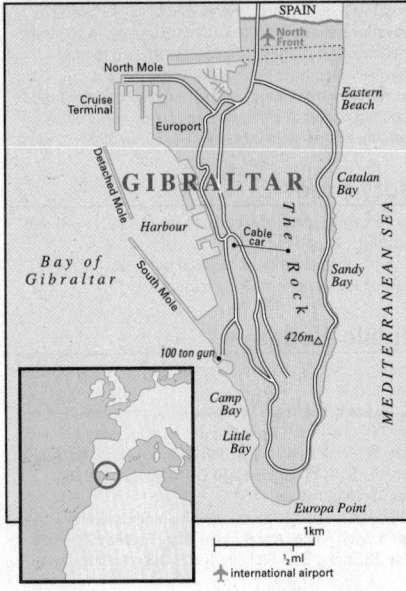

Location: Western entrance to the Mediterranean, southern tip of Europe.

Time: GMT + 1 (GMT + 2 from last Sunday in March to last Sunday in October).

Gibraltar is a British Crown Colony, and is represented abroad by British Embassies – see *United Kingdom* section.

Overview

Gibraltar derives from Gibel Tariq – Tariq's Mountain – which is named after Tariq Ibn Zeyad who led the eighth-century conquest of Spain by a combined force of Arabs and Berbers crossing from Africa. Gibraltar's unusual status was not acquired until almost 1000 years later, long after the Islamic invaders had been driven out by the Spanish, as a consequence of the 1713 Treaty of Utrecht which brought to an end the War of the Spanish Succession and gave the territory to Britain. The British interpretation of the treaty moreover holds that the territory was ceded to them indefinitely. The presence of a foreign-owned mini-state on the Spanish mainland has been an irritant to Anglo-Spanish relations ever since.

The current Spanish position was first outlined by Felipe González, Spain's Socialist Premier during the 1980s, when he suggested joint Anglo-Spanish sovereignty. Successive Spanish Governments, including the present Zapatero administration, have since refined the proposals, allowing for possible EU or NATO involvement. The British have no major objection, in principle, to the Spanish recovering full sovereignty over the territory – provided they are guaranteed continued access to its military base facilities. The problem is that the Gibraltarians are having none of it. In response to the latest round of talks between London and Madrid which began in 2001 and explored in detail possible joint sovereignty models, the Gibraltar Government led by Peter Caruana organised a referendum in November 2002 to assess the popular mood. As expected, it returned a huge majority in favour of the status quo.

Known as the the 'Rock', Gibraltar contains 143 caves, over 48km (30 miles) of road and miles of tunnels. From rock touring, to sailing, diving, fishing and bird watching, visitors will be pleasantly surprised with the diverse range of attractions on offer in Gibraltar. Located at the southernmost tip of the Iberian Peninsula, where Europe meets Africa, visitors are also assured of breathtaking scenery, wildlife and architecture, that captures the unique flavour of this Mediterranean city. As a VAT-free jurisdiction, Gibraltar's popularity with visitors is further enhanced by its value added shopping experience in famed Main Street.

General Information

AREA: 6.5 sq km (2.5 sq miles).
POPULATION: 28,231 (2001).
POPULATION DENSITY: 4343.23 per sq km.
CAPITAL: Gibraltar.
GEOGRAPHY: Gibraltar is a large promontory of jurassic limestone, situated in the western entrance to the Mediterranean. The rock is 5km (3 miles) long and the highest point is 426m (1400ft) above sea level. An internal self-governing British Crown Colony, Gibraltar has given its name to the Bay and the Straits, which it overlooks. Spain is to the north and west, and Morocco is 26km (16 miles) to the south.
GOVERNMENT: British Crown Colony since 1713. **Head of State:** HM Queen Elizabeth II, represented locally by Governor Sir Francis Richards since 2003. **Head of Government:** Chief Minister Peter Caruana QC since 1996, re-elected in 2003. **Recent history:** Gibraltar is a British Crown Colony, where the British monarch is represented by a Governor, currently Sir Francis Richards who assumed the post in 2003. The Chief Minister, currently Peter Caruana, presides over the Council of Ministers which administers domestic affairs. The 17-member House of Assembly, which represents the population's local interests, comprises 15 elected members. The ex-officio members are the Attorney General and the Financial and Development Secretary. Britain is responsible for defence and foreign affairs. Peter Caruana, the leader of the Gibraltar Social Democrats, won a third term in office in elections in November 2003. Mr Caruana strongly opposes the idea of shared sovereignty with Spain and oversaw a 2002 referendum that roundly rejected the concept.
LANGUAGE: English is the official language. Most Gibraltarians are bilingual in English and Spanish.
RELIGION: Roman Catholic majority, also Church of England, Church of Scotland, Jewish, Hindu and other minorities.
ELECTRICITY: 220/240 volts AC, 50Hz. UK-style three-pin plugs are in use.
SOCIAL CONVENTIONS: Gibraltar is a strongly traditional society with an attractive blend of British and Mediterranean customs.

Climate

Warm throughout the year, with hot summers and mild winters. Summer (May to September) can be very hot and humid.
Required clothing: Lightweights for summer and mediumweights for winter months.

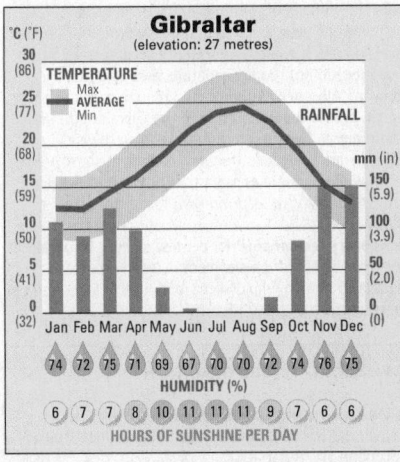

Communications

Telephone: IDD is available. Country code: 350.
Mobile telephone: Coverage spans the whole of Gibraltar and a large part of the sea around. Handsets can be hired from Gibtel, at 25 South Barracks Road.
Internet: There is at least one Internet cafe – *Cyber World*, Ocean Heights Gallery, Queensway.
Post: Airmail within Europe takes one to five days. Airmail flights are usually daily. Post office hours: Mon-Fri 0900-1630 (0900-1415 in summer), Sat 1000-1300.
MEDIA: Television and radio services are operated by the Gibraltar Broadcasting Corporation (GBC). The broadcaster's services are partly funded by TV licence fee revenues. Radio and TV stations based in Spain, and broadcasts for British forces in the territory, can be received.
Press: Newspapers are in English; some have Spanish sections. *The New People, Panorama* (website: www.panorama.gi) and *Vox* are published weekly. *The Gibraltar Chronicle* (established 1801) is the only daily (website: www.chronicle.gi).

A B C D E F G H I J K L M N O P Q R S T U V W X Y Z

TV: *GBC TV* is provided by the Gibraltar Broadcasting Corporation.
Radio: The local radio station is *Radio Gibraltar. BFBS Radio Gibraltar* is for British forces.

Passport/Visa

	Passport Required?	Visa Required?	Return Ticket Required?
Full British	Yes	No	No
Australian	Yes	No	No
Canadian	Yes	No	No
USA	Yes	No	No
Other EU	1	No	No
Japanese	Yes	No	No

Note: *Regulations and requirements may be subject to change at short notice, and you are advised to contact the appropriate diplomatic or consular authority before finalising travel arrangements. Any numbers in the chart refer to the footnotes below.*

PASSPORTS: Required by all except: **1.** EU nationals in possession of a valid national identity card.
VISAS: Required by all except the following:
(a) nationals of countries referred to in the chart above;
(b) nationals of Commonwealth countries (except nationals of Bangladesh, Cameroon, Fiji, Gambia, Guyana, India, Jamaica, Kenya, Mozambique, Nigeria, Pakistan, Sierra Leone, Sri Lanka, Tanzania, Uganda and Zambia who *do* need a visa to enter Gibraltar);
(c) nationals of Andorra, Argentina, Bolivia, Chile, Costa Rica, East Timor, El Salvador, Federated States of Micronesia, Guatemala, Honduras, Iceland, Israel, Korea (Rep), Liechtenstein, Marshall Islands, Mexico, Monaco, Nicaragua, Norway, Panama, Paraguay, San Marino, Switzerland, Uruguay and Venezuela.
Note: Transit visas are not required by passengers continuing their journey by the same or first connecting aircraft, provided holding valid onward or return documentation and not leaving the airport.
Types of visa and cost: *Tourist, Business* and *Transit*. All visas cost £28.
Application to: Any British visa-issuing post abroad or in the UK, or the visa section of the UK Passport Service in London (see *Passport/Visa Information* section).
Application requirements: (a) One application form. (b) Valid passport with two clear pages. (c) Proof of hotel reservation. (d) Fee. (e) Return ticket.
Working days required: Applications are referred to Gibraltar and are normally processed within 20 days.
Note: (a) Holders of multiple-entry UK visas valid for a period of one year or more, and persons with indefinite leave to remain who do not require separate UK entry clearance, do not require separate visas to enter Gibraltar. All other nationals who require a visa to enter the UK need a separate visa to enter Gibraltar. (b) Visa requirements for other nationals wishing to visit Gibraltar are subject to frequent change at short notice and travellers should contact the UK Passport Service (see *Passport/Visa Information*) for up-to-date information.
Temporary residence: Prior permission must be obtained from the Ministry of Employment in New Harbours, Gibraltar if seeking employment (nationals of EU countries are exempt).

PASSPORT/VISA INFORMATION

UK Foreign and Commonwealth Office
Overseas Territories Department, King Charles Street, London SW1A 2AH, UK
Tel: (020) 7008 1500 (general enquiries) *or* 8438 (visa enquiries) *or* 0117 (services for Britons overseas) *or* (0870) 606 0290 (travel advice).
Website: www.fco.gov.uk
Handles Gibraltar's foreign affairs. All other enquiries should be made to the Gibraltar Tourist Board.

The UK Passport Service
London Passport Office, Globe House,
89 Eccleston Square, London SW1V 1PN, UK
Tel: (0870) 521 0410 (24-hour national advice line) *or* (020) 7901 2150 (visa enquiries for British Overseas Territories).
Website: www.passport.gov.uk *or* www.ukpa.gov.uk
Opening hours: Mon-Fri 0730-1900; Sat 0900-1600.
Regional offices in: Belfast, Durham, Glasgow, Liverpool, Newport and Peterborough.
Personal callers for visas should go to the agency window in the collection room of the London office.

Money

Currency: Gibraltar Pound (GIP; symbol £) = 100 new pence. The Gibraltar government issues banknotes of Gib£50, 20, 10 and 5 for local use only. Coinage is the UK coinage with a different reverse design. The Gibraltar government also issues its own coins in denominations of Gib£5, 2 and 1, and 50, 20, 10, 5, 2 and 1 pence. All UK notes are accepted. For exchange rates, see *United Kingdom* section. Most establishments accept Euros and some accept US Dollars.
Currency exchange: Tourists from the UK are strongly advised to change their unspent Gibraltar pounds into UK currency at parity in Gibraltar before departure as UK banks charge for exchanging the Gibraltar Pound.
Credit & debit cards: All major cards accepted. Check with your credit or debit card company for details of merchant acceptability and other services which may be available.
Traveller's cheques: Widely accepted. To avoid additional exchange rate charges, travellers are advised to take traveller's cheques in Pounds Sterling.
Currency restrictions: There are no restrictions on the import or export of either local or foreign currency.
Banking hours: Mon-Thurs 0900-1530, Fri 0900-1630.

Duty Free

The following goods may be taken into Gibraltar without incurring customs duty:
A reasonable quantity of tobacco products, alcoholic beverages and perfume for personal use.

Public Holidays

Below are listed Public Holidays for the January 2006-June 2007 period.
2006: Jan 1 New Year's Day. **Mar 8** Commonwealth Day. **Apr 14** Good Friday. **Apr 17** Easter Monday. **May 1** May Day. **May 29** Spring Bank Holiday. **Jun 12** Queen's Birthday. **Aug 28** Summer Bank Holiday. **Sep 10** Gibraltar National Day. **Dec 25-26** Christmas.
2007: Jan 1 New Year's Day. **Mar 8** Commonwealth Day. **Apr 6** Good Friday. **Apr 9** Easter Monday. **May 7** May Day. **May 28** Spring Bank Holiday. **Jun 11** Queen's Birthday.

Health

	Special Precautions?	Certificate Required?
Yellow Fever	No	No
Cholera	No	No
Typhoid & Polio	No	N/A
Malaria	No	N/A

Note: *Regulations and requirements may be subject to change at short notice, and you are advised to contact your doctor well in advance of your intended date of departure. Any numbers in the chart refer to the footnotes below.*

Food & drink: Mains water is normally chlorinated. Bottled water is available and is advised for the first few weeks of the stay. Milk is pasteurised and dairy products are safe for consumption. Local meat, poultry, seafood, fruit and vegetables are generally considered safe to eat.
Other risks: Visitors to forested areas should consider vaccination for *tick-borne encephalitis*.
Health care: European Economic Area (EEA) and Switzerland:
If you or any of your dependants are suddenly taken ill or have an accident during a visit to an EEA country or Switzerland, free or reduced-cost necessary treatment is available – in most cases on production of a valid European Health Insurance Card (EHIC). Each country has different rules about state medical provision. In some, treatment is free. In many countries you will have to pay part or all of the cost, and then claim a full or partial refund. The EHIC gives access to state-provided medical treatment only and the scheme gives no entitlement to medical repatriation costs, nor does it cover ongoing illnesses of a non-urgent nature, so comprehensive travel insurance is advised. Note that the EHIC replaces the Form E111, which will no longer be valid after 31 December 2005.
Gibraltar is a British Crown Colony; therefore, UK citizens are entitled to free treatment in public wards at St Bernard's Hospital and at Casemates Health Centre on presentation of a UK passport during stays of up to 30 days in the colony. Other EEA nationals are similarly entitled on presentation of a European Health Insurance Card. Under the Group Medical Scheme, treatment is free and available at the Primary Care Centre, a small charge is payable for each medicine prescribed. The scheme applies to emergency cases but not dental treatment. Dental treatment must also be paid for but extractions are undertaken for a nominal charge at St Bernard's Hospital during normal weekday working hours. Visitors are only eligible for treatment if their illness or condition arises during a short visit to Gibraltar.
Note: Passengers travelling from Gibraltar to Spain or Morocco are advised to refer to the *Health* sections for those countries.

Travel - International

AIR:
British Airways (BA) (website: www.britishairways.com), operated by the independent carrier GB Airways Ltd and *Monarch Airlines (ZB)* (website: www.flymonarch.com) operate daily direct services from the UK.
Approximate flight times: From Gibraltar to *London* is two hours 30 minutes.
Main airports: *Gibraltar (GIB)* (North Front) is 1km (0.6 miles) north of the town centre. *To/from the* airport: A bus to the centre departs every 15 minutes from 0800-2030. Return is from the Market Place bus stop. Bus no. 3, which runs every 30 minutes, also goes to the airport. Taxis and courtesy coaches are available. The airport is only a 10 minute walk from the city centre. *Facilities*: Restaurants, banks/bureaux de change, tourist information, duty free shops and car hire.
SEA:
Main port:
The port of *Gibraltar* (website: www.gibraltarport.com). Many international cruise ships stop in Gibraltar. There is a regular ferry service to Tangier, Morocco as well as a catamaran service running from the new ferry terminal to Tangier (travel time – 75 minutes).
ROAD:
The only international land access is the frontier with Spain at La Linea.
RAIL:
No railway systems operate in Gibraltar; however, the neighbouring towns of San Roque and Algeciras, in Spain, are only a few minutes drive away and are both serviced by the national rail network of Spain, RENFE (website: www.renfe.es).

Travel - Internal

ROAD:
Traffic drives on the right. The speed limit is 50kph (31mph), except where otherwise indicated. Seatbelts are compulsory and it is compulsory to drive with dipped headlights at night. **Bus:** There are good local bus services operating at frequent intervals. **Taxi:** There are plenty of taxis and the driver is required by law to carry and produce on demand a copy of the taxi fares. **Car hire:** Both self-drive and chauffeur-driven cars are available. Touring outside Gibraltar can also be arranged. **Documentation:** Third Party insurance is compulsory. Valid national driving licences are accepted. A certificate of registration is required. Vehicles must have a national number plate.
Travel times: The following chart gives approximate travel times (in hours and minutes) from **Gibraltar** to major foreign cities.

	Air	Road	Rail	Sea
London	2.30	-	-	-
Tangier	0.20	-	-	2.00
Malaga	-	2.00	-	-
Madrid	-	12.00	10.00	-

Travel Advice

Most visits to Gibraltar are trouble-free but you should be aware of the global risk of indiscriminate international terrorist attacks, which could be against civilian targets, including places frequented by foreigners.

Credit: ©Gibraltar Tourist Board

This advice is based on information provided by the Foreign and Commonwealth Office in the UK. It is correct at time of publishing. As the situation can change rapidly, visitors are advised to contact the following organisations for the latest travel advice:

British Foreign and Commonwealth Office
Tel: (0845) 850 2829.
Website: www.fco.gov.uk

US Department of State
Website: http://travel.state.gov/travel

Accommodation

HOTELS: Hotels range from luxury establishments with lounges, terrace shops, bars and swimming pools, to more modest hotels. Summer rates are in force from 1 April to 31 October. Hotels are inspected annually and given a star or diamond rating. Hostel accommodation is also available in Gibraltar. More information may be obtained from the Gibraltar Tourist Board on request (see *Top Things To Do*).

CAMPING/CARAVANNING: Camping is not permitted; however, beach tents or beach umbrellas may be rented at Catalan Bay. These will include two deck chairs. There are no caravan sites in Gibraltar, and there are strict regulations concerning caravans and trailers. Camper vans are not allowed into the upper rock area or at most tourist sites and parking is prohibited. Caravans may only be imported as long as a licence is obtained from HM Customs Gibraltar (tel: 78879). Sleeping in vehicles is not permitted. There are several campsites with excellent facilities over the border in Spain.

Top Things To See

- Do not miss **St Michael's Cave**, situated 300m (1000ft) above sea level. This was known to the Romans for its spectacular stalactites and stalagmites. It is part of a complex series of interlinked caves including Leonora's Cave and Lower St Michael's Cave. Today, it is used for concerts and ballet. The Upper Galleries, hewn by hand from the Rock in 1782, house old cannons and tableaux evoking the Great Siege (1779-1783).
- In the **Apes' Den**, take pictures of the famous Barbary apes, which are in fact not apes but Macaque monkeys without tails. The Barbary apes are the only wild primates in Europe.
- In the **Gibraltar Museum**, see a replica of the Gibraltar Skull, the first Neanderthal skull found in Europe (1848) and caveman tools and ornaments excavated from the Rock's caves. There are also exhibits from the Phoenician, Greek, Roman, Moorish, Spanish and British periods of the Rock's history; a comprehensive collection of prints and lithographs; a collection of weapons from 1727 to 1800; a large-scale model of the Rock made in 1865; and displays of fauna and flora. The museum itself was built above a spectacular and complete 14th-century **Moorish Bath House**.
- Other sites of interest are: the 14th-century keep of the much rebuilt **Moorish Castle**; the **Shrine of Our Lady of Europe**, a mosque before conversion to a Christian chapel in 1462, housing the 15th-century image of the Patroness of Gibraltar; the **Lighthouse** and **Mosque**, beautifully designed blending classic Islamic designs with modern facilities; the ancient **Nun's Well**, a Moorish cistern; **Parson's Lodge Battery** (1865), above Rosia Bay; the **Rock Buster**, a 100-ton gun; the 18th-century **Garrison Library**; the only **Lime Kiln** in Gibraltar dating back to the late 19th-century or early 20th-century; **Trafalgar Cemetery**; **Alameda Gardens**; and **Europa Point**, the southernmost tip of Europe and just 26km (16 miles) from Africa. Situated at the site is the **Trinity Lighthouse** which can be seen for 30 miles.

Top Things To Do

- Take a **cable-car** trip to the top of the Rock; built in 1966, the Top Station is on the summit of the Rock, from where visitors can see Spain to the north and southwards to Africa. The cable-car journey stops at the Apes' Den.
- Attend the **Changing of the Guards,** which takes place several times daily at the **Convent**, residence of the Governor, and formerly a 16th-century Franciscan Monastic house.
- Go on a guided walking tour around the almost complete **city walls**, every Friday at 1030.
- The **Mediterranean Steps Walk** which starts at **O'Hara's Battery** (the highest point in Gibraltar), snakes down the eastern cliff and around the southern slopes to the western side of the Rock.
- You can also opt for the 90-minutes-long **Official Rock Tour** which takes visitors to the various attractions around the Rock.

- **Marina Quay** and **Queensway Quay** (two modern marina developments) provide visitors with the chance to indulge in some serious people watching while sampling delicious seafood in one of the many attractive harbour side restaurants.
- Relax on one of Gibraltar's beaches. On the east side are **Eastern Beach**, **Catalan Bay** and, towards the south, **Sandy Bay**, where the Rock is very sheer and parking difficult. **Little Bay**, a pebble beach, and **Camp Bay/Keys Promenade** are on the western coast. Pier fishing facilities are available. **Scuba-diving, parasailing** and **water-skiing** can also be practised in Gibraltar.
- The Bay of Gibraltar is home to a large population of **dolphins** and **whales**, and tourists can take boat trips to view these fascinating creatures.
- **Birdwatching** can be undertaken in spring and autumn, when thousands of migrating birds on their way between their breeding grounds in northern Europe and their wintering areas in Africa stop at the Rock. Owls, eagles, harriers, hoopoes, buzzards and black kytes join resident species such as Peregrine falcons, Blue Rock thrush and Barbary partridge. A large area of the upper rock has been declared a nature reserve, and since 1991 new species of plants have been planted to create **botanical gardens**.
- Go on a **day trip** to Ronda, Malaga and Jerez in Andalucia (the Spanish province) (see the *Spain* section for further information on Andalucia); day trips by air to Tangier and other Moroccan cities (see the *Morocco* section) can also be arranged.

TOURIST INFORMATION

Gibraltar Tourist Board in the UK
Arundel Great Court, 178/9 The Strand,
London WC2R 1EL, UK
Tel: (020) 7836 0777.
Website: www.gibraltar.gov.uk

Gibraltar Government Office in the USA
1156 15th Street, NW, Suite 1100,
Washington, DC 20005, USA
Tel: (202) 452 1108.
Website: www.gibraltar.gov.gi

Entertainment

FOOD & DRINK: There are bars and bistros throughout the town and at the two marinas, operating under Mediterranean licensing hours and selling British beer. Restaurants cover the whole price range. Gibraltar's geographical location and its history as a British colony means that it can offer a large selection of British dishes as well as French, Spanish, American, Moroccan, Italian, Chinese and Indian cuisine.
Spirits and tobacco are substantially cheaper than in the UK for identical brands. All types of alcoholic drinks are served, including draught beer.
National specialities:
- *Spinach tortilla.*
- *Calentita* and *panissa* (both are like quiche but are made from chick pea flour).
Tipping: Normally 10 to 15 per cent.
NIGHTLIFE: Gibraltar has a number of discos and nightspots open until the early hours of the morning. The casino complex includes a restaurant, nightclub, roof restaurant (summer) and gaming rooms, and is open from 0900 to the early hours.
SHOPPING: All goods are sold in Gibraltar at reduced-tax prices and free of VAT. The majority of shops are in or near Main Street. Silk, linen, cashmere, jewellery, glassware, porcelain, perfumes, carvings, radios, leatherwork, electronic and photographic equipment and watches can be bought.
Shopping hours: Mon-Fri 0930-1930, Sat 1000-1300. Some shops open Sunday.

Business

- **GDP:** £470 million.
- **Main imports:** Fuels, manufactured goods and foodstuffs.
- **Main exports:** Petroleum and manufactured goods.
- **Main trade partners:** France, Germany, Greece, Italy, Russia, Spain, Switzerland, Sweden, Turkmenistan, UK and USA.

ECONOMY: The main sources of income are tourism and offshore financial services, principally banking, insurance and shipping-related services. The industrial economy is based on ship repair, construction and small-

Credit: ©Gibraltar Tourist Board

scale manufacturing. The British armed forces – historically the main source of revenue through their base facilities on the Rock – sharply reduced their presence from 1994 onwards and now provide less than 10 per cent of GDP. Since then, concessionary tax and corporate facilities for foreign companies have boosted the financial services sector. Since 1998, a substantial gambling industry has developed, servicing punters from throughout Europe – again the consequence of a favourable tax regime – and it now makes a significant contribution to employment and government revenue. The economy as a whole is sensitive to the state of relations with Spain and, in particular, restrictions on border crossings since a significant number of Spaniards have jobs on the Rock.
BUSINESS ETIQUETTE: English is normally used for business, but Spanish may be used for business connected with Spain. **Office hours:** Mon-Fri 0900-1700; 0800-1400 in summer. **Government office hours:** Generally Mon-Fri 0845-1315 and 1415-1730, but hours vary according to department and season.
CONFERENCES/CONVENTIONS: Europort Gibraltar, an 82,000 sq metre (212,000 sq ft) financial complex, offers extensive office and conference facilities in addition to Gibraltar's recently refurbished hotels. St Michael's Cave (see *Top Things To See*) offers an absolutely unique and scenic location for meetings.

COMMERCIAL INFORMATION

Gibraltar Chamber of Commerce
PO Box 29, Watergate House, 2-6 Casements,
Gibraltar
Tel: 78376.
Website: www.gibraltarchamberofcommerce.com

Gibraltar Government Office in the UK
Tel: (020) 7836 0777.
Website: www.gibraltar.gov.uk

Gibraltar Tourist Board in the UK (Conference and Incentive Division)
Tel: (020) 7836 0777.
E-mail: info@gibraltar.gov.uk

Credit: ©Gibraltar Tourist Board

Greece

Location: Southeast Europe.

Time: GMT + 2 (GMT + 3 from last Sunday in March to last Sunday in October).

Overview

Greece was the birthplace of European civilisation. The period from 700BC saw the rise of the great city states of Athens, Corinth and Sparta, frequently engaged in long struggles for supremacy, and uniting only when faced with the common threat of invasion by the Persian Empire. The zenith was reached in the fifth century BC when Athens became the cultural and artistic centre of the Mediterranean, producing magnificent works of architecture, sculpture, drama and literature.

Greece today offers the traveller the comforts of modern Europe in close proximity to the stark beauty of the ancient world. There is no denying the historical and cultural heritage of Greece continues to resonate throughout the modern Western world - in its literature, art, philosophy and politics. All over Greece are reminders of the country's glory – from Athens' Parthenon and Delphi's Temple of Apollo, to the ruins on Crete of the Minóan city of Knossós, a civilisation reaching even further back into history.

Scattered throughout the calm blue waters of the Aegean are Greece's 1400 islands, the largest of which is Crete, each with its own special story. The serenity of islands like Skópelos contrasts with the hedonistic party islands such as Myknos and Páros where the worship of Dionysus the god of revelry continues to the beat of garage and house music. Athens's previous glory in sports was restored when the Olympic Games returned home in 2004.

Since Greece won her independence in 1830 from the Turkish Ottoman Empire, there have been problems in the relationship between the two neighbours. Achieving a political settlement in Cyprus remains a key concern of Greece's foreign policy. The situation seems to have improved following the accession of Greek-controlled Cyprus to the EU in 2004 which may act as a catalyst to a final resolution of that problem. Greece has now explicitly backed Turkey's own EU application.

General Information

AREA: 131,957 sq km (50,949 sq miles).

POPULATION: 11 million (UN estimate 2005).

POPULATION DENSITY: 83.4 per sq km.

CAPITAL: Athens. **Population:** 750,000 (2004 estimate); Greater Athens 3.3 million (2004 estimate).

GEOGRAPHY: Greece is situated in southeast Europe on the Mediterranean. The mainland consists of the following regions: Central Greece, Peloponnese, Thessaly (east/central), Epirus (west), Macedonia (north/northwest) and Thrace (northwest). Euboea, the second-largest of the Greek islands, lying to the east of the central region, is also considered to be part of the mainland region. The Peloponnese peninsula is separated from the northern mainland by the Isthmus of Corinth. The northern mainland is dissected by high mountains (such as the Pindus) that extend southwards towards a landscape of fertile plains, pine-forested uplands and craggy, scrub-covered foothills. The islands account for one-fifth of the land area of the country. The majority are thickly clustered in the Aegean between the Greek and Turkish coasts. The Ionian Islands are the exception; they are scattered along the west coast in the Ionian Sea. The Aegean archipelago includes the Dodecanese, lying off the Turkish coast, of which Rhodes is the best known; the Northeast Aegean group, including Chios, Ikaria, Lemnos, Lesvos and Samos; the Sporades, off the central mainland; and the Cyclades, comprising 39 islands (of which only 24 are inhabited). Crete, the largest island, is not included in any formal grouping. For fuller descriptions of these regions and islands, see *Top Things To See/Do*.

GOVERNMENT: Republic. **Head of State:** President Karolos Papoulias since May 2005. **Head of Government:** Prime Minister Costas Karamanlis since March 2004. **Recent history:** The Greek conservative New Democracy Party led by Costas Karamanlis took over the reins of government from the Pan Hellenic Socialist Movement (Pasok) in elections in early March 2004. Pasok had been in government for over 10 years. Since he came to power, Mr Karamanlis has faced industrial action due to high unemployment and rising inflation as well as Government plans for pension and labour reforms. He is also under pressure from the European authorities to cut the budget deficit which is in excess of the level permitted under the euro zone stability pact. Despite common membership of NATO, bilateral relations between Turkey and Greece have historically been among the worst between any two European countries. The principal causes are the continuing division of Cyprus (see *Cyprus* section) and control of territorial waters in the Aegean Sea.

LANGUAGE: Greek (Ellenika). Most people connected with tourism and those of a younger generation will speak some English, French, German or Italian.

RELIGION: 98 per cent Greek Orthodox, with Muslim, Roman Catholic and Jewish minorities.

ELECTRICITY: 220 volts AC, 50Hz. Round two-pin plugs are used.

SOCIAL CONVENTIONS: Visitors to Greece will find the Greeks to be well aware of a strong historical and cultural heritage. Traditions and customs differ throughout Greece, but overall a strong sense of unity prevails. The Greek Orthodox Church has a strong traditional influence on the Greek way of life, especially in more rural areas. The throwing back of the head is a negative gesture. Dress is generally casual. Smoking is prohibited on public transport and in public buildings.

Climate

Greece has a warm Mediterranean climate. In summer, dry hot days are often relieved by stiff breezes, especially in the north and coastal areas. Athens can be stiflingly hot, so

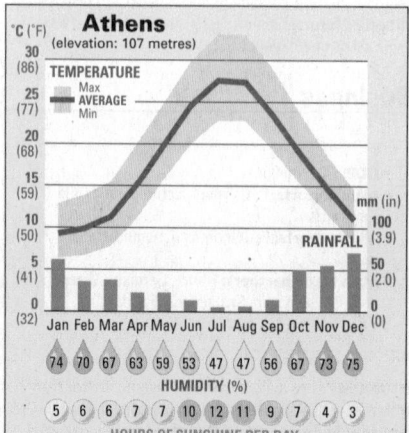

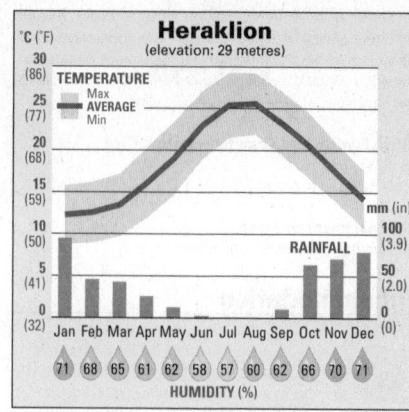

visitors should allow time to acclimatise. The evenings are cool. Winters are mild in the south but much colder in the north. November to March is the rainy season.

Required clothing: Lightweight clothes during summer months, including protection from the midday sun. Light sweaters are needed for evenings. Rainproofs are advised for autumn. Winter months can be quite cold, especially in the northern mainland, so normal winter wear will be required.

Communications

Telephone: Country code: 30, followed by (2100) for Athens, (2310) for Thessaloniki and (2810) for Heraklion (all area codes are prefixed with 2 and end with 0). IDD is available throughout the mainland and islands.

Mobile telephone: Roaming agreements exist with most international mobile phone companies. Coverage is excellent.

Internet: Internet cafes are available in the main cities, including Athens, Thessaloniki and the islands Crete, Kos, Mykonos and Rhodes.

Post: All letters, postcards, newspapers and periodicals will automatically be sent by airmail. Airmail to Europe takes five days; six to North America; seven to Australia. Post office hours: Mon-Fri 0730–1400, Sat 0800–1400.

MEDIA: A free press operates in Greece, although material deemed offensive to the president or religious beliefs can lead to the prosecution of editors and publishers. It was only in the late 1980s that the virtual monopoly of state-run broadcasters came to an end, with the introduction of new commercial TV services. Peak-time TV schedules are dominated by news, domestically-made variety programmes, comedies and game shows. The country hosts about 1700 private radio and TV stations, many of which are unlicensed, since broadcasting in Greece is relatively unregulated by European standards. An attempt made in 2001 to better regulate the FM dial in Athens resulted in a political row.

Press: There are numerous daily newspapers in Athens including *Eleftherotypia*, *Kathimerini* (in English) and *Ta Nea*. *Athens News* is published weekly in English.

TV: Publicly-owned *ERT* operates *ET1*, *NET* and *ET3*. Commercial channels include *Alpha TV*, *Antenna TV* and *Mega TV*.

Radio: Publicly-owned *ERA* operates *ERA1*, *ERA2* (entertainment), *ERA3* (culture) and *ERA4* (sport and music). Commercial stations include *Antenna FM*, *Skai 100.3* and *Sfera 102.2*. Municipal Athens station *Athena 98.4* was one of the first non-state radio stations.

Passport/Visa

	Passport Required?	Visa Required?	Return Ticket Required?
Full British	1	No	No
Australian	Yes	No	Yes
Canadian	Yes	No	Yes
USA	Yes	No	Yes
Other EU	1	No	No
Japanese	Yes	No	Yes

Note: *Regulations and requirements may be subject to change at short notice, and you are advised to contact the appropriate diplomatic or consular authority before finalising travel arrangements. Any numbers in the chart refer to the footnotes below.*

Note: Greece is a signatory to the 1995 **Schengen Agreement**. For further details about passport/visa regulations within the Schengen area, see the introductory section, *How to Use this Guide*.

Entry restrictions: (a) Greece refuses admission and transit to holders of travel documents issued by Macedonia (Former Yugoslav Republic), unless accompanied by a special visa form; holders of Somalian passports issued or extended after 31 January 1991; Norwegian Fremmedpass or Reisbevis; Ethiopian emergency passports; holders of travel documents issued by the area of Cyprus not controlled by the Government of Cyprus; holders of UN laissez-passers; and holders of Turkish travel documents with visas or stamps indicating previous or planned visits to Cyprus. (b) Some nationals may have to register with the Aliens Department of the nearest police station within 48 hours of arrival. It is advised to contact the nearest Embassy/Consulate to determine whether this is necessary prior to travel.

PASSPORTS: Passport valid for at least three months after period of intended stay required by all except:
(a) **1.** EU/EEA nationals (EU+ Iceland, Liechtenstein, Norway) and Swiss nationals holding a valid national ID card.
Note: EU and EEA nationals are only required to produce evidence of their EU/EEA nationality and identity in order to be admitted to any EU/EEA Member State. This evidence can take the form of a valid national passport *or* national identity card. Either is acceptable. Possession of a return ticket, any length of validity on their document, sufficient funds for the length of their proposed visit should *not* be imposed.
(b) nationals of Monaco, holding a valid national ID card.

VISAS: Required by all except the following:
(a) nationals of the countries referred to in the chart above for stays of up to 90 days;
(b) nationals of Andorra, Argentina, Bolivia, Brazil, Brunei, Bulgaria, Chile, Costa Rica, Croatia, El Salvador, Honduras, Hong Kong (SAR) (blue and red passport holders), Iceland, Israel, Korea (Rep), Liechtenstein, Macau (SAR), Malaysia, Mexico, Monaco, New Zealand, Nicaragua, Panama, Paraguay, Romania, San Marino, Singapore, Switzerland, Uruguay, Vatican City and Venezuela for stays of up to 90 days;
(c) those continuing their journey to a third country within 48 hours, provided holding tickets with reserved seats and other documents for their onward journey, except: nationals of Afghanistan, Angola, Bangladesh, Congo (Dem Rep), Eritrea, Ethiopia, Ghana, India, Iran, Iraq, Nigeria, Pakistan, Somalia, Sri Lanka, Sudan, Syrian Arab Republic and Turkey who always need a visa, even if transiting by the same aircraft.

Types of visa and cost: A uniform type of visa, the *Schengen* visa, is issued for tourist, business and private visits. There are three types of *Schengen* visa. *Short-stay, Transit* and *Airport Transit*: £25.50. Prices depend on exchange rates. Contact the Consulate/Consular section at Embassy for further details.
Note: Spouses and children of EU nationals (providing spouse's passport and the original marriage certificate, or child's original birth certificate (with certified translation into English, if applicable), are produced), and nationals of some other countries, receive their visas free of charge (enquire at Embassy for details). Minors under 18 years should be accompanied by both parents. Otherwise, a letter from both parents or legal guardians is needed, authorising the minor to travel and stay in Greece, appointing a person responsible for the minor during stay (authenticated by man of law *or* consular officer of applicant's nationality), parents' passports, birth certificate of the minor and proof of legal guardianship enclosed.
Validity: Depends on nationality.
Application to: Consulate (or Consular section at Embassy); see *Passport/Visa Information*. Travellers visiting just one Schengen country should apply to the Consulate of that country; travellers visiting more than one Schengen country should apply to the Consulate of the country chosen as the main destination *or* the country they will enter first (if they have no main destination).
Application requirements: (a) Passport or travel document valid for at least three months after expiry date of visa, with blank pages to affix visa, showing valid Residence Permit. (b) Completed application form (signed by legal guardian in case of minors). (c) Two recent passport-size photos. (d) Fee (payable in cash or postal order only). (e) Return or onward ticket (necessary for transit and airport transit visas, which also require a visa for onward country to be submitted, if applicable) or proof of booking/itinerary from travel agent. If visiting friends or relatives, a letter duly certified by a police station in Greece must be submitted. (f) Proof of sufficient funds to cover stay (bank statement or travellers cheques). (g) Proof of reason for visit; a letter of reference from employer detailing wages, and letter of invitation from Greek company for business trips; a letter from school for school trip. If self-employed, a letter from a solicitor or an accountant. (h) Original and photocopy of proof of travel insurance to cover intended stay in Greece. (i) Transport documentation, eg air ticket, confirmed ferry booking or, if driving, registration document, proof of legal ownership of vehicle and insurance certificate. (j) Those who claim visas in the UK and live more than 200 miles from London do not have to collect their visas in person at the London Embassy but may supply a Special Delivery self-addressed envelope instead.
Note: Applications can be made in person only.

Credit: ©Annie Launois

Appointments must be made through the automated booking service for those residing in the UK and in the vicinity of London (tel: (09065) 540 744). A limited number of visas are issued each day on a first-come, first-served basis. All documents must be submitted both in their original form and with photocopy.
Working days required: At least two weeks.
Note: Nationals from the following countries should allow several weeks from the date of appointment for the processing of their application: Afghanistan, Algeria, Armenia, Bahrain, Belarus, Burundi, China (PR), Colombia, Egypt, Georgia, Guinea, Indonesia, Iran, Iraq, Jordan, Kazakhstan, Korea (Dem Rep), Kuwait, Lebanon, Libya, Moldova, Oman, Palestinian Authority passport holders, Pakistan, The Philippines, Qatar, Russian Federation, Rwanda, Saudi Arabia, Somalia, Sudan, Surinam, Syrian Arab Republic, Taiwan (China), Ukraine, United Arab Emirates and Yemen.
Temporary residence: Apply to the Aliens Department in Athens.
Important note: Persons arriving in and departing from Greece on a charter flight risk having the return portion of their ticket invalidated by the authorities if, at any time during their stay, they leave Greece and remain overnight or longer in another country.

PASSPORT/VISA INFORMATION

Embassy of Greece (Hellas) in the UK
1A Holland Park, London W11 3TP, UK
Tel: (020) 7229 3850 *or* 7221 6467 (visa section) *or* 7313 5600 (visa helpline) *or* (09065) 540 744 (visa appointment booking line).
Website: www.greekembassy.org.uk
Opening hours: Mon-Fri 0930-1300.

Embassy of Greece (Hellas) in the USA
2221 Massachusetts Avenue, NW,
Washington, DC 20008, USA
Tel: (202) 939 1300 *or* 1318 (consular section).
Website: www.greekembassy.org

Money

Single European currency (Euro): The Euro is now the official currency of 12 EU member states (including Greece). The first Euro coins and notes were introduced in January 2002; the Greek Drachma was in circulation until February 28 2002, when it was completely replaced by the Euro. Euro (€) = 100 cents. Notes are in denominations of €500, 200, 100, 50, 20, 10 and 5. Coins are in denominations of €2, 1 and 50, 20, 10, 5, 2 and 1 cents.
Currency exchange: Foreign currency can be exchanged at all banks, savings banks and bureaux de change. Exchange rates can fluctuate from one bank to another. Many UK banks offer differing exchange rates depending on the denominations of currency being bought or sold. Check with banks for details and current rates.
Credit & debit cards: American Express, Diners Club, MasterCard, Visa and other major credit cards are widely accepted (although less so in petrol stations), as well as Eurocheque cards. Check with your credit or debit card company for details of merchant acceptability and other services which may be available.
Traveller's cheques: All major currencies are widely accepted and can be exchanged easily at banks. Generally, banks in Greece charge a commission of 2 per cent with a minimum of €0.15 and a maximum of €13.21 on the encashment of traveller's cheques. To avoid additional exchange rate charges, travellers are advised to take traveller's cheques in Euros, Pounds Sterling or US Dollars.
Currency restrictions: There are no restrictions on the import or export of either local or foreign currency.
Banking hours: Mon-Thurs 0800-1430, Fri 0800-1400. Banks on the larger islands tend to stay open in the afternoon and some during the evening to offer currency exchange facilities during the tourist season. The GNTO bureau in Athens can give full details.
Exchange rate indicators:
Rate at time of publishing

£1.00=	€1.46
$1.00=	€0.82

Duty Free

The following goods may be imported into Greece by visitors without incurring customs duty by:
(a) Passengers arriving from within the EU:
800 cigarettes or 200 cigars or 400 cigarillos or 1kg of tobacco; 10l of alcoholic beverage or 90l of wine and 110l of beer; there is no limit for perfume.
(b) Passengers arriving from non-EU countries within Europe:
200 cigarettes or 50 cigars or 100 cigarillos or 250g of tobacco; 1l of alcoholic beverage over 22 per cent or 2l of alcohol beverages of 22 per cent or less and 2l of wine and liqueurs; 50g of perfume and 250ml of eau de cologne; gifts up to a value of €175 per person and €90 if under 15.
(c) Passengers arriving from outside Europe:
400 cigarettes or 100 cigars or 200 cigarillos or 500g of tobacco; 1l of alcoholic beverage over 22 per cent or 2l of alcohol beverages of 22 per cent or less and 2l of wine and 2l of still table wine; 50g of perfume and 250ml of eau de cologne.
Note: The tobacco and alcohol allowances listed above are not available to passengers under the age of 18.
Restricted items: It is forbidden to bring in plants with soil. One windsurfboard per person may be imported/exported duty free, if registered in the passport on arrival. The export of antiquities is prohibited without the express permission of the Archaeological Service in Athens; those who ignore this will be prosecuted.
Abolition of duty free goods within the EU: On 30 June 1999, the sale of duty-free alcohol and tobacco at airports and at sea was abolished in all of the original 15 EU member states. Of the 10 new member states that joined the EU on 1 May 2004, these rules already apply to Cyprus and Malta. There are transitional rules in place for visitors returning to one of the original 15 EU countries from one of the other new EU countries. But for the original 15, plus Cyprus and Malta, there are now no limits imposed on importing tobacco and alcohol products from one EU country to another (with the exceptions of Denmark, Finland and Sweden, where limits *are* imposed). Travellers should note that they may be required to prove at customs that the goods purchased are for personal use *only*.

Public Holidays

Below are listed Public Holidays for the January 2006-June 2007 period.
2006: Jan 1 New Year's Day. **Jan 6** Epiphany. **Mar 6** Orthodox Shrove Monday. **Mar 25** Independence Day. **Apr 21** Orthodox Good Friday. **Apr 24** Orthodox Easter Monday. **May 1** Labour Day. **Jun 12** Day of the Holy Spirit. **Aug 15** Assumption. **Oct 28** Ochi Day. **Dec 25** Christmas Day. **Dec 26** Boxing Day.
2007: Jan 1 New Year's Day. **Jan 6** Epiphany. **Feb 19** Orthodox Shrove Monday. **Mar 25** Independence Day. **Apr 9** Orthodox Easter Monday. **May 1** Labour Day. **May 28** Day of the Holy Spirit.

A B C D E F G H I J K L M N O P Q R S T U V W X Y Z

Health

	Special Precautions?	Certificate Required?
Yellow Fever	No	1
Cholera	No	No
Typhoid & Polio	No	N/A
Malaria	No	N/A

Note: *Regulations and requirements may be subject to change at short notice, and you are advised to contact your doctor well in advance of your intended date of departure. Any numbers in the chart refer to the footnotes below.*

1: A yellow fever vaccination certificate is required from all travellers over one year of age coming from infected areas.
Food & drink: Water quality varies from area to area, depending on the source, but in most regions is excellent. Bottled water is available and is advised for the first few weeks of the stay. Milk is pasteurised and dairy products are safe for consumption. Local meat, poultry, seafood, fruit and vegetables are considered safe to eat.
Other risks: Visitors to forested areas should consider vaccination for *tick-borne encephalitis*.
Health care: European Economic Area (EEA) and Switzerland:
If you or any of your dependants are suddenly taken ill or have an accident during a visit to an EEA country or Switzerland, free or reduced-cost necessary treatment is available - in most cases on production of a valid European Health Insurance Card (EHIC). Each country has different rules about state medical provision. In some, treatment is free. In many countries you will have to pay part or all of the cost, and then claim a full or partial refund. The EHIC gives access to state-provided medical treatment only and the scheme gives no entitlement to medical repatriation costs, nor does it cover ongoing illnesses of a non-urgent nature, so comprehensive travel insurance is advised. Note that the EHIC replaces the Form E111, which will no longer be valid after 31 December 2005. Some restrictions apply, depending on your nationality.
Local chemists can diagnose and supply a wide selection of drugs. There are often long waits for treatment at public hospitals. Hospital facilities on outlying islands are sometimes sparse, although many ambulances without adequate facilities have air-ambulance backup. For emergencies, ring 166 (public ambulance).
Consultations and treatment with dentists and doctors are free. However, you will have to pay part of the cost of secondary examinations, such as X-rays. You will also have to pay for supplementary treatment, such as physiotherapy, and for dentures. For prescribed medicines, hand the prescription to any chemist in the IKA scheme - IKA offices will provide a list. You will have to pay a small standard charge, plus 25 per cent of the actual cost of the medicine, which is non-refundable. If you are charged in full, obtain a receipt and ask for the prescription back. Keep the self-adhesive labels from the medicines. If you obtain medicines or any kind of treatment privately, you must pay the full cost. Take the original receipts and your European Health Insurance Card (EHIC) to the IKA within one month, and they will reimburse you up to the limit allowed for similar treatment by the IKA. If you are staying in a remote part of the country or on a small island, there may be no IKA office or facilities within easy reach. In this case you must pay the full cost of private treatment and apply for a refund on return to the UK. If you are charged in full, you will need the original prescription and receipt. The self-adhesive labels from the medicines should be stuck on to the prescription - you will not get a refund without them. Hospital treatment: following an IKA doctor's diagnosis you must ask for a 'ticket', which is your approval of admittance to a hospital within the IKA scheme. If you go into the hospital before obtaining the 'ticket', show the administration your EHIC and ask them to contact the IKA. More information can be obtained from IKA (Social Insurance Institute), 8 Aghiou Constantinou Street, Athens.

Travel - International

AIR:

The national airline is *Olympic Airlines (OA)* (website: www.olympic-airways.com). *British Airways* makes scheduled flights to Greece. *Delta Airlines* operates flights four times a week from New York to Athens.
Note: Please note *Olympic Airlines* is facing bankruptcy as of November 2005. *Aegean Airlines* (website: www.aegeanair.com) is an alternative, but has limited destinations. Please check with the tourist board before travelling.
Approximate flight times: From Athens to *London* is five hours; from Rhodes is five hours 15 minutes; from Corfu is four hours; from Heraklion is eight hours; and from Skiathos is six hours (all flight times include a stopover). From Athens to *Los Angeles* is 15 hours; to *New York* is 13 hours; to *Singapore* is 13 hours; to *Sydney* is 24 hours 30 minutes.
Main airports: *Athens (ATH) (Elfetherios Veniselos)* (website: www.aia.gr) is located 33km (23 miles) northeast of the city. *To/from the airport*: There is a six-lane motorway linking the city and the airport, and regular airport buses running 24 hours from the centre and the port of Piraeus. *Facilities*: Duty free shops, car hire, banks, cash machines, bureaux de change, bar and restaurant facilities, post office, business centre and hotel.
Thessaloniki (SKG) (Macedonia) is 16km (10 miles) from the city. *To/from the airport*: Regular coach and taxi services are available. *Facilities*: Duty free shops, restaurants, bars, banks/bureaux de change, car hire and a post office.
Corfu (CFU) (Kerkira) is 3km (2 miles) from the city. *To/from the airport*: Regular coach, taxi and local bus services are available. *Facilities*: Duty free shop, cafe, bar and car hire.
Rhodes (RHO) (Paradisi) is 16km (10 miles) from the city. *To/from the airport*: Coach, taxi and local bus services are available. *Facilities*: Duty free shop, car hire, bank, bureau de change, cafe and bar.
There are also international airports at *Chania (CHQ), Heraklion* (Crete) *(HER), Kalamata (KLX), Karpathos (AOK), Kavala (KVA), Kefalonia (EFL), Kos (KGS), Lesbos* (Mytilini) (MJT), *Mykonos (JMK), Preveza* (Lefkos) (PVK), *Samos (SMI), Skiathos (JSI), Thessaloniki (SKG), Thira* (Santorini) *(JTR)* and *Zakynthos (ZTH)*, most of which serve predominantly summer traffic.
Departure tax: €12 (when arriving at Athens airport an additional €11.20 is payable).

SEA:

Main ports: *Corfu, Heraklion, Igoumenitsa, Patras, Piraeus* (Athens), *Rhodes, Thessaloniki* and *Volos*. Shipping and ferryboat lines link these ports with Italy, Croatia, Cyprus, Russia and Turkey. Greek ports are used by a number of cruise lines including *Celebrity Cruises, Costa Cruises, Crystal Cruises, Festival Cruises, Holland America Line, Princess Cruises, Silversea* and *Swan Hellenic*. The Greek/Hellenic National Tourism Organisation can give full details (see *Top Things To Do*). A car ferry links the Italian ports of Brindisi, Venice, Trieste and Ancona with Igoumenitsa and Piraeus. There are also services from Corfu to Ancora, Bari, Brindisi and Trieste; and from Rhodes to Marmaris (Turkey). During the summer months there are services from Ithaca and from Cephalonia to Brindisi.

RAIL:

The national railway company is *Hellenic Railways Organisation Ltd (OSE)* (website: www.osenet.gr). A good way to travel from the UK is to take the *Eurostar* through the channel tunnel, from London to either Brussels or Paris, both of which have onward connections to Greece. *Eurostar* is a service provided by the railways of Belgium, the UK and France, operating direct high-speed trains from London (*Waterloo International*) to Paris (*Gare du Nord*) and to Brussels (*Midi/Zuid*). It takes two hours 40 minutes from London to Paris (via Lille) and two hours 20 minutes to Brussels. For further information and reservations, contact *Eurostar* (tel: (0870) 600 0792 (travel agents) or (08705) 186 186 (public; within the UK) or +44 (1233) 617 575 (public; outside the UK); a £5 booking fee applies to all telephone bookings; website: www.eurostar.com); *or Rail Europe* (tel: (08705) 848 848; website: www.raileurope.co.uk).
Rail passes: The *Inter-Rail* pass offers unlimited second-class train travel in up to 29 European countries (includes Morocco and Turkey) split into eight zones (A-H). Three different tickets are available: a ticket covering one zone (two to six countries, 16 days' validity), a ticket covering two zones (six to 10 countries, 22 days' validity) and an *All Zone Pass* (29 countries, one month's validity). Ferry services between Italy and Greece are included. Passengers must be resident in Europe for at least six months before the pass is used. Travel is not allowed in the passenger's country of residence. Travellers under 26 years receive a reduction of about 30 per cent. Children's tickets are reduced by about 50 per cent. Supplements are required for some high-speed services, seat reservations and couchettes. Discounts are offered on *Eurostar* and some ferry routes. Available from *Inter Rail* (website: www.interrailnet.com).
The *Eurailpass* offers unlimited first-class train travel in 17 European countries. Tickets are valid for 15 days, 21 days, one month, two months or three months. The *Eurailpass Saver* ticket offers discounts for two or more people travelling together. The *Eurailpass Youth* ticket is available to those aged under 26 and offers unlimited second-class train travel. The *Eurailpass Flexi* allows either 10 or 15 travel days within a two-month period. The *Eurail Selectpass* is valid in three, four or five bordering countries and allows five, six, eight or 10 travel days (or 15 for five countries) in a two-month period. The *Eurail Regional Pass* allows four to 10 travel days in a two-month period in one of nine regions (usually two or more countries). Children receive a 50 per cent reduction. The passes cannot be sold to residents of Europe, Turkey, Morocco, Algeria, Tunisia or the Russian Federation. Available from *The Eurail Group* (website: www.eurail.com).

ROAD:

It is possible to ferry cars and caravans across to one of the major ports of entry or to enter overland. Points of overland entry are from the Macedonia (Former Yugoslav Republic of) via Evzoni, and Niki; from Bulgaria via Promahonas or Kastanies and Kipi. From Serbia and Montenegro, the route is via Italy (Trieste), Austria (Graz) and Belgrade. The journey from northern France to Athens is over 3200km (2000 miles). For car ferry information, see details under *Sea* above. **Bus:** There are routes from Athens via Thessaloniki to Dortmund, Istanbul, Paris and Sofia. Information and bookings are available from terminals in Athens at 6 Sina Street (tel: (210) 362 4402; 1 Karolou Street (tel: (210) 529 7777) and 17 Filellinon Street (tel: (210) 323 6747); also at Thessaloniki rail station.

Travel - Internal

AIR:

Olympic Airlines flies from *Athens* to Alexandroupolis, Astypalaia, Chania (Crete), Chios, Heraklion, Ikaria, Ioannina, Karpathos, Kassos, Kastellorizo, Kastoria, Kavala, Kefaloniá, Kerkira (Corfu), Kithira, Kos, Kozani, Lemnos, Leros, Milos, Mykonos, Mytilini, Paros, Preveza, Rhodes, Samos, Sitia, Skiathos, Skiros, Thessaloniki, Thira (Santorini) and Zakinthos. There are also routes from Rhodes. **Note:** Please note *Olympic Airlines* is facing bankruptcy at the time of publishing. Please check with the tourist board before travelling. *Aegean Airlines* flies from Athens to Alexandroupolis, Chios, Heraklion, Ioannina, Kavala, Kerkira (Corfu), Kos, Mykonos, Mytilini, Rhodes, Santorini (Thira) and Thessaloniki. Private charter flights are also available.
Departure tax: €12.

SEA:

It is both cheap and easy to travel around the islands. There are ferry services on many routes, with sailings most frequent during the summer. The main ports are Attica, Piraeus and Rafina, although there are regular sailings to the islands from the smaller ports of Alexandroupolis, Igoumenitsa, Kavala, Kyllini, Patras, Thessaloniki and Volos. Tickets can be bought from the shipping lines' offices located around the quaysides. In major ports the larger lines have offices in the city centre. There are two classes of ticket (First Class and Economy Class) which offer varying degrees of comfort; couchette cabins can be booked for the longer voyages or those wishing to avoid the sun. Most ships have restaurant facilities. During high season it is wise to buy tickets in advance, as inter-island travel is very popular.
Routes from Piraeus: There are regular sailings to the following ports: *Dodecanese*: Astypalaia, Chalki, Kalymnos, Karpathos, Kassos, Kastelorizo, Kos, Leros, Lipsi, Nissiros, Patmos, Rhodes, Symi and Tilos. *Cyclades*: Aegiali and Katapola (both on Amorgos), Anafi, Donoussa, Folegandros, Heraklia, Ios, Kimolos, Koufonissia, Kythnos, Milos, Mykonos, Naxos, Paros, Santorini, Schinoussa, Serifos, Sifnos, Sikinos, Siros and Tinos. *Peloponnese*: Gytheion, Hermioni, Kithira, Methana, Monemvassia and Porto Heli. *Saronic Gulf Islands*: Aegina, Hydra, Poros and Spetses. *Crete*: Agios Nikolaos, Chania, Heraklion, Kastelli, Rethymnon and Sitia. *Samos*: Karlovassi and Vathi. *North Eastern Aegean Islands*: Agios Kirykos (Ikaria), Chios, Evdilos (Ikaria), Limnos, Mitilini (Lesvos) and Psara. *Northern Greece*: Kavala and Thessaloniki. Check sailing times either with individual lines, the Greek/Hellenic National Tourist Organisation, or in Piraeus upon arrival in Greece. **Routes from Rafina:** There are local services from Rafina (near Athens) to: Agios Efstratios, Amorgos, Andros, Chalkida (summer only), Chios, Donoussa, Heraklia, Karistos (Evia), Kavala, Koufonissi, Kythnos, Limnos, Marmari (Evia), Milos, Mykonos, Naxos, Schinoussa, Serifos, Sifnos, Syros, Thessaloniki and Tinos. **Other routes:** These include Agia Marina–Nea Styra; Perama–Salamis; Rio–Antirio; Aedipsos–Arkitsa; Eretria–Oropos; Glifa–Agiokambos; Patras–Ithaca; Patras–Kefalonia (Sami); Patras–Corfu; Patras–Paxi; Preveza–Aktion; Igoumenitsa–Corfu; Corfu–Paxi; Kyllini–Zante; Kyllini–Cephalonia (Poros); Kavala–Thassos (Limenas); Kavala– Thassos (Prinos); Keramoti–Thassos; Alexandroupolis– Samothrace and Limnos. **Hydrofoil:** A hydrofoil service (also called the Flying Dolphins) offers a fast and efficient service from Piraeus, travelling to many of the nearby islands. Although this is somewhat more expensive than travelling by ferry, journey times are cut drastically. There are also fast hydrofoil services from Agios, Gytheion, Kimi (Evia), Konstandinos, Lavrion, Thessaloniki, Volos and Zea Marina (Piraeus). For further information on various ferry and hydrofoil timetables, visit www.gtp.gr. **Yachts:** Numerous types of yachts and sailing vessels can be chartered or hired with or without crews. 'Flotilla holidays' are popular, and the *Greek/Hellenic National Tourism Organisation* (see *Top Things To Do*) has a full list of companies running this type of holiday.

RAIL:

The two main railway stations in Athens are Larissa (with trains to northern Greece, Evia and Europe) and Peloponnissos (with trains to the Peloponnese). Train information and tickets are available from the *Hellenic Railways Organisation (OSE)* in Athens (tel: (210) 529 7633 *or* 1110 *or* 1440 (customer services and recorded train departure timetable, in Greece only) *or* in Thessaloniki (tel: (310) 599 143; website: www.ose.gr). Travelling north, there are regular daily trains from Athens to Thessaloniki, Livadia, Paleofarsala, Larissa, Plati, Edessa, Florina, Seres, Drama, Komotini and Alexandroupolis (connections from Thessaloniki and Larissa). Travelling south, there are regular daily trains from Athens to Kiato, Xylokastra, Diakofto, Patras, Olympia, Argos, Tripoli, Megalopolis and Kalamata.

Rail passes: The *EuroDomino* pass enables holders anything from three to eight days' extensive travel within a one-month period on the entire rail network of their chosen country. It is valid in 28 European countries and North Africa, including the ferry service from Brindisi (Italy) to Igoumenitsa (Greece). To purchase a *EuroDomino* pass you must have been resident in Europe for at least six months and a passport number is required at time of booking. It is not permitted to purchase a pass for travel within your own country of residence.

To qualify for the youth rates, you must be under 26 years on the first date of validity of the pass. Children aged four to 11 years inclusive pay half the adult fares rounded up to the nearest pound. Children under four years travel free.

Seat reservations, couchette and sleeper charges are not included in the cost of the pass and are payable at the normal rate. Passholder fares are payable on some services. Reservation/Supplement charges are payable on all trains within Spain.

Available from *Rail Europe* (website: www.raileurope.co.uk/railpasses/eurodomino.htm). *Vergina Flexipass* offers unlimited rail travel in Greece for three, five or 10 days within one or two months in either first or second class, depending on the choice of ticket. *Greek Flexipass* offers unlimited rail travel in Greece for three or five days within one month in first class. Students may be entitled to a 25 per cent reduction in the price of domestic rail fares. For further information on the above schemes, contact the *Hellenic Railways Organisation (OSE)*.

ROAD:

 Greece has a good road network on the whole, totalling approximately 117,000km (73,000 miles), mostly paved. Traffic drives on the right.

Examples of some distances from Athens: to Thessaloniki, 512km (319 miles); to Corinth, 80km (50 miles); to Igoumenitsa, 560km (350 miles); and to Delphi, 165km (103 miles). **Bus:** Buses link Athens and all main towns in Attica, northern Greece and the Peloponnese. Service on the islands depends on demand, and timetables should be checked carefully. Some islands do not allow any kind of motorised transport, in which case islanders use boats, or donkeys and carts to travel around. Fares are low. The Greek/Hellenic Railways Organisation Ltd (OSE) runs bus services to northern Greece from the Karolou Street terminus and to the Peloponnese from the Sina Street station. **Bus information:** There are two long-distance bus terminals in Athens: Terminal A and Terminal B. For information on long-distance buses, run by KTEL, from Athens to the provinces, enquire at Terminal A, 100 Kifissou Street, Athens (tel: (210) 512 4910) *or* Terminal B, 260 Liossion Street, Athens. Further information can be obtained from KTEL offices (website: www.ktel.org). **Taxi:** Rates are per km and are very reasonable, with extra charge for fares to/from stations, ports and airports. Taxis run on two tariffs: tariff 1 is the day rate from 0500 to 2400; tariff 2 is the night rate from 2400 to 0500. **Car hire:** Most car hire firms operate throughout Greece. For details, contact the Greek/Hellenic National Tourism Organisation (see *Top Things To Do*). Reservations can be made by writing or telephoning the car hire agency direct. **Regulations:** The minimum age for driving is 18. Children under 10 must sit in the back seat. Seat belts must be worn. There are fines for breaking traffic regulations. The maximum speed limit is 120kph (75mph) on motorways, 110kph (60mph) outside built-up areas and 50kph (30mph) in built-up areas. There are slightly different speed limits for motorbikes. It is illegal to carry spare petrol in the vehicle. EU nationals may import a foreign-registered car, caravan, motorcycle, boat or trailer for a maximum of six months. This period may be extended to 15 months for a fee and further paperwork. **Documentation:** A national driving licence is acceptable for EU nationals. EU nationals taking their own cars to Greece are advised to obtain a Green Card, to top up the insurance cover to that provided by the car owner's domestic policy. It is no longer a legal requirement for visits of less than three months, but without it insurance cover is limited to the minimum legal cover in Greece. The car registration documents have to be carried at all times. Nationals of non-EU countries may need an International Driving Permit and should contact *ELPA* (Automobile and Touring Club of Greece). **Road assistance:** A breakdown service is available on main roads, conditions of which have vastly improved. For details, contact ELPA, Athens Tower, Messogion 2-4, 115 27 Athens (tel: (210) 779 1615; website: www.elpa.gr). Emergency breakdown services can be contacted toll-free by dialing 104. There are good repair shops in big towns and petrol is easily obtainable.

URBAN:

 Buses: There are several services around Athens and Attica. The terminal at Mauromateon Street, Areos Park, Athens has regular services to *Amfiaraio, Marathonas, Nea Makri, Porto Rafti, Ramnous* and *Sounio*. Trolley buses (ILPAP) and regular buses (ETHEL) have frequent links to tourist attractions and places of interest. Tickets for buses and trolley buses can be purchased from the Athens Urban Transport Organisation (*OASA*) at various booths and kiosks situated around the city. For further information contact OASA at 15 Metsovou Street, 106 82 Athens (tel: (210) 883 6076; website: www.oasa.gr). **Metro:** Athens has a reliable underground system (ISAP) that consists of three major lines. The old line runs north–south between Athens (suburb of Kifissia) and Piraeus daily 0500-0015. There are two other lines: Line 2 runs between Aghios Antonios and Aghios Dimitrios and line 3 runs between Monastiraki and the airport. Tickets can be purchased at every Metro and ISAP station. Information on timetables and schedules can be found from Athens Metro (website: www.ametro.gr) *or* OASA (see address details above). **Tram:** The tram system in Athens cuts through the city from Syntagma Square right through to the coast and runs a pleasant route from Peace and Friendship Stadium all the way to the most southern point of Glyfada. Tickets can be booked at all stations and trams connect with the Metro at Neos Kosmos and Neo Faliro (website: www.tramsa.gr). **Travel times:** The following chart gives approximate travel times (in hours and minutes) from **Athens** to other major cities/islands in Greece.

	Air	Road	Sea
Corfu	0.50	11.00*	-
Crete	0.50	-	6-12.00
Rhodes	0.55	-	14.00
Thessaloniki	0.50	8.00	14.00

Note: *The travel time by road to Corfu includes a sea crossing from Patras.

Travel Advice

Most visits to Greece are trouble-free but you should be aware of the global risk of indiscriminate international terrorist attacks, which could be against civilian targets, including places frequented by foreigners.

This advice is based on information provided by the Foreign and Commonwealth Office in the UK. It is correct at time of publishing. As the situation can change rapidly, visitors are advised to contact the following organisations for the latest travel advice:

British Foreign and Commonwealth Office
Tel: (0845) 850 2829.
Website: www.fco.gov.uk

US Department of State
Website: http://travel.state.gov/travel

Accommodation

HOTELS:

 The range of hotels can vary greatly both among the islands and on the mainland, from high class on larger islands and the mainland to small seasonal chalets. Booking for the high season is essential. Xenia hotels are owned and often run by the Greek/Hellenic National Tourism Organisation. Small family hotels are a friendly alternative to the hotel chains. Hotel reservations can be made by writing directly to the hotels, through a travel agent, or by contacting the Hellenic Chamber of Hotels (at least one month beforehand). **Grading:** Hotels are all officially classified as **Luxury** or rated on a scale from **1** to **5** (star ratings). The category denotes what facilities must be offered and the price range that the hotelier is allowed to charge.

SELF-CATERING:

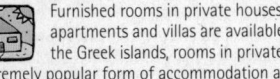 Furnished rooms in private houses, service flats, apartments and villas are available. On most of the Greek islands, rooms in private homes are an extremely popular form of accommodation and can usually be arranged on the spot. All types of accommodation can be arranged through tour operators in this country. The Greek/Hellenic National Tourism Organisation can provide further information on request.

TRADITIONAL SETTLEMENTS:

 Known also as *paradosiakoi oikismoi* in Greek, these traditional hostels can be found throughout the country, notably in Areopolis (Mani), Gythion (Peloponnese), Ia (Santorini), Koriskades (Central Greece), Makrinitsa (Pelion), Mesta (Chios), Milies (Pelion), Monemvasia (Peloponnese), Papingo (Epirus), Psara Island, Vathia (Mani), and Vizitsa (Pelion). This type of accommodation normally offers single, double or triple bedrooms with shower, or a four-bed house.

CAMPING/CARAVANNING:

 There is a wide network of official campsites (website: www.panhellenic-camping-union.gr). For details, contact the Greek/Hellenic National

Tourism Organisation (see *Top Things To Do*). **Note:** It is not permitted to camp anywhere except registered sites.

YOUTH HOSTELS:

 Greece has only six youth hostels recognised by the International Youth Hostel Federation: four in Athens, one in Corfu and one in Santorini. The original Athens hostel is on 16 Victor Hugo Street, 104 38 Athens (tel (210) 523 2540; website: www.interland.gr/athenshostel). A number of youth hostels belong to the Greek Youth Hostels Association. Other youth hostels exist in Crete, the Cyclades and the Peloponnese. For further details, contact the Greek Youth Hostel Association.

ACCOMMODATION INFORMATION

Greek Youth Hostel Association
75 Damareos Street, Athens, Greece
Tel: (210) 751 9530.
E-Mail: y-hostels@otenet.gr *or* skokin@hol.gr

Hellenic Chamber of Hotels
24 Stadiou Street, 105 64 Athens, Greece
Tel: (210) 331 0022.
Website: www.grhotels.gr

Top Things To See

- In **Athens**, the capital and the country's largest city, it is impossible to miss the flat-topped hill of the **Acropolis**, site of the 2400-year-old **Parthenon**, one of the most famous classical monuments in the world. The ruins of the civic, political and commercial centre of the **Ancient Agora** can be visited, as can the reconstructed **Hellenistic Stoa of Attalos**, which houses the **Agora Museum**. Most artefacts are displayed in the **National Archaeological Museum** on Patission Street.
- Then head for the Athens **Parliament Building** on Syntagma Square. Built in 1840 and originally a royal palace, this enormous building was badly damaged by fire in the early 20th century and was rebuilt for the National Assembly. One of the main highlights at the Parliament Building in Athens is the hourly **changing of the guard** at the front of the building.
- Visit the **Panathenaic Stadium** in Athens, which hosted the first modern day Olympic games of 1896. The current stadium was constructed on the site of the original stadium, which was built almost 2,300 years ago.
- Drive or take a train to **Olympia**, the original site of the Olympic Games in the Peloponnese, which began in 776 BC, and the site where the Olympic Flame is still lit today. The site is a mass of marble inscriptions, restored temples and civic buildings, including the **Temple of Zeus**, which once housed the colossal gold and ivory statue of Zeus, one of the 'Seven Wonders of the Ancient World' (later taken to Constantinople and destroyed in a fire). There is also a good **Archaeological Museum** on the site, and a **Museum of the Olympic Games** located in the modern town of Olympia. Southeast of Olympia at **Bassae** (**Vasses**) is the well-preserved monumental **Temple of Apollo Epicurius**, dating back to the fourth century BC.
- Bordering onto Albania, Macedonia (Former Yugoslav Republic of) and Bulgaria, **Macedonia**'s scenery and climate have more in common with the adjoining Balkans. The region's capital, **Thessaloniki**, is the second-largest city in Greece. A modern industrial port, partly protected by impressive city walls, it is home to the superb **Archaeological Museum**, housing the 'Treasures of Ancient Macedonia'. On the seafront, the imposing 16th-century **White Tower**, built by the Ottomans as part of the city's defence system, houses an excellent Byzantine Art Collection. Tha main ancient sites are the **Arch of Galerius** and the ruins of the **Roman Agora**.
- Southeast of Thessaloniki are the three mountainous peninsulas of **Halkidiki**: Kassandra, Sithonia and Agio Oros (Mount Athos). **Mount Athos**, with its renowned monasteries, is undoubtedly the region's highlight.
- **Crete** (Piraeus, 174 nautical miles) is the largest and most southerly Greek island. Despite a busy tourist industry concentrated along the north coast, Crete has preserved its unspoilt nature, local traditions and ancient monuments. In the capital and main port, **Heraklion** (**Iraklio**), the old town lies within the 16th-century Venetian city walls, while the harbour is protected by **Koules**, an imposing Venetian Fortress. The **National Archaeological Museum** is one of the country's top museums, displaying finds from the Minoan era, and the **History Museum** tells the island's story from Byzantine times up to the present day. Close to town stand three wonderful Minoan sites - **Knossos**, **Malia** and **Phaestos**.
- Lying south of Athens and to the east of the Peloponnese, the **Saronic islands** are within easy reach of the capital, with regular ferry and hydrofoil services running from the port of Piraeus. **Aegina, Hydra, Poros, Salamis** and **Spetses** are the most popular islands. A barren, rocky, car-free island, **Hydra (Idra)** (Piraeus, 42 nautical miles) is

popular with artists and jet-setters, primarily for the beauty of its chief settlement and port, **Hydra Town**. Built into the hill overlooking the harbour, Hydra Town is a labyrinth of steep cobbled streets, filled with chic bars, restaurants and art galleries. 500m (1640ft) above town stands a **monastery**, offering fantastic views out over the sea.

- Located off the west coast of mainland Greece, the seven **Ionian Islands** (**Cephalonia, Corfu, Ithaki, Kythira, Lefkada, Paxi** and **Zakinthos**) are comparatively isolated from one another. Consequently, through the centuries each one has developed its own identity.

- The northernmost island of western Greece, **Corfu** is the best-known, busiest and most cosmopolitan of the Ionian islands. The capital, **Corfu Town**, is presided over by two imposing **Venetian fortresses** and gives onto a series of pretty harbours and bays. Worth visiting are the **Archaeological Museum**, which houses finds from local excavations; the **Byzantine Museum**, with a fine collection of icons; and the **Museum of Asiatic Art**. The **Town Hall**, a splendid example of 17th-century Venetian architecture, and the 12th-century Byzantine **Church of St Jason and Sosipater** and the **Church of St Spyridon** are also of interest. At **Kanoni**, on the tip of a small peninsular south of the town centre, a narrow causeway leads to the much photographed **Monastery of Vlacherna**. South of Corfu Town, at **Gastouri**, romantics will be delighted by the sight of the 19th-century **Achillion**, the summer palace of Empress Elizabeth of Austria, surrounded by beautiful Italian-style gardens.

- Best known as the setting of Louis de Bernières' *Captain Corelli's Mandolin*, **Cephalonia** (Patras, 53 nautical miles) is the biggest Ionian island. The mountainous scenery, culminating with the 1600m (5250ft) **Mount Enos**, is dramatic. The chief settlement, **Argostoli**, was largely destroyed in the disastrous 1953 earthquake. However, the **Archaeological Museum** and **Folk Art Museum** are both worth visiting.

- Lying east of the Peloponnese and southeast of the coast of Attica in the Aegean, a total of 39 islands make up the **Cyclades**, the best-known being **Mykonos** and **Santorini**. Other popular islands are **Andros, Delos, Naxos, Paros** and **Tinos**.

- Take a ferry to the most visited and most expensive of all the Greek islands, **Mykonos**, known for its lively nightlife and some of Greece's best discos. **Mykonos Town** (also known as **Hora**) comprises a modern harbour, whitewashed houses and churches, shops selling local arts and crafts, small tavernas and cafes, and is backed by a hill with five thatched windmills. The **Paraportiani Church**, a complex of four chapels, is considered to be an architectural masterpiece. The **Archaeological Museum** exhibits finds excavated from the necropolis on the nearby islet of **Rhenia**. Go on an excursion to the monasteries of **Agios Panteleimon**, close to Mykonos Town, and the **Tourliani Monastery**, close to the old fishing village of **Ano Mera**.

- From Mykonos, take a boat to the tiny and today unhabited island of **Delos**, the religious and political centre of the Aegean in ancient times, also said to have been the birthplace of Apollo and Artemis. Star attractions include the **Avenue of the Lions**, featuring five crouching stone lions, guardians of the Sacred Lake, and the **Sanctuary of Apollo**, made up of three temples. The **Archaeological Museum** exhibits archaic, Classical, Hellenistic and Roman sculptures, including the **Archaic Sphinx of the Naxians** and **Acroteria** (**Victories**) from the **Temple of the Athenians**, found in excavations on the site.

- Considered by many as the most dramatically beautiful of all the Greek islands, **Santorini** (also known as Thira) was formed by the eruption of a now dormant volcano around 1600 BC. Arrival by ferry brings one to the west side of the island, with the whitewashed cliff top villages of **Fira** (the capital) and **Ia** (the Aegean's most photographed town) overlooking the circular *caldera* (a huge depression created by a volcanic explosion). A steep winding path leads up from the harbour of **Skala** to **Fira**, where one finds many excellent hotels, chic restaurants and bars, and a vibrant nightlife. The **Archaeology Museum**, displaying finds from the excavations at **Akrotiri**, is worth a visit. On the east side of the island lie the archaeological remains of **Ancient Thira**, a Dorian city dating back to the ninth century BC.

- The four most popular islands of the **Northeast Aegean Islands** are **Chios, Lemnos, Lesbos** and **Samos**, all of which lie fairly far apart in the waters of the northeast Aegean, close to Turkey. **Lesbos**, home of the ancient poet Sappho, is the largest island in this group, with vast olive groves, shady pinewoods, and picturesque monasteries. The capital, **Mitilini**, is dominated by a 14th-century castle.

- East of the Thessaly region on mainland Greece lie the four islands of the **Sporades** – **Alonissos, Skiathos, Skiros** and **Skopelos**.

- Planted with pine trees and olive groves, **Skiathos** is a popular tourist destination, thanks to its indented coast with numerous sandy coves. The capital, **Skiathos Town**, was built in 1830 on two low hills. The seafront is lined with cafes and seafood restaurants, and there is a good marina. Boat trips take tourists around the island to visit

the **Blue Cave**, the ruins of the medieval walled town of **Kastro** on the south coast, and the pebble beach of **Lalaria**.

- The largest of the Sporades, **Skiros** lies far out from Volos and is most easily accessed from Kimi on Euboea. The main settlement, **Skiros Town** (also known as **Horio**), is made up of whitewashed cottages and narrow winding alleys, crowned by the hilltop Venetian **Kastro** (fortress). Visit the **Folklore Museum** which gives an excellent presentation of local handicrafts, and includes a reconstruction of a traditional house.

- The **Dodecanese Islands** is a cluster of 12 (*dodeca*) islands lying east of Peloponnese, closer to Turkey than to mainland Greece. All the islands can be reached by ferry from Piraeus, and distances between them are fairly small, so visitors can easily hop from one to another, swapping the relative sophistication of Rhodes and Kos for the calmer and simpler life on Tilos or Astipalaia.

- **Rhodes** is one of the most popular and best-developed islands in the Mediterranean. The capital, **Rhodes Town**, is made up of two distinct parts – an old town and a new town. The old town, contained within the walls of a medieval fortress, centres of the **Avenue of the Knights**, lined with magnificent medieval buildings, including the monumental 14th-century **Palace of the Grand Masters**. The 15th-century **Knight's Hospital** now houses the **Archaeological Museum**. 2km (1.2 miles) west of the town walls lies the **Acropolis of Ancient Rhodes**. Many impressive ruins can still be seen, including the **Temple of Apollo**, and a theatre and stadium dating back to the second century BC.

Top Things To Do

- Attend an open-air performance of the *International Athens Festival* at the **Odeon of Herodes Atticus** (from June to September). Alternatively, opt for the *Epidaurus Festival* which offers performances of ancient Greek dramas in the magical setting of the open-air **Epidaurus Theatre**, East of Nafplio (every weekend from late June to August). Open-air performances are also held during the summer at Dodoni's well-conserved theatre, dating back to the third century BC.

- Wander around the old quarter of Athens, **Plaka**, which spreads around the Acropolis. The area is picturesque with its famed flea market, small tavernas, craft shops and narrow winding alleys.

- Close to Arahova, on the main road from Athens to Delphi, lie the southern slopes of **Mount Parnassus**, which towers 2457m (8061ft) over the Gulf of Corinth. Through winter (December to April) the mountain hosts a number of well-equipped **ski resorts**, and the area is popular with **hikers** during spring and autumn.

- **Mount Olympus**, home of Zeus and the immortal gods and land of the Centaurs, is Greece's highest mountain, standing 2917m (9570ft). Walking tours depart from the village of **Litohoro**, where one finds hostels, hotels and *tavernas*. Climbing is also popular on the island of **Euboea**.

- Access the incredible cliff-top monasteries of the **Meteora** by a series of steep steps carved into the rocks. Perched upon bizarre vertical rock formations of up to 300m (984ft) high, a total of 24 monasteries, some with beautiful Byzantine frescoes, can be found to the west, above the Pinios Valley and the town of **Kalambaka**. Several are open to the public, notably **Megalo Meteoro** and **Varlaam Monastery**.

- Treat yourself in **Methana**, an important spa town since ancient times, located east of Epidaurus, with sulphuric waters and modernised hydrotherapy installations.

- East of Patras, travel through the deep **Vouraikos Gorge**, taking a spectacular train journey from **Diakofto** to **Kalavrita**.

- South of Hania (Crete), the beautiful **Samaria Gorge**, declared a **National Park**, is the longest gorge in Europe. Keen hikers will be able to walk the 18km (11.2 miles) length in a day, while the less sporting can join an organised tour, departing from Hania.

- On Tinos, the island's largest settlement, **Tinos Town**, is best known as a pilgrimage site. Each year on 25 March and 15 August, join thousands of believers who gather here to pay their respect to an icon of *Our Lady* (said to perform miracles) kept in the **Church of the Annunciate Virgin** (**Evangelistria**).

- There are over 7000 karstic cave formations in the country, the majority in Crete. In the **Mani** peninsula, go to the semi-abandoned village of Vathia where the **Caves of Dirou** are located. The caves consist of a vast network with underground channels and huge caverns, which can be visited by boat. On the east coast of Cephalonia, the **Cave of Melissani**, noted for its extraordinary colours caused by the reflection of the sun's rays through the sea, can also be visited by boat. The **Cave of St Sophia** in Milopotamos on Ythera island, has frescoes, stalactites and stalagmites. On Milos island, take a boat to **Sikia** (also known as the Blue Cave) and **Kleftiko**. Further information on these caves is available from the Hellenic Speleological Society, 32 Sina Street, 106 72 Athens (tel: (210) 361 7824; website: www.speleologicalsociety.gr).

- There are excellent facilities along all coastlines of the mainland and particularly in the islands for **watersports**. The **Apollo Coast**, a highly developed tourist area stretching from Piraeus to Cape Sounio, is dotted with exclusive resorts such as **Glifada** (17km/11 miles from Athens) and **Vouliagmeni** (24km/15 miles from Athens), offering marinas, well-kept beaches, modern hotel complexes, seafood tavernas and luxury-class restaurants and nightclubs. Near Delphi lie the seaside towns of **Itea** and **Galaxidi**. **Euboea** is an island of great natural beauty and scenic variety, with sandy beaches and secluded coves. There are also plenty of good beaches and seaside resorts on the stretch of coast south of **Kyllini** as far as **Kiparissia**. On **Mystras** island, **Vassiliki** is also popular with surfers. **Kassandra** and **Sithonia** shelter Northern Greece's best beaches. North of Corfu town lie the popular resorts of **Ipsos, Kassiopi and Sidari**. In Cephalonia, the best beaches can be found a little south from **Lixouri**. **Kythera** has often been portrayed as a 'Garden of Paradise' and has some beautiful beaches. On Mykonos island, beaches range from cosmopolitan to secluded, the most popular being **Agios Stefanos** and **Platis Gialos**. On the south side of the island lie several unspoilt nudist beaches, the best known being **Paradise** and **Super Paradise**, which can be reached by boat from Plati Gialos. **Naxos**, the largest in the Cyclades islands, is particularly noted for its numerous sand beaches. For unspoilt beaches, go to **Chios, Tilos or Halki**. In **Rhodes**, just outside Rhodes Town lie the main tourist complexes of **Falikari, Ixia** and **Ialissos** (also known as **Trianda**), all with numerous hotels and good beaches. To see sandy beaches, some of black volcanic sand, go to **Kos**. East of Heraklion (Crete), **Agios Nikolaos**, one of the island's best-known holiday resorts, overlooks the **Gulf of Mirambello** and several fine beaches. East from here stands **Sitia**, another popular resort with bars, restaurants, hotels and a Venetian fortress.

Note: Independent **scuba-diving** is strictly forbidden, in order to guard against the pilfering of underwater antiquities. Divers may only venture out under the auspices of a recognised diving school. For further information, contact the Hellenic Federation of Underwater Activities, West Terminal Post Office, Agios Cosmos, 166 04 Hellenikon, Athens, Greece (tel: (210) 981 9961; website: www.sportsnet.gr).

TOURIST INFORMATION

Greek/Hellenic National Tourism Organisation in the UK
4 Conduit Street, London W1S 2DJ, UK
Tel: (020) 7495 9300.
Website: www.gnto.co.uk
Also deals with enquiries regarding conferences and conventions.

Greek/Hellenic National Tourism Organisation in the USA
Olympic Tower, 645 Fifth Avenue, 9th Floor, Suite 903, New York, NY 10022, USA
Tel: (212) 421 5777.
Website: www.greektourism.com *or* www.gnto.gr

Entertainment

FOOD & DRINK: Restaurant and taverna food tends to be very simple, rarely involving sauces but with full use of local olive oil and charcoal grills. All restaurants have a standard menu which includes the availability and price of each dish. A good proportion of the restaurants will serve international dishes. Hours are normally 1200-1500 for lunch and 2000-2400 for dinner.Opening hours vary according to the region and local laws. Waiter service is usual.

National specialities:
- *Dolmades* (stuffed vine leaves).
- *Moussaka* (aubergine casserole with minced lamb, cinnamon, red wine and olive oil).
- *Kebabs* and *avgolemono* (chicken broth with rice, eggs, salt and lemon juice).
- *Taramasalata* (a dip made from fish roe, bread, onion, olive oil and lemon juice).
- Squid (*kalamari*) or octopus.
- *Keftedes* (hot spicy meatballs).
- *Tzatziki* (a dip made from yoghurt, olive oil, garlic, shredded cucumber and dill).
- Salads (*feta* cheese, tomato, cucumber and fresh olive oil).
- *Gigantes* (large white beans).
- *Kolokithakia* (small boiled courgette with oil and lemon).
- *Baklavas* (filo pastry filled with almonds and topped with honey, vanilla and sugar).
- *Loukoumades* (honey-drenched pastry puffs).

National drinks:
- *Retsina* wine (made with pine-needle resin).
- *Ouzo* (an aniseed-based clear spirit to which water is added).

- Local brandy (sharp and fiery).
- Greek coffee (thick and strong, and sugared according to taste).
- Greek beer is a light *Pilsner* type.

Tipping: 12 to 15 per cent is usual.

NIGHTLIFE: This is centred in main towns and resorts with concerts and discos. Athens offers many local tavernas, particularly in the Plaka area, and *ouzeris* (typical Greek bars). Regular concerts and evening shows are also held at the Odeion of Herodes in Attica. Nightclubs featuring Greek *bouzouki* music are extremely popular. There are some casinos in Greece, such as the Mount Parnes Casino in Athens, the Corfu Casino in Corfu and the Casino at the Grand Hotel Astir in Rhodes.

SHOPPING: Special purchases include lace, jewellery, metalwork, pottery, garments and knitwear, furs, rugs, leather goods, local wines and spirits. Athens is the centre for luxury goods and local handicrafts. The flea markets in Monastiraki and Plaka, below the Acropolis, are all crowded in high season. Regional specialities include silver from Ioannina, ceramics from Sifnos and Skopelos, embroidery and lace from Crete, the Ionian Islands, Rhodes and Skiros, fur from Kastoria, alabaster from Crete and *flokati* rugs from the Epirus region. **Note:** (a) Visitors should be aware that many 'antiques' sold to tourists are fake; it is illegal to export any item of real antiquity without a special permit from the Export Department of the Ministry of Culture. (b) Non-EU citizens can get a refund on Greek VAT (4 per cent on books and 18 per cent on nearly everything else); the process is fairly complex, but well worth it. Non-EU visitors may buy goods from certain shops bearing the sign 'Member of the Tax-Free Club' and have the VAT refunded, in cash, at special refund points at the airport. Ask store owners and tourist information offices for details.

SHOPPING HOURS: These vary according to the season, location and type of shop, but a rough guide follows: Mon, Wed, and Sat 0900-1430, Tues, Thurs and Fri 0900-1430 and 1730-2030. **Note:** Most holiday resort shops stay open late in the evening.

Business

- **GDP:** US$226.4 billion (2004).
- **Main exports:** Food, beverages, manufactured goods, petroleum, chemicals and textiles.
- **Main imports:** Machinery, transport equipment, fuels and chemicals.
- **Main trade partners:** Germany, Italy, UK, Japan, Russia and France.

ECONOMY: Traditionally agricultural, accession to the EU gave a new impetus to the Greek economy, particularly the industrial sectors of textiles, clothing and shoes, cement, mining and metals, chemicals, steel and processed agricultural products. Nonetheless, 20 per cent of the working population still work the land – a very high proportion by EU standards. Tourism, the most important service industry, has boomed since the 1980s, with upwards of 10 million tourists now visiting the country annually. Shipping is also an important source of income: Greece has one of the largest merchant fleets in the world. Greek enterprises have consistently encountered difficulty penetrating European markets, however, because of the comparatively small size of the majority of businesses and high transport costs (owing to its geographical position). Nonetheless, the country exports large quantities of wheat, barley, maize, tobacco and fruit to the rest of the EU and elsewhere. The Greeks have benefited substantially from transfers of funds within the EU and support for its large public-sector debt. Growth is around 3.5 per cent, with inflation nearly 3 per cent, and unemployment hovering around 10 per cent in 2005. Greece's huge public-sector deficit prevented it from meeting the convergence criteria for the European single currency and the country entered the Euro zone in January 2001. The EU accounts for about 65 per cent of Greek trade.

BUSINESS ETIQUETTE: Formal suits are expected. French, German and English are often spoken as well as Greek.

CONFERENCES/CONVENTIONS: Greece has many convention centres and hotels with conference facilities, in locations ideal for post-conference tours, eg Athens, Corfu, Crete, Halkidiki, Metsovo (Epirus) and Rhodes. It also has ships equipped for 'floating conferences', sailing between the islands. For further enquiries, contact the Greek/Hellenic National Tourism Organisation (see *Top Things To Do*).

COMMERCIAL INFORMATION

Athens Chamber of Commerce & Industry (ACCI)
7 Akademias Street, 106 71 Athens, Greece
Tel: (210) 362 5342.
Website: www.acci.gr

Greenland

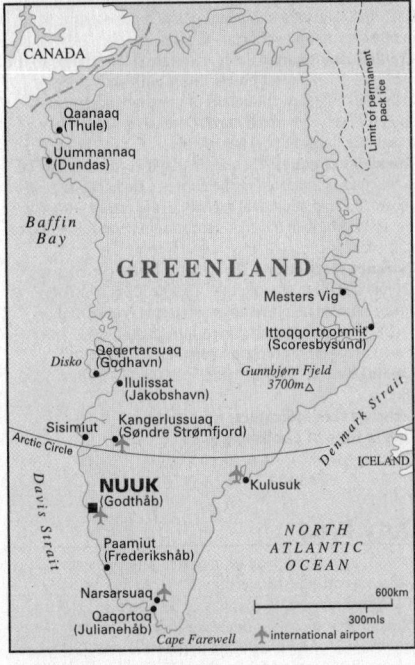

Location: South Arctic/North Atlantic.

Time: Central/ Southern Greenland: GMT - 3 (GMT - 2 from last Sunday in March to last Sunday in October).
Eastern Greenland: GMT - 1 (GMT from last Sunday in March to last Sunday in October).
West Greenland: GMT - 4 (GMT - 3 from last Sunday in March to last Sunday in October).

Greenland is part of the Kingdom of Denmark, and is represented abroad by Danish Embassies – see *Denmark* section.

Overview

Some might be surprised to learn that Greenland is the world's biggest island. Its large and impressive island terrain is therefore marked by the kind of topography that you might expect: surrounding sea, hills and wildlife. Yet the sea is either permanently frozen or chilled by the mainly cold currents. Its hills are framed by wild and rugged scenery and clear, clean air. In the centre of the country, ice can be up to 3km (2 miles) thick. It is no wonder that most of its population huddles around the ice-free coastal region. Indeed, 'Greenland' is a bit of a misnomer, drummed up by Eric the Red - son of a Norwegian chieftain banished from his home in Iceland for murder - in the year 982 AD to attract settlers.

Eric the Red's strategy worked for a short while. By the 10th century, the first European settlements of Greenland had been established. The colonists accepted Norwegian sovereignty around 1260, which lasted until the marginal lifestyle of the settlements finally led to their collapse in the 16th century. The territory was then unoccupied by Europeans until Denmark took possession of it in the early 18th century. It became an integral part of the Danish realm in 1953. A referendum in 1979 approved internal autonomy within the Kingdom of Denmark. In 1982, in another referendum, the population voted by a narrow majority to leave the EC (as it then was), which they had joined as part of Denmark in 1972. Greenland is now an overseas territory in association with the EU. Another source of conflict between Greenland and Denmark has been the presence of a major American military radar installation at Thule in the north, which may be involved in a future US missile defence system. While most of the population would prefer it removed, the Danish Government says that it is bound by treaty obligations. But, for now, relations between Greenland and Denmark are relatively tranquil.

Those still wondering why anyone would want to inhabit such unforgiving terrain are ignorant of the beautiful sights that Greenland grants. The arctic nights in the winter concoct a wondrous continuous twilight and, in the far north of the country, complete darkness, coupled with Northern Lights that drench the sky in effulgence. Greenland's quality of light attracts aspiring photographers from all around the world. The profusion of snow creates the perfect conditions for activities such as dog sledging and tour cruises, which interweave in and out of Greenland's dazzling array of fjords, mountains, islands and icebergs. The wildlife does not disappoint, either: there are abundant opportunities to view creatures such as whales, seals and birds.

In short, Greenland is not a country for those seeking an ordinary holiday. Those seeking an extraordinary holiday might have found the right place.

General Information

AREA: 2,166,086 sq km (836,330 sq miles).
POPULATION: 56,375 (2005 estimate).
POPULATION DENSITY: 0.026 per sq km.
CAPITAL: Nuuk (Godthåb). **Population:** 15,000 (2005).
GEOGRAPHY: Greenland is the world's biggest island. The surrounding seas are either permanently frozen or chilled by the mainly cold currents caused by the meeting of the Arctic and the North Atlantic oceans. The inland area is covered with ice, stretching 2500km (1500 miles) north–south and 1000km (600 miles) east–west. In the centre, the ice can be up to 3km (2 miles) thick. The ice-free coastal region, which is sometimes as wide as 200km (120 miles), covers a total of 410,449 sq km (158,475 sq miles), and is where all of the population is to be found. This region is intersected by deep fjords which connect the inland ice area with the sea. The Midnight Sun can be seen north of the Arctic Circle; the further north you are, the longer the period of the Midnight Sun. The arctic night in the winter results in a continuous twilight and, in the far north of the country, complete darkness. The Northern Lights can be seen during the autumn, winter and early spring.
GOVERNMENT: Part of the Kingdom of Denmark. **Head of State:** HM Queen Margarethe II since 1972. **Head of Government:** Prime Minister Hans Enoksen since 2002.
Recent history: Coalition Governments have controlled Greenland for the last 20-odd years. These have proved generally stable, but 2003 was an exception. The December 2002 election had returned *Siumut* as the largest party, forming a coalition Government with *Inuit Ataqatigiit* (Inuit Brotherhood; IA) under the premiership of *Siumut* leader Hans Enoksen. However, the Government fell after a month under farcical circumstances, relating to the activities of a faith-healer apparently hired to purge Government offices of evil spirits. *Siumut* and Enoksen remained in power, with Attasut as its coalition partner, but this Government was also short-lived. It collapsed after eight months following a dispute over miscalculation of the territory's budget. The IA has now rejoined *Siumut* in Government.
Executive power rests with the five-member *Landsstyre*, excepting defence, foreign affairs and constitutional affairs for which the Danish Government is responsible. Its members are drawn from the local legislature, the *Landsting* (known also by its Inuit title *Inatsi-Satut*), which has 31 members elected for four years.
LANGUAGE: The official languages are Greenlandic, an Inuit (Eskimo) language and Danish. Greenlanders connected with tourism will normally speak English.
RELIGION: Evangelical Lutheran Church of Denmark majority, with small groups of Roman Catholics and other Protestant denominations.

Credit: Greenland Tourism/Filippo Barbanera

A B C D E F G H I J K L M N O P Q R S T U V W X Y Z

ELECTRICITY: 220 volts AC, 50Hz.

SOCIAL CONVENTIONS: Life is generally conducted at a more relaxed pace than is usual in northern Europe, as exemplified by the frequent use of the word *immaqa* – 'maybe'. Until recently, foreign visitors were very rare. The name of the country in Greenlandic is *Kalaallit Nunaat*, meaning 'Land of the People'. **Photography:** Throughout the country there is a ban on taking photographs inside churches or church halls during services. A UV or skylight filter and a lens shade should always be used. In winter, the camera must be polar-oiled. It is advisable to bring your own film. Film cannot always be developed in Greenland.

Climate

Greenland has an Arctic climate, but owing to the size of the country there are great variations in the weather. As the climate graph shows, winters can be severe and the summers comparatively mild, particularly in areas which are sheltered from the prevailing winds. Precipitation, mostly snow, is moderately heavy around the coast. The north of the country, and much of the interior, enjoys true Arctic weather, with the temperature only rising above freezing for brief periods in the summer.

Note: Conditions in all parts of the country can become hazardous when there is a combination of a low temperature and a strong wind. Local advice concerning weather conditions should be followed very carefully. Nevertheless, the summer months are suitable for a wide range of outdoor activities.

Required clothing: Good-quality windproof and waterproof clothes, warm layers and moulded sole shoes at all times of the year; also some slightly thinner clothes – it is important to be able to change clothing during a day's climbing as temperatures can vary greatly during one day. Sunglasses and protective sun lotion are strongly advised. In July and August, mosquitoes can be a problem, especially inside the fjords and so a mosquito net can prove indispensable. Extra warm clothes are necessary for those contemplating dog-sledge expeditions. Extra clothes are not always available for hire in Greenland.

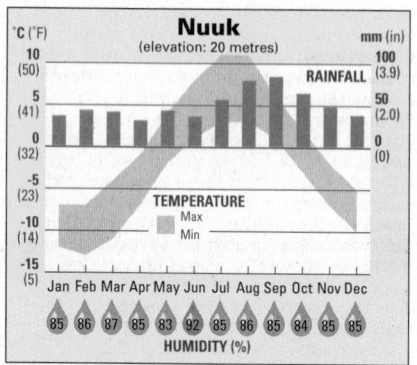

Nuuk (elevation: 20 metres)

Communications

Telephone: IDD is available. Country code: 299. There are no area codes. There are no telephone boxes in Greenland, but calls can be made from hotels.

Mobile telephone: Handsets can be hired at *TELE Greenland* shops (in all cities). A deposit of DKK10,000 is required. Roaming agreements exist with some international mobile phone companies. Coverage is limited to main towns.

Internet: At present, there are Internet cafes in many towns. Access is available in some public libraries.

Post: Greenland produces its own stamps which are popular among collectors. Post from Greenland takes about four to five days to reach Europe. Post office hours: Mon-Fri 0900-1500.

MEDIA: Press: There are no daily newspapers in Greenland, but *Atuagagdliutit/Gronlandsposten* is published twice a week, *Sermitsiaq* is the main weekly publication and *Niviarsiaq* is published monthly. There are no English language newspapers.

TV and Radio: *Kalaallit Nunaata Radio* (Radio Greenland) broadcasts radio and television programmes in Greenlandic and Danish.

Passport/Visa

The regulations for Tourist and Business visas are the same as for Denmark (see *Passport/Visa Information* in the *Denmark* section). Visitors should specify that they wish to visit Greenland when they make their application. Special permits are necessary for persons wishing to transit in Pittuffik (Thule Airbase), as it is a North Atlantic Territory. Further information and application requirements may be obtained from the Nordic Countries, Faroe Islands and Greenland Office at the Ministry of Foreign Affairs, Asiatisk

Plads 2, DK-1448 Copenhagen, Denmark (tel: 3392 0000); website: www.um.dk). Visitors who wish to explore the glaciers and mountains or visit the National Park also require a special permit. Applications should be made to the Danish Polar Centre, Strandgade 100H, DK-1401 Copenhagen, Denmark (tel: 3288 0100; website: www.dpc.dk).

Money

Currency: Danish Krone (DKK) = 100 øre. Notes are in denominations of DKK1000, 500, 200, 100 and 50. Coins are in denominations of DKK20, 10, 5, 2 and 1, and 50 and 25 øre.

Note: There is no banking service in Søndre Strømfjord at present.

Currency exchange: Cheques drawn on Danish banks or on Eurocheque cards can be cashed at banks and cash can also be exchanged. Postal cheques can be cashed at all post offices. There are two banks in Greenland: *Grønlandsbanken* (PO Box 1033, DK-3900 Nuuk) and *Nuna Bank* (PO Box 1031, DK-3900 Nuuk). *Nuna Bank* has branches in Nuuk, Sisimiut, Oaqortoq, Ilulissat and Maniitsoq. *KNI* represents the banks in other towns and villages.

Credit & debit cards: Credit cards are still restricted to the major towns and most hotels. Check with your credit or debit card company for details of merchant acceptability and other services which may be available. Some major towns, like Ilulissat, now have ATMs.

Traveller's cheques: Cheques in major currencies may be exchanged as indicated in the currency exchange section above. To avoid additional exchange rate charges, travellers are advised to take traveller's cheques in Pounds Sterling or US Dollars.

Currency restrictions: The import of local currency is unlimited; export of more than DKK50,000 is allowed provided it can be proved this amount was imported or obtained by changing imported foreign currencies. The import and export of foreign currencies is unlimited.

Banking hours: Mon-Wed and Fri 1000-1600; Thurs 1000-1800.

Exchange rate indicators:
Rate at time of publishing
£1.00= DKK11.04
$1.00= DKK6.34

Duty Free

The following goods may be imported into Greenland without incurring customs duty:

200 cigarettes or 100 cigarillos or 50 cigars or 250g of tobacco; 1l of alcoholic beverages over 22 per cent volume or 2l of fortified wine between 15 and 22 per cent volume; 2.25 litres of table wine; 50g perfume and 250ml toilet water; goods up to a value of DKK700; 1kg of coffee or tea; up to 2kg of chocolate or sweets.

Note: These goods must be carried by the traveller personally. Alcohol allowances are for travellers aged over 18 only.

Prohibited items: (a) Fresh food. (b) Pistols, fully- or semi-automatic weapons. A permit is required from the carrying airline to bring a hunting rifle to Greenland, but hunting is only permitted on special hunting trips organised by a tour operator who has been authorised by the Home Rule Government to do so. (c) Narcotics. (d) Most live animals (guide dogs for the blind are an exception).

Note: Special permission is needed to export souvenirs of whales' teeth and walrus tusks. Authorisation forms are available from shops and tourist offices in Greenland.

Public Holidays

Below are listed Public Holidays for the January 2006-June 2007 period.

2006: Jan 1 New Year's Day. **Jan 6** Epiphany. **Apr 13** Maundy Thursday. **Apr 14** Good Friday. **Apr 17** Easter Monday. **May 12** Great Prayer Day. **May 25** Ascension. **Jun 5** Whit Monday. **Jun 21** National Day. **Dec 24-26** Christmas. **Dec 31** New Year's Eve.
2007: Jan 1 New Year's Day. **Jan 6** Epiphany. **Apr 5** Maundy Thursday. **Apr 6** Good Friday. **Apr 9** Easter Monday. **May 4** Great Prayer Day. **May 17** Ascension. **May 28** Whit Monday. **Jun 21** National Day.

Health

	Special Precautions?	Certificate Required?
Yellow Fever	No	No
Cholera	No	No
Typhoid & Polio	No	N/A
Malaria	No	N/A

Note: *Regulations and requirements may be subject to change at short notice, and you are advised to contact your doctor well in advance of your intended date of departure. Any numbers in the chart refer to the footnotes below.*

Other risks: *Hepatitis A* occurs. *Hepatitis B* is endemic. *TB* may occur. Extreme cold during the winter months is another potential risk to travellers.
Rabies is present. For those at high risk, vaccination before arrival should be considered. If you are bitten, seek medical advice without delay. For more information, consult the *Health* appendix.

Health care: There are hospitals and dentists in all towns. Although medical services are generally free, medical insurance is advisable, particularly as charges are made for dental treatment. Travellers are also advised to bring their own medicines and prescribed drugs, as these can often be difficult to obtain in Greenland.

Travel - International

Note: The arctic weather conditions in Greenland may cause delays and interruptions in transport services or changes to planned itineraries. Visitors are advised to leave enough time for possible disruptions to flights and check with their airline or tour operator before flying.

AIR:
 The national airline is *Air Greenland* (website: www.airgreenland.gl). Flying to Greenland by scheduled services will usually involve a stopover in Iceland or Denmark. *Air Iceland (NY)* also serves Greenland.

Approximate flight times: From Greenland to *London* is five hours 30 minutes (including stopover in Copenhagen).

Main airports: There are international airports at: *Kangerlussuaq (Søndre Strømfjord) (SFJ)*, served from Copenhagen by *Air Greenland*.
Kulusuk (KUS), served from Iceland by *Air Iceland*; *Narsarsuaq (UAK)*, served from Copenhagen by *Air Greenland* and from Iceland by *Air Iceland*; *Nuuk (GOH)*, served from Copenhagen by *Air Greenland*. Other international airports include *Neerlerit Inaat (CNP)* and *Pituffik (THU)*.

Departure tax: None.

Travel - Internal

AIR:
 Air Greenland serves all towns on the west coast, from Nanortalik in the south to Thule/Qaanaq in the north. The frequency of departure on all routes is variable, and it is advisable to make reservations well in advance. Reservations made outside Greenland will take some time to confirm. *Air Greenland* and *Air Alpha* serve other areas by helicopter.

SEA:
 It is generally cheaper to sail than to fly. *Arctic Umiaq Line* operates services along the west coast between Nanortalik and Upernavik. In addition, all villages are served by local boats connecting them with the nearest town, but space may be limited. Boats in some towns may be available for hire, with a skipper. *Coastal Cruise Greenland* offers cruises with all-inclusive flights. During the summer months, visitors are advised to book their journeys in advance as this is the time when Greenlanders travel. For further information, contact Arctic Umiaq Line A/S, PO Box 608, 3900 Nuuk (tel: 349 900; website: www.aul.gl) or Greenland Tourism (see *Top Things To See & Do*).

ROAD:
The only places that are connected by road are Ivituut and Kangilinnguit. The harsh landscape and weather conditions make road building elsewhere a virtually impossible task. Air and sea travel are the recommended ways of getting around.

RAIL:
There are no railways between towns in Greenland.

Dog sledges: These can be hired for the day, or for longer periods. Sledging is possible in all towns on the east coast and on the west coast north of the polar circle. It is important to remember that sledge dogs are usually only semi-tame. This is just one reason why dog sledges should be given right of way at all times. Take particular care, as they are almost totally silent.

Travel times: The following chart gives approximate travel times (in hours and minutes) from **Kangerlussuaq** to other regions in Greenland:

	Air
Disko Bay	0.50
South Greenland	1.30
East Greenland	1.10

Travel Advice

Most visits to Greenland are trouble-free but you should be aware of the global risk of indiscriminate international terrorist attacks, which could be against civilian targets, including places frequented by foreigners.
This advice is based on information provided by the Foreign and Commonwealth Office in the UK. It is correct at time of publishing. As the situation can change rapidly, visitors are advised to contact the following organisations for the latest travel advice:

British Foreign and Commonwealth Office
Tel: (0845) 850 2829.
Website: www.fco.gov.uk

US Department of State
Website: http://travel.state.gov/travel

Accommodation

HOTELS: There are hotels in the major towns, but only those in Ammassalik, Ilulissat, Maniitsoq, Narsaq, Narsarsuaq, Nuuk, Qaqortoq, Qasigianguit, Sisimiut, Søndre, Strømfjord and Ummannaq approach European standards. There is no public accommodation in Scoresby Sund, Thule or Upernavik. All reservations should be made in advance; contact Greenland Tourism or Greenland Tourism in Copenhagen (see Top Things To See & Do) for information. A star-grading system is in place. Hotels are classified by Greenland Tourism, and gradings are roughly equivalent to those in Denmark.

CAMPING: There are no official campsites, but most places have specific areas for pitching tents. Camping is permitted everywhere except on ruins and on cultivated land in south Greenland. Booking is not essential. Local tourist offices have the latest information and will be able to advise on the nearest site.
IGLOOS: An 'igloo hotel' is constructed in winter each year in Kangerlussuaq. A large central igloo is connected to four to six smaller ones via ice tunnels. The complex features a bar, decorative ice sculptures and ice furniture.

YOUTH HOSTELS: Major towns in Greenland have youth hostel accommodation with good facilities and you may come across student accommodation which doubles up as youth hostels during the summer. Elsewhere in south Greenland a number of farmers have installed accommodation attached to their sheep farming stations, but do not expect luxury. Contact Greenland Tourism in Copenhagen for more information (see Top Things To See & Do).
SEAMEN'S HOMES: Originally used by seafarers when their ship was in port, seamen's homes are these days used as simple accommodation with basic facilities. En-suite rooms are rare but there is often a cafe attached.
CHALETS/CABINS: A network of remote cabins can be found throughout most of Greenland. They are available to all and there is usually no charge to stay overnight. Mainly used by locals on hunting trips, they are rarely locked, well-kept or clean but should be regarded as a 'roof over your head'. Visitors are advised to have their own map with updated information drawn on as a number of chalets have disappeared and others may not be marked on as existing. Chalets of a higher standard, such as summer cottages, can be rented through local tourist offices.

Top Things To See & Do

- See **Nuuk**, one of the world's smallest capitals, with a population of about 15,000. It was founded in 1728 by Norwegian missionary, **Hans Egede**, as the very first town of Greenland. His former home now holds the reception room for Greenland's **Home Rule Parliament**. The town is overlooked by **Sermitsiaq Mountain**, and is a popular destination for visitors. Also in the town is a **cathedral**, **university** and **seminary**.
- Take a look at the mummies of a group of women and children who were thought to have died in about 1475 when their boat capsized at **Greenland National Museum**, one of the major attractions is Nuuk. The museum is in the oldest part of the city where buildings date back to 1728.
- Attend the annual **Snow Sculpture Festival**, held in Nuuk (website: www.snow.gl). Here, you will see some spectacular sculptures, which in the moonlight, look almost ethereal.
- **Ilulissat** is one of the country's growth areas and the gateway to **Disko Bay** and the whole of northern Greenland. Originally named Jakobshavn in honour of its Danish founder Jakob Sverin (1691-1753), the Greenlandic name Ilulissat (meaning iceberg) is now more commonly used. Local history, however, dates much further back than the founding of **Jakobshavn**. **Sermermiut**, a settlement situated a few kilometres southwest of the town, shows traces of habitation as early as 2000 BC. With a population of approximately 4700, Ilulissat boasts many modern as well as traditional buildings surrounded by breathtaking scenery. The famous explorer Knud Rasmussen was born here in 1879 and the house where he grew up has been transformed into the interesting **Knud Rasmussen Museum**.
- Visit **Narsarsuaq** and **Qassiarsuk** in southern Greenland, situated in the area first settled by the Viking Eric the Red 1000 years ago. Many ruins from this epoch of Greenland's history still survive.
- **Qaqortoq** is the largest town in South Greenland and

the area's administrative centre. The **town square**, situated close to the harbour, holds the country's oldest **fountain** and is encircled by some of the most well-preserved buildings of the colonial era, dating back 200 years. Throughout the town there are examples of a unique art project called **'Stone and People'** where sculptures are carved into granite.
- There is a small **Inuit** (**Eskimo**) **Museum** at **Qaqortoq**, which includes an exact copy of a turf-built house. There are minor local museums in most towns. The country also has many ruins of old Norse settlements and Inuit houses.
- **Nanortalik** is Greenland's southernmost town and is surrounded by the **Nanortalik Skyscrapers**, steep peaks and sheer mountain walls lining fjords. **Ketil Mountain** and **Ulamertorsuaq** should only be attempted by experienced climbers.
- Venture into either **Qaanaaq**, the world's most northerly municipality, or **Siorapaluk**, the northernmost inhabited place on Earth.
- Watch for gigantic fin whales, especially around **Qeqertarsuaq**, **Aasiaat** and **Qasigianguit**.
- In **Disko Bay** is Greenland's **oldest wooden house**, dating back to 1734, which is now the town's **museum**.
- Over 2700 km (1600 miles) of the East Coast contains only two towns but also the **world's largest national park**.
- **Ittoqqortoormiit** is one of the youngest towns in Greenland and the most isolated - the municipality is about the size of Great Britain but also just happens to hold the largest fjord in the world, **Scoresby Sund**, and also makes up the largest fjord complex in the world with its number of side fjords. The area is ideal for expedition trips in **kayaks** or on **dog sledges** and it is also the departure point for the national park, for which permits are required.
- Guided **tours** for **mountain walking** are available. Greenland Tourism has published colour-coded hiking maps and guides for **Qaqortoq**, **Narsaq**, **Narsarsuaq** in South Greenland and **Ammassalik** in the east. Mountain huts are often available, particularly in the region of the Narsaq and Qaqortoq peninsulas and **Vatnahverfi**.
- Play **golf** on metre-thick ice in **Uummannaq**.

TOURIST INFORMATION

Danish Tourist Board in the UK
55 Sloane Street, London SW1X 9SY, UK
Tel: (020) 7259 5959 (Mon, Wed and Fri 1000-1300).
Website: www.visitdenmark.com

Danish Tourist Board in the USA
PO Box 4649, Grand Central Station,
New York, NY 10163, USA
Tel: (212) 885 9700.
Website: www.goscandinavia.com
Also deals with enquiries relating to Canada.
Not open to personal callers.

Greenland Tourism in Denmark
PO Box 1139, Strandgade 91,
DK-1010 Copenhagen K, Denmark.
Tel: 3283 3880.
Website: www.greenland.com

Entertainment

FOOD & DRINK: Most hotels have restaurants of a good standard, where Danish food and Greenland specialities are served. Prices are expensive but similar to Denmark.
National specialities:
- Reindeer meat (caribou).
- Seal.
- Whale meat.
- Musk ox.
- Fowl.
- Shrimps and fish.
Pubs are open to people over the age of 18 and some have discos or live bands.
Tipping: Service charge is usually added to the bill. Tips are not expected.
SHOPPING: The range of goods available is similar to that in an ordinary Danish provincial town, but prices are, in general, slightly higher. Alcohol, tobacco, fruit and vegetables are expensive. Special purchases include bone and soapstone carvings, skin products and beadwork. "The Board" is the local term for Kalaaliavaq, the markets which can be found in all Greenlandic towns. Here you can buy the day's harvest such as seal, whale, musk, reindeer, fish and berries straight from the hunter, fisherman or picker. They are usually situated close to the town's port. The Greenland Home Rule Administration can provide information on claiming tax back on items purchased in Greenland.
Shopping hours: Mon-Thurs 1000-1730, Fri 1000-1800 and Sat 0900-1300. Smaller grocery shops and kiosks may open for longer but these will vary from region to region.

Business

- **GDP:** US$1.1 billion (2001 estimate).
- **Main imports:** Machinery and transport equipment, manufactured goods, food and petroleum products.
- **Main exports:** Fish and fish products.
- **Main trade partners:** China, Denmark, Japan, Norway and Sweden.

ECONOMY: Greenland withdrew from the European Community (now the European Union) in February 1985 over the issue of the fisheries policy. EU member states are allowed to fish within Greenland's maritime exclusion zone in exchange for an annual cash payment; this compensates, in part, for the loss of development aid which Greenland would otherwise have received. It also enjoys preferential access to EU markets. Although there are plans to develop the island's mineral deposits of iron ore, uranium, zinc, lead and coal, the economy ultimately depends on large subsidies from the Danish central Government. The KNI – Royal Greenland Trade Department – organises transport, supplies and production in the country.
BUSINESS ETIQUETTE: Suits should be worn. A knowledge of Danish is extremely useful. **Office hours:** Mon-Fri 0900-1700 or 0800-1600.

COMMERCIAL INFORMATION

Cultural Conference Centre in Katuaq (**Information on Conferences and Conventions**)
PO Box 1622, DK-3900 Nuuk, Greenland
Website: www.katuaq.gl

Credit: ©Greenland Tourism/Karsten Bidstrup

Grenada

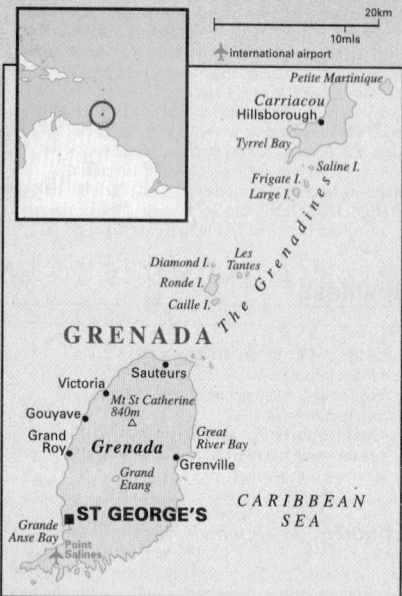

Credit: ©Grenada Board of Tourism

environments in the Caribbean, including crater lakes, as well as a variety of plant and animal life. Dwarf forests high atop Mount St Catherine descend to the rainforests of middle altitudes, which give way in turn to the dry forests of the lowlands. Those forests shift to mangrove at the coast, giving way to stunning white sand beaches, brilliant blue water and exquisite coral reefs.

Just as there is often spice in the air, there is music if you seek it. With Grenada's African origins, Calypso is the music of the native Grenadian. Modern music has infiltrated in the form of reggae and pop but Carnival is still awash with traditional rhythms. West Indian rhythms also translate into West Indian dishes, with Grenada's palate-tempting foods such as *callaloo* soup (much like spinach), seafood and seasoned meats.

However, Grenada's history is not as sweet as its spices, nor as harmonious as its music. Arawak Indians were displaced by Caribs some time before AD 1300, who fiercely resisted settlement until 1650, when the French claimed the island, then taken by the British in 1783. Until emancipation, Grenada was an important centre in the slave trade between Africa and the sugar plantations of the West Indies. Later, trade union organisation, promoted by Eric Gairy, a firebrand ex-teacher, took root among the workforce. Gairy ultimately led Grenada into independence from the UK in 1974, and subsequently won three elections. Among his opponents was the New JEWEL Movement (Joint Endeavour for Welfare, Education and Liberation), a group of mainly young, educated left-wingers, led by Maurice Bishop. In the spring of 1979, the NJM deposed Gairy in a bloodless coup. The USA believed that the NJM wanted to turn Grenada into a mini-Cuba, and from 1980 onwards, increased political pressure against the Government. This led to the military coup of October 1983 in which Bishop was killed, providing a pretext for US invasion and restoration of the pre-NJM system under US tutelage. Four existing political parties allied to form the New National Party (NNP), which has dominated politics ever since. In recent years, hurricanes like Hurricane Ivan and Hurricane Emily have struck the spice island, causing damage and raising fears. However, for now, neither its history, nor environmental threats, can damage the beauty of Grenada – the spirits of its people are as high as their rum is potent.

General Information

AREA: 344.5 sq km (133 sq miles).
POPULATION: 89,211 (2002, estimate).
POPULATION DENSITY: 266.7 per sq km.
CAPITAL: St George's. **Population:** 3908 (2001).
GEOGRAPHY: Grenada is located in the Caribbean. The island is of volcanic origin and is divided by a central mountain range. It is the most southerly of the Windward Islands. Agriculture is based on nutmeg, cocoa, sugar cane and bananas. Tropical rainforests, gorges and the stunning beauty of dormant volcanoes make this a fascinating and diverse landscape with some of the finest beaches in the world. Carriacou and some of the other small islands of the Grenadines are also part of Grenada.
GOVERNMENT: Constitutional monarchy. **Head of State:** HM Queen Elizabeth II, represented locally by Governor-General Sir Daniel Williams since 1996. **Head of Government:** Prime Minister Keith Mitchell since 1995.

Recent history: Four existing political parties allied to form the New National Party (NNP) in 1983, under the leadership of the veteran politician Herbert Blaize. At the General Election in December 1984, the NNP won handsomely. The NNP has dominated Grenadian politics ever since, and won the most recent election in November 2003, when it swept the board for the House of Representatives. Party leader Keith Mitchell is now into his third term as Prime Minister. Mitchell's Government continues the NNP tradition of very close relations with the USA, although a sharp drop in financial support led Mitchell, along with other East Caribbean leaders, to seek economic assistance elsewhere. The Organisation of East Caribbean States plays an important part in Grenada's foreign policy. A proposed political union comprising the member of the organisation has aroused fierce opposition because of historic inter-island rivalries, although its supporters (who include the Mitchell Government) feel it essential to the future prosperity and security of the region.

Grenada is a Dominion within the British Commonwealth; the Head of State is the British Monarch, represented locally by a Governor. Executive power rests with the Cabinet while responsibility for legislation rests with a bicameral parliament comprising the 13-member Senate and the 15-member House of Representatives.
LANGUAGE: English. French African patois is also spoken by some of the population.
RELIGION: Roman Catholic 53 per cent, Anglican 13.8 per cent, as well as other smaller Protestant denominations, 33.2 per cent.
ELECTRICITY: 220 volts AC, 50Hz.
SOCIAL CONVENTIONS: Local culture reflects the island's history of British and French colonial rule and, of course, the African cultures imported with the slaves – African influence is especially noticeable on the island of Carriacou in the Big Drum and in Grenada with the Shango dance. The Roman Catholic Church also exerts a strong influence on the way of life. Local people are generally friendly and courteous. Dress is casual and informal but beachwear is not welcome in town.

Location: Caribbean, Windward Islands.

Time: GMT - 4.

Overview

Grenada is often referred to as 'Spice Island', and with more spices per square mile than anywhere else on the planet, it is indeed true that the sweet scents of nutmeg, cinnamon, ginger and vanilla often linger in this clement climate. This adds an 'air' of exoticism to the Caribbean country, which actually consists of three islands: Grenada, Carriacou and Petite Martinique.

Grenada is by far the largest, with a width of 12 miles (18km) and a length of 21 miles (34km), comprising mountainous, volcanic terrain. This topography provides Grenada with one of the loveliest and most varied

Climate

Tropical. The dry season runs from January to May. The rainy season runs from June to December. The average temperature is 28°C (82°F).
Required clothing: Tropical lightweights and cool summer clothing.

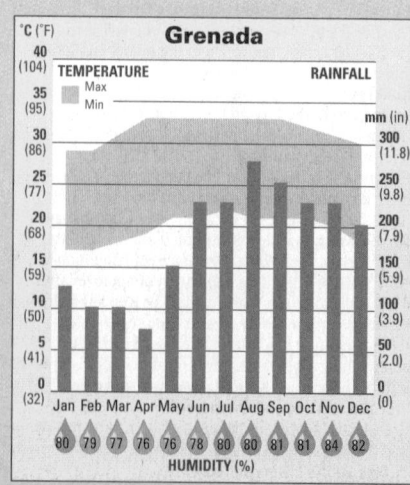

Credit: ©Grenada Board of Tourism

Credit: ©Grenada Board of Tourism

Communications

Telephone: Full IDD service. Country code: 1 473. No area codes are in use. Coin and telephone card payphones are available. Telephone cards can be purchased at the offices of *Cable & Wireless Grenada* and from other agents. International dialling is available from most hotel rooms.

Mobile telephone: Roaming is available to all mobile phones that are TDMA digital network compatible. Contact Cable & Wireless in Grenada for further detail (tel: 440 1000). Coverage is variable.

Internet: Internet is widely available throughout Grenada; there are Internet cafes in St George's.

Post: The main post office is in St George's (on Lagoon Road). Post office hours: Mon-Thurs 0800-1600, Fri 0800-1630 (closed weekends).

MEDIA: Grenada's media are free, as is stipulated in law. No daily newspapers exist, and weeklies are privately owned and freely criticise the Government. The Grenada Broadcasting Network, jointly owned by the Caribbean Communications Network and the Government, runs the main radio and television stations.

Press: All newspapers are in English, and are printed weekly or monthly. They include *Grenada Times*, *Grenada Today* and *The Grenadian Voice*.

TV: There are currently three TV stations; these include *MTV* (a private station) and *GBN TV* (operated by the Grenada Broadcasting Network).

Radio: There are currently five radio stations: *Klassic*

Radio (speech and music, operated by GBN), *Sun FM* (music, targeted at younger listeners, operated by GBN), *Spice Capital Radio* (private FM station), *Harbour Light of the Windwards* (Christian station) and *Voice of Grenada* (private FM station, with music and news).

Passport/Visa

	Passport Required?	Visa Required?	Return Ticket Required?
Full British	Yes	No	Yes
Australian	Yes	No	Yes
Canadian	Yes	No	Yes
USA	Yes	No	Yes
Other EU	Yes	No	Yes
Japanese	Yes	No	Yes

Note: *Regulations and requirements may be subject to change at short notice, and you are advised to contact the appropriate diplomatic or consular authority before finalising travel arrangements. Any numbers in the chart refer to the footnotes below.*

PASSPORTS: Passport valid for six months from date of departure from Grenada required by all.

VISAS: Required by all except the following:
(a) nationals of countries shown in the chart above including Australian External Territories, French Overseas

Dependencies and Netherlands Associated Territories;
(b) nationals of Commonwealth countries, British Dependent Territories and New Zealand Associated and Dependent Territories;
(c) nationals of Argentina, Bulgaria, Chile, China (PR), CIS countries, Korea (Rep), Iceland, Israel, Liechtenstein, Norway, Romania, Taiwan (China) and Venezuela.

Note: Visitors may be required to deposit an amount equal to the fare of their return passage.

Types of visa and cost: *Visitor:* £35, in local currency only.

Validity: Up to three months.

Application to: Consulate (or consular section at Embassy or High Commission) well in advance of intended day of departure; see *Passport/Visa Information* for details.

Application requirements: (a) Valid passport. (b) Completed application form. (c) Two passport-size photos. (d) Return or onward ticket. (e) Fee payable by cash or postal order (to include additional £4 fee to cover postage if required, no foreign currency is accepted). (f) For postal applications, a recorded delivery envelope. (g) Confirmation of hotel reservation. (h) For Business visits, letter from contact in Grenada.

Working days required: Three to four working days.

PASSPORT/VISA INFORMATION

Grenada High Commission in the UK
5 Chandos Street, London W1G 9DG, UK
Tel: (020) 7631 4277.
Opening hours: Mon-Fri 0900-1700; 1000-1400 (consular section).

Embassy of Grenada in the USA
1701 New Hampshire Avenue, NW, Washington, DC 20009, USA
Tel: (202) 265 2561.
Website: www.grenadaconsulate.org *or* www.grenadaembassyusa.org

---

Money

Currency: East Caribbean Dollar (XCD; symbol EC$) = 100 cents. Notes are in denominations of EC$100, 50, 20, 10 and 5. Coins are in denominations of EC$1, and 50, 25, 10, 5, 2 and 1 cents.

Note: The East Caribbean Dollar is tied to the US Dollar.

Note: The East Caribbean Dollar is tied to the US Dollar.

Currency exchange: Barclays Bank, Grenada Bank of Commerce, Grenada Co-operative Bank, National Commercial Bank and Scotia Bank are all found on the island. It is advised to exchange currency at banks to obtain the most favourable exchange rates.

Credit & debit cards: American Express, Diners Club, MasterCard and Visa and other major cards are accepted by most shops, car hire companies and hotels. Check with your credit or debit card company for details of merchant acceptability and other services which may be available. ATMs are available.

Traveller's cheques: Widely accepted. To avoid additional exchange rate charges, travellers are advised to take traveller's cheques in US Dollars.

Currency restrictions: There are no restrictions on the import or export of reasonable quantities of local or foreign currency.

Banking hours: Mon-Thurs 0800-1500, Fri 0800-1700.

Exchange rate indicators:
Rate at time of publishing:
£1.00=   EC$4.69
$1.00=   EC$2.66

Duty Free

The following goods may be imported into Grenada without incurring customs duty:
200 cigarettes or 50 cigars or 250g of tobacco; 1l of wine or spirits.

Prohibited items: Narcotics; arms and ammunition; fruit, vegetables, meat and soil.

Note: Licensed firearms must be declared. A local licence can be obtained from the police.

Public Holidays

Below are listed Public Holidays for period January 2006-June 2007 period.

2006: Jan 1 New Year's Day. **Feb 7** Independence Day. **Apr 14** Good Friday. **Apr 17** Easter Monday. **May 1** Labour Day. **Jun 5** Whit Monday. **Jun 15** Corpus Christi. **Aug 7** Emancipation Day. **Aug 14-15** Carnival. **Oct 25** Thanksgiving Day. **Dec 25-26** Christmas.

2007: Jan 1 New Year's Day. **Feb 7** Independence Day. **Apr 6** Good Friday. **Apr 9** Easter Monday. **May 1** Labour Day. **May 28** Whit Monday. **Jun 7** Corpus Christi.

Credit: ©Grenada Board of Tourism

Health

	Special Precautions?	Certificate Required?
Yellow Fever	No	1
Cholera	No	No
Typhoid & Polio	No	N/A
Malaria	No	N/A

Note: *Regulations and requirements may be subject to change at short notice, and you are advised to contact your doctor well in advance of your intended date of departure. Any numbers in the chart refer to the footnotes below.*

1: A *yellow fever* vaccination certificate is required from all travellers over one year of age coming from infected areas.

Food & drink: Mains water is normally chlorinated and relatively safe, but there is still some risk of diarrhoea, particularly in rural areas. Bottled water is available. Milk is pasteurised and dairy products are safe for consumption. Local meat, poultry, seafood, fruit and vegetables are generally considered safe to eat.

Other risks: Immunisation against *hepatitis A, B* and *diphtheria* is sometimes recommended.

The *Dengue* mosquito is found throughout Grenada. There is a high prevalence of *HIV/AIDS* virus.

Rabies is present. For those at high risk, vaccination before arrival should be considered. If you are bitten, seek medical advice without delay. See the *Health* appendix for further details.

Health care: There is a general hospital in St George's and small hospitals in Mirabeau and Carriacou. Health insurance is strongly recommended.

Travel - International

AIR:

The main airlines serving Grenada are *British Airways (BA)*, which offers a direct flight from London twice weekly; *Virgin Atlantic* (website: www.virgin-atlantic.com), which flies direct from London once a week; *Excel Airways* (website: www.xl.com), which flies once a week from London; *BWIA International* (website: www.bwee.com), which offers daily flights from London, Toronto, New York and Miami to Trinidad with connections to Grenada; and *Air Jamaica* (website: www.airjamaica.com), *American Airlines* (website: www.aa.com), *Caribbean Star* (website: www.flycaribbeanstar.com), *LIAT* (website: www.liatairline.com), *SVG Air* (website: www.svgair.com) and *US Airways* (website: www.usairways.com), which offer connections with Grenada from other Caribbean islands.

Approximate flight times: From Grenada to *London* is 10 hours, to *Los Angeles* is 11 hours and to *New York* is seven hours (including stopovers).

Main airports: *Grenada International Airport* (*Point Salines*) (*GND*) is 11km (8 miles) south of St George's. *To/from the airport:* Taxis are available. *Facilities:* Duty free shops, bureaux de change, car hire, book shop, bar, cafe, restaurants, tourist information and VIP lounge.

Departure tax: EC$50 per adult, payable in cash (local currency only). EC$25 for children five to 12 years of age. Children under five are exempt.

SEA:

Main ports: St George's, considered the most picturesque port in the Caribbean, is a port of call for many cruise lines, including *Costa* and *Cunard*. *Geest Line* (website: www.geestline.co.uk) sails from the UK via Martinique, Antigua, St Lucia and Barbados. Around 70 per cent of tourist arrivals are cruise-ship passengers. *To/from the port:* There is a daily shuttle boat service to Carriacou and Petite Martinique; boats can be hired for access to Isle de Ronde. Check at a local tourist office for times and fares.

Travel - Internal

AIR:

Lauriston Airport (CRU) in Carriacou is serviced daily by the main regional carrier *SVG Air* (website: www.svgairlines.com). Flights are from Grenada and St Vincent. The airport accommodates light aircraft only. *To/from the airport:* There are no buses available, taxis can be called. *Facilities:* Washroom and waiting room only.

SEA:

Main ports: Water-taxis are available from *St George's* across the Carenage to the Esplanade or Grand Anse Beach. There is a ferry service from the *Carenage*, Grenada to *Carriacou*, which runs there every day except Monday and back every day except Tuesday. There is also a daily ferry service from Grenada to Carriacou, *Petite Martinique* and back. A large number of yachts and boats are available to charter. Arrangements can be made via the Grenada Board of Tourism (see *Top Things To Do*).

Credit: ©Grenada Board of Tourism

ROAD:

There is a network of approximately 1046km (650 miles) of paved roads. Most main roads are in good condition but they are narrow and winding. Traffic drives on the left. **Bus:** These are cheap but slow. The main bus terminal is located at the west end of Granby Street. Buses run on Grenada to Annadale, Concorde, Grand Anse, Grand Etang, Grenville, Gouyave, La Sagesse, Sauters, Victoria and Westernhall. On Carriacou, buses run from Hillsborough to Harvey Vale and Windward. Minibuses run between Hillsborough, Windward and Tyrell Bay. **Taxi:** Taxis are the most efficient means of transport. They are available from the airport, the Carenage and most hotels. *Mandoo's Taxi Service* is a fully insured sightseeing and taxi service, recommended by the Board of Tourism (website: www.grenadatours.com). **Car hire:** A large range of vehicles are available in St George's, Grande Anse or St Andrew's. Credit cards are not always accepted by car hire companies. To hire a vehicle, drivers must be over the age of 25. Some rental firms have a minimum rental period of three days during peak periods. **Documentation:** A temporary licence to drive is available from the traffic department at the central police station on Carenage or from most car hire companies, on presentation of a valid driving licence. The cost is approximately EC$30. An International Driving Permit is recommended, although it is not legally required.

Travel times: The following chart gives approximate travel times (in hours and minutes) from **St George's** to other towns/islands in Grenada.

	Air	Road	Sea
Grenville	-	0.35	-
Carriacou	0.20	-	1.30

Travel Advice

Most visits to Grenada are trouble-free but you should be aware of the global risk of indiscriminate international terrorist attacks, which could be against civilian targets, including places frequented by foreigners.

Hurricane Emily caused some damage on 14 July 2005, particularly in the northern half of Grenada and more extensive damage on the islands of Carriacou and Petite Martinique. Despite the damage in the north and the islands, the situation in Grenada has returned to normal and tourist facilities are functioning. The airport on Grenada is operating normally.

This advice is based on information provided by the Foreign and Commonwealth Office in the UK. It is correct at time of publishing. As the situation can change rapidly, visitors are advised to contact the following organisations for the latest travel advice:

British Foreign and Commonwealth Office
Tel: (0845) 850 2829.
Website: www.fco.gov.uk

US Department of State
Website: http://travel.state.gov/travel

Accommodation

HOTELS:

Grenada offers a variety of modern, luxurious hotels. Pre-booking is essential. An 8 per cent Government tax is added to all hotel and restaurant bills, and a 10 per cent service charge is added to the bill by many hotels and restaurants. Contact the Board of Tourism for details and exact price listings (see *Top Things To Do*).

GUEST HOUSES:

There are several guest houses, some of which offer self-catering facilities.

SELF-CATERING:

There are a growing number of apartments and villas available for hire. Contact the Grenada Board of Tourism for details (see *Top Things To Do*).

Credit: ©Grenada Board of Tourism

A B C D E F G H I J K L M N O P Q R S T U V W X Y Z

Grenada

Credit: ©Grenada Board of Tourism

CAMPING:
Camping is not permitted because there are no proper camping facilities. However, it is possible to camp in certain places but only with the prior permission of the landowner.

LUXURY RESORTS:
There are many high-quality luxury resorts on the islands that offer wedding packages and will make all the necessary legal arrangements. These resorts offer excellent facilities for weddings, watersports, dining and excursions.

ACCOMMODATION INFORMATION

Grenada Hotel Association
Ocean House Buildings, Po Box 440, Grande Anse, St George's, Grenada
Tel: 444 1353.
Website: www.grenadahotelsinfo.com

Top Things To See

- Since Grenada is widely known as the '**spice** island', you would do well to visit the **Gouyave Nutmeg Processing Station**, the largest nutmeg processing factory on the Island, where spices are sorted, dried and milled, hidden among the red roofs of **Gouyave**. The **Dougaldston Estate** is a traditional plantation in the centre of the nutmeg- and cocoa-growing region. Most of the traditional spice factories offer tours of the grounds.
- From the rock of **Le Morne des Sauteurs**, the last of the island's Carib Indians plummeted to their deaths in 1650. The **Carriacou Museum** in **Hillsborough** has an impressive collection of Amerindian artefacts and mementoes dating back to occupation by the French and British.
- See the **River Sallee boiling springs** in the north east of the island, of spiritual importance to the local residents. Throw a coin into the fountain and make a wish.
- Many **national parks** have been developed in the last decade and a half, and the protection of both rain forest and coral reefs continues to be a high priority. The **Oyster beds** can be reached by a trail from **Tyrrel Bay**, followed by a short boat ride to the middle of one of the most pristine ecosystems in the region. **La Sagesse Nature Reserve**, located in the south, is a protected bird sanctuary with several rivers, mangroves and salt lakes.
- Before you leave, you must witness **hashing**. Hashing takes place every Saturday and involves participants running around the island following a trail of flour; it is followed by drinking lots of locally made rum.
- Participate in the colourful splendour and riotous joy of Grenada's annual **carnival** in August, involving lively street parties, street theatre, steel bands and calypso competitions.

Top Things To Do

- Luxuriate on the southwest coast on one of the island's best **beaches** at **Grande Anse**; another is at **Levera Bay** near the island's northern tip. The beaches on neighbouring **Morne Rouge** are stunning, as are the deserted beaches on the southern coast. Levera Bay is also a favourite **surfing** spot.

Credit: ©Grenada Board of Tourism

- Grenada is filled with dramatic **volcanic scenery** that is worth your while exploring. **Hikes** range from easy 15-minute jaunts to rigorous expeditions of several hours. The road to the park passes by the northwestern edge of the extinct volcano, **Mount Sinai** (703m/2306ft), which cradles its beautiful 30 acre- (12 hectare-) crater lake, the **Grand Etang**. The **Grand Etang National Park and Forest Reserve** contains numerous marked trails. The park contains a wealth of interesting flora and fauna, and there are spectacular flower displays depending on the season. Another volcanic crater lake, **Lake Antoine**, is located in the **Levara National Park**, a well-known destination for **bird watching**.
- There are several waterfalls in Grenada, the most spectacular of which are the **Annandale Falls**, a 15m- (50ft-) cascade that flows into a mountain stream, and the **Mount Carmel Waterfall**, the island's highest waterfall, which has two falls cascading over 21m (70ft) to clear pools below. Apart from in the sea, **swimming** is also possible at several of the islands' rainforest pools and lakes, many of which are formed by waterfalls, such as the **Concord Falls**.
- Stroll around the **Carenage**, a picturesque inner **harbour** with 18th-century warehouses and restaurants, and **Fort George** (built by the French in 1705) - both are worth a visit. See also the outer harbour, **St Andrew's Presbyterian Church** and **Fort Frederick**. Harbours are important here, since Grenada is considered a yachtsman's paradise. A number of major **yacht** races and regattas are held throughout the year, notably the **January Sailing Festival** (lasting five days) and the sailing regatta in **Tyrell Bay** on **Carriacou**. Particularly popular **sailing** destinations in the area include the **Grenadine islands**, **Sugar Loaf**, **Green Island** and **Sandy Island**. A variety of small and large craft may be hired. Contact the Grenada Board of Tourism for details. Visitors can also make **boat trips** on traditional wooden *schooners*, which is a popular way to cross the 5km- (3-mile) distance between the islands of Carriacou and Petit Martinique.
- **Rum** continues to be made on the Islands in the traditional way. The main rum distilleries have guided tours. At the **Grenada Sugar Factory** visitors can purchase its rum products and enjoy a guided tour of the site.
- **White Island Marine Park** is ideal for picnics and is the first call for excellent snorkelling. **Diving** and **snorkelling** can be practised widely, with the **Grande Anse** beach being the starting point for many diving trips to the nearby reefs and islands. Many of the resorts organise diving excursions to the best sites. Most dive sites are easily accessible from the coast. Some of the best are **Molinière Reef**, located approximately 5km (3 miles) from St George's; **Martin's Bay**, close to Grand Anse, also a popular snorkelling spot; and **Channel Reef**. The neighbouring island of Carriacou, part of the Grenadines, is known as the 'island of coral reefs' and offers ideal diving conditions, with a rich marine life. The islands' waters are the sites of many wrecks; the **Bianca C** is the largest wreck in the Caribbean.

TOURIST INFORMATION

Grenada Board of Tourism in the UK
c/o Representation Plus, 11 Blades Court,
121 Deodar Road, London SW15 2NU, UK
Tel: (020) 8877 4516.
Website: www.grenadagrenadines.com

Caribbean Tourism Organisation in the UK
22 The Quadrant, Richmond, Surrey TW9 1BP, UK
Tel: (020) 8948 0057.
Website: www.doitcaribbean.com *or* www.onecaribbean.org

Grenada Board of Tourism in the USA
PO Box 1668, Lake Worth, FL 33460, USA
Tel: (561) 588 8176.
Website: www.grenadagrenadines.com

Entertainment

FOOD & DRINK: Most hotels and restaurants offer international cuisine, serving a large variety of tropical fish and English, Continental, American and exotic West Indian food. Bars are stocked with the most popular wines and spirits, including various brands of whisky, rum and brandy.

National specialities:
- Seafood, such as crabs and *lambi* (conches).
- *Calaloo* (a leafy vegetable similar to spinach) soup.
- *Oildown* is the national dish consisting of stew made with salted meat, breadfruit, onion, celery, carrot, *daheen* (a root vegetable grown locally) and dumplings all slowly steamed in coconut milk until the liquid is absorbed.
- Nutmeg ice cream.

National drinks:
- Rum is made locally using traditional methods.
- The local beer, *Carib*, is excellent.
- Local fruit juices and nectars.

Tipping: A 10 per cent service charge is added by most hotels and restaurants. If no charge is added, it is customary to leave a 10 per cent tip. There is also an 8 per cent Government tax to pay at hotels and restaurants.
NIGHTLIFE: Home to the vibrant calypso and reggae music, Grenada offers a good mix of local and international restaurants and bars. Many resorts provide night-time entertainment, such as discos, organised shows and cabarets. The Reno Cinema has recently been refurbished and hosts many multi-cultural events as well as showing films. The Grenadian Jazz Society holds concerts several times a year in a number of hotels.
SHOPPING: Special purchases include leather crafts, jewellery, spices, straw goods and *batik* (printed cotton and other fabrics). There are a number of duty free shops selling quality goods from all over the world. A craft and spice market has now opened close to the Grand Anse Beach with scores of vendors offering various goods and services.
Shopping hours: Mon-Fri 0800-1600, Sat 0800-1300. Supermarkets are usually open Mon-Sat 0900-1900. Craft and souvenir shops will open Sundays and bank holidays especially if cruise ships are in port.

Business

- **GDP:** US$439 million (2003 estimate).
- **Main exports:** Nutmeg, bananas, cocoa, fruit and vegetables, clothing and mace.
- **Main imports:** Food, manufactured goods, machinery, chemicals and fuel.
- **Main trade partners:** Trinidad & Tobago, USA, St Lucia, Antigua & Barbuda, The Netherlands, St Kitts & Nevis, Dominica, Germany, UK and France.

ECONOMY: The main sources of employment are agriculture, construction and tourism. Grenada's agricultural economy is centred on the production of spices; however, the importance of agriculture has been reduced over the last decade with natural disasters, declining international prices and disease affecting the sector. There are extensive timber reserves but exploitation is being strictly controlled to prevent deforestation. The fishing industry has grown in recent years and now generates one-sixth of export earnings. There are thought to be some oil and gas deposits off the southern coast of Grenada, and attempts to locate them continue. Industry is confined to production of nutmeg oil and rum, as well as drinks, paint and paper. Tourism (particularly stopover and cruise-ship visitors) has developed gradually since the mid-1980s but the industry is now the island's leading foreign exchange earner. This has, to some extent, eased the depressed condition of the economy which has suffered from the general low level of world commodity prices during the last 10 years or so. Hurricane Ivan in September 2004 badly damaged the tourist infrastructure. Although cruise ships have returned to Grenada and many hotels have reopened it will take some time for the industry to fully recover. Grenada has also developed a sizeable financial services industry in recent years, but has fallen foul of global efforts to tighten regulation.
The other main source of income for the island has been remittances from the estimated 100,000 Grenadians working abroad, mainly in the USA, Canada and Europe. Grenada also relies on foreign aid from the USA, the UK, Canada and the EU. This has declined in recent years and the Government has been looking elsewhere (including Libya) for financial support. Grenada is a member of the Caribbean trade bloc, CARICOM (website: www.caricom.org), and the Organisation of East Caribbean States (website: www.oecs.org).
BUSINESS ETIQUETTE: All correspondence and trade literature is in English. **Office hours:** Mon-Thurs 0800-1500; Fri 0800-1700. Government offices are generally open Mon-Fri 0800-1600 but are closed 1200-1300 for lunch.

COMMERCIAL INFORMATION

Grenada Chamber of Industry and Commerce
PO Box 129, Decaul Building, Mount Gay, St George's, Grenada
Tel: 440 2937 *or* 440 8858.
Website: www.spiceisle.com

Eight hotels offer meeting facilities, seating from 25 to 300 persons. For details, contact Grenada Board of Tourism (see *Top Things To Do*).

A B C D E F G H I J K L M N O P Q R S T U V W X Y Z

326

World Travel Guide 2006-2007

Guadeloupe

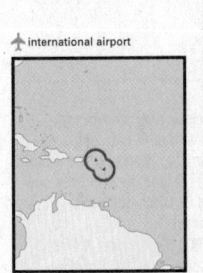

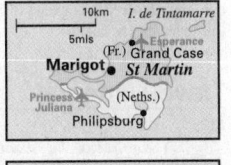

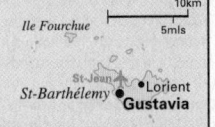

+ international airport

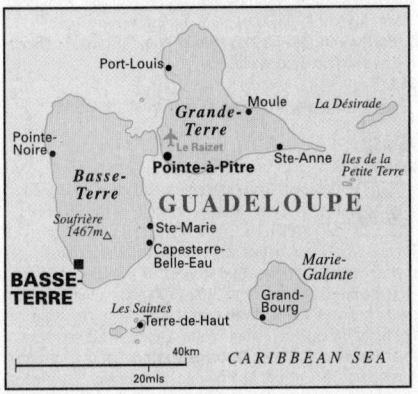

Location: Caribbean, at the arc of the Leeward group of islands of the Lesser Antilles.

Time: GMT - 4.

Guadeloupe is an Overseas Department of the Republic of France, and is represented abroad by French Embassies – see *France* section.

Overview

Guadeloupe was among the islands charted by Columbus in 1493. French colonies were established in 1635. The British made brief attempts to occupy the islands during the 18th and 19th centuries, but they have always remained under French control and, in 1946, the islands were given the status of Overseas Departments. Following President Mitterand's decentralisation policy in the 1980s, Guadeloupe became an administrative region in its own right and is represented in the French National Assembly by four Deputies.

Guadeloupe still retains that enchanting mixture of French and Creole influence, apparent even down to the mix of flavours and ingredients in its cuisine. This Caribbean paradise comprises Basse-Terre, Grande-Terre and five smaller islands, all of which vary quite substantially in scenery. Those considering Guadeloupe to merely possess a few pretty beaches may be surprised to learn that it also boats a wildlife-infested rainforest and the highest waterfall in the Caribbean. Basse-Terre has a rough volcanic relief whilst Grande Terre features rolling hills and flat plains. There are also many lush mountainous areas with stunning and unspoiled tropical scenery. The beautiful beaches vary too, from the white palm-fringed to the volcanic-created black sand.

As might be deemed more typical of the Caribbean, Guadeloupe boasts plenty of restaurants, bars and discos, with displays of local dancing and music. The famous dance of the island is called the *Biguine*, where colourful and ornate Creole costumes are still worn. Biguine is a form of clarinet and trombone music with nasal vocals and improvised instrumental solos, and roots in West African dance. It has long since evolved into embracing more wide-reaching genres such as jazz and pop. If you do not feel your toes tapping, then rest

assured that one or two of Guadeloupe's renowned rum punch cocktails (a brew of rum, lime, bitter and syrup) will almost certainly get you up and dancing beneath the stars. Yet Guadeloupe is a fantastic destination because there is also extreme quietude available, from St Barthélemy to the outlying islands of Marie-Galante, La Désirade and Les Saintes, undeveloped and attractive, with old and crumbling mills frequent reminders of Guadeloupe's historical connections as a major sugar plantation. Sometimes all you need is some twinkling clear waters to snorkel or dive in, exploring colourful flora and fauna, in what the famous diver Jacques Cousteau considered amongst the top 10 dive sites in the world.

General Information

AREA: Total: 1621 sq km (628 sq miles). **Basse-Terre:** 839 sq km (324 sq miles). **Grand-Terre:** 564 sq km (218 sq miles). **Marie-Galante:** 150 sq km (58 sq miles). **La Désirade:** 29.7 sq km (11.5 sq miles). **Les Saintes:** 13.9 sq km (5.4 sq miles). **St-Barthélemy:** 13 sq km (8 sq miles). **St-Martin** (which shares the island with St Maarten, part of the Netherlands Antilles): 86 sq km (33 sq miles) (the French side: 52 sq km (20 sq miles); the Dutch side: 34 sq km (13 sq miles)).

POPULATION: 448,713 (official estimate 2005).

POPULATION DENSITY: 247.8 per sq km.

CAPITAL: Basse-Terre (administrative). **Population:** 12,410 (1999). Pointe-à-Pitre, on Grande-Terre (commercial centre). **Population:** 20,948 (1999).

GEOGRAPHY: Guadeloupe comprises Guadeloupe proper (Basse-Terre), Grande-Terre (separated from Basse-Terre by a narrow sea channel) and five smaller islands. Basse-Terre has a rough volcanic relief whilst Grande Terre features rolling hills and flat plains. All the islands have beautiful white- or black-sand palm-fringed beaches. There are also many lush mountainous areas with stunning and unspoiled tropical scenery.

GOVERNMENT: Guadeloupe is an Overseas Department of France and as such is an integral part of the French Republic. **Head of State:** President Jacques Chirac since 1995, represented locally by Prefect Paul Girot de Langlade since 2004. **Head of Government:** President of the General Council Jacques Gillot since 2001. **Recent history:** Guadeloupe's political life has been characterised by apathy and disillusionment among the electorate. Since the 1990s, elections have barely attracted more than 15 per cent of the population. All four major parties maintain branches on Guadeloupe, although the Socialist party is split between official and dissident factions and the fierce enmity between them allowed the right to take control of the Regional Council in 1992: since 1992 this has been run by Lucette Michaux-Chévry, who is also a deputy in the French National Assembly. The most recent poll for the General Council, held in March 2004, returned Jacques Gillot as President of the Council.

The Government Commissioner on Guadeloupe represents France, and the islands send four representatives to the National Assembly in Paris. There is a 42-member General Council and a 41-member Regional Council which have local legislative and executive powers on the islands and are directly elected for a maximum of six years.

LANGUAGE: The official language is French. The *lingua franca* is Creole. English is spoken by professionals and those in the tourism industry.

RELIGION: The majority are Roman Catholic, with a minority of predominantly Evangelical Protestant groups.

ELECTRICITY: 220 volts AC, 50Hz.

SOCIAL CONVENTIONS: The atmosphere is relaxed and informal. Casual dress is accepted everywhere, but formal dress is needed for dining out and in nightclubs.

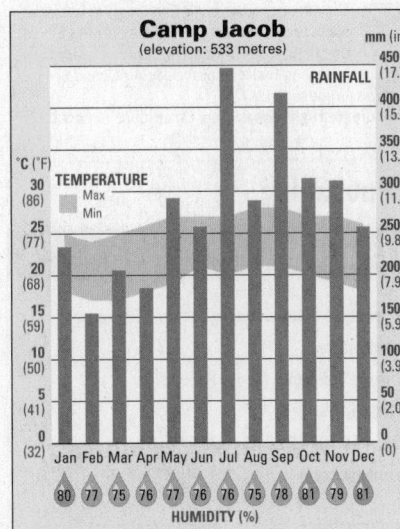

Camp Jacob
(elevation: 533 metres)

Climate

Warm weather throughout the year with the main rainy season occurring from June to October. Showers can, however, occur at any time although they are usually brief. The humidity can be exceedingly high at times. **Required clothing:** Lightweights with warmer top layers for the evenings; showerproofs are advisable.

Communications

Telephone: Country code: 590. Good internal network. There are no area codes. Phonecards (*télécartes*) are necessary to make calls from public telephones. **Mobile telephone:** Roaming agreements exist with some international mobile phone companies. Analogue networks are compatible with most US handsets, which can be activated on the island by dialling 0 or by registering online. Coverage is generally good. **Internet:** Available in Internet cafes at Saint-Francois, Sainte Anne, Mare-Gaillard and Pointe-a-Pitre; there are also terminals in some larger post offices and public buildings.

Post: Airmail takes about one week to reach Europe. Postal rates are the same as metropolitan France. **MEDIA: Press:** Newspapers are all in French. The main daily is *France-Antilles. Journal de St Barths* is in French and English.

TV: RFO is the main broadcasting company in Guadeloupe and is a public service.

Radio: *Radio Caraibes International* is the local radio station and is privately operated, as is *NRJ Antilles. RFO*, a public broadcaster, also operates.

Passport/Visa

	Passport Required?	Visa Required?	Return Ticket Required?
Full British	Yes	No	Yes
Australian	Yes	No	Yes
Canadian	Yes	No	Yes
USA	Yes	No	Yes
Other EU	Yes/1	No	Yes
Japanese	Yes	No	Yes

Note: *Regulations and requirements may be subject to change at short notice, and you are advised to contact the appropriate diplomatic or consular authority before finalising travel arrangements. Any numbers in the chart refer to the footnotes below.*

PASSPORTS: Passport valid for at least three months beyond applicant's last day of stay required by all except the following:
1. nationals of Belgium, France, Germany, Greece, Italy, Luxembourg, Monaco, The Netherlands, Portugal, Spain and Switzerland, who are holders of national identity cards.

VISAS: Required by all except the following:
(a) nationals of countries referred to in the chart above for stays of up to three months;
(b) nationals of Andorra, Argentina, Bolivia, Brunei, Bulgaria, Chile, Costa Rica, Croatia, El Salvador, Guatemala, Honduras, Hong Kong (SAR), Iceland, Korea (Rep), Liechtenstein, Macau (SAR), Malaysia, Mexico, Monaco, New Zealand, Nicaragua, Norway, Panama, Paraguay, San Marino, Singapore, Switzerland, Uruguay, Vatican City and Venezuela for stays of up to three months;
(c) transit passengers continuing their journey by the same or first connecting aircraft provided holding valid onward or return documentation and not leaving the airport.

Note: (a) Nationals of the EU and EEA, and of the Holy See, Liechtenstein and Monaco do not need a a Long Stay visa (trips exceeding three months). (b) Nationals of Canada, Cyprus, Japan, Korea (Rep), Malaysia, Malta, Mexico, Singapore, USA and Venezuela should apply for a visa if they are to receive a salary, even if their trip is a Short Stay. (c) US nationals need a visa if they are crew members, or journalists on assignments, or students enrolled at schools and universities in any of the French Overseas Departments.

Types of visa and cost: All visas, regardless of duration of stay and number of entries permitted, cost €35. In most circumstances, no fee applies to students, recipients of government fellowships and citizens of the EU and their family members.

Validity: *Short-stay* visas (up to 30 days): valid for two months (single- and multiple-entry). *Short stay* visas (31 to 90 days and double- or multiple-entry): valid for a maximum of six months from date of issue. *Transit* visas: valid for single- or multiple-entries of maximum five days per entry, including the day of arrival.

Application to: French Consulate General (for personal visas), or Consular section at Embassy (for diplomatic or service visas); see *Passport/Visa Information* for *France*. All applications must be made in person.

Application requirements: (a) Valid passport with blank page to affix the visa. Minors travelling alone must submit notarised parental authorisation, signed by both parents, plus one copy. (b) Up to two completed application forms. (c) One passport-size photo on each form. (d) Fee, to be paid in cash only if paying by person. If not, fee should be paid by cheque or postal order. (e) Evidence of sufficient funds for stay (two last bank statements, plus copy, or other proof of funds equivalent to US$100 for each day of trip). (f) Letter from employer, or proof of stay in country of residence. (g) Proof of address. (h) Medical insurance. (i) Return ticket and travel documents for remaining journey. (j) Proof of accommodation during stay. (k) Registered self-addressed envelope, if applying by post. (l) Detailed itinerary, including reservations and round trip airline tickets (only required when visa is issued), plus one copy. (m) Proof of employment (eg last payslip or letter from employer). (n) Proof of valid health/travel insurance with worldwide coverage, plus copy. *Business:* (a)-(n) and, (o) Business invitation guaranteeing payment of travel expenses, plus one copy.

Working days required: One day to three weeks depending on nationality.

Temporary residence: If intending to work or stay for longer than 90 days, nationals should contact the Long Stay visa section of the Consulate General or Embassy (tel: (020) 7073 1248).

PASSPORT/VISA INFORMATION

French Consulate General in the UK
12 Cromwell Road, London SW7 2EN, UK
Visa section: 6A Cromwell Place, London SW7 2EW, UK
Tel: (020) 7073 1200 (Consular section) *or* 1250 (visa section) *or* (09065) 508 940 (visa information service; calls cost £1 per minute) *or* (09065) 266 654 (24-hour visa application form request service; calls cost £1.50 per minute) *or* (09065) 540 700 (24-hour automated visa appointment booking service).
Website: www.ambafrance-uk.org *or* www.consulfrance-londres.org
Consulate General also in: Edinburgh.
Opening hours: Mon-Wed 0845-1500, Thurs and Fri 0845-1200 (general enquiries); Mon-Thurs 0845-1200, Fri 0845-1130 (visa applications).

Money

Currency: Since January 2002 the Euro has been the official currency for the French Overseas Departments, French Guiana, Guadeloupe, Martinique and Réunion. For further details, exchange rates and currency restrictions, see *France* section.

Currency exchange: All banks and most hotels will change traveller's cheques and foreign currency. All the major French banks are represented on the island. ATMs are available in every town.

Credit & debit cards: American Express, Diners Club, MasterCard and Visa are accepted. Check with your credit or debit card company for details of merchant acceptability and other services which may be available.

Traveller's cheques: Accepted in most places. Their use may qualify visitors for discounts on luxury items. To avoid additional exchange rate charges, travellers are advised to take traveller's cheques in Euros. US and Canadian Dollar cheques are also accepted in some places.

Banking hours: Mon-Fri 0800-1200 and 1400-1600, some are open on a Saturday 0800-1300 (closed Wednesday afternoons).

Duty Free

Guadeloupe is an Overseas Department of France, and the duty free allowances are the same as for France.

Note: Plants and vegetables of any sort are prohibited, as are animals and food of animal origin from Haiti.

Public Holidays

Below are listed Public Holidays for the January 2006-June 2007 period.

2006: Jan 1 New Year's Day. **Jan 6** Epiphany. **Apr 17** Easter Monday. **May 1** Labour Day. **May 8** Victory Day. **May 25** Ascension. **Jun 5** Whit Monday. **Jul 14** Bastille Day. **Aug 15** Assumption. **Nov 1** All Saints' Day. **Nov 11** Remembrance Day. **Dec 25** Christmas Day.
2007: Jan 1 New Year's Day. **Jan 6** Epiphany. **Apr 9** Easter Monday. **May 1** Labour Day. **May 8** Victory Day. **May 17** Ascension. **May 28** Whit Monday.

Health

	Special Precautions?	Certificate Required?
Yellow Fever	No	1
Cholera	No	No
Typhoid & Polio	2	N/A
Malaria	No	N/A

Note: *Regulations and requirements may be subject to change at short notice, and you are advised to contact your doctor well in advance of your intended date of departure. Any numbers in the chart refer to the footnotes below.*

1: A yellow fever vaccination certificate is required by travellers over one year of age arriving from an infected or endemic zone within six days.
2: Vaccination against typhoid and polio is recommended.
Food & drink: Mains water is chlorinated and whilst relatively safe, may cause mild abdominal upsets. Bottled water is available and is advised for the first few weeks of stay. Drinking water outside main cities and towns may be contaminated and sterilisation is advised. Milk is pasteurised and dairy products are safe for consumption. Local meat, poultry, seafoods and fruit are generally considered safe to eat.
Other risks: *Bilharzia* (schistosomiasis) is present. Avoid swimming and paddling in fresh water; swimming pools that are well maintained and chlorinated are safe. *Hepatitis A* can occur.
The sap of the manchineel tree is toxic and causes burns to the skin. Travellers should avoid contact with its leaves and fruit, and should not stand under the tree when it is raining. These trees, which look similar to apple trees, are often marked with a red sign on the trunk.
Health care: Health care is of a good standard, but health insurance is advisable to cover costs as the reciprocal health agreement between the UK and France may not apply in Guadeloupe. There is a University Hospital Centre in Pointe à Pitre, on Grande-Terre, and a hospital on Basse-Terre as well as a number of clinics. On St-Martin there are four hospitals and several pharmacies and General Practitioners. St-Barthélemy has one small hospital, but is it possible to buy short-term evacuation medical insurance and be flown to a hospital of your choice.

Travel - International

AIR:

 The national airline is *Air Caraïbes (TX)* (website: www.aircaraibes.com). *Air France* operates at least one flight a day to Pointe-à-Pitre from Paris (ORY). Other airlines serving Guadeloupe include *Air Canada*, *American Airlines* and *LIAT*.

Approximate flight times: From Guadeloupe to *London* is

12 hours 40 minutes (including a stopover time of one hour in Paris), to *Los Angeles* is nine hours and to *New York* is six hours.
Main airports: *Pointe-à-Pitre (PTP) (Le Raizet)* (website: www.guadeloupe.aeroport.fr), 3km (2 miles) from Pointe-à-Pitre. The airport has two international terminals: *Guadeloupe Pôle Caraïbes* and *Le Raizet*. *To/from the airport:* Buses and taxis to the city are available. Car hire is available. *Facilities:* Banks/ bureaux de change, ATM, duty free shops, hairdresser, post office, restaurants/bars and tourist information.
Departure tax: None.

SEA:

 Guadeloupe is a point of call for the following international cruise operators: *Cunard, Holland America, Royal Caribbean, Royal Olympic* and *Princess Cruises*. Many ships ply between Guadeloupe and Martinique, and also connect with Miami and San Juan (Puerto Rico). Ferries and catamarans sail regularly from Pointe-à-Pitre to Dominica, Martinique and St Lucia. *Compagnie Générale Maritime* has weekly 'banana boats' carrying passengers between Guadeloupe and Martinique, Dominica and St Lucia.

Travel - Internal

AIR:

 Air Caraïbe, Air Guadeloupe, Air Martinique, Air St Barth, Air St Martin and *LIAT* connect Guadeloupe with the smaller islands in the group. *Air France* also offers a limited inter-island service. There are domestic airports on the islands of La Désirade, Marie-Galante, St-Barthélemy and St-Martin.
Domestic airports: *St-Martin (SFG) (Espérance)* is 4km (3 miles) from Marigot. The airport is served by *Air Caraïbes*. *To/from the airport:* Buses and taxis are available. *Facilities:* A bar.
St-Barthélemy (SBH) is 2km (1 mile) from Gustavia. *To/from the airport:* Taxis are available.

SEA:

 Regular ferry services ply around the islands.

ROAD:

 The roads in Guadeloupe are of good quality and the Point de la Gabare bridge over the Rivière Salée connects Grande-Terre and Basse-Terre. There is a good public **bus** service which arrives at most towns every 15 minutes. **Taxi** services are available but fares increase by 40 per cent from 2100-0700 and on Sundays and public holidays. **Car** and **van rental** is available. Driving is on the right. Buses depart from Pointe-à-Pitre and Basse-Terre to all towns and villages. **Documentation:** National driving licence is sufficient, but at least one year's driving experience is required. An International Driving Permit is advised.
St-Barthélemy: The only way to see the island is to drive; car rental agencies are available and everywhere can be reached within 20 minutes. Compared to the main islands the roads are of poor quality. There are two petrol stations on the island; both of them are closed on Sundays. St-Barthélemy has two taxi stations, one at the airport and one at the public dock in Gustavia.
St-Martin: There are two tourism buses available on St-Martin provided by *Transco* and *Winston Sightseeing Tours* (for contact details see St-Martin Tourist Information, see *Tourist Information* section). Car hire is also in plentiful supply as are two-wheel rental firms. There are a number of taxi companies.

Travel Advice

Most visits to Guadeloupe are trouble-free but you should be aware of the global risk of indiscriminate international terrorist attacks, which could be against civilian targets, including places frequented by foreigners.
This advice is based on information provided by the Foreign and Commonwealth Office in the UK. It is correct at time of publishing. As the situation can change rapidly, visitors are advised to contact the following organisations for the latest travel advice:

British Foreign and Commonwealth Office
Tel: (0845) 850 2829.
Website: www.fco.gov.uk

US Department of State
Website: http://travel.state.gov/travel

Accommodation

HOTELS:

There is a good selection of hotels on Guadeloupe, ranging from first-class beach resorts to country inns. Visitors can also stay in traditional small hotels known as *Relais Créoles*. Most accommodation is to be found on the south coast of Grande-Terre. Accommodation

---

on the outlying islands can be interesting, but may be very basic. At present there are over 4000 rooms throughout the group. The tax on hotel rates is usually inclusive. A standard charge of US$1.50 per day is levied by many hotels. Additional service charges can range between 15 and 30 per cent depending on the time of year. The Relais de la Guadeloupe provides a central booking service. The grading system is quite complicated: 3- and 4-star hotels offer sporting and cultural activities in addition to board and lodging; there are also two particular categories of hotel, Hibiscus (H) and Alamandas (A) (Hibiscus hotels are 2- or 3-star establishments usually run as a family affair whilst Alamandas hotels are sophisticated 1- or 2-star establishments); and many hotels in the Caribbean offer accommodation according to a plans system, such as FAP (Full American Plan), which is a room with all meals, down to EP (European Plan), which is for a room only.

SELF-CATERING:
Villas and cottages may be rented. It is also possible for visitors to stay in traditional accommodation, known as *gîtes ruraux*, which are small furnished apartments or villas located away from major resorts owned by Guadeloupe hosts.

CAMPING:
There is only one campsite in Guadeloupe at present.

ACCOMMODATION INFORMATION

Office du Tourime in Guadeloupe
5 square de la Banque,
97166 Pointe-à-Pitre, Guadeloupe
Tel: (590) 820 930.
Website: www.lesilesdeguadeloupe.com

St-Barthélemy Office du Tourisme
Quai du Général de Gaulle, Gustavia,
St-Barthélemy, Guadeloupe
Tel: (590) 278 727.
Website: www.st-barths.com

St-Martin Tourist Office
Route Sandy Ground, Marigot,
97150 St-Martin, Guadeloupe
Tel: (590) 875 721.
Website: www.st-martin.org

Top Things To See

- **Pointe-à-Pitre**, the commercial capital of Guadeloupe, is situated on the island of **Grande-Terre**. This gracious town has a pleasant square at its core, the **Place de la Victoire**, which is surrounded by a busy market and, further out, the docks. It is an active, lively port with many narrow streets to explore. The **Pavillion d'Exposition de Bergevin** and the **Centre Cultural Rémy Nainsouta** are two interesting museums in the town. The **Schoelcher Museum**, dedicated to Victor Schoelcher who is accredited for his work in abolishing slavery, is in the capital, also. At **Fort Fleur d'Épée**, there are some fascinating underground caves. The **Guadeloupe Aquarium** is just off the main highway, and to the north of these is the old sugar town of **Sainte-Anne**.
- On Grande-Terre, the **Porte d'Enfer** (**Gate of Hell**) is a jagged piece of coastline with a stunning view. Further on, **La Pointe de la Grande Vigie** also overlooks a spectacular scene of white cliffs by the ocean.
- See the **Sainte-Marie de Capesterre** and the Hindu temple to its south in **Basse-Terre**, where it may be possible to see religious ceremonies taking place.
- On Basse-Terre, visitors must venture into the **National Park of Guadeloupe** near **St-Claude**. This 74,000-acre park, of great natural beauty, is situated at the base of **La Soufrière**, a dormant volcano. In the rainforests there are some good walking and picnic areas which make a pleasant alternative to lying on the islands' fine beaches. Sites of interest include the **Cascade Ecrévisses**, **Parc Bras David**, a **zoo** and some **botanical gardens**.
- Explore the town of **Basse-Terre** itself, a beautiful old French colonial town, situated at the foot of La Soufrière. The **St-Charles Fort** is of French military architecture, built in 1605, and now restored and converted into a museum. The cathedral and market place are also worth seeing. Three monuments of interest in the town are **The Prefecture**, the **General Council** and the **Palace of Justice**.
- Travel westwards on the island of Basse-Terre and discover the tallest waterfalls in the Caribbean: the three **Chutes de Cabet** are an impressive 350ft (107m) tall.
- Wander around the **Domaine de Valombreuse**, near **Petit Bourg** on Basse-Terre, which offers a 6-acre (2.4-hectare) park of over 100 different species of plants and flowers.
- Go to the **beach**! For some quietude, head for any of the 14 stunning white sand beaches on the small island of **St-Barthélemy**, which is formed from steep hills and corresponding steep valleys that are rich in vegetation and flora. The former capital, **Le Moule**, on Grande-Terre also possesses one of Guadeloupe's most beautiful beaches.
- **Marigot** is the French capital of the island of **St-Martin** and is a haven of Creole architecture. **Grand Case** is another small Creole village by the sea with traditional gourmet and arts and crafts. In Marigot, the **Fort Louis** was built in 1765 to protect the town from the English but now has a superb lookout point. It has a bustling **market** selling fruits, vegetables, fishes, spices and arts and crafts.
- Look out from **Paradise Peak**, the highest point on St-Martin (424m/1391 ft), situated halfway between Grand Case and Marigot. Leading to the peak is **Lottery Farm**, which has mountain landscapes and rainforest and is home to thousands of plant species as well as iguanas, humming birds, monkeys and mongoose.
- Not to be missed is the **Butterfly Farm** at **Galion** on St-Martin. In the specially built butterfly sphere there are landscaped gardens, waterfalls, ponds, Japanese fish and beautiful music. Early in the morning it may be possible to see butterflies emerging from their chrysalis and taking their first flight.

Top Things To Do

- Guadeloupe's beaches are good for **swimming**, and the sand varies depending on the area: **Grande-Terre** has white sand, and the sand on the **leeward coast** is brown, while black-sand beaches can be found on the western end of **Basse-Terre**. Nude and topless **sunbathing** is restricted to just a few beaches.
- **Snorkelling** and **diving** can be practised widely, and there are several commercial operators offering equipment hire, courses and diving trips. Snorkellers can usually access **coral reefs** directly from the beaches. Divers should note that harpoons and artificial lights are strictly prohibited. Glass-bottomed boats operate at several marine nature reserves on **Petite-Terre** and Basse-Terre. Marine species such as lobsters and sea turtles are protected, and visitors should familiarise themselves with Guadeloupe's conservation policies upon arrival. The best places to dive or snorkel are around the preserved underwater sanctuary of the **Pigeon Isles** in the crystal-clear **Cousteau Reserve**, which is filled with multicoloured fauna.
- Guadeloupe hosts a number of regional and international **sailing** competitions and there are sailing schools throughout the islands. Pleasure sailing boats do not require a licence.
- The **National Park of Guadeloupe** provides around 300km (188 miles) of marked **trails** leading into the **rainforest**, where visitors can observe many tropical animals and plants. The scenery on these **walks** often includes waterfalls (such as the **Cascade aux Ecrevisses**) or lakes (such as the **Grand Etang**). On Grande-Terre, hiking trails lead through the mangrove or along the cliffs of the Atlantic coast. For further information, contact the Office du Tourisme (see *Tourist Information*).
- Attend **The Festival of Women Cooks** (or the **Fête des Cuisinières**), a culinary nirvana proclaimed as one of Guadeloupe's most spectacular events, and usually held in **Pointe-á-Pitre** in August. The festival features a banquet open to all that lasts for hours, and traditional Creole costume is prevalent. Dancing and parades proceed the event. Belying its dual roots, Creole foods and French foods intermix.
- On Basse-Terre, sample some free Caribbean **rum** at the **Rum Museum**, situated close to **St Rose**.

TOURIST INFORMATION

Office du Tourime in Guadeloupe
5 square de la Banque,
97166 Pointe-à-Pitre, Guadeloupe
Tel: (590) 820 930.
Website: www.lesilesdeguadeloupe.com

St-Barthélemy Office du Tourisme
Quai du Général de Gaulle, Gustavia,
St-Barthélemy, Guadeloupe.
Tel: (590) 278 727.
Website: www.st-barths.com

St-Martin Tourist Office
Route Sandy Ground, Marigot,
97150 St-Martin, Guadeloupe
Tel: (590) 875 721.
Website: www.st-martin.org

Maison de la France (French Government Tourist Office) in the UK
178 Piccadilly, London W1J 9AL, UK
Tel: (09068) 244 123 (information line; calls cost 60p per minute) *or* (020) 7399 3520 (travel trade only).
Website: www.franceguide.com

Caribbean Tourism Organisation
22 The Quadrant, Richmond, Surrey, TW9 1BP, UK
Tel: (020) 8948 0057.

Entertainment

FOOD & DRINK: Predominantly seafood, cooked in French, Creole, African or South-East Asian styles. The spicy flavour of Creole cuisine is unique. Dishes include lobster, turtle, red snapper, conch and sea urchin. The more formal restaurants will require appropriate dress.

Things to know: The legal drinking age is 18 and there are no licensing restrictions.

Island specialities:
- Stuffed crab.
- Stewed conch.
- Roast wild goat.
- Jugged rabbit.
- Broiled dove.

Island drinks:
- *Rum punch* (a brew of rum, lime, bitter and syrup).
- French wines.
- Champagnes.
- Liqueurs.

Tipping: 15 per cent is sometimes included on the bill. 10 per cent is normal.

NIGHTLIFE: There are plenty of restaurants, bars and discos, with displays of local dancing and music. The famous dance of the island is called the *Biguine*, where colourful and ornate Creole costumes are still worn. There are two casinos on Guadeloupe and opening hours are 2100-0300, which are extended on Fridays and Saturdays.

SHOPPING: Worthwhile purchases are French imports, including perfume, wine, liqueurs and Lalique crystal. Local items include fine-flavoured rum, straw goods, handmade lace, bamboo hats, voodoo dolls, and objects of aromatic Vetevier root. Traveller's cheques give a 20 per cent discount in some shops. **Shopping hours:** Mon-Fri 0830-1800, Sat 0830-1300.

Business

- **GDP:** US$3.5 billion (2004 estimate).
- **Main imports:** Foodstuff, fuel, vehicles, consumer goods and construction materials.
- **Main exports:** Bananas, sugar and rum.
- **Main trade partners:** France, Germany, Japan, Martinique, Netherlands Antilles and USA.

ECONOMY: Guadeloupe's economy is relatively diverse by regional standards – with agriculture, light industry and tourism as its main components – but remains heavily dependent on French aid and is vulnerable to the vagaries of the Caribbean climate. Bananas and sugar are the main export commodities, accounting for over one-third of total foreign earnings (although the banana trade is threatened by a World Trade Organization ruling preventing preferential access to European markets). Coffee, cocoa and vanilla are the other important cash crops. Industry is largely devoted to processing agricultural products and light manufactured goods such as boats. Tourism is a key and fast-growing sector; mainly ecotourism and a growing market for cruise ship stopovers. France supplies most of the island's imports and takes three-quarters of its exports.

BUSINESS ETIQUETTE: Lightweight suits, safari suits, and shirt and tie are recommended for business meetings. Best times to visit are January to March and June to September. Much of the island's business is connected to France. **Office hours:** Mon-Fri 0800-1200 and 1400-1800.

COMMERCIAL INFORMATION

Chambre de Commerce et d'Industrie de Pointe-à-Pitre
Rue Félix Eboué, 97159 Pointe-à-Pitre, Guadeloupe
Tel: (590) 937 600.
Website: www.cci-pap.org

Chambre de Commerce
6 Rue Victor Hugues, 97100 Basse-Terre, Guadeloupe
Tel: (590) 994 444.
Website: www.basseterre.cci.fr

Guam

Location: Western Pacific, Micronesia.

Time: GMT + 10

Guam is an External Territory of the United States of America and is represented abroad by US Embassies – see *USA* section.

Overview

Guam is the largest and most southerly island of the Marianas Islands, which were occupied by the Chamorro Indians from 1500 BC. It was claimed by the Spanish in 1565 and ruled by Madrid until the Spanish-American War of 1898. The Spanish Governor was unaware of the war and, when a US frigate entered Hagåtña harbour with guns blazing, he apologised to the captain for not having a reciprocal salute ready. He surrendered the island the next day. US rule was interrupted by the Japanese invasion of 1941, to be reinstated after fierce fighting three years later. The island has been an important US strategic base since then.

Due to the large US Naval presence, the island is cosmopolitan and energetic. Hagåtña, the capital, has many historic buildings dating from the Spanish period. Tumon Bay, just up the coast from Hagåtña, is the main tourist centre.

General Information

AREA: 549 sq km (212 sq miles).
POPULATION: 168,000 (UN, 2005).
POPULATION DENSITY: 306 per sq km.
CAPITAL: Hagåtña. Tamuning is the commercial centre.
Population: 1122 (2000) in Hagåtña and 10,833 in Tamuning.
GEOGRAPHY: Guam is a predominantly hilly island and its northern end is a plateau of rolling hills and cliffs rising 152m (500ft) above sea level. The cliffs are tunnelled with caves. The island narrows in the middle, with the southern half widening into a land of mountains and valleys cut by streams and waterfalls. The most sheltered beaches are on the western coast.
GOVERNMENT: US External Territory (Unincorporated). Gained internal autonomy in 1982. **Head of State:** George W Bush since 2001. **Head of Government:** Governor Felix Camacho since 2003.
LANGUAGE: English and Chamorro are the official languages. Japanese is also spoken - particularly by the older generation who were alive during the Japanese occupation.
RELIGION: Christian; 90 per cent Roman Catholic.
ELECTRICITY: 120 volts AC, 60Hz.
SOCIAL CONVENTIONS: Western customs are well understood – for the visiting Westerner it is quite likely that it will not be the customs of the locals that have to be observed, but those of the visiting Japanese who make up around 90 per cent of the island's tourists. The most evident

Chamorro legacy is the Chamorro language and a range of facial expressions, called 'Eyebrow', which virtually constitutes a language of its own.

Climate

Tropical, with dry and rainy seasons. The hottest months precede the rainy season, which is July to November. The temperature ranges from 26-30°C (75-86°F).
Required clothing: Casual lightweight clothing, with waterproof wear needed for the rainy season.

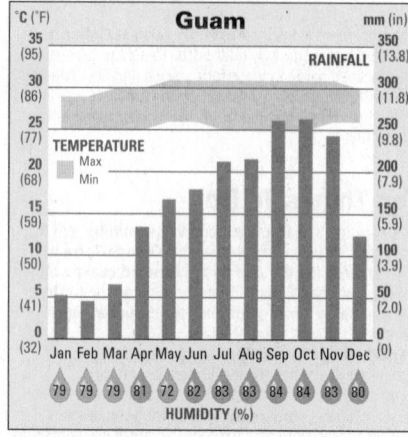

Communications

Telephone: Direct dial overseas telecommunications facilities are available to all overseas points 24 hours a day. Country code: 671.
Mobile telephone: Roaming agreements exist with some international mobile phone companies.
Internet: There are WIFI (wireless) hotspots provided by IT&E situated at the International Airport, Micronesia Mall and some other locations. Internet cafes can be found in the Tumon area.
Post: The main post office hours are Mon-Sat 0800-1500. The Guam Main Facility branch is open Mon-Fri 0930-1700, Sat 1300-1600.
MEDIA: Broadcasting is regulated by the US Federal Communications Commission (FCC).
Press: The English-language daily newspaper is *The Pacific Daily News*.
TV: *Kuam* is a commercial channel.
Radio: *K57* (*KGUM*), commercial; *KPRG*, public.

Passport/Visa

Note: Visa requirements for Guam are the same as for mainland USA; travellers require a visa or, if qualified, may travel visa free under the US Visa Waiver Program. If applying for a visa, application procedures are also the same (see *Passport/Visa* in *US* section). However, there is also a Visa Waiver Program specifically for Guam, the regulations for which are printed in this section.

	Passport Required?	Visa Required?	Return Ticket Required?
Full British	Yes	No/1	Yes
Australian	Yes	No/1	Yes
Canadian	Yes	Yes	Yes
USA	1	No	No
Other EU	Yes	Yes/1	Yes
Japanese	Yes	No/1	Yes

Note: *Regulations and requirements may be subject to change at short notice, and you are advised to contact the appropriate diplomatic or consular authority before finalising travel arrangements. Any numbers in the chart refer to the footnotes below.*

Restricted entry: The following are not eligible to receive a USA entry visa:
(a) people afflicted with certain serious communicable diseases or disorders deemed threatening to the property, safety or welfare of others;
(b) anyone who has been arrested (except for very minor driving offences) or who has a criminal record;
(c) narcotics addicts or abusers and drug traffickers;
(d) anyone who has been deported from or denied admission to the USA.
Note: Those who are ineligible may be eligible for a waiver of ineligibility.
PASSPORTS: Required by all except **1.** US citizens entering Guam from the US mainland or a US territory, provided they hold proof of citizenship and valid photo ID card.
Note: All visitors must now hold a machine-readable passport (MRP).

VISAS: 1. UK, Australian, Japanese and some EU nationals travel visa free for visits or 90 days under the USA Visa waiver Program (see *Passport/Visa US* section).
A US visitor visa is required by all except the following for stays of up to 15 days:
Citizens of Indonesia, Korea (Rep.), Malaysia, Nauru, Papua New Guinea, Solomon Islands, Taiwan*, Vanuatu, or Western Samoa.
* Taiwanese nationals are only visa exempt if in possession of a Taiwanese National ID card and they begin their journey in Taiwan and travel directly to Guam.
Note: The nationals listed above are declared visa-exempt under the Guam Visa Waiver Program on the following conditions: (a) Purpose of visit is for business, touristic or transit purposes only. (b) The air carrier is a participant in the Guam visa waiver programme. (c) All visitors are in possession of a completed and signed visa waiver form, I-736 (obtainable from the airline).
Note: Travellers who enter Guam visa free are not eligible to travel onward to the USA.
Types of visa and cost: *Non-immigrant* (business or tourist): £60. There are several other types of visa; enquire at local US Consulate (or consular section at Embassy); see *Top Things To Do*. Some nationals may also have to pay a reciprocal visa issuance fee – details are available from the State Department (website: www.travel.state.gov).
Validity: Validity varies but visas have a maximum validity of 10 years. The Embassy no longer issues visas "indefinitely".
Application to: US Consulate (or consular section at Embassy). See *Passport/Visa Information* in *USA* section.
Application requirements: (a) Completed visa application form DS-156. (b) Passport valid six months after visit and with at least one blank page. (c) Two passport-size colour photo. (d) Fee, payable by embassy supplied paying in slip only, which must be paid and endorsed at the bank prior to application. (e) Documentation of intent to return to country of residence. Evidence of compelling social and economic ties abroad. (f) Supporting documents (such as purpose of visit), where relevant. (g) Proof of financial status. (h) Self-addressed, special delivery envelope.
Note: (a) Most non-immigrant visa applicants are required to schedule an appointment for a visa interview with a consular officer, and may have to undergo a medical examination, for which there is an additional fee. (b) The six month requirement does not apply to United Kingdom passports. (c) Nationals of Cuba are required to complete two DS-156 application forms and provide two colour passport-size photos. (d) Male applicants aged 16-45 regardless of nationality are required to complete a supplemental DS-157 application form. (e) Nationals of China (PR), Cuba, Iran, Korea (DPR), Libya, Russian Federation, Somalia, Sudan, the Syrian Arab Republic and Vietnam are required to complete one DS-157 application form. Nationals of Korea (DPR), Cuba, Iran, Libya, Syria and Sudan must apply in person. (f) Nationals of Northern Cyprus are also required to provide four colour passport-size photos.
Please note that requirements are subject to change at short notice and any applicant should check with the US Embassy (website: www.usembassy.org.uk).
Working days required: Routine applications can take at least five days after the interview has taken place, but more complex applications can take several months. Applications lodged during the peak travel season may take longer.
Temporary residence: The individual must obtain a work or immigrant visa or be petitioned by a US citizen. Contact the US Consulate (or consular section at Embassy).

Money

Currency: US Dollar (USD; symbol US$) = 100 cents. Notes are in denominations of US$100, 50, 20, 10, 5, 2 and 1. Coins are in denominations of US$1, and 50, 25, 10, 5 and 1 cents. For exchange rates and currency restrictions, see the *USA* section.
Currency exchange: There are numerous US and international banks on the island. ATMs are available at the airport, some hotels, shopping malls and grocery stores. *Cirrus*, *Plus* and *Star* allow international financial transactions.
Credit & debit cards: Most major credit and charge cards are widely accepted on Guam. Check with your credit or debit card company for details of merchant acceptability and other services which may be available.
Traveller's cheques: Traveller's cheques are accepted. To avoid additional exchange rate charges, travellers are advised to take traveller's cheques in US Dollars.
Banking hours: Mon-Thurs 1000-1500, Fri 1000-1800, Sat 0900-1200. Hours may vary slightly.

Duty Free

The following may be imported into Guam without incurring customs duty:
200 cigarettes or 50 cigars or 200g of tobacco (or a combination of the three); three bottles of spirits; a

reasonable amount of perfume for personal use; goods up to the value of US$1000.
Restricted items: Fruit, vegetables, flowers and plants; livestock and meat products; narcotics; items in breach of US copyright law.
Note: Prescription medication should indicate the medicine is used under the doctor's supervision.

Public Holidays

Below are listed the Public Holidays for the January 2006-June 2007 period:
2006: Jan 1 New Year's Day. **Jan 16** Martin Luther King Day. **Feb 13** President's Day. **Mar 6** Guam Discovery Day. **Apr 14** Good Friday. **May 30** Memorial Day. **Jul 4** Independence Day. **Jul 21** Liberation Day. **Sep 21** Labour Day. **Oct 9** Columbus Day. **Nov 2** All Souls' Day. **Nov 11** Veterans Day. **Nov 24** Thanksgiving Day. **Dec 8** Lady of Camarin Day. **Dec 25** Christmas Day. Christmas Day.
2007: Jan 1 New Year's Day. **Jan 15** Martin Luther King Day. **Feb 12** President's Day. **Mar 5** Guam Discovery Day. **Apr 6** Good Friday. **May 28** Memorial Day.

Health

	Special Precautions?	Certificate Required?
Yellow Fever	No	No
Cholera	No	No
Typhoid & Polio	1	N/A
Malaria	No	N/A

Note: Regulations and requirements may be subject to change at short notice, and you are advised to contact your doctor well in advance of your intended date of departure. Any numbers in the chart refer to the footnotes below.

1: *Poliomyelitis* has not been reported for more than six years, although precautions should be taken against typhoid fever.
Food & drink: Mains water is normally chlorinated, and whilst relatively safe may cause mild abdominal upsets. Bottled water is available. Milk is pasteurised and dairy products are safe for consumption. Local meat, poultry, seafood, fruit and vegetables are generally considered safe to eat. There is, however, a risk of biointoxication from raw or cooked fish or shellfish.
Other risks: *Hepatitis B, hepatitis A* and *TB* also occur. *Dengue* fever, *diphtheria* and *Japanese encephalitis* can occur in epidemics. Jellyfish might also pose some threat.
Health care: Health insurance is strongly advised, owing to the high cost of health care. There is one civilian hospital, the Guam Memorial Hospital, and a number of private clinics, as well as some medical facilities run for US military personnel.

Travel - International

AIR:
Virgin Atlantic (website: www.virgin-atlandtic.com) flies regularly to Narita (Tokyo, Japan), where passengers can connect with a *Continental Micronesia* (website: www.continental.com) flight to Guam. Other airlines serving Guam include *Air Japan, All Nippon Airways* (website: www.ana.com), *Korean Air* (website: www.koreanair.com), *Northwest Airlines* (website: www.nwa.com) and *Philippine Airlines* (website: www.philippineairlines.com).
Approximate flight times: From Guam to *London* is 14 hours 30 minutes.
Main airports: *Antonio B Won Pat International Guam Airport (GUM)* (website: www.airport.guam.net) is 11km (7 miles) from the city. *To/from the airport*: Taxis are available, most hotels have courtesy vehicles for airport transfers. *Facilities*: Bureau de change, free hotel telephones, duty free shop, car hire, restaurant, coffee shop and cocktail lounge. The terminal has recently been renovated to improve cargo and passenger facilities and there are plans to add a further runway.
Departure tax: None.
SEA:
Main ports: *Apra Harbour* is the principal port in Micronesia and a port of call for the following shipping lines: *American President* (website: www.apl.com), *Kyowa* (website: www.kyowa-line.co.jp), *Micronesia Transport* and *Maersk Sea-Land Services* (website: www.maersksealand.com).

Travel - Internal

ROAD:
Bus: The *Guam Mass Transit Authority* operates buses on nine routes, connecting nearly all the villages on the island. Buses do not run on Sundays or public holidays. Discount fares are available for under 18's and over 55's. In addition to the Guam mass Transit Authority transportation there is a bus route to select areas including most major shopping centres as well as the hotels in Tumon and Hagåtña. To identify pick up and drop off points look for the bus signs. **Taxi:** Fares are metered. Taxis are available near major shopping centres and at hotels. **Car hire:** Available through most major companies. Hire can be arranged at offices throughout the island including the airport and hotel lobbies. Charges are based on time and mileage plus insurance. Most accept credit cards.
Documentation: An International Driving Permit or a US licence is required.

Travel Advice

Most visits to Guam are trouble-free but you should be aware of the global risk of indiscriminate international terrorist attacks, which could be against civilian targets, including places frequented by foreigners.
This advice is based on information provided by the Foreign and Commonwealth Office in the UK. It is correct at time of publishing. As the situation can change rapidly, visitors are advised to contact the following organisations for the latest travel advice:

British Foreign and Commonwealth Office
Tel: (0845) 850 2829.
Website: www.fco.gov.uk

US Department of State
Website: http://travel.state.gov/travel

Accommodation

HOTELS:
Over the past few years, tourism has been growing rapidly and, to cater for this, numerous hotels have been built offering a good range of facilities to suit most tastes and pockets. Many hotels cater almost exclusively for Japanese tourists. There is now a good range of accommodation on offer. A number of business hotels and family style accommodation are located in Hagåtña, Maite, Tamuning and Mangilao. As the island is small, most of these properties are close to the airport. Tumon bay is the Islands premier resort destination. For more details, contact the Guam Hotel & Restaurant Association, PO Box 8565, Tamuning 96931 (tel: 649 1447; website: www.ghra.org) *or* the Guam Visitors Bureau (see *Top Things To See & Do*).
CAMPING:
Camping is permitted on some beaches and parks; but not all places are suitable so you should seek advice first. Information can be obtained from the Guam Visitors Bureau (see *Top Things To See & Do*).

Top Things To See & Do

- Spain ruled the islands for 333 years and **Hagåtña**, the capital, has many historic buildings dating from this era. Also of interest are the relics of the Chamorro period (a culture which remains alive today, albeit much modified, in about 55,000 persons).
- **Tumon Bay**, just up the coast from **Hagåtña**, is the main tourist centre. There are fine coral reefs around the coast. The interior is mountainous, particularly in the south. There are several spectacular cliffs on the north coast.
- There are three botanical gardens in Guam: the **Inarajan Shore Botanical Garden** by the sea in the southern part of the island; the **Nano Fall Botanical Gardens** in **Agat**, where swimming can be enjoyed in the Nano River under rushing cascades; and the **Pineapple Plantation** in **Yigo**.
- The **South Pacific Memorial Park** in Yigo commemorates those killed in World War II, and the **War in the Pacific National Historical Park** is the location of five World War II battle sites with a museum of war photos and relics. Guam has another small museum with sections dedicated to the Chamorro culture and the Japanese soldier who hid in the interior until 1972, unaware that the war was over. As most tourists to Guam are Japanese, many sites commemorate the war. Other parks include **Latte Park**, located at the bottom of Kasamata Hill; and **Merizo Pier Park**, with recreational facilities for watersports and the location of the annual **Merizo Water Festival**, is a one acre resort surrounded by a clear lagoon and accessible by speedboat. Beach parks include **Talofofo Bay Beach Park**, located at the mouth of the Talofofo River and a surfers' paradise; and **Ipao Beach Park**, once the location of an ancient Chamorro settlement, later a penal and leper colony, and now one of Guam's most popular recreational areas.
- Attractions for **divers** include World War II wrecks, reefs and a variety of marine flora and fauna. A type of dolphin, the spinner dolphin, inhabits the island's shallow bays. A number of creatures which hide in the corals during the day can be seen on night dives. Fully-equipped boats may be chartered for **skindiving** and **snorkelling**. **Surfing** facilities are available at coastal resorts. Most hotels have **swimming** pools, and there is a public pool in Hagåtña; the west coast offers safe bathing.
- **Reef fishing** with net and rod is popular, as is spearfishing for groupers and skipjacks and deep-sea fishing for marlin, tuna, wahoo, barracuda, bonito and sailfish.

TOURIST INFORMATION

Guam Visitors Bureau
401 Pale San Vitores Road, Tamuning, GU 96913, Guam
Tel: 646 5278/9.
Website: www.visitguam.org

Guam Visitors Bureau in the USA
North America Office, E-agency, 291 Third Street, Oakland, CA 94607, USA
Tel: (510) 496 2300.
Website: www.visitguam.org

Entertainment

FOOD & DRINK: The wide selection of restaurants features American, Chinese, European, Filipino, Indonesian, Japanese, Korean and Mexican food. Guamanian cooking is very similar to Spanish cuisine.
National specialities:
- Red rice.
- Shrimp patties.
- *Kelagven* (a dish of chopped chicken, lemon juice, grated coconut and hot peppers).

NIGHTLIFE: A range of nightclubs feature music and dancing. Major hotels frequently stage shows with musicians from the US mainland, or local performers including the *Guam Symphony & Choral Society*. There are a number of cinemas in Tamuning, including at least one 14-screen cinema, most showing recent US films. Dinner shows featuring the traditional dances are held nightly in several hotels. There are also facilities that specialise in Chamorro and other forms of Micronesian Island dances. The Tumon bay SandCastle is a world class performance and entertainment facility and has a multilevel New York style disco. Other hotels also have discos and Karaoke bars are also popular.
SHOPPING: There are many shopping centres in Agaña, Tumon, Tamuning and Dededo that offer an array of retail items. The main malls include the *Hagåtña Shopping Centre* and *Guam Premium* Outlets. Micronesia *Mall* has recently undergone expansion and has the distinction of being the island's first indoor mall. Most hotels in Tumon Bay have a lobby arcade and other speciality shops within walking distance. Dededo flea market is held every Saturday and Sunday at 0600. The Islands duty free status means that name brand merchandise are often less expensive than their country of origin. Good buys in Guam include watches, perfume, jewellery, alcohol, china, stereo equipment and cameras. **Shopping hours:** Generally Mon-Sat 1000-2100, Sun 1200-1800 but hours do vary from centre to centre. **Tipping:** 10-15 per cent is standard for taxi drivers, in restaurants and hotels. Where a 10 per cent service charge has already been added to the bill, tipping is optional. Guam hotel occupancy tax is 11 per cent.

Business

- **GDP:** US$3.2 billion.
- **Main exports:** Re-exports of petroleum-based products, construction materials, fish, food and beverage products.
- **Main imports:** Petroleum and petroleum products, food and manufactured goods.
- **Main trade partners:** Japan, Singapore, Korea (Rep.), Hong Kong and the Philippines.

ECONOMY: The main components of Guam's economy are tourism and the US military for whom the island is a vital staging post for operations through the Pacific region. Tourism has expanded rapidly despite the island's remote location and small size: Guam now receives over one million visitors annually, of whom 90 per cent come from Japan. A range of crops, including maize, cassava, bananas and coconuts, are grown for domestic consumption. Guam is also an important re-export centre for distribution of goods throughout the Pacific, particularly to Micronesia. Government policy presently concentrates on attracting foreign investment, principally from Asia, and has been examining the country's potential as an offshore financial centre. However, the development of the latter is not favoured by the extensive competition in the Pacific and Guam's tax laws.

COMMERCIAL INFORMATION

Guam Chamber of Commerce
173 Aspinall Avenue, Ada Plaza Center, Suite 101, Hagåtña, GU 96910, Guam
Tel: 472 6311 *or* 472 8001.
Website: www.guamchamber.com.gu

Guatemala

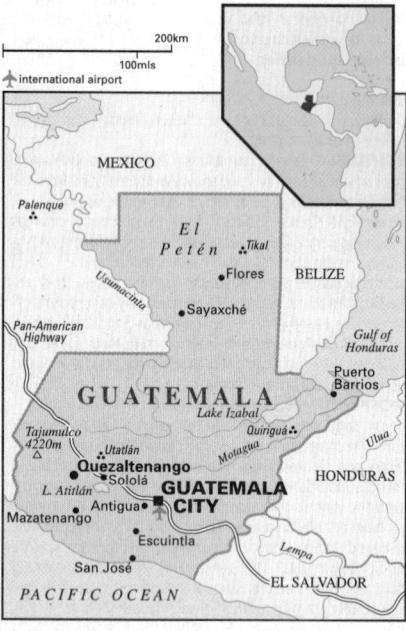

Location: Central America.

Time: GMT - 6.

Overview

Antiquity is at the heart of Guatemala: the country incorporates some of the most spectacular Mayan archaeological sites and the pineforested hills of the Highlands are home to Mayan communities that still wear their traditional weavings. Guatemala has around 21 different ethnic groups, speaking some 23 languages. The staggering Mayan monuments alert the visitor to a mystery that hangs in the air: the Mayans were dominant through much of Central America from the fifth until the eighth centuries, when their civilisation rapidly declined and a variety of other ethnic groups moved into the region. Guatemala was one of the territories overrun by the Spanish conquistador Cortés in the 17th century. Pressure on their empire during the early 19th century forced the Spanish to concede independence to their American colonies, principally Mexico, into which Guatemala was briefly incorporated in 1822. Guatemala then enjoyed comparative stability under a series of dictators who were content to keep the country under a quasi-feudal regime. Eventually, the country slid into almost perpetual civil war between a series of right-wing military Governments and various leftist guerrilla movements: a major figure during this period was the former general Efrain Rios Montt, who as army chief of staff and (briefly) President during the 1970s and 80s, presided over a vicious counter-insurgency campaign whose savagery was exceptional. Only now has the Government admitted that its predecessors were responsible for massive human rights abuses, perhaps because of the findings of a UN-sponsored investigation into the estimated 200,000 killings. This investigation also drew attention to the complicity and active assistance of successive American Governments in the counter-insurgency campaign, for which the then-US president, Bill Clinton, apologised. Under the terms of the deal that ended civil war, the culprits go unpunished.

Even Guatemala's cities have been subject to cataclysm. Three attempts to establish a capital were made before Guatemala City was founded in 1775. The first colonial settlement was built in 1524 but continuing battles with

Cakchiquel warriors necessitated relocation in 1527 near present-day San Miguel Escobar. An earthquake destroyed this in 1541. A third capital was then established on the present site of La Antigua Guatemala and survived until 1773, when it was hit by a huge earthquake and eventually abandoned. The former capital was thereafter known as La Antigua Guatemala, or Old Guatemala.

But nature wields a double-edged sword in Guatemala, and as much as its effects have scathed Guatemalan infrastructure and land, it has also formed some astonishing sights, such as volcanic peaks, subtropical forests and ancient, sulphurous lakes. Orchids spring out of soil, exotic creatures roam it, and exotic birds soar above it. And equally, just as Guatemala's human history contains some savage chapters, a visitor is still frequently greeted by sincere friendliness. The indigenous Guatemalan culture also persists, and those thinking that the Mayans were totally eradicated centuries ago may be surprised to bump into a few on their travels – they constitute almost half the population.

General Information

AREA: 108,889 sq km (42,042 sq miles).

POPULATION: 13 million (UN, 2005).

POPULATION DENSITY: 119.3 per sq km.

CAPITAL: Guatemala City. **Population:** 942,348 (2002).

GEOGRAPHY: Guatemala is located in Central America and shares borders to the north and west with Mexico, to the southeast with El Salvador and Honduras, to the northeast with Belize and the Caribbean sea and to the south with the Pacific ocean. The landscape is predominantly mountainous and heavily forested. A string of volcanoes rises above the southern highlands along the Pacific, three of which are still active. Within this volcanic area are basins of varying sizes which hold the majority of the country's population. The region is drained by rivers flowing into both the Pacific and the Caribbean. One basin west of the capital has no river outlet and thus has formed Lake Atitlán, which is ringed by volcanoes. To the northwest, bordering on Belize and Mexico, lies the low undulating tableland of El Petén, 36,300 sq km (14,000 sq miles) of almost inaccessible wilderness covered with dense hardwood forest. This area covers approximately one-third of the national territory, yet contains only 40,000 people.

GOVERNMENT: Republic. Gained independence from Spain in 1821. **Head of State and Government:** President Oscar Berger Perdomo since 2003. **Recent history:** The most recent polls in December 2003 brought victory for the *Frente Republicano - Guatemalteco* (FRG) for a second consecutive term. The FRG and the *Plan por el Adelantamiento Nacional* (National Advance Party, PAN) now dominate Guatemalan politics. Only now has the Government been prepared to admit that its predecessors, especially the Rios Montt regime, were responsible for massive human rights abuses: this is still a central and highly sensitive issue in Guatemalan domestic politics. Abroad, the main issue facing the country remains the dispute with neighbouring Belize, over which Guatemala has territorial claims; 1993 saw the signing of a non-aggression pact by the two Governments, and as a concession, Belize granted the Guatemalans access to its maritime facilities. The following year, however, the Guatemalan government reasserted its territorial claim at the UN; in 2000, it did so again, claiming half of Belize's current territory. Despite international mediation efforts, relations between the two remained tense. Then, in September 2002, the Organisation of American States (the main pan-regional political alliance) brokered a draft settlement of the dispute which may form the basis for a permanent accord.

Under the 1986 constitution, legislative power is vested in a single-chamber elected assembly with 80 members directly elected every four years. The President, also elected every four years, holds executive power.

LANGUAGE: The official language is Spanish. English is widely spoken in tourist areas and major hotels and restaurants. 22 indigenous languages are also spoken.

RELIGION: The constitution guarantees freedom of worship, but 60 per cent of the population are Catholic. Most of the remaining population are Protestant. Some indigenous communities hold services combining Catholicism with pre-Columbian rites.

ELECTRICITY: 115-125 volts AC, 60Hz. There are some regional variations.

SOCIAL CONVENTIONS: Guatemala is the most populated of the Central American republics and is the only one which is predominantly Indian, although the Spanish have had a strong influence on the way of life. Full names should be used when addressing acquaintances, particularly in business. Dress is conservative and casual wear is suitable except in the smartest dining rooms and clubs.

Photography: Locals are often suspicious of foreigners taking photographs, particularly of young children. Before approaching children for photos, or even just to talk to them, you should check with an an adult that this is acceptable. However, if you are in any doubt, refrain from doing so. You may be asked to pay a small amount of money to take photographs of both children and adults.

Credit: ©Sarah Logan

Climate

Guatemala's climate varies according to altitude. The coastal regions and the northeast are hot throughout the year with an average temperature of 20°C (68°F) sometimes rising to 37°C (99°F). Generally, nights are clear all year round. In higher climes, near the centre of the country, the rainy season, running from May to September, is characterised by clear skies after abundant rainfall in the afternoons and evenings. Temperatures fall sharply at night.

Required clothing: Lightweight tropical clothing. Jacket or light woollens for the evening.

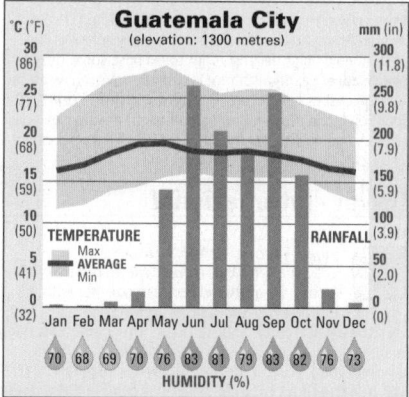

Communications

Telephone: IDD is available. Country code: 502. Telephone calls to Europe are slightly cheaper between 1900 and 0700.

Mobile telephone: Roaming agreements exist with some international mobile phone companies. Coverage is increasing in Guatemala; consult network operator for details.

Internet: Internet is available in large towns; there are several Internet cafes in Guatemala City and the main tourist areas.

Post: Regular airmail to Europe takes 12 days.

MEDIA: Freedom of press is good in Guatemala and the press tends to freely criticise Government policies. However, journalists may face intimidation because of their reporting, such as anonymous threats. Media is dominated by privately-run outlets. Four of the country's national TV channels share the same owner, thus perhaps biasing TV broadcasting. They have also been criticised for being pro-Government.

Press: Publications include *Diario Centroamérica*, *La Hora*, *El Periódico*, *Prensa Libre* and *Siglo Veintiuno*. English-language publications include *Central America Report*, *Guatemala Weekly*, *The Review* and *Siglo News*.

TV: *Canal 3 Radio-TV Guatemala*, *Teleonce*, *Televisiete* and *Trecevision* are commercial channels in Guatemala.

Radio: *La Voz de Guatemala* is a Government-owned radio station. *Emisoras Unidas de Guatemala*, *Radio Continental*, *Radio Nuevo Mundo* and *Radio Panamericana* are commercial stations.

Passport/Visa

	Passport Required?	Visa Required?	Return Ticket Required?
Full British	Yes	No	No
Australian	Yes	No	No
Canadian	Yes	No	No
USA	Yes	No	No
Other EU	Yes	No	No
Japanese	Yes	No	No

Note: *Regulations and requirements may be subject to change at short notice, and you are advised to contact the appropriate diplomatic or consular authority before finalising travel arrangements. Any numbers in the chart refer to the footnotes below.*

Restricted entry: Entry and transit is refused to deportees of other countries who are not nationals of Guatemala. Nationals of some countries require special authorisation from the Department of Immigration in Guatemala before they are granted a visa; nationals of these countries will need to make their application in Guatemala, through a person, company or institution that will be responsible for that person's stay in Guatemala. Authorisation from Guatemala will take two to five weeks and applicants are also required to attend an interview at the Consulate. For an up-to-date list of nationalities, enquire at the nearest Consulate (or Consular section at Embassy).

PASSPORTS: Passport valid for at least six months required by all.

VISAS: Required by all except the following:
(a) nationals of countries referred to in the chart above (also including French Overseas Territories);
(b) nationals of Andorra, Antigua & Barbuda, Argentina, Bahamas, Bahrain, Barbados, Belize, Brazil, Brunei, Bulgaria, Chile, Costa Rica, Croatia, El Salvador, Guam, Honduras, Hong Kong (SAR), Iceland, Israel, Korea (Rep), Kuwait, Liechtenstein, Macedonia (Former Yugoslav Republic of), Madagascar, Malaysia, Marshall Islands, Mexico, Monaco, New Zealand, Nicaragua, Norway, Panama, Paraguay, Qatar, Romania, St Kitts & Nevis, St Lucia, St Vincent & the Grenadines, San Marino, São Tomé e Príncipe, Singapore, Solomon Islands, South Africa, Switzerland, Taiwan (China), Trinidad & Tobago, Turkey, Tuvalu, Uruguay, Vanuatu, Vatican City and Venezuela;
(c) transit passengers continuing their journey to a third country by the same or first connecting aircraft within eight hours, provided holding tickets with confirmed onward reservations and not leaving the transit area.

Types of visa and cost: *Visitor/Tourist:* £25 (single-entry); £50 (multiple-entry). *Business:* £50 (multiple-entry). *Transit:* £10.

Validity: *Visitor/Tourist:* 90 days from date of entry. *Business:* 180 days from date of entry. Visas must be used within 30 days of issue.

Application to: Consulate (or Consular section at Embassy); see *Passport/Visa Information*.

Application requirements: *Visitor/Tourist:* (a) Two application forms. (b) Two passport-size photos. (c) Valid passport. (d) Onward or return ticket. (e) Stamped, self-addressed, registered envelope (if applying by post). (f) Bank or credit card statements for at least three months. *Business:* (a)-(e) and, (f) Letter from applicant's company in duplicate, indicating the nature and status of the company as well as the applicant's planned activities.

Working days required: Two to three.

PASSPORT/VISA INFORMATION

Embassy of the Republic of Guatemala in the UK
13 Fawcett Street, London SW10 9HN, UK
Tel: (020) 7351 3042.
Opening hours: Mon-Fri 0900-1700; 1000-1300 only for walk in queries (consular section).
The Embassy also handles tourism queries.

Embassy of the Republic of Guatemala in the USA
2220 R Street, NW, Washington, DC 20008, USA
Tel: (202) 745 4952.
Website: www.guatemala-embassy.org

Money

Currency: Quetzal (GTQ) = 100 centavos. Notes are in denominations of GTQ100, 50, 20, 10 and 5. Coins are in denominations of GTQ1, and 50, 10, 5 and 1 centavos. The US Dollar also became an official currency in 2001.
Currency exchange: The Quetzal is extremely difficult to obtain outside Guatemala or exchange after leaving Guatemala, and visitors are strongly advised to exchange

Credit: ©Sarah Logan

local currency before departure. It may be difficult to negotiate notes which are torn. Unused local currency can be exchanged at the bank at the airport (opening hours: Mon-Fri 0800-2000). ATMs are common throughout the country.
Credit & debit cards: American Express and Visa are accepted, whilst Diners Club and MasterCard have a more limited acceptance. Check with your credit or debit card company for details of merchant acceptability and other services that may be available.
Traveller's cheques: Accepted by most banks and good hotels, although visitors may experience occasional problems. To avoid additional exchange rate charges, travellers are advised to take traveller's cheques in US Dollars.
Currency restrictions: The import and export of local currency is prohibited. The import and export of foreign currency is unlimited.
Banking hours: Mon-Fri 0900-1700 (some banks offer external windows until 1900); Sat 0900-1300.
Exchange rate indicators:
Rate at time of publishing
£1.00= GTQ13.28
$1.00= GTQ7.63

Duty Free

The following goods may be imported into Guatemala by persons over 18 years of age without incurring customs duty:
80 cigarettes or 100g of tobacco; 1.5l of alcoholic beverages; two bottles of perfume.

Public Holidays

Below are listed Public Holidays for the January 2006-June 2007 period.
2006: Jan 1 New Year's Day. **Apr 13-16** Holy Week. **May 1** Labour Day. **Jun 30** Army Day. **Aug 15** Assumption (Guatemala City only). **Sep 15** Independence Day. **Oct 20** Revolution Day. **Nov 1** All Saints' Day. **Dec 24** Christmas Eve (afternoon only). **Dec 25** Christmas Day. **Dec 31** New Year's Eve (afternoon only).
2007: Jan 1 New Year's Day. **Apr 5-8** Holy Week. **May 1** Labour Day. **Jun 30** Army Day.

Health

	Special Precautions?	Certificate Required?
Yellow Fever	No	1
Cholera	Yes	2
Typhoid & Polio	3	N/A
Malaria	4	N/A

Note: *Regulations and requirements may be subject to change at short notice, and you are advised to contact your doctor well in advance of your intended date of departure. Any numbers in the chart refer to the footnotes below.*

1: A yellow fever vaccination certificate is required from travellers over one year of age coming from countries with infected areas.

2: Following WHO guidelines issued in 1973, a cholera vaccination certificate is no longer a condition of entry into Guatemala. However, cases of cholera were reported in 1996 and precautions are essential. Up-to-date advice should be sought before deciding whether these precautions should include vaccination as medical opinion is divided over its effectiveness. See the *Health* appendix for further information.
3: Typhoid occurs.
4: Malaria risk exists throughout the year below 1500m (4921ft), especially in Alta Verapaz, Baja Verapan, Ixcan, Petén and San Marcos. Chloroquine is the recommended prophylaxis. There is no risk in Antigua or Lake Atitlán.
Food & drink: Bottled water is available everywhere. Other water sources may be contaminated, and water used for drinking, brushing teeth or making ice should have first been boiled or otherwise sterilised. Milk may be unpasteurised and should be boiled. Powdered or tinned milk is available and is advised, but make sure that it is reconstituted with pure water. Avoid dairy products which are likely to have been made from unboiled milk. Only eat well-cooked meat and fish, preferably served hot. Pork, salad and mayonnaise may carry increased risk. Vegetables should be cooked and fruit peeled.
Other risks: *Onchocerciasis* (river blindness) occurs in localised foci in rural areas. *Dengue fever* may occur. *Dysentery* and *diarrhoeal diseases* are common. *Visceral, cutaneous and mucocutaneous leishmaniasis* occur. *Filariasis* and *American trypanosomiasis* are diseases carried by insects in the region. *Myiasis* (botfly) is endemic in Central America. *Hepatitis A* occurs and inoculation is recommended. *Altitude sickness* may be experienced in higher places such as volcanoes and mountains, and exertion should be avoided.
Rabies occurs. For those at high risk, vaccination before arrival should be considered. If you are bitten, seek medical advice without delay. For more information, consult the *Health* appendix.
Health care: There are both public and private medical facilities in Guatemala City, but comprehensive travel and medical insurance is strongly advised before travelling. Some hotels offer doctor's services to their guests.

Travel - International

AIR:
 The national airline is *TACA* (website: www.taca.com). *American Airlines* operates daily flights to Guatemala, via Miami or Dallas. Other airlines serving Guatemala include *British Airways, Continental Airlines, Iberia* (regular flights from London via Madrid) and *United Airlines.*
Approximate flight times: From Guatemala to *London* is 11 hours (plus stopover time in USA or Madrid), to *Los Angeles* is six hours, to *New York* is six hours and to *Miami* is two hours 30 minutes.
Main airports: *Guatemala City (GUA)* (la Aurora) is 6km (4 miles) south of the city. *To/from the airport:* A bus runs to the city. Taxi services to Guatemala City are available (travel time – 20 minutes). *Facilities:* Car hire, duty free shop, bar, buffet, post office, restaurant, bank, tourist information, telephones and bureaux de change.

A
B
C
D
E
F
G
H
I
J
K
L
M
N
O
P
Q
R
S
T
U
V
W
X
Y
Z

Credit: ©Sarah Logan

Flores (FRS) is located an hour from the UNESCO Tikal Archaelogical Park. Regular flights operate to Belize.
Departure tax: US$30. 24-hour transit passengers are exempt.

SEA:

Main ports: *Santo Thomás de Castilla, Puerto Quetzal, San José, Puerto Barrios* and *Champerico*. There are also a number of marinas on the *Rio Dulce*.There are several international passenger services from North America, the Far East and Europe to Santo Tomás de Castilla and Puerto Quetzal. Cruise companies which make a port of call in Guatemala include *Holland American Line*. Cargo services run to the Pacific ports of San José and Champerico.

RAIL:

Ferrovias Guatemala (FVG) is a 497-mile (800km) railroad connecting Guatemala City with Mexico, El Salvador and ports on the Atlantic and Pacific coasts. Restoration of the railroad is currently underway after the devastation caused by Hurricane Mitch in 1999. Currently, 200 miles (322km) of the railroad is in operation.

ROAD:

The Pan-American Highway runs through Guatemala from Mexico in the north and El Salvador in the south covering 511km (318 miles). Access is also possible from Belize. You should exercise particular care when travelling in the Belize/Guatemala border area because of the ongoing dispute between the two countries. Travellers are strongly advised to use only the officially recognised border crossings. **Bus:** There are bus services from Mexico and El Salvador, Nicaragua, Costa Rica and Panama. Border crossings can be subject to considerable delays. The buses used by some companies are comfortable and air conditioned, but it is vital to book as far in advance as possible for every stage of the journey.

Travel - Internal

AIR:

Air transport is by far the most efficient means of internal travel since there are over 380 airstrips. *Tikal Jets* (website: www.tikaljets.com) run daily flights from Guatemala City to El Petén. *Inter*, a subsidiary of TACA, runs scheduled flights to several towns. Private charter flights are available. A travel tax of GTQ5 per person is applied to internal flights and payable at the check-in desks.

ROAD:

Traffic drives on the right. There is an extensive road network but less than a third of the roads are all-weather. Many of the roads are made from volcanic ash, and therefore very muddy during the rains. There are, however, about 13,000km (8000 miles) of first- and second-class roads in the country with paved highways from Guatemala City to the principal towns in the interior and to both the Atlantic and Pacific ports. Seatbelts must be worn at all times but there are no laws regarding the use of child safety seats. Speed limits vary depending on the condition of the road but they are rarely enforced. Driving under the influence of alcohol or drugs is illegal and those caught may be jailed. Travellers should avoid driving to Panajachel via Patzun as the road is badly maintained and criminals take advantage of these conditions to hold up travellers. The road from the El Salvador border to Cuilapa and from the Belize border to El Cruce are major danger spots for bus-jacking and there are also similar incidents on the main Pan-American Highway near Solola. **Bus:** The network of regular bus services between major towns is cheap but crowded and road accidents are common. Slightly more expensive air-conditioned services are available. *Transportes Litegua* operates regular buses along the Caribbean Highway from Guatemala City, Rio Dulce and Morales to Puerto Barrios. The Guatemala City Council no longer permits inter-urban buses to enter the city centre; passengers are dropped at various points on the outskirts. **Taxi:** Flat rate for short or long runs within the city although prices tend to be high. Cars can also be hired by the hour. Vehicles may be summoned by phone or in the street. There are ranks at the main international hotels. Tipping is discretionary (5 to 10 per cent). **Car hire:** International and local firms provide services in Guatemala City. Rates are low, but insurance is extra. It is possible to hire a car for up to 30 days with either an International Driving Permit or national licence. It is also possible to hire motorcycles. Regulations may vary from company to company. **Documentation:** A local licence will be issued on production of the visitor's own national driving licence. Adequate car insurance is essential.

URBAN:

Guatemala City and major towns have limited, but cheap and regular, bus services. New circulating taxi services have been introduced in the capital.

Travel Advice

Travellers should avoid travelling at night or visiting remote places unaccompanied.
Travellers should avoid travelling on some roads in Guatemala, because of criminal attacks on cars and buses. The threat from terrorism is low, but you should be aware of the global risk of indiscriminate terrorist attacks which could be against civilian targets, including places frequented by foreigners.
This advice is based on information provided by the Foreign and Commonwealth Office in the UK. It is correct at time of publishing. As the situation can change rapidly, visitors are advised to contact the following organisations for the latest travel advice:

British Foreign and Commonwealth Office
Tel: (0845) 850 2829.
Website: www.fco.gov.uk

US Department of State
Website: http://travel.state.gov/travel

Accommodation

HOTELS:

There are many first-class hotels in Guatemala City and throughout the country. Many offer excellent service in restaurants, bars and nightclubs. La Antigua Guatemala (the capital until largely destroyed by earthquakes in 1773, a fate which also befell the present capital in 1976) also has a good choice of hotels. Chichicastenango, Cobán, Panajachel (near Lake Atitlán), Puerto Barrios, and Quetzaltenango also have a reasonable selection of hotels, although elsewhere accommodation is more limited. Throughout the country standards are inconsistent. Registered hotels are required to display room rates; the Tourist Office in Guatemala City will deal with complaints. A 10 per cent tip is normal in hotels where service has not been included. Most hotels charge a 20 per cent room tax.

PENSIONS & GUEST HOUSES:

Most large towns have guest houses and boarding houses offering inexpensive accommodation.

CAMPING:

There are a few campsites dotted around the country but facilities are usually basic. A popular excursion is to stay overnight in camping grounds on the still active Pacaya volcano to see the glow of the ashes and lava from the volcano's eruptions. Around Lake Atitlán, camping is permitted only in designated areas.

ECO-ACCOMMODATION:

Los Tarrales, situated on the south slope of the Atitlan volcano, was declared a protected area in 2000. It offers an eco-lodge, two tree houses and a campsite.

ACCOMMODATION INFORMATION

Guatemala Tourist Commission (INGUAT)
Centro Cívico, 7A Avenida 1-17, Zona 4,
Guatemala City 01004, Guatemala
Tel: 2421 2810 *or* (800) 464 8281 (24-hour toll-free number in the USA *or* (801) 464 8281 (24-hour toll-free number in Guatemala).
Website: www.visitguatemala.com

Los Tarrales Reserve
Tel: (502) 2478 4867 *or* 5208 0940.
Website: www.tarrales.com

Top Things To See

- See the sights of **Guatemala City**, the capital, which include **Parque Central**, bordered by the **National Palace**, the **Cathedral** and the **National Library**. **Kaminal Juyú** is a city buried under one of the most commercial areas of Guatemala City. Also not to be missed is the **Relief Map of the Republic** in **Minerva Park**. It is the largest of its kind in the world measuring 1800 sq m (5905 sq ft). Some of the most interesting religious buildings (mainly either neo-classical or Baroque) include the 17th-century **Hermitage of El Carmen** and the churches of **La Merced, Santo Domingo, Santuario Expiatorio, Las Capuchinas, Santa Rosa** and **Capilla de Yurrita** (built in the first half of the 20th century). In the south of the city, close to the airport and the national racecourse, are **Parque la Aurora**, which contains the **zoo**, the **Museum of Archaeology and Ethnology** and the **Ixchel Museum**, housing a good collection of handwoven textiles. Other museums with fine collections include the **Popol Vuh Museum** (a private collection of Mayan and Spanish colonial art) and the **National Museum of Modern Art**. Guatemala City lies at the edge of a plateau cut by deep ravines in the **Valley of the Hermitage**.
- See one of the most ancient lakes in the world - **Lake Amatitlan** . The surrounding rim of this lake, 11 km (7 miles) long and 3.5km (2.2 miles) wide, contains archaeological remains dating back to 2000 BC. Alternatively, another lake definitely worth seeing is **Lake Atitlán**. The road through **Sololá** winds down to this beautiful, volcanic lakeland area, much praised by Aldous Huxley, and is surrounded by purple highlands, olive-green mountains and three distinctive volcanoes – **Tolimán, Atitlán** and **San Pedro**. Although there are some small hotels around the edge of the lake, most visitors stay at **Panajachel**, the key tourist centre, with a long strip of guest houses, restaurants, bookshops, cafes and banks. Water-skiing, swimming and boating are all available on the lake, which is 19km (12 miles) in length and between 6.5km (4 miles) and 12km (7.5 miles) wide.
- Despite widespread devastation in recurrent catastrophes, a trip to **La Antigua Guatemala**, the former capital (originally called **Santiago de los Caballeros Guatemala**), is a must. Antigua is situated southwest of Guatemala City, and was considered to be one of the most splendid cities in Central America before its partial destruction in the earthquake of 1773. Further devastation was wreaked in the massive earthquake in 1976 and the town is now a UNESCO Cultural Heritage Site. Despite the damage of countless earthquakes, floods and fires, Antigua is a beautiful place of multi-coloured,

single-storey buildings, tropical gardens, plazas, fountains and cobbled streets. A popular tourist centre, it has several good hotels, restaurants and bookshops with a fairly lively nightlife. Monuments, former palaces, convents and churches that have survived in varying degrees of intactness include the **Main Square**, **Cathedral**, **Palace of the General Captains**, **University of San Carlos** (containing the **Museum of Colonial Art**), and the churches of **La Merced**, **Santa Clara**, **Las Capuchinas**, **La Recolección** and **San Francisco**. The **Casa Santa Domingo** is a former convent that is now a smart hotel. Two small but fine collections are housed in the **Colonial** and **Archaeological** museums.

- Guatemala has 33 **volcanoes**, three of which are still active. Although not the highest, one of the most dramatic is the **Pacaya Volcano** (2252m/7388ft), which is located about halfway between Guatemala City and **Escuintla** in the **Escuintla Department**. During periods of activity, guided tours are organised to watch the eruptions and the lava flows. When inactive, an ascent of the volcano can be made by a marked route from **San Francisco de Sales**. Northwest of Escuintla are the sugarcane fields of **Santa Lucía Cotzumalguapa**. The remains of great stone heads and other carved reliefs are dotted throughout the fields belonging to three *fincas* (plantations) – **Bilbao**, **El Baúl** and **las Ilusiones**. South from here is the site of **La Democracia**, which contains dramatic basalt sculptures of heads with closed eyes and furrowed brows.
- Survey the superb **craftsmanship** at towns like **Jocotenango** (a centre for ceramics) and **San Antonio Aguascalientes** (a centre of beautiful handwoven textiles). Salamá, the attractive Departmental capital of **Baja Verapaz**, is a good place to buy souvenirs handcrafted from silver, clay and leather. The villages, forests and mountains of **Mataquescuintla** are home to the **Pocomam Indians** who produce some outstanding textiles and ceramics. **San Cristóbal Totonicapán** has a market day on Thursday, which is the best time to purchase outstanding ceramics. It is also an important centre for textiles. **Momostenango** (City of Altars), in the north, is the centre for traditional handwoven **ponchos**.
- Visit the major **Mayan sites**, most found in the vast tropical lowland jungles of the **Petén Department**, which shares borders with Belize to the east and Mexico to the north and west. Many visitors exploring the Mayan sites in all three countries tend to fly directly from either Mexico or Belize into the international airport at **Flores**. Flores is a former Mayan ceremonial centre built on an island in the middle of **Lake Petén Itza**. None of the Mayan structures survived the arrival of the conquistadors who built their main plaza, church and government building on the top of the hill in the centre of the island. A causeway connects Flores to the mainland town of **Santa Elena**, where the banks and main shops are located. Buses run throughout the day from both Santa Elena and Flores to Tikal. The spectacular Mayan ruins of **Tikal** (**City of Voices**) encompass vast pyramidal temples, ball courts, causeways, plazas and public buildings that extend over some 16 sq km (6 sq miles). While there are about 3000 known structures, many more lie buried under dense jungle vegetation. First occupied in about 800 BC, this great city was eventually abandoned around 1000 years later. Copies of some of the more elaborate friezes, stelae, sculptures and bas-reliefs are found in the **Sylvanus Morley Museum**, which is near the entrance. At least two days are recommended to see all of the archaeological sites. Visitors can stay in the park lodges, in Flores, Santa Elena or **El Remate** - a pleasant lakeside town - and guided tours around the ruins can be arranged both for the evening and at sunrise. Several other Mayan sites in north Petén are currently under excavation, one of the most impressive being **El Mirador**, about 4km (2.5 miles) from the Mexican border. Also in the northern part of the Department, **Uaxactún** (Eight Stones) shows how developed the Mayan civilisation had become by the ninth century AD. **Building E-VII-B** was used for determining the precise dates of the equinoxes and the solstices. **Ixlú** was an important lake port, situated in between the **Petén Itza** and **Salpetén** lagoons. Further east, on the edge of the **Yaxhá Lagoon**, **Yaxhá** (Green Water) is an extensive Mayan site of terraces, plazas and causeways. North from here are the smaller sites of **Nakum** and **Naranjo**. Sayaxché is a town in the southern part of the Petén Department that provides a good starting point for exploring other major Mayan sites. **Ceibal**, southeast of Sayaxché, has a small observatory that was designed to pinpoint the location of galaxies, planets and stars. It is also where some of the finest post-classical stelae (AD 900 to 1523), carved with large anthropomorphist clay figures, were recovered. Other impressive stelae representing battle scenes were found at **Dos Pilas**. Southeast from here, the post-Classical site of **Aguateca** was once an important ceremonial centre. In other Departments, there are landmarks such as the remarkable UNESCO Cultural Heritage Site of **Quiriguá**. The nine Maya-carved stelae around a central plaza are the largest stelae ever discovered in the Mayan world. They are carved with intricate detail, revealing much of their beliefs, animal deities, battles, the feats of their kings and cosmology. **Stela E**, at 8m high (26ft), is one of the tallest that has been recovered across the former Mayan Empire.
- For **wildlife**, head for the **Tikal National Park**, where there are over 50,587 hectares (125,000 acres) of rare forest (kapoka, breadnut, mahogany and cedar) and tropical vegetation. Wildlife that can be seen there includes howler monkeys, tropical birds, ocelots, jaguars and brocket deer. Tikal National Park is itself situated in the much larger **Mayan Biosphere Reserve**. Also accessible from Flores is the **Cerro Cahuí Biosphere** – a 600-hectare (1482-acre) nature reserve that contains cedar, sapodilla, indigo and mahogany trees, orchids and ferns as well as white-tailed deer, armadillos, spider monkeys, hawks, parrots and toucans. From October to April, hundreds of migratory birds settle in the reserve. Some 200km (124 miles) from Cobán is the **National Park of Lanchúa**, which is a very humid, subtropical rainforest teeming with many species of mammals and amphibians. Visitors to the park will need a guide and full camping equipment. The town of **Purulhá** is the location for the **Mario Dary Biotape Reserve**, which was set up to protect the Quetzal, Guatemala's national bird and a symbol of liberty. Two walking trails cut through the cloudforest, where visitors can see about 50 different types of trees and a variety of tropical birds such as toucans, hummingbirds and macaws. **Montecristo National Park** (the Tri-State Park) is located in the **Chiquimula Department** and extends over the borders of three countries. Over half of its 12,000 hectares (29,652 acres) of humid and subtropical forest are in Guatemala.
- In **Cobán**, capital of the **Alta Verapaz Department**, are the **Semuc Champey Waterfalls**, which are formed as the **Cahabón River** falls some 300m (985ft) across rocks and ledges. Around 10km (6 miles) further on, the river enters the **Languin Caves**, parts of which can be explored with a guide, either on foot or by boat. From the **Lanchuá Lagoon**, it is possible to take a boat to explore parts of the **Caves of Candelaria**. These ancient caves were considered sacred by the Maya and remnants of ceremonial altars and pots have been found here.
- See two of the finest examples of 16th-century Baroque architecture in **El Progreso**: the parish churches of **San Agustín Acasaguastlán** and **San Cristóbal Acasaguastlán**
- The town of **Esquipulas** in the Chiquimula Department is one of the most significant in Central America. Second only in importance to the shrine of the Virgin of Guadalupe outside Mexico City is the **Basílica of Esquipulas** with its **Icon of the Black Christ** that dates back to 1594. Pilgrims from all over Central America gather here on the feast day of 15 January. Esquipulas is also the seat of the **Central American Parliament** and, given its location just a short distance from the borders with Honduras and El Salvador, it has also been the place where several important peace agreements have been signed. Other attractions include the **Franciscan Sanctuary**, **Belén Convent** and colonial **Little Bridge** (**Puente Chiquito**).
- In the **Santa Rosa Department**, located near **Pueblo Nuevo Viñas** and surrounded by mountains and forests, is the sulphurous **Lake Ixpaco**, which is the site of many springs that are believed to have healing properties. Northwest through a landscape of pine forests and low subtropical mountains is **Ayarza Lagoon**, also slightly sulphurous but with shoals of tilapias and mojarras.
- For a surreal intermixture of the historical and enjoyably tacky, venture to the the **Xocomil Aquatic Park** – a theme park with pools and waterslides built around replica Mayan temples, palaces and sanctuaries. The **Retalhuleu Department** is also home to **El Asintal** and the site of **Abaj Takalik** ('standing stone' in the Quiché language). This is one of the few sites to have remnants of terraces, carved stones, inscribed altars and calendars from two civilisations: the Mayan and the **Olmec**, who preceded the Mayas.
- Explore the unique highlands region of Western Guatemala - known in Spanish as **El Altiplano**. The towns and villages there are inhabited by the greatest number of modern day, indigenous Mayan groups – many of whom still speak the languages and uphold the sacred rituals of their ancestors. Although this practice is gradually dying out, many of the villagers in more remote areas still wear traditional handwoven garments and market days or fiesta celebrations are the best times for visitors to appreciate their vibrant colours. While the main towns are connected with paved highways, some of the outlying villages are accessible only by 4-wheel vehicles. Tourism infrastructure, however, is developing all the time.
- After the capital, the second most important city in Guatemala, set amongst a group of high mountains and volcanoes, is **Quetzaltenago**, in **Northern Guatemala**. Quetzaltenago (often referred to as *Xela*) is quite modern, but it also contains narrow colonial streets, broad avenues, fine public buildings such as the neoclassical **City Hall**, **Municipal Theatre** and **Natural History Museum**, and a magnificent central plaza.

Credit: ©Sarah Logan

- See **traditional garb** in the villages around Lake Atitlán. In each, inhabitants wear differently coloured, densely embroidered clothes. **Santiago Atitlán** is the largest of these. **Easter Week** is famous for combining two traditions – the Catholic Easter procession and the rival procession conducted by the **cofradía** (religious brotherhood). Their idol is **Maximón** – a black-suited figure with a moustache that combines physical characteristics and attributes of St Simón, Mam (a Mayan god), Alvarado (the Guatemalan conquistador) and Judas Iscariot. Inside the church, a little Maximón figure is carved into the altar, as is a scene showing the feast day of the *cofradía*. Some of the women in Santiago still wear traditional headdresses that are made from long lengths of cloth wound repeatedly around the back of the head (a visual reference to **Ixchel**, the snake goddess of weaving). In **San Antonio Palopó**, the women weave on long rectangular backstrap looms. The men use the standing loom introduced by the Spanish and wear a type of wrap-around brown and white kilt. Both men and women in **San Catarina Palopó** wear shirts, *huipiles* (blouses), skirts and trousers embroidered with colourful geometric designs.

Top Things To Do

- Go **mountaineering** on and around Guatemala's many **volcanoes**. At 4200m (13,776ft) above sea level, the **Tajumulco** in the **San Marcos** region is the highest volcano in Central America. In spite of this, it is technically an easy climb. Those requiring something more challenging can try the **Tolimán**, with its 3158m- (10,358ft-) twin peak summit. An easier climb is the **San Pedro** volcano, whose summit can be reached in about six hours. One of the most visited volcanoes, given its proximity to Guatemala City, is **Pacaya** at 2252m (7386ft). Excursions to this constantly erupting volcano must be made in a group and with a guide. The ascent of the **Agua** (or *Hunapu*) volcano at 3776m (1233ft) gives the opportunity to spend the night in the crater where there is a refuge for 30 people. **Aktun Kan**, **Jobtzinaj**, **Lanquín** and **La Candelaria** are principal locations for **caving**.
- There is plenty of opportunity to dabble in some **watersports**: **Río Dulce** and **Lakes Izabal** and **Atitlán** are good for **windsurfing**, with Lake Atitlán also popular for **diving**. Guatemala's fast-moving **rivers**, including **El Cahabón**, **El Chiquibul**, **El Motagua**, **La Pasión** and **El Usamacinta** are ideal for **boating** and **rapids shooting**. Lakes and rivers suitable for **fishing** include **El Lago de Izabal**, **El Petén**, **Río Dulce** and the rivers of **Alta Verepaz**. The **Pacific Coast** is one of the best places worldwide for **sports fishing**. **San José** is the country's second-largest port, which is connected to **Guatemala City** in the north by Highway CA9 (more commonly known as the Pan American Highway). The waters here have abundant marine life (such as red snapper, tarpon, bass and sailfish) and the **sea fishing** is rated very highly. **Caribbean Guatemala** has strong Afro-Caribbean influences as black Afro-Guatemalans known as *Garífunas*, the descendants of former African slaves who intermarried with the indigenous Maya, settled here.

Caribbean traditions remain evident in the area's music, festivals and cooking (in dishes such as *tapado* – made with fresh fish, coconut milk and green bananas). **Sailing**, fishing, **swimming** and scuba-diving are all popular activities and trips to the **Belize Keys** (such as the **Cayos Sapodillas**) are possible.

- Take a **boat trip** from **Livingston**, taken along the Río Dulce, a jungle river that has its source in Lake Izabal and winds its way between steep cliffs and dense vegetation, through the lake of **El Golfete**, to flow into the **Amatique Bay**. Along the river, near **Frontera**, is the fort of **San Felipe**, which was constructed by the Spanish in the 17th century as a defence against pirate attacks. The waterways of the river also pass through the mangrove swamps and lagoons of the **Chocón Machacas Biosphere**. This is a habitat for the endangered **manatee** (**sea cow**), which is Guatemala's largest aquatic mammal. North of Livingston is the **Siete Altares**, a series of waterfalls and pools, which have been formed where the Río Dulce empties into the Caribbean.

- In towns like **La Antigua Guatemala**, **Easter** is when locals and visitors flock to see spectacular processions; huge litters bearing religious icons are carried over carpets of flowers and coloured sawdust.

- Drink some **coffee** in either **Cobán**, capital of the **Alta Verapaz Department**, or Antigua – both vying for title of the most delicious coffee in Guatemala.

- Embark on the adventurous **Spanish Rural Tourism Plan**; visitors can travel on horseback, by bicycle, on foot or by 4-wheel drive vehicle from **Quetzaltepeque** through **San Luis Jiltepeque** to the attractive departmental capital of **Jalapa**, staying in family homes en route.

- Take a beautiful **drive** into the mountains in the Departmental capital of **Huehuetenango**. Here lies the isolated village of **Todos Santos Cuchumatán**. The men's traditional costumes of high-necked red shirts, red and white-striped trousers, black capes and red fabric tied under straw hats are particularly smart and should definitely be seen. On the **Day of the Dead** (**All Souls' Day**) on 1 November, a traditional horse race takes place in the village. Fuelled by *quetzalteca* (the local sugar cane spirit), the riders in traditional costume race up and down a dirt track at the far end of the village. The winner is the last man still on his horse. The Day of the Dead festival is celebrated in **Santiago Sacatepéquez** with hundreds of multi-coloured circular or hexagonal kites, made from bamboo or tissue paper (increasingly polyester or plastic), flown in honour of the dead.

- Visit **Totonicapan** during the week celebrating the feast days of **San Miguel Arcangel** (24-30 September) when traditional dances (**morerías**) are held here, with descriptive titles such as *Mexicans* and *The Deer and the Monkey*.

TOURIST INFORMATION

Guatemala Tourist Commission (INGUAT)
Centro Cívico, 7A Avenida 1-17, Zona 4,
Guatemala City 01004, Guatemala
Tel: 2421 2810 *or* (800) 464 8281 (24-hour toll-free number in USA) *or* (801) 464 8281 (24-hour toll-free number in Guatemala).
Website: www.visitguatemala.com

Entertainment

FOOD & DRINK: There is a variety of restaurants and cafes serving a wide selection of cooking styles including American, Argentinian, Chinese, French, Italian, Japanese, Mexican and Spanish. There are many fast-food chains and continental-style cafes. The visitor should note that food usually varies in price rather than quality and some of the cheap eateries are amongst the best.

National specialities:
- *Kac lc* (soup made from turkey and seasoned with *samat* (a herb from Alta Verapaz).
- *Guacamole*.
- *Flan de naranja* (orange-flavoured flan).

National drinks:
- Coffee.
- *Quetzalteca* (an extremely potent raw cane spirit).

Tipping: 10 per cent is normal in restaurants where service has not been included.

NIGHTLIFE: In Guatemala City in particular, there are nightclubs and discos with modern music and dance, featuring national and international artists. Guatemala is the home of *marimba* music, which can be heard at several venues. In the cities, the *marimba* is a huge elaborate xylophone with large drum sticks played by four to nine players. In rural areas the sounding boxes are made of different shaped gourds (*marimbas de tecomates*). There are regular concerts throughout Guatemala. There are also theatres and numerous plays in English and other cultural

performances. Films with English and Spanish subtitles are often shown in major towns. The most important museums and art galleries are found in Guatemala City, La Antigua Guatemala and Tikal National Park.

SHOPPING: Special purchases include textiles, handicrafts, jewellery, jade carvings, leather goods, ceramics and basketry. Markets are best for local products and bargaining is necessary. Ceramics can be purchased cheaply in many places including Villa de Chinautla, San Luis Jilotepeque and Rabinal. Cobán is the cheapest place to buy silverware. The Central Market in Guatemala City and the Craft Market provide a range of crafts combining traditional and modern styles. Guatemala City contains many modern shopping centres and malls. Gran Centro Comercial Los Proceres, Galerias La Pradera, Plaza Cemaco and Geminis International Mall are all located in Zone 10. In addition, visitors may make use of the facilities at Tikal Futura, Peri-Roosevelt Shopping Mall and the Century Shopping Centre.
Shopping hours: Mon-Sat 0930-1930. Malls are also open on Sunday.

Business

- **GDP:** US$23.3 billion (2004).
- **Main imports:** Fuel, machinery and transport equipment, construction materials, grain, fertiliser and electricity.
- **Main exports:** Coffee, sugar, petroleum, clothing, bananas, shrimps, fruit and vegetables and cardamom.
- **Main trade partners:** China, El Salvador, Honduras, Japan, Korea (Rep), Mexico and the USA.

ECONOMY: Coffee is the leading export in this largely agricultural economy, accounting for about one-third of foreign earnings. Other major crops are sugar cane, bananas, cardamom and cotton. Guatemala boasts the largest manufacturing sector in Central America, accounting for 20 per cent of GDP, and produces processed foods, textiles, paper, pharmaceuticals and rubber goods. Oil deposits, first discovered in the mid-1970s, are being exploited by French and American concerns but the country remains a marginal producer and continues to rely heavily on imported oil. There is a small mining industry producing marble, copper, lead, zinc and other metals.

Although Guatemala has received solid support from the USA and international institutions such as the Inter-American Development Bank and the IMF, its economic development in the last 25 years has been undermined by chronic internal conflict, exacerbated by several major natural disasters and low prices for Guatemala's main export commodities. Nonetheless, the economy has grown steadily in the last few years and annual growth is currently 4 per cent.

Guatemala is a member of the Central American Common Market.

BUSINESS ETIQUETTE: Guatemalan businesspeople tend to be rather formal and conservative. Normal courtesies should be observed and appointments should be made. Punctuality is appreciated and calling cards can be useful.
Office hours: Mon-Fri 0800-1800, Sat 0800-1200.
CONFERENCES/CONVENTIONS: Guatemala has the facilities and hotel infrastructure for conventions, conferences and business meetings. The Centro Cultural Miguel Angel Asturias and other modern conference centres are available for such events, often quite close, or accessible to Guatemala's beauty spots.

COMMERCIAL INFORMATION

Cámara de Comercio de Guatemala (Chamber of Commerce)
10A Calle 3-80, Zona 1, Guatemala City, Guatemala
Tel: 253 5353.
Website: www.negociosenguatemala.com

Cámara de Industria (Chamber of Industry)
Ruta 6 9-21, Zona 4, Edificio Cámara de Industria,
01004 Guatemala City, Guatemala
Tel: 334 0850.
Website: www.industriaguate.com

Guatemala Tourist Commission (Information on Conferences/Conventions)
Centro Cívico, 7A Avenida 1-17, Zona 4,
Guatemala City 01004, Guatemala
Tel: 2421 2810 *or* (800) 464 8281 (24-hour toll-free number in USA) *or* (801) 464 8281 (24-hour toll-free number in Guatemala).
Website: www.visitguatemala.com

Guinea Bissau

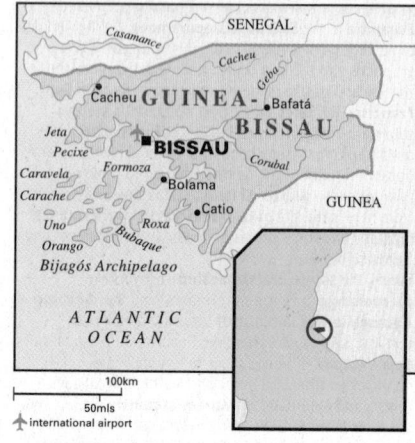

Location: West Africa.

Time: GMT.

Overview

Guinea-Bissau is a small coastal country just to the South of Senegal where the people speak a host of local languages and Creole together with Portuguese and a little bit of French.

Until recently, Guinea-Bissau was well off the tourist route. Struggles for independence and a civil war in 1998-99 devastated the economy. Tourist facilities and infrastructure remain, in general, very limited but efforts have been made to encourage visitors to this undiscovered gem of West Africa.

Although a relatively small country, Guinea-Bissau's beaches and wildlife are exceptional while West African traditions and Portuguese colonial remains can still be seen. On the coast, one finds fishing villages surrounded by forests, whereas further inland the country is dry and dusty. The islands off the coast of Guinea-Bissau (the Bijagos Archipelago) are of exceptional beauty. These islands are home to a group of indigenous people. Turtles, sharks, manatees, and a very special and very rare form of hippopotamus that lives mostly in salt-water can all be seen here.

For those willing to go off the beaten track, Guinea-Bissau has a lot going for it.

General Information

AREA: 36,125 sq km (13,948 sq miles).
POPULATION: 1.4 million (official estimate 2002).
POPULATION DENSITY: 40.1 per sq km.
CAPITAL: Bissau. **Population:** 197,610 (1991).
GEOGRAPHY: Guinea-Bissau (formerly Portuguese Guinea) is located in West Africa, and is bordered to the north by Senegal and to the south and east by the Republic of Guinea. It encompasses the adjacent Bijagós Islands and the island of Bolama. The country rises from a coastal plain broken up by numerous inlets through a transitional plateau to mountains on the border with Guinea. Thick forest and mangrove swamp cover the area nearest to the Atlantic Ocean. Savannah covers the inland areas.
GOVERNMENT: Republic. Gained independence from Portugal in 1973. **Head of State:** Joao Bernardo Vieira since 2005. **Head of Government:** Prime Minister Aristides Gomes since November 2005. **Recent history:** In September 1974, Portugal formally recognised the independence of Guinea-Bissau. The leader of the *Partido Africano da Independencia da Guine e Cabo Verde* (PAIGC) was Joao Vieira, formerly chief of the armed forces, who went on to run the country for the next 25 years. Guinea-Bissau functioned as a typical one-party state until the beginning of the 1990s when the government began a process of political reform which led to multi-party elections being held in 1994. The PAIGC secured a clear majority in the National People's Assembly while Vieira

secured the presidency at the run-off stage.
The Vieira Government was unable to tackle the country's poor and worsening economic situation. It also became embroiled in a series of disputes with Senegal over territorial waters and alleged support for secessionist rebels in the Senegalese region of Casamance. Although these were settled by external mediation, bilateral relations are still brittle. The Csamance guerrillas' main supporter in Guinea-Bissau was Brigadier Ansumane Mane, a politically ambitious officer who in 1998 staged a rebellion against his own government. Vieira survived the attempted coup on this occasion but in May the following year, Mane managed to take power. Elections were held six months later, and the PAIGC lost control of both the presidency and the national assembly at the hands of the *Partido para a Renovacao Social* (PRS). PRS leader Kumba Yala, who took over as President, was quite incapable of tackling the country's enormous problems: he too was overthrown by the military at what was at least the third attempt in September 2003. Henrique Pereira Rosa became President and then later Carlos Gomes Junior became Prime Minister in May 2004.
The situation has remained volatile throughout 2005. In April, Joao Bernardo Vieira, the former military ruler toppled in the 1999 rebellion, returned from exile in Portugal. In May, the former President Kumba Yala, who was deposed in 2003, declared that he was still the rightful Head of State and staged a brief occupation of the presidency building.
On 10 August 2005 Joao Bernardo Vieria was declared the winner of a July presidential runoff election over Malam Bacai Sanha in an election judged by international observers to be free and fair. Vieria dismissed the government of Carlos Gomes Junior in November 2005, appointing Aristides Gomes in his place.
LANGUAGE: Official language is Portuguese. The majority of the population speak Guinean Creole. Balante and Fulani languages are also spoken.
RELIGION: Mainly animist and Muslim. There is a small minority of Roman Catholics and other Christians.
ELECTRICITY: Limited electricity supply on 220 volts AC, 50Hz.
SOCIAL CONVENTIONS: Casual wear is widely accepted. Social customs should be respected, particularly in Muslim areas. Petty thievery and pickpocketing are increasingly common, particularly at the airport, in markets and at public gatherings. **Photography:** Visitors should request permission from security personnel before photographing military or police installations.

Climate

The climate is tropical, with a wet season from June to October. The dry season is from December to April, with hot winds from the interior. Humidity is high from July to September. Temperatures vary with altitude and distance from the coast.
Required clothing: Tropical lightweight cotton clothes and raincoat for the rainy season.

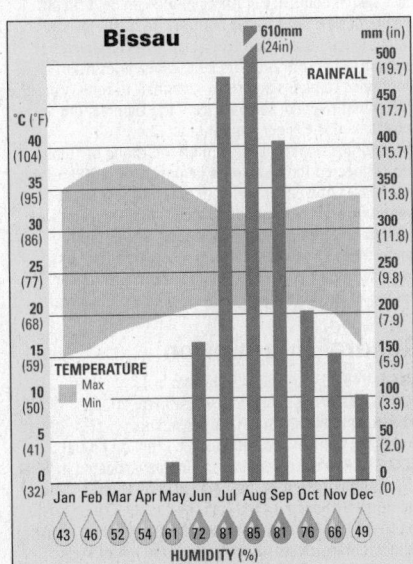

Communications

Telephone: IDD is available. Country code: 245. Outgoing international calls must go through the operator. It is difficult to find public telephones or to receive international calls. Telephone services are also expensive.
Mobile telephone: Guinetel plans to launch its services in March 2006. No roaming agreements have been announced yet.

Internet: Very limited Internet access is available in Bissau.
Post: There is a limited postal service.
MEDIA: Since the overthrow of Kumba Yala in 2003, the media scene has been less repressive. The lack of a reliable power supply is still a problem. Private radio stations operate alongside the state-run broadcaster. There are few private newspapers, essentially due to financial constraints rather than to Government interference.
Press: There are no English-language papers. *Journal Nô Pintcha* is a state-run newspaper published daily; *Banobero*, *Correio-Bissau* and *Fraskera* are private weekly publications.
TV: *Radio Televisao de Guinea-Bissau* (RTGB) is state-run; *RTP Africa*, operated by Portuguese public broadcaster RTP, is run by local management; its studios and infrastructure are funded by Portugal.
Radio: *Radio Nacional* is a state-run station; *Radio Pindjiguiti*, *Bombolom FM* and *Voice of Quelele* are private stations.

Passport/Visa

	Passport Required?	Visa Required?	Return Ticket Required?
Full British	Yes	Yes	Yes
Australian	Yes	Yes	Yes
Canadian	Yes	Yes	Yes
USA	Yes	Yes	Yes
Other EU	Yes	Yes	Yes
Japanese	Yes	Yes	Yes

Note: *Regulations and requirements may be subject to change at short notice, and you are advised to contact the appropriate diplomatic or consular authority before finalising travel arrangements. Any numbers in the chart refer to the footnotes below.*

PASSPORTS: Passport valid for six months required by all.
VISAS: Required by all except the following:
(a) nationals of ECOWAS member countries for a maximum stay of one month (exceptions are possible, check with nearest Consulate);
(b) transit passengers continuing their journey by the same or first connecting aircraft provided holding valid onward or return documentation and not leaving the airport.
Types of visa and cost: *Tourist*, *Business*: €50 (single-entry). Multiple-entry and *Transit* only available on request. An extra €5 is needed for postal applications.
Validity: Single-entry visas are normally valid for up to 45 days; multiple-entry visas are valid for up to 90 days within a period of six months. *Transit* visas are valid for up to five days. Extensions are then granted at the discretion of the Immigration Authorities.
Application to: Consulate (or Consular section at Embassy); see *Passport/Visa Information*.
Application requirements: (a) Two completed application forms. (b) Two passport-size photos. (c) Valid passport. (d) Return ticket. (e) Fee. Business: (a)-(e) and, (f) Confirmation of a job placement.
Working days required: Five. Urgent visas can be handled within 24-48 hours.

PASSPORT/VISA INFORMATION

Embassy of Guinea-Bissau in France
94 Rue St Lazare, 75009 Paris, France
Tel: (1) 4526 1851. Fax: (1) 4526 6059.

Embassy of Guinea-Bissau in the USA
15929 Yukon Lane, Rockville, MD 20855, USA
Tel/Fax: (301) 947 3958.

Money

Currency: CFA (*Communauté Financiaire Africaine*) Franc (XOF) = 100 centimes. Notes are in denominations of XOF10,000, 5000, 2500, 1000 and 500. Coins are in denominations of XOF250, 100, 50, 25, 10 and 5. Guinea-Bissau is part of the French Monetary Area. Only currency issued by the *Banque des Etats de l'Afrique de l'Ouest* (Bank of West African States) is valid; currency issued by the *Banque des Etats de l'Afrique Centrale* (Bank of Central African States) is not. The CFA Franc is tied to the Euro.
Currency exchange: US currency in small denominations is the most useful for exchange. Inter-bank fund transfers are frequently difficult and time-consuming to accomplish.
Credit & debit cards: Very limited use. Check with your credit or debit card company for details of merchant acceptability and other services which may be available.
Travellers cheques: These are rarely accepted. They can sometimes be cashed at banks. There is a fixed rate of commission on all transactions.
Currency restrictions: Import and export of local currency

is prohibited. Import of foreign currency is unlimited, provided declared on arrival; export of foreign currency is limited to the amount declared on arrival.
Banking hours: Mon-Fri 0730-1430.
Exchange rate indicators:
Rate at time of publishing
£1.00= XOF970.85
$1.00= XOF557.61

Duty Free

The following goods can be imported into Guinea-Bissau without incurring customs duty:
A reasonable quantity of tobacco products; 2.5l of alcoholic beverages (non-Muslims only); and a reasonable quantity of perfume in opened bottles.

Public Holidays

Below are listed Public Holidays for the January 2006-June 2007 period.
2006: Jan 1 New Year's Day. **Jan 10** Tabaski (Feast of the Sacrifice). **Jan 20** Death of Amilcar Cabral. **Mar 8** International Women's Day. **May 1** Labour Day. **Aug 3** Anniversary of the Killing of Pidjiguoiti. **Sep 24** National Day. **Oct 22-24** Korité (end of Ramadan). **Dec 25** Christmas Day. **Dec 31** Tabaski (Feast of the Sacrifice).
2007: Jan 1 New Year's Day. **Jan 20** Death of Amilcar Cabral. **Mar 8** International Women's Day. **May 1** Labour Day.
Note: Muslim festivals are timed according to local sightings of various phases of the moon and the dates given above are approximations. During the lunar month of Ramadan that precedes Korité, Muslims fast during the day and feast at night and normal business patterns may be interrupted. Many restaurants are closed during the day and there may be restrictions on smoking and drinking. Some disruption may continue into Korité itself. Korité and Tabaski may last anything from two to 10 days, depending on the region. For more information, see the *World of Islam* appendix.

Health

	Special Precautions?	Certificate Required?
Yellow Fever	Yes	1
Cholera	Yes	2
Typhoid & Polio	3	N/A
Malaria	4	N/A

Note: *Regulations and requirements may be subject to change at short notice, and you are advised to contact your doctor well in advance of your intended date of departure. Any numbers in the chart refer to the footnotes below.*

1: A yellow fever vaccination certificate is required from travellers over one year of age coming from infected areas (contact the nearest Embassy for latest details). Travellers arriving from non-endemic zones should note that a vaccination is strongly recommended for travel outside the urban areas, even if an outbreak of the disease has not been reported and they would normally not require a vaccination certificate to enter the country.
2: Following WHO guidelines issued in 1973, a cholera vaccination certificate is no longer a condition of entry to Guinea-Bissau. However, cholera is a serious risk in this country and precautions are essential. Since June 2005, a cholera outbreak has affected over 10,000 people in Bissau, Biombo and Cachea districts; over 200 people have died, but it is now considered to be under control. Up-to-date advice should be sought before deciding whether these precautions should include vaccination as medical opinion is divided over its effectiveness. See the *Health* appendix for more information.
3: Immunisation against typhoid and poliomyelitis is often advised.
4: Malaria risk, predominantly in the malignant *falciparum* form, exists all year throughout the country. Resistance to chloroquine has been reported.
Food & drink: All water should be regarded as being potentially contaminated. Water used for drinking, brushing teeth or making ice should have first been boiled or otherwise sterilised. Only eat well-cooked meat and fish, preferably served hot. Pork, salad and mayonnaise may carry increased risk. Vegetables should be cooked and fruit peeled.
Other risks: *Diarrhoeal* diseases, including *giardiasis*, and *typhoid fevers* are common. *Bilharzia* (schistosomiasis) is present. Avoid swimming and paddling in fresh water; swimming pools which are well chlorinated and maintained are safe. *Onchocerciasis* (river blindness) and *trypanosomiasis* (sleeping sickness) are present. *Hepatitis A* and *E* are widespread. *Hepatitis B* is hyperendemic. *TB* occurs. Epidemics of *meningococcal disease* may occur,

particularly in the savannah areas and during the dry season. Immunisation against *diphtheria* is sometimes recommended.

Rabies is present. For those at high risk, vaccination before arrival should be considered. If you are bitten, seek medical advice without delay. For more information, consult the *Health* appendix.

Health care: Medical facilities are extremely limited and medicines often unavailable. Doctors and hospitals often expect immediate cash payment for health services. Health insurance is essential. Most doctors work in the public service and have their private clinic in the afternoon and evening. There are few specialists. Several foreign aid agencies have their own doctor and medical facilities, including the French Mission and the Swedish Embassy. There is also a UN clinic. All these clinics will receive visitors in an emergency, but none of them have surgical facilities.

Travel - International

AIR:

 The national airline is *Guiné Bissau Airlines (G6)*. Other airlines that fly direct to Bissau include *Aeroflot* and *TAP Air Portugal*.

Approximate flight times: From Bissau to *London* is 10 hours 20 minutes (including stopover of one hour 30 minutes, usually in Lisbon). There are daily flights to *Lisbon*.

Main airports: *Bissau (OXB)* (Bissalanca) is 11km (7 miles) from the city. *To/from the airport:* Taxi service is available to the city (travel time – 30 minutes).

Departure tax: None.

SEA/RIVER:

 Ferries running between coastal and inland ports form an important part of the transport system, especially as roads are often impassable (see *Sea/River* in *Travel – Internal* section). The main port is Bissau. This and four inland ports are currently being expanded and upgraded. A new commercial river port is being constructed at N'Pungda.

ROAD:

 Travellers should check that overland entry is allowed and travelling is safe before embarking (the usual route of entry is by plane from Conakry in Guinea Republic); entry from Senegal is not recommended.

Travel - Internal

AIR:

 There are 10 small internal airports. The national airline provides internal flights, including to the outlying islands.

SEA/RIVER:

 Most towns are accessible by ship. Riverboats can reach almost all areas; there are ferries from Bissau to Bolama (often irregular owing to tides) and Bissau to Bafatá, calling at smaller towns en route. Coast-hopping ferries go from the north coast to Bissau.

ROAD:

 There are about 4150km (2578 miles) of roads, one-fifth tarred and a similar proportion improved for all-weather use. Improvements are planned. There are local and long-distance **taxis** and **buses** (the latter offer limited services). Traffic drives on the right.

Documentation: An International Driving Permit is recommended, although it is not legally required. A temporary driving licence is available from local authorities on presentation of a valid UK driving licence.

Travel Advice

Travellers should avoid political demonstrations or rallies. The threat from terrorism is low.

There are occasional outbreaks of cholera. Travellers are advised to drink only bottled water.

This advice is based on information provided by the Foreign and Commonwealth Office in the UK. It is correct at time of publishing. As the situation can change rapidly, visitors are advised to contact the following organisations for the latest travel advice:

British Foreign and Commonwealth Office
Tel: (0845) 850 2829.
Website: www.fco.gov.uk

US Department of State
Website: http://travel.state.gov/travel

Accommodation

HOTELS:

 A range of hotels is on offer, some of international standard and others that are small and inexpensive. Accommodation should be

booked in advance. Tariffs are liable to change at any time, therefore confirmation of booking is essential.

CAMPING:

 With the exception of Bolama, there are no designated campsites and camping is not recommended.

Top Things To See & Do

• Enjoy the relaxed atmosphere of **Bissau**, the capital, a town of approximately 200,000 inhabitants. The Portuguese quarter, with its winding streets and Mediterranean-style houses, is worth a visit.

• Visit the **Museum of African Artefacts,** which is a treasure trove of traditional sculpture, pottery, weaving and basketware.

• Enjoy the lively ambience and colourful stalls of Bissau's covered central **market.**

• Go off the beaten track to the **Bijagós Archipelago,** which comprises a group of small islands, several of which are uninhabited, and most of which are very rarely visited by foreigners. The easiest ones to reach are Bolama and Bubaque. **Bolama**, the original capital of Guinea-Bissau, is now a rather attractive ruin, and the island is worth seeing, with several good beaches. There is no accommodation, but camping is an option. The unspoilt island of **Bubaque** is easily accessible from Bissau and offers accommodation in the town.

• Encounter thousands of birds, big mammals and other native fauna which are living freely in the **wildlife breeding River Zoo Farm.** The farm owns a 500-acre (200-hectare) area which is bordered by two freshwater rivers and a lake. The farm ground is registered as an official fauna reserve (website: (www.riverzoofarm.com/the_farm.htm).

• Visit the **Cantanhez Natural Park** in Jemberem. This community-based conservation project was initiated to protect birds, monkeys and chimpanzees (although there is a debate as to whether they are present in the country or not). You can arrange a guided tour through the local chief.

TOURIST INFORMATION

Centro de Informação e Turismo
CP 294, Bissau, Guinea-Bissau
Tel: 213 905 *or* 212 844 (Government office).

Entertainment

FOOD & DRINK: Guinea-Bissau's few hotels and restaurants offer excellent food, though some places are expensive. Local specialities include *jollof rice*, chicken and fish dishes. Staples are cassava, yams and maize. **Tipping:** 10 per cent is an acceptable amount, although not encouraged.

SHOPPING: Locally-made artefacts and carvings can be found in the markets. There are also some modern shops in Bissau. **Shopping hours:** Mon-Fri 0730-1230 and 1430-1830.

Business

ECONOMY: Rice is the staple food in this poor, largely subsistence economy. The main cash crops are groundnuts, cashew nuts and palm kernels. Timber is the only significant industry. An attempt to revive cotton production has received EU assistance; sugar refining and fishing have also undergone major development. Planned developments of oil and bauxite deposits have not progressed as far as had been hoped.

Guinea-Bissau is a member of the West African Economic Community (ECOWAS) and joined the CFA Franc Zone in May 1997. Since then, the country has been recovering from internal conflicts which cut economic output by up to one-third and damaged much of the country's already limited infrastructure. In the short term, Guinea-Bissau will continue to rely on large quantities of foreign aid, of which it is among the highest per capita recipients in the world. France, Portugal, Italy and Thailand are Guinea-Bissau's largest trading partners.

BUSINESS ETIQUETTE: Businesspeople wear safari suits (bush jackets without a tie). A knowledge of Portuguese is useful as only a few executives speak English. Visits during Ramadan should be avoided. **Office hours:** Mon-Fri 0730-1400.

COMMERCIAL INFORMATION

For further information contact the Embassy (or Consular section at Embassy); see *Passport/Visa Information.*

Guinea, Republic of

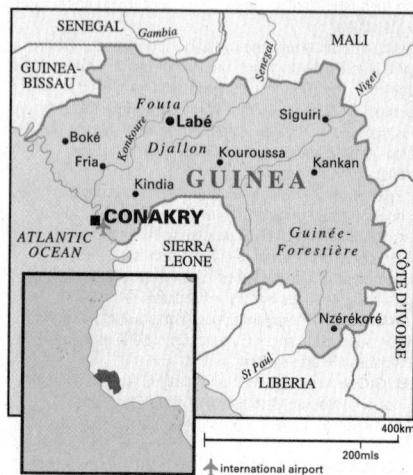

Location: West Africa

Time: GMT.

Overview

The Republic of Guinea is bordered by Guinea-Bissau, Senegal, Mali, Côte d'Ivoire, Liberia and Sierra Leone. In 1958, when it declared independence from France and voted in a staunchly socialist one-party Government, Guinea became an isolated and secretive country. However, after the death of the dictator Sekou Touré in 1984, Guinea began, slowly, to allow tourists through its once stubbornly closed doors. Even so, it is still one of the least visited countries in Africa and it can be difficult, despite declarations to the contrary, to acquire visas. Guinea's main attraction to tourists is its relatively undisturbed countryside. Its landscape varies from mountains to plains and from savannah to forest, and the three great rivers of West Africa – the Gambia, the Senegal and the Niger – all originate here.

The capital, Conakry, is located on the island of Tumbo and connected to the Kaloum Peninsula by a 300m-long (984ft) pier. The city is well laid out, its alleys shaded by mangrove and coconut palm trees. One dish visitors are likely to be offered is hot maize soup, served from calabashes. Guinea has a strong music tradition and Conakry, in particular, is a dynamic centre for music. The singing of the Kindia people is especially renowned.

General Information

AREA: 245,857 sq km (94,926 sq miles).
POPULATION: 8.8 million (UN estimate 2005).
POPULATION DENSITY: 38 per sq km.
CAPITAL: Conakry. **Population:** 1.1 million (2002).
GEOGRAPHY: The Republic of Guinea is located in West Africa and bordered to the northwest by Guinea-Bissau, the north by Senegal and Mali, the east by Côte d'Ivoire, the south by Liberia and the southwest by Sierra Leone. Guinea's many rivers supply water to much of West Africa. The River Niger flows north from the southern highlands into Mali before turning south again through Niger and Nigeria. The coastal plain is made up of mangrove swamps, while inland are the Fouta Djalon hills which form several distinct ranges and plateaux over the whole of western Guinea. In the northeast, savannah plains of the Sahel region stretch into Mali. To the south are mountains known as the Guinea Highlands.
GOVERNMENT: Republic since 1958. Gained independence from France in 1958. **Head of State:** President Lansana Conté since 1984. **Head of**

Government: Cellou Dalein Diallo since December 2004.
Recent history: A new constitution, known as the Third Republic, was accepted by national referendum in December 1990. The first Presidential elections under the new constitution were held in December 1993 and won by Conté. At the beginning of February 1996, Conté survived an attempted coup, after which he assumed personal control of the country's armed forces. He also appointed a Prime Minister, Laimine Sidimé, for the first time. (Sidimé was replaced by Francois Lonseny Fall in February 2004 who then fled the country and resigned in April of the same year. He is currently living in exile claiming his life would be in danger if he returned). The position has since been filled by Cellou Dalein Diallo in December 2004. Conté was elected for a third term as President in December 2003 (after first holding a referendum in 2001 that officially removed the two-term limit on presidency). In March 2006, President Conté was flown to Switzerland for medical treatment. Opposition parties called for the formation of an interim Government.
LANGUAGE: French is the official language. Susu, Malinké and Fula are local languages.
RELIGION: The majority of the population are Muslim, with animist and Christian minorities.
ELECTRICITY: 220 volts, 50Hz.
SOCIAL CONVENTIONS: Although Muslim customs are less strict than in the Arab world, beliefs and traditions should be respected by tourists. Casual dress is acceptable. Street crime is relatively common. It is important to greet people and ask them how they are before starting a conversation. Guineans always use titles when addressing others, so the visitor should do likewise (Monsieur, Madame, Mademoiselle etc). **Photography:** A permit (applied for in advance) has to be obtained from the *Ministère de l'Intérieur et de la Sécurité* when photographing Government buildings, military and transportation facilities or public works. It is inadvisable to photograph buildings at present, and visitors should always ask local people if they want to photograph them.

Climate

The climate is tropical and humid with a wet and a dry season. Guinea is one of the wettest countries in West Africa. The monsoon rainy season with a south-westerly wind lasts from June to November; the dry season with a north-easterly wind lasts from December to May.
Required clothing: Tropical or washable cottons throughout the year. A light raincoat or umbrella is needed during the rainy season.

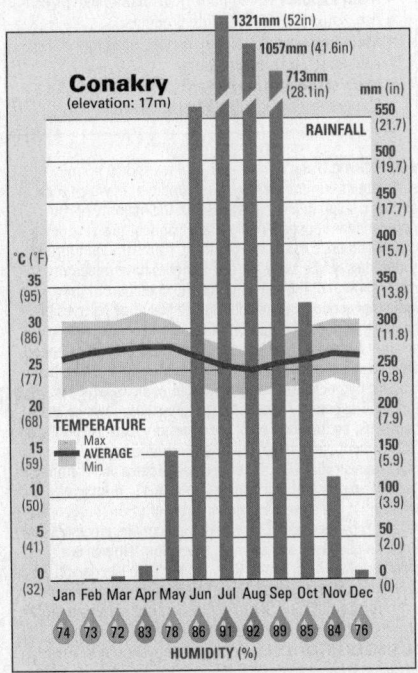

Communications

Telephone: IDD service is available. Country code: 224. The communication is relatively poor and outgoing international calls must be made through the operator. Limited telephone and fax lines are usually available 1800-0600.
Mobile telephone: There are several mobile phone operators. No roaming agreements have been declared.
Internet: Internet cafes are available in Conakry and Souleyman.
Post: There are numerous post offices in the capital.

MEDIA: Press: Newspapers include *Horoya* (official, daily), *Le Lynx* (satirical, weekly), *L'Indépendant* and *La Lance* (weekly), *Journal Officiel de Guinée* (official, fortnightly) and *L'Evénement de Guinée* (monthly).
TV and Radio: *Radiodiffusion-Television Guineenne (RTG)* is the state-run national television and radio braodcaster.

Passport/Visa

	Passport Required?	Visa Required?	Return Ticket Required?
Full British	Yes	Yes	No
Australian	Yes	Yes	No
Canadian	Yes	Yes	No
USA	Yes	Yes	No
Other EU	Yes	Yes	No
Japanese	Yes	Yes	No

Note: *Regulations and requirements may be subject to change at short notice, and you are advised to contact the appropriate diplomatic or consular authority before finalising travel arrangements. Any numbers in the chart refer to the footnotes below.*

PASSPORTS: Passports valid for a minimum of six months beyond date of departure required by all.
VISAS: Required by all except the following: Nationals of Benin, Burkina Faso, Cape Verde, Côte d'Ivoire, Gambia, Ghana, Guinea-Bissau, Liberia, Mali, Niger, Nigeria, Senegal, Sierra Leone and Togo for stays of up to 90 days.
Types of visa and cost: *Tourist* and *Business*: £65 (single-entry for a stay of up to one month); £90 (multiple-entry for a stay of up to three months).
Application to: Consulate (or Consular section at Embassy). UK nationals may apply to the Chancery Consulate General of the Republic of Guinea in London (see *Passport/Visa Information*).
Application requirements: (a) Two application forms. (b) Two passport-size photos. (c) Passport with a remaining validity of six months after intended length of stay. (d) Proof of sufficient funds. (e) Letter of invitation or hotel reservation. *Business:* (a)-(e) and (f) Letter from the applicant's company. (g) Letter from the sponsoring company in Guinea.
Working days required: Two to three.

PASSPORT VISA INFORMATION

Consulate General of the Republic of Guinea in the UK
83 Victoria Street, London, SW1H 0HW, UK
Tel: (020) 7078 6087.
E-mail: ambaguineeuk@yahoo.co.uk

Embassy of the Republic of Guinea in the USA
2112 Leroy Place, NW, Washington, DC 20008, USA
Tel: (202) 986 4300.
Fax: (202) 986 4800.

Money

Currency: Guinea Franc (GNF) = 100 centimes. Notes are in denominations of GNF5000, 1000 and 500. Coins are in denominations of GNF25, 10, 5 and 1.
Currency exchange: Hotels will accept some foreign currencies in payment. Inter-bank fund transfers are frequently difficult, if not impossible, to accomplish.
Credit & debit cards: Limited acceptance. Check with your credit or debit card company for details of merchant acceptability and other services which may be available. Guinea has a cash economy. ATMs are not available.
Traveller's cheques: To avoid additional exchange rate charges, travellers are advised to take traveller's cheques in US Dollars or Euros. These are only accepted in some banks and hotels.
Currency restrictions: It is possible to import up to GNF1000 providing you have a valid export declaration for that amount. Import of foreign currency is unlimited, provided declared on arrival; export is limited to the amount declared on arrival.
Note: It is compulsory to exchange a certain amount of foreign currency. The amount depends on the length of stay specified in the visa, and is at the discretion of the immigration authorities. Unused currency can sometimes be re-exchanged – again at the discretion of the authorities. Travellers are advised to check that the amounts exchanged have been entered correctly onto the declaration form.
Banking hours: Mon-Fri 0800-1230 and 1430-1700.
Exchange rate indicators:
Rate at time of publishing
£1.00= GNF6998.71
$1.00= GNF4065.00

Duty Free

The following goods may be imported into Guinea without incurring customs duty:
1000 cigarettes or 250 cigars or 1kg of tobacco; 1 bottle of alcoholic beverage (opened); a reasonable quantity of perfume.

Public Holidays

Below are listed Public Holidays for the January 2006-June 2007 period.
2006: Jan 1 New Year's Day. **Jan 10** Eid al-Adha (Feast of the Sacrifice). **Apr 14** Easter Monday. **May 1** Labour Day. **Apr 10** Mouloud (Birth of the Prophet). **May 25** Ascension. **Aug 15** Assumption. **Aug 27** Anniversary of Women's Revolt. **Sep 28** Referendum Day. **Oct 2** Republic Day. **Oct 22-24** Eid al-Fitr (End of Ramadan). **Nov 1** All Saints' Day. **Nov** Laila toul Kadir (day after the night's vigil)/Day of 1970 Invasion. **Dec 25** Christmas Day. **Dec 31** Eid al-Adha (Feast of the Sacrifice). **2007: Jan 1** New Year's Day. **Mar 31** Mouloud (Birth of the Prophet). **Apr 9** Easter Monday. **May 1** Labour Day. **May 17** Ascension.
Note: Muslim festivals are timed according to local sightings of various phases of the moon and the dates given above are approximations. During the lunar month of Ramadan that precedes Eid al-Fitr, Muslims fast during the day and feast at night and normal business patterns may be interrupted. Many restaurants are closed during the day and there may be restrictions on smoking and drinking. Some disruption may continue into Eid al-Fitr itself. Eid al-Fitr may last anything from two to 10 days, depending on the region. For more information, see the *World of Islam* appendix.

Health

	Special Precautions?	Certificate Required?
Yellow Fever	Yes	1
Cholera	2	No
Typhoid & Polio	3	N/A
Malaria	4	N/A

Note: *Regulations and requirements may be subject to change at short notice, and you are advised to contact your doctor well in advance of your intended date of departure. Any numbers in the chart refer to the footnotes below.*

1: A yellow fever vaccination certificate is required from travellers over one year of age coming from infected areas. Travellers arriving from non-endemic zones should note that vaccination is strongly recommended for travel outside the urban areas, even if an outbreak of the disease has not been reported and they would normally not require a vaccination certificate to enter the country.
2: Following WHO guidelines issued in 1973, a cholera vaccination certificate is no longer a condition of entry to Guinea. However, cholera is a serious risk in this country and precautions are essential. Up-to-date advice should be sought before deciding whether these precautions should include vaccination as medical opinion is divided over its effectiveness. See the *Health* appendix for more information.
3: Immunisation against typhoid and poliomyelitis is often recommended.
4: A malaria risk, predominantly in the malignant *falciparum* form, exists all year throughout the country. Resistance to chloroquine has been reported.
Food & drink: All water should be regarded as being potentially contaminated. Water used for drinking, brushing teeth or making ice should have first been boiled or otherwise sterilised. Only eat well-cooked meat and fish, preferably served hot. Pork, salad and mayonnaise may carry increased risk. Vegetables should be cooked and fruit peeled.
Other risks: *Diarrhoeal diseases*, including *giardiasis*, and *typhoid fevers* are common. *Bilharzia* (schistosomiasis) is present. Avoid swimming and paddling in fresh water; swimming pools which are well chlorinated and maintained are safe. *Onchocerciasis* (river blindness) and *trypanosomiasis* (sleeping sickness) are present. *Hepatitis A, C* and *E* are widespread. *Hepatitis B* is hyperendemic. Epidemics of *meningococcal disease* may occur, particularly in the savannah areas and during the dry season. *Dengue fever* and TB both occur. Immunisation against *diphtheria* is sometimes recommended.
Rabies is present. For those at high risk, vaccination before arrival should be considered. If you are bitten, seek medical advice without delay. For more information, consult the *Health* appendix.
Health care: Health insurance is essential. Travel insurance which covers travellers for repatriation to their country is advisable. There are rudimentary medical, dental and optical facilities in Conakry. Medical facilities are

poorly equipped and extremely limited. Some private facilities provide a better range of treatment options, but are still well below global standards. There are no ambulance or rescue emergency services available. Doctors and hospitals expect immediate cash payment for health services.

Travel - International

AIR:

Air France (website: www.airfrance.com) flies regularly from London to Conakry, via Paris. *KLM* (website:www.klm.com) and *Brussels Airlines* (website: www.flysn.com) also fly direct from Europe. *Air Afrique* (www.airafrique.com) operates from New York to Dakar, from where connecting flights to Guinea are available.

Approximate flight times: From Conakry to *London* is 11 hours (including a stopover time in Paris or Brussels of up to three hours).

Main airports: *Conakry (CKY)* is 15km (10 miles) southwest of the city. *To/from the airport*: Taxis are available to the city. *Facilities*: Bank and car hire.

Note: Foreigners at Conakry Airport are particular targets for pickpockets and persons posing as officials who will offer assistance and then make off with bags, purses and wallets. Being met at the airport by travel agents, business contacts, family members or friends lessens the risk of this.

Departure tax: None.

SEA/RIVER:

The fast hydrofoil service along the coast from Conakry to Freetown in Sierra Leone has been stopped due to the civil war, but will resume once Freetown is rebuilt. There is also a ferry to Mali which operates when the river is high enough.

ROAD:

There are road links with Danané (Côte d'Ivoire), Bamako (Mali) and Tambacounda (Senegal). Bus services are available to the neighbouring countries, but services can be unreliable and timetables may be purely theoretical (see also *Travel – Internal* section). Visitors should also note that political instability is persisting in some neighbouring countries - notably in Guinea-Bissau. Check with an embassy or relevant organisation for up-to-date travel advice.

Travel - Internal

AIR:

Guinee Airlines operates internal services to some of the main towns, such as Boké, Conakry, Labé, Kankan, Kissidougou, Koundarg and Siguiri. Schedules are erratic.

RAIL:

Despite the existence of rail lines and plans to upgrade them, there are currently no rail services in Guinea.

ROAD:

Many roads are in poor condition and the minor roads are often overgrown with bush. Livestock and pedestrians create road hazards, so extra caution is to be taken while driving at night. Travel by road is often impossible in the rainy season (Jun-Nov). The roads between Conakry (via Kindia) and Kissidougou and from Boké to Kamsar are both paved. Traffic drives on the right. In an effort to counter urban crime, the Guinean Government maintains roadblocks from 2200-0600. **Bus:** The Government bus company, *SOGETRAG*, operates services from Conakry to most other towns. The buses are fairly comfortable and good value. **Taxi:** These are available, although fares should be negotiated in advance. Bush taxis usually cover smaller distances than buses and can take up to seven passengers.

URBAN:

Guinea has no public transport but there are local vans which pick people up along many routes. Buses and taxis operate cheaply within Conakry, but are poorly maintained and tend to be overcrowded.

Travel Advice

Travellers are advised against all but essential travel to the areas bordering Liberia, Sierra Leone and Côte d'Ivoire. Travellers should avoid all demonstrations and political rallies.

Petty crime is common in Guinea. Travellers should take sensible precautions and maintain a high level of vigilance in public.

The threat from terrorism is low.

This advice is based on information provided by the Foreign and Commonwealth Office in the UK. It is correct at time of publishing. As the situation can change rapidly, visitors are advised to contact the following organisations for the latest travel advice:

British Foreign and Commonwealth Office
Tel: (0845) 850 2829.
Website: www.fco.gov.uk

US Department of State
Website: http://travel.state.gov/travel

Accommodation

HOTELS:

In Conakry there are a few fairly expensive hotels of a good standard. In addition, the city centre also has a number of good-value hotels with basic, but adequate, facilities. Outside the city centre, accommodation gets sparser, but there are hotels available, for instance in Labé, Katikan, Kindia and Dalaba. Visitors are advised to book in advance and obtain written confirmation.

REST HOUSES: These are available in most of the major towns; enquire locally.

Top Things To See & Do

- The capital, **Conakry**, is located on the island of Tumbo and is connected to the Kaloum Peninsula by a 300m-long (984ft) pier. It is a city noted for its botanical gardens. The **Cathedral**, built in the 1930s and located in the town centre, is well worth viewing. There is also a **National Museum** (**Musée National**), whose collection of masks, statues and musical instruments is completely free to the public and definitely worth your time. The **Palais du Peuple** is a large, Chinese-built auditorium that is home to two national ballet troupes. Plenty of restaurants line the main north-south street, the **Autoroute** (**Route du Niger**).
- The **Kakimbon Caves** in the village of Ratoma, now a suburb of Conakry, are the source of many interesting legends and are bestowed with great religious significance by the local Baga people. The **Îles de Los**, off the Kaloum Peninsula some 10km (6 miles) southwest of Conakry, are recommended as a tourist destination and are easily accessible from Conakry. Good beaches can also be found at the **Île de Roume** and **Île de Kassa**, the latter being accessible via a public boat service. Approximately 150km (93 miles) outside Conakry is the picturesque **Le Voile de la Mariée**, nestled at the bottom of a 70m- (230ft-) high rock from which the **River Sabende** plunges, amidst lush vegetation, into a deep pond. In **Pita**, located between Dalaba and Labé, the **Kinkon Falls** can be found which produce 150m (492ft) of cascading water. The town of **Katikan** is interesting for its open air markets and **Great Mosque**, along with the **Presidential Palace**. A medium-length excursion from Conakry is the town of Kindia, renowned for its quality of cloth and weaving - an indigo dyeing centre and a cloth market grace the centre.
- If Guinea has a 'party town', it is probably going to be **Faranah**. When the sun sets, this town buzzes with people frequenting the area's cafes and restaurants, usually well within the budget range. Its great mosque, villas, wine boulevards and markets make this an interesting stop along the **source of the Niger**. Indeed, the source of the Niger is an interesting excursion. The river flows from **Foroknia** north to **Bamako**. The whole area is privy to many sacred peoples but the area is quite a sensitive one and local guides should be hired.

Known as the land of waters, fruit, faith and freedom, the **Fouta Djalon** highlands are renowned for their picturesque hills, offering superb views, and the rolling valleys and waterfalls, which are all presided over by the mostly Muslim population of Fula herders and farmers. These highlands are ideal for hiking. **Mamou** is a good nearby town, which also has some good facilities, and excellent street food. In the eastern region of Guinea lie many historical towns with echoes and remnants of medieval empires. Along a road following the **Nimba Range**, which stretches from Guinea to the Côte d'Ivoire, small groups of round houses nestle in traditional African villages. In the south is the **Guinée Forestière**, a highland area of rainforest and old pre-Islamic tribes.

- There are no national parks in Guinea, but wildlife can be best seen in the northeast savannahs between the **Tinkisso River** and the Mali border, in the foothills of the Fouta Djalon highlands and in the southeast.
- The best beaches for **swimming** are on the **Îles de Los** (which lie just off the coast near Conakry), the **Île de Roume** and the **Île de Kassa**, but currents can be strong and swimmers are advised to exercise care and follow local advice. Trekking and hiking are available in Labé, Pita and Dalaba; the largest cities in the **Fouta Djalon** region.

TOURIST INFORMATION

Office National du Tourisme in Guinea
BP 1275, 6 Avenue de la République,
Immeuble Al-Iman, Conakry, Guinea
Tel: 455 163.
Website: www.guinee.gov.gn *or* www.mirinet.net.gn/ont

Entertainment

FOOD & DRINK: Restaurants, except in the capital where Western-style food is available, generally serve local dishes. Main hotels, mostly in the capital, have reasonable restaurants where a wide variety of alcoholic beverages are served. Conakry has several French pâtisseries selling coffee and cakes.

National specialities:
- *Jollof rice*.
- Stuffed chicken with groundnuts.
- Fish (served with rice).
- Cassava, yams and maize.
- Maize soup.
- Brochettes.
- Fruit (coconut and bananas).

National drinks:
- Beer (West African brands).
- Fresh fruit juice.

Tipping: A 10 per cent service charge will usually be included in the bill.

NIGHTLIFE: Although there are theatres, nightclubs and cinemas, Guineans prefer to make their own entertainment. In the streets people can often be seen gathered together to dance, sing and play traditional musical instruments or home-made guitars. Conakry is a dynamic centre for music and the singing of the Kindia people is renowned. There is also an open air cinema in the small town of Mamou.

SHOPPING: Although department stores in the major cities are poorly stocked, local markets sell a unique display of goods. Special purchases include brightly coloured, distinctive Guinean clothes, woodcarvings, leather rugs in bold black-and-white designs, skins, locally produced records, calabashes and jewellery. Gueckedou is well known for its enourmous market where travellers can buy absolutely anything. **Shopping hours:** Mon-Sat 0900-1800.

Business

- **GDP**: US$4 billion (2004).
- **Main exports**: Aluminium, gold, diamonds, coffee, fish, bauxite and agriculture products.
- **Main imports**: Petroleum, metals, transport equipment, textiles and grain.
- **Main trade partners**: France, Côte d'Ivoire, USA, Cameroon, China, Korea (Rep) and Russia.

ECONOMY: Given its resources, Guinea should not be suffering its current impoverished condition in which the annual per capita income is US$460. The majority of the population is engaged in subsistence agriculture, producing cassava and rice as staples, plus fruit, palm, groundnuts and sometimes coffee as cash crops. Fisheries have undergone major growth in the last 10 years. The main part of the industrial economy is mining. Guinea has huge reserves of bauxite (perhaps one-quarter of the world's total) which account for more than 90 per cent of export earnings; there are also substantial diamond deposits. Guinea also boasts massive hydroelectric power potential, some of which has been tapped. The country's economic progress has, however, been hampered by the absence of the necessary legal, corporate and Governmental machinery, allied to corruption and maladministration. For the time being, Guinea will continue to depend on substantial foreign aid, principally from France, although it is also deriving growing benefit from burgeoning regional co-operation: Cameroon, for example, processes much Guinean bauxite ore to produce aluminium. Guinea is a member of both the Mano River Union (with Liberia and Sierra Leone) and of the Gambia River Development Organisation (with The Gambia and Senegal). The country is also a member of the West African economic community, ECOWAS.

BUSINESS ETIQUETTE: Appointments should be made in advance. Tropical-weight suits and ties are worn by some business visitors, but these are not essential. A knowledge of French is helpful. **Office hours:** Mon-Thurs 0800-1630, Fri 0800-1300.

COMMERCIAL INFORMATION

Chambre de Commerce d'Industrie et d'Agriculture de Guinée
BP 545, Conakry, Guinea
Tel: 454 516.
Fax: 454 517.

Guyana

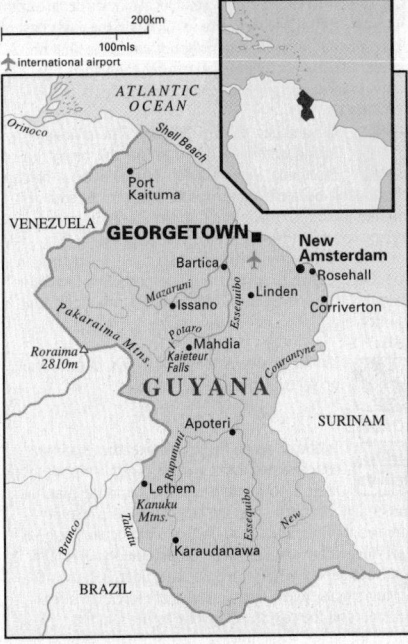

Location: South America, northeast coast.

Time: GMT - 4.

Overview

When Columbus reached the northern coast of South America at the beginning of the 16th century, the area that is now Guyana was inhabited by two distinct groups, the Arawak who lived along the coast and the Carib who lived in the interior. The Spanish were not attracted by the region, however, and it was the Dutch who first established a European presence around 1616. At the heart of it was the trading post at the mouth of the Essequibo River, which was controlled, along with other posts established later on, by the Dutch West India Company. The Dutch remained in undisputed control until the end of the 18th century when the outbreak of the Napoleonic Wars brought a period of turmoil during which the territory changed hands several times between the Dutch, British and French. The British ultimately prevailed following the defeat of Napoleon in 1815. The territory was then declared the colony of British Guiana, a status which it retained until independence in 1996. After the abolition of slavery in 1834, the plantation owners imported labourers from India. Indians now form the largest racial group, with most living in the agricultural areas, particularly around Demerara. Other immigrants were Americans, Europeans (Portuguese, British and Dutch) and Chinese. Guyana's attractions range from the 19th-century stilted wooden houses of its capital, Georgetown, to the awesome natural splendour of the towering Kaieteur Falls along the Potaro River, five times the height of Niagara. The country's mixture of rainforests, beaches, savannah and rivers draws adventure tourists hoping to camp, trek, fish or perhaps be lucky enough to spot a jaguar. Guyana may be in a forgotten corner of South America, but it is a destination which should not be ignored.

General Information

AREA: 214,969 sq km (83,000 sq miles).

POPULATION: 768,000 (UN, 2005).

POPULATION DENSITY: 3.6 per sq km.

CAPITAL: Georgetown. **Population:** 250,000 (2005 estimate).

GEOGRAPHY: Guyana lies in the northeast of South America, bordered by Venezuela to the west, Surinam to the southeast

and Brazil to the south. It is bordered by the Atlantic Ocean to the north and east. The word 'Guiana' (the original Amerindian spelling) means 'land of many waters' and the name was well chosen, for there are over 1600km (965 miles) of navigable rivers in the country. The interior is either high savannah uplands (such as those along the Venezuelan border, called the Rupununi, and the Kanuku Mountains in the far southwest), or thick, hilly jungle and forest, which occupy over 83 per cent of the country's area. The narrow coastal belt contains the vast majority of the population, and produces the major cash crop, sugar, and the major subsistence crop, rice. The country has 322km (206 miles) of coastline. More than 25 per cent of the population lives in or near Georgetown.

GOVERNMENT: Republic. **Head of State:** President Bharrat Jagdeo since 1999. **Head of Government:** Prime Minister Samuel A Hinds since 1997.

LANGUAGE: English is the official language, but Creole, Hindi, Urdu and Amerindian dialects are also spoken.

RELIGION: 50 per cent Christian, 33 per cent Hindu, less than 10 per cent Muslim.

ELECTRICITY: 110 and 220 volts AC, 60Hz.

SOCIAL CONVENTIONS: Hospitality is important to the Guyanese and it is quite common for the visitor to be invited to their homes. Informal wear is widely acceptable, but men should avoid wearing shorts.

Climate

Guyana's climate is warm and tropical throughout the year. The rainfall is generally high for most of the year, as is the humidity. December to January and May to June are the rainy seasons, while in coastal areas the climate is tempered by sea breezes.

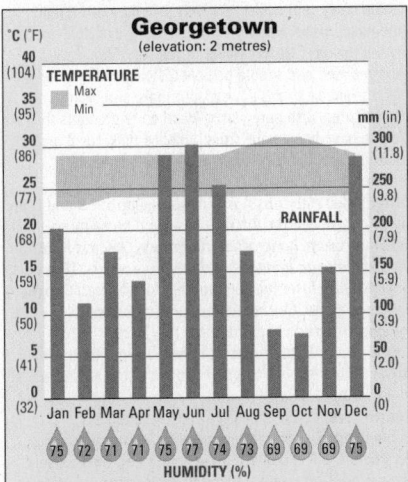

Communications

Telephone: IDD is available to main towns and cities. Country code: 592.

Mobile telephone: Network providers include *Cel Star Guyana Inc* and *Guyana Telephone and Telegraph Company* (GT&T) (website: www.gtt.co.gy). Mobile phones can be hired from *GT&T*.

Internet: Internet cafes are available in Georgetown.

Post: Post offices are found across the country.

MEDIA: Press: The daily state-owned newspaper is *The Guyana Chronicle* (website: www.guyanachronicle.com). The independent *Stabroek News* (website: www.stabroeknews.com) and the *Kaieteur News* are published weekdays. On weekends, there are also *The Mirror*, *The Sunday Chronicle* and *The Sunday Stabroek*.

TV: *Guyana Television (GTV)* is government-owned.

Radio: Local radio can be heard on www.homeviewguyana.com. *Guyana Broadcasting Corporation* is government-owned and runs three radio channels: *Hot FM*, *Radio Roraima* and *Voice of Guyana*.

Passport/Visa

	Passport Required?	Visa Required?	Return Ticket Required?
Full British	Yes	No	Yes
Australian	Yes	No	Yes
Canadian	Yes	No	Yes
USA	Yes	No	Yes
Other EU	Yes	No/1	Yes
Japanese	Yes	No	Yes

Note: *Regulations and requirements may be subject to change at short notice, and you are advised to contact the appropriate diplomatic or consular authority before finalising travel arrangements. Any numbers in the chart refer to the footnotes below.*

PASSPORTS: Passport valid for at least six months beyond intended stay required by all.

VISAS: Required by all except the following:
(a) **1.** nationals mentioned in the chart above for stays of up to 90 days (except nationals of Austria, Cyprus, the Czech Republic, Estonia, Hungary, Latvia, Lithuania, Malta, Poland, Slovak Republic and Slovenia who *do* need a visa);
(b) persons of Guyanese birth with foreign passports provided their passports clearly indicate place of birth or they have other satisfactory documentary evidence;
(c) nationals of Antigua & Barbuda, The Bahamas, Barbados, Belize, Dominica, Grenada, Jamaica, Korea (Dem Rep), Korea (Rep), Montserrat, New Zealand, Norway, St Kitts & Nevis, St Lucia, St Vincent & the Grenadines, South Africa, Surinam, Switzerland and Trinidad & Tobago, provided they hold onward or return tickets and sufficient funds for the duration of stay;
(d) transit passengers continuing their journey to a third country by the same aircraft or by first connecting aircraft within seven hours, without leaving the airport.

Note: Those with Guyanese parentage may enter Guyana visa-free, provided they can submit original birth certificate, and birth certificate/passport of Guyanese parent(s). This will also have to be submitted to the Immigration Officer upon arrival.

Types of visa and cost: *Tourist*: £20. *Business*: £20 (single-entry); £25 (one-year multiple-entry). *Courtesy* visas are issued free of charge to spouses or close relatives of Guyanese citizens, provided they supply documentary proof.

Validity: Visas are usually valid for three months from the date of issue. However, the length of stay and extension is at the discretion of the Immigration Office.

Application to: Consulate (or Consular section at Embassy or High Commission); see *Passport/Visa Information*.

Application requirements: (a) Three application forms. (b) Three passport-size photos. (c) Evidence of sufficient funds to cover length of stay or proof of other satisfactory arrangement for support while in Guyana, in the form of a letter of invitation from Guyana, a recent bank statement, a letter from employer, or a business letter with a certificate from the Chamber of Commerce. (d) Passport valid for at least six months prior to travel. (e) Return or onward ticket. (f) Fee. *Business*: (a)-(f) and, (g) Letter of approval from the Minister of Home Affairs, Guyana, or other appropriate evidence.

Working days required: Applicants should contact Embassy or High Commission at least one week in advance of travel to Guyana. If passport is to be returned by a courier service, pre-paid arrangements (making sure to include own account number) must be made by the applicant.

Temporary residence: Permission must be obtained from the Minister of Home Affairs, Guyana.

Note: Long-term visitors are advised to register their presence with the British High Commission in Georgetown.

PASSPORT/VISA INFORMATION

Guyana High Commission in the UK
3 Palace Court, Bayswater Road, London W2 4LP, UK
Tel: (020) 7229 7684.
E-mail: ghc.1@ic24.net
Opening hours: Mon-Fri 0930-1730 (except national and UK holidays); Mon-Fri 0930-1430 (consular enquiries).

Embassy of the Republic of Guyana in the USA
2490 Tracy Place, NW, Washington, DC 20008, USA
Tel: (202) 265 6900.
Website: www.guyana.org

Money

Currency: Guyanese Dollar (GYD; symbol G$) = 100 cents. Notes are in denominations of G$1000, 500, 100 and 20. Coins are in denominations of G$10, 5 and 1. US Dollars are widely accepted throughout Guyana.

Currency exchange: Banks offer exchange facilities. Bureaux de change (cambios) offer free conversion of currencies.

Credit & debit cards: American Express, Diners Club, MasterCard and Visa are accepted by most larger hotels, restaurants, car hire and tour operators. Check with your credit or debit card company for details of merchant acceptability and other services which may be available. Foreign credit cards cannot be used in Guyanian ATMs.

Traveller's cheques: Accepted but not recommended for those who may wish to change money in a hurry. To avoid additional exchange rate charges, travellers are advised to take traveller's cheques in US Dollars. Visitors are advised to bring traveller's cheques to cover the entirity of their stay.

Currency restrictions: The import and export of local currency is limited to G$200. The import of foreign currency is unlimited, provided declared in writing on arrival. The

Credit: ©Kaieteur National Park

export of foreign currency is limited to the amount imported and declared. The Guyanese Dollar is not negotiable abroad.

Banking hours: Mon-Fri 0800-1230 and Friday 1500-1700.

Exchange rate indicators:

Rate at time of publishing

£1.00= G$313.45
$1.00= G$180.00

Duty Free

The following goods can be imported into Guyana by travellers aged 16 years or over without incurring customs duty:

200 cigarettes or 50 cigars or 225g of tobacco; spirits not exceeding 750ml; wine not exceeding 750ml; computers; a reasonable amount of perfume for personal use.

Public Holidays

Below are listed Public Holidays for the January 2006-June 2007 period.

2006: Jan 1 New Year's Day. **Jan 10** Eid al-Adha (Feast of the Sacrifice). **Feb 23** Republic Day (Mashramani). **Mar 14** Phagwah (Holi). **Apr 10** Yum an-Nabi (Birth of the Prophet). **Apr 14** Good Friday. **Apr 17** Easter Monday. **May 1** Labour Day. **May 5** Indian Heritage Day. **May 26** Independence Day. **Jul 3** Caricom Day. **Aug 1** Freedom Day. **Oct 21** Diwali (Hindu Festival of Light). **Oct 22-24** Eid Al Fitr. **Dec 25-26** Christmas. **Dec 31** Eid al-Adha (Feast of the Sacrifice).

2007: Jan 1 New Year's Day. **Feb 23** Republic Day (Mashramani). **Mar 3** Phagwah (Holi). **Mar 31** Yum an-Nabi (Birth of the Prophet). **Apr 6** Good Friday. **Apr 9** Easter Monday. **May 1** Labour Day. **May 5** Indian Heritage Day. **May 26** Independence Day.

Note: (a) Muslim festivals are timed according to local sightings of various phases of the moon and the dates given above are approximations. For more information, see the *World of Islam* appendix. (b) Hindu festivals are declared according to local astronomical observations and it is only possible to forecast the month of their occurrence.

Health

	Special Precautions?	Certificate Required?
Yellow Fever	Yes	1
Cholera	No	No
Typhoid & Polio	2	N/A
Malaria	3	N/A

Note: *Regulations and requirements may be subject to change at short notice, and you are advised to contact your doctor well in advance of your intended date of departure. Any numbers in the chart refer to the footnotes below.*

1: A yellow fever vaccination certificate is required from travellers over one year of age coming from infected areas and from the following countries: Angola, Benin, Burkina Faso, Burundi, Cameroon, Central African Republic, Chad, Congo (Dem Rep), Congo (Rep), Côte d'Ivoire, Gabon, The Gambia, Ghana, Guinea, Guinea-Bissau, Kenya, Liberia, Mali, Niger, Nigeria, Rwanda, São Tomé e Príncipé, Senegal, Sierra Leone, Somalia, Tanzania, Togo and Uganda; and in Latin America: Belize, Bolivia, Brazil, Colombia, Costa Rica, Ecuador, French Guiana, Guatemala, Honduras, Nicaragua, Panama, Peru, Surinam and Venezuela. Travellers arriving from non-endemic zones should note that vaccination is strongly recommended for travel outside the urban areas, even if an outbreak of the disease has not been reported and they would normally not require a vaccination certificate to enter the country.

2: Typhoid is a risk.

3: Malaria risk exists in all parts of the interior and there have been sporadic cases along the coastal regions. Chloroquine-resistant *falciparum* is reported. The recommended prophylaxis is mefloquine unless contra-indicated, in which case use chloroquine plus proguanil plus protection against mosquito bites.

Food & drink: Mains water is normally chlorinated in main cities, and whilst relatively safe may cause mild abdominal upsets. Bottled water is readily available and is advised for the first few weeks of the stay. Milk is unpasteurised and should be boiled. Powdered or tinned milk is available and is advised, but make sure that it is reconstituted with pure water. Avoid dairy products that are likely to have been made from unboiled milk. Local meat, poultry, seafood, fruit and vegetables are generally considered safe to eat.

Other risks: *Hepatitis A* is common. *Hepatitis B* and *D* are highly endemic in the Amazon basin and precautions should be taken. *Bancroftian filariasis* is endemic in certain parts and *mucocutaneous leishmaniasis* occurs. *TB* occurs. *Jungle yellow fever* may be found in forest areas. *Dengue fever* may occur. *Onchocerciasis* and *American trypanosomiasis* (chagas disease) may occur.

Rabies occurs. For those at high risk, vaccination before arrival should be considered. If you are bitten, seek medical advice without delay.

Health care: Comprehensive health insurance is recommended. Hospital treatment in Georgetown is free, but doctors will charge for an appointment. Medical care and prescription drugs are limited and sanitary conditions are poor in many medical facilities. Travellers are advised to bring prescription medicines sufficient for their length of stay.

Travel - International

AIR:

Air France (AF) (website: www.airfrance.com) operates a daily flight to Cayenne in French Guiana. There are no direct flights from Europe. Airlines serving Trinidad & Tobago, from where connecting flights can be made, include *BWIA (British West Indies Airways)*.

Approximate flight times: From Georgetown to *London* is 10 hours (via Antigua, Barbados or Trinidad & Tobago). There are no direct flights.

Main airports: *Georgetown (GEO)* (Cheddi Jagan International) is 40km (26 miles) from the city (travel time - 45 minutes). *To/from the airport:* An irregular and crowded bus service to the city is available. Taxis meet every plane (fare: approximately G$3500). *Facilities:* Duty free shop, gift shop, restaurants, bars and post office.

Departure tax: G$4000 or equivalent in US Dollars; transit passengers and children under seven years of age are exempt.

Note: Outward flights should be confirmed 48 hours defore departure.

SEA/RIVER:

Main ports: Georgetown.

Numerous schooners sail between Guyana and the Caribbean islands, but schedules are erratic. For details, contact local ports. Cargo vessels run by the *Guyana National Shipping Corporation* ply from Miami to Georgetown and vessels run by the *Demerara Shipping Company* ply between European ports and Georgetown weekly. Following recent improvements in relations with Surinam, a ferry service across the Courantyne River now links the two countries. This is the only mode of transport that should be used when crossing the river; travellers using water taxis could be arrested.

RAIL:

There are no passenger rail services.

ROAD:

There is a soft road from Georgetown via Kurupukari to Lethem to Brazil. The journey will take at least 12 hours in a 4-wheel drive vehicle. Improvements have been made to many roads in recent years and travel during the rainy season is now possible - although care should still be taken to avoid potholes. Buses travel from Boa Vista in Brazil to Lethem and then onwards to Georgetown. Borders with Surinam and Venezuela are in dispute; although these disputes are on a back burner, travellers should be aware of the problems.

Travel - Internal

AIR:

The only reliable means of travelling into the interior is by air. Several local airlines depart from both *Ogle Aerodrome (OGL)* on the east coast of Demerara and from *CBJ International Airport* in Timehri. A number of different airlines and charter companies offer flights to most destinations; enquire locally for details.

SEA/RIVER:

Guyana has 1077km (607 miles) of navigable inland waterways, the most notable being the Essequibo, Demerara and Berbice rivers which are all navigable by oceangoing vessels. Government steamers communicate with the interior up the Essequibo and Berbice rivers, but services can be irregular owing to flooding. The Government also runs a coast-hopping service from Georgetown to several northern ports. Smaller craft operate where there is sufficient demand throughout the country.

RAIL:

Mining concerns operate railways, but there are no scheduled passenger services.

ROAD:

Traffic drives on the left. All-weather roads are concentrated in the eastern coastal strip, although there is now a road inland as far as the Brazilian border and a bridge linking the two countries is nearing completion. The coastal road linking Georgetown, Rosignol, New Amsterdam and Crabwood Creek (Corentyne) is fairly good, but generally road conditions are poor. Because of Guyana's many rivers, most journeys of more than a few miles outside the capital will involve ferries and the attendant delays. Avoid driving at night. Seatbelts must be worn at all times; this law is enforced and failure to abide could lead to a fine. **Bus:** Georgetown's Stabroek Market is the terminus for minibuses. These are regular but generally crowded. Buses run to all areas, departing whenever they are full. The first buses leave at around 0500, and services continue until about 2100. Within Georgetown, buses run all night. Services from Vreed-en-Hoop to Parika operate in conjunction with the passenger-ferry service across the Demerara to Georgetown; services from New Amsterdam to Crabwood Creek operate in conjunction with ferries across the Berbice River. **Taxi:** At night, it is advisable to travel by taxi. Vehicles are plentiful. There is a standard fare for intercity travel; night fares are extra. For longer trips, fares should be agreed before departure. A 10 per cent tip is usual in taxis. Travellers are advised to only use taxis from reputable companies and not to hail one from the roadside. **Car hire:** Limited availability from local firms in Georgetown as well as *Hertz*. **Documentation:** An International Driving Permit is recommended. A one-month local driving permit can be obtained from the 'Licence and Revenue Office,' in Georgetown, after showing a valid foreign licence.

Travel Advice

Most visits to Guyana are trouble-free, but crime levels are high especially in Georgetown and towns in the coastal regions. Visitors to the eco-sector (which excludes Georgetown and the coastal regions) generally experience no problems.

The risk of terrorism is low but you should be aware of the global risk of indiscriminate terrorist attacks which could be against civilian targets, including places frequented by foreigners.

This advice is based on information provided by the Foreign and Commonwealth Office in the UK. It is correct at time of publishing. As the situation can change rapidly, visitors are advised to contact the following organisations for the latest travel advice:

British Foreign and Commonwealth Office
Tel: (0845) 850 2829.
Website: www.fco.gov.uk

US Department of State
Website: http://travel.state.gov/travel

Accommodation

HOTELS:

Hotels in Georgetown range from good to reasonable. There are no high-season charges. Nature lovers can stay in cabins at the interior resorts and camps. As power cuts are common, it is advisable to take a torch.

GUEST HOUSES:

There is a variety of nature resorts, ranches and lodges which offer unusual accommodation. There are also numerous camps, for instance Maparri Wilderness Camp which overlooks the crystal clear river and waterfall, and the Shell Beach Camp at Almond Beach where turtles nest between April and August.

ACCOMMODATION INFORMATION

Wilderness Explorers
Cara Suites, 176 Middle Street, Georgetown, Guyana
Tel: 227 7698.
Website: www.wilderness-explorers.com

Tourism and Hospitality Association of Guyana
157 Waterloo Street, North Cummingsburg, Georgetown, Guyana
Tel: 225 0807 or 225 6699.
Website: www.exploreguyana.com

Amazon Advertures
212 Duncan Street, Lamaha Gardens, Georgetown, Guyana
Tel: (529) 231 7141.
Email: amazon@guyana.net.gy

Dagron International
35 Main Street, Georgetown, Guyana
Email: dagron@solutions2000.net

Evergreen Adventures
159 Charlotte Street, Georgetown, Guyana.
Email: evergreen_adventures@webworksgy.com

Top Things To See & Do

- The 19th-century wooden houses supported on stilts and charming green boulevards laid out along the lines of the old Dutch canals give **Georgetown**, the capital, a unique character. Some of the more impressive wooden buildings dating from the colonial past include the city hall, **St George's Cathedral**, the **Law Courts** and the **State House**. The **Botanical Gardens and Zoo**, covering 120 acres (48.6 hectares), have a fine collection of palms, orchids and lotus lilies; nearby is the **Cultural Centre**, which contains what is probably the best theatre in the Caribbean. Also worth visiting are the **Natural History Museum**, which contains an up-to-date display of all aspects of Guyanese life and culture, and the **Walter Roth Anthropological Museum**.
- At the junction of the **Essequibo** and **Mazaruni** rivers, **Bartica** is the 'take-off' town for the gold and diamond fields, **Kaieteur Falls** and the rest of the interior. A visit to the Kaieteur Falls in the **Kaieteur National Park** is

particularly recommended; situated on the **Potaro River**, it ranks with Iguazú, Niagara and Victoria in majesty and beauty. The National Park is situated on the Guiana Shield, a plateau that is one of the world's oldest and most remote geological formations located in a biodiverse rainforest. There are numerous beaches in Guyana; these include **Almond Beach**, **Shell Beach**, **No 63 Beach** and **Saxacalli Beach**. There are rainforests in **Iwokrama** with a **Canopy Walkway** and the **Pakaraima** mountains. **Surama**, set in savannah surrounded by forest-covered mountains, is home to the Amerindian community of the Macushi tribe, which welcomes tourists. **Rupununi** is the oasis in the desert with the **Rockview Nature Resort** and the ranches of **North** and **South Rupunini**, **Karanambo** and **Dadanawa**.
- The rivers and the interior abound in **game fish**, the best known of which is the man-eating piranha (locally called *perai*). The most sought after by the sportsman is the *lucanni*, a fish similar to the large-mouth bass. Most of the interior rivers are difficult for the more casual visitor to get to, but those who book in advance can reach them by air. Some of the coastal rivers within reach of Georgetown are also good for fishing, although it is wise to stay overnight in the fishing grounds, as the best are four to five hours' drive from the city. Fishing licences are required.
- **Camping** treks, **hiking** and **whitewater rafting** have become increasingly popular over recent years. **Horse riding** is available at Manari Ranch in the Rupununi Savannahs. **Cricket** and **hockey** are both popular. Guyana is hosting the Cricket World Cup in 2007. **Birdwatching** is also very good in some parts of the country.

TOURIST INFORMATION

Guyana Tourism Authority
National Exhibition Centre, Sophia, Greater Georgetown, Guyana
Tel: 223 6351.
Website: www.guyana-tourism.com

Tourism and Hospitality Association of Guyana
157 Waterloo Street, North Cummingsburg, Georgetown, Guyana
Tel: 225 0807 or 225 6699.
Website: www.exploreguyana.com

Caribbean Tourism Organisation in the UK
22 The Quadrant, Richmond, Surrey, TW9 1BP, UK
Tel: (020) 8948 0057.
Website: www.caribbean.co.uk

Entertainment

FOOD & DRINK: The food in hotels and restaurants reflects the range of influences on Guyanese society. On the menus of most restaurants you will often find chicken, pork and steak and, most of the time, shrimp. The best Chinese food in the country can be found in Georgetown. It is best to drink bottled water in Guyana.
National specialities:
- Curry, especially mutton, prawn or chicken.

- Foo-foo (plantains made into cakes).
- *Metamgee* (dumplings made from cornflour, eddews, yams, cassava and plantains cooked in coconut milk and grated coconut).
- Portuguese garlic pork.
- Amerindian pepperpot.
National drinks:
- Local rum.
- Demerara rum.
- *Banks* is the local beer.
Tipping: 10 per cent at hotels and restaurants.
NIGHTLIFE: There are numerous nightclubs and bars in Georgetown.
SHOPPING: Hibiscus Plaza outside the post office in Georgetown has a wide variety of local arts and crafts including straw hats, baskets, clay goblets and jewellery. On Sundays, the Parika Market, on the west coast of Demerara, sells a variety of goods and is worth a visit. Other shops sell Amerindian bows and arrows, hammocks, pottery and salad bowls. Government-run shops sell magnificent jewellery, utilising local gold, silver, precious and semi-precious stones. Prices are very reasonable for the quality of the goods. It is absolutely essential to ensure that receipts and correct documentation are retained, otherwise visitors may experience difficulty when clearing customs. **Shopping hours:** Mon-Fri 0800-1200 and 1300-1630, Sat 0800-1200.

Business

- **GDP:** US$742million.
- **Main imports:** Manufactured goods, machinery, petroleum and food.
- **Main exports:** Sugar, gold, bauxite/aluminium, rice, shrimp, molasses, rum and timber.
- **Main trade partners:** Belgium, Canada, Cuba, Jamaica, Portugal, Trinidad and Tobago, UK and USA.

ECONOMY: Agriculture allows Guyana to be self-sufficient in sugar, rice, vegetables, fruit, meat and poultry, as well as to make major export earnings from the first two. Although 80 per cent of the land area is covered by forest, timber has only very recently assumed any economic significance (subject to internationally backed restrictions on logging). Bauxite mining is the main industry, and responsible for one-third of export earnings. The mining sector also produces gold and diamonds, almost all of which are exported. Gold production has increased sharply since the opening of a new mining complex in 1992. Imported oil meets most of the country's energy requirements, although Guyana and Surinam have begun joint exploration projects.
Guyana has been a beneficiary of a debt write-off which has saved more than £100 million annually in debt-servicing payments, following the Government's implementation of a major economic reform programme. Since 1997, many formerly state-owned assets and industries have been sold, and deregulation measures introduced, as part of that programme. A major obstacle to Guyana's future economic progress is a shortage of trained personnel, especially in the fields of management and technical expertise; the emigration rate remains high, and only serves to compound this long-term problem. Guyana is a founder member of the regional trading bloc CARICOM.
BUSINESS ETIQUETTE: Appointments should be made and punctuality is appreciated. Calling cards are useful. The pace of business and general attitudes are very Caribbean-orientated. It is, however, wise to bear in mind that the country is very much part of South America, the ties with the Caribbean being more a hangover from British colonial days than a reflection of Guyanese popular consciousness.
Office hours: Mon-Fri 0800-1200 and 1300-1630.

COMMERCIAL INFORMATION

Guyana Manufacturer's Association
National Exhibition Centre, Sophia, Georgetown, Guyana
Tel: 227 4295.
Website: www.gma.org.gy

Georgetown Chamber of Commerce and Industry
PO Box 10110, 156 Waterloo Street, North Cummingsburg, Georgetown, Guyana
Tel: 225 5846.
Website: www.georgetownchamberofcommerce.org

Ministry of Tourism, Industry and Commerce
229 South Road, Georgetown, Guyana
Tel: 226 2505.
Website: www.mintic.gov.gy

Credit: ©Kaieteur National Park

Location: Caribbean, island of Hispaniola.

Time: GMT -5.

Overview

A mostly mountainous country with a tropical climate, Haiti's location, history and culture once made it a potential tourist hot spot. Instead, decades of poverty, instability and violence, especially since the 1980s, have all but killed off this prospect and left it as the poorest nation in the Americas.

In 1697, the Spanish ceded the western half of the island to France, who turned their new territory into a major centre for the slave trade. In what was to be the only successful slave rebellion, the French were defeated in a 12-year campaign, led by Toussaint L'Ouverture and others, which ended in 1804.

During the rest of the 19th century, Haiti was under the control of a succession of dictators, none of whom had the wherewithal to resolve the conflict between the country's two main ethnic groups: the mulattos, who held political power, and the blacks. To this day, the huge wealth gap between the impoverished Creole-speaking black majority and the French-speaking mulattos, one per cent of whom own nearly half the country's wealth, remains unaddressed.

Haiti achieved notoriety during the brutal dictatorships of the voodoo physician, Francois 'Papa Doc' Duvalier, and his son, Jean-Claude, known as 'Baby Doc'. With the help of a private militia known as the *Tontons Macoutes* (the Creole phrase for 'bogeymen'), political dissent was systematically eradicated and opponents jailed or murdered. Hopes that the election in 1990 of Jean-Bertrand Aristide, a former priest, would herald a brighter future were dashed when he was overthrown by the armed forces a short time later.

Although economic sanctions and US-led military intervention forced a return to constitutional government in 1994, Haiti's fortune did not improve, with allegations of electoral irregularities, ongoing torture and brutality. In 2003, a wave of protests against Aristide quickly spread throughout the country plunging Haiti into chaos. By 2004, armed rebels had seized control of many towns and violence spread across the island. In February 2004, Aristide fled the country. An interim government took over and a UN stabilisation force was deployed to restore order. But Haiti remains plagued by violent confrontations between rival gangs and political groups. The UN has described the human rights situation as 'catastrophic'.

General Information

AREA: 27,750 sq km (10,714 sq miles).

POPULATION: 8.13 million (official estimate 2001).

POPULATION DENSITY: 293 per sq km.

CAPITAL: Port-au-Prince. **Population:** 917,112 (official estimate 1997).

GEOGRAPHY: Haiti is situated in the Caribbean and comprises the forested mountainous western end of the island of Hispaniola, which it shares with the Dominican Republic. Its area includes the Île de la Gonâve, in the Gulf of the same name; among other islands is La Tortue off the north peninsula. Haiti's coastline is dotted with magnificent beaches, between which stretches lush subtropical vegetation, even covering the slopes which lead down to the shore. Port-au-Prince is a magnificent natural harbour at the end of a deep horseshoe bay.

GOVERNMENT: Republic. Gained independence from France in 1804. **Head of State:** President René Préval since 2006. **Head of Government:** Interim Prime Minister Gerard Latortue. **Recent history:** Despite the presence of the UN peacekeepers, the country has continued to be blighted by political and criminal violence and instability. Killings and kidnappings are now a daily occurrence in the capital. The most recent Presidential and Parliamentary elections took place on February 7 2006. The polls, originally set for November 2005, had been postponed four times because of security and organisational issues. The elections were the first since President Jean-Bertrand Aristide was ousted from power nearly two years earlier. For Haiti's poor, former President René Préval was seen to be the solution to the country's problems. Initially it appeared Préval had not won the 50 per cent needed to be elected outright. Préval alleged massive electoral fraud and crowds of his supporters took to the streets in protest. However, following an agreement between the Government and electoral officials, under which blank ballots were subtracted from the total number of votes counted, it was announced that Préval had gained 51.15 per cent, thus eliminating the need for a second round run-off.

LANGUAGE: The official languages are French and Creole. English is spoken in tourist areas.

RELIGION: The official religions are Roman Catholicism (75 per cent) and Voodooism (70 per cent); most Haitians practise both. Voodooism is a polytheistic folk religion, manifested by a series of complex ritual drawings, songs and dances. It is an African religion, and not incompatible with a shared belief in Christianity. There are Protestant minorities.

ELECTRICITY: 110 volts AC, 60Hz.

SOCIAL CONVENTIONS: Informal wear is acceptable, although scanty beachwear should be confined to the beach or poolside. Only the most elegant dining-rooms encourage guests to dress for dinner.

Climate

Tropical, with intermittent rain throughout the year. Much cooler temperatures exist in hill resorts and there is a high coastal humidity.

Required clothing: Tropical lightweights with rainwear and warm clothing for hill regions.

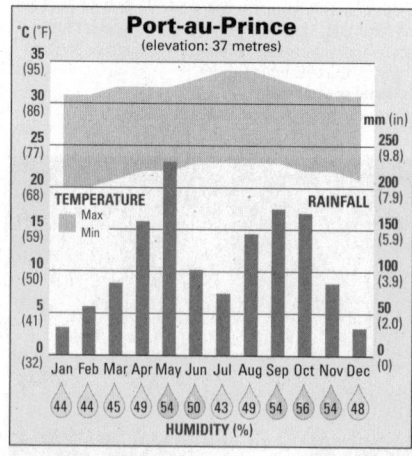

Communications

Telephone: IDD available. Country code: 509. There are no area codes. The internal service, operated by *Telecommunications d'Haiti (Teleco)*, is reasonable. There are telephone booths in the towns which take cards.

Mobile telephone: The GSM network is run by *Haitel*. Handsets can be hired locally.

Internet: Internet cafes can be found in towns and cities. ISPs include *Compa*, *Hintelfocus* and *Netcom*.

Post: Airmail to Europe takes up to one week. The main post office in Port-au-Prince, Cité de l'Exposition, is in place d'Italie. Post office hours: Mon-Fri 0800-2000, Sat 0830-1200. Letters posted after 0900 will not be despatched until the following working day.

MEDIA: Press: The two main dailies, *Le Matin* and *Le Nouvelliste*, are published in French. *Haiti Progres*, also in French, is published weekly.

TV: *PVS Antenne*, private; *Television Nationale d'Haiti*, Government-owned channel.

Radio: Radio is Haiti's most important source of information. There are more than 250 private radio stations. Radio stations include *Radio Metropole*, *Radio Galaxie* and *Radio Caraibes FM*.

Passport/Visa

	Passport Required?	Visa Required?	Return Ticket Required?
Full British	Yes	No	Yes
Australian	Yes	No	Yes
Canadian	Yes	No	Yes
USA	Yes	No	Yes
Other EU	Yes	No	Yes
Japanese	Yes	No	Yes

Note: Regulations and requirements may be subject to change at short notice, and you are advised to contact the appropriate diplomatic or consular authority before finalising travel arrangements. Any numbers in the chart refer to the footnotes below.

PASSPORTS: Passport valid for six months from date of entry required by all.

VISAS: Not required for touristic stays of up to six months except for nationals of China (PR), Colombia, Dominican Republic and Panama who *do* require a tourist visa.

Types of visa and cost: *Visitor Visa:* US$46.

Note: It is possible for visas to be extended under certain circumstances; contact the nearest Consulate/Embassy for further information.

Application to: The Consulate or consular section at the Embassy (see *Passport/Visa Information*).

Application requirements: (a) Valid passport. (b) One completed application form. (c) One passport-size photo. (d) Fee payable by postal order only. (e) Self-addressed, stamped and registered envelope, if applying by post.

Working days required: One week.

Temporary residence: Contact the Consulate (or Consular section at Embassy).

PASSPORT/VISA INFORMATION

Embassy of the Republic of Haiti and Tourist Office in France
10 rue Théodule Ribot, BP275, Cedex 28, 75017 Paris, France
Tel: (1) 4763 4778.
E-mail: haiti01@francophonie.org
Opening hours: Mon-Thurs 1000-1300 and 1400-1700; Fri 1000-1500.

Embassy of the Republic of Haiti in the USA
2311 Massachusetts Avenue, NW, Washington, DC 20008, USA
Tel: (202) 332 4090.
Website: www.haiti.org

Consulate General of Haiti in the USA
271 Madison Avenue, 5th Floor, New York, NY 10016, USA
Tel: (212) 697 9767.
E-mail: info@haitianconsulate-nyc.org

Money

Currency: Gourde = 100 centimes. Notes are in denominations of Gourde500, 250, 100, 50, 25, 10, 5, 2 and 1. Coins are in denominations of Gourde5 and 1, and 50, 20, 10 and 5 centimes. US currency also circulates.

Currency exchange: US Dollars are accepted and exchanged everywhere. Other foreign currencies are accepted for exchange only by some banks.

Credit & debit cards: American Express is widely accepted; Diners Club has more limited use. Check with your credit or debit card company for details of merchant acceptability and other services which may be available.

Travellers cheques: Accepted by most major shops and banks. To avoid additional exchange rate charges, travellers are advised to take travellers cheques in US Dollars.

Currency restrictions: There are no restrictions on the import and export of foreign or local currency. However, amounts in excess of Gourde 200,000 or equivalent must be declared.

Banking hours: Mon-Fri 0900-1630. Some banks open in the afternoons and Sat 0900-1300.

Exchange rate indicators:
Rate at time of publishing
£1.00= HTG73.35
$1.00= HTG42.12

Duty Free

The following goods can be imported into Haiti without incurring customs duty:

200 cigarettes or 50 cigars or 1kg of tobacco; 1l of spirits; small quantity of perfume or eau de toilette for personal use.

Note: In addition, Haitian nationals and foreign residents may bring in, once a year and for their personal use, new goods with a total value not exceeding US$200.

Prohibited items: Coffee, matches, methylated spirits, pork, all meat products from Brazil and the Dominican Republic, drugs and firearms (except sporting rifles with relevant permit).

Public Holidays

Below are listed Public Holidays for the January 2006-June 2007 period.

2006: Jan 1 Independence Day. **Jan 2** Ancestors' Day. **Feb 27-Mar 1** Carnival. **Apr 14** Good Friday; Pan-American Day/Bastilla's Day. **May 1** Labour Day. **May 18** Flag and University Day. **May 25** Ascension. **Jun 15** Corpus Christi. **Aug 15** Assumption. **Oct 17** Anniversary of the Death of Dessalines. **Oct 24** United Nations Day. **Nov 1** All Saints' Day. **Nov 2** All Souls' Day. **Nov 18** Battle of Vertières Day. **Dec 25** Christmas Day.

2007: Jan 1 Independence Day. **Jan 2** Ancestors' Day. **Feb 19-21** Carnival. **Apr 9** Good Friday. **Apr 14** Pan-American Day/Bastilla's Day. **May 1** Labour Day. **May 17** Ascension. **May 18** Flag and University Day. **Jun 7** Corpus Christi.

Health

	Special Precautions?	Certificate Required?
Yellow Fever	Yes	1
Cholera	No	No
Typhoid & Polio	2	N/A
Malaria	3	N/A

Note: *Regulations and requirements may be subject to change at short notice, and you are advised to contact your doctor well in advance of your intended date of departure. Any numbers in the chart refer to the footnotes below.*

1: A yellow fever vaccination certificate is required from travellers arriving within six days from infected areas.
2: Typhoid occurs in rural areas.
3: Malaria risk, in the malignant *falciparum* form, exists throughout the year in certain forest areas in Chantal, Gros Morne, Hinche, Jacmel and Maissade and all other areas below 300m. In the other cantons, risk is estimated to be low. Chloroquine is the recommended prophylaxis.

Food & drink: All water should be regarded as being potentially contaminated. Water used for drinking, brushing teeth or making ice should have first been boiled or otherwise sterilised. Milk is unpasteurised and should be boiled. Powdered or tinned milk is available and is advised, but make sure that it is reconstituted with pure water. Avoid dairy products which are likely to have been made from unboiled milk. Only eat well-cooked meat and fish, preferably served hot. Pork, salad and mayonnaise may carry increased risk. Vegetables should be cooked and fruit peeled.

Other risks: *Hepatitis A* and *Bancroftian filariasis* occur. *Tularaemia* and seasonal *meningococcal meningitis* have been reported. Outbreaks of *dengue fever* occur in the area. *Rabies* is present. For those at high risk, vaccination before arrival should be considered. If you are bitten, seek medical advice without delay. For more information, consult the *Health* appendix.

Health care: Health insurance providing cover for repatriation in the event of serious illness is strongly recommended. Medical facilities are fairly good. The local herb tea is said to be good for stomach upsets.

Travel - International

AIR:

 There are good connections with the USA, the French West Indies and France. *American Airlines* (website: www.aa.com) operates daily flights from London to Port-au-Prince via New York. *Air Canada* (website: www.aircanada.ca) operates flights from London to Port-au-Prince via Montréal at weekends.

Approximate flight times: From Port-au-Prince to *London* is 11 hours (not including overnight stop in New York), to *Los Angeles* is 10 hours, to *New York* is four hours, to *Miami* is two hours and to *Singapore* is 33 hours (with good connections).

Main airports: *Port-au-Prince (PAP)* (Mais Gaté) is 13km (8 miles) from the city. There is a snack bar, duty-free shop, bank, bar and car hire facilities. Taxis are available to the city.

Cap-Haïtien (CAP) is Haiti's second international airport and is approximately 10km (6 miles) from the town.

Departure tax: US$30 plus Gourde10 (security charge); transit passengers and children under two years of age are exempt.

SEA:

 Labadee is a port of call for several cruise lines, including *Royal Caribbean*.

ROAD:

 There are bus services from the Dominican Republic.

Travel - Internal

AIR:

 There are scheduled routes, operated by *Caribintair*, between Port-au-Prince and Cap-Haïtien, Hinche and Jérémie. Reservations should be double-checked as delays and cancellations are common. Planes may be chartered.

SEA:

 Sailing trips can be arranged from Port-au-Prince to beaches around the island. Glass-bottomed boat trips over Sand Cay Reef are available. Cargo ships operating between Jérémie, Cap-Haïtien and Port-au-Prince can take passengers between these ports.

ROAD:

During the 1980s, all-weather roads were constructed from Port-au-Prince to Cap-Haïtien and Jacmel. Driving is on the right. **Bus:** Services depart from Port-au-Prince to Cap-Haïtien, Les Cayes, Jacmel, Jérémie, Hinche and Port-de-Paix on an unscheduled basis. **Taxi:** Station-wagons (*camionettes*) run between Port-au-Prince and Pétionville, as well as some other towns. **Car hire:** Available independently in Port-au-Prince and Pétionville, or through hotels and the airport. Petrol can be very scarce outside Port-au-Prince. All hired cars' registration numbers begin with 'L'. **Documentation:** An International Driving Permit is required.

URBAN:

Bus: *Tap-taps*, which run within Port-au-Prince with a standard rate for any journey, are colourful but crowded. **Taxi:** Unmetered, with fixed route prices, otherwise fares agreed in advance. Taxi licence plates begin with the letter 'P'. Shared taxis (*publics*) are the cheapest form of taxi service in the towns. Drivers can be hired for tours by the hour or the day with price negotiated.

Travel Advice

Travellers are advised against all but essential travel to Haiti, because of the increasing threat to personal security. Incidences of violence and kidnappings for ransom, specifically targeting foreigners are on the increase. The kidnappings are taking place mainly in Port-au-Prince. The threat from external terrorism is low.

This advice is based on information provided by the Foreign and Commonwealth Office in the UK. It is correct at time of publishing. As the situation can change rapidly, visitors are advised to contact the following organisations for the latest travel advice:

British Foreign and Commonwealth Office
Tel: (0845) 850 2829.
Website: www.fco.gov.uk

US Department of State
Website: http://travel.state.gov/travel

Accommodation

Accommodation is limited in Haiti. Existing facilities include modest small inns, guest houses and palatial-style hotels. The majority of accommodation is in Port-au-Prince and Pétionville, while the beach hotels are north of the capital on the road to St Marc or west towards Petit-Gonâve. Accommodation is also to be found in Cap-Haïtien, Les Cayes, the Gonâve Bay area, Jacmel and the Petit-Gonâve beach area. Swimming pools and air conditioning are essential in central hotels where the heat can become severe. All resorts offer substantial reductions between 16 April and 15 December. A 10 per cent room tax is added to all hotel bills.

Note: It is vital to make reservations well in advance for the Carnival period.

Top Things To See & Do

- **Port-au-Prince:** The capital is a bustling city with a population of almost 1 million. Places to visit include the busy **Iron Market**, the two cathedrals, the **Museum of Haitian Art**, the **Statue of the Unknown Slave**, the **Gingerbread Houses** and the **Defly Mansion**. The hillside suburb of **Pétionville** offers a calmer respite and some of the city's best dining, gallery-hopping and nightlife. For views over Port-au-Prince and the Gulf of Gonâve, visitors should head for the suburb of **Boutillier**, high in the mountains.

- **Cap-Haïtien and the North coast:** On Christmas Eve 1492, Columbus ran aground on the north coast of Hispaniola near the present-day site of Cap-Haïtien. The wreck of the **Santa Maria** lies nearby. Today, communications in the region are more convenient, and Cap-Haïtien is only 40 minutes by plane from the capital. Nestling at the foot of lush green mountains and surrounded by several fine beaches, the town has a more laid-back air than the capital and features many fine Spanish-style buildings. Haiti's beautiful **Citadelle**, built by Henri Christophe after the French were overthrown, is not to be missed – a remarkable fortress in the mountains, 40km (25 miles) south of Cap-Haïtien, and the nearby ruins of **Sans Souci Palace**. A half-hour drive leads to the village of **Milot**, gateway to the Citadelle and site of the palace ruins. Versailles was the model for **Sans Souci**, and the ruins still suggest a link.

- **Jacmel and the South coast:** Since the completion of the well-marked road over the mountains, the drive to Jacmel is a pleasant two hours or less through spectacular scenery. Jacmel itself is an elegant town of Victorian stuccoed palaces adorned with filigree balconies. It is an important centre for voodoo and there are several interesting temples to visit. Artists come from all over Europe, America and the Caribbean to work in Jacmel, providing a lively Arts scene that is further enhanced at Carnival time, when dancers in *papier maché* costumes parade the streets and a host of street theatre performances take place. There are several beaches in this region. High in the mountains, south of the capital, is the town of **Kenscoff**, much favoured by Haitians as a summer resort. **Parc Macaya** is perhaps Haiti's most famous national park, offering the visitor trails through spectacular mountain scenery covered in lush rainforest. 12 km outside Jacmel lie the **Bassins Bleus**, a series of three pools joined by waterfalls; the best way to reach the pools is on horseback from Jacmel.

- **Kyona** and **Ibo** beaches (Ibo is on Cacique Isle) are best for **swimming**, **snorkelling**, **spearfishing**, **sailing**, **boomba racing** in dugout canoes and **water-skiing**. La Gonâve is a popular location for **fishing**.

- The national parks of **La Visite** and **Parc Macaya** offer excellent **hiking** opportunities.

TOURIST INFORMATION

Embassy of the Republic of Haiti and Tourist Office in France
10 rue Théodule Ribot, BP275, Cedex 28, 75017 Paris, France
Tel: (1) 4763 4778.
E-mail: haiti01@francophonie.org
Opening hours: Mon-Thurs 1000-1300 and 1400-1700; Fri 1000-1600.

Caribbean Tourism Organisation in the UK
22 The Quadrant, Richmond, Surrey TW9 1BP, UK
Tel: (020) 8948 0057.
Website: www.doitcaribbean.com or www.onecaribbean.org

Entertainment

FOOD & DRINK:

National specialities:
- Guinea hen with sour orange sauce.
- *Tassot de dinde* (dried turkey).
- *Grillot* (fried island pork).
- *Diri et djondjon* (rice and black mushrooms).
- *Riz et pois* (rice and peas).
- *Langouste flambé* (local lobster).
- *Ti malice* (sauce of onions and herbs).
- *Piment oiseau* (hot sauce).
- *Grillot et banane pese* (pork chops and island bananas).

National drinks:
- French wine is available in the better restaurants.
- The island drink is rum and the best is probably. 'Barbancourt', made by a branch of Haiti's oldest family of rum and brandy distillers.

Tipping: 10 per cent service charge is added to hotel and restaurant bills. Taxi drivers do not expect tips.

NIGHTLIFE: There is plenty of choice ranging from casinos to African drum music and modern Western music and dance. There is something happening in at least one major hotel every evening with the main attraction being folkloric groups and voodoo performances. On Saturday nights *bamboche*, a peasant-style dance, can be seen in one of the open-air dance halls. Hotels often have the most up-to-date information on local nightlife.

SHOPPING: Bargaining is recommended at the Iron Market, where both good- and bad-quality local items can be bought, including carvings, printed fabrics, leatherwork, paintings (particularly in the *naïf* style, for which Haiti is famous), straw hats, seed necklaces and jewellery, cigars and foodstuffs. Port-au-Prince has a good selection of shops and boutiques selling a wide range of local and imported items. Bargaining is an accepted practice. **Shopping hours:** Mon-Fri 0800-1200 and 1300-1600, Sat 0800-1200.

Business

ECONOMY: Haiti's average annual income of about US$500 per head is the lowest in the western hemisphere; moreover, vast disparities exist between the incomes of rich and poor. The World Bank estimates that 85 per cent of the people live below the absolute poverty line. Two-thirds of the employed population work in agriculture, mainly in the coffee plantations which generate 25 per cent of Haiti's export earnings, although these have suffered from periodic droughts and persistently low world prices. Sugar cane, sweet potatoes, cocoa and sisal are also grown for export. The mining industry extracts marble, limestone and clay; there are also unexploited deposits of copper, silver and gold. The rest of the manufacturing sector involves food processing, metal products and textiles. Tourism, once promising, has all but vanished thanks to the country's chronic political instability. Haiti's problems are so intractable that even after repeated, large injections of foreign aid and an IMF-approved economic plan, the economy remains stubbornly inert. The appalling state of the country's infrastructure has much to do with this. Haiti's major trading partners are the USA followed by Japan, France, Italy and Belgium. Haiti joined the Caribbean trading bloc CARICOM as a provisional member in 1997 and became a full member in 2002.

BUSINESS ETIQUETTE: It is usual to wear a suit for initial or formal calls. The British Trade Correspondent can put visitors in touch with a reliable English–French translator if required. Business visitors are generally entertained to lunch or dinner by their agents or important customers and should return invitations either at their hotel or a restaurant. Best time to visit is November to March. **Office hours:** Mon-Fri 0800-1600.

COMMERCIAL INFORMATION

Chambre Haïtienne de Commerce et d'Industrie
BP 982, Boulevard Harry Truman, Port-au-Prince, Haiti
Tel: 223 0786 *or* 222 8661.

Chambre Franco-Haïtienne de Commerce et d'Industrie
Le Plaza, 10 rue Capois, Champs-de-Mars, Port-au-Prince, Haiti
Tel: 223 8424.
E-mail: ccih@compa.net

Honduras

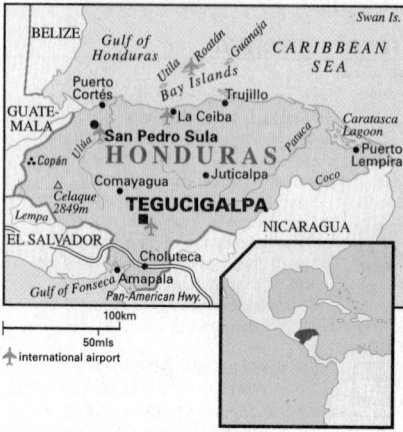

Location: Central America.

Time: GMT - 6.

Overview

Mayan civilisation reached the region that is now western Honduras around the fifth century AD. The Mayas remained in control for the next 300 years, after which several different ethnic groups moved into the area from Mexico and Colombia. Contact with Europeans began soon after Christopher Columbus landed on the Honduran coast in 1502. During the early 1520s, the region was subjugated by a variety of conquistador expeditions, each of which laid claim to a part of it. Cortés, who arrived in 1525 via Mexico, imposed some order on the squabbling groups but after his departure, the local conflicts resumed as before. Only after the discovery of gold and silver deposits in the 1540s was some order imposed on the region; large numbers of slaves from Africa were then imported to work the mines.

Once the deposits were exhausted at the end of the 16th century, Honduras became a colonial backwater. As Spanish power disintegrated in the wake of the Napoleonic wars, the Central American territories were in disagreement as to whether to join Mexico or establish their own federation of states. The latter course was chosen, with the acquiescence of Mexico. During the early 20th century, Honduras was governed by a series of *caudillos*, notably President Carias during the 1930s and 1940s. From the late 1950s onwards, weak civilian Governments prompted the army to assume a greater role, launching several coups in the process. Honduran politics became particularly important during the 1980s, when Honduras was the main base for the US-backed 'Contra' rebels fighting the Sandanista Government in Nicaragua. Soon after the end of that war in 1989, the Partido Liberal (PL) party has dominated Honduran politics, on and off. That Government faced repeated outbreaks of civil and labour unrest throughout the late 1990s as it tried to introduce austerity measures. There have also been persistent domestic and international pressure to address the numerous human rights abuses that have continued. Among those who suffered most at the hands of the military were the indigenous Indian population. In 1994, the Government offered them a long-overdue package of rights and assistance: not unreasonably, it was rejected as inadequate and relations between the communities and the Government remain poor.

Honduras is a country of lowlands and fertile valleys and, indeed, La Ceiba - a major banana port - even looks to tourism as a future major industry. There are good hotels and beaches, and an international airport to boot. Trujillo itself was once a thriving port, with a fascinating pirate history and superb tropical beaches. Hurricane Mitch devastated much of the island in 1998 but an international effort quickly rebuilt much of the country's infrastructure. However, the economy is still very weak. Many people live in poverty and crime levels and drug trafficking have soared. Everywhere lurks touristic potential but Honduras must help its own people before it becomes a playground for holidaymakers.

General Information

AREA: 112,492 sq km (43,433 sq miles).

POPULATION: 7.2 million (UN, 2005).

POPULATION DENSITY: 64 per sq km.

CAPITAL: Tegucigalpa. **Population:** 1.2 million (2005).

GEOGRAPHY: Honduras shares borders in the southeast with Nicaragua, in the west with Guatemala, and in the southwest with El Salvador. To the north lies the Caribbean and to the south the Pacific Ocean. The interior of the country comprises a central mountain system running from east to west, cut by rivers flowing into both the Caribbean and Pacific. The lowlands in the south form a plain along the Pacific coast. The Gulf of Fonseca in the southwest contains many islands which have volcanic peaks. The large fertile valleys of the northern Caribbean lowlands are cultivated with banana plantations. However, large areas of land in Honduras are unsuitable for cultivation. The majority of the population lives in the western half of the country, while the second-largest concentration of people is in the Cortés area which extends northwards from Lake Yojoa towards the Caribbean.

GOVERNMENT: Republic. **Head of State and Government:** President Manuel Zelaya Rosales since 2006.

Recent history: President Ricardo Maduro was elected in 2002 and immediately began an offensive against Honduras' soaring crime rates. Despite his efforts, crime has continued to rise with street gangs (known as *maras*) being blamed. Drug trafficking and gang violence are major problems in the country and the economy is struggling. Strikes and demonstrations are common. This may be why opposition candidate Manuel Zelaya Rosales was declared winner of the November 2005 Presidential elections, defeating former communist Porfirio Lobo. The new Honduran President, Manuel Zelaya, was sworn in on January 2006. Standing for the Liberal Party, he has pledged to tackle the worsening crime problem by maintaining life sentences for the most serious offences and doubling police on the streets. He also vowed to tackle poverty in one of central America's poorest nations.

Under the provisions of the 1982 constitution, modified in 1997, an executive President is elected by popular vote every four years. There are also four-yearly elections for the unicameral 128-seat National Assembly.

LANGUAGE: The official language is Spanish. English is widely spoken by the West Indian settlers in the north and on the Bay Islands off the Caribbean coast.

RELIGION: Roman Catholic majority.

ELECTRICITY: 110/120/220 volts AC, 60Hz.

SOCIAL CONVENTIONS: There are strong Spanish influences, but the majority of the population is mestizo, mainly leading an agricultural way of life with a low standard of living. Many rural communities can still be found living a relatively unchanged, traditional lifestyle. Social courtesies should be observed. It is customary for a guest at dinner or someone's home to send flowers to the hostess, either before or afterwards. Conservative casual wear is widely acceptable with dress tending to be less conservative in coastal areas. Beachwear and shorts should not be worn away from the beach or poolside. Men are required to wear dinner jackets for formal social occasions. Hotels, restaurants and shops include a 12 per cent sales tax on all purchases.

Climate

The climate is tropical with cooler, more temperate weather in the mountains. The north coast is very hot with rain throughout the year, and though the offshore breezes temper the climate, the sun is very strong. The dry season is from November to April and the wet season runs from May to October.

Required clothing: Lightweight cottons and linens; warmer clothes are recommended between November and February and in the mountains. Waterproofs are needed for the wet season.

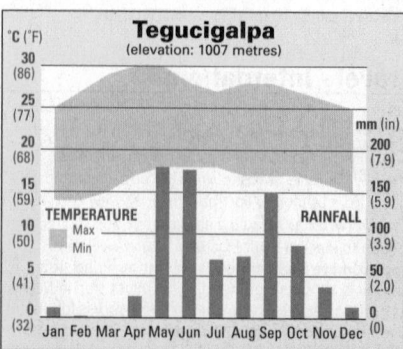

Communications

Telephone: IDD is available. Country code: 504.
Mobile telephone: Roaming agreements with international mobile phone companies exist.
Internet: Internet cafes exist in major towns.
Post: Airmail to Western Europe takes between four and seven days. Post office hours: Mon-Sat 0800-1200 and 1400-1800.
MEDIA: Media freedom in Honduras is restricted by punitive defamation laws, which also require journalists to reveal sources in certain cases. Journalists tend to exercise self-censorship in order to avoid offending the political or economic interests of media owners, and there have also been cases of journalists accepting bribes from officials who wish to influence coverage.
Press: Daily newspapers are in Spanish, and include *El Heraldo* (website: www.elheraldo.hn), *La Prensa* (website: www.laprensahn.com), *El Tiempo* (website: www.tiempo.hn) and *La Tribuna* (website: http://tribuna.prohospedaje.com). The weekly *Honduras This Week* (website: www.marrder.com) is published in English.
TV: *Televicentro* operates *Telesistema Hondureno, Canal 5 El Lider* and *Telecadena 7 y 4*. Other networks are: *CBC Canal 6, Vica TV* and *SOTEL Canal 11*.
Radio: *Radio America* and *Radio HRN*.

Passport/Visa

	Passport Required?	Visa Required?	Return Ticket Required?
Full British	Yes	No	No
Australian	Yes	No	No
Canadian	Yes	No	No
USA	Yes	No	No
Other EU	Yes	No	No
Japanese	Yes	No	No

Note: *Regulations and requirements may be subject to change at short notice, and you are advised to contact the appropriate diplomatic or consular authority before finalising travel arrangements. Any numbers in the chart refer to the footnotes below.*

PASSPORTS: Passport valid for three months from date of arrival required by all.
Note: It is advisable to have a return ticket, but not obligatory. However, visitors may be asked to prove how they plan to leave the country.
VISAS: Required by all except the following:
(a) nationals of countries referred to in the chart above;
(b) nationals of Andorra, Antigua & Barbuda, Argentina, The Bahamas, Bahrain, Barbados, Belize, Brazil, Brunei, Bulgaria, Chile, Costa Rica, Croatia, El Salvador, Former Yugoslav Republic of Macedonia, Guatemala, Iceland, Israel, Korea (Rep), Kuwait, Liechtenstein, Madagascar, Marshall Islands, Malaysia, Mexico, Monaco, New Zealand, Nicaragua, Norway, Panama, Paraguay, Qatar, Romania, St Kitts & Nevis, St Lucia, St Vincent & the Grenadines, San Marino, São Tome and Principé, Saudi Arabia, Singapore, Soloman Islands, South Africa, Switzerland; Trinidad & Tobago, Turkey, Tuvalu, United Arab Emirates, Uruguay and Vanuatu, Vatican City and Venezuela;
(c) those in transit continuing their journey within 48 hours, except for those nationals who require special authorisation.
Note: For certain nationalities, authorisation will have to be obtained from Honduras before a visa can be issued.
Types of visa and cost: *Tourist* and *Business*: £10 (single-entry); £35 (multiple-entry).
Validity: Single-entry: up to 90 days. Multiple-entry: up to one year. A visa extension may be obtained in Honduras at the Immigration Authorities for both tourism and business.
Application to: Consulate (or Consular section at Embassy); see *Passport/Visa Information*.
Note: Applications must be made in person, postal applications are not accepted.
Application requirements: (a) Two passport-size photos. (b) Valid passport. (c) Completed application form. (d) Fee, payable by cash or cheque but the visa will only be issued after the cheque has cleared. *Tourist*: (a)-(d) and where possible, (e) Return tickets and travel itinerary. (f) Bank statements. *Business*: (a)-(d) and, (e) Company letters giving purpose of visit and confirming financial responsibility for the applicant.
Working days required: One to two, unless approval is needed from the Ministry of Foreign Affairs in Honduras, which can take up to 10 days.

PASSPORT/VISA INFORMATION

Embassy of the Republic of Honduras and Consulate General in the UK
115 Gloucester Place, London W1U 6JT, UK
Tel: (020) 7486 4880.
E-mail: hondurasuk@lineone.net
Opening hours: Mon-Fri 1000-1600.

Embassy of the Republic of Honduras in the USA
3007 Tilden Street, NW, Suite 4M, Washington, DC 20008, USA
Tel: (202) 966 7702 *or* 737 1972 (Consular section).
Website: www.hondurasemb.org

Money

Currency: Lempira (HNL) = 100 centavos. Notes are in denominations of HNL500, 100, 50, 20, 10, 5, 2 and 1. Coins are in denominations of 50, 20, 10, 5, 2 and 1 centavos. A real is one-eighth of a Lempira, and is used colloquially, though there is no such coin.
Currency exchange: Sterling cannot normally be exchanged, except at branches of Lloyds Bank; visitors should therefore take US Dollars.
Credit & debit cards: American Express, Diners Club, MasterCard and Visa are accepted. Some banks offer cash withdrawal with Visa or Mastercard. Check with your credit or debit card company for details of merchant acceptability and other services which may be available.
Traveller's cheques: To avoid additional exchange rate charges, travellers are advised to take traveller's cheques in US Dollars.
Currency restrictions: There are no restrictions on the import and export of local or foreign currency, but it is advisable to declare US Dollars.
Banking hours: Mon-Fri 0900-1600 (some banks open until 1800). Some branches open Sat 0900-1200.
Exchange rate indicators:
Rate at time of publishing
£1.00= HNL34.70
$1.00= HNL19.71

Duty Free

The following goods may be imported into Honduras without incurring customs duty:
200 cigarettes or 100 cigars or 450g of tobacco; two bottles of alcoholic beverages; a reasonable amount of perfume for personal use; gifts up to a total value of US$50.

Public Holidays

Below are listed Public Holidays for the January 2006-June 2007 period.
2006: Jan 1 New Year's Day. **Apr 13** Maundy Thursday. **Apr 14** Good Friday; Day of the Americas. **May 1** Labour Day. **Sep 15** Independence Day. **Oct 3** Soldier's Day. **Oct 12** Americas Day. **Oct 21** Armed Forces Day. **Dec 25** Christmas Day.
2007: Jan 1 New Year's Day. **Apr 5** Maundy Thursday. **Apr 6** Good Friday. **Apr 14** Day of the Americas. **May 1** Labour Day.

Health

	Special Precautions?	Certificate Required?
Yellow Fever	Yes	1
Cholera	2	No
Typhoid & Polio	3	N/A
Malaria	4	N/A

Note: *Regulations and requirements may be subject to change at short notice, and you are advised to contact your doctor well in advance of your intended date of departure. Any numbers in the chart refer to the footnotes below.*

1: A yellow fever vaccination certificate is required from all travellers arriving from areas in the endemic zone
2: Following WHO guidelines issued in 1973, a cholera vaccination certificate is no longer a condition of entry into Honduras. However, cases of cholera were reported in 1996 and 1999 and precautions are essential. Up-to-date advice should be sought before deciding whether these precautions should include vaccination as medical opinion is divided over its effectiveness.
3: Typhoid may be a risk in rural areas.
4: Malaria risk, in the benign *vivax* form, exists throughout the year in 80 per cent of the municipalities, especially in the rural areas such as Roatán and the other Bay Islands.
Food & drink: All water should be regarded as being potentially contaminated. Water used for drinking, brushing teeth or making ice should first be boiled or otherwise sterilised. Milk is unpasteurised in rural areas and should be boiled. Powdered or tinned milk is available and is advised, but make sure that it is reconstituted with pure water. Avoid dairy products that are likely to have been made from unboiled milk. Only eat well-cooked meat and fish, preferably served hot. Pork, salad and mayonnaise may carry increased risk. Vegetables should be cooked and fruit peeled.
Other risks: *Visceral, cutaneous* and *mucocutaneous leishmaniasis* and *hepatitis A* and *B* all occur. *Dengue fever, filariasis, onchocerciasis* and *American trypanosomiasis* (Chagas Disease) may also occur. *Paragonimiasis* (oriental lung fluke) has been reported. *Hepatitis B* is present.
Rabies is present. For those at high risk, vaccination before arrival should be considered. If you are bitten, seek medical advice without delay. For more information, consult the *Health* appendix.
Health care: Health insurance is recommended. There are hospitals in Tegucigalpa and all the large towns. Mosquito nets are recommended for coastal areas.

Travel - International

AIR:
American Airlines operates daily flights to Honduras with a one-night stopover in Miami. A sales tax of 10 per cent is payable on international bookings for tickets issued in Honduras.
Approximate flight times: From Tegucigalpa to *London* is 15 hours. (There are no direct flights to London; connections are generally via Miami, Houston, Los Angeles or New York.) From Tegucigalpa to *New York* is four hours 30 minutes (not including stopovers).
Main airports: *Tegucigalpa (TGU)* (Toncontín) is 5km (3 miles) southeast of the city. *To/from the airport*: Taxis and buses are available to the city. *Facilities*: Bar, restaurant, duty free shop, bank, car hire, post office and first aid facilities.
There are also international airports at *San Pedro Sula (SAP)* (La Mesa International Airport), at *La Ceiba (LCE)* (Golosón) and at *Roatán (RTB)* (Dr Juan Manuel Galvez).
Departure tax: US$25 is levied on all passengers aged 12 years of age and over.
SEA:
Main ports: *Amapala, El Henecan, La Ceiba, Puerto Cortés, Tela* and *Trujillo*. There is a ferry service between Port Isabel in Texas and Puerto Cortés. Ships operated by *Carol Line, Cie Generale Transatlantique, Hapag-Lloyd* (website: www.hapag-lloyd.com), *The Royal Netherlands Steamship Company* and vessels owned or chartered by the *Standard Fruit Company* and *United Fruit Company* sometimes have limited passenger accommodation.
RAIL:
There are no rail services between Honduras and neighbouring countries.
ROAD:
Road routes run from El Salvador and Nicaragua via the Pan-American Highway, and from Guatemala on the Western Highway. Visas must be obtained before the journey is undertaken. Border crossings can be fraught with long delays. Areas around the border can be dangerous. **Bus:** The *Ticabus* company (website: www.ticabus.com) runs international services to all Central American capitals, but these comfortable coaches are often booked days in advance.

Travel - Internal

AIR:
The three local airlines (*Isleña Airlines* (website: www.flyislena.com), *Sosa Airlines* (website: www.laceibaonline.net/aerososa/sosaingl) and *Rollins Air* operate daily services which link Tegucigalpa and other principal towns. *Isleña Airlines* and *Sosa Airlines* run services to Utila, the cheapest Bay Island (off the Caribbean coast). Over 30 small airfields handle light aircraft and commercial aviation. This mode is especially more convenient for business visitors.
Departure tax: There is an airport tax on internal journeys of $1.30.
SEA:
Ferries operate between ports on the Pacific and Caribbean coastlines. For details, contact local port authorities. There are sailings from La Ceiba and Puerto Cortés to the Bay Islands several times a week, schedules regularly change. Arrangements must be made with local boat owners.

RAIL:

There are only three railways, confined to the northern coastal region and mainly used for transport between banana plantations. Visitors can, however, take a trip from San Pedro Sula on a banana train, and from La Ceiba on a tourist train.

ROAD:

Traffic drives on the right. An all-weather road exists from Tegucigalpa to San Pedro Sula, Puerto Cortés, La Ceiba and towns along the Caribbean coast, as well as to the towns around the Gulf of Fonseca in the south. Some minor roads are still being repaired after Hurricane Mitch in 1998. **Bus:** Local lines run regular services to most large towns, but the services are well used and booking in advance is essential. On the whole the services are very cheap. **Taxi:** Not metered, and run on a flat rate within cities. For other journeys, fares should be agreed before commencing journey. **Car hire:** Self-drive cars are available at the airport. Travellers are recommended not to drive at night as many vehicles drive without lights on and animals wander onto the road.

Documentation: Both international and foreign driving licences are accepted.

Travel times: The following chart gives approximate travel times (in hours and minutes) from **Tegucigalpa** to other major cities/towns in Honduras.

	Air	Road
Comayagua	-	1.00
Bay Islands	0.40	7.00*
Sta Rosa de Copán	6.00	-
Puerto Cortés	-	4.00

Note: *Includes sea crossing of two hours.

Travel Advice

Travellers should take precautions against widespread petty and violent crime in Honduras., especially in the Bay Islands.

Honduras is recovering from the effects of Hurricane Beta and Tropical Storm Gamma. Flooding has caused damage in the Caribbean coastal areas of Colon, Atlantida, Yoro and Cortes where disruption to transport can be expected. You are advised to check the latest situation locally, prior to travelling to the affected areas.

The threat from terrorism is low, but you should be aware of the global risk of indiscriminate terrorist attacks, which could be against civilian targets, including places frequented by foreigners.

This advice is based on information provided by the Foreign and Commonwealth Office in the UK. It is correct at time of publishing. As the situation can change rapidly, visitors are advised to contact the following organisations for the latest travel advice:

British Foreign and Commonwealth Office
Tel: (0845) 850 2829.
Website: www.fco.gov.uk

US Department of State
Website: http://travel.state.gov/travel

Accommodation

HOTELS:

Reasonable hotels are available in both Tegucigalpa and San Pedro Sula (where the rates are lower, but standards equivalent to those in the capital are maintained). Elsewhere both rates and standards of comfort are somewhat lower. The Instituto Hondureño de Turismo (see *Top Things To Do*) can supply lists of hotels with accommodation details.

Grading: Hotels are split into three categories (upper, middle and lower) according to standard.

Top Things To See & Do

- Honduras' capital city, **Tegucigalpa**, has never been subjected to the disasters of earthquake or fire and so retains many traditional features. The most recent monument is **Christ of the Picacho**, a massive image of Christ that overlooks the city from Picacho Park on a mountaintop. Near the monument there is also a small zoo and a spectacular view of the city. However, even better is neighbouring **Comayagua**, former capital of Honduras and now a colonial masterpiece of cobbled streets, tiny plazas and whitewashed houses.

- See the ancient city of **Copán**, where the **Copán Ruins Archaeological Park** remains the best remaining testament to the culture of the Mayan Indians. Among the best of the ruins are the magnificent **Acropolis** composed of courts and temples, the **Great Plaza**, a huge amphitheatre, and the **Court of the Hieroglyphic Stairway**. Near the **Great Acropolis**, recent archaeological work has brought to light invaluable excavations. The majority of the site's original sculptures are on display at the **Copán Sculpture Museum**, the four-storey centrepiece of which is the **Rosalita** temple, a full-scale replica of a temple recently excavated beneath the Acropolis.

- On Honduras' gorgeous **Caribbean Coast**, **Trujillo** was once a thriving port and the old capital of colonial Honduras. Trujillo is today home to many old Spanish buildings, a fascinating pirate history and - of course - superb tropical beaches. New resorts and subdivisions are continually opening in the Trujillo area. The **Cuyamel Caves** are also nearby and are well worth a visit - though they are so difficult to find you may need help finding them!

- Off the Caribbean coast of Honduras lies the exotic archipelago of the **Bay Islands**. Consisting of three major islands (**Guanaja**, **Roatan** and **Utila**) and several smaller islands, the Bay Islands have a history that spans the ancient Mayan civilisation, early Spanish exploration, colonial buccaneers and the British Empire. **Guanaja** and **Roatán** are hilly, tropical islands, protected by a great coral reef that provides fine **diving**. **Utila** offers wide expanses of sandy beach and is ringed by tiny cays surrounded by palm trees.

- Take a holiday with an **ecotourism** theme: the exciting, unspoilt landscape of Honduras and the multitude of **flora and fauna** that can be found there offer much interest to nature lovers. There are **wildlife refuges** and **national parks** all over the country. Cloud forests, mountains, dry forests, pine forests and huge rivers are among the natural features to be enjoyed. The coastal wetlands are home to monkeys and manatees, and visitors can take boat rides through the swamps to view these animals. Toucans and orchids are amongst the attractions of the cloud forests. The centre for activities focusing on ecotourism is **La Ceiba** and, particularly, the nearby Pico Bonito National Park, which offers excellent opportunities for **hiking** through the rainforest. It also offers spectacular scenery, full of steep slopes and numerous waterfalls. For **birdwatching**, the premier destination is **Lake Yojoa** in the west of the country. Wildlife enthusiasts can also take **boat trips** along the winding canals of the **Cuero y Salado Wildlife Refuge**, which provides a habitat for numerous animal species (including monkeys, alligators and manatees) and dozens of waterbirds.

- Try **canopy touring**: a series of cables are fixed from tree to tree, and attached to a pulley while wearing a harness one can 'fly' through the canopy of the rainforest.

- There is good **fishing** on both coasts and Lake Yojoa offers some of the best bass fishing in the world.

TOURIST INFORMATION

Instituto Hondureño de Turismo
Apartardo Postal 3261, Edificio Europa, Colonia San Carlos, Tegucigalpa, Honduras
Tel: 222 2124 ext. 502 *or* 503.
Website: www.letsgohonduras.com

Entertainment

FOOD & DRINK: There is a wide variety of restaurants and bars in Tegucigalpa and the main cities.

National specialities:
- *Curiles* (seafood).
- *Tortillas*.
- *Enchiladas*.
- Fruits: mangoes, papayas, pineapples, avocados and bananas.

Tipping: Service is included in most restaurant bills. In hotels, cafes and restaurants, 10 per cent of the bill is customary where service is not included. Porters and cab drivers should be tipped when helping with the luggage (La0.50 to La1). Hotels, travel agencies and tour operators charge an extra 4 per cent for tourism services.

NIGHTLIFE: There are cinemas and discos in the main cities. There are also casinos in the major cities, plus many bars, some of which offer happy hours.

SHOPPING: Visit the local markets where local craftsmanship is excellent and inexpensive. Typical items include woodcarvings, cigars, leather goods, straw hats and bags, seed necklaces and baskets. **Shopping hours:** Mon-Fri 0800-1200 and 1330-1800, Sat 0800-1700.

Business

- **GDP:** US$17.46 billion.
- **Main imports:** Fabric, yarn, machinery, chemicals, petroleum, vehicles, processed food, metal, agricultural products and plastic and paper articles.
- **Main exports:** Coffee, bananas, shrimp, lobster, meat, zinc and timber.
- **Main trade partners:** Costa Rica, El Salvador, Germany, Guatemala, Mexico, UK and USA.

ECONOMY: The economy of Honduras, which is one of the poorest nations in the western hemisphere, relies on agriculture and timber. The main agricultural products are bananas, beans, coffee, cotton, maize, rice, sorghum and sugar; there is also some dairy and beef farming, and a trade in shellfish. Apart from wood and wood products, light industries produce a variety of consumer goods. There is a small mining industry which produces lead, zinc and silver for export. The economy draws heavily on various forms of US-sponsored aid – both direct and multilateral (through the IMF, Inter-American Development Bank and others). Export earnings have been badly hit in recent years by low world prices and slack demand within the Central American Common Market, of which Honduras is a member. To compound its difficulties further, Honduras was badly affected by Hurricane Mitch in 1998, which caused an estimated US$3 billion worth of damage.

BUSINESS ETIQUETTE: It is customary to address a professional person by his or her title, particularly on first meeting or during early acquaintance. Businesspeople are generally expected to dress smartly and some dining rooms require men to wear a jacket. There are very few local interpreter or translation services available. Though many businesspeople throughout the country also speak English, correspondence should be in Spanish. **Office hours:** Mon-Fri 0800-1200 and 1400-1700, Sat 0800-1100. Government offices: Mon-Fri 0830-1200 and 1300-1630.

COMMERCIAL INFORMATION

Cámara de Comercio Hondureño-Americana
Sección Comercial Hotel Honduras Maya, Apdo 1838, Tegucigalpa, Honduras
Tel: 232 7043;
Website: www.amcham.hn2.com

Cámara de Comercio e Industrias de Tegucigalpa
Bulevar Centroamérica, Apdo 3444, Tegucigalpa, Honduras
Tel: 232 4200.
Website: www.ccit.hn

Hungary

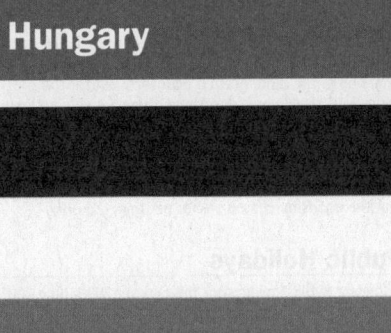

Credit: © Hungarian National Tourist Office

Location: Central Europe.

Time: GMT + 1 (GMT + 2 from last Sunday in March to Saturday before last Sunday in October).

Overview

Hungary has a complex sense of identity, not generally regarding itself as Balkan or Slavic, but Western. The country's assortment of cultures can be traced back through its history.

During the ninth century, Finno-Ugriar nomads came into Hungary via south Russia. The Arpád Dynasty ruled until the end of the 13th century, when Hungary was devastated by a Mongol invasion. Hungary fell under Turkish sovereignty during the 16th century, re-establishing independence after the Thirty Years' War. Hungary then formed an alliance with Austria and was ruled by a Magyar aristocracy. It remained an essentially feudal state until 1914 (under monarchic and republican regimes), with an antiquated (by European standards) social system that was not fully dismantled until after World War II.

Being landlocked, this mosaic of cultures and lineage can also be explained by the country's shared borders with the Slovak Republic, Ukraine, Romania, Croatia, Serbia, Austria and Slovenia. Yet despite being landlocked, Hungary contains some beautiful stretches of water - such as Lake Balaton - and pulsates with hot, medicinal springs. Hungary has also managed to retain its unique language and customs. Immense pride in their homeland may lead Hungarians to persuade the tourist in Budapest to spend some time also exploring Hungary's thousands of acres of vineyards and orchards, plus 11 national parks and hundreds of protected areas.

Nevertheless, Budapest is a fantastic capital city in its own right, situated on a beautiful stretch of the Danube. The city is made up of two parts – Buda, the older, more graceful and cobbled part, and Pest, the commercial centre. The capital is a lively city that has long been a haven for writers, artists and musicians. And Hungary has a lot of them, with rich traditions in folk and classical music, the birthplace of Liszt and Bartok. Budapest is also filled with the strains of much more modern music, which spills out of nightclubs, trendy bars and discos.

Yet beneath this glossy surface lurks the remembrance of how Hungary sided with Nazi Germany during World War II. Once the Germans were driven out by the Russians in 1945, Hungary became a Soviet-style Socialist state, a member of the Warsaw Pact, and a People's Republic. Although the Hungarian regime was, by the 1970s, the most liberal of all Soviet bloc systems, the Socialists nonetheless maintained a firm grip on the country's political and economic life. Finally, Kádár, the Hungarian Communist leader, was removed from the ruling Politburo in 1988 and Hungary began the transition to a pluralistic political system. The first elections were held in the spring of 1990.

Such history is gradually being ebbed away. Gigantic Communist statues have been dumped in Szoborpark (Statue Park), on the outskirts of Budapest. Hungary is now a member of the EU. Such integration has brought both further touristic development and keen preservation of what is wonderful about this country.

General Information

AREA: 93,030 sq km (35,919 sq miles).

POPULATION: 9.8 million (UN estimate 2005).

POPULATION DENSITY: 92 per sq km.

CAPITAL: Budapest. **Population:** 1.8 million (2005).

GEOGRAPHY: Hungary is situated in Central Europe, sharing borders to the north with the Slovak Republic, to the northeast with Ukraine, to the east with Romania, to the south with Croatia and Serbia and to the west with Austria and Slovenia. There are several ranges of hills, chiefly in the north and west. The Great Plain (*Nagyalföld*) stretches east from the Danube to the foothills of the Carpathian Mountains in the CIS, to the mountains of Transylvania in Romania, and south to the Fruska Gora range in Croatia. Lake Balaton is the largest unbroken stretch of inland water in Central Europe.

GOVERNMENT: Republic. **Head of State:** President Laszlo Solymon since 2005. **Head of Government:** Prime Minister Ferenc Gyurcsany since 2004. **Recent history:** In May 2002, the Hungarian Socialist Party (*Magyar Szocialista Part*, MSzP) replaced the right-wing Alliance of Young Democrats (Fiatal Demokratak Szövetsege, FIDESz)-led coalition as the governing party. There have been a few re-shuffles in Parliament since then, most recently when opposition-backed Laszlo Solyman was chosen as the next President, after the Socialists' candidate was blocked - but the coalition has survived. The character of the two main parties is quite different. The Socialists are essentially a party of technocrats with little ideological fervour. By contrast, FIDESz is a populist party with a highly motivated support base. Nevertheless, there are few significant differences to the main agendas of the two parties. The overriding priority is the pursuit of full membership of the European Union, which in itself places major constraints on Government spending irrespective of the party in power. Hungary achieved its other main objective – membership of NATO – in 1999. Along with Poland and the Czech Republic, Hungary was admitted after a two-year period of negotiation and a national referendum which approved future membership by a six-to-one margin. Hungary has also joined with the Czech Republic, Poland and Slovakia in the Visegrad group, which was established to promote political and economic cooperation in central Europe. Abroad, Hungary has had some involvement in the Balkan conflicts of the 1990s. Its calculations must always take account of the sizeable ethnic Hungarian minorities in the Serbian autonomous region of Vojvodina (400,000), north-eastern Romania (1.7 million), the Slovak Republic (550,000) and Ukraine. Hungary clearly believes, however, that NATO is the best guarantor of stability in the region.

Legislative power is held by the 386-seat National Assembly, the *Orszaggyules*, which is elected for four years (176 members come from single seat constituencies, 152 by proportional representation in multi-seat constituencies, and 58 members by proportional representation on a national basis). The Council of Ministers, the highest executive organ, is elected by the assembly on the advice of the president, who is also elected by the National Assembly for a four-year term, and may serve two terms. In April 1995, a 53-member National Autonomous Authority of the Romany Minority was ratified, with the power to administer funds disbursed by the central Government.

LANGUAGE: Hungarian (Magyar) is the official language. German and English are widely spoken. Some French is also spoken, mainly in western Hungary.

RELIGION: 52 per cent Roman Catholic, 16 per cent Calvinist, 3 per cent Lutheran. Christian, Eastern Orthodox and Jewish minorities. There is no official national religion.

ELECTRICITY: 220 volts AC, 50Hz. European-style two-pin plugs are used.

SOCIAL CONVENTIONS: Most Hungarians enjoy modern music and dance, although older people still preserve their traditions and culture, particularly in small villages. Handshaking is customary. Both Christian name and surname should be used. Normal courtesies should be observed. At a meal, toasts are usually made and should be returned. A useful word is *egészségünkre* (pronounced ay-gash-ay-gun-gre), meaning 'your health'. Few people speak English outside hotels, big restaurants and tourist offices. A knowledge of German is very useful. Gifts are acceptable for hosts as a token of thanks, particularly when invited for a meal. Casual wear is acceptable in most places, with the exception of expensive restaurants and bars. Formal attire should be worn for important social functions, but it is not common practice to specify dress on invitations. Smoking is prohibited on public transport in towns and public buildings. Travellers may smoke on long-distance trains. **Photography:** Military installations should not be photographed; other restrictions are usually signposted.

Climate

There are four seasons, with a very warm summer from June to August. Spring and autumn are mild, while winters are very cold. Rainfall is distributed throughout the year with snowfalls in winter.

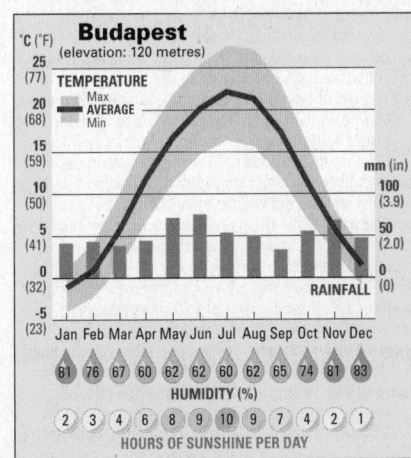

Budapest (elevation: 120 metres)

Communications

Telephone: IDD available. Country code: 36. Public telephones are operated by Ft100, Ft50, Ft20 and Ft10 coins or by telephone cards.

Mobile telephone: Roaming agreements exist with international mobile phone companies. Coverage is good.

Internet: Internet is available; there are Internet cafes in larger towns.

Post: Airmail takes three days to one week to reach other European destinations. In addition to the main post office, the offices at West and East railway stations in Budapest are open daily 0700-2100. Stamps are available from tobacconists as well as post offices. Post office hours: Mon-Fri 0800-1800, Sat 0800-1300.

MEDIA: Hungary's private broadcast media compete with state-run radio and TV, and the state-run broadcaster has faced financial struggles, dwindling audiences and allegations of political influence. Public radio services operated by Hungarian Radio compete with numerous local radio stations and national commercial services. Hungary's national and local newspapers are privately-owned, some of them by foreign groups and investors.

Press: National dailies include *Magyar Hírlap*, *Népszabadság* and *Népszava*. English-language newspapers include the *Budapest Business Journal*, *Budapest Week*, *Courier Diplomatique*, *The Budapest Sun*, *The Hungarian Economy*, *The Hungarian Observer* and *The Hungarian Quarterly*.
TV: Public stations include *Magyar Televizio* (operating two channels) and *Duna TV* (satellite). Private stations include *TV2* and *RTL Klub*.
Radio: Public radio broadcasters include *Hungarian Radio* (operating *Kossuth*, *Petofi* and *Bartok* networks, plus *Radio Budapest*, an external service). Private broadcasters include *Danubius Radio*, *Slager Radio* (owned by the Emmis Group) and *Juventus Radio* (owned by the Metromedia group).

Passport/Visa

	Passport Required?	Visa Required?	Return Ticket Required?
Full British	No	No	Yes
Australian	Yes	No	Yes
Canadian	Yes	No	Yes
USA	Yes	No	Yes
Other EU	1/2	No	Yes
Japanese	Yes	No	Yes

Note: Regulations and requirements may be subject to change at short notice, and you are advised to contact the appropriate diplomatic or consular authority before finalising travel arrangements. Any numbers in the chart refer to the footnotes below.

PASSPORTS: Passport valid for three months required by all, except:
(a) **1.** nationals of EU or EEA member states holding a passport (must be valid for entire duration of stay) or national identity card;
(b) **2.** nationals of Croatia and Switzerland holding valid ID cards but *only* when staying for up to 90 days for touristic purposes, with return ticket and proof of sufficient funds.
VISAS: Required by all except the following:
(a) nationals of countries referred to in the chart above for stays of up to 90 days (nationals of the UK and Ireland for stays of up to six months, and nationals of Cyprus, Latvia, Malta and Slovenia for stays up to 30 days).
(b) nationals of Andorra, Argentina, Bolivia, Brazil, Brunei, Bulgaria, Chile, Costa Rica, Croatia, El Salvador, Guatemala, Honduras, Hong Kong (SAR), Iceland, Israel, Korea (Rep), Liechtenstein, Macau (SAR), Malaysia, Mexico, Monaco, New Zealand, Nicaragua, Norway, Panama, Paraguay, Switzerland, Uruguay, Vatican City and Venezuela (tourist visits only) for stays of up to 30 days;
(c) nationals of Bosnia & Herzegovina, Nicaragua, Romania, San Marino and Singapore for stays of up to 30 days;
(d) persons continuing their journey to a third country within 24 hours, provided not leaving the airport and holding valid onward tickets and documentation. However, nationals who are not eligible for visa exemptions and are non-residents of the UK may need to acquire an *airport transit* visa in all circumstances; contact nearest Embassy/Consulate for further details.
Note: The length of stay which nationals of the exempted countries are allowed is subject to frequent change; contact the embassy for more information.
Types of visa and cost: All visas, regardless of type and duration of stay allocated, cost £25. However, long-term visas cost £35. Multiple-entry visas are only valid for business travellers and for those possessing a long-term visa. Visas for children under seven years, or school children (elementary and high school) travelling in a group of five or more persons on a shool trip, cost £13.
Note: (a) Nationals of Serbia & Montenegro and Ukraine, and family members of UK nationals (eg husband/wife and children under 21 years), can obtain visas free-of-charge. (b) If the visa has to be issued on a separate sheet (because there is no free page in the passport), an additional fee is payable of £17.
Validity: *Single-entry* (*tourist* and *business*): Valid for 90-day stay within six months of the date of issue. *Double-entry*: Valid for 90-day stay taken *twice* within six months from date of issue. *Multiple-entry*: Valid for multiple 90-day stays in Hungary within one year from the date of issue. Validity subject to frequent change according to nationality. *Transit*: Valid for five days within six months from date of issue. *Double-transit*: Maximum of five days *twice* within six months from date of issue.
Application to: Consulate (or Consular section at Embassy; see *Passport/Visa Information*). Visas are not issued at road border points or at Budapest Airport.
Application requirements: (a) Passport valid for at least six months (with at least one blank page). (b) Completed application form. (c) One passport-size photo. (d) Fee (non reimbursable), payable in cash (personal applications) or postal order only. (e) Return ticket or ticket reservation and travel insurance. (f) For postal applications, a pre-paid special delivery return envelope. (g) Confirmation of accommodation in Hungary, or letter of invitation from friends or relatives living in Hungary (copy of the ID cards of the inviting party must be attached; if travelling on a travel document and not a passport, nationals must seek endorsement from the local Hungarian migration authority). (h) Recent bank statement or payslip. *Business* (or just for business purposes, eg a trip to attend a conference): (a)-(h) and, (i) Written invitation from host organisation or company. *Transit*: (a)-(h) and, (i) Valid visa for country of destination.
Working days required: Two, or seven for postal applications and if applicant is applying with a travel document and not a passport.

PASSPORT/VISA INFORMATION

Embassy of the Republic of Hungary in the UK
35 Eaton Place, London SW1X 8BY, UK
Tel: (020) 7235 5218.
Consular section: Tel: (020) 7235 2664 *or* (09065) 508 936 (visa enquiries; calls are charged at the rate of £1 per minute).
Website: www.huemblon.org.uk
Opening hours: Mon-Fri 0930-1200.

Embassy of the Republic of Hungary in the USA
3910 Shoemaker Street, NW, Washington, DC 20008, USA
Tel: (202) 362 6730.
Website: www.huembwas.org

Money

Currency: Hungarian Forint (HUF) = 100 fillér. Notes are in denominations of HUF20,000, Ft10,000, 5000, 2000, 1000, 500 and 200. Coins are in denominations of HUF100, 50, 20, 10, 5, 2 and 1. A large number of commemorative coins in circulation are legal tender.
Currency exchange: Currency can be exchanged at hotels, banks, bureaux de change, airports, railway stations, travel agencies and some restaurants throughout the country. Automatic exchange machines are available in Budapest and other main tourist centres. Credit and debit cards can be used to withdraw money from ATMs, which operate 24 hours. Visitors should retain all exchange receipts, as it is illegal to change money on the black market.
Credit & debit cards: It is possible to withdraw cash by credit card at more than 3200 post offices. American Express, Cirrus, Diners Club, MasterCard, Visa, Eurocard, JCB and EnRoute are accepted. Check with your credit or debit card company for details of merchant acceptability and other services which may be available.
Traveller's cheques: Accepted in some stores and banks, but not all. To avoid additional exchange rate charges, travellers are advised to take traveller's cheques in US Dollars or Pounds Sterling.
Currency restrictions: The import of local currency is limited to Ft200,000, provided the amount is declared on arrival. The export of local currency is limited to Ft200,000 and must be declared. The import of foreign currency is unlimited, provided amounts greater than Ft1,000,000 are declared. The export of foreign currency is limited to the amount declared on import and should be made no longer than three months after import. There is no compulsory money exchange. Hungarian currency can be re-exchanged for up to 50 per cent of the officially exchanged sum (but not more than US$450) at any authorised office or branch of the National Savings Bank.
Banking hours: Mon-Fri 1030-1400 (Hungarian National Bank); Mon-Thurs 0800-1500, Fri 0800-1300 (merchant banks).
Exchange rate indicators:
Rate at time of publishing

£1.00=	HUF368.33
$1.00=	HUF211.57

Duty Free

The following may be imported into Hungary by persons over 16 years of age without incurring customs duty:
250 cigarettes or 50 cigars or 250g of tobacco; 1l of spirits, 1l of wine and 5l of beer; gifts to the value of Ft27,000; up to 1kg each of coffee, tea, cocoa and other spices (excluding paprika and paprika mixtures); photo cameras, non-professional video camera, laptop computer, portable typewriter, portable musical equipment with disks, records and photographic films (up to 10 rolls).
Note: Pets must have health and vaccination certificates, dated no more then one week prior to arrival.
Abolition of duty free goods within the EU: On June 30 1999, the sale of duty-free alcohol and tobacco at airports and at sea was abolished in all of the original 15 EU member states. Of the 10 new member states that joined the EU on May 1 2004, these rules already apply to Cyprus and Malta. There are transitional rules in place for visitors returning to one of the original 15 EU countries from one of the other new EU countries. But for the original 15, plus Cyprus and Malta, there are now no limits imposed on importing tobacco and alcohol products from one EU country to another (with the exceptions of Denmark, Finland and Sweden, where limits *are* imposed). Travellers should note that they may be required to prove at customs that the goods purchased are for personal use *only*.

Public Holidays

Below are Public Holidays for the January 2006-June 2007 period.
2006: Jan 1 New Year's Day. **Mar 15** Anniversary of 1848 uprising against Austrian rule. **Apr 17** Easter Monday. **May 1** Labour Day. **Jun 5** Whit Monday. **Aug 15** Assumption. **Aug 20** National Day (Feast of St Stephen). **Oct 23** Republic Day (Anniversary of 1956). **Nov 1** All Saints' Day. **Dec 25-26** Christmas. **Dec 31** New Year's Eve.
2007: Jan 1 New Year's Day. **Mar 15** Anniversary of 1848 uprising against Austrian rule. **Apr 9** Easter Monday. **May 1** Labour Day. **May 28** Whit Monday.

Health

	Special Precautions?	Certificate Required?
Yellow Fever	No	No
Cholera	No	No
Typhoid & Polio	No	N/A
Malaria	No	N/A

Note: Regulations and requirements may be subject to change at short notice, and you are advised to contact your doctor well in advance of your intended date of departure. Any numbers in the chart refer to the footnotes below.

Food & drink: Mains water is normally chlorinated, and whilst relatively safe may cause mild abdominal upsets. Bottled water is available and is advised for the first few weeks of the stay. Milk is pasteurised and dairy products are safe for consumption. Local meat, poultry, seafood, fruit and vegetables are generally considered safe to eat.
Other risks: *Hepatitis A* occurs. *Tick-borne encephalitis* occurs in forested areas. Vaccination is advisable.
Rabies, although on the decrease, is present. For those at high risk, vaccination before arrival should be considered. If you are bitten, seek medical advice without delay. For more information, consult the *Health* appendix.
Health care: European Economic Area (EEA) and Switzerland:
If you or any of your dependants are suddenly taken ill or have an accident during a visit to an EEA country or Switzerland, free or reduced-cost necessary treatment is available – in most cases on production of a valid European Health Insurance Card (EHIC). Each country has different rules about state medical provision. In some, treatment is free. In many countries you will have to pay part or all of the cost, and then claim a full or partial refund. The EHIC gives access to state-provided medical treatment only and the scheme gives no entitlement to medical repatriation costs, nor does it cover ongoing illnesses of a non-urgent nature, so comprehensive travel insurance is advised. Note that the EHIC replaces the Form E111, which will no longer be valid after 31 December 2005. Some restrictions apply, depending on your nationality.
For emergencies, call 104. Chemists are generally open from 0800-1800. There are chemists with a 24-hour emergency service open in every district. You can get treatment only from surgeries that have a sign saying they are contracted with the National Health Insurance Fund (Országos Egészségbiztosítasi Pénztár or OEP). Doctors' consultations are free, and emergency dental treatment is generally free. Any charges you pay are not refundable. Some prescription drugs are free; for others you pay all or some of the cost. These charges are not refundable. In-patient and out-patient hospital treatment is normally provided through a referral from a GP. Treatment is free of charge, although you will be charged for any extra services you request, for example, obtaining prescription treatment without a referral from a primary healthcare provider; using a healthcare provider other than the one specified by the prescribing doctor; unnecessarily changing the contents of prescription treatment, causing extra costs; or a better room, meals or conditions. Charges for extra services are not refundable. Ambulance travel is free of charge. More information can be obtained from Országos Egészségbiztosítasi Pénztár (National Health Insurance Fund), Department of International Relations and EU Integration, Vaci Street 73/a, 1139 Budapest (tel: (1) 350 1618; website: www.dh.gov.uk).

Travel - International

AIR:

The national airline is *Malév (MA)*, operating flights to more than 40 cities. For further information, contact Malév Hungarian Airlines (tel: 0870 9090 577; website: www.malev.com). Other airlines serving Budapest include *Air France, British Airways, EasyJet, KLM, Lufthansa* (website: www.lufthansa.com), *Sky Europe, Swiss, United Airlines* and *Wizz Air*.

Approximate flight times: From London to *Budapest* is two hours 20 minutes.

Main airports: *Budapest Ferihegy (BUD)*, (website: www.bud.hu) 16km (10 miles) from the city (travel time – 45 minutes). There are three passenger terminals - 1, 2A and 2B. *To/from the airport:* Regular coach and bus services are available to the city, costing around Ft800 for the Centrum bus and approximately Ft2100 or Ft3600 return for the airport minibus, which runs to and from any address in the city. The 93 bus runs an express service between the underground terminus at Kobánya-Kispest and the Ferihegy terminals, however you need a pre-purchased or season ticket. Taxis are available at all times. The major car hire companies are represented. *Facilities:* Duty free shop, florist, newsagent, restaurants and bar, bureaux de change, banks, tourist information centre, gift shop and post office.

Departure tax: None.

RIVER:

From April to October there is a daily hydrofoil service run by *MAHART* between Vienna, Bratislava and Budapest. The journey costs approximately €79 for a single ticket and takes approximately six hours. Reservations must be made in advance. 20kg of luggage may be carried free of charge. Passengers arriving by boat are advised to reserve a taxi through the shipping line, as none are readily available on the dock. For further details, contact MAHART at Belgrád rakpart, 1056 Budapest (tel: (1) 484 4013; website: www.mahartpassnave.hu).

RAIL:

Direct rail links connect Hungary to 16 European cities and there are dozens of international trains daily to Budapest. Inter-Rail, Eurotrain and RES concessions are valid on the Hungarian State Railways (MÁV). Between Dresden and Budapest there is a car transport system. The *Wiener Waltzer* from Basel travels via Zurich, Salzburg and Vienna to Budapest. First- and second-class day carriages run from Basel through to Budapest and both sleeping cars and couchettes (the latter is second-class only) as far as Vienna. There is a minibar service in Switzerland and Austria, and a dining car in Hungary. There are two main routes from London: via Paris or Brussels (*Eurostar* connection from London) to Vienna (including a Paris-Vienna EuroNight service), where several direct trains run daily to Budapest-Keleti; or via Brussels (Eurostar connection from London) to Munich, where several direct trains run daily to Budapest-Keleti (including a EuroNight service). **Luggage allowances:** 35kg for adults, 15kg for children.

Rail passes: The *Inter-Rail* pass offers unlimited second-class train travel in up to 29 countries (includes Morocco and Turkey) split into eight zones (A-H). Three different tickets are available: a ticket covering one zone (two to six countries, 16 days' validity), a ticket covering two zones (six to ten countries, 22 days' validity) and an *All Zone Pass* (29 countries, one month's validity). Ferry services between Italy and Greece are included. Passengers must be resident in Europe for at least six months before the pass is used. Travel is not allowed in the passenger's country of residence. Travellers under 26 years receive a reduction of about 30 per cent. Children's tickets are reduced by about 50 per cent. Supplements are required for some high speed services, seat reservations and couchettes. Discounts are offered on *Eurostar* and some ferry routes. Available from *Inter Rail* (website: www.interrailnet.com).

The *Eurailpass* offers unlimited first-class train travel in 17 European countries. Tickets are valid for 15 days, 21 days, one month, two months or three months. The *Eurailpass Saver* ticket offers discounts for two or more people travelling together. The *Eurailpass Youth* ticket is available to those aged under 26 and offers unlimited second-class train travel. The *Eurailpass Flexi* allows either 10 or 15 travel days within a two-month period. The *Eurail Selectpass* is valid in three, four or five bordering countries and allows five, six, eight or 10 travel days (or 15 for five countries) in a two-month period. The *Eurail Regional Pass* allows four to 10 travel days in a two-month period in one of nine regions (usually two or more countries). Children receive a 50 per cent reduction. The passes cannot be sold to residents of Europe, Turkey, Morocco, Algeria, Tunisia, or the Russian Federation. Available from *The Eurail Group* (website: www.eurail.com).

The *EuroDomino* pass enables holders anything form three to eight days' extensive travel within a one-month period on the entire rail network of their chosen country. It is valid in 28 European countries and North Africa, including the ferry service from Brindisi (Italy) to Igoumenitsa (Greece). To purchase a *EuroDomino* pass you must have been a resident in Europe for at least six months and a passport number is required at time of booking. It is not permitted to purchase a pass for travel within your own country of residence. To qualify for the youth rates, you must be under 26 years on the first date of validity of the pass. Children aged four to eleven years inclusive pay half the adult fares rounded up to the nearest pound. Children under four years travel for free. Seat reservations, couchette and sleeper charges are not included in the cost of the pass and are payable at the normal rate. Passholder fares are payable on some services. Reservation/Supplement charges are payable on all trains within Spain. Available from *Rail Europe* (website: www.raileurope.co.uk/railpasses/eurodomino.htm).

Note: Travellers leaving Hungary by train must pay their fare in convertible currency. Most generally recognised international concessionary tickets are accepted in Hungary. For further details contact MÁV at Budapest VI, Andrássy út 35 (tel: (1) 461 5500 (international timetables) or (1) 461 5400 (internal timetables); website: www.mav.hu). Seat reservations are strongly advised for all services.

ROAD:

Route via The Netherlands, Belgium and Austria and from Vienna via the E5 Transcontinental Highway which passes near Bratislava (Slovak Republic). Bus connections are available from most major European cities, check for further details with *Volanbusz* (tel: (1) 382 0888; website: www.volanbusz.hu). Eurolines, departing from Victoria Coach Station in London, serves destinations in Hungary. For further information, contact *Eurolines*, 52 Grosvenor Gardens, London, SW1V 0AU (tel: (08705) 143 219; website: www.eurolines.com). The *National Express* (Ensign court, 4 Vicarage Road, Edgbaston, Birmingham B15 3ES; tel: 08705 808 080; website: www.national express.com) run regular coach services from the UK to Hungary. Travellers can either choose Mini-Pass breaks or book a 15-, 30- or 60-day pass. The six Mini-Passes give travellers the freedom to visit three cities, with prices starting from £55. Travellers can stay as long as they like in each city. **The Channel Tunnel:**

Eurotunnel operates trains 24 hours per day through the Channel Tunnel between Folkestone in Kent (with direct access from the M20) and Calais in France. All vehicles from motorcycles to campers can be accommodated. Eurotunnel operates two to three passenger trains per hour at peak times. The journey takes approximately 35 minutes. For further information contact Eurotunnel Reservations (tel: (08705) 353 535; website: www.eurotunnel.co.uk).

Travel - Internal

AIR:

There are currently no scheduled internal air services in Hungary. Some are planned for the near future, however.

RIVER/LAKE:

There are regular services on the Danube and Lake Balaton from spring to late autumn. *MAHART* and the *Budapest Travel Company (BKV)* (website: www.bkv.hu) also operate ferries in the city centre, the Roman Embankment (*Római Part*) and at some crossing points. On Lake Balaton, a ferry operates during the year between Balatonföldvár and Tihany, and between Révfülöp and Balatonboglér. Contact *MAHART* for further details (see *Travel – International* section for contact details).

RAIL:

Services are operated by *MÁV*. All main cities are linked by efficient services but facilities are often inadequate. Supplements are payable on IC and express trains. Reservations are compulsory for IC trains and recommended for express trains, particularly in summer. Tickets can be bought 60 days in advance on electric railway lines, as can seat reservations. The most popular tourist rail routes are: Budapest-Kecskemet-Szeged–Budapest and Budapest-Siofok-Lake Balaton.
Rail-bus services are available between the main railway stations within Budapest at fixed rates (tel: (1) 353 2722; website: www.mav.hu). There are also narrow-gauge railways in operation in many parts of the country. The website www.elvira.hu has up-to-date travel information and timetables.

Cheap fares: Concessions are available for groups (minimum of 10 persons), children, students, families and

Credit: © Hungarian National Tourist Office

Credit: © Hungarian National Tourist Office

pensioners. Children under six and pensioners over 70 travel free. Children aged six to 15 pay approximately half of the full fare. Balaton and Tourist Season Tickets (seven to 10 days) are also available. Contact *MÁV* for details (see *Travel – International* section for contact details). The *Hungarian Flexipass*, sold by travel agents worldwide and by Rail Europe, offers unlimited first-class train travel for five days in a 15-day period or for 10 days in a 30-day period. The *Hungarian Tourist Card* offers discounts on rail, bus, taxi and ship services, as well as accommodation, restaurants and museums. The Hungarian National Tourist Office can provide further information (see *Top Things To Do*).

ROAD: Traffic drives on the right. There are eight arterial roads in the country: all but the M8 start from central Budapest. Tolls are payable on some roads and all motorways. Season tickets can be purchased. From Budapest the two main highways are the M1 to Györ and Vienna and the M7 along Lake Balaton. The M3 connects Budapest with eastern Hungary. Generally the road system is good. **Bus:** Budapest is linked with major provincial towns. Tickets are available from *Volán* long-distance bus terminal, Budapest, and at *Volán* offices throughout the country. A bus season ticket is also available. **Car hire:** Available at Ferihegy Airport or at Volán and Budapest tourist offices as well as at major hotels. **Regulations:** Speed limits are 50kph (31mph) in built-up areas, 90kph (50mph) on main roads, 110kph (62mph) on highways and 130kph (75mph) on motorways. Seat belts are compulsory. Children of 16 years and under must sit in the rear seats. Petrol stations are frequent and there are no special tourist petrol coupons. There is a total alcohol ban when driving; severe fines are imposed for infringements. It is obligatory to keep headlights dipped at all times when on the open road. Mobile phones are allowed only with headsets. Child seats are compulsory. **Breakdowns:** The Hungarian Automobile Club operates a breakdown service on main roads at weekends and a 24-hour service on motorways. For further details contact the Hungarian Automobile Club, Rómer Flóris utca 4/A, H-1024 Budapest (tel: (1) 345 1800 *or* 1755 (24-hour emergency helpline); website: www.autoklub.hu). **Documentation:** Pink format EU licence accepted but International Driving Permit required if green licence held.

URBAN:

 There is good public transport in all the main towns. Budapest has bus, trolleybus, tramway, suburban railway (*HEV*), a three-line metro and boat services. The metro has ticket barriers at all stations. The bus-trolleybus-tramway system has pre-purchase flat fares with ticket puncher on board. Day passes are available for all the transport modes in the city. Trams and buses generally run from about 0430-2300. Some night services also operate. The metro runs from 0430-2310 and stations can be identified by a large 'M'. There is also a cogwheel railway (Városmajor–Széchenyi Hill), a Childrens' Railway (Hüvösvölgy–Széchenyi Hill), a chairlift and a funicular. There are tramways in some of the other towns, or else good bus services. Day passes and season tickets are available in Budapest.

Travel times: The following chart gives approximate travel times (in hours and minutes) from **Budapest** to other major cities/towns in Hungary.

	Road	Rail
Sopron	3.00	2.25
Miskolc	2.30	1.55
Szeged	2.30	2.20
Lake Balaton	2.00	2.30

Travel Advice

Most visits to Hungary are trouble-free but you should be aware of the global risk of indiscriminate international terrorist attacks, which could be against civilian targets, including places frequented by foreigners. This advice is based on information provided by the Foreign and Commonwealth Office in the UK. It is correct at time of publishing. As the situation can change rapidly, visitors are advised to contact the following organisations for the latyest travel advice:

British Foreign and Commonwealth Office
Tel: (0845) 850 2829.
Website: www.fco.gov.uk

US Department of State
Website: http://travel.state.gov/travel

Accommodation

Note: The *Hungarian Tourist Card* provides discounts on accommodation including hotels, guest houses and youth hostels (the Hungarian National Tourist Office can provide further information *or* visit the website www.budapestinfo.hu).

HOTELS:

 In all classes of hotel, visitors from the West can expect to be made very welcome and service will usually be friendly and smooth. In addition to hotels, there are Tourist Hostels, which provide simple accommodation usually in rooms with four or more beds. The HNTO also issues a brochure with listings of hotels, guest houses and tourist hotels. Hungarian hotels are classified by use of a star rating system from **5-** and **4-star** hotels, of luxury class, to **2-** and **1-star** hotels, generally adequate and clean.

GUEST HOUSES:

 Available almost everywhere. Paying-guest accommodation is an inexpensive and excellent way of getting to know the people. Renting often includes a bathroom but not breakfast. Such accommodation should be reserved well in advance. Further information can be obtained from the Hungarian National Tourist Office (see *Top Things To Do*).

SELF-CATERING:

 Bungalows with two rooms, fully equipped, can be rented at a large number of resorts. Full details and rates can be obtained from the Hungarian National Tourist Office (see *Top Things To Do*).

CAMPING/CARAVANNING:

 Camping is forbidden except in specially designated areas. Booking is through the Hungarian Camping and Caravanning Club. Further information can also be obtained in a special catalogue published by the Hungarian National Tourist Office (see *Top Things To Do*) and there is an online booking facility (website: www.travelport.hu). Most of the sites cater only for campers bringing in their own equipment. Caravans are permitted in all sites that have power points; a parking charge is made. There is no charge for children under the age of six and young people between six and 16 years of age pay half price. There are four categories of site, designated **I**, **II**, **III** and **IV**, according to the amenities provided, and most are open from May to September.

YOUTH HOSTELS: Available in Budapest and other towns. Hostels are open all day and beds cost around £8. For further information, contact Express Travel Bureau *or* Hungarian Youth Hostel Association.

Top Things To See

- Visit Budapest, the capital city, which was originally two cities on each side of one of the most beautiful stretches of the Danube river – **Buda**, the older, more graceful part, with cobbled streets and medieval buildings, and **Pest**, the commercial centre. The 'Pearl of the Danube' is a lively city which has long been a haven for writers, artists and musicians. In Buda, **Gellért Hill** gives a wonderful view of the city, river and mountains. On the hill is the **Citadella**, a fort built after the unsuccessful 1848 uprising, and a number of thermal baths including the great **Gellért Baths** adjoining the hotel of that name. The **Royal Palace**, fully reconstructed after being bombed during World War II, houses the **National Gallery**, with collections of fine Gothic sculpture and modern Hungarian art, and the **Historical Museum of Budapest**, containing archaeological remains of the old city as well as furnishings, glass and ceramics from the 15th century. Also on this side of the Danube is the rampart of **Halászbástya** (**Fisherman's Bastion**), so called because it was the duty of the city's fishermen to protect the northern side of the Palace during the Middle Ages, and the great **Mátyás templon** (**church**) with its multicoloured tiled roof. On the Pest side are the **Parliament**; the **Hungarian National Museum**, containing remarkable treasures ranging from the oldest skull found in Europe to Franz Liszt's gold baton; the **Belvárosi Templom**, Hungary's oldest church, dating from the 12th century, the **Museum of Fine Arts** housing European paintings and the **Ethnographic Museum**. **Margaret Island**, connected to both Buda and Pest by bridges, is a park with a sports stadium, swimming pool, spas, a rose garden and fountains. Budapest has about 100 hot springs.

- Follow the **Danube Bend** upstream, and see the unusual layout of **Szentendre**, an old market town, originally inhabited by Serbian refugees fleeing from the Turks: unusual because churches had to face east regardless of their position on the streets. The Serbian house styles also add greatly to the village's charm. Due to trade restrictions and floods, the town was abandoned, only to be rediscovered and settled by Hungarian artists in the 1920s. The **Margit Kovács Museum** has a remarkable display of the work of Hungary's greatest ceramicist, the **Béla Czóbel Museum** shows paintings from the 1890s and the **Károly Ferenczy Museum** contains historical, archaeological and ethnographic collections as well as paintings. The **Serbian Museum for Ecclesiastical History** contains many fine examples of ecclesiastical art from the 14th to the 18th centuries. The **Ethnographic Museum** (**skanzen**) is a large open-air addition from the 1960s, still being added to, of reconstructed folk villages from all over the country.

- Originally a Roman outpost, **Esztergom** later became the country's capital from the 11th to the 14th centuries and remains at the heart of the country's Catholicism. Hungary's largest Basilica, the Palace ruins, the **Museum of the Stronghold of Esztergom** and the **Christian Museum of Esztergom**, containing some of Hungary's finest art collections, are all important attractions.

- **Sopron**, close to the Austrian frontier, is built on old Roman foundations, and reminders of the region's history are still very much in evidence in the town's 240 listed buildings. Among the sights here are the **Firewatch Tower**, **Storno House** showing Roman, Celtic and Avar relics as well as mementos of Franz Liszt, the **Gothic**

Goat Church and the gargoyled Church of St Michael.

- Behold the Baroque Esterházy Palace at Fertöd, designed to rival Versailles; Josef Haydn was music master here at the end of the 18th century.
- Szombathely claims to be the oldest town in Hungary and has some excellent Romanesque stonework to admire.
- Fertő-Hanság National Park, the main areas of which are Lake Fertő, the westernmost steppe lake in Eurasia, and the Hanság, an area of wetlands, adjoins the Austrian National Park Neusiedlersee-Seewinkel. Birdwatching, cycling and hiking are popular, and there is a permanent wildlife and ethnographic museum at Öntésmajor.
- See some of the pretty towns along Lake Balaton, and their attractions, such as Tihany's Benedictine Abbey, founded in 1055, Belső-tó Lake and the Aranyház geyser cones. Veszprém, 10km (6 miles) north of Lake Balaton, is a pretty town with cobbled streets, built on five hills. It is the home of the Var Museum, an Episcopal Palace and the 13th-century Gizella Chapel.
- The Kiskunság National Park preserves parts of the Danube Tisza Floodplain of Central Hungary in seven disconnected areas including swamps, alkali plateaus and lakes. The famous Bugac Puszta stretches out here as well. The Hortobágy National Park, the 'Hungarian Puszta', also contains the alkali plains that begin the Asian steppes.
- Szeged is an economic and cultural hub housing Hungary's finest Greek Orthodox (Serbian) church.
- Pécs, one of Transdanubia's largest towns, was colonised by the Romans, and has the fifth-oldest university in Europe (1367) and the finest Hungarian examples of Ottoman architecture from Turkish occupancy (1543-1686). Important tourist sites include the Cathedral, the Mosque of Gazi Kasim Pasha, and the Archaeological Museum. The Danube-Drava National Park encompasses the area between these two rivers and includes Mohács on the Danube, with the battlefield – now a memorial park – where, in 1526, the Turks gained control of the country, and Kalocsa, noted for its folk museums. South of the town is the attractive Forest of Gemenc which can be explored by boat or narrow-gauge train.
- Near Miskolc, Hungary's second-largest city, are the beautiful forested Bükk National Park, part of the Northern Hill Range, which is also an area of karst topography, including the country's deepest caves at Lillafüred; many traces of Neanderthal man have been found here. North of Bükk, the Aggtelek National Park is part of the Gömör Torna Karst area of cave systems which extends into the Slovak Republic. Caving, fishing and riding are popular, and there are many cultural monuments, masterpieces of folk architecture, ruins recalling the atmosphere of the Middle Ages, old churches, graveyards and locally surviving farming techniques.
- Eger should be seen since it is one of the country's oldest and most colourful cities, with nearly 200 historical monuments, including its 14-sided Minaret.
- Gaze at the spectacular Sárospatak Castle, one of Hungary's greatest historical monuments.
- Hungary's many wetlands, rivers and lakes attract large numbers of water birds, and birdwatching is popular. A particularly good area for this is Hortobágy National Park in the Great Plain in the east of the country, where different types of storks, warblers, eagles and herons can be seen. A guide is required for visits to some parts of the park, and motor vehicles are not permitted. Other wildlife to be found in the country includes rare wild cats and lake bats, while species such as boar, otter and deer are common.

Top Things To Do

- Hikers can head for the mountains in the north and northwest of the country. The Börzsöny, Mátra and Pilis ranges not far to the north of Budapest are popular, with the Mátra mountains containing Hungary's highest peak, Kékestetö (1015m/3329ft). Less strenuous walking is possible around Lake Balaton and in the hills in the south of the country.
- The River Tisza, by the Kisköre reservoir, is regarded by many as Europe's second-best angling area (after the Danube Delta). Accommodation for anglers is readily available, and guides can be hired if required. Species such as carp, bream, pike, trout and tench are abundant. There are rules and regulations governing fishing seasons and licences.
- Budapest alone has over 100 thermal springs and scores of swimming pools and medicinal baths. The culture of bathing has been established since Roman times, and today a wide variety of therapeutic treatments, both ancient and modern, is on offer. Some of Hungary's bath houses are also of great architectural

interest: the Király Medicinal Baths, for example, date from the Middle Ages, while the Rudas Medicinal Baths feature a fine dome dating from the 16th century. Outside Budapest, notable spa resorts include Debrecen in the far east; Hévíz, near Lake Balaton; Harkány in the south; and Eger, northwest of Budapest. Treatment is cheaper than in western Europe or North America, and many foreign insurers will pay part of the cost.

- With its long tradition of equestrianism, horse riding is particularly good in Hungary. Long-distance riding in areas such as the Great Plain with its wide open spaces is popular, and riders are well catered for. Hungary is the only European country, apart from Ireland, which places no restrictions on riders. There are many riding schools all over the country, which can organise all types of excursions. The Great Plain contains several famous stud farms, and horse shows take place regularly.
- Go bathing in the popular sandy beaches (strands) and shallow waters of Lake Balaton. The surrounding countryside consists mainly of fertile plains dotted with old villages. Siófok, on the south shore of the lake, has some of the sandiest beaches and best facilities for tourists.
- Drink from the vineyards of the Szépasszony Valley, where visitors can sample the famous Bikavér (Bull's Blood) wine. Due east is Tokaj, the equivalent of Champagne as a wine-producing area.

TOURIST INFORMATION

Hungarian National Tourist Office (HNTO) in the UK
46 Eaton Place, London SW1X 8AL, UK
Tel: (020) 7823 1032 or 1055 or (09001) 171 200 (recorded information; calls cost 60p per minute).
Website: www.hungary.com or www.hungarywelcomesbritain.com

Hungarian National Tourist Office (HNTO) in the USA
150 East 58th Street, 33rd Floor, New York, NY 10155, USA
Tel: (212) 355 0240.
Website: www.gotohungary.com

Entertainment

FOOD & DRINK: A good range of restaurants are available. Table service is common, although there are many inexpensive self-service restaurants. A typical menu offers two or three courses at inexpensive rates. Fine dairy and pastry shops (cukrászda) offer light meals. Eszpresszó coffee bars and Drink bars offer refreshments. Gerbeaud's is probably Budapest's most famous coffee-house.
Things to know: There are no licensing hours, but the legal age for drinking in a bar is 18 years. Minors are allowed to go into bars but will not be served alcohol.
National specialities:
- Halászlé (fish soups).
- Goulash gulyás soup (Western goulash is called pörkölt or tokány).
- Stuffed vegetables.
- Sweet cakes.
- Gundel palacsinta (pancake).
- Goose liver.
- Paprikás csirke (paprika chicken).
- Kolbasz (spicy sausage).
- Samlói galuska (a sponge, chocolate, rum and cream dessert).
National drinks:
- Tokaji (strong dessert wine).
- Bull's Blood (strong red wine).
- Pálinka or barack (apricot brandy).
Tipping: 10 to 15 per cent is expected for nearly all services in restaurants, bars, clubs, taxis and so on.
NIGHTLIFE: Budapest has many nightclubs, bars, discos and casinos. Cinemas in major towns show many English-language films. During the summer months the popular Lake Balaton resort has a lively nightlife. Western Hungary in particular has a lot of very good wine cellars. Visitors would do well to search out traditional folk music and dancing, as the gypsy music which is so common in restaurants is not considered the 'true' folk tradition of the country. The magnificent Budapest Opera House stages regular performances, and seats are (by Western standards) exceedingly cheap.
SHOPPING: Special purchases include embroideries, Herend and Zsolnay porcelain and national dolls. **Shopping hours:** Department stores are open from Mon-Sat 1000-1800. Food shops are open from Mon-Sat 0700-1800. Some shops open on Sundays.

Business

- **GDP:** $149.3 billion (2004).
- **Main exports:** Machinery and equipment, foodstuff, raw material, fuels and electricity.
- **Main imports:** Machinery and equipment, foodstuff, raw material, fuels and electricity.
- **Main trade partners:** Germany, Austria, Russian (Federation), Italy, China (PR), France and The Netherlands.

ECONOMY: Hungary is poor in natural resources other than bauxite, natural gas and some oil. For this reason, it relies heavily on foreign trade, which accounts for half of its GDP. The country has a fairly well-developed industrial economy concentrated in chemicals, plastics, pharmaceuticals, fertilisers, computers and telecommunications, mining, construction and aluminium (from bauxite deposits). It has also been an exporter of agricultural produce, particularly fruit and vegetables, maize and wheat, sugar beet, potatoes and livestock.

Before the political upheaval in Eastern Europe during 1989, Hungary had gone the furthest of all the socialist-bloc countries towards decentralising and deregulating the economy. In the 1990s, it eschewed the Polish-style 'big bang' road to capitalism and opted for a more gradual transition. Price controls were removed, and a programme of privatisation was implemented, starting with the retail and property sectors. By 1995, small business privatisation was more or less complete, while sales of the larger state-owned concerns proceeded apace. Current estimates put 80 per cent of the economy under private ownership. Hungary's economic performance is currently steady: growth is 3.9 per cent, and inflation 7 per cent.

Foreign investment has picked up, largely as a result of the liberalisation of trade through agreements with the EU, EFTA and the Visegrad mechanism, although in recent years there has been a mild backlash against the extent to which foreign companies have penetrated the Hungarian economy. EU membership was a high priority for the Hungarian Government and Hungary became a full member of the EU, along with nine other countries, on May 1 2004. The country's principal trading partners are Germany, Austria, Italy, the Russian Federation and the Czech Republic. Outside Europe, there are important links with the USA, Japan and Brazil.
BUSINESS ETIQUETTE: Businesspeople are expected to dress smartly. Local businesspeople are generally friendly and hospitable and it is usual for visitors to be invited to lunch or dinner in a restaurant. Business cards are widely distributed and visitors are well advised to have a supply available in Hungarian. Best months for business visits are September to May. Appointments should always be made. Interpreter and translation services may be booked through travel agents.
Office hours: Mon-Fri 0800-1600.

COMMERCIAL INFORMATION

Budapest Kereskedelmi és Iparkamara (Budapest Chamber of Commerce and Industry)
Krisztina Krt 99, H-1016 Budapest, Hungary
Tel (1) 488 2173.
Website: www.bkik.hu

Hungarian Convention Bureau
Vérmező út. 4, 1012 Budapest, Hungary
Tel: (1) 488 8642.
Website: www.hcb.hu

TD Hungary in the UK
46 Eaton Place, London SW1X 8AL, UK
Tel: (020) 7235 8767.
Website: www.itd.hu or www.hungarytrade.co.uk

Credit: © Hungarian National Tourist Office

Iceland

Location: North Atlantic, close to Arctic Circle.

Time: GMT.

Overview

Iceland is a large island in the North Atlantic close to the Arctic Circle. The landscape is wild, rugged and colourful, with black lava, red sulphur, hot blue geysers, rivers, waterfalls and green valleys. Its coastline is richly indented with bays and fjords. Iceland is one of the most volcanically active countries in the world. Hekla, in the south of Iceland, has erupted no fewer than 16 times, and was once described by clergymen as the gateway to Hell. Certainly, Iceland's seething mountains contribute towards this sense of otherworldliness.

Yet around the coastal regions, Iceland is a bustle of activity, particularly in the capital city, Reykjavik, where more than half of Iceland's population lives. Reykjavik is set on a broad bay, surrounded by mountains, and is in an area of geothermal hot springs, creating a natural central heating system and pollution-free environment. It is a busy city combining old-fashioned wooden architecture and modern buildings. Despite being a relatively small capital city, Reykjavik has managed to forge a reputation for partying, and its nightclubs and bars are regularly filled with hordes of fun-loving citizens.

Nevertheless, the traditional side of Iceland prevails, as does the Icelander's repute as hardy and proud. Indeed, much of the fascination surrounding Iceland resides with the Icelanders themselves. Their descendents propagated the notion of the 'Viking poet', as unveiled in their heroic sagas: an intoxicating brew of brute force and sensitivity. In the mid-13th century, the islanders submitted to the authority of the King of Norway, and when Norway came under the control of Denmark in 1380, Iceland did too. In 1814, Norway became independent, but Iceland remained a Danish territory. In 1840, Iceland was granted its own constitution – effectively allowing internal self-government. Full independence was granted in 1918, although Iceland continued to recognise the Danish Monarch as head of state. It was not until 1944 that Iceland became a fully independent nation with its own head of state. It is therefore understandable that Icelanders now so ardently champion their heritage. Many long-established foods are still chomped with relish, and much traditional entertainment remains.

Perhaps, also, the Icelanders' character has been as shaped by the scenery as the scenery has been shaped by volatile forces of earth and elements. What is better is that whether you wish to exploit such stunning natural isolation and quietly watch for birds or whales, or whether you wish to go skiing, glacier skidooing or horse riding, Iceland amply provides for both. Although you may not go so far as to believe in magic and elves – over half of the population still do – you will certainly leave believing that Iceland is magical.

General Information

AREA: 103,000 sq km (39,769 sq miles).

POPULATION: 294,000 (UN, 2005).

POPULATION DENSITY: 2.85 per sq km.

CAPITAL: Reykjavík. **Population:** 112,554 (2002).

GEOGRAPHY: Iceland is a large island in the North Atlantic close to the Arctic Circle and includes islands to the north and south. The landscape is wild, rugged and colourful, with black lava, red sulphur, hot blue geysers, grey and white rivers with waterfalls and green valleys, its coastline richly indented with bays and fjords. The whole of the central highland plateau of the island is a beautiful but barren and uninhabitable moonscape - so much so that the first American astronauts were sent there for pre-mission training. Five-sixths of Iceland is uninhabited, the population being concentrated on the coast, in the valleys and in the plains of the southwest and southeast of the country. More than half the population live in or around Reykjavik, the capital. Iceland is one of the most volcanically active countries in the world. Hekla, in the south of Iceland, is the most famous and magnificent volcano of them all. It has erupted no fewer than 16 times since Iceland was settled, and throughout the Middle Ages was considered by European clergymen as one of the gateways to Hell itself. Another volcano, Snæfellsnes, fired Jules Verne's imagination to use its crater as the point of entry for his epic tale, *Journey to the Centre of the Earth*. Iceland's highest and most extensive glacier is Vatnajökull; at 8500 sq km (3280 sq miles), it is the largest in Europe, although it is now reported to be melting.

GOVERNMENT: Republic. Gained full independence from Denmark in 1944. **Head of State:** President Ólafur Ragnar Grimsson since 1996. **Head of Government:** Prime Minister Halldór Ásgrimsson since 2004. **Recent history:** At the General Election in April 1991, the Independence Party (IP) emerged as the largest grouping in the *Althing* and formed a coalition administration with the smaller SDP. The ex-Mayor of Reykjavik, David Oddsson, who had successfully taken over the leadership of the IP, was made Prime Minister. Oddsson was re-elected at the 1995 General Election, but a decline in support for the IP later forced him to form a coalition administration with the Progressive Party (PP). At the most recent poll in 2003, Oddsson retained his position as Prime Minister in the coalition Government. However, in 2004, Oddsson handed over premiership to former Foreign Minister Halldór Asgrimsson. Meanwhile, Icelandic foreign policy is dominated by two factors: fishing and relations with Atlantic powers. Iceland is a member of NATO, the Nordic Council and of the Council of Europe. Ties with NATO have been loosening since before the end of the Cold War – in May 1985, the Althing declared Iceland a 'nuclear-free zone' – and this process has accelerated since the reduction of the large NATO base at Keflavik. Iceland has historically eschewed membership of the European Union but, since Sweden, Finland and Denmark have joined up, it is Iceland's opposition to the EU's fisheries policy of stock management by quotas that is now the decisive influence. Both main parties strongly oppose the Common Fisheries Policy, so it seems unlikely that Iceland will apply for EU membership in the foreseeable future. On the issue of whaling, Iceland has been among the few objecting to the International Whaling Commission's (IWC) ban: in 1992, the Government withdrew from the IWC. In 2001, it applied to rejoin but, having declared its intention to resume commercial whaling, was only granted observer status.

Executive power is vested in the President and Government, while legislative authority rests jointly with the President and the 63-member Althing (Parliament). Both are elected for four-year terms. The Althing has recently been reduced from two houses to one.

LANGUAGE: The official language is Icelandic, which has remained virtually unchanged since the Vikings settled Iceland in the 9th and 10th centuries. The Icelandic language refuses to accept foreign words, preferring instead to coin new words from ancient Viking roots. The word for computer thus becomes *tölva*, a hybrid made up of the old words for 'number' and 'prophetess'. English (which is taught in schools) and Danish are widely spoken.

RELIGION: Lutheran, with a Catholic minority.

ELECTRICITY: 220 volts AC, 50Hz. Plug fittings are normally two-pin with round section pins 4mm in diameter with centres 2cm apart. Lamp fittings are screw-type. Power is generated by a mix of geothermal and hydroelectric stations.

SOCIAL CONVENTIONS: Visitors will find Iceland is a classless society with a strong literary tradition. Handshaking is the normal form of greeting. An Icelander is called by his first name because his surname is made up of his father's Christian name plus 'son' or 'daughter' (eg John, the son of Magnus, would be called John Magnusson, while John's sister, Mary, would be known as Mary Magnusdóttir). People are addressed as *Fru* (Mrs) and *Herra* (Mr). Visitors will often be invited to homes, especially if on business, and normal courtesies should be observed. Icelanders pay careful attention to their appearance and, as for most Western countries, casual wear is widely acceptable although unsuitable for smart and social functions.

Climate

Iceland's climate is tempered by the Gulf Stream. Summers are mild and winters rather cold. The colourful *Aurora Borealis* (Northern Lights) appear from the end of August. From the end of May to the beginning of August, there are nearly 24 hours of perpetual daylight in Reykjavik, while in the northern part of the country the sun barely sets at all. Winds can be strong and gusty at times and there is the occasional dust storm in the interior. Snow is not as common as the name of the country would seem to suggest and, in any case, does not lie for long in Reykjavik; it is only in northern Iceland that skiing conditions are reasonably certain. However, the weather is very changeable at all times of the year, and in Reykjavík there may be rain, sunshine, drizzle and snow in the same day. The air is clean and free of pollution.

Required clothing: Lightweights in warmer months, with extra woollens for walking and the cooler evenings. Medium- to heavyweights are advised in winter. Waterproofing is recommended throughout the year.

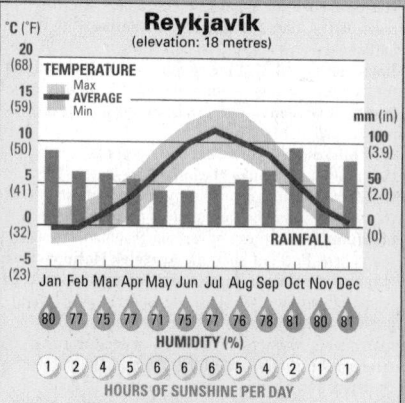

Reykjavík
(elevation: 18 metres)

Communications

Telephone: Full IDD service is available. Country code: 354. Direct dial international calls can be made from all parts of the country.

Mobile telephone: *Siminn* has roaming agreements with roughly 250 telecommunication companies in roughly 100 countries. *Og Vodaphona* and *Viking Wireless* also have agreements. Most mobile phones from the US will not work as Iceland uses the European system. Phones can be rented.

Internet: Internet cafes provide public access to e-mail and Internet services. Many Internet cafes can be found, especially in Reykjavik.

Post: There is an efficient airmail service to Europe. Post office hours: Mon-Fri 0830-1630. The post office at Grensásvegir is also open Sat 1000-1400 year-round.

MEDIA: National radio and TV services are provided by the Icelandic National Broadcasting Service (RUV), a public-service broadcaster owned by the state. The RUV is obliged to promote the Icelandic language and the nation's history and cultural heritage. Its services are funded by a licence fee and advertising revenues. The Icelandic constitution guarantees press freedom. There is a wide range of publications, which includes privately-owned and party-affiliated newspapers.

Press: The most popular newspapers are *DV* (evening daily), *Fréttabladid* (daily) and *Morgunbladid* (morning daily). International English-language newspapers and magazines are available. Online, www.icelandreview.com is an English-language site with news updates.

TV: *Stod 2* is the main private station but other ones include *Syn* and *Skjar einn*. The *Icelandic National Broadcasting Service* operates the public network, *Sjonvarpid*.

Radio: *Bylgjan* is the main private station. The *Icelandic National Broadcasting Service* operates two national networks and four regional stations of public radio.

A B C D E F G H I J K L M N O P Q R S T U V W X Y Z

Passport/Visa

	Passport Required?	Visa Required?	Return Ticket Required?
Full British	Yes	No	No
Australian	Yes	No	Yes
Canadian	Yes	No	Yes
USA	Yes	No	Yes
Other EU	Yes/1/2	No	No
Japanese	Yes	No	Yes

Note: *Regulations and requirements may be subject to change at short notice, and you are advised to contact the appropriate diplomatic or consular authority before finalising travel arrangements. Any numbers in the chart refer to the footnotes below.*

Note: Iceland is a signatory to the 1995 **Schengen Agreement**. For further details about passport/visa regulationswithin the Schengen area, see the introductory section, *How to Use this Guide*.

PASSPORTS: Passport valid for at least three months after intended date of departure required by all, except:
(a) **1.** nationals of the Nordic countries, Denmark, Finland, Norway and Sweden with a valid ID card;
(b) **2.** nationals of Austria, Belgium, France, Germany, Greece, Italy, Liechtenstein, Luxembourg, The Netherlands, Portugal, Spain and Switzerland with a valid ID card.
Please consult the nearest Danish embassy for further details.

VISAS: Required by all except the following for stays of up to three months:
(a) nationals of countries referred to in the chart above;
(b) nationals of Andorra, Argentina, Bolivia, Brazil, British Overseas Territories, Brunei, Bulgaria, Chile, Costa Rica, Croatia, El Salvador, Guatemala, Honduras, Hong Kong (SAR), Israel, Korea (Rep), Liechtenstein, Macau (SAR), Malaysia, Mexico, Monaco, New Zealand, Nicaragua, Norway, Panama, Paraguay, Romania, San Marino, Singapore, Switzerland, Uruguay, Vatican City and Venezuela.

Note: (a) Nationals of the following countries require an airport transit visa (holders of travel documents issued by these countries are also subject to such requirements): Afghanistan, Bangladesh, Congo (Dem Rep), Eritrea, Ethiopia, Ghana, Iran, Iraq, Nigeria, Pakistan, Somalia and Sri Lanka. (b) These nationals do not require an airport transit visa if they hold a valid residence permit for an EU or EEA country, Andorra, Canada, Japan, Monaco, San Marino, Switzerland and the USA. (c) An airport visa is not required by nationals of India in possession of a valid visa to an EU or EEA country, USA or Canada.

Types of visa and cost: *Airport transit*: £7 (single-, double- or multiple-entry); *Short stay*: £15 (up to 30 days); *Short stay* (up to 90 days): £20 plus £3 for additional entries; *Multiple-entry* (valid for one year): £33; *Multiple-entry* (valid for five years): £33 plus £20 for each additional year; *Group visa for transit or airport transit visa*: £7 plus £1 per person (five to 50 people); *Group short stay* (valid for 30 days): £20 plus £1 per person; *Group short stay* (valid for 30 days for additional entries, for five to 50 people): £20 plus £2 per person. An additional fee of £11 is payable for applications lodged at Honorary Consulates.

Note: (a) Visas are issued free of charge to spouses of EU or EEA nationals, or persons related in direct line of ascent or descent to such nationals or their spouses, if they are supported by the national in question and if they have legal residence in the UK. Relevant documentation must be produced in such cases, including an original marriage certificate, the passport of the EU citizen and the EU citizen's residence permit and evidence of an EEA residence permit in the UK, plus proof of joint household. Further documentation may be requested in addition to this.

Validity: Up to three months. For extensions, apply to the Immigration authority in Iceland.

Application to: Icelandic Consulates no longer issue visas. For visa information, contact the Royal Danish Embassy (see *Denmark* section). Applications cannot be made by post. Appointments must be made in advance by calling (09065) 540 755 (automated; 24-hour). Travellers visiting just one Schengen country should apply to the Consulate of that country; travellers visiting more than one Schengen country should apply to the Consulate of the country chosen as the main destination *or* the country they will enter first (if they have no main destination).

Application requirements: (a) Completed visa application form. (b) One colour passport-size photo on a light background. (c) Valid passport or travel document, if applicable, with a blank page to affix the visa. (d) Fee, payable by cash or cheque (non-refundable). (e) Proof of purpose of visit and accommodation such as a letter of invitation from relatives or a hotel reservation. (f) Evidence of sufficient funds to cover the duration of stay, such as bank statements, traveller's cheques or credit card statements (with credit limit). (g) Proof of means of transport. (h) A pre-paid self-addressed envelope for registered post, if you would like your visa to be sent to your home address. (i) Evidence of occupation/student status, eg an original letter from an employer or solicitor; if unemployed, a social benefit booklet; if a student, an original letter from the appropriate school/university. (j) Valid health insurance. *Business*: (a)-(j) and, (k) Letter of invitation from a business contact in Iceland stating nature and duration of stay, type of visa and accommodation. Please note, in some cases, further documents and guarantees may be required.

Working days required: Varies according to nationality, may take several weeks.

Temporary residence: Enquire at Embassy of the Republic of Iceland.

PASSPORT/VISA INFORMATION

Embassy of Iceland in the UK
2A Hans Street, London SW1X 0JE, UK
Tel: (020) 7259 3999 *or* (0906) 554 0755 (for visa appointments via the Danish embassy).
Website: www.iceland.org/uk
Opening hours: Mon-Fri 0930-1600.

Embassy of Iceland in the USA
1156 15th Street, NW, Suite 1200, Washington, DC 20005-1704, USA
Tel: (202) 265 6653.
Website: www.iceland.org/us

Money

Currency: Icelandic Krona (ISK) = 100 aurar. Notes are in denominations of ISK5000, 2000, 1000, 500, 100, 50 and 10. Coins are in denominations of ISK100, 50, 10, 5 and 1.

Currency exchange: Foreign currencies can be exchanged in all major banks, some of which (such as the Landesbanki at Reykjavík airport) are open 24 hours. Most hotels also provide their guests with exchange services. Exchange services are also available from The Change Group, which has offices at Reykjavík airport, the Tourist Information Centre and in central Reykjavík. ATMs are also available throughout the country, especially Reykjavík.

Credit & debit cards: American Express, Diners Club, Europay, MasterCard and Visa are widely accepted. Check with your credit or debit card company for details of merchant acceptability and other services which may be available.

Traveller's cheques: Widely used. To avoid additional exchange rate charges, travellers are advised to take traveller's cheques in US Dollars.

Currency restrictions: The import and export of local currency is unrestricted. When entering Iceland a tourist may bring an unlimited amount of domestic or foreign currency; the same applies when leaving Iceland.

Banking hours: Mon-Fri 0915-1600.

Exchange rate indicators:
Rate at time of publishing
£1.00= ISK105.98
$1.00= ISK61.04

Duty Free

The following goods may be imported into Iceland by persons over 18 years (tobacco products) or 20 years of age (alcoholic beverages) without incurring customs duty:
200 cigarettes or 250g of tobacco products; 1l of spirits and 1l of wine or 1l of spirits and 6l of beer or 1l of wine and 6l of beer or 2.25l of wine.

Note: Travellers may bring in goods free of duty up to the value of ISK46,000. The value of each single item must not exceed ISK23,000.
All fishing equipment, including waders and rubber boots and riding equipment, must be disinfected and a certificate of disinfection issued by an official veterinary authority presented on arrival.

Prohibited and restricted items: Drugs, firearms, telephones and other communications equipment, unpasteurised milk and dairy products, poultry, eggs and uncooked meats.

Public Holidays

Below are listed Public Holidays for the January 2006-June 2007 period.

2006: Jan 1 New Year's Day. **Apr 13** Maundy Thursday. **Apr 14** Good Friday. **Apr 17** Easter Monday. **Apr 20** First Day of Summer. **May 1** May Day. **May 25** Ascension. **Jun 5** Whit Monday. **Jun 17** National Day. **Aug 7** Commerce Day. **Dec 24-26** Christmas. **Dec 31** New Year's Eve (from noon).
2007: Jan 1 New Year's Day. **Apr 5** Maundy Thursday. **Apr 6** Good Friday. **Apr 9** Easter Monday. **Apr 19** First Day of Summer. **May 1** May Day. **May 17** Ascension. **May 28** Whit Monday. **Jun 17** National Day.

Credit: © Icelandic Tourist Board

Health

	Special Precautions?	Certificate Required?
Yellow Fever	No	No
Cholera	No	No
Typhoid & Polio	No	N/A
Malaria	No	N/A

Note: *Regulations and requirements may be subject to change at short notice, and you are advised to contact your doctor well in advance of your intended date of departure. Any numbers in the chart refer to the footnotes below.*

Other risks: Care should be taken as *hypothermia* is a real risk.

Health care: European Economic Area (EEA) and Switzerland:
If you or any of your dependants are suddenly taken ill or have an accident during a visit to an EEA country or Switzerland, free or reduced-cost necessary treatment is available – in most cases on production of a valid European Health Insurance Card (EHIC). Each country has different rules about state medical provision. In some, treatment is free. In many countries you will have to pay part or all of the cost, and then claim a full or partial refund. The EHIC gives access to state-provided medical treatment only and the scheme gives no entitlement to medical repatriation costs, nor does it cover ongoing illnesses of a non-urgent nature, so comprehensive travel insurance is advised. Note that the EHIC replaces the Form E111, which will no longer be valid after 31 December 2005. Some restrictions apply, depending on your nationality. Please note that Swiss nationals are not covered by the EHIC in Iceland. People who do not have UK, EU or EEA nationality are covered for emergency treatment only.
There are medical centres and hospitals in all major towns and cities. Go to a health centre or a doctor registered within the state scheme. You will have to pay a fee of IKR 700, which is not refundable. You will have to pay the full cost of any dental treatment. Children under 16 have to pay only 25 per cent. Prescribed medicines can be obtained from any pharmacy. You must show your European Health Insurance Card (EHIC). You will be charged a set amount depending on the type of medication prescribed. Ask the doctor for a generic drug if possible, as these are generally cheaper than brand name medicines. Patients can be admitted to hospitals only when they are referred by a doctor. However, in emergencies, patients may be admitted immediately to whichever hospital is serving as the emergency hospital at the time. Hospital inpatient treatment is free if you present your EHIC. Otherwise, you will be charged. All hospitals have excellent standards of medical service. Patients must pay the full cost of ambulance transportation within Reykjavík. Elsewhere, the cost of ambulance transportation is limited to a maximum of IKR 2,400. Non-EEA nationals resident in the UK may also be covered for emergency health treatment in Iceland under a separate agreement. You will need to produce your NHS medical card. The emergency number for medical assistance is 112 (open 24 hours). More information can be obtained from the State Social Security Institute, Laugavegur 114, Reykjavík (tel: 560 4400).

A B C D E F G H I J K L M N O P Q R S T U V W X Y Z

Credit: © Icelandic Tourist Board

Travel - International

AIR:

The national airline, *Icelandair (FI)* (website: www.icelandair.net), operates direct flights all-year-round to Reykjavík (Keflavík) from Amsterdam, Baltimore, Boston, Copenhagen, Frankfurt, Glasgow, Halifax, London, Minneapolis, New York, Orlando, Oslo, Paris, Stockholm and Washington, plus other destinations in the summertime only. *Iceland Express* (website: www.icelandexpress.com) flies from London, Frankfurt Hahn and Copenhagen. Other, predominantly Scandinavian, carriers also operate services.

Approximate flight times: From Iceland to *London* is three hours; to *Paris* is three hours and 25 minutes; to *Frankfurt* is three hours and 45 minutes and to *New York* is five hours and 30 minutes.

Main airports: *Reykjavík (Keflavík) (REK/KEF)* is 51km (32 miles) southwest of Reykjavík (travel time – 45 minutes). *To/from the airport*: *Flybus* (website: www.re.is) operates after each flight, making trips to all major hotels in Reykjavík, the camping ground, the youth hostel in Laugardalun and Icelandair's domestic terminal. One-way tickets are ISK1150, children aged four to 12 travel half-price. A taxi service is also available. *Facilities:* Duty free shop; banking and exchange facilities, open on arrival of all Icelandair flights; information desk; post office; restaurants and bars and car hire (*Avis*, *Budget*, *Europcar* and *Hertz*).

Departure tax: There is a security fee of IKR620 for all travellers over 12 years of age (children ages two to 12 pay IKR285), to be paid by all departing from Iceland.

SEA:

Main ports: *Keflavík, Rekjavík and Seydisfjördur*. There is no longer a direct service between the UK and Iceland. Sea passengers must travel from Aberdeen, with a three-day stopover in the Faroe Islands on the return journey. This is a costly and aggravating route, not recommended by travel agents. A few ferry companies also operate services to Iceland from Denmark, Germany and Norway. Although most of these are mainly cargo ships, they have comfortable and modern facilities for passengers. *Smyril Line* (website: www.smyril-line.com), the Faroe Island's ferry service, runs a weekly passenger and car ferry service between the Shetland Islands, Denmark, Norway and Seydisfjördur in Iceland via the Faroe Islands during the summer months. Many cruises also stop in Iceland. Operators include *Crystal* (website: www.crystalcrusies.com), *Cunard* (website: www.cunard.com), *Princess* (website: www.princess.com), *Seabourn* (website: www.seabourncruiseweb.com) and *Silversea* (website: www.silversea.com).

Travel - Internal

AIR:

Air Iceland (formed through merging with *Icelandair Domestic* and *Norlandair*) runs domestic services throughout the island to 10 major destinations which link up with regional carriers in the west, north and east of the country. For further details, contact the local office or check online (website: www.airiceland.is).

Departure tax: None.

SEA:

Ferry services serve all coastal ports in summer, although weather curtails timetables in winter. There is a tunnel between Reykjavík and Akranes.

RAIL:

There is no railway system in Iceland.

ROAD:

Roads serve all settlements. The 12,000km (7500 miles) of roads are mostly gravel rather than tarred. The Ring Road is approximately 1430km (894 miles) long, of which 80 per cent is tarred. Traffic drives on the right. It is obligatory to use headlights at all times of the day and night and to wear safety belts, both in the front and back seats. The Icelandic Tourist Board publishes a useful brochure, *The Art of Driving on Icelandic Roads*. **Bus:** Services are efficient and cheap, connecting all parts of the island during the summer. In winter, buses operate to a limited number of destinations. Holiday tickets (*Omnibus Passport*) and *Air/Bus Rovers* are valid for unlimited travel by scheduled bus services; also *Full-Circle Passports* are available, valid for circular trips around Iceland (without any time limit). **Taxi:** Available from all hotels and airports. **Car hire:** Car rental services are available from Reykjavík, Akureyri and many other towns.

Documentation: Drivers must be over 20 years of age. An International Driving Permit is recommended, although it is not legally required. A temporary driving licence is available from local authorities on presentation of a valid UK driving licence.

Travel times: The following chart gives approximate travel times (in hours and minutes) from **Reykjavík** to other major cities/towns in Iceland.

	Air	Road	Sea
Isafjördur	0.50	9.00	-
Akureyri	0.55	5.00	-
Husavik	1.00	6.00	-
Höfn	0.65	9.30	-
Westmann Is.	0.30*	1.00	6.00

Note: *To Thorlakshofn, then sea crossing.

Travel Advice

Most visits to Iceland are trouble-free but you should be aware of the global risk of indiscriminate international terrorist attacks, which could be against civilian targets, including places frequented by foreigners.

This advice is based on information provided by the Foreign and Commonwealth Office in the UK. It is correct at time of publishing. As the situation can change rapidly, visitors are advised to contact the following organisations for the latest travel advice:

British Foreign and Commonwealth Office
Tel: (0845) 850 2829.
Website: www.fco.gov.uk

US Department of State
Website: http://travel.state.gov/travel

Accommodation

HOTELS:

The most deluxe hotels are in the capital Reykjavík and some of them also have hairdressers, shops and beauty parlours. Hotel or hostel accommodation is available in most areas.

Grading: All accommodation is classified from **5 star** (luxurious) to **1 star** (basic) and is managed by the Icelandic Tourist Board. Visitors should look for the blue and red sign near the entrance to a hotel for the current grading. For a complete list of classified accommodation contact the Icelandic Tourist Board (see *Contact Addresses* section).

PENSIONS & GUEST HOUSES:

These are available in the larger towns. Rooms are also available in private houses with breakfast included in the cost.

FARMHOUSE HOLIDAYS:

Fairly widely available; contact the Icelandic Tourist Board for details. Full board (three meals daily) is included. Reductions are available for children. Further information is available from Icelandic Farm Holidays, Sidumuli 13, 108 Reykjavík (tel: 570 2700; fax: 570 2799; e-mail: ifh@farmholidays.is; website: www.farmholidays.is).

CAMPING/CARAVANNING:

There are approximately 125 registered camping sites. Due to unpredictable weather conditions, camping grounds are normally only open between June and late August or mid-September. The best-equipped camping grounds are to be found in Akureyri, Eglisstadir, Husafell, Isafjördur, Jokulsargljufur, Laugarvatn, Myvatn, Reykjavík, Skaftafell, Thingvellire and Varmahlid. In some places camping is restricted to certain specially marked areas. Prices are approximately US$5-7 and it is also possible to camp in National Parks that are supervised by the Convention Council. Campers, however, must request permission from the local farmer to camp on any fenced and/or cultivated land. For further information contact the Icelandic Tourist Board (see *Contact Addresses* section).

YOUTH HOSTELS:

A total of 24 youth and family hostels are open, including Fossholl, Hrauneyjar, Leirubakki, Njardvik, Reykholt, Reykjavík, Stafafell and Stykkisholmur. Many country hostels provide overnight accommodation for travellers bringing their own sleeping bags or bedrolls for a fee. In uninhabited areas there are a number of huts where travellers can stay overnight. They must observe regulations posted in the huts and bring their own sleeping bags and food. For more information, contact the Icelandic Youth Hostel Association, Sundlaugavegi 34, 105 Reykjavík (tel: 553 8110; fax: 588 9201; e-mail: info@hostel.is; website: www.hostel.is). The Youth Hostel Association also offers a travel service to help with bookings, tours and travel arrangements.

Top Things To See

- See the world's most northerly capital, **Reykjavík**. The city was named after a geothermal stream and actually means 'Smoky Bay'. It is set on a broad bay, surrounded by mountains, and is in an area of geothermal hot springs providing it with a natural central heating system and pollution-free environment. The city has a wonderful mix of natural beauty and lively sophistication. There are plenty of parks and wild outdoor areas for hiking, walking and exploring, but enough nightlife, shopping and museums to keep the chic city-dweller happy. Reykjavík is a busy city of around 100,000 inhabitants, with a combination of old-fashioned wooden architecture and modern buildings. To ensure that all the sights of the city are explored many guided tours are available. The **National Museum** has reopened and houses 2000 objects and 1000 photos of the heritage and history of Iceland; it is free to visitors on Wednesdays. It is the starting point for many tours encompassing different themes, seeing sights such as waterfalls, spouting geysers and glaciers, horse riding, whale watching and sea angling. Tour brochures are available from the Tourist Information Centre on Adalstraeh 2, in Reykjavík.
- If you want to soak up some Scandinavian cliché, visit the **Viking Village** just outside Reykjavík, where Viking performances are held and guests are 'kidnapped' from the tour bus. This delightfully fun experience includes historically accurate combat demonstrations. This is followed by a chance to sample Icelandic Schnapps and *harofiskur* (hard fish), sun-dried fillets of haddock. There is also a hotel with a geothermal tub and two restaurants at the village. The **Viking Festival** is held here in June.
- **Thingvellir National Park**, **Gullfoss** (**Golden Falls**) and **Geysir**, with its geothermal fields and views of the active volcano **Mount Hekla**, are all part of Iceland's **Golden Circle** of natural attractions and historical sites. Thingvellir is the site of the **Althing**, a general assembly established around 930 AD and where Icelanders continued to convene until 1798: in fact, it is widely claimed to be the oldest parliament in the world. All major events in the history of Iceland have taken place at Thingvellir. Today, Thingvellir is a national park where the protected area shall always be the property of the Icelandic nation, under the preservation of the Althing. There is also much natural beauty, such as that of **Lake Thingvallavatn**. Gullfoss consists of two separate waterfalls that churn out a dramatic gush of water. And,

Credit: © Icelandic Tourist Board

Credit: © Icelandic Tourist Board

lastly, Iceland's Geysir is the geyser that lent its name to this phenomenon in a variety of languages. At its most spectacular, the Geysir spurts a steaming jet of water 200ft into the air. However, in recent years, the Geysir has been fairly quiet. If this proves the case, you are advised to travel to nearby **Strokkur**, which reliably spouts hot water up to 100ft skywards every five minutes.

- Look upon Iceland's well-known colourful houses in Reykjavík, or beautifully preserved old houses in the southerly charming villages of **Stokkseyri** and **Eyrarbakki**.
- When people think of fjords, they often think of Iceland's Scandinavian rival, Norway. Yet Iceland's **Western Fjords** are spectacular, and easily accessible by coach from Reykjavik. Such fjords include **Holmavik**, **Isafjördur**, **Kroksfardarnes**, **Korksfjaroarnes** and **Orlygshofn**. This area of Iceland is full of lava formations and geothermal activity. There is some fine woodland, lakes and rivers, as well as breathtaking chasms and waterfalls, overlooked by glaciers. Iceland's highest waterfall, **Glymir**, is found here. **Isafjördur** is the region's main town and has plenty of social and cultural facilities, as well as being a starting point for tours of the region. Travelling around this area, the road takes you over mountain passes between each new fjord. The Western Fjords are renowned for wizards and sorcerers, and the town of **Hólmavik** hosts an exhibition on witchcraft and witch hunts. **Hornstrandir Nature Reserve**, in the region's northern edge, is both breathtakingly raw and astonishingly rich in vegetation.
- Go to **Eiriksstadir** in the Western Fjords, birthplace of Leif the Lucky, who discovered America in AD 1000, and see a replica Viking Age farmstead.
- Visit **Lake Myvatn**, an important bird sanctuary with many rare species, surrounded by lava formations, volcanoes and craters. It has been designated as Iceland's winter sports centre. In the **Myvatn** district are hot pools for bathing. The temperature of some of these pools is now too high for bathing, but others are still usable.
- **Jökulsárgljúfur National Park** in northern Iceland stretches along an awesome canyon that includes **Dettifoss**, Europe's most powerful waterfall.
- See the largest **glacier** in Europe, **Vatnajökull**. **Höfn** is the main starting point for trips to the nearby glacier and visitors can indulge in ice-climbing, skiing, riding snow scooters and hiking. Höfn's multimedia **Glacier Centre** gives information about the geology, formation, history and potential of glaciers. Also on the edge of this region is the scenically stunning **Skaftafell National Park**. It is made up of woodlands and black mountains and a sheer white glacier lying in the shadow of **Hvannadalshnukur**, the country's highest peak.

Top Things To Do

- If you are in Iceland on March 1, then a swig of beer is practically compulsory. March 1 is **Beer Day**, when Icelanders celebrate the day in 1989 when a 75-year prohibition of beer was lifted. Nightlife in the major towns is usually particularly wild on this night. You will almost certainly have a night of fun to remember – so long as you forget that you were spending Icelandic prices on each beer!
- A number of travel agencies and tour operators can organise trips to Iceland's **glaciers**, which cover 11 per cent of the country. Transport is by **4-wheel-drive vehicles**, **snow cats** or – the most popular option – **snowmobiles** (also called **skidoos**). The best time for skidooing is between January and March when the snow is fresh and plentiful. The most visited glaciers are **Drangajökull**, **Glerádalsjökull**, **Snaefellsjökull** and **Vindheimajökull**. A list of tour operators can be obtained from the Icelandic Tourist Board.
- Go skiing, Iceland's most popular winter sport. Ski resorts offering both **downhill skiing** and **cross-country skiing** can be found throughout the country. Several Alpine-style resorts are located near **Akureyri (Hlitharfjall)**,

Ísafjördur and Reykjavik (**Bláfjöll**). These resorts are equipped with standard lifts and facilities. Many good ski slopes are just 30 minutes' drive from Reykjavik. The main skiing season is normally from January until May or June. Summer skiing is possible on the glaciers. **Myrdalsjökull** has a ski lift which is open throughout summer. Equipment hire is available in resorts.
- Bathe - and maybe even cover yourself with the mineral-rich mud - in the **Blue Lagoon** near Reykjavik, heated by geothermal springs. The Blue Lagoon is located in the middle of a lava field in the Icelandic wilderness and is known for its special properties and beneficial effect on the skin. The warm waters of the lagoon – approximately 35°C (90°F) all year round – are one of Iceland's most popular tourist attractions. Another natural spring is **Krysuvik**. Most towns and cities have outdoor and indoor pools filled with water from natural hot springs (water temperature in the pools averages around 29°C/85°F). Many places also have saunas, jacuzzis and hot pots with water temperatures of up to 44°C/112°F.
- Play **golf** during the **Midnight Sun** period (end of May to the beginning of August): there is something unbeatable about playing golf at three-in-the-morning when the sun is still high in the sky. The **Akureyri Golf Club** in the north hosts the yearly **Arctic Open International Golf Tournament**, a competition at the end of June which climaxes with a tee-off at midnight continuing until the early morning hours.
- Watch for **birds** in the **Westmann Islands**, particularly good for spotting seabirds as well as being home to the world's largest puffin population. **Lake Myvatn** in northern Iceland is apparently the most fertile spot on the globe at that latitude and is also a favourite breeding ground for many species of birdlife, particularly waterfowl. Southern Iceland is known for its great skua colony living on the sands. **Latrabjorgin** in the **Western Fjords** is the largest bird cliff in the world, where the largest colony of Razorbills in the world can be found. There are safari and Puffin Island tours from Reykjavik harbour.
- Go **whale watching**. On **Skjalfandi Bay** lies the town of **Husavik**, which is becoming Europe's main whale watching centre. Tours to other spots around the coast are widely available. Minke, humpback and killer whales, **dolphins** and **seals** can be seen.
- When the Vikings created Iceland's (and the world's) first Parliament in 930, one of their acts was to prohibit further import of **horses**. More than 10 centuries later, the Icelandic horse breed remains pure. This small but sturdy and sure-footed horse is reputed for its friendliness and willingness to carry riders over even the roughest terrain. Horses are available for hire near most towns, with experienced guides if required.
- Attend the **Reykjavik Arts Festival** in May/June, or participate in Reykjavik's **Cultural Night** in mid-August. If you do so, you will gain a taste of the Icelander's lust for the literary, their appetite for the arts. There are many nightclubs, cafes, art galleries and museums in the major cities, as well as numerous bookshops selling books in English, German and Icelandic. Icelanders are said to be among the most prolific readers and writers in the world, and literature plays an important part in Icelandic culture and history. The *Icelandic Sagas*, the oldest of which was written in AD 930 as a chronicle of Iceland's history, are still very much alive in Iceland today. The language used over 1000 years ago in the sagas remains virtually unchanged.
- Take a '**safari**' in the mountainous interior of the **Central**

Highlands in specially constructed overland buses. These are camping tours, and tents are provided. Sleeping bags can be bought or hired. Visitors are advised to take warm clothing, hiking shoes, rubber boots and swimsuits for bathing in the warm pools. The tours go through lava beds, sandy deserts and barren wilderness, passing glacial lakes with floating icebergs, glaciers, vast icefields, mountain ranges, crevasses and extinct volcanoes, plus **Skaftafell National Park**. Tours range from all-in package tours or a one- or two-day trip.
- The district of **Skagafjordur** is an area of outstanding natural beauty, with glacial rivers, highlands, lush green valleys and mountains. It is, not surprisingly, a very popular area for **river rafting**.
- Sample some adventurous grub at the ancient Viking feast of **Thorrablot**, now a popular feature at many restaurants during January and February in Reykjavik, but also many other towns and villages. The feast usually includes a hefty lot of meat – and we are not simply talking rare steak. You might be offered anything from an animal's eyeballs to their pickled testicles. A side-dish might consist of blódmör: congealed sheep's blood intermixed with lard and wrapped up in the animal's stomach. Wash this down with some Black Death brew and you may or may not be able to 'stomach' joining in in the singing and dancing that usually follows such a banquet.

TOURIST INFORMATION

Icelandic Tourist Board
Laekjargata 3, 101 Reykjavik, Iceland
Tel: 535 5500.
Website: www.icetourist.is

Icelandic Tourist Board in the USA
c/o The Scandinavian Tourist Board, 655 Third Avenue, New York, NY 10017, USA
Tel: (212) 885 9700.
Website: www.icelandtouristboard.com *or* www.goscandinavia.com

Entertainment

FOOD & DRINK: Icelandic food in general is based on fish and lamb, as well as owing much to Scandinavian and European influences. Fishing is Iceland's most important export, accounting for some 80 per cent of the country's Gross National Product. There is also a heavy emphasis on vegetables grown in greenhouses heated by the natural steam from geysers. There have been some welcome additions to the selection of eating places in Reykjavik and there is now a small but attractive choice of restaurants to cater for all pockets with new tourist menus. Bars have table and/or counter service, and will serve coffee as well as alcohol. Beer was prohibited in Iceland for 75 years and was finally legalised in March 1989. Alcohol is generally expensive (a small beer costs approximately US$8). In coffee shops you pay for the first cup then help yourself to subsequent cups. There is a wide selection of European spirits and wines.

National specialities:
- The salmon of Iceland is a great delicacy, served in many forms, one of the most popular being *gravlax*, a form of marinating.

- *Hangikjot* (smoked lamb).
- *Hardfiskur* (dried fish).
- *Skyr* (curds).
- *Icelandic sild* (herring marinated in various flavours).
- *Slátur*, for the more adventurous, literally means slaughter and is similar to Haggis.
- A delicacy not for the squeamish is rotten shark, cured by burying and washed down with a shot of *Black Death Schnapps*.

National drinks:
- *Brennivin* (a potent variation of aquavit made from potatoes) is a local drink.

Tipping: Service charges are included in most bills and extra tips are not expected.

NIGHTLIFE: There are plenty of nightclubs, bars, cafes and cinemas in Iceland, most of them in the capital. Reykjavik is renowned as one of Europe's hottest nightspots where the friendly pubs and nightlife scene lasts through the night. Icelandic nightlife is particularly vibrant from June to August when there is nearly 24 hours of perpetual daylight (Icelanders call this period the 'White Nights'). Leading theatres are the National Theatre and the Reykjavík City Theatre, closed in summer, but during the tourist season there is an attractive light entertainment show in English called 'Light Nights' with traditional Icelandic stories and folk songs. The *Iceland Symphony Orchestra* gives concerts every week. Iceland also has its own opera company, performing in the smallest (400 seat) and most northernmost opera house in the world. Performances run throughout the winter. Iceland has a vibrant music scene that has produced, amongst others, the internationally acclaimed artist Björk and, reportedly, Brad Pitt's favourite band, Sigur Rós. This has, in turn, attracted a number of British and American pop stars to Iceland, such as Damon Albarn from the British band Blur, who opened his own cafe, the *Kaffibarinn*, in Reykjavík.

SHOPPING: Fluffy, earth-coloured *Lopi* wool blankets and coats, jackets, hats and handknits are synonymous with Iceland. Several local potters handthrow earthenware containers in natural colours. Crushed lava is a common addition to highly glazed ceramic pieces, which are popular as souvenirs. The duty free shop at Keflavík Airport sells all of these products. Laugavegur is Reykjavík's main shopping street. The shops along Skolavordustigur is good for art lovers. *Kringlan* is Reykjavik's world-class shopping mall. Bargain hunters should visit the indoor market in Reykjavik called *Kolaportid*, held every weekend 1100-1700. Great buys on handmade Icelandic jumpers, food and toys can be found. **Shopping hours:** Mon-Fri 1000-1800, Sat 1000-1400, with variations from shop to shop. Shopping malls are open Mon-Wed 1000-1830, Thur 1000-2100, Fri 1000-1900, Sat 1000-1600 and Sun 1300-1700. On the first Saturday of the month, shops open 1000-1800.

Business

- **GDP:** ISK 806,439 million (2003).
- **Main exports:** Fish, fish products, aluminium, animal products, ferrosilicon and diatomite.
- **Main imports:** Machinery and equipment, petroleum products, foodstuffs and textiles.
- **Main trade partners:** UK, Germany, Denmark, France, Sweden, USA, Japan and Norway.

Credit: © Icelandic Tourist Board

ECONOMY: Icelanders enjoy a per capita income that is amongst the highest in the world at US$38,620. Iceland is short of indigenous raw materials and thus relies heavily on foreign trade to keep its relatively successful economy ticking over. Exports of goods and services account for more than one-third of GNP. The largest proportion of these derives from fisheries and related products such as fishmeal and oil. The economy is thus particularly susceptible to fluctuating world prices in this commodity and maintains a broad fisheries exclusion zone (320km/200 miles) to protect its earnings. As several European governments (including the British) have discovered to their cost, the Icelanders are fiercely determined and quite capable of defending their perceived territorial rights. Other sources of revenue come from the sale of minerals such as aluminium, ferrosilicon, cement and nitrates used in fertilisers, although these have lately been affected by low demand. Light industry produces knitwear, blankets, textiles and paint. There is a burgeoning advanced technology sector involved in software and biotechnology, and an embryonic financial services industry. After a period of high inflation and recession in the 1980s and 1990s, Iceland entered a positive economic period; economic growth in 2003 was at 4 per cent and unemployment at 4 per cent in the second quarter of 2004. Tourism is now a major earner, with recent estimates showing that whale watching alone contributes £12 million to the economy per year.

Accession to the European Economic Area (an amalgam of the EU and the European Free Trade Association; Iceland belongs to the latter) effected a wholesale liberalisation of trade among the member states and caused some disruption to the Icelandic economy. This highlighted the fact that Iceland's economy is too dependent on its fishing industry and needs to diversify in areas that will allow it to compete in international markets.

BUSINESS ETIQUETTE: Businesspeople are expected to dress smartly. Local businesspeople are conservative but very friendly and most speak English. Previous appointments are not generally necessary, but visits between May and September should be planned in advance as many local businesspeople travel abroad at this time. The telephone directory is listed by Christian name. **Office hours:** Mon-Fri 0800-1600 (summer) and 0900-1700 (winter). Most offices are closed Saturday and Sunday.

CONFERENCES/CONVENTIONS: There are several large hotels in Reykjavík equipped for conferences and business meetings, while smaller conferences may be held at venues outside the capital.

COMMERCIAL INFORMATION

Iceland Chamber of Commerce
House of Commerce, 7th floor, Kringlan 7, 103 Reykjavík, Iceland
Tel: 510 7100.
Website: www.chamber.is

Iceland Convention & Incentive Bureau
Laekjargata 3, 101 Reykjavík, Iceland
Tel: 562 6070.
Website: www.icelandconvention.com

Credit: © Icelandic Tourist Board

Credit: © Icelandic Tourist Board

HIGHLANDERS
ADVENTURE IN ICELAND

PARADISE
FOR OUTDOOR EXPLORERS

Highlanders is an ideal company for people who like to travel in a different way. We are committed to helping you plan the perfect vacation to Iceland's best destinations.

Our experienced staff work with you to make your travel dreams a reality. All of our tours are fully guided and focus on both seeing Iceland and offering a true learning experience.

We operate throughout the year and offer a variety of activities: day and sport tours, incentive events, company services and teambuilding. We also run tours for groups with special vehicles and driver guide to make sure you have a real Icelandic quality adventure.

Highlander has built a reputation for innovation, quality and unforgettable travel experiences. Today our range of trips is greater than ever before.

HAPPY CUSTOMERS
Highlanders have operated quality tours and programmes with great success. Clients from Discovery Channel, Toyota, Becker, Miss Norway, MTV, ZDF, BNN, National Geographic, CBNC, TV2 Norway, the 007 James Bond production company and many others have all enjoyed Highlanders excellent programs.

- Day Tours • Longer Tours • Snowmobile • Incentive / Team building
- Sport tours • Filming tours • Custom tours • Whale Watching
- Horse Riding Tours • Rafting

Join Highlanders for 'Super Jeep' and 'Super Truck' tours, a bath in the Blue Lagoon, river rafting, snowmobiling and glacier seafood buffet and team building glacier games.

Highlanders

Akralind 8

IS-201 Kópavogur, Iceland

Tel.: +354 568 3030 Fax: +354 565 5030 | www.hl.is www.incentive.is | E-mail: info@hl.is

More than 30 years experience

PERSONAL SERVICE – THE KEY TO HOLIDAY SUCCESS FOR YOUR CUSTOMERS IN ICELAND

FOR BOOKINGS AND INFORMATION
www.exoticiceland.is · info@exoticiceland.is

EXOTIC ICELAND

India

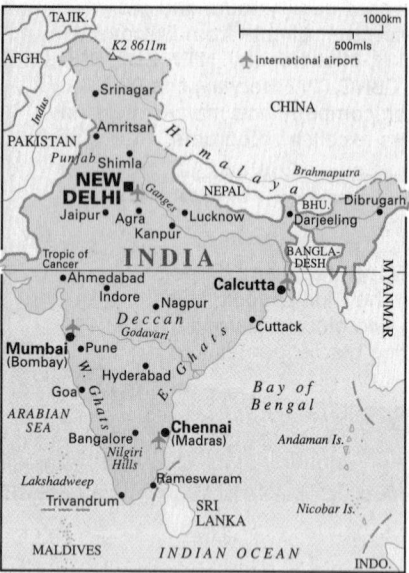

Location: South Asia.

Time: GMT + 5.5.

Overview

India is a mystical land of seductive images. Hinduism is practised by 85 per cent of Indians, the religious rites and red-letter days woven into the fabric of everyday life. It is also India's vastness that challenges the imagination: the subcontinent is home to one sixth of the world's population, a diverse culture and an intoxicatingly rich history.

Perhaps this is because Indian civilisation can be traced back to at least 2500 BC. The first known civilisation settled along the Indus River in what is now Pakistan. Between 521 and 486 BC, under Darius, the area became part of the Persian Empire. India's two great religions, Hinduism and Buddhism, developed, and various dynasties emerged.

The invasion of the White Huns fragmented northern India, only reunified with the arrival of Muslims from the west. The next major influx was the Moghuls in the 1520s from Central Asia, who maintained effective control of the north until the mid-18th century. But by the time of the British conquest, at the end of the 18th century, the Moghul Empire was already in severe decline. The British, motivated by trade and geopolitics, managed to take effective control of the subcontinent using the telegraph and the railways – both of which they built; for the first time, the many and varied provinces of India were administered by a single alien power. The indigenous campaign for independence began with the formation of the Indian National Congress in 1885, but it made little progress until after the end of World War I, when Mahatma Gandhi led the Congress and began the policy of non-cooperation with the British. The colonial authorities were gradually persuaded that reforms were needed, but the Congress itself was split on a key issue – the Muslims, under Muhammad Ali Jinnah, claimed a separate homeland in provinces such as the Punjab and East Bengal, where they formed a majority, but Gandhi wanted India to be a unified and secular state. Jinnah's view prevailed and in August 1947, the independent states of India and Pakistan came into being (Pakistan was divided into two parts, East and West). Since this time, India has been a democratic republic.

Such a rich history has spawned palaces, temples and monuments. Indeed, the most frequently visited part of India is the Golden Triangle. The unfairly maligned great cities of

Mumbai and Kolkata have a bustling, colourful charm, while the holy city of Varanasi or the awe-inspiring temples of Tamil Nadu are worthy objects of pilgrimage. For those who prefer more sybaritic pleasures, tackle the palm-fringed beaches of Goa. And for solitude, India ripples with mountains and hills, from the towering beauty of the Himalayas to pine forests, lakes and babbling streams. One of the fascinations of India is the juxtaposition of old and new; centuries of history rubbing shoulders with the computer age; and Bangalore's 'Silicon Valley' is as much a part of the world's largest democracy as its remotest village.

General Information

AREA: 3,166,414 sq km (1,222,582 sq miles).
POPULATION: 1.1 billion (UN, 2005).
POPULATION DENSITY: 347 per sq km.
CAPITAL: New Delhi. **Population:** 19.8 million (2001).
GEOGRAPHY: India shares borders to the northwest with Pakistan, to the north with China, Nepal and Bhutan, and to the east with Bangladesh and Myanmar. To the west lies the Arabian Sea, to the east the Bay of Bengal and to the south the Indian Ocean. Sri Lanka lies off the southeast coast, and the Maldives off the southwest coast. The far northeastern states and territories are all but separated from the rest of India by Bangladesh as it extends northwards from the Bay of Bengal towards Bhutan. The Himalayan mountain range to the north and the Indus River (west) and Ganges River (east) form a physical barrier between India and the rest of Asia. The country can be divided into five regions: Western, Central, Northern (including Kashmir and Rajasthan), Eastern and Southern.
GOVERNMENT: Republic since 1947. **Head of State:** President APJ Abdul Kalam since 2002. **Head of Government:** Prime Minister Manmohan Singh since 2004.
Recent history: In May 2004, Manmohan Singh became Prime Minister after the Congress Party won the General Election. Singh took the position after the President of the party, Sonia Gandhi, widow of former Prime Minister Rajiv Gandhi, declined the post. Singh vowed to tackle poverty and to create economic reforms and better relations with India's neighbours, especially Pakistan. In his first year as Prime Minister, Singh held together a coalition which included communist allies and ministers accused of corruption and oversaw the introduction of nuclear non-proliferation legislation. His promises to raise the poorest citizens out of poverty has yet to be realised. Meanwhile, Indian foreign policy continues to be dominated by relations with Pakistan. The main cause of friction is the status of Kashmir, most of which was awarded to India in 1947. Both sides claim the entire region and both insist their claim is 'non-negotiable'. Separatist guerrillas, backed by Pakistan, have waged a steady campaign against Indian forces which shows no sign of resolution despite regular initiatives. Given the nuclear capabilities of both countries, and their proven delivery systems, this is now viewed as a major potential flashpoint and is closely watched by the world's major powers. In the spring of 2002, following a spurt of guerrilla activity in Kashmir and intercommunal violence between Muslims and Hindus in the western Indian state of Gujarat, the two countries came close to war. Only frantic international diplomacy calmed the situation. Historically, the USA and China had backed Pakistan while India had close relations with the Soviet Union. The demise of the Soviet Union has not, however, damaged India excessively: it still enjoys close links with Moscow and is concerned only by the possibility of instability in central Asia spilling southwards. China has long viewed India as a rival, and the main irritant is the presence of the exiled Tibetan opposition leader, the Dalai Lama, in northwest India. Nevertheless, the two Governments have signed a major trade agreement and relations are steadily improving. As for the Americans, India moved quickly to support the Bush administration's plan for ballistic missile defence in the hope that the remaining sanctions from 1998 will be lifted.

India is a federal republic with certain powers reserved to the 25 states. There are seven Union Territories (Andaman and Nicobar Islands; Chandigarh; Dadra and Nagar Haveli; Delhi; Goa, Daman and Diu; Lakshadweep; and Pondicherry), which are governed from Delhi. Central Government comprises a bicameral Parliament and Cabinet of Ministers. Each of the states also has an elected Assembly. The bicameral National Parliament consists of the lower house, the *Lok Sabha*, which has 542 members popularly elected for a five-year term and the upper house, the *Rajya Sabha*, which has 245 members indirectly elected by the State Assemblies to serve six years. The Head of State is the President, while executive power is vested in the Prime Minister who is the head of the Cabinet and is normally the leader of the largest party in the *Lok Sabha*.
LANGUAGE: The official language is Hindi which is spoken by about 30 per cent of the population; English is also often used for official or commercial purposes. In addition, 17 regional languages are recognised by the Constitution. These include Bengali, Gujarati, Oriya and Punjabi which are widely

Credit: © Bruce Logan

used in the north, and Tamil and Telegu, which are common in the south. Other regional languages are Kannada, Malayalam and Marathi. The Muslim population largely speak Urdu.
RELIGION: About 82 per cent Hindu, 11 per cent Muslim with Sikh, Christian, Jain and Buddhist minorities.
ELECTRICITY: Usually 220 volts AC, 50Hz. Some areas have a DC supply. Plugs used are of the round two- and three-pin type.
SOCIAL CONVENTIONS: The Indian Hindu greeting is to fold the hands and tilt the head forward to *namaste*. Indian women prefer not to shake hands. All visitors are asked to remove footwear when entering places of religious worship. The majority of Indians remove their footwear when entering their houses. Because of strict religious and social customs, visitors must show particular respect when visiting someone's home. Many Hindus are vegetarian and many, especially women, do not drink alcohol. Sikhs and Parsees do not smoke. Small gifts are acceptable as tokens of gratitude for hospitality. Women are expected to dress modestly. Short skirts and tight or revealing clothing should not be worn, even on beaches. Businesspeople are not expected to dress formally except for meetings and social functions. English-speaking guides are available at fixed charges at all important tourist centres. Guides speaking French, German, Italian, Japanese, Russian or Spanish are available in some cities. Consult the nearest Incredible India office. Unapproved guides are not permitted to enter protected monuments. Tourists are advised to ask for guides with certificates from the Ministry of Tourism or Incredible India (see *Top Things To Do*). **Photography:** Formalities mainly concern protected monuments and the wildlife sanctuaries. Special permission of the Archaeological Survey of India, New Delhi, is necessary for the use of tripod and artificial light to photograph monuments. Photography at many places is allowed on payment of a prescribed fee, which varies. Contact the nearest Government of India Tourist Office.

Climate

Hot tropical weather with variations from region to region. Coolest weather lasts from December to February, with cool, fresh mornings and evenings and dry, sunny days. Really hot weather, when it is dry, dusty and unpleasant, is between March and May. Monsoon rains occur in most regions in summer between June and September.
Western Himalayas: Srinagar is best from March to October; July to August can be unpleasant; cold and damp in winter. Simla is higher and therefore colder in winter. Places like Gulmarg, Manali and Pahalgam are usually under several feet of snow (December to March) and temperatures in Ladakh can be extremely cold. The road to Leh is open from June to October.
Required clothing: Light- to mediumweights are advised from March to October, with warmer wear for winter. Weather can change rapidly in the mountains and therefore it is important to be suitably equipped. Waterproofing is advisable.
Northern Plains: Extreme climate, warm inland from April to mid-June, falling to almost freezing at night in winter between November and February. Summers are hot with monsoons between June and September.
Required clothing: Lightweight cottons and linens in

Credit: © Bruce Logan

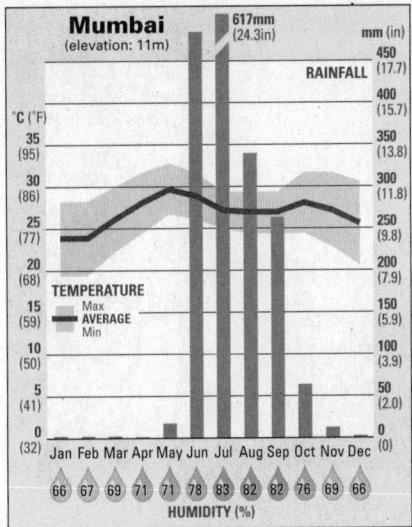

Mumbai
(elevation: 11m)

617mm
(24.3in)

RAINFALL

TEMPERATURE
Max
AVERAGE
Min

Jan Feb Mar Apr May Jun Jul Aug Sep Oct Nov Dec

66 67 69 71 71 78 83 82 82 76 69 66

HUMIDITY (%)

Credit: © Bruce Logan

summer with warmer clothes in winter and on cooler evenings. Waterproofing is essential during monsoons.

Central India: Madhya Pradesh State escapes the very worst of the hot season, but monsoons are heavy between July and September. Temperatures fall at night in winter. *Required clothing:* Lightweights are worn most of the year with warmer clothes during evenings, particularly in winter. Waterproofed clothing is advised during monsoon rains.

Western India: November to February is most comfortable, although evenings can be fairly cold. Summers can be extremely hot with monsoon rainfall between mid-June and mid-September.
Required clothing: Lightweight cottons and linens are worn most of the year with warmer clothes for cooler winters, and waterproofing is essential during the monsoon.

Southwest: The most pleasant weather is from November to March. Monsoon rains between late April and July. Summer temperatures hot as high as Northern India although humidity is extreme. Cooling breezes on coast. Inland, Mysore and Bijapur have pleasant climates with relatively low rainfall.
Required clothing: Lightweight cottons and linens. Waterproofing is necessary during the monsoon. Warmer clothes are worn in the winter, particularly in the hills.

Southeast: Tamil Nadu experiences a northeast monsoon between October and December and temperatures and humidity are high all year. Hills can be cold in winter.
Required clothing: Lightweight cottons and linens. Waterproofing is necessary during the monsoon. Warmer clothes are worn in the winter, particularly in the hills.

Northeast: March to June and September to November are the driest and most pleasant periods. The rest of the year has extremely heavy monsoon rainfall and it is recommended that the area is avoided.
Required clothing: Lightweight cottons and linens. Waterproofing is advisable throughout the year and essential in monsoons, usually from mid-June to mid-October. Warmer clothes are useful for cooler evenings.

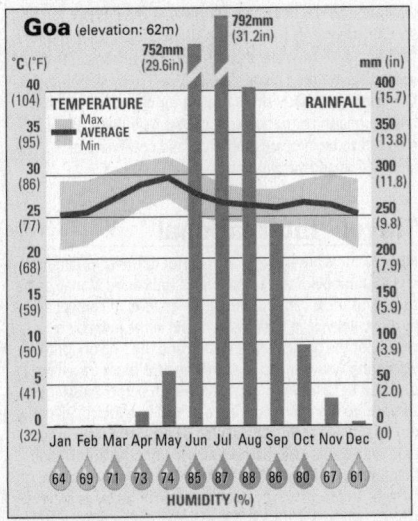

Goa (elevation: 62m)

792mm
(31.2in)

752mm
(29.6in)

TEMPERATURE
Max
AVERAGE
Min

RAINFALL

Jan Feb Mar Apr May Jun Jul Aug Sep Oct Nov Dec

64 69 73 74 85 87 88 86 80 67 61

HUMIDITY (%)

New Delhi
(elevation: 218 metres)

TEMPERATURE
Max
AVERAGE
Min

RAINFALL

Jan Feb Mar Apr May Jun Jul Aug Sep Oct Nov Dec

57 51 36 27 28 45 67 72 62 44 41 56

HUMIDITY (%)

Communications

Telephone: Country code: 91. IDD service is widely available all over India. Otherwise calls must be placed through the international operator.

Mobile telephone: Roaming agreements exist with most international mobile phone companies. Coverage is limited to major towns.

Internet: E-mail can be accessed from Internet cafes accross the country.

Post: Airmail service to Western Europe takes up to one week. Stamps are often sold at hotels.

MEDIA: The state's TV monopoly was broken in 1992, resulting in a boom of private channels. News and entertainment shows are especially popular, with news programmes often attracting the larger audiences. A number of 24-hour news channels operate in India. Public TV is run by *Doordarshan*, while *STAR Plus*, owned by *News Corporation*, is one of the most popular private channels. Private radio stations were sanctioned in 2000, but only public *All India Radio* is allowed to broadcast news. Newspaper circulation has risen, thanks to a growing middle class, as has the number of Internet users.

Press: There are numerous local dailies published in several languages. Many newspapers are in English; the most important include *The Economic Times, The Hindu, Hindustan Times, Indian Express, Navbharat Times, Punjab Kesari, Deccan Herald, The Statesman, Pioneer* and *The Times of India.*

TV: *Doordarshan Television* operates 21 national, regional and local services throughout India. *Zee TV* and *Star TV* are satellite and cable TV services. *Aaj Tak* is a 24-hour news channel, *New Delhi TV (NDTV)* operates *NDTV-India* and *NDTV 24x7* news channels. *Sun Network* is a commercial broadcaster.

Radio: Stations include *All India Radio, All India Radio External Service* (offering broadcasts in local and regional languages, Arabic and English), *Radio Mirchi* (a commercial network in Mumbai, Delhi and other cities), *Radio City* (a commercial station in Mumbai and other cities), and commercial network *Red FM.*

www.gocoti.com

Passport/Visa

	Passport Required?	Visa Required?	Return Ticket Required?
Full British	Yes	Yes	No
Australian	Yes	Yes	No
Canadian	Yes	Yes	No
USA	Yes	Yes	No
Other EU	Yes	Yes	No
Japanese	Yes	Yes	No

Note: *Regulations and requirements may be subject to change at short notice, and you are advised to contact the appropriate diplomatic or consular authority before finalising travel arrangements. Any numbers in the chart refer to the footnotes below.*

PASSPORTS: Passport valid for at least six months required by all.

VISAS: Required by all.

Types of visa and cost: The following prices are for UK nationals only; prices for other nationals vary. *Tourist:* £30. *Business:* £30 (three/six months); £50 (one year); £90 (two years). *Transit:* £8. *Student:* £30 (six months); £50 (one year); £55 (more than one year).

Note: (a) Non-UK nationals applying in the UK need to pay an additional £10 (amounts charged may also vary according to nationality and type of passport held) unless holding proof of at least one-year residence in the UK. (b) A £1 fee may be required for postal applications, depending on consulate.

Validity: *Transit:* 15 days. *Business:* three or six months, or up to two years for multiple entry.

Application to: Embassy or High Commission (or Consular section at Embassy or High Commission); see *Passport/Visa Information.*

Application requirements: (a) Passport valid for up to six months with at least two blank pages. (b) Completed application form. Nationals of Bangladesh and Pakistan must complete special application forms. Personal interviews in some cases may also be necessary. (c) Two passport-size photos. Nationals of Pakistan will require five. (d) Fee (bank draft or postal orders only). (e) Stamped addressed special delivery envelope. *Business:* (a)-(e) and, (f) A letter from their employer stating the reason of the visit and an invitation from the company in India and a letter of introduction from UK company addressed to the Embassy. *Transit:* (a)-(e) and, (f) Proof of onward travel. *Student:* (a)-(e) and, (f) Proof of admission to appropriate university/educational institution with duration of course.

Working days required: Personal applications can normally be processed the same day. Postal applications may take up to 15 working days or longer (early September to February). Those requiring an additional fee may need a minimum of seven working days and possibly much longer for their visa application to be processed.

Temporary residence: Prior permission should be sought before entry into India.

Restricted and protected areas: Certain parts of the country have been designated protected or restricted areas that require special permits and in some cases prior government authorisation. Intent to visit a specific restricted region should be indicated when applying for a visa and a permit will be granted to visit that region only. Passengers are advised to check with India Tourism for up-to-date information before departure. The following states are subject to some restrictions: Andaman & Nicobar Islands, Arunachal Pradesh, borders areas of Jammu and Kashmir, Manipur, Meghalaya, Sikkim and the Union Territory of Laccadives Island (Lakshadweep).

Credit: © Bruce Logan

PASSPORT/VISA INFORMATION

Office of the High Commissioner for India in the UK
India House, Aldwych, London WC2B 4NA, UK
Tel: (020) 7836 8484.
Website: www.hcilondon.net
Opening hours: Mon-Fri 0830-1200 (visa enquiries);
0915-1730 (visa applications and collections;
telephone enquiries).

Embassy of India in the USA
Chancery: 2107 Massachusetts Avenue, NW,
Washington, DC 20008, USA
Consulate: 2536 Massachusetts Avenue, NW,
Washington, DC 20008, USA
Tel: (202) 939 7000 *or* 9806 (consular section).
Website: www.indianembassy.org

Money

Currency: Rupee (INR) = 100 paise. Notes are in denominations of INR1000, 500, 100, 50, 20, 10, and 5. Coins are in denominations of INR5, 2 and 1, and 50, 25, and 10 paise.
Currency exchange: Currency can be changed at banks, airports or authorised money changers. It is illegal to exchange money through unauthorised money changers. US Dollars and Pounds Sterling are the easiest currencies to exchange.
Credit & debit cards: American Express, Diners Club, MasterCard and Visa are accepted. Check with your credit or debit card company for details of merchant acceptability and other services which may be available.
Traveller's cheques: These are widely accepted and may be changed at banks. To avoid additional exchange rate charges, travellers are advised to take traveller's cheques in US Dollars or Pounds Sterling. Some banks may refuse to change certain brands of traveller's cheques which others exchange quite happily.
Currency restrictions: Import of local currency is prohibited. Export of local currency is also prohibited, except for passengers proceeding to Nepal (excluding notes of denominations of INR100 or higher), Bangladesh, Pakistan or Sri Lanka (up to INR20 per person). Foreign currency may be exported up to the amount imported and declared. All foreign currency must be declared on arrival if value is over US$5000, and when exchanged the currency declaration form should be endorsed, or a certificate issued. The form and certificates must be produced on departure to enable reconversion into foreign currency. Changing money with unauthorised money changers is not, therefore, advisable.
Banking hours: Mon-Fri 1000-1400, Sat 1000-1200.
Exchange rate indicators:
Rate at time of publishing
£1.00=   INR78.71
$1.00=   INR45.94

Duty Free

The following goods may be imported into India by persons over 17 years of age without incurring customs duty:
200 cigarettes or 50 cigars or 250g of tobacco; alcoholic liquor or wine (2l); 60ml of perfume and 250ml of eau de toilette; goods for personal use; travel souvenirs (differing amounts according to nationality and duration of stay); reasonable quantities of medicines.
Note: Import by non-residents is only permitted if the national has entered India for a stay of not less than 24 hours and not more than six months, provided they visit not more than once a month. Domestic pets (cats, dogs, birds etc) are permitted to be imported into India.
Prohibited items: Livestock and pigs and pig meat products.

Public Holidays

Below are listed the Public Holidays for the January 2006-June 2007 period.
2006: Jan 10 Idu'z Zuha/Bakrid (Feast of the Sacrifice).
Jan 26 Republic Day. **Jan 31** Muharram (Islamic New Year).
Feb 26 Mahavir Jayanthi. **Mar 14** Holi. **Apr 6** Sri Rama Navami (Birthday of Sri Rama). **Apr 10** Milad-Un-Nabi (Birth of the Prophet). **Apr 14** Good Friday. **May 13** Buddha Purnima. **Aug 15** Independence Day. **Sep 2** Vijaya Dasami/Dussera. **Oct 2** Mahatma Gandhi's Birthday.
Oct 24-26 Eid al-Fitr (End of Ramadan). **Nov 21** Diwali.
Dec 31 Idu'z Zuha/Bakrid (Feast of the Sacrifice).
2007: Jan 26 Republic Day. **Jan 20** Muharram (Islamic New Year). **Mar 3** Holi. **Mar 8** Mahavir Jayanthi. **Mar 27** Sri Rama Navami (Birthday of Sri Rama). **Mar 31** Milad-Un-Nabi (Birth of the Prophet). **Apr 6** Good Friday. **Apr 14** Baisakhi, Vishu/Bahag, Mesadi, Maghi. **May 2** Buddha Purnima.
Notes: (a) Public holidays in India tend to be observed on a strictly regional basis. Only the secular holidays of Republic Day, Independence Day and Mahatma Gandhi's Birthday are universally observed. The above dates are Government of India holidays, when government offices will be closed nationwide. In addition, there are numerous festivals and fairs which are also observed in some States as holidays, the dates of which change from year to year. For more details, contact Incredible India (see *Top Things To Do*). (b) Muslim festivals are timed according to local sightings of various phases of the moon and the dates given above are approximations. During the lunar month of Ramadan that precedes Eid al-Fitr, Muslims fast during the day and feast at night and normal business patterns may be interrupted. Many restaurants are closed during the day and there may be restrictions on smoking and drinking. For more information see the *World of Islam* appendix.

Health

	Special Precautions?	Certificate Required?
Yellow Fever	Yes	1
Cholera	Yes	2
Typhoid & Polio	3	N/A
Malaria	4	N/A

Note: *Regulations and requirements may be subject to change at short notice, and you are advised to contact your doctor well in advance of your intended date of departure. Any numbers in the chart refer to the footnotes below.*

1: Any person (including infants over six months old) arriving by air or sea from an infected country must obtain a yellow fever certificate (includes passengers who have been transit in a country in the endemic zone). Otherwise, isolated detainment may occur for up to six days. Those countries that are considered infected are all African countries (except Algeria, Botswana, Djibouti, Egypt, Eritrea, Lesotho, Libya, Malawi, Mauritania, Morocco, Mozambique, Namibia, South Africa, Swaziland, Tunisia and Zimbabwe) and all South American countries (except Argentina, Chile, Paraguay and Uruguay). When a case of yellow fever is reported from any country, that country is regarded by the government of India as being infected.
2: Following WHO guidelines issued in 1973, a *cholera* vaccination certificate is not a condition of entry to India. However, cholera is a serious risk in this country and precautions are essential. Up-to-date advice should be sought before deciding whether these precautions should include vaccination, as medical opinion is divided over its effectiveness.
3: *Poliomyelitis* is widespread. Immunisation is generally recommended. Typhoid can be contracted and there have been recent reports of typhoid drug resistance.
4: *Malaria* risk exists, mainly in the benign *vivax* form, throughout the year in the whole country below 2000m excluding parts of the states of Himachal Pradesh, Jammu and Kashmir and Sikkim. High resistance to chloroquine and sulfadoxine-pyrimethamine is reported in the malignant *falciparum* form. The recommended prophylaxis is chloroquine plus proguanil in risk areas and mefloquine in Assam.

Food & drink: All water should be regarded as being potentially contaminated. Well water near the Ganges and in West Bengal may contain traces of arsenic chemical. Water used for drinking, brushing teeth or making ice should have first been boiled or otherwise sterilised. Milk is unpasteurised and should be boiled. Powdered or tinned milk is available and is advised, but make sure that it is reconstituted with pure water. Avoid dairy products that are likely to have been made from unboiled milk. Only eat well-cooked meat and fish, preferably served hot. Pork, salad and mayonnaise may carry increased risk. Vegetables should be cooked and fruit peeled.
Other risks: *Visceral leishmaniasis* occurs in rural areas of eastern India. *Cutaneous leishmaniasis* occurs in Rajasthan. *Filariasis* is common throughout India and sandfly fever is increasing. An outbreak of *plague* occurred in 1994 and was contained by adequate Government measures. *Tick-borne relapsing* fever is reported, as is *typhus*, and outbreaks of *haemorrhagic dengue fever* have occurred in eastern India. *Tick-borne haemorrhagic fever* has been reported in the forest areas in Karnataka State. *Hepatitis A* and *E* are common. *Hepatitis B* is endemic. *Leptospirosis* is a bacterial infection that can be contracted from water. Outbreaks of *Japanese encephalitis* occur, particularly in eastern coastal areas. *Meningococcal meningitis* is present in Delhi from November to May. Vaccination is advisable.
Rabies is present. For those at high risk, vaccination before arrival should be considered. If you are bitten, seek medical advice without delay. For more information, consult the *Health* appendix.
Note: All visitors aged between 18 and 70 years of age who are wishing to extend their visa for one year or more are required to take an AIDS test.
Health care: India has seen a massive growth in the voluntary and private health sector in the last few years; however, health care facilities are limited and travellers are strongly advised to take out full comprehensive medical insurance before departing for India. It is advisable to bring specific medicines from the UK. There are state-operated facilities in all towns and cities and private consultants and specialists in urban areas.
On leaving India: Visitors leaving for countries which impose health restrictions on arrivals from India are required to be in possession of a valid certificate of inoculation and vaccination.

Travel - International

Note: Visitors are strongly advised not to travel to Jammu and Kashmir (with the exceptions of Ladakh via Manali or air to Leh), as there continues to be a high level of conflict and terrorist violence in Kashmir. All travel in the immediate vicinity of the border with Pakistan and the Line of Control (excepting Amritsar and Jaisalmer and for those travelling overland to Pakistan through the Wagah border crossing), and all travel to Manipur and Tripura should be avoided. All but essential travel to Srinagar should be avoided. If you believe that your visit is essential seek advice from the British High Commission in New Delhi before undertaking the journey. Parts of the southern coast of India were hit by a tsunami caused by the Asian earthquake in December 2004.

AIR:

The national airlines are *Air India (AI)* (website: www.airindia.com) and *Jet Airways (India)* (website: www.jetairways.com). *British Airways* and *Virgin Atlantic* fly to India from the UK; *Delta Airlines* and *United Airlines* fly from the USA.

Approximate flight times: From *London* to Delhi is eight hours 35 minutes, to Kolkata (Calcutta) is nine hours 45 minutes, to Chennai is 11 hours and to Mumbai is eight hours 30 minutes. From *Los Angeles* to Delhi is 20 hours 30 minutes. From *New York* to Delhi is 15 hours 30 minutes. From *Singapore* to Delhi is five hours 40 minutes. From *Sydney* to Delhi is 13 hours.

Main airports: *New Delhi (DEL)* (Indira Gandhi International) is 23km (14 miles) south of the city (travel time - 45 minutes). *To/from the airport:* There are coach, bus and taxi services to the city. *Facilities*: Duty free shops, banks/bureaux de change, post office, restaurants and car hire.

Mumbai (BOM) (Chhatrapati Shivayi International) is 35km (22 miles) north of the city (travel time - 50 to 75 minutes). *To/from the airport*: Taxi services go to the city. Taxi fares should have fixed rates from the airport to the city. Public transport is also available in the form of the EATS bus service and local buses. There is also a railway system connecting with the Metro rail system. *Facilities*: Bank/bureau de change, post office, nursery, restaurant and shops.

Kolkata (Calcutta) *(CCU) (Netaji Subhash Chandra Bose International)* is 20km (13 miles) northeast of the city (travel time - 40 to 70 minutes). *To/from the airport*: There is a 24-hour coach service to Indian Airlines city office and major hotels. A bus goes every 10 minutes, 0530-2200. Taxi services go to the city. *Facilities*: Post office, bank, bars, duty free shops and restaurants.

Chennai (MAA) (Madras International) is 14km (9 miles) southwest of the city (travel time - 20 minutes). *To/from the airport*: A coach meets all flight arrivals 0900-2300. There is a train every 20 to 30 minutes from 0500-2300. Bus 18A runs every 25 minutes from 0500-2200. Taxi services go to the city. *Facilities*: Money exchange facilities, tourist information offices and hotel reservation services.

Amritsar (ATQ) (Raja Sansi International) is 11km (7 miles) from the city. *To/from the aiport*: Car hire, taxis and hotel pick ups can be arranged from the airport. *Facilities*: Money exchange facilities, tourist information offices and hotel reservation services.

Departure tax: £10. (£8 for neighbouring countries only.)

SEA:

Main ports: *Calicut, Kochi, Kolkata* (Calcutta), *Mumbai, Panaji* (Goa) and *Rameswaram* (the main departure point for the sea crossing to Sri Lanka; passenger services are presently suspended owing to the political situation in Sri Lanka). Indian ports are also served by several international shipping companies and several cruise lines. There are, however, no regular passenger liners operating to South-East Asia.

Departure tax: Seaports levy the following departure tax: INR500 (for journeys to Afghanistan, Bangladesh, Bhutan, Maldives, Myanmar, Nepal, Pakistan and Sri Lanka); INR750 (all other destinations).

RAIL:

This section gives details of the major overland routes to neighbouring countries (where frontiers are open); in most cases these will involve road as well as rail travel. Details should be checked with Incredible India as they may be subject to change (see *Top Things To Do*).

Connections to Pakistan: All travel is advised against in the immediate vicinity of the border with Pakistan other than across the international border at Wagah. Approaching the border away from the official crossing point could be dangerous.

Connections to Nepal: The most practical and popular route to Nepal is by train to Raxaul (Bihar) and then by bus to Kathmandu or by train to Gorakphur (or by bus if coming from Varanasi) and then by bus to Kathmandu crossing the border at Sunauli; also, by train to Nantanwa (UP) and then by bus to Kathmandu/Pokhara, or Bhairawa to Lumbini for Pokhara. It is also possible to make the crossing from Darjeeling by bus to Kathmandu across the southern lowlands.

Connections to Bhutan: The best way of reaching Bhutan is by train to Siliguri, then bus to Phuntsholing. There is also an airlink from Kolkata (Calcutta) to Paro by *Druk Air*.

Connections to Bangladesh: The best route to Bangladesh is Kolkata (Calcutta) to Bongaon (West Bengal) by train, rickshaw across the border to Benapol, with connections via Khulna or Jessore to Dhaka. Another route is from Darjeeling via Siliguri, then train or bus from Jalpaiguri to Haldibari.

Currently, no land frontiers are open between India and Myanmar or India and China (PR).

Credit: © Bruce Logan

ROAD:

Of late, the overland route from Europe to India has become very popular, but travellers should have accurate information about border crossings, visa requirements and political situations en route. The most popular border crossings into India are Sunauli (for Delhi and northwest India), Birganj (for Kolkata (Calcutta) and east India) and Kakarbhitta (for Darjeeling). Several 'adventure holiday' companies arrange overland tours and buses to India. A **bus** service between New Delhi and Lahore (Pakistan) has recently been launched (the first one in 50 years). The journey takes roughly 10 hours and there are four weekly return trips available. For information on this and other overland routes to neighbouring countries, contact Incredible India (see *Top Things To Do*).

Travel - Internal

Note: Travel in rural areas during the monsoon season can be hazardous and care should be taken. Monsoon rains cause flooding and landslides that can cut off some towns and villages for days at a time.

AIR:

The domestic airline is *Indian Airlines (IC)* (website: www.indian-airlines.nic.in). The network connects over 70 cities. Indian Airlines also operates regular flights to the neighbouring countries of Bangladesh, Malaysia, the Maldives, Myanmar, Nepal, Pakistan, Singapore, Sri Lanka, Thailand and the Middle East. Domestic airlines include *Alliance Airlines (3A)*, a subsidiary of *Indian Airlines*, *Jet Airways (9W)* and *Air Sahara (S2)* (website: www.airsahara.net).

Special fares: There are various special *Indian Airlines* fares available to foreign nationals and Indian nationals residing abroad. All are available throughout the year, and may be purchased either abroad or in India, where payment is made in a foreign convertible currency (such as US Dollars or Pounds Sterling). With the exception of the Youth Fare India (see below), discounts of 90 per cent are available for children under two years of age, and of 50 per cent for children aged two to 12. Full details of all the special fares are contained in the *India* brochure, available from Incredible India. A summary of each is given below. Group discounts of up to 30 per cent are also available.

Discover India: There are three types of ticket available; a 21-day ticket costs US$850, a 15-day ticket costs US$600 and a 7-day ticket costs US$400. These offer unlimited economy-class travel on all domestic *Indian Airlines* services. No stop may be visited more than once, except for transfer.

Youth Fare India: This is valid for three months, offering a 25 per cent discount on the normal US Dollar fare. It is available to those aged 12 to 30 at the commencement of travel for journeys on economy/executive class of domestic air services and Indo-Nepal services.

India Wonder Fares (North, South, East and West): Cost US$320 and are valid for seven days, offering unlimited economy-class travel within the north, south, east or western regions of India. No town may be visited more than once, except for transfer. Details of the main air centres included in the deal can be obtained from *Indian Airlines* offices.

Departure tax: £8.

SEA/RIVER:

There are ships from Kolkata (Calcutta) and Chennai to Port Blair in the Andaman Islands, and from Kochi and Calicut to the Lakshadweep Islands. Services are often seasonal, and are generally suspended during the monsoon. There is a catamaran service from Mumbai to Goa. One particularly attractive boat journey is the 'backwaters' excursion in the vicinity of Kochi in Kerala. Several local tours are available.

RAIL:

The Indian internal railway system is state-run by *Indian Railways* (website: www.indianrail.gov.in). It is the largest rail system in Asia and the second-largest in the world. There are over 62,000km of track, over 7030 stations and over 11,200 locomotives, including many steam engines. Its trains carry over 12 million passengers every day. The network covers much of the country and is a quintessential part of the fabric of India, as well as being relatively inexpensive. Express services link all the main cities and local services link most other parts of the country. Buses connect with trains to serve parts of the country not on the rail network. Children five to 11 years old pay half price, children under five travel free. There are six classes of travel: first-class air conditioned, first-class sleeper, second-class air conditioned, second-class sleeper, third-class air conditioned and air conditioned chair car. Major trains carry restaurant cars.

Indrail Pass: This special pass consists of a single non-transferable ticket which enables a visitor to travel on any train without restriction within the period of validity. First-class sleeper tickets are: US$135 for seven days; US$185 for 15 days; US$198 for 21 days; US$248 for 30 days; US$400 for 60 days and US$530 for 90 days. A/C tickets are twice as much and second-class tickets are much cheaper. Children under five travel free; children aged five to 12 are entitled to half-price fares. It is sold only to foreign nationals and Indians residing abroad holding a valid passport, and replaces all other concessional tickets. Payment is accepted only in foreign currency (US Dollars or Pounds Sterling). Refunds can be given only if cancellation is made before the starting date. Validity period is from the date of commencement of the first journey up to midnight of the date on which validity expires. A ticket can be used within one year of its issue. Advance reservation is essential, particularly on overnight journeys, arranged through travel agents. Reservations are on a first-come, first-served basis. Indrail passes can be reserved in the UK from *SD Enterprises Ltd* (tel: (020) 8903 3411; website: www.indiarail.co.uk). The passes can also be purchased in India at all the main railway stations and authorised agents.

Special trains: The **Palace on Wheels** is an expensively decorated Edwardian-style luxury steam train with 14 coaches, which travels to Rajasthan. Each coach consists of a saloon, four sleeping compartments with upper and lower berth, bathroom, shower, toilet and small kitchen. Room service is available. There is a dining car, a bar, a lounge area, an observation car and a fully-equipped first aid centre. Modern amenities include air conditioning, four-channel music and telephone intercom throughout the train. Tariff includes cost of travel; full catering; elephant, camel and boat rides; conducted sightseeing tours; and entrance fees. *Itinerary:* Delhi-Jaipur-Jaisalmer-Jodhpur-Ranthambae-Chittaurgarh-Udaipur-Bharatpur-Agra-Delhi. *Bookings:* Several tour operators/travel agents organise escorted tour facilities which include the Palace on Wheels. **Royal Orient**

Credit: © Bruce Logan

Express: This luxury train journeys through Gujarat and Rajasthan taking in the sights of Chittargarh, Udaipur, Palitana, Ahmedabad and Jaipur. The trip takes eight days and accommodation is in furnished carriages with lounge, minibar and kitchenette. Multi-cuisine restaurants and a library are also available. Contact *Indian Railways* for further information. The **Fairy Queen** is the oldest steam engine in the world. The journey is a 2-day round trip from Delhi to Alwar. Guests are taken to Sariska Tiger Reserve for a jeep safari and stay overnight in a hotel. The **Darjeeling Himalayan Railway** operates from Newjalpoiguri to Darjeeling. It climbs 500ft/152.5m. The service is subject to the local weather. **Hill Trains:** Narrow-gauge rail lines completed in the 19th century linking numerous hill stations and various mountain landscapes. For example, the Kolkata (Calcutta)-Darjeeling route takes eight hours, crosses over 500 bridges and offers ample opportunity for photos as the pace is leisurely.
Other trains: The **Rajdhani Express** trains are deluxe super-fast trains connecting Delhi with Mumbai, Kolkata (Calcutta), Chennai, Bangalore, Bhubhaneswar, Guwahati, Jammu Tawi, Secunderabad, Thiruvananthapuram, Ahmedabad, Ajmer and many others. **Shatabdi Express:** Super-fast trains connecting major and secondary city centres. Visitors can travel chair-car or executive class. Snacks and meals are provided. **Konkan Express:** This route (Mumbai-Goa-Mangalore) includes 72 tunnels and many bridges often crossing ravines of over 50m deep.

ROAD:

Traffic drives on the left. An extensive network of **bus** services connects all parts of the country, and is particularly useful for the mountainous regions where there are no rail services. However, public transport is often crowded and can be uncomfortable. Details of routes may be obtained from the local tourist office. Outside the major cities main roads and other routes are poorly maintained and congested with poor visibility and inadequate warning markers. **Tourist cars:** There are a large number of chauffeur-driven tourist cars (some air conditioned) available in the main tourist centres. These unmetered tourist cars run at a slightly higher rate than the ordinary taxis, and are approved by Incredible India. Travellers should ask drivers to maintain a safe speed and wear a seat belt where available. Self-drive cars are not generally available. Driving around India is not recommended due to the erratic nature of Indian driving standards. **Documentation:** An International Driving Permit is required. A green card is required if importing your own car into India.

URBAN:

Taxis and **auto rickshaws** are available in large cities and fares should be charged by the kilometre. They do not always have meters but, where they do, visitors should insist on the meter being flagged in their presence. Fares change from time to time and therefore do not always conform to the reading on the meter, but drivers should always have a copy of the latest fare chart available for inspection. Kolkata (Calcutta) has a 16.45km (10 mile) underground railway.
Travel times: The following chart gives approximate travel times (in hours and minutes) from **Delhi** to other major cities/towns in India.

	Air	Road	Rail	Sea
Mumbai	1.50	28.00	17.30a	-
Kolkata	2.00	30.00	18.00b	-
Chennai	3.00	45.00	32.00	-
Port Blair	5.05	c	-	d

Note: a. Time by express (not daily); normal train takes 23 hours. **b.** Time by express (not daily); normal train takes 25 hours. **c.** Does not include stopover in Chennai. **d.** Boat journey from Chennai takes three to four days.
Note: Further information (including route maps, times of express trains and more detailed travel-time charts) may be found in the official India brochure, available free from Incredible India (see *Top Things To Do*).

Travel Advice

Travellers are advised against all travel to or through rural areas of Jammu and Kashmir (other than Ladakh) and all but essential travel by air to Srinagar. There is a high level of conflict and terrorist violence in Jammu and Kashmir (excluding Ladakh). Jammu City is somewhat safer but attacks still occur.
On 8 October 2005, a large earthquake hit north west India, northern Pakistan and Afghanistan, with the epicentre near Muzaffarabad (Pakistani-administered Kashmir). The earthquake has caused widespread damage and extensive disruption to transport services in the region. The main area hit in Indian-administered Kashmir is Uri (particularly around the town of Kupwara).
On 26 December 2004 a massive earthquake registering 9.0 on the Richter scale struck off the west coast of Indonesia. The quake created a tsunami – a series of huge waves that spread destruction across many parts of Asia and reached as far as the east coast of Africa. The coastal areas of Tamil Nadu and Andhara Pradesh in Southern India have been badly affected. Floodwaters washed over some of the Andaman and Nicobar Islands contaminating fresh water sources and ruining large areas of arable land. Travel elsewhere in India is unaffected. Those wishing to travel to affected areas should check with the relevant tour operator, tourist board or embassy for the latest advice prior to travel.
Travellers are advised against all but essential travel to Imphal (by air) and against all travel in the rest of Manipur and Tripura. Kidnapping, banditry and insurgency are rife throughout the north-eastern region. There have also been occasional skirmishes on the India/Bangladesh border.
On 7 March 2006, there were three bomb explosions in Varanasi, Uttar Pradesh. There have also been terrorist attacks in other parts of India, including major cities of Delhi and Mumbai. Indian security has been raised in Delhi and other major cities. you should be vigilant in all parts of India.
Penalties for trafficking, dealing and using illegal drugs are severe.
This advice is based on information provided by the Foreign and Commonwealth Office in the UK. It is correct at time of publishing. As the situation can change rapidly, visitors are advised to contact the following organisations for the latest travel advice:

British Foreign and Commonwealth Office
Tel: (0845) 850 2829.
Website: www.fco.gov.uk

US Department of State
Website: http://travel.state.gov/travel

Accommodation

HOTELS:

Modern Western-style hotels are available in all large cities and at popular tourist centres. Usually they offer a choice of first-class Western and Indian cuisine. The well-known Taj Group offers accommodation in either eight grand luxe hotels or in its many superb business hotels. Several beach resorts, so-called palace hotels, garden retreats and hotels in areas of cultural significance are also part of the international group. Hotel charges in India are moderate compared to those in many other countries. Hotel bills may be subject to a 10 per cent expenditure tax, 7 to 15 per cent luxury tax and a variable service charge. Hotels range from old palace buildings that have been converted into **Heritage Hotels**, **5-star deluxe**, **5-** and **4-star** hotels, which are fully air conditioned with all luxury features, **3-star** hotels, which are functional and have air conditioned rooms, to **2-** and **1-star** hotels, which offer basic amenities.
TOURIST BUNGALOWS: There are tourist bungalows (known as holiday homes in Maharashtra and Gujarat, and tourist lodges in West Bengal) at almost every tourist centre in the country, under the control of the respective State Government Tourist Development Corporation, except in the metropolitan cities of Delhi, Kolkata (Calcutta), Chennai, Mumbai (Bombay) and Bangalore. These include a clean single, double and family room, most with a bath and general canteen. At holiday homes and certain tourist cottages there are kitchen facilities. Bookings should be made (a deposit will be required) with the managing director of the respective corporation, or with the manager of the bungalow.

CAMPSITES:

These are to be found throughout India. Full addresses may be obtained from Incredible India (see *Top Things To Do* below).

YOUTH HOSTELS:

These provide a convenient and cheap base for organised tours, trekking, hiking or mountaineering. The Department of Tourism has set up several hostels, spread throughout every region, ideally placed for exploring both the plains and the hill stations. Each has a capacity for about 40 beds or more, segregated roughly half and half into male and female dormitories. Beds with mattresses, bedsheets, blankets, wardrobe with locks, electric light points, member kitchen utensils and parking areas are available at each hostel.

ACCOMMODATION INFORMATION

Youth Hostels Association of India
5 Nyaya Marg, Chanakyapuri, New Delhi 110 021, India
Tel: (11) 2611 0250.
Website: www.yhai.org

Federation of Hotel and Restaurant Associations of India
B-82, 8th Floor, Himalaya House, 23 Kasturba Gandhi Marg, Connaught Place, New Delhi 110001, India
Tel: (11) 2331 8781/2 *or* 2332 2634/47 *or* 3770.
Website: www.fhrai.com
Contact for a full list of Government-approved hotels and palace hotels.

Top Things To See

- **Delhi** has two parts: **New Delhi**, India's capital and the seat of Government, is a modern city, offering wide tree-lined boulevards, spacious parks and the distinctive style of Lutyens' architectural design; **'Old' Delhi**, on the other hand, is a city several centuries old, teeming with narrow winding streets, temples, mosques and bazaars. Must sees include the **Red Fort** and the nearby **Jama Masjid** (India's largest mosque) both built in the mid-17th century at the height of the Moghul Empire. Also of note is the **Qutab Minar's** soaring tower built in 1200AD by Qutab-ud-din immediately after the defeat of Delhi's last Hindu kingdom. At the base of the tower is the **Quwwat-ul-Islam Mosque**, built in the same period using stone from demolished Hindu temples.
- Gaze at the sacred **River Ganges**. Built along its bank is the wondrous city of **Varanasi**, India's holiest Hindu location. The town itself is a maze of winding streets, dotted with temples and shrines. Lining the river are a series of *ghats* which, at dawn, are thronged with pilgrims and holy men performing ritual ablutions and prayers. Set high in the **Garhwal Himalayas**, **Garhwal** (sometimes referred to as the Uttarakhand) is the source of this life-giving 'Ganga' and abounds in myths and legends of the Indian gods. Indeed, many of the great rivers of northern India have their headwaters in this land of lush valleys and towering snow-ridged peaks.
- Discover a host of historical gems – **Delhi**, for instance, lies at the apex of the **'Golden Triangle'**, an area filled with ancient sites and monuments. In the southeast lies **Agra**, city of the fabled **Taj Mahal**, one of the seven wonders of the world. This magnificent mausoleum was built by Shah Jahan as a monument to his love for his wife, Mumtaz, who died in childbirth in 1631. Shah Jehan was later imprisoned by his own son in the nearby **Red Fort**, another major attraction whose massive red sandstone walls rise over 65 feet and measure 1.5 miles in circumference. Other important landmarks are **Akbar's Palace**, the **Jahangir Mahal**, the octagonal tower **Mussumman Burj** and the **Pearl Mosque**. The southwestern pivot of the triangle is **Jaipur**, gateway to the desert state of **Rajasthan**. Known as the 'Pink City' because of the distinctive colour of its buildings painted in preparation for the visit of Prince Albert, Consort of Queen Victoria, in 1883, Jaipur is a town of broad, open avenues and many palaces. The **Amber Palace**, just outside the city is spectacular and the facade of the **Palace of the Winds** within the city walls is an essential photo stop. To the south of the 'Golden Triangle' is the huge state of **Madhya Pradesh**. Its greatest attractions lie close to the northern frontier. Less than 160km (100 miles) from Agra is the great ruined fortress at **Gwalior**. To the east lies **Khajuraho** with its famous temples and friezes of sensuously depicted figures – a must for any visitor. The State of **Karnataka** has a number of important religious and historical sites, including the ruins at **Hampi** to the north of Bangalore, and the vast statue of Lord Bahubali at **Sravanabelagola**, north of **Mysore**.
- Visit the most romantic city in Rajasthan, **Udaipur**, built around the lovely **Lake Pichola** and famed for its **Lake Palace Hotel**, and dubbed the 'Venice of the East'.
- The **Hill Stations** of India are an enchanting must-see. They have long been popular among Indians and foreign

visitors alike for providing a relaxing and salubrious retreat from the heat of the plains. Less than 320km (200 miles) to the north of Delhi is **Shimla**, the greatest of all hill stations, surrounded by finely scented pine forests and the rich beauty of the **Kullu Valley**. Southeast of Mumbai are several fine hill stations, notably **Matheran** with its narrow gauge trains, and Mahabaleshwar. **Mahabaleshwar** is in the north of the range of the **Western Ghats**, running parallel to the west coast of India from the **River Tapti** to the southernmost tip of the subcontinent. The mountains are lush and thickly forested.

- The **temples** of **Rambireshwar** and **Raghunath** in **Kashmir** number among its most impressive sights. **Jammu** is the railhead for **Srinagar**, the ancient capital of Kashmir, and favourite resort of the Mughal emperors. It was they who built the many waterways and gardens around **Lake Dal**, complementing the natural beauty of the area. Among the attractions are the houseboats where visitors can live on the lakes surrounded by scenery so beautiful it is known as 'paradise on earth'. Kashmir is an extravagantly beautiful land of flower-spangled meadows, wild orchards, spectacular coniferous forests, icy mountain peaks and clear streams and rivers.
- Escape any Indian stereotypes by entering the principal metropolis of Western India, **Mumbai**: the capital of the state of **Maharashtra**, a bustling port and the commercial centre of India, with plate-glass skyscrapers and modern industry that jostles alongside bazaars and a hectic streetlife. Many of the country's films are made in the famous Mumbai studios. Welcome to 'Bollywood'.
- Enjoy the sights and sounds of India's **beaches**. Mumbai has a pleasant seafront with a palm-lined promenade and attractive beaches such as **Juhu**, **Versova**, **Marve**, **Madh** and **Manori**. **Goa**'s 100km- (60 mile-) long coastline offers some of the finest beaches in the subcontinent. Goa was Portuguese until 1961, and there is also a charming blend of Latin and Indian cultures. Goa's infamous hippies are being replaced by backpackers, Indian visitors and package tourists. If you are looking for beautiful, quiet beaches head for the South between **Benaulim** and **Palolem**. Accommodation in the region includes the luxury resort of **Aguada**, the Taj holiday village and the Aguada hermitage. There are also good, simple hotels and cottages for rent in villages along the coastline, notably **Calangute**, **Baga** and **Colva**. **Marina Beach** in **Chennai** is the second-largest beach in the world. The state of **Kerala** is where many of India's major coastal resorts are to be found. Among the finest is **Kovalam**, offering unspoilt beaches with increasingly modern amenities. Further to the north is the state of Karnataka, which has fine, unexplored beaches at **Karwar**, **Mahe** and **Udupi**.
- Observe some outstanding rock-cut temples, such as the Buddhist cave temples at **Ajanta**, which date back at least 2000 years. Cut into the steep face of a deep rock gorge, the 30 caves contain exquisite paintings depicting daily life at that time. The caves at **Ellora** depict religious stories and are Hindu, Buddhist and Jain in origin.
- The regional capital is **Chennai** (formerly Madras), India's fourth-largest city and capital of the state of **Tamil Nadu**. Chennai is the cradle of the ancient Dravidian civilisation, one of the oldest articulate cultures in the world. It is also home of the classical style of Indian dancing and a notable centre of temple sculpture art. Sprawling over 130 sq km (50 sq miles), the metropolis has few tall buildings and enjoys the relaxed ambience of a market town rather than the bustle of a huge city. From **Chennai Lighthouse** there is a fine view of the city that includes many churches which tell of the city's strong Christian influence, first introduced in AD 78 when the apostle St Thomas was martyred here.
- Witness the remnants of colonial heritage, most prevalent in the largest city in India and hub of the east, **Kolkata**, the capital of **West Bengal**. Established as a British trading post in the 17th century, it grew rapidly into a vibrant centre. Its colonial heritage is reflected in the buildings of **Chowringhee Street** and **Clive Street**, now **Jawaharlal Nehru Road** and **Netaji Subhash Road**. The city is filled with life and energy. It is a major business centre and offers fine markets and bazaars. It is also the centre of much of the country's creative and intellectual activity, including the subcontinent's best film-makers. **Central Kolkata** (**Calcutta**) is best viewed from the **Maidan**, the central area of parkland where early morning yoga sessions take place. The city's **Indian Museum** is one of the finest in Asia.
- If you want temples, in the state of **Orissa** are three **temple cities**. Foremost is **Bhubaneswar**, a town in which there once stood no less than 7000 temples, 500 of which have survived. Largest of these is the great **Lingaraja Temple**, dedicated to Lord Shiva. A short journey away to the south of **Bhubaneswar** lies **Puri**, one of the four holiest cities in India, now being developed as a beach resort. In June and July, Puri stages one of India's most spectacular festivals, the **Rath Yatra** or **'Car Festival'**, at which pilgrims pay homage to images of gods drawn on massive wooden chariots. A short distance along the coast to the north is **Konarak**, known for its **'Black Pagoda'** – a huge solitary temple to the sun god in the form of a chariot drawn by horses. The sculpture has a sensuous nature similar to that of Khajuraho, and is counted amongst the finest in India.
- The Indian peninsula is a continent in itself, the geographical diversity of which has resulted in a vast range of wildlife, with over 350 species of mammals and 1200 species of birds in the country. There are over 70 national parks, 400 **wildlife** sanctuaries (including **bird sanctuaries**) and 24 tiger reserves in the country. Two of India's most impressive animals, the Bengal (or Indian) tiger and the Asiatic elephant are still found in most regions, though their population has shrunk drastically. In **Kaziranga**, it is possible to see the one-horned rhinoceros of India. **Dachigam Wildlife Sanctuary** (Kashmir) is a broad valley with a variety of vegetation, including rare hangul deer, jackal, leopard, himalayan weasel and wild boar. **Govind National Park** (Himachal Pradesh) has snowclad peaks and glaciers, which contain snow leopard, brown and black bear and musk deer. **Corbett National Park** (Uttar Ranchal) is in the Himalayan foothills and is home to tiger, elephant, sloth bear and rich birdlife. **Dudhwa National Park** (Uttar Pradesh) on the Nepal border withholds tiger, sloth bear, rhino and rich birdlife. **Sariska Wildlife Sanctuary** (Rajasthan) contains sambhar (largest Indian deer), chital (spotted deer), nilgai (Indian antelope), black buck, leopard and tiger. **Ranthambhor** (Sawai Madhopur – Rajasthan) has hill forest, plains and lakes, privy to sambar, chinkara (Indian gazelle), tiger, sloth bear, crocodiles and migratory water-birds. **Bharatpur National Park** (Keoloadeo Ghana Bird Sanctuary) (Rajasthan) is India's most outstanding bird sanctuary; many indigenous water-birds; huge migration from Siberia and China; crane, goose, stork, heron, snakes, etc. **Bandhavgarh National Park** (Madhya Pradesh) has a wide variety of wildlife, including panther, sambar and gaur. **Kanha National Park** (Madhya Pradesh) is filled with sal forest and grassland; home of barasingha (swamp deer), tiger, cheetal and gaur. **Shivpuri National Park** (Madhya Pradesh) contains chinkara, chowsingha (four-horned antelope), nilgai, tiger, leopard and water-birds. In the enclosures of **Tadoba National Park** (Maharashtra) are tiger, leopard wild boar and gaur. **Gir National Park** (Gujarat) is the home of Asiatic lion, sambar, chowsingha, nilgai, leopard, chinkara and wild boar. The best viewings are at dawn and dusk. **Periyar Wildlife Sanctuary** (Kerala) has a large artificial lake, and elephant, monkey, gaur, wild dog, black langur, otters, tortoises and rich birdlife. **Vedanthangal Water Birds Sanctuary** (Tamil Nadu) is one of the most spectacular breeding grounds in India. Cormorant, heron, stork, pelican, grebe and many others can be found here. **Dandeli National Park** (Karnataka) is a park with bison, panther, tiger, sloth bear and sambar, and is easily accessible from Goa. **Wayanad** (Kerala) is extensively mixed forest and contains the largest elephant population in India, with leopard, gaur, sambar, muntjac and giant squirrel. Birds include racquet-tailed drongo, trogon and barbet. **Kaziranga National Park** (Assam) contains elephant grass and swamps, one-horned Indian rhinoceros, water buffalo, tiger, leopard, elephant, deer and rich birdlife. **Sundarban National Park** (West Bengal) is home to tiger, fishing cat, deer, crocodile, dolphin and rich birdlife. **Jaldapara Wildlife Sanctuary** (West Bengal) is tropical forest and grassland with rhino, elephant and rich birdlife. This list of sanctuaries and national parks are only a fraction of the wildlife-viewing opportunities available in India.
- **Ranikhet**, with a magnificent view of the central Himalayas, is the base for treks to **Kausani**. The view from here is one of the most spectacular in India, and inspired Mahatma Gandhi to pen his commentary on the Gita-Anashakti Yoga.
- The **Aravallis** are remnants of the oldest mountain range in the subcontinent, and resemble outcroppings of rocks rather than mountains, virtually barren except for thorny acacias and date palm groves found near the oases. The main resort in the region, **Mount Abu**, stands on an isolated plateau surrounded by rich green forest. A variety of one-day treks are available from here, all of which afford the opportunity to visit some of the remarkable temples in the region, notably **Arbuda Devi Temple**.

Credit: © Bruce Logan

Top Things To Do

- Listen to some of the celebrated sounds of Indian **music**, such as the *sitar*, *sarod* and the subtle rhythm of the *tabla*. Cities like **Delhi** are full of such sounds and are also host to an enthralling variety of **dance forms**, each with its own costumes and elaborate language of gestures.
- Watch some of the exciting camel fairs and treks in India's desert. Near **Ajmer** is the small lakeside town of **Pushkar**, a site of religious importance for Hindus and host every November to the fascinating **Camel Fair**. Stumble into the **Rajasthan desert** and you will discover **Jaisalmer**, a charming oasis town, once a resting place on the old caravan route to Persia which boasts among its attractions the camel treks out into the surrounding desert, and the **Desert Festival** held in January/February each year with **camel racing** and a 'Mr Desert' contest.
- Play **golf** on the highest golf course in the world, at **Gulmarg**. From here there are good views of **Nanga Parbat**, one of the highest mountains in the world.
- Although smaller and less authentic than in the heady days of the 1960s, there are still some fabulous **full moon parties** to go to in **Anjuna** in Goa.
- Whilst in **Goa**, attend the spectacular **Carnival**, held on the three days leading up to Ash Wednesday. This colourful festival is jam-packed with bustling fun, as crowds throng to watch the lavish floats pass by, and dance to music that continually rents the air.
- **Snorkel** in the the **Andaman Islands**, in the **Bay of Bengal**, a lushly forested archipelago that has exotic plant life and a wide variety of corals and tropical fish.
- Take one of the great railway journeys of the world, to the north of Kolkata (Calcutta) - the **'Toy Train'** to **Darjeeling**. The last part of the line runs through jungle, tea gardens and pine forests. Darjeeling straddles a mountain slope which drops steeply to the valley below, and commands fine views of **Kanchenjunga** (8586m/28,169ft), the third-highest mountain in the world. It is the headquarters of the Indian Mountaineering Institute, as well as the birthplace of Sherpa Tenzing. It is also a world-renowned tea-growing centre.
- Since India has a profusion of mountains, why not try some **mountaineering**, or **trekking** for the cautious? Trekking is the main activity for visitors in the mountain state of **Sikkim**. Trekking is allowed only in groups, while individuals may only visit **Gangtok**, **Rumtek** and **Phodom**. Treks from **Manali** include the **Bhaga River** to **Keylong**, and then on to the **Bara Shigri** glacier or over the **Baralacha Pass** to **Leh**. **Kullu**, in the centre of the province, is set in a narrow valley between the towering Himalayas and the **River Beas**, and is famous for its temples and religious festivals. Treks from here traverse terraced paddy fields and on to remoter regions of snow and ice. The view from the **Rohtang Pass** is particularly spectacular. The town of **Dharamsala**, in the **Kangra Valley** area, is the base for treks into the **Bharmaur Valley** over the **Indrahar Pass**, and on to other still higher passes beyond. **Chamba**, situated on a mountain above the **Ravi River**, is named after the fragrant trees which flourish around its richly carved temples. Treks from the nearby town of **Dalhousie** lead to the glacial lake of **Khajjiar** and to the passes of **Sach** and **Chini**. **Shimla**, once the summer capital of the British, is a high hill station and the base for treks into **Kullu Valley** via the **Jalori Pass** and on to the **Kalpur** and **Kinnaur valleys**. The region of **Kumaon** stretches from the Himalayas in the north to the green foothills of **Terai** and **Bhabar** in the south, and consists of the three northeastern Himalayan districts of **Uttar Pradesh**, all of which are particularly rich in wildlife. One of the major trekking centres is **Almora**, an ideal base for treks into pine and rhododendron forests with dramatic views of stark, snow-

capped mountains. The **Pindiri Glacier** and the valley of **Someshwar** can be reached from here. Another base is **Nanital**, a charming, orchard-rich hill station. It is the base for short treks to **Bhimtal**, **Khurpatal** and **Binayak Forest**. The town of **Darjeeling** is the home of the Everest-climber Tenzing Norgay and also of the Himalayan Mountaineering Institute, and is the base for both low- and high-level treks. Destinations include **Tiger Hill** (offering a breathtaking view of the Himalayas), and the peaks of **Phalut**, **Sandakphu**, **Singalila** and **Tanglu**. Other popular bases and trekking destinations include **Lonavala**, **Khandala**, **Matheran** and **Bhor Ghat**, a picturesque region of waterfalls, lakes and woods. Further south in Karnataka is **Coorg**, perched on a green hilltop and surrounded by mountainous countryside. **Madikeri** is a take-off point for treks in this region. The **Upper Palani** hills in **Tamil Nadu** are an offshoot of the Ghats, covered in rolling downs and coarse grass. **Kodaikanal** is the attractive base for two short treks to **Pilar Rock** and **Green Valley View**.

TOURIST INFORMATION

Incredible India in the UK
7 Cork Street, London W1S 3LH, UK
Tel: (020) 7437 3677 *or* (0870) 010 2183 (brochure request line).
Website: www.incredibleindia.org

Incredible India in the USA
Suite 1808, 1270 Avenue of the Americas, New York, NY 10020-1700, USA
Tel: (212) 586 4901.
Website: www.incredibleindia.org
Office also in: Los Angeles.

Entertainment

FOOD & DRINK: The unforgettable aroma of India is not just the heavy scent of jasmine and roses on the warm air. It is also the fragrance of spices so important to Indian cooking – especially to preparing curry. The word 'curry' is an English derivative of *kari*, meaning spice sauce, but curry does not, in India, come as a powder. It is the subtle and delicate blending of spices such as turmeric, cardamom, ginger, coriander, nutmeg and poppy seed. Like an artist's palette of oil paints, the Indian cook has some 25 spices (freshly ground as required) with which to mix the recognised combinations or *masalas*. Many of these spices are also noted for their medicinal properties and, like the basic ingredients, vary from region to region. Although not all Hindus are vegetarians, vegetable dishes are more common than in Europe, particularly in southern India. Broadly speaking, meat dishes are more common in the north.

Things to know: Bottled water, essential for visitors, is sold everywhere in India, but make sure the bottles are properly sealed. Restaurants have table service and, depending on area and establishment, will serve alcohol with meals. Most Western-style hotels have licensed bars. Visitors will be issued All India Liquor Permits on request by Indian Embassies/High Commissions, Missions or Tourist Offices. Various states impose prohibition but this may change; check with the Tourist Office for up-to-date information. In almost all big cities in India, certain days in the week are observed as dry days when the sale of liquor is not permitted. Tourists may check with the nearest local tourist office for the prohibition laws/rules prevailing in any given state where they happen to be travelling or intend to travel.

National specialities:

- *Dal* (crushed lentil soup with various additional vegetables).
- *Dahi* (the curd or yoghurt which accompanies the curry).
- *Kulfi* (Indian ice cream).
- *Rasgullas* (cream cheese balls flavoured with rose water).
- *Gulab Jamuns* (flour, yoghurt and ground almonds).
- *Jalebi* (pancakes in syrup).
- Fruit – mango, pomegranate, melon, apricot, apple and strawberry.
- *Pan* (betel leaf in which are wrapped spices such as aniseed and cardamom; it is common to finish the meal by chewing *Pan* as a digestive).

Regional specialities:

North:

- *Rogan josh* (curried lamb).
- *Gushtaba* (spicy meat balls in yoghurt).
- *Biryani* (chicken or lamb in orange-flavoured rice, sprinkled with sugar and rose water).
- *Tandoori* cooking (chicken, meat or fish marinated in herbs and baked in a clay oven).
- Kebab.
- Flat breads, such as *pooris*, *chapatis* and *naan*.

South:

- *Bhujia* (vegetable curry).
- *Dosa*, *idli* and *samba* (rice pancakes, dumplings with pickles, and vegetable and lentil curry).
- *Raitas* (yoghurt with grated cucumber and mint).
- Coconut is a major ingredient of southern Indian cooking.

West coast:

- *Mumbai duck* (curried or fried bombloe fish).
- *Pomfret* (Indian salmon).
- *Parsi dhan sak* (lamb or chicken cooked with curried lentils).
- *Vindaloo*.

Bengali:

- *Dahi maach* (curried fish in yoghurt flavoured with turmeric and ginger).
- *Malai* (curried prawn with coconut).

National drinks:

- *Chai* (tea) is India's favourite drink. It will often come ready-brewed with milk and sugar unless 'tray tea' is specified.
- Coffee is increasingly popular.
- *Nimbu Pani* (lemon drink).
- *Lassi* (iced buttermilk).
- Coconut milk straight from the nut is cool and refreshing.
- Indian beer (in many varieties).
- Indian-made gin, rum, brandy and wine.

Tipping: Taxis and restaurants do not expect to be tipped, however, hotel and airport porters should be tipped around INR20, and guides and drivers INR100 per day where service is not included (equalling roughly 10 per cent where appropriate).

NIGHTLIFE: India has generally little nightlife as the term is understood in the West, although in major cities a few Western-style shows, clubs and discos are being developed. In most places the main attraction will be cultural shows featuring performances of Indian dance and music. The Indian film industry is the largest in the world, now producing three times as many full-length feature films as the USA. Mumbai (Bombay) and Kolkata (Calcutta) are the country's two 'Hollywoods'. Almost every large town will have a cinema, some of which will show films in English. Music and dancing are an important part of Indian cinema, combining with many other influences to produce a rich variety of film art. Larger cities may have theatres staging productions of English-language plays.

SHOPPING: Indian crafts have been perfected over the centuries, from traditions and techniques passed on from generation to generation. Each region has its own specialities, each town its own local craftspeople and its own particular skills. Silks, spices, jewellery and many other Indian products have long been acclaimed and are widely sought after; merchants would travel thousands of miles, enduring the hardships and privations of the long journey, in order to make their purchases. Nowadays, the marketplaces of the subcontinent are only eight hours away, and for fabrics, silverware, carpets, leatherwork and antiques, India is a shopper's paradise. Bargaining is expected, and the visitor can check for reasonable prices at state-run emporia. **Fabrics:** One of India's main industries is textiles; its silks, cottons, and wools rank amongst the best in the world. Of the *silks*, the brocades from Varanasi are among the most famous; other major centres include Kanchipuram, Murshidabad, Patna and Surat. Rajasthan cotton with its distinctive 'tie and dye' design is usually brilliantly colourful, while Chennai cotton is known for its attractive 'bleeding' effect after a few washes. Throughout the country may be found the *himroo* cloth, a mixture of silk and cotton, often decorated with patterns. Kashmir sells beautiful *woollens*, particularly shawls. **Carpets:** India has one of the world's largest carpet industries, and many examples of this ancient and beautiful craft can be seen in museums throughout the world. Each region will have its own speciality, such as the distinctive, brightly coloured Tibetan rugs, available mainly in Darjeeling. **Clothes:** Clothes are cheap, and can be quickly tailor-made in some shops. Cloth includes silks, cottons, *himroos*, brocades, chiffons and *chingnons*. **Jewellery:** This is traditionally heavy and elaborate. Indian silverwork is world-famous. Gems include diamonds, lapis lazuli, Indian star rubies, star sapphires, moonstones and aquamarines. Hyderabad is a leading pearl centre. **Handicrafts and leatherwork:** Each area has its speciality; the range includes bronzes, brasswork (often inlaid with silver), canework and pottery. Woven rugs and *papier mâché* (some decorated in gold leaf) are a characteristic Kashmir product. Inlaid marble and alabaster are specialities of Agra. Rajasthan is known for its colourful fabrics and silks. Leatherwork includes open Indian sandals and slippers. **Woodwork:** Sandalwood carvings from Karnataka, rosewood from Kerala and Chennai. **Other goods:** Pickles, spices, Indian tea, perfumes, soap, handmade paper, Orissan playing cards and musical instruments. **Shopping hours:** Mon-Sat 0930-1700 in most large stores.

Note: There is a veto on the export of antiques, art objects over 100 years old, animal skins and objects made from skins.

Business

- **GDP:** US$759 billion (2005 estimate).
- **Main exports:** Textiles, gems & jewellery, engineering goods, chemicals and leather manufactures.
- **Main imports:** Crude oil, machinery, gems, fertiliser and chemicals.
- **Main trade partners:** Belgium, China (PR), Hong Kong (SAR), Japan, Russian Federation, Switzerland, United Arab Emirates, the UK and the USA.

ECONOMY: India's industrial economy, which has invested much in advanced technology initiatives such as digital communications and space research, contrasts with the poverty that persists, particularly in rural areas. The country ranks among the top dozen in the world by gross national product. Roughly two-thirds of the population are involved in agriculture, both subsistence – mainly cereals – and cash crops including tea, rubber, coffee, cotton, jute, sugar, oil seeds and tobacco. Growth in this sector has been steady despite frequent damage through drought and flooding. India's energy requirements are met by oil, most of which is imported despite the growth of indigenous production, and hydroelectric schemes, mostly based amid the powerful northern rivers. Mining is a relatively small sector, but does produce iron ore and cut diamonds for export. India's main industrial development has been in engineering, especially transport equipment (a major export earner), iron and steel, chemicals, electronics and textiles. Economic reforms were put into effect throughout the 1990s, under which trade has been liberalised, the sprawling public sector cut back, and state-owned industries sold off. The plan was approved with the IMF, which supplied substantial credits to the Indian treasury. After the hiatus following the 1997 Asian financial crisis, the economy has resumed its healthy growth rate, currently just under 7 per cent per annum, while inflation is just 4 per cent. Indian colleges and universities are turning out large numbers of graduates with advanced technology skills who are now the target of employers in Europe and North America (where there is a shortage of qualified IT workers): the Indian economy is as yet not sufficiently developed to absorb this resource. Further reforms, especially improvements to the national infrastructure and basic services, are now seen as the priority for central and regional governments. Foreign direct investment has reached an all-time peak of over US$4 billion annually and is set to continue rising.

BUSINESS ETIQUETTE: English is widely used in commercial circles, so there is little need for interpreter and translation services. Business cards are usually exchanged and should be presented with both hands. When introduced to someone, wait to see if your host greets you with a *Namaste*, the traditional Indian greeting in which hands are clasped as if in prayer in front of the chest accompanied by a little bow, or offers the hand. When eating, visitors should wait to see if their host uses fingers or cutlery, and follow suit (it is essential that only the right hand is used for eating). All weights and measures should be expressed in metric terms. Indian businesspeople welcome visitors and are very hospitable. Entertaining usually takes place in private clubs. The best months for business visits are October to March, and accommodation should be booked in advance.

Office hours: Mon-Fri 0930-1700, Sat 0930-1300.

CONFERENCES/CONVENTIONS: The main congress and exhibition centres in the country are Agra, Bangalore, Bhubeneswar, Chennai, Delhi, Hyderabad, Jaipur, Kolkata (Calcutta), Mumbai, Panaji, Udaipur and Varanasi. In addition, top-class hotels and auditoria with convention and conference facilities are found throughout the country. *Air India*, *Indian Airlines* and leading hoteliers and travel agents are members of the International Congress and Conference Association (ICCA) and together they provide all the services required for an international event, including the organising of pre- and post-conference tours.

COMMERCIAL INFORMATION

Ministry of External Affairs
South Block, New Delhi 110 011, India
Tel: (11) 2301 2318 *or* 1165.
Website: http://meaindia.nic.in

Associated Chambers of Commerce and Industry of India (ASSOCHAM)
147B Gautam Nagar, Gulmohar Enclave, New Delhi 110 049, India
Tel: (11) 2651 2477/9.
Website: www.assocham.org

Federation of Indian Chambers of Commerce and Industry (FICCI)
Federation House, Tansen Marg, New Delhi 110 001, India
Tel: (11) 2373 8760/70.
Website: www.ficci.com.

Indonesia

Location: South-East Asia.

Time: Indonesia spans three time zones:
Bangka, Balitung, Java, West and Central Kalimantan, Madura and Sumatra: GMT + 7 (West), GMT + 8 (Central), GMT + 9 (East).
Bali, Flores, South and East Kalimantan, Lombok, Sulawesi, Sumba, Sumbawa and Timor: GMT + 8.
Aru, Irian Jaya, Kai, Moluccas and Tanimbar: GMT + 9.
Indonesia does not operate Daylight-Saving Time.

Overview

The islands of the Indonesian archipelago are strung like beads across the equator. Clear blue seas lap pristine beaches, gentle breezes carry scents of spices and flowers, and divers are entranced by the ocean's riches. Inland, dramatic volcanic ranges tower above a green mantle of terraced hillsides and lush rainforest. Bali offers an image of paradise: stunning scenery, gentle sarong-clad people and sunsets of legendary glory. On peaceful Lombok, life moves at a slower pace, while bustling Jakarta exhibits Indonesia's cosmopolitan, modern face. Komodo Island's 'living dinosaurs' and the entrancing 'sea gardens' of Suwalesi invite exploration, as do Borobudur's architectural treasures, which include 5km (3 miles) of Buddhist relief carvings. Adventure-seekers head for Kalimantan's remote jungle interior or explore Sumatra, with its teeming wildlife and wealth of tribal groups. Yet modern Indonesia's amalgam of more than 17,500 islands and a wide variety of cultural and religious traditions, stemming from 1000 years of maritime trade, have triggered troubles. The main independence movement, the Indonesian Nationalist Party (PNI), emerged in the 1920s under the leadership of Ahmed Sukarno and, by 1949, finally claimed the country's sovereignty. Such sovereignty did not get off to a good start - previous colonial powers had depleted much of Indonesia's wealth while contributing little to its development. The Sukarno Government also had to forge a national consciousness among dozens of mutually suspicious tribes and ethnic groups. The leaders therefore chose as their national motto the phrase *Bhineka Tunggalika*, meaning 'unity in diversity'.
Yet these fabled isles of sunshine and spices have long been stalked by security issues, fired up by governmental corruption. The powerful Indonesian Communist Party (PKI) almost won a coup in 1965, but was defeated by an army led by General Suharto, wielding Western support. Between 400,000 and one million were massacred by that army in the aftermath of the coup. Sukarno, politically crippled, was replaced by Suharto, who remained President until his (forced) resignation in May 1998. Under the Suharto Government, the army always held ultimate political power while a technocrat class was left to run the country day-to-day. Since then, militant Islam has been threatening to tear the archipelago apart. Examples of inter-fighting include the Moluccan Islands, one of the few parts of Indonesia with a majority Christian population: since the beginning of 1999, they have been engaged in an increasingly violent struggle with Muslim militants that has claimed thousands of lives. Suicide bombing has occurred in Bali, most recently on 1 October 2005, and there remains a high threat from terrorism in Indonesia. The cataclysmic tsunami that occurred on 26 December 2004 further hampered Indonesia's economic and touristic progress. However, from such a devastating tsunami also came a much-needed glimmer of hope: a peace agreement with separatist rebels was reached just as 2006 dawned, resulting in the withdrawal of state security forces from the Aceh province. In return, Free Aceh Movement rebels began disarmament and vowed to abolish their armed wing. Such withdrawal effectively ended a 29-year conflict that had claimed thousands upon thousands of lives.

However, until such a catalogue of problems are fully resolved, many tourists will be deterred from travelling to Indonesia and will therefore miss out on its myriad marvels; and many of its residents will remain living amidst poverty, corruption and peril.

General Information

AREA: 1,922,570 sq km (742,308 sq miles).
POPULATION: 241.9 million (UN estimate 2005).
POPULATION DENSITY: 131 per sq km.
CAPITAL: Jakarta (Java). **Population:** 13.2 million (UN estimate 2005).
GEOGRAPHY: Indonesia lies between the mainland of South-East Asia and Australia in the Indian and Pacific oceans. It is the world's largest archipelago state. Indonesia is made up of five main islands – Sumatra, Java, Sulawesi, Kalimantan (part of the island of Borneo) and Irian Jaya (the western half of New Guinea) – and 30 smaller archipelagos. In total, the Indonesian archipelago consists of about 17,508 islands; 6000 of these are inhabited and stretch over 4828km (3000 miles), most lying in a volcanic belt with more than 300 volcanoes, the great majority of which are extinct. The landscape varies from island to island, ranging from high mountains and plateaux to coastal lowlands and alluvial belts.
GOVERNMENT: Republic. Declared independence from The Netherlands in 1945. **Head of State and Government:** President Susilo Bambang Yudhoyono since 2004. **Recent history:** The trigger for the fall of General Suharto, leader of the powerful Indonesian Communist Party (PKI), was the Asian financial crisis of 1997. Suharto's deputy, Jusuf Habibie, took over until Presidential elections were held under new rules in November 1999; National Assembly elections were held five months earlier, in June. These saw *Partai Golongan Karya* pushed into second place by the principal opposition party, the *Partai Demokrasi Indonesia Perjuangan* (PDIP, the Indonesian Democratic Party of Struggle), headed by the daughter of former President Sukarno, Megawati Sukarnoputri. Sukarnoputri was expected to win the November Presidential poll. Instead, she suffered from a lack of support in crucial parts of the new electoral college which now selects the President. Her opponents settled on the veteran cleric Abdurrahman Wahid, leader of the third-largest party in the assembly, the *Partai Kebangkitan Bangsa* (PKB, National Awakening Party). He garnered sufficient support to defeat Sukarnoputri in the electoral college. Sukarnoputri secured the Vice-Presidency. It was not a good choice. In his first 12 months in office, apparently stricken by inertia and indecisiveness, Wahid proved incapable of tackling the mess left behind by Suharto. In April 2001, Wahid himself was impeached for alleged corruption – a matter of a few million dollars – and by July had been forced out of office. As Vice President, Sukarnoputri took over. Sukarnoputri faced a huge task. The corruption that typified the Suharto regime continued much as before, despite the implication and arraignment of a series of leading political figures. Sukarnoputri was then herself defeated in 2004 and replaced by the new President, Susilo Bambang Yudhoyono. On taking office, the retired general and former security minister vowed to set an ambitious agenda for reform.
The 1000-member People's Consultative Assembly is the country's highest political institution. It agrees the broad outlines of state policy and selects the President and Vice-President. Its membership comprises all the members of the National Assembly (see below), representatives of the armed forces, the country's main political organisations, and delegates from the regions. The President, who serves a five-year term, holds executive power. The Parliament, the *Dewan Perwakilan Rakyat* (People's Representative Assembly), has 500

members. Of these, 462 are directly elected by proportional representation, while the other 38 are appointed as representatives of the army and security forces. Members of the Assembly serve a five-year term.
LANGUAGE: Bahasa Indonesia is the official national language. It is similar to Malay and written in the Roman alphabet. All together, there are an estimated 583 languages and dialects spoken in the archipelago. Many local languages are further divided by special forms of address depending on social status, and all languages are spoken in a variety of local dialects. English is the most widely used foreign language for business and tourism, and many people in the more remote areas have a basic command of English. The older generation still speaks Dutch as a second language and French is spoken at some of the better hotels and restaurants.
RELIGION: There is a Muslim majority of approximately 90 per cent, with Christian, Hindu (mainly in Bali) and Buddhist minorities. Animist beliefs are held in remote areas.
ELECTRICITY: Generally 220 volts AC, 50Hz, but 110 volts AC, 50Hz, in some rural areas.
SOCIAL CONVENTIONS: Indonesia encompasses at least 583 separate languages and dialects, many of them as different from each other as Welsh is from English. Since independence, many people have developed a strong sense of national pride, and maintain traditions of dance, painting, woodcarving and stonecarving. Social courtesies are often fairly formal. In particular, when drink or food is served, it should not be touched until the host invites the guest to do so. Never pass or accept anything with the left hand. Public displays of affection between men and women are frowned upon and kissing in public will attract a great deal of unwanted attention. Touching a stranger of the same sex while in conversation is very common. Pointing is considered impolite and patting children on the head should be avoided. Indonesians are polite and will extend endless courtesies to visitors whom they trust and like. Smiling is a cultural tradition and Indonesians smile frequently, even in an uncomfortable or difficult situation. Visitors should avoid the temptation of losing their temper. When invited home, a gift is appreciated (as long as it is given with the right hand). Informality is normal, but a few smart establishments encourage guests to dress for dinner. Safari suits are acceptable on formal occasions and for business wear. Muslim customs, especially those concerning female clothes, should be observed.

Climate

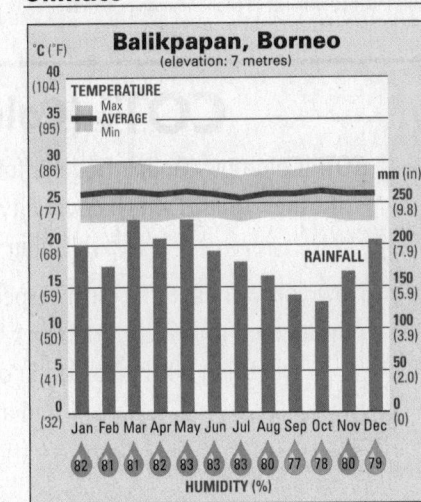

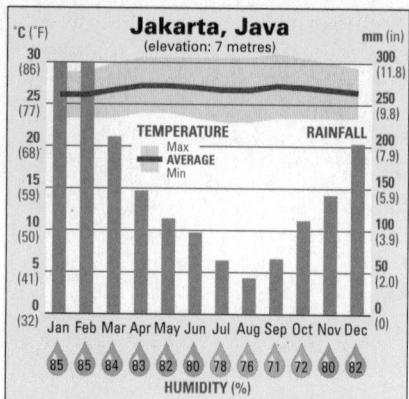

Jakarta, Java (elevation: 7 metres)

TEMPERATURE / RAINFALL

HUMIDITY (%): 85 85 84 83 82 80 78 76 71 72 80 82

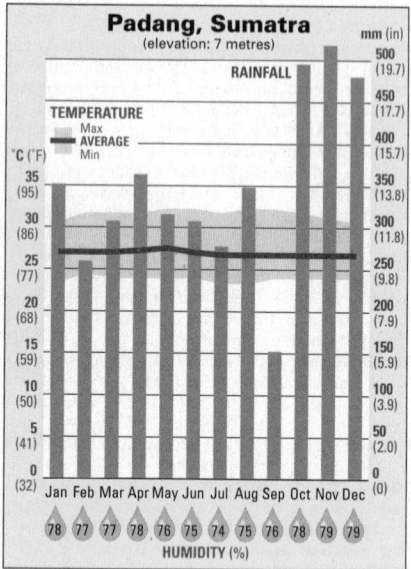

Padang, Sumatra (elevation: 7 metres)

RAINFALL / TEMPERATURE

HUMIDITY (%): 78 77 77 78 76 75 74 75 76 78 79 79

Tropical climate varying from area to area. The eastern monsoon brings the driest weather (June to September), while the western monsoon brings the main rains (December to March). Rainstorms occur all year. Higher regions are cooler.

Required clothing: Lightweights with rainwear. Warmer clothes are needed for cool evenings and upland areas. Smart clothes such as jackets are required for formal occasions, and it is regarded inappropriate to wear halter-neck tops and shorts anywhere other than the beach or at sports facilities.

Communications

Telephone: IDD is available to main cities. Country code: 62 (followed by 22 for Bandung, 21 for Jakarta, 61 for Medan and 31 for Surabaya). Many hotel lobbies have public phones which take credit cards and phone cards. State-operated phone booths (WARTEL), which work on a pay-as-you-leave basis, can be found throughout the country.

Mobile telephone: Roaming agreements exist with some international mobile phone companies. Coverage may be limited to main towns and cities.

Internet: There are Internet cafes in all major cities and tourist destinations.

Post: Airmail to Western Europe takes up to 10 days; USA and Australia seven to 14 days. Internal mail is fast and generally reliable by the express service (*Pos KILAT*), but mail to the outer islands can be subject to considerable delays.

MEDIA: Media freedom increased considerably after the end of President Suharto's rule, during which the now-defunct Ministry of Information monitored and controlled domestic media and restricted foreign media.

Press: There are several English-language newspapers in Jakarta and on the other islands, notably *Bali Post*, *Indonesian Observer*, *The Jakarta Post*.

TV: *Televisi Republik Indonesia* (*TVRI*) is a public broadcaster that operates two networks. Other private stations operate such as *Metro TV* and *Surya Citra Televisi Indonesia* (*SCTV*).

Radio: *Radio Republik Indonesia* (*RRI*) is a public broadcaster that operates six national networks, regional and local stations, and the external service, *Voice of Indonesia*.

Passport/Visa

	Passport Required?	Visa Required?	Return Ticket Required?
Full British	Yes	Yes/1	Yes
Australian	Yes	Yes/1	Yes
Canadian	Yes	Yes/1	Yes
USA	Yes	Yes/1	Yes
Other EU	Yes	Yes/1	Yes
Japanese	Yes	Yes/1	Yes

Note: *Regulations and requirements may be subject to change at short notice, and you are advised to contact the appropriate diplomatic or consular authority before finalising travel arrangements. Any numbers in the chart refer to the footnotes below.*

Restricted entry: Nationals of Afghanistan, Albania, Angola, Bangladesh, Cameroon, Cuba, Ethiopia, Ghana, Iran, Iraq, Israel, Nigeria, Korea (Dem Rep), Pakistan, Somalia, Sri Lanka, Tanzania and Tonga will be refused entry unless they have applied to the Immigration Office in Indonesia, prior to travelling, to obtain a special permit.

PASSPORTS: Passport valid for at least six months from date of entry required by all.

VISAS: Required by all except nationals of Brunei, Chile, Hong Kong (SAR), Macau (SAR), Malaysia, Morocco, Peru, The Philippines, Singapore, Thailand and Vietnam, provided that they enter through one of the authorised airports, seaports or Etikong overland port, for tourist stays of up to 30 days.

Note: 1. Nationals of Argentina, Australia, Austria, Belgium, Brazil, Canada, Denmark, Finland, France, Germany, Hungary, India, Ireland, Italy, Japan, Korea (Rep), Kuwait, Luxembourg, New Zealand, Norway, Oman, Portugal, Qatar, Russian Federation, Saudi Arabia, Spain, South Africa, Switzerland, Taiwan (China), United Arab Emirates, UK and USA can apply for a *Tourist* visa, valid for 30 days (non-extendable), on arrival, provided that they enter through one of the authorised airports or seaports.

Warning: Visitors who exceed their visa-free stay will be given severe fines and possibly deported or imprisoned.

Types of visa and cost: *Single-entry*: £35. *Multiple-entry*: £125 (*business* only). *Transit*: £15. Fees are non-refundable.

Validity: *Single-entry*: Three months from date of issue for a maximum stay of 60 days. *Multiple-entry*: One year, with each stay lasting no longer than 60 days. The first entry must be within three months of date of issue. *Transit*: Three months from the date of issue for a maximum stay of 14 days.

Application to: Visa section at Embassy; see *Passport/Visa Information*. All visitors are advised to process their visas at the visa section at the Embassy before entry to Indonesia.

Application requirements: (a) Passport valid for at least six months from date of entry. (b) One (double-sided) application form (the original not a photocopy, signed by the applicant). (c) One recent colour passport-size photo. (d) Proof of sufficient funds (£1000 for touristic stays); for instance, a bank statement less than one month old or traveller's cheques. (e) Fee, payable in cash or by postal order only. (f) For postal applications, a pre-paid special delivery envelope. *Tourist*: (a)-(f) and, (g) Travel itinerary. (h) Hotel reservation. (j) Letter, less than one month old from applicant's employer certifying the applicant's obligation to return (if self-employed, from solicitor, accountant or bank manager, if a student, from school, college or university). *Business*: (a)-(f) and, (g) Letter from the applicant's company in home country and the sponsor/ counterpart in Indonesia stating the reason and duration of the visit and guarantee of financial responsibility and responsibility for arrangement of accommodation. *Social Visit*: (a)-(f) and, (g) Letter of invitation from the applicant's family, friends or relatives in Indonesia stating the reason and duration of the visit and details of accommodation, and a photocopy of their passport/ID.

Working days required: Five to six. Applications for multiple-entry business visas and applications from nationals of certain countries will need to be referred to the authorities in Indonesia and may take two months or more. There is an additional £5 fee in this case.

Temporary residence: People wishing to stay and work in Indonesia must apply directly to the Immigration Office in Indonesia for a temporary stay visa.

PASSPORT/VISA INFORMATION

Embassy of the Republic of Indonesia in the UK
38 Grosvenor Square, London W1K 2HW, UK
Consular section: 38A Adam's Row, London W1X 9AD, UK
All post should be addressed to 38 Grosvenor Square.
Tel: (020) 7499 7661.
Website: www.indonesianembassy.org.uk
Opening hours: Mon-Fri 0900-1700 (general and tourist enquiries); 1030-1300 (visa applications) and 1430-1600 (visa collections).

Embassy of the Republic of Indonesia in the USA
2020 Massachusetts Avenue, NW, Washington, DC 20036, USA
Tel: (202) 775 5200.
Website: www.embassyofindonesia.org

Consulate General of Indonesia in the USA
5 East 68th Street, New York, NY 10021, USA
Tel: (212) 879 0600.
Website: www.indony.org

Money

Currency: Rupiah (IDR) = 100 sen. Notes are in denominations of IDR100,000, 50,000, 20,000, 10,000, 5000, 1000, 500 and 100. Coins are in denominations of IDR1000, 500, 100, 50 and 25.

Currency exchange: Although there should be no difficulty exchanging major currencies in the main tourist centres, problems may occur elsewhere. The easiest currency to exchange is the US Dollar.

Credit & debit cards: American Express, MasterCard, Visa, Diners Club and Eurocard are widely accepted in Jakarta and the main tourist areas. In more remote areas, it is best to carry cash in small denominations. Check with your credit or debit card company for details of merchant acceptability and other services which may be available. ATMs are available.
Traveller's cheques: Limited merchant acceptance but can be easily exchanged at banks and larger hotels. To avoid additional exchange rate charges, travellers are advised to take traveller's cheques in US Dollars or Pounds Sterling. Amex are more widely accepted.
Currency restrictions: There are no restrictions on the import or export of foreign currency. The import and export of local currency is limited to IDR50,000, which must be declared; more than IDR10,000,000 needs authorisation. Failure to declare amounts in excess of IDR10,000,000 may result in heavy fines. Local currency may be exchanged on departure.
Banking hours: Mon-Fri 0830-1530/1730; Sat 0930-1230.
Exchange rate indicators:
Rate at time of publishing
£1.00= IDR17310.34
$1.00= IDR10062.93

Duty Free

The following goods may be imported into Indonesia by persons over 18 years of age without incurring customs duty:
200 cigarettes or 50 cigars or 100g of tobacco; 2l of alcohol (opened); a reasonable quantity of perfume; gifts up to a value of US$250 per person or US$1000 per family.
Note: Cameras must be declared on arrival. Video cameras, portable radios, tape recorders, binoculars, sport equipment and typewriters may be imported provided exported on departure. Motion-picture film, video tapes, video laser discs, records and computer software must be screened by the censor board. Fresh fruits and animals must have a valid quarantine permit.
Prohibited items: Weapons, firearms and ammunition, non-prescribed drugs, narcotics, TV sets, Chinese publications and medicines, pornography, and any commercial or merchandised goods as part of baggage (infringements will be charged Rp25,000 per piece).

Public Holidays

Below are listed Public Holidays for the January 2006-June 2007 period.
2006: Jan 1 New Year's Day. **Jan 10** Eid al-Adha (Feast of the Sacrifice). **Jan 29** Chinese New Year. **Jan 31** Muharram (Islamic New Year). **Mar 30** Nyepi (Hindu New Year). **Apr 11** Mouloud (Birth of the Prophet). **Apr 14** Good Friday.
May 13 Waisak Day (Buddha's Birthday). **May 25** Ascension. **Aug 17** Indonesian Independence Day. **Aug 22** Lailat al Miraj (Ascension of the Prophet). **Oct 22- 24** Eid al-Fitr (End of Ramadan). **Dec 25** Christmas Day. **Dec 31** Eid al-Adha (Feast of the Sacrifice).
2007: Jan 1 New Year's Day. **Jan 20** Muharram (Islamic New Year) **Feb 18** Chinese New Year. **Mar 20** Nyepi (Hindu New Year). **Mar 31** Mouloud (Birth of the Prophet). **Apr 6** Good Friday. **May 2** Waisak Day (Buddha's Birthday). **May 17** Ascension.
Note: (a) Muslim festivals are timed according to local sightings of various phases of the moon and the dates given above are approximations. During the lunar month of Ramadan that precedes Eid al-Fitr, Muslims fast during the day and feast at night and normal business patterns may be interrupted. Many restaurants are closed during the day and there may be restrictions on smoking and drinking. Some disruption may continue into Eid al-Fitr itself. Eid al-Fitr and Eid al-Adha may last anything from two to 10 days, depending on the region. For more information, see the *World of Islam* appendix. (b) Buddhist festivals are also timed according to phases of the moon and variations may occur.

Health

	Special Precautions?	Certificate Required?
Yellow Fever	No	1
Cholera	Yes	2
Typhoid & Polio	3	N/A
Malaria	4	N/A

Note: *Regulations and requirements may be subject to change at short notice, and you are advised to contact your doctor well in advance of your intended date of departure. Any numbers in the chart refer to the footnotes below.*

1: A *yellow fever* vaccination certificate is required from travellers coming from infected areas. The countries and areas included in the yellow fever endemic zones are considered by Indonesia as infected areas. For a map of yellow fever endemic zones, see the *Health* appendix.
2: Following WHO guidelines issued in 1973, a *cholera* vaccination certificate is no longer a condition of entry to Indonesia. However, cholera is a serious risk in this country and precautions are essential. Up-to-date advice should be sought before deciding whether these precautions should include vaccination as medical opinion is divided over its effectiveness; see the *Health* appendix.
3: *Typhoid* occurs. *Poliomyelitis* transmission has been interrupted in Indonesia.
4: *Malaria* risk exists throughout the year everywhere except in the main tourist resorts of Java and Bali, Jakarta municipality and other big cities where risk is only slight. The malignant form *falciparum* is reported to be highly resistant to chloroquine and sulfadoxine-pyrimethane. The benign form *vivax* is reported to be resistant to chloroquine. The recommended prophylaxis in risk areas is mefloquine.
Food & drink: All water should be regarded as a potential health risk. Water used for drinking, brushing teeth or making ice should have first been boiled or otherwise sterilised. Milk is unpasteurised and should be boiled. Powdered or tinned milk is available and is advised, but make sure that it is reconstituted with pure water. Avoid dairy products that are likely to have been made from unboiled milk. Only eat well-cooked meat and fish, preferably served hot. Salad and mayonnaise may carry increased risk. Vegetables should be cooked and fruit peeled.
Other risks: *Amoebic* and *bacillary dysenteries* occur. *Hepatitis A* and *E* occur and *hepatitis B* is highly endemic. *Dengue fever*, *giardiasis*, *Japanese Encephalitis* and *Parityphoid* can occur. *Tuberculosis* and *diphtheria* vaccinations are sometimes recommended. *Bilharzia* (schistosomiasis) is present in central Sulawesi. Avoid swimming and paddling in fresh water; swimming pools which are well chlorinated and maintained are safe.
Rabies is present. For those at high risk, vaccination before arrival should be considered. If you are bitten, seek medical advice without delay. For more information, consult the *Health* appendix.
There have been renewed outbreaks of *avian influenza* (bird flu) amongst poultry and a small number of pig farms throughout west and central Indonesia. There have been a number of human fatalities in this latest outbreak. The World Health Organisation is still investigating the possibility of human-to-human transmission. Travellers to Indonesia are unlikely to be affected, but should avoid visiting live animal markets, poultry farms and other places where they may come into close contact with wild or caged birds; and ensure poultry dishes are thoroughly cooked.
Health care: Health insurance to include emergency repatriation cover is strongly advised. Adequate routine medical care is available in all major cities, but emergency services are generally inadequate outside major cities. Doctors and hospitals often expect immediate cash payments before any treatment is given. Although medical costs are relatively cheap, drugs can be expensive.

Travel - International

AIR:
The national airlines are *Garuda Indonesia (GA)* (website: www.garuda-indonesia.com) and *Merpati Nusantara Airlines (MZ)*. Other major airlines that serve Indonesia include *Air France* (website: www.airfrance.com), *Air India* (website: www.airindia.com), *Cathay Pacific* (website: www.cathaypacific.com), *Emirates* (website: www.emirates.com), *Gulf Air* (website: www.gulfairco.com), *Japan Airlines* (website: www.jal.com), *KLM* (website: www.klm.com), *Lufthansa* (website: www.lufthansa.com), *Qantas* (website: www.quantas.com), *Singapore Airlines* (website: www.singaporeair.com) and *Thai Airways International* (website: www.thaiairways.com).
Approximate flight times: From *London* to Jakarta is 20 hours 20 minutes and to Bali is 22 hours 15 minutes (with a good connection in Jakarta). From *Los Angeles* to Jakarta is 24 hours 20 minutes. From *New York* to Jakarta is 30 hours via Europe or 31 hours via Los Angeles. From *Singapore* to Jakarta is one hour 35 minutes. From *Sydney* to Jakarta is seven hours 55 minutes.
Main airports: *Jakarta (CGK)* (Soekarno-Hatta) is 20km (13 miles) northwest of the city (travel time – 45 minutes). *To/From the airport*: A bus goes to the city every 30 to 60 minutes. Buses leave Jakarta from Gambir railway station and from Rawamangun, Blok M and Pasar Minguu bus stations. Taxis are also available to the city centre. *Facilities*: Banks/bureaux de change, a post office, duty free shops, gift shops, restaurants, snack bars, car hire and medical/vaccination facilities.
Halim Perdana Kusuma (HLP), 13km (8 miles) southeast of the city (travel time – 45 to 60 minutes).
Denpasar (DPS) (Ngurah Rai), 13km (8 miles) southwest of the city, is the main airport on Bali (travel time – 30 minutes). *To/From the airport*: A bus goes to the city centre. Taxis are available to the city and to Kuta, Urud, Nusadua and Sanur. *Facilities*: Restaurant/bar, newsagent, bank, post office and car hire.
Departure tax: IDR100,000; infants under the age of two are exempt.
Note: For a list of the air- and seaports which may be used to enter and exit Indonesia, see the *Passport/Visa Information*.
SEA:
High-speed ferries run between Sumatra and Malaysia-Singapore. Routes are either Medan–Penang or Dumai–Malacca. There are also services between Mandalo (Sulawesi) and The Philippines. Many cruise lines serve Indonesia.
RAIL:
There is a daily sea and rail service between Belawan and Penang (West Malaysia) operated by *National Railroad of Indonesia*.
ROAD:
Indonesia's international land borders are between Kalimantan and the Malaysian states of Sarawak and Sabah on the island of Borneo, and Papua and Papua New Guinea. There are no road links with Sabah and the few (poorly maintained) roads to Sarawak are not recognised as gateways to Indonesia.

Travel - Internal

AIR:
Indonesia has a good internal air system linking most of the larger towns to Jakarta. Domestic flights from Jakarta depart from Terminal 1 at *Soekarno-Hatta International Airport* (except *Garda Airlines'* flights, which leave from Terminal 2). Domestic operators include: *Bouraq Indonesia Airlines (BO)*, *Garuda Indonesia (GA)* and *Merpati Nusantara Airlines (MZ)* (website: www.merpati.co.id).
Cheap fares: The *Asean Air Pass* offers special fares on domestic flights and gives access to varying numbers of cities depending on the ticket bought. Passes must be bought at Garuda Indonesia offices in Australia, Europe, Japan or the USA (not available inside Indonesia). For prices and further information, contact *Garuda Indonesia* (tel: (020) 7467 8600; website: www.garuda-indonesia.com).
Departure tax: IDR8-30,000 depending on airport of departure; infants under the age of two are exempt.
SEA:
Main ports: Soekarno-Hatta (Jakarta), Ngurah Rai (Bali), Polonia (Medan) and Sekupang (Batam). *PELNI* (website: www.merpati.co.id), the state-owned shipping company, has 23 luxurious passenger liners serving all the main ports across the archipelago. Foreign cruise liners also operate on an irregular basis. Luxury cruise ships offer trips to various destinations, including the eastern islands (leaving from Bali). For further details, contact the Indonesia Tourism Promotion Office (see *Top Things To Do*).
RAIL:
Children under three travel free. Children aged three to seven pay half fare. There are nearly 7000km (4350 miles) of track on Java, Madura and Sumatra. In Sumatra, trains connect Belawan, Medan and Tanjong Balai/Rantu Prapet (two or three trains daily) in the north, and Palembang and Panjang (three trains daily) in the south. An extensive rail network runs throughout Java. The *Bima Express*, which has sleeping and restaurant cars, links Jakarta and Surabaya; there are also other express services. There are three classes of travel, but first-class exists only on principal expresses. There is some air-conditioned accommodation.
ROAD:
Traffic drives on the left. There are over 378,000km (234,360 miles) of roads in the country, of which about 28,500km (17,670 miles) are main or national roads and 200km (125 miles) are motorway. Nearly half of the network is paved. There are good road communications within Java and, to a lesser extent, on Bali and Sumatra. The other islands have poor road systems, although conditions are improving with tourism becoming more important. Road tolls are in operation on some major city roads and need to be paid for by visitors if using a taxi. Chauffeur-driven cars are widely available, with rates varying according to the type of destination. Driving at night can be dangerous due to locals often driving without their lights on. During the rainy season the roads are almost impossible to pass. **Bus:** The 'Big Bird' chartered buses have been serving Indonesia since 1979. There are regular services between most towns. Bus trips can be made from Jakarta to Bali (two days) and as far as Sumatra. Indonesia is the land of *jam karet* (literally 'rubber time'), and complicated journeys

involving more than a single change should not be attempted in a day. Bus fares are relatively low, but most are fixed with a higher price for the air-conditioned buses. Vehicles can be extremely crowded, as they tend to the transportation needs of Jakarta's major schools and workforce. Many of the buses are air conditioned and can hold from 12 to 54 passengers. The crew includes a conductor. There are 'Bis Malam' night buses on a number of routes, running in competition with the railways. Pre-booking is essential. Special 'travel minibuses' offering a door-to-door service are also available in cities and major tourist areas. Visitors should note that Indonesian bus drivers are notorious for reckless driving. **Taxi:** Widely available in most large cities and some smaller towns. Metered taxis are usually only found in the main cities and major tourist areas. Taxi drivers do not always know how to get to the desired destination and passengers may have to tell them. Like all public transport vehicles, taxis have yellow number plates (for private and rented vehicles, the number plates are black, while Government vehicles have red plates). **Car hire:** Available from a number of companies and from taxi firms, some of which also provide a limousine service. **Documentation:** An International Driving Permit is required.

Alternative transport: There are two forms of tricycle **rickshaws** available in Indonesia: the motorised version is called *bajaj* (pronounced 'baj-eye'), which is a bright orange colour and seats two passengers, with the driver in front; and the *becak* (pronounced 'be-chak') is pedal-powered by a rider sitting behind a maximum of two passengers. Fares should be negotiated in advance. Rickshaws are an extremely popular and cheap form of transport and can be hired almost everywhere (although becaks have now been banned from Jakarta city centre). **Motorcycles** and **bicycles** can be rented on a daily or weekly basis; for motorcycles, an International Driving Licence is recommended and a helmet should be worn. **Bemos** and **Colts** are small buses, seating up to 10 people, and can be chartered on a daily or weekly basis for travel away from the city centres; fares should be negotiated in advance. **Horse carts** may still be hired in rural areas (though they are no longer available in Jakarta). **River taxis** are popular in Jakarta amongst the older locals. These boats allow passengers to cross the river from a major road to the other side, without going the long way around.

URBAN:

Jakarta is the only city with an established conventional bus service of any size. Double-deckers are operated.

Travel Advice

On 26 December 2004, a massive earthquake registering 9.0 on the Richter scale struck off the west coast of Indonesia. The quake created a tsunami – a series of huge waves that spread destruction across many parts of Asia and reached as far as the east coast of Africa. Both the west and north coasts of the province of Aceh on the island of Sumatra were badly affected by damage caused by the tidal waves and flooding. Those wishing to travel to affected areas should still check with a relevant tour operator, tourist board or embassy for the latest information prior to travel.

Visitors are advised against all travel to Aceh, except for those involved in post-tsunami humanitarian and reconstruction work or in the Aceh Monitoring Mission. Parts of Aceh remain affected by a long running internal conflict. Visitors should exercise caution when travelling to remote areas.

Visitors are advised against travel to Maluku Province, especially Ambon, and some parts of Central Sulawesi Province, which are experiencing civilian unrest.

There remains a high threat from terrorism in Indonesia. Attacks could occur at any time, anywhere in Indonesia and are likely to be directed against locations and buildings frequented by foreigners.

If you intend to travel to Indonesia in the immediate future or you are already in Indonesia, you should exercise caution at all times. You should review thoroughly the latest information on the situation, including media reports; keep in close contact with your tour operator; and follow any advice from local authorities. If you are travelling to, or resident in Indonesia, you should ensure that you are comfortable with, and regularly review, your and your family's security arrangements.

Visitors should exercise caution when visiting places of worship and other locations known to be frequented by foreigners or where large groups of people gather.

Terrorists have shown in previous attacks, like the attack on the Australian Embassy, the Marriott Hotel, Jakarta and both the Bali bombings, that they have the means and the motivation to carry out successful attacks.

There have been outbreaks of Avian Influenza (Bird Flu) amongst poultry and a small number of pig farms in 23 of Indonesia's 33 provinces, including on the islands of Java, Sumatra, Bali, Kalimantan, Sulawesi and Nusa Tengarra. There have been a number of human fatalities in this latest outbreak. The World Health Organisation is still investigating the possibility of human-to-human transmission. If you are travelling to Indonesia, you should consult your usual healthcare provider for travel medical advice before departure. The risk from Avian Influenza is believed to be very low, provided you avoid visiting live animal markets, poultry farms and other places where you may come into close contact with domestic, caged or wild birds; and ensure poultry and egg dishes are thoroughly cooked.

This advice is based on information provided by the Foreign & Commonwealth Office in the UK. It is correct at time of publishing. As the situation can change rapidly, visitors are advised to contact the following organisations for the latest travel advice.

British Foreign and Commonwealth Office
Tel: (0845) 850 2829.
Website: www.fco.gov.uk

US Department of State
Website: http://travel.state.gov/travel

Accommodation

HOTELS:

International hotels are found only in major towns and tourist areas. Several of these have business centres with a variety of services. High hotel taxes are charged (10 per cent service, plus 11 per cent Government tax). However, hotels of all grades from deluxe to standard can be found in most towns around the country. Resort hotels on Bali vary from international class, luxury hotels to beach cottages along the shore. Most hotels have pools and can supply most leisure equipment. All hotels are graded according to facilities.

SELF-CATERING:

Available in Bali.

ACCOMMODATION INFORMATION

Indonesian Hotel & Restaurant Association
JL RP Soeroso no. 27 GHI, Jakarta 10350, Indonesia
Tel: (21) 310 2922.
Website: www.ihra.co.id

Top Things To See

- See the modern **Istiqlal Mosque** in **Jakarta**, **Java** - it is one of the largest in the world.
- In Jakarta, see the wonderful fabrics and weavings of **batik**: **Karet** is home to a large factory.
- Witness **puppet shows** staged throughout Java, in which traditional **wayang golak** and *wayang kulit* marionettes act out stories based on well-known legends; performances can sometimes last all night. ~
- Visit the **Prambanan temple complex**, built in honour of the Hindu gods Brahma, Shiva and Vishnu, which includes the 10th-century **Temple of Loro Jonggrang**, said to be the most perfectly proportioned Hindu temple in Indonesia. At the temple there are also open-air performances of **Ramayana ballet** which involve hundreds of dancers, singers and *gamelan* musicians. Perched on a hill to the west of Yogyakarta is **Borobudur**, probably the largest Buddhist sanctuary in the world, which contains more than 5km (3 miles) of relief carvings.
- Wallow in the beauty of **Sulawesi**, unofficially known as '**Orchid Island**'. Sulawesi is a land of high mountains, misty valleys and lakes. In the south is **Bantimurung Nature Reserve**, which has thousands of exotic **butterflies**. The island has **geysers** and **hot springs**, the most celebrated of which are at **Karumengan**, **Kinilow**, **Lahendong**, **Leilem** and **Makule**.
- Go to **Torajaland** , known as the '**Land of the Heavenly Kings**', on Sulawesi, and note the inhabitants' richly ornamented houses and custom of burying the dead in vertical cliffside tombs.
- **Sumatra** is the second-largest island in Indonesia, straddling the Equator, and teems with indigenous **wildlife**. **Bengkulu**, **Gedung Wani** and **Mount Loeser Reserve** organise supervised safaris enabling visitors to see tigers, elephants, tapirs and rhinos at close hand.
- Be surprised to see an inhabited island in the middle of **Lake Toba**, which was once a volcanic crater, 900m (3000ft) above sea level in Sumatra.
- Luxuriate on the **beach** and soak up the scene as well as the sea water. The best beaches can be found at: the east coast of Sumatra; **Sanur Beach** and **Kuta**, which lie on a narrow isthmus in Bali; **Nusa Dua** in Bali; **Banda**, in the middle of the Banda Sea, often referred to as the original '**Spice Island**' and famous as a nutmeg-growing centre; **Tukang Besi**, a group of isolated atolls that epitomise a tropical paradise; **Nusa Penida**, at one time a penal colony but now attracting visitors to its dramatic seascapes and beaches; **Padangbai** on Bali, a beautiful tropical coastal village, where lush vegetation backs a curving stretch of white, sandy beach; the **Terawangan Islands**, with their beautiful beaches and coral gardens; and on **Lombak** are some glorious beaches, some of white sand, others, such as those near **Ampenan**, of black sand.
- Perceive the signs of **Hinduism** on **Bali**, the '**Island of the Gods**'. This is unlike the rest of Indonesia; here, the predominant form of Hinduism practised is *Agama-Hindu*.
- Behold the chain of volcanic mountains on Bali, stretching from east to west across the island, dominated by the mighty **Gunung Agung** (**Holy Mountain**), whose conical peak soars more than 3170m (10,400ft) into the sky.
- See some of Bali's thousands of temples – the exact number has never been counted. They range from the great 'Holy Temple' at **Besakih** to small village places of worship.
- Travel to the **Sea Temple of Tanah Lot** on the west coast (a short drive from **Kediri**), one of the most breathtaking sights of Bali.
- See some of Bali's fantastic wildlife, from **Serangan Island**, also known as **Turtle Island** because of the turtles kept there in special pens, to the sacred **monkey forest** at **Sangeh**, a forest reserve which, as well as being the home of a variety of exotic apes, also has a temple.
- Go to **Penelokan** for views of the **black lava streams** from **Mount Batur**.
- Don't miss Bali's **Pura Besakih**, a temple that dates back originally to the 10th century and stands high on the volcanic slopes of **Gunung Agung**. Nowadays, it is a massive complex of more than 30 temples, and the setting for great ceremonial splendour on festival days.
- If you dare, enter **Goa Lawah**, which lives up to its name ('**bat cave**' in the local tongue), a safe and holy haven for thousands of bats which line every inch of space on its walls and roof. Look up and see what is either terrific or terrible, depending on your feelings towards these nocturnal creatures. Indeed, non bat-lovers should avoid moonlight strolls in the area, as the animals leave for food sorties at night.
- Gaze out at an unusual sight in a tropical landscape: **Lake Bratan** is reached via a winding road from **Budugul** and exemplifies shimmering, cool beauty, fringed by pine-forested hillsides.
- Look at some **Indonesian art**: the village of **Ubud** is the centre of Bali's considerable art colony and contains the galleries of the most successful painters, including those of artists of foreign extraction who have settled on the island. Set in a hilltop garden is the **Museum Puri Lukistan** (**Palace of Fine Arts**) with its fine display of sculpture and paintings in both old and contemporary styles. **Kamasan**, near **Klungkung**, is another centre, but the painting style of the artists is predominantly *wayang* (highly stylised). Other artistic centres include **Celuk** (gold and silver working), **Denpasar** (woodworking and painting) and **Batubulan** (stone carving).
- On Lombak, a 15-minute flight (or ferry trip) away from Bali and an unspoilt island whose name means 'chilli pepper', glimpse one of the highest volcanic mountains in the Indonesian archipelago, **Mount Rindjani**, whose cloud-piercing peak soars to 3745m (12,290ft).
- **Mount Keli Mutu** is one of Indonesia's most spectacular natural sights, famous for its **three crater lakes**, whose striking colours change with the light of the day.

Top Things To Do

- The Indonesian archipelago is one of the world's top **surfing** destinations. The best time to surf is from April to September with the best waves generally found on islands facing south and southwest, including **Bali**, **Flores**, **Java**, **Lombok**, **Sumatra**, **Sumba** and **Sumbawa**. Some well-known surfing beaches, such as **Ulu Watu** on Bali, tend to get overcrowded, but organised trips to isolated areas are widely available. Surf camps such as those at **Cempi Bay** (Sumbawa) or **Lagundri Bay** (**Nias**) offer basic accommodation and simple food.
- Tens of thousands of kilometres of coastline are reputed to contain 15 per cent of the world's **coral reefs**. In spite of the obvious opportunities, Indonesia's **diving** industry is still relatively young, though the number of companies offering courses and excursions is rising rapidly. On Java island, the best diving is on the west coast, where three volcanic islands mark the remains of the **Krakatoa volcano** (which last erupted in 1883). Bali's tourist stronghold in the **Kuta**, **Nusa Dua** and **Suar triangle** offers easy and moderate diving, with easily accessible reefs. Tours to more remote (and less busy) areas are available. On the northern tip of Sulawesi island, the **Taman Nasional Laut Bunaken Manado Tua** is a national marine reserve with particularly steep coral walls; international air connections to the island facilitate access.

Further north, the lesser-known **Sangihe-Talaud** and **Togian** islands are reached by live-aboard dive boats. In the south, **Take Bone Rate** is the world's third-largest atoll, while the **Tukang Besi** islands have featured extensively in the films by the French underwater explorer Jacques Cousteau. Nusa Tenggara's most popular sites are the three **Gili** islands near Lombok, whose calm shallow waters are ideal for beginners. **Maluku** consists of approximately 1000 islands and has only recently been discovered as a top diving destination. Southeast of Ambon, the **Bandana** islands are accessible by air and offer a number of sites suitable for beginners and experienced divers. The major resort in the Sumatra and **Riau** islands is **Bintan**, easily accessible from Singapore. The clearest and most colourful dive sites are in **Pulau Sikuai** off the **Padang coast** (western Sumatra) and *Pulau Weh* off **Banda Aceh** (northern Sumatra). **Irian Jaya** also offers good diving around the famous **Mapia Atoll** (where dolphins and killer whales can sometimes be spotted) and the waters of **Cenderawasih Bay** off the western end of **Bird's Head peninsula**.

- Indonesia's most accessible **caves** are on the island of Java and include **Luweng Jaran**, stretching over 20km (125 miles) beneath the **Gunung Seuw mountain range**; **Gua Barat**, which has the longest underground river system in the southern hemisphere; and **Gombong**, whose stone towers rise spectacularly to some 40m (132ft) above sea level. On **Kalimantan island**, **Mangkalihat** offers a rarely visited underground world of giant limestone corridors. Even less explored are the isolated caves near **Wamena** on the remote Bird's Head peninsula in Irian Jaya.
- **River tours** up the great **Mahakam River** on the island of **Kalimantan**, which is dissected by a network of rivers running from the mountainous interior to the coasts, are billed as a trip into the 'heart of darkness'. Starting from the port city **Samarinda**, such tours last for several days (with onboard accommodation available) and continue deep into the upper jungle reaches, where tribal communities have largely preserved their traditions.
- Indonesia has around 130 active volcanoes and numerous **volcano treks** are possible: on Java island, popular volcanic destinations include Krakatoa (reached by a five-hour boat trip followed by a 30-minute climb), **Mount Bromo** (the most visited of Indonesia's volcanoes) and **Kawah Ijen** (whose crater is filled by a turquoise-blue lake). Those preferring dormant volcanoes may head to **Gunung Agung** in Bali (known as the 'Navel of the World'), **Gunung Rinjani** on Lombok island (which has hot springs at the top and is revered for its mystical qualities) and **Keli Mutu** on **Nusa Tenggara Barat** (whose crater contains three spectacular mineral lakes).
- **Jungle trek** through the Indonesian rainforest; the islands of Irian Jaya, Kalimantan and Sumatra offer the most remote and untouched terrain. The best trails include trips to **Bukit Barisan National Park**, a remote and beautiful peninsula in Sumatra (with routes leading through tropical rainforest onto a beach inhabited by turtles); the **Muller Mountain** on **Kalimantan** (with a trail following the traditional jungle route used by the native Iban people); and **Lake Habbema** on Irian Jaya (a week-long trek to remote villages and mountains).
- Having been criticised in the past for the destruction of large areas of its rainforest through forest exploitation, the Indonesian Government is now keen to encourage an **environmentally friendly tourism** policy. The growing trend for back-to-nature holidays means that numerous types of **eco-tours** are available. In the **Tukangbeshi archipelago** near Sulawesi, tourists have the opportunity to participate in **coral reef preservation** projects by helping to collect scientific data.
- During August and September, **Madura** is a venue for a series of **bullock races**, which culminate in a 48-hour non-stop carnival celebration in the town of **Pamekasan**.
- Visit the internationally recognised **Konservatori Kerawitan**, one of the major centres of **Balinese dancing**.
- Enjoy the supposedly curative properties of the **Holy Springs of Tampaksiring**, which attract thousands of visitors each year.

TOURIST INFORMATION

Indonesia Culture and Tourism Board Data and Information Centre
Sapta Pesona Building, 21st Floor, Jalal Medan Merdeka Barat 17, Jakarta 10110, Indonesia
Tel: (21) 383 8717.
Website: www.budpar.go.id

Indonesian Tourism Promotion Board (ITPB)
Wisma Nugra Santana Building, 9th Floor, Jalan Jend Sudirman Kav 7-8, Jakarta 10220, Indonesia
Tel: (21) 570 4879.
Website: www.tourismindonesia.com

Entertainment

FOOD & DRINK: The staple diet for most Indonesians is rice (*nasi*), which is replaced on some islands with corn, sago, cassava and sweet potatoes. Indonesia's spices make its local cuisine unique. Almost every type of international cuisine is available in Jakarta, the most popular being Chinese, French, Italian, Japanese and Korean. Indonesians like their food highly spiced and the visitor should always bear this in mind. In particular, look out for the tiny and fiery hot, red and green peppers often included in salads and vegetable dishes. Seafood is excellent and features highly on menus (with salt and freshwater fish, lobsters, oysters, prawns, shrimp, squid, shark and crab all available). Coconuts, which are found everywhere, are often used for cooking. Vegetables and fresh fruit, such as bananas, papaya, pineapple and oranges, are available throughout the year; some tropical fruits such as mango, watermelon and papaya are seasonal. A feature of Jakarta are the many *warungs* (street stalls). Each specialises in its own dish or drink, but travellers are probably best advised not to try them without the advice of an Indonesian resident. There are restaurants in the hotels which, along with many others, serve European, Chinese and Indian food.

National specialities:
- *Campur*, *nasi uduk* and *rasirames* (rice dishes).
- *Rijstafel* (a Dutch concoction consisting of a variety of meats, fish, vegetables and curries).
- *Sate* (chunks of beef, fish, pork, chicken or lamb cooked on hot coals and dipped in peanut sauce).
- *Sate ajam* (broiled, skewered marinated chicken).
- *Ajam ungkap* (Central Java; deep-fried, marinated chicken).
- *Sate lileh* (Bali; broiled, skewered fish sticks).
- *Ikan acar kuning* (Jakarta; lightly marinated fried fish served in a sauce of pickled spices and palm sugar).
- *Soto* (a soup dish with dumpling, chicken and vegetables).
- *Gado-gado* (Java; a salad of raw and cooked vegetables with peanut and coconut milk sauce).
- *Babi guling* (Bali; roast suckling pig).
- *Opor ajam* (boiled chicken in coconut milk and light spices).

National drinks:
- *Brem* (rice wine).
- *Tuak* (a famously potent local brew).

Tipping: Tipping is normal and 10 per cent is customary, except where a service charge is included in the bill. Taxi fees should be rounded up to the nearest number. Small change is rarely given and visitors should carry a supply of their own.

NIGHTLIFE: Jakarta nightclubs feature international singers and bands and are open until 0400 during weekends. Jakarta has loads of cinemas and some English-language and subtitled films are shown. There are also casinos, and theatres providing cultural performances. Dancing is considered an art, encouraged and practised from very early childhood. The extensive repertoire is based on ancient legends and stories from religious epics. Performances are given in village halls and squares, and also in many of the leading hotels by professional touring groups. The dances vary enormously, both in style and number of performers. Some of the more notable are the *Legong*, a slow, graceful dance of divine nymphs; the *Baris*, a fast moving, noisy demonstration of male, warlike behaviour; and the *Jauk*, a riveting solo offering by a masked and richly costumed demon. Many consider the most dramatic of all to be the famous *Cecak* (Monkey Dance) which calls for 100 or more very agile participants. Many of the larger hotels, particularly in Bali, put on dance shows accompanied by the uniquely Indonesian Gamelan Orchestras.
Throughout the year, many local moonlight festivals occur; tourists should check locally. Indonesian puppets are world famous and shows for visitors are staged in various locations.

SHOPPING: Favourite buys are batik cloth, woodcarvings and sculpture, silverwork, woven baskets and hats, bamboo articles, *krises* (small daggers), paintings and woven cloth. At small shops, bartering might be necessary. **Shopping hours:** Mon-Sun 0900-2100. Most local markets open either very early in the morning or at dusk. In the smaller towns, shops may close between 1300 and 1700.

Business

- **GDP**: US$67 billion.
- **Main exports**: Oil, gas, electrical appliances, plywood, textiles and rubber.
- **Main imports**: Chemicals, foodstuff, fuel, machinery and equipment.
- **Main trade partners**: Singapore, Saudi Arabia, Japan, China (PR), Thailand, Australia, Korea (Rep) and the USA.

ECONOMY: 'The most dramatic economic collapse anywhere in the past five decades' is how one World Bank official described the calamitous disintegration of the Indonesian economy in the autumn of 1997. In 1998, economic output in Indonesia declined by more than 12 per cent and the national currency, the Rupiah, lost 80 per cent of its value. The crash occurred after more than a decade of uninterrupted growth at between 8 and 10 per cent annually. In January 1998, the IMF was forced into arranging its largest-ever financial rescue package, totalling US$43 billion, in order to prevent total economic collapse. During 1999, the economy stabilised and, since 2000, has resumed steady annual growth of around 5 per cent. Inflation has now stabilised at around 6 per cent; unemployment remains relatively high at 9 per cent of the workforce. The value of the Rupiah has also settled down. Nonetheless, only limited measures have been taken to deal with the structural problems which previously blighted the economy. The Suharto era's system of 'crony capitalism' still prevails, and essential reforms to the country's financial system have yet to be effected.
Thirty years earlier, as Indonesia's economic expansion began in earnest after the upheavals of the mid-60s, the country was far less developed than many of its neighbours. However, it was able to exploit its considerable mineral resources as a foundation on which to build an industrial economy. Oil and natural gas are the most important raw materials produced by Indonesia; it is still one of the largest exporters of liquefied natural gas. The country is also the second-largest producer of tin and extracts substantial quantities of other metals and metal ores (bauxite, copper, silver, gold and nickel) as well as coal and rubber. Much of the processing of these products is now done within the country. The agricultural sector (including fishing and forestry) remains important but more as a source of employment – it accounts for half the work force – than for its contribution to the economy. The service sector grew rapidly from the beginning of the 1980s onwards. Tourism has become a major industry and a vital source of foreign exchange (though likely to suffer in the wake of the Bali bomb attacks). Transport and communications, financial services and international freight traffic also made important contributions. However, it was the manufacturing industry, which developed from virtual non-existence in 1965 to its mid-90s position of providing one quarter of economic output, which received most attention from the Government (as well as outsiders) and announced Indonesia's arrival as a fully fledged 'Asian Tiger' economy. Despite the high profile of the vehicle, aerospace and electronics industries, Indonesia's manufacturing success was rooted in less glamorous areas such as textiles, food processing, tobacco and timber products.

BUSINESS ETIQUETTE: Business dealings should be conducted through an agent and tend to be slow. Visiting cards are widely used. It is conventional to shake hands and give a slight bow with the head on meeting and taking leave. Literature should be in English, but prices should be quoted in US Dollars as well as Pounds Sterling. **Private office hours:** Mon-Fri 0900-1700. **Government office hours:** Mon-Fri 0800-1600.

CONFERENCES/CONVENTIONS: The Balai Sidang Jakarta Convention Centre has the capacity for up to 5000 people. For information or assistance in organising a conference or convention in Indonesia, contact the Directorate-General of Tourism *or* the Indonesia Tourism Promotion Board *or* a representative IPTO office.

COMMERCIAL INFORMATION

Kamar Dagang dan Industri Indonesia (KADIN) (Indonesian Chamber of Commerce and Industry)
3rd-5th Floors, Chandra Building, Jalan M H Thamrin 20, Jakarta 10350, Indonesia
Tel: (21) 324 000.

Iran

Location: Middle East.

Time: GMT + 3.5 (GMT + 4.5 from 21 March to 23 October).

Overview

Iran is located in the Middle East, bounded by Turkmenistan and the Caspian Sea, Afghanistan, Pakistan, the Persian Gulf, the Gulf of Oman, Iraq and Turkey. The centre and east of the country is largely barren desert with mountainous regions in the west. Tehran, the capital, is essentially a modern city, but the best of the old has been preserved. The Shahid Motahari Mosque has eight minarets, from which the city can be viewed. The Bazaar is one of the world's largest. More traditional towns, such as Rey, Varamin, Qazvin and Shemshak are within easy reach of Tehran. The town of Tabriz is known for its restored blue mosque built in 1465. The covered Qaisariyeh Bazaar dates back to the 15th century. The Golden Triangle is the name popularly given to the region enclosed by the ancient cities of Hamadan, Kermanshahan and Khorrambabad. For many centuries the Silk Road passed through the pleasant rolling countryside of the region. Local dishes include *chelo khoresh* (rice topped with vegetables and meat in a nut sauce) and *morgh polo* (chicken and pilau rice).

General Information

AREA: 1,648,043 sq km (636,313 sq miles).

POPULATION: 66.47 million (official estimate 2003).

POPULATION DENSITY: 40.3 per sq km.

CAPITAL: Tehran. **Population:** 7,04 million (UN estimate, including suburbs, 2001).

GEOGRAPHY: Iran is located in the Middle East, bordered to the north by Turkmenistan and the Caspian Sea, the east by Afghanistan and Pakistan, the south by the Persian Gulf and the Gulf of Oman, and the west by Iraq and Turkey. The centre and east of the country are largely barren undulating desert, punctured by *qanats* (irrigation canals) and green oases, but there are mountainous regions in the west along the Turkish and Iraqi borders and in the north where the Elburz Mountains rise steeply from a fertile belt around the Caspian Sea.

GOVERNMENT: Islamic Republic since 1979. **Head of State:** Supreme Leader (Rahbar-e Moazam) Seyyed Ali Khameni since 1989. **Head of Government:** President Mahmoud Ahmadinejad since June 2005.

LANGUAGE: Persian (*Farsi*) is the most widely spoken language. Arabic is spoken in Khuzestan in the southwest, and Turkish in the northwest around Tabriz. English, French and (to a lesser extent) German are spoken by many businesspeople and officials.

RELIGION: Predominantly Islamic; mostly Shi'ite, with a minority of Sunnis. The 1976 census recorded 300,000 Christians, 80,000 Jews and 30,000 Zoroastrians.

TIME: GMT + 3.5 (GMT + 4.5 from 20 March to 21 September).

ELECTRICITY: 230 volts AC, 50Hz. Plugs are of the round two-pin type.

SOCIAL CONVENTIONS: Feelings about certain countries (such as the USA and the UK) run high, so the visitor should avoid contentious subjects. The Westernisation of the Iranian way of life has been arrested since the fall of the Shah, and Koranic law exercises a much more traditional influence over much of the populace. In general, Western influences are now discouraged. Handshaking is customary, but not with members of the opposite sex. It must be remembered that intimate relations between non-Muslim men and Muslim women is illegal, and may incur imprisonment. Visitors should address hosts by their surname or title. Iranians are very hospitable and like to entertain. It is also customary to be offered tea, and guests are expected to accept such offers of hospitality. Because of Islamic customs, dress should be conservative and discreet, especially women's. This has been especially enforced of late; women should cover their heads when in the public sphere, wear loose-fitted clothing, and ensure that their arms and legs are also concealed. Businesspeople are expected to wear a suit and more formal attire is also needed in smart dining rooms and for important social functions. During Ramadan, smoking, eating and drinking in public are prohibited between sunrise and sunset; however, facilities are always available in major hotels.

Climate

Dry and hot in summer, harsh in winter. Low annual rainfall. Iran is highly prone to earthquakes and tremors.

Required clothing: Tropical attire is worn from April to October. Mediumweights are advised from November to March.

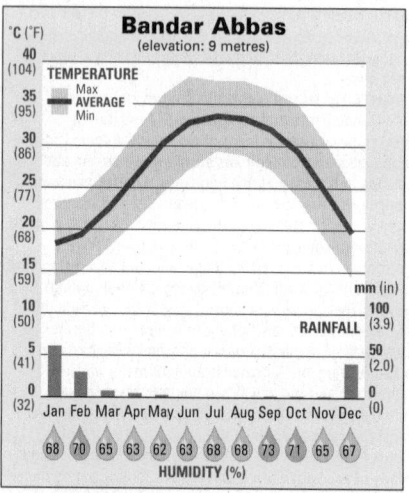

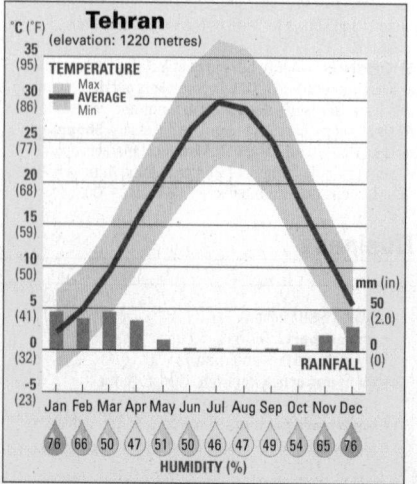

Communications

Telephone: IDD service available. Country code: 98. Telephone booths are yellow.

Mobile telephone: GSM 900 network. Main network operators include *MTCE* (website: www.mtce.ir), *TCI* and *TKC* (website: www.tkckish.com).

Internet: There are Internet cafes in Tehran and other cities.

Post: Airmail to Western Europe can take at least two weeks. There are 10 main post offices in Tehran. Post boxes are yellow. Stamps can be bought at some cigarette kiosks. Post office hours: Generally Sat-Thurs 0730-1500, but some main post offices stay open until 2100.

MEDIA: Press: The main English-language papers are the *Iran News*, *Kayhan International* and *Tehran Times*.

TV: *IRIB*, state-run, operates four national networks, as well as international services.

Radio: *IRIB* operates eight national networks, provincial services and an external service.

Passport/Visa

	Passport Required?	Visa Required?	Return Ticket Required?
Full British	Yes	Yes	No
Australian	Yes	Yes	No
Canadian	Yes	Yes	No
USA	Yes	Yes	No
Other EU	Yes	Yes	No
Japanese	Yes	Yes	No

Note: *Regulations and requirements may be subject to change at short notice, and you are advised to contact the appropriate diplomatic or consular authority before finalising travel arrangements. Any numbers in the chart refer to the footnotes below.*

Restricted entry: Nationals of Israel or holders of passports containing a visa for Israel (either valid or expired) will be refused entry under all circumstances. Women judged to be dressed immodestly will be refused entry.

PASSPORTS: Passport valid for six months beyond stay required by all.

VISAS: Required by all except the following:
(a) nationals of Turkey for stays of up to three months;
(b) nationals of Malaysia and Singapore may obtain a visa on arrival, free of charge, for stays of up to two weeks;
(c) transit passengers continuing their journey within 12 hours provided holding valid onward or return documentation and not leaving the airport. Transit passengers continuing their journey within 48 hours (under the above conditions) can obtain a transit visa on arrival against a fee of US$40, or within 72 hours for US$30.

Types of visa and cost: *Tourist/Business/Pilgrimage*: £61 (single-entry); £68 (double-entry). *Business* (multiple-entry): £79 (three months); £90 (six months); £90 (one year). *Transit*: £61. The above prices are for UK nationals; fees vary according to nationality of applicant.

Validity: *Tourist*, *Business* and *Pilgrimage* visas are issued for stays of up to one month and are valid for three months from date of authorisation. *Transit* visas are valid for five days. Applications for renewal or extension should be made to the Iranian Embassy.

Application to: Consulate (or consular section at Embassy); see *Passport/Visa Information* for details.

Application requirements: (a) Valid passport with a minimum of two blank pages to affix visa. (b) Two application forms. (c) Two passport-size photos (women should be photographed wearing the *hejab* – Islamic head dress). (d) For postal applications, self-addressed registered delivery envelope. (e) Proof of fee payment (payable by postal order or banker's draft to the 'Embassy of the Islamic Republic of Iran', *or* by direct payment into the Embassy bank account at Melli Bank plc, 98A Kensington High Street, London W8 4SG, UK, or by credit card, form to be filled in and sent with application). *Pilgrimage*: (a)-(e) and, (f) Letter of introduction signed by the Head of an Islamic Centre. *Business*: (a)-(e) and, (f) Letter of invitation from the sponsoring company in Iran, authorised and given a reference number by the Iranian Ministry of Foreign Affairs. The applicant should allow five working days before contacting the appropriate Embassy/Consulate with this reference number.

Working days required: A minimum of four weeks. A *pilgrimage* visa may only take two weeks to process.

Temporary residence: All visitors wishing to stay for more than three months must obtain a residence permit. Application must be made within eight days of arrival to Police Headquarters or the Ministry of Foreign Affairs in Tehran.

PASSPORT/VISA INFORMATION

Embassy of the Islamic Republic of Iran in the UK
16 Prince's Gate, London SW7 1PT, UK
Tel: (020) 7225 3000.
Website: www.iran-embassy.org.uk
Opening hours: Mon-Fri 0900-1700.

Iranian Consulate in the UK
50 Kensington Court, Kensington High Street, London W8 5DB, UK
Tel: (020) 7937 5225 *or* (0906) 302 0600 (visa section).
Website: www.iran-embassy.org.uk
Opening hours: Mon-Thurs 0900-1300, Fri 0900-1200.

Permanent Mission of the Islamic Republic of Iran to the United Nations
622 Third Avenue, 34th Floor, New York, NY 10017, USA
Tel: (212) 687 2020.
Website: www.un.int/iran

Interests Section of the Islamic Republic of Iran in the USA
c/o The Embassy of Pakistan, 2209 Wisconsin Avenue, NW, Washington, DC 20007, USA
Tel: (202) 965 4990.
Website: www.daftar.org

Money

Currency: Iranian Rial (IRR) = 100 dinars. Notes are in denominations of IRR10,000, 5000, 2000 and 1000. Coins are in denominations of IRR250, 100, 50, 20, 10 and 5.
Currency exchange: It is advisable to bring hard currency for exchange purposes.
Credit & debit cards: MasterCard is accepted in some places, but credit cards should not be relied on as the sole means of payment. Be aware that if the card was issued in the USA, it may not be usable due to the US trade embargo.
Traveller's cheques: It is not possible to exchange traveller's cheques.
Currency restrictions: The import and export of local currency is limited to IR500,000. Any amount larger than this requires authorisation from the Central Bank. The import of foreign currency is unlimited, provided declared on arrival (there is a special form). The export of foreign currency is limited to the amount declared on arrival. There are no ATMs.
Banking hours: Sat-Wed 0800-1600; some branches are open 0800-2000. Most banks are closed Thurs-Fri.
Exchange rate indicators:
Rate at time of publishing
£1.00= IRR15723.18
$1.00= IRR9058.00

Duty Free

The following goods may be imported into Iran without incurring customs duty:
A reasonable quantity of cigarettes; reasonable quantity of perfume for personal use; gifts on which the import duty/tax does not exceed US$80.
Prohibited items: Alcoholic beverages; all horticultural and agricultural goods including seeds and soil; living (or collection); bacteria, fungi, insects, nematodes or viruses; old books or magazines; live birds, animals and their products.
Penalties for being in possession of narcotics are very severe.

Public Holidays

Below are listed Public Holidays for the January 2006-June 2007 period.
2006: Jan 10 Eid al-Adha (Feast of the Sacrifice). **Jan 19** Eid al-Ghadir-al Khom. **Jan 31** Islamic New Year. **Feb 9** Ashoura. **Feb 11** Victory of the 1979 Islamic Revolution. **Mar 20** Oil Nationalisation Day. **Mar 21** Nowrooz (Iranian New Year). **Mar 29** Death of the Prophet and Martyrdom of Imam Hassan. **Apr 1** Islamic Republic Day. **Apr 2** Sizdah-Bedar (Public Outing Day to end Nowrooz). **Apr 11** Prophet's Birthday and Imam Sadeq. **Jun 4** Death of Imam Khomeini. **Jun 5** Anniversary of Uprising Against the Shah. **Aug 8** Birthday of Iman Ali. **Aug 22** Leilat al-Meiraj (Ascension of the Prophet). **Sep 9** Birthday of Imam Mahdi. **Oct 15** Martyrdom of Imam Ali. **Oct 20** Quds Day. **Oct 22-24** Eid al-Fitr (End of Ramadan). **Nov 18** Martyrdom of Imam Sadeq. **Dec 31** Eid al-Adha (Feast of the Sacrifice).
2007: Jan 20 Islamic New Year. **Jan 30** Ashoura. **Feb 11** Victory of the 1979 Islamic Revolution. **Mar 20** Oil Nationalisation Day. **Mar 21** Nowrooz (Iranian New Year). **Mar 31** Prophet's Birthday and Imam Sadeq. **Apr 1** Islamic Republic Day. **Apr 2** Sizdah-Bedar (Public Outing Day to end Nowrooz). **Jun 4** Death of Imam Khomeini. **Jun 5** Anniversary of Uprising Against the Shah.
Note: Some extra dates in 2007 to be confirmed.
Note: Muslim festivals are timed according to local sightings of various phases of the moon and the dates given above are approximations. During the lunar month of Ramadan that precedes Eid al-Fitr, Muslims fast during the day and feast at night and normal business patterns may be interrupted. Many restaurants are closed during the day and there may be restrictions on smoking and drinking. Some disruption may continue into Eid al-Fitr itself. Eid al-Fitr and Eid al-Adha may last anything from two to 10 days, depending on the region. For more information see the *World of Islam* appendix.

Health

	Special Precautions?	Certificate Required?
Yellow Fever	Yes	1
Cholera	2	No
Typhoid & Polio	3	N/A
Malaria	4	N/A

Note: Regulations and requirements may be subject to change at short notice, and you are advised to contact your doctor well in advance of your intended date of departure. Any numbers in the chart refer to the footnotes below.

1: A *yellow fever* vaccination certificate is required from all travellers coming from infected areas.
2: Following WHO guidelines issued in 1973, a *cholera* vaccination certificate is no longer a condition of entry to Iran. However, *cholera* is a serious risk in this country and precautions are essential. Up-to-date advice should be sought before deciding whether these precautions should include vaccination as medical opinion is divided over its effectiveness; see the *Health* appendix for further information.
3: Immunisation against *typhoid* is advised.
4: Limited malaria risk exists from March to November in rural areas of the provinces of Sistan-Baluchestan, Hormozgan and Kerman (tropical part); in some areas north of the Zagros mountains and in western and southwestern regions during the summer months. Resistance to chloroquine and sulfadoxine-pyrimethamine has been reported in the malignant *falciparum* strain. The recommended prophylaxis is chloroquine in the *vivax* risk areas; chloroquine plus proguanil in the *falciparum* risk areas.
Food & drink: Mains water is normally chlorinated, and whilst relatively safe, may cause mild abdominal upsets. Bottled water is available and is advised for the first few weeks of the stay. Pasteurised milk is available; unpasteurised milk should be boiled. Powdered or tinned milk is available and is advised, but make sure that it is reconstituted with pure water. Avoid dairy products which are likely to have been made from unboiled milk. Only eat well-cooked meat and fish, preferably served hot. Salad and mayonnaise may carry increased risk. Vegetables should be cooked and fruit peeled.
Other risks: *Bilharzia* (*schistosomiasis*) is present in southwestern Iran. Avoid swimming and paddling in stagnant water; swimming pools which are well chlorinated and maintained are safe. *Diarrhoeal diseases* such as *dysentery*, *giardiasis* and *typhoid fever* are common. *Tick-borne relapsing fever*, *cutaneous leishmaniasis* and *hepatitis A* and B occur. *Trachoma* is reported to be common.
Rabies is present. For those at high risk, vaccination before arrival should be considered. If you are bitten, seek medical advice without delay. For more information, consult the *Health* appendix.
Health care: Health facilities are limited in remote areas. Medical insurance is essential.

Travel - International

AIR:
The national airline is *Iran Air (IR)* (website: www.iranair.com), which operates three/four direct flights per week to Tehran from London (Heathrow). *British Mediterranean* (a franchise partner of *British Airways*) operates four services a week from London to Tehran. Other airlines serving Iran include *Emirates, Gulf Air, KLM, Lufthansa* and *Turkish Airlines*.
Approximate flight times: From Tehran to *London* is six hours.
Main airports: *Tehran (THR)* (Mehrabad) is 5km (3 miles) west of the city. Airline buses are available to the city (travel time - 45 minutes) for approximately IRR200-500. Taxis are also available to the city centre for approximately IRR10,000 (travel time - 30 minutes). Airport facilities include a bank, post office, restaurants and snack bar, duty-free shop, gift shops, tourist information and first aid/vaccination facilities.
Departure tax: IRR70,000.
SEA:
The main port was Khorramshahr until its destruction during the war with Iraq. It is currently under reconstruction. The ports of Abbas and Bushehr are to be found in the Persian Gulf and Nowshahr and Anzelli on the Caspian Sea. *P&O Ferries* connects Iranian ports with Persian Gulf States and Karachi.
RAIL:
RAJA Trains (part of *Iranian Islamic Republic Railways*) operates passenger services from Tehran to Isanbul (Turkey) and Damascus (Syrian Arab Republic); from Tabiz to Djolfa (for the CIS) and Van (Turkey); and from Zahedan to Quetta (Pakistan). The Qom-Zahedan Line, when completed, will link Europe with India. Contact *RAJA Trains* (c/o Iranian Islamic Republic Railways) (website: www.irirw.com) for details.
ROAD:
No reliable international through-road links. There are various routes possible from Turkey and Pakistan, but these are not recommended. Cars can also be put on boats at Venice or Brindisi and picked up at Ezmir. For details of political conditions governing access, contact the Embassy.

Travel - Internal

AIR:
Iran Air runs services to Ahwaz, Esfahan, Kish, Mashhad, Shiraz, Tabriz, Tehran and Zahedan and other major cities. *Aseman Air* also runs services to the major cities. The vast size of Iran makes internal flights the most practical method of transport.
RAIL:
RAJA Trains run a fairly comprehensive internal rail network. Major intercity trains operate on five main regional routes: Azarbaijan route (Tehran - Jolfa); Golestan route (Tehran - Gorgan); Hormozgan route (Tehran - Bandar-e-Abbas); Khorasan route (Tehran - Mashhad); and Khozetan route (Tehran - Khorramshahr). There are many areas in the mountains and the desert which can only be reached by rail. There are some air-conditioned trains, and sleeping and dining cars on many trains. For further details, contact RAJA Trains (c/o Iranian Islamic Republic Railways) (see *Travel – International* section) for details.
ROAD:
The road network is extensive, with more than 51,300km (31,800 miles) of paved roads and 490km (304 miles) of motorways, but the quality is unreliable. The two main roads, the A1 and A2, link the Iraqi and Pakistani borders and the Afghan and Turkish borders. Traffic drives on the right. **Bus:** Widespread, cheap and comfortable, although services tend to be erratic. **Taxi:** Available in all cities. The urban taxis (orange or blue) will carry several passengers at a time and are much cheaper than the private taxis which only carry one person. Unofficial taxis should be avoided; use only legitimate taxis or those ordered through legitimate agencies. Group taxis for up to 10 people are available for intercity travel. Prices are negotiated beforehand and tipping is not necessary. **Car hire:** Available in most cities and from airports.
Documentation: An International Driving Permit is recommended but it is not a legal requirement. Personal insurance is required. All motorists entering Iran must possess a *Carnet de Passage en Douane* and an International Certificate of Vehicle ownership.
URBAN:
Tehran has an extensive bus system, including double-deckers. Tickets are bought in advance at kiosks.
Travel times: The following chart gives approximate travel times (in hours and minutes) from Tehran to other major cities/towns in Iran.

	Air	Road	Rail
Ahvaz	1.30	17.00	19.00
B. Abbas	1.55	28.00	-
Esfahan	1.00	8.00	9.00
Kerman	1.30	20.00	18.00
Mashhad	1.30	14.00	15.00

Travel Advice

Travellers are strongly advised against all travel to the border areas with Afghanistan, Pakistan and Iraq. Westerners have been the target of kidnaps by armed gangs in southeast Iran. Travellers should not travel overland to Pakistan or Afghanistan.

Iran

There is a threat from terrorism and violent protests in Iran. Attacks could be directed at Western interests. On 2 August 2005, a small device was set off inside a building in Tehran, which houses foreign commercial offices. Iran is prone to earthquakes. Small tremors occur frequently but many people have lost their lives in Iran in large earthquakes in recent years.

There have been reports that the runway at the new Imam Khomeni International Airport in Tehran may not yet be suitable for use. Until the situation has been clarified, travellers are advised to travel by flights using the existing (Mehrabad) airport.

This advice is based on information provided by the Foreign and Commonwealth Office in the UK. It is correct at time of publishing. As the situation can change rapidly, visitors are advised to contact the following organisations for the latest travel advice:

British Foreign and Commonwealth Office
Tel: (0845) 850 2829.
Website: www.fco.gov.uk

US Department of State
Website: http://travel.state.gov/travel

Accommodation

HOTELS:

A number of hotels are available and there is a fair range of accommodation. Student accommodation is available in small hotels. Schools and private houses also offer accommodation. For more information contact the Iran Tourist Company or the Iran Touring and Tourism Organisation (ITTO) (see *Top Things To See and Do*).

CAMPING/CARAVANNING:

There are limited camping facilities and off-site camping is discouraged. Registration with the police is required if camping.

Top Things To See & Do

- **Tehran:** The capital is essentially a modern city, but the best of the old has been preserved. The **Shahid Motahari Mosque** has eight minarets, from which the city can be viewed. The **Bazaar** (open every day except Friday and religious holidays) is one of the world's largest; another bazaar, catering mainly for local communities, can be found in the **Tajrish** suburb. Located in the north of the capital, an endless maze of vaulted alleys, everything from fine carpets to silver- and copperware to exotic aromatic spices can be found here. There is a separate section for each trade practised and craftsmen can be seen at their work. Tehran has several good museums, including the **Abgineh Museum of Iranian Pottery**; the **Rea Abbasi Museum**, housing a rare collection of Iranian calligraphy and paintings; the **National Museum of Iran (Iran Bastan Museum)**, which displays mostly archaeological and anthropological exhibits; the **Rassam Cultural and Art Foundation of Carpet**, which includes a carpet museum and carpet weaving school; the **Carpet Museum**, whose oldest carpet is 450 years old; and the **Anthropological Museums** in Golestan Place and Saad Abad. Iran's capital also has a number of cultural centres (including Azadi, Bahman and Khavaran) as well as a **National Library**, a **City Theatre**, a **Zoo** and a **University**.
- The **Alborz** mountain chain is a popular destination for excursions from Tehran. There are numerous mountain resorts offering cable car facilities as well as skiing slopes (the season running from January to March). Within easy reach of Tehran are the towns of **Rey**, **Varamin**, **Qazvin** and **Shemshak**, which have preserved much of their original character.
- The country's second-largest city, **Tabriz**, has a ruined but restored fine blue mosque built in 1465. The covered **Qaisariyeh Bazaar** dates back to the 15th century. About 22km (14 miles) from the salt lake is the town of **Uromieh**, which claims to be the birthplace of Zoroaster. Other towns worth visiting include **Ardabil**, **Astara**, **Bandar-e Anzali** and **Rasht**.
- **The Golden Triangle** is the name popularly given to the region enclosed by the ancient cities of Hamadan, Kermanshah and Khorramabad. This is a part of Iran which is particularly rich in historical associations; for many centuries the **Silk Road** passed through the pleasant rolling countryside of the region, and there are several indications of settlements dating back over 6000 years. **Hamadan** was the summer capital of the Persian Emperors, although one of the few easily visible signs of the city's antiquity is the **Stone Lion**, dating back to the time of Alexander the Great. **Kermanshah** is a good base for visiting the **Taghe Bostan Grottoes**, which

have several excellent bas-relief carvings. The site of the **Seleucid Temple of Artemis** is in **Kangavar**; it consists of massive fallen columns and is now being reconstructed.
- **Esfahan** is the former capital of Persia and has been designated by UNESCO as a World Heritage Site. The city's most remarkable feature is its magnificent central square which is roughly seven times larger than San Marco in Venice. The mosques, palaces, bridges and gardens also deserve a visit. The **Friday Mosque** (Masjid-e Jomeh) is one of Iran's finest buildings. The **Shaikh Lotfullah Mosque** is famous for the stalactite effect of its northern entrance. There are also several good bazaars.
- **Shiraz** is the capital of the Fars Province, and another of the country's ancient cities. Several of the buildings date back to the ninth century, and there are many excellent parks and gardens. About 50km (30 miles) away is **Persepolis**, also on the UNESCO World Heritage list, and famous for the Ceremonial Seat of Darius, built on an enormous platform carved out of the Kuhe Rahmat. Another UNESCO-listed archaeological site can be found at **Changha Zanbil**, 40km (25 miles) southeast of **Susa**.
- **Khorasan** is a large province in the east where a great revival of learning occurred in the early Middle Ages. **Mashhad**, a former trading post on the Silk Road, is the capital of the region.
- The city of **Kerman** in the southern desert region has several stunning mosques and a ruined citadel, although visitors are advised to exercise caution and only travel on tours organised through Iranian government-approved tourist organisations.
- **Water-skiing** facilities are available at the **Karadj Dam** near Tehran.
- **Fishing:** Many streams are well stocked with trout including the Djaje-Rud, the Karadje and the Lar. The dammed lakes of the Karadje River and the Sefid Rud are also filled with fish. The Caspian Sea is another good choice, with large numbers of bream, mullet, salmon and sturgeon.
- **Wintersports:** The skiing season is from January to March in the Alborz Mountains. Resorts include **Abe Ali**, 62km (38 miles) east of Tehran; the Noor Slope, 71km (44 miles) from the capital; **Shemshak**, 59km (37 miles) from Tehran, and **Dizine** near the town of Gatchsar.
- *Iran Air* operates **trekking** and **climbing** package holidays, which can be booked at any of their offices throughout the world.

TOURIST INFORMATION

Iran Touring and Tourism Organisation (ITTO)
238 Sindokht Street, Fatemi Avenue, Tehran, Iran
Tel: (21) 643 5650.
Website: www.itto.org

Iran Tourist Company
257 Ostad Motahari Avenue, Ghaem Magham Farahni Street, Cross Road, Tehran, Iran
Tel: (21) 873 9819 or 6762-5.
Website: www.irantouristco.com

Entertainment

FOOD & DRINK:
Things to know: Most Iranian meals are eaten with a spoon and fork, but visitors may choose a Western dish and eat with a knife and fork. The consumption of alcohol is strictly forbidden.

National specialities:
Rice is the staple food and the Iranians cook it superbly.
- *Chelo khoresh* (rice topped with vegetables and meat in a nut sauce).
- *Polo chirin* (sweet-sour saffron-coloured rice with raisins, almonds and orange).
- *Adas polo* (rice, lentils and meat), *morgh polo* (chicken and pilau rice), *chelo kababs* (rice with skewered meats cooked over charcoal). *kofte* (minced meat and formed into meatballs).
- *Khoreshe badinjan* (mutton and aubergine stew), *mast-o-khier* (cold yoghurt-based soup flavoured with mint, chopped cucumber and raisins) and *dolmeh* (stuffed aubergine, courgettes or peppers).

National drinks:
- Fruit and vegetable juices are popular, as are sparkling mineral waters.
- Tea is also popular and drunk in the many tea-houses (*ghahve khane*).

Tipping: In large hotels, a 10 to 15 per cent service charge is added to the bill. In restaurants (*chelokababis*) it is usual to leave some small change. Tipping is not expected in tea-houses or small hotels.

SHOPPING: While the shops offer a wide selection of quality goods, local items can be bought in the many bazaars. Purchases include hand-carved, inlaid woodwork, carpets, rugs, silks, leather goods, mats, tablecloths, gold, silver, glass and ceramics. Bargaining is customary. There are restrictions on which items may be taken out of the country; see *Duty-Free* section for details. **Shopping hours:** Generally 0900-1300 and 1500-2000.

Business

ECONOMY: Iran's main sources of income are its huge oil and gas deposits, which are among the world's largest. The agricultural sector is important for the numbers employed, although output has been depressed by drought and migration of rural labour to the cities. Both subsistence crops, mainly wheat, barley and sugar, and cash crops are grown. The manufacturing sector, which accounts for about one-sixth of total output, produces textiles, food-processing and transport equipment. Apart from hydrocarbons, Iran also has viable deposits of coal, magnesium ores and gypsum. Government policy has sought to promote the agricultural and light industry in order to reduce the economy's dependence on oil and increase the influence of the private sector – about 80 per cent of economic activity is state controlled. The economy is performing fairly steadily at present: annual growth is about 5 per cent and inflation is 12 to 15 per cent. As in other areas, economic policy is dominated by fundamental difference of approach between the elected government and the ruling clergy. On the trade front, Iran has developed important new links with the newly independent states of central Asia as well as Turkey and China but, more importantly, existing trade with traditional partners in Europe, Japan and the Middle East have been restored. Bilateral trade with the US remains, not surprisingly, at a low level.

BUSINESS ETIQUETTE: Most Iranian businesspeople speak English and are polite and conservative in manner and expect an appropriate response from visitors. Exchanging calling cards is normally restricted to senior people. Appointments should be made and punctuality is expected for business meetings. Business gifts are quite acceptable. **Office hours:** Sat to Wed 0800-1600, Thurs 0900-1200 (some offices may close all day).

COMMERCIAL INFORMATION

Export Promotion Centre
PO Box 1148, Tadjrish, Dr Chamran Highway, Tehran, Iran
Tel: (21) 21911.
Website: www.iran-export.com

Iranian Trade Association in the USA
PO Box 927743, San Diego, California 92192, USA
Tel: (619) 368 6790.
Website: www.iraniantrade.org

Iraq

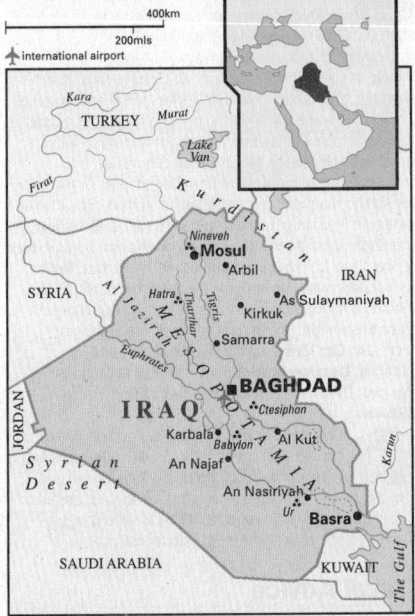

Location: Middle East.

Time: GMT + 3 (GMT + 4 from 1 April to 1 October).

Overview

The media depiction of Iraq is of a place where humanity is found at its most ugly; a land of violent insurgency, kidnappings and religious intolerance and extremism. Yet this is also where humanity at its most tremendous once lived. The core of modern Iraq was Mesopotamia, at the heart of the Sumerian, Babylonian and Assyrian empires between the seventh century BC and AD 100. Many great civilisations were cradled in often verdant arms here - amidst huge and unforgiving desert terrain snakes stupendous rivers such as the Euphrates and Tigris. This country supposedly contained the glorious Garden of Eden and Babylon's bountiful Hanging Gardens. Ancient Baghdad was a focal point of learning, a major stop along the Silk Road. Such cultural leanings can still be seen in the Iraq of today, museums crammed with astonishing artefacts and relics.

However, Iraq has been blighted by resurgent conflict: from the Arab Caliphate to Mongols, and from the Timur Empire to the Ottoman Empire. In 1920, the Hashemite Amir Faisal ibn Hussain was proclaimed King; Independence came in 1932. In 1958, the Hashemite Dynasty disintegrated via murder and coup. Iraq's final coup in recent history came in 1968, bringing the Ba'ath Party to power.

In 1979, Saddam Hussein became President and Party Leader of the Ba'ath Party. Iraqis hoped to resolve a long-running territorial dispute with Iran over the Shatt al-Arab waterway, and a full-scale invasion of Iran was launched in 1980. The war degenerated into one of attrition, lasting until 1988, when the two exhausted nations sued for peace. Despite minor territorial gains, the Iraqi economy was crippled and incurred an enormous foreign debt, mainly owed to neighbouring Kuwait. Insistent Kuwaiti demands for repayment, Iraq's historical claim over Kuwaiti territory, and a dispute over oil reserves provided the main pretext for the Iraqi invasion of Kuwait in 1990. The US-led response to the invasion, with firm backing from the UN, ensured that Iraq suffered a massive defeat. The Iraqi regime was seriously threatened by armed opposition

elements among the Shia of southern Iraq and the Kurds in the north. However, the superior firepower of Iraqi troops and the Western refusal to provide effective backing for the rebels resisted this.

Thereafter, the USA and others used several means to constrain Iraq, such as a complete trade embargo - excepting a strictly controlled regimen of oil sales with which the Iraqi Government could buy food and medicine. Arguably, ordinary Iraqis were worst hit by such sanctions. A few years later, the USA would lead the war against Iraq that has generated such fiercely mixed reactions, from relief that Hussein's brutal regime was toppled, to anger at the flimsy lies surrounding the now officially non-existent 'weapons of mass destruction' and Hussein's alleged connections with Al-Qaeda.

With time, the shackles of war will hopefully be dismantled, and Iraq shall pave itself a future as grand as was its past.

General Information

AREA: 438,317 sq km (169,235 sq miles).
POPULATION: 26.5 million (UN, 2005).
POPULATION DENSITY: 60.4 per sq km.
CAPITAL: Baghdad. **Population:** 5.7 million (2004 estimate).
GEOGRAPHY: Iraq shares borders with Turkey, Iran, the Gulf of Oman, Kuwait, Saudi Arabia, Jordan and the Syrian Arab Republic. There is also a neutral zone between Iraq and Saudi Arabia administered jointly by the two countries. Iraq's portion covers 3522 sq km (1360 sq miles). The country's main topographical features are the two rivers, the Euphrates and the Tigris, which flow from the Turkish and Syrian Arab Republic borders in the north to the Gulf in the south. The northeast is mountainous, while the country in the west is arid desert. The land surrounding the two rivers is fertile plain, but the lack of effective irrigation has resulted in flooding and areas of marshland.
GOVERNMENT: Iraqi Transitional Government. **Interim President:** Jalal Talabani. **Interim Prime Minister:** Ibrahim Jaafari. **Recent history:** Since March 2003 when the US-led coalition declared war on Iraq and successfully ousted the regime of Saddam Hussein, the country has been in a period of transition. After much anticipation, the transferral of power was finally granted to a new Iraqi Government in mid-2004. This was supplemented by countrywide elections on 30 January 2005 to appoint a 275-member National Assembly, of which the majority of seats were democratically assigned to the Shia United Iraqi Alliance (although, contentiously, some people were unable to vote due to dangerous conditions and many Sunni Muslims did not participate in the electoral process for various reasons). This Assembly elected a President, Jalal Talabani, and two deputies, Ghazi Yawer and Adel Abdul Mahdi, who, in turn, designated Ibrahim Jaafari as Prime Minister responsible for the day-to-day running of Iraq. Iraq's future, despite the hope that elections in early 2005 gave to some, remains highly uncertain. In November 2005, UN Security Council Resolution 1637 (2005) extended backing for the Multinational Force's role in Iraq for a further year. Parliamentary elections took place on 15 December 2005.
LANGUAGE: 80 per cent Arabic, 15 per cent Kurdish. Assyrian and Armenian may also be spoken.
RELIGION: More than 50 per cent Shia Muslim, with the remaining Sunni Muslim, and Druze and Christian minorities.
ELECTRICITY: 230 volts AC, 50Hz. Various two- and three-pin plugs are in use. Electricity supplies were severely affected in the recent conflict.
SOCIAL CONVENTIONS: Owing to a long and varied history, Iraq is a culturally rich country. Today, traditional Islamic culture predominates, with Koranic law playing an active role in the day-to-day life of the country, and visitors should be careful to respect this and act accordingly. Visitors should always address their hosts by full name and title. Traditional Arab hospitality is followed as a rule, in accordance with religious law. Conservative and discreet dress should be worn in observance of local Islamic laws.
Photography: The summary execution of journalist Farzad Bazoft exemplifies the need for extreme caution when photographing anything of a sensitive nature. This includes photographs of local people (the Muslim religion does not allow the representation of human or animal images in any form); and, most importantly, any Government installations, buildings or indeed anything else that may be considered off-limits to visitors. If in any doubt, do not take a photo.

Climate

Summers are very hot and dry. Winters are warm with some rain.
Required clothing: Tropical attire is worn in summer months. Mediumweights are advised during the winter.

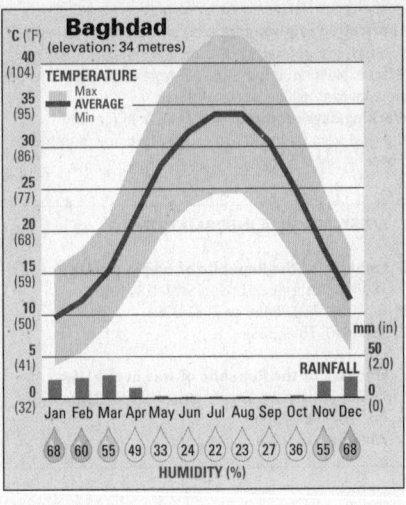

Baghdad (elevation: 34 metres)

Communications

Telephone: IDD service available, but services were severely disrupted following the conflict and are only gradually returning. Country code: 964.
Mobile telephone: Roaming agreements with international mobile phone companies are still in progress. There is extremely limited coverage.
Internet: There are no ISPs in Iraq at present. However, although connectivity within the home is rare, Internet access is sprouting everywhere via cafes and hotels, mainly in Baghdad.
Post: All mail may take several weeks to process and is inadvisable.
MEDIA: There has been a surge of media outlets since the downfall of Saddam Hussein. During his dictatorship, satellite TV was banned.
Press: Newspapers published in Arabic include *Al Mada* (website: www.almadapaper.com), *Al Mashriq* and *Al Dustur*. *Al-Sabah* (website: www.alsabaah.com) is the main English-language daily , *Al-Zaman* (website: www.azzaman.com) is a London based daily printed in Baghdad and Basra and *Iraq Today* (website: www.iraq-today.com) is an English-language daily.
TV: *Al-Iraqiya, Al Sharquiya, Kurdistan Satellite Channel* and *KurdSat*.
Radio: *Republic of Iraq Radio, Radio Nahrain, Voice of Iraq, Hot FM* and *Radio Dijla*.

Passport/Visa

Note: Iraq continues to undergo a period of transition following the end of the US-led war against Saddam Hussein's regime in March/April 2003. Most of the country's political, social, physical and economic infrastructures have, by and large, been destroyed and need to be rebuilt, are in the process of being so, or have only just initiated recovery. As a result of the uncertain situation, some of the following information may be unreliable or inaccurate. All travel to Iraq is ill-advised unless for relief purposes.
Any British nationals travelling to Iraq for essential reasons should register their presence with the British Embassy.

	Passport Required?	Visa Required?	Return Ticket Required?
Full British	Yes	Yes	Yes
Australian	Yes	Yes	Yes
Canadian	Yes	Yes	Yes
USA	Yes	Yes	Yes
Other EU	Yes	Yes	Yes
Japanese	Yes	Yes	Yes

Note: *Regulations and requirements may be subject to change at short notice, and you are advised to contact the appropriate diplomatic or consular authority before finalising travel arrangements. Any numbers in the chart refer to the footnotes below.*

PASSPORTS: Passport valid for at least six months from date of issue of visa required by all.
Note: At time of publishing, non-Iraqi Arab passport holders cannot enter Iraq.
VISAS: Required by all.
Types of visa and cost: *General:* £25.
Validity: Three months.
Application to: Consulate (or consular section at

Embassy); see *Passport/Visa Information* for details.
Application requirements: (a) Valid passport. (b) Two passport-size photos. (c) One application form. (d) Fee. (e) Letter explaining purpose of visit from company for whom the applicant will be working in Iraq.
Working days required: One week from receipt of approval from Baghdad (which may take one month or more).

PASSPORT/VISA INFORMATION

Embassy of the Republic of Iraq in the UK
169 Knightsbridge, London SW7 1DW, UK
Tel: (020) 7602 8456 *or* 7581 2264.
Fax: (020) 7589 3356.

Embassy of the Republic of Iraq in the USA
1801 P Street, NW, Washington, DC 20036, USA
Tel: (202) 483 7500.
Website: www.iraqiembassy.org

Money

Currency: The new Iraqi Dinar was introduced in October 2003. Iraqi Dinar (IQD) = 20 dirhams = 1000 fils. Notes are in denominations of IQD25,000, 10,000, 5000, 1000, 500, 250 and 50. Coins are in denominations of IQD100 and 25. This information is subject to frequent change in the current conditions.
Currency exchange: Foreign currency can be used at special duty-free shops in Baghdad up to a value of US$200. To obtain this concession, goods must be purchased within 20 days of arrival and passports must be produced.
Credit & debit cards: Not widely used.
Traveller's cheques: These are not generally accepted.
Currency restrictions: The import of local currency is allowed up to IQD25 and export up to IQD5. The import of foreign currency is unlimited, provided declared on arrival. The export of foreign currency is limited to the amount imported and declared.
Banking hours: Sat-Wed 0800-1230, Thurs 0800-1100. Banks close at 1000 during Ramadan.
Exchange rate indicators:
Rate at time of publishing
£1.00=   IQD2590.17
$1.00=   IQD1470.00

Duty Free

The following goods may be imported into Iraq without incurring customs duty:
200 cigarettes or 50 cigars or 250g tobacco; one bottle of wine and one bottle of spirits with a total volume of not more than 1l; 500ml of perfume (two small opened bottles); gifts to the value of IQD10.
Note: (a) The total value of the above goods may not exceed IQD100. (b) Travellers who have not left the country within 120 days must report to customs.
Prohibited items: Electrical appliances other than personal effects, souvenirs in quantities considered to have commercial value, many types of fruits and plants.

Public Holidays

Below are listed Public Holidays for the January 2006-June 2007 period.
2006: Jan 1 New Year's Day. **Jan 6** Army Day. **Jan 10** Eid al-Adha (Feast of the Sacrifice). **Jan 31** Islamic New Year. **Feb 8** Ramadan Revolution. **Feb 9** Ashoura. **Apr 11** Mouloud (Birth of the Prophet Muhammad). **Apr 17** FAO Day. **May 1** Labour Day. **Jul 14** National Day. **Jul 17** Republic Day. **Aug 8** Ceasefire Day (End of Iran-Iraq War). **Oct 22-24** Eid al-Fitr (End of Ramadan). **Dec 31** Eid al-Adha (Feast of the Sacrifice).
2007: Jan 1 New Year's Day. **Jan 6** Army Day. **Jan 20** Islamic New Year. **Jan 30** Ashoura. **Feb 8** Ramadan Revolution. **Mar 31** Mouloud (Birth of the Prophet Muhammad). **Apr 17** FAO Day. **May 1** Labour Day.
Note: Muslim festivals are timed according to local sightings of various phases of the moon and the dates given above are approximations. During the lunar month of Ramadan that precedes Eid al-Fitr, Muslims fast during the day and feast at night and normal business patterns may be interrupted. Many restaurants are closed during the day and there may be restrictions on smoking and drinking. Some disruption may continue into Eid al-Fitr itself. Eid al-Fitr and Eid al-Adha may last anything from two to 10 days, depending on the region. For more information, see the *World of Islam* appendix.

Health

	Special Precautions?	Certificate Required?
Yellow Fever	No	1
Cholera	No	No
Typhoid & Polio	2	N/A
Malaria	3	N/A

Note: *Regulations and requirements may be subject to change at short notice, and you are advised to contact your doctor well in advance of your intended date of departure. Any numbers in the chart refer to the footnotes below.*

1: A *yellow fever* vaccination certificate is required from travellers coming from infected areas.
2: Vaccination against *typhoid* is advised.
3: *Malaria* risk is almost entirely in the benign *vivax* form and exists from May to November principally in areas in the north below 1500m (4920ft) – Basra, Duhok, Erbil, Ninawa, Sulaimaniya and Ta'min Province. The recommended prophylaxis is chloroquine.
Food & drink: All water should be regarded as being potentially contaminated. Water used for drinking, brushing teeth or making ice should have first been boiled or otherwise sterilised. Milk is unpasteurised and should be boiled. Powdered or tinned milk is available and is advised, but make sure that it is reconstituted with pure water. Avoid dairy products which are likely to have been made from unboiled milk. Only eat well-cooked meat and fish, preferably served hot. Pork, salad and mayonnaise may carry increased risk. Vegetables should be cooked and fruit peeled.
Note: (a) All travellers entering Iraq are required to take an AIDS test. A fee will be charged for this. (b) Travellers suffering from *AIDS*, *tuberculosis*, *syphilis* or *leprosy* will be deported.
Other risks: *Bilharzia* (schistosomiasis) is present. Avoid swimming and paddling in fresh water; swimming pools which are well chlorinated and maintained are safe. *Diarrhoeal diseases*, including *giardiasis*, *dysentery* and *typhoid fever* are common. *Hepatitis B* is endemic and *hepatitis A* is widespread. *Visceral leishmaniasis* is common in central Iraq. *Cutaneous leishmaniasis* is reported. *Crimean-Congo haemorrhagic fever* has been reported. *Tick-borne relapsing fever* may occur. Venomous snakes, scorpions and spiders are present in Iraq, and if you are bitten or stung, seek medical advice without delay. Temperatures can reach 40 degrees Celsius, so dehydration is a problem. *Rabies* is present. For those at high risk, vaccination before arrival should be considered. For more information, consult the *Health* appendix.
Health care: Health insurance including emergency repatriation cover is essential. Only limited facilities are available and evacuation by air ambulance may be required; therefore, insurance should have provision for this. Doctors and hospitals often expect immediate cash payment for services.

Travel - International

AIR:

The national airline is *Iraqi Airways (IA)*. At time of publication, there are no scheduled civilian flights into Iraq.
Approximate flight times: From Baghdad to *London* is six hours.
Main airports: *Baghdad International Airport (BGW)* is 18km (11 miles) south of the city (travel time – 20 minutes). *To/from the airport*: Taxi services go to the city with rates negotiable for shared taxis. There is a surcharge after 2200. Coach service is available to the city and returns from Damascus Street (100 minutes before flight departure). Car hire is also available. *Facilities*: Banks, bureaux de change, post office, duty free shops, bars, restaurants, snack bar, shops and first aid.
Note: Due to the airport being repeatedly targeted by rocket and mortar attacks, at time of publication, the British Embassy in Iraq no longer uses the Baghdad to Baghdad International Airport road.
Departure tax: IQD2000.
SEA:

At present, all ports in Iraq are closed.

RAIL:

There is a rail journey between Istanbul (Turkey) and Baghdad. All other overland routes may not be accessible to foreigners.
ROAD:

At time of publication non-Iraqi Arab passport holders can not enter Iraq.
Before the Gulf War, principal international routes ran through Jordan, Syrian Arab Republic and Turkey. Work on the Express Highway, an attempt to link Iraq with Jordan, Kuwait and Syrian Arab Republic has been suspended for the time being. For further information, contact the Iraqi Interests Section for up-to-date political conditions and border details.

Travel - Internal

AIR:

Aircraft are not normally allowed into Baghdad. However, before sanctions there were regular flights between Baghdad, Al Basrah and Mosul.
RAIL:

Rail services are operated by the *State Enterprise for Iraqi Railways*. The country has over 2000km (1242 miles) of track, most of which is standard gauge. A further 300km (200 miles) or so is under construction. The principal route is from the Syrian Arab Republic border at Tel-Kotchek to Mosul, Baghdad and Al Basrah. Trains also run from Baghdad to Kirkuk and Arbil. A service operates three times daily between Baghdad and Al Basrah. Some sleeping cars, restaurants and air-conditioned coaches are available.
Note: Many tracks were destroyed during the fighting and it is uncertain if any passenger services are running at all.
ROAD:

Travel by road is not wholly recommended at present, due to the continuing threat of car-jacking, robbery and random attacks; these have often occurred on highways 1, 5, 10 and 15. It is recommended to travel in convoys of at least four per vehicle in daylight hours only. Road closures must also be expected. Improvised Explosive Devices (IEDs) and/or mines are used on some roads. Traffic drives on the right. Some cars do not use lights during the night and some urban street lighting may be broken. Road congestion is a problem. Principal routes are from Baghdad to Kirkuk, Arbil and Zakho; Baghdad to the Jordanian frontier; Baghdad to Kanaquin (Iranian border); Baghdad to Hilla and Kerbela; and Baghdad to Al Basrah and Safwan (Kuwait border). **Bus:** Services run from Baghdad and other main cities. **Taxi:** Services are available both in cities and for transit. Fares should be negotiated in advance. Metered taxis charge twice the amount shown on the meter. Tipping is not necessary. **Car hire:** Available at the airport and in Baghdad. **Documentation:** International Driving Permit required. Third Party insurance is necessary.
URBAN:

Baghdad has an extensive bus system with double-deckers, and also private minibuses and share-taxis. Buses are poorly maintained and they are often involved in accidents. Services are irregular and frequently change route. Bus tickets should be pre-purchased at kiosks. A metro is under construction.

Travel Advice

All travel to Baghdad and the adjacent provinces of Al Anbar, Salah Ad Din, Diyala, Wasit and Babil is advised against. The security situation is dangerous and there continues to be widespread outbreaks of violence. Even the most essential of travel to Iraq should be delayed, if possible. There has been a steady increase in the number of attacks against non-Iraqi civilians, including British nationals. A number of British nationals have been killed and many others have been seriously injured in terrorist incidents since the beginning of March 2004. If in Iraq, security arrangements should be carefully reviewed. Terrorists are actively targeting British, international and other interests in Iraq. Targets include hotels where UK and other nationals may stay, as well as civilian vehicles and aircraft. Attacks have often involved the use of firearms and explosives. There is a continuing threat from kidnapping. There have been numerous kidnappings of non-Iraqi civilians, particularly in the region surrounding Fallujah and Al Ramadi and on the Baghdad-Amman highway. However, this threat applies to all nationals.
The security situation is dangerous. There continues to be widespread outbreaks of violence against foreign nationals and targets have included hotels, civilian vehicles and aircraft, and attacks have occurred in the International Zone.
There has been an increase in fatal roadside bombings around Basra, where both civilian and military vehicles have been targeted. Travellers should be aware of the increased danger by road travel in Basra.
There have been numerous kidnappings of foreign nationals across Iraq. Some of those kidnapped have been killed by their captors.
Curfews exist in many areas of Iraq. Travellers should ensure that they adhere to all curfew times.
This advice is based on information provided by the Foreign and Commonwealth Office in the UK. It is correct at time of publishing. As the situation can change rapidly, visitors are advised to contact the following organisations for the latest travel advice:

British Foreign and Commonwealth Office
Tel: (0845) 850 2829.
Website: www.fco.gov.uk

US Department of State
Website: http://travel.state.gov/travel

Accommodation

HOTELS:

 Accommodation is mainly for business travellers. Hotel accommodation is limited and bookings should be made in advance. Small hotels are also available for low budgets, but with a lower standard of facilities. Hotel bills are payable in foreign currency but operate on a cash-only basis. A 10 per cent service charge is usually added to the bill.

Top Things To See & Do

• See the ruins of some historic buildings in **Baghdad**, such as the **Ike Abbasid Palace**.

• Browse some of Iraq's long-established markets that mostly still trade, even in Baghdad.

• Explore some of Iraq's fantastic museums, such as the museums of **Iraqi Folklore** and **Modern Art** in Baghdad.

• Travel to **Babylon**, the great Biblical city once ruled by the Semitic King Hammirabi. The city, and particularly the famous **Hanging Gardens**, are now being restored. Around here, you should also gaze up at the **Great Mosque** of **Samara**, a memorable and magnificent swirling piece of architecture. The minaret was built around 850 AD and is a 52m-tall spiral. This mosque deliberately alludes to the medieval image of the Biblical **Tower of Babel**, which is said to have once stood tall on this soil. This is also, depending on your theistic beliefs, the area of the **Garden of Eden**.

• The **Northern/Kurdish region** is a mountainous and forested area. **Mosul** is the main northern town, with the 13th-century **Palace of Qara Sariai** and the old **Mosque of Nabi Jirjis**. **Nineveh** is an ancient and rich archaeological site near Mosul.

• Visit what is probably the oldest continuously inhabited city in the world: **Arbil**.

• Watch the '**Eternal Fires**' of **Kirkuk**: the endless burning of gas seepage.

• Discover **Ur**, which was supposedly the birthplace of Abraham, an extremely significant figure in the region, miraculously linking up Christianity (who considers Abraham a model of perfect faith), Judaism (for whom Abraham is a patriarch) and Islam (who considers Abraham to have been a very important prophet). With no real 'modern' village to speak of, the centrepiece of Ur is the pyramid-shaped **ziggurat**, which commands a great view of the surrounding area, and is rumoured to include the remains of many past royals.

• For a macabre but telling insight into the man who ruled Iraq for decades - Saddam Hussein - then look no further than some of the **Presidential palaces** on display all around Baghdad (and some in **Tikrit**, too). Many of these palaces were destroyed in the 2002 US-led war, and some are simply in alternative use now, such as Coalition headquarters. But those that are available to the public are all characterised by overly-lavish interiors that form a poignant contrast with Iraqi poverty elsewhere. The rapidly diminishing murals in honour of Hussein also elucidate the mindset of this past leader and his regime.

• Located in a near-silent desert, **Hatra** is considered by many to contain the most beautiful ancient monuments in Iraq. This archaeological treasure-trove is thought to have flourished as a trading post along the Silk Route, and also at one point governed by Arab leaders. Fortified with two city walls and citadels, the centre of Hatra consists of a cluster of impressive temples. Although some statues were damaged or destroyed in the US-led war against Iraq, Hatra's historic and elegant beauty is still secure - and palpable.

Entertainment

Things to know: There is strict adherence to Islamic laws on the consumption of alcohol, which is available within the limits of religious laws. A permit for alcohol may be necessary, although this may only be valid at international hotels. Certain hotels prohibit the consumption of alcohol by visitors. During the lunar month of Ramadan, smoking and drinking in public is not permitted. Waiter service is usual.

FOOD & DRINK:

National specialities:
• *Dolma* (vine leaves, cabbage, lettuce, onions, aubergine, marrow or cucumbers stuffed with rice, meat and spices).
• *Tikka* (small chunks of mutton on skewers grilled on a charcoal fire).
• *Quozi* (small lamb boiled whole and grilled, stuffed with rice, minced meat and spices and served on rice) and *masgouf* (fish from the Tigris, cooked on the river bank).

Tipping: Normal limit is 10 to 15 per cent. Taxi drivers need not be tipped since the fare is agreed before the journey.

NIGHTLIFE: Baghdad has nightclubs with cabaret, music and dancing, as do other main towns. There are also cinemas, theatres and bars.

SHOPPING: The long-established town markets sell copperware, silver, spices, carpets and brightly coloured rugs. In Baghdad the copper market is a centre of noisy activity with coppersmiths beating their pots into shape.

Shopping hours: Sat-Thurs 0830-1300 and 1700-1900.

Business

• **GDP:** US$24.3 billion (2005 estimate).
• **Main imports:** Food, medicine and manufactures.
• **Main exports:** Crude oil, crude materials excluding fuel, food and live animals.
• **Main trade partners:** Canada, Germany, Italy, Japan, Jordan, Spain, Syrian Arab Republic, Turkey and USA.

ECONOMY: With proven deposits of over 110 billion barrels – about 10 per cent of the total – Iraq has the world's second-largest oil reserves. Oil income drove Iraq's rapid post-war development until the end of the 1970s. However, the Iran-Iraq war, which lasted from 1980 until 1988, brought Iraq's growth to a halt. Now that Iraq's US-led occupation has formally ended and the transferral of power to a new Iraqi government has been instigated, perhaps a glimmer of economic optimism can be permitted, although the situation remains perilous and eminently unstable. As reconstruction progresses, the country's economic momentum should recover, although the scale of destruction and dilapidation is such that this continues to be a lengthy process.

The agricultural sector by contrast fared relatively well, at least during the early sanctions period as Iraq sought to grow more food in order to compensate for the absence of imported produce. However, light industry, which the government originally promoted as part of an import substitution programme, operated far below the levels of the 1980s. The all-important oil industry meanwhile was constrained by limits imposed by the UN sanctions. But gradually the Iraqis developed an extensive network of smuggling routes and 'illicit' markets; indeed, the scale of these was such that by 2001, the Iraqis announced that they were no longer prepared to abide by the agreement with the UN and withdrew entirely from the international market.

But there was no disguising the decline which the Iraqi economy had undergone, especially during the previous 10 years. Accurate figures about the Iraqi economy are inevitably hard to come by. There were several bouts of hyperinflation during the 1990s, and the Iraqi dinar lost 90 per cent of its value during the decade. The economy contracted at an estimated average annual rate of 5 per cent during the same period. In 2002, inflation was 70 per cent, and the economy contracted by 6.5 per cent. Iraq also has a vast external debt in the region of US$200 billion, the majority of which is owed to Kuwait and Saudi Arabia. Hopes that the economy might grow in 2003 were dashed by both the extent of the rehabilitation needed by the oil industry and the consequences of the US-led war against Iraq.

In the year ending May 2005, inflation was 33 per cent. However, the rebuilding of oil, electricity and other production sources is proceeding effectively. The International Monetary Fund (IMF) has loaned US$685 million towards rebuilding Iraq.

NOTE: Any companies with involvement or planned involvement in re-construction projects in Iraq should contact the Iraq Unit at UK Trade and Investment (tel: (020) 7215 8893; e-mail: iraqunit@uktradeinvest.gov.uk).

BUSINESS ETIQUETTE: Formal courtesies are common and expected. Visiting cards are regularly exchanged and these are often printed in Arabic and English. Meetings may not always be on a person-to-person basis and it is often difficult to confine items to the business in progress as many topics may be discussed in order to assess the character of colleagues or traders. **Office hours:** Sat-Thur 0800-1400. Friday is the weekly day of rest when offices tend to be closed. During the month of Ramadan, hours are reduced.

A B C D E F G H I J K L M N O P Q R S T U V W X Y Z

Ireland

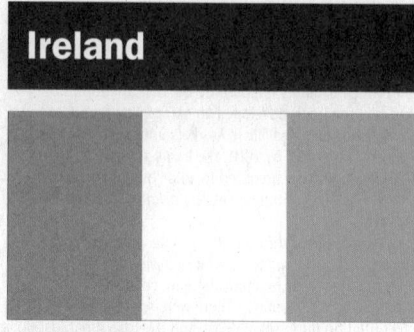

Location: Europe, off the west coast of Great Britain.

Time: GMT (GMT + 1 from last Sunday in March to Saturday before the last Sunday in October).

Overview

The most enduring features of the history of Ireland are, firstly, an unswerving commitment to Catholicism, the origins of which can be traced back to the pioneering monastic orders of the fifth and sixth centuries. Secondly, the frequent instability governing Anglo-Irish relations: Ireland was never so fully conquered that it absorbed the culture and way of life of its larger neighbour.

After the monastic age, Viking invaders built heavily fortified ports, laying the foundations of some major Irish cities. War between Irish chieftains and Vikings first led to the involvement of the English. Richard of Clare, Earl of Pembroke (nicknamed Strongbow), was invited by one of the chieftains to support his claims, but instead conquered almost the entire country in 1169-70. Many Norman families moved across the Irish Sea, effectively colonising the country. The turbulent and increasingly polarised political life of Ireland took a new and bitter twist after the English Civil War, when the Irish rose in favour of the deposed monarchy in 1649. The victorious Oliver Cromwell ruthlessly put down the rebellion. All Catholic land was expropriated and given to a new wave of Protestant immigrants. The subsequent Act of Union, passed in 1801, incorporated the whole of Ireland, along with England, Scotland and Wales, into the UK. However, the grossly inadequate response of the Government to the potato famine of 1845/6, which decimated the Irish population through death and emigration, highlighted its lack of interest in the welfare of the Irish people. Various independence movements struggled until Home Rule was granted in 1920. The terms of independence partitioned Ireland into two parts because, in the northern provinces, mostly Protestants settlements fiercely opposed to being ruled by a Government drawn from a Catholic majority. Six of the nine counties of the historic province of Ulster therefore remained in the UK; the other 26 counties became the Irish Free State, given full sovereignty within the Commonwealth in 1937, and remaining links with Britain dissolved.

In 1973, Ireland became a member of (as it then was) the EEC and adopted the Euro in 2002. European membership has proved to be of huge economic benefit. But this might not be the only reason behind the good cheer of the Irish. Besides a fantastic capital city, Dublin, bound in rich layers of history and now overflowing with trendy bars and nightclubs, are mountains, heather moors, coastline, valleys, waterfalls and lakes, dotted with prehistoric and religious sites and a wealth of dramatic castles.
Yet certain issues still dominate the political agenda. The first concerns the orthodox morality of the Catholic Church; abortion contentiously remains illegal, despite divorce being legalised after a referendum in 1995. Equally contentious is the future of Northern Ireland. Ironically, for now, the Republic is more prosperous than the North, and the Irish are happy to forget any troubles with some good, hearty *craic*.

General Information

AREA: 70,182 sq km (27,097 sq miles).
POPULATION: 4 million (UN, 2004).
POPULATION DENSITY: 56.9 per sq km.
CAPITAL: Dublin. **Population:** 1 million.
GEOGRAPHY: The Republic of Ireland lies in the north Atlantic Ocean and is separated from Britain by the Irish Sea to the east. The northeastern part of the island (Northern Ireland) is part of the United Kingdom. The country has a central plain surrounded by a rim of mountains and hills offering some of the most varied and unspoilt scenery in Europe – quiet sandy beaches, semi-tropical bays warmed by the Gulf Stream, and rugged cliffs make up the 5600km (3500 miles) of coastline.
GOVERNMENT: Republic. **Head of State:** President Mary McAleese since 1997. **Head of Government:** Prime Minister Bertie Ahern since 1997. **Recent history:** At the 1997 election for the *Dáil* (lower chamber of Parliament), once again no single party secured an overall majority. Fianna Fáil leader Bertie Ahern formed a new Government in alliance with the support of the small Progressive Democrats (a split from Fianna Fáil) and several independents. Ahern's new administration officially took office at the end of June with Mary Harney of the PD as Deputy Prime Minister (Tanaiste), the first woman ever to hold the position. Ahern's relatively successful tenure ensured that the electorate returned his Fianna Fáil-led coalition with an increased majority at the most recent poll in May 2002.
Since 1949, Ireland has been a republic with a bicameral legislature: the lower house, the Dáil, has 166 members and is directly elected by universal adult suffrage every five years; the 60-strong Senate has 49 directly elected members with the balance made up of political appointees. Executive power is vested in the Taioseach (Prime Minister) who presides over a Cabinet of Ministers. The cabinet is responsible to the Dáil for its actions.
LANGUAGE: Irish (Gaelic) is the official language, spoken as a first language by about 55,000 people (mostly in the west). The majority speak English. Official documents are printed in both languages.
RELIGION: Roman Catholic 91.6 per cent, the remainder being Protestant, with Jewish and Islamic minorities.
ELECTRICITY: 220 volts AC, 50Hz. Three-pin plugs are in use.
SOCIAL CONVENTIONS: The Irish are gregarious people, and everywhere animated *craic* (talk) can be heard. Oscar Fingal O'Flahertie Wills (better known as Oscar Wilde) once claimed: 'We are the greatest talkers since the Greeks.' Close community contact is very much part of the Irish way of life and almost everywhere there is an intimate small-town atmosphere. Pubs are often the heart of a community's social life. Visitors will find the people very friendly and welcoming no matter where one finds oneself in the country. A meal in an Irish home is usually a substantial affair and guests will eat well. Dinner is the main meal of the day and is now eaten in the evening. Even in cities there is less formal wear than in most European countries and casual dress is widely acceptable as in keeping with a largely agricultural community. Women, however, often dress up for smart restaurants and social functions. Handshaking is usual, and modes of address will often be informal. Smoking is banned in all public enclosed/working spaces, including pubs, bars and restaurants.

Climate

The temperate climate is due to mild southwesterly winds and the Gulf Stream. Summers are warm, while temperatures during winter are much cooler. Spring and autumn are very mild. Rain falls all year.
Required clothing: Lightweights during summer with warmer mediumweights for the winter. Rainwear is advisable throughout the year.

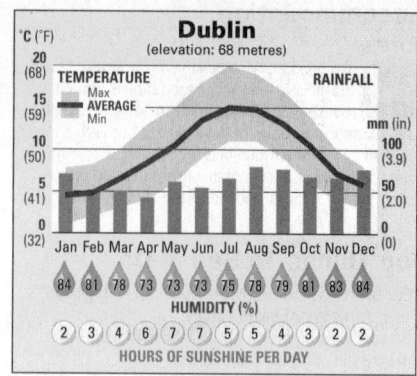

Communications

Telephone: IDD is available. Country code: 353 followed by the area code, omitting the initial zero.
Mobile telephone: Roaming agreements exist with a wide range of international mobile phone carriers. Coverage is good.
Internet: Internet is readily available; Internet cafes exist in nearly every town.
Post: Post office hours: Mon-Fri 0900-1730/1800, Sat 0900-1300. Sub-post offices close at 1300 one day a week. The Central Post Office is in O'Connell Street, Dublin.
MEDIA: The national public broadcaster *Radio Telefis Eireann* (RTE) dominates the radio and TV sector. It provides a comprehensive service in both English and Irish. The Irish print and broadcast media operate freely within the confines of the law. Broadcasting is regulated by a commission appointed by the Department of Communications. The Competition Authority safeguards against unfair competition in the press sector. Cross-media ownership is permitted within certain limits - press groups may own up to 25 per cent of local radio and TV stations.
Press: There are several daily newspapers published in Dublin including *Evening Herald*, the *Irish Independent* (website: www.unison.ie/irish_independent) and *The Irish Times* (website: www.ireland.com); and two in Cork (*Evening Echo* and *Irish Examiner* (website: www.irishexaminer.com). British dailies and Sunday papers are available.
TV: *RTE* is a public broadcaster and operates three networks, including an Irish-language station *TG4*.
Radio: *Radio RTE* is a public broadcaster and operates four networks, including the flagship station *Radio 1*, a pop music station; *Raidio na Gaeltachta* operates an Irish-language station; and *Lyric FM* is a classical and cultural station. *Today FM* is the national commercial network.

Passport/Visa

	Passport Required?	Visa Required?	Return Ticket Required?
Full British	1	No	No
Australian	Yes	No	No
Canadian	Yes	No	No
USA	Yes	No	No
Other EU	2	No	No
Japanese	Yes	No	No

Note: *Regulations and requirements may be subject to change at short notice, and you are advised to contact the appropriate diplomatic or consular authority before finalising travel arrangements. Any numbers in the chart refer to the footnotes below.*

PASSPORTS: Valid passport required by all except:
(a) **1.** persons born in the UK travelling direct from the UK (applicable to British passport holders only).
Note: Whilst UK citizens do not require a passport or visa to enter Ireland, most carriers by air or sea now require some form of identification with photograph, usually a passport or driving license with photo. Visitors should check what form of ID is required with the individual airline, ferry company or travel agent before travelling.
VISAS: Required by all except the following for stays of up to 90 days:
(a) nationals of countries referred to in the chart above;
(b) nationals of Andorra, Antigua & Barbuda, Argentina, The Bahamas, Barbados, Belize, Bolivia, Botswana, Brazil, British Overseas Territories, Brunei, Chile, Costa Rica, Croatia, Dominica, El Salvador, Fiji, Grenada, Guatemala, Guyana, Honduras, Hong Kong (SAR), Iceland, Israel, Kiribati, Korea (Rep), Lesotho, Liechtenstein, Macau (SAR), Malawi, Malaysia, The Maldives, Mauritius, Mexico, Monaco, Nauru,

Credit: All images © Tourism Ireland

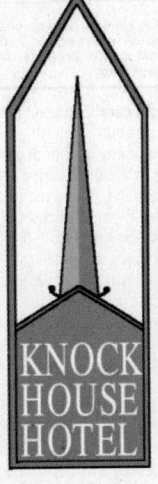

A B C D E F G H I J K L M N O P Q R S T U V W X Y Z

New Zealand, Nicaragua, Norway, Panama, Paraguay, St Kitts & Nevis, St Lucia, St Vincent & the Grenadines, San Marino, Seychelles, Singapore, Solomon Islands, South Africa, Swaziland, Switzerland, Tonga, Trinidad & Tobago, Tuvalu, Uruguay, Vanuatu, Vatican City, Venezuela and Western Samoa;
(c) transit passengers continuing their journey within 24 hours by the same or first connecting flight provided holding valid onward or return documentation and not leaving the airport. However, the following nationals *do* always require a transit visa: Afghanistan, Albania, Bulgaria, Cuba, Congo (Dem Rep), Eritrea, Ethiopia, Ghana, Iran, Iraq, Lebanon, Moldova, Nigeria, Romania, Serbia & Montenegro, Somalia, Sri Lanka and Zimbabwe.
Types of visa and cost: *Single-entry*: €60. *Multiple-entry*: €100. *Transit*: €25. Nationals of some countries receive visas free of charge. Enquire at Consulate/Consular Section of Embassy for further details (see *Passport/Visa Information*).
Application to: Consulate (or consular section at Embassy); see *Passport/Visa Information* for details.
Application requirements: (a) Valid passport. (b) One completed application form. (c) Fee. (d) Letters of reference to substantiate purpose of visit or confirmation of hotel booking containing dates of proposed stay. (e) Three passport-size photos. (f) Evidence that applicant is obliged to return to country of residence, eg letter from current employer stating when applicant is due to return to work. (g) Evidence of sufficient funds or letter of reference from resident in Ireland claiming full financial responsibility for applicant, with proof they have sufficient funds to do so (eg bank statement). *Student*: (a)-(g) and, (h) Letter of acceptance from place of study (must be full-time and at least 15 hours' study time per week). (i) Proof of paid fees and sufficient funds for duration of course. (j) Copies of educational qualifications. *Business*: (a)-(g) and, (h) Letter of invitation from company in Ireland/conference host.
Working days required: Six to eight weeks.

PASSPORT/VISA INFORMATION

Embassy of the Republic of Ireland in the UK
17 Grosvenor Place, London SW1X 7HR, UK
Tel: (020) 7235 2171.
Opening hours: Mon-Fri 0930-1300, 1415 - 1700.
Passport and Visa office: Montpelier House, 106 Brompton Road, London SW3 1JJ, UK
Tel: (020) 7225 7700.
Opening hours: Mon-Fri 1000-1200 (Visa section); 0930-1630 (Passport section).

Embassy of the Republic of Ireland in the USA
2234 Massachusetts Avenue, NW, Washington, DC 20008, USA
Tel: (202) 462 3939.
Website: www.irelandemb.org

Money

Single European currency (Euro): The Euro is now the official currency of 12 EU member states (including Ireland). The first Euro coins and notes were introduced in January 2002; the Irish Punt was completely replaced by the Euro on 9 February 2002. Euro (€) = 100 cents. Notes are in denominations of €500, 200, 100, 50, 20, 10 and 5. Coins are in denominations of €2 and 1, and 50, 20, 10, 5, 2 and 1 cents.
Currency exchange: Available in banks, airports and in bureaux de change. ATMs are widely available, catering for Cirrus and Maestro symbols.
Credit & debit cards: American Express, MasterCard and Visa are all widely accepted. Check with your credit and debit card company for details of merchant acceptability and other services which may be available.
Traveller's cheques: Accepted throughout Ireland. To avoid additional exchange rate charges, travellers are advised to take traveller's cheques in Euros, Pounds Sterling or US Dollars.
Currency restrictions: There are no restrictions on the import or export of either local or foreign currency, although declarations of more than €6350 are advised.
Banking hours: Mon-Fri 0930-1630. In Dublin, banks stay open Thurs until 1700; there are also late opening nights in other parts of the country, but the day will vary.
Exchange rate indicators:
Rate at time of publishing
£1.00= €1.46
$1.00= €0.82

Duty Free

The following goods may be imported by persons over 17 years of age without incurring customs duty if obtained duty- and/or tax-free outside the EU:
200 cigarettes or 100 cigarillos or 50 cigars or 250g of tobacco; 1l of spirits and distilled beverages (more than 22 per cent) or 2l of other alcoholic beverages with an alcoholic strength not exceeding 22 per cent, including sparkling or fortified wine, plus 2l of table wine; 50g of perfume and 250ml of eau de toilette; other dutiable goods to the value of €175, or €90 if under 15 years old.
Prohibited items: Firearms, ammunition, explosives, offensive weapons, indecent/obscene material, plants or bulbs, live or dead animals, bird or poultry, endangered species, meat and meat products and hay or straw (even if used as packing).
Abolition of duty free goods within the EU: On June 30 1999, the sale of duty free alcohol and tobacco at airports and at sea was abolished in all of the original 15 EU member states. Of the 10 new member states that joined the EU on May 1 2004, these rules already apply to Cyprus and Malta. There are transitional rules in place for visitors returning to one of the original 15 EU countries from one of the other new EU countries. But for the original 15, plus Cyprus and Malta, there are now no limits imposed on importing tobacco and alcohol products from one EU country to another (with the exceptions of Denmark, Finland and Sweden, where limits *are* imposed). Travellers should note that they may be required to prove at customs that the goods purchased are for personal use *only*.

Public Holidays

Below are listed Public Holidays for the January 2006-June 2007 period.
2006: Jan 1 New Year's Day. **Mar 17** St Patrick's Day. **Apr 14** Good Friday. **Apr 17** Easter Monday. **May 1** Bank Holiday. **Jun 5** Bank Holiday. **Aug 6** Summer Bank Holiday. **Oct 30** Halloween Bank Holiday. **Dec 25** Christmas Day. **Dec 26** St Stephen's Day.
2007: Jan 1 New Year's Day. **Mar 17** St Patrick's Day. **Apr 6** Good Friday. **Apr 9** Easter Monday. **May 7** Bank Holiday. **Jun 6** Bank Holiday.

Health

	Special Precautions?	Certificate Required?
Yellow Fever	No	No
Cholera	No	No
Typhoid & Polio	No	N/A
Malaria	No	N/A

Note: *Regulations and requirements may be subject to change at short notice, and you are advised to contact your doctor well in advance of your intended date of departure. Any numbers in the chart refer to the footnotes below.*

Health care: European Economic Area (EEA) and Switzerland:
If you or any of your dependants are suddenly taken ill or have an accident during a visit to an EEA country or Switzerland, free or reduced-cost necessary treatment is available - in most cases on production of a valid European Health Insurance Card (EHIC). Each country has different rules about state medical provision. In some, treatment is free. In many countries you will have to pay part or all of the cost, and then claim a full or partial refund. The EHIC gives access to state-provided medical treatment only and the scheme gives no entitlement to medical repatriation costs, nor does it cover ongoing illnesses of a non-urgent nature, so comprehensive travel insurance is advised. Note that the EHIC replaces the Form E111, which will no longer be valid after 31 December 2005. Some restrictions apply, depending on your nationality.
If you need a doctor or a dentist, contact the local Health Board, which will arrange for you to see a public health service doctor or dentist. Make it clear to the practitioner that you wish to be treated under the EU's social security arrangements. You may be asked to complete a simple statement. Emergency treatment and medicines are free if you go to a General Medical Services (GMS) doctor and the prescription is on GMS paper. If you require hospital treatment, a doctor will arrange for you to be admitted to a health service hospital, where treatment in public wards is normally free. If you can't contact a doctor before admission, explain to the hospital authorities that you wish to be treated under the EU arrangements. If you need emergency medication on discharge from a public hospital, you must go to a Health Board doctor for the prescription, otherwise you may have to pay a charge. More information can be obtained from www.irlgov.ie/healthboards.htm.

Travel - International

AIR:
The national airline is *Aer Lingus (EI)* (website: www.aerlingus.com). *Aer Lingus* provides a service from Los Angeles and New York's JFK to Shannon and Dublin. *Delta Air Lines* operates a service from New York's JFK Airport to Shannon and Dublin. Services to London are frequent and moderately priced. There is a wide range of promotional air fares to Ireland from main cities in the UK, and an ever-increasing number of airlines connect regional UK airports with Ireland.
Approximate flight times: From Dublin to *London* is one hour 20 minutes, to *New York* is seven hours 30 minutes.
Main airports: *Dublin Airport (DUB)* (website: www.dublin-airport.com) is 10km (6 miles) north of the city. *To/from the airport*: Taxis into the city centre cost approximately €15; passengers may be charged extra for large luggage. An aircoach service runs to and from the airport, 24 hours per day. *Citylink* runs a service from Galway to Dublin Airport (travel time - 3 hours). *Dublin Bus* offers many routes throughout Dublin to the airport, including an *AirLink Express* bus from Heuston and Connolly railway stations. *Facilities*: Duty free shop, car hire, bank, bureau de change, bars, restaurants, tourist information centre and chemist.
Shannon Airport (SNN) (website: www.shannonairport.com) is 24km (15 miles) north of Limerick City (travel time - 25 minutes). *To/from the airport*: Bus services are available to and from both Limerick and Clare, approximately every hour. A daily express coach travels between Limerick and Shannon, plus to Ennis bus station. *Citylink* operates a service from Galway to Shannon Airport (travel time - one hour and 15 minutes). Taxi services are available, 24 hours, to Limerick City. *Facilities*: Outgoing duty free shop, bank, bureau de change, bar, restaurant and tourist information centre.
Cork Airport (ORK) (website: www.corkairport.com) is 8km (5 miles) southwest of the city. *To/from the airport*: Buses travel between the city centre and airport (travel time - 15 minutes), a single journey costs €3.70 and a return costs €6. *Facilities*: Outgoing duty free shop, car hire, bar and restaurant.
Knock International Airport (NOC) (website: www.knockairport.com) is 11km (7 miles) north of Claremorris (Co Mayo) and receives scheduled international flights from the UK only: *Ryanair* from London Stansted, *Bmibaby* from Birmingham and Manchester, *Loganair* from Dublin, *Easyjet* from London Gatwick and *British Airways* from London Gatwick via Dublin. At other times of the year, chartered flights operate between Knock and a number of European destinations, such as Salzburg, Majorca, Crete and Lisbon. *To/from the airport*: Taxi services are available to Claremorris, where onward rail and bus connections are available to the rest of the country. *Facilities*: Duty free shop, bar, restaurant and car hire (pre-booking advised).
Departure tax: €10 at Knock International Airport only, payable by everyone over 12 years.
SEA:
Main ports: *Baltimore*, *Dublin* (website: www.dublinport.ie), *Galway*, *Kinsale* and *Wexford*.
In addition to conventional ferry crossings, many ferry companies now offer high-speed services as well as upgraded, state-of-the-art craft on many Irish sea routes. Fares will vary by season and promotional offers are available. Routes from Britain and France include:
From England: *Liverpool–Dublin* (travel time - eight hours); *Fleetwood–Larne* (Northern Ireland, travel time - eight hours). From the Isle of Man: *Douglas–Dublin* (travel time - two hours 45 minutes, summer only, or four hours 45 minutes on conventional ferries); *Douglas–Belfast* (Northern Ireland, travel time - two hours 45 minutes).
From Scotland: *Cairnryan–Larne* (Northern Ireland, travel time - one hour on fast ferries and one hour 45 minutes on conventional ferries); *Troon–Belfast* (Northern Ireland, travel time - two hours 35 minutes); *Stranraer–Belfast* (travel time - one hour 45 minutes on fast ferries and three hours 15 minutes on conventional ferries).
From Wales: *Holyhead (Isle of Anglesey)–Dublin* (travel time - one hour 50 minutes on fast ferries and minimum three hours 15 minutes on conventional ferries); *Holyhead (Isle of Anglesey)–Dun Laoghaire* (travel time 1 hour 40 minutes on fast ferries); *Fishguard–Rosslare* (travel time - one hour 40 minutes on fast ferries and three hours 30 minutes on conventional ferries); *Swansea–Cork* (seasonal, travel time - 10 hours); *Pembroke–Rosslare* (travel time - three hours 45 minutes).
From France: Irish Ferries operate at least four direct ferry crossings a day between France and Ireland. The routes are *Cherbourg–Rosslare* (travel time - 19 hours); *Roscoff–Rosslare* (travel time - 18 hours); *Roscoff-Cork* (travel time - 13 hours 30 minutes).
For information on routes, fares and reservations, contact one of the following: *Brittany Ferries* (tel: (08703) 665 333; website: www.brittany-ferries.com); *Irish Ferries* (tel: (08705) 171 717 (UK office) *or* (1) 855 222 (Dublin office); website: www.irishferries.com); *Isle of Man Steam Packet* (tel: (01624) 661 661; website: www.steam-packet.com); *P&O Irish Sea* (tel: (0870) 242 4777; website: www.poirishsea.com); *Stena Line* (tel: (08705) 707 070;

A B C D E F G H I J K L M N O P Q R S T U V W X Y Z

Ireland

website: www.stenaline.co.uk); and *Swansea-Cork Ferries* (tel: (01792) 456 116).
Most ferry companies now also offer an online booking facility on their website.

RAIL:
Rail links serve Ireland from all the above ferry ports, as well as from Northern Ireland.
Rail passes: The *Inter-Rail* pass offers unlimited second-class train travel in up to 29 European countries (includes Morocco and Turkey) split into eight zones (A-H). Three different tickets are available: a ticket covering one zone (two to six countries, 16 days' validity), a ticket covering two zones (six to 10 countries, 22 days' validity) and an *All Zone Pass* (29 countries, one month's validity). Ferry services between Italy and Greece are included. Passengers must be resident in Europe for at least six months before the pass is used. Travel is not allowed in the passenger's country of residence. Travellers under 26 years receive a reduction of about 30 per cent. Children's tickets are reduced by about 50 per cent. Supplements are required for some high-speed services, seat reservations and couchettes. Discounts are offered on *Eurostar* and some ferry routes. Available from *Inter Rail* (website: www.interrailnet.com). The *Eurailpass* offers unlimited first-class train travel in 17 European countries. *Saver* tickets are valid for 15 days, 21 days, one month, two months or three months. The *Eurailpass Saver* ticket offers discounts for two or more people travelling together. The *Eurailpass Youth* ticket is available to those aged under 26 and offers unlimited second-class train travel. The *Eurailpass Flexi* allows either 10 or 15 travel days within a two-month period. The *Eurail Selectpass* is valid in three, four or five bordering countries and allows five, six, eight or 10 travel days (or 15 for five countries) in a two-month period. The *Eurail Regional Pass* allows four to 10 travel days in a two-month period in one of nine regions (usually two or more countries). Children receive a 50 per cent reduction. The passes cannot be sold to residents of Europe, Turkey, Morocco, Algeria, Tunisia or the Russian Federation. Available from the *Eurail Group* (website: www.eurail.com). The *EuroDomino* pass enables holders anything from three to eight days' extensive travel within a one-month period on the entire rail network of their chosen country. It is valid in 28 European countries and North Africa, including the ferry service from Brindisi (Italy) to Igoumenitsa (Greece). To purchase a *EuroDomino* pass you must have been resident in Europe for at least six months and a passport number is required at time of booking. It is not permitted to purchase a pass for travel within your own country of residence. To qualify for the youth rates, you must be under 26 years on the first date of validity of the pass. Children aged four-11 years inclusive pay half the adult fares rounded up to the nearest pound. Children under four years travel for free. Seat reservations, couchette and sleeper charges are not included in the cost of the pass and are payable at the normal rate. Passholder fares are payable on some services. Reservation/Supplement charges are payable on all trains within Spain. Available from *Rail Europe* (Website: www.raileurope.co.uk/railpasses/eurodomino.htm).

Travel - Internal

AIR:
Aer Lingus (as well as several other carriers) operates services throughout the country. Charter flights are also available. The Aran Islands are served by *Aer Arann* (website: www.aerarann.ie) via a 15-minute flight from Connemara Regional Airport (located 27km/17 miles west of Galway city).
Domestic airports: *Galway (GWY)* is approximately 8km (5 miles) from the city centre. *To/from the airport*: Bus and taxi services are available into Galway centre.
Sligo (SXL) (website: www.sligoairport.com) is 8km (5 miles) from Sligo. *To/from the airport*: Taxis need prior booking. Bus and taxi services are available into Sligo.
Carrickfinn (CFN) is in Co Donegal.
Kerry (Farranfore) (KIR) (website: www.kerryairport.ie) in Co Kerry is 19km (12 miles) from both Killarney and Tralee. *To/from the airport*: Taxi services are available to both these towns and to the nearby railway station. Car hire is also available.
As well as the airports listed above (and in *Travel – International*), there are various small licensed airstrips which receive passenger services; enquire at Tourism Ireland for details of operators and routes (see *Top Things To Do*).

SEA:
Ferry services run to the various west coast islands; enquiries should be made locally.

RAIL:
Rail services in the Republic are owned by *Iarnród Eireann (Irish Rail)* (website: www.irishrail.ie) and express trains run between the main cities. There are two classes of accommodation, with restaurant and buffet cars on some trains. Children under five travel free. Children aged five to 15 pay half fare. A range of rail-only and combined rail and bus tickets are available for unlimited travel within the Republic of Ireland. The *Britrail* and *Eurorail* card systems are valid in Ireland (see *Travel - International*).

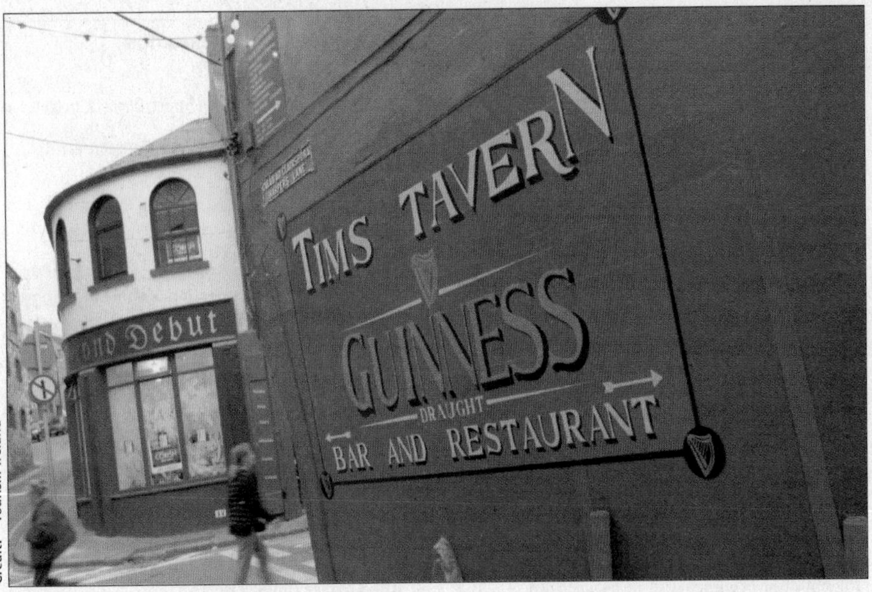

Credit: © Tourism Ireland

ROAD:
The network links all parts of Ireland. Traffic drives on the left. Ireland changed all road signs from imperial to metric measurements on 20 January 2005. **Bus:** Internal bus services are run by *Bus Eireann (Irish Bus)* (website: www.buseireann.ie) which has a nationwide network of buses serving all the major cities and most towns and villages outside the Dublin area. Bus services in remote areas are infrequent. An 'Expressway' coach network complements rail services. The central bus station is in Store Street, Dublin. A variety of special passes are available, including the *Irish Rambler*, which offers unlimited travel for three, eight or 15 days. *Irish Explorer* offers unlimited intercity and suburban rail services, as well as the Bus Eireann Expressway and local and city services. The *Emerald Card* offers services in Northern Ireland as well as in the Republic of Ireland. Several independent bus companies, which are often cheaper, faster and more frequent than Bus Eireann, operate regular, scheduled services to and from Dublin. Further information can be found in local papers. **Coach tours:** Many companies offer coach tours, varying in length and itinerary. Full-day and half-day guided tours are organised from the larger towns and cities. These run from May to October. Full details are available from *Bus Eireann* and *CIE Tours International*. **Taxi:** Service is available in major cities. Taxis are metered in Cork, Dublin, Galway and Limerick. In other areas is it advised to agree on a fare beforehand. Cruising taxis are infrequent. Places to get taxis are at hotels, rail and bus stations or taxi stands. **Car hire:** Available from all air- and seaports as well as major hotels. All international hire companies are represented in Ireland, as well as local operators. Age requirements vary from a minimum of 21 to a maximum of 70 years. A full licence from the driver's home country is required, and the driver will normally be required to have had at least two years' experience. It is advisable to book hire cars in advance, especially in the peak season, and a child seat should be ordered in advance also. Advise the car hire company if the car will be driven into Northern Ireland. The *'Guide to Touring Ireland by Car'* is available from the Tourism Ireland (see *Top Things To Do*). **Bicycle hire:** Ask for a Tourist Board leaflet. **Regulations:** Speed limits: 50 k/h (30mph) in towns and cities, 80 k/h (50mph) on local roads (this is displayed on white signs) and 100 k/h (60mph) on national roads (this is displayed on green signs). Seatbelts should be worn at all times and it is illegal to drive while under the influence of alcohol or drugs. **Documentation:** EU nationals taking cars into the Republic require: motor registration book (or owner's authority in writing); full EU driving licence or International Driving Permit; nationality coding stickers; and insurance cover valid for the Republic. A Green Card is strongly recommended, as without it, insurance cover is limited to the minimum legal requirement in Ireland – the Green Card tops this up to the cover provided by the visitor's domestic policy.

URBAN:
Extensive bus services operate in Dublin. There is a fast suburban rail service (*DART*, Dublin Area Rapid Transport), travelling from Malahide in the north to Greystones in the south. Buses in the city are run by DublinBus; they operate from 0600-2330 during weekdays with a limited night bus service on Thursday, Friday and Saturday departing the city every 20 minutes, 0030-0430. Dublin also has its own tram system, *LUAS*, which is a high-speed service with convenient stop locations throughout the city. Taxis can be hailed or hired at a taxi rank: the three main taxi ranks in the city are O'Connell Street, Dame Street and St Stephens Street.
Travel times: The following chart gives approximate travel times (in hours and minutes) from **Dublin** to other major cities/towns in Ireland.

	Air	Road	Rail
Cork	**0.40**	**3.00**	**2.40**
Limerick	-	**3.30**	**2.10**
Shannon Airport	**0.35**	**3.00**	-
Kilkenny	-	**2.00**	**1.45**

Travel Advice

Most visits to Ireland are trouble-free but you should be aware of the global risk of indiscriminate international terrorist attacks, which could be against civilian targets, including places frequented by foreigners.
This advice is based on information provided by the Foreign and Commonwealth Office in the UK. It is correct at time of publishing. As the situation can change rapidly, visitors are advised to contact the following organisations for the latest travel advice:

British Foreign and Commonwealth Office
Tel: (0845) 850 2829.
Website: www.fco.gov.uk

US Department of State
Website: http://travel.state.gov/travel

Accommodation

EDITOR'S CHOICE: CABIN CRUISING

There are five main waterways in Ireland made up of connecting canals, lakes, rivers and inlets. Barges can be hired, usually on a weekly basis, with two, six, eight or 10 berths (beds). Previous experience of operating a barge is not essential as full training is provided, so a license is not required. The cost of hiring a barge varies depending on the season.

HOTELS:
There are over 800 hotels inspected, approved and graded by Fáilte Ireland (Tourism Ireland in Ireland) and prices are fixed by Fáilte Ireland. Fáilte Ireland registers and grades hotels from **5-star** (highest) to **1-star** (lowest).

GUEST HOUSES:
Guest houses are smaller, more intimate establishments often under family management. There are over 490 guest houses registered and inspected by Fáilte Ireland. These range from converted country houses to purpose-built accommodation. Meals range from bed & breakfast to full board. The minimum number of bedrooms is five and the availability of meals is not a requirement. Fáilte Ireland registers and grades guest houses from **4-star** (very high standard) to **1-star** (clean and comfortable). Hot and cold running water in all

A B C D E F G H I J K L M N O P Q R S T U V W X Y Z

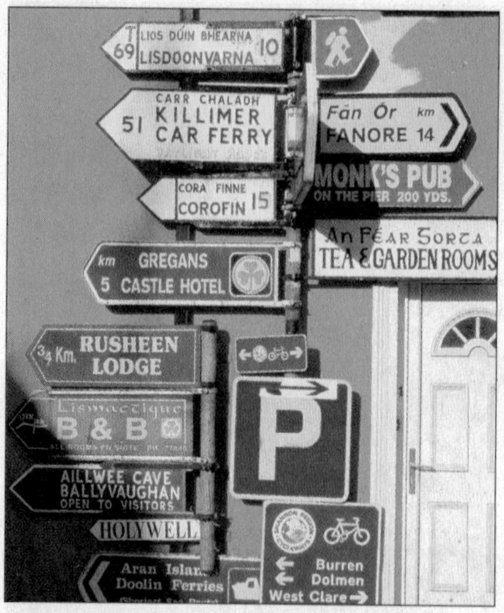

Credit: © Tourism Ireland

bedrooms. Adequate bathroom and toilet facilities. **Ungraded premises** are hotels and guest houses not sufficiently long in operation, so are left ungraded.

FARMHOUSES/TOWN & COUNTRY HOMES:

There are hundreds of town or country homes and farmhouses offering bed & breakfast on a daily or weekly basis with other meals often provided. This informal type of accommodation gives visitors the opportunity to share in the life of an Irish family in an urban or country setting. They may live in a Georgian residence, a modern bungalow or a traditional cottage. A farmhouse holiday again gives scope for meeting people and is especially suitable for children. Visitors can forget about city life and enjoy the everyday life of the farm. Either way it will be a relaxing and friendly holiday.

All homes and farmhouses that have been inspected and approved by Fáilte Ireland are listed in the official guide, available from the Tourist Board. In addition to this, the Town and Country Homes Association and Fáilte Tuaithe (pronounced Foil-tya Too-ha), the Irish Farmhouse Association, produce their own annual guides to their members' houses. These are also available from Tourism Ireland in Britain and from tourist information offices throughout Ireland.

SELF-CATERING:

There are self-catering establishments scattered throughout Ireland, listed by Fáilte Ireland. Self-catering holidays are available for those who like to come and go as they please without any restrictions. There is self-catering accommodation to suit all tastes, including houses, self-contained apartments, cottages and caravans. There are even traditional-style thatched cottages which are fully equipped and located in carefully selected beauty spots.

CAMPING/CARAVANNING:

Ireland's caravan and camping parks are inspected by Fáilte Ireland. Those that meet minimum requirements are identified by a special sign and listed in an official guide which shows the facilities at each park. Firms offering touring caravans, tents and camping equipment for hire are included in the listing. There are over 100 caravan and campsites. The majority are open from May to September.

YOUTH HOSTELS:

A total of 24 youth hostels are operated by *An Oige* (Irish Youth Hostel Association). They provide simple dormitory accommodation with comfortable beds and facilities for cooking meals. Usage is confined to members of *An Oige* or other youth organisations affiliated to the International Youth Hostel Federation. Non-members can buy stamps at hostels entitling them to further hostel use. A *Youth Hostel Accommodation Guide* is available.

HOLIDAY HOSTELS:

There are registered holiday hostels offering privately-owned accommodation at reasonable prices. Dormitory-style sleeping accommodation and/or private bedrooms are available, with fully-equipped kitchens. No membership is required. Some provide meals, others breakfast only.

HOLIDAY CENTRES:

These centres offer a comprehensive holiday with a wide variety of amenities and facilities including self-catering units, indoor heated swimming pool and restaurant facilities. The centres are registered with Fáilte Ireland.

OTHER ACCOMMODATION:

Student accommodation is available at many of Ireland's universities during the holidays. There are a number of **health farms** throughout Ireland, which offer spa baths, massage clinics and beauty salons as well as accommodation.

ACCOMMODATION INFORMATION

Fáilte Ireland
Baggot Street Bridge, Baggot Street, Dublin 2, Ireland
Tel: (1) 602 4000.
Website: www.ireland.ie *or* www.failteireland.ie

Irish Hotels Federation
13 Northbrook Road, Dublin 6, Ireland
Tell: (1) 497 6459.
Website: www.irelandhotels.com

Distinction World (A selection of some of the finest hotels in Ireland)
Website: www.distinctionworld.com

Fáilte Tuaithe (Irish Farm Holidays)
2 Michael Street, Limerick, Ireland
Tel: (61) 400 700.
Website: www.irishfarmholidays.com

Town and Country Homes Association
Belleek Road, Ballyshannon, Co Donegal, Ireland
Tel: (71) 982 2222.
Website: www.townandcountry.ie

Irish Cottage Holiday Homes
Central Reservations Office, Bracken Court, Bracken Road, Sandyford, Dublin 18, Ireland
Tel: (1) 205 2777.
Website: www.irishcottageholidays.com

Irish Caravan and Camping Council
PO Box 4443, Dublin 2, Ireland
Website: www.camping-ireland.ie

***An Oige* (Irish Youth Hostel Association)**
61 Mountjoy Street, Dublin 7, Ireland
Tel: (1) 830 4555.
Website: www.irelandyha.org *or* www.anoige.ie

Waterways Ireland
Tel: (1) 965 0787.
Website: www.waterwaysireland.org

Healthfarms of Ireland
Website: www.healthfarmsofireland.com

Top Things To See

- Artists and writers have thrived in Ireland, and their legacy is apparent everywhere. Founded during the reign of Elizabeth I, **Trinity College** is Dublin's most famous landmark, and was a symbol of English dominance to which, until 1873, admission was restricted to Protestants. Many of the college's students have achieved a measure of fame, notably Oscar Wilde, Bram Stoker, Samuel Beckett and Jonathan Swift. The **Old Library** houses a number of important manuscripts in its Treasury, among which the Book of Kells is the best known. **Merrion Square** is the city's most elegant place, lined with classical Georgian houses with stunning doorways, canopies and fanlights. Oscar Wilde lived at 1 Merrion Square, Daniel O'Connell at 58, with WB Yeats only a few doors higher, at 82. For those wanting an insight into the life of an author, head for the **James Joyce Centre** in **North Great George's Street**. A short excursion from Dublin, the **James Joyce Tower and Museum**, at **Sandycove**, encloses many personal effects of James Joyce, including a first edition of *Ulysses*. Further afield in the Midlands, in **County Longford**, **Ballymahon** is famed for Oliver Goldsmith, author of *She Stoops to Conquer* and the classic poem *The Deserted Village*. He was born at **Pallas**, a few miles to the east. **County Sligo** may be worth a visit, too: WB Yeats, the Nobel Prize winner, used to visit here with his artist brother, Jack.
- Ireland is a country of castles. West of Trinity College in Dublin stands **Dublin Castle**, the seat of British rule in Ireland, and worth a visit for its beautiful state apartments. Three castles at nearby **Dalkey** survive from the 15th and 16th centuries: **Bullock Castle** (not open to the public), **Archbold's Castle**, now the town hall, and **Goat Castle**, housing the **Dalkey Heritage Centre**. **Malahide Castle**, north of the city, was built in the 12th century and houses some lovely furniture and a portrait gallery with paintings by Irish and British artists. In **Counties Louth and Meath**, **King John's Castle** is a small stronghold overlooking the sea, and **Taaffe's Castle** is one of many fortified residences in the area dating from the 16th century. The thriving market town of **Enniscorthy**, by far the most attractive in **County Wexford**, was established by the Normans – it is still dominated by the Norman castle and the much later **St Aidan's Cathedral**. The castle houses the **Wexford County Museum**. **County Westmeath** contains the beautiful grounds of **Tullynally Castle** at **Castlepollard**, the family seat of the earls of Longford.
- Wander around and take in the sights of Dublin's **Phoenix Park** - the largest city park in Europe, and a good place to watch the city going about its business. **Dublin Zoo** is in the southeast corner of the park.
- Explore some of Ireland's watery wonderlands: Counties Louth and Meath share the **River Boyne**, which is wide, gentle and very beautiful; in **County Wicklow**, a pleasant footpath leads to the **Powerscourt Waterfall**, the highest falls in Ireland, formed by the **Dargle River** which drops over cliffs 122m (400ft) high; in **County Monaghan**, **Castleblaney** lies at the head of **Lough Muckno**, the county's largest lake and a source of excellent coarse fishing; and **Killarney National Park** in **County Kerry** embraces three lakes all linked by a river.
- Much of Ireland's land is significant for the battles and war scenes that took place there. River Boyne, in counties Louth and Meath, is famous for the **Battle of the Boyne** in 1690, when James II sought to regain the English throne, but was out-manoeuvred by William of Orange. Astride the Boyne, **Drogheda**, the harbour town of County Louth, holds an important place in the history of medieval Ireland. It was besieged by Oliver Cromwell in 1649, who massacred or transported most of the inhabitants. In County Wexford, Enniscorthy's moment of fame arrived in 1798 in the form of the **Battle of Vinegar Hill**, when the United Irishmen made their last stand against the British.
- See some sights of great antiquity. The prehistoric burial sites of **Brú na Bóinne**, west of Drogheda in Counties Louth and Meath, number more than 40 and predate the pyramids. Among these, **Newgrange** is western Europe's most outstanding chambered tomb, built around 5000 years ago. In **County Kildare**, **Naas** (pronounced Nace) is a small industrial town on the edge of the **Wicklow Mountains**. Once the seat of the kings of the **Province of Leinster**, Naas was the heart of the ancient Irish kingdom of **Ui Dunlainge**. **Cavan**, in **County Cavan**, has nearby **Clough Oughter**, a circular tower castle, which tells of a time when this was the stronghold of the O'Reillys, the princes of **Breffni**. A short way out of Cavan, is a group of standing stones, **Finn MacCool's Fingers**, said to be the place where the princes were crowned. More than 2000 stone forts litter the landscape of County Clare, a county that would be virtually unknown were it not for **The Burren**, a beautiful limestone district overlooking **Galway Bay** and formed around an ancient barony of that name. Along the north **Mayo** coast is the archaeological site known as the **Céide Fields**, supported by an imaginative visitor centre that explains the 5000 years of settlement in this part of Ireland. **Carrowmore** in **County Sligo** is an important prehistoric site with a vast number of stone circles and dolmens.
- Whether you seek religious or mystical monuments, the enchanting **Emerald Isle** has them in hordes. **Monasterboice** in Counties Louth and Meath was formerly a sixth-century monastery, and in the cemetery stand three of the finest High Crosses in the country. For centuries, County Wicklow was a stronghold of Celtic Christianity, with a focal point around **Glendalough**. Glendalough, the glen of the two lakes, is a place of holiness among the hills and a place of pilgrimage, where St Kevin founded a monastery in AD 570. The tall round tower is a familiar landmark, variously used as a look-out post, a grain store and a belfry. The cathedral is now in ruins, but is no less evocative for that. Down towards the river is **St Kevin's Church**, a modest building with a chimney-shaped belfry. **Kells Priory**, south of **Kilkenny**, the site of an Augustinian priory, is little known in Ireland, but is one of the most beautiful and finest ruins in the country. **Jerpoint Abbey**, south of **Thomastown**, is a remarkable Cistercian ruin, famed for the carvings on its tombs. It dates from 1158, but was embraced by Henry VIII's dissolution of the monasteries. In **County Westmeath**, in **Crookedwood** village, stmands **St Munna's Church**, the stuff of fairytales, complete with 15th-century tower and battlements and a lakeside setting. One of Ireland's most holy places, **Clonmacnoise**, in **Counties Offaly and Laios**, was founded in AD 548 by St Ciaran at a strategic crossing point of the **Shannon**. During medieval times, it developed into a great seat of learning, acknowledged by kings. **County Mayo**'s topography rises to the sacred mountain of **Croagh Patrick**, an annual place of pilgrimage. In County Mayo, the small town of **Knock** has an internationally recognised **Marian shrine**. Approximately 1.5 million pilgrims visit the shrine annually. **Costelloe Memorial Chapel** in **County Leitrim** has a strange claim to fame: it claims to be the second-smallest chapel in the world.
- Gaze out at some gorgeous, white sandy beaches: **Dunmore East**, in County Waterford, is a charming village close to safe bathing beaches and attractive coves, including **Ladies Cove**, a neat sandy bay popular with local people and tourists, whilst **Tramore** is one of Ireland's main holiday resorts and has a 4.8km- (3 mile-)

sandy beach caressed by the Gulf Stream, whilst **Ardmore** is renowned for its long, fine beach set against high cliffs and its place in Irish history as an important ecclesiastical site based on a seventh-century monastic settlement founded by St Declan; **County Cork** has a very attractive coastline, from **Kinsale**, a pretty seaside town at the mouth of **Bandon River**, to **Kilbrittain**, **Timoleague** and **Courtmacsherry**, all unspoilt in lovely settings, to **Bantry**, ideal for exploring **Bantry Bay** and the **Sheep's Head Peninsula**; the **Dingle Peninsula** in **County Kerry** has some lovely beaches and the fine town of **Dingle** itself, the westernmost town in Europe; not to be missed is **Brandon Mountain** and **Brandon Bay**; **Ventry** has a lovely white-sand strand, on which legend claims the King of the Other World landed to subjugate Ireland; **St John's Point** sticks out on a limb in **County Donegal**; and **Slieve League** is outstanding, from the cliffs of **Bunglass** to the glorious sands of **Silver Strand**.

- Gaze at what are arguably the most beautiful gardens in the southeast of Ireland, and not to be missed: **Kilmokea Gardens** in County Wexford.
- Explore **Dunmore Cave** in **County Kilkenny**, one of the most famous caves in Ireland, notable for its great beauty. In the past, people took refuge here from the Vikings, not always successfully.
- Ireland isn't just rolling green hills and beaches in widescreen – it also has its fair share of dramatic mountains. **County Tipperary**'s **Slievenamon** is called the mountain of the fairies. Northwards, amid farmlands, rises the limestone **Rock of Cashel**, and to the south are the **Comeragh Mountains**, amidst countryside dotted with Norman castles and churches, and Stone and Iron Age sites. The **Comeragh** and **Knockmealdown mountain ranges** are vast uplands of forest and bog, but easy to explore either by car or on foot. **County Offaly** shares with **County Laios** the beautiful glens of the **Slieve Bloom Mountains** which, in spite of a low elevation and a distinctly boggy feel about them, nevertheless convey a sense of grandeur and remoteness. And County Kerry has the highest mountain of them all: **Carrantoohill**.
- Spend a day absorbing the delights of **Cork**. Remember that the name *Corcaigh* means 'swamp', a reminder that Cork is built on the marshy ground flanking the River Lee. The city is lively, buzzing with industry, academia and, invariably, the sound of impromptu music recitals. The main part of the city is squashed onto an elongated island linked by elegant bridges. **Paul Street** is the trendy part of Cork. Other places worth taking in are the tower of **St Anne's Shandon**, the **Butter Exchange**, which houses the **Shandon Craft Centre**, **Cork City Gaol**, **Elizabeth Fort** (now a Garda station), the **Cork Public Museum** in **Fitzgerald Park** and **St Fin Barre's Cathedral**. Cork was designated the **European Capital of Culture** in 2005.

Top Things To Do

- Equestrianism is one of Ireland's principal tourist attractions and facilities for **horse riding** are found all over the country. The principal racecourses are at **Leopardstown**, **Fairyhouse** (**Irish Grand National** every year), **The Curragh** (**Irish Sweeps Derby**) and **Punchestown** (an international cross-country and three-day-event riding course).
- Ireland's sparsely populated countryside makes it ideal for **walkers** of all levels. The mild climate means that the mountains are accessible all year round. The more mountainous areas are towards the coast, which makes for dramatic seascapes, especially by the Atlantic Ocean. More adventurous walkers may want to tackle Ireland's highest peak, **Carrauntoohil** (1041m/3415ft) in **Macgillycuddy's Reeks**, in the far southwest of the country. Across the shadow of MacGillycuddy's Reeks is the finest ridge walk in Ireland. Other notable mountains include **Croagh Patrick** (765m/2510ft) near **Westport** in **County Mayo**, a holy mountain and, on the last Sunday in July, a place of pilgrimage. Its distinctive conical summit is silhouetted against the horizon for miles, acting as a beacon to pilgrims. St Patrick is supposed to have driven all the snakes out of Ireland from this mountain. The **12 Bens** in **Connemara** offer lovely hill walking, with views over towards the jagged coastline. The beautiful scenery of the **Wicklow Mountains** is barely one hour's drive from Dublin. There are 28 national waymarked ways in the country, including the **North Kerry Way**, the **Beara Way** and the **Wicklow Way**. Tailor-made tours with a local guide can be arranged through Walking Cycling Ireland (website: www.irelandwalkingcycling.com). There are many gentle walks for the less energetic. Public transport is increasing its capacity to carry bikes and accommodation is being upgraded so that bikes are stored securely.
- Although some of Ireland's coastal parts are mountainous, the sheltered valleys and the gently undulating central plain are excellent for easy **cycling**. Roads are well-maintained and most are very quiet. Inland, the landscape is dotted with small farms, and one is never too far away from some form of civilisation if one requires it. There are a surprisingly high number of pre-Celtic monuments in lonely places; owing to old Irish superstitions, these were not cleared away when the land was farmed. The **Boyne Valley** alone contains over 300.
- Being blessed with miles of rivers and streams and over 5500km (3500 miles) of coastline, Ireland offers excellent **fishing**. **Carrick-on-Shannon** is the centre of **river cruising** on the **Shannon**, and heavily geared up to all aquatic pursuits, with over 40 lakes where fishing is unrestricted. There is no closed season for **freshwater angling**, but March to October are the most suitable months for bream, rudd, roach, dace and perch. For **coarse angling**, there are new regulations regarding share certificates. **County Cavan** is known to anglers as a place of lakes and rivers and the very best in coarse fishing. **County Longford** holds great appeal for all anglers, sitting in the middle of Ireland, lying in the catchments of the **River Shannon**. Lakes abound, notably **Lough Gowna** in the north and **Lough Kinale** in the east. **Westport** even holds an annual **Westport Sea Angling Festival**. The **sea angling** in **Clew Bay**, meanwhile, is reputedly the finest in Europe. **Game fishing** requires a licence and, generally, also a permit. The brown trout season is usually from mid-February or March until 30 September. Open salmon season is 1 January to 7 September, according to district. The best sea trout period is from June to 30 September or 12 October in some areas. Salmon licences/permits also cover sea trout. Along the Atlantic coast, sea angling is possible from piers, rocks, in the surf or during a day's boat fishing excursion (which can be organised locally).
- **Dolphins** can be seen off the coast of Shannon. This area of the Atlantic is home to around 100 wild dolphins.
- Drink a pint of *Guinness*, one of the most famous, popular and distinctive drinks in the world, whilst indulging in some *craic* (see Social Conventions). **Dublin** is the ideal city to do this, with a palpable buzz of excitement, especially around **Temple Bar**. Indeed, the whole city boasts fashionable pubs, good places to eat, discos and inordinate *joie de vivre*.
- Taste some succulent **oysters** in the place where they are famed – **Carlingford**, which looks across the lough to the **Mourne Mountains**.
- Kiss the **Blarney Stone** at **Blarney Castle** in **County Cork** and get the 'gift of the gab'.
- The **Ring of Kerry** is a stunning, 180km- (112 mile-) scenic **drive** around the **Iveragh Peninsula**, with numerous diversions along coastal roads and out to islands like **Skellig Michael**. A drive through the hills, via **Ballaghbearna Gap** and the **Ballaghisheen Pass**, promises rugged landscapes studded with lakes and carved by rivers. The Atlantic Drive is also a wonderful drive, beginning from the village of **Mulrany**. The **Arigna Scenic Drive** is highly regarded for its fine views of **Lough Key**.
- Go **birdwatching** in the uninhabited **Saltee Islands**, one of Ireland's most important bird sanctuaries, off **County Wexford**. In this county are also the mudflats of the **Slaney Estuary** (known as 'slobs'), which make up the **Wexford Wildfowl Reserve**, at its best between October and April when wildfowl are here.
- Although now celebrated in various places around the world, there is still nothing better than partaking in the revels of **St Patrick's Week** (website: www.stpatricksday.ie) in Ireland itself. Usually held in March, Ireland observes its patron Saint, who brought Christianity to the pagan Celts almost 1500 years ago, with a flurry of raucous activities, from fireworks, exhibitions, funfairs and treasure hunts in Dublin, the capital city, plus a spectacular 3km-long **St Patrick's Day Festival Parade**, to food markets and street theatre in **Cork**.

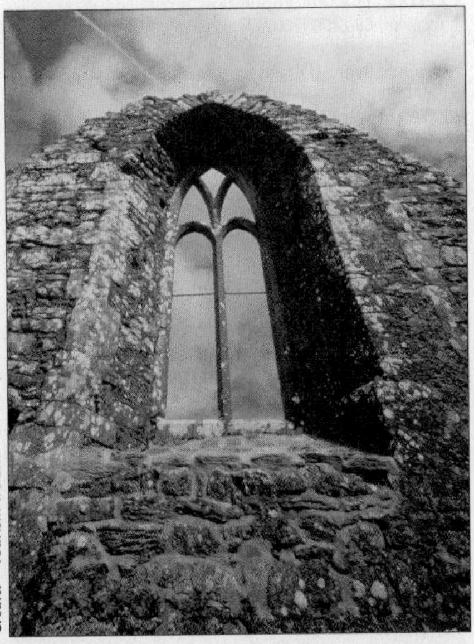

Credit: © Tourism Ireland

TOURIST INFORMATION

Tourism Ireland in the UK
Nations House, 103 Wigmore Street, London
W1U 1QS, UK
Tel: (0800) 039 7000 (travel enquiries) *or*
(020) 7518 0800 (trade enquiries).
Website: www.tourismireland.com

Tourism Ireland in the USA
345 Park Avenue, 17th Floor, New York, NY 10154, USA
Tel: (212) 418 0800 (general enquiries) *or*
(800) 223 6470 (toll-free brochure request line) *or*
669 9967 (toll-free for travel trade in USA and Canada).
Website: www.tourismireland.com

Entertainment

FOOD & DRINK: Ireland is a farming country noted for its meat, bacon, poultry and dairy produce. The surrounding sea, inland lakes and rivers offer fresh fish including salmon, trout, lobster, mussels and periwinkles. Dublin has a wide selection of restaurants and eating places to suit every pocket, as do the other major towns.

Cooking courses: Ireland has recently become a must-visit destination for food lovers. Cookery courses are available throughout the country. They vary from formal teaching in schools which offer classes all year round, to smaller, informal courses run by enthusiastic chefs in rural restaurants.

Things to know: Table and self-service are both common. 'Tea' is often almost a full meal with sandwiches and cakes. Pubs, of which Ireland has plenty, are sometimes called 'lounges' or 'bars' and there is often a worded sign outside the premises rather than the traditional painted boards found in Britain. Pubs and bars have counter service. The measure used in Ireland for spirits is larger than that used in Britain, for example an Irish double is equal to a triple in Britain.

National specialities:
- Dublin Bay prawns.
- Oysters (served with *Guinness* and wholemeal bread).
- Irish stew (traditionally made with mutton or old sheep, now mostly made with lamb or juicy beef, this dish is usually served with potatoes, stock, onions, carrots and garlic).
- *Crubeens* (pigs' trotters).
- *Colcannon* (a mixture of potatoes and cabbage cooked together).
- Soda bread.
- Soufflé made with *carrageen* (a variety of seaweed).

The two most internationally distinctive alcoholic products are *whiskey* (spelt with an 'e') and *stout*. Irish whiskey has a uniquely characteristic flavour and is matured in a wooden barrel for a minimum of seven years. Certainly as popular as whiskey is stout which is bottled or served from the tap.

National drinks:
- *Whiskey*: popular brands are: *Jamesons, John Powers Gold Label, Hewitts, Midleton, Old Bushmills, Paddy, Reserve* and *Tullamore Dew*.
- *Irish coffee* is popular (a glass of strong black coffee, brown sugar and whiskey with cream).
- *Guinness*, one of the most famous, popular and distinctive drinks in the world, is found everywhere.
- One of the most popular lighter ales is *Smithwick's* or *Harp Lager*, also available everywhere.
- Liqueurs such as *Bailey's* and *Irish Mist* are both made from a base of Irish whiskey.

Licensing hours: Mon-Wed 1030-2330, Thurs-Sat 1030-0030 and Sun 1030-2300.

Legal drinking age: 18, although some bars will insist that patrons are over 21 and carry ID. Children under 18 years must leave establishments by 2100.

Tipping: The customary tip in Ireland is 10 to 12 per cent. Many hotels and restaurants add this in the form of a service charge indicated on the menu or bill. It is not customary to tip in bars unless you have table service when a small tip is advised. Tipping porters, taxi drivers, hairdressers etc is customary but not obligatory.

NIGHTLIFE: Most towns in Ireland have clubs, bars and pubs with live music. It is quite common to find pubs holding *seisun*, playing traditional Irish music with traditional instruments. The dancehalls and discos of previous eras have now been replaced with clubs similar to those found throughout the UK and Western Europe. Special events and themed nights often take place at special attractions such as the medieval banquet at Bunratty Castle. There is still a good choice of theatres and cinemas.

SHOPPING: Special purchases include hand-woven tweed, hand-crocheted woollens and cottons, sheepskin goods, gold and silver jewellery, Aran knitwear, linen, pottery, Irish crystal and basketry. Ideal gifts include: a copy of *Ulysses* from an Irish bookshop, a bottle of *Jameson* or *Bushmills* whiskey from the distillery or Irish Salmon. **Shopping hours:** Mon-Sat 0900-1730/1800. Many towns have a late night opening on Thursday or Friday until 2000/2100 and smaller towns may have one early closing day a week. On Sunday, main shopping centres and some of the larger deprtment stores open from 1200 - 1700/1800. Many smaller supermarkets in towns and villages also open.
Note: Under the 'Retail Export Scheme', it is possible to claim VAT back on goods bought in Ireland on leaving the EU. For further information, contact the VAT Administration Branch, Stamping Building, Dublin Castle, Dublin 2 (tel: (1) 674 8858; website: www.revenue.ie).

Business

- **GDP:** US$159.88 billion.
- **Main imports:** Data processing equipment, other machinery and equipment, chemicals, petroleum and petroleum products, textiles and clothing.
- **Main exports:** Machinery and equipment, computers, chemicals, pharmaceuticals, live animals and animal products.
- **Main trade partners:** Belgium, France, Germany, Italy, The Netherlands, UK and USA.

ECONOMY: Ireland's recent economic history is characterised by what is now the cliché of the 'Celtic Tiger'. Fuelled by EU membership and effective investment promotion policies, the Irish economy has been transformed over a period of two decades from a European backwater into the fastest-growing economy in the EU.
Hitherto Ireland had not been industrialised to the same degree as the rest of Europe, and only recently has agriculture been overtaken as the largest single contributor to the national product. It remains a key sector, and the Government is seeking to consolidate its role within the economy by modernisation and expansion of food-processing industries. Beef and dairy dominate the sector, but there is also large-scale production of potatoes, barley and wheat. Ireland's recent industrial development has been achieved by a deliberate policy of promoting export-led and advanced technology businesses, partly by offering attractive packages for foreign investors. Textiles, chemicals and electronics have performed particularly strongly. Most of Ireland's economic development in the 1990s, however, was in the service sector. Banking and finance have grown to the extent that Dublin now supports a sizeable international financial centre, while tourism has become a substantial foreign exchange earner.
The statistics of Ireland's remarkable development show an average GDP growth of between 7 and 10 per cent since the mid-1990s, while inflation and unemployment were kept consistently below five per cent. However, there has been a slowdown of late with GDP growth in 2004 being 1.4 per cent. The Irish are famously enthusiastic about Europe and there is little of the scepticism so prevalent in Britain. Ireland joined EMU with the majority of EU members in the first wave at the beginning of 1999, despite some concern about the consequences of Britain's non-membership. Trade with the UK, which provides 30 per cent of total imports and takes 20 per cent of Ireland's exports, remains important but the proportion is declining gradually as other EU countries assume greater significance.
BUSINESS ETIQUETTE: Businesspeople should wear formal clothes for meetings. Local businesspeople are very friendly and an informal business approach is most successful. However, it is advisable to make prior appointments and to allow enough time to complete business matters. Avoid business visits in the first week of May, during July, August and at Christmas or New Year.

BUSINESS INFORMATION

Fáilte Ireland
Bord Fáilte, Baggot Street Bridge, Dublin 2, Ireland
Tel: (1) 602 4000.
Website: www.conference-ireland.ie

Chambers of Commerce of Ireland
17 Merrion Square, Dublin 2, Ireland
Tel: (1) 661 2888.
Website: www.chambers.ie

Israel

Location: Eastern Mediterranean.

Time: GMT + 2. Israel operates Daylight-Saving Time which is 3 hours ahead of Greenwich Mean Time (GMT+3). According to the Office of the Secretary General of the Ministry of Interior, there is no set rule for Daylight-saving time changes. One thing that is entrenched in law is that there must be at least 150 days of Daylight-Saving Time annually.

Overview

Regarded by many as the Holy Land, Israel is a remarkable, fascinating and controversial country.
The history of Israel may be traced back to 2000 BC, though the earliest recorded event derives from the era of Moses (around 1300 BC) when elements of the tribes of Israel escaped to Palestine from serfdom in the eastern Nile Delta. After 1291, the Jews continued to spread across Europe, North Africa and the Middle East (and later the Americas) and few countries today lack a community descended from Jewish settlers. The Zionist movement emerged in the 19th century with the aim of re-establishing a separate Jewish nation in Palestine, building on the common sense of identity of the scattered Jewish communities and the insecurity caused by frequent persecution.
The aspirations of the Zionist movement were ultimately recognised by the British government in the Balfour Declaration of 1917, which followed Britain's occupation of Palestine during World War I. The Balfour Declaration formed the basis of the 1920 mandate granted by the League of Nations, which acceded to British rule over the territory. The mandate laid the foundations of the modern Arab-Israeli conflict as the British struggled to balance their commitment to the Jews against their parallel promises to the indigenous Arab population.
The Jewish leaders inaugurated the State of Israel in May 1948, bringing an immediate conflict with the Arab population, which escalated into full-scale war. Much of the history of the region since that time has been one of

---

Credit: © Israel Government Tourist Office/www.fotoseeker.com

conflict between Israel and the Palestinians, represented by the Palestine Liberation Organisation (PLO). Many Palestinians were displaced and several wars were fought which also involved Egypt, Jordan, Syria and Lebanon. Palestinians in the West Bank, including east Jerusalem, have lived under Israeli occupation since 1967. Although Egypt and Israel signed a peace agreement in 1979, a peace process only began with the Palestinians in the early 1990s after years of uprising or intifada. Israel evacuated its settlers from the Gaza Strip in 2005 and withdrew its forces, ending almost four decades of military occupation. A final status agreement has yet to be reached. Following the death of the Palestinian leader Yasser Arafat, there is now hope that this calamity may compel some sort of closure to this lengthy conflict and the world waits with bated breath to observe Mahmoud Abbas's strategies. Although visitors are advised to check official government advice before travelling to the Palestinian National Authority Region or to Jerusalem, owing to political tension, Israel is a world-class destination which offers numerous cultural and religious attractions, spas and renowned sea resorts - all within an atmosphere that combines the very ancient with the ultra high-tech. The Dead Sea is a very popular attraction. An inland lake lying in the lower Jordan Valley, flanked by the Judean and Moab Mountains, it has minerals and high salt content renowned worldwide for their health-giving properties.

General Information

AREA: 22,145 sq km (8550 sq miles; includes East Jerusalem and the Golan sub-district).
POPULATION: 6.7 million (UN, 2005).
POPULATION DENSITY: 302.6 per sq km.
CAPITAL: Jerusalem. **Population:** (including East Jerusalem) 680,400 (2002). The Israeli government has designated Jerusalem as the capital, although this is not recognised by the UN, and most foreign embassies are based in Tel Aviv.
GEOGRAPHY: Israel is on the eastern Mediterranean, bordered by Lebanon and the Syrian Arab Republic to the north, Jordan to the east, and Egypt to the south. The autonomous Palestinian Authority Region lies mostly on the west bank of the River Jordan. Part of the Gaza strip, in the south of the country, is also administered by the Palestinians. The country stretches southwards through the Negev Desert to Eilat, a resort town on the Red Sea. The fertile Plain of Sharon runs along the coast, while inland, parallel to the coast, is a range of hills and uplands with fertile valleys to the west and arid desert to the east. The Great Rift Valley begins beyond the sources of the River Jordan and extends south through the Dead Sea (the lowest point in the world), into the Red Sea, continuing on into Eastern Africa.
GOVERNMENT: Republic. The state of Israel was founded in 1948. **Head of State:** Moshe Qatzav since 2000. **Head of Government:** Acting Prime Minister Ehud Olmert took control in March 2006 from former Primer Minister Ariel Sharon who became unconscious on 4 January 2006 having suffered a significant stroke. **Recent history:** Ariel Sharon was elected in the midst of the second Palestinian *intifada* (uprising) on a pledge to ensure total security for Israel. One

of the principal catalysts of the intifada was Mr Sharon's controversial visit to Jewish holy sites on Jerusalem's Temple Mount (or Haram al-Sharif to the Palestinians), an area of the old city considered to be Islam's third holiest site. In 2002, despite international criticism, Mr Sharon's government decided to build a 640 km (440 mile) West Bank barrier to protect Israel from Palestinian suicide bombers. In 2005, Mr Sharon also pursued a plan to evacuate more than 8,000 Israeli settlers from the Gaza Strip despite anger among pro-settlement activists, with a view to reviving an international peace plan.
In November 2005, a new twist in Israeli politics saw Ariel Sharon quitting the *Likud* party which he had helped found in 1973. Frustrated by the more right-wing Likud MPs' refusal to accept his ministerial nominees and their disapproval of the forced removals of Jewish settlers from the Gaza Strip, Sharon announced he would create a new centre party, bringing with him 14 members of Likud. This party is called *Kadima*. Sharon asked President Moshe Katsav to dissolve Parliament and call an early election. Acting Israeli Prime Minister Ehud Olmert was declared winner of the March 2006 election. His *Kadima* party, founded by now coma-stricken Ariel Sharon, won but by less than predicted. He has vowed to push ahead with plans to define Israel's final borders.
Palestinian Leader: Former Palestinian Prime Minister Mahmoud Abbas. **Palestinian Prime Minister (outgoing):** Ahmed Qurei, from the *Fatah* faction, resigned on 26 January 2006 because of the *Hamas* Parliamentary victory (see *Recent History*, below). Possible replacements for Prime Minister now include Gaza political leader Ismail Haniya or Mahmoud Zahhar, also based in Gaza, a co-founder of the organisation with Sheikh Ahmad Yassin, who would possibly be a more hardline choice. **Recent history:** Mahmoud Abbas, candidate of the ruling Fatah faction, won the January 2005 poll to replace the late Palestinian leader, Yasser Arafat. Regarded as a moderate, he has condemned the armed Palestinian uprising and favours the resumption of negotiations with Israel. But his primary challenge at the moment is to deal with the militant Islamic group, Hamas, who scored a stunning win in January 2006 Parliamentary elections - the first that the group had ever taken part in. Abbas must now appoint the Prime Minister in accordance with the largest party in Parliament - Hamas. This dominance of Hamas has met with worldwide controversy, with many nations, such as the US and Italy, refusing to negotiate with any party advocating the wipeout of Israel or who condone terrorist activity, and the EU, for example, threatening to sever financial aid. Meanwhile, others have argued that it is hypocritical for countries such as the USA to promote democracy and then refute the outcome of democratic procedure when it does not meet their approval. This is only the beginning of a colossal shift in Palestinian affairs, and only time will tell how the situation changes, and whether Hamas will adapt its policies within a democratic context.
LANGUAGE: Hebrew is the official language, spoken by about two-thirds of the population. Arabic is spoken by around 15 per cent of the population. English is spoken in most places and other languages, including French, German, Hungarian, Polish, Romanian, Russian, Spanish and Yiddish are widely used.
RELIGION: 77 per cent Jewish, 15 per cent Muslim, with Christian, Druze and other minorities.
ELECTRICITY: 230 volts AC, 50Hz. Three-pin plugs are standard; if needed, adaptors can be purchased in Israel.
SOCIAL CONVENTIONS: Israelis are usually very informal but in keeping with the European style of hospitality. Visitors should observe normal courtesies when visiting someone's home and should not be afraid to ask questions about the country as most Israelis are happy to talk about their homeland, religion and politics. Often the expression *shalom* ('peace') is used for hello and goodbye. Dress is casual, but in Christian, Jewish and Muslim holy places, modest attire is worn. For places such as the Wailing Wall, male visitors are given a smart cardboard *yarmulke* (scull cap) to respect the religious importance of the site. Businesspeople are expected to dress smartly, while plush restaurants, nightclubs and hotel dining rooms may require guests to dress for dinner. Formal evening wear is usually specified on invitations. It is considered a violation of the *Shabbat* (Saturday) to smoke in certain restaurants and many hotels. There is usually a sign to remind the visitor, and to disregard this warning would be regarded as discourteous to Orthodox Jews.

Climate

Mediterranean, with a pleasant spring and autumn. Winters in the north can be cool. Rain in winter is widespread, particularly in Jerusalem. Snow is rare. Summers can be very hot, especially in the south. The Red Sea resort of Eilat has a good climate for beach holidays all the year round.
Required clothing: Lightweight cottons and linens for warmer months are required. Mediumweights are recommended for winters, although on the Red Sea coast they are unlikely to be necessary during the day.

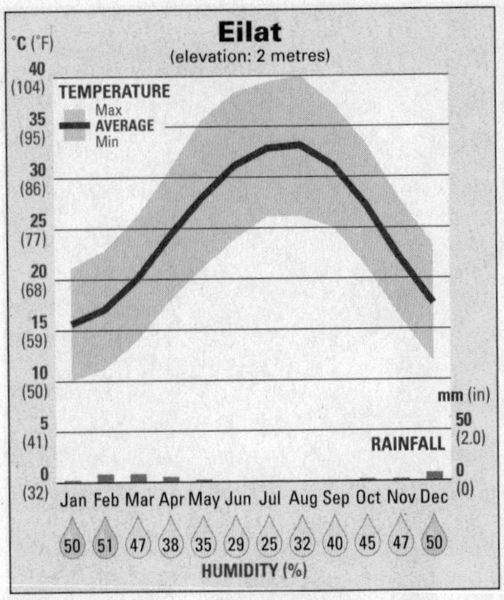

Eilat
(elevation: 2 metres)
°C (°F)
TEMPERATURE
Max
AVERAGE
Min
40 (104)
35 (95)
30 (86)
25 (77)
20 (68)
15 (59)
10 (50)
5 (41)
0 (32)
mm (in)
50 (2.0)
0 (0)
RAINFALL
Jan Feb Mar Apr May Jun Jul Aug Sep Oct Nov Dec
50 51 47 38 35 29 25 32 40 45 47 50
HUMIDITY (%)

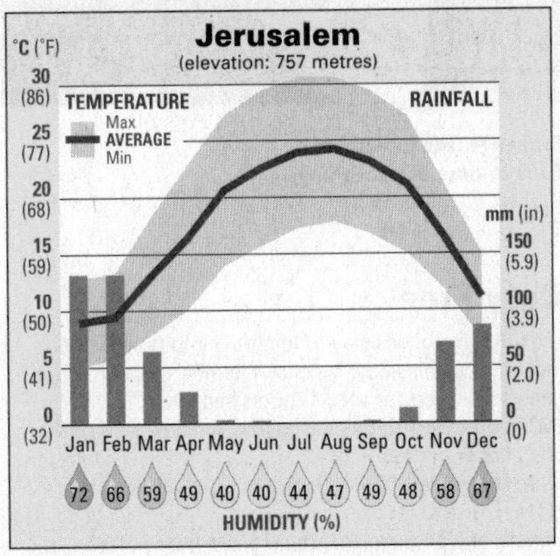

Jerusalem
(elevation: 757 metres)
°C (°F)
TEMPERATURE
Max
AVERAGE
Min
RAINFALL
30 (86)
25 (77)
20 (68)
15 (59)
10 (50)
5 (41)
0 (32)
mm (in)
150 (5.9)
100 (3.9)
50 (2.0)
0 (0)
Jan Feb Mar Apr May Jun Jul Aug Sep Oct Nov Dec
72 66 59 49 40 40 44 47 49 48 58 67
HUMIDITY (%)

Communications

Telephone: Full IDD service. Country code: 972. Local telephone directories are in Hebrew, but there is a special English-language version for tourists.
Mobile telephone: Roaming agreements exist with most international mobile phone companies. There is coverage practically all over the country, including over parts of the sea. Visitors should note that it is illegal to drive whilst holding a mobile telephone.
Internet: There are many Internet cafes.
Post: Airmail to Europe takes up to one week. Post office hours: May vary but are generally Sun-Tues and Thurs 0800-1200 and 1530-1830, Wed 0800-1330 and Fri 0800-1200. All post offices are closed on *Shabbat* (Saturday) and holy days, although central telegraph offices are open throughout the year.
MEDIA: Israel's media scene is varied. The Israel Broadcasting Authority (IBA) operates public radio and TV services and is funded mainly by licence fees on TV sets. *Channel 2* and *Channel 10* are the main commercial TV networks. Most Israeli households subscribe to cable or satellite TV. Commercial radio arrived in 1995, but faces competition from a proliferation of pirate radio stations, some carrying ultra-Orthodox programme material. All Israeli newspapers are privately-owned. Newspapers are printed in a variety of languages, including English. Political and religious affiliations are common.
Press: The main dailies are *Ha'aretz*, *Ma'ariv* and *Yedioth Aharonoth*. The English-language daily is the *Jerusalem Post*. The *Jerusalem Post International Edition* is published weekly and goes out to 95 countries.
TV: The Israel Broadcasting Authority operates public TV channel *Channel 1*; *Channel 2* and *Channel 10* are national, commercial channels.
Radio: The Israel Broadcasting Authority operates public radios, including speech-based *Reshet Aleph*, news-based *Reshet Bet*, music-based *Reshet Gimmel* and Arabic-language *Reshet Dalet*; *Galei Zahal* is Israel Defence Forces (IDF) radio; it broadcasts news and music to a mostly-civilian audience and operates the music and traffic news network *Galgalatz*.
PALESTINIAN MEDIA: Most people in the Palestinian areas get information from television and satellite dishes are common. Pan-Arab broadcasters, particularly Qatar's *Al-Jazeera TV*, are popular among viewers. There are dozens of private radio stations and a handful of private TV stations. Jordanian TV is widely-watched in the West Bank. The Palestinian authorities limit freedom of speech and self-censorship by Palestinian journalists is widespread. Control of the official radio and TV was transferred from the PLO and the Palestinian Authority to the Information Minister in 2005. But media analysts questioned how far the measure represented a real step towards creating a public-service broadcaster. Palestinian media outlets were badly damaged by Israeli military operations in the wake of the second *intifada*.
Press: Jerusalem-based *Al-Quds* is the largest-circulation Palestinian daily; *Al-Ayyam* is a Ramallah-based daily; *Al-Hayat Al-Jadidah* is the Palestinian National Authority daily.
Radio *Voice of Palestine* is the official radio station.
TV: *Palestine TV* and Gaza-based *Palestine Satellite Channel* are official channels; private channels include *Al-Quds Educational TV, Al-Mahd TV, Al-Majd TV, Al-Nawras TV, Al-Sharq TV, Amwaj TV, Bayt Lahm TV, Shepherds TV* and *Watan TV*.

Passport/Visa

	Passport Required?	Visa Required?	Return Ticket Required?
Full British	Yes	No	Yes
Australian	Yes	No	Yes
Canadian	Yes	No	Yes
USA	Yes	No	Yes
Other EU	Yes	1	Yes
Japanese	Yes	No	Yes

Note: *Regulations and requirements may be subject to change at short notice, and you are advised to contact the appropriate diplomatic or consular authority before finalising travel arrangements. Any numbers in the chart refer to the footnotes below.*

PASSPORTS: Passport valid for a minimum of six months beyond intended date of arrival required by all.
Note: (a) Persons wishing to proceed to an Arab country other than Egypt or Jordan after visiting Israel should ensure their passport does not contain an Israeli visa or stamp. However, persons permitted to stay in Israel for a period of three months or more will be required to have an extension stamped in their passport. (b) Former nationals of Israel holding a foreign passport must have written proof of having given up Israeli identity, otherwise, they may be required to obtain a new Israeli passport or renew their original one.
VISAS: All nationals require a stamp on arrival. Visas are required by all except the following:
(a) **1.** nationals of countries mentioned in the chart above (*except* nationals of Germany if born before 1 January 1928 who *do* require a visa);
(b) nationals of Argentina, The Bahamas, Barbados, Bolivia, Brazil, Central African Republic, Chile, Colombia, Costa Rica, Croatia, Dominican Republic, Ecuador, El Salvador, Fiji, Gibraltar, Guatemala, Haiti, Hong Kong (SAR), Iceland, Jamaica, Korea (Rep), Lesotho, Liechtenstein, Malawi, Mauritius, Mexico, Micronesia (Federated States of), Monaco, Mongolia, New Zealand, Norway, Panama, Paraguay, The Philippines, St Kitts & Nevis, San Marino, South Africa, St Lucia, Surinam, Swaziland, Switzerland, Trinidad & Tobago, Uruguay and Vanuatu;
(c) transit passengers continuing their journey within 24 hours by the same or first connecting flight provided holding valid onward or return documentation and not leaving the airport.
Note: It is advisable to check with nearest Consulate (or consular section at Embassy) for visa requirements before travelling to Israel as requirements may vary for some nationals.
Types of visa: *Tourist/Entry*: £11 (cash only, or £12 postal order). These fees are for UK nationals; prices vary according to nationality. Cruise ship passengers visiting Israel will be issued *Landing Cards*, allowing them to remain in the country for as long as the ship is in port. No visa applications are required.
Validity: Three months but varies according to nationality. Visas may be extended (for a nominal fee) at offices of the Ministry of the Interior in the following locations: Afula, Akko (Acre), Ashqelon, Be'ersheba, Eilat, Hadera, Haifa, Herzrelia, Holon, Jerusalem, Nazareth, Netanya, Petah Tiqva, Ramat Gan, Ramla, Rehovot, Safed, Tel Aviv and Tiberias.
Application to: Consulate (or consular section at Embassy); see *Passport/Visa Information* for details.
Application requirements: (a) Valid passport. (b) Application form. (c) One passport-size photo. (d) Return ticket. (e) A copy of tenancy agreement or mortgage arrangements. (f) Bank statement for last three months. (g) Self-addressed envelope and a day time telephone number. (h) Invitation from company/friends/contact in Israel (i) Letter from travel agent confirming itinerary, reservation of return ticket, hotel and medical insurance. (i) Letter from employer/university specifying period of time you have

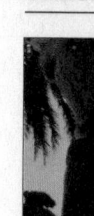

Credit: © Israel Government Tourist Office/www.fotoseeker.com

worked with them and that you will be returning after trip. (j) Fee, payable by postal order or cash.

Note: Different application requirements, and advice on crossing the border, will almost certainly apply to those travelling on to Egypt or Jordan; it is essential that the Embassy/Consulate be consulted beforehand.

Working days required: Depends on nationality. Some visas will require authorisation from Israel and so it is advisable to contact the Embassy before booking travel tickets.

Temporary residence: Apply to the Ministry of the Interior in Israel.

Note: As a concession to travellers intending to travel at a later date to countries with entry restrictions for visitors to Israel, entry stamps will, on request, be entered only on the entry form AL-17 and not on the passport. This facility is not available to those required to obtain their Israeli visas in advance.

PASSPORT/VISA INFORMATION

Embassy of Israel in the UK
2 Palace Green, London W8 4QB, UK
Tel: (020) 7957 9500.
Website: http://london.mfa.gov.il
Opening hours: Mon-Thurs 0900-1730, Fri 0830-1330.
Consular section: 15a Old Court Palace, London W8 4QB, UK
Tel: (020) 7957 9576/9627/9680.
Opening hours: Mon-Thurs 1000-1330, Fri 1000-1230.

Embassy of Israel in the USA
3514 International Drive, NW, Washington, DC 20008, USA
Tel: (202) 364 5500 or 5527 (consular section).
Website: www.israelemb.org

Money

Currency: New Shekel (ILS) = 100 agorot (singular, agora). Notes are in denominations of ILS200, 100, 50, and 20. Coins are in denominations of ILS100, 50, 10, 5, 1 and half and 50 and 10, 5 and 1 agorot.

Currency exchange: Foreign currency can only be exchanged at authorised banks, hotels and change shops. Change shops found in most cities charge no commission and equal the bank exchange rates. It is advisable to leave Israel with the minimum of Israeli currency. Payment in foreign currency exempts tourists from VAT on certain purchases and services, and is sometimes preferred by shop keepers. A maximum of US$500 worth of new shekels can be reconverted to foreign currency by travellers leaving Israel.

Credit & debit cards: All major credit cards are accepted. ATMs are widely available.

Traveller's cheques: These are widely accepted. To avoid additional exchange rate charges, travellers are advised to take traveller's cheques in US Dollars.

Currency restrictions: There are no restrictions on the import of local or foreign currency. Travellers planning to export local currency should apply to a local bank before departure from Israel. The export of foreign currency is limited to the amount imported.

Banking hours: Sun-Fri 0830-1200 and Sun, Tues, Thurs 1600-1800.

Exchange rate indicators:
Rate at time of publishing
£1.00=   ILS8.14
$1.00=   ILS4.69

Duty Free

The following goods may be imported into Israel without incurring customs duty (alcohol and tobacco can only be imported by persons aged 17 years and over):

250 cigarettes or 250g of tobacco products; 1l of spirits and 2l of wine; 250ml of eau de cologne or perfume; gifts up to the value of US$150.

Note: Provided for personal use and re-exported, one video camera, one photographic camera, one movie camera, one tape recorder and up to a value of US$250 in film and video cassettes may be imported; subject to high deposits paid in cash or VISA credit card only. For flowers, plants and seeds, a health certificate is required.

Prohibited: Fresh meat, bananas and pineapples; fruit and vegetables from the African continent, especially South Africa; and dogs and cats aged under three months.

Public Holidays

Below are listed Public Holidays for the January 2006-June 2007 period.
2006: Mar 14 Purim. **Apr 12-19*** Pesach (Passover). **May 3** Yom Ha'Atzmaut (Israel Independence Day). **Jun 2** Shavu'ot (Pentecost). **Sep 24-25** Rosh Hashana (New Year). **Oct 2** Yom Kippur (Day of Atonement). **Oct 6-13*** Sukkot (Tabernacles). **Oct 14** Shemini Atzeret (Celebration of Renewal and Thanksgiving). **Dec 14-16** Chanukah (Feast of the Lights).
2007: Mar 4 Purim. **Apr 3-9*** Pesach (Passover). **Apr 23** Yom Ha'Atzmaut (Israel Independence Day). **May 23** Shavu'ot (Pentecost). **Mar 4** Purim. **Apr 2-9*** Pesach (Passover). **May 3** Yom Ha'Atzmaut (Israel Independence Day). **May 23** Shavu'ot (Pentecost).
Note: *Only the first and last days of Passover and Sukkot are officially recognised as national holidays, but there may be some disruption on intermediate dates; many shops and businesses may open but close early. Jewish festivals commence on the evenings before the dates given above. The Jewish religious day is Saturday – Shabbat – and begins at nightfall on Friday until nightfall on Saturday. Most public services and shops close early on Friday as a result. Muslim and Christian holidays are also observed by the respective populations. Thus, depending on the district, the day of rest falls on Friday, Saturday or Sunday.

Health

	Special Precautions?	Certificate Required?
Yellow Fever	No	No
Cholera	No	No
Typhoid & Polio	1	N/A
Malaria	No	N/A

Note: Regulations and requirements may be subject to change at short notice, and you are advised to contact your doctor well in advance of your intended date of departure. Any numbers in the chart refer to the footnotes below.

1: Immunisation against typhoid and poliomyelitis is sometimes recommended.

Food & drink: Mains water is normally chlorinated, and whilst relatively safe, may cause mild abdominal upsets. Bottled water is available and is advised for the first few weeks of the stay. Drinking water outside main cities and towns may be contaminated and sterilisation is advisable. Milk is pasteurised and dairy products are safe for consumption. Local meat, poultry, seafood, fruit and vegetables are generally considered safe to eat.

Other risks: Hepatitis A and B occur. West Nile fever has been seen recently. Tick-borne relapsing fever may occur. Rabies is present. For those at high risk, vaccination before arrival should be considered. If you are bitten, seek medical advice without delay. For more information, consult the Health appendix.

Health care: Israel has excellent medical facilities and tourists may go to all emergency departments and first-aid centres. However, any medical form of treatment can be expensive. Health centres are marked by the red Star of David on a white background. Medical insurance is recommended.

Travel - International

AIR: The national airline is El Al Israel Airlines (LY) (website: www.elal.co.il).
Approximate flight times: From London to Tel Aviv is four hours 30 minutes and to Eilat is five hours. From Los Angeles to Tel Aviv is 17 hours, from New York is 11 hours, from Singapore is 10 hours 55 minutes and from Sydney is 14 hours 35 minutes.
Main airports: Tel Aviv (TLV) (Ben Gurion International) is 20km (12 miles) southeast of the city. To/from the airport: There is a bus service from the airport to Shohom, Midi'in and Be'er Sheva. The airport has a train station located on level five. There is also a taxi service (travel time – 20 minutes). A shared sherut (taxi service) is available, charging a fixed rate per passenger. The El Al airline bus goes to the airport terminal in Tel Aviv. Departure depends on El Al flights. The best way to travel to Jerusalem, which is 50km (31 miles) away, is by sherut. Facilities: Banks, restaurants, duty-free shops, general shops, tourist information and VIP lounge.
Eilat Central Airport (ETH) is 20 minutes from the city. To/from the airport: Buses and taxis and limousines are available to the city (travel time – 15 minutes). Facilities: Duty free shop, light refreshments, a souvenir shop and car hire.
Departure tax: None.

SEA: **Main ports:** Ashdod and Haifa. Foreign yachts sailing to Israel may use these ports of entry as well as Eilat and the marinas of Ashkelon, Herzliya and Tel-Aviv. There are regular sailings of car/passenger ferries from Greece (Piraeus) and Cyprus to Haifa. Cruise lines run to Haifa and Ashdod from Athens and other Mediterranean ports.

ROAD: On the whole, road access to Israel is somewhat limited. There are two crossing points from Egypt into Israel. Travellers are permitted to cross the border on foot, by bus or in privately owned cars only; taxis and hired cars may not cross. Rafiah (Rafah), the main point of entry, is located some 50km (31 miles) southwest of Ashqelon (open 0900-1700). Four bus companies maintain services between Cairo and Tel Aviv and Jerusalem via Rafiah. EGGED Bus no. 362 leaves Tel Aviv for the Rafiah terminal daily and Rafiah for Tel Aviv at Taba, just south of Eilat, is open 24 hours a day. A regular bus service is available between Taba, Santa Katerina (Sinai) and Cairo.
It is possible to enter Jordan via the Allenby Bridge near Jericho, about 40km (25 miles) from Jerusalem. The Allenby Bridge border opening hours are Sun-Thurs 0800-0000, Fri 0800-1500. EGGED buses and taxi services are also available to the bridge. At present, every tourist passing through here must obtain an entry visa to and an exit visa from Jordan. Exit fees are only payable on leaving for Jordan. Nationals of countries who are required to obtain an Israeli visa in advance should do so before visiting Jordan, as such visas cannot be obtained at the Allenby Bridge.
The Arava Checkpoint crossing is situated 4km (3 miles) north of Eilat. It is possible to cross the border in both directions. Nationals should check whether visas are required for this crossing with their local Embassy. The opening hours for the Arava border checkpoint are Sun-Thurs 0630-2230, Fri-Sat 0800-2000 (closed on Yom Kippur and the Muslim festival of Eid al-Adha).
The Jordan River Crossing (Sheikh Hussein Bridge) can be crossed by holders of UK passports valid for at least six months from the date of entry and persons with dual nationality as individuals or in groups. Entry visas for Jordan or Israel can either be organised through travel agents who will make the necessary arrangements or can be provided on arrival for all those who have organised pre-arranged visas (except for Israeli passport holders who must make arrangements through travel agents). Travel agents are requested to coordinate the arrival time of buses with the

A B C D E F G H I J K L M N O P Q R S T U V W X Y Z

management of the crossing point. All UN cars (on official business or not) and vehicles with foreign registration will be permitted to cross freely without paying any fees; however, Israeli cars with diplomatic plates will not be permitted to cross the border. Transfer of passengers between the Israeli and Jordanian checkpoints will be carried out by shuttle service. Transfers on foot will not be permitted. The Jordan River (Sheikh Hussein) border crossing hours are Sun-Thurs 0630-2200, Fri-Sat 0800-2000 (closed on Yom Kippur and the Jordanian festival on the first day of the Hijirah Calendar). There is no access to the Syrian Arab Republic and Lebanon. Mobile telephones are not allowed on buses crossing the border.

Travel - Internal

AIR:

A comprehensive service linking Tel Aviv with Eilat and all major cities is run by *Arkia/Israel Inland Airways (IZ)* (website: www.arkia.co.il) and by *Israir (6H)* (website: www.israirairlines.com). Flights operate daily except on Friday evenings and Saturday mornings and afternoons.

SEA/LAKE:

Ferries run across the Lake Tiberias (Sea of Galilee) from Tiberias on the west side to Ein Gev kibbutz on the eastern shore. Coastal ferries serve all ports. For details, contact local port authorities.

RAIL:

Israel Railways (website: www.israrail.org.il) operates four suburban train lines and runs regular services between Akko (Acre), Ashdod, Binyamina, Hadera, Haifa, Herzliya, Netanya, Nahariya, Krayat, Petah, Rehovot, Rosh Ha'ayin, Tel Aviv and Tikva. There is also a service between Tel Aviv and Jerusalem, which follows a particularly scenic route. Reserved seats may be ordered in advance. There is no railway service on *Shabbat* (Saturday) and major holidays.

ROAD:

Traffic drives on the right. An excellent system of roads connects all towns. However, driving is erratic and there are frequent accidents. Radar speed traps operate and fees for speeding are high. Distances by road from Jerusalem to other cities are as follows: Tel Aviv 62km (39 miles), Tiberias 157km (97 miles), Eilat 312km (194 miles), Netanya 93km (58 miles), Dead Sea 104km (65 miles), Zefat 192km (120 miles) and Haifa 159km (99 miles). **Bus:** Two national bus systems, run by the *DAN* and *EGGED* cooperatives, provide extensive services. The service is fast and efficient as well as cheap. With a few exceptions, services are suspended on religious holidays, and between sunset on Friday and sunset on Saturday (*Shabbat*). **Sherut:** Unique to Israel, these limousines seat seven to 10 passengers and follow intercity and local bus routes. Prices are around 30 per cent higher than the bus. **Taxi:** Services are either run by companies or by individuals. There are both shared taxis (*sheruts*) and ordinary taxis. Taxi drivers are required by law to operate a meter and are recommended for short journeys only. **Car hire:** Available in major cities. Hire fees are not cheap. **Documentation:** Full driving licence and insurance are required. An International Driving Permit is recommended.

URBAN:

Bus companies *DAN* and *EGGED* provide good local services in the main towns. Taxis are available.

Travel Advice

Visitors are advised against all travel to the Occupied Territories (including the West Bank and Gaza).
Visitors are advised against all but essential travel along Israel's border with Lebanon, and close to the Israeli side of the Israel/Gaza Strip border. Visitors should take care at crossing points between Israel and Jordan.
While there was a reduction in the level of violence in 2005, a high threat from terrorism and military activity in Israel and in the Occupied Territories remains.
If you are planning to travel to Israel, you should be very careful about your personal security arrangements throughout your visit. Developments in the region could affect the security situation.
This advice is based on information provided by the Foreign & Commonwealth Office in the UK. It is correct at time of publishing. As the situation can change rapidly, visitors are advised to contact the following organisations for the latest travel advice:

British Foreign and Commonwealth Office
Tel: (0845) 850 2829.
Website: www.fco.gov.uk

US Department of State
Website: http://travel.state.gov/travel

Accommodation

EDITOR'S CHOICE: KIBBUTZ GUEST HOUSE

For a holiday with a difference, unique to Israel, there are *kibbutz country inns* in all parts of the country where one can find relaxed informality in delightful rural surroundings. Kibbutz Fly-Drive holidays are very popular and so are discovery tours by air-conditioned coach, staying at different hotels and kibbutzim to see the whole country. All are clean and comfortable with modern dining rooms. Most have swimming pools (though it is wise to check that this facility is open to visitors) and provide a valuable insight into the style and aims of kibbutz life. Approximately 130 out of the 300 kibbutzim have guest houses and each is located in a rural or scenic part of the country and is usually open all year. Further information is available from the Israel Kibbutz Hotels Chain, the Kibbutz Artzi Federation (see *Accommodation Information*) and the Israel Government Tourist Office.

HOTELS:

There are over 350 hotels listed for visitors by the Ministry of Tourism. Prices vary according to season and region. It is best to book months in advance for Israel's high season (usually July to August, though this varies according to the region) and for religious holiday seasons. 350 hotels are members of the Israel Hotel Association, see *Accommodation Information*.

HOLIDAY/RECREATION VILLAGES:

Located on the Mediterranean or the Red Sea Gulf, these villages provide accommodation usually in the form of small two-bed cabins and bungalows. The standard fittings often include full air conditioning and facilities. Most are only open between April and October and the emphasis is on casual living.

SELF-CATERING:

Apartments and individual rooms are available on a rental basis throughout the country.

CHRISTIAN HOSPICES: Throughout the country, some 30 Christian hospices (operated by a variety of denominations) provide rooms and board at low rates. Although preference is given to pilgrimage groups, most will accommodate general tourists. They vary greatly in size and standards but all offer tourists basic accommodation in situations where hotels are full. Details are available from the Israel Government Tourist Office.

CAMPING/CARAVANNING:

The fine climate means Israel is a good country for camping, with campsites providing a touring base for each region. They offer full sanitary facilities, electric current, a restaurant and/or store, telephone, postal services, first-aid facilities, shaded picnic and campfire areas and day and night watchmen. They can be reached by bus, but all are open to cars and caravans. Most have tents and cabins, as well as a wide range of equipment for hire. All sites have swimming facilities either on-site or within easy reach. Hitchhiking is not recommended.

YOUTH HOSTELS:

Hostels in Israel can be dormitory, family bungalows, guest house standard rooms, huts or modern cubicles and they are scattered all over the country in both urban and rural areas. For further details, write to the IYHA, see *Accommodation Information*.

ACCOMMODATION INFORMATION

Israel Hotel Association
PO Box 50066, 29 Hamered Street, Tel Aviv 61500, Israel
Tel: (3) 517 0131.
website: www.israelhotels.org.il

Israel Youth Hostelling Association (IYHA)
Binyanei Ha'mah, PO Box 6001, Jerusalem 91060, Israel
Tel: (2) 655 8400/6.
website: www.youth-hostels.org.il

Kibbutz Hotel Chain
41 Montefiore Street, Tel Aviv, Israel
Tel: (3) 560 8118.
Website: www.kibbutz.co.il

Kibbutz Artzi Federation
Website: www.kba.org.il/eng/welcome.htm

Information is also available from the Israel Government Tourist Office see *Top Things To Do*.

Top Things To See

- For Christians, Jews and Muslims, **Jerusalem** is one of the most revered cities on earth. Attractions range from religious emblems and relics of antiquity to modern items of interest. For centuries, Jerusalem's **Old City**, framed by massive stone turreted walls, has comprised four distinct neighbourhoods, known as the Jewish, Christian, Muslim and Armenian Quarters (website: www.jerusalem.muni.il/english).
- See the eight gates piercing Jerusalem's Old City walls, with the **Jaffa Gate** being the most trafficked entry.
- In the Armenian quarter, discover the majestic **St James Cathedral**.
- In the Jewish quarter, do not miss the **Herodian Quarter/Wohl Archaeological Museum**. This recent excavation unearthed a 9000 sq m (30,000 sq ft) area, formerly the exclusive residential community from the Second Temple period, two thousand years ago. Six villas and one mansion can be toured, each with a ritual bath decorated in ceramic tiles and collections of household antiquities on display.
- Walk down the **Street of the Chain** and come to the world's holiest Jewish site, **The Western Wall**. The Wall, 20.2m (67ft) high and 27.7m (91ft) long, is a place symbolic of strength and ritual and is a must see for every visitor to Israel. Once called the Wailing Wall because of tearful worshipers, a constant flow of people and commotion can always be found here. Write a prayer and place it into the cracks between the giant yellow stones worn smooth from years of caresses.
- Climb the pathway to the right of The Western Wall and enter **The Temple Mount.** Existing as a place of worship since the tenth century BCE, when Solomon built the First Temple there, this is a site holy to Jews, Christians, and Muslims.
- Be inspired by the **Dome of the Rock**, an octagonal mosque built on the remains of The Great Temple of the Jews. This landmark, with its gilded dome and vibrant blue tiles, is the holiest Islamic place of worship in Israel, and a major photo opportunity.
- Near **The Lions Gate**, also known as **St Stephen's Gate**, is the peaceful garden setting of the **Pools of Bethesda** and **St Anne's Church**, traditionally known as the

Credit: © Israel Government Tourist Office/www.fotoseeker.com

Credit: © Israel Government Tourist Office/www.fotoseeker.com

birthplace of Mary. The pools at one time appeared to have been almost 9m (30ft) deep and are sites of healing described by John in the New Testament. St Anne's is the best preserved Crusader built church in all of Israel.
- Veer off the Via Dolorosa and enter the **Church of The Holy Sepulchre**, a centre of Christian worship in Jerusalem. Though it is impossible to see the many domes of the church from the street, they are stunning viewed from inside. The recently restored great dome beams glorious paths of sun rays through stained glass windows drenching the formerly gloomy interior with light.
- See the *Dead Sea Scrolls* at the **Israel Museum** in Jerusalem.
- Pay tribute to the six million Jews who died in the Holocaust at **Yad Vashem**, Jerusalem's memorial.
- Go on a religious tour from West Jerusalem to **Mount Zion** and the **Tomb of David**.
- Discover **Jaffa**'s archaeological finds reaching back to the third century BC.
- In Galilee and the North, places of interest are **Lake Tiberias** (the **Sea of Galilee**) itself, **Nazareth** (especially the **Church of the Annunciation**), the **Bet She'arim Catacombs**, **Megiddo**, **Tiberias** and the **Mount of Beatitudes**. The **Museum of Mediterranean Archaeology** celebrates many finds in the region.
- See the ancient fortress of **Haifa**, Israel's leading seaport.
- South from Haifa, visit the artists' colony of **En Hod** and the Roman ruins at **Caesarea**.
- Enjoy breathtaking views of the Dead Sea and the pink mountains of Moab from the once luxurious **Palace of King Herod**, perched on a clifftop in **Masada** (**Mezada**). It can be reached by cable car or a winding footpath.
- Other interesting sights around the Dead Sea include **Mount Sodom**, a 13km- (8 mile-) long mountain range made up of pure salt which has many caves with extraordinary hanging salt formations, and **Qumran**, where the *Dead Sea Scrolls*, written by Essene scribes, were discovered in ancient pottery jars in 1947. Excavations at the site found more than 900 pieces of scrolls in more than 30 caves.

THE PALESTINE NATIONAL AUTHORITY REGION
- Do not miss **Bethlehem**, most famous for being the birthplace of Christ. A major attraction is the **Church of the Nativity** at the **Manger Square**, built over the cave where Jesus was born. The city is also well known for **olive woodcarving** and **mother-of-pearl jewellery**, which, today, has developed into a modern industry.
- One of the prime sites of interest in the region for historians and visitors alike is the ancient town of **Jericho**, which dates back more than 10,000 years and lies 260m (853ft) below sea level, 36km (22.5 miles) east of Jerusalem. Known as the 'City of Palms', Jericho is one of the world's oldest continuously inhabited sites. The walls and towers of Jericho are 4000 years older than the pyramids of Egypt. Excavations at **Tel al-Sultan ruins** show Jericho settlements as early as 10000BC. Visit the **Monastery of St George, Wadi Qelt, Nabi Musa, the Mount of Temptation**, where Jesus spent 40 days and nights fasting and meditating and where a monastery was later built, **the Sycamore Tree** and **Hisham's Palace**.
- The city of **Hebron** lies in the mountainous region south of Jerusalem, at an altitude of 1000m (3280ft). Hebron is an unspoiled town, with many narrow and winding

streets, flat-roofed stone houses and old bazaars, where pottery, glassware and other inventive arts can be found. Hebron is the burial place of Abraham Al-Khalil. The **Abraham Mosque** which houses the tombs of the Patriarchs dominates the city centre.
- Be enthralled with the **Roman Theatre** near the heart of the city of **Nablus**, the major commercial, industrial and agricultural centre in the northern West Bank. Other archaeological sites in various stages of excavation can be seen here.
- **Gaza**, located on the western Mediterranean coast, 32km (22.4 miles) north of the Egyptian border is a long-established economic regional centre for trade in citrus fruits and other goods. Gaza is also known for its archaeological resources. See splendid mosaics in the **Byzantine ruins** and tombs recently excavated in the northern part of Gaza. Other interesting sites include: the **Great Omari Mosque, Napoleon's Fort** and the **Sayyed Hashem Mosque**.
- **Note:** For further information about the Palestinian National Authority Region, contact the Palestinian Ministry of Tourism (see *Tourist Information*).

Top Things To Do

- In **Tel Aviv, attend a concert** by the Israeli Philharmonic Orchestra, which draws audiences from all over the world. Israel has an international standard Opera Company, The New Israeli Opera (website: www.israel-opera.co.il), four full-time symphony orchestras (including the Israel Philharmonic, founded in 1936; website: www.ipo.co.il), as well as dozens of theatre, dance, chamber music and contemporary music companies.
- From the Jaffa Gate in **Jerusalem**'s Old City, walk straight ahead onto David Street and prepare yourself for the **souk**. Enjoy the buzz of the bustling **Carmel Market** in **Tel Aviv** or the **flea market** in **Jaffa** (Jaffa was united with Tel Aviv in 1950 and is situated a mile from the city).
- Follow the **Via Dolorosa** in Jerusalem's Old City and trace the traditional path Jesus walked from judgment to crucifixion. The path has been followed by hundreds of millions of pilgrims over 1500 years. There are nine 'stations' along the route leading to five more in the Christian Quarter's Church of the Holy Sepulchre, traditionally recognized as the site of the death, burial, and resurrection of Jesus.
- The **Negev**, once largely a desert, is now being irrigated and farmed in a settlement movement started by, amongst others, David Ben Gurion. **Beersheba** and **Dimona** are both of interest. Underwater enthusiasts will enjoy the seaside resort of **Eilat**.
- Become acquainted with Israel's culture, religions, history and society by trying the unique experience of living in a **Kibbutz**. See the *Accommodation* section. For more information, contact the The Kibbutz Artzi Federation (website: www.kba.org.il/eng/welcome.htm).
- Nature lovers will have plenty of opportunity to discover fauna and flora at Israel's 50 national parks such as **Baram National Park, Corazim National Park, Gamla Nature Reserve** and **Ahziv National Park**; many are also home to historic sites (website: www.parks.org.il/ParksENG).
- Take a ride across the **River Jordan**, the river in which Jesus was baptised.

- In **Nablus**, in the northern West Bank, sample *Kenafa*, a tasty oriental pastry, made from a delicate combination of melted cheese, shredded grain and a sugary honey sauce.
- Enjoy the cool climate of the twin cities of **Ramallah**, also known as **the 'Bride of Palestine'** and **El-Bireh**. Attend dance and folklore festivals throughout the Summer in Ramallah.
- 60km (41 miles) long and 17km (11 miles) wide, the **Dead Sea** is an inland lake lying 400m (1320ft) below sea level in the lower part of the **Jordan Valley**, flanked by the **Judean Mountains** to the west and the **Moab Mountains** to the east. It has more minerals and salt than any other body of water in the world. Treat yourself to a a variety of treatments, including mud packs, salt massages and salt water pools at a number of **health spas** and resorts in the area.
- **Fishing, sailing, surfing, swimming, water-skiing** and **yachting** are all available. **Haifa** is Israel's leading seaport. There are marinas in **Akko, Eilat, Jaffa** and **Tel Aviv**. **Skindiving** and **aqualung diving** are especially popular in **Eilat**, the best-equipped seaside resort in the Middle East, on the Red Sea coast with an excellent underwater observatory descending to the floor of the coral reef near the town. Eilat is a particularly good destination for winter sun for visitors from Western Europe.
- **Note:** The Red Sea coastline has been designated a preservation area and any tourists found with 'souvenirs' such as coral will suffer severe fines from both the Israeli and Egyptian authorities.
- To many people's surprise, there is a full **skiing** season at **Mount Hermon**, on the northern border.

TOURIST INFORMATION

Israel Government Tourist Office in the UK
UK House, 180 Oxford Street, London W1D 1NN, UK
Tel: (020) 7299 1100/10/11.
Website: www.go-israel.org

Israel Government Tourist Office in the USA
800 Second Avenue, 16th Floor, New York, NY 10017, USA
Tel: (212) 499 5660 *or* (888) 77 477 235 (toll-free in USA and Canada).
Website: www.goisrael.com

Entertainment

FOOD & DRINK: Israeli cuisine is essentially a combination of Oriental and Western cuisine, plus an additional distinct flavour brought by the many and varied nationalities which make up the Israelis. Some restaurants are expensive, though a high price does not necessarily mean a high standard. Table service is usual. There are many snack bars. Restaurants, bars and cafes catering for tourists usually have menus in two languages (Hebrew plus French or English).

Things to know: The Hebrew word *kosher* means food conforming to Jewish religious dietary laws. Milk, cream or cheese may not be served together with meat in the same meal. Pork and shellfish are officially prohibited, but it is possible to find them on many menus in non-kosher restaurants.

National specialities:
- *Falafel*, deep fried mashed chickpeas.
- *Humus*, ground chickpea dip.
- *Tahini*, sesame seed paste.
- *Shishlik*, charcoal grilled meet on a skewer.
- *Kebabs*, meat usually served in a pita bread.
- *Gefilte fish*, a traditional Jewish white fish dish.
- Chopped liver and chicken soup.

National drinks:
- The wines of Israel range from light white to dry red and sweet rosé.
- *Gold Star* and *Maccabee*, Israeli beer.
- *Arak* (an anise drink).
- *Hard Nut* (a walnut concoction of Eliaz winery)
- *Sabra* (chocolate and orange liqueur). A centre for liqueurs is the monastery at Latrun on the road between Jerusalem and Tel Aviv.

Tipping: A 15 per cent service charge is added to restaurant, cafe and hotel bills by law.

NIGHTLIFE: There are nightclubs and discos in most cities. Israel's club scene, particularly Tel Aviv and Jeruslem draw DJs and club fans from the USA and Europe. Tel Aviv has a wealth of entertainment to divert the visitor and there are rock, jazz, folk and pop music clubs in all the main cities and resorts. Israeli folklore and dance shows can be seen everywhere, especially in the kibbutzim. The Israeli Philharmonic Orchestra can be heard at the ICC Binaynei

Ha'uma Hall in Jerusalem during the winter. A summer attraction is the *Israel Festival of International Music*. The *New Israel Opera* hosts an annual season at the Tel Aviv Performing Arts centre. The season runs from October to July. Cinema is popular in Israel and many cinemas screen three daily shows of international and local films (all Hebrew films are subtitled in English and French). Tickets for all events and even films can be bought in advance from ticket agencies and sometimes from hotels and tourist offices.

SHOPPING: There is a wide choice for shoppers in Israel; and in certain shops, especially in Arab markets, visitors can - and should - bargain. Tourists who buy leather goods at shops listed by the Ministry of Tourism and pay for them in foreign currency are exempt from VAT and receive a 25 per cent discount on leather goods if these are delivered to them at the port of departure. Special purchases include jewellery, diamonds and other precious stones, ceramics, embroidery, glassware, wines, religious articles and holy books. 'Cashback' on purchased items can be claimed from the Customs Office at the airport. The best place to buy food is outdoor markets or *Shuk*; the produce is cheaper and fresher. **Shopping hours:** Sun-Fri 0800-1900; some shops close 1300-1600 and some early on Friday. Remember that shopping facilities are both Israeli and Arabic, and are therefore governed by two different sets of opening hours and methods of business. Jewish stores observe closing time near sunset Friday evenings before *Shabbat* (Saturday) and Arabic stores close Friday. It takes a while to realise that Sunday is a normal working day unlike in Western countries. For shoppers, Jewish stores are therefore open Friday, Arab markets Saturday and both are open Sunday when Christian stores close. Shops in hotels are often open until midnight.

Business

- **GDP:** US$129 billion (2004).
- **Main exports:** Machinery and equipment, software, cut diamonds, agricultural products, chemicals, textiles and apparel.
- **Main imports:** Raw materials, military equipment, investment goods, rough diamonds, fuel, grain and consumer goods.
- **Main trade partners:** USA, Belgium, Germany, Switzerland, UK and Hong Kong.

ECONOMY: Israel has a diverse and sophisticated manufacturing economy that, in many respects, rivals that of western Europe (this much is recognised by the IMF which in 1997 reclassified Israel's economy as 'industrial' rather than 'developing'). Agriculture is relatively small – about 4.2 per cent of GDP – with citrus fruit as the main commodity and export earner. The industrial sector is concentrated on engineering, aircraft, electronics, chemicals, construction materials, textiles and food-processing. Mining is also small but set to expand through production of potash and bromine. There is a small indigenous oil industry. The infrastructure is well-developed and tourism, in which there has been considerable investment, has become an important sector of the economy.

Israel's economic difficulties, which were particularly serious during the 1970s and 1980s, were largely the product of political circumstances: specifically very heavy defence expenditure (estimated at around 40 per cent of GDP) and the cost of resettling Jewish arrivals. Other important factors are a large and relatively inefficient state sector and a substantial annual aid package from the USA, estimated at around US$10 billion per year. Israel is the single largest recipient of US aid, which accounts for about 10 per cent of GDP. The economy performed relatively well during the 1990s in the wake of economic reforms introduced at the beginning of the decade, including deregulation and some privatisation. However, Israel was experiencing serious recession by 2000. This lasted until 2002 when the economy contracted by 1 per cent; since then a mild recovery has been under way: growth for 2003 was 0.8 per cent. However, given favourable conditions positive growth could return, but the outlook is heavily dependent on development in the conflict with the Palestinians and on political and security developments in the region more generally. Under the Sharon Government, economic reforms have continued unevenly, and it remains to be seen whether this will remain the case, with Sharon all but officially having stepped down as Prime Minister following his stroke in early January 2006. Israel has free trade agreements with the EU and the USA.

The areas under the control of the Palestinian Authority have not shared in Israeli prosperity; economic

Credit: © Israel Government Tourist Office/www.fotoseeker.com

development under the Palestinian Authority was managed in a haphazard and often corrupt manner, especially regarding the use of foreign aid. Since the Sharon administration came to power in Israel, the Palestinian areas have been effectively sealed off; the wall currently under construction around the West Bank (at huge cost) merely confirms that strategic decision. Large areas under nominal Palestinian control have been completely destroyed and those remaining are barely able to function economically. Equally damaging, Palestinians with jobs in the Israeli territory have been unable to pursue them properly through punitive security measures. Much of the population now relies on assistance from aid organisations. Following the win of Hamas in Parliamentary elections in January 2006, and much condemnation worldwide of this militant Islamic party, it remains to be seen whether this much-needed financial aid continues or whether sanctions will be imposed.

BUSINESS ETIQUETTE: Business can be frustrating, as in many instances it is difficult to get a direct reply to a question. Appointments are usual, as is the use of business cards. Normal courtesies should be observed, although business meetings tend to be less formal than in Britain. **Office hours:** Business hours vary owing to the different religions practised. Some offices are open half a day on Friday.

CONFERENCES/CONVENTIONS: The Ministry of Tourism's brochure, *Israel Conventions & Congresses 1996-2000*, states that "about 2000 years ago, some of the greatest conventions were held near Tiberias where it was recorded that 5000 were amply catered for". Israel's record as a contemporary international conference centre began in 1963, and the country now attracts about 150 international meetings a year with 50,000 delegates; scientific and academic meetings account for about half the meetings, though religious and sporting events are on the increase. 55 per cent of meetings are held in Jerusalem. Apart from hotels and convention centres in Jerusalem, Eliat and Tel Aviv, opportunities also exist to hold meetings in kibbutzim.

COMMERCIAL INFORMATION

Federation of Israeli Chambers of Commerce
PO Box 20027, 84 Haashmonaim Street, Tel Aviv 67132, Israel
Tel: (3) 563 1010.
Website: www.chamber.org.il

Jerusalem International Convention Centre (JICC)
Binyaney Ha'ooma, PO Box 6001, Jerusalem 91060, Israel
Tel: (2) 655 8558.
Website: www.iccjer.co.il

International Conventions Department – Ministry of Tourism
5 Bank Israel Street, B Genri Building, Jerusalem 91009, Israel
Tel: (2) 666 4200.
Website: www.tourism.gov.il

Italy

400km
200mls
✈ international airport

Location: Western Europe.

Time: GMT + 1 (GMT + 2 from the last Sunday in March to last Sunday in October).

Overview

Although Italy has only been unified since 1861, the rich and complex history of the peninsula has, perhaps more than that of any other country, influenced the course of European development, particularly in the fields of culture and political thought.

The most important early settlers in the area were the Etruscans, who had established settlements in northern Italy by the sixth century BC. By the third century BC, the city state of Rome, having subdued most of the peninsula, was intent on extending its influence elsewhere.

At its greatest extent, the Empire (so called after 30 BC) made the Mediterranean a Roman lake and for several centuries conferred on its inhabitants the benefits of the Pax Romana: culture (mainly Hellenic in origin), law, relative peace and comparative prosperity.

In the 12th century, the kingdom was one of the greatest centres of culture in Europe, particularly under Roger II. The popes played a leading role in the tortuous diplomacy of 15th-century Italy. The period arguably witnessed the greatest ever flowering of art and culture (the Italian Renaissance), associated with writers such as Machiavelli, Aristio and Guicciardini and notable patrons such as the Medici family and several popes supporting a wealth of artists including Fra Angelico, Raphael, Botticelli, Michelangelo and Leonardo da Vinci.

Today, besides the renowned cities of Venice, Genoa and Naples, each with its own unique identity and architecture, Italy features romantic Medieval hill towns, such as San Gimignano in Tuscany, and unspoilt fishing villages, like the unforgettable Positano on the Amalfi coast. Indeed Italy combines art, history and contemporary fashion with stunning natural landscapes: the turquoise waters of the Costa Smeralda offer one of Europe's most beautiful stretches of sand, sea and sunshine, while the snow-covered slopes of the Dolomite mountains are a haven for winter sports enthusiasts. Visit vineyards and cellars to taste the very best regional wines: the Veneto, famed for the sparkling white prosecco, and Tuscany, home of the highly acclaimed robust red, Brunello di Montalcino. And to really get away from it all, take a boat to the islands of Sicily or Sardinia to experience rural hospitality in the blissful Mediterranean. Italy: still so much more to discover.

General Information

AREA: 301,338 sq km (116,346 sq miles).
POPULATION: 57.2 million (UN, 2005).
POPULATION DENSITY: 189 per sq km.
CAPITAL: Rome. **Population:** 2.6 million (2005)
GEOGRAPHY: Italy is situated in Europe and attached in the north to the European mainland. To the north, the Alps separate Italy from France, Switzerland, Austria and Slovenia. **Northern Italy:** The Alpine regions, the Po Plain and the Ligurian-Etruscan Appennines. Piedmont and Val d'Aosta contain some of the highest mountains in Europe and are good areas for winter sports. Many rivers flow down from the mountains towards the Po Basin, passing through the beautiful Italian Lake District (Maggiore, Como, Garda). The Po Basin, which extends as far south as the bare slopes of the Appennines, is covered with gravel terraces and rich alluvial soil and has long been one of Italy's most prosperous regions. To the east, where the River Po flows into the Adriatic Sea, the plains are a little higher than the river itself; artificial (and occasionally natural) embankments prevent flooding. **Central Italy:** The northern part of the Italian peninsula. Tuscany (Toscana) has a diverse landscape with snow-capped mountains (the Tuscan Appennines), lush countryside, hills and a long sandy coastline with offshore islands. Le Marche, lying between the Appennines and the Adriatic coast, is a region of mountains, rivers and small fertile plains. The even more mountainous regioni (administrative districts) of Abruzzo and Molise are bordered by Marche to the north and Puglia to the south, and are separated from the Tyrrhenian Sea and to the west by Lazio and Campania. Umbria is known as the 'green heart of Italy'; hilly with broad plains, olive groves and pines. Further south lies Rome, Italy's capital and largest city. Within its precincts is the Vatican City.
Southern Italy: Campania consists of flat coastal plains and low mountains, stretching from Baia Domizia to the Bay of Naples and along a rocky coast to the Calabria border. Inland, the Appennines are lower, mellowing into the rolling countryside around Sorrento. The islands of Capri, Ischia and Procida in the Tyrrhenian Sea are also part of Campania. The south is wilder than the norh, with mile upon mile of olive trees, cool forests and rolling hills. Puglia, the 'heel of the boot', is a landscape of volcanic hills and isolated marshes. Calabria, the 'toe', is heavily forested and thinly populated. The Calabrian hills are home to bears and wolves. **The Islands:** Sicily (Sicilia), visible across a 3km- (2 mile-) strait from mainland Italy, is fertile but mountainous with volcanoes (including the famous landmark of Mount Etna) and lava fields, and several offshore islands. Sardinia (Sardegna) has a mountainous landscape, fine sandy beaches and rocky offshore islands.
For more information on each region, see the *Resorts & Excursions* section.
GOVERNMENT: Unification in 1861. Republic since 1946.
Head of State: President Carlo Azeglio Ciampi since 1999.
Head of Government: Prime Minister Silvio Berlusconi since 2001. **Recent history:** Silvio Berlusconi is Italy's longest serving post-war Premier. He and his centre-right coalition won the 2001 general election. Following the April 2005 regional elections, he was forced to resign after the collapse of his centre-right coalition but was immediately reappointed and formed a new Government with representatives from all the parties of the governing coalition.
LANGUAGE: Italian is the official language. Dialects are spoken in different regions. German and Ladin are spoken in the South Tyrol region (bordering Austria). French is spoken in all the border areas from the Riviera to the area north of Milan (border with France and Switzerland). German is spoken around the Austrian border. English, French and German are also spoken in the biggest cities and in tourism and business circles.
RELIGION: 90 per cent Roman Catholic with Protestant minorities.
ELECTRICITY: 230 volts AC, 50Hz.
SOCIAL CONVENTIONS: The social structure is heavily influenced by the Roman Catholic church and, generally speaking, family ties are stronger than in most other countries in Western Europe. Normal social courtesies should be observed. Dress is casual in most places, though beachwear should be confined to the beach. Conservative clothes are expected when visiting religious buildings and smaller, traditional communities. Formal wear is usually indicated on invitations. Smoking is prohibited in some public buildings, transport and cinemas. Visitors are warned to take precautions against theft, particularly in the cities.

Climate

Summer is hot, especially in the south. Spring and autumn are mild with fine, sunny weather. Winter in the south is much drier and warmer than in northern and central areas. Mountain regions are colder with heavy winter snowfalls.

Required clothing: Lightweight cottons and linens are worn during the summer, except in the mountains. Light- to mediumweights are worn in the south during winter, while warmer clothes are worn elsewhere. Alpine wear is advised for winter mountain resorts.

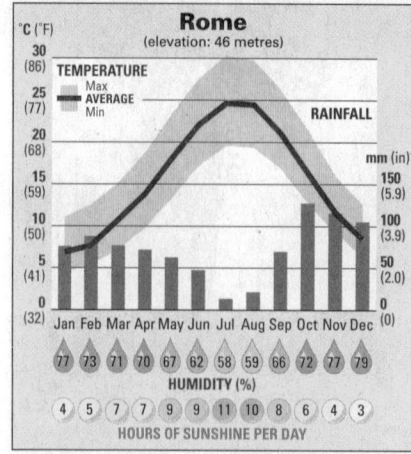

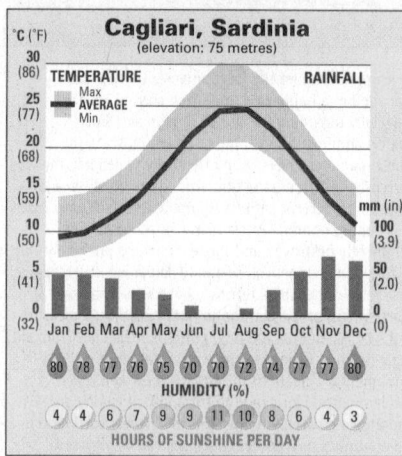

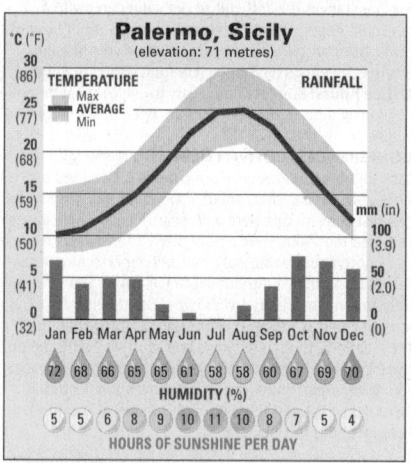

Communications

Telephone: Full IDD service available. Country code: 390 (followed by 6 for Rome, 2 for Milan, 11 for Turin, 81 for Naples, 41 for Venice and 55 for Florence). Outgoing international code: 00. Telephone kiosks now only accept phonecards, which can be purchased at post offices, tobacconists and certain newsagents.
Mobile telephone: Roaming agreements exist with most international mobile phone companies. Coverage is good.
Internet: Public access is available in Internet Corner Kiosks operated by *Telecom Italia*. Kiosks have been installed at airports, major hotels and in other public places. There are also Internet cafes in all main towns.
Post: The Italian postal system tends to be subject to delays. Letters between Italy and other European countries usually take seven to 10 days to arrive. Stamps are sold in post offices and tobacconists. Post office hours: Mon-Fri 0830-1400, central offices are open until 1700.
MEDIA Press: Among the most important Italian dailies are *Corriere della Sera* (Milan) (website: www.corriere.it), *Il*

Messaggero (Rome) (website: http://ilmessaggero.caltanet.it), *La Repubblica* (Rome) (website: www.repubblica.it) and *La Stampa* (Turin) (website: www.lastampa.it). *Il Sole 24 Ore* is the daily financial publication (website: www.ilsole24ore.com). *The Informer* (website: www.informer.it) is a useful English-language online guide for expatriates living in Italy. The main towns publish a weekly booklet with entertainment programmes, sports events, restaurants, nightclubs, etc. There are several English-language publications: monthly magazines *Enigma Roma* (Rome), *Grapevine* (on the Luca area) (website: www.lucagrapevine.com) and *Hello Milano* (Milan), as well as *Wanted In Rome* (website: www.wantedinrome.com), published twice-monthly.
TV: Rai is the public broadcaster; television stations include: *Rai Uno, Rai Sue, Rai Tre* and *Rai News 24*. Mediaset is Italy's largest private television broadcaster and operates stations such as: *Italia 1, Rete 4* and *Canale 5*.
Radio: Rai is the public broadcaster, stations include *Radio 1, Radio 2, Radio 3* and *GR Parlamento*. Commercial stations include: *Radio 24, Radio 101* and *Radio Italia*.

Passport/Visa

	Passport Required?	Visa Required?	Return Ticket Required?
Full British	No	No	No
Australian	Yes	No	No
Canadian	Yes	No	No
USA	Yes	No	No
Other EU	1	No	No
Japanese	Yes	No	No

Note: *Regulations and requirements may be subject to change at short notice, and you are advised to contact the appropriate diplomatic or consular authority before finalising travel arrangements. Any numbers in the chart refer to the footnotes below.*

Note: (a) Italy is a signatory to the **1995 Schengen Agreement**. For further details about passport/visa regulations within the Schengen area, see the introductory section, *How to Use this Guide*. (b) The regulations stated below also apply to San Marino and the Vatican City.
PASSPORTS: Passport valid for at least three months beyond length of stay required by all except:
(a) 1. EU/EEA nationals (EU + Iceland, Liechtenstein, Norway) and Swiss nationals holding a valid national ID card.
Note: EU and EEA nationals are only required to produce evidence of their EU/EEA nationality and identity in order to be admitted to any EU/EEA Member State. This evidence can take the form of a valid national passport or national identity card. Either is acceptable. Possession of a return ticket, any length of validity on their document, sufficient funds for the length of their proposed visit should not be imposed.
(b) nationals of Croatia and San Marino holding a valid national ID card.
VISAS: Required by all except the following for stays of up to 90 days:
(a) nationals of countries referred to in the chart above;
(b) nationals of Andorra, Argentina, Bolivia, Brazil, Brunei, Bulgaria, Chile, Costa Rica, Croatia, El Salvador, Guatemala, Honduras, Hong Kong (SAR), Iceland, Israel, Korea (Rep), Liechtenstein, Macau (SAR), Malaysia, Mexico, Monaco, New Zealand, Nicaragua, Norway, Panama, Paraguay, Romania, San Marino, Singapore, Switzerland, Uruguay, Vatican City and Venezuela;
(c) airport transit passengers continuing their journey to a third country by the same or connecting aircraft within 48 hours, provided holding tickets with reserved seats and valid documents for onward travel (except certain nationals who *always* require a visa.
Types of visa and cost: *Airport Transit, Transit, Tourism, Business, Study. Schengen short-stay:* £24.40. Fees should be paid in the exact money as change is not available. Payment is by cash only.
Visas are free of charge to the spouses and dependents of EU nationals.
Note: Spouses and children of EU nationals (providing spouse's passport and the original marriage certificate is produced), and nationals of some other countries, receive their visas free of charge (enquire at Embassy for details).
Validity: *Schengen short-stay:* up to 90 days. *Long term:* up to one year.
Application to: Consulate (or consular section at nearest Embassy); see *Passport/Visa Information*. Postal applications are not accepted. Because of the high volume of visa applications an appointment system has been introduced. Appointments must be made via the 24-hour call line 09065 540 707 (UK) (call charged at £1 per minute). Admission without an appointment is not permitted. Travellers visiting just one Schengen country should apply to the Consulate of that country at least six weeks in advance; travellers visiting more than one Schengen country should apply to the Consulate of the country chosen as the main destination *or* the country they will enter first (if they have no main destination).
Application requirements: *Tourism:* (a) Valid passport, with one blank page to affix the visa. (b) Completed

Credit: © Fototeca ENIT

application form. (c) One passport-size photograph. (d) Health insurance. (e) Proof of sufficient funds to cover duration of stay. (f) Fee. (g) Proof of means of onward/return travel. (h) Proof of accommodation. (i) Proof of occupation, eg letter from employer, solicitor or Chamber of Commerce. *Business*: (a)-(g) and, (h) Proof of business status. (i) Evidence of business contact(s) in Italy. *Student*: (a)-(f) and, (g) Letter from Italian university addressed to the Italian Consulate General confirming acceptance of the application, explaining details of the course (duration, programme etc). *Airport Transit/Transit*: (a)-(g) and, (h) Proof of the need for transit.
Note: (a) Minors under 18 years of age not travelling with their parents require a declaration from both parents or their legal guardian authorising their travel. (b) Visa officers may also ask for additional documents.
Working days required: Usually two. Certain nationals may take up to 21 days.
Temporary residence: Enquire at Consulate (or consular section at Embassy); see *Passport/Visa Information*

PASSPORT/VISA INFORMATION

Italian Embassy in the UK
14 Three Kings Yard, London W1K 4EH, UK
Tel: (020) 7312 2200.
Website: www.embitaly.org.uk
Political enquiries only.

Italian Consulate General in the UK
136 Buckingham Palace Road, London SW1W 9SA, UK
Tel: (020) 7235 9371 *or* 7823 6519 (visa section) *or* (09001) 600 340 (recorded visa information; calls cost 60p per minute).
Website: www.embitaly.org.uk
Opening hours: Mon-Fri 0900-1200.

Embassy of the Italian Republic in the USA
3000 Whitehaven Street, NW, Washington, DC 20008, USA
Tel: (202) 612 4400 *or* 4405/7 (visa section).
Website: www.italyemb.org

Consulate General of Italy in the USA
690 Park Avenue, New York, NY 10021, USA
Tel: (212) 439 8600.
Website: www.italconsulnyc.org

Money

Single European currency (Euro): The Euro is now the official currency of 12 EU member states (including Italy). The first Euro coins and notes were introduced in January 2002; the Italian Lira was still in circulation until 28 February 2002, when it was completely replaced by the Euro. Euro (€) = 100 cents. Notes are in denominations of €500, 200, 100, 50, 20, 10 and 5. Coins are in denominations of €2 and 1, and 50, 20, 10, 5, 2 and 1 cents.
Currency exchange: Traveller's cheques, cheques and foreign money can be changed at banks, railway stations and airports, and very often at major hotels (generally at a less convenient rate). Many UK banks offer differing exchange rates depending on the denominations of currency being bought or sold. Check with banks for details and current rates.
Credit & debit cards: Diners Club, MasterCard and Visa are widely accepted, as well as Eurocheque cards. Check with your credit or debit card company for merchant acceptability and other facilities that may be available.
Traveller's cheques: Traveller's cheques are accepted almost everywhere. To avoid additional exchange rate charges, travellers are advised to take traveller's cheques in Euros, Pounds Sterling or US Dollars.
Currency restrictions: Check with the Embassy before departure. Import and export of both local and foreign currency is limited to €12,500. If it is intended to import or export amounts greater than this, the amount should be declared and validated in Italy on form V2.
Banking hours: These vary from city to city but, in general, Mon-Fri 0830-1330 and 1500-1600.
Exchange rate indicators:
Rate at time of publishing
£1.00= €1.46
$1.00= €0.82

Duty Free

The following goods may be imported into Italy from outside the EU by persons over 17 years of age without incurring customs duty:
200 cigarettes or 50 cigars or 100 cigarillos or 250g of tobacco; 2l of wine and 1l of spirits (over 22 per cent) or 2l of fortified or sparkling wine; 50g of perfume and 250ml of eau de toilette; 500g of coffee or 200g of coffee extract (if over 15 years of age); 100g of tea or 40g of tea extract; gifts not exceeding €89.96 (if entering from an EU country), €175 (if entering from a non-EU country).
Abolition of duty free goods within the EU: On June 30 1999, the sale of duty free alcohol and tobacco at airports and at sea was abolished in all of the original 15 EU member states. Of the 10 new member states that joined the EU on May 1 2004, these rules already apply to Cyprus and Malta. There are transitional rules in place for visitors returning to one of the original 15 EU countries from one of the other new EU countries. But for the original 15, plus Cyprus and Malta, there are now no limits imposed on importing tobacco and alcohol products from one EU country to another (with the exceptions of Denmark, Finland and Sweden, where limits *are* imposed). Travellers should note that they may be required to prove at customs that the goods purchased are for personal use *only*.

Public Holidays

Below are listed Public Holidays for the January 2006-June 2007 period.
2006: Jan 1 New Year's Day. **Jan 6** Epiphany. **Apr 17** Easter Monday. **Apr 25** Liberation Day. **May 1** Labour Day. **Jun 2** Anniversary of the Republic. **Aug 15** Assumption. **Nov 1** All Saints' Day. **Nov 7** World War 1 Victory Anniversary Day. **Dec 8** Immaculate Conception. **Dec 25** Christmas Day. **Dec 26** St Stephen's Day.
2007: Jan 1 New Year's Day. **Jan 6** Epiphany. **Apr 9** Easter Monday. **Apr 25** Liberation Day. **May 1** Labour Day. **Jun 2** Anniversary of the Republic.
Note: In addition, local feast days are held in honour of town patron saints, generally without closure of shops and offices. These include:
Turin/Genoa/Florence: Jun 24 (St John the Baptist). **Milan:** Dec 7 (St Ambrose). **Siena:** Jul 2 and Aug 16, Palio horserace. **Venice:** Apr 25 (St Mark). **Bologna:** Oct 4 (St Petronius). **Naples:** Sep 19 (St Gennaro). **Bari:** Dec 6 (St Nicholas). **Palermo:** Jul 15 (St Rosalia). **Rome:** Jun 29 (St Peter). **Trieste:** Nov 3.

Health

	Special Precautions?	Certificate Required?
Yellow Fever	No	No
Cholera	No	No
Typhoid & Polio	No	N/A
Malaria	No	N/A

Note: *Regulations and requirements may be subject to change at short notice, and you are advised to contact your doctor well in advance of your intended date of departure. Any numbers in the chart refer to the footnotes below.*

Food & drink: Tap water is generally safe to drink. Bottled water is available. The inscription 'Acqua Non Potabile' means water is not drinkable. Milk is pasteurised and dairy products are safe for consumption. Local meat, poultry, seafood, fruit and vegetables are considered safe to eat.
Other risks: *Leishmaniasis* (*cutaneous* and *visceral*), *sandfly fever*, *typhus* and *West Nile virus*, though rare, may occur along the Mediterranean coast. *Echinococcosis* and *brucellosis* also occur, although rarely. There have been some outbreaks of *Legionnaires disease* in tourist resorts. *Rabies* is present. For those at high risk, vaccination before arrival should be considered. If you are bitten, seek medical advice without delay. For further information, see the *Health* appendix.
Health care: European Economic Area (EEA) and Switzerland:
If you or any of your dependants are suddenly taken ill or have an accident during a visit to an EEA country or Switzerland, free or reduced-cost necessary treatment is available – in most cases on production of a valid European Health Insurance Card (EHIC). Each country has different rules about state medical provision. In some, treatment is free. In many countries you will have to pay part or all of the cost, and then claim a full or partial refund. The EHIC gives access to state-provided medical treatment only and the scheme gives no entitlement to medical repatriation costs, nor does it cover ongoing illnesses of a non-urgent nature, so comprehensive travel insurance is advised. Note that the EHIC replaces the Form E111, which will no longer be valid after 31 December 2005. Some restrictions apply, depending on your nationality.
Make sure the doctor you go to is a national health service (Servizio Sanitario Nazionale or SSN) doctor. Their services are normally free. Surgeries are open from Monday to Friday but times vary. At weekends and on weekdays between 8pm and 8am, emergency services are available through the Guardia Medica. If you pay any charges, keep the original receipts and apply at the local health authority (Azienda Unità Sanitaria Locale or ASL) for a refund. Most dentists are private. To get state treatment you will need to go to a national health service hospital or a dentist who is working in an ASL-managed centre. If an SSN doctor issues you with a prescription, take it and your European Health Insurance Card (EHIC) to the pharmacy. Some medicines are free; for others you will be charged a standard fee, which is non-refundable. The cost of medicines bought over the counter is not refundable. The ASL can supply a list of SSN hospitals or private hospitals that are affiliated to the state scheme. Depending on the region you are in, you may or may not have to pay for medicines prescribed in a hospital or for your ambulance travel. If you can't contact the ASL beforehand, show the hospital authorities your EHIC and ask them to contact the local office at once about your right to treatment under the state healthcare scheme. You can obtain the ASL number from a telephone directory or, in an emergency, by dialling 118.

Travel - International

AIR:
The national airline is *Alitalia (AZ)* (website: www.alitalia.it). A great number of major international airlines operate direct flights to various destinations in Italy from Australia, Canada, Europe and the USA. Owing to the number of flights available, ticket prices vary greatly and there is a wide range of discount fares and special tickets available. Further information can be obtained from the airline or a travel agent.
Approximate flight times: From Rome to *London* is two hours 50 minutes, to *Los Angeles* is 15 hours 55 minutes, to *New York* is nine hours 45 minutes, to *Singapore* is 13 hours 55 minutes and to *Sydney* is 23 hours 35 minutes.
Main airports: *Rome (FCO)* (Fiumicino) (website: www.adr.it), 26km (16 miles) southwest of the city (travel time – 30 to 55 minutes). *To/from the airport*: There is a direct rail link to Termini Station in central Rome and a bus service every 15 minutes. Taxis are also available to the city. *Facilities*: Outgoing duty free shop, car hire, bank and bureau de change and bar/restaurant.
Rome (CIA) (Ciampino) (website: www.adr.it), 32km (15 miles) from the city (travel time – 60 minutes). *To/from the airport*: Buses are available to the underground station Anagnina. Taxis are also available. *Facilities*: A bank/bureau de change, duty free shop and souvenir shop and cafe.
Florence (FLR) (Amerigo Vespucci) (website: www.aeroporto.firenze.it), 4km (2.4 miles) north of the city (travel time – 20 minutes). *To/from the airport*: Buses and taxis are available to the city. *Facilities*: Banks, bureaux de change, left luggage, bars and restaurants and duty free facilities.
Milan (MXP) (Malpensa) (website: www.sea-aeroportimilano.it) is 45km (29 miles) northwest of the city (travel time – 30 minutes). *To/from the airport*: The Malapensa Express connects terminal one with the centre of Milan, the journey takes 40 minutes. A free shuttle bus connects the airport terminals. Taxis are available into Milan, the journey will cost approximately €70. *Facilities*: Duty free.
Venice (VCE) (Marco Polo) (website: www.veniceairport.it) is 10km (6 miles) northwest of the city (travel time – 20 minutes). *To/from the airport*: Buses and taxi services run to Piazzale Roma and the railway station. Water taxis operate to San Marco. *Facilities*: Bank, duty free shops, bars and restaurants.
Note: People travelling to Florence can fly to Pisa and then take the train service directly from Pisa Airport to Florence (travel time – 60 minutes). The railway station in Pisa is practically inside the airport. Rail services connect with arrivals and departures of all international flights and major domestic services.
Departure tax: None.
SEA:
Main ports: *Ancona* (website: www.autoritaportuale.ancona.it/), *Brindisi* (website: http://www.porto.br.it), *Naples* (website: www.porto.napoli.it) and *Venice* (website: www.port.venice.it). International sailings to Italy run from Albania, Croatia, Cyprus, the Far East, France, Greece, Libya, Malta, Portugal, South America, Spain, Tunisia, Turkey and West Africa.

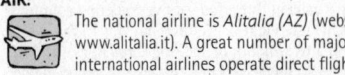

RAIL:
Italian State Railways run regular services covering national and international routes (website: www.trenitalia.com/en). The *Artesia Service*, in conjunction with SNCF and Trenitalia, is the fastest overnight and daytime railway link between France and Italy. It operates from Paris and Dijon to most Italian destinations. The *Venice Simplon-Orient-Express* operates services from London and Paris to Venice and Rome, as well as Istanbul, Budapest and Vienna. Travelling by train from the UK, the quickest way is by *Eurostar* (see *France* section).
Rail passes: The *Inter-Rail* pass offers unlimited second-class train travel in up to 29 European countries (includes Morocco and Turkey) split into eight zones (A-H). Three different tickets are available: a ticket covering one zone (two to six countries, 16 days' validity), a ticket covering two zones (six to ten countries, 22 days' validity) and an *All Zone Pass* (29 countries, one month's validity). Ferry services between Italy and Greece are included. Passengers must be resident in Europe for at least six months before the pass is used. Travel is not allowed in the passenger's country of residence. Travellers under 26 years receive a reduction of about 30 per cent. Children's tickets are reduced by about 50 percent. Supplements are required for some high-speed services, seat reservations and couchettes. Discounts are offered on *Eurostar* and some ferry routes. Available from *Inter Rail* (website: www.interrailnet.com).
The *Eurailpass* offers unlimited first-class train travel in 17 European countries. Tickets are valid for 15 days, 21 days, one month, two months or three months. The *Eurailpass Saver* ticket offers discounts for two or more people travelling together. The *Eurailpass Youth* ticket is available to those aged under 26 and offers unlimited second-class train travel. The *Eurailpass Flexi* allows either 10 or 15 travel days within a two-month period. The *Eurail Selectpass* is valid in three, four or five bordering countries and allows five, six, eight or 10 travel days (or 15 for five countries) in a two-month period. The *Eurail Regional Pass* allows four to 10 travel days in a two-month period in one of nine regions (usually two or more countries). Children receive a 50 per cent reduction. The passes cannot be sold to residents of Europe, Turkey, Morocco, Algeria, Tunisia or the Russian Federation. Available from the *Eurail Group* (website: www.eurail.com).
The *Greece 'n Italy Pass* offers four to 10 days rail travel over a two-month period on all *Trenitalia* trains within Italy, on Greek railway trains *(OSE)* and a return sea journey with *Superfast Ferries* or *Blue Star Ferries* operating between Italy and Greece.
The *EuroDomino* pass enables holders anything from three to eight days' extensive travel within a one-month period on the entire rail network of their chosen country. It is valid in 28 European countries and North Africa, including the ferry service from Brindisi (Italy) to Igoumenitsa (Greece). To purchase a *EuroDomino* pass you must have been resident in Europe for at least six months and a passport number is required at time of booking. It is not permitted to purchase a pass for travel within your own country of residence. To qualify for the youth rates, you must be under 26 years on the first date of validity of the pass. Children aged four-11 years inclusive pay half the adult fares rounded up to the nearest pound. Children under four years travel for free. Seat reservations, couchette and sleeper charges are not included in the cost of the pass and are payable at the normal rate. Passholder fares are payable on some services. Reservation/supplement charges are payable on all trains within Spain. Available from Rail Europe (website: www.raileurope.co.uk/railpasses/eurodomino.htm).
ROAD:
Routes to Italy run through Austria, France, Slovenia and Switzerland and most routes use the tunnels under the Alps and Apennines. From the UK, the quickest way to travel by car is via Eurotunnel to France (see *France* section). *Italian State Railways* run regular daily services called *auto el seguito* (trains carrying cars), especially during the summer holiday season covering national and international routes. These services operate from special railway stations and are generally bookable at the departure station. Owners must travel on the same train. The documents required are the log-book, valid driving licence with Italian translation, Green Card insurance and national identity plate fixed to the rear of the vehicle. For more information on routes, contact the Italian State Tourist Board (see *Top Things To Do*). For more information on required documentation and traffic regulations in Italy, see *Travel – Internal* section. **Coach:** There are numerous and excellent road links with all neighbouring countries. *Eurolines* (52 Grosvenor Gardens, London SW1W 0AU; tel: (08705) 143 219; website:www.eurolines.com) and *National Express* (Ensign Court, 4 Vicarage Road, Edgbaston, Birmingham B15 3ES; tel: 08705 808 080; website: www.nationalexpress.com) run regular coach services from the UK to Italy.
Travellers can either choose Mini-Pass breaks or book a 15-, 30- or 60-day pass. The six Mini-Passes give travellers the freedom to visit three cities, with prices starting from £55. Travellers can stay as long as they like in each city.

Travel - Internal

AIR:
Alitalia (AZ) and other airlines run services to all the major cities. There are over 30 airports. For details, contact the airlines direct or *ENIT*, the Italian State Tourist Office (see *Top Things To Do*).
SEA:
Main ports: *Cagliari* (website: www.porto.cagliari.it), *Civitavecchia* (website: www.port-of-rome.org), *Genoa* (website: www.porto.genova.it), *Livorno* (website: www.portauthority.li.it) and *Naples* (website: www.porto.napoli.it). A number of car and passenger ferries operate throughout the year linking Italian ports.
Ferries: Regular boat and hydrofoil services run to the islands of Capri, Elba, Giglio, Sardinia, Sicily and the Aeolian Islands. There are also some links along the coast.
Note: Travellers on public transport should be aware that tickets for public transport need to be endorsed in a ticket machine before the journey. Machines are located in entrances to platforms in railway and metro stations and on-board buses and trams. Failure to do so could lead to an on-the-spot fine of up to 60.
RAIL:
The *Italian State Railways (FS)* (website: www.fs-on-line.com) run a nationwide network at very reasonable fares, calculated on the distance travelled, and there are a number of excellent reductions. The *Trenitalia Pass* is the only pass available to people resident outside of Italy. This allows from three to 10 days of unlimited travel within a two-month period. Any train in Italy can be used, although a small supplement is payable on Eurostar Italia services. The pass also entitles the holder to discounts on some Italy-Greece ferry routes, hotels and other special offers. *Basic*, *Youth* and *Saver* passes are available.
For further information, contact *Trenitalia* (website: www.trenitalia.com) *or Railchoice* (tel: (020) 8659 7300; website: www.railchoice.co.uk); *or Freedom Rail* (tel: (0870) 757 9898; website: www.freedomrail.com).
ROAD:
There are more than 300,000km (185,500 miles) of roads in Italy, including over 6000km (3700 miles) of motorway (*autostrada*) which link all parts of the country. Tolls are charged at varying distances and scales, except for the Salerno–Reggio Calabria, Palermo–Catania and Palermo–Mazara Del Vallo stretches, which are toll-free. Secondary roads are also excellent and require no tolls. Road signs are international. Many petrol stations are closed 1200-1500. Visitors are advised to check locally about exact opening times. More information on the Italian motorway network is available from the *Società Autostrade* (website: www.autostrade.it).
Traffic regulations: Traffic drives on the right. Speed limits are 50kph (30mph) in urban areas, 90/110kph (55/65mph) on country roads, 130kph (80mph) on motorways. Undipped headlights are prohibited in towns and cities, but are compulsory when passing through tunnels. All vehicles must carry a red warning triangle, available at border posts.
Note: Fines for speeding and other driving offences are on-the-spot and particularly heavy. **Breakdown service:** In case of breakdown on any Italian road, dial 116 at the nearest telephone box. Tell the operator where you are, your plate number and type of car and the nearest *Automobile Club of Italy (ACI)* (website: www.aci.it) office will be informed for immediate assistance.
Customs regulations: Driving licences, log books and other motoring documents are only accepted if they are accompanied by a translation into Italian or an international driving licence. Visitors must carry their log-book, which must either be in their name as owner, or have the owner's written permission to drive the vehicle. Customs documents for the temporary importation of motor vehicles (also aircraft and pleasure-boats) have been abolished. **Bus:** Good coach services run between towns and cities and there are also extensive local buses, including good services on Sicily and Sardinia. In more remote areas, buses will usually connect with rail services. **Taxi:** Services are available in and between all cities. **Car hire:** Self-drive hire is available in most cities and resorts. Many international and Italian firms operate this service with different rates and conditions. With the larger firms, it is possible to book from other countries through the car hire companies, their agents or through the air companies. Generally, small local firms offer cheaper rates, but cars can only be booked locally. Many car hire agencies have booths at the airport or information in hotels. Many special-rate fly/drive deals are available for Italy.
Documentation: A UK driving licence and EU pink format licences are valid in Italy but green-coloured licences must be accompanied by an International Driving Permit. Visitors must carry their log-book, which must either be in their name as owner, or have the owner's written permission to drive the vehicle.
A driving licence or a motorcycle driving licence is required for motorcycles over 49cc. Passengers are required by law to

Credit: © Fototeca ENIT

wear seat belts. Customs documents for the temporary importation of motor vehicles (also aircraft and pleasure-boats) have been abolished.
URBAN:
All the big towns and cities (Genoa, Milan, Naples, Rome, Turin and Venice) have good public transport networks. **Underground:** In Rome there are two underground lines – Metropolitana A from Via Ottaviano via Termini station to Via Anagnina and also connecting with the new Ottaviano-San Pietro link; and Metropolitana B, which runs between Termini Station, via Exhibition City (EUR) (Via Laurentina) and then onwards to Rebibbia. The underground is open from 0530 to 2330 every day. Both day and monthly passes are available. Line B was expanded considerably at the beginning of the 1990s, when 10 new stations were added to its network. Line A has been expanded much more recently to include five new stations via the Ottaviano-San Pietro connection. Milan also has a three-line underground system, with tickets useable on both underground and bus. **Tram:** There is a 28km- (17-mile) network consisting of eight routes in Rome; Milan, Messina and Turin also have tram services. **Bus:** Services operate in all main cities and towns. In Rome, the network is extensive and complements the underground and tram systems, the bus 590 follows the same route as the Metropolitana A and has disabled access. The fare structure is integrated between the various modes. Flat-fare tickets and weekly passes can be bought in advance from roadside or station machines or from tobacconists (*tabacchi*). A 'hop-on, hop-off' bus service is available for €13 per day. Information is available from the ATAC booth in front of the Termini station. Trolleybuses also run in a number of other towns. In larger cities, fares are generally pre-purchased from machines or tobacconists (*tabacchi*). Bus fares – generally at a standard rate per run – can be bought in packets of five or multiples and are fed into a stamping machine on boarding the bus. **Taxi:** Available in all towns and cities. Government-regulated taxis are either white or yellow. Visitors should avoid taxis that are not metered. In Rome, they are relatively expensive, with extra charges for night service, luggage and taxis called by telephone. All charges are listed on a rate card displayed in the cab with an English translation. Taxis can only be hailed at strategically located stands or booked by telephone. A 10 per cent tip is expected by taxi drivers and this is sometimes added to the fare for foreigners.
City tours: *Rome:* Run by many travel agencies, these tours allow first-time visitors to get a general impression of the main sights and enable them to plan further sightseeing. Information is available from the local tourist office. Horse-drawn carriages are available in Rome. Boating trips on the River Tiber are available. A day ticket costs €2.30, a cruise tour costs €10 and an evening dinner cruises costs €43. Panoramic flights and hot air balloon flights are available. Charges are high. *Venice:* Privately hired boats and gondolas are available, as well as a public ferry service.
Travel times: The following chart gives approximate travel times (in hours and minutes) from **Rome** to other major cities/towns in Italy.

	Air	**Road**	**Rail**
Florence	**0.45**	**2.30**	**2.30**
Milan	**0.65**	**6.00**	**6.00**
Naples	**0.45**	**2.00**	**2.30**
Cagliari	**0.55**	**-**	**-**

Italy

Travel Advice

Most visits to Italy are trouble-free but you should be aware of the global risk of indiscriminate international terrorist attacks, which could be against civilian targets, including places frequented by foreigners.
There continues to be isolated cases of domestic terrorism in Italy by extreme left wing and seccessionist groups which are aimed primarily at official Italian targets.
Visitors should be alert to the dangers of car and street crimes in cities.
There continues to be non-violent volcanic activity on the island of Stromboli. Italy is in an earthquake zone.
Visitors to ski resorts should take advice on weather and avalanche conditions before they travel and should make themselves aware of local skiing laws and regulations throughout their visit (see: http://www.goski.com/italy.htm and http://www.avalanches.org).
This advice is based on information provided by the Foreign & Commonwealth Office in the UK. It is correct at time of publishing. As the situation can change rapidly, visitors are advised to contact the following organisations for the latest travel advice.

British Foreign and Commonwealth Office
Tel: (0845) 850 2829.
Website: www.fco.gov.uk

US Department of State
Website: http://travel.state.gov/travel

Accommodation

HOTELS:

There are more than 30,000 hotels throughout the country. Every hotel has its fixed charges agreed with the provincial tourist board. Charges vary according to class, season, services available and locality. The Italian State Tourist Board publishes the official list of all Italian hotels and pensions (*Annuario Alberghi*) every year, which can be consulted through a travel agent or ENIT, the Italian State Tourist Board (see *Top Things To Do*). In all hotels and pensions, service charges are included in the rates. VAT (*IVA* in Italy) operates in all hotels at 10 per cent (19 per cent in deluxe hotels) on room charges only. Visitors are now required by law to obtain an official receipt when staying at hotels. Rome is well provided with hotels, but it is advisable to book in advance. Rates are high with added extras. To obtain complete prices, ask for quotations of inclusive rates. Many luxury hotels are available. Cheap hotels, which usually provide basic board (room plus shower), offer an economical form of accommodation throughout Italy, and there is a wide choice in the cities. Again, especially in the main cities, it is wise to book in advance (bookings should always be made through travel agents or hotel representatives).
Grading: Hotels are graded on a scale of **1** to **5 stars**.

MOTELS:

Located on motorways and main roads.

SELF-CATERING:

Villas, flats and chalets are available for rent at most Italian resorts. Information is available through daily newspapers and agencies in the UK and from the Italian State Tourist Office or the Tourist Office (*Azienda Autonoma di Soggiorno*) of the locality concerned. The latter are also able to advise about boarding with Italian families.

TOURIST VILLAGES: These consist of bungalows and apartments, usually built in or near popular resorts. The bungalows vary in size but usually accommodate four people and have restaurant facilities.

CAMPING/CARAVANNING:

Camping is very popular in Italy. The local Tourist Office in the nearest town will give information and particulars of the most suitable sites. On the larger campsites, it is possible to rent tents/caravans. There are over 2300 campsites and full details of the sites can be obtained in the publication *Campeggi e Villaggi Turistici in Italia*, published by the Touring Club Italiano (TCI) and Federcampeggio. A campsite review, *Guida Camping d'Italia*,' is published bi-monthly.
The tariffs at Italian campsites vary according to the area and the type of campsite. There are discounts for members of the AIT, FICC and FIA. Usually there is no charge for children under three years of age. The Touring Club Italiano offers campsites already equipped with fixed tents, restaurants, etc.

YOUTH HOSTELS:

There are over 100 youth hostels run by the Italian Youth Hostels Association (see *Accommodation Information*). During the summer season in the major cities, reservations are essential and must be applied for directly from the hostel at least 15 days in advance, specifying dates and numbers. There are also student hostels in several towns.

ACCOMMODATION INFORMATION

Federalberghi (National Hotel Association)
Via Toscana 1, 00187 Rome, Italy
Tel: (06) 4274 1151.
Website: www.italyhotels.it

Italian Confederation of Campers
via Vittorio Emanuele 11, 50041 Calenzano (Firenze), Italy
Tel: (055) 882 391.
Website: www.federcampeggio.it

Touring Club Italiano
Corso Italia 10, 20122 Milano, Italy
Tel: (02) 85261.
Website: www.touringclub.it

Centro Internazionale Prenotazioni Campeggio
Casella Postale 23, 50041 Calenzano (Firenze), Italy
To book places in advance on campsites belonging to the 'International Campsite Booking Centre'. Ask for a list of the campsites and a booking form.

Associazione Italiana Alberghi per la Gioventù (Italian Youth Hostels Association)
Via Cavour 44, 00184 Rome, Italy
Tel: (06) 487 1152.
Website: www.ostellionline.org

Top Things To See

- Be fascinated by **Rome**'s numerous relics and monuments, the hectic buzz of swarming scooters, bellowing motorists and animated street cafes. Roman streets contain reminders of all the eras in Rome's rich history – the **Colosseum** and the **Forum** are the most famous from the classical period and ancient basilicas bear witness to the early Christian era. **Via del Corso**, Rome's main thoroughfare, cuts through the length of the city centre from **Piazza Venezia** in the south, with the vast marble **Vittorio Emanuele Monument** (erected to commemorate the unification of Italy and honour her first king), to emerge in **Piazza del Popolo** in the north, beyond which lies the cool green refuge of the **Villa Borghese**. East of Via del Corso lie the elegant shopping streets including **Via Borgognona** and **Via Condotti** which lead up to **Piazza di Spagna** (the famous Spanish Steps). At the nearby **Trevi Fountain**, visitors guarantee their return to Rome by throwing a coin into the waters. West of Via del Corso, a maze of narrow streets winds its way down to the **River Tiber**. It is here, in the historic centre of Rome, that the most complete ancient Roman structure is found: the **Pantheon**, on **Piazza della Rotonda**, built by Emperor Hadrian and completed in AD 125. Monumental in scale, the diameter of the dome and its height are precisely equal, while the interior is illuminated by sunlight entering through a 9m (30ft) hole in the dome's roof. Just beyond the Pantheon lies **Piazza Navona**, a long thin square, on a classical site, rebuilt in the 17th century in High Baroque style. Close by stands the circular hulk of **Castel Sant'Angelo**, burial place of Emperor Hadrian and the papal city's main fortified defence in later times.
- On the west bank of the Tiber, the **Vatican City** is an independent sovereign state, best known for the magnificent **St Peter's Basilica**. The Basilica is approached through the 17th-century **St Peter's Square**, a superb creation by Bernini, enclosed by two semi-circular colonnades, with an Egyptian obelisk in the centre. To the right of St Peter's stands the **Vatican Palace**, the Pope's residence. Among the principal features of the Palace are the **Sistine Chapel** and the **Vatican Museum**. The **Vatican Gardens** can be visited only by those on guided tours. For further information, see the separate *Vatican City* country section.
- Probably the highlight of any tour of Italy, **Venice (Venezia)** is a must. The city's main monuments – **St Mark's Basilica** and the **Doge's Palace** overlooking **St Mark's Square** – have gained fame through innumerable paintings by such artists as Canaletto, but the whole city is in many ways a work of art. The city's most important thoroughfare is the **Grand Canal**, lined with fine Gothic and Renaissance *palazzi* (buildings) and crossed by the bustling **Ponte di Rialto** (Rialto Bridge) and the wooden **Ponte dell'Accademia** (Academy Bridge). Nearby, the **Galleria dell'Accademia** displays hundreds of Venetian paintings dating from between the 14th and 18th centuries. The Venetian islands of **Burano** (famous for lacemaking), **Murano** (famous for glassmaking) and **Torcello** (noted for the magnificent Byzantine **Basilica of Santa Maria Assunta**) can be visited by boat.

Note: The city is linked to **Mestre**, on the mainland, by a causeway which can be crossed by road or rail. Although there is a large car park in Venice, at the end of the causeway, it is easier and cheaper to park in Mestre and continue by train.

- Visit **Turin**, also known as *La Parigi d'Italia* (the Italian Paris). Uptown Turin is centred on the main shopping street, **Via Roma**, which links the city's favourite square, the **Piazza Castello**, with its most dramatic building, the **Baroque Palazzo Madama**, which houses the **Museum of Ancient Art**, and the **Egyptian Museum**, the second-largest in the world after Cairo. The famous **Turin Shroud** may be viewed in the 15th-century white marble Cathedral.
- In **Milan (Milano)**, appreciate the delicate and ethereal beauty of the splendid Gothic **Duomo** (Cathedral), one of the world's largest churches. The **Castello Sforzesco**, in the west of the city, is a massive fortified castle, which now houses a number of museums. Leonardo da Vinci's masterpiece, *The Last Supper*, may be viewed at the convent of **Santa Maria della Grazie**. The **Teatro della Scala** (Scala Theatre) remains the undisputed world capital of opera and is well worth viewing for its magnificent opulence.
- In Lombardy, discover **Cremona**, the birthplace of the Stradivarius violin. A walk around the Medieval **Piazza del Comune** offers various architectural treats. There are also two interesting museums: the **Museo Stradivariano**, housing a wealth of Stradivarius musical instruments, and the **Museo Civico**, displaying mosaics and relics from the Romanesque period.
- Discover the beauty of the great **northern lakes** which lie in a series of long, deep valleys running down onto the plains from the Alps. **Lake Como** is perhaps the most attractive, **Lake Maggiore** the most elegant (and populous) and **Lake Garda** the wildest and most spectacular.
- Visit **Genoa (Genova),** capital of Liguria, and the birthplace of Christopher Columbus. The Medieval district of the city holds many treasures, such as the **Church of Sant'Agostino** (next to the **Museo dell'Architettura e Scultura Ligure**), the beautiful **Church of San Donato**, the 12th-century **Church of Santa Maria di Castello**, the **Gothic Cathedral** of San Lorenzo and the **Porta Soprana** (the old stone entrance gate to the city). The **Doge's Palace** was built in the 17th-century. It holds the **Doge's Chapel**, the **Grimaldi Tower**, the **Hall of the Minor Consiglio** and the **Hall of the Maggior Consiglio.** The **Acquario** (Aquarium) presents underwater ocean life, with 1000 species housed in 71 vast tanks, making it the largest centre of its kind in Europe.
- Immerse yourself in the Shakespearian world by going to **Verona,** the setting of Shakespeare's *Romeo and Juliet*. The **Casa di Giulietta** (Juliet's House), a small Medieval home with a balcony and courtyard, attracts thousands of visitors each year. The other big attraction is the well-preserved **Roman Arena**, built in AD 290 and able to accommodate over 20,000 spectators. An opera festival, with open-air night-time performances, is staged here throughout summer.
- Discover a profusion of early Byzantine and Christian monuments decorated with stunning mosaics in **Ravenna**, notably the splendid **Mausoleum of Galla Placidia**, the octagonal **Basilica di San Vitale**, and the churches of **San Apollonare Nuovo** and **Sant'Apollinare** in **Classe**, all of which are UNESCO-listed World Heritage Sites.
- Visit the principal Tuscan city, **Florence (Firenze),** the world's most celebrated storehouse of Renaissance art and architecture. Brunelleschi's revolutionary design for the dome of the **Duomo** (Cathedral) is generally accepted as the first expression of Renaissance ideas in architecture. Between the **Piazza del Duomo** at its feet and the river are many of the best-loved *palazzi* (palaces), whilst close by to the north are the churches of **San Lorenzo** and **Santa Maria Novella**. The shop-lined **Ponte Vecchio** bridge scans the river to arrive at **Palazzo Pitti** and the **Boboli Gardens**. The **Uffizi Gallery** houses one of the world's most celebrated art collections including masterpieces such as Botticelli's *Birth Of Venus*, Leonardo da Vinci's *Annunciation*, Michelangelo's *Holy Family* and Titian's *Urbino Venus*. Michelangelo's famous statue of *David* may be viewed at the **Accademia di Belle Arti** near the University.
- Take a picture of the famous **Leaning Tower,** a free-standing *campanile* or bell tower in **Pisa**, north of Siena. Next to the tower, on **Campo dei Miracoli**, stand the elegant 11th-century Gothic **Cathedral** and the **Baptistry**.
- Visit the place where pizza was invented, **Naples**. Frequently criticised for urban decay and delinquency, it is a city where splendid churches and palaces stand aside squalid tenement blocks. Notable monuments include the 17th-century **Palazzo Reale**, built by the Bourbons, the massive stone **Castel Nuovo**, overlooking the sea, and the **San Carlo Opera House**. The impressive **Museo Archeologico Nazionale** houses an excellent collection of Greco-Roman artefacts, including mosaics from Pompeii and Herculaneum.

A B C D E F G H I J K L M N O P Q R S T U V W X Y Z

Credit: © Fototeca ENIT

- Enjoy fantastic views of the **Bay of Naples, Pompeii** and the **Tyrrhennian Sea** from Mount Vesuvius, still an active volcano.
- Understand how the ordinary first-century Romans lived their daily lives at the remains of **Pompeii** and **Herculaneum**, engulfed in the great eruption of AD 79. Moulds of people and animals found well-preserved, buried under the burning ash, can be seen at Pompeii, and the decoration in some of the excavated villas is amazingly intact, including numerous wall paintings of gods and humans in scenes ranging from the heroic to the erotic.
- Visit the 13th-century **Basilica di San Francesco**, one of Italy's best-loved and most-visited churches, located in the picturesque Medieval hilltown of Assisi, famous as the birthplace of St Francis, founder of the Franciscan order of monks. The life of St Francis is commemorated in frescoes by Giotto in the basilica.
- Pay a visit to **Castelgandolfo**, on the western side of the Italian 'boot'. The city overlooks the spectacular **Lake Albano**, and is dominated by the **Palazzo Pontificio**, the Pope's summer retreat.
- In **Matera**, visit the extraordinary **Sassi**, a vast troglodyte settlement of houses and churches carved into tufa rock. Home to 15,000 residents until the 1950s, this is now a UNESCO-listed World Heritage Site.
- **Sicily** is littered with the remains of successive invading cultures. The most important ancient Greek sites are: the temples of the **Valle dei Templi** at **Agrigénto**, said to be better preserved than any in Greece itself; the **Greek Theatre** at **Syracuse** (where there is also a Roman Amphitheatre); and the vast **Temple of Apollo** at **Selinunte**. In the capital, **Palermo**, notable buildings include the **Cathedral**, the **Martorana**, the **Palazzo dei Normanni, San Cataldo, San Giuseppe dei Teatini** and **Santa Maria di Gesù** churches. The catacombs at the **Capuchin Monastery** contain thousands of mummified bodies.
- There are many Bronze Age remains, the best known being the *nuraghi* - circular (sometimes conical) stone dwellings throughout **Sardinia**. The largest collection may be found at **Su Nuraxi**, about 80km (50 miles) north of **Cagliari**, the island's capital.

Top Things To Do

- In **Rome**, wander around the district of **Trastevere**, the city's alternative focus which is home to numerous bars, restaurants and nightclubs.
- In **Turin (Torino)**, the focus of the Italy's automobile industry, go on a guided tour of the **Fiat headquarters**, where a full-scale test track may be found on the roof, while the **Museo dell'Automobile** (Automobile Museum), traces the history of the car on an international level.
- Gamble at one of Italy's few casinos at **St Vincent**.
- Go shopping in **Milan (Milano)**, Italy's most sophisticated city.
- Practice your Italian or develop your art skills. Italian **language** and **art** courses are available throughout Italy. Language courses are often complemented by subjects

such as **cooking** or **architecture**. Well known institutions offering a range of art courses include the *Palazzo Spinelli* and *Università Internazionale dell'Arte* in Florence; the *Accademia Italia* in Rome; the *Centro Internazionale degli Studi per l'Insegnamento del Mosaico* in Ravenna for **mosaic making**; and, for **music** courses, the *Accademia Chigiana* in Siena. Further information can be obtained from the Italian Cultural Institute in London (tel: (020) 7235 1461; website: www.italcultur.org.uk) or the Italian State Tourist Board (see *Tourist Information*).
- Rejuvenate at one of Italy's thermal spas, some famous since the Roman era. The most important and best-equipped health resorts in Italy are **Abano Terme** and **Montegrotto Terme (Veneto), Acqui Terme (Piedmont), Chianciano Terme** and **Montecatini Terme (Tuscany), Fiuggi (Lazio), Porretta Terme** and **Salsomaggiore Terme (Emilia-Romagna), Sciacca Terme (Sicily)** and **Sirmione (Lombardy)**. At **Merano (Alto Adige)**, it is possible to have a special grape-diet treatment. More information on health spas in Italy is available from *La Federterme* (Italian Federation of Thermal Industries and Curative Mineral Waters; website: www.federterme.it).
- Do not miss the chance to wear an elaborate costume and mask at the **Venice Carnival** (end of January).
- Italy has some 8500km (5345 miles) of coastline and remains one of Europe's favourite destinations for beach holidays. All types of **watersports** are available at major resorts. The enduring appeal of the **Italian Riviera in Liguria** (a 350km-/219 mile-stretch from France to Tuscany), or of the **Adriatic** and **Amalfi coasts**, the latter known for its steeply terraced villages clinging to a rocky coastline **(Positano)**, is witnessed by the ever-growing number of visitors. Less busy are the beaches on the islands, in **Sicily**, which has large sandy stretches on the southern coast, and in **Sardinia**, much of which is still relatively untouched. Many of Italy's best **dive** sites are located in Sardinia, and underwater Italy's first **surfing** school is based in Mauro. Diving courses and equipment hire are also available on the **Tremiti Islands (Puglia)** in the Adriatic and along the coasts of Tuscany and Liguria. In **Capri**, one of Italy's most visited islands, take a boat trip from the Marina Grande to the main tourist attraction, the **Blue Grotto**. **Ischia**, an island on the west side of Naples, is well visited by the locals who appreciate its calm and scenic beauty.
- **Fishing** is excellent throughout **Sardinian** and **Sicilian waters** (also renowned for their healthy lobster population), while the **rivers in northern Italy, Umbria** and **Tuscany** can offer particularly scenic fishing holidays. For sea fishing, private or chartered boats can be rented. **Genoa** has frequent **yachting** regattas, as does **Santa Margherita Ligura**, where a canoe and small boat regatta is held in July. **Sailing** is popular on Italy's five major lakes near the Alps in the north – **Como, Garda, Iseo, Lugano and Maggiore**.
- Go **skiing** in the Italian Alps. To the west of Turin, in the Piedmont region, major resorts include **Bardonechia, Sauze d'Oulx** and **Sestriere**. Further north, the Aosta Valley has 28 resorts, such as **Cervinia, Courmayeur** and **La Thuile**, which can be easily reached from France (via the Mont Blanc tunnel from Chamonix) or from Switzerland (via the St Bernard tunnel). Driving can be difficult in the Dolomites, further east, but the beautiful scenery more than makes up for it, helping to make this one of Italy's prime skiing destinations; major resorts include **Cortina D'Ampezzo** (Italy's most upmarket resort), **Madonna di Campiglio, Merano** and **Selva/Sella Ronda**. Skiing is also possible in Central Italy, in resorts such as **Abetone (Tuscany), Campo Imperatore (Abruzzo)**, and in several other places in **Abruzzo**, down to **Mount Etna** in Sicily.
- In the **Valle d'Aosta** region, go **hillwalking** or **climbing** in the **Gran Paradiso National Park** and **Mont Avic Regional Park**, home to wildlife including the chamois and ibex. The **Dolomites** on the Swiss border is also ideal for hiking and climbing.
- See Marsican brown bears (unique to Italy), wolves, chamois and eagles in the **National Park of Abruzzo**. In the Molise region, the **Matese mountain range** is still the haven of wolves and various birds of prey.
- Make sure to see a bareback horserace on **Piazza del Campo** in Siena. A special event since the 13th century, the race, known as *Palio*, is held here twice a year, in July and August, and attracts crowds from all over the world.
- Go **mushroom picking** in Calabria, the toe of the 'boot', a spectacularly beautiful region of high mountains and dense forests. *Porcini* (boletus edulis), fresh, dried and pickled, naturally adorn the shelves of all the speciality shops of the region.
- Visit **wine cellars** in **Tuscany**. The landscape of Tuscany is, typically, one of vine-covered hills, cypress woods, fields of sunflowers and remote hilltop villages. *Chianti*, the best-known Italian wine, is made in the area north of Siena, and several wine cellars are open to the public.

TOURIST INFORMATION

Italian State Tourist Board (ENIT) in the UK
1 Princes Street, London W1B 2AY, UK
Tel: (020) 7408 1254 or 7399 3550 (brochure request).
Website: www.enit.it

Italian Government Tourist Board (ENIT) in the USA
630 Fifth Avenue, Suite 1565, New York, NY 10111, USA
Tel: (212) 245 5618 or 4827.
Website: www.italiantourism.com

Entertainment

FOOD & DRINK: Table service is most common in restaurants and bars. There are no licensing laws. Pasta and pizza plays a substantial part in Italian recipes, but nearly all regions have developed their own special dishes. Examples of regional dishes are listed below. Italy has over 20 major wine regions, from Valle d'Aosta on the French border to Sardinia and Sicily in the south.

National specialities:
Rome:
- *Abbacchio* (suckling lamb in white wine flavoured with rosemary).
- *Gnocchi alla romana* (semolina dumplings).
- Cheeses the best include *mozzarella, caciotta romana* (semi-hard, sweet sheep cheese), *pecorino* (hard, sharp sheep's milk cheese) and *gorgonzola*.

Piemonte:
- *Bagna caoda* (a traditional anchovy soup, served with vegetables).
- *Bonet* (a chocolate cake made with coffee and local biscuits).

Valle d'Aosta:
- *Fonduta* (a hot dip with Fontina cheese, milk and egg yolks sprinkled with truffles and white pepper).
- *Lepre piemontese* (hare cooked in Barbera wine and sprinkled with herbs and bitter chocolate).

Lombardy:
- *Risotto alla milanese* (rice with saffron and white wine).
- *Panettone* (Christmas cake with sultanas and candied fruit).

Trentino and Alto Adige:
- Some excellent sausages and hams come from these regions.

Veneto:
- *Fegato alla veneziana* (calves' liver thinly sliced and cooked in butter with onions).
- *Radicchio rosso di treviso* (wild red chicory with a bitter taste).

Friuli-Venezia Giulia:
- *Prosciutto di San Daniele* (raw ham).

Liguria:
- *Pesto* (sauce made of basil, garlic, pine nuts and pecorino cheese with pasta).
- *Pandolce* (sweet cake with orange flavour).

Emilia-Romagna:
- *Parmigiano* (parmesan cheese).
- *Prosciutto di Parma* (Parma ham).

Tuscany:
- *Bistecca alla fiorentina* (thick T-bone steak grilled over charcoal, sprinkled with freshly ground black pepper and olive oil).

Marche:
- *Brodetto* (a thick soup made from many varieties of fish, similar to chowder).

Abruzzo-Molise:
- Lamb is a favourite ingredient in many dishes.

Umbria:
- Fish from Lake Trasimeno and the River Nera
- *Porchetta alla perugina* (suckling pig).

Campania:
- *Sfogliatelle* (sweet ricotta cheese turnovers).

Puglia:
- *Ostriche* (fresh oysters baked with bread crumbs).

Calabria and Basilicata:
- *Sarde* (fresh sardines with olive oil and oregano).
- *Alici al limone* (fresh anchovies baked with lemon juice).

Sicily:
- *Pesce spada* (swordfish stuffed with brandy, mozzarella and herbs, grilled on charcoal).
- *Pasta con le sarde* (pasta with fresh sardines).

Sardinia:
- *Burrida* (fish stew with dogfish and skate).
- *Calamaretti alla sarda* (stuffed baby squid).

National drinks:
Wines are named after grape varieties or after their village or area of origin. The most widespread is the *Chianti* group of vineyards, governed by the Chianti Classico quality controls (denoted by a black cockerel on the neck of each

bottle). The Chianti area is the only area in Italy with such quality controls. *Denominazione di origine controllata* wines come from officially recognised wine-growing areas (similar to *Appellation Contrôlée* in France), while wines designated *Denominazione controllata e garantita* are wines of fine quality.

- Roman wines include *Albano, Frascati,* and *Velletri* (whites); *Cesanese, Marino* and *Piglio* (reds). *Grumello* in Lombardy. *Barolo* and *Barbera* in Valle d'Aosta. *Valpolicella* in Veneto. *Pinot Bianco, Pinot Grigio* and *Tokai* (whites); *Cabernet, Merlot* and *Pinot Nero* (reds) in Friuli-Venezia. *Chianti* and *Vernaccia* in Tuscany. The Abruzzo-Molise district is home to *Montepulciano d'Abruzzo* (red) and *Trebbiano d'Abruzzo* (dry white). The district is also home of a strong liqueur known as *Centerbe*.
- Vermouths from Piemonte vary from dry and light pink to dark-coloured and sweet.
- Aperitifs such as *Campari* and *Punt e Mes* are excellent appetisers.
- Italian liqueurs include *Amaretto, Galliano, Sambuca* and *Strega*.

Tipping: Service charges and state taxes are included in all hotel bills. It is customary to give up to 10 per cent in addition if service has been particularly good.

NIGHTLIFE: Nightclubs, discos, restaurants and bars with dancing can be found in most major towns and tourist resorts. In the capital, English-language films can be found at the Pasquine Cinema, *Vicolo della Paglia*, just off Santa Maria in Trastevere. Restaurants and cafes throughout Italy will invariably have tables outside. Open-air concerts in summer are organised by the *Academy of St Cecilia* and the *Opera House*, while there is open-air theatre at the *Baths of Caracalla*. Jazz, rock, folk and country music can all be heard at various venues.

SHOPPING: Many Italian products are world-famous for their style and quality. Care should be taken when buying antiques since Italy is renowned for skilled imitators. Prices are generally fixed and bargaining is not general practice, although a discount may be given on a large purchase. Florence, Milan and Rome are famous as important fashion centres, but smaller towns also offer good scope for shopping. It is advisable to avoid hawkers or sellers on the beaches. Some places are known for particular products, eg Carrara (Tuscany) for marble, Como (Lombardy) for silk, Deruta (Umbria) and Faenza (Emilia-Romagna) for pottery, Empoli (Tuscany) for the production of bottles and glasses in green glass and Prato (Tuscany) for textiles. Alghero (Sardinia) and Torre Annunziata (Campania) are centres for handicraft products in coral, and in several parts of Sardinia business cards and writing paper made of cork are produced. Cremona (Lombardy) is famous for its handmade violins. Castelfidardo (Marche) is famous for its accordion factories, and for its production of guitars and organs. Two small towns concentrate on producing their speciality: Valenza (Piedmont), which has a large number of goldsmith artisans, and Sulmona (Abruzzo), which produces 'confetti', sugar-coated almonds used all over Italy for wedding celebrations. Vietri sul Mare (Campania) is one of the most important centres of ceramic paving-tiles, and Ravenna (Emilia-Romagna) is famous for mosaics. Main shopping areas are listed below.

Rome: Offers a wide choice of shops and markets. Every shop in the fashionable Via Condotti–Via Sistina area offers a choice of styles, colours and designs rarely matched, but at very high prices. Equally expensive are shops along Via

Credit: © Fototeca ENIT

Vittorio Veneto, a street famous for its outdoor cafes. Old books and prints can be bought from bookstalls of Piazza Borghese. Rome's flea market is at Porta Portese in Trastevere on Sunday mornings, selling everything from second-hand shoes to 'genuine antiques'.

Milan: The city's industrial wealth is reflected in the chic, elegant shops of Via Montenapoleone. Prices tend to be higher than in other major cities.

Venice: Is still famous for its glassware and there is a great deal of both good and bad glass; that made on the island of Murano, where there are also art dealers and skilful goldsmiths, has a reputation for quality. Venetian lace is also exquisite and expensive; however, most of the lace sold is no longer made locally (only lace made on the island of Burano may properly be called Venetian lace).

Florence: Boasts some of the finest goldsmiths, selling from shops largely concentrated along both sides of the Ponte Vecchio bridge. Florentine jewellery has a particular quality of satin finish called *satinato*. Much filigree jewellery can also be found. Cameos are another speciality of Florence, carved from exotic shells.

Southern Italy: In the south, there are still families handmaking the same local products as their ancestors: pottery, filigree jewellery and products of wrought iron and brass in Abruzzo; products in wood in Calabria; corals and cameos in Campania; a variety of textiles, including tablecloths, in Sicily and Sardinia. In Cagliari, it is possible to find artistic copies of bronze statuettes from the Nuraghe period of the Sardinian Bronze Age. In the larger towns, such as Bari, Cagliari, Calabria, Naples, Palermo and Reggio, there are elegant shops with a whole range of Italian products. Many smaller towns have outdoor markets, but souvenirs sold there are sometimes of very low quality, probably mass-produced elsewhere.

SHOPPING HOURS: Mon-Sat 0830-1230 and 1530-1930, with some variations in northern Italy where the lunch break is shorter and the shops close earlier. Food shops are often closed on Wednesday afternoons.

Business

- **GDP:** US$1.3 trillion (2004).
- **Main imports:** Engineering products, chemicals, transport equipment, energy products, minerals and nonferrous metals, textiles and clothing, food, beverages and tobacco.
- **Main exports:** Engineering products, textiles and clothing, production machinery, motor vehicles, transport equipment, chemicals, food, beverages, tobacco, minerals and nonferrous metals.
- **Main trade partners:** Belgium, China, France, Germany, Netherlands, Spain, Switzerland, UK and USA.

ECONOMY: Traditionally agricultural, Italy industrialised rapidly after 1945, particularly in manufacturing and engineering, to the point where less than five per cent of the population is now engaged in agriculture. The majority of these live in the south of Italy, which is substantially poorer than the centre and north of the country. The principal crops are sugar beet, wheat, maize, tomatoes and grapes (many are used for wine, of which Italy is a leading producer). As with most Western European economies, the tourism industry now enjoys a major position in the economy alongside other service industries such as financial services and communications media. Italy continues to rely heavily on the export of manufactured goods, particularly of industrial machinery, vehicles, aircraft, chemicals, electronics, textiles and clothing. Its particular strengths are in advanced manufacturing techniques and systems, high-quality design and precision engineering.

Italy's historic trade performance has been all the more impressive given the dearth of raw materials, in particular the fact that all of the country's oil and many of its raw materials must be imported. The economy has been sluggish since the turn of the millennium with growth in 2004 less than one per cent. Inflation is just under three per cent; unemployment has fallen slightly to just under nine per cent. In Europe, despite some doubts about the size of its budget deficit, Italy was among the founding members of the Euro-zone in 1999. The current Berlusconi government is trying to implement a programme of tax cuts and labour reform which are intended to boost economic performance but it has been hamstrung by political difficulties.

BUSINESS ETIQUETTE: A knowledge of Italian is a distinct advantage. Prior appointments are essential. Visitors should remember that ministries and most public offices close at 1345 and, except by special appointment, it is not possible to see officials in the afternoon. Genoa, Milan and Turin form the industrial triangle of Italy; Bologna, Florence, Padua, Rome, Verona and Vicenza also have important business centres. In all the above cities, major trade fairs take place throughout the year.
Office hours: Mon-Fri 0900-1700.
CONFERENCES/CONVENTIONS: There are many hotels with facilities.

COMMERCIAL INFORMATION

Unione Italiana delle Camere di Commercio, Industria, Artigianato e Agricoltura (Italian Union of Chambers of Commerce, Industry, Crafts and Agriculture)
Piazza Sallustio 21, 00187 Rome, Italy
Tel: (06) 47041.
Website: www.unioncamere.it

Credit: © Fototeca ENIT

A B C D E F G H I J K L M N O P Q R S T U V W X Y Z

Jamaica

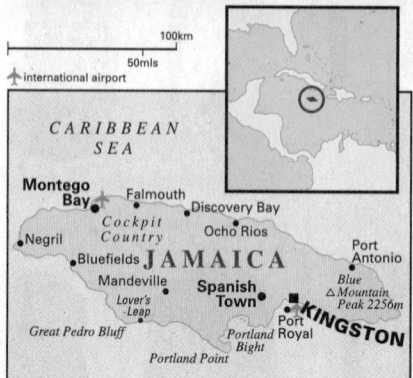

100km
50mls

✈ international airport

CARIBBEAN
SEA

**Montego
Bay** • Falmouth
• Discovery Bay
Cockpit • Ocho Rios
• Negril Country
Bluefields JAMAICA Port
• Mandeville Antonio
Lover's Blue
Leap Spanish △ Mountain
Town Peak 2256m
Great Pedro Bluff Port KINGSTON
Portland Royal
Bight
Portland Point

Location: Caribbean.

Time: GMT - 5.

Overview

Jamaica was inhabited by Arawak Indians prior to the arrival of Christopher Columbus in 1494. Although Columbus was in the habit of declaring that each new island he chanced upon was more beautiful than the last, he seems to have maintained a lifelong enthusiasm for the beauty of Jamaica.

A few years later, it was formally colonised by the Spanish whose rule lasted until 1655. They were displaced by the British who turned Jamaica into the most important of the British Caribbean slaving colonies. Within 100 years, virtually the whole island had been divided up into large plantations owned by absentee landlords and worked by forced labour imported from West Africa.

After the abolition of slavery in 1834, Jamaica became relatively prosperous under orthodox colonial rule until the early 20th century when a spate of natural disasters, compounded by the depression of the 1930s, sent the economy into decline.

The 1930s also saw the rise of black political activity and trade union organisation, forming the rivalries that characterise modern Jamaican politics in the process. Jamaica became independent in 1962.

Everybody knows Jamaica as the home of Bob Marley, but there is more to it than just reggae and Rastafarians. The third-largest island in the Caribbean offers excellent tourist facilities. It has wonderful white-sand beaches, mountains, waterfalls, wildlife and the best coffee in the world. The island's luxuriant tropical and subtropical vegetation is probably unsurpassed anywhere in the Caribbean. Kingston is its lively capital, surprising visitors with elegant, old colonial houses against the stunning backdrop of the Blue Mountains.

Jamaica has gained a reputation for violence, and there certainly are no-go areas in Kingston, but most Jamaicans are overwhelmingly friendly and fun-loving.

The two main tourist resorts are Negril and Montego Bay, Jamaica's second city – known to one and all as Mo' Bay. Negril boasts one of the longest beaches in the country, some 11km (7m) of it, with all the watersports one would expect in a lively resort. But just a little way along the coast, one will find 'the real Jamaica' with fishing villages like Treasure Beach, Port Antonio and Oracabessa providing quieter retreats.

Tourism grows, encouraged by the governing People's National Party. Many visitors return as they succumb to Jamaica's charms, the beautiful scenery, the warmth of the people; and of course, wherever you go, there is always music, music, music.

Columbus Travel Publishing

booksales@nexusmedia.com

General Information

AREA: 10,991 sq km (4244 sq miles).
POPULATION: 2.7 million (UN, 2005).
POPULATION DENSITY: 245.65 sq km.
CAPITAL: Kingston. **Population**: 660,000.
GEOGRAPHY: Jamaica is the third-largest island in the West Indies and is a narrow outcrop of a submerged mountain range. The island is crossed by a range of mountains reaching 2256m (7402ft) at the Blue Mountain Peak in the east, and descending towards the west with a series of spurs and forested gullies running north and south. Most of the best beaches are on the north and west coasts. The island's luxuriant tropical and subtropical vegetation is probably unsurpassed anywhere in the Caribbean.
GOVERNMENT: Constitutional monarchy. Gained independence from the UK in 1962. **Head of State**: HM Queen Elizabeth II, represented locally by Governor General Sir Felixe Cook. **Head of Government**: Prime Minister Portia Simpson Miller since 2006. **Recent history:** The People's National Party (PNP, social democrat) has held power since February 1989, first under Michael Manley and, since March 1992, PJ Patterson. Elections were held in October 2002, when the People's National Party (PNP) won a fourth consecutive term in office, giving PJ Patterson an unprecedented fourth term as Prime Minister. He has successfully tackled Jamaica's rampant inflation through tight monetary and fiscal policies and has sought to reduce the state's debt by privatising state enterprises. PJ Patterson stepped down in March 2006, after 14 years as Prime Minister. Portia Simpson Miller, the newly-elected leader of the ruling People's National Party (PNP), automatically succeeded him, becoming Jamaica's first female Prime Minister.
LANGUAGE: The official language is English. Local *patois* is also spoken.
RELIGION: Protestant majority (Anglican, Baptist, Church of God and Methodist) with Roman Catholic, Jewish, Muslim, Hindu and Bahai communities. Rastafarianism, a religion based on belief in the divinity of the late Emperor of Ethiopia, Haile Selassie (Ras Tafari), is also widely practised.
ELECTRICITY: 110 volts AC, 60Hz, single phase. American two-pin plugs are standard, but many hotels offer, in addition, 220 volts AC, 50Hz, single phase, from three-pin sockets.
SOCIAL CONVENTIONS: Handshaking is the customary form of greeting. As tourism is a major industry in Jamaica, the visitor is well catered for, and hotel and restaurant staff are generally friendly and efficient. Outside Kingston, the pace of life is relaxed and people are welcoming and hospitable. Normal codes of practice should be observed when visiting someone's home. It may be common to see signs on the island referring to 'Jah lives', Jah being the name given to God by the Rastafarians. Casual wear is suitable during the day, but shorts and swimsuits must be confined to beaches and poolsides. Evening dress varies from very casual in Negril to quite formal during the season in other resorts, where some hotels and restaurants require men to wear jackets and ties at dinner. Possession of marijuana may lead to imprisonment and deportation.

Climate

Tropical all year. Temperate in mountain areas. The rainy months are May and October, but showers may occur at any time. Prone to Hurricanes during the rainy season, between June and November. Jamaica also lies within the earthquake zone. Cooler evenings.
Required clothing: Lightweight cottons and linens; lightwoollens are advised for evenings. Avoid synthetics. Waterproofing is necessary all year round.

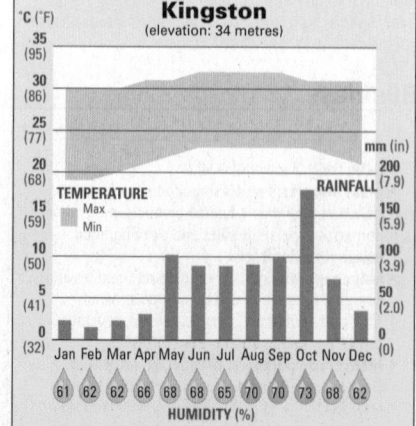

Kingston
(elevation: 34 metres)

°C (°F)
TEMPERATURE
Max
Min
RAINFALL mm (in)

Jan Feb Mar Apr May Jun Jul Aug Sep Oct Nov Dec

61 62 62 66 68 65 67 70 70 73 68 62

HUMIDITY (%)

Communications

Telephone: Full IDD is available. Country code: 1 876. There are no area codes.
Mobile telephone: Roaming agreements exist with many international mobile phone companies.
Internet: There are several free Internet kiosks at shopping centres in Kingston. Internet cafes exist mainly in the Kingston area. Internet is also available in many hotels and parish libraries.
Post: Airmail to Europe takes up to four days. Post office hours: Mon-Fri 0830-1630.
MEDIA: Jamaica enjoys a free press. The broadcast media are predominantly commercial and the main newspapers are privately-owned.
Press: Daily papers are *The Jamaica Gleaner* (website: www.jamaica-gleaner.com), *The Daily Star* and *The Jamaica Observer* (website: www.jamaicaobserver.com).
Radio: Radio Jamaica Ltd (RJR) operates three commercial networks: *RJR 94 FM*; entertainment station *FAME-FM*; music and sports station *Radio 2 FM*. Other commercial stations include *Irie FM, reggae Hot 102, KLAS FM* and *Power 106. Roots 96.1 FM* is a community station. *BBC Caribbean Service* and *World Service* radio programmes are available via the *BBC 104 FM* network.
TV: *Jamaica Broadcasting Corporation* became *Television Jamaica Limited (TVJ)* when it was privatised in 1997. Other channels include private channel *CVM Television* and religious channel *Love TV*.

Passport/Visa

	Passport Required?	Visa Required?	Return Ticket? Required?
Full British	Yes	No	Yes
Australian	Yes	No	Yes
Canadian	Yes	No	Yes
USA	No/1	No	Yes
Other EU	Yes	No/2	Yes
Japanese	Yes	No	Yes

Note: *Regulations and requirements may be subject to change at short notice, and you are advised to contact the appropriate diplomatic or consular authority before finalising travel arrangements. Any numbers in the chart refer to the footnotes below.*

Restricted entry: Jamaica does not recognise passports issued by the Palestinian Government.
PASSPORTS: Passport valid for at least six months required by all except the following:
(a) **1**. nationals of the USA holding a certified copy of a birth certificate and photo identification (eg driver's licence or student ID).
VISAS: Required by all except the following:
(a) nationals of countries referred to in the chart above, except **2**. nationals of Czech Republic, Estonia, Hungary, Latvia, Lithuania, Poland, Slovak Republic and Slovenia who can obtain their visas on arrival;
(b) nationals of Commonwealth countries, except nationals of Cameroon, Mozambique, Nigeria, Pakistan and Sri Lanka who *do* need visas prior to arrival;
(c) nationals of Argentina, Brazil, Chile, Costa Rica, Ecuador, Iceland, Israel, Korea (Rep), Liechtenstein, Mexico, Norway, San Marino, Surinam, Switzerland, Turkey, Uruguay, Venezuela and Zimbabwe for stays not exceeding 90 days.
Note: (a) All of the above *must* have evidence of sufficient funds and a return or onward-bound ticket for their next destination. (b) Except for persons in certain categories, a work permit is required for a business visit. The Consulate (or Consular section at Embassy or High Commission) can advise. (c) Nationals of the following countries can obtain a visa on arrival, provided holding valid onward or return tickets and evidence of sufficient funds: Albania, Andorra, Bosnia & Herzegovina, Bulgaria, CIS, Croatia, Macedonia (Former Yugoslav Republic of), Monaco, Romania, Serbia & Montenegro, Turkmenistan, Taiwan. These visas cost US$20.
Types of visa and cost: *Entry* and *Transit*: £25.
Application to: Consulate (or Consular section at Embassy or High Commission); see *Passport/Visa Information*.
Application requirements: (a) One passport-size photo. (b) Valid passport. (c) Completed application form. (d) Fee, payable in cash or postal orders only. (e) For postal applications, £5 for return postage. (f) Travel itinerary. *Business*: (a)-(f), (g) Letter from company and, (h) Work permit.
Working days required: 48 hours, but up to three weeks in cases where applications are referred to Immigration Authorities in Kingston.
Temporary residence: Enquire at High Commission.

Credit: ©Jamaica Tourist Board

PASSPORT/VISA INFORMATION

Jamaica High Commission in the UK
1-2 Prince Consort Road, London SW7 2BZ, UK
Tel: (020) 7823 9911.
Website: www.jhcuk.com
Opening hours: Mon-Thurs 0900-1700, Fri 0900-1600
(High Commission); Mon-Fri 1000-1530 (Consulate).

Jamaican Embassy in the USA
1520 New Hampshire Avenue, NW,
Washington, DC 20036, USA
Tel: (202) 452 0660-9.
Website: www.emjamusa.org

Jamaican Consulate General in the USA
767 Third Avenue, 2nd Floor,
New York, NY 10017, USA
Tel: (212) 935 9000.
Website: www.congenjamaica-ny.org

Money

Currency: Jamaican Dollar (JMD; symbol J$) = 100 cents.
Notes are in denominations of J$1000, 500, 100 and 50.
Coins are in denominations of J$20, 10, 5 and 1, and 25, 10
and 1 cents.
Currency exchange: Money can be exchanged at the
airport as well as at banks, hotels and bureaux de change.
Receipts must be retained, as changing money on the black
market is illegal. Many Jamaican ATMs accept international
bank cards.
Credit & debit cards: American Express, Diners Club,
MasterCard and Visa are all widely accepted as well as other
cards with the Cirus or Plus logo. Banks give credit card
advances. Check with your credit or debit card company for
details of merchant acceptability and other services which
may be available.
Traveller's cheques: To avoid additional exchange rate
charges, travellers are advised to take traveller's cheques in
US Dollars.
Currency restrictions: The import and export of local
currency is prohibited; that of foreign currency is
unrestricted, subject to declaration.
Banking hours: Mon-Thurs 0900-1400, Fri 0900-1200 and
1430-1700.
Banking hours: Mon-Thurs 0900-1400, Fri 0900-1200 and
1430-1700.
Exchange rate indicators:
Rate at time of publishing
£1.00=   J$114.36
$1.00=   J$64.50

Duty Free

The following goods may be imported into Jamaica without
incurring customs duty:
*200 cigarettes or 50 cigars or 225g of tobacco; 1l of spirits
and all other goods including gifts and souvenirs
amounting to £145.*
Prohibited items: Indecent or obscene articles. All
publications of *de Laurence Scott and Company* or *Red
Star Publishing Company* of Chicago, in the USA, relating
to divination, magic, cultism or supernatural arts. Goatskin
articles.
Restricted items: Meat, fruit and vegetables, ground
provisions, pharmaceuticals, chemicals, herb teas, firearms,
used tyres, two-way radios, coconut derivatives, oil
producing seeds, edible oils, detergents, motor vehicles,
explosives, alcohol in bulk, sugar, human remains, pesticides
and live animals.

Public Holidays

Below are listed the Public Holidays for the January 2006-
June 2007 period.
2006: Jan 1 New Year's Day. **Mar 1** Ash Wednesday. **Apr 14**
Good Friday. **Apr 17** Easter Monday. **May 22** Labour Day.
Aug 1 Emancipation Day. **Aug 6** Independence Day. **Oct 17**
National Heroes' Day. **Dec 25-26** Christmas.
2007: Jan 1 New Year's Day. **Feb 21** Ash Wednesday. **Apr 6**
Good Friday. **Apr 9** Easter Monday.

Health

	Special Precautions?	Certificate Required?
Yellow Fever	No	1
Cholera	No	No
Typhoid & Polio	No	N/A
Malaria	No	N/A

Note: *Regulations and requirements may be subject to change at short
notice, and you are advised to contact your doctor well in advance of
your intended date of departure. Any numbers in the chart refer to the
footnotes below.*

1: A yellow fever vaccination certificate is required from
travellers over one year of age coming from infected areas.
Food & drink: Mains water is normally chlorinated and,
whilst relatively safe, may cause mild abdominal upsets.
Bottled water is available. Milk is pasteurised and dairy
products are safe for consumption. Local meat, poultry,
seafood, fruit and vegetables are generally considered safe
to eat.
Other risks: *Hepatitis A* occurs. *Leptospirosis* and *toxic
fish poisoning* occurs. There is a high prevalence of
HIV/AIDS and precautions should be undertaken to avoid
exposure.
Health care: Health insurance is recommended, since
medical treatment can be expensive. There are 16 public
and six private hospitals. Standards vary hugely.

Travel - International

AIR:

The national airline is *Air Jamaica (JM)*
(website: www.airjamaica.com).
Approximate flight times: From Kingston or
Montego Bay to *London* is 10 hours, to *Los Angeles* is 6
hours and to *New York* is 3 hours 40 minutes.
Main airports: *Norman Manley International (KIN)*
(Kingston) is 18km (11 miles) southeast of the city.
To/from the airport: Coach, bus and taxis depart to the
city (travel time – 30 to 60 minutes). *Facilities:*
Banks/bureaux de change, bars, restaurants, shops, duty-
free, and car hire.
Montego Bay (MBJ) (International) is 3km (2 miles) north
of the city. *To/from the airport:* Air Jamaica Express runs
shuttle services between the airports. *Facilities:* Duty-free
facilities.
Departure tax: J$1000.
SEA:

Main ports: *Montego Bay* and *Ocho Rios* are
ports of call for several cruise lines. Other
passenger/freight lines (Geest) sail from North,
South and Central American ports.

Travel - Internal

AIR:

The *Air Jamaica Express* (website:
www.airjamaica.com) runs services to and from
Kingston, Montego Bay, Negril, Ocho Rios and
Port Antonio. During the winter season, there are frequent
daily flights. For more information, contact the airline (tel:
923 6664 *or* (800) 523 5585, toll-free in North America
and the Caribbean).
SEA:

There are a number of local operators running
yacht tours around the island, as well as cruises.
Boats and yachts can also be hired on a daily or
weekly basis. Contact the Jamaica Tourist Board for details
(see *Top Things To Do*).
RAIL:
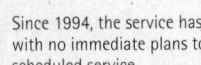
Since 1994, the service has been suspended
with no immediate plans to resume a daily
scheduled service.
ROAD:

There is a 17,000km (11,000mile) road network,
one-third tarred. Traffic in Jamaica drives on
the left. Speed limits are 30mph (48kph) in
towns and 50mph (80kph) on highways. **Bus:** Reliable
service in Kingston and Montego Bay; less reliable for
trans-island travel. Coach and minibus tours are bookable

at most hotels. *JUTA* (tel: 952 0813) is the main provider
of scheduled and unscheduled bus/minibus and vehicle
charter services. **Taxi:** Route taxis drive designated courses
and pick up passengers on the way; they are the cheapest
and quickest way of getting around the island. These have
red plates marked PP (Public Passenger). They charge fixed
rates, and it is best to check standard charges prior to
embarkation. A 10 per cent tip is usual. It is recommended
that only taxis authorised by the Jamaica Union of
Travellers Association and ordered from hotels (unshared)
should be used. **Car hire:** Most major towns, as well as
airports, have hire facilities, both local and international.
Hire can also be arranged via hotels. Drivers must be aged
25 or over. There is a general consumption tax of 15 per
cent on all car hire transactions. **Regulations:** Seat belts
must be worn at all times and children under 3 years must
sit in a child seat. **Documentation**: A full UK driving
licence is valid for up to 12 months.
URBAN:

Most transport in the capital is by private
minibus.

Travel Times: The following chart gives approximate
travel times (in hours and minutes) from **Montego Bay** to
other major cities/towns in Jamaica.

	Air	Road
Kingston	0.30	3.00
Negril	0.20	1.30
Ocho Rios	0.30	2.00
Port Antonio	0.40	4.30

Travel Advice

Travellers should be aware that there are high levels of
crime and violence, particularly in the Kingston area and
tourists should avoid certain routes.
The threat from terrorism is low. Most visits to Jamaica are
trouble-free but you should be aware of the global risk of
indiscriminate international terrorist attacks, which could
be against civilian targets, including places frequented by
foreigners.
This advice is based on information provided by the
Foreign and Commonwealth Office in the UK. It is correct
at time of publishing. As the situation can change rapidly,
visitors are advised to contact the following organisations
for the latest travel advice.

British Foreign and Commonwealth Office
Tel: (0845) 850 2829.
Website: www.fco.gov.uk

US Department of State
Website: http://travel.state.gov/travel

Accommodation

HOTELS:

There are over 144 hotels and guest houses
throughout the island; all are subject to 15 per
cent general consumption tax. There is an
annual 'Spring Break' over March/April, during which
students holidaying in Jamaica are offered discount rates
at selected hotels. Contact the Jamaica Tourist Board for
details (see *Top Things To Do*). **Grading:** Hotels are
government-controlled in four categories: **A**, **B**, **C** and **D**.
SELF-CATERING:

There are over 800 cottages for rent on the
island. Information is available from the
Jamaica Tourist Board (see *Top Things To Do*).
The properties range from small apartments to houses
with several bedrooms. Some tour operators can arrange
villa accommodation including car hire and tours, as well
as travel to and from the villa.
CAMPING/CARAVANNING:
The island has many campsites, including the
eco-tourist Sonrise Beach Retreat (formerly
known as 'Strawberry Fields') which offers all
types of facilities, including the hiring of tents and
ancillary equipment.

ACCOMMODATION INFORMATION

**Jamaican Association of Villas & Apartments
Ltd (JAVA)**
PO Box 298, Ocho Rios, Jamaica
Tel: 974 2508 *or* 974 2763.
Website: www.villasinjamaica.com

Jamaica Hotel & Tourist Association
2 Ardenne Road, Kingston 10, Jamaica
Tel: 926 3635.
Website: www.jhta.org

A B C D E F G H I J K L M N O P Q R S T U V W X Y Z

Credit: ©Jamaica Tourist Board

Top Things To See

- In **Kingston**, Jamaica's capital city and cultural centre, visit the **National Gallery of Art,** which has a colourful display of modern art. **Hope Botanical Gardens** contain a wide variety of trees and plants and are particularly famous for orchids. The **Port Royal**, on top of the peninsula bordering **Kingston Harbour**, is a museum to the time when Port Royal (Jamaica's ancient capital city that was submerged under the sea after an earthquake in 1692) was known as the 'richest and wickedest city on earth' under the domination of Captain Morgan and his buccaneers. In the **White Marl Arawak Museum**, see artefacts and relics of the ancient culture of the Arawak Indians.
- A short drive to the west of Kingston, **Spanish Town** is the former capital of Jamaica. Go to the **Spanish Town Square**, which is said to be one of the finest examples of Georgian architecture in the Western hemisphere. The Spanish **Cathedral of St Jago de la Vega** is the oldest in the West Indies.
- **Montego Bay** (or Mo'Bay, as it is more colloquially called) is the capital of Jamaican tourism and market town for a large part of western Jamaica. From Gloucester and Kent Avenues, there are superb views onto the clear Caribbean waters and the long reef protecting the bay.
- **Ocho Rios** lies roughly 108km (67 miles) east of Montego Bay. The name is said to have come from the old Spanish word for *roaring river* or, in modern Spanish, *eight rivers.* Do not miss one of the most stunning sights in Jamaica, **Dunn's River Falls**, a crystal water stairway which leads to the nearby botanical gardens. Ocho Rios is known as the garden-lover's paradise, and the **Shaw Park Botanical Gardens** exhibit the fascinating variety of the area's exotic flora, for which the town is celebrated.
- Visit the 24-hour open-air museum and and see relics of Jamaican history at **Columbus Park, Discovery Bay**, which commemorates Columbus' arrival in Jamaica.
- Discover the **Blue Mountains** at **Port Antonio**, which is set on one of the Caribbean's most beautiful bays. The town dates back to the 16th century, and sights include **Mitchell's Folly**, a two-storey mansion built by the American millionaire Dan Mitchell in 1905, and the ruins of the 60-room **Great House**.

Top Things To Do

- Go to the **crafts market** on King Street in **Kingston**.
- On the south coast, relax at the **Milk River Spa**, a naturally radioactive mineral bath with waters at a temperature of 33°C (86°F).
- In **Montego Bay**, chill out at the town's three main beaches: **Doctor's Cave Beach** (so named because it was once owned by a Dr McCatty and had a cave that has since eroded away) which has beautiful white sand, and where the exceptionally clear water is believed to be fed by mineral springs; **Walter Fletcher Beach**, nearest the centre and a short walk from the Upper Deck Hotel; and **Cornwall Beach**, which is a few yards from the local Tourist Board Office. A short way inland from the Bay is **Rose Hall**, a restored Great House on a sugar plantation.
- The best beaches for **bathing** are mainly on the northern

coast. **Surfing** is also best on the north coast, east of **Port Antonio**, where long lines of breakers roll into Boston Bay. Jamaica has many attractions for **divers**, including close-to-shore wrecks, sponge forests, underwater caves and coral reefs. In some areas, visibility is exceptional, reaching 30.5m (100ft). Popular dive sites include the **Throne Room** near **Negril**, where it is possible to see corals, sponges, nurse sharks and cubera snapper; **Ricky's Reef**, with brightly coloured fish; and the wreck of the *Kathryn*. **Sailing, water-skiing, deep-sea fishing, scuba diving, parasailing and windsurfing** are also available at **Negril**. Beaches in the Port Antonio area include **San San** and **Boston** (where the Jamaican 'jerk pork' is found). The **Blue Lagoon** is a salt-water cove offering **fishing, swimming** and **water-skiing** and is considered one of the finest coves in the Caribbean.
- Fresh- and sea-water **fishing** are popular. Mountain mullet, hognose mullet, drummer and small snook are caught in rivers. Spearfishing is permitted among the reefs. No licence is needed. Take part in a **fishing tournament** in **Port Antonio**. The surrounding sea is rich in game fish, such as kingfish, yellowtail, wahoo and bonito. Blue marlin, however, are the great prize. An annual **Blue Marlin Tournament**, run alongside the **Jamaica International Fishing Tournament** in Port Antonio, takes places every autumn.
- Go on a tour to **Runaway Bay**, which has fine **beaches**, excellent **scuba diving** and **horse riding**; and the **Runaway Caves** nearby, which offer a boat ride 35m (120ft) below ground on a lake in the limestone **Green Grotto**.
- **Rafting** is available on the **Rio Grande**, comprising two-hour trips on two passenger bamboo rafts, which begin high in the Blue Mountains at **Berrydale**, sail past plantations of bananas and sugar cane, and end up at **Margaret's Bay**. The scenic **Somerset Falls** nearby are a popular picnic spot.
- From **Falmouth**, a delightful harbour resort, 42km (26 miles) east of Montego Bay, visit **Rafters Village** for rafting on the **Martha Brae**, and a fascinating crocodile farm called **Jamaica Swamp Safaris**. There is also a plantation mansion, **Greenwood Great House**, once owned by the Barrett Brownings. The **Church of St Paul** has Sunday services, where visitors can listen to the choir singing.
- For those keen on **mountain climbing** and **hiking**, the **Blue Mountains**, which reach above 2134m (7000ft), offer unspoilt scenery and a variety of flora and fauna. It is best to go hiking with a guide.
- At **Rocklands Feeding Station**, discover some of the most exotic birds in the world, such as the mango hummingbird, orange quit and the national bird of Jamaica, the Doctor Bird. Visitors are allowed to feed the birds at certain times of the day. Very popular is a motor coach ride through thick mountain forests into the interior, passing through banana and coconut plantations and **Ipswich Caves** (a series of deep limestone recesses) to the sugar estate of the famous **Appleton Rum Factory** and onwards to **Catadupa**, where shirts and dresses are made to measure.
- Go on a tour to working plantations at **Brimmer Hall** and **Prospect** where sugar, bananas and spices are still grown and harvested, using many of the traditional skills handed down through generations. Any sightseeing itinerary should include a drive along **Fern Gully**, a road running along an old river-bed that winds through a 6.5km (4 mile) valley of ferns.
- Another tour is the **Jamaica Night** on the **White River**, a canoe ride up the torchlit river to the sound of drums. Dinner and an open-air bar is available on the riverbank (Sunday evenings).
- Mix with the locals at **Rick's Café**, located at **West Point** (which is as far west as Jamaica goes), famous as the place from which to observe the sun going down.

TOURIST INFORMATION

Jamaica Tourist Board in the UK
1-2 Prince Consort Road, London SW7 2BZ, UK
Tel: (020) 7225 9090.
Website: www.visitjamaica.com

Jamaica Tourist Board in the USA
5201 Blue Lagoon Drive, Suite 670, Miami, Florida, 33126, USA
Tel: (305) 665 0557 *or* (800) 233 4582 (toll-free in the US only).
Website: www.visitjamaica.com

Caribbean Tourist Organisation in the UK
22 The Quadrant, Richmond, Surrey TW9 1BP, UK
Tel: (020) 8948 0057.
Website: www.doitcaribbean.com *or* www.onecaribbean.org

Entertainment

FOOD & DRINK: Jamaican food is full of fire, taking advantage of pungent spices and peppers.

Things to know: Bars have table and/or counter service. The legal drinking age is 18. There are no licensing hours and alcohol can be bought all day.

National specialities:
- 'Rice and peas', a tasty dish with no peas at all but with kidney beans, white rice, coconut milk, scallions (spring onions) and coconut oil.
- Salt fish (dried cod) and *ackee* (the cooked fruit of the ackee tree).
- Jamaican pepperpot soup (salt pork, salt beef, *okra* and Indian kale known as *callaloo*).
- Chicken fricassée Jamaican-style (a rich chicken stew with carrots, scallions, yams, onions, tomatoes and peppers prepared in unrefined coconut oil).
- Roast suckling pig (a three-month-old piglet which is boned and stuffed with rice, peppers, diced yam and thyme mixed with shredded coconut and corn meal).

National drinks:
- Jamaican rum is world famous, especially *Gold Label* and *Appleton*.
- *Rum Punch.*
- *Rumona* is a delicious rum cordial.
- *Red Stripe* beer.
- *Tia Maria* (a Blue Mountain coffee and chocolate liqueur).
- Blue Mountain coffee.

Tipping: Most Jamaican hotels and restaurants add a service charge of 10 per cent; otherwise 10 to 15 per cent is expected. Chambermaids, waiters, hotel bellboys and airport porters all expect tips.

NIGHTLIFE: There is no shortage of night-time entertainment on the island that is the home of reggae music. Every town or village has some sort of nightlife, and there are regular street dances. Folkloric shows at larger resort hotels are held and steel bands often play. At least once a week, there is a torchlit, steel band show with limbo dancing and fire-eating demonstrations. Nightclubs feature jazz, soca, reggae and other music. For details of events, visitors should consult local newspapers. The Jamaica Tourist Board arranges 'Meet the People' evenings in various scenic locations throughout the island. Contact the Tourist Board in Kingston, Montego Bay, Ocho Rios or Port Antonio.

SHOPPING: Special purchases are locally made items and duty free bargains. Crafts include hand-loomed fabrics, embroidery, silk screening, woodcarvings, oil paintings, woven straw items and sandalmaking. Custom-made rugs and reproductions of pewter and china from the 17th-century ruins of the ancient submerged city of Port Royal can be bought in the In-Craft workshop. At *Highgate Village* in the mountains, Quakers run a workshop specialising in wicker and wood furniture, floor mats and other tropical furnishings. Jamaican rum, the *Rumona* (see *National drinks*) and *Ian Sangsters Rum Cream* are unique purchases. Other local specialities are *Pepper Jellies*, jams and spices. The most famous produce market in Jamaica is *Coronation Market*, Kingston. Other markets: *Linstead Market*, St Catherine; *Brownstown Market*, St Anne; the *Savanna-la-mar Market*, Westmoreland; and the *Albert George Market*, Falmouth. There are shops offering facilities for 'in-bond' shopping, which allows visitors to purchase a range of international goods free of tax or duty at very competitive prices. These goods are sealed (hence the 'bond') and, because goods are tax- or duty free, can only be opened once away from Jamaican waters or territory. All goods must be paid for in Jamaican currency.

Shopping hours: Mon-Fri 0800-1600, Sat 0800-1300. Some shops close half day Wednesday in Kingston, and Thursday in the rest of the island.

Business

- **GDP:** US$8 billion (2004).
- **Main imports:** Food and other consumer goods, industrial suppliers, fuel, parts and accessories of capital goods, machinery and transport equipment, construction materials.
- **Main exports:** Alumina, bauxite, sugar, bananas, rum, coffee, yams, beverages, chemicals, wearing apparel and mineral fuels.
- **Main trade partners:** Canada, China, France, Germany, Japan, The Netherlands, Norway, Trinidad and Tobago, UK and USA.

ECONOMY: Jamaica is one of the world's largest producers of bauxite, which accounts for half of the country's export earnings, but, despite expanding production, low world prices and falling demand have kept revenues static. After a period of rapid expansion in the mid-1970s, tourism has become the major source of foreign exchange. Agriculture (principally sugar cane, bananas, coffee and cocoa) has also been largely stagnant, with improved efficiency and production methods offset by climatic conditions and the state of the world markets. The manufacturing sector produces cement, textiles, tobacco and other consumer goods among its products. Imported oil and gas account for the bulk of the island's energy requirements.

Economic policy has pursued a familiar course of privatisation of state-owned enterprises, deregulation, tight budgetary controls, and reform of the tax and banking systems. The process was supervised by the IMF and aimed principally at reducing Jamaica's large debt burden. These measures improved Jamaica's financial position, but with little benefit to the population who still suffer from high inflation and unemployment. The economy as a whole has contracted by an average of one per cent annually since the mid-1990s. This trend then reversed causing the economy to grow slowly. Hurricane Ivor, in 2004, destroyed infrastructure and disrupted Jamaica's agriculture, especially the production of bananas. Storm rains of the 2005 hurricane season caused further damage. Jamaica is a member of the Caribbean trading bloc, CARICOM, and of the Inter-American Development Bank.

BUSINESS ETIQUETTE: The traditional 'shirtjac' (jacket without a tie), also known locally as a *kareba*, which was popular until the 1970s, has been replaced by a suit, jacket and tie. Usual formalities are required and appointments and business cards are normal. Samples of non-commercial value are allowed into the country without a licence prior to arrival, although it may still be necessary to visit the office of the Trade Administrator to exchange the licence copy for a clearance copy, which the customs authorities demand before clearing the goods.
Office hours: Mon-Fri 0830-1700.

COMMERCIAL INFORMATION

The American Chamber of Commerce of Jamaica
81 Knutsford Blvd, Kingston 5, Jamaica
Tel: 929 7866.
Website: www.amchamjamaica.org

Trade Board Ltd
107 Constant Spring Road, Kingston 10, Jamaica
Tel: 969 0883/3228/2785.
Website: www.tradeboard.gov.jm
Contact to obtain an import licence for trade samples.

Jamaica Conference Centre
Duke Street, Kingston, Jamaica
Tel: 922 9160.
Email: jccgm@cwjamaica.com

The Jamaica Tourist Board (see *Top Things To Do*) can supply information on conferences.

Credit: ©Jamaica Tourist Board

Japan

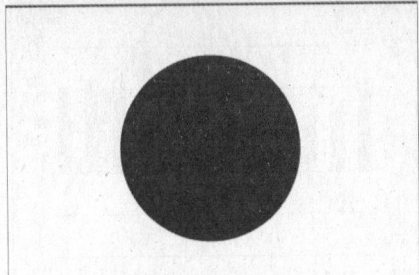

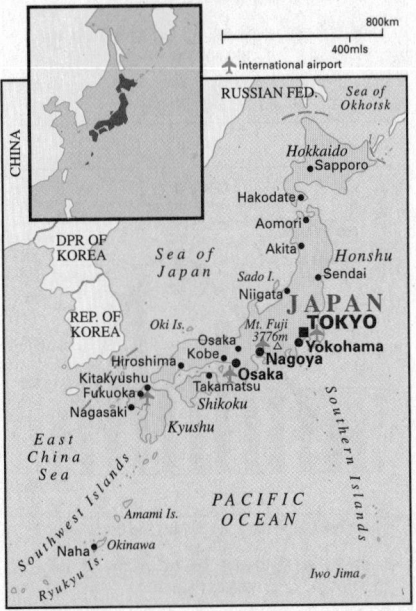

800km
400mls
✈ international airport

Location: Far East.

Time: GMT + 9.

Overview

The earliest recorded history of Japan dates back to the reign of the emperor Jimmu during the sixth century BC. Political and economic power was in the hands of a group of noble dynasties that operated on a largely feudal basis. The 12th century AD saw the emergence of the *shogun*, a military governor drawn from one of the great families, who ruled with the consent of the others. Only an external threat such as the attempted Mongol invasions in the late 13th century would unite the various families against the common enemy. This helped create a latent national consciousness which slowly developed over the next 300 years.

The actual unification of Japan began during the Tokugawa period (1600-1868). During this period, the shogun retained supreme executive power, retaining Japan's unyielding resistance to foreign influence. However, in the late 19th century, a new breed of rulers took control and embarked on a programme of rapid industrialisation, establishing a Western-style system of administration.

The military was the main driving force behind this process but formal executive power was in the hands of the Emperor, who inherited his position and was treated by most of his subjects as a demi-god. Japan's imperial ambitions in the Far East developed, resuming after World War I (which Japan took little part in) with China as the main target. Japan's subsequent collision with the British, who had substantial political and economic interests in China, contributed to her alliance with Germany in World War II.

Between 1938 and 1941, Japan's forces occupied China and South-East Asia. At its zenith, the Japanese empire, which carried the Orwellian title 'Co-Prosperity Zone', stretched as far south as Indonesia and eastwards far into the Pacific. The American response to the Japanese attack on Pearl Harbor slowly pushed back the Japanese over the following four years, on the brink of surrendering when the devastating nuclear attacks on Hiroshima and Nagasaki sealed the outcome. Japan was occupied by American troops who imposed the constitution in 1946 that governs Japan today. Throughout the East-Asian region lingers

Credit: ©Japan National Tourist Organisation

strong resentment at Japan's brutal treatment of its subject populations, compounded by the fact that Japan was - and is - in denial about its history.

Since 1950, Japan has overseen exceptional economic growth, becoming one of the world's most powerful economies. Tokyo dazzles with bright lights and high-tech gadgetry. Bustling cities burst with skyscrapers, bullet trains, trendy nightlife and rampant consumerism. Yet beneath the brash modernity beats an ancient heart. This is still the realm of the exquisite art of the geisha and the skill of the sumo wrestler; where ancient festivals are celebrated and food is elevated to an art form. And Japan is still a land of great natural beauty, from the snow festivals and lavender farms of the northern isle of Hokkaido to the sun-drenched beaches of the subtropical south. Whether you choose to climb Mount Fuji or relax at volcanic hot spring resorts, Japan is unforgettable.

General Information

AREA: 377,864 sq km (145,894 sq miles).
POPULATION: 127.9 million (UN, 2005).
POPULATION DENSITY: 338.48 per sq km.
CAPITAL: Tokyo. **Population**: 8.1 million (2000).
GEOGRAPHY: Japan is separated from the Asian mainland by 160km (100 miles) of sea. About 70 per cent of the country is covered by hills and mountains, a number of which are active or dormant volcanoes. A series of mountain ranges runs from northern Hokkaido to southern Kyushu. The Japanese Alps (the most prominent range) run in a north-south direction through central Honshu. The highest mountain is Mount Fuji at 3776m (12,388ft). Lowlands and plains are small and scattered, mostly lying along the coast and composed of alluvial lowlands and diluvial uplands. The coastline is very long in relation to the land area, and has very varied features. The deeply indented bays with good natural harbours tend to be adjacent to mountainous terrain.
GOVERNMENT: Constitutional monarchy. **Head of State**: Emperor Akihito since 1989. **Head of Government**: Prime Minister junichiro Koizumi since 2001. **Recent history:** After scraping through the November 2000 general election, the LDP (Liberal Democratic Party, or Jiyu Minshu-to) was about to recall their leader, the deeply unpopular ex-finance minister Ryutaro Hashimoto, when an unlikely would-be saviour appeared in the form of Junichiro Koizumi, a former minister with a huge popular following by virtue of his flamboyant personal style and evident determination to break with the past. The LDP's overwhelming victory in upper house parliamentary elections in July 2001 secured his position. In October 2002, the Koizumi government finally unveiled plans to tackle the country's financial crisis. Barring unemployment, which reached an unprecedented 6 per cent, the programme had begun to show results by late 2003 as Government measures began to take effect. This was the main reason for Koizumi's successful re-election campaign that saw the LDP returned as the largest party. Koizumi also won an overwhelming victory in lower house elections in September 2005, giving his party and its coalition ally a key two-thirds majority in the new Parliament. Mr Koizumi promised to push on with post office reform, which he had put at the heart of his campaign. He said he still intended to step down in September 2006, when his term as President of the ruling Liberal Democratic Party (LDP) ends. The Japanese parliament is the bicameral Kokkai (or *Diet*). The upper house (*Sangi-in*) has 252 members directly elected from constituencies for six-year terms (half of which are renewed every three years). The lower house (*Shugi-in*) has 500 members elected for four-year terms partly by single-seat constituencies, partly by proportional representation. The Diet approves the appointment of a Prime Minister who holds executive power with the assistance of a cabinet of ministers. The appointment of the Prime Minister is formally entrusted to the Emperor who is head of State but has negligible constitutional powers.
LANGUAGE: Japanese is the official language. Some English is spoken in major cities.
RELIGION: Shintoism and Buddhism (most Japanese follow both religions) with a Christian minority. In Okinawa, however, people believe in Niraikanai, the realm of the dead beyond the sea.

Credit: ©Japan National Tourist Organisation

ELECTRICITY: 100 volts AC, 60Hz in the west (Osaka); 100 volts AC, 50Hz in eastern Japan and Tokyo. Plugs are flat two-pin and light bulbs are screw-type.

SOCIAL CONVENTIONS: Japanese manners and customs are vastly different from those of Western people. A strict code of behaviour and politeness is recognised and followed by almost all Japanese. However, they are aware of the difference between themselves and the West and therefore do not expect visitors to be familiar with all their customs but expect them to behave formally and politely. A straightforward refusal does not form part of Japanese etiquette. A vague 'yes' does not really mean 'yes' but the visitor may be comforted to know that confusion caused by non-committal replies occurs between the Japanese themselves. Entertaining guests at home is not as customary as in the West, as it is an enterprise not taken lightly and the full red-carpet treatment is given. Japanese men are also sensitive lest their wives be embarrassed and feel that their hospitality is inadequate by Western standards; for instance, by the inconvenience to a foreign guest of the custom of sitting on the floor. Bowing is the customary greeting but handshaking is becoming more common for business meetings with Westerners. The honorific suffix *san* should be used when addressing all men and women; for instance Mr Yamada would be addressed as *Yamada-san*. When entering a Japanese home or restaurant it is customary to remove shoes. Table manners are very important, although the Japanese host will be very tolerant towards a visitor. However, it is best if visitors familiarise themselves with basic table etiquette and use chopsticks. It is customary for a guest to bring a small gift when visiting someone's home. Exchange of gifts is also a common business practice and may take the form of souvenir items such as company pens, ties or high-quality spirits. Smoking is only restricted where notified.

Climate

Except for the Hokkaido area and the subtropical Okinawa region, the weather is mostly temperate, with four seasons. Winters are cool and sunny in the south, cold and sunny around Tokyo (which occasionally has snow), and very cold around Hokkaido, which is covered in snow for up to four months a year. Summer, between June and September, ranges from warm to very hot, while spring and autumn are generally mild throughout the country. Rain falls throughout the year but June and early July is the main rainy season. Hokkaido, however, is much drier than the Tokyo area. Rainfall is intermittent with sunshine. Typhoons are only likely to occur in September or October but rarely last more than a day.

Required clothing: Lightweight cottons and linens are required throughout summer in most areas. Light- to mediumweights during spring and autumn; medium- to heavyweights for winter months, according to region. Much warmer clothes will be needed in the mountains all year round. There is much less rainfall than in Western Europe.

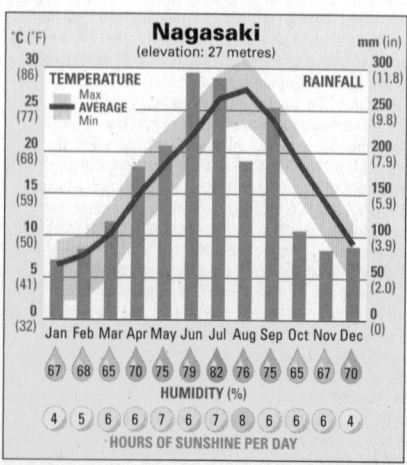

Nagasaki
(elevation: 27 metres)

HUMIDITY (%)
67 68 65 70 75 79 82 76 65 65 67 70

HOURS OF SUNSHINE PER DAY
4 5 6 6 7 8 6 6 6 4

Communications

Telephone: Full IDD service. Country code: 81. Three companies provide international communications services: KDDI, IDC and ISD, each possessing their own international access number (001 010, 0061 and 0041, respectively). Credit cards can also be used directly in some phone boxes. Phone boxes are found virtually everywhere in Japan. They are green and grey, and accept ¥10 coins, ¥100 and magnetic pre-paid cards. IC phone boxes accept IC cards only.

Mobile telephone: The Japanese mobile network uses PDC (Personal Digital Cellular System) technology, which is not compatible with GSM or other mobile services. Visitors can hire handsets from companies such as NTT, Mover Rental Centre, 2-2-1 Marunouchi, Chiyoda-ku, Tokyo 100-8019 (tel: (3) 3282 0100) or Sony Finance, Rental Sales Department, Minamiaoyama, Minato-ku, Tokyo (tel: (3) 3475 5721). For UK travellers, mobiles can also be hired before departure from Adam Phones (tel: (0800) 123 000), Cellhire PLC (tel: (0800) 610 610; e-mail: london@cellhire.com) or Mobell Communications (tel: (01543) 426 999). Coverage is good.

Internet: Internet is available; there are many Internet cafes in Tokyo and in the main cities in Japan. Some hotel telephones and the new grey telephones have modular sockets for computer network access.

Post: Letters can be taken to the Central Post Office in front of Tokyo Station or the International Post Office, near exit A-2 Otemachi subway station, which provide English-speaking personnel. Airmail to Europe takes four to six days. Post office hours: Mon-Fri 0900-1700. Some main post offices are open daily.

MEDIA: Japan's broadcasting scene is advanced and vibrant, and very competitive, with established public and commercial outlets competing for audiences. Many millions now watch satellite and cable pay-TV services, including those provided by NHK. High-definition TV (HDTV) now has an NHK channel dedicated to such transmissions. Digital terrestrial TV broadcasting is in the process of being introduced, also. Newspaper readership is extremely high, and national dailies have circulations in the millions.

Press: The English-language daily newspapers in Tokyo include Daily Sports, Yomiuri Shimbun, The Japan Times and The Mainichi Daily News.

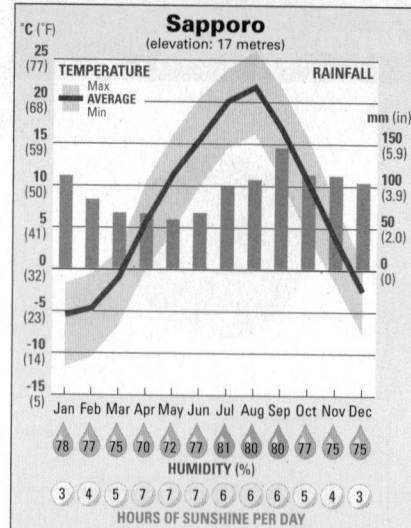

Sapporo
(elevation: 17 metres)

TEMPERATURE
Max
AVERAGE
Min

RAINFALL

HUMIDITY (%)
78 77 75 70 72 77 81 80 80 77 75 75

HOURS OF SUNSHINE PER DAY
3 4 5 7 7 7 6 6 6 5 4 3

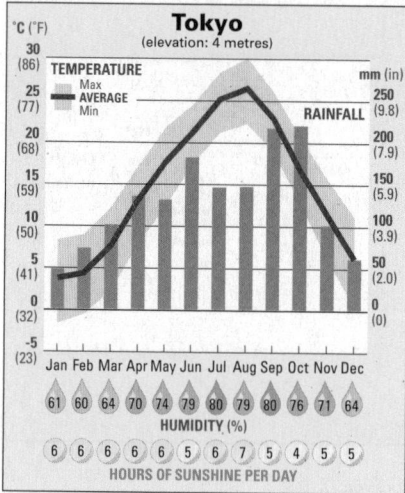

Tokyo
(elevation: 4 metres)

TEMPERATURE
Max
AVERAGE
Min

RAINFALL

HUMIDITY (%)
61 60 64 70 74 79 80 79 80 76 71 64

HOURS OF SUNSHINE PER DAY
6 6 6 6 6 5 5 6 5 4 5 5

TV: National commercial networks include TV Asahi, Fuji TV, Nippon TV (NTV) and the Tokyo Broadcasting System (TBS). NHK is a public broadcaster, and operates general and educational TV channels, as well as satellite channels and a high-definition TV network.

Radio: NHK is a public broadcaster that operates a news- and speech-based radio station, as well as a cultural and educational network, a classical-music-based network and an external service, Radio Japan. Inter FM, J-Wave and Tokyo FM are all commercial stations. TBS Radio is operated by the Tokyo Broadcasting System.

Passport/Visa

	Passport Required?	Visa Required?	Return Ticket? Required?
Full British	Yes	No/1	Yes
Australian	Yes	No	Yes
Canadian	Yes	No	Yes
USA	Yes	No	Yes
Other EU	Yes	No/1	Yes
Japanese	N/A	N/A	N/A

Note: Regulations and requirements may be subject to change at short notice, and you are advised to contact the appropriate diplomatic or consular authority before finalising travel arrangements. Any numbers in the chart refer to the footnotes below.

PASSPORTS: Passport valid for the duration of intended stay in Japan required by all.

Note: Whether or not they hold a visa, visitors who do not possess visible means of support for their stay, onward or return tickets, or other documents for their next destination, may be refused entry.

VISAS: Required by all except the following for tourism, short-term business meetings or to attend a conference: (a) **1.** nationals of countries referred to in the chart for up to 90 days (except nationals of Austria, Germany, Ireland, Liechtenstein, Mexico, Switzerland and the UK who although initially granted a 90-day stay may apply, while in Japan, to the local Immigration Department for an extension of up to a further 90 days, making the visa-free stay up to six months; (b) nationals of Andorra, Argentina, Barbados, Bahamas, Bulgaria, Chile, Costa Rica, Croatia, Dominican Republic, El Salvador, Guatemala, Honduras, Hong Kong (SAR), Iceland, Israel, Korea (Rep) (visa exemption extended to Feb 2006), Lesotho, Macau (SAR), Federated States of Macedonia, Mauritius, Monaco, New Zealand, Norway, San Marino, Singapore, Surinam, Taiwan (Republic of China, Taiwan passports with ID number), Tunisia, Turkey and Uruguay for up to three months; (c) nationals of Brunei for stays of up to 14 days.

Types of visa and cost: Temporary Visitor: £15 (single-entry) and £31 (multiple-entry) for all except nationals of the following countries; Britain (except for BNO): £6 (single and multiple-entry); Iran: £26 (single-entry) and £51 (multiple-entry); India: £4 (single and multiple-entry). Transit: £4 for all except nationals of the following countries; India: £0.50; Iran: £26; Britain: £1. Visas are free of charge to some nationalities; charges also vary according to the exchange rate and nature of intended visit.

Validity: Transit: 15 days. Temporary Visitor: 15, 30 or 90 days. College Student: One or two years.

Application to: Consulate (or consular section at Embassy); see Passport/Visa Information. Applications for all visas must be made in person.

Application requirements: Temporary Visitor/Transit: (a) Valid passport. (b) One or two completed application forms depending on nationality. (c) One or two passport-size photos depending on nationality. (d) Proof of sufficient funds for stay (eg recent bank statement). (e) Fee (cash only). (f) Return air/sea ticket or copy. (g) Original letter from employer or college. (h) Letter of invitation from Japan or hotel booking. (i) Personal itinerary or schedule for the proposed trip. College Student: (a)-(e) and, (f) Copy of certificate of admission to Japanese educational institution.

Note: All visas must be applied for in person by each applicant. Once a visa has been issued, passports may be returned via post if a pre-paid, self-addressed, special delivery envelope is submitted. Further documents maybe required from applicants of certain nationalities; please contact the Embassy visa section for further information.

Working days required: Five working days for applications that do not need referral to the Ministry of Foreign Affairs in Tokyo. Up to four weeks if referral is needed. For those nationals that possess a Certificate of Eligibility, the processing time will be reduced to three days. Some types of visa may take three months or longer. Contact the nearest Consulate (or Consular section of the Embassy) for more information.

Temporary residence: Contact the nearest Consulate (or Consular section of the Embassy) for more information.

PASSPORT/VISA INFORMATION

Embassy of Japan in the UK
101-104 Piccadilly, London W1J 7JT, UK
Tel: (020) 7465 6500 *or* 6565 (visa section).
Website: www.uk.emb-japan.go.jp
Opening hours: Mon-Fri 0930-1300 and 1430-1730; 0930-1330 and 1430-1630 (consular section).

Embassy of Japan in the USA
2520 Massachusetts Avenue, NW, Washington, DC 20008, USA
Tel: (202) 238 6700.
Website: www.us.emb-japan.go.jp

Money

Note: Japan has a strong cash culture, and it is usual to see people carrying large amounts of cash with them because of the low crime rate. It is only recently that credit cards have begun to become more popular. However, travellers may still encounter difficulties with foreign credit cards.
Currency: Japanese Yen (JPY; symbol ¥). Notes are in denominations of ¥10,000, 5000, 2000 and 1000. Coins are in denominations of ¥500, 100, 50, 10, 5 and 1.
Currency exchange: All money must be exchanged at an authorised bank or money changer.
Credit & debit cards: American Express, Diners Club, MasterCard, Visa and other major credit cards are widely accepted in towns. Check with your credit or debit card company for merchant acceptability. ATMs are widely available although many do not accept foreign credit or debit cards, and are harder to find outside of towns. They only operate during normal banking hours and weekend services can be restricted to Saturday morning. ATMs are available in towns and they are generally open Mon-Fri 0700-2300, Sat-Sun 0900-1900. *Citibank* machines also accept foreign credit cards and are often open 24 hours.
Traveller's cheques: These can be exchanged at most major banks, larger hotels and some duty free shops. To avoid additional exchange rate charges, travellers are advised to take traveller's cheques in Japanese Yen or US dollars.
Currency restrictions: The import and export of local and foreign currency is unrestricted, subject to declaration of amounts equivalent to ¥1,000,000 or above.
Banking hours: Mon-Fri 0900-1500.
Exchange rate indicators:
Rate at time of publishing

£1.00=	¥204.38
$1.00=	¥117.72

Duty Free

The following goods may be imported into Japan without incurring customs duty:
400 cigarettes or 100 cigars or 500g of tobacco or 500g of a combination of these; three bottles (approximately 0.76l each) of spirits; 56ml of perfume; gifts up to the value of ¥200,000.
Note: There is no duty free allowance for alcohol or tobacco products for travellers aged 19 years or younger. Oral declaration is necessary on arrival at customs.
Prohibited items: Counterfeit, altered or imitated coins, paper money, banknotes or securities; all plants with soil; most meats and fruits (prohibited meats include eggs, bones, horns etc of cows, goats, sheep, bees, chickens, dogs, ducks, geese, horses, rabbits and turkeys); animals without health certificates; firearms and ammunition; narcotics; obscene articles and publications (including films).

Public Holidays

Below are listed Public Holidays for the January 2006-June 2007 period.
2006: Jan 1 New Year's Day. **Jan 2** Bank Holiday. **Jan 3** Bank Holiday. **Jan 9** Coming of Age Day. **Feb 11** National Foundation Day. **Mar 20** Vernal Equinox. **May 3** Constitution Memorial Day. **May 4** Greenery Day. **May 5** Children's Day. **Jul 17** Maritime Day. **Aug 6** Hiroshima Peace Festival (Hiroshima only). **Aug 9** Nagasaki Memorial Day (Nagasaki only). **Sep 18** Respect for the Aged Day. **Sep 23** Autumnal Equinox. **Oct 9** Health and Sports Day. **Nov 3** Culture Day. **Nov 23** Labour Thanksgiving Day. **Dec 23** Birthday of the Emperor. **Dec 31** Bank Holiday.
2007: Jan 1 New Year's Day. **Jan 2** Bank Holiday. **Jan 3** Bank Holiday. **Jan 8** Coming of Age Day. **Feb 11** National Foundation Day. **Mar 20** Vernal Equinox. **Apr 29** Greenery Day. **May 3** Constitution Memorial Day. **May 5** Children's Day.
Note: (a) With the exception of New Year Bank Holidays, if a holiday falls on a Sunday, the following day is treated as a holiday instead. (b) When there is a single day between two national holidays, it is also taken as a holiday. (c) Between 29 December and 3 January government offices and many shops and offices are closed.

Health

	Special Precautions?	Certificate Required?
Yellow Fever	No	No
Cholera	No	No
Typhoid & Polio	1	N/A
Malaria	No	N/A

Note: *Regulations and requirements may be subject to change at short notice, and you are advised to contact your doctor well in advance of your intended date of departure. Any numbers in the chart refer to the footnotes below.*

1: It is sometimes recommended to be vaccinated against typhoid.
Food & drink: Food and drink are generally considered safe but there is risk of parasitic infection and toxins from raw seafood.
Other risks: Vaccination against *Hepatitis A* is sometimes recommended; *hepatitis C* also occurs. *Typhus* occurs in some river valleys. *Japanese encephalitis* may occur and *paragonimiasis* has been reported. *TB* occurs.
Health care: Health insurance is strongly recommended, owing to the high cost of treatment. The International Association for Medical Assistance to Travellers provides English-speaking doctors. There are hospitals in all major cities.

Travel - International

AIR:

The largest national airline is *Japan Airlines (JAL)* (website: www.jal.co.jp).
Approximate flight times: From Tokyo to *London* is 12 hours; to *New York* is 12 hours 30 minutes; to *Los Angeles* is nine hours 30 minutes; to *Hong Kong* is five hours; to *Sydney* is nine hours 30 minutes.
Main airports: *Tokyo Narita Airport (NRT) (Narita City)* (website: www.narita-airport.or.jp) is 65km (40 miles) east of Tokyo (travel time - one hour 10 minutes). *To/from the airport*: Luxury coaches depart regularly from the airport to city-centre hotels. There is also a limousine bus to the Tokyo City Air Terminal (TCAT). A shuttle bus links the airport with major hotels in the city centre. Tickets for all services can be bought in the terminals. Japan Railways' reservation-only *Narita Express* line runs from Narita station terminal located beneath the airport to Tokyo station (travel time - one hour), Shinjuku (travel time - 90 minutes) and Yokohama (travel time - 105 minutes) every 30 minutes from 0745-2145. *JR* also operates a slower, cheaper service that departs every 45 minutes (travel time - one hour 20 minutes). First-class and private compartments are available. *Keisei Electric Railway* also runs from the airport terminal to Keisei Ueno station in central Tokyo (travel time - one hour) from 0920-2200. There are taxis to the city, with a surcharge after 2200 (travel time - 60 to 70 minutes). Travellers should note that these are five times as expensive as the trains. There is a free shuttle bus connecting both terminals every 10 to 15 minutes (travel time - 10 minutes). *Facilities*: Duty free shops, bank/bureau de change, car hire, restaurants, a tourist information centre with multilingual staff located in both terminals, post office, cellular phone and video camera hire and internet facilities.
(Osaka) Kansai International (KIX) (Kansai) (website: www.kansai-airport.or.jp) is 50km (31 miles) southwest of Osaka. To/from the airport: There is a bus to the city every 30 minutes from 0800-2120 (travel time - one hour). The *Nankai RR* service goes to Namba station every 15 minutes (travel time - 30 minutes). The *JR West* service goes to JR Osaka station every 30 minutes (travel time - one hour 10 minutes). Taxis are available to the city (travel time - 60 minutes), although a surcharge may be imposed after 2200. It is also possible to take the jetfoil from Kansai Airport to Kobe's Port Island (travel time - 32 minutes). *Facilities*: Duty free shops, car hire (includes Japaren, Nippon, Nissan and Toyota), banks/bureaux de change, tourist information and bar/restaurant.
Fukuoka International (FUK) is 20 minutes' travel time from Fukuoka City. *Facilities*: Outgoing duty free shop, car hire, bank/bureau de change and bar/restaurant.
Nagoya International (NGO) is 10km (6 miles) north of the city and has flights to 29 international destinations, including: Bangkok, Brisbane, Frankfurt/M, Hong Kong City, Honolulu, Melbourne, Paris, Seoul, Singapore, Sydney and Taipei.
Departure tax: Depends on airport; ¥2040 from Narita Airport. Children under 12 are charged half price; children under two are exempt. Departure tax is usually paid when purchasing tickets and not at the airport.
SEA:

Main ports: Japan is easily accessible by sea, and passenger ships include the major ports on their schedules. Ferries operate daily from *Osaka* and *Kobe* to Shanghai (China) and weekly from Kobe to Tanggu (near Tianjin, China). For Taiwan, ferries depart from *Okinawa*. The Shimonoseki-Busan ferry runs nightly across the Sea of Japan to Korea (Rep). Links to the Russian Federation include weekly services between *Yokohama* and Nakhoda (near Vladivostok). Alternatively, there is a twice-weekly service to *Wakkanai* in Hokkaido from Korsakov in the Russian Federation. There are cruises between the Japanese islands en route to Shanghai and Hong Kong.
RAIL:

The Trans-Siberian route to Japan is an interesting and very well organised, if lengthy, trip. Connections can be made daily from London (Liverpool Street) via Harwich or London (Victoria) via Dover through Europe to Moscow. There are sleeping cars four times a week from Hook of Holland to Moscow, and twice a week from Ostend to Moscow. The Trans-Siberian railway departs regularly from Moscow (see *Russian Federation* section).

Travel - Internal

AIR:

All Nippon Airways (ANA), *Japan Air Systems (JAS)* and *Japan Airlines (JAL)* and several other airlines maintain an extensive network covering Japan proper and its islands. Tokyo's domestic airport is *Haneda (HND)*. A monorail service runs from Hamamatsu-cho to Haneda. One international airline, *China Airlines*, serves Haneda. Other international flights to and from Haneda are made via Fukuoka, Nagoya, Osaka or Tokyo airports. Main routes are Tokyo-Sapporo; Tokyo-Fukuoka; Tokyo-Osaka; and Tokyo-Naha. Tickets can be purchased at automatic machines at Tokyo International Airport's domestic departure counter, and at Osaka International Airport.
SEA:

There are frequent services by high-speed boat, ferry or hydrofoil to Japan's islands. Popular routes include Tokyo-Hokkaido (in the north) and Tokyo-Okinawa (in the south). Major sea routes include Awaji Island: Akashi- Iwaya; Shodo Island: Himeji-Fukuda, Okayama-Tonosho and Takamatsu-Tonosho; Shiraishijima and Manabejima Islands: Kasaoka-Shiraishijima-Manabejima; Ikuchijima and Omishama Islands: Mihara-Setoda. Bullet train services travel frequently to ports.
RAIL:

The *Japan Railways Group (JR)* runs one of the best rail networks in the world, and is widely used for both business and pleasure. Express and 'limited express' trains are best for intercity travel. Very frequent services run on the main routes. *Shinkansen*, the 'Bullet Train', are the fastest, with compartments for wheelchair passengers, diners and buffet facilities. Supplements are payable on the three classes of express train and in 'Green' (first-class) cars of principal trains, for which reservations must be made. Other types of train include *Kyuko* (Express), *Tokkyu* (Limited Express), *Kaisoku* (Rapid Train) and *Futsu* (Local Train). For short-distance trains, tickets can only be bought at vending machines outside train stations. For route maps, timetables, fares and reservations, see online (website: www.japanrail.com).
Discount fares: The *Japan Rail Pass*, an economical pass for foreign tourists which must be purchased before arrival in Japan, can be obtained from *Japan Airlines* (*JAL* users only); contact the Tourist Board for other vendors. It can be used on all trains except the new Nozomi super express trains, and also on Japan Rail buses and Japan Rail ferries. A *Japan Rail Pass* brochure is available from the Japan National Tourist Organisation (see *Top Things To Do*). A seven-day basic pass currently costs ¥28,300, a 14-day pass ¥45,100 and a 21-day pass ¥57,700. For travellers with a Japan Rail Pass, there are various other discounts in operation including a 10 per cent discount at any JR Group Hotel. Other rail passes include the *JR East Pass*, *JR Kyushu Rail Pass*, *JR West Rail Pass*, *Kansai Passport* and the *Hokkaido Rail Pass*. For details of other discount fares, contact the Japan Railways Group (website: www.japanrail.com).
ROAD:

Driving in Japan is complicated for those who cannot read the language as it will be a problem to understand the road signs. Traffic in cities is often congested. Traffic drives on the left. The Keiyo Highway, Meishin Expressway, Tohoku Expressway and the Tomei Expressway link Japan's major Pacific coastal cities, passing through excellent scenery. **Documentation**: An International Driving Permit is required.
URBAN:

Public transport is well developed, efficient and crowded. The underground systems and privately run suburban rail services, which serve all the main cities, are very convenient but best avoided in rush hours. Tokyo also has a good network of trams. **Bus**: These can be confusing and are best used with someone who knows the system. Otherwise visitors should get exact

details of their destination from the hotel. Fares systems are highly automated, but passes may be available. On buses, payment may be made on leaving. **Metro**: All of Japan's largest cities have subway systems. Tokyo has two underground systems: the Tokyo Metro Co Ltd operates the nine Tokyo Metro lines (TRTA), and the Tokyo Metropolitan Government (TBTMG) operates the four lines on the Toei Subway. Tickets for Toei lines are not valid for the Tokyo Metro and vice versa, so a transfer ticket must be bought. A variety of tickets can be bought including a monthly open pass, one-day open ticket, 14 tickets for the price of 10, and a Tokyo Combination ticket; this can be bought six months in advance and entitles the passenger to unlimited travel on all the lines on the subway, JR rail, Toei buses and street cars for one day within the six months. Kyoto also has its own subway system with two major lines: the Karasuma and Tozai lines. Kyoto Sightseeing Passes can be bought enabling unlimited rides on buses and the underground. **Taxi**: These can be expensive, particularly in rush hour (0730-0930 and 1700-1800). There is a minimum charge for the first 2km (1.2 miles) and there is a time charge in slow traffic. It is advisable for visitors to have prepared in advance the name and address of their destination in Japanese writing, together with the name of some nearby landmark; a map may also help. Hotels can provide this service.

Travel times: The following chart gives approximate travel times (in hours and minutes) from **Tokyo** to other major cities/towns in Japan.

	Air	Road	Rail	Sea
Nagoya	-	4.00	2.00	-
Nagasaki	1.40	18.00	9.00	-
Osaka	1.00	6.00	3.15	-
Sapporo	1.25	-	14.00	-

Travel Advice

Most visits to Japan are trouble-free but you should be aware of the global risk of indiscriminate international terrorist attacks, which could be against civilian targets, including places frequented by foreigners.

Do not become involved with drugs. Possession of small amounts will lead to detention and prosecution. Possession of large amounts earns long sentences of rigorous imprisonment and very heavy fines.

This advice is based on information provided by the Foreign & Commonwealth Office in the UK. It is correct at time of publishing. As the situation can change rapidly, visitors are advised to contact the following organisations for the latest travel advice:

British Foreign and Commonwealth Office
Tel: (0845) 850 2829.
Website: www.fco.gov.uk

US Department of State
Website: http://travel.state.gov/travel

Accommodation

Note: The *Welcome Card* (Culture Card) offers reductions for foreign visitors on accommodation, meals, shopping and entertainment. It is available free of charge at JNTO's Tokyo Tourist Information Centres, or for ¥700 from information centres at Kansai International Airport, Kobe City Information Centre, Kyoto City Information Centre and Kyoto Prefectural Information Centre.

Accommodation tax: The Tokyo Metropolitan Government enforces an 'Accommodation Tax' on hotels and *ryokan* (inns) around the city that charge over ¥10,000 per room. The tax is ¥100 on rooms costing between ¥10,000 and ¥14,999 per night, and ¥200 for rooms costing ¥15,000 and over. For more information check online (website: www.tax.metro.tokyo.jp).

HOTELS:

Hotels are 'Western' or 'Japanese' style. Western-style accommodation (ranging from deluxe hotels to pensions) are much like any modern US or European hotel. Japanese-style hotels (*ryokan*) provide exciting new experiences: guests receive kimonos and wooden clogs and rooms come equipped with Japanese bathtubs and paper sliding doors. Many non-obligatory extras are available. Service charges of 10 to 20 per cent are added to the bill. No accommodation grading system operates in Japan.

GUEST HOUSES:

Minshuku, often found in resorts and vacation spots, are the Japanese equivalent of guest home-type lodging. Rates are moderate, and visitors should expect considerably fewer amenities than *ryokan* or Western-style hotels. Visitors are expected to fold up their bedding in the morning and stow it away in a closet, and towels are usually not provided. No shoes are worn in the house as slippers are provided. Small gifts or a 5 per cent tip may be given with the bill. The price usually includes two meals per day.

YOUTH HOSTELS:

There are roughly 400 youth hostels throughout Japan. Many require visitors to be a member of the International Youth Hostel Federation, although a guest card can be bought in advance at the Tokyo National Headquarters.

PENSIONS:

These are 'Bed & Breakfast' style lodges which offer a comfortable atmosphere. They are often located near ski resorts, lakesides or in more rural areas.

SHUKUBO: Some temples offer temple lodging (*Shukubo*). Guests may have to join in the routines of the monks (getting up early, chanting, doing chores etc) and facilities may be basic. The JNTO can provide a list (see *Top Things To Do*).

ACCOMMODATION INFORMATION

Japan Ryokan Association
Website: www.ryokan.or.jp

Japan Hotel Association
Shin Otemachi Building, 2-2-1 Otemachi, Chiyoda-ku, Tokyo 100-0004, Japan
Tel: (3) 3279 2706.
Website: www.j-hotel.or.jp

Japan Hotel Network
Akae Machi, Hanagashima Cho, Miyazaki City 880-0036, Japan
Website: www.japanhotel.net

Tokyu Hotel Chain Co Ltd
10-3 Nagata-Cho, 2-Chome, Chiyoda-Ku, Tokyo 100-0014, Japan
Tel: (3) 3581 8655.
Website: www.tokyuhotelsjapan.com

Japan Youth Hostels Inc
2-20-7 Misaki-Cho, Chiyoda-ku, Tokyo 100-0006, Japan
Tel: (3) 3288 1417.
Website: www.jyh.or.jp

Top Things To See

• Enjoy the mix of old and new in Japan's capital city, **Tokyo**. Stroll into the **Kabukiza Theatre** and observe the **Imperial Palace** (open to the public on special occasions) with its impressive moat and **East Garden** (**Higashi Gyoen**). *Tokyo Tower* affords excellent views of the bay and the space-age architecture on **Rainbow Town** (*O-daiba*), a reclaimed island. **West Shinjuku** is Tokyo's high-rise metropolis with its 'Gotham City' skyscrapers and plazas. The **Tokyo Metropolitan Government Building** is a twin-tower edifice that soars high above the the Shinjuku district and is now an iconic feature of the skyline. To the east, Shinjuku's bustling shopping and neon-lit nightlife districts contrast strongly with the calm beauty of the neighbouring **Shinjuku Gyoen National Garden**. For a taste of 'Old Tokyo', the downtown **Shitamachi** area is the place to head for, particularly in the summer when three enormous festivals attract vast crowds of revellers and spectators. The **Asakusa-Kannon Temple** is the area's main tourist draw, a vibrant Buddhist complex approached via a colourful shopping lane. Across the river, **Ryogoku** is the location of the excellent **Edo-Tokyo Museum** and the renowned **National Sumo Stadium**. **Ueno** is famous for its large park containing several important art museums and cultural venues.

• Two hours north of Tokyo in **Nikko**, the extraordinary **Toshogu Shrine** complex is situated with the mausoleum of the founder of Japan's Tokugawa Shogunate.

• The coastal town of **Kamakura**, one hour south of Tokyo, was the seat of Japan's medieval feudal government and abounds in historic sights. Highlights include the giant bronze **Great Buddha**, colourful **Hachimangu Shrine** and picturesque **Enoshima Island**.

• See the foreboding sight of Japan's highest mountain at 3776 metres tall, **Mount Fuji**, which may be climbed during the high summer.

• Gaze out at the volcanic landscapes of the **Bandai-Asahi National Park**, a favourite with hikers, as is the dramatic **Dewa Sanzan** area and **Mount Zao**, which transforms into one of Japan's top ski resorts in winter. To the very north of **Honshu**, the stunning volcanic crater of **Lake Towada** is surrounded by the alpine landscapes of the **Towada-Hachimantai National Park**, also known for its hot springs and ski resorts.

• Historic **Hiraizumi** is of interest for the fabulously ornate **Chusonji Temple**.

• Step onto the island of **Hokkaido** - for a long time, Japan's 'Wild West', and still retaining a distinct pioneer feel. Hokkaido is home to the last of Japan's indigenous Ainu people, and the remnants of their distinct culture are a must-see. As is the scenery - large parts of Hokkaido are protected as National Parks, full of fantastic volcanic scenery, 'bottomless' crater lakes, hot springs and numerous mountain and ski resorts. **Furano**, in particular, is renowned for its summer flower fields and winter skiing. During the winter visitors flock to see two of Hokkaido's outstanding natural phenomena: 'dancing' cranes and hot-spring-bathing monkeys. The port city of **Hakodate** was one of the first of Japan's ports to open to foreign trade. Known for its historic **Goryokaku Fort** and gorgeous night views, the city displays a notable Russian influence.

• **Nagoya** is Japan's fourth-largest city, noted for its porcelain industry, textile and lacquer crafts. **Nagoya Castle** is an impressive sight, as is **Atsuta Jingu**, one of Japan's most important shrines. **Meiji Mura** is an extensive outdoor museum of characteristic buildings from the Meiji period. Japan's pre-eminent Shinto shrine is the revered **Ise Grand Shrine**, located one hour 30 minutes from Nagoya.

• See the three famous cities of **Kyoto**, **Nara** and **Osaka** in the **Kansai** area of central **Honshu**; each has contributed distinctive elements towards Japanese history and culture. Capital of Japan for over 1000 years, Kyoto remains Japan's star attraction. Founded in AD 794, the city's vast number of temples, shrines, museums and historical sites acts as a textbook to Japanese history, while her arts, crafts and cuisine rank among the country's finest. 'Must see' sights include the **Golden Pavilion** (**Kinkakuji**), the minimalist Zen rock garden of **Ryoanji**, impressive **Kiyomizu Temple** and the Imperial gardens and villas of **Katsura** and **Shugakuin** (permit required). The splendid medieval **Nijo Castle**, the vermilion-lacquered **Heian Shrine** and the Buddhist art treasures of **Sanjusangendo Temple** are also well worth visiting. The city's many historical neighbourhoods, such as the rural temples of **Arashiyama**, the textile workshops of **Nishijin** and the **Gion geisha district**, are best explored on foot. Nara, one hour south of Kyoto, is a major Buddhist centre and acted as Japan's capital during the eighth century AD. Visitors flock to see the famous 'great Buddha' of **Todaiji Temple**, the world's largest wooden structure at 57 metres high, ancient **Kasuga Shrine** and the Buddhist sculptures of **Kofukuji Temple**. The beautiful expanses of **Nara Park** are home to hundreds of sacred deer. Nearby, the venerable **Horyuji Temple** dates back to the seventh century AD and is the world's oldest wooden structure, and Japan's oldest existing Buddhist temple. One of Japan's largest cities, prosperous and commercial Osaka is renowned for its abundance of excellent restaurants, historic **Osaka Castle** and the performing arts of Kabuki and Bunraku. The city also boasts an impressive aquarium and superb **Museum of Oriental Ceramics**. The city's busy **Namba** and **Umeda districts** are renowned for their nightlife and the **Dotonburi area** is particularly vibrant after dark. **Universal Studios Japan**, a 140-acre theme park in Osaka, is enormously popular.

• In **Western Honshu**, along the coasts, the gleaming white walls of **Himeji Castle**, which dominate the city of **Himeji**, can be found. Known as the 'White Heron Castle', it is the best-preserved and most beautiful castle in Japan.

• The pleasant city of **Okayama** is known for its **black castle** and the **Korakuen Stroll Garden**, considered one of the three most beautiful in the country.

• Go to the beautiful island of **Miyajima** and see its famous red **Shinto** *torii* gateway, which seemingly floats on the sea at high tide. **Itsukushima Shrine**, the cable car up the central mountain for panoramic views and the tame deer are all major attractions.

• Along the northern coastline, make sure you see the **sand dunes of Tottori**, ancient **Izumo Taisha Shrine** and the famous coastal panorama of **Amanohashidate**.

• The historic **Ritsurin Park** in **Shikoku** is considered among the most beautiful in Japan and the mountaintop **Kotohira Shrine**, about one hour away, is extremely impressive.

• **Dogo Spa** is famous as being among the oldest in Japan. **Ibusuki Spa**, on the southern tip of **Kyushu**, also boasts some of the most famous hot springs in Japan and is renowned for its hot-sand saunas.

• On **Okinawa**, **Iriomote Island** is known for its mangrove swamps, jungle interior and rare wildlife such as the **Iriomote Wildcat**, while tiny **Taketomi** retains its rural charm.

• In the **Tohoku** region, in between bathing at medicinal **hot springs**, be dazzled by the sights of other watery paradises on display. Lake **Towada**, in the centre of **Towada-Hachimantai National Park**, is one of the most picturesque lakes in Japan, fringed by dense woods and dotted with crystal-clear waterfalls. Meanwhile, the **Zao** mountain range contains *Okama*, a mystical caldera lake, shaped like a cauldron and full up to the brim with emerald water.

Japan

Top Things To Do

- Watch some Japanese **martial arts** – or take part, if you're feeling brave. In terms of ceremonial wrestling, **sumo** and **judo** are Japan's national sports, both drawing huge crowds. There are six sumo tournaments a year, each of which lasts for 15 days. Three of them are held in **Tokyo**, and the others take place in **Fukuoka**, **Nagoya** and **Osaka**. Matches by senior wrestlers begin at 1500. Sumo training sessions can be observed between 0500 and 1030 at Kasungo Stable in Tokyo (tel: (3) 3631 1871). Judo enthusiasts can visit the Kodokan Judo Hall, 1-16-30, Kasuga, Bunkyo-ku, Tokyo (tel: (3) 3818 4172), where there is a spectators' gallery. There are opportunities for the visitor to purchase a costume and learn some of the techniques. There are separate classes for men and women and English is spoken in most large schools. More information can be obtained from the All Japan Judo Federation (website: www.judo.or.jp). **Karate**, the art of self-defence, is taught at schools in Japan and has become a very popular sport since it was introduced into the country in 1922. For further information, contact the Japan Karatedo Federation (website: www.karatedo.co.jp). **Kendo**, Japanese fencing, is practised in numerous clubs and college halls. In December, the All-Japan Championships are held in Tokyo. **Kyudo**, Japanese archery, is one of the oldest martial arts. It is closely associated with Zen Buddhism. Unlike many martial arts, it is pursued by almost as many female students as males. *Yabusame*, or archery on horseback, which was originally performed by courtiers or imperial guards in the seventh century, is today a Shinto rite for ensuring peace and good harvests. It is staged by horse riders in colourful costumes who gallop down a narrow 250m course shooting at small wooden targets set up at 80m intervals. The best-known events are at **Tsurugaoka Hachmagu shrine** in **Kamakura** on the third Sunday in April and on 16 September and at the **Shimogano Shrine** in **Kyoto** on 3 May.
- There are dozens of major **ski** resorts in Japan, especially in the **Japanese Alps** and on the northern island of **Hokkaido**. One of the great attractions is the prevalence of hot springs in the skiing areas. Various resorts at **Nagana** in **Central Honshu** offer facilities for **night-skiing**. The southernmost natural ski slope in Japan is the **Gokase Highland Ski**, in the north **Miyazaki** prefecture, which offers grass skiing out of season between late-April and late-November. Transport connections are very good, and there are sometimes railway stations within a few minutes' walk of the slopes. During the ski season, it is necessary to reserve seats on trains and buses. Although equipment is easy to hire, it can sometimes be a problem to obtain ski boots in larger sizes; skiers should telephone the resort in advance in order to check on availability.
- For **beach resorts**, on **Shikoku** is **Inland Sea National Park**, whose 600 islands are popular summer destinations, filled with enticing water. The 161 islands that make up **Okinawa** lie to the far south of Japan, like stepping stones between Kyushu and Taiwan. The subtropical climate, clear turquoise seas and many fine beaches mean that the islands have also long been a holiday favourite among the Japanese. Recently, several of the islands have also started to become well known as eco-destinations. Numerous coral reefs offer excellent **diving** opportunities, with many resorts catering to enthusiasts. Okinawa Island, the main island of the group, has a number of famous resorts such as **Manza Beach** and **Onna Beach**, offering white sands and **watersports**. The fantastic formations of the **Gyokusendo Caves** are also a popular attraction. The island retains many reminders of the fierce fighting that took place there during World War II, and the southern coastline is dotted with war memorials. **Ishigaki Island** has great diving, **snorkelling** and folkcrafts and is a good base from which to explore the remoter islands.
- Between January and March, take a **whale**- and/or **dolphin-watching** tour, departing from the town of **Kasasa**.
- **Cycle** through fields during the **cherry blossom season** in April and May, or October and November when autumnal colours adorn Japan. During this time, **flower festivals** occur everywhere.
- **Sapporo**, Hokkaido's vibrant capital, is famous for its great nightlife and the extraordinary **Snow Festival** in February, which lasts for seven days, and is marked by huge, elaborate snow and ice sculptures.
- Book a seat to see some *bunraku*, a unique form of **puppet theatre**, and the very best in traditional entertainment. Here, the conflicts between established ethical ideas and the reality of love and life amongst ordinary folk is depicted, all performed along with a ballad-chanting *joruri*, which accompanies three-stringed *shamisen* instruments. For more traditional forms of theatre, *can noh* and *kabuki* are dramatic forms that can be seen in certain towns sporadically, with participants attired in medieval costumes. Kabuki is usually performed on a magnificently colourful stage. Noh is highly stylised theatre, exuding the world of *yugen*, a deeply aesthetic value based on a profound and refined beauty that goes beyond words and concrete shapes.
- The most fascinating and colourful of Japan's religious festivals takes place in Kyoto, the old imperial capital. The **Gion Festival** reaches its climax on 16-17 July. A street parade takes place with the participants dressed in fine costumes and carrying portable shrines. This is the largest festival in Kyoto and dates back to the ninth century. The large floats depict ancient themes. The **Aoi** (or **Hollyhock**) **Festival** on 15 May dates back to the sixth century. The procession, consisting of imperial messengers in oxcarts followed by a retinue of 600 people dressed in traditional costume, leaves at around 1000 from the imperial palace and heads for the **Shimogamo-jinja shrine** where ceremonies take place. It then proceeds to **Kamigamo-jinja shrine**. The **Jidai Festival** (**Festival of the Ages**) is of more recent origin, though still splendid to watch. More than 2000 people parade through the town dressed in costumes dating from different periods.
- Japan offers the very best of **shopping** experiences. In Tokyo alone, the **Ginza** is one of Asia's shopping paradises. Prices are high but the selection and presentation are superb. There are also plenty of markets for the budget-minded, such as the massive waterfront **Tsukiji Fish Market**. Cheap eats and bargains galore are also to be found at the raucous **Ameyoko Market**.
- Go **hiking** in areas such as the **Nikko National Park**, full of mountain hot springs, the **Fuji-Hakone-Izu National Park**, a recreational paradise offering hot spring resorts and good facilities for camping, **Honshu Island**, known as 'the Roof of Japan' and a popular natural playground, and the beautiful, mountainous island of **Yakushima**, a National Park renowned for its primeval cedar forests and hiking trails.
- At **Hakone**, take a **cable car** over volcanic landscapes of boiling mud; look down and see sightseeing boats ply scenic **Lake Ashi**.
- At **Sendai**, a lively, modern city, watch the famous **Tanabata Star Festival**, when numerous bamboo branches are decorated with colourful paper stripes.
- Traverse **Sado Island**: rural, unspoilt, and home to the world-famous **Kodo Drummers**. The Kodo Drummers have often been referred to as 'samurai percussionists', since their world-famous troupe is selected on the basis of a rigorous two-year training apprenticeship in a remote area deep in the mountains, and adherence to a strict way of personal conduct.
- Have a night out on the town in Tokyo, especially in **Akasaka** and **Roppongi**, playgrounds for the nearby banking and governmental districts which offer vibrant **nightlife** of every kind, from **geisha tea houses** to discos. For youth culture, fashion and trendy dining, **Harajuku** and **Shibuya** are the places to see and be seen.
- Take part in a **Japanese tea ceremony**; you can arrange to do so through the tourist information centres in Kyoto and Tokyo. It takes place in a room designed and designated for tea, called a *chashitsu*. The small number of guests are first led to a water-sprinkled garden devoid of flowers, called a *roji*. Here, the guests are encouraged to rid themselves of the main dust of the world. No words are spoken as the guests are led, after a short while, through the *chumon*, a door that signifies the exit from the coarse physical world into the spiritual world of tea. The door is particularly low so that all guests must bow and crouch to enter. Inside the actual teahouse, there is usually little decoration except for a *kakemono* (scroll painting), which reveals the theme of the ceremony. Once guests are seated, greetings are exchanged and incense and a fire may be lit. A meal called a *chakaiseki* may be served, often involving sake and grilled foods. Tea is then served, steeped in symbolism long entrenched in the ceremony's traditions. Upon conclusion, guests usually politely express their admiration for their tea and the art of their host.

TOURIST INFORMATION

Japan National Tourist Organisation (JNTO) in the UK
Heathcoat House, 20 Saville Row, London W1S 3PR, UK
Tel: (020) 7734 9638.
Website: www.seejapan.co.uk

Japan Information and Culture Center in the USA
Lafayette Center III, 1155 21st Street,
NW, Washington, DC 20036, USA
Tel: (202) 238 6949.
Website: www.us.emb-japan.go.jp/jicc

Japan National Tourist Organisation (JNTO) in the USA
1 Rockefeller Plaza, Suite 1250, New York, NY 10020, USA
Tel: (212) 757 5640.
Website: www.japantravelinfo.com

Credit: ©Japan National Tourist Organisation

Entertainment

FOOD & DRINK: Japanese cuisine, now popular in the West, involves very sensitive flavours, fresh crisp vegetables and an absence of richness. The best place to try sushi is a *Kaiten Sushi Bar*, where many varieties pass the customer on a conveyor belt allowing complete choice over which delicacies to try, at more reasonable prices than a traditional Sushi Bar. Fine Oriental food (Korean – very hot – and Chinese) is served in restaurants. An amazing number and variety of international restaurants are also available, catering for every possible taste and budget, from French and Italian to Chinese, Indian and Thai. Western dishes in expensive places are good, but cheaper restaurants may be disappointing. The Japanese are very fond of original Scotch whisky, but this is both very expensive and highly sought after, therefore Japanese versions of this drink are often served.

Things to know: Restaurants have table service and in some places it is customary to remove footwear. Waiter service is common in bars. There are no licensing hours. Drinking is subject to long-standing rituals of politeness. The hostess will pour a drink for the visitor, and will insist on the visitor's glass being full. It is also appreciated if the visitor pours drinks for the host, but it is bad manners for a visitor to pour one for himself.

National dishes:
- *Teriyaki* (marinated beef/chicken/fish seared on a hot plate).
- *Sukiyaki* (thin slices of beef, tofu and vegetables cooked in soy sauce and then dipped in egg).
- *Tempura* (deep fried seafood and vegetables).
- Sushi (slices of raw seafood placed on light and vinegary rice balls – very tasty and refreshing).
- *Sashimi* (slices of raw seafood dipped in soy sauce).

National drinks:
- Green tea is by far the most popular beverage amongst the Japanese. The quality of the tea varies greatly from *houjicha* (a common brown-coloured tea) to *matcha* (a bitter green tea used in tea ceremonies).
- *Sake*, rice wine served hot or cold according to the season, is strong and distinctively fresh tasting. • *Shochu*, a strong aquavit, is an acquired taste.
- Japanese wines are worth trying once.
- Beer – similar to lager – is recommended. Popular brands are *Asahi*, *Kirin*, *Sapporo* and *Suntory*.

Tipping: Tips are never expected since a 10 to 15 per cent service charge is added to the bill at hotels, ryokan and restaurants; where a visitor wishes to show particular appreciation of a service, money should not be given in the form of loose change but rather as a small financial gift. Special printed envelopes can be bought for financial gifts of this type.

NIGHTLIFE: Tokyo has an abundance of cinemas, theatres, bars, coffee shops, discos and nightclubs. A wide range of bars are available, from the upmarket and stylish to cheap street stalls. In the summer, rooftop beer gardens are popular. Some clubs have hostesses who expect to be bought drinks and snacks. In bigger nightclubs and bars, a basic hostess charge is levied. However, there are thousands of other bars and clubs. In Tokyo there are concerts of all styles of music almost every night. Foreign opera companies, ballet companies, orchestras and rock/pop stars visit Japan all year round. Some live jazz houses are also available. For those who would like to try the traditional Japanese performing arts, there is *kabuki* and *noh* theatre in Tokyo. It is advisable to purchase the tickets in advance because shows are quickly sold out. *Karaoke* bars are a very popular form of entertainment in Japan.

SHOPPING: A blend of Oriental goods and Western sales techniques confronts the shopper, particularly at the big department stores, which are more like exhibitions than shops. Playgrounds for children are available. Special purchases include *kimonos*, *mingei* (local crafts including kites and folk toys); *Kyoto* silks, fans, screens, dolls; religious articles such as Shinto and Buddhist artefacts; paper lanterns; lacquerware; hi-fi equipment, cameras, televisions and other electronic equipment. Bargaining is not usual.

Tax exemptions: These are available in authorised tax-free stores. Certain items costing more than ¥10,000 are exempt from tax. **Shopping hours**: 1000-1900/2000 every day of the week and on public holidays.

A B C D E F G H I J K L M N O P Q R S T U V W X Y Z

Credit: ©Japan National Tourist Organisation

Business

- **GDP:** US$4295 billion (2003).
- **Main exports:** Transport equipment, motor vehicles, semi-conductors, electrical machinery and chemicals.
- **Main imports:** Machinery and equipment, fuel, foodstuffs, chemicals, textiles and raw materials.
- **Main trade partners:** USA, China (PR), Taiwan (China), Korea (Rep), Germany and Hong Kong (SAR).

ECONOMY: After suffering massive destruction during World War II, Japan was the economic phenomenon of the late 20th century. At US$4000 billion, the country's GDP ranks second in the world after the USA. This has been achieved through several decades of sustained growth (although this period has now ended – see below) driven by judicious application of import controls and consistently high domestic investment, coupled with an aggressive export drive orchestrated by the powerful Ministry of International Trade and Industry (MITI). The structure of the Japanese domestic economy revolves around a group of large multi-product corporations (many of which have since become global household names), linked in loose alliances (known as *keiretsu*) with banks and finance houses. The corporations are serviced with components and raw materials by a plethora of small firms with low overheads and labour costs, and a well-honed distribution system (many of these lower-level processes are now carried out in the 'tiger economies' of the Pacific Basin).
The model worked superbly until the early 1990s, when competition from abroad and excessive lending by the banks began to put the Japanese economy under a set of pressures to which it has proved quite unable to respond. The extent of the problem became apparent initially with the 1991 property crash and, more spectacularly, with the 1997 Asian financial crisis. In the following years the economy has stagnated, often struggling to reach 1 per cent growth annually. Unemployment, a comparative novelty in a country where jobs were typically guaranteed for life, reached 6 per cent. Successive Governments made little more than token efforts at structural reform. The financial sector continues to operate much as before. The Koizumi Government has tabled a set of proposals, which include deregulation and much-needed reform as well as a package designed to kick-start the economy and create 5 million jobs. Unfortunately, its plans are being undermined by the Government's poor fiscal position (Government debt is 150 per cent of GDP – by way of comparison, conditions for Eurozone countries require that the figure not exceed 60 per cent). The economy is now recovering strongly; over the past year, the growth rate has averaged four per cent due to booming exports and business investment, plus solid growth in private consumption. Unemployment has also begun to fall, dwindling to 4.7 per cent in 2004.
Agriculture is the only sector of the economy that does not measure up to Western standards in terms of technology and management, and remains relatively inefficient and heavily protected by the Government. (This is a quirk of the

Japanese electoral system, which affords a disproportionate number of parliamentary seats to rural areas.) Rice, potatoes, sugar and citrus fruits are the main crops. The manufacturing industry is still important, particularly vehicles and electronic goods, although traditional industries such as coal mining, shipbuilding and steel are also sizeable and, unlike many of their Western counterparts, profitable. Overall, industry contributes 35 per cent of economic output – a larger proportion than the world's other leading economies. The service sector grew rapidly in the 1980s as the economy matured and Japan became a major force in the international economy. The emphasis in Japanese trade thus switched from manufactured goods to export of services and 'invisibles', such as finance and insurance. In the international arena, Japan is a leading member of the Organisation of Economic Co-operation and Development (OECD) and the Asia-Pacific Economic Co-operation (APEC) forum.
BUSINESS ETIQUETTE: A large supply of visiting cards printed in English and Japanese is essential. Cards can be quickly printed on arrival with Japanese translation on the reverse side. Appointments should be made in advance and, because of the formality, visits should consist of more than a few days. Punctuality is important. Business discussions are often preceded by tea and are usually very formal.
Office hours: Mon-Fri 0900-1700. Some offices are open Sat 0900-1200.
CONFERENCES/CONVENTIONS: The Japan Convention Bureau is a division of the Japan National Tourist Organisation (see *Top Things To Do*); its *Convention Planner's Guide to Japan* lists 35 cities with conference facilities including Hiroshima, Kyoto, Nagasaki, Osaka, Tokyo and Yokohama. Kyoto has proved to be one of the most popular locations for international meetings over the last few years.

COMMERCIAL INFORMATION

Japanese Chamber of Commerce in the UK
Salisbury House, 29 Finsbury Circus,
London EC2M 5QQ, UK
Tel: (020) 7628 0069.

Nippon Shoko Kaigi-sho (The Japan Chamber of Commerce and Industry)
2-2 Marunouchi 3 Chome, Chiyoda-ku, Tokyo 100-0005, Japan
Tel: (3) 3283 7824.
Website: www.jcci.or.jp

JETRO (Japan External Trade Organisation)
Ark Mari Building, 6F 12-32, Akasaka 1-Chrome, Minato-Ku, Tokyo 107-6006, Japan
Tel: (3) 3582 5511.
Website: www.jetro.go.jp

Japan Convention Bureau
2-10-1 Yurakucho, Chiyoda-ku,
Tokyo 100-0006, Japan
Tel: (3) 3216 2905.
Website: www.jnto.go.jp

Jordan

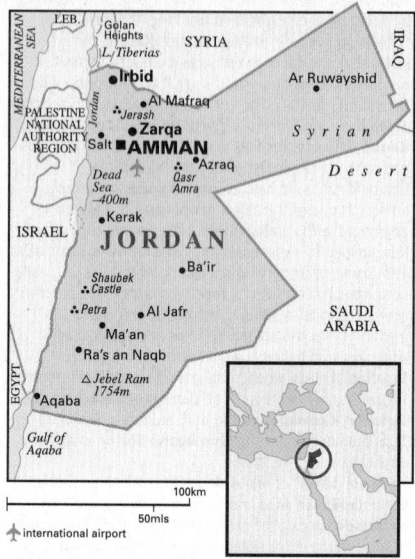

Location: Middle East.

Time: GMT + 2 (GMT + 3 between October and March - dates vary).

Overview

Although a small country, the Hashemite Kingdom of Jordan has played a significant role in the struggle for power in the Middle East, partly because of its strategic location at the crossroads of what Christians, Jews and Muslims call the Holy Land.
After World War I, the area east of the Jordan River, known as Transjordania, fell to the British. Their mandate ceased in 1946, at which point Transjordania attained full independence.
Jordanian history and politics since independence have been dominated by the Palestinian issue and relations with Israel. When war broke out in 1948 between the newly-declared state of Israel and the Palestinians, backed by the forces from neighbouring Arab countries, the Jordanian army occupied a 6000sq km area of Palestine bounded by the west bank of the River Jordan.
Until a major change in Jordanian policy in 1988, the West Bank comprised three of Jordan's eight provinces, while over half of the Jordanian population claimed Palestinian origin. Jordan lost the West Bank after the Six-Day War of 1967, and gained thousands of Palestinian refugees.
Then in 1990, another of Jordan's other neighbours, Iraq, became the cause of major problems for the Jordanians when Saddam Hussein invaded Kuwait. The ensuing Gulf War of 1991 proved a political and economic disaster for Jordan. Traditionally friendly to both the US and Iraq and, economically reliant on both, Jordan lost out with both sides through its failure to give wholehearted support for the US-led coalition, and by accepting large numbers of Iraqi refugees. The arrival of King Abdullah to the throne in 1999 meant that the long-awaited call for political, social and economic reform could be put in place.
Unlike many of its neighbours, Jordan does not have any oil and the economy depends largely on services and tourism. The country is dense with history. Above the layers of antiquity lies a land of mesmerising beauty and contrast. The fertile Jordan Valley and the remote and immense desert canyons are not to be missed. Here are splendid castles and hunting lodges, the haunting wilderness of Wadi Rum and restful spas. Here, too, are monuments from every age of humanity, crowned by the rock-carved city of Petra, a UNESCO World Heritage Site.
Jordan also boasts another wonder of the Middle-Eastern world: the Dead Sea, 392m (1286ft) below sea level, and the lowest point on earth, where even the non-swimmer can float.

General Information

AREA: 89,342 sq km (34,495 sq miles; not including West Bank).

POPULATION: 5.7 million (UN, 2005). The West Bank is now administered by the Palestinian National Authority; see *Israel* section for details of area and population.

POPULATION DENSITY: 63.8 per sq km.

CAPITAL: Amman. **Population:** 2.02 million (2002).

GEOGRAPHY: Jordan shares borders with Israel, the Syrian Arab Republic, Iraq and Saudi Arabia. The Dead Sea is to the northwest and the Red Sea to the southwest. A high plateau extends 324km (201 miles) from the Syrian Arab Republic to Ras en Naqab in the south with the capital of Amman at a height of 800m (2625ft). Northwest of the capital are undulating hills, some forested, others cultivated. The Dead Sea depression, 400m (1300ft) below sea level in the west, is the lowest point on earth. The River Jordan connects the Dead Sea with Lake Tiberias (Israel). To the west of Jordan is the Palestinian National Authority Region. The east of the country is mainly desert. Jordan has a tiny stretch of Red Sea coast, centred on Aqaba.

GOVERNMENT: Constitutional Monarchy since 1952. **Head of State:** King Abdullah Ibn al-Hussein al-Hashimi since 1999. **Head of Government:** Prime Minister Dr Adnan Badran since 2005. **Recent history:** Weeks before his death, King Hussein made his eldest son, Abdullah, Crown Prince. He ascended the throne on King Hussein's death on 7 February 1999. King Abdullah has gone to great lengths to plan long-term improvements to the economy of Jordan. He is one of a new generation of Arab leaders in favour of social and economic reform. He has backed the promotion of women's rights, information technology, democracy, liberal economic policies and integration with the rest of the world. Parliamentary elections last took place in June 2003 under a one-person-one-vote multi-member constituency system with quotas for women, minority ethnic and religious groups. On 5 April 2005, Faisal al-Fayez resigned as Prime Minister. The King appointed Dr Adnan Badran, a former Minister of Higher Education, as the new Prime Minister. He soon appointed a new Cabinet.

LANGUAGE: Arabic is the official language. English is widely spoken in the cities. French, German, Italian and Spanish are also spoken.

RELIGION: Over 90 per cent Sunni Muslim, with Christian and Shi'i Muslim minorities.

ELECTRICITY: 220 volts AC, 50Hz. Round two-pin plugs are used. Lamp sockets are screw-type, and there is a wide range of wall sockets.

SOCIAL CONVENTIONS: Handshaking is the customary form of greeting. Jordanians are proud of their Arab culture, and hospitality here is a matter of great importance. Visitors are made to feel very welcome and Jordanians are happy to act as hosts and guides, and are keen to inform tourists about their traditions and culture. Islam always plays an important role in society and it is essential that Muslim beliefs are respected (see the *World of Islam* appendix). Arabic coffee will normally be served continuously during social occasions. To signal that no more is wanted, slightly tilt the cup when handing it back, otherwise it will be refilled. A small gift is quite acceptable in return for hospitality. Women are expected to dress modestly and beachwear must only be worn at the beach or poolside. **Photography:** It is polite to ask permission to take photographs of people and livestock; in some places photography is forbidden.

Climate

Hot and dry summers with cool evenings. The Jordan Valley below sea level is warm during winter and extremely hot in summer. Rain falls between November and March, while colder weather conditions occur in December/January.

Required clothing: Lightweight cottons and linens are advised between May and September. Warmer clothes are necessary for winter and cool summer evenings. Rainwear is needed from November to April.

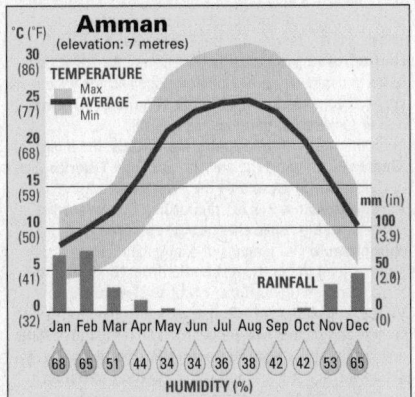

Amman (elevation: 7 metres)

Communications

Telephone: IDD service is available within cities, with direct dialling to most countries. Country code: 962 (followed by 6 for Amman). There are telephone and facsimile connections to Israel from Jordan. Card phones are available in most big cities and major tourist sites, cards can be purchased at numerous shops. International calls from hotels and post offices carry a three-minute minimum charge.

Mobile telephone: Roaming agreements exist with many international mobile phone companies. Coverage is good.

Internet: There are Internet cafes in Amman, Aqabam Jerash and Jordan.

Post: Packages should be left opened for customs officials. The Central Post Office in Amman is the only post office where packages can be sent. Airmail to Western Europe takes three to five days. For a higher charge, there is a rapid service guaranteeing delivery within 24 hours to around 22 countries. Post office hours: Sat-Thurs 0800-1800 in summer and 0700-1700 in winter, Fri 0700-1300.

MEDIA: Jordan is trying to persuade Arab commercial satellite broadcasters to relocate to its media free zone, though investors remain concerned about safeguards against censorship. In 2003, the government repealed legislation that provided for jail terms for harming the King's reputation or for inciting strikes, criminal activity or 'illegal' gatherings.

Press: Arabic-language daily publications include *Ad Dustour*, *Al Ra'y*, *Al Ghadd* and *Al Arab al Yawm*. The English-language newspapers are *The Jordan Times* (daily) and *The Star* (weekly).

TV: State-run Jordan Radio and Television operates main network *Channel One*, sports network *Channel Two*, film network *Channel Three* and *Jordan Satellite Channel*.

Radio: State-run *Jordan Radio and Television* provides services in Arabic, English and French. *Radio Fann* is an FM entertainment station run by armed forces. *Mood FM* and *Play 99.6* are private, pop music stations. The *BBC Arabic Service* and *Radio Monte Carlo Middle East* are available on FM in Amman and in northern Jordan.

Passport/Visa

	Passport Required?	Visa Required?	Return Ticket? Required?
Full British	Yes	Yes/1	No
Australian	Yes	Yes/1	No
Canadian	Yes	Yes/1	No
USA	Yes	Yes/1	No
Other EU	Yes	Yes/1	No
Japanese	Yes	Yes/1	No

Note: *Regulations and requirements may be subject to change at short notice, and you are advised to contact the appropriate diplomatic or consular authority before finalising travel arrangements. Any numbers in the chart refer to the footnotes below.*

PASSPORTS: Passport valid for six months required by all.

VISAS: Required by all except the following:
(a) nationals of Bahrain, Egypt, Iraq, Kuwait, Oman, Qatar, Saudi Arabia, Syrian Arab Republic, United Arab Emirates and Yemen for maximum stays of one month (extensions may be obtained at the nearest police station);
(b) transit passengers continuing their journey to another country by the same or first connecting aircraft within 24 hours provided holding valid onward or return documentation and not leaving the airport. Transit visas can only be issued at Jordanian airports/airlines and not at embassies or consulates.

Note: 1. (a) Nationals of certain countries – including all European Union countries, Australia, Canada, Japan, New Zealand and the USA – can obtain visas on arrival at the airport in Jordan. Multiple-entry visas can only be obtained at the nearest Embassy/Consulate. (b) For information about land border crossings, see the *Travel - International* section or contact the Embassy.

Types of visa and cost: *Tourist*, *Transit* and *Business*: £11 (single-entry); £21 (multiple-entry).

Validity: Validity varies according to nationality. For Australian, Canadian, UK and US nationals, visas are valid as follows: *Tourist*: Three months for single-entry if obtained from the Embassy or two weeks if obtained at the airport, these can be extended at any Jordanian police station; Multiple-entry are valid for six months; *Business*: Three months. After the first two weeks of stay, all visitors holding a visa must report to the nearest police station.

Application to: Consulate (or Consular section at Embassy); see *Passport/Visa Information*.

Application requirements: (a) Completed application form. (b) Passport valid for at least six months with at least one blank page. (c) One recent passport-size photo. (d) Stamped, self-addressed, recorded or registered envelope if applying by post. (e) Fee (only cash or postal orders are accepted). *Business* (a)-(e) and, (f) Company letter supporting application.

Working days required: Two if applying in person; two weeks by post once application has been received.

Note: Nationals of Afghanistan, Albania, Angola, Bangladesh, Belize, Benin, Bosnia & Herzegovina, Botswana, Burkina Faso, Burundi, Cambodia, Cameroon, Central African Republic, Chad, China, Congo (Dem Rep), Congo (Rep), Colombia, Côte d'Ivoire, Cuba, Djibouti, Eritrea, Ethiopia, Gabon, Gambia, Ghana, Guinea, Guinea-Bissau, Guyana, India, Iran, Laos, Lebanon, Liberia, Kenya, Macedonia (Former Yugoslav Republic of), Madagascar, Maldives, Mali, Mauritania, Mongolia, Mozambique, Namibia, Niger, Nigeria, Pakistan, Papua New Guinea, The Philippines, Senegal, Sierra Leone, Somalia, Sri Lanka, Sudan, Tanzania, Thailand, Togo, Uganda, Vietnam Zaire and Zambia are required to seek approval from the Ministry of Interior in order to obtain a visa and therefore should allow six to eight weeks for their applications to be processed. Contact the Embassy for further information (see *Passport/Visa Information*).

Temporary residence: Apply to Embassy; see *Passport/Visa Information*.

PASSPORT/VISA INFORMATION

Embassy of the Hashemite Kingdom of Jordan in the UK
6 Upper Phillimore Gardens, London W8 7HA, UK
Tel: (020) 7937 3685.
Website: www.jordanembassyuk.org
Opening hours: Mon-Fri 0900-1200 (consulate enquiries); 1400-1500 (visa collection).

Embassy of the Hashemite Kingdom of Jordan in the USA
3504 International Drive, NW,
Washington, DC 20008, USA
Tel: (202) 966 2664 *or* 966 2861 (consular section).
Website: www.jordanembassyus.org

Money

Currency: Dinar (JOD) = 100 piaters or 1000 fils. Notes are in denominations of JOD50, 20, 10, 5 and 1, and 500 fils. Coins are in denominations of 1JOD, 500, 250, 100, 50, 25, 10 and 5 fils.

Currency exchange: Foreign currencies can be exchanged easily in banks and bureaux de change. Most hotels also provide exchange facilities. The daily exchange rates are published in local newspapers.

Credit & debit cards: American Express, Visa, Diners Club and MasterCard are accepted in hotels restaurants and larger shops. Check with your credit and debit card company for details of merchant acceptability and other services which may be available. There are some ATMs but only some accept foreign cards.

Traveller's cheques: Those issued by UK banks are accepted by licensed banks and bureaux de change. To avoid additional exchange rate charges, travellers are advised to take traveller's cheques in US Dollars.

Currency restrictions: The import and export of local or foreign currency is unrestricted.

Banking hours: Sat-Thurs 0830-1500. Hours during Ramadan are 0830-1000, although some banks open in the afternoon.

Exchange rate indicators:
Rate at time of publishing
£1.00=   JOD1.26
$1.00=   JOD0.71

Duty Free

The following goods may be imported into Jordan by people 18 years of age and older without incurring customs duty:

200 cigarettes or 25 cigars or 200g of tobacco (a charge of JD3.75 for each additional 200 cigarettes, up to a maximum of 2000); 1l of alcohol (a charge of JD2.91 for each additional litre, up to a maximum of 4l); one or two opened bottles of perfume and a reasonable amount of eau-de-cologne or lotion in opened bottles for personal use only; gifts up to the value of JD50 or the equivalent of US$150.

Prohibited items: Narcotics.

Restricted items: Firearms, sporting guns and other weapons require prior approval from both country of origin and destination. They may be carried as checked baggage only.

Public Holidays

Below are listed Public Holidays for the January 2006-June 2007 period.

2006: Jan 1 New Year's Day. **Jan 10** Eid al-Adha (Feast of the Sacrifice). **Jan 31** Islamic New Year. **Apr 11** Mawlid al-Nabi (Birth of the Prophet). **Apr 14** Good Friday. **Apr 17** Easter Monday. **May 1** Labour Day. **May 25** Independence Day. **Jun 9** Accession of HM King Abdullah. **Jun 10** Army Day. **Sep 12** Isra wa al-Miraj (Prophet's Night Journey). **Oct 22-24** Eid al-Fitr (End of Ramadan). **Nov 14** King Hussein Remembrance Day. **Dec 25** Christmas. **Dec 31** New Year's Eve; Eid al-Adha (Feast of the Sacrifice).

2007: Jan 1 New Year's Day. **Jan 20** Islamic New Year. **Mar 31** Mawlid al-Nabi (Birth of the Prophet). **Apr 6** Good Friday. **Apr 9** Easter Monday. **May 1** Labour Day. **May 25** Independence Day. **Jun 9** Accession of HM King Abdullah. **Jun 10** Army Day.

Note: (a) Christmas and Easter holidays are only observed by Christian business establishments. (b) Muslim festivals are timed according to local sightings of various phases of the moon and the dates given above are approximations. During the lunar month of Ramadan that precedes Eid al-Fitr, Muslims fast during the day and feast at night and normal business patterns may be interrupted. Many restaurants are closed during the day and there may be restrictions on smoking and drinking. Some disruption may continue into Eid al-Fitr itself. Eid al-Fitr and Eid al-Adha may last anything from two to 10 days, depending on the region. For more information, see the *World of Islam* appendix.

Health

	Special Precautions?	Certificate Required?
Yellow Fever	No	1
Cholera	No	No
Typhoid & Polio	2	N/A
Malaria	No	N/A

***Note:** Regulations and requirements may be subject to change at short notice, and you are advised to contact your doctor well in advance of your intended date of departure. Any numbers in the chart refer to the footnotes below.*

1: A yellow fever vaccination certificate is required from travellers over one year of age coming from infected areas.
2: Immunisation against typhoid and poliomyelitis is often recommended.

Food & drink: Water that is not bottled should never be drunk unless it has first been boiled or otherwise sterilised. Milk should not be consumed unless bought in a container stating that it has been pasteurised. Avoid dairy products which are likely to have been made from unboiled milk. Food and water in rural areas may carry increased risk. Only eat well-cooked meat and fish, preferably served hot. Salad and mayonnaise may carry increased risk. Vegetables should be cooked and fruit peeled.

Other risks: *Hepatitis A* may occur, *hepatitis B* is endemic. Inoculations for *tetanus* are also recommended. *Heat* and *dehydration* may become a health hazard for pilgrims on their way to Mecca and Medina. Precautions should be taken.

Rabies is present. For those at high risk, vaccination before arrival should be considered. If you are bitten, seek medical advice without delay. For more information, consult the *Health* appendix.

Health care: Health insurance is recommended. There are excellent hospitals in large towns and cities, with clinics in many villages.

Notes: An HIV test is mandatory for anyone planning to stay longer than 14 days.

Travel - International

AIR:

The national airline is *Royal Jordanian Airlines (RJ)* (website: www.rja.com.jo). There are flights to 50 destinations in the Middle East, Europe, North America, the Far East and Asia.

Approximate flight times: From *London* to Amman is five hours.

Main airport: *Queen Alia International (AMM)* is 35km (22 miles) southeast of the capital. *To/from the airport*: The airport is connected by a good highway (travel time - approximately 40 minutes). There is a regular bus service to Amman every 30 minutes (travel time - approximately 50 minutes), and taxis are also available. *Facilities*: Duty free shops, bank/bureau de change, eating and shopping facilities and car hire.

Departure tax: JD5 for individual tourists which is included in the airline ticket, JD25 for Jordanian nationals on international departures. Transit passengers are exempt.

SEA:

The only port is *Aqaba*, which is on the cruise itineraries for *Cunard*, *P&O* and *Swan Hellenic*. Car and passenger ferries from Aqaba to Cairo and Aqaba to Nuweiba operate twice-daily and there is also a high-speed hydrofoil service. There is a weekly passenger service to Suez and Jeddah. Contact *Telstar Maritime Agencies* (tel: (6) 462 4104; website: www.telstarmaritime.com).

Departure tax: JD5 for foreigners and JD6 for nationals of Jordan.

RAIL:

The Hijaz Railway operates twice a week on the old Ottoman track between Amman and Damascus (Syrian Arab Republic).

ROAD:

There are roads into the Syrian Arab Republic via Ramtha or Jaber. The route to/from the Syrian Arab Republic to Western Europe is through Turkey. Driving time from Amman to Damascus is four hours. From Egypt, there is a ferry connection from Nuweiba to Aqaba (visa should be obtained in advance). Multiple-entry visas may be needed. A coach service runs from Damascus to Irbid or Amman. There is a share-taxi service from Amman to Damascus. Public buses and coaches run from Amman to Damascus, Baghdad, Cairo, Egypt, Iraq, Istanbul, Saudi Arabia and Syria daily, as well as to Allenby Bridge for the crossing to the Palestinian National Authority Region. To cross, a visa is required, and it should be obtained in advance. Further border crossings to Israel are at Sheikh Hussein Bridge (Jordan River Crossing) near Lake Tiberias in the north and Wadi Arabah (Arava Crossing) in the south, the latter linking Jordan to the Israeli Red Sea resort of Eilat. Most nationalities can obtain a visa at the border; for information on which nationals require a visa, contact a travel agent in Jordan. Some cars are permitted to cross these two borders, subject to various rules and regulations; for further details, contact the Jordanian authorities.

Road departure tax: JD4.

Travel - Internal

AIR:

Royal Wings operates regular flights from Amman to Aqaba (tel: (6) 487 5201; website: www.royalwings.com.jo). It is also possible to hire executive jets and helicopters.

RAIL:

There is no longer a reliable public railway service.

ROAD:

Main roads are good (there are nearly 3000km (1900 miles) of paved roads in the country), but desert tracks should be avoided. It is important to make sure that the vehicle is in good repair if travelling on minor roads or tracks. Take plenty of water and follow local advice carefully. In case of breakdown, contact the Automobile Association. **Regulations**: Traffic drives on the right. Speed limits are 60kph/38mph (cities), 80 kph/50mph (country roads) and 120kph/75mph (motorways). There are frequent passport controls along the Red Sea and travellers are advised to have their papers ready. **Bus**: Services are efficient and cheap. *Alpha*, *JETT* and *Petra* all operate modern, air-conditioned fleets. **Taxi**: All taxis operate a meter and can be hired for the day. Share-taxi service to all towns on fixed routes is also available and can be hired for private use. Share-taxis to Petra should be booked in advance owing to demand. **Car hire**: Major international car rental companies and a number of local companies operate services in the main towns, including Amman and Aqaba, available also from hotels and travel agents. Drivers are available for the day. **Documentation**: National driving licences are accepted if they have been issued at least one year before travel. However, an International Driving Permit is recommended. Visitors are not allowed to drive a vehicle with normal Jordanian plates unless they have a Jordanian driving licence.

Note: When using routes which go near the Israeli border (and even when sailing or swimming in the Red Sea without a guide), the traveller should always have all papers in order and within reach.

URBAN:

There are conventional buses and extensive fixed-route 'Servis' (share-taxis, most seating up to seven) in Amman. The 'Servis' are licensed, with a standard fare scale, but there are no fixed pick-up or set-down points. Vehicles often fill up at central or outer terminal points and then run non-stop.

Travel Advice

Most visits to Jordan are trouble-free. However, there is a high threat from terrorism.

Travellers planning to travel to Jordan should take sensible precautions for their personal security arrangements throughout their visit.

Developments in the region could affect the security situation.

Travellers should take extra care at the borders with Israel and Iraq. Travellers should take particular care when using Jordanian service taxis to cross into neighbouring countries. This advice is based on information provided by the Foreign & Commonwealth Office in the UK. It is correct at time of publishing. As the situation can change rapidly, visitors are advised to contact the following organisations for the latest travel advice:

British Foreign and Commonwealth Office
Tel: (0845) 850 2829.
Website: www.fco.gov.uk

US Department of State
Website: http://travel.state.gov/travel

Accommodation

There are several high-standard hotels throughout the country, most of which are run by well-known international chains. Amman and Aqaba, in particular, have a good choice of hotels. Hotels are fully booked during business periods so reservations are advised. Rates can be negotiated in Winter. All rates are subject to 20 per cent tax and service. There are serviced apartments available. **Grading**: Hotels are graded from **5- to 1-star**. 5- and 4-star hotels have discos and nightclubs with live music. Prices are fixed by the Ministry of Tourism, which can also deal with complaints. For further information, contact the Ministry of Tourism or the Jordan Tourism Board (see *Top Things To Do*).

Top Things To See

- The capital since 1921, **Amman**, often referred to as the 'white city', features remains from the Roman, Greek and Ottoman Turk occupations. Do not mis the main attraction, the **Roman amphitheatre** from the second century AD in the centre of the city. Then head to the **Jebel el Qalat** (citadel) which houses the **Archaeological Museum**, the **National Gallery of Fine Arts** and the **Jordan Museum of Popular Traditions**.
- There are three routes from Amman to Aqaba, the most picturesque being the **King's Highway**, the whole length of which is dotted with places of interest. **Madaba** and nearby **Mount Nebo**, where Moses is said to have struck the rock, were both flourishing Byzantine towns and have churches and well-preserved mosaics. In Madaba, there are also ancient maps of sixth-century Palestine, a museum and an old family carpet-making industry which uses ancient looms.
- Off the Highway is **Mukawir**, a small village near the ruins of **Machaerus of Herod Antipas**, where Salome performed her fateful dance. From the summit of nearby **Qasr al-Meshneque**, where St John was beheaded, is a magnificent view of the Dead Sea, and sometimes even of Jerusalem and the Mount of Olives.
- Nearby, see the hot mineral water springs of **Zarqa Main**. Rugged scenery characterises this area: deep gorges, waterfalls, white rocks, small oases, birds and wild flowers.
- Further south, on the Highway, discover **Karak**, a beautiful medieval town surrounded by high walls and with one of the Crusader Castles.
- Other places of historical, scenic or religious interest along the route before Petra include **Mazar** and **Mutah**, **Edomite Qasr Buseirah**, **Tafila** and the magnificent crusader hill fortress, **Shaubek Castle**.
- At **Iraq al-Amir**, see the only **Hellenistic palace** still to be found in the Middle East.
- Go to **Jerash**, a magnificent Graeco-Roman city on an ancient site, beautifully preserved by the desert sands. Jerash is justly famous for the **Triumphal Arch**, the **Hippodrome**, the great elliptical forum, the theatres, baths and gateways, the Roman bridge and the wide street of columns that lead to the **Temple of Artemis.** *Son et lumière* programmes are available.
- In the far north of the country, **Umm Qais**, the Biblical '**Gadara**', dominates the area around **Lake Tiberias** (Sea of Galilee). Be impressed by the town's ruins: the **Acropolis** built in 218 BC, the forum, the colonnaded street with still-visible chariot tracks and the **Nymphaeum** and remains of a large basilica.
- Return along the northwest border from Umm Qais to Jerash through the lush scenery of the **Jordan River Valley**, stopping at **Al Himma**, a town known for its hot springs and mineral waters. Visitors can also stop at **Pella**, once a city of the **Roman Decapolis**, now being excavated, and the hilltop castle of **Qalaat al-Rabadh** built by the Arabs in defence against the Crusaders. The

scenery in this surprisingly fertile part of Jordan is often very beautiful, especially in the spring when the Jordan Valley and surrounding area is covered in flowers.

- In the east are the desert **Umayyad** castles (Qasr) of **Al-Kharanah** and **Amra**. Built as hunting lodges and to protect caravan routes, they are well preserved with frescoes and beautiful vaulted rooms.

- Make a point of seeing **Petra**, one of the wonders of the Middle-Eastern world and now a UNESCO world heritage site: a gigantic natural amphitheatre hidden in the rocks out of which a delicately coloured city with immense facades has been carved; it was lost for hundreds of years and only rediscovered in 1812. The temples and caves of Petra rest high up above a chasm, with huge white rocks forming the *Bab*, or gate, of the *Siq*, the narrow entrance which towers over 21m (70ft) high. Most of this unique city was built by the Nabatean Arabs in the fifth and sixth centuries BC as an important link in the caravan routes. It was added to by the Romans who carved out a huge theatre and, possibly, the spectacular classical facade of the **Khazneh** (treasury). Away from the road, it is only possible to reach Petra on horseback. This city of rock stairs, rock streets, rock-carved tombs and dwellings and temples has among its other attractions the **Qasr al-Bint** castle shrine and the **Al-Habis** caves and museums. There is a rest house in Petra built against the rock wall near the beginning of the Siq, where it is advisable to book early in season, but is bitterly cold in winter.

- A short distance away from the more commercialised site of Petra is **Al-Barid** where a number of tombs lie in solitude and tranquility among the rocks.

Top Things To Do

- Get a taste of traditional **Amman** by going to the **central market** (*souk*).
- The coast south of **Aqaba**, on the shores of the Gulf of Aqaba, is teeming with tropical fish and coral and is renowned for its excellent year-round **diving** and **snorkelling**. Aqaba's beaches, notably the **Aquamarine** or **Holiday Beach**, offer good **swimming**. **Dolphin-**, **shark-** and **whale-watching** trips can also be arranged. **Note:** It is forbidden to remove coral or shells, or to use harpoon guns and fishing spears.
- Float freely in the rich salt water of the **Dead Sea**. Supporting no life and having no outlet, the Dead Sea, 392m (1286ft) below sea level and the lowest point on earth, glistens by day and night in an eerie, dry landscape. The Biblical cities of **Sodom** and **Gomorrah** are thought to be beneath its waters.
- One of the best destinations to go **hiking** is **Wadi Rum**, a vast area of dry riverbeds, mountains, black hills and sand dunes, located some 50km (30 miles) northeast of Aqaba, and a location for the film *Lawrence of Arabia*.
- Alternatively, opt for a **camel trek** or a **jeep trip** into the desert, or a **hot-air balloon trip** over Wadi Rum's **Valley of the Moon**.
- There are 10 designated wildlife reserves in Jordan, the best being the **Azraq Wetland Wildlife Reserve**, and the **Shaumari Wildlife Reserve**. Animals that can be seen include hyenas, red wolves, jerboas, gazelles, ostriches and Arabian oryxes. Both reserves are run with the help of the World Wide Fund for Nature. Wild animals once native to Jordan, such as the oryx and gazelle, are being re-introduced, while the wetlands are visited by thousands of migratory birds each year. The Shaumari was opened in October 1983 in an attempt to protect the country's dwindling oryx population.
- **Stay with a Bedouin tribe**. Trips into the desert can be arranged in **Wadi Rum**, about five hours from Amman by road. The small Bedouin village includes the Desert Patrol Fort (now a Badiya or Desert Police station); it was built to defend the valley in a great plain of escarpments and desert wilderness, and is a place strongly associated with TE Lawrence (Lawrence of Arabia). The men of the Desert Police are a spectacle in themselves, traditionally dressed and many still ride camels. Many Bedouins, of a tribe thought to be descended from Muhammad, still live in the valley in tents.

Credit: ©Bruce Logan

Entertainment

FOOD & DRINK: The cuisine varies, although most restaurants have a mixed menu which includes both Arabic and European dishes.

National specialities:
- *Meze* (small starters such as *fool*, *humus*, *kube* and *tabouleh*).
- *Kebabs*.
- *Mahshi Waraq 'inab* (vine leaves stuffed with rice, minced meat and spices).
- *Musakhan* (chicken in olive oil and onion sauce roasted on Arab bread).
- *Mensaf* (stewed lamb in a yogurt sauce served on a bed of rice), a dish which is normally eaten with the hand.
- *Baklava* (pastry filled with nuts or honey).
- *Kanafa* (pastry filled with nuts or goats cheese).
- *Ataif* (small fried pancakes filled with nuts or cheese and traditionally eaten during Ramadan).
- *Mohallabiya* (milk-based pudding perfumed with rose water or orange).

National drinks:
- Drinking Arabic coffee is a ritual. Coffee tends to be very strong and is served in small cups (with plenty of coffee grounds at the bottom).
- Local beer, wine and other types of alcohol are served in most restaurants and bars, except during the fasting month of Ramadan (non-Arabic nationals can drink alcohol only in hotels during Ramadan).
- *Araq* is a local liquor similar to Greek Ouzo, usually mixed with water and ice.

Tipping: 10 to 12 per cent service charge is generally added in hotels and restaurants, and extra tips are discretionary. Porters' and drivers' tips are about 8 per cent.

NIGHTLIFE: There are nightclubs, theatres and cinemas in Amman, while some other major towns have cinemas. Often clubs will only admit couples or mixed groups. Many of the 4- and 5-star hotels have popular clubs and bars.

SHOPPING: Every town will have a *souk* (market), and there are also many good craft and jewellery shops. There is a particularly good gold and jewellery market in Amman. Special items include: Hebron glass; mother-of-pearl boxes; pottery; backgammon sets; embroidered tablecloths; jewelled rosaries and worry beads; nativity sets made of olive wood; leather hassocks; old and new brass and copper items; and caftans hand-embroidered with silver and gold thread. Jordan is famous for its gold and silver; the centre of Amman has a gold *souk* with over 50 shops. Necklaces with a small golden coffee pot (*dalleh*) – a national symbol – are popular and widely available. **Shopping hours**: Sat-Thurs 0930-1330 and 1530-1800, some open as early as 0800 and close at 2000. Shops are closed Friday except for the souk.

Business

- **GDP:** US$25.5 billion (2004 estimate).
- **Main exports:** Phosphates, potash, fertilisers, chemicals and pharmaceuticals.
- **Main imports:** Crude oil, wheat, sugar, meat, machinery, transport equipment and spare parts.
- **Main trade partners:** USA, Saudi Arabia, Iraq, China (PR), India and Germany.

ECONOMY: Jordan's agricultural sector has never recovered from the loss of the West Bank after the 1967 Middle East war, which deprived Jordan of 80 per cent of its fruit-growing area and a proportionate amount of export revenue. Tomatoes, citrus fruit, cucumbers, watermelons, aubergines and wheat are the principal commodities grown in the remaining, mostly desert, area. Phosphate mining and potash extraction from the Dead Sea area are the longest established industries; to these, oil refining, chemical manufacturing, food processing, and the production of metals and minerals have since been added. Other commercial enterprises include paints, plastics and cement production. The ongoing search for exploitable oil deposits - unsuccessful thus far - continues, and attempts have been made to develop alternative sources of power. The service sector, which accounts for around two-thirds of total output, covers wholesale and retail trading, finance, transport and tourism. This sector has been especially badly hit by events in Iraq, Jordan's eastern neighbour, which accounted for some 20 per cent of Jordan's total pre-sanctions trade. UN sanctions against Iraq curtailed much Iraqi transit trade that would otherwise have come through the Jordanian port of Aqaba. Cheap oil supplies from Iraq have been made up, but only in part, by shipments from other Arab countries.

During the latter years of King Hussein's rule, some economic reforms based on the customary package of deregulation and privatisation were instituted. These brought the country's rampant inflation under control but failed to dent the country's massive unemployment problem. These reforms have, by and large, continued under King Abdullah. Many Jordanian workers have moved abroad in search of employment and their remittances are an essential means of support for many families. Jordan is a member of various pan-Arab economic bodies, notably the Council of Arab Economic Co-operation and the Arab Monetary Fund. The Government liberalised the trade regime sufficiently to secure Jordan's membership of the World Trade Organisation (WTO) in 2000, a free trade accord with the US and an association agreement with the EU in 2001; these measures have helped to improve productivity.

BUSINESS ETIQUETTE: English is widely spoken in business circles. Avoid Friday appointments. A good supply of visiting cards is essential. Formality in dress is important and men should wear a suit and tie for business meetings. **Office hours**: Sun-Thurs 0930-1330 and 1530-1800. **Government office hours**: Sun-Thurs 0800-1500. During the month of Ramadan, working hours are greatly reduced (see *Public Holidays* section).

A B C D E F G H I J K L M N O P Q R S T U V W X Y Z

Kazakhstan

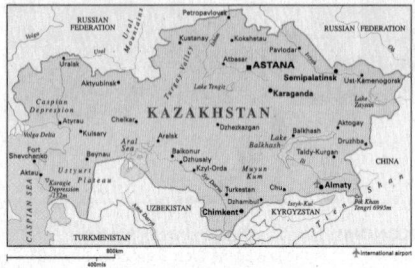

Location: Central Asia, north of Uzbekistan.

Time: Kazakhstan is divided into three time zones:
Eastern zone: GMT + 6.
Central zone (including Astana): GMT + 5.
Western zone: GMT + 4.

Overview

Kazakhstan is bordered by the Russian Federation, the Caspian Sea, Turkmenistan, Uzbekistan, Kyrgyzstan and China. For centuries, Kazakhstan's vast plains were home only to nomads and they are still virtually empty. Most settlements are concentrated in the southeast and the east of the Republic. South Kazakhstan is a focus of Central Asian history and there are many famous monuments in the region. It is a scenically diverse region where the snow-capped peaks, lakes and glaciers of the Tian Shan range give way to steppe and desert. The desert is home to the Singing Barkhan – a sand dune 3.2km (2 miles) long, which, as it crumbles, produces a peculiar singing sound. Almaty was until very recently the former capital of Kazakhstan and it enjoys a beautiful setting between mountains and plains. It is a city of modern architecture, cool fountains, parks and spectacular mountain views. Kazakh dishes include *kazi, chuzhuk, suret* and *besbarmak* (made from horse meat or mutton). There are a number of nightclubs and casinos in the main cities.

General Information

AREA: 2,717,300 sq km (1,049,150 sq miles).
POPULATION: 14.8 million (2002).
POPULATION DENSITY: 5.5 per sq km.
CAPITAL: Astana (formerly called Akmola). **Population:** 328,000 (UN estimate 2001).
GEOGRAPHY: Five times the size of France and half the size of the USA, Kazakhstan is the second largest state in the Commonwealth of Independent States, and is bordered by the Russian Federation to the north and west, the Caspian Sea, Turkmenistan and Uzbekistan to the southwest, Kyrgyzstan to the south and China to the southeast. 90 per cent of the country is made up of steppe, the sand massives of the Kara Kum and the vast desert of Kizilkum, while in the southeast of the country the mountains of the Tian Shan and the Altai form a great natural frontier with tens of thousands of lakes and rivers. The Aral Sea and Lake Balkhash are the country's largest expanses of water.
GOVERNMENT: Republic. **Head of State:** President Nursultan A Nazarbayev since 1991. **Head of Government:** Prime Minister Daniyal Akhmetov since 2003. **Recent history:** Following the attempted coup against Gorbachev in August 1991, Nursaltan Nazarbayev quickly guided Kazakhstan to independence within the Commonwealth of Independent States, while the Kazakh Communist Party split from the Moscow-based Communist Party and re-established itself as the Socialist Party of Kazakhstan (SPK).

Although the SPK was ordered to cease functioning, Nazarbayev used many of the old personnel and party structures to maintain a firm grip on power (the SPK was later allowed to reform, but Nazarbayev had by then established his own political vehicle, the People's Unity Party, PUP - later the Republican Party). As the only candidate at the presidential election in December 1991, Nazarbayev won 98 per cent of the vote. Following the introduction of a new constitution in 1995, a new set of political forces emerged in Kazakhstan. However, this made little difference to the distribution of power. The PUP took control of the Supreme Kenges while Nazabayev has been re-elected three times (in 1995, 1999 and 2005). In June 1997, Nazarbayev also managed to realise his pet project, the inauguration of a new capital city at Astana, based on a former Cossack fortress and located 750 miles north of the old capital, Almaty. In the most recent elections in December 2005, Nazabayez won over 90 per cent of the vote, an election which the opposition claimed to be rigged.International observers also reported serious flaws in the electoral process.
LANGUAGE: The official language is Kazakh, a Turkic language closely related to Uzbek, Kyrgyz, Turkmen and Turkish. The Government has begun to replace the Russian Cyrillic alphabet with the Turkish version of the Roman alphabet. Meanwhile, the Cyrillic alphabet is in general use and most people in the cities can speak Russian, whereas country people tend to only speak Kazakh. English is usually spoken by those involved in tourism. Uygur and other regional languages and dialects are also spoken.
RELIGION: Mainly Sunni Muslim. There are Russian Orthodox and Jewish minorities. There are 10 independent denominations of Christianity. The Kazakhs do not express their religious feelings fervently – Kazakhstan is an outlying district of the Muslim world and a meeting point of Russian, Chinese and Central Asian civilisations. Islam plays a minor role in policy and there are no significant Islamic political organisations in the country.
ELECTRICITY: 220 volts AC, 50Hz. Round two-pin continental plugs are standard.
SOCIAL CONVENTIONS: Kazakhs are very hospitable. When greeting a guest, the host gives him/her both hands as if showing that he/she is unarmed. When addressing a guest or elder, a Kazakh may address him/her with a shortened form of the guest's or elder's name and the suffix 'ke'. For example, Abkhan may be called Abeke, Nursultan can be called Nureke. This should be regarded as indicating a high level of respect for the visitor. At a Kazakh home, the most honoured guest, usually the oldest, is traditionally offered a boiled sheep's head on a beautiful dish as a further sign of respect. National customs forbid young people whose parents are still alive from cutting the sheep's head. They must pass the dish to the other guests for cutting. Inside mosques, women observe their own ritual in a separate room, and must cover their heads and their arms (see the *World of Islam* appendix for more information). Formal dress is often required when visiting the theatre, or attending a dinner party. Shorts should not be worn except on the sports ground.

Climate

Continental climate with cold winters and hot summers. Although Kazakhstan has some of the highest peaks in the CIS, the climate is fairly dry. The hottest month is July (August in mountain regions).

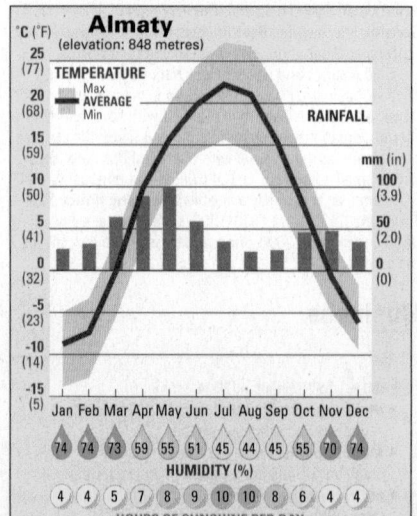

Almaty (elevation: 848 metres)

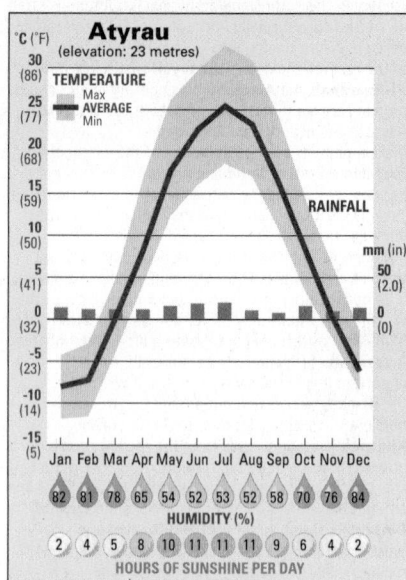

Atyrau (elevation: 23 metres)

Communications

Telephone: Country code: 7. Area code for Almaty: 3272. International calls can be made at a reduced rate from 2000-0800 local time. International calls should be made from a telephone office; these are usually attached to post offices.
Mobile telephone: Dual band 900 networks in use. Coverage is good around the main cities. Network providers include *K'CELL* (website: www.kcell.kz) and *K-MOBILE* (website: www.k-mobile.kz/ru).
Internet: ISPs include *Astel* (website: www.astel.kz) and *Parasang* (website: www.ricc.kz). There are Internet cafes in most towns and cities.
Post: Full postal facilities are available at main post offices in the cities, which are open 24 hours a day, seven days a week. The main post office in Almaty is located on Ulitsa Kurmangazy. International postal communication is undertaken by the firms *Blitz-Pochta*, *International Press* (e-mail: mpress87@hotmail.com) and *Press Limited*. Delivery within the republic takes three to five days. Post to Western Europe and the USA takes between two to three weeks. Mail addresses should be laid out in the following order: country, postcode, city, street, house number and, lastly, the person's name. Post office hours: Mon-Fri 0900-1800. Visitors can also use post offices located within major hotels.
MEDIA: Press: There are 70 newspapers and 50 magazines in German, Kazakh, Korean, Russian and Uygur published in the country. The most popular dailies are *Ekspress K*, *Kazakhstanskaya Pravda* and *Yegemen Kazakhstan*.
TV: *Kazakh TV* is State owned. Private channels include Kazakh commercial TV and *Channel 31 TV*.
Radio: *Kazakh Radio* is state owned. Private stations include *Europa Plus* and *Khabar Hit FM*.

Passport/Visa

	Passport Required?	Visa Required?	Return Ticket? Required?
Full British	Yes	Yes	No
Australian	Yes	Yes	No
Canadian	Yes	Yes	No
USA	Yes	Yes	No
Other EU	Yes	Yes	No
Japanese	Yes	Yes	No

Note: *Regulations and requirements may be subject to change at short notice, and you are advised to contact the appropriate diplomatic or consular authority before finalising travel arrangements. Any numbers in the chart refer to the footnotes below.*

PASSPORTS: Passport valid for at least six months required by all.
VISAS: Required by all except the following:
(a) nationals of CIS holding passports, and holders of valid passports issued by the former Soviet Union and registered in the CIS (nationals of Ukraine do not require a visa for stays of up to three months; nationals of Turkmenistan *always* require a visa);
(b) nationals of Turkey for stays of up to one month.
Note: Nationals of the following countries may apply for a single-entry tourist visa without obtaining an invitation letter validated by the Kazakhstan Ministry of Interior: nationals of countries referred to in the chart above (except

nationals of Cyprus, Czech Republic, Estonia, Hungary, Latvia, Lithuania, Malta, Poland, Slovak Republic and Slovenia) and nationals of Iceland, Korea (Rep), Liechtenstein, Malaysia, Monaco, New Zealand, Norway, Singapore, and Switzerland, who must instead provide a letter of introduction explaining the purpose of the visit.
Types of visa and cost: *Tourist*: £23 (single-entry); £33 (double-entry). *Business* and *Private*: £33 (single-entry); £43 (double-entry); £73 (triple-entry); £133 (multiple-entry, up to one year); £263 (multiple-entry, up to two years). *Transit*: £13.
Validity: *Tourist*: one month (single-entry); two months (double-entry). *Business* and *Private*: three months (single-, double- and triple-entry); one or two years (multiple-entry). *Transit*: five days
Application to: The Consulate (or Consular section at Embassy), see *Passport/Visa Information* section.
Application requirements: (a) Completed application form. (b) Valid passport with one blank page to affix visa. (c) One recent passport-size photo. (d) Letter of invitation with reference number, validated by the Kazakhstan Ministry of Interior (not required by certain nationals - see note above). (e) Fee, payable by personal cheque or postal order (not cash). (f) Self-addressed, stamped registered envelope, if applying by post. *Business*: (a)-(f) and, (g) Letter of invitation from host organisation in Kazakhstan with registration number approved by the Ministry of Foreign Affairs in Kazakhstan. (h) Letter from own business company with details of the purpose of the visit and name and address of partner organisation. *Transit*: (a)-(f) and, (g) Valid visa for country of final destination. (h) Air or railway ticket to third country.
Note: (a) All nationals staying longer than five days must register with an OVIR office and pay a registration charge. Failure to do so will result in penalties on departure.
Working days required: One day.
Temporary Residence: Enquire at Embassy.

PASSPORT/VISA INFORMATION

Embassy of the Republic of Kazakhstan in the UK
33 Thurloe Square, London SW7 2SD, UK
Tel: (020) 7581 4646 (ext 207/8 for visa section) *or* (09065) 508 978 (recorded visa information; calls cost £1 per minute).
Website: www.kazakhstanembassy.org.uk
Opening hours: Mon-Fri 0830-1830; Mon-Fri 0900-1200 (consular section, closed Wednesdays except for nationals of Kazakhstan).

Embassy of the Republic of Kazakhstan in the USA
1401 16th Street, NW, Washington, DC 20036, USA
Tel: (202) 232 5488.
Website: www.kazakhembus.com

Money

Currency: Tenge (KZT) = 100 tiyin. Notes are in denominations of KZT10,000, 5000, 2000, 1000, 500, 200, 100, 50, 20, 10, 5, 3 and 1, and 50, 20, 10, 5, 2 and 1 tiyin. Coins are in denominations of KZT100, 50, 20, 10, 5, 2 and 1.
Currency exchange: The national currency, the Tenge, may only be obtained within Kazakhstan. Conversion of the Tenge back into hard currency may prove difficult. Foreign currency should only be exchanged at official bureaux and all transactions must be recorded on the currency declaration form that is issued on arrival. It is wise to retain all exchange receipts, although they are seldom inspected. Unless travelling with a licensed tourist company (in which case, accommodation, transport and meals are paid before departure), money should be brought in US Dollars cash and exchanged when necessary.
Credit & debit cards: Major European and international credit cards, including Diners Club and Visa, are accepted in the larger hotels in Almaty and in major shops and restaurants. Facilities exist for credit card cash withdrawals in Kazakhstan.
Traveller's cheques: To avoid additional exchange rate charges, travellers are advised to take traveller's cheques in US Dollars.
Currency restrictions: The import and export of local currency and import of foreign currency is unlimited provided declared on arrival. The export of foreign currency is limited to the amount imported. Special bank permission is required for all amounts exceeding this.
Banking hours: Mon-Fri 0930-1730. Banks close for lunch 1300-1400. All banks are closed Sat-Sun.
Exchange rate indicators:
Rate at time of publishing

£1.00=	KZT 233.38
$1.00=	KZT 134.44

Duty Free

The following goods may be imported into Kazakhstan by persons over 16 years of age without incurring customs duty:
1000 cigarettes or 1kg of tobacco products; 2l of spirits or 2l of wine; a reasonable quantity of perfume for personal use; gifts up to the value of US$500 for personal use only.
Note: On entering the country, tourists must complete a customs declaration form, which must be retained until departure. This allows the import of articles intended for personal use, including currency and valuables, which must be registered on the declaration form. They must be exported at the end of the stay. Customs inspection can be long and detailed. It is advisable to keep receipts for items bought in Kazakhstan in order to avoid difficulties at customs on departure.
Prohibited imports: Military weapons and ammunition; narcotics; pornography; live animals (unless with special permit); photographs or other printed materials aimed against Kazakhstan; pigeons; loose pearls; anything owned by a third party that is to be carried in for that third party.
Prohibited exports: As prohibited imports, as well as annulled securities, state loan certificates, lottery tickets, works of art and antiques (unless permission has been granted by the Ministry of Culture), saiga horns, Siberian stag, punctuate and red deer antlers (unless on organised hunting trip), and punctuate deer skins.

Public Holidays

Below are listed Public Holidays for the January 2006-June 2007 period.
2006: Jan 1-2 New Year. **Mar 8** International Women's Day. **Mar 22** Nauryz Meyrami (Traditional Spring Holiday). **May 1** Kazakhstan People's Unity Day. **May 9** Victory Day. **Aug 30** Constitution Day. **Oct 25** Republic Day. **Dec 16** Independence Day.
2007: Jan 1-2 New Year. **Mar 8** International Women's Day. **Mar 22** Nauryz Meyrami (Traditional Spring Holiday). **May 1** Kazakhstan People's Unity Day. **May 9** Victory Day.

Health

	Special Precautions?	Certificate Required?
Yellow Fever	Yes	1
Cholera	Yes	2
Typhoid & Polio	Yes	N/A
Malaria	No	N/A

Note: *Regulations and requirements may be subject to change at short notice, and you are advised to contact your doctor well in advance of your intended date of departure. Any numbers in the chart refer to the footnotes below.*

1: A yellow fever vaccination certificate is required from travellers arriving within six days from infected areas (children under one year are exempt).
2: Following WHO guidelines issued in 1973, a cholera vaccination certificate is no longer a condition of entry to Kazakhstan. However, cholera is a serious risk in this country and precautions are essential. Up-to-date advice should be sought before deciding whether these precautions should include vaccination as medical opinion is divided over its effectiveness; see the *Health* appendix for further information.
Food & drink: All water should be regarded as being a potential health risk. Water used for drinking, brushing teeth or making ice should have first been boiled or otherwise sterilised. Milk is pasteurised and dairy products are safe for consumption. Only eat well-cooked meat and fish, preferably served hot. Pork, salad and mayonnaise may carry increased risk. Vegetables should be cooked and fruit peeled.
Other risks: *Hepatitis A*, *B* and *E* occur. *Diphtheria* outbreaks have been reported in the area. *Giardiasis*, *echinococcosis*, *typhus* (tick-borne), *Crimean-Congo haemorrhagic fever*, *trechinellosis*, *leishmaniasis* and *brucellosis* can also occur. Although rare, foci of *plague* exist. *Tuberculosis* and *typhoid* are increasing throughout. Increased cases of *meningitis* and *encephalitis* have also been reported in Almaty.
There is some presence of *Rabies*. For those at high risk, vaccination before arrival should be considered. If you are bitten, seek medical advice without delay. For more information, consult the *Health* appendix.
Note: Foreign visitors (except nationals of CIS countries) staying in Kazakhstan for longer than three months may be required to take an AIDS test.
Health care: There is a large network of hospitals, emergency centres and pharmacies. The largest include the Central Hospital, the Maternity and Childhood Institute Clinic and the Medical Teaching Institute Clinic in Almaty, and the Spinal Centre and Hospital of Rehabilitation Treatment in Karaganda. However, standards within the public healthcare system have declined significantly since the Soviet era. It is hard to ascertain the level of expertise of the doctors, and visitors cannot rely on the availability of western medicines. Medical insurance is strongly recommended and should include Medevac insurance.

Travel - International

AIR:
Almaty is rapidly gaining importance as an international hub. It has air links with many cities in the CIS. *British Airways* flies direct from London to Almaty three times a week. Connections from London can also be made on *Austrian Airlines* (via Vienna), *KLM* (via Amsterdam), *Lufthansa* (via Frankfurt/M) and *Turkish Airlines* (via Istanbul). There are no direct flights from Australia or the USA. Further connections are offered by *Aeroflot* from Almaty to Urumchi (China), from where there are connections to Beijing. New direct routes from Almaty to Delhi, Tehran and Tel Aviv are planned.
Approximate flight times: From *London* to Almaty is eight hours, from *Istanbul* is six hours, from *Ulgi* (Mongolia) is four hours and from *Hanover* and *Frankfurt/M* is 10 hours.
Main airports: *Almaty (ALA)* is located 10km (6 miles) northeast of the city. *To/from the airport*: Bus nos. 38, 446 and 492 connect the airport with the city centre (travel time - 20 minutes). Taxis are also available at the airport for transport into the city centre. *Facilities*: Car hire, duty free shops, restaurant and post office.
Departure tax: None.
SEA:
Freight is carried on the Caspian Sea to Iran and the Russian Federation.
RAIL:
There are international rail connections with China, the Russian Federation, Turkmenistan and Uzbekistan. Services run regularly from Almaty to Urumchi in China and daily to Moscow (travel time - three days) and connect with the entire Russian Federation railway network. The *Tashkent–Novosibirsk Express* passes through Almaty each day in both directions. The lines from Almaty in the north connect with the *Trans-Siberian Railway* running west to Chimkent and finally to Orenburg in the Russian Federation. A new railway line is being built to connect Kazakhstan to Iran and Turkey. Foreign visitors should exercise caution when using trains other than the Almaty–Moscow train; violent crime against westerners is on the increase.
ROAD:
There are good road connections into the Russian Federation, the other Central Asian states and China. **Bus:** Buses leave Chimkent for Tashkent every 25 minutes 0700-1925. The journey is 160km (100 miles) (travel time - three hours). There are also buses from Chimkent to Bishkek.

Travel - Internal

AIR:
There are frequent flights from Almaty to Astana, Chimkent (four times a day), Dzhambul, Karaganda, Kzil-Orda, Pavlodar, Semipalatinsk and Ust-Kamenogorsk. Flights also leave Chimkent for Almaty, Karaganda and Semipalatinsk. Travellers should note that maintenance procedures for aircraft operating internally may not conform to internationally accepted standards.
Domestic airports: *Chimkent* has an airport offering mostly domestic flights. However, there are also services to Moscow (four times a week) and Novosibirsk (Russian Federation), and to Tashkent (Uzbekistan) (daily). Bus no. 12 runs from the city centre to the airport.
Semipalatinsk has a domestic airport with flights to Almaty, Chimkent, Dzhambul, Karaganda and Ust-Kamenogorsk. However, it also receives flights from Bishkek, Krasnoyarsk, Moscow (four times a week), Omsk, Tashkent and Tomsk.
The airport at *Ust-Kamenogorsk* receives flights from Almaty and a few other Kazakh cities, as well as from Moscow, Novosibirsk and a few other Siberian cities. Bus no. 12 runs to the Hotel Ust-Kamenogorsk in the city centre.
RIVER:
River trips can be taken in Semipalatinsk on the River Irtysh.
RAIL:
There are two *TurkSib* trains leaving Chimkent daily, one to Tashkent (Uzbekistan) and the other to Novosibirsk (Russian Federation), stopping at destinations in between. The cost of rail travel in Kazakhstan is minimal in comparison with Western Europe and there are regular connections between all the main centres. Queues at stations to buy a ticket can be long and passengers should bring their own food and drink for the journey. It may be advisable for foreign visitors to travel by bus between cities, owing to an increase in robberies on trains.

A B C D E F G H I J K L M N O P Q R S T U V W X Y Z

ROAD:

Traffic drives on the right. There is a reasonable network of roads in Kazakhstan connecting all the towns and regional centres. Petrol supplies are reasonably reliable in comparison with other Central Asian republics. **Bus:** There are regular bus connections between all the main cities of Kazakhstan. **Taxi:** These are available in all Kazakh cities. **Car hire:** Available in Almaty and Astana and at the airports. **Documentation:** An International Driving Permit is required.

URBAN:

Almaty is served by trolleybuses and buses.

Travel Advice

Most visits to Kazakhstan are trouble-free but you should be aware of the global risk of indiscriminate international terrorist attacks, which could be against civilian targets, including places frequented by foreigners.

This advice is based on information provided by the Foreign and Commonwealth Office in the UK. It is correct at time of publishing. As the situation can change rapidly, visitors are advised to contact the following organisations for the latest travel advice:

British Foreign and Commonwealth Office
Tel: (0845) 850 2829.
Website: www.fco.gov.uk

US Department of State
Website: http://travel.state.gov/travel

Accommodation

HOTELS:

Most towns in Kazakhstan have a limited supply of reasonable accommodation. It is advisable to make reservations in advance, either directly or through a travel agency. Most hotels deliver a basic level of comfort, although Western standards should not be expected.

Grading: A star-grading system is in use. There are at least two 5-star hotels in Almaty, as well as numerous new hotels of a reasonable standard. Classification of tourist hotels and campsites is carried out by the Department of Tourism (see *Contact Addresses* section); classification of other forms of accommodation is carried out by the local authorities.

TURBAZAS:

These 'tourist bases' are an alternative to hotel accommodation. For a small fee, visitors have access to basic bungalow accommodation and three meals a day.

CAMPING:

The only designated campsites are the permanent base camps from which the high peaks of Kazakhstan are climbed. Travellers pitch their tents in other localities at their own risk, although there are no regulations against it.

Top Things To See

• **South Kazakhstan** is a focus of Central Asian history and culture and there are many famous monuments in the region. It is a scenically diverse region in which all four seasons can be experienced in the space of a day, as the snow-capped peaks, lakes and glaciers of the **Tien Shan range** give way to steppe and desert land which stretches for thousands of kilometres. The desert is home to the Singing Barkhan – a sand dune 80m (260ft) high and 3km (2 miles) long, which, as it crumbles and shifts, produces a peculiar sound reminiscent of loud singing.

• **Almaty** (formerly Alma Ata) enjoys a beautiful setting between mountains and plains. It is a city of modern architecture, wide streets, cool fountains, parks and squares and spectacular mountain views and, particularly in spring and autumn, is an attractive place despite the inevitable legacy of Soviet architecture. Attractions in the city include the **Panfilov Park**, which is dominated by one of the world's tallest wooden buildings, built at the turn of the 20th century without using a single nail, and the **Zenkov Cathedral**. This served in Soviet times as a concert and exhibition hall, but is currently standing empty, whilst the Christians of Almaty worship at St Nicholas Cathedral. Other sights include **New Square**, which is usually the location for national ceremonies and parades and is overlooked by the **City Hall** (the President's official residence) and the **Obelisk of Independence.** Almaty boasts several fine museums including the **Museum of Kazakh National Instruments**, the **Central State Museum** and the **State Art Museum** which has, among its exhibits, traditional Kazakh rugs, jewellery and clothing. The **Arasan Baths**, in the western area of Panfilov Park, have Eastern, Finnish and Russian saunas.

• 160km (100 miles) from Chimkent (travel time – two hours 30 minutes) is the 14th-century **Kodja Ahmed Yasavi Mausoleum** in Turkestan; built under Tamerlane, this mausoleum has the largest dome in Central Asia. **Dzhambul**, too, is an industrial city in the region with some reproductions of ancient remains from when it was known as Taraz – these are housed in the Karakhan and the **Daudbek Shahmansur Mausoleums**. The nearby village of **Golovachovka**, 18km (11 miles) to the west, has authentic remains from Taraz, including the 11th-century **Babadzi-Khatun Mausoleum** and the 12th-century **Mausoleum Aisha Bibi**. Another ancient historical centre is **Taldikorgan**. Much of this region was crossed by the **Great Silk Road**.

• Central Kazakhstan has one of the largest lakes in the world. The unique **Lake Balkhash** is half saline, half fresh water. Some archaeological and ethnographic sites have been preserved in central Kazakhstan. There are Bronze Age and Early Iron Age sites and New Stone Age and Bronze Age settlements in the **Karkarala Oasis**. The **Bayan-Aul National Park** has rock drawings, stone sculptures, clean, sparkling lakes and pines clinging to the rocks. The **Baikonur Cosmodrome**, located 5km (3 miles) from the garrison city of Leninsk and 230km (143 miles) from Kzil-Orda, is the Central Asian answer to Cape Canaveral – tours are available, during which visitors can witness space launches. It was from here, on 12 April 1961, that Yuri Gagarin, the world's first cosmonaut, took off, and it is still a point of departure for space launches.

• West Kazakhstan marks the southern convergence of Europe and Asia in the basin of the Caspian Sea. The region's **Karagie Depression**, 132m (433ft) below sea level, is the lowest point in the world after the Dead Sea in Sinai. There are many architectural heritage sites in this region, including the subterranean cross-shaped **Shakpak-Ata Mosque** (12th-14th century) which is hewn out of rock.

• **Astana** was made Kazakhstan's new capital in 1997, as its location was thought to be more accessible to the Russian Federation and less earthquake-prone than Almaty (the former capital), where foreign embassies and consulates are still based. Although a small and friendly town and an important centre for the production of grain, it has little else to recommend it. The nature reserve of **Kurgaldjino** in the north of Kazakhstan houses the most northerly settlement of pink flamingoes in the world, while another nature reserve, **Naurzum**, offers a rich landscape of geographical contrasts – salt lakes ringed by forests, the remains of ancient pines strewn amongst sand dunes, pine forests growing out of salt-marsh bedsm, vast meadows, and rare animals such as hisser swans and grave eagles.

• East Kazakhstan offers a colourful landscape of snow-capped mountain peaks, plunging forested canyons and picturesque cedar forests. **Lake Marakol** rivals Baikal in beauty. It is 35km (22 miles) long and 19km (12 miles) wide and lies 1449m (4754ft) above sea level. The city of **Semipalatinsk**, 30km (19 miles) from Siberia, was a Russian place of exile; Dostoyevsky was exiled here from 1857-1859 and his house is preserved as a museum – exhibits include notes for Crime and Punishment and The Idiot. Other museums in the city include the **Abai Kununbaev Museum**, commemorating the Kazakh poet, and the **History Museum**. Nuclear tests were carried out southwest of Semipalatinsk until 1990, although background radiation today is easily within reach of internationally accepted levels. The town of **Ust-Kamenogorsk** is a mining and smelting town and is the gateway to the **Altai Mountains**.

• **Nature Reserves: Aksu-Jabagli**: A UNESCO biosphere reserve in southern Kazakhstan, situated 1000 to 4000m (3280 to 3120ft) above sea level, and home to 238 species of birds, 42 species of animals and 1300 species of plants.
Almaty: Located in the southern Tian Shan Mountains and home to snow leopards, jeirans, gazelles, arkhars and the unique Tjan-Shan fir tree.
Barsa Kelmes: Translated as 'the land of no return', this island, off the northwestern Aral Sea coast, is the home of the rarest hoofed animal in the world – the kulan.
The West-Altai: Situated in the Altai Mountains and home to 16 types of forest, 30 species of mammals and 120 species of birds.
Kurgaldjino: Located in central Kazakhstan, this A-class nature reserve is of international importance, and its feather-grass steppe is home to 300 types of plant and the most northerly settlement of flamingos in the world.
Marakol: Home to 232 species of bird, 50 species of animal and 1000 types of plant, the reserve is set in the southern foothills of the Altai Mountains.
Naurzum: Located in northern Kazakhstan and home to such rare animals as white herons, jack-bustards, hisser swans and grave eagles.
Ustiurt: Situated in west Kazakhstan in the Karagie Depression, 132m (433ft) below sea level, this chalk-cliffed reserve is the largest in the country.
Bayan-Aul National Nature Park: Known as 'the museum of nature', the reserve is located in central Kazakhstan.

Top Things To Do

• Kazakhstan has a wide range of spas offering various treatments. There are 98 sanatoria holiday hotels and 115 preventative medicine sanatoria. Most are located in areas with much to interest the tourist, such as sports, cultural events, historical and archaeological sites, and offer developed excursion facilities. The most internationally renowned resorts include **Sari Agach** (in the south), **Mujaldi** (in the Pavlodar region), **Arasan-Kapal** (in the Taldikorgan region), **Jani-Kurgan** (in the Kzil-Orda region), **Kokshetau and Zerenda** (in the Kokshetau region) and those located in **Zaili Alatau**.

• **Hiking and trekking:** Due to the country's rugged landscape and incredible mountain ranges, mountain climbing and trekking are becoming increasingly popular with visitors. The best season for trekking is between June and September. **Horse riding** is also popular in Kazakhstan. Visitors may either take part in or view competitions of the many Kazakh equestrian sports, such as *baiga*, *kiz-kuu* and *kokpar*.

• **Wintersports:** The 4000m- (1310ft-) high **Zaili Alatau Mountains** near Almaty offer numerous opportunities all year round for sports and recreation. Near Almaty, 12km (7 miles) from the city centre, surrounded by mountains, the **Medeu ice-skating rink** is the largest speed-skating rink in the world and is very popular with all the inhabitants of the capital. Over 120 world records in ice skating and ice hockey have been set at Medeu. **Ice hockey** games can be viewed at the rink in **Ust-Kamenogorsk**. On a spur of **Zaili Alatau**, 7km (4 miles) to the south, the wintersports complex of **Chimbulak** offers some of the finest skiing in the CIS and many ski competitions take place here. **Shymbulak** is a popular ski resort, located near Medeu ice rink, with a 1.6km- (1mile-) long chair lift.The **Tien Shan Mountains** in the southeast of Kazakhstan stretch for more than 1500km (932 miles). The highest peaks are **Pobeda Peak** (7439m/24,406ft) and **Khan-Tengri Peak** (7010m/23,000ft), a snow-white, marble-like pyramid. The huge **Inylchek Glacier**, reaching almost 60km (37 miles) in length, splits the summits and the beautiful **Mertzbakher Lake** lies at its centre. The **Kolsai Lakes** are three blue mountain lakes, known as the 'pearls of the northern Tien-Shan', that lie within the ridges of the Kungei Alatau range at heights of up to 2700m (8858ft) above sea level. The **Khan-Tengri International Mountaineering Camp** provides experienced mountain guides to take visitors on organised climbing and trekking programmes.

• **Watersports:** All the regional centres boast sport complexes, swimming pools and training halls. **Rafting** and **canoeing** can be easily arranged through local travel agents. The **Ili river** between Lake Qapshaghay and Lake Balhash is a good place for this.

TOURIST INFORMATION

State Agency for Tourism and Sport
473000 Astana, Mukhtar Auezor 126, Kazakhstan
Tel: (3272) 396 638.
Website: www.kazsport.kz

Hotel Complex Otrar and Travel & Air Agency
ul Gogolya 73, Hotel Otrar, Almaty 480002, Kazakhstan
Tel: (3272) 506 806/40 *or* 848.
Website: www.group.kz

Entertainment

FOOD & DRINK: Beer, vodka, brandy and sparkling wines are available in many restaurants.

National specialities:
• *Kazi*.
• *Chuzhuk*.
• *Suret*.
• *Besbarmak* (made from horse meat or mutton).
• *Shashlyk* (skewered chunks of mutton barbecued over charcoal).
• *Lepeshka* (round unleavened bread) are often sold on street corners and make an appetising meal.
• *Plov* is made up of scraps of mutton, shredded yellow turnip and rice, and is a staple dish in all the Central Asian republics.
• Other mutton dishes such as *laghman* and *beshbermak* include long thick noodles garnished with a spicy meat sauce.
• *Manty* (boiled noodle sacks of meat and vegetables), *samsa* (samosas).
• *Chiburekki* (deep-fried dough cakes) are all popular as snacks.
• Almaty is renowned for its apples – indeed the city was named after them.

National drinks:
• Kazakh tea or *chai* is very popular and there are national cafes called *Chai-Khana* (tea-rooms) where visitors may sip this Kazakh speciality. It is drunk very strong with cream.
• *Kumis*, fermented mare's milk. Cafes where this can be ordered are called *Kumis-Khana*. Refusing it when offered may cause offence.

• In the steppe and desert regions where camels are bred, the camel's milk, called *shubat*, is offered to guests.

Tipping: This is not customary at restaurants and cafes, but is increasingly common in international hotels. A service charge is included in hotel and restaurant bills. There is also a fixed charge in taxi and railway transport.

NIGHTLIFE: There are a number of nightclubs and casinos in Almaty and several other cities. Many restaurants play music after 2000. Kazakhstan's most reknowned concert halls and theatres are all located in Almaty.

SHOPPING: Located north of Panfilov Park, Almaty has a bazaar, where a diverse range of items can be bought.

Shopping hours: Mon-Sat 0900-2000.

Business

ECONOMY: Kazakhstan has enormous natural deposits: iron, nickel, zinc, manganese, coal, chromium, copper, lead, gold and silver are presently being mined. The coalfields of the Karaganda are some of the largest in Asia. There are substantial oil and gas deposits, many of which have only recently been located and the Kazakh Government has signed joint production deals with US and European consortia. New pipeline projects agreed with the Russian Federation and Oman will offer further outlets for Kazakh oil and boost national revenues. The rapid increase in the size of the sector mainly accounts for the country's recent healthy growth, which saw GDP increase by around 10 per cent annually since 2000 (9.5 per cent in 2002). Inflation and unemployment in the same year were 6 and 9 per cent respectively. The Government's economic policy has limited the involvement of foreign investors (the oil and gas industry apart). A privatisation programme has seen the bulk of the country's commercial enterprises transferred to the domestic private sector. The Government has established a strong financial position, albeit at the expense of much-needed investment in Kazakhstan's decaying infrastructure.

Other than oil and gas, stone, such as marble and granite, is produced in large quantities. The country's industries are predominantly concerned with processing these raw materials. Domestic production also fulfils Kazakhstan's own energy needs. Agriculture still accounts for half of economic output. The main commodities are wheat, meat products, wool and a variety of crops: sugar beet, potatoes, cereals, cotton, fruit and vegetables. Livestock rearing is also important in this very arid region. However, one of the consequences of extensive cultivation has been heavy demand on water supplies, most particularly the rivers of Kazakhstan and its neighbour Uzbekistan: this was the major cause of one of the greatest ecological disasters of recent times – the shrinking of the Aral Sea.

Since independence, Kazakhstan has joined the IMF, World Bank and the European Bank for Reconstruction and Development, and has signed a partnership and co-operation agreement with the EU. It also belongs to the main regional economic co-operation venture, the Central Asian Economic Union (ECO). Since the dissolution of the Soviet Union, the Kazakhs have sought economic independence from the Russian Federation but find that they are still affected by developments in their larger neighbour. The Russian Federation remains Kazakhstan's largest trading partner, followed by China (PR), Germany, the US and Italy. In 1993, the Kazakh exchequer introduced a new currency, the *Tenge*, to replace the Rouble.

CONFERENCES/CONVENTIONS: Many international business events are held in the Alatau Winter Resort near Almaty, by such organisations as UNESCO, ICF and others, . There is an annual International Exhibition Fair called *Karkara* held at the Exhibition Complex of the Business Cooperation Centre in Almaty every September. Businesspeople from all over the world meet here to make contacts and conclude business contracts. Other large industrial towns, such as Chimkent, Karaganda and Pavlodar, have conference and convention facilities and other industrial exhibitions and fairs are held here.

COMMERCIAL INFORMATION

Trading House of the Republic of Kazakhstan in the UK
58 Ribblesdale Avenue, London N11 3BQ, UK
Tel: (020) 8368 4348.
E-mail: thrk@dircon.co.uk

Ministry of Economy and Trade
Ministry House, Astana 47330, Kazakhstan
Tel: (3172) 117 511 *or* 118 146/145.

Union of Chambers of Commerce and Industry of the Republic of Kazakhstan
Masanchi Street 26, Almaty 480091, Kazakhstan
Tel: (3272) 920 052.
Website: www.ccikaz.kz

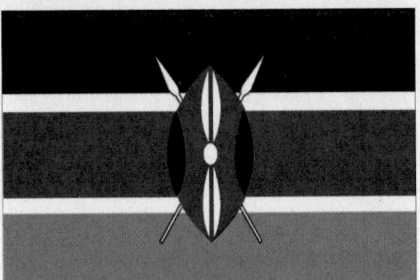

Kenya

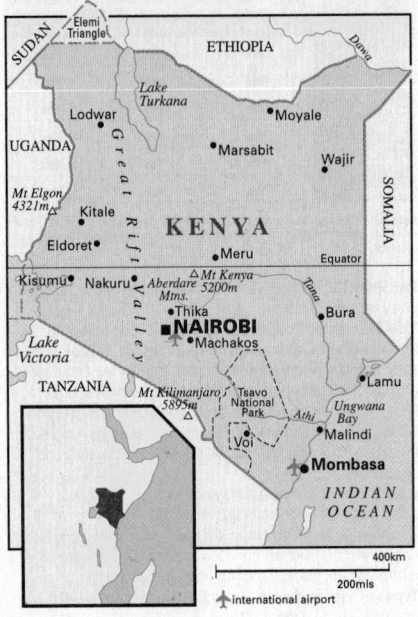

Location: East Africa.

Time: GMT + 3.

Overview

Excavations in Kenya suggest that the region is the cradle of humanity, the home some 3.25 million years ago of *Homo habilis*, from whom *Homo sapiens* descended. What is certain is that, in more recent times, Kenya was the settling place of a huge number of tribes from all over Africa, with a long history of migration, settlement and conflict. During the following centuries, the region became prosperous on the profits of trade, and also as an entrepôt for commerce from the Indian Ocean.

Today, Kenya, regarded by many as the 'jewel of East Africa', has some of the continent's finest beaches, most magnificent wildlife and scenery and an incredibly sophisticated tourism infrastructure. It is a startlingly beautiful land, from the coral reefs and white sand beaches of the coast to the summit of Mount Kenya, crowned with clouds and bejewelled by strange giant alpine plants. Above all, Kenya is a place for safaris. Between these two extremes is the rolling savannah that is home to game parks such as Amboseli, the Masai Mara, Samburu and Tsavo; the lush, agricultural highlands with their sleek green coat of coffee and tea plantations; and the most spectacular stretch of the Great Rift Valley, the giant scar across the face of Africa. One-tenth of all land in Kenya is designated as national parks and reserves. Over 50 parks and reserves cover all habitats from desert to mountain forest, and there are even six marine parks in the Indian Ocean.

Kenya also has a fascinatingly diverse population with around 40 different tribes, all with their own (often related) languages and cultures. The major tribes include the Kikuyu from the central highlands, the Luyia in the northwest, and the Luo around Lake Victoria. Of them all, however, the most famous are the tall, proud, beautiful red-clad Masai, who still lead a traditional semi-nomadic lifestyle of cattle-herding along the southern border.

Kenya does have its downside as a tourist destination. Rampant corruption means that many of the roads are in poor condition and driving can be a chore. Urban crime is high and continuing inter-tribal skirmishes and banditry are a threat in some areas of the North. More prosaically, the tourist trade has taught people there to think of foreigners as open wallets. Prices for everything from park fees to

Credit: ©Kenya Tourist Board

hotel rooms are set way above the local level. There is enormous pressure to buy anything and everything, often at ridiculously inflated prices, and even taking a photograph in the local market is likely to incur a cost. But despite this, the people are friendly, and the tourist trade is supremely well organised and professional. For those in search of a little adventure, this can be an ideal holiday destination.

General Information

AREA: 582,646 sq km (224,961 sq miles).

POPULATION: 32.8 million (UN, 2005).

POPULATION DENSITY: 56.29 per sq km.

CAPITAL: Nairobi. **Population:** 2.14 million (1999).

GEOGRAPHY: Kenya shares borders with Ethiopia in the north, Sudan in the northwest, Uganda in the west, Tanzania in the south and Somalia in the northeast. To the east lies the Indian Ocean. The country is divided into four regions: the arid deserts of the north; the savannah lands of the south; the fertile lowlands along the coast and around the shores of Lake Victoria; and highlands in the west, where the capital Nairobi is situated. Northwest of Nairobi runs the Rift Valley, containing the town of Nakuru and Aberdare National Park, overlooked by Mount Kenya (5200m/17,000ft), which also has a national park. In the far northwest is Lake Turkana (formerly Lake Rudolph). Kenya is a multicultural society; in the north live Somalis and the nomadic Hamitic peoples (Rendille, Samburu and Turkana), in the south and eastern lowlands are Kamba and Masai and the Luo live around Lake Victoria. The largest group is the Kikuyu who live in the central highlands and have traditionally been dominant in commerce and politics, although this is now changing. There are many other smaller groups and, although Kenya emphasises nationalism, tribal and cultural identity is a factor. A small European settler population remains in the highlands, involved in farming and commerce.

GOVERNMENT: Republic. Gained independence from the UK in 1963. **Head of State and Government:** President Emilio Mwai Kibaki since December 2002. **Recent history:** With former President Daniel arap Moi constitutionally barred from contesting the December 2002 election, Mwai Kibaki – the most prominent opposition politician – made his second attempt at the presidency and was elected President. His National Rainbow Coalition (Narc) won a parliamentary majority. He promised that his main objective would be to fight against corruption. However, both former and current ministers have become embroiled in a recent corruption scandal, involving a multi-million dollar scam. Furthermore, voters rejected a draft constitution in a referendum in late 2005. While the President presented it as a modernising measure, his opponents said that it would have left too much power in the hands of the President.

LANGUAGE: Swahili is the national language and English is the official language. There are over 42 ethnic languages spoken, including Kikuyu and Luo.

RELIGION: Mostly traditional but there is a sizeable Christian population (both Catholic and Protestant) and a small Muslim community.

ELECTRICITY: 220/240 volts AC, 50Hz. Plugs are UK-type square three-pin. Bayonet-type light sockets exist in Kenya.

SOCIAL CONVENTIONS: Western European habits prevail throughout Kenya as a result of British influences in the country. Kenyans are generally very friendly. Dress is informal, and casual lightweight clothes are accepted for all but the smartest social occasions.

Climate

The coastal areas are tropical, but tempered by monsoon winds. The lowlands are hot but mainly dry, while the highlands are more temperate with four seasons. Nairobi has a very pleasant climate throughout the year due to its altitude. Near Lake Victoria, the temperatures are much higher and rainfall can be heavy.

Required clothing: Lightweight cottons and linens with rainwear are advised for the coast and lakeside. Warmer clothing is needed in June and July and for the cooler mornings on the coast. Lightweights are needed for much of the year in the highlands. Rainwear is advisable between March and June and October and December.

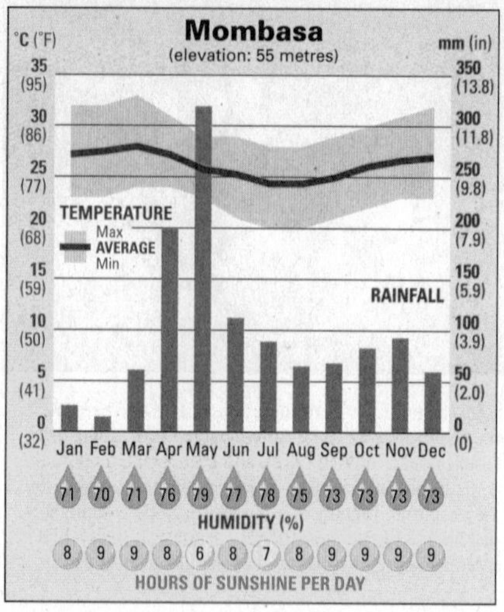
°C (°F)
Mombasa
(elevation: 55 metres)
mm (in)
35 (95) 30 (86) 25 (77) 20 (68) 15 (59) 10 (50) 5 (41) 0 (32)
350 (13.8) 300 (11.8) 250 (9.8) 200 (7.9) 150 (5.9) 100 (3.9) 50 (2.0) 0 (0)
TEMPERATURE
Max
AVERAGE
Min
RAINFALL
Jan Feb Mar Apr May Jun Jul Aug Sep Oct Nov Dec
71 70 71 76 79 77 78 75 73 73 73 73
HUMIDITY (%)
8 9 9 8 6 8 7 8 9 9 9 9
HOURS OF SUNSHINE PER DAY

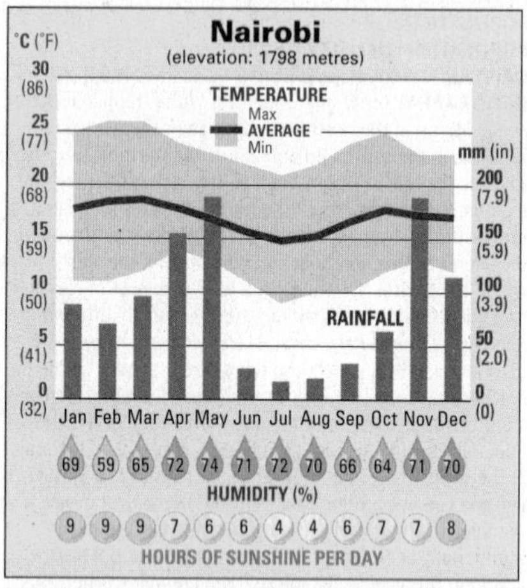
°C (°F)
Nairobi
(elevation: 1798 metres)
30 (86) 25 (77) 20 (68) 15 (59) 10 (50) 5 (41) 0 (32)
TEMPERATURE
Max
AVERAGE
Min
mm (in)
200 (7.9) 150 (5.9) 100 (3.9) 50 (2.0) 0 (0)
RAINFALL
Jan Feb Mar Apr May Jun Jul Aug Sep Oct Nov Dec
69 59 65 72 74 71 72 70 66 64 71 70
HUMIDITY (%)
9 9 9 7 6 6 4 4 6 7 7 8
HOURS OF SUNSHINE PER DAY

Communications

Telephone: IDD service is available to the main cities. Country code: 254 (followed by 20 for Nairobi, 41 for Mombasa and 51 for Nakuru). International calls can sometimes be made direct or operator-assisted by dialling 0196. Public telephones work with coins or with phone cards (which may be purchased from post offices or from international call services in major towns); coin-operated phone booths are painted red, card-operated booths are painted blue. Major hotels also offer an international phone service, but they usually charge up to 100 per cent more. In larger towns, private telecommunication centres offer international services. For local calls, it is useful to have plenty of small change available.
Mobile telephone: Roaming agreements exist with international mobile phone companies. The main network providers are *Celtel* (website: www.celtel.com), which has extensive coverage in the south west and around the coast and Mombasa, and *Safaricom* (website: www.safaricom.co.ke), with coverage in from Mombasa to Nairobia and in the south east.
Internet: There are Internet cafes in major cities and hotels.
Post: Post offices are identified by *Telkom Kenya* (Kenya Posts & Telecommunications Corporation). Post boxes are red. Stamps can usually be bought at post offices, stationers, souvenir shops and hotels. Airmail to Western Europe takes up to four days, and the service is generally reliable. Post office hours: Mon-Fri 0800-1700, Sat 0900-1200 (main post offices).
MEDIA: Kenya enjoys a more diverse media scene than many other African countries, although some media have been harrassed for upsetting the government. Most Kenyans rely on the broadcast media, particularly radio, for news. The print media is dominated by two publishing houses, the Nation Media Group and Standard, which also have broadcasting interests.
Press: The main dailies (all published in English) include *Daily Nation, The East African Standard, Kenya Times* and *The People Daily. Taifo Leo* is the only Swahili-language daily, published by the Nation Media Group. Nairobi is the main publishing centre.
TV: State-owned *Kenya Broadcasting Corporation (KBC)* has channels in English and Swahili. *Kenya Television Network* was the first TV station to break the state broadcasting monopoly; it is available in Nairobi, Mombasa, Nakuru, Eldoret, Kisumu. *Nation TV* is a Nairobi-based station operated by the Nation Media Group. Other private channels include: Nairobi-based station *Citizen TV* and *Stella TV (STV)*.
Radio: *Kenya Broadcasting Corporation (KBC)* is state-owned, with language-based networks in English, Swahili and 15 other indigenous languages. *Metro FM* is a national music-based station operated by KBC. *Coro FM* is a KBC-operated Kikuyu-language station in Nairobi. *Capital FM* and Kiss FM are music stations. *Radio Citizen* is a private station with wide coverage which also operates Kikuyu-language *Inooro FM* and *Luo-language*. Full-time FM relays of the *BBC World Service* are on the air in Nairobi, Mombasa and Kisumu, and some BBC programmes are also rebroadcast by private *Kameme FM*. *The Voice of America* has an FM relay in Nairobi and *Radio France Internationale* is relayed on FM in Mombasa.

Passport/Visa

	Passport Required?	Visa Required?	Return Ticket? Required?
Full British	Yes	Yes	Yes
Australian	Yes	Yes	Yes
Canadian	Yes	Yes	Yes
USA	Yes	Yes	Yes
Other EU	Yes	Yes	Yes
Japanese	Yes	Yes	Yes

Note: *Regulations and requirements may be subject to change at short notice, and you are advised to contact the appropriate diplomatic or consular authority before finalising travel arrangements.*

PASSPORTS: Passport valid for three months from date of entry required by all.
VISAS: Required by all except nationals of the following:
(a) nationals of Commonwealth countries for stays of up to three months *except* those nationals listed in the chart above, and nationals of Bangladesh, Cameroon, Dominica, Guyana, India, Mozambique, New Zealand, Nigeria, Pakistan, South Africa, Sri Lanka and St Kitts & Nevis who *do* require a visa;
(b) nationals of Ethiopia, San Marino, Turkey, Uruguay and Zimbabwe;
(c) nationals of Malaysia if staying less than 30 days;
(d) all holders of a re-entry pass to Kenya;
(e) transit passengers continuing their journey by the same or first connecting aircraft provided holding valid onward or return documentation and not leaving the airport.
Types of visa and cost: *Entry*: £30 (single-entry); £60 (multiple-entry). *Transit*: £10.
Note: If the application is referred to Immigration in Nairobi, an additional £7 will be payable. Nationals of Rwanda will receive visas gratis.
Validity: *Single-entry*: up to three months from date of issue; *Multiple-entry*: up to 12 months from date of issue. Renewals (up to six months) or extensions can be made at Immigration in Nyayo House, Uhuru Highway, Nairobi or at Kisumu and Mombasa. The period of stay in Kenya can be given at the port of entry (maximum three months).
Note: Multiple-entry visas may only be issued to nationals of the United Kingdom.
Application to: Consulate (or Consular section at Embassy or High Commission); see *Passport/Visa Information*.
Application requirements: (a) Valid passport with at least one blank page. (b) Completed application form. (c) One recent passport-size photo. (d) Fee, payable by postal order or bank cheque if applying by post, or cash if applying in person. (e) Holiday itinerary or business letter. (f) For postal applications, include a self-addressed stamped, registered envelope for return of passport and daytime telephone number.
Working days required: Three (applying in person) or one week from date of receipt (postal applications). If the visa has to be referred to Nairobi it will take at least eight weeks.
Note: The following nationals will automatically be referred to the Principal Immigration Officer in Nairobi before a visa can be granted: nationals of Afghanistan, Armenia, Azerbaijan, Cameroon, Iraq, Jordan, Korea (Dem Rep), Lebanon, Mali, Nigeria, Senegal, Somalia, the Syrian Arab Republic and Tadjkistan.
Temporary residence: Apply to Principal Immigration Officer, PO Box 30191, Nairobi.

PASSPORT/VISA INFORMATION

Kenya High Commission in the UK
45 Portland Place, London W1B 1AS, UK
Tel: (020) 7636 2371/5.
Website: www.kenyahighcommission.com
Opening hours: Mon-Fri: applications 0930-1400, collections 1400-1530.

Kenya Embassy in the USA
2249 R Street, NW, Washington, DC 20008, USA
Tel: (202) 387 6101.
Website: www.kenyaembassy.com

Money

Currency: Kenyan Shilling (KES) = 100 cents. Notes are in denominations of KES1000, 500, 200, 100 and 50. Coins are in denominations of KES20, 10 and 5.
Currency exchange: Currency can be exchanged at the major banks, bureaux de change or authorised hotels. The bank at Jomo Kenyatta International Airport and Moi International Airport have 24-hour exchange services. The easiest currencies to exchange are US Dollars, Pounds Sterling and Euros. There are over 140 ATMs.
Credit & debit cards: American Express, Diners Club, MasterCard and Visa are all widely accepted. Major hotels now also accept payment by credit card, as do major safari companies, travel agencies and restaurants. Check with your credit or debit card company for details of merchant acceptability and other services which may be available.
Traveller's cheques: These can be changed at banks, and are widely accepted. To avoid additional exchange rate charges, travellers are advised to take traveller's cheques in US Dollars or Pounds Sterling.
Currency restrictions: There is no restriction on the import and export of local or foreign currency. However, authorisation from the Central Bank is required for amounts of 500,000 KES and above.
Banking hours: Mon-Fri 0900-1500; 0900-1100 on the first and last Saturday of each month. National and international banks have branches in Mombasa, Nairobi, Kisumu, Thika, Eldoret, Kericho, Nyeri and in most other major towns. Banks in Mombasa and the coastal areas open and close half an hour earlier. Many of the banks and bureaux de change at the international airports open 24 hours every day.
Exchange rate indicators:
Rate at time of publishing
£1.00= KES129.59
$1.00= KES74.65

Duty Free

The following goods may be imported into Kenya by passengers over 16 years of age without incurring customs duty:
200 cigarettes or 50 cigars or 250g of tobacco; 1l of spirits or 2l of wine; perfume and toilet water not exceeding in all 0.5l of which not more than a quarter may be perfume.
Note: Firearms and ammunition require a police permit. Pets require a good health certificate, a rabies certificate and an import permit.
Prohibited items: The import of fruit, plants, seeds, children's toys and imitation firearms. The export of gold, diamonds and wildlife skins or game trophies not obtained from the authorised Kenyan government department is also prohibited.

Public Holidays

Below are listed Public Holidays for the January 2006-June 2007 period.
2006: Jan 1 New Year's Day. **Apr 14** Good Friday. **Apr 17** Easter Monday. **May 1** Labour Day. **Jun 1** Madaraka Day. **Oct 10** Moi Day. **Oct 20** Kenyatta Day. **Oct 22-24** Eid al-Fitr (End of Ramadan). **Dec 12** Independence Day. **Dec 25-26** Christmas.
2007: Jan 1 New Year's Day. **Apr 6** Good Friday. **Apr 9** Easter Monday. **May 1** Labour Day. **Jun 1** Madaraka Day.
Note: (a) Holidays falling on a Sunday are observed the following Monday. (b) Muslim festivals are timed according to local sightings of various phases of the moon and the dates given above are approximations. During the lunar month of Ramadan that precedes Eid al-Fitr, Muslims fast during the day and feast at night and normal business patterns may be interrupted. Many restaurants are closed during the day and there may be restrictions on smoking and drinking. Some disruption may continue into Eid al-Fitr itself. Eid al-Fitr may last anything from two to 10 days, depending on the region. For more information, see the *World of Islam* appendix.

Health

	Special Precautions?	Certificate Required?
Yellow Fever	Yes	1
Cholera	Yes	2
Typhoid & Polio	3	N/A
Malaria	4	N/A

Note: *Regulations and requirements may be subject to change at short notice, and you are advised to contact your doctor well in advance of your intended date of departure. Any numbers in the chart refer to the footnotes below.*

1: A *yellow fever* vaccination certificate is required from travellers over one year of age arriving from infected areas;

those countries formerly classified as endemic zones are considered to be still infected by the Kenyan authorities. Travellers arriving from non-endemic zones should note that vaccination is strongly recommended for travel outside the urban areas, even if an outbreak of the disease has not been reported and they would normally not require a vaccination certificate to enter the country.
2: Following WHO guidelines issued in 1973, a *cholera* vaccination certificate is no longer a condition of entry to Kenya. However, cholera is a serious risk in this country and precautions are essential. There was an outbreak of cholera in the Eastleigh area of Nairobi in June 2005. Up-to-date advice should be sought before deciding whether these precautions should include vaccination, as medical opinion is divided over its effectiveness; see the *Health* appendix for further information.
3: Immunisation against *typhoid* and *poliomyelitis* is recommended.
4: *Malaria* risk exists throughout the year in the whole country. There is usually less risk in Nairobi and in the highlands (above 2500m/8200ft) of the Central, Eastern Nyanza, Rift Valley and Western Provinces. The predominant *falciparum* strain has been reported as highly resistant to chloroquine and resistant to sulfadoxine/pyrimethamine. Mefloquine, doxycycline or malarone are the recommended prophylaxis.
Food & drink: Mains water is normally chlorinated and relatively safe. Bottled water is available and is advised for the first few weeks of the stay. Drinking water outside main cities and towns is likely to be contaminated and sterilisation is considered essential. Milk is pasteurised and dairy products are safe for consumption. Local meat, poultry, seafood, fruit and vegetables are generally considered safe to eat. Food prepared by unlicensed vendors should be avoided at all times.
Other risks: *Dysenteries* and *diarrhoeal diseases* are common. *Hepatitis B* is hyperendemic; *hepatitis A* and *E* are widespread. *Meningococcal meningitis* is a risk, particularly in the savannah in the dry season; long-staying visitors and backpackers should consider vaccination. *Bilharzia* (schistosomiasis) is present. Avoid swimming and paddling in fresh water; bathing in rivers and lakes is forbidden in national parks and is best avoided elsewhere due to dangers from wildlife and water borne diseases; swimming pools which are well chlorinated and maintained are safe. *Dengue fever* is present, as are *leishmaniasis*, *trypanosomiasis* (sleeping sickness) and *filariasis*. Avoid sandfly, mosquito and tsetse fly bites, and wear shoes to protect against hookworm. *Relapsing fever* and *typhus* are present. In June 2004, there were 141 suspected cases, including six deaths, of *leptospirosis* in a high school in the Bungoma district. A nearby primary school also reported two deaths. Travellers should be aware of these developments when within the Bungoma district.
Rabies is present. For those at high risk, vaccination before arrival should be considered. If you are bitten, seek medical advice without delay. See the *Health* appendix for further information.
Note: There is a risk of contracting *AIDS* if the necessary precautions are not taken. It is advisable to take a kit of sterilised syringe needles for any possible injections needed, as well as drip needles for emergencies.
Health care: Health insurance is essential. *East African Flying Doctor Services* have introduced a special Tourist Membership which guarantees that any member injured or ill while on safari can call on a flying doctor for free air transport. There are good medical facilities in Mombasa and Nairobi. The Kenya Tourism Federation (KTF) safety communication centre (24-hour) help tourists in difficulty (tel: (20) 604 767 in emergenmcies *or* 604729 *or* 601343 *or* 604730; e-mail: safetour@wananchi.com).

Travel - International

AIR:
The national airline is *Kenya Airways (KQ)* (website: www.kenya-airways.com).
Approximate flight times: From Nairobi to *London* is nine hours 30 minutes; to *New York* is 18 hours; to *Los Angeles* is 20 hours; to *Singapore* is 21 hours; and to *Sydney* is 25 hours.
Main airports: *Nairobi (NBO)* (Jomo Kenyatta International) is 16km (10 miles) southeast of the city. *To/from the airport*: A *Kenyan Bus Services* bus and a *Kenyan Airways* bus leave every 20 minutes (travel time - 40 minutes). Scheduled bus service to and from the town centre is available at unit 1 and 2 bus stops. Taxis are readily available, but the fare should be established before getting into the vehicle (travel time - 15 minutes). The state-controlled *Kenacto* taxis work on a fixed rate as do the British-style black cabs, and *Dial a Cab*, which are legally required to charge per kilometre. *Facilities*: Duty free shop, hotel reservation, bank/bureau de change, post office, restaurant/bar, car hire, internet cafe and wireless hotspots. *Mombasa (MBA)* (Moi International) is 13km (8 miles) west of the city. *To/from the airport*: There is a regular bus service by *Kenya Airways* to their city centre office in Mombasa (travel time - 20 minutes). Taxis are also available. Fares should be negotiated in advance. State-controlled *Kenacto* taxis and British-style black cabs work on a fixed rate. *Facilities*: Duty-free shop, bank, restaurant/bar, tourist information and car hire.
Note: Immigration procedures in Kenyan airports are likely to be extremely slow, so it is advisable to arrive early.
Departure tax: None.
SEA/LAKE:
Main ports: *Mombasa*. Short-distance ships sail between Mombasa, Mauritius, the Seychelles and Zanzibar. The ports in the Lake Victoria passenger service include *Homa Bay*, *Mfangano* and *Port Victoria/Kisumu*. The ferries in Lake Victoria connect Kisumu in Kenya to Mwanza, Musoma and Bukoba in Tanzania. Fares are paid for in the currency of the port of embarkation. It is also possible to get ferries from Mombasa to Pemba and Zanzibar in Tanzania, and also to Chiamboni in Somalia. Enquire locally for details.
RAIL:
Kenya is serviced by a single railway system running from Mombasa through Nairobi to Uganda, with branches to Nanyuki, Kitale and Kisumu. Another branch connects Kenya to Tanzania through to Taveta. Train services operate between Voi and Moshi (Tanzania) and between Nairobi and Kampala (Uganda). The sea port of Mombasa is linked to surrounding areas of Kenya and Uganda by rail. Travellers should check beforehand as these rail services may be subject to disruption. For more information contact Kenya Railways, PO Box 30121, Nairobi (tel: (20) 221 211).
ROAD:
The main crossing points from Tanzania are at Lunga Lunga and Namanga, with smaller posts at Isebania and Taveta. Some direct coach services operate. From Uganda there are crossing points at Buisa and Malaba. Note that at Malaba, the Kenyan and Ugandan customs posts are about 1km (0.6 miles) apart and no transport between them is available. For all road frontier crossings, it is advisable to contact the Kenya AA, PO Box 40087, Embakasi, Nairobi (tel: (20) 825 060-6) prior to departure from the country of origin for up-to-date information concerning insurance requirements and conditions.

Travel - Internal

AIR:
Kenya Airways (website: www.kenya-airways.com) operates an extensive network of flights, which includes scheduled services to Eldoret, Kisumu (on the shore of Lake Victoria), Lamu Island, Lockichogio, Malindi and Mombasa. *Air Kenya* (website: www.airkenya.com) offers scheduled flights from Nairobi to Amboseli, Kilimanjaro, Kiwayu, Lamu, Malindi, Masai Mara, Mombasa, Nanyuki and Samburu. Air Kenya also operates into all of Kenya's game parks. *Regional Air* also operates from Nairobi. There are also private airlines operating light aircraft to small airstrips. Planes can be chartered and are useful for transport into game parks.
Departure tax: None.
SEA:
Local ferries run between Mombasa, Malindi and Lamu. For details, contact local authorities and tour operators. It is also possible to hire a traditional Kenyan sailing boat (*dhow*) in Lamu, Malindi and Mombasa. This is a very basic form of sea travel which requires travellers to take their own food and drinking water. Trips can be arranged directly with the captain or through local travel agencies. There are several popular anchorage points for yachts at Mtwapa, Kiliti, Mnaroni and Lamu.
RAIL:
Kenya Railways Corporation runs passenger trains between Mombasa and Nairobi; trains generally leave in the evening and arrive the following morning after a journey of around 13 to 14 hours. There are also branches connecting Taveta and Kisumu to the passenger network. There is a daily train in each direction on the Nairobi-Kisumu route, and also an overnight service (travel time - approximately 14 hours). There is also a service through to Kampala. Trains are sometimes delayed, but most of the rolling stock is modern and comfortable, and most trains have restaurant cars. There are three classes: first class is excellent, with two-berth compartments, wardrobe, etc; second class is more basic but comfortable; third is basic. In first and second class, doors can be locked from the inside but when leaving the compartment valuables should not be left unattended. The dining-car service on the Nairobi-Mombasa route is very highly regarded. Sleeping compartments should be booked in advance. Sexes are separated in first and second class. Children under three years of age travel free. Children between three and 15 years of age pay half fare. Tickets can be booked at Nairobi railway station or through local travel agencies. For further information contact Kenya Railways (see address in *Travel – International* section).

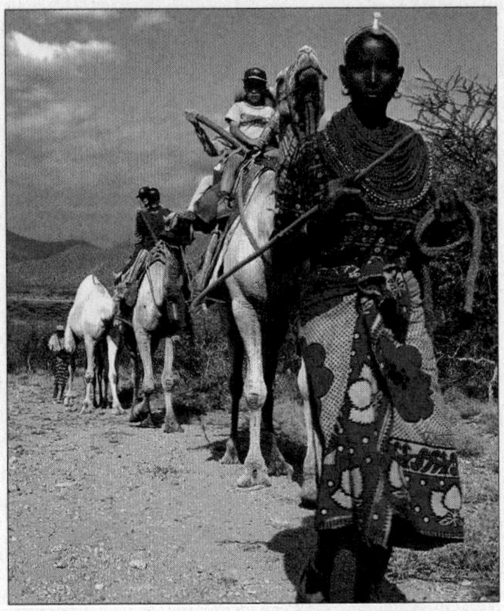
Credit: ©Kenya Tourist Board

ROAD:
Traffic drives on the left. All major roads are paved and many of the others have been improved, particularly in the southwest, although vast areas of the north still suffer from very poor communications. Care should be taken when leaving trunk roads as the surfaces of the lesser roads vary greatly in quality, particularly during the rainy season. There are petrol stations on most highways. The Kilifi Bridge linking Mombasa to Malindi serves as an alternative to the Kilifi ferry, and eases traffic flows to the northern circuit. **Bus:** Buses run regularly between most cities and towns. City buses operate in Nairobi and Mombasa at reasonable prices. Peak hours should be avoided as buses get very crowded. Buses also run across the borders to Uganda, tanzania and Ethiopia. Fares are paid to the conductor. There is a network of regular buses and shared minibuses (*Matatu*); the fares do not vary greatly, but buses tend to be the safer method of transport. All bus companies are privately run. Local advice should be taken for bus companies with a better safety record and reputation. In some towns the different bus services and the *matatu* share the same terminus. **Taxi:** Kenya is very well served by long-distance taxis, carrying up to seven passengers. The best services are between the capital and Mombasa and Nakuru. Taxis are not metered and a price must be agreed before departure. Taxis and minibuses are a convenient method of travel on the coast.
Car hire: Self-drive and chauffeur-driven cars may be hired from a number of travel agents in Malindi, Mombasa and Nairobi. This can be expensive, and rates - particularly the mileage charges - can vary a good deal. Most companies insist that only 4-wheel-drive vehicles should be rented.
Tours and safaris: Many tour companies in Nairobi offer package arrangements for visits to the game parks and other attractions. Before booking it is very important to know exactly what the all-in price provides. For further information contact Kenya Association of Tour Operators (KATO), PO Box 48461, 00100 Nairobi (tel: (20) 713 348 *or* 713 386; website: www.katokenya.org). **Documentation:** Visitors bringing in vehicles with registration other than Ugandan or Tanzanian must obtain an 'International Circulation Permit' from the Licensing Officer in Nairobi. This will be issued free of charge on production of a permit of customs duty receipt and a certificate of insurance. A full British driving licence is valid, otherwise an International Driving Permit is required. For further details, apply to the Registrar of Motor Vehicles in Nairobi.
URBAN:
Bus: Nairobi and Mombasa have efficient bus systems. Single tickets are sold (by conductors), but monthly bus passes are also available from the Kenya Bus Offices in the city centre. There are also unregulated *Matatu*, 12- to 25-seat light pick-ups and minibuses. These are often severely overloaded and badly driven and therefore should be used with caution. The three-wheel Bajaj Auto Rickshaw or *Tuk tuk* of South East Asia is becoming increasingly popular. In Kisumu, cycle rickshaws and bicycle taxis are popular. They are locally known as *Boarder-boarders*. **Taxi:** *Dial a Cab*, *Jatco* and *Kenatco* run fleets of taxis and these are usually very reliable. The older yellow-band taxis do not have meters, so fares should be agreed in advance. A 10 per cent tip is expected. Taxis cannot be hailed in the street. Hotels and restaurants can order taxis.
Travel times: The following chart gives approximate travel times (in hours and minutes) from **Nairobi** to other major cities/towns in Kenya.

	Air	Road	Rail
Kisumu	1.05	7.00	14.00
Mombasa	1.00	6.00	14.00
Nakuru	0.30	3.00	5.00
Eldoret	1.15	7.00	9.00

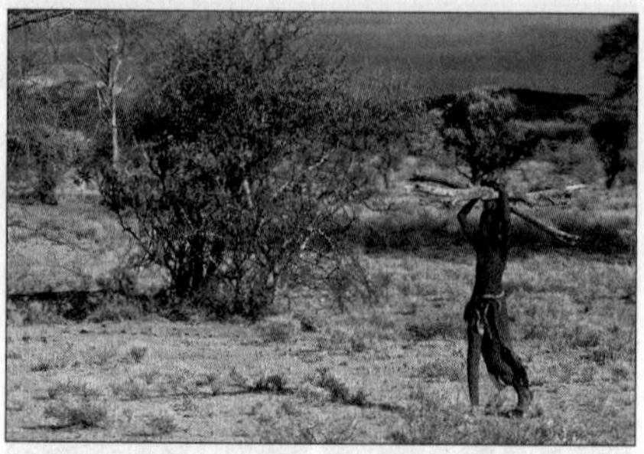
Credit: ©Kenya Tourist Board

Travel Advice

Kenya shares with neighbouring countries a high threat from terrorism. Previous attacks have been against civilian or visibly Western targets where foreigners have been present. These have included bomb attacks on a hotel and a western Embassy, both of which resulted in significant loss of life, and an unsuccessful attempt to bring down a civilian airliner in Mombasa.

Recently there have been skirmishes and inter-clan fighting in the North Eastern Province, along the Somalia border. People have been killed. Travel in the northeast should only be undertaken with care and after consulting the police. There have been a number of violent attacks and murders of non-indigenous residents in recent years. Muggings and armed attacks are also prevalent, particularly in Nairobi and Mombasa.

This advice is based on information provided by the Foreign and Commonwealth Office in the UK. It is correct at time of publishing. As the situation can change rapidly, visitors are advised to contact the following organisations for the latest travel advice:

British Foreign and Commonwealth Office
Tel: (0845) 850 2829.
Website: www.fco.gov.uk

US Department of State
Website: http://travel.state.gov/travel

Accommodation

EDITOR'S CHOICE: GAME LODGES/SAFARI TENTS

Many safari operators offer camping safaris. Vehicles, tents, guides and equipment are provided. The type of accommodation available on a safari depends on the type of safari booked. Upmarket safaris offer overnight stays in luxurious game lodges and luxury tented camps. These are often situated in beautiful or dramatic surroundings, with animals sometimes roaming around the grounds freely. Camping safaris are also available – but only travellers willing to live without luxuries such as running water or flushing toilets should consider this. The Kenya Wildlife Service recently completed the rehabilitation of selected self-catering *bandas* (cabins) in various national parks. These are privately owned country bush homes usually in spectacular locations, major cities or on main tour circuits. Most travel agents in Nairobi can arrange stays.

For further information, contact the Kenya National Tourist Office, the Kenya Wildlife Service (see *Top Things To Do*) or KATO (see *Travel – Internal* section).

HOTELS:
Many of Nairobi's hotels are of top international standards, and some of them are still in the colonial style. Cheaper hotels are also available. Small boutique hotels are becoming increasingly popular in Nairobi, on the coast and in wilderness areas. Hotel bills must be paid in foreign currency or Kenyan Shillings. Almost all towns in the country offer basic budget hotels and lodgings, and in many tourist areas private campsites offer budget rates for backpackers. **Grading:** Accommodation in Kenya is divided into groups: town hotels, vacation hotels, lodges and country hotels. Within each group, grading is according to amenities and variety of facilities. For further information, contact the Kenya Association of Hotel Keepers & Caterers, PO Box 46406, Nairobi (tel: (20) 726 640/2).

CAMPING/CARAVANNING:
There are no restrictions on camping in Kenya. However, visitors should be aware that camping in remote regions can be dangerous, owing to wild animals and to *shifta* (armed bandits); the latter are a hazard particularly in the far north. If camping in the vicinity of a village, culturally sensitive behaviour must be practised. Visitors intending to camp in remote areas should contact the Kenya Association of Tour Operators (see *Travel – Internal* section) or Kenya Wildlife Service (KWS) (see *Top Things To Do*). Most game reserves and national parks have camp grounds and basic facilities. Clear tent space and long drop latrines are often available.

YOUTH HOSTELS:
There are youth hostels in all major towns. For further information, contact the Kenya Youth Hostels Association, Ralph Bunche Road, PO Box 48661, Nairobi (tel: (20) 723 012; e-mail: kyha@africaonline.co.ke).

SELF CATERING:
Apartments ranging from luxury villas to basic beach cottages can be rented. Assistance with domestic chores can also be arranged.

HOME STAY:
Home stays with Kenyan families can be arranged for visitors wishing to discover the way of life in a typical home.

Top Things To See

- In **Mombasa**, enjoy the city's Arab flavour in the **Old Town** with its narrow, crowded streets and street vendors selling all manner of local and imported craftwork; continue to **Fort Jesus**, now a museum, with *son et lumière* shows; the **Old Harbour** is an interesting place for early morning and late afternoon strolls, and is often filled with sailing *dhows* from the Yemen and Persian Gulf. Excellent information about the city can be found online (website: www.mombasaonline.com).
- In **Nairobi**, the 'Green City in the Sun', see the ethnographic and archaeological exhibits of the **Kenya National Museum** (this is where many of the earliest human remains, discovered by the Leakeys at Olduvai, Koobi Fora and other well-known prehistoric sites, are displayed). In the suburb of Karen, go to the **Karen Blixen Museum,** which occupies the farmhouse made famous by the author's book, *Out of Africa*.
- In the **Bomas of Kenya**, a short distance outside Nairobi's city centre, see displays of **traditional dancing**. On **Lamu Island**, see dancing and other celebrations at a week-long festival on the Prophet's Birthday.
- In **Lamu Town**, a Swahili town on **Lamu Island**, see many mosques and fine old Arab houses with impressive carved wooden doors. Go to the **Lamu Museum** and the **Swahili House Museum**. The **Fortress** is also open to the public. Other attractions in the city include the **Hindu Temple** in Mwagogo Road, off Treasury Square, and the bazaars. Day trips to the 14th- and 15th-century ruins on the nearby islands of **Manda** and **Pate** can be arranged with local boat owners.
- Close to **Watamu**, in the town of **Gedi,** see the well-preserved ruins of a Swahili city, founded in the 13th century and destroyed by Somali raiders in the 17th century. The **Arabuko-Sokoke Forest**, south of Watamu, and the little village of **Mambrui**, north of Malindi, are also worth a visit.
- In the **Amboseli Park**, which lies on the Tanzanian border 220km (140 miles) from Nairobi, see fine views of snow-capped **Mount Kilimanjaro**, Africa's highest mountain (5895m/19,340ft).
- North of Nairobi, take the road through the suburb of **Thika** to discover excellent views of the **Great Rift Valley**. The eastern wall of the Rift is made up by the **Aberdare Mountains**, while further east still looms the vast bulk of **Mount Kenya**. Between the two are several attractive small towns such as **Nyeri**; **Nyahururu**, home of the **Thomson's Falls**; **Muranga'a**, whose cathedral tells the story of the Mau Mau rebellions in a series of colourful murals.
- In **Aberdare National Park**, be enchanted by the sight of many waterfalls, the greatest being **Guru Falls**, which drops over 300m (1000ft). The western face of the mountain range is the sheer **Mau Escarpment**, which falls dramatically to the floor of the **Great Rift Valley**.

Top Things To Do

- Skate on East Africa's first **ice skating** facility. The Solar Ice Rink, which opened in December 2005, at the Panari Hotel in Nairobi, can accommodate 200 skaters and measures 15,000 square feet.
- Take a **dhow** (traditional Arab sailing ship) **trip** from **Mombasa**.
- Go shopping with atmosphere in **Mombasa**. **Biashara Street** is probably the best place to go to buy *kikoi* and *khanga* cloths; the main city market is the **Makupa Market**, off Mwembe Tayari and there is a floating market at **Tudor Creek**, to the north of the city. Serious souvenir shoppers should head for **Bombolulu Workshops** and **Cultural Village**, where 260 disabled men and women produce high-quality leatherwork, jewellery and other crafts. In the **Masai Mara**, buy traditional bead necklaces and decorated gourds from the Masai tribespeople, who will also be very keen to pose for tourist cameras in return for a fee.
- Close to Mombasa, visit the **Kenya Marineland and Snake Park**, **Bamburi Quarry Nature Trail**, which also has a butterfly farm, the **Mamba Crocodile Village** in **Freretown**, and the **Ngomongo Villages** cultural park, showing off the lifestyle of 11 different Kenyan tribes.
- West of the Mara, on the Ugandan border, **Lake Victoria** is the largest lake in Africa. Take an unforgettable **sunset boat trip** through the channel between Mbasa and Mholo Island.
- Go **scuba diving**, **snorkelling**, **sailing**, **water-skiing**, **swimming** and **surfing** on Kenya's **Coral Coast**, north and south of Mombasa. The most popular resorts include **Bamburi**, which is undertaking a project to protect the turtle nesting sites, **Kikambala**, **Kilifi**, **Malindi**, **Nyali**, **Shanzu**, **Lamu Island** and **Wasini Island**. Along the South Coast, one of the the best and most famous beach is the 10km long, dazzlingly white **Diani Beach**, some 40km (24 miles) south of Mombasa.
- The coast around **Malindi** is renowned for **game fishing**. **Trout fishing** in the lakes (notably at **Lake Naivasha** and **Lake Victoria**) is particularly good between November and March. **Deep-sea fishing** is good along the coast between July and April. Sailfish, marlin, wahoo, swordfish, kingfish, barracuda and tuna are all available. **Lake Turkana**, recently designated a UNESCO World Heritage Site, contains many unique species of fish and marine plants.
- Climb **Mount Kenya**, an extinct volcano, and at 4986m (16,358ft) above sea level, the second-highest mountain in Africa. The lower slopes are one of the last haunts of the black leopard and the black and white colobus monkey. *A Rockclimber's Guide to Mount Kenya and Mount Kilimanjaro* can be bought from the Mountain Club of Kenya, PO Box 45741, Nairobi 00100 (tel: (20) 602 330 (evenings); website: www.mck.or.ke).
- In the **Great Rift Valley**, escarpment walls 2000m high plunge to the flat-bottomed valley floor, decorated by a small string of volcanoes and brackish soda lakes. Walk up **Mount Longonot**, a dormant volcano (2885m/9466ft), that has recently been gazetted as a national park. At the top, enjoy the wildlife and the final spectacular views of the crater and along the Rift. There are also possibilities for **abseiling**.
- The most common way to see Kenya's rich wildlife is to go on a **safari**. For those staying on the coast, the **Shimba Hills National Reserve** is the most accessible place to see big game, leopard and Kenya's only population of sable antelope . There is also the **Mwalu-Ganje Elephant Sanctuary**. The largest park in Kenya, **Tsavo** covers a mammoth 21,000 sq km (8000 sq miles). The **Taita Hills** are the setting for most of the local game lodges. See large herds of elephants, buffaloes, a few rhinos, lions, antelopes, gazelles, giraffes and zebras. Crocodiles and hippos can be seen at **Mzima Springs** in the northwest of the park. **Tsavo** also has a wealth of birds, with over 440 species recorded. Just 8km (5 miles) from Nairobi city centre, **Nairobi National Park** was Kenya's first national park and today still looks much as it did in the early photographs – wild, undulating pasture dotted with every kind of East African plain-dwelling animal except elephants. At the gates to the park is the **Animal Orphanage**. Also near here, the **Langata Giraffe Centre** offers the enchanting opportunity of hand-feeding the resident Rothschild giraffes. The **Sheldrick Elephant Orphanage** is also nearby. In **Aberdare National Park**, get close to elephants, rhinos, dik-dik, leopards, lions and monkeys as well as rare forest antelopes such as the bongo, giant forest pigs, baboons and buffaloes. In **Lake Nakuru National Park**, see pink flamingos, along with hundreds of other species of bird. Above all, it is one of Kenya's rhino sanctuaries. In the **Masai Mara National Reserve**, in the southwest corner of the country, be fascinated by the spectacular setting for the great migration, the constant clockwise motion of an estimated two million wildebeests and zebra who arrive in the Mara from late June onwards, heading south again in September. The Masai Mara has the largest population of lions. Other animals to be seen, at any time of the year, include elephants, cheetahs, baboons, gazelles, giraffes, jackals, hyenas, water buffaloes, ostriches and several types of antelope. Due north of the Central Highlands are several game-rich, if less visited, national parks, including **Samburu, Meru and Kora**. There are several parks and reserves in the far north of Kenya, gathered around **Lake Turkana** (formerly Lake Rudolph).
  Each park or game reserve offers different types of animals and vegetation. For further details, contact the Kenya Wildlife Service (see *Tourist Information*). A list of safari tour operators can be obtained from the Kenya Association of Tour Operators, KATO (see *Travel - Internal* section).
- **Aeroplane** or **hot-air balloon trips** are available at the **Masai Mara National Reserve**. **Camel safaris** can be organised in the **Samburu and Turkana** areas between Isiolo and Lake Turkana.

TOURIST INFORMATION

Kenya Tourist Development Corporation
PO Box 42013, Utalii House, Uhuru Highway,
Nairobi-00100, Kenya
Tel: (20) 229 751 or 311 474.

Kenya Wildlife Service
PO Box 40241, Nairobi, Kenya
Tel: (20) 600 800.
Website: www.kws.org

Kenya Tourist Board in the UK
c/o Hills Balfour, Notcutt House,
36 Southwark Bridge Road, London SE1 9EU, UK
Tel: (020) 7202 6373 (dial 1).
Website: www.magicalkenya.com

Kenya Tourist Board in the USA
2249 R Street, NW, Washington, DC 20008, USA
Tel: (202) 387 6101.
Website: www.kenyaembassy.com

Credit: ©Kenya Tourist Board

Entertainment

FOOD & DRINK: Kenya's national dishes appear on most hotel menus. The country's beef, chicken, lamb and pork are outstandingly good, as is the wide variety of tropical fruits. Local trout, Nile perch and lobster, shrimps and Mombasa oysters are included on menus in season. Indian and Middle Eastern food is available in most areas. There is a wide range of restaurants in Nairobi and Mombasa, otherwise hotels in smaller towns offer restaurant service.
National specialities:
• Some game-park lodges serve game, including buffalo steaks marinated in local liqueurs and berries, often garnished with wild honey and cream.
• *Nyma Choma* literally means roasted meat, and is one of Kenya's best known specialities.
• Most Kenyans eat maize, beans and maize meal.
• At the small 'hotelis', *chai* (tea boiled with milk and sugar) and *mandazi* (doughnuts) are popular.
National drinks:
• Locally brewed beer (*Tusker* and *White Cap*) and bottled sodas may be found throughout the country.
• *Kenya Cane* (spirit distilled from sugar cane).
• *Kenya Gold* (a coffee liqueur).
• Traditional beer made with honey (*uki*).
• Locally made spirit distilled from maize (*changaa*) may sometimes be found.
Tipping: This is not required. Most hotels include a 10 per cent service charge in the bill. If the service charge has not been included, a KES20 tip is usual, although the amount is entirely at the visitor's discretion.
NIGHTLIFE: Most of the major hotels in Nairobi and the tourist resorts have dancing with live bands or discos each evening. There are also a few nightclubs. There is a large selection of cinemas in Nairobi which show mainly British, European and US films. Theatre is popular in Nairobi. There is a National Theatre and several small groups of dramatic companies, probably the best known of which are the *Phoenix Players*.
SHOPPING: *Khanga*, *kitenge* and *kikoi* cloths may be bought in markets. The Masai market is held in Nairobi city centre on Tuesdays. There is a particularly good cooperative shop in Machakos which sells *kiondos*, bags stained with natural dyes and with strong leather straps. *Makonde* woodcarvings are sold throughout the country, and young Kamba and Masai men sell carvings and necklaces on the beaches of the south coast. **Shopping hours:** Mon-Sat 0830-1230 and 1400-1730.
Note: The sale of souvenirs made of wildlife skins (this includes reptiles) and shells is forbidden.

Business

• **GDP:** US$13.8 billion (2004).
• **Exports:** Tea, horticultural products, coffee, petroleum products, fish and cement.
• **Imports:** Machinery and transportation equipment, petroleum products, motor vehicles, iron and steel, resins and plastics.
• **Main trade partners:** Africa (Uganda and Tanzania mainly), EU (UK mainly), and the Far East.

ECONOMY: The Kenyan economy is largely agricultural – 80 per cent of the population are dependent on the land, contributing around 30 per cent of national output. The main cash crops are tea and coffee, although pyrethrum, sisal, sugar and cotton are also important. Kenya is one of the few African countries with a significant dairy industry. Hydroelectric plants meet 80 per cent of the country's

energy requirements. The remainder comes from imported oil, which is also used for one of the country's principal industries, the manufacture of petroleum-based products such as plastic and chemicals. Kenya, which has one of Africa's largest manufacturing sectors, also produces cement, paper, drinks, tobacco, textiles, rubber and metal products, ceramics, and electrical and transport equipment. The mining industry, however, is very small. In the service sector, tourism is the largest industry and the country's principal source of foreign exchange; this increased significantly in 2004 with a 51.9 per cent increase in earnings over 2003.
Like many African countries, Kenya signed up to an IMF-imposed Structural Adjustment Programme in the mid-1990s but it lapsed following policy disagreements between the Fund and the Kenyan government. Further concerns, mainly concerning political reform and widespread corruption, disrupted Kenyan relations with its other major Western aid donors. The IMF and World Bank withdrew support entirely in January 2000. However, following introduction of anti-corruption measures and the privatisation of several major state-owned enterprises, the IMF is now expected to resumed its support by the end of 2003. The IMF approved the new Poverty Reduction and Growth Facility. The 2005/6 budget gave new emphasis to economic recovery strategies, with particular emphasis on increasing expenditure on health, education and infrastructure. In addition, for the first time, foreign investors have been allowed to take controlling stakes in Kenyan companies.
Overall economic performance has been disappointing due to the persistent Government failures and slow pace of reform. Since the election of the Narc Government, pace has begun to pick up. Economic growth reached 4.3 per cent in 2004. An estimated two million Kenyans are unemployed and the new Government, elected in 2003, plans to create 500,000 new jobs. Along with Tanzania, Kenya and Uganda have explored plans to establish a customs union as the first step towards an east African regional trading bloc (a previous effort collapsed in 1977).
BUSINESS ETIQUETTE: Lightweight suits are recommended for all occasions. Prior appointments are necessary. Although Swahili is the national language, English is the official language and is widely spoken. **Office hours:** Mon-Fri 0900-1300 and 1400-1700.
CONFERENCES/CONVENTIONS; Main urban centres, such as Mombasa and Nairobi, and most international hotels have conference facilities.

COMMERCIAL INFORMATION

Kenya National Chamber of Commerce and Industry
PO Box 47024, Ufanisi House, Hailé Sélassie Avenue, Nairobi, Kenya
Tel: (20) 220 867.
Website: www.kncc.org

Investment Promotion Centre
PO Box 55704, 8th Floor, National Bank Building, Harambee Avenue, Nairobi City Square 00200, Nairobi, Kenya
Tel: (20) 221 401-4.
Website: www.investmentkenya.com

The Kenyatta International Conference Centre (Information on Conferences/Conventions)
PO Box 30510, Nairobi, Kenya
Tel: (20) 332 383.

Kiribati

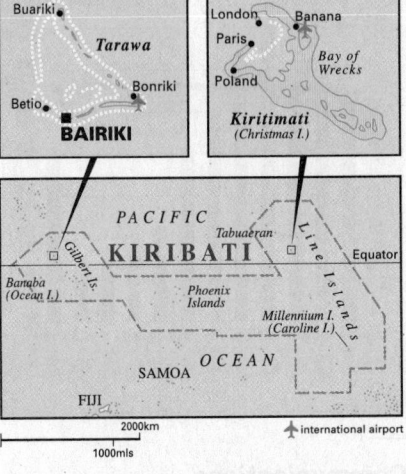

Location: South Pacific, Micronesia.

Time: Christmas (Line) Islands: GMT + 14.
Phoenix Islands: GMT + 13.
Gilbert Islands (including Tarawa): GMT + 12.

Overview

Kiribati is remote and tourism is very much in its infancy. However, after Kiribati changed the International Dateline to make its uninhabited Caroline Island the 'first to see the year 2000' (causing hefty arguments with neighbouring 'first-dawn' contenders Fiji and Tonga in the process), the country has moved further into the tourist spotlight. The islands boast superb white sandy beaches and crystal-clear lagoon waters.

General Information

AREA: 810.5 sq km (312.9 sq miles).
POPULATION: 87,400 (official estimate 2002).
POPULATION DENSITY: 104.2 per sq km.
CAPITAL: South Tarawa atoll (including Bairiki, the capital town). **Population:** 36,717(2000).
GEOGRAPHY: Kiribati (pronounced 'Kiribass', formerly the Gilbert Islands) consists of three groups in the central Pacific: Kiribati (including Banaba, formerly Ocean Island), the Line Islands and the Phoenix Islands. The 33 islands, scattered across 2 million square miles of the central Pacific, are low-lying coral atolls with coastal lagoons. The exception is Banaba, which is a coral formation rising to 80m (265ft). The soil is generally poor, apart from Banaba, and rainfall is variable. Coconut palms and pandanus trees comprise the main vegetation. There are no hills or streams throughout the group. Water is obtained from storage tanks or wells.
GOVERNMENT: Republic. Gained independence from the UK in 1979. **Head of State and Government:** President Anote Tong since July 2003. **Recent history:** The most recent Presidential elections were held in July 2003, in which Anote Tong defeated his older brother, Harry. The President has identifitied rising population levels, youth unemployment and the threat from climate change as the country's key issues.
LANGUAGE: Kiribati and English.
RELIGION: Christianity (53.4 per cent Roman Catholic and 39.2 per cent Kiribati Protestant), the Bahai Faith and Islam.
ELECTRICITY: 240 volts AC, 50Hz.
SOCIAL CONVENTIONS: Like the other Pacific islanders, the people are very friendly and hospitable and retain much of their traditional culture and lifestyle. In this casual

atmosphere, European customs still prevail alongside local traditions. Although in official correspondence the Western convention of signing names with initials is adopted, it is more polite (and customary) to address people by their first name. Bikinis should not be worn except on the beach. Nudity and overly scant swimming costumes are forbidden by local law.

Climate

Maritime equatorial in the central islands of the group. The islands to the north and south are more tropical. The trade winds blow between March and October, making this the most pleasant time of the year, while the highest rainfall (December to May) is concentrated on the northern islands. November to February is more wet and humid than the rest of the year.

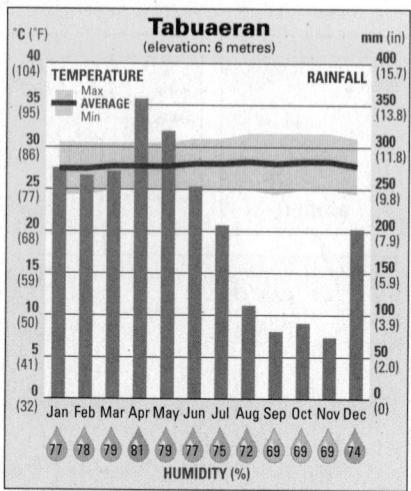

Tabuaeran (elevation: 6 metres)

TEMPERATURE — Max — AVERAGE — Min — RAINFALL

Jan Feb Mar Apr May Jun Jul Aug Sep Oct Nov Dec

HUMIDITY (%): 77 78 79 81 79 77 75 72 69 69 69 74

Communications

Telephone: Country code: 686. Most international calls from Kiribati have to go through the operator. IDD is available throughout urban Tarawa. Radio telephone calls can be arranged to most outer islands.
Mobile telephone: GSM 900 network in use. Network provider is *Telecom Services Kiribati Ltd* (website: www.tskl.net.ki).
Internet: There are currently no Internet cafes in Kiribati.
Post: Airmail to Western Europe takes up to two weeks. There is a weekly postal service for overseas mail. Post office hours: Mon-Fri 0900-1500.
MEDIA: Press: The weekly papers are *Kiribati Newstar* and *Te Uekera*, published in English and Kiribati. *Kiribati Business Link* is published in English.
Radio: *Radio Kiribati* is state run.

Passport/Visa

	Passport Required?	Visa Required?	Return Ticket? Required?
Full British	Yes	1	Yes
Australian	Yes	Yes	Yes
Canadian	Yes	2	Yes
USA	Yes	Yes	Yes
Other EU	Yes	1	Yes
Japanese	Yes	Yes	Yes

Note: *Regulations and requirements may be subject to change at short notice, and you are advised to contact the appropriate diplomatic or consular authority before finalising travel arrangements. Any numbers in the chart refer to the footnotes below.*

PASSPORTS: Passport valid for six months required by all.
VISAS: Required by all except the following:
(a) **1.** nationals of Spain, Sweden and the UK (irrespective of endorsement in passport regarding national status) for stays of up to 28 days; all other EU nationals *do* require a visa;
(b) **2.** nationals of Canada for stays of up to 28 days;
(c) nationals of Antigua & Barbuda, The Bahamas, Barbados, Botswana, Cyprus, Fiji, Grenada, Guyana, Hong

Kong (SAR), Iceland, India, Jamaica, Kenya, Lesotho, Liechtenstein, Malaysia, Malta, New Zealand, Norway, St Kitts & Nevis, St Lucia, Samoa, San Marino, Seychelles, Sierra Leone, Singapore, Solomon Islands, Switzerland, Tonga, Trinidad & Tobago, Tunisia, Tuvalu, Uruguay, Vanuatu and Zimbabwe for up to 28 days;
(d) nationals of Korea (Rep) and Nauru for up to 30 days;
(e) nationals of the The Philippines for up to 21 days;
(f) nationals of American Samoa, Ecuador, Guam, Marshall Islands, Pacific Islands of Micronesia and Palau for up to 20 days;
(g) transit passengers continuing their journey by the same or first connecting aircraft, provided holding onward or return documentation and not leaving the airport (some nationalities *always* require a transit visa; enquire at the Consulate).
Note: (a) Nationals of the following countries require permission to enter the country from the Principal Immigration Officer: Albania, Algeria, Bahrain, Bosnia & Herzegovina, Bulgaria, Cambodia, China (PR), CIS (except nationals of Belarus), Croatia, Cuba, Czech Republic, Egypt, Hungary, Iraq, Jordan, Korea (Dem Rep), Kuwait, Laos, Lebanon, Libya, Macedonia (Former Yugoslav Republic of), Mongolia, Morocco, Poland, Saudi Arabia, Serbia & Montenegro, Slovak Republic, Slovenia, South Africa, Sudan, Syrian Arab Republic, United Arab Emirates, Vietnam and Yemen. Visa application will take an additional two weeks. The nationals of some countries require references along with their visas; check details with the Consulate (or the Consular section at the Embassy or High Commission). (b) On arrival, visitors may apply for a Visitor's Permit to stay for a maximum of four months; a visa, return or onward travel tickets and sufficient funds for the duration of stay are required.
Types of visa and cost: *Tourist* and *Business*: A$50 (single- and multiple-entry).
Validity: From 20 days to four months depending on nationality. Enquire at nearest Consulate (or Consular section at Embassy or High Commission).
Application to: The Honorary Consulate or Consular section at the Embassy (see *Passport/Visa Information*).
Application requirements: (a) Completed application form. (b) Passport. (c) Travel itinerary. (d) Stamped and self-addressed envelope. (e) Appropriate letters from company/sponsors if on business. (f) Fee.
Working days required: Allow three weeks for postal applications. An additional two weeks is required when permission needs to be obtained from the Principal Immigration Officer in Tarawan.

PASSPORT/VISA INFORMATION

South Pacific Tourism Organisation in Fiji
Street address: Level 3 FNPF Place, 343-359 Victoria Parade, Suva, Fiji
Postal address: PO Box 13119, Suva, Fiji
Tel: 330 4177.
Website: www.tcsp.com

Honorary Consulate of Kiribati in the UK
The Great House, Llanddewi Rhydderch, Monmouthshire NP7 9UY, UK
Tel/Fax: (01873) 840 375.
E-mail: michael.walsh@sema.co.uk
Visas issued by appointment only.

Money

Currency: Australian Dollar (AUD; symbol A$) = 100 cents. Notes are in denominations of A$100, 50, 20, 10 and 5. Coins are in denominations of A$2 and 1, and 50, 20, 10 and 5 cents.
Currency exchange: Currency may be exchanged at the Bank of Kiribati Ltd or local hotels. There are ATMs at branches of the Bank of Kiribati/ANZ in Betio, Bairiki and Bikenibeu (all on Tarawa atoll).
Credit & debit cards: MasterCard and Visa have very limited acceptance. Check with your credit or debit card company for details of services which may be available.
Travellers cheques: Accepted in hotels, some shops and at the Bank of Kiribati Ltd. To avoid additional exchange rate charges, travellers are advised to take travellers cheques in Australian Dollars.
Currency restrictions: There are no restrictions on the import or export of either local or foreign currency.
Banking hours: Mon-Fri 0930-1500. The Bikenibeu branch is open 0900-1400.
Exchange rate indicators:
Rate at time of publishing
£1.00= A$2.38
$1.00= A$1.37

Duty Free

The following goods may be imported into Kiribati without incurring customs duty:
200 cigarettes or 225g tobacco or cigars; 1l of spirits and 1l of wine (only if aged 21 years and older); a reasonable amount of perfume for personal use (subject to declaration); one pair of binoculars, one camera and six rolls of film, one cine camera and 200m of film, one radio, one broadcast receiver, one tape recorder, one typewriter (subject to declaration); reasonable quantity of sports equipment for personal use (subject to declaration).

Public Holidays

Below are listed Public Holidays for the January 2006-June 2007 period.
2006: Jan 1 New Year's Day. **Apr 14** Good Friday. **Apr 18** Health Day. **Jul 12** Independence Day. **Aug 7** Youth Day. **Dec 25-26** Christmas.
2007: Jan 1 New Year's Day. **Apr 9** Good Friday. **Apr 18** Health Day.

Health

	Special Precautions?	Certificate Required?
Yellow Fever	No	1
Cholera	No	No
Typhoid & Polio	2	N/A
Malaria	No	N/A

Note: *Regulations and requirements may be subject to change at short notice, and you are advised to contact your doctor well in advance of your intended date of departure. Any numbers in the chart refer to the footnotes below.*

1: A yellow fever vaccination certificate is required from travellers over one year of age arriving within six days from infected areas.
2: Immunisation against typhoid and poliomyelitis is often recommended.
Food & drink: All water should be regarded as a potential health risk. Water used for drinking, brushing teeth or making ice should have first been boiled or otherwise sterilised. Only eat well-cooked meat and fish, preferably served hot. Pork, salad and mayonnaise may carry increased risk. Vegetables should be cooked and fruit peeled.
Other risks: *Hepatitis A* and *B* are reported. *Diarrhoeal diseases* are common. *Dengue fever*, including its haemorrhagic form, occurs in epidemics. *Diphtheria* and *tuberculosis* may all occur.
Health care: Health insurance is strongly recommended. Tungaru Central Hospital on Tarawa provides medical service to all the islands. Government dispensaries on all islands are equipped to handle minor ailments and injuries. Visitors should bring their own supply of basic medicines with them.

Travel - International

AIR:
 Kiribati is mainly served by *Air Fiji, Air Marshall Islands* and *Air Nauru*. The national airline is *Air Kiribati. Air Kiribati* flies to Honolulu (Hawaii) and Fiji and provides a weekly connection between Christmas Island and Honolulu.
Approximate flight times: From *London* to Tarawa via Sydney and Nauru is 30 hours 30 minutes.
Main airports: *Tarawa (Bonriki)* (TRW) lies 11km (7 miles) northeast of Bikenibeu. *To/from the airport:* Buses operate every three to four minutes from the airport to the capital. Other airports include *Christmas Island (CXI)*.
Departure tax: A$20; children under two years of age and transit passengers are exempt.
SEA:
 Main ports: *Banaba, Christmas Island* and *Tarawa*. Kiribati is served by *Norwegian Cruise Lines*, which call at Fanning Island.

Travel - Internal

AIR:
 Air Kiribati operates an internal scheduled service to nearly all outer islands, linking them with Tarawa.
SEA:
 Several passenger ferries run between the smaller islands. Boats are available for hire.

ROAD:

Traffic drives on the left. All-weather roads are limited to urban Tarawa and Christmas Island. Privately owned **buses** and **taxis** are available on urban Tarawa only. Buses are fairly cheap (A$15 is the maximum fare), but taxis are expensive (A$25 for a journey from the airport to urban Tarawa). **Car hire**: Available on urban Tarawa and Christmas Island only. **Documentation**: International Driving Permit required.

Travel Advice

There is some petty theft and you should take care with personal possessions.

Women travelling on their own should exercise caution, particularly at'night.

Most visits to Kiribati are trouble-free but you should be aware of the global risk of indiscriminate international terrorist attacks, which could be against civilian targets, including places frequented by foreigners.

This advice is based on information provided by the Foreign and Commonwealth Office in the UK. It is correct at time of publishing. As the situation can change rapidly, visitors are advised to contact the following organisations for the latest travel advice:

British Foreign and Commonwealth Office
Tel: (0845) 850 2829.
Website: www.fco.gov.uk

US Department of State
Website: http://travel.state.gov/travel

Accommodation

HOTELS:

There are few hotels in Kiribati, the major ones being on Tarawa, Christmas Island and Abemama. The small island of Kirimati also has a few hotels.

Accommodation is good although not luxurious, but there are plans to build a luxury 150-room hotel on Christmas Island. A 10 per cent service charge is added to all hotel bills. Further information is available from the South Pacific Tourism Organisation or the Honorary Consulate (see *Passport/Visa Information*).

REST HOUSES:

Inexpensive rest houses can be found on all the other islands - for example, Abemama, Captain Cook, Christmas Island, Otintai, Robert Louis Stevenson and Tarawa. However, cooking facilities are limited and visitors should take what they need with them. Prices for accommodation in rest houses vary considerably.

Top Things To See & Do

- The capital of Kiribati, **Tarawa** is fast becoming one of the most densely populated areas in the Pacific, being similar in density to Hong Kong. **The President's Office**, **Parliament** building and International Airport are all situated on **Bonriki**. A number of war relics can be seen on **Betio** and visits to World War II battlegrounds and natural history expeditions can be organised. Stretching for almost half the land mass of Kiribati, **Christmas Island** is covered in lakes and ponds and boasts some of the largest colonies of birds.
- Trips with studies of the local birdlife are available.
- Game fishing is extremely popular on the island. There are also trips to see outrigger canoe races and dancing contests.
- The main towns are **London**, **Paris** and **Banana**.
- Or visit the *maneaba*, a community meeting house, where visitors may enjoy traditional dancing, singing and storytelling.
- A fine way to get the whole picture of Kiribati is to take

a 'flight-seeing' trip on board frighteningly small planes. Tours take in the islands of **Abaiang**, **Abemama**, **Maiana** and **Tarawa** – other islands can be visited on request.

- The islands boast superb white sandy beaches and crystal-clear lagoon waters. However, swimming in south Tarawa Lagoon is not advisable due to the extent of its pollution, and extreme caution is recommended on oceanside reefs. There are excellent facilities for **snorkelling** and **deep-sea fishing**. It is also possible to charter boats for sailing across the **Tarawa Lagoon**. **Game fishing** on Christmas Island is also popular. A fishing licence is unnecessary and charters are easily available.
- **Birdwatching** is popular, especially on Christmas Island where millions of birds swarm everywhere.

TOURIST INFORMATION

South Pacific Tourism Organisation in Fiji
Street address: Level 3 FNPF Place, 343-359 Victoria Parade, Suva, Fiji
Postal address: PO Box 13119, Suva, Fiji
Tel: 330 4177.
Website: www.tcsp.com

Commonwealth Resource Centre in the UK
The British Empire and Commonwealth Museum Resource Library, The British Empire and Commonwealth Museum, Clock Tower Yard, Temple Meads, Bristol BS1 6QH, UK
Tel: (0117) 925 4980.
Website: www.empiremuseum.co.uk
Provides information on Kiribati.

Entertainment

FOOD & DRINK: Restaurants are few in number and are situated mainly in the larger towns. Local specialities in the southern islands include the boiled fruit of *pandanus* (screwpine), sliced thinly and spread with coconut cream. A Kiribati delicacy is *palu sami*, which is coconut cream with sliced onion and curry powder, wrapped in taro leaves and pressure cooked in an earth-oven packed with seaweed. It can be eaten on its own or served with roast pork or chicken. As in many of the islands of the South Pacific, there is a tendency amongst local people to regard imported canned products as luxuries.

Tipping: Not expected.

NIGHTLIFE: There are 'Island Nights' which feature traditional Polynesian music and dancing, film shows and feasts in *maneabas* (local meeting houses), which can be found throughout the islands.

SHOPPING: Handicrafts include baskets, table mats, fans and cups made from pandanus leaves, coconut leaves, coconut shells and sea shells. Sea-shell necklaces are popular, as are models of Gilbertese canoes and houses. A prized item is the Kiribati shark-tooth sword made of polished coconut wood with shark teeth, filed to razor sharpness, lashed to the two edges. These days, most examples are modern reproductions. **Shopping hours**: Mon-Sat 0800-1900 (some shops open until 2030), Sun 0800-1900 (most small shops).

Business

ECONOMY: The main agricultural crop is coconut, from which copra, the principal export commodity, is derived. Bananas, breadfruit and papayas are also produced, largely for domestic consumption. The local fishing industry has declined drastically, particularly after the closure of the state fishing company, but the sale of licences to foreign fleets is an important source of government revenue. Despite its remoteness, Kiribati has managed to develop a tourism industry which now accounts for about one-fifth of GDP. Kiribati remains heavily dependent on foreign aid and remittances from the many islanders of working age employed overseas.

Kiribati is a member of the Pacific Community, the South Pacific Forum and the Asian Development Bank. Kiribati is also involved with various regional initiatives to promote economic development. Most trade takes place with Australia, New Zealand, the UK, Japan, the USA, Papua New Guinea and Fiji. Kiribati is also one of the 14 signatories to the Pacific Islands Countries Trade Agreement, agreed in 2001, which plans measures to boost regional trade.

BUSINESS ETIQUETTE: Shirt and smart trousers or skirt will suffice most of the time; ties need only be worn for formal occasions. **Office hours**: Mon-Fri 0800-1230 and 1330-1615.

Korea (Democratic People's Republic of)

Location: Far East.

Time: GMT + 9.

Overview

The Democratic People's Republic of Korea shares borders with China, the Sea of Japan, the Yellow Sea and the demilitarised zone (separating it from the Republic of Korea). North Korea's capital, Pyongyang, was completely rebuilt after the Korean War as a city of wide avenues, neatly designed parks and enormous marble public buildings. The Palace of Culture, the Grand Theatre, the Juche Tower and the Ongrui Restaurant epitomise the Korean variant of Communist architecture. The Gates of Pyongyang and the Arch of Triumph (built in honour of Kim Il-Sung's 70th birthday) are particularly impressive. Many ancient buildings in Kaesong (six hours from the capital by train) bear witness to Korea's 500-year-old imperial history. The town is surrounded by beautiful pine-clad hills. Kumgangsan is the country's largest national park, consisting of a range of mountains (known as 'the Diamond Mountains') along the east coast of the country. A night at the opera provides a unique experience. There are also circuses and musical events of a high quality.

Please note that only travel companies officially recognised by the North Korean Authorities are permitted to bring groups of tourists to Korea (Dem Rep). Independent tourism is not permitted, and foreigners must be accompanied by a guide at all times.

General Information

AREA: 122,762 sq km (47,399 sq miles).

POPULATION: 22.5 million (UN estimate 2002).

POPULATION DENSITY: 183.6 per sq km.

CAPITAL: Pyongyang. **Population:** 2.7 million (1993).

GEOGRAPHY: The Democratic People's Republic of Korea shares borders in the north with China, in the east with the Sea of Japan, in the west with the Yellow Sea, and in the south with the demilitarised zone (separating it from the Republic of Korea). Most of the land consists of hills and low mountains and only a small area is cultivable. Intensive water and soil conservation programmes, including land reclamation from the sea, are given high priority. The eastern coast is rocky and steep with mountains rising from the water and this area contains most of the waterways.

GOVERNMENT: Communist Republic. **Head of State**: President Kim Jong-Il since 1994. Jong-Il is officially known

as Chairman of the National Defence Commission, with the deceased Kim Il-Sung regarded as the 'Eternal President'.
Head of Government: Prime Minister Pak Pong-Ju since 2003.
LANGUAGE: Korean.
RELIGION: Buddhism, Christianity and Chundo Kyo are officially cited as the main religions.
ELECTRICITY: 110/220 volts AC, 60Hz.
SOCIAL CONVENTIONS: Discretion and a low political profile are advised. **Photography**: It is strongly advised to ask permission before taking a photo. Photographs of Korean officials or guarded buildings should be avoided.

Climate

Moderate with four distinct seasons. The hottest time is July to August, which is also the rainy season; coldest is from December to January, winters in the far north can be very severe. Spring and autumn are mild and mainly dry.
Required clothing: Lightweight cottons and linens are worn during the summer. Light- to mediumweights are advised in the spring and autumn, and medium- to heavyweights in the winter. Waterproofs are advisable during the rainy season.

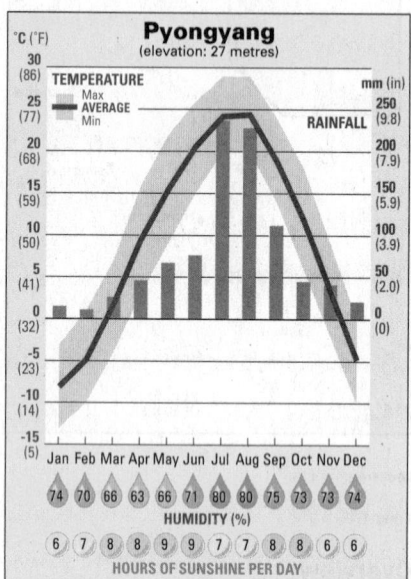

Pyongyang (elevation: 27 metres)

Communications

Telephone: IDD to the country is available, although there is a very sparse internal network. Some hotels in Pyongyang provide direct international calls although this may be expensive. Country code: 850.
Mobile telephone: Limited GSM 900 network. *SUNNET* is the only network provider.
Internet: Access to the internet is unavailable.
Post: Services are extremely slow and limited outside the capital. Airmail takes about 10 days to reach Western Europe. Post office hours: Mon-Sat 0900-2100.
MEDIA: Press: *Rodong Sinmun* (Labour Daily) is the organ of the Korean Workers' Party; other publications include *Joson Inmingun* (Korean People's Army Daily), *Minju Choson* (Democratic Korea), which is Government-owned and *Rodongja Sinmum* (Workers' Newspaper), the organ of the trade union federation.
TV: *Korean Central TV* is the TV channel of the Korean Workers' Party; *Mansudae TV* is a cultural channel.
Radio: *Korean Central Broadcasting Station* is the radio station of the Korean Workers' Party; *Voice of Korea* is a state-run external service, via shortwave.

Passport/Visa

	Passport Required?	Visa Required?	Return Ticket? Required?
Full British	Yes	Yes	Yes
Australian	Yes	Yes	Yes
Canadian	Yes	Yes	Yes
USA	Yes	Yes	Yes
Other EU	Yes	Yes	Yes
Japanese	Yes	Yes	Yes

Note: Regulations and requirements may be subject to change at short notice, and you are advised to contact the appropriate diplomatic or consular authority before finalising travel arrangements. Any numbers in the chart refer to the footnotes below.

Note: Tourism in Korea (Dem Rep) is currently permitted only in officially organised groups. Visas can be obtained through officially recognised travel companies or the nearest Korea (Dem Rep) Embassy.
Passports: Valid passport required by all, including nationals of Korea (Dem Rep).
VISAS: Required by all, including nationals of Korea (Dem Rep).
Types of visa and cost: *Ordinary* and *Tourist*: £30.
Application to: Consular section of the General Delegation of the DPRK or of the nearest Korean (Dem Rep) Embassy. Applications should be made by an officially recognised tour operator.
Application requirements: (a) Valid passport. (b) One passport-size photo. (c) One completed application form. (d) Tour confirmation from recognised travel company. (e) Proof of sufficient funds to cover stay. (f) Copy of applicant's passport.
Working days required: Approximately 20 days.
Note: For stays of over 24 hours registration with the MFA is required, although most hotels and travel agents will automatically do this for the visitor. It is advisable to contact the nearest Embassy prior to departure for further details.

> **PASSPORT/VISA INFORMATION**
>
> **Embassy of the Democratic People's Republic of Korea in the UK**
> 73 Gunnersbury Avenue, Ealing, London W5 4LP, UK
> Tel: (020) 8992 4965. Fax: (020) 8992 2053.

Money

Currency: Won (KPW) = 100 chon. Notes are in denominations of KPW100, 50, 10, 5 and 1. Coins are in denominations of KPW1, and 50, 10, 5 and 1 chon.
Note: Hotels tend to only accept cash payments in local currency whilst shops prefer US Dollars.
Currency exchange: Currencies may be changed at the Trade Bank (Mon-Sat 0900-1200 and 1400-1700) or at some hotels. Convertible currencies include Australian, Hong Kong and US Dollars, Euros, Pounds Sterling and Yen.
Credit & debit cards: Main hotels in Pyongyang will accept credit and debit cards such as Mastercard and Visa. However, American Express is not usually accepted.
Traveller's cheques: Generally not accepted. However, US Dollars are often accepted as an alternative method of payment.
Currency restrictions: The import and export of local currency is prohibited. The import and export of foreign currency is unrestricted, subject to declaration on arrival.
Exchange rate indicators:
Rate at time of publishing
£1.00= KPW3.82
$1.00= KPW2.20

Duty Free

The following goods may be imported into Korea (Dem Rep) without incurring customs duty:
A reasonable amount of tobacco and alcoholic beverages.
Prohibited items: Binoculars, arms, ammunition, explosives, drugs, any books or literature in Korean language, and seeds. Animals, plants and all groceries require certificates of entry.
Note: Gifts, precious metals and personal items such as cameras, watches and tape recorders must be declared.

Public Holidays

Below are listed Public Holidays for the January 2006-June 2007 period.
2006: Jan 1 New Year's Day. **Feb 16** Kim Jong-Il's Birthday. **Apr 15** Day of the Sun/Kim Il-Sung's Birthday. **Apr 25** Foundation of the People's Army. **May 1** International

Workers' Day. **Jul 27** Victory Day. **Aug 15** Anniversary of Liberation. **Sep 9** Independence Day. **Oct 5-7** Ch'usok (Harvest Moon Festival). **Oct 10** Foundation of the Korean Workers' Party. **Dec 27** Constitution Day.
2007: Jan 1 New Year's Day. **Feb 16** Kim Jong-Il's Birthday. **Apr 15** Day of the Sun/Kim Il-Sung's Birthday. **Apr 25** Foundation of the People's Army. **May 1** International Workers' Day. **Jul 27** Victory Day. **Aug 15** Anniversary of Liberation. **Sep 9** Independence Day. **Sep 24-26** Ch'usok (Harvest Moon Festival). **Oct 10** Foundation of the Korean Workers' Party. **Dec 27** Constitution Day.

Health

	Special Precautions?	Certificate Required?
Yellow Fever	No	No
Cholera	1	No
Typhoid & Polio	2	N/A
Malaria	3	N/A

Note: Regulations and requirements may be subject to change at short notice, and you are advised to contact your doctor well in advance of your intended date of departure. Any numbers in the chart refer to the footnotes below.

1: Following WHO guidelines issued in 1973, a cholera vaccination certificate is not a condition of entry to the Democratic People's Republic of Korea. However, cholera is a risk in this country and precautions are essential. Up-to-date advice should be sought before deciding whether these precautions should have a vaccination, as medical opinion is divided over its effectiveness; see the *Health* appendix.
2: Immunisation against typhoid is highly recommended, and against poliomyelitis is generally advised.
3: Malaria risk is low and exists mainly in the benign vivax form.
Food & drink: All water should be regarded as a potential health risk. Water used for drinking, brushing teeth or making ice should have first been boiled or otherwise sterilised. Bottled water is widely available and considered fine to drink. Milk is unpasteurised and should be boiled. Powdered or tinned milk is available and is advised, but make sure that it is reconstituted with pure water. Avoid dairy products which are likely to have been made from unboiled milk. Only eat well-cooked meat and fish, preferably served hot. Pork, salad and mayonnaise may carry increased risk. Vegetables should be cooked and fruit peeled.
Other risks: Diarrhoeal diseases including *giardiasis*, *dysentery* and *typhoid fever* are common. *Hepatitis B* is endemic in the area. *Hepatitis A* and *E* also occur along with tuberculosis. Epidemics of *Japanese encephalitis* and *dengue fever* may occur.
Rabies is present. For those at high risk, vaccination before arrival should be considered. If you are bitten, seek medical advice without delay.
Health care: 'People's Hospitals' and clinics are found throughout the country, but resources can be limited and basic. At present, emergency medical flights are not permitted into the country. Tourist sites generally provide medical facilities. International travellers are strongly advised to take out health insurance.

Travel - International

AIR: The national airline is *Air Koryo (JS)*. During the summer months *China Northern Airlines (CJ)* also serves Korea (Dem Rep). Direct flights run four times a week from Beijing (China) with both airlines, and *Air Koryo* also operates weekly flights to Beijing and Shenyang (China), Bangkok (Thailand), Macau (SAR) and Moscow and Vladivostok (Russian Federation).
Approximate flight times: From Pyongyang to *London* is 13 hours.
Main airports: *Pyongyang (FNJ)* (Sunan) is 24km (15 miles) from the city (travel time – 45 minutes). *Facilities*: Bars, restaurants and duty free shops.
Departure tax: None.
SEA: **Main ports:** *Chongjin, Haeju, Hungnam, Kimchaek, Kosong, Najin, Sinuiju, Sonbong, Songnim, Unsang, Wonsan, Nampo* and *Pyongyang.*
RAIL: The country has a relatively good rail network with connections to China and the Russian Federation. The *Trans-Mongolian Railway* and *Trans-China Railway* runs between Shineuiju and China. Namyang connects with the *Trans-Manchurian Railway* and *Trans-Siberia Railway* links Rajin with the Russian Federation. There are no routes to the Republic of Korea, although it is hoped that these may open sometime in the future, following negotiations between the two countries.

ROAD:
There are roads from Dandong, Lu-ta, Liaoyang, Jilin and Changchun in China and Vladivostock in the Russian Federation, but foreigners are only permitted to enter the country by rail or by air.

Travel - Internal

AIR:

There are flights from Chongjin, Hamhung, Kaesong, Kanggye, Kiliju, Pyongyang, Sinuiju and Wonsan, although foreigners are not allowed to use these.

RAIL:

The extensive rail network built by the Japanese during World War II has been broken by the separation of North and South Korea, but the main passenger routes run from Pyongyang to Sinuiju, Haeju and Chongjin. Service, however, is slow. Timetables are not published and it is advised to purchase tickets through a travel agent.

ROAD:

Traffic drives on the right. The quality of major roads is good; many are dual carriageways. All roads leading out of Pyongyang have police security checkpoints where identity documents must be produced before continuing the journey. There are no buses between cities. There are very few road signs. International driving licences are not accepted and in order to drive within the country it is necessary to sit a local driving test and obtain a local licence.

URBAN:

Pyongyang has a two-line metro and regular bus services.
Travel times: The following chart gives approximate travel times (in hours and minutes) from **Pyongyang** to other major cities/towns in the Democratic People's Republic of Korea.

	Road	Rail
Diamond Mt	10.00	-
Kaesong	8.00	6.00
Nampo	1.30	8.00

Travel Advice

It is not possible to enter the Korea (Dem Rep) from the Republic of Korea (South Korea).
The threat from terrorism in Korea (Dem Rep) is low, but you should be aware of the global risk of indiscriminate terrorist attacks, which could be against civilian targets, including places frequented by foreigners.
Travellers should register with their Embassy in Pyongyang on arrival.
Travel within Korea (Dem Rep) is severely restricted.
This advice is based on information provided by the Foreign and Commonwealth Office in the UK. It is correct at time of publishing. As the situation can change rapidly, visitors are advised to contact the following organisations for the latest travel advice:

British Foreign and Commonwealth Office
Tel: (0845) 850 2829.
Website: www.fco.gov.uk

US Department of State
Website: http://travel.state.gov/travel

Accommodation

Pyongyang has a few first-class hotels where foreign visitors stay, although groups cannot know in advance which one will be used. All other towns have at least one first-class hotel for use by groups. Visitors must stay in designated tourist hotels (rather than in local *yogwan*). These are generally of reasonable standard, and are graded as deluxe, first, second and third class.

Top Things To See & Do

- Korea (Dem Rep)'s capital, **Pyongyang**, was completely rebuilt after the Korean War as a city of wide avenues, neatly designed parks and enormous marble public buildings, leading to its alternative name of the 'youthful city'. The **Palace of Culture**, the **Grand Theatre**, the **Juche Tower** and the **Ongrui Restaurant** epitomise the Korean variant of Communist architecture. The **Gates of Pyongyang** and the **Arch of Triumph** (built in honour of Kim Il-Sung's 70th birthday) are particularly impressive, while **Morangborg Park** and **Taesongsan Recreation Ground** (with its fairground attractions) offer relaxation. For the (mainly communist) *13th World Festival of Youth and Students* in 1989, a 150,000-seat stadium was built in Pyongyang.
  Mangyongdae, Kim Il-Sung's birthplace, is a national shrine. His family's thatched cottage, now a museum, overlooks the **Taedong River** and the capital.

- Many ancient buildings in **Kaesong** (six hours from the capital by train), bear witness to Korea's 500-year imperial history. The town is surrounded by beautiful pine-clad hills.
- **Kumgangsan** is the country's largest national park, consisting of a range of mountains (known as 'the Diamond Mountains') along the east coast of the country. Its unspoilt, diverse environment is popular with birdwatchers, photographers and botanists.
- **Myohyangsan**, whose name means 'exotic fragrant mountain', offers pleasant walks and climbs through a contrasting scenery of waterfalls, woods and Buddhist pagodas, just 120km (75 miles) northeast of the capital. The **Exhibition Centre**, with its imposing 4-tonne bronze doors, houses thousands of gifts presented by foreigners to Kim Il-Sung and his son.

TOURIST INFORMATION

The National Tourism Administration of the DPRK
Central District, Pyongyang, Korea (Dem Rep)
Tel: (2) 381 8901.
E-mail: nta@silibank.com

Kumgangsan International Tourist Company
Central District, Pyongyang, Korea (Dem Rep)
Tel: (2) 31562. Fax: (2) 381 2100.

Entertainment

FOOD & DRINK: Reasonable restaurants can be found in the main towns and cooking is usually based on the staple food: rice. In hotels and restaurants it is better to stick to the Chinese, Japanese or Korean items on the menu as experience of Western and Russian cooking is limited. Eating out is arranged by the guide.
Tipping: Officially frowned upon although some hotel staff may expect a tip.
NIGHTLIFE: A night at the revolutionary opera provides a unique experience. There are also circuses and musical events of a high quality.

Business

ECONOMY: The Democratic People's Republic of Korea has a Soviet-style command economy based on heavy industry. The country has rich mineral deposits, including most of the major base metals, as well as gold, silver and tungsten. Since the main industrial infrastructure was developed in the 1950s, development resources have gradually shifted to light industry and latterly concentrated on automation and modernisation. Most trade is conducted with the Russian Federation, Japan and China, where a number of joint industrial ventures have been set up. These measures have only partially compensated, however, for the serious loss of trade with the former Soviet Union, which precipitated Korea (Dem Rep)'s economic decline during the 1990s. Estimated at 4 per cent per annum, this contraction has been compounded by a series of serious floods. Although most evidence is anecdotal – in the absence of detailed official information – it is clear that the North Korean people have recently suffered severe shortages and, in some areas, starvation.
The North Koreans have yet to adopt political or economic reforms on the scale seen in China, the Russian Federation and Eastern Europe. China is the most likely model, but so far Korea (Dem Rep) has gone no further than devaluing the Won (a largely artificial measure since the Won is not convertible) and cutting the subsidies on some basic goods. Pyongyang has pinned its hopes on an improvement of relations with the South. There is $300 million of trade between the two countries, conducted at present through intermediaries. In August 2003, an economic and trade agreement was signed under which South Korean companies manufacture products in the North (where labour costs are much lower). The major obstacle is political: Washington is still hostile to Korea (Dem Rep)'s nuclear ambitions.
BUSINESS ETIQUETTE: Suits are required. Business transactions will take place outside the office, generally in the evening, as visitors are not allowed to enter offices.

COMMERCIAL INFORMATION

DPRK Committee for the Promotion of External Economic Cooperation
Jungsongdong, Central District, Pyongyang, Democratic People's Republic of Korea
Tel: (2) 381 6163.

Korea (Republic of)

Location: Far East.

Time: GMT + 9.

Overview

The first civilisation in Korea was centred on the state of Choson which developed in the northwest corner of the peninsula in the second century BC.
During the 19th century, Korea became a geopolitical pawn in the burgeoning regional competition between China, Japan and the encroaching European powers (plus the USA). After the 1895 Treaty of Shimonoseki, which ended the First Sino-Japanese war, Japan established a firm hegemony over Korea. Over the next 15 years, Korea entered one of the darkest periods of its history. The deep suspicion which continues to affect Japanese-Korean relations to this day dates from this period.
At the end of World War II, as Japan was stripped of its colonial territories, the Soviets and Americans agreed to divide Korea along latitude 38°N (the 38th parallel). As the Cold War evolved, the Korean border – one of the few direct meeting points between the Soviet and American spheres of influence – became a key flashpoint. Cross-border incursions increased until full-scale war broke out between the two sides in 1950. The three-year war which followed engaged all the major powers and came closer than is often realised to provoking a nuclear conflagration. By 1953, a stalemate had been reached and an armistice was signed (although the war was never officially brought to an end). For the next three decades, locked into opposing Cold War blocs, the two Koreas went their separate ways. Relations with its northern neighbour remain a major concern in Seoul and the border between the two countries is closed. Korea is a mountainous peninsular, which boasts breathtaking mountain scenery and a ruggedly scenic coastline.
Seoul's many attractions and excellent transport links make it the country's number one destination for foreign visitors and the logical place from which to embark on a tour of the country.
The country also has several dozen National and Provincial Parks, renowned for their natural beauty and numerous temples.

Korea (Republic of)

Credit: ©Boris Sedacca

Finally, The Republic of Korea also has considerable experience in hosting major international sporting events, notably the 1986 Asian Games, the 1988 Olympic Games in Seoul, the 2002 Asian Games and the 2002 FIFA World Cup, which it co-hosted together with Japan – the first time this major sporting event has taken place in an Asian country. Visitors will benefit from sports facilities of a generally high standard, particularly in Seoul and in the larger cities.

General Information

AREA: 99,313 sq km (38,345 sq miles, excluding demilitarised zone).

POPULATION: 48.2 million (UN, 2005).

POPULATION DENSITY: 485.3 per sq km.

CAPITAL: Seoul. **Population:** 9,853,972 (2000).

GEOGRAPHY: The Republic of Korea (South Korea) shares borders to the north with the demilitarised zone (separating it from the Democratic People's Republic of Korea), to the east with the Sea of Japan (East Sea), to the south with the Korea Strait (separating it from Japan), and to the west with the Yellow Sea. There are many islands, bays and peninsulas in the Korea Strait. The volcanic island of Cheju-do lies off the southwest coast. Most of the country consists of hills and mountains and the 30 per cent of flat plain contains the majority of the population and cultivation. Most rivers rise in the mountains to the east, flowing west and south to the Yellow Sea. The Naktong River flows into the Korea Strait near the southern port of Busan. The eastern coast is rocky and steep with mountains rising from the sea.

GOVERNMENT: Republic since 1945. **Head of State:** President Roh Moo-Hyun since 2002. **Head of Government:** Prime Minister Han Myung-Sook since 2006.

Recent history: Roh Moo-Hyun won closely-fought Presidential elections in 2002. A liberal reformer, he favours the 'Sunshine Policy' of constructive engagement with North Korea. The leaders of South and North Korea shook hands at Pyongyang airport in June 2000, while still technically at war since their conflict ended in 1953 without a peace agreement. Despite this historic handshake, relations with its northern neighbour remain a major concern in Seoul, particularly over the North's fragile economy and its nuclear ambitions. However, South Korea has resisted international calls for sanctions against the North. Following a scandal over illegal election funds, the Parliament voted to impeach Roh Moo-Hyun in 2004 but the move was overturned two months later by the Constitutional Court and he was reinstated. South Korea's President nominated Han Myung-Sook to become the country's first female Prime Minister in March 2006. She replaced Lee Hae-chan, who resigned. Ms Han has a reputation as a moderate. The Prime Minister's job is largely ceremonial in South Korea, where the President holds most important powers. Legislation is the responsibility of the unicameral Kuk Hoe (National Assembly): of the assembly's 273 members, 227 are elected in single-seat constituencies; the remaining 46 are chosen by proportional representation. Members of the assembly serve four-year terms.

LANGUAGE: Korean.

RELIGION: Mahayana Buddhism with a large Christian minority. Also Confucianism and Chundo Kyo, which is peculiar to Korea and combines elements of Shamanist, Buddhist and Christian doctrines.

ELECTRICITY: 110/220 volts AC, 60Hz. Government policy is to phase out the 110 volt supply and many hotels now have a 220 volt supply.

SOCIAL CONVENTIONS: Shoes should be removed before entering a Korean home. Entertainment is usually lavish and Koreans may sometimes be offended if their hospitality is refused. Customs are similar to those in the West. Small gifts are customary and traditional etiquette requires the use of the right hand for giving and receiving. Dress should be casual and practical clothes are suitable. Traditional costume, or *hanbok*, is mainly worn on holidays and special occasions. For men it consists of a short jacket and loose trousers, called *baji*, that are tied at the ankles. Women's hanboks comprise a wrap-around skirt and a bolero-style jacket and is often called a *chima-jeogori*. Both ensembles may be topped by a long coat called a *durumagi*.

Climate

Moderate climate with four seasons. The hottest part of the year is during the rainy season between July and August, and the coldest is December to February. Spring and autumn are mild and mainly dry and are generally considered the best times to visit.

Required clothing: Lightweight cottons and linens are worn during summer, with light- to mediumweights in spring and autumn. Medium- to heavyweights are advised during the winter.

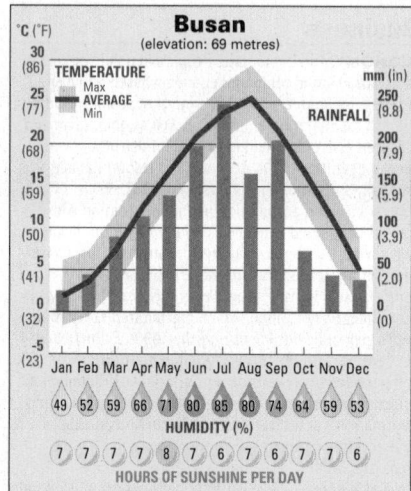

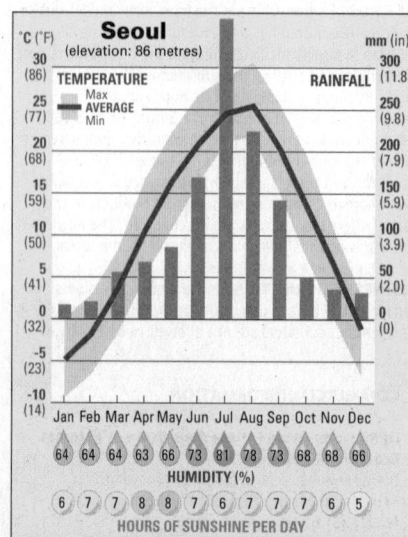

Communications

Telephone: IDD is available to Seoul and other major cities. Country code: 82.

Mobile telephone: Roaming agreements exist with some mobile phone companies. Coverage is sporadic. It is possible to rent a handset to use whilst in Korea (Rep); pre-booking is recommended (contact *SK Telecom* (website: www.sktelecom.co.kr) or *KT ICOM* (website: www.ktf.com).

Internet: Internet is available; there are Internet cafes in Seoul, and one in Taejon.

Post: Airmail to Western Europe takes up to 10 days. Post office hours: Mon-Fri 0900-1800. Gwanghwamun post office: Mon-Fri 0900-2000; Sat-Sun 0900-1800.

MEDIA: The major terrestrial TV networks dominate viewing and advertising revenue. Many South Koreans are connected to cable TV services and a digital satellite TV service competes for multichannel subscribers. There are more than 100 daily titles with national or local coverage.

Press: English-language national dailies include *Korea Daily News* (website: www.kdaily.com), *The Korea Herald* (website: www.koreaherald.co.kr) and *The Korea Times* (http://times.hankooki.com). Other newspapers include *Hankook Ilbo* (website: www.hankooki.com), *Hangyore Sinmun* (website: www.hani.co.kr) and *Munhwa Ilbo* (website: www.munhwa.com).

TV: Public operator Korea Broadcasting System (KBS) operates two networks. *Munhwa Broadcasting Corporation (MBC)* and *Education Broadcasting System (EBS)* are public. *Seoul Broadcasting System (SBS)* and Inchon-based *Inchon Television (iTV)* are private. *SkyLife* is a digital satellite TV operator.

Radio: Public operator Korea Broadcasting System (KBS) operates six networks. Public operator Munhwa Broadcasting Corporation operates *MBC Radio* and music-based *MBC FM*. Seoul Broadcasting System operates *SBS-FM*. *Buddhist Broadcasting System (BBS)* is a Buddhist network and *Far East Broadcasting Corporation (FEBC)* also has religious content. *American Forces Network Korea (AFN Korea)* is a station aimed at US military personnel.

Passport/Visa

	Passport Required?	Visa Required?	Return Ticket? Required?
Full British	Yes	No	Yes
Australian	Yes	No	Yes
Canadian	Yes	No	Yes
USA	Yes	No	Yes
Other EU	Yes	No/1	Yes
Japanese	Yes	No	Yes

Note: *Regulations and requirements may be subject to change at short notice, and you are advised to contact the appropriate diplomatic or consular authority before finalising travel arrangements. Any numbers in the chart refer to the footnotes below.*

PASSPORTS: Passport valid for a minimum of three months required by all.

VISAS: Required by all except the following:
(a) nationals of countries referred to in the table above except **1.** nationals of Latvia and Slovak Republic, who *do* need a visa;
(b) nationals of Albania, Andorra, Argentina, Antigua & Barbuda, The Bahamas, Bangladesh, Barbados, Brazil, Brunei, Bulgaria, Chile, Colombia, Costa Rica, Croatia, Dominica, Dominican Republic, Egypt, El Salvador, Federated States of Micronesia, Fiji, Grenada, Guam, Guatemala, Haiti, Honduras, Hong Kong (SAR), Iceland, Israel, Jamaica, Kiribati, Kuwait, Lesotho, Liberia, Liechtenstein, Macau (SAR), Malaysia, Marshall Islands, Mexico, Monaco, Morocco, Nauru, New Caledonia, New Zealand, Nicaragua, Norway, Oman, Palau, Panama, Paraguay, Peru, Qatar, Romania, Serbia & Montenegro, St Kitts & Nevis, St Lucia, St Vincent & the Grenadines, San Marino, Saudi Arabia, Singapore, Solomon Islands, South Africa, Surinam, Swaziland, Switzerland, Taiwan, Thailand, Trinidad & Tobago, Tunisia, Turkey, United Arab Emirates, Uruguay, Vatican City, Venezuela and Yemen.

Types of visa and cost: *Single-entry* (up to 90 days): £16.20. *Single-entry* (more than 90 days): £28. *Multiple-entry*: £45. The same fees apply for both business and tourist visas. Nationals of Italy, Japan, Spain, Sweden, Taiwan (China), Thailand and UK can obtain a visa valid up to six months free of charge.

Validity: 30-, 60- or 90-days.

Application to: Consulate (or Consular section at Embassy); see *Passport/Visa Information* for details.

Application requirements: These may vary according to visa required and nationality of applicant. (a) Valid passport. (b) Completed application form. (c) One recent passport-size colour photo. (d) Fee, payable by cash or postal order (but not cheque). (e) Stamped, self-addressed envelope, if applicable. (f) Proof of sufficient funds (a bank statement for £1000 if not working in the UK and a company letter if working in the UK). *Short-term business*: (a)-(f) and, (g) Substantiating documents for the activity of the applicant, eg letter of invitation from the host company in the Republic of Korea, business-related documents etc. *Private visit*: (a)-(f) and, (g) A certificate for confirmation of visa issuance, obtained by the person in Korea with whom the applicant will be staying. *Student*: (a)-(f) and, (g) Standard admission letter for students, substantiating the educational ability and coverage of the expense of the applicant, issued by the president or a dean of the University. (h) Substantiating documents for researchers, including a reference, if applicable.

Note: (a) For a national who cannot fulfill the necessary requirements and entry conditions (such as the expiration of passport validity) due to unavoidable circumstances, or is required for further review before a visa can be issued, a conditional entry permit may be granted with a validity of up to 72 hours. In regard to this permit, the chief of a district or branch office may impose conditions such as a reference, financial guarantee, restriction on duration of stay, a duty to obey summons or other necessary conditions, and, if deemed necessary, a monetary deposit not exceeding 10 million Won (US$10,000). (b) When a short-term visitor or unregistered national who visited Korea (DPR) re-enters the Republic of Korea, an immigration officer shall issue the same visa which was granted, minus the duration of stay in Korea (DPR). If a national's duration of stay on the visa expired whilst in Korea (DPR), or the remaining period is less than 30 days, a new visa may have to be granted. (c) A national who wishes to enter the Republic of Korea via Korea (DPR) must carry a valid passport and visa. If the national has a visa waiver agreement with the Republic of Korea, they must present a passport, a written paper outlining the reason for visiting Korea (DPR) and E/D Card (Immigration Card) to the Immigration officer at an inspection counter.

Working days required: Five.

Temporary residence: Applications for a residence certificate or for a stay of more than 90 days should be made to the Immigration Office in Seoul. For details contact the Consulate (or Consular section at Embassy); see *Passport/Visa Information*.

PASSPORT/VISA INFORMATION

Embassy of the Republic of Korea in the UK
60 Buckingham Gate, London SW1E 6AJ, UK
Tel: (020) 7227 5500 *or* 5505 (consular section).
Website: www.korea.embassyhomepage.com
Opening hours: Mon-Fri 0930-1230, 1400-1730.

Embassy of the Republic of Korea in the USA
2450 Massachusetts Avenue, NW,
Washington, DC 20008, USA
Consular section: 2320 Massachusetts Avenue, NW,
Washington, DC 20008, USA
Tel: (202) 939 5600 *or* 5661-3 (consular section).
E-mail: consular_usa@mofat.go.kr (consular section).

Money

Currency: Won (KRW). Notes are in denominations of KRW10,000, 5000 and 1000. KRW1000 is called *Chon Won* in Korean (*chon* means 'one thousand'). Coins are in denominations of KRW500, 100, 50 and 10.

Currency exchange: Foreign banknotes and travellers cheques can be exchanged at foreign exchange banks and other authorised money changers. ATMs are available in all major cities, but all instructions are in Korean.

Credit & debit cards: American Express, Diners Club, MasterCard and Visa are widely accepted at major hotels, shops and restaurants in the larger cities. Check with your credit or debit card company for details of merchant acceptability and other services which may be available.

Traveller's cheques: Accepted, but may be difficult to change in smaller towns. To avoid additional exchange rate charges, travellers are advised to take traveller's cheques in US Dollars.

The Korea Travel Card (KTC): This is a multi-purpose, pre-paid travel card sold by the Korean National Tourism Office, Shinhan Card and the Shinhan Bank, only to foreign tourists or residents. This card provides discounts on currency charges, international and national calls and provides free travel insurance. The card can be bought in denominations of KRW100,000, 200,000, 300,000, 500,000 or in a customised amount between KRW100,000 and 500,000.

Currency restrictions: The import and export of local currency is allowed up to KRW8,000,000. The import of foreign currency is unlimited, provided amounts greater than US$10,000 (including traveller's cheques) are declared on arrival. Export of foreign currency is limited to the amount declared on arrival.

Banking hours: Mon-Fri 0900-1700.

Exchange rate indicators:
Rate at time of publishing

£1.00=	KRW1824.09
$1.00=	KRW1029.02

Duty Free

The following goods may be imported into the Republic of Korea by persons aged 19 and over without incurring customs duty:

200 cigarettes or 50 cigars or 250g of other tobacco products; one bottle (not exceeding 1l) of alcoholic beverage; 57g of perfume; gifts up to the value of US$400.

Prohibited items: Narcotics, drugs, fruit, hay, seeds; printed material, films, records or cassettes considered by the authorities to be subversive, obscene or harmful to national security or public interests; products originating from communist countries.

Restricted items: Firearms, explosives and other weapons and ammunition, even for sporting purposes, unless prior police permission is obtained, and item(s) is/are declared on arrival; plants and and plant products require a phytosanitary certificate issued by the plant quarantine office of the country of origin.

Public Holidays

Below are listed Public Holidays for the January 2006-June 2007 period:

2006: Jan 1 New Year. **Jan 29-31** Sollal (Lunar New Year). **Mar 1** Independence Movement Day. **Apr 5** Arbor Day. **May 5** Children's Day. **May 13** Birth of Buddha. **Jun 6** Memorial Day. **Jul 17** Constitution Day. **Aug 15** Liberation Day. **Sep 26-28** Harvest Moon (Chusok). **Oct 3** National Foundation Day. **Dec 25** Christmas Day.
2007: Jan 1 New Year. **Jan 18-20** Sollal (Lunar New Year). **Mar 1** Independence Movement Day. **Apr 5** Arbor Day. **May 5** Children's Day. **May 2** Birth of Buddha. **Jun 6** Memorial Day.

Health

	Special Precautions?	Certificate Required?
Yellow Fever	Yes	No
Cholera	No	1
Typhoid & Polio	No	N/A
Malaria	2	N/A

Note: *Regulations and requirements may be subject to change at short notice, and you are advised to contact your doctor well in advance of your intended date of departure. Any numbers in the chart refer to the footnotes below.*

1: Following WHO guidelines issued in 1973, a cholera vaccination certificate is not a condition of entry to the Republic of Korea. However, cholera may be a risk in this country and precautions are essential. Up-to-date advice should be sought before deciding whether these precautions should include a vaccination, as medical opinion is divided over its effectiveness; see the *Health* appendix.
2: Malaria risk, exclusively in the benign vivax form, is limited to the demilitarised zone and to rural areas in northern parts of Kyonygo and the Kangwon province.

Food & drink: Mains water is normally chlorinated and, whilst relatively safe, may cause mild abdominal upsets. Bottled water is available and is advised for the first few weeks of stay. Powdered or tinned milk is available and is advised, but make sure that it is reconstituted with pure water. Avoid dairy products which are likely to have been made from unboiled milk. Only eat well-cooked meat and fish, preferably served hot. Vegetables should be cooked and fruit peeled.

Other risks: *Japanese encephalitis* may be transmitted by mosquitoes between June and the end of October in rural areas. A vaccine is available, and travellers are advised to consult their doctor prior to departure. *Hepatitis A* is common; *B* is highly endemic, as is *Korean haemorrhagic fever*. TB occurs.
Rabies may be present. For those at high risk, vaccination should be considered. If you are bitten, seek medical advice without delay. For more information consult the *Health* appendix.

Note: There were 19 cases of Avian Influenza (AI) reported in ROK between 10 December 2003 and 20 March 2004, in a number of areas including Eumsung, Chunan, Kyungju, Naju, Icheon, Hincheon, Ulsan, Yangsan, Asan and Yangju. The ROK authorities took immediate action by slaughtering five million birds, and no further cases have been reported since that time. No human infections or deaths have been reported in ROK.
Travellers wishing to stay for more than three months may need to supply a certificate showing they have tested HIV negative, issued within one month before their arrival in Korea. Ask at the Consulate (or Consular section at Embassy) for details.

Health care: Comprehensive health insurance is recommended. There are facilities in all tourist areas, and hotels will recommend a local doctor. International clinics at large general hospitals like Severance Hospital, Asan Medical Centre or Samsung Medical Centre are recommended. Almost all hospitals require payment and registration prior to

treatment. Most nurses and receptionists do not speak English; writing words out on paper can help in an emergency.

Travel - International

AIR:
The national airlines are *Asiana Airlines (OZ)* (website: http://us.flyasiana.com) and *Korean Air (KE)* (website: www.koreanair.com).
Approximate flight times: From Seoul to *London* is 11 hours; add one hour if flying to any other main European city. From Seoul to *New York* is 13 hours 30 minutes. From Seoul to *Los Angeles* is 10 hours 30 minutes. From Seoul to *Sydney* is 10 hours 30 minutes.
Main airports: Seoul (SEL) Incheon International Airport (ICN) (website: www.airport.or.kr) is located 40km (25 miles) west of Seoul on Yongion. *To/from the airport:* Limousine buses, taxis and coaches operate regular routes between the main urban area (travel time – 90 minutes). A ferry service operates a daily service (0500-2130) every 15 to 20 minutes between the airport ferry pier and Wolmido/Yuldo on the coast of Incheon city (travel time – 15 to 20 minutes). The Korea Train Express (KTX) has two lines (the Honam line, running from Seoul to destinations such as Cheonana, Iksan and Mokpo; and the Gyeongbu line, running from Seoul to destinations such as Gwangmyeong and Busan) to transport people from the airport. *Facilities:* Left luggage, banks/bureaux de change, chemist, duty free shops, post office, restaurants and tourist information.
Busan (PUS) (Kimhae) is 27km (17 miles) from Busan (in the far south). The airport receives flights from Fukuoka, Osaka and Tokyo. *To/from the airport:* There are bus, subway, coach and taxi services to the town. *Facilities:* Currency exchange, post office, duty free shop, snack bar, gift shop, restaurant, travel information service and car hire.
Jeju (CJU) (Jeju), located on the island of Jeju, is 4km (2.5 miles) from the town centre. *To/from the airport:* Buses and coaches are available to the town and leave every 10 minutes (0610-2230). Limousine buses and taxis are also available from the airport terminal. *Facilities:* Currency exchange, post office, duty free shop, snack bar, gift shop and travel information service.
Note: Seoul (SEL) Gimpo (GMP) airport is the main domestic airport, although a few international flights (mainly to Hong Kong) do still depart from there (see *Travel Internal* section).
Departure tax: KRW10,000. Transit passengers and infants under two years old are exempt.

SEA:
Main ports: *Busan* (in the far south) and *Incheon* (due west of Seoul). Passenger lines that sail to Japan are *Bugwan Ferry, Korea Ferry* and *Korea Marine Express. Jinchon Ferry* and *Weidong Ferry* sail regularly to China. Cargo/passenger lines include *Yellow Sea Ferry.* Weekly trips from the USA are offered by *CP Ships*. Under an agreement reached between Korea (Dem Rep) and Korea (Rep) tour operators, groups of tourists are now allowed to travel to Korea (Dem Rep) on cruise ships leaving from the port of Tonghae, in Korea (Rep), and sailing to the port of Changjon (see *Top Things To Do*).

RAIL/ROAD:
The Republic of Korea's only land frontier with Korea (Dem Rep) remains closed, although a limited number of tourists are now allowed to travel to the north via certain cruise ships (see *Sea* above).
Discount tickets: The *Korea-China Through-ticket* and *Korea-Japan Through-ticket* provide discounts on travel between the countries, including transport by ferry and train. For more information, contact KNTO (see *Top Things To Do*).

Travel - Internal

Note: It is not possible for British nationals to travel directly to the Democratic People's Republic of Korea (North Korea) from the Republic of Korea.

AIR:
Asiana Air and *Korean Air* run frequent services between Seoul and Busan, Taegu, Cheju, Ulsan and Kwangju, linking the Republic of Korea's 16 major cities.
The main domestic airport is *Seoul Gimpo (GMP)*, located 17km (10 miles) from the city. *To/from the airport:* Limousine buses depart to the city every five to 10 minutes from 0700-2215 (travel time – 40 minutes). *Airport Express* buses depart every 12 minutes. A subway line 5 runs to the city centre (travel time – 40 minutes). Taxis to the city are also available. The first phase of a railway link between Incheon Airport and Gimpo Airport (41 km/26 miles) was completed in 2005. In 2008, the second phase of the project, a 20.5km (12.5 miles) stretch between Gimpo and Seoul, will be complete. *Facilities:* Currency exchange, pharmacy, children's restroom, post office, gift shop, duty free shop, car hire, local products' shop, restaurant and travel information desk.
Departure tax: KRW3000-5000.

Credit: ©Boris Sedacca

SEA/RIVER: There are ferry terminals at: Mokpo, Yeosu, Jeju, Gunsan, Wando, Tongyeong, Pohang, Geoje, Donghae and Boryeong. Ferries connect Busan with Jeju-do Island. Car ferries also operate this route. *Han River Land Company* operates a cruise service on the Han-Gang River in Seoul, which runs through the centre of the capital. Children pay half fare and night cruises are available.

RAIL: *Korean National Railroads* connect major destinations. There are three classes of trains: Super-Express, Express and Local. Super-Express trains operate on Seoul–Mokpo, Seoul–Busan, Seoul–Chungju–Yosu, Seoul–Incheon (particularly scenic) and Seoul–Onyang (second-class only) routes. Some have air conditioning and restaurant cars. A supplement is payable for better-quality accommodation on some trains. Station signs in English are common and English translations of timetables are usually available. Children under six travel free and children six to 12 years old pay half fare. Timetables and fares are accessible online (website: www.korail.go.kr).

Korea Rail Pass: The Korea Rail Pass allows visitors free travel with reserved seats on any KR train (except subways) within a three-, five-, seven- or 10-day period. *Saver* passes are available for groups of between two and five people, and *Youth* passes for people aged between 13 and 25 years old. A Korea Rail Pass voucher can be purchased at certain offices and travel agencies abroad and exchanged for the actual pass at Korean railway stations. The voucher must be exchanged within 60 days from the date of purchase. For further details, contact the Korea National Tourist Organisation (see *Top Things To Do*).

Korea Rail Pack: This is a rail pass which includes accommodation and sightseeing services as well as the actual rail journey. Packs are available for two-, three- or five-days and include a free pick-up/drop-off service for major hotels in downtown Seoul, hotel accommodation with breakfast and an English-speaking guide throughout. Routes covered include: Seoul-Gyeongju, Seoul-Gyeongju-Busan, Seoul-Andong and Busan-Seoul. Children under three years travel free of charge and children under 10 years get a 30 per cent discount. Pre-booking is essential and the money for the journey must be received at least two weeks before departure (website: www.korail.go.kr).

ROAD: Cars drive on the right. Over half of the roads are paved. Excellent motorways link all major cities, but minor roads are often badly maintained. Road signs are usually written in both Korean and English.

Bus: Local and express buses are inexpensive, though local buses within cities are often crowded and make no allowances for English-speakers. Hotel staff will be able to assist in choosing the correct bus and stop. Air-conditioned city-express buses, called *Chwasok* buses in Korean and much more comfortable than local buses, operate in competition with trains for connections to major cities. Towns and villages are linked by local bus services. Fares are paid in change into the coin box to the right of the driver upon boarding. To stop the bus at your destination, push one of the stop buttons located along the length of the bus.

Taxi: Cheap and a good way to travel. There are also deluxe-taxis (*mobom* taxis) that are black with a yellow sign on top. Taxi drivers tend to speak little or no English. It is recommended that destinations are written in Korean and that you have a map of private addresses. **Car hire**: There are numerous car hire companies operating, including the major international ones. Some hotels and travel agents also provide a car hire service. **Regulations:** Seat belts are mandatory. Driving under the influence of alcohol or drugs is a serious offence.

Documentation: International Driving Permit required. Drivers must have more than one year's driving experience, be in possession of a valid passport and be over 25 years of age.

URBAN: Seoul has underground and suburban railways and well-developed bus services, all of which are very crowded during the rush hour. Underground station names, ticket counters and transfer signs are clearly marked in English as well as Korean. Underground lines are colour-coded, and all trains have multilingual announcements. Fares are relatively cheap, but do vary with service areas. The base fare for 12km is KRW800, 13 to18 year olds pay KRW640 and seven to12 year olds pay KRW400. Taxis are widely available. Good bus services also operate in other cities.

Travel times: The following chart gives approximate travel times (in hours and minutes) from **Seoul** to other major cities/towns in the Republic of Korea.

	Air	Road	Rail
Kwangju	0.50	3.55	4.20
Chonju	1.10	3.00	3.20
Kyongju	-	4.40	3.30
Ulsan	0.50	4.40	4.00

Additional times: From Busan to Cheju by sea is 11 hours (three hours 30 minutes via the super-express ferry). From Mokpo to Cheju by sea is five hours 30 minutes. From Busan to Kyongju is one hour by road and 40 minutes by rail.

Travel Advice

Most visits to the Republic of Korea are trouble-free but you should be aware of the global risk of indiscriminate international terrorist attacks, which could be against civilian targets, including places frequented by foreigners. Developments in the Democratic People's Republic of Korea (DPRK) (North Korea) could potentially give rise to regional tension.

It is recommended that British nationals coming to the ROK for longer than two weeks should register with the Consular Section of the British Embassy.

This advice is based on information provided by the Foreign and Commonwealth Office in the UK. It is correct at time of publishing. As the situation can change rapidly, visitors are advised to contact the following organisations for the latest travel advice:

British Foreign and Commonwealth Office
Tel: (0845) 850 2829.
Website: www.fco.gov.uk

US Department of State
Website: http://travel.state.gov/travel

Accommodation

EDITOR'S CHOICE: YOGWANS

These are Korean motels, very reasonable and considered by many travellers as the 'only place to stay'. Sleeping arrangements consist of a small mattress and a firm pillow on the *ondol*, the hot floor-heating system which is traditional in Korea. Some have Western-style rooms, but it is wise to check beforehand if it is required. KNTO can provide a list of yogwans throughout Korea (see *Top Things To Do*).

HOTELS: There are many modern tourist hotels in the major cities and tourist areas. All of these are registered with the Government. Most rooms have private baths as well as heating and cooling systems. Facilities in most tourist hotels include dining rooms, convention halls, bars, souvenir shops, cocktail lounges, barber and beauty shops and recreation areas. For further information and reservations, contact the Korea National Tourism Organisation (see *Top Things To Do*). A service charge of 10 per cent and 10 per cent VAT are included in hotel bills; tipping is not necessary. All registered hotels are classified according to their standard and quality of service. Hotels range from **5-Star** (super deluxe) to **1-Star** (third class). For further information, contact Korea National Tourism Organization, KNTO (see *Top Things To Do*).

GUEST HOUSES: This is an inexpensive way to experience Korean culture and meet other tourists. Many are re-modelled family homes and so have a shared bathroom.

COTTAGES (PENSIONS)/CONDOMINIUMS: Pensions are relatively new to Korea (Rep). They are often European-style villas and are usually located in tourist areas. They are especially popular with couples and families. Condominiums are apartment-style lodgings usually situated near ski resorts, famous mountains, parks and beaches.

LOG CABINS/MOUNTAIN HUTS: Situated in recreational forests and amusement parks, log cabins are ideal for families and groups. They are fully furnished with all services and amenities provided. Mountain huts and shelters (*daespiso*) are located in national parks and tend to be frequented by hikers. They have basic amenities: beds, light meals, clean drinking and bathing water, and are especially busy during the summer and autumn. From Nov 15 to Dec 15, they are closed to the public to prevent wild fires.

HOMESTAY PROGRAMME: This programme is supported by the Korea National Tourism Organization, offering visitors the chance to stay with a host family in Korea. For more information, contact the KNTO (see *Top Things To Do*).

HANOK (TRADITIONAL HOME) STAY: This type of accommodation is an ideal way to sample traditional life in Korea (Rep). All of the interior accurately reproduces a traditional Korean home with traditional sleeping pads and quilts provided. Some hanoks are located inside a hanok village.

CAMPING: Campsites are located throughout the country in national parks, recreational forests and amusement parks. Services such as 'tent rent' is provided as well as shower facilities and bathrooms. Contact KNTO for details (see *Top Things To Do*).

YOUTH HOSTELS: At present there are 52 youth hostels in Korea (Rep), mainly located in Busan, Kyongju, Puyo, Seoul, Sokcho and vicinities.

TEMPLE STAYS: There is also a Temple Stay Programme where visitors can, as the name suggests, stay in temples and see what goes on. Further information can be obtained from the KNTO (see *Top Things To Do*).

ACCOMMODATION INFORMATION

Korea Hotel Reservation Center
PO Box 1099, Fort Lee, NJ 07024, USA
Tel: (845) 426 7335.
Website: www.khrc.com

Korean Youth Hostels Association
Room 409, Jeokseon Hyundai Building, 80 Jeokseon-dong, Jongno-gu, Seoul, Korea (Republic of)
Tel: (2) 725 3031.
Website: http://yh.kyha.or.kr

Temple Stay Korea
Website: www.templestaykorea.com

Top Things To See

- In the capital **Seoul**, go to the **Changdeokung Palace**, surrounded by the picturesque **Secret Gardens**; the nearby **Chongmyo Shrine**, set in wooded grounds, contains the ancestral tablets of the Kings of the Joseon Dynasty. The **Museum of Modern Arts** is within the grounds of **Toksukung Palace**, a former royal villa. **Kyongbokkung Palace**, the most impressive of the palaces, dates in part to 1394 and has the excellent **National Folk Museum** and temporary displays of treasures from the fantastic collection of the **National Museum of Korea** within its grounds. See the symbol of Seoul, the **Great South Gate** (Namdaemun), which was the main gate in the city's 15th-century defences. For fine city panoramas, ascend **Seoul Tower** (236.7meters/ 776ft), which sits atop landscaped **Namsan Mountain**. Visit the **War Memorial and Museum** on **Yongsan-gu** military base which traces the history of conflict on the Korean Peninsular.
- See the impressively preserved and UNESCO-listed city walls and defences of **Suwon City**.
- Towards the centre of the country, **Mount Songnisan National Park** is another area renowned for its natural beauty. In the area there is **Mount Songnisan** and the **Hwayang**, **Seonyu** and **Ssanggok valleys** in the middle of the **Sobaeksanmaek Mountains**. See the impressive pagoda, and a number of art treasures such as the largest Buddha statue in the world (**Cheongolongmireukbul**) at the famous **Beopjusa Temple** (AD 553).
- Known as Korea's 'museum without walls', **Gyeongju** is a repository of ancient Korean history and Buddhist culture and has been designated by UNESCO as one of the world's 10 most historically significant sites. Discover the most impressive structure to survive, the seventh-century **Chomseongdae**, an observatory that ranks amongst the oldest in Asia. Nearby, **Tumuli Park** contains 20 tomb mounds of Shilla Royalty, one of which, the **Heavenly Horse Tomb**, can be entered. Many treasures of the area, including golden crowns excavated from the tombs, can be seen in the **Gyeongju National Museum**.
- Near the **Bomun Lake Resort**, visit the **Bulguksa Temple,** one of the country's most famous and a major

tourist draw. This large wooden temple is beautifully painted and very atmospheric and the stone foundations and pagodas date back to the sixth century.

- High on the mountain above **Bulguksa**, be fascinated by the **Seokguram Grotto**, an ancient and highly complex cave-like structure containing a large granite Buddha and wall carvings of guardian deities, all of great artistic importance.
- 50km west of **Taegu City** is the **Mount Gayasan National Park**, at the centre of which is **Haeinsa**, Korea's best-known temple. Built in AD 802, it houses the extraordinary **Tripitaka Koreana**, a set of over 80,000 wooden printing blocks engraved with the complete Buddhist scriptures. Completed in 1252 after 16 years of work, they are still in perfect condition.
- In **Busan**, on South Korea's southeastern coast, enjoy great views from the **Busan Tower**. The city's attractions include **Beomeosa Temple**, **Geumjeong Mount Fortress** and **Jagakhi Fish Market**, Korea's largest fish market.
- The **Kumgang Park** features unusual rock formations and historic monuments, including a pagoda and several temples.
- Located on the flank of **Mount Jirisan**, **Hwaeomsa Temple** is famous for its ancient pagodas and annual lantern festival.
- In South Korea's western area, head for the **Mount Gyeryongsan National Park** which includes the two beautiful temples of **Gapsa** and **Donghaksa**. 35km (20 miles) apart, both **Gongju** and **Buyeo** were once capital of the ancient **Baekje** kingdom. Today, numerous burial mounds are still to be found in the area and both towns boast branches of the **National Museum** featuring fine displays of artefacts dating back over 1000 years. The **Gyeongju National Museum** also houses the crowns and other treasures excavated from the tomb of King Muryeon. Nearby, a reconstruction of the tomb is open to visitors.
- **Mount Maisan Provinical Park** is renowned for its 80 unique pagodas, as well as mysterious happenings that occur on the mountain.

Top Things To Do

- Learn about Korea's Buddhist heritage by going on a **historical and cultural tour**. The country has over 10,000 temples and 20,000 monks. Korean monks are now opening their temples and monasteries to tourists. More dedicated seekers can enrol in Buddhist retreats to practise silence, meditation and prayer for periods lasting anything from three weeks to several years.
- Korea (Rep) has a reputation as a shoppers' paradise, with many shops providing special duty free prices for foreigners. (For further details on shopping, see the *Social Profile* section.) Fashion, antiques, medicine, herbs and spices, electronics and wedding clothes feature highly on Korea's shopping itinerary; organised tours often combine souvenir and bargain hunting with sightseeing. The best shopping districts and markets are in the capital, Seoul. Bargain hunters will enjoy the city's huge markets such as the daily **East Gate (Dongdaemun) Market**, while for fashion shopping, the **Itaewon** district is the place to head for. **Myeongdong** is renowned for quality brand-name shops and restaurants. Here, you will also find the headquarters of all the major banks. **Seoul**'s traditional shopping area of **Insadong** offers everything from antiques to calligraphy brushes.
- Enjoy yourself at the **Everland leisure complex**, one hour from Seoul, which features a huge theme park, a zoo and a speedway-racing track. Also part of the complex, the superb treasures of the **Hoam Art Museum** will appeal to anyone interested in Korean art.
- In **Incheon**, a major seaport famous for the 1950 'Incheon Landings' of UN troops during the Korean War, spend time in the many shopping malls, amusement park and waterfront attractions of the **Wolmido Island** (1km from the Incheon coast).
- Go on an excursion to the truce village of **Panmunjeom**, one hour from Seoul, on the border with **North Korea**, where the 1953 armistice negotiations took place. Access is possible only on an official tour, but many will find the sight of the North Korean landscape and soldiers well worth it.
- Observe craftspeople at their trade in the **Suwon Korean Folk Village**, a functioning rural community and wonderful reconstruction of the past, located south of Seoul.
- Take part in a **Lantern Festival** at the **Hwaeomsa Temple**, located on the flank of **Mount Jirisan,** also famous for its ancient pagodas. The lantern festival is Korea's most significant festival, celebrating Buddha's Birthday, during which the 'Feast of Lanterns' is performed in the Republic of Korea's streets. Many other annual village festivals take place during which mountain spirits, great generals and royalty of the past are remembered and celebrated. Towards the centre of the country, the **Andong Hahoe Village** is particularly known for its mask-makers and dancers. There are also festivals that mark the changing seasons and festivals of prayer for a good harvest. All are characterised by processions, masked and costumed local people, music, dancing, battles and sports. For more details and exact dates, contact the Korea National Tourism Organisation (see *Tourist Information*).
- Go **bird-watching** at world-class sites such as **Saemangeum, Geum Estuary** and **Suncheon Bay**. The **Eulsukdo Bird Sanctuary** is also in Korea (Rep).
- Go **hiking** or **camping** in Korea's national parks. Three parks, **Seoraksan**, **Odaesan** and **Chuwangsan**, are accessible from the East Coast highway. **Seoraksan National Park**, the northernmost, is widely considered to offer the most beautiful scenery in Korea with its rugged peaks, waterfalls, forests and temples. Hike to the **Osaek Springs** luxury hot spring resorts. In the South, **Jirisan National Park** is also a fine hiking and mountaineering destination.
- For wintersports, the **Alps Ski Resort** is well known. **Odaesan National Park** is also famous for its ski resorts, as is the **Dragon Valley** (**Yongpyong**) area further south. Rock climbers will enjoy the challenges of the **Chiaksan** area. There are 13 ski resorts all within four or five hours of Seoul. An e-book entitled *Winter in Korea* is available from the Korea National Tourism Organisation (see *Tourist Information*).
- Go on **honeymoon** to the scenic resort island of **Jeju-do**, off the southwest coast. Follow the trail to the summit of **Mount Hallasan,** Korea's highest mountain at 1950m (6400ft). The **Jungmun** tourist complex offers watersports, a golf course and a 'Pacific'-themed leisure centre. Numerous natural attractions include the **Manjanggul Cave**, three spectacular waterfalls and the volcanic scenery of **Seongsan Ilchulbong Peak**. Tour the many **tangerine orchards** and visit **Seongeup Folk Village**. renowned is also famous for its seafood, some of which is still harvested by traditional *renowned* women divers.
- Eastern Korea's mountains run down to the sea along much of the 390km- (240 mile-) east coast but are interspersed by harbours, fishing villages and long, sandy beaches, such as the popular resort of **Hwajinpo**. Relax on the beautiful beaches of the **Samchok** area, which range from tiny, undiscovered coves to large resorts. The incredibly scenic volcanic island of **Ulleungdo** lies 130km (80 miles) off the coast and is accessible by ferry.
- Korea's southwestern area offers dramatic coastal scenery, most notably the 1000-plus islands that make up the **Dadohae Marine National Park**. Of the islands that offer accommodation and facilities for visitors, scenic **Hongdo** and craggy **Heuksando** are two of the most popular. The coastal town of **Mokpo** is the departure point for ferries to many of the National Park's islands and also for Jeju-do Island.
- **Jeju-do Island** is also the most popular destination for **scuba diving** enthusiasts; the waters surrounding the island are considered exceptionally good for **deep-sea fishing** too. Standard facilities for **windsurfing**, **water-skiing** and **boating** are widely available in all coastal resorts.
- Watch Korean traditional sports: **T'aekwondo** is the main martial art practised in Korea. The traditional Korean sport, **Ssirum** (Korean wrestling), is similar to Sumo wrestling and is a big spectator sport in Korea. **Kite-flying** and **archery** are also popular traditional games.
- Participate in **ancient pottery-making** techniques. Organised tours to Korea's pottery and ceramics centres are available.

TOURIST INFORMATION

Korea National Tourism Organization (KNTO) in the UK
3rd Floor, New Zealand House, Haymarket,
London SW1Y 4TE, UK
Tel: (020) 7321 2535 *or* 7925 1717.
Website: www.tour2korea.com

Korea National Tourism Organization (KNTO) in the USA
2 Executive Drive, Suite 750, Fort Lee, NJ 07024, USA
Tel: (201) 585 0909 *or* (800) 868 7567 (toll-free in USA).
Website: http://english.tour2korea.com/newyork

Entertainment

FOOD & DRINK: Korea has its own cuisine, quite different from Chinese or Japanese. Rice is the staple food and a typical Korean meal consists of rice, soup, rice water and eight to 20 side dishes of vegetables, fish, poultry, eggs, bean-curd and sea plants. Most Korean soups and side dishes are heavily laced with red pepper.
Things to know: There is waiter as well as counter service. Most major hotels will offer a selection of restaurants, serving Korean, Japanese and Chinese cuisine or more Western-style food. *Korean Food* is a 44-page e-book available from Korea National Tourism Organisation's website (see *Top Things To Do*). The most common type of drinking establishment is the *suljip* (wine bar), but there are also beer houses serving well-known European brands. Koreans offer glasses of liquor to each other as a gesture of camaraderie. When someone offers you an empty glass you are expected to hold it out and receive a fill-up and then to drink it empty. Juniors pour for seniors.
National specialities:
- *Bibimbap* (boiled rice mixed with vegetables).
- *Kimchi* (Korean national dish, highly spiced pickle of Chinese cabbage or white radish with turnips, onions, salt, fish, chestnuts and red pepper).
- *Bulgogi* (marinated, charcoal-broiled beef barbecue).
- *Grilled galbi* (seasoned ribs).
- *Haemultang* (seafood stew).

National drinks:
- *Yakju* (refined pure liquor fermented from rice).
- *Soju* (like vodka and made from potatoes or grain).
- Korean beer: *Cass*, *Hite* and *OB*.
- *Makgeolli* and *donggongju* (milky liquor).
- *Ginseng* wine is strong and sweet, similar to brandy, but varies in taste according to the basic ingredient used.
- Tea: *nokcha* (green tea), *insamcha* (ginseng tea) and many other varieties.

Tipping: Although not a Korean custom, most hotels and other tourist facilities add a 10 per cent service charge to bills. Taxi drivers are not tipped unless they help with the luggage.
NIGHTLIFE: Korea's nightlife successfully blends the traditional with increasing external influences. Yong-Dong and Itaewon are areas of Seoul with nightclubs catering largely to visitors, many with cabaret evenings. Some hotels also have nightclubs but these tend to be expensive. Larger hotels have their own private theatre restaurants. Beer halls, many decorated along a European theme, are popular places to drink and meet friends. Visitors are expected to eat as well as drink. There are also many cinemas. Operas, concerts and recitals can be seen at the *National Theatre* and performances of Korean classical music, dances and plays can be seen at *Korea House*. For daily listings of events, consult Korea's English-language papers. Several licensed state-of-the-art casinos operate at various locations throughout the country.
SHOPPING: The country has a reputation as a shoppers' paradise, with many shops providing special duty free prices for foreigners. Fashion, antiques, medicine, herbs and spices, electronics and wedding clothes feature highly on Korea's shopping itinerary. The best shopping districts and markets are in the capital, Seoul, and include: *Namdaemun* (Korea's largest general wholesale market); *Tongdaemun* (one of Seoul's oldest markets, good for bargains); *Myong-dong* (Korea's fashion district); *Insa-dong* (antiques and art); *Changanp'yong* (one of the largest antiques markets in the Far East); *Itaewon* (modern shopping district particularly popular with foreign tourists); *Noryargjin* (fish market); *Yongsan Electronics Market* (largest electronics and computer market in Korea); *Koyndang* (Oriental medicine, spices and herbs market); *Hwangkhak-dong* (flea market, good for second-hand shopping); *Ahyon-dong* (the 'wedding street', featuring over 120 wedding boutiques); and *Shinch'on* (a shopping street popular with young people, good for accessories and fashion).
Favourite buys to look for are hand-tailored clothes, sweaters (plain, embroidered or beaded), silks, brocades, handbags, leatherwork, gold jewellery, topaz, amethyst, amber, jade and silver, ginseng, paintings, costume dolls, musical instruments, brassware, lacquerware, woodcarvings, baskets, scrolls and screens. Prices are fixed in department stores, but may be negotiated in arcades and markets. Major cities have foreigners' duty free shops where people can use foreign currency with a valid passport. **Shopping hours**: Mon-Sun 1030-2000.
Note: For visitors who purchase goods worth more than KRW50,000 at stores with 'Tax Free Shopping' signs or goods over KRW30,000 at outlets with 'Tax Refund Shopping' signs, 70 to 80 per cent of the paid VAT (Value Added Tax) and SET (Special Excise Tax) will be refunded in cash at the airport. Only visitors staying less than three months are eligible. Purchases and receipts may need to be shown to the customs officer.

Business

- **GDP:** US$605 billion.
- **Main imports:** Machinery, electronics, electrical equipment, oil, steel, transport equipment, organic chemicals and plastics.
- **Main exports:** Semi-conductors, wireless telecommunications equipment, motor vehicles, computers, steel, ships and petrochemicals.
- **Main trade partners:** China, Hong Kong (SAR), Japan, Saudi Arabia and USA.

ECONOMY: Korea (Rep) is one of the so-called 'tiger economies' of the Pacific Rim, which underwent rapid growth and industrialisation from the 1960s onwards and forged a major presence in world export markets. The Republic of Korea's strength came from four main areas: shipbuilding, steel, consumer goods and construction. The agricultural sector, dominated by rice-growing and fisheries, is an important export earner as well as meeting domestic demand. Tourism dominates the service sector, which is still relatively small but received a boost from the success of the 2002 World Cup football competition, which Korea (Rep) co-hosted. Compared with the North, which has extensive coal and mineral deposits, the South is relatively poor in natural resources, although there have been recent offshore discoveries of natural gas which should help to reduce South Korea's dependence on imported energy. The financial crisis which struck Asia in the autumn of 1997 had a very serious effect on the South Korean economy and raised major concerns about the long-term viability of the *chaebol* – the large conglomerates that form the foundations of Korea (Rep)'s industrial economy – and the stability of the finance sector, which had assumed increasing importance. The economy was saved from further damage at the beginning of 1998 by a US$60 billion financial rescue package put together by the IMF which kick-started a strong recovery by the South Korean economy. After settling down, the economy is now accelerating again: growth in 2002 increased to 6.3 per cent on the back of an increase in exports and investment, although did slow down in the following years. In 2003 it was 3.1 per cent and in 2004 it rose to 4.6 per cent. The Korean Development Institute estimates that 5.2 per cent average growth will be possible until 2011. The Republic of Korea (Rep) continues with its economic reforms. Inflation for 2004 was between 2.5 and 3.5 per cent. The Government has successfully dealt with important structural weaknesses in the financial sector, but has yet to tackle the chaebol. The slow thaw in relations with the North has also seen a growth of economic links between the two parts of Korea.

BUSINESS ETIQUETTE: Businessmen are expected to wear a suit and tie. English is widely spoken in commercial and official circles. Prior appointments are necessary and business cards are widely used. The use of the right hand when giving and receiving particularly applies to business cards. Best months for business visits are February to June. **Office hours:** Mon-Fri 0900-1800.

COMMERCIAL INFORMATION

Korean Chamber of Commerce and Industry (KCCI)
PO Box 25, 45 4-ga, Namdaemun-ro, Chung-gu, Seoul 100-743, Korea (Republic of)
Tel: (2) 316 3114.
Website: www.kcci.or.kr

Korea Trade Centre in the UK
1st Floor, Brettenham House North, Lancaster Place, London WC2E 7EN, UK
Tel: (020) 7520 5300.
Website: www.kotra.or.kr/london

Korea Exhibition Centre (COEX)
World Trade Center, 159 Samsong-dong, Kangnam-ku, Seoul 135-731, Korea (Republic of)
Tel: (2) 6000 0114.
Website: www.coex.co.kr

Korea Convention and Coordinating Committee (Information on Conferences/Conventions)
PO Box 903, c/o Korea National Tourism Organization (see *Top Things To Do*),

International Convention Centre Jeju
2700 Jungmun-dong, Seoguipo City, 697-120 Jeju, Korea (Republic of)
Tel: (6) 4735 1000.
Website: www.iccjeju.co.kr

Kuwait

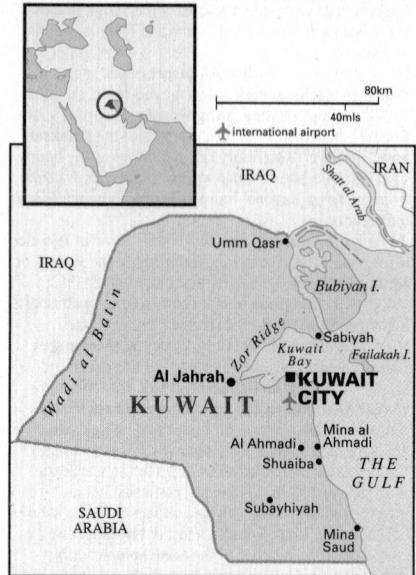

Location: Middle East.

Time: GMT + 3.

Overview

The area that became Kuwait was controlled by the main regional powers in the Gulf, principally various dynasties based in Mesopotamia and Persia. The most influential of these were the Safavids, a Persian dynasty which moved into the region around 1500 and established a commercial empire along the eastern seaboard of the Arabian peninsula. Later on in the 16th century, the northeastern corner of the Arabian peninsula became part of the Turkish Ottoman Empire. It remained so until the latter part of the 19th century when the Al-Sabah family steered the country into a semi-autonomous position. However, fearing that the Turks would try to reassert their control, the Kuwaitis made an agreement with the British allowing for British control of Kuwaiti foreign affairs in exchange for military protection. This danger passed with the collapse of the Ottoman Empire at the end of World War I, although Kuwait remained a British protectorate until 1961, when the country was granted full independence.

Since then, Kuwait has remained a puzzling but intriguing mix of Western liberalism and strict Islam. The capital, Kuwait City, is a bustling metropolis full of the high-rise buildings and luxury hotels that you would expect. Yet the country is also host to elaborate and opulent mosques and palaces, and its religion is an integral part of its affairs.

This juxtaposition perhaps stems from Kuwait's marrying of Islamism with oil-wealth, mostly traded with Western superpowers. Upon independence, Sheikh Abdullah assumed Head of State, adopting the title of Emir. The large revenues from oil production allowed Independent Kuwait to build up its economic infrastructure and institute educational and social welfare programmes. In the early 1990s, the Emir established a National Assembly (*Majlis*), which placed limits on the power of the ruling family. Since then, the National Assembly has clashed several times with the Emir and the Cabinet (which is still dominated by the Al-Sabah family) over misuse of state funds and poor management of the all-important oil industry. Underlying these disputes is the growing impression that the ageing and increasingly infirm Al-Sabah clan is no longer capable of running the country. However, they continue to dominate Kuwaiti policies. Surrounded by three major Middle Eastern powers, the main threat to the country came from the renewal of Iraqi territorial claims over Kuwait (along with the overdue repayment of some US$40-60 billion on the part of Iraq), which led to the Iraqi invasion of Kuwait in 1990. The Kuwaitis later recovered their country by virtue of a US-led, UN-backed multinational military force. After a period of euphoria, the Kuwaitis had to address a number of difficult questions; the future security of the country was dealt with by the signing of defence and security pacts with the USA, the UK and Kuwait's Gulf allies. More recently, Kuwait was one of the first countries to join Operation Iraqi Freedom following the US-led war against Iraq, and provided aid and support during Iraq's (ongoing) process of reconstruction.

General Information

AREA: 17,818 sq km (6880 sq miles).
POPULATION: 2.4 million (official estimate 2002).
POPULATION DENSITY: 135.8 per sq km.
CAPITAL: Kuwait City. **Population:** 28,747 (1995).
GEOGRAPHY: Kuwait shares borders with Iraq and Saudi Arabia. To the southeast lies the Persian Gulf, where Kuwait has sovereignty over nine small islands (the largest is Bubiyan and the most populous is Failaka). The landscape is predominantly desert plateau with a lower, more fertile coastal belt.
GOVERNMENT: Traditional Arab monarchy. Gained full independence from the UK in 1961. **Head of State**: Sheikh Sa'ad Al Abdullah Al Salim Al-Sabah since January 2006. **Head of Government**: Prime Minister Sheikh Sabah Al-Ahmad Al-Sabah. **Recent history**: Following the death of His Highness Sheikh Jaber A- Ahmad Al-Jaber Al-Sabah, Emir of the State of Kuwait, his Highness Sheikh Sa'ad Al-Abdullah Al-Salim Al-Sabah became Emir of the State of Kuwait in January 2006. He is also ill and Prime Minister Sheikh Sabah Al-Ahmad Al-Sabah is likely to effectively run the country.
LANGUAGE: Arabic, but English is widely understood, especially in commerce and industry.
RELIGION: 95 per cent Muslim (mostly of the Sunni sect), with Christian and Hindu minorities.
ELECTRICITY: 240 volts AC, 50Hz; single phase. UK-type flat three-pin plugs are used.
SOCIAL CONVENTIONS: Handshaking is the customary form of greeting. It is quite likely that a visitor will be invited to a Kuwaiti's home, but entertaining is also conducted in hotels and restaurants. A small gift promoting the company, or representing your own country, is always welcome. The visitor will notice that most Kuwaitis wear the national dress of long white *dishdashes* and white headcloths, and that many women wear *yashmaks*. It is important for women to dress modestly according to Islamic law. Men do not usually wear shorts in public and should not go shirtless. All other Islamic rules and customs must be respected. Convicted users of narcotics can expect to receive a sentence of up to five years' imprisonment, plus a heavy fine. 'No Smoking' signs are posted in many shops. It is greatly appreciated if visitors learn at least a few words of Arabic.

Climate

Kuwait shares European weather patterns but is hotter and drier. Summers (April to October) are hot and humid with very little rain. Winters (November to March) are cool with limited rain. Springs are cool and pleasant.

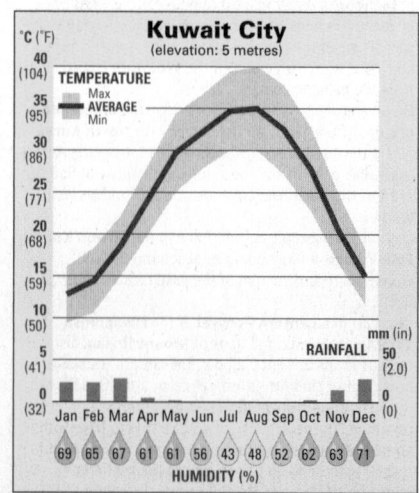

Communications

Telephone: Full IDD is available. Country code: 965.
Mobile telephone: GSM 900 and 1800 networks. Network operators include *Mobile Telecom* (website: www.mtc-vodafone.com) and *National Mobile Telecom* (website: www.wataniya.com).
Internet: Internet cafes throughout Kuwait provide public access to e-mail and Internet services. ISPs include *Gulfnet International* (website: www.zajil.com) and *QualityNet*.
Post: Airmail to Western Europe takes about five days. Post office hours: Sat-Wed 0700-1400, Thurs 0700-1200.
MEDIA: Press: The English-language newspapers are the *Arab Times* and the *Kuwait Times*. Although remaining loyal to the ruling family, the press enjoys a fair degree of freedom.
TV: *Kuwaiti TV* is state-run. Private channels include *Al-Rai* and *Flash TV*.
Radio: *Radio Kuwait* is state-run and *Marina FM* is a private music station.

Passport/Visa

	Passport Required?	Visa Required?	Return Ticket? Required?
Full British	Yes	Yes	No
Australian	Yes	Yes	No
Canadian	Yes	Yes	No
USA	Yes	Yes	No
Other EU	Yes	Yes	No
Japanese	Yes	Yes	No

Note: *Regulations and requirements may be subject to change at short notice, and you are advised to contact the appropriate diplomatic or consular authority before finalising travel arrangements. Any numbers in the chart refer to the footnotes below.*

PASSPORTS: Passport valid for at least six months required by all.
Note: Married women and children (except nationals of Iran and Iraq) may travel on the passport of their husband or father.
VISAS: Required by all except nationals of Bahrain, Oman, Qatar, Saudi Arabia and the United Arab Emirates for an unlimited period.
Types of visa and cost: *Business, Visitor* and *Transit*. Transit visas are not required provided passengers hold onward tickets and do not leave the airport. The fee for a visa depends on the applicant's nationality. For UK nationals the fees are as follows: *Single-entry*: £30 (for three months); £48 (for six months). *Multiple-entry*: £66 (for six months); £75 (for one year); £96 (for two years); £135 (for five years).
Validity: Depends on nationality and purpose of visit. Validity of the visa is usually three months from date of issue. Enquire at Consulate (or Consular section at Embassy) for further details.
Application to: Consulate (or Consular section at Embassy); see *Passport/Visa Information* for details.
Note: Nationals of Andorra, Australia, Brunei, Canada, China (PR), nationals of the EU (except nationals of Cyprus, Czech Republic, Estonia, Hungary, Ireland, Latvia, Lithuania, Malta, Poland, Slovak Republic and Slovenia), Hong Kong (SAR), Iceland, Japan, Korea (Rep), Liechtenstein, Malaysia, Monaco, New Zealand, Norway, San Marino, Singapore, Switzerland, USA and the Vatican City can now obtain visas for entry into Kuwait upon arrival at the port of entry.
Application requirements: (a) Valid passport. (b) One completed application form. (c) One passport-size photo. (d) Fax or other confirmation of invitation from sponsor/contact in Kuwait. This should be faxed directly to the Embassy; see *Passport/Visa Information* for fax numbers (not required for visa on arrival - see above). (e) Covering letter from employer in home country detailing evidence of position and status within company, purpose of visit, length of stay. (f) Registered, self-addressed envelope if applying by post. (g) Fee.
Working days required: 10.
Temporary residence: Enquire at Embassy. Note that UK nationals who wish to take up employment will eventually require a *Residence Permit*. This must be obtained before arrival in Kuwait as it is not possible to transfer status from 'visitor' to 'temporary resident' without first leaving Kuwait.

PASSPORT/VISA INFORMATION

Embassy of the State of Kuwait in the UK
2 Albert Gate, London SW1X 7JU, UK
Tel: (020) 7590 3400.
Website: www.kuwaitinfo.org.uk
Opening hours: Mon-Fri 0900-1230 and 1400-1600 (visa collection only).

Embassy of the State of Kuwait in the USA
2940 Tilden Street, NW, Washington, DC 20008, USA
Tel: (202) 966 0702. Fax: (202) 966 0517.

Money

Currency: Kuwait Dinar (KWD) = 1000 fils. Notes are in denominations of KWD20, 10, 5 and 1, and 500 and 250 fils. Coins are in denominations of 100, 50, 20, 10, 5 and 1 fils.
Credit & debit cards: American Express, Diners Club, MasterCard and Visa are accepted. Check with your credit or debit card company for details of merchant acceptability and other services which may be available.
Traveller's cheques: Widely accepted. To avoid additional exchange rate charges, travellers are advised to take traveller's cheques in US Dollars or Pounds Sterling.
Currency restrictions: The import and export of local and foreign currency is not restricted.
Banking hours: Sun-Thurs 0800-1200.
Exchange rate indicators:
Rate at time of publishing
£1.00 = KWD0.51
$1.00= KWD0.29

Duty Free

The following goods may be imported into Kuwait without incurring customs duty:
500 cigarettes or 2lb of tobacco.
Prohibited items: Alcohol, narcotics, unsealed milk products, unsealed salty fish, unsealed olives and pickles, food prepared abroad, fresh vegetables, shellfish and its products, fresh figs and mineral water. Penalties for attempting to smuggle restricted items are severe.

Public Holidays

Below are listed Public Holidays for the January 2006-June 2007 period.
2006: Jan 1 New Year's Day. **Jan 10** Eid al-Adha (Feast of the Sacrifice). **Jan 31** Islamic New Year. **Feb 25** National Day. **Feb 26** Liberation Day. **Apr 11** Mouloud (Birth of the Prophet). **Aug 22** Al-Esra Wa Al-Meraj (Ascension of the Prophet). **Oct 22-24** Eid al-Fitr (End of Ramadan). **Dec 31** Eid al-Adha (Feast of the Sacrifice).
2007: Jan 1 New Year's Day. **Jan 20** Islamic New Year. **Feb 25** National Day. **Feb 26** Liberation Day. **Mar 31** Mouloud (Birth of the Prophet).
Note: (a) Muslim festivals are timed according to local sightings of various phases of the moon and the dates given above are approximations. During the lunar month of Ramadan that precemdes Eid al-Fitr, Muslims fast during the day and feast at night and normal business patterns may be interrupted. Many restaurants are closed during the day and there may be restrictions on smoking and drinking. Some disruption may continue into Eid al-Fitr itself. Eid al-Fitr and Eid al-Adha may last anything from two to 10 days, depending on the region. For more information see the appendix *World of Islam*.
(b) If a holiday falls on a Friday, a day is given in lieu.

Health

	Special Precautions?	Certificate Required?
Yellow Fever	No	No
Cholera	No	No
Typhoid & Polio	1	N/A
Malaria	No	N/A

Note: *Regulations and requirements may be subject to change at short notice, and you are advised to contact your doctor well in advance of your intended date of departure. Any numbers in the chart refer to the footnotes below.*

1: Vaccination against typhoid and poliomyelitis is sometimes advised.
Food & drink: Mains water is normally chlorinated and, whilst relatively safe, may cause mild abdominal upsets. Bottled water is available and is advised for the first few weeks of the stay. Milk is pasteurised and dairy products are safe for consumption. Local meat, poultry, seafood, fruit and vegetables are generally considered safe to eat.
Other risks: *Diarrhoeal diseases* such as *giardiasis*, *dysentery* and *typhoid fever* are common. *Hepatitis A* occurs and *hepatitis B* is endemic in the region. *Cutaneous leishmaniasis* is reported. *Tick-borne relapsing fever* may occur.
Rabies is present. For those at high risk, vaccination before arrival should be considered. If you are bitten, seek medical advice without delay. For more information, consult the *Health* appendix.
Health care: Medical insurance is essential. Both private and government health services are available.

Travel - International

Note: Following the military action in Iraq, there is an increased risk of terrorism in Kuwait. For further advice visitors should contact the relevant local government travel advice department.
AIR:

The national airline, *Kuwait Airways (KU)* (website: www.kuwait-airways.com) operates daily non-stop flights to Kuwait from London. Other airlines serving Kuwait include *Air France, British Airways, Emirates, Gulf Air, KLM, Lufthansa* and *United Airlines.*
Approximate flight times: From Kuwait to *London* is seven hours 30 minutes, to *New York* is 15 hours, to *Los Angeles* is 19 hours, to *Singapore* is eight hours 30 minutes and to *Sydney* is 27 hours.
Main airports: *Kuwait (KWI)* (website: www.kuwait-airport.com.kw) lies 16km (10 miles) south of Kuwait City (travel time - 20 minutes). *To/from the airport*: Reliable transport to and from the city is available, including a bus (travel time - 30 minutes) departing every 45 minutes (0600-2300), and taxi service costing KWD4. *Facilities*: Restaurants, shops, cafe, bank/bureau de change, car hire, conference room and post office.
Departure tax: KWD2; transit passengers not leaving the airport transit area and children under 12 are exempt.
SEA:

More than 30 shipping lines call regularly at Kuwait City, Kuwait's major port. Most traffic is commercial.
ROAD:

All road links with Iraq, and therefore through to the Syrian Arab Republic and Jordan, are advised against due to political instability within Iraq. It is also wise to check with the Embassy before considering travelling to Lebanon.
There are **bus** services between Kuwait City and Cairo (Egypt), via Aqaba in Jordan and Nuweiba in Egypt. Buses also operate to Damman in Saudi Arabia. The main land route into Saudi Arabia is Beirut-Damascus-Amman-Kuwait, which follows the Trans-Arabian Pipeline (TAP line) through Saudi Arabia.

Travel - Internal

SEA:

Dhows and other small craft may be chartered for trips to the offshore islands.
ROAD:

There is a good road network between cities. Driving is on the right. **Bus:** *Kuwait Transport Company* operates a nationwide service which is both reliable and inexpensive. **Taxi:** These are recognisable by red licence plates and may be hired by the day, in which case fares should be agreed beforehand. Share-taxis are also available. Taxis can be phoned and this service is popular and reliable. A standard rate is applicable in most taxis, but those at hotel ranks are more expensive. Tipping is not expected. **Car hire:** Self-drive is available. If you produce an International Driving Permit, the rental company will, within five days, grant a temporary local licence valid for one month. **Documentation**: International Driving Permit required. A temporary driving licence is available from local authorities on presentation of a valid British or Northern Ireland driving licence. Insurance must be arranged with the Gulf Insurance Company or the Kuwait Insurance Company.

Travel Advice

There is a high threat from terrorism. Al Qaeda continues to issue statements threatening to carry out attacks in the Gulf region. These include references to attacks on Western interests, including residential compounds, military, oil, transport and aviation interests.
In early 2005, Kuwaiti security forces mounted operations against suspected militants and their safe houses, during which several suspected militants were killed or arrested. The security forces discovered bomb-making equipment and material linked with planned kidnaps. It is believed that individuals associated with these incidents are still at large and remain a threat to Western interests.
This advice is based on information provided by the Foreign and Commonwealth Office in the UK. It is correct at time of publishing. As the situation can change rapidly, visitors are advised to contact the following organisations for the latest travel advice:

British Foreign and Commonwealth Office
Tel: (0845) 850 2829.
Website: www.fco.gov.uk

US Department of State
Website: http://travel.state.gov/travel

Accommodation

HOTELS:
Hotels range from deluxe to first and second class. Many top hotels in Kuwait City feature sport complexes, restaurants and shopping malls. Serviced apartments, some with hotel-style room service, are also available. Prices are generally high. All rates are subject to a 15 per cent service charge.

Top Things To See & Do

- **Kuwait City** is a bustling metropolis of high-rise office buildings, luxury hotels, wide boulevards and well-tended parks and gardens. Its seaport is used by oil tankers, cargo ships and many pleasure craft. Its most dominant landmark is **Kuwait Towers**, and its oldest is **Seif Palace**, built in 1896, the interior of which features original Islamic mosaic tilework, though these suffered badly during the Iraqi occupation. The **Kuwait National Museum** was also stripped of many artefacts – part of it has been renovated and is now open to the public. The **Sadu House**, near the museum, is made of coral and gypsum and is used as a cultural museum to protect the arts and crafts of Bedouin society. It is an ideal place to purchase Bedouin goods. The huge **Grand Mosque** in the centre is also worth visiting.
- A port with many old *dhows*, **Failakai Island** can be reached by regular ferry services. There are also some Bronze Age and Greek archaeological sites well worth viewing, including the island's Greek temple. Traditional-style *boums* and *sambuks* (boats) are still built in **Al Jahrah**, although, nowadays, vessels are destined to work as pleasure boats rather than pearl fishing or trading vessels. **Mina Al Ahmadi**, lying 12 miles south of Kuwait City, is an oil port with immense jetties for supertanker traffic. The **Oil Display Centre** pays homage to the work of the Kuwait Oil Company.
- **Swimming, sailing** and **scuba diving** are available. **Powerboating** is a Kuwaiti passion. **Horse riding** clubs flourish in the winter.

TOURIST INFORMATION

Touristic Enterprises Company of Kuwait
PO Box 23310, Safat 13094, Kuwait City, Kuwait
Tel: 565 3771 *or* 2775.
Website: www.kuwaittourism.com

Kuwait Information Centre in the UK
Hyde Park House, 60/60A Knightsbridge, London
SW1X 7JX, UK
Tel: (020) 7235 1787.
Website: www.kuwaitinfo.org.uk

Entertainment

FOOD & DRINK: There is a good choice of restaurants serving a wide choice of international and Arab cuisine, prices are reasonable. Typical Middle-Eastern food includes *hummus*, *falafel* and *foul*. Everything is eaten with *aish* (Arabic flat bread).
Alcohol is totally prohibited in Kuwait.
Tipping: A service charge of 15 per cent is usually added to bills in hotels, restaurants and clubs. Otherwise 10 per cent is acceptable.

NIGHTLIFE: Several cinemas in Kuwait City show recent films. Two theatres often put on very good amateur productions.
SHOPPING: Numerous large shopping complexes have recently been built. The *Souk Sharp Complex* is an extensive centre near the waterfront in Kuwait City, and contains Western chain stores as well as Kuwaiti shops. Other centres include the *Al-Fanar Shopping Centre* and the *Leila Gallery*. Boutiques and small general stores in Kuwait City sell all the basic and most luxury goods.
Shopping hours: Sat-Thurs 0830-1230 and 1630-2100, Fri 1530-2030.

Business

ECONOMY: Kuwait's considerable wealth is the result of the country's vast oil deposits, estimated at 100 billion barrels (9 per cent of the world's total known reserves). With production of over two million barrels daily, oil now accounts for about half of total output, 90 per cent of export income and three-quarters of Government revenue. The economy has long since recovered from the extensive and systematic looting conducted by Iraqi troops during the occupation of 1990-1. This was estimated to have cost Kuwait US$170 billion, and the extent of the reconstruction was reflected in the fact that Kuwait was obliged to liquidate a large proportion of its overseas investment portfolio. These holdings, which are administered by the Kuwait Investment Office, are used partly to meet the country's running costs (free education and social services) and partly lodged in the Fund for Future Generations. During the 1990s, Kuwait, not surprisingly, invested large sums in building up a military apparatus.
There has been some diversification of the economy, promoted and funded by the Government. Heavy industrial projects have been eschewed in favour of light manufacturing industries such as paper and cement production. There is a small fishing industry and some agriculture. The Government has tabled a privatisation programme both as a means to raise revenue and as an instrument of economic policy. A free-trade zone has also been established. Kuwait is a member of OPEC and of the Gulf Co-operation Council. The re-emergence of OPEC as a major influence appears to have triggered some disputes inside the Kuwaiti Government over oil production and pricing policy. Japan, The Netherlands and Italy are the main markets for Kuwaiti oil. The principal exporters to Kuwait are Japan, the USA, Germany and the UK.
BUSINESS ETIQUETTE: Men are expected to wear suits and ties for business and formal social occasions. English is widely spoken in business circles, although a few words or phrases of Arabic are always well received. Visiting cards are widely used. Some of the bigger hotels have translation and bilingual secretarial services. **Government office hours**: Sat-Wed 0700-1300 (winter); 0730-1330 (summer). **Office hours**: Sat-Wed 0730-1230 and 1600-1900.

COMMERCIAL INFORMATION

Kuwait Chamber of Commerce and Industry
PO Box 775, Safat 13008, Kuwait City, Kuwait
Tel: 805 580 ext. 555.
Website: www.kcci.org.kw

Kyrgyzstan

Location: Central Asia, north of Afghanistan and Tajikistan.

Time: GMT + 6.

Overview

The main attraction of Kyrgyzstan lies in the breathtaking landscape of mountains, glaciers and lakes; their isolation ensures that they have been almost forgotten by the crowds. The lakes and mountainous terrain provide excellent opportunities for trekking, skiing, climbing, sailing and swimming.
For more ambitious travellers, it is possible to follow the route of the old Silk Road to Kashgar in China, crossing the border at the Torugart Pass, near Lake Chatyr-Kul. Trekking tours and adventure holidays in this region are offered by a growing number of companies.

General Information

AREA: 199,900 sq km (77,182 sq miles).
POPULATION: 5.1 million (UN estimate 2002).
POPULATION DENSITY: 25.3 per sq km.
CAPITAL: Bishkek (called Frunze from 1926 to 1991).
Population: 736,000 (UN estimate 2001).
GEOGRAPHY: Kyrgyzstan is bordered by Kazakhstan, Uzbekistan, Tajikistan and China. The majestic Tian Shan (Heavenly Mountains) range occupies the greater part of the area. Its highest peak is Pik Pobedy at 7439m (24,406ft).
GOVERNMENT: Republic. Gained independence from the Soviet Union in 1991. **Head of State and Government**: President Kurmanbek Bakiev since 2005. **Prime Minister**: Felix Kulov since 2005.
LANGUAGE: The official language is Kyrgyz, a Turkic language closely related to Uzbek, Kazakh, Turkmen and Turkish. Any attempt by a foreigner to speak Kyrgyz will be greatly appreciated. In deference to the large Russian population of Kyrgyzstan, Russian is also protected under law. In 1993, the Government undertook to replace the Russian Cyrillic Alphabet with the Turkish version of the Roman alphabet. Meanwhile, most people can speak Russian, and do so, especially in the north. English is widely spoken by those involved in tourism. Uzbek, Kazakh, Tajik and various other regional languages and dialects are also spoken.
RELIGION: The major religion is Islam with the majority of Kyrgyz being Sunni Muslim with Christian and Russian Orthodox minorities.
ELECTRICITY: 220 volts AC, 50Hz. Round two-pin continental plugs are standard.

Climate

Kyrgyzstan has a continental climate with relatively little rainfall. It averages 247 sunny days a year. In the summer, in the mountains, the mornings are generally fine and the afternoons hazy with occasional rain. In the lowlands, the temperature ranges between -4° and -6°C (21-24°F) in January to 16 and 24°C (61-75°F) in July. In the highlands, the temperatures range from -14° and -20°C (6.8° and -4°F) in January to 8-12°C (46-54°F) in July. There are heavy snowfalls during winter.

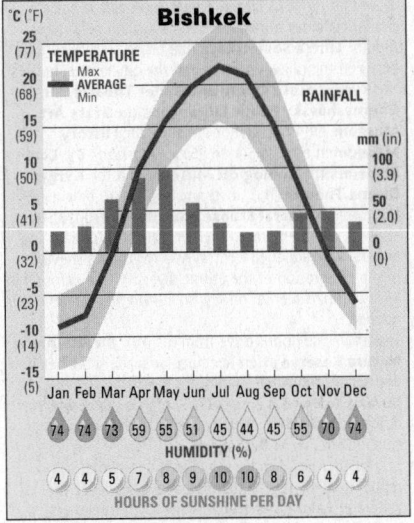

Communications

Telephone: Country code: 996 (312 for Bishkek). International calls should be made from a telephone office which will usually be found attached to a post office; they can also be made from some hotels by asking at reception. All international calls from Kyrgyzstan have to go through the operator. Local calls (within the city) are free of charge if made from private telephones; hotels sometimes levy a small charge. Direct-dial calls within the CIS are obtained by dialling 8 and waiting for another dial tone and then dialling the city code followed by the number.
Mobile telephone: GSM 900 network in use. The main provider is *Bitel Ltd* (website: www.bitel.kg).
Internet: ISPs include *Asiainfo* (website: www.asiainfo.kg), *ElCat* (website: www.elcat.kg) and *Intra Net* (website: www.intranet.kg). There are two Internet cafes on ul Sovetskaya in Bishkek, amongst others.
Post: Letters to and from Western Europe and the USA can take anything between two weeks and two months. Stamped envelopes can be bought from post offices. Mail to recipients within Kyrgyzstan should be addressed in the following order: country, postcode, city, street, house number and, lastly, the person's name. Visitors can also use post offices located within some major hotels. Post office hours: Mon-Fri 0900-1800.
MEDIA: Press: The *Bishkek Observer*, *Kyrgyzstan Chronicle*, *Times of Central Asia* and *Zaman Kyrgyzstan* are published weekly in English. The main dailies are published in Bishkek and include *Kyrgyz Tuusu* (both in Kyrgyz), and *Delo No*, *Slovo Kyrgyzstana* and *Vechernii Bishkek* (in Russian).
TV: State-run *Kyrgyz National TV and Radio Broadcasting Corporation* operates two networks. Private channels include *Pirimida* and *Osh TV*.
Radio: *Kyrgyz National TV and Radio Broadcasting Corporation* runs two networks. private stations include *Almaz* and *Europa Plus*.

Passport/Visa

	Passport Required?	Visa Required?	Return Ticket? Required?
Full British	Yes	Yes	No
Australian	Yes	Yes	No
Canadian	Yes	Yes	No
USA	Yes	Yes	No
Other EU	Yes	Yes/1	No
Japanese	Yes	No	No

Note: *Regulations and requirements may be subject to change at short notice, and you are advised to contact the appropriate diplomatic or consular authority before finalising travel arrangements. Any numbers in the chart refer to the footnotes below.*

PASSPORTS: Passport required by all.
VISAS: Required by all except the following:
(a) nationals of CIS countries (except Turkmenistan and Uzbekistan who *do* require a visa), provided residing in country of nationality;
(b) nationals of Malaysia and Turkey for stays of up to 30 days;
(c) **1.** nationals of Albania, Bosnia & Herzegovina, Bulgaria, Croatia, Cuba, Czech Republic, Japan, Korea (Dem Rep), Macedonia, Mongolia, Poland, Romania, Serbia & Montenegro, Slovak Republic, Slovenia and Vietnam travelling as tourists (provided they are permanent residents of their country);
(d) transit passengers continuing their journey by the same or first connecting aircraft within 48 hours, provided holding onward or return documentation and not leaving the airport
Note: Nationals of the following countries may apply for a visa valid for one month or less without providing a letter of support from Kyrgyzstan: nationals of countries referred to in the chart above (except countries who do not require a visa, as listed above, and nationals of Estonia, Hungary, Latvia and Lithuania, who do need to provide an invitation letter), and nationals of Iceland, Israel, Korea (Rep), Liechtenstein, Monaco, New Zealand and Norway.
Types of visa and cost: *Business, Private Trip, Tourist* and *Transit. Single-entry:* £40 (one month). *Multiple-entry:* £100 (six months); £125 (one year). *Transit:* £20 (one week). *Express:* double the price. Multiple-entry visas can only be issued with authorisation from the Ministry of Foreign Affairs of the Kyrgyz Republic.
Validity: Up to three months from date of issue. Multiple-entry visas are valid for six months.
Application to: Consulate (or Consular section at Embassy); see *Passport/Visa Information*. Those resident in the UK can also obtain visas from Russia House (for address, see *Russian Federation* section).
Application requirements: (a) Completed application form. (b) One passport-size photo. (c) Valid passport (must be an original, not a photocopy) with one blank page to affix visa. (d) Stamped self-addressed, registered envelope. (e) Fee, payable by cash, cheque or bank transfer. (f) Letter of support from Kyrgyzstan, authorised by the Ministry of Foreign Affairs (not required by certain nationals - see note above).
Working days required: Five; one for Express visa applications.
Temporary residence: Enquire at Embassy for details (see *Contact Addresses* section).

PASSPORT/VISA INFORMATION

Embassy of the Kyrgyz Republic in the UK
Ascot House, 119 Crawford Street, London W1U 6BJ, UK
Tel: (020) 7935 1462.
Website: www.kyrgyz-embassy.org.uk
Opening hours: Mon-Fri 0900-1800; 0930-1230 (visa section).

Embassy of the Kyrgyz Republic in the USA
1732 Wisconsin Avenue, NW, Washington, DC 20007, USA
Tel: (202) 338 5141.
Website: www.kyrgyzstan.org

Money

Currency: Kyrgyz Som (KGS) = 100 tyin. Notes are in denominations of KGS1000, 500, 200, 100, 50, 20, 10, 5 and 1, and 50, 10 and 1 tyin.
Currency exchange: Foreign currencies can be exchanged at commercial banks and at authorised bureaux de change. The US Dollar is the easiest currency to exchange.
Credit & debit cards: Credit cards are accepted in some of the larger hotels in Bishkek and can also be used at banks to withdraw cash from the counter. Check with your credit or debit card company for merchant acceptability and other services which may be available.
Traveller's cheques: There is limited acceptance of these, but some banks in Bishkek accept traveller's cheques, with US Dollars probably the best option; commission charges are high. Cash is recommended.
Currency restrictions: There are no restrictions on the import or export of foreign currency, provided declared on arrival. The import and export of local currency is unlimited for Kyrgyz residents only.
Banking hours: Usually Mon-Fri 0930-1730.
Exchange rate indicators:
Rate at time of publishing
£1.00=   KGS70.92
$1.00=   KGS40.85

Duty Free

The following goods may be imported into Kyrgyzstan by travellers of 16 years or over without incurring customs duty:
1000 cigarettes or 1000g of tobacco products; 1.5l of alcoholic beverages and 2l of wine; a reasonable quantity of perfume for personal use.
Note: On entering the country, tourists must complete a customs declaration form which must be retained until departure, and then handed over on the international flight leaving any CIS country. This allows the import of articles intended for personal use, including currency and valuables which must be registered on the declaration form. Customs inspection can be long and detailed.
Prohibited imports: Military weapons and ammunition (subject to special permit); narcotics; fruit and vegetables; live animals (subject to special permit); photographs and printed matter directed against Kyrgyzstan; anything owned by a third party that is to be carried in for that third party. If there are any queries regarding items that may be imported, an information sheet is available on request from Intourist.
Prohibited exports: As prohibited imports, as well as precious metals and articles, works of art and antiques (unless permission has been granted by the Ministry of Culture), furs.

Public Holidays

Below are listed Public Holidays for the January 2006-June 2007 period.
2006: Jan 1 New Year's Day. **Jan 7** Russian Orthodox Christmas. **Jan 10** Kurban Ait (Feast of the Sacrifice). **Mar 8** International Women's Day. **Mar 21** Nooruz (Kyrgyz New Year). **May 1** Labour Day. **May 5** Constitution Day. **May 9** Victory Day. **Aug 31** Independence Day. **Oct 22-24** Eid al-Fitr (End of Ramadan). **Dec 31** Kurban Ait (Feast of the Sacrifice).
2007: Jan 1 New Year's Day. **Jan 7** Russian Orthodox Christmas. **Mar 8** International Women's Day. **Mar 21** Nooruz (Krygyz New Year). **May 1** Labour Day. **May 5** Constitution Day. **May 9** Victory Day.

Health

	Special Precautions?	Certificate Required?
Yellow Fever	No	No
Cholera	Yes	1
Typhoid & Polio	2	N/A
Malaria	3	N/A

Note: *Regulations and requirements may be subject to change at short notice, and you are advised to contact your doctor well in advance of your intended date of departure. Any numbers in the chart refer to the footnotes below.*

1: Following WHO guidelines issued in 1973, a *cholera* vaccination certificate is not a condition of entry to Kyrgyzstan. However, cholera is common in this country and precautions are essential. Up-to-date advice should be sought before deciding whether these precautions should include vaccination, as medical opinion is divided over its effectiveness. For more information, see the *Health* appendix.
2: *Typhoid* is common in rural areas. Polio eradication is underway, rapidly reducing the risk of infection with the disease.
3: A *malaria* risk, exclusively in the *vivax* form, exists from June to September in some southern and western parts of the country - mainly in Batken, Osh amd Zhele-Abudskaya provinces, in areas bordering Tajikistan and Uzbekistan.
Food & drink: The water has been tested by the US-based Center for Diseases Control and found to be generally bacteria-free; however, it does have a high metal content. Milk is pasteurised and dairy products are safe for consumption. Only eat well-cooked meat and fish, preferably served hot. Pork, salad and mayonnaise may carry increased risk. Vegetables should be cooked and fruit peeled.
Owing to the difficulty of obtaining a balanced diet in some parts of Kyrgyzstan, visitors are recommended to take vitamin supplements.
Other risks: *Diphtheria* outbreaks have been reported in the area. *Hepatitis A* and E are common. *Hepatitis B* is endemic. On 28 September 2005, an outbreak of anthrax near Kara-Su in the south was reported. Some villages have been quarantined and on 13 October 2005, Uzbekistan closed its border at Kara-Su as a a result. *Rabies* is present. For those at high risk, vaccination before arrival should be considered. If you are bitten, seek medical advice without delay. For more information, consult the *Health* appendix.
Note: HIV testing is required for visits of over one month.

Health care: There is no reciprocal health agreement with the UK. Medical services offered to foreigners, except emergency care, require immediate cash payment and are somewhat limited. There is a severe shortage of basic medical supplies, including disposable needles, anaesthetics and antibiotics, and travellers are advised to bring any necessary medication or equipment. Elderly travellers and those with existing health problems may be at risk owing to inadequate medical facilities. The US Embassy maintains a list of English-speaking physicians in the area. Medical insurance is strongly recommended.

Travel - International

Note: All but essential travel to the south and west of Osh and to the Ferghana Valley region is advised against, due to the history of terrorist activity and armed violence, and to the threat of landmines in the Batken region and along the Kyrgyz-Uzbek border that Kyrgyzstan shares with other countries in Central Asia. However, this should not deter travel since most visits to Kyrgyzstan are trouble-free.

AIR:

The national airline is *Kyrgyzstan Airlines (R8)*, which operates direct flights to Bishkek from Germany, India, Russian Federation and Turkey (Istanbul). *British Airways* operates a direct flight from London to Bishkek. *British Mediterranean* (a franchise partner of British Airways) operates services three times a week from London to Bishkek. *Turkish Airlines* also flies to Bishkek from London, with a stopover in Istanbul. In addition, there is a number of direct flights from Europe to Almaty, in neighbouring Kazakhstan. The connection from there to Kyrgyzstan is via frequent bus services to Bishkek (travel time - four hours). Other European airlines flying direct to Almaty include *KLM* (from Amsterdam) and *Lufthansa* (five weekly flights from Frankfurt/M). There are also direct flights to Bishkek from Moscow and St Petersburg (Russian Federation) and from Tashkent (Uzbekistan).

Approximate flight times: From *London* to Bishkek is nine hours. From *London* to Almaty (Kazakhstan) is six hours 30 minutes, from *Istanbul* to Almaty is five hours 30 minutes and from *Frankfurt/M* to Almaty is seven hours.

Main airports: *Bishkek Manas Airport (FRU)* is 30km (18 miles) north of Bishkek. *To/from the airport*: There is a minibus shuttle service to the city centre when the airport is open (travel time - 30 minutes). Taxis are available 24 hours. There is also the bus service 153 every 30 minutes (travel time - 45 minutes). *Facilities*: Left luggage, crèche, bars, restaurant, chemist, bank and bureau de change.

Departure tax: US$10.

RAIL:

There are rail connections with the Russian Federation (travel time to Moscow is three days) and with other Central Asian Republics. However, tourists are advised that robberies on trains have been reported.

ROAD:

The main international road links are with Kazakhstan and there is presently one crossing point into China (PR); visitors should note that the Chinese authorities normally require proof of an invitation by a Chinese tour operator as a condition of entry. There are regular **bus** links from Bishkek to Tashkent (Uzbekistan) (travel time - 10 to 12 hours) and Almaty (Kazakhstan) (travel time - six hours); services leave the long-distance (*zapadni*) bus station in Bishkek. There is also a direct service to Osh from Tashkent (Uzbekistan) via the Fergana Valley, but road conditions are very poor on this route (see also *Uzbekistan* section). Generally, roads can be affected by landslides (especially during spring in the mountain areas), while winter may cause hazardous conditions on a number of roads (especially on mountain passes, some of which may be closed during certain periods); visitors should also note that garage services are very limited.

Travel - Internal

AIR:

There are internal connections from Bishkek to Cholpan-Ata, Kara-Kol, Naryn and Osh. Travellers should note that maintenance procedures for aircraft operating internally may not conform to internationally accepted standards. Access to the Central Tien-Shan region is via helicopter, which takes climbers up the Inylchek Valley.

RAIL:

There is only one railway line, which runs from Bishkek to Balikchi at the western end of Lake Issyk-Kul. Osh, in the south of the country, can be reached by rail via Tashkent (Uzbekistan). A new North-South railway is currently planned. Travellers are advised that robberies on trains have been reported.

ROAD:

Kyrgyzstan has 28,400km (17,400 miles) of roads. Traffic drives on the right. Visitors should note that roads are poorly maintained and badly signposted. **Bus:** There are regular bus connections to all parts of Kyrgyzstan. Buses are crowded. The FCO currently advises against the use of local buses/minibuses due to their commonly poor maintenance. **Taxi:** Taxis can be found in all major towns. Many are unlicensed, and fares should be agreed in advance. As many of the street names, particularly in the capital, have changed since independence, visitors are advised to ask for both the old and the new names when seeking directions. **Car hire:** Car hire is not available. It is possible to hire cars with drivers for long-distance journeys, but because of the shortage of petrol, it is generally an expensive option. Foreigners are generally expected to pay in US Dollars. **Documentation:** Licences for long-stay residents intending to buy or import a car can be obtained from the Protocol Department of the Foreign Ministry. An International Driving Permit and two photos are required.

URBAN:

There are bus and trolleybus services around the capital.

Travel times: The following chart gives approximate travel times from **Bishkek** (in hours and minutes) to other towns in Kyrgyzstan.

	Road
Osh	**12.00**
Tokmak	**1.00**
Balikchi	**2.30**
Kara-Kol	**5.30**

Travel Advice

After the peaceful Presidential elections on 10 July, the political situation remains calm though still uncertain throughout the country. Travellers should check the current situation before travelling and avoid any political demonstrations or large crowds while in Kyrgyzstan. Travellers should be aware of the continuing threat from terrorism, which Kyrgyzstan shares with other countries in Central Asia.

Tensions also exist over recognition of the Kyrgyz-Uzbek borders and all visitors choosing to travel there should ensure that they only use officially recognised border crossings. These tensions have been heightened following the recent events in Andijan in Uzbekistan. There is a risk that uncontrolled border areas may be landmined.

On 28 September 2005, an outbreak of anthrax near Kara-Su in the south was reported. Some villages have been quarantined and on 13 October 2005, Uzbekistan closed its border at Kara-Su as a result.

Most visits to Kyrgyzstan are trouble-free. However, there have been incidents of Westerners being targeted for theft.

This advice is based on information provided by the Foreign and Commonwealth Office in the UK. It is correct at time of publishing. As the situation can change rapidly, visitors are advised to contact the following organisations for the latest travel advice:

British Foreign and Commonwealth Office
Tel: (0845) 850 2829.
Website: www.fco.gov.uk

US Department of State
Website: http://travel.state.gov/travel

Accommodation

HOTELS:

Accommodation is limited outside the capital and visitors should not expect Western standards of comfort (although hotels are generally clean). Hotels charge considerably higher prices for individual tourists from non-CIS countries. Foreign tour operators booking for their clients are usually offered a preferential rate. Some hotels in more remote areas may still be wary of accepting foreigners travelling independently.

TURBAZAS:

These 'tourist bases' are an alternative to hotel accommodation. For a dollar or two in local currency, visitors have access to basic bungalow accommodation and three meals a day. Homestays are also possible throughout the country as are stays in camps made of *yurts* - the traditional Kyrgyz nomadic tents.

SANATORIA:

Since the break-up of the Soviet Union, the sanatoria on the shores of Lake Issyk-Kul - originally built by cooperatives and trade unions for fatigued workers - have started to take in tourists, but the atmosphere may not be to everyone's taste.

MOUNTAINEERING CAMPS:

Various private companies run a number of camps for mountaineers attempting to climb the many peaks in Kyrgyzstan's mountains. For further details, contact the State Committee for Tourism, Sport and Youth Policy *or* Regent Holidays (see *Top Things To See & Do*).

Top Things To See & Do

- The capital **Bishkek** was founded in 1878 on the site of a clay fort built by the Khan of Kokand and destroyed by the Russians, and sits at the foot of the *Tian Shan* mountain range. A largely Soviet-built city, it has a similar spacious atmosphere to its Kazakh neighbour, Almaty. **Ulitsa Sovietskaya**, the broad tree-lined road between the railway station and the city centre, houses the **Kyrgyz State Opera and Ballet Theatre**, the **Chernyshevsky Public Library** and the **State Art Museum**. Other attractions include the **History Museum** in the Old Square (*Stary Ploshad*), the **Lenin Museum**, the **Zoological Museum** and the **Kyrgyz Drama Theatre**. The Government plans to redevelop the former **General Frunze Museum** on Frunze Street - which commemorated the Kyrgyz-born Russian general who subdued Central Asia for the Bolsheviks - into a celebration of the ethnic diversity that is found in Kyrgyzstan. A section on Jewish culture has already been opened.
- Less than one hour's drive from Bishkek, the **Ala-Archa Nature Reserve** offers spectacular scenery for trekking and skiing. A further 50 minutes east from the city, the **Burana Tower** is a 25m- (82ft-) high minaret which dates from the 11th century and is all that remains of the ancient city of **Balasagun**.
- Still further east lies the jewel in the crown of the republic. Lying 1600m (5249ft) above sea level, the saltwater **Lake Issyk-Kul** was closed to foreigners during the Soviet era. Both its Kyrgyz name and Chinese name (Ze-Hai) mean warm sea, as it never freezes over, despite the altitude. Surrounded by snow-capped mountains and ringed with sandy beaches, the lake has a pristine and outstanding beauty. On the north shore, the town of **Cholpan-Alta** is a spa town which was a former retreat for the Communist Party elite. The resort of Issyk-Kul is now open to anyone, although it is very busy during the summer season and visitors are advised to book in advance. In the **Kungay Ala-Too Mountains** behind it, four trekking routes start, leading eventually to Medeo, outside Almaty (Kazakhstan), four to six days away. For scuba-diving enthusiasts, there is spectacularly clear water and a 12th-century town that lies 2 to 3m (6 to 10ft) below the surface of the lake near **Ulan**, 18km (11 miles) from Balikchi.
- At the southeast end of the lake is the town of **Kara-Kol**, with its attractive houses and tree-lined streets, and behind it are the **Terskay Ala-Too Mountains**, an unspoilt wilderness populated only by nomadic shepherds, and only then during the summer. There are few roads and little accommodation. Around 16km (10 miles) outside Kara-Kol is the health resort of **Ak-Soo** with hot mineral springs.
- **Osh,** Kyrgyzstan's second city is in the south, on the Uzbek border. Although it is 2500 years old, few traces of its ancient history remain. Since the 10th century, pilgrims have come to visit the **Suleiman Gora**, a hill in the middle of the city where legend has it that the Prophet once prayed. Childless women come here in the hope that they may conceive (the hill is supposed to look like a pregnant woman lying on her back). Other attractions include the **Museum of Local Studies** and the bazaar.
- North of Osh is the town of **Uzgen** where there is a mausoleum that is supposed to have contained the body of the Kyrgyz hero Manas. East of Osh is the **Sary-Chelek Nature Reserve**, which includes the stunning **Lake Sary-Chelek**.
- **The Silk Road:** This ancient trading route was used by silk merchants from the second century AD until its decline in the 14th century, and is open in parts to tourists, stretching from northern China through bleak and foreboding desert and mountainous terrain to the ports on either the Caspian Sea or Mediterranean Sea. For further details of the route, see the *Silk Road* in the China section. The main attraction of the route in Kyrgyzstan is the amazing alpine scenery including the **Kyrgyz Altau** and **Tian Shan** mountain ranges and **Issyk-Kul Lake** (the world's second-largest alpine lake). The difficult but exhilarating journey between Bishek and Kashgar (China) via the **Torugart Pass** is a popular trekking route. Travel along the Silk Road can be quite difficult due to the terrain, harsh climate and lack of developed infrastructure. Visitors to the region are advised to travel with an organised tour company or travel agent.
- Kyrgyzstan's reputation as a **trekking** and **climbing** destination has improved considerably in recent years and a growing number of tour operators now offer

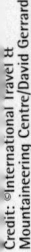

Credit: ©International Travel &
Mountaineering Centre/David Gerrard

walking, mountaineering and heli-skiing tours
throughout Kyrgyzstan and the neighbouring republics;
these companies can also arrange entry formalities for
border crossings into China and other CIS countries
where visas may be required. Mountaineering camps are
available: the *Ala-Archa camp*, 40km (25 miles) from
Bishkek, offers over 160 routes and is the base for
attempts to climb the Kyrgyz range (highest point:
4876m/15,997ft). In the south, the *Pamir camp* offers
opportunities on the peaks of the *Pamir Mountains*.

• **Horse riding:** The national sports reflect the importance
of the horse in Kyrgyz culture. *Ulak Tartysh* is a team
game in which two mounted teams attempt to deliver
the carcass of a goat weighing 30 to 40kg over the
opposition's goal line. Players are allowed to wrestle the
goat from an opponent, but physical assault is frowned
upon. Each game is 15 minutes long. **Aht Chabysh** are
horse races held over distances varying between 4 and
50km (2.5 to 31 miles). Competitors under 13 years of
age are barred from entering. *Udarysh* is a competition
on horseback in which two riders or two teams of riders
attempt to wrestle each other, and frequently their
mounts, to the ground.

TOURIST INFORMATION

Ministry of Tourism
ul Togolok Moldo 17, 720033 Bishkek, Kyrgyzstan
Tel: (312) 220 657.
E-mail: gatiskr@bishkek.gov.kr

Regent Holidays (UK) Limited
15 John Street, Bristol BS1 2HR, UK
Tel: (0117) 921 1711.
Website: www.regent-holidays.co.uk

Entertainment

FOOD & DRINK: Kyrgyz food shows the effect of its
location and history; befitting a nation descended from
nomadic herdspeople, mutton is the staple meat,
enlivened with Chinese influences. *Shashlyk* (skewered
chunks of mutton barbecued over charcoal) and *lipioshka*
(round unleavened bread) are often sold on street corners.
Plov, rice fried with shredded turnip and scraps of mutton,
served with bread, is a Central Asian staple. *Laghman* is a
noodle soup with mutton and vegetables that was
originally imported from Chinese Turkestan. *Beshbarmak*
is noodles with shredded, boiled meat in bouillon. Around
Lake Issyk-Kul, the noodles are sometimes served with
jellied potato starch rather than meat. *Shorpur* is a meat
soup with potatoes and other vegetables. *Manty* (steamed
noodle sacks of meat and vegetables), *samsa* (samosas)
and *chiburekki* (deep-fried dough cakes) are all popular as
snacks. The Kyrgyz and the Kazakhs are almost alone
among Central Asian people in eating horse meat; only
young mares are used and they are fed on the Alpine
grasses, which are thought to impart a particularly good
flavour. Restaurants in the capital tend to stop serving at
2200.
Black or green tea is the most popular drink. *Koumys*
(fermented mares' milk) is mildly alcoholic and can still be
found in the countryside; refusing an offer of *koumys*
may cause offence. Other local specialities include *dzarma*
(fermented barley flour) and *boso* (fermented millet,
resembling beer). During the summer, *chai khanas* (open-
air tea houses) are popular. Beer, vodka and local brandy
are all widely available in restaurants.
Tipping: This is becoming more customary, especially in
international hotels.
NIGHTLIFE: There are performances of both Russian and
European operas and ballets in the State Opera House in
Bishkek. Local music and theatre has enjoyed a strong
revival since independence and excerpts from the *Manas*,
the Kyrgyz national epic about the eponymous warrior
that runs to some 500,000 lines, play to packed houses.
The *Manas* was originally handed down orally, but was
written down in the early part of the 19th century.
SHOPPING: In Bishkek, Osh and Al-Medin bazaars are
popular for food and handicrafts. There is also a shop in
the Art Gallery that sells paintings and traditional Kyrgyz
products. Particularly popular are embroidered Kyrgyz felt

hats (*kalpak*), felt carpets and chess sets with traditional
Kyrgyz figures. **Shopping hours:** Mon-Sat 0900-1700.

Business

ECONOMY: Like the other central Asian States, the
Government of Kyrgyzstan inherited a seriously unbalanced
and dysfunctional economy from the Soviet Union. It chose
a policy of rapid change, including privatisation and a freely
floating and convertible currency (the Som, introduced in
1993) which has, by and large, been reasonably successful in
ensuring steady economic growth. This was also an
important factor in attracting foreign aid and investment,
which has done much to bolster the economy.
Despite the relatively small area of fertile land, agriculture
remains the largest employer, occupying almost half of the
working population and contributing a similar proportion of
GDP. Half of the irrigated agricultural land is devoted to
livestock, which is the mainstay of the farming sector. Other
agricultural products include grain, potatoes, fruit and
vegetables, cotton and tobacco. Kyrgyzstan's economic
potential lies in its mineral resources: there are known
deposits of iron ore, copper, lead, zinc, mercury, antimony,
tin, bismuth, vanadium, bauxite, molybdenum, manganese,
silver and gold. Oil reserves, provisionally thought to be
sufficient to cover domestic needs for 20 years, were located
in 2001. There are also large amounts of stones such as
marble, granite and limestone.
The industrial sector was the main casualty of the post-
Soviet era and output of metal goods, machinery, electronics
and textiles has declined over the last decade. In the service
sector, tourism has future potential but, given the dearth of
necessary infrastructure, this must be considered a long-
term objective. Finance grew quickly during the late 1990s
following reform of the banking industry. In November 2000,
the privatisation of several major state enterprises (including
telecommunications, air transport and energy) was agreed
by the Government despite serious domestic opposition.
Kyrgyzstan belongs to the Central Asian Economic Union
(ECO) which aims to promote regional economic co-
operation and trade among the former Soviet republics and
their neighbours. Kyrgyzstan is a member of the World Bank,
the IMF (which in October 2001 agreed a US$100 million
loan), the European Bank for Reconstruction and
Development (as a 'country of operation') and the Asian
Development Bank. The United Nations Development
Programme has also been active in Kyrgyzstan.
BUSINESS ETIQUETTE: Kyrgyzstan is actively seeking
overseas partners to modernise its industry and introduce
new technology. To this end, it has enacted a number of laws
to encourage and protect foreign investors; the law on
property extends to all foreign investors the rights granted
to Kyrgyz citizens with respect to ownership; foreigners are
allowed to purchase businesses and buildings to carry out
their activities, but the Government reserves the exclusive
right to own land, natural resources, water, agriculture and
livestock. There are significant tax holidays for foreign
investors. In order to invest in Kyrgyzstan, foreigners must be
registered with the Ministry of Economy and Finance.
Applications to set up in Kyrgyzstan should be sent in the
first instance to the State Committee on Foreign
Investments and Economic Assistance (Goskominvest). The
Government is particularly interested in encouraging
investment in mining, industry (including electronics, light
agricultural machinery and pharmaceuticals), petroleum,
hydroelectricity and agriculture. **Office hours:** Mon-Fri
0900-1800, Sat 0900-1300 (Mar-Oct). **Government office
hours:** Mon-Fri 0900-1700, Sat 0900-1300 (Nov-Feb).

COMMERCIAL INFORMATION

**State Technical Committee of the Kyrgyz
Republic on Foreign Investments and Economic
Development**
Room 210, ul Erkindik 58A,
720040 Bishkek, Kyrgystan
Tel: (312) 223 292.

Ministry of Finance
Prospekt Erkindik 58, 720040 Bishkek, Kyrgystan
Tel: (312) 228 922.

**Kyrgyz Chamber of Commerce and Industry,
Foreign Affairs Department**
Kievskaya 107, 720001 Bishkek, Kyrgystan
Tel: (312) 210 565.
Website: www.ihk-kg.de

**US Department of Commerce International
Trade Administration**
USA Trade Centre, 1401 Constitution Avenue,
Washington, DC 20230, USA
Tel (202) 482 4655.
Website: www.bisnis.doc.gov

Laos

Location: South-East Asia.

Time: GMT + 7.

Overview

Laos is one of the few Communist countries left in the
wold. Until 1988 tourists were not allowed access to Laos,
but the country has now opened up and it is perfectly
feasible to travel all over the country, preferably with a
recognised tour company. The number of tourists is
expected to continue increasing over the next few years.

General Information

AREA: 236,800 sq km (91,400 sq miles).
POPULATION: 5.5 million (2002).
POPULATION DENSITY: 23.3 per sq km (2002).
CAPITAL: Vientiane. **Population:** 663,000 (UN estimate
2001).
GEOGRAPHY: Laos is a landlocked country bordered to the
north by China, to the east by Vietnam, to the south by
Cambodia, and to the west by Thailand and Myanmar. Apart
from the Mekong River plains, along the border of Thailand
the country is mountainous, particularly in the north, and in
places is densely forested.
GOVERNMENT: People's Republic since 1975. Gained
independence from France in 1953. **Head of State:**
Khamtai Siphandon since 1998. **Head of Government:**
Prime Minister Boungnang Volachit since 2001.
LANGUAGE: The official language is Lao, however, many
tribal languages are also spoken. French, Vietnamese and
some English are in circulation.
RELIGION: The Laos-Lum (Valley Laos) people follow the
Hinayana (Theravada) form of Buddhism. The religions of
the Laos-Theung (Laos of the mountain tops) range from
traditional Confucianism to animism and Christianity.
ELECTRICITY: 230 volts AC, 50Hz.
SOCIAL CONVENTIONS: Religious beliefs should be
respected. Lao people should not be touched on the head.
Handshaking is not that usual; Lao people greet each other
with their palms together and a slight bowing of the head.
Take care when discussing politics and related subjects in
conversation so as not to cause offence. Shorts or revealing
clothes are not always acceptable.

A B C D E F G H I J K L M N O P Q R S T U V W X Y Z

Climate

Throughout most of the country, the climate is hot and tropical, with the rainy season between May and October when temperatures are at their highest. The dry season runs from November to April.
Required clothing: Lightweights and rainwear, with a sweater for winter and upland areas.

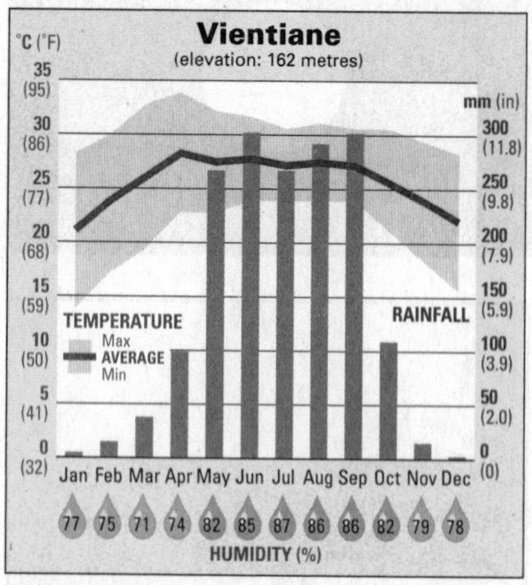
Vientiane
(elevation: 162 metres)
°C (°F)
35 (95)
30 (86)
25 (77)
20 (68)
15 (59)
10 (50)
5 (41)
0 (32)
mm (in)
300 (11.8)
250 (9.8)
200 (7.9)
150 (5.9)
100 (3.9)
50 (2.0)
0 (0)
TEMPERATURE
Max
AVERAGE
Min
RAINFALL
Jan Feb Mar Apr May Jun Jul Aug Sep Oct Nov Dec
77 75 71 74 82 85 87 86 86 82 79 78
HUMIDITY (%)

Communications

Telephone: Restricted IDD available. Country code: 856.
Mobile telephone: Coverage is sporadic and mainly, though not exclusively, situated around Vientiane.
Internet: Internet cafes are located in the major towns.
MEDIA: The ruling party maintains strict control over the media. The Govenment owns all newspapers and broadcast media.
Press: English-language newspapers include the *Vientiane Times*.
TV: *Laos National TV* and *Laos Television 3*.
Radio: *Lao national Radio*.

Passport/Visa

	Passport Required?	Visa Required?	Return Ticket? Required?
Full British	Yes	Yes	Yes
Australian	Yes	Yes	Yes
Canadian	Yes	Yes	Yes
USA	Yes	Yes	Yes
Other EU	Yes	Yes	Yes
Japanese	Yes	Yes	Yes

Note: *Regulations and requirements may be subject to change at short notice, and you are advised to contact the appropriate diplomatic or consular authority before finalising travel arrangements. Any numbers in the chart refer to the footnotes below.*

PASSPORTS: Passport with at least six months remaining validity required by all.
VISAS: Required by all.
Types of visa and cost: *Tourist, Business*: US$50 (including service and document fees). Families may only be charged US$50 per family if all living at the same address, and same surname is indicated on passports.
Validity: Validity starts from day of entry into Laos. *Tourist/Business*: 30 days (can be extended twice in Vientiane for 30 days). Visas must be used within three months of being issued.
Application to: Consulate (or consular section at Embassy) *or* an officially recognised tour operator. A visa valid for Laos can also be obtained from travel agencies in Bangkok (Thailand) or on arrival (see above). Visas are issued on arrival at 14 international checkpoints throughout Laos, including Luang Prabang Airport, Pakse Airport and (Wattay) Vientiane International Airport for stays of 15 days and costs US$30. For further details, contact the nearest Embassy.
Application requirements: (a) One passport-size photo. (b) One signed and completed application form. (c) Valid passport. (d) Fee payable by cash or cheque. (e) Postal applications should include an additional US$5 (inside France) or US$10 (international), to cover postage. *Business*: (a)-(e) and, (f) Letter from sponsor in Laos.
Working days required: Three.
Temporary residence: Enquire at nearest Embassy or Consulate. For extension of visa, consult the Immigration Office (tel: (21) 512 012); neglecting to do so will result in a fine of US$10 per day until leaving the country.

PASSPORT/VISA INFORMATION

Embassy of the Lao People's Democratic Republic in France
74 Avenue Raymond Poincaré, 75116 Paris, France
Tel: (1) 4553 0298.
Website: www.laoparis.com

Embassy of the Lao People's Democratic Republic in the USA
2222 S Street, NW, Washington, DC 20008, USA
Tel: (202) 332 6416.
Website: www.laoembassy.com

Money

Currency: Lao Kip (LAK) = 100 cents. Notes are in denominations of LAK5000, 2000, 1000, 500 and 100.
Currency exchange: Thai Baht and US Dollars are the easiest currencies to exchange. They are also widely accepted in shops, markets and hotels in Vientiane and Luang Prabang.
Credit & debit cards: Major credit cards are accepted in the more upmarket hotels and restaurants. Check with your credit or debit card company for details of merchant acceptability and other services which may be available.
Traveller's cheques: Limited acceptance. To avoid additional exchange rate charges, travellers are advised to take traveller's cheques in US Dollars or Thai Baht.
Currency restrictions: The import and export of local currency is prohibited. There are no restrictions on the import or export of foreign currency, but amounts greater than US$2000 must be declared.
Banking hours: Mon-Fri 0800-1200 and 1330-1730.
Exchange rate indicators:
Rate at time of publishing
£1.00= LAK18077.27
$1.00= LAK10415.85

Duty Free

The following goods may be imported into Laos, from countries not bordering Laos, without incurring customs duty:
500 cigarettes or 100 cigars or 500g of tobacco; one bottle of alcoholic beverage and two bottles of wine; personal jewellery up to 500g.

Public Holidays

Below are listed Public Holidays for the January 2006-June 2007 period.
2006: Jan 1 New Year's Day. **Jan 6** Pathet Lao Day. **Jan 20** Army Day. **Jan 29** Chinese New Year. **Mar 8** International Women's Day. **Mar 22** Day of the People's Party. **Apr 13-15*** Lao New Year (Pi Mai). **May 1** Labour Day. **May 13** Birth of Buddha. **Jul 11** Khao Pansa (Buddhist Fast begins). **Jun 1** Children's Day. **Aug 13** Lao Issara (Day of the Free Laos). **Oct 2** Bouk ok Pansa (Buddhist Fast ends). **Oct 12** Day of Liberation. **Dec 2** National Day.
2007: Jan 1 New Year's Day. **Jan 6** Pathet Lao Day. **Jan 20** Army Day. **Feb 18** Chinese New Year. **Mar 8** International Women's Day. **Mar 22** Day of the People's Party. **Apr 13-15*** Lao New Year (Pi Mai). **May 1** Labour Day. **May 2** Birth of the Buddha. **Jun 1** Children's Day. **Jun/Jul** Khao Pansa (Buddhist Fast begins).
Note: *Variations may occur.

Health

	Special Precautions?	Certificate Required?
Yellow Fever	No	1
Cholera	Yes	2
Typhoid & Polio	3	N/A
Malaria	4	N/A

Note: *Regulations and requirements may be subject to change at short notice, and you are advised to contact your doctor well in advance of your intended date of departure. Any numbers in the chart refer to the footnotes below.*

1: A *yellow fever* vaccination certificate is required from travellers arriving from infected areas.
2: Following WHO guidelines issued in 1973, a *cholera* vaccination certificate is not a condition of entry to Laos. However, *cholera* is a serious risk in this country and precautions are essential. Up-to-date advice should be sought before deciding whether these precautions should include vaccination, as medical opinion is divided over its effectiveness; see the *Health* appendix.
3: *Typhoid* may occur. *Polio virus* transmission has been interrupted, but complete eradication is not yet certain.
4: *Malaria* risk exists throughout the year in the whole country, except in Vientiane. The malignant *falciparum* form is prevalent and is reported to be highly resistant to chloroquine. The recommended prophylaxis is mefloquine.
Food & drink: All water should be regarded as being potentially contaminated. Water used for drinking, brushing teeth or making ice should have first been boiled or otherwise sterilised. Milk is unpasteurised and should be boiled. Powdered or tinned milk is available and is advised, but make sure that it is reconstituted with pure water. Avoid dairy products that are likely to have been made from unboiled milk. Only eat well-cooked meat and fish, preferably served hot. Pork, salad and mayonnaise may carry increased risk. Vegetables should be cooked and fruit peeled.
Other risks: *Hepatitis A* and *E* occur; *hepatitis B* is highly endemic. *Dengue fever, diphtheria, tuberculosis* and *Japanese encephalitis* occur. Some vaccinations may be advised. *Liver fluke* (opisthorchiasis) is present; travellers should avoid eating raw or undercooked fish.
Rabies is present. For those at high risk, vaccination before arrival should be considered. If you are bitten, seek medical advice without delay. For more information, consult the *Health* appendix.
Health care: Any treatment must generally be paid for in cash. Health insurance is essential and should include cover for air evacuation.

Travel - International

Note: Penalties for illegal drug importation and use are severe and can include the death penalty. Over the past year there have been explosions in the capital Vientiane and attacks on buses, resulting in injury and death. There are also reports of banditry in rural areas and unexploded ordnance is an ongoing danger. It is illegal not to carry an ID document or a passport, and fines for not having one for presentation on demand can be high. The Lao Government prohibits sexual relationships, including sexual contact between foreign citizens and Lao nationals, except when the two parties have been married in accordance with Lao family law. Penalties for failing to register a relationship range from fines to imprisonment. Most visits to Laos are trouble-free.
AIR:
The national airline of Laos is *Lao Aviation (QV)* which serves the international routes from Vientiane to Hanoi and Ho Chi Minh City (Vietnam), Bangkok and Chiang Mai (Thailand), Phnom Penh (Cambodia) and Kunming (China). *Thai Airways International* (website: www.thaiair.com) flies from Bangkok; *Vietnam Airlines* (website: www.vietnamairlines.com) flies from Hanoi.
Main airports: *Vientiane (VTE)* (Wattay) is 3km (2 miles) from the city (travel time - 20 minutes). *To/from the airport*: Taxis cost US$5, on average. *Facilities*: Bank/bureaux de change, bars, post office, restaurants and car hire.
Departure tax: US$10; children under two years of age and transit passengers are exempt.
RAIL:
There are no railways in Laos, but the Thai system stretches from Bangkok via Nakhon Ratchasima to Nong Khai on the Laos/Thailand border. A ferry and a bridge link the Lao side of the Mekong, 19km (12 miles) east of Vientiane.
ROAD:
It is possible to enter Laos from Thailand at Nong Khai over the Friendship Bridge. Other border crossings include Chiang Kong (Thailand)-Houei Xay (Laos) in the north; Mukdahan (Thailand)-Savannakhet (Laos); Chong Mek (between Pakse and Ubon Ratchathani); Nakorn Phanom (Thailand)-Tha Kek (Laos) and Jouay Kone (Thailand)-Xaingnabouri (Laos). It is possible to enter Laos by road from Vietnam either at Lao Bao or at the new border post of Lak Xao near Vinh. Laos can also be entered from China, from Mengla in Yunnan province to Luang Nam Tha. Overland travel to Cambodia and Myanmar is not feasible owing to security risks. Internally, the road link between Vientiane and Luang Prabang to the north has been upgraded.

Travel - Internal

AIR:
Domestic air services run from Vientiane to Houayxai, Luang Nmatha, Luang Prabang, Oudomxai, Sam Neua and Sayabouti in the north *and* Pakse and Savanakhet in the south. Private charter flights are also available through *Westcoast Helicopters*.
RIVER:
The Mekong and other rivers are a vital part of the country's transport system. The choice is between irregular (and very basic) slow ferries and exciting but noisy and hazardous speedboats. Both services run from Vientiane to Luang Prabang and Luang Prabang to Huay Xai. Ferries often depart early in the

mornings and can take several days, whilst speedboats run more regularly and take approximately eight hours for each leg of the journey. Times and prices alter according to demand. Private jet boats can be hired from *Lao River Exploration Services*. For further details, contact Lao National Tourism Authority (see *Top Things To See & Do*).

ROAD:
Traffic drives on the right. Many of the roads have been paved in recent years, including the main highway from the Thai border at Savannakhet to the Vietnamese border. However, few main roads are suitable for all-weather driving. In the north of the country, there is a road link between Vientiane and Luang Prabang, and from Vientiane to Nam Dong and Tran Ninh. **Bus:** Services link all major towns and cities. Buses can vary from the more traditional type to the converted pick-up truck. **Car hire:** It is not recommended to hire cars in Laos as driving standards are low. However, it is possible to hire cars with a driver through hotels or tourist agencies. *Asia Vehicle Rental Co Ltd* in Vientiane can help visitors with all their rental needs (tel: (21) 217 493 (and fax) *or* 223 867; website: www.avr.laopdr.com). **Documentation:** International Driving Permit recommended, although it is not legally required.

URBAN:
There is a mixture of old and metered taxis in Vientiane that can usually be located at Wattay Airport, the Friendship Bridge and the Morning market. Taxis can also be hired for approximately US$20 per day. Converted motorcycles, known as *tuk-tuks* or *jumbos*, are available in all major towns and cities and are perfect for shorter journeys around town. Bargaining is expected. Motorcycles and bicycles can be hired for the day in Vientiane and Luang Prabang.
Note: Travel outside Vientiane should be prearranged with a tour company.

Travel Advice

Most visits to Laos are trouble-free but you should be aware of the global risk of indiscriminate international terrorist attacks, which could be against civilian targets, including places frequented by foreigners.
In 2004, there were explosions in the capital Vientiane and attacks on buses, resulting in injury and death.
Penalties for illegal drug importation and use are severe and can include the death penalty. Banditry has also been reported in rural areas and unexploded ordnance is an ongoing danger.
This advice is based on information provided by the Foreign and Commonwealth Office in the UK. It is correct at time of publishing. As the situation can change rapidly, visitors are advised to contact the following organisations for the latest travel advice:

British Foreign and Commonwealth Office
Tel: (0845) 850 2829.
Website: www.fco.gov.uk

US Department of State
Website: http://travel.state.gov/travel

Accommodation

HOTELS:
There are good hotels and guest houses in Luang Prabang, Vang Vieng and Vientiane, but facilities are sparse elsewhere. Local village hostels are available, but with few amenities. For more details of prices and location, contact a tour company with experience in Laos.

CAMPING:
There are no facilities for camping in Laos.

ECOLODGES:
Laos is eager to promote ecotourism and visitors can stay in specially constructed ecolodges in either **Laopako**, one hour 30 minutes from Vientiane on the **Nam Mgum river**, or the Boat Landing in **Luang Namtha** province.

Top Things To See & Do

- One of Asia's most relaxed and quiet capital cities, **Vientiane** is nestled in fertile plains on the banks of the **Mekong River**. Many buildings reflect the country's past links with Europe, such as the old French colonial houses and the capital's **Victory Monument**, which bears a striking, if somewhat *rococo*, similarity to the *Arc de Triomphe* in Paris. An important national monument is the 16th-century **That Luang** (Royal Stupa) that symbolises Buddhist and Lao union. Other interesting sights include the **Lao Revolutionary Museum**; **Wat Ho Prakeo**, a former royal temple; **Wat Sisaket**, one of the capital's oldest temples; **Wat Xieng Khouang** (Buddha Park), situated 24km (15 miles) south of the city and displaying fascinating Buddhist and Hindu structures.
- **Xiang Khouang** province in the northeast of the country is characterised by lush green mountains and Karst limestone. The capital, **Phonsavan**, enjoys a favourable climate being at an altitude of 1200m (3937ft). The unusual **Plain of Jars** is accessible from the city and offers the mysterious sight of hundreds of stone jars, some weighing up to 6 tonnes, scattered over the landscape. The jars are over 2000 years old and legend says that they were used to ferment rice wine in the sixth century in order to celebrate a victory in battle. Some 52km (32 miles) north of Phonsavan, visitors can enjoy bathing in two hot springs: **Bo Noi** and **Bo Yai**.
- **Luang Prabang:** This ancient royal city has been a UNESCO World Heritage Site since 1995. Located between the Mekong and **Khan River**, it is the cultural and religious centre of the country, boasting 32 large temple complexes. **Wat Xieng Thong** is one of the most impressive temples, decorated with coloured glass and gold. Testament to the fact that it had been the royal capital until 1975, the royal palace there contains fine artwork and gifts made for former kings. Nearby, in the town centre, visitors can ascend **Mount Phousi** for a panoramic view of the city and surrounding rivers. Also worth seeing is the **Palace Museum** (the former royal palace), easily recognisable by its golden-spired stupa, which houses an impressive collection of artefacts from old rulers of the Kingdom of **Lane Xang**.
- Close by is **Ban Phanom Village**, famous for its weavings, which offers the opportunity to visit a traditional community and to purchase bargain-priced silk and embroideries. Around 25km (16 miles) along the Mekong river lie the fascinating **Pak Ou Caves**, that can be easily reached by speedboat from Luang Prabang. The two caves, **Tham Ting** and **Tham Phun**, are full of Buddha images that have been left there over hundreds of years by worshippers. Further downriver is the small village of **Ban Xang Hai**, famous for its production of rice whisky. Also worth seeing are the **Kuang Si Waterfalls**, situated 30km (19 miles) from Luang Prabang. Visitors can swim in the lower pools.
- Situated in the far northwest of Laos, **Luang Namtha** province is a mountainous region, with areas of tropical rainforest and over 39 ethnic minority groups. An ecotourism project for the region has been proposed by UNESCO. **Muang Xing** is a small town on the river plains which used to be an outpost for an ancient southern Chinese empire. A number of guest houses can offer hiking trips starting from here.
- **Khammouane** province in Southern Laos is accessible from Vientiane by bus. The region is currently being explored for its potential as a place for ecotourism, and its amazing limestone formations, caves, rivers and jungle make it a unique environment. Its capital, **Tha Kek**, is a good place to reach other sights, such as the **Tham Xieng Lap Caves** and the **That Skihotabang**, a stunning stupa built by King Nanthasen in around the 10th century.
- Within easy reach by bus from Khammouane is **Savannakhet** province. Positioned between Thailand and Vietnam, the province acts as a useful trading junction between the two. Most of the town's architecture is French colonial, including a large Catholic church, although there are several Buddhist temple buildings worth seeing, such as **Wat Sainyaphum**. It is possible to walk the **Ho Chi Minh Trail**, a former clandestine route used by the North Vietnamese Army to transport military gear to South Vietnam. The trail was bombed by the USA during the Vietnam War and parts of this devastation can still be viewed. However, the trail *must* be seen with a guide as large parts of the route still contain unexploded bombs.
- **Pakse**, capital of Champassak province, is easily reached by air from Vientiane. Pakse is home to many ethnic minority groups, much of the **Bolaven Plateau** and the famous, although relatively unvisited, Wat Phu temple. **Wat Phu** was constructed around the fifth century on a mountain top near fresh spring water by the Khmer Hindus, who went on to settle their empire at its former capital – *Ankor Wat* (Cambodia). There are breathtaking views across the Mekong Valley from the temple. The complex can be reached by chartered boat along the Mekong River. Other excursions worth making are to the Bolaven Plateau, where visitors can enjoy elephant riding and trekking, and to **Sii Pan Dan** (Four Thousand Islands), where islands are formed during the rainy season on the Mekong river. There is the opportunity to see spectacular waterfalls and the endangered *irriwaddy* dolphins.
- **Wildlife:** Laos's pristine landscape hosts a variety of flora and fauna, including rare primates, mammals and birds. Freshwater dolphins can be found in the Mekong river. There is still some unexploded ordnance in the countryside, and official advice should be taken about which areas to avoid.
- **Trekking:** Travellers can head to the hills independently or take part in locally organised guided tours.
- **Mountain biking:** The lack of cars makes cycling a good proposition. Terrain can be difficult, however, and there are not many roads. Visitors are advised to bring their own bicycles, though there are some for hire in the larger towns.

TOURIST INFORMATION

Lao National Tourism Authority (LNTA)
PO Box 3556, Lane Xang Avenue, Hadsady, Chanthaboury, Vientiane, Laos
Tel: (21) 222 971.
Website: www.visit-mekong.com/laos

Adventure World Ltd in Australia
Street Address: 179 Progress Drive, Bibra Lake, 6163 Western Australia, Australia
Postal Address: PO Box 1186, Bibra Lake, 6965 WA, Australia
Tel: (8) 5417 9666.
Website: www.adventureworld.net.au

Entertainment

FOOD & DRINK: Rice, especially sticky rice, is the staple food and dishes will be Indo-Chinese in flavour and presentation. Lao food can be found on the stalls in the markets. There are several fairly good French restaurants in Vientiane, catering mainly for the diplomatic community. Baguettes and croissants are normally eaten for breakfast. Rice whisky, *lao lao*, is popular and there are two brands available. The beer is also good.
Tipping: Practised modestly in hotels and restaurants.
NIGHTLIFE: There are several discos in Vientiane that tend to have live Lao bands. Most large hotels will have their own nightclubs.
SHOPPING: The markets in Vientiane and Luang Prabang (about 40 minutes by air from Vientiane) are worth visiting. Silk, silver jewellery and handmade shirts are good buys. Although the majority of shops have fixed prices, bartering is still advisable for antiques and other art objects. **Shopping hours:** Mon-Fri 0800-1600; Mon-Sat 0900-2100 (private shops).

Business

ECONOMY: Laos is one of the world's poorest countries, and its predominantly agricultural economy operates almost entirely at subsistence level. Rice, the main crop, is grown in several different varieties; other crops include maize, cassava, pulses, groundnuts, fruits, sugar cane, tobacco and coffee. Though little known outside the region, Laotian coffee is highly rated among connoisseurs and is now the country's single largest export commodity. The country has considerable, though largely untapped, reserves of tin, lead and zinc, as well as iron ore, coal and timber. Industry is mostly concerned with processing raw materials, principally timber and food; textiles and basic consumer goods are also produced. Despite its relative obscurity and secretive nature, a tourism industry has developed which is now Laos' single largest source of income. Development is hampered by chronic shortages of skilled labour and foreign exchange, and the Laotian economy relies heavily on foreign aid (80 per cent of public sector investment is financed by aid) from Japan and Scandinavia, and more recently Thailand, Taiwan and Australia.
Economic reforms began in the early 1990s and included an extensive programme of privatisation. These initially attracted the support of the IMF but the Government's failure to meet successive financial targets led to a withdrawal of the Fund's support in 1998. Compounded by the regional financial crisis, the economy was in serious difficulties by the beginning of 1999 with 100 per cent annual inflation, a collapsed currency value and a desperate shortage of foreign and domestic currency. Since then, something of a recovery has taken place: the economy is now growing at around 6 per cent annually while inflation has been cut to a more manageable 25 per cent. Nonetheless, the country's economic prospects are uncertain. Laos is a member of the Asian Development Bank and the Colombo Plan, which promotes economic and social development in Asia and the Pacific.
BUSINESS ETIQUETTE: Punctuality is appreciated. Lightweight suits, shirt and tie should be worn. English is not spoken by all officials and a knowledge of French is useful. Business cards should have a Laotian translation on the reverse. Best time to visit is during the dry season, from November to April. **Office hours:** Mon-Fri 0800-1200 and 1330-1730.

COMMERCIAL INFORMATION

Lao National Chamber of Commerce and Industry
BP 4596, Sihom Road, Ban Haisok, Vientiane, Laos
Tel/fax: (21) 219 223.
E-mail: ccilcciv@laotel.com

Ministry of Finance
Luang Prabang Road, Ban Phonxang, Vientiane, Laos
Tel: (21) 412 401.

Latvia

200km
100mls
✈ international airport

BALTIC SEA

ESTONIA

Gulf of Riga

• Ventspils

VIDZEME

Sigulda

Valmiera

LATVIA

Jurmala

• Liepaja

KURZEME

• Jelgava

ZEMGALE

RIGA

LATGALE

Rezekne

Daugavpils

LITHUANIA

BELARUS

RUSSIAN FED.

Location: Northern Europe.

Time: GMT + 2. (GMT + 3 from last Sunday in March to last Sunday in October.)

Overview

Latvia is a small country on the Baltic Sea with ancient history and traditions. If you want to enjoy nature, there is not only the serene Gulf of Riga and the open Baltic Sea, but also nature parks, lakes and beautiful forests. In Old Riga, you will find not only fabulous architectural monuments but also various nightclubs and pubs. According to legend, once every 100 years, the devil rears his head from the waters of Riga's River Daugava and asks whether Riga is 'ready' yet. If the answer is 'yes', the now nearly 900-year-old city will be condemned to sink into the waters.

Yet Latvia has resisted doom and disarray for centuries. The largest of the three Baltic Republics, Latvia has often been an important trading centre and strategic pawn in the Baltic region. The various Latvian tribes were self-governing until the end of the 13th century when conquered by the German Teutonic Knights. Latvia was then subject to sporadic invasions by the Poles and the Swedes until the 18th century when Russia, under Peter the Great, emerged as a major European power and subsumed Latvian territory. The Bolshevik revolution of 1917 heralded the end of Russian suzerainty. Once Germans were expelled too, Latvians asserted their independence for the first time in more than 600 years. However, World War II again threatened the country with foreign domination and, in 1940, the Russians took over once more. Latvia had, that same year, signed a bilateral non-aggression pact with the Germans and a pact with Moscow. The Russians were driven out by the Nazi invasion of the Soviet Union in 1941, but returned three years later, after which Latvia was incorporated into the Soviet Union along with Estonia and Lithuania as one of the 15 Soviet republics. The process that led eventually to Latvia's present independence began with the accession of Mikhail Gorbachev as Soviet leader in 1985.

What has remained since such recent times is a tricky relationship with the Russian Federation, which is shown in microcosm via ethnic Russians who live in Latvia. The suppression of Latvian language and culture during the Soviet era has left a legacy of hostility which is only gradually being overcome, but Russians now feel subject to discrimination in certain areas.

For now, however, there is no chance of Latvia being 'ready' to sink. Long the Baltic favourite, it is now also beginning to emerge as a tourist destination further afield, championed as one of Europe's hidden treasures. Those who visit will appreciate the small picturesque medieval towns, country castles, museums and folk parks, ruined fortresses and, occasionally, grand palaces. They will also appreciate the little Latvian quirks still entrenched in customs, crafts and culture. Rather than sinking, Latvia is truly in ascension.

General Information

AREA: 64,589 sq km (24,938 sq miles).

POPULATION: 2.3 million (UN, 2005).

POPULATION DENSITY: 35.6 per sq km.

CAPITAL: Riga. **Population:** 739,232 (2003).

GEOGRAPHY: Latvia is situated on the Baltic coast and borders Estonia in the north, Lithuania in the south, the Russian Federation in the east and Belarus in the southeast. The coastal plain is mostly flat but, inland to the east, the land is hilly with forests and lakes. There are about 12,000 rivers in Latvia, the biggest being the River Daugava. The ports of Riga, Liepaja and Ventspils often freeze over during the winter.

GOVERNMENT: Republic. Gained independence from the Soviet Union in 1991. **Head of State:** President Vaira Vike-Freiberga since 1999. **Head of Government:** Prime Minister Aigars Kalvitis since 2004. **Recent history:** The present administration is headed by Indulis Emsis, who was appointed and approved by the *Saiema* (National Assembly) in early 2004. Emsis's Government is another centre-right Government; a coalition of the Union of Famers and Greens (Emsis's own), the People's Party and the Latvia First Party. The President of the republic, who also chairs the Saiema, is Vaira Vike-Freiberga; she was elected to a second term in June 2003. A little less than a year later, Latvia also joined - along with nine other applicants, including its Baltic neighbours - the European Union.

Under the current constitution, legislative power is vested in the elected 100-member *Saiema* (Supreme Council) which is elected for a four-year term by proportional representation. Executive power is held by the Prime Minister who heads an appointed Cabinet of Ministers. The Head of State, the President, is elected by - and chairs - the *Saiema*.

LANGUAGE: Latvian is the official language. It is an Indo-European, non-Slavic and non-Germanic language and is similar only to Lithuanian. Russian is the mother tongue of over 30 per cent of the population and is understood by most people. English and German may also be understood.

RELIGION: Predominantly Protestant (Lutheran) with 19 per cent of the population being Roman Catholic. There is also a Russian Orthodox minority.

ELECTRICITY: 220 volts AC, 50Hz. European-style two-pin plugs are in use.

SOCIAL CONVENTIONS: Handshaking is customary. Normal courtesies should be observed. The Latvians are somewhat reserved and formal, but nevertheless very hospitable. They are proud of their culture and visitors should take care to respect this sense of national identity.

Climate

Temperate climate, but with considerable temperature variations. Summer is warm with relatively mild weather in spring and autumn. Winter, which lasts from November to mid-March, can be very cold. Rainfall is distributed throughout the year with the heaviest rainfall in August. Snowfall is common in the winter months.

Required clothing: Light- to mediumweights are worn during summer months. Medium- to heavyweights are needed during winter. Rainwear is advisable all year.

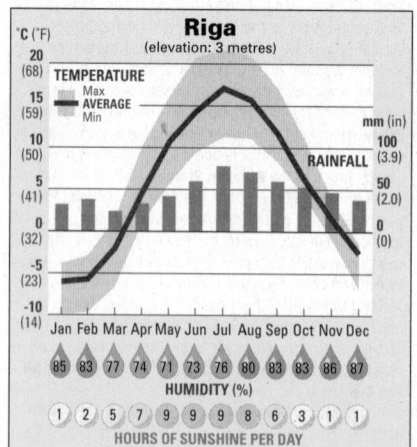

Riga
(elevation: 3 metres)

°C (°F)
TEMPERATURE
Max
AVERAGE
Min

RAINFALL

mm (in)

Jan Feb Mar Apr May Jun Jul Aug Sep Oct Nov Dec

85 83 77 74 71 73 76 80 83 83 86 87
HUMIDITY (%)

1 2 5 7 9 9 9 8 6 3 1 1
HOURS OF SUNSHINE PER DAY

Communications

Telephone: IDD is available. Country code: 371. Directory enquiries: 09. International calls can be made from telephone booths. Payphones are operated by phonecards which can be purchased at kiosks, post offices and in some shops.

Mobile telephone: Roaming agreements exist with international mobile phone companies. It is illegal to use a mobile telephone while driving.

Internet: There are many Internet cafes in Riga and some in other towns.

Post: The main post office is at Brivibas bulvaris 19 (open 24 hours). Postboxes are yellow. Airmail to Western Europe takes five to seven days. Post office hours: Mon-Fri 0900-1800 and Sat 0900-1300.

MEDIA: The media operate freely with few legal restrictions on their work.

Press: There are Latvian and Russian newspapers - *Diena*, *Neatkariga Rita Avize* and *Vakara Zinas* being the most popular Latvian titles.

TV: *Latvian Television* (*LTV*) is a publicly owned channel which operates *LTV1* and *LTV7*. *Latvian Independent Television* (*LNT*) is the main commercial terrestrial channel.

Radio: The privately owned *Latvian Radio* operates four national networks.

Passport/Visa

	Passport Required?	Visa Required?	Return Ticket? Required?
Full British	1	No	No
Australian	Yes	No	No
Canadian	Yes	No	No
USA	Yes	No	No
Other EU	1	No	No
Japanese	Yes	No	No

Note: *Regulations and requirements may be subject to change at short notice, and you are advised to contact the appropriate diplomatic or consular authority before finalising travel arrangements. Any numbers in the chart refer to the footnotes below.*

PASSPORTS: Passport valid for at least three months beyond length of stay required by all except:
(a) **1.** EU/EEA nationals (EU+ Iceland, Liechtenstein, Norway) and Swiss nationals holding a valid national ID card.

Note: EU and EEA nationals are only required to produce evidence of their EU/EEA nationality and identity in order to be admitted to any EU/EEA Member State. This evidence can take the form of a valid national passport *or* national identity card. Either is acceptable. Possession of a return ticket, any length of validity on their document, sufficient funds for the length of their proposed visit should *not* be imposed.

VISAS: Required by all except the following for a stay of up to 90 days within any six-month period:
(a) nationals of countries mentioned in the table and under passport exemptions above;
(b) nationals of Andorra, Argentina, Bolivia, Brazil, Brunei, Bulgaria, Chile, Costa Rica, Croatia, El Salvador, Guatemala, Honduras, Hong Kong (SAR), Israel, Korea (Rep), Macau (SAR), Malaysia, Mexico, Monaco, New Zealand, Nicaragua, Panama, Paraguay, Romania, San Marino, Singapore, Switzerland, Uruguay, Vatican City and Venezuela;
(c) transit passengers continuing their journey by the same or first connecting aircraft, provided holding onward or return documentation and not leaving the airport, except citizens of: Afghanistan, Bangladesh, Congo (Dem Rep), Eritrea, Ethiopia, Ghana, Iran, Iraq, Nigeria, Pakistan, Somalia and Sri Lanka who must obtain an airport transit visa issued prior to arrival.

Note: Nationals of countries who require an airport transit visa can cross the transit zone without one provided that they: (a) hold a valid residence permit, entry visa or transit visa for Latvia; (b) hold a valid entry visa or residence permit issued by a member of the EU or Schengen Agreement; (c) hold a valid residence permit issued by Andorra, Canada, Japan, Liechtenstein, Monaco, San Marino, Switzerland, USA and the Vatican City, guaranteeing the right to return; (d) the national is a crew member of an aeroplane or citizen of a country which is a member of the December 7th 1944 International Civil Aviation Convention.

Types of visa and cost: *Short-term*: £23 (single- and double-entry); £40 (multiple-entry). Visas for children under 16 are free of charge.

Note: There is no separate category for a 'Business' visa. If travelling to Latvia for business purposes, please consult the Latvian Embassy (see *Passport/Visa Information*) for the requirements and cost of a tourist visa.

Validity: *Short-term*: from one day to 12 months.
Transit: Three days (foreign sailors may be issued with a transit visa entitling them to remain in the country for five days).

Application to: Consulate (or consular section at Embassy); see *Passport/Visa Information*.

Application requirements: (a) Passport valid for at least three months beyond expiry of visa, with at least two blank pages. (b) One completed application form. (c) One passport-size photo. (d) Valid travel health insurance policy guaranteeing coverage of costs associated with health care (except for nationals of Estonia, Finland, Sweden and Ukraine). (e) Fee, cash only. *Short-term*: (a)-(e) and, (f) An invitation to visit Latvia, approved by the

A B C D E F G H I J K L M N O P Q R S T U V W X Y Z

Office of Citizenship and Migration Affairs at the Ministry of Interior in Riga (see below for address). *Transit* and *Airport Transit*: (a)-(e) and, (f) Valid visa for the country to be entered after Latvia, if required.
Note: (a) Additional documents, such as return or onward tickets, confirmed hotel reservation and proof of sufficient funds, may also be requested. (b) All invitations must be registered by the Office of Citizenship and Migration Affairs, Alunāna Str. 1, Riga LV-1050 (tel: 721 9656; website: www.pmlp.gov.lv).
Working days required: Usually seven; however in some cases processing may take longer.

PASSPORT/VISA INFORMATION

Embassy of Latvia in the UK
45 Nottingham Place, London W1U 5LY, UK
Tel: (020) 7312 0040.
Website: www.london.am.gov.lv
Opening hours: Mon-Fri 0830-1700; 1000-1300 (consular section).

Embassy of Latvia in the USA
2306 Massachusetts Avenue, NW, Washington, DC 20008, USA
Tel: (202) 328 2840.
Website: www.latvia-usa.org
Opening hours: Mon 1400-1600 and Tues-Thur 1000-1200.

Money

Currency: Latvian Lat (LVL) = 100 santims. Notes are in denominations of LVL500, 100, 50, 20, 10 and 5. Coins are in denominations of LVL2 and 1, and 50, 20, 10, 5, 2 and 1 santims.
Currency exchange: Bureaux de change are found all over main towns, including inside shops, hotels, post offices and train stations. These tend to close at 1900. Currency may also be obtained at ATMs in towns and cities. The most convenient currencies to exchange are Euros and the US Dollar.
Credit & debit cards: American Express, Diners Club, Eurocard, JCB, MasterCard and Visa are accepted by most hotels, restaurants and supermarkets. Some shops in Riga also accept credit cards. Check with your credit or debit card company for details of merchant acceptability and other services which may be available.
Traveller's cheques: To avoid additional exchange rate charges, travellers are advised to take traveller's cheques in US Dollars or Pounds Sterling.
Currency restrictions: There are no restrictions on the import and export of either local or foreign currency.
Banking hours: Mon-Fri 0900-1700. Some banks are open Sat 0900-1300.
Exchange rate indicators:
Rate at time of publishing

£1.00=	LVL1.04
$1.00=	LVL0.60

Duty Free

The following goods may be imported into Latvia without incurring customs duty by persons aged 17 years and over arriving from countries outside the EU:
200 cigarettes, 100 cigarillos, 50 cigars or 250g of tobacco; 1l of alcoholic beverages exceeding 22 per cent volume, up to 2l of spirits or aperitifs less than 22 per cent volume; 2l of still wine; up to 50g of perfume; 250g of eau de toilette; medication for personal use up to three months, provided it is accompanied by documentary confirmation; other goods up to a value of €175.
Prohibited items: Narcotics; guns and ammunition (without a police import permit).
Note: (a) It is advisable to declare expensive items such as jewellery and furs. (b) A certificate must be obtained from the Latvian authorities in order to export pieces of art over 50 years old.
Abolition of duty free goods within the EU: On June 30 1999, the sale of duty free alcohol and tobacco at airports and at sea was abolished in all of the original 15 EU member states. Of the 10 new member states that joined the EU on May 1 2004, these rules already apply to Cyprus and Malta. There are transitional rules in place for visitors returning to one of the original 15 EU countries from one of the other new EU countries. But for the original 15, plus Cyprus and Malta, there are now no limits imposed on importing tobacco and alcohol products from one EU country to another (with the exceptions of Denmark, Finland and Sweden, where limits *are* imposed). Travellers should note that they may be required to prove at customs that the goods purchased are for personal use *only*.

Credit: ©Patricia Tourist Office, Riga – www.rigalatvia.net

Public Holidays

Below are listed Public Holidays for the January 2006-June 2007 period.
2006: Jan 1 New Year's Day. **Apr 14** Good Friday. **Apr 17** Easter Monday. **May 1** May Day. **Jun 23** Ligo Day. **Jun 24** St John's Day (Summer Solstice). **Nov 18** National Day (Proclamation of the Republic). **Dec 25-26** Christmas (Winter Solstice). **Dec 31** New Year's Eve.
2007: Jan 1 New Year's Day. **Apr 6** Good Friday. **Apr 9** Easter Monday. **May 1** May Day. **Jun 23** Ligo Day. **Jun 24** St John's Day (Summer Solstice).

Health

	Special Precautions?	Certificate Required?
Yellow Fever	No	No
Cholera	No	No
Typhoid & Polio	No	N/A
Malaria	No	N/A

Note: *Regulations and requirements may be subject to change at short notice, and you are advised to contact your doctor well in advance of your intended date of departure. Any numbers in the chart refer to the footnotes below.*

Food & drink: Water used for drinking, brushing teeth or making ice should have first been boiled or otherwise sterilised.
Other risks: *Tick-borne encephalitis* is present, particularly in forested areas. Campers and trekkers should wear protective clothing; immunisation is strongly advisable as reported cases have increased in recent years. *Diphtheria* and *hepatitis A* have been reported in the area. *Diphyllobothriasis* (fish tapeworm) can be ingested from freshwater fish caught around the Baltic Sea area. *Tuberculosis* has been reported and precautions are necessary. *Trichinellosis* has been reported after the consumption of contaminated pork products at the beginning of 2005. Ensure pork products are well cooked before consumption.
Some types of fish may contain poisonous biotoxins even when cooked. Barracuda should never be eaten. Red Snapper, Grouper, Amberjack and Sea bass may also be affected.
Rabies is present. For those at high risk, vaccination before arrival should be considered. If you are bitten, seek medical advice without delay. For more information, consult the *Health* appendix.
Health care: European Economic Area (EEA) and Switzerland:
If you or any of your dependants are suddenly taken ill or have an accident during a visit to an EEA country or Switzerland, free or reduced-cost necessary treatment is available – in most cases on production of a valid European Health Insurance Card (EHIC). Each country has different rules about state medical provision. In some, treatment is free. In many countries you will have to pay part or all of the cost, and then claim a full or partial refund. The EHIC gives access to state-provided medical treatment only and the scheme gives no entitlement to medical repatriation costs, nor does it cover ongoing illnesses of a non-urgent nature, so comprehensive travel insurance is advised. Note that the EHIC replaces the Form E111, which is no longer valid since 31 December 2005. Some restrictions apply, depending on your nationality.
You will be charged a standard fee for seeing a doctor. Children under 18 and pregnant women getting treatment relating to their pregnancy will not be charged. Any dentist you see must be contracted with a Sickness Insurance Fund or with the Compulsory Health Insurance State Agency. You will have to pay for most dental services. For children up to 18, most treatments are free. The dental surgery at Stabu iela 9 has an emergency service from 2000-0800. Medicines are prescribed by doctors and dispensed by pharmacies. You may have to pay a prescription charge. A full range of medicines is available at pharmacies; however, it is advisable to bring any medicines necessary, as instructions on the packet are in Latvian, and familiar brands may not be available. In an emergency you can go directly to a hospital. Otherwise, for in-patient treatment, you will need a referral from a GP or medical specialist. There is a hospital admission fee and a daily charge for in-patient treatment from the second day of an admission (up to a maximum limit). The reception of the City Clinical Hospital No 1 at Bruninieku iela 8 is open 24 hours. Ambulance travel is free provided it is requested by the public health service in an emergency. More information can be obtained from the Latvian Compulsory Health Insurance State Agency (*VOAVA*) (website: www.voava.gov.lv/eng/).

Travel - International

AIR:
Airlines serving Riga include *Austrian Airlines* (website: www.ava.com), *British Airways* (website: www.british-airways.com), *Czech Airlines* (website: www.csa.cz), *Finnair* (website: www.finnair.com), *LOT Polish Airlines* (website: www.lot.com.pl), *Lufthansa* (website: www.lufthansa.com) and *SAS* (website: www.scandinavian.net).
Approximate flight times: From Riga to *Frankfurt/M* is two hours 10 minutes, to *London* is two hours 30 minutes, and to *New York* is approximately 14 hours (via Helsinki).
Main airports: *Riga (RIX) (Spilve)* is 8km (5 miles) from the city. *To/from the airport*: Bus no. 22 runs every 20 to 30 minutes to the city centre (0530-2240), costing LVL 0.20 (travel time - 30 minutes). Bus no. 22a runs to various hotels in the city. Several hotels provide a shuutle bus to and from the airport. Taxis are also available, costing LVL 0.40 plus LVL 0.35 per kilometre, taxis to the city centre cost around LVL5 (travel time – 15 minutes). *Facilities*: Duty free shop, car hire, restaurant, bar/cafe and post office.
There is an international airport at *Liepaja (LPX)*, with flights to Europe and CIS countries.
Departure tax: None.
SEA:
Main ports: *Liepaja*, *Riga* and *Ventspils*. There are ferry connections from *Riga* to Stockholm with *Monolines* (travel time – 18 hours) and to Köln in Germany. There are direct ferries from Travemunde in Germany and Stockholm in Sweden. There are also connections from *Liepaja* to Rostock in Germany and to Karlshamm in Sweden. Ships run regularly from *Ventspils* to Vöstervik in Sweden. Several shipping lines run cruises on the Baltic Sea calling at Riga.
RAIL:
Latvia has links with Belarus, the Russian Federation, Estonia to the north, and Lithuania to the south. The main route into Western Europe runs from Riga to Berlin via Warsaw and Vilnius.
ROAD:
The road network is relatively well developed and there are good routes through to Belarus and to the neighbouring two Baltic Republics. Entry by car is possible from the Russian Federation, Estonia, Belarus or Lithuania. Border posts between Poland and Lithuania: Ogrodniki–Lazdijai; between Poland and Belarus: Terespol–Brest. Recent changes in Eastern Europe have opened a new highway through the Baltic countries, known as the *Via Baltica*. To drive along the Via Baltica is to discover places that were closed to Western tourists for decades. Services along this highly attractive route are improving all the time. Both the road network and signposting are being modernised; the service station network is represented by both local and foreign companies (many of which are open 24 hours). *Eurolines*, departing

Credit: ©Patricia Tourist Office, Riga – www.rigalatvia.net

from Victoria Coach Station in London, serves destinations in Latvia. For further information, contact *Eurolines* (website: www.eurolines.com *or* www.gobycoach.com).

Travel - Internal

RAIL:

Latvia's reasonably well-developed rail network includes routes from Riga to all other major towns in the country. The railway terminal is at Stacijas laukums. For information about trains, contact LDZ (tel: 723 4940 *or* 4208; website: www.ldz.lv).

ROAD:

There are reasonable connections to all parts of the country from Riga. Traffic drives on the right. **Bus:** Buses are a better form of transport than trains in Latvia. The Central Bus Station is at Pragas iela 1. **Car hire:** Available through hotels and directly from car hire companies, reservations are recommended. Drivers can also be hired. **Traffic regulations:** Seat belts must be worn. Speed limits on highways are 90kph (56mph) and 50kph (32mph) in cities. It is compulsory to drive with headlights on 24 hours a day all year round. The consumption of alcohol by drivers is strictly forbidden as is the use of mobile telephones while driving. **Documentation:** European nationals should be in possession of an EU pink format licence, otherwise an International Driving Permit is required.

URBAN:

Public transport in Riga runs from 0530-0000. Taxis in Riga are cheap, but prices are rising. All taxis are now privately run and all have meters. There is a 50 per cent surcharge at night. All parts of the city can also be reached by bus, tram and trolleybus. Tickets should be bought on board from the conductor and retained for inspection. Share-taxis (*taksobussi*) also operate but are slightly more expensive than ordinary buses. Fines for fare dodging are common.

Travel Advice

Most visits to Latvia are trouble-free but you should be aware of the global risk of indiscriminate international terrorist attacks, which could be against civilian targets, including places frequented by foreigners.

This advice is based on information provided by the Foreign and Commonwealth Office in the UK. It is correct at time of publishing. As the situation can change rapidly, visitors are advised to contact the following organisations for the latest travel advice:

British Foreign and Commonwealth Office
Tel: (0845) 850 2829.
Website: www.fco.gov.uk

US Department of State
Website: http://travel.state.gov/travel

Accommodation

HOTELS:

Owing to the present level of bed capacity, early reservation is absolutely necessary. Since independence, there has been a scramble from Western firms to turn the old state-run hotels into modern Western-standard enterprises. Several of the main hotels in Riga have been renovated in joint ventures with Western firms. A number of newer hotels, including representatives of the major international chain hotels, have recently opened. Many more such joint ventures with firms from all over Western Europe and the USA have ensured that the standard of accommodation in Latvia has reached Western European levels. Outside Riga, which for the time being is the main location of the current expansion in hotel accommodation, Latvia enjoys a good range of modest accommodation, left over from the pre-independence days, including large hotels and smaller pension-type establishments.

RURAL ACCOMMODATION:

Advice on farm holidays, Bed & Breakfast and self-catering cottages may be obtained from the Latvian Country Tourism Association, see *Accommodation Information.*

CAMPING:

Most of Latvia's campsites are located along main highways and the Gulf of Riga, especially the resort of Jurmala. For more details, contact the Latvian Camping Association (see *Accommodation Information*), the Latvian Embassy or the Tourist Office (see *Top Things To Do*).

YOUTH HOSTELS:

There are 10 hostels in the network. Information on youth accommodation is available from Hostelling Latvia (see *Accommodation Information*).

ACCOMMODATION INFORMATION

Hotels in Latvia
A. Ėaka iela 55-218, LV-1011 Riga, Latvia
Tel: 701 4131.
Website: www.hotelsinlatvia.lv

Latvian Country Tourism Association
Kugu iela 11, LV-1048 Riga, Latvia
Tel: 761 7600.
Website: www.celotajs.lv

Latvian Camping Association
Alksnu iela 30, Jurmala, Latvia
Tel: 773 2350.
Website: www.camping.lv

Hostelling Latvia
Tel: 921 8560.
Website: www.hostellinglatvia.com

Top Things To See & Do

- Visit the capital, **Riga**, and be dazzled by its rich history and culture, reflected in its remarkable range of architectural styles, with Gothic, Baroque, Classical and Art Nouveau buildings. The centre of the city is considered to contain the finest concentration of Art Nouveau buildings in Europe and has been declared a UNESCO World Heritage Site. **Old Riga** contains a remarkable diversity of architectural styles, perhaps best epitomised by the **Dome Cathedral**. The cathedral's **organ**, with nearly 7000 pipes, is recognised as one of the world's greatest musical instruments and concerts are regularly performed here. The numerous other historical buildings in Riga bear witness to Latvia's chequered history. Since its restoration after World War I, the old quarter of the city has been a protected area. The one surviving town gate is the so-called **Sweden Gate**, whilst the symbol of Riga, the 137m- (450ft-) high tower of **St Peter's Church**, rises above the city. The **St John's Church** of the former Dominican monastery was built in the 14th century and is one of several interesting churches in this former Episcopal seat. The Catholic **St Jacob's Church** was built in 1226 and is a fine example of Gothic architecture. The delightful **Viestura Garden** is ideal for relaxation. Its foundations were laid by Peter the Great who planted the first tree, an event commemorated by a flagstone in the park. **Alexander Gate**, the entrance to the park, was erected to mark the Russian victory over Napoleon's army. At the end of the 18th century, Katharina II built the **Peter and Paul Church** north of the castle. Merchants' houses from the Middle Ages such as the **Three Brothers** and the 24 **warehouses** in the old quarter are also picturesque examples of Latvian architecture. The residence of Peter I near the Cathedral has been dramatically altered and rebuilt. In central Riga, the **Freedom Monument** (*Brivibas Piemineklis*) is a very significant site for Latvians. Built in 1935, the monument is a striking obelisk crowned by a female figure with upstretched arms holding three stars which represent the three historic regions of Latvia: Kurzeme, Latgale and Vidzeme. Reminiscent of the famous Statue of Liberty in New York, though much smaller at 42m (138ft), the statue ranks among the most distinguished monuments in Europe. Another place of interest is the **Warriors' Cemetery** which was designed by the sculptor Zale, the architect Birznieks and the landscape gardener Zeidaks. Approximately 2000 graves from World War I are divided into three sections.
- Luxuriate in the health resort that is **Sigulda**, about 53km (33 miles) from Riga. Situated on the picturesque banks of the **River Gauja**, the town has been established since the 13th century and attractions here include the ruins of the castle and local caves. In the **National Park** that is situated here, **Turaida Castle** (13th century) and its museum can be visited, as well as a sculpture park where Latvian folk poetry has been captured in stone. There is good downhill **skiing** in winter, and Sigulda is a popular **boating** spot in summer.
- Nature enthusiasts will enjoy the rich **flora and fauna** in the regions of **Kurzeme**, **Latgale** and **Vidzeme**, which are also favourites with **hikers**. Throughout the country, the landscape is dotted with picturesque villages such as **Bauska**, **Cesis**, **Kolka** and **Talsi**, where life generally follows a very relaxed pace amidst beautiful countryside. In summer, **hikers** can take to the trails in the national parks and protected areas. **Gauja National Park**, located 32km (20 miles) north of Riga between Sigulda and Valmiera, is the country's biggest. Covering an area of nearly 94km (58 miles) around the River Gauja, it features caves, rocks and dense woods. Wildlife includes elk, deer, brown bears and wolves. There are special nature trails to introduce walkers to the plants and animals. **Kemeri National Park** is also rich in flora and fauna. Other hiking trails include the **Amber Trail** along the western coast of **Courland**.
- **Picnic** besides Latvia's highest **waterfall** at **Kuldiga**, situated on the banks of the **River Venta**.
- Go **birdwatching** since Latvia's wetlands and traditionally cultivated farmland attract significant populations of interesting and rare birds. The country's many meadows and pastures are a prime habitat for the corncrake, now rare in other parts of Europe. White storks are common in agricultural areas near wetlands. Northern European birds such as red-throated and black-throated divers and Slavonian grebes breed in the open water. Reed marshes harbour bitterns and marsh harriers, while ospreys and the large white-tailed eagle can be seen by lakes and rivers. The forests contain a variety of birds including hazelhens, black storks, pygmy owls and three-toed woodpeckers. Local operators can arrange birdwatching trips. For more information, contact the Latvian Ornithological Society, AK 1010, Riga 1050 (tel: 722 1580; website: www.lob.lv).
- Holiday in the **Jurmala** region, which abounds with fresh pine forest-scented air, sun and endless sandy beaches, with an appeal for all age groups. Drivers entering Jurmala need to purchase a special ticket; the fee is used to sponsor ecological programmes in the area. The area is connected by roads and the commuter railway, which takes about 15 minutes from Riga.

TOURIST INFORMATION

Latvia Tourism Development Agency
Pils Lauqums 4, LV-1050 Riga, Latvia
Tel: 722 9945.
Website: www.latviatourism.lv

Entertainment

FOOD & DRINK: Hors d'oeuvres are very good and often the best part of the meal. Overall, cuisine can be heavy but almost always tasty and nourishing.

National specialities:

- *Kotletes* (meat patties).
- *Skabu kapostu zupa* (cabbage soup).
- *Alexander Torte* (raspberry- or cranberry-filled pastry strips).
- Sweetbread soup with dried fruit.
- *Piragi* (pastry filled with bacon and onions).
- Sorrel soup with boiled pork, onions, potatoes and barley.
- There is a large selection of excellent dairy products on offer, such as *skabs krejums* (sour cream).

National drinks:

- Riga's *Black Balsam* is a thick, black alcoholic liquid which has been produced since 1700. The exact recipe is a closely guarded secret, but some of the ingredients include ginger, oak bark, bitter orange peel and cognac. It is drunk either with coffee or mixed with vodka.

- There are several good local beers, including the dark beer *Bauskas Tumsais* and the pale *Gaisais*.
- *Kvass* is a refreshing summer drink.
- Sparkling wine is popular.

Tipping: Taxi fares and restaurant bills usually include a tip. It is customary to give a little extra for good service.

NIGHTLIFE: Riga has a good range of excellent restaurants, bars and cafes.

SHOPPING: Amber is of high quality and a good buy. Other purchases include folk art, wicker work and earthenware. **Shopping hours:** Mon-Fri 0900/1000-1800/1900, Sat 0900/1000-1600/1700. Some smaller shops may be closed for an hour or two between 1200 and 1500 for lunch. Food shops open 0800/0900-2000/2100. Some shops are open 24 hours.

Business

- **GDP:** US$14 billion (2004).
- **Main exports:** Timber and wood products, fish and fish products.
- **Main imports:** Machinery and equipment, chemicals, fuels and vehicles.
- **Main trade partners:** EU (mainly Germany, Sweden, Lithuania and the UK) and Russia.

ECONOMY: With few raw materials, the Latvian economy is principally dependent on producing manufactured goods from imported materials. Key industries include vehicle and railway rolling stock manufacture, electronics, and the production of fertilisers, chemicals, timber and wood products, light machinery and food processing, which draws on Latvia's own dairy and fisheries products as well as imported raw materials from the Russian Federation. The infrastructure is, in common with the other Baltic States, comparatively well developed. Latvia relies on power supplies from its Baltic neighbours and on imported fuel from the Russian Federation to meet its energy needs; energy imports account for one-third of Latvia's total import bill. Through the Ventspils Nafta terminal on the Baltic coast, Latvia is one of the major outlets for Russian oil exports. In the service sector, Riga is now an important regional financial centre. Latvia has pursued economic reform in a gradual manner. The Government's reform programme during the 1990s was limited by political opposition which prevented, for example, the sale of major state enterprises. The economy performed steadily during most of the 1990s, although the effects of the immediate post-Soviet period and the 1998 Russian economic crisis meant there was an overall contraction between 1990 and 2000 of about 20 per cent. Since 2000, annual growth has accelerated to its current level of about 8.5 per cent, possibly conferring on Latvia the status of a 'Baltic tiger'. The country introduced its own currency, the Lat, in 1993: this is now the sole legal tender. The following year, a free trade zone was established with Estonia and Lithuania. In June 1995, Latvia signed an Association Agreement with the European Union, as the first stage on the path towards joining the EU - a major objective of successive Governments since independence. Negotiations proceeded more rapidly and successfully than had been expected, and Latvia was able to join the EU, along with nine other countries (including both of Latvia's Baltic neighbours), on 1 May 2004. Latvia had previously been admitted to the European Bank for Reconstruction and Development in 1991, then in 1996 to the World Bank and IMF (which in 2001 provided a loan of US$40 million to finance structural reforms). The EU - especially Germany, Sweden and Finland - now accounts for half of total Latvian trade; the Russian Federation and the other Baltic states are the other main trade partners.

BUSINESS ETIQUETTE: Business cards are exchanged. Appointments should be arranged in advance. In general, business is conducted in a fairly formal manner. **Office hours:** Mon-Fri 0830-1730.

COMMERCIAL INFORMATION

Latvian Chamber of Commerce and Industry
Valdemara Street 35, Riga LV-1010, Latvia
Tel: 722 5595.
Website: www.chamber.lv

Latvian Development Agency
Perses iela 2, Riga LV-1042, Latvia
Tel: 703 9400.
Website: www.lda.gov.lv

The Association of Latvian Travel Agents (Information on Conferences/Conventions)
PO Box 59, Riga LV-1010, Latvia
Tel: 721 0065.
Website: www.alta.net.lv

Lebanon

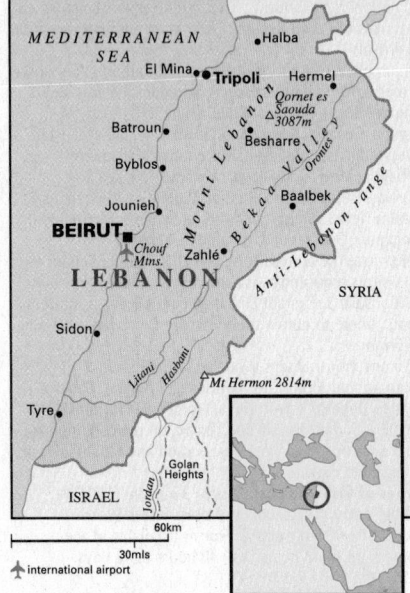

Location: Middle East.

Time: GMT + 2 (GMT + 3 from last Sunday in March to last Saturday in October).

Overview

Lebanon, over the course of history, provided an inaccessible haven for tribes and religious groups escaping from repression and persecution in other parts of the Middle East: the Maronites, Christians; the Greek Orthodox Christians; the Shia Muslims; and the Druze, a heretical Muslim sect founded in the 10th century.

Since its independence from France in 1943, these disparate communities cohabited in relative peace with political power divided between Christians, Shia and Sunni Muslims. On this basis, Lebanon developed a thriving economy based on providing business services for other countries in the region. This situation prevailed until the 1970s when the Palestine Liberation Organisation (PLO), which had been expelled from Jordan in 1971, established itself in Lebanon with the tacit agreement of the Lebanese. The influx of a large new community with a powerful armed wing upset the relatively fragile political balance in Lebanon. The PLO's presence ultimately led to the Israeli invasion of Lebanon in 1978 and 1982.

By then Lebanon had been engulfed in a six-year civil war between right-wing Christian militias (the Falange and the southern militia led by Saad Haddad, and later the forces led by General Michel Aoun) and various alignments of Muslim and Palestinian forces. Among the latter, the most important were the Amal movement and the more radical, Iranian-inspired Hezbollah organisation. Syrian troops also moved in shortly after the war started.

The Israelis withdrew in early 1985 to a self-declared 'security zone' in the south from which they withdrew in 2000. Despite still having a strong influence in Lebanon, Syria withdrew its troops out of the country in 2005, ending a 29-year military presence.

Lebanon's diverse patchwork of Mediterranean-lapped coast, rugged alpine peaks and green, fertile valleys is packed into a parcel of land some 225km long and 46km wide.. Once known as the 'Paris of the East', Beirut commands a magnificent position, thrust into the Mediterranean. Behind the city are towering mountains, visible when the traffic haze settles down. The Corniche

seafront boasts beaches, restaurants, theatres and a dazzling variety of shops and restaurants. Beirut suffered greatly from Lebanon's 16-year civil war, but following an impressive and ongoing process of reconstruction, the city is once again one of the most popular tourist and business destinations in the Middle East. Beirut's Central District, known as Solidere (the company in charge of the reconstruction programme), is seeing a spectacular number of modern buildings and office blocks springing up everywhere. After massive landfill, two new marinas, a new seaside promenade and a green park are also planned. The cities and ruins of Aanjar, Baalbeck, Byblos, Tyre and the Qadisha Valley/Cedars Forest are listed as UNESCO World Heritage sites and are also worth visiting.

General Information

AREA: 10,452 sq km (4036 sq miles).
POPULATION: 3.8 million (UN, 2005).
POPULATION DENSITY: 363.6 per sq km.
CAPITAL: Beirut. **Population:** 1.17 million (2003).
GEOGRAPHY: Lebanon lies to the east of the Mediterranean, sharing borders to the north and east with the Syrian Arab Republic, and to the south with Israel/Palestinian Territory. It is a mountainous country and between the two mountain ranges of Jebel Lubnan (Mount Lebanon), Mount Hermon and the Anti-Lebanon range lies the fertile Bekaa Valley. Approximately half of the country lies at an altitude of over 900m (3000ft). Into this small country is packed such a variety of scenery that there are few places to equal it in beauty and choice. The famous cedar trees grow high in the mountains, while the lower slopes bear grapes, apricots, plums, peaches, figs, olives and barley, often on terraces painstakingly cut out from the mountainsides. On the coastal plain, citrus fruit, bananas and vegetables are cultivated, with radishes and beans grown in tiny patches.

GOVERNMENT: Republic. **Head of State:** President Emil Jamil Lahoud since 1998. **Head of Government:** Prime Minister Fouad Siniora since 2005. **Recent history:** General Emile Lahoud was unanimously elected President by the Lebanese Parliament in October 1998. Rafic Hariri became Prime Minister (for the second time) in August 2000. Under Syrian pressure, Emile Lahoud's term as President, originally set to end in late 2004, was extended for a further three years when Parliament approved a controversial constitutional amendment allowing him to remain in office. Hariri resigned in October 2004 and was replaced by former Prime Minister Omar Karameh. Prior to the extension of President Lahoud's mandate, the UN Security Council adopted resolution 1559 (UNSCR 1559) on 2 September 2004. This resolution called for respect for the sovereignty, territorial integrity, unity and political independence of Lebanon under the sole and exclusive authority of the Government of Lebanon throughout Lebanon; all remaining foreign forces to withdraw from Lebanon; and the disbanding of all Lebanese and non-Lebanese militia. A UN verification team reported on 23 May 2005 that all Syrian troops had withdrawn from Lebanon but it was uncertain whether all intelligence personnel had. Former Prime Minister Rafic Hariri was assassinated in a bomb attack on 14 February 2005. In Lebanon, it is widely believed that Syria was involved in this attack. Since the assassination, an anti-Syrian majority has formed in Parliament and the Lebanese opposition parties have worked closely together to demand a full investigation into the attack and the full implementation of the Taif Accord. On 28 February 2005, in the face of public protests, including a general strike, the Lebanese Government resigned. Elections in May and June 2005 saw an anti-Syrian alliance led by Saad al-Hariri, son of the assassinated ex-PM Rafik Hariri, win control of Parliament. For the first time in a decade and a half, the Assembly was dominated by members opposed to Syrian influence. All but two members of the new Parliament nominated former Finance Minister and Hariri ally Fouad Siniora as Premier during the May and June 2005 elections. Mr Siniora promised to carry out a reform and development programme initiated by Rafik Hariri. Members of his Cabinet were drawn mainly from groups which opposed Syrian involvement in Lebanon and included - for the first time - a Minister from the Hezbollah movement.

LANGUAGE: The official language is Arabic, followed by French as the second language; English is widely spoken. Armenian is spoken by a small percentage of the population.

RELIGION: Islam and Christianity are the main religions. Islam (predominantly Shi'ite) accounts for approximately 40 per cent of the population's beliefs. Christian denominations, mainly Greek Orthodox, Maronite, Armenian and Protestant, account for another 40 per cent. Other religions account for the remaining 20 per cent (including a very small Jewish community).

ELECTRICITY: 230 volts AC, 50Hz.

SOCIAL CONVENTIONS: Lebanese people are known for their hospitality. Handshaking is the normal form of greeting. It is acceptable to give a small gift, particularly if invited home for a meal. As far as dress is concerned, casual dress is suitable for daytime wear, except in main towns where dress tends to be rather formal. Smarter hotels and restaurants often require guests to dress for dinner. Since Lebanon is almost evenly divided between those adhering to the Muslim faith, and those adhering to the Christian faith, visitors should dress according to the custom of the majority in the individual places being visited. Smoking is common and acceptable unless specified otherwise.

Climate

There are four seasons. Summer (June to September) is hot on the coast and cooler in the mountains. Spring and autumn are warm and pleasant. Winter (December to mid-March) is mostly rainy, with snow in the mountains.

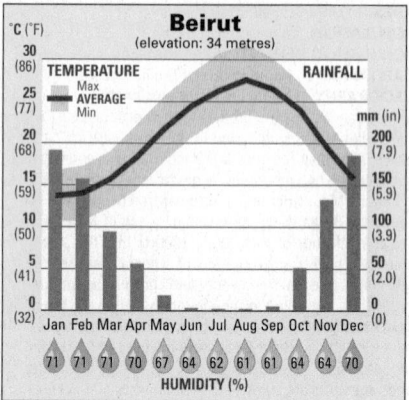

Communications

Telephone: IDD is available. Country code: 961. Telephone booths are accessible for local and international calls. Payphone cards are available from post offices and kiosks.
Mobile telephone: Roaming agreements exist with most international mobile phone companies. Cellular phones are widely used and are available for hire to visitors.
Internet: There are Internet cafes in Beirut, Tripoli and most major towns.
Post: Post to Europe and the USA usually takes from one to two weeks.
MEDIA: Lebanon's broadcasting scene is well-developed and diverse, reflecting the country's pluralism and divisions. Lebanon was the first Arab country to permit private radio and television stations. But the Government has a say over who may operate stations and whether or not they can broadcast news. Several stations are owned by leading politicians.
Press: There are more than 30 daily newspapers published in Arabic, Armenian and French and over 100 publications appear on a weekly or monthly basis. *The Daily Star* is published in English and there are several English-language weeklies, primarily *Monday Morning*. The best-selling Arabic dailies are *Al Anwar, Al Dyar, Al-Mustaqbal, An Nahar* and *Al Safir*. The most important daily in French is *L'Orient-Le Jour*.
TV: *Tele-Liban* is state-run; *Lebanese Broadcasting Corporation (LBC)* is the commercial, market leader and pan-regional broadcaster; *Al-Manar TV* is a pro-Hezbollah channel; *Future TV* is a commercial channel.
Radio: *Radio Liban* is state-run. *Voice of Lebanon, Radio Delta* and *Radio One* are commercial stations.

Passport/Visa

	Passport Required?	Visa Required?	Return Ticket? Required?
Full British	Yes	Yes/1	Yes
Australian	Yes	Yes/1	Yes
Canadian	Yes	Yes/1	Yes
USA	Yes	Yes/1	Yes
Other EU	Yes	Yes/1	Yes
Japanese	Yes	Yes/1	Yes

Note: *Regulations and requirements may be subject to change at short notice, and you are advised to contact the appropriate diplomatic or consular authority before finalising travel arrangements. Any numbers in the chart refer to the footnotes below.*

Restricted entry: The Government of Lebanon refuses entry to holders of Israeli and Palestinian passports, holders of passports containing a visa for Israel, valid or expired, used or unused and passports with entry stamps to Israel.

PASSPORTS: Passport valid for six months required by all except nationals of the Syrian Arab Republic arriving from their country with a valid national ID.
VISAS: Required by all except the following:
(a) nationals of the Syrian Arab Republic for unlimited stays, provided arriving directly from the Syrian Arab Republic (check with Embassy for current regulations);
(b) nationals of Bahrain, Jordan (who hold a passport with a national serial number), Kuwait, Oman, Qatar, Saudi Arabia and the United Arab Emirates for stays of up to three months;
(c) transit passengers continuing their journey by the same or first connecting aircraft, provided holding onward or return documentation and not spending the night at, or leaving, the airport.
Note: 1. The following can obtain their visas on arrival at Beirut International Airport or any other port of entry at the Lebanese border, providing passport holders do not possess an Israeli stamp, and they hold return or onward tickets:
(a) nationals of countries listed in the chart above, except nationals of Czech Republic, who must obtain a visa prior to arrival;
(b) nationals of Andorra, Antigua and Barbuda, Argentina, Armenia, Azerbaijan, Bahamas, Barbados, Belarus, Belize, Bhutan, Brazil, Bulgaria, Chile, China (PR), Costa Rica, Croatia, Georgia, Hong Kong (SAR), Iceland, Kazakhstan, Kyrgyzstan, Liechtenstein, Macedonia, Macau (SAR), Malaysia, Mexico, Moldova, Monaco, New Zealand, Norway, Panama, Peru, Russian Federation, Singapore, St Kitts & Nevis, Samoa, San Marino, Serbia & Montenegro, Singapore, Switzerland, Ukraine, Uzbekistan and Venezuela. The above list is subject to frequent changes. All visitors requiring a visa should contact the Consulate (or Consular section at Embassy) before leaving for details about where to obtain their visa; see *Passport/Visa Information*.
(c) a one month visa is available at the Beirut International Airport, for nationals of Algeria, Comoro Islands, Djibouti, Egypt, Libya, Morocco, Mauritania, Somalia, Sudan, Tunisia and Yemen, on the condition they hold a return ticket, hotel reservation and $2000 in cash or legalised cheque.
Types of visa and cost: *Visitor 3 month*: L£50,000 (single-entry); L£100,000 (multiple-entry). *Visitor 1 month*: free (single entry). *Transit* (available at the border): up to 48 hours free; 48 hours to 15 days: L£25,000.
Validity: Visitor visas are generally issued for stays of up to three months.
Application to: Consulate (or consular section at Embassy); see *Passport/Visa Information*.
Application requirements: (a) Valid passport. (b) Two completed application forms. (c) Two passport-size photos. (d) Fee payable by cash or postal order only. (e) For *Visitor* visas, a letter of invitation from Lebanese host or confirmation of accommodation booking from travel agent. (f) For *Business* visas, a letter of invitation from the Lebanese host company and/or the applicant's company in country of origin. (g) Stamped, self-addressed, registered envelope for postal applications.
Note: Children under 18 years old require written consent from their parents/guardian before their visa can be processed.
Working days required: Depends on nationality of applicant; please contact the Embassy (see *Passport/Visa Information*) for the specific number of days required for processing applications.
Temporary residence: Formalities for temporary residence will be arranged in Lebanon. For details of student and employment visas, enquire at Consulate (or consular section at Embassy); see *Passport/Visa Information*.

PASSPORT/VISA INFORMATION

Embassy of the Republic of Lebanon in the UK
21 Palace Gardens Mews, London W8 4QM, UK
Tel: (020) 7727 6696 *or* 7229 7265 (consular section).
E-mail: emb_leb@btinternet.com
Opening hours: Mon-Fri 0930-1230 (visa applications); 1400-1500 (visa collection). Closed Tuesday and Wednesday.

Embassy of the Republic of Lebanon in the USA
2560 28th Street, NW, Washington, DC 20008, USA
Tel: (202) 939 6300.
Website: www.lebanonembassyus.org

Consulate General of the Republic of Lebanon in the USA
9 East 76th Street, New York, NY 10021, USA
Tel: (212) 744 7905.
Website: www.lebconsny.org

Money

Currency: Lebanese Pound (LBP; symbol L£) = 100 piastres. Notes are in denominations of L£100,000, 50,000, 20,000, 10,000, 5000, 1000, 500, 250 and 100. Coins are in denominations of L£500, 250, 100 and 50.
Currency exchange: There are a large number of banks in Beirut where international currencies can be exchanged. Numerous licensed exchange shops also operate and some hotels offer exchange services. US Dollars are best and do not need to be exchanged as they are accepted even in small shops.
Credit & debit cards: All major credit cards are widely accepted. Check with your credit or debit card company for details of merchant acceptability and other services which may be available. ATMs are widely available in Beirut and larger cities.
Traveller's cheques: Limited acceptance, as major banks only accept certain types of traveller's cheques. Traveller's cheques also require up to two weeks to clear and are therefore generally not recommended.
Currency restrictions: There are no restrictions on the import or export of local or foreign currency.
Banking hours: Mon-Fri 0800-1230, Sat 0800-1200. Some banks stay open until 1700.
Exchange rate indicators:
Rate at time of publishing
£1.00= 2601.78
$1.00= 1510.22

Duty Free

The following goods may be imported into Lebanon by residents and non-residents over 18 years of age without incurring customs duty:
800 cigarettes or 50 cigars or 100 cigarillos or 1000g of tobacco; 2l of champagne, whisky or cognac or a maximum of 4l of other alcoholic beverages; 1l of eau de cologne and 100g of perfume; personal belongings not exceeding L£2,000,000; prescribed dosages for medicine.
Note: Those aged under 18 years are permitted half the specified quantities for duty free except tobacco and alcoholic beverages, which are forbidden.
Restricted items: Arms, ammunition, narcotics, immoral publications and recordings.
Prohibited: Antiques without an export licence.

Public Holidays

Below are listed Public Holidays for the January 2006-June 2007 period.
2006: Jan 1 New Year's Day. **Jan 6** Orthodox Armenian Christmas. **Jan 10** Eid al-Adha (Feast of the Sacrifice). **Jan 31** Islamic New Year. **Feb 9** Feast of St Maroun/Ashoura. **Apr 11** Mawlid (Prophet's Birthday). **Apr 6** Good Friday. **Apr 9** Easter. **Apr 21** Orthodox Good Friday. **Apr 23** Orthodox Easter. **May 1** Labour Day. **May 6** Martyrs' Day. **May 25** Liberation of the South. **Aug 15** Assumption. **Nov 1** All Saints' Day. **Oct 22-24** Eid al-Fitr (End of Ramadan). **Nov 22** Independence Day. **Dec 25** Christmas Day. **Dec 31** Eid al-Adha (Feast of the Sacrifice).
2007: Jan 1 New Year's Day. **Jan 6** Orthodox Armenian Christmas. **Jan 20** Islamic New Year. **Jan 29** Ashoura. **Feb 9** Feast of St Maroun. **Mar 31** Mawlid al-Nabi (Prophet's Birthday). **Apr 6** Good Friday, Orthodox Good Friday. **Apr 9** Easter Sunday, Orthodox Easter. **May 1** Labour Day. **May 6** Martyrs' Day. **May 25** Liberation of the South.
Note: Muslim feasts are timed according to local sightings of various phases of the moon and the dates given above are approximations. During the lunar month of Ramadan that precedes Eid al-Fitr, Muslims fast during the day and feast at night and normal business patterns may be interrupted. Many restaurants are closed during the day and there may be restrictions on smoking and drinking. Some disruption may continue into Eid al-Fitr itself. Eid al-Fitr and Eid al-Adha may last anything from two to 10 days, depending on the region. For more information, see the *World of Islam* appendix.

Health

	Special Precautions?	Certificate Required?
Yellow Fever	No	1
Cholera	No	No
Typhoid & Polio	2	N/A
Malaria	No	N/A

Note: *Regulations and requirements may be subject to change at short notice, and you are advised to contact your doctor well in advance of your intended date of departure. Any numbers in the chart refer to the footnotes below.*

1: *A yellow fever vaccination certificate is required from travellers from infected areas.*
2: *Typhoid occurs in rural areas.*

Food & drink: Mains water is normally chlorinated and, whilst relatively safe, may cause mild abdominal upsets. Bottled water is recommended. Drinking water outside main towns and cities is likely to be contaminated and sterilisation is considered essential. Milk is pasteurised and dairy products are safe for consumption. Local meat, poultry, seafood, fruit and vegetables are generally considered safe to eat.

Other risks: *Hepatitis A* and *B* are present but rare. Rabies is present. For those at high risk, vaccination before arrival should be considered. If you are bitten, seek medical advice without delay. For more information, consult the *Health* appendix.

Health care: Health insurance is essential. Lebanese hospitals are very modern and well equipped and many doctors are highly qualified, reputed to be among the best in the world. All doctors speak either English or French. The majority of hospitals in the region are private and require proof of the patient's ability to pay the bill before providing treatment (even in emergency cases). Visitors who are not insured and require hospitalisation should contact their Embassy for advice. Standards at Lebanon's public hospitals are much lower. The two best hospitals in the country are the Hôtel Dieu in Achrafieh, Beirut, and the American University/AUB Hospital in Hamra, Beirut.

Credit: ©Ministry of Tourism, Lebanon

Travel - International

AIR:

The national airline is *Middle East Airlines (MEA)* (website: www.mea.com.lb).

Main airports: *Beirut International (BEY)* (Khaldeh) is 8km (5 miles) south of the city (travel time – 20 minutes). *To/from the airport*: A bus service operates to the city centre (0600-2000), leaving every 30 minutes. Taxis are also available (*Allô Taxi, New Taxi* or *Premier Taxi*). *Facilities*: Tourist information desk, duty free shops, post office, restaurants, bars, hotel reservations, bank/bureau de change, car hire and a VIP lounge.

Departure tax: L£100,000 for first class; L£75,000 for business class; and L£50,000 for economy class.

SEA:

Main ports: *Beirut, Jounieh, Tripoli, Sidon* and *Tyre*. Several steamship lines connect Beirut, Jounieh and Tripoli with the rest of the world. Cruise lines operating to Lebanon include *Fred Olsen* (website: www.fredolsencruises.com) and *Louis Cruise Lines* (website: www.louiscruises.com). The sea connection between the Cypriot port of Larnaca and Jounieh in Lebanon may be closed and travellers considering that route are advised to check with the Ministry of Tourism or the Embassy.

RAIL:

There are no passenger services operating at present.

ROAD:
Best international routes are via Turkey and Aleppo–Homs and Lattakia in the Syrian Arab Republic along the north–south coastal road, and also the Beirut–Damascus trunk road. Bus services are available from Europe. For details, contact the Ministry of Tourism or the Embassy (see *Top Things To Do*).

Travel - Internal

AIR:

There are no internal flights.

SEA:

Ports are served by coastal passenger ferries. For details, contact the Embassy (see *Passport/Visa Information*).

ROAD:
Traffic drives on the right. Speed limit signs, traffic police and traffic lights are present but may not always be respected and driving, particularly in Beirut, can be quite unpredictable. As public transport is limited, roads in Beirut are over-congested. The worst times for traffic jams are 0730-0930 and 1630-1900. **Bus:** Intercity buses run by private companies are cheap and efficient. Many hotels also offer complimentary bus and other transport services. **Taxi:** Intercity taxis operate throughout Beirut and Lebanon. Travel is normally shared. Prices are negotiated in advance. Town taxis have red licence plates and an official tariff. There is a surcharge of 50 per cent after 2200. **Car hire:** Self-drive cars are available, but chauffeur-driven vehicles are recommended: check with the Ministry of Tourism. It should be noted that the price of petrol is very expensive in Lebanon. **Documentation:** An International Driving Permit and Green Card are required.

URBAN:

Public bus services are available in Beirut, where bus services have recently been expanded, although service taxis remain the most widely used option.

Travel Advice

Caution is advised when travelling in the northern Beka'a Valley, the mountainous areas bordering Syria and areas of southern Lebanon close to the border with Israel south of a line between Tyre and Marjayoun.

There is a high threat of terrorism in Lebanon. There was a spate of bomb explosions in and around Beirut in 2005. Travellers are advised to maintain a high level of vigilance in public places, including tourist sites, and should avoid military sites and Palestinian refugee camps.

Travellers are also advised to avoid any political gatherings and/or demonstrations.

Unexploded mines and ordnance pose a danger to travellers throughout the country especially in the part of South Lebanon occupied by Israel until May 2000. Travellers should seek local advice before venturing off well-worn tracks.

This advice is based on information provided by the Foreign and Commonwealth Office in the UK. It is correct at time of publishing. As the situation can change rapidly, visitors are advised to contact the following organisations for the latest travel advice:

British Foreign and Commonwealth Office
Tel: (0845) 850 2829.
Website: www.fco.gov.uk

US Department of State
Website: http://travel.state.gov/travel

Accommodation

HOTELS:

Following the large-scale destruction during the civil war, Beirut's hotels have now all been rebuilt, and a number of new ones added. Lebanon today offers accommodation to suit all budgets and the Ministry of Tourism publishes an annual hotel guide which lists most of the hotels in the country. Outside Beirut, however, hotels are few and far between, particularly in the South. Visitors are advised to check reservations through a Lebanese representative at home before departing. Winter and summer rates are the same. Accommodation rates are normally subject to a 15 per cent service charge. **Grading:** Hotels are classified from **1** to **4** stars (**A** and **B** within each class) and **luxury**. Prices are usually quoted in US Dollars and only hotels with rooms costing more than US$50 tend to accept credit cards.

GUEST HOUSES:

Local hostels are available in coastal and mountain villages at reasonable prices.

SELF-CATERING:

Furnished and other apartments are available for rent.

CAMPING/YOUTH HOSTELS:
There are a number of campsites throughout Lebanon, notably in Amchite, near Byblos, and particularly in mountainous regions, such as Barouk and Chouk. For further information on campsites, cheap rooms, youth hostels and work camps, contact the Ministry of Tourism (see *Top Things To Do*).

ACCOMMODATION INFORMATION

Lebanese Hotels Owners Association
Sodeco Street, PO Box 166011, Beirut, Lebanon
Tel: (1) 202 059 *or* 329 095/6.
E-mail: synhotlb@cyberia.net.lb

Ministry of Tourism
Street address: 550 rue de la Banque Centrale, Hamra, Beirut, Lebanon
Postal address: PO Box 11-5344, Beirut, Lebanon
Tel: (1) 340 940-4.
Website: www.destinationlebanon.com

Top Things To See

• Head for **Hamra** in West **Beirut**, where the **American University** is located along with the majority of hotels. The other centre is **Achrafieh** in East Beirut, home to the **Université St Joseph** and an increasing number of smart shops and expensive restaurants. In Beirut's Central District, known as **Solidere** (the company in charge of the reconstruction programme), be amazed at the spectacular number of modern buildings and office blocks springing up everywhere. While many of the new buildings look very modern, Beirut's old *souks* (covered markets) are being reconstructed in an authentic way. The **Turkish bath** at **Al-Nouzha** provides another glimpse of the old Beirut. The **Beirut National Museum**, has been rehabilitated and is constantly updating its interesting collection. On the western tip of Beirut, **Raouche** is an increasingly popular district with a lively seaside promenade. Its famous landmark, the **Pigeon Rocks**, are huge formations standing like sentinels off the coast.

• The country's second city, **Tripoli** is Lebanon's most Arabian city and retains much of its provincial charm. Tripoli's old medieval centre at the foot of the **Crusader castle** has a number of interesting mosques, including the **Al-Muallaq Burtasiyat Madrassa**, **Al-Qartâwiyat Madrassa**, **Great Mosque** and **Taynâl**.

• Just off Tripoli, see green turtles and rare birds on the **Island of Palm Trees**, listed by UNESCO as a nature reserve.

• Discover **Tyre's** archaeological sites: area one is located on what was the Phoenician Island and contains ruins of the large district of civic buildings, public baths and mosaic streets; area two contains an extensive network of Romano-Byzantine roads and other installations; area three is most notable for containing one of the largest Roman hippodromes ever found.

• **Byblos** is reputed to be the oldest town in the world, with excavations unearthing artefacts dating back to Neolithic times as well as from Canaanite, Phoenician, Hellenistic, Roman and Crusader periods. Fishing boats and pleasure craft ply the old harbour.

• In the small port city of **Sidon**, discover the sea castle built of stone from Roman remains.

• **Beiteddine**, in the **Chouf Mountains**, is the site of the **palace** built by the Amir Basheer in the 19th century. Visit the courtyard and state rooms.

• Near the Syrian border, in **Baalbek**, see one of the best-preserved temple areas of the Roman world still in existence. It is, in fact, a complex of several temples behind which soar the columns of the **Temple of Jupiter**.

• In **Besharre**, to the northwest, best known as the birthplace of the famous Lebanese poet Khalil Gibran, author of *The Prophet*, visit the **Gibran museum**. The town is also a gateway to the mountainous region, famous for its many cedar trees.

Top Things To Do

- Around 20km (13 miles) north of Beirut, visit the spectacular **Jeita caverns**. The caverns are on two levels, and the lower gallery includes an underground waterway which can be visited by boat (but may be closed during winter).
- In **Tripoli**, shop at the old *souks* (covered markets). Tripoli is famous for its sweets and traditional olive oil-based soap. In the port area, known as **Al Mina**, enjoy delicious Lebanese food at the city's numerous seafood restaurants and fish markets.
- Go **scuba diving** and **snorkelling**. The waters near the ancient city of **Tyre** offer some interesting underwater archaelogical ruins, which divers may explore. **Swimming** is generally popular and many beaches offer full facilities, with guest memberships and freshwater pools provided to supplement the sea. Other watersports that can be practised in Lebanon incude **water-skiing** and **sailing**.
- Despite its Mediterranean setting, **skiing** is possible in Lebanon and is actually quite popular. Mountain resorts such as **Bakish**, **The Cedars**, **Faqra**, **Faraya**, **Laklouk** and **Zarour** offer excellent accommodation and facilities. These mountains and gorges also present excellent terrain for **hiking**.

TOURIST INFORMATION

Ministry of Tourism
Street address: 550 rue de la Banque Centrale, Hamra, Beirut, Lebanon
Postal address: PO Box 11-5344, Beirut, Lebanon
Tel: (1) 340 940-4.
Website: www.destinationlebanon.com

Embassy of the Republic of Lebanon in the UK
21 Palace Gardens Mews, London W8 4QM, UK
Tel: (020) 7727 6696 *or* 7229 7265 (consular section).
E-mail: emb_leb@btinternet.com
Opening hours: Mon-Fri 0930-1230 (visa applications); 1400-1500 (visa collection). Closed Tuesday and Wednesday.
Also deals with tourism enquiries.

Entertainment

FOOD & DRINK: Lebanese cuisine is widely acknowledged to be the finest in the Middle East. The country's gastronomic tradition is characterised by the use of an extremely wide variety of locally-produced, and therefore extremely fresh, vegetables served in all forms and shapes with an abundance of fresh herbs (mostly coriander, parsley and mint). A meal is always concluded with a wide range of fresh fruit, including melon, apples, oranges, persimmon, tangerines, cactus fruit, grapes and figs, which are all grown locally. Excellent Lebanese food is available everywhere. Beirut also offers a large choice of international restaurants which offer dishes from all over the world. Bars have table and/or counter service. Alcohol is not prohibited.
National specialities:
- *Kebbeh*, made of lamb pounded to a fine paste, with *burghul* or cracked wheat, and served raw or baked in flat trays or rolled into balls and fried.
- *Mezza*, a range of up to 40 small dishes served as hors d'oeuvres with *arak*.
- *Lahm mishwi* (pieces of mutton with onions, peppers and tomato) is popular.
- *Tabbouli*.
- *Houmos*.
- *Mtabbal*.
- Lebanese palates also favour pastries with local varieties of baked doughs flavoured with nuts, cream and syrup.

National drinks:
- *Arak*, a wine traditionally produced and aged for five to 10 years before being redistilled with anis seeds.
Tipping: In hotels and restaurants, a tip of between 5 and 10 per cent of the bill is expected. It is not necessary to tip taxi drivers.
NIGHTLIFE: Nightclubs spice up the evenings in Beirut and mountain resorts. Entertainment ranges from solo guitarists to orchestras and floor shows. Some British-style pubs can be found in Beirut. There are many cinemas presenting the latest films from all over the world. The internationally renowned Casino du Liban in Maameltain (22km/14 miles north of Beirut) is equipped with lavish gambling halls, luxurious restaurants and a cabaret.
SHOPPING: Lebanon's traditional *souks* or markets are found all over the country offering decorative and precious handmade items at very low prices. Special purchases include traditional pottery and glassware, as well as cutlery made of tempered steel or copper with ram or buffalo bone handles shaped in the form of beautiful

and colourful birds' heads. Brass and copper goods include braziers, bowls, fluted jugs, ashtrays, swords and doorstops, all attractively designed and hand engraved. Cloth, silk and wool kaftans, *abayas* (embroidered nightwear) and table linen are popular, as are handworked gold and silver. Shops sell the latest Western goods including clothes, cosmetics, furniture and electrical appliances. **Shopping hours:** Mon-Sat 0800-1800.

Business

- **GDP:** US$18.2 billion.
- **Main exports:** Authentic jewellery, inorganic chemicals, consumer goods, fruit, tobacco, construction materials, electric power, machinery and switchgear, textile fibres and paper.
- **Main imports:** Petroleum products, cars, medicinal products, clothing, meat and live animals, consumer goods, paper, textile fabrics and tobacco.
- **Main trade partners:** Syria, Italy, France, UAE, Germany, Turkey, Switzerland, China, USA, Saudi Arabia and UK.

ECONOMY: The 15-year civil war from 1976 to 1991 all but completely destroyed the economy; Beirut's position as a major financial and commercial centre for the Middle East was lost. Since then, both Lebanon and its capital have gone a long way to re-establishing themselves. Agriculture now accounts for about 10 per cent of GDP, with citrus fruit, olives and cereals as the main products. Light industries include textiles, processed foods and industrial machinery. There are no significant mineral resources, but the manufacturing industry is growing rapidly. In the all-important service sector, the two main components, banking and transit trade (both of which were almost wiped out during the civil war) have recovered reasonably well. Essential reconstruction, financed by expatriate capital, international aid and foreign investment, began with infrastructural projects. However, by the late-1990s, the Government's failure to control the budget deficit and external debt was causing serious difficulties. Annual growth had fallen from an average 4 per cent during most of the 1990s to just over 1 per cent by 2000. At the end of 2000, the Government introduced a major reform programme based on privatisation and promotion of foreign investment. However, it was at pains to do so outside the normal channels of the IMF and World Bank which, the Government felt, imposed unacceptable constraints on its freedom of manoeuvre on economic policy-making. To that end, in November 2002, Lebanon successfully raised a $4 billion loan package from a consortium including a dozen Governments (notably excluding the US) and a number of investment banks and multinational funds. However, the debt burden has continued to climb. Lack of confidence and speculation about the risk of devaluation placed the currency under considerable pressure as local investors switched to the American Dollar. Lebanon has a major bilateral trade deal with the EU.
BUSINESS ETIQUETTE: Businesspeople usually wear a jacket and tie. English is spoken by many local businesspeople and normal courtesies are observed. Appointments and business cards are used. **Office hours:** Mon-Fri 0800-1330 and 1500-1800. **Government office hours:** Mon-Thurs 0800-1400, Fri 0800-1100, Sat 0800-1300.
CONFERENCES/CONVENTIONS: Beirut is an increasingly popular business destination and a number of companies offer extensive conference and exhibition facilities.

COMMERCIAL INFORMATION

Chamber of Commerce, Industry and Agriculture of Beirut and Mount Lebanon
PO Box 11-1801, Rue Sanayeh, Sanayeh, Beirut, Lebanon
Tel: (1) 353 390 *or* 744 160.
Website: www.ccib.org.lb

Ministry of Economy and Trade
Artois Street, Hamra, Beirut, Lebanon
Tel: (1) 345 178
Website: www.economy.gov.lb

Euro Info Correspondence Centre (EICC)
PO Box 11-1801, 1 Rue Justinien, Sanayeh, Beirut, Lebanon
Tel: (1) 744 163.
Website: www.euroinfocentre.net

Lesotho

Location: Southern Africa.

Time: GMT + 2.

Overview

Civil unrest throughout 1999 caused some destruction in most of the town centres and the country is still in the process of rebuilding. Maseru, Lesotho's capital, is the obvious stepping-off point for a holiday.

General Information

AREA: 30,355 sq km (11,720 sq miles).
POPULATION: 2.2 million (official estimate 2002).
POPULATION DENSITY: 67.0 per sq km.
CAPITAL: Maseru. **Population:** 271,000 (UN estimate 2001, including suburbs).
GEOGRAPHY: Lesotho is a landlocked country surrounded on all sides by South Africa. It is a mountainous kingdom situated at the highest part of the Drakensberg escarpment on the eastern rim of the South African plateau. Its mountainous terrain is cut by countless valleys and ravines, making it a country of great beauty. To the west, the land descends through a foothill zone of rolling hills to a lowland belt along the border where two-thirds of the population live. Three large rivers, the Caledon, the Orange, and the Tugela, rise in the mountains.
GOVERNMENT: Kingdom. Gained independence from the UK in 1966. **Head of State:** King Letsie III since 1996.
Head of Government: Prime Minister Bethuel Pakalitha Mosisili since 1998.
LANGUAGE: Sesotho and English.
RELIGION: 90 per cent Christian; mainly Anglican, Roman Catholic and Lesotho Evangelical. The remainder belong to other denominations, including Islam.
ELECTRICITY: 220 volts AC, 50Hz.
SOCIAL CONVENTIONS: If spending some time in rural villages, it is polite to inform the Head Chief. It is likely that he will be very helpful. Normal social courtesies and a friendly, warm approach will be greatly appreciated. Dress should be practical and casual but local customs should be respected (including those regarding modesty in dress). Religion plays an important part in daily life.
Photography: Photographs must not be taken of the following: the palace, police establishments, Government offices, the airport or monetary authority buildings.

Climate

Temperate climate with well-marked seasons. Summer is the rainy season; 85 per cent of rainfall occurs from October to April, especially in the mountains. Snow occurs in the highlands from May to September. The hottest period is from January to February. Lesotho is a land of clear blue skies and more than 300 days of sunshine a year.

Required clothing: During the summer, lightweight cottons with warmer wear for the evenings is needed. In winter, medium- to heavyweight clothes are advised. Waterproofing is necessary during the rainy season.

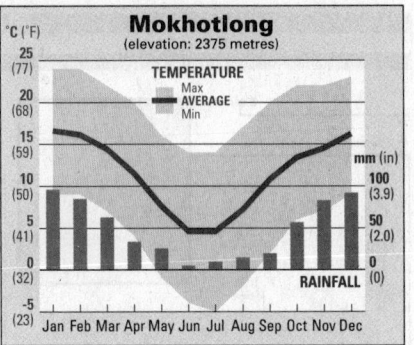

Mokhotlong (elevation: 2375 metres)

Communications

Telephone: IDD is available to some cities. Country code: 266 (no area codes). There is a limited internal telephone network.
Mobile telephone: Coverage is limited to main urban areas.
Internet: There are Internet cafes in Maseru. ISPs include *LEO Internet Services* (website: www.lesoff.co.za).
Post: Post office hours: Mon-Fri 0800-1300 and 1400-1630, Sat 0800-1200.
MEDIA: The Government operates a range of media. South African radio and TV stations can also be received in Lesotho.
Press: *Makatolle, MoAfrica* and *Mohlanka* are weekly publications; *The Mirror* is published in English.
TV: *Lesotho Television* is state-run.
Radio: *Radio Lesotho* is state-run; *MoAfrika FM* is private; Other stations include *People's Choice FM, Joy Radio FM* and *Catholic Radio FM*.

Passport/Visa

	Passport Required?	Visa Required?	Return Ticket Required?
Full British	Yes	No	Yes
Australian	Yes	No	Yes
Canadian	Yes	No	Yes
USA	Yes	No	Yes
Other EU	Yes	No/1	Yes
Japanese	Yes	No	Yes

Note: Regulations and requirements may be subject to change at short notice, and you are advised to contact the appropriate diplomatic or consular authority before finalising travel arrangements. Any numbers in the chart refer to the footnotes below.

Note: Visitors travelling via South Africa will need to comply with South African passport/visa regulations.
PASSPORTS: Required by all.
VISAS: Required by all except the following for stays of up to three months:
(a) nationals referred to in the chart above except
1. nationals of Czech Republic, Estonia, Hungary, Latvia, Lithuania, Poland, Slovak Republic and Slovenia who *do* need a visa;
(b) nationals of Commonwealth countries, except for nationals of Bangladesh, Cameroon, Fiji, Ghana, India, Mozambique, Nigeria, Pakistan and Sri Lanka who *do* require a visa;
(c) nationals of Iceland, Israel, Madagascar, Norway, Switzerland and Zimbabwe.
Types of visa and cost: *Tourist/Business*: £30 (single-entry); £50 (multiple-entry).
Validity: *Single-entry*: up to three months. *Multiple-entry*: up to six months.
Application to: Consulate (or consular section at Embassy or High Commission); see *Passport/Visa Information*.
Application requirements: (a) Valid passport. (b) Two application forms. (c) Two passport-size photos. (d) Return ticket. (e) Fee. *Business*: (a)-(e) and, (f) Letter from sponsor.
Working days required: One.
Temporary residence: Apply to the Ministry of Home Affairs, Maseru. Enquire at Embassy for details.

Money

Currency: Loti (LSL) = 100 lisente. Notes are in denominations of LSL200, 100, 50, 20 and 10. Coins are in denominations of 500, 200, 100, 50, 25, 10, 5, 2 and 1 lisente. The plural of 'loti' is 'maloti' and the singular of 'lisente' is 'sente'. The South African Rand is accepted as legal currency on a par with the Loti (Rand R1 = 100 cents).
Credit & debit cards: Limited acceptance of Diners Club, MasterCard and Visa. Check with your credit or debit card company for details of merchant acceptability and other services which may be available.
Traveller's cheques: These are widely accepted. To avoid additional exchange rate charges, travellers are advised to take traveller's cheques in US Dollars or Pounds Sterling.
Currency restrictions: The import and export of local and foreign currency is unrestricted.
Banking hours: Mon-Tues and Thurs-Fri 0830-1530, Wed 0830-1300, Sat 0830-1100.
Exchange rate indicators:
Rate at time of publishing
£1.00=   LSL11.73
$1.00=   LSL6.75

Duty Free

The following goods may be imported into Lesotho without incurring customs duty:
400 cigarettes and 50 cigars and 250g of tobacco; 1l of spirits and 2l of wine (irrespective of age); 50ml of perfume and 250ml of eau de toilette; gifts up to value of LSL500.
Note: (a) Goods with serial numbers must be declared. (b) No alcohol may be imported by South African nationals.

Public Holidays

Below are listed Public Holidays for the January 2006-June 2007 period.
2006: Jan 1 New Year's Day. **Mar 11** Moshoeshoe Day. **Apr 4** Heroes' Day. **Apr 14** Good Friday. **Apr 17** Easter Monday. **May 1** Workers' Day. **May 28** Ascension. **Jul 17** King Letsie III's Birthday. **Oct 4** Independence Day. **Dec 25-26** Christmas.
2007: Jan 1 New Year's Day. **Mar 11** Moshoeshoe Day. **Apr 6** Good Friday. **Apr 9** Easter Monday. **Apr 4** Heroes' Day. **May 1** Workers' Day. **May 20** Ascension.

Health

	Special Precautions?	Certificate Required?
Yellow Fever	Yes	1
Cholera	No	No
Typhoid & Polio	2	N/A
Malaria	No	N/A

Note: Regulations and requirements may be subject to change at short notice, and you are advised to contact your doctor well in advance of your intended date of departure. Any numbers in the chart refer to the footnotes below.

1: A *yellow fever* vaccination certificate is required from all travellers arriving from infected areas, even if they do not leave the airport.
2: *Typhoid* fever is common in some areas. *Poliomyelitis* has very nearly been eradicated, so risk of infection is very low.
Food & drink: Tap water is considered safe to drink. However, drinking water outside main cities and towns may be contaminated and sterilisation is advisable. Milk is pasteurised and dairy products are safe for consumption. Local meat, poultry, seafood, fruit and vegetables are generally considered safe to eat.
Other risks: *Hepatitis A* and B occur. Lesotho is free of *bilharzia* (schistosomiasis) and people may swim in fresh water without danger. There is a high incidence of *HIV/AIDS*.
Health care: Health insurance is recommended.
Note: Since the most practical way to reach Lesotho is to go through South Africa, it will also be necessary to conform to South African health regulations.

Travel - International

AIR:

Lesotho's national airline has closed down. *South African Airways (SA)* has daily flights to Maseru from Johannesburg (flight time is approximately one hour 10 minutes), where connections to the rest of the world can be made.
Approximate flight times: From Maseru to *London* is 14 hours (including a stopover of two hours).
Main airports: *Maseru (MSU)* (Moshoeshoe International) is 18km (11 miles) south of Maseru. Buses go to the city (travel time – 30 minutes). Airport facilities include a bank and bureau de change (with limited opening hours on Tuesday and Friday), bar, restaurant, flight information, left luggage facilities, car hire and post office.
Departure tax: LSL20; transit passengers and children under five years are exempt.
ROAD:

There are three major road links to South Africa: at Caledonsport, Ficksburg Bridge and Maseru Bridge. Other crossing points exist, but the road surfaces are not as good. Maseru Bridge and Ficksburg Bridge are open 24 hours a day. Caledonsport is open by 0800 but may close as early as 1600. **Bus:** Minibuses run regularly between Maseru and Johannesburg.
Road tax: LSL5, payable by all travellers leaving Lesotho by road.
RAIL:

Lesotho is linked with the South African railway system by a short line (2.6km/1.6 miles) from Maseru to Marseilles, on the Bloemfontein/Natal main line. However, this is only used for goods trains at present.

Travel - Internal

ROAD:

Traffic drives on the left. The road system is underdeveloped and few roads are paved. The main road which runs through the towns from the north to the western and southern borders is tarred, but other roads can be impassable during the rainy season. There are **minibuses** in the lowlands. **Car hire** is available in Maseru. It is advised not to drive in rural areas at night (or even walk around Maseru at night). There have been incidents of mugging and vehicle hijacking. **Documentation:** An International Driving Permit is recommended. National driving licences are normally valid, provided that they are either in English or accompanied by a certified translation. Enquire at the High Commission or Embassy for details.
Travel times: The following chart gives travel times (in hours and minutes) from **Maseru** to other towns in Lesotho.

	Road
Teyateyaneng	-
Mokhotlong	7.00
Qachas Nek	8.00
Mohales Hoek	1.30
Mafeteng	1.00

Travel Advice

Most visits to Lesotho are trouble-free but there have been incidents of muggings and vehicle hijacking in the past 12 months (some involving firearms). There have also been incidents of armed robbery in Maseru. Sporadic demonstrations are possible.
Do not walk around Maseru at night; and avoid driving in rural areas at night.
The threat from terrorism is low. But you should be aware of the global risk of indiscriminate terrorist attacks, which could be against civilian targets, including places frequented by foreigners.
This advice is based on information provided by the Foreign and Commonwealth Office in the UK. It is correct at time of publishing. As the situation can change rapidly, visitors are advised to contact the following organisations for the latest travel advice:

British Foreign and Commonwealth Office
Tel: (0845) 850 2829.
Website: www.fco.gov.uk

US Department of State
Website: http://travel.state.gov/travel

Accommodation

HOTELS: There are hotels of varying quality in the main towns and mountain lodges giving access to the wilder regions. There are several hotels in Maseru of international standard. Further information can be obtained from the Lesotho Tourist Board (see *Top Things To See & Do*).

LODGES: Commercial concerns have built several lodges (mostly self-catering) providing bungalow accommodation.

Top Things To See & Do

- **Maseru,** Lesotho's capital is the obvious stepping-off point for a holiday. There are local highlights to visit such as the historic cemetery and the fascinating architecture of the **King's Palace** and the **Prime Minister's Residence**. From Maseru, you can take many day trips, either independently or by luxury minibus, visiting surrounding points of interest.
- Near Maseru, the **Ha Khotso Bushmen Rock Paintings** make an interesting visit. Also nearby is **Thaba Bosiu**, a flat-topped hill where the Basotho made a last heroic stand against the Boers. Many of their chiefs are buried here.
- The southern region of Lesotho is being promoted for tourism, with hotels at **Moyeni** and **Mohales Hoek** offering facilities for horse riding, mountain climbing and hiking. Worth visiting in the district are the **Motlejoeng Caves**, 2km (1.2 miles) south of Mahale's Hoek; the dinosaur footprints at **Moyeni**; the **Masitise Cave House** and the petrified forest on the mountain of **Thaba-Ts'oeu**. In the southeast, in the region bordering South Africa, is one of the most beautiful parts of Lesotho - if not southern Africa. It is ideal for **trekking**. Places of most interest include **Ramanbanta**, **Semonkong** (where the **Maletsunyane Waterfalls** can be visited) and the **Sehlabathebe National Park**.
- **Pony trekking:** At the moment three treks are on offer, two of them covering the great falls at **Ribaneng**, **Ketane** and **Maletsunyane**, the latter being particularly noteworthy as it is the highest single-drop fall in southern Africa. There is a choice of return, once Semonkong has been reached, between going back to Maseru by road on the fourth day or continuing the pony ride for another two days to Ha Ramabanta, where motor transport is available for the return to Maseru. The other route is the **Molimo Nthuse** circular trip, starting at the **Molimo Nthuse** ('God Help Me') **Centre** (the actual base for the Basotho Pony Trekking Centre) and going over **Thaba Putsoa** ('Blue Mountain') *Pass* to reach Ha Marakabei-Senqunyane Lodge on the second day. The return trip via Molikaliko and **Qiloane Falls** reaches Molimo Nthuse from a different direction on the fifth day. Unlike the three falls of the first trip, Qiloane is a wide fall with several smaller drops. Overnight stops are usually made in the rural areas in the huts of the remote Basotho where a taste of real Basotho life is experienced. All the routes pass through magnificent countryside.
- **Skiing:** In conjunction with a private company, the Lesotho Government has developed a modern ski resort in the heart of the Lesotho highlands. Just four-and-a-half hours' drive from Johannesburg, the resort aims to attract skiers from both Southern Africa and Europe (website: www.afriski.co.za).
- **Mountain climbing:** Mountain climbing is a popular and ideal way of seeing the rugged beauty of the land.
- **Birdwatching:** As many as 279 species of birds have been recorded and keen birdwatchers should take a trip along the Mountain Road to see birds rare to southern Africa.
- **Fishing:** Lesotho's dams and rivers contain local and imported fish. Brown and rainbow trout and carp provide satisfying sport for anglers.
- For **swimming**, bilharzia-free rivers and lakes and hotel pools are available for bathing.

TOURIST INFORMATION

Ministry of Tourism, Sports and Culture
PO Box 52, Maseru 100, Lesotho
Tel: (22) 313 034.
Website: www.lesotho.gov.ls

Entertainment

FOOD & DRINK: The main hotels in Maseru serve international food, but there are also some interesting places to dine in the main towns. Hotels and restaurants in Lesotho cater for all nationalities. There are *halal* foods and seafood. Cooking styles include French, Italian, Continental and Chinese in Maseru. Much food has to be imported from South Africa, but freshwater fish is in abundant supply.
Good beer is widely available and better establishments will have a good choice of beers, spirits and wines.
Tipping: It is customary in restaurants and hotels to give a tip as a reward for good service.
NIGHTLIFE: Some hotels and restaurants have live entertainment. There are also several cinemas in Maseru and there are casinos at the two major international hotels.
SHOPPING: There are many handicraft shops and centres selling items including Lesotho's famous conical hats; grass-woven articles (mats, brooms and baskets); pottery; wool and mohair rugs; tapestries and other textiles; rock painting reproductions; traditional seed, clay bead and porcupine quill jewellery; silver and gold items; copper work (particularly chess sets of African design) and ebony items. **Shopping hours:** Mon-Fri 0800-1700, Sat 0800-1500.

Business

ECONOMY: The earnings of the estimated 150,000 Lesotho nationals working in South Africa account for a substantial proportion of the country's income. Inside the country, 40 per cent of the workforce are engaged in agriculture, farming maize, wheat and other crops. Wool, mohair and hides are important exports. Nonetheless, Lesotho's vulnerability to drought means that over half the country's food must be imported from South Africa: this was particularly apparent during mid-2002, when large-scale famine was narrowly averted. There are reserves of ores and minerals, including diamonds, uranium, lead and iron ore, but little exploitation has taken place. Light manufacturing, meanwhile, has grown steadily with food, drink and textiles as the main products. Tourism is a major source of foreign exchange. Lesotho's Government has historically relied on foreign aid, particularly for infrastructure programmes (large parts of which were destroyed during a major civil insurrection in 1998). The most important infrastructure project of recent years has been Lesotho Highlands Water Project, which aims to deliver water to South Africa and provide 60 per cent of Lesotho's electricity supply. South Africa is Lesotho's major trading partner and the Southern African Customs Union provides over 95 per cent of the country's imports. Unfortunately, Lesotho and South Africa also share the scourge of the region, HIV/AIDS, which has infected over one-third of Lesotho's productive labour force.
BUSINESS ETIQUETTE: Lightweight suit, shirt and tie should be worn for business meetings. English will be spoken by most businesspeople. Usual business formalities should be observed, but expect a casual atmosphere and pace. **Office hours:** Mon-Fri 0800-1245 and 1400-1630, Sat 0800-1300. **Government office hours:** Mon-Fri 0800-1245 and 1400-1630.
CONFERENCES/CONVENTIONS: The Lesotho Tourist Board can provide advice (see *Top Things to See and Do*).

COMMERCIAL INFORMATION

Ministry of Trade, Industry and Marketing
PO Box 747, Maseru 100, Lesotho
Tel: 312 938.

Lesotho National Development Corporation
Private Bag A96, Development House, Block A, Kingsway Street, Maseru 100, Lesotho
Tel: 312 012.
Website: www.lndc.org.ls

Lesotho Chamber of Commerce and Industry
PO Box 79, Kingsway Avenue, Maseru 100, Lesotho
Tel: 323 482.

Liberia

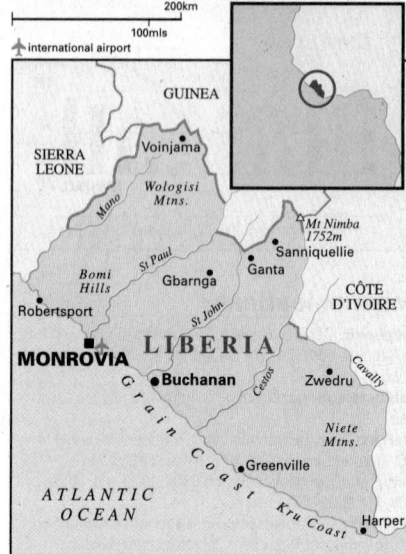

Location: West Africa.

Time: GMT.

Overview

The most evocative description of Liberia can be found in Graham Greene's *Journey without Maps*, an account of his overland trip across the country in 1935. Although it can now hardly pretend to be an up-to-date guide book, the descriptions and the atmosphere of the country it creates – particularly when dealing with the mysterious and jungle-rich interior – make the book a valuable and entertaining introduction for anyone planning to visit the country. However, foreigners are currently advised against all but essential travel to Monrovia and the rest of Liberia: the security situation is volatile and flights out of the country are intermittent. There is sporadic fighting and looting.

General Information

AREA: 97,754 sq km (37,743 sq miles).
POPULATION: 3.2 million(2003).
POPULATION DENSITY: 33.1 per sq km.
CAPITAL: Monrovia. **Population:** 550,200 (2003).
GEOGRAPHY: Liberia borders Sierra Leone, Guinea Republic and Côte d'Ivoire. The Atlantic coastline to the west is 560km (348 miles) long, of which over half is sandy beach. Lying parallel to the shore are three distinct belts. The low coastal belt is well watered by shallow lagoons, tidal creeks and mangrove swamps, behind which rises a gently undulating plateau, 500 to 800m (1640 to 2625ft) high, partly covered with dense forests. Inland and to the north is the mountain region which includes Mount Nimba at 1752m (5748ft) and Waulo Mountain at 1400m (4593ft). About half of the country's population are rural dwellers.
GOVERNMENT: Republic. Declared independence in 1847.
Head of State and Government: President Ellen Johnson-Sirleaf since January 2006. **Recent history:** Elections resulted in a run-off between ex-footballer George Weah and Johnson-Sirleaf, a former World Bank economist. Johnson-Sirleaf won with 59 per cent of the vote. International observers declared the election to be free and fair, despite Weah's allegations of electoral fraud. She is Africa's first elected female ruler. She pledged to unite her country, which has been struggling for peace after nearly 25 years of coups and civil wars.
LANGUAGE: English is the official language. The main local languages are Bassa, Dan (Gio), Kpelleh, Kru, Lorma and Mano. There are 16 major languages and dialects.
RELIGION: Officially a Christian state, with more than 30 denominations represented; Islam is practised in the north and traditional animist beliefs exist throughout the country.
ELECTRICITY: 110 volts AC, 60Hz.

SOCIAL CONVENTIONS: In Muslim areas, the visitor should respect the conventions of dress and the food laws, since failure to do so will be taken as an insult. Dress is casual and must be practical, but smarter dress will be expected in hotel dining rooms and for important social functions. The visitor should be aware that the cost of living is high. Sending flowers or chocolates to hosts is inappropriate; a letter of thanks is all that is required.

Climate

Hot, tropical climate with little variation in temperature. The wet season runs from May to October. The dry *harmattan* wind blows from December to March, making the coastal belt particularly arid.

Required clothing: Lightweight cottons and linens are worn throughout the year, with waterproofing advised during the wet season.

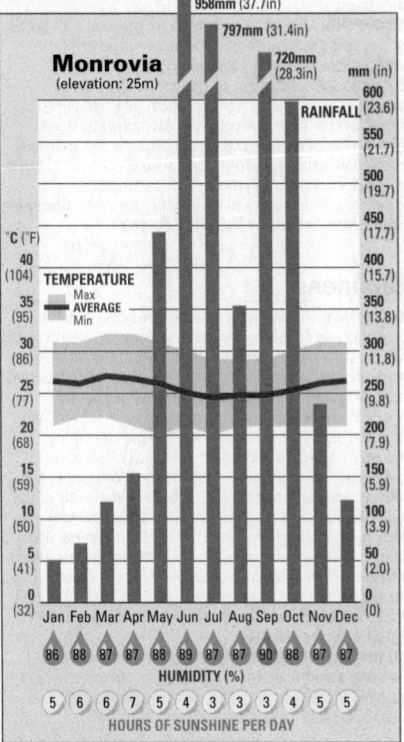

Communications

Telephone: IDD service to some cities. Country code: 231 (no area codes). The internal network in Monrovia is gradually being extended over the country.

Mobile telephone: GSM 900 networks operated by *Comium* (website: www.comium.com), *Libercell* and *LonestarCell*.

Internet: There are a few Internet cafes in Monrovia. ISPs include *Africalink* (website: www.africalink.com).

Post: Airmail to Europe takes up to one month.

MEDIA: Following years of civil war, Liberia's broadcasters and publishers are still struggling to find resources to pay their staff. The state-run broadcaster has no television service and operates a single radio service, which does not have national coverage.

Press: Private daily newspapers include *The Inquirer*, *The News* and *The Analyst*. Weekly publications include *The Heritage*.

TV: *DC TV* is private.

Radio: State run ELBC is operated by Liberian Broadcasting System. Many stations are run with the support of international agencies. *Star Radio* is an FM and shortwave station, operated in partnership with Swiss-based Hirondelle Foundation; *UNMIL Radio* is operated by the United Nations mission.

Passport/Visa

	Passport Required?	Visa Required?	Return Ticket? Required?
Full British	Yes	Yes	No
Australian	Yes	Yes	No
Canadian	Yes	Yes	No
USA	Yes	Yes	No
Other EU	Yes	Yes	No
Japanese	Yes	Yes	No

Note: *Regulations and requirements may be subject to change at short notice, and you are advised to contact the appropriate diplomatic or consular authority before finalising travel arrangements. Any numbers in the chart refer to the footnotes below.*

PASSPORTS: Passport valid for a minimum of six months from date of entry required by all.

VISAS: Required by all except the following:
(a) nationals of ECOWAS countries, Israel, Korea (Rep) and Thailand;
(b) transit passengers continuing their journey by the same or first connecting aircraft within 48 hours, provided holding onward or return documentation and not leaving the airport.

Types of visa and cost: *Tourist/Business:* £30 (single-entry); £60 (multiple-entry).

Validity: *Single-entry:* three months from date of issue; *multiple-entry:* six months from date of issue. Visas may be extended at the Immigration Office in Monrovia.

Application to: Consulate (or consular section at Embassy); see *Passport/Visa Information*.

Application requirements: (a) Valid passport. (b) Completed application form. (c) Two passport-size photos attached to each form. (d) International *yellow fever* vaccination certificate. (e) Letter stating purpose of visit and name of contact in Liberia. Applicants must produce proof of financial status while in the country. (f) For business trips, a letter from company, or statement giving purpose of visit.

Working days required: One.

Temporary residence: Application should be made prior to arrival to the Ministry of Foreign Affairs, Monrovia.

Note: All visitors holding a visa issued abroad and intending to stay in Liberia for more than 15 days must report within 48 hours of their arrival to the Immigration Office, Broad Street, Monrovia. Two passport-size photos must be submitted.

PASSPORT/VISA INFORMATION

Embassy of the Republic of Liberia in the UK
23 Fitzroy Square, London W1 6EW, UK
Tel: (020) 7388 5489.
Opening hours: Mon-Fri 1300-1600; Mon-Thurs 1030-1500 (visa section).

Embassy of the Republic of Liberia in the USA
5201 16th Street, NW, Washington, DC 20011, USA
Tel: (202) 723 0437.
Website: www.embassyofliberia.org

Money

Currency: Liberian Dollar (LRD; symbol L$) = 100 cents. Notes are in denominations of L$100, 50, 20, 10 and 5. US Dollar notes are in circulation in the following denominations: US$100, 50, 20, 10, 5 and 1.

Note: The Liberian Dollar is tied to the US Dollar.

Currency exchange: Money can be exchanged at the Liberia Bank for Development and Investment (LBDI), on the corner of Randall and Ashmun Streets in Monrovia. LBDI also incorporates a Western Union office, which can receive urgent money transfers from abroad (though the procedure is lengthy and will take approximately one day).

Credit & debit cards: Not generally accepted.

Traveller's cheques: These are generally not accepted.

Currency restrictions: There are no restrictions on the import or export of local currency. The import of foreign currency over the equivalent of US$10,000 should be declared or heavy fines may be imposed. The export of foreign currency is permitted up to US$7500; more may be exported only as bank drafts, traveller's cheques or money orders.

Banking hours: Mon-Thurs 0900-1200, Fri 0800-1400. Some banks may open on Saturday.

Exchange rate indicators:
Rate at time of publishing
£1.00=   L$86.77
$1.00=   L$50.00

Duty Free

The following goods may be imported into Liberia without incurring customs duty:
200 cigarettes or 25 cigars or 250g tobacco products; 1l of spirits and 1l of wine; 100g of perfume and 1l of eau-de-toilette; goods to the value of US$125.

Public Holidays

Below are listed Public Holidays for the January 2006-June 2007 period.

2006: Jan 1 New Year's Day. **Feb 11** Armed Forces Day. **Mar 8** Decoration Day. **Mar 15** J J Roberts' Birthday. **Apr 12** National Redemption Day. **Apr 14** Fast and Prayer Day. **May 6** Samuel K Doe's Birthday. **May 14** National Unification Day. **May 25** Africa Day. **Jul 26** Independence Day. **Aug 24** Flag Day. **Oct 29** Youth Day. **Nov 23** Thanksgiving Day. **Nov 29** President Tubman's Birthday. **Dec 25** Christmas Day.
2007: Jan 1 New Year's Day. **Feb 11** Armed Forces Day. **Mar 8** Decoration Day. **Mar 15** J J Roberts' Birthday. **Apr 12**

National Redemption Day. **Apr 14** Fast and Prayer Day. **May 6** Samuel K Doe's Birthday. **May 14** National Unification Day. **May 25** Africa Day.

Health

	Special Precautions?	Certificate Required?
Yellow Fever	Yes	1
Cholera	2	No
Typhoid & Polio	3	N/A
Malaria	4	N/A

Note: *Regulations and requirements may be subject to change at short notice, and you are advised to contact your doctor well in advance of your intended date of departure. Any numbers in the chart refer to the footnotes below.*

1: A *yellow fever* vaccination certificate is required from all travellers over one year of age. Note that the certificate must be presented with all visa applications.

2: Following WHO guidelines issued in 1973, a *cholera* vaccination certificate is not a condition of entry to Liberia. However, *cholera* is a serious risk in this country and precautions are essential. Up-to-date advice should be sought before deciding whether these precautions should include vaccination, as medical opinion is divided over its effectiveness; see the *Health* appendix.

3: *Typhoid* is widespread and poliomyelitis is still endemic.

4: *Malaria* risk, predominantly in the malignant *falciparum* form, exists all year throughout the country. High resistance to chloroquine and resistance to sulfadoxine-pyrimethamine has been reported. The recommended prophylaxis is mefloquine.

Food & drink: All water should be regarded as being potentially contaminated. Water used for drinking, brushing teeth or making ice should have first been boiled or otherwise sterilised. Milk is unpasteurised and should be boiled. Powdered or tinned milk is available and is advised, but make sure that it is reconstituted with pure water. Avoid dairy products which are likely to have been made from unboiled milk. Only eat well-cooked meat and fish, preferably served hot. Pork, salad and mayonnaise may carry increased risk. Vegetables should be cooked and fruit peeled.

Other risks: *Bilharzia (schistosomiasis)* is present. Avoid swimming and paddling in fresh water; swimming pools which are well chlorinated and maintained are safe. *Meningococcal meningitis* is a risk, depending on the area visited and time of year. *Cutaneous* and *visceral leishmaniasis* occur. *Trypanosomiasis* (sleeping sickness) is reported. *Hepatitis B* is hyperendemic, and *hepatitis A* and *E* are widespread.

Rabies is present. For those at high risk, vaccination before arrival should be considered. If you are bitten, seek medical advice without delay. For more information, consult the *Health* appendix.

Health care: International travellers are strongly advised to take out full medical insurance before departure. Hospitals are gradually re-emerging in Liberia, but some patients may still need evacuation to medical facilities in Côte d'Ivoire.

Travel - International

Note: Foreigners are advised against all but essential travel to Monrovia and the rest of Liberia; the security situation is volatile and flights out of the country are intermittent. There is sporadic fighting and looting. For further advice, potential visitors should contact their local Government travel advice department. It is recommended that visitors, should they choose to visit Liberia, do not stay overnight outside the city.

AIR:

 Main airlines serving Liberia include *Air Afrique (RK)* and *Ghana Airways (GH)*. *Air Ivoire* operates flights between Monrovia and Abidjan (Côte d'Ivoire). *Weasua Air Transport (XA)* operates flights between Monrovia and Freetown (Sierra Leone) (tel: 275 440; fax: 226 067).

Approximate flight times: From Monrovia to *New York* (via Dakar) is nine hours; to *London* (via Brussels) is 11 hours.

Main airports: *Monrovia (ROB)* (Roberts International) is 60km (36 miles) southeast of the city. There are bus services and taxis to and from the city. Airport facilities are limited, but include restaurant and first aid facilities.

No airlines currently land at *Spriggs Payne Airport (MLW)* which is in the city itself.

Departure tax: None.

SEA:

There are unscheduled freighter services with passenger accommodation from European ports. The main Liberian ports are Monrovia, Buchanan, Greenville, Harper and Robertsport. The port in Monrovia is being expanded.

A B C D E F G H I J K L M N O P Q R S T U V W X Y Z

ROAD:

Best routes to Liberia are through Guinea Republic and Côte d'Ivoire, but they are impassable during the rainy season. The northeastern route to Sierra Leone (via Kolahun and Kailahun) is currently closed.

Travel - Internal

AIR:

There are 60 airfields for small aircraft.

SEA/RIVER:

There is a passenger service between Monrovia and Buchanan. There is also a boat service which runs weekly between Harper and Greenville. Unscheduled coastal steamers may sometimes take passengers. Small craft are used for local transportation on Liberia's many rivers. **Canoe safaris:** Between December and March, specialist companies arrange canoe trips upriver from Greenville, a small seaport 200km (125 miles) southeast of Monrovia. Contact the Ministry of Information, Culture and Tourism for further details (see *Contact Addresses* section).

RAIL:

No service at present.

ROAD:

Traffic drives on the right. Difficulties in bypassing lagoons and bridging river estuaries often result in long detours and delays along the coast. Main roads are from Monrovia to Buchanan and from Monrovia to Sanniquellie with branches to Ganta and Harper. Many of the smaller roads are still untarred. Vehicle transport is limited. **Bus:** No services between main towns at present. **Car hire:** Self-drive or chauffeured cars may be hired in Monrovia. **Documentation:** An International Driving Permit is recommended, although it is not legally required. A temporary licence to drive is available from local authorities on presentation of a valid British, Northern Ireland or US driving licence and is valid for up to 30 days.

URBAN:

Taxis are available and tipping is unnecessary.

Travel Advice

Travellers are advised against all but essential travel to Liberia. UN peacekeepers are deployed to the main population centres and patrol major roads, but the security situation remains unpredictable, with sporadic unrest and violence.

For those deciding to travel outside Monrovia, it is recommended that they do not overnight outside the city and that they check the security situation before travelling. The threat from terrorism is low.

This advice is based on information provided by the Foreign and Commonwealth Office in the UK. It is correct at time of publishing. As the situation can change rapidly, visitors are advised to contact the following organisations for the latest travel advice:

British Foreign and Commonwealth Office
Tel: (0845) 850 2829.
Website: www.fco.gov.uk

US Department of State
Website: http://travel.state.gov/travel

Accommodation

HOTELS:

Hotel accommodation can be quite expensive, but is not extortionate by international standards. It is advisable to book well in advance, whatever the category of accommodation. There are a few air-conditioned hotels of international standard and a range of inexpensive hotels and motels. The top hotels charge from US$110 a night. Hotels in the mid-range charge from US$60 and tend to provide the bare minimum.

GUEST HOUSES:

There are several mission guest houses with both cooking and laundry facilities about 4km (2 miles) from the city centre.

CAMPING:

There are few official sites. Camping is free but caution should be exercised when choosing where to camp. Specialist operators run sites near national parks.

YOUTH HOSTELS:
The YMCA is cheap, but often full, and is located on the corner of Broad and McDonald Streets.

Top Things To See & Do

• **Monrovia**, the capital is a sprawling city on the coast divided by inlets, lagoons and rocky headlands. The city has several nightclubs, restaurants and bars, centred on the area around Gurley Street. There are several good sandy beaches near the capital.

• Around 80km (50 miles) from the capital is **Lake Piso**, ideal for fishing and watersports. Conducted tours of the **Firestone Rubber Plantation**, one of the largest in the world, make an interesting day excursion, situated only 50km (30 miles) from Monrovia. Some of the country's most beautiful beaches can be found at **Robertsport**. The **Kpa-Tawe Waterfalls** are four hours 30 minutes' drive away from Monrovia (a 4-wheel-drive vehicle is recommended).

• For wildlife and nature enthusiasts, the **Sapo National Park** has much to offer: located in Sinoe County, this pristine forest wilderness is home to a great variety of plants and animal species (including elephant, leopard, giant forest hog and the rare pygmy hippo). The park is only accessible on foot (there are no roads) and consists largely of rainforest, which has never been logged, and hence makes it Western Africa's largest untouched tract of rainforest. The park's western boundary is formed by the **Sinoe River** and river trips on the Sinoe River are also available. For further information, contact the Ministry of Information, Culture and Tourism (see *Tourist Information*).

• **Swimming** and **boating** are popular at Liberia's many sandy beaches. These include **Bernard's Beach**, **Caesar's Beach**, **Cedar Beach**, **Cooper's Beach**, **Elwa Beach**, **Kendaje Beach**, **Kenema Beach and Sugar Beach**, all of which charge a small entrance fee. The skindiving season is from December to May, when the sea is at its clearest. There is good **fishing** in the **Mesurado and Saint Paul** rivers, along the coast and at Lake Piso, where there are traditional fishing villages.

TOURIST INFORMATION

Ministry of Information, Cultural Affairs and Tourism (MICAT)
110 United Nations Drive, PO Box 10-9021, Capitol Hill, 1000 Monrovia, Liberia
Tel: 226 269. Fax: 226 069.

Embassy of the Republic of Liberia in the UK
23 Fitzroy Square, London W1 6EW, UK
Tel: (020) 7388 5489. Fax: (020) 7380 1593.
Opening hours: Mon-Fri 1300-1600; Mon-Thurs 1030-1500 (visa section).
Also deals with tourism enquiries.

Embassy of the Republic of Liberia in the USA
5201 16th Street, NW, Washington, DC 20011, USA
Tel: (202) 723 0437.
Website: www.embassyofliberia.org

Entertainment

FOOD & DRINK: Liberia's hotels, motels and restaurants serve a variety of American, European, Asian, Chinese, Lebanese and African dishes, as well as the more predictable fare of hotel dining rooms. Here, as well as in the smaller towns of the north and east, the visitor should enjoy sampling some of the more unusual West African foods in 'cookhouses' which serve rice with traditional Liberian dishes. Liberia produces a lot of its own brands of alcoholic drink, which are readily available – some of the beers are excellent; wines and imported beverages are also available.
Tipping: There is no need to tip taxi drivers, but other tips are normally around 10 per cent.
NIGHTLIFE: In Monrovia, nightlife is extensive with dozens of crowded nightclubs, discos and bars open until the early hours. Most of the nightlife centres on Gurley Street. Providence Island has a bandstand and an amphitheatre where performances of traditional African music and dance are staged.
SHOPPING: Monrovia's sidestreets are crowded with tailors selling brightly coloured tie-dyed and embroidered cloth which they will make up immediately into African or European styles. Monrovia offers the shopper elegant boutiques and shops as well as modern, air-conditioned supermarkets which compete with old-fashioned stores. Liberian handicrafts include carvings in sapwood, camwood, ebony and mahogany, stone items, soapstone carvings (such as fertility symbols from the Kissi), ritual masks, metal jewellery and figurines and reed dolls of the Loma. **Shopping hours:** Mon-Sat 0800-1300 and 1500-1800.

Business

ECONOMY: The civil war caused severe damage to the economy and, following the peace settlement, reconstruction has been the highest priority. 70 per cent of the population work the land, producing rice and cassava as staple foods and palm oil, coffee and cocoa as cash crops. The country's principal export commodities are iron ore and rubber. Some gold and diamonds are also mined. The manufacturing industry – still operating far below capacity – produces cement and other building materials, chemicals, drinks and tobacco and consumer products. Liberia operates one of the longest established open registry (flag of convenience) merchant shipping fleets. This continues to be an essential source of foreign exchange and Government revenue. Liberia relies heavily on international aid and financial support. It is a member of the West African trading bloc ECOWAS. The USA is Liberia's largest trading partner, followed by Germany, Belgium, France and Italy.
BUSINESS ETIQUETTE: Business dress is informal – normally a shirt and tie is acceptable. The language used in business circles is English. **Office hours:** Mon-Fri 0800-1200 and 1400-1700.

COMMERCIAL INFORMATION

Liberia Chamber of Commerce
PO Box 92, Monrovia, Liberia
Tel: 222 040 *or* 223 738.

Libya

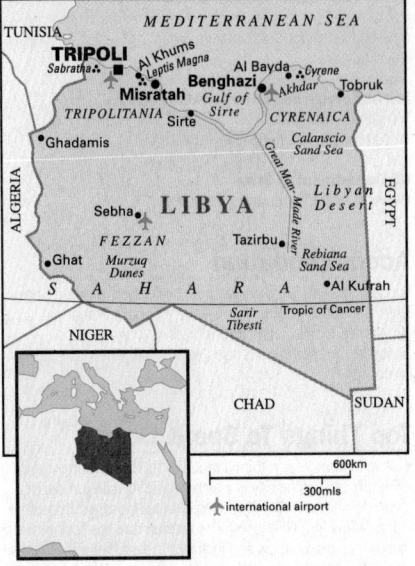

Location: North Africa.

Time: GMT + 2.

Overview

Present-day Libyans descend almost entirely from the Arabian incursion of the 11th century AD, with a few black Africans from the south and indigenous Berbers in the west. Although traditionally the rural people have been nomadic shepherds, since the discovery of oil there has been a drift into the towns. Once one of Italy's few colonies, Libya was occupied by the British and French during World War II. Under the United Nations' direction, the country was granted full independence in 1951. In 1969, a military coup, led by Colonel Muammar al-Gadhafi, occurred that not only radically altered Libyan politics, but brought the country to world attention. Domestically, Gadhafi embarked on the so-called Green Revolution (this was before the colour had become unequivocally associated with the worldwide environmental movement), whose ultimate aim is the creation of a *Jamahiriya* – literally a 'state of the masses'. Following the Libyan Government's political and practical support for a variety of revolutionary and terrorist groups, and its complicity in various acts of terrorism in the West, Libya became ostracised from the international community. The most serious of these were the destruction of two airliners: one French over the Sahara in 1987, the other American over the Scottish town of Lockerbie the following year. The West's response was to impose economic sanctions and to engage in a series of attempts to dispose of Gadhafi, all of which have failed. The Libyan Government has now made some reparations for its alleged misdeeds. By 2003, almost all sanctions had been lifted. Libya had opened up a number of new channels to the West. The most important of these is with Italy, with which Libya has important historic and economic links.

Just emerging from years of international isolation, Libya's beauty and diversity are still relatively unknown and, as a result, the country remains largely unspoilt by tourism. Visitors will enjoy exploring the bustling souks and Italian streets and squares of Tripoli and will be amazed by the spectacular remains of the Roman cities of Leptis Magna and Sabratha, testaments to ancient civilisations. They will also have plenty of opportunity to travel through the vast Saharan desert and camp amongst great sand seas, while appreciating Berber hospitality in Western Libya.

General Information

AREA: 1,775,500 sq km (685,520 sq miles).
POPULATION: 5.7 million (2003).
POPULATION DENSITY: 3.2 per sq km.
CAPITAL: Tripoli (Tarabulus). **Population:** 1.1 million (2003).
GEOGRAPHY: Libya consists mostly of huge areas of desert. It shares borders with Tunisia and Algeria in the west and Egypt in the east, while the Sahara extends across the southern frontiers with Niger, Chad and the Sudan. There are almost 2000km (1250 miles) of Mediterranean coast, with a low plain extending from the Tunisian border to the Jebel Akhdar (Green Mountain) area in the east. Inland the terrain becomes more hilly. Agriculture has developed mainly on the coast between Zuwarah and Misratah and from Marsa Susa to Benghazi in the east. In the uplands of the old province of Cyrenaica and on Jebel Akhdar the vegetation is more lush. With the exception of the 'Sand Sea' of the Sarir Calanscio, and the Saharan mountains of the Sarir Tibesti, there are oases scattered throughout the country.
GOVERNMENT: Jamahiriya (state of the masses). Gained independence from Italy in 1951. **Head of State:** Muammar al-Qadhafi (Leader of the Revolution) since 1969. **Head of Government:** Prime Minister Baghdadi Mahmudi replaced Shukri Muhammad Ghanim (Secretary of the General People's Committee) as Prime Minister in March 2006.
LANGUAGE: Arabic (which must be used for all official purposes), with some English or Italian. All road, shop and other signs are in Arabic. English is normally understood by people working in hotels, restaurants and shops.
RELIGION: Sunni Muslim.
ELECTRICITY: 220 volts AC, 40Hz. All services may be intermittently disrupted by power cuts.
SOCIAL CONVENTIONS: Life in Libya is regulated fairly strictly along socialist/Islamic principles; in general, Arab courtesies and social customs prevail and should be respected. Women do not generally attend typical Arab gatherings; see the *World of Islam* appendix for further information. In religious buildings and small towns, women should dress modestly. Beachwear must only be worn on the beach. Smoking is common and codes of practice concerning smoking are the same as in Europe.
Photography: It is unwise to use or carry cameras.

Climate

Summers are very hot and dry; winters are mild with cooler evenings. The desert has hot days and cold nights.

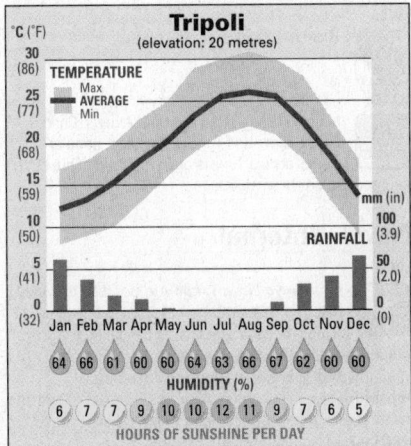

Tripoli
(elevation: 20 metres)

Communications

Telephone: IDD service is available. Country code: 218.
Mobile telephone: GSM 900 and 1800 networks in use. Network providers include *General Post* and *Telecommunications Company*, *El Madar* and *Orbit*.
Internet: ISPs include *Libya Telecom* and *Technology* (website: www.lttnet.com). There are Internet cafes in Tripoli and some other towns.
Post: Postal services are available in all main towns, but services are generally poor and erratic, and mail may be subject to censorship. Airmail to Europe takes approximately two weeks.
MEDIA: The state owns and controls all media. Criticism of Government policies is not allowed.
Press: There are several newspapers and periodicals, but none are published in English. The main dailies are *Al-Fajir al-Jadid* and *Az-zahf al-Akhdar*.
TV: *Great Jamahiriyah TV* is state-run and is available terrestrially and via satellite.
Radio: *Great Jamahiriyah Radio* is state-run; *Voice of Africa* is a state-run service, broadcasting in Arabic, English, French.

Credit: ©Bruce Logan

Passport/Visa

	Passport Required?	Visa Required?	Return Ticket? Required?
Full British	Yes	Yes	Yes
Australian	Yes	Yes	Yes
Canadian	Yes	Yes	Yes
USA	Yes	Yes	Yes
Other EU	Yes	Yes	Yes
Japanese	Yes	Yes	Yes

Note: *Regulations and requirements may be subject to change at short notice, and you are advised to contact the appropriate diplomatic or consular authority before finalising travel arrangements. Any numbers in the chart refer to the footnotes below.*

Restricted entry: (a) Holders of Israeli passports, or holders of passports containing a valid or expired visa for Israel will be refused entry or transit. (b) Children of nationals of Arab League countries will be refused entry if they are travelling alone, unless they are met at the airport by their husband/father or unless they are holding a 'No Objection Certificate', issued by the Libyan Immigration Department, and are met at the airport by the resident relative who made the application.
PASSPORTS: Passport valid for a minimum of six months required by all except Algeria, Bahrain, Egypt, Kuwait, Mauritania, Morocco, Oman, Qatar, Saudi Arabia, Tunisia and United Arab Emirates holding ID cards.
VISAS: Required by all except the following:
(a) nationals of Algeria, Bahrain, Egypt, Kuwait, Mauritania, Morocco, Oman, Qatar, Saudi Arabia, Sudan, Tunisia and United Arab Emirates;
(b) nationals of Jordan and the Syrian Arab Republic, provided arriving from their country of origin;
(c) transit passengers continuing their journey by the same or first connecting aircraft within 24 hours provided holding valid onward or return documentation and not leaving the airport.
Types of visa and cost: *Tourist/Business:* £20.
Validity: 45 days.
Application to: Any of Libya's diplomatic representatives in the relevant country or abroad (such as the Libyan People's Bureau in London; see *Passport/Visa Information*). Nationals of Germany must obtain their visas in Bonn/Berlin. Nationals of Canada *must* obtain their visas in Brussels, Belgium.
Application requirements: (a) One completed visa application form. (b) Four recent passport-size photos. (c) Valid passport. (d) Visa authorisation telex/invitation with reference number from Libya or travel agent. *Business:* (a)-(d) and, (e) Proof that they are sponsored by a Libyan company which will organise the issue of the visa.
Working days required: Two to three.

PASSPORT/VISA INFORMATION

Embassy of the Socialist People's Libyan Arab Jamahiriya in France
2 Rue Charles-Lamoureux, Paris 75116, France
Tel: (1) 4704 7160.

Libyan People's Bureau in the UK
61-62 Ennismore Gardens, London SW7 1NH, UK
Tel: (020) 7589 6120.
Opening hours: Mon-Wed 1000-1100 (visa application); Thurs 1400-1500 (visa collection).

Permanent Mission of the Great Socialist People's Libyan Arab Jamahiriya to the United Nations
309-315 East 48th Street, New York, NY 10017, USA
Tel: (212) 752 5775.
Website: www.libya-un.org

Money

Currency: Libyan Dinar (LYD) = 1000 dirhams. Notes are in denominations of LYD10, 5 and 1, and 500 and 250 dirhams. Coins are in denominations of 100, 50, 20, 10, 5 and 1 dirhams. Visitors must possess the foreign currency equivalent of at least LYD500 on arrival. ATMS in Tripoli are unreliable.
Credit & debit cards: Cash is almost always used. Limited acceptance of Diners Club and Visa. Check with your credit or debit card company for details of merchant acceptability and other services which may be available.
Traveller's cheques: Traveller's cheques are generally not accepted, owing to US government sanctions.
Currency restrictions: Free import of foreign currency, subject to declaration. Export of foreign currency is limited to the amount declared on arrival. The import and export of local currency is prohibited.
Banking hours: Sat-Wed 0800-1200 (winter); Sat-Thurs 0800-1200 and Sat-Wed 1600-1700 (summer).
Exchange rate indicators:
Rate at time of publishing
£1.00= LYD2.29
$1.00= LYD1.32

Duty Free

The following goods may be imported into Libya without incurring customs duty:
200 cigarettes or 250g of tobacco or 250g cigars; 250ml of perfume.
Prohibited items: All alcohol is prohibited, as is the import of obscene literature, pork, pork products and any kind of food (including tinned). All goods made in Israel or manufactured by companies that do business with Israel are prohibited, for instance Coca Cola and certain makes of CDs and tapes. For a full list of prohibited items, contact the nearest Libyan diplomatic representative.

Public Holidays

Below are listed Public Holidays for the January 2006-June 2007 period.
2006: Jan 10 Eid al-Adha (Feast of the Sacrifice). **Jan 31** Islamic New Year. **Feb 9** Ashoura. **Mar 3** Declaration of the Authority's Power. **Mar 28** British Evacuation Day. **Apr 11** Mouloud (Prophet's Birthday). **Jun 11** Evacuation Day. **Jul 23** Revolution Day. **Sep 1** National Day. **Oct 7** Italian Evacuation Day. **Oct 22-24** Eid al-Fitr (End of Ramadan). **Dec 31** Eid al-Adha (Feast of the Sacrifice).
2007: Jan 20 Islamic New Year. **Jan 29** Ashoura. **Mar 3** Declaration of the Authority's Power. **Mar 28** British Evacuation Day. **Mar 31** Mouloud (Prophet's Birthday). **Jun 11** Evacuation Day.
Note: Muslim festivals are timed according to local sightings of various phases of the moon and the dates given above are approximations. During the lunar month of Ramadan that precedes Eid al-Fitr, Muslims fast during the day and feast at night and normal business patterns may be interrupted. Many restaurants are closed during the day and there may be restrictions on smoking and drinking. Some disruption may continue into Eid al-Fitr itself. Eid al-Fitr and Eid al-Adha may last anything from two to 10 days, depending on the region. For more information see the *World of Islam* appendix.

Health

	Special Precautions?	Certificate Required?
Yellow Fever	No	1
Cholera	2	No
Typhoid & Polio	3	N/A
Malaria	4	N/A

Note: Regulations and requirements may be subject to change at short notice, and you are advised to contact your doctor well in advance of your intended date of departure. Any numbers in the chart refer to the footnotes below.

1: A *yellow fever* vaccination certificate is required from travellers arriving from infected areas.
2: Following WHO guidelines issued in 1973, a *cholera* vaccination certificate is not a condition of entry to Libya. However, cholera is a risk in this country and precautions are essential. Up-to-date advice should be sought before deciding whether these precautions should include vaccination, as medical opinion is divided over its effectiveness; see the *Health* appendix.
3: Immunisation against *typhoid* and *poliomyelitis* is often recommended.
4: A very limited *malaria* risk exists in the southwest of the country from February to August. No indigenous cases have been reported in recent years.
Food & drink: Mains water is normally chlorinated and, whilst relatively safe, may cause mild abdominal upsets. Bottled water is available and is advised for the first few weeks of the stay. Drinking water outside main cities and towns is likely to be contaminated and sterilisation is considered essential. Milk is unpasteurised and should be boiled. Powdered or tinned milk is available and is advised, but make sure that it is reconstituted with pure water. Avoid dairy products which are likely to have been made from unboiled milk. Only eat well-cooked meat and fish, preferably served hot. Salad and mayonnaise may carry increased risk. Vegetables should be cooked and fruit peeled.
Other risks: *Dysenteries, typhoid fever* and other *diarrhoeal diseases* are common. *Hepatitis A* and *E* occur throughout the area. *Bilharzia* (schistosomiasis) is present. Avoid swimming and paddling in fresh water; swimming pools which are well chlorinated and maintained are safe. Cases of *meningococcal meningitis* have been reported in the Sebha region.
Health care: Medical facilities outside the main cities are limited. Full health insurance is recommended.

Travel - International

AIR:
The national airline is *Jamahiriya Libyan Arab Airlines (LN)*. Other airlines that serve Libya include *Alitalia, British Airways, Lufthansa* and *Royal Jordanian*.
Approximate flight times: From Tripoli to *London* is four hours.
Main airports: *Tripoli International (TIP)* is 35km (22 miles) south of the city. Bus and taxi services are available to the city (travel time - 40 minutes). Airport facilities include chemist, post office, light refreshments, duty free shops, banks, restaurants and shops.
Benghazi International (BEN) is 19km (12 miles) from Benghazi city centre.
Sebha (SEB) is 11km (7 miles) from the town.
Departure tax: LYD6; children under two years of age and transit passengers, provided not leaving the airport and departing within 24 hours, are exempt.
SEA:
The main ports are Es-Sider, Benghazi, Darna, Mersa Brega, Misurata, El Mina and Tripoli. Several shipping lines operate services from Europe to Libya. A car ferry operated by the Libyan Government shipping line sails regularly from Tripoli to Malta and several Italian ports. Italian lines *Grimaldi* and *Tirrenia* run similar services from Genoa, Trapani and Naples to Tripoli and Benghazi. Other cruise lines include *P&O* and *Swan Hellenic*.
RAIL:
There is no passenger rail system.
ROAD:
Main routes to Libya are from Algeria, Chad, Egypt, Niger and Tunisia. The most popular routes are via Tunisia or Egypt. Several buses and taxis operate on these routes.

Travel - Internal

AIR:
Jamahiriya Libyan Arab Airlines (LN) provides fast and frequent internal services between Tripoli, Benghazi, Sebha, Al Bayda, Mersa Brega, Tobruk, Misratah, Ghadamis and Al Khufrah. They also offer an hourly shuttle between Tripoli and Benghazi.
Departure tax: LYD3; children under two years of age and transit passengers, provided not leaving the airport and departing within 24 hours, are exempt.
ROAD:
The main through-road follows the coast from west to east. Main roads are Al Qaddahia-Sebha, Sebha-Ghat, Tripoli- Sebha, Agedabia-Al Khufrah, Garian-Jefren, Tarhouna-Homs, Mersa Susa-Ras, Hilal-Derna and Tobruk-Jaghboub. Since 1969, signposts other than those in Arabic script have been prohibited; signs and house numbers are, in any case, rare outside the main towns. Petrol is available throughout Libya and is very reasonably priced. There are no reliable town maps. Spare parts are often difficult to obtain; in particular, automatic transmissions can prove almost impossible to repair. The quality of servicing is generally poor by European standards, as is the standard of driving. Traffic drives on the right. **Bus & taxi:** There are bus services between Tripoli and Benghazi and other major urban areas. A minibus service operates from Benghazi to Tobruk. Taxi fares can be quite expensive and should be agreed in advance. **Car hire:** Self-drive cars are available in Tripoli and Benghazi.
Documentation: National driving licence valid for three months. After this time, a Libyan licence must be obtained.
Note: Travellers visiting the desert regions require permission (a desert pass) from the Libyan authorities in advance. Tour operators can usually obtain these. Oil companies will provide passes for their employees.
URBAN:
A substantial publicly owned bus system operates in Tripoli. Fares are charged on a three-zone basis. There is a similar system in operation in Benghazi. Services are generally irregular and overcrowded.

Travel Advice

Travellers are advised against all but essential travel to areas bordering Chad and Sudan, because of instability in the region.
Libya shares with the rest of the North Africa region a threat from terrorism. Attacks could be indiscriminate and against civilian targets, including places frequented by foreigners. Travellers should avoid desert areas where oil extraction is in operation.
This advice is based on information provided by the Foreign and Commonwealth Office in the UK. It is correct at time of publishing. As the situation can change rapidly, visitors are advised to contact the following organisations for the latest travel advice:

British Foreign and Commonwealth Office
Tel: (0845) 850 2829.
Website: www.fco.gov.uk

US Department of State
Website: http://travel.state.gov/travel

Accommodation

Tripoli and Benghazi have several comfortable modern hotels. There are hotels in Al Bayda, Cyrene (Shahat), Derna, Ghadamès, Homs, Sabha and Tobruk.
Hostel accommodation is also available and there are some campsites.

Top Things To See & Do

- Libya's capital has retained much of its historical heritage; Tripoli's old walled city is a picturesque African jumble of narrow alleyways leading to traditional mosques, houses and *khans* (public houses). The architecture is a fusion of the country's many rulers and includes Turkish, Spanish, Maltese and Italian influences. Worth seeing is the ancient **Marcus Aurelian Arch**, the **Al Nagha** and **Ahmed Pash** mosques, and some of the many vibrant *souks* (markets) in the heart of **Medina** (Tripoli's centre).
- Situated on a promontory above the city is **Assai al-Hamra** (Red Castle); a spectacular fortress stretching over an area of approximately 13,000 sq metres, that houses a maze of courtyards and buildings. Next to the castle on the **Green Square** is the **Jamahiriya Museum** that was designed in conjunction with UNESCO. Classical artefacts such as ancient mosaics and statues are among the extensive collection displayed here. Visitors to the city can also enjoy a number of beautiful Mediterranean beaches.
- **Leptis Magna:** This historical town lies 120km (75 miles) east of Tripoli overlooking the Mediterranean. This incredible archaeological site was originally a port, built by the Phoenicians in the first millennium BC. After that it became a Roman settlement and today many of the ruins from that time remain preserved. Among the things to see are the **Severan Arch** (erected in honour of Emperor Septimus Severus), the marble- and granite-lined **Hadrianic Baths**, a detailed basilica and an amphitheatre.
- In the Eastern region, **Benghazi** is Libya's second-largest city, located on the Eastern edge of the Gulf of Sirte. Far more commercial and less aesthetically pleasing than Tripoli, Benghazi is nevertheless a popular tourist spot due to its close proximity to a number of beautiful beaches. **Ras Alteen** is a nearby beach with pristine white sands. It has recently been the location of an amazing archaeological discovery where Greek and Byzantine graves from a colossal underwater city were recovered. Other historical sites include the battlefield of **Tobruk**, 140km east of Ras Alteen, and the town of **Cyrene**, 245km east of Benghazi. The lush forested range of the Green Mountains is easily reached from Benghazi and Ras Alteen and is a great area for walking. A suspended cave named after the apostle Mark, who was thought to have been raised in the **Green Mountains**, can be found in the **Marcus Valley**.
- In the Western region, **Ghadames**, known as the 'Pearl of the Desert', is a unique desert oasis town 800km (500 miles) southwest of Tripoli. The old town's unique architecture consists of white-washed mud walls and covered labyrinthine walkways that are only lit by overhead skylights and open squares. Worth seeing are the **D'jmaa al-Kabir** mosque, where the minaret can be climbed for a wonderful panorama of the city; **Mulberry Square**, site of the old slave market; and the **House Museum**, that displays traditional mercantile furnishings.
- Nearby are the **Zallaf Sand Dunes**, home to the native Tuareg tribe. Saline lakes with high mineral content and palm trees surround the dunes. In this unusual environment visitors can enjoy relaxing sand baths and salt-lake bathing.
- There are good beaches for **swimming** away from the municipal beaches of Tripoli and Benghazi.

Credit: ©Bruce Logan

TOURIST INFORMATION

Embassy of the Socialist People's Libyan Arab Jamahiriya in France
2 Rue Charles-Lamoureux, Paris 75116, France
Tel: (1) 4704 7160.

Entertainment

FOOD & DRINK: Since alcohol was banned by the Government in 1969, many restaurants have closed, and those remaining are very expensive. Hotel restaurants, although not particularly good, are therefore often the only eating places. Most restaurants have table service and, although food is traditionally eaten with the right hand only, knives and forks will generally be available.

National specialities:
- *couscous*, a dish based on savoury semolina that can be combined with chicken, lamb or vegetables and is a staple dish in many northern African countries.
- *Ruuz*, a rice dish with a variety of spices, meat and vegetables.

Tipping: A tip of 10 to 20 per cent is usually included in hotel and restaurant bills.

NIGHTLIFE: All nightclubs and bars have been closed. There are several cinemas in major towns, some showing foreign films. There are no theatres or concert halls.

SHOPPING: *Souks* in the main towns are the workplaces of many weavers, copper-, gold- and silversmiths and leatherworkers. There are numerous other stalls selling a variety of items including spices, metal engravings and various pieces of jewellery.

Business

ECONOMY: Oil- and gas-related industries account for the bulk of Libya's economy; 95 per cent of export earnings come from oil. The high quality of Libyan oil has produced strong demand from consumers so that, despite relatively small reserves, Libya has been able to sustain high production levels of around 1.5 million barrels per day. The recent discovery of large deposits is a further bonus. Oil revenues have enabled the Government to build up the country's economic infrastructure virtually from scratch since the early 1970s. However, low world oil prices and UN sanctions brought the economy to a virtual standstill during the 1990s, undermining economic development and forcing the cancellation of a number of large projects. By 2003 though, the Libyan Government's rapprochement with the international community, and more favourable conditions in the world oil market, had allowed the resumption of economic growth. Outside the oil and gas industry, agriculture is almost entirely geared to domestic consumption: animal husbandry is the most important part of this, but crops including barley and wheat are also grown in the country's few fertile areas. An industrial sector producing petrochemicals, iron, steel and aluminium has also been developed. Libya is a member of the Arab Development Bank, the Union of the Arab Maghreb and various other pan-Arab economic organisations. It is also a member of the Organisation of Petroleum Exporting Countries (OPEC). Italy and Germany are Libya's major trading partners.

BUSINESS ETIQUETTE: Shirt sleeves are acceptable business wear in hot weather. Suits and ties are worn for more formal occasions. Most business dealings take place with state organisations and English is often understood. It is, however, Government policy for official documents to be in Arabic (or translated into Arabic) and for official business to be conducted in Arabic. Business visitors need to be fully prepared for this. Appointments are necessary and business cards are useful, though not widely used. Hours for businesses and Government offices fluctuate, but the working day starts early. **Office hours:** Generally Sat-Wed 0700-1400.

COMMERCIAL INFORMATION

Tripoli Chamber of Commerce, Industry and Agriculture
PO Box 2321, Tripoli, Lybia
Tel: (21) 333 3755.

Liechtenstein

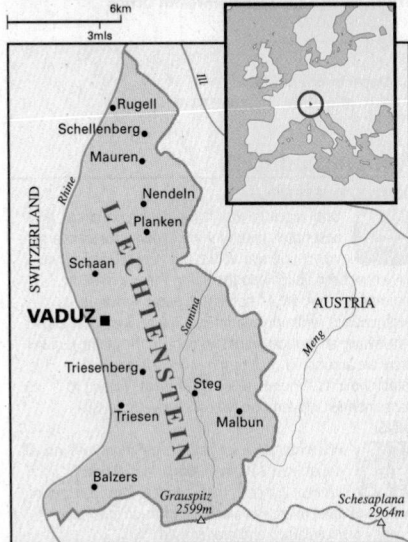

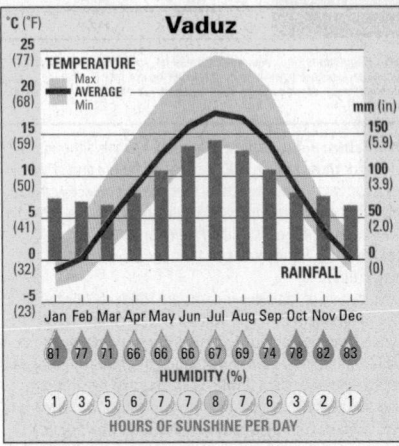

Location: Western Europe.

Time: GMT + 1 (GMT + 2 from last Sunday in March to last Sunday in October).

Overview

The Principality of Liechtenstein covers both lowlands – including part of the fertile Rhine Valley and the steep western slope of the Three Sisters massif – and mountains. The latter are in the eastern part of the country and are accessible through three high valleys, the best known being that of Malbun, Liechtenstein's premier ski resort. Like neighbouring Austria and Switzerland, Liechtenstein has excellent wintersports facilities (though on a comparatively small scale).

In summer, hikers and ramblers may wish to explore Liechtenstein's vineyards, forests and nature reserves. The principality's mountains attract climbers of all abilities. For the less energetic, there are several tourist sites of interest.

General Information

AREA: 160 sq km (61.8 sq miles).
POPULATION: 34,294 (2004).
POPULATION DENSITY: 211.6 per sq km.
CAPITAL: Vaduz. **Population:** 5,038 (2002).
GEOGRAPHY: Liechtenstein shares borders with Austria and Switzerland and lies between the upper reaches of the Rhine Valley and the Austrian Alps. The principality is noted for its fine vineyards.
GOVERNMENT: Imperial Principality with a hereditary constitutional monarchy. Principality established in 1719.
Head of State: Prince Hans Adam II since 1989. **Head of Government:** Prime Minister Otmar Hasler since 2001.
LANGUAGE: German; a dialect of Alemannish is widely spoken. English is also widely spoken.
RELIGION: Christian, predominantly Roman Catholic (78 per cent).
ELECTRICITY: 230 volts AC, 50Hz. European two-pin plugs are used.
SOCIAL CONVENTIONS: Similar to northwest Europe. Regulations concerning smoking are becoming increasingly strict.

www.gocoti.com

Climate

Liechtenstein has a temperate, alpine climate, with warm, wet summers and mild winters.

Required clothing: Mediumweights with some lightweight clothing is advised for summer. Warmer heavyweights are worn in winter. Waterproofs are needed throughout the year.

Communications

Telephone: Full IDD service. Country code: 423. Outgoing international code: 00.
Mobile telephone: GSM 900/1800 network. Handsets can be hired at the Telecom shop in Vaduz. Main network operators include *Mobilkom* (website: www.mobilkom.li), *Orange, Swisscom Mobile* (website: www.swisscom-mobile.ch) and *Tele2* (website: www.tele2.li).
Internet: Internet access is available in phone booths operated by Swisscom. Charges are payable by phonecard or credit card. Public access is also available at the Telecom shop in Vaduz. ISPs include *LIE-NET* (website: www.lie-net.li).
Post: Post office hours: Mon-Fri 0730-1200 and 1345-1830, Sat 0800-1100, (Mon-Fri 0745-1800, Sat 0800-1100 in Vaduz). Post to European destinations takes three to four days.
MEDIA: Viewers rely on foreign and satellite broadcasters for most services.
Press: There are two daily newspapers, *Liechtensteiner Vaterland* and *Liechtensteiner Volksblatt*, and two weekly papers, *Apotheke und Marketing* and *Liechtensteiner Wochenzeitung*. All are published in German.
Radio: *Radio Liechtenstein*.

Passport/Visa

The passport and visa requirements for persons visiting Liechtenstein are the same as for Switzerland. For further details, see the *Switzerland* section.

Money

Currency: Swiss Franc (CHF) = 100 centimes. For further information on currency, currency exchange, credit cards, traveller's cheques, exchange rates and currency restrictions, see the *Switzerland* section.
Banking hours: Mon-Fri 0830-1630.

Duty Free

The customs regulations for persons visiting Liechtenstein are the same as for Switzerland. For further details, see the *Switzerland* section.

Public Holidays

Below are listed Public Holidays for the January 2006-June 2007 period.
2006: Jan 1 New Year's Day. **Jan 2** St Berchtold's Day. **Jan 6** Epiphany. **Feb 2** Candlemas. **Feb 28** Shrove Tuesday. **Mar 19** Feast of St Joseph. **Apr 14** Good Friday. **Apr 17** Easter Monday. **May 1** Labour Day. **May 25** Ascension. **Jun 5** Whit Monday. **Jun 15** Corpus Christi. **Aug 15** Assumption. **Sep 8** Nativity of Our Lady. **Nov 1** All Saints' Day. **Dec 8** Immaculate Conception. **Dec 25** Christmas Day. **Dec 26** St Stephen's Day. **Dec 31** New Year's Eve.
2007: Jan 1 New Year's Day. **Jan 2** St Berchtold's Day. **Jan 6** Epiphany. **Feb 2** Candlemas. **Feb 20** Shrove Tuesday. **Mar 19** Feast of St Joseph. **Apr 6** Good Friday. **Apr 9** Easter Monday. **May 1** Labour Day. **May 20** Ascension. **May 28** Whit Monday. **Jun 7** Corpus Christi.

A B C D E F G H I J K L M N O P Q R S T U V W X Y Z

A B C D E F G H I J K L M N O P Q R S T U V W X Y Z

Health

	Special Precautions?	Certificate Required?
Yellow Fever	No	No
Cholera	No	No
Typhoid & Polio	No	N/A
Malaria	No	N/A

Note: *Regulations and requirements may be subject to change at short notice, and you are advised to contact your doctor well in advance of your intended date of departure. Any numbers in the chart refer to the footnotes below.*

Other risks: *Rabies* is present in some animals although risk is low. For those at high risk, vaccination before arrival should be considered. If you are bitten, seek medical advice without delay. Post-exposure treatment should be readily available. For more information, consult the *Health* appendix.

Health care: European Economic Area (EEA) and Switzerland:

If you or any of your dependants are suddenly taken ill or have an accident during a visit to an EEA country or Switzerland, free or reduced-cost necessary treatment is available – in most cases on production of a valid European Health Insurance Card (EHIC). Each country has different rules about state medical provision. In some, treatment is free. In many countries you will have to pay part or all of the cost, and then claim a full or partial refund. The EHIC gives access to state-provided medical treatment only and the scheme gives no entitlement to medical repatriation costs, nor does it cover ongoing illnesses of a non-urgent nature, so comprehensive travel insurance is advised. Note that the EHIC replaces the Form E111, which is no longer valid since 31 December 2005. Some restrictions apply, depending on your nationality. All other international travellers are strongly advised to take out full medical insurance before departure.Please note that Swiss nationals and people who do not have UK, EU or EEA nationality are not covered by the EHIC in Liechtenstein.

You can see any doctor covered by a contract with the public healthcare scheme. You will have to pay a standard fee. There is no state dental treatment, and you will have to pay the costs of private treatment in full. There is only one hospital in Liechtenstein, but the standard of medical facilities is very good. The competent authority should approve your admission, although no approval is needed in an emergency. More information can be obtained from *Amt für Volkswirtschaft* (National Office of Economy), Austrasse 15, 9490 Vaduz.

Travel - International

AIR:

The nearest international airport (and the most convenient for travel from the UK) is Zurich. For details of airlines serving the airport, see *Switzerland* section.

Approximate flight times: From Zurich to *London* is one hour 30 minutes.

Main airports: *Zurich (ZRH)* (Kloten) (website: www.zurich-airport.com) is approximately 130km (81 miles) from Vaduz. Travel to Liechtenstein from Zurich can be continued by rail, bus or road. An autoroute connects the city with Liechtenstein (first exit: Balzers; further exits: Vaduz, Schaan, Bendern and Ruggell). Cars can be hired through agencies at the airport for this journey, and in Liechtenstein.

Departure tax: None.

RAIL:

The best rail access is via the Swiss border stations at Buchs (SG) or Sargans (easier and closer when coming from Zurich) or the Austrian station at Feldkirch. All are well served by express trains and connected with Vaduz by bus. From Buchs it takes only 15 minutes by bus or 10 minutes by taxi.

ROAD:

An autoroute (N13) runs along Liechtenstein's Rhine frontier to Lake Constance, Austria and Germany in the north, and southwards past Chur towards St Moritz. To the west, there are autoroutes to Zurich, Berne and Basel. Traffic drives on the right. *Eurotunnel* operates trains 24 hours per day through the Channel Tunnel between Folkestone in Kent (with direct access from the M20) and Calais in France, from where you can drive to Liechtenstein. For further information, see *Travel - International* in the France section or contact Eurotunnel Reservations (tel: (08705) 353 535; website: www3.eurotunnel.com). **Bus:** Local buses operate between all 11 villages, and to the Liechtenstein alpine area.

Documentation: A national driving licence is sufficient.

Travel times: The following chart gives approximate travel times (in hours and minutes) from **Vaduz** to major cities in Europe.

	Road	Rail
Zurich	1.30	1.30
Geneva	4.00	5.00
Munich	3.00	4.30
Milan	4.30	5.30
Paris	10.00	9.00

Travel Advice

Most visits to Liechtenstein are trouble-free but you should be aware of the global risk of indiscriminate international terrorist attacks, which could be against civilian targets, including places frequented by foreigners.

This advice is based on information provided by the Foreign and Commonwealth Office in the UK. It is correct at time of publishing. As the situation can change rapidly, visitors are advised to contact the following organisations for the latest travel advice:

British Foreign and Commonwealth Office
Tel: (0845) 850 2829.
Website: www.fco.gov.uk

US Department of State
Website: http://travel.state.gov/travel

Accommodation

HOTELS/GUEST HOUSES:

Until recently, with few notable exceptions, the best hotels (although none of deluxe standard) were in or near Vaduz, but new establishments have now been built along the Rhine Valley and in the mountains. There are 44 hotels and guest houses in Liechtenstein, with approximately 1300 beds in total. Eight hotels have an indoor swimming pool. In the alpine region, there are around 40 chalets and other self-catering establishments. Around 165 establishments belong to Gastronomie Liechtenstein (website: www.hotels.li).

INNS:

A Liechtenstein speciality is the mountain inn. All are at least 1200m (4000ft) up, but easily accessible by car. They are ideal for those seeking peace and quiet and clean air. Some of these inns have recently been enlarged and modernised.

ALPINE HUTS:

There are alpine huts at: Gafadura, 1428m (4284ft) high, which accommodates 47; Bettlerjoch Pfälzer-Hütte, 2111m (6333ft) high, which accommodates 80; and at Triesenberg-Malbun which sleeps 45; check online (website: www.alpenverein.li).

CAMPING:

Campsites exist at Mittagspitze, FL-9495 Triesen (tel: 392 2311 *or* 392 3677) and Bendern, FL-9487 Bendern.

HOLIDAY APARTMENTS/CHALETS:

Contact the local tourist offices in Malbun, Triesenberg or Vaduz for information.

YOUTH HOSTELS:

Liechtenstein's only youth hostel, Youth Hostel Schaan-Vaduz, is between Schaan and Vaduz, 500m (1640ft) away from the main road. It has sleeping accommodation for 110 in a variety of room sizes.

Top Things To See & Do

- In the capital, **Vaduz**, the **Postage Stamp Museum (Postal Museum)**, the **National Library**, the **Ski Museum**, and the **National Museum** are worth visiting. The **Liechtenstein Art Museum**, housed in a specially designed building, contains the treasures of the Prince's collection, including works by Rembrandt, Rubens and Van Dyck, as well as modern art from the former Liechtenstein State Art Collection. Wine tasting groups of 10 or more people are welcome in the **Prince's Wine Cellars** in Vaduz, subject to reservation (tel: 232 1018; fax: 233 1145; e-mail: office@hofkellerei.li; website: www.hofkellerei.li). A 'City Train' will take visitors around the sights on a 30-minute tour.
- There are local museums in **Triesenberg** (the **Walser Museum**) and **Schellenberg-Ruggell**. **Schaan** is noted for its theatre, its Roman excavations, the **St Maria zum Trost Chapel** and **DoMus – Museum and Gallery of the Community of Schaan**. Also of interest are the **Gutenberg Castle** and **St Peter's Chapel** at Balzers; the **St Mamerten** and **Maria Chapels** and the old part of the village in **Triesen**; the **Chapel of St Joseph** in **Planken**; the Roman excavations at **Eschen-Nendeln**; the parish churches in **Bendern**, **Mauren** and **Ruggell**; and the ruins of the upper and lower **Burg Schellenberg**.
- The winter sports area is concentrated around **Malbun** at 1600m (5250ft) and **Steg** at 1300m (4250ft). At Malbun, there are two chair lifts, four ski lifts and a natural ice rink. Steg has become famous for its popular cross-country skiing loop with three distances – 4km (2.5 miles), 12km (7 miles), 12.5km (7.8 miles) – which is also equipped for use at night. Steg also has a ski lift and sledge-run.
- In the summer, all the resorts are good starting points for **walking tours**. **Gaflei** at 1500m (4920ft) is the starting point for the Fürstensteig, a path along the high ridge dividing the Rhine and Samina valleys. **Cycling** is possible in the valleys and lower-lying areas, and there are 96km (56 miles) of cycling trails on both sides of the River Rhine. **Mountain bikers** may also use the hiking trails. Bicycles can be hired at cycling shops. **Paragliding** is gaining in popularity. Excursions can be arranged with specialist operators; contact the tourist board for further information.

TOURIST INFORMATION

Switzerland Tourism in the UK
30 Bedford Street, London WC2E 9ED, UK
Tel: (00800) 1002 0030 (toll-free in Europe) *or* (020) 7420 4900.
Website: http://uk.myswitzerland.com
Opening hours: Mon-Fri 0900-1700; Thurs 1000-1700.

Switzerland Tourism in the USA
608 Fifth Avenue, New York, NY 10020, USA
Tel: (212) 757 5944 *or* (877) 794 8037 (toll-free in USA) *or* (011800) 1002 0030 (toll-free international) *or* (800) 794 7763 (travel trade).
Website: www.myswitzerland.com

Entertainment

FOOD & DRINK: The cuisine is Swiss with Austrian overtones and there are numerous restaurants. All internationally known beverages are obtainable. There are strict laws against drinking and driving.

National specialities:
- *Käseknöpfle*, small dumplings with cheese.

National drinks:
- *Vaduzer* (red wine). **Tipping:** A service charge will be included in most bills.

NIGHTLIFE: There are cinemas at Vaduz and Balzers. Dancing can be enjoyed at the *Maschlina-Bar* and the *Hubraum* in Triesen; *Tiffany* in Eschen; *Derby* in Schaanwald; and *Pacha* and *Schlosshof* at Balzers.

SHOPPING: Prices and the range of goods are the same as in Switzerland. Specialist buys include handmade ceramics, pottery and Liechtenstein postage stamps. **Shopping hours:** Generally Mon-Fri 0800-1200 and 1330-1830, Sat 0800-1600. From April to October, souvenir stores in Vaduz are open Sunday and holidays.

Business

ECONOMY: The population of Liechtenstein is amongst the world's most prosperous. Financial services are the main component of the economy: over 75,000 foreign corporations have taken advantage of the principality's banking secrecy laws to establish nominee companies which pay low taxes on both income and profits. Fees from these companies provide about one-third of Government revenues. Since the mid-1990s, Liechtenstein has come under sustained pressure to deal with money laundering and other financial malpractice. In April 2002, Liechtenstein was strongly condemned by the Organisation for Economic Co-operation and Development (the 24-strong club of industrialised nations) as one of seven countries worldwide which had refused to cooperate properly and continually faces economic sanctions.

The country has vital economic links with Switzerland, based upon a customs union, and uses the Swiss franc as currency. Other than Switzerland, most of Liechtenstein's trade is conducted with members of the EU.

BUSINESS ETIQUETTE: Personal visits and the following of all business formalities are very important. Times to avoid business visits include the Easter holiday, the second half of July and August, and the week after Christmas. **Office hours:** Generally Mon-Fri 0800-1200 and 1400-1700.

CONFERENCES/CONVENTIONS: Although there is no conference association in Liechtenstein, a number of hotels have conference facilities and can organise conventions: Löwen in Vaduz, Schaanerhof in Schaan, Meierhof in Triesen, Kulm in Triesenberg, Gorfion and Malbuner-Hof in Malbun/Triesenberg. Website: www.lihk.li

COMMERCIAL INFORMATION

Liechtensteinische Industrie und Handelskammer (Chamber of Industry and Commerce)
Josef Rheinberger-Strasse 11, FL-9490 Vaduz, Liechtenstein
Tel: 237 5511.

Lithuania

Location: Northern Europe.

Time: GMT + 2 (GMT + 3 from last Sunday in March to last Sunday in October).

Overview

Present-day Lithuanians are descendants of the Balts, an Indo-European ethnic group that settled on the Baltic coast 4000 years ago. At the Union of Lublin in 1569, a full-scale merger between Lithuania and Poland took place. However, the ensuing centuries showed that this was insufficient to protect Lithuania from the territorial ambitions of other regional powers. At the end of the 18th century, the Joint Republic was carved up and occupied in successive partitions. Russia took possession of part of Lithuania in 1795 (the western region was claimed by Prussia) and held on to it until the early 20th century. The Russians were driven out by the German army during World War I and the Lithuanian Council declared independence in February 1918. In 1921, Lithuania joined the League of Nations. Although the Lithuanians had settled their differences with the Russians, temporarily at least, the Poles continued to occupy Vilnius, the Lithuanian capital, in defiance of Allied demarcation which had awarded the city to the Lithuanians. The capital of the new state was therefore established at Kaunas. The Lithuanian constitution in 1922 declared Lithuania to be a parliamentary republic. However, a military coup in 1926 brought Antanas Smetona to power at the head of an authoritarian regime. The status of Lithuania was again altered following the Nazi-Soviet Pact of 1939, whose secret protocols allowed for a Soviet takeover of all three Baltic Republics. Lithuania was occupied by the German Army in 1941 until its re-annexation by the Soviets three years later.
When Mikhail Gorbachev came to power in the Kremlin in 1985, pressure for political and economic reform in Lithuania grew. This was spearheaded by the *Sajudis*, the Lithuanian Reform Movement. Moscow responded initially with selective economic sanctions, and then military deployments to deter the pro-independence elements. Despite occupying radio, TV and other key installations, the Soviet forces were forced to back down in the face of a referendum on independence which won 90 per cent support. This decisive period in recent Lithuanian history finished with the failed coup against Gorbachev in August 1991 and the effective end to Soviet Government. Lithuanian independence followed immediately, unopposed and by default.
The transition to a full market economy began; by 1995 it had been more or less completed. The long-running border dispute with Poland was settled with the signing of a friendship and co-operation treaty in January 1992, and

negotiations with Russia led to the withdrawal of the remaining Russian troops in Lithuania in August 1993. Such events have led up to the country joining the EU in May 2004. EU membership has catapulted Lithuania onto the global stage, with more and more people becoming aware of the country's rich panoply of castles, lakes and forests, and more people flocking to see Vilnius, one of Europe's most enchanting cities.

General Information

AREA: 65,300 sq km (25,212 sq miles).
POPULATION: 3.43 million (Census, 2005).
POPULATION DENSITY: 52.5 per sq km.
CAPITAL: Vilnius. **Population:** 541,300 (Census, 2005).
GEOGRAPHY: Lithuania is situated on the eastern Baltic coast and borders Latvia in the north, the Kaliningrad region of the Russian Federation and Poland in the southwest, and Belarus in the southwest and east. The geometrical centre of Europe lies in eastern Lithuania near the village of Bernotai, 25km (16 miles) north of Vilnius. The landscape alternates between lowland plains and hilly uplands and has a dense, intricate network of rivers, including the Nemunas and the Neris. 1.5 per cent of the country's territory is made up of lakes, of which there are over 2800. The majority of these lie in the east of the country and include Lake Druksiai and Lake Tauragnas.
GOVERNMENT: Republic. Gained independence from Russia/Germany 1918-1940, and then from the Soviet Union in 1990. **Head of State:** President Valdas Adamkus since 2004. **Head of Government:** Prime Minister Algirdas Mykolas Brazauskas since 2001. **Recent history:** Domestic politics in the immediate post-Soviet era were dominated by the struggle between the Democratic Labour Party – which grew out of the former Lithuanian Communist Party – and centre-right, liberal and nationalist groupings based around *Sajudis*, the Lithuanian Reform Movement, which put forward a programme of democratic and national rights coupled with support for an independent Lithuania in the mid-1980s. More recently, new political formations have tended to organise around a prominent individual, such as Algirdas Brazauskas who has given his name to the four-party social democratic coalition which won the most recent *Seimas* (Parliament) Election in October 2000. In 2001, Brazauskas recovered the Premiership personally and has since held onto the post. The Presidency was most recently contested in December 2002. The incumbent Valdas Adamkus, a recent returnee from the United States who was the surprise winner in 1998, was the clear leader after the first round. However, at the second stage run-off the following month, he was surprisingly defeated by a former Soviet aerobatics champion, Rolandas Paksas.
Under the constitution adopted in October 1992, legislative authority rests with the popularly elected *Seimas*, the Parliament, with 141 Government members. The President is the Head of State and is elected for a five-year term by universal adult suffrage. Executive power is vested in the Government, consisting of the Prime Minister, who is appointed by the President with approval of the *Seimas* and his cabinet.
LANGUAGE: Lithuanian is the official language. Lithuania has a large number of dialects for such a small territory, including High Lithuanian (*Aukstaiciai*) and Low Lithuanian (*Zemaiciai*).
RELIGION: Predominantly Roman Catholic with Evangelical Lutheran, Evangelical Reformist, Sunite, Baptist, Muslim, Judaic, Karaite and others.
ELECTRICITY: 220 volts AC, 50Hz. European two-pin plugs are in use.
SOCIAL CONVENTIONS: Handshaking is customary. Normal courtesies should be observed. The Lithuanians are proud of their culture and their national heritage and visitors should take care to respect this sense of national identity.

Climate

Temperate climate, but with considerable temperature variations. Summer is warm with relatively mild weather in spring and autumn. Winter, which lasts from November to mid-March, can be very cold. Rainfall is distributed throughout the year with the heaviest rainfall in August. Heavy snowfalls are common in the winter months.

Credit: ©Lithuanian State Dep't of Tourism

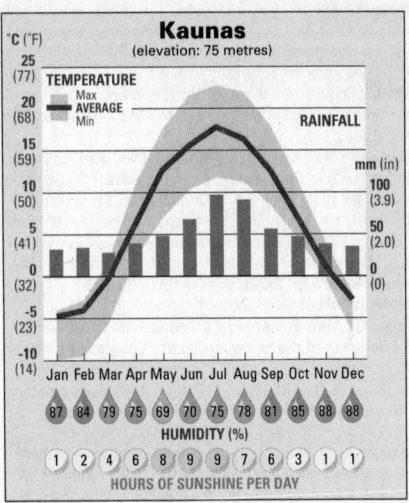

Communications

Telephone: IDD is available. Country code: 370. City codes: 2 for Vilnius, 7 for Kaunas, 6 for Klaipeda. There are two kinds of payphone: rectangular telephones which take magnetic strip cards and rounded telephones which take chip cards. Phonecards are sold at kiosks and post offices. Plans are underway to introduce one type of phonecard, compatible with both phones.
Mobile telephone: Roaming agreements exist with most international mobile phone companies. Coverage is very good country-wide.
Internet: Internet is available; public access is at the Lithuanian National Library and increasingly at Internet centres and cafes in main cities and towns.
Post: Post to Western Europe takes up to six days. There is a variety of private companies offering express mail services.
MEDIA: Lithuania's TV market is dominated by commercial channels. The radio market is similarly competitive, with more than 30 stations competing for listeners and advertisers. Lithuania's media are free and operate independently of the state, and there are no Government-owned newspapers. However, politicians do occasionally attempts to influence editorial policy.
Press: Newspapers are published in Lithuanian and some in Russian or Polish. The major dailies are *Kauno Diena*, *Lietuvos Rytas*, *Respublika* and *Lietuvos Zinios*.
TV: Public broadcaster *Lithuanian National Radio and Television* (*LRT*) operates one national TV channel. In early 2003, LRT launched a cultural TV channel, initially available in Vilnius and Kaunas. Commercial stations include *LNK TV*, *TV3* and *TV4*.
Radio: *LRT* operates two national radio networks. Commerical radio stations include *M-1* (pop music and news), *Radiocentras* (pop music) and *Pukas*.

Passport/Visa

	Passport Required?	Visa Required?	Return Ticket? Required?
Full British	1	No	No
Australian	Yes	No	No
Canadian	Yes	No	No
USA	Yes	No	No
Other EU	1	No	No
Japanese	Yes	No	No

Note: Regulations and requirements may be subject to change at short notice, and you are advised to contact the appropriate diplomatic or consular authority before finalising travel arrangements. Any numbers in the chart refer to the footnotes below.

PASSPORTS: Passport valid for at least three months beyond the length of stay required by all except:
(a) **1.** EU/EEA nationals (EU+ Iceland, Liechtenstein, Norway) and Swiss nationals holding a valid national ID card.
Note: EU and EEA nationals are only required to produce evidence of their EU/EEA nationality and identity in order to be admitted to any EU/EEA Member State. This evidence can take the form of a valid national passport *or* national identity card. Either is acceptable. Possession of a return ticket, any length of validity on their document, sufficient funds for the length of their proposed visit should *not* be imposed.
Note: There is now a new application form that those seeking visas must fill out, consistent with the visa forms of other European Union member states, which Lithuania

joined on May 1 2004. At present, the Lithuanian visa will only be valid for travelling to Lithuania but will become valid for travelling to other *Schengen* countries once Lithuania joins the *Schengen* area.

VISAS: Required by all except the following:
(a) nationals listed in the chart above for tourist stays of up to 90 days;
(b) nationals of Andorra, Argentina, Bolivia, Brazil, Brunei, Bulgaria, Chile, Costa Rica, Croatia, El Salvador, Guatemala, Honduras, Hong Kong (SAR), Iceland, Israel, Korea (Rep), Liechtenstein, Macau (SAR), Malaysia, Mexico, Monaco, New Zealand, Nicaragua, Norway, Panama, Paraguay, Romania, San Marino, Singapore, Switzerland, Uruguay, Vatican City and Venezuela for tourist stays of up to 90 days.

Note: (a) Nationals of South Africa holding valid Estonian or Latvian visas *do not* need a separate visa for Lithuania. (b) Nationals of the following countries may apply for a Lithuanian visa without first obtaining an invitation endorsed by the Lithuanian Migration Authorities: Belarus (maximum of 30 days), Bermuda, Ecuador, Kazakhstan (maximum of 30 days), Moldova, Russian Federation (maximum of 30 days), South Africa, Taiwan (maximum of 30 days) and Ukraine (maximum of 30 days). Nationals of Belarus, Kazakhstan, Taiwan, the Russian Federation and Ukraine are required to present proof of sufficient funds (minimum €40 or £27 per day), via traveller's cheques, credit cards and bank statements. Enquire at the Consulate/Embassy for details.

Types of visa and cost: *Short-stay*, *Airport-transit* and *Transit*: €35; *Long-stay* (single-entry) and *Special-entry* (for employment or studies): €60; *Group single-entry* (five to 30 members with appointed guide and on the condition that group have same purpose of visit, follow same travel itinerary with same arrivals, departures and locations): €35 plus €1 per person. Consular fees are waived in certain circumstances; consult Embassy/Consulate for details. There is no Consular fee for members for certain charity missions, official delegations, those aged under 16 years, and Lithuanians travelling with foreign passports.

Validity: *Single-* and *Multiple-entry*: Three months. In some cases, a multiple-entry visa may be issued for up to one or even five years. Documents must be submitted that prove the need for a multiple-entry visa and warrant amount of validity allocated. *Transit*: No more than five days each stay. *Airport Transit*: 48 hours.

Application to: Consulate (or Consular section at Embassy); *Passport/Visa Information*.

Application requirements: (a) Passport valid for at least three months after expiry of visa. (b) One passport-size photo. (c) Completed application form. (d) Letter of invitation endorsed by the Lithuanian Migration Authorities (not required by certain nationals - see note above). (e) Fee. (f) Other documents, such as hotel reservations, tickets, right to return country form/right to travel to onward country, documents certifying payment of consular fee, and bank statements may be required. (g) Valid health and travel insurance. *Transit* and *Airport Transit*: (a)-(g) and, (h) Visa and/or other documents granting right to enter country of destination.

Working days required: Five. Visas can be obtained within 24 or 72 hours for an additional charge; consult nearest Embassy/Consulate for further details. This service is not available to all nationalities/passport holders.

PASSPORT/VISA INFORMATION

Embassy of the Republic of Lithuania in the UK
84 Gloucester Place, London W1U 6AU, UK
Tel: (020) 7486 6401 *or* 6404 (visa section).
Website: http://amb.urm.lt/jk
Opening hours: Mon-Fri 0900-1300 (consular section); Mon, Wed & Fri 1500-1600 (visa section; appointments not necessary).

Embassy of the Republic of Lithuania in the USA
2622 16th Street, NW, Washington, DC 20009, USA
Tel: (202) 234 5860 (ext. 127 for visa section).
Website: www.ltembassyus.org

Money

Currency: Litas (LTL) = 100 centas. Notes are in denominations of LTL500, 200, 100, 50, 20, 10, 5, 2 and 1. Coins are in denominations of LTL5, 2 and 1, and the worthless 50, 20, 10, 5, 2 and 1 centas. The Litas is pegged to the Euro.

Currency exchange: Currency can be exchanged at banks and bureaux de change. ATMs are available in most cities. There are 24-hour exchange bureaux at Gelezinkelio 6, near the main railway station and at Lietuvos Taupomasis Bankas, Savanoriu 15A in Vilnius.

Credit & debit cards: Major credit cards are accepted in the main hotels, restaurants, shops and in some petrol stations. Check with your credit and debit card company for details of merchant acceptability and other services which may be available.

Traveller's cheques: These are not accepted by retailers and can only be exchanged at a few outlets. To avoid additional exchange rate charges, travellers are advised to take traveller's cheques in US Dollars.

Currency restrictions: The import of local and foreign currency is unlimited. The export of local currency is limited to LTL5000. The export of foreign currency is unlimited. Any amount exceeding LTL40,000 or equivalent must be declared.

Banking hours: Mon-Fri 0900-1700. Some banks also open Sat 0900-1300.

Exchange rate indicators:
Rate at time of publishing
£1.00= LTL5.11
$1.00= LTL2.94

Duty Free

The following goods may be imported into Lithuania by persons over 17 years of age without incurring customs duty:
200 cigarettes or 100 cigarillos or 50 cigars or 250g of tobacco or combination, provided amount does not exceed 250g; 1l of spirits exceeding 22 per cent volume or 2l of spirits, wine-based spirits or alcohol below 22 per cent volume or 2l of sparkling wine or 2l of spirited wine or 2l of non-sparkling wine; 250g of eau de toilette or 50g of perfume; 500g of coffee or 200g of extract and essences; 100g of tea or 40g of tea extract and essences.

Prohibited: Ethyl alcohol and homemade alcoholic beverages; meat, meat products, meat sub-products, dairy products and eggs; military weapons, hunting guns, ammunition, electric fishing equipment, drugs and psychotropic substances, radioelectronic equipment, colour photocopying equipment (all require a permit).

Abolition of duty free goods within the EU: On June 30 1999, the sale of duty free alcohol and tobacco at airports and at sea was abolished in all of the original 15 EU member states. Of the 10 new member states that joined the EU on May 1 2004, these rules already apply to Cyprus and Malta. There are transitional rules in place for visitors returning to one of the original 15 EU countries from one of the other new EU countries. But for the original 15, plus Cyprus and Malta, there are now no limits imposed on importing tobacco and alcohol products from one EU country to another (with the exceptions of Denmark, Finland and Sweden, where limits *are* imposed). Travellers should note that they may be required to prove at customs that the goods purchased are for personal use *only*.

Public Holidays

Below are listed Public holidays for the January 2006-June 2007 period.

2006: Jan 1 New Year's Day. **Feb 16** Independence Day. **Mar 11** Restoration of Lithuania's Statehood. **Apr 17** Easter Monday. **May 1** International Labour Day. **Jun 24** St John's Day (Midsummer's Day). **Jul 6** Anniversary of the Coronation of King Mindaugas. **Aug 15** Assumption. **Nov 1** All Saints' Day. **Dec 25-26** Christmas.

2007: Jan 1 New Year's Day. **Feb 16** Independence Day. **Mar 11** Restoration of Lithuania's Statehood. **Apr 9** Easter Monday. **May 1** International Labour Day. **Jun 24** St John's Day (Midsummer's Day).

Health

	Special Precautions?	Certificate Required?
Yellow Fever	No	No
Cholera	No	No
Typhoid & Polio	No	N/A
Malaria	No	N/A

Note: *Regulations and requirements may be subject to change at short notice, and you are advised to contact your doctor well in advance of your intended date of departure. Any numbers in the chart refer to the footnotes below.*

Food & drink: Water supplies are generally reliable in cities, though it has a high mineral content and can be cloudy. Bottled or filtered water is preferable for these reasons. If travelling in rural areas, drink only bottled water. Milk is pasteurised and dairy products are generally safe for consumption. Local meat, poultry, seafood, fruit and vegetables are generally considered safe to eat, although there is some risk of fish tapeworm from freshwater fish. Exercise food and drink hygiene precautions, especially in rural areas.

Other risks: *Hepatitis A* and *B*, and *diphtheria* are present. *TB* may be a threat. *Tick-borne encephalitis* occurs in forested areas, and vaccination is strongly advisable. *Rabies* is present. For those at high risk, vaccination before arrival should be considered. If you are bitten, seek medical advice without delay. For more information, consult the *Health* appendix.

Health care: European Economic Area (EEA) and Switzerland:
If you or any of your dependants are suddenly taken ill or have an accident during a visit to an EEA country or Switzerland, free or reduced-cost necessary treatment is available - in most cases on production of a valid European Health Insurance Card (EHIC). Each country has different rules about state medical provision. In some, treatment is free. In many countries you will have to pay part or all of the cost, and then claim a full or partial refund. The EHIC gives access to state-provided medical treatment only and the scheme gives no entitlement to medical repatriation costs, nor does it cover ongoing illnesses of a non-urgent nature, so comprehensive travel insurance is advised. Note that the EHIC replaces the Form E111, which is no longer valid since 31 December 2005. Some restrictions apply, depending on your nationality.
You can get treatment only from doctors or dentists contracted to a Territorial Patient Fund. Doctors' consultations and treatment are free of charge. There is no charge for a dentist's consultation but you will have to pay for any materials the dentist uses. Most dentists - 80 per cent - practise privately. If you see a doctor or dentist privately, you can't claim any money back. You can get prescriptions from a doctor. You will need to show your European Health Insurance Card (EHIC). Some medicines are provided free of charge; for others you will have to pay between 10 and 50 per cent of the cost. This is not refundable. If you are prescribed a medicine that is not available under the state scheme, you will have to pay for it yourself. You can get treatment in the emergency section of a hospital. You can also be referred to a hospital for in-patient or out-patient treatment by a doctor. There are no charges for in-patient or out-patient hospital treatment. If you are treated privately in a hospital, you will have to pay. This is not refundable. Ambulance travel is free. More information can be obtained from Vilnius Territorial Patient Fund, Placioji g. 10 Vilnius 2600 (tel: (5) 266 1364).

Travel - International

AIR:

The national airline, *FlyLAL(TE)* (website: www.lal.lt), flies from Vilnius to Amsterdam, Frankfurt/M, Helsinki, Kiev, London, Moscow, Paris and Stockholm. For further information, contact *FlyLAL* in the UK (tel: (01293) 579 900); or *FlyLAL* in Palanga (tel: 460 42300; website: www.lal.lt). *FlyLAL* offers flights from Palanga to London.

Approximate flight times: From Vilnius to *London* is three hours, to *Copenhagen* is one hour 30 minutes and to *Berlin* is one hour 20 minutes.

Main airports: *Vilnius Airport (VNO)* (website: www.vilnius-airport.lt) is situated approximately 6km (3.5 miles) southeast of the city centre. *To/from the airport*: There are taxi and bus services to the city (travel time - 10 minutes). These depart every 10 to 15 minutes. Bus 1 travels between the airport and station and bus 2 travels from the city centre and the airport. Minibuses also run every five to 15 minutes. *Facilities*: Duty free shop, banks/bureaux de change, refreshments, tourist information, travel agencies, hotel, VIP lounge and car rental (*Avis*, *Budget* and *Hertz*). There are also international airports in *Kaunas (KUN)* and *Palanga (PLQ)*; the latter serves the whole of the Baltic coast.

Departure tax: LTL60.

SEA:

Main ports: *Klaipeda* is connected by trade routes with 200 foreign ports. There are seven ferry services to Denmark, Kaliningrad (Russian Federation), Germany, Poland and Sweden. There is also a cruise ship terminal. For information on ferry services from Klaipeda, contact Krantas Shipping (tel: (6) 395 233; website: www.krantas.lt *or* www.lisco.lt *or* www.scandlines.lt). At present, there are services to Karlshamm in Sweden; Aarhus and Aabenraa in Denmark; and to Kiel and Sassnitz in Germany.

RAIL:

Lithuania has a well-developed rail network and Vilnius is the focal point for rail connections in the region. Major routes go to Kaliningrad, Lviv (Ukraine), Minsk, Moscow, Riga, St Petersburg and Warsaw.

ROAD:

Lithuania has a good network of roads connecting the country with all neighbouring states. The crossing points on the Lithuanian-Polish border are Ogrodniki (Poland)–Lazdijai (Lithuania) and for trucks at Kalvarija (Lithuania). There are numerous crossing points with Latvia, Belarus and the Kaliningrad region of the Russian Federation. The international road Via Baltica goes from Tallinn to Warsaw through Latvia and Lithuania, thus connecting Scandinavia with Western Europe. **Coach:** There are passenger coaches from Vilnius to cities including Berlin, Gdansk, Kaliningrad, Minsk, Moscow, Prague, Riga, Tallinn, Vienna and Warsaw. Charter buses go to all Western European countries. *Eurolines*, departing from Victoria Coach Station in London, serves destinations in Lithuania. For further information, contact *Eurolines* (52 Grosvenor Gardens, London SW1; tel: (08705) 143 219; website: www.eurolines.com *or* www.nationalexpress.com).

Travel - Internal

AIR:

There are domestic airports at Kaunas, Palanga and Siauliai. There are not many domestic flights.

WATER:

Local ferries connect Klaipeda and the Curonian Spit. Klaipeda is home to two yacht clubs.

RAIL:

There are good connections from Vilnius to Kaunas, Klaipeda and Siauliai. Twice-daily passenger trains (including a sleeper train) connect Vilnius with the Baltic coast. Though the train does not stop in Palanga, the major resort on the Baltic coast, passengers to Palanga usually get off at Kretinga station or in Klaipeda, and then reach Palanga by bus. Passengers to Neringa (Nida, Juodkrante) can go to Klaipeda by train, and then take a bus. Suburban trains going to Ignalina connect Vilnius with the popular lake district of the National Park. The ancient Trakai Castle can be reached by taking the suburban train going to Trakai.

ROAD:

There is a good network of roads within the country. Modern four-lane motorways connect Vilnius with Klaipeda, Kaunas and Panevezys.

Traffic regulations: Seat belts must be worn. The speed limit is 110kph (68mph) on motorways, 90kph (56mph) on country roads and 60kph (44mph) inside towns. The Vilnius-Kaunas highway has a speed limit of 100kph (60mph). Traffic drives on the right. **Bus:** Generally, buses are more frequent and quicker than domestic trains and serve almost every town and village. Kautra (website: www.kautra.lt) has services from Kaunas to almost all the major cities in Lithuania. Tickets are sold to as many passengers as wish to travel and more buses are assigned as necessary. **Car hire:** *Avis*, *Europcar* and *Hertz* can provide chauffeur-driven or self-drive cars. **Documentation:** Most European nationals should be in possession of EU pink format driving licences. Otherwise, a national driving licence is sufficient, if supported by photo-bearing ID.

URBAN:

Public transport in urban districts includes **buses** and **trolleybuses**, which usually run from 0500-2300, but times do vary between routes. Transport coupons can be bought either at news kiosks before boarding or from the driver. Minibuses are less crowded but more expensive. **Taxi:** These display illuminated *Taksi* signs and can be hailed in the street, found at taxi ranks or ordered by phone.

Travel Advice

Most visits to Lithuania are trouble-free but you should be aware of the global risk of indiscriminate international terrorist attacks, which could be against civilian targets, including places frequented by foreigners.

This advice is based on information provided by the Foreign & Commonwealth Office in the UK. It is correct at time of publishing. As the situation can change rapidly, visitors are advised to contact the following organisations for the latest travel advice:

British Foreign and Commonwealth Office
Tel: (0845) 850 2829.
Website: www.fco.gov.uk

US Department of State
Website: http://travel.state.gov/travel

Accommodation

HOTELS:

Since independence, Western-style hotels and motels have been built in Lithuania in cooperation with foreign firms. Modernisation and renovation programmes are generally concentrated in Vilnius. All major hotels in Kaunas are concentrated in the centre of the town. Meanwhile, Vilnius and the other major centres in the country enjoy an adequate range of good accommodation including large hotels and smaller pensions. A star grading system is in force. For further details, contact the Lithuanian State Department of Tourism (see *Top Things To Do*)

PRIVATE ROOMS:

Travel agencies can arrange rental of rooms in private homes as well as houses. This is especially popular in resort regions.

Self-catering apartments in Vilnius can also be rented (website: www.oldtown-apartments.com).

CAMPING:

Campsites are not numerous. The majority of them are located in the most picturesque regions: Palanga (on the shore of the Baltic Sea), Trakai (lake district) and near larger towns. Pitching a tent is permitted at the majority of Lithuanian lakes and rivers (including the National Park) for a small fee, but almost no other facilities are provided at these sites. A star grading system is used.

YOUTH HOSTELS:

There are currently about four hostels in Lithuania. For further information, contact Lithuanian Youth Hostels (see *Accommodation Information*).

ACCOMMODATION INFORMATION

Lithuanian Hotel and Restaurant Association
Jasinsjio 16, LT-2001 Vilnius, Lithuania
Tel/fax: (5) 249 7478.
Website: www.lvra.lt

Lithuanian Youth Hostels
Ausros Vartu 20-15, 2001 Vilnius, Lithuania
Tel: (5) 262 5357.
Website: www.lithuanianhostels.org

Top Things To See & Do

- Various **Mardi Gras** festivities are held in various Lithuanian cities and small towns, but what happens in Vilnius Old Town at the beginning of February remains the most renowned. See off the winter like Lithuanians do and witness the procession of feasts in colourful masks, dances around fire, pancake and the burning of the winter symbol.
- The historic city of **Vilnius** (founded in 1323) is the capital of Lithuania. Surrounded on three sides by wooded hills and situated in a picturesque valley formed by the **rivers Neris** and **Vilnia**, the ancient yet modern centre of the city lies on the southern or left bank of the river. Vilnius' **Old Town** is the biggest in Europe and is also a UNESCO World Heritage Site. Unlike Riga and Tallinn in the other Baltic Republics, Vilnius is not of Germanic origin, although like these other cities it has a large old quarter which is gradually being restored. Almost all major European architectural styles are represented, although ultimately it was the Baroque which came to dominate. The heart of the capital is the beautiful and spacious **Gediminas Square**, the main feature of which is the **Cathedral** built in the Classical style. Other interesting churches are the Gothic **St Ann's Church** and the **St Peter and St Paul's Church**, which houses the body of St Casimieras, one of the most revered of Lithuania's dukes. It also includes some fine sculptures. Any itinerary of the city should include the historic University of Vilnius, which was granted its charter in 1579, the Golden Age in the city's history. The university is among the oldest in Central Europe and has a distinctly Renaissance feel with its inner courtyards and arcades. To enjoy a view of the whole city, visitors should climb the **Gediminas Tower**. High on a hill in the centre of the city, it rises above Vilnius and is the symbol of the Lithuanian capital. Go during the **Days of the Capital festival** in September, and you will also be spoilt with carnivals, fairs, concerts and fireworks, taking place in all streets and squares of the capital (website: www.vilniusfestivals.lt).
- Why not visit **Trakai**, an ancient capital of Lithuania? Situated on the shore of the picturesque **Lake Galve**, on which boat rides are available, the city has a castle dating from the 14th century.
- Be cultural, and amble around **Kaunas**, Lithuania's 'city of museums', which boasts, amongst others, the **Devil Museum** and a memorial to those who suffered during the Nazi occupation. The most famous museum is dedicated to the works of the Lithuanian painter Ciurlionis. Kaunas also numbers three **theatres**, some 11th-century **castle ruins** and the old **City Hall** among its attractions.
- Five strange grassy mounds mark Lithuania's ancient capital at **Kernave**, one of Lithuania's UNESCO World Heritage sites. Much mystery surrounds the spot, which is steeped in epic history. • Have some old-fashioned fun in popular seaside resorts that include **Palanga** and **Kursiu Nerija** (with the settlements of **Nida** and **Juodkrante**), famous for their clean white sand beaches, natural sand dunes and pine forests. Palanga also boasts the **Amber Museum-Gallery** (website: www.ambergallery.lt) and an interesting botanical park. To the south lies the city of **Klaipeda**, an important seaport as well as the main centre for ferry connections from Lithuania.
- Lithuania is a predominantly flat country, a quarter of which is covered by forests. There are five national parks and numerous other conservation areas. **Hiking** trails can be found all over the country. One of the highlights is the **Curonian Spit National Park** (another UNESCO World

Credit: ©Lithuanian State Department of Tourism

Heritage Site), on the peninsula separating the **Curonian Lagoon** from the **Baltic Sea**, where visitors can explore a range of large sand dunes and several pine forests. Rare **flora** and **fauna** are to be found here. **Trakai National Park** contains many **lakes** while **Aukstaitija** and **Zemaitija National Parks** feature hills, lakes and uplands. **Cycling** is also popular.
- **Nida** makes a true paradise for **sailing**, **windsurfing** and also **paragliding** and **kiting**. Nida is the last village on the Lithuanian half of the spit surrounded by endless stretches of clean white sand. A **lighthouse** from 1874 can be visited here, as can the **Thomas Mann Cultural Centre**, situated in the house where the German writer spent his holidays between 1930 and 1932. There is the award winning **Park of Soviet Sculptures at Gruto Parkas**, which reminds visitors of some of Lithuania's grim past.
- There are opportunities for more **extreme sports** in Lithuania, such as **hot-air ballooning**, **gliding**, or, for the ultimate experience, the chance to leap off Vilnius' TV Tower, the tallest **bungee jump** of its kind in Europe!
- The **International Folklore Festival** (**Skamba Skamba Kankliai**) is now in its third decade since inception. During the festival, everyone may visit craft fairs, taste traditional dishes, join song and glee parties, enjoy the concerts given by guests, listen to psalms, and have fun at the night of dances and various exhibitions. The festival is held in Vilnius Old Town in May.

TOURIST INFORMATION

Lithuanian State Department of Tourism
A. Juozapavicius Street 13, 09311 Vilnius, Lithuania
Tel: (5) 210 8796.
Website: www.tourism.lt

Entertainment

FOOD & DRINK: Waiter service is the norm in restaurants and cafes, but self-service restaurants, bistros and snack bars are numerous.

National specialities:
- *Skilandis* (smoked meat).
- *Salti barsciai* (cold soup).
- *Cepelinai* (made from grated potatoes with a minced meat filling).
- *Vedarai* (potato sausage) and *bulviniai blynai* (potato pancakes).
- Smoked eel is a famous Baltic delicacy.
- It is highly recommended to try the mild white curd cheese, best served with honey.

National drinks:
- Local brands of beer and imported drinks are popular.
- A famous Lithuanian spirit is *midus*, a mild alcoholic beverage made from honey.

Tipping: Taxi fares and restaurant bills include a tip. Otherwise, tips are discretionary.

NIGHTLIFE: Cinemas can be found in all towns. Lithuanian theatres, most of which are concentrated in the capital, are also renowned. The Jaunimo *teatras* (website: www.jaunimoteatras.lt) in Vilnius are famous throughout the country. Opera and ballet are staged in the city at the Vilnius Opera Theatre and Kaunas has a Musical Theatre. Puppet shows are staged for children in Vilnius and Kaunas. There are restaurants with live music as well as numerous discos and nightclubs with variety shows in the larger towns.

SHOPPING: Amber, linen goods and local crafts are good buys. National artists sell their works in specialised art galleries in major towns. **Shopping hours:** Grocery shops open Mon-Fri 0800-2000.

Business

- **GDP:** US$22.23 billion (2004).
- **Main exports:** Mineral products, textiles and clothing, machinery and equipment, chemicals, wood and wood products, and foodstuffs.
- **Main imports:** Mineral products, machinery and equipment, transport equipment, chemicals, textiles and clothing, and metals.
- **Main trade partners:** Russian Federation, Germany, Poland, Latvia, The Netherlands, France, UK, Sweden, Estonia, Denmark, USA and Switzerland.

ECONOMY: Lithuania has historically been the least developed of the Baltic republics, with a smaller industrial base and greater dependence on agriculture, prior to rapid industrialisation during the Soviet era. Sugar beet, cereals, potatoes and vegetables are the main crops. Electrical, electronic and optical goods and light machinery are the main industrial products. Food processing is also an important industry, with an ample supply of agricultural products from Lithuania's own farming and fisheries sector and more recently from Russia. Timber production has expanded on the back of growing trade links with Scandinavia. Lithuania's other major economic asset is the Baltic's only naturally ice-free port (other than Kaliningrad) at Klaipeda. Lithuania is a founder member of the regional cooperation organisation for Baltic littoral states, the Council of Baltic Sea States. The Government has largely completed the dismantling of the old Soviet-style command economy, introducing a market system and liberalising foreign trade. Domestic political factors stalled some parts of the otherwise rapid privatisation programme, especially the key energy industries as well as the finance and banking sector. Action in the energy field is further complicated by the fact that 80 per cent of Lithuania's energy comes from nuclear power (the highest figure of any country in the world): the Government plans to reduce the percentage but faces major problems regarding waste disposal and alternative energy sources. Further privatisations of state assets, principally in the banking and transport sectors, were completed in 2002.
Lithuania's trade patterns have gradually shifted during the 1990s towards the West, and the European Union now accounts for just under half of all Lithuanian trade. Lithuania has recovered from the serious knock-on effects of the 1998 Russian financial crisis, and growth was 6.7 per cent in 2004. The country joined the IMF and World Bank in 1992, as well as the European Bank for Reconstruction and Development as a Country of Operation. A convertible currency, the Litas, was introduced in 1993. Membership of the European Union has been a high priority for Lithuania since independence. Accession negotiations began in October 1999 and progressed well. Following a 90 per cent endorsement in a national referendum held in May 2003, Lithuania – along with nine other countries, including both its Baltic neighbours – joined the EU on May 1 2004.
BUSINESS ETIQUETTE: Business is conducted in a fairly formal manner and a smart appearance is important. Appointments should be made in advance. English is used for international commerce. A knowledge of German, Russian or Polish may also be useful. **Office hours:** Mon-Fri 0900-1300 and 1400-1800.

COMMERCIAL INFORMATION

Association of Lithuanian Chambers of Commerce, Industry and Crafts
J Tumo-Vaizganto 9/1-63A, 01108 Vilnius, Lithuania
Tel: (5) 261 2102.
Website: www.chambers.lt

European Committee of the Government of the Republic of Lithuania
Gedimino ave 11, LT-01103 Vilnius, Lithuania
Tel: (5) 266 3827.
Website: www.euro.lt

LITEXPO (Information on Conferences/Conventions)
Laisves pr 5, LT 04215 Vilnius, Lithuania
Tel: (5) 245 1800.
Website: www.litexpo.lt

Luxembourg

Location: Western Europe.

Time: GMT + 1 (GMT + 2 from last Sunday in March to last Sunday in October).

Overview

Luxembourg owes its continued existence to a mixture of good fortune and good diplomacy, which have prevented it from being permanently absorbed into the territories of its larger neighbours. By the time that Luxembourg's independence was finally confirmed in 1867, however, the Grand Duchy was left with such a tiny territory that its people had to look across its borders for economic survival. This has resulted in a cosmopolitan attitude, which has survived to the present day and is exemplified not only by the fact that the country has the highest percentage of foreigners of any EU country, but also by the trilingual ability of its people.
Luxembourg is an attractive country with a green and picturesque landscape and many historical sites within easy reach of one another. The central and southern part of the country that surrounds the capital, known as 'the Good Land', consists mainly of rolling farmland and woods. To the northeast is the Müllerthal, characterised by sandstone rock formations and forests, while the northern third of the country is the Ardennes, set in beautiful forested hills and valleys. South of the capital is the Land of the Red Rocks, so named from its 'red earth', rich in iron. The southeast frontier is marked by the Moselle Valley, famous for its wines.
The capital, Luxembourg-Ville, is split into two districts: the delightful old centre, complete with fortress towers, turrets and winding, cobblestone streets; and the modern downtown area on the plâteau du Kirchberg. The entire old part of Luxembourg-Ville was declared a World Heritage Site by UNESCO in 1994. In contrast, the myriad of new modern office complexes being built in the modern district on the Plâteau du Kirchberg testify to Luxembourg's reputation as a major international financial centre. The country's geographical position at the 'heart of Europe', its strict banking secrecy laws and fiscal legislation are amongst the reasons why Luxembourg is the country with the highest banking concentration in Europe. Proud of its role as a founding member of the EU, Luxembourg sees itself as playing a prominent position in European affairs and there are a number of European Union institutions based in Luxembourg-Ville.

General Information

AREA: 2586 sq km (999 sq miles).
POPULATION: 465,000 (UN estimate 2005).
POPULATION DENSITY: 179 per sq km.
CAPITAL: Luxembourg-Ville. Population: 82,000 (2005).
GEOGRAPHY: The Grand Duchy of Luxembourg shares borders to the north and west with Belgium, to the south with France and to the east with Germany. One-third of the country is made up of the hills and forests of the Ardennes, while the rest is wooded farmland. In the southeast is the rich wine-growing valley of Moselle. The capital, Luxembourg-Ville, is built on a rock overlooking the Alzette and Petrusse valleys.
GOVERNMENT: Constitutional monarchy. Luxembourg is a founding member of the European Union and the only Grand Duchy in the world. **Head of State:** Grand Duke Henri since 2000. **Head of Government:** Prime Minister Jean-Claude Juncker since 1995. **Recent history:** Jean-Claude Juncker, of the conservative Christian Social Party, has been Prime Minister since 1995 when his predecessor, Jacques Santer, became President of the European Commission. His party had originally formed a coalition Government with the Democratic Party. Following the June 2004 general elections, he formed a coalition with the Socialist Workers Party.
LANGUAGE: Lëtzeburgesch, a German-Moselle-Frankish dialect, became the officially recognised national language in 1984. French and German are generally used for administrative and commercial purposes. Many Luxembourgers also speak English.
RELIGION: Around 88 per cent Roman Catholic, with Protestant, Anglican, Jewish and Muslim minorities.
ELECTRICITY: 220 volts AC, 50Hz.
SOCIAL CONVENTIONS: Handshaking is the normal greeting. The code of practice for visiting someone's home is similar to other Western European countries: it is acceptable to give gifts or flowers if invited for a meal. Smart-casual dress is widely acceptable, but some dining rooms, clubs and social functions will demand formal attire. Evening wear, black tie (for men) is usually specified on invitation if required. Smoking is prohibited where notified and is becoming increasingly unacceptable.

Climate

Warm weather from May to September and snow likely during winter months. The north (the Ardennes region) tends to be wetter and colder than the south.
Required clothing: Waterproofs are advisable at all times of the year.

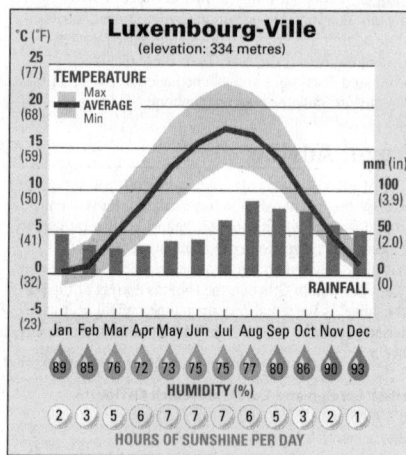

Communications

Telephone: Full IDD is available. Country code: 352 (no area codes). International phones have a yellow sign showing a telephone dial with a receiver in the centre.
Mobile telephone: Roaming agreements exist with most international mobile phone companies. Coverage is excellent.
Internet: There are Internet cafes in Luxembourg City.
Post: Post to other European destinations takes two to four days. Post office hours: Mon-Fri 0800-1200 and 1330-1700. The Luxembourg-Ville main office (opposite the railway station) is open Mon-Fri 0600-1900, Sat 0600-1200. Smaller offices may open for only a few hours.
MEDIA: Luxembourg has a long tradition of operating radio and TV services for pan-European audiences, including those in France, Germany and the UK thanks to the Luxembourg-based media group RTL. Today, RTL's television and radio stations remain key players in media markets across Europe. The country is also home to Europe's largest satellite operator, Société Européenne des Satellites (SES), which operates the Astra satellite fleet. Freedom of speech

is guaranteed by the constitution.

Press: There are several daily newspapers including the *Lëtzebuerger Journal, Luxemburger Wort, Tageblatt/Zeitung fir Letzebuerg* and *Zeitung vum Lëtzebuerger Vollek.* 352 is a weekly publication in English.

TV: *RTL Tele Letzeburg* is RTL's domestic network; *Nordliicht TV* broadcasts in northern Luxembourg.

Radio: *RTL Radio Letzeburg* is RTL's domestic network; *Den Neien Radio* is a commercial network; *Radio ARA* broadcasts a variety of music and some English-language programmes; *EldoRadio* broadcasts pop music; *Honnert,7 (100.7)* is a public, cultural station.

Passport/Visa

Credit: ©Luxembourg National Tourist Office

	Passport Required?	Visa Required?	Return Ticket? Required?
Full British	1	No	No
Australian	Yes	No	2
Canadian	Yes	No	2
USA	Yes	No	2
Other EU	1	No	No
Japanese	Yes	No	2

Note: *Regulations and requirements may be subject to change at short notice, and you are advised to contact the appropriate diplomatic or consular authority before finalising travel arrangements. Any numbers in the chart refer to the footnotes below.*

Note: Luxembourg is a signatory to the **1995 Schengen Agreement**. For further details about passport and visa regulations in the Schengen area see the introductory section *How to Use This Guide*.

PASSPORTS: Passport valid for at least three months beyond the length of stay required by all except:
(a) **1.** EU/EEA nationals (EU+ Iceland, Liechtenstein, Norway) and Swiss nationals holding a valid national ID card.
Note: EU and EEA nationals are only required to produce evidence of their EU/EEA nationality and identity in order to be admitted to any EU/EEA Member State. This evidence can take the form of a valid national passport *or* national identity card. Either is acceptable. Possession of a return ticket, any length of validity on their document, sufficient funds for the length of their proposed visit should *not* be imposed.
(b) nationals of Andorra, Monaco, and San Marino, holding a valid national ID card.
Note: 2. It is advisable to have a return ticket, but not obligatory. If a visitor is not in possession of a return ticket, proof of sufficient means of support may be required.
VISAS: Required by all except the following nationals for periods not exceeding three months and as long as the passport is still valid for three months beyond length of stay:
(a) nationals referred to in the chart above;
(b) nationals mentioned under passport exemptions above;
(c) nationals of Argentina, Bolivia, Brazil, Brunei, Bulgaria, Chile, Costa Rica, Croatia, El Salvador, Guatemala, Honduras, Hong Kong (SAR), Iceland, Israel, Korea (Rep), Macau (SAR), Malaysia, Mexico, New Zealand, Nicaragua, Norway, Panama, Paraguay, Romania, Singapore, Uruguay, Vatican City and Venezuela;
(d) passengers continuing their journey by the same or first connecting aircraft within 72 hours provided holding valid onward or return documentation and not leaving the airport (except nationals of certain countries who *always* need an airport transit visa). Please contact the Consulate for details.
Types of visa and cost: A uniform type of visa, the *Schengen* visa, is issued for tourist, business and private visits. All *Schengen* visas, regardless of the duration of stay and whether single- or multiple-entry, are available for approximately £27, although prices are subject to change.
Note: Spouses and children of EU nationals (providing spouse's passport and the original marriage certificate is produced) receive their visas free of charge (enquire at Embassy for details).
Validity: Short-stay visas are valid for up to six months from date of issue for single- or multiple-entries of maximum 90 days in total. Transit visas are valid for single- or multiple-entries of maximum five days per entry, including the day of arrival. Long-stay visas are valid for up to one year. Visas cannot be extended; a new application must be made each time.
Application to: Applications must be made in person to the Consulate (or Consular section at Embassy) of the Benelux country which the applicant will enter first.
Application requirements: (a) One completed application form. (b) One passport-size photo. (c) Passport valid for at least three months longer than the validity of the visa (with a blank page to affix visa stamp). (d) Proof of the purpose of visit (official letter of invitation/confirmed hotel booking; onward or return ticket). (e) Evidence of sufficient funds to cover the duration of stay. (f) Evidence of medical coverage for the Schengen countries (eg form E111). (g) Fee.

Working days required: Two days to three weeks depending on purpose of visit and nationality.
Temporary residence: Enquire about special application procedures at Consulate (or Consular section at Embassy); see *Passport/Visa Information*.

PASSPORT/VISA INFORMATION

Embassy of the Grand Duchy of Luxembourg in the UK
27 Wilton Crescent, London SW1X 8SD, UK
Tel: (020) 7235 6961.
E-mail: amb.lux@virgin.net
Opening hours: Mon-Fri 0900-1230 and 1330-1700; 1000-1145 (visa section; applications).

Embassy of the Grand Duchy of Luxembourg in the USA
2200 Massachusetts Avenue, NW, Washington, DC 20008, USA
Tel: (202) 265 4171/2.
Website: www.luxembourg-usa.org

Money

Single European currency (Euro): Single European currency (Euro): The Euro is now the official currency of 12 EU member states (including Luxembourg). The first Euro coins and notes were introduced in January 2002; the Luxembourg Franc was completely replaced by the Euro on 28 February 2002. Euro (€) = 100 cents. Notes are in denominations of €500, 200, 100, 50, 20, 10 and 5. Coins are in denominations of €2 and 1, and 50, 20, 10, 5, 2 and 1 cents.
Currency exchange: Foreign currencies, traveller's cheques and cheques can be exchanged at banks, bureaux de change, the airport, railway stations, the post office and major hotels (generally at a less advantageous rate).
Credit & debit cards: American Express, Diners Club, MasterCard, Visa and others are all widely accepted, as well as Eurocheque cards. Many retailers require a minimum (eg €10 to 25) before accepting credit/debit cards. Check with your credit or debit card company for details of merchant acceptability and other services which may be available. ATMs are widely available.
Traveller's cheques: Widely accepted. To avoid additional exchange rate charges, travellers are advised to take traveller's cheques in Euros, Pounds Sterling or US Dollars.
Currency restrictions: There are no restrictions on the import and export of either local or foreign currency.
Banking hours: Generally Mon-Fri 0830-1630, with limited hours on Saturday.
Exchange rate indicators:
Rate at time of publishing
£1.00   €1.46
$1.00   €0.82

Duty Free

The following goods may be imported into Luxembourg without incurring customs duty by travellers arriving from countries outside the EU:
200 cigarettes or 100 cigarillos or 50 cigars or 250g of tobacco; 1l of spirits or 2l of sparkling wine or 2l of liqueur wine and 2l of non-sparkling wine; 50g of perfume and 250ml of eau de toilette; 500g of coffee and 200g of coffee extract; 100g of tea and 40g of tea extract; other goods to the value of €175 for passengers over 15 years and €90 for passengers under 15.
Note: Alcohol and tobacco products are only available to passengers of 17 years of age or over.
Abolition of duty free goods within the EU: On June 30 1999, the sale of duty free alcohol and tobacco at airports and at sea was abolished in all of the original 15 EU member states. Of the 10 new member states that joined the EU on May 1 2004, these rules already apply to Cyprus and Malta. There are transitional rules in place for visitors returning to one of the original 15 EU countries from one

of the other new EU countries. But for the original 15, plus Cyprus and Malta, there are now no limits imposed on importing tobacco and alcohol products from one EU country to another (with the exceptions of Denmark, Finland and Sweden, where limits *are* imposed). Travellers should note that they may be required to prove at customs that the goods purchased are for personal use *only*.

Public Holidays

Below are listed Public Holidays for the January 2006-June 2007 period.
2006: Jan 1 New Year's Day. **Feb 27** Carnival. **Apr 17** Easter Monday. **May 1** May Day. **May 25** Ascension. **Jun 5** Whit Monday. **Jun 23** National Day. **Aug 15** Assumption. **Sep 1*** Luxembourg City Kermesse. **Nov 1** All Saints' Day. **Dec 25** Christmas Day. **Dec 26** St Stephen's Day.
2007: Jan 1 New Year's Day. **Feb 19** Carnival. **Apr 9** Easter Monday. **May 1** May Day. **May 17** Ascension. **May 28** Whit Monday. **Jun 23** National Day.
Note: (a) *Applies to the City of Luxembourg only. (b) Official Public Holidays falling on a Sunday may be deferred to the following Monday, for a maximum of two holidays. Exact details should be confirmed with the National Tourist Office or the Embassy (see *Top Things To Do*).

Health

	Special Precautions?	Certificate Required?
Yellow Fever	No	No
Cholera	No	No
Typhoid & Polio	No	N/A
Malaria	No	N/A

Note: *Regulations and requirements may be subject to change at short notice, and you are advised to contact your doctor well in advance of your intended date of departure. Any numbers in the chart refer to the footnotes below.*

Food & drink: Tap water is considered safe to drink. Milk is pasteurised and dairy products are safe for consumption. Local meat, poultry, seafood, fruit and vegetables are generally considered safe to eat.
Other risks: *Rabies* may be present in wildlife. For those at high risk, vaccination before arrival should be considered. If you are bitten, seek medical advice without delay. For more information, consult the *Health* appendix.
Health care: European Economic Area (EEA) and Switzerland:
If you or any of your dependants are suddenly taken ill or have an accident during a visit to an EEA country or Switzerland, free or reduced-cost necessary treatment is available – in most cases on production of a valid European Health Insurance Card (EHIC). Each country has different rules about state medical provision. In some, treatment is free. In many countries you will have to pay part or all of the cost, and then claim a full or partial refund. The EHIC gives access to state-provided medical treatment only and the scheme gives no entitlement to medical repatriation costs, nor does it cover ongoing illnesses of a non-urgent nature, so comprehensive travel insurance is advised. Note that the EHIC replaces the Form E111, which is no longer valid since 31 December 2005. Some restrictions apply, depending on your nationality.
You can go to any doctor. You must pay for treatment and prescribed medicines. Make sure you get receipts for everything you pay for. You will be able to get a refund, although not always for the full amount. If a doctor thinks you need hospital treatment, they will issue a certificate which you should give to the hospital authorities. Treatment is normally free but you must pay a non-refundable daily charge. If you can't contact a doctor before being admitted, show your European Health Insurance Card (EHIC) to the hospital authorities and ask them to contact the Sickness Insurance Fund. More information can be obtained from *Caisse de Maladie des Ouvriers* (Sickness Insurance Fund for Manual Workers), 125 Route d'Esch, L-1471 Luxembourg Ville.

Travel - International

AIR:

The national airline is *Luxair (LG)* (website: www.luxair.lu).
Approximate flight times: From *London* to Luxembourg is one hour.
Main airports: *Luxembourg (LUX)* (Findel) is 5km (3.5 miles) northeast of the city (travel time - 20 minutes).
To/from the airport: Coaches and buses run regular services to the city. Buses cost about €1.20. Taxis are also available (travel time - 10 minutes), costing between €15 to 25. *Facilities*: Outgoing duty free shop, car hire, bank/bureau de change and a tourist information office.
Departure tax: None.

RAIL:

Eurostar: The quickest route by train from the UK is through the Channel Tunnel with connections from Paris *Gare de l'Est* (journey time: three and a half to four hours) or Brussels to Luxembourg.
There is an inter-city train from Brussels to Luxembourg (travel time: three hours) and a night train to Luxembourg-Ville leaving at 1910 (travel time:14 hours).
Eurostar is a service provided by the railways of Belgium, the UK and France, operating direct high-speed trains from London (*Waterloo International*) to Paris (*Gare du Nord*) and to Brussels (*Midi/Zuid*). It takes two hours 40 minutes from London to Paris (via Lille) and two hours 20 minutes to Brussels. For further information and reservations, contact *Eurostar* (tel: (0870) 600 0792 (travel agents) or (08705) 186 186 (public; within the UK) or +44 (1233) 617 575 (public; outside the UK); a £5 booking fee applies to all telephone bookings; website: www.eurostar.com); or *Rail Europe* (tel: (08705) 848 848; website: www.raileurope.co.uk).
Rail passes: The *Inter-Rail* pass offers unlimited second-class train travel in up to 29 countries (includes Morocco and Turkey) split into eight zones (A-H). Three different tickets are available: a ticket covering one zone (two to six countries, 16 days' validity), a ticket covering two zones (six to ten countries, 22 days' validity) and an *All Zone Pass* (29 countries, one month's validity). Ferry services between Italy and Greece are included. Passengers must be resident in Europe for at least six months before the pass is used. Travel is not allowed in the passenger's country of residence. Travellers under 26 years recieve a reduction of about 30 per cent. Children's tickets are reduced by about 50 per cent. Supplements are required for some high speed services, seat reservations and couchettes. Discounts are offered on *Eurostar* and some ferry routes. Available from *Inter Rail* (website: www.interrailnet.com).
The *Eurailpass* offers unlimited first-class train travel in 17 European countries. Tickets are valid for 15 days, 21 days, one month, two months or three months. The *Eurailpass Saver* ticket offers discounts for two or more people travelling together. The *Eurailpass Youth* ticket is available to those aged under 26 and offers unlimited second-class train travel. The *Eurailpass Flexi* allows either 10 or 15 travel days within a two month period. The *Eurail Selectpass* is valid in three, four or five bordering countries and allows five, six, eight or 10 travel days (or 15 for five countries) in a two-month period. The *Eurail Regional Pass* allows four to 10 travel days in a two-month period in one of nine regions (usually two or more countries). Children recieve a 50 per cent reduction. The passes cannot be sold to residents of Europe, Turkey, Morocco, Algeria, Tunisia, or the Russian Federation. Available from *The Eurail Group* (website: www.eurail.com).
The *EuroDomino* pass enables holders anything from three to eight days' extensive travel within a one-month period on the entire rail network of their chosen country. It is valid in 28 European countries and North Africa, including the ferry service from Brindisi (Italy) to Igoumenitsa (Greece). To purchase a *EuroDomino* pass you must have been a resident in Europe for at least six months and a passport number is required at time of booking. It is not permitted to purchase a pass for travel within your own country of residence. To qualify for the youth rates, you must be under 26 years on the first date of validity of the pass. Children aged four-eleven years inclusive pay half the adult fares rounded up to the nearest pound. Children under four years travel for free. Seat reservations, couchette and sleeper charges are not included in the cost of the pass and are payable at the normal rate. Passholder fares are payable on some services. Reservation/Supplement charges are payable on all trains within Spain. Available from *Rail Europe* (website: www.raileurope.co.uk/railpasses/eurodomino.htm).

ROAD:

Luxembourg is easily reached within one day from the UK, via Belgium or France. The quickest way to cross the channel is by driving the car onto *Eurotunnel* trains. **The Channel Tunnel:** *Eurotunnel* runs shuttle trains for cars, bicycles, motorcycles, coaches, minibuses, caravans, campervans and other vehicles over 1.85m (6.07ft) between Folkestone in Kent, with direct road access from the M20, and Calais, with links to the A16/A26 motorway (Exit 13). All road vehicles are carried through the tunnel in shuttle trains running between the two terminals. Terminals and shuttles are well-equipped for disabled passengers. Passenger Terminal buildings contain a variety of shops, restaurants, bureaux de change and other amenities. The journey takes about 35 minutes from platform to platform and around one hour from motorway to motorway. There are up to four passenger shuttles per hour at peak times, 24 hours per day and services run every day of the year. Motorists pass through customs and immigration before they board, with no further checks on arrival. Fares are charged according to length of stay and time of year and whether or not you have a reservation. The price applies to the car, regardless of the number of passengers or size of the car. Promotional deals are frequently available, especially outside the peak holiday seasons. Tickets may be purchased in advance from the travel agents, or from Eurotunnel Customer Services in France or the UK with a credit card. For further information, brochures and reservations, contact *Eurotunnel Customer Services UK*, Customer Relations Department, Saint Martin's Plain, Cheriton, Folkestone, Kent CT19 4QD (tel: 08705) 353 535; website: www.eurotunnel.com). For further information about departure times of shuttles at the French terminal, contact *Eurotunnel Customer Information* in Coquelles (tel: France +33 (3) 2100 6543). **Car ferries:** For drivers not using the shuttle through the channel tunnel, car ferries operate frequently between Dover and Calais (regular ferries and Hovercraft services) and Dover and Ostend (regular ferries as well as Catamaran and Hoverspeed services). See United Kingdom - *Travel International* section.
Luxembourg-Ville is approximately 320km (200 miles) from Ostend, and 420km (260 miles) from Calais. From Calais, the quickest route is to take the motorway to Brussels via Lille (A25, then head south through Namur along the E411 to Luxembourg; from Ostend, take the E40 motorway to Brussels, then the E411 to Luxembourg. In total, the journey from London (including the ferry crossing) takes approximately eight hours.
Coach: *Eurolines* runs a limited service to Luxembourg from London. For further information contact Eurolines in the UK (52 Grosvenor Gardens, London SW1; tel: (08705) 143 219; website: www.eurolines.com or www.nationalexpress.com).
Travel times: The following chart gives approximate travel times (in hours and minutes) from **Luxembourg-Ville** to other major cities/towns in Europe.

	Air	Road	Rail
Amsterdam	0.45	5.30	6.30
Brussels	0.45	2.00	2.30
Paris	1.00	4.00	4.00
London	1.00 1.00	*8.00	**6.30

Note: *Includes ferry crossing from Dover (via Calais or Ostend); **Eurostar via Bruxelles-Midi (Brussels).

Travel - Internal

RAIL:

The national railway company, *Chemins de Fer Luxembourgeois (CFL)*, runs an efficient rail service which is fully integrated with the bus network. CFL has recently introduced a so-called *horaire cadencé* schedule, meaning there is now at least one train every hour to every station at the same time in every hour. Reductions are offered for weekend and holiday return tickets. CFL rail services and *CFL/CRL* buses in Luxembourg are covered by the *Benelux Tourrail* rail pass covering Belgium, Luxembourg and The Netherlands. This gives unlimited travel on any five days within a one-month period throughout the year. *Rail/Coach Rover Tickets* are valid for both networks. The *Luxembourg Card* gives unlimited travel on public transport for a period of one to three days, with free entrance to up to 40 attractions. There is also an *Öko Pass*, which is a single-day ticket for unlimited travel on all forms of public transport (not valid on sightseeing buses), with concessions for senior citizens. For further information, contact CFL (tel: 49901 *or* 4990 5572 website: www.cfl.lu).

ROAD:

As in the rest of Western Europe, there is an excellent network of roads and motorways in Luxembourg. Traffic drives on the right. **Bus:** Cross-country buses are punctual and operate between all major towns. For information on passes, see the *Rail* section. **Taxi:** These are metered. There is a minimum charge and a 10 per cent surcharge is applied from 2200-0600. There is also an extra 25 per cent surcharge all-day on Sundays. Taxis are plentiful but cannot be hailed in the street. A 10 per cent tip is usual for taxi drivers. **Car hire:** All the main agencies operate in Luxembourg. **Traffic regulations**: The minimum age for driving is 18. It is obligatory to carry €15 at all times for the payment of on-the-spot fines; there are stiff drinking/driving spot fines. The wearing of seat belts is compulsory in the front seat and in the back, where seat belts are fitted. Children under 12 years of age must travel in the back seats, unless they are 1.5m (5ft) or taller, or if the front seat is fitted with an appropriate ECE-approved child seat. Motorcyclists must use a dipped beam even by day. The speed limit is 50kph (31mph) in built-up areas, 90kph (56mph) outside built-up areas, and 120kph (74mph) on motorways. For more details, contact Automobile Club du Grand-Duché de Luxembourg, 54 route de Longwy, L-8007 Bertrange, Luxembourg-Helfenterbruck (tel: 450 045 -400; website: www.acl.lu). **Documentation:** Third Party insurance is necessary. A Green Card is not obligatory but is strongly recommended. Without it, visitors have only the minimum legal cover in Luxembourg (if they have motor insurance at home). The Green Card tops this up to the level of cover provided by the visitor's domestic policy. A valid national driving licence is sufficient.

URBAN:

Luxembourg-Ville has municipal bus services, for which single-journey flat-fare tickets may be purchased. This 'short distance' ticket is valid for one hour (or for a maximum of 10km/6 miles) from purchase on the whole of Luxembourg's public transport network, and also allows transits between city and country buses and trains. Ten-journey tickets are also available, but must be purchased in advance. There is no underground or tramway service.

Travel Advice

Most visits to Luxembourg are trouble-free but you should be aware of the global risk of indiscriminate international terrorist attacks, which could be against civilian targets, including places frequented by foreigners.
This advice is based on information provided by the Foreign and Commonwealth Office in the UK. It is correct at time of publishing. As the situation can change rapidly, visitors are advised to contact the following organisations for the latest travel advice.

British Foreign and Commonwealth Office
Tel: (0845) 850 2829.
Website: www.fco.gov.uk

US Department of State
Website: http://travel.state.gov/travel

Accommodation

HOTELS:

Luxembourg has a wide range of hotels, more than half of which are classified according to the Benelux system. **Grading**: Standard of accommodation is indicated by a row of 3-pointed stars from the highest (5 stars) to the minimum (1 star). However, membership of this scheme is voluntary and there may be first-class hotels which do not have a classification.

HOLIDAY APARTMENTS:

A number of holiday flats and chalets are available throughout the country. A free pamphlet giving location and facilities is published by the National Tourist Office (see *Top Things To Do*).

CAMPING:

There are over 108 campsites throughout the country. According to Government regulations, campsites are ranged in three different categories and the tariff in each camp is shown at the entrance. The National Tourist Office publishes a free, comprehensive brochure giving all relevant information concerning campsites.

YOUTH HOSTELS:

There are youth hostels at Beaufort, Bourglinster, Echternach, Hollenfels, Larochette, Lultzhausen, Luxembourg-Ville, Vianden and Wiltz. A *Youth Hostel Guide* may be obtained free of charge from the National Tourist Office in London or the Centrale des Auberges de Jeunesses Luxembourgeoises.

ACCOMMODATION INFORMATION

National Hotel Association
Horesca 7 rue Alcide de Gasperi, PO Box 2524, L-1025 Luxembourg
Tel: 421 351-5.
Website: www.horesca.lu

Centrale des Auberges de Jeunesses Luxembourgeoises
24-26 place de la Gare, L-616 Luxembourg
Tel: 2629 3500.
E-mail: information@youthhostels.lu

Credit: ©Luxembourg National Tourist Office

Top Things To See

- Discover the delightful old centre of the capital, **Luxembourg-Ville**. See the **fortress towers**, **turrets** and winding, **cobblestone streets**. The fortress was dismantled in 1867 but many of the old fortifications remain well preserved to this day. The Luxembourg City Tourist Office (whose main office is on the Place d'Armes) can provide details and maps for numerous walks taking visitors past the city's medieval remains and historic sites. Visit the underground tunnels, known as *casemates*. Hop on the special open-air tourist train called the 'Petrusse Express', which offers frequent guided tours through the **Petrusse Valley** (from which many of the remaining fortifications can easily be viewed). The train departs from underneath one of the arches of the **Pont Adolphe** viaduct. Most of the city's historical sites are easily visited on foot and a walk through the Petrusse and Alzette valleys (which are spanned by several bridges) offers excellent views of the ancient fortifications.
- Observe the changing of the guard at the **Palais Grand Ducal**, the official residence of the Grand Duke. Other attractions in **Luxembourg-Ville** include the **Place Guillaume** (also called *Knuedler*) and its twice-weekly market (Wednesday and Saturday); and, near the **Place Guillaume**, the 17th century **Notre Dame Cathedral**. Art lovers will find numerous galleries in the capital. Interesting museums include the **National Museum of Natural History**, the **National Museum of History and Art** and the **Museum of the City of Luxembourg** (whose architecture interestingly combines the 'old' and the 'new' and which displays a very detailed and informative account of Luxembourg's colourful history).
- Alternatively, head for the modern district on the **Plateau du Kirchberg** (reached via the **Pont Grand Duchesse Charlotte** – the most impressive of the many bridges in the capital). Luxembourg's main cinema complex, **Utopolis**, is located here, next to the country's biggest shopping complex. The myriad of new modern office complexes being built on the plateau Kirchberg testify to Luxembourg's reputation as a major international financial centre. The Kirchberg is also home to numerous European institutions.
- Further east, in the town of **Echternach**, see a colourful religious dancing **procession**, which takes place annually on Whit Tuesday and attracts pilgrims from all over the world. The town's **Benedictine Abbey** (which was founded in the seventh century by St Willibrord and now also houses a museum) and, in particular, the **St Willibrord Basilica** (with its crypt as a centrepiece) are well worth visiting. Echternach also has a distinctive 15th-century **Town Hall** overlooking the market square.
- In **Vianden**, crossed by the **River Our**, be impressed by a magnificent **castle**, built between the 11th and 14th centuries and one of Luxembourg's major tourist attractions. The castle overlooks the town from a 450m-(1476ft-) elevation that can be reached by the country's only chairlift. Vianden also has a **wild boar sanctuary**. Another castle can be visited at **Bourscheid** nearby.
- Further north, in the medieval market town of **Clervaux**, visit the 12th-century **Castle**, which now houses the offices of the local Government, the reception of the local tourist office (*syndicat d'initiative*), a small war museum exhibiting weapons and souvenirs from the 1944-1945 Ardennes offensive (the famous 'Battle of the Bulge'), and the renowned collection of documentary art photography, the *Family of Man*, by Edward Steichen.

Top Things To Do

- In **Luxembourg-Ville's** main square, the **Place d'Armes**, enjoy the charm of the city's outdoor cafes and restaurants. The area known as the *Grund*, near the River Alzette, has many lively cafes and restaurants; it can be reached via a lift going down through the ancient rock (with the entrance located on the square **Fëschmaart** above).
- Approximately 30km (19 miles) north of the capital, the **Müllerthal** region is frequently referred to as Luxembourg's 'Little Switzerland'. Hundreds of footpaths through densely wooded forests (many of which have vast expanses of needle trees), crystal-clear brooks and spectacular rock formations combine to make this one of the country's most popular areas for **walking** and **hiking**. Coach tours to the Müllerthal, also known as the **Germano-Luxembourg Natural Park**, leave daily from the main bus station in Luxembourg-Ville. The main resorts are **Beaufort** and **Larochette**, both of which also have castles located on a hilltop offering good views. Another well-known resort in the area is **Berdorf**.
- Almost one-third of Luxembourg's total land area consists of forest and it is particularly the north (a region known as the Luxembourg **Ardennes** referred to locally as *Eisléck*) which offers the best natural attractions. The scenic beauty and quiet of this region, which consists of forested plateaux, wooded hills and lush valleys, attracts many nature and outdoor enthusiasts. Head for the small town of **Esch-sur-Sûre**, a well-known regional resort which is entirely surrounded by the natural moat of the **River Sûre** (*Sauer*).
- **Rock climbing** is available near **Berdorf** in the Müllerthal region. Permission is required and can be obtained by writing to Eaux et Forêts, Diekirch, PO Box 30, L-920, Diekirch.
- A few miles further upstream is the country's drinking water reservoir, where a barrage dam (the *Staudamm*) makes a beautiful lake, used extensively for many types of **watersports**, and located within the **Upper Sûre National Park**, an area of outstanding natural beauty.
- In the southeast, the **River Moselle** (a tributary to the Rhine) flows through the lush valleys of Luxembourg's main wine-producing region (referred to as 'the Moselle' or *d'Musel* in Luxembourgish). Go on a wine tasting tour in **Grevenmacher** and in the nearby towns of **Remerschen**, **Remich** and **Wormeldange**. **Boat-cruises** on the Moselle are also available.
- In the towns of **Diekirch** and **Wiltz**, visit **breweries**.
- In the spa town of **Mondorf-les-Bains**, enjoy **thermal health treatments** as well as sports and leisure facilities. The town also has a casino.
- Visit the the small village of **Schengen**, where the Moselle marks the meeting of three countries (Luxembourg, France and Germany), which has become internationally known after the 'Schengen Agreement' was signed there in 1995.

Entertainment

FOOD & DRINK: Luxembourg cooking combines German heartiness with Franco-Belgian finesse. The preparation of trout, pike and crayfish is excellent, as are the pastries and cakes. Delicious desserts are prepared with local liqueurs, and a dash of *quetsch*, *mirabelle* or *kirsch* will be added to babas or fruit cups. Most aspects of restaurants and bars are similar to the rest of Europe. Luxembourg's white Moselle wines resemble those of the Rhine, but are drier than the fruitier wines of the French Moselle. Beer is another speciality and is a traditional industry. **Minimum drinking age**: The minimum age for drinking in bars is 17, and anyone younger than 17 must be accompanied by an adult in cafes and bars. Hours are generally from 0700-2400 (weekdays) and until 0300 (weekends and public holidays). Nightclubs are generally open until 0300.

National specialities:
- *Carré de porc fumé* (smoked pork and broad beans or sauerkraut).
- *Cochon de lait en gelée* (jellied suckling pig).
- *Jambon d'Ardennes* (famous smoked Ardennes ham).
- *Tarte aux quetsches*.
- *Omelette soufflée au kirsch*.

National drinks:
- *Bofferding*, *Diekirch Mousel* and *Simon* (beer).
- *Eau de vie* (45 to 50 per cent alcohol).

Tipping: Bills generally include service, but a rounding up is often given. Taxi drivers expect 10 per cent of meter charge.
NIGHTLIFE: Visitors to Luxembourg can enjoy a variety of evening entertainment from theatre performances, classical music concerts, opera and ballet, to nightclubs, cinemas and discos. For more information, contact the Luxembourg City Tourist Office (see *Top Things To Do*).
SHOPPING: Special purchases include beautiful porcelain and crystal. Villeroy & Boch's crystal factories in Septfontaines are open to visitors. A regional speciality is earthenware pottery from Nospelt, where in August there is a fortnight's exhibition of local work. **Shopping hours:** Mon 1400-1800, Tues-Sat 0800-1800.

Business

- **GDP**: US$27.2 billion.
- **Main exports**: Machinery and equipment, steel products, chemicals, rubber products and glass.
- **Main imports**: Minerals, metals, foodstuff and quality consumer goods.
- **Main trade partners**: Belgium, Germany, China, UK, France, The Netherlands, Italy and Spain.

ECONOMY: Luxembourg is one of the most prosperous countries in Western Europe. Two very different industries – banking and steel – have historically been the mainstays of the economy. The steel industry has ceased to be so dominant as other industries, notably chemicals, rubber, plastics, metal products and light manufacturing (textiles, paper, electronic equipment), have prospered. The banking and finance sector is also in a healthy condition: companies originally attracted to Luxembourg by favourable banking secrecy laws and low taxation have prospered despite the gradual harmonisation of taxes and tariffs across the EU. There is also a small but healthy agricultural sector mainly producing crops. In 2005, growth was 2.3 per cent, with inflation at 2.4 per cent. The Luxembourgeois economy has long been linked with that of Belgium, initially through the 1921 economic union, supplemented by a further treaty in 1958 and latterly, by mutual membership of the EU. Luxembourg was an inaugural adopter of the Euro at the beginning of 1999.
BUSINESS ETIQUETTE: Businesspeople are expected to wear suits. It is advisable to make prior appointments and business cards are often used. Avoid business visits during Christmas and New Year, Easter week and July and August.
Office hours: Generally Mon-Fri 0830-1200 and 1400-1800.
CONFERENCES/CONVENTIONS: The location of the Grand Duchy of Luxembourg at the heart of the EU ensures its status as one of the most popular destinations for conferences and conventions in Western Europe.

Credit: ©Luxembourg National Tourist Office

Macedonia

SERBIA & MONTENEGRO

Kosovo

BULGARIA

Kumanovo

SKOPJE

Tetovo · Delčevo

Korab · Gostivar Veles · Kočani
2764m

Debar · Kičevo MACEDONIA Štip

Strumica

Prilep

Lake Dojran

Ohrid Bitola

Lake Ohrid Lake Prespa Mt Kajmakčalan
2524m

ALBANIA GREECE

80km

40mls

✈ international airport

Location: Former Yugoslav Republic; southeastern Europe.

Time: GMT + 1 (GMT + 2 from last Sunday in March to last Sunday in October).

Overview

Macedonia (Former Yugoslav Republic of) is a mountainous land right at the heart of the Balkans. Its churches and mosques contain many fine examples of art and architecture from the Byzantine and Ottoman periods.

General Information

AREA: 25,713 sq km (9928 sq miles).
The former Yugoslav republic of 'Macedonia' is only one of three areas of the historical region of 'Macedonia', which includes Pirin Macedonia (Bulgaria) and Aegean Macedonia (Greece), with a total area of 66,600 sq km (25,700 sq miles), most of which is in Greece. In deference to Greek sensibilities, the United Nations and other international organisations have formally recognised Macedonia under the interim name of 'The Former Yugoslav Republic of Macedonia'; however this is gradually reverting to 'The Republic of Macedonia'.
POPULATION: 2 million (official estimate 2002).
POPULATION DENSITY: 79.7 per sq km.
CAPITAL: Skopje. **Population:** 467,257 (2002).
GEOGRAPHY: Roughly rectangular in shape, and on the strategic Vardar Valley north–south communications route, Macedonia (Former Yugoslav Republic) is landlocked, bordering Serbia & Montenegro to the north, Albania to the west, Greece to the south and Bulgaria to the east.
GOVERNMENT: Republic since 1991. Gained independence from Yugoslavia (now Serbia and Montenegro) in 1991. **Head of State:** President Branko Crvenkovski since 2004. **Head of Government:** Premier Vlado Buckovski since 2004.
LANGUAGE: Macedonian (a slavonic language using the Cyrillic script) is the most widely used language. Albanian, Turkish and Serbo-Croat are also used by ethnic groups. English, French and German are widely spoken.
RELIGION: 67 per cent of the population are Eastern Orthodox Macedonians and around 23 per cent are Muslim Albanians. There are also Muslim Turks and Serbian Orthodox minorities. As elsewhere in the former Yugoslav federation, local politics are now strongly divided along national confessional lines.
ELECTRICITY: 220 volts AC, 50Hz.
SOCIAL CONVENTIONS: Handshaking is the common practice on introduction. Local business protocol is fairly informal, but things go very slowly or not at all owing to the local bureaucracy and the more recent general socio-economic collapse in the Republic.

Climate

Macedonia has a pronounced continental climate, with very cold winters and hot summers.
Required clothing: Mediumweight clothing and very warm overcoats in winter; lightweight clothing and raincoats required for the summer.

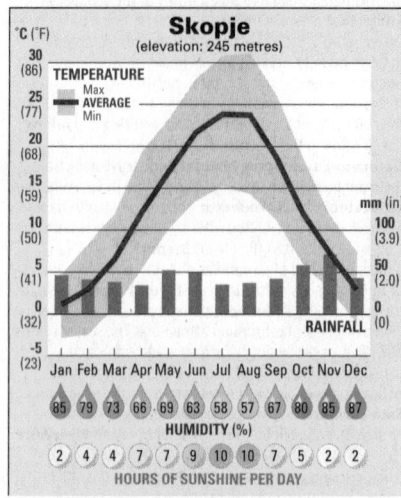

Skopje (elevation: 245 metres)

TEMPERATURE
Max
AVERAGE
Min

RAINFALL

Jan Feb Mar Apr May Jun Jul Aug Sep Oct Nov Dec

HUMIDITY (%)
85 79 73 66 69 63 58 57 67 80 85 87

HOURS OF SUNSHINE PER DAY
2 4 4 7 7 9 10 10 7 5 2 2

Communications

Telephone: IDD is available. Country code: 389. All telecommunications services are generally working normally.
Mobile telephone: Coverage is limited to the main towns.
Internet: There are a few Internet cafes in the main towns.
Post: Services work normally.
MEDIA: The constitution guarantees freedom of speech.
Press: The main daily newspapers are *Dnevnik*, *Flaka e Vëllazërimit*, *Nova Makedonija* and *Vecer* (an evening paper). Weekly papers include *Fokus* and *Puls*.
TV: *MTV* operates three national networks.
Radio: *Macedonian Radio* is state owned. *Kanal 77* and *Antenna 5* are private stations.

Passport/Visa

	Passport Required	Visa Required?	Return Ticket Required?
Full British	Yes	No	No
Australian	Yes	Yes	No
Canadian	Yes	Yes	No
USA	Yes	No	No
Other EU	Yes	No/1	No

Note: *Regulations and requirements may be subject to change at short notice, and you are advised to contact the appropriate diplomatic or consular authority before finalising travel arrangements. Any numbers in the chart refer to the footnotes below.*

PASSPORTS: Passport with at least three to six months' validity (depends on the individual case) required by all.
VISAS: Required by all except the following:
(a) **1.** nationals referred to in the chart above (except Australia, Canada, Czech Republic, Estonia, Hungary, Latvia, Lithuania, Poland, Slovak Republic and Slovenia) for tourist and business stays of up to three months;
(b) nationals of Barbados, Bosnia & Herzegovina, Botswana, Croatia, Cuba, Iceland, Israel, Liechtenstein, Monaco, New Zealand, Norway, San Marino, Switzerland and the Vatican City for tourist and business stays of up to three months;
(c) nationals of Serbia & Montenegro and Turkey for tourist and business stays of up to 60 days;
(d) nationals of Bulgaria and Malaysia for tourist and business stays of up to one month;
(e) nationals of CIS countries, except nationals of Moldova and Uzbekistan, can travel without a visa for purposes such as organised tourism and visiting relatives.
Note: (a) Nationals of the following countries need to obtain official approval from the Ministry of the Interior in (Former Yugoslav Republic of) Macedonia. in order to obtain visas: Afghanistan, Algeria, Bangladesh, Burundi, Cameroon, Chile, China (PR), Congo (Rep), Egypt, Ethiopia, Gabon, Ghana, Guatemala, Guinea, Guinea-Bissau, Honduras, Hong Kong (SAR), India, Iran, Iraq, Jordan, Lebanon, Libya, Morocco, Niger, Nigeria, Oman, Pakistan, The Philippines, Rwanda, Saudi Arabia, Senegal, Somalia, Sri Lanka, Sudan, Syrian Arab Republic, Tunisia, United Arab Emirates, Vietnam and Yemen. Their visas must also be issued at an Embassy (including for nationals of Czech Republic, although they do not need prior approval). All other nationals require visas, but their applications do not need to be referred to Skopje. (b) Any

holders of travel documents other than a passport must also require approval from (Former Yugoslav Republic of) Macedonia.
Types of visa: *Single-entry:* £13 (£21*); *Double-entry:* £17 (£25*); *Multiple-entry:* £24 (£32*).
* These prices are for those nationals that require approval from the Macedonian authorities. Visas are issued free of charge to nationals of the CIS (except nationals of Moldova and Uzbekistan).
Validity: Valid for 30 days. Transit visas valid for up to five days.
Application to: Nearest Diplomatic or consular mission (see *Passport/Visa Information*).
Application requirements: (a) Valid passport. (b) Application form, which must be submitted in person. (c) One passport-size photo. (d) Fee payable in cash. *Tourist:* (a)-(d) and, (e) Hotel reservation. *Business:* (a)-(d) and, (e) Letter of invitation from Macedonian company. (f) Business letter from the applicant's company. *Transit:* (a)-(d) and, (e) Visa for next country, if required.
Working days required: Usually one to three, although if approval is needed from (Former Yugoslav Republic of) Macedonia (see above), can take a minimum of 10 days.

PASSPORT/VISA INFORMATION

Embassy of (Former Yugoslav Republic of) Macedonia in the UK
Suite 2.1 & 2.2, 2nd Floor, Buckingham Court, Buckingham Gate, London SW1E 6BE, UK
Tel: (020) 7976 0535 *or* 0538 (consular section).
Website: www.macedonianembassy.org.uk
Opening hours: Mon-Fri 0930-1730; Mon, Wed and Fri 1200-1500 (for personal callers).

Embassy of (Former Yugoslav Republic of) Macedonia in the USA
1101 30th Street, Suite 302, NW Washington, DC 20007, USA
Tel: (202) 337 3063.
E-mail: rmacedonia@aol.com

Money

Currency: Macedonian Denar (MKD) = 100 deni. Notes are in denominations of MKD5000, 1000, 500, 100, 50 and 10. Coins are in denominations of MKD5, 2 and 1, and 50 deni.
Currency exchange: All major currencies may be exchanged, but Euros are easiest to exchange.
Credit & debit cards: Very limited acceptance. Check with your credit or debit card company for details of merchant acceptability and other services which may be available.
Traveller's cheques: To avoid additional exchange rate charges, travellers are advised to take cheques in US Dollars or Euros.
Currency restrictions: There are no restrictions on the import and export of local or foreign currency.
Banking hours: Mon-Fri 0700-1900; Sat 0700-1300.
Exchange rate indicators:
Rate at time of publishing
£1.00= MKD89.45
$1.00= MKD51.55

Duty Free

The following goods may be imported into Macedonia (Former Yugoslav Republic) without incurring customs duty:
one box of cigarettes; one bottle of alcohol; gifts to the value of €30.70.

Public Holidays

Below are listed Public Holidays for the January 2006-June 2007 period.
2006: Jan 1 New Year's Day. **Jan 6-7** Orthodox Christmas. **Mar 8** International Women's Day. **May 1** May Day. **May 24** St Cyrilus and St Methodius Day. **Aug 2** Ilinden (National Holiday). **Sep 8** Independence Day.
2007: Jan 1 New Year's Day. **Jan 6-7** Orthodox Christmas. **Mar 8** International Women's Day. **May 1** May Day. **May 24** St Cyrilus and St Methodius Day.

Health

	Special Precautions?	Certificate Required?
Yellow Fever	No	No
Cholera	No	No
Typhoid & Polio	No/1	N/A
Malaria	No	N/A

Note: *Regulations and requirements may be subject to change at short notice, and you are advised to contact your doctor well in advance of your intended date of departure. Any numbers in the chart refer to the footnotes below.*

1: An outbreak of *poliomyelitis* occurred in the region in 1996, and immunisation is advisable. Vaccination against *typhoid* is also advised.
Food & drink: Mains water is normally chlorinated and, whilst relatively safe, may cause mild abdominal upsets. Bottled water is available and is advised for the first few weeks of the stay. Milk is pasteurised and dairy products are safe for consumption. Local meat, poultry, seafood, fruit and vegetables are generally considered safe to eat.
Other risks: *Hepatitis A* and *brucellosis* are endemic. *Rabies* is present. For those at high risk, vaccination before arrival should be considered. If you are bitten, seek medical advice without delay. For more information, consult the *Health* appendix.
Health care: Prescribed medicines must be paid for. There is a reciprocal health agreement with the UK but health insurance with emergency repatriation is strongly recommended.

Travel - International

AIR:
The national airline is *Macedonian Airlines – MAT (IN)*. Other airlines serving Skopje are *Adria Airways, Austrian Airlines, Croatia Airlines* and *KLM*. Connections are available to Austria, Croatia, Denmark, Germany, The Netherlands, Italy, Serbia & Montenegro, Slovenia, Sweden, Switzerland and Turkey.
Approximate flight times: From Skopje to *London* is approximately four hours.
International airports: *Skopje (SKP)* (website: www.airports.com.mk) is 25km (16 miles) from the city. Taxis are available to the city centre (travel time – 25 to 30 minutes). Airport facilities include duty-free shop, bar and restaurant, bank/bureau de change, baggage facilities, post office and car hire. There is also an airport at *Ohrid*.
Departure tax: None.
RAIL:
Intercity trains operate five times a day between Skopje and Belgrade (Serbia) via Nijs. Trains also run twice daily between Skopje and Thessaloniki (Greece).
ROAD:
Bus: The international bus station in Skopje serves buses destined for Tirana (Albania), Sofia (Bulgaria), Belgrade (Serbia) and Istanbul (Turkey), which run daily, and buses to Germany, which run twice weekly.

Travel - Internal

AIR:
There are no regularly scheduled domestic flights – however, there are occasional flights between Ohrid and Skopje.
RAIL/ROAD:
All the main internal road and rail services are operating normally, with links from Skopje to Kumanovo in the north, to Stip in the east, to Veles and Gevgelija in the south, and to Prilep and Bitola in the southwest. **Buses:** The bus network in (Former Yugoslav Republic of) Macedonia is well developed with frequent services from Skopje to Ohrid and Bitola. Long-distance buses need to be booked well in advance.

Travel Advice

Most visits to Macedonia are trouble-free but you should be aware of the global risk of indiscriminate terrorist attacks, which could be against civilian targets, including places visited by foreigners.
Travellers intending to travel to the northern and western border regions of Macedonia should exercise caution. Sporadic acts of violence do still occur in Macedonia, particularly in the north, but also including Skopje.
This advice is based on information provided by the Foreign and Commonwealth Office in the UK. It is correct at time of publishing. As the situation can change rapidly, visitors are advised to contact the following organisations for the latest travel advice:

British Foreign and Commonwealth Office
Tel: (0845) 850 2829.
Website: www.fco.gov.uk

US Department of State
Website: http://travel.state.gov/travel

Accommodation

HOTELS:
Macedonia (Former Yugoslav Republic) has one deluxe/A-class hotel. There are B-class hotels in Skopje and the Ohrid Lake tourist area on the border with Albania and Greece.

Top Things To See & Do

- **Skopje**, (Former Yugoslav Republic of) Macedonia's capital is largely new, owing to an earthquake in 1963. **Skopje Old Town** is the most attractive quarter of the city. It is full of shops and restaurants. Here is the **Church of the Holy Saviour** with its intricately carved *iconostasis* (a screen in orthodox churches on which icons are hung). Also to be found in the Old Town are the **Kursumli An** (16th-century) and the **Suli An** (15th-century) *caravanserais* and the **Daut Pasha Baths** with its two large and 11 small domes. It now houses the **Art Gallery**. There are a number of mosques dating from the Ottoman period, particularly the 15th-century **Mustafa Pasha Mosque**, as well as the old 10th-century **Kale Fortress** and a magnificent footbridge spanning the **River Vardar**. Near Skopje is the **Nerezi Monastery** with the accompanying 12th-century Church **of St Pantelejmon** housing magnificent Byzantine frescoes.
- Located 18km (11 miles) from the Greek border, **Bitola** has the ruins of the ancient city of **Heraclea** nearby.
- Situated on **Lake Ohrid**, **Ohrid** is probably the most attractive town in (Former Yugoslav Republic of) Macedonia. The walls of the fortress still survive and now provide a venue for summer concerts, operas and plays. Near the old fortress are the remains of a classical theatre. Dotted around this beautiful town are a number of ancient churches, particularly the **Cathedral of St Sophia** containing some magnificent 11th-century frescoes.

TOURIST INFORMATION

Tourist Association of Skopje
Street address: Dame Gruev Gradski Blok 3, 1000 Skopje, (Former Yugoslav Republic of) Macedonia
Postal address: PO Box 399, Skopje, (Former Yugolav Republic of) Macedonia
Tel: (2) 3118 498.

Entertainment

FOOD & DRINK: Macedonian cuisine is similar to that of Turkey and Greece. Different varieties of kebab can be found almost everywhere, as can dishes such as *moussaka* (aubergines and potatoes baked in layers with minced meat). National specialities are *gravce tavce* (beans in a skillet) and the delicious Ohrid trout.
SHOPPING: Shopping hours: Mon-Fri 0800-2000 and Sat 0800-1500.

Business

ECONOMY: As the smallest of the six former Yugoslav republics, Macedonia accounted for just 6 per cent of total Yugoslav output. It was the most dependent on federal Government subsidies but these vanished along with guaranteed markets in Yugoslavia (now Serbia & Montenegro) when the old central economic planning system ceased in 1991. Since then the economy has been further undermined by regional strife – the civil war in the neighbouring Serbian province of Kosovo, instability in Albania and, most recently, the conflict between the Government and Albanian nationalists – which has also deterred investment from the region. The economy shrank consistently throughout the 1990s; in 2001, it contracted by 5 per cent.
(Former Yugoslav Republic of) Macedonia has a predominantly agricultural economy in which the main products are rice, wine and wheat (for export), fruit and vegetables, cheese, lamb and tobacco for domestic consumption. Food processing is a major component of the industrial sector, which also produces metal goods, chemicals and textiles. Many families are dependent for their survival on remittances from émigré Macedonians working elsewhere in Europe. Unemployment remains exceptionally high at around 40 per cent, with the result that a thriving black economy – a characteristic of most of the southern Balkans – is operating. Reconstruction in (Former Yugoslav Republic of) Macedonia is closely linked to a number of factors: the settlement of the territorial dispute with Greece; the cancellation of old debts from the Yugoslav era; and the resolution of the conflict with Albanian nationalists. All have improved (Former Yugoslav Republic of) Macedonia's economic prospects. Thus, in the spring of 2002, international donors, including the IMF, the World Bank and the European Union, were able to authorise a US$500 million aid package.
BUSINESS ETIQUETTE: Suits and ties are correct attire for men, with skirt, blouse and tights the accepted attire for women. English, French and German are spoken in most business circles. **Office hours:** Mon-Fri 0730-1530.

COMMERCIAL INFORMATION

Economic Chamber of Macedonia
PO Box 324, St Dimitrie Cupovski br. 13, 1000 Skopje, (Former Yugoslav Republic of) Macedonia
Tel: (2) 3116543.
Website: http://info.mchamber.org.mk.

Madagascar

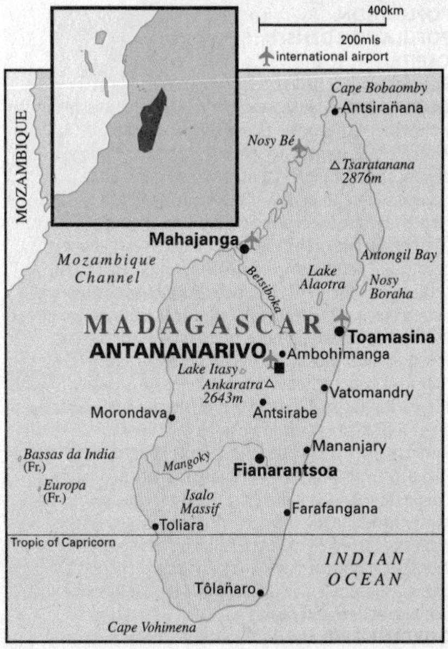

Location: Indian Ocean, 500km (300 miles) off the coast of Mozambique.

Time: GMT + 3.

Overview

Madagascar is a beautiful island, ringed by golden beaches and palm trees, and with an interior that is resplendent in its variety, from grassy plateaus to volcanoes and opaque forests and natural reserves.
According to local legend, the island was first inhabited by the Vazimba, a race of white pygmies. These people, if they existed, were displaced by successive waves of Polynesian migrants from the Malayo-Indonesian archipelago, from as early as the sixth century AD. In the ninth century, Madagascar was a major trading power in the western Indian Ocean. Moreover, ancient ruins indicate an extensive Arab presence on the island around that time. Bantu tribes from mainland Africa later settled on the west coast. The first Europeans arrived in the mid-17th century. Several French settlements were established on the south-east coast but were destroyed within 30 years.
At the time, Madagascar supported several kingdoms along its coastline and, in the central highlands, the kingdom of the Merina, which was the dominant ethnic group. From their fortress city of Antananarivo, the 19th-century kings gradually conquered the coastal kingdoms and by 1830 most of the island was under unified Merina control. The success of the Merina was partly due to a well-worked strategy of playing off rival European colonists against each other: in particular, the British and the French. However, the UK – with copious commitments elsewhere – was content by the end of the 19th century to leave the southern Indian Ocean to the French. Without a counter-balancing power, Madagascar was vulnerable to French takeover, which duly occurred in 1896 when the Merina kingdom was overthrown by a French military force. In 1948, the Malagasy people sought to re-establish their independence through armed insurrection. They were unsuccessful, but the uprising paved the way for independence, which came in 1960. Philibert Tsirana's PSD Party ruled with the support of France and the people of the coastal regions until 1972, when highland agitation against French influence prompted the Army Chief of Staff, Major-General Ramanantsoa, to assume executive power for the purpose of pursuing a more nationalistic policy. Three years later the military

Government resigned after selecting Lt-Commander Didier Ratsiraka as Head of State. A gradual civilianisation of the Government culminated in 1977 in elections to the National People's Assembly, which were won by the sole legal party, Avant-garde de la Révolution Malgache (AREMA).

Recent years have been marred by political, economic and meteorological crises. Indeed, some may be deterred by the levels of poverty on this island and the enormous gap between rich and poor. Nevertheless, Madagascar dazzles with its rich wildlife, with a large majority of its species unique to the island, and found nowhere else on earth. Of the popular creature, the lemur, there are over 10 different species alone. The island is also a mass of unusual and colourful flowers and other flora. In terms of biodiversity alone, Madagascar really is one of a kind.

General Information

AREA: 587,041 sq km (226,658 sq miles).
POPULATION: 18.4 million (UN, 2005).
POPULATION DENSITY: 31.34 per sq km.
CAPITAL: Antananarivo (formerly Tananarive).
Population: 1.5 million (estimate, 2003).
GEOGRAPHY: Madagascar, the fourth-largest island in the world, lies in the Indian Ocean off the coast of Mozambique. It includes several much smaller islands. A central chain of high mountains, the Hauts Plateaux, occupies more than half of the main island and is responsible for the marked differences – ethnically, climatically and scenically – between the east and west coasts. The narrow strip of lowlands on the east coast, settled from the sixth century by Polynesian seafarers, is largely covered by dense rainforests, whereas the broader west-coast landscape, once covered by dry deciduous forests, is now mostly savannah. The east coast receives the monsoon and, on both coasts, the climate is wetter towards the north. The southern tip of the island is semi-desert, with great forests of cactus-like plants. The capital, Antananarivo, is high up in the Hauts Plateaux near the island's centre. Much of Madagascar's flora and fauna is unique to the island. There are 3000 endemic species of butterfly; the many endemic species of lemurs fill the niches occupied elsewhere by animals as varied as racoons, monkeys, marmots, bushbabies and sloths. There is a similar diversity of reptiles, amphibians and birds (especially ducks), and also all levels of plant life.
GOVERNMENT: Republic since 1992. Gained independence from France in 1960. **Head of State:** President Marc Ravalomanana since 2002. **Head of Government:** Prime Minister Jacques Sylla. **Recent history:** In 1992, under intense domestic and international pressure, Ratsiraka conceded the introduction of a genuinely democratic constitution. The first Presidential poll under the new system, held in 1993, saw Ratsiraka defeated by Albert Zafy. Three years later, however, Ratsiraka recovered the office and held on to it until 2001. The old highland/lowland rivalry which previously characterised the country's politics had by now evolved into an urban/rural split. This emerged at the 2001 election. This time Ratsiraka's opponent was a businessman, Marc Ravalomanana, who drew his main support from urban areas. There was no question that Ravalomanana topped the first round of polling: in dispute was whether or not he had reached the 50 per cent threshold required to claim victory without a second-round run-off (which would have been against Ratsiraka). Both sides mobilised their supporters and a bizarre but violent stand-off followed: the capital was effectively cut off from the rest of the country; roads and bridges were destroyed and suppliers of food and essential goods were unable or unwilling to sell their goods in the capital. With both sides spurning mediation, the outcome depended upon who gained the support of the army. Most senior officers sided with Ravalomanana and, by July 2002, he had secured control over the whole country. Ratsiraka went into exile and was later convicted in his absence of embezzlement. The crisis left Madagascar in a fragile political and economic condition; the country's difficulties have since been compounded by severe drought, especially in the southern part of the island.
Under the terms of a new constitution adopted by popular referendum in August 1992, legislative power resides in a bicameral legislature, comprising a partially-elected Senate and fully-elected National Assembly, each of which has a four-year term. A Council of Ministers is appointed by the Prime Minister. The President is elected by popular vote for a five-year term. The Prime Minister is appointed by the President from a list of candidates nominated by the National Assembly. Executive power rests with the Prime Minister.
LANGUAGE: The official languages are Malagasy (which is related to Indonesian) and French. Local dialects are also spoken. Very little English is spoken.
RELIGION: 51 per cent follow animist beliefs; about 43 per cent Christian; remainder Muslim.
ELECTRICITY: Mostly 220 volts AC, 50Hz. Plugs are generally two-pin.

SOCIAL CONVENTIONS: The Madagascans are extremely hospitable and welcoming, although their relaxed attitude to time (public forms of transport, for example, will not generally move until they are full – no matter how long it takes to fill the last seat) may be frustrating. Dress is casual, except for the very smartest hotel and restaurant functions. Visitors are advised not to wear any military-style clothing; locally it is disapproved of and could lead to detention. Entertaining is done in restaurants and bars, and a good degree of acquaintance is necessary before being invited to a family home. Gifts should be offered if staying at a local village, particularly to the village headman, although monetary contributions will be seen as an insult. Respect should be paid to the many local taboos (*fady*) – but as these vary from region to region this is not always easy; however, it is clear that advice should be sought before approaching tombs and graves. It remains the practice in some regions (though it is increasingly rare due to the enormous cost) to invite an ancestor to a village celebration, disinterring the body so that the ancestor may attend physically, and later re-interring the body with new shrouds; this traditional observance (known as *famadihana*) demonstrates the continuing hold of traditional beliefs. Visitors invited to such an occasion should consider it a great honour. **Photography:** Do not photograph military or police establishments.

Climate

Hot and subtropical climate, colder in the mountains. Rainy season: November to March. Dry season: April to October. The south and west regions are hot and dry. Monsoons bring storms and cyclones to the east and north from December to March. The mountains, including Antananarivo, are warm and thundery from November to April and dry, cool and windy the rest of the year.
Required clothing: Lightweights are worn during the summer on high central plateaux and throughout the year in the north and south. Warmer clothes are advised for during the evenings and winter in mountainous areas. Rainwear is advisable.

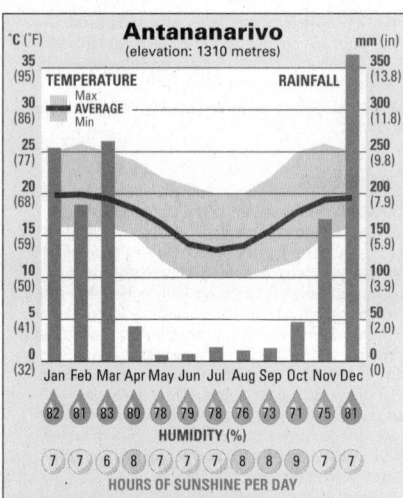

Communications

Telephone: IDD is available to major towns. Country code: 261, followed by a two-digit number for an access provider, but a standard dialling code is expected to be introduced soon. After the international and access codes, numbers should be seven digits including two initial digits for the geographical area. The cheapest way to make phone calls is to use a telephone card and call from a telephone booth. Telephone cards can be purchased at post offices and most hotels.
Mobile telephone: Roaming agreements exist with international mobile phone companies. Coverage reaches major cities and main roads.
Internet: Public Internet access exists in large cities; there are a few Internet cafes in Antananarivo.
Post: Airmail to Europe takes at least seven days and surface mail three to four months.
MEDIA: Mr Ravalomanana owns the private Malagasy Broadcasting System, which operates the *MBS TV* and *Radio MBS* networks. Although nationwide radio and TV broadcasting remain the monopoly of the state, there are hundreds of private local radio and TV stations.
Press: There are no English-language newspapers; six dailies are published in French and/or Malagasy. The main papers include *La Gazette de la Grande Ile*, *Madagascar Tribune* and *Midi Madagasikara*.
TV: *Television Malagasy* (TVM) is state-owned. *Radio-Television Analamanga* is privately run, as is *Madagascar TV*. The commercial *MBS TV* is owned by Ravalomanana.

Radio: Many private radio stations in the capital are owned by pro-Ravalomanana politicians. However, a boom in privately-owned FM radio stations and more critical political reporting by the print media followed 1990's law on press freedom. *Malagasy National Radio* (RNM) is state-owned; privately owned stations include *Radio Don Bosco* (Roman Catholic FM station), *Radio Tsioka Vao* and *Radio Korail*; *Radio MBS* is commerical and owned by Ravalomanana.

Passport/Visa

	Passport Required?	Visa Required?	Return Ticket Required?
Full British	Yes	Yes	Yes
Australian	Yes	Yes	Yes
Canadian	Yes	Yes	Yes
USA	Yes	Yes	Yes
Other EU	Yes	Yes	Yes
Japanese	Yes	Yes	Yes

Note: *Regulations and requirements may be subject to change at short notice, and you are advised to contact the appropriate diplomatic or consular authority before finalising travel arrangements. Any numbers in the chart refer to the footnotes below.*

Passports: Passports valid for six months after date of entry required by all.
VISAS: Required by all except:
Transit passengers continuing their journey by the same or first connecting aircraft within 24 hours provided holding onward or return documentation and not leaving the airport.
Types of visa and cost: *Tourist*: £40 (single-entry); £50 (multiple-entry). *Business*: £55 (single-entry); £65 (multiple-entry).
Validity: Visas are issued for stays of up to 90 days and are valid for six months from date of issue.
Application to: Consulate (or consular section at Embassy). Some nationalities are able to get a visa at Antananarivo airport on arrival; however it is strongly recommended to obtain a visa prior to this. Contact the Embassy for further information before departure.
Application requirements: (a) Valid passport. (b) One application form and one copy. (c) Two passport-size photos. (d) Return ticket or confirmation of booking from travel agent. (e) Fee payable by cheque or cash. (f) If applying by post enclose pre-paid, next-day special delivery envelope. *Business*: (a)-(f) and, (g) Letter of recommendation and confirmation of employment on company-headed notepaper with details about the applicant's business activity, stating the company or individual responsible for expenses and the name of correspondent in Madagascar.
Working days required: Same day (personal applications); up to five days (postal applications).
Temporary residence: Enquire at Consulate (or Consular section at Embassy).

PASSPORT/VISA INFORMATION

Honorary Consulate of the Republic of Madagascar in the UK
16 Lanark Mansions, Pennard Road, London
W12 8DT, UK
Tel: (020) 8746 0133.
Website: www.madagascar.org.uk
Opening hours: Mon-Fri 0930-1300.

Embassy of the Republic of Madagascar in the USA
2374 Massachusetts Avenue, NW, Washington, DC
20008, USA
Tel: (202) 265 5525-7.

Money

Currency: The pre-colonial Ariary (MGA) has been reintroduced to replace the Malagasy Franc (MGF). Notes are in denominations of MGA10,000, 5000, 2000, 1000, 500, 200 and 100. Coins are in denominations of MGA50, 20, 10 and 5. Malagasy Francs are no longer legal tender but can be exchanged at banks until 2009.
Currency exchange: Malagasy Francs can be bought only at banks and official bureaux de change in hotels and at the airport in Antananarivo. Hotels have a less favourable exchange rate. A few ATMs have now been installed in Antananarivo. The Ariary is a non-convertible currency and cannot be exchanged back into tradable currency. Therefore it is a good idea to exchange currency as required.
Credit & debit cards: American Express, Diners Club, MasterCard and Visa are accepted at top-end hotels in Tana and the provincial capitals. These and other cards have

limited use elsewhere in the country. Check with your credit or debit card company for details of merchant acceptability and other services which may be available.

Traveller's cheques: These can be exchanged in banks and major hotels. To avoid additional exchange rate charges, travellers are advised to take traveller's cheques in Euros or US Dollars.

Currency restrictions: The import of local currency is limited to MGA1000. The export of local currency is prohibited to non-residents. The import and export of foreign currency is unlimited, subject to declaration.

Banking hours: Mon-Fri 0800-1100 and 1400-1600.

Exchange rate indicators:

Rate at time of publishing

£1.00= MGA3140.84
$1.00= MGA1810.05

Duty Free

The following goods can be imported into Madagascar without incurring customs duty by persons 21 years of age and over:

500 cigarettes or 25 cigars or 500g of tobacco; one bottle of alcoholic beverage.

Note: All perfume is subject to duty. All vegetables must be declared and import permit received before travel. Animals need a detailed veterinary certificate. Dogs and cats must be vaccinated against rabies. Arms and ammunition require an exit permit. Tourists should be aware that many items on sale may have been manufactured illegally and may not be taken out of the country, with or without a permit.

Public Holidays

Below are listed Public Holidays for the January 2006-June 2007 period.

2006: Jan 1 New Year's Day. **Mar 29** Commemoration of the 1947 Rebellion. **Apr 14** Good Friday. **Apr 17** Easter Monday. **May 1** Labour Day. **Jun 26** Independence Day. **Aug 15** Assumption. **Sep 27** St Vincent de Paul's Day. **Nov 1** All Saints' Day. **Dec 25** Christmas Day. **Dec 30** Anniversary of the Republic of Madagascar.

2007: Jan 1 New Year's Day. **Mar 29** Commemoration of the 1947 Rebellion. **Apr 6** Good Friday. **Apr 9** Easter Monday. **May 1** Labour Day. **Jun 26** Independence Day.

Health

	Special Precautions	Certificate Required?
Yellow Fever	Yes	1
Cholera	Yes	2
Typhoid & Polio	3	N/A
Malaria	4	N/A

Note: *Regulations and requirements may be subject to change at short notice, and you are advised to contact your doctor well in advance of your intended date of departure. Any numbers in the chart refer to the footnotes below.*

1: A *yellow fever* vaccination certificate is required from travellers arriving from, or having passed through, an area considered by the Malagasy authorities to be infected within six days; enquire at Embassy.

2: A *cholera* vaccination certificate is recommended for travellers arriving from, or having passed through, an area considered by the Malagasy authorities to be infected; enquire at Embassy.

3: Immunisation against *typhoid* and *poliomyelitis* is often recommended.

4: *Malaria* risk, predominantly in the malignant *falciparum* form, exists all year throughout the country and is highest in coastal areas. Resistance to chloroquine has been reported. The recommended prophylaxis is mefloquine.

Food & drink: All water should be regarded as being potentially contaminated. Water used for drinking, brushing teeth or making ice should have first been boiled or otherwise sterilised. Milk is unpasteurised and should be boiled. Powdered or tinned milk is available and is advised, but make sure that it is reconstituted with pure water. Avoid dairy products that are likely to have been made from unboiled milk. Only eat well-cooked meat and fish, preferably served hot. Pork, salad and mayonnaise may carry increased risk. Vegetables should be cooked and fruit peeled.

Other risks: *Bilharzia (schistosomiasis)* is present. Avoid swimming and paddling in fresh water; swimming pools which are well chlorinated and maintained are safe. *Hepatitis A, B,* and *E* are endemic and precautions are advised. *Dysenteries* and *diarrhoeal diseases* are common. Many *viral diseases* including severe *haemorrhagic fevers* have been reported. Natural foci of plague occur. *Rabies* is present. For those at high risk, vaccination before arrival should be considered. If you are bitten, seek medical advice without delay. For more information, consult the *Health* appendix.

Health care: Health insurance is strongly recommended; it should include cover for emergency repatriation. Private and public healthcare is available, but public facilities can be very limited. It is highly recommended that visitors bring medication for stomach upsets.

Travel - International

AIR:

 Madagascar's national airline is *Air Madagascar (MD)* (website: www.airmadagascar.mg).
Approximate flight times: From Antananarivo to *London* is 13 hours 50 minutes (including connection in Paris). There are regular flights from Madagascar to the Comoro Islands, Kenya, Mauritius, Réunion, the Seychelles and Tanzania.

Main airports: *Antananarivo (TNR)* is 17km (11 miles) from the city. *To/from the airport:* Taxis asking special higher rates are available at the airport. *Air Madagascar* provide a regular bus service to Antananarivo. *Facilities:* Restaurant, bureau de change and car hire.
Further airports are at *Arivonimamo* (international standby airport), which is 45km (28 miles) from the capital, *Mahajanga* (links to East Africa and the Comoro Islands), *Nossi Bé* (links to the Seychelles) and *Toamasina* (links to Mauritius and Réunion islands).

Departure tax: None.

SEA:

 Main port: *Toamasina.* International tour operators promote Madagascar as a stopping place on extended cruises of the Indian and western Pacific Oceans. Expensive private cruises can be arranged from Europe and the USA.

Travel - Internal

AIR:

 Most of Madagascar can be reached by air, the exceptions being a few towns in the central highlands. *Air Madagascar* flies to 51 towns and localities in the island and they offer a 50 per cent discount on domestic flights to passengers using the airline to travel to Madagascar.

SEA/RIVER/CANAL:

 Madagascar has a strong maritime tradition and there are many coastal transport services. Rapids render many of the rivers unnavigable; local tour operators can organise small-boat safaris on the Betsiboka and the Tsiribihina. The Pangalanese Canal runs for almost 600km (370 miles) along the east coast. Much of it is currently too clogged with silt for commercial traffic; the Tourist Board can arrange sailing holidays.

RAIL:

 There are five railway links on the island, Antananarivo to Toamasina and Fianarantsoa to Manakara travel through mountains, rainforests and quaint villages. Other links are Antananarivo to Antsirabe and Moramaga to Lake Alaotra. The only regular passenger rail service runs from Antananarivo to Moramanga and Lake Alaotra. Services leave every Tuesday, Thursday and Saturday, returning on Wednesday, Friday and Sunday. First-class carriages are air conditioned. Light refreshments are sometimes available. The rail service is intermittent in that trains arrive on one day and return on the following day. Children under four years old travel free. Children aged four to six years old pay half fare.

ROAD:

 The road network is in need of repair. Tarred roads of varying quality link the main towns in the central highlands and continue to the most populous parts of the east and northwest coasts. The Government have given priority to road building and improvement. There is a new route from Antananarivo to Toliara which has reduced travel time between these destinations from three to two days. There are isolated sections of tarred road, but dirt tracks are more common. Many roads are impassable in the rainy season (November to March). In 1988, the World Bank approved a US$140-million loan to rehabilitate the network. Traffic drives on the right. **Bus:** A flat fare is charged, irrespective of the distance travelled. Services can be unreliable and buses tend to be crowded. **Taxi:** Flat fares apply except in Antananarivo and Fianarantsoa, where fare is calculated according to whether the ride is confined to the 'lower town' or goes on to the 'upper town'. There are two types of taxi: the *taxi-be*, which is quick and comfortable, and the *taxi-brousse* (bush taxi), which is cheaper, slower, makes more stops and generally operates on cross-country routes. Fares should be agreed in advance and tipping is unnecessary. **Rickshaw:** The *pousse-pousse* (rickshaw) takes passengers except where traffic or gradient renders it impractical. Prices are not controlled and vary according to distance. **Stagecoach:** A few covered wagons continue to take passengers in Antananarivo. **Car hire:** This is not widespread and car hire agencies can only be found in the main tourist towns. It is advisable to make enquiries in advance about insurance requirements for car hire. **Motorbike hire:** Available from several companies in Madagascar. **Documentation:** A national driving licence is sufficient.

Travel Advice

Most visits to Madagascar are trouble-free but you should be aware of the global risk of indiscriminate international terrorist attacks, which could be against civilian targets, including places frequented by foreigners.
Travellers should avoid walking in city centres after dark. There have been reports of hold-ups at night on some of the major roads.
This advice is based on information provided by the Foreign and Commonwealth Office in the UK. It is correct at time of publishing. As the situation can change rapidly, visitors are advised to contact the following organisations for the latest travel advice:

British Foreign and Commonwealth Office
Tel: (0845) 850 2829.
Website: www.fco.gov.uk

US Department of State
Website: http://travel.state.gov/travel

Accommodation

HOTELS/YOUTH HOSTELS:

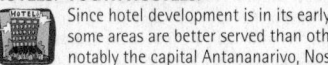 Since hotel development is in its early stages, some areas are better served than others, notably the capital Antananarivo, Nossi Bé and Toamasina. However, recent projects aimed at increasing the number of international-standard establishments have led to the opening of national tourism centres where good- to medium-standard accommodation is now available at moderate prices. As well as classified or classifiable accommodation, group and youth lodging is available. European-style accommodation is scarce outside the larger towns, and those visiting remote areas should travel with an open mind. Enquiries should be addressed to the Tourism Office in Antananarivo or *Air Madagascar* agencies. The *Guide to Madagascar* by Hilary Bradt provides excellent information on hotels and is available through the Madagascan Consulate in the UK or through bookshops.
Hotels are classified from **1** to **5 stars** (5-star being equivalent to an international standard of about 3 stars); a secondary system of **ravinala** (travellers' palms) is used for more 'rustic' accommodation. More information is available from the Ministry of Tourism (see *Top Things To See & Do*).

Top Things To See & Do

- Visit **Antananarivo**, often abbreviated to **Tana**, for its distinctively French flavour and atmosphere: French is widely spoken, and road as well as shop signs are mostly in French. The city is built on three levels. Dominating the city is the **Queen's Palace** and associated Royal Village or **Rova**. Now a national monument, it was once the residency of the Merina Dynasty which, in the 19th century, united all Madagascar for the first time. The **Tsimbazaza Zoological and Botanical Garden** is open Thursday, Sunday and holidays 0800-1100 and 1400-1700. The Tourist Information Office is nearby. It is wise not to wander too far after dark.

- The birthplace of the Malagasy state, **Ambohimanga** is 20km (12 miles) from the capital. Known variously as 'the blue city', 'the holy city' and 'the forbidden city', it is surrounded by forests. The citadel was an important Merina stronghold and retains several structures associated with their ceremonies. Its main gate is an enormous stone disc; 40 men were needed to roll it into position.

- Explore some of Madagascar's impressive National Parks and nature reserves. Spread across 152,000 hectares, the **Tsingy de Bemaraha Strict Nature Reserve** is located 60 to 80km inland from the west coast in the northern sector of the Anstingy region of the **Bemaraha Plateau**, north of the **Manambolo River Gorge**. Undisturbed forests, lakes and mangrove swamps are home to a variety of rare and endangered birds and lemurs. Rocky landscapes and limestone uplands are cut into large peaks with a mass of limestone needles. Rivers flow on the plateau and springs arise on each flank of the **Tsingy**, making this an important water catchment area. Ancient cemeteries can also be found in the Gorge. Visitors are currently restricted to the pinnacle region to the south or to the forests in the north; both of these areas are accessible overnight with guides based at **Antsalova** and **Bekopaka**. **Ampefy**, 90km (60 miles) from the capital, is a volcanic region with spectacular waterfalls and geysers. Dams are used here to catch eels. **Perinet**, 140km (90 miles) from the capital, is a nature reserve, home of the *indri* (a tail-less lemur) and many species of orchid. Also known as *Andasibe*, **Antsirabe**, 170km (110 miles) from the capital, is a thermal spa and Madagascar's main industrial centre. The volcanic hills surrounding the town are dotted with crater lakes. Madagascar's second-highest mountain, **Tsiafajovona**, may be seen to the west of the road from Antananarivo. In the **Central Highlands** is the **Hauts Plateaux**, a chain of rugged, ravine-riven mountains that run from north to south down the centre of Madagascar. Meanwhile, the lush north is dominated by two great mountains. **Tsarantanana**, the island's highest at 2880m (9450ft), is covered with the giant ferns and lichens peculiar to high-altitude rainforests. **Montagne d'Arbre** (1500m/4900ft) is a national park and is famous for its orchids and lemurs. The monsoon falls in the north between December and March. On the East Coast, the **Ivolina Zoological Park and Botanical Gardens** contain every kind of vegetable species from the eastern forests and many varieties of animal life. Local tour operators can organise a variety of **trekking** and **hiking** trips in many different parts of the country. They are generally designed to cater for specific interest groups – speleologists, mineralogists, ethnologists, ornithologists, those who wish to see rare orchids or lemurs, etc.

- Many towns have municipal pools. **Sea-bathing** along the east coast is not advised due to sharks. The main **diving** centres are **Nossi Bé** (with its neighbouring islands, **Nossi Mitsio**, **Nossi Radama** and **Tanikely**; exotic perfume plants such as ylang-ylang, vanilla, lemongrass and patchouli are grown here), **Nossi Lava**, **Toliara** (excellent bathing beaches and opportunities for skindiving, fishing, sailing and other watersports) and **Ile Ste-Marie** (**Nossi Boraha**; known for its beautiful white-sand beaches and coral reefs). **Scuba-diving** centres are located on the west and west coasts. **Water-skiing** and **sailing** centres are located at **Ambohibao** (**Lake Mantasoa**), **Antsiralse** (on **Andraikiba Lake**) and **Ramona**. **River-rafting** can be done in the **Highlands** and on the **East Coast**. Other excellent beaches include: fine grottoes at **Anjohibe**, 90km (60 miles) inland; Antseranana (formerly Diégo Suarez), a cosmopolitan seaport overlooking a beautiful gulf at the northernmost tip of the island with many lakes, waterfalls and grottoes in the rainforests above the port, and wildlife and flora including lemurs, crocodiles and orchids; and the good sandy beach at **Ramena** (but sharks may be a problem).

- Stroll around one of Madagascar's lively **markets**. **Toamasina** is the country's main port and a provincial capital. It is an eight-hour drive from Antananarivo and, like the capital, it has several busy markets, including the **Bazary Be**. In the actual capital, the **Zoma Market** claims to be the second-largest in the world and is certainly worth a visit - it is held daily. Other areas where you can stumble across some wonderful arts and crafts are **Fianarantsoa**, an important centre for wine and rice production and a good base for exploring the southern highlands, and the **Zafimaniny** village, where intricate marquetry products are made.

- Dabble in the macabre by visiting the fascinating **Amabalavao**, said to be the 'home of the departed', where *antemore* paper and *lamba aridrano* silk are made; nearby are **Ambondrome** and **Ifandana** crags, where the revered bones of exhumed ancestors may be seen (the latter was the site of a mass suicide in 1811).

TOURIST INFORMATION

Ministère de la Culture et du Tourisme de Madagascar (Ministry of Culture & Tourism)
PO Box 610, Rue Fernand Kasanga, Tsimbazaza, 101 Antananarivo, Madagascar
Tel: (2022) 66805.
Website: www.tourisme.gov.mg

Entertainment

FOOD & DRINK: In Madagascar, eating well means eating a lot. Malagasy cooking is based on a large serving of rice with a dressing of sauces, meat, vegetables and seasoning. The people of Madagascar enjoy very hot food and often serve dishes with hot peppers. Local restaurants are often referred to as *hotely*.
The choice of beverages is limited. The national wine is acceptable.

National specialities:
- *Ro* (a mixture of herbs and leaves with rice).
- Beef and pork marinated in vinegar, water and oil, then cooked with leaves, onion, pickles and other vegetables and seasoned with pimento.
- *Ravitoto* (meat and leaves cooked together).
- *Ramazava* (leaves and pieces of beef and pork browned in oil).

- *Vary amid 'anana* (rice, leaves or herbs, meat and sometimes shrimps), often eaten with *kitoza* (long slices of smoked, cured or fried meat).

National drinks:
- Malagasy drinks include *litchel* (an aperitif made from lychees).
- *Betsa* (fermented alcohol).
- *Toaka gasy* (distilled from cane sugar and rice).
- *Three Horses* lager.
- Non-alcoholic drinks include *ranon 'apango* or *rano vda* (made from burnt rice) and local mineral waters.

Tipping: Not customary, although waiters expect 10 per cent of the bill. In European-style hotels and restaurants, the French system of tipping is followed. One should also tip in Chinese and Vietnamese establishments.

NIGHTLIFE: There are a few discos, sometimes with bands and solo musicians. Casinos can be found at Antananarivo, Toamasina and on Nossi Bé. Most main towns have cinemas and theatres, and touring theatre groups perform local plays throughout the country. Traditional dance troupes can also be seen.

SHOPPING: Handicrafts include *lamba* (traditional squares of cloth in various designs and woven materials); *zafimaniny* marquetry, which is applied to furniture, chessboards and boxes; silverwork such as *mahafaly* crosses and *vangavanga* bracelets; jewellery made from shells and precious stones; items woven from reeds, raffia and straw; *antemore* paper decorated with dried flowers; and embroidery. All products incorporating Malagasy flora or fauna (including dried flowers) often require export permits (see *Duty Free* section). **Shopping hours:** Mon-Fri 0800-1200 and 1400-1800.

Business

- **GDP:** US$3.9 billion (2004).
- **Main exports:** Coffee, shellfish, vanilla, fish, textiles and garments (free zone), cloves, pepper, cotton, chromite, graphite and sapphires.
- **Main imports:** Machinery and transport equipment, mineral fuels, foodstuffs and consumer goods.
- **Main trade partners:** France, USA, Germany, Mauritius and China.

ECONOMY: Madagascar's mainly agricultural economy relies heavily on coffee production to earn foreign exchange, and this has suffered lately from a decline in world demand and prices. Rice and cassava are produced primarily for domestic staple consumption. Fishing is underdeveloped thus far: the Government, which still exercises extensive control over the economy, is hoping to improve its performance. The country has appreciable mineral deposits of chromium ore, bauxite and titanium ore, all of which are being exploited. The recent discovery of oil deposits is set to bring about further development as well as hopefully resolve Madagascar's energy problems. 15 per cent of GDP derives from the manufacturing industry, mainly textiles and food processing. The service sector is relatively underdeveloped at present. The Government has been looking at ways of developing the tourism industry, and has focused on the island's abundance of exotic wildlife as a major attraction. Although the Madagascan economy has considerable potential, there are major problems to overcome. There is little that can be done about the climate; Madagascar suffers from frequent cyclones which have done severe damage to agriculture, especially in the last few years. More seriously, political instability afflicted Madagascar throughout 2002 and threatened to undermine the economy. In 2004, economic growth resumed, reaching 5.3 per cent. The country continues to rely heavily on loans and grants from the EU (especially France) and the World Bank: these were among a consortium of donors which in July 2002 agreed a major aid package worth $2.3 billion over four years. France accounts for about 30 per cent of all Madagascar's trade.

BUSINESS ETIQUETTE: Tropical lightweight suits are appropriate wear. If arranged far enough in advance, the Embassy can arrange interpreters for business meetings.
Office hours: Mon-Fri 0800-1630.

COMMERCIAL INFORMATION

Fédération des Chambres de Commerce d'Industrie et d'Agriculture de Madagascar
20 Rue Paul Dussac, Antaninarenina, Antananarivo 101, BP 166, Madagascar
Tel: (2022) 20211.
Website: www.tana-cciaa.org

Malawi

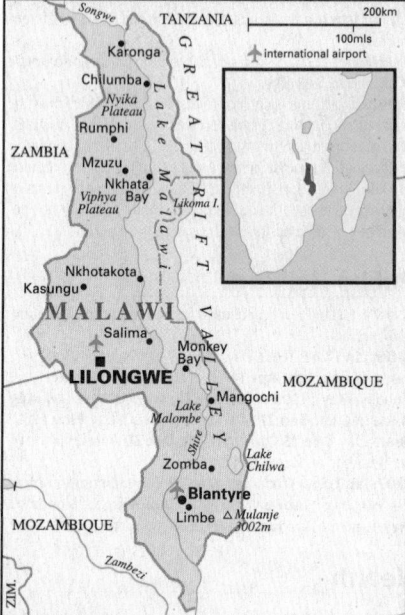

Location: Southeast Africa.

Time: GMT + 2.

Overview

Malawi is becoming well known for the number of activities it can offer visitors. Wildlife and game viewing in the national parks are especially attractive to those wanting to experience trekking and viewing in entirely natural surroundings without tarred roads filled with convoys of 4-wheel drive vehicles. Malawi has nine national parks and wildlife reserves but six are especially recommended for visitors. There are also many attractive and accessible forest reserves. All the parks and reserves are uncrowded and give visitors an excellent experience of unspoilt wilderness.

General Information

AREA: 118,484 sq km (45,747 sq miles).
POPULATION: 11.9 million (UN estimate 2002).
POPULATION DENSITY: 100.2 per sq km.
CAPITAL: Lilongwe. **Population:** 440,471 including suburbs (1998). Blantyre, with a population of 502,053 (1998), is the largest city in the country.
GEOGRAPHY: Malawi shares borders to the north and northeast with Tanzania, to the south, east and southwest with Mozambique and to the west with Zambia. Lake Malawi, the third largest lake in Africa, is the dominant feature of the country, forming the eastern boundary with Tanzania and Mozambique. The scenery varies in the country's three regions. The Northern Region is mountainous, with the highest peaks reaching over 2500m (8200ft), and features the rolling Nyika Plateau, rugged escarpments, valleys and the thickly forested slopes of the Viphya Plateau. The Central Region is mainly a plateau, over 1000m (3300ft) high, with fine upland scenery. This is the country's main agricultural area. The Southern Region is mostly low-lying except for the 2100m– (6890ft–) high Zomba Plateau south of Lake Malawi and the huge, isolated Mulanje Massif (3000m/10,000ft) in the southeast. The variety of landscape and the wildlife it supports make this relatively unspoilt country particularly attractive to visitors.

GOVERNMENT: Republic since 1966. Gained independence from the UK in 1964. **Head of State and Government:** President Bingu Wa Mutharika since 2004.
LANGUAGE: The national language is the widely spoken Chichewa but the official language, and that of the business community, is English.
RELIGION: 80 per cent are Christian, 13 per cent Muslim, 7 per cent follow traditional beliefs and there is a small Hindu minority.
ELECTRICITY: 230 volts AC, 50Hz. The standard plug is square three-pin.
SOCIAL CONVENTIONS: Despite the large number of tribal backgrounds in the Malawi population, integration is well established and visitors need not be aware of any social differences. The white population is very small in number. There are some religious differences, most noticeable among the Muslim population and especially as far as alcohol consumption is concerned. Malawians place emphasis on the importance of shaking hands on meeting and departing. The special handshake, which includes grasping the thumb and putting the other hand on the forearm, is best avoided unless practised. Children and some women may curtsey as a greeting or if being made a presentation. Offering a soft drink to a visitor is common at meetings. Malawians tend to be conventional rather than casual in their dress, especially in formal gatherings. The strict dress code of Dr Banda's days are gone but modest dress should be worn unless at the beach or playing sport.

Climate

Varies from cool in the highlands to warm around Lake Malawi. Winter (May to July) is dry and nights can be chilly, particularly in the highlands. The rainy season runs from November to March. Around Lake Malawi, in winter, the climate is particularly dry with pleasant cooling breezes.

Required clothing: Lightweights are worn all year in the Lake Malawi area, with warmer clothes advised in the mountains, particularly during winter and on chilly evenings elsewhere. Visitors to Nyika and Zomba should note that the nights can be cold. Dark or 'natural' coloured clothing should be worn for game viewing.

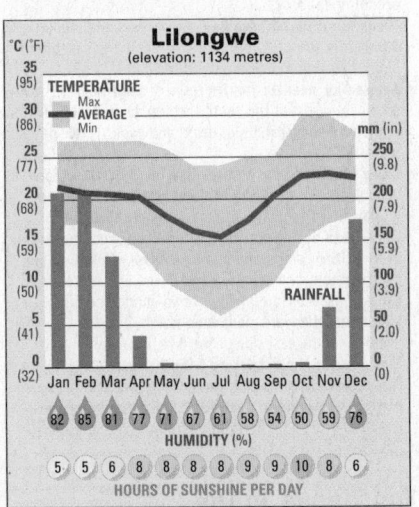

Lilongwe
(elevation: 1134 metres)

Communications

Telephone: IDD is available. Country code: 265 (no area codes). Outgoing international code: 101. The digits 01 were added to the beginning of each land telephone number in 2002; the zero should be omitted when calling from outside Malawi. The number of landlines has doubled in the past three years.
Mobile telephone: Roaming agreements currently exist with Vodafone.
Internet: Services are available in business centres in hotels, and there are a few Internet cafes.
Post: Letters take about seven to 10 days to reach Europe by airmail. Post office hours: generally Mon-Fri 0730-1200 and 1300-1700. Post offices in some of the larger towns may be open Sun 0900-1000, but only to sell stamps or to accept telegrams.
MEDIA: Radio is the main source of information.
Press: There are two main daily English-language newspapers, *The Daily Times* and *The Nation*. *The Malawi News* and *The Nation* are published weekly, and a number of other newspapers are published periodically, including the news magazine, *Malawi First*.
TV: Television Malawi is state run.
Radio: *Malawi Broadcasting Corporation* is the main national broadcaster.

Passport/Visa

	Passport Required?	Visa Required?	Return Ticket Required?
Full British	Yes	No	Yes
Australian	Yes	No	Yes
Canadian	Yes	No	Yes
USA	Yes	No	Yes
Other EU	Yes	Yes/1	Yes
Japanese	Yes	No	Yes

Note: *Regulations and requirements may be subject to change at short notice, and you are advised to contact the appropriate diplomatic or consular authority before finalising travel arrangements. Any numbers in the chart refer to the footnotes below.*

PASSPORTS: Passport valid for at least six months beyond date of intended departure required by all.
VISAS: Required by all except the following:
(a) nationals of countries referred to in the chart above, except **1.** nationals of Austria, Czech Republic, Estonia, Greece, Hungary, Latvia, Lithuania, Poland, Slovak Republic and Slovenia, who *do* need a visa
(b) nationals of Commonwealth countries (except Cameroon, India, Nigeria and Pakistan who *do* require a visa);
(c) nationals of Iceland, Israel, Madagascar, Norway, San Marino and Zimbabwe;
(d) foreign nationals in transit who are continuing their journey by the same or connecting aircraft to a third country within 24 hours. Permission must be obtained to leave the airport, however.
Types of visa and cost: *Single-entry:* £45. *Multiple-entry:* £70 (up to six months); £90 (up to one year). Transit: £32.
Validity: Three months from date of issue.
Application to: Consulate (or consular section at Embassy or High Commission); see *Passport/Visa Information*.
Application requirements: (a) Valid passport. (b) Two application forms. (c) Two passport-size photos. (d) Fee. (e) Onward or return air ticket. (f) Proof of means of support during residence in country. (g) Confirmed hotel booking or host address of where visitor may stay. (h) Letter from company/sponsor, where required. (i) For postal applications, pre-paid recorded delivery envelope.
Working days required: In most cases, applications will be processed within five working days, but for nationals of India, Nigeria and Pakistan, applications may take two to three weeks.
Temporary residence: Application should be made prior to arrival. Contact the Controller of Immigration Services, PO Box 331, Blantyre, Malawi.

PASSPORT/VISA INFORMATION

High Commission for the Republic of Malawi and Malawi Tourist Office in the UK
33 Grosvenor Street, London W1K 4QT, UK
Tel: (020) 7491 4172/7.
E-mail: tourism@malawihighcomm.prestel.co.uk (tourism section).
Opening hours: Mon-Fri 0930-1600.

Embassy of the Republic of Malawi in the USA
1156 15th Atreet, Suite 320, NW, Washington, DC 20005, USA
Tel: (202) 721 0270.

Money

Currency: Kwacha (MWK) = 100 tambala. Notes are in denominations of MWK500, 200, 100, 50, 20, 10 and 5. Coins are in denominations of MWK1 and 50, 20, 10, 5, 2 and 1 tambala.
Currency exchange: US Dollars, Pounds Sterling, Euros or South African Rand are readily exchanged but lesser-known currencies may prove difficult to exchange.
Credit & debit cards: Acceptance of credit and debit cards is very limited, although in Lilongwe and Blantyre and in main hotels, American Express, Diners Club, MasterCard and Visa can be used. Check with your credit or debit card company for details of merchant acceptability and other services which may be available.
Traveller's cheques: Traveller's cheques can be exchanged in banks, hotels and other institutions. In remote areas, the Treasury Office of Local District Commissioner's offices will cash traveller's cheques. To avoid additional exchange rate charges, travellers are advised to take traveller's cheques in US Dollars, Euros, Pounds Sterling or South African Rand.
Currency restrictions: The import of local currency is unlimited. The export of local currency is limited to K200. The import of foreign currency is unlimited on arrival. The export of foreign currency is allowed up to the amount imported and declared on entry.

Banking hours: Mon-Fri 0800-1400.
Exchange rate indicators:
Rate at time of publishing
£1.00= MWK214.24
$1.00= MWK123.46

Duty Free

The following goods may be imported into Malawi by passengers without incurring customs duty:
200 cigarettes or 225g of tobacco in any form; for those over 16 years of age, also 1l of spirits and 1l of beer and 1l of wine.
Prohibited items: The import of firearms is prohibited unless a permit has been bought in advance from the Registrar of Firearms, Box 41, Zomba.

Public Holidays

Below are listed Public Holidays for the January 2006-June 2007 period.
2006: Jan 1 New Year's Day. **Jan 15** John Chilembwe Day. **Mar 3** Martyrs' Day. **Apr 14-17** Easter. **May 1** Labour Day. **Jun 14** Freedom Day. **Jul 6** Republic Day. **Oct 9** Mothers' Day. **Dec 11** Arbor Day. **Dec 25-26** Christmas.
2007: Jan 1 New Year's Day. **Jan 15** John Chilembwe Day. **Mar 3** Martyrs' Day. **Apr 6-9** Easter. **May 1** Labour Day. **Jun 14** Freedom Day.
Note: If a public holiday falls on a Saturday, the preceding day will be a holiday; if on a Sunday, the next day will be a holiday. *Ad hoc* public holidays or extensions may also be declared, sometimes at short notice.

Health

	Special Required?	Certificate Precautions?
Yellow Fever	No	1
Cholera	Yes	2
Typhoid & Polio	3	N/A
Malaria	4	N/A

Note: *Regulations and requirements may be subject to change at short notice, and you are advised to contact your doctor well in advance of your intended date of departure. Any numbers in the chart refer to the footnotes below.*

1: A *yellow fever* vaccination certificate is required from travellers arriving from, or transiting through, infected areas.
2: Following WHO guidelines issued in 1973, a *cholera* vaccination certificate is not a condition of entry to Malawi. However, *cholera* is a risk in this country and precautions are essential. Up-to-date advice should be sought before deciding whether these precautions should include vaccination, as medical opinion is divided over its effectiveness; see the *Health* appendix.
Note: It has been reported that cholera vaccination certificates have been demanded at the border with Tanzania; if immunisation is necessary, avoid the use of local needles under all circumstances.
3: *Typhoid* may occur in rural areas.
4: *Malaria* risk exists all year throughout the country. The predominant malignant *falciparum* strain is reported to be highly resistant to chloroquine and resistant to sulfadoxine-pyrimethamine. The recommended prophylaxis is mefloquine.
Food & drink: All water should be regarded as being potentially contaminated. Water used for drinking, brushing teeth or making ice should have first been boiled or otherwise sterilised. Milk is unpasteurised and should be boiled. Powdered or tinned milk is available and is advised, but make sure that it is reconstituted with pure water. Avoid dairy products which are likely to have been made from unboiled milk. Only eat well-cooked meat and fish, preferably served hot. Pork, salad and mayonnaise may carry increased risk. Vegetables should be cooked and fruit peeled.
Other risks: *Bilharzia (schistosomiasis)* is present, and has been confirmed to occur in some parts of Lake Malawi. Avoid swimming and paddling in slow-moving or stagnant fresh water; swimming pools which are well chlorinated and maintained are safe. *Trypanosomiasis* (sleeping sickness) is reported. *Hepatitis A, B, C* and *E* and *TB* are all present. *Meningococcal meningitis* can occur, especially in the dry season. Avoid tick and insect bites, as they can result in viral diseases. *HIV* infection is a risk. *Rabies* is present. For those at high risk, vaccination before arrival should be considered. If you are bitten, seek medical advice without delay. For more information consult the *Health* appendix.
Health care: Health insurance is essential. It is advisable to take personal medical supplies, including needles.

Travel - International

AIR:

For intercontinental flights from Europe, *British Airways* (with *Regional Air*) has a weekly service via Nairobi, as well as operating in conjunction with *Air Malawi (QM)* via the regional hubs of Dar es Salaam, Harare, Johannesburg, Lusaka and Nairobi. *Air Zimbabwe, Ethiopian Airlines, Kenya Airways, KLM* and *South African Airways* (five flights a week via Johannesburg) offer similar connecting services. Regional links between Malawi and Kenya, South Africa, Tanzania and Zimbabwe are provided by *Air Malawi* and the various national airlines.

Approximate flight times: From Lilongwe to *London* is approximately 12 hours.

International airports: *Lilongwe (LLW)* (Lilongwe International) is 26km (16 miles) from the city (travel time – 25 to 30 minutes). Taxis and a bus service are available to the city from the airport. Airport facilities include a duty free shop, post office, local travel agents, car hire, bank/bureau de change, restaurant and bar. Blantyre (BLZ) (Chileka) is 13km (8 miles) from the city. There is a coach service to the city. Airport facilities include car hire, restaurant and bar.

Departure tax: A passenger service charge of US$30 (payable in US currency) is levied on all international flights. Malawi passport holders can pay in local currency (MWK950). Children under two years of age and transit passengers are exempt.

ROAD:

There are road connections with Mozambique at Mwanza in southwestern Malawi and at Chiponde in the east; with Tanzania at the Songwe River Bridge in the far northwest of the country; and with Zambia on the main Lilongwe–Lusaka highway near Chipata in the west. A luxury coach service connects Blantyre with Johannesburg (South Africa).

Travel - Internal

AIR:

Air Malawi's domestic network provides regular links between Blantyre, Lilongwe, Mzuzu, Club Makokola (southern lakeshore) and Liwonde National Park. *Jakamaka Air Charters* serves the main tourist destinations in the country.

Departure tax: K150 is payable on domestic flights.

LAKE:

Cruises on Lake Malawi are available by local steamer. Food and cabins are available. For details contact local travel bureaux.

RAIL:

Malawi Railways operates the lines in the country. The main route connects Mchinji, Lilongwe, Salima, Chipoka, Blantyre, Limbe and Nsanje. For further information, contact Malawi Railways, PO Box 5144, Limbe (tel: 01 640 844; fax: 01 643 496 *or* 640 683). Trains tend to be slow and crowded and are little used by tourists.

ROAD:

Traffic drives on the left. There are over 13,500km (8400 miles) of roads in the country. All major roads are tarmac and most secondary roads are all-weather. **Bus:** There is a good bus system, including an express service, connecting main towns. The journey from Mzuzu to Karonga is particularly spectacular. Luxury coaches connect Blantyre to Lilongwe and Mzuzu.

Car hire: This is becoming increasingly available, with a number of companies offering a wide choice of vehicles. Standards do vary (even with the internationally franchised chains) so it is worth seeking a recommendation. Nonetheless, cars should be reserved well in advance as they are very much in demand. Chauffeur-driven cars are also available. **Documentation:** An International Driving Permit is required.

URBAN:

Bus: There are services in all major cities. **Taxi:** These are in short supply and cannot be hailed on the street. Taxi drivers expect a tip.

Travel times: The following chart gives approximate average travel times (in hours and minutes) from **Lilongwe** to other major cities/towns in Malawi.

	Air	Road
Blantyre	0.40	4.00
Mzuzu	1.00	5.00
Zomba	-	4.00
Karonga	1.30	6.30
Mangochi	1.00	4.30

Travel Advice

Most visits to Malawi are trouble-free but you should be aware of the global risk of indiscriminate international terrorist attacks, which could be against civilian targets, including places frequented by foreigners.

Driving can be hazardous. Travellers should drive carefully, avoid travelling after dark and should always wear seat belts. There have been armed car-jackings, especially of four wheel drive vehicles. Travellers are warned not to resist. In Lilongwe, the majority of attacks on visitors take place on Kenyatta Drive and around the bus station. Travellers should take care when visiting these areas.

This advice is based on information provided by the Foreign and Commonwealth Office in the UK. It is correct at time of publishing. As the situation can change rapidly, visitors are advised to contact the following organisations for the latest travel advice:

British Foreign and Commonwealth Office
Tel: (0845) 850 2829.
Website: www.fco.gov.uk

US Department of State
Website: http://travel.state.gov/travel

Accommodation

HOTELS:

There is a range of hotels in the main towns: Lilongwe, Blantyre/Limbe and Mzuzu. The same is true along the lakeshore with a concentration in the south between Monkey Bay, Mangochi and Senga Bay. Zomba Plateau has a luxury hotel. For further information, see the *Resorts & Excursions* section.

REST HOUSES: A programme of privatisation has seen many of the rest houses and forest reserve lodges transformed into luxury or mid-range lodges, the equivalent of established hotels.

LAKESIDE LODGES: There is a scattering of small luxury and mid-market lodges along the western shore of Lake Malawi and on Likoma Island. Most offer the same facilities as the larger hotels with watersports and excellent private beaches. Some accommodation is on islands and lake safaris are catered for.

SAFARI CAMPS/LODGES: Recent years have seen a transformation in four of the parks and reserves: Liwonde, Kasungu, Nyika and Vwasa. Single privately-run safari camps/lodges have replaced Government camps in all of these parks. New luxury en-suite accommodation is provided in permanent tents, rondavels, log cabins or bamboo huts. There is also good-quality, mid-price accommodation and camping. Full catering is available. Booking ahead is important especially at weekends and in holiday periods. See also *National Parks* in the *Resorts & Excursions* section.

CAMPING:

There are campsites along the lakeshore, often near the hotels, and elsewhere in the resort and forest areas. Most game parks and reserves have campsites. Sites are usually well equipped and camping is excellent during the dry season which runs from April to November.

Top Things To See

- The capital of the northern region, **Mzuzu**, has one major hotel and several smaller establishments. The town is approached from the south by a road across the rolling hills of the **Viphya Plateau** or by the lakeshore road. There are two game areas in the region: the beautiful and unique plateau of **Nyika National Park** and the **Vwasa Marsh Wildlife Reserve**. Both have new luxury lodges as well as simpler accommodation. Also in the region is the famous **Livingstonia Mission** with its interesting museum. Access is difficult up the escarpment road but the Mission can also be reached from the east via **Rumphi**. Nearby, the **Manchewe Falls** spill off the escarpment.
- Malawi's capital, **Lilongwe**, is in the central region, 90 minutes' drive inland from **Lake Malawi**. Alongside the traditional Old Town, with its interesting markets, is the modern city and seat of Government with its imaginative architecture in a garden setting. There is a wide range of hotels in Lilongwe.
- Northwest of the capital is the vast **Kasungu National Park** with a variety of wildlife and good accommodation. North of Lilongwe is the famous **Kamuzu Academy** (the 'Eton of Africa'). This is also the region supplying much of the country's important tobacco crop.
- **Blantyre,** Malawi's commercial capital and largest town was established at the end of the 19th century. It is really two towns: Blantyre and **Limbe**, joined by a development corridor. Visits can be made to the **National Museum**, to **St Michael and All Angels Church** (associated with Dr David Livingstone) and to **Mandala House** (the oldest European building in Malawi).
- North of Blantyre is the university town and former capital, **Zomba**. Towering above the town is the 2100m- (6890ft-) **Zomba Plateau** with its vast forests and waterfalls. There is a newly rebuilt luxury hotel as well as lodges and two campsites. The views from the plateau are stunning and it is possible to drive around or walk on the

plateau top. There is also a trout farm which is now rehabilitated and has a very nice picnic area.
- Large tea estates, which offer accommodation, lie to the southeast of Thyolo, overshadowed by the magnificent **Mulanje Massif**, a huge block of mountains of more than 640 sq km (250 sq miles) rising to over 3000m (10,000ft) at its highest point at **Sapitwa**. For the tourist, **Mulanje** offers a wide variety of activities, from rock climbing and mountain walking to the more leisurely pursuit of trout fishing. Much of the massif is accessible and guides can be hired. Forest huts provide simple accommodation. Mulanje is best visited between April and November.

The **Lower Shire Valley** is different from the rest of the country, as it is low lying, hotter, and dominated by the great river which drains Lake Malawi. There are vast sugar plantations at **Sucoma**.
- **Lake Malawi:** This vast lake stretches from the northern tip of the country to **Mangochi** in the south. The surface area of the lake covers nearly 24,000 sq km (15,000 sq miles), and lies in the deep, trough-like rift valley which runs the length of the country. The shores of the lake are generally sandy and the resort areas are largely bilharzia-free. There are no tides or currents. Most of the hotels provide pleasure craft enabling visitors to enjoy water-skiing, sailing, fishing, snorkelling and windsurfing. Lake Malawi is known to contain more species of fish than any other lake in the world: over 500 and up to a possible 1000 at the latest estimate. Some of the rarest tropical fish in the world are unique to the lake, which is also the home of fish eagles, black eagles, several varieties of kingfisher, tern and many other birds. One of the best ways of seeing Lake Malawi is to cruise in the 630-ton *Ilala II*, the lake's mini-liner, which cruises the lake between **Monkey Bay** and **Karonga** in the north of the country. The 1052km- (654 mile-) voyage gives the passenger the opportunity to visit lake ports and to view the spectacular mountain scenery. Luxury yacht chartering is also available.
- **Nkhotakota**, on the central lake shore, is one of Africa's oldest market towns and was once a centre of the slave trade. There are mid-range lodges here from which one can visit the nearby wildlife reserve. The beautiful Chintheche Strip has excellent small lodge accommodation.

Further north is **Nkhata Bay**, a busy port and market and a favourite stopping place for visitors. There is plenty of budget accommodation around the bay.
- **Senga Bay**, near the market town of **Salima**, is the main lakeshore resort of the central region. **Lizard Island**, home to many varieties of lizard and eagle, is one of the many off-shore islands.
- **Cape Maclear**, near Monkey Bay, has a beautiful sandy beach and is in the **Lake Malawi National Park**, the world's first freshwater reserve. It is here that the fish-rich lake is seen at its best. There is top-class accommodation at the island camps, and at a new lodge offering sailing in luxury yachts, and kayaking and diving are offered from the islands. There are plenty of mid-range and budget lodges and there are plans for a hotel.
- Located on the east side of the lake, near the Mozambique shore, **Likoma Island** is worth a visit - there is excellent swimming off the beaches and a very interesting **Anglican Cathedral**, built by missionaries over 100 years ago. Accommodation is limited but includes a luxury lodge.

Top Things To Do

- Malawi is becoming well known for the number of activities it can offer visitors. **Wildlife and game viewing** in the national parks are especially attractive to those wanting to experience trekking and viewing in entirely natural surroundings without tarred roads filled with convoys of 4-wheel drive vehicles.
- **Nyika National Park:** Situated in the far north of the country, the park's unique rolling grassland covers most of the Nyika Plateau, which lies at an altitude of 2500m (8200ft). The whaleback hills are broken by deep valleys and occasional patches of evergreen, natural forest and bubbling streams. Nyika is known to sustain many rare birds and butterflies, game and a multitude of flowers, including an incredible range of orchids. At **Chelinda** there is a variety of accommodation, including new luxury log cabins. The lodges and camps are set high up on the edge of a pine forest, overlooking trout-filled lakes. The enormous plateau has zebra, antelope, leopard and hyena as well as elephants on the lower slopes. A speciality of Chelinda is its horse safaris. There is an airstrip for visitors arriving by air.
- **Vwasa Marsh Wildlife Reserve:** Located to the west of Mzuzu. A camp with luxury reed huts has been established, overlooking **Lake Kazuni**. There is a variety of game including elephant, buffalo and hippos, as well as a large number of bird species. There is a mix of woodland, open grassland and marsh. This is a totally unspoilt reserve.

- **Kaslungu National Park:** Situated in the northwest of the central region, 154km (96 miles) from Lilongwe, Kasungu National Park consists of some 2000 sq km (770 sq miles) of woodland. The park is best known for its elephants, which appear in the early morning and evening to drink from *dambos* (river channels). The grasslands support large herds of buffalo, as well as a variety of antelope such as kudu and reedbuck. Predators such as lion and leopard may be seen. Accommodation in the park is easily accessed at *Lifupa*, where there are luxury rondavels as well as a separate self-catering camp.
- **Liwonde National Park:** Situated in the Shire Valley, south of Lake Malawi and north of Zomba, Liwonde is the most popular of the national parks. The River Shire flows along the eastern border of the park allowing for boat safaris. The river is frequented by vast numbers of hippo, and elephants and crocodiles can also be seen. There is a wide range of game in the park, including rhino and various antelope. Through introductions, Liwonde now has the 'big five' for visitors to see. The birdlife includes one of the greatest variety of species in Africa. There is accommodation in the park at **Mvuu**, including a luxury lodge and a separate permanent camp and camping site. Walking, boating and driving safaris (in 4-wheel-drive vehicles) are on offer. There is a landing strip for visitors coming by air. A second safari lodge has been opened on a hill site in the southern part of the park.
- **Lake Malawi National Park:** Close to **Monkey Bay**, this reserve lies towards the southern extremity of the lake. Opened in 1980, it was the world's first freshwater national park and its setting and attractions are world-renowned. Tropical fish, which can be viewed by snorkelling or scuba-diving, are a speciality of the park, while further inland klipspringer, bushbuck and vervet monkeys may be seen. Access to the park is easy throughout the year. In the past, only budget accommodation was available but there are now excellent camps on two deserted islands in the park, as well as a luxury guest house, which is also linked to an upmarket yachting operation. Many visitors make day-trips from the hotels on the lakeshore south of Monkey Bay.
- **Lengwe National Park:** Lengwe National Park is in the Lower Shire Valley and is only 130 sq km (80 sq miles) large. The park has the distinction of being the farthest point north where the rare Nyala antelope can be found. Also here is the diminutive Livingstone's Suni, one of the smallest of antelopes, as well as the rare Blue or Samango monkey.

These and other game can be viewed from concealed hides. New accommodation is being developed here and it is possible to visit the park in a daytrip from Blantyre.
- Of the other wildlife reserves, the vast **Nkhotakota Wildlife Reserve** is little developed and lacks drivable tracks. However, there is a good range of game including lion and elephant. Accommodation can be had nearby along the lakeshore. **Majete** and **Mwabvi Wildlife Reserves** are in the Lower Shire Valley. Majete has little viewable game and Mwabvi is difficult to access.
- **Lake Malawi** offers a range of **watersports** along its whole length. **Snorkelling** and **scuba-diving** are increasingly popular in Lake Malawi because of the attraction of seeing the brilliantly coloured fish, the *mbuna*. Instruction in these sports for beginners as well as for experienced practitioners is possible at many resorts. **Swimming**, **water-skiing**, **sailing** and **kayaking** are all available along the lakeshore. The Lake Malawi 500km *Sailing Marathon*, which is the world's longest freshwater sailing race, is held each year in July and attracts an international entry field. The risk of contracting bilharzia when engaging in watersports in Lake Malawi is minimised if sensible precautions are taken: bathers should swim only at the resort areas known to be free of bilharzia, avoiding parts of the lake where there is still water or close human habitation. Many areas of the lake are bilharzia-free.
- **Fishing** is especially attractive on the southern lakeshore north of **Mangochi** and at **Senga Bay**. Tournaments take place each year and catches include the delicious Sungwa. There are also opportunities to fish for yellow fish, lake salmon and lake tiger. Elsewhere, angling for trout is easily arranged at Chelinda on **Nyika Plateau** and on **Zomba Plateau**. There is also good fishing for lake-salmon (*mpasa*) in the rivers of the **Nkhotakota Game Reserve**.
- The **Nyika Plateau** is popular for **trekking** and **walking**. Guides and porters are available for one to six-day wilderness hikes. The same arrangements apply on **Mount Mulanje** where huts are available for hire. There is excellent walking on the Zomba and Viphya Plateaux. There is plenty of scope for **climbing**. Rising to a height of 3000m (9850ft), **Mount Mulanje** is the highest mountain in central Africa and has proved to be an irresistible lure to climbers. The massif has the longest sheer rock face in Africa. Dedza, south of Lilongwe, and **Michiru**, **Ndirande** and **Chiradzulu**, near Blantyre, also offer challenging slopes.

- **Horse riding** is a speciality on **Nyika Plateau**, where safaris on horseback are popular, and on **Zomba Plateau**, where there is a dressage school.
- **Cycling** has more recently been added to Malawi's list of activities for tourists and has also attracted the interest of charity organisations. Popular areas include **Nyika**, **Luwawa Forest** and along the lakeshore.
- **Dance** plays a part in most ceremonies in Malawi, an important dance being the **Gule Wamkulu** (performed by the Chewa and Mang'anja), with its heavily carved masks, feathers and skin paint. For further information on events in Malawi, contact the Malawi Tourism Information Service.

TOURIST INFORMATION

Ministry of Tourism, Parks and Wildlife
Street address: Tourism House, off Convention Drive, Lilongwe, Malawi
Postal address: P/Bag 326, Lilongwe 3, Malawi
Tel: (0) 177 1295/5499/2702.
Website: www.tourismmalawi.com

Malawi Tourism Information Service in the UK
4 Christian Fields, London SW16 3JZ, UK
Tel: (0115) 982 1903.
Website: www.malawitourism.com

Entertainment

FOOD & DRINK:
Hotel restaurants and many of those in the cities are of a good standard. They offer a wide choice of dishes including European, Korean and Chinese as well as authentic Malawi dishes and *haute cuisine*.

National specialities:
- Fresh fish from Lake Malawi is the country's speciality, *chambo* (Tilapia fish) being the main lake delicacy.
- Trout from streams on the Zomba, Mulanje and Nyika plateaux.
- Poultry and dairy produce are plentiful and tropical fruits are abundant in season.

National drinks:
- The local beer is very good and imported beer and soft drinks are widely available.

• Malawi gin and tonic is well known and inexpensive, with almost cult status.

Tipping: Generally not expected, but some employees who are very poorly paid might appreciate a small tip for good service.

NIGHTLIFE: There is little nightlife in the European or US sense. Some restaurants have entertainment as do some of the hotels but outside Blantyre and Lilongwe this will usually take the form of a display of dancing during or after dinner at the lakeshore hotels.

SHOPPING: Malawi produces a variety of colourful arts and crafts. Items are invariably handmade and there is no factory production of curios. Purchases include woodcarvings, wood and cane furniture, soapstone carvings, decorated wooden articles, colourful textiles, pottery, beadwork, cane and raffia items. The standard of woodcarving is one of the highest in Africa. The *Mua Mission*, south of Salima, where carvers are trained, has an excellent shop. Traditional musical instruments are also sold throughout Malawi. **Shopping hours:** Mon-Sat 0800-1700. Markets and roadside stalls function every day.

Business

ECONOMY: The economy is almost entirely agricultural, with both subsistence and cash crops including tobacco, sugar, tea and maize being farmed. The manufacturing industry now accounts for about 15 per cent of economic output, and is concentrated in light industrial import substitution projects such as textiles, chemicals, agricultural implements and processed foodstuffs. Tourism is intended to become a major source of foreign exchange but this will depend on improvements in basic infrastructure and political stability in the region. The overall economy is weak with inflation around 30 per cent and negative growth of 1.5 per cent in 2001. Recent economic policy has followed an orthodox course of privatisation, deregulation and Government spending cuts. The latter have had a severe impact on the country's already limited basic services, especially healthcare, which Malawi can ill afford as the HIV/AIDS pandemic continues to devastate the population. Between one-third and one-half of the working population are thought to be infected, with the inevitable economic consequences.
Malawi is normally self-sufficient in food, especially maize, the main staple. But it also has a vast balance of payments deficit and is heavily dependent on foreign aid, both bilateral and from the World Bank. In 2000, in a development which had repercussions across Africa, Malawi was pressurised by international financial institutions due to the surplus from its bumper maize crop to meet debt repayments. Two years later, there was a disastrous harvest, but no reserves to meet the shortfall - and Malawi was forced to call upon emergency food aid. Malawi is a member of the Southern African Development Community and, in 1993, signed the treaty establishing a Common Market for Eastern and Southern Africa (COMESA). The UK is Malawi's most important single trading partner, taking one-third of the country's exports and providing 15 per cent of Malawi's imports. South Africa, Japan, Germany and The Netherlands are Malawi's other important trading partners.

BUSINESS ETIQUETTE: Suits or a jacket and tie are suitable for business meetings in cities. Similar to the European system, appointments should generally be made and business cards are used. Offices tend to open early in Malawi. Best months for business visits are May to July and September to November. **Office hours:** Mon-Fri 0730-1700.

CONFERENCES/CONVENTIONS: Malawi's only dedicated conference centre is the Kwacha International Conference Centre in Blantyre, with seating for up to 500 people. Details of this and hotels with conference facilities can be obtained from the Malawi Tourism Information (see *Top Things To Do*).

COMMERCIAL INFORMATION

Malawi Confederation of Chambers of Commerce and Industry
PO Box 258, Chichiri Trade Fair Grounds, Blantyre, Malawi
Tel: 167 1988.
Website: www.mccci.o

Malaysia

Location: South-East Asia.

Time: GMT + 8.

Overview

Malaysia is the rising star of South-East Asian tourism, a nation looking to the future while cherishing the ways of the past. Centuries of trade have resulted in a vibrant mix of Malay, Chinese, Indian and indigenous tribal cultures, creating a veritable melting pot of peoples, traditions and religions. The region now known as Malaysia was first mentioned in Chinese and Sanskrit records of the seventh and eighth centuries. In subsequent centuries the area was under the influence and loose control of various Thai and Indonesian empires, including the great Sumatra-based civilisation of Sri Vijaya. This was followed in the 14th century by the Majapahit Empire based in Java. Sri Vijaya and Majapahit, Buddhist and Hindu respectively, both left a mark on the peninsula. But, even by the 14th century, Islam was steadily spreading eastwards. In the 16th century, the Portuguese moved in and, after capturing Malacca, established a number of fortified bases in the region. Sultan Mahmud was unable to recapture it immediately but his successors formed an alliance with Dutch arrivals to expel the Portuguese in 1641. Dutch expansion eventually produced the Dutch East Indies, the heart of a prosperous colonial trading operation. The British were relatively late arrivals to the region in the late-18th century, but they played a key role following the

European wars of the 1790s and, in particular, the defeat of The Netherlands by France in 1795. Rather than hand them to the French, the Dutch passed control of some valuable resources to the British. Gradually, during the 19th century, the British took control of the peninsula using economic pressure. The Federated Malay States were created in 1895, and remained under British colonial control until the Japanese invasion of 1942. After Japanese defeat in 1945, the 11 states were once again incorporated as British Protectorates and, in 1948, became the Federation of Malaya. In the same year, communist guerrillas – the bulk of whom were ethnic Chinese – launched an armed struggle aimed at establishing an independent socialist state. 'The Emergency', as colonial authorities dubbed it, lasted formally until 1960. In 1963, the Federation of Malaya merged with Singapore and the former British colonies of Sarawak and Sabah (North Borneo) to form Malaysia. Singapore seceded to become an independent state in its own right in 1965, leaving Malaysia in its present form.
Such history highlights why Malaysia is so ethnically and culturally diverse. Even better, the magnificent landscape is no less diverse – dense jungles, soaring peaks and lush tropical rainforests harbour an abundant flora and fauna. Tropical island resorts and endless white, sandy beaches offer a taste of paradise, while beneath warm coral seas, world-class dive sites await exploration. Orang-utans, the oldest rainforest in the world, city skyscrapers, majestic mosques and temples plus a gorgeous coastline.are enough to tempt even the most jaded visitor.

General Information

AREA: 329,847 sq km (127,355 sq miles).
POPULATION: 25.3 million (UN, 2005).
POPULATION DENSITY: 76.7 per sq km.
CAPITAL: Kuala Lumpur. **Population:** 1.4 million including suburbs (UN estimate 2002).
GEOGRAPHY: Malaysia is situated in central South-East Asia, bordering on Thailand in the north, with Singapore and Indonesia to the south and The Philippines to the east. It is composed of Peninsular Malaysia and the states of Sabah and Sarawak on the north coast of the island of Borneo, 650 to 950km (404 to 600 miles) across the South China Sea. Peninsular Malaysia is an area of forested mountain ranges running north-south, on either side of which are low-lying coastal plains. The coastline extends some 1900km (1200 miles). The west coast consists of mangrove swamps and mudflats which separate into bays and inlets. In the west, the plains have been cleared and cultivated, while the unsheltered east coast consists of tranquil beaches backed by dense jungle. Sarawak has alluvial and, in places, swampy coastal plains with rivers penetrating the jungle-covered hills and mountains of the interior. Sabah has a narrow coastal plain which gives way to mountains and jungle. Mount Kinabalu, at 4094m (13,432ft), is the highest peak in Malaysia. The major islands are Langkawi (a group of 99 islands), Penang and Pangkor off the west coast; and Tioman, Redang, Kapas, Perhentian and Rawa off the east coast.
GOVERNMENT: Constitutional monarchy since 1963. Gained independence from the UK in 1957.
Head of State: King Syed Sirrajuddin ibni al-Marhum Syed Putra Jamalullail since 2002.
Head of Government: Prime Minister Datuk Abdullah Ahmad Badawi since 2003.
Recent history: The dominant political organisation in Malaysia has long been the United Malay National Organisation (UMNO), which allied itself with several smaller formations to create the *Barisan Nasional* (NF, National Front). In 1982, the NF won the General Election scheduled for that year under the new leadership of Mahathir Mohammed. Mahathir's style was characterised by maverick policy-making, an acerbic tongue, strident nationalism, acute political antennae and a ferocious intolerance of opposition from any quarter. In his two decades in power, he stamped his authority on Malaysian politics. His ruthlessness was exemplified after falling out with his former deputy and heir apparent, Anwar Ibrahim, over Malaysia's handling of the 1997 Asian financial crisis. Anwar was framed for alleged homosexuality (which is illegal in Malaysia) and corruption; after a show trial he was then imprisoned for 15 years. Although the NF had comfortably won every poll in the 1980s and '90s, many people, including influential figures within UMNO, believed that Mahathir had finally overreached himself. The acid test came at the general election of November 1999. In the event, Mahathir ran a well-judged campaign which returned the NF to office with, once again, a substantial majority. Both the democratic opposition, organised around residual supporters of Anwar, and the Islamist opposition centred on the Pan-Malaysian Islamic Party (PAS) were comfortably dealt with. In particular, Mahathir made effective use of the '9/11' attacks in the US to demonise his Islamist opponents. With his political position now all but unassailable, Mahathir's announcement in June 2002 of his intention to resign the following year was a huge surprise. The shock was followed by scepticism, and then by a further surprise in October 2003 when Mahathir did indeed stand down. The main political task for his chosen successor, Abdullah Ahmad Badawi – formerly a senior civil servant – is to prevent any further progress by the Islamist PAS. The

General Election on 21 March 2004 resulted in a landslide win by the Barisan Nasional.

Malaysia has a complex federal political system, with extensive local power still in the hands of nine hereditary Sultans, who elect the Head of State (entitled HM the Yang di-Pertuan Agong) every five years from among their number. There are 13 states plus two 'Federal Territories' (Kuala Lumpur and the island of Labuan). Legislative power is in the hands of the bicameral Parliament, comprising the *Dewan Rakyat* (House of Representatives) with 192 members directly elected for a five-year term, and the 70-strong Dewan Negara (Senate), of which 40 members are appointed by the Head of State and 30 members elected by the country's 13 regional assemblies. Executive power is held by the Prime Minister, who is formally appointed by the head of state but in practice by the leader of the largest party in the Dewan Rakpat. The Prime Minister governs with the assistance of an appointed ministerial Cabinet.

LANGUAGE: Bahasa M is the national and official language, but English is widely spoken. Other languages such as Chinese (Cantonese and Hokkien), Iban and Tamil are spoken by minorities.

RELIGION: Muslim (52 per cent) and Buddhist (17 per cent) majorities. The remainder are Christian, Taoist, Confucianist, Hindu and animist.

ELECTRICITY: 220-240 volts AC, 50Hz. Square three-pin plugs and bayonet-type light fittings are generally used.

SOCIAL CONVENTIONS: Malaysia's population is a mixture of diverse cultures and characters. In general, the racial groups integrate, but keep to their individual traditions and lifestyles. Malays still form more than half of the total population and lead a calm life governed by the authority of elders and a strong sense of respect and etiquette. The Indian, Pakistani and Sri Lankan members of the population originally came to Malaysia to take up positions in the civil service, police and local Government departments, as well as in the new rubber plantations, but many are now among the professional classes. European influences (British, Dutch and Portuguese in particular) are also very evident in Malaysia, although the European section of the population is now small. As far as greetings are concerned, the Malaysian equivalent of 'hello' is the Muslim 'peace be with you'. Malay men are addressed *Encik* (pronounced Enchik) with or without the name; Malay women should be called *Cik* (pronounced Che) if they are single and *Puan* if they are married. Touching the hand to the chest is a sign of respect and a relaxed wrist and gentle touch should be adopted when shaking hands. Chinese and Indians usually use Western forms of address. Hospitality is always warm, lavish and informal. When eating food by hand, only the right hand should be used. Visitors should respect religious beliefs and follow the Malaysian example, such as wearing appropriate clothing. Footwear should be taken off at the door when entering a house or temple. Dress should be informal, but not over-casual. Within towns, smoking has now become the subject of Government disapproval and fines are levied in a number of public places,

Climate

Tropical without extremely high temperatures. Days are very warm, while nights are fairly cool. The main rainy season in the east runs between November and February, while August is the wettest period on the west coast. East Malaysia has heavy rains (November to February) in Sabah and in Sarawak. However, it is difficult to generalise about the country's climate, as rainfall differs on the east and west coasts according to the prevailing monsoon winds (northeast or southwest).

Required clothing: Lightweight cottons and linens are worn throughout the year. Waterproofing is advisable all year.

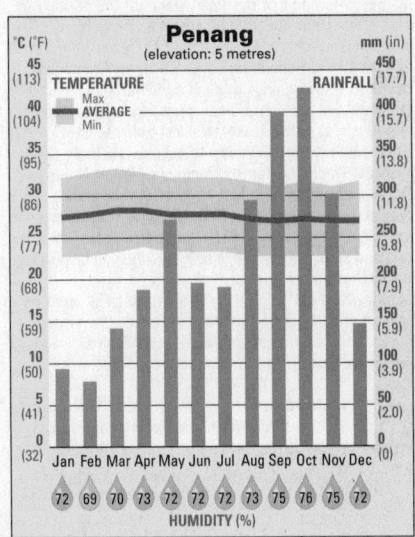

Communications

Telephone: Full IDD is available. Country code: 60. International calls can be made from public telephones with card facilities or at any *Telekom* office. Public coin-operated phones can be found in many areas, such as supermarkets and post offices. Cards can be purchased at airports, petrol stations and some shops. There are currently two types – *Kadfon* and *Unicard* – and these can only be used in their appropriate phone booths.

Mobile telephone: Roaming agreements exist with some international mobile phone companies. Coverage is good, though sporadic.

Internet: Internet is available; there are numerous Internet cafes. Hotels and hostels often have facilities.

Post: There are post offices in the commercial centre of all towns. Post office hours: Mon-Sat 0800-1700.

MEDIA: Malaysia has some very tough censorship laws. Authorities exert substantial control over the media and restrictions may be imposed in the name of 'national security'. The Government strives hard to shield the Malaysian population from foreign influences that are deemed 'harmful'. News is subject to censorship, as are other programmes and films, particularly those showing swearing or kissing. Private radio stations broadcast in Malay, Tamil, Chinese and English. Newspapers renew their publication licences annually, and the danger of suspension or abolition always lurks.

Press: The English-language dailies printed in Peninsular Malaysia are the *Business Times*, *The Edge*, *Malay Mail*, *Malaysiakini*, *New Straits Times* and *The Star*. There are also several English-language Sunday newspapers and periodicals. English-language newspapers available in Sarawak include the *Borneo Post* and *Sarawak Tribune*. English-language dailies in Sabah include the *Borneo Mail*, *Daily Express* and *Sabah Times*.

TV: *Radio Television Malaysia* (RTM) is state-run and operates *TV1* and *TV2* networks. *TV3*, *ntv7* and *8TV* are all commercial networks.

Radio: *Radio Television Malaysia* (RTM) operates some 30 state-run radio stations across the country, plus an external service. *Time Highway Radio* is a private FM station in Kuala Lumpur; *Era FM* is another private FM station in Malaysia.

Passport/Visa

	Passport Required	Visa Required	Return Ticket? Required
Full British	Yes	No	Yes
Australian	Yes	No	Yes
Canadian	Yes	No	Yes
USA	Yes	No	Yes
Other EU	Yes	No/1	Yes
Japanese	Yes	No	Yes

Note: *Regulations and requirements may be subject to change at short notice, and you are advised to contact the appropriate diplomatic or consular authority before finalising travel arrangements. Any numbers in the chart refer to the footnotes below.*

Restricted entry: (a) Certain nationals have to apply for a visa with a reference/approval from the Immigration Department in Malaysia, rather than through an Overseas Mission in their country of residence. (b) Foreign women who are at least six months pregnant (unless in transit) may be denied entry. (c) Nationals of Israel and Serbia & Montenegro require special approval from the Ministry of Home Affairs, and must be travelling for a special reason.

PASSPORTS: A valid passport or other travel documents recognised by the Malaysian Government required by all. The former must have enough pages for the embarkation stamp upon arrival and be valid for at least six months at date of entry. The latter should be endorsed with a valid re-entry permit. If not in possession of a passport or travel document, a Document in lieu of Passport must be obtained from any Malaysian Representation Office. Holders of travel documents such as a Certificate of Identity, a Laisser Passer, a Titre de Voyage or a Country's Certificate of Residence must ensure guarantee of return to country that issued the documents or the national's country of residence.

Note: All visitors must also have proof of adequate funds and an onward or return sea or air ticket.

VISAS: Visas are required by all except the following:
(a) **1.** nationals of countries referred to in the chart above for stays of up to three months, except nationals of Cyprus, Estonia, Greece, Lithuania, Malta, Portugal and Slovenia who may stay for up to one month, and nationals of Latvia, who do require a visa;
(b) nationals of Albania, Algeria, Argentina, Bahrain, Bosnia & Herzegovina, Brazil, Croatia, Cuba, Egypt, Iceland, Japan, Jordan, Korea (Rep), Kuwait, Kyrgyzstan, Lebanon, Liechtenstein, Morocco, New Zealand, Norway, Oman, Peru, Qatar, Romania, San Marino, Saudi Arabia, South Africa, Switzerland, Tunisia, Turkey, Turkmenistan, United Arab Emirates, Uruguay and Yemen for social visits of up to three months;
(e) nationals of Iran, Libya, the Syrian Arab Republic, and holders of Palestinian travel documents or a Macau Travel Permit for social visits of up to 14 days;
(f) nationals of all countries other than those mentioned above for stays of up to one month, except for nationals of Afghanistan, Angola, Bangladesh, Benin, Bhutan, Botswana, Burkina Faso, Burundi, Cameroon, Central African Republic, China (PR), Colombia, Congo (Dem Rep), Congo (Rep), Côte D'Ivoire, Djibouti, Equatorial Guinea, Eritrea, Ethiopia, Ghana, Guinea-Bissau, India, Iraq, Israel, Latvia, Liberia, Mali, Mozambique, Myanmar, Nepal, Niger, Nigeria, Pakistan, Rwanda, Serbia & Montenegro, Sierra Leone, Sri Lanka, Taiwan and Western Sahara who *always* require a visa.

Note: Certain nationals can only enter Malaysia through airports and not seaports. Nationals may still require a pass upon arrival, even if they are permitted to enter Malaysia visa-free.

Types of visa and cost: *Single-entry:* £10. Prices are subject to change. *Student:* MYR60 per year, available only in Malaysia. Enquire at the Malaysian High Commission for details.

Validity: One to three months from date of issue. Multiple-entry visas are valid for up to three months; in certain cases, validity of up to 12 months may be granted. Extensions are also possible. Enquire at the Malaysian High Commission for further details. *Transit:* five days. The validity of the visa can also vary from nationality to nationality in accordance with whether a reference from the Immigration Department is obtained.

Application and enquiries to: Malaysian High Commission; see *Passport/Visa Information*.

Application requirements: (a) Valid passport. (b) Two identical passport-size photos. (c) Fee (payable in cash or postal order only). (d) Two completed application forms. (e) Proof of sufficient funds (eg most recent bank statement). (f) Onward or return ticket or travel itinerary from travel agent. (g) Letter of introduction (and copy) from applicant's employer, college or university. For the spouse who is not working, a marriage certificate, photocopy of other spouse's passport and a letter of introduction from their spouse's employer must be submitted. (h) Self-addressed envelope (recorded delivery) if applying by post. *Student:* (a)-(h) and, (i) Letter of acceptance and covering letter from educational

A B C D E F G H I J K L M N O P Q R S T U V W X Y Z

institution in Malaysia. (j) Stamped personal bond.
Working days required: Same day – morning submission of the application (0915-1215) and afternoon collection (1530-1630). Times apply to the Malaysian High Commission in London. Applications by post take approximately two weeks. Students who apply for a student pass on arrival will usually obtain one within two weeks.

> **PASSPORT/VISA INFORMATION**
>
> **Malaysian High Commission in the UK**
> 45 Belgrave Square, London SW1X 8QT, UK
> Tel: (020) 7235 8033 *or* 7930 7932 (tourist board).
> E-mail: mwlondon@btinternet.com
> Opening hours: Mon-Fri 0900-1300 and 1400-1700; 0915-1215 (Consular section).
> *Also deals with tourism enquiries.*
>
> **Embassy of Malaysia in the USA**
> 3516 International Court, NW, Washington, DC 20008, USA
> Tel: (202) 572 9700.
> E-mail: malwash@kln.gov.my

Money

Currency: Ringgit (MYR) = 100 sen. Notes are in denominations of MYR1000, 500, 200 100, 50, 20, 10, 5, 1. The MYR1000 and MYR500 notes are now being phased out. Coins are in denominations of 50, 20, 10, 5 and 1 sen. There are also many commemorative coins in various denominations which are legal tender. The Ringgit is often referred to as the Malaysian Dollar.
Currency exchange: The best currency for exchange is the Pound Sterling, but US Dollars are also widely accepted. All commercial banks are authorised foreign exchange dealers; major hotels are only licensed to buy or accept foreign currency in the form of notes and traveller's cheques. Although all major currencies can be exchanged easily in the main tourist centres, problems may occur elsewhere. It is difficult to exchange Malaysian currency outside of Malaysia, Singapore or Indonesia. All visitors need to fill in a Travellers Declaration Form (TDF); see below for details.
Credit & debit cards: American Express, Diners Club, MasterCard, Visa and Eurocard are accepted. Check with your credit or debit card company for details of merchant acceptability and other services which may be available.
Traveller's cheques: Accepted by all banks, hotels and large department stores. To avoid additional exchange rate charges, travellers are advised to take traveller's cheques in Pounds Sterling, US Dollars or Australian Dollars.
Currency restrictions: All visitors entering Malaysia (including children) must declare amounts over MYR1000 that they have in their possession (local and equivalent in foreign currencies) on a Travellers Declaration Form (TDF), which can be obtained at the airport or Malaysian Embassies, High Commissions and Tourist Offices. On departure, the TDF has to be filled in prior to immigration clearance.
The import and export of local currency is limited to MYR1000. The import of foreign currency is unlimited. The export of foreign currency is limited to the amount imported on arrival.
Banking hours: Mon-Fri 0930-1600, Sat 0930-1130 (closed on the first and third Saturday of each month). Banks in Sabah open at 0800 and usually break for lunch (1200-1400).
Exchange rate indicators:
Rate at time of publishing

£1.00=	MYR6.63
$1.00=	MYR3.78

Duty Free

The following goods may be imported into Malaysia without incurring customs duty:
200 cigarettes or 50 cigars or 225g of tobacco; 1l of spirits or wine or malt liquor; cosmetics, perfumery, soaps and dentifrices up to the value of MYR200; gifts and souvenirs not exceeding a total value of MYR200 (except goods from Langkawi and Labuan, up to a value of MYR500); 100 matches; a total of MYR75 for dutiable food preparations; a maximum three pieces of new wearing apparel, plus one pair of new footwear; one unit of each portable electrical or battery-operated appliance for personal care and hygiene.
Prohibited items: It is prohibited to import any goods from South Africa and Israel. Non-prescribed drugs, weapons and any imprint or reproduction of any currency note or coin are prohibited. Drug-smuggling carries the death penalty.

Public Holidays

Below are listed Public Holidays for the January 2006-June 2007 period.
2006: Jan 1 New Year's Day. **Jan 10** Hari Raya Qurban (Feast of the Sacrifice). **Jan 29-30** Chinese New Year. **Jan 31** Hari Raya Tussa (Islamic New Year). **Apr 11** Mawlid al-Nabi (Birth of the Prophet Muhammad). **May 1** Labour Day. **May 13** Vesak Day (Birth of the Buddha). **Jun 3** Official Birthday of HM the Yang di-Pertuan Agong. **Aug 31** National Day. **Oct 21** Deepvali Festival. **Oct 22-24** Hari Raya Puasa (End of Ramadan). **Dec 25** Christmas Day. **Dec 31** Hari Raya Qurban (Feast of the Sacrifice).
2007: Jan 1 New Year's Day. **Jan 20** Hari Raya Tussa (Islamic New Year). **Feb 18** Chinese New Year. **Mar 31** Mawlid al-Nabi (Birth of the Prophet Muhammad). **May 1** Labour Day. **May 2** Vesak Day (Birth of the Buddha). **Jun 4** Official Birthday of HM the Yang di-Pertuan Agong.
Note: (a) Muslim festivals are timed according to local sightings of various phases of the moon and the dates given above are approximations. During the lunar month of Ramadan that precedes Hari Raya Puasa, Muslims fast during the day and feast at night and normal business patterns may be interrupted. Some restaurants are closed during the day and there may be restrictions on smoking and drinking. Some disruption may continue into Hari Raya Puasa itself and Hari Raja Haji may last anything from two to 10 days, depending on the region. For more information see the *World of Islam* appendix. (b) Buddhist festivals are also timed according to phases of the moon and variations may occur.

Health

	Special Precautions	Certificate Required
Yellow Fever	No	1
Cholera	Yes	2
Typhoid & Polio	3	N/A
Malaria	4	N/A

Note: Regulations and requirements may be subject to change at short notice, and you are advised to contact your doctor well in advance of your intended date of departure. Any numbers in the chart refer to the footnotes below.

1: A *yellow fever* vaccination certificate is required from travellers over 1 year of age arriving within six days from infected areas. Those countries formerly classified as endemic by the WHO are considered by the Malaysian authorities to be infected areas.
2: Following WHO guidelines issued in 1973, a *cholera* vaccination certificate is not a condition of entry to Malaysia, although it may be required if travelling on to a cholera-infected country. However, outbreaks have been reported in Semphorna and Pulau Gaya, Sabah, in May 2005; see the *Health* appendix.
3: *Typhoid* risk exists, especially in rural areas. Vaccination again *poliomyelitis* and *typhoid* is recommended. There was an outbreak of *typhoid* in Kelantan in April 2005.
4: *Malaria* risk exists only in certain isolated inland regions. Urban and coastal areas are safe. The *falciparum* strain is reported to be highly resistant to chloroquine and resistant to sulfadoxine/pyrimethamine. The recommended prophylaxis is mefloquine.
Food & drink: All water should be regarded as being potentially contaminated. Water used for drinking or making ice should have first been boiled or otherwise sterilised. Milk is unpasteurised and should be boiled. Powdered or tinned milk is available and is advised, but make sure that it is reconstituted with pure water. Avoid dairy products that are likely to have been made from unboiled milk. Only eat well-cooked meat and fish, preferably served hot. Pork, salad and mayonnaise may carry increased risk. Vegetables should be cooked and fruit peeled.
Note: It is generally considered safe to drink water straight from the tap; however, as no authority is absolutely clear on this matter, the above advice is included as it reflects the necessity for caution for visitors who are unused to the Malaysian way of life.
Other risks: *Hepatitis A*, *C* and *E* occur and *hepatitis B* is hyperendemic. Epidemics of *dengue fever* and *Japanese encephalitis* can occur in both urban and rural areas. Immunisation against *tetanus*, *TB*, *diphtheria*, *hepatitis A* and *E* is recommended. Outbreaks of *meningococcal meningitis* can occur.
There may be some risk of *rabies* in certain areas. For those at high risk, vaccination before arrival should be considered. If you are bitten, seek medical advice without delay. For more information, consult the *Health* appendix.
Malaysia has periodic problems with air quality reaching hazardous levels because of smoke haze. For more information on the air quality in Malaysia please visit the Malaysian Department for the Environment's website at: www.jas.sains.my/jas/Air+Pollutant+Index
In November 2004, there were outbreaks of *Avian Influenza* (also known as *Bird Flu*) in poultry in Kelantan State in peninsular Malaysia. In February 2006, local health authorities confirmed the presence of the virus in 40 chickens that died in villages on the outskirts of Kuala Lumpar. No human infections or deaths have been reported. The risk to humans from Avian Influenza is believed to be very low. As a precaution, visitors should avoid visiting live animal markets, poultry farms and other places where they may come into close contact with domestic, caged or wild birds; and ensure poultry and egg dishes are thoroughly cooked.
There have been large-scale outbreaks of *Hand, Foot and Mouth Disease (HFMD)* across Sarawak in early 2006. HFMD is a communicable disease, which affects all age groups, but children are particularly vulnerable. The disease usually causes mild illness but may occasionally take a more serious form, sometimes resulting in death. For further information on HFMD please visit the NaTHNac website: www.nathnac.org/pro/clinical_updates/HFMD_140306.htm
Health care: Health insurance is recommended. Hospitals are found in all the main cities and can deal with all major needs. Private hospitals, some managed and staffed by British-trained doctors and nurses, provide a high standard of medical care and include Gleneagles Intan Medical Centre in Kuala Lumpur and Ampang Puteri Specialist Hospital, Selangor. Smaller towns and rural areas have private clinics. In an emergency, dial 999.

Travel - International

AIR:
The national airline is *Malaysia Airlines (MH)* (website: www.malaysiaairlines.com), which is southeast Asia's biggest airline and flies to over 110 cities across six continents. Further details can be obtained from the London office of *Malaysia Airlines* (tel: (0870) 607 9090). *Singapore Airlines*, *Royal Brunei* and *Thai International* operate flights to certain Malaysian destinations.
Approximate flight times: From Kuala Lumpur to *London* is 14 hours.
Main airports: *Kuala Lumpur International Airport (KUL)* (Sepang) (website: www.klia.com.my) is 55 km (34 miles) south from Kuala Lumpur and near Putra Jaya, Malaysia's future administrative capital. It currently handles 25 million passengers a year and is served by all major international airlines. *To/from the airport*: Kuala Lumpur's city centre is accessible via the Kuala Lumpur–Seremban Highway/KLIA interchange and the Shah Alam/North-South Central Link Expressway (travel time – 45 minutes). Taxis must be pre-paid in the Arrivals Area at the airport (travel time – 40 minutes). *KL City Buses* operates an Express Bus Service to the Airport Bus Terminal, Hentian Duta, Kuala Lumpur city centre; the journey takes approximately one hour. Regular feeder buses travel from Hentian Duta to Lot 10 on Jalan Sultan Ismail in the city centre between 0800 and 2430 (travel time – 30 minutes). The cheapest way to travel to the city is by combined bus and train. The *Stage Bus Service*, which operates 0715-2230, leaves the airport every 30 minutes for Nilai KTM Station (travel time – 30 minutes). From Nilai, trains travel to Kuala Lumpur Railway Station 0644-2244 every 20 to 30 minutes (travel time – 1 hour). The *KLIA Express* and *KLIA Transit* train link the airport to Kuala Lumpur (KL Sentral); Express trains depart every 15 minutes and the Transit trains every 30 minutes. *Facilities*: ATMs, bureaux de change, shopping, duty free, restaurants, postal services, tourist information, hotel reservations, medical service, left-luggage, prayer rooms and car hire. Business facilities include executive lounges, shower facilities, limousine services to the city and business centres, which provide telephone, fax, computers, internet, teleconferencing, postal and secretarial services and even golf putting.
Penang (PEN) (Bayan Lepas) is 16km (10 miles) south of Georgetown, capital of this small island off the northwest coast of the peninsula. Though not receiving as many international flights as Kuala Lumpur, there are connections from the UK via Hong Kong (SAR), Singapore or Bangkok. *Facilities*: Incoming and outgoing duty-free shop, restaurant and bar, bank/bureau de change and car hire.
Kota Kinabalu (BKI) is 6.5km (4 miles) from the city. Situated on the northern coast of Sabah state (the northeastern part of Borneo Island), this airport is the international gateway to East Malaysia (Sabah and Sarawak) and receives international flights from all over the world. Connections from the UK go via Singapore, Hong Kong and Kuala Lumpur. *Facilities*: Bank/bureau de change facilities, restaurant and bar.
Kuching (KCH) is 11km (7 miles) from the city. Situated in the west of Sarawak on the island of Borneo, the airport receives a limited number of international flights.
Departure tax: MYR45 for international departures.
SEA:
Main Ports: *Georgetown (Penang)*, *Port Kelang* and *Westport (for Kuala Lumpur)* and, in East Malaysia (for Sabah and Sarawak), *Bintulu*, *Kota Kinabalu*, *Kuching*, *Lahad Datu*, *Rejang*, *Sandakan* and *Tawau*. Shipping lines with passenger services to Malaysia include *Blue Funnel*, *P&O* and *Straits Shipping*. Cargo/passenger lines are *Austasia*, *Knutsen*, *Lykes*,

Neptune Orient, *Orient Overseas* and *Straits Shipping*. *Star Cruises* (Singapore) organises luxury cruises from Westport. Other lines that offer cruises from this port include *Coral Princess* and *Gemini*. *Norwegian Cruise Lines*, *Royal Caribbean* and *Seabourn Cruise Lines* also call at Malaysia. There is also a ferry service to Tanjung from Changi port in Singapore.

RAIL:
Through services operate to and from Singapore via Kuala Lumpur and between Butterworth and Bangkok (Thailand). There is also a 41-hour round trip available from the *Eastern and Oriental Express*, a luxury train service modelled on the famous Orient Express, which leaves from Singapore, journeys through Kuala Lumpur and heads north to Bangkok from where it returns to Singapore.

ROAD:
Peninsular Malaysia is linked by good roads to Thailand and (via two causeways) to Singapore. Toll fees are levied on all highways throughout Malaysia. Road connections between the two eastern states, Sarawak and Sabah, and their neighbours on Borneo, Brunei and the Indonesian state of Kalimantan are fairly good.

Travel - Internal

Note: During major festivals (especially *Hari Raya Pusa*, the *Chinese New Year* and *Hari Raya Haji*), internal travel becomes extremely difficult unless tickets have been pre-booked long in advance. Domestic express bus tickets often go on sale up to two months before the festivals and sell out within one or two weeks. Even domestic flights tend to be packed during these periods.

AIR:
Malaysia Airlines (MH) (website: www.malaysiaairlines.com) serves numerous commercial airports in Peninsular Malaysia. In East Malaysia, *Malaysia Airlines* crisscrosses both Sabah and Sarawak and also flies to Brunei.

Air Passes: *Discover Malaysia Pass* can be purchased for US$199 and is valid for 28 days from the date of issue; pass holders can make up to five flights to any Malaysian destination.

Domestic airports: *Kuala Lumpur Subang (KUL)* is 22 km (14 miles) west from the city. Previously the main international airport, it is now mainly used for domestic flights. Most Malaysian states have domestic airports and plans are underway for the further development of several airports.

Departure tax: MYR6.

SEA/RIVER:
Coastal ferries sail frequently between Penang and Butterworth and there is a scheduled passenger service linking Port Kelang with both Sarawak and Sabah. Small rivercraft often provide the most practical means of getting about in East Malaysia, even in the towns, and they are the only way to reach the more isolated settlements (unless one has access to a helicopter). A modern ferry service runs between Kuala Perlis, Kuala Kedah and Pulau Langkawi. Regular boat services also connect Lumut to Pangkor Island and Tunjung Gemak or Mersing to Tioman Island. In Sabah, long boats connect Labuen to Menumbak. In rural Sarawak the major means of transport are air-conditioned express boats. Boats may easily be chartered and river buses and taxis are plentiful.

RAIL:
Malayan Railway (Keretapi Tanah Melayu Berhad *or* KTM) at Jalan Sultan Hishamuddin, 50621 Kuala Lumpur (tel: (3) 2263 1111; website: www.ktmb.com.my) operates nearly 2092km (1300 miles) of line. There are three classes of train: Deluxe or First Class (with upholstered seats), Eksekutif or Second Class (with padded leather seats) and Ekonomi or Third Class (with cushioned plastic seats). The fast daytime *Express Rakyat* runs from Singapore to Butterworth, and continues on to Thailand. Express trains are modern, and some have sleeping berths and buffet cars. Some trains are air conditioned. East Malaysia has one railway line, known by travellers as the Jungle Railway, which is the main overland route for the Taman Negara National Park; it runs along the coast from Kota Kinabalu (Sabah), then inland up a steep jungle valley to the small town of Tenom. Other than this line, there are two main lines operated for a passenger service. One runs along the west coast and from Singapore, which runs northwards to Kuala Lumpur and Butterworth, meeting the Thai railways at the border. The other line separates from the west coast line at the town of Gemas and takes a northeastern route to Kota Bharu and Tenom. There is also a passenger service to two of Malaysia's seaports – Penang and Padang Besar on the west coast. The *KTM Komuter*, a commuter service, runs from Kuala Lumpur to Port Klang (west), Rawang (north) and Seremban (south). There are no rail services in Sarawak.

Cheap fares: Children under four travel free; children aged four to 11 pay half fare. For further information on discount fares available to passengers, contact Malayan Railway (see address details above).

Special tickets: The *Malayan Railway Pass* is available in 10- and 30-day tickets, giving unlimited travel on all trains through Peninsular Malaysia and Singapore and can be purchased from train stations in Butterworth, Johor Bahru, Kuala Lumpur, Padang Besar, Port Kelang, Rantau Panjang, Singapore and Wakaf Bharu. However, reservations must be made in advance for seats in first-class, air-conditioned trains and a supplement is charged. Reservations may be made up to three months in advance with the Director of Commerce, Malayan Railway, Jalan Sultan Hishamuddin, Kuala Lumpur. Enquire at Tourism Malaysia for further details.

ROAD:
Traffic drives on the left. Most roads in the peninsular states are paved and signs leading to the various destinations are well placed and clear. The north–south expressway, spanning 890km (553 miles) from Bukit Kayu Hitam (on the Kedah–Thailand border) to Johor Bahru is fully open to traffic. The dual carriageway will provide shorter travel times between towns. **Bus:** Local bus networks are extensive, with regular services in and between all principal cities. 4-wheel-drive buses are used in rural areas of Sabah and Sarawak.

Trishaw: Available in Penang and Malacca, these are inexpensive for short trips. Fares should be negotiated in advance. **Taxi:** Shared and normal taxis are a fast means of inter-town travel, but delays may be encountered whilst drivers get their passenger load before moving off. Ask drivers to turn the meter on before starting the journey. There is a 50 per cent surcharge for fares between 0000-0600 and an extra MYR1 is charged for taxis booked by phone. Taxi coupons providing fixed prices to specific destinations can be purchased at the Kuala Lumpur railway station and the airport. **Car hire:** This is available through several agencies. Some agencies provide cars on an unlimited mileage basis. Cars with driver are also available.

Documentation: An International Driving Permit is required. For UK citizens, a national driving licence is sufficient, but it has to be endorsed by the Registrar of Motor Vehicles in Malaysia.

URBAN:
Parking in the centre of Kuala Lumpur and other towns is restricted to spaces for which a charge is made and a receipt is given. Public transport services in Kuala Lumpur are provided by conventional buses and by 'Bas Mini' fixed-route minibuses, taxis and pedi-cabs (trishaws) licensed by the Government. Bus fares vary, but the 'Bas Mini' have flat rates. These are used for shorter journeys, and tend to be crowded. The *PUTRA Light Rail Transit (LRT)* is a quick way to get around the city and provides links to the eastern and western suburbs of Kuala Lumpur. Routes and timetables are indicated in stations with an LRT logo.

Travel times: The following chart gives approximate travel times (in hours and minutes) from **Kuala Lumpur** to other major centres in Malaysia.

	Air	Road	Rail
Penang	**0.45**	**5.00**	**9.30**
Alor Setar	**0.45**	**7.00**	**7.30**
Johor Bahru	**0.35**	**3.00**	**6.00**
Singapore	**0.45**	**6.00**	**7.00**

Travel Advice

Malaysia shares with the rest of South East Asia a threat from terrorism. Attacks could be indiscriminate and against civilian targets, including places frequented by foreigners. It is believed that terrorists and criminal elements are continuing with plans to kidnap foreign tourists from the islands and coastal areas of Eastern Sabah. Boats travelling to and from offshore islands and dive sites are possible targets. Travellers wishing to visit resorts on, and islands off, Eastern Sabah, should exercise extreme caution.

Travellers planning to cross the border to Thailand should be aware that there has been a resurgence of terrorism in southern Thailand, particularly in the far southern provinces of Pattani, Yala, Narathiwat and Songkhla. All but essential travel to these Thai provinces is advised against. Since the beginning of 2004, over 800 people have been killed and several hundred injured.

Travellers should not become involved with drugs of any kind: possession of even very small quantities can lead to imprisonment or the death penalty.

On 26 December 2004 a massive earthquake registering 9.0 on the Richter scale struck off the west coast of Indonesia. The quake created a tsunami – a series of huge waves that spread destruction across many parts of Asia and reached as far as the east coast of Africa. The north west coast of the Malaysian peninsular (including Langkawi and Penang) was affected by the tidal waves which destroyed many buildings. However, the destruction has been far less severe than in other neighbouring countries. Travel in Malaysia has largely been unaffected but those wishing to travel to Malaysia should still check with a relevant tour operator, tourist board or Embassy for the latest advice prior to travel (see *Top Things To Do*).

This advice is based on information provided by the Foreign and Commonwealth Office in the UK. It is correct at time of publishing. As the situation can change rapidly, visitors are advised to contact the following organisations for the latest travel advice:

British Foreign and Commonwealth Office
Tel: (0845) 850 2829.
Website: www.fco.gov.uk

US Department of State
Website: http://travel.state.gov/travel

Accommodation

EDITOR'S CHOICE: HOMESTAY PROGRAMMES

Increasing in popularity in many states, Malaysian Homestay Programmes combine budget accommodation with the opportunity to experience typical Malaysian life.

HOTELS:
Malaysia has many luxury and economy class hotels. Many new luxury hotels have recently been built in Kuala Lumpur. It is necessary to book well in advance, especially during school and public holidays when the Malaysians take their holidays in the popular resorts, notably Penang, Langkawi and the highlands. The more basic hotels have little in the way of modern washing or bathing facilities, often only a water trough instead of a bath or shower. Government tax of 5 per cent and a service charge of 10 per cent are added to bills. Tips are only expected (on the basis of good service) for room service and porterage. Laundry service is available in most hotels.

GOVERNMENT REST HOUSES: These are subsidised, moderately priced hotels. They are basic, but always clean and comfortable, with full facilities and usually good restaurants. As they are primarily travelling inns they tend to fill up quickly, so it is advisable to telephone and reserve a room.

CAMPING:
There are camping facilities in the Taman Negara or national parks. Here jungle lodges provide tents, camp beds, pressure lamps and mosquito nets for trips into the rainforests.

YOUTH HOSTELS:
Malaysia is a full member of the International Youth Hostel Federation. There are not many youth hostels, but they are very cheap. Accommodation is in dormitories and meals can be arranged. Visitors must register at the hostel from 1700-2000. Hostels are to be found in Cameron Highlands, Kuala Lumpur, Kuantan, Malacca, Penang and Port Dickson.

ACCOMMODATION INFORMATION

Malaysian Association of Hotels
C5-3, Wisma MAH Jalan Ampang Utama 1/1, 1 Ampang Avenue, 68000 Ampang, Kuala Lumpur
Tel: (3) 4251 8477.
Website: www.hotels.org.my

Malaysian Youth Hostel Association
Kuala Lumpur International Youth Hostel, 21 Jalan Kg Attap, 50460 Kuala Lumpur, Malaysia
Tel: (3) 2273 6870.

Association of Homestay Programmes
Tel: (3) 3263 0048.
E-mail: araitu@mapro.or.ja

Top Things To See

- Malaysia is, surprisingly for some, enriched by modern, daring architecture. Nowhere is this better observed than in **Kuala Lumpur** (or **KL**, as it is locally known), Malaysia's hub; a huge, bustling, cosmopolitan city that is the business heart of the nation. Here, the voluminous **Petronas Twin Towers** dominate the city at a height of 436m (1453ft): they are amongst the tallest buildings in the world. From the viewing level of the Towers, the city unfolds with its old mosques and ramshackle buildings, contrasting with the gleaming skyscrapers that have sprouted as Malaysia has become one of the regional economic powerhouses. The Menara Kuala Lumpur is the tallest telecommunication tower in South-East Asia and the fourth-tallest in the world. **Merdeka Square** is at the very heart of old Malaysia, with the stunning highlight, the **Sultan Abdul Samad Building**, which bizarrely blends Victorian and Moorish architectural styles. The **Tasek Perdana Lake Gardens** are one of the city's best-known natural landmarks, a popular spot for picnics and

A B C D E F G H I J K L M N O P Q R S T U V W X Y Z

walking. Within the gardens are **Parliament House** and the **National Monument**. The National Monument, an impressive brass sculpture, is one of the world's largest free-standing sculptures. Outside of Kuala Lumpur, however, the trend continues. In **Ipoh**, Malaysia's third-largest city and dubbed the 'City of Millionaires', the ghosts of its grand colonial days ensure a mixture of colonial and modern architecture. Thirty minutes' drive from Ipoh, near **Batu Gajah**, stands the impressive **Kellie's Castle**. Surrounded by rubber plantations, the magnificent ruins of the unfinished castle are all that remains of Scotsman William Kellie Smith's nostalgic ambition to recreate an authentic piece of his Scottish homeland. Work halted with the sudden demise of Smith in 1926 and, since his death, the rumours and mystique surrounding the castle have intensified. Reputed to be haunted, the castle is also believed to possess secret rooms and tunnels, undetected to this day.

Credit: ©Tourism Malaysia

- Mosques are to Islam what cathedrals are to Christianity: you would be foolish to miss out on the sights of these wonderful and varied tributes to religion and, indeed, you often will not be able to miss out on them, such is their visual prominence. Malaysia has some mosques of the very highest standard. In Kuala Lumpur, the **National Mosque** is surrounded by lawns ornamented with fountains. This modern mosque, built in 1965, gleams every bit as brightly as any of Kuala Lumpur's skyscrapers. The main dome is moulded in the shape of an 18-point star to represent the 13 states of Malaysia and the five central Pillars of Islam. The huge main prayer hall can hold up to 10,000 worshippers, although this section of the mosque is closed to non-worshippers. Also in the capital, the **Friday Mosque** is situated astride the confluence of the **Klang** and **Gombak Rivers** at the point where the first Europeans scrambled ashore, and is the most stunning and popular sight in the city. The best time to visit is at sunset or during the muezzin's call to prayer, which echoes around the ornate domes and palm trees, lending the mosque an air of calm amidst the skyscrapers. Other mosques worth visiting or inspecting throughout Malaysia are **Kuala Kangsar**; the **Ubudiah Mosque**; the **State Mosque** in **Seremban**, which has nine pillars to represent the nine districts of the state, and which overlooks the tranquil **Lake Gardens**, which include two beautiful lakes and a floating stage where cultural shows are performed; the **Tranquerah Mosque**, one of the oldest in the country, in **Malacca**; **Kuching**'s **Sarawak State Mosque**, with its magnificent gilt domes; and the many religious buildings of **Labuan**, which include the **An'nur Jamek Mosque**, which has a progressive futuristic design.
- See some of Malaysia's dazzling caves. The **Batu** are large natural caves that can be reached by 272 steps, and which house the Hindu shrine of Lord Subramaniam. Nearby is the **Museum Cave**, a fascinating display of brightly coloured statues and murals from Hindu mythology. Meanwhile, just north of Ipoh at **Jalan Kuala Kangsar**, **Perak Tong**, a limestone cave temple, houses over 40 statues of Buddha. In a cave behind the main altar 385 steps lead up to a magnificent viewpoint, from where one can survey the surrounding countryside. **Sam Poh Tong** and **Kek Lok Tong**, near **Gunung Rapat**, are impressive cave temples where statues of Buddha stand alongside magical stalactites and rock formations. Both temples have Buddhist vegetarian restaurants in the temple grounds. **Gunung Mulu National Park** is a World Heritage Site and amongst its thousands of different plant species and abundance of wildlife are some magnificent limestone caves – these just happen to be the most extensive cave system in the world, including the **Deer Cave**, **Clearwater Cave** and **The Cave of the Winds**. The park is also home to Sarawak's last nomadic tribe. Elsewhere, the **Niah Caves** are also worth a visit, showing evidence of human existence dating back to 5000 BC. The caves are valued for their guano and bird's nests, the latter being used to make soup. Many of the caves – and some are more easily accessible than others – may be visited with a guide.
- Traverse Malaysia's stunning **rainforests** and **jungles** to obtain different vistas of beauty. **Templar Park**, 22km (14 miles) north of Kuala Lumpur, is a well-preserved tract of primary rainforest, which is rich in scenic beauty. Jungle paths, swimming lagoons and waterfalls all lie within the park boundaries. Malaysia's largest national park of them all is **Taman Negara**. Surrounded by the world's oldest tropical forest (supposedly 130 million years old), the park has remained virtually untouched and is a favourite haunt for outdoor enthusiasts, especially birdwatchers. The journey to the park headquarters involves travel by train, road and a three-hour boat ride. Accommodation is mostly modest and the more comfortable lodgings are limited.
- If you are keen to watch for birds, head to Ipoh where the **Kuala Gula Bird Sanctuary** is host to over 150 different species of birds; lucky visitors may see smooth otters, long-tailed macaque and ridge-back dolphins. The best time to visit is between September and December when many migratory birds arrive at the sanctuary. **Penang Bird Park** is also a must for bird lovers and horticultural enthusiasts alike. This landscaped park in **Seberang Jaya** is home to over 400 species of birds with specially designed aviaries placed among manmade islands with waterfalls and gardens ablaze with ornamental flowers and tropical greenery.
- If you come to Malaysia on holiday, chances are that you will want to see some of its stunning **beaches**. The island of **Penang** has long been eulogised as the 'Pearl of the Orient', lying just off the northwest coast of Peninsular Malaysia. Recently a network of expanded tourist facilities has been created, which have ruined many of the island's main beach charms, but most of the island is still a beautiful tropical oasis of palm trees and sandy beaches. It was the natural harbour that first attracted the British to Penang in the late 18th century, and the port is still one of the most important in the country today. More than 100km (60 miles) north of Penang lie the 104 islands, many of which are just outcrops of coral, that make up Langkawi. The largest, **Langkawi Island**, is the only one with sophisticated tourist facilities (it has been declared a free port and duty free shopping is available). Several international hotels and resorts have opened as the Government and international developers flood into what is set to become Malaysia's premier island beach resort. The island's many coves, lagoons and inlets make it ideal for all kinds of watersports. The state of **Kelantan** also has many clean and unspoilt beaches and the sea is ideal for swimming, diving and fishing. The coastal **Port Dickson** is about one-and-a-half hour's travelling time from Kuala Lumpur and Malaysians flock here from the city at weekends - but with 18km (11 miles) of beach, there is always plenty of room. The bays are fine for all kinds of watersports and fishing. However, the water quality is not always good and the sea around the beaches is often too shallow for decent swimming. Nevertheless, they are certainly scenic. **Desaru** is one of Johor's newest resorts and boasts unspoilt beaches and jungle. However, it is probably Malaysia's **East Coast** that contains many of the finest beaches in the country, including some of the least spoilt in southern Asia. In effect, the whole east coast is one huge beach, backed by jungle. **Kuantan**, the state capital of **Pahang**, is fast gaining popularity as a beach resort. **Telek Chempadek**, just 5km (3 miles) north of Kuantan, is another popular beach resort with a wide range of watersports available, including windsurfing, water-skiing and sailing. It has a good selection of restaurants along the seafront. Asia's first Club Mediterranée holiday village is in **Cherating**, about 45km (30 miles) north of Kuantan. The beaches at Cherating are some of the finest on the east coast and conditions are particularly favourable for windsurfing. The island of **Tioman**, in the South China Sea off the coast of Pahang, will be familiar to fans of the film *South Pacific*, as it was here that the film-makers found their mythical Bali Hai. The sweeping palm trees and luxuriously white beaches are still there, but fame has come at a price with a rush of development, which on one side has brought the ease of direct flights and express boats from the mainland, but also a raft of accommodations, not all of them of the same quality and aesthetic standards. Tioman is the largest of a group of 64 volcanic islands, and also the largest island on Malaysia's east coast. The three most popular resorts are **ABC**, **Salang** and **Juara**. Tioman is also one of the best destinations in Malaysia for scuba diving and snorkelling. The state of **Terengganu** has 225km (140 miles) of white sandy beaches. Swimming and all forms of watersports are favourite pastimes. And the twin islands of **Perhentian Besar** and **Perhentian Kecil** are certainly worth a mention, considered to be the two most beautiful islands in the country by many. They both boast pristine white beaches, crystal clear waters and are still relatively unexploited. The strict local beliefs mean that alcohol is not common and this has helped deter major companies from setting up here, leaving the islands in their natural state for those who do choose to visit. The islands are popular for scuba diving and snorkelling with easy access to reefs and good visibility.
- For an unusual attraction, go to the **Snake Temple** in Penang, which swarms with poisonous snakes, their venomous threat countered by heavily drugging them with incense.
- Malaysia is not all jungle and coastline – it also has its very own highlands to explore. In the **Central Highlands**, dotted about the mountain range that runs down the spine of Malaysia, are several hill resorts. All are situated more than 1400m (4500ft) above sea level and offer cool, pleasant weather after the humidity of the plain and the cities. Still further north are the **Cameron Highlands**. These are among the best-known mountain resorts in Asia, and consist of three separate townships: **Brinchang**, **Tanah Rata** and **Ringlet**. An international-standard hotel and many bungalows are set around a golf course in lush green surroundings. From here you can visit **Gunung Brinchang**: at 2064m (6773ft) above sea level, it is the highest inhabited point in Peninsular Malaysia and therefore a magnificent viewpoint.
- In the southern state of **Johor**, **Johor Bahru** is Malaysia's southernmost gateway. In this state, be sure to watch the trance-inducing *Kuda Kepang* dances in Muar, accompanied by the euphony of *ghazal* music and devotional chanting To elaborate, Kuda Kepang is a puppet shaped like a legless horse that is straddled by performers – usually a troupe of around 15 people – and then harnessed in a sort of repetitive, bobbing movement. The dance is particularly likely to be performed at cultural or personal celebrations, such as festivals or weddings. It is believed to have originated as a means of spreading the religion of Islam by Muslim missionaries in the 14th century.
- In the interior of Pahang, visit Malaysia's answer to Loch Ness: **Lake Chini**'s waters are said to contain mythological monsters that guard the entrance to a legendary sunken city.
- Do not miss the opportunity to see **orang-utans** in their natural environment. In **Sabah**, on the northern tip of **Borneo**, some of the world's oldest jungles and South-East Asia's highest peaks are home to such creatures. The **Sepilok Orang-Utan Rehabilitation Centre** in **Sandakan** has many of these 'wild men of Borneo' – in fact, it has the world's largest orang-utan population. The sanctuary is a rehabilitation centre where orang-utans reap the benefits of inhabiting virgin rainforest in a protected environment. Now one of Sabah's top tourist attractions, the centre is no flippant tourist site as it actively manages to take in injured or orphaned orang-utans and return them to the wild once they are rehabilitated. There is no guarantee of seeing an orang-utan, but they usually turn up for their twice-daily feedings.

Top Things To Do

- Go to one of Malaysia's annual festivals, which celebrate significant religious events and public holidays and are staged throughout the year, magnificent spectacles that burst with vibrancy and colour. Each of the different communities has its own customs, traditions and festivals. **Kelantan** is a state especially renowned for its many cultural festivals. **Puja Umur** (the birthday of the Sultan) is celebrated with a week-long festival, beginning with a parade in **Kota Bharu**. The **Annual Penang International Dragon Boat Festival** is another colourful, popular event (website: www.penangdragonboat.com).
- The tropical waters off peninsular Malaysia and **Borneo** offer ideal conditions for **scuba diving**. Water visibility is often greater than 30m (100ft). The best dive sites include: **Layang Layang**, located northwest of **Kota Kinabulu** off the coast of **Sabah** and accessible by air, a coral atoll consisting of 13 coral reefs linked together, with an amazing array of marine life and cliffs that plunge 2000m to the ocean bed; **Miri**, located north of **Kuching** off the coast of **Sarawak**, Borneo, with popular dive sites that include a Japanese World War II shipwreck and **Scubasa Reef**, a shallow reef which provides refuge for migrating turtles during August each year; **Pulau Redang**, home to Malaysia's first protected marine park, the **Terengganu Marine Park**, located north of **Kuala Terengganu** and an archipelago that contains nine islands; **Pulau Sipadan**, Malaysia's only oceanic island, renowned for its wide range of rare marine species; **Pulau Tioman**, located within the **Pahang Marine Parks**, consisting of eight islands and with one of the best dive sites being **Tiger Reef**, which has a particularly high number of sea fans; **Tunku Abdul Rahman Park**; **Pulau Tenggol**, a popular weekend getaway for Malaysians, located south of **Terengganu**, accessible by air and with waters protected by marine park status; **Pulau Paya Marine Park**; **Pulau Perhentian**, located in the South China Sea, off the coast of **Kelantan**, rich in giant soft corals, large schools of pelagic fish and nocturnal shellfish, plus surrounded by beautiful beaches and a tropical interor filled with wildlife such as monkeys, flying squirrels and butterflies; **Tunku Abdul Rahman Marine Park**; and **Labuan Island**, a popular wreck-diving destination, with two wrecks from ships sunk in World War II, and one recent Malaysian wreck.

- Nearly 75 per cent of Malaysia is covered in forests, of which the rainforest is reputedly the world's oldest (130 million years). Many of the parks offer excellent **trails** for **jungle trekking**, particularly at **Taman Negara National Park** (peninsular Malaysia). The best time to visit is between February and September (dry season). There are many clearly marked trails including a **canopy walkway**. Expert guides should be hired from the Wildlife Department at the **Taman Negara Resort** at **Kuala Tahan**, the park's headquarters. Tour packages lasting from one to three days are available. Kuala Tahan is reached by a three-hour riverboat trip from **Kuala Tembeling**, but there is also a daily shuttle bus from Kuala Lumpur. Treks up **Gunung Tahan mountain** (2187m/7174ft) are also possible; a guide is compulsory and the trip takes several days. In East Malaysia, the best treks are in Sarawak, Borneo and **Gunung Mulu National Park**, which is renowned amongst caving enthusiasts. The recently discovered **Sarawak Chamber** and the 51km- (32 mile-) long **Clearwater Cave** (accessible by boat only) are favourite destinations. Permits for Gunung Mulu National Park must be obtained in Miri, reached either by a short flight or a couple of three-hour boat trips. Adventurous trekkers may wish to explore the **Kelabit Highlands** around nearby **Bario**, but these are quite demanding and should only be undertaken in the company of a local guide. Another famous trekking destination is the **Kinabalu National Park**, located in the state of Sabah, whose centrepiece, **Mount Kinabulu** (4101m/13,452ft), is South-East Asia's highest peak. Despite its size, Kinabulu is very easy to climb. No skills are required, but a guide and a climbing permit (which can be bought on location) are still compulsory. The climb involves an overnight stay in one of the resthouses along the route. Owing to the altitude, people with high blood pressure or heart problems should not attempt the climb.
- Participate in one of Malaysia's **traditional**, unusual **sports**, including **Gasing-top spinning** (called **Main Gasing**), which uses tops fashioned from hardwood and delicately balanced with lead. **Wau-kite flying** is another favourite pastime. *Sepak Takraw* is a game like volleyball, played with a ball made of rattan strips. Players may use their heads, knees and feet but not their hands.
- Stay in **Malaysian longhouses**, which are common along the rivers in Sarawak and Sabah, and are really entire villages housed under one single roof, inhabited by native communities. For some years now, Tourism Malaysia has been promoting these characteristic habitations to tourists who are welcome to stay free of charge (although small gifts as a sign of appreciation are recommended). Visitors should be accompanied by a local guide who can also take them on a jungle walk.
- Malaysia's central **railway** travels largely through areas of dense jungle. It commences near **Kota Bahru** and continues via **Kuala Krai**, **Gua Musang**, **Kuala Lipis** and **Jerantut** to meet the Singapore-KL railway line at **Gemas**. Take this route and you will find yourself enjoying rail travel with a difference.
- Explore Malaysia's experiments with **ecotourism**. The Forestry Research Institute, 15km northwest of **Kuala Lumpur**, is a genuine example of ecotourism in that it is a stretch of jungle that has been protected and is now being used to study how this unique eco-system works. The centre also looks at ways of sustainable development and at ways of protecting this environment. There are a number of **low eco-impact trails** that visitors can explore.
- Bathe in the restorative waters of the **Pedas Hot Springs**, 30km (18 miles) south of **Seremban**. Visitors will find bathing enclosures, dining and recreational facilities.
- Step back in time with a trip to the city of **Malacca**, only two hours by road south of Kuala Lumpur, but centuries away in ambience. Founded in the early 15th century, Malacca remains predominantly a Chinese community, although there are many reminders of periods under Portuguese, Dutch and British rule; some of these can be seen in the Malacca Museum. Old men in fishing boats still cruise up through the centre of the modern city with the catch of the day, which can be enjoyed in the city's excellent restaurants. **River cruises** that open up the city's history are justifiably popular.

TOURIST INFORMATION

Tourism Malaysia in the UK
Malaysia House, 57 Trafalgar Square, London WC2N 5DU, UK
Tel: (020) 7930 7932.
Website: www.malaysiatrulyasia.co.uk
Opening hours: Mon-Fri 0900-1700.

Tourism Malaysia in the USA
120 East 56th Street, Suite 810, New York, NY 10022, USA
Tel: (212) 754 1113-5.
Website: www.tourismmalaysia.gov.my

Entertainment

FOOD & DRINK: In multiracial Malaysia, every type of cooking from South-East Asia can be tasted. Malay food concentrates on subtleties of taste using a blend of spices, ginger, coconut milk and peanuts. There are many regional types of Chinese cooking including Cantonese, Peking, Hakka, Sichuan and Taiwanese. Indian food is also popular, with curries ranging from mild to very hot indeed. Vegetarian food, chutneys and Indian breads are also available. Indonesian cuisine also combines the use of dried seafoods and spiced vegetables with the Japanese method of preparation with fresh ingredients cooked to retain the natural flavour. Korean and Thai food are available in restaurants. Western food is served throughout the country and includes US, Spanish, Italian and French cuisine. Kuala Lumpur has several restaurants which rival the high standards set by established Western restaurants in Singapore and Hong Kong. Although the country is largely Islamic, alcohol is available.
Things to know: Table service is normal, and chopsticks are customary in Chinese restaurants. Indian and Malay food is eaten with the fingers. Set lunches, usually with four courses, are excellent value for money.

Credit: ©Tourism Malaysia

National specialities:
- *Sambals* (a paste of ground chilli, onion and tamarind) is often used as a side dish.
- *Blachan* (a dried shrimp paste) is used in many dishes.
- *Ikan bilis* (dried anchovies) are eaten with drinks.
- Popular Malay dishes include *satay*, which consists of a variety of meats, especially chicken, barbecued on small skewers with a spicy peanut dipping sauce and a salad of cucumber, onion and compressed rice cakes. The best sauce often takes several hours to prepare to attain its subtle flavour.
- *Gula Malacca* (a firm sago pudding in palm sugar sauce) is also served in restaurants.
- Japanese-style seafood such as *siakaiu beef* (grilled at the table).
- *Tempura* (deep-fried seafood) and *sashimi* (raw fish with salad) are excellent.
- Amongst Malaysia's exotic fruits are starfruit, durian, guavas, mangos, mangosteen and pomelos.

National drinks:
- Local beers such as *Tiger* and *Anchor* are recommended.
- The famous *Singapore Gin Sling*.
- International beers are also available.

Tipping: 10 per cent service charge and 5 per cent Government tax are commonly included in bills. Taxi drivers are not tipped..
NIGHTLIFE: Kuala Lumpur has a selection of reputable nightclubs and discos, most belonging to the big hotels. Nightclubs generally stay open until 0500 or 0600 and usually request a cover charge which includes the first drink free. Many of Kuala Lumpur's bars have a 'Happy Hour', offering two drinks for the price of one, between 1700-2000/2100. *Bintang Walk* is a lively spot and has a good selection of al fresco bars and coffee shops. Penang is also lively at night, larger hotels having cocktail lounges, dining, dancing and cultural shows. There are night markets in most towns, including both Kuala Lumpur and Penang Chinatown. Malay and Chinese films often have English subtitles and there are also English films. The national lottery and Malaysia's only casino at *Genting Highlands* are Government-approved and visitors are not supposed to gamble elsewhere. *Keno* and Chinese *Tai Sai*, roulette, baccarat, French bull and blackjack are played at the casino. Dress is relatively formal and visitors must be over 21 years of age.
SHOPPING: Shopping in Malaysia ranges from exclusive department stores to street markets. Bargaining is expected in the markets, unless fixed prices are displayed. Kuala Lumpur is a popular shopping destination, rivalling Singapore and Hong Kong. *Suria KLCC*, a shopping mall with a spectacular fountain, gardens and a beautiful piazza, houses a great selection of leading couture outlets. *Star Hill* and *Lot 10* are popular shopping malls and there were plans underway to develop and finish an additional mall – *Times Square*. The islands of Labuan and Langkawi are duty free zones. Cameras, pens, watches, cosmetics, perfume and electronic goods are available duty free throughout Malaysia. Malaysian speciality goods include pewterware, silverware and brassware; batik; jewellery; pottery; and *songket*. Enquire at Malaysian Royal Customs and Excise about claiming cashback on duty free goods. **Shopping hours:** Most shops keep their own opening hours, usually within the range of 1000-2200.

Business

- **GDP:** US$103.7 billion (2003).
- **Main exports:** Electrical equipment, petroleum and liquefied natural gas, wood and wood products, palm oil, rubber, textiles and chemicals.
- **Main imports:** Electronics, machinery, petroleum products, plastics, vehicles, iron and steel products and chemicals.
- **Main trade partners:** USA, Japan, Singapore, Taiwan (China), Hong Kong (SAR), Thailand, Korea (Rep), Germany and Indonesia.

ECONOMY: A fully-fledged 'tiger' economy, from the 1970s onwards Malaysia grew rapidly at around 10 per cent annually. This extraordinary economic development had been achieved through the familiar East Asian combination of a strong state allied to unfettered capitalism. The Government plays a central role in guiding the country's economic progress – the New Development Policy was unveiled in 1991 as the country's economic blueprint for the following 20 years. However, in 1997 the Asian financial crisis brought this process to a shuddering halt. Malaysia has recovered reasonably well since then, although the headlong pre-1997 expansion has been replaced by a more measured pace of growth of between 4 and 4.5 per cent per annum in 2002 and 2003. Inflation was a respectable 1.8 per cent in 2002 and Malaysia enjoys a substantial trade surplus ($18 billion in 2002). Growth topped 7 per cent in 2004. Healthy foreign exchange reserves, low inflation and a small external debt are all strengths that make it unlikely that a financial crisis similar to 1997 will re-occur. The Ringgit/US Dollar peg was abolished in July 2005. This has not resulted in any significant change to the exchange rate. The manufacturing sector produces electronics, transport equipment, machinery steel and textiles. There are also reserves of oil and natural gas and mineral deposits of tin (of which it is a major producer), bauxite, copper, iron and gold. In the agricultural sector palm oil, of which Malaysia is the world's leading producer, is a major export commodity. Timber production remains important although it has been limited by the introduction of conservation measures in the mid-1990s. Other cash crops include rubber (again, Malaysia is one of the world's top producers), cocoa and pepper. Tourism dominates the service sector.
Malaysia is a member of the Pacific Rim organisation APEC (Asia-Pacific Economic Forum). The essential stability of Malaysia's financial sector meant that, although it suffered short-term damage, it was able to recover quickly.
BUSINESS ETIQUETTE: Suits or safari suits are acceptable for business meetings. Business visitors should remember that the Malay population is predominantly Muslim and religious customs should be respected and normal courtesies observed, eg appointments, punctuality and calling cards. **Office hours:** These vary between Peninsular Malaysia and East Malaysia. In general most private sector offices are open Mon-Fri 0900-1700 and Sat 0900-1300. Government office hours: 0830-1630. Many private sector companies operate a five-day week.
CONFERENCES/CONVENTIONS: Many conferences and conventions are held in Malaysia each year. Apart from the dedicated facilities at the Putra World Trade Centre in Kuala Lumpur, many hotels have facilities. For further information contact Tourism Malaysia, Convention Promotion Division (see *Top Things To Do*).

COMMERCIAL INFORMATION

Malaysian Trade Commission in the UK
17 Curzon Street, London W1J 5HR, UK
Tel: (020) 7499 5255.

National Chamber of Commerce and Industry of Malaysia
37 Jalan Kia Peng, 50450 Kuala Lumpur, Malaysia
Tel: (3) 241 9600.
Website: www.nccim.org.my

Malaysian International Chamber of Commerce and Industry (MICCI)
PO Box 12921, 50792 Kuala Lumpur, Malaysia
Tel: (3) 6201 7708.
Website: www.micci.com

Malaysian Industrial Development Authority (MIDA)
Block 4, Plaza Sentral, Jalan Stesen Sentral 5, 50470 Kuala Lumpur, Malaysia
Tel: (3) 2267 3633.
Website: www.mida.gov.my

Maldives

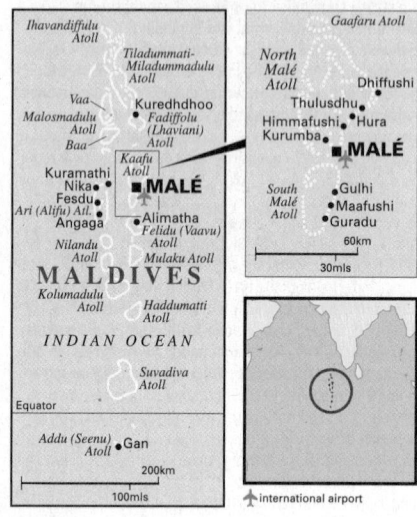

Location: A group of islands in the Indian Ocean, 500km (300 miles) southwest of the southern tip of India.

Time: GMT + 5.

Overview

For a long time, the Republic of the Maldives was one of the best-kept secrets in the world; a beautiful string of low-lying coral islands in the Indian Ocean, a paradise for watersports enthusiasts and sunseekers alike. Now the tourism potential of the country has developed significantly: the islands have become an increasingly popular long-haul destination. However, the Maldives is somewhat divided between being an idyllic tourist destination, and being a country with indigenous people who rarely intermix with the tourists. The Dhivehin, as the islanders are called, are a mixed people of Aryan, Negroid, Sinhalese, Dravidian and Arab descent. The mix reveals their history: the islands were under Muslim control from the 12th century, then Portuguese rule from 1518, a dependency of Ceylon (Sri Lanka) in 1645, then a British Protectorate with an elected Sultan as Head of State in 1887. The islands achieved full Independence as a Sultanate in 1965. Three years later, the Republic of the Maldive Islands established Ibrahim Nasir as President, who was succeeded by Maumoon Abdul Gayoom in 1978, who has been the dominant figure in the islands' politics since then.

Somehow it is difficult to think about the Maldives' history when relaxing on one of the country's 26 natural atolls. The resort islands offer nautical delights from night-fishing trips, windsurfing and scuba diving. Many islands embrace enormous lagoons, where bright blue-green water laps gently. Indeed, photos of the Maldivian sea look doctored: it is only when you travel there that you discover the sea really is that luminous, enchanting colour.

Yet, even in paradise, trouble can bubble beneath the surface. It is precisely because the Maldives are so low-lying (80 per cent of the territory is less than 1m above sea level), so transparent and perfect for snorkelling, that their very existence is especially threatened by global warming. They are also particularly vulnerable to natural catastrophe, as shown in the devastating tsunami on December 26 2004: twenty of The Maldives' 199 inhabited islands were totally destroyed. In addition are human factors: the Maldives continue to spark international outrage for their detention of prisoners of conscience, jailed for journalistic reproach of Governmental conduct. With no formal political parties, there is no credible threat to Gayoom, and dissent is firmly repressed.

All of these factors need to be seriously discussed by the international community in future years. Otherwise, paradise really might be lost.

General Information

AREA: 298 sq km (115 sq miles).
POPULATION: 338,000 (UN, 2005).
POPULATION DENSITY: 1134 per sq km.
CAPITAL: Malé. **Population:** 70,000 (2005).
GEOGRAPHY: The Maldives Republic is located 500km (300 miles) southwest of the southern tip of India and consists of about 1190 low-lying coral islands, of which only 200 are inhabited. Most of the inhabited islands are covered by lush tropical vegetation and palm trees, while the numerous uninhabited islands, some of which are mere sand spits or coral tips, are covered in shrubs. Each island is surrounded by a reef enclosing a shallow lagoon. Hundreds of these islands together with other coral growth form an atoll, surrounding a lagoon. All the islands are low-lying, none more than 2m (7ft) above sea level. The majority of the indigenous population does not mix with the tourist visitors, with the exception of those involved with tourism in the resorts and Malé.
GOVERNMENT: Republic since 1965. Gained independence from the UK in 1965. **Head of State and Government:** President Maumoon Abdul Gayoom since 1978, re-elected 2003. **Recent history:** Islam is a central feature of the country's life and is now supervised by a Supreme Council for Islamic Affairs, working under direct presidential control. With no formal political parties, the Maldives' politics are personality based; no credible threat to President Maumoon Abdul Gayoom has emerged in the 25 years during which he has held power, not least because dissent is firmly repressed by Gayoom's security forces. The only overt sign of discontent in recent years came in September 2003 when the death of several prisoners sparked riots in the capital. Nonetheless, after the riots were quelled, Gayoom – underpinned by his reputation for good economic management – went on to secure a record sixth term of office at the Presidential poll in November 2003. Under the revised constitution which came into effect in 1998, the legislature, or *Majlis*, has 48 members. Of these, 40 are directly elected for a five-year term in multi-seat constituencies, and the remaining eight are Presidential appointees. The President holds executive power assisted by an appointed ministerial Cabinet. Outside the capital, however, considerable power is exercised by the atoll chiefs (Atholhu Verins), who are appointed by the President.
LANGUAGE: The national language is Dhivehi. English is widely used as a business language in Government offices and the commercial sector. Other languages are widely used within tourist areas.
RELIGION: The indigenous population is almost entirely Sunni Muslim.
ELECTRICITY: 230 volts AC, 50Hz. Round-pin plugs are used, although square-pin plugs are now becoming more common.
SOCIAL CONVENTIONS: Dress is informal, but locals who are Muslim will be offended by nudity or scanty clothing in public places, and the Government rigidly enforces these standards. Bikinis and other scanty beachwear are not acceptable in Malé or on any other inhabited island; they should be restricted to resort islands only. When entering a mosque, the legs and the body, but not the neck and the face, should be covered. Handshaking is the most common form of greeting. The indigenous population not involved in the tourist trade lives in isolated island communities maintaining almost total privacy. A large number of locals smoke, but smoking and eating during Ramadan is discouraged.

Climate

The Maldives have a hot tropical climate. There are two monsoons, the southwest from May to October and the northeast from November to April. Generally the southwest brings more wind and rain in June and July. The temperature rarely falls below 25°C (77°F). The best time to visit is November to Easter.

Required clothing: Lightweight cottons and linens throughout the year. Light waterproofs are advised during the rainy season.

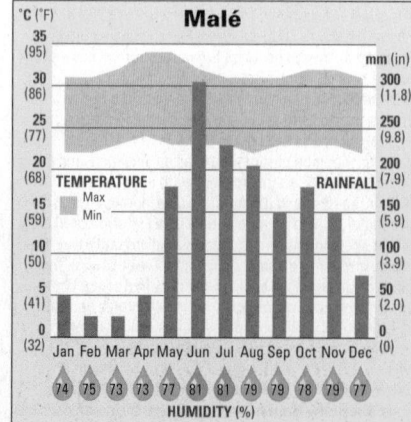

Communications

Telephone: IDD is available. Country code: 960.
Mobile telephone: Roaming agreements exist with a few international mobile phone companies. Handsets can by hired by the day.
Internet: The Internet can be accessed from most areas of the Maldives. Malé, the capital, has an Internet cafe and almost all resorts facilitate the sending and receiving of e-mails.
Post: Airmail to Western Europe takes about one week. Post office hours: Sat-Thurs 0730-1330 and 1600-1750.
MEDIA: Criticism of the state is limited, and the Government occasionally closes media outlets for this reason. Self-regulation by the media has meant that there has been only isolated official action against journalists.
Press: Local dailies which publish in the Dhivehi language have some English-language pages and concentrate on local and regional topics. *The Maldives News Bulletin* is published weekly in English. The other dailies *Aafathis Daily News* (website: www.aafathisnews.com.mv), *Haveeru Daily* (website: www.haveeru.com.mv) and *Miadhu News* (website: www.miadhu.com) have English sections. Information about local events is widely available on all the resort islands.
TV: The Government controls the sole TV service, Television Maldives. *Television Maldives (TVM)* operates two channels.
Radio: The Government decided in 2005 to allow licence applications from would-be private radio broadcasters. The Government controls the state radio station *Voice of Maldives. Radio Eke* is also state-owned.

Passport/Visa

	Passport Required?	Visa Required?	Return Ticket Required?
Full British	Yes	1	Yes
Australian	Yes	1	Yes
Canadian	Yes	1	Yes
USA	Yes	1	Yes
Other EU	Yes	1	Yes
Japanese	Yes	1	Yes

Note: *Regulations and requirements may be subject to change at short notice, and you are advised to contact the appropriate diplomatic or consular authority before finalising travel arrangements. Any numbers in the chart refer to the footnotes below.*

PASSPORTS: Passport valid for six months required by all.
VISAS: 1. Tourist visas for 30 days will be issued on arrival only and are free of charge to all visitors in possession of valid travel documents.
Note: Foreign visitors who enter the Maldives must be in possession of return or onward tickets and sufficient funds to cover duration of stay.
Types of visa and cost: Tourist visas can be extended for a minimum of three months for a fee of MUR750 (£45).
Validity: Three months to one year.
Application to: Visas are issued on arrival at the immigration desk at Maldives International Airport.
Application Requirements: (a) Valid passport and travel documents. (b) Fee. (c) Return or onward ticket. (d) Proof of sufficient funds to cover duration of stay (US$30 per person per day) or a confirmed hotel reservation for the intended period of stay.
Working days required: Visa extensions can be requested on arrival at Maldives International Airport, and will be issued immediately provided nationals are holding valid travel documents.

PASSPORT/VISA INFORMATION

High Commission of the Republic of Maldives in the UK
22 Nottingham Place, London W1U 5NJ, UK
Tel: (020) 7224 2135.
Website: www.maldiveshighcommission.org
Opening hours: Mon-Fri 0930-1700.

Money

Currency: Maldivian Rufiya (MVR) = 100 laari. Notes are in denominations of MVR500, 100, 50, 20, 10 and 5. Coins are in denominations of MVR2 and 1, and 50, 25, 10, 5, 2 and 1 laari.
Currency exchange: Major currencies can be exchanged at banks, tourist resort islands, hotels and leading shops. Payments in hotels can be made in most hard currencies (particularly US Dollars) in cash, traveller's cheques or credit cards.
Credit & debit cards: Most major island resorts, local and souvenir shops will accept American Express, Diners Club, Eurocard, MasterCard and Visa. Arrangements vary from

island to island, and it is advisable to check with your credit or debit card company for details of merchant acceptability and other facilities which may be available. There are ATMs at a few places on the Capital Island.

Traveller's cheques: These are generally accepted in Pounds Sterling and US Dollars. To avoid additional exchange rate charges, travellers are advised to take traveller's cheques in US Dollars.

Currency restrictions: There are no restrictions on import or export of either local or foreign currencies. An explanation must be provided when carrying large quantities of currencies.

Banking hours: Sun-Thurs 0800-1330.

Exchange rate indicators:

Rate at time of publishing

£1.00= MVR23.23

$1.00= MVR13.13

Duty Free

The following goods may be imported into the Maldives without incurring customs duty:

A reasonable amount of cigarettes, cigars and tobacco; a reasonable number of gifts.

Prohibited items: Pornographic literature; idols of worship; dogs, pigs or pork products; explosives and weapons; alcoholic beverages. Drugs are strictly prohibited; the penalty for importing drugs for personal or other use is life imprisonment. Animals require a veterinary certificate. The following may not be exported in any form: tortoise and turtle shells and products made of turtle shell (the Government has banned the killing of turtles), and black coral in whole form.

Note: An official licence is required to import alcohol.

Public Holidays

Below are listed Public Holidays for the January 2006-June 2007 period.

2006: Jan 1 New Year's Day. **Jan 9** Hajj Day. **Jan 10** Eid Al-Adha (Feast of the Sacrifice). **Jan 31** Islamic New Year. **Apr 11** Mawlid al-Nabi (Birth of the Prophet). **Apr 21** National Day. **Jul** Huravee Day. **Jul 26-27** Independence Day. **Sep** Martyrs' Day. **Sep 24** Start of Ramadan. **Oct 22-24** Eid al-Fitr (End of Ramadan). **Nov 3** Victory Day. **Nov 11-12** Republic Day. **Dec 31** Eidal Al-Adha (Feast of the Sacrifice).

2007: Jan 1 New Year's Day. **Jan 20** Hajj Day. **Feb 10** Islamic New Year. **Mar 31** Mawlid al-Nabi (Birth of the Prophet). **Apr 21** National Day.

Note: Muslim festivals are timed according to local sightings of various phases of the moon and the dates given above are approximations. During the lunar month of Ramadan that precedes Eid al-Fitr, Muslims fast during the day and feast at night and normal business patterns may be interrupted. Many restaurants are closed during the day and there may be restrictions on drinking in public places. Some disruption may continue into Eid al-Fitr itself, although this is generally unlikely to affect life on the resort islands. Eid al-Fitr and Eid el-Kebir may last anything from two to 10 days, depending on the region. For more information, see the *World of Islam* appendix.

Health

	Special Precautions?	Certificate Required?
Yellow Fever	Yes	1
Cholera	Yes	2
Typhoid & Polio	3	N/A
Malaria	4	N/A

Note: *Regulations and requirements may be subject to change at short notice, and you are advised to contact your doctor well in advance of your intended date of departure. Any numbers in the chart refer to the footnotes below.*

1: A *yellow fever* vaccination certificate is required from travellers arriving from infected areas.

2: Following WHO guidelines issued in 1973, a *cholera* vaccination certificate is not a condition of entry to the Maldives.

3: *Typhoid* may occur: vaccination is recommended.

4: *Malaria* is disappearing. The risk of infection is very low.

Food & drink: The water provided in the resort areas is generally safe to drink. In other areas, water of uncertain origin used for drinking, brushing teeth or making ice should have first been boiled or otherwise sterilised. Food in hotels and resorts is usually risk free, although visitors should be cautious elsewhere.

Other risks: *Hepatitis A, B,* and *E* can occur. *Tuberculosis* and *diphtheria* vaccines are sometimes advised. *Dengue fever* and *Leptospirosis* occur.

Rabies may be present although there have been no reported incidences in animals or humans since 1996. For those at high risk, vaccination before arrival should be considered. If

you are bitten, seek medical advice without delay. Sensible precautions should be taken to prevent sunburn and dehydration.

For more information, consult the *Health* appendix.

Health care: There are two hospitals on Malé, the Indhira Gandhi Memorial hospital and the ADK private hospital. First-aid facilities are available on all resort islands. A decompression chamber is accessible at most resorts in case of diving emergencies. Medical treatment in the Maldives can be very expensive and comprehensive health insurance is recommended.

Travel - International

AIR:

 The national airline is *Island Aviation Services (Q2)* (website: www.island.com.mv).

Approximate flight times: From Malé to *London* is 10 hours 20 minutes.

Main airports: *Hulule International (MLE)* (Malé) on Hulule Island is 2km (1.2 miles) from Malé (travel time by boat – 15 minutes). *To/from the airport:* Boats travel from the airport to Malé 24 hours per day. They leave every 15 minutes during the day and every 30 minutes after midnight. Boats from the various island resorts meet each arriving plane to take visitors to their accommodation. There is no scheduled transfer from Hulule Island to the other islands. *Maldivian Air Taxi* and *Trans Maldivian Airways* operate special transfer trips to most resorts. If an advance booking has been made, representatives of the resorts will receive tourists at the airport and will take care of all onward transport arrangements.

Facilities: Left luggage, first aid, bank, duty free shops, snack bar, post office and restaurant.

Departure tax: None if airport tax has been paid before; otherwise, US$12.

SEA:

 Many cruise ships stop over at the Maldives islands as part of their itinerary.

Travel - Internal

AIR:

 Internal air services are operated by *Island Aviation Services,* linking Malé with Kaadedhdhoo, Kadhdhoo and Gan. There are also services to Hanimaadhoo in the north, although these islands will not be on most visitors' itineraries.

A number of companies operate twin-otter and float plane services around the Maldives. The transfer from the airport to the resort islands may be an optional extra on the tour. These services are also available for trips around the islands.

SEA:

 Visitors generally remain on their resort island for the duration of their stay, although island-hopping trips by ferries are widely available. Local charter boats are also easily available for hire. High-speed boats meet arrivals at the airport, supplied by the resort they are booked with, and boats are available for hire at the ferry counter near the jetty area. The speedboats connect the airport with Ari Atoll and some outlying islands. The indigenous inhabitants, however, live a parochial life and tend to visit only Malé, and even then irregularly.

ROAD:

 Travel on individual islands does not present any problem since few of them take longer than half an hour to cross on foot. In Malé, it is possible to take taxis.

Travel Advice

The 26 December 2004 tsunami caused damage to a number of islands in the Maldives, including some resort islands. The large majority of resorts are now operating normally.

Travellers should avoid any demonstrations or large gatherings, especially on Malé Island and the Southern Islands where there was some violence in demonstrations in August 2005.

The threat from terrorism is low, but you should be aware of the global risk of indiscriminate terrorist attacks which could be against civilian targets, including places frequented by foreigners.

Petty crime occurs: you should take care of your valuables and other personal possessions.

Possession of illegal drugs carries severe penalties.

Public observance of any religion other than Islam is prohibited.

This advice is based on information provided by the Foreign and Commonwealth Office in the UK. It is correct at time of publishing. As the situation can change rapidly, visitors are advised to contact the following organisations for the latest travel advice:

British Foreign and Commonwealth Office

Tel: (0845) 850 2829.

Website: www.fco.gov.uk

US Department of State

Website: http://travel.state.gov/travel

Accommodation

HOTELS:

 There are four hotels on Malé and one on Gan; there are also a large number of guest houses on Malé, although most visitors stay on resort islands. There are no guest houses or self-catering facilities on any of the resort islands.

RESORTS: There are over 90 resorts which vary from extravagantly luxurious to fairly simple. Accommodation almost invariably consists of thatch-roofed coral cabanas with ensuite facilities. Most of the resorts have air-conditioned rooms with mini-bar, although some of the resorts still have fan-cooled rooms. Many resort groups have recently installed desalination plants to provide clean tap water. The resorts are fully integral communities with sport and leisure facilities including scuba diving and snorkelling, restaurants and bars and, in some cases, a shop and/or disco. A few islands have more than one resort and these generally range in size from six to 250 units, with most having 30 to 100 units. There is a shop on every resort island. Different islands tend to attract different nationalities.

ACCOMMODATION INFORMATION

Maldives Association of Tourism Industry (MATI)

3rd Floor, Gadhamoo Buliding, Malé , Maldives

Tel: 326 640 *or* 321 701.

E-mail: mati@dhivehinet.net.mv

Top Things To See & Do

• Wander around **Malé's National Museum**, located in **Sultan's Park**, which possesses a superb collection of artefacts, including Sultanese thrones and palanquins.

• The Maldives excel in the area of **arts and crafts**, and the **Baa Atoll** is one of the few places where traditional arts and crafts are still practised - and now home to five resorts. Malé, the capital, also has several markets of fresh and wholesome food produce for those wanting to sample local fare.

• Exceptional and easily accessible underwater life makes the Maldives one of the world's top **diving** and **snorkelling** destinations. All of the resorts have professional dive schools with fully qualified multilingual instructors offering a range of courses, from beginners to full PADI certification. Basic diving equipment is provided in all resorts and some also rent out underwater cameras. Dive schools organise daily dive boat trips to sites around the islands throughout the year. Night dives and special trips for more experienced divers are also available. Most of the resorts also offer reef sightseeing trips on glass-bottomed boats. Some of the best dive sites include: **Maldives Victory Wreck** (which sank in 1981), lying on the western side of **Hulule island** (because of strong currents, this dive is for experienced divers only); **Mushimasmingili Thila** (**Shark Thila**), located in the northern section of the **Ari Atoll**, and renowned for its abundance in fish (notably grey reef shark), giant snappers and tropical reef fish; **Guraidhoo Corner**, where powerful currents mean that this is one for experienced divers, who are rewarded with large fish, including grey reef sharks, eagle rays, sailfish and large snappers; **Kuda Rah Thila**, which is good for less experienced divers; **Banana Reef**, where strong currents make for an exceptionally abundant marine life, with reef sharks, bannerfish and oriental sweetlips all present, and with windsurfing skills on most of its resorts. Other islands with good diving and snorkelling include: the oval-shaped **North Baros**, which has one side full of corals and a nearby shallow beach; **Bandos**, with its particularly good diving school and its aptly-named **Shark Point** attraction; **Kurumba**, where colourful fish in the lagoon eat out of your hand; **Kanifinolhu**, which boasts some of the best inside reefs in the country; **Embudu Village**, which has a house reef as well as two wrecks, caves and drop offs; **Vaadhu**, a diving paradise; and immediately south of the **South Kaafu Atoll**, the **Vaavu Atoll** has some of the best diving in the entire archipelago. Visitors should note that the Maldives adhere to a strict reef and marine conservation policy and that severe penalties may be imposed for disrespecting the environment (see also 'Prohibited Items' in the *Duty Free* section).

• For the people of the Maldives, **fishing** has been a lifeline and, with over 99 per cent of the Maldives' total area consisting of water, the country has some of the world's best fishing grounds. Many resorts offer fishing trips on

modern speedboats equipped for big game fishing. **Night fishing** for groupers, snappers, squirrelfish or barracuda is particularly popular. **Fishing trips** will usually end with a barbecue at the resort with the day's catch being cooked and eaten. As a conservation measure, sport fishing is confined to the tag and release method. The use of harpoon guns and hunting of marine mammals such as whales and dolphins and large fish such as the whale shark is strictly prohibited. The fishing and collection of the following is also prohibited: turtle, Napoleon wrasse, berried and small lobster, conch, giant clam and black coral.

- Opt for some **aerial sightseeing** for an astonishing glimpse of a blue panorama. **Photo flights** are also possible, and although all of the islands are beautiful, some respond particularly well to photographic scrutiny. **Ihuru** is a small and gorgeous that is much-photographed. Similarly, **Nakatchafushi**, situated on the west side of the **North Malé Atoll**, boasts the country's largest lagoon and can perhaps take the title of the most photographed of all the islands.

- For real Maldivian-style living, **Reethi Rah** is an untouched and beautiful island to the northwest of the North Malé Atoll, which has **thatched bungalows** and 10 **water bungalows** built on stilts overlooking the lagoon – all of which are influenced by local architectural styles without missing any of the modern comforts. On the **Kaafu (Malé) Atoll**, **Coco Island** has eight two-storey, beautifully furnished thatched huts. **Angaga**, in **Ari Atoll**, is a small island, impressively constructed in traditional Maldivian style and with air-conditioned rooms and fresh hot and cold water. Staying in a water bungalow is particularly recommended: there is something about waking up and seeing a seemingly never-ending stretch of turquoise sea in front of you that is truly breathtaking.

- Some people might presume that facilities are limited on the Maldives' islands, but all of the resort islands have an assortment of traditional and international restaurants. What's more, the island of **Makunudhoo** (reached by a two-hour voyage from the airport) is renowned for the quality of its food. It is also protected on all sides by a beautiful lagoon and accommodation consists of individual thatched bungalows situated in coconut groves leading down to the beach. The catch? It is one of the most expensive island resorts in the Maldives!

- Why not spend a day and a night alone on an **uninhabited island**? You can usually do so as part of an island-hopping tour. Another option is to visit a fishing village with a trip to an uninhabited island (where often a beach barbecue will be served). Traditional boats (*dhoni*) or speedboats can be hired privately.

- If you wish to escape pure sun, sea and sand, then check out the beautiful 17th-century *Hukuru* (or **Friday Mosque**) in Malé. The **Islamic Centre** topped with a magnificent golden dome is worth a visit. Should you wish to visit more mosques, there are over 20 of them scattered around the capital.

TOURIST INFORMATION

Maldives Tourism Promotion Board (MTPB)
3rd Floor, H. Aage 12, Boduthakurufaanu Magu, Malé, Maldives
Tel: 323 228.
Website: www.visitmaldives.com.mv

Entertainment

FOOD & DRINK: Malé, the capital, has a few simple restaurants which serve local and international food. On the other islands, there are a few restaurants in addition to those run by the resorts. Cuisine is international, with all foodstuffs other than seafood imported. There are no bars, except in the resorts, where there is a good range of alcoholic and non-alcoholic drink available, reflecting the demands of the visitors.

Things to know: All bars are situated in tourist resorts (no alcohol is available on Malé). All accept cash, but normally add orders onto the total bill. Locals do not drink at all. During the month of Ramadan (see *Public Holidays*), visitors are not allowed to drink alcohol in public except in the tourist resorts.

National specialities:
- Seafood is widely available, such as tuna, grouper, octopus, jobfish and swordfish.
- *Kavaabu* (deep fried snacks made from rice, tuna, coconut, lentils, and spices).
- Curries, such as chicken or beef, are widely available. Curry leaves are added to a lot of Maldavian dishes.

National drinks:
- *The Maldive Lady* (a powerful and delicious cocktail, whose composition varies from bar to bar and island to island).

Tipping: This is officially discouraged.

Note: All bars are situated in tourist resorts (no alcohol is

---

available on Malé). All accept cash, but normally add orders onto the total bill. Locals do not drink at all. During the month of Ramadan (see *Public Holidays*), visitors are not allowed to drink alcohol in public except in the tourist resorts.

NIGHTLIFE: There is little or no organised nightlife, although most resorts have informal discos around the bar areas, sometimes featuring live bands playing either traditional or Western music. Beach parties and barbecues are also popular. On some evenings, many resorts have cultural shows and some show videos.

SHOPPING: Local purchases include sea shells (only when bought in official shops; they may not be removed from the beach or from the sea), lacquered wooden boxes and reed mats. Jewellery to purchase includes gold, silver, coral, mother-of-pearl and turtle-shell items. However, there are strict prohibitions against the export of coral and turtle-shell. **Shopping hours:** Sat-Thurs 0830-2300, Fri 1330-2300. Shops officially shut for 15 minutes five times a day in deference to Muslim prayer times; however, this rule is not always strictly adhered to in the tourist areas away from the capital.

Business

- **GDP:** US$639.5 million.
- **Main imports:** Petroleum and petroleum products, ships, foodstuff, textiles, clothing, intermediate and capital goods.
- **Main exports:** Fish and clothing.
- **Main trade partners:** Bahrain, Germany, India, Japan, Malaysia, Singapore, Sri Lanka, Thailand, United Arab Emirates, UK and USA.

ECONOMY: Small quantities of cereals, fruit and vegetables are grown on the little fertile land available on the islands. Fishing is far more important: tuna fishing accounts for half of the Maldives' export earnings. The industrial sector has grown substantially since 1980 as a result of major infrastructure investment in desalination plants, refurbished accommodation, generators and air conditioning. Much of this was originally designed for use by the tourism industry, which has also grown rapidly following the decline of shipping, and now accounts for almost one quarter of GDP. Otherwise, there is some light industrial activity, including fish-canning, textiles and boat building, and a small financial services sector which has recently come under scrutiny (along with several dozen other small economies offering 'offshore' services). In general, the islands' economic development has been constrained by their relative isolation and the small size of the domestic market. Hopes that the Maldives might become an oil producer were dashed when a 10-year exploration programme failed to locate deposits in the islands' territorial waters. The Maldives is a member of the Asian Development Bank and the Colombo Plan.

BUSINESS ETIQUETTE: Since the islands import almost everything, business potential is high, but only on Malé. Most business takes place during the morning. An informal attitude prevails. Appointments should be made well in advance. For business meetings, men normally wear a shirt and tie and a lightweight or tropical suit. Women wear a lightweight suit or equivalent. Handshaking is the customary form of greeting. **Office hours:** Sun-Thurs 0730-1430. Friday and Saturday are official rest days.

COMMERCIAL INFORMATION

State Trading Organisation
Boduthakurufaanu Magu, Maafannu, Malé, 20345, Maldives
Tel: (3) 344 333.
Website: www.stomaldives.com

Kurumba Village (Information on Conferences/Conventions)
Universal Enterprises Ltd, 38 Orchid Magu, Malé, Maldives
Tel: 442 324.

Bandos Island Resort (Information on Conferences/Conventions)
North Malé Atoll, Maldives
Tel: 640 088.
Website: www.bandosmaldives.com

Paradise Island (Information on Conferences/Conventions)
Villa Hotels, Villa Building, Ibrahim Hassan Didi Magu, PO Box 2073, Malé 20-02, Maldives
Tel: (960) 331 6161.
Website: www.villahotels.com

Mali

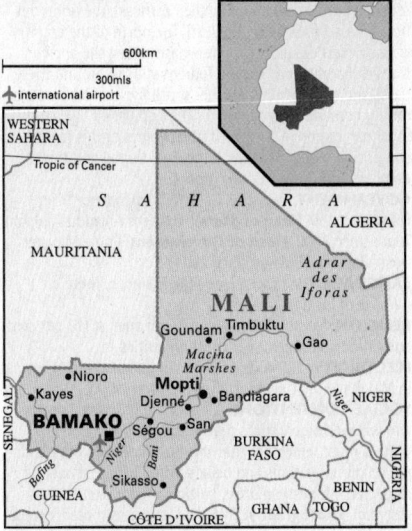

Location: Central West Africa.

Time: GMT.

Overview

The largest country in West Africa, Mali is bordered on the North by Algeria, on the East and Southeast by Niger, on the South by Burkina Faso and Côte d'Ivoire, and on the West by Guinea, Senegal, and Mauritania. In the south, traversed by the Niger and Senegal rivers, are fertile areas where peanuts, rice, and cotton are grown. Elsewhere the country is arid desert or semi desert. Although large swathes of Mali are barren, the country is self-sufficient in food thanks to the fertile Niger river basin in the south and east.

During the Middle Ages, the Moslem empire of Mali covered most of West Africa. For several centuries, Mali was a centre of Islamic culture and prosperity. When Trans Saharan routes were in use by traders in olden days, Mali was a trading centre and a tax collection point. The empires developed because of trade in gold and salt and other goods. Slaves were also transported along this route. Their control of the Trans-Saharan trade route was finally broken by European traders. By the end of the 19th century, France annexed the country, which became independent in 1960.

Today, Mali is one of the poorest countries in the world. But since 1992, when the country's first democratically-elected President took power, Mali has had a civilian Government. Malians continue to draw a sense of national pride from the heritage of the Songay and Malian empires. Visitors can experience the way of living in the Sahara, enjoy the local tribes' songs and dances, and ride camels with the Tuaregs, the 'Blue Princes' of the desert. The hidden city of Timbuktu, the mythical gate of the Sahara, is the last wonder of Western explorers. This old city was a beehive of activity in its heydays in the past. By the 15th century, Timbuktu was a major trading centre for salt and gold on the trans Saharan trade route. Later on it assumed the status of a great Islamic learning centre. There are several beautiful mosques and tombs dating back to the 14th century. Bamako, the capital, is a modern city and the cultural centre of Mali. The main places of interest are the markets, the Botanical Gardens, the Musée National, the zoo and the craft centre at the Maison des Artisans.

Mali is also famous for its music and musicians from the days of the Mali Empire. The traditional music of Mali is based on the songs of the *jalis* (griots), a distinct caste of people in the social structure. Mali still maintains a key role in the contemporary African music scene.

General Information

AREA: 1,240,192 sq km (478,841 sq miles).
POPULATION: 12.6 million (official estimate 2002).
POPULATION DENSITY: 10.2 per sq km.
CAPITAL: Bamako. **Population:** 1 million (1998).
GEOGRAPHY: Mali is a landlocked republic, sharing borders with Mauritania, Algeria, Burkina Faso, Côte d'Ivoire, Guinea, Niger and Senegal. It is a vast land of flat plains fed by two major rivers, the Senegal on its western edge and the great River Niger. On its journey north the Niger converges with the River Bani, and forms a rich inland delta, the marshlands of the Macina, stretching for some 450km (280 miles) along the river's length, in some places 200km (124 miles) wide. The central part of the country is arid grazing land, called the Sahel, which has suffered great drought. At Timbuktu, the Niger reaches the desert and here it turns first to the east, then to the southeast at Bourem, where it heads for the ocean. In the desert, near the Algerian and Niger borders in the northeast, the Adrar des Iforas massif rises 800m (2625ft). The north of the country is true desert except for the few oases along the ancient trans-Saharan camel routes. Tuaregs still live around these oases and camel routes. Further south live the Peulh cattle-raising nomads. The majority of the population lives in the savannah region in the south. The peoples of this region comprise Songhai, Malinke, Senoufou, Dogon and the Bambara (the largest ethnic group).
GOVERNMENT: Republic. Gained independence from France in 1960. **Head of State:** President Amadou Toumani Touré since 2002. **Head of Government:** Prime Minister Ousmane Issoufi Maïga since 2004.
LANGUAGE: The official language is French. There are a number of local languages.
RELIGION: Muslim (80 per cent), with animist (18 per cent) and Christian (under 2 per cent) minorities.
ELECTRICITY: 220 volts AC, 50Hz in Bamako. Larger towns in Mali have their own locally-generated supply.
SOCIAL CONVENTIONS: Malians are hospitable people and will welcome visitors gracefully into their homes. Visitors must remember that this is a Muslim country and the religious customs and beliefs of the people should be respected. Modesty in dress, particularly for women, is essential. **Photography:** This is no longer restricted, except for military subjects. However, interpretation of what is considered off limits tends to vary. Other subjects may be considered sensitive from a cultural or religious point of view and it is advisable to obtain permission before taking photographs in Mali.

Climate

Three main seasons which vary according to latitude. Rainy season runs between June and October, diminishing further north. The cooler season (October to February) is followed by extremely hot, dry weather until June.
Required clothing: Lightweight cottons and linens are worn throughout most of the year, though warmer clothing is needed between November and February. Waterproofing is advised during the rainy season.

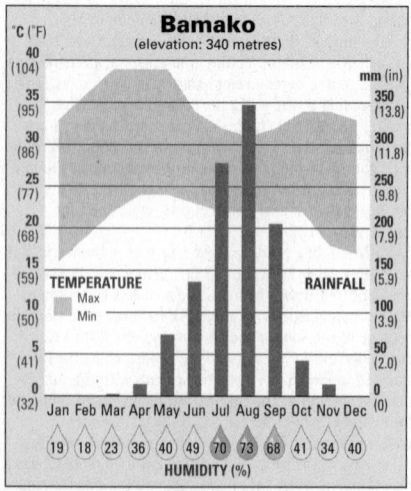

Communications

Telephone: Limited IDD service. Country code: 223. Outgoing international calls must be made via the international operator. These are expensive and collect calls cannot be made from Mali.
Mobile telephone: GSM 900 network exists. Operators are *Ikatel* (website: www.ikatel.net) and *Malitel-SA* (website: www.malitel.com).
Internet: Main ISPs include private companies *Cefib* (website: www.cefib.com), *Datatech* (website:

www.datatech.toolnet.org) and *Spider* (website: www.spider.toolnet.org). There is an Internet cafe in Bamako.
Post: International post is limited to main towns and the central post office. Airmail to Europe takes approximately two weeks. For further details, contact the Embassy.
MEDIA: Mali's media are amongst the freest in Africa.
Press: There are no English-language newspapers. The dailies, including *Les Echos*, *L'Essor* (website: www.essor.gov.ml), *Info Matin* and *Le Républicain*, are published in French.
TV: *Office de la Radiodiffusion Television du Mali* (ORTM), Multi Canal and Tele Kledu.
Radio: *Office de la Radiodiffusion Television du Mali* (ORTM); commercial stations include: *Radio Liberte*, *Radio Kledu* and *Radio Patriote*.

Passport/Visa

	Passport Required?	Visa Required?	Return Ticket Required?
Full British	Yes	Yes	Yes
Australian	Yes	Yes	Yes
Canadian	Yes	Yes	Yes
USA	Yes	Yes	Yes
Other EU	Yes	Yes	Yes
Japanese	Yes	Yes	Yes

Note: *Regulations and requirements may be subject to change at short notice, and you are advised to contact the appropriate diplomatic or consular authority before finalising travel arrangements. Any numbers in the chart refer to the footnotes below.*

PASSPORTS: Passport valid for at least six months from date of entry required by all except the following in possession of a valid ID card:
(a) nationals of ECOWAS countries;
(b) nationals of Algeria, Andorra, Cameroon, Chad, The Gambia, Monaco, Morocco and Tunisia.
VISAS: Required by all except the following for stays of up to three months:
(a) nationals of the countries referred to under passport exemptions above;
(b) transit passengers continuing their journey by the same or first connecting aircraft within 24 hours provided holding onward or return documentation and not leaving the airport.
Types of visa and cost: *Tourist*, *Business* and *Transit*: *single entry*: US$80 (three months); *multiple entry*: US$110 (three months); US$200 (six months); US$370 (one year).
Validity: One month from the date of entry, although visas can be extended in Mali, either in Bamako at the Immigration Service or at any police station. Visas may be obtained up to three months in advance of travelling to Mali.
Application to: Consulate (or consular section at Embassy); see *Passport/Visa Information*.
Application requirements: (a) Valid passport. (b) Two application forms (must be completed in block capitals and returned to the consulate with several photocopies of the form). (c) Two passport-size photos. (d) Stamped, self-addressed envelope for postal applications (which must be sent by registered post). (e) Fee; payable in cash, company cheque or postal order (personal cheques are not accepted). (f) Copy of airline itinerary or flight ticket(s). (g) *Yellow fever* certificate, if travelling from an infected area. (h) Proof of hotel reservation. *Business*: (a)-(h) and, (i) Letter of invitation from company, stating purpose of trip. *Transit*: (a)-(h) and, (i) Copies of onward tickets and visas to further destinations.
Working days required: Five. Visas can be issued more quickly (in three days) for an additional fee of US$10.
Temporary residence: Enquire at Embassy.

PASSPORT/VISA INFORMATION

Embassy of the Republic of Mali in Belgium
Avenue Molière 487, 1050 Brussels, Belgium
Tel: (2) 345 7432.

Embassy of the Republic of Mali in the USA
2130 R Street, NW, Washington, DC 20008, USA
Tel: (202) 332 2249.
Website: www.maliembassy.us

Money

Currency: CFA (*Communauté Financiaire Africaine*) Franc (XOF) = 100 centimes. Notes are in denominations of XOF10,000, 5000, 2000 and 1000. Coins are in denominations of XOF500, 200, 250, 100, 50, 25, 10 and 5. Mali is part of the French Monetary Area. Only currency issued by the *Banque des Etats de l'Afrique de l'Ouest* (Bank of West African States) is valid; currency issued by the

Banque des Etats de l'Afrique Centrale (Bank of Central African States) is not. The CFA Franc is tied to the Euro.
Currency exchange: Possible at main banks in Bamako, but this can be a slow process and exchange rates are often out of date.
Credit & debit cards: Diners Club, MasterCard and Visa are accepted in two hotels in Bamako. Cash advances on credit cards are available at only one bank in Mali, the BMCD Bank in Bamako, and only with a Visa credit card. Check with your credit or debit card company for details of merchant acceptability and other services which may be available.
Traveller's cheques: Can be exchanged at banks. To avoid additional exchange rate charges, travellers are advised to take traveller's cheques in US Dollars or Euros.
Currency restrictions: The import and export of local currency is unlimited. The import and export of foreign currency is unlimited provided amounts exceeding XOF25,000 are declared.
Banking hours: Mon-Thurs 0730-1200 and 1315-1500, Fri 0730-1230.
Exchange rate indicators:
Rate at time of publishing
$1.00=   XOF559.17
£1.00=   XOF970.20

Duty Free

The following items may be imported into Mali without incurring customs duty:
1000 cigarettes or 250 cigars or 2kg of tobacco; two bottles of alcoholic beverage; a reasonable amount of perfume for personal use.
Note: (a) Cameras and films must be declared. An import permit is needed for sporting guns. Plants, except fruit and vegetables, need a certificate. (b) Authorisation from the National Museum in Bamako must be obtained when exporting certain Malian archaeological objects, particularly those from the Niger River Valley.

Public Holidays

Below are listed Public Holidays for the January 2006-June 2007 period.
2006: Jan 1 New Year's Day. **Jan 10** Tabaski (Feast of the Sacrifice). **Jan 20** Armed Forces Day. **Mar 26** Day of Democracy. **Apr 11** Mawloud (Prophet's Birthday). **Apr 17** Easter Monday. **May 1** Labour Day. **May 25** Africa Day. **Sep 22** Independence Day. **Oct 22-24** Korité (End of Ramadan). **Dec 25** Christmas Day. **Dec 31** Tabaski (Feast of the Sacrifice).
2007: Jan 1 New Year's Day. **Jan 20** Armed Forces Day. **Mar 26** Day of Democracy. **Mar 28** Easter Monday. **Mar 31** Mawloud (Prophet's Birthday). **May 1** Labour Day. **May 25** Africa Day.
Note: Muslim festivals are timed according to local sightings of various phases of the moon and the dates given above are approximations. During the lunar month of Ramadan that precedes Korité (Eid al-Fitr), Muslims fast during the day and feast at night and normal business patterns may be interrupted. Many restaurants are closed during the day and there may be restrictions on smoking and drinking. Some disruption may continue into Korité itself. Korité and Tabaski (Eid al-Adha) may last anything from two to 10 days, depending on the region. For more information, see the *World of Islam* appendix.

Health

	Special Precautions?	Certificate Required?
Yellow Fever	Yes	1
Cholera	Yes	2
Typhoid & Polio	3	N/A
Malaria	4	N/A

Note: *Regulations and requirements may be subject to change at short notice, and you are advised to contact your doctor well in advance of your intended date of departure. Any numbers in the chart refer to the footnotes below.*

1: A *yellow fever* vaccination certificate is required by all travellers over one year of age arriving from all countries.
2: Following WHO guidelines issued in 1973, a *cholera* vaccination certificate is not a condition of entry to Mali. However, *cholera* is a serious risk in this country and precautions are essential. There was, for instance, a recent outbreak in the Segou district, central Mali. Up-to-date advice should be sought before deciding whether these precautions should include vaccination, as medical opinion is divided over its effectiveness; see the *Health* appendix for further information.
3: *Typhoid* is widespread and appropriate precautions should be taken. *Polio* is endemic.
4: *Malaria*, mainly in the malignant *falciparum* form, is present all year throughout the country. Resistance to

chloroquine and sulfadoxine-pyrimethamine has been reported. The recommended prophylaxis is mefloquine.
Food & drink: All water should be regarded as being potentially contaminated. Water used for drinking, brushing teeth or making ice should have first been boiled or otherwise sterilised. Milk is unpasteurised and should be boiled. Powdered or tinned milk is available and is advised, but make sure that it is reconstituted with pure water. Avoid dairy products which are likely to have been made from unboiled milk. Only eat well-cooked meat and fish, preferably served hot. Pork, salad and mayonnaise may carry increased risk. Vegetables should be cooked and fruit peeled.
Other risks: *Bilharzia* (schistosomiasis) is present. Avoid swimming and paddling in fresh water; swimming pools which are well chlorinated and maintained are safe. The following health risks have been reported from the area: many *viral diseases* (transmitted by mosquitoes, ticks and sandflies), *meningococcal meningitis* (particularly in the savannah areas and during the dry season), *dysenteries, diarrhoeal diseases, diphtheria, tuberculosis, hepatitis A, B* and *E* (all widespread) and *trachoma*.
Rabies is also present. For those at high risk, vaccination before arrival should be considered. If you are bitten, seek medical advice without delay. For more information, consult the *Health* appendix.
Health care: Medical facilities are very limited and inadequate for dealing with emergencies. Health insurance (including adequate medical evacuation) is therefore essential. Many medicines are unavailable, and doctors and hospitals expect immediate cash payment for health care services.

Travel - International

AIR:

Mali's national airline is *Air Mali (L9)*. Mali also has a share in the multinational airline, *Air Afrique (RK)*. Airlines operating between Mali and Europe include *Aeroflot* and *Air France*. *Air Afrique* also operates flights between Mali and New York via Dakar (Senegal) or Abidjan (Côte d'Ivoire). There are three weekly flights between Mali and Niger.
Approximate flight times: From Bamako to *London* is 11 hours (including stopover in Brussels or Paris).
International airports: *Bamako (BKO)* is 15km (9 miles) from the city (travel time - 20 minutes). A bus service into the city is available.
Departure tax: XOF10,000; for destinations in Africa XOF8000. Children under two years are exempt.

RAIL:

There is a twice-weekly service from Bamako to Dakar (Senegal) which has air conditioning, sleeper facilities and restaurant cars (travel time - 35 hours). It will also carry cars. There are also plans to extend rail links into Guinea.

ROAD:

The best road connections are from Côte d'Ivoire and Burkina Faso. There are also road links with Senegal, Guinea, Niger and Mauritania. The all-weather road follows the Niger as far as Niamey (Niger). Travel via the Algerian border is currently considered dangerous and not recommended. **Bus:** Services operate from Kankan (Guinea) to Bamako, as well as from Bobo Dioulasso (Burkina Faso) to Ségou and Mopti, and Niamey (Niger) to Gao. From Côte d'Ivoire, there are three buses per week (travel time - at least 36 hours). From Niger, the national bus line SNTN operates three weekly buses to Mali.

Travel - Internal

AIR:

Some domestic flights are provided by *Air Mali*. Light aircraft can also be chartered from the *Société des Transports Aériens (STA)*.
Departure tax: XOF2500.
RIVER: Between July and December, there are weekly services between Bamako and Gao via Timbuktu along the River Niger. However, because of drought in the Sahel desert, services are sometimes suspended. The journey is approximately 1300km (800 miles) and takes five or six days. Between December and March, travel is only possible between Mopti and Gao. Food is available on the boats and first-class cabins can be booked in advance. Motorised and non-motorised *pirogues* and *pinasses* (types of river boat) are available for hire between Timbuktu and Mopti. Since the completion of the Manantali Dam in 1988, work has continued to improve the navigability of the River Senegal.

RAIL:

There is a daily service from Bamako to Kayes, en route to Dakar on the Senegal coast. There are two trains, one Malian and one Senegalese - the Senegalese train is far superior, with air conditioning and buffet car. The railway line is Mali's most important method of transport, over and above the road link. There is also a daily service from Bamako to Koulikoro.

ROAD:

Traffic drives on the right. Roads in Mali range from moderate to very bad. Particular care should be taken if driving in Bamako. The main road runs from Sikasso in the south to Bamako, and to Mopti and Gao. The roads from Bamako to Mopti, Douentza, Koutiala, Sikasso and Bougouni, along with a few other roads, are paved. Between Mopti and Gao, travel can be difficult during the rainy season (mid-June to mid-September) when the Niger, at its confluence with the Bani, splits into a network of channels, and floods its banks to form the marshlands of the Macina. Stops at customs and police checkpoints are frequent on major roads and driving is particularly hazardous after dark. **Bus:** Services run between the main towns. **Documentation:** International Driving Permit recommended, although not legally required. Insurance and a *carnet de passage* are also needed.
Note: Visitors are advised to keep to the main roads, otherwise they should travel in convoy. Caution should be exercised when travelling at night. Visitors should be aware of the recent violent incidents which have occurred in northern Mali and the Mauritanian border.

URBAN:

Taxi: Collective taxis in cities are very cheap. The taxis charge a standard fare regardless of the distance travelled. Tipping is not expected.

Travel Advice

Travellers are advised against all travel to the north of Timbuktu, the western border area with Mauritania and the eastern border with Niger, due to banditry.
You should be aware of the global risk of indiscriminate terrorist attacks which could be against civilian targets, including places frequented by foreigners.
This advice is based on information provided by the Foreign and Commonwealth Office in the UK. It is correct at time of publishing. As the situation can change rapidly, visitors are advised to contact the following organisations for the latest travel advice:

British Foreign and Commonwealth Office
Tel: (0845) 850 2829.
Website: www.fco.gov.uk

US Department of State
Website: http://travel.state.gov/travel

Accommodation

HOTELS:

Only Bamako has hotels that meet international standards, but other main towns have hotels of an adequate standard and some have air conditioning. Accommodation tends to be expensive and difficult to obtain at short notice - advance booking is recommended. Further information can be obtained from the *Office Malien du Tourisme et de l'Hôtellerie* (see *Contact Addresses* section).

LODGES/CAMPING:

There are a number of *campements* in the National Park of La Boucle du Baoule. The reserve is 120km (75 miles) from Bamako.

Top Things To See & Do

- **Bamako, t**he capital is a modern town and the educational and cultural centre of Mali. The main places of interest are the markets, the **Botanical Gardens**, the **Musée National**, the zoo and the craft centre at the **Maison des Artisans**.
- Known as the 'Jewel of the Niger', **Djenné** was founded in 1250. It has a beautiful mosque, the **Grande Mosquée**, and it is one of the oldest trading towns along the Trans-Saharan caravan routes. **Old Djenné** is located about 5km (3 miles) from Djenné and was founded around 250BC. The town quickly developed into a market centre and important link in the Trans-Saharan gold trade. In the 15th and 16th centuries, it became one of the spiritual centres for the dissemination of Islam. Nearly 2000 of its traditional houses, built on hillocks (*toguere*) and adapted to the seasonal floods, have survived. Old Djenné is today listed by UNESCO as a World Heritage Site.
- The centre of Mali's tourist industry, **Mopti** is located at the confluence of the Bani and the Niger and is built on three islands joined by dykes. There is another fine mosque here. The market in the town centre, **Marché des Souvenirs**, and the area surrounding the port are also worth visiting.
- Southeast of Mopti is the **Bandiagara** country, peopled by the Dogons, whose ancient beliefs have remained largely untouched by Islam. Visitors should treat villagers with respect. The **Cliffs of Bandiagara** have been listed by UNESCO as a World Heritage Site. The Dogon people are believed to have been the original inhabitants of the Niger river valley and, for thousands of years, inhabited villages cut into the cliffs of the 200km- (80mile-) long Bandiagara escarpment. Although most of the Dogons have now relocated to the plains, the ancient villages on the cliffs are still standing.
- **Timbuktu** is a name that has passed into English vernacular as a byword for inaccessibility and remoteness. It is, however, neither of these things owing to the magnificent camel caravans (some of them comprising over 3000 animals) which arrive every year from the Taoudenni salt mines to distribute their produce throughout the Sahel. By the 15th century, Timbuktu was the centre of a lucrative trade in salt and gold, straddling the Trans-Saharan caravan routes, as well as being a great centre of Islamic learning. Much of this ancient city is in decay, but it is the site of many beautiful mosques (**Djingerebur**, **Sankore** and **Sidi Yahaya** for example) and tombs, some dating back to the 14th century.
- Another ancient city which had its heyday in the 15th century is **Gao**. Gao houses the mosque of **Kankan Moussa** and the tombs of the Askia Dynasty. There are also two excellent markets. The city has recently undergone much urban development. **San** and **Ségou** are both interesting towns. The **National Park of La Boucle de Baoule** contains an array of southern Sahelian species of wildlife, including giraffe, leopard, lion, elephant, buffalo and hippo.
- A good area for **trekking** is the Bandiagara escarpment in the Dogon country, with Bandiagara, Bankass and Mopti being the main starting points for trekking trips. Guides are available and recommended; travellers should check that guides have an official identification card.

TOURIST INFORMATION

Office Malien du Tourisme et de l'Hôtellerie (Tourist Office of Mali)
Street address: Rue Mohamed V., Bamako, Mali
Postal address: BP 191, Bamako, Mali
Tel: 222 5673.
Website: www.malitourisme.com

Entertainment

FOOD & DRINK: Several of the hotels have restaurant and bar facilities of international standard, serving international cuisine, and most towns have small restaurants serving local and north African dishes. Hotel restaurants are open to non-residents. There is a limited choice of restaurants. Alcohol is available in bars (with very late opening hours), but since the majority is Muslim, there is a good range of fresh fruit juices. Most people tend to drink fruit juice rather than alcohol.

National specialities:
• *La Capitaine Sangha*, a kind of Nile perch served with hot chilli sauce, whole fried bananas and rice.

National drinks:
• Malian tamarind and guava juices are delicious.
• Malian tea which should be drunk in three stages; the first is very strong ('as bitter as death'); the second is slightly sweetened ('just like life'); the third is well sugared ('as sweet as love'). Visitors to Mali may be invited to partake in this tea ritual.

Tipping: A 10 per cent tip is customary in restaurants and bars, but is not normal for taxi drivers. Porters receive XOF100 per piece of luggage.

NIGHTLIFE: Bamako has a good selection of nightclubs with music and dancing.

SHOPPING: Traditional crafts range from the striking masks of the Bambara, Dogon and Malinko peoples, to woodcarvings, original designs in ebony and bronze, woven cloth, and mats, gold and silver jewellery and copperware. Excellent pottery is made in the Ségou region, while Timbuktu is a good centre for iron and copper articles, including swords, daggers and traditional household utensils.

Business

ECONOMY: Mali is one of the poorest countries in the world with an average per capita annual income of about US$200. The economy is almost entirely agricultural even though less than 2 per cent of the land is cultivable. Livestock and subsistence crops such as millet, sorghum, maize and rice are raised for domestic consumption. The main cash crop is cotton, of which Mali is one of Africa's largest producers and exporters, along with groundnuts, fruit and vegetables. The Malian cotton industry, upon which one-third of the population depend for their livelihood, is in serious difficulty because of exceptionally low world prices, caused in part by subsidies provided to cotton growers in the industrialised world (in 2003, this was the subject of a major dispute at the World Trade Organisation). Local manufacturing has grown steadily, albeit from a very low level, and is mostly concerned with the processing of agricultural produce: food, drinks and tobacco are the main products. Construction materials are also produced locally. There is a small but fast-growing mining sector centred on Mali's recently discovered gold deposits. Mali is now the third-largest gold producer in Africa after South Africa and Ghana, and the growth in this sector largely accounts for the country's rapid 2002 growth rate of 9 per cent. Marble, salt and phosphates are also being exploited; there are also known reserves of iron ore and uranium. Much of the economy has been privatised and deregulated since 1997 under the supervision of the IMF with which Mali presently enjoys good relations. Mali has also been one of the main beneficiaries of the debt cancellation for the poorest countries, and it continues to rely on foreign aid and remittances from émigrés. France is Mali's major trading partner, providing a quarter of imports and taking a similar proportion of exports, followed by Côte d'Ivoire, Senegal, Germany and Switzerland. Mali is a member of ECOWAS and various other West African multinational economic organisations.

BUSINESS ETIQUETTE: The forms of address are those of France, eg Monsieur le Directeur. Lightweight or tropical suit and tie are advised for only the smartest meetings. Otherwise, a light, open-neck shirt is worn. It is essential to be able to speak French for business purposes.

Office hours: Mon-Thurs 0730-1230 and 1300-1600, Fri 0730-1230 and 1430-1730.

CONFERENCES/CONVENTIONS: Information can be obtained from the Ministry of Foreign Affairs (Protocol Section), Kounoulba, Bamako (tel: 225 489; fax: 228 559 *or* 225 226).

COMMERCIAL INFORMATION

Chambre de Commerce et d'Industrie du Mali
BP 46, Place de la Liberté, Bamako, Mali
Tel: 222 5036 *or* 222 9645.

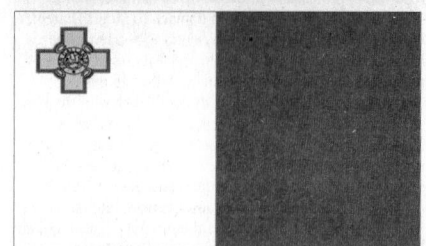

Malta

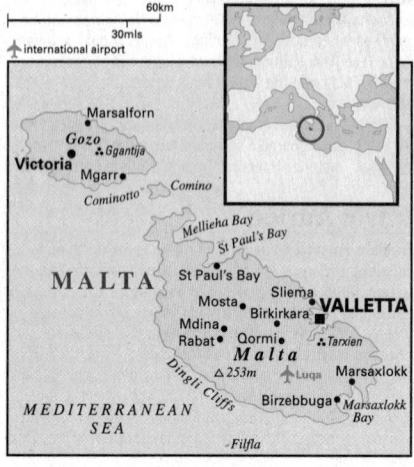

Location: Mediterranean, south of Sicily.

Time: GMT + 1 (GMT + 2 from the last Sunday in March to last Sunday in October).

Overview

The Maltese archipelago, situated almost at the centre of the Mediterranean, includes the islands of Malta, Gozo, Comino, Comminotto and Filfla. Its situation in the central Mediterranean has made it an important strategic base since the earliest days of navigation. The first civilisation to leave any significant remains flourished in the third millennium BC, building many megalithic temples. Later the island was occupied by the Phoenicians, the Carthaginians and the Romans.

Independence from Britain was achieved in 1964, and forty years on Malta was the smallest of the 10 countries to join the EU in May 2004.

Each year, the population of Malta is tripled by an influx of tourists - the nation's main source of income. The Maltese islands offer the attraction of clear blue waters, secluded bays and sandy beaches while, in the towns, medieval walled citadels and splendid baroque churches and palaces reflect the rich history of the islands. The Maltese Islands have indeed been described as one big 'open-air museum'. What makes them unique is that so much of their past is visible today. It is easy to delve into the islands' mysterious prehistory, retrace the footsteps of St Paul or see where the Knights of St John defended Christendom. Worlds apart from the main resorts and the capital Valletta, are the Islands' villages, which are the soul of the islands' past. Yet with their lively festas and unique everyday life, they are very much part of the islands' culture today. Then there are the seaside villages, where the rhythm of life is dictated by fishing.

General Information

AREA: 316 sq km (122 sq miles).

POPULATION: 397,000 (UN, 2005).

POPULATION DENSITY: 1256 sq km.

CAPITAL: Valletta. **Population:** 7173 (2002).

GEOGRAPHY: The Maltese archipelago is situated in the middle of the Mediterranean, with the largest inhabited island, Malta, lying 93km (58 miles) south of Sicily and 290km (180 miles) from North Africa. Gozo and Comino are the only other inhabited islands. The landscape of all three is characterised by low hills with terraced fields. Malta has no mountains or rivers. Its coastline is indented with harbours, bays, creeks, sandy beaches and rocky coves. Gozo is connected to Malta by ferry and is more thickly vegetated, with many flat-topped hills and craggy cliffs. Comino, the smallest island, is connected to Malta and Gozo by ferry and is very sparsely populated.

GOVERNMENT: Republic. Gained independence from the UK in 1964. **Head of State:** President Fenech Adami since

---

2004. **Head of Government:** Prime Minister Lawrence Gonzi since 2004. **Recent history:** Lawrence Gonzi took office in March 2004, a few weeks before Malta's entry into the European Union. Mr Gonzi said Malta should seize the opportunities afforded by its imminent EU membership and promised to boost tourism and to create favourable conditions for investment

LANGUAGE: Maltese (a Semitic language) and English are the official languages. Italian is also widely spoken.

RELIGION: 91 per cent Roman Catholic.

ELECTRICITY: 240 volts AC, 50Hz. UK-style three-pin plugs are in use.

SOCIAL CONVENTIONS: The usual European courtesies are expected, but the visitor should also bear in mind the tremendous importance of Roman Catholicism; if visiting a church, for instance, modest dress covering the shoulders and legs will be expected. Smoking is prohibited on public transport and in some public buildings, including cinemas.

Climate

Warm most of the year. The hottest months are between July and September, but the heat is tempered by cooling sea breezes. Rain falls for very short periods, mainly in the cooler winter months.

Required clothing: Lightweight cottons and linens are worn between March and September, although warmer clothes may occasionally be necessary in spring and autumn and on cooler evenings. A light raincoat is advisable for winter.

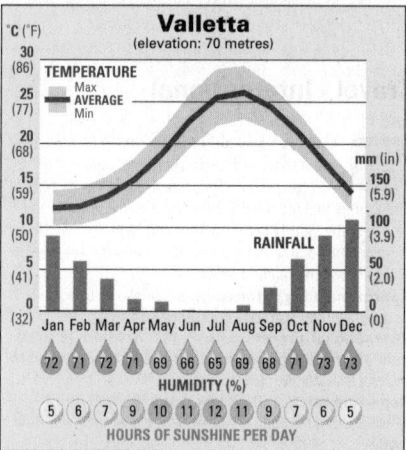

Communications

Telephone: IDD is available. Country code: 356. There are no area codes. Public telephone booths are widely available.

Mobile telephone: Roaming agreements exist with most international mobile phone companies. Coverage is good.

Internet: There are a few Internet cafes.

Post: Good postal services exist within the island.

MEDIA: Daily and weekly publications appear in both Maltese and English. Italian television and radio are also received. Italian TV channels are still very popular in Malta.

Press: Maltese dailies include *In-Nazzjon Taghna* and *L'Orizzont*. The daily English-language newspapers published on the island are *The Malta Independent* and *The Times of Malta* (website: www.timesofmalta.com). *Malta Today* (website: www.maltatoday.com.mt), *The Malta Business Weekly*, *The Malta Independent on Sunday* and the *Sunday Times* are also available.

Radio: Networks include *Radio Malta*, *Super One Radio*, owned by the Malta Labour Party, *Radio 101*, owned by the Nationalist Party; *Bay Radio* is a commercial station and *RTK* is a Catholic Church station.

TV: *Television Malta (TVM)*, *Super One TV*, owned by the Malta Labour Party and *Net TV*, owned by the Nationalist Party.

Passport/Visa

	Passport Required?	Visa Required?	Return Ticket Required?
Full British	1	No	Yes
Australian	Yes	No	Yes
Canadian	Yes	No	Yes
USA	Yes	No	Yes
Other EU	1	No	Yes
Japanese	Yes	No	Yes

Note: *Regulations and requirements may be subject to change at short notice, and you are advised to contact the appropriate diplomatic or consular authority before finalising travel arrangements. Any numbers in the chart refer to the footnotes below.*

PASSPORTS: Passport valid for at least three months beyond the length of stay required by all except:
(a) **1.** EU/EEA nationals (EU+ Iceland, Liechtenstein, Norway) and Swiss nationals holding a valid national ID card.
Note: EU and EEA nationals are only required to produce evidence of their EU/EEA nationality and identity in order to be admitted to any EU/EEA Member State. This evidence can take the form of a valid national passport *or* national identity card. Either is acceptable. Possession of a return ticket, any length of validity on their document, sufficient funds for the length of their proposed visit should *not* be imposed.
VISAS: Required by all except the following for stays of up to three months:
(a) nationals of countries referred to in the chart above;
(b) nationals of Andorra, Argentina, Bolivia, Brazil, Brunei, Bulgaria, Chile, Costa Rica, Croatia, Cyprus, Czech Republic, Denmark, El Salvador, Estonia, Finland, Guatemala, Honduras, Hong Kong (SAR), Hungary, Iceland, Ireland, Israel, Korea (Rep), Latvia, Liechtenstein, Lithuania, Malaysia, Mexico, Monaco, New Zealand, Nicaragua, Norway, Panama, Paraguay, Romania, San Marino, Singapore, Slovak Republic, Sweden, Switzerland, Uruguay, Vatican City and Venezuela;
(c) nationals of UK Overseas Territories;
(d) nationals of Macau, provided in possession of passports bearing 'Regio Administrativa Especial de Macao';
(e) transit passengers continuing their journey by the same or first connecting aircraft within 24 hours provided holding valid onward or return documentation and not leaving the airport except nationals of Afghanistan, Bangladesh, Congo (Dem Rep), Eritrea, Ethiopia, Ghana, Iran, Iraq, Nigeria, Pakistan, Somalia and Sri Lanka, who need a transit visa.
Types of visa and cost: *Entry*: £23.50 (single-entry); for Algerian and Moroccan nationals: £15.50; for Libyan nationals: £11.50. *Transit*: £17.50. Multiple-entry visas for one year are issued only by the Immigration Police in Malta. Sudanese nationals en route for Libya via Malta require a transit visa and a valid residence permit for Libya.
All visa applicants, except nationals of Libya, Tunisia and Turkey (for whom there is no visa fee), are subject to an administrative charge of MTL4 (except nationals of Libya who must pay MTL10), even if a visa is not issued.
Note: Visitors requiring an entry visa to Malta and undertaking day trips of less than 24 hours to another country do not need to pay for another entry visa on their return to Malta.
Validity: *Single-entry visa*: one month; *Transit visa*: 24 hours. For renewal, apply to the High Commission or Embassy. For extension, apply to the Principal Immigration Officer at the Immigration Office, Police Headquarters, Floriana, Malta.
Application to: Consulate (or consular section at Embassy or High Commission); see *Passport/Visa Information*. If there is no Embassy/Consulate in the applicant's country of residence, the applicant must contact either an Honorary Consul or directly contact the Immigration Police in Malta.
Application requirements: (a) Valid passport with at least one blank page. (b) Application form. (c) Two recent passport-size photos. (d) Fee (payable in cash or by postal order only). (e) £3.75 (UK) is required to cover postage costs, if not collecting visa in person. These can be handed in at the High Commission or Embassy. (f) Self-addressed envelope for applications by post. (g) Other documents may be required in certain cases, including invitation from host, proof of financial means, proof of means of transport and valid health insurance.
Working days required: 15.
Temporary residence: Apply to Principal Immigration Officer, Immigration Office, Police Headquarters, Floriana, Malta.

PASSPORT/VISA INFORMATION

Malta High Commission in the UK
Malta House, 36-38 Piccadilly, London W1V 0PQ, UK
Tel: (020) 7292 4800.
Website: www.gov.mt
Opening hours: Mon-Fri 0900-1700.

Embassy of Malta in the USA
2017 Connecticut Avenue, NW, Washington, DC 20008, USA
Tel: (202) 462 3611.
Website: www.gov.mt

Money

Currency: Maltese Lira (MTL) = 100 cents = 1000 mils. Notes are in denominations of MTL20, 10, 5 and 2. Coins are in denominations of MTL1, and 50, 25, 10, 5, 2 and 1 cents. A number of gold and silver coins are also minted.
Currency exchange: Money can be changed at banks, bureaux de change, some hotels, and larger shops and restaurants. Automated foreign exchange machines and ATMs are available at various locations on the islands. Exchange bureau are often open 24-hours per day. Many hotels, larger shops and restaurants accept foreign currency.
Credit & debit cards: American Express, Diners Club, MasterCard and Visa are accepted. Check with your credit or debit card company for details of merchant acceptability and other services which may be available.
Traveller's cheques: Exchanged in the normal authorised institutions.
Currency restrictions: The import of local currency is limited to MTL5000. The export of local currency is limited to MTL5000. The import and export of foreign currency is unlimited, subject to declaration if contemplating re-export up to amount imported.
Banking hours: Mon-Fri 0830-1230, Sat 0830-1130. Some work longer hours and summer and winter hours may differ.
Exchange rate indicators:
Rate at time of publishing

£1.00=	MTL0.63
$1.00=	MTL0.36

Duty Free

The following items may be imported into Malta without incurring customs duty from non-EU countries:
200 cigarettes or 100 cigarillos or 50 cigars or 250g tobacco; 1l of spirits and 1l of wine; 60ml of perfume and 250ml of eau de toilette; gifts to a value not exceeding Lm50.
The following items may be imported into Malta without incurring customs duty from EU countries:
800 cigarettes, 400 cigarillos (cigars not weighing more than 4g each), 200 cigars, 1kg of tobacco; 10l of spirits, 20l of fortified wine, 90l of wine (including a maximum 60l of sparkling wine), 10l of beer; gifts to a value not exceeding Lm50.
Note: It is advisable to declare any larger or unusual items of electrical equipment brought into the islands (such as video cameras, portable televisions or video recorders), as this will prevent duty being levied on these items when leaving the country. Those under 17 cannot bring in alcohol or tobacco.
Prohibited items: Firearms and ammunition; counterfeit goods; unlicensed drugs; obscene literature and other media; animals and birds (dead or alive); transmitting apparatus; plants and meat products (without import licence).
Abolition of duty free goods within the EU: On June 30 1999, the sale of duty free alcohol and tobacco at airports and at sea was abolished in all of the original 15 EU member states. Of the 10 new member states that joined the EU on May 1 2004, these rules already apply to Cyprus and Malta. There are transitional rules in place for visitors returning to one of the original 15 EU countries from one of the other new EU countries. But for the original 15, plus Cyprus and Malta, there are now no limits imposed on importing tobacco and alcohol products from one EU country to another (with the exceptions of Denmark, Finland and Sweden, where limits *are* imposed). Travellers should note that they may be required to prove at customs that the goods purchased are for personal use *only*.

Public Holidays

Below are listed the Public Holidays for the January 2006-June 2007 period.
2006: Jan 1 New Year's Day. **Feb 10** Feast of St Paul's Shipwreck. **Mar 19** St Joseph's Day. **Mar 25** Good Friday. **Mar 31** Freedom Day. **May 1** Labour Day. **Jun 7** Sette Giugno (Commemoration of 1919 Riot). **Jun 29** Feast of St Peter and St Paul. **Aug 15** Assumption. **Sep 8** Feast of Our Lady of Victories. **Sep 21** Independence Day. **Dec 8** Immaculate Conception. **Dec 13** Republic Day. **Dec 25** Christmas Day.
2007: Jan 1 New Year's Day. **Feb 10** Feast of St Paul's Shipwreck. **Mar 19** St Joseph's Day. **Mar 31** Freedom Day. **Apr 6** Good Friday. **May 1** Labour Day. **Jun 7** Sette Giugno (Commemoration of 1919 Riot). **Jun 29** Feast of St Peter and St Paul.

Health

	Special Precautions?	Certificate Required?
Yellow Fever	No	1
Cholera	No	No
Typhoid & Polio	No	N/A
Malaria	No	N/A

Note: *Regulations and requirements may be subject to change at short notice, and you are advised to contact your doctor well in advance of your intended date of departure. Any numbers in the chart refer to the footnotes below.*

1: A *yellow fever* vaccination certificate is required from travellers over nine months of age arriving from infected areas. If indicated on epidemiological grounds, infants under nine months of age are subject to isolation or surveillance if arriving from an infected area.
Food & drink: Mains water is normally chlorinated and, whilst safe, may cause mild abdominal upsets. Bottled water is available and is advised for the first few weeks of the stay. Milk is pasteurised and dairy products are safe for consumption. Local meat, poultry, seafood, fruit and vegetables are generally considered safe to eat.
Health care: European Economic Area (EEA) and Switzerland:
If you or any of your dependants are suddenly taken ill or have an accident during a visit to an EEA country or Switzerland, free or reduced-cost necessary treatment is available – in most cases on production of a valid European Health Insurance Card (EHIC). Each country has different rules about state medical provision. In some, treatment is free. In many countries you will have to pay part or all of the cost, and then claim a full or partial refund. The EHIC gives access to state-provided medical treatment only and the scheme gives no entitlement to medical repatriation costs, nor does it cover ongoing illnesses of a non-urgent nature, so comprehensive travel insurance is advised. Note that the EHIC replaces the Form E111, which is no longer valid since 31 December 2005. Some restrictions apply, depending on your nationality.
Emergency medical treatment is available free from doctors in Government health centres. Acute emergency dental treatment is provided free of charge in hospital out-patient wards or Government health centres, but is not widely available. Most dentists practise privately. Any prescription charges incurred are not refundable. Emergency treatment in the accident and emergency department of a Government hospital is free for both in-patients and out-patients. Any medication prescribed during in-patient treatment, or for the first three days after you are discharged, is free, but you will be charged in full for anything prescribed after this period. These charges are not refundable. The principal hospitals are St Luke's, Guardamangia in Malta and Craig Hospital, Victoria in Gozo. Ambulance travel is free in an emergency, as long as you can prove that you are entitled to treatment. More information can be obtained from Entitlement Unit, Ministry of Health, 24 St John's Street, Valletta CMR02 (tel: 2299 2345 *or* 2299 2346).
Note: Malta has a reciprocal health agreement with Australia; residents from Australia visiting for no longer than one month are also entitled to free medical hospital care in Malta.

Travel - International

AIR:
The national airline is *Air Malta (KM)* (website: www.airmalta.com).
Approximate flight times: From Luqa to *London* is three hours and 10 minutes.
Main airports: *Malta International (MLA)* (Luqa) (website: www.maltairport.com), 5km (3 miles) south of Valletta (travel time – 15 minutes). *To/from the airport:* Buses depart regularly to and from Valletta City Gate. There is a regular service to the main bus terminal in Valletta. There is a full, 24-hour, taxi service to all parts of Malta, fares are charged at a fixed rate. *Facilities:* Incoming and outgoing duty-free shops, car hire, bank, bureau de change, left luggage and restaurant/bar.
Departure tax: None.
SEA:
Main ports: *Valletta, Marsaxlokk* and *Mgarr/Gozo*. Services operate to the Sicilian ports of Catania and Pozzallo. These routes are served by high-speed hydrofoils and catamarans (travel time – one hour 30 minutes) and car ferries (travel time – three hours). There are also sailings to Italy (to Reggio Calabria, Genoa and Salerno). For information on the ports in Malta, contact the Malta Maritime Authority, Marina Pinto,Valletta VLT 01, Malta; tel: 2122 2203; website: www.mma.gov.mt.

Travel - Internal

AIR:
There is a helicopter service operating all year round between Malta International Airport and Xewkija, Gozo. A quick alternative to the ferry service, it takes only 10 to 15 minutes.
SEA: A passenger car ferry operates several times daily between Cirkewwa in Malta and Mgarr in Gozo. Crossing time is about 30 minutes. Services to Comino operate from mid-March to mid-November. For further information, contact the *Gozo Channel Company*, Hay Wharf, Sa Maison, Malta (tel: 2124 3964-6; website: www.gozochannel.com). The *Comino Hotel* runs a ferry service to the island which stops at Mgarr, Gozo and Cirtewwa. The service is free to residents of the hotel and there is a small charge for non-residents. *Paradise Diving*, in Cirkewwa, offers a daily service to Blue Lagoon from May to October.

ROAD: Driving is on the left. Speed limit is 80kph (50mph) on highways and 50kph (30mph) in residential areas. **Bus:** Good local services operate from Valletta and Victoria (Gozo) to all towns. **Taxi:** Identifiable by their all-white livery. Although taxis are under meter charge at Government-controlled prices, it is best to agree prices before departure. **Car hire:** A number of car hire firms offer self-drive cars. Both *Avis* and *Hertz* have desks at the airport. Rates on Malta are among the cheapest in Europe. **Documentation:** Valid international driving licence required.

Travel Advice

Most visits to Malta and Gozo are trouble-free but you should be aware of the global risk of indiscriminate international terrorist attacks, which could be against civilian targets, including places frequented by foreigners. This advice is based on information provided by the Foreign and Commonwealth Office in the UK. It is correct at time of publishing. As the situation can change rapidly, visitors are advised to contact the following organisations for the latest travel advice:

British Foreign and Commonwealth Office
Tel: (0845) 850 2829.
Website: www.fco.gov.uk

US Department of State
Website: http://travel.state.gov/travel

Accommodation

Accommodation in Malta is provided in hotels, holiday complexes, guest houses, hostels or self-catering flats. Many hotels offer substantial reductions, particularly during the low season. For further information, contact the Malta Tourism Authority (see *Top Things To Do*).
Grading: Gradings range from **2** to **5 stars**, indicating the level of standards, facilities and services offered by the hotel.

YOUTH HOSTELS:

There are five youth hostels in Malta, four of which are located in Malta, and one in Gozo (with a minimum of two hostels open at any time of the year).

ACCOMMODATION INFORMATION

NSTS Student and Youth Travel
220 St Paul Street, Valletta VLT 07, Malta
Tel: 2124 4983.
Website: www.nsts.org

Top Things To See

- In **Valetta** (Malta island), see some of the finest examples of Maltese-style Baroque architecture in the islands in **Merchants Street**. Visit the **Co-Cathedral of St John**, the **Grand Master's Palace** in Republic Street which houses a group of tapestries originally designed for Louis XIV and an armoury which has one of the best collections in existence, the **National Museum of Fine Art**, housed in an 18th-century palace, the **Church of Our Lady of Victories** and at the nearby **Auberge de Provence,** the **National Museum of Archaeology**.
- In **Mdina** (Malta island), the **citadel** is one of the finest surviving examples of a medieval walled city. Of particular interest is the Norman-style **Palazzo Falzon** which has a collection of antique weapons and pottery, a cathedral, and a museum that still houses a magnificent collection of art treasure. From **Bastion Square**, see breathtaking view of the surrounding fields and villages, and also of **St Paul's Bay**.
- In **Rabat** (Malta island), see fine Baroque churches, **St Paul's** and **St Agatha's Catacombs** and the **Roman Villa**. On the southwest shore is the **Blue Grotto** where, legend reports, sirens bewitched seafarers with their songs. Four caves reflect the brilliant colours of the corals and minerals in the limestone. The most spectacular is the Blue Grotto itself, which is best viewed in the early morning with a calm sea.
- Within close proximity to Paola are the archaeological sites of **Tarxien**, with its neolithic temple; **Hypogeum**, a complex of ancient underground burial chambers on three levels dating back 3000 years; and **Ghar Dalam (Dark Cave)** where the remains of now extinct birds and animals such as dwarf hippos and elephants have been found.
- In **Hagar Qim** on the south of the island, see a **neolithic temple** dating back 3000 years and constructed from huge closely-fitting stones decorated in a very ornate style.

- Also at **Marsaxlokk** is the recently discovered **Temple of Juno**, which was originally used by the Greeks as a place of worship to the goddess of fertility.

Top Things To Do

- On Malta island, see performances of opera, theatre, music and ballet (between October and May) at **Valletta's Manoel Theatre**, the second-oldest theatre in Europe.
- **Swimming**, **scuba diving** and **snorkelling** is possible all-year-round. On **Malta** island, the best dive sites are located around the northern part, the many caves and steep drop-offs, such as **Qawra Point** and **Cirkewwa**, being a particular attraction; **Wied Iz-Zurrieq** is good for night dives. The most popular beach area is also along the north coast and the best beaches are at **Paradise Bay**, **Golden Bay**, **Mellieha Bay**, **Armier Bay** and **Ghajn Tuffieha Bay**. On **Gozo** island, one of the most spectacular sites is **Dwejra Point**, which features a 35m (115ft) tunnel. The most important beaches are **il-Qawra** (better known as the inland sea, with a secluded pebbly bathing pool, crystal clear water and sheer cliffs), an unspoilt sandy beach known as **Ir-Ramla il-Wamra** and **Xlendi Bay**. **Marsalforn** is a fishing village on the north coast which has become one of Gozo's most popular seaside resorts.

Credit: ©Malta Tourism Authority

- **Windsurfing** has become very popular, especially in **Mellieha Bay**, **St Pauls Bay** and **Bahar Ic-Caghaq**.
- Attend **rowing** regattas, held in the Grand Harbour during April and September. The *Valletta Yacht Club* is at Couvre Port, Manoel Island, in Marsamxetto Harbour (temporary members accepted).
- Buy some of the **local crafts**, lace and knitwear, from the doorways of houses and on the streets of **Gozo** island, the second-largest island of the archipelago.
- In summer attend a **festival** with fireworks and horseracing in the streets of **Gozo**.
- Chill out on the island of **Comino**, which is inhabited by probably no more than a dozen farmers. Paths which wind through the unusual rock formations provide the only communication links and the island is ideal for anyone seeking a very quiet holiday. A few sandy coves and small bays, such as **Blue Lagoon**, are the main attractions. The **St Marija Caves** offer interesting cave diving.
- Typical Maltese fishing communities such as **Marsaxlokk**, **Birzebbugia** and **Marsacala** are sprawled along the coves and inlets at the southernmost tip of Malta. **Eat fresh fish** at the family-run tavernas while enjoying the sights of nets and colourfully painted boats crowding the waterfronts.

TOURIST INFORMATION

Malta Tourist Office in the UK
Unit C, Parkhouse, 14 Northfields, London SW18 1DD, UK
Tel: (020) 8877 6990.
Website: www.visitmalta.com

Entertainment

FOOD & DRINK: There is a very good choice of restaurants and cafes from deluxe to fast food (hamburgers and fish and chips), including Chinese, fish and beachside bars. Table service is normal, but many bars and cafes have table and/or counter service. The best Maltese fruits are oranges and grapes; also delicious are strawberries, melons, mulberries, tangerines, pomegranates and figs.
National specialities:
- *Lampuki pie* (fish pie).
- *Bragoli* (beef olives).
- *Fenek* (rabbit cooked in wine).
- Ricotta sweets are popular.

- *Helwa tat-Tork* (a sweet sugary mixture of crushed and whole almonds, offered to diners after a meal).
National drinks:
- Maltese beer is excellent.
- Maltese wine.
- Maltese spirits.
Licensing hours of bars, restaurants and cafes are usually 0900-0100 and beyond. Most hotel bars close between 1300 and 1600 and then reopen after 1800.
Tipping: 10 to 15 per cent is expected in hotels and restaurants when not included in the bill. Taxi drivers are usually tipped 10 per cent of the fare.
NIGHTLIFE: There are several discos, bars and nightclubs. Roulette, baccarat, blackjack and boule can be played at the 'Dragonara' casino, St Julian's or at the Casino de Venezia in Vittoriosa. The Manoel Theatre is one of the oldest in Europe. Cinemas show mainly English and American films.
SHOPPING: Special purchases include Malta weave, pottery, blown glass, ceramics, dolls, lace, copper and brass items. Malta is renowned for its gold and silver filigree work and handmade lace. **Shopping hours:** Mon-Sat 0900-1300 and 1600-1900.

Business

- **GDP:** US$7 billion (2005).
- **Main imports:** Machinery and transport equipment, manufactured and semi-manufactured goods, food, drink and tobacco.
- **Main exports:** Potatoes, machinery and transport equipment.
- **Main trade partners:** France, Germany, Italy, Singapore, UK and USA.

ECONOMY: The agricultural sector is small, with potatoes being the only major export commodity. Although Malta is an island, the fishing industry is also relatively insignificant. With few natural resources, Governments have sought to develop the economy through tourism and export-dedicated manufacturing. Tourism now accounts for over a quarter of Malta's foreign exchange earnings. The industrial sector includes textiles, footwear and clothing (the most important of the new industries), plastics, printing, electronic components and electrical equipment. The old naval dockyards used by the British have now converted to operate as a commercial shipyard. Malta has developed close economic links with Libya, which has invested heavily in property and commerce on the island as well as supplying the bulk of the oil that meets the island's energy needs. France has become the principal market for exports, followed by the USA, Germany, Singapore, the UK and Italy. The main economic policy issue under debate in Malta is relations with the EU and the country's application for membership. The conservative Nationalist Party (PN) favoured joining while the Maltese Labour Party was strongly opposed to membership. After a sudden withdrawal in 1996 of its original application, the PN administration reapplied in 1998. The PN went on to win the 2003 poll, and Malta's membership was endorsed in March 2003 by popular referendum. Negotiations progressed fairly smoothly and Malta joined the EU, along with nine other countries (mostly from Eastern Europe), in May 2004.
BUSINESS ETIQUETTE: English is widely spoken in business circles and, on the whole, Maltese businesspeople have a conservative approach to business protocol. Punctuality is expected and appreciated and dress must be smart. The best months for business visits are October to May. Office hours: Mon-Fri 0830-1245 and 1430-1730, Sat 0830-1200. Some smaller offices close 1300-1600, opening again later.

COMMERCIAL INFORMATION

Ministry of Foreign Affairs
Palazzo Parisio, Merchants' Street, Valletta, Malta
Tel: 2124 2191.
Website: www.foreign.gov.mt

Malta Chamber of Commerce
Exchange Buildings, Republic Street, Valletta VLT05, Malta
Tel: 2123 3873
Website: www.chamber.org.mt

Conference and Incentive Travel Division of the Malta Tourism Authority
'Auberge d'Italie', Merchants Street, Valletta, CMR 02, Malta
Tel: 2291 5204.
Website: www.maltaconferences.com

A
B
C
D
E
F
G
H
I
J
K
L
M
N
O
P
Q
R
S
T
U
V
W
X
Y
Z

Martinique

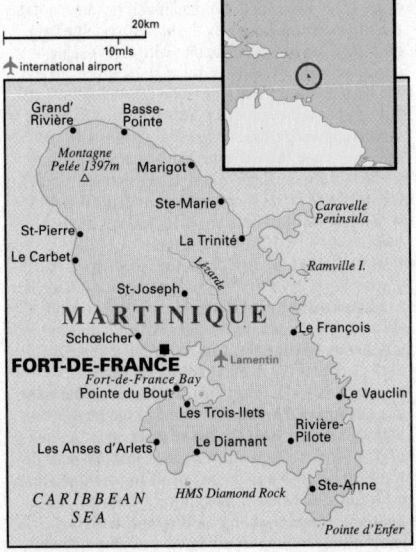

Location: Caribbean, northernmost of the Windward group of islands.

Time: GMT - 4.

Overview

When he discovered Martinique in 1493, Christopher Columbus, said it was 'the most beautiful country in the world', naming it in honour of St Martin. Before then, the area was inhabited by Arawak and Carib Indians and was called *Madinina* ('island of flowers') by the native population.

Though the British made brief attempts to occupy the island during the 18th and 19th centuries, it has remained under French control since 1635 (along with Guadeloupe). Tourism represents a major part of the economy. Each year, hundreds of thousands of visitors are drawn to Martinique's picturesque volcanic landscape, its fine black, white or peppered sand beaches surrounded by sugar, palm, banana and pineapple plantations. The island's location also makes it a stopping-off point for cruise ships.

Visitors will appreciate Martinique's French and Creole heritage, which is mirrored in its customs, food and languages. Most Martiniquais are of mixed ancestry, being the descendants of 17th century French settlers and slaves brought from Africa to work on the island's plantations. In addition, visitors won't escapte *zouk*, the lively, two-beat local music similar to merengue but unique to the French West Indies. Martinicans are very proud of it and it can be heard everywhere. Finally, one should not leave the island without tasting its rum, considered among the best in the world. It was awarded the prestigious French label *'appellation d'origine contrôlée'* previously only reserved for French cheeses and wines.

General Information

AREA: 1100 sq km (424.7 sq miles).

POPULATION: 382,000.

POPULATION DENSITY: 346.8 per sq km.

CAPITAL: Fort-de-France. **Population:** 93,000 (UN estimate 2001).

GEOGRAPHY: The French Overseas Department of Martinique, a volcanic and picturesque island, is the northernmost of the Windward Caribbean group. The island is noticeably more rocky than those of the Leeward group, with beaches (of fine black or white or peppered sand) surrounded by sugar, palm, banana and pineapple plantations.

GOVERNMENT: Martinique is an Overseas Department of France and as such is an integral part of the French Republic. **Head of State:** President Jacques Chirac since 1995, represented locally by Prefect Yves Dassonville since 2004. **Head of Government:** Claude Lise, President of the General Council since 1992. **Recent history:** The Prefect on Martinique represents France, and the island sends four representatives to the French National Assembly and two to the Senate. The 45-seat General Council and the 41-seat Regional Council administer the island's local affairs; both are elected every six years.

LANGUAGE: The official language is French; a Creole patois is widely used.

RELIGION: The majority of the population is Roman Catholic.

ELECTRICITY: 220 volts AC, 50Hz.

SOCIAL CONVENTIONS: The atmosphere is generally relaxed and informal. Casual dress is acceptable everywhere, but formal attire is needed for dining out and nightclubs.

Climate

Warm weather throughout the year, with the main rainy season occurring in the autumn. Showers can occur at other times of the year, but they are usually brief. Cooler in the upland areas.

Required clothing: Lightweight, with waterproof wear advised for the rainy season.

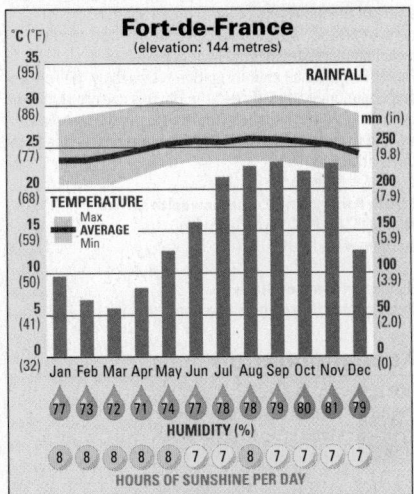

Communications

Telephone: IDD is available. There are both payphones and card phones on the island. *Télécartes* (phonecards) are sold at post offices, newsagents and kiosks. There are only card phones at the airport.

Mobile telephone: Roaming agreements exist with international mobile phone companies. Coverage extends throughout the French Antilles and in French Guiana.

Internet: There are a few internet cafes in Martinique, predominantly in the cities such as Fort de France and main tourist areas.

Post: Letters take about a week to reach Europe. Post office hours: Mon-Fri 0700-1800 and Saturday mornings.

MEDIA: TV and radio services are provided by the French public overseas broadcaster, RFO, and by private operators.

Press: Newspapers are in French and vary in their political bias. The main dailies are *Carib Hebdo* and *France Antilles*. Other newspapers are imported into Martinique, such as the *Washington Post*.

TV: *RFO Martinique* is a public channel, operated by Réseau France Outre-Mer; Antilles TV is a private channel.

Radio: *RFO Martinique* is a public station, operated by Réseau France Outre-Mer; *Radio Caraibes International* and *NRJ Antilles* are private stations.

Passport/Visa

	Passport Required?	Visa Required?	Return Ticket Required?
Full British	Yes	No	Yes
Australian	Yes	No	Yes
Canadian	Yes	No	Yes
USA	Yes	No	Yes
Other EU	Yes/1	No	Yes
Japanese	Yes	No	Yes

Note: *Regulations and requirements may be subject to change at short notice, and you are advised to contact the appropriate diplomatic or consular authority before finalising travel arrangements. Any numbers in the chart refer to the footnotes below.*

PASSPORTS: Passport valid for at least three months beyond applicant's last day of stay required by all except the following:
1. nationals of Belgium, France, Germany, Greece, Italy, Luxembourg, Monaco, The Netherlands, Portugal, Spain and Switzerland, who are holders of national identity cards and are citizens of that country.

VISAS: Required by all except the following:
(a) nationals of countries referred to in the chart above for stays of up to three months;
(b) nationals of Andorra, Argentina, Bolivia, Brunei, Bulgaria, Chile, Costa Rica, Croatia, El Salvador, Guatemala, Honduras, Hong Kong (SAR), Iceland, Korea (Rep), Liechtenstein, Macau (SAR), Malaysia, Mexico, Monaco, New Zealand, Nicaragua, Norway, Panama, Paraguay, San Marino, Singapore, Switzerland, Uruguay, Vatican City and Venezuela for stays of up to three months;
(c) transit passengers continuing their journey by the same or first connecting aircraft provided holding valid onward or return documentation and not leaving the airport.

Note: (a) Nationals of the EU, the EEA, the Holy See, Liechenstein and Monaco do not need a long stay visa (for trips exceeding three months). (b) Nationals of Canada, Cyprus, Japan, Korea (Rep), Malaysia, Malta, Mexico, Singapore, USA and Venezuela should apply for a visa if they are to receive a salary, even if their trip is a short stay. (c) US nationals need a visa if they are crew members, or journalists on assignments, or students enrolled at schools and universities in any of the French Overseas Departments.

Types of visa and cost: All visas, regardless of duration of stay and number of entries permitted, cost €35. In most circumstances, no fee applies to students, recipients of Government fellowships and citizens of the EU and their family members.

Validity: *Short-stay* visas (up to 30 days): valid for two months (single- and multiple-entry). *Long stay* visas (31 to 90 days and double- or multiple-entry): valid for a maximum of six months from date of issue. *Transit* visas: valid for single- or multiple-entries of maximum five days per entry, including the day of arrival.

Application to: French Consulate General (for personal visas), or consular section at Embassy (for diplomatic or service visas); see *Passport/Visa Information* for France. All applications must be made in person.

Application requirements: (a) Valid passport with blank page to affix the visa. Minors travelling alone must submit notarised parental authorisation, signed by both parents, plus one copy. (b) Up to two completed application forms. (c) One passport-size photo on each form. (d) Fee, to be paid in cash only if paying by person. If not, fee should be paid by cheque or postal order. (e) Evidence of sufficient funds for stay (last two bank statements, plus copy, or other proof of funds equivalent to US$100 for each day of trip). (f) Letter from employer, or proof of stay in country of residence. (g) Proof of address. (h) Medical insurance. (i) Return ticket and travel documents for remaining journey. (j) Proof of accommodation during stay. (k) Registered self-addressed envelope, if applying by post. (l) Detailed itinerary, including reservations and round-trip airline tickets (only required when visa is issued), plus one copy. (m) Proof of employment (eg last payslip or letter from employer). (n) Proof of valid health/travel insurance with worldwide coverage, plus copy. *Business:* (a)-(n) and, (o) Business invitation guaranteeing payment of travel expenses, plus one copy.

Working days required: One day to three weeks depending on nationality.

Temporary residence: If intending to work or stay for longer than 90 days, nationals should contact the Long Stay visa section of the Consulate General or Embassy (tel: (020) 7073 1248).

PASSPORT/VISA INFORMATION

Martinique is an Overseas Department of the Republic of France and does not maintain overseas missions. Addresses of French Embassies, Consulates and Tourist Offices may be found in the *France* section.

Money

Currency: Since January 2002 the Euro has been the official currency for the French Overseas Departments (*Départements d'outre-mer*), French Guiana, Guadeloupe, Martinique and Réunion. For further details, exchange rates and currency restrictions, see *France* section. US Dollars are also accepted in some places.

Currency exchange: All major currencies can be exchanged at banks and bureaux de change.

Credit & debit cards: American Express, Diners Club and Visa are accepted in the major tourist areas. MasterCard has limited acceptance. Cards can also be used in cash dispensers. Check with your credit or debit card company for details of merchant acceptability and other services which may be available.

Traveller's cheques: Accepted in most places, and may qualify for discounts on luxury items. To avoid additional exchange rate charges, travellers are advised to take traveller's cheques in Euros or US Dollars.
Banking hours: Mon-Fri 0800-1200 and 1430-1630.

Duty Free

The island of Martinique is an Overseas Department of France, and therefore duty-free allowances are the same as those for France; see *France* section.

Public Holidays

As for France (see *France* section) with the following dates also observed until June 2007.
2006: Feb 25-Mar 1 Carnival. **Apr 14** Good Friday. **May 22** Slavery Abolition Day. **Jul 21** Schoelcher Day.
2007: Feb Carnival. **Apr 6** Good Friday. **May 22** Slavery Abolition Day.

Health

	Special Precautions?	Certificate Required?
Yellow Fever	No	No
Cholera	No	No
Typhoid & Polio	1	N/A
Malaria	No	N/A

Note: *Regulations and requirements may be subject to change at short notice, and you are advised to contact your doctor well in advance of your intended date of departure. Any numbers in the chart refer to the footnotes below.*

1: Immunisation against typhoid and poliomyelitis is recommended.
Food & drink: Mains water is normally chlorinated and, whilst relatively safe, may cause mild abdominal upsets. Bottled water is available and is advised for the first few weeks of the stay. Drinking water outside main cities and towns may be contaminated and sterilisation is advisable. Milk is pasteurised and dairy products are safe for consumption. Local meat, poultry, seafood, fruit and vegetables are generally considered safe to eat.
Other risks: *Bilharzia* (*schistosomiasis*) is present. Avoid swimming and paddling in fresh water; swimming pools which are well chlorinated and maintained are safe. *Typhoid, hepatitis A, hepatitis B, diphtheria* and *tuberculosis* immunisations are occasionally recommended. *Dengue* and *leptospirosis* are present. *Rabies* is present, particularly in the mongoose. For those at high risk, vaccination before arrival should be considered. If you are bitten, seek medical advice without delay. For more information, consult the *Health* appendix.
Health care: A reciprocal health agreement exists between France and the UK. However, the benefits which go with this agreement may not be fully available in Martinique. Check with your doctor before departure. Martinique has 18 hospitals and several specialists and clinics.

Travel - International

AIR:

Martinique's national airline is *CTA Air Martinique*.
Approximate flight times: From Martinique to *London* is 12 hours (including an average stopover time of three hours in Paris); to *Los Angeles* is nine hours (excluding two stopovers); to *New York* is six hours and to *Singapore* is 25 hours.
Main airports: *Fort-de-France (FDF)* (Lamentin) is 11km (7 miles) from the city. *Facilities*: Restaurants, banks and bureaux de change, shops, tourist information and car hire.
Departure tax: None.

SEA:

Main port: *Fort-de-France*. The Pointe Simon cruise dock, nearer the city centre, accommodates larger cruise ships. Regular high-speed catamaran services run to Guadeloupe, St Lucia and Dominica. For more information, contact either *Express des Îles* (tel: (596) 631 212; e-mail: info@express-des-iles.com) *or Brudey Frères* (tel: (596) 700 850; fax: (596) 705 375). *Caribbean Ferries* sail to and from Dominique, St Lucia and Guadeloupe (tel: (596) 636 868). Other ships sail from Miami and San Juan (Puerto Rico).

Travel - Internal

AIR:

Aeroplanes and helicopters may be chartered from *Air Martinique*.

SEA/RIVER:

Scheduled ferries ply between Fort-de-France and the main resorts of Trois Îlets and Sainte-Anne via Anse Mitan, Pointe du Bout, Anse à l'Âne and Anses d'Arlet. Children's tickets are half price.

ROAD:

Traffic drives on the right. The road system is well developed and surfaced. **Bus:** A limited although inexpensive service is provided within the communes. Most of Martinique's public transport is served by communal taxis, denoted by the sign TC. TCs depart at frequent intervals from Pointe Simon (by the waterfront in Fort-de-France) to destinations all over the islands, making stops along the way. Fares are fixed and are reasonable. TCs run from early morning until 1800. **Taxi:** Government-controlled, plentiful and reasonably cheap if shared. The majority of taxis are Mercedes-Benz. There is a 40 per cent surcharge at night (2000-0600). Main taxi stands are at major hotels, resorts and the airport. **Car hire:** The island has excellent car hire facilities. 50cc mopeds do not need a licence. Bicycles can also be hired. **Documentation:** An International Driving Permit is recommended, but a national driving licence is sufficient, provided the driver has at least one year's experience. The minimum driving age is 21.

Travel Advice

Most visits to Martinique are trouble-free but you should be aware of the global risk of indiscriminate international terrorist attacks, which could be against civilian targets, including places frequented by foreigners.
This advice is based on information provided by the Foreign and Commonwealth Office in the UK. It is correct at time of publishing. As the situation can change rapidly, visitors are advised to contact the following organisations for the latest travel advice:

British Foreign and Commonwealth Office
Tel: (0845) 850 2829.
Website: www.fco.gov.uk

US Department of State
Website: http://travel.state.gov/travel

Accommodation

HOTELS:

There is a good selection of hotels on Martinique; 10 per cent service is charged, sometimes with other Government taxes added. The Relais de la Martinique is an association of small hotels, often called *Relais Créoles*, and guest houses offering special reservation and tour facilities. Hotels range from deluxe, to medium- and low-priced. For further information, contact the tourist office, *or* Maison de la France (see *Top Things To See and Do*).

SELF-CATERING:

Gîtes (furnished apartments or bungalows) are widely available.

CAMPING AND CARAVANNING:

Visitors can pitch a tent almost anywhere in Martinique: mountains, forests and most beaches. *Tropicamp* at Gros Raisins Plage and *Nid Tropical* at Anse à L'Âne are two sites offering full amenities for campers.

ACCOMMODATION INFORMATION

Centrale de Réservation Martinique
Immeuble le Beaupré, Pointe de Jahan 97233 Schoelcher, Martinique
Tel: (596) 616 177.
Website: www.martinique.org

Relais des Gîtes de France – Martinique
BP 1122, Maison du Tourisme Vert, 9 boulevard du Général-de-Gaulle, 97248 Fort-de-France, Martinique
Tel: (596) 737 474.
Website: www.itea.fr/GDF/972

Top Things To See & Do

- Be delighted by the winding streets and colourful markets of **Fort-de-France**, the island's capital. In the centre of the town, go to the park of **La Savanne** where a statue commemorates Napoleon's Empress Joséphine, a native of Martinique. Her home, **La Pagerie**, is one of the main tourist attractions. Near **Trois-Îlets**, across the bay from Fort-de-France is Joséphine's birthplace, **La Pagerie**, which has a museum chock full of her mementos; nearby is the **Parc des Floralies**, a peaceful and pretty botanical park. Also of note in the vicinity is the **Pottery Centre**.
- Pay a visit to the **Musée Départemental**, which has remains of the predominantly Arawak and Carib Indian prehistory of the island. There is an interesting **Caribbean Arts Centre**.
- See the **Cathedral of St-Louis**, a late-17th-century cathedral with a Roman-style bell tower. Many governors of Martinique are buried inside.
- The 1430m (4700ft) volcanic mountain in the north, **Montagne Pelée**, last erupted in 1902 (in a unique explosion which literally ripped the summit off), destroying the city of **St Pierre** and its entire population of 30,000. The remains of St Pierre, once a beautiful and remarkable city known as the 'pearl of the Caribbean', are now a tourist attraction. The **Musée Volcanologique** contains exhibits, photographs and documents that tell the story of the disaster. Today, St Pierre is Martinique's second city and, although run down, still shows some signs of its former glory: the old **stone stairways** and **bridges** still exist, and the ruins of the **theatre** are a prominent feature. Some of the historic buildings are being rebuilt and restored, notably the **old customs house** by the waterfront. The long grey-sand beach is very popular with local people. It is possible to visit the wrecks of the ships which were in the harbour on the day Montagne Pelée erupted – all but one of them went down in the disaster. Special submarines with glass windows take tourists to view the wrecks and the colourful fish which swim around them. It is also possible to dive to see them. The best way to see St Pierre is on the *Cyparis Express* train which takes visitors on a one-hour journey around the town.
- Near **Le Carbet**, where Columbus landed on his fourth voyage in 1502, visit the restored plantation of **Leyritz**. The **Centre d'Art Paul Gauguin** may be found in Le Carbet itself. It contains exhibits relating to the painter's stay in the area and the work he did while there.
- In the south of the island is **Pointe du Bout**, Martinique's major resort area. **Ste Anne**, **Le Diamant** and **Les Anses d'Arlets** have some of the island's best bathing beaches. **HMS Diamond Rock**, 4km (2.5 miles) off Diamant, is a rock which was designated a man-of-war by the British during the Napoleonic wars and rates a 12-gun salute from passing British warships.
- **Swimming**, **water-skiing**, **sailing**, **scuba diving**, **snorkelling** and **spearfishing** are available at many coastal resorts. Take part in the **aqua-festival**, a sailing event held each year around the **Bay of Robert**.
- **Horse riding** is a very enjoyable way to see Martinique's lovely countryside. There is also horseracing at the Carère track at **Lamentin**. **Hiking**, **mountain climbing** and **mountain biking** are also catered for.
- Do no leave the island without sampling the island **rum**. As rich as the island's history is the island's soil. Rum distilleries abound throughout Martinique and all of them welcome visitors for a sampling of their product. The **St. James Distillery** at **Sainte-Marie** in the north operates the **Musée du Rhum** (nearby is Morne des Esses, a straw-weaving centre). The charming **Rhum Clement Domaine Acajou**, in **Le François** on the east coast, recently added a fine contemporary museum. The **Fonds Saint-Jacques**, a historically important 17th-century sugar estate in the north, attracts visitors with its **Musée du Père Labat**. Finally, there is the **Maison de la Canne**, a modern museum devoted to sugar and rum just outside **TroÎs-Ilets**.

TOURIST INFORMATION

Office du Tourisme de la Martinique (Martinique Tourist Office)
2 Rue des Moulins, 75001 Paris, France
Tel: (1) 4477 8600.
Website: www.touristmartinique.com

Maison de la France (French Government Tourist Office in the UK)
178 Piccadilly, London W1Y 0AL, UK
Tel: (09068) 244 123 (information line; calls cost 60p per minute) *or* (020) 7399 3500.
Website: www.franceguide.com

Martinique Promotion Bureau in the USA
444 Madison Avenue, 16th Floor, New York, NY 10022, USA
Tel: (212) 838 7800.
Website: www.martinique.org

Caribbean Tourism Organisation in the UK
22 The Quadrant, Richmond, Surrey TW9 1BP, UK
Tel: (020) 8948 0057.
Website: www.doitcaribbean.com *or* www.onecaribbean.org

Entertainment

FOOD & DRINK: The island's cuisine is characterised by French and Caribbean influences. Creole cuisine is also widely available and is an original combination of French, Indian and African traditions seasoned with exotic spices.

National specialities:
- Lobster, red snapper, conch and sea urchin.
- Stuffed crab.
- Stewed conch.
- Colombo (dish of goat, chicken, pork or lamb in a thick curry sauce).

National drinks:
- 'Ti punch (a brew of rum, lime juice, bitters and syrup).
- Shrub (a Christmas liqueur consisting of rum and orange peel).
- Planteur (made from rum and fruit juice).
- Guava, soursop, passionfruit, mandarin and sugar-cane juices.

Minimum drinking age: 18 years.

Things to know: There are no licensing restrictions. Meals are ended with tropical fruit.

Tipping: 10 per cent is acceptable.

NIGHTLIFE: There are plenty of restaurants, bars and discos and some displays of local dancing and music. The Ballet Martiniquais is one of the world's most prestigious traditional ballet companies. Limbo dancers and steel bands often perform at hotels in the evenings. The local music, zouk, lively, two-beat music similar to merengue but unique to the French West Indies, can be heard everywhere. Martinicans are very proud of it. There are two casinos, the Casino de la Batelière Plazza, in Schoelcher, and there is one in the Méridien Hotel. The Fort-de-France City Hall is now a municipal theatre. The local guide, Choubouloute, contains information on local entertainment and is sold at newsagents.

SHOPPING: French imports are worthwhile purchases, especially wines, liqueurs and crystal. Local items include rum, straw goods, bamboo hats, creole dolls, creole jewellery, baskets and objects of aromatic vetiver roots. A discount of 20 per cent is given if payment is made by traveller's cheques in some tourist shops. **Shopping hours:** Mon-Fri 0830-1800.

Business

- **GDP:** US$37 million.
- **Main exports:** Petroleum products, bananas, sugar, cut flowers, rum and pineapples.
- **Main imports:** Petroleum products, crude oil, foodstuffs, construction materials, vehicles, clothing and other consumer goods.
- **Main trade partners:** France, Germany, Guadeloupe, Italy, Venezuela and the USA.

ECONOMY: In the agricultural sector, sugar cane and bananas are the main cash crops; a range of fruit is also grown for domestic consumption and export. Cut flowers have also become an important export earner. The processing of agricultural goods and refining of imported oil (which is also the main source of energy) are the island's main industries. The most important part of the economy is tourism, both as a major employer and a vital source of foreign exchange – worth some US$400 million a year to the economy. Martinique also enjoys substantial material benefits from being an integral part of the French nation, receiving financial support both from Paris and the EU. France accounts for more than 75 per cent of Martinique's foreign trade, with the remainder of the import market captured by the major EU economies and the USA.

BUSINESS ETIQUETTE: Lightweight suits and safari suits are recommended. The best time to visit is January to March and June to September. A command of French is essential, as most of the island's business is connected with France. Office hours: Mon-Fri 0800-1200 and 1400-1800.

CONFERENCES/CONVENTIONS: Facilities for business conferences are available at the Palais des Congrès Convention Centre.

COMMERCIAL INFORMATION

Chambre de Commerce et d'Industrie de la Martinique
BP 478, 50 Rue Ernest Deproge, 97241 Fort-de-France, Martinique
Tel: 552 800.
Website: www.martinique.cci.fr

Palais des Congrès (Convention Centre)
Schoelcher Commune, Madiana, Martinique
Tel: 721 515.

Mauritania

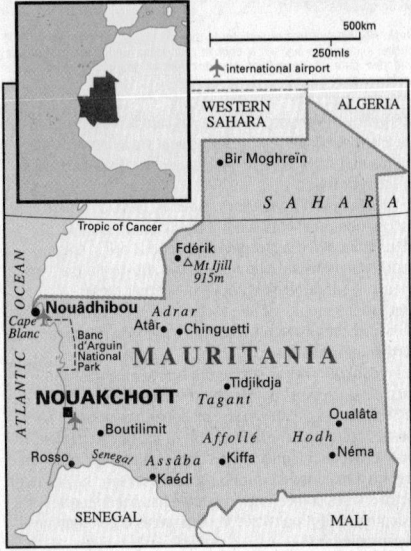

500km
250mls
✈ international airport

Location: West Africa.

Time: GMT.

Overview

Much of the land is dry and inhospitable and many locations are difficult to reach without long journeys in 4-wheel drive vehicles. Mauritania's coast is essentially an 800km-(500 mile-) long sandy beach, all but devoid of vegetation but supporting an astonishingly large and varied population of birds. Drawbacks aside, Mauritania is a fascinating country with a colourful, indigenous Moorish population.

General Information

AREA: 1,030,700 sq km (397,950 sq miles).

POPULATION: 2.8 million (UN estimate 2004).

POPULATION DENSITY: 2.7 per sq km.

CAPITAL: Nouakchott. **Population:** 611,883 (2001).

GEOGRAPHY: Mauritania is bordered by Algeria, Mali, Western Sahara (Sahrawi Arab Democratic Republic) and Senegal. To the west lies the Atlantic Ocean. Mauritania consists mainly of the vast Saharan plain of sand and scrub. Most of this area is a sea of sand dunes, but in places the land rises to rocky plateaux with deep ravines leaving isolated peaks. The Adrar plateau in the central region rises to 500m (1640ft), and the Tagant further south to 600m (1970ft). The area is scattered with towns, small villages and oases. The northern bank of the Senegal River, which forms the country's southern border, is the only area in the country with any degree of permanent vegetation and it supports a wide variety of wildlife.

GOVERNMENT: Republic. Gained independence from France in 1960. **Head of State:** Military Leader Ely Ould Mohammed Vall since 2005. **Head of Government:** Prime Minister Sidy Mohamed Ould Boubacar since 2005.

LANGUAGE: The official language is Arabic. The Moors of Arab/Berber stock, speaking Hassaniya dialects of Arabic, comprise the majority of the people. Other dialects include Soninke, Poular and Wolof. French and English are increasingly spoken.

RELIGION: Islam is the official religion. Despite ethnic and cultural differences among Mauritanians, they are all bound by a common Muslim attachment to the Malekite sect.

ELECTRICITY: 220 volts AC, 50Hz. Round two-pin plugs are normal.

SOCIAL CONVENTIONS: Islam has been the major influence in this country since the seventh and eighth

---

centuries and visitors should respect the religious laws and customs. Dress for women should be uncompromisingly modest. Nearly all the population have traditionally been nomadic herdsmen. The bulk of the population is divided into two main Moorish groups, the Bidan (55 per cent) and the Harattin (20 per cent), with the non-Moorish population concentrated in the Senegal River area. Different classes and tribes tend to be contiguous.

Climate

Most of the country is hot and dry with practically no rain. In the south, however, rainfall is higher with a rainy season which runs from July to September. The coast is tempered by trade winds and is mild with the exception of the hot Nouakchott region (where the rainy season begins a month later). Deserts are cooler and windy in March and April.

Required clothing: Lightweight cottons and linens, with a warm wrap for cool evenings. Waterproofs are necessary for the rainy season.

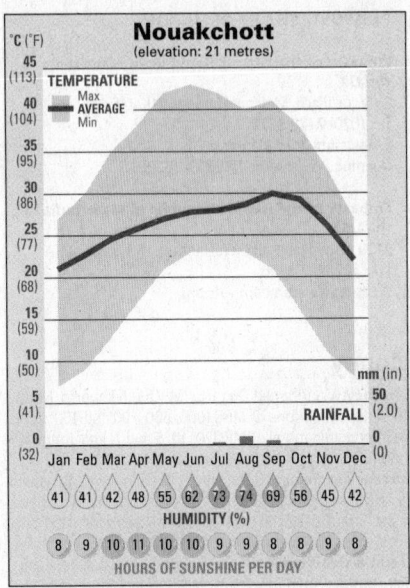

Communications

Telephone: IDD is available in Nouakchott and Nouadhibou. Country code: 222 (no area codes). Outgoing international calls must go through the operator.

Mobile telephone: GSM 900 network operators include Mattel and Mauritel (website: www.mauritelmobiles.mr).

Internet: ISPs include Mauritel (website: www.mauritel.mr).

Post: International postal facilities are limited to main cities. Airmail to Europe takes approximately two weeks.

MEDIA: Mauritania's TV and radio stations are state-owned.

Press: Newspapers are in French and Arabic. The dailies are Châab and Nouakchott-Info. The main weeklies include Le Calame, L'Eveil-Hebdo and Rajoul Echarée.

TV: Mauritanian TV broadcasts programmes in Arabic, French and other local languages.

Radio: Radio Mauritania.

Passport/Visa

	Passport Required?	Visa Required?	Return Ticket Required?
Full British	Yes	Yes	Yes
Australian	Yes	Yes	Yes
Canadian	Yes	Yes	Yes
USA	Yes	Yes	Yes
Other EU	Yes	Yes	Yes
Japanese	Yes	Yes	Yes

Note: Regulations and requirements may be subject to change at short notice, and you are advised to contact the appropriate diplomatic or consular authority before finalising travel arrangements. Any numbers in the chart refer to the footnotes below.

PASSPORTS: Valid passports required by all except nationals of some other ECOWAS countries (Burkina Faso, Cape Verde, Côte d'Ivoire, Gambia, Ghana, Guinea, Mali, Niger, Senegal and Sierra Leone) and Cameroon, Central African Republic, Chad, Congo (Rep), Gabon and Madagascar holding a valid national ID card.

VISAS: Required by all except the following:
(a) nationals of Algeria, Benin, Burkina Faso, Cameroon, Cape Verde, Central African Republic, Chad, Congo (Rep), Côte d'Ivoire, Gabon, Gambia, Ghana, Guinea, Guinea-Bissau,

Liberia, Libya, Madagascar, Mali, Niger, Nigeria, Romania, Senegal, Sierra Leone, Togo and Tunisia; (b) transit passengers continuing their journey by the same or first connecting aircraft provided holding onward or return documentation and not leaving the airport.

Types of visa and cost: *Tourist* or *Business*: £42. All visas are multiple-entry.

Validity: Three months.

Application to: Consulate (or consular section at Embassy); see *Passport/Visa Information.*

Application requirements: (a) Valid passport. (b) Application form. (c) Two passport-size photos. (d) Fee. (e) For Business visas, a letter of invitation from sponsor may be required. (f) Stamped, self-addressed envelope if applying by post.

Working days required: Usually takes 72 hours to be processed.

Temporary residence: Applications should be made to the Home Ministry in Mauritania.

PASSPORT/VISA INFORMATION

Embassy of the Islamic Republic of Mauritania in the UK
8 Carlos Place, Mayfair, London W1K 3AS, UK
Tel: (020) 7478 9323.
E-mail: ambarim@aol.com
Opening hours: Mon-Fri 0930-1630.

Embassy of the Islamic Republic of Mauritania in the USA
2129 Leroy Place, NW, Washington, DC 20008, USA
Tel: (202) 232 5700.
Website: www.ambarim-dc.org

Money

Currency: Mauritanian Ouguiya (MRO) = 5 khoums. Notes are in denominations of MRO1000, 500, 200 and 100. Coins are in denominations of MRO20, 10, 5 and 1, and 1 and 0.2 khoums.

Currency exchange: Currency declaration forms are issued on arrival and should be kept. Currencies can be exchanged at the airport or at the main banks in Nouakchott. It is illegal to exchange money on the black market.

Credit & debit cards: Generally not accepted. American Express is accepted in a few hotels in Nouakchott and Nouadhibou. Check with your credit or debit card company for details of merchant acceptability and other services which may be available.

Traveller's cheques: Limited use. To avoid additional exchange rate charges, travellers are advised to take traveller's cheques in US Dollars.

Currency restrictions: The import and export of local currency is prohibited. There is no restriction on the import of foreign currency provided the amount is declared on arrival. The balance of foreign currency not spent but declared on entry may be exported, but the import declaration must be produced.

Banking hours: Sun-Thurs 0800-1600.

Exchange rate indicators:
Rate at time of publishing
£1.00=	MRO495.31
$1.00=	MRO285.50

Duty Free

The following items can be imported into Mauritania by persons of 18 years of age and over without incurring customs duty:

200 cigarettes or 25 cigars or 450g of tobacco (women – cigarettes only); 50g of perfume and 250ml eau de toilette; one still camera, one cinecamera and one wireless set; one projector (tourists only).

Note: Sporting guns require an import and gun licence, obtained prior to arrival from the Home Ministry.

Prohibited items: Alcohol.

Public Holidays

Below are listed Public Holidays for the January 2006-June 2007 period.

2006: Jan 1 New Year's Day. **Jan 10** Tabaski (Feast of the Sacrifice). **Jan 31** Islamic New Year. **Apr 11** Mouloud (Prophet's Birthday). **May 1** Labour Day. **May 25** African Liberation Day (Anniversary of the OAU's Foundation). **Jul 10** Armed Forces Day. **Oct 22-24** Korité (End of Ramadan). **Nov 28** Independence Day. **Dec 31** Tabaski (Feast of the Sacrifice).
2007: Jan 1 New Year's Day. **Jan 20** Islamic New Year. **Mar 31** Mouloud (Prophet's Birthday). **May 1** Labour Day. **May 25** African Liberation Day (Anniversary of the OAU's Foundation).

Note: Muslim festivals are timed according to local sightings of various phases of the moon and the dates

given above are approximations. During the lunar month of Ramadan that precedes Korité (Eid al-Fitr), Muslims fast during the day and feast at night and normal business patterns may be interrupted. Many restaurants are closed during the day and there may be restrictions on smoking and drinking. Some disruption may continue into Korité itself. Korité and Tabaski (Eid al-Adha) may last anything from two to 10 days, depending on the region. For more information, see the *World of Islam* appendix.

Health

	Special Precautions?	Certificate Required?
Yellow Fever	Yes	1
Cholera	2	No
Typhoid & Polio	3	N/A
Malaria	4	N/A

Note: *Regulations and requirements may be subject to change at short notice, and you are advised to contact your doctor well in advance of your intended date of departure. Any numbers in the chart refer to the footnotes below.*

1: A *yellow fever* vaccination certificate is required from all travellers over one year of age, except travellers arriving from a non-infected area and staying less than two weeks in the country.

2: Following WHO guidelines issued in 1973, a *cholera* vaccination certificate is not a condition of entry to Mauritania. However, *cholera* is a serious risk in this country and precautions are essential. Up-to-date advice should be sought before deciding whether these precautions should include vaccination, as medical opinion is divided over its effectiveness; see the *Health* appendix for further information.

3: Immunisation against *typhoid* is recommended and vaccination against *poliomyelitis* is sometimes advised.

4: *Malaria* risk, mainly in the malignant *falciparum* form, exists throughout the year except in the northern areas of Dakhlet-Nouadhibou and Tiris-Zemour. In Adrar and Inchiri, there is a malaria risk during the rainy season (July through October). Resistance to chloroquine has been reported. The recommended prophylaxis in these areas is chloroquine plus proguanil.

Food & drink: All water should be regarded as being potentially contaminated. Water used for drinking, brushing teeth or making ice should have first been boiled or otherwise sterilised. Milk is unpasteurised and should be boiled. Powdered or tinned milk is available and is advised, but make sure it is reconstituted with pure water. Avoid dairy products that are likely to have been made from unboiled milk. Only eat well-cooked meat and fish, preferably served hot. Vegetables should be cooked and fruit peeled.

Other risks: *Bilharzia (schistosomiasis)* exists. Avoid swimming or paddling in fresh water; swimming pools that are well chlorinated and maintained are safe. Also present are *hepatitis A* and *E. Hepatitis B* is hyperendemic. *Rift Valley fever* is present in the Trarza region. Epidemics of *meningococcal meningitis* may occur, particularly in the savannah areas and during the dry season.
Rabies is present. For those at high risk, vaccination before arrival should be considered. If you are bitten, seek medical advice without delay. For more information, consult the *Health* appendix.

Health care: Medical facilities are very limited. Nouakchott boasts the country's best medical facilities with many doctors, most in private practices or clinics, and plenty of chemists stocking most existing French medicines. The hospital in the capital has 450 beds; there are fewer than 100 other beds elsewhere. Health insurance, to include cover for emergency repatriation, is essential.

Travel - International

AIR:

Mauritania's national airline is *Air Mauritanie (MR)*. *Air France* operates weekly flights from London to Nouakchott via Paris. Other airlines serving Mauritania include *Air Algerie, Delta Air Lines, Royal Air Maroc* and *Tunis Air.*

Approximate flight times: From Nouakchott to *London* is seven hours (via Paris).

International airports: *Nouakchott (NKC)* is 5km (3 miles) east of the city (travel time – 20 minutes). Taxis are available. Facilities include shops and restaurants. *Nouâdhibou (NDB)* is 4km (2.5 miles) from the city. Taxis are available.

Departure tax: MRO560 for those departing for countries in Africa. MRO860 for all other countries.

SEA:

The principal port is Nouadhibou and there is a small port at Nouakchott, while St Louis in Senegal also serves Mauritania.

ROAD:

The most reliable way into Mauritania overland is from Senegal. From Dakar, the journey to Nouakchott is along a 575km- (360 mile-) tarred road (travel time – approximately eight hours). The River Senegal has to be crossed by ferry at Rosso. A service operates daily 0730-1200 and 1500-1800. There is also a paved road from Mali. Travellers intending to drive into Mauritania from the north should contact the nearest Mauritanian diplomatic mission for an assessment of political conditions in the Western Sahara; the *Route de Mauritanie* via Algeria and Senegal is out of service. The border with Algeria is currently closed.

Travel - Internal

AIR:

Air Mauritanie (MR) operates internal flights between Nouakchott and Atâr, Nouâdhibou (daily), Ayoûn el Atroûs, Tidjikja, Kaédi, Néma and Zouérat. It is possible to charter light aircraft.

Departure tax: MRO270.

RAIL:

The only line runs between Nouâdhibou and Zouérat and is provided by the national mining company, SNIM, to serve the ore mines. Services are free but booking in advance is advisable; journeys are long and arduous and not recommended.

ROAD:

Traffic drives on the right. There are adequate roads linking Nouakchott with Rosso in the south of the country, Néma in the southeast and Akjoujt in the north. A paved highway, namely *La Route de l'Espoir*, runs east from Nouakchott to Mali. All other routes are sand tracks necessitating the use of 4-wheel drive vehicles. In some regions during and after the rainy season roads may become impassable. Similarly, in the dry season tracks can be obscured by drifting sand; a guide is highly recommended, if not essential. **Car hire:** Available in Nouakchott, Nouâdhibou and Atâr. 4-wheel drive vehicles with a driver can be hired and are recommended, but they are expensive. **Documentation:** An International Driving Permit is recommended, although it is not legally required. **Note:** Travellers should never attempt any desert journey without a full set of spare parts and essential safety equipment. The Direction du Tourisme in Nouakchott, part of the Ministère du Commerce de l'Artisanat et du Tourisme, can give further information and advice on road travel (see *Contact Addresses* section).

URBAN:

Taxis are plentiful but very expensive in the towns (Nouakchott and Nouadhibou). Fares are set, not metered, and a small tip is expected.

Travel Advice

A coup occurred in Mauritania on 3 August 2005. The situation in the country appears to have stabilised somewhat, but further instability cannot be ruled out. Travellers to Mauritania are advised to exercise caution, and pay close attention to developments in the country. Travellers should be flexible, and be prepared to alter their plans at short notice.

Mauritania shares with the rest of the region a threat from international terrorism to visibly Western interests. Travellers should be aware of the global risk of indiscriminate attacks, which could be against civilian targets, including places frequented by foreigners.

This advice is based on information provided by the Foreign and Commonwealth Office in the UK. It is correct at time of publishing. As the situation can change rapidly, visitors are advised to contact the following organisations for the latest travel advice:

British Foreign and Commonwealth Office
Tel: (0845) 850 2829.
Website: www.fco.gov.uk

US Department of State
Website: http://travel.state.gov/travel

Accommodation

HOTELS:

Hotel accommodation is very limited in Mauritania and visitors are advised to book well in advance. The larger hotels in Nouakchott are comfortable and have air conditioning but, even in the capital, accommodation is limited and expensive. Bills normally include service and local tax.

REST HOUSES:

There are numerous Government rest houses throughout the country, bookable through the Ministère du Commerce de l'Artisanat et du Tourisme.

Top Things To See & Do

- **Nouakchott**, the capital of Mauritania is a new city created in 1960. It lies near the sea in a desert landscape of low dunes scattered with thorn bushes, on a site adjoining an old Moorish settlement, the **Ksar**. The modern buildings maintain the traditional Berber style of architecture. The following places are worth visiting: the **Plage du Wharf**, the mosque, the Ksar and its market, the African market and the camel market, the crafts centre, the **Maison de la Culture** and the carpet factory.
- **Parc National du Banc d'Arguin:** Possibly Mauritania's best attraction, this national park is a vast area of islands and coastline located on the Atlantic desert coast midway between Nouakchott and Nouâdhibou. The park, which was declared a World Heritage Site by UNESCO, is one of the world's largest bird sanctuaries and provides a shelter for over two million migrant birds from northern Europe. There are also several archaeological sites on the islands.
- Mauritania's coast is essentially an 800km-(500 mile-) long sandy beach, all but devoid of vegetation but supporting an astonishingly large and varied population of birds. The waters are equally rich in fish and, consequently, despite the shortage of fresh water, some coastal stretches are inhabited by people. A growing port and centre of the fishing industry, **Nouâdhibou** is situated on a peninsula at the northern end of the **Bay of Levrier**. Inland, the landscape is empty desert. One tribe, halfway between Nouakchott and **Nouâdhibou**, survives through a symbiotic relationship with wild dolphins: the marine mammals drive fish towards the shore, the tribesmen swim out with nets, and both get their share. Foreign trawlers, however, are rapidly depleting offshore fish stocks.
- **Adrar Region:** It is important to check on conditions for travel before setting out for this region as Government permission may be necessary. The Adrar is a spectacular massif of pink and brown plateaux gilded with dunes and intersected by deep canyons sheltering palm groves. It lies in the north central part of the country, and begins about 320km (200 miles) northeast of Nouakchott. **Atâr**, capital of the region, is an oasis lying on the route of salt caravans. It is the market centre for the nomads of northern Mauritania and has an old quarter, the **Ksar**, with flat-roofed houses and a fine palm grove. The oasis of **Azoughui** was the Almoravid capital in the 11th and 12th centuries, and remains of fortified buildings from this period can still be seen. A whole-day excursion from Atâr leads over the breathtaking mountain pass of **Homogjar** to **Chinguetti**, a holy city of Islam, founded in the 13th century, and now listed by UNESCO as a World Heritage site. The city has a medieval mosque and a library housing ancient manuscripts, but much of the old town is disappearing under the encroaching drifts of sand.
- It is worth making a tour of the **Affolé** and **Assaba** regions, south and southeast of the Tagant, via **Kiffa**, **Tamchakett** and **Ayoun el Atrous**, to the wild plateaux of **El Agher**. The interesting archaeological sites include **Koumbi Saleh**, once capital of the Ghana Empire, 70km (45 miles) from Timbedra along a good track. Near Tamchakett is **Tagdawst**, which has been identified as 'Aoudaghost', an ancient capital of a Berber empire. **Oualata** lies 100km (60 miles) from **Néma** at the end of a desert track. Declared a World Heritage Site by UNESCO, Oualata was at one time among the greatest caravan *entrepôts* of the Sahara. A fortified medieval town built in terraces up a rocky peak, it has for centuries been a place of refuge for scholars and has a fine library. The Muslim cemetery of **Tirzet** is nearby.
- There are some good spots for **fishing** and even **surfing** along the coast in the west. **Swimming** is also possible, but travellers should note that pickpocketing and crime is reported to be rife on Mauritania's beaches. Remote and deserted beaches can be found near Nouâdhibou, although travellers should beware of landmines in the area.

TOURIST INFORMATION

Office National du Tourisme
BP 246, Nouakchott, Mauritania
Tel: 525 3572.

Entertainment

FOOD & DRINK: Moroccan, Lebanese, Chinese and French restaurants can be found in the capital, especially in hotels. Local cuisine, based on lamb, goat and rice can be sampled throughout the country. Consumption of alcohol is prohibited by the Islamic faith, but alcoholic beverages may be found in hotel bars.
National specialities:
- *Mechoui* (whole roast lamb).
- Dates.
- Spiced fish and rice with vegetables,.
- Couscous.
National drinks:
- *Zrig* (camel's milk) is a common drink.
- Sweet Arab tea with mint.

Tipping: 12 to 15 per cent is normal.
SHOPPING: Handicrafts such as dyed leather cushions and some engraved silver items, rugs and woodcarvings can be bought on the open market. A fine selection of silver jewellery, daggers, wood and silver chests, carpets and decorated nomad tents can be bought in the crafts centre in Nouakchott. Unique to the Tagant region are neolithic arrowheads, awls and pottery, while at Boutilimit in the south is a Marabout centre (Institute of High Islamic Studies) where fine carpets of goat and camel hair are made.
Shopping hours: Sat-Thurs 0800-1200 and 1400-1900.

Business

ECONOMY: Successive years of drought and encroaching desert have consumed large areas of Mauritania's cultivable land. More than half the population is engaged in subsistence agriculture, producing vegetables, millet, rice and dates, and rearing livestock, mostly in the area south of the Senegal River. The quantities produced are insufficient to meet domestic needs and Mauritania relies on imports of basic foodstuffs.
Fishing is essential both to domestic needs and the country's export income, also for the revenue from licences granted to foreign fleets from Korea, Japan and Russia. Mining is Mauritania's principal industry: the main products are iron ore (output of which has been cut due to falling demand), gypsum and gold. There are plans to exploit the country's copper reserves, which were long thought uneconomic, as well as newly located diamond deposits. Offshore drilling for oil and gas fields has recently begun. Nonetheless, Mauritania will remain an exceptionally poor country for the foreseeable future and a major aid recipient, with other Arab countries as the main donors. The economy grew by 5 per cent in 2002; inflation was 3 per cent in the same year. The IMF and World Bank have given some economic support in exchange for the standard economic reform programme. Current economic growth is around 5 per cent annually. Nonetheless, Mauritania's financial position remains precarious. Japan and the southern EU countries are the main export markets, while the major exporters to Mauritania are France, Spain, Germany, The Netherlands and the USA. Mauritania is a member of the Union of the Arab Maghreb. It was also a member of the Economic Community of West African States (ECOWAS) until its withdrawal from the organisation in 2000.
BUSINESS ETIQUETTE: Use forms of address as for France, eg 'Monsieur le Directeur'. It is essential that businesspeople have a sound knowledge of French, as very few executives speak English. Office hours: Sun-Thurs 0800-1500.

COMMERCIAL INFORMATION

Chambre de Commerce, d'Agriculture, d'Elevage, d'Industrie et des Mines de Mauritanie
Avenue de la Republique, BP 215, Nouakchott, Mauritania
Tel: 252 214.

Mauritius

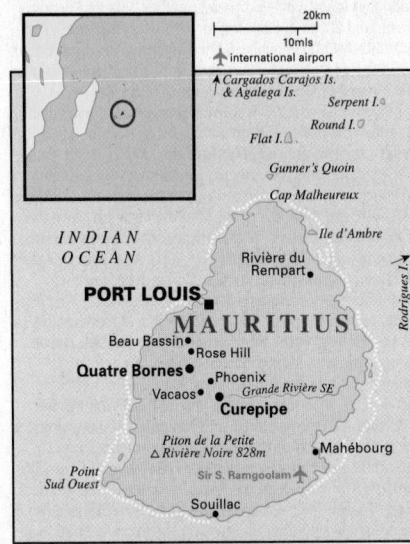

Location: Indian Ocean, off southeast coast of Africa; due east of Madagascar.

Time: GMT + 4.

Overview

This island group was uninhabited until the 16th century, when it was occupied by a small Dutch force that named it after Prince Maurice of Nassau. It was abandoned in 1710 and then re-occupied five years later by the French who imported African slaves to work on the sugar plantations. Mauritius and its neighbouring islands were captured by the British in 1810 and formally ceded by the 1814 Treaty of Paris. After the abolition of slavery in the 1830s, Indian labourers were imported and their descendants now comprise more than two-thirds of the population. Incorporated into the British Empire, Mauritius remained a colony until 1957, when it was granted internal self-government with an electoral system based on the Westminster model. Full independence was granted in 1968, but the British kept a number of smaller islands, which were hived off as the British Indian Ocean Territory.
These connections to the Dutch, the British, the Indian and the African, have all contributed towards Mauritius' refreshing brand of multiculturalism, which lingers within a social climate as peaceful and warm as its meteorological one. The friendliness of the Mauritian people is renowned, and you may even find yourself invited to dance the Sega, their indigenous dance, with them beneath star-filled skies. Dwarfed by other countries in factors such as total area and oil reserves, Mauritius remains colossal in terms of economic growth and political stability – and social stability.
The Mauritian climate also complements Mauritius' deep limpid blue waters, coral reefs and silky blonde piles of sand. For a while, Mauritius was a relatively unknown tourist destination, as were many islands of the Indian Ocean, but now – like most of them – it is regarded as a tropical paradise at an often-bargain price.
Concern that touristic development might impede the country's ecological progress led to an eco-touristic expansion, an earnest preservation of Mauritius' nature parks and hiking trails. There are strict policies that ensure that divers and snorkellers do not disturb Mauritius' delicate coral reefs. Officials have guaranteed that fishing and construction work will not be executed in excess. Mauritius' ecological decisions are usually under scrutiny, since this is an island made famous for its extinct bird, the Dodo, wiped out when human arrivals on the island brought livestock, which hunted the Dodo, and cleared forest space, destroying the Dodo's home. Now,

Mauritius is full of birdwatching spots, where rare and interesting birds can be glimpsed, and this is a side of the island that has been eagerly promoted.
Mauritius more than anywhere deserves such gentle care of its landscape, since its stunning landscape ripples with volcanic skylines and pulsates with streams and waterfalls.

General Information

AREA: 2040 sq km (788 sq miles).
POPULATION: 1.2 million (UN, 2005).
POPULATION DENSITY: 588.24 per sq km.
CAPITAL: Port Louis. **Population:** 146,319.
GEOGRAPHY: Mauritius, a volcanic and mountainous island in the Indian Ocean, lies 2000km (1240 miles) off the southeastern coast of Africa, due east of Madagascar. The island state stands on what was once a land bridge between Asia and Africa called the Mascarene Archipelago. From the coast, the land rises to form a broad fertile plain on which sugar cane flourishes. Some 500km (310 miles) east is Rodrigues Island, while northeast are the Cargados Carajos Shoals and 900km (560 miles) to the north is Agalega.
GOVERNMENT: Republic. Gained independence from the UK in 1968. **Head of State:** President Sir Anerood Jugnauth since 2003. **Head of Government:** Prime Minister Navin Ramgoolam since 2005. **Recent history:** Post-independence Mauritian politics have been dominated by Ramgoolam, and then by the two principal figures of the Mauritian Left, Paul Bérenger and (later Sir) Anerood Jugnauth. The charismatic Bérenger made a dramatic contrast to the cautious, pragmatic Jugnauth, and the focus of the Mauritian political scene has often been the personal and political clash between the two. Jugnauth withdrew from politics in 2003. After over a decade of dominating Mauritian politics, Jugnauth handed the Premiership over to Bérenger (who thus became the first non-Hindu to hold the post), and the leadership of the Socialists to his son, Pravind. In the most recent election in 2005, Navin Ramgoolam won his second non-consecutive term.
Under constitutional amendments that came into effect in March 1992, Mauritius is now a Republic. Legislative power rests with the unicameral 62-seat National Assembly, which is elected by universal suffrage for a five-year term. Four additional members are appointed by the Supreme Court. The National Assembly elects the President of the Republic who is Head of State. The President appoints the Prime Minister from the Assembly and other ministers on the recommendation of the Prime Minister.
LANGUAGE: The official languages are English and French (with French being the most popular), the most commonly used are Creole (a mixture of French and African languages), Hindi and Bhojpuri. Urdu and Chinese are also spoken.
RELIGION: 52 per cent Hindu, 28 per cent Christian, 17 per cent Muslim.
ELECTRICITY: 220 volts AC, 50Hz. UK-type three-pin plugs are commonly used in hotels.
SOCIAL CONVENTIONS: Handshaking is the customary form of greeting. Visitors should respect the traditions of their hosts, particularly when visiting a private house. The type of hospitality the visitor receives is determined by the religion and social customs of the host, which are closely related. It is appropriate to give a gift as a small token of appreciation if invited for a meal. Dress is normally informal although men will need to wear a suit for particularly formal occasions.

Climate

Warm coastal climate (particularly January to April), with relatively little seasonal variation in temperatures, although they are generally slightly lower inland, with more rain on the plateau around Curepipe. Cyclones may occur between November and February. Sea breezes blow all year, especially on the east coast.
Required clothing: Tropical lightweights, with warmer wear for evenings and winter months (July to September). Rainwear advisable all year round. In the summer months, sun-care products and a hat are advisable.

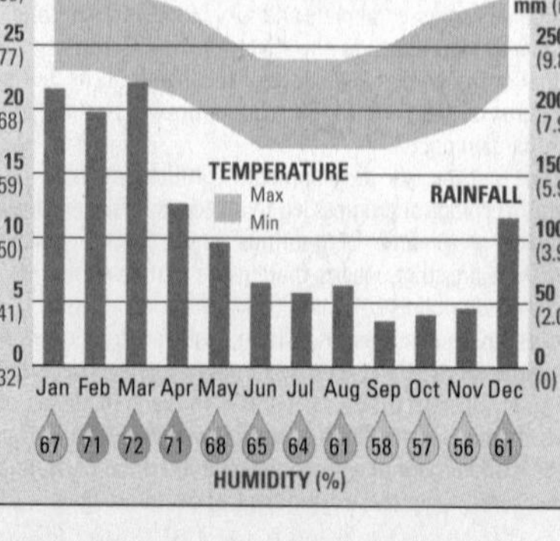

Communications

Telephone: IDD is available. Country code: 230. There are no area codes. There are a limited number of public telephone booths, mainly at the airport and in major hotels.
Mobile telephone: Roaming agreements with international mobile phone companies are available and coverage extends over the entire island.
Internet: There are Internet cafes in Phoenix, Vaoas and other main towns. Most hotels offer Internet facilities.
Post: Airmail to Western Europe usually takes five days; by sea, mail takes four to six weeks. Post office hours: Generally Mon-Fri 0815-1115 and 1200-1600, Sat 0800-1145.
MEDIA: Press: Of the 10 daily newspapers, two are published in Chinese and the remainder in French and English. *L'Express* (website: www.lexpress.mu), *Le Mauricien* (website: www.lemauricien.com) and *Le Matinal* (website: www.lematinal.com) have the highest circulation.
TV: *MBC* is state-run and operates three channels.
Radio: *MBC* stations include *Kool FM, Radio Maurice 1* and *2, One World FM* and *Taal FM* . Other stations include *Radio One, Radio Plus* and *Top FM*.

Passport/Visa

	Passport Required?	Visa Required?	Return Ticket Required?
Full British	Yes	No	Yes
Australian	Yes	No	Yes
Canadian	Yes	No	Yes
USA	Yes	No	Yes
Other EU	Yes	No	Yes
Japanese	Yes	No	Yes

Note: *Regulations and requirements may be subject to change at short notice, and you are advised to contact the appropriate diplomatic or consular authority before finalising travel arrangements. Any numbers in the chart refer to the footnotes below.*

PASSPORTS: Passport valid for at least six months from date of entry required by all. Passports issued by the Government of Taiwan and the Turkish Republic of Cyprus are not recognised. The holders of such documents can apply for an entry permit to the Passport and Immigration Officer (see address below).
Note: All visitors must hold valid tickets and documents for their onward or return journey and adequate funds for their intended length of stay.
VISAS: Required by all except the following:
(a) nationals of countries referred to in the chart above for stays of up to three months;
(b) nationals of Commonwealth countries, except nationals of India (see below) and nationals of Bangladesh, Cameroon, Fiji, Nigeria, Pakistan, Sri Lanka and Swaziland, who *do* require a visa for stays of up to three months;
(c) nationals of Bahrain, Hong Kong (SAR), Israel, Kuwait, Liechtenstein, Monaco, Norway, Oman, Qatar, San Marino, Saudi Arabia, Switzerland, Tunisia, Turkey, United Arab Emirates, Vatican City and Zimbabwe for stays of up to three months;
(d) nationals of China (PR), India, Jordan and Lebanon for touristic stays of up to 15 days;
(e) transit passengers continuing their journey to a third country within 24 hours provided holding valid onward or return documentation and not leaving the airport.
Types of visa and cost: *Tourist*, *Business* and *Social*, each available as single- or multiple-entry. Visas are issued free of charge.
Validity: *Tourist/Business* visas: Up to three months. Applications for extensions should be made to the relevant authority (see below).
Application to: Consulate (or consular section at Embassy or High Commission); see *Passport/Visa Information*.
Note: (a) Nationals of Argentina, Brazil, Chile and Paraguay can obtain a visa on arrival for stays of up to three months. (b) Nationals of Korea (Rep) can obtain a visa on arrival for stays of up to 16 days. (c) Nationals of Albania, Bulgaria, CIS, Comoro Islands, Fiji, Madagascar and Romania can obtain a visa on arrival for stays of up to two weeks. Extensions are possible. These visas can be issued from Sir Seewoosagur Ramgoolam International Airport or the Passport and Immigration Office in Port Louis (see *Passport/Visa Information*). (d) Nationals of Afghanistan, Algeria, Congo (Dem Rep), Iraq, Iran, Liberia, Libya, Nigeria, Sudan and Yemen should obtain a visa before travelling to Mauritius, even if they are in transit.
Application requirements: (a) Valid passport. (b) Completed application form. (c) Two passport-size photos. (d) Photocopy of passport page with date of birth. (e) Proof of sufficient funds (at least US$50 per day or equivalent, or at least US$100 per day for some other nationals). (f) Proof of accommodation such as hotel booking or letter of invitation. (g) Self-addressed stamped envelope. (h) Appropriate documents for the next destination, including return or onward tickets.
Working days required: Varies according to nationality of applicant. Most can be issued within seven days but can take up to one month.
Temporary residence: Residence permits are issued by the Passport and Immigration Officer, Sterling House, Lislet Geoffrey Street, Port Louis (tel: 210 9312-9). Work permits are necessary for those taking up employment.

PASSPORT/VISA INFORMATION

Mauritius High Commission in the UK
32-33 Elvaston Place, London SW7 5NW, UK
Tel: (020) 7581 0294.
E-mail: londonmhc@btinternet.com
Opening hours: Mon-Fri 0930-1200 (consular section); 0930-1700 (general enquiries).
Also deals with tourism enquiries.

Embassy of Mauritius in the USA
4301 Connecticut Avenue, Suite 441, NW, Washington, DC 20008, USA
Tel: (202) 244 1491/2.
Website: http://ncb.intnet.mu

Money

Currency: Mauritian Rupee (MUR) = 100 cents. Notes are in denominations of MUR2000, 1000, 500, 200, 100, 50 and 25. Coins are in denominations of MUR10, 5 and 1, and 50, 20, 10, and 5 cents.
Currency exchange: Available in banks and at bureaux de change. A better rate of exchange can be obtained on traveller's cheques than on cash.
Credit & debit cards: American Express, Diners Club, MasterCard and Visa are accepted by most banks, hotels, restaurants and tourist shops. Check with your credit, or debit card company for details of merchant acceptability and other services which may be available. ATMs are available.
Traveller's cheques: May be exchanged at banks, hotels and authorised dealers.
Currency restrictions: There are no limits on the import or export of local or foreign currency.
Banking hours: Mon-Thurs 0915-1515, Fri 0915-1530, Sat 0915-1115 (except for Bank of Mauritius). Some banks may open Mon-Fri 0900-1700. Banks are also open to coincide with the arrival and departure of international flights at the Sir Seewoosagur Ramgoolam Airport.
Exchange rate indicators:
Rate at time of publishing

£1.00=	MUR54.62
$1.00=	MUR30.94

Duty Free

The following goods may be imported into Mauritius by persons 18 and over without incurring customs duty:
200 cigarettes or 250g of tobacco products or 50 cigars; 1l of spirits and 2l of wine or beer; 250ml of eau de toilette and 100ml of perfume for personal use.
Restricted items: Vegetables, fruit, flowers, plants, bulbs and seeds must be declared (all require permit from the Ministry of Agriculture), as must firearms and ammunition. Imported animal products also require a permit and a health certificate from the country of origin.
Prohibited items: Sugarcane and related parts thereof, soil micro-organisms and invertebrate animals.

Public Holidays

Below are listed Public Holidays for the January 2006-June 2007 period.
2006: Jan 1-2 New Year. **Jan 29** Chinese New Year. **Feb 1** Abolition of Slavery Day. **Feb 11** Thaipoosam Cavadee. **Feb 26** Maha Shivaratri. **Mar 12** National Day. **Mar 30** Ougadi. **May 1** Labour Day. **Aug 15** Assumption of the Blessed Virgin Mary. **Aug 29** Ganesh Chaturthi. **Nov 2** Arrival of Indentured Labourers. **Oct 21** Diwali. **Oct 22-24** Eid al-Fitr (End of Ramadan). **Dec 25** Christmas Day.
2007: Jan 1-2 New Year. **Jan** *or* **Feb** Thaipoosam Cavadee. **Feb 1** Abolition of Slavery Day. **Feb 16** Maha Shivaratri. **Feb 18** Chinese New Year. **Mar 12** National Day. **Mar** *or* **Apr** Ougadi. **May 1** Labour Day.
Note: (a) Hindu festivals are timed according to local sightings of various phases of the moon. The dates given above are approximations. (b) There is a diversity of cultures in Mauritius, each with its own set of holidays. (c) Muslim festivals are timed according to local sightings of various phases of the moon and the dates given above are approximations. During the lunar month of Ramadan that precedes Eid al-Fitr, Muslims fast during the day and feast at night and normal business patterns may be interrupted. Some disruption may continue into Eid al-Fitr itself. Eid al-Fitr may last from two to 10 days, depending on the town

or region. For more information, see the *World of Islam* appendix. (d) Chinese festivals are declared according to local astronomical observations and it is often only possible to forecast the approximate time of their occurrence.

Health

	Special Precautions?	Certificate Required?
Yellow Fever	No	1
Cholera	No	No
Typhoid & Polio	2	N/A
Malaria	3	N/A

Note: *Regulations and requirements may be subject to change at short notice, and you are advised to contact your doctor well in advance of your intended date of departure. Any numbers in the chart refer to the footnotes below.*

1: A yellow fever vaccination certificate is required of travellers over one year of age arriving from infected areas. The Mauritius Government considers those countries and areas classified as yellow fever endemic to be infected.
2: Immunisation against typhoid and poliomyelitis is sometimes advised.
3: Malaria risk, exclusively in the benign *vivax* form, exists throughout the year in northern rural areas, except on Rodrigues Island.
Food & drink: Water used for drinking should have first been boiled or otherwise sterilised. Bottled water is readily available. Milk is unpasteurised and should be boiled. Powdered or tinned milk is available and is advised, but make sure that it is reconstituted with pure water. Avoid dairy products which are likely to have been made from unboiled milk. Vegetables should be cooked and fruit peeled.
Other risks: *Diarrhoeal diseases, giardiasis, dysentery* and *typhoid fever* are common. *African trypanosomiasis* (African sleeping sickness), *Rift Valley fever, bilharzia* (schistosomiasis), *leishmaniasis, dengue fever, filariasis* and *onchocerciasis* are present. Rickettsial infections can be contracted. *Meningococcal meningitis* is a risk from December to June. Avoid swimming and paddling in fresh water; swimming pools which are well chlorinated and maintained are safe. *Hepatitis A, B* and *E* occur.
Health care: Public medical facilities are numerous and of a high standard and there are several private clinics. All treatment at state-run hospitals is free for Mauritians, but foreign visitors have to pay. There is no reciprocal health agreement with the UK; health insurance is advised.
Note: For travellers applying for a working visa or permanent residence, an HIV test will be required.

Travel - International

AIR:

The national airline is *Air Mauritius (MK)* (website: www.airmauritius.com).
Approximate flight times: From Mauritius to *London* is 12 hours 15 minutes (non-stop).
Main airports: *Mauritius (MRU)* (Sir Seewoosagur Ramgoolam) is 48km (30 miles) southeast of Port Louis. *To/from the airport:* Taxis are available to the city (travel time – 45 minutes). *Facilities:* Duty free shops, banks/bureaux de change, snack bar, post office, shops and car hire.
Departure tax: None.
SEA:

Port Louis is the main port. It is primarily commercial but there is a limited passenger service to Madagascar, Réunion and Rodrigues Island.

Travel - Internal

AIR:

Air Mauritius operates daily flights connecting Plaisance Airport and Rodrigues Island (flight time – one hour 15 minutes). Three helicopters are available for transfers and for sightseeing tours. For more information contact *Air Mauritius Helicopter* (tel: 603 3754; email: helicopter@airmauritius.intnet.mu).
SEA:

Coraline sails once a week to Rodrigues Island from Port Louis. Contact Mauritius Shipping, Suite 417-418, St James Court, St Denis St, Port Louis, Mauritius (tel: 210 5944 *or* 6120).
ROAD:
There is a good network of paved roads covering the island. Traffic drives on the left. **Bus:** There are excellent and numerous bus services to all parts of the island. **Taxi:** These have white registration plates with black figures. Taxis are metered. **Car hire:** There are numerous car hire firms. Most require drivers to be over 23 years old. **Documentation:** International Driving Permit recommended, although a foreign licence is accepted. A

temporary driving licence is available from local authorities on presentation of a valid British or Northern Ireland driving licence.
URBAN:

Bus and taxi services are available in urban areas. Bicycles and boats are also available to hire.
Travel times: The following chart gives approximate travel times (in hours and minutes) from **Port Louis** to other major cities/towns in Mauritius.

	Road
Curepipe	0.20
Grand Bay	0.30
St Geran	1.00
Souillac	1.00

Travel Advice

Most visits to Mauritius are trouble-free but you should be aware of the global risk of indiscriminate international terrorist attacks, which could be against civilian targets, including places frequented by foreigners.
Drug trafficking carries severe penalties.
This advice is based on information provided by the Foreign and Commonwealth Office in the UK. It is correct at time of publishing. As the situation can change rapidly, visitors are advised to contact the following organisations for the latest travel advice:

British Foreign and Commonwealth Office
Tel: (0845) 850 2829.
Website: www.fco.gov.uk

US Department of State
Website: http://travel.state.gov/travel

Accommodation

HOTELS:

There is an abundance of hotels throughout the island and a number of smaller family holiday bungalows. From June to September, and during the Christmas season, reservations should be made in advance. A 10 per cent tax is added to all hotel bills. For more information, contact the Tourist Office (see *Top Things To See & Do*).

ACCOMMODATION INFORMATION

Association des Hôteliers et Restaurateurs de l'Ile Maurice (AHRIM)
Level 7, Travel House, Sir William Newton Street, Port Louis, Mauritius
Tel: 211 6105 *or* 637 3782 (desk at the airport).
Website: www.mauritius.net/ahrim

Top Things To See & Do

• Glimpse Mauritius' **colonial history** in the resplendent **Port Louis**, capital and main port of the country. Its **harbour** is sheltered by a semicircle of mountains. Off the main square, the palm-lined **Place d'Armes**, there are some particularly fine French colonial buildings, especially **Government House** (built in 1738) and the **Municipal Theatre**, built around the same time. South of Port Louis is **Le Réduit**, the French colonial residence of the President of Mauritius, set in magnificent gardens.
• Gawk at Mauritius' most famous bird, the **Dodo** – although, since the Dodo is famous for being extinct, you are best advised to head for Port Louis' **Natural History Museum** and its wonderful exhibit. Or, for birds besides the notorious Dodo, make your way to **Casela Bird Park**, set in the district of the **Rivière Noire**, which stretches over 20 acres of land and contains more than 140 varieties, amounting to 2500 birds. Specimens from the five continents may be seen there, but the main attraction is the **Mauritian Pink Pigeon**, which is one of the rarest birds in the world. Other attractions are the fish ponds, tortoises, monkeys and orchids (seasonal). Trees, streams and small cascades all add to the remarkably peaceful atmosphere.
• The **Domaine Les Pailles nature park** nestling at the foot of the **Moka mountain range** covers an area of 3000 acres (1214 hectares). Among the attractions are a natural spring, a spice garden, a replica of a sugar mill and an old rum distillery. Trips through the park in 4-wheel-drive vehicles or trains are available – or, particularly recommended, glide along through the landscape on a horse-drawn carriage. Alternatively, you may want to trek through this nature park. Indeed, there are many opportunities for trekking in the interior of the island. Many of the best walks are in the **Réserve Forrestière Macchabée** and **Rivière Noire National Park**.
• Southern Mauritius' **Domaine des Grands Bois** covers over 2000 acres (over 800 hectares) of magnificent parkland, rich in lush and exotic **fauna**. Ebony, eucalyptus, palm trees and wild orchids provide the backdrop for

stags, deer, monkeys and other **wildlife**. Near **Souillac**, in the wild south, **La Vanille Crocodile Park** breeds Nile crocodiles imported from Madagascar. The site offers a vast park with a nature walk through luxuriant forest studded with freshwater springs. A small zoo of animals found in the wild in Mauritius is also located here.
• To the north of Port Louis are the **Pamplemousses Gardens**. These, created at the end of the 18th century, are known to naturalists throughout the world for their large collection of indigenous and exotic plants, including the giant Victoria regia water lilies and many species of palm trees. Of particular interest is the talipot palm, which is said to flower once, after 60 years, and then die. There are also tortoises here, some of them over 100 years old.
• Visit the **Aquarium**, facing the calm water of the lagoon between **Pointe aux Piments** and **Trou aux Biches** and populated by 200 species of fish, invertebrates, live coral and sponges, all originating from the waters around the island. An open-circuit seawater cycle of 1 million litres (220,000 gallons) runs through the 36 tanks every day. The aquarium offers a unique opportunity to admire the colourful treasures of the Indian Ocean.
• Admire a spectacular view of the island – from the rim of a dramatic crater, the product of a now-extinct volcano, measuring 85m (280ft) deep and more than 180m (600ft) wide. The volcano in question is **Trou aux Cerfs**, between **Curepipe** and **Floreal**.
• The tiny, rugged, volcanic **Rodrigues Island** is situated 550km (340 miles) northeast of Mauritius, and is a beautiful and relaxing refuge for travellers. The island is covered in coconut palms, casuarina trees and pink-flowered bushes known as *vieilles filles* (spinsters). The capital, Port Mathurin, is the main port of entry and the 'Mauritius Pride' sails regularly to and from Mauritius. Here, you can truly believe you have stumbled across your own desert island. The island also has some lovely **hiking** country, with coastal and mountain walks, notably to the island's highest points, **Mount Limon** and **Mount Malartic**.
• Within a short distance of **Bois Cheri**, **Grand Bassin** rests in the crater of an extinct volcano, and this is one of the island's two natural **lakes**. Its beauty truly is humbling, which may explain why this is a place of **pilgrimage** for a large number of Mauritians of the Hindu faith.
• **Beaches**, **lagoons** and **inlets** around the coast offer plenty of opportunity for safe **swimming**, supplemented by hotel swimming pools. **Grand Baie**, north of Pamplemousses Gardens, is a popular beach for **diving**. Around this northern-coastline area are the beaches of **Baie du Tombeau**, **Pointe aux Piments**, famous for its underwater scenery, **Trou aux Biches**, with its fringe of *filaos* (casuarina) and coconut palms and its splendid Hindu temple, and **Choisy**, one of the most popular beaches on the island, offering facilities for safe bathing, **sailing**, **windsurfing** and **water-skiing**. Further good dive sites can be found around **Flic-en-Flac** on the west coast of Mauritius, and on Rodrigues Island. The Mauritian Scuba Diving Association can provide further information (tel: 454 0011; website: www.msda-cmas.org). Lying in the shadow of the **Rivière Noire Mountains**, **Tamarin** has a fine lagoon which is split in two by the Rivière Noire **estuary**. The bathing at this point is a big attraction, and amenities for surfing in the big ocean swells are available. **Péreybère** is a delightful little cove midway on the coast road between Grand Baie and **Cap Malheureux**. The deep, clear water makes it one of the very best bathing places on the whole island. Cap Malheureux is a fishing village in the extreme north, with a magnificent view of **Flat Island**, **Round Island** and **Gunner's Quoin**, which are islands of volcanic origin, rising from the light-green sea. Further along the coast is **Grand Gaube**, a charming fishing village where fishermen have earned a well-deserved reputation for their skill in the making of sailing craft and of **deep-sea fishing**. Roches Noires/Poste Lafayette are both favoured seaside resorts, especially in the hotter months, because of the fresh prevailing winds that blow almost all the year round from the sea. **Belle Mare** is a beautiful white sandy beach with fine bathing. The coast, with its white sweep of sands at **Palmar** and **Trou d'Eau Douce**, stretches out lazily to **Grand Port**, a quaint little village by the sea. There, the beach narrows and the road follows the coastline closely to **Mahébourg**. **Pointe d'Esny**, the adjoining white sandy beach with its string of bungalows, leads to Blue Bay. In a semicircle of filao trees lies one of the finest bathing spots on the island. Situated on the southeast coast, not far from **Mahébourg**, **Blue Bay** offers a fine stretch of white sandy beach, and a deep, clear, light-blue bathing pool.

TOURIST INFORMATION

Mauritius Tourism Promotion Authority in the UK
32 Elvaston Place, London SW7 5NW, UK
Tel: (020) 7584 3666.
Website: www.mauritiustourism.co.uk

Entertainment

FOOD & DRINK: Standards of cuisine, whether French, Creole, Indian, Chinese or English, are generally very high but fruit, meat, vegetables and even fresh seafood are often in short supply and restaurants must usually depend on imports.
National specialities:
- Venison (in season).
- *Camarons* (freshwater prawns) in hot sauces.
- Octopus.
- Fresh pineapple with chilli sauce.
- Rice with curry.
- *Dholl purri* is a wheat pancake stuffed with *dholl* and dipped in tomato sauce.
- *Samosas*.

National drinks:
- Rum.
- Beer.
- *Alouda* (almond drink).
- Fresh coconut milk.

Things to know: Waiter service is normal in restaurants and bars.
Tipping: 10 per cent is usual in most hotels and restaurants. Tips are not customary for taxi drivers.
NIGHTLIFE: In Grand Baie and some towns there are discos and nightclubs with music and dancing. Rivière Noire is a Creole fishermen's district where *sega* dancing is especially lively on Saturday nights. *Sega* troupes give performances at most hotels. Gamblers are lavishly catered for; casinos in the island's hotels are amongst the island's attractions.
SHOPPING: The Central Market in Port Louis is full of beautifully displayed goods, including fruit, vegetables, spices, fish, meat and handicrafts. Island crafts include jewellery, Chinese and Indian jade, silks, basketry and pottery. Shopping centres are located at Quatre-Bornes and Rose-Hill. There is no duty payable on a number of products, including textiles. Shop signs may be in English, French or Chinese. Beside the Museum in Mahébourg, on the southeast coast of the island, is a handicraft village.
Shopping hours: Ranges from Mon-Sat 0930-1930. Some shops are open until 1200 on Sundays and public holidays. There are no shops open on Rose-Hill, Curepipe and Quatre-Bornes on Thursday afternoons.

Business

- **GDP:** US$6 billion.
- **Main imports:** Manufactured goods, capital equipment, foodstuff, petroleum products and chemicals.
- **Main exports:** Clothing and textiles, sugar, cut flowers and molasses.
- **Main trade partners:** Bahrain, China, France, India, Italy, Japan, Madagascar, South Africa, UK and USA.

ECONOMY: Sugar dominates Mauritius' agricultural economy: raw and processed sugar accounts for one-quarter of the island's export earnings. Tobacco and tea are the other main cash crops. Since independence in 1968, the government has deliberately sought to develop the industrial and service components of the economy. The island's industrial capacity is centred on a number of Export Processing Zones whose main products are clothing and textiles, consumer and industrial electronics, flowers and jewellery. Mauritius' service economy is based on tourism and financial services. Tourism is well established and now worth over US$500 million annually. The growth of financial services arose from a government initiative implemented in 1989; as a result, the island has since attracted more than US$1 billion of investment, mainly from South Africa and the Indian subcontinent. The overall economy grew at 4.6 per cent in 2004.
The Government's economic policy aims to counter the threat to the two largest sectors of the economy – sugar and textiles – from new regulations introduced by the World Trade Organization. The centrepiece of its strategy is the creation of a custom-built 'cyber-city', based on similar development in India, using high-speed communications links to offer e-commerce and financial transactions. Mauritius is a member of the Indian Ocean Commission, which promotes regional economic cooperation, and of the Southern African Development Community.
BUSINESS ETIQUETTE: Suits are often worn in business circles. **Office hours:** Mon-Fri 0900-1600, Sat 0900-1200 (some offices only).

COMMERCIAL INFORMATION

Mauritius Chamber of Commerce and Industry
3 Royal Street, Port Louis, Mauritius
Tel: 208 3301.
Website: www.mcci.org

Mexico

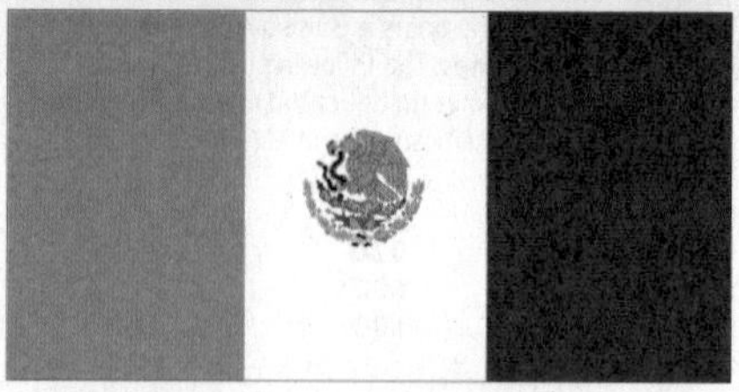

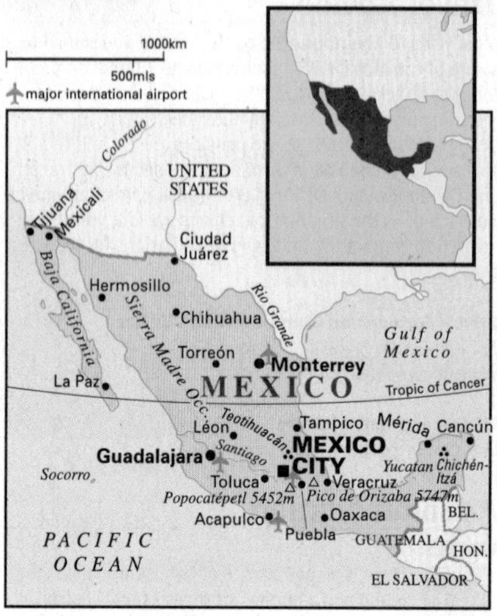

Location: Central America

Time: Central Standard Time: GMT - 6. (GMT - 5 from first Sunday in April to last Sunday in October.)
Mountain Standard Time: GMT - 7 (GMT - 6 from first Sunday in April to last Sunday in October.)
Pacific Standard Time: GMT - 8 (Pacific Time). (GMT - 7 from first Sunday in April to last Sunday in October.)

Overview

Almost 500 years on, the impact of Spanish conquistadores can be seen in the tall, ornate churches that crown the hillsides and plazas of Mexico's cities and whitewashed walls of haciendas. But traces of earlier inhabitants remain in the remarkable temples and pyramids at Palenque and Teotihuacán, and in the traditions of dozens of indigenous cultures. Accompanying it all are the subtle spices of Mexico's famous tortillas, *tamales* and enchiladas, washed down with bold red wines and heady tequila and mescal.
Mexico's earliest known civilisation was the Olmec in the second century BC, a Mayan culture advanced in religion, architecture and mathematics, who reached their height between AD 600-900. The Toltecs were the predominant civilisation of this time. Known for their fine architecture, elegant speech and intellectual pursuits, they were the ancestors of the famous Aztecs. In 1519, a Spaniard named Hernan Cortés arrived from Cuba with a 550-strong crew. The Aztec Empire controlled vast territories from the Yucatán peninsula to the Pacific, with over 370 individual nations under their authority. Ruling from their capital city, Tenochtitlan, the Aztecs demanded heavy tribute from their subjects, which caused some to side with Cortés. The other factor on Cortés' side was the lucky coincidence that 1519 was the exact year when legend had it that the Aztec god, Quetzalcoatl, would return from the east and so Cortés was mistaken for a god. After two years of fighting, the Aztecs were defeated. Mexico later achieved independence after the wars of 1810-21.
In Mexico City is the Plaza de las Tres Culturas, which celebrates the three major cultures that have shaped Mexico: there are Aztec ruins, the 17th-century colonial church of San Diego and several late 20th-century buildings. Mexico's capital city is one of speeding VW taxis and bustling marketplaces, countered by colourful Aztec dancers and *panaderías* with freshly baked pastries. Mexico City has a peculiar charm, possessing Mexico in microcosm: pollution and poverty intermingled with streets named after philosophers. Mexico City itself provides a contrast with the country's arresting topography: its Sierre Madre mountains, volcanoes, national parks and beaches.
History comes to life in Mexico: the scars of recent history are still apparent. In 1847, Mexico was forced to cede half of its territory to the USA. In 1861, Benito Juárez was elected President and announced a two-year moratorium on the payment of foreign debts, causing a series of civil wars and conflicts with European and US Governments for the next 30 years. Later came Porfirio D'az's dictatorship of 1876-1910, revolutions and coups, and the one-party state of the PRI until the mid-1970s. Mexico's largely oil-based economy brought Mexico to the verge of bankruptcy in the 1970s/80s due to corruption and mismanagement, a collapse of oil prices, and political crisis. Some areas of Mexico are, indeed, still blighted by crime and destitution. But, for the most part, Mexico remains a fascinating amalgam of antiquity and forward-looking vigour.

General Information

AREA: 1,959,248 sq km (758,449 sq miles).
POPULATION: 106.4 million (UN, 2005).
POPULATION DENSITY: 54.3 per sq km.
CAPITAL: Mexico City. **Population:** 21 million (2003 estimate).
GEOGRAPHY: Mexico is at the southern extremity of North America and is bordered to the north by the USA, northwest by the Gulf of California, west by the Pacific, south by Guatemala and Belize, and east by the Gulf of Mexico and the Caribbean. Mexico's geographical features range from swamp to desert, and from tropical lowland jungle to high alpine vegetation. Over half the country has an altitude above 1000m (3300ft). The central land mass is a plateau flanked by ranges of mountains to the east and west that lie roughly parallel to the coast. The northern area of this plateau is arid and thinly populated, and occupies 40 per cent of the total area of Mexico. The southern area is crossed by a range of volcanic mountains running from Cape Corrientes in the west through the Valley of Mexico to Veracruz in the east, and includes the magnificent volcanoes of Cofre de Perote, Ixtaccíhuatl, Matlalcueyetl, Nevado de Toluca, Orizaba and Popocatépetl. This is the heart of Mexico and where almost half of the population lives. To the south, the land falls away to the sparsely populated Isthmus of Tehuantepec whose slopes and flatlands support both commercial and subsistence agriculture. In the east, the Gulf Coast and the Yucatán peninsula are flat and receive over 75 per cent of Mexico's rain. The most productive agricultural region in Mexico is the northwest, while the Gulf Coast produces most of Mexico's oil and sulphur. Along the northwest coast, opposite the peninsula of Baja California, and to the southeast along the coast of Bahía de Campeche and the Yucatán peninsula, the lowlands are swampy with coastal lagoons.
GOVERNMENT: Republic since 1917. Gained independence from Spain in 1821. **Head of State and Government:** President Vicente Fox Quesada since 2000.
Recent history: Carlos Salinas de Gortari's first term of office began in 1988. The new Government embarked on a major economic reform programme comprising a package of devaluation, tax reform, privatisation and deregulation. The programme, dubbed 'Cactus Thatcherism', also included an application to join GATT (the General Agreement on Tariffs and Trade, forerunner of the World Trade Organisation) and the instigation by Salinas of a free-trade treaty with the USA and Canada. This eventually led to the creation of the North American Free Trade Agreement (NAFTA), which was ratified by the three countries during 1993. The Salinas Government also improved its standing in Washington by cracking down on drug trafficking. Popular as all this was overseas, Mexicans saw little benefit as living standards for most people fell sharply. The traditional political opposition was all but emasculated by PRI's stranglehold over the country, but at the beginning of 1994, in the impoverished southern state of Chiapas, an armed insurrection started with land reform at the heart of its aims.

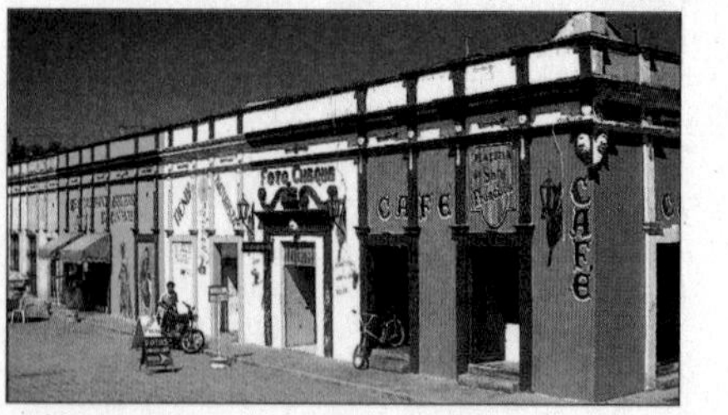

Credit: ©Mexico Tourism Board

The guerrillas described themselves as 'Zapatistas' (after Mexican revolutionary hero Emiliano Zapata, who also fought primarily on the issue of land ownership). The Mexican Government initially waged a classic counter-insurgency war, using a mixture of force and incentives on the largely pro-guerrilla peasant population. This was a problem that Salinas was happy to leave to his successor, Ernesto Zedillo Ponce de Leon, who won the next round of Presidential elections, held in August 1994. After six years of struggle and bouts of negotiation, the Zapatistas and the Government reached a deal – the San Andreas accord – conceding autonomy to the region. Whether or not the Government had any intention of honouring the agreement is unclear: it certainly met furious opposition from within PRI and the military, and none of its provisions were put into effect. Disillusioned, the Zapatistas returned to guerrilla war and waited for a more receptive administration to take office. Meanwhile the *Partido Revolucionario Institucional* (Institutional Revolutionary Party, PRI) had other matters on its mind. In 2000, the PRI had overtaken the Soviet Communist Party's 70-year longevity record for a ruling political party. But it was deeply unpopular and, that very year, it lost control of both the Presidency and the National Assembly to the centre-right *Partido Acción Nacional* (PAN, National Action Party). Vicente Fox Quesada took over the Presidency. Fox re-engaged with the Zapatistas, and some elements of the San Andreas deal have now been put into effect. Fox has also managed to open up one of the murkier episodes in recent Mexican history. During the 1960s and 70s, as in Argentina, Chile and Brazil, the security forces had engaged in a 'dirty war' against trades unionists and activists: thousands were detained without trial, tortured, murdered or 'disappeared'. Some perpetrators are now being brought to account. Despite this, economic problems have undermined Fox's popularity and, as he reached the middle of his six-year term, the PAN lost control of the National Assembly to the PRI.

Mexico is a federal Republic with 31 states and one federal district. The bicameral National Congress is elected by universal adult suffrage. The 64 members of the Senate (two per state plus two for the federal district) serve for a term of six years. The 500-seat Chamber of Deputies consists of members elected for three years, 300 from single-member constituencies with the remaining 200 allocated to minority parties on the basis of proportional representation. The President, who appoints a Cabinet, has executive power and serves a term congruent with that of the Senate. Each state has its own Governor and elected Chamber of Deputies.

LANGUAGE: Spanish is the official language (spoken by more than 90 per cent). English is widely spoken. 8 per cent speak indigenous languages, of which Nátinate is most widely spoken.

RELIGION: 89 per cent Roman Catholic, five per cent Protestant and six per cent other denominations.

ELECTRICITY: 110 volts AC, 60Hz. US two-pin (flat) plugs are usual.

SOCIAL CONVENTIONS: Handshaking is the most common form of greeting. Casual sportswear is acceptable for daytime dress throughout the country. At beach resorts, dress is very informal for men and women. In Mexico City, however, dress tends to be smart in elegant restaurants and hotel dining rooms. Smoking is unrestricted except where notified. Mexicans regard relationships and friendships as the most important thing in life next to religion and they are not afraid to show their emotions. A large Mexican family always seems to find room for one more and a visitor who becomes friends with a Mexican will invariably be made part of the family. Visitors should always remember that local customs and traditions are important.

Climate

Climate varies according to altitude. Coastal areas and lowlands (*tierra caliente*) are hot and steamy with high humidity, while the central plateau is temperate even in winter. The climate of the inland highlands is mostly mild, but sharp changes in temperature occur between day and night. The cold lands (*tierra fría*) lie above 2000m (6600ft). Rainfall varies greatly from region to region. Only the Sierra Madre Oriental, the Isthmus of Tehuantepec and the state of Chiapas in the far south receive any appreciable amount of rain during the year, with the wet season running between June and September. All other areas have rainless seasons, while the northern and central areas of the central plateau are dry and arid. There is some snow in the north in winter. The dry season runs from October to May.

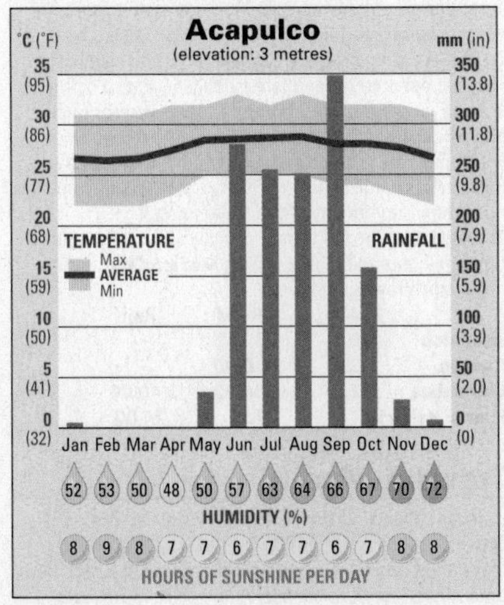
°C (°F)
Acapulco
(elevation: 3 metres)
mm (in)
TEMPERATURE
Max
AVERAGE
Min
RAINFALL
Jan Feb Mar Apr May Jun Jul Aug Sep Oct Nov Dec
52 53 50 48 50 57 63 64 66 67 70 72
HUMIDITY (%)
8 9 8 7 7 6 7 7 6 7 8 8
HOURS OF SUNSHINE PER DAY

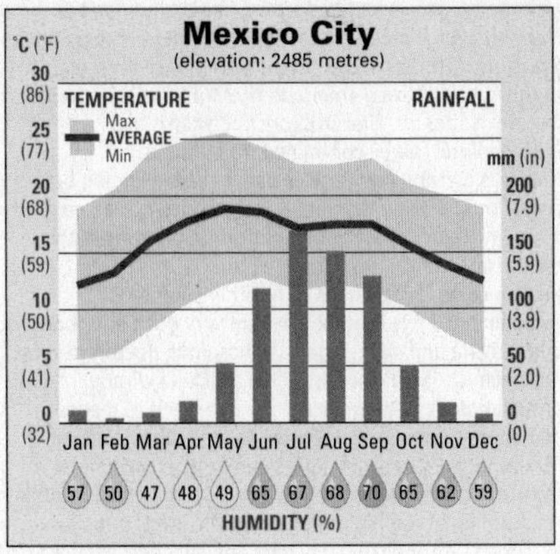
°C (°F)
Mexico City
(elevation: 2485 metres)
TEMPERATURE
RAINFALL
Max
AVERAGE
Min
mm (in)
Jan Feb Mar Apr May Jun Jul Aug Sep Oct Nov Dec
57 50 47 48 49 65 67 68 70 65 62 59
HUMIDITY (%)

Communications

Telephone: IDD is available. Country code: 52. Long-distance calls are very expensive.

Mobile telephone: Roaming agreements exist with a few international mobile phone companies. Handsets can be hired. Coverage is variable.

Internet: Internet is available in all regions, particularly the main tourist areas.

Post: Airmail to Europe takes about six days. Surface mail is slow. Within the capital, there is an immediate delivery (*entrega inmediata*) service, which usually takes two or three days.

MEDIA: Press: The major daily newspapers published in Spanish are *Esto*, *Excélsior* (website: www.excelsior.com.mx), *EL Financiero* (website: www.elfinanciero.com.mx), *El Heraldo de México*, *Le Jornada* (website: www.jornadaunam.mx), *La Prensa* and *El Universal* (website: www.eluniversal.com.mx). The English-language papers available are *Mexico City Times*, *New York Times* (website: www.nytimes.com), *The News* and *USA Today* (website: www.usatoday.com).

TV: *Televisa* operates four networks throughout Mexico. *TV Azteca* operates two networks and local stations.

Radio: *Grupo ACIR* has stations in Mexico City and across the country. *MVS Radio* operates in the capital and elsewhere. *Grupo Radio Centro* operates a large network of stations.

Passport/Visa

	Passport Required?	Visa Required?	Return Ticket Required?
Full British	Yes	No	Yes
Australian	Yes	No	Yes
Canadian	Yes	No	Yes
USA	Yes	No	Yes
Other EU	Yes	No	Yes
Japanese	Yes	No	Yes

Note: *Regulations and requirements may be subject to change at short notice, and you are advised to contact the appropriate diplomatic or consular authority before finalising travel arrangements. Any numbers in the chart refer to the footnotes below.*

Note: Non-compliance with visa regulations will result in fines and transportation (at the carrier's expense) to the visitor's country of origin.

PASSPORTS: Passport valid for at least six months after date of entry required by all.

VISAS: Required by all except the following, who can obtain a Blue Tourist Card for touristic purposes from their airline on direct flights, at port of entry, or from the Mexican Consulate before travelling:

(a) nationals of countries referred to in the chart above for 180 days (except nationals of Australia, Austria, Cyprus, Czech Republic, Estonia, France, Greece, Hungary, Italy, Latvia, Lithuania, Malta, Poland, Portugal, Slovak Republic and Slovenia who can stay for up to 90 days);

(b) nationals of Andorra, Argentina, Bermuda, Chile, Costa Rica, Liechtenstein, New Zealand, Norway, San Marino, Singapore, Switzerland and Uruguay for stays of up to 180 days;

(c) nationals of Hong Kong (SAR), Iceland, Israel, Korea (Rep) and Monaco for up to 90 days;

(d) nationals of Venezuela for stays of up to 30 days.

Note: (a) Applicants for Blue Tourist Cards should have a valid passport, return/onward ticket and proof of financial means. (b) Tourist Cards must be kept by the visitor during the entire length of stay as they will have to be presented and stamped on leaving. (c) Nationals of the following countries travelling to Mexico on business on one entry and for less than 30 days do not need a business visa: Argentina, Australia, Austria, Belgium, Canada, Costa Rica, Chile, Czech Republic, Denmark, Finland, France, Germany, Greece, Hungary, Italy, Israel, Ireland, Japan, Luxembourg, New Zealand, Norway, Poland, Portugal, Korea (Rep), Singapore, Spain, Sweden, Switzerland, The Netherlands, UK, USA and Uruguay.

Types of visa and cost: *Tourist*: £21.10. *Business*: £57.40. Visa prices fluctuate according to the exchange rate.

Validity: *Tourist*: Up to six months (single-entry, but double- and multiple-entry in particular circumstances). *Business Visitor*: Up to one year. Visas must be used within 90 days of issue. Extensions for visas must be submitted 30 days before the expiration of the allocated visa.

Application requirements: *Tourist*: (a) Valid passport with photocopy. (b) Completed application form. (c) One passport-size photo. (d) Fee (payable by cash or postal order only). (e) Proof of sufficient funds (eg last three bank statements and letter stating current salary, or original letter from the person who financially supports the traveller. (f) Letter specifying the purpose of the trip and the dates of entry and departure. (g) Dependent on nationality, either reference letter from employer/educator or original and photocopy of return, or onward, ticket. (h) Proof of permanent residence in country where application is being made. *Business Visitor Carnet (FM3)*: (a)-(b) and, (c) Two identical passport-size photos. (d) Letter from applicant's employer accepting financial responsibility to cover the applicant's stay, which also states the nature of business to be undertaken. (e) Letter from company in Mexico to be visited, explaining purpose of visit. (f) Fee (payable in cash, postal order or company cheque). (g) Postal applications must be accompanied by a stamped, self-addressed envelope with recorded delivery.

Note: a) Non-British nationals seeking to visit Mexico on business are advised to check with the Consulate regarding visa requirements and fees. (b) Vaccinations against cholera and yellow fever are required by the Mexican Immigration Office if the visitor has been in an infected area two weeks prior to entry into Mexico. They are not required for transit passengers remaining in the airport.

Application to: Consulate (or consular section at Embassy); see *Passport/Visa Information*.

Working days required: Two in person; one week by post. Applications should be made in good time as it may take up to four weeks for some nationals.

Temporary residence: Application should be made to the Mexican Home Office with proof of sufficient funds to cover length of stay without working. Contact the Consulate (or consular section at Embassy) for further details; see *Passport/Visa Information*.

PASSPORT/VISA INFORMATION

Mexican Embassy in the UK
16 St George Street, Hanover Square,
London W1S 1LX, UK
Tel: (020) 7499 8586 *or* 7201 0961-3 (visa section).
Website: www.embamex.co.uk

Mexican Consulate in the UK
8 Halkin Street, London SW1X 7DW, UK
Tel: (020) 7235 6393 *or* (0906) 550 8969 (recorded visa information; calls cost £1 per minute).
Website: www.mexicanconsulate.org.uk
Opening hours: Mon-Fri 0930-1300.

Mexican Embassy in the USA
1911 Pennsylvania Avenue, NW,
Washington DC 20006
Tel: (202) 728 1600.
Website: www.embassyofmexico.org

Mexican Consulate in the USA
2827 16th Street, NW, Washington DC 20009, USA
Tel: (202) 736 1000/2.
Website: www.embassyofmexico.org

Money

Currency: New Peso (MXN; symbol ME$) = 100 centavos. Notes are in denominations of ME$500, 200, 100, 50 and 20. Coins are in denominations of ME$20, 10, 5, 2 and 1, and 50, 20, 10 and 5 centavos.

Currency exchange: Currency may only be exchanged at authorised banks. The exchange rate of the Mexican peso against Sterling and other hard currencies has, in recent years, been subject to considerable fluctuation.

Credit & debit cards: MasterCard and Visa are the two most widely accepted cards. American Express and Diners Club are accepted on a smaller scale. Check with your credit or debit card company for details of merchant acceptability and other services which may be available. There is a Government tax of 6 per cent on such transactions. There are ATMs nationwide.

Traveller's cheques: Traveller's cheques or letters of credit in US Dollars issued by well-known banks or travel organisations are readily negotiable in banks and hotels. Sterling traveller's cheques are not readily negotiable except at head offices of banks in the capital, and may be subject to a considerable discount. To avoid additional exchange rate charges, travellers are advised to take traveller's cheques in US Dollars.

Currency restrictions: Local currency may be imported and exported up to the equivalent of US$10,000; larger amounts must be declared. The import of foreign currency is unlimited, provided declared. Foreign currency may be exported up to the amount imported and declared. The export of gold coins is prohibited.

Banking hours: Mon-Fri 0900-1600; some banks are open longer hours and others are open on Saturday afternoon.

Exchange rate indicators:
Rate at time of publishing
£1.00=   ME$19.03
$1.00=   ME$10.76

Duty Free

The following goods may be imported into Mexico by persons over 18 years of age without incurring customs duty:

400 cigarettes or 25 cigars or 200g of pipe tobacco; 3l of wine, spirits or beer; a reasonable amount of perfume or eau de toilette or lotions for personal use; a photo, movie or video camera for non-residents and up to 12 unexposed rolls of film or video cassettes; goods (not including beer, alcoholic drinks and tobacco) up to the value of US$300 or equivalent, or US$50 per person if travelling into Mexico by land.

Prohibited items: Any uncanned food, pork or pork products; certain fish and fish products; plants, fruits, vegetables, flowers, seeds (except if special permit is obtained prior to arrival) and their products; insecticide. Canned food is permitted, provided it is not pork or pork products. Firearms and ammunition need an import permit. Archaeological relics may not be exported.

Public Holidays

Below are listed the Public Holidays for the January 2006-June 2007 period.
2006: Jan 1 New Year's Day. **Feb 5** Constitution Day. **Mar 21** Birthday of Benito Juárez. **Apr 13-16** Easter. **May 1** Labour Day. **May 5** Anniversary of Battle of Puebla. **Sep 16** Independence Day. **Oct 12** Día de la Raza (Columbus Day). **Nov 2** Día de los Muertos (Day of the Dead). **Nov 20** Anniversary of the Mexican Revolution of 1910. **Dec 12** Day of Our Lady of Guadalupe. **Dec 25** Christmas Day. **2007: Jan 1** New Year's Day. **Feb 5** Constitution Day. **Mar 21** Birthday of Benito Juárez. **Apr 5-8** Easter. **May 1** Labour Day. **May 5** Anniversary of Battle of Puebla.

Note: (a) In addition there are many local holidays. For details, contact the Mexico Tourism Board. (b) Holidays falling at the weekend are not celebrated on the previous or following weekday.

Health

	Special Precautions?	Certificate Required?
Yellow Fever	No	No
Cholera	1	No
Typhoid & Polio	2	N/A
Malaria	3	N/A

Note: *Regulations and requirements may be subject to change at short notice, and you are advised to contact your doctor well in advance of your intended date of departure. Any numbers in the chart refer to the footnotes below.*

1: Cholera is a risk in Mexico.
2: Immunisation against typhoid is sometimes recommended.
3: Malaria risk, almost exclusively in the benign *vivax* form, exists in rural areas of the following states (in decreasing order of risk): Chiapas, Quintano Roo, Sinaloa, Tabasco, Chihuahua, Durango, Nayarit, Oaxaca, Sonora, Campeche, Guerrero, Michoacán and Jalisco. The recommended prophylaxis is chloroquine.

Food & drink: Water supplied in bottles and from taps marked 'drinking/sterilised water' in hotels can be drunk without precautions. All other water should be regarded as being potentially contaminated. Water used for drinking, brushing teeth or making ice should have first been boiled or otherwise sterilised. Milk in major cities, hotels and resorts is pasteurised. Otherwise, milk is unpasteurised and should first be boiled. Powdered or tinned milk is available and is advised, but make sure that it is reconstituted with pure water. Avoid dairy products which are likely to have been made from unboiled milk. Only eat well-cooked meat and fish, preferably served hot. Pork, salad and mayonnaise may carry increased risk. Vegetables should be cooked and fruit peeled.

Other risks: *Visceral* and *mucutaneous leishmaniasis* occur. *Dysenteries* and *diarrhoeal diseases* are present.

Hepatitis A occurs and *hepatitis E* has been reported. *Dengue fever* is predominant in the northern border states. Cases of *gnathostomiasis* (roundworm) have been reported in the Acapulco area. *American trypanosomiasis* (chagas disease) is present. *Filariasis, onchocerciasis* and *leishmaniasis* can be contracted from insects. *Rabies* is present. For those at high risk, vaccination before arrival should be considered. If you are bitten, seek medical advice without delay. For more information, consult the *Health* appendix.

Health care: Comprehensive health insurance is recommended. Medical facilities are very good and there are both private and state-organised hospitals, doctors, clinics and chemists. Medicines are often available without prescriptions, and pharmacists are permitted to diagnose and treat minor ailments. Owing to the high altitude of Mexico City, visitors may take some time to acclimatise to the atmosphere, particularly since its geographical location results in an accumulation of smog. The levels of pollution in Mexico City are extremely high and are considered a health threat, so precautions should be taken.

Travel - International

AIR:

The national airlines are *Aeroméxico (AM)* (website: www.aeromexico.com) and *Mexicana (MX)* (website: www.mexicana.com).

Approximate flight times: From Mexico City to *London* is 11 hours 40 minutes; to *Los Angeles* is six hours 30 minutes; to *New York* is four hours 40 minutes; to *Singapore* is 22 hours 45 minutes; and to *Sydney* is 19 hours.

Main airports: *Mexico City (MEX)* (Benito Juárez) (website: www.aeropuertosmexico.com) is 13km (8 miles) south of the city. *To/from the airport:* Buses run to and from the city at regular intervals (travel time – 35 minutes). Underground trains and taxis are also available. *Facilities:* Duty free shops, restaurants, bank/bureau de change, bar, snack bar, chemist, shops, tourist information, left luggage, post office, first aid (with vaccinations for cholera and yellow fever available) and car hire.

Guadalajara (GDL) (Miguel Hidalgo) is 20km (12 miles) southeast of the city (travel time – 35 minutes). *Facilities:* Restaurant, bar, snack bar, bank, post office and shops. *Acapulco (ACA)* (General Juan N Alvarez) is 26km (16 miles) southeast of the city (travel time – 35 minutes). *To/from the airport:* Coaches and taxi services run to the city. *Facilities:* Restaurant, bank, post office and car hire. *Monterrey (MTY)* (General Mariano Escobedo) is 24km (15 miles) northeast of the city (travel time – 45 minutes). *To/from the airport:* Coach and taxi services run to the city. *Facilities:* Restaurant, bar, bank, post office, shops and car hire.

Departure tax: Departure tax US$13, airport tax US$8.50 (varies according to airport). Children under two years and transit passengers are exempt. The tax is sometimes included in the price of the ticket.

SEA/RIVER:

Main ports: *Acapulco, Cabo San Lucas, Cozumel, Manzanillo, Mazatlán, Puerto Vallarta, Tampico* and *Zihuatanejo/Ixtapa.* Regular passenger ships run from the USA and South America. *Carnival, Celebrity, Fred Olsen Cruise Lines, P&O Cruises, Princess Cruises* and *Royal Caribbean* all operate cruise services to Mexico. There are also riverboat services from Flores and Tikal (Guatemala) to Palenque, Chiapas in Mexico; enquire locally for details.

RAIL:

Railway connections with Mexico can be made from any city in the USA or Canada. All trains are provided with pullman sleepers, restaurant cars, lounge observation and club cars. Most trains are air-conditioned.

ROAD:

Main points of entry from the USA are Mexicali from San Diego; Nogales from Phoenix/Tucson; El Paso/Ciudad Juárez from Tucson and Alberquerque; Eagle Pass/Piedras Negras from Del Río, San Angelo and El Paso; Laredo/Nuevo Laredo from Houston, San Antonia and Del Río; and Brownsville/Matamoros from Houston and Galveston. From Guatemala, there are two main roads into Mexico. The Pan American Highway crosses into Mexico from Guatemala and continues through Central America and South America. There is also a road border crossing point from Belize near Chetumal and Corozal.

Travel - Internal

AIR:

There is an excellent network of daily scheduled services between principal commercial centres operated by *Aero California, Aeroméxico* and *Mexicana.* Many of the smaller airports also have capacity for large planes and some international flights. Flights between Mexico City and Guadalajara take about 70 minutes, and those between Mexico City and Monterrey about 80 minutes.

Departure tax: Departure tax US$13, airport tax US$8.50 (varies according to airport).

SEA:

Steamer ferries operate regularly between Mazatlán and La Paz (Baja California) daily; between Guaymas and Santa Rosalia, across the Gulf of California; between La Paz and Topolobampo three or four times weekly; and from Puerto Vallarta to Cabo San Lucas twice-weekly. Some west coast cruises include Pacific ports such as Mazatlán, Puerto Vallarta and Acapulco. There are also regular ferries from the mainland to the Caribbean Islands of Isla Mujeres and Cozumel.

RAIL:

Mexico has a good railway network and trains link all the main towns in the country. A spectacular route is the *Chihuahua-Pacific Railway* that runs between Chihuahua and Los Mochis and includes a stop in the Copper Canyon region (travel time- 14 to 16 hours). However, most people travel by bus since it is considerably faster and provides a more extensive service. Children under five travel free, provided they are accompanied by a parent. Children aged five to 11 pay half-fare.

ROAD:

Traffic drives on the right. Only half of Mexico's road network is paved. A toll is charged for use of the expressways, which are managed by *Caminos y Puentes Federales de Ingresos y Servicios Conexos.* The amount you will pay on a particular toll road depends on how far you travel along it; payment booths are set out at major towns or turn-off points. Every time you go through a toll booth you pay a fee covering the cost to the next toll booth. It is advised to pay in cash, as only some booths have credit/debit card payment facilities. Rest areas at toll sites also provide ambulance and breakdown services. An organisation known as 'Angeles Verdes' (Green Angels) has 15 vehicles providing breakdown assistance to tourists on the highways free of charge except for petrol, oil and spare parts. Car use in Mexico City is restricted so as to reduce pollution. The last digit of the car number plate determines when that car *cannot* be driven. **Bus:** Mexico is linked by a good and very economical bus system. There are first-class and deluxe coaches as well as ordinary buses. First-class buses only travel on toll roads, making the journey quicker and more comfortable. Central bus terminals in major cities provide service and information on fares and schedules. **Car hire:** Self-drive cars are available at airports, city centres and resorts. When driving around Mexico it is advised that car doors and windows are locked and closed at all times, especially at traffic lights.

Documentation: An International Driving Permit or a full British driving licence is required for locally registered vehicles. Minimum driving age is 18. Payment is by credit card. Mexican car insurance is essential and can usually be purchased at the borders. It is relatively cheap and drivers only need a copy of their current car registration and a valid driving licence.

URBAN:

There is an excellent and cheap metro system in Mexico City with frequent trains and flat fares. However, it is often crowded and some familiarity with the city is necessary to use it successfully. The metro opens Mon-Sat at 0600 (Sun 0700) and closes at about midnight; there is an unlimited distance fare. There is also a small tramway network, and extensive bus and trolley bus services. The latter system has recently been modernised, and also has a flat fare. There is a state-run bus and trolley bus service in Guadalajara, with trolley buses running in tunnels, and also extensive private bus services.

Taxi: Four different types of taxi operate in Mexico City. Yellow and white taxis (usually Volkswagens) are metered, as are orange taxis (*sitio*), which are available at taxi-stands. These charge slightly more, and it is advisable to agree on the fare before starting the journey. *Turismo* taxis with English-speaking drivers are available outside main hotels. They are not metered and fares should be agreed before starting journey as rates can be excessive. *Peseros* (green and white) are share-taxis travelling on fixed routes, for which fares are charged according to the distance travelled. Radio taxis charge double fee but are very secure. Tipping is not compulsory for any of the taxi services.

Travel times: The following chart gives approximate travel times (in hours and minutes) from **Mexico City** to other major cities/towns in Mexico.

	Air	Road	Rail
Acapulco	0.35	3.30	-
Cancún	2.15	30.00	-
Chihuahua	2.15	34.00	40.00
Puerto Vallarta		1.55	14.00

Travel Advice

Hurricane Wilma hit the Yucatan Peninsula in Mexico between 21-23 October 2005, including Cancún, Riviera Maya and Cozumel. Cancún airport, many hotels and most other tourist facilities are operating normally. For latest updates issued by the Mexican authorities on services and hotel availability, please consult the website www.caribemexicano.gob.mx.

Most visits to Mexico are trouble-free, but be warned that street crime and kidnappings are on the increase. Travellers should be particularly alert in tourist areas (especially on public transport and when dealing with real or purported policemen) and exercise caution when withdrawing money from cashpoints or exchanging money at bureaux de change. The threat from terrorism is low but you should be aware of the global risk of indiscriminate terrorist attacks, which could be against civilian targets, including places frequented by foreigners.

This advice is based on information provided by the Foreign and Commonwealth Office in the UK. It is correct at time of publishing. As the situation can change rapidly, visitors are advised to contact the following organisaions for the latest travel advice:

British Foreign and Commonwealth Office
Tel: (0845) 850 2829.
Website: www.fco.gov.uk

US Department of State
Website: http://travel.state.gov/travel

Accommodation

HOTELS:

The enormous growth of tourism in Mexico is reflected in the wide range of hotels from the modern, elegant and expensive to the clean and modest. There are a variety of chain hotels throughout Mexico as well as 'dude' ranches, thermal spas and resorts that feature specific facilities. Reservations should be confirmed by hotels in writing at the time of booking as hotel tariffs are liable to alteration at any time; it is especially important to make reservations when travelling in the high season. There is a wide range of prices with plenty of choice throughout the country; every hotel is required to display officially approved rate schedules, but the visitor should note that most rates do not include meals. There are also a number of more modest guest houses (*casas de huespedes*). Mexico operates a 5-star grading system similar to that in Europe, with an additional Gran Turismo category. All hotels are covered.

CAMPING/CARAVANNING:

The Pico de Orizaba and Cofre de Perote National Parks near Xalapa have camping areas, but the the most popular regions for camping are the Baja California peninsula, Sonora, Chihuahua and Coahuila. The forests of Campeche and Chiapas also offer beautiful settings to pitch a tent. The western Pacific coast has excellent caravan 'hookups' while Baja California is far more informal and isolated. The number of caravan parks along Mexico's major motorways is growing, and there is no difficulty in locating places to park.

ACCOMMODATION INFORMATION

Mexican Hotel and Motel Association
CP 11590, Thiers 83, Colonia Anzurez,
México DF, Mexico
Tel: (5) 203 0466/6946.
Website: www.hotelesenmexico.com.mx

Top Things To See

- There are some stunning cathedrals and churches in Mexico. In **Mexico City**, Mexico's capital, well worth worth visiting is the **Basilica of Nuestra Señora de Guadalupe**. The shrine that is built around **Tepeyac hill** signifies the spot where the Virgin Mary is said to have appeared to the Indian Juan Diego in 1531. It is also a major pilgrimage site. Each year, on 12 December, millions of devout pilgrims from all over Mexico, many shuffling forward on their knees, congregate at the Basilica to worship their patron saint. Built in 1976, it has a capacity of 10,000 inside plus another 25,000 outside when the 70 surrounding portals are opened. Puebla's **Cathedral**, meanwhile, is one of the oldest in Mexico, with 14 chapels and built of blue-grey stone. Its towers, at 69m (226ft), are the highest in Mexico. The building thus dominates the arcade-lined *zócalo* with its beautiful gardens and **Fuente de San Miguel** (**Saint Michael Fountain**), the patron saint of the city. The **Church of Santo Domingo**, also in **Puebla**, is famous for its **Capilla del Rosario** (**Rosary Chapel**), a breathtaking masterpiece in goldleaf that was consecrated in 1690. **Colima**, the capital of the state of the same name, is located near Mexico's mid-Pacific coast. Founded in the 11th century, when it was known by the Aztec word 'Cajitlán', one of its principal sights is the **Cathedral** whose twin towers were constructed out of volcanic stone quarried from the local **Volcán de Colima National Park**, one of whose peaks, the **Volcán del Fuego de Colima**, last erupted in 1991.

- You will see a heap of interesting sights, preservations and curios in Mexico's world-class **museums**, which mostly fixate around Mexico City. In Mexico City, make every effort to enter the **Museo Nacional de Antropología** in **Chapultepec Park** ('Grasshopper Hill' in the Nahuatl language), which holds an enormous and absolutely fascinating collection of Pre-Hispanic artefacts within 12 halls on the first floor, including the 24-ton Aztec Sun Stone – the Calendar Stone. Ethnological exhibits on the second floor illustrate life today in Mexico's indigenous communities. Other museums in Mexico City that contain outstanding collections include: the **Museo Franz Mayer** (16th- to 19th-century European, Asian and Mexican fine and applied arts, displayed in a restored 16th-century hospital); **Museo de Arte Moderno** (a collection of some of the major works from 20th-century Mexican and Latin American artists); **Museo Frida Kahlo** (examples of the artist's work, her own art collection and belongings displayed in her former home and studio); and **Museo Anahuacalli** (an extraordinary volcanic stone-clad house, designed by Diego Rivera to house his extensive collection of pre-Hispanic artefacts).

- Gaze at the oldest university in the Americas and one of the largest in the world, the **Ciudad Universitaria** (**University City**) in Mexico City, located in **Pedregal Square**. It is a remarkable architectural complex dating back to the 1950s. Among its landmark buildings is the library – a tower encased in an astonishing natural stone, glass and tile mural, which was designed by Juan O'Gorman to illustrate key chapters in Mexico's history.

- Visit **Teotihuacán**, The 'City Where the Gods are born', 48km (30 miles) northeast of Mexico City, which was built about 2000 years ago. It was the largest pre-Hispanic city in Mexico and, at the height of its power, controlled most of Mexico. Visitors to the site can see the **Pyramids of the Sun and Moon**, the **Citadel** with the **Temple of Quetzalcoatl** (the plumed serpent) and the **Palace of Quetzalpapálotl** (the plumed butterfly), all found in a mile-long stretch called the **Calle de los Muertos** (**Great Way of the Dead**).

- Amble around **Tepoztlán** ('Place of Copper'), an attractive, relaxed town in a spectacular natural setting. Spread out across the valley floor, it is surrounded by steep, jagged cliffs that glow pink in the afternoon sun. It is also the legendary birthplace of Quetzalcóatl, the Aztec serpent god. Set on a cliff, 400m (1312ft) above the town, is a pyramid dedicated to Tepoztécatl, god of the harvest, fertility and pulque (a light alcoholic drink). The hour-long climb to the summit is a strenuous one, but well worth it for the extensive views that are afforded over the town, valley and surrounding hills. Dominating the town centre is the fortress-like **Dominican church** and **monastery**. From the market side, the entrance to the churchyard has an arch which is decorated with a golden mural depicting local gods and history, and crafted entirely from seeds, stones and other natural products.

- **Taxco** has been classed as a national monument. The town's fortune was made from the silver mines and the selling of silverware and jewellery is still a thriving local trade. As well as numerous interesting, narrow and winding cobbled streets, the **Church of Santa Prisca and San Sebastián** is a jewel of Churrigueresque architecture, with a reredos decorated with gold leaf and a wealth of statues and ornaments. A cable-car runs from **Los Arcos**, at the northern end of the town, to the summit of **Monte Taxco**. The view over the valley and surrounding mountains from the top are spectacular. Best of all are the **Cacahuamilpa Caves** to the north of Taxco.

- For spectacular colonial architecture, venture no further than Puebla, nestled in the foothills of the **Sierra Madre**. Its buildings include astonishing glazed tiles (known as *talavera* after a town in Spain), which cover most of the church domes and house walls; the town is still full of skilled craftspeople who produce them. Tiles and other ceramics can be purchased in **El Parián market** and in the street leading to **Plazuela de los Sapos**. The **Convention Centre**, a modern building of striking elegance and clean lines, reflects its artistic heritage in its choice of tiles and use of natural materials found within the state. This juxtaposition of ancient and modern is made explicit with a walkway that literally bridges the convention centre and the **Barrio del Artista** (**Artists' Quarter**). In 1988, UNESCO declared Puebla part of the 'Cultural Heritage of Mankind'. Puebla's colonial heritage is also expressed in the architectural riches of its former monasteries and *casonas* (mansions). Two of the best examples of colonial mansions are the **Casa de los Muñecos** (**Dolls' House**), the tiles on the façade depicting the Labours of Hercules (the building is now the **University Museum**), and the **Casa del Alfeñique** (**Sugar Paste House**), which displays craftware and regional costumes.

- Watch the sun set over **Monte Albán**, a sacred city in prehistoric times and the religious centre of the Zapotec culture, which flourished 2000 years ago. The remarkable **Central Plaza**, the **Ball Court**, and many of the tombs, are open to the public. It is an amazing complex situated on a levelled mountain top. Aldous Huxley wrote that 'even today this high place of the Zapotecs remains extraordinarily impressive...Monte Albán is the work of men who knew their architectural business consummately well'. There is nothing more tranquil than watching the light change on the buildings as the sun climbs and falls.

- **Hierve el Agua** ('boiling water'), near **San Lorenzo Albarradas**, is a natural, warm, mineral-rich spring that contains air trying to escape. As the water runs off of the edge of the nearby cliff, calcium carbonate and magnesium in the water create a petrified waterfall. There are only two such sites in the world, the other one being in Turkey.

- For Mexican history of a slightly more modern nature than some of its ruins, travel along the famous **Independence Route**, a road 1400km (875 miles) in length, along which can be traced Mexico's historic struggle for independence. Designated a UNESCO World Heritage Site, **Guanajuato**, a town situated on this route, preserves a colonial charm. The parish **Church of Dolores Hidalgo** is of great significance, being the place where, in 1810, Father Miguel Hidalgo raised the 'Grito de Dolores', the cry of rebellion against the Spanish when, with 80,000 armed supporters, he commenced the independence struggle.

- Soak in the sun-drenched panorama of some of Mexico's best **beach resorts**. On the **Baja Peninsula**, **Cabo San Lucas** and **San José del Cabo** are the main tourist destinations, offering miles of excellent beaches. At Cabo San Lucas on the tip of the peninsula, 260km (162 miles) from **La Paz**, seals may often be seen. **Puerto Vallarta** is the largest town in the immense **Bahía de Banderas** resort area (one hour 10 minutes by air from Mexico City). It is situated on the Bahía de Banderas, which is the largest natural bay in Mexico. There are 160 km (100 miles) of coastline with many sandy beaches and facilities for parasailing, shooting, scuba diving, sailboarding, fishing, golf and tennis. Boat trips provide opportunities to explore the coast. For the visitor who would relish the experience of journeying in a dugout canoe, there is the chance to visit **Yelapa**, a Polynesian-style village which cannot be visited in any other way. The mountains behind the bay may be explored on horseback. **Acapulco** is probably the most famous beach resort in Mexico. The town stretches for over 16km (10 miles) round the bay. It has many beaches as well as numerous top-class hotels. The *malecón* (seaside promenade) runs along the beaches. There is a square in the centre of the old town to the west of the bay. This lively and fashionable resort offers a range of activities, plus the unique spectacle of the Quebrada divers. The waters of the bay are famous for their calmness and safety, though the beach of **La Condesa** has rougher waters and good surf for those who want it.

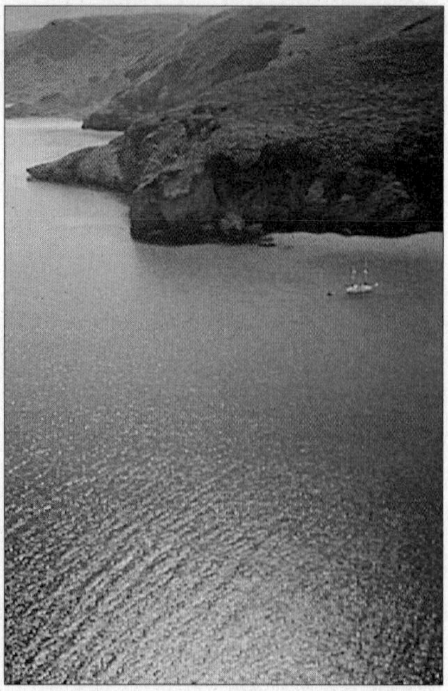

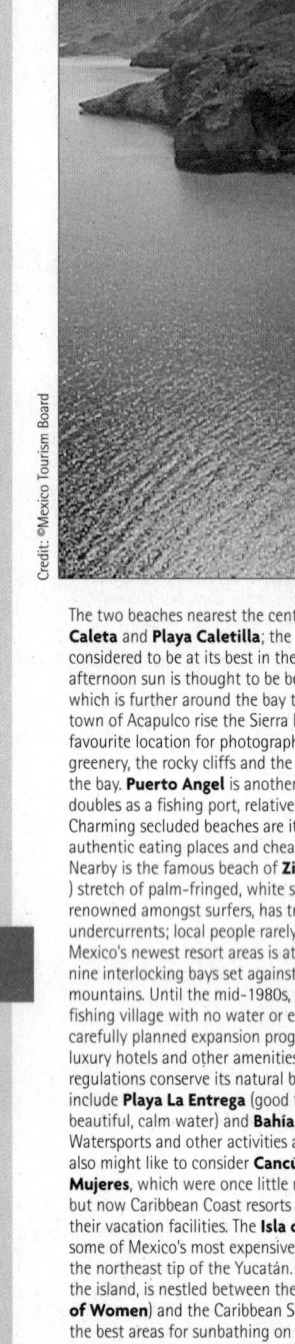

Credit: ©Mexico Tourism Board

The two beaches nearest the centre of the town are **Playa Caleta** and **Playa Caletilla**; the sun on these is considered to be at its best in the morning. The late afternoon sun is thought to be best on **Playa Hornos**, which is further around the bay to the east. Behind the town of Acapulco rise the Sierra Madre Mountains, a favourite location for photographers who relish the greenery, the rocky cliffs and the breathtaking views over the bay. **Puerto Angel** is another lovely beach, which doubles as a fishing port, relatively low-key and sleepy. Charming secluded beaches are its main attraction, plus authentic eating places and cheap accommodation. Nearby is the famous beach of **Zipolite**, a 2km- (1.2 mile-) stretch of palm-fringed, white sand, which, although renowned amongst surfers, has treacherous undercurrents; local people rarely swim there. One of Mexico's newest resort areas is at **Huatulco**, a group of nine interlocking bays set against rainforest-covered mountains. Until the mid-1980s, this area was a sleepy fishing village with no water or electricity. However, a carefully planned expansion programme has brought luxury hotels and other amenities to the area, while strict regulations conserve its natural beauty. The beaches include **Playa La Entrega** (good for snorkelling with beautiful, calm water) and **Bahía Tangolunda**. Watersports and other activities are easily arranged. You also might like to consider **Cancún**, **Cozumel**, and **Isla Mujeres**, which were once little more than sleepy villages, but now Caribbean Coast resorts world-renowned for their vacation facilities. The **Isla de Cancún**, made up of some of Mexico's most expensive beachfronts occupies the northeast tip of the Yucatán. The *punta*, or point of the island, is nestled between the **Bahía de Mujeres** (**Bay of Women**) and the Caribbean Sea and boasts some of the best areas for sunbathing on the Peninsula.
At the tip of the point is **Playa Chac Mool**, a public beach area offering comfortable dining and shopping. Although the beaches of Cancún are known for their powder white sand and exquisite beauty, the waters along the east edge of the island are subject to strong undertow and should be treated with caution. Lifeguards are posted on the beaches fronting most of the major hotels and swimming is encouraged in these areas only. On the west side of the island are the shimmering waters of **Laguna Nichupté** (**Nichupté Lagoon**) and **Laguna Río Inglés** (**English River Lagoon**), which are home to 200 species of birds and host a number of watersports. The Ciudad de Cancún borders the west side of the lagoons, and is a good place for shopping. South of the point lies the **Zona Arqueológica El Rey**, with a small collection of Mayan ruins. The reefs of **Los Manchones**, **Cuevones**, **Chital** and **La Bandera** are prized diving spots, known for their extraordinary marine life and unusual cave structures. South of Cancún is the equally prized beach resort of Cozumel, with its extraordinary coral reefs, gentle currents and exceptional diving.

- Visit the ruins of the Totonac city of **El Tajín**, one of Mexico's most impressive ancient sites. Most of the buildings to be seen on this extensive site date from AD 600-700, while the Totonac civilisation was at its height at around AD 600-900. Abandoned around 1200, El Tajin was rediscovered by the Spaniards in 1785. The central edifice is the **Piramide de los Nichos**, so-called because of the 365 square niches on the sides of the building, representing the solar year. Around the pyramid are 11 ball courts whose walls are carved with bas-reliefs depicting human sacrifices, warriors and ball games. Behind this edifice is a network of buildings, **El Tajín Chico**, which is dominated by the **Edificio de las Columnas**, featuring massive columns covered in mosaics. An ancient Totonac ritual is performed daily at about noon by the 'voladores' of Papantla. Five men in traditional dress climb to a small platform at the top of a pole where one of them performs a dance in honour of the sun god, accompanying himself on the drum and whistle. Meanwhile, the other four wrap themselves in rope fastened to a suspended frame. At a given signal, they launch themselves gracefully into space, rotating exactly 13 times, arms outstretched to greet the sun while the rope unwinds. The exact significance of this ritual is unknown, though it is thought to relate to a pre-Hispanic calendar.
- If you visit Mexico, make a point of heading towards the Yucatán Peninsula at some point on your trip. More than 3000 years ago, there emerged a highly sophisticated civilisation, the Mayas, remnants of which provide a feast for the eyes in this Mexican area. At the height of their development (AD 250-900), the Mayans built extraordinary temples and ceremonial centres, many now engulfed by the rainforest. The capital of Yucatan State is **Mérida**, the 'White City', founded in 1542 on the site of an ancient Mayan town. It has an air of elegant, faded grandeur, a legacy of its once worldwide importance as a centre of *henequén* (sisal used in the manufacture of rope) production. Above all, it is a good base for excursions. Nestled in the foothills at the edge of the **Chiapas rainforest** lies **Palenque**. This small but important Mayan site is one of the most aesthetically appealing sites of the Mayan world, with its exquisite stucco facades. The **Temple of Inscriptions** (above the crypt of a Maya king), the **Multileveled Palace** and the **Temple of the Count** are other highlights. It is easily reached in a couple of hours' drive from **Villahermosa** or **San Cristobal de las Casas**. The site of **Bonampak**, 150km (90 miles) southeast of Palenque, is famous for the finest Mayan murals ever to be discovered. Housed in the **Temple of Frescoes**, the multicoloured murals depict scenes of Mayan warfare, sacrifice and celebration. The famous archaeological and UNESCO World Heritage Site of **Chichén-Itzá**, 120km (75 miles) south of Mérida, contains the **Pyramid of Kukulcan** (**El Castillo**), where one can find the 'Red tiger with jade eyes'. During the spring and autumn equinoxes (21-22 March and 21-22 September), huge crowds gather to see a unique spectacle, when shadows create the illusion of a serpent descending the northern staircase. Of interest are also the snaking columns of the **Temple of the Warriors**, a ball court in perfect condition, **El Caracol** (the observatory), the **Caves of Balankanche and the Sacred Cenote** (where bejewelled young girls were thrown into the well as sacrifices to the rain god Chac). The elaborate stucco work and detailed facades of **Uxmal**, 80km (50 miles) south of Mérida, have led to a comparison of the city with Rome. Among the fine stonework are the entwined serpents in the **Nun's Quadrangle**, the **House of Pigeons** and the **Ball Court**. The walled fortress of **Tulum**, 131km (78 miles) south of Cancún, has been described as one of the most dramatic sites of the pre-Hispanic world. Perched atop rugged cliffs on the coast, this last outpost of the Maya civilisation commands a breathtaking view of the Caribbean. Settlement here dates from AD 900-1500 and sights include the **Temple of the Descending God**, **El Castillo** and the **Temple of the Frescoes**. **Coba**, 38km (24 miles) north of Tulum, is possibly the largest archaeological site on the Yucatán peninsula. This town, set amongst dense jungle and marshlands and including four lakes, dates from the classical period and is believed to have been occupied during the time of the conquest. The most significant groupings of sites are the **Coba Group**, **Las Pinturas**, the **Macanxoc Group**, the **Crossroad Pyramid** and the **Chumuc Mul Group**. It also houses the tallest structure in Yucatán, the **Nohoch Mul Pyramid**.
- Mexico's variety of landscape is matched by its abundance of **flora and fauna**, unrivalled anywhere else in the continent. There are 58 national parks and biosphere reserves where the flora and fauna receive special protection. The country boasts approximately 176 kinds of orchids and more species of birds than exist in the USA and Canada combined. **Birdlife** includes toucans, parrots and macaws, hummingbirds and others. The **Wildlife Reserve of Contoy Island** is the resting and nesting place for hundreds of migrant and resident birds. The upland **cloud-forests** are home to the multicoloured guacamayas as well as the resplendent and elusive *quetzal*, an emerald-coloured bird with trailing feathers considered sacred by the Mayan Indians. The coast also supports a wealth of birdlife, as well as alligators and manatee, a rare aquatic animal distantly related to the elephant, which can be found in the coastal lagoons. The **manatee sanctuary** protects over 694,000 acres (281,000 hectares) of land and water ecosystems in Mexico and has the largest population of Caribbean manatee in the world. Guided 'ecotourist excursions' with multilingual professional guides can be arranged. Transportation is via kayak, mountain bike, jeep or on horseback. If visitors care to venture out alone, updated information on protected camping sites and special permits is provided by tourism offices in each state. Those wishing to observe sea life can go to **Guerrero Negro** in Baja California, home to one of Mexico's prime **whale watching** spots, the **Parque Natural de la Ballena Gris** (**Grey Whale National Park**), where grey whales breed near the shores of **Scammon's Lagoon** from November through March. The small town of **San Ignacio** (145 km (90 miles) to the southeast) is noted for its nearby **San Ignacio Lagoon**, where whales are reputed to be so 'friendly' that they swim close enough to be petted. **Puerto Lopez Mateos** on **Magdalena Bay** is another good spot for whale watching; it is here that the whales give birth and rear their newborns from January to March each year. Several islands in **Baja California** host colonies of sea lions and sea birds. Monarch butterflies are a must-see in the region of **Michoacán**, as is the tortoise sanctuary at **Oaxaca**. The lowland **rainforest** of Chiapas, **Campeche** and **Quintana Roo** is home to such exotic **wildlife** as ocelots, margays, whitetail deer, anteaters, peccaries, tapirs, howler and spider monkeys and jaguars, the largest wildcats in the Americas. Even the underwater world can offer a richness of species such as marlin, snapper, grouper, bonito, wahoo, shrimp, lobster, octopus and sailfish, and the beaches are important nesting places for sea turtles during the summer months.

Top Things To Do

- **Climb** the high **volcanic peaks** of **Popocatépetl** and **Nevado de Toluca**, and then go **scuba-diving** in their craters.
- Almost all Mexican resorts have facilities for the full range of **watersports**, including **jet-skiing**, **windsurfing** and **sea kayaking**. **Surfing** can be enjoyed on the pacific breakers and **parasailing** is another exciting sport. Equipment can be hired at hotels or through watersports centres. **Acapulco** has particularly good facilities for **water-skiing**. Visitors can marvel at the skill of the professional divers that **swallow-dive** from the cliffs at Acapulco. All over Mexico, there are excellent facilities for **sailing**, with modern marinas sited around the coasts. Most resort hotels will rent small sailing boats to guests. **Diving** is particularly popular in two areas: the **Sea of Cortés** and the **Yucatán Peninsula**'s east coast. In these areas, the sea is clear and placid, and facilities are outstanding. The Yucatán Peninsula features the second-largest **coral reef** in the world. **Snorkelling** enthusiasts may like to head for the **Puerto Vallarta** area on the Pacific coast, where resorts include **Punta Mita**, **Guayabitos**, **Mismaloya** and **Los Arcos**. In **Zihuatanejo**, **Playa Las Gatas** and **Ixtapa Island** offer good conditions and in **Huatulco**, the bays of **La Entrega** and **Tangolunda** are very suitable.
- Go on a **spa holiday**: it might not be the first thing that crosses your mind when you think of Mexico but the Aztecs, Tarascans and other native peoples used to frequent the countless hot springs which abound in the country, especially in the area around Mexico City. Nowadays, there are many resorts with high-class facilities offering a range of treatments. Visitors can choose from spiritual retreat spas, with a New Age bias and a meditation programme, mineral water spas, hot springs and 'upscale spas', which are mini-resorts offering complete packages based on weight reduction, stress management and body fitness.

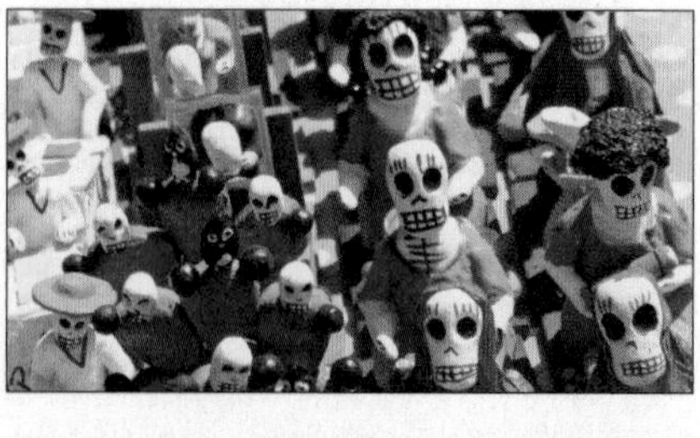

Credit: ©Mexico Tourism Board

- Put on your best outfit and descend into the carousing of Mexican nightlife. Exceptionally vibrant and exciting, nightlife in Mexico is likely to incorporate everything from top-name entertainers, international shows, jazz groups, rock groups, traditional Mexican music and dancing, Spanish flamenco dancers and gypsy violinists. Acapulco in particular is known as 'the city that never sleeps' with bars and discos lining the streets. Do not forget to have a shot of that Mexican tipple, **tequila**, for added energy! Some of the recommended night-time things to do include: a trip to see the **Ballet Folklórico** perform every Wednesday and Sunday at **Mexico City**'s **Palacio de Bellas Artes** (**Palace of Fine Arts**) near **Alameda Central**

Mexico

(**Central Park**), a beautiful arts centre and concert hall, sculptured out of white Carrara marble, built between 1900-34 in neo-classical, art nouveau and art deco styles, where the Ballet Folklórico blend ancient Mayan and Aztec ritual, dramatised episodes from Mexican history, as well as current songs and dances from all over Latin America; also in Mexico City, visit the **Plaza Garibaldi**, where *mariachis* from all over Mexico, usually dressed in ornate clothes and giant sombreros, play for the public their hugely popular and sentimental Mexican music; lastly, listen to Mexico's famed *marimba* music in places such as **Tuxtla Gutierrez**.

- Hire a brightly painted **trajinera** (**gondola**), usually accompanied by mariachis, to cruise the tree-lined canals and Aztec-engineered floating gardens of **Xochimilco**.
- Go **shopping** in **Oaxaca**, known as the 'Jade City' due to the green tinge in the stone used in the construction of many of its buildings. This culturally diverse city is capital of a state whose pre-Hispanic, colonial and indigenous roots are vividly expressed through its architecture, craft traditions, Zapotec and Mixtec archaeological sites, gastronomy and festivals – the **Noche de Rábanos** (**Night of the Radishes**) and the **Guelaguetza** in particular reflect age-old traditions. Within its 95,364 sq km (59,258 sq miles) live 16 ethnic groups, each with its own dialect or language, making the state one of the most linguistically and culturally varied of any in Mexico. In 1987, UNESCO declared both Oaxaca city and the Zapotec site of **Monte Albán**, 9km (5.5 miles) away, to be a 'Cultural Heritage of Humanity'. Traditional arts and crafts – hand-woven and hand-embroidered clothing, alebrijes (painted wooden figures and fantastical creatures), rugs, gold jewellery and distinctive, shiny black pottery – reflect the vibrancy and skill of modern artists who have built on, and refined, older artistic traditions. Works by Oaxacan artists, particularly those of Rufino Tamayo, Francisco Toledo and Rodolfo Morales, are recognised internationally, and several galleries within the town specialise in modern art; it is possible to visit artists in their homes to purchase paintings. Many of the villages surrounding Oaxaca also have weekly markets where fantastic food and craft products can be bought, of which the following are the most notable: **Tlaxiaco** (blankets); **Tlacolula** (rugs and ceramics); **Miahuatlán** (mescal, leather goods and bread); **Santa Ana del Valle** (a general market); **Etla** (flowers, cheese and meat); **Ejutla** (embroidered clothes and mescal); **Ocotlán** (pottery, flowers and textiles); and **Oaxaca** (crafts of all descriptions). Villages where the actual manufacture of local crafts can be seen include the *barro negro brillante* (black, shiny pottery) of **San Bartolo Coyotepec** and the beautiful woven rugs stained with natural dyes at **Teotitlán del Valle**.
- Grasp the **Column of Life** to determine how long you will live: this curious relic is situated in the prehistoric site of **Mitla**, full of numerous Mixtec remains.
- During the annual **October Festival**, horsemanship and bullfighting can be seen at the **charreada** (**rodeo**) in **Guadalajara**. The famous '**Mexican Hat Dance**' originated in this area - locally, it is called *Jarabe Tapatio*.
- Take a ride on the remarkable **Copper Canyon Railway**, which passes through **Chihuahua** on its way from **Ojinaga** on the **Río Grande** to the **Gulf of California**. It is an engineering miracle in itself and also provides a good way of seeing the canyons, mesas and bare peaks of the **Sierra Madre Occidental**. The view at the **Barranca del Cobre**, where the **Urique River** has cut a 1840m- (6136ft-) deep chasm through the mountains, rivals the Grand Canyon. The journey lasts about 13 hours.
- Celebrate the notorious Mexican **Day of the Dead** on November 1 (and also sometimes on November 2). It is celebrated on the Island of **Janitzio** like nowhere else in Mexico, but celebrations occur throughout the country. It is a celebration of dead ancestors that is now steeped in Catholic tradition, linked to All Saints and All Souls Day, because of a process of syncretism that occurred when Spanish conquistadors first arrived in Mexico and were shocked at the pagan rituals in place. A large number of people mark the day(s) by visiting cemeteries and laying flowers on graves, lighting candles and praying. However, the occasion is not cause for morbidity, and Mexicans celebrate joyously, with parades and special events always on the agenda.

TOURIST INFORMATION

Mexico Tourism Board in the UK
Wakefield House, 41 Trinity Square,
London EC3N 4DJ, UK
Tel: (020) 7488 9392.
Website: www.visitmexico.com

Mexican Government Tourism Office in the USA
375 Park Avenue, Floor 19, Suite 1905,
New York, NY 10152, USA
Tel: (212) 308 2110.
Website: www.visitmexico.com

Entertainment

FOOD & DRINK: Self-service (fast food) is available but table-service is usual. Bars have table- and/or counter-service. There are laws relating to minors and licensing on civic holidays. Every region of Mexico has its own dishes. International cuisine is available at most hotels in the larger cities, and at most restaurants. Imported spirits are expensive; local spirits probably give better value for money. The best buys are rum and gin. European aperitifs are produced in Mexico and are of excellent quality; and, of course, Mexico is a producer of good beer; both the dark beers and the light beers are worth sampling. All the big supermarkets sell spirits, beer and wine.

Things to know: The legal drinking age is 18.

National specialities:

- *Turkey mole*, a sauce containing a score of ingredients, including several sorts of chilli, tomatoes, peanuts, chocolate, almonds, onions and garlic.
- *Guacamole* incorporates avocados, red peppers, onions and tomatoes.
- *Tortillas* (pancakes made with maize).
- *Enchiladas* and *tacos* (maize pancakes served with pork, chicken, vegetables or cheese and chilli).
- Exotic fruits such as papayas, mangoes, guavas, *zapotes* (brown fruit resembling an avocado), pineapples and *tunas* (juicy prickly pears, fruit of the cactus).

National drinks:

- *Tequila* (made from *maguey*, a variety of cactus).
- *Hidalgo*, *Domecq* and *Derrasola* are good Mexican white wines.
- *Los Reyes* and *Calafia* are excellent red wines.
- Mexico's coffee liqueur, *kahlúa*, is world-famous.

Tipping: Service charges are rarely added to hotel, restaurant or bar bills and many of the staff depend on tips for their livelihood. 15 per cent is expected and 20 per cent if the service has been very good.

NIGHTLIFE: The Mexican nightlife is very vibrant and exciting and features a large variety of top-name entertainers, international shows, jazz groups, rock groups, traditional Mexican music and dancing, Spanish flamenco dancers and gypsy violinists. With a range of settings from panoramic restaurants to intimate bars, Mexico City offers excellent music and assorted cuisine, with some of the best bars and restaurants located in hotels. The main nightspots are on Avenida Insurgentes, the longest avenue in the capital. For a more cosy atmosphere with nice coffee shops and restaurants, visit the Condesa district. Acapulco is known as 'the city that never sleeps' with bars and discos lining the streets. Worth seeing is the impressive light show, with accompanying sound show at the archaeological site of Teotihuacán. The history and mythology of this ancient civilisation are recreated through a gorgeous display of coloured lights, poetic dialogue and music. The season runs from October to May.

SHOPPING: Good buys include silverware, ceramics and locally made pottery, woven wool blankets (*sarapes*), brightly coloured scarves in wool or silk (*rebozos*), richly embroidered charro hats, straw work, blown glass, embossed leather, hard- and semi-precious stones, gold and silver jewellery, finely pleated men's shirts in cotton voile (*guayaberas*), white dresses embroidered with multi-coloured flowers (*huipiles*), which are sold in the markets, and hammocks. The best shopping is in Mexico City, Acapulco, Campeche, Cuernavaca, Guadalajara, Mérida, Oaxaca, San Miguel de Allende and Taxco. **Shopping hours:** Mon-Sun 1000/1100-2000/2200 (big towns and cities); Mon-Fri 0900-1400/1600 (rest of the country). Check locally for details.

Business

- **GDP:** US$615 billion.
- **Main imports:** Metalworking machines, steel mill products, agricultural machinery, electrical equipment, car parts of assembly, repair parts for motor vehicles, aircraft and aircraft parts.
- **Main exports:** Manufactured goods, oil and oil products, silver, fruit, vegetables, coffee and cotton.
- **Main trade partners:** Canada, China, Japan, Spain and USA.

ECONOMY: The agricultural sector produces various staple crops, including sorghum, wheat, maize, rice, beans and potatoes largely for domestic consumption; while coffee, sugar cane, fruit and vegetables are grown for export. The contribution made by agriculture (including fishing, which is a major employer in coastal areas) has declined since the 1980s; it now employs about 20 per cent of the workforce and accounts for about 5 per cent of GDP.

Manufacturing has grown considerably during the last 20 years. The main products are vehicles, processed foods, iron and steel, chemicals and machinery. Many companies in this sector are located in so-called *maquiladora* plants, where semi-finished goods or raw materials from the southern USA are shipped across the border into Mexico, completed, and then (for the most part) returned to the USA. The system allows American companies to take advantage of lower wages and running costs, as well as a less stringent regulatory regime. NAFTA (see below) has also contributed substantially to the growth of this part of the Mexican economy. Mexico also has a sizeable mining sector, producing a wide range of minerals including silver, bismuth, arsenic and antimony; there are also smaller deposits of sulphur, lead, zinc and cadmium. However, the largest single natural resource, and the source of much of Mexico's revenue in recent years, is oil. In some respects this has been a mixed blessing: Mexico has suffered several economic crises in which over-reliance on oil income was at least a contributory factor. In the service sector, tourism is the most important single industry, although it suffered a serious downturn in the wake of the '9-11' catastrophe and has yet to fully recover. As for the overall economy, after a mild recession in 2001/02, estimated Mexican GDP growth for 2003 was 1.5 per cent; this rose to 4.2 per cent in 2004. In 2004, inflation was over 5 per cent.

Under the statist policies of the PRI, the Government was always in firm control of economic policy. However, once the party's stranglehold had been broken, Mexico embarked on the type of reform process familiar throughout the world: privatisation of state-controlled industries, deregulation and removal of tariffs and subsidies, and the opening of the economy to foreign investment. The reform process has been somewhat spasmodic and piecemeal, however, as a result of continuous political disputes. In 1993, Mexico signed the North American Free Trade Agreement (NAFTA), which created a free trade bloc among the USA, Canada and Mexico of a size to rival the EU in both population and economic output. Mexican trade with its fellow NAFTA members increased threefold, and accounts for 80 per cent of the total trade volume. Nor has Mexico neglected trade links with its fellow Latin American countries: there are free-trade agreements with Central America, Colombia and Venezuela. Mexico is also a member of the Inter-American Development Bank, the Association for Latin American Integration (ALADI) and, most recently, the Asian-Pacific Economic Forum (APEC).

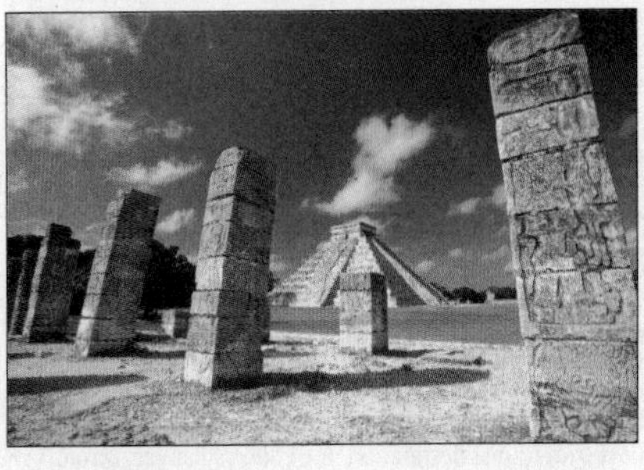

Credit: ©Mexico Tourism Board

BUSINESS ETIQUETTE: English is widely spoken in business circles although it is preferable for the visitor to be able to speak Spanish. Letters written in Spanish should be replied to in Spanish. Business wear is formal. Mexicans attach much importance to courtesy and the use of titles. Prior appointments are necessary and if in doubt about a correct title it is advisable to use *licenciado* in place of *señor*. Best months for business visits are January to June and September to November. Avoid the two weeks before and after Christmas and Easter. **Office hours:** These vary considerably, but are usually Mon-Fri 0900-1800; lunch breaks usually last an hour but some business lunches can go on for longer.

CONFERENCES/CONVENTIONS: The meetings, conventions, exhibitions and incentives planner's kit issued by the Mexico Tourism Board (see *Top Things To Do*) lists over 70 convention venues in Mexico City, Acapulco, Taxco, Morelia, Puerto Vallarta, Ixtapa, Guadalajara, Mazatlán, Cancún and Mérida. Taxco, Acapulco, Morelia and Cancún have dedicated centres, the largest of which, in Acapulco, can seat up to 8000 people.

COMMERCIAL INFORMATION

Confederación de Cámaras Nacionales de Comercio (Confederation of National Chambers of Commerce)
Servicios y Turismo (CONCANACO),
3rd Floor, Balderas 144, Col. Centro,
06079 México DF, Mexico
Tel: (55) 5722 9300.
Website: www.concanacored.com

Trade Commission of the Mexican Embassy (BANCOMEXT) in the UK
1 Angel Court, 19th Floor, London EC2R 7HJ, UK
Tel: (020) 7726 4442.
Website: www.buyinmexico.com.mx *or* www.investinmexico.com.mx.

A B C D E F G H I J K L M N O P Q R S T U V W X Y Z

Moldova

100km
50mls
✈ international airport

UKRAINE

Edineţ
Soroca
Dniester
Bălţi · Răbniţa
Prut
MOLDOVA
Orhei · Dubăsari
CHIŞINĂU
Tiraspol
Tighina
Basarabeasca
ROMANIA
UKRAINE
Cahul
Lake Yalpuh
Danube
BLACK SEA
Danube Delta

Location: Southeastern Europe.

Time: GMT + 2 (GMT + 3 from last Sunday in March to last Sunday in October).

Overview

Although Moldova is a picturesque country with an interesting history and many places to visit, it remains a fairly unknown tourist destination. The country has very strong links with Russia and Romania. The decision to ally with one or the other of its two more powerful neighbours dominated Moldovan politics during the 20th century. Moldova next experienced a period of independence in 1918, in the course of the Russian Revolution, when they voted to become part of Romania. However, the Soviet Union objected and brought it within the Soviet orbit. It was then occupied by Soviet forces in 1940 under the terms of the Nazi-Soviet Pact. The German invasion of the Soviet Union put Moldova back under Nazi control; a brief period of unification with Romania followed before the Red Army overran it in 1944.

The Moscow Government pursued a policy of attempting to detach Moldova – which was now confirmed as one of the 15 constituent republics of the Soviet Union – from its Romanian roots. This policy was pursued with notable vigour by Leonid Brezhnev, the Communist party leader in Moldova in the early 1950s, who later rose to become leader of the Soviet Union. Gorbachev's reform programme reversed the suppression of national characteristics within the Soviet Union and, by the late 1980s, Romanian was in common and official use in Moldova. Along with the other peripheral Soviet republics, Moldova started to move towards independence from 1991 onwards.

The terrain consists of rolling steppe with a gradual slope towards the Black Sea. The proximity to the Black Sea provides Moldova with a mild and sunny climate though winters can be cold. The fertile soil of the river valleys supports wheat, corn, barley, tobacco and sugar beet. Moldova is a wine-growing country and the vineyards and wine cellars of Mileshti and Krikova-Veki are famous throughout the region and popular tourist destinations.

General Information

AREA: 33,800 sq km (13,050 sq miles).
POPULATION: 4.3 million (UN estimate 2005).
POPULATION DENSITY: 127.2 per sq km.
CAPITAL: Chisinau (Kishinev). **Population:** 662,200 (official estimate 2004).
GEOGRAPHY: Moldova is a small landlocked state in southeastern Europe – one of the most highly populated republics of the former USSR. To the north, east and south Moldova is bound by Ukraine; to the west by Romania. The River Prut constitutes the border with Romania. The country has rich pastures and wooded slopes, ideal for wine-growing.
GOVERNMENT: Republic since 1991. Gained independence from the Soviet Union in 1991. **Head of State:** President Vladimir Voronin since 2001. **Head of Government:** Prime Minister Vasile Tarlev since 2001. **Recent history:** The Communist party came to power in 2001 and were winners again in the most recent Parliamentary elections in March 2005. The Moldovan Parliament then returned President Voronin for a second term in April 2005, at which point he said he would focus on European integration, resolving the ongoing conflict with Transnistria and raising the standard of living.
LANGUAGE: The Constitution of 1994 described the official language as 'Moldovan' although it is considered to be virtually identical to Romanian. In 1940, after Soviet annexation, the Cyrillic script was introduced and was referred to as Moldavian up until 1989 when the Latin alphabet was reintroduced. Russian is still the most widely spoken language. The ethnic and linguistic make-up of Moldova is as follows: Moldovans 64.5 per cent, Ukrainians 13.8 per cent, Russians 13 per cent, Gagauz 3.5 per cent, Bulgarians 1.5 per cent, others 3.7 per cent.
RELIGION: Mostly Eastern Orthodox Christian and other Christian denominations. A small amount of the population are Jewish.
ELECTRICITY: 220 volts AC, 50Hz.
SOCIAL CONVENTIONS: Dress should be casual but conservative. For official engagements, men should wear a jacket and tie. The country is famous for its tradition of folk arts and there are many lively musical groups (*Tarafs*), which play a variety of rare folk instruments including the *tsambal* (not unlike a dulcimer), *cimpoi* (bagpipe), *fluier* and *nai*.

Climate

Very mild and pleasant. Temperate with warm summers 20-23°C (68-73°F), crisp, sunny autumns and cold, sometimes snowy, winters.
Required clothing: Mediumweights, heavy topcoat and overshoes for winter; lightweights for summer. A light raincoat is useful.

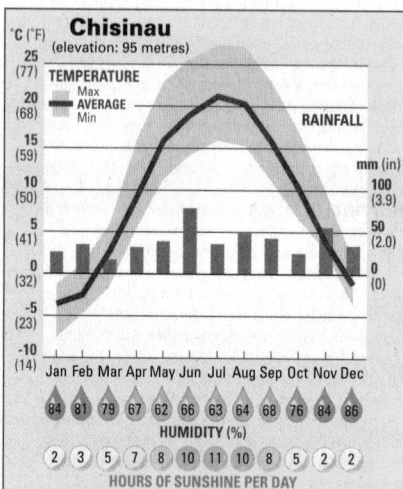

Chisinau (elevation: 95 metres)

TEMPERATURE
Max
AVERAGE
Min
RAINFALL

HUMIDITY (%)
84 81 79 67 62 66 63 64 68 76 84 86

HOURS OF SUNSHINE PER DAY
2 3 5 7 8 10 11 10 8 5 2 2

Communications

Telephone: IDD is available to major towns. Country code: 373. There are two types of payphone: Soviet ones (taking tokens) and modern ones (taking cards).
Mobile telephone: Roaming agreements exist with most international mobile phone operators. Coverage extends over the central area of the country.
Internet: There are Internet cafes in main towns.
Post: All mail to and from Moldova may be subject to long delays. The postal and telecommunication systems are being modernised. The main post office is at 73 Stefan cel Mare boulevard, 277012 Chisinau. Post office hours: Mon-Sun 0900-2000. There are express mail services in Chisinau.
MEDIA: Press: The press is generally uncensored. There are more than a dozen daily newspapers in Moldova, the most popular being *Moldova Suverana* published in Romanian. Other main papers include *Dnestrovskaya Pravda*, *Nezavisimaya Moldova* (published in Russian), *Trudovoi Tiraspol* and *Viata Satului*. English-language publications can sometimes be found at major hotels in Chisinau. Western press deliveries are erratic.
TV: State-run Teleradio-Moldova operates *Moldova One*. *Pro TV Chisinau* is a commercial channel.
Radio: Teleradio-Moldova runs *Radio Moldova*. *Radio Nova* is a commercial station.

Passport/Visa

	Passport Required?	Visa Required?	Return Ticket Required?
Full British	Yes	Yes	No
Australian	Yes	Yes	No
Canadian	Yes	Yes	No
USA	Yes	Yes	No
Other EU	Yes	Yes/1	No
Japanese	Yes	Yes	No

Note: *Regulations and requirements may be subject to change at short notice, and you are advised to contact the appropriate diplomatic or consular authority before finalising travel arrangements. Any numbers in the chart refer to the footnotes below.*

PASSPORTS: Passport valid for at least six months required by all.
VISAS: Required by all except the following for stays of up to 90 days:
(a) nationals of the CIS, except nationals of Turkmenistan who *do require a visa;*
(b) **1.** nationals of Poland;
(c) nationals of Romania.
Types of visa and cost: *Tourist, Simple, Service* (Business) and *Transit*. All may be issued on a single-, double- or multiple-entry basis. Costs vary depending on nationality of applicant and type of visa. Contact Embassy for further details.
Validity: *Tourist:* One month from date of issue.
Application to: Consulate (or Consular section at Embassy); see *Passport/Visa Information*.
Application requirements: (a) Passport with blank pages to affix the visa. (b) One application form. (c) One passport-size photo. (d) Fee payable by money order or cheque only. (e) For postal applications, a self-addressed return envelope should also be submitted. (f) Letter of invitation from Moldova, authorised by the Department of Migration in Moldova, or a tourist voucher issued by a Moldovan tourist agency. *Transit:* (a)-(e) and, (f) Entry documents for next country. (g) Onward tickets.
Note: (a) Nationals of EU countries, Bulgaria, Canada, Croatia, Israel, Japan, Norway, Switzerland, Turkey and the USA do not need to submit an invitation to obtain a visa for stays of up to 90 days. (b) All foreign visitors must register with the police within three days of arrival.
Working days required: Five; same day for urgent visas with surcharge of 50 per cent of visa price.
Temporary residence: Apply to the Foreign Ministry in Moldova.

PASSPORT/VISA INFORMATION

Embassy of the Republic of Moldova in the UK
5 Dolphin Square, Edensor Road, London W4 2ST, UK
Tel: (020) 8995 6818.
E-mail: movilamd@mail.md

Embassy of the Republic of Moldova in the USA
2101 S Street, NW, Washington, DC 20008, USA
Tel: (202) 667 1130 *or* 1137 (ext. 15 for consular section).
E-mail: embassyofmoldova@mcihispeed.net

Money

Currency: Leu (MDL) = 100 bani. Notes are in denominations of MDL500, 200, 100, 50, 20, 10, 5 and 1. Coins are in denominations of 50, 25, 10, 5 and 1 bani.
Currency exchange: Foreign currencies can be exchanged in hotels or bureaux de change. Moldova is essentially a cash-only economy. There are three ATMs in Chisinau where local currency can be withdrawn using Visa cards.
Credit & debit cards: Credit cards are only accepted by a few banks. Check with your credit or debit card company for details of merchant acceptability and other services which may be available.
Traveller's cheques: Traveller's cheques are not generally accepted, though a few banks may exchange them.
Currency restrictions: The import of local and foreign currency is unlimited. The export of local currency is unlimited. The export of foreign currency is limited to amount imported.
Banking hours: Mon-Fri 0930-1730.
Exchange rate indicators:
Rate at time of publishing
£1.00= MDL21.91
$1.00= MDL12.63

Duty Free

The following goods may be imported into Moldova by persons of 18 years of age or older without incurring customs duty:
200 cigarettes; 1l of spirits and/or wine; a reasonable quantity of perfume for personal use.

Public Holidays

Below are listed Public Holidays for the January 2006-June 2007 period.
2006: Jan 1 New Year's Day. **Jan 7-8** Moldovan Christmas. **Mar 8** International Women's Day. **Apr 24** Easter Monday (Orthodox). **Apr 18** Memorial Day. **May 1** Labour Day. **May 9** Victory and Commemoration Day. **Aug 27** Independence Day. **Aug 31** Limba Noastra (National Language Day). **Oct 13-14** National Day of Wine and Wine Festival.
2007: Jan 1 New Year's Day. **Jan 7-8** Moldovan Christmas. **Mar 8** International Women's Day. **Apr 9** Easter Monday (Orthodox). **May 1** Labour Day. **May 8** Memorial Day. **May 9** Victory and Commemoration Day.

Health

	Special Precautions?	Certificate Required?
Yellow Fever	No	No
Cholera	Yes	No
Typhoid & Polio	1	N/A
Malaria	No	N/A

Note: *Regulations and requirements may be subject to change at short notice, and you are advised to contact your doctor well in advance of your intended date of departure. Any numbers in the chart refer to the footnotes below.*

1: Immunisation against typhoid is sometimes recommended.
Food & drink: Mains water is normally chlorinated but bottled water is available and advised. Local meat, poultry, fruit and vegetables are generally considered safe to eat.
Other risks: There is a small risk of *hepatitis A* in rural areas. Cases of *diphtheria* have also been reported.
Rabies is present and casual exposure to stray dogs is common throughout Chisinau. Vaccination before arrival should be considered. If you are bitten, seek medical advice without delay. For more information, consult the *Health* appendix.
Health care: A number of large medical institutions operate in Chisinau, including the Republican Clinical Hospital. Elderly travellers and those with existing health problems may be at risk owing to inadequate medical facilities. There is a reciprocal health agreement with the UK for urgent medical treatment. Otherwise, all services and prescriptions are charged for and doctors and hospitals often expect immediate cash payment; medical insurance is strongly recommended.
Note: Travellers staying longer than three months may be required to produce proof of HIV-negative status.

Travel - International

AIR:
The national airlines are *Air Moldova (9U)* and *Air Moldova International (RM)*. *Moldovian Airlines*, *Tarom* (Romania's national airline), *Transaero* (Russian airline) and *Tyrolean Airlines* fly regularly to Moldova. There are also charter airlines operating between Chisinau and some major destinations in the CIS, France, Germany, Hungary, Israel, The Netherlands, Romania and Turkey.
Approximate flight times: From *London* to Chisinau is approximately seven hours, with a stopover in Moscow. From *Moscow* to Chisinau is two hours, from *Kiev* is one hour 30 minutes and from *St Petersburg* is three hours.
Main airports: *Chisinau International (KIV)* is 14km (8.5 miles) from the city centre (travel time - 15 to 25 minutes). *To/from the airport:* There is a regular bus service to the city. Taxis are also available. *Facilities:* Bank, post office, left-luggage and duty free shops.
Departure tax: US$12.
RAIL:
There are daily train services between Chisinau and Moscow, Russian Federation (travel time - 22 hours), Odessa, Ukraine (travel time - five hours) and Bucharest, Romania (travel time - 13 hours). Other, less frequent, destinations include Minsk (Belarus) and St Petersburg.
ROAD:
Moldova can be entered from Ukraine (although the self-proclaimed 'Republic of Transnistria' area around Tiraspol should be avoided at present) and also from Romania via the border crossing at Leusheni, Sculeni and Giurgiulesti. From Chisinau to Odessa is 183km (114 miles).

Travel - Internal

RAIL:
There are over 1145km (715 miles) of railway track in use in Moldova. Trains run daily to Ocnita, Tighina and Ungheni, and there are connections to most areas of the country. For more details, contact the information service of Moldovan Railways (tel: (22) 252 737/5; website: www.railway.md).
ROAD:
The road network covers 13,622km (8500 miles). **Bus:** These run between most of the larger towns and cities. For further information, contact either Chisinau Main Bus Station (tel: (22) 542 185) or South East Bus Station (tel: (22) 723 983). **Taxi:** These can be found everywhere. Fares should be negotiated in advance, though drivers prefer to charge per hour. Taxis are requested by calling 900 or 905-8. **Car hire:** Self-drive cars can be obtained for self-drive or with an English-speaking driver.
Documentation: An International Driving Permit is required.
URBAN:
Buses, trolleybuses and minibuses are cheap but notoriously crowded and unreliable. They all operate from 0500-2400 with services every 15 minutes. Tickets for buses and trolleybuses can be purchased from kiosks or on board the vehicle. Minibus tickets are bought from the driver.

Travel Advice

Travellers to Moldova should be aware of the global risk of indiscriminate international terrorist attacks, which could be against civilian targets, including places frequented by foreigners.
Caution is advised if considering travelling to Transnistria. Transnistria (northeast Moldova) is not under Moldovan government control and seeks autonomous status. There was tension between the Moldovans and Transnistrians in summer 2004 and relations remain poor. It is very important to avoid getting into difficulty with the Transnistrian authorities.
This advice is based on information provided by the Foreign and Commonwealth Office in the UK. It is correct at time of publishing. As the situation can change rapidly, visitors are advised to contact the following organisations for the latest travel advice:

British Foreign and Commonwealth Office
Tel: (0845) 850 2829.
Website: www.fco.gov.uk

US Department of State
Website: http://travel.state.gov/travel

Accommodation

HOTELS:
There is a small selection of hotels in the capital Chisinau, most of which are located close to the railway station and in the city centre. There are some low-grade hotels in other towns.
Grading: From **1-star** (basic facilities) to **4-stars** (larger capacity and greater facilities of a higher standard).

Top Things To See & Do

- The Moldovan capital of **Chisinau** (formerly Kishinev) stands on the banks of the small **River Byk**. The city was founded around 1470 and the history and life of Moldova through the centuries is best presented in the **History and Regional Lore Museum**, a beautiful Turkish-style complex. The **Fine Arts Museum** houses good examples of Russian, West European and Moldovan paintings, sculpture and applied arts. The **Pushkin House** is the place where the great Russian poet spent his days in exile between 1820-23. The museum is famous as the place where Pushkin began working on his epic poem *Eugene Onegin*. There are also two old cemeteries in Chisinau, the **Armenian Cemetery** and the **Jewish Cemetery**. The latter is famous as the burial place for the victims of the Chisinau Pogrom in 1903; in the 1960s, the lower part of the cemetery was deliberately razed by the authorities. Owing to massive Jewish emigration from Moldova during the 1980s and the beginning of the 1990s, the state of the cemetery has significantly deteriorated. The only working synagogue in Chisinau is situated not far from the city centre, on Habad-Liubavici str. The former Chisinau Choral Synagogue today houses the **Chekhov Drama Theatre**. The **Monument of Stefan cel Mare** (Stefan the Great) is situated at the entrance to the well-tended Pushkin Park. He was Moldova's *Gospodar* (ruler) between 1457-1504 during a time of brief independence, thus securing him a special place in Moldova's history. The monument by the sculptor Plamadeala was unveiled in 1927. In 1990-91, the monument was the focal point of meetings and violent clashes between Moldova's Nationalists and pro-Soviet supporters. Just outside the park is an impressive building housing the largest cinema, **Patria** (Fatherland), which was built in 1947 by German POWs.
- Picturesque bathing beaches line the manmade **Chisinau Lake** (formerly Komsomol Lake). Boats can also be hired. There are two parts to the complex: the **Exhibition of Achievements** and the open-air **Green Theatre** with a seating capacity of 7000.
- **Benderi** (Tighina) is one of the oldest towns in Moldova. Its beautiful 17th-century fortress, as well as the town itself, were seriously damaged during the recent fighting.
- Approximately 160km (100 miles) south of Chisinau is **Cahul**. The town is famous for its thermal spas and mud treatments and there is a small hotel in the town. There is also a good local theatre. **Hirjauca** is a renowned spa in the area.
- Moldova is a wine-growing country and the vineyards and wine cellars of **Mileshti** and **Krikova-Veki** are famous throughout the region.

TOURIST INFORMATION

National Tourism Agency
180 Stefan cel Mare Street, Office 901,
Chisinau MD 2004, Moldova
Tel: (22) 210 774.
Website: www.turism.md

Entertainment

FOOD & DRINK: There are plenty of small restaurants and coffee shops. The service tends to be slow, but the cuisine is delicious. Local specialities include *mititeyi* (small grilled sausages with onion and pepper) and *mamaliga* (thick, sticky maize pie) which is served with *brinza* (feta cheese). *Tocana* (pork stew) should be tried with sweet-and-sour watermelons and apples. There are more than 100 varieties of excellent wines produced in Moldova. White wines include *Aligote*, *Riesling* and *Sauvignon*. *Moldovan Cabernet* and *Merlot* are noteworthy reds. *Doina* or *Nistru* brandy is an ideal accompaniment with desserts.
Tipping: 5 to 10 per cent will be gladly accepted.
NIGHTLIFE: In Chisinau, there is a good selection of theatres and concerts halls, which includes an opera house. The *Eminescu Music and Drama Theatre* specialises in Romanian productions, as does the *Youth Theatre Luceafarul* (Poetic Star). All performances in the Chekhov Drama Theatre are exclusively in Russian (the building used to be the Chisinau Choral Synagogue). The Philharmonia Concert Hall houses *Moldova's Symphony Orchestra*. It is also the base for the folklore *Doina Choir*, the internationally renowned *Zhok National Dance Ensemble* and the *Fluerash Orchestra of National Music*. Russian and Romanian productions can be seen in the puppet theatre Licurici (Glow-worm).
SHOPPING: Good buys are the vividly coloured costumes, handmade carpets and locally produced wines and brandies. The main open-air market or *tolchok* is on Calea Mosilor, about 10 minutes' drive away from central Chisinau. Although crowded, it sells everything and is a good place for bargains. **Shopping hours:** Larger shops open 0800-2000; all others open 0900-1700.

Business

ECONOMY: Moldova's economy is dominated by agriculture, food processing and related industries which account for over half of total output. The land is very fertile: some 85 per cent is cultivated. The republic was the largest wine-growing region in the former Soviet Union and this is still a major source of revenue. It also grows fruit, vegetables, tobacco and grain, and produces dairy and meat products in large quantities. Other than food and drink processing, Moldova's industrial sector is dominated by metals and machinery, textiles and footwear. The once thriving electronics industry has declined due to the dissolution and/or contraction of its major clients in the Russian space and defence sector. Under the Soviet system of economic planning, Moldova exported much of its output to other Soviet republics in exchange for raw materials and fuel products. The demise of the Soviet system triggered a major collapse which saw Moldovan economic output decline by 15 per cent annually during the early 1990s. This catastrophic decline has been arrested but there are few signs of economic growth, and Moldova is now one of the poorest countries in an already impoverished region. In 1992, Moldova joined the IMF, World Bank and the European Bank for Reconstruction and Development (EBRD) as a 'Country of Operation'. After an uncertain start, a reform programme got under way in Moldova and by 1999 much of the economy had been privatised and deregulated. However, the IMF and World Bank then cut off financial support when the Government refused to sell off the key tobacco and wine industries. Following some shifts in policy, the Government has since been able to secure funding from the EBRD and occasional small packages from the IMF and World Bank. But relations with the latter pair are still difficult. At the beginning of 2003, the Government announced its intention to liberalise the economy further.
The national currency, the Leu, introduced in November 1993, has been reasonably stable apart from the period immediately after the 1998 Russian financial crisis. Russia remains Moldova's largest trading partner, followed by the Belarus, Romania, Ukraine and Germany. In May 2001, Moldova joined the World Trade Organization. Moldova eventually hopes to join the European Union. That aspiration depends on the results of the 2004 expansion and Moldova's own economic performance.

COMMERCIAL INFORMATION

Chamber of Commerce and Industry of the Republic of Moldova
151 Stefan cel Mare St., Chisinau, MD 2004, Moldova
Tel: (22) 221 552.
Website: www.chamber.md

Monaco

Location: Western Europe.

Time: GMT + 1 (GMT + 2 from last Sunday in March to last Sunday in October).

Overview

The history of Monaco is inseparable from that of the House of Grimaldi. At various times, they were to be found allied with almost every power in the region, particularly during the Italian Wars in the late 15th and early 16th centuries. Monaco's geographical position left them ideally placed to either help or hinder the repeated and largely unsuccessful attempts by the kings of France to conquer Italy. This Machiavellian approach – indeed, Machiavelli himself was in Monaco in the early 16th century to sign a treaty on behalf of Florence – paid dividends in 1612 when Honoré II was granted the title of prince by the French crown. He signed a treaty of friendship with France, and the Principality remained independent from that time on, despite a brief interruption during the French Revolution. The family's motto – 'Deo Juvante' (With God's Help) – provides another possible explanation for the survival of this tiny country. Monaco became an independent state under French protection in 1861.

Monaco survives principally by providing tax concessions and discreet banking facilities for wealthy foreigners, and this has recently led to spats with France and difficulties with the wider world. Despite being 'named and shamed' by inclusion on an Organisation for Economic Cooperation and Development 'blacklist' of seven countries that have failed to take adequate measures to deal with the money-laundering and multi-national fraud problems in April 2002, Monaco attracts many extremely wealthy individuals as residents. In the main harbour, expensive luxury yachts and boats, which are a permanent fixture, corroborate Monaco's reputation as a glamorous destination for the rich and famous. Monaco's pleasant climate, reputation and environment as well as the absence of income or inheritance tax and lack of financial reporting requirements all contribute to this situation. Tourism is also a major source of revenue, contributing about 25 per cent of government revenue, as well as being the mainstay of local retail businesses.

Although the second-smallest independent state in the world, Monaco benefits from an excellent climate and beautiful settings on the Côte d'Azur. From the heights of the Tête de Chien or Mont Agel, or from lower down from the Moyenne-Corniche at the level of the entrance to the Jardin Exotique, there are a number of panoramic viewpoints looking out over exceptional scenery. Gamblers

flock to the Place du Casino in Monte-Carlo and every May the principality hosts the renowned Monaco Grand Prix. Monaco is also well located for exploring both Provence, the French Riviera and Italy.

General Information

AREA: 1.95 sq km (0.75 sq miles).

POPULATION: 32,000 (2005).

POPULATION DENSITY: 16,435 per sq km.

CAPITAL: Monaco-Ville. **Population:** 1034 (2000).

GEOGRAPHY: Monaco is second only to the Vatican as the smallest independent state in Europe. Set on the Mediterranean coast of France just a few miles from the Italian border, the principality is a constitutional monarchy and relies largely on foreign currency for an economic base. Its principal industry is tourism. The country is a narrow ribbon of coastline backed by the Alpes-Maritimes foothills, creating a natural amphitheatre overlooking the sea, with the population centred in four districts. Monaco-Ville is set on a rocky promontory dominating the coast. The Palace is the home of the Grimaldi family, the oldest ruling house in Europe. Monaco-Ville also boasts a fine Romanesque cathedral among its other attractions. La Condamine is the area around the Port, while Monte-Carlo is the main centre for business and entertainment. Fontvieille has been set aside as an area for new light industrial and residential development.

GOVERNMENT: Constitutional Monarchy. **Head of State:** Prince Albert II since 2005. **Head of Government:** Minister of State Jean Paul Proust. **Recent history:** Following the death of Prince Rainier in April 2005, his son Prince Albert II was enthroned in November 2005, ending a process that began when he was sworn in before his subjects in July. The Government of the Principality is controlled by the hereditary ruler Prince Albert II, under whom executive authority is exercised by a Minister of State. The Monegasque electorate elects the 18-member *Conseil National* (National Council) for a five-year term; the Council and the Prince share legislative power.

LANGUAGE: French. Monégasque (a mixture of French Provençal and Italian Ligurian), English and Italian are also spoken. Native Monégasques make up only a minority of Monaco's population.

RELIGION: 95 per cent Roman Catholic (Monaco has a Catholic Bishop), with Anglican minorities.

ELECTRICITY: 220 volts AC, 50Hz. Round two-pin plugs are in use.

SOCIAL CONVENTIONS: Casual wear is acceptable for daytime and dress is the same as for the rest of the French Riviera. Smart restaurants, dining rooms, clubs and the Casino's private rooms require more formal attire. Handshaking and, more familiarly, kissing both cheeks, are accepted forms of greeting.

Climate

Monaco has a mild climate throughout the year, the hottest months being July and August, and the coolest being January and February. Rain mostly falls during the cooler winter months and there is an average of only 60 days' rain per year.

Required clothing: Lightweights are worn, with a warm wrap for cooler summer evenings. Light- to mediumweights are advised for winter.

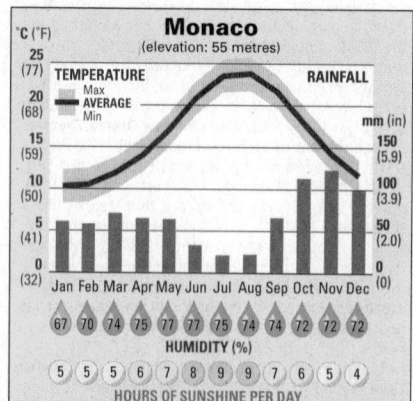

Communications

Telephone: Full IDD is available. Country code: 377.

Mobile telephone: Roaming agreements exist with international mobile phone companies. Good coverage.

Internet: There are several Internet cafes.

Post: Same rates as France. The main post office is at The Scala Palace, Beaumarchais Square. Post office hours: Mon-Fri 0800-1900, Sat 0800-1200. There are special Monégasque stamps.

MEDIA: The influence of Monaco's broadcast media extends far beyond its borders. Since the 1960s, *Radio Monte-Carlo* has reached listeners across much of France, and in the 1970s broadcasts to Italy began.

Press: There are no daily newspapers in Monaco, but French papers - and the tabloid magazines, cover news from the principality. The principal regional daily is *Nice-Matin* (which includes two pages on Monaco). Weekly publication, the *Monaco Hebdo* covers Monaco's current affairs. The *Journal de Monaco* (website: www.gouv.mc/Dataweb/journmon) an internal Government journal, is published weekly. Other newspapers include *Gazette Monaco-Côte d'Azur*, *Monaco Actualité* and *Monte Carlo Méditerranée*. French newspapers are widely available, as are English books and magazines. The *Riviera Reporter*, the only English-language magazine for residents in the French Riviera, is published every two months.

TV: TV Monte-Carlo (TMC).

Radio: *Radio Monte-Carlo (RMC) Info* is a French-language network. *Radio Monte-Carlo (RMC)* is an Italian-language network. *Riviera Radio* is a privately run English-language network. *Radio Monte-Carlo Moyen Orient* is a pan-Arab station, now based in Paris and operated by *Radio France Internationale*.

Passport/Visa

The passport and visa requirements for persons visiting Monaco as tourists are the same as for France. For further details, see the *France* section. Monaco is not a member of the EU, however, so residency and long-stay requirements differ and are liable to change. For further details, contact any French Consulate (or Consular section at Embassy).

Money

Currency: The first Euro coins and notes were introduced in January 2002. For details of the Euro currency, exchange rates and currency restrictions, see *France* section.

Credit & debit cards: All major credit cards are widely accepted. Check with your credit or debit card company for details of merchant acceptability and other services which may be available.

Traveller's cheques: Widely accepted. To avoid additional exchange rate charges, travellers are advised to take traveller's cheques in Euros, US Dollars or Pounds Sterling.

Banking hours: Mon-Fri 0900-1200 and 1400-1630.

Duty Free

See *France* section for details.

Public Holidays

Below are listed Public Holidays for the January 2006-June 2007 period.

2006: Jan 1 New Year's Day. **Jan 27** Saint-Devote's Day. **Apr 17** Easter Monday. **May 1** Labour Day. **May 25** Ascension. **Jun 5** Whit Monday. **Jun 15** Corpus Christi. **Aug 15** Assumption. **Nov 1** All Saints' Day. **Nov 19** Monaco National Day. **Dec 8** Immaculate Conception. **Dec 25** Christmas Day. **2007: Jan 1** New Year's Day. **Jan** Saint-Devote's Day. **Apr 9** Easter Monday. **May 1** Labour Day. **May 17** Ascension. **May 28** Whit Monday. **Jun 7** Corpus Christi.

Health

	Special Precautions?	Certificate Required?
Yellow Fever	No	No
Cholera	No	No
Typhoid & Polio	No	N/A
Malaria	No	N/A

Note: *Regulations and requirements may be subject to change at short notice, and you are advised to contact your doctor well in advance of your intended date of departure. Any numbers in the chart refer to the footnotes below.*

Health care: Health insurance is recommended. There are high standards of medical care.

Travel - International

AIR:

There is no airport in Monaco. The nearest airport is *Nice* (NCE) (Nice-Cote d'Azur) (website: www.nice.aeroport.fr), 22km (14 miles) from Monaco. *To/from the airport:* There is a direct bus service from Nice Airport to Monaco, which stops at major hotels. The return journey stops at slightly fewer hotels and takes passengers to Terminals 1 and 2 at Nice airport (travel time – 45 minutes). A helicopter service run by *Héli-Air Monaco (YO)* links Monaco with the airport (journey time– seven minutes); the cost is from €80 for a one-way ticket. *Héli-Air*

Monaco

also serves points along the Côte d'Azur and in Italy. There are free shuttle links from the heliport to hotels in the principality. For more information, contact *Héli-Air Monaco*, Monaco Heliport, Quartier de Fontvieille, 98000 Monaco (tel: 9205 0050; website: www.heliairmonaco.com). *Facilities*: Restaurants/bars, Internet facilities, shops, car hire and a business centre.

Departure tax: None.

SEA:

The main harbours are at *Condamine (Hercule port)* and *Fontvieille*, which are equipped to handle yachts of all tonnages. Intercontinental liners are able to anchor in the bay of Monaco.

RAIL:

An extensive train service, including daily and overnight through-trains, runs through the Principality to all neighbouring towns. The *TGV Méditerranée* line runs between Paris and Monaco (travel time – six hours five minutes). High-speed trains on this route run through the beautiful Burgundy and Provencal countryside. For more information, contact *Rail Europe* (tel: (0870) 830 2000; website: www.raileurope.co.uk). Trains run to Genoa, Milan and Basel. Night trains are available to Strasbourg, Paris, Toulouse, Irun, Port-Bou, Milan, Venice, Pisa and Rome. The *Regional Express Trains (TER)* connect with all the towns on the Riviera. *SNCF Métrazur* summer service runs every 30 minutes, stopping at all towns on the Côte d'Azur between Cannes and the Italian frontier at Vintimille, including Monaco. For more information, contact *French Railways* (SNCF) (tel: (8) 3635 3535; website: www.sncf.com).

Rail passes: The *Inter-Rail* pass offers unlimited second-class train travel in up to 29 European countries (includes Morocco and Turkey) split into eight zones (A-H). Three different tickets are available: a ticket covering one zone (two-six countries), 16 days' validity); a ticket covering two zones (six to 10 countries, 22 day's validity) and an *All Zone Pass* (29 countries, one month's validity). Ferry services between Italy and Greece are included. Passengers must be resident in Europe fro at least six months before the pass is used. Travel is not allowed in the passenger's country of residence. Travellers under 26 years receive a reduction of about 30 per cent. Children's tickets are reduced by about 50 per cent. Supplements are required for some high-speed services, seat reservations and couchettes. Discounts are offered on *Eurostar* and some ferry routes. Available from *Inter Rail* (website: www.interrailnet.com).

The *Eurailpass* offers unlimited first-class train travel in 17 European countries. Tickets are valid for 15 days, 21 days, one month, two months or three months. The *Eurailpass Saver* ticket offers discounts for two or more people travelling together. The *Eurailpass Youth* ticket is available to those aged under 26 and offers unlimited second-class train travel. The *Eurailpass Flexi* allows either 10 or 15 travel days within a two-month period. The *Eurail Selectpass* is valid in three, four or five bordering countries and allows five, six, eight or 10 travel days (or 15 for five countries) in a two-month period in one of nine regions (usually two or more countries). Children receive a 50 per cent reduction. The passes cannot be sold to residents of Europe, Turkey, Morocco, Algeria, Tunisia or the Russian Federation. Available from *The Eurail Group* (website: www.eurail.com).

ROAD:

Cannes and Nice are 50km (31 miles) and 18km (11 miles) west of Monaco. The French/Italian border and Menton are 12km (7 miles) and 9km (6 miles) east of Monaco. No formalities are required to cross the frontier between France and the Principality of Monaco. The European motorway network is 8km (5 miles) away from the city centre linking Monaco with France, Spain, Italy, Germany, Benelux, Austria and the UK. Between Monaco and Nice there are three attractive roads: highway 98, *Basse Corniche*; highway 7, *Moyenne Corniche*; and the Great Coastal Road, *Grande Corniche*. **Bus:** There are good connections with the surrounding areas, with regular services as outlined. *Nice*: Seaside route with stops at Cap d'Ail, Eze-sur-Mer, Beaulieu-sur-Mer and Villefranche-sur-Mer. Service from 0600-2100 approximately every 30 minutes. Middle Corniche route with stops at Cap d'Ail, Eze-Village and Col de Villefranche. Services from 0600-1815 (Sat-Sun 2000) approximately every hour. *Menton*: Seaside route with stops in Roquebrune and Cap-Martin (service from 0530-2100) approximately every 30 minutes. Service to Saint Roman/Rocher de Monaco, Jardin Exotique/Rocher de Monaco, Gare SNCF/Larvotto Beach and Rocher de Monaco/Parking Touristique Fontvieille. Buses run approximately every five minutes between Monaco-Ville and the Casino, every 10 minutes towards Saint Roman or the Jardin Exotique and between the Railway Station and beaches (Larvotto). **Taxi:** Available from Casino Square, Monaco Monte-Carlo Railway Station, avenue Princesse Grace, Fontvieille, Métropole, Place des Moulins and the Post Office of Monte-Carlo. There is a surcharge after 2200. Taxi drivers are usually tipped 15 per cent of the fare.

Documentation: As for France, a national driving licence will suffice.

Travel Times: The following chart gives approximate travel times (in hours and minutes) from **Monaco** to a selection of other cities in Europe.

	Air	Road	Rail	Sea
Paris	1.15	-	-	-
Nice	*0.07	0.45	0.30	0.20
London	1.55	20.00	11.00	-
Rome	1.00	-	-	-

* Time by helicopter; see above under *Air*.

Travel Advice

Most visits to Monaco are trouble-free but you should be aware of the global risk of indiscriminate international terrorist attacks, which could be against civilian targets, including places frequented by foreigners.

This advice is based on information provided by the Foreign and Commonwealth Office in the UK. It is correct at time of publishing. As the situation can change rapidly, visitors are advised to contact the following organisations for the latest travel advice:

British Foreign and Commonwealth Office
Tel: (0845) 850 2829.
Website: www.fco.gov.uk

US Department of State
Website: http://travel.state.gov/travel

Accommodation

HOTELS:

Some of the most luxurious hotels and conference facilities are centred in Monte Carlo, and all are equipped with extensive modern amenities. Hotels in Monaco are graded **1-** to **4-star deluxe**.

SELF-CATERING:

Apartments are available to let. For further details, contact the Monaco Government Tourist & Convention Office (see *Top Things To Do*).

YOUTH HOSTELS:

There is one youth hostel in Monaco, Hotel le Versailles. It is located close to the railway station and overlooks the bay.

ACCOMMODATION INFORMATION

Association de l'Industrie Hôtelière Monégasque
Hôtel Tulipin, 9 avenue Prince Pierre,
MC 98000, Monaco
Tel: 9205 6491.
Website: www.monte-carlo.mc

Top Things To See

- At **Monte Carlo**'s spiritual heart is **Monaco-Ville** (old town) where the **Place du Palais** houses the **Prince's Palace and State Apartments** (open daily 0930-1830 (June to September), 1000-1700 (October)). Built around 1215, the palace's focal points are the **Throne Room** and the **Main Courtyard** with its horse-shaped marble staircase, adorned with millions of geometric patterns. Attend the **Changing of the Palace Guard** (admission free), which takes place daily, just before noon (1155).
- There are a number of museums of varying degrees of interest located in the Old Town, including the **Oceanographic Museum and Aquarium**, whose grandiose facade rises spectacularly out of the sea and houses a world-renowned collection of marine fauna and interactive exhibits. Other museums and attractions include the **Museum of Napoleonic Souvenirs and Collection of the Palace's Historic Archives**, which exhibits thousands of objects relating to the First Empire (Napoleon I) and provides a colourful history of Monaco; the **Wax Museum of the Princes of Monaco**, Monaco's answer to London's Madame Tussaud's and the **Monte Carlo Story**, a multivision show about Monaco's history.
- Chill out at the serene and sea-facing **Saint-Martin Gardens** (also in the Old Town), which inspired the poet Guillaume Apollinaire between 1887 and 1889.
- Alternatively, visit the **Japanese Gardens**, right next to the sea; the **National Museum of Dolls and Clockwork Exhibits of Yesteryear**; the **Exotic Garden** from where excellent **views** of **Monte-Carlo's harbour** and its usual armada of luxury yachts can be enjoyed; the **Observatory Caves and Museum of Prehistoric Anthropology** (located in Moneghetti); and the **Condamine Market**, a covered market next to one of Monaco's best shopping districts (the pedestrianised **Rue Princesse Caroline** and the **Rue Grimaldi**).
- In the **Fontvieille** area, discover more than 180 varieties of rose at the **Princess Grace Rose Garden**. The **Museum of Stamps and Coins** features rare philatelic items from the postal history of the Principality. The permanent exhibition of **Prince Rainier III's Private Collection of Classic Cars**, with over 100 classic cars, is nearby. The **Naval Museum** and the **Zoological Terraces** are also located here.

Top Things To Do

- In **Monaco-Ville** (the Old Town), hop on the **Azur Express Tourist Train**, which offers commentaries in French, Italian, German and English.
- Attend the world-famous **Monaco Grand Prix Formula One race**, which takes place every year in the Principality's narrow winding streets, attracting thousands of spectators. Another favourite is the **Historic Grand Prix**, which is held every other year.
- Practise all types of watersports, with facilities for **water-skiing**, **skindiving**, **parasailing** and **windsurfing** all provided. **Swimming** in the sea is safe (although the beaches tend to be crowded). The Diving Club of Cap d'Ail (outside Monaco) organises **diving** sessions (tel: (4) 9378 3174). **Sailing** and **yachting** are generally popular and the *Yacht Club de Monaco* offers sailing lessons during July and August, while the harbour also offers extensive facilities.

Credit: ©Monaco Government Tourist & Convention Office

- **Gamble** in style at the **Grand Casino** in **Monte Carlo**. The casino is located in Monaco's most famous *quartier* known as the **Golden Circle**, where all the most luxurious and fashionable hotels, restaurants and boutiques can also be found (including the famous Hôtel de Paris). The casino was originally built in 1863 and demolished in 1878, but was then replaced six months later by a new structure according to the plans of Charles Garnier, the architect of the Paris Opera House. The style is distinctively grand and luxurious and the casino is linked to the **Salle Garnier Opera House** (closed for refurbishment until 2007) by an impressive atrium lined with 28 Ionic columns made of onyx. Public slot machines open daily from 1400, private gambling rooms from 1500. An admission fee is charged. The minimum age for entering any of Monte Carlo's casinos is 21.
- Relax at Monaco's health **spas** and beauty centres, the most famous one being the **Thermes Marins de Monte Carlo** (website: www.montecarlospa.com).
- Take a **panoramic flight** over the Principality and the surrounding area with *Heli-Air Monaco* (tel: 9205 0050; website: www.heliairmonaco.com). Trips last from 10 to 40 minutes.

TOURIST INFORMATION

Monaco Government Tourist and Convention Office in the UK
The Chambers of Chelsea Harbour, London SW10 0XF, UK
Tel: (020) 7352 9962 *or* (0500) 006 114 (toll-free in the UK).
Website: www.monaco-tourisme.com

Consulate General of the Principality of Monaco and Monaco Government Tourist Office in the USA
23rd Floor, 565 Fifth Avenue, New York, NY 10017, USA
Tel: (212) 286 3330 (tourist office) *or* 286 0500 (consular section) *or* (800) 753 9696 (toll-free).
Website: www.visitmonaco.com (tourism) *or* www.monaco-consulate.com (consular section).

Entertainment

FOOD & DRINK: Restaurants in Monaco offer a wide choice of food. Service and standards are excellent. Cuisine is similar to France.

National specialities:

- *Barbagiuan* (a type of pastry filled with rice and pumpkin).
- *Fougasse* (fragrant orange flower water pastries decorated with nuts, almonds and aniseed).
- *Socca* (chick-pea flour pancakes).
- *Stocafi* (dried cod cooked in a tomato sauce).

Tipping: Hotel and restaurant bills generally include a 15

A B C D E F G H I J K L M N O P Q R S T U V W X Y Z

per cent service charge; however, where this is not added it is customary to leave a 15 per cent tip.

NIGHTLIFE: The world-famous Monte Carlo Casino is a perennial attraction. The building also houses the Casino Cabaret and the *Salle Garnier*, the delightful gilded Opera House offering a winter season of ballet, opera and music. There are further gambling venues in the Monte Carlo Grand Hotel and the Monte Carlo Sporting Club and the Café de Paris. There are also several nightclubs, cinemas, discos and variety shows.

SHOPPING: Monégasque products include perfume, chocolates, ceramics, clothing, hosiery, shoes, books, jewellery and embroidery. Handcrafted items are sold at Boutique du Rocher, a charity of the late Princess Grâce de Monaco. Monégasque stamps are highly prized by collectors. **Shopping hours:** Mon-Sat 0900-1230 and 1500-1830.

Business

- **GDP:** Not published by Government
- **Main exports:** Pharmaceuticals, perfumes and clothing.
- **Main imports:** Electricity.
- **Main trade partners:** France and Italy.

ECONOMY: Service industries, especially property and financial services, account for the bulk of Monaco's economy. Tourism is also a major source of revenue, contributing about 25 per cent of Government revenue, as well as being the mainstay of local retail businesses. There is also a highly successful, custom-built business conference venue. The dearth of land precludes any agriculture, but there is some light industry, the main products of which are pharmaceuticals, plastics, electronics, paper and textiles. Monaco attracts many extremely wealthy individuals as residents, by virtue of its pleasant climate, reputation and environment as well as the absence of income or inheritance tax and lack of financial reporting requirements. Migrant, non-resident labour supplies the menial workforce. Since the late 1990s, concerted international efforts to tackle the global problem of money laundering and tax evasion have been led by the Organisation of Economic Cooperation and Development (the group of 24 leading industrial countries) and its Financial Action Task Force (FATF). The FATF has set down a number of criteria covering disclosure which 'offshore' financial centres must meet. Most centres have cooperated with the new FATF regime. Monaco is one of seven which, by the deadline in April 2002, had failed to do so: future developments rely on the actions of Monaco's ruling Grimaldi family (itself implicated in a major fraud inquiry) and the attitude of the French Government. Almost all the Principality's external trade is conducted with France – and France, along with Italy, supplies the bulk of Monaco's visitors (both as tourists and foreign labour).

BUSINESS ETIQUETTE: A suit should be worn and prior appointments are necessary. Business meetings are formal. It is considered impolite to begin a conversation in French and then revert to English. **Office hours:** Mon-Fri 0900-1200 and 1400-1700.

CONFERENCES/CONVENTIONS: Monaco is a year-round leisure and business destination and there are extensive conference facilities. The Forum Grimaldi Cultural and Exhibition Centre, one of Europe's largest venues for conference events, provides three terraced auditoria, the largest with 1900 seats and two massive exhibitions halls. Large parts of the new complex are built under water. Other conference venues include the 1100-capacity Convention Centre and Auditorium (built on land reclaimed from the sea), including technical support and exhibition areas; the International Conference Centre (with a capacity for 450 persons); and the Meridien Beach Plaza Club, which can seat up to 1624 people. For further information, contact the Direction du Tourisme (see *Top Things To Do*).

COMMERCIAL INFORMATION

Conseil Economique et Social (Consultative organisation dealing with all aspects of the national economy)
8 rue Louis Notari, MC 98000, Monaco
Tel: 9330 2082.

Grimaldi Forum Monaco (Information on Conferences/Conventions)
BP 2000, 10 avenue de la Princesse Grace, MC 98001, Monaco
Tel: 9999 2000.
Website: www.grimaldiforum.com

Mongolia

Location: Central Asia.

Time: GMT + 8 (GMT + 9 from the last Saturday in March to last Saturday in September.)
Bayan Ulgii, Uvs & Khovd Aimags in western Mongolia: GMT + 7 (GMT + 8 from last Saturday in March to last Saturday in September).

Overview

Mongolia is a far-flung, little visited destination, with much to offer in terms of scenery, wildlife, and historic and cultural sites. Outside the main cities, Mongolians continue to live the traditional life of *malchin* (herdsmen), and many are nomadic. With one of the world's lowest population densities, Mongolia's vast areas of wilderness, desert, lakes and mountains offer plenty of scope for adventurous outdoor enthusiasts. Although independent travel is now becoming more common, travel outside the capital is usually by prior arrangement.

General Information

AREA: 1,564,116 sq km (603,909 sq miles).
POPULATION: 2.5 million (official estimate 2002).
POPULATION DENSITY: 1.6 per sq km.
CAPITAL: Ulaanbaatar. **Population:** 869,900 (2004).
GEOGRAPHY: Mongolia has a 3485km- (2165 mile-) border with the Russian Federation in the north and a 4670km- (2902 mile-) border with China in the south. From north to south, it can be divided into four areas: mountain-forest steppe, mountain steppe and, in the extreme south, semi-desert and desert (the latter being about 3 per cent of the entire territory). The majority of the country has a high elevation, with the principal mountains concentrated in the west. The highest point is the peak of Tavan Bogd, in the Altai Mountains, at 4374m (14,350ft) high. The lowest point, Khukh Nuur lake, in the east, lies at 560m (1820ft). There are several hundred lakes in the country and numerous rivers.
GOVERNMENT: Republic. Declared independence from China in 1921. **Head of State:** President Nambaryn Enkhbayar since 2005. **Head of Government:** Prime Minister Miyeegombo Enkhbold since 2006. **Recent history:** The Mongolian Parliament chose the former mayor of Ulaanbaatar, Miyeegombo Enkhbold, as the new Prime Minister in the January 2006 elections. Mr Enkhbold was the widely expected choice, being the Mongolian People's Revolutionary Party (MPRP) candidate. Mongolia was plunged into crisis weeks before the election when the MPRP withdrew from the governing coalition, causing Prime Minister Tsakhia Elbegdorj to resign.
LANGUAGE: Khalkh Mongolian is the official language. Kazakh is spoken by 5 per cent of the population. There are also many Mongolian dialects.
RELIGION: Buddhist Lamaism is the main religion, although there is no state religion.
ELECTRICITY: 230 volts AC, 50Hz.

SOCIAL CONVENTIONS: Religious customs should be respected. Mongolia has a large number of customs and traditions. Further details can be obtained from the Mongolian Tourism Association (see *Top Things To See & Do*). Visitors are requested to familiarise themselves with these customs. **Photography:** Not permitted in temples and monasteries. A fee is payable for photography in protected areas, although this regulation is often not enforced. Caution should be exercised when photographing Government buildings, military establishments and border crossings.

Climate

A dry climate with short, mild summers and long, severe winters (October to April). Some rain falls during summer and there is snow during winter.
Required clothing: Mediumweights are worn during summer, with very warm heavyweights advised for winter.

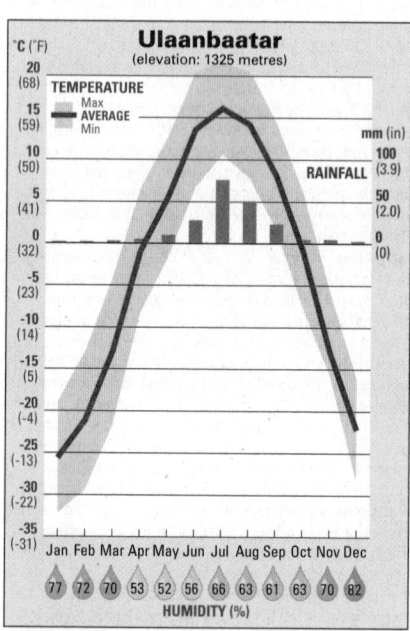

Communications

Telephone: An Asiasat Earth station has provided international telecommunications with Mongolia since 1994. Country code: 976. Area codes: Ulaanbaatar: 11, Darkhan: 01-372, Erdenet: 01-352, Khovd: 01-432. International calls can be made from telephone exchanges in Ulaanbaatar.
Mobile telephone: Roaming agreements exist with some international mobile phone operators. Coverage is limited to urban areas.
Internet: Access is available in Ulaanbaatar at business centres (often located in hotels), Internet cafes and at the telephone exchange on Suhkbaatar Square.
Post: Airmail abroad can be very slow. There is an express mail service available for a limited number of countries.
MEDIA: Press: The main newspapers include *Odriin Sonin*, *Ünen* and *Zuuny Medee*. The English-language papers published in Mongolia include *The Mongol Messenger* and *The UB Post*, both of which are published weekly.
TV: State-run television is operated by *Mongolteleviz*. MN Channel 25 is a private channel in Ulaanbaatar.
Radio: State-run national radio is operated by *Mongolradio*. Private stations include *Radio Ulaanbaatar*.

Passport/Visa

	Passport Required?	Visa Required?	ReturnTicket Required?
Full British	Yes	Yes	No
Australian	Yes	Yes	No
Canadian	Yes	Yes	No
USA	Yes	1	No
Other EU	Yes	Yes	No
Japanese	Yes	Yes	No

Note: *Regulations and requirements may be subject to change at short notice, and you are advised to contact the appropriate diplomatic or consular authority before finalising travel arrangements. Any numbers in the chart refer to the footnotes below.*

PASSPORTS: Passport valid for at least six months required by all.
VISAS: Required by all except the following:

(a) nationals of Kazakhstan for stays of up to three months;
(b) **1.** nationals of the USA, if entering the country as a tourist, for stays of up to three months;
(c) nationals of Cuba, Israel and Malaysia for up to one month;
(d) nationals of The Philippines for stays of up to three weeks;
(e) nationals of Hong Kong and Singapore for stays of up to 14 days.

Types of visa and cost: *Business* and *Ordinary: Single-entry/Exit:* £35. *Double-entry/Exit:* £50. *Multiple-entry/Exit:* £65. *Single-transit:* £30. *Double-transit:* £35. *Multiple-transit:* £40.

Validity: Visas are generally valid for 30 days from date of entry (and three months from date of issue) and can be extended in Mongolia by a maximum of 30 days.

Application to: Consulate (or Consular section at Embassy); see *Passport/Visa Information*. If travelling on an organised tour, visas can be obtained through tourism companies or travel agencies. A group visa in the name of the tour leader is valid for all tourists on the list attached, provided relevant details (nationality, sex, date of birth, passport numbers, and dates of issue and expiry) are given at the time of application.

Note: All foreign nationals staying in Mongolia for longer than 30 days are required to register with the police within 10 days of arrival.

Application requirements: (a) Valid passport. (b) Application form. (c) One passport-size photo. (d) Fee, payable by cash or cheque; there is an additional £5 fee for postal applications. *Business* (and any visas valid more than one month): (a)-(d) and, (e) Invitation letter from Mongolia.

Working days required: Two to five. An express service is available which costs an additional £10.

Temporary residence/work permit: Enquire at the Mongolian Embassy.

PASSPORT/VISA INFORMATION

Embassy of Mongolia in the UK
7-8 Kensington Court, London W8 5DL, UK
Tel: (020) 7937 0150 ext. 29 (visa section).
Website: www.embassyofmongolia.co.uk
Opening hours: Mon-Fri 1000-1230 (visa section).

Embassy of Mongolia in the USA
2833 M Street, NW, Washington, DC 20007, USA
Tel: (202) 333 7117.
Website: www.mongolianembassy.us

Money

Currency: Tugrik (MNT). Notes are in denominations of MNT10,000, 5000, 1000, 500, 100, 50, 20, 10, 5 and 1. Coins are in denominations of MNT500, 200, 100, 50 and 20.
Currency exchange: Official organisations authorised to exchange foreign currency include commercial banks in Ulaanbaatar and bureaux de change at certain hotels. The easiest currency to exchange is the US Dollar.
Credit & debit cards: Accepted by main commercial banks, large hotels and a few shops and restaurants in Ulaanbaatar. Credit card cash advances can be obtained at the Trade and Development Bank.
Traveller's cheques: American Express Traveller's Cheques are most widely accepted although Thomas Cook cheques are accepted by the Trade and Development Bank. To avoid additional exchange rate charges, travellers are advised to take traveller's cheques in US Dollars. Traveller's cheques can be difficult to exchange outside the capital.
Currency restrictions: The import of local currency is limited to MNT815, provided declared on arrival. Bank certificates must be shown. The import of foreign currency is limited to US$2000 or equivalent. The export of local and foreign currency is limited to the amount declared on arrival.
Banking hours: Mon-Fri 0930-1230 and 1400-1500.
Exchange rate indicators:
Rate at time of publishing
£1.00=   MNT2057.94
$1.00=   MNT1186.00

Duty Free

The following goods may be imported into Mongolia without incurring customs duty:
200 cigarettes or 50 cigars or 250g of tobacco; 1l of vodka and 2l of wine and 3l of beer; personal effects; goods up to a value of US$1000.
Prohibited items: Guns, weapons and ammunition without special permission; explosive items; radioactive substances; narcotics; pornographic publications; any publications, records, films and drawings critical of Mongolia; palaeontological and archaeological findings without special permission; collections of various plants and their seeds; birds and wild or domestic animals; wool, raw skins, hides and furs without permission from the appropriate authorities.
Note: (a) Every tourist must fill in a customs declaration,

---

which should be retained until departure. This allows for the free import and re-export of articles intended for personal use for the duration of stay. (b) Visitors intending to export antiques and fossils must have official permission. Some shops will supply the necessary documents upon purchase; otherwise, permission should be obtained from the Ministry of Enlightenment. (c) Goods to the value of Tg20,000 are allowed to be exported from Mongolia.

Public Holidays

Below are listed Public Holidays for the January 2006-June 2007 period.
2006: Jan 1 New Year's Day. **Jan 28-30** Tsagaan Sar (Lunar New Year). **Jun 1** Mothers and Children's Day. **Jul 11-13** Naadam. **Nov 26** Independence Day.
2007: Jan 1 New Year's Day. **Jan** or **Feb** Tsagaan Sar (Lunar New Year). **Jun 1** Mothers and Children's Day.

Health

	Special Precautions?	Certificate Required?
Yellow Fever	No	No
Cholera	1	No
Typhoid & Polio	2	N/A
Malaria	No	N/A

Note: *Regulations and requirements may be subject to change at short notice, and you are advised to contact your doctor well in advance of your intended date of departure. Any numbers in the chart refer to the footnotes below.*

1: There may be some risk of cholera; precautions should be considered.
2: Typhoid is a risk.
Food & drink: All water should be regarded as being potentially contaminated. Water used for drinking, brushing teeth or making ice should have first been boiled or otherwise sterilised. Some milk is unpasteurised and should be boiled. Powdered, long-life or tinned milk is available and is advised, but make sure that it is reconstituted with pure water. Avoid dairy products which are likely to have been made from unboiled milk. Only eat well-cooked meat and fish, preferably served hot. Pork, salad and mayonnaise may carry increased risk. Vegetables should be cooked and fruit peeled.
Other risks: Diarrhoeal diseases and outbreaks of *meningococcal meningitis* occur. There is some risk of *plague.* Immunisation against *Hepatitis A* and *TB* is recommended. *Hepatitis B* is highly endemic and *Hepatitis C* also occurs.
Rabies is present. For those at high risk, vaccination before arrival should be considered. If you are bitten, seek medical advice without delay. For more information, see the *Health* appendix.
Health care: There are almost 23,000 hospital beds and over 5000 doctors in Mongolia. However, health-care facilities available to foreigners are limited. All Mongolian hospitals are very short of most medical supplies, including basic care items, drugs and spare parts for medical equipment. Reciprocal agreements with the UK or USA are not available and US medical insurance is not valid in Mongolia. Doctors and hospitals expect immediate cash payment for health services. Visitors are urged to have health insurance including cover for evacuation to Hong Kong and to take any regular medication with them. Emergency care is available at the Russian Hospital, although a translator is essential.

Travel - International

AIR:

The national airline, *MIAT – Mongolian International Air Transport (OM)* (website: www.miat.com), operates flights to Ulaanbaatar from Beijing, Berlin, Moscow and Seoul all year round, and to and from Hong Kong and Osaka in the summer months. Other airlines serving Mongolia include *Aeroflot, Air China* and *Korean Air.*
Approximate flight times: To Ulaanbaatar from *London* is 14 hours including stopovers.
Main airports: *Ulaanbaatar (ULN)* (*Chinggis Khaan*) is 15km (9 miles) from the city. *To/from the airport:* Buses run to the city centre (travel time – 30 minutes). Taxis are also available (travel time – 15 minutes). *Facilities:* Bank, duty free shops, car hire, post office and a restaurant.
Departure tax: US$12.
RAIL:

Ulaanbaatar is linked to the Russian Federation and China by the *Trans-Mongolian Railway.* An express train runs once a week between Moscow, Ulaanbaatar and Beijing. Trains on international routes have sleeping and restaurant cars. There are also other weekly trains from Ulaanbaatar to Beijing and Ulaanbaatar to Moscow.
Note: At present, there are problems reported on buying

---

train tickets to Ulaanbaatar for the Trans-Mongolia train. Although the trains certainly stop in Ulaanbaatar, tickets are only being sold to Chinese or Russian destinations. Therefore, a passenger wishing to travel from Beijing to Ulaanbaatar will have to pay for a ticket to Ulaan Ude, just over the Russian border. The other trains between Moscow and Ulaanbaatar, and Beijing and Ulaanbaatar are unaffected.
ROAD:

There are several international road links; the principal route is via Irkutsk (East Siberia) to Ulaanbaatar. Travellers are not normally allowed to enter Mongolia by road unless they obtain prior permission from the Mongolian authorities.

Travel - Internal

AIR:

Internal flights are operated by *MIAT – Mongolian International Air Transport (OM)*. This is the recommended means of travelling to remote areas.
RAIL:

There are 1815km (1127 miles) of track. The main line runs from north to south: Sukhbaatar–Darkhan–Ulaanbaatar–Sainshand. Branch lines serve the principal industrial regions.
ROAD:

Paved roads are to be found only in or near major cities. **Bus:** There are frequent bus services between major towns, but the roads are mostly unpaved. **Car hire:** Available through tourism companies (although self drive is not available since most roads are unpaved, maps are poor and there are no road signs). Jeeps, camels or horses are available for hunters, trekkers and special-interest travellers.
URBAN:

There are frequent bus and trolleybus services in the city.
Travel times: The following chart gives approximate travel times (in hours and minutes) from **Ulaanbaatar** to other major cities/towns in Mongolia.

	Air	Road
Erdenet	0.45	9.00
Dalanzadgad	1.20	14.00
Darkhan	-	5.00
Khovd	4.00	4/5 days

Travel Advice

Most visits to Mongolia are trouble-free but you should be aware of the global risk of indiscriminate international terrorist attacks, which could be against civilian targets, including places frequented by foreigners.
Communications and health facilities in Mongolia, particularly outside Ulaanbaatar, can be poor.
Travellers entering Mongolia by road should be aware that only a few specified border crossings are open to foreigners. This advice is based on information provided by the Foreign and Commonwealth Office in the UK. It is correct at time of publishing. As the situation can change rapidly, visitors are advised to contact the following organisations for the latest travel advice:

British Foreign and Commonwealth Office
Tel: (0845) 850 2829.
Website: www.fco.gov.uk

US Department of State
Website: http://travel.state.gov/travel

Accommodation

HOTELS:

There are six major hotels in Ulaanbaatar, offering over 1000 beds. There are also many smaller hotels, guest houses and hostels of varying standards. There is suitable accommodation for backpackers. Outside the capital, hotels are basic and few in number. Most provide full board, daily excursions and entrance fees to museums and the services of a guide or interpreter. Accommodation can be arranged through tourism companies or directly with the hotels.
Grading: There is currently no official grading system for accommodation in Mongolia.
RESORT SPAS: There is limited accommodation for visitors. Prices are available on request.
CAMPING:

There are now 95 tourist *ger* camps spread throughout the countryside. The accommodation is in *gers* (round felt tents used by nomadic herders). In most cases, there are also restaurants, bars, toilets and showers. *Ger* camps are usually open from May to October. Tourists with their own tents have the opportunity to camp almost anywhere they want although there are restrictions in protected areas and it is advisable to avoid settlements.

ACCOMMODATION INFORMATION

Mongolian Hotels Association
Children's Palace, Door No 27, Ulaanbaatar, Mongolia
Tel: (11) 450 683.
Fax: (11) 684 595.

Top Things To See & Do

• The capital, **Ulaanbaatar**, is the country's political, commercial and cultural centre. There are a number of museums in the city, the largest being the **Museum of Natural History**. The palaeontological section has a magnificent display of the skeletons of giant dinosaurs. Others include the **Zanabazar Museum of Fine Arts**, the **National Museum of Mongolian History** and the **Military Museum**. There are also several Buddhist temple museums, and the still-functioning **Gandan Monastery** is worth a visit. Ulaanbaatar also has several theatres and theatre groups, such as the *State Opera and Ballet Theatre*, the *State Drama Theatre* and the *Folk Song and Dance Ensemble*. The Ulaanbaatar **State Public Library** has a unique collection of 11th-century Sanskrit manuscripts.

• Coaches take parties to the country's tourist camps. The nearest to Ulaanbaatar is **Terelj**, 85km (50 miles) from the capital, where the **Gorki Mountains**, the **Turtle Rock** and the **Terelj River** may be seen.

• **Khangai** is a mountainous region with more than 20 hot springs renowned for their healing properties. Another therapeutic spring can be found in **Khujirt**, where the ruins of the world-renowned **Kharakhorum**, capital of the Great Mongolian Empire of the 13th century, can also be found.

• The Mongolian Tourism Association will be able to put you in touch with Mongolian tour operators that can arrange itineraries and special-interest tours, including visits with nomadic herdsmen and overnight stays in *gers*. Activity tours available include **trekking**, **mountaineering**, **birdwatching**, **horse riding**, **rafting**, **camel riding**, **yak caravan** and overland **motorcycle** tours. Many of these tours focus strongly on **ecology** and **wildlife**, and almost all of them include the **Gobi Desert** as one of their destinations; apart from its numerous native animal species (including Bactrian wild camels, snow leopards, Prezwalsky horses and Gobi bears), the desert is famous for its fossilised dinosaur bones and eggs. Mongolia's **lakes** (notably the huge **Khuvsgul Nuur**) represent another good hiking destination, as do the **Four Holy Peaks** surrounding Ulaanbaatar or the **Gobi Gurvansaikhan National Park**, in the South Gobi. Visitors should note that the weather, although milder than expected, can vary greatly, especially in the mountains and in the Gobi Desert; it is recommended to bring a warm sweater and raincoat for any time of the year.

• **Skiing** and **cross-country skiing** are possible around **Ulaanbaatar**.

TOURIST INFORMATION

Mongolian Tourism Association
Room 318, Trade Union Building,
Sukhbaatar Square-11,
Ulaanbaatar - 38, 210628, Mongolia
Tel: (11) 327 820.
Website: www.travelmongolia.org

Mongolian National Ecotourism Society
PO Box 72, Ulaanbaatar 210520, Mongolia
Tel: (11) 318 099.
Website: www.owc.org.mn/ecobund

Mongolian Youth Tourism Association
BCC Company, Sukhbaatar Street, Youth Avenue 7/4,
PO Box 72, Ulaanbaatar 210520, Mongolia
Tel: (11) 350 615.
E-mail: aroundworld@hotmail.com

Runwild (ecotourism and adventure tours)
40 Miangat Street, Bldg. 68, Sukhbaatar District,
Ulaanbaatar, Mongolia
Tel: (11) 315 374.
Website: www.runwild.co.uk

Entertainment

FOOD & DRINK: Meat is the basis of the diet, primarily beef and mutton. The local cooking is quite distinctive. Traditional meals generally consist of boiled mutton with lots of fat and flour with either rice or dairy products. One local speciality is *Boodog*; this is the whole carcass of a goat roasted from the inside – the entrails and bones are taken out through the throat, the carcass is filled with burning hot stones and the neck tied tightly, and thus the goat is cooked from the inside to the outside. Fish is also beginning to be widely available.
Mongolian tea (*suutei tsai*), meaning salty tea with milk, is very popular. Mongolian vodka is excellent, as is the beer (although it is expensive). Hot and cold beverages are not normally included in meals and many restaurants will add on a 13 per cent sales tax.

Tipping: Not customary, but this is changing and, if leaving a tip, 10 per cent is the norm.

NIGHTLIFE: There are evening performances at the *State Opera and Ballet Theatre*, *State Drama Theatre* and *Puppet Theatre*. The *Folk Song and Dance Ensemble* and *People's Army Song and Dance Ensemble* are in the capital. Other major towns also have theatres. Circus entertainment is also very popular. There is also one cinema featuring English-language films, and large numbers of bars, nightclubs and restaurants that offer dancing or live entertainment (bands).

SHOPPING: In Ulaanbaatar, there are a few duty free shops and restaurants where convertible currencies are accepted. In all other shops, local currency must be used. The best buys include pictures, cashmere garments, camel-wool blankets, national costumes, boots, jewellery, carpets, books and handicrafts. The notorious *black market* on the outskirts of Ulaanbaatar is a large, crowded flea market which sells a huge variety of items. Suitable for the adventurous traveller, it is patronised mainly by local people. Pickpockets can be a problem. **Shopping hours:** Mon-Sun 1000-1800 as a general guide although times and days vary considerably.

Business

ECONOMY: The vast bulk of Mongolia's working population is engaged in animal herding. Otherwise, large farms (formerly state owned) produce crops for domestic consumption, principally cereals, potatoes and vegetables. Industrial activity is dominated by production of food, hides and wool, especially high-quality cashmere – much of which is consigned for export – and mining. There are large deposits of coal which meet most of Mongolia's energy requirements, as well as copper, fluorspar, tungsten, tin, gold, lead and molybdenum, a rare metal of which Mongolia is one of the world's largest producers. The output of the copper-molybdenum mine at Erdenet accounts for around half of Mongolia's export earnings. It is likely that there are other large deposits as yet undiscovered. Limited oil production began in 1997, but Mongolia still relies on Russia to meet most of its domestic needs. Textiles and light engineering complete Mongolia's main economic activities. The country suffered badly from the collapse of the former Soviet Union: while Mongolia was not a constituent part of the Soviet Union, its economy was especially dependent on the USSR, with which it did 80 per cent of its trade; most of the rest was with its fellow members of the Council for Mutual Economic Assistance (COMECON). After some initial resistance by the MPRP (Mongolia's historic ruling party), most of the economy has been steadily transferred to the private sector. This process was still underway in 2001 when a diverse collection of two dozen enterprises was earmarked for complete or partial sale.
Unfortunately, structural difficulties and an unprecedented two consecutive years of the *zhud* (a uniquely Mongolian climatic phenomenon associated with very severe winters) set back the country's economic development. Russia and China are now Mongolia's principal trade partners and South Korea is a major investor. In 1991, Mongolia joined the IMF and World Bank; in 2000, it became a shareholder (but not a 'country of operation') in the European Reconstruction and Development Bank. The EBRD provides support through the Mongolian Co-operation Fund. It is also a member of the Asian Development Bank and receives aid from the EU's technical assistance programme.

BUSINESS ETIQUETTE: Suits are recommended; mediumweight for summer, and heavyweight for winter. Translator services should be arranged prior to departure for Mongolia, although an increasing number of executives speak English, and Russian is widely spoken. **Office hours:** Mon-Fri 0900-1800.

CONFERENCES/CONVENTIONS: For further information, contact the Mongolian Chamber of Commerce and Industry (see *Commercial Information* below).

COMMERCIAL INFORMATION

Mongolian Chamber of Commerce and Industry
Freedom Square 1, Democracy Street 1,
Ulaanbaatar 210538, Mongolia
Tel: (1) 312 371 *or* 501.

Montserrat

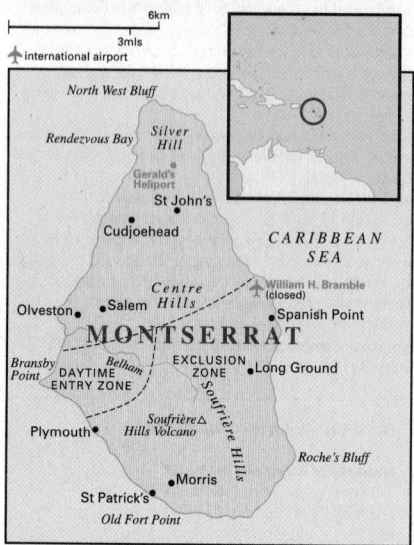

Location: Leeward Islands, Caribbean.

Time: GMT - 4.

Montserrat is a British Overseas Territory, and is represented abroad by British Embassies – see *United Kingdom* section.

Overview

Arawak and Carib Indians were the first residents of Alliouagana, 'land of the prickly bush', until Christopher Columbus claimed it for Spain in 1493, whereupon he named the island Santa Maria de Montserrat. It was not until 1632 that the British colonised the island, which is still a British Overseas Territory. The actual settlers were mainly of Irish Catholic origin, who appreciated the presence of an ocean between them and Oliver Cromwell. Irish surnames among the present population reflect this history. Between 1871 and 1956 the island was administered as part of the Federal Colony of the Leeward Islands.
At this point the federation was dissolved; since then Montserrat has been a British colony administered by a Governor appointed by the British Government (see *General Information* section).
There remains uncertainty about the island's economic future. The main reason is its vulnerability to the elements; Montserrat is located in the Caribbean hurricane zone and has suffered repeated assaults from tempests. However, the damage caused was nothing compared to that wrought by the eruption of a previously dormant volcano, Soufrière, in August 1997.
This rendered almost half the island uninhabitable, and much of the 12,000 population left the island. Many original inhabitants have returned to Montserrat, but the island has been left more dependent than ever on aid and support from the British Government. The southern part of the island, which bore the brunt of the eruption, has been partially repopulated, but the overriding priority for the Government has been to bring economic and social life back to the devastated island. Although this has been a difficult and gradual process, hampered by disagreements, Montserrat continues to welcome visitors to the northern part of the island where economic development is now being planned.

General Information

AREA: 102 sq km (39.5 sq miles).
POPULATION: 4482 (2001).
POPULATION DENSITY: 43.9 per sq km.
CAPITAL: Plymouth, the former capital, was mostly destroyed by pyroclastic flows in August 1997. Brades is currently the interim capital.

GEOGRAPHY: Montserrat is one of the Leeward Islands group in the Eastern Caribbean. It is a volcanic island with black sandy beaches and lush tropical vegetation. There are three main volcanic mountains on the island and Chances Peak is its highest point at 915m (3002ft). The Soufrière group of hills houses the volcano which began erupting in July 1995 and to date is continuously active. The Great Alps Waterfall, previously one of the most spectacular sights in the West Indies, has been destroyed by the volcano.

GOVERNMENT: British Overseas Territory since 1632. **Head of State:** HM Queen Elizabeth II, represented locally by Governor Deborah Barnes Jones since 2004. **Head of Government:** Chief Minister Dr John A Osborne since 2001. **Recent history:** The island's internal politics during the last four decades have been dominated by the struggle between a small number of key individuals around whom political parties have been organised. The dominant figure has been John Osborne, whose People's Liberation Movement was the largest single party in the Legislative Council between 1978 and 1991. Osborne himself served as Chief Minister throughout this period. In September 1991, Osborne's great rival, Reuben Meade, leader of the other main party on the island, the National Progressive Party (NPP), took over as Chief Minister following the election held that month.

The NPP remained in power throughout the 1990s, but the 'New' People's Liberation Movement was returned to office – Osborne still at its helm – with a substantial majority on the Legislative Council in 2001. In 2004, Deborah Barnes Jones took over from Osborne as leader of NPLM. For the most part, the major political issue since 1960 has been independence. While a significant minority has backed this option, it has failed to attract a majority owing to uncertainty about the island's economic future.

LANGUAGE: English.
RELIGION: Roman Catholic, Anglican, Methodist and other Christian denominations.
ELECTRICITY: 110/220 volts AC, 60Hz.
SOCIAL CONVENTIONS: Casual clothes are acceptable. Beachwear should be confined to the beach or poolside. The lifestyle is generally peaceful, combining many English influences with West Indian. The people are usually friendly and relaxed. All visitors are made welcome.

Climate

The climate is subtropical, tempered by trade winds. There is little climatic variation throughout the year. The heaviest rainfall occurs between September and November; however, the heavy cloudbursts serve to refresh the atmosphere and once they are over the sun reappears.

Required clothing: Tropical lightweights are worn, with light woollens for cooler evenings. A light raincoat or an umbrella is useful.

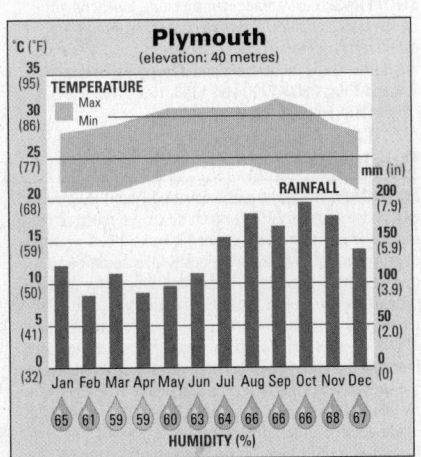

Plymouth (elevation: 40 metres)

Communications

Telephone: Full IDD is available. Country code: 1 664. Phone booths are operated by coins and phonecards.
Mobile telephone: TDMA network not compatible with GSM handsets. Coverage extends over the northern half of the island. Handsets can be hired from the network provider, *C&W Caribbean Cellular*. GSM 850 network operates, provided by *Cable & Wireless West Indies*.
Internet: Internet access is available at *Andy's Internet Cafe*.
Post: The main post office in Brades is open Mon-Fri 0815-1555
MEDIA: Press: *The Montserrat Reporter* and *The Montserrat Times* are both in English and published weekly.
TV: *Cable TV of Montserrat* is privately operated.
Radio: *ZJB Radio Montserrat* is a public station.

Passport/Visa

	Passport Required?	Visa Required?	Return Ticket Required?
Full British	Yes	No	Yes
Australian	Yes	No	Yes
Canadian	Yes	No	Yes
USA	Yes	No	Yes
Other EU	Yes	No/1	Yes
Japanese	Yes	No	Yes

Note: *Regulations and requirements may be subject to change at short notice, and you are advised to contact the appropriate diplomatic or consular authority before finalising travel arrangements. Any numbers in the chart refer to the footnotes below.*

PASSPORTS: Valid passport required by all.
VISAS: Required by all except the following:
(a) nationals of countries referred to in the chart above, except **1.** nationals of Czech Republic, Estonia, Hungary, Latvia, Lithuania, Slovak Republic and Slovenia who *do* need a visa;
(b) nationals of Commonwealth countries, except nationals of Cameroon and Mozambique who *do* need a visa;
(c) nationals of UK Overseas Territories;
(d) nationals of French Dependent Territories;
(e) nationals of Algeria, Andorra, Argentina, Bahrain, Bolivia, Brazil, Central African Republic, Chile, Colombia, Costa Rica, Côte d'Ivoire, Dominican Republic, Ecuador, El Salvador, Guatemala, Haiti, Honduras, Iceland, Israel, Liechtenstein, Mexico, Monaco, Morocco, Nicaragua, Nigeria, Norway, Panama, Paraguay, Peru, The Philippines, San Marino, Surinam, Tunisia, Turkey, United Arab Emirates, Uruguay, Vatican City and Venezuela.
Types of visa and cost: *Tourist* and *Transit*; £28.
Validity: Three months.
Application to: UK Passport Service (see *Passport/Visa Information*) or nearest British Consulate.
Application requirements: (a) Completed application form. (b) Valid passport. (c) Evidence of accommodation. (d) Photocopy of travel itinerary. (e) Fee.
Working days required: Three weeks to one month.
Note: All passengers must hold a return or onward ticket to a country to which they have a legal right of entry and sufficient funds to cover the period of their stay. Passengers not in possession of a return or onward ticket may be required to leave a deposit on arrival. Passengers not complying with any of the entry regulations listed above may be deported.
Temporary residence: Enquire at Chief Immigration Officer, Police Headquarters, Brades, Montserrat (tel: 491 2555).

PASSPORT/VISA INFORMATION

The UK Passport Service
London Passport Office, Globe House, 89 Ecclestone Square, London SW1V 1PN, UK
Tel: (0870) 521 0410 (24-hour passport advice line).
Website: www.passport.gov.uk or www.ukpa.gov.uk
Opening hours: Mon-Fri 0745-1845, Sat 0900-1500 (appointment only).
Personal callers for visas should go to the agency window in the collection room of the London office.

Montserrat Government in the UK
7 Portland Place, London W1B 1PP, UK
Tel: (020) 7031 0317.
Website: www.montserratfirst.com

Money

Currency: East Caribbean Dollar (XCD; symbol EC$) = 100 cents. Notes are in denominations of EC$100, 50, 20, 10 and 5. Coins are in denominations of EC$1, and 25, 10, 5, 2 and 1 cents. US Dollars are also accepted.
Note: The East Caribbean Dollar is tied to the US Dollar.
Currency exchange: There are three banks on Montserrat.
Credit & debit cards: Major credit and debit cards are accepted.
Travellers cheques: Widely accepted. To avoid additional exchange rate charges, travellers are advised to take travellers cheques in US Dollars.
Currency restrictions: There are no restrictions on the import of local or foreign currency if declared. Export of local and foreign currency is limited to the amount imported and declared.
Banking hours: Mon-Thurs 0800-1500, Fri 0800-1500, depending on the bank.
Exchange rate indicators:
Rate at time of publishing
£1.00=   EC$4.69
$1.00=   EC$2.66

Duty Free

The following goods may be imported into Montserrat without incurring customs duty:
200 cigarettes or 50 cigars*; wines and spirits not exceeding 1.14l*; 168g of perfume; gifts up to a value of EC$250 (only once per 12 months).
Note: Tobacco products and alcoholic beverages are only available to passengers 17 years of age or over.

Public Holidays

Below are listed Public Holidays for the January 2006-June 2007 period.
2006: Jan 1 New Year's Day. **Mar 17** St Patrick's Day. **Apr 14-17** Easter. **May 1** Labour Day. **Jun 5** Whit Monday. **Aug 7** August Monday. **Dec 25-26** Christmas. **Dec 31** Festival Day.
2007: Jan 1 New Year's Day. **Mar 17** St Patrick's Day. **Apr 6-9** Easter. **May 1** Labour Day. **May 28** Whit Monday.

Health

	Special Precautions?	Certificate Required?
Yellow Fever	No	No
Cholera	No	1
Typhoid & Polio	No	N/A
Malaria	No	N/A

Note: *Regulations and requirements may be subject to change at short notice, and you are advised to contact your doctor well in advance of your intended date of departure. Any numbers in the chart refer to the footnotes below.*

1: Following WHO guidelines issued in 1973, a cholera vaccination certificate is not normally a requirement of entry to any country. However, Montserratian authorities may require one from travellers arriving from infected areas. See the *Health* appendix for further information about the cholera vaccination.
Food & drink: Mains water is normally chlorinated, and is safe to drink. Bottled water is available. Milk is pasteurised and dairy products are safe for consumption. Local meat, poultry, seafood, fruit and vegetables are generally considered safe to eat.
Other risks: *Bacillary* and *amoebic dysenteries* are common. *Hepatitis A* is present. Outbreaks of *dengue fever* may occur. After an ash fall, the ash-laden air may cause breathing problems for persons suffering from respiratory problems such as *asthma*.
Health care: There is a well-equipped 30-bed hospital, providing 24-hour casualty service. Montserrat is a UK Dependency and a limited reciprocal health agreement exists with the UK. On presentation of proof of UK residence, free treatment is available at the general hospital and at state-run clinics to those aged over 60 and under 16. Dental treatment is also free for school-age children. Private health insurance is recommended. For specialist treatment, visitors are required to travel to neighbouring islands (eg Antigua or Guadeloupe).

Travel - International

AIR:

The nearest international gateway is Antigua. All information on transport and current time tables can be verified with Montserrat Aviation Services (MAS) (tel: 491 2362; fax: 491 7186).
Approximate flight times: From Montserrat to *London* is eight hours 30 minutes, including an hour's stopover in Antigua; to *Los Angeles* is nine hours; to *New York* is six hours and to *Singapore* is 33 hours.
Main airports: *Gerald's International Airport (MNI)* opened in 2005. *WinAir* (website: www.fly-winair.com) operates several daily flights from Antigua and St Maarten. *WH Bramble Airport* has been closed since August 1997 owing to volcanic activity. *Carib Aviation* runs charter flights. *Caribbean Helicopters* also flies from Antigua.
Departure tax: US$13 for CARICOM nationals and US$21 for all other nationals. Children under 12 years of age and transit passengers who continue their journey within 24 hours are exempt.

SEA:

A high-speed ferry service operates regular services six days a week between Little Bay, Montserrat and Heritage Quay, Antigua (travel time – one hour).

Travel - Internal

SEA:

Charter yachts are available. The main harbour is at Little Bay where a new jetty has been constructed.

Credit: ©John Cole

ROAD:

Traffic drives on the left. There are good road networks to all towns. Montserrat has 203km (126 miles) of well-paved roads, but driving can be difficult for those not used to winding mountain roads. Speed limits are restricted to 20mph (32 kph). **Bus:** Minibuses are available for sightseeing. A bus service between villages and the town is provided by privately owned minibuses. **Taxi:** There are fixed rates for standard journeys. Drivers can act as guides and a number of different tours can be arranged. **Car hire:** A number of car hire companies operate on the island. **Documentation:** A valid foreign licence can be used to purchase a temporary licence at either the heliport or any police station. This costs EC$50 and the licence is valid for three months.

Travel Advice

Montserrat is still experiencing volcanic activity at the Soufrière Hills (which began erupting in 1995), causing the capital, Plymouth, to be closed and the relocation of businesses and residents living on the southern and eastern sides of the island to the northern side. Montserrat continues to welcome visitors to the northern part of the island where economic development is now being planned. Following a recent lull in volcanic activity the previously designated Day Time Entry Zone (DTEZ) has been rescinded and these areas are now open for 24-hour occupancy. However, at present, there are no utilities in these areas and roads are in poor condition. Anyone visiting these areas should drive with extreme caution, especially when crossing the Belham Valley due to a danger from mudflows. A small portion of the previously designated Exclusion Zone incorporating St George's Hill has been re-designated a DTEZ and entry is permitted in this area between the hours of 06:00 and 18:00, seven days a week.

Credit: ©Montserrat Tourist Board

A major part of the island is still a total Exclusion Zone where no entry is permitted. Maps showing the designated zones are available at points of entry and at local police stations. There are three designated Maritime Exclusion Zones and visiting yachtsmen should avoid these waters. The Montserrat Port Authority can advise on these areas (tel: +1 664 491 2791). Though the crime rate is very low, travellers should take sensible precautions against petty crime.

Most visits to Montserrat are trouble-free but you should be aware of the global risk of indiscriminate international terrorist attacks, which could be against civilian targets, including places frequented by foreigners.

This advice is based on information provided by the Foreign and Commonwealth Office in the UK. It is correct at time of publishing. As the situation can change rapidly, visitors are advised to contact the following organisations for the latest travel advice:

British Foreign and Commonwealth Office
Tel: (0845) 850 2829.
Website: www.fco.gov.uk

US Department of State
Website: http://travel.state.gov/travel

Accommodation

HOTELS:

The Vue Pointe is still operating. An 18-room hotel, the Tropical Mansion Suites, is open. There are a small number of bed & breakfast establishments. Some hotels have had to close due to sporadic volcanic activity. Contact Montserrat Tourist Board for more information (see *Top Things To See & Do*).

SELF-CATERING:

Villas and apartments are available throughout the island; Montserrat Tourist Board can provide a list. All accommodation bookings must be confirmed with a 20 per cent deposit. A service charge of 10 per cent and a 7 per cent government occupancy tax is added to all accommodation bills.

Top Things To See & Do

Many of the previously famous sights on Montserrat, including the capital Plymouth, have been either destroyed by the Soufrière Hills volcano or are currently off-limits. However, there are still opportunities for quiet beach holidays, watersports, ecotourism and volcano viewing. Check with the Montserrat Tourist Board for information.

- The island offers diverse and beautiful beaches in a quiet and friendly atmosphere. **Rendezvous Bay** contains the only white (coral) sand beach in Montserrat; sand in the other bays is of volcanic origin and may be grey or black. Several bays offer excellent opportunities for snorkelling and a variety of watersports; others are totally undeveloped (though plans for some of them exist, and those who like their scenery untouched should make the most of current opportunities).

- **Pelican Point** on the east coast is home to the island's only breeding colony of the spectacular Frigate birds.

- Montserrat's national bird, the *icterus oberi* (a species of oriole), can be seen at **Centre** and **Silver Hill** in the north of the island.

- **Hiking:** The Montserrat Forest rangers offer a wide range of guided walks and hiking tours in the northern part of the island. Popular routes include the *Cot trail* (which runs through an oki banana plantation to a historic family house), *Runaway Ghaut*, the *Centre Hills trail*, and the *Silver Hills trail* (which passes through one of the island's oldest volcanic centres). Trained guides are available to inform hikers about the flora and fauna. Contact Montserrat Tourist Board for further details (see *Tourist Information*).

- **Volcano viewing:** Day tours of the volcano area are available. Experienced guides take the visitor to safe vantage points from which they can observe the *Soufrière Hills* volcano. The Montserrat Volcano Observatory can also be visited (tel: (664) 491 5647; website: www.mvo.ms). *Caribbean Helicopters* offer helicopter tours around the volcano (tel: (268) 460 5900 (flight information); website: www.caribbeanhelicopters.net).

- **Watersports:** The surrounding waters are excellent for **scuba-diving**. Both deep and shallow dives are available. Equipment may be hired or purchased on the island. **Snorkelling** equipment is available in resorts. Villa owners or agents can arrange professional instruction, and the tourist board can give details of dive schools. **Sea-fishing** trips can be organised through hotels or directly with specialist operators.

TOURIST INFORMATION

Montserrat Tourist Board
PO Box 7, Farare Plaza, Brades, Montserrat, West Indies
Tel: 491 2230 *or* 8730.
Website: www.visitmontserrat.com

Caribbean Tourism Organisation in the UK
22 The Quadrant, Richmond, Surrey, TW9 1BP, UK
Tel: (020) 8948 0057.
Website: www.doitcaribbean.com *or* www.onecaribbean.co.uk

Caribbean Tourism Organisation in the USA
32nd Floor, 80 Broad Street, New York, NY 10004, USA
Tel: (212) 635 9530.
Website: www.doitcaribbean.com *or* www.onecaribbean.com

Entertainment

FOOD & DRINK: Dining options in Montserrat are varied, with a choice of international or local specialities. The island specialities are fresh seafood and *mountain chicken* – not actually chicken, but the leg from a local species of large frog (Dominica is the only other island where these frogs can be found). Barbecues are popular and other local dishes include pumpkin soup, goat water (comparable to Irish stew), aubergine patties, salt fish, crêpes and dishes made from abundant local fruits. Waiter service is normal.

Most bars serve imported beers, spirits and wines. The local rum punch liqueur is *Monserrat Rum Punch*. There is also an abundance of local fruit drinks available.

Tipping: Service charge and Government tax are added to restaurant and hotel bills.

NIGHTLIFE: There are numerous clubs open in the evenings and at weekends.

SHOPPING: Locally made items include jewellery, needlework, ceramics, glassware and some interesting artefacts made from coconut. Local arts and crafts shops are dotted throughout the island. **Shopping hours:** Mon, Tue and Thurs 0800-1200 and 1300-1600, Wed and Sat 0800-1300, Fri 0800-1700.

Business

ECONOMY: The island was recovering from the volcanic explosion of January 1997, which destroyed much of the island's productive capacity, when it was hit by a new series of eruptions in July 2003. Previously, Montserrat had a diverse if fragile economy. The agricultural sector produced vegetables, cotton and livestock. The industrial sector, which employed one-third of the workforce and earned the bulk of Montserrat's export income, was concentrated in food processing and the assembly of electronic components. In the service sector, e-commerce and financial services were two important growth areas. After the 1997 eruption, the island became largely dependent on foreign aid – in particular, a US$125 million aid package from the UK. However, following the latest series of eruptions, Montserrat is reaching the point where the economy is no longer viable.

BUSINESS ETIQUETTE: A short- or long-sleeved shirt or safari suit is suitable for most business visits. **Office hours:** Mon-Fri 0800-1600.

CONFERENCES/CONVENTIONS: Contact Montserrat Tourist Board for further details (see *Top Things to See & Do*).

COMMERCIAL INFORMATION

Development Unit
PO Box 292, Brades, Montserrat
Tel: 491 2066.
Website: www.devunit.gov.ms

Morocco

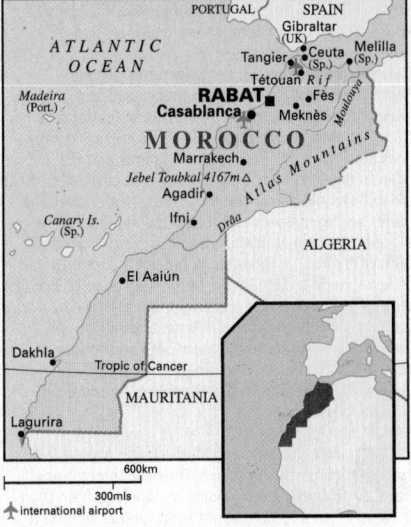

Location: North Africa.

Time: GMT.

Overview

The original inhabitants of Morocco, the Berbers, have experienced a series of invaders over the centuries. The first Arabs arrived from the west in 682 AD and established a series of dynasties which have ruled Morocco ever since. As in much of North Africa, the conflict between Arabs and Berbers has been a central feature of the country's history.

Morocco achieved independence from the French in 1956 and despite some progress, today two territorial disputes remain: in the Sahrawi region (previously known as Spanish Sahara), claimed by indigenous guerrilla movement, the Polisario Front, and in the Spanish-occupied enclaves of Ceuta and Melilla, on Morocco's Mediterranean coast.

Modern Morocco is an initiation into the exotic magic of the Islamic, Arabic, African world - the world of medinas and minarets, desert and mountain; yet it almost touches western Europe and, for all the differences, retains a European patina, the legacy of the French Protectorate. To imbibe the spirit of Morocco, wander the streets of the great cities. Fès - the ancient capital – has a stunning array of medieval buildings, while Marrakech compels attention, its world-famous souk selling a bewildering array of goods; both hark back to the Arab dynasties that ruled the country from the Muslim conquest. Casablanca, a thriving commercial centre, and Rabat, the capital, reflect their modern French origins; Tangier is mildly seedy, slightly melancholy. All Moroccan cities are crowded, the hustlers a fact of life.

Morocco's charm lies in its diversity. For sun-worshippers, there are miles of beaches, while inland lies Berber country where, among the snow-capped Atlas Mountains, the energetic can walk or trek. Beyond the Atlas are the fringes of the Sahara, where the caravans once stopped on their way south to trade in spice and ivory.

Whether scaling distant ridges, idling by the sea, haggling for exotic artefacts, gazing at ancient wonders or marvelling at the pink and indigo of a desert dawn, you will be mesmerised.

General Information

AREA: 710,850 sq km (274,461 sq miles).

POPULATION: 31.6 million (UN, 2005).

POPULATION DENSITY: 44.4 per sq km.

CAPITAL: Rabat. **Population:** 1.3 million (1994).

GEOGRAPHY: Morocco is located on the westernmost tip of north Africa, bordering Algeria to the east and Mauritania to the south and southeast, the Atlantic ocean to the west and the Mediterranean to the north. Running through the middle of the country is the Atlas mountain range, which leads to the fertile plains and sandy beaches of the Atlantic coast. The Middle Atlas range sweeps up from the south, rising to over 3000m (9850ft), covered with woodlands of pine, oak and cedar, open pastureland and small lakes. The Rif Mountains run along the north coast. The ports of Ceuta (Sebta) and Melilla on the north coast are administered by Spain.

GOVERNMENT: Constitutional monarchy since 1956. Gained independence from France in 1956. **Head of State:** King Mohammed VI since 1999. **Head of Government:** Prime Minister Driss Jettou since October 2002. **Recent history:** King Mohammed VI was enthroned in July 1999. He soon embarked on a series of political and economic changes and pursued a modernising course. Although poverty is still widespread and unemployment remains high, one of the King's priorities was to fight poverty. He set up a programme of economic liberalisation to attract foreign investment, eased restrictions on the press and granted more rights to women.

LANGUAGE: The official language is Arabic, but Berber is spoken by a large minority. French is widely spoken throughout the country, except in the northern regions where Spanish is more predominant. English is also understood, particularly in the north and the main tourist areas.

RELIGION: Predominantly Muslim with Jewish and Christian minorities. Morocco's population and culture stems from a cross-section of origins including Berbers, Arabs, Moors and Jews.

ELECTRICITY: 127/220 volts AC, 50Hz, depending on age and location of building.

SOCIAL CONVENTIONS: Handshaking is the customary form of greeting. Many of the manners and social customs emulate French manners, particularly amongst the middle class. The visitor may find, in some social situations, that patience and firmness will pay dividends. Often visitors may find themselves the centre of unsolicited attention. In towns, young boys after money will be eager to point out the way, sell goods or simply charge for a photograph, while unofficial guides will always be offering advice or services. The visitor should be courteous but wary of the latter. Normal social courtesies should be observed in someone's home. Casual wear is widely acceptable, although swimsuits and shorts should be confined to the beach or poolside. Women travelling alone, and/or wearing clothes regarded as provocative (eg strappy tops, short skirts, etc) may attract unwanted attention. Sexual relations outside marriage, and homosexual conduct, are punishable by law. Smoking is widespread and it is customary to offer cigarettes.

Climate

The climate varies from area to area. The coast has a warm, Mediterranean climate tempered on the eastern coast by southwest trade winds. Inland areas have a hotter, drier, continental climate. In the south of the country, the weather is very hot and dry throughout most of the year, with the nights coolest in the months of December and January. Rain falls from November to March in coastal areas. Mostly dry with high temperatures in summer. Cooler climate in the mountains. Marrakech and Agadir enjoy an average temperature of 21°C (70°F) in the winter.

Required clothing: Lightweight cottons and linens are worn during summer, with warm mediumweights for the evenings during winter and in the mountains. Waterproofing is advisable in the wet season, particularly on the coast and in the mountains.

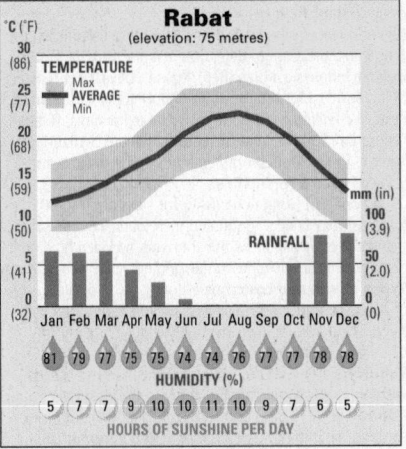

Communications

Telephone: IDD is available. Country code: 212. Privately-run *téléboutiques* can be found through out the country. There is an attendant to provide advice, change and phone cards.

Mobile telephone: Roaming agreements exist with international mobile phone companies. Coverage is mainly available in the cities in the west of Morocco.

Internet: Access is widely available in business centres, hotels and in Internet cafes.

Post: Airmail to Europe takes up to one week and can be unreliable. Post office hours: Mon-Fri 0830-1200 and 1430-1830, Sat 0830-1400.

MEDIA: Although King Mohammed VI eased restrictions on the press when he came to power, some issues such as Western Sahara, the monarchy and corruption remain sensitive topics. The Government owns, or has a stake in, Morocco's two television networks. It plans to allow private investment in state-run broadcasters and the official news agency. Satellite dishes are widely used, giving access to a range of foreign TV stations.

Press: Daily newspapers are published in French and Arabic. The main French newspapers are: *L'Economiste*, *Le Matin*, *Libération* and *Le Journal*. The main Arabic newspapers are *Al Anbaa* and *Assabah*.

TV: *Radio-Television Marocaine (RTM)* is state-run while *2M* is partly state-owned. *Al Maghribiya*, a satellite channel operated by RTM and 2M, is aimed at Moroccans living abroad.

Radio: State-run *Radio-Television Marocaine (RTM)* has regional and national services. Tangier-based *Medi 1* is privately-owned by Moroccan and French concerns and has programmes in Arabic and French.

WESTERN SAHARA: *National Radio of the Saharan Arab Democratic Republic* broadcasts in Arabic and Spanish; the station supports the Polisario Front.

Passport/Visa

	Passport Required?	Visa Required?	Return Ticket Required?
Full British	Yes	No	Yes
Australian	Yes	No	Yes
Canadian	Yes	No	Yes
USA	Yes	No	Yes
Other EU	Yes	No	Yes
Japanese	Yes	No	Yes

Note: *Regulations and requirements may be subject to change at short notice, and you are advised to contact the appropriate diplomatic or consular authority before finalising travel arrangements. Any numbers in the chart refer to the footnotes below.*

PASSPORTS: Passport valid for at least six months from date of entry required by all.
VISAS: Required by all except the following:
(a) nationals of countries shown in the chart above for stays of up to three months;
(b) nationals of Algeria, Andorra, Argentina, Bahrain, Brazil, Bulgaria, Chile, Congo (Rep), Côte d'Ivoire, Croatia, Guinea, Iceland, Indonesia, Korea (Rep), Kuwait, Libya, Liechtenstein, Mali, Mexico, Monaco, New Zealand, Niger, Norway, Oman, Peru, The Philippines, Puerto Rico, Qatar, Romania, Russian Federation, Saudi Arabia, Senegal, Singapore, Switzerland, Tunisia, Turkey, United Arab Emirates and Venezuela for stays of up to three months;
(c) nationals of Hong Kong (SAR) for stays of up to 30 days;
(d) transit passengers continuing their journey by the same or first connecting aircraft within 24 hours, provided holding onward or return documentation and not leaving the airport.
Types of visa and cost: *Single-entry*: £16; *Double-entry* or *Multiple-entry* (both business only): £25. Prices may fluctuate in accordance with the exchange rate and must be paid by postal order only.
Validity: Entry visas are valid for three months; visitors wishing to stay longer should apply to the local police station within 15 days of arrival. For other visa enquiries, contact the Embassy (see *Passport/Visa Information*). Extensions can be applied for with the Directorate General of National Security in Morocco.
Application to: Consular section at Embassy (*not* the Consulate for those residing in London); see *Passport/Visa Information*.
Application requirements: (a) One completed application form. (b) Four passport-size photos taken within the previous six months. (c) Valid passport with at least one blank page, and with a photocopy of the relevant data pages. (d) Fee, payable by postal order only. (e) Photocopy of all flight bookings. (f) Photocopy of hotel reservation. (g) Letter from employer or educator. (h) Self-addressed, stamped, registered envelope for postal applications (for those living outside London only).
Working days required: Normally four, upon receipt of all necessary documents. Some nationals should note that their application forms are sent to Morocco for clearance and processing and may take up to two months.

PASSPORT/VISA INFORMATION:

Embassy of the Kingdom of Morocco in the UK
49 Queen's Gate Gardens, London SW7 5NE, UK
Tel: (020) 7581 5001/4.
Website: www.mincom.gov.ma
Opening hours: Mon-Fri 0930-1700; 1000-1300 (visa section); closed UK and Moroccan national holidays (open until 3pm during Ramadan).

Embassy of the Kingdom of Morocco in the USA
1601 21st Street, NW, Washington, DC 20009, USA
Tel: (202) 462 7979.

Money

Currency: Moroccan Dirham (MAD) = 100 centimes. Notes are in denominations of MAD200, 100, 50, 20 and 10. Coins are in denominations of MAD10, 5 and 1, and 50, 20, 10 and 5 centimes.
Currency exchange: Moroccan Dirhams can only be obtained in Morocco. National currencies should be exchanged at official bureaux de change only (identified by a golden sign); changing money in the street is illegal. There is no commission charge and visitors will be issued with a receipt which they must keep in order to exchange Moroccan currency back into the original national currency upon departure. Money can be withdrawn in banks with a credit card and a cheque book or directly from an ATM in some larger towns.
Credit & debit cards: Some credit cards are accepted. Check with your credit or debit card company for details of merchant acceptability and other services which may be available.
Traveller's cheques: To avoid additional exchange rate charges, travellers are advised to take traveller's cheques in Pounds Sterling or US Dollars.
Currency restrictions: The import and export of local currency is prohibited; all local currency must be reconverted prior to departure. The import and export of foreign currency is unlimited but must be declared if in excess of the equivalent of MAD15,000. Upon production of bank vouchers, half the Moroccan currency purchased during a visitor's stay may be re-exchanged for foreign currency (subject to some limitations) and all of it if the stay is less than 48 hours.
Banking hours: Mon-Thurs 0815-1215 and 1415-1715; Fri 0815-1115 and 1430-1730; Sat 0900-1300.
Exchange rate indicators:
Rate at time of publishing

£1.00=	MAD16.04
$1.00=	MAD9.28

Duty Free

The following goods may be imported into Morocco without incurring customs duty:
200 cigarettes or 50 cigars or 400g of tobacco; 1l of spirits and 1l of wine; 5g of perfume.
Restricted items: A special permit is required for sporting guns and ammunition which is obtainable upon arrival from the police authorities if passenger(s) hold a permit from their country of origin.

Public Holidays

Below are listed Public Holidays for the January 2006-June 2007 period.
2006: Jan 1 New Year's Day. **Jan 10** Aïd al-Adha (Feast of the Sacrifice). **Jan 11** Manifesto of Independence. **Jan 31** Fatih Mouharram (Muslim New Year). **Apr 10** Aïd al-Mawlid (Prophet's Birthday). **May 1** Labour Day. **Jul 30** Feast of the Throne. **Aug 14** Fête Oued Eddahab (Oued Eddahab Allegiance Day). **Aug 20** Révolution du Roi et du Peuple (The King and the People's Revolution Day). **Aug 21** King Mohammed's Birthday. **Oct 22-24** Aïd al-Fitr (End of Ramadan). **Nov 6** Marche Verte (Anniversary of the Green March). **Nov 18** Fête de l'Indépendance (Independence Day). **Dec 31** Aïd al-Adha (Feast of the Sacrifice).
2007: Jan 1 New Year's Day. **Jan 11** Manifesto of Independence. **Jan 20** Fatih Mouharram (Muslim New Year). **Mar 31** Aïd al-Mawlid (Prophet's Birthday). **May 1** Labour Day.
Note: Muslim festivals are timed according to local sightings of various phases of the moon and the dates given above are approximations. During the lunar month of Ramadan that precedes Aïd al-Fitr, Muslims fast during the day and feast at night and normal business patterns may be interrupted. Some disruption may continue into Aïd al-Fitr itself. Aïd al-Fitr and Aïd al-Adha may last anything from two to 10 days, depending on the region. For more information, see the *World of Islam* appendix.

Health

	Special Precautions?	Certificate Required?
Yellow Fever	No	No
Cholera	No	No
Typhoid & Polio	1	N/A
Malaria	2	N/A

Note: *Regulations and requirements may be subject to change at short notice, and you are advised to contact your doctor well in advance of your intended date of departure. Any numbers in the chart refer to the footnotes below.*

1: Vaccination against polio and typhoid is advised.
2: A minimal malaria risk, exclusively in the benign *vivax* form, exists from May to October in rural areas of the Chefchaouen province.
Food & drink: Bottled water is available and is advised for the first few weeks of stay. Drinking water outside main cities and towns may be contaminated and sterilisation is advisable. Milk is unpasteurised and should be boiled. Powdered or tinned milk is available and is advised, but make sure that it is reconstituted with pure water. Avoid dairy products which are likely to have been made from unboiled milk. Only eat well-cooked meat and fish, preferably served hot. Salad and mayonnaise may carry increased risk. Vegetables should be cooked and fruit peeled.
Other risks: *Bilharzia* (schistosomiasis) is present in small foci. Avoid swimming and paddling in fresh water; swimming pools which are well chlorinated and maintained are safe. *Soil parasites* are also present; visitors should wear shoes. *Hepatitis A* and *E* also occur. Immunisations are sometimes recommended for *hepatitis B*, *tuberculosis* and *diphtheria*. *Tungiasis* and *Lassa fever* also occur, although rarely.
Rabies is present. For those at high risk, vaccination before arrival should be considered. If you are bitten, seek medical advice without delay. For more information, consult the *Health* appendix.
Health care: There are good medical facilities in all main cities, including emergency pharmacies (sometimes in the Town Hall) outside normal opening hours. Government hospitals provide free or minimal charge emergency treatment. Full health insurance is essential.

Travel - International

AIR:
The national airline is *Royal Air Maroc (AT)* (website: www.royalairmaroc.com). There are frequent direct flights from all major European cities, from North America and from the Middle East.
Approximate flight times: From Casablanca to *London* is three hours; from Tangier is two hours 30 minutes. From Casablanca to *New York* is six hours 30 minutes.
Main airports: *Casablanca (CMN)* (Mohammed V) is 30km (19 miles) south of the city (travel time - 35 minutes). *To/from the airport*: There are taxi services into Casablanca and train services available to Rabat. *Facilities*: Outgoing duty free shop, post office, banking and bureau de change, restaurant, bar, tourist help desk and car hire.
Tangier (TNG) (Boukhalef Souahel) is 11km (7 miles) from the city (travel time - 20 minutes). *To/from the airport*: Bus and taxi services are available into Tangier. *Facilities*: Outgoing duty free shop, banking and bureau de change, restaurant, bar, tourist help desk and car hire.
Other international airports include *Fez (FEZ)*, *Marrakech (RAK)* and *Rabat-Salé (RBA)*.
Departure tax: None.
SEA:
Main ports: *Tangier*, *Casablanca* and *Ceuta*. Lines serving these ports are *Bland Line* (from Spain and Gibraltar), *Comanav* (from France, Spain and Italy), *Compañía Trasmediterránea*, *Limadet*, *Polish Ocean Lines* (from Northern Europe) and *Transtour*.
Car/passenger ferries: Ferry operators include *FerriMaroc* (website: www.ferrimaroc.com) and *Trasmediterranea* (website: www.trasmediterranea.com). There are cheap and regular car- and passenger-ferry links between southern Spain and Tangier and the Spanish enclaves on the north Moroccan coast. Most links are roll-on, roll-off car ferries except where shown. The routes are from Algeciras to Ceuta (Sebta) (car ferry); Algeciras to Tangier (hydrofoil and car ferry); Tarifa to Tangier (hydrofoil); Gibraltar to Tangier (hydrofoil and car ferry); Almería to Melilla (car ferry); Málaga to Melilla (car ferry); Almería to Nador (car ferry); Gênes (Italy) to Tangier; Alicante to Orán and Almería to Al Hoceima. There are also car ferries between Sète on the French coast (between Béziers and Montpellier on the Golfe du Lyon) and Tangier run by *Compagnie Marocaine de Navigation*.
RAIL:
Rail links between Morocco and Algeria are currently suspended. The main international routes are from Oujda to Algiers or from Oran to Algiers. Trains can be caught from London Victoria to Gare du Nord in Paris, and then Gare d'Austerlitz to Algerciras. From here ferries can be caught to Morocco (see Sea section).
Rail passes: The *Inter-Rail Pass* offers unlimited second-class train travel in up to 29 European countries (includes Morocco and Turkey) split into eight zones (A-H). Three different tickets are available: a ticket covering one zone (two to six countries, 16 days' validity), a ticket covering two zones (six to 10 countries, 22 days' validity) and an *All Zone Pass* (29 countries, one month's validity). Ferry services between Italy and Greece are included. Passengers must be resident in Europe for at least six months before the pass is used. Travel is not allowed in the passenger's country of residence. Travellers under 26 years receive a reduction of about 30 per cent. Children's tickets are reduced by about 50 per cent. Supplements are required for some high-speed services, seat reservations and couchettes. Discounts are offered on *Eurostar* and some ferry routes. Available from *Inter Rail* (website: www.interrailnet.com).
ROAD:
The best road link is from southern Spain or France via passenger/car ferries (see above under *Sea*). The road link on the north Algerian border is currently closed. *Eurolines*, departing from Victoria Coach Station in London, serves destinations in Morocco. For further information, contact *Eurolines* (52 Grosvenor Gardens, London SW1; tel: (08705) 143 219; website: www.eurolines.com *or* www.nationalexpress.com).

Travel - Internal

AIR:
Royal Air Maroc (AT) (website: www.royalairmaroc.com) operates regular services from Casablanca airport to Agadir, Dakhla, Fès, Marrakech, Ouarzazate, Oujda and Tangier. Contact *Royal Air Maroc* for further details. *Regional Airlines (FN)* also runs an internal service.
RAIL:
The Moroccan rail system, run by *Office National des Chemins de Fer (ONCF)* (website: www.oncf.org.ma), provides regular and cheap services with first-class travel available between major centres. Rail fares are amongst the cheapest in the world, although a supplement must be paid for air-conditioned trains. Sleeping cars and restaurant cars are available. The network runs from Oujda in the northeast to Casablanca on the west coast, Tangier on the north coast and Fès and Marrakech in the interior. The most useful route is from Fès to Rabat and Casablanca, with five daily and two overnight trains. There are also two daily trains and one overnight train (without sleepers) which run from Casablanca to Marrakech.

Also, from Monday to Friday, a train runs every 30 minutes from Kenitra to Rabat.
Cheap fares: Children under four travel free and children from four to 12 may travel for half fare. The European Inter-Rail pass is valid in Morocco. See *Travel International* section.

ROAD:

Traffic drives on the right. The major Moroccan roads, particularly those covering the north and northwest of the country, are all-weather highways. In the interior, south of the High Atlas Mountains, road travel becomes much more difficult, especially across the Atlas Mountains in winter. **Coach:** The main centres are connected by a wide variety of coach services, many of which are privately run. The two largest firms are *CTM* (covering the whole country) and *SATAS* (between Casablanca, Agadir and south of Agadir). Visitors should bear in mind, however, that Morocco has a poor road safety record; the roads from Agadir to Marrakech, via Imi'n Tanoute and Chichaoua, are particularly hazardous. **Bus:** Connections between most major towns and villages are regular and frequent, although buses can be very crowded and it may be wise to buy tickets in advance and arrive well before departure to secure a seat. The price of tickets is very low, especially with some of the smaller local bus companies. It is customary to tip the guard for loading luggage. For charter purposes, air-conditioned motor coaches are available from several companies. **Taxi:** Those available in major towns, the *petits* taxis, are metered (see below under *Urban*). Other larger taxis, usually Mercedes cars, are used for travel to areas outside towns. These can be shared, but fares should be agreed before departure. **Car hire:** Major hire companies have offices in major towns and cities. Car hire is generally expensive. **Documentation:** Foreign driving licences are accepted, as well as International Driving Permits. Third Party insurance is required. A Green Card is also necessary. Insurance can be arranged locally.

URBAN:

There are extensive bus services in Casablanca and other main towns. Pre-purchase tickets are sold. Urban area *petits* taxis are plentiful and have metered fares. Taxi drivers expect a 10 per cent tip.
Travel times: The following chart gives approximate travel times (in hours and minutes) from **Casablanca** to other major cities/towns in Morocco.

	Air	Road	Rail
Rabat	**0.30**	**1.30**	**1.00**
Marrakech	**0.30**	**4.00**	**4.00**
Tangier	**0.50**	**6.00**	**6.00**
Laayoune	**1.30**	**20.00**	**-**

Travel Advice

Most visits to Morocco are trouble-free, but there is a high threat from terrorism in Morocco.
Violent crime, though not a major problem in Morocco, is growing. There are occasional incidents involving theft at knifepoint in the major cities and along beaches.
Morocco has a poor road safety record. Accidents are frequent, especially on busy major routes. The main road from Agadir to Marrakesh via Imi'n Tanoute and Chichaoua has been reported as particularly hazardous.
This advice is based on information provided by the Foreign and Commonwealth Office in the UK. It is correct at time of publishing. As the situation can change rapidly, visitors are advised to contact the following organisations for the latest travel advice:

British Foreign and Commonwealth Office
Tel: (0845) 850 2829.
Website: www.fco.gov.uk

US Department of State
Website: http://travel.state.gov/travel

Accommodation

EDITOR'S CHOICE: RIADS

Riads are traditional, luxury Moroccan town houses. These are usually found in *Medinas* (old towns) of large cities and can offer excellent self catering accommodation. Meals can be provided. Check whether your accommodation is to be on the top floor, (very hot in summer) or the ground floor (damp in winter).

HOTELS:

Morocco has 100,000 hotel beds to cater for its thriving tourist market. There is quite a wide choice of accommodation in all sizeable centres. The upper end of the market is represented by internationally known hotels in most main towns, notably Agadir, Marrakech and Tangier.
Grading: Hotels are rated from **1** to **5 stars**.

SELF-CATERING:

Self-catering apartments are available in Agadir, Marrakech and Tangier. Full details are available from the Moroccan National Tourist Office (see *Top Things To Do*).

CAMPING/CARAVANNING:

There are established campsites with good facilities in many parts of Morocco. Full details are available in a brochure from the National Tourist Office.

YOUTH HOSTELS:

There are hostels in Asni, Azrou, Casablanca, Fès, Marakech, Meknes and Rabat. There is an International Youth Hostel at 6 Place Abmed Al Bidaoui, Ville Ancienne, Casablanca (tel: (22) 220 551).

ACCOMMODATION INFORMATION

Fédération Nationale de l'Industrie Hôtelière
320 Bd. Zerktouni, Casablanca 20000, Morocco
Tel: (22) 267 313/4.
Website: www.fnih.ma

Fédération Royale Marocaine des Auberges de Jeunesse
BP 15998, Casa Principale, Parc de la Ligue Arabe, Casablanca 21000, Morocco
Tel: (22) 470 952

Top Things To See

- Do not miss **Rabat**'s many monumental gateways, including the **Gate of the Ambassadors** and the **Oudaias Kasbah Gate**. Other attractions include **Hassan Tower**, the grandiose minaret of a vast, uncompleted 12th-century mosque; the **Mohammed V Mausoleum**, an outstanding example of traditional Moroccan architecture; the **Royal Palace**; the **Chellah**, with superb monuments, delightful gardens and Roman ruins; the **Oudaias**; the **Archaeological Museum**; the **National Museum of Handicrafts** and the antique Moorish cafe. Also worth a visit is **Salé**, Rabat's twin city.
- See the the third-century Roman ruins at **Volubilis**, which are on UNESCO's World Heritage list; there is also an interesting archaeological museum.
- Discover the mystery of **Fès,** the most ancient and impressive of the imperial cities. Officially encompassing two cities – **El Bali** and **Jadid** – Fès is famous for the **Nejjarine Square** and **Fountain**, the **Er Rsif** and **Andalous** (Al-Andalus) mosques, the **Royal Palace**, the **Kasbah** and **Karaouine** (Al-Qarawiyin) **University** and the **Dar Batha Museum**. The old part of Fès – **Fès El Bali** – still retains the magical, bustling atmosphere of an ancient time and it is centred around the two famous mosques of **Al-Qarawiyin** and **Al-Andalus**.
- In the valley of **Ouergha** to the north of Fès, see the **Karaouine** (Al-Qarawiyin) **Mosque** and **Mesbahai Medersa**, an old school, remarkable for its traditional architecture and late afternoon auctions in the Kissaria, the shopping area.
- **Marrakech,** the 'Pink City' (due to the colour of the local earth used in its construction), is a city of labyrinthine alleyways, secluded palaces, museums, mosques and markets. After nightfall, head for the **Djemaa el-Fna** (Place of the Dead), the city square, to see an exotic spectacle of street dancers, fortune-tellers, musicians, acrobats, storytellers and snake charmers. Do not miss **Koutoubia**, the 12th-century mosque, which is as tall as the towers of Nôtre Dame in Paris. The **Ben Youssef Medersa** is the largest theological site in the Mahgreb. It forms part of Marrakech's UNESCO-listed *medina*, now a World Heritage site, crammed with architectural masterpieces. Other interesting places to see are the sumptuous **Bahia Palace**; the beautiful **Saadian Tombs** housing the remains of rulers of the Saadian Dynasty; the **Dar Sisaid Museum**; the **Menara** and **Aquedal gardens** and the famed **camel market**.
- In **Tangier**, visit the **Mendoubia Gardens**, the **Sidi Bou Abid Mosque**, the **Moulay Ismail Mosque**, the **Forbes Museum** and the **Merinid College**.
- In the newer city of **Casablanca,** do not miss the **Hassan II Mosque**, the world's largest mosque with one of the world's tallest minarets.
- On the road between **Er Rachidia** and **Erfoud,** look for the 'Blue Springs' at **Meski** and the natural amphitheatre of **Cirque de Jaffar** near **Midelt**. **Tinerhir**, once a garrison of the French Foreign Legion, is worth visiting for its kasbahs. Near Tinerhir is the outstanding scenery of the **Drâa Valley** (famous for its red-earthern kasbahs) and the magnificent **Todra** gorge.
- Of particular interest in **Ouarzazate** in **The Deep South** is the kasbah of **Taourirt**, the **Museum of Arts and Crafts** and the **Carpet Weavers' Co-operative Shop**.
- About 30km (19 miles) from Ouarzazate lies the exotic and UNESCO World-Heritage-listed **Ksar of Aït-Ben-Haddou**. The Ksar is a traditional pre-Saharan habitat and consists of a group of earthen buildings surrounded by high walls. Aït-Ben-Haddou has featured in several films, including *Lawrence of Arabia*.
- Do not miss one of Morocco's highlights, the magnificent ochre-coloured cliffs and rock formations of the **Dadès Gorge**, approximately 100km (63 miles) east of Ouarzazate.

Top Things To Do

- The old part of **Fès** – **Fès El Bali** is a huge maze of winding streets and covered bazaars. At the *medina* (market), one of the largest in the world and on UNESCO's World Heritage list, buy carpets, rugs and ornate metalwork. As in all of Morocco, the market business is conducted in a leisurely, although deadly earnest way, with the accompaniment of endless glasses of sweet mint tea. The valley of **Ouergha** to the north of Fès is also famed for its *souks* and Morocco's most celebrated gathering of riders. **Meknes**, whose old town is listed by UNESCO as a World Heritage Site, also has a wonderful *souk*. **Tangier** has a picturesque market called the **Grand Socco**.
- Try **golfing**, which is very popular in Morocco, partly because King Hassan II was an internationally ranked practitioner of the game. Some of the best-known of the country's 16 golf courses are located at the **Royal Dar es Salaam Golf Club** in Rabat, which has three courses and annually hosts the internationally renowned *Hassan II Trophy*.
- With its four distinct mountain ranges – the **Rif**, the **Middle Atlas**, the **High Atlas** and the **Anti-Atlas** – Morocco offers outstanding opportunities for **hiking**, **trekking** and **camping** trips. One of the most popular treks in the High Atlas is the ascent of **Jebel Toubkal** (4167m/6668ft), North Africa's highest peak. The Toubkal area is about a one-hour drive from Marrakech and the usual starting point for this trek is the picturesque village of **Imlil**. Trekking is possible all year round, but the best time is from April to October. The canyons and gorges are best tackled from June to October (in summer, storms can make the gorges impassable).
- Several clubs organise **pony treks** in the Middle Atlas. The combination of travelling by mule and skiing (known as **mule-skiing**) is characteristic to the High Atlas and can be carried out from February to April. A useful brochure, *The Great Trek through the Moroccan Atlas*, is available from the Moroccan Ministry of Tourism or the Moroccan National Tourist Office (see *Tourist Information*). **Camel riding** (*méharrées*) is also available, both in the Atlas mountains and around the Sahara Desert area in the southwest.
- **Ski** in **Ifrane** in the Middle Atlas and **Oukaïmeden** in the High Atlas (70km/44 miles from Marrakech). Other ski resorts include **Mischliffen** in the Middle Atlas, on the doorstep of Fès and Meknes. **Mount Tidiquin** in the Ketama district and **Djebel Bou Volane** in the Middle Atlas are popular areas for **expedition-type skiing** and **walking trips**.
- Sandy beaches offer safe **swimming**, although the Atlantic can be cold even in summer. **Mohammedia, Agadir, El Jadida, Oualidia, Safi** and **Essaouira** are all good bathing resorts. The Mediterranean coast in the north, opposite Spain, is being developed; resorts include **Cabonegro** (14km/23 miles from Tetouan), **Al Hoceima** and **Mdiq.**
- Go **whitewater rafting** on the rivers in the High and Middle Atlas ranges, particularly the **Oum-er-Rbia.**
- Go **deep-sea fishing** at **Dakhla** in the Sahara or **Mohammedia** near Casablanca.
- Go on a **4-wheel-drive tour** to natural and cultural sights such as the 300m- (984ft-) deep **Gorge of Todra,** the massive sand dunes of **Merzouga** and the Berber region of **Ouarzazate**. Most of these tours feature typical Moroccan feasts and barbecues. Try to see the famous *Paris-Dakar* motor rally which passes through Morocco every year.

TOURIST INFORMATION

Moroccan National Tourist Office in the UK
205 Regent Street, 2nd Floor, London W1B 4HB, UK
Tel: (020) 7437 0073.
Website: www.visitmorocco.org

Moroccan National Tourist Office in the USA
20 East 46th Street, Suite 1302,
New York, NY 10017, USA
Tel: (212) 557 2520.

Entertainment

FOOD & DRINK: Morocco's traditional *haute cuisine* dishes are excellent and good value for money. They are often exceedingly elaborate, based on a diet of meat and sweet pastries. Hotel restaurants usually serve French cuisine. Restaurants offer a good selection of food, including typical Moroccan dishes, French, Italian or Spanish meals. The three-course fixed menus are not expensive. Many of the *souks* have stalls selling kebabs (*brochettes*) often served with a spicy sauce. Most restaurants have waiter service. Bars can have either waiter or counter service. Laws on alcohol are fairly liberal (for non-Muslim visitors) and bars in most tourist areas stay open late. Wines, beers and spirits are widely available. Locally produced wines, beers and mineral waters are excellent and good value, but imported drinks tend to be expensive.

National specialities:
- *Harira*, a rich soup.
- *Pastilla*, a pigeon-meat pastry made from dozens of different layers of thick flaky dough.
- *Couscous*, a dish based on savoury semolina that can be combined with egg, chicken, lamb or vegetables.
- *Tajine* is a stew, often rich and fragrant, using marinated lamb or chicken.
- *Hout* is a fish version of the same stew.
- *Djaja mahamara* is chicken stuffed with almonds, semolina and raisins.
- Also popular are *mchoui*, pit-roasted mutton.
- *Kab-el-ghzal*, almond pastries.

National drinks:
- Mint tea made with green tea, fresh mint and sugar. It is very refreshing and its consumption is an integral part of Moroccan social courtesy.
- Coffee is made very strong, except at breakfast.

Tipping: Service charges are usually included in hotel bills; it is customary to tip hairdressers, cinema usherettes and waiters MAD1-2.

NIGHTLIFE: Morocco offers a variety of entertainment from casinos, bars, discos, restaurants and nightclubs, often with belly dancing. There are modern nightclubs in all the cities and resorts around the country. There are casinos in Marrakech, Mohammedia, Tangier and Agadir. Traditional Moroccan entertainment, such as folk dancing, can be seen in every town.

SHOPPING: The co-operative shops of Moroccan craftspeople, *coopartim*, operate under state control selling local handicrafts at fixed prices and issue an authenticity receipt or a certificate of origin for customs when exporting. *Souks* are also worthwhile places to visit for local products. Special buys are leather, tanned and dyed in Fès; copperware; silver; silk or cotton garments; and wool rugs, carpets and blankets. Bargaining is essential, and good buys generally work out at around a third of the asking price. In the south, there are Berber carpet auctions, especially in Marrakech, Taroudannt and Tiznit. Visitors will need a guide to make the best of these occasions. **Shopping hours:** Mon-Thurs 0830-1200 and 1430-1830, and Fri 0830-1100 and 1500-1830; large stores are open Mon-Sat 0900-1300 and 1500-1900; *souks* (traditional markets) are open Mon-Sun 0830-1300 and 1430-1800.

Business

- **GDP:** US$50.1 billion (2004).
- **Main exports:** Clothing, fish, inorganic chemicals, transistors, crude minerals, fertilisers, petroleum products, fruit and vegetables.
- **Main imports:** Crude petroleum, textile fabric, telecommunications and equipment, wheat, gas and electricity, transistors and plastics.
- **Main trade partners:** Spain, France, USA and UK.

ECONOMY: Agriculture employs one-fifth of the working population, the principal crops being cereals, vegetables and citrus fruits (of which Morocco is one of the world's largest exporters), and accounts for about 20 per cent of GDP. Livestock farming produces enough meat to fulfil domestic needs. Fishing is vital to both the domestic and export markets, as well as for the revenue accruing from the sale of licences allowing foreign fleets to fish in Moroccan territorial waters. Mining is the country's principal industry. Morocco is the world's largest exporter of phosphate rock, both in raw and processed form (such as fertilisers), and this is the principal source of export revenue. It has substantial other mineral assets including iron ore, coal, lead, zinc, cobalt, copper, silver and manganese. Morocco has small reserves of oil and gas, but must import the bulk of its needs. The main components of the manufacturing sector are food processing, textiles and the production of leather goods. In the service sector, tourism has grown rapidly and is now worth almost US$2 billion annually. The tourism industry has benefited from Morocco having one of the best infrastructures on the African continent; this is also an important consideration for foreign investors. Remittances from Moroccan workers abroad (mostly in Europe) are another major source of revenue. During the last 10 years, the government has introduced a series of IMF-sponsored reforms, including trade liberalisation and public expenditure cuts in exchange for successive assistance programmes. This has reduced the size of the public sector and contributed towards easing Morocco's huge foreign debt but at the cost of increased unemployment. Almost half the workforce are officially unemployed. A trade agreement with the EU was signed in 1995 under which all tariff barriers will be removed by 2012. Morocco is also part of a planned Free Trade Zone (including Jordan, Tunisia and Egypt) which will offer preferential access to EU markets. The Moroccan Government formed a free trade agreement with the US in 2004. Finally, Morocco is now the largest single recipient of aid from the EU. Morocco is also a member of the African Development Bank, the Islamic Development Bank and a founder member of the Union of the Arab Maghreb. In 2004, GDP growth reached 3.5 per cent.

BUSINESS ETIQUETTE: Businesspeople should be of a smart appearance, although a suit is not necessary in very hot weather. Appointments should be made in advance. Negotiations often involve a great deal of bargaining and a visitor should expect to deal with a number of people.

Office hours: Government offices Mon-Thurs 0830-1200, 1430-1830 and Fri 0830-1100 and 1500-1830. Commercial offices Mon-Thurs 0830-1200, 1430-1830 and Fri 0830-1100 and 1500-1830.

CONFERENCES/CONVENTIONS: The Pullman Conference Centre in Marrakech provides meeting facilities for up to 5000 people. Additional facilities can be found at the Palais des Congrès. Further information and a special brochure on conferences and conventions, Morocco, A Feast for the Senses, can be obtained from the Moroccan National Tourist Office (see *Top Things To Do*).

COMMERCIAL INFORMATION

Fédération des Chambres de Commerce et d'Industrie du Maroc
6 rue d'Erfoud, BP 218, Hassan-Rabat, Morocco
Tel: (37) 767 881 *or* 051.
E-mail: fccism@ccis.ma

Mozambique

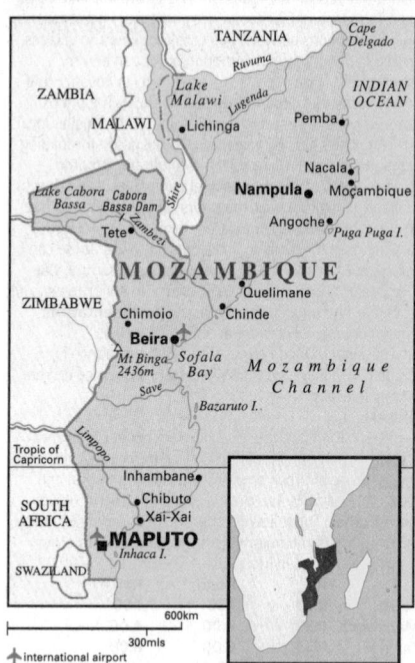

Location: Southeast Africa.

Time: GMT + 2.

Overview

The country is opening up to tourism but, at present, it is mainly in the form of package tours. Independent travellers are relatively few in number. There are many beaches and lagoons with safe bathing and there is good fishing. There is also good hiking but advice and extreme caution should be taken due to the large amount of leftover landmines in the country. Birdwatching is excellent.

General Information

AREA: 799,380 sq km (308,641 sq miles).
POPULATION: 18.1 million (official estimate 2002).
POPULATION DENSITY: 22.6 per sq km.
CAPITAL: Maputo. **Population:** 1.1 million (UN estimate 2001).
GEOGRAPHY: Mozambique borders Tanzania to the north, Zambia and Malawi to the northwest, Zimbabwe to the west, and South Africa and Swaziland to the southwest. To the east lies the Indian Ocean and a coastline of nearly 2500km (1550 miles) with beaches bordered by lagoons, coral reefs and strings of islands. Behind the coastline, a vast low plateau rising towards mountains in the west and north accounts for nearly half the area of Mozambique. The landscape of the plateau is savanna – more or less dry and open woodlands with tracts of short grass steppe. The western and northern highlands are patched with forest. The Zambezi is the largest and most important of the 25 main rivers which flow through Mozambique into the Indian Ocean. The major concentrations of population (comprising many different ethnic groups) are along the coast and in the fertile and relatively productive river valleys, notably in Zambezia and Gaza provinces. The Makua-Lomwe, who belong to the Central Bantu, live mainly in the area north of Zambezia, Nampula, Niassa and Cabo Delgado provinces. The Tsonga, who are the predominant race in the southern lowlands, provide a great deal of the labour for the South African mines. In the Inhambane coastal district are the Chopi and Tsonga, while in the central area

are the Shona. The Makonde inhabit the far north. Mestizos and Asians live in the main populated area along the coast and in the more fertile river valleys.
GOVERNMENT: Republic since 1990. Gained independence from Portugal in 1975. **Head of State:** President Armando Guebuza since 2005. **Head of Government:** Prime Minister Luisa Diogo since 2004. **Recent history:** President Chissano stepped down in December 2004 and his hand-picked successor, Armando Guebuza, took over the position early in 2005. However, it was widely believed that the National Resistance Movement (RENAMO) leader, Afonso Dhlakama, would finally be voted in as president and there were disputes over allegations of election rigging.
2004 was a significant year for Mozambique, heralding the appointment of their first-ever female Prime Minister, former Finance Minister, Luisa Diogo. The priority now for Diogo and the Guebuza government is the state of the economy. The country is still recovering from catastrophic flooding in the spring of 2001 which caused huge damage to the agricultural sector. Economic problems in neighbouring Zimbabwe and South Africa, upon both of whom Mozambique relies heavily, have had a serious impact.
LANGUAGE: Portuguese is the official language. Many local African languages, such as Tsonga, Sena Nyanja, Makonde and Macua, are also spoken.
RELIGION: Christian (mainly Roman Catholic), Muslim and Hindu. Many also follow traditional beliefs.
ELECTRICITY: 220/240 volts AC, 50Hz.
SOCIAL CONVENTIONS: Shaking hands is the customary form of greeting. The courtesies and modes of address customary in Portugal and other Latin countries are still observed. Casual wear is acceptable. Formal dress is seldom required. **Photography:** Visitors should not take photographs of soldiers, airports, bridges or government/public buildings, since this is illegal. Only photos of beaches and other tourist sites may be taken.

Climate

Climate varies according to area. Inland is cooler than the coast and rainfall higher as the land rises, with most rain between January and March. Hottest and wettest season is October to March. From April to September the coast has warm, mainly dry weather tempered by sea breezes.
Required clothing: Tropical lightweights, with warmer clothing for evenings. Rainwear advisable all year round.

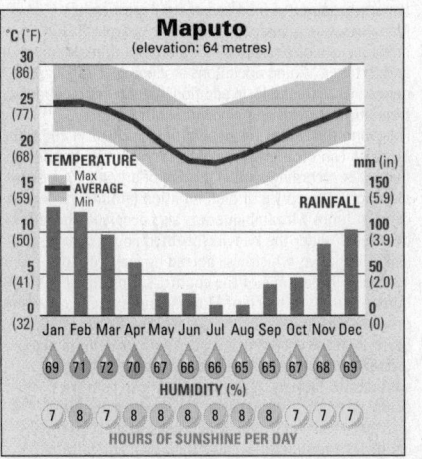

Communications

Telephone: IDD is available. Country code: 258. Outgoing international calls must go through the operator, although direct dialling is available to South Africa and Swaziland; there may be some delay.
Mobile telephone: Roaming agreements exist with most international mobile phone operators. Coverage is expanding to all main cities in most provinces.
Internet: There are at least two Internet cafes in Maputo (one in Avenida Julius Nyerere).
Post: Postal services are available in main centres. Airmail to Europe usually takes five to seven days, but sometimes longer.
MEDIA: Press: There are no English-language newspapers published in Mozambique. The daily papers are *Correio da Manha, Diário de Moçambique* and *Notícias. Express da Torde, Imparcial Fax* and *Mediafax* are news sheets available by fax.
TV: *Televisao de Mozambique (TVM)* is state-run, while *Radio-Televisao Klint (RTK)* is a private broadcaster.
Radio: State-run Radio Mozambique operates national network *Antena Nacional*, as well as provincial and local channels. *RTK* broadcasts privately-run services.

Passport/Visa

	Passport Required?	Visa Required?	Return Ticket Required?
Full British	Yes	Yes	Yes
Australian	Yes	Yes	Yes
Canadian	Yes	Yes	Yes
USA	Yes	Yes	Yes
Other EU	Yes	Yes	Yes
Japanese	Yes	Yes	Yes

Note: *Regulations and requirements may be subject to change at short notice, and you are advised to contact the appropriate diplomatic or consular authority before finalising travel arrangements. Any numbers in the chart refer to the footnotes below.*

PASSPORTS: Passport valid for a minimum of six months beyond intended date of departure required by all.
VISAS: Required by all.
Types of visa and cost: *Tourist* and *Business*: £40 (single-entry); £70 (multiple-entry). *Express service*: £50 (single-entry); £100 (multiple-entry). *Same-day express service*: £60 (single-entry); £110 (multiple-entry). *Transit*: £40.
Validity: *Single-entry*: One day to one month from date of entry, renewable to a maximum of three months. *Multiple-entry*: One to six months from date of issue. *Transit*: On request.
Application to: Mozambique Embassies, High Commissions, Consulates; or Empresa Nacional de Turismo (see *Passport/Visa Information*).
Note: A visa can sometimes be obtained through a contact living in Mozambique or at the airport, although processing is often subject to delay. Apply to nearest High Commission for more information.
Application requirements: (a) Official application form. (b) Two passport-size photos. (c) Valid passport. (d) Return or onward ticket or flight confirmation slip. (e) Evidence of booked hotel/hostel accommodation *or* sufficient financial means. (f) Fee payable in cash or by cheque (made payable to the Mozambique High Commission). (g) Stamped, self-addressed registered envelope for postal applications. *Business*: (a)-(g) and, (h) Letter of invitation to Mozambique and/or introduction from an official or business institution.
Working days required: Three. Visas can be processed within 24 hours (express service) or within 90 minutes (same-day express service) for an additional fee.
Temporary residence: Apply to the Embassy or High Commission (see *Passport/Visa Information*).

PASSPORT/VISA INFORMATION

Mozambique High Commission in the UK
21 Fitzroy Square, London W1T 6EL, UK
Tel: (020) 7383 3800.
Website: www.mozambiquehc.org.uk
Opening hours: Mon-Fri 0930-1300; 1400-1600 (consular section).

Embassy of the Republic of Mozambique in the USA
1990 M Street, NW, Suite 570, Washington, DC 20036, USA
Tel: (202) 293 7146/9.
Website: www.embamoc-usa.org

Money

Currency: Mozambique Metical (MZM) = 100 centavos. Notes are in denominations of MZM100,000, 50,000, 20,000, 10,000, 5000 and 1000. Coins are in denominations of MZM5000, 1000, 500, 100, 50, 20, 10, 5 and 1.
Currency exchange: There are bureaux de change at the airports. Money can also be changed at banks. It is advisable to take US Dollars or South African Rand.
Credit & debit cards: These are rarely used in shops. However, money can be obtained from some ATMs using Visa credit or debit cards.
Traveller's cheques: High rates of commission are often charged on these. To avoid additional exchange rate charges, travellers are advised to take traveller's cheques in Pounds Sterling, US Dollars or South African Rand.
Currency restrictions: The import and export of local currency is prohibited. The import of foreign currency is unlimited, subject to declaration. The export of foreign currency is limited to the amount declared on import.
Banking hours: Mon-Fri 0730-1530.
Exchange rate indicators:
Rate at time of publishing
£1.00= MZM46418.93
$1.00= MZM26750.00

Duty Free

Duty-Free: The following goods may be imported into Mozambique, by persons irrespective of age, without incurring customs duty:
200 cigarettes or 250g of tobacco; 0.75l of spirits; a reasonable quantity of perfume (opened).
Prohibited/restricted items: Narcotics are prohibited. Firearms require a permit.

Public Holidays

Below are listed Public Holidays for the January 2006-June 2007 period.
2006: Jan 1 New Year's Day. **Feb 3** Heroes' Day. **Apr 7** Day of the Mozambican Woman. **May 1** Workers' Day. **Jun 25** Independence Day. **Sep 7** Lusaka Agreement Day. **Sep 25** Armed Forces Day. **Dec 25** National Family Day/Christmas Day.
2007: Jan 1 New Year's Day. **Feb 3** Heroes' Day. **Apr 7** Day of the Mozambican Woman. **May 1** Workers' Day. **Jun 25** Independence Day.

Health

	Special Precautions?	Certificate Required?
Yellow Fever	No	1
Cholera	Yes	2
Typhoid & Polio	3	N/A
Malaria	4	N/A

Note: *Regulations and requirements may be subject to change at short notice, and you are advised to contact your doctor well in advance of your intended date of departure. Any numbers in the chart refer to the footnotes below.*

1: A yellow fever vaccination certificate is required of travellers over one year of age arriving from countries with infected areas.
2: Following WHO guidelines issued in 1973, a cholera vaccination certificate is not a condition of entry to Mozambique. However, cholera is a serious risk in this country and precautions are essential. The last major outbreak was in March 2004. Up-to-date advice should be sought before deciding whether these precautions should include vaccination, as medical opinion is divided over its effectiveness. For more information, see the *Health* appendix.
3: Immunisation against typhoid and poliomyelitis is often advised.
4: Malaria risk exists throughout the year, particularly in the north. The predominant *falciparum* strain is reported to be highly resistant to chloroquine and resistant to sulfadoxine-pyrimethamine. Travellers should bring a mosquito net. The recommended prophylaxis is mefloquine.
Food & drink: All water should be regarded as being potentially contaminated. Water used for drinking, brushing teeth or making ice should have first been boiled or otherwise sterilised. Some milk is unpasteurised and should be boiled. Powdered or tinned milk is available and is advised, but make sure that it is reconstituted with pure water. Avoid dairy products which are likely to have been made from unboiled milk. Only eat well-cooked meat and fish, preferably served hot. Pork, salad and mayonnaise may carry increased risk. Vegetables should be cooked and fruit peeled.
Other risks: *Diarrhoeal diseases, giardiasis, dysentery* and *typhoid fever* are all common. *Bilharzia* (schistosomiasis) is present. Avoid swimming and paddling in fresh water; swimming pools which are well chlorinated and maintained are safe. *Hepatitis A, B* and *E* are present. *Meningococcal meningitis* may occur. *Human trypanosomiasis* (sleeping sickness) has been reported. Plague has been reported in remote areas. Visitors should also be wary of the dangers of *tetanus*. There is a high level of *HIV/AIDs* reported; travellers should take all necessary precautions. Rabies is present. For those at high risk, vaccination before arrival should be considered. If you are bitten, seek medical advice without delay. For more information, see the *Health* appendix.
Health care: Full health insurance, preferably including Medevac, is essential. Medical facilities are scarce. Many rural health centres were forced to close during the conflict with the MNR rebels. It is advisable to carry basic medical supplies including medications and sterile syringes.

Travel - International

AIR:

The national airline is *LAM-Linhas Aéreas de Moçambique (TM)*. Other airlines serving Mozambique include *Air France, Air Mauritius, Ethiopian Airlines, South African Airways* and *TAP Air Portugal*.
Approximate flight times: From Maputo to *London* is 14 hours, including stopover in Johannesburg.
Main airports: *Maputo International (MPM)* (Maputo) is

3km (1.8 miles) northwest of the city. *To/from the airport:* Bus and taxi services run to the centre (travel time - 15 minutes).*Facilities:* Bank, restaurant, bar, snack bar, car hire and post office.
Beira (BEW) is 13km (8 miles) from the city (travel time - 15 minutes). Beira receives flights from Continental Europe, other African countries and America. *Facilities:* Restaurant, shops and a post office.
Departure tax: US$20 if destination is outside Africa; US$10 if destination is within Africa. Infants under two years of age and transit passengers are exempt.
SEA:
British, European, American, Japanese and South African cargo vessels call at Maputo and Beira, but there are no regular passenger services.
RAIL:
A train runs six times a week from Johannesburg to the Mozambique border at Komatipoort where there is a connection to Maputo (travel time - 15 hours). An overnight train runs regularly from Durban to Maputo. There is a service from Harare to Beira. There are connections from Malawi to Beira (although the border still has to be crossed on foot).
Note: Rail services are sometimes sporadic and unreliable.
ROAD:
There are good road links with all neighbouring countries except Tanzania. However, road travel can be dangerous and should only be undertaken in daylight. Highjacking and robberies are rife and travellers should be aware of the possiblilty of unexploded landmines on the lesser-used roads. **Bus:** There is a daily bus service from Maputo to Johannesburg, and there are good bus links to other South African cities. Minibuses run between Maputo and towns in Swaziland, crossing the border at Namaacha. For further information about entry requirements and routes for border crossing, contact the High Commission (see *Passport/Visa Information*).

Travel - Internal

AIR:
There are flights linking Maputo with Beira, Blantyre (Malawi), Inhambane, Lichinga, Nampula, Pemba, Quelimane and Tete. Flights depart from Maputo between 0500 and 0730 and are subject to seasonal alterations. Flights are frequently delayed or cancelled and baggage is often lost or tampered with. Air-taxi services are also available, and are the safest means of transport outside the main cities.
Departure tax: US$7.
RAIL:
There is no rail connection between Maputo and Beira. There is a rail link between Beira and Tete and lines from the towns of Moçambique and Nacala, via the junction at Monapo, to Nampula and Lichinga. Trains also run from Maputo to Goba and Ressano Garcia, and northwards on the line to Zimbabwe. Most trains have three classes, but there are few sleepers and no dining or air-conditioned cars. For seats and sleepers, it is necessary to book in advance. All train services are subject to disruption.
ROAD:
There are an estimated 29,810km (18,631 miles) of roads in Mozambique. Tarred roads connect Maputo with Beira and Beira with Tete. It is now possible to travel by road in southern Mozambique though flood damage can still cause serious delays. Traffic drives on the left. **Bus:** There are regular services covering most of the country. In more rural areas, road passage can only be undertaken by converted passenger trucks known as *chapas*. It is advisable to carry food and water on long journeys. There are occasional controls on the roads to check papers, especially in the north and near the border with Zimbabwe. Bus travel is the cheapest form of transport in the country and is, on the whole, fairly reliable. **Taxi:** Rarely available outside large towns. **Car hire:** Cars can be hired from international and national agencies in Maputo and Beira. Only hard currency is accepted. **Documentation:** International Driving Permit is recommended.
Note: Landmines may make travel by road outside the capital risky, and up-to-date travel advice should be sought. Driving after dark can be hazardous owing to vehicles travelling without headlights. Hijacking occurs.
URBAN:
Bus services in Maputo have been improved with the introduction of new vehicles, and there are now fairly extensive services. Taxis are metered. Taxi drivers expect a tip.

Travel Advice

Travellers should be aware of the risks of violent crime, poor road safety standards and minimal health facilities.
Women should not walk alone on the beach anywhere in Mozambique.
Travellers should also be aware of the global risk of indiscriminate terrorist attacks which could be against civilian targets, including places frequented by foreigners. This advice is based on information provided by the Foreign and Commonwealth Office in the UK. It is correct at time of publishing. As the situation can change rapidly, visitors are advised to contact the following organisations for the latest travel advice:

British Foreign and Commonwealth Office
Tel: (0845) 850 2829.
Website: www.fco.gov.uk

US Department of State
Website: http://travel.state.gov/travel

Accommodation

HOTELS:
Hotels of international standard are found mainly in the cities of Maputo and Beira. Accommodation in smaller towns is generally of a lower standard.
GUEST HOUSES:
It is possible to rent holiday cottages, bungalows and *rondavels* cheaply.
CAMPING/CARAVANNING:
There are campsites along the beaches, and a rest camp with a restaurant in Gorongosa Game Park. Camping is also permitted at various Catholic and Protestant missions in the country.

Top Things To See & Do

- **Beira** has lovely beaches and is the base for trips to **Gorongosa National Park** (see below). Amongst the numerous beaches in Mozambique are **Ponta do Ouro**, **Malugane** (in the south), **Inhaca Island** (near Maputo), **Inhambane** with its beach resort of **Tofo** (about 400km/250 miles north of the capital), **Xai-Xai**, **Vilankulo**, **São Martino do Bilene** and **Chonguene**. There are many beaches and lagoons with safe **bathing**; however, there is a danger of occasional sharks in the warm Indian Ocean. Some resorts have facilities and excellent clear waters full of underwater sights for **divers** or **snorkellers** to explore. **Zavora**'s coral reef is outstanding.
- There is good **fishing** for marlin, barracuda, sailfish and swordfish.
- There is also good **hiking** but advice and extreme caution should be taken due to the large amount of leftover landmines in the country. **Birdwatching** is excellent.
- The museum in **Maputo** (the capital) houses paintings and sculptures by well-known local artists. The gallery in the **Ministry of Labour** building is also worth a visit, as is the **market**.
- **Ilha de Moçambique** (Mozambique Island), near Nampula in the north, is a fascinating place, dotted with 17th- and 18th-century buildings, many of them from the colonial Portuguese period. There are also some interesting mosques dating from that period. It has been declared a UNESCO World Heritage Site.
- Regions that are being promoted as tourist resorts include the **Bazaruto Archipelago** (780km/485 miles north of Maputo), consisting of four islands plus surrounding islets and reefs. This beautiful area features inviting sandy beaches and offers excellent opportunities for game fishing.
- There are three good national parks in Mozambique. The **Gorongosa National Park** is open from the beginning of May to the end of October. Visits can be booked through the LAM office in Maputo. Access is provided by an airstrip at Chitengo. Guides and cars are available inside the park. The **Maputo Elephant Park** is on the right bank of the Maputo River. The **Marromeu National Park** is at the mouth of the **Zambesi River**.

TOURIST INFORMATION

Fundo Nacional do Turismo (FUTUR) (National Tourism Fund)
Avenida 25 de Setembro 1203, PO Box 4758,
Maputo, Mozambique
Tel: (1) 307 320.
Website: www.futur.org.mz

Entertainment

FOOD & DRINK: The cuisine is mainly Portuguese with Far Eastern influences. Specialities are *piri-piri* chicken, Zambesi chicken, shellfish, including Delagoa Bay prawns (which are grilled and served with piri-piri sauce), *matapa* (sauce of ground peanuts and cassava leaves) with rice or *wusa* (stiff maize porridge). Restaurants are to be found in main towns, as well as hotel dining rooms.
Tipping: Not generally expected outside Maputo. In Maputo and other tourist-exposed areas, around 5 per cent of the bill is normal (depending on standards of service and the place itself).
NIGHTLIFE: Maputo has a lively nightlife, particularly on weekends. *Feira Popular* is the main forum of evening activity with various bars and discos, some with live music. The style of music in clubs varies from typical Mozambican rhythms to Western pop music. The *National Company of Song & Dance* has rehearsals which are open to the public. Most major towns have cinemas.
SHOPPING: Special purchases include basketwork, reed mats, woodcarvings, masks, printed cloth and leather articles. **Shopping hours:** Mon-Fri 0800-1230 and 1400-1730, Sat 0800-1800.

Business

ECONOMY: Agriculture, which employs 80 per cent of the working population, is the mainstay of the economy. Cash crops include cashew nuts (see below), tea, sugar, sisal, maize, cotton, copra, oil seeds and some citrus fruit. Forestry is increasing in importance. Fishing is both an important source of food and a vital export earner. Manufacturing industry produces one quarter of GDP: products include processed foods, textiles, drinks, cement and fertiliser. Mining operations produce coal, salt, bauxite, gemstones and marble. In addition, natural gas is extracted from onshore fields and piped to South Africa.
Following the end of the debilitating civil war in 1994, the Mozambican economy picked up strongly over the next five years, recording annual growth of around 10 per cent, although at the price of high inflation (around 35 per cent) at times. Mozambique was also deemed eligible for debt relief under the Heavily Indebted Poor Countries (HIPC) initiative, which was agreed by major donors in 1999 and lifted some of the country's substantial debt burden. However, much of Mozambique's fragile economic progress was undone by the devastating floods of 2000. Since then the economy has been further undermined by drought and trade-related disputes over the issue of subsidies to farmers. A number of African countries complain of the international financial community's insistence that they remove subsidies while Western countries continue to support their own agricultural sector. (Mozambique points to the near-collapse of its once thriving cashew nut industry.) In 2002, Mozambique was once again obliged to call upon its aid donors for emergency food aid. Mozambique is a member of the Southern African Development Conference. South Africa, the USA and Portugal are Mozambique's most important trading partners.
BUSINESS ETIQUETTE: Safari suits are advised for the hot season, while lightweight suits or jackets should be worn for the rest of the year. Prior appointments are recommended. A knowledge of Portuguese is normally necessary for business dealings, although there are translation facilities available in Maputo. January is the main holiday month, so this should be avoided for business trips. **Office hours:** Mon-Fri 0730-1230 and 1400-1730.

COMMERCIAL INFORMATION

Câmara de Comércio de Moçambique
CP 1836, Rua Mateus Sansão Mutemba 452,
Maputo, Mozambique
Tel: (1) 491 970.

Myanmar

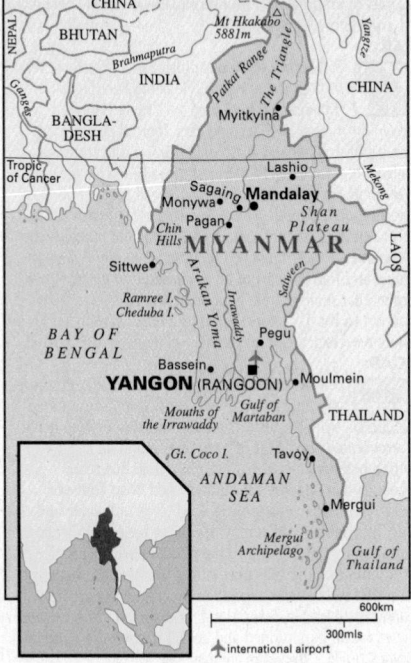

Location: South-East Asia.

Time: GMT+6.5.

Overview

Tourist numbers are steadily rising. Certain areas in Upper and Lower Myanmar are currently out of bounds owing to the past civil war. Most coastal resorts have now been opened to tourists and Sunday round-trip flights are arranged by Myanmar Travel and Tours to Napali and Sandoway beaches during the dry season. Myanmar was affected by the 2004 tsunami which struck off the west coast of Indonesia but the damage was far less severe in Myanmar than in other countries and travel, for the most part, has been unaffected.

General Information

AREA: 676,552 sq km (261,218 sq miles).

POPULATION: 48.9 million (UN estimate 2002).

POPULATION DENSITY: 72.2 per sq km.

CAPITAL: Yangon (Rangoon). The authorities plan to move the seat of Government to Pyinmana. **Population:** 4.5 million (UN estimate 2001).

GEOGRAPHY: Myanmar is a diamond-shaped country extending 925km (575 miles) from west to east and 2100km (1300 miles) from north to south. It is bounded by China, Laos and Thailand in the east, by Bangladesh and India in the north and by the Indian Ocean in the west and south. The Irrawaddy River runs through the centre of the country and fans out to form a delta on the south coast; Yangon stands beside one of its many mouths. North of the delta lies the Irrawaddy basin and central Myanmar, which is protected by a horseshoe of mountains rising to over 3000m (10,000ft), creating profound climatic effects. To the west are the Arakan, Chin and Naga mountains and the Patkai Hills; the Kachin Hills are to the north; to the east lies the Shan Plateau, which extends to the Tenasserim coastal ranges. Intensive irrigated farming is practised throughout central Myanmar, and fruit, vegetables and citrus crops thrive on the Shan Plateau, but much of the land and mountains are covered by subtropical forest.

GOVERNMENT: Socialist Republic since 1974. Power assumed by the army in 1988. **Head of State:** Senior General Than Shwe since 1992. **Head of Government:**

Prime Minister Soe Win since 2004.

LANGUAGE: The official language is Myanmar (Burmese). There are over 100 dialects spoken in Myanmar. English is spoken in business circles.

RELIGION: 87 per cent Theravada Buddhist. The remainder are Hindu, Muslim, Christian and animist.

ELECTRICITY: 230 volts AC, 50Hz.

SOCIAL CONVENTIONS: Handshaking is the normal form of greeting. Full names are used, preceded by *U* (pronounced *oo*) in the case of an older or well-respected man's name, *Aung* for younger men and *Ko* for adult males; a woman's name is preceded by *Daw*. Courtesy and respect for tradition and religion is expected; for instance, shoes and socks must be removed before entering any religious building and it is customary to remove shoes before entering a traditional home (in most modern residences this is no longer observed except in bedrooms). When sitting, avoid displaying the soles of the feet, as this is considered offensive. Small presents are acceptable and appreciated, although never expected. Shorts and mini-skirts should not be worn. Penalties for drug-trafficking range from five years' imprisonment to a death sentence. Homosexuality is illegal.

Climate

A monsoon climate with three main seasons. The hottest period is between February and May, with little or no rain. Rainy season exists from May to October and dry, cooler weather from October to February.

Required clothing: Lightweight cottons and linens throughout most of the year are required. A light raincoat or umbrella is needed during the rainy season. Warmer clothes are advised for coolest period and some evenings.

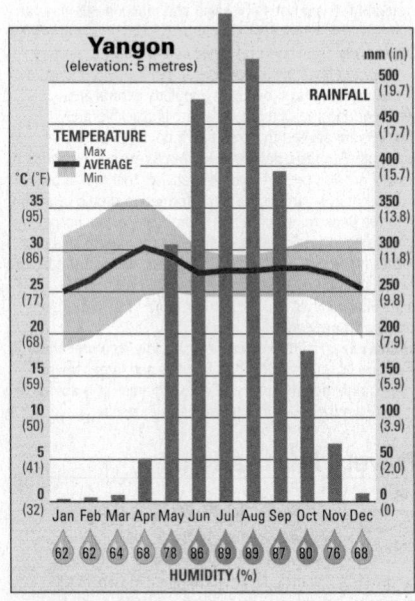

Communications

Telephone: IDD is available to the main cities. Country code: 95. For emergencies, dial 199 (police), 191 (fire) and 192 (ambulance). There is a limited public internal service. Only larger cities can be dialled direct from within Myanmar; smaller towns still use manual switchboards and callers need to ask the operator to connect them to a specific town operator. The *Central Telephone & Telegraph (CTT)* office on the corner of Pansodan and Mahabandoola Streets is the only public place in the country where international telephone calls can be conveniently arranged. The office is open Mon-Fri 0800-1600 and weekends and holidays 0900-1400.

Mobile telephone: GSM 900 network is operated by *Myanmar Posts and Telecommunications*. Fees are high and coverage limited. Note: All visitors who want to use communication devices such as mobile phones and receivers must first apply for permission from the Government of the Union of Myanmar. Without prior permission granted, mobile phones will be temporarily held by Customs on arrival.

Internet: There are a few Internet cafes, but access to many free international e-mail services is blocked. All Internet use is monitored by the Government and is usually expensive.

Post: Service to Europe takes up to one week and letter forms are quicker than ordinary letters. To ensure despatch, it is advisable to go to the post office personally to obtain a certificate of posting, for which a small fee is charged.

MEDIA: Press: The only English-language newspapers are the *Guardian* and the *New Light of Myanmar*. Myanmar Travel & Tours also publishes a tourist publication, *Today*, in English.

TV: *TV Myanmar* is state-run.

Radio: *Radio Myanmar* is state-run. *Democratic Voice of Burma* is an opposition station based in Norway and broadcasts via shortwave.

Passport/Visa

	Passport Required?	Visa Required?	Return Ticket Required?
Full British	Yes	Yes	No
Australian	Yes	Yes	No
Canadian	Yes	Yes	No
USA	Yes	Yes	No
Other EU	Yes	Yes	No
Japanese	Yes	Yes	No

Note: *Regulations and requirements may be subject to change at short notice, and you are advised to contact the appropriate diplomatic or consular authority before finalising travel arrangements. Any numbers in the chart refer to the footnotes below.*

Entry restrictions: Holders of passports issued by the government of the Chinese Taipei, if not holding a special affidavit issued by a diplomatic representation of Myanmar abroad.

PASSPORTS: Passport valid for at least six months beyond date of intended departure required by all.

VISAS: Required by all except transit passengers continuing their journey by the same or first connecting aircraft, provided holding valid onward or return documentation and not leaving the airport.

Note: A separate visa is required for each child over seven years of age, even if travelling on their parent's passport.

Types of visa and cost: *Tourist* (Foreign Independent Travellers - FIT): £14. *Business* and *Social*: £20.

Validity: Tourist visas are valid for two months from the date of issue for stays of 28 days in Myanmar. This can be extended for an additional 14 days. Business visas are valid for three months from date of issue for stays of 10 weeks, extendable for up to 12 months on an individual basis. Transit visas are valid for 24 hours.

Application to: Consulate (or consular section at Embassy; see *Passport/Visa Information*).

Application requirements: (a) One application form. (b) Two passport-size photos. (c) Valid passport. (d) Fee (cash accepted if applying in person; cheque or postal order only if applying by post). (e) Self-addressed, stamped enveloped for postal applications with sufficient postage (registered post is recommended). *Social Visit* (visiting friends or relatives in Myanmar): (a) Two application forms (can be photocopied). (b) Three passport size photos. (c) Valid passport. (d) Fee (cash or postal order). (e) Self-addressed stamped envelope for postal applications with sufficient postage (registered post is recommended). (f) Letter of invitation from friends or relatives in Myanmar. *Business*: (a)-(e) and (f) Company letter explaining purpose of visit. (g) Letter of invitation from company in Myanmar.

Working days required: Normally three.

Temporary Residence: It is possible to get a stay permit once in Myanmar at the Immigration Department.

PASSPORT/VISA INFORMATION

Embassy of the Union of Myanmar in the UK
19A Charles Street, Berkeley Square, London W1J 5DX, UK
Tel: (020) 7499 4340 *or* (0906) 550 8924 (recorded visa and tourism information; calls cost £1 per minute).
Website: www.myanmar.com
Opening hours: Mon-Fri 0930-1630.

Embassy of the Union of Myanmar in the USA
2300 S Street, NW, Washington, DC 20008, USA
Tel: (202) 332 9044/5.
Website: www.mewashingtondc.com *or* www.myanmar.com

Money

Currency: Kyat (MMK) = 100 pyas. Notes are in denominations of MMK1000, 500, 200, 100 and 90 pyas. Coins are in denominations of MMK1, and 50, 25, 10, 5 and 1 pyas. MMK100,000 is known as a *lakh*, and MMK10 million as a *crore*. Kyat is pronounced like the English word 'chat'. To combat the black market and limit the financial power of dissident groups, currency denominations are occasionally declared invalid without prior notice. Limited refunds are usually allowed for certain sectors of the population.

Currency exchange: FECs, which are printed in China, are Myanmar's second legal currency and are issued by the Bank of Myanmar specifically for visiting tourists. They come in denominations equivalent to US$20, 10, 5 and 1. Payment for FECs is *only* accepted in US Dollars. One US Dollar equals one FEC. FECs can be exchanged into Kyats at officially authorised banks, bureaux de change, hotels and Myanmar Travel and Tours offices and can be spent anywhere in the country. Cash payments can also be made in US Dollars, but *only* at establishments (eg hotels, railway stations, airlines) that have an official licence allowing them to accept dollars. Wherever possible, it is advisable to change US Dollars into Kyats rather than FECs, as FECs usually have a poorer exchange rate than Kyats. However, US Dollar traveller's cheques can only be exchanged into FECs and not directly into Kyats unlike US Dollar cash. It is also recommended to carry small change as large notes may be difficult to change.

Euros are now also accepted in all banks and currency exchange bureaux. There are no ATMs.

Credit & debit cards: It is unlikely that credit or debit cards will be accepted; it is best to check with your card company prior to travel.

Traveller's cheques: Accepted, although probably not by all establishments. To avoid additional exchange rate charges, travellers are advised to take traveller's cheques in US Dollars or Pounds Sterling.

Currency restrictions: The import and export of local currency is prohibited. There are no import limits on foreign currencies, but any amounts must be declared on arrival and the declaration certificate kept safe – on departure, foreign currencies are checked with the amounts declared on entry. There are regular customs checks at Yangon airport, aimed at curbing black-market activities; this makes it essential to keep all receipts in order to account for money spent while in the country.

Banking hours: Mon-Fri 1000-1400.

Exchange rate indicators:

Rate at time of publishing

£1.00 =	MMK10.31
$1.00 =	MMK5.95

Duty Free

The following goods may be taken into Myanmar by persons over 17 years of age without incurring customs duty:

200 cigarettes or 50 cigars or 250g tobacco; 1l of alcohol; 0.5l of perfume or eau de cologne.

Prohibited and restricted items: Playing cards, gambling equipment, antiques, archaeological items and pornography are prohibited. Jewellery, electrical goods and cameras must be declared; failure to do so may result in visitors being refused permission to export it on departure. Video cameras will be held in safe custody at the airport and will be returned on departure.

Note: All gems, jewellery and silverware purchased from authorised shops can be taken out of the country.

Public Holidays

Below are listed Public Holidays for the January 2006-June 2007 period.

2006: Jan 4 Independence Day. **Jan 10** Eid Al Adha (Feast of the Sacrifice). **Feb 12** Union Day. **Mar 2** Peasants' Day (anniversary of the 1962 coup). **Mar 13** Full Moon of Tabaung. **Mar 27** Armed Forces Day. **Apr 13-16** Maha Thingyan (Water Festival). **Apr 17** Myanmar New Year. **May 1** May Day. **May 11** Full Moon of Kasone. **Jul 9** Full Moon of Waso (Beginning of Buddhist Lent). **Jul 19** Martyrs' Day. **Oct 6** Full Moon of Thadingyut (End of Buddhist Lent). **Oct 21** Deepavali. **Nov 14** Tazaungmon Full Moon Day. **Dec 6** National Day. **Dec 23** Kayin New Year. **Dec 25** Christmas Day. **Dec 31** Eid Al Adha (Feast of the Sacrifice).

2007: Jan 4 Independence Day. **Feb** *or* **Mar** Full Moon of Tabaung. **Feb 12** Union Day. **Mar 2** Peasants' Day (anniversary of the 1962 coup). **Mar 27** Armed Forces Day. **Apr** *or* **May** Full Moon of Kasone. **Apr 13-16** Maha Thingyan (Water Festival). **Apr 17** Myanmar New Year. **May 1** May Day.

Note: Buddhist holidays are determined according to lunar sightings, and dates given here are approximations only. Other festivals celebrated by minorities include the Islamic observance of Bakri Idd in late November; Christmas and Easter; and the Karen New Year in early January. For further information, contact the Embassy (see *Passport/Visa Information* section) or see the *World of Buddhism* appendix.

Health

	Special Precautions?	Certificate Required?
Yellow Fever	Yes	1
Cholera	Yes	2
Typhoid & Polio	3	N/A
Malaria	4	N/A

Note: *Regulations and requirements may be subject to change at short notice, and you are advised to contact your doctor well in advance of your intended date of departure. Any numbers in the chart refer to the footnotes below.*

1: A yellow fever vaccination certificate is required from all travellers arriving from infected areas. Nationals and residents of Myanmar are required to possess certificates of vaccination on their departure to an infected area.

2: Following WHO guidelines issued in 1973, a cholera vaccination certificate is no longer a condition of entry to Myanmar. However, cholera is a serious risk in this country and precautions are essential. Up-to-date advice should be sought before deciding whether these precautions should include vaccination, as medical opinion is divided over its effectiveness. For more information, see the *Health* appendix.

3: Immunisation against typhoid and poliomyelitis is strongly advised.

4: Malaria risk (predominantly in the malignant *falciparum* form) exists below 1000m (3281ft) in the following areas: (a) throughout the year in Karen State; (b) from March to December in Chin, Kachin, Kayah, Mon, Rakhine and Shan States, in Pegu Division, and in Hlegu, Hmawbi and Taikkyi townships of Yangon Division; (c) from April to December in rural areas of Tenasserim Division; (d) from May to December in the Irrawaddy Division and rural areas of Mandalay Division; (e) from June to November in rural areas of Magwe Division and in Sagaing Division. The *falciparum* strain is reported to be highly resistant to chloroquine and resistant to sulfadoxine/pyrimethamine. Mefloquine resistance is reported in the eastern part of the Shan state. Reduced sensitivity to chloroquine in the *vivax* form is reported. The recommended prophylaxis is mefloquine, and doxycycline in the eastern part of the Shan state.

Food & drink: All water should be regarded as being potentially contaminated. Water used for drinking, brushing teeth or making ice should have first been boiled or otherwise sterilised. Milk is unpasteurised and should be boiled. Powdered or tinned milk is available and is advised, but make sure that it is reconstituted with pure water. Avoid dairy products which are likely to have been made from unboiled milk. Only eat well-cooked meat and fish, preferably served hot. Pork, salad and mayonnaise may carry increased risk. Vegetables should be cooked and fruit peeled.

Other risks: *Diarrhoea, amoebic* and *bacillery dysentery* and *typhoid fever* are all common. *Japanese encephalitis* may be caught via mosquito bites, particularly in rural areas between June and October. A vaccine is available, and travellers are advised to consult their doctor prior to departure. *Filariasis, dengue fever, trachoma* and *Hepatitis A, B* and *E* are also present. The WHO advises that foci of plague are present in Myanmar. Further information should be sought from the Department of Health or from any of the hospitals specialising in tropical diseases listed in the *Health* appendix. *Rabies* is present. For those at high risk, vaccination before arrival should be considered. If you are bitten, seek medical advice without delay. For more information, see the *Health* appendix.

Health care: Health insurance is strongly recommended. There are hospitals and clinics in cities and larger towns, and regional health centres in outlying areas. It is advisable to carry a remedy against minor enteric upsets.

Travel - International

AIR:

The national airline is *Myanmar Airways International (UB)* (website: www.maiair.com). Yangon has direct air links with Bangkok, Bangladesh, Calcutta, Jakarta, Kunming, Moscow and Singapore. Airlines serving Myanmar include *Air China, Austrian Airlines, Bangladesh Airlines, Indian Airlines, Lufthansa, Silk Air* and *Thai Airways International.*

Main airports: *Yangon (RGN)* is 19km (12 miles) from the city. *To/from the airport:* Buses go to the city (travel time - 30 minutes). Taxis are also available (travel time – 45 minutes). *Facilities:* Restaurant, bar, snack bar, bank, post office, duty free shop and tourist information.

Departure tax: US$10, payable also in FECs (Foreign Exchange Certificates; see also *Money* section for details). Passengers in direct transit are exempt.

SEA:

Cruise ships call at *Yangon Port.*

ROAD:

Overland entry with a border pass is, in theory, permitted at the following border check points: Kyukoke, Namkhan and Muse on the Myanmar-Yunnan (People's Republic of China) border; and Tachileik, Myawaddy and Kawthaung on the Mynamar-Thailand border. Generally speaking, however, foreigners are only allowed to travel as part of an organised group. Owing to continuing political instability, borders may periodically close. Contact the nearest Embassy for up-to-date details.

Note: It is recommended to use only air travel as a means of access into Myanmar.

Travel - Internal

AIR:

Air travel is the most efficient way of moving within Myanmar and the only permissible means of transport for independent travellers, but there is a rather limited schedule of flights, and a rather less than perfect safety record. The British Embassy in London bans its staff from using *Myanmar Airways* for this reason; although the staff *do* use *Myanmar Airways International. Air Mandalay* and *Air Yangon* operate internal flights. Internal security can restrict ease of movement. There are daily flights to most towns; charter flights are also available. There are over 60 airstrips in the country. For tickets and information, contact Myanmar Travel and Tours (see *Top Things To Do*).

Internal flight times: From Yangon to *Mandalay* is two hours 10 minutes; to *Pagan* is one hour 30 minutes; and to *Heho* is one hour 25 minutes.

SEA/RIVER:

The best way of seeing Myanmar is by boat, particularly between Bhamo–Mandalay and Mandalay–Pagan. Myanmar has about 8000km (5000 miles) of navigable rivers. Trips can only be arranged as part of an organised tour group. It is generally necessary to provide one's own food.

RAIL:

Myanmar Railways provides services on several routes, the principal line being Yangon to Mandalay (travel time - 12 to 14 hours). Overnight trains have sleeping cars. There is also a good service from Mandalay–Lashio–Myitkyina. The state-run railway has 4300km (2700 miles) of track and serves most of Myanmar. First class is available but, with the exception of the Yangon to Mandalay line, services are regularly afflicted with delays caused by climatic, technical and bureaucratic difficulties. Tickets must be purchased through Myanmar Travel and Tours as part of an organised tour group. There are regular services from Yangon to Mandalay and from Yangon to Thazi. Visitors should be aware that much railway equipment is decrepit and some accidents are unreported.

ROAD:

Traffic drives on the right. There has been some modernisation of Myanmar's once antiquated vehicles. Visitors must remember that, under Burmese law, the driver of a car involved in an accident with a pedestrian is *always* at fault. **Bus:** Buses are generally operated by the state-owned Road Transport Enterprise. Public bus services tend to be unreliable and uncomfortable; visitors may pay using the Kyat currency on certain lines only. Owing to the ongoing privatisation programme of the transport industry, a fleet of privately operated buses is also available. The main lines are from Yangon to Meiktila, Pyay, Mandalay and Taunggyi. Private buses are air conditioned and accept payment in Kyat, US Dollars or FECs. **Bicycles** are available for hire.

Documentation: An International Driving Permit is required. This must be presented to the police, who will endorse it or issue a visitor's licence. Otherwise, Burmese driving licences, valid for two years, are issued without test on production of a valid British driving licence and payment of a fee of FEC50/MMK150.

URBAN:

Yangon has a circular rail service. There are also antiquated and overcrowded bus services in all cities. Yangon has blue Government taxis with set fares. Unmetered three- and four-wheel taxis are available in cities, as are rickshaws; it is wise to pre-arrange fares. Taxi drivers do not expect a tip.

Travel Advice

Travellers should exercise caution on visits to Myanmar, and avoid all but essential travel to the Myanmar side of the Myanmar/Thai border.

Travellers should be aware of the threat from terrorism in Myanmar. There have been a number of recent bomb explosions in public places. Targets have included commercial interests and places tourists may visit as well as public transport.

The political situation in Myanmar remains unsettled and there are stringent restrictions on freedom of movement and speech.

This advice is based on information provided by the Foreign and Commonwealth Office in the UK. It is correct at time of publishing. As the situation can change rapidly, visitors are advised to contact the following organisations for the latest travel advice:

British Foreign and Commonwealth Office
Tel: (0845) 850 2829.
Website: www.fco.gov.uk

US Department of State
Website: http://travel.state.gov/travel

Accommodation

HOTELS:

Since the privatisation of the hotel industry in 1993, a large number of new hotels and guest houses have been completed or are under construction, particularly in Yangon. Advance booking is

A B C D E F G H I J K L M N O P Q R S T U V W X Y Z

advisable, particularly from November to March. There are also hotels at the resorts of Sandoway, Taunggyi and Pagan. For further details, contact Myanmar Travel and Tour (see *Top Things To Do*).

Grading: An increasing number of hotels are divided into three categories: luxury, first class and lower.

INNS: These are another option for visitors. Although reserved for state officials in many towns, inns will often accommodate travellers who have been granted official permission. Visitors travelling away from the normal tourist routes should carry sleeping bags or blankets, as pagodas, temples and monasteries will usually only accommodate visitors for a night or two.

Top Things To See

- **Yangon** (or *Rangoon*), the capital, is a city of Buddhist temples, open-air markets, food stalls and ill-repaired colonial architecture. It has a population of over 2 million. Although most of the city has been built in the last hundred years, and although it suffered considerable damage during World War II, there are still several examples of a more ancient culture. These include the golden **Shwedragon Pagoda**, one of the most spectacular Buddhist shrines in Asia and reputedly 2500 years old (although rebuilt in 1769); the **Sule Pagoda**, also over 2000 years old; the **Botataung Pagoda**, hollow inside with a mirrored maze; and the **Maha Pasan Guha**, or 'Great Cave'.
- Outside the capital, places worth visiting include the **Naga-Yone** enclosure near **Myinkaba**, with a Buddha figure entwined and protected by a huge cobra – a combination of Buddhism and Brahman astrology; **Kyaik Tyo** and its 'Golden Rock Pagoda', a 5.5m (18ft) shrine built on a gold-plated boulder atop a cliff; and **Pegu**, founded in 1573, with its golden **Shwemawdaw Pagoda** and market. Just northeast of Pegu is the **Shwethalyaung Buddha**, revered as one of the most beautiful and lifelike of reclining Buddhas, which was lost and totally overgrown by jungle after the destruction of Pegu in 1757. It was rediscovered in the British era, during the construction of the railway line.
- **Pagan** is one of the greatest historical areas in the country. It is best seen at sunrise or sunset. More than 13,000 pagodas were once spread over this dry plain during the golden age of the 11 great kings (roughly 1044-1287); this came to an end with the threat of invasion by Kublai Khan from China, and this extraordinary area was abandoned. Now there are fewer than 3000 pagodas. The actual village of Pagan has a museum, market and places to eat and stay; within walking distance of Bagan, there are lacquerware workshops and an attractive temple. There are dozens of open temples in the Pagan area (about 40 sq km/15 sq miles), but places of special interest include the **Shwegugyi Temple**, built in 1311 and noted for its fine stucco carvings; the **Gawdawpalin Temple**, badly damaged in the 1975 earthquake, but still one of the most impressive of the Pagan temples; and the **Thatbyinnyu Temple**, which is the highest in Bagan.
- **Mandalay:** This old royal city is rich in palaces, stupas, temples and pagodas (although the city has suffered several bad fires which have destroyed some buildings), and is the main centre of Buddhism and Burmese arts. There are some excellent craft markets and there are thriving stone-carving workshops and gold-leaf industries. Taking its name from **Mandalay Hill** (rising about 240m/787ft to the northeast of the palace), the city was founded by King Mindon in 1857, the old wooden palace buildings at **Amarapura** being moved and reconstructed. Sights of interest include the huge **Shweyattaw Buddha**, close to the hill, with its outstretched finger pointing towards the city; the **Eindawya Pagoda**, built in 1847 and covered in gold leaf; the **Shwekyimyint Pagoda**, containing the original Buddha image consecrated by Prince Minshinzaw during the Pagan period; and the **Mahumuni Pagoda** or 'Great Pagoda', housing the famous and revered Mahumuni image. Covered in gold leaf over the years by devout Buddhists, this image was brought from Arakan in 1784, although it is thought to be much older. The base, moat and huge walls are virtually all that remain of the once stupendous **Mandalay Palace**, which was an immense walled city (mostly of timber construction) rather than a palace. It was burnt down in 1942. A large-scale model gives an indication of what it must have been like. The **Shwenandaw Kyaung Monastery** was at one time part of the palace complex and was used as an apartment by King Mindon and his chief queen. Like the palace, the wooden building was once beautifully gilded. There are some extraordinary carved panels inside and also a photograph of the **Atumashi Kyaung Monastery**, destroyed by fire in 1890. The ruins can be seen to the south of the **Kuthodaw Pagoda**, called 'the world's biggest book' because of the 729 marble slabs that surround the central pagoda – they are inscribed with the entire Buddhist canon.

- The area around Mandalay contains several older, abandoned capital cities. **Sagaing** is easily accessible to the visitor, and contains interesting pagodas at **Tupayon**, **Aungmyelawka** and **Kaunghmudaw**. Sagaing was, for a time, the capital of an independent Shan Kingdom. In the 15th century, **Ava** was chosen as the kingdom's new capital and it remained so until well into the 19th century, when the kingdom vanished; the old city walls can still be traced. **Mingun** (a pleasant river trip from Mandalay) possesses the famous **Mingun Bell**, supposedly the largest uncracked hung bell in the world. It was cast in 1790 by King Bodawpaya to be hung in his giant pagoda, which was never finished, due to the king's death in 1819. The base of the pagoda alone is about 50m (165ft) high. **Amarapura**, south of Mandalay, was founded by Bodawpaya in 1783 and the city is famous for its cotton and silk weaving.
- **The East & the Northwest** region of the country offers the visitor opportunities for walking and rock-climbing, and the various hill stations, such as **Kalaw**, provide a pine-forested escape from the heat and humidity of Yangon. The caves and lake at **Pindaya** are famous; the caves contain thousands of Buddha images. Near the village of **Yengan** are the **Padah-Lin Caves**, containing prehistoric paintings. **Inlay Lake** on the Shan Plateau is famous for its floating gardens and leg-rowing fishermen. **Maymyo** is a charming British hill station further north, with attractive waterfalls and a pleasant climate because of its high altitude. Difficult communications usually prevent tourists from visiting the largely tribal Northwest. Many of Myanmar's minority peoples live here.

Top Things To Do

- A large number of **Buddhist festivals**, many timed to coincide with the full moon, are held annually in Myanmar and provide an interesting way for visitors to experience local traditions and culture. Any visitor would be unlucky not to be able to enjoy at least one during their stay: *Amanda Pagoda Festival* in January/February; *Pindaya Cave Festival* in March; *Maha Thingyan* (New Year) in March; or *Thihoshin Pagoda Festival*, Pakkoku, in June/July.
- **Traditional sports:** The national game is **Chinglone**; played in teams of six, the object of the game is to keep a cane ball in the air for as long as possible using any part of the body except the hands. Burmese boxing is another popular sport; it can appear extremely vicious to the uninitiated spectator. Many Western sports are also played.
- For serious practitioners, there are several centres for the study and practice of **Theravada Buddhism**, the most famous of which is the *Mahasi Meditation Centre* in Yangon. The centre was founded in 1947 by Mahasi Sayadaw, one of Myanmar's greatest meditation teachers. Visitors wishing to participate in Buddhist **retreats** need to obtain a special, long-stay entry visa (allowing stays of up to 12 weeks). The application procedure takes up to 10 weeks. For further details about the necessary application requirements, contact the Embassy or Consular section at the Embassy (see *Passport/Visa Information*).
- Visitors can also attend performances of Myanmar's traditional popular **theatre**, known as *pwe* (show). Performances take place in a variety of contexts, including religious festivals, weddings, sporting events or even funerals, and sometimes last for an entire night. Of further interest are performances of traditional **dance** forms (*nat pwes*), which pay homage to the spirit world, or **marionette theatre** (*yok-thei pwe*), widely practised during the late 18th century in Mandalay and one of the most characteristic forms of national cultural expression.
- **Ecotourism:** This is encouraged by Myanmar Travel and Tours and there are a number of national parks and wildlife sanctuaries which also offer **trekking** and **safaris**. The best parks are the **Alaungdaw Kathapa National Park** (located northwest of Monywa); **Hlawga National Park** (near Yangon, good for birdwatching); **Popa Mountain Park** (extinct volcano covered in forests in the desert area of central Myanmar); **Lampi Island** (Myeik Archipelago) (which can be reached by boat trips from Myeik and Kawthaung); and **Shwesettaw Wildlife Sanctuary** (located in Minbu).
- **Swimming** and other types of watersports are possible on the following beaches: **Kanthaya Beach** (located on the Rakhine coast); **Maung-ma-gan Beach** (located on the Taninthayi coast in the south and reached from Dawei); **Ngapali Beach** (located on the Rakhine coast); and **Chaung-tha Beach** (located west of Pathein).

TOURIST INFORMATION

Myanmar Tourism Promotion Board
c/o Traders Hotel, Level 3, Business Centre,
223 Sule Pagoda Road, Yangon, Myanmar
Tel: (1) 242 800.
Website: www.myanmar-tourism.com

Myanmar Travel and Tours
77-91 Sule Pagoda Road, Yangon, Myanmar
Tel: (1) 252 859 *or* 371 910 *or* 371 927.
Website: http://myanmartravelandtours.com

Entertainment

FOOD & DRINK: The regional food is hot and spicy. Fish, rice, noodles and vegetables spiced with onions, ginger, garlic and chillies are the common local ingredients. Local dishes include *lethok son* (a sort of spicy vegetarian rice salad), *mohinga* (fish soup with noodles) and *oh-no khauk swe* (rice noodles, chicken and coconut milk). The avocados by Inle Lake are very good. Delicious fruits are available in the markets and food stalls appear on the corners of most large towns. Chinese and Indian cuisine is offered in many hotels and restaurants.

Tea is a popular drink; the spices which are added to it can make the tongue turn bright red. Locally produced soft drinks are generally of poor quality and rather expensive. Coffee is not common. Locally produced beer, rum, whisky and gin are generally available. **Tipping:** It is usual to give 5 to 10 per cent on hotel and restaurant bills. Taxi drivers do not expect a tip.

NIGHTLIFE: Western-style nightlife is almost non existent, although there are occasional performances in Yangon's three theatres as well as a number of rock and pop groups gaining in popularity. Cinemas are popular and seven of Yangon's 50 cinemas regularly show English-language films.

SHOPPING: Souvenirs include handicrafts and jewellery. In Yangon, a good place to shop is Bogyoke Aung San Market, which sells luxury items, handicrafts, food stuffs, clothing, jewellery and consumer goods. It is open from 0800-1800 (except Sunday and public holidays) but the best time to visit is around 1000. Mandalay is a good place for traditional handicrafts which can be purchased at Zegyo Market. Phatahe Bazaar sells Buddhist articles of worship. **Shopping hours:** Mon-Sun 0800-2200.

Business

ECONOMY: The largest single sector of Myanmar's economy is agriculture, mainly livestock and fishing, but it continues to rely on traditional non-mechanised methods. Rice, generally the principal export earner, has diminished in importance in line with the continually depressed state of the world market in the commodity. Teak wood is the country's other main export (much of it felled and traded illegally). Other crops include oil seeds, sugar cane, cotton, jute and rubber. Myanmar has significant deposits of tin, copper, zinc, gemstones, silver and coal: commercial exploitation has recently begun. Although Myanmar's oil production, never substantial, has been falling during the last 10 years, there are thought to be large untapped reserves of both oil and gas inland. Domestically produced gas meets about half of the country's energy needs; hydroelectric power covers most of the rest. A wide range of manufactured goods is assembled locally but the majority are imported. Otherwise, Myanmar's industrial sector is mostly concerned with processing domestically produced raw materials. Further significant sources of revenue include opium trafficking and gemstone mining, both of which are largely controlled by the military Government and have been mainly used to finance substantial arms purchases. There are few reliable economic statistics for Myanmar; inflation in 2004 was an estimated 27 per cent. After years of political isolation, Myanmar became a member of ASEAN in July 1997. The Government has tried to attract foreign investment by relaxing its previous tight controls over commercial activity. However, many potential investors are deterred by the Government's appalling human rights record and the prospect of widespread international opprobrium. Myanmar's economic future depends largely on political developments.

BUSINESS ETIQUETTE: Lightweight suits are recommended during the day; jackets are needed for top-level meetings. Most commercial business transactions will be conducted in English. Business cards in Burmese script can be useful. The best time to visit is October to February. **Office hours:** Mon-Fri 0930-1630.

COMMERCIAL INFORMATION

There are over 20 Government Corporations dealing with all aspects of business. The Inspection and Agency Corporation in Yangon promotes business with foreign companies. For further information, contact the commercial section of the Embassy (see *Passport/Visa Information*).

Namibia

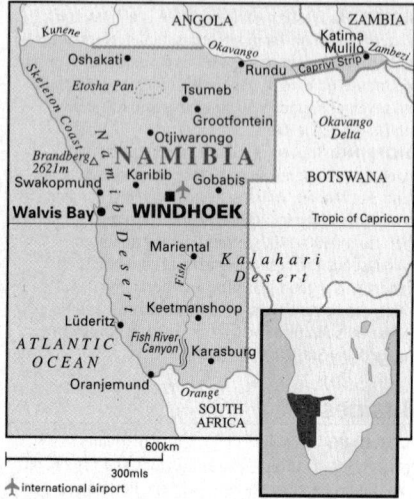

Location: Southwest Africa.

Time: GMT + 1 (GMT + 2 from the first Sunday in September to the first Sunday in April).

Overview

Although not as well known as some of its African neighbours, Namibia is a gem for those in search of the wilderness.

Before achieving independence in 1990, Namibia was subject to German influence in the 19th century; the territory was then occupied by the South Africans during World War I.

Today Namibia is peaceful and is better off economically than many other countries of the region because of its productive mining, farming, fishing and tourism industries. However, little change in the pattern of ownership has been achieved since independence and the issue of land reform will need to be addressed as half of the country's agricultural land is still owned by a few thousand white farmers.

Essentially a desert country, Namibia offers contrasting landscapes. The desolate Namib Desert is said to be the oldest in the world, with its high dunes and awe-inspiring sense of space. The central plateau, with its thorn bush savannah and rugged mountains, rising abruptly from the plains, gives way to the majestic Fishriver Canyon in the south. In the north of the country, landscapes range from dense bush and open plains of the great Etosha Pan, to woodland savannah and lush vegetation.

The Etosha national park, the third largest in Africa, owes its unique landscape to the Etosha Pan, a vast shallow depression. A series of waterholes along the southern edge of the pan guarantee rewarding and often spectacular game viewing. Germanic influence can still be found in the country's good road infrastructure, well-equipped rest camps throughout the country and most cities' architecture. The perfect choice for nature lovers and amateur photographers alike.

General Information

AREA: 824,292 sq km (318,261 sq miles).
POPULATION: 2 million (UN estimate 2005).
POPULATION DENSITY: 2.43 per sq km.
CAPITAL: Windhoek. **Population:** 223,364 (2001).
GEOGRAPHY: Namibia is in southwest Africa. It is a large and mainly arid country sharing borders with Angola to the north, Botswana to the east, South Africa to the south and, in the Caprivi Strip, a narrow panhandle of Namibian territory jutting from the northeast corner of the country, with Zambia and Zimbabwe. To the west is 1280km (795 miles) of some of

the most desolate and lonely coastline in the world. The port of Walvis Bay, situated roughly halfway down Namibia's coast, was returned by South Africa to Namibian jurisdiction in February 1994. Along its entire length, the vast shifting sand dunes of the Namib Desert spread inland for 80 to 130km (50 to 80 miles). In the interior, the escarpment of a north-south plateau slopes away to the east and north into the vast interior sand basin of the Kalahari. In the far northwest, the 66,000 sq km (25,500 sq miles) of the Kaokoland mountains run along the coast, while further inland lies the Etosha Pan (a dried-out saline lake), surrounded by grasslands and bush which support a large and varied wildlife. The Etosha National Park & Game Reserve is one of the finest in Africa, in that it remains, to a large extent, free of human influence.
GOVERNMENT: Republic. Gained independence from South Africa in 1990. **Head of State**: President Hifikepunye Pohamba since 2005. **Head of Government**: Prime Minister Nahas Angula since 2005. **Recent history:** Hifikepunye Pohamba, representing the ruling Swapo party, won a landslide victory in Presidential elections in November 2004 and was inaugurated in March 2005. He promised to pursue the land reforms proposed by his predecessor President Nujoma.
LANGUAGE: English is the official language. Afrikaans is spoken by most people. German, Herero, Kavango, Nama and Ovambo (51 per cent) are also spoken.
RELIGION: Christian majority (90 per cent).
ELECTRICITY: 220 volts AC, 50hz. Outlets are of the three-pin type.
SOCIAL CONVENTIONS: Western customs prevail; normal courtesies should be shown when visiting someone's home.

Climate

The cold Benguela current keeps the coast of the Namib Desert cool, damp and free of rain for most of the year, with a thick coastal fog. Inland, all the rain falls in summer (November to April). Summer temperatures are high while the altitude means that nights are cool. Winter nights can be fairly cold, but days are generally warm and pleasant.
Required clothing: Light cottons, with slightly heavier cottons or light woollens for evening. Inland, shoes are essential during the day as the ground is very hot.

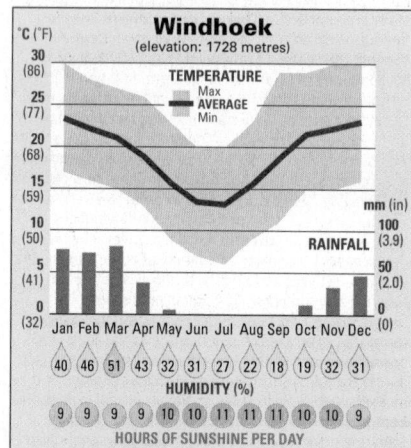

Communications

Telephone: IDD is available. Country code: 264.
Mobile telephone: Roaming agreements exist with most international mobile phone operators. Coverage is limited to urban areas.
Internet: There are Internet cafes in Walvis Bay and Windhoek.
Post: Good postal service. Airmail to Europe takes approximately four days to two weeks.
MEDIA: Press freedom is provided for by the constitution and largely respected by the Government. Opposition views are broadcast.
Press: Newspapers are printed Monday to Friday. English-language dailies include *The Namibian*, *The Namibian Economist* and *New Era*; weeklies include the *Windhoek Observer*. *Die Republikein* is a daily Afrikaans-language newspaper. *Allgemeine Zeitung* is published daily in German.
TV: The state-owned *Namibian Broadcasting Corporation* (NBC) broadcasts nationwide. *Desert TV* is a Windhoek-based private station.
Radio: State-run radio is operated by NBC. Private music stations include *Radio Kudu*, *Radio Wave* and *Radio Energy*. *Katutura Community Radio* (KCR) broadcasts some BBC World Service programmes in Windhoek.

Passport/Visa

	Passport Required?	Visa Required?	Return Ticket Required?
Full British	Yes	No	Yes
Australian	Yes	No	Yes
Canadian	Yes	No	Yes
USA	Yes	No	Yes
Other EU	Yes	No/1	Yes
Japanese	Yes	No	Yes

Note: *Regulations and requirements may be subject to change at short notice, and you are advised to contact the appropriate diplomatic or consular authority before finalising travel arrangements. Any numbers in the chart refer to the footnotes below.*

PASSPORTS: Passport valid for a minimum of six months after the date of departure from Namibia required by all.
VISAS: Required by all except the following for stays of up to 30 days:
(a) **1.** nationals of countries shown in the chart above, except nationals of Cyprus, Czech Republic, Estonia, Greece, Hungary, Latvia, Lithuania, Malta, Poland, Slovak Republic and Slovenia who *do* require a visa;
(b) nationals of Angola, Botswana, Brazil, Cuba, Iceland, Kenya, Lesotho, Liechtenstein, Malawi, Malaysia, Mozambique, New Zealand, Norway, Russian Federation, Singapore, South Africa, Swaziland, Switzerland, Tanzania, Zambia and Zimbabwe;
(c) those continuing to a third country and not leaving the airport transit area.
Types of visa and cost: *Tourist, Business* and *Transit*: £20
Validity: Valid up to three months from date of issue for stays of up to three months from date of entry. Extensions for a further three months are available from the Ministry of Home Affairs in Windhoek.
Application to: Consulate (or consular section at High Commission); see *Passport/Visa Information*.
Application requirements: (a) Valid passport. (b) Completed application form. (c) Two passport-size photos. (d) Return or onward ticket or proof of accommodation. (e) Fee. *Private:* (a)-(e) and, (f) Letter of invitation from Namibian resident. *Business:* (a)-(e) and, (f) Company letter. (g) Letter from sponsoring company in Namibia.
Working days required: Three.
Temporary residence: Apply to the High Commission or Embassy; see *Passport/Visa Information*.

PASSPORT/VISA INFORMATION

High Commission for the Republic of Namibia in the UK
6 Chandos Street, London W1G 9LU, UK
Tel: (020) 7636 6244.
Opening hours: Mon-Fri 0900-1300 and 1400-1700.

Embassy of the Republic of Namibia in the USA
1605 New Hampshire Avenue, NW,
Washington, DC 20009, USA
Tel: (202) 986 0540.
Website: www.namibianembassyusa.org

Money

Currency: The Namibian Dollar (NAD; symbol N$) is in note denominations of N$200, 100, 50, 20 and 10. Coins are in denominations of N$5, N$1, 50 cents, 10 cents and 5 cents. It is linked to the South African Rand (R) on a 1:1 basis (South African Rand = 100 cents). The South African Rand is also acceptable as currency in Namibia.
Currency exchange: Available in banks and at bureaux de change. A better rate of exchange can be obtained on traveller's cheques than on cash.
Credit & debit cards: American Express, Diners Club, MasterCard and Visa are accepted. Check with your credit or debit card company for details of merchant acceptability and other services which may be available. Credit cards are not usually accepted at petrol stations.
Traveller's cheques: To avoid additional exchange rate charges, travellers are advised to take traveller's cheques in US Dollars or South African Rand.
Currency restrictions: The import and export of local currency is limited to N$50,000. The import of foreign currency is unlimited, provided declared on arrival. Export of foreign currency is unlimited up to amount imported and declared as long as the departure is within 12 months. No limits exist for travel between Botswana, Lesotho, Namibia, South Africa and Swaziland as these countries are members of the same common monetary area.
Banking hours: Mon-Fri 0900-1530, Sat 0900-1100.
Exchange rate indicators:
Rate at time of publishing
£1.00=   N$11.72
$1.00=   N$6.76

Duty Free

The following may be imported into Namibia by persons over 16 years of age without incurring customs duty: *400 cigarettes and 50 cigars and 250g of tobacco; 2l of wine and 1l of spirits; 50ml of perfume and 250ml of eau de toilette; gifts to the value of N$50,000 (including value of imported duty free items).*

Restricted items: Hunting rifles need a permit, issued by customs when entering the country. Handguns are not allowed.

Public Holidays

Below are listed Public Holidays for the January 2006-June 2007 period.
2006: Jan 1 New Year's Day. **Mar 21** Independence Day. **Apr 14-17** Easter. **May 1** Workers' Day. **May 4** Cassinga Day. **May 25** Ascension/Africa Day (Anniversary of the OAU's Foundation). **Aug 26** Heroes' Day. **Dec 10** International Human Rights Day. **Dec 25** Christmas Day. **Dec 26** Family Day.
2007: Jan 1 New Year's Day. **Mar 21** Independence Day. **Apr 6-9** Easter. **May 1** Workers' Day. **May 4** Cassinga Day. **May 17** Ascension. **May 25** Africa Day (Anniversary of the OAU's Foundation).

Health

	Special Precautions?	Certificate Required?
Yellow Fever	Yes	1
Cholera	No	No
Typhoid & Polio	2	N/A
Malaria	3	N/A

Note: *Regulations and requirements may be subject to change at short notice, and you are advised to contact your doctor well in advance of your intended date of departure. Any numbers in the chart refer to the footnotes below.*

1: A yellow fever vaccination certificate is required from travellers arriving from infected areas. Those countries or parts of countries that are included in the endemic zones in Africa and South America are regarded by the Namibian authorities as infected. Travellers on scheduled airlines whose flights have originated outside areas regarded as infected but have passed through such areas in transit are not required to possess a certificate, provided they have remained at the scheduled airport or in the adjacent town during transit. All passengers with unscheduled airlines whose flights originated or passed in transit through an infected area are required to possess a certificate. The certificate is not insisted upon in the case of children under one year of age, but such infants may be subject to surveillance.
2: Typhoid may occur.
3: Malaria risk exists in Oshana, Oshikoto, Omusati, Ohangwenga, Otjozondjupa and Omaheke from November to June and along the Kunene river and in Kavango and Caprivi regions throughout the year. The predominant *falciparum* strain is reported to be resistant to chloroquine. The recommended prophylaxis is either mefloquine, doxycycline or atovaquone/proguanil.

Food & drink: Mains water is normally chlorinated and, whilst safe, may cause mild abdominal upsets. Bottled water is available and is advised for the first few weeks of the stay. Drinking water outside main cities and towns may be contaminated and sterilisation is advisable. Milk is pasteurised and dairy products are safe for consumption. Local meat, poultry, seafood, fruit and vegetables are generally considered safe to eat.
Other risks: *Bilharzia* (schistosomiasis) is endemic. Avoid swimming and paddling in fresh water (also because of the presence of crocodiles); swimming pools which are well chlorinated and well maintained are safe. *Natural foci* of plague have been reported in Namibia. *Hepatitis A* can occur. *Hepatitis B* is hyperendemic. An increase in *rabies* amongst dogs in Windhoek was reported in late 2005 and early 2006.
Health care: Anti-bite serums for snakes and scorpions are advised. Health insurance is essential.

Travel - International

AIR:
 The national airline is *Air Namibia (SW)* (website: www.airnamibia.com.na).
Approximate flight times: From *London* to Windhoek is 11 hours 15 minutes. From *Frankfurt* to Windhoek is 11 hours.
Main airports: *Windhoek (WDH)* (Hosea Kutako International Airport) is 40km (25 miles) from the city (travel time - 35 minutes). *To/from the airport:* Buses go to the city. Taxis and minivans are also available (travel time - 40 minutes). *Facilities:* Restaurant, bars, snack bar, duty free shops, post office, bureau de change and car hire.
Departure tax: None.

SEA:
 Main ports: There is a modern deep-water harbour at *Walvis Bay*. There is also a small port at *Lüderitz*.
RAIL:
 TransNamib (website: www.transnamib.com.na) runs a train from Windhoek to Upington, just across the border in South Africa. However, there are no onward trains from Upington to other South African destinations.
ROAD:
 A tarred road runs from the south through Upington in South Africa to Grünau, where it connects with the tarred road from Cape Town. The trans-Kalahari highway, which was completed in 1998, links Walvis Bay and Windhoek with Gaborone, Botswana and Gauteng, South Africa. The trans-Caprivi highway runs through the Caprivi strip and via Botswana into Zimbabwe.
Bus: *Intercape Mainliner* (website: www.intercapemainliner.co.za) runs direct overnight services from Windhoek to Cape Town four times a week, as well as services to Johannesburg via Upington. Other bus services go to Botswana and Zambia.

Travel - Internal

Note: If travelling along the Caprivi Strip, stay on the tarred road. Wildlife and livestock pose a serious hazard, so it is best to avoid driving at night.
AIR:
 Flying is the quickest and often the most economical way to travel around the country. *Air Namibia (SW)* links all of the major towns in the territory. Planes can also be chartered.
RAIL:
 The main rail routes in Namibia are Windhoek-Keetmanshoop-Upington, South Africa, Walvis Bay-Swakopmund-Tsumeb, Windhoek-Tsumeb and Lüderitz-Keetmanshoop. First- and second-class carriages are available on these routes. Light refreshments are offered on some services. On overnight voyages, seats in first-class compartments convert to four couchettes and those in second class to six couchettes. Local passenger and goods trains run daily. Children under two years of age travel free and children aged two to 11 pay half fare. The *Desert Express*, a luxury train aimed at tourists, runs between Swakopmund and Windhoek. The 19-hour 30-minute journey includes several stops which give travellers the opportunity to watch lions feeding, see the Namib Desert, walk in the sand dunes and admire the stars. A three-course dinner and overnight accommodation are included in the ticket price. More details on rail services are available from *TransNamib* (website: www.transnamib.co.na).
ROAD:
 Traffic drives on the left. Roads are generally well maintained. There are 64,799km (40,266 miles) of road, of which 7841km (4872 miles) are tarred.
Bus: There is a local bus service in Windhoek, and **taxis** are also available. A luxury bus service exists between Windhoek and all major centres in Namibia and South Africa. **Car hire**: Self-drive cars are available at the airport and Windhoek city centre, as well as some other major centres.
Documentation: An International Driving Permit is required.

Travel Advice

Most visits to Namibia are trouble-free but you should be aware of the global risk of indiscriminate international terrorist attacks, which could be against civilian targets, including places frequented by foreigners.
If travelling along the Caprivi Strip, travellers should stick to the well-travelled routes.
Wildlife and livestock pose a serious hazard; travellers should avoid driving at night.
This advice is based on information provided by the Foreign and Commonwealth Office in the UK. It is correct at time of publishing. As the situation can change rapidly, visitors are advised to contact the following organisaions for the latest travel advice.

British Foreign and Commonwealth Office
Tel: (0845) 850 2829.
Website: www.fco.gov.uk

US Department of State
Website: http://travel.state.gov/traveloek

Accommodation

HOTELS:
 There are good-quality hotels both in Windhoek and Swakopmund, and some scattered throughout the country. There are a number of 4-star hotels providing modern conference facilities. Hotel accommodation is limited and visitors are advised to book well in advance. For further information, contact the Hospitality Association of Namibia (see *Accommodation Information*). **Grading**: Hotels are graded on a scale of **1 to 5 stars**.
LODGES:
 In the Etosha National Park and other game reserves, there are well-equipped rest camps with comfortable accommodation. Reservations for the national parks can be made with Namibia Wildlife Resorts Ltd (see *Accommodation Information*).
CAMPING:
 Some of the national parks have camping facilities, notably the Etosha National Park & Game Reserve. There is also camping at Ai-Ais, a hot-spring area towards the South African border, Hardap Dam in the south, Gross Barmen near Okahandja, Popa Falls in Kavango, in the Namib-Naukluft Park and at various places along the coast.
GUEST FARMS:
Visitors can experience life on a working farm by staying at one of the many guest farms offering overnight accommodation. Contact the Hospitality Association of Namibia (see *Accommodation Information*) for details.

ACCOMMODATION INFORMATION

Hospitality Association of Namibia (HAN)
PO Box 86078, Windhoek, Namibia
Tel: (61) 222 904.
Website: www.hannamibia.com

Namibia Wildlife Resorts Ltd
Website: www.nwr.com.na

Top Things To See & Do

- In **Windhoek**, the attractive capital of the country, surrounded by mountains, see several examples of German colonial architecture, including the **Alte Feste**, the **Christuskirche** and the **Tintenpalast** (Ink Palace), the former colonial administrative building. Relax at **Gross Barmen**, a hot-spring resort to the north.
- The **Etosha National Park** is one of the most famous game sanctuaries in the world and remains largely free of human influence. Its 22,270 sq km (8599 sq miles) are located in the north around the Etosha Pan. This depression is 1065m (3494ft) above sea level, forming a huge, salty hollow which is only occasionally filled with water and surrounded by grasslands and bush. Encounter vast stocks of **wildlife**, particularly elephants, lions, zebras, giraffes, wildebeest, springboks, kudus, gemsboks or oryxes, hyenas, jackals, leopards and cheetahs. There are well-equipped camps with comfortable rondavel accommodation and camping facilities.
- **Waterberg Plateau Park,** Namibia's only mountain resort, has striking red sandstone cliffs and is home to many rare and endangered species of game. It is a popular stopover for visitors on their way to Etosha National Park. There are good facilities here for **game viewing** and a number of **hiking** trails.
- Also en route to Etosha is **Lake Otjikoto**, 24km (15 miles) northeast of the mining town of **Tsumeb**. Once fabled to be bottomless, it is now known to be 55m (140ft) deep and contains some rare fish. Northeast of here is **Kaudom Game Reserve** in Kavango, where there are two camping areas and where blue wildebeest, elephants, lions, cheetahs, leopards and various species of antelope wander.
- Further northeast, stop at the **Popa Falls Rest Camp**, a popular haven on the banks of the **Okavango River**, where crocodiles and hippos bask in the water. About 12km (7 miles) to the south is **Mahango Game Reserve**, catering to day visitors only, with elephants, buffalo and lechwe.
- Head still further northeast to **East Caprivi**, bordered by the **Kwando**, **Linyanti**, **Chobe** and **Zambezi** rivers. This region of swamps and flood plains has several safari lodges and offers **boat trips**, **fishing**, **hiking** and **game viewing**, particularly in the **Mudumu** and **Mamili National Parks**.
- Purchase various **handicrafts** such as baskets, bracelets, malachite and soapstone carvings at **Katima Mulilo's Arts Centre**, on the banks of the **Zambezi River**. Flights to **Victoria Falls**, less than one hour's flight away, are available from Katima Mulilo.
- In the south of the country, be amazed by the size of **Fish River Canyon**, which is only second in dimensions to the Grand Canyon. Situated between Seeheim and **Ai-Ais** (a hot spring resort), the gigantic cleft stretches for 150km (93 miles) and is up to 27km (17 miles) wide and up to 550m (1804ft) deep in parts. Trips are best arranged from **Keetsmanshoop**. Situated on the **Fish River** is Hardap Dam.
- In the **Kokerboom** (**Quiver Tree**) **Forest**, located 14km (9 miles) northeast of Keetmanshoop on Gariganus Farm, discover *kokerbooms*, which belong to the aloe family and grow up to 8m (26ft). They were often used by the San people to make quivers for their arrows (thus 'quiver trees').

The trees create a bizarrely elegant effect and are now a protected plant in Namibia.

- Enjoy the charm of **Lüderitz**, a small port in the southern Namib region, with atmosphere from bygone days of diamond prospecting.
- The **Namib Desert** appears more like the surface of the moon with its towering sand dunes (some of them 300m (1000ft) high), and is believed to be the oldest desert in the world. Visit **Namib Naukluft Park**, at 49,768 sq km (19,215 sq miles), the fourth-largest conservation area in the world. **Camp** at **Sesriem**, where the **Tsauchab River** disappears down a deep gorge in the plain (leaving pools of water where many animals feed) and in the Naukluft. **Climb** some of the **world's highest sand dunes** at the nearby **Sossusvlei**.
- Pay a visit to the delightful little seaside resort of **Swakopmund**, which is situated in the middle of Namibia's coastline and is surrounded by desert and sea.
- Further north, visit the seal colony at Cape Cross on the **Skeleton Coast,** a strange desert shoreline with massive dunes and treacherous rocks. The name relates to the number of ships wrecked and lost in the vicinity.
- Inland, the **Brandberg/Twyfelfontein** area has some very ancient rock engravings and paintings, of which the **White Lady of the Brandberg** is the best known.
- Walk in the 3-million-year-old **Petrified Forest**.

TOURIST INFORMATION

Namibia Tourism in the UK
Suite 200, Parkway House, Sheen Lane,
London SW14 8LS, UK
Tel: (0870) 330 9333.
Website: www.namibiatourism.com.na

Entertainment

FOOD & DRINK: Restaurants and cafes reflect the German influence on Namibia, and most dining rooms offer a reasonable choice of local and continental cuisine.
National specialities:
- *Biltong* (air-dried meat).
- *Rauchfleisch* (smoked meat).
- Asparagus.
- Kalahari truffle.
- Seafood, especially oysters.
National drinks:
- *Tafel* lager.
- *Windhoek* lager.
Tipping: 10 per cent is customary.
NIGHTLIFE: In the central area of Windhoek, there are restaurants, cafes, a cinema and a theatre.
SHOPPING: Windhoek has a selection of fashionable shops. Local crafts can be bought in some specialised shops and at the Windhoek Street Market, held every second Saturday. Good buys include diamonds and semi-precious stones, *Herero* dolls, hand-carved wooden objects, jewellery, *karosse* rugs, liqueur chocolates made in Windhoek and Swakara garments.
Shopping hours: Mon-Fri 0900-1700, Sat 0900-1300. Some supermarkets are also open Sun 1100-1300 and 1600-1900.

Credit: ©Namibia Tourism – www.fotoseeber.com

Business

- **GDP:** US$5.5 billion (2004).
- **Main exports:** Minerals, beef, cattle and fish.
- **Main imports:** Foodstuffs, construction material and manufactured goods.
- **Main trade partners:** South Africa, UK, Spain, Japan and USA.

ECONOMY: The mining industry is the strongest part of the economy, the kernel of Namibia's export economy, and accounts for about 20 per cent of GDP. Extracted minerals include silver, copper, lead, zinc, tungsten and uranium, and Namibia is also the source of some of the world's highest-quality diamonds. A much larger proportion of the workforce – 45 per cent against 4 per cent engaged in mining – is engaged in agriculture and fishing. Livestock dominates the agricultural sector, although a substantial proportion of the agricultural workforce is engaged in subsistence farming of crops such as wheat, maize and millet. Agriculture is becoming increasingly difficult over time as the desert encroaches on previously fertile soil; it has also suffered chronic damage from the recurrent drought afflicting the whole region. Namibia enjoys exceptionally rich fishing grounds, although stocks of pilchard – the main species in the area – have been depleted by uncontrolled fishing in the period before Namibian independence. Commercial shipping activity has picked up since the return of Walvis Bay, the best deep-water port in Africa on the Atlantic side, to Namibian jurisdiction (the apartheid government in Pretoria tried to hang on to the port, even after independence). The establishment of a free-trade zone at Walvis Bay has further enhanced its status as a centre for regional trade. Manufacturing is mainly devoted to processing of raw materials and agricultural produce. Most of the country's trade is with South Africa, essentially involving the exchange of raw materials for manufactured goods. Recent economic policy has seen many former state enterprises transferred to the private sector. The economy has performed reasonably well during the last decade. Annual growth in 2004 was 5.7 per cent and inflation was 4.1 per cent. However, unemployment hovers at around 35 per cent.
BUSINESS ETIQUETTE: Suits should be worn in winter, safari suits in summer. Prior appointments are necessary. English is widely spoken in business circles. The best times for business are February to May and September to November. **Office hours**: Mon-Fri 0800-1700.

COMMERCIAL INFORMATION

Namibia Chamber of Commerce and Industry
PO Box 9355, Windhoek, Namibia
Tel: (61) 228 809.
Website: www.ncci.org.na

Nauru

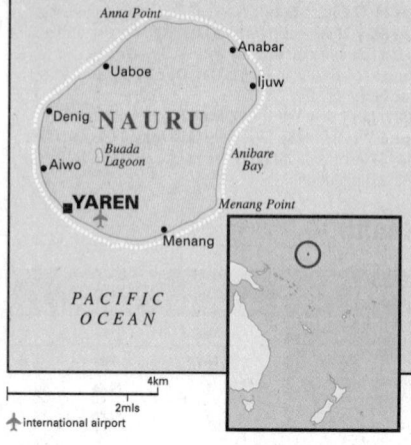

Location: Central Pacific.

Time: GMT + 12.

Overview

Since the extensive phosphate fields were found in the 1900s, the island has been mainly used for the mining of the natural fertiliser. The Nauru Phosphate Corporation is the largest employer. The population lives mainly on the coast or on the shore of Buada Lagoon, the remainder of the island being used for phosphate extraction. As yet, little is given over purely to tourism, although the situation is slowly changing.

General Information

AREA: 21.3 sq km (8.2 sq miles).
POPULATION: 11,845 (official estimate 2000).
POPULATION DENSITY: 556 per sq km.
CAPITAL: Aiwo. **Population:** 600 (1992).
GEOGRAPHY: Nauru, the world's smallest republic, is an oval-shaped outcrop, situated in the Central Pacific, west of Kiribati, surrounded by a reef which is exposed at low tide. Although there is no deep-water harbour on the island, offshore moorings are reputedly the deepest in the world. A century of phosphate mining has stripped four-fifths of the land area, and has left the central plateau, which rises to 56m (213ft), infertile and unpopulated: a barren terrain of jagged coral pinnacles which stand 15m (49ft) high. The island has a fertile coastal strip 150 to 300m (492 to 984ft) wide, where there are coconut palms, pandanus trees and indigenous hardwoods such as the tomano. On the land surrounding Buada lagoon, bananas, pineapples and some vegetables are grown. Some secondary vegetation grows over the coral pinnacles which intersperse the island's beaches.
GOVERNMENT: Republic. Gained independence from Australia in 1968. **Head of State and Government**: President Ludwig Scotty since 2004.
LANGUAGE: Nauruan and English are spoken.
RELIGION: Christian, mostly Nauruan Protestant Church. There is also a significant Roman Catholic minority.
ELECTRICITY: 240 volts AC, 50Hz.
SOCIAL CONVENTIONS: The island has a casual atmosphere in which diplomacy and tact are always preferable to confrontation; European customs continue alongside local traditions.

Climate

A maritime, equatorial climate tempered by northeast trade winds from March to October. The wettest period is during the westerly monsoon from November to February. If global warming causes sea levels to rise, the habitable low-lying land areas will be at risk from tidal surges and flooding.
Required clothing: Lightweight cottons and linens with waterproofing all year.

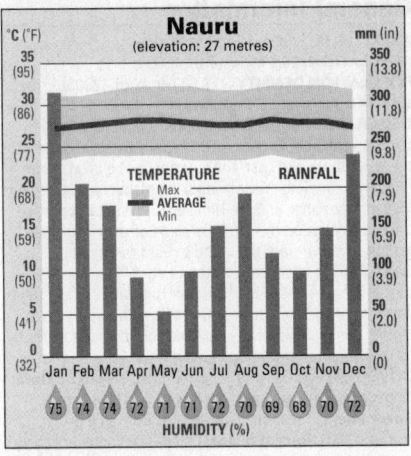

Nauru (elevation: 27 metres)

°C (°F) / mm (in)

TEMPERATURE — Max, AVERAGE, Min
RAINFALL

HUMIDITY (%): 75 74 74 72 71 71 72 70 69 68 70 72

Communications

Telephone: IDD is available. Country code: 674. Outgoing international calls must be made through the operator.
Mobile telephone: Although an AMPS network is in operation, there are no facilities at the moment for travellers to use their handsets on the island.
Internet: Internet: There is one Internet cafe on the island, and access to the Internet may be available in hotels.
Post: Airmail to Europe takes up to one week.
MEDIA: Press: The main newspaper is the *Nasero Bulletin*, published fortnightly in Nauruan and English. Others are the *Central Star News* and *The Nauru Chronicle*.
TV: *Nauru Television (NTV)* is Government-owned.
Radio: *Radio Nauru* is a non-commercial Government-owned station.

Passport/Visa

	Passport Required?	Visa Required?	Return Ticket Required?
Full British	Yes	Yes/1	Yes
Australian	Yes	Yes/1	Yes
Canadian	Yes	Yes/1	Yes
USA	Yes	Yes/1	Yes
Other EU	Yes	Yes/1	Yes
Japanese	Yes	Yes/1	Yes

Note: *Regulations and requirements may be subject to change at short notice, and you are advised to contact the appropriate diplomatic or consular authority before finalising travel arrangements. Any numbers in the chart refer to the footnotes below.*

PASSPORTS: Passport valid for six months from the date of entry required by all.
VISAS: Required by all except the following:
(a) nationals of New Zealand for stays of up to three months and Korea (Rep) for stays of up to 14 days;
(b) transit passengers continuing their journey by the same or first connecting aircraft, provided they hold onward or return documentation and do not leave the airport.
Note: 1. Nationals of the following countries may obtain a tourist visa on arrival for stays of up to 30 days, provided holding valid passport, return or onward tickets, sufficient funds and a confirmed hotel booking: Australia, The Bahamas, Barbados, Canada, Cayman Islands, Fiji, Guam, Ireland, Japan, Korea (Rep), Montserrat, Peru, St Kitts & Nevis, St Lucia, St Vincent & the Grenadines, Sierra Leone, Singapore, Turks & Caicos Islands, the UK and the USA.
Types of visa and cost: *Visitor* and *Business*. Visitor's visas should be organised by the sponsor in Nauru. Passport details should be given so that a visa letter may be sent directly. Visas are issued free of charge.
Validity: 30 days.
Application to: Consulate General.
Application requirements: (a) Letter giving details such as purpose of visit and dates of intended stay. There is no application form. (b) Proof of return or onward ticket and valid documents for next destination. (c) Evidence of prearranged hotel booking or details of other accommodation. (d) Valid passport (should not be sent with application, but presented on arrival). (e) For business visas, letter from Nauruan company or individual.
Working days required: Four to five (tourist visas); five to six (business visas); it is, however, recommended that applications are made at least two weeks prior to date of travel.
Temporary residence: Contact the Principal Immigration Officer in Nauru (tel: (674) 444 3133). A visa can be sent by post; no fee is charged.

PASSPORT/VISA INFORMATION

Consulate General of the Republic of Nauru in Australia
Level 7, 128 Exhibition Street, Melbourne, Victoria 3000, Australia
Tel: (3) 9653 5709.
Website: www.dfat.gov.au/geo/nauru

Nauru Permanent Mission of the Republic of Nauru to the United Nations in the USA
800 2nd Avenue, Suite 400A,
New York, NY 10017, USA
Tel: (212) 937 0074.
Website: www.un.int/nauru

Money

Currency: The Australian Dollar (AUD; symbol A$) is legal tender. For further information and exchange rates, see *Australia* section.
Currency exchange: Available in banks. There are no ATMs on the island.
Credit & debit cards: American Express, Diners Club and Visa are accepted. Check with your credit or debit card company for details of merchant acceptability and other services which may be available.
Traveller's cheques: These can be exchanged in banks and some hotels.
Currency restrictions: The import of local and foreign currency (including travellers cheques) is unlimited, provided declared on arrival. The export of local currency is limited to A$2500; severe penalties can be incurred if this rule is infringed and the proper authority from the Bank of Nauru is not obtained. The export of foreign currency is unlimited.

Duty Free

The following goods may be imported into Nauru by those over 16 years of age without incurring customs duty:
400 cigarettes or 50 cigars or 450g of tobacco; three bottles of alcoholic beverage (if visitor is over 21 years of age).
Prohibited items: Explosives, firearms and pornography, drugs and weapons, dangerous drugs, pornographic films and literature.
Restricted exports: Nauruan artefacts may not be exported without a licence.

Public Holidays

Below are listed Public Holidays for the January 2006–June 2007 period.
2006: Jan 1 New Year's Day. **Jan 31** Independence Day. **Apr 14-17** Easter. **May 17** Constitution Day. **Oct 26** Angam Day. **Dec 25-26** Christmas.
2007: Jan 1 New Year's Day. **Jan 31** Independence Day. **Apr 6-9** Easter. **May 17** Constitution Day.

Health

	Special Precautions?	Certificate? Required?
Yellow Fever	No	1
Cholera	No	2
Typhoid & Polio	3	N/A
Malaria	No	N/A

Note: *Regulations and requirements may be subject to change at short notice, and you are advised to contact your doctor well in advance of your intended date of departure. Any numbers in the chart refer to the footnotes below.*

1: A yellow fever vaccination certificate is required from travellers over one year of age coming from infected areas. (This includes transit passengers not leaving the airport.)
2: Vaccination may be required.
3: Typhoid may occur in rural areas with poor sanitation. Immunisation is advised.
Food & drink: Mains water is normally chlorinated and, whilst relatively safe, may cause mild abdominal upsets. Bottled water is available and is advised for the first few weeks of stay. Drinking water outside main cities and towns may be contaminated and sterilisation is advisable. Local meat, poultry, seafood, fruit and vegetables are generally considered safe to eat.
Other risks: Immunisations are sometimes recommended for *hepatitis A, B, TB* and *diphtheria*. Outbreaks of *dengue fever* and *Japanese encephalitis* have also been reported. *Sea snakes, poisonous fish* and *corals* may present hazards to bathers.
Health care: Nauru has 14 GPs, all of whom work at either one of the two hospitals – Nauru General Hospital or Nauru Phosphate Corporation Hospital. There are no medical specialists, and serious or complicated cases are sent to Australia for treatment via *Air Nauru*. Travellers are advised to take out full health insurance prior to departure.

Travel - International

AIR:
 The national airline is *Air Nauru (ON)*; its destinations include Brisbane and Melbourne in Australia, Guam and Fiji. It also offers charter services to Sydney, Australia and Norfolk Island. There are a number of passes available, including the *Pacific Air Pass* and the *Pacific Wanderer Pass*.
The Visit the South Pacific Pass is valid for many airlines operating in the South Pacific, including most of the larger ones, such as *Air Caledonie, Air Marshall Islands, Air Nauru, Air Niugingi, Air Pacific, Air Vanuatu, Polynesian Airlines, Qantas, Royal Tongan Airlines* and *Solomon Airlines*. Offering reductions of up to 40 per cent on normal airfares, this sector-based pass allows for flexible island-hopping between the destinations of the Cook Islands, Fiji, Nauru, New Caledonia, Samoa, Tahiti, Tonga, Vanuatu and the more remote Melanesian and Micronesian islands, together with major cities in Australia (Brisbane, Melbourne and Sydney) and New Zealand (Auckland, Christchurch and Wellington). It is only available for people resident outside of the South Pacific. The journey must be started outside of the South Pacific and only one stopover in Australia is allowed. A minimum of two sectors must be bought before departure (extra sectors can be purchased en route). There is a maximum of one pass per person, and passes must be used within six months of the first day of travel. Children under 12 years of age pay 75 per cent of the adult fare. For details and conditions, contact the South Pacific Tourist Organisation (see *Top Things To See & Do*).
Approximate flight times: From *London* to Nauru Island is 31 hours, including stopovers in Hong Kong, Manila, Guam and Pohnpei.
Main airports: *Nauru International Airport (INU)*.
To/from the airport: There are buses to the town available after every arriving flight, costing approximately A$1. Taxis are also available. *Facilities:* Snack bar, gift shops and tourist information.
Departure tax: A$25 per person on departure. Transit passengers and those under 12 years of age are exempt.
SEA:
 The international port is Nauru. Main sealinks are with Australia, New Zealand and Japan. Coastal hazards force commercial vessels to moor some way offshore.

Travel - Internal

RAIL:
There are just over 5km (3 miles) of railway to serve the phosphate mining area.
ROAD:
A sealed road, 19km (12 miles) long, circles the island and there are several miles of road running inland to Buada District and the phosphate areas. Traffic drives on the left. The island speed limit is 50kmph (30 mph). **Bus:** Buses run from the hotels. **Car hire:** This is available. **Documentation:** A national driving licence will suffice.

Travel Advice

Most visits to Nauru are trouble-free but you should be aware of the global risk of indiscriminate international terrorist attacks, which could be against civilian targets, including places frequented by foreigners.
This advice is based on information provided by the Foreign and Commonwealth Office in the UK. It is correct at time of publishing. As the situation can change rapidly, visitors are advised to contact the following organisations for the latest travel advice:

British Foreign and Commonwealth Office
Tel: (0845) 850 2829.
Website: www.fco.gov.uk

US Department of State
Website: http://travel.state.gov/travel

Accommodation

HOTELS:
 There are a few hotels on Nauru situated on both the east and west coasts. Facilities include restaurants and nearby shops. Contact the South Pacific Tourism Organisation for further details (see *Top Things To See & Do*).

Top Things To See & Do

- In **Yaren**, there are remains of Japanese guns, bunkers and pillboxes left over from World War II.
- **Anibore Bay** is probably the most beautiful beach on the island, although the sea currents are dangerous. **Fishing**

by net or by line is, of course, an essential part of life, and **swimming** is possible at either of the two channels cut into the surrounding reef and in the boat harbour when the ships are not being handled. A coral reef, along with shipwrecks from World War II, provides good **diving**.
- The national game is **Australian rules football**, which is played all through Saturday on the sports field just north of Buada Lagoon.
- The **Frigate bird game** is the most distinctive of the traditional sports.
- In recent years, Nauru's international success in **weightlifting** has created a national interest.

TOURIST INFORMATION

South Pacific Tourism Organisation in Fiji
Street address: Level 3, FNPF Place, 343-359 Victoria Parade, Suva, Fiji
Postal address: PO Box 13119, Suva, Fiji
Tel: (679) 330 4177.
Website: www.spto.org

Entertainment

FOOD & DRINK: Cultivation is difficult on Nauru owing to the poor soil, irregular rainfall and the impact of mining. There are no local fruit or vegetables and most of the available food is canned, refined and imported. Fresh food is limited to a small amount of fish and, very occasionally, beef. The island is, however, very well served with restaurants with a wide range of international dishes, especially Chinese, but little is fresh. Most international brands of alcohol are available. **Tipping**: Not generally practised.
NIGHTLIFE: This mostly revolves around the dining rooms and bars. There is one cinema located in the southern part of the island.
SHOPPING: There are a number of shops on the island, although service and goods at government shops tend to be of poor quality. There are numerous supermarkets, the largest being Capelle's, but visitors should buy essential goods in advance. There are no sales taxes but customs duties are now levied on a range of goods. **Shopping hours**: Mon-Fri 0900-1700, Sat 0900-1300.

Business

ECONOMY: Until a few years ago, Nauru's economy depended almost entirely on the extraction and sale of phosphates, over which the Nauru Phosphate Corporation has a monopoly. Much of the revenue was invested in anticipation of the eventual exhaustion of the resource. Now that this has occurred, the Government, in common with a number of other small island states, looked to offshore financial services to sustain the economy. However, the laxity of Nauru's newly established tax and financial disclosure arrangements attracted much foreign money of allegedly uncertain or dubious origin. From 1997 onwards, the OECD (Organisation for Economic Co-operation and Development, the organisation representing the world's richest two dozen economies) took the lead in constructing an international regime to crack down on money-laundering. Most of the several dozen countries loosely described as 'tax havens' have complied with the new system: Nauru is one of the seven which have refused to do so. Accordingly, in April 2002, it was 'named and shamed' and subject to a number of sanctions. There was some hope that a fishing industry could be developed following the completion of a new harbour, but the industry has failed to take off and Nauru accrues more revenue from selling licences to foreign fleets.
Nauru has few other strings to its economic bow and in 2004 was facing chaos amid political strife and the collapse of the island's telecommunications system. There is some agriculture, exploiting what little fertile land is available. Although the island has a benign climate and attractive features (those remaining after the damage done during the phosphate mining era), the potential of any tourism industry is limited by Nauru's remoteness and lack of infrastructure. In 2002, Nauru found a novel source of income by accepting asylum seekers (mostly from Iraq and Afghanistan) who had been rejected by Australia. Nauru took 400 of them, and was paid A$30 million by Canberra. Australia and New Zealand are the island's main trading partners, and supply almost all basic and capital goods. There are now serious questions about the long-term viability of Nauru's economy.
BUSINESS ETIQUETTE: Shirt and smart trousers or skirt will suffice; more formal wear is needed only for very special occasions. English and French are widely spoken. The best time to visit is May to October. **Office hours**: Mon-Fri 0800-1200 and 1330-1630.

COMMERCIAL INFORMATION

Bank of Nauru
PO Box 289, Civic Centre, Nauru
Tel: 444 3238 *or* 3267.

Nepal

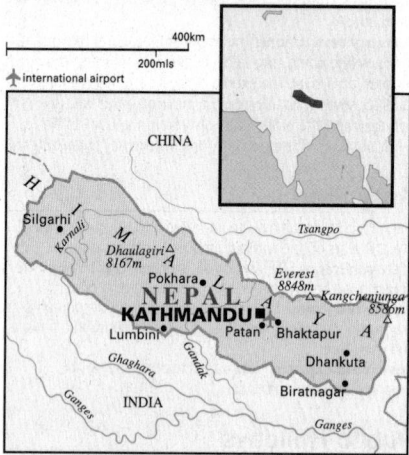

Location: South Asia.

Time: GMT + 5.45.

Overview

Nepal was created from an amalgam of small principalities in 1768 under King Prithvi Narayan Shah. Under the control of a hereditary king, Nepal then became a 'buffer state' between the British empire and the territories to the north. The main instrument of British rule from the mid-19th century onwards was a hereditary Prime Minister drawn from the Rana family. The country became formally independent in 1923, but it was not until 1947 (the year of Indian independence) and the total withdrawal of the British from the region that Nepal achieved genuine independence.
Nepal is known as the abode of the gods. For many years a secret, unknown country, it was, in the 1950s, faced with making a leap from the 11th century to modern times. Visited first by mountaineers and trekkers, it later became the haunt of hippies. In 1989, restrictions barring several areas to tourists were lifted.
Despite being one of the poorest countries in the world, a situation made worse by an ongoing Maoist rebellion (Communist Party of Nepal), which has left more than 12,000 people dead, and more than 100,000 displaced since it started in 1996, the country is a potentially very popular tourist destination. In addition to a distinctive ancient Hindu and Buddhist culture, Nepal has the world's highest mountain, Everest, and spectacular scenery and wildlife. For walkers and trekkers, Nepal is a true paradise: the picturesque hamlets and mountain villages are linked by hundreds of trails that have been used for centuries, with little change noticeable even today. Numerous temples and Buddhist shrines can be also be discovered en route. The Nepalese Government has also set aside more than 35 per cent of the total area of the country as natural sanctuaries. There are now nine national parks and three wildlife reserves, located both in the mountainous zones as well as in the tropical plains. The Terai lowlands in the south form the richest habitat in the country.

General Information

AREA: 147,181 sq km (56,827 sq miles).
POPULATION: 26.3 million (UN, 2005).
POPULATION DENSITY: 178.69 per sq km (2005).
CAPITAL: Kathmandu. **Population**: 1.5 million (2005).
GEOGRAPHY: Nepal is a landlocked kingdom sharing borders with Tibet to the north and northwest, and India to the west, south and east. The country can be divided into five zones: the Terai, the Siwaliks, the Mahabharat Lekh, the Midlands or Pahar, and the Himalayas. The greater part of the country lies on the southern slope of the Himalayas, extending down from the highest peaks through hill country to the upper edge of the Ganges Plain. The hilly central area is crossed by the Lower Himalayas, where there are eight of the highest peaks in the world, leading up to Mount Everest. Wildlife in Nepal includes tigers, leopards, gaur, elephants, buffalo, deer and rhinos.
GOVERNMENT: Constitutional monarchy. **Head of State**: King Maharajadhira Gyanendra since 2001. **Head of Government**: The Prime Minister was dismissed on 1 February 2005. **Recent history**: King Gyanendra ascended the throne in June 2001 soon after then Crown Prince Dipendra gunned down his parents King Birendra and Queen Aishwarya and seven other royals before killing himself. King Gyanendra became well known for his conservation work. He is also interested in developing the kingdom's tourism potential. On 1 February 2005 the King dismissed Prime Minister Sher Bahadur Deuba and his Government for failing in its mandate to hold elections and to restore peace. He took power directly himself. His move was also accompanied by a state of emergency, which included a number of measures including censorship of the press and suspension of many fundamental rights. He subsequently appointed a mainly pro-monarchist cabinet to govern under him, largely drawn from the pre-democratic Panchayati era.
LANGUAGE: The official language is Nepali (spoken by 49 per cent). There are many other languages, including Maithili and Bhojpuri. English is spoken in business circles and by people involved in the travel trade.
RELIGION: Mainly Hindu (81 per cent) and Buddhist (11 per cent), with a small Muslim minority (4 per cent).
ELECTRICITY: 220 volts AC, 50Hz. There are frequent power cuts.
SOCIAL CONVENTIONS: As a foreign visitor, one must be careful to respect local customs in order not to cause offence. The following are some local conventions it is advisable to adhere to: never step over the feet of a person, always walk round; never offer food and drink which is 'polluted', in other words, food that you have tasted or bitten; never offer or accept anything with the left hand, use the right or both hands. It is rude to point at a person or statue with a finger (or even with a foot). Often when people shake their head, it means 'yes.' Shoes and footwear should be removed when entering houses or shrines. Kitchens and eating areas of houses should also not be entered with footwear, as the hearth of a home is sacred. Do not stand in front of a person who is eating as this means your feet will be next to his food; squat or sit by his side. Local *Chorten* are built to pacify local demons or dead persons and should be passed by in a clockwise direction, as should temples; the earth and universe revolve in this direction. Small flat stones with inscriptions and supplications next to the *Chorten* should not be removed as souvenirs; this is considered sacrilege by the Nepalese. Avoid touching a Nepalese dressed all in white; his dress signifies a death in the family. Shaking hands is not a common form of greeting; the normal greeting is to press the palms together in a prayer-like gesture (*Namaste*). A gift given to a host or hostess will probably be laid aside unopened; to open a parcel in the presence of a guest is considered uncivil. Casual wear is suitable except for the most formal meetings or social occasions. Bikinis, shorts, bare shoulders and backs may not be appreciated. Men only remove their shirts when bathing. Overt public displays of affection, especially near religious places, are inappropriate. Seek permission before entering a temple; some do not allow westerners or non-Hindus to enter. Do not take leather articles into a temple. Nepalese cities are generally safe, but take sensible precautions with personal possessions. **Photography:** Always ask permission first. In general, it is allowed outside temples and at festivals, but not at religious ceremonies or inside temples; however, there is no hard and fast rule and the only way to be sure of not giving offence is to ask first and accept the answer.

Climate

Nepal's weather is generally predictable and pleasant. There are four climatic seasons: March to May (spring), June to August (summer), September to November (autumn) and December to February (winter). The monsoon is approximately from the end of June to the middle of September. About 80 per cent of the rain falls during that period, so the remainder of the year is dry. Spring and autumn are the most pleasant seasons; winter temperatures drop to freezing with a high level of snowfall in the mountains. Summer and late spring temperatures range from 28°C (83°F) in the hill regions to more than 40°C (104°F) in the Terai. In winter, average maximum and minimum temperatures in the Terai range from a brisk 7°C (45°F) to a mild 23°C (74°F). The central valleys experience a minimum temperature often falling bellow freezing point and a chilly 12°C (54°F) maximum. Much colder temperatures prevail at higher elevations. The Kathmandu Valley, at an altitude of 1310m (4297ft), has a mild climate, ranging from 19-27°C (67-81°F) in summer, and 2-20°C (36-68°F) in winter.

Required clothing: Lightweight and tropical clothes with umbrella are advised for June to August. Between October and March, lightweight clothes are worn in Kathmandu, with a coat for evenings and warm clothing for the mountains.

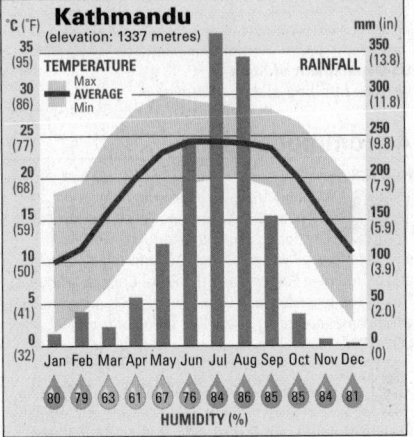

Communications

Telephone: IDD is available to all major cities. Country code: 977. The Telecommunication Office, Tripureshwar, deals with telephone calls and cables. The International Telephone Office is open Mon-Thurs 0900-1400 and Fri 0900-1330. Hotels and private communication centres provide long-distance telephone services (ISD, STD).
Mobile telephone: Roaming agreements exist with some international mobile phone companies. Coverage is sporadic and variable.
Internet: There are Internet cafes in Kathmandu, Patan and Pokhara. Internet services are also provided by hotels.
Post: Postal services are available in most centres. Make sure that letters are hand-cancelled at the post office (post boxes should not be used for important communications). The general post office in Kathmandu (near the Dharahara Tower) is open Mon-Fri 0900-1700. Main hotels will also handle post.
MEDIA: The Maoist rebellion in Nepal, and the efforts to suppress it, have had a profound impact on the media. Media rights groups say attacks on media workers have been perpetrated by both sides in the conflict. It is reported that in 2004, for the third consecutive year, more journalists had been arrested in Nepal than in any other country. Press freedoms were suspended under a state of emergency invoked by King Gyanendra in February 2005. The restrictions were enshrined in a media law in October. As a result, some newspapers have left their editorial pages blank, or have published editorials on deliberately bland topics. Up to 60 private FM radio stations have been ordered not to broadcast political news and to restrict their coverage to sport, education, environment and health matters. The government publishes a Nepali-language daily and an English-language newspaper. It operates national radio and TV services.
Press: English-language newspapers available in Nepal are *The Himalayan Times* (website: www.thehimalayantimes.com), *The Kathmandu Post* (website: www.kantipuronline.com) and *Rising Nepal*. Other dailies include *Kantipur* and *Annapurna Post*. *The International Herald Tribune*, *Newsweek* and *Time* can all be found in Kathmandu. State-owned *Gorkhapatra* is Nepal's oldest newspaper.
TV: *Nepalese Television Corporation (NTV)* is state-run. Private channels include *Kantipur TV*, *Image Channel TV* and *Channel Nepal*.
Radio: *Radio Nepal* is state-run. *HBC 94 FM* is operated by the Himalayan Broadcasting Company. FM station *Radio Sagarmatha* is a public, community station. *Kantipur FM*, *Image FM* and *Hits FM* are commercial stations. *BBC World Service* is available on FM in Kathmandu.

Passport/Visa

	Passport? Required	Visa Required?	Return Ticket Required?
Full British	Yes	Yes	No
Australian	Yes	Yes	No
Canadian	Yes	Yes	No
USA	Yes	Yes	No
Other EU	Yes	Yes	No
Japanese	Yes	Yes	No

Note: *Regulations and requirements may be subject to change at short notice, and you are advised to contact the appropriate diplomatic or consular authority before finalising travel arrangements. Any numbers in the chart refer to the footnotes below.*

PASSPORTS: Valid passport required by all except nationals of India holding proof of identity and arriving from India. (Acceptable proofs include Voter's Identity Card issued by the Election Commission of India or Photo Identity Card issued by the state or central Government of India or Temporary Photo ID issued by the Indian Diplomatic Mission in Nepal.)
Note: Children under 10 years old travelling from India to Nepal are not required to produce photo identification.
VISAS: Required by all except the following:
(a) nationals of India;
(b) transit passengers continuing their journey by the same or first connecting aircraft on the same day provided holding valid onward or return documentation and not leaving the airport.
Types of visa and cost: *Tourist:* £20 (single-entry); £55 (multiple-entry). *Business:* applications can be made on arrival which need to be approved by the Ministry of Industry.
Note: (a) All nationals may obtain tourist visas on arrival at the airport. Two passport-size photos are required. (b) Business can be conducted on a Tourist visa for up to 30 days.
Validity: Visas are valid for up to six months from date of issue. Visas are valid for 60 days on first visit to Nepal in a visa year, but only valid for 30 days when national is visiting Nepal for the second or more time in a visa year (Jan 1-Dec 31). They may be extended in Nepal at the Department of Immigration, Kathmandu (tel: 494 273 *or* 337), or the Immigration Office, Pokhara. Maximum stay in Nepal is 150 days in any calendar year. For full conditions on visa extension (including charges and conditions), contact the Consulate (or Consular section at Embassy); see *Passport/Visa Information*.
Application to: Consulate (or Consular section at Embassy). Visas can also be obtained on arrival from the Immigration authorities at all entry points (with fees payable in US Dollars) provided travellers are in possession of valid travel documents, two passport photos and the relevant fee. Applications for business visas must be made to the Department of Immigration (see above under *Validity* for address).
Application requirements: (a) One completed application form. (b) Passport valid for at least six months. (c) One passport-size photo. (d) Fee (in cash, postal order or bank draft). (e) A stamped-addressed envelope if applying by post. Business: (a)-(e) and, (f) Letter from company explaining purpose of visit, accompanying application made direct to Department of Immigration in Nepal (as above).
Working days required: Minimum 24 hours if applying in person; two weeks if applying by post.

PASSPORT/VISA INFORMATION

Royal Nepalese Embassy in the UK
12A Kensington Palace Gardens, London W8 4QU, UK
Tel: (020) 7229 1594 *or* 6231.
Website: www.nepembassy.org.uk
Opening hours: Mon-Fri 0900-1700; 1000-1200 (consular section).

Royal Nepalese Embassy in the USA
2131 Leroy Place, NW, Washington, DC 20008, USA
Tel: (202) 667 4550.
Website: www.nepalembassyusa.org

Royal Nepalese Consulate General in the USA
820 Second Avenue, Suite 17B, 17th Floor,
New York, NY 10017, USA
Tel: (212) 370 3988/9.

Money

Currency: Nepalese Rupee (NPR) = 100 paisa. Notes are in denominations of NPR1000, 500, 100, 50, 20, 10, 5, 2 and 1. Coins are in denominations of 50, 25 and 10 paisa.
Note: Visitors should bear in mind that foreign visitors

other than Indian nationals are required to pay their airline tickets, trekking permits and hotel bills in foreign currency.
Currency exchange: It is illegal to exchange currency with persons other than authorised dealers in foreign exchange (banks, hotels and licensed money changers). Visitors should obtain Foreign Exchange Encashment Receipts when changing currency and keep them, as these will help in many transactions, including getting visa extensions and trekking permits.
Credit & debit cards: American Express is widely accepted, with MasterCard and Visa in tourist shops, hotels, restaurants and agencies. Check with your credit or debit card company for details of merchant acceptability and other services which may be available. ATMs are widely available in Nepal.
Traveller's cheques: Accepted at banks and major hotels. If trekking, it is important to bear in mind that cash is necessary. To avoid additional exchange rate charges, travellers are advised to take traveller's cheques in US Dollars or Pounds Sterling.
Currency restrictions: Import of local and Indian currency is prohibited, except for nationals of Nepal and India. Foreign currency is unlimited but must be declared. Export of local and foreign currency is limited to the amounts declared on arrival. Only 10 per cent of the amount exchanged into local currency will be reconverted into foreign currency on departure and all exchange receipts must be retained.
Banking hours: Banks in the Kathmandu valley are open Mon-Fri 0900-1530. In other areas, opening hours are usually Sun-Thurs 1000-1500 and Fri 1000-1200. Licensed money changers are open 12 hours per day.
Exchange rate indicators:
Rate at time of publishing
£1.00=   NPR132.78
$1.00=   NPR75.38

Duty Free

The following goods may be imported into Nepal without incurring customs duty:
200 cigarettes, 50 cigars or equivalent of other tobacco articles; 1x1.5l bottles of alcoholic beverage; a reasonable amount of perfume for personal use.
Note: (a) All baggage must be declared on arrival and departure. (b) Certain goods including cameras, videos and electronic goods may only be imported duty free if they are exported on departure. They may not be left in Nepal. (c) It is illegal to export goods over 100 years old. (d) Export certificates need to be obtained from the Department of Archaeology for the export of any metal statues, sacred paintings and similar objects.

Public Holidays

Below are listed Public Holidays for the January 2006-June 2007 period.
2006: Feb 2 Vasant Panchami. **Jan 11** National Unity Day. **Jan 29** Martyrs' Day. **Feb 19** Rashtriya Prajatantra Divas (National Democracy Day). **Feb 26** Shivaratri (in honour of Lord Shiva). **Mar 8** Nepalese Women's Day. **Mar 14** Holi. **Mar 29** Ghode Jatra (Festival of Horses). **Apr 5** Chaite Dashain. **Apr 7** Ram Nawami (Birthday of Lord Ram). **Apr 14** Navabarsha (New Year's Day). **May 13** Buddha Jayanti (Birthday of Lord Buddha). **Jul 7** HM King's Birthday. **Aug 9** Rakshya Bandhan (Janai Purnima). **Aug 10** Gai Jatra (Procession of Cows). **Aug 16** Krishna Asthami (Birthday of Lord Krishna). **Aug 26** Teej (Festival of Women). **Sep 6** Indra Jatra (Festival of Rain God). **Oct 2-3** Dasain (Durga Puja Festival). **Oct 21** Deepawali (Festival of Lights). **Nov 9** Constitution Day.
2007: Jan 11 National Unity Day. **Jan 23** Vasant Panchami. **Jan 29** Martyrs' Day. **Feb 16** Shivaratri (in honour of Lord Shiva). **Feb 19** Rashtriya Prajatantra Divas (National Democracy Day). **Mar 4** Holi. **Mar 8** Nepalese Women's Day. **Mar** Ghode Jatra (Festival of Horses). **Mar/Apr** Chaite Dashain. **Mar/Apr** Ram Nawami (Birthday of Lord Ram). **Apr 14** Navabarsha (New Year's Day). **May 2** Buddha Jayanti (Birthday of Lord Buddha).
Note: Some of the above are Hindu festivals, which are declared according to local astronomical observations. It is not possible to predict the exact dates of festivals occuring and the dates published are approximations. Travellers should check locally nearer the time for precise dates.

Health

	Special Precautions?	Certificate Required?
Yellow Fever	No	1
Cholera	Yes	2
Typhoid & Polio	3	N/A
Malaria	4	N/A

Note: *Regulations and requirements may be subject to change at short notice, and you are advised to contact your doctor well in advance of your intended date of departure. Any numbers in the chart refer to the footnotes below.*

1: A yellow fever vaccination certificate is required of travellers arriving from infected areas.
2: Following WHO guidelines issued in 1973, a cholera vaccination certificate is not a condition of entry to Nepal. However, cholera is a serious risk in this country and precautions are essential. Up-to-date advice should be sought before deciding whether these precautions should include vaccination, as medical opinion is divided over its effectiveness. For more information, see the *Health* appendix.
3: Typhoid is common and there are reports of resistance to anti-typhoid drugs.
4: Malaria risk, mainly in the benign *vivax* form, exists throughout the year in rural areas of the Terai districts (including forested hills and forest areas) of Bara, Dhanukha, Kapilvastu, Mahotari, Parsa, Rautahat, Rupendehi, Sarlahi, and especially along the Indian border. There is no risk in areas higher than 1200 metres. Chloroquine is not an effective anti-malaria drug.
Food & drink: All water should be regarded as being potentially contaminated. Water used for drinking, brushing teeth or making ice should have first been boiled or otherwise sterilised. Milk is unpasteurised and should be boiled. Powdered or tinned milk is available and is advised, but make sure that it is reconstituted with pure water. Avoid dairy products which are likely to have been made from unboiled milk. Do not buy food from street vendors. Only eat well-cooked meat and fish, preferably served hot. Pork, salad and mayonnaise may carry increased risk. Vegetables should be cooked and fruit peeled.
Other risks: *High altitude sickness* is a hazard for trekkers, so it is important to be in good health before travelling. Advice can be obtained from the Himalayan Rescue Association near the Kathmandu Guest House, Thamel. It is advisable, particularly when in rural areas, to carry a medical kit containing items such as rehydration mixture for the treatment of severe diarrhoea and 'dry spray' for cuts and bruises. There is an increased risk of sunburn in higher regions. Avoid walking barefoot. Contact the Nepal Tourism Board for advice (see *Top Things To Do*).
Giardiasis, dysenteries and *diarrhoeas* are all common. *Japanese encephalitis* occurs in southern lowland rural areas. *Hepatitis A, B* and *E* occur. *Meningitis* has been reported in some areas. There has been a sharp rise in *visceral leishmaniasis*, and *trachoma* is fairly common. *Rabies* is present. For those at high risk, vaccination before arrival should be considered. If you are bitten, seek medical advice without delay. For more information, see the *Health* appendix.
Health care: The most convenient hospital for visitor care is Patan Hospital in Lagankhel. Other hospitals include the Western Regional Hospital and the Manipal Hospital in Pokhara and the Mission Hospital in Tansen. Most hospitals have English-speaking staff and larger hotels have doctors. Pharmacies in Kathmandu, mainly along New Road, offer a wide range of Western drugs at low prices. In Kathmandu, you can get certain vaccinations free of charge at the Infectious Diseases Clinic. Full medical insurance is essential.

Travel - International

AIR:

The national airline is *Royal Nepal Airlines (RA)* (website: www.royalnepal.com). It operates flights to Bangkok, Delhi, Frankfurt/M, Hong Kong, Mumbai, Osaka, Paris, London, Shanghai and Singapore.
Approximate flight times: From Kathmandu to *London* is 10 hours 55 minutes (non-direct).
Main airports: *Kathmandu (KTM)* (Tribhuvan) (website: www.tiairport.com) is 5.5km (3.5 miles) east of the city (travel time - 20 minutes). *To/from the airport*: Buses and taxis to the city are available. *Facilities*: Bank/bureau de change, duty free shop, post office, refreshments and tourist information.
Departure tax: NPR1356 for international flights to the SAARC region (the South Asian Association for Regional Cooperation), which includes Bangladesh, Bhutan, India, the Maldives, Pakistan and Sri Lanka; NPR1695 for flights to all other countries. Children under two years are exempt.
Note: Foreign nationals must pay for airfares in foreign currency. Only Nepalese and Indian nationals are allowed to pay in Nepalese Rupees for air passage between Nepal and India.

RAIL:

Two stretches of the Indian Railway Line run to the border with Nepal, where cycle-rickshaws are available for onward journeys.

ROAD:

Kathmandu is connected with India and Tibet by new and picturesque highways through the fertile plains of the Terai. Bus services operate from all border points to Kathmandu. However, during the monsoon season, landslides can often make border points impassable. Visitors are permitted to drive their own cars provided they are in possession of an international carnet. For information on how to obtain an international carnet, visitors should contact their national Automobile Association. See also *Travel - Internal* section for required documentation.
Note: All visitors entering Nepal by land must use one of the following entry points: Belhiya (Bhairahawa), Birgunj, Dhangadi, Kakarbhitta, Mahendra Nagar and Nepalgunj (all on the Nepal-India border); and Kodari (on the Nepal-China border). If entering overland by car, an international carnet is required (enquire at Embassy for details); see *Top Things To Do*.

Travel - Internal

AIR:

There is a network of domestic flights linking major towns, radiating from Kathmandu. Many of these offer spectacular views across the mountains. *Royal Nepal Airlines* operates an extensive range of scheduled flights to around 32 destinations in the interior parts of Nepal. Other domestic airlines provide regular and charter services to popular destinations. Helicopters can be chartered for various purposes. Nepal's domestic air service is known to be punctual and reliable.
Departure tax: NPR165 for all domestic flights.
Note: Air fares must be paid in foreign currency by foreign nationals. Only Nepalese and Indian nationals are allowed to pay in Nepalese Rupees.

RAIL:

Nepal Janakpur-Jayanager Railways (NJJR) operates a freight and passenger service in the eastern Terai.

ROAD:

Traffic drives on the left. The interior parts of the country are linked with a number of motorable roads. The road system is of unpredictable quality. Many of the mountain and hill roads are impassable during the monsoon season (June to September). **Bus:** There are regular bus services to Kathmandu from all the border points. Tickets may be booked in advance. Buses for the different parts of the country are available at the Gongabu bus terminal, which is located near Balaju. Services are operated by the *Transport Corporation of Nepal* and by private operators. Deluxe tourist buses are available from Kathmandu to Pokhara and Chitwan. Most of them depart at 0700 from near Thamel in the city centre. Six-seater *sumo tato* vans, 12-seater vans and air-conditioned minibuses are also available for long distance travel. Visitors should, however, be aware that multiple-fatality accidents on buses are common. **Bicycles and motorcycles**: These can be hired cheaply from Thamel, Rani Pokhari and Jhochhen. Motorcyclists require a driving licence. Cyclists should make sure they have a working bell. **Car hire:** Cars can be hired in Kathmandu. Chauffeur-driven cars can only be hired in the Kathmandu Valley. **Documentation:** An International Driving Permit is valid in Nepal for 15 days, after which a local licence is required. The minimum driving age is 18. A temporary licence to drive is available from local authorities on presentation of a valid national driving licence.

URBAN:

There are bus services in the populous areas around Kathmandu, which include the neighbouring cities of Patan and Bhaktapur. A trolleybus route provides frequent journeys over the 11km (7-mile) Kathmandu- Bhaktapur road. Private minibuses feed the trolleybus route from nearby villages. On buses and trolleybuses belonging to the *Transport Corporation of Nepal*, a 4-stage fare system applies, with colour-coded tickets issued by conductors. 'Microbuses' also operate. **Taxi**: Metered taxis are plentiful in Kathmandu; at night, the meter reading plus 50 per cent is standard. Private taxis are more expensive and fares should be agreed before departure. **Tempos**: These are metered 3-wheel scooters, which work out slightly cheaper than taxis. **Rickshaws**: These operate throughout the city. Fares should be negotiated in advance. **Bicycles and motorcycles**: These can be hired cheaply from Thamel, Rani Pokhari and Jhochhen. Motorcyclists require a driving licence. Cyclists should make sure they have a working bell.

Travel Advice

The political situation in Nepal remains tense and unpredictable following the end of the Maoist ceasefire and elections, which took place on 8 February 2006. There is a possibility of further violence and disturbances with planned blockades in Kathmandu and other regional centres from 14 March onwards, and an indefinite nationwide Bandh (shutdown) from 3 April onwards. Travellers are advised to take extreme caution if travelling in Nepal during this period.
The Maoist's unilateral four-month ceasefire ended on 2 January 2006. Since the end of the ceasefire, hostilities have resumed and there have been a number of small bomb explosions in Pokhara, Butwal and Bhairahawa, all aimed at Government and municipal buildings.
The situation outside the Kathmandu Valley remains unpredictable and travel by road can be difficult, even when a bandh is not officially in operation.
There is a high threat from terrorism in Nepal. In recent months, Maoist rebels have carried out a large number of attacks, including bombings and shootings, even in areas frequented by foreigners.
Visitors are advised to exercise extreme caution and vigilance throughout their visit.
It is strongly recommended that trekkers travel in a group with an experienced guide. Travelling in groups will make them less vulnerable to theft and assault and will assist visitors greatly in the event of an accident. It also helps not to be alone in the face of Maoist demands for money on the main trekking routes.
This advice is based on information provided by the Foreign & Commonwealth Office in the UK. It is correct at time of publishing. As the situation can change rapidly, visitors are advised to contact the following organisations for the latest travel advice:

British Foreign and Commonwealth Office
Tel: (0845) 850 2829.
Website: www.fco.gov.uk

US Department of State
Website: http://travel.state.gov/travel

Accommodation

HOTELS:

Kathmandu has an increasing number of international-class hotels, which are particularly busy during spring and autumn, when it is advisable to book well in advance. Comfortable hotels can also be found in Pokhara, and the Royal Chitwan National Park in the Terai Jungle. A Government tax is added to bills, which varies according to the star rating of the hotel.

LODGES:

Besides the officially recognised hotels, there are a number of lodges or hostels. In Kathmandu, these are located in the old part of the town, in the streets around the Durbar Square or in the Thamel district. Lodges are available outside the main towns, and provide suitable accommodation for mountaineers and trekkers. For a list of approved hostels and lodges, contact the Nepal Tourism Board in Kathmandu or one of their representatives abroad (see *Top Things To Do*).

ACCOMMODATION INFORMATION

Hotel Association of Nepal (HAN)
PO Box 2151, Kamalpokhari, Kathmandu, Nepal
Tel: (1) 412 705 *or* 410 522.
Website: www.hotelassociation.org.np

Top Things To See

- Enjoy the magic of **Kathmandu**, the capital and also the cultural, commercial and business hub of the Kingdom. In **Durbar Square,** discover a wonderful collection of temples and shrines, both Buddhist and Hindu, the old **Royal Palace**, and the **Statue of Hanuman the Monkey God**, clad in a red cloak. Here also is the house of the living goddess - the **Kumari.**
- Climbing upwards from Kathmandu, reach the famous Buddhist stupa of **Swayambhunath**, popularly known as the **Monkey Temple**, and see the temple's large staring eyes. There are a great many steps leading up to the temple, which is frequented by an even greater number of monkeys. There are also a number of monasteries in the area.
- Just 5km (3 miles) west of the city, below the **Nagarjun Forest**, head for the **Balaju Water Gardens**, with a reclining statue of Lord Vishnu and a 22-headed sea-dragon fountain.
- Around 19km (12 miles) south of Kathmandu, and accessible by taxi, in the **Godavari Royal Botanical Gardens** see beautiful trees, shrubs and orchids in an idyllic setting.
- In **Bhaktapur** (also known as the 'temple city'), have a look at unusual, colourful animal paintings in the **National Art Gallery**, located in the old **Malla Palace.** Other museums in Bhaktapur are the **National Woodworking Museum**, showing fine examples of Newari woodcarving (for which the city is renowned), and the **Brass and Bronze Museum**, both in Dattatreya Square.
- In **Patan,** discover ancient historic and artistic landmarks, including **Patan Durbar Square** (also the location for the interesting **Patan Museum**), **Krishna Mandir**, the **Royal Bath**, the **Kumbheshwor Temple** and the **Golden Temple**. See exotic South-Asian animals in the **Jawalakhel Zoo.**
- There are shrines for every purpose in the valley, such as the **Shrine of Ganesh the Elephant God**, reputed to bring good luck. There are four Ganesh temples in the valley, each a masterpiece of Nepalese architecture - one in Kathmandu's Durbar Square, one in **Chabahil**, one in

A B C D E F G H I J K L M N O P Q R S T U V W X Y Z

Chobar and one near Bhaktapur. **Lumbini**, being the birthplace of Lord Buddha, is one of the world's most important pilgrimage sites.

- Get spectacular views of **Mount Everest**, mist permitting, in **Nagarkot Village**, situated on rice steppes in magnificent countryside.
- In the secluded town of **Pokhara** in the centre of Nepal on **Lake Phewa**, get the best view of the Himalayas. It was at one time the home of JRR Tolkien.

Top Things To Do

- Buy Tibetan handicrafts and artefacts in the hugely impressive **Bodnath Stupa**, a centre of Tibetan exile culture, a few kilometres from Kathmandu. Alternatively, visit the lively **bazaar** in the hill town of **Gorkha**, the ancestral home of the Shah Dynasty and residence of the original Gurkha soldiers.
- Go on an elephant ride in the **Royal Chitwan National Park**, Nepal's first national park, which is a jungle overflowing with wildlife.
- Take a **scenic flight** over **Mount Everest**. Most of the domestic airlines arrange flights in light aircraft. Flights are also available from **Pokhara** and other locations west of the capital, flying over the spectacular **Annapurna** range.
- **Go river rafting**: Rafting permits are not required for the general areas; however, to raft the Himalayan rivers, a permit must be obtained from the Ministry of Culture, Tourism and Civil Aviation (tel: (1) 425 6232 or 6231 or 6228).
- **Go ballooning** or **hang-gliding** in Kathmandu. Hang-gliding is popular in **Pokhara** and in the **Langtang** region. **Paragliding** and **power paragliding** are available in Pokhara.
- Try to find the **Nepal Yeti**: the existence of the famous Nepal Yeti, a giant, gorilla-sized hairy snowman that eats yaks and sheep, remains strongly questionable. Only a few people, including the father of Tenzing Norgay (the first Sherpa to conquer Mount Everest), claim to have seen it. Popular myth recounts that those who did spot the creature got sick and died within a few days. For Yeti enthusiasts wishing to try their luck, the abominable snowman is said to make random appearances around the **Khumbu** region (in the foothills of Mount Everest).
- One of the principal reasons for visiting Nepal must be either to see or to **climb the mountains**, especially **Mount Everest**, Sagarmatha ('Head of the Sky') in Nepalese. At an altitude of 8848m (29,022ft), Everest is the world's highest peak and has been opened for commercial mountaineering for decades. **Note**: To scale any of the mountain peaks in Nepal, climbing permits are required. They can be obtained from the Ministry of Culture, Tourism and Civil Aviation (tel: (1) 425 6232 or 6231 or 6228) or the Nepal Mountaineering Association (NMA) (tel: (1) 434 525; website: www.nma.com.np). Further information can also be obtained from the Nepal Tourism Board (see Tourist Information).
- For **walkers** and **trekkers**, Nepal is a true paradise. The trekking season is generally from September to May, but the best periods are October to December and March to April. Different types of trips with varying degrees of difficulty can be arranged. Some foreign travel agencies can book trekking packages in advance in collaboration with the Nepalese trekking agencies. In Kathmandu, there are many local officially registered trekking agencies that can provide a fully organised trek, complete with porters, guide, cook, food tents, sleeping bags, mattresses, transport to and from the starting and finishing points,

flight arrangements, permits and insurance. They also provide participants with a choice of itineraries. Pony treks are also available and follow nearly the same routes as normal treks and are offered mostly in the western region around **Pokhara**, as well as in the hinterlands of **Dolpo** and **Lo Manthang**. Trekking permits are no longer required for the general trekking areas designated by the Department of Immigration (such as the Annapurna, the Everest, the Langtang and Rara). For all other areas, a permit is still required and can be obtained from the Department of Immigration located at New Baneshwar, Kathmandu (see Passport/Visa Information for further details) or trekking agencies and tour operators. Trekking to Dolpa, Kanchanjunga, Makalu and Upper Mustang can only be undertaken through a registered trekking agency. Entrance fees are levied for the national park areas and wildlife reserves; these range from NPR500 to NPR2000 per person per day. Children under 10 are exempt. Higher fees are payable for filming and helicopter landing permits. Further information can be obtained from the Nepal Tourism Board (see Tourist Information).The Nepal Tourism Board gives the following advice to trekkers: use authorised guides and porters; be careful with matches around wooded or grassy areas as forest fires can cause serious damage; be economical with all fuel, especially local firewood (campfires are not recommended); prioritise tour companies and lodges which do not use firewood; trekkers are strictly forbidden to cut any green forest reserve or kill any wildlife; use washing and toilet facilities provided or, if none are available, make sure to be at least 30 metres away from any water source; use biodegradable items as much as possible; when visiting temples or Buddhist shrines, respect local religious customs; take necessary precautions when suffering from altitude sickness (for details, see the Health section).

TOURIST INFORMATION

Nepal Tourism Board
Bhrikuti Mandap, PO Box 11018, Kathmandu, Nepal
Tel: (1) 425 6909 or 6229.
Website: www.welcomenepal.com

Entertainment

FOOD & DRINK:
National specialities:
- Dal Bhat (lentils and rice).
- Tarkan (spiced vegetables).
- Gurr (a Sherpa dish of raw potatoes, pounded with spices, then grilled like pancakes on a hot, flat stone ground and mixed with milk, tea or water).
- Rotis (flat pancake-like bread made from wheat or rice flour).

National drinks:
- Chiya (tea brewed with milk, sugar and spices; in the mountains it is salted with yak butter).
- Arak (potato alcohol).
- Raksi (wheat or rice spirit).
- Chang (beer made from fermented barley, maize, rye or millet).

Tipping: Only usual in tourist hotels and restaurants. Taxi drivers need only be tipped when they have been particularly helpful. 10 per cent is sufficient for all three services. Elsewhere, tipping should be avoided.

NIGHTLIFE: Kathmandu has a few cinemas featuring

mainly Indian films. For Western films, see the programmes of the European and US cultural centres. Most people are asleep by 2200. Nightlife is fairly limited; a few temples and restaurants offer entertainment and some tourist hotels stage Nepalese folk dances and musical shows. There are casinos with baccarat, chemin de fer and roulette, open 24 hours a day, every day, at some 5-star hotels in Kathmandu.
SHOPPING: There are bargains for those careful to avoid fakes and the badly made souvenirs sold by unscrupulous traders. Popular buys include locally made clothes such as lopsided topis (caps), knitted mittens and socks, Tibetan dresses, woven shawls, Tibetan multicoloured jackets and men's diagonally fastened shirts; and pashmina (fine goat's-wool blankets), khukri (the national knife), saranghi (a small, four-stringed viola played with a horse-hair bow), Tibetan tea bowls, papier mâché dance masks, Buddhist statuettes and filigree ornaments, bamboo flutes and other folk objects. **Shopping hours**: Sun-Fri 1000-2000 (shops are usually closed on Saturday).

Business

- **GDP:** US$6.7 billion (2004).
- **Main imports:** Gold, machinery and equipment, petroleum products and fertiliser.
- **Main exports:** Clothing, carpet, leather, jute goods and grain.
- **Main trade partners:** China, Germany, India, Saudi Arabia, United Arab Emirates and USA.

ECONOMY: Nepal is one of the world's least developed countries with an average annual income of just US$200 per annum. Although little of the land can be cultivated, 90 per cent of the working population finds employment in agriculture and forestry. Foodstuffs and live animals provide about 30 per cent of Nepal's export earnings. The principal crops are maize, rice, barley, wheat, sugar cane, potatoes and fruit. The manufacturing sector is very small and concentrated in light industries such as construction materials, food processing, textiles and carpet-making (the latter being an important export earner).
The country has a considerable hydroelectric potential which would save Nepal from having to import much of its energy requirements, but the sector is as yet underdeveloped. There is some mining of mica and small quantities of lignite, copper, coal and iron ore. The main service industry, tourism, has gone into decline since the late 1990s. In 2002, bad weather and the effects of the Maoist insurgency caused the economy to contract by 0.5 per cent. The sustained expansion of the 1990s has clearly ended and the Nepalese economy is highly vulnerable. It relies on substantial amounts of foreign aid, especially food aid (international donors provide about 30 per cent of the Government's budget) and runs a large external debt. India is the main trading partner, although following the 1989/90 dispute which led to the closure of the border between the two countries, Nepal has actively pursued trade links elsewhere. Agreements have also been signed with several other governments, of which that with China (PR) is the most important. Nepal is a member of the Asian Development Bank and the Colombo Plan, both of which aim to promote regional economic cooperation.
BUSINESS ETIQUETTE: Tropical-weight suits or shirt and tie are recommended. Best time to visit is October to May.
Government office hours: Kathmandu Valley: Mon-Fri 0900-1700 (winter), 0900-1600 (summer). Other areas: Sun-Fri 1000-1700 (winter), 1000-1600 (summer). **Private office hours**: Sun-Fri 0930-1700.

COMMERCIAL INFORMATION

Nepal Chamber of Commerce
PO Box 198, Kantipath, Kathmandu, Nepal
Tel: (1) 222 890.
Website: www.nepalchamber.org

Federation of Nepalese Chambers of Commerce and Industry
PO Box 269, Pachali Shahid Shukra, Milan Marg, Teku, Kathmandu, Nepal
Tel: (1) 426 2061 or 2218 or 6889.
Website: www.fncci.org

Nepal-Britain Chamber of Commerce & Industry
British Embassy Premises, PO Box 106, Lainchaur, Kathmandu, Nepal
Tel: (1) 410 738 or 588 or 583.
Website: www.nbcci.org.np

Nepal Incentive and Convention Association (Information on Conferences/Conventions)
PO Box 4258, Kathmandu, Nepal
Tel: (1) 494 491.

Credit: ©Nepal Tourism Board

The Netherlands

Location: Northwest Europe.

Time: GMT + 1 (GMT + 2 from last Sunday in March to last Sunday in October).

Overview

The Netherlands has almost dispelled the notion of simply being an archaic land of clogs and windmills with its string of exciting conurbations, including the cosmopolitan capital, Amsterdam – one of Europe's great cities. Even towns such as Eindhoven, The Hague, Utrecht and Rotterdam are instilled with a genuine buzz.

Away from the cities, the idyllic land of windmills and tulips still exists in the bucolic splendour of the countryside, as do a number of stunning medieval towns and beach resorts on its wide swathe of coastline. The Netherlands is renowned for being unremittingly flat, but this does have its advantages, providing excellent terrain for cycling and walking, plus opening up sweeping, vast skies that celebrated painters past and present – of which The Netherlands boasts many – have sought to capture on canvas. Essentially, what The Netherlands offers is high culture in low land. Amsterdam alone enables you to delve through centuries of history aboard a canal boat or explore an exhaustive array of museums and galleries.

The Netherlands' roots in the arts stem from the 17th century, the so-called 'Golden Age', which placed this tiny but rich country at the forefront of European culture. The gaining of the upper hand by imperial influence and the annexing of The Netherlands to the far-flung empire of the Hapsburgs in the 16th century resulted in the rebellion of the largely Protestant northern provinces of the Low Countries, led by William of Orange and Nassau – this struggle for independence would last until 1648. This was compounded by a remarkable growth in Dutch sea power, as many Spanish and Portuguese possessions in the New World and East Asia were seized. This reached its acme in 1689 when William III of Orange became King of England - although the association was severed on his death in 1702. William III of Orange's death portended The Netherlands' 18th-century wane and its eventual absorption into Napoleon's empire. The whole area of the Low Countries was briefly reunited (1814-30) and, in 1848, the constitution was amended, leaving the Monarch only

limited powers. The Netherlands took no part in World War I but suffered badly as a result of the Nazi invasion of 1940. Post-war Dutch diplomacy has concentrated on increasing European unity: the Dutch are enthusiastic Europeans and the EU is the main focus of Dutch foreign policy. Although recent years have seen bad publicity surrounding the rise and murder of far-right politician Pim Fortuyn in 2002, and increased public debate about tighter immigration controls (somewhat denting the city's reputation for tolerance), The Netherlands – in particular, Amsterdam – is still a haven for many nationalities, sexualities and radically different political and religious persuasions. It also just happens to be incredibly exciting, enchanting and interesting.

General Information

AREA: 41,528 sq km (16,034 sq miles).

POPULATION: 16.3 million (UN, 2005).

POPULATION DENSITY: 392.5 per sq km.

CAPITAL: Amsterdam. **Population**: 735,562 (2003). **Seat of Government**: The Hague. **Population**: 463,826 (2003).

GEOGRAPHY: The Netherlands shares borders to the south with Belgium and to the east with Germany, while the North Sea lies to the north and west. Large areas of The Netherlands have been reclaimed from the sea and consequently one-fifth of the country lies below sea level. The country is flat and level and is criss-crossed by rivers and canals. Areas reclaimed from the sea, known as *polders*, are extremely fertile. The landscape is broken by the forest of Arnhem, the bulb fields in the west, the lakes of the central and northern areas, and coastal dunes that are among the most impressive in Europe.

GOVERNMENT: Constitutional monarchy since 1848.

Head of State: Queen Beatrix Van Oranje Nassau since 1980. **Head of Government**: Prime Minister Jan Peter Balkenende since 2002. **Recent history:** Various political groupings occasionally have registered strong electoral showings and managed minor representation in Government. These include the ecologist Green Party, the radical *Democraten 66* (D66) and, most recently, the *List Pim Fortuyn*, which emerged at the election of May 2002. Taking its name from its charismatic leader, Pim Fortuyn, the List campaigned on a far-right anti-crime, anti-immigration platform. This struck a chord with a disillusioned electorate and coincided with the resurgence of the far right throughout Western Europe. At the poll, List Pim Fortuyn emerged as the second-largest party and entered Government in coalition with the *Christen-Democratisch Appel* (Christian Democratic Appeal, CDA). However, during the campaign, Fortuyn himself was assassinated. A common feature of European far-right parties is the influence of a single dominant personality which guarantees the party's cohesion – for example, Jean-Marie Le Pen of the French Front Nationale, or Jorg Haider, leader of Austria's Freedom Party – and a propensity for self-destructive internal feuding. Once in office, without Fortuyn, the List almost immediately fell apart, causing the collapse of the Government. New elections were called. Held in January 2003, the CDA was returned as the largest party; it now governs in coalition with *Volkspartij voor Vrijheid en Democratie* (People's Freedom and Democracy, VVD) and D66 with CDA party leader Jan Peter Balkenende as Premier. The List Pim Fortuyn was reduced to a handful of seats but it has left its mark on Dutch politics in the form of a hardening of the official attitude towards immigrants and asylum seekers.

The Netherlands is a constitutional Monarchy with a bicameral multiparty legislature: the First (Lower) Chamber has 150 members, elected for a four-year term; and the Second (Upper) Chamber has 75 members, indirectly elected by provincial councils for the same length of term.

LANGUAGE: Dutch is the official language. English, German and French are widely spoken.

RELIGION: 31 per cent Roman Catholic, 21 per cent Protestant; 40 per cent do not profess any religion.

ELECTRICITY: 220 volts AC, 50Hz. Two-pin European-style plugs are in use.

SOCIAL CONVENTIONS: It is customary to shake hands. English is spoken as a second language by many and is willingly used; many Dutch people will also speak German and French. Hospitality is very much the same as for the rest of Europe and the USA. It is customary to take a small gift if invited for a meal. Casual wear is widely acceptable. Men are expected to wear a suit for business and social functions. Formal wear may be required for smart restaurants, bars and clubs. Evening dress (black tie for men) is generally specified on invitation.

Climate

Mild, maritime climate. Summers are generally warm with changeable periods, but excessively hot weather is rare. Winters can be fairly cold with the possibility of some snow. Rainfall is prevalent all year.

Required clothing: European according to season, with light-to mediumweights worn in warmer months and medium- to heavyweights in winter. Rainwear is advisable all year.

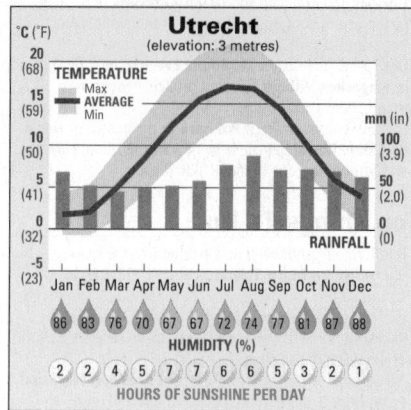

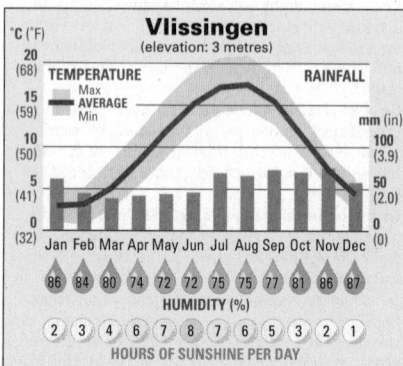

Communications

Telephone: Full IDD is available. Country code: 31 (followed by 20 for Amsterdam, 10 for Rotterdam and 70 for The Hague). Telephone information is given in French, English and German. There is a cheaper rate from Mon-Fri 2000-0800. Calls can be made from public booths or post offices. Most booths only accept cards, which can be bought at post offices, VVV offices, and shops displaying the *PTT-telephone card* poster; and, sometimes, coins.

Credit: ©Netherlands Board of Tourism and Conventions

Mobile telephone: Roaming agreements exist with many international mobile phone companies. Coverage is good.

Internet: Internet is available; there are many Internet cafes and some Internet access centres. Business centres also provide public access. Using the Internet is very straightforward in Amsterdam, where computers are available to use free of charge in libraries and public buildings.

Post: Stamps are available from all post offices as well as from tobacconists and kiosks selling postcards and souvenirs. Mail within Europe takes approximately five days. Post office hours: Mon-Fri 0900-1700. Some post offices in major towns are also open on late shopping nights (Thursday or Friday night) and Sat 0900-1200/1230. There are all-night post offices in Amsterdam and Rotterdam.

MEDIA: The Dutch have a unique approach to public broadcasting. Programmes are made by a variety of groups, some reflecting political or religious currents in society, others representing interest groups. These organisations are allocated airtime on TV and radio, in line with the number of members they have. The TV market is very competitive, with many private stations also currently flourishing. The Dutch also have one of the highest cable take-up rates in Europe. Every province has at least one local public TV channel. Freedom of press and free speech is guaranteed by the constitution. Newspaper ownership, however, is highly concentrated, and most titles are broadsheets.

Press: The main newspapers are *NRC Handelsblad* (an evening paper), *De Telegraaf*, *Trouw* and *De Volkskrant*.

Foreign newspapers are widely available.

TV: *NOS* oversees the country's three national public networks; *RTL* operates commercial channels, as does *SBS*.

Radio: *NOS* oversees public radio stations, including news and information station *Radio 1*, music network *Radio 2*, pop station *3FM* and cultural station *Radio 4*. *Radio Netherlands* is an international broadcaster.

Passport/Visa

	Passport Required?	Visa Required?	Return Ticket Required?
Full British	1	No	No
Australian	Yes	No	No
Canadian	Yes	No	No
USA	Yes	No	No
Other EU	1	No	No
Japanese	Yes	No	No

Note: *Regulations and requirements may be subject to change at short notice, and you are advised to contact the appropriate diplomatic or consular authority before finalising travel arrangements. Any numbers in the chart refer to the footnotes below.*

Note: The Netherlands is a signatory to the **1995 Schengen Agreement**. For further details about passport/visa regulations within the Schengen area, see the introductory section in *How to Use this Guide.*

PASSPORTS: Passport valid for at least three months beyond the length of stay required by all except:
(a) **1.** EU/EEA nationals (EU+ Iceland, Liechtenstein, Norway) and Swiss nationals holding a valid national ID card.
Note: EU and EEA nationals are only required to produce evidence of their EU/EEA nationality and identity in order to be admitted to any EU/EEA Member State. This evidence can take the form of a valid national passport *or* national identity card. Either is acceptable. Possession of a return ticket, any length of validity on their document, sufficient funds for the length of their proposed visit should *not* be imposed.
(b) nationals of Andorra, Monaco and San Marino holding a valid national ID card.
Note: It is now dutch law that everyone over the age of 14 must produce a valid identity document to police officers and other law enforcement authorities on their request.
VISAS: Required by all except the following for stays of up to three months:
(a) nationals referred to in the chart and under passport exemptions above;
(b) nationals of Andorra, Argentina, Bolivia, Brazil, Brunei, Bulgaria, Chile, Costa Rica, Croatia, El Salvador, Guatemala, Honduras, Iceland, Israel, Korea (Rep), Liechtenstein, Malaysia, Mexico, Monaco, New Zealand, Nicaragua, Norway, Panama, Paraguay, Romania, San Marino, Singapore, Switzerland, Uruguay, Vatican City and Venezuela;
(c) transit passengers continuing their journey to/from other *Schengen* countries within 72 hours by the same or first connecting aircraft, provided holding onward or return documentation and not leaving the airport.
Note: Nationals of Afghanistan, Angola, Bangladesh, Congo (Dem Rep), Eritrea, Ethiopia, The Gambia, Ghana, Guinea, Iran, Iraq, Nigeria, Pakistan, Sierra Leone, Somalia, Sri Lanka, Sudan and the Syrian Arab Republic passing through The Netherlands *always* require an airport transit visa even though they do not actually enter Dutch territory, unless holding a Residence Permit for the USA or EEA countries, or temporary residence permit for Canada and the USA, valid on the departure date from The Netherlands, with a confirmed onward ticket and are not leaving the transit lounge. Transit passengers are advised to check transit regulations with the relevant Embassy or Consulate before travelling.
Types of visa and cost: A uniform type of visa, the *Schengen* visa, is issued for the relevant Schengen member nationals, for tourist, business and private visits. *Short-stay* (for up to three months), *Multiple-entry* (for three months, one year *or* five years) and *Transit* visas are available for a handling fee of approximately €35, although prices are subject to change. You may also have to pay other costs incurred in processing the application. Costs must be paid in local currency. The Consulate (or Consular section at Embassy) can be contacted for further details.
Note: Spouses and children (under 21 years) and/or dependents of EU nationals (providing spouse's passport and the original marriage/birth certificate, mentioning name of parents with certified translation in English for Embassy in London are produced) receive their visas free of charge (enquire at Embassy or Consulate for details). Nationals of the Dominican Republic, Ghana, India, Nigeria and Pakistan should have their marriage and birth certificates verified and legalised by the relevant Netherlands Embassy or a visa fee will be charged.
Validity: Visas are normally valid for the duration of stay, with a maximum of three months (90 days) per six months. The visa issuing authorities will want to see the flight tickets to check arrival and departure dates. Transit visas are valid for single- or multiple-entries of maximum five days

per entry, including the day of arrival. Visas cannot be extended; a new application must be made each time.
Application to: Consulate (or Consular section at Embassy); see *Passport/Visa Information*. Applications should be made in person. Travellers visiting just one Schengen country should apply to the Consulate of that country; travellers visiting more than one Schengen country should apply to the Consulate of the country chosen as the main destination *or* the country they will enter first (if they have no main destination).
Application requirements: (a) Passport (valid for at least three months longer than the validity of the visa requested) containing a blank page to affix the visa, or official travel document accepted by *Schengen* countries. If travelling on a new passport, the old one must also be submitted. A residence permit should be endorsed in your current valid passport and must still be valid on departure from the *Schengen* area. (b) Completed application form, listing full address and daytime telephone number. For minors under 18 years, it is necessary to submit approval from both parents or legal guardians, submitting a copy of each parent's/guardian's passport. (c) One passport-size photo. (d) Fee, where applicable (payable in cash or by postal order). (e) Travel insurance policy covering medical expenses, including emergency hotel treatment and repatriation, taken out in the UK, valid for the duration of stay and with a minimum cover of €30,000. (f) Evidence of sufficient funds for period of stay (eg bank statements or traveller's cheques). The amount considered 'enough' will depend on the purpose of visit, accommodation and duration of visit, but is usually €34 per person per day *or* a letter of guarantee from a national of the Netherlands who has a net annual income of €11,000; some Consulates may require both. *Business*: (a)-(f) and, (g) An invitation from a Dutch company confirming duration and purpose of stay, and a recent letter from the applicant's employer, solicitor, bank manager or local Chamber of Commerce, plus last payslip. If unemployed, submit a letter from a solicitor, accountant or Company House or Social Security booklet. *Student*: (a)-(f) and, (g) A letter from the applicant's school, college or university. *Airport Transit*: (a)-(f) and, (g) Confirmed non-refundable and non-endorsable airline ticket.
Note: (a) The number of forms and photos required may vary according to the nationality of the applicant. (b) The applicant may also be asked to provide further relevant documentation in certain cases. (c) Applications must be made in person for those residing in the vicinity of London, UK, and appointments to do so must be made in advance by telephoning the automated telephone appointments booking service (tel: (09065) 540 720; calls cost £1 per minute). For those married to a Dutch national, it is not necessary to telephone the automated booking service. Those married to Dutch nationals may visit the Embassy in London from 0900-1100 on any working day, or visit another of the Dutch Consulates in the UK. An original marriage certificate and original passport of Dutch spouse must be submitted. Postal applications are not accepted.
Working days required: Normally processes within 48 hours, but can take up to two months for certain nationals. It is essential to apply with plenty of time to spare (three weeks at the very least).
Temporary residence: Work permit and residence permit required for non-EU nationals. Enquire at Consulate (or Consular section at Embassy) for further information; see *Passport/Visa Information or* visit Ministrie van Justice, Immigratie-en Nationalisatiedienst (website: www.ind.nl).

PASSPORT/VISA INFORMATION

Royal Netherlands Embassy in the UK
38 Hyde Park Gate, London SW7 5DP, UK
Tel: (020) 7590 3200 *or* (09065) 508 916 (visa information line; calls cost £1 per minute).
Website: www.netherlands-embassy.org.uk
Opening hours: Mon-Fri 0900-1700; 0900-1200 (passport and visa section; by appointment only).
The passport and visa section is closed on the first Wednesday of every month.

Royal Netherlands Embassy in the USA
4200 Linnean Avenue, NW,
Washington, DC 20008, USA
Tel: (202) 244 5300.
Website: www.netherlands-embassy.org

Consulate General of The Netherlands in the USA
1 Rockefeller Plaza, 11th Floor,
New York, NY 10020, USA
Tel: (212) 246 1429.
Website: www.cgny.org

Money

Single European currency (Euro): The Euro is now the official currency of 12 EU member states (including The Netherlands). The first Euro coins and notes were introduced in January 2002; the Dutch Guilder was in circulation until 28 January 2002, when it was completely replaced by the Euro. Euro (€) = 100 cents. Notes are in denominations of €500, 200, 100, 50, 20, 10 and 5. Coins are in denominations of €2 and 1, and 50, 20, 10, 5, 2 and 1 cents.
Currency exchange: Exchange offices are indicated by the letters GWK. GWK is a national organisation with currency exchange offices at major railway stations, at Schiphol Airport and at the border crossings with Germany and Belgium. Hotels tend to charge high commissions. *Verkoopt* means sell, while *Koopt* means buy.
Credit & debit cards: American Express, Diners Club, MasterCard and Visa are accepted, as well as Eurocheque cards. Check with your credit or debit card company for details of merchant acceptability and other services which may be available. ATMs are widely available.
Traveller's cheques: Widely accepted. To avoid additional exchange rate charges, travellers are advised to take traveller's cheques in Euros, Pounds Sterling or US Dollars.
Currency restrictions: There are no restrictions on the import and export of either local or foreign currency.
Banking hours: Mon 1300-1600; Tues-Fri 0900-1600. GWK offices are open seven days a week.
Exchange rate indicators:
Rate at time of publishing
£1.00= $1.46
$1.00= €0.82

Duty Free

The following goods may be imported into The Netherlands without incurring customs duty by travellers from non-EU European countries and countries outside of Europe:
200 cigarettes or 50 cigars or 100 cigarillos or 250g of tobacco; 1l of liquor or 2l of sparkling wine or liqueur wines and 2l of non-sparkling wine; 50g of perfume and 250ml of eau de toilette; 500g of coffee or 200g of coffee extract; 100g of tea or 40g of tea extract; other goods to the value of €175 (if bought outside Europe).
Note: (a) Goods must be purchased in non-EU countries. (b) The above allowances are only for travellers aged 17 years and above. (c) Enquiries concerning current import regulations should be made to the Royal Netherlands Embassy in the country of departure, or to the national Chamber of Commerce. (d) The import of firearms and ammunition requires a licence.
Abolition of duty free goods within the EU: On June 30 1999, the sale of duty free alcohol and tobacco at airports and at sea was abolished in all of the original 15 EU member states. Of the 10 new member states that joined the EU on May 1 2004, these rules already apply to Cyprus and Malta. There are transitional rules in place for visitors returning to one of the original 15 EU countries from one of the other new EU countries. But for the original 15, plus Cyprus and Malta, there are now no limits imposed on importing tobacco and alcohol products from one EU country to another (with the exceptions of Denmark, Finland and Sweden, where limits *are* imposed). Travellers should note that they may be required to prove at customs that the goods purchased are for personal use *only*.

Public Holidays

Below are listed Public Holidays for the January 2006-June 2007 period.
2006: Jan 1 New Year's Day. **Apr 14-17** Easter. **Apr 29** Queen's Day. **May 5** Liberation Day. **May 25** Ascension. **Jun 5** Whit Monday. **Dec 25** Christmas Day. **Dec 26** Boxing Day. **2007: Jan 1** New Year's Day. **Apr 6-9** Easter. **Apr 30** Queen's Day. **May 5** Liberation Day. **May 17** Ascension. **May 28** Whit Monday.

Health

	Special Precautions?	Certificate Required?
Yellow Fever	No	No
Cholera	No	No
Typhoid & Polio	No	N/A
Malaria	No	N/A

Note: *Regulations and requirements may be subject to change at short notice, and you are advised to contact your doctor well in advance of your intended date of departure. Any numbers in the chart refer to the footnotes below.*

Other risks: *Rabies* may be present in animals, although risk to travellers is very rare. For those at high risk, vaccination before arrival should be considered. If you are bitten, seek medical advice without delay. For more information, consult the *Health* appendix.

Health care: European Economic Area (EEA) and Switzerland: If you or any of your dependants are suddenly taken ill or have an accident during a visit to an EEA country or Switzerland, free or reduced-cost necessary treatment is available – in most cases on production of a valid European Health Insurance Card (EHIC). Each country has different rules about state medical provision. In some, treatment is free. In many countries you will have to pay part or all of the cost, and then claim a full or partial refund. The EHIC gives access to state-provided medical treatment only and the scheme gives no entitlement to medical repatriation costs, nor does it cover ongoing illnesses of a non-urgent nature, so comprehensive travel insurance is advised. Note that the EHIC replaces the Form E111, which will no longer be valid after 31 December 2005. Some restrictions apply, depending on your nationality.

Outside of the EU, The Netherlands has reciprocal health agreements with Cape Verde, Morocco, Serbia & Montenegro, Tunisia and Turkey. All other travellers are advised to take out full medical insurance. For police, fire or ambulance emergencies, dial 112 anywhere in the country. Make sure you see a doctor who is part of the health insurance scheme. Treatment is usually free. State dental care in the Netherlands is limited to treatment for children. Some prescribed medicines are free, for some you pay part of the cost, and for others you will have to pay the full cost. These charges are not refundable. Certain strong medicines can be taken to The Netherlands if they are accompanied by a doctor's prescription. Doctors will need authorisation from *AGIS Verzekeringen* for you to get free hospital in-patient treatment. If you cannot contact a doctor before being admitted, show the hospital authorities your European Health Insurance Card (EHIC) and ask them to contact *AGIS Verzekeringen* in Utrecht immediately. Ambulance travel is free only if a doctor agrees that it is necessary. The standard of health care (and other social services) is very high, with an unusually high proportion of the national income devoted to public health. More information can be obtained from *AGIS Verzekeringen*, PO Box 8261, 3503 RG Utrecht, The Netherlands (tel: (30) 233 0600).

Travel - International

AIR:

The national airline is *KLM-Royal Dutch Airlines (KLM)* (website: www.klm.com). *KLM* flies direct to all major European, North American and Asia-Pacific cities. Most major international airlines, and some low-cost carriers fly to Amsterdam.

Approximate flight times: From Amsterdam to *Belfast* is one hour; to *London* is one hour 20 minutes; to *Manchester* is one hour 15 minutes and to *New York* is seven hours (including stopover in London).

Main airports: *Amsterdam (AMS)* (Schiphol) (website: www.schiphol.nl) is 15km (9 miles) southwest of the city (travel time by train – 20 minutes). *To/from the airport*: KLM buses provide a daily service from 0600-0000 departing every 15 to 30 minutes, stopping at a selection of major hotels and returning to Schiphol. The Schiphol Hotel Shuttle operates between 0600-2100 and travels to almost all hotels in Amsterdam (tel: (0) 38 339 4741). There are many public buses available from the airport to major towns. There is a direct rail link between the airport and Amsterdam *Centraal Station*, with trains every 10 to 20 minutes from 0600-0000 and every hour through the night. Trains to *Zuid Station* (Amsterdam South) run every 15 minutes from 0525-0015; return is from *Zuid Station*, Parnassusweg/ Minervalaan (via tram no 5 from the city centre) from 0545-0040. There is also a service to the RAI Congress Centre every 15 minutes from 0525-0012. Return is from RAI station (via tram no 4 from the city centre) from 0545-0040. Plentiful taxis are available to the city.
Facilities: Restaurants, duty free shops, currency exchange machines (able to convert 17 different currencies), banks, an art gallery, baby rooms, showers, a business centre (with fax, personal computer and telephone facilities), conference rooms and car hire.
Rotterdam (RTM) (Zestienhoven) (website: www.rotterdam-airport.nl) is 8km (5 miles) northwest of the city (travel time – 15 minutes). *To/from the airport*: Bus no 33 departs every 10 minutes. Return is from Central Station (travel time – 20 minutes). Taxis to the city are also available.
Facilities: Restaurant, bank, outgoing duty free shop, wireless Internet, meeting facilities and car hire.
Eindhoven (EIN) (Welschap) (website: www.eindhovenairport.nl) is 8km (5 miles) from the city. *To/from the airport*: Coaches run every 15 minutes and taxis to the city are also available. Express buses run after each *Ryanair* flight (except those from London Stansted and Corendon Istanbul flights) to Amsterdam Central Station. *Facilities*: ATMs, restaurants, car rental, wireless Internet and outgoing duty free shops.
Maastricht (MST) (Aachen) (website: www.maa.nl) is 8km (5 miles) from the city. *To/from the airport*: From the Maastricht Aachen Airport bus stop, take bus no 61 (no 51 on Sundays) to Sittard Station and Maastrict Station.

Facilities: Restaurant, bar and outgoing duty free shop.
Groningen (GRQ) (Eelde) (website: www.groningenairporteelde.nl) is 9km (6 miles) from the city.
Enschede (ENS) (Twente) (website: www.enschede-airport.nl) is 8km (5 miles) from the city.
Departure tax: None.

SEA:

Main ports: Hook of Holland (*Hoek van Holland*), *Rotterdam* and *Vlissingen*. Regular car and passenger ferries are operated from the UK to The Netherlands via the following routes and shipping lines:
Stena Line (tel: (08705) 707 070; website: www.stenaline.co.uk): Harwich to Hook of Holland; travel time – three hours 40 minutes (day), six hours 15 minutes (night); four sailings daily.
P&O Ferries (tel: (08705) 202 020; website: www.ponsf.com): Hull to Rotterdam (Europoort); travel time – 12 hours; one sailing daily.
DFDS Seaways (tel: (08705) 333 000 (within the UK) *or* (01255) 240 240 (outside the UK); website: www.dfdsseaways.co.uk): Newcastle to Amsterdam; travel time – 16 hours.
Note: *Hoverspeed UK* and *P&O European Ferries* run services to The Netherlands via Belgium. French ports also provide connections.

RAIL:

Eurostar is a service provided by the railways of Belgium, the UK and France, operating direct high-speed trains from London (*Waterloo International*) to Paris (*Gare du Nord*) and to Brussels (*Midi/Zuid*). It takes two hours 40 minutes from London to Paris (via Lille) and two hours 20 minutes to Brussels. For further information and reservations, contact *Eurostar* (tel: (0870) 600 0792 (travel agents) or (08705) 186 186 (public; within the UK) or +44 (1233) 617 575 (public; outside the UK); a £5 booking fee applies to all telephone bookings; website: www.eurostar.com); *or Rail Europe* (tel: (08705) 848 848; website: www.raileurope.co.uk). *Thalys International* runs six daily trains (seven in summer) from Brussels to Amsterdam and other Dutch destinations.
Rail passes: The *Inter-Rail* pass offers unlimited second-class train travel in up to 29 European countries (includes Morocco and Turkey) split into eight zones (A-H). Three different tickets are available: a ticket covering one zone (two to six countries, 16 days' validity), a ticket covering two zones (six to 10 countries, 22 days' validity) and an *All Zone Pass* (29 countries, one month's validity). Ferry services between Italy and Greece are included. Passengers must be resident in Europe for at least six months before the pass is used. Travel is not allowed in the passenger's country of residence. Travellers under 26 years receive a reduction of about 30 per cent. Children's tickets are reduced by about 50 per cent. Supplements are required for some high-speed services, seat reservations and couchettes. Discounts are offered on *Eurostar* and some ferry routes. Available from *Inter Rail* (website: www.interrailnet.com). The *Eurailpass* offers unlimited first-class train travel in 17 European countries. Tickets are valid for 15 days, 21 days, one month, two months or three months. The *Eurailpass Saver* ticket offers discounts for two or more people travelling together. The *Eurailpass Youth* ticket is available to those aged under 26 and offers unlimited second-class train travel. The *Eurailpass Flexi* allows either 10 or 15 travel days within a two-month period. The *Eurail Selectpass* is valid in three, four or five bordering countries and allows five, six, eight or 10 travel days (or 15 for five countries) in a two-month period. The *Eurail Regional Pass* allows four to 10 travel days in a two-month period in one of nine regions (usually two or more countries). Children receive a 50 per cent reduction. The passes cannot be sold to residents of Europe, Turkey, Morocco, Algeria, Tunisia or the Russian Federation. Available from *The Eurail Group* (website: www.eurail.com).

ROAD:

The Netherlands is connected to the rest of Europe by a superb network of motorways. All roads are well signposted with green 'E' symbols indicating international highways, red 'A's indicating national highways, and smaller routes indicated by yellow 'N's. The national speed limit is 120kph (75mph). Although frontier formalities between The Netherlands, Germany and Belgium have now all but vanished, motorists – particularly on smaller roads – should be prepared to stop when asked to do so by a customs official. The yellow cars of the *ANWB/Wegenwacht* (Royal Dutch Touring Club) (tel: (70) 314 1420) patrol major roads 24 hours a day with qualified mechanics equipped to handle routine repairs. In case of emergencies, assistance is available (tel: 60888 within The Netherlands only).
The Channel Tunnel: *Eurotunnel* runs shuttle trains for cars, bicycles, motorcycles, coaches, minibuses, caravans, campervans and other vehicles over 1.85m (6.07ft) between Folkestone in Kent, with direct road access from the M20, and Calais, with links to the A16/A26 motorway (Exit 13). All road vehicles are carried through the tunnel in shuttle trains running between the two terminals. Terminals and shuttles are well-equipped for disabled passengers.

Passenger Terminal buildings contain a variety of shops, restaurants, bureaux de change and other amenities. The journey takes about 35 minutes from platform to platform and around one hour from motorway to motorway. There are up to four passenger shuttles per hour at peak times, 24 hours per day and services run every day of the year. Motorists pass through customs and immigration before they board, with no further checks on arrival. Fares are charged according to length of stay and time of year and whether or not you have a reservation. The price applies to the car, regardless of the number of passengers or size of the car. Promotional deals are frequently available, especially outside the peak holiday seasons. Tickets may be purchased in advance from travel agents, or from Eurotunnel Customer Services in France or the UK with a credit card. For further information, brochures and reservations, contact *Eurotunnel Customer Services UK*, Customer Relations Department, Saint Martin's Plain, Cheriton, Folkestone, Kent CT19 4QD (tel: (08705) 353 535; website: www.eurotunnel.com). For further information about departure times of shuttles at the French terminal, contact *Eurotunnel Customer Information* in Coquelles (tel: France +33 (3) 2100 6543).
Coach: *Eurolines* (52 Grosvenor Gardens, London SW1W 0AU; tel: (08705) 143 219; website: www.eurolines.com) and *National Express* (Ensign Court, 4 Vicarage Road, Edgbaston, Birmingham B15 3ES; tel: 08705 808 080; website: www.nationalexpress.com) run regular coach services from the UK to The Netherlands and other European cities.
Passes: Travellers can either choose Mini-Pass breaks or book a 15-, 30- or 60-day pass. The six Mini-Passes give travellers the freedom to visit three cities, with prices starting from £55. Travellers can stay as long as they like in each city. **Car hire:** Major companies can be found in all the main cities.

Travel - Internal

AIR:

KLM Cityhopper (WA) (website: www.klmcityhopper.nl) operates between seven airports in Holland. *Transavia Airlines (HV)* (website: www.transavia.com) (80 per cent of which is owned by KLM) also runs scheduled flights. *Martinair Holland (MP)* (website: www.martinair.com) operates passenger and cargo charter services. Enquire at KLM offices or at The Netherlands Board of Tourism for further information (see *Top Things To Do*).

SEA:

There are regular ferry services to the Wadden Islands (Ameland, Schiermonnikoog, Terschilling, Texel and Vlieland) across the Ijsselmeer (former Zuyder Sea) and Schelde Estuary. There is also a service to the Frisian Islands across the Waddenzee. *Boat Tours* runs excursions from Amsterdam, Arnhem, Delft, Giethoorn, Groningen, Maastricht, Rotterdam and Utrecht. Note: No cars are permitted to Vlieland.
Wadden Ticket: For travellers wanting to visit any of the five Wadden Islands, the Wadden Ticket allows return travel by bus, train and ferry to an island of choice. The pass is valid for one day of the departure journey and one day of the return journey, although the period between the two must not exceed one year. Contact The Netherlands Board of Tourism for further details (see *Top Things To Do*).

RAIL:

The highly developed rail network, of which about 70 per cent is electrified, is efficient and cheap, and connects all towns. Both intercity and local trains run at least half-hourly on all principal routes. Rail and bus timetables are integrated, and there is a common fare structure throughout the country. *NV Nederlandse Spoorwegen* (website: www.ns.nl) is the state-owned rail company and operates all lines within the country. Regional railway companies include Syntus (website: http://www.syntus.nl) and Noordned (website: http://www.arriva.nl).
Cheap fares: *Holland Rail Pass* allows unlimited travel in the Netherlands for either three or five days within one month. Reduced rates exist for senior citizens (over 60), travellers under 26 years and children. Every second person travels half-price. Tickets must be purchased from International Rail before travel.
Summer Trip Passes are available between July and August and give two people three days of unlimited travel within a period of 10 days for only a single fare. *Summer Trip Plus Passes* cover unlimited travel on all public transport buses and trams in town and country, and on the underground system in Amsterdam and Rotterdam. Tickets for two cost €69 (€49 per person).
Euro Passes are available for travel in The Netherlands, or The Netherlands and Belgium. Three- to eight-day passes are available. *The Benelux Tourrail Card* allows unlimited travel for any five days within a one-month period, covering The Netherlands, Belgium and Luxembourg. *Inter-Rail* passes are also valid in The Netherlands.

Children under four years of age travel free on all journeys within The Netherlands. *Child's Railrunner* tickets, which cost €1, are available for children aged between four and 11 years travelling with a fare-paying adult (19 years or older), and include up to three children travelling with any one adult. Contact the railway authority of any of the participating countries for prices and further information.

ROAD:

There is an excellent road system. Visitors to The Netherlands may use credit cards when obtaining petrol. The motoring association in The Netherlands is the *ANWB* (Royal Dutch Touring Club), PO Box 93200, 2509 BA The Hague (tel: (263) 860 249). **Bus:** Extensive regional bus networks exist. Long-distance coaches also operate between the cities, but costs are generally on a par with trains. **Taxi:** Taxis have an illuminated 'taxi' sign on the roof and there are taxi ranks at railway stations and at various other points in the cities. Rather than hailing taxis in the street, it is more usual in The Netherlands to order a taxi by phone. Taxis should have meters inside to indicate the fare, including the tip. Taxi Trains (*Treintaxis*) are taxis shared with others at a reduced price per person. These run between 59 railway stations. **Car hire:** Available from airports and main hotels. All European car hire companies are represented. **Bicycle hire:** Bicycles can be hired from all main railway stations, but must be returned to the station from which they are hired. A refundable deposit is required. **Driving regulations:** Driving is on the right. Drivers should be particularly aware of cyclists; often there are special cycle lanes. There is a chronic shortage of parking space in central Amsterdam, and the rush hours (0700-0900 and 1700-1900) should be avoided throughout the whole country. Parking fines are severe. Headlights should be dipped in built-up areas, but it is prohibited to use sidelights only. Children under 12 years of age should not travel in the front seat. Seat belts are compulsory. Speed limits are 80kph (50mph) on major roads, 120kph (75mph) on motorways and 50kph (30mph) in towns. **Documentation:** An International Driving Permit is not required, as long as a driving licence from the country of origin is held. EU pink format licences are accepted. However, it is sometimes advised for non-members of the EU. Trailers and caravans are allowed in without documents. A Green Card is advisable, but not compulsory. Without it, drivers with motor insurance policies in their home country are granted only the minimum legal cover in The Netherlands; the Green Card tops this up to the level of cover provided by the driver's own policy.

URBAN:

Public transport is very well developed in the cities and large towns. A *strippenkaart* national fares system exists – strips of 15 tickets each are widely available at railway stations, post offices and some tourist offices. These are accepted anywhere in payment of standard zonal fares. There are also individual and multi-day tickets for the cities. For more detailed information on travel within Amsterdam, The Hague and Rotterdam, see below. **Amsterdam:** The Amsterdam Card offers free travel on trains, buses, the subway and a 25 per cent discount on train tickets to Schiphol airport. Price per person is €33 for 24 hours, €43 for 48 hours and €53 for 72 hours. Amsterdam has an extensive network of buses, trams and underground (*GVB*), with frequent services from early morning to about midnight. There are less frequent services throughout the night at a higher fare. Full information on services (including a map), day tickets and *strippenkaart* (strip-tickets) can be obtained from the GVB office in front of the Central Station, the GVB Central Office at Prins Hendrikkade 108-114 or post offices, department stores and tobacconists. They can be purchased on board trams and buses but at a higher price. **Tram:** Amsterdam's 17 tram lines provide a fast, frequent and reliable service, making the tram the best way to travel around the capital. Trams operate from Mon-Fri 0600-2400 (from 0630 Saturday and 0730 Sunday). The tram system (as well as the buses and the underground) enables reasonably quick travel even during the busiest periods of the day. Trams leave from Central Station: 1 and 2 traverse the main canals, 19 takes a route to Museumplein and Concertgebouw and 9 and 14 to the Muziektheater and Waterlooplein market. The Circle Tram operates through central Amsterdam, taking in major attractions and hotels. **Underground:** Amsterdam's underground lines all originate at the Central Station and serve the southeastern business district and the suburbs. Trains run from Mon-Fri 0600-0015, from Sat 0630 and from Sun 0730. The GVB is easy to use. **Car hire:** The major European firms are represented. Cars can also be hired through most hotels. Parking regulations are quite strict and failure to park in prescribed areas or to pay the parking fee can result in a fine and the prospect of the car being clamped or towed away. **Water travel:** Canal Buses (every 25 to 45 minutes between Central Station and Rijksmuseum; children under the age of four travel free); Watertaxis (carrying eight to 44 passengers); Museum Boats (departing from Prins Hendrikkade every 30 minutes in summer and every 45 minutes in winter) and Waterbikes (for two to four people, with a route map provided) are all

available. **Boat hire:** Visitors can hire pedalos (also known as canal bikes) and boats to explore the canals. **Bicycle hire:** This is an excellent way to travel around Amsterdam, and it seems nearly everyone is doing it. Cycle lanes are clearly marked by white lines – but visitors are advised to watch out for trams, cars and pedestrians. There are numerous companies hiring out bikes.
Rotterdam: The city has excellent bus and tram services and a two-line underground network, which all work on a zonal system. Information is available from the Central Station. **Car hire:** The major European firms and other international agencies are represented.
The Hague: The Hague has bus and tram services. Information is available from the Central Station, Koningin Julianaplein. **Car hire:** The major firms are represented.
Travel Times: The following chart gives approximate travel times (in hours and minutes) from **Amsterdam** to other major cities in The Netherlands.

	Air	Road	Rail
The Hague	-	0.40	0.44
Rotterdam	-	1.00	1.00
Groningen	-	2.00	2.20
Maastricht	0.40	2.30	2.30
Eindhoven	0.30	1.30	1.25

Travel Advice

Most visits to The Netherlands are trouble-free but you should be aware of the global risk of indiscriminate international terrorist attacks, which could be against civilian targets, including places frequented by foreigners. This advice is based on information provided by the Foreign and Commonwealth Office in the UK. It is correct at time of publishing. As the situation can change rapidly, visitors are advised to contact the following organisations for the latest travel advice:

British Foreign and Commonwealth Office
Tel: (0845) 850 2829.
Website: www.fco.gov.uk

US Department of State
Website: http://travel.state.gov/travel

Accommodation

HOTELS:

The Netherlands has a wide range of accommodation, from luxury hotels in big towns to modern motels along motorways. The Netherlands Board of Tourism issues a shield to all approved hotels by which they can be recognised. This must be affixed to the front of the hotel in a conspicuous position. Hotels which display this sign conform to the official standards set by Dutch law on hotels, which protects the tourist and guarantees certain standards of quality. Hotels are also graded according to the *Benelux* system, in which the standard is indicated by a row of 3-pointed stars from the highest (**5-star**) to the minimum (**1-star**). However, membership of this scheme is voluntary, and there may be first-class hotels that are not classified in this way. For further information, contact The Netherlands Board of Tourism (see *Top Things To Do*).
GUEST HOUSES:

These are called *pensions* and rates vary. Book through local tourist offices.

BED & BREAKFAST:

Not as common a form of accommodation as it is in the UK.

SELF-CATERING:

Farmhouses for groups can be booked months in advance via the local tourist offices. Holiday chalets, especially in the relatively unknown parts of Zeeland, can be booked through the local tourist office. Bungalow parks throughout the country can be booked through The Netherlands Reserverings Centrum (NRC). Most bungalow resorts offer a full range of recreational facilities including swimming pools, golf and tennis. Prices depend on size, quality of amenities and the time of year. To order a self-catering brochure, call The Netherlands Board of Tourism (see *Top Things To Do*).
CAMPING/CARAVANNING:

There are some 2500 registered campsites in Holland. Only 500 offer advanced booking, the others operate on a first-come, first-served basis. Off-site camping is not permitted. Prices are fairly high and it is often far better value to stay more than one night. A list is available from The Netherlands Board of Tourism (see *Top Things To Do*) and reservations can be made through the Stichting Vrije Recreatie.
YOUTH HOSTELS:

There are around 30 hostels in various surroundings, from castles to modern buildings. People with a Hostelling International card receive a discount of €2.50 for an overnight stay including

breakfast. Information is obtainable from Stayokay (the Dutch Youth Hostel Association/Stichting Nederlandse Jeugdherberg Centrale).

ACCOMMODATION INFORMATION

The Netherlands Reservation Centre (NRC) (Netherlands Reserverings Centrum)
Plantsoengracht 2, 1441 DE Purmerend, The Netherlands
Tel: (299) 689 144.
Website: www.hotelres.nl

Bed & Breakfast Service Nederland (Online Reservations)
Website: www.bedandbreakfast.nl

Stichting Vrije Recreatie (Information on Camping/Caravanning)
Scr Broakseweg 75-77,
4231 VD Meerkerk, The Netherlands
Tel: (183) 352 741.
Website: www.svr.nl

Stayokay (the Dutch Youth Hostel Association/Stichting Nederlandse Jeugdherberg Centrale)
Tel: (10) 264 6064.
Website: www.stayokay.com

Top Things To See

• See the pretty **canals** of **Amsterdam**, the capital of The Netherlands (though not the seat of Government), and one of Europe's great destinations, as popular with tourists as it is with businesspeople. Amsterdam's lifeblood is water, which courses through the city in a concentric network of canals and waterways spanned by more than 1000 bridges. As Amsterdam is inextricably linked with water, one of the most attractive ways of viewing the city is on a canal tour. Many of the houses date back to The Netherlands' golden age in the 17th century. These narrow-fronted merchants' houses are characterised by the traditionally Dutch ornamented gables. The oldest part of the city is **Nieuwmarkt**, located near the first canals – **Herengracht**, **Keizersgracht** and **Prinsengracht** – built to protect the city against invasion. In the 17th century, Amsterdam gained a reputation for religious tolerance, which attracted thousands of Flemish, Walloon and French Protestants, as well as Jewish merchants from Spain, Portugal and Central Europe. In towns such as **Giethoorn** in the province of **Overijssel**, small canals take the place of streets, and all transport is by boat.
• The Netherlands provides a veritable feast for those artistically-inclined. In conjunction with The Netherlands having produced many great cultural figures, including artists such as Rembrandt and Van Gogh, Amsterdam alone boasts 53 museums, 61 art galleries, 12 concert halls and 20 theatres. A special canal boat (the 'museum boat') links 20 of the major museums. A special Museum Pass which entitles holders to free entry to over 400 museums is available from participating museums and local tourist offices. One of the city's cultural Meccas is the **Rijksmuseum**, a voluminous art gallery that is home to the works of many of the country's artistic luminaries, as well as numerous European masters. The highlight for many visitors is Dutch master Rembrandt's epic Night Watch, though the list of the gallery's treasures is almost endless. Van Gogh is also celebrated throughout the city, with the **Rembrandt House Museum**, housed in the historical building where the great artist used to live and work. The **Stedelijk Museum of Modern Art**, a collection of Dutch and international art from 1850 onwards, includes works by Cézanne, Chagall, Monet and Picasso, as well as photography, video, film and industrial design.
• See The Netherlands' many **tulips**; most spectacular glimpses of these flowers can be seen in **Haarlem**, 20km (12 miles) west of Amsterdam. Haarlem's surrounding countryside affords a fine view of the bulb fields from the end of March to mid-May. The town itself has a beautiful 16th- and 17th-century town centre and two fine museums. There is also a famous **Flower Auction** in Aalsmeer, open weekday mornings, the **Keukenhof Gardens**, which have a **lily show** in late May, and the renowned **fruit trees** of Boskoop, which is especially delightful during the blossom season.
There are also some spectacular flower markets in Amsterdam, such as the famous **Bloemenmarkt** along the **Singel canal**, which is a major tourist attraction. Delft and Utrecht also have lovely flower markets. Dutch flower bulbs are available for sale but it is essential to make sure the vendor sells them with an official export certificate. There are also various colourful flower parades (*corso*), notably the **Bollenstreek flower parade** (the country's biggest). Many parades display spectacular flower 'floats' made of hyacinths, daffodils and daliahs. The **Floriade**, held every 10 years in The Netherlands, is one of the world's most famous flower exhibitions. Last held in 2002 (from mid-

April to mid-October), the city of **Haarlemmermeer** hosted this prestigious horticultural event. Visitors may also visit one of the country's unique flower auctions, such as the **Flower Auction Holland** near The Hague and Rotterdam in the Westland.

- Explore the many churches of **Utrecht**, a city that is a favourite destination with the Dutch, offering Amsterdam's charms on a smaller scale without the tourist hordes that fill the capital for much of the year. During the Middle Ages, Utrecht was often an imperial residence, and the city's bishops regularly played an important role in the secular affairs of Europe. The city's prosperity allowed the construction of its beautiful churches, which include, in particular, the **Cathedral of St Michael** (13th century), **St Pieterskerk** and **St Janskerk** (both 11th century) and **St Jacobkerk** (12th century). The best way to explore Utrecht is by canal boat, which takes visitors on a loop of the city that opens up its different districts.
- See the seat of the Dutch Government, home to over 60 foreign embassies, the International Court of Justice and the capital of the province of **Zuid-Holland**: **The Hague**. The central part of the **Old Town** is the **Binnenhof**, an irregular group of buildings surrounding an open space. Walking around the old parts of town is a joy in itself – the local tourist office publishes a map that opens up the city and also includes most of the many antique shops in The Hague. The **Parliament Buildings** and **Knight's Hall** are 13th-century buildings where there are regular tours and slide shows that illuminate their history, while the **Royal Cabinet of Paintings**, housed in the **Mauritshuis**, is a collection that includes the *Anatomical Lesson of Dr Tulp* by Rembrandt, and other 17th-century Dutch works.
- Watch the **windmills** of **Kinderdijk**, which can be visited during the week. **Leiden**, 20km (12 miles) northeast of The Hague, 40km (25 miles) north of Rotterdam), was not only the birthplace of Rembrandt, a famous weaving town during the Middle Ages, and a large-part player in the wars of independence against Spain in the 16th century, but also boasts one of the most charming windmills in the country, set in a park overlooking water.
- If you decide to explore The Netherlands' maritime history, your first stop should be **Rotterdam**. Rotterdam is Europe's largest and, indeed, the world's second-largest, port and is the hub of the Dutch economy, but it is now also emerging as a tourist destination in its own right. Much of the city was obliterated during World War II, and only small parts of the old city remain. The best place to get an idea of the city layout is from the viewing level of the **Euromast & Space Tower**, which at 185m (605ft) is the highest point in The Netherlands. Rotterdam's pride in its maritime heritage is on show at the **Maritiem Museum Prins Hendrik**, where outdoor and indoor exhibits include ships, barges, harbour cranes and marine archaeological artefacts. Regular boat tours also now take tourists around the city's abundance of channels and waterways. Boat tours (*Spido*) through the harbour of Rotterdam are available throughout the year. In the summer, there are excursions to **Europoort**, the **Delta Project**, as well as evening tours, and there are also luxury motor cruisers for hire. A drive through the harbour of Rotterdam is also possible; the 100 to 150km (60- to 90-mile) journey takes in almost every aspect of this massive harbour. The route passes wharves and warehouses, futuristic grain silos and loading equipment, cranes and bridges, oil refineries, powerstations and lighthouses, all of which create a skyline of awesome beauty, particularly at sunset. The docks, waterways, canals and ports-within-ports are interspersed with some surprising and apparently incongruous features; at one point the route passes a garden city built for shipyard workers, while further on there is a village and, at the harbour's westernmost point, a beach. A visit to **Rotterdam harbour** is recommended. Other interesting places to visit include the 17th-century houses in the Delfshaven quarter of the city; the **Pilgrimskerk**; collections of maps and seacharts at the **Delfshaven Old Town Hall**; many traditional workshops for pottery, watchmaking and woodturning. Rotterdam has also become something of a Mecca for designers and architects, who have flocked to the city to take part in its massive rebuilding programme, and their work is often showcased both in the buildings they create and also in temporary exhibits. Today, the waterfront is increasingly being transformed into a leisure oasis.
- See the largest Cathedral in the country, **St Jan's Cathedral** in **'s-Hertogenbosch** (non-Dutch speaking visitors will welcome the use of 'Den Bosch' as a widely accepted abbreviation).
- Visit the province of **Zeeland**'s several medieval harbour towns, where some of the best seafood in Europe can be found. Most of the province lies below sea level and has been reclaimed from the sea. The region also includes several islands and peninsulas in the southwest Netherlands (Walcheren, Goeree-Overflakkee, Schouwen-Duiveland, Tholen, St Filipsland and North and South Beveland). The small town of Veere, 8km (5 miles) to the north, retains many buildings from its golden age in the early 16th century. The North Sea port of **Flushing** (**Vlissingen**) is, for many British travellers arriving by boat, their first sight of The Netherlands. It is also the country's first town in another sense; in 1572 it became the first place to fly the free Dutch flag during the War of Independence.

Top Things To Do

- The Netherlands is rightly known as 'the land of bicycles': around 15 million Dutch people regularly travel by bicycle and there are an estimated 12 million cycles in use. The popularity of **cycling** is perhaps mainly due to the country's geography: distances between the cities are short and the countryside is almost totally flat, except for a few rolling hills in the east and south (the highest of which is a mere 321m/1053ft). Not surprisingly, cycling facilities are outstanding and there are approximately 17,000km (10,625 miles) of special cycling lanes and paths available. Detailed cycling maps (recommended) can be obtained for every province from local tourist information offices; as well as indicating cycling routes and tracks, the maps provide route descriptions and guides. Cycling lanes are recognisable by a round blue sign with a white bicycle in the middle. Most itineraries are circular routes, starting and ending at the same place. The province of **Gelderland** has the highest number of marked cycling routes. Landscapes vary from spectacular dunes (on the **Duinroute** in the north of the country) to wilderness and forests (on the route across the **Hoge Veluwe nature reserve** in the Gelderland Valley). Long-distance routes (such as the 270km (169-mile) North Sea route LF1 between the Belgian border and the northern Dutch town of **Den Helder**) are also available. Bicycles can be hired virtually everywhere and a list of local hire companies is available from The Netherlands Board of Tourism (see *Tourist Information*). The Netherlands Railways also offer bike-rental vouchers, which can be bought at railway ticket offices. Vouchers can be used at bicycle depots at over 100 train stations throughout the country. Over 300 stations offer the facility to take bicycles onto the train. The classic Dutch upright single-speed hub-brake bicycle is the most frequent, but other types of bicycles (including mountain bikes, children's bicycles and tandems) are also available.
- In The Netherlands, **walking** holidays are also very popular; the 300km- (188 mile-) long coast has a number of scenic walks through sand dunes and nature reserves. Visitors can obtain maps with walking routes from the Foundation for Long Distance Walks (Stitching Lange-Afstand-Wandelpadsen), PO Box 846, 3800 AV Amersfoort (tel: (33) 465 3660). Visitors can also join the annual six-day walking event (beginning of August), where participants walk from Hook of Holland to Den Helder. At **Wadden Sea National Park** (Europe's largest continuous national park), there is also the opportunity to take part in various types of mud walking trips on the bottom of the Wadden sea, whose shallows fall dry at low tide.
- Party hard in Amsterdam, justifiably famous for its nightlife. Within a few blocks, well-heeled couples idle away an evening in a canal-side gourmet restaurant, and a group of backpackers stumble across the cobbles after a night in a cheery pub, as just around the corner the local trendies pose their way through an evening in a new-style bar. Then there is the **Opera House**, the string of concert venues, the football stadium, some of Europe's best nightclubs and the jazz cafes, to name a few other nocturnal pastimes in Amsterdam. And, of course, there are the other ways to spend an evening, either exploring the infamous coffee shops of a city where soft drugs are not only allowed, but are sold over the counter, and the **Red Light District**, a nefarious playground where all sorts of characters mingle with the curious and the downright bizarre. Wherever tourists spend their evening, there is the same relaxed, live-and-let-live ambience of a city where almost anything goes.
- Throughout The Netherlands are frequent markets, ranging from farmer's produce to knick-knacks. Amongst the best include a famous **cheese market** at **Waagplein**, open every Friday from mid-April to mid-September and another famous cheese market at **Gouda**, 20km (12 miles) southeast of Rotterdam.

TOURIST INFORMATION

Netherlands Board of Tourism & Conventions (NBTC) in the UK
PO Box 30783, London WC2B 6DH, UK
Tel: (020) 7539 7950 *or* (09068) 717 777 (brochure line; calls cost 60p per minute).
Website: www.holland.com/uk

Netherlands Board of Tourism & Conventions (NBTC) in the USA
355 Lexington Avenue, 19th Floor, New York, NY 10017, USA
Tel: (212) 370 7360.
Website: www.holland.com

Entertainment

FOOD & DRINK: There are few dishes that can be described as quintessentially Dutch, and those that do fall into this category are a far cry from the elaborate creations of French or Italian cuisine. Almost every large town, however, has a wide range of restaurants specialising in their own brands of international dishes including American, Balkan, British, Chinese, French, German, Italian and Spanish. Indonesian cuisine, a result of the Dutch colonisation of the East Indies, with its use of spices and exotic ingredients, is particularly delicious. Restaurants usually have table service. Bars and cafes generally have the same, though some are self-service. There are no licensing laws and drink can be bought all day. Bars open later and stay open until the early hours of the morning at weekends.

National specialities:

- A typical Dutch breakfast usually consists of several varieties of bread, thin slices of Dutch cheese, prepared meats and sausage, butter and jam or honey and often a boiled egg.
- A working lunch would be *koffietafel*, once again with breads, various cold cuts, cheese and conserves. There will often be a side dish of omelette, cottage pie or salad.
- *Broodjes* (sandwiches) are a common daytime snack, served in the sandwich bars – *broodjeswinkels*.
- Lightly salted 'green' herring can be bought from street stalls (they are held by the tail and slipped down into the throat).
- *Erwtensoep* (thick pea soup served with smoked sausage, cubes of bacon, pig's knuckle and brown or white bread).
- *Groentensoep* (clear consommé with vegetables, vermicelli and meatballs).
- *Hutspot* (potatoes, carrots and onions).
- *Klapstuk* (an accompaniment of stewed lean beef).
- *Boerenkool met rookworst* (frost-crisped kale and potatoes served with smoked sausage).
- Seafood dishes are often excellent, particularly in Amsterdam or Rotterdam, and include *gebakken zeetong* (fried sole), *lekkerbekjes* (fried whiting), royal imperial oysters, shrimps, mussels, lobster and eel (smoked, filleted and served on toast or stewed or fried).
- *Flensjes* or *pannekoeken* (25 varieties of Dutch pancake) are a favourite Dutch dessert.
- *Wafels met slagroom* (waffles with whipped cream).
- *Offertje* (small dough balls fried and dusted with sugar).
- *Spekkoek* (alternate layers of heavy buttered sponge and spices from Indonesia), which translated means 'bacon cake'.

National drinks:

- Coffee, tea, chocolate and fruit juice are drunk at breakfast.
- The local spirit is *jenever* (Dutch gin), normally taken straight and chilled as a chaser with a glass of beer, but it is sometimes drunk with cola or vermouth; Favoured brands are *Bols*, *Bokma*, *Claeryn* and *De Kuyper*.
- Dutch beer is excellent. It is a light, gassy *pils* type beer, always served chilled, generally in small (slightly under half a pint) glasses. The most popular brand in Amsterdam is *Amstel*. Imported beers are also available, as are many other alcoholic beverages.
- Dutch liqueurs are excellent and include *Curaçao*, *Parfait d'Amour*, *Triple Sec* (similar to Cointreau) and Dutch-made versions of crème de menthe, apricot brandy and anisette.

Tipping: All hotels and restaurants include 15 per cent service and VAT. It is customary to leave small change when paying a bill. €0,5-1,00 is usual for porters and doormen, and around 10 per cent for taxi drivers and waiters. Hairdressers and barbers have inclusive service prices.

NIGHTLIFE: Large cities have sophisticated nightclubs and discos, but late opening bars and cafes are just as popular in provincial towns. There are theatres and cinemas in all major towns. Amsterdam is a cosmopolitan city, with some of the liveliest nightlife in Europe. There are legal casinos in Amsterdam, Breda, Eindhoven, Den Haag, Groningen, Nijmegen, Rotterdam, Scheveningen, Valkenburg and Zandvoort; all have an age limit of 'over 18' (passports must be shown).

SHOPPING: Special purchases include Delft (between The Hague and Rotterdam) blue pottery and pottery from Makkum and Workum, costume dolls, silverware from Schoonhoven, glass and crystal from Leerdam and diamonds from Amsterdam. **Shopping hours**: Mon 1100-1800; Tues-Fri 0900-1800; Sat 0900-1700. In Amsterdam, Rotterdam and other big cities, supermarkets are open from 0800-2000/2100. In large city centres, shops are open Sun 1200-1700. Shopping malls are also open on Sunday. Some cities also have late-night shopping on Thursdays or Fridays.

Note: Bulbs and plants may not be exported except by commercial growers, or by individuals with a health certificate from the Plant Disease Service. A reasonable number of bulbs for own personal use are allowed.

Business

- **GDP:** US$606.7 billion (OECD, 2004).
- **Main exports:** Machinery and equipment, chemicals, fuels and foodstuffs.
- **Main imports:** Machinery and transport equipment, chemicals, fuels, foodstuffs and clothes.
- **Main trade partners:** EU countries (mainly Germany, France, UK and Belgium).

ECONOMY: The Netherlands has a typical developed European economy. It is also the world's third-largest exporter of farm produce (after the USA and France), accounting for 16 per cent of total export earnings. Dairy products, meat, vegetables and flowers are the main products. Industry is concentrated in petrochemicals and plastics, pharmaceuticals, synthetic fibres and food processing. There is also a wide range of light industries, including the manufacturing of electronic goods, although the historically strong textiles has been in long-term decline. By contrast, The Netherlands has developed a strong base in advanced technological industries including computing, telecommunications and biotechnology. Deposits of natural gas (the only mineral resource of any size) meet much of the country's energy needs. Service industries are also important, representing 70 per cent of the economy, notably transport through the world's busiest container port at Rotterdam. The Netherlands has derived substantial benefits from its membership of the EU, with whose members the bulk of its trade takes place. It has generally been a strong proponent of further economic integration within Europe and joined the Eurozone upon its inception in January 1999. In 2003, the government was forced to increase taxes and cut spending in order to stay within the limits imposed by Maastricht criteria which govern the operation of the Eurozone. The global economic slow-down which took hold in 2001 reduced annual GDP growth to 1.5 per cent, and in the following year to just 0.2 per cent. In 2003, the Dutch economy contracted but in 2004 growth improved to 1.2 per cent. Inflation has declined from 5.1 per cent in 2001 to its present level of 1.25 per cent; unemployment has climbed gently to 6.75 per cent. The Netherlands is a founder member of the Benelux Economic Union and of the European Bank for Reconstruction and Development.

Appointments are necessary and visiting cards are exchanged. The Dutch expect a certain standard of dress for business occasions. Best months for business visits are March to May and September to November. Practical information can be obtained from the Economic Information Service in The Hague (tel: (70) 379 8933; website: www.hollandtrade.com). The majority of Dutch businesspeople speak extremely good English, and promotional literature can be disseminated in English. However, interpreters can be booked through Conference Interpreters, Jan van Goyenkade 11, NL-1075 HP Amsterdam (tel: (20) 625 2535; website: www.conferenceinterpreters.com). Alternatively, they can be booked through The Netherlands Chamber of Commerce in the country of departure. (There are Netherlands-British Chambers of Commerce in London, Manchester and The Hague, and Netherlands-US Chambers of Commerce in New York and Chicago.) There are also many secretarial agencies in The Netherlands, such as International Secretaries, who will be able to supply short-term help to visiting business travellers. The principal venue for trade fairs is the RAI Exhibition Centre in Amsterdam. **Office hours**: Mon-Fri 0830-1700.

CONFERENCES/CONVENTIONS: The largest conference and exhibition centres are RAI in Amsterdam and the Jaarbeurs in Utrecht. There are smaller centres in The Hague, Rotterdam and Maastricht, as well as many hotels with facilities. The fourth-largest conference centre in The Netherlands is Noordwijk, where the largest hotel has a helipad; this small seaside town has won prizes for its clean beaches. Amsterdam and The Hague both have business centres. For further information, contact The Netherlands Board of Tourism in London (see *Top Things To Do*).

COMMERCIAL INFORMATION

The Hague Chamber of Commerce and Industry
Konigskade 30, 2502 LS Gravenhage,
The Hague, The Netherlands
Tel: (70) 328 7100.
Website: www.denhaag.kvk.nl

Amsterdam Chamber of Commerce and Industry
De Ruyterkade 5, 1000 CW Amsterdam,
The Netherlands
Tel: (20) 531 4000.
Website: www.amsterdam.kvk.nl

The Netherlands Chamber of Commerce in the UK
Imperial House, 7th floor, 15-19 Kingsway,
London WC2B 6UN, UK
Tel: (020) 7539 7960.
Website: www.nbcc.co.uk

The Hague Convention Bureau
PO Box 85456, 2508 CD The Hague, The Netherlands
Tel: (70) 361 8888.
E-mail: conventionbureau@spdh.net

New Caledonia

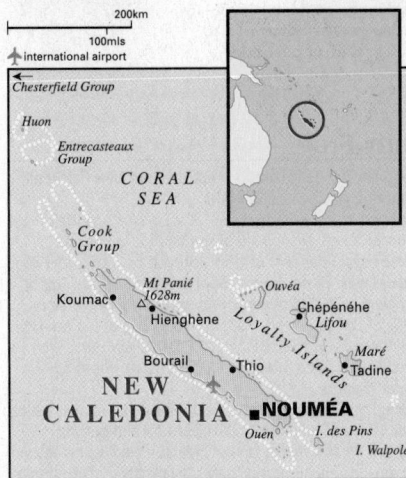

Location: South Pacific.

Time: GMT + 11.

Overview

New Caledonia is the third largest island in the Pacific Region after Papua New Guinea and New Zealand and has been a French colony since 1853. It became a French Overseas Territory in 1946. From time to time, attempts have been made by the indigenous population to free themselves from French rule. The most serious of these was the Kanak Revolt of 1878. In recent years, intermittent conflicts have flared up between the Melanesians and the French, reflecting the widely differing attitudes that exist towards the various plans for self-government. In France itself, the traditional consensus between Gaullists and Socialists on colonial matters has broken down as regards New Caledonia, although both parties recognise the strategic importance of the island for nuclear testing.

Unlike its volcanic neighbours, New Caledonia is a fragment of an ancient continent which drifted away some 250 million years ago. Its flora and fauna evolved in isolation, and are now quite unique: 3500 recorded species of plants, three quarters of which occur only here; 4300 species of land animals, 1000 species of fish and 6500 species of marine invertebrates. New Caledonia offers an endless variety of landscapes, from some of the best white sand beaches in the Pacific to spectacular mountain retreats. Surrounded by a 1600km- (1000 mile-) long coral reef, New Caledonia also boasts the largest lagoon in the world. The reef can be as close as a few kilometres from the coast in some places and as far as 65km (41 miles) in others - with an average depth of 40m (131ft).

General Information

AREA: 18,575 sq km (7172 sq miles).
POPULATION: 220,000 (official estimate 2000).
POPULATION DENSITY: 10.6 per sq km.
CAPITAL: Nouméa. **Population:** 196,836 (1996).
GEOGRAPHY: New Caledonia consists of the Mainland, the Isle of Pines to the south of the Mainland, the Loyalty Islands to the east of the Mainland (Maré, Lifou, Tiga and Ouvéa), the Belep Archipelago in the northwest, and numerous islands and islets (Huon & Surprise, Christfield, Walpole, Beautémps-Beaupré, Astrolabe and the Bellona reef); a total surface area of 19,000 sq km (16,372 for the Mainland alone, which is 400km long). The Mainland is divided by a range of mountains (Chaîne

Centrale), the highest points of which are Mount Pancé in the north (1629m) and Mount Humboldt in the south (1618m). Various species of trees can be found here. This unusual relief divides the Grande Terre/Mainland into the East coast (humid and open to trade winds; fertile and exotic with lush tropical vegetation) from the West coast (dry and temperate; filled with *niaouli* trees, cattle and beautiful beaches).
GOVERNMENT: French Overseas Territory since 1957.
Head of State: President Jacques Chirac, represented locally by High Commissioner Daniel Constantin since 2002. **Head of Government:** Marie-Noelle Themereau since 2004. **Recent history:** A referendum on independence was held in November 1998 and produced a vote of 70 per cent in favour of independence. However, since then, the two main parties and the French Government have been engaged in a complex and often devious political struggle, which has persuaded many Kanaks (Melanesians) that Paris had no intention of allowing the colony to become independent. Moreover, during the 1990s, New Caledonia's economic difficulties led to a growth of labour unrest and the assumption by local trade unions of the major role in the campaign to reform New Caledonia's social and economic system and achieve independence. The present Government is headed by Marie-Noelle Themereau, from the anti-independence Avenir Ensemble (Future Together) party, who was elected President in June 2004.
LANGUAGE: French is the official language, but there are approximately 30 different Melanesian languages. English and Japanese are also widely spoken.
RELIGION: Vast Christian majority, with 59 per cent Roman Catholic.
ELECTRICITY: 220 volts AC, 50Hz. European-style, two-pin plugs are in use.
SOCIAL CONVENTIONS: There is a casual atmosphere, and local traditions still prevail alongside European customs. Casual wear is the norm, but smart restaurants require a more formal style of dress. Long trousers are required for men at night in restaurants and casinos.

Climate

Warm, subtropical climate. The cool season is from April to August and the hottest period is from September to March. The main rains are between January and March. The seasons are less defined on the east coast than the west. Climate is tempered by trade winds.
Required clothing: Tropical lightweights, with jackets and sweatshirts for evenings.

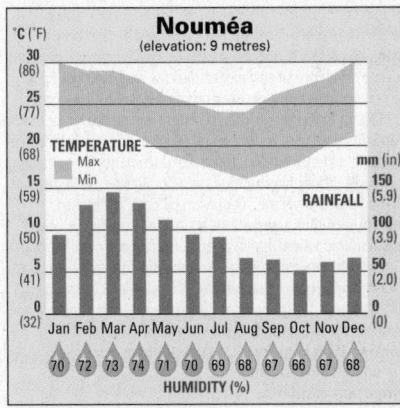

Communications

Telephone: IDD is available. Country code: 687. There is a 24-hour service for international calls. International calls are bookable at the post office (0745-1115 and 1215-1530) or through hotels. Most hotels have direct dial facilities.
Mobile telephone: Roaming agreements exist with some international mobile phone companies.
Internet: Public access is available in several Internet cafes and at 'cyber points' (computers available for public use in local businesses/ISPs).
Post: Airmail to Western Europe takes up to one week. The post office, located on rue Eugène Porcheron, is open Mon-Fri 0745-1115 and 1215-1530.
MEDIA: Press: Newspapers are published in French and include *Les Nouvelles Calédoniennes* (daily) and *L'Hebdo*, *Les Infos* and *Télé 7 Jours* (weekly).
TV: *RFO Nouvelle Caledonie* is a public channel. *Canal+ Caledonie* is a pay TV service.
Radio: *RFO Nouvelle Caledonie* is publicly-run, while private stations include *NRJ Nouvelle Caledonie*, *Radio Djiido* and *Radio Rythme Blue*.

Passport/Visa

	Passport Required?	Visa Required?	Return Ticket Required?
Full British	Yes	No	No
Australian	Yes	No	No
Canadian	Yes	No	No
USA	Yes	No	No
Other EU	Yes/1	No	No
Japanese	Yes	No	No

Note: Regulations and requirements may be subject to change at short notice, and you are advised to contact the appropriate diplomatic or consular authority before finalising travel arrangements. Any numbers in the chart refer to the footnotes below.

PASSPORTS: Passport valid for at least six months, except for the following:
1. nationals of Belgium, Germany, Greece, Italy, Luxembourg, Monaco, The Netherlands, Portugal, Spain and Switzerland, who are holders of national identity cards.
VISAS: Required by all except the following:
(a) nationals of the EU (except **1.** nationals of the Czech Republic, Estonia, Latvia and Lithuania who *do* require a visa) and nationals of Andorra, Chile, Iceland, Liechtenstein, New Zealand, Norway, St Maarten, Switzerland and the Vatican City;
(b) nationals of Argentina, Bermuda, Brunei, Croatia, Malaysia, Mexico, Uruguay and Venezuela for stays of up to one month;
(c) transit passengers continuing their journey by the same or first connecting aircraft, provided holding valid onward or return documentation and not leaving the airport.
Types of visa and cost: All visas, regardless of duration of stay and number of entries permitted, cost €35. In most circumstances, no fee applies to students, recipients of Government fellowships and citizens of the EU and their family members.
Validity: *Short-stay* (up to 30 days): valid for two months (single- and multiple-entry). *Short stay* (31 to 90 days and double- or multiple-entry): valid for a maximum of six months from date of issue. *Transit*: valid for single- or multiple-entries of maximum five days per entry, including the day of arrival.
Application to: French consulate General (for personal visas), or consular section at Embassy (for diplomatic or service visas); see *Passport/Visa Information* for France. All applications must be made in person.
Application requirements: (a) Valid passport with blank page to affix the visa. Minors travelling alone must submit notarised parental authorisation, signed by both parents, plus one copy. (b) Up to two completed application forms. (c) One passport-size photo on each form. (d) Fee, to be paid in cash only if paying by person. If not, fee should be paid by cheque or postal order. (e) Evidence of sufficient funds for stay (two last bank statements, plus copy, or other proof of funds equivalent to US$100 for each day of trip). (f) Letter from employer, or proof of stay in country of residence. (g) Proof of address. (h) Medical insurance. (i) Return ticket and travel documents for remaining journey. (j) Proof of accommodation during stay. (k) Registered self-addressed envelope, if applying by post. (l) Detailed itinerary, including reservations and round-trip airline tickets (only required when visa is issued), plus one copy. (m) Proof of employment (eg last payslip or letter from employer). (n) Proof of valid health/travel insurance with worldwide coverage, plus copy. *Business*: (a)-(n) and, (o) Business invitation guaranteeing payment of travel expenses, plus one copy.
Working days required: One day to three weeks, depending on nationality.
Temporary residence: If intending to work or stay for longer than 90 days, nationals should contact the Long Stay visa section of the French Consulate General or Embassy (tel: (020) 7073 1248). Nationals of the EU may gain long-stay status in New Caledonia on the condition that they have independent means and are self-employed (proof must be submitted).

PASSPORT/VISA INFORMATION

Office of the High Commissioner
Street address: 1 avenue du Maréchal Foch, Nouméa, New Caledonia
Postal address: BP C5, 98848 Nouméa, New Caledonia
Tel: 266 300.
Website: www.etat.nc

Money

Currency: French Pacific Franc (XPF). Notes are in denominations of XPF10,000, 5000, 1000 and 500. Coins are in denominations of XPF100, 50, 20, 10, 5, 2 and 1. New Caledonia is part of the French Monetary Area. Australian and New Zealand dollars are widely accepted in shops, hotels and restaurants. The French Pacific Franc is tied to the Euro. For further details on the Euro, see *France* section.
Currency exchange: Exchange facilities are available at the airport and at main branches of banks, but may charge a steep commission. ATMs are available in Nouméa, but sometimes have a maximum weekly withdrawal limit.
Credit & debit cards: American Express and Visa are widely accepted; Diners Club and MasterCard have more limited use. Check with your credit or debit card company for details of merchant acceptability and other services which may be available.
Traveller's cheques: To avoid additional exchange rate charges, travellers are advised to take traveller's cheques in Euros. There is, however, a charge of XPF515, including tax, for each transaction.
Currency restrictions: Any amount of money in excess of XPF909,000, being carried by a person in their baggage, must be declared to customs. This does not engender supplementary costs.
Banking hours: Mon-Fri 0730-1545.
Exchange rate indicators:

Rate at time of publishing	
£1.00=	XPF1.48
$1.00=	XPF0.84

Duty Free

The following goods may be imported into New Caledonia without incurring customs duty:
200 cigarettes or 50 cigars or 100 cigarillos or 250g of tobacco; 2l of wine plus 1l of spirits and liquors not exceeding 22 per cent alcohol content, or 2l of spirits and liquors with 22 per cent alcohol content or less; 50ml of perfume or 250ml of eau-de-toilette; 500g of coffee or 200g of coffee essence; 100g of tea or 50g of tea essence; other goods up to a value of XPF30,000 per passenger aged 15 years and older, and XPF15,000 for those aged under 15 years.
Note: Those importing duty free alcohol and tobacco must be aged 18 years and older. If taking personal and everyday goods, such as cameras, tape recorders and radios, it is advised to carry documents providing legal justification of ownership.
Prohibited items: Plants, flowers, seeds and earth (except on import permit); meat and other animal products (except with prescribed sanitary certificate).

Public Holidays

Below are listed Public Holidays for the January 2006-June 2007 period.
2006: Jan 1 New Year's Day. **Apr 17** Easter Monday. **May 1** Labour Day. **May 8** 1945 Victory Day. **May 25** Ascension. **Jul 14** Bastille Day. **Aug 15** Assumption. **Sep 24** New Caledonia Day. **Nov 1** All Saints' Day. **Nov 11** Armistice Day. **Dec 25** Christmas Day. **Dec 31** New Year's Eve.
2007: Jan 1 New Year's Day. **Apr 9** Easter Monday. **May 1** Labour Day. **May 8** 1945 Victory Day. **May 17** Ascension.

Health

	Special Precautions?	Certificate Required?
Yellow Fever	No	1
Cholera	No	2
Typhoid & Polio	3	N/A
Malaria	No	N/A

Note: Regulations and requirements may be subject to change at short notice, and you are advised to contact your doctor well in advance of your intended date of departure. Any numbers in the chart refer to the footnotes below.

1: A yellow fever vaccination certificate is required from travellers over one year of age arriving from infected areas.
2: Travellers arriving from infected areas do not require cholera vaccination and will not be given chemoprophylaxis. They are required, however, to fill out a form for use by the Health Service.
3: Typhoid is reported. Visitors may wish to ensure up-to-date polio vaccinations have been administered prior to travel.
Food & drink: Mains water is normally chlorinated and generally regarded as safe to drink. Bottled water is available and is advised for the first few weeks of the stay. Milk is pasteurised and dairy products are safe for consumption. Local meat, poultry, seafood, fruit and vegetables are considered safe to eat.
Other risks: *Hepatitis A* and *C* occur and *hepatitis B* is endemic. *Dengue fever* occurs. Immunisations against *diphtheria*, *tuberculosis* and *tetanus* are sometimes advised.
Health care: New Caledonia offers a wide range of efficient medical services in both public and private hospitals, and an adequate selection of chemists. Hotels can generally recommend an English-speaking doctor or dentist. Health insurance is advised.

Travel - International

AIR:
The national airline is *Aircalin (Air Calédonie International) (SB)*. Other airlines serving New Caledonia include *Air New Zealand*, *KLM* and *Qantas*. The *Oceania Pass* is available in Economy class on the *Aircalin* network within the Southwest Pacific, but is limited to non-residents, and must be purchased prior to departure (for details and conditions, see website: www.aircalin.nc). Air travel is by far the easiest and most rapid means of transport to New Caledonia.
Approximate flight times: From Nouméa to *London* is 26 hours, including stopovers, but this may increase to 30 hours, depending on the day of travel; to *Los Angeles* is 18 hours (via Tahiti); to *Sydney* is two hours 30 minutes.
Main airports: *Nouméa (NOU)* (La Tontouta) is 50km (31 miles) from the city (travel time – 45 minutes). *To/from the airport:* Taxi and coach services are available to the city. It is advisable to book transfers before arrival in New Caledonia. *Facilities:* Post office, bureau de change, duty-free shops (available for scheduled flights), bar, restaurant and car hire.
Departure tax: None.
SEA:
International port is *Nouméa*, served by shipping lines including *CTC*, *P&O* and *Princess Cruises*.

Travel - Internal

AIR:
Domestic flights are run by *Air Calédonie (TY)* (website: www.air-caledonie.nc), maintaining regular services from Nouméa to airfields on the island, and the other smaller islands. The principal local airport is *Magenta Airport*, 6km (4 miles) from Nouméa city centre. From here, *Air Calédonie* operates regular flights to Touho (east coast), Koné, Koumac, Belep (west coast), and to the neighbouring Ile des Pins and the Loyalty Islands: Maré, Ouvéa, Lifou and Tiga. The airport has been extended in order to increase capacity. Light aircraft and helicopters are available from *Air Alizé*, *Aviazur*, *Helicocean* and *Helitourisme*.
Approximate flight times: From Nouméa to *Ile des Pins* is 25 minutes; to *Lifou* is 40 minutes; to *Maré* is 40 minutes; to *Ouvéa* is 40 minutes; to *Tiga* is one hour 25 minutes (including stopover); to *Koné* is 45 minutes; to *Touho* is 45 minutes; to *Koumac* is one hour five minutes and to *Belep* is one hour 45 minutes (including stopover).
SEA:
An inter-island, high-speed catamaran 'Betico' runs regularly to Ile des Pins and Loyalty Islands from Grande Terre; for further details, contact *Armement Loyaltien*, Quai des Caboteurs, Centre Ville, BP 2217-98845, Nouméa Cedex (tel: 260 100; fax: 289 897). Boats can be hired or chartered to visit smaller islands.
ROAD:
The road network consists of 5000km (3125 miles) of paved and unpaved roads. Traffic drives on the right. Petrol costs the same at all petrol stations.
Bus: Buses are available throughout the island. There are regular services in Nouméa which run every 15 to 30 minutes from 0500-1900. The Green Line travels between Kuendu Beach, the city centre and other beach resorts. The Blue Line travels to Tjibaou Cultural Centre. A tourist day pass can be bought for XPF650, which allows the visitor unlimited travel on the buses for one day. **Taxi**: Charges are for time and distance. There is a surcharge after 1900 and on Sundays. **Car hire**: International and local companies all have representatives in the capital. **Bicycle hire**: Bicycles, motorcycles and motorscooters may also be hired. **Documentation**: International Driving Permit is required. Drivers must be aged 21 or over (in some cases, 25 or over).
Travel Times: The following chart gives approximate travel times (in hours and minutes) from **Nouméa** to other major localities/villages in New Caledonia.

	Air	Road
Bourail	-	2.10
Hienghene	-	5.10
Koné	0.45	3.30
Poindimie	-	4.10
Thio	-	2.00
Tontouta	-	0.45
Touhó	0.45	4.40

Travel Advice

Most visits to New Caledonia are trouble-free but you should be aware of the global risk of indiscriminate international terrorist attacks, which could be against civilian targets, including places frequented by foreigners. This advice is based on information provided by the Foreign and Commonwealth Office in the UK. It is correct at time of publishing. As the situation can change rapidly, visitors are advised to contact the following organisations for the latest travel advice:

British Foreign and Commonwealth Office
Tel: (0845) 850 2829.
Website: www.fco.gov.uk

US Department of State
Website: http://travel.state.gov/travel

Accommodation

There is a very good selection of accommodation available with hotels, country inns and rural lodgings.

HOTELS:
Hotels are mostly small and intimate. Prices range from moderate to expensive. Modern **3-** and **5-star** hotels have been built or fully renovated at Anse Vata and there is also bungalow-style accommodation in remoter parts of the main island and in the outer islands.

TRADITIONAL HOMESTAYS: Visitors interested in experiencing the traditional way of life can arrange to stay in Melanesian-style bungalows or huts. Home-cooked meals may be booked in advance. Payment is usually made in cash as credit cards are not accepted.

FARM HOLIDAYS:
These are regulated by the Chamber of Agriculture.

CAMPING:
Major camping sites are in the rural lodging area. Most sites include washrooms, toilets, barbecue facilities and mini-supermarkets. Permission should be sought from landowners before setting up camp.

YOUTH HOSTELS:
Situated in Nouméa is a hostel with dormitories and communal facilities at reasonable rates. Non-YHA members are also accommodated.

ACCOMMODATION INFORMATION

Association des Hôtels de Nouvelle Calédonie
c/o Paillottes de la Ouenghi,
98812 Boulouparis, New Caledonia
Tel: 351 735.
Website: www.hotels-nc.com

Association of International Hotel Chains (ACHI)
c/o Le Meridien Hotel, PO Box 1915,
Nouméa, New Caledonia
Tel: 265 000.
E-mail: gm.noumea@meridien.nc

Chambre d'Agriculture de Nouvelle Calédonie
Antenne de Bourail, BP 847,
98870 Bourail, New Caledonia
Tel: 442 348.
Website: www.bienvenue-a-la-ferme.com

Association des Auberges de Jeunesse de Nouvelle Calédonie
51 bis rue Pasteur Marcel Ariege, BP 767,
98845 Nouméa, New Caledonia
Tel: 275 879.
E-mail: yha.noumea@lagoon.nc

Top Things To See

Grande Terre

- **NOUMÉA:** The capital, near the southeastern tip of Grande Terre, overlooks one of the world's largest sheltered natural harbours. Nouméa is a busy little city with a population composed of many racial groups: French, Melanesian, Polynesian and Vietnamese, amongst others. The main square, the **Place des Cocotiers**, has undergone extensive restoration. Minibuses, the **Nouméa Explorer** and **Le Petit Train** are probably the best ways of seeing the city and its suburbs. The centre of the network is the bus station on the **Place des Cocotiers**. Attractions in the city include **St Joseph's Cathedral**, museums, the market, many old colonial houses and the **Aquarium**, one of the world's leading centres of marine scientific research. Nearby, the **South Pacific Commission Building** houses a collection of native handicrafts from all over the South Seas. The **New Caledonia Museum** is open Tuesday to Saturday, and also contains many local handicrafts and ornaments. The new **Museum of Maritime History** (whose exhibits include artefacts from numerous local wrecks) is situated by the port in Nouméa. The **Tjibaou Cultural Centre** in Nouméa is a new venue for concerts, plays and exhibitions celebrating indigenous cultural traditions.
- **Excursions:** Approximately 4km (2.5 miles) from the city centre is the **Botanical and Zoological Gardens**, home to over 700 species of animals. Also near Nouméa is the **Amedée Lighthouse**, constructed in Paris during the reign of Napoleon III and shipped to New Caledonia in pieces. It is located in a coral reef, 18km (11 miles) from the capital. The lagoon, which is the biggest in the world, offers good opportunities for swimming and scuba-diving. East of the capital is **Mont-Dore**, a mountain surrounded by magnificent coastal scenery. On the way, stops can be made at the Melanesian village of **St Louis** and the **Plum Lookout** for a spectacular view across the surrounding reef. The **Blue River Provincial Park** is well worth a visit. Day trips are available from the capital.
- **THE WEST COAST:** Some 170km (105 miles) from Nouméa is **Bourail**, where there are many elaborate and beautiful caves and rock formations shaped by the Pacific breakers. Further north is the ancient site of **Koné**, where decorated pottery dating back to the 10th century BC has been discovered. From the town of **Koumac**, a new road has been constructed which loops round the top of the island. The scenery consists of pure white sand beaches and offshore atolls, backed by dense rainforest.
- **THE EAST COAST:** The new road takes one to **Hienghéne**, which has a lagoon surrounded by 120m-(400ft-) high black cliffs. **Poindimié**, the main town of the east coast, is further south. Nearby is **Touho**, overlooked by a 500m (1640ft) peak. The region is dotted with churches and Melanesian villages, forests, coconut palms and beautiful beaches. At the southern point of this coast is **Yaté**, a village surrounded by lakes, waterfalls and rich wooded countryside.

Outlying Islands

- **ILE DES PINS:** Discovered and named the Isle of Pines by Captain Cook in 1774, Ile des Pins lies some 70km (45 miles) off the southeast coast of Grande Terre. This exceedingly beautiful island has many white sand beaches and turquoise lagoons and is lush with rainforests, pines, orchids and ferns. Archaeological excavations have revealed settlements 4000 years old. The island was also briefly used as a convict settlement during the 19th century following the Paris Commune. The ruins of the jail can still be seen amongst the dense vegetation. Day trips are available from Nouméa to the Ile des Pins.

Top Things To Do

- **Snorkelling** and **diving** are very popular. The New Caledonian authorities have created marine reserves on several islets to protect marine fauna and flora. There are also sunken shipwrecks, which act as artificial reefs. Some of the best dive sites include: around Nouméa, the **Amédée Lighthouse Reserve** (including shark feeding), **La Dieppoise** (shipwreck of a Royal Navy patrol ship sunk in 1988), and **Ilot Maître**; to the south, the **Prony Needle**; to the north, the **Tenia Horn** (near Boulouparis), the **Fault** (near Bourail) and the **Hienghene Reef**; and **Lifou** in the **Loyalty Islands**. For a list of diving centres, contact New Caledonia Tourism (see *Tourist Information*). **The Bay of Anse Vata** and **Côte Blanche**, both in Nouméa, are the favourite locations for **windsurfing**. International competitions such as the *Trophée des Alizés* attract some of the world's top competitors.
- **Fishing** is one of the locals' favourite pastimes, which visitors can participate in by accompanying them on fishing expeditions to catch tuna, marlin or snapper. Chartered fishing boats can also be hired. The coral barrier reef off the shore of Nouméa is excellent for underwater spearfishing. The **Loyalty Islands**, 100km (60 miles) off the east coast of New Caledonia, are superb for scuba-diving and spear-fishing. **Ouvéa Island** is 130 sq km (50 sq miles), but is rarely more than 3 or 4km (2 or 2.5 miles) wide. The lagoon is rich in fish. The main location for freshwater fishing is **Yaté Lake**, which is open from January to October.
- **Whale watching:** From July to September, humpback whales can be spotted during the mating season in the bays of the southern lagoon and Lifou. Excursions are organised from Nouméa and from the south of the mainland to spot them. The whales may also be seen during scuba diving trips.
- **Boat trips:** Excursions in Melanesian **outrigger canoes** are organised at the **Isle of Pines**. Several operators offer trips to the coral reefs in **glass-bottomed boats** from which visitors can observe the marine life. Reservations can be made from *gîtes* or hotels on the islands. **Sailing boats** can be chartered with or without a skipper. **Kayaks** or **canoes** can be rented to explore New Caledonia's network of rivers, streams and lakes.
- **Hiking:** Arrangements can be made in the capital for trips into the interior. Botanical excursions through the forest of **Mount Koghi** (with French- or English-speaking guides) are also available.
- **Horse riding:** Excursions are organised from **Nouméa, Dumbea, La Foa, Bourail, Thio** and the **Koné** villages. These vary from simple rides to major expeditions to the local bush (which involve crossing the mountain range, mustering cattle and camping in the mountains).

TOURIST INFORMATION

New Caledonia Tourism South
Street address: 20 rue Anatole France,
Immeuble Nouméa-Centre, Place des Cocotiers,
Nouméa, New Caledonia
Postal address: BP 688, 98845 Nouméa Cédex,
New Caledonia
Tel: 242 080.
Website: www.nctps.com

New Caledonia Tourism South in France
7 rue du Général Bertrand, 75007 Paris, France
Tel: (1) 4273 6980.
Website: www.nctps.com

South Pacific Tourism Organisation in Fiji
Street address: Level 3, FNPF Place,
343-359 Victoria Parade, Suva, Fiji
Postal address: PO Box 13119, Suva, Fiji
Tel: (639) 330 4177.
Website: www.spto.org

Entertainment

FOOD & DRINK: The choice of eating places and food on New Caledonia is excellent; costs vary from moderate to expensive. Gourmet restaurants and bistros serve African, Chinese, French, Indonesian, Italian and Spanish cooking. Dishes include Pacific spiny lobsters, prawns, crabs or mangrove oysters and salads of raw fish (marinated in lime juice). An island speciality is *bougna*: fish or chicken wrapped in banana leaves and cooked on hot stones covered with sand. First-class delicatessens and grocers in Nouméa and at Anse Vata Beach provide a wide choice of picnic fare. There is a good selection of French wine available. **Tipping**: There is no tipping.

NIGHTLIFE: There are plenty of discos and also two casinos, situated in the Anse Vata area. Nightclubs in Nouméa are lively with both European and local floorshows. There are also several cinemas, which show French films.

SHOPPING: In Nouméa, boutiques sell fashionable French clothes, mainly casual but sometimes *haute couture*. Other purchases include luxury French goods such as perfume, jewellery and footwear, and silk scarves, sandals and handbags from France and Italy can also be found. Duty free items are also sold. Local items include curios made of shells, coral, woodcarving, ceramics, hand-painted materials and aloha shirts. **Shopping hours**: Mon-Fri 0730-1100 and 1400-1800, Sat 0730-1100.

Business

ECONOMY: The mainstays of the country's economy are mining, tourism and, to a lesser degree, agriculture and fishing. The agricultural sector produces cereals, fruit and vegetables, as well as copra and coffee for export. The fishing industry trawls primarily for shrimp and tuna, the bulk of which is sold to Japan. A small light-industrial sector has grown up in the last two decades, producing building materials, furniture and processed foods, largely for domestic consumption. In the mining sector, New Caledonia is the world's largest producer of nickel after Canada and the USA, and has about one-quarter of the world's known deposits; this generates 90 per cent of the country's export revenue. There are also deposits of cobalt, iron, manganese, lead and zinc. Tourism is the major service industry and remains the most dynamic sector in terms of economic development. Subventions from France are essential to the territory's economic well-being. And, by virtue of its link with France, New Caledonia is an Associate Member of the EU. France is the largest trading partner, accounting for approximately half of all imports and exports, followed by Australia, Germany, Japan and the USA.

BUSINESS ETIQUETTE: Appointments should be made. Businesspeople generally work long hours and take long lunch breaks, but business lunches are rare as most businesspeople go home at lunchtime. Prices should be quoted in Euros or French Pacific Francs. The best time to visit is May to October. **Office hours**: Mon-Fri 0730-1130 and 1330-1730; Sat 0730-1130.

CONFERENCES/CONVENTIONS: Conferences and conventions take place at major hotels such as Le Meridien, Park Hotel and Novotel Surf Nouméa, as well as at the Chamber of Commerce (see *Commercial Information*), the Tjibaou Cultural Centre and the South Pacific Commission, all situated in Nouméa.

COMMERCIAL INFORMATION

Chambre de Commerce et d'Industrie
BP M3, 15 rue de Verdun,
98849 Nouméa Cédex, New Caledonia
Tel: 243 100.
Website: www.cci.nc

New Zealand

Location: South Pacific.

Time: New Zealand: GMT + 12 (GMT + 13 from the first Sunday in October to the third Sunday in March).
Chatham Island: GMT + 12.45 (GMT + 13.45 from the last Sunday in October to the last Sunday in March).

Overview

New Zealand was first settled at least 1000 years ago by the Polynesian Maori, a well ordered tribal society led by hereditary chiefs and a powerful priesthood.

The first European arrival was Dutchman Abel Tasman in 1642, although it was not until the voyages of Captain James Cook, in 1769 and 1779, that the islands were charted and explored. The Treaty of Waitangi (1840) signed between representatives of the British Crown and Maori chiefs formed the basis of the British annexation of New Zealand. However, conflicting land claims gave rise to the 'New Zealand Wars', an issue which has remained controversial until today.

New Zealand was granted internal self-government in 1852. The later years of the century saw a rapid growth in investment, communications and agricultural production. In 1893, New Zealand became the first country in the world to extend the vote to women.

Today, New Zealand is a unique land of breathtaking scenery and tourism is on the rise. Visited are drawn by the country's craggy coastlines, sweeping golden beaches, verdant forests, snow-capped alpine mountains, gurgling volcanic pools, flashing fish-filled rivers and glacier-fed lakes, all beneath a brilliant blue sky.

New Zealand is spread over three relatively small islands with modern and efficient transport, quiet roads, plenty of flights and two stunningly scenic rail journeys.

Other pluses are friendly, English-speaking people, a low crime rate, and a trio of rich cultural influences – adventurous Polynesian navigators (Maori), pioneering European settlers who followed a thousand years later, and modern Pacific Rim immigrants.

The plant and animal life are also excellent offering opportunities to see the varied birdlife (including kiwis), seals, dolphins and whales.

Enjoy the chance to explore two of the richest New World wine regions on the planet, taste wonderful cuisine, stroll on moody beaches, tramp through the national parks or over alpine passes.

The county is also perfect for every kind of outdoor activity and not surprisingly, some of the world's most cutting-edge

adventure activities originated in New Zealand. Try bungee jumping, caving or whitewater rafting.

If that is not your bag, immerse yourself in culture in the museums and galleries of New Zealand's main cities – Auckland, Christchurch and the capital Wellington. New Zealand's time as an original, fully fledged tourist haven has come and the country's isolation, once a bane, is now a boon.

General Information

AREA: 270,534 sq km (104,454 sq miles).
POPULATION: 4 million (Statistics New Zealand, 2004).
POPULATION DENSITY: 14.8 per sq km.
CAPITAL: Wellington. **Population:** 423,765 (2003). Auckland, with a population of 1.3 million (2005), is the largest urban area in the country.
GEOGRAPHY: New Zealand is 1930km (1200 miles) southeast of Australia and consists of two major islands, the North Island (116,031 sq km/44,800 sq miles) and the South Island (153,540 sq km/59,283 sq miles), which are separated by Cook Strait. Stewart Island (1750 sq km/676 sq miles) is located immediately south of the South Island, and the Chatham Islands lie 800km (500 miles) to the east of Christchurch. Going from north to south, temperatures decrease. Compared to its huge neighbour Australia, New Zealand's three islands make up a country that is relatively small (about 20 per cent more land mass than the British Isles). Two-thirds of the country is mountainous, a region of swift-flowing rivers, deep alpine lakes and dense subtropical forest. The country's largest city, Auckland, is situated on the peninsula that forms the northern part of the North Island. The southern part of the North Island is characterised by fertile coastal plains rising up to volcanic peaks. Around Rotorua, 240km (149 miles) south of Auckland, there is thermal activity in the form of geysers, pools of boiling mud, springs of hot mineral water, silica terraces, coloured craters and hissing fumaroles, which make Rotorua a world-famous tourist attraction. The South Island is larger, although only about one-third of the population lives there. The Southern Alps extend the whole length of the island, culminating in Mount Cook, the country's highest peak. In the same region are the Franz Josef and Fox glaciers.

There are also four Associated Territories: **The Cook Islands**, about 3500km (2175 miles) northeast of New Zealand; **Niue**, 920km (570 miles) west of the Cook Islands (area 260 sq km/100 sq miles); **Tokelau**, three atolls about 960km (600 miles) northwest of Niue (area 12 sq km/4 sq miles), and the **Ross Dependency**, which consists of over 700,000 sq km (270,270 sq miles) of the Antarctic.
Cook Islands and **Niue** have separate individual sections in the World Travel Guide.
GOVERNMENT: Constitutional monarchy since 1907.
Head of State: HM Queen Elizabeth II since 1952, represented locally by Governor-General Dame Silvia Cartwright since 2001. **Head of Government:** Prime Minister Helen Clark since 1999. **Recent history:** Helen Clark became New Zealand's first woman Deputy Primer Minister in 1989 and Prime Minister in 1999. She was re-elected as Prime Minister for a third time in September 2005. Her Labour Party won 50 seats in Parliament and formed a coalition with the Progressive Party. Her Government voted a number of controversial measures such as the decision to legalise prostitution. The Government's opposition to the invasion of Iraq in 2003 raised tensions with the US, one of the country's main trading partner.
LANGUAGE: English is the common and everyday language, but other languages are also spoken, including Maori, which is New Zealand's second official language (spoken by the indigenous Maori people who constitute approximately 15 per cent of the population).
RELIGION: 60 per cent Christian: Anglican, Presbyterian, Roman Catholic and Methodist are all represented.
ELECTRICITY: 230 volts AC, 50Hz. Most hotels provide 110-volt AC sockets (rated at 20 watts) for electric razors only.
SOCIAL CONVENTIONS: Should a visitor be invited to a formal Maori occasion, the *hongi* (pressing of noses) is common. Casual dress is widely acceptable. New Zealanders are generally very relaxed and hospitable. Stiff formality is rarely appreciated and, after introductions, first names are generally used. Smoking is restricted where indicated. It is banned in pubs and restaurants.

Climate

Subtropical in the North and temperate in the South. The North has no extremes of heat or cold but winter can be quite cool in the South, with snow in the mountains. The eastern areas often experience drought conditions in summer; the West, particularly in the South Island, has more rain.
Required clothing: Lightweight cottons and linens are worn in the North Island most of the year and in summer in the South Island. Medium weights are worn during winter in the South Island. Rainwear is advisable throughout the year, and essential if visiting the South Island's rainforest areas.

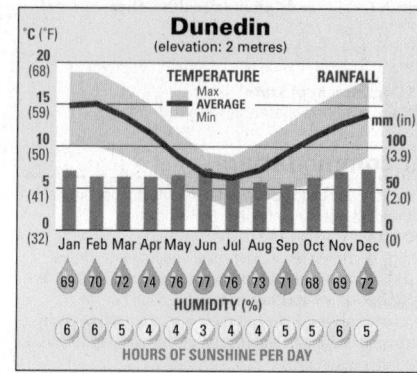

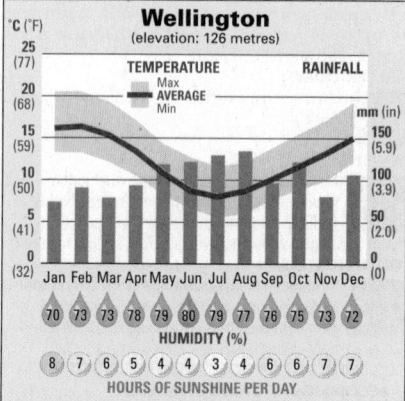

Communications

Telephone: IDD is available. Country code: 64. Most public phones take cards purchased from bookstalls; some also accept credit cards, but very few still accept coins.
Mobile telephone: Roaming agreements exist with most international mobile phone companies. Coverage is good.
Internet: There are Internet cafes in cities and smaller town central business districts. Travellers may access the Internet at many hotels and youth hostels.
Post: Post offices are open Mon-Fri 0900-1700. Airmail to Western Europe takes four to five days and to the USA three to 10 days.
MEDIA: New Zealand's media scene is very liberal. The broadcasting sector was deregulated in 1988.
Press: The English-language daily newspapers with the highest circulation include the *New Zealand Herald* (website: www.nzherald.co.nz), the *Dominion Post*, *Otago Daily Times*, and *The Press*.
Radio: Public broadcaster *Radio New Zealand* runs three networks: *National Radio*, *Concert FM* and *The AM Network*. *Radio New Zealand International* broadcasts to the South Pacific region, *Niu Mai* is Maori-owned and Radio Works' stations include *Radio Pacific*.
TV: State-owned Television New Zealand (TVNZ) operates *TV1* and *TV2*. *TV3* and *Prime TV* are private networks. *Sky TV* is a pay-TV operator. *Maori Television* is public.

Passport/Visa

	Passport Required?	Visa Required?	Return Ticket Required?
Full British	Yes	No	Yes
Australian	Yes	No	No
Canadian	Yes	No	Yes
USA	Yes	No	Yes
Other EU	Yes	No	Yes
Japanese	Yes	No	Yes

Note: *Regulations and requirements may be subject to change at short notice, and you are advised to contact the appropriate diplomatic or consular authority before finalising travel arrangements. Any numbers in the chart refer to the footnotes below.*

PASSPORTS: Passport valid for at least three months beyond the intended period of stay required by all. Some governments are not recognised by New Zealand and citizens in doubt should check with the New Zealand Immigration Service (see *Passport/Visa Information*).
VISAS: Required by all except the following:
(a) nationals of the EU and nationals of countries referred to in the chart above for stays of up to three months, except nationals of the UK who may stay for up to six months and nationals of Australia who may stay indefinitely;

(b) nationals of Andorra, Argentina, Bahrain, Brazil, Brunei, Chile, Hong Kong (SAR), Iceland, Israel, Korea (Rep), Kuwait, Liechtenstein, Malaysia, Mexico, Monaco, Norway, Oman, Qatar, San Marino, Saudi Arabia, Singapore, South Africa, Switzerland, United Arab Emirates, Uruguay and Vatican City for stays of up to three months;
(c) transit passengers continuing their journey by the same or first connecting aircraft within 24 hours, providing they hold onward or return documentation and are not leaving the airport and are not transiting to or from a South Pacific Island or a national of the Kingdom of Nepal;
(d) those in transit whose next or final destination is Australia and the traveller holds a current Australian visa.
(e) nationals travelling on a UN laissez-passer for stays of up to three months.
Types of visa and cost: *Visitor:* £50. *Transit:* £55. *Student:* £80. Business visitors discussing or negotiating business arrangements and staying for up to three months can travel using a visitor visa.
Validity: *Visitor Permit:* nine months in any 18-month period. This can be extended by a further three months in certain circumstances. Visitors must then remain outside New Zealand for a period of time equal to that they spent inside New Zealand, before applying for another visa.
Application to: Consulate (or consular section at Embassy or Immigration Service at High Commission); see *Passport/Visa Information.*
Application requirements: *Visitor Permit/Transit Visa:* (a) Completed application form. (b) One recent passport-size photo of each person named in the application. (c) Passport valid for three months beyond the date of departure. (d) Proof of sufficient funds for duration of stay, approximately NZ$1000 per person per month, or NZ$400 per person per month when accommodation has been paid for in advance (eg recent bank statements). (e) Onward or return ticket, or declaration by New Zealand sponsor that cost of travel back to home country will be met. (f) Fee (payable in cash or by bank/building society cheque, credit card accepted by some offices, money order or bank draft). *Student:* (a)-(f) and, (i) Confirmation of placement and payment of fees at an approved educational institution.
Note: Applicants must prove themselves to be in good health (ie not suffering from ill health that may become a burden to the New Zealand health services) and of good character (by providing a police certificate showing a good record. Those applying for a visa may also be asked to undergo an interview and/or a medical examination prior to travel, or by the Immigration Officer at port of entry.
Working days required: Two weeks, but this may vary depending on type of visa required and nationality of the applicant.
Temporary residence: Enquire at the nearest New Zealand High Commission or Immigration Service for details.

PASSPORT/VISA INFORMATION

New Zealand Immigration Service in the UK
Mezzanine Floor, New Zealand House, 80 Haymarket, London SW1Y 4TE, UK
Tel: (09069) 100 100 (visa information and immigration service; calls cost £1 per minute).
Opening hours: Mon-Fri 1000-1545.
Website: www.immigration.govt.nz

New Zealand High Commission in the UK
Second Floor, New Zealand House, 80 Haymarket, London SW1Y 4TQ, UK
Tel: (020) 7930 8422.
Website: www.nzembassy.com
Opening hours: Mon-Fri 0900-1700.

New Zealand Embassy in the USA
37 Observatory Circle, NW, Washington, DC 20008, USA
Tel: (202) 328 4800.
Website: www.nzemb.org

Money

Currency: New Zealand Dollar (NZD; symbol: NZ$) = 100 cents. Notes are in denominations of NZ$100, 50, 20, 10 and 5. Coins are in denominations of NZ$2 and 1, and 50, 20, 10 and 5 cents.
Currency exchange: Exchange facilities are widely available throughout New Zealand.
Credit & debit cards: American Express, Diners Club, MasterCard and Visa are widely accepted. Check with your credit or debit card company for details of merchant acceptability and other services that might be available.
Traveller's cheques: Can be exchanged at official rates at trading banks, large hotels and some shops. To avoid additional exchange rate charges, travellers are advised to take traveller's cheques in US Dollars, Pounds Sterling or Australian Dollars.
Currency restrictions: There are no restrictions on the import and export of foreign or local currency.

Banking hours: Mon-Fri 0900-1630.
Exchange rate indicators:
Rate at time of publishing
£1.00=   NZ$2.45
$1.00=   NZ$1.42

Duty Free

The following items may be imported into New Zealand by persons of 17 years of age and over without incurring customs duty:
200 cigarettes or 50 cigars or 250g tobacco or a mixture of all three weighing no more than 250g; 4.5l of wine or beer; 1.125l or 40oz of spirits or liqueurs; goods to a total value of NZ$700.
Prohibited items: Because of the importance of agriculture and horticulture to the New Zealand economy, it is illegal to import most foodstuffs (meat, meat products, honey, fruit and dairy). Take care when importing wood products, such as golf clubs, shoes and items made from animal skin. For further information, contact the nearest Embassy, High Commission or Consulate. The import of the following items is also prohibited: firearms and weapons (unless a special permit is obtained from the New Zealand police); ivory in any form; tortoise or turtle shell jewellery and ornaments; medicines using musk, rhinoceros or tiger derivatives; carvings or anything made from whalebone or bone from any other marine animals; cat skins or coats and certain drugs (eg diuretics, depressants, stimulants, heart drugs, tranquillisers, sleeping pills) unless covered by a doctor's prescription.

Public Holidays

Below are listed Public Holidays for the January 2006-June 2007 period.
2006: Jan 1-3 New Year. **Feb 6** Waitangi Day. **Apr 14-17** Easter. **Apr 25** ANZAC Day. **Jun 5** Queen's Birthday. **Oct 23** Labour Day. **Dec 25** Christmas Day. **Dec 26** Boxing Day.
2007: Jan 1-2 New Year. **Feb 6** Waitangi Day. **Apr 6-9** Easter. **Apr 25** ANZAC Day. **Jun 4** Queen's Birthday.
Note: Each region also observes its particular anniversary day as a holiday.

Health

	Special Precautions?	Certificate Required?
Yellow Fever	No	No
Cholera	No	No
Typhoid & Polio	No	N/A
Malaria	No	N/A

Note: Regulations and requirements may be subject to change at short notice, and you are advised to contact your doctor well in advance of your intended date of departure. Any numbers in the chart refer to the footnotes below.

Food & drink: Mains water is considered safe to drink. Milk is pasteurised and dairy products are safe for consumption. Local meat, poultry, seafood, fruit and vegetables are generally considered safe to eat.
Other risks: There are no snakes or dangerous wild animals in New Zealand. Sandflies are prevalent in Fiordland, but these can be effectively countered with insect repellent. The only poisonous creature is the very rare katipo spider.
Health care: Medical facilities, both public and private, are of a high standard. Telephone numbers for doctors and hospitals are listed at the front of the white pages of local telephone directories. Should visitors need drugs or pharmaceutical supplies outside normal shopping hours, they should refer to 'Urgent Pharmacies' in the local telephone directory for the location of the nearest pharmacy or check with their hotel. Many hotels have doctors on call. Long-staying visitors with a valid permit to stay for two or more years are entitled to health care services on the same basis as New Zealand citizens. There is a reciprocal health agreement with the UK, which entitles short-term British visitors to publicly funded health treatment. They will receive free treatment as a hospital inpatient, but must pay some charges for any services provided by outpatients and private doctors. Comprehensive medical insurance is strongly recommended before travelling to cover any additional charges. If you intend to participate in adventure activities, such as bungee jumping or white water rafting, you should ensure that your travel insurance covers these types of activities. You should check any exclusions, and that your policy covers you for the activities you want to undertake.

Travel - International

AIR:

The national airline is *Air New Zealand (NZ)* (website: www.airnz.co.nz).
Approximate flight times: From Auckland to

London is 25 hours, from Wellington is 29 hours and from Christchurch is 30 hours. From Auckland to *Los Angeles* is 12 hours, to *New York* is 20 hours, to *Singapore* is 10 hours 30 minutes, and to *Sydney* is three hours.
Main airports: *Auckland (AKL)* (website: www.auckland-airport.co.nz) is 22.5km (14 miles) south of the city (travel time – 40 minutes). *To/from the airport:* Airbus runs an efficient service between the international terminal and the city centre. These operate from 0600 until the last flight and cost NZ$15/single and NZ$22/return (student and child discounted fares are available). *Rideline* operates from 0700-1800 and costs NZ$4 (travel time – approximately 60 minutes) from the city centre to the airport. Take buses 363, 364, 374 or 375. In addition to regular taxis, there is a shuttle taxi service which operates 24 hours; the fare is approximately NZ$40 depending on the number of passengers. *Heletranz* has a helicopter service from Auckland's North Shore and city to the airport (travel time - 12 minutes). An inter-terminal bus operates 0600-2230 daily. *Facilities:* Duty free shopping, banks/bureaux de change, post office, restaurants and cafes, car hire and baggage facilities/left luggage. There is a wide selection of hotels near the airport.
Christchurch (CHC) (website: www.christchurch-airport.co.nz) is 10km (6 miles) northwest of the city (travel time – 20 minutes). *To/from the airport:* Buses operate all day, every half hour (less regular at weekends) from the city centre to the airport at a cost of NZ$7 (travel time - 40mins). A door-to-door shuttle service operates; it costs from NZ$12. A journey into the city centre by taxi takes approximately 20 minutes and costs NZ$25. *Facilities:* Currency exchange, ATM, mobile phone rental and bank. Good hotels are within 10km (6 miles).
Wellington (WLG) (website: www.wellington-airport.co.nz) is 8km (5 miles) southeast of the city (travel time – 30 minutes). *To/from the airport:* Stagecoach Flyer operates a bus service to the city centre every 30 minutes (fare NZ$3-8). The shuttle service operates on demand (maximum 10 persons) and costs NZ$12-14 accordingly. Taxis are available from outside the terminal. *Facilities:* Duty free, bar, restaurant, ATM and currency exchange.
Queenstown International Airport (ZQN) (website: www.queenstownairport.co.nz). *To/from the airport:* A taxi into the town centre takes 10 minutes and costs approximately NZ$18. Shuttle buses are available for NZ$8 (a discount is available for more than one passenger) and the journey lasts 15 minutes. For NZ$5, a bus takes passengers into town and will also pick up from some hotels (travel time - 20 minutes). *Facilities:* Duty free, currency exchange and baggage storage.
Departure tax: Up to NZ$25 (depending on airport) plus NZ$5 security tax; children aged under 12 are exempt (except at Wellington where only passengers under two years of age are exempt and passengers aged two to 11 pay NZ$10). Transit passengers are exempt for 24 hours.
SEA:

Main ports: *Auckland, Christchurch, Dunedin, Lyttelton, Opua, Picton* and *Wellington.* They are served by international shipping lines sailing from the USA and from Europe. A few cruise ships, such as *P&O, Cunard* and *Princess* Cruises, visit New Zealand, but there are no regular passenger ship services. For further details, contact Tourism New Zealand (see *Top Things To Do*).

Travel - Internal

AIR:

Air New Zealand (NZ) and *Qantas Airways* operate domestic flights between the major airports (see *Travel – International* section). Several smaller airlines, including *Air Nelson, Eagle Air* and *Mount Cook Airlines,* are wholly owned by *Air New Zealand* and have been grouped together as *Air New Zealand Link.* They serve many of the 27 other airports throughout the two islands.
SEA:

The North and South Islands are linked by modern ferries operating between Wellington and Picton, carrying passengers and vehicles across Cook Strait. The *Interislander* (travel time - three hours) and *The Lynx* (travel time - two hours 15 minutes) make several daily crossings with long-distance train connections from Wellington and Picton railway stations (website: www.interislander.co.nz); Reservations on all ferry services are highly recommended, particularly for visitors taking their vehicles. Information can be obtained from Tourism New Zealand (see *Top Things To Do*) or via the Toll New Zealand reservation line; see the *Rail* section for further details.
RAIL:
Toll New Zealand (formerly *Tranz Rail Ltd*) operates a reliable rail service with many routes of great scenic attraction. *Tranz Scenic* operates eight scenic long-distance trains. The *Overlander* runs between Auckland and Wellington (daytime and overnight) with good views of forests, gorges and volcanic peaks. The

Transcoastal runs between Christchurch and Picton along the east coast between the snow-capped Kaikoura Mountains and past the Kaikoura coast, which is famous for whale-watching. The *TranzAlpine* runs between Christchurch and Greymouth through spectacular landscapes of gorges and river valleys and across the snow-capped Southern Alps. There are buffet cars on all trains, but there are no sleeping cars on overnight services. All services are one-class travel only. For further information, contact *Toll New Zealand* (tel: (4) 498 3000; website: www.tollnz.co.nz); or *Tranz Scenic* (tel: (4) 495 0775 *or* (0800) 277 482 (toll free in New Zealand); website: www.tranzscenic.co.nz).

Travel passes: *Travelpass New Zealand* offers a 2-in-1, 3-in-1 or 4-in-1 travel pass. The 2-in-1 pass offers unlimited coach travel and one ferry journey. The 3-in-1 pass offers unlimited coach travel, one ferry journey and one train journey. The 4-in-1 pass offers unlimited coach travel, one ferry journey, one train journey and one domestic flight. *InterCity* coaches, *Tranz Scenic* trains and *Interislander* ferry services across Cook Strait are available with the pass. It is issued for periods between five and 15 days; extra days cost NZ$50 each. The pass can be bought outside New Zealand from any InterCity Coachlines office, Toll New Zealand travel centre or accredited travel agency. The *Scenic Rail Pass* is available for seven days or one month and includes a journey on the *Interislander* ferry. A seven-day pass costs NZ$299, a one-month pass costs NZ$499. For further information, contact Tourism New Zealand (see *Top Things To Do*).

The *Kiwi Experience* is a coach transport network for backpackers and independent travellers.

ROAD:

Traffic drives on the left. **Coach**: *InterCity Coachlines* (website: www.intercitycoach.co.nz) operates scheduled services throughout the country. Coach passes are available. *Newmans Coach Lines* (website: www.newmanscoach.co.nz) operates services in both islands. It is advisable to make reservations for seats.

Bus: There are regional bus networks which serve most parts of the country and are on the whole friendly and cheaper than the larger companies. **Taxi**: There are metered taxis throughout the country. **Car hire**: Major international firms and local firms have offices at airports and most major cities and towns. It is recommended to hire vehicles from members of the *New Zealand Vehicle Rental & Leasing Association*.

Regulations: The minimum age for driving a rented car is 21. The legal speed limit is 100kph (60mph) on the open road and 50kph (30mph) in built-up areas. Distances are indicated in kilometres. Both driver and passengers are legally required to wear seat belts at all times. For further information, contact *The New Zealand Automobile Association* (tel: (9) 966 8800 *or* (800) 500 222 (toll free in New Zealand); website: www.aa.co.nz). **Documentation**: All international driving licences are recognised by New Zealand. And, although not compulsory, an International Driving Permit is recommended. Motor insurance is not a legal requirement in

New Zealand because New Zealand law has removed the right of accident victims to sue a third party in the event of an accident. For further information, contact Tourism New Zealand (see *Top Things To Do*).

URBAN:

Good local bus services are provided in the main towns; there are also trolley buses in Wellington. Both Auckland and Wellington have zonal fares with pre-purchase tickets and day passes. *Rideline* (website: www.rideline.co.nz) houses all the bus, train and ferry information about travelling around Auckland. Positively Wellington Tourism (website: www.wellingtonnz.com) has information about getting around.

Travel Times: The following chart gives approximate travel times (in hours and minutes) from **Wellington** to other major cities/towns in New Zealand:

	Air	Road	Rail
Auckland	1.00	9.00	10.00
N. Plymouth	1.00	8.30	-
Christchurch	0.45	*7.20	*5.20
Dunedin	1.20	*12.20	-

Note: *Plus ferry crossing of three hours.

Travel Advice

Travellers visiting remote areas should ensure that their journey details are made known to local authorities or friends/relatives before setting out. New Zealand weather can be treacherous, especially in winter.

Most visits to New Zealand are trouble-free but you should be aware of the global risk of indiscriminate international terrorist attacks, which could be against civilian targets, including places frequented by foreigners.

This advice is based on information provided by the Foreign and Commonwealth Office in the UK. It is correct at time of publishing. As the situation can change rapidly, visitors are advised to contact the following organisations for the latest travel advice:

British Foreign and Commonwealth Office
Tel: (0845) 850 2829.
Website: www.fco.gov.uk

US Department of State
Website: http://travel.state.gov/travel

Accommodation

MOTELS & HOTELS:

New Zealand offers a wide range of top-class hotels, exclusive retreats, motels, moderately priced accommodation and guest houses. Rates on the whole are cheaper in rural areas, while every city and town also offers a choice of budget hotels and motels. Budget accommodation, often with self-catering facilities, is increasingly popular. **Disabled travellers**: Every new building and every major reconstruction is required by law

to provide reasonable and adequate access for people with disabilities. The law specifies that every motel and hotel must provide a certain number of units with accessible facilities. New Zealand is recognised as a world leader in providing accessibility for the disabled. **Grading**: Hotels are graded from **1 to 4 stars**. Motels are graded on a separate scale of **1 to 5 stars**.

GUEST HOUSES & PRIVATE HOTELS:

Usually located in restored, older buildings, guest houses and private hotels offer moderately priced accommodation, often with shared bathroom facilities, but with generally high standards.

Country pubs: The cheapest type of accommodation and particularly popular on the west coast of the South Island.

Farm and home stays: A number of established companies can arrange farm holidays, where visitors stay with a family as a guest, sharing bathroom facilities. Many farms are conveniently located for outdoor activities such as fishing, skiing and horse trekking. Prices usually include breakfast and dinner. **Bed and breakfast**: There is an eclectic mix of hosts and homes to stay in. Guests will have their own room and are served breakfast in the morning. **Boutique accommodation**: This type of accommodation is almost always in a historic or heritage building or landmark. They offer a high standard of amenities and individual flair and breakfast is often served to guests in the morning. **Lodges**: These are small, intimate establishments with up to 20 rooms offering breakfast and dinner.

CAMPING/CARAVANNING:

There are many campsites throughout New Zealand, which is reputed to have some of the world's best camping grounds. Rates and facilities vary considerably. It is advisable to make advance reservations from December to Easter. **Motorcamps, holiday parks, cabins** and **tourist flats**: These are characteristic of New Zealand. Motorcamps and holiday parks provide sites for tents, caravans and campervans. Many also have cabins, self-contained motels and backpackers lodges. Some are powered, others are non-powered and there is usually access to a shared kitchen, bathroom, dining area, TV lounge and other amenities such as a swimming pool. Visitors are required to provide their own tents and equipment, which can be hired from a number of companies. Occupants are usually required to supply their own linen, blankets and cutlery. Cabins are ideal for budget travellers and contain only beds and rudimentary furniture (visitors need to bring their own bedding). Tourist flats are at the top end of the cabin scale and usually offer sheets and bedding as well as fully equipped kitchens. Full details can be obtained from Tourism New Zealand (see *Top Things To Do*).

HOLIDAY HOMES: Many New Zealanders have a family holiday home which they rent out to friends and others. The homes come in a variety of guises from tiny cottages to large homes. Hiring a holiday home is an ideal way to experience true 'kiwi' living.

YOUTH HOSTELS:

The Youth Hostel Association runs 62 hostels throughout the country, and reservations can be made in advance from December to March.

BACKPACKER HOSTELS: There are over 350 backpacker hostels located all over the country. Budget Backpacker Hostels (BBH) issues a backpacker card costing NZ$40, which entitles the holder to discounted transport within New Zealand as well as NZ$20 of pre-paid telephone calls.

ACCOMMODATION INFORMATION

Motel Association of New Zealand
PO Box 27-245, 79 Boulcott Street,
Wellington, New Zealand
Tel: (4) 499 6415.
Website: www.nzmotels.co.nz

Hospitality Association of New Zealand
Level 2, Radio Network House,
Corner Abel Smith and Taranaki Streets, PO Box 53,
Wellington, New Zealand
Tel: (4) 385 1369.
Website: www.hanz.org.nz

Boutique Lodgings
Website: www.lodgings.co.nz

Youth Hostel Association
PO Box 436, Christchurch, New Zealand
Tel: (3) 379 9970 *or* (0800) 278 299 (toll free in New Zealand)
Website: www.yha.org.nz

Budget Backpacker Hostels (BBH)
99 Titiraupenga Street, Taupo, New Zealand
Tel: (7) 377 1568.
Website: www.backpack.co.nz.

Credit: ©Tourism Auckland

Top Things To See

- In **Auckland**, enjoy fantastic views of the city, its beaches, the coast, and the mountains from the distinctive **Sky Tower**, a casino with a glorious circular, glass viewing gallery at its bulbous summit. It is also possible for the particularly brave tourist to abseil down the side of the building to the street, a drop of over 100m (328ft).
- In **Rotorua's arts centre,** see how young Maori learn the skills of traditional bone, wood and greenstone carving. There is also the opportunity to visit a *Marae* (a Maori meeting house usually forbidden to *pakeha*, foreigners) and enjoy a concert of traditional songs, the *haka* (a Maori challenge usually witnessed before All Black rugby matches) and a *hangi* (a delicious feast cooked in an earth oven).
- In **Napier**, immerse yourself in art deco. The city was razed by an earthquake in 1931 and subsequently rebuilt in the art deco style of the time. Today, it boasts one of the world's finest collections of lovingly preserved art deco buildings.
- To the south, on the edge of the flat patchwork quilt of the **Canterbury Plains**, lies the 'Garden City' of **Christchurch**, whose Neo-Gothic architecture is reminiscent of an old English university town. About 500m (1640ft) from the square is the vast expanse of **Hagley Park**, on the borders of which are the **Old Canterbury University/Arts Centre**, the **Canterbury Museum**, the **Robert McDougall Art Gallery**, the botanical gardens and **Christ's College**. Just a short walk along the river, discover **St Michael and All Angels Church,** an unusually beautiful wooden Neo-Gothic building combining French and English styles and containing a mixture of Maori and Catholic elements.
- Discover New Zealand's **wildlife**: As New Zealand was separated from other land masses some 100 million years ago, many plant and animal species are unique to the country. This is particularly true in the case of birds, which attract **birdwatching** enthusiasts from all over the world. Owing to the lack of predators, many of the country's birds never fully developed wings and, hence, live on the ground. The best-known native bird is the *kiwi*, also the country's unofficial national symbol. Others include the *kea* and *weka*, as well as the endangered *kakapo*, the world's largest parrot. Famous locations for birdwatching include **Taiaroa Head** (near **Dunedin**), known for colonies of royal albatrosses and **Stewart Island**, where kiwis can be observed at night. **Cape Kidnappers** in Hawkes Bay is the only gannet colony in the world, and is well worth a visit at low tide when it is possible to walk along the beach or take a tractor ride. In **Dunedin**, in the **Otago Peninsula**, a glorious natural thumb poking out into the **Pacific**, see rare yellow-eyed penguins (Maori name *hoihoi*, meaning noise maker), enormous yet graceful royal albatross, and basking on the rocks around the peninsula – fur seals.
- See **Wellington**'s star attraction, the spectacular **Te Papa Museum of New Zealand**, on the city's pretty waterfront. The museum combines cultural and historical exhibitions with education and entertainment (website: www.tepapa.govt.nz).
- In the forests of the **Northland Forest Park**, see some of the world's oldest trees, including the famous *kauri*, many of which date back centuries.

Top Things To Do

- Have a go at some of the world's most cutting-edge adventure activities. **Bungee jumping** was first commercialised by New Zealanders and the country remains the world's prime destination for the sport. Famous jump-off points include the **Kawarau River Bridge**, the **Skippers Bridge**, the **Pipeline**, the **Ledge** (near **Queenstown**), **Taupo** and **Mangaweka** (in the **North Island**), **Hanmer Springs** (in the **South Island**) and the **Bungee Rocket** (at New Brighton Pier).
- Choose **rap jumping**, which consists of abseiling headfirst down a cliff, and is currently popular in **Auckland, Bay of Islands, Queenstown,** also known as New Zealand's 'adventure capital', and **Wanaka**.
- Go **river sledging** which involves riding down a river holding on to a polystyrene sledge or boogie board, in **Queenstown** (South Island) and on the **Rangitaiki River** near Rotorua (North Island).
- Test your **paragliding** skills (also referred to as 'parapenting'); beginner's courses are available near **Queenstown** and **Wanaka**, while experienced paragliders tend to head to **Christchurch**, the **Daney Pass** or **Wanaka**. Queensland is also a good place to experiment **zorbing**, which involves being strapped into an inflatable transparent plastic ball, which is then rolled down a grassy hill or onto a river.
- Opt for **jetboating**, another New Zealand invention, which consists of high-speed boat trips in special power boats. It is available to people of all ages and popular on many of the country's best-known rivers.
- **Surf rafting** invites visitors to accompany experienced rafters through crashing waves while simultaneously being offered a commentary on the coastline nearby. Best locations are the **Otago Peninsula** (near Dunedin, South Island) and **Piha Beach** (near Auckland, North Island).
- New Zealand's coastline stretches for a total of roughly 16,000km (10,000 miles) and the conditions for **swimming, diving** and **windsurfing** are ideal. Many dive spots are easily accessible from the shore, particularly those in **Northland** (North Island). The **Poor Knights Islands** (near Whangarei) are particularly renowned among divers (Jacques Cousteau cited them as one of the world's top diving destinations). Many different types of diving are available, including kelp forests at **Stewart Island** (home to the huge Paua shellfish), black and red coral in **Fiordland**, and wreck-diving, notably at the *Rainbow Warrior*, the famous Greenpeace boat which was sunk off the Bay of Islands. A detailed brochure with information on New Zealand's best dive sites can be obtained from New Zealand Underwater, PO Box 875, Auckland (tel: (9) 623 3252; website: www.nzunderwater.org.nz).
- Go **surfing** on New Zealand's long coastlines, with some of the best breaks located at **Mahia Peninsula** (near **Gisborne**), **Murawai, Palliser Bay** (near **Wellington**), **Piha** and **Raglan**.
- Go **swimming with dolphins** in the **Bay of Islands** (north of Auckland), the **Coromandel Peninsula, Kaikoura** (South Island) and **Whakatane.**
- **Whale watching** is possible on the eastern coast of **South Island** all year round (with the greatest number of sightings in winter, from April to August). For further information and details of prices, contact Whale Watch (website: www.whalewatch.co.nz).
- Go **sailing** and **yachting** in **Auckland** – 'the city of sails'. Excursions to the remote maritime reserves in the **Bay of Islands, Hauraki Gulf** and **Marlborough Sounds** are also possible.
- Seek the thrill of **whitewater rafting**. Trips ranging from a couple of hours to five days are available on many rivers, including the **Wairora** (near Tauranga), the **Mohaka** (in Hawke's Bay) and the **Kaituna** (near Rotorua), which also features the world's highest commercially rafted waterfall at 7m (23ft). **Blackwater rafting** trips through underground caves are also available.
- New Zealand offers good **skiing**, **snowboarding** and **mountaineering**, with ideal conditions from June to October. On the North Island, the best ski regions are **Whakapapa and Turoa** (both located on **Mount Ruapehu**). Other good ski slopes can be found in the **Southern Lakes region** (particularly **Queenstown** and **Wanaka**) and **Mount Hutt**. **Glacier skiing** and **glacier walking** can be enjoyed at the **Fox, Franz Josef** and **Tasman glaciers** in the Southern Alps.
- Go **caving**: The **Waitomo Caves**, whose 'Lost World' cave can be abseiled into through shafts of sunlight, are the most visited. Other ways to explore the country's many underground caves are through **cave rafting** or **tubing**, where participants are kitted out with a wetsuit and helmet (complete with light) and then float through the cave system on custom-made tyres.
- Go **fishing**: Brown and rainbow trout are particularly popular. Salmon fishing is best in the **Rakaia, Rangitata, Waimakariri** and **Waitaki** rivers on the East Coast (the season lasts from mid-December to late April). Permits are *only* required for trout and salmon fishing and there is a special Tourist Licence (available only from the Tourism Rotorua Information Office) which allows holders to fish anywhere in the country for a one-month period. For further information, contact the New Zealand Professional Fishing Guides Association, PO Box 16, Motu, Gisborne (tel: (6) 863 5822; website: www.nzpfga.com).
- **Walk** though beautiful national parks or protected forest areas. The Department of Conservation (DOC) has singled out eight different walks which are generally the best known and most popular, including the **Abel Tasman Coastal Track** (New Zealand's most widely used recreational track), the **Lake Waikaremoana Track** (in **Te Urewara National Park**), the **Milford Track** (the country's most famous track in World-Heritage-listed **Fiordland Park**) and the **Rakiura Track** (a remote walk on **Stewart Island** to New Zealand's southernmost parts). These tracks generally take from one to several days, with accommodation provided en route, either in the form of basic camping and huts or comfortable lodges. For further information, contact the Department of Conservation in Wellington (tel: (4) 471 0726; website: www.doc.govt.nz).
- Visit the wine growing region of **Hawke's Bay**. Around 70 wineries (ranging from large commercial estates to small boutiques) are open for free wine tasting. This area is best known for its red wines, particularly Pinot Noir. The **Marlborough province** also has world-class, new-world wineries such as **Cloudy Bay, Le Brun,**

Fromm, Highfield, Hunters and **Montana**. The best wines from this area tend to be white, sharp Chardonnay and crisp Sauvignon Blanc.
- In **Dunedin** (which is Gaelic for Edinburgh), visit the **Wilson's Whisky Distillery**, reputedly the world's southernmost distillery. Dunedin and **Invercargill** are located in the green and fertile province of Southland at the bottom of the South Island (both of which have strong Scottish roots and retain a distinctive Celtic flavour). The **Emmerson's** and **Speights** breweries are also located in Dunedin.
- In **Wellington**, attend the **New Zealand International Festival of the Arts**, the country's main cultural event including street theatre, comedy, music and film festivals.

TOURIST INFORMATION

Tourism New Zealand in the UK
Level 7, New Zealand House, 80 Haymarket, London SW1Y 4TQ, UK
Tel: (0906) 601 3601 (60p per minute; call centre) or (0906) 910 0100 (immigration).
Website: www.newzealand.com (consumer information) or www.tourismnewzealand.com (trade information).

Tourism New Zealand in the USA
501 Santa Monica Boulevard, Suite 300, Santa Monica, CA 90401, USA
Tel: (310) 395 7480 or (866) 639 9325 (toll-free inside USA only).
Website: www.newzealand.com or www.tourisminfo.govt.nz

Entertainment

FOOD & DRINK: New Zealand has a reputation as a leading producer of meat and dairy produce with lamb, beef and pork on most menus. Venison is also widely available. Locally produced vegetables, such as *kumara* (a natural sweet potato), are good. There is also a wide range of fish available, including snapper, grouper and John Dory. Seasonal delicacies such as whitebait, oysters, crayfish, scallops and game birds are recommended. New Zealand is also establishing a reputation for French-type cheeses: *bleu de Bresse, brie, camembert* and *montagne bleu*.

National specialities:
- *Kumara* (native sweet potato) in Auckland.
- *Feijoa* (local fruit) and *golden-fleshed Zespri Gold kiwi fruit* from the Bay of Plenty.
- Battered fish and chips from Gisbourne.
- *Pavlova* (a large roundcake with a meringue base topped with cream and fruit) from Taranaki.
- Salmon and mussels from Marlborough.
- Yams, seaweed and crayfish from Canterbury.
- Whitebait from the West Coast.
- *Koura* (freshwater crayfish) from Central Otago.
- Bluff oysters and muttonbird from Southland.

Things to know: Many picnic areas with barbecue facilities are provided at roadside sites. Restaurants are usually informal except for very exclusive ones. Waiter service is normal, but self-service and fast-food chains are also available. Some restaurants invite the customer to 'BYO' (bring your own liquor).

National drinks:
New Zealand boasts world-class domestic wines and beers, some of which have won international awards. A wide range of domestic and imported wines, spirits and beers is available from hotel bars, 'liquor stores' and wine shops.
- Merlot (Auckland and Wairarapa), Chardonnay (Bay of Plenty, Gisbourne, Wairarapa and Canterbury), Pinot Gris and Noir (Auckland, Wairarapa, Marlborough and Central Otago), Sauvignon Blanc (Marlborough and Wairarapa).
- New Zealand draught beer and lager.

Things to know: Bars have counter service and public bars are very informal. Lounge bars and 'house bars' (for hotel guests only) are sometimes more formal and occasionally have table service. The minimum drinking age in a bar is 18. There is some variation in licensing hours in major cities and some hotel bars open Sunday, providing a meal is eaten. In most hotels and taverns, licensing hours are 1100-2300 except Sunday.

Tipping: Service charges and taxes are not added to hotel or restaurant bills. Tips are not expected.

NIGHTLIFE: New Zealand has an active and varied entertainment industry. Theatres offer good entertainment ranging from drama, comedy and musicals to pop concerts and shows. Concert tickets can be booked online (website: www.ticketek.com). In large cities, there are often professional performers or guest artists from overseas. Visitors should check 'What's On' in local papers. There are also cinemas and a small selection of nightclubs in larger cities.

SHOPPING: Special purchases include distinctive jewellery made from New Zealand *greenstone* (a kind of jade) and from the beautiful translucent *paua* shell. Maori arts and crafts are reflected in a number of items such as the carved greenstone *tiki* (a unique Maori charm) and intricate woodcarvings often inlaid with *paua* shell. Other items of note include woollen goods, travel rugs, lambswool rugs, leather and skin products. **Shopping hours**: All shops and businesses are open Mon-Sat 0900-1700, as a minimum; there are local variations but many stores and most malls are also open Sun 1000-1300. In resorts, most shops are also open in the evenings.

Business

- **GDP:** US$99.69 billion (2005).
- **Main imports:** Machinery and equipment, vehicles and aircraft, petroleum, electronics, textiles and plastics.
- **Main exports:** Dairy, meat, wood and wood products, fish and machinery.
- **Main trade partners:** Australia, China, Germany, Japan, UK and USA.

ECONOMY: New Zealand is primarily thought of as an agricultural country and, although the sector employs less than 10 per cent of the workforce and contributes just 8 per cent of GDP, it accounts for 40 per cent of the country's export income, primarily from wool, meat and dairy, and woods products. Barley, wheat, maize and fruit are the main crops. There is also a sizeable fishing industry. Energy-related natural resources, principally coal but also natural gas, have been heavily developed. There are also deposits of iron, gold and silica. From the late 1970s, a new generation of industrial enterprises centred on these natural resources was established to replace the declining traditional industries.
Between the mid-1980s and the mid-1990s, New Zealand underwent one of the most radical economic transformations of any Western industrialised country, with wholesale privatisation, the abolition of subsidies, tariff barriers and corporate regulations, and the dismantling of many welfare systems (although spending has risen sharply of late as the Government tackles the pensions crisis afflicting the developed world). The reforms have also meant that New Zealand is much more dependent on foreign trade. Recent economic performance has seen annual growth grow slightly to 3.5 per cent in 2004, mainly due to a fall in agricultural exports. Inflation was 1.8 per cent in 2004.
Unemployment has hovered around the 5 per cent mark for several years, although much of it is concentrated in particular areas where it remains a major problem.
Australia is New Zealand's largest trading partner, and the two Governments have established a completely free trading regime between them. New Zealand is a member of the Organisation for Economic Co-operation and Development (OECD, the international forum for the world's main industrialised economies), the South Pacific Forum (which aims to promote economic co-operation in the region) and the recently established Asian-Pacific Economic Co-operation (APEC) forum.
BUSINESS ETIQUETTE: Businesswear is generally conservative and both sexes tend toward tailored suits. Appointments are necessary and punctuality is appreciated. Calling cards are usually exchanged. The business approach is fairly conservative and visitors should avoid the period from Christmas to the end of January. The best months for business visits are February to April and October to November. **Office hours**: Mon-Fri 0900-1700.
CONFERENCES/CONVENTIONS: The largest centres are in Auckland, Christchurch and Wellington. Many hotels also have facilities. There are over 20 regional convention bureaux in New Zealand, most of which are members of NZ Convention Association (Inc).

COMMERCIAL INFORMATION

Wellington Chamber of Commerce and Industry
PO Box 1590, Level 9, 109 Featherson Street,
Wellington, New Zealand
Tel: (4) 914 6500.
Website: www.wgtn-chamber.co.nz

NZ Convention Association (Inc)
PO Box 331-202, Suite 3, Level 1, 15 Huron Street,
Takapuna, Auckland, New Zealand
Tel: (9) 486 4128.
Website: www.conventionsnz.com.
The organisation is also known as Conventions and Incentives New Zealand.

Nicaragua

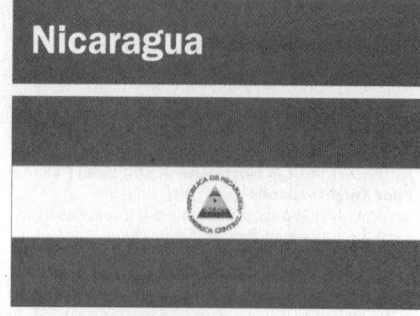

Location: Central America.

Time: GMT - 6.

Overview

Nicaragua remains undiscovered by the tourist hordes, with misconceptions still lingering in the popular consciousness. During the 19th century, the American William Walker took effective control of Nicaragua's Government and national army, with the plan of remodelling Nicaragua as a slave colony annexed to the US. Walker was defeated after a bitter struggle and eventually executed in 1865. Much later, in 1912, the USA were called upon by conservatives to intervene to resolve Nicaragua's serious domestic upheaval, resolving around issues such as the failure to secure the construction of an Atlantic-Pacific canal. The Americans maintained a constant military presence for the next two decades, and most Nicaraguan politicians acquiesced to American will. However, a radical group, led by Augusto César Sandino – who gave his name to the Sandinista movement – launched an effective guerrilla campaign that forced the Americans' departure in 1933. But a new power had arisen in the form of the paramilitary National Guard, led by General Anastasio Somoza Garcia. Sandino and his senior commanders were arrested by Somoza and executed in early 1934; Somoza was soon elected President, duly establishing a military dictatorship characterised by brutality, despotism and systematic corruption. Upon assassination in 1956, his son, Luis Somoza Delbaye, immediately took over; but, at the turn of the 1960s, a rebel movement called the Frente Sandinista de Liberación Nacional (FSLN) began a guerrilla campaign, which finally overthrew the Somozas in 1979.
The 'Sandinistas' established a Junta of National Reconstruction and began a programme of agrarian reform, nationalisation of industry and massive health and literacy schemes. However, in 1981, following the election of Ronald Reagan as US President, the Americans – under the banner of fighting communism – began a programme of destabilisation in Nicaragua, helping 'Contra' guerrilla forces in Honduras and Costa Rica and mounting an economic boycott. Repeated attempts to negotiate a settlement were opposed by the USA, determined to topple the Sandinistas. Finally, in 1989, a deal was agreed to end the insurgency. Years of turmoil and austerity had damaged Sandinista popularity and Violeta Chamorro, widow of Chamorro killed by the Somoza regime, won the election in 1990, representing the combined opposition, UNO Alliance. The disintegration of this artificially-created UNO coalition in the mid-1990s was to be expected. More of a surprise

was the split in the traditionally disciplined Sandinistas. The days of the Contra war and the Sandinistas are over, no more than fascinating graffiti and gunfire stuck stubbornly on walls. And, although certain parts of Nicaragua are best avoided, it is actually one of the safest countries in Central America, enhanced by its friendly, welcoming people. Although certain areas lack tourist facilities, some do not – and those that do, are arguably better for their untouched beauty and 'off the beaten track' appeal. This appeal, should you visit, is instantly evident: Nicaragua incorporates three stunning eco-regions (Pacific, Central and Atlantic), containing everything from volcanoes, tropical forests, beaches, and agricultural land.

General Information

AREA: 120,254 sq km (46,430 sq miles).
POPULATION: 5.7 million (UN estimate 2005).
POPULATION DENSITY: 47.4 per sq km.
CAPITAL: Managua. **Population:** 1.37 million (official estimate 2003).
GEOGRAPHY: Nicaragua borders Honduras to the north and Costa Rica to the south. To the east lies the Caribbean, and to the west the Pacific. In the north are the Isabella Mountains, while the country's main feature in the southwest is Lake Nicaragua, 148km (92 miles) long and about 55km (34 miles) at its widest. The island of Ometepe is the largest of the 310 islands on the lake. These islands have a reputation for great beauty and are one of the country's main tourist attractions. Lake Managua is situated to the northwest. Volcanoes, including the famous Momotombo, protrude from the surrounding lowlands northwest of the lakes. The country's main rivers are the San Juan, the lower reaches of which form the border with Costa Rica, and the Rio Grande. The Corn Islands (Islas del Maiz) in the Caribbean are two small beautiful islands fringed with white coral and palms. They are very popular as holiday resorts with both Nicaraguans and tourists. The majority of Nicaragua's population lives and works in the lowland between the Pacific and western shores of Lake Nicaragua, the southwestern shore of Lake Managua and the southwestern sides of the range of volcanoes. It is only in recent years that settlers have taken to coffee growing and cattle farming in the highlands around Matagalpa and Jinotega.
GOVERNMENT: Republic. Gained independence from Spain in 1821. **Head of State and Government:** President Enrique Bolaños Geyer since 2001. **Recent history:** In 1996, Daniel Ortega was defeated by Arnoldo Aleman Lacayo, leading an alliance of liberal and centrist parties, and then in the most recent poll in 2001 by Aleman's vice-president, Enrique Bolaños Geyer. By this time, the rebel movement, the Frente Sandinista de Liberación Nacional (FSLN), had restyled themselves as Convergencia and adopted a 'Blairite' Christian Democrat programme. The Bolaños Government which took office in 2001 has a tiny majority in the National Assembly, and its work was initially hamstrung by a dispute over the fate of his predecessor, Arnoldo Aleman. The former President had been arraigned for corruption during his term of office, but was protected by his Parliamentary immunity. His immunity was eventually removed in September 2002. Fourteen months later, Aleman was convicted and sentenced to 20 years' imprisonment. The Government received some welcome good news at the start of 2004, however, when, following protracted negotiations, the World Bank agreed to write off 80 per cent of the country's debt to the institution – a sum of around US$3 billion.
The President, who is elected for a five-year term, wields executive power and is assisted by a Deputy and Cabinet of Ministers. Legislative power rests with the National Assembly, whose 92 members (reduced from 96 in 1990) are popularly elected by proportional representation. Under the terms of constitutional amendments adopted in July 1995, the President and legislature's mandate was established as five years.
LANGUAGE: Spanish. Along the Mosquito Coast (*Costa de Mosquito*), there are English-speaking communities in which African or mixed African and indigenous Indians predominate.
RELIGION: 85 per cent Roman Catholic; 14 per cent Protestant.
ELECTRICITY: 110 volts AC, 60Hz.
SOCIAL CONVENTIONS: Dress is informal. **Photography:** Avoid photographing military sites or personnel.

Climate

Tropical climate for most of the country. The dry season is from December to May, and the rainy season is from June to November. The northern mountain regions have a much cooler climate.
Required clothing: Lightweight cottons and linens are required throughout the year. Waterproofs are advisable during the rainy season. Warmer clothes are advised for the northern mountains.

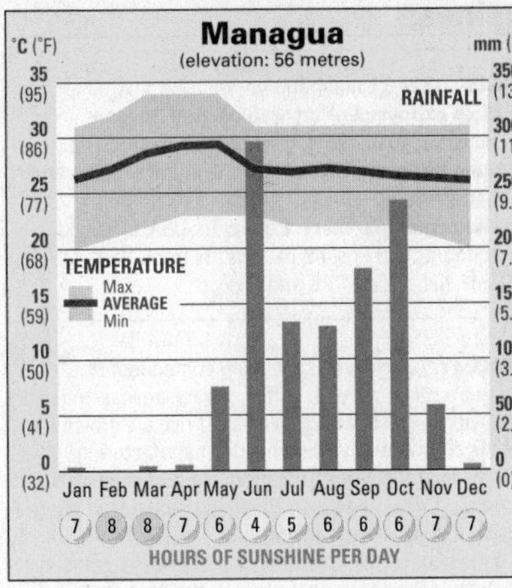

Managua
(elevation: 56 metres)
°C (°F)
mm (in)
RAINFALL
TEMPERATURE
Max
AVERAGE
Min
35 (95)
30 (86)
25 (77)
20 (68)
15 (59)
10 (50)
5 (41)
0 (32)
350 (13.8)
300 (11.8)
250 (9.8)
200 (7.9)
150 (5.9)
100 (3.9)
50 (2.0)
0 (0)
Jan Feb Mar Apr May Jun Jul Aug Sep Oct Nov Dec
7 8 8 7 6 4 5 6 6 6 7 7
HOURS OF SUNSHINE PER DAY

Communications

Telephone: IDD is available. Country code: 505. Outgoing international calls may be made via the international operator or through direct dialling.
Mobile telephone: Roaming agreements exist with some international mobile phone companies. Check with your provider before travelling. Coverage is limited to urban areas.
Internet: Internet cafes in Nicaragua provide public access to Internet and e-mail services.
Post: Most larger towns have an Enitel telecommunications and postal office. Airmail to Europe takes up to two weeks. Post office hours: Mon-Sat 0900-1730.
MEDIA: Nicaraguan media represents both pro- and anti-Government views. There are several television networks and over 100 radio stations. Cable TV is available in most urban areas.
Press: Main publications include the *Confidencial, Nuevo Diario* and *La Prensa*.
TV: Channels include state-owned *Canal 6*, as well as commercial broadcasters *Nicavision Canal 12, Telenica Canal 8* and *Televicentro Canal 2*.
Radio: *Radio Nicaragua* is state-owned, while commercial stations include *Radio Corporación* and *Radio Mundial*.

Passport/Visa

	Passport Required?	Visa Required?	Return Ticket Required?
Full British	Yes	No/1	Yes
Australian	Yes	No/1	Yes
Canadian	Yes	No/1	Yes
USA	Yes	No/1	Yes
Other EU	Yes	No/1	Yes
Japanese	Yes	No/1	Yes

Note: *Regulations and requirements may be subject to change at short notice, and you are advised to contact the appropriate diplomatic or consular authority before finalising travel arrangements. Any numbers in the chart refer to the footnotes below.*

PASSPORTS: Passport valid for at least six months from the date of arrival required by all.
VISAS: Required *only* by nationals of the following countries: Afghanistan, Albania, Algeria, Angola, Armenia, Bangladesh, Bosnia and Herzegovina, Cameroon, China (PR), Congo (Dem Rep), Congo (Rep), Cuba, East Timor, Eritrea, Ethiopia, Ghana, Haiti, India, Indonesia, Iran, Iraq, Jordan, Korea (Dem Rep), Laos, Lebanon, Liberia, Libya, Mali, Mozambique, Nepal, Nigeria, Pakistan, Palestine National Authority, Sierra Leone, Somalia, Sri Lanka, Sudan, the Syrian Arab Republic, Vietnam and Yemen.
Note: 1. All other nationals can obtain a **Tourist Card** on arrival for approximately US$10 for touristic stays of one month, provided they are holding valid travel documents and, in the case of business travellers, a letter from their employer and/or company in Nicaragua.
Types of visa and cost: *Tourist* and *Business*: £18.
Validity: One month from date of issue. Visas can be extended for up to 30 more days. Applications should be made to the Immigration Office in Managua.
Application to: Consulate (or consular section at Embassy); see *Passport/Visa Information*. Tourist Cards can be obtained on arrival.
Application requirements: (a) Valid passport and a photocopy of passport required. (b) Completed application form. (c) Two passport-size photos. (d) Fee. (e) Onward or return ticket; including any travel documents needed for previous and next destination.
Working days required: Confirmation for visas can take six to eight weeks as special authorisation from the Nicaraguan Ministry of Foreign Affairs may be required.
Temporary residence: Enquire at Embassy.
Note: Applicants need to have lived in Nicaragua for at least one year before applying.

PASSPORT/VISA INFORMATION

Embassy of the Republic of Nicaragua in the UK
Vicarage House, Suite 31,
58-60 Kensington Church Street, London W8 4DB, UK
Tel: (020) 7938 2373.
Website: http://freespace.virgin.net/emb.ofnicaragua
Opening hours: Mon-Fri 1000-1230.

Embassy of the Republic of Nicaragua in the USA
1627 New Hampshire Avenue, NW,
Washington, DC 20009, USA
Tel: (202) 939 6570.

Money

Currency: Nicaraguan Gold Córdoba (NIO) = 100 centavos. Notes are in denominations of NIO500, 100, 50, 20 and 10. Coins are in denominations of NIO5 and 1, and 50, 25, 10 and 5 centavos.
Note: Frequent adjustments to the traded value of the Nicaraguan Gold Córdoba, and the various exchange systems that have been used, make it impossible to make meaningful comparative assessments over successive years.
Currency exchange: Foreign currencies can be exchanged at the airport, at banks and at official bureaux de change in major cities.
Credit & debit cards: American Express, Diners Club, MasterCard and Visa are accepted on a limited basis. Check with your credit or debit card company for details of merchant acceptability and other services which may be available.
Traveller's cheques: Accepted in a number of places.
Currency restrictions: There are no restrictions on the import or export of local or foreign currency. Amounts over US$10,000 or equivalent must be declared.
Banking hours: Mon-Fri 0830-1830, Sat 0830-1230; some may close for an hour over lunch.
Exchange rate indicators:
Rate at time of publishing

£1.00=	NIO30.68
$1.00=	NIO17.20

Duty Free

The following items can be imported into Nicaragua without incurring customs duty:
400 cigarettes or 50 cigars or 500 prepared sheaves of tobacco; 5l of alcoholic beverage; clothing, personal items and medicines for personal use; a camera or video recorder; a portable audio recorder and player; a portable computer; goods up to the value of US$500.
Restricted imports: Canned or uncanned meats, leather and dairy products. A licence is required for firearms.
Prohibited exports: Archaeological items, artefacts of historical or monetary value, and gold.

Public Holidays

Below are listed Public Holidays for the January 2006-June 2007 period.
2006: Jan 1 New Year's Day. **Apr 13** Holy Thursday. **Apr 14** Good Friday. **May 1** Labour Day. **Jul 19** Liberation Day. **Sep 14** Battle of San Jacinto. **Sep 15** Independence Day. **Nov 2** All Souls' Day. **Dec 8** Immaculate Conception. **Dec 25** Christmas Day.
2007: Jan 1 New Year's Day. **Apr 5** Holy Thursday. **Apr 6** Good Friday. **May 1** Labour Day.
Note: A considerable number of local holidays are also observed.

Health

	Special Precautions?	Certificate Required?
Yellow Fever	No	1
Cholera	2	No
Typhoid & Polio	3	N/A
Malaria	4	N/A

Note: *Regulations and requirements may be subject to change at short notice, and you are advised to contact your doctor well in advance of your intended date of departure. Any numbers in the chart refer to the footnotes below.*

1: A yellow fever vaccination certificate is required from all travellers aged one year and over arriving within six days from infected areas.
2: Following WHO guidelines issued in 1973, a cholera vaccination certificate is not a condition of entry to Nicaragua. However, cholera is a risk in this country, especially after outbreaks in 1999 in Jinotega, Managua, Nueva Segovia and RAAN areas. Precautions are essential. Up-to-date advice should be sought before deciding whether these precautions should include vaccination, as medical opinion is divided over its effectiveness; see the *Health* appendix.
3: Immunisation against typhoid is strongly recommended.
4: Risk of malaria, predominantly in the benign *vivax* form, exists throughout the year in 119 municipalities, with the highest risk in Chinandega, Jinotega, Nueva Segovia, RAAN, RAAS and San Juan. In the other 26 municipalities, in the departments of Carazo, Madriz and Masaya, transmission risk is low or negligible. Malaria risk is higher during the rainy season. Chloroquine chemoprophylaxis is recommended.
Food & drink: All water should be regarded as being potentially contaminated. Water used for drinking, brushing teeth or making ice should have first been boiled or otherwise sterilised. Milk in rural areas may be unpasteurised and should be boiled. Powdered or tinned milk is available and is advised, but make sure that it is reconstituted with pure water. Avoid dairy products which are likely to have been made from unboiled milk. Only eat well-cooked meat and fish, preferably served hot. Pork, salad and mayonnaise may carry increased risk. Vegetables should be cooked and fruit peeled.
Other risks: *Amoebic* and *bacillary dysenteries, diarrhoeal diseases, typhoid fever* and *hepatitis A* are common throughout the country. *Cutaneous* and *visceral leishmaniasis* occur. *Dengue fever* may occur. There are occasional cases of *leptospirosis*.
Rabies is present. For those at high risk, vaccination before arrival should be considered. If you are bitten, seek medical advice without delay. For more information, consult the *Health* appendix.
Health care: Each department of Nicaragua has a public hospital. These do not charge for emergency services, but will charge for supplies and medicines. There is an extensive network of health posts and health centres in rural areas, however, their resources can be limited. There are about 10 private hospitals/clinics in Managua. Many doctors and hospitals will require payment in cash before treatment, although some private hospitals may accept credit cards. International travellers are strongly advised to take out full medical insurance before departure.

Travel - International

AIR:
The national airline is *Nicaraguenses de Aviación (NICA)*, which is now a member of the *Taca International Airlines (TA)* (website: www.taca.com). Other airlines serving Nicaragua are *American Airlines, Continental* and *Iberia*. Services are available to Canada, Costa Rica, El Salvador, Guatemala, Honduras, Mexico, Panama, Spain and the USA.
Approximate flight times: From Managua to *London* is 14 hours 30 minutes, including one stopover in Miami; to *Madrid* is 13 hours; to *Miami* is two hours 30 minutes.
Main airports: *Managua International Airport (MGA)* (website: www.eaai.com.ni) is 12km (7 miles) north of the city (travel time - 15 minutes). *To/from the airport*: Bus and taxi services run to the city. *Facilities*: Bank, bars, post office, tourist information, restaurants, duty free shop, pharmacy and car hire.
Departure tax: None. (The US$35 departure tax is included in the ticket as of January 2006; children under two years and passengers leaving within eight hours of arrival are exempt.)
SEA:
Main ports: *Corinto, El Bluff, Puerto Cabezas* and *Puerto Sandino*, which are served by shipping lines from Nicaragua, as well as Central American, North American and European countries.
ROAD:
The Pan-American Highway runs through Nicaragua via Esteli and Managua. **Bus**: There are daily bus services between Managua and Tegucigalpa (Honduras), San Salvador (El Salvador) and San José (Costa Rica) (travel time - nine hours). Services are provided by *King-Quality, Nicabus, Ticabus* (website: www.ticabus.com) and *Transnica* (website: www.transnica.com).

Travel - Internal

AIR:
Given the relative size of the country and the difficulty of some ground travel routes, internal flights are worth considering. *La Costeña* and *Atlantic Airlines* cover a wide range of internal routes.
Note: Managua International Airport charges an airport management fee of US$1.50 or local equivalent for travellers on domestic routes.
SEA:
A twice-weekly boat service runs between Bluefields and the Corn Islands. It is also possible to visit the 300 or so islands on Lake Nicaragua, which are very beautiful.

A B C D E F G H I J K L M N O P Q R S T U V W X Y Z

RAIL:
There is no passenger rail service at present.

ROAD:
Lack of road safety is probably the biggest single hazard to travellers in Nicaragua. There is a network of 18,447km (11,463 miles) of roads of which 1749km (1087 miles) are paved. Traffic drives on the right. **Bus**: There is a service to most large towns. Booking seats in Managua in advance is advisable. **Taxi**: Available at the airport or in Managua. Prices should be agreed before departure. A map of each area in the city determines taxi prices. No tip is expected. **Car hire**: Available in Managua or at the airport. This is often the best way of travelling, as public transport is slow and overcrowded. **Documentation**: National licences are only valid for 30 days.

URBAN:
The bus and minibus services in Managua are cheap, but they can be both crowded and confusing.

Travel times: The following chart gives approximate travel times (in hours and minutes) from **Managua** to other major cities/towns in Nicaragua.

	Road
Granada	**1.00**
Esteli	**2.15**
Matagalpa	**1.45**
Rivas	**1.30**

Travel Advice

Only essential travel to the North Atlantic Autonomous Region (RAAN) should be undertaken. There have been occasional incidents of violent crime in Bonanza, La Rosita, Siuna and Little Corn Island. It is not recommended to walk alone after dark. The security situation here is poor and several armed gangs operate in the region.
Managua is prone to strikes and demonstrations, which have occasionally turned violent and affected access to the airport. Road blocks may occur on main roads. Further demonstrations are likely in Managua and could take place elsewhere in Nicaragua. It is advised to avoid all public gatherings or demonstrations.
Road safety, or lack of it, is probably the single-biggest hazard to travellers in Nicaragua. Due to recent assaults on vehicles travelling from Managua airport via Tipitapa to Granada, travellers should avoid use of this route after dark. Travellers are strongly advised not to hike without an experienced guide on volcanoes or in remote areas.
The threat from terrorism is low but you should be aware of the global risk of indiscriminate terrorist attacks, which could be against civilian targets, including places frequented by foreigners.
This advice is based on information provided by the Foreign and Commonwealth Office in the UK. It is correct at time of publishing. As the situation can change rapidly, visitors are advised to contact the following organisations for the latest travel advice:

British Foreign and Commonwealth Office
Tel: (0845) 850 2829.
Website: www.fco.gov.uk

US Department of State
Website: http://travel.state.gov/travel

Accommodation

HOTELS/SELF-CATERING/JUNGLE LODGES/GUEST HOUSES:
Managua has several 4-star hotels with conference facilities. A 15 per cent tax is levied on all hotel bills. Self-catering apartments are also available in Managua. There are motels along the Pan-American Highway and modern resort hotels along the west coast, offering a good standard of accommodation. Ecotourism is also developing in the country where some excellent hacienda-style accommodation and jungle lodges can be found. Guest houses are found throughout the country. Accommodation is graded using a star rating system. For more information, contact the Nicaraguan Institute of Tourism (INTUR); see *Top Things To See & Do*.

Top Things To See & Do

- There are several **volcanic crater lagoons** in the environs of **Managua** – centres of **watersports** and residential development with **boating**, **fishing** and **picnicking** facilities. **Laguna de Xiloa** is the most popular of these lagoons. Hire a boat on the shores of **Lake Managua** for visiting the still-smoking **Momotombo volcano** and the shore villages. You can also take a safe and refreshing dip in Nicaragua's volcanic crater lagoons. Bathing in Lake Managua should be avoided due to contamination, although steps to clean up the lake are being taken. Bathing is possible in the Laguna de Tiscapa. Meanwhile, a **canopy tour** above **Tiscapa Lagoon** flies visitors across the crater from platforms connected by zip lines.
- Discover **León**, the intellectual capital of Nicaragua. It contains a university, religious colleges, the largest cathedral in Central America and several colonial churches. Also worth visiting is the **Ruben Dario Museum**, which unveils the history of poet Ruben Dario at his childhood home. Colourful, provocative and revolutionary graffiti graces the city walls, and the whole of the city is charged with an artistic buzz. North of León are the **Hervideros de San Jacinto**, natural sulphuric hot springs fed by an underground river which is heated by the **Telica volcano**.
- Located at the foot of the **Mombacho volcano**, **Granada** has many beautiful buildings to walk around, and has faithfully preserved its Castilian traditions. The cathedral has been rebuilt in neo-classical style. Also of interest are the **Church of La Merced**, the **Church of Jalteva** and the **fortress-church of San Francisco**.
- **Kayak** on **Ometepe Island**, since this offers a good chance of spotting **monkeys** hanging from the trees!
- **Beaches** on the Pacific coast offer safe **swimming**, as do those on the Caribbean, including the popular **Corn Islands**. You can get here by boat from the small but important port of **Bluefields**, and the beautiful, coral-fringed Corn Islands (**Islas del Maiz**) are worth it. The larger of the islands make a popular Nicaraguan holiday resort, with good surfing and bathing facilities. Elsewhere, one hour's drive from Managua are the **Masachapa** and **Pochomil** beaches. **Montelimar Beach Resort** is the largest of its kind in Central America. A visit to the **El Velero** beach is recommended, where **surfing** is excellent. The Pacific coast has a number of fine beaches, including **El Coco**, **Marsella**, **Ocotal**, **San Juan del Sur** and many others which are located in the south of Nicaragua in the department of **Rivas**. These beaches are distinguished by their unique and beautiful surroundings, and a number of touristic developments are underway in this region.
- **Hike** in the **Mombacho Volcano Natural Reserve** – a wonderful experience that should not be missed. It is possible to see a wide variety of **orchids** in the **cloud forest**. **Climbing** the volcano itself leads to spectacular panoramic views.
- Take to the skies onboard a **hot air balloon** for the best aerial view of Nicaragua's volcanic craters.

TOURIST INFORMATION

Nicaraguan Institute of Tourism (INTUR)
Hotel Crowne Plaza, 1 cuadra al sur, 1 cuadra al oeste, Managua, Nicaragua
Tel: 254 5191.
Website: www.visit-nicaragua.com

Entertainment

FOOD & DRINK: Restaurants, particularly in Managua, serve a variety of cooking styles including Chinese, French, Italian, Latin American and Spanish.
Things to know: There are a number of cheap but good restaurants/bars (*coreders*) where beer, often the cheap local brand, is available. At the other end of the scale, the few plush hotels have sophisticated restaurant/bars with a choice of international cuisine and beverages.
National specialities:
- *Gallopinto* (fried rice and pinto beans).
- *Mondongo* (tripe soup).
- Plantain is used in many dishes.
- *Picadillo* (shredded beef dish).
- *Ajiaco* (pork and tortilla dish).
- *Nacatamal*.
- *Indio viejo*.
- *Quesillo*.
- *Vigorón*.
- *Rosquillas* (a type of cheese and cornmeal biscuit).
- Food is often scooped up in *tortillas* instead of using cutlery.
- Roast corn on the cob is sold on the streets.
- Seafood.

National drinks:
- Fresh tropical fruit juice.
- *Chicha de maíz* and *de jengibre* (fermented corn or ginger drink).
- *Tiste* (corn and cocoa drink).

Tipping: 10 to 15 per cent of the bill is customary in hotels and restaurants.
NIGHTLIFE: Managua has several nightclubs, some offering live music. There are also cinemas with English, French and Spanish films. Other cities, such as Granada, Léon, Masaya, Matagalpa and Rivas, also offer nightlife entertainment.
SHOPPING: Local items include goldwork, hand-carved wood, embroidery, shoes and paintings. Traditional crafts are available, particularly in Masaya, at the handicrafts market. **Shopping hours**: Mon-Fri 0900-1900, Sat 0900-1800.

Business

- **GDP:** US$4.3 billion (2004).
- **Main exports:** Coffee, seafood, beef, sugar, industrial goods, gold, bananas and sesame.
- **Main imports:** Petroleum, agricultural supplies and manufactured goods.
- **Main trade partners:** Exports to: USA, El Salvador, Honduras and Costa Rica. Imports from: USA, Venezuela, Costa Rica and Mexico.

ECONOMY: Agriculture is the main component of Nicaragua's economy, with coffee, sugar, bananas and meat the principal exports. Maize, beans and rice are grown for domestic consumption. The principal manufacturing industries are food, drinks, the production of chemicals and oil refining. There is also a small mining industry working deposits of gold, silver, lead and zinc.
Nicaragua's economic travails during the last 20 years have left it among the poorest countries in the Americas. Some key industrial operations were nationalised following the 1979 Sandinista revolution but the bulk of the economy was left in private hands.
Unfortunately, domestic mismanagement, Western economic sanctions and the cost of the civil war against the 'contras' meant that the Sandinista period was one of continuous economic decline. However, the economy has fared little better since then. During the 1990s, Nicaragua implemented a Structural Adjustment programme supervised by the IMF. It also required several injections of emergency aid after a series of major natural disasters – floods and droughts – which caused huge damage to the agricultural economy. Low commodity prices and the pressure of a substantial foreign debt exacerbated the country's economic difficulties. In 2001, Nicaragua was a beneficiary of the Heavily Indebted Poor Countries (HIPC) initiative which wrote off part of the debt. It reached completion point in January 2004, resulting in an 80 per cent reduction in external debt. Annual growth in 2004 was 4.2 per cent, while inflation was 9.3 per cent. Nicaragua is a member of the Central American Common Market and the Inter-American Development Bank.
BUSINESS ETIQUETTE: Businessmen wear business suits with ties, or long-sleeved shirts and smart trousers; businesswomen wear business dresses. A knowledge of Spanish is an advantage, although some businesspeople speak English. Enquire at the Embassy for interpreter services. The best time to visit is November to March.
Office hours: Mon-Fri 0800-1700. Some offices close for an hour at lunchtime (1230-1330).

COMMERCIAL INFORMATION

Cámara de Comercio de Nicaragua
PO Box 135-C-001, Managua, Nicaragua
Tel: 268 3505 *or* 3514.

NicaExport, Centro de Promoción de Exportaciones
Street address: Km 4 Carretera a Masaya, Esquina Sur, Edificio Delta, 1 cuadra al este, 1/2 cuadra al norte, Managua, Nicaragua
Postal address: Apartado Postal 5932, Managua, Nicaragua
Tel: 252 5747.
Website: www.nicaexport.com.ni *or* www.cei.org.ni

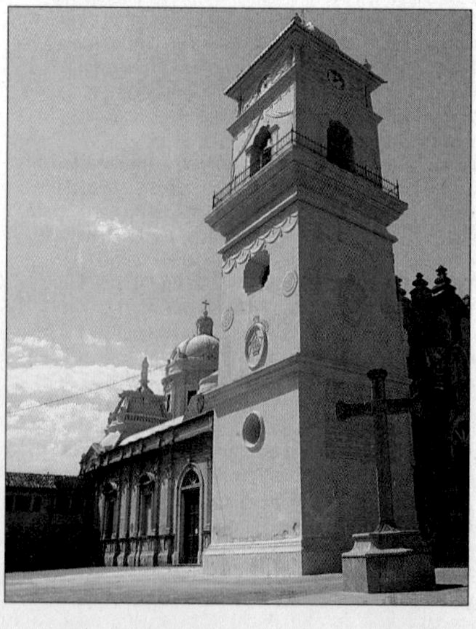
Credit: ©Nicaragua Institute of Tourism

Niger

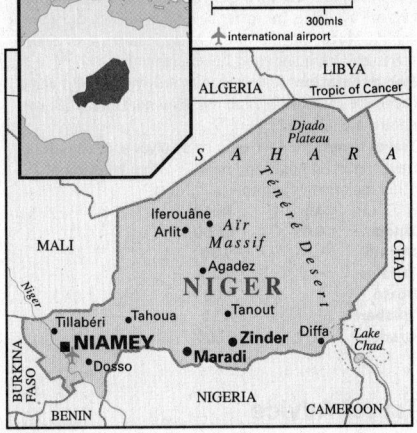

Location: Central Africa.

Time: GMT + 1.

Overview

Up until the 19th century, power in the region was based on control of the great trans-Saharan trade routes, mostly dominated by the Hausa Kingdom until the advent of European traders. Then colonised by the French, Niger was part of French West Africa until 1958, and achieved Independence in 1960. Hamani Diori was elected Head of State presided over a period of stability until its latter stages when severe drought from 1968 onwards brought about widespread civil unrest.

In 1974, the army staged a military coup under Lieutenant Colonel Seyni Kountché. By 1983, the legislative Council of Ministers was entirely composed of civilians. Kountché died in 1987, to be replaced by Ali Seibou. Seibou established the Mouvement Nationale pour une Société de Développement (MNSD), which became the sole legitimate political party.

In the early 1990s, the Government came under internal and external pressure to introduce democratic Government. After some uncertainty and opposition, the Government installed an interim administration, prior to multi-party elections and the introduction of a new constitution. The National Assembly poll saw a victory for the six-party coalition, the *Alliance des Forces de Changement* (AFC). The Presidential election was then won by Mahamane Ousmane of the AFC coalition. Apart from the economy, the new Government's main problem was a series of clashes between security forces and guerrillas belonging to the nomadic Tuareg people. The Tuareg had left Niger to escape the chronic Sahel drought of the 1980s. A series of agreements were brokered, providing for Tuareg land rights and defined future relations between the Tuareg and central Government. Despite occasional problems, the agreement has held.

Following the January 1995 legislative elections, MNSD recovered control of the National Assembly and the Government under ex-World Bank official Amadou Aboubacar Cissé. Friction between the Cissé government and President Ousmane steadily worsened until, exactly one year later, the military stepped in once again. Army chief of staff Colonel Ibrahim Baré Mainassara took control of the country. Under strong external pressure, particularly from Niger's main Western financial backers, the military moved quickly to restore a veneer of civilian Government. In April 1999, Mainassara was killed by his own head of security, after an escalating series of disputes with his erstwhile military colleagues. The uncertain political situation was resolved with the holding of simultaneous Presidential and legislative elections in November that year. The MNSD, the country's historic ruling party, recovered control of both the Presidency – via Mamadou Tandja – and the National Assembly. Since then, the Government has continued to be mired in mutiny and controversy.

Behind environmental and Governmental crises, however, are the faces of Niger's ordinary people, who exude exceptional politeness and affability. These people mostly see past the barrenness and instead see a country with outstanding national parks, prolific wildlife, cambers of sand, black volcanic mountains and green oases. The gentle remoteness of Niger wraps itself around you like a swirling sandstorm.

General Information

AREA: 1,267,000 sq km (489,191 sq miles).

POPULATION: 11.5 million (official estimate 2002).

POPULATION DENSITY: 9.1 per sq km.

CAPITAL: Niamey. **Population:** 550,000 (1988).

GEOGRAPHY: Niger has borders with Libya and Algeria to the north, Chad to the east, Nigeria and Benin to the south, and Mali and Burkina Faso to the west. The capital, Niamey, stands on the north bank of the Niger River and has long been a major trading centre on this important navigable waterway. The river meanders for 500km (300 miles) through the southwestern corner of the country. To the east is a band of semi-arid bush country along the border with Nigeria, shrinking by 20km (12 miles) every year as over-grazing claims more land for the Ténéré Desert, which already occupies over half of Niger. This desert is divided by a range of low mountains, Aïr ou Azbine, in the eastern foothills of which lies the city of Agadez. Surrounded by green valleys and hot springs amid semi-desert, this regional capital is still a major terminus for Saharan caravans. The desert to the west of the mountains is a stony plain hosting seasonal pastures; to the north and west are mostly vast expanses of sand. There is arable land beside Lake Chad in the extreme southeastern corner of the country. The Hausa people live along the border with Nigeria and most are farmers. The Songhai and Djerma people live in the Niger valley and exist by farming and fishing. The nomadic Fulani have spread all over the Sahel. The robed and veiled Tuaregs once dominated the southern cities; the few who remain are camel herders and caravanners on the Saharan routes. The Manga (or Kanun) live near Lake Chad and are well known for their colourful ceremonies in which pipes and drums accompany slow, stately dancing.

GOVERNMENT: Republic since 1960. **Head of State:** President Mamadou Tandja since 1999. **Head of Government:** Prime Minister Hama Amadou since 2000.

Recent history: In 2002, the Government faced a series of mutinies by soldiers demanding better pay and conditions; these were put down by other units loyal to the Government. The following year, the United States and Britain claimed that Niger had sold uranium ore to the former Iraqi dictator Saddam Hussein in the course of his efforts to build nuclear weapons. The claim was subsequently proven to have been based on forged documents but the case drew unwelcome attention to Niger and its dependence on sales of the ore.

LANGUAGE: The official language is French. Also spoken are Hausa (by half of the population), Djerma, Fulani, Manga, Zarma and Tuareg dialects.

RELIGION: Approximately 95 per cent Muslim, with Christian and animist minorities.

ELECTRICITY: 220 volts AC, 50Hz.

SOCIAL CONVENTIONS: Handshaking is customary. Casual wear is widely suitable. Women should avoid wearing revealing clothes. Traditional beliefs and Muslim customs should be respected. **Photography:** Permits are required for photography and filming, and can be obtained from police stations. Tour operators and tourist bureaux are often able to make arrangements. Film is expensive and local facilities for processing film are not always good. Ask local people for permission before taking their photographs. Military installations, airports and administrative buildings (including the Presidential Palace) should not be photographed.

Climate

Summers are extremely hot. The dry season is from October to May. Heavy rains with high temperatures are common in July and August.

Required clothing: Lightweight cottons and linens are required most of the year. Warmer clothes during the cool evenings, especially in the north, are essential. Rainwear is advisable.

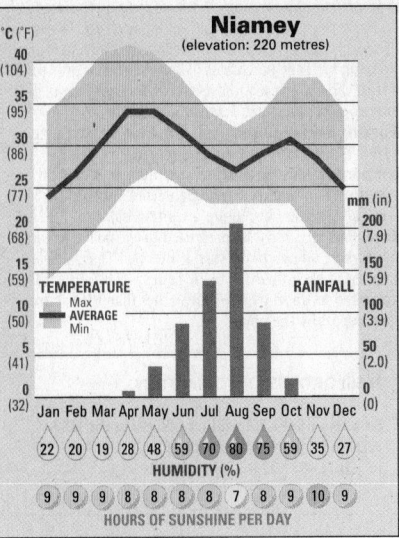

Niamey (elevation: 220 metres)

Communications

Telephone: IDD is available. Country code: 227 (no area codes). Telephone services are provided by Société Nigérienne des Télécommunications (SONITEL).

Mobile telephone: Roaming agreements exist with some international mobile phone companies. Coverage is limited to urban areas.

Internet: Internet access can be found in major urban areas.

Post: Airmail to Western Europe takes up to two weeks. Post office hours: generally 0730-1230 and 1530-1800.

MEDIA: Press: All newspapers are published in French; most are weeklies.

TV: *Tele-Sahel* is state-run. *Tenere TV* is private and *Telestar* runs a pay TV service.

Radio: *La Voix du Sahel* is a state-run, national station. Private stations include *Anfani FM*, *Horizon FM* and *Tenere FM*.

Passport/Visa

	Passport Required?	Visa Required?	Return Ticket Required?
Full British	Yes	Yes	Yes
Australian	Yes	Yes	Yes
Canadian	Yes	Yes	Yes
USA	Yes	Yes	Yes
Other EU	Yes	1	Yes
Japanese	Yes	Yes	Yes

Note: *Regulations and requirements may be subject to change at short notice, and you are advised to contact the appropriate diplomatic or consular authority before finalising travel arrangements. Any numbers in the chart refer to the footnotes below.*

PASSPORTS: Passport valid for six months required by all, except holders of National ID Cards issued to Benin, Burkina Faso, Côte d'Ivoire, Mali, Mauritania, Nigeria, Senegal and Togo, and holders of a UN laissez-passer.

VISAS: Required by all except the following:

(a) **1.** nationals of Benin, Burkina Faso, Cape Verde, Central African Republic, Chad, Côte d'Ivoire, Denmark, Finland, The Gambia, Ghana, Guinea, Guinea-Bissau, Liberia, Mali, Mauritania, Morocco, Nigeria, Norway, Rwanda, Senegal, Serbia & Montenegro, Sierra Leone, Togo and Tunisia;

(b) alien residents holding a valid 'Permis de Séjour' or 'Visa de Séjour';

(c) transit passengers continuing their journey within 24 hours and who do not leave the airport. Some nationals *do* require a visa for transit. Contact Consular section at Embassy for further information.

Note: Visa exemptions generally apply for periods of up to three months. However, it is advised to contact the nearest Embassy/Consulate for further details as this may vary according to nationality.

Types of visa and cost: *Ordinary:* €50 (up to three-month stay).

Validity: Up to three months, depending on purpose of stay.

Application to: Nearest Consulate (or consular section at Embassy); see *Passport/Visa Information.*

Application requirements: (a) Valid passport. (b) Three completed and signed application forms. (c) Three passport-size photos. (d) A return or onward ticket. (e) Proof of sufficient funds (eg bank letter). (f) Yellow fever vaccination certificate (cholera also required if travelling from a neighbouring country which has reported an outbreak). (g) Postal applications should be accompanied by a stamped, self-addressed, registered envelope. (h) Fee, payable by cash or money order. *Tourist*: (a)-(h) and, (i) Copy of letter from travel agent certifying round-trip ticket has been purchased. (j) Bank statement or proof of at least US$500 (for road travellers). *Transit*: (a)-(i) and, (j) Photocopy of round-trip ticket and/or itinerary.

Working days required: Two. A visa can be processed within 24 hours for an extra fee of €16.

Exit permit: Must be obtained from the Immigration Department in Niamey before departure (except for nationals who do not require an entry visa).

Note: Passports must be presented to the police in each town where an overnight stay is intended. Passports are stamped at each town, so blank pages will be required. It is prohibited to travel by any route other than that stamped in the passport by the police.

PASSPORT/VISA INFORMATION

Embassy of the Republic of Niger in the USA
2204 R Street, NW, Washington, DC 20008, USA
Tel: (202) 483 4224/5/6/7.
Website: www.nigerembassyusa.org

Money

Currency: CFA (Communauté Financiaire Africaine) Franc (XOF) = 100 centimes. Notes are in denominations of XOF10,000, 5000, 2500, 1000 and 500. Coins are in denominations of XOF250, 100, 50, 25, 10, 5 and 1. Niger is part of the French Monetary Area. Only currency issued by the Banque des Etats de l'Afrique de l'Ouest (Bank of West African States) is valid; currency issued by the Banque des Etats de l'Afrique Centrale (Bank of Central African States) is not. The CFA Franc is tied to the Euro.

Currency exchange: Currency can be exchanged at the airport as well as at main banks and hotels.

Credit & debit cards: Diners Club and MasterCard are both accepted on a limited basis. Check with your credit or debit card company for details of merchant acceptability and other services which may be available.

Traveller's cheques: Accepted by hotels, restaurants, most shops and airline offices. To avoid additional exchange rate charges, travellers are advised to take traveller's cheques in Euros.

Currency restrictions: The import of local currency is unrestricted. Export of local currency is limited to XOF25,000. The import and export of foreign currency is unlimited.

Banking hours: Mon-Fri 0800-1100 and 1600-1700.

Exchange rate indicators:
Rate at time of publishing
£1.00=   XOF970.66
$1.00=   XOF559.53

Duty Free

The following items may be imported into Niger by passengers of 15 years of age or older without incurring customs duty:

200 cigarettes or 100 cigarillos or 25 cigars or 250g of tobacco; one bottle of spirits and one bottle of wine; 500ml of eau de toilette and 250ml of perfume.

Restricted items: A licence is required for sporting guns. Customs must authorise their temporary admission. Digging up or attempting to export ancient artefacts is prohibited. Pornography is prohibited. Apparatus for transmission or reception needs special authorisation (as does photographic equipment, see *Photography* in the *General Information* section). Selling cars without permission is prohibited.

Public Holidays

Below are listed Public Holidays for the January 2006-June 2007 period.

2006: Jan 1 New Year's Day. **Jan 10** Tabaski (Feast of the Sacrifice). **Apr 11** Mouloud (Birth of the Prophet Mohammed). **Apr 17** Easter Monday. **Apr 24** National Concord Day. **May 1** Labour Day. **Aug 3** Independence Day. **Oct 22-24** Eid al-Fitr (End of Ramadan). **Dec 18** Republic Day. **Dec 25** Christmas Day. **Dec 31** Tabaski (Feast of the Sacrifice).

2007: Jan 1 New Year's Day. **Mar 31** Mouloud (Birth of the Prophet Mohammed). **Apr 9** Easter Monday. **Apr 24** National Concord Day. **May 1** Labour Day.

Note: (a) Muslim festivals are timed according to local sightings of various phases of the moon and the dates given above are approximations. During the lunar month of Ramadan that precedes Eid al-Fitr, Muslims fast during the day and feast at night and normal business patterns may be interrupted. Many restaurants are closed during the day and there may be restrictions on smoking and drinking. Some disruption may continue into Eid al-Fitr itself. Eid al-Fitr and Tabaski may last anything from two to 10 days, depending on the region. For more information, see the *World of Islam* appendix. (b) Niger's small Christian community also

observes Easter, Whitsun, Ascension, Assumption, All Saints' Day and Christmas.

Health

	Special Precautions?	Certificate Required?
Yellow Fever	Yes	1
Cholera	Yes	2
Typhoid & Polio	3	N/A
Malaria	4	N/A

Note: *Regulations and requirements may be subject to change at short notice, and you are advised to contact your doctor well in advance of your intended date of departure. Any numbers in the chart refer to the footnotes below.*

1: A yellow fever vaccination certificate is required of all travellers over one year of age arriving from all countries: it is also recommended for all travellers leaving Niger.
2: Following WHO guidelines issued in 1973, a cholera vaccination certificate is not a condition of entry to Niger. However, cholera is a serious risk in this country and precautions are essential. Up-to-date advice should be sought before deciding whether these precautions should include vaccination as medical opinion is divided over its effectiveness; see the *Health* appendix for further information.
3: Polio and typhoid both occur.
4: Malaria risk, predominantly in the malignant *falciparum* form, exists all year throughout the country. Chloroquine resistance has been reported.

Food & drink: All water should be regarded as being potentially contaminated. Water used for drinking, brushing teeth or making ice should have first been boiled or otherwise sterilised. Milk is unpasteurised and should be boiled. Powdered or tinned milk is available and is advised, but make sure that it is reconstituted with pure water. Avoid dairy products which are likely to have been made from unboiled milk. Only eat well-cooked meat and fish, preferably served hot. Pork, salad and mayonnaise may carry increased risk. Vegetables should be cooked and fruit peeled.

Other risks: *Bilharzia* (schistosomiasis) is present; avoid swimming and paddling in fresh water. Swimming pools which are well chlorinated and maintained are safe. *Filariasis, trypanosomiasis* and *leishmaniasis* are also reported; avoid insect bites. Long-staying visitors, particularly backpackers and those living with local people, should consider *meningococcal meningitis, diphtheria* and *hepatitis B* vaccinations. *Hepatitis A, C* and *E* are widespread. *HIV* is a danger.
Rabies may be present. For those at high risk, vaccination before arrival should be considered. If you are bitten, seek medical advice without delay. For more information, consult the *Health* appendix.

Health care: The two main hospitals are in Niamey and Zinder. Only the main centres have reasonable medical facilities. Personal medicines should be brought in as these can be difficult or impossible to obtain in Niger. Full health insurance is essential and should include cover for emergency repatriation.

Travel - International

AIR:

Most international flights are operated by *Air Afrique (RK)*. Other airlines serving Niger include *Air Algerie, Air France, Royal Air Maroc* and *Sudan Airways*. (There are no direct flights to Niger from the UK.)

Approximate flight times: From *London* to Niamey is six hours, excluding stopover time in Paris.

Main airports: *Niamey (NIM)* is 12km (7.5 miles) southeast of the city (travel time – 10 minutes). *To/from the airport:* Taxi services are available to the city. Hotels have their own vehicles and provide free transport for their clients between the hotel and the airport. *Facilities:* Bars, shops, post office, currency exchange and car hire.

Departure tax: None.

ROAD:

There are main roads from Kano (Nigeria) to Zinder, and from Benin, Burkina Faso and Mali. The principal trans-Sahara desert track runs from Algiers to Asamakka and Arlit, with a paved road to Agadez. Desert driving can be difficult, marker beacons may not always be visible, and petrol is not always available.

Bus: Services operate from Benin, Burkina Faso and Mali.

Travel - Internal

Note: It is essential that all visitors report to the police station in any town where they are making an overnight stop; see *Passport/Visa Information*.

AIR:

Air Niger runs services from Niamey to Agadez, Arlit, Maradi and Zinder. Charter flights can be arranged; contact *Air Niger* or *Transniger* in Niamey.

ROAD:

Certain roads are permanently closed to tourists without special authorisation. Traffic drives on the right. There are an estimated 13,808km (8580 miles) of classified roads, 3256km (2020 miles) of which are main roads. Principal internal roads are from Niamey to Zinder, Tahoua, Arlit and Gaya. Many tracks are impassable during heavy rain. The best season for road travel is from December to March. Petrol stations are infrequent and garages are extremely expensive. It is prohibited to travel by a different route than the one entered in the passport by the police at the previous town. It is necessary to pay a toll on main routes. **Bus:** There are reasonable services between the main centres, even though many roads have been sealed. Coach services operate from Niamey to Agadez, N'guemi, Tera and Zinder. Elsewhere, it is common practice to pay for rides in cross-country lorries; note that this can be an extremely slow and uncomfortable means of transport and that extra payment is expected of those who wish to ride in the cab. **Car hire:** Self-drive and chauffeur-driven cars are available, the latter being compulsory outside the capital. **Note:** Much of the country requires 4-wheel-drive vehicles, guides and full equipment.

Documentation: An International Driving Permit and a Carnet de Passage are required. Minimum age is 23. Two photos are required.

Travel times: The following chart gives approximate travel times (in hours and minutes) from **Niamey** to other major cities and towns in Niger.

	Air	Road
Zinder	0.45	12.00
Maradi	-	9.00
Tahoua	-	7.00
Dosso	-	1.00
Tillabéri	-	4.50
Agadez	-	17.00

Travel Advice

Travellers are advised against all travel to the Aïr Massif, Ténéré and Kaouar regions due to clashes between the Nigerien security forces and armed groups. It is possible, however, to travel north from Agadez as far as the tree of Ténéré and south as far as the Termit Massif. Travellers are advised against all travel to the Azawagh area, particularly the area between the Malian and Algerian borders and the Nigerien towns of Tahoua and Ingall, and to the east of the Aïr Massif and the area north of Iferouane up to the Algerian border.

Border areas are generally insecure and travellers are advised to avoid a 200km-deep zone along the borders with Mali, Algeria/Libya and Chad.

Travellers are advised against all but essential travel on the Agadez-Arlit road. Certain roads are permanently closed to tourists without special authorisation.

Travellers should always use local guides and seek local advice when travelling outside of the main towns and in desert areas, and avoid travelling after dark.

Niger is facing a serious food crisis affecting up to 2.5 million people. A major international relief operation is underway. Visitors considering travelling outside major towns should ensure they take adequate provisions.

Terrorists are active in countries neighbouring Niger, including Algeria and Chad. Travellers should be aware of the global risk of indiscriminate terrorist attacks, which could be against civilian targets, including places frequented by foreigners.

This advice is based on information provided by the Foreign and Commonwealth Office in the UK. It is correct at time of publishing. As the situation can change rapidly, visitors are advised to contact the following organisations for the latest travel advice:

British Foreign and Commonwealth Office
Tel: (0845) 850 2829.
Website: www.fco.gov.uk

US Department of State
Website: http://travel.state.gov/travel

Accommodation

HOTELS:

Hotel accommodation is difficult to obtain and reservations for major international hotels should be booked prior to arrival. All reservations should be made well in advance. There are good hotels in Agadez, Ayorou, Maradi, Niamey, La Tapoa and Zinder. There are also 'Encampments' in Agadez, Boubon, Namaro and Tillabéri. Local hotels are available on a first-come, first-served basis. For further information, contact the National Tourist Office (see *Top Things To See & Do*).

Top Things To See & Do

- The Peulh people celebrate the end of the rainy season with a lively **festival**. Also of interest is the *Cure Salée*, when the nomads gather their cattle to lead them to the new pastures; a highlight of this is the *gerewol* festival of the nomadic Wodaabé tribe.
- Spread along the northern bank of the **River Niger**, **Niamey** is a sprawling city with a modern centre and shanty towns on the outskirts. The two markets, the Small and Great markets, are worth a visit. Other places of interest include the **Great Mosque**, the **National Museum** (including a large park with botanical gardens and a zoo, and an artisan/crafts area), the **Franco-Nigerian Cultural Centre** and the **Hippodrome** where horse and camel races often take place on Sundays. Tours of the city are available.
- Outside Niamey is the famous **'W' National Park**, with its abundant wildlife including buffalos, elephants, lions, hyenas, jackals and baboons. The birdlife is also prolific.
- **Agadez:** This beautiful old Tuareg capital is still a caravan trading city: it also has a thriving tourist trade. Beautiful silver and leatherwork can be bought in the back streets and the minaret of the mosque can be climbed at sunset for a spectacular view of the town.
- North of Agadez, the **Air Mountains** enjoy slightly more rain than the surrounding semi-desert lowlands and were, until recently, home to many species of animals not generally seen at this latitude, including leopards, lions and giraffes. However, the drought has even taken hold here and the stranded populations are dwindling rapidly. Special permission may be required to visit the region.
- Expeditions can be arranged through the mountains to the springs at **Igouloulef** and **Tafadek** or the prehistoric site at **Iferouane** and beyond the **Ténéré Desert** and the **Djado Mounta**.
- The town of **Zinder** was the capital of Niger until 1927. The old part of the town is a compact maze of alleyways, typical of a Hausa town. Near the centre is the **Sultan's Palace** and the mosque, which offers a good view from the minaret. The part of the town known as **Zengou** was formerly a caravan encampment. There is an excellent market here on Thursdays, selling beautiful leatherwork.
- On the route from Niamey to Zinder is the town of **Dosso**, founded in the 13th century by the Zarmas after the fall of Gao. It has an exceptional palace, a lively village square and celebrates many festivals with parades and official ceremonies. Niger's economic centre is **Maradi**, where the people are engaged in various activities from agriculture to diverse crafts. The **Sultanate** and the **Mosque** are well worth viewing.
- The **Ayorou** region on the Mali frontier is an old trading station where a market is held every Sunday. In the region around **Tillabéri**, giraffes are often encountered. Two-day tours are available from the capital.
- Visitors can take **canoes** or **motorboats** along the **Niger River** to the Mali border of the **'W' Game Park**. There are several **swimming** pools in Niamey and Agadez, but it is not advisable to swim in the lakes or rivers. **Fishing** is possible throughout the year, the main season being from April to September. Big-game hunting has been outlawed.

Entertainment

FOOD & DRINK: Although Niger has concentrated on improving its agriculture, shortages of locally produced foodstuffs are common, owing to drought. Traditional dishes tend to be less varied than in countries further south and are usually based around millet, rice or *niebé*, a type of bean that has become an important crop. Beef and mutton are common in the Hausa country and the nomadic regions of the north. In both areas, brochettes are sold in the streets. *Foura*, which consists of small balls of ground and slightly fermented millet crushed with milk, sugar and spices, is a speciality. African, Asian and European dishes are also served, particularly in Niamey, using local fish, meat and vegetables.

Niger's most popular drink is tea, which is available everywhere from street stalls. There is also a good selection of imported beverages. Alcohol is available, but there are restrictions because of Muslim beliefs and traditions.
Tipping: Expected for most services, usually 10 per cent. Most hotels add a 10 to 15 per cent service charge.
NIGHTLIFE: In Niamey, there are several nightclubs with music and dancing. There are also three open-air cinemas in the capital.
SHOPPING: Markets in the main towns, notably Niamey and Agadez, sell a range of local artefacts. The Centre des

Métiers d'Art de Niger, close to the National Museum, is worth visiting, as a wide range of local goods can be bought there. Courteous bargaining is expected and items include multicoloured blankets, leather goods, engraved calabashes, silver jewellery, swords and knives. **Shopping hours**: Mon-Fri 0800-1200 and 1600-1900, Sat 0800-1200.

Business

ECONOMY: Niger is one of the world's poorest countries, with a per capita annual income of around US$200. 90 per cent of the country's inhabitants are employed on the land, although less than 5 per cent of the actual land area is cultivated. This already difficult situation is exacerbated by the ever-expanding Saharan desert, drought and problems with pest control. Less than one-tenth of the crops grown are cash crops (cotton and groundnuts), while the rest (sorghum, millet and rice) are staples grown for domestic consumption. Livestock rearing is very important, especially among the country's nomadic population. In a good year, Niger is self-sufficient in basic foodstuffs; otherwise, the country needs food aid. Niger's most valuable commodity is its uranium deposits – the country is one of the world's largest producers. France and Japan buy the bulk of the uranium output but falling demand has reduced Niger's receipts from this mineral. (Alleged attempts by Iraq to procure uranium from Niger were the subject of controversy in 2003). Gypsum, coal and tin ore are also extracted in commercial quantities and there are proven deposits of other minerals, including copper, manganese, lithium, lead and tungsten. Oil deposits are also thought to exist. Niger has a little light industry, which produces food and drinks, textiles and cement.
From 1997 onwards, the Government embarked on a programme of privatisation of the major public utilities at the behest of the IMF and World Bank. The process was delayed by the 1999 coup but several major sales have since gone through, along with an overhaul of the country's financial systems. The following year, Niger was a beneficiary of the Heavily Indebted Poor Countries (HIPC) debt relief programme, while the World Bank and IMF have provided occasional packages of financial support. In the period since 2001, after several years of sluggish performance, the economy has grown, although not achieving such strong growth in 2004, at only 3.8 per cent. Membership of the CFA Franc Zone affords some monetary stability. France is the country's most important trading partner, followed by Nigeria, Côte d'Ivoire, Japan and Germany. Niger is a member of the West African trading bloc, ECOWAS, as well as various other regional bodies concerned with economic co-operation.
BUSINESS ETIQUETTE: A lightweight suit and tie are generally acceptable. A knowledge of French is essential, as interpreters are not readily available and executives seldom speak English. **Office hours**: Mon-Fri 0730-1230 and 1500-1800, Sat 0730-1230 (winter); Mon-Fri 0730-1230 and 1530-1830, Sat 0730-1230 (summer).

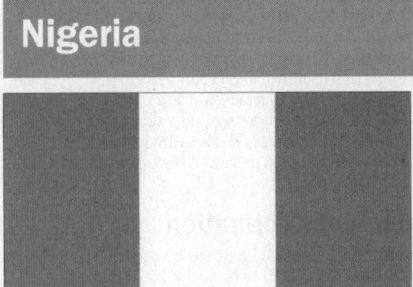

Nigeria

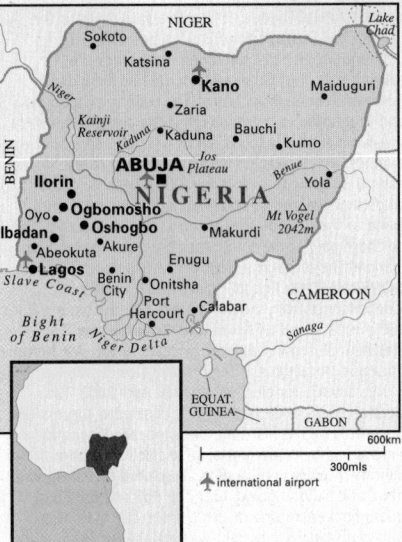

Location: West Africa.

Time: GMT + 1.

Overview

The history of the Nigerian people is a long and involved one. The states of Kanem and Borno, which flourished on the shores of Lake Chad from about AD 10 onwards, were the first imperial states in the region. Their wealth was founded on control of trans-Saharan trade routes. From the 11th to 14th centuries, the Islamic Hausa city-states were also a dominant influence, while in the southwest, the Yoruba cities became major trading centres. In the 15th century, the Portuguese began trading but, by the end of the 19th century, the British had conquered present-day Nigeria. After gradual internal self-government, full independence was achieved in 1960. Since then, the country has endured numerous changes of Government. Since then, Nigeria's army has chosen to intervene on several occasions to thwart a perceived threat to the integrity of the nation. The greatest crisis came about in the mid-1960s, when the eastern part of the country – styling itself the 'Republic of Biafra' – attempted to secede. A three-year (1967-70) civil war followed, at the end of which the secessionists were defeated. Nevertheless, military overthrow, coups and assassination followed over many years. After the annulled 1993 elections, Sani Abacha emerged as the new military strongman and presided over an increasingly oppressive regime. Then, in 1998, Abacha suddenly died. Another member of the military junta, General Abdulsalam Abubakar, took over and moved quickly to shed the country's pariah status by organising elections. The victor, standing for the People's Democratic Party (PDP), was the former military ruler of the 1970s, Olusegun Obasanjo.
The inexperienced civilian Government faced a formidable task. Apart from the dire economic situation, there was growing religious conflict. A particular problem was the decision of several local and regional Governments in the mainly Muslim north to introduce a version of Islamic Shari'a law, very unpopular amongst non-Muslim minorities. Hundreds were killed in inter-communal clashes in 2000 and again in 2002. Tensions have been so high that almost any dispute can set off a spate of violence. Yet, for all its domestic difficulties, Nigeria remains the major regional power and its troops intervened in a number of conflicts throughout West Africa during the 1990s. Regional stability of the West African region has become a major international issue in recent years since the discovery of new oil and gas deposits in West African waters, and recent events in the

Nigeria

Middle East.

As has been illustrated, Nigeria's greatest asset – its wealth of native races and religions, its vibrant population, the largest of any country in Africa – have also proven its downfall on countless explosive occasion. It is a shame that Nigeria is not currently able to entice visitors other than those seeking a slice of the oil dollar. After all, this country is blessed with hundreds of miles of coastline, national parks and fascinating ancient sites.

General Information

AREA: 923,768 sq km (356,669 sq miles).

POPULATION: 130.2 million (UN, 2005).

POPULATION DENSITY: 140.9 per sq km.

CAPITAL: Abuja. **Population:** 403,000 (1999).

GEOGRAPHY: Nigeria has borders with Niger to the north, Chad (across Lake Chad) to the northeast, Cameroon to the east and Benin to the west. To the south, the Gulf of Guinea is indented by the Bight of Benin and the Bight of Biafra. The country's topography and vegetation vary considerably. The coastal region is a low-lying area of lagoons, sandy beaches and mangrove swamps, which merges into an area of rainforest where palm trees grow to over 30m (100ft). From here, the landscape changes to savannah and open woodland, rising to the Central Jos Plateau at 1800m (6000ft). The northern part of the country is desert and semi-desert, marking the southern extent of the Sahara.

GOVERNMENT: Republic since 1963. Gained independence from the UK in 1960. Military regime from 1983-1999. **Head of State and Government:** President Matthew Olusegun Obasanjo since 1999. **Recent history:** Olusegun Obasanjo and the People's Democratic Party (PDP) came up for election again in April 2003. The election was a tense one since, if concluded successfully, this would be the first time since Independence that Nigeria had held two consecutive elections without military intervention. Despite allegations of widespread fraud and ballot-rigging, both the PDP and President Obasanjo were returned with comfortable majorities. (Obasanjo's main opponent was yet another ex-military dictator, Mohammed Buhari.)

Under the provisions of the constitution announced by the Government in late 1998, executive power is vested in the President of the Republic. Legislative responsibilities are entrusted to the bicameral National Assembly, comprising the 360-member House of Representatives and the 109-member Senate. Members of both houses serve a four-year term.

LANGUAGE: The official language is English. A variation of English (Pidgin English) is also spoken. The three main Nigerian languages are Yoruba, Ibo (also spelt Igbo) and Hausa; another 400 languages are also spoken in the country.

RELIGION: 50 per cent Muslim (mainly in the north and west of the country), 40 per cent Christian (mostly in the south) and 10 per cent traditional beliefs.

ELECTRICITY: 240 volts AC, 50Hz. Single phase.

SOCIAL CONVENTIONS: Shaking hands with everyone is customary on meeting and departing. In Yorubaland, it is a sign of respect for women to curtsey when introduced and to enquire after relations, even if this is a first meeting. Unless the visitor knows someone well, it is unusual to be invited to a Nigerian's home. Most entertaining, particularly in Lagos, takes place in clubs or restaurants. A small gift of appreciation is always welcome and business souvenirs bearing the company logo are also acceptable. Casual wear is suitable and a lightweight suit and tie are only necessary for businesspeople on formal meetings; on most other occasions men will not need to wear a jacket, although a tie might be expected. Women should dress modestly, and respect local customs regarding dress, particularly in the Muslim north. It is inadvisable for women to wear trousers. There are over 250 tribes in Nigeria, the principal groups being the Hausa in the north, the Ibo (or Igbo) in the southeast and the Yoruba in the southwest. The larger of the minor groups are the Fulani, Idoma, Igala, Igbirra, Kanuri, Tiv and Nupe in the north; the Efik, Ekoi, Ibibio and Ijaw in the east; and the Edo, Itsekiri, Ijaw and Urhobo in the west. A result of this ethnic variety is the diversity of art, dance forms, language, music, customs and crafts. Nigerians have a very strong sense of ethnic allegiance.

Climate

Varies from area to area. The southern coast is hot and humid with a rainy season from March to November. During the dry season, the *Harmattan* wind blows from the Sahara. The north's rainy season is from July to September. Nights can be cold in December and January.

Required clothing: Lightweight cottons and linens are worn, with a warm wrap advisable in the north. Rainwear is essential during the rainy season.

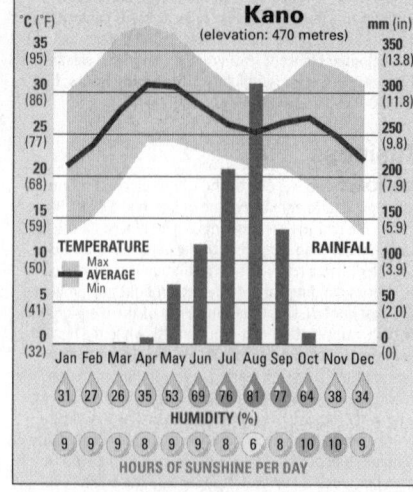

Kano (elevation: 470 metres)

HUMIDITY (%): Jan 31, Feb 27, Mar 26, Apr 35, May 53, Jun 69, Jul 76, Aug 81, Sep 77, Oct 64, Nov 38, Dec 34

HOURS OF SUNSHINE PER DAY: 9 9 9 8 8 8 9 8 8 10 10 9

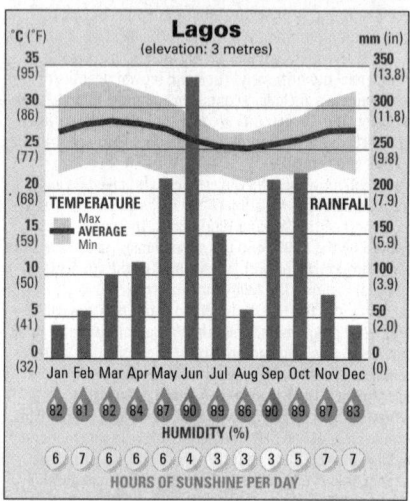

Lagos (elevation: 3 metres)

HUMIDITY (%): Jan 82, Feb 81, Mar 82, Apr 84, May 87, Jun 90, Jul 89, Aug 86, Sep 90, Oct 89, Nov 87, Dec 83

HOURS OF SUNSHINE PER DAY: 6 7 6 6 6 4 3 3 5 7 7

Communications

Telephone: Full IDD is available. Country code: 234.

Mobile telephone: Roaming agreements exist with some international mobile phone companies. Coverage is average.

Internet: Internet and e-mail services are available in Internet cafes in Lagos.

Post: Airmail to Europe is unreliable and takes up to three weeks. Delivery may be more reliable through international couriers who are represented in major towns.

MEDIA: Nigeria's media scene is one of the most vibrant in Africa. State-run radio and TV services reach virtually all parts of the country and operate at a federal and regional level. All 36 states run their own radio stations, and most of them operate TV services. Despite high levels of violence, the private press still occasionally criticises the Government.

Press: English-language newspapers include the the *Daily Times*, the *Guardian*, *New Nigerian*, *This Day* and the *Vanguard*.

TV: *Nigerian Television Authority* (*NTA*) is state-run and operates national and regional stations; *Degue Broadcasting Network* (*DBN*) is a commercial station, as are *AIT* (which broadcasts in Lagos and Abuja via satellite), *Minaj TV* (serves eastern Nigeria), *Galaxy TV* (serves western Nigeria) and *Channels TV*.

Radio: This is the main medium of information for most Nigerians. The state-run *Federal Radio Corporation of Nigeria* operates *Radio Nigeria* stations in Abuja, Lagos, Ibadan, Kaduna and Enugu. *Ray Power* is commercial and mainly music- and speech-based.

Passport/Visa

	Passport Required	Visa Required	Return Ticket? Required
Full British	Yes	Yes	Yes
Australian	Yes	Yes	Yes
Canadian	Yes	Yes	Yes
USA	Yes	Yes	Yes
Other EU	Yes	Yes	Yes
Japanese	Yes	Yes	Yes

Note: Regulations and requirements may be subject to change at short notice, and you are advised to contact the appropriate diplomatic or consular authority before finalising travel arrangements. Any numbers in the chart refer to the footnotes below.

PASSPORTS: Passport valid for a minimum of six months beyond the date of departure required by all.

VISAS: Required by all except the following:
(a) nationals of Benin, Burkina Faso, Cameroon, Cape Verde, Chad, Côte d'Ivoire, The Gambia, Ghana, Guinea, Guinea-Bissau, Liberia, Mali, Mauritania, Niger, Senegal, Sierra Leone and Togo for stays of up to 90 days;
(b) transit passengers continuing their journey by the same or first connecting aircraft, provided holding valid onward or return documentation and not leaving the airport, except for nationals of the USA who require a transit visa.

Note: Children under 16 years of age accompanying their parents residing in Nigeria (provided the name of such a child is entered in the passport of one of the parents) do not require visas, but must, however, complete one application form accompanied by a photo. All children holding their own passport must have separate visas or re-entry permits.

Types of visa and cost: *Tourist*, *Business*: £40 (single-entry); £70 (six-month multiple-entry); £90 (one-year multiple-entry); £120 (two-year multiple-entry). *Transit*: £40. The prices quoted are for UK nationals; visa costs depend on nationality. Nationals of some African countries receive visas free of charge. Contact High Commission or Consular section at Embassy for further information.

Application to: Consulate (or consular section at Embassy or High Commission); see *Passport/Visa Information*.

Application requirements: (a) One completed application form. (b) Valid passport. (c) One passport-size photo. (d) Fee, payable by postal order or credit/debit card. (e) Onward or return ticket for *Tourist* visas. (f) Paid and registered return-postage envelope if applying by post. (g) Letter of invitation from Nigeria, addressed to Visa Section, Nigeria High Commission, London, accepting full immigration responsibility for applicant; any Nigerian inviting a visitor must attach photocopies of the first five pages of his/her passport. (h) Evidence of sustaining self while in Nigeria. This should be in the form of traveller's cheques to be cashed in Nigeria. *Business*: (a)-(f) and, (g) Letter of introduction from a company or a resident of Nigeria, accepting immigration responsibility for applicant; any Nigerian inviting a visitor must attach photocopies of the first five pages of his/her own passport, while a resident must enclose a copy of his/her residence permit.

Note: In addition to the normal visa requirements, minors must also provide: original birth certificate plus one photocopy; a letter of consent from parents; and photocopies of parents' passports.

Working days required: Two if applying in person; 10 for postal applications.

PASSPORT/VISA INFORMATION

High Commission for the Federal Republic of Nigeria in the UK
9 Northumberland Avenue, London WC2N 5BX, UK
Tel: (020) 7839 1244.
Website: www.nigeriahc.org.uk
Opening hours: Mon-Fri 1000-1200 (visa submission); 1530-1630 (visa collection).

Nigerian Consular Section in the UK
56-57 Fleet Street, London EC4 1BT, UK
Tel: (020) 7353 3776.
Website: www.nigeriahc.org.uk
Opening hours: Mon-Fri 1000-1200 (visa submission); 1530-1630 (visa collection).

Embassy of Nigeria in the USA
3519 International Court, NW, Washington, DC 20008, USA
Tel: (202) 986 8400 (ext 1005 for Consular and immigration section).
Website: www.nigeriaembassyusa.org

Nigerian Consulate General in the USA
828 Second Avenue, 10th Floor, New York, NY 10017, USA
Tel: (212) 850 2200.
Website: www.nigeria-consulate-ny.org

Money

Currency: Naira (NGN) = 100 kobo. Notes are in denominations of NGN500, 200, 100, 50, 20, 10 and 5. Coins are in denominations of NGN1 and kobo 25, 10, 5 and 1.

Currency exchange: The Government of Nigeria has fixed an artificially high rate for local currency (the Naira) in terms of its value in exchange for foreign currencies. However, trading on the black market is extremely dangerous and could lead to arrest. Therefore, visitors are advised to exchange currency at the official rate and at approved exchange facilities, which often include major hotels. Inter-bank transfers are frequently difficult, if not impossible, to accomplish.

Credit & debit cards: American Express, Diners Club, MasterCard and Visa are rarely accepted in Nigeria and, because of the prevalence of credit card fraud, their use is ill-advised.

Traveller's cheques: Facilities for changing traveller's cheques are limited to Abuja and larger towns.

Currency restrictions: Import of local currency is limited to NGN20 in notes and must be declared on arrival. Export of local currency is restricted to NGN20 in notes. Import of foreign currency is unlimited, but it must be declared on arrival; export is limited to NGN100 per adult over 16 and must be declared. Penalties for black market transactions are severe.

Banking hours: Mon 0800-1500, Tue-Fri 0800-1330. The Government owns a large percentage of all foreign banks.

Exchange rate indicators:
Rate at time of publishing
£1.00= NGN226.37
$1.00= NGN130.50

Duty Free

The following goods may be imported into Nigeria by persons over 18 years of age without incurring customs duty:
200 cigarettes or 50 cigars or 200g of tobacco; 1l of spirits and 1l of wine; 284ml of perfume; gifts to the value of NGN300 (excluding jewellery, photographic equipment, electronics and luxury goods).

Note: (a) If more than each of the above is imported, duty will be levied on the whole quantity. Heavy duty will be levied on luxury items such as cameras or radios unless the visitor's stay is temporary. (b) It is forbidden to buy or sell antiques from or to anyone other than the Director of Antiquities or an accredited agent; visitors should obtain a clearance permit from one of the above before presenting antiques, artefacts or curios at the airport.

Prohibited items: Champagne, sparkling wine, beer, mineral water and soft drinks; fruits, vegetables, cereals and eggs, whether fresh or preserved; jewellery and precious metals; textile fabrics and mosquito netting.

Public Holidays

Below are listed Public Holidays for the January 2006-June 2007 period.
2006: Jan 1 New Year's Day. **Jan 10** Eid al-Kabir (Feast of the Sacrifice). **Apr 11** Mouloud (Birth of the Prophet). **Apr 14-17** Easter. **May 1** Workers' Day. **Oct 1** Independence Day. **Oct 22-24** Eid al-Fitr (End of Ramadan). **Dec 25-26** Christmas. **Dec 31** Eid al-Kabir (Feast of the Sacrifice).
2007: Jan 1 New Year's Day. **Apr 6-9** Easter. **Mar 31** Mouloud (Birth of the Prophet). **May 1** Workers' Day.
Note: Muslim festivals are timed according to local sightings of various phases of the moon and the dates given above are approximations. During the lunar month of Ramadan that precedes Eid al-Fitr, Muslims fast during the day and feast at night and normal business patterns may be interrupted. Many restaurants are closed during the day and there may be restrictions on smoking and drinking. Some disruption may continue into Eid al-Fitr itself. Eid al-Fitr and Eid al-Kabir (Eid al-Adha) may last anything from two to 10 days, depending on the region. For more information, see the *World of Islam* appendix.

Health

	Special? Precautions?	Certificate Required?
Yellow Fever	Yes	1
Cholera	Yes	2
Typhoid & Polio	3	N/A
Malaria	4	N/A

Note: *Regulations and requirements may be subject to change at short notice, and you are advised to contact your doctor well in advance of your intended date of departure. Any numbers in the chart refer to the footnotes below.*

1: A yellow fever vaccination certificate is required by travellers over one year of age arriving within six days from infected areas. Travellers arriving from non-endemic zones should note that vaccination is strongly recommended for travel outside the urban areas, even if an outbreak of the disease has not been reported and they would normally not require a vaccination certificate to enter the country. The risk of contracting yellow fever is highest in Lagos and Kaduna states. Contact Embassy/High Commission for exact details of vaccination requirements prior to travel.
2: Following WHO guidelines issued in 1973, a cholera vaccination certificate is not a condition of entry to Nigeria. However, evidence of cholera vaccination is required by certain nationals before they may enter the country (check with the nearest Nigerian Embassy) and vaccination is therefore advised.

Cholera is a serious risk in this country and precautions are essential. Up-to-date advice should be sought before deciding whether these precautions should include vaccination, as medical opinion is divided over its effectiveness; see the *Health* appendix for further information.
3: Polio and typhoid both occur.
4: Malaria risk exists all year throughout the country. The predominant *falciparum* strain has been reported to be resistant to chloroquine.

Food & drink: All water should be regarded as being potentially contaminated. Water used for drinking, brushing teeth or making ice should have first been boiled or otherwise sterilised. Milk is unpasteurised and should be boiled. Powdered or tinned milk is available and is advised, but make sure that it is reconstituted with pure water. Avoid dairy products which are likely to have been made from unboiled milk. Only eat well-cooked meat and fish, preferably served hot. Pork, salad and mayonnaise may carry increased risk. Vegetables should be cooked and fruit peeled.
Other risks: *Bilharzia* (schistosomiasis) is present. Avoid swimming and paddling in fresh water; swimming pools which are well chlorinated and maintained are safe. *Hepatitis A, B, C* and *E* are present; precautions should be taken. *Meningococcal meningitis, leishmaniasis, trypanosomiasis* and *onchocerciasis* (river blindness) occur. TB and *dengue fever* also occur and *HIV* is a risk.
Rabies is present. For those at high risk, vaccination before arrival should be considered. If you are bitten, seek medical advice without delay. For more information, consult the *Health* appendix.
Health care: The Government-provided health care facilities are of a poor standard and are subject to shortages of drugs, equipment, materials and even electricity. It is advisable to take a sufficient supply of drugs or medication to meet personal needs. However, there are some adequate private facilities where the standards approach those of Europe. Doctors and hospitals often expect immediate cash payment for health services. There is no reciprocal health agreement with the UK. Medical insurance is essential.

Travel - International

AIR:

The national airline is *Virgin Nigeria* (website: www.virginnigeria.com); flights began in June 2005 and operate between Lagos, London, Accra (Ghana), Johannesburg (South Africa) and Doula (Cameroon).
Approximate flight times: From Lagos to *London* is seven hours 25 minutes and to *New York* is 12 hours 10 minutes.
Main airports: *Lagos (LOS)* (Murtala Muhammed) is 22km (13 miles) north of Lagos (travel time – 40 minutes).
To/from the airport: Taxis to the city are available.
Facilities: Restaurant, bar, snack bar, bank, post office, bureau de change, duty free shop and car hire.
Kano (KAN) is 8km (5 miles) north of Kano (travel time – 25 minutes). *To/from the airport:* Taxis are available.
Facilities: Restaurant, bank, post office, duty free shop and car hire.
Abuja (ABV) is 35km (22 miles) from the city. *To/from the airport:* Taxis are available.
Note: Pickpockets and confidence tricksters, some posing as local immigration and other Government officials, are especially common at Murtala Muhammed Airport.
Departure tax: None.
SEA:

Main ports: *Lagos, Port Harcourt* and *Calabar.* Other important ports include *Warri* and *Sepele.*
ROAD:

Links are with Benin, Cameroon, Chad and Niger. The principal trans-Saharan routes pass through Nigeria from Niger. The principal link with Benin is via the Idoroko border point along the good coast road to Lagos.

Travel - Internal

AIR:

The former national carrier, *Nigeria Airways,* has now been liquidated but the new airline *Virgin Nigeria* (website: www.virginnigeria.com) operates domestic flights to Abuja and Port Harcourt. Charter facilities are available in Lagos from *Aero Contractors* (website: www.acn.aero). It is advisable to book internal flights well in advance. There is often considerable delay in internal air services. Lack of fuel sometimes disrupts internal commercial air travel and flights may be cancelled at short notice.
SEA:

Ferry services operate along the south coast and along the Niger and Benue rivers. For timetables and prices, enquire locally.
RAIL:

The two main routes are from Lagos to Kano (via Ibadan–Oyo–Ogbombosho–Kaduna–Zaria); and from Port Harcourt to Maiduguri (via Aba–Enugu–Makurdi–Jos). These two lines link up Kaduna

and Kafanchan. There is also a branch line from Zaria to Gusau and Kaura Namoda. A daily service runs on both main routes. Sleeping cars are available, which must be booked in advance. There are three classes and some trains have restaurant cars and air conditioning. Trains are generally slower and less reliable than buses, but cheaper.
ROAD:

Traffic drives on the right. The national road system links all the main centres, although in some areas secondary roads become impassable during the rains. Reports of armed robberies in broad daylight on rural roads in the northern half of Nigeria have been reported and appear to be increasing. **Buses** and **taxis** (or 'bush taxis' in the shape of Ford Transit vans) run between the main towns. **Car hire** is not difficult to obtain in Lagos and Abuja, but it is best to go through hotels. Chauffeur-driven cars are advised. **Documentation**: An International Driving Permit is required, accompanied by two passport-size photos.
URBAN:

Public transport in Lagos operates in rather chaotic conditions. The city suffers from chronic traffic congestion, which makes it impossible for buses and taxis to operate efficiently, especially during the rush hours. There are many private bus companies and several thousand private minibuses. Taxis in Lagos are yellow and both fares and tip should be agreed in advance. A ferry service runs to Lagos Island.

Travel Advice

All travel to the Bakassi Peninsula is advised against. All but essential travel by boat and road to the riverine areas in Rivers, Bayelsa and Delta States is also advised against. Localised outbreaks of civil unrest can occur at short notice. Violent crime is prevalent in the south of the country, including Lagos.
Travellers should be aware of the threat from terrorism in Nigeria. A statement issued by Osama Bin Laden in February 2003 called for an uprising by Muslims in a number of countries including Nigeria.
Travellers should be aware of the global risk of indiscriminate terrorist attacks, which could be against civilian targets.
This advice is based on information provided by the Foreign and Commonwealth Office in the UK. It is correct at time of publishing. As the situation can change rapidly, visitors are advised to contact the following organisations for the latest travel advice:

British Foreign and Commonwealth Office
Tel: (0845) 850 2829.
Website: www.fco.gov.uk

US Department of State
Website: http://travel.state.gov/travel

Accommodation

HOTELS:
There are first-class hotels in Lagos and in the major towns, but they are heavily booked and advance reservation is essential. Lagos is one of the most congested cities in Africa, and the majority of good hotels are on Lagos Island. Hotels are generally very expensive, but there is a variety of alternative accommodation. Further information can be obtained from the Nigeria Tourism Development Corporation (see *Top Things To See & Do*).
CATERING REST-HOUSES/CHRISTIAN MISSIONS/GUEST HOUSES/SPORTING CLUBS:
Government-run **catering rest-houses** are scattered throughout the country and offer accommodation in colonial-style rest-houses. In many towns, **Christian missions** are able to offer good basic accommodation at a reasonable price. The universities have **guest houses** for visiting academics, but may be able to accommodate other visitors. Most of the big towns have **sporting clubs** which offer cheap accommodation and eating facilities, and can be used by visitors who take temporary membership. Port Harcourt is the centre of the national oil industry and offers a large selection of accommodation to the industry, which is also available to tourists.

Top Things To See & Do

- In the predominantly Muslim north, the most important festival is **Sallah**, celebrated three months after the feast of Eid al-Fitr (End of Ramadan), particularly in the towns of **Kano**, **Katsina**, **Maiduguri** and **Zaria**. Every family is required to slaughter a ram and festivities last for several days, with horseback processions, musicians and dancers. Featured also in northern communities are *Durbars*, long lines of horsemen led by a band, the horses in quilted armour with the riders wearing quilted coats and wielding ceremonial swords.
- Watch out for Nigeria's wonderful selection of homemade **crafts**. The **National Museum** at **Onikan** on **Lagos Island**

houses numerous exhibits of Nigeria's ancient civilisations and has a craft centre which sells examples of Nigerian craft at fixed prices. In the **Jankara Market** on Lagos Island, you can bargain for locally dyed cotton and handwoven cloth, herbs and leather goods. In the southwest, meanwhile, **Ibadan** has a **market** that is reputedly one of the biggest in Nigeria. Many of the villages in **Cross River State** at the Mouth of the Niger are of interest for their handicrafts and traditions of magic, but may only be accessible by foot or canoe. **Abaraka**, **Auchi**, **Sapele**, **Sapoba** and **Warri**, however, can be reached by road. **Ikot Ekepne** is the centre for beautiful baskets and carvings, and at **Oron** there is a museum renowned for its exhibits of Ibibio and Efik carvings. In the north in Kano, **Kurmi Market** has many tourist souvenirs, including the richly embroidered *Fulani* horse blankets and decorations used at festivals. The famous **dye pits** (**Kofar Mata**) are still in use and apparently some of the oldest in Africa.

- Walk where the capital of the **Yoruba Empire** once was, and admire **Oyo**'s old Portuguese-style houses. Worship the Yoruba goddess of fertility in **Oshogbo**, the founding centre of the internationally renowned school of Oshogbo art and home of the shrines and grove of Oshun. The famous **Oshun Shrine** is to be found here. The **Oshun Festival** takes place towards the end of August each year (at the end of the rainy season, during which thousands of childless women seek the help of the Yoruba goddess of fertility). **Ile-Ife**, the ancient name of the town of **Ife**, is another recess of Yoruba culture, and includes the **Ife Museum**, which has many fine bronze and terracotta sculptures dating back to the 13th century. Modern **Benin City** is a rapidly developing metropolis, but there are a few reminders of its long Yoruba history. The old city's moat and wall survive in places and the **National Museum** houses an interesting collection of Benin royal art. The **Oba's Palace** is worth visiting, although permission needs to be obtained in **Lagos**.
- Marvel at some of Nigeria's magnificent views: **Akure** is a good base from which to explore the seven **Olumirin Waterfalls**; **Calabar** is a pleasant town in a beautiful setting, high on a hill above the **Calabar River**; **Abuja**'s outlook across the savannah; and the striking and fascinating mountain scenery enjoyed around **Biu** and towards the Cameroon border.
- Journey through the **Cross River National Park**. The best base from which to do so is the town of **Ikom**, on the road to Cameroon, which has curious carved **monoliths** set in circles, believed to be ancient monuments assembled in reverence to ancestors. The Cross River National Park piques a curiosity in nature, rather than humanity. In the Rainforest Conservation area, this is a place of majestic mountains and rolling hills, with **wildlife** including leopards, buffaloes, chimpanzees, gorillas, baboons and elephants. Elsewhere, the **Yankari National Park** in the eastern half of the country is particularly good for **birdwatching**. Animals which can be viewed here include elephants, crocodiles and monkeys. The park has accommodation, restaurants and a swimming pool. The title of Nigeria's most scenic national park might also go to the **Gashaka Game Reserve** near **Yola**, which provides opportunities to view birds and animals and is home to some highly endangered species.
- Circumnavigate the walled old town of Kano, formerly the largest of the ancient Hausa cities, and soak up its lingering medieval atmosphere. Despite this atmosphere, reinforced by the wall, Kano was founded at least 1000 years ago, being of strategic importance on the trans-Saharan trade routes. The **Emir's Palace** remains an outstanding example of Hausa architecture.
- **Picnic** without breaking a sweat in **Jos**, a favourite holiday centre on account of its location (1200m (3900ft) above sea level) and consequent pleasantly cool climate. The nearby **Assob Falls** and many streams and dams make this an extremely pretty area.

TOURIST INFORMATION

Nigeria Tourism Development Corporation
Old Secretariat, Area 1, Garki, PMB 167, Abuja, Nigeria
Tel: (9) 234 2764.
Website: www.nigeriatourism.net

Entertainment

FOOD & DRINK: There are restaurants of all varieties in Lagos and the major towns. European and Oriental food is readily available. Although there are self-service cafes, mainly in department stores, most restaurants have table service. Nigerian food is typical of that found throughout West Africa, with regional variations. In the north, meat is more popular than in other areas. Spirits are expensive. Larger hotels and clubs have bars and cocktail lounges.
National specialities:
- Yam.
- Sweet potatoes.
- Plantain and pepper soup.
- *Suya* (barbecued liver and beef on sticks) and *kilishi* (spiced dried meat).
- In the east *egussi soup* (stew of meat, dried fish and melon seeds).
- In the south, goat meat and bush meat - particularly antelope - are considered a delicacy.

National drinks:
- There are many brands of locally brewed and bottled beer which are very good.
- Nigerian-brewed Guinness is available.

Tipping: Unless a service charge has been included, 10 per cent is expected for most services.
NIGHTLIFE: There are nightclubs in many of the hotels in Lagos and in the Surulere district. Some clubs have live entertainment, details of which are given in the local newspapers. North of Oyo in Ogbomosho, there is a lively market, particularly in the evenings. Local festivals which generally take place in the summer months provide a good opportunity to see dancing, music and traditional costumes.
SHOPPING: Markets are the most interesting places to shop. Special purchases include *adire* (patterned, indigo-dyed cloth), batiks and pottery from the southwest, leatherwork and *kaduna* cotton from the north and carvings from the east. Designs vary greatly, many towns having their own distinctive style. Other purchases include herbs, beadwork, basketry and ceremonial masks such as those of the Ekpo.
Shopping hours: Mon-Fri 0800-1700, Sat 0800-1630.

Business

- **GDP:** US$65.2 billion (2004).
- **Main exports:** Petroleum and related products, cocoa and rubber.
- **Main imports:** Machinery, chemicals, transport equipment, manufactured goods, food and live animals.
- **Main trade partners:** USA, Brazil, China (PR), UK, Spain, The Netherlands, France, Germany and Italy.

ECONOMY: Nigeria is Africa's largest oil producer; the industry earns 90 per cent of the country's export income and has underpinned its economy for decades. Nigeria also has commercially viable quantities of tin, coal, iron ore, zinc and some uranium, plus substantial but as yet largely untapped reserves of natural gas and coal. Agriculture occupies well over half of the population, who produce rice, maize, cassava, sorghum and millet as staples, as well as groundnuts, cocoa, palm oil and rubber as cash crops. Timber and livestock rearing have both developed during the last 20 years. Nonetheless, successive governments have failed to restore Nigeria's one-time self-sufficiency in food. Manufacturing was established during the 1960s, principally with oil money, and now includes food processing and the production of vehicles, textiles, pharmaceuticals, paper and cement. Despite its abundance of natural resources, Nigeria has suffered an almost permanent economic crisis during the last 10 years, due to political instability, mismanagement and corruption. Per capita GDP is around US$650 annually, which is improved but still not desirable. The country is weighed down by a massive foreign debt. Reduction negotiations have been completed with the 'Paris Club' of leading creditors. As a condition of the rescheduling, the new civilian Government has begun to put into effect economic reforms, including the sale of major state-owned industries. Recent economic performance has been determined mainly by the state of the world oil market. Governmental deregulation of fuel prices and the privatisation of Nigeria's four oil refineries in 2003, coupled with the rise in oil production, meant that recent GDP growth has been good, estimated at around 4.6 per cent in 2005. Nigeria is the dominant member of the West African economic cooperation organisation, ECOWAS, as well as a leading member of the oil producers' cartel, OPEC.
BUSINESS ETIQUETTE: English is spoken in business circles. It is common for business meetings to take place without a prior appointment, although these should be made for Government visits. Business deals will often progress at a slower pace than is common in Europe. Owing to the prevalence of commercial fraud targeting foreigners, business travellers should contact both their local Nigerian Embassy and Chamber of Commerce before travelling to Nigeria.
Office hours: Mon-Fri 0800-1600 (Government offices); 0830-1700 (private businesses). However, offices in the northern States may close at 1300 as Muslim workers take part in *Jumat* services at 1400: business resumes after this.

COMMERCIAL INFORMATION

Nigerian High Commission's Nigerian Information Service Center
9 Northumberland Avenue, London WC2N 5BX, UK
Tel: (020) 7839 1244.
Website: www.nigeriahc.org.uk

Niue

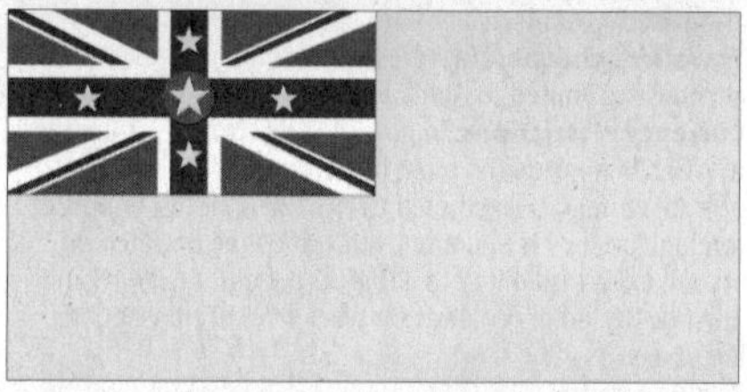

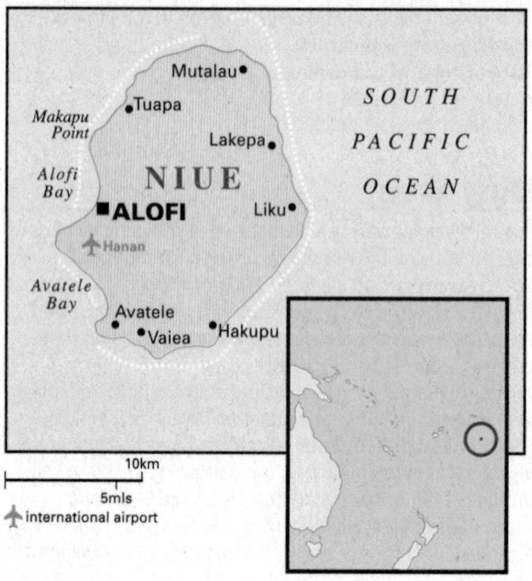

Location: South Pacific.

Time: GMT - 11.

Overview

Most of the inhabitants of Niue descend from settlers from Tonga, Samoa and Fiji, who arrived between AD 600-1000, developing their own particular culture. The first Europeans reached Niue in the wake of Captain Cook's expedition to the region in 1774. Administered by the London Missionary Society from 1846, it became a British Protectorate in 1900. The island was then formally annexed to New Zealand in 1901, as part of the Cook Islands. In October 1974, Niue was granted 'self-government in free association with New Zealand', making it the smallest self-governing state with that status. This also allows Niueans to retain New Zealand citizenship while maintaining self-government in their own country. The major problems facing Niue are chronic population decline caused by emigration and the fragility of the island's status as an offshore tax haven, which is under threat from new measures designed to tackle international money laundering. Niue is also vulnerable to Pacific cyclones: in January 2004, the island suffered serious damage from Cyclone Heta. Reputedly the world's largest coral island, Niue's rugged coastline and reef offer excellent fishing, diving and snorkelling opportunities. Parakeets, white-tailed terns, weka and other exotic birds live on this island and butterflies are a common sight darting among the hibiscus and orchids. The island is well off the beaten track but tourist numbers are steadily increasing with 2758 tourist arrivals by air recorded for 2003 - significantly more than the island's permanent population.

General Information

AREA: 262.7 sq km (101.4 sq miles).
POPULATION: 1761 (official estimate 2004).
POPULATION DENSITY: 6.7 per sq km.
CAPITAL: Alofi. **Population**: 404 (2004).
GEOGRAPHY: Niue is an isolated island located 480km (298 miles) east of Tonga, 560km (348 miles) southeast of Western Samoa, 980km (609 miles) west of Rarotonga and 2400km (1500 miles) northeast of New Zealand. Affectionately known as 'the rock', Niue is reputedly the largest upraised coral atoll in the world. It has 6178 acres (2500 hectares) of the most undisturbed forests in the world, designated tapu areas by the locals, where no humans were allowed to set foot for centuries. Now all the tapu forests, except the one controlled by Hakupu village, are penetrable. These forests are full of lush undergrowth, coconut palms and some of the oldest-known ebony trees on earth. Light and scattered forest covers approximately 34,594 acres (14,000 hectares). At the edge of the forest, the coast gives way to coral outcrops.
GOVERNMENT: Self-governing state in 'free association' with New Zealand. (New Zealand retains responsibility for external affairs.) **Head of State**: HM Queen Elizabeth II, represented locally by High Commissioner Sandra Lee. **Head of Government**: Premier Young Vivian since 2002. **Recent history:** The only formal political party is the Niue People's Party

(NPP), which has dominated politics on the island since its formation in 1987. Although it has not always enjoyed an absolute majority, it has been able to govern with the support of independents. The current premier is the veteran Mititaigimimene Young Vivian who took over following the most recent poll in April 2002.
LANGUAGE: Niuean and English.
RELIGION: Most people belong to the Ekalesia Niue, a Protestant denomination; also Apostolic, Bahaii Faith, Christian Outreach Church, Latter Day Saints (Mormon), Jehovah's Witness, Roman Catholic and Seventh Day Adventist.
ELECTRICITY: 240 volts AC, 50Hz. Plugs are the standard three-pin type.
SOCIAL CONVENTIONS: Niuean children are bestowed with gifts of money or handmade mats and cloths from their relatives upon coming of age, when girls have their ears pierced and boys receive their first haircut. It is polite to ask permission before entering private land. Niueans consider Sunday as a serious day of rest and most attend church both in the morning and afternoon. While many people play golf, go swimming or sightsee, certain activities, such as boating and fishing, are not allowed on Sunday. For further information on Sunday protocol, contact the Niue Tourism Office (see *Top Things To See & Do*). Clothing is usually casual, cool and comfortable but women often wear a hat and cover their shoulders for church and men wear long trousers. Swimming attire is not acceptable in towns or villages.

Climate

Tropical climate bathed by southeast trade winds, Niue has warm days and pleasantly cool nights.
Required clothing: Cotton shorts and shirts (or cotton dresses for women) with a wrap for the evenings.

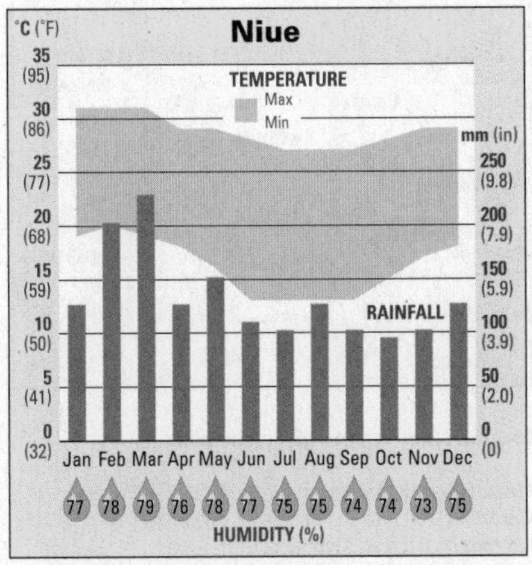

Communications

Telephone: IDD and local facilities are available. Country code: 683. International calls can also be made directly from the telephone or with the assistance of an operator. There are telephones in hotels, motels and guest houses. Services are run by the Telecommunications Department located at the Commercial Centre in Alofi, which also provides fax facilities, and is open 24 hours a day.
Internet: The island has a wireless Internet service provided by the Niue Internet Users Society.
Post: The Niue post office is open Mon-Fri 0830-1500.
MEDIA: Press: The *Niue Star* is published weekly in English and Niuean.
TV: *Television Niue* broadcasts in English and Niuean five evenings a week but other programming is available outside of these times.
Radio: Radio Sunshine is operated by Niue Broadcasts Corporation

Passport/Visa

	Passport Required?	Visa Required?	Return Ticket Required?
Full British	Yes	1	Yes
Australian	Yes	1	Yes
Canadian	Yes	1	Yes
USA	Yes	1	Yes
Other EU	Yes	1	Yes
Japanese	Yes	1	Yes

***Note:** Regulations and requirements may be subject to change at short notice, and you are advised to contact the appropriate diplomatic or consular authority before finalising travel arrangements. Any numbers in the chart refer to the footnotes below.*

PASSPORTS: Required by all.
VISAS: Required by all except:
(a) nationals of New Zealand;
(b) **1.** bona fide tourists staying less than 30 days with return or onward tickets, all documents required for the next destination and sufficient funds for length of stay. However an *Entry Permit* is required by all nationals, which is granted on arrival;
(c) those who are in transit, continuing their journey by the first or connecting aircraft and not leaving the airport.
Note: Visas *are* required for all nationals staying for 30 days or longer.
Entry permit requirements: (a) Valid passport. (b) Sufficient funds for duration of stay. (c) Return or onward ticket.
Types of visa: *Ordinary* and *Transit*. Transit visas are not required by nationals of New Zealand or by other nationals continuing their journey by the same or first connecting aircraft, provided they hold valid onward documentation and are not leaving the airport.
Validity: Entry Permit: 30 days. Extensions are available from the Immigration Office, PO Box 69, Alofi, Niue (tel: 4349 *or* 4333; fax: 4336).
Application to: Consulate or High Commission (see *Passport/Visa Information*).
Temporary residence: Check with the Immigration Office.

PASSPORT/VISA INFORMATION

Niue High Commission in New Zealand
Level 1, Gleneagles Building, 71 The Terrace, Wellington, PO Box 10-123, New Zealand
Tel: (4) 499 4515.

Money

Currency: The New Zealand Dollar (NZ$) is legal tender (see *New Zealand* section). Niue sometimes produces commemorative coins which, when available, may be obtained at the treasury.
Currency exchange: The Bank of the South Pacific in Alofi, the only commercial bank in Niue, can exchange currency.
Credit & debit cards: American Express, Diners Club, MasterCard and Visa are accepted in most hotels and resorts. Contact your credit or debit card company for details of merchant acceptability and other services which may be available.
Currency restrictions: There are no restrictions on the import of local or foreign currency. However, there are restrictions on postal notes, money orders, cheques or promissory notes in New Zealand currency, which must be declared to the Westpac Banking Corporation in Niue. Export of local currency is restricted to NZ$10,000. Export of foreign currency is restricted to the amount declared on arrival and authorisation from a bank is required.
Banking hours: Mon-Thurs 0900-1500, Fri 0830-1500.
Exchange rate indicators: See *New Zealand* section.

Duty Free

The following items can be imported into Niue by persons of 18 years of age or older without incurring customs duty:
400 cigarettes or 50 cigars or 500g of tobacco or a combination of each with a maximum weight of 0.5lb; 3.5l of spirits, liquor or wine; other goods to the value of NZ$250.
Restricted imports: Firearms and ammunition are prohibited unless permission is received from the Chief of Police at the Police Department of Niue. A maximum of one of each of the following: radio, personal stereo, tape recorder, laptop computer, pair of binoculars, photo or video camera.
Restricted exports: Artefacts, coral and valuable shells.

Public Holidays

Below are listed Public Holidays for the January 2006-June 2007 period.
2006: Jan 1 New Year's Day. **Jan 4** Takai Commission Holiday. **Feb 6** Waitangi Day. **Apr 14-17** Easter. **Apr 25** ANZAC Day. **Jun 5** Queen's Birthday. **Oct 16-19** Constitution Celebrations. **Oct 17** Peniamina's Day. **Dec 25-26** Christmas.
2007: Jan 1 New Year's Day. **Jan 4** Takai Commission Holiday. **Feb 6** Waitangi Day. **Apr 6-9** Easter. **Apr 25** ANZAC Day. **Jun 4** Queen's Birthday.

Health

	Special Precautions?	Certificate Required?
Yellow Fever	Yes	1
Cholera	No	No
Typhoid & Polio	2	N/A
Malaria	Yes	N/A

***Note:** Regulations and requirements may be subject to change at short notice, and you are advised to contact your doctor well in advance of your intended date of departure. Any numbers in the chart refer to the footnotes below.*

1: A yellow fever certificate is required from all travellers over one year of age arriving from infected areas.
2: Typhoid is not currently a concern on the island. However, if coming from an infected area it is advised to take the necessary precautions.
Food & drink: Drinking water is from natural spring and rainwater, but it is also recommended that you boil water prior to drinking. Imported bottled water is also available. There is a low risk of travellers' diarrhoea; exercise moderate food caution. Milk is pasteurised and dairy products are safe for consumption. Local meat, poultry, seafood, fruit and vegetables are generally considered safe to eat.
Other risks: *Hepatitis A* occurs and *hepatitis B* is endemic.
Health care: The Niue Health Centre offers medical and dental treatment. There is a 24-hour on-call emergency service. Patients will be asked for on-the-spot payment. Complicated cases will be sent overseas to New Zealand. International travellers are strongly advised to take out full medical insurance before departure.
Note: Medical charges for overseas patients: Consultation fee: NZ$25; diving certificate: NZ$50; dressings: NZ$10.

Travel - International

AIR:
Polynesian Airlines (website: www.polynesianairlines.com) flies to Niue from Auckland, New Zealand and from Apia, Samoa.
Main airports: *Niue International (IUE)* (Hanan) is 7km (4 miles) north of Alofi. *To/from the airport:* Transfer buses are available from the airport to all tourist accommodations. *Facilities:* There are some shops at the airport, open for scheduled flights.
Departure tax: NZ$25.
SEA:
It is possible to visit Niue by yacht; weekday arrivals are preferred. Moorings and buoys are available.

Travel - Internal

ROAD:
There are 123km (76 miles) of paved roads in Niue. Driving is on the left. There is no organised public transport on Niue. **Car hire:** Cars can be hired on the island although it is best to make reservations before arrival. A limited number of mountain bikes can also be hired on the island. **Documentation:** Along with their national driving licence, visitors must obtain a local licence from the Niue Police Department.

Travel Advice

Most visits to Niue are trouble-free but you should be aware of the global risk of indiscriminate international terrorist attacks, which could be against civilian targets, including places frequented by foreigners.
This advice is based on information provided by the Foreign and Commonwealth Office in the UK. It is correct at time of publishing. As the situation can change rapidly, visitors are advised to contact the following organisations for the latest travel advice:

British Foreign and Commonwealth Office
Tel: (0845) 850 2829.
Website: www.fco.gov.uk

US Department of State
Website: http://travel.state.gov/travel

Accommodation

ANAIKI MOTEL: Located next to the Avaiki Caves at Makefu. This accommodation has five units in a long block (single/double/triple), breakfast included. A hot plate is provided for heating up simple meals.
CORAL GARDENS MOTEL: Five self-contained studio-room chalets adjoining Sails Restaurant. Situated near a tropical coral garden close to Alofi and Makefu and in close proximity to popular reefs and swimming pools.
HUVALU FOREST CAMP: Set in the beautiful Huvalu Forest near Hakupu village, this camp offers very basic accommodation with shared bathroom and cooking facilities and bunkhouse-style sleeping arrangements.
KOLOLI'S MOTEL: Built in the centre of Alofi, it provides a range of rooms, including a large bedroom suite, a large double bedroom, two double rooms and a twin room with shared bathroom facilities. There is a kitchen and barbecue area, or meals can be provided.
MATAVAI RESORT: Situated on a cliff top, with views overlooking Dolphin Bay and the bays of Avatele and Tamakautoga, this resort is just 10 minutes from Alofi, has 24 rooms and two executive suites. The main building houses a restaurant, two bars, conference facilities and two freshwater swimming pools. They also offer wedding packages.

NAMUKULU MOTEL: With sea and reef views, this motel is situated a 10-minute drive from Alofi and a few minutes walk from Limu. It consists of three self-contained chalets which can sleep up to four people. There is a licensed restaurant and bar nearby, as well as opportunities for snorkelling, swimming and cycling.

PELENI'S GUEST HOUSE: A former family home in the centre of Alofi, it consists of three bedrooms with shared cooking, bathroom and lounge facilities. Meals can be provided.

Top Things To See & Do

- Every month sees a traditional **haircutting and ear-piercing ceremony** held in various locations in Niue. However, prior permission must be sought.
- Recommended sites in **Alofi** include the **Women's Club Town Hall**, with a craft shop featuring various handicrafts for sale; and **Alofi Market** open on Fridays. *Note*: The **Huanaki Cultural Centre** and the **Huanaki Museum** were completely destroyed by Cyclone Heta in January 2004.
- Some 5km (3 miles) north of Alofi, near **Makapu Point**, **Peniamina's Grave**, the resting place of the Niuean who first brought Christianity to the island, can be found in a small clearing on the left side of the road. The **Experimental Farm**, a centre for animal husbandry and plant testing, is another popular destination for visitors. **Opaahi** is the site of Captain Cook's landing where he received a hostile reception from the local people and was almost hit by a spear. There are good swimming holes at **Vaitafe**, 800m (2625ft) south of **Fulala** and 2.5km (1.5 miles) north of **Lakepa**, at **Avaiki**, and at **Limu**, perhaps the most beautiful on the north coast with its colourful coral and its wide variety of marine life (thatched cottages and a barbecue area can also be found here).
- **Avatele Bay** is another excellent location for swimming and snorkelling and visitors may watch the many fishermen in their canoes and dinghies who fish the bay's waters for tuna, wahoo and marlin, as well as the spectacular sunsets that set over the bay.
- An interesting excursion is to the deserted village of **Fatiau Tuai**, 1600m (5249ft) from the main road on the seaward side of **Vaiea Village**. The original inhabitants suffered from an eye disease and the entire population was moved by the Government to Vaiea. The coastline here is stunning for its rough surf crashing against the shore and shooting up through blowholes.
- Chasms are another of Niue's natural wonders. The amazing **Vaikona Chasm** can be reached by the Namuke sea track from the main road about 4km (2.5 miles) south of **Liku**. **Togo Chasm** is also popular. Located on the eastern side of the island, 4km (2.5 miles) north of **Hakupu**, it is one of Niue's most magnificent scenic areas with a tropical rainforest, towering coral pinnacles and an oasis of white sand, coconut palms and a pond hidden beneath overhanging cliffs (guide recommended).
- **Matapa Chasm** is another well-known scenic attraction, reached by road from the foot of **Hikutavake Hill**. **Vaotoi Pool**, 3km (2 miles) north of Hakapu, is the scene of the wreck of a Japanese fishing vessel which was beached during a storm in 1967. However, access to many of the chasms and pools are along difficult paths and an experienced guide is usually considered necessary.
- There are hundreds of **caves** and grottoes which are excellent for land explorations or dive sites. Various caves are used as repositories for canoes as well as for the bones of dead ancestors. **Avaiki Cave** is reported to be where the first settler's canoe landed. **Talava – The Arches** are a group of extraordinary arches and caverns, many containing stalactites and stalagmites, which may be visited at low tide. Other caves known for their spectacular formations are **Ulupaka Cave**, reached by a track 800m (2625ft) south of Lakepa, and Palaha Caves, 180m (591ft) north of Palaha. **Anatoloa Cave**, 1600m (5249ft) north of Lakepa and a five-minute walk from the main road, is hard to find but is well worth the effort. Niuean mythology cites it as being the home of a dangerous god and human bones have been found within it.
- Surrounded on all sides by the crystal clear and unpolluted waters of the Pacific Ocean, Niue is an ideal destination for **swimming**, **scuba-diving** and **snorkelling**. Snorkellers and divers have the opportunity to encounter humpback whales and dolphins in Niuean waters. For further information as well as bookings of twin-hulled dive boats, scuba and snorkelling gear and PADI certification courses, contact Niue Dive, PO Box 140, Alofi, Niue (tel: 4311; website: www.dive.nu). The best diving sites in Niue are **Limu** (Ana Mahaga), **The Dome, The Chimney,** the **Bubble Cave, Egypt** and **Snake Gully**. Generally the most popular of the dive sites, Snake Gully gets its name from the large concentration of sea snakes found in the area.
- Because of the sheer drops from reefs into deep ocean, land-based game **fishing** is a unique experience for many. Red bass, wahoo (also known locally as *paala*), tuna, sailfish and marlin abound. Traditional outrigger canoes and motor boats can be arranged for line-fishing expeditions.

TOURIST INFORMATION

Niue Tourism Office
PO Box 42, Alofi, Niue Island
Tel: 683 4224.
Website: www.niueisland.com

South Pacific Tourism Organisation in Fiji
Street address: Level 3, FNPF Place,
343-359 Victoria Parade, Suva, Fiji
Postal address: PO Box 13119, Suva, Fiji
Tel: (679) 330 4177.
Website: www.spto.org

Niue Tourism Office in New Zealand
PO Box 68716, Newton, Auckland, New Zealand
Tel: (64) 585 1493.
Website: www.niueisland.com

Entertainment

FOOD & DRINK: Many ceremonies and social events stem from the processing of food. One community ritual is based on the extraction of *nu pia* starch from arrowroot, which is used in traditional dishes and soups and often given as a gift. Another ritualised ceremony surrounds *ti* root, which is made into a sweet drink or eaten as a sweet with coconuts. The *luku* fern is another indigenous plant used in Niuean cooking and is boiled, stir-fried or baked in an earth oven with coconut cream and chicken or corned beef. Other popular foods include taro, kumara, coconuts, pawpaw, bananas, tomatoes, capsicum and many varieties of yam. Restaurants in Niue include the Matavai Resort and Sails Restaurant. Jenna's is open for dinner but bookings are required. Lunch is available at Taki's Cafe and Tavana's Snack Bar. Restaurants do not have service charge or tax. *Note*: Some establishments were put out of business by Cyclone Heta in 2004. This information is subject to change.
Tipping: Not encouraged.

NIGHTLIFE: There are a number of enjoyable nightclubs. Hakupu Village also hosts a traditional cultural night once a week beginning with a tour of the village, followed by a traditional feast with dancing and singing (advance booking is recommended).

SHOPPING: Niuean women are especially regarded for the quality of their weaving, producing hats, baskets, handbags and mats from indigenous plants, such as pandanus, which make excellent buys for the visitor. These are available to visitors at Hinapoto Handcrafts at the Cultural Centre but can also be found at village show days. **Shopping hours**: Mon-Fri 0800-1600, Sat 0800-1600. There are generally one or two small stores in most villages around the island which are open in the evenings and during weekends.

Business

ECONOMY: There is a small amount of agriculture, producing coconuts and honey – some of which is exported – as well as yams, cassava and sweet potatoes for domestic consumption. But the weather is inclement (cyclones are a major problem) and two-thirds of the land surface is unsuitable for cultivation. Some livestock is reared, again for local consumption. Tourism is worth about US$1 million annually and brings in foreign exchange; postage stamps are another valuable source of revenue. However, there is still a budgetary shortfall, which is made up for by aid from New Zealand and, more recently, Australia. In common with other small and remote Pacific island states, Niue has opted for the development of an 'offshore' financial services industry to boost the economy. The necessary legislation was passed by the Assembly in 1994, although little progress has been made, not least due to the intense competition from other Pacific island economies who have adopted the same strategy. Niue continues to suffer a drain on its resources as its younger, educated population leaves for New Zealand in search of work.

BUSINESS ETIQUETTE: Shaking hands is the usual form of greeting and leaving. Lightweight or tropical suits are recommended for business. Official invitations will always state the dress code required: 'formal' means a jacket and tie for men and 'fiafia' means casual dress is acceptable.
Office hours: Mon-Fri 0730-1530 or 0800-1600.

CONFERENCES/CONVENTIONS: Matavai Resort conference rooms can seat 50 to 60 people or 120 theatre-style.

COMMERCIAL INFORMATION

Matavai Resort (Information on Conferences/Conventions)
PO Box 133, Alofi, Niue
Tel: 4360.
E-mail: matavai@niue.nu

Norway

Location: Northern Europe, Scandinavia.

Time: Norway Mainland: GMT + 1 (GMT + 2 from last Sunday in March to last Sunday in October).
Jan Mayen Islands, Svalbard: GMT + 1.

Overview

The breathtaking fjords of the southwest are Norway's most dramatic features, but there are many other reasons to visit this sparsely populated land on the northern fringe of Europe. The North Cape's midnight sun is rightly famous – here, far above the Arctic Circle, lies the spectacularly situated town of Tromsø, where the sun never rises in winter, nor sets in midsummer. And each of Norway's three major cities offers distinct appeal – Oslo as present-day capital, Bergen as major trading port and Trondheim as long-established centre of Christian pilgrimage.

In the wilderness that lies between the main urban centres are such delights as Jostedalsbreen, Europe's largest glacier. There are opportunities to indulge in outdoor activities including skiing, hunting, fishing and rock-climbing. Even the less energetic can marvel at the awesome beauty of the Norwegian countryside, with its countless steep-sided valleys, high mountain lakes and unbelievable views.

For those who hike this stunning landscape, there emerges a thrill from following the footsteps of Norwegian ancestors. The known history of the country begins in the 9th century AD and is based on the sagas, supported by archaeological evidence, and the explorations of Viking adventurers. Norway itself was divided into a number of fiefdoms; the unification process began with King Harald Fairhair, who defeated the major northern tribes at the battle of Hafrsfjord in 872. Over the next two centuries, Christianity gradually supplanted traditional belief in Norse gods. By 1060, the country was unified. From 1200 onwards, the twin powers of church and crown took control. The arrival of bubonic plague (The Black Death) in Norway in 1350 killed half the Norwegian population. The Norwegians and Swedes had already established a joint Monarchical structure which lasted between 1319 and 1343. Following the ravages of the Black Death, Norway entered into a political union with Denmark in 1380 through intermarriage between the countries' ruling families. The alliance was intended to be one of equals; in practice, Denmark was the dominant partner, and in 1536, Norway became formally subservient to the Danish crown. Thus, when the 17th-century rivalry between Denmark and Sweden – the two dominant powers in the Baltic – broke out into warfare, the vanquished Danes handed over parts of Norwegian territory to Sweden.

The link between Denmark and Norway was finally broken in 1815 at the end of the Napoleonic wars. Denmark/Norway had sided with France. After the defeat of Napoleon, Norway was handed over to the Swedes. The Norwegians were allowed their own Parliament, the Storting, which repeatedly clashed with the Swedish Government. This was officially and peacefully dissolved in 1905 following a referendum at which just 200 people – from a franchise of about 400,000 – voted in favour of retaining the union. The Swedes accepted the decision and Norway achieved true independence in 1905.

Norway is foremost a land for those who love nature. However, it also offers a rich cultural experience, as would be expected of such varied history, from the Vikings to later luminaries such as artist Edvard Munch.

General Information

AREA: 323,759 sq km (125,004 sq miles).
POPULATION: 4.6 million (UN estimate, 2005).
POPULATION DENSITY: 15 per sq km.
CAPITAL: Oslo. **Population:** 533,000 (2005).
GEOGRAPHY: Norway is bordered to the north by the Arctic Ocean, to the east by Finland, the Russian Federation and Sweden, to the south by the Skagerrak (which separates it from Denmark) and to the west by the North Sea. The coastline is 2735km (1700 miles) long, its most outstanding feature being the fjords. Most of them are between 80 to 160km (50 to 100 miles) long, and are often very deep and surrounded by towering mountains. Much of northern Norway lies beyond the Arctic Circle and the landscape is stark. In the south, the landscape consists of forests with many lakes and rivers.
GOVERNMENT: Constitutional monarchy. Declared independence from Sweden in 1905. **Head of State:** King Harald V since 1991. **Head of Government:** Prime Minister Kjell Jens Stoltenberg since September 2005. **Recent history:** The minority centre-right coalition (Christian Democrats, Conservatives and Liberals), which took office after the last election in 2001, was led by Prime Minister Kjell Magne Bondevik, and lost the general election in September 2005. A new majority centre-left 'red-green' coalition made up of the Labour Party, Centre Party and Socialist Left was formed in October 2005, led by Labour Party leader Jens Stoltenberg. Norway is a constitutional Monarchy with a unicameral 165-seat Parliament, the *Storting*, elected by proportional representation in multi-seat constituencies for a four-year term. The Prime Minister is the supreme executive authority. The Monarch, currently King Harald V, is Head of State.
LANGUAGE: Norwegian (Bokmål and Nynorsk). Sami is spoken by the Sami population in the north. English is widely spoken.
RELIGION: Approximately 86 per cent Evangelical Lutherans; plus other Christian denominations.
ELECTRICITY: 220 volts AC, 50Hz. Plugs are of the European round two-pin type.
SOCIAL CONVENTIONS: Normal courtesies should be observed. It is customary for the guest to refrain from drinking until the host toasts their health. Casual dress is normal. Lunch generally takes place between 1200 and 1300 and dinner usually takes place at 1700. It is customary for an invited guest to offer gifts to the host/hostess of a meal. Punctuality is expected if invited out for dinner. Smoking is prohibited in all public places.

Climate

Coastal areas have a moderate climate owing to the Gulf Stream and North Atlantic Drift. Inland temperatures are more extreme with hot summers and cold winters (November to March). In general, the lowlands of the south experience colder winters and warmer summers than the coastal areas. Rain is distributed throughout the year with frequent inland snowfalls during the winter.

The northern part of the country inside the Arctic Circle has continuous daylight at midsummer, and twilight all day during winter.
Required clothing: European according to the season. Light- to mediumweights are worn in summer. Warmer clothing is required during the winter. Waterproofing is advisable throughout the year.

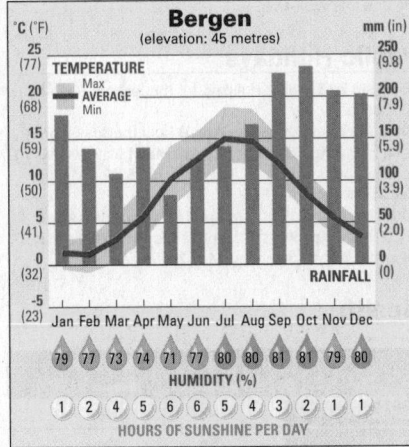

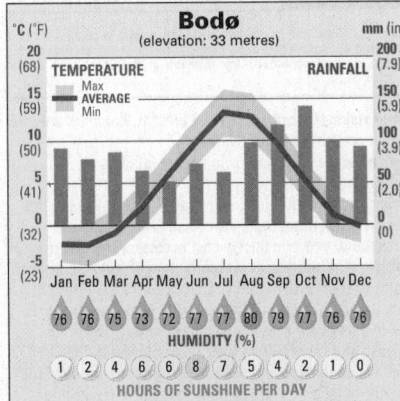

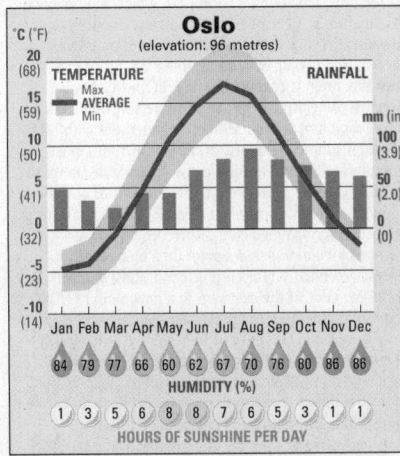

Communications

Telephone: IDD is available. Country code: 47.
Mobile telephone: Roaming agreements deal with many international mobile phone companies. Mobile phones cannot be hired. Coverage is mostly good, but may be patchy in rural areas.
Internet: There are many Internet cafes throughout Norway and the Internet can also be accessed via public libraries.
Post: Hotel receptions, shops and kiosks selling postcards will sell stamps. Airmail within Europe takes two to four days. Post office hours: These vary from place to place but are generally Mon-Fri 0830-1600 and Sat 0800-1300.
MEDIA: Norway's public broadcaster, *NRK*, has had competition from private local and national stations since the heady days of monopoly. Press freedom is guaranteed by the constitution and public radio and TV broadcast without interference from the Government.
Press: Norwegians are among the world's keenest newspaper readers. The number of publications is impressive, given the country's small population. Most of the press is privately-owned and openly partisan. The national newspapers published in Oslo are *Aftenposten*, *Dagbladet* and *Verdens Gang*. There are no English-language newspapers although English newspapers are readily available (one day after publication in the UK).
TV: NRK operates national channels *NRK-1* and *NRK-2*; *TV2* is national and commercial; NRK's main competitor is the commercial *TV3 Norge*.
Radio: *Radio NRK* is a public broadcaster, operating three national stations and local services; *P4* is national and commercial, as is *Kanal 24*; *Radio 1* is commercial but is essentially a music-based radio station.

Passport/Visa

	Passport Required?	Visa Required?	Return Ticket Required?
Full British	1	No	No
Australian	Yes	No	No
Canadian	Yes	No	No
USA	Yes	No	No
Other EU	1	No	No
Japanese	Yes	No	No

Note: *Regulations and requirements may be subject to change at short notice, and you are advised to contact the appropriate diplomatic or consular authority before finalising travel arrangements. Any numbers in the chart refer to the footnotes below.*

Note: On 25 March 2001 Norway became a signatory to the 1995 **Schengen Agreement**. For further details about passport/visa regulations within the Schengen area, see the introductory section, *How to Use this Guide*.
PASSPORTS: NORWAY
Passport valid for at least three months beyond length of stay required by all except:
1. EU/EEA nationals (EU + Iceland, Liechtenstein, Norway) and Swiss nationals holding a valid national ID card.
Note: EU and EEA nationals are only required to produce evidence of their EU/EEA nationality and identity in order to be admitted to any EU/EEA Member State. This evidence can take the form of a valid national passport or national identity card. Either is acceptable. Possession of a return ticket, any length of validity on their document, sufficient funds for the length of their proposed visit should not be imposed.
VISAS: Required by all except the following for stays of up to three months:
(a) nationals shown in the chart above;
(b) nationals of Andorra, Argentina, Bermuda (only holders of BDTC (Bermuda) passports), Bolivia, Brazil, Brunei, Bulgaria, Chile, Costa Rica, Croatia, El Salvador, Guatemala, Honduras, Hong Kong (SAR), Israel, Korea (Rep), Liechtenstein, Macau (SAR), Malaysia, Mexico, Monaco, New Zealand, Nicaragua, Panama, Paraguay, Romania, San Marino, Singapore, Switzerland, Uruguay, Vatican City and Venezuela;
(c) nationals of Nordic countries (including Faroe Islands, Greenland and Iceland).
Types of visa and cost: A uniform type of visa, the *Schengen* visa, is issued for tourist, business and private visits. The cost of a visa is £25 but prices are subject to frequent change against the exchange rate. Fee is payable when visa is issued. Enquire at the nearest Embassy for further details.

See beautiful Oslo

Note: Spouses and children of EU or EEA nationals (providing spouse's/dependent's passport and birth certificate and [if applicable] the original marriage certificate are produced), and nationals of some other countries, receive their visas free of charge (enquire at Embassy for details).
Validity: Up to three months in any six-month period. For renewal or extension, apply to Embassy.
Application to: Consulate (or Consular section at Embassy); see *Passport/Visa Information*. An appointment must first be booked (tel: (09065) 540 725; for UK residents not residing in Scotland or Northern Ireland). If applying in the UK and living within the London area, all applications *must* be lodged in person at the Embassy. Travellers visiting just one *Schengen* country should apply to the Consulate of that country; travellers visiting more than one *Schengen* country should apply to the Consulate of the country chosen as the main destination or the country they will enter first (if they have no main destination).
Application requirements: (a) Valid passport with at least one blank page (this should not be submitted until the applicant is informed that a visa has been granted). (b) One completed application form. (c) Two recent passport-size photos. (d) Fee, payable in cash (exact money only), cheque supported by a cheque card or postal order (visa fees are non-refundable and payable on submission of the visa application). (e) Further documentation such as a letter of invitation, proof of accommodation or a letter from an employer explaining nature and duration of stay may be required, depending on purpose of visit. (f) Evidence of sufficient funds for stay (recent original bank statement, traveller's cheques or credit card with credit limit statement; cash not accepted). (g) Parental consent for minors (under 18 years of age). (h) Evidence of occupation/student status. If unemployed, social security booklet must be submitted. (i) Proof of adequate and valid travel insurance (valid throughout the *Schengen* territory).
Working days required: The total length of processing time depends on nationality and individual circumstances.
Temporary residence: Apply to Embassy for residence and work permit if the stay exceeds three months.

PASSPORT/VISA INFORMATION

Royal Norwegian Embassy in the UK
25 Belgrave Square, London SW1X 8QD, UK
Tel: (020) 7591 5500.
Website: www.norway.org.uk
Opening hours: Mon-Fri 1000-1200 (visa section), 1330-1500 (visa telephone enquiries).

Royal Norwegian Embassy in the USA
2720 34th Street, NW, Washington, DC 20008, USA
Tel: (202) 333 6000.
Website: www.norway.org

Money

Currency: Norwegian Krone (NOK) = 100 øre. Notes are in denominations of NOK1000, 500, 200, 100 and 50. Coins are in denominations of NOK20, 10, 5 and 1, and 50 øre.
Currency exchange: Eurocheque cards allow encashment of personal cheques. ATMs are widely available.
Credit & debit cards: All major credit and debit cards are widely accepted. Check with your credit or debit card company for details of merchant acceptability and other services which may be available.
Traveller's cheques: Accepted in banks, hotels, shops and by airlines.
Currency restrictions: The import and export of local currency is limited to NOK25,000. The export of foreign currency is unlimited, provided proof is shown that the currency was imported or obtained by conversion of other currencies.
Banking hours: Mon-Thur 0900-1600, Fri 0900-1700 and Sat 0900-1200.
Exchange rate indicators:
Rate at time of publishing

£1.00=	NOK11.51
$1.00=	NOK6.55

Duty Free

The following items can be imported into Norway without incurring customs duty by:
(a) Residents of European countries:
200 cigarettes or 250g of tobacco products and 200 leaves of cigarette paper (travellers over 18 years of age); 1l of spirits and 1l of wine or 2l of wine and 2l of beer (travellers over 20 years of age); other goods to the value of NOK3000-6000; a small amount of perfume and eau de cologne.
(b) Residents of non-European countries:
400 cigarettes or 500g of tobacco products and 200 leaves of cigarette paper (travellers over 18 years of age); 1l of spirits and 1l of wine or 2l of wine and 2l of beer (travellers over 20 years of age); 50g of perfume and 50cl of eau de cologne; other goods (not to be resold) to the value of NOK3000-6000.
Prohibited items: Spirits over 60 per cent volume (120 per cent proof), certain foodstuffs (including eggs, potatoes, meat, meat products, dairy products and poultry), narcotics, firearms and explosives.

Public Holidays

Below are listed Public Holidays for the January 2006-June 2007 period.
2006: Jan 1 New Year's Day. **Apr 13** Holy Thursday. **Apr 14** Good Friday. **Apr 17** Easter Monday. **May 1** May Day. **May 17** Constitution Day. **May 25** Ascension. **Jun 5** Whit Monday. **Dec 25-26** Christmas.
2007: Jan 1 New Year's Day. **Apr 5** Holy Thursday. **Apr 6** Good Friday. **Apr 9** Easter Monday. **May 1** May Day. **May 17** Ascension/Constitution Day. **May 28** Whit Monday.

Health

	Special Precautions?	Certificate Required?
Yellow Fever	No	No
Cholera	No	No
Typhoid & Polio	No	N/A
Malaria	No	N/A

Note: *Regulations and requirements may be subject to change at short notice, and you are advised to contact your doctor well in advance of your intended date of departure. Any numbers in the chart refer to the footnotes below.*

Other risks: *Hepatitis C* may be present. *Rabies* is only present on the islands of Svalbard.
Health care: European Economic Area (EEA) and Switzerland:
If you or any of your dependants are suddenly taken ill or have an accident during a visit to an EEA country or Switzerland, free or reduced-cost necessary treatment is available – in most cases on production of a valid European Health Insurance Card (EHIC). Each country has different rules about state medical provision. In some, treatment is free. In many countries you will have to pay part or all of the cost, and then claim a full or partial refund. The EHIC gives access to state-provided medical treatment only and the scheme gives no entitlement to medical repatriation costs, nor does it cover ongoing illnesses of a non-urgent nature, so comprehensive travel insurance is advised. Note that the EHIC replaces the Form E111, which will no longer be valid after 31 December 2005. Some restrictions apply, depending on your nationality. Please note that Swiss nationals and people who do not have UK, EU or EEA nationality are not covered by the EHIC in Norway.
Standards of health care are high. Make sure you see a doctor who has a reimbursement arrangement with the National Insurance Administration. This includes most medical practitioners. There is a non-refundable standard fee. You will usually have to pay the full cost of any dental treatment. Chemists are called *Apotek*. You will have to pay for most prescribed medicines. However, if you are prescribed medication by a doctor on a blue prescription (generally medication for chronic conditions) you will pay only 36 per cent of the costs, up to a maximum of NOK 360 per prescription. Charges are payable for specialist hospital consultations and out-patient treatment. Normally, a GP will refer you to hospital. In an emergency, you can get treatment from the nearest public hospital. Hospital in-patient treatment, including necessary medication, is free of charge. More information can be obtained from *Folketrygdkontoret for Utenlandsaker* (National Office for Social Insurance Abroad), PO Box 8138, Dep 0033, Oslo 1, Norway (tel: 2331 1300).

Travel - International

AIR:

Norwegian air travel is served by *Braathens SAFE (BU)* (website: www.braathens.no) and *SAS Scandinavian Airlines (SK)* (website: www.sas.se). *Ryanair* also operates services to Norway.
Approximate flight times: From *London* to Oslo is three hours 15 minutes, to Bergen is three hours 10 minutes and to Stavanger is three hours. From *New York* to Oslo is 10 hours 45 minutes (including stopover in London).
Main airports: *Oslo International Airport (OSL)* (Gardermoen) (website: www.osl.no) is 47km (30 miles) north of Oslo. It is the largest land-based development project in Norway. *To/from the airport*: The high-speed airport express trains *Flytoget* leave every 10 minutes to/from Oslo's central station (travel time – 20 minutes). Buses serving the airport include the *SL buses* and *Bussekspress* which stop in front of the terminal building and take approximately 45 minutes to Oslo. There is a new bus station for regional services located within walking distance of the terminal. Access by car is also facilitated by the construction of new roads (regional no. 174 from Jessheim) and the widening of two others (regional no. 120 from Erpestad and national no. 6 from Tangerud). There is a taxi rank at the terminal building. Travellers are advised to order a taxi from the airport reception and ask for a fixed price. Otherwise, prices will vary. In addition to regular taxis, there are 'airport taxis', cheaper taxis which must be ordered in advance by groups of up to three people, and wheelchair taxis. *Facilities*: Duty free shopping, banks/bureaux de change, restaurants and cafes, car hire, lost luggage, information kiosks as well as laundry/dry cleaning, shoe repair and key-cutting services.
Stavanger (SVG) (Sola) is 14.5km (9 miles) southwest of the city (travel time – 20-30 minutes). *To/from the airport*: There is a coach to the Royal Atlantic Hotel, Jembaneveien 1. Bus no. 40 goes every 20 minutes (0620-2400) for a fare of approximately NOK21 (travel time – 30 minutes). Taxi services are available to the city with a surcharge after 2200 (travel time – 15 minutes). *Facilities*: Duty free shops, bar, restaurant, snack bar, many shops, tourist information, post office, banks/bureaux de change, left luggage, lockers and car hire.
Bergen (BGO) (Flesland) is 19km (12 miles) south of the city (travel time – 25 minutes). *To/from the airport*: Bus service (*Flybussen*) leaves for the city every 20 minutes (0645-2130). Return is from various points in the city centre. Taxi services are available to the city for a fare of approximately NOK170 with a surcharge after 2200 (travel time – 25 minutes). *Facilities*: Left luggage, lockers, banks, bureaux de change, post office, duty free shops, bar, cafes, shops, tourist information, nursery and car hire.
Departure tax: None.

SEA:

Main ports: *Bergen, Kristiansand, Larvik, Oslo* and *Stavanger*. The main sea routes from the UK, operated by *Fjord Line* and *DFDS Seaways* respectively, are from Newcastle to Bergen (travel time – 25 hours 30 minutes) and to Kristiansand (travel time – 19 hours). Services from Newcastle to Bergen via Stavanger are also operated by *Fjord Line*, a Norwegian line operating a number of fjord cruises within Norway (in UK tel: (0191) 296 1313; website: www.fjordline.co.uk). *Fjord Line* also operates services from Bergen to Hanstholm (Denmark). *Smyril Line* operates services from Bergen to Iceland via the Shetland Islands and the Faroe Islands in the summer (tel: (298) 345 900; website: www.smyril-line.no).

RAIL:

Connections from the UK are from London via Dover/Ostend (via Denmark, Germany, The Netherlands and Sweden) or Harwich/Hook of Holland, or from Newcastle to Bergen via Stavanger. There are two principal routes to Sweden, with daytime and overnight trains from Copenhagen, Malmö and Stockholm.
Rail passes: The *Inter-Rail* pass offers unlimited second-class train travel in up to 29 countries (includes Morocco and Turkey) split into eight zones (A-H). Three different tickets are available: a ticket covering one zone (two to six countries, 16 days' validity), a ticket covering two zones (six to ten countries, 22 days' validity) and an *All Zone Pass* (29 countries, one month's validity). Ferry services between Italy and Greece are included. Passengers must be resident in Europe for at least six months before the pass is used. Travel is not allowed in the passenger's country of residence. Travellers under 26 years receive a reduction of about 30 per cent. Children's tickets are reduced by about 50 per cent. Supplements are required for some high speed services, seat reservations and couchettes. Discounts are offered on *Eurostar* and some ferry routes. Available from *Inter Rail* (website: www.interrailnet.com).
The *Eurailpass* offers unlimited first-class train travel in 17 European countries. Tickets are valid for 15 days, 21 days, one month, two months or three months. The *Eurailpass Saver* ticket offers discounts for two or more people travelling together. The *Eurailpass Youth* ticket is available to those aged under 26 and offers unlimited second-class train travel. The *Eurailpass Flexi* allows either 10 or 15 travel days within a two month period. The *Eurail Selectpass* is valid in three, four or five bordering countries and allows five, six, eight or 10 travel days (or 15 for five countries) in a two-month period. The *Eurail Regional Pass* allows four to 10 travel days in a two-month period in one of nine regions (usually two or more countries). Children receive a 50 per cent reduction. The passes cannot be sold to residents of Europe, Turkey, Morocco, Algeria, Tunisia, or the Russian Federation. Available from *The Eurail Group* (website: www.eurail.com).
The *ScanRail* pass can be used for extensive travel for five or 10 days in two months or 21 consecutive days across Denmark, Finland, Norway and Sweden. Payment of a supplement is required on some trains. Seat reservations, couchettes, sleeper or cabin charges are not included in the cost of the pass and are payable at the normal rate. The

ScanRail pass also entitles holders to free travel on some ferry and bus routes as well as up to 50 per cent discount on ferries, buses and private railways throughout Scandinavia, free or discounted admission (up to 50 per cent off) to railway museums in Denmark, Finland, Norway and Sweden and reduced room rates at 160 hotels throughout Scandinavia. Available from *Rail Europe* (website: www.raileurope.co.uk/railpasses/scanrail.htm).

ROAD:

The only international routes are from Sweden or Finland in the far north. Camping trailers up to 2.3m (7.5ft) wide, with number plates, are permitted on holiday visits. *Eurolines* (52 Grosvenor Gardens, London SW1W 0AU; tel: (08705) 143 219; website: www.eurolines.com) and *National Express* (Ensign Court, 4 Vicarage Road, Edgbaston, Birmingham B15 3ES; tel: 08705 808 080; website: www.nationalexpress.com) run regular coach services from the UK to Norway and other European cities. Passes: Travellers can either choose Mini-Pass breaks or book a 15-, 30- or 60-day pass. The six Mini-Passes give travellers the freedom to visit three cities, with prices starting from £55. Travellers can stay as long as they like in each city.

Travel - Internal

AIR:

Domestic flights are run by *Braathens ASA (BU)*, *Norwegian Air Shuttle (DY)*, *SAS Scandinavian Airlines (SK)* and *Widerøe's Flyveselskap (WF)*. A total of 50 airports with scheduled services exist in the fjord country of western Norway and along the remaining coast. Charter sea or land planes are available at most destinations. Reduced airfare tickets are available for families, children under 12 years of age (who pay half price), groups and pensioners. For further information, contact *Widerøe Flyveselskap A/S* (tel: 8100 1200; website: www.wideroe.no).

SEA:

All coastal towns are served by ferries, catamarans and hydrofoils. The Hurtigruten (express) from Bergen to Kirkenes (near the Russian border) takes 12 days round trip, leaving daily and stopping at 34 ports on the west coast. Various ferry trips are available (half price in spring and autumn). There are also numerous companies operating cruises on Norway's spectacular fjords, one of which is *Norway Fjord Cruise AS*, Sagnefjordvegen 40, N-6863, Leikanger, Norway (tel: 5765 6999; website: www.fjordcruise.com).

RAIL:

All services are run by NSB (*Norwegian State Railways*) (tel: 8150 0888 (dial '4' for an English-speaking operator); website: www.nsb.no). The main internal rail routes are: Oslo–Trondheim (*Dovre Line*); Trondheim–Bodø (*Nordland Railway*); Oslo–Bergen (*Bergen Railway*); and Oslo–Stavanger (*Sorland Railway*). There are also services to Charlottenburg (Stockholm) and Halden (Malmö) on routes to Sweden. Seats on express trains must be reserved. There are buffet/restaurant cars on some trains, and sleepers on long-distance overnight services. Heavy luggage may be sent in advance. Children under four years of age travel free; children four to 14 years of age pay half fare. For further information, contact *NSB* (*Norwegian State Railways*) (telephone number above) or the Norwegian Tourist Board (see *Top Things To Do*).

Rail passes: The *EuroDomino* pass enables holders anything form three to eight days' extensive travel within a one-month period on the entire rail network of their chosen country. It is valid in 28 European countries and North Africa, including the ferry service from Brindisi (Italy) to Igoumenitsa (Greece). To purchase a *EuroDomino* pass you must have been a resident in Europe for at least six months and a passport number is required at time of booking. It is not permitted to purchase a pass for travel within your own country of residence. To qualify for the youth rates, you must be under 26 years on the first date of validity of the pass. Children aged four-eleven years inclusive pay half the adult fares rounded up to the nearest pound. Children under four years travel for free. Seat reservations, couchette and sleeper charges are not included in the

cost of the pass and are payable at the normal rate. Passholder fares are payable on some services. Reservation/Supplement charges are payable on all trains within Spain. Available from *Rail Europe* (website: www.raileurope.co.uk/railpasses/eurodomino.htm).

ROAD:

Traffic drives on the right. The road system is of variable quality (especially under freezing winter conditions in the north), but supplemented by numerous car ferries across the fjords. **Bus**: Principal long-distance internal bus routes are from Bø (in Telemark) to Haugesund (travel time – eight hours); and from Ålesund–Molde–Trondheim (travel time – eight hours) with links to the Bø line in the north. *Inter-Nordic* runs from Trondheim to Stockholm. There are also extensive regional local bus services, some of which are operated by companies with interests in the ferries. Visitors can contract *NOR-WAY Bussekspress AS* for seat reservations and route information (tel: 8154 4444; website: www.nor-way.no). The official *Rutehefte* is a must for anyone using public transport, and gives extensive timetable information and maps of all bus, train, ferry and air routes. **Taxi**: In most cases, fares are metered. Taxis can be found at ranks or booked by telephone. It is not customary to tip taxi drivers. **Car hire**: Available in airports and most towns, but costly; in general, problems of cost and parking make public transport more practical and convenient. It is also possible to hire bicycles. **Regulations**: The minimum age for driving is 18. Tolls, ranging from NOK5-50, are charged on certain cross-country roads, underwater tunnels and in certain cities such as Bergen, Oslo and Trondheim. There are severe penalties for drink-driving and illegal parking. Seat belts are compulsory. Children under 12 years of age must travel in the back of the car. It is obligatory for all vehicles to drive with dipped headlights at all times, even on the brightest summer day. This includes motorcycles and mopeds. Carrying spare headlight bulbs is recommended. Speed limits are 80 to 90kph (49 to 56mph) outside built-up areas and 50kph (31mph) in built-up areas. Snow chains or studded winter tyres are advised during the winter. Petrol stations are numerous, although tourists are only able to use credit cards in some of them. The contact for AIT (Alliance Internationale de Tourisme) is the Norwegian Automobile Association (NAF), PO Box 6682 Etterstad, 0609, Norway (tel: 2234 1400; website: www.naf.no). **Documentation**: International Driving Permit or national driving licence and log book are required. A Green Card is strongly recommended (for those with more than Third Party cover on their domestic policy). Without it, visitors with motor insurance in their own countries are allowed the minimum legal cover in Norway; the Green Card tops this up to the level of cover provided by the visitor's own policy. The maximum legal blood to alcohol ratio is 0.5 per cent.

URBAN:

Good public transport systems operate in the main towns. Oslo has bus, rail, metro and tramway services. Tickets are pre-purchased and self-cancelled, and there is one hour's free transfer between any of the modes. Meters on taxis are obligatory.

Travel times: The following chart gives approximate travel times (in hours and minutes) from **Oslo** to other major cities/towns in Norway.

	Air	Road	Rail
Bergen	0.35	9.00	8.00
Stavanger	0.35	7.00	8.00
Tromsø	1.40	20.00	-
Trondheim	0.40	10.00	8.00

Travel Advice

Most visits to Norway are trouble-free but you should be aware of the global risk of indiscriminate international terrorist attacks, which could be against civilian targets, including places frequented by foreigners.

Travellers should not become involved with drugs of any kind. Possession of even small quantities can lead to heavy fines and/or imprisonment. This applies also to the use, possession and/or importation of khat/qat which is prohibited in Norway, though legal in the UK

This advice is based on information provided by the Foreign and Commonwealth Office in the UK. It is correct at time of publishing. As the situation can change rapidly, visitors are advised to contact the following organisations for the latest travel advice:

British Foreign and Commonwealth Office
Tel: (0845) 850 2829.
Website: www.fco.gov.uk

US Department of State
Website: http://travel.state.gov/travel

Accommodation

EDITOR'S CHOICE: RORBU HOLIDAYS

A rorbu is a hut or shelter used by fishermen during the winter cod-fishing season. Equipped with all the necessary facilities, these are leased to holidaymakers during the summer, providing an inexpensive form of accommodation. They will often be actually over the water. Catching your own fish will further reduce the cost of the holiday.

Credit: ©Terje Rakke/Nordic Life/ Innovation Norway

See beautiful Norway

OSL

HOTELS:

First-class hotels are to be found all over the country. Facilities in all establishments are classified, as hotels must come up to official high standards; for example, there must be a reception service, dining room, and a minimum of 30 rooms, each with full bath or shower. Many hotels are still family-run establishments. Full en pension terms are available to guests staying at the same establishment for at least three to five days. Hotels usually allow a reduction on the same en pension rate according to age. This reduction may only apply when the child concerned occupies an extra bed in the parents' room. There are several schemes which offer visitors reduced rates in selected hotels. A Fjord Pass (which covers two adults with special concessions for children under 15 years of age and is available from Innovation Norway in the UK) is accepted by 170 hotels and is valid all year; reductions of 20 per cent or more are possible. The Nordic Passepartout is a pan-Scandinavian card accepted by over 50 hotels in Norway in the main summer period and at weekends; the visitor's fifth night is free. A Scandinavian Bonus Pass (which covers two adults with special concessions for children under 16 years of age) is accepted by 45 hotels in Norway between 15 May and 1 September and at weekends during winter; a Scanrail railway pass will also be accepted. Scandinavian Hotel Express is a travel club which enables visitors to have reductions of 50 per cent in certain hotels. Roughly 50 per cent of establishments belong to the Norwegian Hospitality Association. There is no grading system, but establishments designated turisthotel or høyfjellshotell must meet specified standards.

GUEST HOUSES AND MOUNTAIN LODGES:

Guest houses (*pensjonat*) and mountain lodges are generally smaller in size and offer less elaborate facilities than hotels, although many establishments can offer the same standard as those officially listed as hotels.

FARMHOUSE HOLIDAYS:

These are working farms and anyone who wants to can join in the work, but guests are at liberty to plan their own day, and the hosts will generally be able to suggest tours, excursions and other activities. Contact the Norwegian Tourist Board for further information. The tour operator *Trollsykling* offers many farmhouse holidays, and a programme printed in English, German and Norwegian is available from *Trollsykling A/S*.

SELF-CATERING:

Chalets, log cabins and apartments are available for rent by groups and will generally work out less expensive per head than other kinds of holiday. Most chalets have electric lighting, heating and hot plates; some have kerosene lamps, calor gas for cooking and wood fires, while water will often have to be fetched from a nearby well or stream. Chalets are grouped near a central building which may contain such facilities as a cafe, lounges, TV rooms, sauna, a grocer's shop, and in some cases a swimming pool. All chalets and apartments are regularly inspected by responsible rental firms. Bookings can be made by writing to various firms.

CAMPING/CARAVANNING:

Offsite camping is permitted in uninhabited areas (not lay-bys), but fires are illegal in field or woodland areas between 15 April and 15 September. Farmers must be asked for permission for farmland camping. Further details and a manual are available from the Norwegian Automobile Association (NAF) (see *Road* section for contact details). **Grading**: There are over 1000 authorised sites in Norway, classified according to standards and amenities from **1-** to **5-star** camps, with charges varying accordingly. Notice of available amenities is posted in each camp.

YOUTH HOSTELS:

There are over 100 youth hostels spread all over Norway, some of which are open all year round. Others are in apartment houses attached to schools or universities and are open only during the summer season. Sleeping bags can be hired if necessary. Groups must always make advance bookings. All are welcome, but members of the Norwegian Youth Hostel Association (NUH), or similar associations in other countries, have priority. International membership cards can be bought at most youth hostels. Hostels vary from **1-** to **3-star** establishments. Breakfast is usually NOK50-60.

ACCOMMODATION INFORMATION

Norwegian Hospitality Association
PO Box 5465, Majorstua, 0305 Oslo, Norway
Tel: (22) 2308 8620.
Website: www.rbl.no

Bed & Breakfast Norway AS
PO Box 92, N-6659 Rindal, Norway
Tel: 9923 7799.
Website: www.bbnorway.com

Trollsykling A/S (Information on Farmhouse Holidays)
PO Box 373, Elvegaten 19, 2602 Lillehammer, Norway
Tel: 6128 9970.
Website: www.norske-bygdeopplevelser.no

Den Norske Hytteformidling A/S (Information on Chalet Holidays)
PO Box 309, 0103 Oslo, Norway
Tel: 8154 4270.
Website: www.novasol.com

Fjordline in the UK (Information on Self-Catering Holidays)
Tel: (0191) 296 1313.
Website: www.fjordline.com

Destinasjon Lofoten (Information on Rorbu Holidays)
PO Box 210, 8301 Svolvær, Norway
Tel: (76) 069 800.
Website: www.lofoten-tourist.no

Norske Vandrerhjem (Information on Youth Hostels)
Torggata 1, N-0181 Oslo, Norway
Tel: 2313 9300.
Website: www.vandrehjem.no

Top Things To See

- **Oslo** is Norway's most populous district, providing a home for more than one-tenth of the country's inhabitants in a mere 700th of its total area. For all this, urban and industrial development only occupies one-eighth of the land within the city boundaries, the rest consisting mainly of woods, islands in Oslo Fjord, and lakes. The city has a strong arts culture, with a good choice of museums and galleries. The **Munch Museum** is the main draw among these, and others include the **National Gallery**; the **Norwegian Museum of Applied Arts**; the **Thor Heyerdahl Kon-Tiki Museum** and the **Norwegian Folk Museum**, both on **Bygdøy Island** to the west of the city centre; the **Viking Ships Museum**; **Oslo City Museum**; and the **Norwegian Home Front Museum**, which tells the story of the country's occupation during World War II. Principal architectural interest in Oslo focuses on the **Kongelige Slott** (**Royal Palace**), **Stortinget** (**Parliament Building**), the **Cathedral** and **Åkershus Castle**. Oslo's entertainment centres include the **Norwegian National Theatre**; the **New Theatre**; the **Norwegian Opera House**; **Konserthuset** (the **Concert House**); and **Oslo Spektrum**, the main rock and pop concert venue.

- For those seeking a literary treat, **Skien** was the birthplace of Ibsen and his childhood home provides many insights into the life of this distinguished Norwegian playwright, including a multimedia exhibition.

- Former Hanseatic port and medieval Norwegian capital, **Bergen**'s appeal centres on the **Hanseatic Bryggen** harbour-side district, a UNESCO World Heritage Site with many buildings dating from the 17th century and earlier. Board a cable car to the summit of **Mount Ulriken** or a funicular railway to **Mount Fløyen** to see outstanding views over the city and coastline. Museums abound, and there is a large aquarium. Additionally, a broad choice of boat excursions plies the waters around the city, which is Norway's busiest tourist destination.

- Go to **Old Stavanger** and see Europe's largest collection of wooden buildings.

- Founded in 997 AD as Kaupangr, and later called Nidaros, Norway's early capital of Trondheim has a number of major attractions, not least the **Nidarosdomen Cathedral**, which dates from the late 11th century. Built over **St Olav's grave**, it has been a centre of pilgrimage since medieval times.

- One of just four UNESCO World Heritage Sites in Norway, **Røros** is a small but picturesque mountain town near the Swedish border; from the 17th century until the 1980s it had been a copper mining and smelting settlement. Dsicover the **Old Town**, the wooden church and the **Mining Museum**. Close to Røros is **Olavsgruva**, an early mine now open to visitors.

- Observe the summer **Midnight Sun** at the **North Cape**. The **North Cape Hall**, built into the side of a mountain, and with panoramic views out to sea, is the main visitor centre here.

- Observe the world's most powerful **maelstrom**, **Saltstraumen**, 33km (21 miles) east of **Bodø**; a multimedia visitor centre is dedicated to the phenomenon. Saltstraumen is a strong tidal current located some 30km (19 miles) east of the city of Bodø. It is the strongest tidal current in the world. Vortices up to 10m (33ft) in diameter and 5m (16.5ft) in depth are

formed when the current is at its strongest; this feature is commonly known as a whirlpool. However, there are short periods of time when the current is calm and vessels can pass through this area. The waters are also abundant in marine life, and **fishing** is very popular here.

Top Things To Do

- **Tromsø** boasts the world's most northerly brewery, so if you are feeling thirsty and you happen to be traversing these near-Arctic traditions, you know where to head!
- Unquestionably, **Fjordland** and the **Southwest** is Norway's most important tourist area, due to its scenery. Many visitors arrive on cruise ships working their way north along the coast from **Stavanger** via **Haugesund** to **Bergen** and the best known fjord of all, **Sognefjorden**, **Førdefjorden**, **Hardanger Fjord** and **Nordfjord** are among other notable scenic attractions in the region. Near **Sogndal**, at the head of **Sognefjorden**, lies **Urnes**, whose wooden stave-built church is a UNESCO World Heritage Site.
- Inland are the **Hardangervidda Mountains**, which rise to over 1700m (5600ft) and incorporate the National Park of the same name. To the north of Sognefjorden lies Europe's biggest glacier, the **Jostedalsbreen**, and its surrounding **National Park** of the same name. Daily **glacier walks** are organised in summer in the company of experienced guides. For information about organised glacier walks, contact the glacier centre at Jostedalsbreen (tel: 5787 7200; website: www.fjordinfo.no *or* www.jostedalsbre.no) or consult *Breoppleving* for glacier tours (tel: 5787 6800; website: www.bre.no). Immediately to the east of this area is the **Jotunheimen National Park**, which contains Norway's highest mountain, **Galdhøpiggen** (2469m/8100ft). Fjords elsewhere include the fjord near **Trondheim**, the country's third largest city, **Trondheimsfjorden**, which although not spectacular scenically when compared to the fjords of the southwest, is one of the largest, stretching more than 70km (44 miles) inland. For easy access from the capital, the **Oslo Fjord** area is dotted with historic and prehistoric sites of varying importance, along with manor houses, stone churches (most are built of wood in Norway) and fortifications.
- Norway claims to be the birthplace of skiing. The country has about 30,000km (18,750 miles) of marked ski trails, winding their way through unspoiled scenery. Both **cross-country** and **downhill skiing** are available from November until the end of May. Although skiing is at its best just before Easter, when the days are getting longer, it is possible to ski for long hours in the winter, since many of the tracks are illuminated. In summer, it is possible to go skiing in several parts of Norway. For further information about summer skiing, contact Stryn Sommerskisenter (tel: 5787 4040; website: www.strynefjellet.com). The centres of **Elverum**, **Hamar**, **Kongsvinger** and **Lillehammer** (site of the 1994 Winter Olympics) are all suitable for those seeking solitude, wilderness and wintersports facilities. Lillehammer stands on the banks of the **Mjøsa Lake**, Norway's largest, with an area of 362 sq km (140 sq miles), and which reputedly conceals a 'Loch Ness' monster. Hamar contains the **Olympic Hall**, which staged skating events during the 1994 Winter Olympics. To the south of Trondheim, the mountain village of **Oppdal** is an excellent skiing resort.

Credit: ©Jens Henrik Nybo/Innovation Norway

TOURIST INFORMATION

Innovation Norway in the UK
Charles House, 5 Lower Regent Street,
London SW1 4LR, UK
Tel: (020) 7389 8800 *or* (09063) 022 003 (brochure request line).
Website: www.visitnorway.com

Innovation Norway in the USA
800 Third Avenue, 23rd Floor,
New York, NY 10022, USA
Tel: (212) 421 9210.
Website: www.invanor.no/usa

Entertainment

FOOD & DRINK: Breakfasts are often enormous with a variety of fish, meat, cheese and bread served from a cold buffet with coffee and boiled or fried eggs. Open sandwiches are topped with meat, fish, cheese and salads. Alcohol tends to be limited and expensive, although beer and wine are generally served in restaurants. Bars have table and counter service. Licensing laws are strict and alcohol is sold only by the State through special monopoly. Licensing hours are also enforced.

National specialities:
- *Koldtbord* (cold table), with smoked salmon, fresh lobster, shrimp and hot dishes.
- Roast venison.
- *Ptarmigan* in cream sauce.
- Wild cranberries.
- *Multer* (a berry with a unique flavour).
- *Lutefisk* (a hot, highly flavoured cod fish)
- Herring.
- Reindeer meat.
- Shrimps.

National drinks:
- *Aquavit* (schnapps).

Tipping: Waiters expect a tip of no more than 5 per cent of the bill; porters at airports and railway stations charge per piece of luggage. Hotel porters are tipped NOK5-10 according to the number of pieces of luggage.

NIGHTLIFE: Several hotels and restaurants in Oslo stage cabaret programmes and floor shows. Venues change so it is best to check in the local newspaper. Theatres, cinemas, nightclubs and discos are located in major centres. Resorts have dance music, and folk dancing is popular.

SHOPPING: Most towns and resorts have a shop where typical Norwegian handicrafts are on sale. Silversmiths and potteries are numerous and worth visiting. Traditional items include furs, printed textiles, woven articles, knitwear, woodcarving, silver, enamel, pewter, glass and porcelain. Tax-free cheques can be obtained from any of the 3000 shops carrying the sticker 'Tax free for tourists'. These shops save visitors 11 to 18 per cent of the price paid by residents. VAT refunds are paid in cash at airports, ferries, cruise ships and border crossings. **Shopping hours**: Mon-Wed and Fri 0900-1700/1800, Thurs 0900-2000, Sat 0900-1300/1500.

Business

- **GDP:** US$238 billion (2004).
- **Main exports:** Crude oil, natural gas, refined petroleum products, machinery and transport equipment and manufactured goods.
- **Main imports:** Machinery and transport equipment, manufactured goods and chemical and related products.
- **Main trade partners:** UK, Germany, The Netherlands, France and Sweden.

ECONOMY: The Norwegian economy is dominated by its oil and gas industry, which accounts for nearly 20 per cent of GDP and 60 per cent of export earnings. There is little cultivable land in Norway, however many farmers breed livestock, combining this with forestry to supply Norway's numerous sawmills. Consequently, wood products and paper are both thriving industries. Offshore fishing has been in decline for some time, although a large number of fish farms have been established, making Norway by far the world's largest supplier of salmon. Heavy engineering industries, principally shipbuilding and machinery, have also declined (although Norway retains a large merchant fleet). Nonetheless, the country has sustained its economic prosperity outside the European Union (see below) through development of an exceptionally strong energy sector. As well as oil and gas, Norway has abundant hydroelectric resources: the development of these has allowed much-reduced overheads for heavy industries such as aluminium production while freeing oil and gas products for export. Norway has been a major oil and gas exporter since the mid-1970s, after discovering large deposits of both in the North Sea. Proven oil reserves are around 11 billion barrels (one-tenth of Saudi reserves and 1 per cent of the world total). Much of the income is invested in a fund, now worth over US$40 billion, for such time (perhaps 15-20 years) as the oil and gas last. The country also has deposits of various iron ores plus copper, lead and zinc, which feed the country's metallurgical and chemical industries. Recent years have seen the emergence of advanced technological industries.

The UK, Germany and Sweden are Norway's principal trading partners. Norway is a member of the European Free Trade Association (EFTA) and hence the so-called 'European Economic Area', which is an amalgam of EU and EFTA members united in a free-trade zone and created in 1991. Concern about the possible effects on the fishing and farming industries lay behind the Norwegians' decision – registered in two referendums, in 1973 and 1994 – to reject EU membership. Nonetheless, with the exception of these two industries, Norway enjoys a wholly liberalised trade regime with EU members, and conducts 70 per cent of its trade with the EU.

BUSINESS ETIQUETTE: Businesspeople are expected to dress smartly. Prior appointments are necessary. Norwegian businesspeople tend to be reserved and formal. English is widely spoken. Punctuality is essential. Calling cards are common. The best months for business visits are February to May and October to December.

Office hours: Mon-Fri 0800-1600.

COMMERCIAL INFORMATION

Innovation Norway
PO Box 448 Sentrum, 0104 Oslo, Norway
Tel: 2200 2500.
Website: www.ntc.no

Innovation Norway in the UK
5th Floor, Charles House, 5 Lower Regent Street,
London SW1Y 4LR, UK
Tel: (020) 7389 8800.
Website: www.norway.org.uk

A B C D E F G H I J K L M **N** O P Q R S T U V W X Y Z

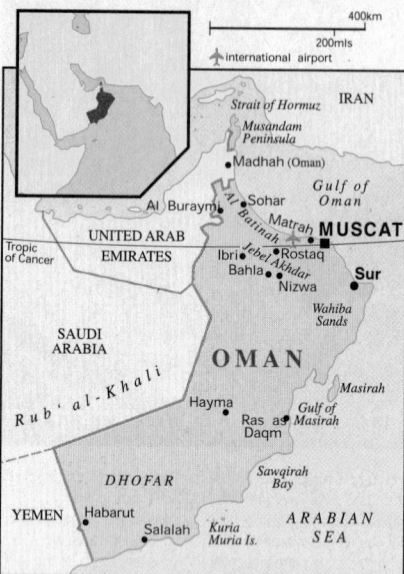

Location: Middle East, southeastern tip of Arabian Peninsula.

Time: GMT + 4.

Overview

During the 18th and 19th centuries, the Sultans of Muscat (Oman) were often powerful figures in Arabia and East Africa, who often came into conflict with the colonial powers in the region, particularly the Portuguese, who first settled in the 16th century, in an attempt to protect their eastern trade routes.

Close ties with Britain were established in 1798, when a treaty of friendship was concluded. British influence remains strong, though the number of British advisers occupying key positions in Omani Government Departments has steadily declined. During the early years of his reign, which began in 1970, Sultan Qaboos' overriding priority was to deal with an insurgency in the western part of his kingdom, conducted by the Popular Front for the Liberation of Oman (PFLO) with the backing of the People's Democratic Republic of Yemen (South Yemen; since unified with North Yemen). The defeat of the insurgents served to increase both domestic and foreign pressure on Qaboos to introduce democratic reforms. A series of incremental measures were introduced to modernise and liberalise this previously autocratic regime. Two Consultative Assemblies, the Majlis as-Shura and the Majlis al-Dawlah, were groomed to assume the functions of a Bicameral Parliament at the turn of the millennium, but this has not yet happened. The two Majlis have some influence over domestic affairs but no say in foreign and defence matters. The most recent poll for the Majlis as-Shura in November 2003 registered little change in its make-up: no formal political parties are allowed but supporters of the Sultan are in the majority.

In recent years, Omani concerns have been focused further afield. In 1981, Oman was a founder member of the Gulf Co-operation Council and has played a leading role in promoting its increasing involvement in regional security issues. The country's strategic importance to the West has been underlined throughout the last two decades as it has been used as a staging post for Anglo-American military, naval and air operations, most recently in both assaults on Afghanistan and Iraq. In 1994, Oman was also the first Gulf state to establish official relations with Israel. It has managed to, under politically delicate circumstances, also foster cordial relations with countries such as Iran, now extending as far as mutual security co-operation in the Gulf. Oman is a chameleon of a country: whatever you want it to be, it will become. If you are seeking a modern country, you will spot its cosmopolitan shopping malls and well-equipped watersports facilities. If you are seeking antiquity and tradition, you will observe ancient trading towns and smell the aroma of frankincense. Very much still an Islamic country, resplendent mosques jostle alongside large hotel complexes. Oman is a beautiful country, and, moreover, very unspoiled – whatever you are looking for, you are sure to find it here.

General Information

AREA: 309,500 sq km (119,500 sq miles).

POPULATION: 3 million (UN, 2005).

POPULATION DENSITY: 9.69 per sq km.

CAPITAL: Muscat. **Population:** 1.65 million (including the Batinah coastal plain, northwest of Muscat).

GEOGRAPHY: The Sultanate of Oman occupies the southeastern tip of the Arabian Peninsula with almost 1700km (1062 miles) of coastline stretching along the Indian Ocean and the Arabian Gulf. It is bordered by the Kingdom of Saudi Arabia to the west and the Republic of Yemen to the south. The United Arab Emirates lies to the northwest of Oman and to the east lies the Arabian Sea and the Gulf of Oman.

GOVERNMENT: Sultanate since 1744. **Head of State and Government:** Sultan Qaboos bin Sa'id since 1970.

LANGUAGE: Arabic is the official language. English is widely spoken. Swahili is also spoken by the population from East Africa. German and French are spoken by some hotel staff.

RELIGION: Predominantly Ibadi Muslim, with Shi'ite Muslim, Sunni Muslim and Hindu minorities.

ELECTRICITY: 220/240 volts AC, 50Hz.

SOCIAL CONVENTIONS: Shaking hands is the usual form of greeting. A small gift, either promoting your company or country, is well received. As far as dress is concerned, it is important that women dress modestly, ie long skirts or dresses (below the knee) with long sleeves, men should wear trousers and shirts with sleeves. Tight-fitting clothes must be avoided and although this is not strictly followed by Westerners, it is far better to adopt this practice and avoid causing offence. Shorts should never be worn in public and beachwear is prohibited anywhere except the beach. Collecting sea shells, abalone, corals, crayfish and turtle eggs is also prohibited. Dumping litter is forbidden. It is polite not to smoke in public, but generally no-smoking signs are posted where appropriate. Homosexual behaviour is illegal. **Photography:** Visitors should ask permission before attempting to photograph people or their property. 'No Photography' signs exist in certain places and must be observed.

Climate

The months between May and August are particularly hot. The climate is best from September through to April. Rainfall varies according to the region. During the period June to September there is a light monsoon rain in Salalah.

Required clothing: Lightweights are worn throughout the year, with a warm wrap for cooler winter evenings. Light rainwear is advisable.

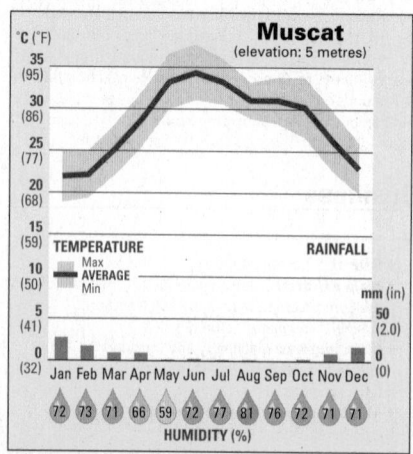

Communications

Telephone: IDD is available. Country code: 968.

Mobile telephone: Roaming agreements exist with international mobile phone companies. Coverage is variable.

Internet: There are Internet cafes in the cities of Nizwa and Muscat.

Post: Airmail to Western Europe takes three to four days.

MEDIA: The Government operates Oman's TV and radio stations. However, private, Omani-owned radio and TV stations are now emerging. The use of satellite dishes is permitted. A press act allows the Government to censor publications for political or cultural reasons.

Press: English-language newspapers include *The Oman Daily Observer* (website: www.omanobserver.com) and *The Times of Oman* (website: www.timesofoman.com). There are more than 20 publications, including dailies and weeklies.

TV: *Oman TV* is a state-run network.

Radio: *Radio Oman* is a state-run network in Arabic and English.

Passport/Visa

	Passport Required?	Visa Required?	Return Ticket Required?
Full British	Yes	Yes	Yes
Australian	Yes	Yes	Yes
Canadian	Yes	Yes	Yes
USA	Yes	Yes	Yes
Other EU	Yes	Yes	Yes
Japanese	Yes	Yes	Yes

Note: *Regulations and requirements may be subject to change at short notice, and you are advised to contact the appropriate diplomatic or consular authority before finalising travel arrangements. Any numbers in the chart refer to the footnotes below.*

PASSPORTS: Passport valid for at least six months required by all except the following:
(a) nationals of Bahrain, Kuwait, Qatar, Saudi Arabia and the United Arab Emirates (Gulf Cooperation Council States) holding national identity cards;
(b) holders of Macau (SAR) Travel Permit.

VISAS: Required by all except nationals of the Gulf Cooperation Council States.

Note: (a) Nationals of the following countries may apply for a visa (at a cost of OMR6 for single-entry visas and OMR10 for multiple-entry visas; children 17 years and younger are exempt from paying a fee) on arrival at Oman Seeb International Airport for a maximum stay of one month: Andorra, Argentina, Australia, Bolivia, Brazil, Brunei, Canada, Chile, Colombia, Croatia, Ecuador, EU nationals, (Former Yugoslav Republic of) Macedonia, Hong Kong (SAR), Iceland, Indonesia, Japan, Korea (Rep), Lebanon, Liechtenstein, Malaysia, Moldova, Monaco, New Zealand, Norway, Paraguay, Peru, Romania, San Marino, Seychelles, Singapore, South Africa, Surinam, Switzerland, Taiwan (China), Thailand, Tunisia, Turkey, USA, Uruguay, Vatican City and Venezuela. (b) Travellers who have resided in one of the Gulf Cooperation Council countries for at least one year and who hold a valid residence permit and labour card may obtain a tourist visa on arrival, provided they meet certain conditions regarding professional status. Contact Embassy/Consulate for further details. (c) For minors (under 18 years) travelling unaccompanied, a consent letter is required from one of their parents. (d) Any other visitors arriving in Oman without a tourist or a sponsored visa will be refused entry. Visitors are not allowed to enter Oman by road unless their visa states such validity and a designated point of entry. A sponsored visa is obtainable from the Royal Oman Police Immigration Department.

Types of visa and cost: Cost may vary according to nationality, but generally is as follows for tourist/business/ sponsored visas: *Single-entry*: £12 (generally for all European and Latin American countries, and the USA; enquire at the Embassy/Consulate for specific details as certain countries may also be/not be eligible); £14 (other countries). *Multiple-entry* (see the list of countries eligible for discounted single-entry): £20. Visitors are advised to contact the Embassy. Fees may be paid by cheque if application is made in person.

Validity: *Single-entry*: One-month stay from date of entry for those listed (can be extended for one-month when in Oman). *Multiple-entry*: 12 months from date of issue, for stays up to three weeks on each visit (cannot be extended).

Application to: Consulate (or Consular section at Embassy); see *Passport/Visa Information* for details. Applications are referred to Muscat.

Application requirements: (a) Completed application form (preferably typed) and signed. (b) Valid passport with a blank page to affix the visa. (c) Fee; cash not accepted and cheques must be supported by a cheque guarantee card from bank. (d) Details of travel plans. (e) Evidence of employment or proof of sufficient funds for period of stay, eg bank statement or last two payslips. (f) Business letter, if applicable, detailing purpose of visit and requested travel date. (g) Self-addressed envelope with stamp sufficient to cover cost of posting passport and other documents if applying by post, sent by special or recorded delivery.

Note: Passengers who have a new passport, but whose visa is entered in a previous passport, should also carry their previous passport. Passports must have spare pages.

Working days required: Two to five. Postal applications take longer.

PASSPORT/VISA INFORMATION

Embassy of the Sultanate of Oman in the UK
167 Queen's Gate, London SW7 5HE, UK
Tel: (020) 7225 0001 *or* (0906) 550 8964 (recorded visa information; calls cost £1 a minute).
Opening hours: Mon-Fri 0900-1530; 0930-1230 (visa section).

Embassy of the Sultanate of Oman in the USA
2535 Belmont Road, NW,
Washington, DC 20008, USA
Tel: (202) 387 1980.

Money

Currency: Omani Rial (OMR) = 1000 baiza. Notes are in denominations of OMR50, 20, 10, 5 and 1, and 500, 250, 200 and 100 baiza. Coins are in denominations of 50, 25, 10 and 5 baiza.
Credit & debit cards: American Express is accepted, as are other major credit cards. Check with your credit or debit card company for details of merchant acceptability and other services which may be available. There are over 70 ATMs in Oman.
Traveller's cheques: Easily exchanged. To avoid additional exchange rate charges, travellers are advised to take traveller's cheques in US Dollars.
Currency restrictions: There are no restrictions on the import or export of local or foreign currency. Israeli currency, however, is prohibited.
Banking hours: Sat-Wed 0800-1200, Thurs 0800-1130.
Exchange rate indicators:
Rate at time of publishing
£1.00=   OMR0.68
$1.00=   OMR0.38

Duty Free

The following items may be imported per family into Oman without incurring customs duty:
Up to 2l of alcoholic beverages (non-Muslims only); a reasonable quantity of tobacco products; 227ml perfume; eight video tapes for personal use.
Restricted items: Meat and meat products have the same regulations as when importing pets; an Islamic slaughter certificate is required.
Prohibited items: Narcotics, non-canned food products (including vegetables, fruit and non-alcoholic beverages), bees (unless clearance is given), dates (including shoots of palm date, coconut and ornamental palm trees), firearms (including toys and replicas) and obscene films/literature. Videos are subject to censorship.
Note: The import and use of narcotics and obscene material are forbidden and can lead to imprisonment. There are severe penalties for drug offences including, in some cases, the death penalty. "Soft" drugs are treated as seriously as "hard" drugs. The possession of small quantities of cannabis can lead to a 12-month prison sentence and deportation.

Public Holidays

Below are listed Public Holidays for the January 2006-June 2007 period.
2006: Jan 1 New Year's Day. **Jan 10** Eid al-Adha (Feast of the Sacrifice). **Jan 31** Muharram (Islamic New Year). **Apr 11** Mouloud (Birth of the Prophet). **Aug 22** Leilat al-Meiraj (Ascension of the Prophet). **Oct 22-24** Eid al-Fitr (End of Ramadan). **Nov 18** National Day and birthday of HM Sultan Qaboos. **Dec 31** Eid al-Adha (Feast of the Sacrifice).
2007: Jan 1 New Year's Day. **Jan 20** Muharram (Islamic New Year). **Mar 31** Mouloud (Birth of the Prophet).
Note: Muslim festivals are timed according to local sightings of various phases of the moon and the dates given above are approximations. During the lunar month of Ramadan that precedes Eid al-Fitr, Muslims fast during the day and feast at night and normal business patterns may be interrupted. Many restaurants are closed during the day and there may be restrictions on smoking and drinking. Some disruption may continue into Eid al-Fitr itself. Eid al-Fitr and Eid al-Adha may last anything from two to 10 days, depending on the region. For more information, see the *World of Islam* appendix.

Health

	Special Precautions?	Certificate Required?
Yellow Fever	No	1
Cholera	No	No
Typhoid & Polio	2	N/A
Malaria	3	N/A

Note: *Regulations and requirements may be subject to change at short notice, and you are advised to contact your doctor well in advance of your intended date of departure. Any numbers in the chart refer to the footnotes below.*

1: A yellow fever vaccination certificate is required from travellers arriving within six days from infected areas.
2: Typhoid may occur in rural areas.
3: Malaria is a limited risk in remote areas of Musandam Province. No anti-malarial drugs are needed.
Food & drink: All water outside the capital area should be regarded as being potentially contaminated. Water used for drinking, brushing teeth or making ice should have first been boiled or otherwise sterilised. Bottled water is available and is advised throughout Oman. Food bought in the main supermarkets can be regarded as safe. Outside the capital area, milk may be unpasteurised and if so, should be boiled. Powdered or tinned milk is available and is advised, but make sure that it is reconstituted with pure water. Avoid dairy products which are likely to have been made from unboiled milk. Only eat well-cooked meat and fish, preferably served hot. Salad and mayonnaise may carry increased risk. Vegetables should be cooked and fruit peeled.
Other risks: *Hepatitis A* and *B*, *leishmaniasis* and *lymphatic filariasis* all occur.
Rabies is present. For those at high risk, vaccination before arrival should be considered. If you are bitten, seek medical advice without delay. For more information, consult the *Health* appendix.
Health care: Oman has an extensive public health service (free to Omani nationals), with around 46 hospitals, 86 health centres and 65 preventative health centres. Treatment varies according to the location. Hospital emergency treatment is available. Doctors and hospitals often expect cash for services, and costs can be high for foreigners. Health insurance is essential.

Travel - International

AIR:

 The national airlines of Oman are *Gulf Air (GF)* (website: www.gulfairco.com), which it jointly owns with the governments of Abu Dhabi, Bahrain and Qatar; and *Oman Air (WY)* (website: www.oman-air.com).
Approximate flight times: From Muscat to *London* is nine hours (excluding stopover), to *Singapore* six hours 30 minutes and to *Sydney* 16 hours.
Main airports: *Muscat (MCT)* (Seeb International), 40km (25 miles) west of the city (travel time – 15 to 30 minutes). *To/from the airport:* Taxis and buses to the city are available. *Facilities:* Bank/bureau de change, duty free shops, bar and light refreshments, restaurants and tourist information as well as post office and car hire.
Departure tax: OMR5 for all departures (this has usually already been collected at ticket issuance). Children under two years old are exempt.

SEA:

 Main ports: *Salalah* (website: www.salalahport.com) and *Sultan Qaboos.* Traffic is mainly commercial.

ROAD:

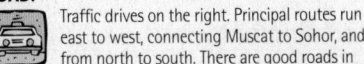 Travel into Oman by land is only possible with prior Government permission. The best route is the north-south road from Muscat to Salalah, a journey of some 10 to 12 hours. Road travel through Saudi Arabia and the United Arab Emirates is extremely limited. There is no access from Yemen. The import (even temporary) of right-hand vehicles is not allowed.

Travel - Internal

AIR:

 Oman Air (WY) runs domestic flights to Salalah and Khasab from Seeb airport; the approximate flight time to Salalah is 90 minutes.

ROAD:

Traffic drives on the right. Principal routes run from east to west, connecting Muscat to Sohor, and from north to south. There are good roads in Muscat and between Muscat and other major towns in Oman. Driving at night can be dangerous because of the risk of hitting camels that stray on the roads outside Muscat. Whilst driving at night it is advised to keep doors locked and windows closed. **Bus:** The state-owned *Oman National Transport Company* has been developing a network of services in Muscat and north Oman using modern, air-conditioned vehicles. Seventeen long-distance routes now exist. There are daily departures from Runi (Muscat) to Nizwa, Bahla, Ibri, Dhank, Yanqui, Ibra, Sohar, Shinas, Buraimi, Fahud, Dubai, Abudhabi and Salalah. There is competition from taxis and pick-up trucks converted for passenger service. **Taxi:** Prices are high and fares should be agreed in advance. Shared taxis are also available. **Car hire:** Available from international firms which have offices at hotels throughout the country.
Regulations: Traffic laws are strictly imposed. Heavy penalties are imposed for drinking and driving; 48-hour prison sentences are imposed if traffic offences are caused by driving under the influence of alcohol. Seat belts should be worn at all times. On-the-spot fines are imposed if caught using a mobile phone whilst driving. It is also forbidden to drive on the beaches.

Documentation: A local licence must be obtained from the police by presenting a national driving licence or International Driving Permit. Police passes may be required if travelling via the United Arab Emirates.

Travel Advice

There is a high threat from terrorism. Al Qaeda continues to issue statements threatening to carry out attacks in the Gulf region. These include references to attacks on Western interests, including residential compounds, military, oil, transport and aviation interests.
Travellers should review their security arrangements carefully and should remain vigilant, particularly in public places. This advice is based on information provided by the Foreign and Commonwealth Office in the UK. It is correct at time of publishing. As the situation can change rapidly, visitors are advised to contact the following organisations for the latest travel advice:

British Foreign and Commonwealth Office
Tel: (0845) 850 2829.
Website: www.fco.gov.uk

US Department of State
Website: http://travel.state.gov/travel

Accommodation

HOTELS:

There is a good selection of hotels to suit all budgets. Smaller hotels are cheaper but facilities are more limited. There are very few hotels in provincial areas but a large hotel-building programme has been initiated. The Shangri-La luxury hotel chain has recently opened a **6-star** resort and spa in Oman. Booking well in advance is strongly recommended. All rates are subject to a 10 per cent service charge.

ACCOMMODATION INFORMATION

Barr Al Jissah Resort and Spa (6-star)
PO Box 644, Postcode 113, Muscat, Oman
Tel: 2477 6666.
Website: www.shangri-la.com

Top Things To See

• Explore Oman's capital, divided into three main districts: **Muscat**, **Mutrah** and **Ruwi**. Muscat, the old walled port town, is dominated by the **Sultan's palace**, buildings of the **Royal Court** and Government offices. Two well-preserved 16th-century Portuguese forts, **Al Jalali** and **Mirani**, guard the entrance to Muscat, and the **city walls** contain three beautifully carved original gates. The town's old houses and narrow streets are overlooked by the hillside **Mutrah Fort**. The **Ali Mosque, Sultan Qaboos Grand Mosque** and the **New Mosque** beside the sea add to the district's charm. Mutrah port is the capital's commercial centre and its **fish market**, **souk** and many **bazaars** are well worth visiting. **Ruwi** is the capital's business district and has excellent streets for shopping. The **National Museum**, featuring fine displays of Omani silverwork, and the **Sultan's Armed Forces Museum**, which outlines Omani history, are located here.
• Catch the **monsoon** in **Salalah**, the capital of the southern region and a city set amongst coconut groves and banana plantations, sprawled along sandy beaches that run the length of its plain. The lush vegetation makes Salalah seem almost tropical, particularly as it is one of the only places in the Arabian peninsular where the monsoon occurs. The **Al-Balid** and **Samhuram ancient cities** are a major tourist attraction. **Nabi Ayoub** (Jacob) **Tomb** and **Tomb of Prophet Omran** are interesting to visit.
• Wander around the old town of **Sur**, famous for its traditional shipbuilding. Sur started trading along the African coast as early as the sixth century. It is constructed around winding streets, full of carved wooden doors and old Arabesque buildings.
• Peer into Oman's past in **Nizwa**, the main town in the interior province, with an immense palm oasis stretching for 13km (8 miles) along the course of two wadis. Nizwa was once the country's capital during the sixth and seventh centuries. Famous for its copper and silver handicrafts, the centre of the town is dominated by the huge circular tower of one of Oman's oldest and largest castles.
• For a splendid view across the desert to the mountains, look out from the 17th-century fortified **palace** in **Jabrin** (notable for its painted wooden ceilings).
• Visit the World Heritage Site of **Bahla**, which dates back to the third millennium BC, an ancient town with seven miles of ancient defensive **walls**. There is a good souk here and the town is known for its **pottery**. The picturesque village of **Al Hamra** can be found nearby.
• For those craving greenery, head to **Jebel Akhdar**, noted

Credit: © Oman Tourism

for its date palm groves, valleys and terraced villages, and rising to nearly 3000m (10,000ft); it literally translates as 'The Green Mountain'. On the northern slopes of the Jebel Akhdar are the fortress of **Al Hazm**, built in 1708, and the oasis town of **Rostaq**, containing the tombs of Oman's early rulers. On the side of a deep wadi on the south slope of the Jebel Akhdar, sits **Misfah**, one of the most picturesque villages in Oman.

Top Things To Do

- There are many sandy **beaches** offering good **bathing**, **diving** and **sailing** facilities. **Surfing** is popular around **Masirah Island** where waves are normally four to six feet high - it is also good for **windsurfing**. The **Bander al-Rowdha Marina** has a purpose-built watersports complex, with landscaped beach area, swimming pool and restaurants. Some recommended, stunning beaches include **Qurum Beach**, **Bandar**, **Al-Jissah** and **Yeti**, as well as **Ain Sahnot**, **Ain Rzat** and **Ain Hamran**, with parks and gardens surrounding them.
- Take a **dhow cruise** along the palm-fringed coast of **Qurum**, which encapsulates Oman's archaeology, history and culture. The **National Museum** here has a collection of silver, jewellery, weapons and ancient stone artefacts.
- Watch for **spinner-**, **common-** and **bottlenose dolphins**, regularly seen off the coast of Oman. **Whales** are also occasionally spotted. **Fahal Island** is an especially good site to watch for them.
- Where better to go **caving** than in **Majlis al-Jhinn**, the world's second-largest cave? Its long passages, crystal-clear streams, canals and drip curtains extend throughout its 4 million cubic metre expanse.
- Spectate at Oman's popular **camel races**, held on Fridays and public holidays at a variety of locations. If you are brave, and want to hop on a camel yourself, this option is available at some locations on **desert safaris**, such as from **Shargiyah Sands** to **Al-Rub'a**.
- Go **birdwatching**: species from Europe, Africa and Asia can be spotted in Oman, especially from October to April.

Herons, ospreys, laughing doves and Egyptian vultures can be seen. The best sites are the **Al-Ansab lagoons**, **Qurum National Park** and the **Arabian Oryx Sanctuary**.
- **Swim** in the crystal-clear beauty of the **Bimmah Sinkole**, located on the coastal road from **Muscat** to **Sur**. The colours of its water have to be seen to be believed.

TOURIST INFORMATION

Oman Tourism in the UK
c/o Representation Plus, 11 Blades Court,
121 Deodar Road, London, SW15 2NU, UK
Tel: 020 8877 4524.
Website: www.omantourism.gov.om

Entertainment

FOOD & DRINK: Numerous restaurants have opened in recent years, but many people retain the habit of dining at hotels. There is a wide variety of cuisine on offer, including Arabic, Indian, Oriental, European and other international dishes. Coffee houses are popular.

Things to know: Waiter service is usual. Muslim law forbids alcohol, but most hotel bars and restaurants serve alcohol. Visitors are only allowed to drink alcohol in licensed hotels and restaurants. To buy alcohol for home consumption, Western nationals must obtain a licence from their Embassy.

National specialities:
- *Shuwa* (meat cooked slowly (up to two days) in underground clay ovens with herbs and spices).
- *Mashuai* (spit-roasted kingfish served with lemon rice).
- *Maqbous* (rice dish with saffron cooked over spicy red or white meat).
- *Halwa* (sticky, sweet, gelatinous substance made from brown sugar, eggs, honey and spices).
- *Lokhemat* (balls of flour and yeast flavoured with cardamom and deep fried, served with sweet lime and cardamom syrup).

National drinks:
- *Kahwa* (coffee; a strong, bitter drink flavoured with cardamom, served with *halwa* and *lokemat*). **Tipping**: Becoming more common and 10 per cent should be given.

NIGHTLIFE: There are a few nightclubs and bars in Muscat, mostly in the hotels. There are three air conditioned cinemas in Ruwi and an open-air cinema at the al-Falaj Hotel showing Arab, Indian and English films.

SHOPPING: The modern shops are mostly in Ruwi and Qurum. The two main *souks* (markets) are located in Matrah and Nizwa. Traditional crafts include silver and gold jewellery, *khanjars* (Omani daggers), coffeepots, saddles, frankincense, handwoven textiles, carpets, baskets and camel straps. Antique khanjars (over 50 years old) may not be exported. It is wise to check with the Ministry of National Heritage and Culture for the necessary documentation before purchasing. **Shopping hours**: Sat-Thurs 0800-1300 and 1600-2000. *Souks* open 0800-1100 and 1600-1900. Many shops close on Friday. Opening hours are one hour later during Ramadan.

Credit: © Oman Tourism

Business

- **GDP:** US$21.58 billion.
- **Main imports:** Machinery, transport equipment, manufactured goods, food, livestock and lubricants.
- **Main exports:** Petroleum, fish, metals and textiles.
- **Main trade partners:** China (PR), Japan, Korea (Rep), Thailand and United Arab Emirates.

ECONOMY: Oman was acutely underdeveloped until the discovery of oil and natural gas in the early 1970s; in 2004, this accounted for 56 per cent of the country's export earnings. Agriculture, owing to Oman's desert land, is confined to the coastal plain and a few irrigated areas in the interior. Dates, limes and alfalfa are the main products; some livestock is also bred. There are mineral deposits of copper, chromite, marble, gypsum and limestone, manganese ore and coal. The Government has used some of its oil revenues to develop indigenous industries such as construction, agriculture and tourism, and to build up the country's infrastructure; these projects are incorporated in the Vision 2020 economic development programme. In the late 1990s, Oman started to privatise major government-owned parts of the economy and introduce a legislative framework to encourage foreign investment. The economy has been growing at around 7 per cent annually and enjoys low inflation. Unemployment is about 15 per cent. Oman is a member of various pan-Arab political and economic organisations. However, it is not a member of the Organisation of Petroleum Exporting Countries (OPEC) – although its pricing policy tends to follow that of OPEC fairly closely.

BUSINESS ETIQUETTE: Men should wear suits and ties for business and formal occasions. English is usually spoken in business circles, but a few words or phrases of Arabic will be useful and welcome. Appointments are essential and punctuality is gradually becoming more important in business circles. Visiting cards are widely used. **Office hours**: Sat-Wed 0800-1300 and 1600-1900, Thurs 0800-1300. Government office hours: Sat-Wed 0730-1430, and sometimes half-day Thursday. All offices are closed Friday. Office hours are shorter during Ramadan.

COMMERCIAL INFORMATION

Ministry of Commerce and Industry
PO Box 550, Postal Code 113, Muscat, Oman
Tel: 771 7085.
Website: www.mocioman.gov.om

Oman Chamber of Commerce and Industry
PO Box 1400, Postal Code 112, Ruwi, Oman
Tel: 2470 7674/84/94.
Website: www.chamberoman.com

The Pacific

The Pacific
Most of the countries in the Pacific have their own entries elsewhere; consult the *Contents*.

Overview

The vast, sparsely populated region of the Pacific Ocean, which covers one-quarter of the Earth's surface, has been the subject of growing interest in the last few years. It is neither easy nor especially useful to make generalisations about the area and the myriad small islands peppered across it. All have unique features of geography, economy and, not least, political history. Some are genuinely independent, some are internally self-governing with foreign and security policies controlled elsewhere, while a handful remain simple colonies. There are, nevertheless, global political and economic trends that are certain to create a substantial impact throughout the Pacific.
A notable feature of the 1970s and 1980s was the growing militarisation of the Pacific. This trend, while yet to be reversed, has at least halted. Its most obvious and damaging manifestation – the nuclear tests run by the French and the Americans – ended in the mid-1990s, at least for the time being. But the region still hosts a large number of airfields, storage depots, port complexes, intelligence-gathering, early-warning and other 'support' facilities. The host Governments are often in two minds about their presence – the bases put these small nations in a diplomatic straitjacket, as well as offer a series of targets for hostile forces. On the other hand, they are guaranteed military protection and a steady rental income, plus essential economic aid.
But the islands are well aware that they must develop their own economic systems in order to survive in the long term and have focused on three principal areas in which they hope to progress.
One of these is tourism. Much of the region is currently within reach of the North American traveller but further exploitation of its tourism potential is dependent either on the development of cheaper, faster and perhaps less-polluting forms of long-distance transport to bring the Pacific within reach of Europe, or on a substantial increase in the disposable incomes of the populations of Asia and South America. Neither of these is likely to be realised in the short term.
Another economic asset that might produce more immediate dividends is the Pacific's awe-inspiring wealth of natural resources. Many Pacific nations are just a few score square kilometres of land, however, their boundaries enclose hundreds of thousands of square kilometres of ocean. Commercial fishing, notably by Japan, has long been carried out on a huge scale but has yet to make any real impact on the ocean's deep-sea fish stocks. The region also has enormous mineral potential. Much attention has been given to developing commercially viable methods of harvesting the mineral-rich manganese nodules that cover much of the ocean's abyssal plains, although there are believed to be other mineral deposits of great value. Additionally, the whole Pacific Rim has great potential as an energy source, initially from geothermal installations, later perhaps from deep-sea tidal and temperature gradient devices.
Finally, the islands stand to benefit from the rapidly growing Pacific trade axis as Japan and the Pacific Rim countries link up with the west coast of the Americas. This offers opportunities for developing transit facilities for shipping and 'offshore' financial services of the type that have long been offered by, for example, Jersey and the Cayman Islands. The islands will need more than this type of business to sustain a healthy economy and it remains to be seen whether or not they are able to develop their undoubted assets without becoming excessively dominated by foreign commercial interests.
On a darker note, one problem that has arisen in the last few years and is worrying several Pacific Governments, concerns the possible consequences of global warming on sea levels. A number of islands face a serious threat to their land masses. Some, such as Nauru, could disappear altogether – it already has lost one, albeit uninhabited, island. The Pacific islands are consequently an increasingly vocal presence at international forums discussing global environmental questions.

www.gocoti.com

The Pacific Islands of Micronesia

(Islands formerly comprising the US-administered Pacific Trust Territory.)

Location: This region was administered by the USA on behalf of the United Nations until 1990. It includes the Federated States of Micronesia, the Republic of the Marshall Islands, the Northern Mariana Islands and the Republic of Palau. The Northern Marianas have had US Commonwealth status since 1986. Under the terms of the Compacts of Free Association between the USA and the other former territories, each is a sovereign self-governing state pursuing its foreign policy along agreed guidelines, with the USA retaining responsibility for defence in exchange for economic aid. The Federated States of Micronesia and the Republic of the Marshall Islands became members of the UN in 1991 and Palau became a member in 1994.

Time: See individual sections.

Overview

Micronesia comprises four archipelagos: the Federated States of Micronesia (Caroline Islands), the Republic of the Marshall Islands, the Northern Mariana Islands and the Republic of Palau.
The area has a turbulent history of foreign control and political change. Despite upheavals and foreign influences from Spanish, German, Japanese and US Governments, many people of this vast island area have maintained much of their cultural heritage and traditions, while others have lifestyles inspired mainly by the teachings of 19th-century missionaries. Having come under UN Trusteeship, administered by the USA, at the end of World War II, all of the Pacific Micronesian states have now reached final political settlements.
See individual country sections for further details.

General Information

AREA: 7,800,000 sq km (3,000,000 sq miles) of which 1846.3 sq km (721.2 sq miles) is land.
POPULATION: See individual entries.
GEOGRAPHY: Each archipelago is composed of hundreds of island groups, within which there are many islands varying widely in topography. A more detailed description is given under the individual section for each country. There are three distinct population groups: Malayans who passed through Indonesia and The Philippines; Melanesians coming from the islands of the southwest Pacific; and Polynesians who inhabited the South Pacific.
LANGUAGE: English, Japanese and nine local languages.
RELIGION: Roman Catholic and Protestant with Mormon and Baha'i minorities.
ELECTRICITY: 110/120 volts AC, 60Hz. Plugs are the US flat two-pin type.
SOCIAL CONVENTIONS: The Western understanding of private property is alien to many parts of Micronesia and personal possessions should be well looked after, though not necessarily under lock and key; outside main tourist areas, where normal precautions apply, it is usually sufficient just to keep items out of sight. All land, however, does have an owner and before using it, protocol in many areas demands that permission is sought; in places this includes use of footpaths as there is not necessarily immediate right of way. A clearly expressed desire to be courteous will usually see the visitor through; see individual sections for further details.

Climate

With 2000 islands spread over 7.8 million sq km (3 million sq miles) of the Pacific Ocean, the islands have a variety of weather. The period from autumn to winter (November to April) is the most pleasant time, while May to October is the wet season. The climate can generally be described as tropical in this part of the world, but the cooling sea breezes prevent really extreme temperatures and humidity. For regional climate charts, see under the individual sections.
Required clothing: Lightweight cottons and linens and rainwear.

Communications

Telephone: IDD is available to any of the islands. See individual entries for country codes.
Internet: There is basic access and services on the islands. See individual entries.
Post: Airmail to Europe takes approximately 10 days. Post offices are located in the centre of each state.
MEDIA: Press: *The Pacific Daily News* (Guam) is the main English-language daily newspaper in the region and is distributed throughout all the islands. Further information is provided under individual entries.
TV: Cable TV is available on Pohnpei and Chuuk.
Radio: The state Governments and a religious organisation operate radio stations throughout the Pacific Islands of Micronesia.

Passport/Visa

Note: (a) Each of the four constitutional Governments is responsible for its own tourism policies, and regulations may be subject to change. (b) On many islands, especially the remoter ones, it is not the possession of documents (necessary though they are) that secures access, but the consent of the islanders. For more details, see the individual sections.

Money

Currency: US Dollar (USD; symbol US$) = 100 cents. Notes are in denominations of US$1000, 500, 100, 50, 20, 10, 5, 2 and 1. Coins are in denominations of US$1 and 50, 25, 10, 5 and 1 cents. Japanese yen are accepted on many islands.
Currency exchange: Foreign exchange services are limited on some islands.
Credit & debit cards: American Express, MasterCard and Visa are accepted in most hotels and tourist-oriented facilities. Check with your credit or debit card company for details of merchant acceptability and other services which may be available.
Traveller's cheques: US Dollar traveller's cheques are advised.
Currency restrictions: These vary; see individual sections for details.
Banking hours: Mon-Thurs 1000-1500, Fri 1000-1800. There are some local variations.
Exchange rate indicators:
Rate at time of publishing
£1.00= US$1.77

Public Holidays

Some US public holidays are observed in addition to regional public holidays, though there are variations from island to island; see individual sections for main holidays in each region.

Health

	Special Precautions?	Certificate Required?
Yellow Fever	1	1
Cholera	2	2
Typhoid & Polio	3	N/A
Malaria	No	N/A

Note: Regulations and requirements may be subject to change at short notice, and you are advised to contact your doctor well in advance of your intended date of departure. Any numbers in the chart refer to the footnotes below.

1: See individual sections for information about yellow fever vaccination requirements.
2: A cholera vaccination is a condition of entry to some of the Pacific Islands of Micronesia; see individual sections for details.
3: Typhoid and para-typhoid vaccinations are strongly recommended.
Food & drink: Mains water is normally chlorinated, and whilst relatively safe may cause mild abdominal upsets. Drinking water outside main towns may be contaminated and sterilisation is advisable. Bottled water is available and is advised for the first few weeks of the stay. Milk is pasteurised and dairy products are safe for consumption. Local meat, poultry, seafood, fruit and vegetables are generally considered safe to eat.
Other risks: *Hepatitis A* and *B* may occur on some islands and precautions should be taken. *Tetanus* vaccination is also advised. *Dengue fever*, including its haemorrhagic form, can occur in epidemics in most islands. Colenterates, poisonous fish and sea snakes can present hazards to bathers.
Health care: Health insurance is recommended. There are nine hospitals in the region.

Travel - International

AIR:
The region's major airline is *Continental Micronesia (CS)*. Consult individual entries for further information.
Approximate flight times: Flight durations from London to destinations in the Pacific vary considerably depending on the route taken. The most common route would include stopovers in Los Angeles and Honolulu; eg the flight time from London to Honolulu is 19 hours 30 minutes and from

A B C D E F G H I J K L M N O P Q R S T U V W X Y Z

Honolulu to the Marshall Islands four hours 30 minutes.
Main airports: Guam (GUM), Koror Babeldaob (ROR) and Saipan (SPN) when entering from the north and west, Pohnpei (PNI) from the south, and Majuro (MAJ) from the south and east.

Regional airlines: Scheduled inter-island travel, charters and sightseeing are offered by several local airlines. There is excellent provision for travelling from Guam, Majuro and Saipan to the various islands.

Flights between the islands tend to be rarer. Airlines include: Air Marshall Islands (CW): This Government-owned airline runs charters, sightseeing tours and point-to-point flights between Majuro and other islands in the Marshalls; also international flights to Fiji, Honolulu, Kiribati and Tuvalu. Continental Micronesia (CS): Operates between islands in all four groups, and to Guam, Hawaii, Japan and The Philippines. Several smaller airlines fly to Guam.

Air passes: The Visit South Pacific Pass is valid for many airlines operating in the South Pacific, including most of the larger ones, such as Air Caledonie, Air Marshall Islands, Air Nauru, Air Niugingi, Air Pacific, Air Vanuatu, Polynesian Airlines, Qantas, Royal Tongan Airlines and Solomon Airlines. Offering reductions of up to 40 per cent on normal airfares, this sector-based pass allows for flexible island-hopping between the destinations of the Cook Islands, Fiji, Nauru, New Caledonia, Samoa, Tahiti, Tonga, Vanuatu and the more remote Melanesian and Micronesian islands, together with major cities in Australia (Brisbane, Melbourne and Sydney) and New Zealand (Auckland, Christchurch and Wellington). It is only available for people resident outside of the South Pacific. The journey must be started outside the South Pacific and only one stopover in Australia is allowed. A minimum of two sectors must be bought before departure (extra sectors can be purchased en route). There is a maximum of one pass per person, and passes must be used within six months of the first day of travel. Children under 12 years of age pay 75 per cent of the adult fare. For details and conditions, contact the South Pacific Tourist Organisation.

SEA:

The major ports are Koror, Majuro, Pohnpei, Saipan, Tuik and Yap.
The following cargo/passenger lines serve the islands: Daiwa Navigation Co, Nauru Pacific, Oceania Line Inc, P&O, Royal Shipping Co, Saipan Shipping Co and Tiger Line.

There are numerous boats for touring, ranging from small speed boats to large glass-bottomed boats for fishing, sightseeing, sunset cruising, scuba-diving and short-distance travel. A ferry provides service between Saipan and Tinian. Inter-island vessels provide limited and irregular service between Saipan and the smaller islands. Requests for reservations should be directed to the Office of the Government of the following: Saipan, Commonwealth of the Northern Marianas; Office of Transportation in Majuro, Marshall Islands; Koror, Palau; Kolonia, Pohnpei; Moen, Chuuk and Colonia, Yap. Cabin space is limited, and passengers may be required to sleep on deck (bring own mat). The field trip ships are leased by the Governments to private firms, and rates are subject to change.
Cruise lines: Norwegian American, Princess, Royal Viking and Small Ship currently offer cruises to the islands.

Travel - Internal

ROAD:

Good roads are limited to the major island centres. **Bus:** There are no local bus systems other than tourist services. However, public transport is widely available in all the Micronesian district centres in the form of sedans, pickups and jeepneys. **Taxi:** Inexpensive taxis are available throughout Micronesia. **Car hire:** Each major centre offers rental cars, either through international or local agents. **Documentation:** A valid national driving licence is required.

Accommodation

HOTELS:

Accommodation is extremely varied. Rooms are scarce in some districts and single guests may be required to share twin-bedded rooms with other single guests.

Top Things To See & Do

• There is excellent fishing, hiking and watersports. The islands are particularly appealing for skindivers, as the surrounding waters offer unsurpassed underwater scenery and marine life; see individual sections.

Entertainment

FOOD & DRINK: Most hotels serve continental, Chinese, Japanese, Western-style and local cuisine.
Things to know: Although some dining rooms serve buffet-style fare, table service is usual and operates at a leisurely pace; see individual sections for further details.
National specialities:
• On some remote islands, the arrival of a stranger calls for a feast of fish, clams, octopus, langusta, sea-cucumber and eels.
• Breadfruit (pounded, boiled, baked or fried).
• Taro, rice and cassava (tapioca).
• Coconut crabs.
• Mangrove clams.
NIGHTLIFE: Some hotels have cocktail lounges with live entertainment. In Saipan there are nightclubs featuring music and dancing. Throughout Micronesia there are cinemas in major areas. However, tourists seek their own entertainment for the most part; see individual sections for further details.

Business

ECONOMY: In all four territories, subsistence agriculture is a key employer. Copra, coconuts, cassava and sweet potatoes are the major crops: yields are sufficient in some cases to sustain export markets. Fishing is similarly important. The Marshalls and Palau have developed small-scale light industries engaged in food-processing, boat-building and the like. Service economies based on tourism and financial services have generally proved difficult to establish owing to the remoteness of the territories and the lack of infrastructure. Micronesia and the Northern Marianas have gone furthest in their efforts to overcome these obstacles, but the region as a whole continues to rely heavily on foreign aid, mostly from the USA. As members of the Pacific Islands Forum, the islands have agreed to participate in a free trade zone, known as PICTA (Pacific Island Countries Trade Agreement), set up in 2002. Supporters of the Agreement contend that it will bring much-needed trade to the region; critics maintain that the islands are being run over by the globalisation bandwagon and small, fragile economies are being forced to open up before they are ready.
BUSINESS ETIQUETTE: Lightweight suits or shirt and tie are usually worn. Appointments should be made and calling cards are exchanged. The best time to visit is May to October. **Office hours:** Mon-Fri 0800-1700. **Government office hours:** Mon-Fri 0800-1200 and 1300-1700. There may be some local variations.

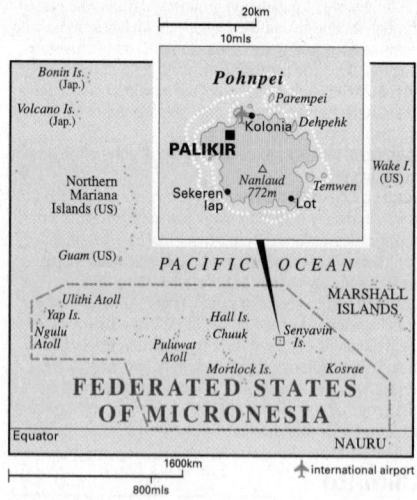

Federated States of Micronesia

Location: Western Pacific Ocean.

Time: Owing to the vast area covered by the islands, Micronesia spans two time zones:
Chuuk and Yap: GMT + 10.
Kosrae and Pohnpei: GMT + 11.

Overview

The Federated States of Micronesia became a US-administered Trust Territory of the Pacific Islands in 1947. This followed successive colonisation by the Portuguese, Spanish and Germans and, latterly, Japanese rule between the two World Wars, under a mandate from the League of Nations (a forerunner of the United Nations). In November 1986, the Federated States signed a Compact of Free Association with the USA, allowing for near-independence with US defence support. Admission to and support from the South Pacific Forum – an association that groups Australasia with the smaller Pacific island nations – has been particularly valuable. Other than political matters, successive Governments have been pre-occupied with the economic situation, as the Federated States suffer from remoteness and lack of industry and infrastructure. There is some development potential, but Micronesia has some way to go before it ceases to be dependent on aid from the USA. Perhaps tourism is one industry that can boost the fiscal situation of this spate of islands.

It certainly boasts some tantalising attributes: some of the most clear-blue seas you will ever see, with white, crumbly sand. In islands like Chuuk are shallow and vast lagoons of monumental beauty, filled with shipwrecks and a kaleidoscope of hard and soft corals. These islands constitute paradise for divers, and many argue that the diving and snorkelling on offer here ranks among the best in the world. Yet what also makes the the Federated States of Micronesia truly special are those idiosyncrasies that indicate that, despite being economically and politically interlinked with the USA, the States are very much socially and culturally independent. The Micronesians are a profusion of languages, customs and folklore. On the island Yap, islanders still trade in the ancient stone currency that many might presume has long been assigned to urban myth. Micronesians may still be glimpsed in traditional garment. Throughout, you are likely to stumble across snatches of unique island music and witness zesty, time-honoured dances.

These idiosyncrasies have remained, in part, because the Federated States of Micronesia have mostly stayed an undiscovered treasure. Some might be worried that any emphasis on enticing more tourists for economic purposes might sever such exquisite isolation. Yet with over 600 islands to this country's name, it looks likely that you will be able to attain some desert island bliss of your own here for a long time yet.

General Information

AREA: Kosrae (five islands) – 110 sq km (42 sq miles); **Pohnpei** (163 islands) – 344 sq km (133 sq miles); **Chuuk** (formerly Truk) (294 islands) – 127 sq km (49 sq miles); **Yap** (145 islands) – 119 sq km (46 sq miles). **Total:** 702 sq km (270.8 sq miles).
POPULATION: 108,105 (2005).
POPULATION DENSITY: 156 per sq km.
CAPITAL: Palikir (Pohnpei). **Population:** 35,000 (2005).
GEOGRAPHY: The Federated States of Micronesia lie 3680km (2300 miles) north of Australia and 4000km (2500 miles) west of Hawaii. They comprise 607 islands scattered over 1.6 million sq km (617,761 sq miles), the most widely spread Pacific Islands group. Yap's uplands are covered by dry meadows and scrub growth. Chuuk lagoon is circled by one of the largest barrier reefs in the world, while Pohnpei has mountains rising to over 600m (2000ft).
GOVERNMENT: Federal Republic since 1980. Gained self-governing status (in free association with the USA) in 1986.
Head of State and Government: President Joseph J Urusemal since 2003. **Recent history:** In 1991, the Federated States of Micronesia were admitted to the UN. Joseph Urusemal was elected in May 2003. In the same year he told the UN General Assembly that the Federated States of Micronesia were under threat from climate change. Aid from the USA amounted to US$1.3 billion between 1986 and 2001.
LANGUAGE: English; Micronesian languages, including Chuukese, Kosrean, Pohnpian and Yapese, are widely spoken.
RELIGION: Mostly Roman Catholic (50 per cent), Protestant (47 per cent) and other Christian denominations (3 per cent).
ELECTRICITY: 120 volts AC, 60Hz. Plugs are of the round two pin type.
SOCIAL CONVENTIONS: There are considerable variations of custom and belief. Approximately 95 per cent of Kosreans are Congregationalists with a deeply held respect for Sunday as a day of rest. Pre-European influences are stronger elsewhere and nowhere more so than in Yap where visitors are only allowed with prior permission. Use of islands, paths, beaches etc may also require permission in many areas; it is best to check beforehand. **Photography:** Permission should always be sought. Though people are friendly, and usually accommodating, not to seek prior permission before taking pictures is considered an insult, especially on some of the more remote islands.

Climate

Tropical with year-round high humidity. The typhoon season is from June to December, therefore there is a threat to low-lying atolls. Rainfall is generally plentiful and Pohnpei is reputedly one of the wettest places on Earth, with up to 330 inches of rain per year.
Required clothing: Lightweight cottons and linens, with light rainwear advisable all year round.

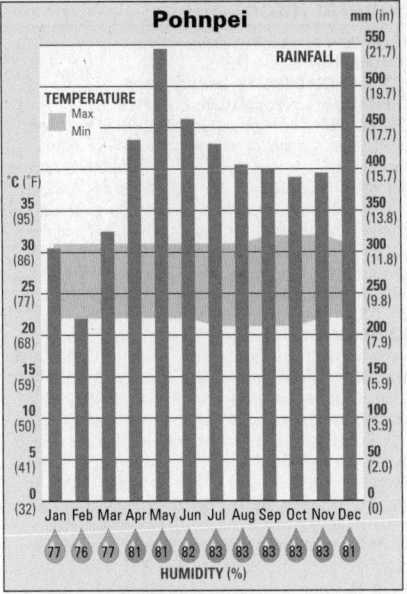

Pohnpei — RAINFALL / TEMPERATURE (Max / Min) — monthly chart (Jan–Dec)

HUMIDITY (%): 77 76 77 81 81 82 83 83 83 83 83 81

Communications

Telephone: IDD is available. Country code: 691.
Internet: Internet services are available.
Post: The US postal service picks up and delivers all mail to each of the states via air service. The Federated States of Micronesia are part of the US zip code system. Codes are: Pohnpei: 96941; Chuuk: 96942; Yap: 96943; and Kosrae: 96944. Rates are the same as the US. Express delivery is provided by a variety of private carriers. Post offices are located in Kolonia for Pohnpei, Moen for Chuuk, Lelu for Kosrae and Colonia for Yap. Post office hours: Mon-Fri 0830-1630. Closed on the weekends.
MEDIA: Press: *Pacific Daily News* (Guam) is the main English-language newspaper in the Federated States of Micronesia. *The Island Tribune* is printed twice weekly.
TV: *WAAB TV* is a Government channel on Yap. *KPON TV* is a commercial channel on Pohnpei. *TTTK TV* is a commercial channel on Chuuk.
Radio: Stations include *V6AH* (Pohnpei), *V6AI* (Yap), *V6AJ* (Kosrae), *V6AK* (Chuuk) and Baptist church-run station *V6A*.

Passport/Visa

	Passport Required?	Visa Required?	Return Ticket Required?
Full British	Yes	1	Yes
Australian	Yes	1	Yes
Canadian	Yes	1	Yes
USA	No	1	Yes
Other EU	Yes	1	Yes
Japanese	Yes	1	Yes

Note: *Regulations and requirements may be subject to change at short notice, and you are advised to contact the appropriate diplomatic or consular authority before finalising travel arrangements. Any numbers in the chart refer to the footnotes below.*

PASSPORTS: Passport valid for at least 120 days beyond the date of entry required by all except nationals of the Marshall Islands, Palau and the USA with acceptable documentation (birth certificate or entry permit issued by Micronesia), if no passport is available.
VISAS: 1. Not required for visits of up to 30 days. For longer stays and for all visits other than touristic visits, an entry permit is required, and should be obtained prior to travel or arrival. Nationals of the passport-exempt countries may stay for one year without an entry permit, if visiting as tourists.
Types of visa and cost: *Entry Permit:* cost on application.
Validity: Normally up to an additional 30 days. May be extended to 60 days, although nationals of passport-exempt countries may apply for an extension of one year's duration.
Application to: Chief of Immigration, Department of Justice, FSM Government Office, PO Box PS 105, Palikir, Pohnpei FSM 96941 (tel: 320 5844 *or* 2605).
Note: All visitors require proof of adequate funds and return or onward tickets.
Working days required: Must apply by post; applications are dealt with on receipt.
Temporary residence: Apply to Division of Immigration (see address above).
Note: Foreign-owned vessels or aircraft are required to have entry permits (visas) applied for and in their possession prior to entering Micronesia or to apply for one immediately on entry into Micronesia.

Money

Currency: The US Dollar (US$) is the official currency. Giant stone money remains in use on Yap, but not for ordinary transactions or any that are likely to involve visitors. Dollar = 100 cents. Notes are in denominations of US$100, 50, 20, 10, 5, 2 and 1. Coins are in denominations of US$1 and 50 25, 10, 5 and 1 cents.
Credit & debit cards: Most major credit cards are accepted at major visitor-orientated businesses.
Traveller's cheques: Exchanged at the larger hotels and businesses.
Currency restrictions: None.
Banking hours: Mon-Thurs 1000-1500, Fri 1000-1800 and Sat 0900-1200.
Note: For information on convertible currency, see *Money* in the *Pacific Islands of Micronesia* section. There are several US FDIC insured banks operating (although there are no banks on Chuuk).

Duty Free

The following goods may be taken into the Federated States of Micronesia without incurring customs duty by travellers aged over 18 years and above:
600 cigarettes or 454g of cigars or tobacco; 2l of alcoholic beverages; a reasonable amount of perfume for personal use.
Note: Alcohol for passengers over 21 years of age only.
Prohibited items: Firearms and ammunition. Plants and animals must be declared and will be subject to restrictions.

Public Holidays

Below are listed Public Holidays for the January 2006-June 2007 period.
2006: Jan 1 New Year's Day. **Jan 11*** Kosrae Constitution Day. **Mar 1*** Yap Day. **Mar 31*** Pohnpei Culture Day. **Apr 14** Good Friday. **May 10** Constitution (Federated States of Micronesia) Day. **Sep 8*** Kosrae Liberation Day. **Sep 11*** Pohnpei Liberation Day. **Oct 24** United Nations Day. **Nov 3** National Day. **Nov 8*** Pohnpei Constitution Day. **Nov 23*** Kosrae Thanksgiving Day. **Dec 24*** Yap Constitution Day. **Dec 25** Christmas Day.
2007: Jan 1 New Year's Day. **Jan 11*** Kosrae Constitution Day. **Mar 1*** Yap Day. **Mar 31*** Pohnpei Culture Day. **Apr 6** Good Friday. **May 10** Constitution (Federated States of Micronesia) Day.
Note: *Variations occur from island to island.

Health

Health care: All the Federated States have good Government hospitals in the main cities. There are also dental services and private health clinics throughout the islands. Be aware that doctors and hospitals may ask for cash payment for health services. Scuba-divers are advised there are only three decompression chambers in the Federated States (Yap, Pohnpei and Chuuk). Their availability varies and there is very little experience in treating dive injuries. Travellers should note that yellow fever certificates and cholera vaccinations are required by anyone arriving from infected countries. Health insurance is highly recommended. Vaccination against *typhoid* and *polio* is advised and *hepatitis A* is present. Certain emergency cases are referred to Hawaii and Guam.

Travel - International

AIR:
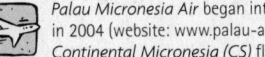
Palau Micronesia Air began international flights in 2004 (website: www.palau-air.com). *Continental Micronesia (CS)* flights link the major islands with Guam, Honolulu, Manila and Tokyo. *Air Nauru* provides weekly services linking Pohnpei to Australia, Fiji, Guam, Manila and Nauru.
Air passes: The *Visit the South Pacific Pass* is valid for many airlines operating in the South Pacific, including most of the larger ones, such as *Air Caledonie, Air Marshall Islands, Air Nauru, Air Niugingi, Air Pacific, Air Vanuatu, Polynesian Airlines, Qantas, Royal Tongan Airlines* and *Solomon Airlines*. Offering reductions of up to 40 per cent on normal airfares, this sector-based pass allows for flexible island-hopping between the destinations of the Cook Islands, Fiji, Nauru, New Caledonia, Samoa, Tahiti, Tonga, Vanuatu and the more remote Melanesian and Micronesian islands, together with major cities in Australia (Brisbane, Melbourne and Sydney) and New Zealand (Auckland, Christchurch and Wellington). It is only available for people resident outside of the South Pacific. The journey must be started outside the South Pacific and only one stopover in Australia is allowed. A minimum of two sectors must be bought before departure (extra sectors can be purchased en route). There is a maximum of one pass per person, and passes must be used within six months of the first day of travel. Children under 12 years of age pay 75 per cent of the adult fare. For details and conditions, contact the South Pacific Tourist Organisation.

Approximate flight times:
See *Pacific Islands of Micronesia* section.
Main airports: *Pohnpei (PNI)* is 5km (3 miles) from Kolonia. *To/from the airport:* Taxis are available. *Facilities:* Car hire, light snacks and tourist information.
Guam (website: www.guamairport.com) is 3km (2 miles) from Tumon Bay (travel time - 10 minutes). *To/from the airport:* Taxis are available, as is car hire. *Facilities:* Fast food outlets, bars, shops for consumer goods, bureaux de change, ATMs, tourist information and car hire.
Departure tax: US$10 for Pohnpei; $15 for Chuuk; $10 Kosrae; no departure tax for Yap.

SEA:

International ports are *Chuuk, Pohnpei* and *Yap*. Inter-island trading ships based in Pohnpei, Yap and Chuuk visit the outlying islands.

ROAD:

There are good roads in and around major island centres, although most roads remain unpaved.
Bus: No scheduled service, although some buses may be available for hire or charter. On Yap, a school bus runs twice daily from Colonia to the villages. **Taxi:** Available throughout Micronesia and inexpensive. **Car hire:** Self-drive cars are available in major towns. **Documentation:** National driving licence or International Driving Permit required.

Travel - Internal

AIR:

Continental Air Micronesia (website: www.continental.com) flies between Pohnpei and the three other States and to neighbouring countries (three-times weekly to Hawaii and four-times weekly to Guam). Travel to the outer islands of Pohnpei State are operated by *Caroline Islands Air*. These services are known to be highly expensive.

SEA:

Pohnpei's State ship, the *Micro Glory*, is in poor condition so these runs are now being handled by the *FSM Voyager* on a quarterly basis between *Colonia (Yap), Kolonia (Pohnpei), Lele* and *Moen*.

Travel Advice

Most visits to Micronesia are trouble-free but you should be aware of the global risk of indiscriminate international terrorist attacks, which could be against civilian targets, including places frequented by foreigners.
Typhoons constitute a threat from June-December annually. These usually effect the low lying atolls. However be aware that the FSM are prone to floods during this period.
This advice is based on information provided by the Foreign and Commonwealth Office in the UK. It is correct at time of publishing. As the situation can change rapidly, visitors are advised to contact the following organisations for the latest travel advice:

British Foreign and Commonwealth Office
Tel: (0845) 850 2829.
Website: www.fco.gov.uk

US Department of State
Website: http://travel.state.gov/travel

Accommodation

HOTELS:

There are hotels in the various island capitals. Parts of Chuuk, Kosrae and Pohnpei have been developed into beach resorts.
CAMPING:
There are no official campsites, but private arrangements can be made with local landowners. For further information, contact the FSM Visitors Board (see *Top Things To See & Do*).
APARTMENTS AND SELF CATERING:
Native-style thatched cottages with beautiful garden showers but limited facilities. Available in the larger States. Prices are cheaper then some of the resorts, but still tend to be expensive.

Top Things To See & Do

- See some of the States' most important historical sites: **The Spanish Wall** ; the **Catholic Bell Tower** in **Pohnpei**; the **Japanese Wartime Communication Centre** at Xavier High School in **Chuuk; the ancient ruins of Nan Madol in Pohnpei**; and the ruins of **INSARU** in **Kosrae**. The **Sokehs Mass Grave** holds the remains of 17 Pohnpeians who were executed by firing squad in 1911 for resisting the German administration.
- Enjoy some cultural delights, such as the small but fascinating **museums** in Chuuk and Kosrae.
- The States are full of nautical treats to explore. Pohnpei has magnificent waterfalls with **pools** that are ideal for **bathing**. Two of the most beautiful **falls** are **Kepirohi**

and **Sahwartik**. A 20-minute ride out of Kolonia takes travellers to the **Nanpil River** and a large natural pool where the river temporarily slows down. Further along the same river are the spectacular **Liduduhniap Twin Waterfalls**, complete with thatched huts where travellers can rest or **picnic** in a natural jungle setting.

- All States have beautiful white sandy **beaches**. In case you tire of relaxing, warm water and spectacular underwater scenery make **diving** an attraction option. Kosrae has over 50 dive sites, each marked with a buoy to prevent improper anchoring. Unspoiled coral reefs close to the shore make the island suitable for both walk-in and boat diving. In neighbouring Pohnpei State, recommended dive sites include the unspoiled **Ant Atoll**, **Pakin Atoll** and **Black Coral**, all a short boat ride away from the main island. The state of Chuuk contains the famous **Truk Lagoon**, where a whole Japanese fleet was sunk during World War II. More than 50 wrecks can be seen here, with various artefacts still intact. Some of the shallower wrecks are suitable for **snorkellers**. The island of **Yap** is notable for its schools of manta rays, which can be seen all year round. Tuna, dolphins and reef fish are also abundant.

- See for yourself the large **eels** that have become a prominent part in Pohnpei's mythological stories at the **Pwudoi Sanctuary**, an eel pool, where visitors can witness locals handling these slippery creatures. The eels are portrayed as both benevolent and as terrifying monsters.

- A moderately difficult **hike** up **Sokehs Mountain** offers breathtaking views of Sokehs rock and Kolonia harbour, tropical vegetation and birds.

- Watch islanders dabble in a game of **baseball**, which is an island-wide passion - as is **volleyball**.

- **Fishing** and **ocean trolling tours** are available. Tuna is abundant in waters off Kolonia and game fish, such as marlin and mahi-mahi, are also found.

TOURIST INFORMATION

FSM Visitors Board
FSM National Government, PO Box PS-12, Palikir, Pohnpei FSM 96941
Tel: 320 5133.
Website: www.visit-fsm.org

Entertainment

FOOD & DRINK: Local specialities include breadfruit (Chuuk) and thin slices of raw fish dipped in a peppery sauce. Pohnpeians have over 100 words for yams and grow them to massive proportions (it may take several men to carry one); yams occupy a central position in local culture. Although some dining rooms serve buffet-style fare, table service is usual and operates at a leisurely pace.

Sakau, as it is known on Pohnpei, or kava, as it is known throughout the rest of Polynesia, is made from the root of a shrub which yields a mildly narcotic substance when squeezed through hibiscus bark. There are several *sakau* bars where visitors can sample it and watch it being made. Alcohol is prohibited on Chuuk (with the consequence that nearby islands are often used as picnic resorts).

National specialities:
- Sweet potatoes.
- Coconut.
- Fish (especially crabs and clams).
- Pork.

National drinks:
- *Sakau* (a traditional drink used in ceremonies).
- Fresh lime juice and water.

Tipping: Visitors to the country are seen as guests and hospitality is an honour in the culture. Therefore tips are neither encouraged nor expected.

NIGHTLIFE: There are good restaurants and a few cinemas in major island centres. Locals and visitors alike enjoy making their own entertainment. Video rentals are a main form of entertainment and a few well stocked DVD and video rental stores are located in Kolonia. *Sakau* drinking is the most frequent evening activity on Pohnpei. Cultural dances can be arranged through tourist offices or hotels. Most hotels have music, dancing and discos. Bars and restaurants open untill 2200 every night.

SHOPPING: Favourite purchases on Chuuk include love sticks and war clubs. Yap people produce colourful grass skirts, *lava-lavas* woven from hibiscus bark, woven baby cradles, betel-nut pouches and stone money. On Pohnpei, there are elaborate, carefully scaled model canoes and woven items. Stores sell handicrafts, canoes, shark, turtle, gecho, manta ray, shampoo, soap and lotion made from fresh coconut. **Shopping hours:** Mon-Fri 0800-1700. On weekends some shops open with limited hours; 0830-1330.

Business

- **GDP:** US$277 million (GDP is supplemented by grant aid averaging US$100 million annually).
- **Main exports:** Fish, garments, bananas and black pepper.
- **Main imports:** Foodstuffs, manufactured goods, machinery and equipment and beverages.
- **Main trade partners:** Australia, Japan and USA.

ECONOMY: Subsistence farming and fishing are of declining importance as tourism has come to dominate the domestic economy and fishing is largely pursued by foreign commercial concerns operating under licence. Mineral resources are limited to a few high-grade phosphate deposits. Sales of these licences account for over one-third of national income. Aid from the USA has been a vital source of income: under the Compact of Free Association between the islands and the USA, Micronesia received US$1.3 billion in bilateral aid over the 15-year period up to 2001. Much of this was sunk into infrastructure projects, principally an airport and harbour on each of the main islands. However, the end of this subvention has depressed the economy and, with few other immediate options, Micronesia's economic prospects are at best uncertain. The Federated States of Micronesia is a member of the South Pacific Commission and the South Pacific Forum. The main industries FSM profit from are tourism, construction, specialised aquaculture, wood, pearls and craft items from shells.

BUSINESS ETIQUETTE: Office hours: Mon-Fri 0800-1200 and 1300-1700.

COMMERCIAL INFORMATION

FSM Visitors Board (Information on Conferences/Conventions)
FSM National Government, PO Box PS-12, Palikir, Pohnpei FSM 96941
Tel: 320 5133.

The Pohnpei State Chamber of Commerce
PO Box 405, 96941, Pohnpei, Kolonia, FSM
Tel: 320 2452.

Marshall Islands

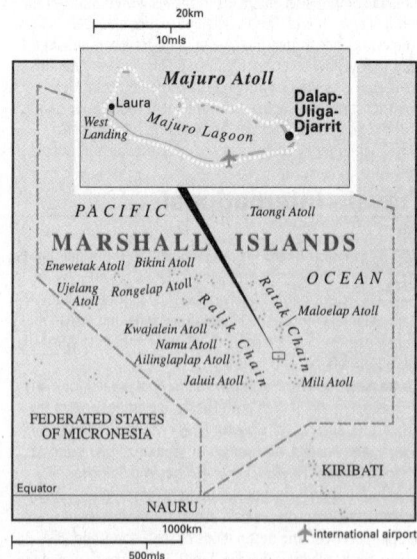

Location: Western Pacific Ocean.

Time: GMT + 12.

Overview

Many of the atolls are dotted with Flame of the Forest, hibiscus and different-coloured plumeria flowers. There are also at least 160 species of coral surrounding the islands. The uninhabited atolls are noted for their coconut and papaya plantations and for pandanus and breadfruit trees.

General Information

AREA: 181.4 sq km (70 sq miles).
POPULATION: 50,848 (1999).
POPULATION DENSITY: 280.3 per sq km.
CAPITAL: Majuro. **Population:** 23,682 (1999).
GEOGRAPHY: The Marshall Islands consist of two almost parallel chains of atolls and islands and lie west of the International Date Line. Majuro Atoll is 2285km (1428 miles) west of Honolulu, 1624km (1015 miles) east of Guam and 2624km (1641 miles) southeast of Tokyo. The eastern *Ratak* (Sunrise) Chain consists of 15 atolls and islands, and the western *Ralik* (Sunset) Chain consists of 16 atolls and islands. Together these two chains comprise 1152 islands and islets dispersed over more than 1,900,000 sq km (500,000 sq miles) of the central Pacific.
GOVERNMENT: Republic since 1990. Gained self-governing status (in free association with the USA) in 1986.
Head of State and Government: President Kessai H Note (since 2000). **Recent history:** Until his death in 1996, Amata Kabua – who was elected to five consecutive terms as president from 1979 – was the dominant political figure on the atoll after independence. The main issues facing successive Governments have been the legacy of the nuclear testing and the state of the economy. Extensive nuclear testing, especially on the Kwajalein Atoll, has resulted in long-term damage to islanders' health and to the environment. The extent and nature of compensation and restitution – in the form of environmental improvement and healthcare – remain sore points in relations between the Marshalls and the USA. Following the death of Amata Kabua, his cousin, Imata Kabua, was elected as his successor in January 1997. Imata Kabua's Government was undermined by allegations of corruption and following elections held at the end of 1999 he was replaced by Kessai Note, who leads a bloc associated with the United Democratic Party, although officially no political parties are represented in the Nitijela. Kessai Note was elected for a second term in 2003.
LANGUAGE: Marshallese and English are the official languages.
RELIGION: Christian, mostly Protestant.
ELECTRICITY: 110 volts AC, 60 Hz. Plugs are US two-pin style.
SOCIAL CONVENTIONS: Informal dress is usual for both business and social occasions. Scanty clothing (including topless bathing) is considered offensive. Use of islands, paths, beaches etc may require permission in many areas; it is best to check locally.

Climate

Tropical, with cooling sea breezes and frequent rain. Trade winds blow steadily from the northeast from December through to March. Wettest months are usually October to November. The average temperature is 27°C (80°F).
Required clothing: Lightweight cottons and linens with rainwear.

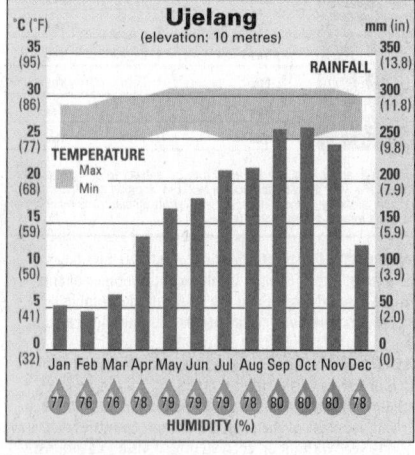

Communications

Telephone: IDD is available. Country code: 692. There are international satellite links. In Majuro, dial 625 3399 *or* 3355 for the hospital; 625 8666 for the fire services; 625 3233 for police; and 625 1411 for general information
Internet: Availabilty and reliability are limited.
Post: US post offices are located in Ebeye, Jaluit and Majuro. Post office hours: Mon-Fri 1000-1530, Sat 0900-1545.
MEDIA: Press: The English/Marshallese-language newspaper is the weekly *Marshall Islands Journal* and the monthly *Marshal Islands Gazette*.
TV: *MBC TV* is state-run, while the US military operates *AFN Kwajalein*.
Radio: State-run *V7AB* is the only nationwide station. *Micronesia Heatwave* is a commercial station.

Passport/Visa

	Passport Required?	Visa Required?	Return Ticket Required?
Full British	Yes	Yes	Yes
Australian	Yes	Yes	Yes
Canadian	Yes	Yes	Yes
USA	Yes	No	No
Other EU	Yes	Yes	Yes
Japanese	Yes	Yes	Yes

Note: *Regulations and requirements may be subject to change at short notice, and you are advised to contact the appropriate diplomatic or consular authority before finalising travel arrangements. Any numbers in the chart refer to the footnotes below.*

PASSPORTS: Passports valid for at least one year from date of arrival required by all.
VISAS: Required by all except the following:
(a) nationals of the USA;
(b) nationals of the Federated States of Micronesia and the Republic of Palau.
Note: Tourist visas are issued on arrival. It may be necessary to obtain a transit visa for the USA first, as flights to the Marshall Islands are via Guam or Hawaii. Contact an airline such as *Air Marshall Islands* or *Continental Micronesia* for further information. All visitors require proof of adequate funds and return or onward tickets.
Types of visa and cost: *Tourist:* Free (up to 30 days); US$25 (up to 90 days). *Business:* US$50.
Validity: 30 days; extensions for up to 90 days are available upon arrival in the Marshall Islands.
Application to: For stays exceeding 30 days, apply to: Attorney General, Office of the Attorney General, PO Box 890, Majuro, Marshall Islands 96960 (tel: 635 8495; fax: 625 5218).
Application requirements: (a) Valid passport. (b) Completed incoming passenger card (available on board ship/aircraft). (c) Return or onward ticket. (d) Sufficient funds to cover stay. (e) For those intending to stay for more than 30 days, an AIDS certificate is required. Contact the Chief of Immigration for latest information.
Working days required: Applications are dealt with on receipt.
Temporary residence: Apply to Attorney General (address above).

> **PASSPORT/VISA INFORMATION**
>
> **Embassy of the Republic of the Marshall Islands in the USA**
> 2433 Massachusetts Avenue, NW, Washington, DC 20008, USA
> Tel: (202) 234 5414.
> Website: www.rmiembassyus.org

Money

For details of currency, credit & debit cards, traveller's cheques, exchange rate indicators and banking hours, see *Pacific Islands of Micronesia* section.
Currency exchange: The banks of Guam and the Marshall Islands have branches on Majuro; those of the Marshall Islands and Guam have branches on Ebeye; and that of Guam has a branch on Kwajalein.
Currency restrictions: There are no limits on the import and export of local and foreign currency, subject to declaration of amounts exceeding US$5000.

Duty Free

The following items may be imported into the Marshall Islands by passengers without incurring customs duty:
600 cigarettes or 454g of cigars or tobacco; 2l of alcoholic beverages (alcohol for passengers over 21 years of age only).
Prohibited items: Firearms, ammunition, drugs and pornographic materials are not permitted. Birds, animals, fruit and plants need certification from the Quarantine Division of the Ministry of Resources and Development. Coral, turtle shells and certain other natural resources cannot be exported. Any artefacts or objects of historical value cannot be taken out of the country.

Public Holidays

Below are listed Public Holidays for the January 2006-June 2007 period.
2006: Jan 1 New Year's Day. **Mar 1** Memorial and Nuclear Victims' Remembrance Day. **May 1** Constitution Day. **Jul 7** Fishermen's Day. **Sep 1** Rijerbal (Labour) Day. **Sep 29** Manit (Custom) Day. **Oct 21** Compact Day. **Nov 17** President's Day. **Dec 1** Gospel Day. **Dec 25** Christmas Day.
2007: Jan 1 New Year's Day. **Mar 1** Memorial and Nuclear Victims' Remembrance Day. **May 1** Constitution Day. **Jul 1** Fishermen's Day.
Note: Separate holidays occur from island to island.

Health

Yellow fever certificates and *cholera* vaccinations are required by all travellers arriving from infected areas. Vaccination against *Hepatitis A* and *B, typhoid, tetanus* and *diphtheria* may be advised. HIV testing is required for temporary visitors staying for more than 30 days. Foreign test results are accepted in certain circumstances but you should check prior to travel.
Health care: Majuro has one private clinic and one public hospital. Ebeye has a public hospital. Most outer islands have medical dispensaries.

Travel - International

AIR:
Air Marshall Islands (CW) provides regular scheduled internal flights to 10 of the atolls in the Marshall Islands and has planes available for charter. Flights are available between Honolulu and the Marshall Islands and to Fiji via Kiribati and Tuvalu. *Continental Micronesia (CS)* stops in Majuro and Kwajalein on its island-hopper service between Guam and Honolulu. *Aloha Airlines* also runs flights to the islands. *Continental Airlines (CO)* also offers weekly flights to and from Guam and Honolulu.
Approximate flight times: From *New York* to Majuro is 14 hours; from *Tokyo* it is 11, from *Guam* it is eight hours to Majuro and five hours from *Honolulu*.
Main airports: *Majuro International Airport (MAJ)*. There are taxis and hotel transport from the airport to the town.
Departure tax: US$20 on international flights.
SEA:
The international port is *Majuro*. Shipping lines servicing the Marshalls include *Daiwa Lines, Matson Lines, Micronesia & Orient Line, Nauru Pacific Line, Philippine* and *Tiger Lines*.
Four Government-owned field ships connect the islands within the Marshalls on a regular schedule. Comfortable passenger cabins are available on these ships and arrangements can be made for charter trips. **Cruise:** *Royal Viking Line* and the *Asuka Cruise Ship* sometimes call at Majuro port, but not on a regular basis. The *Princess Cruise Line* visits Majuro twice a year. Inter-island cruises are available. Boats can be rented from companies on the islands for sightseeing, diving tours, picnics, game fishing, snorkelling, water-skiing and other boating activities.
ROAD:
All the main roads are paved. Driving is on the left. The minimum age is 18. **Taxi:** Plentiful and cheap. Generally used on a seat-sharing basis.
Car hire: These are usually Japanese sedans. Companies include Deluxe Car Rental, Majuro, MH 96960, Marshall Islands (tel: 625 3665; fax: 625 3663). **Documentation:** A national driving licence is valid for 30 days.

Travel Advice

Most visits to the Marshall Islands are trouble-free but you should be aware of the global risk of indiscriminate international terrorist attacks, which could be against civilian targets, including places frequented by foreigners. This advice is based on information provided by the Foreign and Commonwealth Office in the UK. It is correct at time of publishing. As the situation can change rapidly, visitors are advised to contact the following organisations for the latest travel advice:

British Foreign and Commonwealth Office
Tel: (0845) 850 2829.
Website: www.fco.gov.uk

US Department of State
Website: http://travel.state.gov/travel

Accommodation

There is a variety of first-class and budget hotels and some islands have guest houses. Restaurant and bar facilities are available in the more deluxe hotels.
CAMPING:
Facilities are available on Majuro and various other islands. For further information, contact the Visitors Authority (see *Top Things To See & Do*).

Top Things To See & Do

- The first stop in the Marshall Islands should be either **Ebeye** or **Majuro**, although visits to outer islands can be arranged.
- The former capital **Jaluit** (its name meaning both 'come here' and 'beautiful') boasts some of the best scuba-diving and marine life among the islands.
- There are Sunday day trips to **Maloelap** or **Mili** atolls where there are opportunities to snorkel over World War II wrecks, eat local food and watch dancing. There are also many historic sites and buildings.

- Opportunities for **diving** include drop-offs, coral heads, black coral and World War II wrecks. **Fishing** expeditions can be arranged by local hotels or the Marshalls Billfish Club (tel/fax: 625 7491). The club also organises monthly fishing tournaments. For further information, consult the Marshall Islands Journal *or* the Visitors Authority.

Credit: ©Marshall Islands Visitors Authority

- The **Alele Museum** ('alele' meaning a traditional Marshallese basket) has preserved the history and local traditions of the Marshallese culture. The Visitors Authority can provide information on various other sites.

> **TOURIST INFORMATION**
>
> **Marshall Islands Visitors Authority**
> PO Box 5, Majuro, Marshall Islands 96960
> Tel: 625 6482.
> Website: www.visitmarshallislands.com

Entertainment

FOOD & DRINK: There are several restaurants in Majuro, serving Chinese, Marshallese, US and Western specialities. Consumption of alcohol is forbidden on some of the islands.
Tipping: Unnecessary.
NIGHTLIFE: There are several nightclubs on Majuro and Ebeye and some hotels offer traditional dancing.
SHOPPING: Special purchases include *kili* handbags woven by former residents of Bikini, stick charts (once used to navigate long distances between the region's scattered islands), plaited floor mats, fans, purses, shell necklaces and baskets. There is a 3 per cent sales tax in Majuro. **Shopping hours:** Mon-Fri 0800-1700.

Business

ECONOMY: The economy suffers many of the problems faced by the small, remote island states of the Pacific. Aid subventions from the USA remain essential, while repeated and diverse attempts to broaden the base of the economy have met with mixed success. Agriculture is of a subsistence nature, with coconuts, tomatoes, melons and breadfruit as the main products. The fishing industry is dominated by a commercial tuna operation, which includes canning and transhipment. The islands' international shipping registry – a "flag of convenience" – has been a key source of income since the end of the 1980s, when many operators reflagged from Panama. The Government had high hopes for a major tourist development, but the plans have been scaled down following the economic downturn in the Asia-Pacific region and may yet be further undermined by the islands' remote location. There is also an important offshore financial services industry. However, in April 2002 the Marshall Islands were one of seven countries 'named and shamed' by the Organisation for Economic Co-operation and Development, which has spearheaded a global assault on money-laundering, for their failure to tackle the issue. The USA provides around US$65 million annually in aid. The Marshall Islands is a member of the South Pacific Commission and the South Pacific Forum.

> **COMMERCIAL INFORMATION**
>
> **Majuro Chamber of Commerce**
> Majuro MH 96960, Marshall Islands
> Tel: 625 2525.

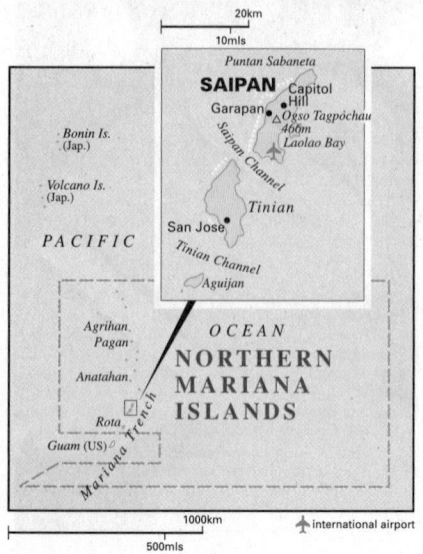

Northern Mariana Islands

The Northern Mariana Islands include Saipan, Tinian and Rota (formerly the Marianas.)

Location: Western Pacific Ocean.

Time: GMT + 10.

Overview

The Northern Marianas consist of a chain of 14 islands nearly 55 miles in length. Volcanic in origin, they host a variety of scenery including beautiful bays, spectacular cliffs, caves and mountains. Because of their location they played a significant part in World War II, and the many shipwrecks around the coast bear witness to this. These, the numerous coral reefs and the clear water make them particularly good for diving.

General Information

AREA: 457 sq km (176.5 sq miles).

POPULATION: 74,151 (official estimate 2002).

POPULATION DENSITY: 162 per sq km (official estimate 2002).

CAPITAL: Saipan. **Population:** 67,011 (2002).

GEOGRAPHY: Located to the south of Japan and to the north of Guam, the Northern Mariana Islands comprise 14 islands, the main ones being Rota, Saipan and Tinian. The group is compact, consisting of a single chain 736km (460 miles) long. The islands have high volcanic cones.

GOVERNMENT: Self-governing US Commonwealth Territory (incorporated). Gained internal autonomy in 1986. **Head of State:** President George W Bush since 2000. **Head of Government:** Governor Juan Babauta since 2002. **Recent history:** Domestic politics traditionally mirrored the Republican–Democrat duopoly until the recent emergence of the Convenant Party, which is independent of both the major US parties. At the most recent elections held in November 2001, the Republican candidate, Juan Babauta, won with 43 per cent of the poll. However, at the most recent poll for the local House of Representatives, the Covenant Party was returned as the largest party.

The islands face significant social and economic problems that are largely attributable to the rapid growth of the population in the last two decades and the lack both of adequate employment opportunities and infrastructure. The constitution, which came into operation in January 1978, allows for an executive Governor and a bicameral legislature consisting of an 18-seat House of Representatives and a nine-member Senate.

LANGUAGE: English, Chamorro and Carolinian are the official languages. Japanese and Korean are widely spoken.

RELIGION: Mostly Roman Catholic.

SOCIAL CONVENTIONS: The Chamorro culture of the original inhabitants can still be traced, although it is overlaid by strong American influences. Western conventions are well understood.

Climate

Tropical climate, tempered by trade winds. The rainy season is July to November.

Required clothing: Lightweight cottons and linens, with light rainwear advisable all year.

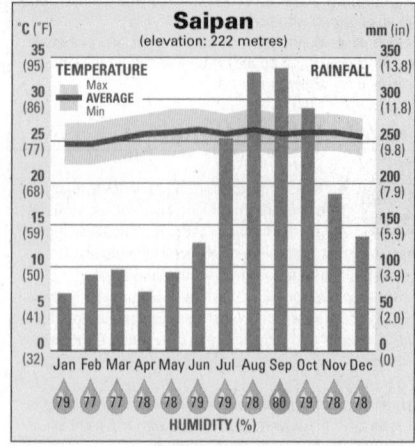

Communications

Telephone: IDD is available. Country code: 1 670. There are payphones in Saipan and most hotels; restaurants and other public facilities have telephones which visitors can use.

Mobile telephone: A GSM 1900 service is scheduled for launch soon by Wave Runner LLC Mariana Islands.

Internet: Availability and reliability is limited.

Post: There are post offices on the three main islands, as well as private postal companies in Saipan. US postal rates apply. Post office hours: Mon-Fri 0900-1600, Sat 0900-1200.

MEDIA: Press: The English-language newspapers include the *Pacific Daily News*, *Pacific Star* (weekly), *Saipan Tribune* (twice weekly) and the *Marianas Variety News and Views* (weekdays).

Passport/Visa

	Passport Required?	Visa Required?	Return Ticket Required?
Full British	Yes	No/3	Yes
Australian	Yes	2/3	Yes
Canadian	Yes	Yes/3	Yes
USA	Yes	No	No
Other EU	Yes	No/1/3	Yes
Japanese	Yes	2/3	Yes

Note: *Regulations and requirements may be subject to change at short notice, and you are advised to contact the appropriate diplomatic or consular authority before finalising travel arrangements. Any numbers in the chart refer to the footnotes below.*

Restricted Entry and Transit: Nationals of the following countries are 'Excluded Locations' and must apply to the Northern Mariana Islands' Attorney General in Saipan for a preliminary waiver that is issued on a case-by-case basis and that necessitates additional documents (including providing, or having a sponsor provide, a bond by an approved bond company for US$5000 or amount decided by Attorney General, and official letter - bearing the seal of the relevant immigration or governmental authority in the particular excluded country - that declares that such country will unconditionally accept the return of the excluded national without delay): Afghanistan, Algeria, Bahrain, Bangladesh*, Cuba, Egypt, Eritrea, Fujian Province of China, Indonesia, Iran, Iraq, Jordan, Korea (Dem Rep), Kuwait, Lebanon, Libya, Morocco, Myanmar, Oman, Pakistan, Qatar, Saudi Arabia, Somalia, Sri Lanka*, Sudan, Syrian Arab Republic, Tunisia, United Arab Emirates and Yemen, unless having a US Visa in their passport, which should be valid for a minimum of 60 days after entry. All aforementioned information should be submitted by fax or post at least four weeks prior to the intended date of departure.

Note: Nationals marked * require a letter guaranteeing expedited return in order to gain a preliminary waiver.

PASSPORTS: Passports valid for at least 60 days after date of entry are required by all.

VISAS: Required by all except the following:
(a) nationals of EU countries (except **1.** Cyprus, Czech Republic, Estonia, Greece, Hungary, Latvia, Lithuania, Malta, Poland and Slovak Republic who *do* require a visa as they are not current participants in the US Visa Waiver Program); (b) **2.** nationals of Andorra, Australia, Brunei, Iceland, Japan, Liechtenstein, Monaco, New Zealand, Norway, San Marino, Singapore and Switzerland.

Note: 3. Nationals of Australia, Canada, Hong Kong (SAR), Ireland, Japan, Korea (Rep) and the UK are exempt from Visitor Entry Permits into the Northern Mariana Islands, although this may be counteracted by individual circumstances.

Types of visa and cost: Various; decided according to individual cases.

Note: All Visitor Entry Permit applications submitted one week or less prior to arrival will be processed at an emergency administrative fee of US$100.

Validity: Various. Visas are generally required for touristic stays of more than 30 days. Stays may be extended by an additional 60 days whilst in the Northern Mariana Islands.

Application to: CNMI Division of Immigration (see *Passport/Visa Information*).

Application requirements: *Visitor Entry Permit*: (a) Possession of Authorization Board letter (approved by the Director of Immigration), including full name, permanent address, telephone number(s), purpose of visit, proof of place of employment, date of arrival and departure, airline carrier and flight number (full itinerary), passport (plus photocopy), proof of sufficient funds and address of intended location. A sponsor must submit a notarised Affidavit of Support letter, including copy of passport valid for at least 60 days after entry date, copy of Driver's License (if applicable), copy of entry permit, copy of two latest paycheck stubs, Business License (if applicable), and if sponsor is a company, a copy of the latest Business Gross Revenue (BGR) tax document. (b) Some individuals will need to submit evidence of police clearance, issued within six months of date of embarkation; contact the Division of Immigration for further information. *Visa*: Individuals will need to submit various documents, including some necessary for Visitor Entry Permits. Individuals should prepare by contacting the Division of Immigration well in advance to negotiate what documents are necessary for the individual processing of their visa.

Note: (a) Nationals of Indonesia and Malaysia *always* require Police Clearance for the processing of a Visitor Entry Permit. (b) Nationals of The Philippines *always* require a National Bureau Investigation (NBI) for the processing of a Visitor Entry Permit.

Working days required: By post: applications are dealt with on receipt. In person: subject to the discretion of the Division of Immigration. Generally, documents needed for the processing of all Visitor Entry Permits should be submitted at least two weeks prior to arrival.

Temporary residence: Apply to CNMI Division of Immigration (see *Passport/Visa Information*).

PASSPORT/VISA INFORMATION

Marianas Visitors Authority
PO Box 500861 Saipan, MP 96950,
Northern Mariana Islands
Tel: 664 3200/1.
Website: www.mymarianas.com

CNMI Division of Immigration
Street address: Afetna Square Building, 2nd Floor,
San Antonio, Saipan MP 96950,
Northern Mariana Islands
Postal address: PO Box 10007, San Antonio,
Saipan MP 96950, Northern Mariana Islands
Tel: 236 0922/23.

Office of the CNMI Resident Representative to the United States
2121 R Street, NW, Washington, DC 20008, USA
Tel: (202) 673 5869.
Website: www.resrep.gov.mp

Money

Currency: The US Dollar is used. For further details of currency, credit & debit cards, traveller's cheques, exchange rate indicators and banking hours, see main *Pacific Islands of Micronesia* section.

Currency exchange: There are several Asian and US banks in the Mariana Islands where currencies from some foreign countries can be exchanged. ATMs are available at most banks and major shopping centres.

Currency restrictions: There are no restrictions on the import and export of local and foreign currency. Amounts exceeding US$10,000, however, must be declared.

Duty Free

The following goods may be imported into the Northern Mariana Islands without incurring customs duty:
600 cigarettes or 454g of cigars or tobacco; 2.3l of alcoholic beverage; 3.8l of wine and Japanese sake; a reasonable quantity of perfume.

Prohibited items: Narcotics and certain cooked and uncooked foods. Enquire at Immigration Office for details (see *Passport/Visa Information*). Firearms require a licence.

Public Holidays

Below are listed Public Holidays for the January 2006-June 2007 period.
2006: Jan 1 New Year's Day. **Jan 9** Commonwealth Day. **Feb 16** President's Day. **Mar 24** Covenant Day. **Apr 14** Good Friday. **May 29** Memorial Day. **Jul 4** US Independence Day. **Sep 4** Labour Day. **Oct 9** Columbus Day. **Nov 4** Citizenship Day. **Nov 11** Veterans Day. **Nov 23** Thanksgiving Day. **Dec 9** Constitution Day. **Dec 25** Christmas Day.
2007: Jan 1 New Year's Day. **Jan 9** Commonwealth Day. **Feb** President's Day. **Mar 24** Covenant Day. **Apr 6** Good Friday. **May 28** Memorial Day.
Note: Variations occur from island to island.

Health

There are no vaccination requirements. *Hepatitis A* and *B*, *dengue fever* and *TB* occur. Rare outbreaks of *Japanese encephalitis* have been reported.
Health care: There is a major, modern hospital on Saipan and routine facilities on Rota and Tinian. Full medical facilities are available but are not free of charge; health insurance is advisable.

Travel - International

AIR:

 Airlines serving the Northern Mariana Islands include *Asiana Airlines (OZ)*, *China Southern Air (CZ)*, *Continental Airlines (CO)*, *Japan Airlines (JL)*, *Korean Airlines (KE)* and *Northwest Airlines (NW)*.
Main airports: Saipan (SPN) is situated 3 miles (5km) south of Chalan Kanoa. *To/from the airport:* Taxis are available to the town (travel time – 15 minutes) and tour buses may meet some flights. *Facilities:* Bureau de change, refreshments and car hire. There are smaller airports at *Rota (ROP)* and *Tinian (TIQ)*.
Departure tax: None.
SEA:

 The international port of the Northern Mariana Islands is *Saipan*. The following lines sail there: *Daiwa Navigation Co*, *Nauru Pacific Line*, *Oceania Line Inc*, *P&O*, *Royal Shipping Co* (PO Box 238, Saipan), *Saipan Shipping Co* and *Tiger Line*.
ROAD:

 There are good roads in and around major island centres. **Bus:** There is a public shuttle bus service to major shopping facilities from hotels. **Taxi:** Available in all main centres. **Car hire:** Self-drive cars are available in towns; US driving laws are followed.
Documentation: International Driving Permit or national licence accepted.

Travel - Internal

AIR:

 Commuter aircraft (from *Pacific Island Aviation* and *Freedom Air*) are available to take visitors from Saipan to Tinian (travel time – 12 minutes) and Rota (travel time – 30 minutes).
SEA:

 There is a ferry from Tinian to Saipan (travel time – 55 minutes).

Travel Advice

Most visits to the Northern Mariana Islands are trouble-free but you should be aware of the global risk of indiscriminate international terrorist attacks, which could be against civilian targets, including places frequented by foreigners.
This advice is based on information provided by the Foreign and Commonwealth Office in the UK. It is correct at time of publishing. As the situation can change rapidly, visitors are advised to contact the following organisations for the latest travel advice:

British Foreign and Commonwealth Office
Tel: (0845) 850 2829.
Website: www.fco.gov.uk

US Department of State
Website: http://travel.state.gov/travel

Accommodation

Hotels in the Northern Mariana Islands vary in standard from luxury to basic. They cater mainly for Japanese and Korean markets.

ACCOMMODATION INFORMATION

Hotel Association of the Northern Mariana Islands (HANMI)
PO Box 501983, Saipan, MP 96950,
Northern Mariana Islands
Tel: 234 3455.
Website: www.marianashotels.org

Top Things To See & Do

• Attend a village **fiesta** in honour of local patron saints.
• The largest island, **Saipan**, is relatively developed, with good amenities and shopping facilities. Its western shore is encircled by a barrier reef, creating a lagoon with white sand beaches. Attractions on Saipan include the last command post of the Japanese Imperial Army known as **Banadero**, with World War II cannons, tanks and artillery preserved in a limestone cave. Japanese and Korean peace memorials commemorate the islands' central role in the war. Spectacular views can be had from the **Puntan Sabaneta** (also known as Banzai Cliff) and **Laderan Banadero** (also known as 'Suicide Cliff' because of the thousands of Japanese soldiers and their families who jumped to their deaths from it in order to avoid capture).
• The island of **Tinian**, 3 miles south of Saipan, has a rugged coastline with tiny coves. At **Abbas** on the northern shore, there are blow holes where incoming waves shoot 20ft into the air. The **House of Taga**, a temple or meeting house associated with the legendary chief Taga, consists of magnificent stone pillars, carved in the traditional way and transported from nearby coastal areas.
• **Rota** is a small and friendly island with a variety of natural attractions. In the main village of **Songsong**, life is conducted at a leisurely pace. Outside Songsong, sights include **Toga Cave**, a huge limestone cavern with stalactites and stalagmites, so large it was used as a wartime hospital. Wedding Cake Mountain, resembling a layered cake, is a fascinating sight. An interesting collection of artefacts can be viewed at the **Rota Cave Museum**, located in a gigantic limestone cave. At the **Taga Stone Quarry**, huge ancient stone remains carved by the Chamorros can be seen.
• **Isleta Maigo Fahang** (also known as Bird Island) and **Managha Island** are beautiful, unspoilt islands, set aside as nature reserves. The former can be visited in a glass-bottomed boat.
• **Watersports:** These are popular, with many suitable **diving** and **snorkelling** locations; **windsurfing** is popular on Saipan. **Parasailing** is available. Local **fishing** competitions are held in several places. Those not wishing to dive to see wrecks and underwater scenery can go on submarine cruises. For details, contact Pacific Subsea Saipan Inc (tel: 322 7746/7; website: www.submarine.co.mp).

TOURIST INFORMATION

Marianas Visitors Authority
PO Box 500861 Saipan, MP 96950,
Northern Mariana Islands
Tel: 664 3200/1.
Website: www.mymarianas.com

Entertainment

FOOD & DRINK: Local specialities include *kelaguin*, a chewy mixture of diced chicken and shredded coconut and thin slices of raw coconut dipped in a peppery sauce. A wide choice of food is on offer, including Chinese, French, Italian, Japanese, Thai and US.
NIGHTLIFE: There are several popular bars in Garapan and a few nightclubs and discos.
SHOPPING: Special purchases here include wishing dolls, coconut masks, coconut-crab decorations and woodcarvings, plus numerous duty free items. **Shopping hours:** Mon-Sun 0800-2100.

Business

ECONOMY: Fruit, vegetables, beef and pork are produced in commercial quantities, with some being exported. Fisheries and copra are other important industries in the agricultural sector. Manufacturing is dominated by textile production. The economy is dominated overall, however, by the service sector, of which tourism is the principal component. The establishment of an air link with Japan gave a major boost to this sector. However, the lack of available workers led to the recruitment of large numbers of foreign workers (which accounts for the huge growth in the islands' population). Bilateral aid from the USA is an important source of income for the Government,

---

particularly monies earmarked for the development of the islands' infrastructure, the poor condition of which is currently holding back further economic growth. The Northern Marianas is a member of the Pacific Community.

COMMERCIAL INFORMATION

Saipan Chamber of Commerce
PO Box 500806 CK, 96950, Saipan MP,
Northern Mariana Islands
Tel: 233 7150.
Website: www.saipanchamber.com

Palau

Palau was formerly part of the Caroline Islands.

Location: Western Pacific Ocean.

Time: GMT + 9.

Overview

Located between Guam, The Philippines and Papua New Guinea, Palau is an archipelago which is more than 640km (400 miles) long and harbours one of the world's greatest concentrations of corals, fish and other marine life. As such, Palau has some of the world's most spectacular snorkelling and diving locations and a well-developed diving infrastructure, with numerous operators offering a wide choice of facilities, including live-aboard dive tours to more remote sites. Palau's coral reefs are home to more than 1500 species of fish and 700 species of corals and sea anemones. Plunging walls, coral gardens and World War II wrecks are all part of the range of diving available. The local marine life is abundant and varies from schools of triggerfish, snappers, butterflyfish, spadefish and barracudas to grouper, Napoleon wrasse and a variety of reef sharks. Manta and eagle rays, cuttlefish, hawksbill and green turtles are also frequently sighted.

General Information

AREA: 508 sq km (196 sq miles), including Babeldaob Island, whose area is 409 sq km (158 sq miles).
POPULATION: 19,129 (2000).
POPULATION DENSITY: 37.7 per sq km.
CAPITAL: Koror. **Population:** 11,560 (1995).
GEOGRAPHY: Palau, the westernmost cluster of the six major island groups that make up the Caroline Islands, lies 1000km (600 miles) east of The Philippines. The archipelago stretches over 650km (400 miles) from the atoll of Kayangel to the islet of Tobi. The Palau islands include more than 200 islands, of which only eight are inhabited. With three exceptions, all of the islands are located within a single barrier reef and represent two geological formations. The largest are volcanic and rugged with interior jungle and

large areas of grassed terraces. The Rock Islands, now known as the Floating Garden Islands, are of limestone formation, while Kayangel, at the northernmost tip, is a classic coral atoll.

GOVERNMENT: Republic since 1947. Gained self-governing status (in free association with the USA) in 1994. **Head of State and Government:** President Tommy Remengesau since 2001. **Recent history:** In 1986, the governments of Palau and the USA agreed the terms of a Compact of Free Association, similar to those reached with other Micronesian Trust members, which allows for virtual independence under a US defence umbrella. The Palau Compact, however, remained unsigned, because of a crucial clause forbidding the presence of any nuclear weapons on the islands, including visits by ships equipped to carry them. This was unacceptable to the USA, which therefore refused to sign the Compact until the clause was rescinded. The dispute over the Compact introduced a violent aspect into Palau's politics – President Haruu Remeliik was assassinated in 1985; his successor, Lazarus Salii, committed suicide in August 1988. At the Presidential election of November 1992, Kuniwo Nakamura won a narrow victory. A decision over the Compact could not be left much longer. The island was faced with a stark choice of accepting it or seeking full independence – a hazardous proposition for economic reasons. In October 1994, the Compact was endorsed and Palau was subsequently admitted to the UN in December 1994 and became a member of the IMF in 1997. Nakamura served a second term between 1996 and 2000, after which he was replaced by the current President, Tommy Remengesau. Economic issues have dominated the political agenda in recent years, as Palau attempts to deal with the typical problems of all Pacific islands – isolation and lack of infrastructure. Executive authority is vested in the President, who is elected for a four-year term. Legislative authority rests with the bicameral National Congress, the Olbiil era Kelulau.

LANGUAGE: English and Palauan.

RELIGION: Roman Catholic majority.

ELECTRICITY: 115/230 volts AC, 60 Hz.

SOCIAL CONVENTIONS: Traditional Palauan society was a complex matriarchal system. The people are now amongst the most enterprising in the region, though a version of traditional beliefs, *Modekngei*, exists alongside the imported Christian beliefs. The political system is modelled on that of the USA, and Western culture is being assimilated – not least because of the many Palauans who continue their education abroad.

Climate

Palau enjoys a pleasantly warm climate all year round with an annual average temperature of 27°C (82°F). The heaviest rainfall takes place between July and October but typhoons are rare.

Required clothing: Lightweight cottons and linens, with light rainwear advisable all year round.

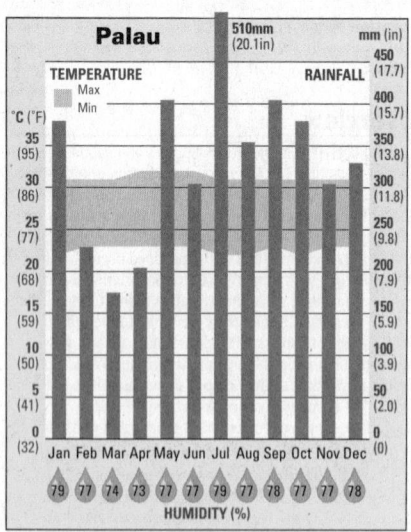

Communications

Telephone: Country code: 680. Phonecards are available and calls can be made from most hotels in Koror.

Internet: Access and reliability is limited.

Post: Post office located in Koror. Post office hours: Mon-Fri 0800-1600, Sat 0900 to 1000.

MEDIA: Press: The main newspaper is *Pacific Daily News* (Guam). The local newspaper, which appears fortnightly, is *Tia Belau*; *Palau Horizon* appears weekly.

TV: There are no television stations based in Palau, but most households receive US TV via cable and satellite.

Radio: *T8AA Eco Paradise* is a Government-run news and talk station. *WWFM* and *KRFM* are private stations.

Passport/Visa

	Passport Required?	Visa Required?	Return Ticket Required?
Full British	Yes	3	Yes
Australian	Yes	3	Yes
Canadian	Yes	3	Yes
USA	1	2	Yes
Other EU	Yes	3	Yes
Japanese	Yes	3	Yes

Note: Regulations and requirements may be subject to change at short notice, and you are advised to contact the appropriate diplomatic or consular authority before finalising travel arrangements. Any numbers in the chart refer to the footnotes below.

PASSPORTS: 1. Passports valid for at least 30 days beyond intended period of stay required by all except US nationals holding proof of citizenship accompanied by any other photo ID document.

VISAS: Required by all except:

(a) **2.** nationals of Marshall Islands, Micronesia and the USA for up to one year;

(b) **3.** all other nationals for stays of up to 30 days; Entry Permits are issued on arrival. For longer stays, permission must be granted from the Chief of Immigration.

Types of visa and cost: *Entry Permit:* US$50. Extension is possible for two times 30 days if application is made no less than seven days beyond expiration of visa. *Extension:* US$100.

Validity: Various.

Application to: Chief of Immigration, Bureau of Legal Affairs, Ministry of Justice, PO Box 100, Koror 96940, Palau.

Note: All nationals staying longer than six months must register with the Chief of Immigration within 30 days after arrival.

Application Requirements: (a) Valid passport. (b) Vaccination certificates from those arriving from infected areas; see the *Health* section for details. (c) Proof of adequate funds (US$200 per week). (d) Return or onward tickets. A bond signed by the Chief of Immigration prior to arrival can be accepted instead of return/onward tickets. (e) All visitors must sign a declaration stating that they are HIV-negative. (f) Fee.

Note: These application requirements do not apply to Government officials, students and nationals of the Marshall Islands, Micronesia and the USA.

Working days required: Postal applications are dealt with on receipt but visas are usually issued on arrival to those who are eligible.

Temporary residence: Apply to Division of Immigration (address above).

PASSPORT/VISA INFORMATION

Chief of Immigration, Bureau of Legal Affairs, Ministry of Justice
PO Box 100, Koror, Palau 96940, Palau

Embassy of the Republic of Palau in the USA
1700 Pennsylvania Avenue, Suite 400, NW, Washington, DC 20006, USA
Tel: (202) 452 6814.
Website: www.palauembassy.com

Money

Currency: The US Dollar is in use. For further information on currency, currency exchange, credit & debit cards, traveller's cheques, exchange rate indicators and banking hours, see main *Pacific Islands of Micronesia* section.

Currency restrictions: There are no limits on the import and export of local or foreign currency, but amounts of more than US$5000 must be declared.

Duty Free

The following goods may be imported into the Republic of Palau without incurring customs duty:
200 cigarettes or 454g of cigars or tobacco; one bottle of liquor.

Note: Alcohol for passengers over 21 years of age only.

Prohibited items: Narcotics, firearms, shells and natural artefacts.

Public Holidays

Below are listed Public Holidays for the January 2006-June 2007 period.

2006: Jan 1 New Year's Day. **Mar 15** Youth Day. **May 5** Senior Citizens' Day. **Jun 1** President's Day. **Jul 9** Constitution Day. **Sep 4** Labour Day. **Oct 1** Independence Day. **Oct 24**

United Nations Day. **Nov 23** Thanksgiving Day. **Dec 25** Christmas Day.

2007: Jan 1 New Year's Day. **Mar 15** Youth Day. **May 5** Senior Citizens' Day. **Jun 1** President's Day.

Health

Vaccination certificates for *yellow fever* and *cholera* are required from all travellers arriving from infected areas. *Hepatitis B* is endemic. *Hepatitis A, typhoid fever* and *dengue fever* can occur.

Health care: Palau has two private medical clinics and a public hospital. As health care is not free, health insurance is recommended.

Travel - International

AIR:

Palau Micronesia Air began international flights in 2004 (website: www.palau-air.com). *Continental Airlines (CO)* operates from Guam. There are twice weekly flights to Manila, from where connections to other destinations can be made. *Japan Airlines (JL)* flies from Nagoya, Japan, and *Far Eastern Airlines (EF)* flies directly from Taipei.

Main airports: *Koror Babeldaob (ROR)* on Babeldaob Island, which is near Koror Island, is situated 12 miles (19km) northeast of Airai. To/from the airport: Buses and taxis are available to Airai and Koror. Travel time to Koror is approximately 30 minutes.

Departure tax: US$20.

SEA:

International cruise lines seldom call at Palau ports. Visitors who sail privately to Palau will find Naval Oceanographic charts to be most useful. US Naval Chart HO 5500 covers the entire region of Micronesia. Unscheduled inter-island boat services are available to Babeldaob and Kayangel. Anguar and Peleliu have scheduled boat services.

ROAD:

The road network is extended beyond Koror to Babeldaob Island with many coral and dirt roads connecting to other states. A 4-wheel-drive car is recommended if you wish to see Babeldaob. Cars can be hired from the airport. Driving is on the right and the speed limit is 40kph (25mph). **Taxi:** There are many taxis in Koror offering comfortable travel. They are not metered and fares are fixed.

Travel Advice

Most visits to Palau are trouble-free but you should be aware of the global risk of indiscriminate international terrorist attacks, which could be against civilian targets, including places frequented by foreigners.

This advice is based on information provided by the Foreign and Commonwealth Office in the UK. It is correct at time of publishing. As the situation can change rapidly, visitors are advised to contact the following organisations for the latest travel advice:

British Foreign and Commonwealth Office
Tel: (0845) 850 2829.
Website: www.fco.gov.uk

US Department of State
Website: http://travel.state.gov/travel

Accommodation

RESORTS/MOTELS:

There is a wide variety of accommodation on Palau and the outlying islands, ranging from first-class luxury resorts with most services, to the mid-priced bungalows and motels. While most resorts are located in Koror, there is quieter and more secluded accommodation available on the southern islands. For more information, contact the Palau Visitors Authority.

Top Things To See & Do

- The capital, **Koror**, is the busiest centre in the islands with many gift shops, restaurants and other resort facilities. For an insight into Palau's history, a visit to the **Palau National Museum** is advised where more than 1000 relics of Palau's past are housed including shell money and traditional weapons.

- **Babeldaob,** Palau's biggest island is about 43km (27 miles) long and 24km (15 miles) across at its widest, and is covered in dense foliage. The terrain is varied with steep mountains, freshwater lakes and sand dunes. Palau's first inhabitants settled along the coastline. Today, visitors can explore the 37 stone monoliths known as *Badrulchau* which are concrete examples of the island's early civilisation. Other remnants of Palau's history are located at **Imeungs** in the southwest of the island. These stone foundations and pillars are all that remain of the political and military centre of this part of the island.

- For sports lovers, the **Rock Islands** offer endless possibilities for **snorkelling, sea kayaking, sailing** and **fishing**. The island of **Peleliu** forms the southern boundary of the Rock Islands. In 1985 it was designated a US National Historic Landmark, owing to the part it played during World War II. Abandoned tanks, helmets and bomb casings are still dotted throughout the island.
- Palau's most popular **dive** sites include **Blue Corner**, where dogtooth tuna, resident Napoleon wrasses, wahoo and other large fish float on the rapid current; **Ngemelis Wall**, commonly referred to as the Big Drop-off, and praised by Jacques Cousteau; the **German Channel**, known for its regular sightings of manta rays; **Siaes Tunnel**, an enormous underwater cavern where white-tip reef sharks can almost always be seen; and **Chandelier Cave**, a series of underwater chambers filled with ancient stalactites. Millions of jellyfish inhabit **Jellyfish Lake**, cut off from the rest of the ocean; snorkellers can get up close as they no longer have their stings.

TOURIST INFORMATION

Palau Visitors Authority
PO Box 256, Koror, Palau 96940
Tel: 488 2793/1930.
Website: www.visit-palau.com

Entertainment

FOOD & DRINK: Many restaurants offer an eclectic mix of cuisine. Fresh local seafood is the highlight of many menus and there are many exotic local dishes in addition to the ubiquitous pizza or traditional American, Chinese or Japanese fare. **Tipping:** Optional.

NIGHTLIFE: There are several open-air cocktail lounges, some offering live entertainment or karaoke.

SHOPPING: Koror has a range of modern shopping facilities on offer. Several small gift shops offer a variety of unusual items, and the Belau National Museum and Ormuul Gift Shop offer authentic handmade local craft items. Palau's best-known art form is the *storyboard*. These are carvings on various lengths of wood, sometimes shaped into crocodiles, turtles or fish and painted. The storyboards depict Palauan stories taken from about 30 popular legends or recorded events. In addition to the storyboards, models of *bais* (men's meeting buses), canoes and sculptured figurines called *dilukai* are also carved. Other gifts include jewellery, etchings and baskets, purses, hats and mats woven from pandanas and palm. In addition to these local crafts, the Palau Pacific Resort has a duty free shop which features locally produced items as well as designer and brand name gift products. **Shopping hours:** Mon-Sat 0800-2100.

Business

ECONOMY: Subsistence agriculture is a vital employer, with cassava, coconuts, bananas and sweet potatoes as the main crops. Fishing is valuable mainly through the sale of licences to large foreign fleets allowing them to operate within Palau's 200-mile territorial limit. Industry is limited to small-scale light manufacturing, such as food-processing and boat-building. Foreign aid, mainly from the US, completes the country's principal sources of revenue. Tourism has grown steadily during the last decade despite problems arising from the islands' inaccessibility and a lack of investment, especially in basic infrastructure. Palau is a member of the two main regional economic organisations, the South Pacific Forum and the South Pacific Commission.

CONFERENCES/CONVENTIONS: The Airai View Hotel in Koror can provide facilities for up to 150 delegates (see *Commercial Information*).

COMMERCIAL INFORMATION

Palau Chamber of Commerce
PO Box 1742, Koror 96940, Palau
Tel: 488 3400.
E-mail: pcoc@palaunet.com.

Airai View Hotel (Information on Conferences/Conventions)
PO Box 8067, Koror, Palau 96940, Palau
Tel: 587 3530/1
Website: www.airaiview.com

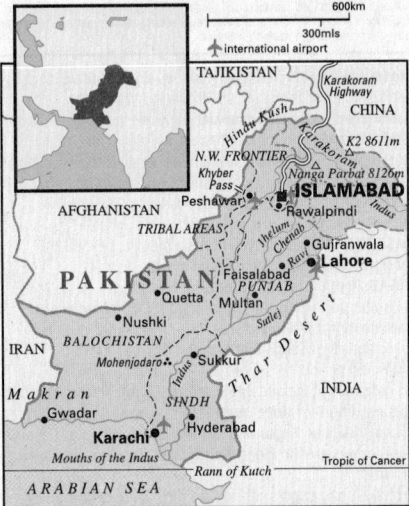

Location: South Asia.

Time: GMT + 5.

Overview

Pakistan encapsulates such variety that it is regretful that it is not top of every traveller's must-see list. Pakistan is enriched by friendly people and magnificent landscapes. Opportunity for adventure is as high as its mighty mountain ranges, with watersports, mountaineering and trekking all popular and rewarding activities. Coupled with this is a profound sense of cultural concoction, Pakistan once being home to several ancient civilisations, and witness to the rise and fall of dynasties.

In ancient times, the area that now comprises Pakistan marked the farthest reaches of the conquests of Alexander the Great. It was also the home of Buddhist Ghandaran culture. It was the independence of India in 1947 that catalysed Pakistan's nationhood. Under pressure from Indian Muslims, the British created a separate Muslim state. Originally, it consisted of two parts, East Pakistan (now Bangladesh) and West Pakistan (now a single unitary state). Mohammed Ali Jinnah, who led the independence struggle, became the new country's first President.

Democracy failed to take root and Pakistan suffered military rule and civil war, eventually securing an independent Bangladesh and truncating Pakistan. Democratic civilian Government followed this defeat and Zulfiqar Ali Bhutto became President. In 1977, the military took power in a coup under General Mohammed Zia ul-Haq. A democratic constitution and civilian Government were re-instituted following his death in 1988. A decade of revolving-door civilian politics ensued between Ali Bhutto's daughter, Benazir, and Mohammed Nawaz Sharif, leader of the Islamic Democratic Alliance, essentially a military creation. Sharif and Bhutto contested four violent elections during the next 10 years, winning two each. Both Bhutto Governments and Sharif's first were dismissed by Presidential decree because of incompetence, nepotism and corruption. The military interceded with Sharif's second because of Pakistan's controversial nuclear weapons programme, designed to ensure parity with India. At the heart of the long-running Indo-Pakistan is the status of Kashmir which, although it has a majority Muslim population, became part of India in 1947. The two sides have nearly come to war on several occasions. However, in early 2004, a "road map" was agreed and tentative commitment to peace established.

Equally troubling is the issue of Pakistan's position in regards to international terrorism. General Musharraf helped the USA against Afghanistan after the '9/11' 2001 attacks, making him extremely unpopular among parts of Pakistani society. Historically, Pakistan had been intimately involved with the creation of the Taleban and the Pathans of Pakistan, well-represented in the military, are closely linked to the Pashtun, Afghanistan's largest ethnic group, who made up most of the Taleban. The US-Pakistani relationship is also controversial since General Musharraf is himself marred by corruption, recently 'awarding' himself further years as President. Pakistan's topography is therefore as fractured and unsettled as its history. Yet its swerving shifts of mountainous land possess great beauty. Visit Pakistan for yourself and begin untangling this complex enigma.

General Information

AREA: 796,095 sq km (307,374 sq miles) excluding data for the disputed territories of Jammu and Kashmir.

POPULATION: 161.1 million (UN, 2005).

POPULATION DENSITY: 202.36 per sq km.

CAPITAL: Islamabad. **Population:** 800,000 (2005).

GEOGRAPHY: Pakistan has borders to the north with Afghanistan, to the east with India and to the west with Iran; the Arabian Sea lies to the south. In the northeast is the disputed territory of Jammu and Kashmir, bounded by Afghanistan, China and India. Pakistan comprises distinct regions. The northern highlands – the Hindu Kush – are rugged and mountainous; the Indus Valley is a flat, alluvial plain with five major rivers dominating the upper region, eventually joining the Indus River and flowing south to the Makran coast; Sindh is bounded on the east by the Thar Desert and the Rann of Kutch, and on the west by the Kirthar Range; the Baluchistan Plateau is an arid tableland encircled by mountains.

GOVERNMENT: Federal Islamic Republic since 1973. Gained independence from the UK in 1947. **Head of State:** President Pervez Musharraf since 2001. **Head of Government:** Prime Minister Shaukat Aziz since 2004.

Recent history: At home, the Musharraf Government sought to establish its popular legitimacy by holding elections for the National Assembly, as well as a referendum on his Presidency, in October 2002. These returned General Musharraf – now partially reinvented as a civilian President – while his supporters took control of the national assembly. However, his pro-American stance has made him extremely unpopular among parts of Pakistani society. In the last two years he has been the target of at least a dozen assassination attempts. Otherwise, his position appears reasonably secure for the time being. Until the emergence of a plausible untainted civilian political leader, Musharraf is probably the best that Pakistan can expect.

The legislature is the bicameral Majlis-I-Shura, comprising the National Assembly and the Senate. The National Assembly has 342 members elected for a five-year term: 272 members are elected in single-seat constituencies; the remaining 70 are reserved for women and national minorities and are chosen by the political parties in proportion to their share of the directly elected seats. The Senate has 100 members selected by each of the four provincial Parliaments, the Federally Administered Tribal Areas and the federal capital.

LANGUAGE: Urdu is the national language. English is widely spoken. Regional languages include Punjabi, which is spoken by 48 per cent of the population (1981), Pushto, Sindhi, Saraiki, and Baluchi. There are numerous local dialects.

RELIGION: 97 per cent Muslim, the remainder are Hindu or Christian.

ELECTRICITY: 220 volts AC, 50Hz. Round two- or three-pin plugs are in use.

SOCIAL CONVENTIONS: The right hand is used both for shaking hands (the usual form of greeting) and for passing or receiving things. Mutual hospitality and courtesy are of great importance at all levels, whatever the social standing of the host. Visitors must remember that most Pakistanis are Muslim and should respect their customs and beliefs.

Smoking is prohibited in some public places and it is polite to ask permission before lighting a cigarette. It is common for visiting businesspeople to be entertained in hotels and restaurants. If invited to a private home, a gift or national souvenir is welcome. Informal dress is acceptable for most occasions. Women should avoid wearing tight clothing and both men and women should ensure that their arms and legs are covered. Pakistani society is divided into classes and within each group there is a subtle social grading. The Koran is the law for Muslims and it influences every aspect of daily life; see the *World of Islam* appendix for more information.

Photography: Do not take photographs at military establishments, airports or of any infrastructure, including dams and bridges or from aircraft. The penalties can be severe.

A B C D E F G H I J K L M N O P Q R S T U V W X Y Z

Pakistan

Climate

Pakistan has three seasons: winter (November to March) is warm and cooled by sea breezes on the coast; summer (April to July) has extreme temperatures and the monsoon season (July to September) has the highest rainfall on the hills. Karachi has little rain. The best time to visit southern Pakistan is between November and March, when the days are cool and clear. The best time to visit northern Pakistan is from April to October.

Required clothing: Lightweights, with warmer clothing for upland areas in the winter. Rainwear is advised for the monsoon season.

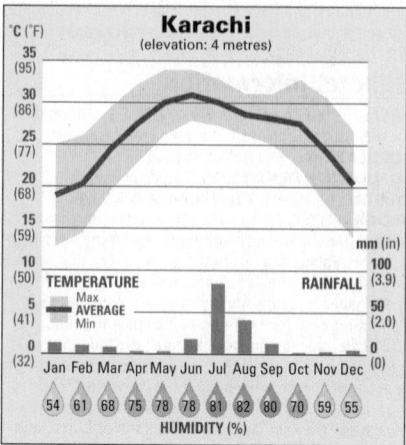

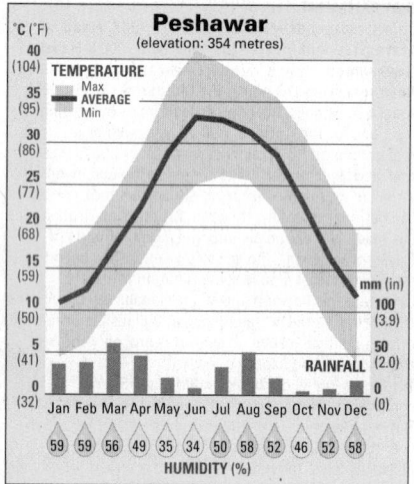

Communications

Telephone: IDD is available. Country code: 92.
Mobile telephone: Roaming agreements exist with some international mobile phone companies. Coverage is largely limited to main cities.
Internet: Internet is available in urban areas where Internet cafes can be found.
Post: Airmail takes four to five days to reach Western Europe. General post offices in major cities offer 24-hour services.
MEDIA: President Pervez Musharraf's rule has been marked by increased freedom for the print media and liberalisation of broadcasting policies; the state's monopoly has been diminished by the expansion of private radio and TV stations. In 2005, issued licenses for private FM radio stations totalled around 100, but private stations are not allowed to broadcast news. Pakistani censorship, however, remains far more rigorous than in India. The Pakistani Government uses a range of legal and constitutional powers to curb press freedom. The country's law on blasphemy has been used against journalists. Nevertheless, Pakistan's print media are among the most outspoken in South Asia.
Press: The English-language press enjoys a great deal of influence in business circles. Dailies include *Business Recorder*, *Dawn* (website: www.dawn.com), *Financial Post*, *Frontier Post* (website: http://frontierpost.com.pk), *Leader*, *Pakistan Observer*, *Pakistan Times*, *Star*, *The Nation* (website: www.nation.com.pk) and *The News* (website: www.jang.com.pk).
TV: *Pakistan Television Corporation Ltd* is a state TV broadcaster that operates *PTV 1*, *PTV 2*, *Channel 3* and *PTV World*. *Geo TV* and *Indus TV* are popular satellite channels. *Shalimar Television Network* (*STN*) has both state-run and privately owned networks.

Radio: *Radio Pakistan* is state-run and operates more than 20 stations nationwide, an external service and the FM 101 network, aimed at younger listeners. *Azad Kashmir Radio* is also state-run, whilst *FM 100* is a commercial, music-based FM network.

Passport/Visa

	Passport Required?	Visa Required?	Return Ticket Required?
Full British	Yes	Yes	Yes
Australian	Yes	Yes	Yes
Canadian	Yes	Yes	Yes
USA	Yes	Yes	Yes
Other EU	Yes	Yes	Yes
Japanese	Yes	Yes	Yes

Note: *Regulations and requirements may be subject to change at short notice, and you are advised to contact the appropriate diplomatic or consular authority before finalising travel arrangements. Any numbers in the chart refer to the footnotes below.*

Note: Travellers are currently advised against travel to certain areas of Pakistan (see *Travel Advice*).
Restricted entry and transit: The Government of Pakistan refuses entry to nationals of Israel, even for transit. Nationals of Afghanistan are refused entry if their passports or tickets show evidence of transit or boarding in India. Holders of Taiwan (China) passports are refused entry except in transit or airport transit.
PASSPORTS: Passport valid for six months beyond the intended length of stay required by all.
VISAS: Required by all except the following:
(a) holders of a Pakistan Origin Card (POC) regardless of nationality for unlimited stay;
(b) nationals of Tonga and Trinidad & Tobago for an unlimited period;
(c) nationals of Iceland, Maldives and Zambia for stays of up to a maximum of three months;
(d) nationals of Nepal and Samoa, and holders of Chinese passports issued in Hong Kong (SAR), for stays of up to 30 days;
(e) transit passengers continuing their journey within 24 hours by the same or first connecting aircraft, provided they are holding onward or return documentation and not leaving the airport;
(f) holders of UN laissez-passer.
Note: Nationals of Algeria, Bangladesh, Bhutan, India, Iraq, Israel, Libya, Nigeria, Palestinian Authority passport holders, Serbia & Montenegro, Somalia, Sri Lanka, Sudan, Tanzania, Uganda and Yemen must report to the nearest Foreigners Registration Office for registration, except for those issued *Work* permits/visas in the managerial category. In certain circumstances, this may also be applicable to other nationals and will be indicated on their passports.
Types of visa and cost: Price of visa varies according to nationality. For UK nationals, prices are: *Single-entry*: £40; *Double-entry*: £54; *Multiple-entry*: £74. These prices are identical to those issued for the *Visa for Media Professionals*, which must be routed through the Information Division of the Pakistan High Commission. For Pakistanis holding dual nationality, prices are: *Adult*: £20; *Child* (up to 18 years old): £10; valid for stays of up to one year. Applicants with parents holding Pakistani passports get the same concession, provided they produce the original detailed birth certificate and their parents' Pakistani passports. *Pilgrim* (*Single-entry*): £45. This is issued to those wishing to visit holy places (Shrines/Gurdawaras) in Pakistan and is allowed for groups of pilgrims, normally restricted to a specified period. *Business*: £68 (*Single-entry*); £90 (*Double-entry*); £122 (*Multiple-entry*).
Note: An 80 pence bank surcharge per application for a visa or passport is required. Certain nationals are issued visas free of charge, but they must be obtained prior to travel. For further information, consult the High Commission or Embassy.
Validity: Single-entry/Double-entry: six months from the date of issue for stays of up to three months. Multiple-entry: six months to one year.
Application to: Consulate (or Consular section at Embassy or High Commission); see *Passport/Visa Information*.
Application requirements: (a) Original valid passport, plus one photocopy. (b) One application form. (c) Two passport-size photos. (d) Confirmed return/onward ticket. (e) Proof of sufficient funds for duration of stay. (f) Fee payable by cash or postal order only. (g) For business trips, a letter of invitation from a company in Pakistan.
Note: There may be slightly different application requirements for Indian nationals and the nearest Consulate/Embassy should be contacted for further information prior to travel.
Working days required: Depends on nationality (in UK, visas are normally granted within 24 to 48 hours). Enquire at the nearest Consulate or Embassy. Pilgrim visas require two months' processing time.

PASSPORT/VISA INFORMATION

High Commission for the Islamic Republic of Pakistan in the UK
34-36 Lowndes Square, London SW1X 9JN, UK
Tel: (020) 7664 9200 or 9204.
Website: www.pakmission-uk.gov.pk
Opening hours: Mon-Fri 0930-1730; 0930-1200 (visa submission); 1600-1700 (visa collection).

Consulate General of Pakistan in the UK
Pakistan House, 137 Dickenson Road, Rusholme, Manchester M14 5JB, UK
Tel: (0161) 225 2005.

Embassy of the Islamic Republic of Pakistan in the USA
3517 International Court, NW, Washington, DC 20008, USA
Tel: (202) 243 6500.
Website: www.embassyofpakistan.org

Consulate General of the Islamic Republic of Pakistan in the USA
12 East, 65th Street, New York, NY 10021, USA
Tel: (212) 879 5800 or 517 7541.
Website: www.embassyofpakistan.org

Money

Currency: Pakistan Rupee (PKR) = 100 paisa. Notes are in denominations of PKR1000, 500, 100, 50, 10 and 5. Coins are in denominations of PKR2 and 1, and 50 and 25 paisa.
Credit & debit cards: American Express is the most widely accepted card. MasterCard and Visa are also good, but Diners Club and other cards have more limited use. Check with your credit or debit card company for details of merchant acceptability and other services which may be available.
Traveller's cheques: Generally accepted at most banks, 4- and 5-star hotels and major shops. To avoid additional exchange rate charges, travellers are advised to take traveller's cheques in US Dollars or Pounds Sterling.
Currency restrictions: The import and export of local currency is limited to PKR100 in denominations of PKR10 or less (the import of banknotes in denominations of PKR50 and PKR100 or more is prohibited). The import and export of foreign currency are unlimited. Up to PKR500 may be reconverted into foreign currency, provided official exchange receipts are shown.
Banking hours: Mon-Sat 0900-1330, Fri 0900-1230.
Exchange rate indicators:
Rate at time of publishing
£1.00= PKR102.93
$1.00= PKR59.71

Duty Free

The following items may be imported into Pakistan without incurring customs duty:
200 cigarettes or 50 cigars or 8oz of tobacco; 250ml of perfume and eau de toilette (opened); gifts up to a value of PKR2000 (for the first visit in a calendar year, PKR100 for the second visit in a calendar year).
Note: * Residents under 18 years old are not allowed any free import.
Prohibited items: The import of alcohol, matches, plants, fruit and vegetables is prohibited. The export of antiques is prohibited.

Public Holidays

Below are listed Public Holidays for the January 2006-June 2007 period.
2006: Jan 13 Eid ul-Azha (Feast of the Sacrifice). **Feb 9** Ashoura. **Mar 23** Pakistan Day. **Apr 11** Eid-e-Milad-un-Nabi (Birth of the Prophet). **Aug 14** Independence Day.
Oct 22-24 Eid al-Fitr (End of Ramadan). **Nov 9** Allama Muhammad Iqbal Day. **Dec 25** Quaid-e-Azam's Birthday. **Dec 31** Eid ul-Azha (Feast of the Sacrifice).
2007: Jan 29 Ashoura. **Mar 23** Pakistan Day. **Mar 31** Eid-e-Milad-un-Nabi (Birth of the Prophet).
Note: (a) Muslim festivals are timed according to local sightings of various phases of the moon and the dates given above are approximations. During the lunar month of Ramadan that precedes Eid al-Fitr, Muslims fast during the day and feast at night and normal business patterns may be interrupted. Most restaurants are closed during the day and there is a restriction on smoking and drinking in public places. Eid al-Fitr and Eid ul-Azha may last from two to four days, depending on the region. For more information, see the *World of Islam* appendix. (b) Christian holidays are observed by the Christian community only.

Pakistan

Health

	Special Precautions?	Certificate Required?
Yellow Fever	No	1
Cholera	2	No
Typhoid & Polio	3	N/A
Malaria	4	N/A

Note: *Regulations and requirements may be subject to change at short notice, and you are advised to contact your doctor well in advance of your intended date of departure. Any numbers in the chart refer to the footnotes below.*

1: Yellow fever vaccination certificate is required of all travellers arriving within six days from any part of a country in which yellow fever is endemic. Infants under six months of age are exempt if the mother's vaccination certificate shows her to have been vaccinated prior to the child's birth. Countries and areas within the endemic zone are regarded as infected.
2: Following WHO guidelines issued in 1973, a cholera vaccination certificate is no longer a condition of entry to Pakistan. However, cholera is a serious risk in this country and precautions are essential. Up-to-date advice should be sought before deciding whether these precautions should include vaccination, as medical opinion is divided over its effectiveness; see the *Health* appendix.
3: Vaccination against typhoid is advised. There are reports of typhoid drug resistance.
4: Malaria risk exists throughout the year in all areas below 2000m (6560ft). The malignant *falciparum* strain is present and has been reported as chloroquine-resistant.
Food & drink: All water should be regarded as being potentially contaminated. Water used for drinking, brushing teeth or making ice should have first been boiled or otherwise sterilised. Milk is unpasteurised and should be boiled. Powdered or tinned milk is available and is advised, but make sure that it is reconstituted with pure water. Avoid dairy products that are likely to have been made from unboiled milk. Only eat well-cooked meat and fish, preferably served hot. Salad and mayonnaise may carry increased risk. Vegetables should be cooked and fruit peeled. Avoid food from street vendors.
Other risks: *Hepatitis A* and *E* occur and *hepatitis B* is endemic. *Trachoma* and *typhoid fever* are common. Between June and January, *Japanese encephalitis* is a risk in rural areas. *Dengue fever* may also occur. Do not walk barefoot.
Rabies is present. For those at high risk, vaccination before arrival should be considered. If you are bitten, seek medical advice without delay. For more information, consult the *Health* appendix.
Health care: Medical facilities can be very limited. There is no reciprocal health agreement with the UK. Travellers are strongly advised to take out full medical insurance before departure. The main hospitals are: Agha Khan Hospital, Karachi; Doctor's Hospital, Lahore; and Shifa International Hospital, Islamabad.
Note: A certificate proving the visitor to be HIV-negative is required if planning on staying over one year in the country.

Travel - International

AIR:
The national airline is *Pakistan International Airlines (PK)* (website: www.piac.com.pk) and links Pakistan with 47 destinations around the world.
Approximate flight times: From Karachi to *London* is eight hours 40 minutes, to *Los Angeles* is 22 hours 30 minutes, to *New York* is 21 hours 40 minutes, to *Riyadh* is three hours 35 minutes and to *Singapore* is seven hours 15 minutes.
Main airports: *Karachi (KHI)* (Jinnah International Airport) (website: www.karachiairport.com) is 15km (10 miles) northeast of the city (travel time - 30 to 45 minutes). *To/from the airport*: Coaches to the city run every 25 minutes. A bus runs from dusk to dawn every 15 minutes. Taxi services to the city are available. *Facilities*: Duty free shops, restaurant, post office, bank and shops.
Lahore (LHE) (website: www.lahore-airport.com) is 18km (5 miles) southeast of the city (travel time - 20 minutes). *To/from the airport*: Coaches and buses leave regularly for the city. Taxi services to the city are also available. *Facilities*: Car hire, bank, restaurant and shops.
Islamabad (ISB) (Islamabad International) is 8km (5 miles) southeast of the city (travel time - 20 minutes). *To/from the airport*: Coach and taxi services to the city are available. *Facilities*: Duty free is available.
Peshawar (PEW) is 4km (2.5 miles) from the city (travel time - 10 minutes). *To/from the airport*: Full bus and taxi services to the city are available.
Departure tax: PKR400-800 depending on the airport and class of travel. Transit passengers and children under two years of age are exempt. Departure tax is payable by cash only; credit cards are not accepted.

SEA:
Main port: *Karachi* (Kemari). It is both Afghanistan's and Pakistan's port for goods, together with Port Qasim. No passenger boats or ships for the general public sail to or from Pakistan at present.

RAIL:
A rail link extends from Quetta (via the border crossing at Taftan) to Zahedan, Iran; the express train (travel time - 27 hours) runs weekly from Quetta, as does the passenger train, which only travels as far as Taftan. For more information contact *Pakistan Railways* (website: www.pakrail.com).

ROAD:
From China: The Khunjerab Pass is often snow-covered and, during the rainy season (December to April), it is closed due to the high risk of mudslides. Transport includes buses, vans and 4-wheel drive vehicles.
From India: Wagha is the only land border open between Pakistan and India (Lahore–Amritsar route). The border post is open daily 0830-1430 from 16 April to 15 October, and 0900-1500 from 16 April to 15 October. A minibus runs from Lahore railway station to Wagha and there are also taxis available (travel time - 30 minutes). The Pakistan Tourism Development Corporation (PTDC) operates two weekly buses from Lahore to Delhi on Friday and Tuesday, returning on Saturday and Wednesday (travel time - 12 hours). The Delhi Transport Corporation (DTC) also operates two weekly services from Delhi.
From Iran: travel is only possible via the Quetta–Taftan–Zahedan route. The border is open from 0900-1300 and 1400-1700. Several buses and coaches leave daily from Quetta to Taftan (travel time - 18 hours). There is also a road from Kabul, Afghanistan to Peshawar.
Note: Visitors exiting Pakistan by land routes are subject to a road toll. Travel to the federally administered tribal areas and the border areas with Afghanistan is not recommended. For further information, visitors should seek official advice.

Travel - Internal

AIR:
Most domestic services are operated by *Pakistan International Airlines (PK)* (website: www.piac.com.pk). Other airlines are *Aero Asia* (website: www.aeroasia.com) and *Bhoja Air* (website: www.bhojaair.com.pk). There are many daily flights between Islamabad, Karachi, Lahore, Multan, Peshawar and Quetta. Air transport is the quickest and most efficient means of travel.
Departure tax: PKR20-40 for internal flights. Children under two years are exempt.

RIVER:
Traffic along the Indus River is almost exclusively commercial. Many goods are carried to Punjab and the north from the main port at Karachi.

RAIL:
Much of Pakistan's extensive rail network is a legacy of British rule. The main line, from Karachi to Lahore, Rawalpindi and Peshawar, has several daytime and overnight trains. Most other routes have several daily trains. Even first-class compartments can be hot and crowded. Travel in air conditioned coaches is advised, as are reservations on long-distance journeys and overnight service. Children under three years of age travel free. Children aged three to 11 years pay half fare. *Pakistan Railways* offer concessions for tourists (on presentation of a certificate issued by PTDC), excluding Indian nationals travelling by rail. A discount of 25 per cent is offered to individuals and groups, and 50 per cent for students. Details are available from railway offices in Pakistan. For more information contact Pakistan Railways (www.pakrail.com).
Approximate rail times: *Karachi* to Lahore is 20 hours, to Rawalpindi is 28 hours and to Peshawar is 32 hours; and *Lahore* to Rawalpindi is five hours.

ROAD:
Traffic drives on the left. The highway network between cities is poorly maintained. Caution should be taken when driving at night as roads are badly lit. It is advised that tourists to Pakistan travel with local drivers or guides. When driving it is advised to keep doors and windows locked at all times. **Bus:** Regular services run between most towns and villages. Lahore–Rawalpindi–Peshawar has an hourly service. Air-conditioned coaches/buses are recommended for long distances. Advance booking is advised. **Car hire:** Available in major cities, as well as at Karachi, Lahore and Rawalpindi airports. Most hotels can book cars for guests.
Documentation: An International Driving Permit or own national licence is required.

URBAN:
Extensive **bus** and **minibus** services operate in Lahore, Karachi and other towns, although services can be crowded. **Taxi:** Reasonably priced and widely available, they are by far the most efficient means of urban travel. Note that they may not operate after sunset during Ramadan. **Auto-rickshaws** are also available.

Travel Advice

Travellers are advised against all travel to the Federally Administered Tribal Areas, including the Khyber Pass (except as part of an organised group); and to other border areas except for official crossing points. Travellers are advised against all but essential travel to the Swat Valley in the North West Frontier Province (NWFP), northern and western Baluchistan and Hub (near Karachi).
Travellers are advised against using the rail network and buses in Baluchistan. If travelling on the Karakoram Highway towards Gilgit and Hunza travellers are advised to join a police guarded convoy and only to travel in daylight.
There is a high threat from terrorism and sectarian violence throughout Pakistan. In 2005 there were a number of bombings in Karachi and Lahore, including at locations frequented by Westerners. On 2 March 2006, a bomb exploded outside the US Consulate in Karachi, killing several and injuring about 50 people. Travellers are advised against all travel to areas where there are ongoing reports of military or militant activity.
Travellers should avoid any large gatherings and demonstrations.
A large earthquake on 8 October 2005, with its epicentre near Muzaffarabad in Pakistani-administered Kashmir, caused severe damage and loss of life. Travellers are advised to consider carefully whether their presence in the region will help the ongoing relief effort. Aid workers in the affected areas should maintain contact with local UN co-ordination officials and Pakistani authorities for the latest security advice.
This advice is based on information provided by the Foreign and Commonwealth Office in the UK. It is correct at time of publishing. As the situation can change rapidly, visitors are advised to contact the following organisaions for the latest travel advice:

British Foreign and Commonwealth Office
Tel: (0845) 850 2829.
Website: www.fco.gov.uk

US Department of State
Website: http://travel.state.gov/travel

Accommodation

HOTELS:
Pakistan offers a wide range of accommodation. Modern well-equipped hotels can be found in most major towns and offer excellent facilities such as swimming pools and sports facilities. There are also cottages, Dak bungalows and rest houses in all principal hill stations and health resorts. A Government room tax of up to 17.5 per cent is added to the cost of accommodation. In all cases it is advisable to book well in advance and check reservations.

HOTELS & MOTELS:
The Pakistan Tourism Development Corporation (PTDC) manages one hotel, *Flashman's* at Rawalpindi, as well as well-furnished and moderately priced motels at Ayubia, Bahawalpur, Balakot, Bamburet, Barseen (Karakoram Highway), Besham, Chitral, Gilgit, Gupis, Hunza, Kalam, Khaplu, Malam Jabba Ski & Summer Resort, Moenjodaro, Naran, PanaKot (Dir), Saidu Sharif, Satpara, Skardu, Sost (Pakistan-China border), Taftan (Pakistan-Iran border), Taxila, Wagha (Pakistan-India border) and Ziarat.
PAKISTAN TOURS LTD (PVT): A subsidiary of PTDC, operating tours and providing ground handling facilities for domestic and foreign tourists throughout Pakistan.

YOUTH HOSTELS:
The Pakistan Youth Hostel Association has 14 hostels throughout the country, available to members of the affiliated International Youth Hostel Federation and young people.

A B C D E F G H I J K L M N O P Q R S T U V W X Y Z

A B C D E F G H I J K L M N O P Q R S T U V W X Y Z

ACCOMMODATION INFORMATION

Associated Hotels of Pakistan
Ground Floor, Sha Court, Mereweather Road, Civil Lines, PO Box 7448, Karachi, Pakistan
Tel: (21) 568 6407.

PTDC Motels (PVT) Reservation Office
Block B-4, Markaz F-7, Bhitai Road, Islamabad 44000, Pakistan
Tel: (51) 920 3223.
E-mail: tourism@comsats.net.pk

Pakistan Tours Ltd (PVT) Head Office
Room 14-15, Flashman's Hotel, The Mall, Rawalpindi, Pakistan
Tel: (51) 927 2017 *or* 2018 *or* 2005.

Pakistan Youth Hostel Association
Shaheed-e Millat Road, Aabpara, Sector G-6/4, Islamabad, Pakistan
Tel: (51) 282 6899.
E-mail: pyha@comsats.net.pk

Top Things To See & Do

- Visit **Karachi**, Pakistan's former capital and its largest city, situated on the shores of the Arabian Sea near the mouth of the Indus. The most magnificent building is the **Quaid-e-Azam's Mazar**, the mausoleum of the founder of Pakistan, made entirely of white marble with impressive north African arches and magnificent Chinese crystal chandeliers. The changing of the guard, which takes place three times a day, is the best time to visit. Other places to visit are the **National Museum**, parks, the zoo and a beach at **Clifton**.
- Tour the **Sindh** region, known for the remarkable quality of its light. The two main places of interest are **Mohenjodaro**, a settlement dating back 5000 years, and **Thatta**, notable for its mausoleums and mosques. There are sporting facilities on **Lake Haleji**.
- Explore **Islamabad**, the capital of Pakistan since 1963, and **Rawalpindi**, both located on the Pothowar Plain. The old part of Rawalpindi boasts fine examples of local architecture and bazaars crammed into the narrow streets where craftspeople still use traditional methods. Islamabad has an air of spaciousness, with parks, gardens and fountains below the silhouette of the **Margalla Hills**. In the midst of these lies **Daman-e-Koh**, a terraced garden with an excellent view over the city. Also in Islamabad is the **Shah Faisal Masjid** (mosque) which can accommodate 10,000 worshippers. The majestic white building comprises four 88m (288ft) minarets and a desert tent-like structure, which is the main prayer chamber.
- Take a day trip. About 8km (5 miles) from the capital is **Rawal Lake** with an abundance of leisure facilities for watersports and a picnic area.
- Discover **The Punjab**. **Lahore** is an historic, bustling city with buildings of pink and white marble. There is plenty to see: bazaars, the **Badshahi Mosque** (one of the largest mosques in the world, and an example of Moghul architecture rivalled only by the Taj Mahal), the beautiful **Shalimar Gardens**, the **National Museum of Archaeology** and the **Gate of Chauburji**. Near **Taxila** are two interesting excavated sites, **Jaulian** and **Sirkap**, dating back to the Buddhist Gandhara period.
- See some of the highest mountains in the world in **Kashmir**, including the famous **Nanga Parbat** and the second-highest mountain in the world, **K2**. The **Baltoro Glacier** and the **Batura Glacier** are the largest outside the polar regions.
- Follow the **Karakoram Highway**. In the 1960s and 70s, the Pakistan and Chinese authorities jointly built an asphalt road between Rawalpindi and Islamabad (Pakistan) and Kashgar (Xinjiang province in China). This unique highway follows the ancient silk road (see China section) over a breathtaking knot of mountain ranges that incorporates the **Himalaya mountains**, **Hindukush**, **Karakorum**, **Kunlun** and **Pamir**. The trail runs along the **Indus River** and to the beautiful **Gilgit** and **Hunza** valleys. Today the highway is popular with tourists wishing to cycle or trek its length and it is still used by *hajis* (Muslims making a pilgrimage to Mecca). The main attractions of the route are undoubtedly its challenging geography, unusual yet spectacular scenery and hospitable local ethnic groups. The best time to travel here is between September and October, and due to its demanding altitude and difficult terrain, it should be undertaken with an organised tour group or travel agent.
- Visit **Peshawar**, the capital of the North West Frontier Province. The city is surrounded by high walls with 20 entry gates. This is the area of the Pashtuns, or Pathans as they are also known. The lawns and parks reflect the former colonial days. Much of the surrounding area is still under the jurisdiction of tribal law. These areas can only be visited with a permit from the relevant authorities. Many of the tribesmen carry firearms, the normal adornment for a Pathan warrior. In the land of the Afridis is the **Khyber Pass**, the 1067m- (3501ft-) high break in the sheer rock wall separating Afghanistan and Pakistan.
- Head north of Peshawar to the wild and beautiful area of **Chitral** in the Hindu Kush Mountains, inhabited by the Kalash people, last of the non-Islamic tribes of Kafiristan. This valley is noted for its hot springs and trout-filled rivers. East of Chitral is the beautiful **Swat Valley**. This is an area of wild mountains and fantastic alpine scenery. It was, in ancient times, the home of the famous Gandhara school of sculpture, a manifestation of Greek-influenced Buddhist forms. The ruins of great Buddhist *stupas*, monasteries and statues are found all over Swat. It is now the home to the Swat Pathans and also boasts popular mountain retreats such as **Behrain**, **Kalam**, **Miandam** and **Mingora**, with **Saidu Sharif** its principal town.
- **Trekking and mountaineering:** Pakistan contains five of the world's highest peaks and several of the world's largest glaciers. The northern areas are the most popular for trekking, with **Gilgit** and **Skardu** being good starting points for trips. The Karakorum Highway is also a popular hiking route. Contact the Pakistan Tourism Development Corporation (see *Tourist Information*) for details on 'open' and 'restricted' zones, permits and regulations.
- Watch a **cricket** or **polo** match. Polo is particularly popular in the northern towns of Gilgit and Chitral.
- **Ski** at the **Malam Jabba** resort in the Karakoram range.
- Go **whitewater rafting** or **canoeing**. Both are increasingly popular on the rivers of the north of the country

TOURIST INFORMATION

Pakistan Tourism Development Corporation (PTDC)
Information Service, P.O. Box 1465, Agha Khan Road, Markaz F-6 (Supermarket), Islamabad 44000, Pakistan
Tel: (51) 921 2760 *or* 920 2766
Website: www.tourism.gov.pk

Entertainment

FOOD & DRINK: Pakistani cuisine is based on curry or *masala* (hot and spicy) sauces accompanying chicken, lamb, shrimps and a wide choice of vegetables.

National specialities:
- *Biryani* (seasoned rice with mutton, chicken and yoghurt).
- *Sag gosht* (spinach and lamb curry).
- *Shish kebabs* (charcoal-grilled meat on skewers).
- *Shami-kebabs* (patties of chopped meat fried in ghee or butter).
- *Halwa* (sweetmeat made with eggs, carrots, maize cream, *sooji* and nuts).
- *Firni* (similar to vanilla custard).

National drinks:
- Tea (drunk strong with milk and often very sweet).

Things to know: Alcohol may be bought at major hotels by visitors who have been issued a Liquor Permit from the Excise and Taxation Office. Wine is expensive and only available in upscale restaurants. Pakistani-brewed beer is widely available, as are canned carbonated drinks. There are no bars since there are strict laws concerning alcohol, and it is illegal to drink in public. Waiter service is provided in the larger hotels and restaurants. Visitors should avoid drinking water from the tap; bottled water is available everywhere, but it is necessary to make sure it comes in properly sealed plastic bottles.
Tipping: Most high-class hotels and restaurants add a 10 per cent service charge. Other tipping is discretionary.
NIGHTLIFE: Top hotels have bars and dancing but there is little Western-style nightlife. Cinemas in the large cities show international as well as Pakistani films. There are plenty of cultural events featuring traditional music and dance organised by the Pakistani Arts Academy throughout the year. Festivals and annual celebrations are colourful and lively.
SHOPPING: Special purchases include carved wooden tabled, trays, screens, silver trinkets, pottery, camel-skin lamps, bamboo decorations, woodwork, brassware, cane items, conch shell ornaments, glass bangles, gold ornaments, hand-embroidered shawls, rugs and carpets, silk, cashmere shawls and *saleem shahi* shoes with upturned toes. While some of the major towns have craft centres where handicrafts from different regions are sold, bazaars often provide the most interesting shopping. It is expected that the customer should bargain for goods. **Shopping hours:** Sat-Thurs 0930-1300 and 1500-1830. Bazaars stay open longer.

Business

- **GDP:** US$59.8 billion.
- **Main imports:** Petroleum and petroleum products, machinery, plastics, transport equipment, edible oils, paper and paperboard, iron, steel and tea.
- **Main exports:** Textiles, rice, leather goods, sports goods, chemicals, manufactures and carpets and rugs.
- **Main trade partners:** China, Germany, Hong Kong (SAR), Japan, Kuwait, Saudi Arabia, UK, United Arab Emirates and USA.

ECONOMY: About half of the Pakistani labour force works in agriculture and about 28 per cent of the land is under cultivation and watered by one of the largest irrigation systems in the world. Wheat, rice, sugar cane and cotton are the main products. Cotton is by far the country's most important export, accounting for almost 60 per cent of revenues. Textiles and leather goods are significant export earners. Pakistan has some reserves of graphite and limestone, as well as gypsum, silica, coal, copper and manganese. It also has a small oil industry, but most of its needs must be imported: together with chemicals and machinery, this accounts for nearly three-quarters of Pakistan's import expenditure. Established manufacturing industries include textiles, food processing and building materials.
The overriding economic problem for the Pakistani economy is its huge foreign debt burden, which is over 90 per cent of GDP and consumes over half of Government revenue to meet interest payments. The situation has been made more difficult by the history of poor relations between Pakistan and the international financial community generally. Sanctions were imposed following Pakistani nuclear tests in 1998, coinciding with the fall-out from the 1997 financial crisis that engulfed the major economies of East Asia. Yet despite these factors, the regional crisis centred on Afghanistan and Iraq, and domestic political instability, the Pakistani economy has performed steadily in the last five years. Both annual economic growth and inflation have been in low single figures for the last few years: the 2004 figures were 5.5 and 5.9 per cent, respectively; unemployment was at a record 7.7 per cent, with a high level of underemployment amongst the workforce. In the first half of 2005 inflation was a concern, rising above the lows of the previous year. In general, economic policy has been determined by the need to comply with conditions laid down by the IMF. An economic reform programme has gradually been implemented, with several major privatisations in recent years.
BUSINESS ETIQUETTE: Ties should be worn for important business appointments. English is commonly used. Appointments should be made, remembering that businesses are usually closed on Muslim holidays. Visiting cards should be used. **Office hours:** Mon-Thurs and Sat 0900-1700, Fri 0900-1230.

COMMERCIAL INFORMATION

Overseas Investors' Chamber of Commerce and Industry
PO Box 4833, Talpur Road, Karachi 74000, Pakistan
Tel: (21) 241 0814.
Website: www.oicci.org

Federation of Pakistan Chambers of Commerce (FPCCI)
PO Box 13875, Federation House, Sharea Firdousi, Main Clifton, Karachi 75600, Pakistan
Tel: (21) 587 3691/93-4.
Website: www.fpcci.com.pk

Panama

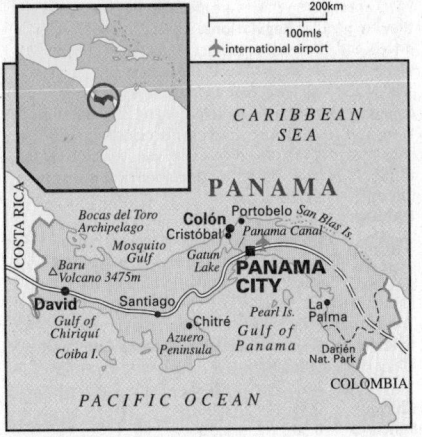

Location: Central America.

Time: GMT - 5.

Overview

Under Spanish rule from 1501, Panama was a pivotal trade route and collection point for commerce from the New World. This abundance of transient wealth also attracted many foreign pirates and buccaneers, such as Henry Morgan and Sir Francis Drake. Panama achieved independence in 1821, as a region of Gran Colombia. However, when Gran Colombia collapsed in 1830, Panama became part of modern Colombia. Unhappy with this, the Panamanians found an ally in the United States, which had strategic interests in the region – specifically, in the construction of an Atlantic-Pacific link, and the construction of the Panama Canal, embarked upon when Panama achieved full independence in 1903.

The Panama Canal Zone, completed in 1914, became an American Protectorate. Panama remained under effective American control until 1939. The country's domestic politics were reasonably stable until the 1968 military coup, led by General Omar Torrijos Herrera. He held effective power until his death by plane crash in 1981. Four years earlier, the Americans agreed to turn over the Canal to full Panamanian control at the turn of the century.

During most of the 1980s, the country was run by the Head of the Armed Forces, Manuel Noriega. The General's policies and his personal activities - including alleged involvement in drug trafficking - produced very strained relations with the USA. US intervention became more likely after the Panamanian Presidential election of May 1989. This was won by the principal opposition candidate, Guillermo Endara Galimany, but the election was annulled. After an attempted coup in October 1989 – believed to have had US backing – Endara was quickly crushed by Noriega's forces. The only means of getting rid of the troublesome dictator was military intervention. So, in December 1989, US President George Bush authorised an invasion. After a few days of fierce fighting, US forces secured control of the country and the capture of Noriega, who was later tried, convicted and sentenced to 40 years of imprisonment on US soil. Guillermo Endara was installed as the head of a new administration drawn from the ADOC coalition, which had won the May 1989 election. By 1999, the defining event in recent Panamanian history took place – the return of the Panama Canal Zone to Panama under the terms of the agreement negotiated by the Panamanians and the US Carter administration in 1980. Quite groundbreaking too was that the event was overseen by Panama's first female President, Elisa Moscoso Rodriguez, who won the race that

same year.

Panama is thus a curious but exhilarating combination of cultural influence. It lies at the centre of the world, its isthmus constituting the last part of a natural land-bridge between the North and South American continents. Its strategic position and glorious terrain – from jungle to beach - suggests that it will remain an important country for a long time yet.

General Information

AREA: 75,517 sq km (29,157 sq miles).

POPULATION: 3.2 million (UN, 2005).

POPULATION DENSITY: 42.3 per sq km.

CAPITAL: Panama City. **Population:** 827,828 (2005).

GEOGRAPHY: Panama forms the land link between the North and South American continents. Panama borders Colombia to the east, Costa Rica to the west, and the Caribbean and the Pacific Ocean to the north and south. The country forms an S-shaped isthmus which runs east–west over a total length of 772km (480 miles) and is 60 to 177km (37 to 110 miles) wide. The landscape is mountainous with lowlands on both coastlines cut by streams, wooded slopes and a wide area of savannah-covered plains and rolling hills called *El Interior* between the Azuero peninsula and the Central Mountains. The Caribbean and the Pacific Ocean are linked by the man-made Panama Canal, cut into a gap between the Cordillera de Talamanca and the San Blas mountain range and stretching for over 65km (40 miles); the length of the Canal is often referred to as 80km (50 miles) as this is the distance between deep-water points of entry. Only about a quarter of the country is inhabited. The majority of the population live either around the Canal and main cities of Panama City and Colón (the two cities which control the entrance and exit of the Canal) or in the Pacific lowlands and the adjacent mountains.

GOVERNMENT: Republic. Gained independence from Colombia in 1903. **Head of State and Government:** President Martin Torrijos since 2004. **Recent history:** At the Presidential election held in 1994, the victor was Ernesto Perez Balladares, backed by a three-party centre-left coalition under the banner of *Pueblo Unido.* Five years later, Panamanians reverted to the conservative bloc, which took control of the National Assembly, where a four-party coalition was in Government. Mireya Elisa Moscoso Rodriguez the leader of the largest party in the coalition, the *Partido Anulfista,* also won the Presidential race. Moscoso thus became Panama's first female President and presided over *the* defining event in recent Panamanian history – the return of the Panama Canal Zone to Panama under the terms of the agreement negotiated by the Panamanians and the US Carter administration in 1980. (The prospect of Noriega enjoying unrestricted control of the canal had been an important reason behind the US invasion.) Despite obvious US irritation at the unusual phenomenon of ceding territory to a foreign Government, the Americans pulled out on schedule in a low-key ceremony in December 1999. After this, the Moscoso Government was subjected to a string of violent street protests against Government corruption and mismanagement of the country's social security fund. And, May 2004, Martin Torrijos (son of the former military leader Omar Torrijos who had been instrumental in negotiating the 1977 treaty with the US to handover the Panama Canal) defeated ex-President Guillermo Endara in the Presidential elections. Torrijos took office in September that year and pledged to pursue a free trade agreement with the USA.

LANGUAGE: The official language is Spanish, but English is widely spoken.

RELIGION: Almost all Christian; 86 per cent Roman Catholic.

ELECTRICITY: 120 volts AC, 60Hz. Plugs are the flat two-pin American type.

SOCIAL CONVENTIONS: Handshaking is the normal form of greeting and dress is generally casual. The culture is a vibrant mixture of American and Spanish lifestyles. The Mestizo majority, which is largely rural, shares many of the characteristics of Mestizo culture found throughout Central America. Only three indigenous tribes have retained their individuality and traditional lifestyles as a result of withdrawing into virtually inaccessible areas.

Climate

Temperatures are high across the whole country throughout the year, though cooler at high altitudes. The rainy season lasts from May to November. Rainfall is twice as heavy on the Pacific coast as it is on the lowlands of the Caribbean coast.

Required clothing: Lightweight cottons and linens are worn, with rainwear advisable, particularly in the rainy season. Warmer clothes are needed in the highlands.

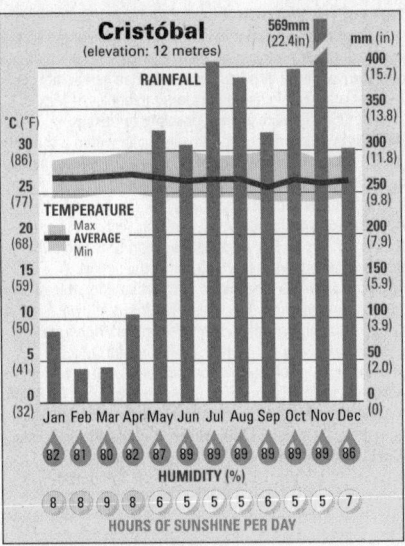

Communications

Telephone: IDD is available. Country code: 507. There are no area codes.

Mobile telephone: Roaming agreements exist with international mobile phone companies. Coverage is good.

Internet: Internet cafes exist in main urban areas.

Post: Airmail to Western Europe takes five to 10 days. Post office hours: Mon-Fri 0800-1600, Sat 0800-1300

MEDIA: Press: *Crítica Libre* (website: www.critica.com.pa), *La Estrella de Panamá* (website: www.estrelladepanama.com), *El Matutino, El Panamá América* (website: http://elpanamaamerica.terra.com.pa), *La Prensa* (website: www.prensa.com), *La República, El Siglo* (website: www.elsiglo.com) and *El Universal* (all in Spanish) are the largest daily newspapers.

TV: *RPC, Telemetro* and *Televisora Nacional (TVN)* are commercial networks. *FETV* is a charitable network.

Radio: *Metro Stereo, Omega Stereo, RPC* and *Super Q* are all commercial networks. *KW Continente* broadcasts come BBC programmes.

Passport/Visa

	Passport Required?	Visa Required?	Return Ticket Required?
Full British	Yes	1	Yes
Australian	Yes	2	Yes
Canadian	Yes	2	Yes
USA	Yes	2	Yes
Other EU	Yes	1/2	Yes
Japanese	Yes	2	Yes

Note: Regulations and requirements may be subject to change at short notice, and you are advised to contact your doctor well in advance of your intended date of departure. Any numbers in the chart refer to the footnotes below.

Note: (a) No brief account of the complex Panamanian visa regulations is likely to be fully successful as passport and visa regulations are liable to change at short notice. (b) Panamanian immigration procedures are rigidly enforced and non-compliance with the regulations may result in transportation at carrier's expense to country of origin. (c) Many nationals requiring visas also require authorisation from the Immigration Authorities in Panama before entry.

PASSPORTS: Passport valid for a minimum of six months required by all.

VISAS: Required by all except the following for stays of up to 90 days (at the discretion of the Immigration Authorities): (a) **1.** nationals of the EU and the UK (except for UK passports issued in Hong Kong (SAR) to those who were born in Hong Kong);

(b) nationals of Andorra, Argentina, Brazil, Bolivia, Chile, Colombia, Costa Rica, El Salvador, Guatemala, Honduras, Iceland, Israel, Liechtenstein, Monaco, Norway, Korea (Rep), Korea (Dem Rep), Nicaragua, Paraguay, San Marino, Singapore, Switzerland, Uruguay and the Vatican City.

Tourist cards: A Tourist Card will be issued in lieu of a visa to the following for stays of up to 30 days (extendable to 90 days at the discretion of the Immigration Authorities): **2.** nationals of Antigua & Barbuda, Aruba, Australia, The Bahamas, Barbados, Belize, Bermuda, Canada, Curacao, Dominica, Grenada, Guyana, Jamaica, Japan, Mexico, New Zealand, St Kitts & Nevis, St Lucia, St Vincent & the Grenadines, Thailand, Taiwan (China), Trinidad & Tobago, USA and Venezuela.

Types of visa and cost: *Tourist:* £30. *Tourist Card:* Prices vary, depending on nationality and also on where the Tourist Card is obtained from (eg prior to departure, on the flight or upon arrival at the airport). Some nationals can obtain the Tourist Card free of charge (including nationals of Mexico and the USA). Enquire at the Consulate for details.

Validity: Visas and Tourist Cards are valid within a three-month period from the date of issue and allow stays for up to 30 days (extendable to 90 days at discretion of Immigration Authorities).

Application to: Consulate (or Consular section at Embassy); see *Top Things To Do*. A Tourist Card can be issued either by the travel agent *or* on the flight *or* at the airport.

Application requirements: (a) Passport valid for at least six months. (b) Two completed application forms. (c) Two passport-size photos. (d) Booking reservation. *For countries requiring special authorisation:* (a)-(c) and, (d) Copies of passport. (e) Copy of return or onward ticket. (f) Letter from the person in Panama taking responsibility for applicant. (g) Proof of financial stability in cash, traveller's cheques or bank statements (at least US$500). (h) Fee, plus postage if necessary.

Working days required: Normally 24 hours if no authorisation is needed; up to 40 days if authorisation (which depends on nationality) is needed.

PASSPORT/VISA INFORMATION

Embassy of the Republic of Panamá in the UK
Panama House, 40 Hertford Street,
London W1J 7SH, UK
Tel: (020) 7493 4646.
Opening hours: Mon-Fri 1000-1700.
Consular Section: Tel: (020) 7409 2255.
Website: www.panaconsul.com
Opening hours: Mon-Fri 0930-1730.
Can also deal with tourism enquiries.

Embassy of the Republic of Panamá in the USA
2862 McGill Terrace, NW,
Washington, DC 20008, USA
Tel: (202) 483 1407.
Website: www.embassyofpanama.org

Money

Currency: Balboa (PAB) = 100 centavos. There is no Panamanian paper currency; coins exist in denominations of PAB10 and 1, and 50, 25, 10, 5 and 1 centavos. US currency was adopted in 1904 and exists alongside the Balboa coinage: PAB1 = US$1.

Currency exchange: Banks and *cambios* are available for changing currency. There is no need to exchange US Dollars.

Credit cards: MasterCard and Visa are the most commonly used, but American Express and Diners Club are also accepted. Check with your credit or debit card company for details of merchant acceptability and other services which may be available.

Traveller's cheques: To avoid additional exchange rate charges, visitors are advised to take traveller's cheques in US Dollars.

Currency restrictions: There are no restrictions on the import and export of either foreign or local currency. However, amounts of over US$10,000 must be declared to immigration upon arrival.

Banking hours: Mon-Fri 0800-1500, Sat 0830-1200.

Exchange rate indicators:
Rate at time of publishing
£1.00= PAB1.85

Duty Free

The following items may be imported into Panama without incurring customs duty:
500 cigarettes or 50 cigars or 500g tobacco; three bottles of alcoholic beverage; perfume and eau de cologne in opened bottles for personal use; gifts up to the value of PAB50.

Prohibited items: Fruit, vegetable and meat animal products including shrimp larvas, post larvas and normal shrimp.

Public Holidays

Below are listed Public Holidays for the January 2006-June 2007 period.
2006: Jan 1 New Year's Day. **Jan 9** National Martyrs' Day. **Feb 28** Carnival Tuesday. **Apr 14** Good Friday. **May 1** Labour Day. **Aug 15** Old Panama City Day (Panama City only). **Nov 3** Independence Day (from Colombia). **Nov 5** Independence Day (Colón City only). **Nov 10** First Call for Independence from Spain. **Nov 27** Independence Day (from Spain). **Dec 25** Christmas Day.
2007: Jan 1 New Year's Day. **Jan 8** National Martyrs' Day. **Feb 20** Carnival Tuesday. **Apr 6** Good Friday. **May 1** Labour Day.
Note: For public holidays falling on a Sunday, the following Monday will be observed as a holiday.

Health

	Special Precautions?	Certificate Required?
Yellow Fever	1	No
Cholera	2	No
Typhoid & Polio	3	N/A
Malaria	4	N/A

Note: *Regulations and requirements may be subject to change at short notice, and you are advised to contact your doctor well in advance of your intended date of departure. Any numbers in the chart refer to the footnotes below.*

1: Yellow fever vaccination is recommended for those over nine months travelling to Darién and Kunayala (San Blas), excluding the canal zone. Travellers arriving from non-endemic zones should note that vaccination is strongly recommended for travel outside the urban areas, even if an outbreak of the disease has not been reported and they would normally not require a vaccination certificate to enter the country.

2: Following WHO guidelines issued in 1973, a cholera vaccination certificate is not a condition of entry to Panama. However, cholera may be a slight risk in this country and precautions are essential. Up-to-date advice should be sought before deciding whether these precautions should include vaccination, as medical opinion is divided over its effectiveness; see the *Health* appendix.

3: Typhoid fevers are common, but polio is not present.

4: There is a low malaria risk, predominantly of the *plasmodium vivax* form in three provinces throughout the year: Bocas de Toro, Darién and San Blas. There is no risk in Panama City or in the former canal zone.

Food & drink: Mains water is normally chlorinated and safe. Bottled water is available. Drinking water outside main cities and towns may be contaminated and sterilisation is advised. Milk is pasteurised and dairy products are safe for consumption. Local meat, poultry, seafood, fruit and vegetables are generally considered safe to eat.

Other risks: *Hepatitis A, B* and *E* occur. *Dengue fever*, *filariasis, leishmaniasis, onchocerciasis* and *American trypanosomiasis* (chagas disease) may occur. *Myiasis* (botfly) is endemic in Central America.
Rabies is present. For those at high risk, vaccination before arrival should be considered. If you are bitten, seek medical advice without delay. For more information, see the *Health* appendix.

Health care: Modern and reliable private medical services are available. According to current legislation covering sanitary matters, Panama offers healthcare facilities to all nationals and foreign travellers who may require them, independent of any reciprocal agreement with a particular country. International travellers are, however, advised to take out medical insurance.

Travel - International

AIR:

The national airline is *Compañia Panameña de Aviación (COPA - CM)* (website: www.copaair.com).

Approximate flight times: From Panama City to *London* is 14 hours and to *Miami* is two hours 45 minutes.

Main airports: *Panamá City (PTY)* (Tocumén) is 27km (17 miles) northeast of the city (travel time – 30 to 60 minutes). *To/from the airport:* Buses and taxis go to the city. *Facilities:* Bank, car hire, chemist, restaurant and full duty free.

Departure tax: PAB20. Children under two years of age and passengers in transit to another country not leaving the airport and remaining for under nine hours are exempt.

SEA:

Main port: *Panama (Balboa),* a port of call for both passenger and freight vessels. The Panama Canal is the major route from the Atlantic to the Pacific Ocean.

RAIL:

There is currently no rail link betwen Panama and other international destinations.

ROAD:

The principal route to Panama is the Pan-American Highway from Costa Rica to Yaviza in Darién Province. Visitors are strongly advised not to use the route to Colombia via Darién Gap for personal safety reasons.

Travel - Internal

AIR:

Smaller airports for internal flights are: *Aeropuerto Marcos A Gelabert* in Albrook and *Enrique Malek* in David, Chiriquí. Internal air services operated by *Aeroperlas, Aerotaxi, Ansa, Aviatur* and *AeroMapiex* include flights from Panama City to all centres in the interior of the country.

RAIL:

The *Ferrocarril de Panamá* currently only operates freight trains and is in the process of selling the national rail service. The *Panamá Canal Railway Company (PCRC)* (website: www.panarail.com) runs a scenic 47-mile passenger route from Panama City to Colón as well as cargo services. Further information can be obtained from the Instituto Panameño de Turismo (see *Top Things To See & Do*).

ROAD:

There is a reasonably good road system throughout Panama. The Trans-Isthman Highway links Panama City and Colón. The *Corredor Norte* toll road has reduced the travel time to Colón by 30 minutes. **Bus:** Traffic drives on the right. There are services between most large towns, but they can be very slow. **Taxi:** Not metered, and fares, though varying considerably, are generally very low. Fares should be agreed in advance. Taxi drivers do not expect tips. **Car hire:** Available in city centres and airport; you must be at least 23 years old to hire a car. Four-wheel drive vehicles are available, but plan ahead as they are popular. **Regulations:** Seatbelts must be worn by drivers and front seat passengers at all times. Children under five years must travel in the back in a fitted child seat. Motor insurance, even third party, is not a legal requirement in Panama; therefore, many Panamanians drive without it. If you are involved in an accident, the law stipulates that you should wait with your vehicle until the traffic police (*transito*) arrive. **Documentation:** A national driving licence is sufficient.

URBAN:

Extensive bus and minibus services run in Panama City. There is a flat fare with coin-operated turnstiles at the entrances of most buses. A single journey will cost about 15 cents per passenger.

Travel times: The following chart gives approximate travel times (in hours and minutes) from **Panama City** to other major cities in Panama.

	Air	Road
Chiriquí	0.45	6.00
Santiago	0.30	3.00
Chitre	0.30	3.10

Travel Advice

Travel to the Darién Province should be conducted only with an organised group, and to recognised tourist destinations protected by the Panamanian police.

There were sporadic demonstrations in Panama City about various social and political issues in 2005. Visitors should avoid all demonstrations and monitor local radio and TV for up-to-date information.

Travellers should be aware of the global risk of indiscriminate terrorist attacks, which could be against civilian targets, including places frequented by foreigners. This advice is based on information provided by the Foreign and Commonwealth Office in the UK. It is correct at time of publishing. As the situation can change rapidly, visitors are advised to contact the following organisations for the latest travel advice:

British Foreign and Commonwealth Office
Tel: (0845) 850 2829.
Website: www.fco.gov.uk

US Department of State
Website: http://travel.state.gov/travel

Accommodation

HOTELS:

Panama has embarked on an extensive hotel expansion programme, not only in Panama City, but also in the countryside and in mountain and seaside areas. Accommodation ranges from international standard to inexpensive country inns, very simple hotels and new resort-style hotels. There is a 10 per cent Government tax added to hotel bills. For further information, contact Instituto Panameño de Turismo (see *Top Things To See & Do*).

CAMPING:

There are a couple of camping resorts in Panama. It is possible to camp on some beaches, and also in the mountainous areas of Boquete and Volván.

YOUTH HOSTELS:

For those travelling on a budget, there are many youth hostels in Panama, including several in Panama City and other main tourist areas. They often come equipped with a kitchen and a living room with cable television. Some even have a swimming pool.

Top Things To See & Do

• Make the most of Panama's excellent **shopping**. Its position as a crossing point between the Atlantic and the Pacific has naturally made it a major commercial route. **Panama City's Central Avenue, Colón's Front Street** and the newer

Panama

shopping sectors around the hotels, and **Tocumen**'s duty free stores have grown because of this trade.

- Attend one of the many **fiestas** in Panama's various cities - in particular, the one at **Panama City** during the **Carnival** is superb. This is held on the four days before Ash Wednesday. Others are held to celebrate local patron saints. **Las Balserías**, a Ngöbé-Bugle Indian celebration held in the **Chiriquí Province** every February, includes feasts and a contest in which the young men toss balsa logs at one another; those who emerge unscathed may choose their partners.
- **Panama City**, the capital, is a curious blend of old Spain, modern America and the bazaar atmosphere of the East. Most of the interesting sights are to be found in the old part of the city with its narrow, cobble-stoned streets and colonial buildings. These include the **Plaza de Francia**, the **Court of Justice Building**, the **Paseo de las Bóvedas** along the massive stone wall, **San José Church**, with its magnificent golden Baroque altar, and the **Santo Domingo Church**, next to which is the **Museum of Colonial Religious Art**. The old historic city with the **Salón Bolivar** is listed by UNESCO as a World Heritage Site. Overlooking the bay is the **President's Palace**, the most impressive building in the city; further along the waterfront is the colourful public market. The most interesting museum in town is the **Museum of the Panamanian Man** north of the market and near the shopping centres. A worthwhile excursion from the city is a visit to **Panama Viejo** and its ruins including the square tower of the old cathedral, 6km (4 miles) away. This is the original Panama City which – like Fort San Lorenzo – was sacked and looted in 1671 by Henry Morgan, the celebrated Welsh buccaneer who helped to undermine Spanish control of their colonies.

Credit: © IPAT

- **Birdwatching** enthusiasts will not be disappointed in Panama: there are about 950 registered species and the country is considered one of the world's best birdwatching spots. Recommended birdwatching sites include the easily accessible strip of rainforest within **Soberanía National Park** (40km (25 miles) north of Panama City), and the **Baru National Park** in the Chiriquí Province, famous for its many Quetzal birds.
- Take a **boat trip** along the **Panama Canal**, to the west of Panama City, 80km (50 miles) long and Panama's main tourist attraction. The scenery is beautiful, and the mechanics of the Canal equally fascinating. There are various types of tours available. Crocodiles, frigate birds and other animals living along the banks and in the surrounding jungle can be observed. Canal tours often aim to provide visitors with a chance to observe one of the many large vessels moving through the canal locks, usually the Miraflores and Pedro Miguel locks. Executive **yacht tours** are available. Also recommended are **bus** or **train rides** alongside the Canal. There is an interesting **Panama Canal Museum** in the **Casco Viejo area**. The Canal was opened in 1914, and an average transit takes eight hours to complete. On 31 December 1999, Panama took over full control of the canal from the USA. Some 50km (30 miles) northwest of the capital lies **Barro Colorado**, the largest island in **Gatun Lake**, a humanmade stretch of water created during the construction of the Panama Canal (and one of the world's largest artificial lakes). The island is a biological reserve managed by the Smithsonian Tropical Research Institute and reputed to be one of the world's leading natural tropical laboratories. Day trips to the island from Panama City take visitors to the small town of **Gamboa** from where special tours (either on foot or by boat) can be arranged.
- Breathe in the sea air of the island of **Taboga**, where fine **beaches** and quality hotels abound. The main method of transport is by water taxi, known locally as *panga*. A longer trip by launch is necessary to get to the **Pearl Islands**, which are visited mainly by sea-anglers. In the **Bocas del Toro Province**, in the Panama Caribbean, an archipelago (of the same name) consists of seven large islands and hundreds of smaller ones. Many of the islands lie in the **Laguna de Chiriqui**, which is particularly popular with **diving** enthusiasts. There are some excellent locations for diving and **snorkelling** in Panama, the best of which include **Isla Grande** near **Portobelo**, where there are a number of dive centres offering excursions to the best reefs; the **Bocas del Toro archipelago**; and the **San Blás Islands** (off the northeast coast). Good sites for **surfing** include **Santa Catalina**, **Venado** and **Rio Mar** in the Pacific and Isla Grande, **Bluf** and **Careneros** in the Atlantic; waves can reach 15ft (4.5 metres). In the **Azuero Peninsula** are charming small colonial towns, quiet villages and near-empty beaches awaiting visitors who do not expect to find big hotels.
- Marvel at the **Chiriquí Province**'s scenery, characterised by volcanic highlands, with many waterfalls, rivers and spectacular mountain scenery, known for its cattle and thoroughbred horses, as well as banana and coffee plantations. The province also contains the dormant **Baru Volcano** (3,475m/11,400 ft), located near the popular resort town of **Boquete** and the mountain resort, **Cerro Punta**. Why not go **horse riding** right up to the Baru Volcano?
- Notice Panama's Spanish legacy, particularly prevalent in **Portobelo**, a Spanish garrison town for two centuries, with three large **stone forts** facing the entrance to the harbour. Also in the town are an **old Spanish cannon**, and the **treasure house** where gold and silver from Perú and Bolivia were stored before being shipped to Spain. Along the Caribbean coast, between Portobelo and **San Lorenzo**, are numerous notable 17th- and 18th-century **military fortifications**.
- Embark on a **tree canopy adventure** in the **El Níspero Botanical Gardens**, where participants are fastened into a harness, pulled up to the treetops and swung from one platform to another in order to enjoy particularly 'green' views. If you fancy green views from groundlevel, Panama is full of ecotouristic opportunities. The **Gamboa Tropical Rainforest Reserve** and the **Soberanía National Park** offer good opportunities for learning about tropical **fauna and flora**. The **Antón Valley** (**El Valle de Antón**), 120km (70 miles) west of Panama City, is famous for its orchids and trips to the famous Smithsonian Tropical Research Institute on **Barro Colorado Island** (which houses a renowned tropical research laboratory) are also possible, although appointments need to be made at least one month in advance. **Darién Gap** is a sparsely populated wilderness area linking central and southern America and also the only break in the Pan-American Highway (which runs from Alaska to Argentina). Much of this region lies within the **Darién National Park**, which contains an exceptional variety of habitats, ranging from sandy beaches, rocky coasts, mangroves and swamps to tropical rainforest. The park is also home to two Choco Indian tribes.

TOURIST INFORMATION

Instituto Panameño de Turismo (IPAT) (Institute of Tourism)
Apartado 4421, Zone 5,
Centro de Convenciones ATLAPA,
Vía Israel, Republic of Panamá
Tel: 226 7000 *or* 3544.
Website: www.ipat.gob.pa *or* www.visitpanama.com

Entertainment

FOOD & DRINK: American, French and Spanish food is available in all restaurants and hotels in Panama City and Colón. There is a huge selection of excellent restaurants in Panama City, as well as other main cities. There are also several Oriental restaurants. Native cooking is reminiscent of creole cuisine, hot and spicy. Seafood is excellent and in abundance. The choice and availability of wines, spirits and beers in hotels, restaurants and bars is unlimited.
Things to know: Waiter service is the norm.
National specialities:

- *Ceviche* (fish marinated in lime juice, onions and peppers).
- *Patacones de plátano* (fried plantain).
- *Sancocho* (Panamanian stew with chicken, meat and vegetables).
- *Tamales* (seasoned pie wrapped in banana leaves).
- *Empanadas* (turnovers filled with meat, chicken or cheese).

Tipping: 10 to 15 per cent is customary in hotels (where it is added automatically) and restaurants.
NIGHTLIFE: Panama City, in particular, has a wide range of nightlife from nightclubs and casinos to folk, ballet, belly dancing and classical theatre. Dancing and entertainment are available in all the big hotels, as well as many clubs. Other large towns and resorts have music, dancing, casinos and cinemas. Further details can be found in local papers.
SHOPPING: Panama is a duty free haven and luxury goods from all over the world can be bought at a saving of at least one-third. Local items include leatherware, patterned, beaded necklaces made by Guaymí Indians, native costumes, jewels and precious stones, straw products, electrical equipment, handicrafts of carved wood, ceramics, *papier mâché* artefacts, macramé and mahogany bowls. **Shopping hours:** Mon-Sat 0900-2000. Some supermarkets are open 24-hours.

Business

- **GDP:** US$13.83 billion.
- **Main imports:** Capital goods, crude oil, foodstuffs, chemicals, other consumer and intermediate goods.
- **Main exports:** Bananas, petroleum products, shrimp, sugar, coffee and clothing.
- **Main trade partners:** Colombia, Costa Rica, Japan, Mexico, The Netherlands, the Netherlands Antilles, Spain, Sweden and USA.

ECONOMY: Panama has a relatively prosperous economy based on agriculture, light industry, revenues from the Panama Canal and the service sector. Over half the land area is given over to agriculture: the main cash crops are sugar cane, coffee and bananas, while the main food crops are rice, maize and beans. Commercial cattle-raising is also prominent. The country has significant reserves of timber, particularly mahogany, and good fishing stocks, shrimp being a major and valuable export earner. Local industries include food processing, clothing, paper and building materials. Panama also exports petroleum refined from imported crude oil. Further revenue is obtained from tolls levied on ships passing through the Panama Canal (which came under full Panamanian control in 2000) and from registration fees for a plethora of 'offshore' companies exploiting Panama's strict banking and commercial secrecy laws (although the Government has recently instituted measures to permit disclosure in suspected cases of money-laundering).
Other important sources of revenue include the Colón Free Trade Zone established near the Canal through which 30 per cent of all Panamanian trade passes, an 'open' shipping registry, and a rapidly growing tourist industry now worth more than US$500 million annually. A major reform programme undertaken during the 1990s saw the privatisation of many state enterprises, reform of the tax and social security systems, and the removal of price controls and import tariffs. Current annual GDP growth is 6 per cent and inflation is around 2 per cent; the official unemployment rate is 12.6 per cent. Panama is a member of the Inter-American Development Bank. About 50 per cent of two-way trade is with the USA and Japan.
BUSINESS ETIQUETTE: Punctuality is appreciated and the exchange of business cards is normal. Suits are necessary for business meetings. **Office hours:** Mon-Fri 0800-1700, Mon-Fri 0730-1630 (Government offices).
CONFERENCES/CONVENTIONS: *Atlapa Convention Centre* in Panama City is the largest convention facility in Central America which has a capacity of 3000 and includes lecture rooms, a theatre/auditorium and exhibition rooms. Other centres include *Figali Convention Centre* and *Vasco Nunez de Balboa Convention Centre*.

COMMERCIAL INFORMATION

Cámara de Comercio Industrias y Agricultura de Panamá (Chamber of Commerce)
Apartado 0816-07517, Avenida Cuba y Ecuador,
Calle 34, Edificio 33 A-18, Panamá 1, Panama
Tel: 227 1233.
Website: www.panacamara.com

Atlapa Convention Centre (Information on Conferences/Conventions)
Instituto Panameno de Turimo, Via Israel,
San Francisco, Panama City, Panama
Tel (507) 226 7000.
Website: www.ipat.gob.pa/atlapa

Figali Convention Centre (Information on Conferences/Conventions)
Tel: (507) 314 1414.
Website: www.panamacanalvillage.com/figalli

Vasco Nunez de Balboa Convention Centre (Information on Conferences/Conventions)
Tel: (507) 215 9286 *or* 269 2917.
Email: banquetes6@elpanama.com
Website: www.elpanama.com

A B C D E F G H I J K L M N O P Q R S T U V W X Y Z

Papua New Guinea

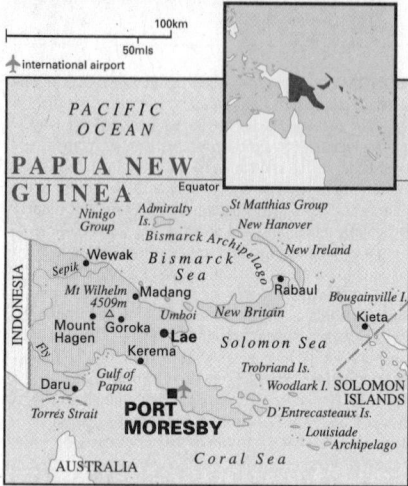

100km
50mls
✈ international airport

Location: South Pacific.

Time: GMT + 10.

Overview

Papua New Guinea consists of over 600 islands and lies in the middle of the long chain of islands stretching from mainland South East Asia. It is situated in the South Pacific, 160km (100 miles) north of Australia. A line of active volcanoes stretches along the north coast of the mainland and continues on the island of New Britain.

The tribal diversity of a country with over 700 languages cannot easily be summarised, although in Papua New Guinea it is the tribal life that is most fascinating to the visitor. Some of the excursions in Papua New Guinea are interestingly different from those offered elsewhere; for example, tourists can be taken to one of the many wrecks of World War II aircraft that lie in the jungle. *Haus Tambarans* ('Spirit Houses') are a feature of many towns and villages in the country, especially in the area of the Sepik River, so only a few of them can be given specific mention. Only initiated men of a tribe can enter (though in places this rule is relaxed for foreigners). They are built in a variety of styles, with massive carved wooden supports being a major feature. Other carvings and masks inside represent spirits. The orator's stools in these places are not used for sitting on; bunches of leaves are slapped down on the stools as the orator makes his points.

General Information

AREA: 462,840 sq km (178,704 sq miles).
POPULATION: 5.6 million (2002).
POPULATION DENSITY: 12.1 per sq km.
CAPITAL: Port Moresby. **Population:** 254,158 (2000).
GEOGRAPHY: Papua New Guinea occupies the eastern half of the second-largest non-continental island in the world, as well as the smaller islands of the Bismarck Archipelago (Admiralty Island, Bougainville, New Britain and New Ireland), the D'Entrecasteaux Island group and the three islands of the Louisiade Archipelago. The main island shares a land border with Irian Jaya, a province of Indonesia. The mainland and larger islands are mountainous and rugged, divided by large fertile upland valleys. Fast-flowing rivers from the highlands descend to the coastal plains. To the north and south of the central mountain range on the main island lie vast stretches of mangrove swamps and coastal river deltas. Volcanoes and

thermal pools are also found in the southeast of other islands. Papua New Guinea offers the greatest variety of terrestrial ecosystems in the South Pacific, including five types of lowland rainforest, 13 types of montane rainforest, five varieties of palm and swamp forest and three different mangrove forests. Two-thirds of the world's species of orchids come from Papua New Guinea. Birds include 38 species of the bird-of-paradise, and the megapode and cassowary. Marsupials and mammals include cuscus, tree kangaroos, wallabies, bandicoots, spiny anteaters and, in the coastal waters, the dugong. There are between 170 and 200 species of frog and 450 species of butterfly.

GOVERNMENT: Constitutional monarchy. Gained independence from Australia in 1975. **Head of State:** HM Queen Elizabeth II, represented locally by Governor General Paulias Matane since 2004. **Head of Government:** Prime Minister Sir Michael Somare since 2002. **Recent history:** Papua's fortunes have improved little in the last few years, and the country seems indefinitely caught up in the spiral of inter-communal violence and economic decline which afflicts much of the south-west Pacific. At the end of 2003, the Australian Government, which is now asserting itself as a regional power, arranged for the despatch of 300 police and security officers to Papua: it was made clear to the Government in Port Moresby that continuing Australian financial aid was conditional of their accepting the security package.

Papua New Guinea has a unicameral Parliamentary system, with executive power nominally held by the British Crown, represented by a Governor General. Legislative power rests with the 109-member parliament. The local Government system underwent extensive reform in 1995, when the 19 directly elected provincial Governments were replaced by new regional authorities.

LANGUAGE: The official language is English, which is widely used in business and Government circles. Pidgin English and Hiri Motu are more commonly used (an estimated 742 other languages and dialects are also spoken).
RELIGION: 90 per cent Christian.
ELECTRICITY: 240 volts AC, 50Hz. Australian-style three-pin plugs are in use. Some hotels provide 110-volt outlets in guest-rooms.
SOCIAL CONVENTIONS: Papua New Guinea's culture still includes elements of a primitive lifestyle. There are universities at Lae (which is a University of Technology with a liberal infusion of Europeans and North Americans) and at Port Moresby. Casual clothes are recommended. Informality is the order of the day and although shorts are quite acceptable, beachwear is usually best confined to the beach. In the evenings some hotels expect men to wear long trousers but ties are rare. A long dress is appropriate for women on formal occasions.

Climate

Hot, tropical climate at sea level, cooling towards the highlands which also cause climatic variation from one area to another, affecting the southeast trade winds and the northwest monsoons. The majority of the rain falls between December and March due to the northwest monsoon, although Port Moresby enjoys a dry season at this time. There is frost and there are occasional snow falls on the highest mountain peaks.
Required clothing: Tropical, lightweights and cottons are recommended. In the highlands, warmer clothing is needed. Rainwear is advised for the monsoon season (December to March).

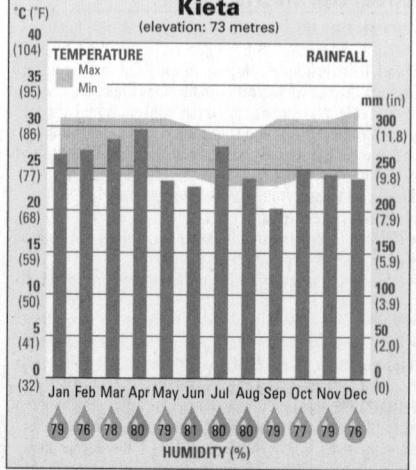

Kieta
(elevation: 73 metres)
TEMPERATURE
Max
Min
RAINFALL
HUMIDITY (%)

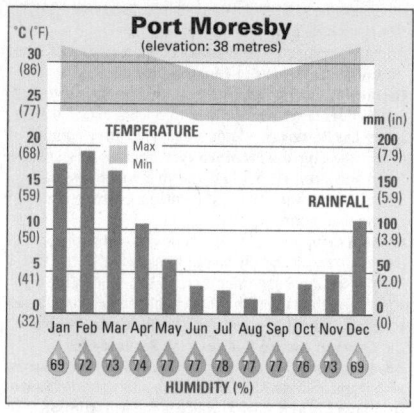

Port Moresby
(elevation: 38 metres)
TEMPERATURE
Max
Min
RAINFALL
HUMIDITY (%)

Communications

Telephone: IDD is available. Country code: 675. There are no area codes in Papua New Guinea.
Mobile telephone: The only network provider is *Pacific Mobile Communications* (website: www.pacificmobile.com.pg). Coverage is likely to be limited.
Internet: Services tend to be slow and sometimes unreliable.
Post: Airmail to Europe takes seven to 10 days. Post office hours: Mon-Fri 0800-1600, Sat 0900-1200.
MEDIA: Press: Two daily newspapers are published in English: *The National* and *Papua New Guinea Post-Courier*. The most popular daily is *Niugini Nius*.
TV: Commercial channel *EMTV* is the only broadcaster.
Radio: The *National Broadcasting Corporation* is a Government-run national station. *NAU FM* is private.

Passport/Visa

	Passport Required?	Visa Required?	Return Ticket Required?
Full British	Yes	Yes	Yes
Australian	Yes	Yes	Yes
Canadian	Yes	Yes	Yes
USA	Yes	Yes	Yes
Other EU	Yes	Yes	Yes
Japanese	Yes	Yes	Yes

Note: *Regulations and requirements may be subject to change at short notice, and you are advised to contact your doctor well in advance of your intended date of departure. Any numbers in the chart refer to the footnotes below.*

Note: On receipt of a stamped, self-addressed envelope, the High Commission can supply information sheets on how to apply for visas for Papua New Guinea. The information below should be considered as a guide, as visa requirements may be subject to change at short notice.
PASSPORTS: Passport valid for at least six months after entry required by all.
VISAS: Required by all.
Types of visa and cost: *Tourist:* £7. *Business* (multiple-entry): £175. Costs vary for special categories of visitors (including consultants, yachtsmen and those engaged in medical, research or expedition activities). There will also be charges for extensions and costs incurred in processing documents.
Validity: Up to 60 days for tourists; up to 12 months for business trips with 60 days maximum per stay. Details of renewals or extensions are available from the Embassy or High Commission.
Application to: Consulate (or Consular section at Embassy or High Commission); see *Passport/Visa Information*. In emergency cases, Tourist visas can be obtained at Jackson International Airport in Port Moresby or at Mount Hagen on arrival, but only for a maximum period of 60 days in any 12-month period, which cannot be extended. However, visitors are strongly advised to obtain visas in advance (which is also the cheaper option).
Application requirements: *Tourist:* (a) Completed application form (one per passport submitted). (b) Two passport-size photos. (c) Passport with minimum one year remaining validity from date of entry. (d) Return ticket. (e) Postal applications should be accompanied by a self-addressed, stamped, registered envelope. (f) Fee, payable by postal order or bank drafts if applying by post or in cash if applying in person. *Business:* (a)-(f) and; (g) Confirmed itinerary from travel agent. (h) Detailed letter in support of application covering curriculum vitae and confirmation of ongoing project in Papua New Guinea. (i) For visas issued at the airport, a letter of guarantee from sponsor must have been sent in advance to the Director of Immigration at the airport. Contact the nearest Papua New Guinea

representative office for further information.

Working days required: 48 hours minimum for Business and Tourist visas. Temporary residence visas take up to six weeks or more. It is advisable for visa applications to be made one week or more before departure date, depending on type of visa.

Temporary residence: Available for those entering for employment purposes, usually professional persons or those undertaking research, consultancy, etc. Applications should be made to the nearest High Commission or Embassy in the first instance.

PASSPORT/VISA INFORMATION

Papua New Guinea High Commission in the UK
14 Waterloo Place, London SW1Y 4AR, UK
Tel: (020) 7930 0922/7.
Opening hours: Mon-Fri 0900-1300 and 1400-1600.

Papua New Guinea Embassy in the USA
1779 Massachusetts Avenue, NW, Suite 805,
Washington, DC 20036, USA
Tel: (202) 745 3680.
Website: www.pngembassy.org

Money

Currency: Kina (PGK) = 100 toea. Notes are in denominations of PGK50, 20, 10, 5 and 2. Coins are in denominations of PGK1, and 50, 20, 10, 5, 2 and 1 toea.

Currency exchange: Exchange facilities are available through trade banks.

Credit cards: American Express is the most widely accepted credit card. Holders of this and other cards should check with their credit or debit card company for details of merchant acceptability and other services which may be available.

Traveller's cheques: Accepted by most shops and hotels. To avoid additional exchange rate charges, traveller's are advised to take traveller's cheques in US Dollars, Pounds Sterling or Australian Dollars.

Currency restrictions: There are no restrictions on the import of local or foreign currency. The export of local currency is restricted to PGK200 and of foreign currency to PGK10,000; if more, approval is required from the Bank of Papua New Guinea.

Banking hours: Mon-Thurs 0845-1500, Fri 0845-1600.

Exchange rate indicators:

Rate at time of publishing
£1.00=   PGK5.26
$1.00=   PGK3.03

Duty Free

The following may be imported into Papua New Guinea by persons over 18 years of age without incurring customs duty: *260 cigarettes or 250g of cigars or tobacco; 1l of alcoholic beverages; a reasonable quantity of perfume; new goods up to a value of PGK200 (PGK100 for persons under 18 years of age) excluding radios, tape recorders, television sets, video cameras, video tapes, record players and associated equipment.*

Prohibited items: Plants and soil, uncanned foods of animal origin (unless from Australia or New Zealand), and all pig meat from New Zealand.

Public Holidays

Below are listed Public Holidays for the January 2006-June 2007 period.
2006: Jan 1 New Year's Day. **Apr 14** Good Friday. **Apr 17** Easter Monday. **Jun 13** Queen's Birthday. **Jul 21** Remembrance Day. **Sep 16** Independence Day; Constitution Day. **Dec 25-26** Christmas.
2007: Jan 1 New Year's Day. **Apr 6** Good Friday. **Apr 9** Easter Monday. **Jun 13** Queen's Birthday.
Note: In addition, there are various regional festivals throughout the year.

Health

	Special Precautions?	Certificate Required?
Yellow Fever	No	1
Cholera	2	No
Typhoid & Polio	3	N/A
Malaria	4	N/A

Note: *Regulations and requirements may be subject to change at short notice, and you are advised to contact your doctor well in advance of your intended date of departure. Any numbers in the chart refer to the footnotes below.*

1: A yellow fever vaccination certificate is required for travellers over one year of age if arriving within six days of leaving/transiting infected areas.
2: Following WHO guidelines issued in 1973, a cholera vaccination certificate is not a condition of entry to Papua New Guinea. However, cholera is a risk in this country and precautions are advisable. Up-to-date advice should be sought before deciding whether these precautions should include vaccination, as medical opinion is divided over its effectiveness; see the *Health* appendix for further details.
3: Vaccination against typhoid is advised.
4: Malaria risk exists all year throughout the country below 1800m (5760ft). The predominant *falciparum* strain is reported to be highly resistant to chloroquine and resistant to sulfadoxine/pyrimethamine.

Food & drink: All water should be regarded as being potentially contaminated. Water used for drinking, brushing teeth or making ice should have first been boiled or otherwise sterilised. Milk is pasteurised and dairy products are safe for consumption. Only eat well-cooked meat and fish, preferably served hot. Pork, salad and mayonnaise may carry increased risk. Vegetables should be cooked and fruit peeled.

Other risks: *Hepatitis A* and *B* are endemic. *Dengue fever* and *typhoid fever* can occur in epidemics. *Japanese encephalitis* occurs sporadically. Poisonous fish and sea snakes are a hazard to bathers.

Health care: The main hospitals are Port Moresby General (Papuan region), Goroka Base (Highlands) and Angau Memorial. Visitors can use any of the private doctors or public consultation clinics. Doctors and hospitals are not free and often expect immediate payment for medical services. Hospitals are poorly equipped and sudden shortages of common medications can sometimes occur; travellers who may need ongoing or routine medical treatment are advised to obtain visas for Australia, where medical facilities are more reliable, before leaving their country of origin. Dental care outside the main centres is limited, but pharmacies in the major centres are well stocked. There is no reciprocal health agreement with the UK. Health insurance is essential and must include evacuation facilities.

Travel - International

AIR:
 The national airline is *Air Niugini (PX)* (website: www.airniugini.com.pg).
Approximate flight times: The total flying time from Port Moresby to *London* is up to 30 hours (using current services and routes), but the journey takes at least two days to complete.

Main airports: Port Moresby (POM) (Jacksons) is 11km (7 miles) from the city. There are direct flights to Australia and Singapore. *To/from the airport:* Buses and taxis are available to the city (travel time – 20 to 60 minutes). *Facilities:* Duty free and banking facilities are available at the airport.

Departure tax: PGK30 is levied on international flights. Children under two years of age and passengers not leaving the airport are exempt.

SEA:
 Main ports: *Alotau, Kieta (North Solomons), Lae, Madang, Momote (Manus), Port Moresby, Rabaul (New Britain)* and *Wewak (Sepik).*
Passenger/cruise lines running regular services include *Lindblad, Peter Deilmann, Society Expeditions* and *World Discoverer.* Main cargo/passenger lines include *Austasia* and *Bank Line.*

Travel - Internal

AIR:
 Services are run by *Air Niugini* to all main centres, but are expensive. Internal services should be booked between November and February. *Air Niugini* flies to over 100 airstrips throughout the country and operates regular services to the 20 major towns of the country. *Air Niugini* also offers reductions for pre-booking excursions. Charter services are also in operation.

SEA:
 Cruises and excursions are available lasting three to 16 days. These go mainly to the islands and some otherwise inaccessible places on the coast. Cargo/passenger services between Lae and Madang are run by *Lutheran Shipping* with facilities including passenger cabins, accommodation and meals.

RIVER:
 For the local people in some regions of the country, rivers, particularly the Sepik, provide the main thoroughfares. In these areas it is possible to hire motorised canoes or obtain passage on a trading boat; however, apart from cruises, there are no regular public transport operators on the rivers.

ROAD:
 Driving is on the left and is not recommended. Owing to the rugged terrain of Papua New Guinea, road development of the interior has

been slow. There are currently 19,736km (12,262 miles) of roads of which 4865km (3023 miles) are highways or trunk roads. There is a network of roads connecting the northern coast towns of Madang and Lae with the major urban centres in the Highlands region. There are few roads connecting the various provinces, however. **Bus:** PMVs (public motor vehicles) operate in the main centres from bus shelters or they can be hailed. **Taxi:** Available in district centres but expensive. Although operated on a metered basis, fares can be negotiated. **Car hire:** Available in principal towns. **Documentation:** A national driving licence is sufficient.

RAIL:
 There is no railway.

Accommodation

Adequate and comfortable accommodation is available throughout Papua New Guinea. Generally, it is more expensive than in most Australasian states.

HOTELS:
 There are hotels of international standard in Lae, Madang, Port Moresby and most major centres. Many motels also offer good value accommodation.

LODGES:
 There is a developing tourist industry and tourist accommodation is increasing in many hitherto inaccessible areas. There are lodges in the Highlands and on the Sepik River, many of which can only be reached by air or river. Generally they consist of bungalows constructed of local materials. Contact the Tourism Promotion Authority for further details (see *Top Things To Do*).

Travel Advice

Law and order remains poor or very poor in many parts of the country. But most visits to Papua New Guinea are trouble-free.
Outbreaks of tribal fighting may occur without warning in the Highland Provinces and in particular in the Southern Highlands and Enga Provinces.
In the cities of Port Moresby, Lae and Mt Hagen armed carjackings, assaults, robbery, random shootings and serious sexual assaults are common. All visitors are advised to be extra vigilant whilst travelling in these cities, particularly during the hours of darkness.
Travellers should be aware of the global risk of indiscriminate terrorist attacks, which could be against civilian targets, including places frequented by foreigners.
This advice is based on information provided by the Foreign and Commonwealth Office in the UK. It is correct at time of publishing. As the situation can change rapidly, visitors are advised to contact the following organisations for the latest travel advice:

British Foreign and Commonwealth Office
Tel: (0845) 850 2829.
Website: www.fco.gov.uk

US Department of State
Website: http://travel.state.gov/travel

Top Things To See

- **Port Moresby**, the capital, is situated on the magnificent **Fairfax Harbour**. It houses the **National Parliament**, the **National Museum**, which contains exhibits of pottery from all the provinces, the **Botanical Gardens** and the **Catholic Cathedral** (which is built in the *Haus Tambaran* style). There are many sporting facilities in Port Moresby, including **scuba-diving, windsurfing, sailing, game fishing, water-skiing, golf, tennis** and **squash**.
- Major attractions in the Port Moresby area include **The Kokoda Trail and Sogeri**, 40km (24 miles) from Port Moresby via the Sogeri road, which offers magnificent views and winds through rubber plantations; and **Village Arts**, a Government-owned artefacts shop with the best artefact collection in the country situated at **Six Mile**, near the airport. Other places of interest near Port Moresby include the **Wairiata National Park**; **Moitaka Crocodile Farm**; **Loloata Island** and the **Sea Park Oceanarium**.
- In **Lae**, the capital of Morobe province, the **Botanical Gardens** are among the best in the country. **Mount Lunaman** in the centre of the town was used by the Germans and the Japanese as a lookout point during World War II. It gives a magnificent view over the **Huon Gulf** and the **Markham Valley**.
- Outside Lae is **Wau**, formerly a gold-mining centre. The **Wau Ecology Institute**, a privately funded organisation, has a small museum and zoo. Visitors can see cassowaries, tree kangaroos, crocodiles, birds of paradise, native butterflies and rhododendrons. Sights near Wau are **McAdam National Park** and **Mount Kaindi**,

A B C D E F G H I J K L M N O P Q R S T U V W X Y Z

Finschhafen (a very pretty coastal town) and the **Tami Islands**, whose people are renowned for their carved wooden bowls. **Sialum** is an attractive area of coastline known for its coral terraces. **White-water rafting** on the **Watut River** is an attraction for the adventurous.

- The capital of Madang Province, **Madang** is an ideal starting place for many of the tours round the islands and up the **Sepik River**. It has a variety of shops, hotels, restaurants and markets, where storyboards depicting myths and legends can be bought. In nearby **Bilbils** and **Yabobs**, traditional pottery-making can be seen.
- From the many villages along the banks of the **Sepik River** come highly-prized examples of primitive art. The *Haus Tambaran* at **Angoram** possesses a display of art from almost the entire length of the river. At **Kambaramba** village, and elsewhere, houses are built on stilts as a protection against flooding and the dugout canoe is still the main local means of transport. Tourists have the option of being taken on a cruise. Woodcarving is one of the main local crafts and its architectural use in gables and posts in houses is a noteworthy feature as can be seen, for instance, at the village of **Tambanum**. **Timbunke** village is a further example of fine construction techniques, including bridge-building.
- The area around the **Chambri Lakes** is home to the diverse species of birds for which Papua New Guinea is famous. These include egrets, pied herons, brahminee kites, whistling kites, jacanas, darters, cormorants and kingfishers. Islands of tangled vegetation and the debris of fallen trees float down the river to the Bismarck Sea. Salt and freshwater crocodiles abound and come out mostly at night. Nightly or early morning excursions into the jungle can be arranged for tourists wishing to experience the unique cacophony of birds preparing for the day's hunting. Tours along the river have a flexible itinerary which is adapted to river conditions and set to coincide with the many local customs and events. Also in the Chambri area can be found a unique pottery-making village, **Aibom**, where clay fireplaces, storage and cooking pots are made by the coil method and fired in the open air by women.
- At **Kanganaman**, a *Haus Tambaran* of national cultural importance is being rebuilt, providing an excellent example of the carvings on the immense *Haus Posts*. **Korogo** is famous for its *Mei Masks*.

In the upper reaches of the Sepik, clan representation and art is characterised by insect totems using praying mantis, rhinoceros-beetle motifs and distinctive insect eyes. Canoe prows are extremely elaborate, as are the tops of stepladders leading into dwellings. At **Waskusk**, the drawings on the ceiling of the *Haus Tambaran* depict a clan leader's dream, but conditions on the river sometimes make this village inaccessible. At **Yigei**, Upper Sepik-style *Garamut Drums* ('Slit Gongs') can be seen (and heard); and there are dramatic designs in white and yellow along the waterway in **Swagap Village**, which also has simple, elegant pottery and fireplaces, and often very fine examples of the canoe-builder's craft.

- In the **Eastern Highlands, Kainantu** is reached from Lae through the **Kassim Pass**. It has a large cultural centre, selling traditional artefacts; it also provides training in print-making and weaving. The largest town is **Goroka**, an agricultural and commercial centre for the entire Highlands region. The **JK McCarthy Museum** has a comprehensive display of regional artefacts; the Leahy wing contains photographs taken by early explorers. In the town centre the **Raun Raun Theatre** company provides contemporary performances of traditional stories and legends. **Bena Bena Village**, 10km (6 miles) from Goroka, is the largest handweaving organisation in the Highlands. Also nearby is **Asaro**, where the men coat themselves with grey mud and re-enact for visitors their historic revenge on a neighbouring village. The legend has it that, having been defeated in battle, the resourceful villagers covered themselves in mud and successfully frightened the opposition, who ran away in fear of being visited by ghosts.
- **Kundiawa**, a small town, is the capital of **Simbu Province**. Some of the local caves are used as burial places; others are popular with cavers. Rafting down the **Wahgi** and **Purari** rivers is also exciting. **Mount Wilhelm**, 4509m (1480ft), is in Simbu Province and is the highest mountain in Papua New Guinea.
- In some ways **Mount Hagen** in the Western Highlands resembles a town from the Wild West. Its expansion is only recent and the local population organise a number of *sing-sing* celebrations to mark a diverse variety of events ranging from payment of a bride-price to the opening of a new road. There is also a cultural centre in the town. The **Baiyer River Wildlife Sanctuary** lies 55km (34 miles) north of Mount Hagen and is one of the best places to see the famous birds of paradise. Possums, tree kangaroos, parrots and cassowaries are also part of the natural habitat.
- The **Mendi Valley** of the Southern Highlands is noted for its spectacular scenery and limestone caves. It is home to the *Huli Wigmen* who wear red and yellow face-paint and elaborately decorated wigs made of human hair.
- **Wabang** in **Enga Province** has a large cultural centre with an art gallery and a museum. Young artists can be seen working on sand paintings. War shields, wigs, weapons and other artefacts from all over Papua New Guinea are on display. Enga is the most primitive of the Highland Provinces.
- **Rabaul** on **New Britain** is the capital of the island and suffered extensive damage in 1994, owing to volcanic activity. During the eruptions most of the town was destroyed and the inhabitants were evacuated to other parts of the island. It is still possible to visit part of the 576km (360-mile) underground tunnel system left by the Japanese.
- **New Ireland** and the **Manus** group of islands are off the general tourist trail. In the northwestern islands of the latter group there are no trees. The islanders have a tradition of making sea-going canoes out of logs that float down the Sepik into the surrounding ocean.
- **Milne Bay**, the islands offshore from Bougainville, are lined with white sandy beaches. The **Trobriands** are the most accessible of the groups of islands in Milne Bay Province, but tourists might feel slightly less welcome than in the main tourist areas. As elsewhere in the islands, swimming and snorkelling enthusiasts are well catered for. The harvesting of yams from May to September is accompanied by extended rituals and celebrations which peak in the months of July and August. The mountainous **D'Entrecasteaux Islands** rise out of the sea. In the centre of **Goodenough Island**, there is a large stone decorated with mysterious paintings.

Top Things To Do

- The beaches and coral reefs around Papua New Guinea offer spectacular **swimming** and **snorkelling** facilities. **Diving** facilities and qualified instructors are available. **Madang, Port Moresby** and **Rabaul** offer a wide variety of dives ranging from wrecks to reefs. Diving holidays can also be arranged at locations such as **Loloaka** and off the island of **New Britain**, the latter being considered one of the best diving areas in Papua New Guinea. There is an underwater club in Port Moresby which is open to visitors.
- **Game fish** are plentiful in **Lae, Madang, Port Moresby, Rabaul** and **Wewak**. Information is available from Port Moresby Game Fishing Club Gantry, PO Box 154, Boroko, Papua New Guinea (tel: 325 4532; website: www.pmgfc.org.pg).
- The Royal Papua Yacht Club (tel: 321 1700; website: www.rpyc.com.pg) makes its extensive **sailing** facilities available to visitors; the season begins in late April.
- There are many **backpacking** and **hiking** tours are on offer, ranging from simple bush walks to extended tours through the rugged interior.

TOURIST INFORMATION

Tourism Promotion Authority
Street address: Pacific MMI Building, Level 5, Champion Parade, Port Moresby, Papua New Guinea
Postal address: PO Box 1291, Port Moresby, Papua New Guinea
Tel: 320 0211.
Website: www.pngtourism.org.pg

South Pacific Tourism Organisation in Fiji
Street address: Level 3, FNPF Place, 343-359 Victoria Parade, Suva, Fiji
Postal address: PO Box 13119, Suva, Fiji
Tel: (639) 330 4177.
Website: www.spto.org

Entertainment

FOOD & DRINK: Hotel dining rooms cater for most visitors and menus in main centres are fairly extensive. The more remote the area, the more likely it is that the menus will be basic. However, increasing use is made of fresh local meat, fish, vegetables and fruit, including pineapples, pawpaws, mangoes, passion fruit and bananas. Traditional cuisine of Papua New Guinea is based on root crops such as taro, kaukau and yams, sago and pig (cooked in the earth on traditional feasts). *Mumu* is a traditional dish combining pork, sweet potatoes, rice and greens. The number of European, Chinese and Indonesian restaurants is rising. Waiter service is usual. Alcohol is readily available and includes Australian and Filipino beers.
Tipping: Not customary and discouraged.
NIGHTLIFE: Several hotels in Port Moresby have dancing in the evenings and some organise live entertainment. The Arts Theatre stages regular performances. The local newspaper advertises programmes. *Sing-sings*, tribal events on a smaller scale than the biannual festival, are sometimes held.
SHOPPING: A wide range of crafts is available in shops; alternatively, visitors can buy directly from villagers. Favourite buys include local carvings of ceremonial masks and statuettes from Angoram and the Sepik, *Buka* basketry, arrows, bows and decorated axes, crocodile carvings from the Trobriands, pottery and local art. The many butterfly farms send specimens of unusual species throughout the world. **Shopping hours:** Mon-Fri 0900-1700, Sat 0900-1300 (some open longer and/or Sunday).

Business

ECONOMY: Although Papua New Guinea has been described as 'a mountain of gold floating on a sea of oil', it is a poor country and most of the population is engaged in subsistence agriculture. The most important commercial cash crops are copra, coffee, cocoa, timber, palm oil, rubber, tea, sugar and peanuts. However, the gradual discovery of exploitable mineral deposits has transformed the country. Papua New Guinea boasts the largest known supply of low-grade copper, the entire production of which is exported to Western Europe and Japan under long-term contract, and accounts for three-quarters of the country's export earnings. Other identified mineral deposits include gold and chromite. Some oil and natural gas has also been located. Light industry has grown steadily, mostly to meet consumer demands: the construction industry, printing, brewing, bottling and packaging are among these. Papua New Guinea's attempts to develop a tourist industry have been undermined by a lack of basic infrastructure and, more importantly, political stability. The country is always subject to the vagaries of the climate and natural phenomena – in recent years, it has suffered drought, flooding and an earthquake. During the past few years, the Government has managed to stabilise the economy, cutting the budget deficit, reducing inflation to around 10 per cent and stabilising the currency. However, growth has been stagnant at best and Papua New Guinea is still burdened by an overseas debt of US$2.5 billion.

Credit: ©Papua New Guinea Tourism Promotion Authority

Papua New Guinea belongs to the Asian Development Bank and the South Pacific Commission. Its largest trading partners are Australia, with 50 per cent of the market, followed by Japan, Singapore and the USA.
BUSINESS ETIQUETTE: Business affairs tend to be conducted in a very informal fashion. A conventional suit will not be required – shirt and tie or safari suit are sufficient. **Office hours:** Mon-Fri 0800-1630.
Government office hours: Mon-Fri 0800-1600.
CONFERENCES/CONVENTIONS: Some hotels provide facilities.

COMMERCIAL INFORMATION

Papua New Guinea Chamber of Commerce and Industry
Tel: 321 3057.
Website: www.pngcci.org.pg

Investment Promotion Authority
Level 3, Credit Corporation House, Cuthbertson St, Port Moresby, Papua New Guinea
Tel: 321 7311.
Website: www.ipa.gov.pg

Paraguay

Location: Central South America.

Time: GMT - 4 (GMT - 3 from the first Sunday in October to the first Sunday in March).

Overview

Paraguay is a little known landlocked country, which has found itself somewhat isolated from even its neighbours in the past by geography and politics. Since 1811, when it became independent, Paraguay has been governed mainly by dictatorships and has endured a number of costly wars against neighbouring countries.

However, Paraguay has taken a number of steps to overcome its political, economic and geographic situation and is building a more welcoming image. The country can boast many attractions: grassy plains and an untamed wilderness of marshes, lagoons, dense forests, jungles, national parks, Jesuit missions and the Chaco, one of South America's great wilderness areas. The country will particularly appeal to travellers who have already been to larger, more varied South American destinations, but who are now ready to experience the more subtle attractions of the Continent such as learning about the Guarani Indians, watching Nanduti lace being made or seeing a jaguar or alligator. In addition, Paraguay boasts breathtaking waterfalls, where the borders of Brazil, Paraguay, and Argentina come together. For all these reasons, Paraguay is definitely a country worth discovering.

General Information

AREA: 406,752 sq km (157,048 sq miles).

POPULATION: 6.2 million (UN, 2005).

POPULATION DENSITY: 15.24 per sq km.

CAPITAL: Asunción. **Population:** 539,000 (2005).

GEOGRAPHY: Paraguay is a landlocked country surrounded by Argentina, Bolivia and Brazil, lying some 1440km (900 miles) up the River Paraná from the Atlantic. The River Paraguay, a tributary of the Paraná, divides the country into two sharply contrasting regions. The Oriental zone, which covers 159,800 sq km (61,700 sq miles), consists of undulating country intersected by chains of hills rising to about 600m (2000ft), merging into the Mato Grosso Plateau in the north; the Paraná crosses the area in the east and south. East and southeast of Asunción lie the oldest centres of settlement inhabited by the greater part of the population. This area is bordered to the west by rolling pastures, and to the south by thick primeval forests. The Occidental zone, or Paraguayan Chaco, covers 246,827 sq km (95,300 sq miles). It is a flat alluvial plain, composed mainly of grey clay, which is marked by large areas of permanent swamp in the southern and eastern regions. Apart from a few small settlements, it is sparsely populated.

GOVERNMENT: Republic since 1967. Gained independence from Spain in 1811. **Head of State and Government:** President Óscar Nicanor Duarte Frutos since 2003. **Recent**

history: Nicanor Duarte, from the ruling Colorado Party, won Presidential elections in April 2003 with 38 per cent of the vote. Desptie a campaign based on promises to crack down on crime and corruption and to create new jobs through public work programmes, corruption remains widespread and Paraguay is a centre for smuggling, money laundering and organised crime. Around 60 per cent of Paraguayans live in poverty.

LANGUAGE: The official languages are Spanish and Guaraní; Guaraní is spoken by most of the rural population. Most Paraguayans are bilingual, but prefer to speak Guaraní outside Asunción.

RELIGION: Mostly Roman Catholic.

ELECTRICITY: 220 volts AC, 50Hz.

SOCIAL CONVENTIONS: Shaking hands is the usual form of greeting. Smoking is not allowed in cinemas and theatres. Dress tends to be informal and sportswear is popular. **Photography:** Avoid sensitive subjects such as military installations.

Climate

Subtropical with rapid changes in temperature throughout the year. Summer (December to March) can be very hot. Winter (June to September) is mild with few cold days. Rainfall is heaviest from December to March.

Required clothing: Lightweight cottons and linens are worn in warmer months, with some warm clothes for spring and autumn. Mediumweights are best for winter. Rainwear is advisable throughout the year.

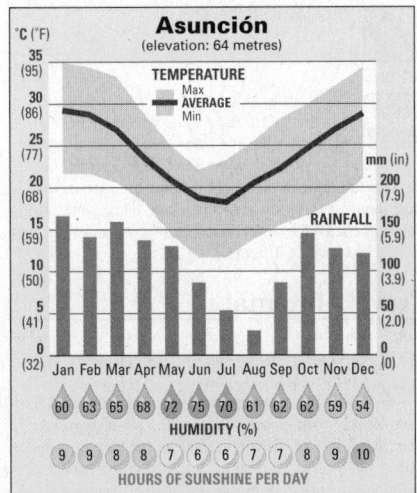

Communications

Telephone: IDD is available. Country code: 595. Moderate internal network apart from the main cities.

Mobile telephone: Roaming agreements exist with international mobile phone companies. Coverage is limited to urban areas.

Internet: Internet cafes are available in main urban areas.

Post: Airmail to Europe takes five days.

MEDIA: Press: The main newspapers are *ABC Color* (website: www.abc.com.py), *La Nación* (website: www.lanacion.com.py) and *Ultima Hora* (website: www.ultimahora.com.py). American newspapers are available.

TV: *Sisitema Nacional de Television* is a commercial network. Other stations include *Canal 2* and *El Trece*.

Radio: *Radio Nacional del Paraguay* is state-run. Other stations include *Radio Canal 100, Radio Cardinal, Radio City, Radio Nanduti* and *Radio Venus*.

Passport/Visa

	Passport Required?	Visa Required?	Return Ticket Required?
Full British	Yes	No	Yes
Australian	Yes	Yes	Yes
Canadian	Yes	Yes	Yes
USA	Yes	Yes	Yes
Other EU	Yes	No	Yes
Japanese	Yes	No	Yes

Note: *Regulations and requirements may be subject to change at short notice, and you are advised to contact your doctor well in advance of your intended date of departure. Any numbers in the chart refer to the footnotes below..*

PASSPORTS: Passport valid for six months after the intended length of stay required by all except nationals of Argentina, Brazil, Chile and Uruguay with valid ID cards entering as tourists directly from their own country.

VISAS: Required by all except the following entering as tourists for stays of up to 90 days:
(a) nationals of countries indicated in the chart above;
(b) nationals of Argentina, Bolivia, Brazil, Chile, Colombia, Costa Rica, Ecuador, El Salvador, Israel, Japan, Liechtenstein, Norway, Panama, Peru, South Africa, Switzerland, Uruguay and Venezuela;
(c) transit passengers continuing their journey by the same or first connecting aircraft within six hours provided holding onward or return documentation and not leaving the airport.

Types of visa and cost: *Tourist* and *Business: Single-entry*: £36. *Multiple-entry*: £52.

Validity: 90 days from date of issue.

Application to: Consulate (or Consular section at Embassy); see *Passport/Visa Information.*

Application requirements: (a) Valid passport (plus two photocopies from page with personal data). (b) Two completed application forms. (c) Two passport-size photos. (d) Self-addressed envelope for postal applications (see *Note* below). (e) Fee, payable in cash, bank transfer (or cheque in Pounds Sterling at the Embassy of Paraguay in London). *The following requirements must be presented with two photocopies:* (f) Proof of adequate funds (bank statement or credit card). (g) Travel tickets and copy of itinerary. *For business visas:* (a)-(g) and, (h) A covering letter from employer including name of contact in Paraguay (two photocopies).

Note: Postal applications are accepted only from Australia, Iceland and New Zealand and will not be processed until return post is paid or a courier service is arranged. A self-addressed envelope must be included with all postal applications.

Working days required: 2 to 3 days. May take 20 to 30 days for countries with no diplomatic relation with Paraguay.

Temporary residence: If you wish to stay longer than three months as a visitor you must produce a '*Certificado de Buena Conducta*' (certificate of good conduct) in order to apply for a permanent residence permit. The certificate must be obtained from a local police station in the UK. It must be issued in the month before leaving the UK and must be valid for six months.

PASSPORT/VISA INFORMATION

Embassy of the Republic of Paraguay in the UK
344 Kensington High Street, 3rd Floor,
London W14 8NS, UK
Tel: (020) 7610 4180.
Website: www.paraguayembassy.co.uk
Opening hours: Mon-Fri 1000-1500.

Embassy of the Republic of Paraguay in the USA
2400 Massachusetts Avenue, NW,
Washington, DC 20008, USA
Tel: (202) 483 6960.
Website: www.embassparusa.gov.py

Money

Currency: Guaraní (PYG). Notes are in denominations of PYG100,000, 50,000, 10,000, 5000, 1000 and 500. Coins are in denominations of PYG500, 100, 50, 10 and 5.

Currency exchange: Paraguay maintains a free monetary exchange policy and the purchase and sale of foreign currencies is not subject to any controls or regulations. US Dollars, which are more easily negotiable than Sterling, are widely accepted throughout the country. Travellers are advised to use an official bureau de change and not deal with people offering services on the street as false banknotes are common. ATMs are widespread; many accept Cirrus, Maestro and Visa cards.

Credit & debit cards: American Express, MasterCard and Visa are widely accepted (though not in smaller hotels), while Diners Club has more limited use. ID is required, such as a passport, when making a purchase with a credit card. Check with your credit or debit card company for details of merchant acceptability and other services which may be available.

Traveller's cheques: US Dollar traveller's cheques are not widely used in Paraguay.

Currency restrictions: There are no restrictions on the import or export of local or foreign currency.

Banking hours: Mon-Fri 0845-1500.

Exchange rate indicators:
Rate at time of publishing
£1.00=   PYG11000
$1.00=   PYG6160

Duty Free

The following items may be imported into Paraguay without incurring customs duty:
A reasonable quantity of tobacco, alcoholic beverages and perfume for personal use; a reasonable quantity of personal and sporting equipment.

Public Holidays

Below are listed Public Holidays for the January 2006-June 2007 period.

2006: Jan 1 New Year's Day. **Mar 1** Heroes' Day. **Apr 13** Maundy Thursday. **Apr 14** Good Friday. **Apr 16** Easter. **May 1** Labour Day. **May 15** Independence Day. **Jun 12** Peace of Chaco. **Aug 15** Founding of Asunción. **Sep 29** Battle of Boquerón. **Dec 8** Immaculate Conception. **Dec 25** Christmas Day.

2007: Jan 1 New Year's Day. **Mar 1** Heroes' Day. **Apr 5** Maundy Thursday. **Apr 6** Good Friday. **Apr 8** Easter. **May 1** Labour Day. **May 15** Independence Day. **Jun 12** Peace of Chaco.

Health

	Special Precautions?	Certificate Required?
Yellow Fever	No	1
Cholera	No	No
Typhoid & Polio	2	N/A
Malaria	3	N/A

Note: *Regulations and requirements may be subject to change at short notice, and you are advised to contact your doctor well in advance of your intended date of departure. Any numbers in the chart refer to the footnotes below.*

1: A yellow fever vaccination certificate is required from travellers over nine months leaving Paraguay to go to endemic areas (forested areas in the east and west of the country). A certificate is also required from travellers coming from endemic areas.

2: Typhoid is a risk in rural areas.

3: Malaria risk, almost exclusively in the benign *vivax* form, is moderate in certain municipalities of Alto Paraná, Caaguazú and Canendiyú. In the other 13 departments, there is a negligible risk.

Food & drink: Mains water is normally chlorinated, and whilst relatively safe, may cause mild abdominal upsets. Bottled water is available and is advised for the first few weeks of stay. Drinking water outside main cities and towns is likely to be contaminated and sterilisation is considered essential. Milk may be unpasteurised and, if so, should be boiled. Powdered or tinned milk is also available and is advised, but make sure that it is reconstituted with pure water. Avoid dairy products which are likely to have been made from unboiled milk. Only eat well-cooked meat and fish, preferably served hot. Pork, salad and mayonnaise may carry increased risk. Vegetables should be cooked and fruit peeled.

Other risks: *Hepatitis B* and *D* are endemic; *hepatitis A* is common; *hepatitis C* occurs. There have been large epidemics of *dengue fever* across the country in the past few years. *Filariasis, leishmaniasis, onchocerciasis* and *American trypanosomiasis* (chagas disease) are present. *TB* occurs.

Rabies is present. For those at high risk, vaccination before arrival should be considered. If you are bitten, seek medical advice without delay. For more information, consult the *Health* appendix.

Health care: Health insurance is essential. There is no reciprocal health agreement with the UK.

Travel - International

AIR:

The national airline is *TAM Mercosur (PZ)* (website: www.tam.com.py). There are also a number of scheduled flights to Asunción from other South American cities, notably Buenos Aires, Santa Cruz (Bolivia) and Santiago (Chile).

Approximate flight times: From Asunción to *London* is 15 to 19 hours, depending on the route taken.

Main airports: *Asunción (ASU) (Silvio Pettirossi)* is 16km (10 miles) from the city (travel time - 20 minutes). *To/from the airport*: A coach and taxi service runs to the city. *Facilities*: Bureau de change, duty free shopping, restaurants and car hire.

Air passes: The *Mercosur Airpass* is valid within Argentina, Brazil, Chile (except Easter Island), Paraguay and Uruguay. Participating airlines include *TAM Mercosur* (PZ), *Pluna* (PU), *TAM Linhas Aéreas* (JJ) and *VARIG* (RG). The pass can only be purchased by passengers who live outside South America, who have a return ticket. Only eight flight coupons are allowed with a maximum of four coupons for each country and it is valid for seven to a maximum of 30 days. At least two countries must be visited and the flight route cannot be changed. A maximum of two stopovers is allowed per country.

The *Visit South America* pass is valid within Argentina, Bolivia, Brazil, Colombia, Chile (except Easter Island), Ecuador, Paraguay, Peru, Uruguay and Venezuela. Participating airlines include *Aer Lingus* (EI), *American Airlines* (AA), *British Airways* (BA), *Cathay Pacific* (CX), *Finnair* (AY), *Iberia* (IB), *LAN* (LA) and *Qantas* (QF). The pass must be bought outside South America in country of residence. It allows unlimited travel to 34 cities. A minimum of three flights must be booked, with no maximum; the maximum stay is 60 days, with no minimum, and prices depend on the amount of flight zones. For further details, contact one of the participating airlines.

Departure tax: US$25 for international departures, US$4 for domestic departures from Asunción airport. Transit passengers are exempt.

RIVER:

There are ferry links with Argentina, Bolivia and Brazil. Travellers using the river to travel to Argentina should note that the Posadas (Argentina)-Encarnación (Paraguay) route is 321km (200 miles) shorter than the more traditional route to Buenos Aires. It traverses the Argentine provinces of Misiones and Corrientes and then proceeds across a bridge over the Paraná River to Resistencia. Those who prefer to continue along the left bank of the Paraná River will have to travel to Paraná, provincial capital of Entre Ríos, crossing under the Paraná River in the tunnel between the cities of Paraná and Santa Fé. It is also possible to reach Paraguay by river from Brazil, in boats which connect Asunción with the Brazilian city of Corumba.

RAIL:

There are no rail services.

ROAD:

The roads from Río and São Paulo to Asunción (via the Iguazú Falls) are paved and generally good, as is the one from Buenos Aires. Another road link to Argentina is via the San Roque González de Santa Cruz bridge in Encarnación across the Paraná river.

Bus: There are daily services from Rio de Janeiro and São Paulo, Buenos Aires (Argentina), Córdoba, Rosario and Santa Fé, and Montevideo (Uruguay).

Travel - Internal

AIR:

Air service is run by *LATN (Líneas Aéreas de Transporte Nacional)* and *TAM Mercosur*. The most popular visitors' flight is to the Iguazú Falls from Asunción with *Varig Airways (RG)*. Air-taxis are popular with those wishing to discover the Paraguayan Chaco. Travel agencies offer daily city tours, but services suffer from frequent disruption by weather conditions.

RIVER:

There are no regular passenger services on the river.

RAIL:

There are no rail services.

ROAD:

Traffic drives on the right. Roads serving the main centres are in good condition and there is an ongoing programme to upgrade the major routes. Potholes are a hazard, especially in Asunción. Unsurfaced roads may be impassable in bad weather, especially between November and April. Approximately 10 per cent of roads are surfaced. A highway links Asunción with Iguazú Falls, a drive of up to six hours. There are regular police checks; it is also advisable to lock doors. Travelling or driving at night are not advisable. **Bus:** Often the best and cheapest method of transport within Paraguay. For longer distances, advance booking may be necessary. There are express links to major centres. **Taxis:** They are readily available and may be called by using telephone numbers listed in the local newspapers. **Car hire:** Cars can be hired at the airport or through local tourist agencies.

Documentation: National driving licence or International Driving Permit are both accepted.

URBAN:

Bus and minibus services are provided by private companies in Asunción, with two-zone fares collected by conductors. The Government-operated tramway runs on two routes.

Travel times: The following chart gives approximate travel times (in hours and minutes) from **Asunción** to other major cities in Paraguay.

	Air	Road	Rail	River
Pedro Juan Caballero	1.15	11.00	-	13.00
Concepción	1.00	12.00	-	14.00
Ciudad del Este	1.05	5.00	-	-
Encarnación	1.10	5.00	14.00	9.00

Travel Advice

Most visits to Paraguay are trouble-free but you should be aware of the global risk of indiscriminate terrorist attacks which could be against civilian targets, including places frequented by foreigners.

Violent crime is increasing, so travellers need to be on their guard and exercise caution at all times, particularly in cities at night.

This advice is based on information provided by the Foreign and Commonwealth Office in the UK. It is correct at time of publishing. As the situation can change rapidly, visitors are advised to contact the following organisations for the latest travel advice:

British Foreign and Commonwealth Office
Tel: (0845) 850 2829.
Website: www.fco.gov.uk

US Department of State
Website: http://travel.state.gov/travel

Accommodation

HOTELS:

All hotels in Asunción are likely to be fully booked throughout the tourist season (July and August). Visitors are advised to consult a reputable travel agent for up-to-date information, or to ascertain the rates with hotels when making reservations. For further information, contact the Secretaría Nacional de Turismo (see *Top Things To See & Do*). Outside the capital, accommodation is fairly limited.

CAMPING AND CARAVANNING:

There are a number of campsites throughout Paraguay.

OTHER ACCOMMODATION: Package tours to national parks in the Chaco or the waterfalls near Ciudad del Este along the Brazilian border include lodgings, but for individual travellers all accommodation must be booked in writing well in advance; details of current prices are available from the Secretaría Nacional de Turismo (see *Top Things To See & Do*).

Top Things To See & Do

- **Asunción**, the capital city, is situated on the **Bay of Asunción**, an inlet off the **Paraguay River**. Planned on a colonial Spanish grid system, it has many parks and plazas. On the way to the waterfront the visitor enters the old part of town, an area of architectural diversity. Enjoy good views of the city from the **Parque Carlos Antonio Lopez**, high above Asunción. The **Botanical Gardens** are situated in a former estate of the Lopez family on the Paraguay River. Among the many religious buildings is the **Metropolitan Cathedral**. Visit the **National Fine Arts Museum**, with its 19th-century paintings and colonial works, the **Visual Arts Museum**, and the **Andres Barbero Museum**, which contains works of anthropological value.
- Stop at **Luque**, near the capital, the home of the famous Paraguayan harps.
- Follow the popular **'Central Circuit'**, a route of some 200km (125 miles) that takes in some of the country's most interesting sites clustered around the capital. Head for **San Lorenzo**, the site of the university halls of residence and an interesting Gothic-style church.
- Founded in 1539 by Domingo Martínez, **Ita**'s main event is the **San Blas festival** in February. Follow the procession through the streets while eating traditional food. Its main craft speciality is handpainted black clay Gallinita hens.
- View the churches of **Yaguarón**, set in an orange-growing district, 48km (29 miles) from the capital. Yaguarón played a part during the Spanish conquest as a base for the Franciscan missions.
- Situated in the foothills of the **Cordillera de los Altos**, the historic village of **Paraguarí** has several old buildings in colonial style.
- Rent a bungalow in the holiday centre of **Chololo**, 87km (54 miles) from the capital.
- Purchase the **Encaje-yú spindle lace**, the **'sixty-stripe' Paraní poncho** and other **handmade** goods in **Piribebuy**, which was the scene of bloody fighting during the war of the triple alliance. It is also famous as a place of worship of the 'Virgin of Miracles'.
- Situated on **Lake Ypacarai**, 47km (29 miles) from the capital, **San Bernardino** is a holiday resort and, owing to its beaches and lake shores, very popular during the summer months. It also has a camping ground, 'Camping 19'.
- The **Chaco** is a vast, scarcely populated area, consisting mainly of empty plains and forests. It covers 61 per cent of the country's total surface, but is inhabited by only 3 per cent of Paraguay's population. The drive from Asunción leads through the Low Chaco, a land of palm forests and marshes, and reaches the Middle Chaco with

its capital **Filadelfia**. Here, Mennonites of German descent have set up farms and other agricultural outlets as well as their own schools and are considered to be the only organised community in the whole of the Chaco region. The Chaco is home to Paraguay's major national parks including the **Defensores del Chaco**, **Tifunque**, **Enciso** and **Cerro Cora**. Wildlife and nature enthusiasts can also visit the area's beautiful biological reserves (in **Itabo**, **Limoy**, **Tati Yupi**) or the protected forests in **Mbaracayu** and **Nacunday**, where over 600 species of birds (including the Chacoan peccary, once thought to be extinct), 200 species of mammals and numerous kinds of reptiles and amphibians live in a natural habitat. For more information on Paraguayan national parks, contact the Dirección de Parques Nacionales y Vida Silvestre, Madame Lynch 3500, casi Primer Presidente, Asunción, Paraguay (tel: (21) 615 812; e-mail: biodiversidad@seam.gov.py).

- Go **fishing**. The *dorado*, found in the Paraguay, Paraná and Tebicuary rivers, can weigh up to 29kg (65lb). International fishing contests are held near Asunción. There are many other smaller fish that are peculiar to Paraguay such as the *surubí*, *pati*, *pacu*, *manguruyus*, *armados*, *moncholos* and *bagres*.
- **Ciudad del Este**, 326km (204 miles) east of the capital, is a good starting point for a visit to the majestic **Monday Falls** and **Iguazú Falls**, which are a 15- to 30-minute drive from the city. Also nearby is the **Italpú Dam**, the largest hydroelectric complex in the world. Stretching over 180km (112 miles), the water reservoir provides a unique ecosystem for **wildlife** and **birds** as well as providing tourists with a number of activities, including **fishing**, **watersports**, **sailing**, **camping** and **walking** tours.
- To the south, walk along the sleepy waterfront area of **Encarnación**. Nearby is the **Roque González de Santa Cruz bridge** linking Paraguay with Posadas in Argentina across the river Paraná.
- In the 16th century, the Company of Jesus started the process of converting the Guaraní people to Christianity. As a result, the native Indians eventually agreed to live in *reducciones*, large villages with a fairly rigid socioeconomic structure based on Jesuit principles and values. Skilled in construction and artistic techniques, the Guaraníes left behind a heritage of churches, religious sculptures and paintings scattered throughout Argentina, Bolivia, Brazil and Paraguay. Seven of the largest **Jesuit missions** remain in Paraguay, and those in **Jesús de Taravangue** and **Trinidad del Paraná** have been declared World Heritage Sites by UNESCO. They can be reached either by plane, car/bus or via light river transport.

TOURIST INFORMATION

Secretaría Nacional de Turismo
Palma 468, casi 14 de Mayo, Edificio Central,
Asunción, Paraguay
Tel: (21) 494 110.
Website: www.senatur.gov.py

Entertainment

FOOD & DRINK: There is a wide choice of restaurants in Asunción, most with table service.
Things to know: There are no strict licensing hours and alcohol is widely available.
National specialities:
- *Chipas* (maize bread flavoured with egg and cheese).
- *Sopa paraguaya* (soup of mashed corn, cheese, milk and onions).
- *Soo-yosopy* (a soup of cornmeal and ground beef).
- *Palmitos* (palm hearts).
- *Surubí* (a fish found in the Paraná).

National drinks:
- *Caña* (distilled from sugar cane and honey).
- *Mosto* (sugar cane juice).
- *Yerba maté* (tea-like drink brewed from dried leaves and stemlets for the Yerba maté tree).

Tipping: 10 to 15 per cent is normally included in hotel, restaurant and bar bills.
NIGHTLIFE: In Asunción, there are numerous bars, casinos and discos. The *parrilladas* or open-air restaurants offer by far the best atmosphere, especially in Asunción. There is a casino in the border towns of Ciudad del Este and Encarnación. The most popular traditional music in Paraguay is *polcas* and *guaranías* which have slow and romantic rhythms and which are used as serenades.
SHOPPING: There are some modern shopping centres in the capital. A popular shopping street is the Calle Palma. Special purchases include *ñandutí* lace, made by the women of Itagua, and *aopoí* sports shirts, made in a variety of colours and designs. Other items include leather goods, wood handicrafts, silver *yerba maté* cups and native jewellery. **Shopping hours:** Mon-Fri 0800-1200 and 1500-1900, Sat 0730-1300.

Business

GDP: US$7.9 billion.
Main imports: Petroleum, machinery, transport equipment, metal and metal products, foodstuff, alcoholic beverages, dairy and other edible animal products and cocoa derivatives.
Main exports: Electricity, charcoal, soya, cotton, timber, oil seed, coffee, orange juice, tobacco, meat, fruit, peel and nuts, organic sugar, leather, rum, pet food, crafts, mineral water and dairy produce.
Main trade partners: Argentina, Brazil, Chile, China, Uruguay and USA.

ECONOMY: Paraguay's agriculture plays an important part in its economy, supplying one-quarter of GNP and almost all the country's export earnings. Production of Paraguay's principal cash crops, cotton and soya, expanded rapidly during the late 1980s and continues to grow annually. Other crops such as sugar cane, maize and wheat are also grown on a commercial scale. Paraguay also has large timber reserves which feed the country's rapidly expanding wood-based industries. Wood and soya oil are the main export products. The main manufacturing industries are textiles, chemicals, and the production of metal goods and machinery. Hydroelectric projects, undertaken jointly with Brazil and including the world's largest hydroelectric dam at Itaipu, have made Paraguay self-sufficient in energy. Although since the early 1990s Paraguay has implemented major economic reforms centred on liberalisation and deregulation of the public sector and large private monopolies, as required by its principal external creditors and donors, the economy has performed poorly in recent years. The main reason is persistently low commodity prices, exacerbated by large-scale corruption and structural weaknesses in the banking sector. External factors, notably the economic crises in Argentina and Brazil, have also played an important role. Annual growth is at around 2 per cent, whilst high unemployment (officially at 18.5 per cent but in reality nearer to 40 per cent) has forced much of the workforce into the unregulated 'black' parts of the economy. In July 2002, the IMF offered a US$200 million support package: the Government was unable or unwilling to meet the loan conditions and relations with the IMF are now effectively frozen. The Government elected in August 2003 faces an urgent task to stimulate the economy.
Paraguay is a member of the 11-strong Latin American Integration Association (*Asociación Latinoamericana de Integración*, ALADI), which seeks to promote free trade and economic development within Latin America, and under which Paraguay, alongside Bolivia, enjoys special tariff concessions. Paraguay is also a founding member to the Mercosur trade bloc of southern Latin American countries.
BUSINESS ETIQUETTE: For formal occasions or business affairs, men should wear lightweight suits and ties or a dinner jacket in the evening; women a lightweight two-piece suit or equivalent. Most businesspeople are able to conduct a conversation in English, but a knowledge of Spanish will be useful. Appointments and normal business courtesies apply. The best time to visit is from May to September. **Office hours:** Mon-Fri 0800-1200 and 1430-1900, Sat 0800-1200.

COMMERCIAL INFORMATION

Cámara Nacional de Comercio y Servicios de Paraguay
Estrella 540-550, Asunción, Paraguay
Tel: (21) 493 321/2.
Website: www.ccparaguay.com.py

PROPARAGUAY (Trade & Investment Promotion Agency)
Edificio Ayfra, 12th Floor, Asunción, Paraguay
Tel: (21) 207 055.
Website: www.proparaguay.gov.py

British Paraguayan Chamber of Commerce
Gral Diaz 521, Edificio Internacional Faro, 2nd Floor, Oficina 2a, Asunción, Paraguay
Tel/fax: (21) 498 274.

Peru

Location: Western South America.

Time: GMT - 5.

Overview

Perhaps no other country has more to offer the visitor than Peru: panoramic mountain ranges, vast deserts, beautiful beaches and tropical jungle. All this combined with a rich historical and archaeological past and enduring indigenous cultures.
The indigenous Inca civilisation of what is now Peru was conquered by Spain in the early 16th century. Spain ruled the country until the early 19th century. The wars of Independence, which expelled the Spanish from virtually the entire South American continent, reached Peru in the early 1820s. After the 1821 declaration of Independence, Peru was challenged by the royalists. The new Government appealed to the revolutionary leader, Simon Bolivar, for assistance, who proceeded to defeat the royalists at the Battle of Ayacucho in December 1824, after which he became Head of State. Relations between Peru and its neighbours were difficult in the early years of Independence. There were border disputes with Brazil and Ecuador, and especially with Chile. The War of the Pacific, which broke out between Peru and Chile in 1879 with a complete victory for Chile and the loss to Peru of some southern territories. Internal problems dominated the agenda for the next 30 years, as a series of Governments struggled to keep the economy, which was almost completely destroyed as a result of the Pacific War, from disintegrating.
The first of Peru's many military coups was in 1914. The junta lasted five years, before giving way to the civilian Government of Augusto Leguia. His tenure ended with another military take-over. While the military has always been a powerful force in Peruvian politics, its principal opponent and the country's largest political party for much of the 20th century was the *Alianza Popular Revolucionaria Americana* (*APRA*), founded by Dr Victor Raul Haya de la Torre in 1924, as a continent-wide anti-imperialist movement. Although increasingly moderate and Peruvian-centred in its appeal, APRA has nevertheless been illegal for much of its history. Politics has also persistently been dogged by alleged – and sometimes proven –

corruption. The 'war on drugs' has long dominated relations between Peru and the USA. Border disputes have also arisen; the most serious of these was with Ecuador over access to the Amazonian river system and control of the potentially mineral-rich Condor mountain range. In early 1995, full-scale fighting broke out after talks broke down, continuing intermittently until a settlement was reached in 1999.

Just as complex is Peru's topography: divided into the three main geographical zones of *costa* (coast); *sierra* (mountains); and *selva* (rainforest). Such diverse landscape generates diverse pleasures; Peru successfully offers history, archaeology, sports, beaches, mountains, medicinal springs, nature, fantastic landscapes, friendly people and mesmeric music. Ancient archaeological remains and Nazca Lines augment Peru's sense of mystery, of possessing an awesomeness of both humankind and nature.

General Information

AREA: 1,285,216 sq km (496,225 sq miles).

POPULATION: 27.15 million (2004 estimate).

POPULATION DENSITY: 21.1 per sq km.

CAPITAL: Lima. **Population:** 8.27 million (2004).

GEOGRAPHY: Peru is a large, mountainous country on the Pacific coast of South America. It has borders with Ecuador and Colombia to the north, Brazil and Bolivia to the east, and Chile to the south. The Pacific Ocean lies to the west. There are three natural zones, running roughly north to south. The *Costa* region, which contains Lima (the capital), is a narrow coastal plain consisting of large tracts of desert broken by fertile valleys. The cotton, sugar and rice plantations and most of the so-far exploited oil fields lie in this area. The *Sierra* contains the Andes, with peaks over 6000m (20,000ft), most of the country's mineral resources (silver, zinc, lead, copper and gold) and the greater part of its livestock. The *Selva*, an area of fertile, subtropical uplands, lies between the Andes and the border with Brazil. Sections of a proposed international highway are at present being built through it, with some sections already in use. The Amazonian jungle has vast natural resources. The absence of land communications, however, left the area largely uncharted until full-scale oil exploration began in 1973. The population is largely Indian and Mestizo with a noticeable influence from African, Chinese and European (mainly Spanish) settlers.

GOVERNMENT: Republic. Gained independence from Spain in 1824, having declared it in 1821. **Head of State:** President Alejandro Toledo Manrique since 2001. **Recent history:** After the comparatively unknown independent centrist candidate, Alberto Fujimori, won the 1995 election, he contrived to stand for an unprecedented third term of office in 2000, which he also won - this time by default when his opponent, Alejandro Toledo, withdrew citing numerous irregularities. Fujimori's triumph, such as it was, was short-lived. During his first two terms, he had relied heavily on the dubious services of his intelligence chief and principal fixer, Vladimir Montesinos. The mysterious appearance of a videotape showing Montesinos bribing an opposition Assembly member to switch sides triggered Montesinos' fall. As investigations into his activities widened, he was found to be implicated in an extraordinary range of illegal activities, including drug trafficking, money laundering and organising death squad killings. He has since been jailed. Montesinos' demise also meant the end for Fujimori, who was implicated in many of the same crimes. He resigned from Presidency in November 2000 and quickly left for Japan due to his dual Japanese/Peruvian nationality. Bizarrely, Fujimori now apparently believes that he can make a political comeback, possibly at the 2006 Presidential election. However, the Peruvian authorities are currently seeking his extradition from Chile, where he is currently being detained by the authorities, to Peru to face trail. Meanwhile, in April 2001, Alejandro Toledo (who had conceded to Fujimori a year earlier) won a new Presidential poll, defeating the *APRA* (American Popular Revolutionary Alliance) candidate, ex-President Alan Garcia. Following simultaneous National Assembly elections, Toledo's party, the centrist *Peru Posible*, leads a governing six-party coalition. Toledo, the first Peruvian President of native Indian origin, has had a difficult time, largely due to the poor economic situation. In June 2002, a state of emergency was declared in the country's second city, Arequipa, after riots broke out. In early 2003, the country was hit by a wave of major storms and floods. At the beginning of 2004, Toldeo carried out yet another Cabinet reshuffle, the seventh, sacking Peru's first woman Prime Minister, Beatriz Merino in favour of Carlos Ferrero.

LANGUAGE: Spanish and Quechua are the official languages. Aymará is spoken in some areas of the region of Puno. Many other dialects exist in the jungle regions. English is spoken in major tourist areas.

RELIGION: 89 per cent Roman Catholic, 7 per cent Evangelical and 4 per cent other denominations.

ELECTRICITY: 220 volts AC, 60Hz. (110 volts AC is available in most 4- and 5-star hotels).

SOCIAL CONVENTIONS: Shaking hands is the customary form of greeting. Visitors should follow normal social courtesies and the atmosphere is generally informal. A small gift from a company or home country is sufficient. Dress is usually informal, although for some business meetings and social occasions men wear a jacket and tie. Life is conducted at a leisurely pace.

Climate

Varies according to area. On the coast winter lasts from June to September. During this period, the mountainous areas are often sunny during the day but cold at night. Heavy rains in the mountains and jungle last from December to April. It never rains in Lima nor most of the coast, except for Tumbes and Piura, which have tropical climates.

Required clothing: Lightweights during summer with warmer clothes worn in upland areas. Mediumweights are advised during cooler months.

Credit: © Alejandro Balaguer / Promperú

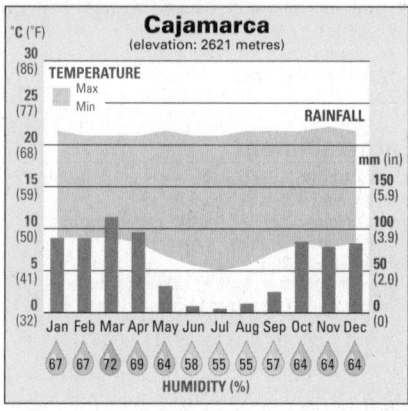

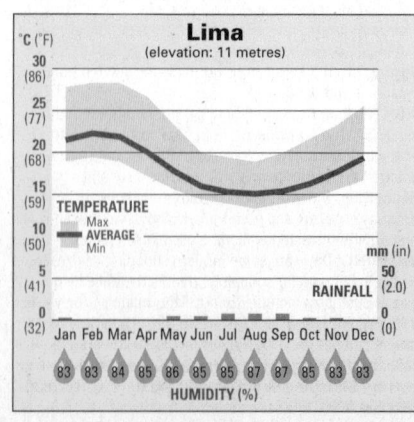

Communications

Telephone: IDD is available. Country code: 51. Telephone cards are available in the main cities from stands and supermarkets.
Mobile telephone: Roaming agreements exist with some international mobile phone companies. Cellular phones can be rented in Lima and the main cities.
Internet: Public Internet booths and Internet cafes are widely available in the main cities. Coverage is sporadic.
Post: Airmail to Western Europe takes up to one week. Postal facilities are limited outside Lima. First-class airmail from Europe or North America addressed to PO boxes in Peru usually takes only a few days, but may be subject to delay. The main post office (*Correo Central de Lima*) is near the Plaza de Armas.
MEDIA: Privately-run broadcasters and newspapers dominate the Peruvian media scene, with the state-run media having relatively small audiences. The airwaves of Lima are home to dozens of radio stations and several TV services. Many radio stations and regional newspapers are available in the provinces. Peru's media have enjoyed greater press freedom since the fall of former President Alberto Fujimori.
Press: Newspapers are in Spanish. Morning dailies include *El Bocón*, *El Comercio*, *Gestión* and *La República*.
TV: *Television Nacional de Peru* is state-owned; *America TV*, *Panamericana* and *Andina TV* are all commercial.
Radio: *Radio Programas de Peru* (RPP) is a popular Lima-based news and talk station; *Radio Panamericana* and *Radio America* are commercial FM stations based in Lima; news and music radio station, *Radio Nacional*, is state-run.

Passport/Visa

	Passport Required?	Visa Required?	Return Ticket Required?
Full British	Yes	1	Yes
Australian	Yes	1	Yes
Canadian	Yes	1	Yes
USA	Yes	1	Yes
Other EU	Yes	1	Yes
Japanese	Yes	1	Yes

Note: *Regulations and requirements may be subject to change at short notice, and you are advised to contact the appropriate diplomatic or consular authority before finalising travel arrangements. Any numbers in the chart refer to the footnotes below.*

PASSPORTS: Valid passport required by all except nationals of Bolivia, Chile and Ecuador entering certain regions of Peru. Citizens of these countries are advised to contact their nearest Peruvian Consulate before travelling.
VISAS: Required by all except the following:
(a) **1.** nationals of countries shown in the chart above travelling as tourists for stays of up to 90 days with the exception of Malta nationals of which *do* require a visa;
(b) nationals of Andorra, Antigua & Barbuda, Argentina, The Bahamas, Barbados, Belarus, Belize, Bolivia, Brazil, Brunei, Bulgaria, Chile, Colombia, Cook Islands, Costa Rica, Croatia, Dominica, Dominican Republic, Ecuador, El Salvador, Federated States of Micronesia, Fiji, Grenada, Guatemala, Guyana, Haiti, Honduras, Hong Kong (SAR), Iceland, Indonesia, Israel, Jamaica, Kiribati, Korea (Rep), Liechtenstein, Macedonia, Malaysia, Malta, Marshall Islands, Mexico, Moldova, Monaco, Nauru, New Zealand, Nicaragua, Niue, Norway, Palau, Panama, Papua New Guinea, Paraguay, The Philippines, Russian Federation, Serbia & Montenegro, St Kitts & Nevis, St Lucia, St Vincent & the Grenadines, Samoa, San Marino, Singapore, Solomon Islands, South Africa, Surinam, Switzerland, Taiwan, Thailand, Tonga, Trinidad & Tobago, Tuvalu, Ukraine, Uruguay, Vanuatu, Vatican City and Venezuela, provided travelling as tourists, for stays of up to 90 days;
(c) transit passengers continuing their journey by the same or first connecting aircraft within 48 hours provided holding valid onward or return documentation and not leaving the airport.
Note: (a) Nationals of Bangladesh, Cuba, China (PR), Iran, Iraq, Lebanon, Morocco, Pakistan and Sri Lanka require special authorisation from the Immigration Office in Lima to obtain a visa. This application could take one month (approximately) to be processed. (b) All visitors must hold return tickets or letter of guarantee from travel agency and sufficient funds for their stay.
Types of visa and cost: *Tourist* and *Business*: £19.20. Costs are subject to change according to exchange rates.
Validity: Up to 90 days.
Note: A Business visa is required for all nationals if the purpose of the visit is business. Any business-related unpaid work can be made on a tourist visa. Upon arrival in Peru, the Business visa holder must register at the *Dirección General de Contribuciones* for taxation purposes. Business visa holders can remain in Peru for 90 days. If wishing to extend the visit, an application must be lodged with the *Dirección General de Migraciones*.
Application to: Consulate (or consular section at Embassy); see *Passport/Visa Information* for details.
Application requirements: (a) Valid passport. (b) Return or through ticket to show the visitor will be leaving Peru. (c) Two passport-size, colour photos. (d) Fee. (e) Two completed application forms. (f) Proof of economic solvency, such as latest bank statement. *Business*: (a)-(f) and, (g) Company letter specifying the reason for the trip, the length of stay and confirming employment status. *Student*: (a)-(f) and, (g) Letter from your centre of studies confirming attendance.
Note: (a) All nationals are advised to check with the Peruvian Consulate prior to departure to obtain current details of any documentation which might be required. Postal visa applications are not accepted unless submitted through a travel agency. (b) Visitors travelling to areas with a tropical climate are advised to have yellow fever, smallpox and malaria vaccinations.
Working days required: At least 24 hours; longer if authorisation from the Immigration Office in Lima is required.

PASSPORT/VISA INFORMATION

Embassy of the Republic of Peru in the UK
52 Sloane Street, London SW1X 9SP, UK
Tel: (020) 7235 1917 *or* 2545.
Website: www.peruembassy-uk.com
Opening hours: Mon-Fri 0930-1700.
Consular section: Tel: (020) 7838 9223.
Opening hours: Mon-Fri 0930-1300 (general enquiries); 1430-1630 (collection point only).

Embassy of the Republic of Peru in the USA
1700 Massachusetts Avenue, NW, Washington, DC 20036, USA
Tel: (202) 833 9860.
Website: www.peruvianembassy.us

Money

Currency: New Sol (PEN) = 100 céntimos. New Sol notes are in denominations of PEN200, 100, 50, 20 and 10. Coins are in denominations of PEN5, 2 and 1, and 50, 20, 10 and 5 céntimos.
Currency exchange: Only a few bureaux de change in Lima will exchange currencies other than US Dollars. Outside Lima, it is virtually impossible. US Dollars can be exchanged everywhere and banks, hotels and shops also readily accept US Dollars (although torn or damaged notes are usually rejected). It is not recommended to exchange money from street vendors. ATMs are now generally regarded as one of the best ways to obtain money in Peru.
Credit & debit cards: All major credit cards are accepted, but usage may be limited outside of Lima. Check with your credit or debit card company for details of merchant acceptability and other services which may be available.
Traveller's cheques: Banks will exchange traveller's cheques although it can be a slow process outside Lima. To avoid additional exchange rate charges, travellers are advised to take traveller's cheques in US Dollars. The ability to use traveller's cheques is also quite limited in some areas so you should check whether or not they will be accepted in the area you are visiting prior to travel.
Currency restrictions: There are no restrictions on the import and export of local currency. The import of foreign currency is unrestricted. The export of foreign currency is limited to the amount imported. Receipts of exchange of foreign currencies into PEN must be presented when exchanging back from PEN into foreign currency.
Banking hours: Mon-Fri 0900-1800, Sat 0900-1300 (may vary during the summer).
Exchange rate indicators:
Rate at time of publishing

£1.00=	PEN5.82
$1.00=	PEN3.36

Duty Free

The following items may be imported by visitors over 18 years of age into Peru without incurring customs duty:
400 cigarettes or 50 cigars or 250g of tobacco; alcoholic beverages not exceeding 2.5l; a reasonable amount of perfume for personal use; gifts or new articles for personal use up to a value of US$300; 2kg of processed food.
Restricted items: If importing sausages, salami, ham or cheese, a sanitary certificate from the manufacturer is required. The import of raw ham from Italy and Portugal is prohibited. The export of artistic or cultural articles is prohibited.

Public Holidays

Below are listed Public Holidays for the January 2006-June 2007 period.
2006: Jan 1 New Year's Day. **Apr 13** Maundy Thursday (half day). **Apr 14** Good Friday. **May 1** Labour Day. **Jun 29** St Peter's and St Paul's Day. **Jul 28-29** Independence Day Celebrations. **Aug 30** St Rosa of Lima Day. **Oct 8** Angamos Battle. **Nov 1** All Saints' Day. **Dec 8** Immaculate Conception. **Dec 24** Christmas Eve (half day). **Dec 25** Christmas Day.
2007: Jan 1 New Year's Day. **Apr 5** Maundy Thursday (half day). **Apr 6** Good Friday. **May 1** Labour Day. **Jun 29** St Peter's and St Paul's Day.

Health

	Special Precautions?	Certificate Required?
Yellow Fever	Yes	1
Cholera	2	No
Typhoid & Polio	3	N/A
Malaria	4	N/A

Note: *Regulations and requirements may be subject to change at short notice, and you are advised to contact your doctor well in advance of your intended date of departure. Any numbers in the chart refer to the footnotes below.*

1: A *yellow fever* vaccination certificate is required for travellers over six months of age arriving from infected areas. Travellers arriving from non-endemic zones should note that vaccination is strongly recommended for travel to areas within the Amazon Basin, even if an outbreak has not been reported and they would normally not require a vaccination certificate to enter the country.
2: Following WHO guidelines issued in 1973, a *cholera* vaccination certificate is no longer a condition of entry to Peru. However, autochthonous cases of *cholera* were reported in 1996. Up-to-date advice should be sought before deciding whether these precautions should include vaccination as medical opinion is divided over its effectiveness; see the Health appendix for more information.
3: Immunisation against *typhoid* is advised.
4: *Falciparum* malaria exists in all areas below 1500m and in the areas of Jaen, Lambayeque, Loreto, Luciano Castillo, Piura, San Martin, Tumbes and Ucayali. All health centres, which are controlled by the Ministry of Health, will provide free information and medication to anyone entering a high risk area.
Food & drink: Drink only bottled water. Pasteurised milk is widely available. Avoid dairy products that are likely to have been made from unboiled milk. Avoid street food vendors and the cheaper restaurants. Only eat well-cooked meat and fish, preferably served hot. Pork, salad and mayonnaise may carry increased risk. Vegetables should be cooked and fruit peeled. Always check the expiry date of processed food.
Other risks: *Hepatitis A* occurs, and *hepatitis B* and *D* are a risk in the Amazon Basin. *Dengue fever* outbreaks are common in the Amazon Basin. In April 2005, there were reported cases of *dengue fever* in the northern outskirts of Lima, isolated parts of the jungle provinces of Loreto, San Martin and Ucayali and in the northern coastal area between Tumbes and La Libertad.
Rabies is present. For those at high risk, vaccination before arrival should be considered. If you are bitten, seek medical advice without delay. For more information, consult the *Health* appendix.
Altitude sickness can be a problem if visiting the highlands. Visitors should take time to acclimatise and avoid doing too much strenuous exercise on the day or arrival.
Insect bites may be a problem in the jungle and the highlands. Insect repellent and long layers for the evening are recommended. *Malaria* is prevalent in northern parts of Peru and in Iquitos (Amazon) particularly, where there is risk of flooding during the Peruvian summer months of November to April.
Health care: International travellers are strongly advised to take out full health insurance and should be prepared to pay up front for medical services.

Travel - International

AIR:
The national airlines are *Lan Perú (LP)* (website: www.lan.com) and *Taca Perú (TA)* (website: www.taca.com).
There are no direct flights from London; however, airlines with regular services to Peru include *Air Canada*, *Air Madrid*, *Alitalia*, *American Airlines*, *Avianca*, *British Airways*, *Continental*, *Iberia*, *KLM*, *Lacsa* and *United Airlines*.
Approximate flight times: From Lima to *London* is 15 hours (including stopover in Madrid), to *Los Angeles* is six hours, to *Miami* is five hours and to *New York* is nine hours. Direct flights from Europe take between 12 hours (from Madrid) and 14 hours (from Frankfurt).
Main airports: *Lima (LIM) (Jorge Chávez International Airport* (website: www.lap.com.pe) is 16km (10 miles) northwest of the city centre (travel time – 25 minutes).
To/from the airport: Taxis to the city centre are available.

Facilities: Duty free and handicrafts shop, banks/bureaux de change, left luggage facility, pharmacy, medical centre, Internet cafe, car hire (*Avis, Budget, Hertz, National* and *Thrifty*), coffee shops, bars and restaurants and tourist information. *Cusco (CUZ)*, located in the south, receives flights from La Paz (Bolivia).
Vist South America Pass: Vist South America Pass: This must be bought outside South America in the country of residence and allows unlimited travel to 34 cities in the following countries: Argentina, Bolivia, Brazil, Colombia, Chile (except Easter Island), Ecuador, Paraguay, Peru, Uruguay and Venezuela. Participating airlines include *Aer Lingus (EI), American Airlines (AA), British Airways (BA), Cathay Pacific (CX), Finnair (AY), IBERIA (IB), LAN-Chile (LA)* and *Qantas (QF)*. A minimum of three flights must be booked, with no maximum; the maximum stay is 60 days, with no minimum, and prices depend on the amount of flight zones covered. Children under 12 years of age are entitled to a 33 per cent discount and infants (under two years old) only pay 10 per cent of the adult fare. For further details, contact one of the participating airlines.
Departure tax: US$28 from Lima's airport. Transit passengers and children under two years of age are exempt. Payment must be paid in cash prior to boarding.

SEA:
Main ports: Callao and San Martin. Some international cruises occasionally call at Callao, such as *Princess Cruises* (website: www.princess.com)

ROAD:
The main international highway is the Pan-American Highway running north-south through the coastal desert of Peru from Tumbes to Tacna. Transport from Argentina, Brazil, Chile, Colombia, Ecuador, Paraguay, Uruguay and Venezuela is available through companies like *Bus Tas Choapa Internacional, Empresa Paraguaya de Transporte, Ormeño, El Rápido* and *Rutas de América*. It is also possible to go from La Paz in Bolivia to Puno on Lake Titicaca (south Peru).

Travel - Internal

AIR:
Aerocóndor, Aviandina, LAN Perú, Star Up, Taca Perú and *TANS* handle virtually all domestic air traffic linking Lima to Andahuaylas, Arequipa, Ayacucho, Cajamarca, Chiclayo, Cusco, Huánuco, Iquitos, Juliaca-Puno, Piura, Pucallpa, Puerto Maldonado, Tacna, Tarapoto, Trujillo, Tumbes and other cities. For information on internal flights, contact the Peruvian Corporation of Airports (Corpac) (website: www.corpac.gob.pe).
Departure tax: US$5. Children under two years of age are exempt. Payment must be paid in cash prior to boarding.

RIVER:
Transportation is available between Pucallpa and Iquitos (approximately five days) and from Iquitos to the border with Brazil and Colombia (two to three days). However, river travel can be long and uncomfortable.

RAIL:
A tourist train operates services between Puno and Cusco and from Cusco to Ollantaytambo and Machu Picchu. There is a daytime connection from Puno and Juliaca to Cusco. From Cusco there is a daily train to Machu Picchu, which takes approximately four hours. There are also three major passenger services in Peru; these run between Arequipa, Puno and Cusco, Cusco and Machu Picchu and Lima and Huáncayo. Please remember that the trains between Arequipa and Puno and Puno to Cusco are the only means of transport for local people, therefore do not expect a luxury trip with good service. Fast and comfortable electric *autovagons* operate on some routes. There are no connections between Lima and Cusco. Always check for revised schedules. For more information, contact Peru Rail in Lima (tel: (01) 444 5020/5; website: www.perurail.com). It is also possible to charter a train from Arequipa to Juliaca for groups of 40 or more.

ROAD:
The *Central Highway* connects Lima with La Oroya and Huancayo. From La Oroya there is a road connecting Cerro de Pasco, Huánuco, Tingo María and Pucallpa on the Ucayali River. Landslides are frequent in the rainy season (December to March), making for slow travel. The *Touring y Automóvil Club del Perú* and the *Instituto Geográfico Nacional* sell maps. Travel guides like *Guía Toyota* and *Guía Inca del Perú* include good road maps. Traffic drives on the right. **Bus:** Operated extensively, providing a very cheap means of travel. Greyhound-type buses are operated by *Cruz del Sur, Enlaces, Express Sud Americano, Ittsa, Oltursa, Ormeño, Perú Bus* and many others. Quality of service varies according to prices. **Taxi:** Many unlicensed taxis companies are in operation and visitors are advised to avoid these. They usually have a red and white taxi sign on the windscreen. Bright yellow taxis are registered with the Metropolitan Lima Taxi Service. These are the only taxis allowed in to downtown Lima. There are taxis at the main hotels and airports. Taxis do not have meters and fares should be agreed before departure (they are relatively inexpensive). There is an extensive and safe taxi service available by telephone in the main cities. Taxi fares increase by 35 to 50 per cent after midnight and on holidays. **Car hire:** Major car hire companies have offices in Lima and provide service to all main cities.
Documentation: Foreign driving permits are valid for 30 days starting the date of arrival. An International Driving Permit is required in case of longer stays. International driving permits in Peru can be obtained through the *Touring y Automóvil Club del Perú*. All foreign vehicles must obtain the appropriate documentation from the National Automobile Association in their own country or on the Peruvian border before entering the country (in this case a 90-day permission will be obtained). You should always carry your driver's licence, a copy of your passport and, if the vehicle is rented, a copy of the rental contract.

URBAN:
Public transport in Lima is provided by conventional buses and by minibuses (*combis*). The minimum rate is US$0.30. These operate from 0600 to 0000 on established routes; wherever possible, try to avoid using bus travel late at night.

Travel times:

	Air	Road
Arequipa	**1.25**	**14.00**
Ica	**-**	**4.00**
Puno (Juliaca)	**1.30***	**24.00**
Tumbes	**1.30**	**18.00**

Note: (a) Approximate travel times are given for travel by bus. (b)* Includes one stopover.

Travel Advice

There has been a significant increase in the number of reported robberies, bag snatches and crimes associated with rogue taxis recently..
Street crime is a problem, particularly in Lima, Cusco, Arequipa and Huaraz.
Travellers should be aware of the global risk of indiscriminate terrorist attacks, which could be against civilian targets, including places frequented by foreigners.
The internal terrorism in Peru of the 1980s and 1990s has largely ended, but has not completely disappeared. States of Emergency remain in force in certain districts.
Street demonstrations, sometimes violent, are a common form of protest in Peru. Travellers should take care to avoid any area in which large crowds are gathering.
Peru is an earthquake zone and tremors are frequent. On 25 September 2005, there was an earthquake measuring 7.5 on the Richter scale north east of Moyobamba in San Martin department. This followed an earthquake on 13 June 2005, on the Peru/Chile border.
On 13 October, a landslide stranded 1400 tourist and residents near the Inca ruins of Machu Picchu. Train services in the area have been affected and it is not clear how long it will take to restore the service.
This advice is based on information provided by the Foreign and Commonwealth Office in the UK. It is correct at time of publishing. As the situation can change rapidly, visitors are advised to contact the following organisations for the latest travel advice:

British Foreign and Commonwealth Office
Tel: (0845) 850 2829.
Website: www.fco.gov.uk

US Department of State
Website: http://travel.state.gov/travel

Accommodation

HOTELS:
Lima has the largest choice of hotels in Peru. Other cities where 5- and 4-star hotels can be found are Arequipa, Cajamarca, Chiclayo, Cusco, Ica, Iquitos, Puno and Trujillo (the grading does not always match international standards). Throughout Lima and in most major towns, there are many economical *pensiones* (guest houses) to be found. The quality of accommodation in the provinces varies considerably, but hotels are frequently of a good standard. Hotel prices in the provinces are lower than in the capital. Hotels are classified by the star system, the highest and most luxurious being 5 stars. The level of comfort, quality of service and general infrastructure are the criteria for inclusion in each grade. Prices vary accordingly. All accommodation prices are subject to 19 per cent tax (IGV). Hotels of the higher categories might also add 1 to 13 per cent service charges. It is advisable to reserve a room during the peak tourist season (June to September).

HOME STAYS:
It is possible to arrange a stay in a Peruvian family home. Promperú are able to offer further information (see *Top Things To Do*).

CAMPING/CARAVANNING:
No formal arrangements exist in Peru.

YOUTH HOSTELS:
There are 34 youth hostels in the country with dormitory, single or twin rooms. They usually have a bar or cafe and a kitchen.

ACCOMMODATION INFORMATION

Asociación Peruana de Hoteles, Restaurantes y Afines (AHORA)
Avenida Avenida Benavides 881, Miraflores, Lima 18, Peru
Tel: (1) 444 4303.

Asociación Peruana de Albergues Turísticos Juveniles (Peruvian Association of Youth Hostels)
Avenida Casimiro Ulloa 328, San Antonio, Miraflores, Lima 18, Peru
Tel: (1) 446 5488.
Website: www.limahostell.com.pe

Top Things To See

- Pizarro chose **Lima**'s palace of local chief Taurí Chusko as the site of the city's inauguration on January 6 1535 - and thus began Lima's colonial history. Such history is reflected in the opulent mansions that grace Lima's plazas, with their Moorish latticed wooden balconies. The main square, **Plaza de Armas**, is a UNESCO World Heritage Site, complete with paths, gardens and an elegant bronze fountain. The impressive **Palacio de Gobierno (Government Palace)**, located at the northern end of the plaza, is another lavish example of colonial opulence. Highlights are the **Grand Salon**, modelled on the Versailles Palace's Hall of Mirrors, the dining room adorned with friezes depicting Inca history and the private theatre. Outside, visitors can admire the elaborate military uniforms in the **Changing of the Guard**.
- See one of the few buildings to withstand the 1746 earthquake in Lima - the **Church of San Francisco**. Recently renovated with the help of UNESCO, this exquisite church has several highlights, including the extraordinary early 17th-century domed cedarwood roof above the broad staircase leading to the cloisters. The library, in its thin, rectangular two-storey salon with twin delicate wooden spiral staircases, houses a collection of some 20,000 volumes, plus masterpieces by Jordeans, Rubens and Van Dyck. Underneath the church are the **catacombs**, complete with ghoulish circular displays of the skulls and bones of some 70,000 souls.
- Unearth some of Peru's many archaeological treasures, such as **Chan Chan**, the largest pre-Inca mud city (20 sq km/7.7 sq miles) declared a World Heritage Site by UNESCO in 1986 and the *huacas* (religious centres) of the **Sun** and the **Moon** (the latter has painted mud walls depicting one of the main deities of the Moche culture). The beautifully restored **Huaca Arco Iris** is covered with pre-Inca hieroglyphics.
- Any trip to Peru must entrail venturing into the capital of the Inca Empire. **Cusco**, founded AD 1100, is today a fascinating mix of Inca and colonial Spanish architecture and was declared a World Heritage Site by UNESCO in 1983. Almost every central street has remains of Inca walls, arches and doorways that serve as the foundation for the colonial and modern buildings. Colourful murals depicting historical scenes can be seen on countless walls and indigenous women with braids and embroidered shawls set up makeshift stalls selling woven blankets and handmade crafts and jewellery.
- The **Church of Santo Domingo** was built on the foundations of the **Inca Temple of the Sun, Qoricancha**, (**Quechua** for golden courtyard: its walls were covered in solid gold sheets, much to the delight of the gold-hungry Spanish invaders). Heavy doors leading into the cloisters are now adorned with Moorish star- and diamond-shape patterns. The cloisters are lined with oil paintings in heavy gilt frames that depict scenes from the life of St Dominic. Remains of the original Inca temple walls are found inside the main courtyard. Huge blocks of green and grey diorite stone were placed together in a perfect fit without mortar, perfectly demonstrating the sophisticated Inca engineering and architectural skills. A further example of Inca skill with polygonal masonry is seen in the **Stone of Twelve Angles**.
- For most visitors, the Inca city of **Machu Picchu** is the highlight of their visit. Revealed to the Western world by the American Hiram Bingham on July 24 1911, and declared a World Heritage Site by UNESCO in 1983, it is probably the most important archaeological site in South America and requires at least one day to explore fully.

Highlights of the site include the **ceremonial baths**, the **Temple of the Sun**, **Temple of the Three Windows** and the **Intihuatana**, or carved rock pillar used by Inca astronomers to predict the solstices.

- A 30-minute walk south from the main complex takes the visitor to the **Inca Bridge**, carved into the vertiginous cliff face. Climb the peak of **Huayna Picchu** that towers over the city.
- **Lake Titicaca** is the highest navigable lake in the world and home to the Uros people, who have for centuries built their homes and boats out on the lake using Totora reeds. Extending over a total surface area of 8379 sq km (3235 sq miles), Lake Titicaca is 180km (112 miles) long and 69km (43 miles) across at its widest point. Around the lake can be found pre-AD 1000 remains from the Pucara and Tiahuanaco cultures. An unforgettable site is the **Yavari Project**, the oldest steamship on Lake Titicaca. The lake forms a natural border between Peru and Bolivia and in this part of Peru the native people are predominantly Aymara and not Quechua speakers.
- Delve into **Manu National Park**, Peru's greatest natural treasure in biodiversity. Located in the rainforests of the Cusco and **Madre de Dios** regions and extending to some 20,000 sq km (7722 sq miles) of tropical rainforest, the area was first earmarked for protection in 1973, declared a UNESCO Biosphere Reserve in 1977 and a World Natural Heritage Site in 1987. The park is inhabited by indigenous people including the Arahuaca, Matiguenka, Piro, Yine and Yora tribes and is divided into three distinct areas. The first section, **Parque Nacional Manu**, can only be entered by scientists and researchers on special permits, while the **Zona Reservada** is accessible to group tours operated by a licensed company and the **Zona Cultural** consists of a few villages that are outside restricted areas. Tourist infrastructure in the Zona Reservada is rustic and made from sustainable materials such as local timber and woven palm fronds for roofing material. Few of the lodges have hot water or electricity and, as such, are packaged as eco-friendly and follow strict environmental practices. Scientists believe that the park is home to more than 2000 species of plants, 1200 species of butterflies, around 800 types of birds and 200 different mammals. The dense carpet of tropical rainforest is irrigated and dissected by several great rivers, including the Madre de Dios, **Manu Panagua** and **Ucayali**. Over time, swamps and *cochas* (oxbow lakes) have formed, sustaining unique types of flora and fauna. In the Manu region, a whole host of birds can be seen including the Amazon kingfisher, harpy eagle, hoatzin, orinoco goose and tiger herons. It is possible to spot various primate groups in the dense tree cover, such as the emperor tamarin, spider and howler monkeys, but less common are the lowland tapir, sloth, jaguar or capybaras.
- If you have time on your travels, you also wish to visit the **Tambopata-Candamo Reserved Zone**, 45km (28 miles) from **Puerto Maldonado** by river, which specialists say contains the largest and richest bio-diversity of the world. The flora and fauna within includes more than 2000 flower varieties, 1000 birds and 900 butterflies and dragonflies.

Top Things To Do

- On 30 August, marvel at the **religious processions** held to honour **Lima**'s patron saint, **Santa Rosa de Lima**. Later, on October 18, a purple haze descends upon the city as the faithful don purple robes to march in processions, praising El Señor de los Milagros.
- Browse for exquisite **handicrafts** in areas like **Ayacucho** (specializing in pottery, leatherwork, textiles and jewellery) or **Cajamarca**. There is also a colourful daily **market** in Lima's **Chinatown** district that should not be missed.
- **Fly** above the **Nazca Lines** and gaze at these large and spectacular geoglyphs below. The Nazca Lines are located 420km (265 miles) south of Lima and are geometric shapes and lines drawn with sand and stone, representing animals (birds, felines and reptiles). They are thought to have been made by three different cultures between 200 BC and AD 600. Although best viewed aerially, they can also be seen from an observation tower. **Ica** is a good point of call for trips to the Nazca Lines.
- Go to **Cajamarca**'s **Carnival**, famous throughout Peru for its annual celebrations that last for an entire month. One word of warning – try to avoid getting soaked with water, since it is the traditional Cajamarca Carnival greeting!
- Nicknamed the 'Peruvian Switzerland' for its glacial lakes and snow-capped peaks, **Huaraz** is the departure point for treks and **expeditions** to the **Callejón de Huaylas**. Huaraz hosts the annual **Semana del Andinismo**, including international **ski** events on the **Pastoruri Glacier**. The **Huascarán National Park**, declared a World Heritage Site by UNESCO in 1985, protects the area's biggest indigenous plants, the Puya Raymondi (giant bromeliads that grow up to 15m high and live for over 40 years) and is the home of the native viscacha,

puma, vicuña and the rare spectacled bear.
- Explore **Sacsayhuamán** on **horseback**. Just outside of Cusco, Sacsayhuamán is the most impressive of four of the city's nearby Inca ruins (the others are **Puca Pucara**, **Qenko** and **Tambo Machay**). This magnificent ceremonial centre, with its three vast ramparts that run parallel for more than 350m (1148ft), was the site of the famous battle between Manco Inca and Juan Pizarro, Francisco's younger brother, in 1536. The boulders used to construct the walls are immense, weighing up to 360 tons and measuring up to 10m (33ft) in height and 4m (13ft) in depth. On June 24 each year, thousands of locals arrive to celebrate the **Inti Raymi festival** with a colourful pageant held at Sacsayhuaman.
- Of course, the most famous **mountain trek** in Peru is probably the **Inca Trail** to **Machu Picchu**, which offers views of snow-capped mountains, high cloud forests and the opportunity to walk past 12 magnificent ancient Inca ceremonial centres, such as those at **Phuyupatamarca** and **Wiñay Wayna**. Other fantastic routes include: the **Cordillera Blanca trail**, which covers the highest tropical mountain range, a 180km-(112.5 mile-) long paradise of snow-capped mountains, glaciers, emerald-green lakes and archaeological sites, containing a wide variety of flora and fauna and practically the entire range lying within the Huascarán National Park; the **Olleros-Chavín Llama Trek** between the attractive town of **Olleros** and the spectacular archaeological site of **Chavín de Huántar**; the **Cordillera Huayhuash** (Huaraz); the **Colca Valley** (164km/102 miles north of Arequipa), where major attractions include snow-capped volcanoes; and **Mount Ausangate** (south of Cusco), a physically demanding eight- to 12-day walk, which requires climbing through high mountain passes and being exposed to changing weather conditions.

TOURIST INFORMATION

PromPerú (Commission for the Promotion of Peru)
Calle 1 Oeste 050, Piso 13, Urbani Cacion, Córpac, San Isidro, Lima 27, Peru
Tel: (1) 224 3131.
Website: www.peru.org.pe

Entertainment

FOOD & DRINK: The hot and spicy nature of Peruvian food, created by *ají* and *ajo* (hot pepper and garlic), has become celebrated at home and abroad. Peruvians enjoy a wide variety of vegetables; there are over 2000 kinds of indigenous and cultivated potatoes alone. Table service is the norm in hotels and restaurants and many of them also offer buffet-type lunches.

National specialities:
- *Ceviche* (uncooked fish marinated in lemon or lime juice and hot chili pepper, served with fried corn, sweet potatoes, onions and flavoured with coriander).
- *Escabeche* is a cooked fish appetiser eaten cold, served with peppers and onions.
- Scallops (*conchitas*), mussels (*choros*), octopus (*pulpo*) and shrimps (*camarones*) are plentiful and delicious.
- *Chupe de camarones* is a chowder-type soup made with shrimps, milk, eggs, potatoes and peppers.
- *Papa a la huancaina* (yellow potato with cheese and chilli sauce).
- *Cau cau* (tripe cooked with potato, peppers and parsley).
- *Tamales* (boiled corn dumplings filled with meat and wrapped in a banana leaf).
- *Anticuchos* (strips of beef or fish marinated in vinegar and spices, then barbecued on skewers).
- *Lomo saltado* (pieces of beef sautéed with onions and peppers, served with fried potatoes and rice).
- Traditional desserts are *arroz con leche* (rice pudding).
- *Alfajores* (wafer-thin spirals of shortbread dusted with icing sugar) and served with *manjar blanco* (a caramel sauce).
- *Mazamorra morada* (purple maize and sweet potato starch jelly cooked with lemons, dried fruits, cinnamon and cloves).

National drinks:
- The most famous drink is *pisco sour*, made from a potent grape brandy.
- Other pisco-based drinks are *algarrobina* (pisco and carob syrup), *chilcano* (pisco and ginger ale) and *capitán* (pisco and vermouth).
- *Chicha de jora* (fermented red or yellow corn juice) and *chicha morada* (non-alcoholic purple corn juice) are popular drinks dating from Inca times.
- Peruvian beers and national wines are good.

Tipping: Service charges of 10 per cent are added to all bills. Additional tips of 5 per cent are expected. Taxi drivers do not generally expect tips. Doorkeepers should be tipped about US$1.

NIGHTLIFE: There are many good bars, pubs, discos and

casinos in the major towns and tourist resorts. *Peñas* always serve snacks and some serve full meals. Here one can enjoy *criolla* or folk music, especially at weekends. Nightlife in Lima and Cusco has a wide array of choices. Most discos, *peñas*, pubs and karaokes are open until 0300 or 0400 in the morning.

SHOPPING: There are many attractive Peruvian handicrafts such as *alpaca* wool sweaters, *alpaca* and *llama* rugs, Indian masks, weaving, jewellery and much more. Galleries and handicraft shops abound in the Miraflores, Pueblo Libre and downtown districts of Lima. Handicrafts markets are located in Miraflores (Petit Thouars Ave, blocks 52 to 53) and Pueblo Libre (La Marina Ave, blocks 8 to 10). Bargaining is an expected practice with beach vendors and at markets and known as 'regateo'.

Shopping hours: Mon-Sat 1000-1300 and 1600-2000 (although many shops are open Mon-Sun 0900-2000).

Business

- **GDP:** US$68.4 billion (2004).
- **Main exports:** Copper, gold, zinc, crude petroleum and petroleum products and coffee.
- **Main imports:** Petroleum and petroleum products, plastics, machinery, vehicles, iron and steel, wheat and paper.
- **Main trade partners:** USA, Chile, China, Spain, UK, Brazil, Colombia and Japan.

ECONOMY: The Peruvian economy is divided into two distinct parts: a relatively modern industrial and service economy concentrated on the coastal plain, and a subsistence agricultural economy in the interior. Inevitably, one consequence has been huge migration from the interior to the coastal cities. About one-third of the workforce is engaged in agriculture, producing rice, maize and potatoes for domestic consumption and coffee as the principal cash crop. There is also a substantial illicit economy based on the production of coca (which has grown recently due to the collapse of world coffee prices). Fisheries are also important, and provide substantial export income. Much of the foreign investment of the early 1990s was directed towards Peru's major industry, mining, which accounts for about half of export earnings. Peru is a major producer of copper; in addition, there are sizeable deposits of lead, zinc, silver, gold, and some oil reserves. Manufacturing is concentrated in processed foods, chemicals, metal products, machinery and textiles. In the service sector, tourism has grown considerably during the last two decades, and now brings in almost US$1 billion annually.

During the early- to mid-1990s, Peru implemented important market-oriented reforms, including a drastic overhaul of the fiscal and monetary systems, privatisation of key industries (mining, telecommunications and energy), trade deregulation and measures to attract investment from abroad. The strategy was reasonably successful, boosting exports and Government tax revenues while attracting foreign capital. The defeat of the *Sendero Luminoso* insurgency also served to boost investor confidence. Throughout most of the decade, Peru was among the most dynamic economies in Latin America, with an average annual GDP growth of around 5 per cent. The economy stalled in 1997 – affected by the Asian and Brazilian financial crises, the effects of *El Niño* (especially upon agriculture) and internal politics – but has since recovered. The official unemployment rate is 9.5 per cent, but it is estimated that up to 40 per cent of the workforce are underemployed. During 2004, annual growth 4.5 per cent. The inflation rate is 4.3 per cent.

Peru is a member of the Andean Treaty and the Latin American Integration Association, ALADI, which promotes trade and economic development in Latin America. Significant new investment opportunities remain in Peru and with the growth of gas production, rising domestic consumption, increasing exports together with the prospect of a free trade agreement with the US, Peru's economy appears to be set on a path of sustainable and stable growth.

BUSINESS ETIQUETTE: Although the majority speak Spanish, many businesspeople speak some English. **Office hours:** Mon-Fri 0900-1800.

COMMERCIAL INFORMATION

Cámara de Comercio de Lima
Avenida Gregorio Escobedo 396, Jesus Maria, Lima 11, Peru
Tel: (1) 463 3434.
Website: www.camaralima.org.pe

A B C D E F G H I J K L M N O P Q R S T U V W X Y Z

The Philippines

500km
250mls
✈ international airport

Batan Is.
Luzon Strait
Babuyan Is.
SOUTH CHINA SEA
Laoag
Baguio
Luzon
PHILIPPINE SEA
Mt Pinatubo△ ·Angeles
MANILA ·Quezon City
PHILIPPINES
Manila Bay
San Pablo ·Laguna de Bay
Calapan·
Mindoro
Busuanga
Culion
Roxas·
Panay
Iloilo·
Bacolod·
Palawan
Puerto
Princesa
Negros
SULU SEA
Mapin
Zamboanga·
Basilan·
MALAYSIA
Sulu Archipelago
Jolo
Tawitawi
Catanduanes
·Legaspi
Masbate
Calbayog
Samar
Visayas
Tacloban
Cebu Leyte
Dinagat
·Siargao
Bohol
Bohol Sea
·Butuan
Iligan·
L. Lanao ·Cagayan de Oro
Moro Mindanao
Gulf ·Davao
Mt Apo
2954m
General
Santos
CELEBES SEA
INDONESIA

Location: South-East Asia.

Time: GMT + 8.

Overview

Although composed of 7107 islands (7108 at low tide), with a total coastline longer than that of the USA, most of the population of The Philippines lives on just 11 of them.

The earliest inhabitants of the Philippines were the Negritos. Other tribes later arrived from Malaysia and Indonesia. The islands were occupied by the Japanese between 1942 and 1945, during World War II, only achieving independence in 1946. During the next two decades, there was a succession of Presidents who maintained strong links with the United States.

In 1965, Ferdinand Marcos of the Nacionalista party won the Presidential elections and began a programme of rapid economic development. By 1972, Marcos had instituted martial law and suppressed all political opposition. He also set about large-scale looting of the country's finances to fill his and his family's own foreign bank accounts.

By the mid-1980s, the New People's Army (NPA), the armed wing of the Communist Party, was able to sustain a major insurrection right across the country in both rural and urban areas. The turning point for the regime came after the assassination of Benigno Aquino upon his return from exile in 1983. Public opinion rallied behind his widow, Corazon Aquino in a massive campaign of demonstrations and non-violent protest, popularly dubbed 'People Power'. Then, US President Ronald Reagan withdrew his backing from Marcos. The Filipino military, Marcos' last bastion of support, followed suit and Marcos left for Hawaiian exile in February 1986. He died there in September 1989.

Even though the current President, Gloria Arroyo – daughter of Diosdado Macapagal, the President during the early 1960s, has promised to create jobs and to improve living standards, poverty and the country's debt burden are still very high. This explains the high number of Filipinos residing abroad. Called *balikbayans*, these prove a steady source of incoming tourists in the country, representing approximately eight per cent of all visitors.

Aware of this situation, WOW Philippines, the cornerstone program of the Department of Tourism, is proving to be successful in attracting both domestic and foreign visitors to the country. With a fresh mandate given to President Gloria Macapagal-Arroyo in 2004, infrastructure projects involving airports, expressways, inter-island transport and even the currently almost non-existent railway system are part of the 10-point development agenda for the Presidency until 2010. Travel and tourism will surely benefit, as airports nationwide are being constructed or renovated to accommodate larger planes and more visitors, attracted by the country's warm tropical waters, coral gardens with beautiful marine life and dramatic drop-offs on the sea bed. Inland, the rich history and culture of the Filipino people, the dramatic landscapes and thriving cities will fascinate the visitor. Manila, the capital of the Philippines is also its heart and soul. It sets the rhythm of life in this archipelago and is a pulsating hub that blends the Oriental with the Occidental, the traditional with the modern, the mundane with extraordinary.

General Information

AREA: 300,000 sq km (115,831 sq miles).

POPULATION: 82.8 million (UN, 2005).

POPULATION DENSITY: 274.3 per sq km.

CAPITAL: Manila. **Population:** 9.9 million (2005 metropolitan area).

GEOGRAPHY: The Philippines lie off the southeast coast of Asia between Taiwan and Borneo in the Pacific Ocean and South China Sea. They are composed of 7107 islands and islets (7108 at low tide), 2773 of which are named. The two largest islands, Luzon in the north and Mindanao in the south, account for 65 per cent of the total land area and contain 60 per cent of the country's population. Between the two lie the Visayas Islands.

GOVERNMENT: Republic since 1935. Gained independence from the USA in 1946. **Head of State and Government:** President Maria Gloria Macapagal Arroyo since 2001. **Recent history:** The constitution adopted in 1987 provides for a dual-chamber congress comprising a 24-member Senate and a House of Representatives with a maximum 250 members, of whom 200 are directly elected. The President, who holds executive power, is elected for a six year term. Gloria Arroyo was elevated from Vice President to President in 2001 after protests led to the ousting of her predecessor, Joseph Estrada. In 2003, she survived an attempt by military mutineers to unseat her. Mrs Arroyo won a second six-year term in June 2004, defeating her main rival, the film star Fernando Poe Junior. Her first term brought mixed success. Her opponents claimed that she had cheated in the 2004 elections and levelled corruption allegations against her husband and other family members. Mrs Arroyo faces the challenge of delivering on her promises to create jobs and to improve living standards. Social and economic reforms introduced during her first term did little to ease poverty and the country's debt burden.

LANGUAGE: Filipino, based on Tagalog, is the national language. English is widely spoken, Spanish less so. There are over 111 cultural and racial groups, each with its own language or dialect; in 1990 there were 988 recorded languages.

RELIGION: Roman Catholic 83 per cent; the rest are made up mostly of Muslims, other Christian denominations, Buddhists and Taoists.

ELECTRICITY: 220 volts (110 volts in Baguio) AC, 60Hz. 110 volts is available in most hotels. Flat and round two- and three-pin plugs are in use.

SOCIAL CONVENTIONS: Government officials are addressed by their titles such as Senator, Congressman or Director. Otherwise, usual modes of address and levels of politeness are expected. Casual dress is acceptable in most places, but in Muslim areas the visitor should cover up. Filipino men may wear an embroidered long-sleeved shirt or a plain white *barong tagalog* with black trousers for formal occasions, women wear cocktail dresses or long gowns. The Philippines are, in many respects, more westernised than any other Asian country, but there is a rich underlay of Malay culture.

Climate

Tropical climate tempered by constant sea breezes. There are three distinct seasons: the rainy season (June to September), cool and dry (October to February), and hot and mainly dry (March to May). Evenings are cooler. Typhoons occasionally occur from June to September.

Required clothing: Lightweight cottons and linens are worn throughout most of the year, with warmer clothes useful on cooler evenings. Rainwear or umbrellas are advisable for the rainy season.

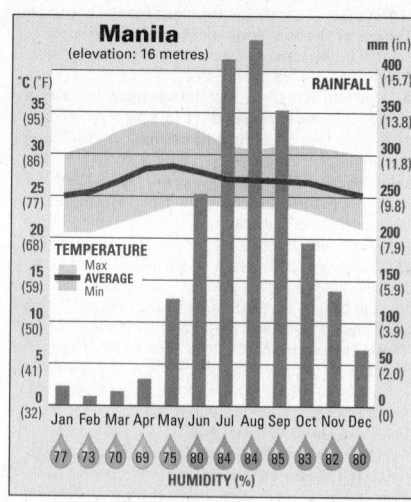

Manila (elevation: 16 metres)
TEMPERATURE Max, AVERAGE, Min
RAINFALL
HUMIDITY (%): 77 73 70 69 75 80 84 84 85 83 82 80

Communications

Telephone: IDD is available to main towns. Country code: 63. International calls to the smaller towns must be booked through the operator.

Mobile telephone: Roaming agreements exist with international mobile phone companies. Coverage is limited to Manila and other main urban areas.

Internet: Internet cafes are available across the country.

Post: Airmail to Europe takes at least five days. Post office hours: Mon-Fri 0800-1700.

MEDIA: Powerful commercial interests control or influence much of the media. The lively TV scene is dominated by the free-to-air networks ABS-CBN and GMA. Many TV broadcasters also operate radio networks. Press freedom is guaranteed under the 1987 constitution.

Press: There are about 17 daily newspapers. English-language daily newspapers include the *Daily Tribune*, *Manila Bulletin* (website: www.mb.com.ph), *Malaya* (website: www.malaya.com.ph), *Manila Times* (website: www.manilatimes.net), *Philippine Daily Inquirer* (website: www.inq7.net) and the *Philippine Star* (website: www.philstar.com).

TV: *IBC* is a Government-owned network. Commercial networks include *ABS-CBN* and *GMA Network*.

Radio: *Philippine Broadcasting Service (PBS)* is a Government-run network operating stations all over the Philippines. *ABS-CBN, GMA Network, Manila Broadcasting Company* and *Radio Mindanao Network* operate stations nationwide.

Passport/Visa

	Passport Required?	Visa Required?	Return Ticket Required?
Full British	Yes	1	Yes
Australian	Yes	1	Yes
Canadian	Yes	1	Yes
USA	Yes	1	Yes
Other EU	Yes	1	Yes
Japanese	Yes	1	Yes

Note: *Regulations and requirements may be subject to change at short notice, and you are advised to contact the appropriate diplomatic or consular authority before finalising travel arrangements. Any numbers in the chart refer to the footnotes below.*

PASSPORTS: Passports valid for a minimum of six months beyond intended length of stay required by all. **Note:** (a) Holders of certificates of identity, travel documents (*titre de voyage*), documents of identity, Taiwanese passports and all stateless persons *do* require visas. (b) All children of Filipino nationality must hold individual passports. (c) Immigration Officers at ports of entry may admit those with passports only valid for at least 60 days after intended length of stay, at their discretion.

VISAS: Required by all except the following:
(a) **1.** bona fide foreign tourists (including business travellers) for stays of less than 21 days provided holding passports valid for a minimum of six months beyond period of stay and return or onward tickets (except nationals of Afghanistan*, Albania, Algeria*, Bangladesh, Belize, Bosnia & Herzegovina, China (PR), CIS, Croatia, Cuba, Egypt*, Estonia, Georgia, India*, Iran*, Iraq*, Jordan*, Korea (Dem Rep), Latvia, Lebanon*, Libya*, Lithuania, Macedonia (Former Yugoslav Republic of), Moldova, Nauru, Nigeria*, Pakistan*, Sierra Leone, Serbia & Montenegro, Slovenia, Sri Lanka*, Sudan*, Syrian Arab Republic*, Tonga, Vanuatu, Yemen* and holders

of Palestinian* passports who *do* require a visa even if staying less than seven days);
(b) transit passengers continuing their journey to a third country within 72 hours provided holding onward or return documentation (some nationals are required to leave by the same or first connecting aircraft; enquire at Embassy for details).
Note: (a)* Nationals of these countries must apply for a Temporary Visitor Visa in their country of origin or place of legal residence. (b) All tourists wishing to stay longer than 21 days need a visa.
Types of visa and cost: *Temporary Visitor:* £22 (three month single-entry); £43 (six month multiple-entry); £65 (one year multiple-entry). *Restricted nationals* (three months): £30. Minors must pay PHP3,120.00 to the Immigration Officer at ports of entry.
Validity: 59 days from date of issue; multiple-entry: between six months and one year from date of issue. Visas normally allow stays of up to 59 days. Extensions are possible at the discretion of the Bureau of Immigration Office, with additional payment to the Emigration Clearance Certificate and corresponding Legal Research Fee.
Application to: Consulate (or consular section at Embassy); see *Passport/Visa Information*.
Application requirements: (a) One application form. (b) One passport-size photo signed on the bottom front, taken in the last six months. (c) Passport valid for at least six months beyond the intended period of stay. (d) Proof of means of support during stay, either by bank statement showing a balance of at least £500 or letter of employment. (e) Fee, in cash or postal order only (if applying by post, fee must be paid by postal order only). (f) If applying by post, a registered, stamped, self-addressed envelope is required and the application should be signed by a notary or commissioner of oaths. (g) Onward or return tickets. (h) A utility bill for proof of address. (i) Business travellers also require a letter from the sponsoring Filipino company or from their employer, stating the purpose of the visit.
(j) Proof of financial capability, eg latest bank statement, employment certificate etc. (k) Minors (under 15 years) must be accompanied by, or joining, parents to/in the Philippines. They must submit to the Immigration Officer at port of entry, an affidavit of request and consent by either parent/legal guardian (authenticated by relevant Embassy), and a clear photocopy of data page of passport of both minor and their parent(s). Application for a non-immigrant visa should be made in person.
Working days required: Two to three. Applications can be made Mon-Fri 0900-1300 and 1400-1700. Visas can be collected between 1600 and 1700.

PASSPORT/VISA INFORMATION

Embassy of the Republic of the Philippines in the UK
9A Palace Green, London W8 4QE, UK
Tel: (020) 7937 1600 *or* (020) 7361 4640/36/42 (consular section).
Website: www.philemb.org.uk
Opening hours: Mon-Fri 0900-1300 and 1400-1700.

Embassy of the Republic of the Philippines in the USA
1600 Massachusetts Avenue, NW, Washington, DC 20036, USA
Tel: (202) 467 9300.
Website: www.philippineembassy-usa.org

Money

Currency: Philippine Peso (PHP) = 100 centavos. Notes are in denominations of PHP1000, 500, 100, 50, 20, 10 and 5. Coins are in denominations of PHP5, 2 and 1, and 50, 25 and 10 centavos.
Currency exchange: Cash in pounds sterling or US dollars can be exchanged in banks, hotels and some retail outlets. Always use authorised money-changers or banks in Manila. Outside the capital there is a shortage of facilities for changing foreign currency and rates may get progressively worse as you travel further away from the city. It is advisable to carry a sufficient amount of Philippine pesos when travelling to other provinces.
Credit & debit cards: American Express, Diners Club, MasterCard and Visa are widely accepted in major establishments throughout the big cities of the Philippines. Check with your credit or debit card company for details of merchant acceptability and other services which may be available. 24-hour ATMs are available.
Traveller's cheques: Traveller's cheques and major foreign currency may be cashed at most commercial banks and Central Bank dealers. They are also accepted in most hotels, restaurants and shops. To avoid difficulties, travellers are advised to carry their receipt of purchase with them. To avoid additional exchange rate charges, travellers are advised to take traveller's cheques in US Dollars.
Currency restrictions: The import and export of local currency is limited to PHP10,000; any amount above this must be authorised by the Central Bank of the Philippines. The import and export of foreign currency is unlimited, but must be declared over PHP10,000.
Banking hours: Mon-Fri 0900-1500.
Exchange rate indicators:
Rate at time of publishing

£1.00=	PHP91.45
$1.00=	PHP53.66

Duty Free

The following items may be imported into The Philippines without incurring customs duty:
400 cigarettes or 50 cigars or 250g of tobacco; 2l of alcoholic beverage of not more than 1l each.
Note: (a) Visitors carrying more than US$3000 are to declare this at the Central Bank of the Philippines counter at customs. (b) Departing passengers cannot take out more than PHP1000 out of the country.
Prohibited items: Firearms, explosives, pornographic material, seditious or subversive material, narcotics and other internationally prohibited drugs (unless accompanied by a medical prescription), gambling articles and machines and misbranded and adulterated foodstuffs.

Public Holidays

Below are listed Public Holidays for the January 2006-June 2007 period.
2006: Jan 1 New Year's Day. **Apr 9** Bataan Day. **Apr 13** Maundy Thursday. **Apr 14** Good Friday. **May 1** Labour Day. **Jun 12** Independence Day. **Aug 31** National Heroes' Day. **Oct 22-24** Eid Ul Fitr (exact date varies). **Nov 1** All Saints' Day. **Nov 30** Bonifacio Day. **Dec 25** Christmas Day. **Dec 30** Rizal Day. **Dec 31** New Year's Eve.
2007: Jan 1 New Year's Day. **Apr 5** Maundy Thursday. **Apr 6** Good Friday. **Apr 9** Bataan Day. **May 1** Labour Day. **Jun 12** Independence Day.
Note: Easter is a major holiday in The Philippines and travel may be disrupted.

Health

	Special Precautions?	Certificate Required?
Yellow Fever	No	1
Cholera	2	No
Typhoid & Polio	3	1
Malaria	4	N/A

Note: *Regulations and requirements may be subject to change at short notice, and you are advised to contact your doctor well in advance of your intended date of departure. Any numbers in the chart refer to the footnotes below.*

1: A *yellow fever* or typhus vaccination certificate is required from travellers over one year of age arriving within six days from infected areas. A certificate is also required by those arriving from small pox or plague infected areas.
2: Following WHO guidelines issued in 1973, a *cholera* vaccination certificate is not a condition of entry to the Philippines, unless travellers arrive from infected areas. However, cholera is a risk in this country and precautions are essential. Up-to-date advice should be sought before deciding whether these precautions should include vaccination, as medical opinion is divided over its effectiveness; see the *Health* appendix for further information.
3: Vaccination against *typhoid* is advised.
4: *Malaria* risk exists throughout the year in areas below 600m (1969ft), except in the Provinces of Aklan, Bilaran, Bohol, Camiguin, Catanduanes, Capiz, Cebu, Guimaras, Iloila, Leyte, Manila, Masbate, North Samar and Sequijor. No risk is considered to exist in urban areas or in the plains. The malignant *falciparum* strain is present and is reported to be resistant to chloroquine.
Food & drink: Water used for drinking, brushing teeth or making ice should have first been boiled or otherwise sterilised. Milk is unpasteurised and should be boiled. Powdered or tinned milk is available and is advised, but make sure that it is reconstituted with pure water. Avoid dairy products which are likely to have been made from unboiled milk. Only eat well-cooked meat and fish, preferably served hot. Pork, salad and mayonnaise may carry increased risk. Vegetables should be cooked and fruit peeled.
Other risks: *Bilharzia* (*schistosomiasis*) is endemic in the south. Avoid swimming and paddling in stagnant fresh water; swimming pools that are well chlorinated and maintained are safe. *Dengue fever* and *filariasis* occur and *plague* is carried by insects. *Hepatitis B* is highly endemic. *Hepatitis A* may occur. *Japanese encephalitis* occurs rarely in western Luzon, Mindoro and Palawan from April to November and throughout the year in other areas, with the highest risk from April to January. *Leptospirosis* is a risk. *Chikungunya fever* is particularly common in urban areas of the central islands, such as Manila. *Gonorrhoea* resistant to penicilin is common in the Philippines, particularly in Manila and Cebu City. *Rabies* is present. For those at high risk, vaccination before arrival should be considered. If you are bitten, seek medical advice without delay. For more information, consult the *Health* appendix.
Health care: There is no reciprocal health agreement with the UK and health insurance is, therefore, essential. Approximately three-quarters of the hospitals are private.
Note: Although there have been no reported cases of Avian Influenza (Bird Flu) in the Philippines during the recent series of outbreaks, the World Health Organisation has confirmed cases elsewhere in the region. If you are travelling to The Philippines you should consult your usual healthcare provider for travel medical advice before departure. The risk from Avian Influenza is believed to be very low provided that live animal markets, poultry farms and other places where there is contact with domestic, caged or wild birds are avoided. Ensure poultry and egg dishes are thoroughly cooked.

Travel - International

AIR:
The national airline is *Philippine Airlines (PR)* (website: www.philippineairlines.com).
Note: The period over Easter, from Good Friday to the following Bank holiday (and sometimes beyond), is a major holiday in The Philippines, as are Christmas and New Year. There may be some difficulty booking a flight during these periods.
Approximate flight times: From Manila to *London* is 18 hours; to *Paris* is 16 hours 20 minutes; to *Los Angeles* is 20 hours 30 minutes; to *New York* is 27 hours; to *Singapore* is three hours 25 minutes; to *Tokyo* is four hours 50 minutes and to *Sydney* is eight hours.
Main airports: *Ninoy Aquino (MNL)* (website: www.miaa.gov.ph) is 12km (7 miles) south of Manila. *To/from the airport*: Bus and taxi services are available to the city (travel time – 60 to 90 minutes by public bus or 25 minutes by taxi). *Facilities*: Banks, post office, medical clinic, baggage deposit area, duty free shops and car hire.
Mactan International Airport (CEB) (Cebu Island) (website: www.mactan-cebuairport.com) is 45km (28 miles) from the city centre. *To/from the airport*: Hotels and tour operators provide their own coaches; taxis can be hired.
Departure tax: PHP550 for international departures. Children under two years of age and transit passengers are exempt.
SEA:
Main ports: *Manila*. The port is a crossroads of trade in the Asia-Pacific region. Shipping lines which call at Manila include *Evergreen Lines, Far Eastern Shipping Company (FESCO)* and *Lloyd Triestino*. Schedules and rates are listed in the shipping pages of daily newspapers. For more information, contact the Philippines Ports Authority (website: www.ppa.gov.ph).

Travel - Internal

AIR:
In addition to *Philippine Airlines (PR)*, there are several other charter airlines, including *Air Ads* (website: www.flyaai.com), *Air Philippines* (website: www.airphils.com), *Asian Spirit* (website: www.asianspirit.com), *Cebu Pacific Air* (website: www.cebupacificair.com) and *Laoag International Airlines*.
Departure tax: PHP100 for internal flights from Manila. Children under two years and passengers in transit remaining in the airport are exempt.
SEA:
Inter-island ships with first-class accommodation connect the major island ports. For details, contact local shipping lines (Aboitiz Transport Systems Corporation, tel: (2) 528 7979 *or* 7171; *or* WG&A Super Ferry, tel: (2) 528 7000; website: www.superferry.com.ph).
RAIL:
The *Metrotren* is recommended for long journeys. The railway is on Luzon Island and stretches as far south as Carmona and Cavite to Meycauayan in the North.
ROAD:
Roads spread among the islands, with highways on the Mindanao, Visayas and Luzon island groups. Further roads are currently being constructed. Traffic drives on the right. Driving off the main highway at night is dangerous and should be avoided. **Bus:** There are bus services between the towns and also widely available *jeepneys*. These are shared taxis using jeep-derived vehicles equipped to carry up to 14 passengers on bench seats. Fares are similar to buses. **Taxi:** Taxis are available in the cities and in many towns. Make sure meters are used, as some taxi drivers will set an exorbitant and arbitrary rate. **Car hire:** Car rentals are available in Manila and in major cities. The minimum age is 18.
Documentation: International Driving Permit required, together with a national driving licence.

URBAN:

A number of bus routes are operated by *Metro Manila Transport* using conventional vehicles, including double-deckers. Most journeys, however, are made by *jeepneys*, of which there are an estimated 30,000 in Manila alone. The *Metro Railway Transit (MTR)* connects North Avenue in Quezon to Taft Avenue in Pasay City, travelling the length of Epifanio delos Santo Avenue (EDSA). The *Light Railway Transit (LRT)*, a light rail transit link, runs from Baclaran terminal in the south to Caloocan terminal in the north. Tricycles (motorbikes with sidecars) and pedicabs (bicycles with a sidecars) are a cheaper alternative for shorter distances around towns. *Calseas* (horse-drawn carriages) are popular with tourists and are a common sight in downtown Manila.

Travel times: The following chart gives approximate travel times (in hours and minutes) from **Manila** to other major cities/towns in the Philippines.

	Air	Road	Sea
Batangas	-	2.00	-
Cagayan de Oro	1.25	-	48.00
Laoag	1.25	7.00	-
Palawan	1.10	-	24.00

Travel Advice

Travellers are advised against all travel to central, southern and Western Mindanao, and the Sulu archipelago including Basilan, Tawi-Tawi and Jolo, where there are ongoing military and police operations against insurgent groups.

The president of the Philippines declared a state of emergency on 24 February 2006, following the arrest of three people for an attempted coup. Public protests are likely. Visitors should avoid political gatherings or demonstrations.

There is a threat of kidnapping throughout the Philippines.

There is a high threat from terrorism throughout the Philippines.

In February 2005, bombs in Manil and Mindanao killed at least nine people and injured over 130 others. Attacks could be indiscriminate and against civilian targets in public places, includung those frequented by foreigners.

Travellers should also be alert to the risk of street crime.

Penalties for illegal drug importation and use are severe and can include the death penalty.

Visitors are advised to obtain comprehensive travel and medical insurance before travelling and to check any exclusions, and that their policy covers them for activities they want to undertake.

This advice is based on information provided by the Foreign and Commonwealth Office in the UK. It is correct at time of publishing. As the situation can change rapidly, visitors are advised to contact the following organisaions for the latest travel advice:

British Foreign and Commonwealth Office
Tel: (0845) 850 2829.
Website: www.fco.gov.uk

US Department of State
Website: http://travel.state.gov/travel

Accommodation

HOTELS:

In Manila, there are over 11,000 first-class hotel rooms. There are numerous smaller hotels, inns, hostels and pensions. Prices are often quoted both in Philippine Pesos and US Dollars. A complete directory of hotels is available from the Department of Tourism. The majority of establishments belong to the Hotel and Restaurant Association of the Philippines (HRAP). In addition, most regions have their own associations. Hotels are graded in the following categories based on standards set by the Office of Tourism Services, Department of Tourism, Manila: Economy, Standard, First Class and Deluxe.

SELF-CATERING:

'Apartels' are available for minimum stays of one week, and palm *nipa* huts can be rented on some islands.

CAMPING/CARAVANNING:

Offered only in a very limited number of places.

HOMESTAY:

This accommodation offers visitors the chance to sample life in a real Filipino home.

ACCOMMODATION INFORMATION

Hotel and Restaurant Association of the Philippines (HRAP)
Unit 701, Golden Rock Building, 168 Salcedo Street, Legaspi Village, Makati City, The Philippines
Tel: (632) 816 2421 *or* 2405 *or* 2422.
Website: www.dotpcvc.gov.ph/hrap/HRAP.html

Credit: © Gunther Deichmann

Top Things To See

- In the oldest part of the capital **Manila (Luzon island)**, see the remains of the massive wall which protected the **Intramuros (Walled City)**. Places of interest include **San Agustin Church** and **Manila Cathedral**, from which there is an excellent view of the 2072 sq km (800 sq miles) of the harbour, the ruins of **Fort Santiago** and **Chinatown** (outside the Intramuros). In the **Luneta Park**, discover the **Rizal Monument**, a memorial to the execution of this great Filipino intellectual of the late 19th century. Other places of interest are the **American Cemetery** and **Coconut Palace**.
- In the Parish of **Las Piñas**, a little way outside Manila, view the famous and unique **bamboo organ** inside the **St. Joseph Church**.
- 250km (150 miles) north of Manila is **Baguio**, 1525m (5000ft) above sea level, a cool haven from the summer heat. Drive up the zigzagging **Kennon Road** to have spectacular views of the countryside. Main attractions include **The Mansion**, summer residence of the Philippine President; **Bell Church**; **Baguio Cathedral**; and the **Crystal Caves**, composed of crystalline metamorphic rocks and once an ancient burial site.
- **Banaue** is a nine-hour bus ride north of Baguio. The beautiful **rice terraces** are the main attraction of this area. A breathtaking sight, they rise majestically to an altitude of 1525m (5000ft), and encompass an area of 10,360 sq km (4000 sq miles). The terraces were hand-carved some 2000 years ago using crude tools cutting into once barren rock, each ledge completely encompassing the mountain. Now listed by UNESCO as World Heritage sites, they offer an unforgettable sight to tourists and trekkers in the area.
- On **Corregidor Island**, 'The Rock', has a famous **memorial** to those who were killed during the Japanese invasion, and is accessible by hydrofoil.
- On **Mindoro** island, reached by ferry from Batangas pier and south of Manila, discover the stunning scenery of **Mount Halcon**, 2695m (8841ft) high, **Naujan Lake** and **Tamaraw Falls**.
- **Cebu City**, on **Cebu** island, is the main resort of the **Visayas**, a group of islands between Luzon and Mindanao. Sights include **Magellan's Cross**, a wooden cross planted by Magellan himself over 450 years ago to commemorate the baptism into the Christian faith of Rajah Humabon and his wife Juana with 800 followers. **Basilica Minor del Santa Niño** houses a baptismal gift that Magellan gave to his wife - a black image of the infant child. **Fort San Pedro**, the oldest and smallest Spanish fort in the country, was built on the orders of Spanish conquistador Miguel Lopez de Legazpi in 1565. The **Taoist Temple** is a reminder the city's Chinese heritage.
- In **Carcar** town, south of Cebu City, view many preserved Castillian houses, gardens and churches. The **Chapel of the Last Supper** in **Mandaue City** features hand-carved life-size statues of Christ and his apostles dating back to Spanish times.
- The **Magellan Monument** on **Mactan Island** was raised in 1886 to mark the spot where Magellan died, felled by the fierce chieftain, Datu Lapu-Lapu, who refused to submit to the Spanish conquerors. There is also a monument to Datu Lapu-Lapu honouring him as the first Filipino patriot. **Maribago** is the centre of the region's guitar-making industry.
- In **Iloilo City**, on **Panay island**, look at the 18th-century **Miagao Church**, a unique piece of Baroque colonial architecture with a facade decorated with impressions of coconut and papaya trees.
- On **Bohol Island**, just across the straits from Cebu in Central Visayas, **see the smallest monkey in the world**, the tarsier, and some of the country's most fascinating natural wonders; hundreds of **limestone hills**, some 30m (100ft) high, that in summer look like oversized chocolate drops, earning them the name '**Chocolate Hills**'. Visit the **Baclayon Church,** probably the oldest stone church in the Philippines, dating back to 1595.
- In **Zamboanga City**, considered by some as the most romantic place in the Philippines, in the southwestern tip of **Mindanao,** discover the island's seashells, unspoiled tropical scenery and magnificent flowers. Zamboanga was founded by the Spanish, and the 17th-century walls of **Fort Pilar**, built to protect the Spanish and Christian Filipinos from Muslim onslaughts, are still standing. **Pershing** and **Pasonanca Park** are worth visiting.
- **Davao** province (Mindanao island) is the site of **Mount Apo**, the highest peak in the country, while the **Apo Range** has spectacular waterfalls, rapids, forests, springs and mountain lakes.
- On the northern coast of Mindanao, **Cagayan de Oro** is the gateway to some of the most beautiful islands in the Philippines. By way of contrast, in **Bukidnon** there are huge cattle ranches and the famous Del Monte pineapple fields, and **Iligan City** is the site of the hydroelectric complex driven by the **Maria Cristina Falls**.
- In the province of **Lanao del Sur** (Mindanao island), characterised by its Muslim community, do not miss **Lake Lanao, Signal Hill,** the **Sacred Mountain,** the native market, **Torongan,** homes of the Maranao royalty, the various Muslim **mosques** on the shores of the lake and examples of the famous brassware industry centred in **Tugaua**.

Top Things To Do

- Go **diving** and explore World War II wrecks on the islands of **Batangas, Bohol, Mindoro** (particularly **Apo Reef Marine Park**) and **Palawan**. **Sicogon Island** is a haven for scuba divers, and has mountains and virgin forests to explore. **Boracay Island** is another such island paradise. A survey considered its powdery-fine white-sand beach to be amongst the best in the world. **Santa Cruz Island** has a sand beach which turns pink when the corals from the sea are washed ashore, and is ideal for **bathing**, **snorkelling** and **scuba diving**. There is also an old Muslim burial ground here. **La Union**, situated on the northwest coast of **Luzon**, has some of the best beach resort facilities on the island. **Boating** enthusiasts can rent traditional canoes (*bancas*) on most beaches. **Surfing** and **windsurfing** are also popular. **Kayaking** and some **rafting** are available in the wet season in the interiors of **Luzon** and **Mindanao**.
- Go on a **fishing** trip. The Philippines' warm waters, incorporating almost 2,000,000 sq km (772,200 sq miles) of fishing grounds, are inhabited by some 2400 fish species, including many game fish such as giant tuna, tanguingue, king mackerel, great barracuda, swordfish and marlin. Game fishing is best from December to August.
- Book an **adventure tour** with an ecological slant, including activities such as **canopy walking** (participants are lifted by pulleys to the canopy on the Philippine rainforest near **Cagayan de Oro**). The best areas for **trekking** and **mountaineering** include the region around **Matulid River**, **Mount Pulog** and **Mount Halcon** as

well as the famous UNESCO World Heritage-listed **rice terraces** in the **Cordillera** mountain range in northern Luzon. **Whale** and **dolphin watching** is popular in the **Tanon Strait** near Bohol Island.

- Watch a traditional game of **Sipa**, played with a small wicker ball, at the **Rizal Court** in Manila.
- In **Baguio** (Luzon island), 250km (150 miles) north of Manila and 1525m (5000ft) above sea level, go **biking, skating, hiking, horseback riding** or **walking** in **Burnham Park**, named after the city's planner, David Burnham.
- In summer, enjoy all kinds of festivities in **Tagaytay** (Luzon island). Buy flowering plants and fruits (in season) at roadside stalls. **Tagaytay Ridge** in **Cavite** overlooks a lake that contains **Taal Volcano**, which itself holds another lake.
- On **Bohol island**, a coconut-growing area, **purchase local handicrafts**, mostly of woven materials: grass mats, hats and baskets.
- In **Zamboanga City** (Mindanao island), visit the **flea market** which sells Muslim pottery, clothes and brassware.
- Visit **Villa Escudero**, an 800-hectare coconut plantation in **Quezon Province** (Luzon island). Less than two hours by road from Manila, it is part of a working plantation, yielding rare glimpses into rural life. Guests are taken on a tour of a typical village on a cart drawn by a **carabao**, or water buffalo.
- A day trip to the town of **Pagsanjan**, 63km (39 miles) southeast of Manila, includes dug-out **canoe rides** down the jungle-bordered river to the **Pagsanjan Falls**. This was a location for the filming of *Apocalypse Now*.
- On **Hundred Islands**, the second-largest marine reservation in the world, teeming with over 2000 species of aquatic life, explore the caves and domes of **Marcos Island** and the **Devil's Kitchen.** The entire province of **Palawan** is a remarkable terrain for adventure and exploration, with its primeval rainforests, **St Paul's Underground River, Tubattaha Reef** and **Tabon Caves** with human fossils dating back 22,000-24,000 years.

TOURIST INFORMATION

Philippine Cultural and Tourism Office in the UK
146 Cromwell Road, London SW7 4EF, UK
Tel: (020) 7835 1100.
Website: www.wowphilippines.co.uk

Entertainment

FOOD & DRINK: Unlike a lot of Asian cooking, Filipino cuisine is distinguished by its moderate use of spices. American, Chinese, Japanese, Malay and Spanish influences have all left their mark in a subtle blending of cultures and flavours. All the regional dishes are available in Manila's excellent restaurants, which, like the restaurants of all the main towns, offer a varied cuisine. For the less adventurous, there are also European-style restaurants and American fast food. Restaurants are generally informal, with table service. Rice is a staple of Filipino cuisine. Fruit is plentiful with mangoes, papayas, bananas, chicos, lanzones, guavas and rambutans. Philippine preserves like *atsara* (a chutney-like vegetable preserve) and numerous native desserts such as *Pili nut brittle bangus* (a crunchy sweet made with the luscious pili nuts found only in the Bicol region) can be purchased in local markets.

Things to know: Waiter service is common in bars and there are no strict regulations regarding the sale of alcohol.

National specialities:
- *Lechon* (roasted whole pig) is prepared for fiestas and family celebrations.
- *Kare-kare* (an oxtail stew in peanut sauce served with *bagoong* (fermented shrimp paste)).
- *Sinigang* (meat or fish in a pleasantly sour broth).
- *Adobo* (braised pork and chicken in a tangy soy sauce with vinegar and garlic).
- Seafoods such as *bangus* (the bony but prized milkfish), crabs, lobsters, prawns, oysters, tuna, freshwater fish and the sweet *maliputo*, found in deep-water lakes. It is freshly harvested and often simply grilled, boiled, fried or steamed and served with *kalamansi* (the local lemon), *bagoong* (a fish paste) or vinegar with *labuyo* (the fiery native pepper).

National drinks:
- Locally brewed beer, such as *San Miguel*.
- Philippine rum.

Tipping: Usually 10 per cent of the bill, unless service charge is included. Hotels generally add a 15 per cent service charge, but it is customary to leave small change.

NIGHTLIFE: The choice of entertainment in Manila displays the Filipino's affinity for music. 5-star hotels offer everything from high-tech discos to lavish cultural songs and dances, as well as superb pop singers and performers, trios, show bands and classical string ensembles. On most evenings there are cultural performances by local artists or foreign groups at the many other venues for the

performing arts. Free concerts are offered by several parks every week, and occasionally by banks and other corporations. The Philippines also have some unusual musical groups like the Pangkat Kawayan bamboo orchestra, which uses bamboo musical instruments, and the Rondalla group which uses tiny guitars like the ukelele. Casinos are located in Cebu, Davao, Ilocos Norte, Iloilo, Manila, Pampanga and Zamboanga.

SHOPPING: The Philippines is a haven for shoppers. Countless bargain opportunities for the handicrafts of the different regions are found in the numerous shopping complexes, which range from sleek air-conditioned department stores and malls to open-air bazaars. Duty Free Philippines near NAIA is the largest in the country. The chain stores offer everything from the famous *barong tagalog* (hand-embroidered dress shirts for men in delicate *jusi* material) to Tiffany lamps made with capiz shells. For local colour, there is nothing like the flea markets where visitors can buy all kinds of cloth weaves, brassware from the south, woodcarvings and other local crafts and souvenirs, like the painted papier-maché horses of Laguna. Some particularly good buys are south-sea pearls, the silver jewellery from Baguio, coral trinket boxes, coral and pearl accessories, rattan furniture, baskets in different designs, woven grass mats (*banig*), antique wooden figurines of saints, ready-to-wear clothes, garments embroidered with the traditional callado, Filipino dresses for women (usually made from banana and pineapple fibres), cigars, terracotta, porcelain and *abaca* placemats. Handicraft stores are found everywhere in the country, especially in cities. Large department stores sell both local and foreign manufactured goods. **Shopping hours:** Mon-Sat 1000-2000, but these can vary. Most department stores and supermarkets are open Sunday and there are some 24-hour convenience stores.

Business

- **GDP:** US$84.2 billion.
- **Main imports:** Raw materials, machinery and equipment, fuels, vehicles, vehicle parts, plastic and chemicals.
- **Main exports:** Electrical equipment, machinery and transport equipment, garments, optical instruments, coconut products, fruit and nuts, copper products and chemicals.
- **Main trade partners:** China (PR), Hong Kong (SAR), Japan, Korea (Dem Rep) Malaysia, The Netherlands, Singapore, Taiwan (China), UK and USA.

ECONOMY: The agricultural sector produces rice, corn, coconuts, copra, sugar cane and bananas as the main crops. Production of timber, formerly a major export earner, has been suspended due to the effects of deforestation. There is a moderately sized mining industry producing copper, gold, silver, nickel and coal. Offshore oil production is due to begin in the next few years. Most of the Philippines' recent economic development has been industrial, with food processing, oil refining, and the production of chemicals, electrical machinery, metal goods and textiles all having been established during the last 20 years.
Broad financial incentives aimed at attracting foreign investment capital, and the creation of five export processing zones (EPZ) with concessionary tax rates and tariffs, prompted strong growth during the early- and mid-1990s. However, it also produced a somewhat skewed economy in which the Manila area, known as the National

Capital Region, now hosts 15 per cent of the population and accounts for one-third of GDP: there are huge income disparities between the capital and the rest of the country. The Philippines' economic growth came to a shuddering halt in late 1997 when the collapse of the region's currencies produced a stock market crash, high inflation, the cessation of foreign investment, and a large budget deficit. *El Niño*, the climatic system which wreaks periodic havoc upon the Philippines, worsened the situation further. The economy has since recovered fairly well. In 2004, growth was 6.1 per cent and it is expected that this was repeated through 2005. Industrial production has picked up after several years of decline. In 2004, foreign investment quadrupled and local investment increased by 50 per cent. Foreign aid (including a US$100 million subvention from the USA in 2002) has helped the country's finances, along with a sharp increase in remittances from the thousands of Filipinos working abroad. Unemployment is still a problem, having grown steadily during the last few years to its current level of 11.4 per cent. The Philippines' longer term economic prospects will depend on the Government's vigour in pursuing essential and overdue reforms to the tax and banking systems, and improvements to the country's shaky infrastructure. The Philippines belong to the Association of South East Asian Nations (the anti-Communist bloc which is now assuming an important economic role) and the Asian Development Bank.

BUSINESS ETIQUETTE: The weather is almost uniformly warm and humid and so short-sleeved shirts, preferably with a tie, can be worn for business visits. However, with most offices being air conditioned, it is best to wear safari suits or a long-sleeved Filipino *barong tagalog* when visiting top business officials and executives. Filipinos have an American business style and English is widely spoken. Best months for business visits are October to November and January to May. Unless you have urgent business matters to attend to, business visits around Christmas and Easter are not recommended as delays tend to be unavoidable. **Office hours:** These vary. Usually Mon-Fri 0800-1700. Some private sector offices are open Sat 0900-1200.

CONFERENCES/CONVENTIONS: Many establishments are members of the Philippine Convention and Visitors Corporation (PCVC). Popular locations for conferences and conventions are the Philippine International Convention Centre and the World Trade Centre. For further general information, contact the PCVC (see *Commercial Information*).

COMMERCIAL INFORMATION

Philippine Trade and Investment Promotion Centre in the UK
1a Cumberland House, Kensington Court, London W8 5NX, UK
Tel: (020) 7937 1898.
E-mail: dtilondon1@aol.com

Philippine Chamber of Commerce and Industry
19/F Salcedo Towers, 169 H.V Del Costa Street, Salcedo Village, Makati City, Philippines 1227
Tel: (2) 844 5713.
Website: www.philippinechamber.com

Philippine Convention and Visitors Corporation
4F Legaspi Towers, 300 Roxas Boulevard, Metro Manila, Philippines 1004
Tel: (632) 525 1255 *or* 9318.
Website: www.dotpcvc.gov.ph

Credit: © Gunther Deichmann

Poland

Location: Central Europe.

Time: GMT + 1 (GMT + 2 from last Sunday in March to last Sunday in October).

Overview

Situated at the centre of Europe, and the largest of the former Eastern European states, Poland's position is crucial. The principal city in the southwest and the capital of Lower Silesia, Wroclaw (Breslau) can claim to be the cradle of the Polish state: it was here that the Polanie tribe built their first fortified settlement (on Ostrow Tumski Island).

The country is best remembered for being the birthplace of the former Soviet bloc's first officially recognised independent mass political movement when strikes at the Gdansk shipyard in August 1980 led to agreement with the authorities on the establishment of the *Solidarnosc* (Solidarity) trade union. Opposition to the regime was significantly led by elements of the industrial work force – in contrast to movements elsewhere in Eastern Europe which were led by intellectuals. It was also supported by the Catholic Church, a major political force in Poland that the communists had never been able to fully suppress.

Elections in summer 1989 ushered in eastern Europe's first post-Communist Government. A member of the European Union, the country has achieved some success in creating a market economy and attracting foreign investment although growth remains low.

Today, Poland is also one of the major destinations for travellers. Its beauty can be admired in both its old cities and in the wild scenery of its national parks and nature reserves. The country's regions are largely divided into horizontal bands: the Baltic Coast and the hilly post-glacial lake district. Central Poland is split into northern lowlands and southern uplands, including the Kraków-Wielun Upland with its limestone areas, caves and medieval castles. The Carpathian Mountains, including the Tatras, lie in the extreme south; their mountain scenery, folklore and sports facilities are important parts of their charm.

Poland is a nation with a proud cultural heritage and strong theatrical and musical traditions. Warsaw and the main cities have theatres and opera companies that put on a whole range of musical and cultural programmes for both locals and visitors.

General Information

AREA: 312,685 sq km (120,728 sq miles).

POPULATION: 38.63 million (official estimate 2005).

POPULATION DENSITY: 122.3 per sq km.

CAPITAL: Warsaw. **Population:** 1.65 million (official estimate 2004).

GEOGRAPHY: Poland shares borders to the east with the Russian Federation, Belarus, Ukraine and Lithuania, to the south with the Czech Republic and the Slovak Republic and to the west with Germany. To the north lies the Baltic Sea. The Baltic coast provides over 500km (300 miles) of sandy beaches, bays, steep cliffs and dunes. Northern Poland is dominated by lakes, islands and wooded hills joined by many rivers and canals. The Mazurian Lake District to the northeast is particularly beautiful. Lake Hancza, the deepest lake in Poland, is located in this district. The River Vistula has cut a wide valley from Gdansk on the Baltic coast to Warsaw in the heart of the country. The rest of the country rises slowly to the Sudety Mountains, which run along the border with the Czech Republic, and the Tatra mountains, which separate Poland from the Slovak Republic. To the west, the River Oder, with Szczecin at its mouth, forms the northwest border with Germany.

GOVERNMENT: Republic since 1918. **Head of State:** President Lech Kaczynski since 2005. **Head of Government:** Kazimierz Marcinkiewicz since September 2005. **Recent history:** President Lech Kaczynski, from the traditionalist Law and Justice party, won a run-off vote in October 2005. Mr Kaczynski, who was Warsaw's Mayor at the time of his election, co-founded Law and Justice with his identical twin brother, Jaroslaw, who heads the party. Under the Polish constitution, the President has fewer powers than the Prime Minister. However, he has a significant say in foreign policy. Kazimierz Marcinkiewicz was nominated as Prime Minister in 2005. He has eight non-party technocrats in his 17-member Cabinet.

LANGUAGE: Polish is the official language. There is a small German-speaking community. English and Russian are also spoken.

RELIGION: More than 95 per cent Roman Catholic; other religions include Polish Autocephalous Orthodox, Russian and Greek Orthodox, Protestant, Jewish and Muslim.

ELECTRICITY: 220 volts AC, 50Hz; continental sockets.

SOCIAL CONVENTIONS: Poles are friendly, industrious people and foreigners are usually made very welcome. There are vast contrasts between urban and rural life and the Polish peasantry is very religious and conservative, maintaining a traditional lifestyle. Roman Catholicism plays an important role in daily life and criticism or jokes about religion are not appreciated, despite the general good humour of the people. Music and art are also important aspects of Polish culture. Shaking hands is the normal form of greeting. Normal courtesies are observed when visiting private homes and it is customary to bring flowers. Fairly conservative casual wear is the most suitable attire, but dress should be formal when specified for entertaining in the evening or in a smart restaurant. Smoking is restricted in some public buildings.

Photography: Military installations such as bridges, ports, airports, border points etc should not be photographed.

Climate

Temperate with warm summers, crisp, sunny autumns and cold winters. Snow covers the mountainous area in the south of Poland (mid-December to April). Rain falls throughout the year.

Required clothing: Light- to mediumweights are worn during warmer months. Medium- to heavyweights are needed during winter. Rainwear is advisable all year.

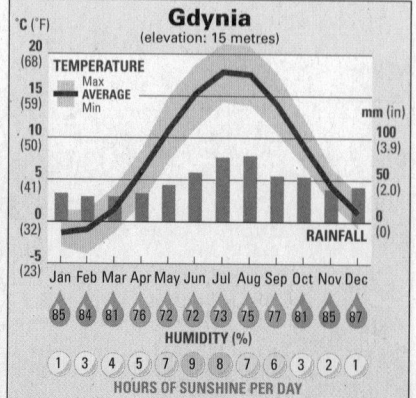

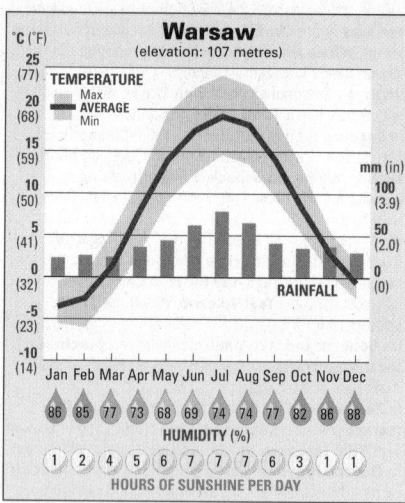

Communications

Telephone: Full IDD is available. Country code: 48. Cheap rate on long-distance calls is available from 1600-0600. Telephone cards can be purchased from post offices, newsagents and hotel receptions for local calls.

Mobile telephone: Roaming agreements exist with international mobile phone companies. Good coverage.

Internet: There are many internet cafes in cities.

Post: Service to Western Europe takes up to four days. Post office hours: Mon-Fri 0800-1800.

MEDIA: State-owned TV (TVP) still has the largest share of the audience with its two national channels. It also operates regional programmes and the international satellite channels. TVN operate the leading commercial TV channels. Polsat also operates a digital pay-TV platform and is present in the Baltic states. Up to a quarter of Poles also watch foreign television channels. State-owned Polish Radio reaches just over half of the population and there are more than 200 stations on the air. There are more than 300 newspapers, most of them local or regional.

Press: The principal dailies are *Gazeta Wyborcza*, *Rzeczpospolita* and *Super Express*. The biggest selling daily, the *Fakt Tabloid*, is a relative newcomer. Weeklies include *Gazeta Polska*, *Polityka* and *Wprost*. English-language publications include *The Warsaw Voice* (weekly).

TV: Public broadcaster *Telewizja Polska (TVP)* operates two national networks, regional services and international satellite channel; Commercial broadcaster *TV Polonia TVN* operates news channel *TVN 24*; *Polsat* is a commercial channel and pay-TV operator; The digital pay-TV platform *Cyfra+* was launched by France's Canal+.

Radio: Public broadcaster Polish Radio operates five national networks and many regional stations; *Radio Polonia* is a public, external service; *RMF FM* and *Radio Zet* are commercial stations.

Passport/Visa

	Passport Required?	Visa Required?	Return Ticket Required?
Full British	1	No	No
Australian	Yes	No	No
Canadian	Yes	No	No
USA	Yes	No	No
Other EU	1	No	No
Japanese	Yes	No	No

Note: *Regulations and requirements may be subject to change at short notice, and you are advised to contact the appropriate diplomatic or consular authority before finalising travel arrangements. Any numbers in the chart refer to the footnotes below.*

PASSPORTS: Passport valid for at least three months beyond the length of stay required by all except:
(a) **1.** EU/EEA nationals (EU+ Iceland, Liechtenstein, Norway) and Swiss nationals holding a valid national ID card.
Note: EU and EEA nationals are only required to produce evidence of their EU/EEA nationality and identity in order to be admitted to any EU/EEA Member State. This evidence can take the form of a valid national passport *or* national identity card. Either is acceptable. Possession of a return ticket, any length of validity on their document, sufficient funds for the length of their proposed visit should *not* be imposed.
VISAS: Required by all except the following for up to 90 days:
(a) nationals of countries referred to in the chart above;
(b) nationals of Andorra, Argentina, Bolivia, Brazil, Brunei,

Bulgaria, Chile, Costa Rica, Croatia, El Salvador, Guatemala, Honduras, Hong Kong (SAR), Iceland, Israel, Korea (Rep), Liechtenstein, Macau (SAR), Malaysia, Mexico, Monaco, New Zealand, Nicaragua, Norway, Panama, Paraguay, Romania, San Marino, Singapore, Switzerland, Uruguay, Vatican City and Venezuela.

Types of visa and cost: *Short-stay*: £26 (single-entry), £34 (double-entry), £42 (multiple-entry). *Long-validity* (more than 90 days): £51 (single-entry), £59 (double-entry), £68 (multiple-entry). *Airport Transit Visa*: £9. *Transit*: £9 (single-entry), £17 (double-entry), £26 (multiple-entry). *Work* (one year maximum, multiple-entry): £94. *Next day service*: additional £22. Payment is non-refundable even if visa is rejected. There is a 50 per cent discount for foreign citizens who have a Polish spouse and a 25 per cent discount for children and students up to the age of 26 (proof of identity is required).

Validity: *Airport Transit*: two days. *Transit*: up to five days. *Short stay*: up to 90 days. *Long validity*: over 90 days. *Work*: maximum one year.

Application to: Consulate (or consular section at Embassy); see *Passport/Visa Information* for details.

Application requirements: (a) Passport valid for three months after planned departure from Poland with blank page to affix visa. (b) Completed application form. (c) One passport-size photo. (d) Evidence of immigration status in country of residence, endorsed in current or previous passport (if applicable). (e) Fee, payable by cash or postal order made payable to 'Consulate General of the Republic of Poland'. *Short-stay*: (a)-(e) and, (f) Confirmation of travel itinerary, accommodation booking or invitation from friends or family in Poland. The invitation should be entered in the register of invitations in a Regional Office. *Long-validity*: (a)-(e) and, (f) Letter from applicant's company or organisation and original of a 'Work Promise'. Self-employed persons should produce an invitation from the business partner from Poland. If studying in Poland, an official letter from a college or university must be produced. *Transit*: (a)-(e) and, (f) Visa for country of destination. (g) Transport documentation, such as a rail or aeroplane ticket.

Note: All visitors must possess sufficient funds to cover the cost of their stay. Foreigners staying in excess of three days must possess; PLN100 per day but no less than PLN500 in total or the equivalent in foreign currency if over 16 years of age; PLN50 per day but no less than PLN300 in total or the equivalent in foreign currency if under 16 years of age. Documents required for proof of funds are: traveller's cheques, credit cards or a bank statement. Additionally, each foreigner needs to have PLN300 for each day of the visit or the equivalent in foreign currency to cover the cost of medical treatment; a letter from the insurer can be used to confirm this.

Working days required: Three. For certain passport holders it may take several weeks. Express visas: the following working-day, for an additional fee of £22. Postal applications may take up to two weeks (no express service available).

Temporary residence: Apply to Consulate.

PASSPORT/VISA INFORMATION

Embassy of the Republic of Poland in the UK
47 Portland Place, London W1B 1JH, UK
Tel: (0870) 774 2700.
Website: www.polishembassy.org.uk
Opening hours: Mon-Fri 0830-1630.

Consulate General of the Republic of Poland in the UK
73 New Cavendish Street, London W1W 6LS, UK
Tel: (0870) 774 2800.
Website: www.polishconsulate.co.uk
Opening hours: Mon-Fri 0930-1230 (Wed 0900-1100 and Thur 1300-1600).

Embassy of the Republic of Poland in the USA
2640 16th Street, NW, Washington, DC 20009, USA
Tel: (202) 234 3800/2.
Website: www.polandembassy.org
Opening hours: Mon- Fri 0900- 1600

Consular Division of the Embassy of the Republic of Poland in the USA
2224 Wyoming Avenue, NW, Washington, DC 20008, USA
Tel: (202) 234 3800.

Money

Currency: Zloty (PLN) = 100 groszy. Notes are in denominations of PLN200, 100, 50, 20 and 10. The new coins are in denominations of PLN5, 2 and 1, and 50, 20, 10, 5, 2 and 1 groszy.

Currency exchange: Foreign currency can be exchanged at all border crossing points, hotels and bureaux de change, some of which are open 24 hours. Cash can also be obtained from Visa credit cards at banks.

Credit & debit cards: American Express, Diners Club, MasterCard and Visa are accepted in larger establishments. Check with your credit or debit card company for details of merchant acceptability and other services which may be available.

Traveller's cheques: Readily exchanged. To avoid additional exchange rate charges, travellers are advised to take traveller's cheques in Pounds Sterling.

Currency restrictions: The import of local currency is allowed up to the equivalent of €10,000. The import of foreign currencies exceeding €10,000 or its equivalent in freely convertible currency must be declared.
Residents and non-residents are allowed to export local currency up to the equivalent of €10,000. Residents are allowed to export foreign currencies up to the equivalent of €10,000. Higher amounts can be exported with permission of the Bank of Poland only. The export of foreign currencies exceeding €10,000 or its equivalent in freely convertible currency by non-residents must be declared. Gold and platinum, metal and articles of gold, platinum or metal are subject to special regulations.

Banking hours: Mon-Fri 0900-1600, Sat 0900-1300 in main cities. In smaller towns, banking hours are more limited.

Exchange rate indicators:
Rate at time of publishing

£1.00=	PLN5.52
$1.00=	PLN3.14

Duty Free

The following items may be imported into Poland by persons of 17 years of age and over without incurring customs duty:
250 cigarettes or 50 cigars or 250g of tobacco; 1l of wine and 1l of spirits; goods up to the value of ¤175.

Prohibited items: The export of all articles of artistic, historical or cultural value is subject to special regulations. Parrots, although in special cases permission is obtainable from the Ministry of Agriculture.

Abolition of duty free goods within the EU: On June 30 1999, the sale of duty-free alcohol and tobacco at airports and at sea was abolished in all of the original 15 EU member states. Of the 10 new member states that joined the EU on May 1 2004, these rules already apply to Cyprus and Malta. There are transitional rules in place for visitors returning to one of the original 15 EU countries from one of the other new EU countries. But for the original 15, plus Cyprus and Malta, there are now no limits imposed on importing tobacco and alcohol products from one EU country to another (with the exceptions of Denmark, Finland and Sweden, where limits *are* imposed). Travellers should note that they may be required to prove at customs that the goods purchased are for personal use *only*.

Public Holidays

Below are listed the Public Holidays for the January 2006-June 2007 period.

2006: Jan 1 New Year's Day. **Apr 17** Easter Monday. **May 1** Labour Day. **May 3** National Day. **Jun 15** Corpus Christi. **Aug 15** Assumption. **Nov 1** All Saints' Day. **Nov 11** Independence Day. **Dec 25-26** Christmas.

2007: Jan 1 New Year's Day. **Apr 9** Easter Monday. **May 1** Labour Day. **May 3** National Day. **Jun 7** Corpus Christi.

Health

	Special Precautions?	Certificate Required?
Yellow Fever	No	No
Cholera	No	No
Typhoid & Polio	No	N/A
Malaria	No	N/A

Note: *Regulations and requirements may be subject to change at short notice, and you are advised to contact your doctor well in advance of your intended date of departure. Any numbers in the chart refer to the footnotes below.*

Food & drink: Mains water is normally chlorinated, and whilst relatively safe may cause mild abdominal upsets. Bottled water is available and is advised for the first few weeks of the stay. Milk is pasteurised and dairy products are safe for consumption. Local meat, poultry, seafood, fruit and vegetables are generally considered safe to eat.

Other risks: *Hepatitis A* and B and *diphtheria* occur. Freshwater fish from the Baltic Sea area could contain fish tapeworm, causing *diphyllobothriasis*. *Tick-borne encephalitis* occurs in forested areas. Vaccination is advisable. Campers and trekkers should wear long trousers when walking near long grass in order to avoid tick bites. *Rabies* is present. For those at high risk, vaccination before arrival should be considered. If you are bitten, seek medical advice without delay. For more information, consult the *Health* appendix.

Health care: European Economic Area (EEA) and Switzerland:
If you or any of your dependants are suddenly taken ill or have an accident during a visit to an EEA country or Switzerland, free or reduced-cost necessary treatment is available – in most cases on production of a valid European Health Insurance Card (EHIC). Each country has different rules about state medical provision. In some, treatment is free. In many countries you will have to pay part or all of the cost, and then claim a full or partial refund. The EHIC gives access to state-provided medical treatment only and the scheme gives no entitlement to medical repatriation costs, nor does it cover ongoing illnesses of a non-urgent nature, so comprehensive travel insurance is advised. Note that the EHIC replaces the Form E111, which will no longer be valid after 31 December 2005. Some restrictions apply, depending on your nationality.
Healthcare in Poland is provided by units that have a contract with the National Health Fund (*Centrala Narodowego Funduszu Zdrowia* or *NFZ*). In an emergency, go to the nearest basic healthcare GP and make sure they are contracted to the *NFZ*. If they are not contracted to the *NFZ*, you will be charged as a private patient and will not be able to get a refund. Check that the dentist you go to is contracted to the *NFZ*, otherwise you will be charged privately. Only basic emergency dental care is provided free of charge. Depending on the medication, you will have to pay between 30 and 50 per cent of the price of prescriptions, the full amount, or a fixed price. These charges are not refundable. You can go directly to a state hospital in an emergency and get free treatment. A GP can also refer you to a hospital and decide if you need an ambulance. Medicines provided in a hospital are free of charge. More information can be obtained from Central *NFZ* (National Health Fund) and regional branches, Ul. Grójecka 186, 02-390 Warszawa (tel: (22) 572 6036 *or* 6112; website: www.nfz.gov.pl/ue).

Travel - International

AIR:

The national airline is *LOT Polish Airlines (LO)* (website: www.lot.com).

Approximate flight times: From Warsaw to *London* is two hours, to *Frankfurt/M* is one hour 50 minutes, and to *Prague* is one hour 20 minutes.

Main airports: *Warsaw (WAW)* (Okecie) is 10km (6 miles) southwest of the city. *To/from the airport*: Buses and taxis are available. Travel time: 20-40 minutes by bus; 20-30 minutes by taxi. *Facilities*: Post office, banks, bureaux de change, bars, restaurants, left-luggage facilities, tourist information services, car hire and duty free shops.
Kraków (KRK) (Balice John Paul II) is 16km (10 miles) west of the city centre. *To/from the airport*: Buses and taxis are available. *Facilities*: Bar, bureau de change and car hire. There are duty free facilities in the departure hall.
Wroclaw (WRO) (Strachowice) (website: www.airport.wroclaw.pl) is 8km (5 miles) from the city centre. *To/from the airport*: Buses, taxis and car hire are available. There is a daily connection to Frankfurt/M and twice weekly connection (Thursday and Sunday) to Düsseldorf. Katowice (KTW) is 34km (21 miles) from the city. There are connections to Copenhagen, Frankfurt/M and Munich daily. *Facilities*: Bank, duty free shop, post office, restaurants and shops.
Gdansk (GDN) (website: www.airport.gdansk.pl) is the most common entry point into northern Poland.

Departure tax: None.

SEA:

Main ports: The Port of *Gdansk* (website: www.portgdansk.pl) is situated at the intersection of the principal European transport routes, providing the most convenient connection between both Central and Eastern Europe and Scandinavia as well as between Western and Eastern Europe. Additionally, for countries such as the Czech Republic, Slovakia, Ukraine, the Belarus Republic and Hungary, the Port of Gdansk provides easy access to the Baltic Sea. *Pol Ferries* operates between Poland and Sweden, Denmark and Finland. For further information, contact the Polish National Tourist Office (see *Top Things To Do*) or Pol Ferries, ul. Chalubinskiego 8, 00-613, Warsaw (tel: (22) 830 0930; website: www.polferries.com). Tickets can also be purchased from travel agents or the ferry terminal (tel: (58) 343 1887).

RAIL:

Polish State Railways (PKP) (website: www.pkp.pl) operates *EuroCity* trains between Poland and a number of major European cities. All services from Western Europe to Poland pass through the Czech Republic, Germany or the Slovak Republic. The main routes link Warsaw with Berlin and Cologne, Budapest, Prague and Vienna. There is a car-sleeper service from the Hook of Holland to Poznan/ Warsaw.

Rail passes: The *Inter-Rail* pass offers unlimited second-class train travel in up to 29 countries (includes Morocco and Turkey) split into eight zones (A-H). Three different tickets are available: a ticket covering one zone (two to six countries, 16 days' validity), a ticket covering two zones (six to ten countries, 22 days' validity) and an *All Zone Pass* (29 countries, one month's validity). Ferry services between Italy and Greece are included. Passengers must be resident in Europe for at least six months before the pass is used. Travel is not allowed in the passenger's country of residence. Travellers under 26 years receive a reduction of about 30 per cent. Children's tickets are reduced by about 50 per cent. Supplements are required for some high speed services, seat reservations and couchettes. Discounts are offered on *Eurostar* and some ferry routes. Available from *Inter Rail* (website: www.interrailnet.com).

The *EuroDomino* pass enables holders anything form three to eight days' extensive travel within a one-month period on the entire rail network of their chosen country. It is valid in 28 European countries and North Africa, including the ferry service from Brindisi (Italy) to Igoumenitsa (Greece). To purchase a *EuroDomino* pass you must have been a resident in Europe for at least six months and a passport number is required at time of booking. It is not permitted to purchase a pass for travel within your own country of residence. To qualify for the youth rates, you must be under 26 years on the first date of validity of the pass. Children aged four-eleven years inclusive pay half the adult fares rounded up to the nearest pound. Children under four years travel for free. Seat reservations, couchette and sleeper charges are not included in the cost of the pass and are payable at the normal rate. Passholder fares are payable on some services. Reservation/supplement charges are payable on all trains within Spain. Available from *Rail Europe* (website: www.raileurope.co.uk/railpasses/eurodomino.htm).

ROAD:

Poland is best reached from the Czech Republic and Germany or the car-sleeper rail service from the Hook of Holland to Poznan/Warsaw. There are extensive **bus** and **coach** services. *Eurolines*, departing from Victoria Coach Station in London, serves destinations in Poland. For further information contact *Eurolines* (tel: (08705) 143 219; website: www.eurolines.com).

Travel - Internal

AIR:

All internal airlines are operated by *LOT Polish Airlines* (website: www.lot.com) and there is a comprehensive network linking all major cities.

RAIL:

Cheap and efficient *InterCity* trains are operated by *Polish State Railways (PKP)* (website: www.pkp.pl) and link all parts of the country in a network radiating from Warsaw. There are two classes of travel. The *Polrailpass* (and *Junior Polrailpass* for travellers under 26) is available for eight, 15, 21 or 30 days. This pass is available from travel agents and international rail ticket outlets, as well as from railway stations and travel agents within Poland. Children under four years of age travel free. Children aged four to 10 pay half fare.

ROAD:

Traffic drives on the right. Poland has a dense network of filling stations. Unleaded petrol is available in most of the petrol stations. Most filling stations located along international routes are open 24 hours a day. The Polish Automobile and Motorway Federation *Polski Zwiazek Motorowy (PZM)* can be called on 9637 nationwide for assistance. Starter emergency breakdown service can be called on (0801) 122 222. For further information, contact Polski Zwiazek Motorowy, ul Kazimierzowska 66, 02-518 Warsaw (tel: (22) 849 9361; website: www.pzm.pl). **Bus:** There are good regional bus and coach services operated by Polish Motor Communications (PKS) as well as the Polski Express connecting most towns. **Car hire:** Self-drive cars are available at the airport or through various car rental offices in town centres. The minimum age is 21. Charges are usually based on a daily rate plus a kilometre charge. **Regulations:** Minimum driving age is 17. The speed limit is 60kph (40mph) in built-up areas, 90kph (57mph) on major roads and 110kph (69mph) on motorways. Seat belts and warning triangles are compulsory. Trams have the right of way. From 1 October to 1 April, all vehicles should have their lights switched on at all times. **Documentation:** Tourists travelling in their own cars should have car registration cards, their national driving licence (driving licences of EU nationals are accepted) and valid Green Card motor insurance. An International Driving Permit is also required.

URBAN:

Bus: There are good services in all towns, with additional trams and trolleybuses operating in a dozen of the larger urban areas. Warsaw has bus, tramway and rail services. A flat fare is charged and there are pre-purchase tickets and passes. **Tram:** Weekend and seven-day tourist tickets can be purchased. Most public transport operates from 0530-2300. **Taxi:** These are available in all main towns. They are usually found at ranks or can be ordered by phone. There is a surcharge from 2300-0500 and for journeys out of town, as well as at weekends. Taxi drivers may insist on payment in hard currency. **Tipping** is welcomed.

Travel times: The following chart gives approximate travel times (in hours and minutes) from **Warsaw** to other major cities/towns in Poland.

	Air	Road	Rail
Kraków	1.40	4.00	2.35
Poznan	1.00	4.00	3.00
Wroclaw	1.15	6.00	4.35
Gdansk	1.00	6.00	3.40

Travel Advice

Most visits to Poland are trouble-free but you should be aware of the global risk of indiscriminate international terrorist attacks, which could be against civilian targets, including places frequented by foreigners.

This advice is based on information provided by the Foreign and Commonwealth Office in the UK. It is correct at time of publishing. As the situation can change rapidly, visitors are advised to contact the following organisations for the latest travel advice:

British Foreign and Commonwealth Office
Tel: (0845) 850 2829.
Website: www.fco.gov.uk

US Department of State
Website: http://travel.state.gov/travel

Accommodation

HOTELS:

Most major international hotel chains are represented in Poland. International Student Hotels offer better facilities than youth hostels and are inexpensive, comfortable and pleasant. **Grading:** Hotels in Poland are graded in five categories: **luxury, 4-star, 3-star, 2-star** and **1-star**. In addition there are tourist hotels, boarding houses and motels, each graded into three or four categories.

GUEST HOUSES:

Three categories are available in all towns and run by regional tourist boards. Reservations can be made from local offices.

CAMPING/CARAVANNING:
There are 213 campsites in Poland, nearly 75 per cent of which are fitted with 220-volt powerpoints and several with 24-volt points for caravans. Facilities also include washrooms, canteens and nearby restaurants and food kiosks. The main camping season is June to August. Holders of an international camping card (FICC) qualify for a 10 per cent rebate on rates. **Grading:** There are two categories. Category I sites cover an area of 100 sq m (10,764 sq ft) and have 24-hour reception and lighting.

YOUTH HOSTELS:

There are 155 hostels in Poland which are open all year round, and 450 only in the summer season.. Addresses can be found in the *Youth Hostel Handbook* published by the Polish Youth Hostels Association.

ACCOMMODATION INFORMATION

Polskie Towarzystwo Schronisk Mlodziezowych (Polish Youth Hostels Association)
Ul. Chocimska 28, 00-791 Warsaw, Poland
Tel: (22) 849 8128.
E-mail: hostellingpol.ptsm@pro.onet.pl

Polish Hotel Association
Ul. Nowogrodzka 44 m 2, 00-695 Warsaw, Poland
Tel: (22) 622 6991-3.
Website: www.hotel.pl

Polska Federacja Campingui I Caravaningu (Polish Federation of Camping and Caravanning)
Ul. Grochowska 331, 03-838 Warsaw, Poland
Tel: (22) 810 6050.
Website: www.pfcc.info

Top Things To See

- Spanning both banks of the **River Wisla (Vistula)**, **Warsaw**, Poland's capital and largest city was almost completely destroyed during World War II. Following massive and painstaking reconstruction, **Warsaw's Old Town (Stare Miasto)** on the west bank was authentically reconstructed from original plans and is now a UNESCO World Heritage Site. The Polish capital plays an important role in the country's cultural life and there are over 32 museums. One of the best is the **Warsaw Historical Museum**, which traces Warsaw's history. The **National Museum** has a superb collection of art and archaeology. **Zamek Królewski**, the reconstructed Royal Castle, is now an important museum of fine and applied arts. The **Wilanów Palace** has a spectacular collection of old paintings and furniture; its **Orangerie** holds the new **Museum of Posters**. For wonderful views over the whole city, go to the enormous **Palace of Culture and Science**, an unwelcome gift from Josef Stalin. The **Lazienki Palace** is set in a lovely park with an open-air Greek theatre and a monument to the famous Polish composer Frederic Chopin.

- See the manor house where Chopin was born in the attractive park of **Zelazowa Wola**, 53km (32 miles) west of Warsaw.

- In **Zamosc's Old Town**, which has been declared a UNESCO World Heritage Site, head for the **Market Square.**

- The old and new **Lublin Gates** indicate the city's former role as an important regional fortress. Lublin is given a southern flavour through the many buildings designed by Bernardo Morando of Padua, and by the many Armenians and Greeks who settled here.

- Immerse yourself in **Krakow**'s charming medieval atmosphere; it is one of UNESCO's 12 most significant historical sites. In the middle of the central **Market Square** – the largest in Europe – is the **Cloth Hall**, which was reconstructed in the 19th century from 14th-century merchants' stalls; this houses the art and sculpture galleries of the **National Museum**. Opposite, discover **St Mary's Church** with its world-famous wooden altar carved by Wit Stwosz. The **Jagiellonian University**, founded in 1364, is one of the oldest in Europe. After many years of neglect, Kraków's former Jewish quarter, **Kazimierz**, is reviving; the **Old Synagogue** (1557) is the oldest surviving in the country. Also in Kazimierz is the country's largest **Ethnographic Museum**. Overlooking the city is **Wawel Castle**, with its marvellous 16th-century tapestries and, beside it, the Gothic **Cathedral**, where many Polish kings are buried. The **Czartoryski Palace** houses the city's best collection of ancient art, European paintings and crafts.

- Discover another of Poland's UNESCO World Heritage Sites, the **cathedral-like salt mines** at Wieliczka, 13km (8 miles) from Kraków. The subterranean route spans 4.5km (2.8 miles) leading to the oldest part of the mine through 14th- and 15th-century chapels and crystal caves.

- See the **Bledowska Desert**, perhaps the only true desert in Europe.

- Visit **Wadowice**, the birthplace of Pope John Paul II.

- See the **Icon of the Black Madonna** in the huge Jasna Góra monastery complex at **Czestochowa**, 100km (60 miles) north of Kraków (reputed to have been painted by St Luke).

- Locate Wroclaw (**Breslau**)'s 100 bridges. Other important sights include the 15th-century **Town Hall**, now the **Historical Museum**; the **Ethnographic Museum** in the **Royal Palace**; and the **Cathedral** on Ostrow Tumski (**Cathedral Island**). The 120m (400ft) by 15m (50ft) tall painting, *Panorama of the Battle of Raclawice*, remains the city's best-loved sight; painted in 1894, it celebrates the Russian army's defeat by Tadeusz Krsciuszko's people's militia.

- In **Poznan**, do not miss the Italianate **Town Hall** in the **Old Market Square**, the **Gorki Palace**, the 12th-century **Church of St John** and **Przemyslaw Castle**, once the seat of the Grand Dukes of Poland. The **National Museum** houses one of the country's few displays of old master paintings.

- The Baltic port of **Gdansk**, formerly known as **Danzig**, is famous for its **Lenin Shipyards** which were the birthplace of **Solidarnosc (Solidarity)** and thus of today's democratic Poland. See the largest Gothic church in Poland – and possibly the largest brick building in the world – the **Church of the Virgin Mary (Kosciol Mariacki)**. The 17th-century **Golden Gate** and the **Court of the Fraternity of St George** can be viewed along the spectacular **Royal Way**, one of Gdansk's most historic streets. The **National Art Museum** has an excellent collection of Gothic art and sculpture. The beach resort at nearby **Sopot** has Europe's longest pier (500m/1640ft). Within easy reach are the forested **Hel Peninsula**, the **Kashubian Lakeland**, and the Teutonic castles at **Malbork (Marienburg)**, **Gniew** and elsewhere. There is also a narrow-gauge railway that runs along the **Vistula Spit** offering an attractive way to see part of the Baltic coast.

- In the heart of the Mazurian forest, at **Ketrzyn (Rastenburg)**, view the site of **Hitler's 'Eagle's Nest'**, the concrete bunker where members of his High Staff attempted to assassinate him in August 1944.

- The medieval walled town of **Torun**, a UNESCO World Heritage Site on the banks of the River Wisla (Vistula), south of Gdansk, was the birthplace of the astronomer Copernicus (Mikolaj Kopernik). The most notable historic sites include **St Mary's Church**, **St John's Church** (where Copernicus was baptised); the striking Gothic **Town Hall** and the **Granaries** (which helped to make Torun a prosperous trade town). Important museums are the **Town Museum** with the

Credit: © Marie Peyre

wonderful stained glass for which the town was known, the **Copernicus Museum**, and the **Ethnographic Museum**.
- In **Szczecin**, 60km (37 miles) upstream from the mouth of the **River Oder**, set your eyes on the Pomeranian princes' 14th-century **Palace** and the 12th-century **Cathedral**. The city was largely rebuilt in the last century taking Paris as a model, and has a spacious feel to it with many wide, tree-lined boulevards.

Top Things To Do

- Go to the theatre. The **National** and the **Polish** are the most renowned of Warsaw's many **theatres**.
- Poland's national parks and nature reserves offer a variety of **hiking** trails through different types of landscapes ranging from dunes, beaches, rivers and lakes to deep forests and high mountains. Nature enthusiasts can visit the **Kampinos National Park**, near Warsaw, where it is possible to see wild boar and elk. The **Bialowieza National Park**, an area of primal forest straddling the border with Belarus, is the last major refuge of the European bison as well as being home to many other forest-dwelling species. **Bieszczadski National Park** is part of the **Carpathian mountain range** and contains the surviving fragments of the **Great Bieszczady Forest**, home to the brown bear, lynx and wildcat.
- Horses have traditionally been popular in Poland and **horseriding** enthusiasts have a large choice of riding schools to choose from. Polish stud farms are internationally renowned and welcome guests; board and lodging is provided and many stables also offer riding instruction. Horse auctions are held at **Janów Podlaski**, **Poznan**, **Racot** and **Walewice**. The main horseracing tracks are **Warsaw (Sluzewiec)**, **Sopot**, **Raculka** (near **Zielona Gora**), **Bialy Bor** (near **Slupsk**) and **Ksiaz** (near **Walbrzych**). Inexperienced riders may prefer riding a *Hucul* – a very rare Polish mountain pony.
- Spread across the northeast is **Mazuria**, a huge, thinly populated area of lakes, dense forests and swamps. It is rich in wildlife, including wild bison and Europe's largest herd of elks, and offers every form of outdoor pursuit – **sailing**, **canoeing**, **camping** and even **mushroom-picking**.
- The **Tatra Mountains** are Poland's main **skiing** destination. Although the 80km of the Tatras in the extreme south are only a small part of the entire range, they attract over 1.5 million visitors every year, with high peaks for **climbing**, excellent **trails**; **cable cars** and superb **wintersports facilities**. **Zakopane**, about 112km (70 miles) south of Kraków in the foothills, is a charming resort and wintersports centre. There is a fairytale atmosphere here, with its 'gingerbread' wooden cottages and many inhabitants who still wear national dress. Organised trips are available to the **Koscieliska Valley**, through beautiful countryside; the mountain of **Kasprowy Wierch** by means of a cable car offering spectacular views; and **Morskie Oko**, the glacial lake which is one of the Tatras' main attractions.
- Another popular wintersport is **ice-boating** on Poland's frozen waterways. **Sleigh rides** used to be popular with the Polish gentry and 'traditional' rides are available in most resorts.
- Relax at the **spas** and health resorts of the **Klodzko Valley**, which are within easy travel from **Wroclaw** (**Breslau**).
- Escape the cities of the north for the beach resorts of the **Pomeranian coast**, such as **Kolobrzeg** (large and fashionable) or **Leba** (a quiet resort with a beach of fabulous

white sand), or the beech woods and islands of the **Wolin National Park**. **Slowinski National Park** is known for its giant 'wandering sand dunes' which can shift several metres each year.
- **Swimming** is also available in the **Mazurian Lake District** (consisting of approximately 3000 lakes), also a favourite **angling** destination. For **sailing**, the **Augustow**, **Ilawa** and **Mazurian lakes** are best. **Canoeists** may also head to the **Brodnica** or **Mysliborz lakelands**, or the rivers **Brda**, **Czarna Hancza** and **Obra** where canoeing trips lasting up to 12 days can be undertaken.
- Pay tribute to the victims of the holocaust at **Oswiecim-Birkenau** (**Auschwitz-Birkenau**) concentration camp, 70km (43 miles) from Kraków. The camp area has been designated as a memorial monument and a World Heritage Site by UNESCO.

TOURIST INFORMATION

Polish National Tourist Office in the UK
Level 3, Westec House, West Gate, London, W5 1YY, UK
Tel: (0870) 0675 010 (brochure line).
Website: www.visitpoland.org

Polish National Tourist Office in the USA
5 Marine View Plaza, Suite 208, Hoboken, New Jersey 07030, USA
Tel: (201) 420 9910.
Website: www.polandtour.org

Entertainment

FOOD & DRINK: Poland has a distinctive cuisine, with typical ingredients being dill, marjoram, caraway seeds, wild mushrooms and sour cream, which is frequently added to soups, sauces and braised meats. Soups play an important part at mealtimes and are usually rich and very thick, and are often served in cups with small hot pasties stuffed with meat or cabbage. Poland is also a good country for fish (*ryba*). Pastries (*ciastka*) are also very good. Table service is the norm in restaurants. Western drinks, such as whisky, gin or brandy, can be obtained in most bars but are expensive. Wine is available but, again, is imported and expensive. Bars have table and/or counter service. Coffee shops are very popular in Poland and are the favourite places for social meetings from early morning to late at night. They do not close during the day and have the same function as do pubs in the United Kingdom. Alcoholic drinks are available throughout the day.

National specialities:
- *Bigos* (sauerkraut, fresh cabbage, onions and any variety of leftover meat).
- Carp served in sweet-and-sour jellied sauce.
- Poached pike with horseradish in cream.
- Salted and rolled herring fillets with pickles and onions.
- *Kulebiak* (a large mushroom and cabbage pasty).
- *Kabanos* (long, thick sausages).
- *Barszcz* (beetroot soup, excellent with sour cream).
- *Zrazy zawijane* (mushroom-stuffed beefsteak rolls in sour cream).

National drink:
- Vodka (*wódka*, in many various flavours).

- The best bottled beer is *zywiec*, a fairly strong lager-type beer.

Tipping: 10 to 15 per cent is customary in restaurants and cafes. Tipping in self-service restaurants is not expected. Tips for porter's services in hotels and train stations are customary but amounts are at the traveller's discretion.

NIGHTLIFE: Warsaw has about 17 theatres and three opera companies. Cinemas in Poland show both Polish and foreign films. There are some discos, as well as a growing number of nightclubs and music bars in Warsaw.

SHOPPING: Special purchases include glass and enamelware, handwoven rugs, silverware, handmade jewellery with amber and silver, dolls in regional costumes, woodcarvings and clay and metal sculptures.

Shopping hours: Mon-Fri 0600-1800/1900, shorter hours on Saturday and Sunday. 'Night shops' open 2000-0800. Supermarkets and department stores open Mon-Sat 0900-2000. Bookshops open Mon-Fri 1100-1900.

Business

- **GDP**: US$463 billion.
- **Main exports**: Machinery, transport, food and live animals.
- **Main imports**: Minerals, fuels, lubricants, chemicals and intermediate manufactured goods.
- **Main trade partners**: Germany, Italy, France, Spain, UK, China and Russian Federation.

ECONOMY: As the largest economy in ex-Soviet eastern Europe, the fate of Poland was, and still is, central to that of the whole region. The economic contribution of the agricultural sector declined steadily throughout the 1990s and now accounts for just 2.9 per cent of the GDP, but still employs one-quarter of the workforce. Livestock and meat are major export earners; rye, wheat, oats, sugar beet and potatoes are the main crops. In the industrial sector, Poland's once substantial coal mining industry – like its counterparts elsewhere in Europe – has been scaled down in recent years. Other important industries are shipbuilding, textiles, steel, cement, chemicals and food processing. Again following the trend across the continent, the industry's contribution to the GDP has declined to 31.3 per cent, while the service sector has seen rapid growth.
With the collapse of the communist system at the end of the 1980s, Poland adopted the 'big bang' strategy of rapid transition to a market economy: price controls (including subsidies) were removed at a stroke; production, distribution and trade were deregulated; large parts of the economy were privatised using a voucher system; the tax and fiscal systems were overhauled; and the national currency (the Zloty) was made fully convertible. The shock of these measures and the collapse of the Comecon trading system threw the economy into temporary crisis, but it recovered quickly and by the mid-1990s was growing strongly. Many of those parts of the economy still under state ownership – including several important industrial enterprises – were privatised, albeit at a more leisurely pace. By 2000, the private sector accounted for 70 per cent of GDP. Over the next two years the economy suffered mild recession, but by the end of 2003, growth had reached 3.4 per cent and is still rising. Inflation is currently 3.4 per cent.
Unemployment, however, has risen consistently since 2000 to its current level of 19.5 per cent, which is one of the highest levels in Europe. This, in turn, has led to the growth of a large informal or 'grey' economy, in which as many as 2 million people may be engaged.
Poland became a full member of the European Union on 1 May 2004 as one of 10 new entrants. The decision to join was endorsed by 77 per cent of the electorate in a June 2003 national referendum. Within the EU, Poland may be expected to work with its fellow members of the 'Visegrad Group' – Hungary and the Czech and Slovak Republics – who are also joining the EU. Where necessary, they will seek to protect their regional interests against the larger and more powerful Western European economies.

BUSINESS ETIQUETTE: In Poland, a formal approach is favoured and it is therefore advisable to give plenty of notice of an intended visit. Employees in state organisations do not take a lunch break, but they have their main meal after 1500. **Office hours:** Mon-Fri 0800-1600.

CONFERENCES/CONVENTIONS: The most popular conference venues are in Warsaw. Events are also hosted in Kraków, while Gdansk, Wroclaw and other towns are used occasionally.

COMMERCIAL INFORMATION

Krajowa Izba Gospodarcza (Polish Chamber of Commerce)
PO Box 361, Trebacka 4, 00-074 Warsaw, Poland
Tel: (22) 630 9600.
Website: www.kig.pl

Portugal

Location: Western Europe.

Time: GMT (GMT + 1 from last Sunday in March to last Sunday in October).

Overview

Often overshadowed by its much larger eastern neighbour, Spain, Portugal is something of an unspoilt jewel on the European tourist map. Portugal is also a country with a rich and turbulent history of seafaring and discovery dating back to the 15th century when Portuguese explorers such as Vasco da Gama put to sea in search of a passage to India. From this point, the Portuguese went on to build a colonial empire in Africa, Latin America, India and the Far East. Because Portugal was a dictatorship for almost half of the 20th century, under the leadership of Antonio de Oliveira Salazar, the rulers' stubborn refusal to relinquish their grip on the former colonies as demands for independence gained momentum there resulted in expensive wars in Africa. This period was brought to an end in 1974 in a bloodless coup, known as the 'Revolution of the Carnations', which ushered in a new democracy. By the end of 1975, all of Portugal's former colonies in Africa were independent of Lisbon but the 200 million Portuguese speakers around the world today are an obvious legacy of Portugal's colonial past.
Today, Portugal remains one of the least spoilt corners of Europe. Yet it contains enough World Heritage Sites and other natural and cultural wonders to keep any visitor busy for a long, long time. It is a country of astonishing beauty and diversity, not to mention clear blue skies and friendly, courteous people. Pick any destination and the view from your window might be a rugged stretch of windswept coastline (Cabo do São Vicente, Castelejo, Cabo Espichel), a pristine beach where fishermen mend their nets beside brightly painted sardine boats (Albufeira, Bordeira, Praia do Camilo) or a cobbled street overlooked by dazzling whitewashed houses with wooden balconies and red-tiled roofs. Portugal is a land of infinite options. You can mingle with the crowds in one of the more sophisticated beach resorts or wander through the medieval quarters of historic cities like Lisbon, Porto, Braga or Coimbra. To explore the

more remote beauty spots (car hire is relatively cheap, driving a delight) stay overnight in a romantic *pousada* - a converted farm, monastery or manor house enjoying a wonderful setting - an amazing bargain. If it is an activity holiday you are looking for, Portugal is one of Europe's premier golfing destinations while the tennis schools are second-to-none. You could try your hand at big game fishing or horseriding, learn how to windsurf or water ski. Other unmissable experiences include *Fado* (Portugal's answer to soul music), country fairs where centuries-old folk traditions are lovingly reenacted, Port wine tastings and mouthwatering fish suppers. Portugal is a country ripe for discovery.

General Information

AREA: 92,345 sq km (35,655 sq miles).
POPULATION: 10.3 million.
POPULATION DENSITY: 112.7 per sq km.
CAPITAL: Lisbon. **Population:** 564,657; 2.5 million in Greater Lisbon.
GEOGRAPHY: Portugal occupies the southwest part of the Iberian Peninsula and shares borders in the north and the east with Spain, while to the south and west lies the Atlantic Ocean. The country is divided into various provinces, including the Atlantic islands of Madeira and the Azores; the latter lying some 1220km (760 miles) due west of Lisbon. The Douro, Guadiana and Tagus rivers flow across the border from Spain. North Portugal is mountainous, the highest part being the Serra da Estrela, a popular area for skiing. South of Lisbon stretch the vast plains of the Alentejo region. A range of mountains divides the Alentejo from the Algarve, which runs along the south coast, and is one of the most popular resort areas with wide sandy beaches and attractive bays.
GOVERNMENT: Republic since 1910. **Head of State:** President Anibal Cavaco Silva since 2006. **Head of Government:** Prime Minister Jose Socrates since 2005.
Recent history: In spite of a successful Presidency of the EU in 2000, the domestic popularity of Portugal's Socialist Government was decreasing, and after Prime Minister Antonio Guterres resigned in December 2001, the centre-right Social Democratic Party (PSD), headed by new Prime Minister Durao Barroso, formed a coalition Government with the Popular Party. Barroso went on to become President of the European Commission in July 2004, but the Government he left had become increasingly unpopular because of escalating unemployment, and in the Autumn of 2004 there were clear signs of its instability, which led President Jorge Sampaio to dissolve Parliament. In the general elections in February 2005, the Socialist Party won its first absolute majority since democracy returned to the country in 1974, and Prime Minister Jose Socrates and his new Cabinet were sworn in. On taking office, Mr Socrates said his priority would be to encourage economic growth and stem the rising unemployment. President Sampaio, a Socialist, has served two five-year terms and was succeeded by the winner of the January 2006 Presidential poll, Anibal Cavaco Silva. Mr Silva, a former Prime Minister, is the first centre-right politician to be President since the coup of 1974. He defeated two Socialist candidates to win a first round election victory.
LANGUAGE: Portuguese. English is widely spoken within the business community.
RELIGION: Roman Catholic.
ELECTRICITY: 220 volts AC, 50Hz. 110 volts in some areas and 230 DC in parts of the south. Continental two-pin plugs are in use.
SOCIAL CONVENTIONS: The Portuguese way of life is leisurely, and old-fashioned politeness is essential. Warm, Latin hospitality is the norm. The country has a deeply individual national character, although each province has its own traditions and folklore. Casual wear is widely acceptable, although beachwear should not be worn in towns. In restaurants, it is usual to smoke only at the end of the meal. Smoking is prohibited in cinemas, theatres and on buses.

Credit: © ITP/ Rui Morais de Sousa

Climate

The northwest has mild winters with high levels of rainfall and fairly short summers. The northeast has longer winters and hot summers. In the south, summers (March to October) are warm with very little rain except in early spring and autumn. High temperatures are moderated by a permanent breeze in Estoril (July to August).
Required clothing: Light- to mediumweights and rainwear are advised.

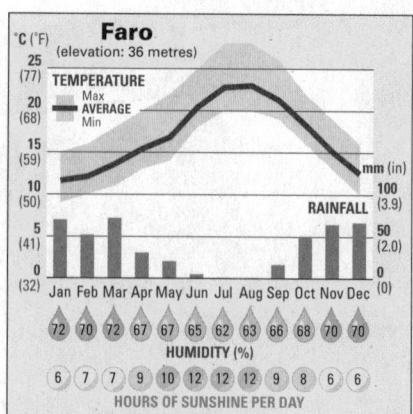

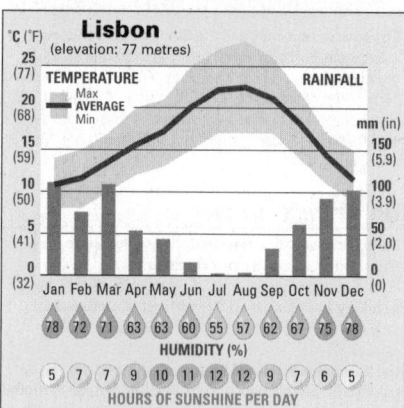

Communications

Telephone: IDD is available. Country code: 351. There are call boxes in most villages and all towns; there are also public telephones in many cafes and bars, from which international calls may be made.
Mobile telephone: Roaming agreements exist with international mobile phone companies. Coverage exists across the whole country.
Internet: Internet cafes exist in all urban areas, and some post offices offer Internet facilities. In various hotels and public facilities, there are areas where it is possible to access wireless Internet.
Post: Post office (*correios*) hours: Usually Mon-Fri 0800-2200, Sat-Sun 0900-1800. The post office at Lisbon Airport is open 24 hours a day. Airmail to European destinations from continental Portugal and the Azores takes three days; from Madeira, up to five days.
MEDIA: Public TV services are operated by *RTP*, which enjoyed a monopoly until the launch of commercial channel *SIC* in 1992. Today, Portugal's commercial TV stations provide tough competition for the public broadcaster.
Press: Each region has its own Portuguese-language dailies. The English-language newspapers published in Portugal include: *Anglo Portuguese News* (Lisbon) and *The Portugal News* (Algarve). Portugese dailies include: *Diario Noticias*, *Publico* and *Expresso*.
TV: *RTP* operates two domestic channels and external services *RTP Africa* and *RTP Internacional*. It had a monopoly position until the commercial channel *Sociedade Independente de Comunicação (SIC)* was launched in 1992. *TVI* is another commercial channel, while *TV Cabo* is the main pay-TV operator. A wide range of domestic and foreign channels are available through *Multichannel TV* - via cable and satellite - in Portugal.
Radio: *Rádio e Televisão de Portugal (RTP)* is Portugal's public broadcasting organisation. It operates public radio networks in the country. *Radio Comercial* and *Radio Clube Portugues* are two of the commercial channels. *Radio Renascenca* is very popular and owned by the Roman Catholic Church. Around 300 local and regional radio stations operate in Portugal.

Passport/Visa

	Passport Required?	Visa Required?	Return Ticket Required?
Full British	1	No	No
Australian	Yes	No	2
Canadian	Yes	No	2
USA	Yes	No	2
Other EU	1	No	No
Japanese	Yes	No	2

Note: *Regulations and requirements may be subject to change at short notice, and you are advised to contact the appropriate diplomatic or consular authority before finalising travel arrangements. Any numbers in the chart refer to the footnotes below.*

Note: Portugal is a signatory to the **1995 Schengen Agreement**. For further details about passport and visa regulations in the Schengen area see the introductory section *How to Use This Guide*.
PASSPORTS: Passport valid for at least three months beyond the length of stay required by all except:
1. EU/EEA nationals (EU+ Iceland, Liechtenstein, Norway) and Swiss nationals holding a valid national ID card.
Note: EU and EEA nationals are only required to produce evidence of their EU/EEA nationality and identity in order to be admitted to any EU/EEA Member State. This evidence can take the form of a valid national passport *or* national identity card. Either is acceptable. Possession of a return ticket, any length of validity on their document, sufficient funds for the length of their proposed visit should *not* be imposed.
Note: Passport validity depends on nationality.
2. A return or onward ticket and funds of €75 plus €40 per day are obligatory.
VISAS: Required by all except the following for stays of up to 90 days:
(a) nationals referred to in the chart and under passport exemptions above;
(b) nationals of Andorra, Argentina, Bolivia, Brazil, Brunei, Bulgaria, Chile, Costa Rica, Croatia, Cyprus, Czech Republic, El Salvador, Estonia, Guatemala, Honduras, Hong Kong (SAR), Hungary, Iceland, Israel, Korea (Rep), Latvia, Liechtenstein, Lithuania, Macau (SAR), Malaysia, Malta, Mexico, Monaco, New Zealand, Nicaragua, Norway, Panama, Paraguay, Poland, Romania, San Marino, Singapore, Slovak Republic, Slovenia, Switzerland, Uruguay, Vatican City and Venezuela;
(c) transit passengers continuing their journey by the same or first connecting aircraft, provided holding onward or return documentation and not leaving the airport. However, nationals of Afghanistan, Bangladesh, Congo (Dem Rep), Eritrea, Ethiopia, Ghana, Iran, Iraq, Liberia, Nigeria, Pakistan, Senegal, Somalia and Sri Lanka *always* require a transit visa, even when not leaving the airport transit area; contact the Consulate (or Consular section at Embassy) for details.
Types of visa and cost: A uniform type of visa, the *Schengen* visa, is issued for touristic, private or business visits. There are three types of Schengen visa: *Short-stay*, *Transit* and *Airport Transit*. Visa costs are dependent on the tariff charges of the issuing country and prices may vary with exchange rates. Check with your local Embassy for the most up-to-date prices.
Note: A Schengen visa will be issued free of charge to the spouse and children of an EU national, upon presentation of the original marriage or birth certificate and a valid EU passport. For children, original full birth certificates are required.
Validity: Transit visas are valid for single or two entries of maximum five days, including the day of arrival. Visas cannot be extended; a new application must be made each time.
Application to: Consulate (or Consular section at Embassy) responsible for your place of residence; see *Passport/Visa Information*. Travellers visiting just one Schengen country should apply to the Consulate of that country; travellers visiting more than one Schengen country should apply to the Consulate of the country chosen as the main destination or the country they will enter first (if they have no main destination).
Application requirements: *Tourism:* (a) Passport or official travel documents accepted by Schengen countries, valid for at least three months longer than the validity of the visa, with blank page for attachment of visa sticker. (b) Application form. (c) One passport-size photo. (d) Proof of purpose of visit in the form of an official letter of invitation from host or business partner, provisional ticket booking and hotel booking where appropriate. (e) Proof of sufficient funds and medical insurance may also be required. (f) Fee (payable in cash or by postal order). (g) For postal applications, a large self-addressed envelope, stamped for registered or recorded delivery. (h) For applicants driving to Portugal, registration document, proof of legal ownership of the vehicle, driving licence and insurance papers. Applicants entering Portugal by land must register with the Police within three days of arrival. *Business:* (a)-(g) and, (h) Letter from employer or, if self-employed, from solicitor, accountant, bank manager or local Chamber of Commerce stating purpose and duration of the visit. This should be faxed to the relevant Consulate at least 48 hours before submitting an application. References may also be required.
Working days required: From a few days to a few weeks. Apply in plenty of time.
Temporary residence: Contact the Consulate (or consular section at Embassy) for further details; see *Passport/Visa Information*.

PASSPORT/VISA INFORMATION

Embassy of the Portuguese Republic in the UK
11 Belgrave Square, London SW1X 8PP, UK
Tel: (020) 7235 5331.
Opening hours: Mon-Fri 0900-1300 and 1400-1730.

Portuguese Consulate General in the UK
3 Portland Place, London W1B 1HR, UK
Tel: (020) 7291 3770 *or* (0906) 550 8948 (recorded visa information; calls cost £1 per minute).
Opening hours: Mon-Fri 0830-1330 (appointment only; closed UK and Portuguese public holidays).

Embassy of the Portuguese Republic in the USA
2012 Massachussetts Avenue, NW, Washington, DC 20008, USA
Tel: (202) 328 8610.

Money

Single European currency (Euro): The Euro is now the official currency of 12 EU member states (including Portugal). The first Euro coins and notes were introduced in January 2002; the Portuguese Escudo was still in circulation until 28 February 2002, when it was completely replaced by the Euro. Euro (€) = 100 cents. Notes are in denominations of €500, 200, 100, 50, 20, 10 and 5. Coins are in denominations of €2 and 1, and 50, 20, 10, 5, 2 and 1 cents.
Currency exchange: Many banks offer differing exchange rates depending on the denominations of Portuguese currency being bought or sold. It is common practice for banks to charge 0.5 per cent commission with a minimum charge of approximately £6/€10. However, some banks do not charge any commission on transactions of less than €24.94. Check with banks for details and current rates. Additionally, ATMs, identified by the symbol MB (MultiBanco), are increasingly being installed and tend to be more efficient and only charge 2 per cent commission. There are also many bureaux de change available.
Credit & debit cards: American Express, MasterCard and Visa are widely accepted, as well as Eurocheque cards. Check with your credit or debit card company for details of merchant acceptability and other services that may be available.
Traveller's cheques: These are readily exchanged. To avoid additional exchange rate charges, travellers are advised to take traveller's cheques in Euros, Pounds Sterling or US Dollars.
Currency restrictions: The import of local or foreign currency in cash or traveller's cheques is unlimited. However, there is an obligation to inform the customs authorities if foreign currencies exceed approximately €4987.98/US$6000. The export of local currency is limited to €498.80. There are no restrictions on the export of foreign currency although currency exchange receipts may be requested for amounts over €4987.98. The export of gold, silver, jewellery and other valuables is limited to a value of €149.64 and subject to special conditions. For details, contact the Embassy; see *Passport/Visa Information*.
Banking hours: Generally, Mon-Fri 0830-1500 (certain banks in Lisbon are open until 1800).
Exchange Rate indicators:
Rate at time of publishing
£1.00= €1.46
$1.00= €0.82

Duty Free

The following items may be imported by visitors over 18 years of age from countries outside the EU without incurring customs duty:
200 cigarettes or 100 cigarillos or 50 cigars or 250g of tobacco; 1l of spirits over 22 per cent or 2l of spirits up to 22 per cent; 2l of wine; 50g of perfume and 250ml of eau de toilette; 500g of coffee or 200g of coffee extract (provided bought in a tax-free shop); 100g of tea or 40g of tea extract (provided bought in a tax-free shop); further goods up to €175 per adult or €90 if under 15 years of age.
Abolition of duty free goods within the EU: On June 30 1999, the sale of duty free alcohol and tobacco at airports and at sea was abolished in all of the original 15 EU member states. Of the 10 new member states that joined the EU on May 1 2004, these rules already apply to Cyprus and Malta. There are transitional rules in place for visitors returning to one of the original 15 EU countries from one of the other new EU countries. But for the original 15, plus Cyprus and Malta, there are now no limits imposed on importing tobacco and alcohol products from one EU country to another (with the exceptions of Denmark, Finland and Sweden, where limits *are* imposed). Travellers should note that they may be required to prove at customs that the goods purchased are for personal use *only*.

Public Holidays

Below are listed Public Holidays for the January 2006-June 2007 period.
2006: Jan 1 New Year's Day. **Feb 28** Mardi Gras (Carnival). **Apr 14** Good Friday. **Apr 25** Freedom Day. **May 1** Labour Day. **Jun 10** Portugal Day. **Jun 15** Corpus Christi. **Aug 15** Assumption. **Oct 5** Republic Day. **Nov 1** All Saints' Day. **Dec 1** Restoration of Independence Day. **Dec 8** Immaculate Conception. **Dec 25** Christmas Day.
2007: Jan 1 New Year's Day. **Feb 20** Mardi Gras (Carnival). **Apr 6** Good Friday. **Apr 25** Freedom Day. **May 1** Labour Day. **May 26** Corpus Christi. **Jun 10** Portugal Day.
Note: Holidays falling on a Sunday are *not* observed on the following Monday.

Health

	Special Precautions?	Certificate Required?
Yellow Fever	No	1
Cholera	No	No
Typhoid & Polio	No	N/A
Malaria	No	N/A

Note: *Regulations and requirements may be subject to change at short notice, and you are advised to contact your doctor well in advance of your intended date of departure. Any numbers in the chart refer to the footnotes below.*

1.: A *yellow fever* vaccination certificate is required from travellers over one year of age arriving in (or going to as a destination) the Azores or Madeira, if coming from infected areas. However, no certificate is required from passengers transiting through Funchal, Porto Santo and Santa Maria.
Health care: European Economic Area (EEA) and Switzerland: If you or any of your dependants are suddenly taken ill or have an accident during a visit to an EEA country or Switzerland, free or reduced-cost necessary treatment is available - in most cases on production of a valid European Health Insurance Card (EHIC). Each country has different rules about state medical provision. In some, treatment is free. In many countries you will have to pay part or all of the cost, and then claim a full or partial refund. The EHIC gives access to state-provided medical treatment only and the scheme gives no entitlement to medical repatriation costs, nor does it cover ongoing illnesses of a non-urgent nature, so comprehensive travel insurance is advised. Note that the EHIC replaces the Form E111, which will no longer be valid after 31 December 2005. Some restrictions apply, depending on your nationality.
If you require a doctor or a dentist in mainland Portugal, go to the nearest health centre (*Centro de Saúde*). Show your passport or European Health Insurance Card (EHIC), and ask to be treated under the EU arrangements. You will be charged a non-refundable standard fee. Dental treatment is limited under the state scheme. You will probably have to pay, and the charges are not refundable. In Madeira, you can get a partial refund if you see a private doctor. Make sure you get an official (green) receipt. For some prescribed medicines, you will have to pay between 30 and 80 per cent of the cost. There is no charge for prescriptions issued for certain serious illnesses ('A Level'). Basic hospital treatment is free, but you will have to pay for secondary examinations, such as X-rays, and laboratory tests. More information can be obtained in Portugal from the nearest *Administração Regional de Saúde* (Regional Health Service Office).

Travel - International

AIR:
The national airline, *TAP Air Portugal (TP)* (website: www.tap.pt), operates direct flights to Faro, Lisbon and Porto from a number of countries, including Canada, France, Spain, the UK and USA. *Portugália Airlines (NI)* (website: www.pga.pt) operates flights from Europe.
Approximate flight times: From Lisbon to *London* is two hours 30 minutes and to *New York* is eight hours.
Main airports: *Lisbon (LIS)* (Portela de Sacavem) (website: www.ana-aeroportos.pt) is 7km (4.5 miles) north of the city (travel time - 35 minutes). *To/from the airport:* Carris buses run from the airport to the city and the main railway stations. A special 'Aerobus' departs to the city centre every 20 minutes from 0745 to 2015. There is an airport shuttle bus that departs daily to Estoril and Cascais, every hour from 0700 to 2230, and an Express bus runs to many

destinations around the country. Taxi services to the city are available, with a 20 per cent surcharge after 2200, at weekends and on holidays. **Facilities:** Bureaux de change, banks, tourist information, post office, duty free shops, showers and car hire.

Faro (FAO) (website: www.ana-aeroportos.pt) is 4km (3 miles) west of the city (travel time – 30 minutes). *To/from the airport:* EVA buses (website: www.eva-bus.com) link the airport with different parts of the city; taxis are available. *Oporto (OPO)* (Oporto Sá Carneiro) (website: www.ana-aeroportos.pt) is 20 km (7 miles) from the city. *To/from the airport:* Buses and taxis to the city are available.

Faro and Oporto airports. **Facilities:** Outgoing duty free shop; bank/bureau de change; car hire and a restaurant/bar.

Departure tax: None.

SEA:

 Main ports: *Lisbon, Leixões* (Oporto), *Funchal* (Madeira) and *Portimão* (Algarve), served by *Cunard* (website: www.cunard.com) and *P&O* (website: www.pocruises.com). For details, contact shipping lines.

RAIL:

 Travelling from the UK, the quickest way is to travel by *Eurostar* through the Channel Tunnel to Paris (travel time – three hours) and, from there, to Portugal. The *Sud-Express* runs between Paris and Lisbon, offering first- and second-class seats, sleepers and a restaurant car. For further information and reservations, contact *Eurostar* (tel: (0870) 6000 792 (travel agents) *or* (08705) 186 186 (public; within the UK) *or* (+44 1233) 617 575 (public; outside the UK only); website: www.eurostar.com); *or Rail Europe* (tel: (08705) 848 848). Travel agents can obtain refunds for unused tickets from Eurostar Trade Refunds, 2nd Floor, Kent House, 81 Station Road, Ashford, Kent TN23 1PD, UK. Complaints and comments may be sent to Eurostar Customer Relations, Eurostar House, Waterloo Station, London SE1 8SE, UK (tel: (020) 7928 5163; e-mail: new.comments@eurostar.co.uk). Rail travellers from the UK not using the Channel Tunnel link need to cross the Channel via some form of sea crossing, usually by ferry or catamaran; for details on sea crossings, see also the *Sea* section above. The cost of the crossing is usually included in the price of the rail ticket. There is a daily service between London, Paris and Lisbon, taking approximately 26 hours. *Caminhos De Ferro Portugueses* (website: www.cp.pt) offers an international rail service to Vigo, Madrid and Paris.

Rail passes: The *Inter-Rail* pass offers unlimited second-class train travel in up to 29 European countries (includes Morocco and Turkey) split into eight zones (A-H). Three different tickets are available: a ticket covering one zone (two to six countries, 16 days' validity), a ticket covering two zones (six to 10 countries, 22 days' validity) and an All Zone Pass (29 countries, one month's validity). Ferry services between Italy and Greece are included. Passengers must be resident in Europe for at least six months before the pass is used. Travel is not allowed in the passenger's country of residence. Travellers under 26 years receive a reduction of about 30 per cent. Children's tickets are reduced by about 50 per cent. Supplements are required for some high-speed services, seat reservations and couchettes. Discounts are offered on *Eurostar* and some ferry routes. Available from *Inter Rail* (website: www.interrailnet.com).

The *EuroDomino* pass enables holders anything from three to eight days' extensive travel within a one-month period on the entire rail network of their chosen country. It is valid in 28 European countries and North Africa, including the ferry service from Brindisi (Italy) to Igoumenitsa (Greece). To purchase a *EuroDomino* pass you must have been resident in Europe for at least six months and a passport number is required at time of booking. It is not permitted to purchase a pass for travel within your own country of residence. To qualify for the youth rates, you must be under 26 years on the first date of validity of the pass. Children aged four-11 years inclusive pay half the adult fares rounded up to the nearest pound. Children under four years travel for free. Seat reservations, couchette and sleeper charges are not included in the cost of the pass and are payable at the normal rate. Passholder fares are payable on some services. Reservation/supplement charges are payable on all trains within Spain. Available from *Rail Europe* (website: www.raileurope.co.uk/railpasses/eurodomino.htm).

ROAD:

 The only land border is shared with Spain. Major border posts are now open around the clock, but smaller ones may close earlier in winter. From the UK, the quickest routes are via the ferry links from Plymouth to Santander and from Portsmouth to Bilbao in northern Spain (which obviates the need to drive through France). Cars can be imported for up to six months. For information on documentation and regulations, see the *Travel - Internal* section. Travelling from the UK, *Eurotunnel* operates trains 24 hours per day through the Channel Tunnel between Folkestone in Kent (with direct access from the M20) and Calais in France. All vehicles, from motorcycles to campers, can be accommodated. For further

information, contact *Eurotunnel Reservations* (tel: (08705) 353 535; website: www.eurotunnel.co.uk). For further details, see also *Travel – International* in the *France* section. For information on required documentation and traffic regulations, see *Travel – Internal* section. **Coach:** *Eurolines* operates an extensive network of coach services to many destinations throughout Europe, including Coimbra, Faro, Lagos, Lisbon and Oporto. For information on timetables and fares, contact Eurolines (tel: (08705) 143 219; website: www.eurolines.com).

Travel - Internal

AIR:

 TAP Air Portugal and *Portugália* run services between Lisbon, Faro, Madeira, Porto Santo, Oporto and the Azores. Charter flights are also available. The airline for the Azores is *SATA* (*Sociedade Acoriana de Transportes Aereos*) (website: www.sata.pt), which operates its *Air Açores* service between the various islands.

SEA/RIVER:

 Transport is available from all coastal ports and along the major rivers: For details, contact local ports.

RAIL:

 Caminhos de Ferro Portugueses (Portuguese Railways) (website: www.cp.pt) provides a rail service to every town. There are a number of options: the top-of-the -range *Alfa Pendular* trains offer the fastest and most comfortable rail link between Lisbon and the Algarve and in the North (Oporto, Braga or Guimarães, with stops in Coimbra and Aveiro); the *Intercidades* (Intercity) service covers Lisbon, Oporto, Alentejo and Lisbon to Algarve routes; the *International Sud-Express* train and *Lusitânia Hotel* train leave from Lisbon and Oporto. There is a vast network of regional, inter-regional and suburban trains covering the country. The tourist areas of Cascais and Sintra are connected to Lisbon by frequent express trains. High-speed *Alfa* trains run between Lisbon and Porto via Coimbra and Aveiro. *Fertagus* trains cross the River Tagus in Lisbon, operating between Entrecampus station to Fogueteiro (on the south bank).

Cheap fares: On 'Blue Days', usually Monday afternoon to Thursday, special rates are available. There are also special fares (with up to 30 per cent reductions) for groups of 10 or more (*Bilhetes de Grupo*), travelling for a minimum distance of 75km/47 miles (single journey) or 150km/94 miles (return journey). Application should be made four days in advance by the group leader. Tourist tickets (*Bilhetes Turisticos*) for seven, 14 or 21 days of unlimited travel are also available. The Rail Cheque (*Cheque Trem*), obtainable in four different values, can be in one name or a company's name and has no time limit; it gives a reduction of 10 per cent and can be used both for purchasing tickets and many other railway services.

An *International Youth Ticket* (*BIJ*) entitles those aged 12 to 26 to a discount (subject to certain conditions) in 25 countries for two months, including Portugal.

Senior citizens are entitled to 50 per cent reduction on production of proof of age. Children under four travel free. Children aged between four and 11 pay half fare.

Euro Domino, Family Card, Inter-Rail Card, Rail Inclusive Tours and *Special Tourist Trips* are amongst other offers from the Portuguese Railways (*Caminhos de Ferro Portugueses*), Calçada do Duque 20, 1249-109 Lisbon Codex (tel: 2132 15700; website: www.cp.pt). Rail information is also available from ICEP/Portuguese Trade and Tourism Office; see *Top Things To Do*.

ROAD:

 Traffic drives on the right. Every town and village can be reached by an adequate system of roads. Petrol stations generally open 0700-2000, although some are open 24 hours. Travel by motorway is subject to a toll according to distance covered and type of vehicle. A small tax may be added to petrol bought with a credit card. **Bus:** There are frequent coach services between all Portuguese cities. For further information, contact *Rede Nacional de Expressos* (website: www.rede-expressos.pt). **Taxi:** Charges are according to distance and taxis are all metered. Taxis are usually painted beige (although some taxis painted in the old colours of green and black still exist). In the city, they charge a standard meter fare; outside the city limits they charge per kilometre and are entitled to charge for the return fare. There is a surcharge for carrying luggage in the cities. **Car hire:** Available from main towns and airports, with or without driver. **Regulations:** Minimum age for driving is 18 (but must be at least 21 to 25 if hiring a car). Cars may be imported for up to six months. Traffic signs are international. Headlights should be dipped in built-up areas and side lights used when parking in badly lit areas. Children should not travel in the front seat. Seat belts should be worn. Warning triangles are compulsory. It is forbidden to carry cans of petrol in vehicles. Speed limits are 50kph (30mph) in built-up areas, 90kph (56mph) outside built-up areas and 120kph (70mph) on motorways. Visitors who passed their driving test less than one year previously must

display a yellow disc with '90' on it on the rear of their vehicle and must not go faster than 90kph (56mph). Permitted speeds will vary if trailers are being used. **Documentation:** International Driving Permits or foreign driving licences are accepted. Third Party insurance is compulsory. Under the requirements of the Portuguese Road Code, those wishing to drive a car must possess a valid national/international driving licence, other official documentation with photograph, log book or rental contract and adequate car insurance. Failure to produce, on request to the authorities, any of the above will result in an on-the-spot cash fine. A *carnet de passage* is needed for a van.

URBAN:

 Lisbon and Oporto have underground systems. Lisbon's underground (*Metropolitano*) (website: www.metrolisboa.pt) is currently being expanded. Oporto's underground (website: www.metro-porto.pt) operates two lines. Trams operate in major Portuguese cities. A tram ride in Lisbon provides a good opportunity to see the city. There is also an extensive bus network in Lisbon (website: www.carris.pt). **Cheap fares:** In Lisbon, a *Tourist Pass* is available for either four or seven days travel on trams, buses and the underground. The *Lisboa Card* (for sightseeing) is valid for 24 or 72 hours and offers unlimited bus, tram and underground travel as well as entry to 25 museums.

Travel times: The following chart gives approximate travel times (in hours and minutes) from **Lisbon** to other major cities/towns in Portugal.

	Air	Road	Rail
Faro	0.35	4.00	5.00
Oporto	0.45	5.00	3.00
Funchal	1.30	-	-

Travel Advice

Most visits to Portugal are trouble-free but you should be aware of the global risk of indiscriminate international terrorist attacks, which could be against civilian targets, including places frequented by foreigners.

Travellers should be aware of serious outbreaks of forest fires in Summer and take every care during their visit to rural areas.

This advice is based on information provided by the Foreign and Commonwealth Office in the UK. It is correct at time of publishing. As the situation can change rapidly, visitors are advised to contact the following organisations for the latest travel advice:

British Foreign and Commonwealth Office
Tel: (0845) 850 2829.
Website: www.fco.gov.uk

US Department of State
Website: http://travel.state.gov/travel

Accommodation

There is a wide range of accommodation available all over the country, ranging from luxury hotels, pensions, boarding houses and inns to simple guest houses, manor houses, campsites and youth hostels. *Pousadas* offer very good value and are often situated in places of scenic beauty in converted castles, palaces or old inns.

EDITOR'S CHOICE: POUSADAS

The *pousadas* are a network of inns housed in historic buildings, castles, palaces and convents, or sometimes built especially for the purpose. They have often been geographically sited in regions not on the usual tourist itinerary to give people the opportunity to visit the whole country. The architecture and design of the *pousadas* has been carefully studied in order to give visitors a better knowledge of the cultural traditions of the various regions of the country, with particular attention paid to handicrafts, cooking and wines.

HOTELS:

Most hotels have a private swimming pool and serve international cuisine as well as some typically Portuguese dishes. During the low season, hotels normally grant substantial reductions. There should be an officially authorised list of prices displayed in every bedroom, and children under eight years of age are entitled to a reduction of 50 per cent on the price of full meals and 50 per cent on the price of an extra bed, if sharing parents' room or apartment. Classification of hotels is according to the international **1- to 5-star** system and their prices are officially approved. Apartment hotels are classified from 2- to 4-star, motels from 2- to 3-star and boarding houses from 1- to 3-star (with 1-star being the best); there are also 4-star *albergarias*.

PRIVATE HOUSES:

Rooms are available in private houses and on farms all over Portugal. Some of the old manor houses are now open to visitors and provide good opportunities for tourists to make contact with Portuguese customs and people.

SELF-CATERING:

There is self-catering tourist accommodation in deluxe, first- and second-class tourist villages and tourist apartments, particularly on the Algarve. Tour operators can arrange a wide variety of villas for self-catering parties.

YOUTH HOSTELS:

Youth hostels are located to give young people the opportunity of visiting towns, countryside, mountains and coastal areas. Tourists can obtain accommodation and meals.

CAMPING/CARAVANNING:

Portugal provides camping and caravan parks near beaches and in thickly wooded areas. Some have model installations including swimming pools, games fields, supermarkets and restaurants. For further information, check online (websites: www.roteiro-campista.pt or www.orbitur.pt).

ACCOMMODATION INFORMATION

Associação Hotéis de Portugal
Avenida Duque d'Ávila 75, 1000 Lisbon, Portugal
Tel: 2135 12360.
Website: www.hoteis-portugal.pt

Pousadas de Portugal
Rua Soares de Passos, 3 Alto de Santo Amaro, 1300-314, Lisbon, Portugal
Tel: 2184 4200.
Website: www.pousadas.pt

MOVIJOVEM (Youth Hostels)
Rua Lucio de Azevedo 27, 1600 Lisbon, Portugal
Tel: 2172 32100.
Website: www.pousadasjuventude.pt

Federação Portuguesa de Campismo
Avenida Coronel Eduardo Galhardo 24D, 1199-007 Lisbon, Portugal
Tel: 2181 26890.
E-mail: campasino@fpcampismo.pt

Top Things To See

- The dramatic setting of **Lisbon** on a series of steep hills at the estuary of the **River Tagus (Tio Tejo)** ensures that any visit to the city will have a sense of excitement. Ascend the highest of the seven hills surrounding the city and discover the magnificent 12th-century **Castle of St George** with its 10 towers. Back in town, check out the fabulous **Lisbon Cathedral** built at the same time as the castle. The exhibition grounds of '**Expo '98**', known as the **Park of Nations**, are still worth exploring. So is the riverside suburb of **Belém** where the ships of Vasco da Gama and other famous explorers were launched in the 15th and 16th centuries. The attractions here include the strikingly beautiful **Torre de Belém** and the architectural wonder that is the **Monastery of the Hieronymites** at the entrance to the harbour, both of which are World Heritage Sites.
- Experience the magic of **Sintra** (also a World Heritage Site), a mountain town full of palaces 25km (15 miles) from Lisbon. A site for lunar cults in ancient times, it boasts the former summer **residence of the Portuguese royal family** and the beautiful **Monserrate gardens**.
- Go further inland and discover **Évora**, a virtual museum of a town that reached its golden age in the 15th century, when it became the residence of the Portuguese kings. Its monuments had a profound influence on Portuguese architecture in Brazil.
- Head north for the **Monastery of Batalha (Mosteiro de Santa Maria)**, another UNESCO World Heritage Site and a breathtaking example of Portuguese Gothic and Manueline architecture, built to commemorate the victory of King João I over a Castilian army in 1385.
- Not far away is the **Monastery of Santa Maria d'Alcobaça**, which was founded in the 12th century by King Alfonso I. This is a masterpiece of Cistercian Gothic art.
- Explore medieval history at its most intriguing at the **Knights Templar castle** and town of **Tomar** built in the 12th century.
- **Porto** is the second-largest city in Portugal. It was nominated European City of Culture for 2001 and the historical centre is a UNESCO World Heritage Site. There are several attractions to explore; the **Stock Exchange Palace**, the Romanesque-Gothic **Cathedral**, the church of **Cedofeita** (Romanesque), the **Clérigos tower** (Porto's ex-libris of Baroque architecture). The old waterfront,

known as the **Cais da Ribeira**, caters for tourists with cafes, restaurants and an open-air market.
- Take the trip north-east from Porto to **Guimarães**, Portugal's medieval capital. An exceptionally well-preserved and authentic example of the evolution of a Medieval settlement into a modern town, it boasts a fine castle, the former palace of the Dukes of Bragança, as well as some attractive squares and churches.
- Vila **Nova de Foz Côa** is the place to go for visits to **Côa Archaeological Park** where along the Côa River an exceptional concentration of rock carvings from the Upper Palaeolithic period (22,000–10,000 B.C.) constitutes what UNESCO has called the most outstanding example of early human artistic activity in this form anywhere in the world.
- **Coimbra** in the Beiras region is one of Europe's oldest university towns. Here students can be heard singing the soulful tones of the '**fado de Coimbra**' (traditional song sung to the sound of guitars) in between visits to the university's sumptuous Baroque library. In the adjacent quarters stand the **Old Cathedral** (Romanesque) and the **Machado de Castro Museum**, built over a Roman cryptoportico. 10 miles to the south lies **Conímbriga**, the most important Roman remains in Portugal.

Top Things To Do

- Join the crowds and enjoy the sun and the excellent **beaches** and rocky coastline of **Algarve**.
- **Watersports** can be enjoyed all along Portugal's coastline - **swimming**, **snorkelling**, **water-skiing**, **sailing** and **windsurfing** are all widely available. For information on **diving**, contact the Portuguese Federation for Underwater Activities (website: www.fpas.pt).
- Big-game **fishing** is another popular option, particularly along the **Algarve** coast (website: www.biggamefishing.info).
- For a genuinely cultural experience, seek out the **Alfama** or **Bairro Alto (Upper Town)** neighbourhoods of **Lisbon** where **Fado**, Portugal's best-known traditional musical form, can be heard in many clubs.
- Lovers of port wine should explore the many opportunities for **wine tasting**, either in **Porto** or across the river in **Gaia**, where all the port-making companies are. The vine district of **Alto Douro** is a World Heritage Site on account of centuries of viticulture that has produced a cultural landscape of outstanding beauty that reflects its technological, social and economic evolution. Since the 18th century, its main product, port wine, has been world famous for its quality.
- The **shrine** at **Fátima** has been an important centre of Roman Catholic **pilgrimage** since 1917 when the Virgin Mary appeared to a group of children. Experience the **torchlight processions** held annually on May 13 and October 13.
- Go on one of the interesting **boat trips** in traditional Portuguese *moliceiros* (gondola-like sailing barges) in the **wetlands** around **Rio de Aveiro** which is crossed by numerous canals.
- Another good **boating** destination is the **Douro Valley**, stretching from Oporto to the Spanish border, where the River Douro is navigable.
- Go **hiking** in the **Peneda-Gerês**, Portugal's only **national park** comprising 170,000 acres (68,798 hectares) of mountainous countryside near the Spanish border. It is popular with hikers, climbers and naturalists, as it has an extraordinary diversity of climate, environment and scenery. **Canoeing** is also available.
- Portugal is a well-known **golfing** destination and the

south in particular has many championship golf courses (19 in the Algarve alone). The climate allows playing all year round. Some of the best-known 18-hole courses include **Estoril**, one of the oldest, close to Lisbon, hosting many major competitions; **Quinta de Marinha**, on the Estoril coast near **Lisbon**, with good views of the **Sintra** mountain range; **Golden Eagle**, near **Rio Maior**, boasting a typically US design, open to non-members; **Ponte de Lima**, a typical mountain course in the northern **Minho** region, close to vineyards, fruit gardens and mountains; **Estela**, on the coast near **Póvoa de Varzim**; **Tróia**, in **Alentejo**, southern Portugal, reputedly the country's most difficult course; and the **Royal Golf Course**, in the **Algarve**, said to be one of the world's most famous and most photographed courses.
- Attend a **race** at world famous race track, **Estoril**, a short distance from Lisbon, on Portugal's Atlantic coast.

TOURIST INFORMATION

Portuguese Trade and Tourism Office in the UK (ICEP)
Portuguese Embassy, 11 Belgrave Square, London SW1X 8PP, UK
Tel: (0845) 3551212 (brochure request and information service; local call rate).
Website: www.visitportugal.com

Portuguese Trade and Tourism Office (ICEP) in the USA
590 Fifth Avenue, 4th Floor, New York, NY 10036, USA
Tel: (212) 723 0200/99.
Website: www.portugal.org

Entertainment

FOOD & DRINK: Seafood is popular, especially in Lisbon. Soup is a main dish. Portugal's sweet pastries are also worth a try.

Things to know: Table service is normal. There are no licensing hours.

National specialities:
- *Sopa de marisco* (shellfish soup cooked and served with wine).
- *Caldo verde* (green soup made with finely shredded green kale leaves in broth).
- *Bacalhau* (dried cod, cooked in over 100 different ways).
- *Caldeirada* is a fish stew with as many as nine kinds of fish, cooked with onions and tomatoes.
- *Carne de porco á Alentejana*, in which bits of fried pork are covered with a sauce of clams stewed with tomato and onions.
- Puddings include *arroz doce* (rice pudding), Madeira pudding and *nuvens* (egg custard).
- Portugal's sweet pastries (available in most cafes) are also worth a try.

National drinks:
Portuguese wines have changed beyond recognition over the past 10 years. Many of these new, modern wines are indigenous varieties with distinctive flavours. Sparkling rosé wines are mostly produced for export.
- *Mateus Rosé* is a famous lightweight rosé.
- Portuguese brandies are also good; the best are produced around Oporto, where Port wines originate.

Tipping: Generally 10 to 15 per cent. Taxi drivers are tipped 10 per cent.

Credit: © ITP/José Manuel

NIGHTLIFE: The large towns offer every kind of entertainment. There are many nightclubs, theatres, cinemas, stage shows, folk dancing and music performances. The traditional *Fado* can be heard in many restaurants, and performances begin at about 2200. Gambling is authorised and Espinho, Estoril, Figueira da Foz and Monte Gordo have casinos. The elegant Estoril Casino is the most renowned.

SHOPPING: Items include leather goods, copper, ceramics, handcrafted silver and gold, embroidery and tapestry, woodcarving, cork products, porcelain and china, crystal and glassware. **Shopping hours:** Generally Mon-Fri 0900-1300 and 1500-1900, Sat 0900-1300 (and 1500-1900 in December). Shopping centres are usually open Mon-Sun 1000-2300.

Business

GDP: € 129.9 billion (2003).
Main exports: Clothing and footwear, machinery, chemicals, cork and paper products, and hides.
Main imports: Machinery and transport equipment, chemicals, petroleum, textiles and agricultural products.
Main trade partners: Spain, Germany, France, UK, Italy and The Netherlands.

ECONOMY: Portugal was traditionally an agrarian economy but since joining the EU in 1986, the industrial and especially the service sectors have grown considerably by comparison. Agriculture still employs 12 per cent of the workforce – unusually high by Western European standards – and contributes 3 per cent of GDP, producing wheat, maize, tomatoes, potatoes and grapes. Production has undergone a relative decline so that Portugal now imports a sizeable proportion of its foodstuffs after having long been self-sufficient. The manufacturing sector is dominated by the textile and footwear industries and automobiles, which now account for 15 per cent of total exports. Other important products are paper, cork and other wood products, electrical appliances, chemicals and ceramics. Both foreign and internal investment have been high, attracted by Portugal's relatively low labour costs and the recent modernisation of much of the country's infrastructure. Many former state-owned industries have been sold off under a gradual privatisation programme which began in 1989. During the last five years, unemployment has hovered around 5 per cent while inflation has fell to 2.4 per cent in 2004. Portugal joined the Eurozone upon its inauguration in 1999. Unfortunately, since then, the economy has stagnated – growth was 1 per cent in 2004. The main reasons have been a reduction in domestic demand and Government spending cuts – required under the terms of Eurozone membership – to tackle the country's large budget deficit.

BUSINESS ETIQUETTE: Businesspeople are expected to dress smartly and formal attire is expected in some dining rooms and for important social functions. English is widely spoken in business circles, although when visiting a small family business it is best to check in advance. Visiting cards are generally only exchanged by more senior members of a company. July and August are best avoided. **Office hours:** Mon-Fri 0900-1300 and 1500-1900.

CONFERENCES/CONVENTIONS: Lisbon is the main centre for conventions, with venues that can seat up to 1500 people. The Lisbon Convention Centre was founded in 1987, and a major Congress centre, fully integrated with the facilities offered by the Lisbon International Fair, opened in 1989. The fair is a department of the Portuguese Industrial Association, which promotes trade fairs, exhibitions and meetings.

After the EXPO '98 in Lisbon, the North International Area became the new Lisbon Exhibition Centre, with an area of 80,000 sq m (743,200 sq ft), also run by the Portuguese Industrial Association. The Lisbon International Fair will now be the major congress centre in Lisbon, with a capacity for events of up to 3000 delegates. The Lisbon Convention Bureau is a non-profit-making association of companies providing support services to conference organisers. Its services directory includes details of the Congress Centre and hotels with conference facilities. Lisbon opened the Belem Cultural Centre in 1992 to coincide with Portugal's EU Presidency; it features high-quality technical equipment and facilities for meetings of up to 1400 delegates. Additionally the former site of the EXPO '98 'Utopia Pavillion' has been converted into the multi-purpose Atlantic Pavillion, which can accommodate up to 16,500 seated spectators. The city of Oporto also has two major international exhibition and congress centres. The Oporto International Exhibition Centre (Exponor) has a total area of 29,500 sq m (274,000 sq ft) with a congress centre that has a capacity for 1000 delegates; the International Congress and Exhibition Centre (Europarque) has a large and flexible exhibition hall that can host receptions for up to 12,000 delegates on a floor space of 7200 sq m (66,890 sq ft).

COMMERCIAL INFORMATION

Associação Comercial de Lisboa
Câmara de Comércio e Indústria Portuguesa, Rua das Portas de Santo Antão 89, 1169-022 Lisbon, Portugal
Tel: 2132 24050.
Website: www.port-chambers.com

Confederação do Comércio e Serviços de Portugal (CCP)
Avenida Dom Vasco de Gama 29, 1449-032 Lisbon, Portugal
Tel: 2130 31380.
Website: www.ccp.pt

Lisbon Convention Bureau
Rua do Arsenal 15, 1100-038 Lisbon, Portugal
Tel: 2103 12700.

Porto Convention Bureau
Av Inferior a Ponte D. Luis 1, 53, 1 4050 Porto, Portugal
Tel: 2233 26751.
Website: www.portocvb.com

Belem Cultural Centre
Praça do Império, 1499-003 Lisbon, Portugal
Tel: 2136 12400.
Website: www.ccb.pt

The Azores

Location: Atlantic, 1220km (760 miles) due west of Portugal.

Time: GMT - 1 (GMT from last Sunday in March to last Sunday in October).

Overview

For more than 500 years, the Azores, an archipelago of nine widely dispersed islands in the middle of the Atlantic, have remained almost completely unspoilt, mainly on account of their remoteness. Volcanic in origin, they are pitted with deep craters, some filled with shimmering lakes, others covered with lush vegetation. Geysers and health-giving sulphur springs abound. The Azores is also characterised by large tracts of arable farmland, sprinkled with tiny settlements of whitewashed houses. The gently sloping hillsides are planted with vineyards and fruit trees. The coastlines tend to be rugged and somewhat forbidding, but there are plenty of bays, and rocky inlets for swimming and sunbathing. Watersports are widely available such as scuba diving and whale watching; equally popular are yachting, horseriding, cycling and hiking. Tourist development throughout is on a modest scale and there are few signs of change.

General Information

AREA: 2333 sq km (868 sq miles).
POPULATION: 241,800 (2001).
POPULATION DENSITY: 103.8 per sq km.
CAPITAL: São Miguel: Ponta Delgada; **Faial:** Horta; **Terceira:** Angra do Heroísmo.
GEOGRAPHY: The Azores are a widely separated group of

nine islands in the Atlantic, due west of mainland Portugal. The islands are Corvo, Faial, Flores, Graciosa, Pico, Santa Maria, São Jorge, São Miguel and Terceira. The islands are mountainous in the interior and forested, leading down to long beaches and fishing harbours. There are several hot springs and spas.
ELECTRICITY: 220/110 volts AC, 50Hz. Round two-pin plugs are in use.

Climate

Subtropical due to the Gulf Stream. Very equable and slightly humid climate. The rainy season is from November to March.
Required clothing: Mid-season clothes are best; the temperatures are mild at all times of the year.

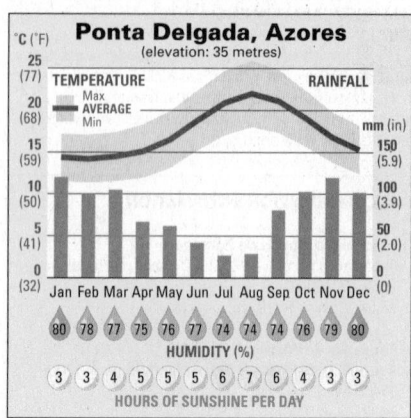

Communications

Telephone and mobile services are similar to, but less extensive than, those offered on mainland Portugal.
Internet: Internet services are widely available in kiosks and hotels.
MEDIA:
Press: *Uniao Acores, Diario Insular* and *Açoreano Oriental* are among the local newspapers available in the Azores.
Radio: Local radio stations include *Radio Acores*.

Travel - International

AIR:
 TAP Air Portugal (TP) operates flights to the Azores from London via Lisbon to Terceira and Faial. The Azores' local airline, *SATA Air Açores (SP)*, runs interconnecting flights between the islands, and operates from Lisbon to Ponta Delgada.
Approximate flight times: From the Azores to *London* is five hours, plus stopover time in Lisbon of two hours.
Main airports: *Ponta Delgada (PDL)* (São Miguel), *Terceira (TER)* (Terceira) and *Faial*.
SEA:
 Main ports: *Ponta Delgada, Horta* and *Faial*. There are regular ferries between Faial, Pico and São Jorge and between Terceira and Graciosa provided by Transmaçor. During the summer, ferries from the Açorline connect all islands except Corvo.

Accommodation

HOTELS:
The main islands have a reasonably good selection of hotel and youth hostel accommodation, and they are rarely full, so although it is a good safeguard, it is not vital to book in advance.

Top Things To See & Do

• Head for **São Miguel**, the largest of the **Eastern Islands** and arguably the most beautiful, and marvel at the most spectacular sight there, **Sete Cidades** - a 40 sq km (15 sq mile) volcanic crater with two lakes, one of deep blue, the other emerald green.
• The former fishing village of **Ponta Delgada** is the administrative and commercial centre of the archipelago with a population of more than 60,000. Enjoy the **historic centre** with its narrow streets and attractive whitewashed houses from the waterfront promenade, the best vantage point.
• At **Furnas**, visitors can explore **Terra Nostra Park**, a tropical garden created in the 18th and 19th centuries, and bathe in therapeutic sulphurous spring water.
• **Graciosa**, one of the **Central Islands**, contains the geological curiosity of **Furna de Enxofre**, a small, warm sulphur lake concealed in a grotto beneath a crater, access to which is via an 80m (270ft) spiral staircase. Graciosa

also boasts a **subterranean lake** (Caldeira) and **hot springs** in the spa village of **Carapacho**.

- Take in the beauty of **Angra do Heroismo** on **Terceira**, a town that was founded in the 15th century and developed into a major commercial outpost for the Portuguese and Spanish empires. It is listed as a UNESCO World Heritage Site.
- The Azores is a well-known destination for **whale** and **dolphin watching** with many species currently identified in the area. The best time to spot them is from June to September when they feed off the waters around the islands of **Faial**, **Pico** and **São Jorge**.
- The abundant marine life around the Azores' nine islands offers excellent **diving** and dive centres can be found on a number of islands, particularly **Faial** and **São Miguel**.
- **Surfing** has recently become popular on **Santa Maria** and **São Miguel** islands while **sailing** clubs, which can be found on all islands (except Corvo), also provide assistance to **windsurfing** enthusiasts.
- An internationally renowned destination for **deep-sea fishing**, the Azores have charter boats available at many coastal resorts, particularly on **Faial** and **São Miguel** where tourist facilities are more developed. **Freshwater fishing** is only allowed in the lakes of the islands of **Flores** and **São Miguel** with a licence.
- There are three 18-hole **golf** courses in the Azores. Two of them (**Furnas** and **Batalha**) are on **São Miguel** island; the third is on **Terceira**. The mild climate allows playing all year round.

Credit: © ITP/ João Paulo

- Home to over 50 native plants as well as many imported ones such as the acacia tree, the Azores attract many **nature** and **plant lovers**. The flowering hydrangeas and azaleas are particularly widespread. The many species of birds also make it an ideal destination for **birdwatching**.
- The volcanic origins of the archipelago provide interesting material for amateur and professional **speleologists** as there are numerous craters and other volcanic phenomena to explore. **Caving** enthusiasts can explore the caves and tunnels of **Algar do Carvão** on **Terceira** island.
- The Azores' rocky landscapes are ideal for **parasailing** and **paragliding**, and operators can be found on **Faial**, **Santa Maria**, **São Miguel** and **Terceira**.

TOURIST INFORMATION

Direcção Regional Turismo Açores
Rua Comendador Ernesto Rebelo 14, 9900-112 Horta, Faial, Azores
Tel: 292 200 500.
Website: www.drtacores.pt

Entertainment

FOOD & DRINK: Generally, the food is Portuguese.
Regional specialities:
- Seafood and cheese.
Regional drinks:
- Locally produced wines are recommended.
- Brandies are distilled on the islands.
SHOPPING: Locally made linens and woollen goods, lace and pottery make good buys.

Madeira

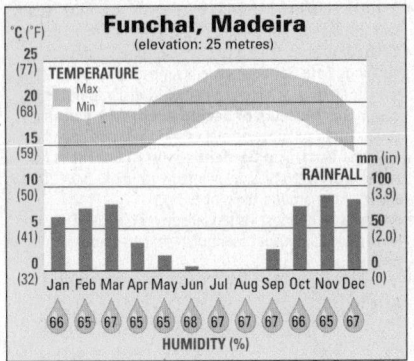

Location: Atlantic Ocean, 990km (619 miles) southwest of Lisbon.

Time: GMT (GMT + 1 from last Sunday in March to last Sunday in October).

Overview

Madeira is a singularly beautiful island. The scenery is memorable and remarkably diverse, especially bearing in mind the island's modest size. Madeira has been described as a 'floating garden', reflecting centuries of cultivation. The rich volcanic soil, mild climate and abundant rainfall (especially in the north) have been responsible for contrasting landscapes: lush river valleys, terraced hillsides planted with vines and bananas and dense primeval forest. The most enjoyable way to explore the island is to follow the course of the levadas (irrigation channels) which crisscross the countryside. The island's burgeoning coastal resorts are geared to the demands of modern tourism and the expansion of Santa Catarina Airport is expected to lead to a marked increase in the number of foreign visitors over the next decade.

General Information

AREA: 779 sq km (301 sq miles).
POPULATION: 245,000 (2001).
POPULATION DENSITY: 314.5 per sq km.
CAPITAL: Funchal. **Population:** 126,889 (1991).
GEOGRAPHY: The group comprises the main island of Madeira, the smaller island of Porto Santo, the three uninhabited islets of Ilheu Chao, Deserta Grande and Ilheu de Bugio, and the Selvagens (a group of uninhabited islets located south of Madeira). The islands are hilly and of volcanic origin and the coast of Madeira is steep and rocky with deep eroded lava gorges running down to the sea. These are particularly impressive on the north coast of Madeira island. The largest of a group of five islands formed by volcanic eruption, Madeira is in fact the summit of a mountain range rising 6.5km (4 miles) from the sea bed. At Cabo Girão, west of the capital of Funchal, is the second-highest cliff in the world. Inland, Pico Ruivo is the island's highest point (1862m/6109ft) with the slightly lower Pico de Arieiro (1810m/5940ft) nearby. Both are destinations for

sightseeing tours, commanding fine views of the surrounding mountains. Madeira's volcanic origin means that it has no sandy beaches, although there is a small beach, Prainha, near the whaling village of Canical on the extreme east of the island. Madeira itself is 58km (36 miles) long and 23km (14 miles) wide. Porto Santo is much smaller, only 14km (9 miles) long and 5km (3 miles) wide, with a long, golden sandy beach, complementing Madeira.
ELECTRICITY: 220 volts AC, 50Hz. Round two-pin plugs are in use.

Climate

Mild subtropical climate with warm summers and extremely mild winters.
Required clothing: Mid-seasonal wear.

Funchal, Madeira (elevation: 25 metres)

Communications

Telephone and mobile services are similar to those offered on the mainland.
Internet: Internet services are widely available in kiosks and hotels.
MEDIA:
Press: *Diario de Noticias* and *Jornal da Madeira* are among the most important local newspapers in Madeira.
Radio: Even some of the small villages in Madeira have their own radio stations; these include *Radio Journal de Madeira*.

Travel - International

AIR:
The airlines serving Madeira are *GB Airways (GT)* (website: www.gbairways.com) and *TAP Air Portugal (TP)*. Air Portugal currently operates two weekly direct flights from London to Madeira, and daily via Lisbon (schedules are subject to changes). There are internal flights between Funchal and Porto Santo.
Approximate flight times: From Funchal to *London* is three hours 40 minutes.
Main airports: *Madeira Intercontinental (FNC)*, 16km (10 miles) from Funchal. *To/from the airport:* Taxis are available. Buses leave from the airport to Funchal. TAP passengers can take the *Aerobus* free of charge; non TAP passengers will have to pay onboard the bus.
Porto Santo (PXO), is served by flights from Funchal and Lisbon. Funchal Airport has a capacity of over 3.5 million passengers per year. *To/From the airport:* Taxis are available.
SEA:
Main ports: *Funchal*. served by *Costa* (website: www.costa.it), *Cunard* (website: www.cunard.com), *Fred Olsen* (website:

Credit: © ITP/ Paulo Magalhães

www.fredolsencruises.com) and *P&O* (website: www.pocruises.com). Ferry services from Madeira to Porto Santo take between two and three hours depending on weather conditions.

Accommodation

HOTELS:

There are many luxury hotels on the island along the coast. These tend to be fully booked during the summer and over the Christmas period, therefore early booking is advisable. Most of the hotels compensate for the lack of beaches on the island of Madeira by providing swimming pools.

Top Things To See & Do

- A trip to **Funchal**, Madeira's capital city, is a must. Nearly half the island's population of 250,000 lives here. The **Cathedral** from 1514 is one of the island's oldest buildings. Late Gothic in style, its most remarkable feature is a geometrical wooden ceiling of Mudejar (Moorish) design. The **Museum of Sacred Art** has a remarkable collection of religious artefacts and paintings. The beautiful **Botanical Gardens** consist of 5 hectares (2 acres) of terraced hillside, planted with more than 2000 species from around the globe.
- **Santana** is the most visited village on the island, best known for its unusual triangular-shaped houses known as **palheiros**.
- It is possible to drive almost to the summit of **Pico do Arieiro** (1818m/5965ft) where the views are spectacular. The island's highest peak, **Pico Ruivo** (1861m/6106ft), is accessible on foot.
- Take the **cable car** from **Funchal** to **Monte**, where the church, **Nossa Senhora de Monte**, becomes a centre of **pilgrimage** on 15 August, when worshippers climb the 74 steps on their hands and knees.
- **Machico** is Madeira's second-largest town. Worth seeing are the 15th-century parish **church**, the **Chapel of Miracles** (a place of **pilgrimage**) and the small but picturesque 18th-century **fort**.
- **Hikers** can enjoy the many paths along the coastline that offer dramatic views from the many steep cliffs, often giving way to tranquil terraced valleys further inland. The **levadas**, a network of ancient irrigation channels stretching some 2130km (1333 miles) across the island's slopes, are particularly popular.
- Try a **toboggan run**. Before motor vehicles, the toboggan was commonly used in Madeira and a number of special 'runs' were constructed. Today, the toboggans carry tourists with two men using ropes to control the wide *carro*, a large wicker basket mounted on wooden runners. The runs are available at the villages of **Monte** or **Terreiro da Luta**, down to **Funchal**.
- Sample some of the distinctive and world-famous Madeira **wine**. The grapes are pressed where they are grown and carried down the hills in goatskin bags by porters. The famous **Madeira Wine Festival** takes place annually in September.

- The **Campo de Golfe do Santo da Serra** (27-hole) and **Palheiro** (18-hole) are the two courses on the island, the former offering spectacular panoramic ocean views from its 500m- (1640ft-) high location. Clubs and trolleys are available for hire. The courses are located within 29km (18 miles) of Funchal. For more information, contact Madeira Island Golf (website: www.madeira-golf.com).
- Madeira has few sandy **beaches** (**Porto Sano** being the exception), but there are plenty of opportunities to go for a **swim** either in the sea or in one of the many swimming pools. There is also a **lido** large enough for 2000 people, with pools, shops and restaurants.
- **Watersports**, including **water-skiing**, **windsurfing**, **snorkelling** and **scuba diving**, can be arranged through some of the hotels on the island.
- Madeira is known for excellent **deep-sea fishing**, particularly blue marlin. A number of companies offer fishing tours to suit all budgets and tastes. Special charters can be arranged for groups.

TOURIST INFORMATION

Direcção Regional de Turismo
18 Avenida Arriaga, 9004-519, Funchal, Madeira
Tel: (291) 211 900.
Website: www.madeiratourism.org

Entertainment

FOOD & DRINK:

Regional specialities:
- *Sopa de tomate e cebola* (tomato and onion soup).
- *Caldeirada* (fish soup).
- *Bife de atum e milho frito* (tuna steak and fried maize).
- *Carne em vinha d'alho* (pickled pork and garlic).
- *Espada* (fresh black sword fish).
- *Espetada* (beef grilled on laurel wood skewers over an open fire).
- *Bolo de mel* (Madeira honey cake).

Regional drinks:
- *Malmsey* (Malvasia), a popular wine.
- *Bual* is a sweet dessert wine.
- *Serceal* is a dry wine.
- Wines, spirits and beers imported from mainland Portugal and Europe are also available.
- *Galão*, a glass of milky coffee, and *bica*, a small cup of black coffee, are popular.

NIGHTLIFE: Some hotels have excellent nightclubs with music for dancing and international cabaret entertainment. Folk entertainment is also included in the weekly programme of these hotels and, in most cases, non-residents are welcome.

SHOPPING: In Funchal, there is a wide variety of shops selling everyday goods, as well as many souvenirs. Special purchases include Madeira folk art such as embroidery, tapestry and wickerwork. Madeira wine is a popular gift.

Credit: © ITP/ José Manuel

Puerto Rico

Location: Caribbean.

Time: GMT - 4.

Overview

The relatively small island of Puerto Rico has a comparatively large array of natural riches. Its central mountain range reaches an altitude of 1338m (4390ft) at Cerro de Punta; it is in possession of the only tropical rainforest in the US National Forest System, El Yunque; and its beaches brag warm, turquoise waters and soft, yellow sand. Indeed, Puerto Rico's bionetwork succeeds in comprising unique characteristics, that are different to what can be found on US soil, despite being a 'commonwealth state' of the USA. This same uniqueness can be discovered in Puerto Rico's culture and way of life. Many of San Juan's buildings have proudly preserved their original Spanish style. This is still an island of fiestas and paella.

Puerto Rico was 'discovered' by Columbus in 1493 on his second voyage to the New World (despite the Taino Indians being the first Puerto Rican inhabitants). It was governed by Ponce de Leon from 1508. There therefore existed many years of Spanish rule before Puerto Rico (Rich Port) was eventually ceded to the USA in 1898 at the end of the Spanish-American War.

In 1917, Puerto Ricans were granted US citizenship and, in 1952, the island became a self-governing 'Commonwealth in association with the USA'. Many people regard this situation as a compromise between full membership to the USA and full independence. In practice, this gives Puerto Ricans an American passport and makes them eligible for military draft but they do not pay US federal taxes and cannot vote in US elections. This 'limbo' situation largely exists with support from the Puerto Ricans. Referendum after referendum has voted towards Puerto Rico retaining the status quo, albeit from sometimes a narrow majority. There is still a vocal lobby for full Independence for Puerto Rico, and the issue remains a sensitive one. However, the country, for the most part, happily juggle both Spanish and US influence, plus the African influence that came when Spaniards shipped African slaves to Puerto Rico. Its geographical position in the centre of the arc of the Antilles, and the outcome of history, has meant that Puerto Rico very much stands as a meeting of Hispanic, African and Anglo culture.

You can also hear the meeting of cultures in island's infectious music, which pounds out the fast-paced rhythm of nightlife in Puerto Rico. Latino beats fuse with West African percussion, which in turn intermingles with swing and big band. What a wonderful way to enjoy multiculturalism!

General Information

AREA: 8959 sq km (3459 sq miles).
POPULATION: 3.91 million (official estimate 2005).
POPULATION DENSITY: 437.1 per sq km.
CAPITAL: San Juan. **Population:** 442,447 (2004).
GEOGRAPHY: Puerto Rico is an island east of the Dominican Republic and west of the British Virgin Islands.

Also included are several smaller islands, such as Culebra, Mona and Vieques. The island is comparatively small, 8959 sq km (3459 sq miles), with a central mountain range reaching an altitude of 1338m (4390ft) at Cerro de Punta, and surrounded by low coastal plains. The capital is on the northeast shore. Much of the natural forest has been cleared for agriculture, but the trees in the northeast are protected as a national park. The other main towns are Aguadilla, Arecibo, Bayamón, Caguas, Carolina, Cayey, Farjardo, Guaynabo, Mayagüez and Ponce.

GOVERNMENT: Self-governing US Commonwealth Territory (incorporated). Gained internal autonomy in 1951.

Head of State: President George W Bush since 2001.

Head of Government: Governor Anibal Acevedo Vila since 2004. **Recent history:** In December 1998, the third referendum in 30 years was held on the issue of whether voters wished Puerto Rico to become the 51st state of the USA, become independent, enter a compact of Free Association (similar to that which operates in a number of Pacific micro-territories) or retain the status quo. By a narrow majority, they voted for the status quo. There is still a strong lobby for full independence for Puerto Rico, and the issue remains a sensitive issue on the island: its advocates received a boost in 2003 when the US military ended its use of the island of Vieques for military exercises after 60 years.

Executive power is held by the Governor, who is elected by universal adult suffrage for a four-year term, assisted by a 15-member Cabinet staffed by appointees. A bicameral Assembly, a scaled-down version of the US Congress, is responsible for legislation. The House of Representatives has 54 members; the Senate has 28.

Puerto Rico has a representative in the US House of Representatives; the inhabitants of the island are US citizens, but they may not vote in Presidential elections. The latest election for Governor, held in November 2000, was a three-way fight between PNP candidate Carlos Pesquera, Sila Maria Calderón of the PPD and Ruben Berrios Martine of the small *Partido Independentista*. Calderon won with just under half the total poll. Elections to the Senate and the House of Representatives on the same day gave the PPD a small majority in both houses. At the end of 2004, Calderón was opposed by Anibal Acevedo Vila. After two months of wrangling and recounts, the leader of the pro-Commonwealth Popular Democratic Party was confirmed as the new Head of Government.

LANGUAGE: Spanish and English are the official languages.

RELIGION: Roman Catholic 85 per cent; the remainder are other Christian denominations and Jews.

ELECTRICITY: 110 volts AC, 60Hz.

SOCIAL CONVENTIONS: Handshaking is the customary form of greeting. Casual dress is acceptable, but shorts should not be worn in hotel dining rooms or casinos, where formal dress is required after 2000. Spanish and American manners and conventions exist side by side on the island. Some hotels require formal dress.

Climate

Hot tropical climate. The temperature varies little throughout the year. Cooler in the upland areas.

Required clothing: Lightweight tropical clothes. Light rainwear required.

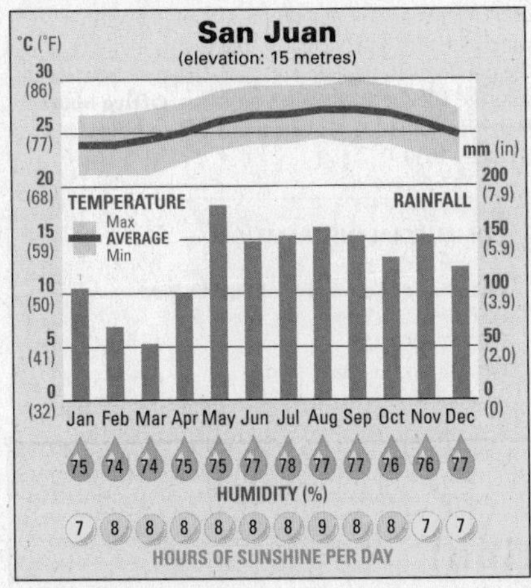
San Juan
(elevation: 15 metres)
°C (°F)
TEMPERATURE
Max
AVERAGE
Min
RAINFALL
mm (in)
Jan Feb Mar Apr May Jun Jul Aug Sep Oct Nov Dec
75 74 74 75 75 77 78 77 77 76 76 77
HUMIDITY (%)
7 8 8 8 8 8 8 9 8 8 7 7
HOURS OF SUNSHINE PER DAY

Communications

Telephone: IDD service is available. Country code: 1787.

Mobile telephone: CDMA/TDMA networks exist that are not compatible with GSM handsets (although there are plans to introduce the network soon).

Internet: Internet is available in limited areas; access can be found in hotels and business centres.

Post: Puerto Rico post is part of the US postal system. Airmail to Western Europe takes up to one week.

MEDIA: Broadcasting is regulated by the US Federal Communications Commission (FCC).

Press: The English-language newspaper published in Puerto Rico is *The San Juan Star*; others include *El Nuevo Dia*, *El Vocero de Puerto Rico* and *Primera Hora*.

TV: Home-grown comedies, talk shows and Spanish-language soaps are staple fare on local TV stations. The multichannel offerings of cable TV are also widely available. Examples of commercial stations include *Telemundo*, *Televicentro* and *Univision*; *TUTV* (Channel 6) is a public station.

Radio: *WIAC Radio Puerto Rico* is a commercial station (news and talk), as is *WPRM Cadena Salsoul* (salsa and tropical music). *WIPR Radio 940* is a public radio station.

Passport/Visa

The passport and visa requirements for entering Puerto Rico are the same as for entering the USA. See *Passport/Visa* in the *USA* section.

Money

Currency: US Dollar (USD; symbol US$) = 100 cents. For exchange rates and currency restrictions, see the *USA* section.

Currency exchange: Foreign currency can be exchanged at banks and bureaux de change. All major ATM services are also available.

Credit & debit cards: All international credit cards, and many leading debit cards are accepted.

Traveller's cheques: Cheques in various currencies are accepted, but US Dollar cheques are preferred.

Banking hours: Mon-Fri 0900-1530. Hours may vary.

Duty Free

As for the USA; see the *USA* section.

Public Holidays

Below are Public Holidays for the January 2006-June 2007 period.

2006: Jan 1 New Year's Day. **Jan 6** Epiphany. **Jan 9** Birthday of Eugenio María de Hostos. **Jan 16** Martin Luther King Day. **Feb 20** President's Day. **Mar 22** Emancipation of the Slaves. **Apr 14** Good Friday. **Apr 21** José de Diego Day. **May 22** Memorial Day. **Jul 4** US Independence Day. **Jul 15** Luis Muñoz Rivera's Birthday. **Jul 25** Constitution Day. **Jul 26** José Celso Barbosa's Birthday. **Sep 4** Labour Day. **Oct 9** Columbus Day. **Nov 11** Veterans' Day. **Nov 19** Discovery of Puerto Rico Day. **Nov 23** Thanksgiving Day. **Dec 25** Christmas Day.

2007: Jan 1 New Year's Day. **Jan 6** Epiphany. **Jan 11** Birthday of Eugenio María de Hostos. **Jan 15** Martin Luther King Day. **Feb 12** President's Day. **Mar 22** Emancipation of the Slaves. **Apr 6** Good Friday. **Apr 16** José de Diego Day. **May 23** Memorial Day.

Note: Each town celebrates a festival or fiesta in honour of a local patron saint. These can last up to 10 days.

Health

	Special Precautions?	Certificate Required?
Yellow Fever	No	No
Cholera	No	No
Typhoid & Polio	No	N/A
Malaria	No	N/A

Note: *Regulations and requirements may be subject to change at short notice, and you are advised to contact your doctor well in advance of your intended date of departure. Any numbers in the chart refer to the footnotes below.*

Food & drink: Water is purified in main areas, although bottled water may be preferable. Mains water is considered safe to drink. Milk is pasteurised and dairy products are safe for consumption. Local meat, poultry, seafood, fruit and vegetables are considered safe to eat.

Other risks: *Hepatitis A* occurs in the northern Caribbean region. The incidence of *dengue fever* has increased in the past few years. *Bilharzia* (*schistosomiasis*) is present. Avoid swimming and paddling in fresh water; swimming pools which are well chlorinated and maintained are safe.

Rabies is present. For those at high risk, vaccination before arrival should be considered. If you are bitten, seek medical advice without delay. For more information, consult the *Health* appendix.

Health care: Health services are good but costly; health insurance is recommended.

Travel - International

AIR:

Airlines serving Puerto Rico include *American Airlines*, *American Trans Air*, *Argentina Airlines*, *Iberia*, *LACSA*, *Martinair*, *Mexicana* and *Northwest Airlines*.

Approximate flight times: From Puerto Rico to *Chicago* is four hours 30 minutes, to *London* is eight hours (direct), to *Los Angeles* is eight hours, to *Miami* is two hours 30 minutes, to *New York* is three hours 30 minutes and to *Washington, DC* is three hours 30 minutes.

Main airports: *Luis Muñoz Marín (SJU)* is 14km (9 miles) northeast of San Juan. *To/from the airport*: Buses and taxis are available (travel time - 20 to 30 minutes.) *Facilities*: Restaurants, bars, bank, post office, hotel reservations, duty free shops and car hire.

Departure tax: None.

SEA:

Main Port: *San Juan*. Cruise lines running services to San Juan include: *Carnival*, *Celebrity*, *Cunard*, *Princess Cruises*, *Radisson Seven Seas Cruises* and *Royal Caribbean*.

Travel - Internal

AIR:

American Eagle and *Vieques Air-Link* (website: www.vieques-island.com) provide domestic air travel within Puerto Rico.

ROAD:

Traffic drives on the right. **Taxi:** A service called a *línea* will pick up and drop off passengers where they wish. Líneas operate between San Juan (from Río Piedras líneas station) and most towns, at a fixed rate. Special black and white *Tourist Taxis* exist. These are part of the Tourist Taxi Program, and charge set rates for travel between the airport and major tourist sites. **Car hire:** Available at the airport and city agencies. Rental companies include: *AAA*, *Afro*, *Atlantic*, *Avis*, *Budget*, *Discount* and *Hertz*. **Documentation:** US or foreign licence accepted for 120 days of stay, after which a national licence will be required.

URBAN:

Bus: San Juan has local bus services (*Guaguas*) and there are bus terminals in Bayamón, Catano, Country Club and Rio Piedras, as well as the capital. Buses usually tend not to run after 2100. There are also coach services. Bus companies offering sightseeing trips include *American Tours of Puerto Rico*, *Normandie Tours*, *Rico Sun Tours*, *Royal Coach* and *Tour Coop*. **Taxi:** *Públicos* (share-taxis) have 'P' or 'PD' at the end of licence plate numbers and run regular routes between established points. They usually operate only during daylight hours and depart from the main *plaza* (central square) of a town. *Públicos* must be insured by law and the Public Service Commission fixes their routes and reasonable rates. Conventional taxis are hired by the hour, and charges are metered except in charter trips outside the usual taxi zones. They can be hailed in the street, or called by telephone. They are available at the airport and at stands at most hotels. Taxi drivers expect a 15 per cent tip.

Travel times: The following chart gives approximate travel times (in hours and minutes) from **San Juan** to other major cities and resorts in Puerto Rico.

	Air	Road	Sea
Ponce	0.30	1.30	-
Mayagüez	0.30	2.30	-
Vieques	0.30	0.45*	2.00
Fajardo	-	0.45	-

Note: *As far as Fajardo and then by sea.

Travel Advice

Most visits to Puerto Rico are trouble-free but you should be aware of the global risk of indiscriminate international terrorist attacks, which could be against civilian targets, including places frequented by foreigners.

This advice is based on information provided by the Foreign and Commonwealth Office in the UK. It is correct at time of publishing. As the situation can change rapidly, visitors are advised to contact the following organisations for the latest travel advice:

British Foreign and Commonwealth Office
Tel: (0845) 850 2829.
Website: www.fco.gov.uk

US Department of State
Website: http://travel.state.gov/travel

Accommodation

HOTELS:

San Juan has modern Americanised hotels and there is similar lodging in Ponce. Outside the main urban areas, there are *Paradores* (Government-sponsored country inns). These are less modern, but of a good standard. For further information, contact the Puerto Rico Hotel and Tourism Association (see *Top Things To Do*).

APARTMENTS & CONDOMINIUMS:

 These are available from a number of companies specialising in renting this type of accommodation. See *Accommodation* in the general introduction to the *USA* section. Condominiums and flats are best around Luquillo Beach to the northeast.

Top Things To See

- **San Juan**, Puerto Rico's capital city, has extremely good museums: the **Pablo Casals Museum** has manuscripts and photographs relating to the work of the famous cellist; **Casa de los Contrafuertes** houses the **African Heritage Museum**; **Casa del Callejón** is a traditional Spanish-style home that holds the **Museum of Colonial Architecture** and the **Museum of the Puerto Rican Family**; **Casa del Libro** holds a rare collection of early manuscripts and books, some dating back to the 15th century; the **San Juan Museum of Art and History** was built in 1855 as a market and restored in 1979 as a cultural centre where the patio is often used for concerts; and **Plaza de San José**, at the 'top' of old San Juan and marked by a statue of Juan Ponce de León, is a picturesque area of small museums and pleasant cafes. There is also a very good **Museum of Art** in Ponce, which contains more than 1000 paintings and 400 sculptures, ranging from ancient classical to contemporary art. Its collection of 19th-century Pre-Raphaelite paintings considered among the best in the Americas.
- In **Old San Juan** is the wonderful **El Morro**, a 16th-century Spanish fortress, and the 18th-century fort of **San Cristobal**, built in 1771. Both buildings are perched on clifftops at the tip of a peninsula. El Morro, in particular, has many exhibits documenting Puerto Rico's role in the discovery of the New World and was instrumental in the defence of San Juan in the 16th century and its continuing survival. The old **San Juan City Wall**, dating from the 1630s, was built by the Spanish and it follows the peninsula contour, providing picturesque vantage points for viewing Old San Juan and the sea.
- Visit **La Fortaleza**, completed in 1540, and now the Governor's residence – the oldest of its kind in the Western hemisphere.
- See the second-oldest church in the Western hemisphere – **San José Church** is where Ponce de León's body was interred until the early 20th century.
- **El Yunque**, east of the capital, is a 28,000-acre **rainforest** (with over 240 species of trees) and a bird sanctuary. It is the only tropical rainforest in the US National Forest System and is located in the **Luquillo Mountains**. This rainforest represents one of the oldest reserves in the Western Hemisphere. Rare wildlife, including the **Puerto Rican Parrot** (one of the ten most endangered species of birds in the world) resides here. **Birdwatchers** in general will enjoy the **Guanica dry forest** or the **Cabezas de San Juan** nature reserve. **Hiking** is permitted in El Yunque, as in other forest reserves in Puerto Rico. Energetic walkers can tackle the mountains in the interior. **Toro Negro**, with its lush forests and marvellous vistas, is recommended, while the highest peak is **Cerro de Punta**. The Guanica dry forest in the southwest has a visitors' centre where trail maps and advice can be obtained. For more advice on hiking, contact the Conservation Trust of Puerto Rico, PO Box 9023554, San Juan PR 00902-3554 (tel: 722 5834; website: www.fideicomiso.org).
- The beautiful town of **Ponce**, on the southern side of the island and connected to the capital by a toll road, is situated near many excellent **beaches**.
- Explore the **Tibes Indian Ceremonial Centre**, a short drive from Ponce, which is an ancient Indian burial ground. A replica of a Taino Indian village has been built near the small museum, reception area and exhibition hall. The **Caguana Indian Ceremonial Park**, south of the Arecibo Observatory, is also worth seeing: it was built by Taino Indians as a site for recreation and worship 800 years ago.

Top Things To Do

- Be dazzled by **Phosphorescent Bay**, near **La Parguera** in the southwest of the island. Here, marine life, microscopic in size, light up when disturbed by fish, boats or any movement at all. The phenomenon – especially vivid on moonless nights – is rarely found elsewhere. Boat trips are available at night. There are other phosphorescent bays in Vieques and Fajardo. In Phosphorescent Bay, you can even have a nighttime **snorkel** in the sea in the right weather conditions. Other recommended areas include the island of **Mona**, just off **Boquerón** on the southwest coast, where the marine life is particularly rich. Because this area is a nature reserve, independent divers require Government permission to dive there. **Desecheo Island**, off the northwest coast, and **Isabela** are also good diving areas.
- Roam the third-largest cave system in the world: the **Camuy Caves**, near **Arecibo** on the north coast. There are well-paved access roads, a reception area, and electric trains to the entrance of the caves. Visitors need to be escorted by a local guide.
- The **Arecibo Observatory** is the site of the largest **radar/radio telescope** in the world. Located in the unusual karst country of Puerto Rico, the 20-acre dish is best seen from a small aeroplane flight between San Juan and **Mayagüez**.
- **Horse ride** on a beach, or even on a mountain trail, which will provide excellent views of the island. Puerto Rico prides itself on its *paso fino* horses, a breed noted for its endurance and the comfort it affords the rider. Beach riding is particularly recommended at **Luquillo** in the northeast or Isabela in the northwest.
- Attend one of Puerto Rico's **Fiestas Patronales** - celebrations that are held in each town's plaza to honour the area's patron saint. These fiestas can last up to 10 days and include religious processions, games, local food and dance. One of many recommended fiestas include **San Juan Bautista Day**, a week of festivities that celebrates San Juan's patron saint.

TOURIST INFORMATION

Puerto Rico Tourism Company in the UK
67a High Street, 2nd Floor, Walton-on-Thames, Surrey KT12 1 DJ, UK
Tel: (01932) 253 302.
Website: www.gotopuertorico.com

Puerto Rico Tourism Company in the USA
666 Fifth Avenue, 15th Floor, New York, NY 10103, USA
Tel: (212) 586 6262 *or* (800) 223 6530 *or* 866 7827 (toll-free in the USA).
Website: www.gotopuertorico.com

Entertainment

FOOD & DRINK: Puerto Rico (and especially San Juan) abounds with good restaurants, catering for all tastes from Spanish to Chinese, French, Greek and Italian. The island cuisine is Spanish-based, with rice and beans as the staple diet.
National specialities:
- *Paella*.
- Chicken dishes.
- Black bean soup.
- *Sancocho* (beef stew).
- *Jueyes* (land crabs).
- *Pan de agua* (native bread).
National drinks:
- *Barrilito* and *Don Q* (Rum).
Tipping: Generally 15 to 20 per cent if not included on the bill.
NIGHTLIFE: Puerto Rico's nightlife is abundant and varied. The streets are lively in the evening. Many shops are open late, and the visitor can sit in the squares of old San Juan and indulge in people-watching. A recommended walk is down *La Princesa Promenade*, lined with antique street lamps. Meeting places include a Bogart-style cigar bar and cocktail bars. Hotels provide some of the entertainment, but there are also different types of clubs, both modern and more mainstream. Many Puerto Ricans favour traditional Latin dance clubs with large dance floors, which often have live bands playing *salsa* and *merengue* music. Puerto Ricans are passionate about their nightlife, and often dress up. Casinos are intimate and friendly, generally opening at noon and closing at around 0400 daily. Hotel casinos are open to guests and non-guests alike.
SHOPPING: Special purchases are cigars, coffee, hammocks, rum, straw weavings, sculpture, *santos* (carved religious figures), festival masks and stringed musical instruments. **Shopping hours:** Mon-Wed and Sat 0900-1900, Thurs-Fri 0900-2100, Sun 1100-1700 (shopping malls). Some shops open on Sunday if cruise liners are in port.

Business

- **GDP**: US$68.95 billion.
- **Main exports**: Chemicals, electronics, tinned tuna, rum and medical equipment.
- **Main imports**: Clothing, petroleum and foodstuffs.
- **Main trade partners**: USA, Ireland, The Netherlands, Japan and the Dominican Republic.

ECONOMY: Puerto Rico has few natural resources, although some nickel and copper have been located. Manufacturing has overtaken agriculture as the main source of income following an intensive programme of industrialisation by the Government. The main products are pharmaceuticals, electrical and electronic equipment, processed food, textiles, clothing, rum, petrochemicals and refined oil. There is a foreign free-trade zone at Mayagüez. In the agricultural sector, dairy and livestock produce is now more important than sugar cane, the island's main crop. Fresh fruit and vegetables are grown for export. Tourism is the main service industry and has undergone steady growth in recent years; the sector is now worth more than US$2 billion annually. Another major source of revenue for the territory derived from a US naval base on the island of Vieques. Although employing over 6,000 people and injecting an estimated $300 million annually into the economy, it was widely unpopular with islanders; after sustained pressure, the closure of the base was announced in 2003.
Puerto Rico has observer status at the Caribbean trading bloc, CARICOM. The USA and its corporations dominate both the domestic economy and overall trade patterns, although Puerto Rico has important trading links of its own with Japan, the Dominican Republic and Venezuela. The US Government is in the process of removing certain tax exemptions enjoyed by US and foreign investors in Puerto Rico; the economic impact of this is as yet unclear but is causing concern in the territory.
BUSINESS ETIQUETTE: A knowledge of Spanish (the official language) is very useful, although English is widely spoken; most people in the tourist industry and the greater metropolitan areas are bilingual. Lightweight suits are advised for business meetings. **Office hours:** Mon-Fri 0900-1800. **Government office hours:** Mon-Fri 0830-1630.

COMMERCIAL INFORMATION

Chamber of Commerce of Puerto Rico
PO Box 9024033, San Juan, Puerto Rico
Tel: 721 6060/82.
Website: www.camarapr.org

Qatar

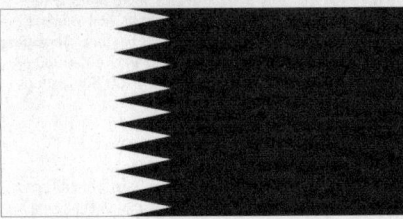

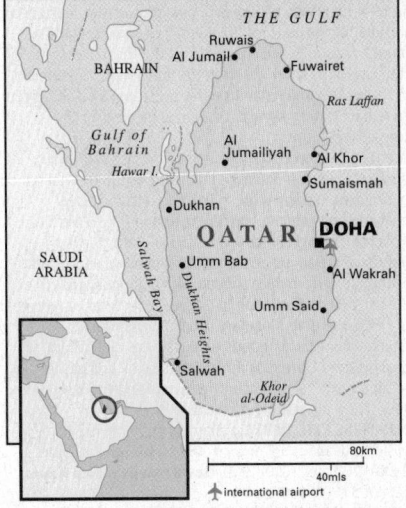

Location: Middle East, Gulf Coast.

Time: GMT + 3.

Overview

Qatar has moved on from being a poor pearl fishing country to become one of the richest Gulf states thanks to the exploitation of oil and gas fields since the 1940s. The majority of the country consists of sand dunes and salt flats. The city of Doha combines a rich mixture of traditional Arabic and modern architecture. The Grand Mosque with its many domes and the Abu Bakir al-Siddiq Mosque are particularly interesting. The north contains most of the historic sites, including Umm Salal Mohammed, a relatively large village dominated by the ruins of a 19th-century fort. Al Khor is the second-largest city, situated around a natural shallow harbour. On the west coast there are fine beaches at Umm Bab ('The Palm Tree Beach'), Dukhan and Salwah near the Saudi border. The south is a region of sand dunes and beaches, offering opportunities to go pearl hunting, or to practise any of a number of watersports. Public entertainment can be rather limited. Live entertainment is infrequent, but some international artists do perform in Qatar.

General Information

AREA: 11,437 sq km (4416 sq miles).
POPULATION: 618,000 (official estimate 2002).
POPULATION DENSITY: 54.0 per sq km.
CAPITAL: Doha. **Population:** 264,009 (1997).
GEOGRAPHY: Qatar is an oil-rich peninsula jutting out into the Gulf between Bahrain and the United Arab Emirates. There are hills in the northwest, but the rest of the country consists of sand dunes and salt flats, with scattered vegetation towards the north.
GOVERNMENT: Emirate since 1971. Gained independence from the UK in 1971. **Head of State:** Crown Prince Sheikh Hamad bin Khalifa al-Thani since 1995. **Head of Government:** Prime Minister Sheikh Abdallah bin Khalifa al-Thani since 1996.
LANGUAGE: Arabic is the official language. Some English is spoken.
RELIGION: Islam.
ELECTRICITY: 220-240 volts AC, 50Hz.
SOCIAL CONVENTIONS: The visitor should be fully aware of Muslim religious laws and customs. Women should always dress modestly. It is also worth noting that, while it is acceptable to cross legs, showing the sole of the foot or unknowingly pointing it at a person is considered an insult. At business and social functions, the traditional Qatari coffee, in tiny handleless cups, will invariably be served. This is a ritual of welcome with strict rules: guests are served in order of seniority – a few drops at first, then, after three or

four others have been served, the server returns to fill the first cup; always hold the cup in the right hand; two cups are polite, but never take only one or more than three. For more information, see the *World of Islam* appendix.

Climate

Summer (June to September) is very hot with low rainfall. Winter is cooler with occasional rainfall. Spring and autumn are warm and pleasant.
Required clothing: Lightweight cottons and linens are worn during summer months, with warm clothes for cooler evenings and during the winter. Rainwear is advisable during winter.

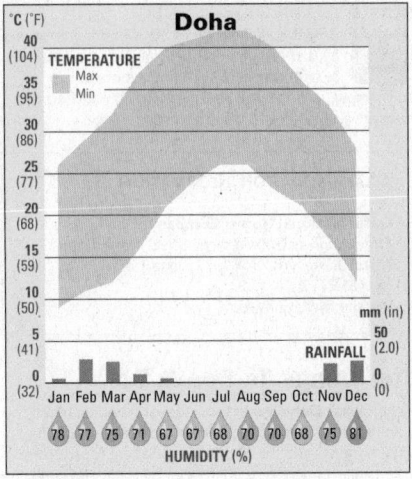

Communications

Telephone: IDD is available. Country code: 974. There are no area codes.
Mobile telephone: GSM 900 network exists. Main network provider is *Q-tel* (website: www.qtel.com.qa).
Internet: Internet cafes exist in Doha.
Post: Airmail to Europe takes up to one week.
MEDIA: There has been no censorship of the media since 1995. Qatar television has been famous worldwide since the launch of *Al Jazeera* in 1997, which is extremely popular in the Arab world.
Press: English-language newspapers include the *Gulf Times* and *The Peninsula*. The main dailies are *Al-'Arab, Ar-Raya* and *Ash-Sharq*.
TV: *Al Jazeera* is a satellite broadcaster financed by the Qatar Government. *Qatar TV* is state run.
Radio: *Qatar Broadcasting Service* (QBS) is state run. The *BBC World Service* is available on FM in Doha.

Passport/Visa

	Passport Required?	Visa Required?	Return Ticket Required?
Full British	Yes	Yes	Yes
Australian	Yes	Yes	Yes
Canadian	Yes	Yes	Yes
USA	Yes	Yes	Yes
Other EU	Yes	Yes	Yes
Japanese	Yes	Yes	Yes

Note: *Regulations and requirements may be subject to change at short notice, and you are advised to contact the appropriate diplomatic or consular authority before finalising travel arrangements. Any numbers in the chart refer to the footnotes below.*

Restricted entry: The Government refuses entry and transit to holders of passports issued by Israel.
PASSPORTS: Passport valid for at least six months required by all.
VISAS: Required by all except the following:
(a) nationals of Bahrain, Kuwait, Oman, Saudi Arabia and United Arab Emirates;
(b) transit passengers whose tickets show they intend to continue their journey from the airport within eight hours.
Note: (a) All visitors require onward or return tickets and sufficient funds for the period of stay. Visa requirements are subject to change, and travellers are strongly advised to contact an Embassy or Consulate of Qatar for up-to-date information.
(b) Nationals of Andorra, Australia, Brunei, Canada, EU countries, Hong Kong (SAR), Japan, Korea (Rep), Liechtenstein, Malaysia, New Zealand, San Marino, Singapore, Switzerland and USA can obtain business and tourist visas upon arrival at the airport in Doha for QAR50 (£10-12).
Types of visa and cost: Prices vary according to

nationality. The following prices are for British nationals: *single-entry:* £36; *multiple-entry:* £50 (six months), £71 (two years), £130 (five years) (depending on validity).
Note: All children included in the same passport of applicant travelling to Qatar must pay the same fees.
Validity: Single-entry visas permit stays of up to three months. Multiple-entry visas permits stays of up to six months, two years and five years.
Application to: Consulate (or consular section at Embassy); see *Passport/Visa Information* for details. Nationals of countries where Qatar has no diplomatic representation should apply for visas through their hotel in Qatar, which will arrange for the visa to be collected on arrival at the airport. Those wishing to visit friends or relatives in Qatar should ask them to apply to the immigration authorities in Qatar on their behalf for a visa. For longer-period visas apply to the Immigration Department, Ministry of the Interior, PO Box 115, Doha (tel: 465 7802; website: www.e.gov.qa). There is now a facility to book all visas online through the Ministry of Interior's website.
Application requirements: (a) Completed application form. (b) Valid passport. (c) Two passport-size photos. (d) Fee (postal order or company cheque only). (e) Name and address of sponsor in Qatar and for American nationals and EU passport holders except nationals from Ireland and the UK. Business visas need to be accompanied by an invitation letter from company and confirmation of hotel booking. (f) Stamped, self-addressed envelope for postal applications.
Working days required: One although it could take as long as three weeks depending on nationality. Applications should be made well in advance of the intended departure date.

PASSPORT/VISA INFORMATION

Embassy of the State of Qatar in the UK
1 South Audley Street, London W1K 1NB, UK
Tel: (020) 7493 2200.
Opening hours: Mon-Fri 0930-1600 (1000-1400 during Ramadan); 0930-1230 (visa section).

Embassy of the State of Qatar in the USA
4200 Wisconsin Avenue, NW, Suite 200, Washington, DC 20016, USA
Tel: (202) 274 1600/3.
Website: www.qatarembassy.net

Money

Currency: Qatari Riyal (QAR) = 100 dirhams. Notes are in denominations of QAR500, 100, 50, 10, 5 and 1. Coins are in denominations of 50, 25, 10, 5 and 1 dirhams; however, only the 50 and 25 coins are in wide circulation, minting of the rest ceased in the 1970s and smaller denominations are becoming ever-scarcer.
Note: The Qatari Riyal is tied to the US Dollar.
Credit & debit cards: American Express, Diners Club, MasterCard and Visa are widely accepted. Check with your credit or debit card company for details of merchant acceptability and other services which may be available.
Traveller's cheques: Widely accepted. To avoid additional exchange rate charges, travellers are advised to take traveller's cheques in US Dollars or Pounds Sterling.
Currency restrictions: There are no restrictions on the import or export of either local or foreign currency. Israeli currency, however, is prohibited.
Banking hours: Sat-Thurs 0730-1330.
Exchange rate indicators:
Rate at time of publishing
£1.00=   QAR6.32
$1.00=   QAR3.64

Duty Free

The following goods may be imported into Qatar without incurring customs duty:
A reasonable amount of tobacco and perfume for personal use.
Prohibited items: All alcohol is prohibited. Firearms can only be imported with a licence obtained in advance from the Ministry of Defence.

Public Holidays

Below are Public Holidays for the January 2006-June 2007 period.
2006: Jan 10-13 Eid al-Adha (Feast of the Sacrifice). **Jan 31** Islamic New Year. **Jun 27** Accession of HH The Amir Sheikh Hamad Bin Khalifa Al-Thani. **Sep 3** Independence Day. **Oct 22-24** Eid al-Fitr (End of Ramadan). **Dec 31** Eid al-Adha (Feast of the Sacrifice).
2007: Jan 20 Islamic New Year. **Jun 27** Accession of HH The Amir Sheikh Hamad Bin Khalifa Al-Thani.
Note: Muslim festivals are timed according to local sightings of various phases of the moon and the dates given above are approximations. During the lunar month of

Ramadan that precedes Eid al-Fitr, Muslims fast during the day and feast at night and normal business patterns may be interrupted. Many restaurants are closed during the day and there may be restrictions on smoking and drinking. Some disruption may continue into Eid al-Fitr itself. Eid al-Fitr and Eid al-Adha may last anything from two to 10 days, depending on the region. For more information, see the *World of Islam* appendix.

Health

	Special Precautions?	Certificate Required?
Yellow Fever	No	No
Cholera	No	No
Typhoid & Polio	1	N/A
Malaria	No	N/A

Note: *Regulations and requirements may be subject to change at short notice, and you are advised to contact your doctor well in advance of your intended date of departure. Any numbers in the chart refer to the footnotes below.*

1: Vaccination against *typhoid* is advised.
Food & drink: All water should be regarded as being potentially contaminated. Water used for drinking, brushing teeth or making ice should have first been boiled or otherwise sterilised. Milk is unpasteurised and should be boiled. Powdered or tinned milk is available and is advised, but make sure that it is reconstituted with pure water. Avoid dairy products which are likely to have been made from unboiled milk. Only eat well-cooked meat and fish, preferably served hot. Salad and mayonnaise may carry increased risk. Vegetables should be cooked and fruit peeled.
Other risks: *Hepatitis A* exists; precautions should be taken. *Hepatitis B* is endemic. *Cutaneous leishmaniasis* occurs. *Rabies* is present. For those at high risk, vaccination before arrival should be considered. If you are bitten, seek medical advice without delay.
Note: Certificates proving the visitor to be HIV-negative may be required if planning on staying more than one month in the country. Check with Embassy (see *Passport/Visa Information*).
Health care: There are several hospitals in Qatar, the most recent and modern being the Hamad General Hospital. The Poly Clinic has good dentists. Charges are high and health insurance is essential. As a precaution against the intense heat, visitors should maintain a high salt and fluid intake.

Travel - International

AIR:
 Gulf Air (GF) and *Qatar Airways (QR)* are the major airlines serving Qatar.
Approximate flight times: From Doha to *London* is eight hours 25 minutes. There are no direct flights from the USA.
Main airports: *Doha (DOH)* is 8km (5 miles) southeast of the city (travel time – 25 minutes). Taxis are available to the city with official rates displayed. Facilities include car hire, banks, restaurant and a duty free shop.
Departure tax: None.
SEA:
 The main international ports are *Doha* and *Umm Said*. The traffic is mostly commercial, but some passenger lines call at Doha.
ROAD:
 Access is possible via both Saudi Arabia and the United Arab Emirates, but the main international route from Saudi Arabia is unreliable and often impassable during the rainy season.

Travel - Internal

ROAD:
 The road system is fair, but conditions are poor during the wet season. Driving is on the right.
Bus: No organised public bus service. **Taxi:** These have black and yellow number plates, are painted orange and white, and are metered. Taxis can be hired on an hourly basis. **Car hire:** Available from local companies at the airport and hotels. **Documentation:** An International Driving Permit is required, but a temporary licence can be obtained on presentation of a valid UK licence.

Travel Advice

There is a high threat from terrorism in Qatar. Al Qaeda continues to issue statements threatening to carry out attacks in the Gulf region. These include references to attacks on Western interests, including residential compounds, military, oil, transport and aviation interests. Travellers should review their security arrangements carefully. They should remain vigilant, particularly in public places.

This advice is based on information provided by the Foreign and Commonwealth Office in the UK. It is correct at time of publishing. As the situation can change rapidly, visitors are advised to contact the following organisations for the latest travel advice:

British Foreign and Commonwealth Office
Tel: (0845) 850 2829.
Website: www.fco.gov.uk

US Department of State
Website: http://travel.state.gov/travel

Accommodation

HOTELS:
 Recent building ensures that Qatar is well served by first-class hotels. There are also a number of **3-** or **4-star** hotels offering reasonable accommodation. Advance booking is strongly advised. All rates are subject to a 15 per cent service charge.

ACCOMMODATION INFORMATION

Qatar National Hotels Company
Street address: 200 Corniche Street, Doha, Qatar
Postal address: PO Box 2977, Doha, Qatar
Tel: 485 7777.
Website: www.qnhc.com

Top Things To See & Do

- The capital, **Doha,** is a rich mixture of traditional Arabic and modern architecture. The **Grand Mosque** with its many domes and the **Abu Bakir al-Siddiq Mosque** are particularly interesting. There is an excellent **National Museum** in Doha tracing the country's development. The modern town clusters around the Grand Mosque, the **New Amir's Palace** and the **Clock Tower**. **Doha** also boasts several marinas, sub-aqua clubs and **sailing** facilities as well as a number of sports clubs which are open to visitors.
- The northern area contains most of the historic sites, including **Umm Salal Mohammed**, a relatively large village dominated by the ruins of a 19th-century fort.
- At **Al Zubara** is the **Qalit Marir Fortress**.
- **Al Khor** is the second-largest city, situated around a natural shallow harbour.
- **Gharya** has a golden sandy beach stretching for miles.
- **Ruwais** boasts a harbour, from where there is an occasional *dhow* service to Bahrain.
- There are also good beaches at **Fuwairat**, on the northeast coast, and **Ras Abruk**, opposite Hawar Island.
- On the West Coast, there are beaches at **Umm Bab** ('The Palm Tree Beach'), **Dukhan** and **Salwah**, near the Saudi border.
- The south is a region of sand dunes and beaches, offering opportunities to go **pearl hunting**, or to practise any number of **watersports**. The 'inland sea' of **Khor al-Odeid** is the centre of a region of outstanding natural beauty, surrounded by the **Sandi Hills**, accessible only to 4-wheel-drive vehicles.
- There are several **camel race** tracks; the main one is found off the road to **Dukhan**, but spectators need a 4-wheel-drive vehicle to follow the race. The graded track is 18km (11 miles) long through the desert and sometimes more than 250 camels take part with big money prizes and prestige at stake. **Desert excursions** can also be arranged.

TOURIST INFORMATION

Qatar Tourist Authority in the UK
Kennedy House, 115 Hammersmith Road, London, W14 0QH, UK
Tel: (020) 7371 1571.
Website: www.experienceqatar.com

Entertainment

FOOD & DRINK: While the best food is generally found in hotels, Chinese, Indian, Persian, Thai, US and Western cuisine is also available. All the major hotels have good public restaurants and most offer outside catering of high quality; waiters, crockery and cutlery will be provided on request. There are a reasonable number of places to eat in Doha, including snack bars serving fast foods, as well as the traditional Levantine *shawarma* and Egyptian *foul* and *taamiyeh*. Restaurants are scarce outside the capital. Alcohol is prohibited and should not be consumed in public, though some international hotels may serve alcohol.
Tipping: Taxi drivers do not expect a tip. A service charge is often added to bills in hotels and most restaurants, otherwise 10 per cent is appropriate.

NIGHTLIFE: Public entertainment is rather limited. Doha has a cinema showing English-language films, and there is also the National Theatre. Live entertainment is infrequent, but some international artists do perform in Qatar.
SHOPPING: There are several large modern malls, with cinemas, restaurants and other facilities as well as brand shops. The old *souks* remain popular for bargains. **Shopping hours:** Generally Sat-Thurs 0800-1200 and 1600-1900 or later, with the malls open until 2100 or 2200. Some shops close on Friday.

Business

ECONOMY: Oil and gas reserves have transformed Qatar from an impoverished outcrop on the Arabian Peninsula into one of the richest countries in the world. The oil deposits located and exploited from the 1970s onwards were of unusually high quality and generated a substantial income for the country. In addition, one of the world's largest natural gas fields, known as the North Field, was discovered in Qatari waters in the late 1980s. Measured by revenue, gas production has now outstripped oil and is set to remain Qatar's principal source of income for the foreseeable future.
Agriculture is necessarily limited by climate and water resources. Some indigenous industry exists, mainly based on petrochemicals and refining but also including steel, concrete and cement, plastics, paint and flour. The Qatari Government has earmarked US$5 billion for further industrialisation projects over the coming years. Current economic performance is good with an annual growth of 8.5 per cent and inflation of 2.3 per cent. Qatar is a member of OPEC, the Arab Monetary Fund and the Islamic Development Bank. It also belongs to the World Trade Organisation. Currently, most of Qatar's oil and gas is sold to Japan and Italy. EU countries, Japan and the USA are the country's main trading partners.
BUSINESS ETIQUETTE: Politeness and patience in business dealings are needed. **Office hours:** Sat-Thurs 0800-1200 and 1600-1900. **Government office hours:** Sat-Wed 0700-1400.
CONFERENCES/CONVENTIONS: Several of Doha's largest hotels provide facilities with extensive support services, including simultaneous translation systems and full audio-visual capability. Contact individual hotels for more information.

COMMERCIAL INFORMATION

Qatar Chamber of Commerce and Industry
PO Box 402, Doha, Qatar
Tel: 462 2538.
Website: www.arab.net/qatar/qr_commerce.htm

Réunion

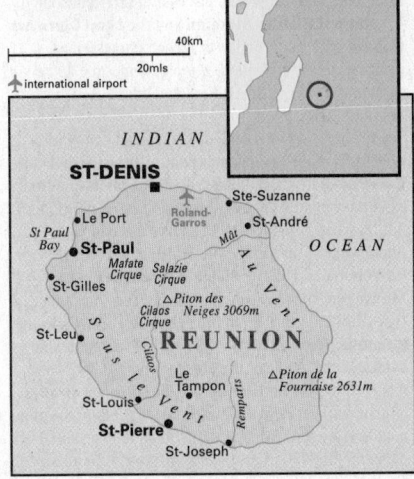

Location: Due east of Madagascar, in the Indian Ocean.

Time: GMT + 4.

Overview

In the 1640s, Réunion was occupied by the French, displacing the Portuguese, who in 1513 had been the first European arrivals on the island. The island became prosperous during the 18th century, along with nearby Mauritius, when it lay on the shipping routes which carried trade between Europe and Asia. Sugar plantations, worked by slaves imported from Africa, formed the other main economic sector. Réunion was ruled as a colony until 1946 when it was granted the status of an Overseas Department of France, under which it is an integral part of the French State, which is represented on the island by a Commissioner. Politics in recent years have been primarily concerned with internal autonomy: most people appear to favour an increase beyond the present level but very few support a complete severing of the link with France, particularly as the island is largely dependent economically on aid from the French Government.

Much French culture has also seeped into the island's day-to-day life, intermixing with Réunion's African, Indian and Chinese influences, and creating a wonderful tropical twist. The predominant spoken language is French, the architecture leans towards the French models; but this is also a land of volcanoes and cyclone seasons. Equally, French dishes may be on the menu but they are usually subverted: you may well be served duck curry rather than the *Canard à L'Orange* you were expecting! It is little wonder that Réunion is a much-kept secret, since the French presumably want to keep this little gem of an island to themselves.

Although this is an island of exceptional and bright turquoise waters, its quantity of sharks mean that swimming and other watersports activities may not be the number-one reason why visitors might want to go to Réunion. Far, far greater are its stupendous trekking routes across mountain terrain. *Cirques* – large volcanic valleys surrounded by mountains, creating a natural amphitheatre of about 10km (6 miles) in diameter – sink into the ground, replete with magnificent waterfalls and other natural features.

It is fortunate that Réunion has so many areas of beauty, since this is a densely populated island that, although once flourishing from the cultivation of sugar cane, is now mostly sustained from its tourist industry – plus financial aid from the hands of France. Nevertheless, economic problems persist, and the large wealth gap on the island has often fuelled social tensions, occasionally spilling into actual violence. Unemployment remains stubbornly high,

and migration is common. Yet, as long as Réunion seek them, tourists will continue to be drawn to the island's unusual and captivating landscape.

General Information

AREA: 2507 sq km (968 sq miles).

POPULATION: 777,000 (UN, 2005).

POPULATION DENSITY: 309.9 per sq km.

CAPITAL: Saint-Denis. **Population:** 131,557 (1999).

GEOGRAPHY: Réunion lies 760km (407 miles) east of Madagascar in the Indian Ocean. Running diagonally across the island is a chain of volcanic peaks, separating a green humid eastern zone (*Le Vent*) from a dry, sheltered south and west (*Sous le Vent*). The majority of the population lives along the coast. Sugar cane production accounts for over half the arable land in a country where many basic foodstuffs are imported.

GOVERNMENT: Réunion is an Overseas Department of France and as such is an integral part of the French Republic. **Head of State:** President Jacques Chirac since 1995, represented locally by Prefect Laurent Cayrel since 2005. **Head of Government:** Nassimah Dindar, President of the General Council. **Recent history:** The most recent elections to the Regional Council and the General Council, held in 1998 and 2000 respectively, were won by a right-wing coalition and the left-wing alliance of Communists and Socialists.

Réunion is an Overseas Department of France. As such, it is an integral part of the French nation and its citizens are able to vote in French national elections. It also enjoys a measure of autonomy in its legislature which comprises the 49-member General Council and the 45-member Regional Council. Both of these bodies are directly elected to serve six year terms.

LANGUAGE: French is the official language. Local Creole *patois* is also spoken.

RELIGION: The majority of the population is Roman Catholic, with a Muslim minority.

ELECTRICITY: 220 volts AC, 50Hz.

SOCIAL CONVENTIONS: The islanders follow French fashion. Normal social courtesies should be observed. The immigrants from India, Pakistan and Europe have retained their cultural identities.

Climate

Hot tropical climate. Temperatures are cooler in the hills, occasionally dropping to freezing point in the mountains at night. The cyclone season (January to March) is hot and wet.

Required clothing: Lightweights, with warmer clothes for the evenings.

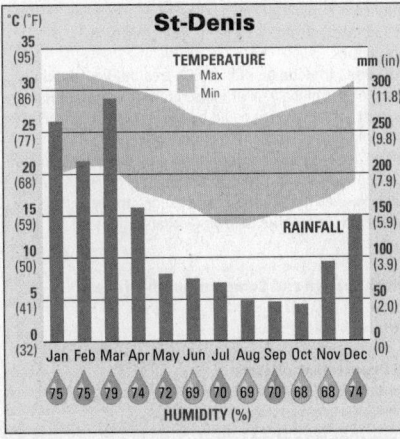

Communications

Telephone: IDD is available. Country code: 262. There are no area codes.

Mobile telephone: Roaming agreements exist with international mobile phone companies.

Internet: There are Internet cafes in towns throughout La Réunion.

Post: Airmail to Western Europe takes up to three weeks.

MEDIA: TV and radio services are provided by the French public overseas broadcaster, RFO.

Press: The two biggest dailies are the *Journal de l'Ile de la Réunion* and the *Quotidien de la Réunion*. Weekly periodicals include *L'Economie de la Réunion* and *Témoignages*. There are no English-language dailies.

TV: *RFO Reunion* is a public service, operated by *Reseau France Outre-Mer*. *Antenne Reunion* is a private broadcaster.

Radio: *RFO Reunion* is a public service that operates radio stations.

Passport/Visa

	Passport Required?	Visa Required?	Return Ticket Required?
Full British	Yes	No/2	Yes
Australian	Yes	No	Yes
Canadian	Yes	No/2	Yes
USA	Yes	No/2/3	Yes
Other EU	Yes/1	No/2	Yes
Japanese	Yes	No/2	Yes

Note: *Regulations and requirements may be subject to change at short notice, and you are advised to contact the appropriate diplomatic or consular authority before finalising travel arrangements. Any numbers in the chart refer to the footnotes below.*

PASSPORTS: Passport valid for at least three months beyond applicant's last day of stay required by all except the following: **1.** nationals of EU, EEA, Monaco and Switzerland, who are holders of national identity cards.

VISAS: Required by all except the following:
(a) nationals of countries referred to in the chart above for stays of up to three months;
(b) nationals of Andorra, Argentina, Bermuda, Brunei, Chile, Costa Rica, Croatia, Ecuador, El Salvador, Guatemala, Honduras, Iceland, Korea (Rep), Liechtenstein, Malaysia, Mexico, Monaco, New Zealand, Nicaragua, Norway, Panama, Paraguay, San Marino, Singapore, Switzerland, Uruguay, Vatican City and Venezuela for stays of up to three months;
(c) holders of French residence permits.

Note: (a) Nationals of the EU, EEA and Monaco do not need a a Long Stay visa (trips exceeding three months). (b) **2.** Nationals of Canada, Cyprus, Japan, Korea (Rep), Malaysia, Malta, Mexico, Singapore, USA and Venezuela should apply for a visa if they are to receive a salary, even if their trip is a Short Stay. (c) **3.** US nationals need a visa if they are crew members, or journalists on assignments, or students enrolled at schools and universities in any of the French Overseas Departments.

Types of visa and cost: All visas, for stays or up to 90 days, regardless of the number of entries permitted, cost €35. For visas valid for more than 90 days, the cost is €99. Visas must be paid for in local currency. In most circumstances, no fee applies to students, recipients of Government fellowships and citizens of the EU and their family members.

Validity: *Short-stay* (up to 30 days). *Short stay* (31 to 90 days and single- or multiple-entry): valid for six months, one year or two to five years from date of issue. *Long stay:* 90 days plus. *Transit* visas: valid for single- or multiple-entries of maximum five days per entry, including the day of arrival. *Airport Transit:* Allows transit through the airport.

Application to: French Consulate General (for personal visas), or Consular section at Embassy (for diplomatic or service visas); see *Passport/Visa Information*. All applications must be made in person.

Application requirements: (a) Valid passport with blank page to affix the visa. Minors travelling alone must submit notarised parental authorisation, signed by both parents, plus one copy. (b) Up to two completed application forms. (c) One passport-size photo on each form. (d) Fee, to be paid in cash or credit card. (e) Evidence of sufficient funds for stay (two last bank statements, plus copy, or other proof of funds equivalent to US$100 for each day of trip). (f) Letter from employer, or proof of stay in country of residence. (g) Proof of address. (h) Medical insurance. (i) Return ticket and travel documents for remaining journey. (j) Proof of accommodation during stay. (k) Detailed itinerary, including reservations and round trip airline tickets (only required when visa is issued), plus one copy. (l) Proof of employment (eg last payslip or letter from employer). (m) Proof of valid health/travel insurance with worldwide coverage, plus copy. *Business:* (a)-(m) and, (n) Business invitation guaranteeing payment of travel expenses, plus one copy.

Working days required: One day to three weeks depending on nationality.

Temporary residence: If intending to work or stay for longer than 90 days, nationals should contact the Long Stay visa section of the Consulate General or Embassy; see *Passport/Visa Information*.

PASSPORT/VISA INFORMATION

French Consulate General in the UK
21 Cromwell Road, London SW7 2EN, UK
Visa section: 6A Cromwell Place, London SW7 2EW, UK
Tel: (020) 7073 1200 (consular section) *or* 1250 (visa section) *or* 7073 1295 (visa applications in progress; 1500-1700 only) *or* (09065) 508 940 (visa information service; calls cost £1 per minute) *or* 266 654 (24-hour visa application form request service; calls cost £1.50 per minute) *or* 540 700 (24-hour automated visa appointment booking service). Website: www.ambafrance-uk.org *or* www.consulfrance-londres.org

Money

Currency: Since January 2002 the Euro has been the official currency for the French Overseas Departments (*Départements d'Outre-Mer*) of French Guiana, Guadeloupe, Martinique and Réunion. For further details, exchange rates and currency restrictions, see the *France* section. US Dollars are also accepted in some places.
Currency exchange: All major currencies can be exchanged at banks and bureaux de change.
Credit & debit cards: American Express, Diners Club and Visa are accepted. MasterCard has limited acceptance. Cards can also be used in ATMs. Check with your credit or debit card company for details of merchant acceptability and other services which may be available.
Traveller's cheques: Accepted in most places. To avoid additional exchange rate charges, travellers are advised to take traveller's cheques in Euros, US Dollars or Pounds Sterling.
Currency restrictions: Same regulations as France; see *France* section.
Banking Hours: Mon-Fri 0800-1600.

Duty Free

The island of Réunion is an Overseas Department of France, and therefore duty free allowances are the same as those for France; see *France* section.
Prohibited items: All plants, vegetables and vegetable products.

Public Holidays

As for France (see *France* section).

Health

	Special Precautions?	Certificate Required?
Yellow Fever	No	1
Cholera	No	2
Typhoid & Polio	3	N/A
Malaria	No	N/A

Note: *Regulations and requirements may be subject to change at short notice, and you are advised to contact your doctor well in advance of your intended date of departure. Any numbers in the chart refer to the footnotes below.*

1: A *yellow fever* vaccination certificate is required from travellers over one year of age arriving from infected areas.
2: A *cholera* vaccination certificate may be required from travellers arriving from infected areas.
3: There is a risk of *typhoid*, but not of *polio*. Immunisation is advised.
Food & drink: All water should be regarded as being potentially contaminated. Water used for drinking, brushing teeth or making ice should have first been boiled or otherwise sterilised. Milk is unpasteurised and should be boiled. Powdered or tinned milk is available and is advised, but make sure that it is reconstituted with pure water. Avoid dairy products which are likely to have been made from unboiled milk. Only eat well-cooked meat and fish, preferably served hot. Pork, salad and mayonnaise may carry increased risk. Vegetables should be cooked and fruit peeled.
Other risks: *Hepatitis A, B* and *E* are present; precautions should be taken. Since 2006, there has been a serious epidemic of the *chikungunya virus*, spread by mosquito bites.
Rabies is present. For those at high risk, vaccination before arrival should be considered. If you are bitten, seek medical advice without delay. For more information, consult the *Health* appendix.
Health care: There are around 10 hospitals and many out-patient clinics. The French national health scheme is in force and there is a reciprocal health agreement with the UK (see *France* section). Facilities are limited and full health insurance is advised.

Travel - International

AIR:

The main airline to serve Réunion is *Air France (AF)* (website: www.airfrance.com). Other airlines operating to Réunion include *Air Madagascar* and *Corsair International*. *Air Austral* and *Air Mauritius* operate daily flights between Réunion and Mauritius (from Saint-Pierre Pierrefonds Airport).
Approximate flight times: From Réunion to *London* is 14 hours 40 minutes (via Paris); to *Paris* is 11 hours.
Main airports: *Saint-Denis de la Réunion (RUN) (Roland-Garros)* is 10km (6 miles) from the town (travel time – 20 minutes). *To/from the airport*: *Cinor* buses run 13 return trips per day between the Roland Garros and Saint Denis; buses run from 0700-2030. *Facilities*: Banks/bureaux de change, ATMs, bars, restaurant, post office and car hire.
Saint-Pierre Pierrefonds (ZSE) is 5km (3 miles) from Saint-Pierre. A shuttle bus service operates to Saint-Peirre, Tampon, Saint-Louis, Entre-Deux, Avirans, Etang-Salé, Saint-Leu, Saint-Philippe, Petite Ile, Saint-Joseph and Cilos. *SEMITTEL* buses run between the airport and Saint Pierre after the arrival of each plane. Taxi services as well as car hire are available at the airport.
Departure tax: None.
SEA:

Main ports: *Port Réunion*. Two boats are currently in operation to Mauritius; the *Mauritius Pride* ferry and the *Ahinora Catamaran*. Both freight and passenger lines (a large number are French) dock at Pointe-des-Galets.

Travel - Internal

AIR:

Aero-clubs at Roland-Garros Airport hire planes for flights over the island, which are well worth the price.

SEA:

Four shipping lines run services around the island.

ROAD:

Roads are in a fair condition. Speed limits are the same as in France. The main road runs on a north-south axis. The island can be easily crossed by bus, taxi or hired car. Car hire is available throughout the island. Further details can be obtained from the Comité du Tourisme de la Réunion. **Bus:** Two types of buses operate on the island: urban buses mainly serve the Saint-Denis area; yellow buses connect main towns. Services are excellent and luxurious, with very comfortable vehicles. Buses stop by request. **Taxis:** Taxi ranks can be found in city centres. Taxis can be hired by telephone (telephone numbers can be obtained from the information points at the airport). There are likely to be extra charges after 2000 Mon-Fri, on Sunday and Bank Holidays. **Car hire:** Available from the airport and from car hire firms in Saint-Denis. Camper-vans can also be rented. Petrol prices are similar to those in France. **Documentation:** An International Driving Permit is recommended, though not legally required.

Travel Advice

Since 2006, Réunion has been affected by a serious epidemic of the mosquito-borne *Chikungunya virus*, with a significant number of cases reported countrywide. Visitors should take precautions against being bitten by mosquitoes.
Most visits to Réunion are trouble-free but you should be aware of the global risk of indiscriminate international terrorist attacks, which could be against civilian targets, including places frequented by foreigners.
This advice is based on information provided by the Foreign and Commonwealth Office in the UK. It is correct at time of publishing. As the situation can change rapidly, visitors are advised to contact the following organisations for the latest travel advice:

British Foreign and Commonwealth Office
Tel: (0845) 850 2829.
Website: www.fco.gov.uk

US Department of State
Website: http://travel.state.gov/travel

Accommodation

HOTELS:

There is a good range of hotels, inns and *pensions*. Prices are high (and plumbing somewhat basic), but the food is often excellent. Tariffs usually include bed and breakfast, tax and service charges. Hotels range from **1** to **4 stars**.
MOUNTAIN LODGES:

Cheap and basic accommodation called *gîtes* favoured by trekkers are available throughout the island. For further information, contact Maison de la Montagne.
YOUTH HOSTELS:

For information, contact Les Auberges de Jeunesse de la Réunion.
OTHER ACCOMMODATION: There are many rooms available in guest houses across the island as well as self-catering studio flats and accommodation in farmhouses. For further information, contact Comité du Tourisme de la Réunion (see *Top Things To See & Do*).

ACCOMMODATION INFORMATION

Maison de la Montagne (Information on Mountain Lodges)
5 rue Rontaunay, 97400 Saint-Denis, Réunion
Tel: 907 878.
Website: www.reunion-nature.com

Les Auberges de Jeunesse de la Réunion (Information on Youth Hostels)
5 rue Rontaunay, 97400 Saint-Denis, Réunion
Tel: 411 534.
Website: www.chez.com/fraj

Top Things To See & Do

- **Saint-Denis**, the capital, is surrounded by mountains on three sides and has several places of interest, including the **Natural History Museum** and the **Léon Dierx Art Gallery** with its collection of French Impressionist paintings. There are various temples, a mosque and a cathedral, a sign of the cultural and religious variety of the island population.
- See the amazing rites of Réunion's Indian community, principally made up of Tamil Hindus. These rites include **Cavadee**, which is an Indian sacrificial procession that essentially involves body piercing and other gruesome but reverential symbolism. This takes place in Saint-André. Other rites include fire-walking.
- Go trekking around the **Plaine d'Affouches** in **La Montagne**, lined by lush tamarind trees and calumets, a type of wild fig tree. From Brûlé, a footpath leads to the **Roche-Écrite**, a 2227m- (7306ft-) high summit which overlooks the whole of the northern part of the island.
- A special feature on Réunion are the so-called **cirques** – large volcanic valleys surrounded by mountains, creating a natural amphitheatre of about 10km (6 miles) in diameter. Day-long sightseeing trips to the cirques may be arranged with travel agents in Saint-Denis. There are over 600km (370 miles) of footpaths leading through the island. The most beautiful cirque is probably **Salazie**, with its magnificent waterfalls, especially those known as **Le Voile de la Mariée** (The Bride's Veil) near Hell-Bourg.
- There are excellent **walking** opportunities in the mountains. The National Forestry Office has provided many sign-posted footpaths throughout the island. Good **climbing** is to be had among the volcanic peaks. **Cilaos**, once infamous as a refuge for escaped slaves, is a lovely mountain area rising to about 1220m (4000ft) with impressive views from **Le Bras Sec** and **Îlet à Cordres**. There is a day-trip to **Grand-Îlet**, taking in some spectacularly rugged scenery. **Piton des Neiges** is the highest point on the island and is an enjoyable hike from **Hell-Bourg**. **Mafate** is the most secluded of the valleys, unconnected by any road with the outside world.
- Take a tour to the island's still-active volcano, **La Fournaise**, which erupted three times in 2005. **Nez-de-Boeuf** (ox's nose) affords a splendid view over the **Rivière des Remparts**, 1000m (3300ft) below, the **Plaine des Sables** and the **Belle Combe** pass. The **Enclos Fouque** crater and the highest peak of the 2631m (8632ft) Fournaise can both be explored on foot. The still active **Bory** and **Brûlant** craters are also interesting excursions.
- See the island's many communities gather together in **St Paul** for the interesting and tasty **street market** (Friday afternoons and Saturday mornings).
- Inhale the scent of Réunion's exquisite tropical flowers, trees and fruit; there are tours which aim to show the visitor some of the many species on the island, before returning to the **Botanical Gardens** at **Saint-Denis**.
- Good swimming and diving are to be found along the **Sous le Vent** coast, especially at **Saint-Gilles-des-Bains**, which has a reef-protected lagoon. On the more remote beaches, sharks may be a danger, so it is best to enquire locally. **Surfing** can be practised in **Saint-Gilles**, **Saint-Paul** and **Saint-Pierre**. Réunion does not have extensive beaches, but those on the leeward west coast are beautiful with yellow, black or white sands. Some of the best beaches are to be found at **Saint-Gilles**, **Saint-Leu and Étang-Sale**. These are mostly shallow coral, running out to the reef. The **Coral Turtle Farm** near Saint-Leu is an interesting place. The coral reefs along the west coast are a protected area, but scuba-diving and snorkelling are available. Also on the west coast is the historic town of **Saint-Paul**, Réunion's original capital, and birthplace of Leconte de Lisle.

TOURIST INFORMATION

Comité du Tourisme de la Réunion (Tourist Office)
Place du 20 Décembre 1848, BP 615, 97472 Saint-Denis, Réunion
Tel: (262) 210 041.
Website: www.la-reunion-tourisme.com

Maison de la France in the UK
178 Piccadilly, London W1J 9AL, UK
Tel: (0906) 824 4123 (consumer information line; calls cost 60p per minute) *or* (020) 7399 3520 (travel trade only).
Website: www.franceguide.com

Business

- **GDP:** US$4.57 billion.
- **Main exports:** Sugar, rum and molasses, perfume essences and lobster.
- **Main imports:** Manufactured goods, food, tobacco, machinery and equipment, raw materials and petroleum products.
- **Main trade partners:** France, Japan, Comoro Islands, Germany and Italy.

ECONOMY: Sugar cane is the principal crop and export earner in this mainly agricultural economy. Other crops include vanilla, tobacco, and plants such as *vétiver* and *ylang-ylang*, used in tropical essences. Sugar and rum production are the principal industries; others include the manufacture of construction materials, metal goods, textiles and electronics. The service sector, including transport, telecommunications, finance and tourism, provides three-quarters of the country's economic output. Tourism has grown particularly rapidly in recent years, and is now worth about US$300 million annually to the island's economy. However, the Réunion economy is far from self-sustaining and relies on large injections of aid from France and, more recently, the European Union, to cover its trade and budgetary deficits (as an integral part of France, Réunion belongs to the EU). The most pressing problem for the Government is a very high level of unemployment, which has been around 35 to 40 per cent for the last decade.
BUSINESS ETIQUETTE: The atmosphere is relaxed and friendly; suits will only be required for the most formal of meetings. A sound knowledge of the French language will be useful, since there are no formal interpreter services available. Prices should be quoted in Euros, and all trade literature should be in French. **Office hours:** Mon-Fri 0800-1200 and 1400-1800.

COMMERCIAL INFORMATION

Chambre de Commerce et d'Industrie de la Réunion
5 bis rue de Paris, BP 120, 97463 Saint-Denis, Réunion
Tel: 942 000.
Website: www.reunion.cci.fr

Délégation Régionale au Commerce, à l'Artisanat et au Tourisme
Préfecture de la Réunion, Avenue de la Victoire, 97400 Saint-Denis, Réunion
Tel: 407 758.

Romania

300km
150mls
✈ international airport

POLAND
SLOVAK REPUBLIC
UKRAINE
Carpathian Mountains
Tisza
HUNGARY
Baia Mare
Moldovita
MOLDOVA
Iaşi
Prut
Oradea
Cluj-Napoca
MOLDAVIA
Dniester
Arad
Bacău
ROMANIA
Timişoara
Mureş
Sibiu
Braşov
Galaţi
Moldoveanu 2544m
Brăila
Transylvanian Alps
Ploieşti
Tulcea
Danube Delta
WALACHIA
YUGOSLAVIA
Craiova
Olt
BUCHAREST
SERBIA
Danube
Giurgiu
Constanţa
Mangalia
BULGARIA
BLACK SEA

Location: Eastern Europe.

Time: GMT + 2 (GMT + 3 from the last Sunday in March to last Sunday in October).

Overview

The largest of the Balkan states, Romania has seen several empires come and go, from the Roman, to the Ottoman to the Austro-Hungarian.
After the Second World War, the Communists gradually established their political hegemony within the Government: in 1947 the Monarchy was deposed and the Government declared the Romanian People's Republic. Nicolae Ceausescu assumed the post of First Secretary of the Romanian Communist Party (RCP) in 1965 and held power in the country until the dramatic, bloody and largely unpredicted revolution during Christmas 1989.
After Ceausescu's death, the new Government, under the provisional leadership of Ion Iliescu (the former Communist Central Committee Secretary) was faced with a number of acute problems: the pacification of the country; the disbanding of the Securitate; the restoration of the economy; and the need to prepare Romania for peaceful multi-party elections. In the following years, economic progress has been patchy while Romania has not advanced as far as its east European counterparts towards its twin principal goals: membership of NATO and of the European Union. Nevertheless, in 2004 Romania was officially welcomed as a new member of NATO. Membership of the EU will take somewhat longer. This will be a difficult process, involving radical and painful reforms of parts of the Romanian economy, but the country is on track to join the EU in 2007/8.
Romania has dramatic mountain scenery including the Carpathian Mountains and Transylvania. The beautiful and densely forested Carpathian Mountains area lends itself to many sporting and leisure activities such as skiing, bobsleighing, horseriding and tennis. Situated in picturesque valleys and on mountain slopes are many health and winter resorts. Since Roman times, the Romanian spas of Transylvania have been known for their miraculous healing powers. The Black Sea Coast, ideal for family holidays with 70km (43 miles) of fine white sandy beaches, boasts many resorts. Transylvania also contains the famous Bran Castle, said to be one of the original abodes of the medieval king known as Vlad the Impaler, who helped inspire Bram Stoker's novel, *Dracula*. Legend says that Bucharest, the Romanian capital was founded by a shepherd called *Bucur*, whose name is recognisable in the

Romanian version of the name *Bucuresti*. Located midway between the Carpathian Mountains and the Black Sea, Bucharest has not earned the nickname 'Paris of the Balkans' by accident. Its astonishing range of architecture – from Wallachian wooden and bell-towered mansions to Byzantine-style chapels, neo-classical buildings, striking 1930s modernism and even the post-Stalinist absurdities of Ceausescu's megalomaniac regime – cannot help but leave the visitor in awe at the varieties of vision that have taken place in this city over the centuries. But Bucharest has also been the epicentre of the country's many upheavals, with the stages of the country's history like vivid tattoos etched across the city's surface, each telling a different chapter of the story.

General Information

AREA: 238,391 sq km (92,043 sq miles).
POPULATION: 22.2 million (UN, 2005).
POPULATION DENSITY: 90.9 per sq km.
CAPITAL: Bucharest. **Population:** 2 million (2005).
GEOGRAPHY: Romania is bordered to the north and east by Moldova and Ukraine, the southeast by the Black Sea, the south by Bulgaria, the southwest by Serbia and Montenegro and in the west by Hungary. The country is divided into four geographical areas. Transylvania (a belt of Alpine massifs and forests) and Moldavia compose the northern half of the country, which is divided down the middle by the north–south strip of the Carpathian Mountains. South of the east–west line of the Carpathians lies the flat Danube plain of Walachia with the capital Bucharest, its border with Bulgaria being defined by the course of the Danube. Romania's coastline is along the Black Sea, incorporating the port of Constanta and the Danube Delta.
GOVERNMENT: Democratic Republic since 1991. **Head of State:** President Traian Basescu since December 2004.
Head of Government: Prime Minister Calin Tariceanu.
Recent history: Traian Basescu, won the second round of Romania's Presidential election in mid-December 2004, defeating incumbent Prime Minister Adrian Nastase of the leftist Social Democratic party. Calin Tariceanu became Prime Minister following Parliamentary elections in November 2004. His Government is an alliance of Liberals and Democrats and has members from four reformist parties. Both men have said that their main objectives will be to focus on the acceleration of reforms aimed at ensuring EU membership for Romania in 2007 and to fight poverty and corruption.
LANGUAGE: Romanian is the official language. Some Hungarian and German are spoken in border areas, while mainly French and some English are spoken by those connected with the tourist industry.
RELIGION: 86 per cent Romanian Orthodox, with Greek and Roman Catholic, Reformed/Lutheran, Unitarian, Muslim and Jewish minorities.
ELECTRICITY: 220 volts AC, 50Hz. Plugs are of the two-pin type.
SOCIAL CONVENTIONS: Handshaking is the most common form of greeting, but it is customary for men to kiss a woman's hand when being introduced. Mr or Mrs should be used when greeting someone for the first time. Visitors should follow normal European courtesies on social occasions. Dress tends to be rather conservative but casual wear is suitable. Beachwear should not be worn away from the beach or poolside. If visiting a home, a small gift should be given to the host, such as flower or chocolates (to women only), wine or liquor. Flowers should be given as a gift in odd numbers only. Many Romanians are smokers and gifts of Western cigarettes are greatly appreciated. Other well-appreciated gifts include toiletries and Western clothing.
Photography: Military installations should not be photographed. Some tourist attractions require visitors to pay a fee of approximately Lei2000 for taking photographs. **Smoking:** The Romanian Government has recently approved legislation that bans smoking in every public place, but, as in many countries in Eastern Europe smokers have little respect for non-smokers and for smoking laws. Smoking is prohibited in all public places including hospitals, concert halls and theatres. Smoking is also forbidden on planes, on buses and on some trains. Luxury hotels have designated no-smoking floors but very few restaurants have no-smoking sections.

Climate

Summer temperatures are moderated on the coast by sea breezes while inland at sea level it is hot. Winters are coldest in the Carpathian Mountains where there is snow from December through to April. Snow also falls throughout most of the country. Winters are mildest on the coast.
Required clothing: Lightweights are worn in summer on the coast and in low inland areas. Warmer clothes are needed in winter and throughout the year in the uplands. Rainwear is recommended throughout the year.

Credit: © Romania National Tourist Office

Bucharest
(elevation: 82 metres)

TEMPERATURE
Max
AVERAGE
Min

RAINFALL

HUMIDITY (%)
86 82 71 63 62 61 58 57 61 73 84 87

2 3 5 6 8 9 11 10 8 5 2 2

HOURS OF SUNSHINE PER DAY

Communications

Telephone: IDD is available. Public telephones are widely available and can be used for direct international calls. Hotels often impose a high service charge for long-distance calls, but usually do not charge for local calls.

Mobile telephone: Roaming agreements exist with many international mobile phone companies. Coverage is good around Bucharest but variable elsewhere.

Internet: *Kappa* and *PC-Net* are two of the largest of the 250-odd ISPs. The former has open-air terminals at Strada Paulescu Nicolae 9, Bucharest, while the latter is at Strada Calderon Jean Louis 1-5, Bucharest. *Sweet Internet Cafe*, Strada Maria Rosetti 7-9, Bucharest (tel: (21) 212 4111) has 24-hour access, as do a couple others of Bucharest's many Internet cafes.

Post: Airmail to Western Europe takes one week. Post offices are open daily, including Saturday mornings.

MEDIA: The media scene is Romania is one of the most dynamic in southeastern Europe. The 1991 constitution upholds freedom of expression, but prohibits 'defamation of the country'. The first private radio stations appeared in 1990; there are now more than 100 of them. State-run *Radio Romania* operates four national networks and regional and local stations. Romania's newspapers thrived after the 1989 revolution, but many subsequently closed because of rising costs.

State-owned *Romania 1* and the private commercial stations *Pro TV* and *Antena 1* command the lion's share of television viewing. There are also many smaller, private TV stations, some of them part of local networks. The state broadcaster, TVR, operates a second national network, *TVR 2*, and a pan-European satellite channel. Pay TV channels have a smaller audience. There are hundreds of cable distributors offering access to Romanian, European and other stations and many households in Bucharest have cable TV.

Press: English newspapers and publications include *Bucharest Business Week*, *Nine O'Clock* (website: www.nineoclock.ro) and *Romanian Economic Daily*. There are a great number of daily and weekly newspapers published in Romanian, Hungarian and German. Daily

papers include *Adevarul, Libertatea, Evenimentul Zillei* and *Romania Libera*.

TV: TVR operated *Romania 1* and *TVR 2*. Commercial networks include: *Antena 1, Pro TV, Prima TV, Acasa TV* and *Realitatea TV*.

Radio: *Radio Romania* is state-owned. Commercial networks include: *Europa FM, Kiss FM, Pro FM* and *Radio 21*. The BBC World Service is available on FM in the capital.

Passport/Visa

	Passport Required?	Visa Required?	Return Ticket Required?
Full British	Yes	No/1	Yes
Australian	Yes	Yes	Yes
Canadian	Yes	No/1	Yes
USA	Yes	No/1	Yes
Other EU	Yes	No/1	Yes
Japanese	Yes	No/1	Yes

Note: *Regulations and requirements may be subject to change at short notice, and you are advised to contact the appropriate diplomatic or consular authority before finalising travel arrangements. Any numbers in the chart refer to the footnotes below.*

PASSPORTS: Passport valid for a minimum of six months after return from Romania required by all with at least one blank page.

VISAS: Required by all except the following:
(a) **1.** nationals mentioned in the chart above for up to 90 days, except nationals of Czech Republic, Poland and Slovak Republic who can stay for up to 30 days; and all nationals of Australia who *do* require a visa;
(b) nationals of Andorra, Costa Rica, Iceland, Korea (Rep), Liechtenstein, Malaysia, Monaco, Republic of Moldova, Norway, San Marino, Switzerland and Venezuela for stays of up to 90 days within six months of date of arrival;
(c) nationals of Uruguay for stays of up to 90 days within 12 months of arrival;
(d) nationals of Bulgaria, Croatia and Singapore for stays of up to 30 days;
(e) transit passengers continuing their journey by the same or first connecting aircraft within 24 hours provided holding valid onward or return documentation and not leaving the airport *except for* nationals of Afghanistan, Bangladesh, Congo (Dem Rep), Eritrea, Ethiopia, Ghana, India, Iran, Iraq, Nigeria, Pakistan, Somalia and Sri Lanka who *always* require transit visas.

Note: All other nationals require a visa which must be applied for prior to arrival. There are no visas issued on arrival.

Special requirements: Nationals of the following need an official notarised invitation from a company or individual in Romania, which may be faxed by the Embassy to the Romanian Passport General Directorate or any of the Romania County Passport Authorities for approval (allow at least 30 days):
Afghanistan, Albania, Algeria, Angola, Armenia, Azerbaidjan, Bangladesh, Belarus, Benin, Bhutan, Burkina Faso, Burundi, Cambodia, Cameroon, Cape Verde, Central African Republic, China (PR), Chad, CIS (except Moldova, Russian Federation and Ukraine), Comoro Islands, Congo (Dem Rep), Congo (Rep), Côte d'Ivoire, Cuba, Djibouti, Dominican Republic, Egypt, Equatorial Guinea, Eritrea, Ethiopia, Fiji, Gabon, The Gambia, Georgia, Ghana, Guinea, Guinea-Bissau, Guyana, Haiti, India, Iran, Iraq, Jordan, Kazakhstan, Kenya, Kirgizstan, Korea (Dem Rep), Laos, Lebanon, Liberia, Libya, Madagascar, Maldives, Mali, Mauritania, Mauritius, Mongolia, Morocco, Mozambique,

Myanmar, Nepal, Niger, Nigeria, Pakistan, Palestine, Papua New Guinea, Peru, The Philippines, Rwanda, São Tomé e Príncipe, Senegal, Sierra Leone, Somalia, Sri Lanka, Sudan, Surinam, The Syrian Arab Republic, Tanzania, Togo, Tunisia, Turkmenistan, Uganda, Uzbekistan, Vietnam, Yemen and Zambia (if these nationals are married to Romanian nationals the relevant certificate should be produced).

Note: Nationals of EU member states, Iceland, Liechtenstein, Norway and Switzerland can extend their stay in Romania by submitting an application to the Romanian authorities 30 days before their initial right to stay expires.

Types of visa and cost: *Single-entry:* £35 (business, conference and family visits or individual tourist). *Transit:* £27 (single-entry); £35 (double-entry). *Multiple-entry:* £60 valid for six months and not renewable. An additional fee of £7 is charged for each person included in the passport if travelling with the owner.

Note: Multiple-entry visas will not be issued to nationals listed under *Special Requirements* above, even if the purpose of their visit is for business.

Validity: *Single-entry:* Six months from date of issue for stays of up to 90 days. *Multiple-entry:* Six months from date of issue for stays of up to 90 days each visit. *Transit:* Five days maximum (for both single- and double-entry).

Application to: Consulate (or consular section at Embassy); see *Passport/Visa Information*. Applicants for multiple-entry business visas must apply in their own country.

Application requirements: (a) Passport valid for at least six months after visa expires with a blank page to affix visa stamp. (b) One completed application form. (c) Two recent passport-size photos. (d) Fee (paid in cash or by postal order only). (e) Postal applications should be accompanied by a registered, self-addressed envelope. (f) Medical Insurance. (g) Proof of financial means in amount of $100 per day or the equivalent value in convertible currency for the entire period of time. *Tourist* (a)-(g) and, (h) Letter from travel agent or a hotel booking in Romania. *Business:* (a)-(g) and, (h) Letter from employer and invitation from company in Romania. *Student:* (a)-(g) and, (h) Evidence of enrolment on course. *Transit:* (a)-(g) and, (h) Ticket for onward travel with visa if required.

Note: All nationals are advised to check with the Romanian Consulate prior to departure to obtain current details of any further documentation which might be required.

Working days required: Visas take up to a maximum of 30 days to be issued, depending on type of visa and nationality. Travellers are advised to apply for a visa at least a month in advance.

Temporary residence: Enquire at Embassy.

PASSPORT/VISA INFORMATION

Embassy of Romania in the UK
Arundel House, 4 Palace Green, London W8 4QD, UK
Tel: (020) 7937 9666/7.
Website: www.roemb.co.uk
Opening hours: Mon-Fri 0900-1700; Mon-Thurs 1000-1300 (visa section).

Embassy of Romania in the USA
1607 23rd Street, NW, Washington, DC 20008, USA
Tel: (202) 332 4846/8.
Website: www.roembus.org

Money

Currency: Leu (plural Lei) = 100 bani;
Old notes are in denominations of Lei1,000,000, 500,000, 100,000, 50,000 and 10,000. Old coins are in denominations of Lei5000, 1000, 500, 100 and 1.
New notes are in denominations of new Lei500, 100, 50, 10, 5 and 1. New coins are in denominations of Bani: 50, 10, 5 and 1.

Note: As of 1 July 2005, Romania's legal tender, previously coded as ROL, has been redenominated so that new Lei 10,000 are exchanged for 1 new Leu (RON). The old Leu will be legal tender until the end of December 2006.

Currency exchange: It is recommended that visitors bring hard currency, particularly US Dollars, as this can be easily and even eagerly exchanged by shops, restaurants and hotels. Sterling can be easily exchanged in most resorts. All hard foreign currencies can be exchanged at banks, larger hotels and airports and at authorised exchange offices (*Birou de Schimb Valutar*). Rates can vary from one place to another, so visitors are advised to shop around for the best rate of exchange. Exchanges on the black market are made frequently, but visitors are advised to exchange money through proper exchange channels and to receive a currency exchange receipt, as certain services require visitors to show the receipt as proof of having made at least one financial transaction. ATMs (*bancomat*) accepting MasterCard and Visa can be found in main banks, airports and shopping centres but should not be relied upon as a sole source of cash.

Credit & debit cards: American Express, Diners Club, MasterCard and Visa are accepted by large hotels, car hire firms and some restaurants and shops. Check with your credit or debit card company for details of merchant acceptability and other services which may be available.
Traveller's cheques: Like credit and debit cards, these are usually only useful in hotels and for obtaining cash at the bank or selected exchange offices. To avoid additional exchange rate charges, travellers are advised to take traveller's cheques in US Dollars or Euros.
Currency restrictions: The import of local currency is prohibited (unless in possession of a special licence); the export of local currency is prohibited. The import of foreign currency is limited to $10,000; the export of foreign currency is limited to the amount imported.
Banking hours: Mon-Fri 0900-1300.
Exchange rate indicators:
Rate at time of publishing
£1.00= Lei5.38
$1.00= Lei3.10

Duty Free

The following items may be imported into Romania without incurring customs duty:
200 cigarettes, 40 cigars or 200g of other tobacco articles; 2l of liquor; 4l of wine or beer; gifts up to a value of Lei2000; 200g of cocoa; 200g of coffee; 20 rolls of camera film and reasonable quantities of perfume, medicines and travel souvenirs.
Prohibited imports: Ammunition, explosives, narcotics, pornographic material, uncanned meats, animal and dairy products.
Prohibited exports: Articles of cultural, historical or artistic value.
Note: Valuable goods, such as jewellery, art, electrical items and foreign currency should be declared on entry. Endorsed customs declarations must be kept, as they must be shown on leaving the country.

Public Holidays

Below are listed Public Holidays for the January 2006-June 2007 period.
2006: Jan 1-2 New Year. **Jan 6** Epiphany. **Apr 24** Easter Monday (Orthodox). **May 1** Labour Day. **Dec 1** National Day. **Dec 25-26** Christmas.
2007: Jan 1-2 New Year. **Jan 6** Epiphany. **Apr 9** Easter Monday (Orthodox). **May 1** Labour Day.

Health

	Special Precautions?	Certificate Required?
Yellow Fever	No	No
Cholera	No	No
Typhoid & Polio	1	N/A
Malaria	No	N/A

Note: *Regulations and requirements may be subject to change at short notice, and you are advised to contact your doctor well in advance of your intended date of departure. Any numbers in the chart refer to the footnotes below.*

1: Vaccination against *typhoid* is advised.
Food & drink: Mains water is normally chlorinated, and whilst relatively safe, may cause abdominal upsets; visitors are thus advised to drink bottled water. Milk is pasteurised and dairy products are safe for consumption. Local meat, poultry, seafood, fruit and vegetables are generally considered safe to eat.
Other risks: *Hepatitis A, hepatitis C* and *tuberculosis* occur and *hepatitis B* is endemic. Rare *West Nile Fever* outbreaks have been reported in the southeast. *Brucellosis* occurs sporadically although risk to the traveller is low. Stray dogs may carry *African Typhus* disease. Ensure booster vaccinations for *tetanus-diphtheria* and *measles* are up-to-date.
Rabies is present. For those at high risk, vaccination before arrival should be considered. If you are bitten, seek medical advice without delay. For more information, see the *Health* appendix.
Note: EU experts have confirmed that the Avian Influenza (Bird Flu) virus has been detected in tests on birds in the Danube Delta. The Romanian authorities have taken measures to prevent an outbreak. No human infections or deaths have been reported. The risk to Avian Influenza is believed to be very low, provided you avoid visiting live animal markets, poultry farms and other places where you may come into close contact with domestic, caged or wild birds; ensure poultry and egg dishes are thoroughly cooked.
Health care: Medical facilities in Romania are poor and there is a serious shortage of basic medical supplies and qualified personnel. Nationals of countries who do not have a reciprocal health agreement with Romania are expected to pay immediate cash for health services. Health insurance is strongly advised.

Travel - International

AIR:
The national airline is *Tarom (RO)* (website: www.tarom.ro).
Approximate flight times: From Bucharest to *London* is three hours and 15 minutes.
Main airports: *Bucharest (BUH)* (Otopeni) (website: www.otp-airport.ro) is 16km (10 miles) north of the city (travel time - 25 minutes). The airport has been greatly modernised in recent years, but some visitors may find it relatively limited compared to Western European or American standards. *To/from the airport:* There is an express bus service (bus no. 783) which runs every 15 minutes between 0530-2330 Mon-Fri and every 30 minutes Sat-Sun and holidays; the journey takes approximately 45 minutes. Taxis, minibuses and limousines are available 24 hours (travel time - 25 minutes).
Facilities: Bar, snack bar, restaurant, left luggage, first aid, post office, bank and ATM, car hire and duty free.
There are also international airports at *Arad (ARW), Cluj (CLJ)* (website: www.airportcluj.ro), *Constanta (CND)* (Mihail Kogalniceanu), *Sibiu (SBZ)* (website: www.sibiu.ro) and *Timisoara (TSR)* (website: www.airotim.ro).
Departure tax: None.
SEA/RIVER:
Main ports: *Constanta* on the Black Sea. **Sea ferries:** Not running at present. Contact the Romanian National Tourist Office for up-to-date information (see *Top Things To Do*). **River cruises:** Sailings from Passau to Constanta on the Black Sea along the Danube are available; these stop at various places of interest, including Vienna, Bratislava, Budapest, Bazias, Giurgiu, Calafat and Bucharest. The cruises incorporate varied itineraries: historic towns, museums, art collections, monasteries, spas, archaeological sites, folk evenings, nature reserves and of course, the dramatic scenery of Eastern Europe, including the 'Iron Gate' through the Carpathians. With the opening of the Main-Danube Canal, some companies now offer travel as far west as Rotterdam along the Rhine. For further information, contact the Romanian National Tourist Office (see *Top Things To Do*).
RAIL:
Romania National Railways (SNCFR) (website: www.cfr.ro) operates services from many European cities to Bucharest. First and second class sleepers are available for journeys longer than 10 hours and for overnight journeys. The main international train from Western Europe to Romania (Bucharest) is the *Wiener Waltzer*, which runs to Bucharest in summer only (June to September) and includes two nights' travel from Basel, arriving in Bucharest two days later. There are no through carriages from Basel, which means moving to the Bucharest coaches in Vienna. As well as day carriages, there are sleeping cars from Vienna to both Bucharest and Constanta on the Black Sea coast. There are also through trains from other Eastern European cities.
Rail Passes: The *Inter-Rail* pass offers unlimited second-class train travel in up to 29 European countries (includes Morocco and Turkey) split into eight zones (A-H). Three different tickets are available: a ticket covering one zone (two to six countries, 16 days' validity), a ticket covering two zones (six to 10 countries, 22 days' validity) and an *All Zone Pass* (29 countries, one month's validity). Ferry services between Italy and Greece are included. Passengers must be resident in Europe for at least six months before the pass is used. Travel is not allowed in the passenger's country of residence. Travellers under 26 years receive a reduction of about 30 per cent. Children's tickets are reduced by about 50 per cent. Supplements are required for some high-speed services, seat reservations and couchettes. Discounts are offered on *Eurostar* and some ferry routes. Available from *Inter Rail* (website: www.interrail.com).
The *EuroDomino* pass enables holders anything from three to eight days' extensive travel within a one-month period on the entire rail network of their chosen country. It is valid in 28 European countries and North Africa, including the ferry service from Brindisi (Italy) to Igoumenitsa (Greece). To purchase a *EuroDomino* pass you must have been resident in Europe for at least six months and a passport number is required at time of booking. It is not permitted to purchase a pass for travel within your own country of residence.
To qualify for the youth rates, you must be under 26 years on the first date of validity of the pass. Children aged four-11 years inclusive pay half the adult fares rounded up to the nearest pound. Children under four years travel for free. Seat reservations, couchette and sleeper charges are not included in the cost of the pass and are payable at the normal rate. Passholder fares are payable on some services. Reservation/supplement charges are payable on all trains within Spain. Available from *Rail Europe* (website: www.raileurope.co.uk/railpasses/eurodomino.htm).
ROAD:
Border crossing between Romania and its western neighbours is just a formality. At the border, drivers need to show vehicle registration, proof of insurance and a Driver's Licence for their home country. Insurance can be bought at any border crossing point. The most direct international routes to Romania are via Austria, Germany and Hungary. The best route from Hungary is the E64 from Budapest to Szeged through Arad, Brasov, Campina and Ploiesti. There is also a route from Szeged to Timisoara. A more frequently used route from Hungary to Germany is via the E60 through Oradea. There are numerous and excellent road links with all neighbouring countries. *Eurolines*, (52 Grosvenor Gardens, London SW1W 0AU; tel (08705) 143 219; website: www.eurolines.com) and *National Express* (ensign Court, 4 Vicarage Road, Edgbaston, Birmingham B15 3ES; tel: 08705 808 080; website: www.nationalexpress.com) run regular coach services from the UK to Romania and other European cities. Travellers can either choose Mini-Pass breaks or book a 15-, 30-, or 60-day pass. The six Mini-passes give travellers the freedom to visit three cities, with prices starting from £55. Travellers can stay as long as they like in each city.

Travel - Internal

AIR:
Carpatair (www.carpatair.com) operates domestic flights from *Timisoara* to Bucharest, Constanta, Bacau, Cluj, Iasi, Oradea, Tirgu-Mures, Satu-Mare, Arad and Suceava. A couple of flights also operate from *Cluj. Tarom (RO)* operates regular services from *Baneasa* (travel time - 20 minutes to Otopeni) to Arad, Baia Mare, Cluj-Napoca, Constanta, Iasi, Oradea, Satu Mare, Sibiu, Suceava, Timisoara and Tirgu Mures.
RIVER:
The Danube Delta is easily explored by boat. Most trips and cruises depart from the ancient city of Tulcea and sail to Sulina.
RAIL:
Bucharest's main station is the Gara de Nord on Calea Grivitei. *Romanian State Railways* (website: www.cfr.ro) runs frequent, efficient and cheap services to most cities, towns and larger villages, some with sleeping and restaurant cars. There are five different types of train, varying in speed from the slow *personal* to the faster *accelerat, rapid* and *express* trains, and the more expensive and comfortable *Inter-City*. The other two types of train have dining cars and sleepers. Supplements are payable on rapid and express trains, for which seats must be reserved in advance. Express routes run from Bucharest to Timisoara, Cluj-Napoca, Iasi, Constanta and Brasov. Rail Inclusive Tour tickets include transport and hotel accommodation. There are no platforms of any great height in Romania, making entering and alighting a little difficult for the elderly or infirm. There is a discount of 25 to 35 per cent for non-express trains. For train enthusiasts, there are nine steam train dating from the 1920s and 1930s, some of which have been restored, that are available to rent to organisations and individuals. Contact the Romanian National Tourist Office for more information (see *Top Things To Do*).
ROAD:
Traffic drives on the right. Road conditions vary widely throughout Romania. While major streets in larger cities and major inter-city roads are in fair to good condition, other roads are in poor repair, badly lit, narrow and often do not have marked lanes. Drivers need to be alert for horse-drawn carts and livestock especially at night. Tolls are charges on motorways and main roads, payable in Euros. Vignettes can be bought for one-week or one-month and can be bought at border points, post offices and at most petrol stations throughout Romania. Fines are charges for those without vignettes. The *Romanian Automobile Club (ACR)* has its headquarters in Bucharest (tel: (21) 212 8247 *or* 223 4525) and offers services through all its branches to AA and RAC members. **Coach:** Several bus companies offer fast and inexpensive connections between Romania's main cities. Inter-city bus stations are usually located next to the train stations. The main coach stations in Bucharest are at 164 Soseaua Alexandriei, 1 Ion Ionescu de la Brad Boulevard, 1 Piata Gãrii Filarest, 221 Soseaua Chitilei, 141 Pacii Boulevard and 3 Gãrii Obor Boulevard. **Taxi:** Metered taxis can be hailed in the street or called from hotels. Prices are relatively low, but drivers expect a 10 per cent tip. Although most drivers are honest, prices should be agreed beforehand, especially at the airport. **Car hire:** Available at hotels and at Bucharest Airport. Driving is very erratic, so it might be advisable to hire a car with a driver. **Regulations:** Children under 12 are not allowed to travel in the front seat and front seat passengers must wear a seatbelt. Speed limits are 50k/h (30mph) in built up areas, 90k/h (56mph) on main roads, and 110 k/h (70mph) on highways. Driving under the influence of alcohol is forbidden. **Documentation:** National driving licence or International Driving Permit are required, as is Green Card insurance. Most Romanian roads

Credit: © Romania National Tourist Office

are best suited to 4-wheel-drive vehicles as they are in poor, potholed condition. Police carry out frequent checks so it is essential that you observe the speed limit, ensure that your vehicle is roadworthy and you have all your car documents.

URBAN:

 Most cities offer efficient and inexpensive bus, trollybus or tram transport. Bucharest has a good bus and tram system and a metro. Tickets are pre-purchased from agents, and there are stamping machines on board buses and trains. There are also daily, weekly and fortnightly passes. A separate minibus network is operated.

Travel Advice

Most visits to Romania are trouble-free but you should be aware of the global risk of indiscriminate international terrorist attacks, which could be against civilian targets, including places frequented by foreigners.

Beware of pickpockets and other petty thieves in crowded areas.

This advice is based on information provided by the Foreign and Commonwealth Office in the UK. It is correct at time of publishing. As the situation can change rapidly, visitors are advised to contact the following organisations for the latest travel advice.

British Foreign and Commonwealth Office
Tel: (0845) 850 2829.
Website: www.fco.gov.uk

US Department of State
Website: http://travel.state.gov/travel

Accommodation

EDITOR'S CHOICE: HOMESTAY

To sample the real Romanian lifestyle opt to stay in someone's home. A room costs from Lei20 to Lei80 per night, which often includes two meals. Rooms are clean but some do not have private bathrooms for guests. Hosts may not speak English.

HOTELS:

 Visitors are advised to book accommodation in advance through a travel agency, particularly for summertime visits to coastal resorts. Room prices in lower-end hotels are very reasonable compared to Western European prices, whereas 4- and 5-star hotels are comparable in both standards and price. Breakfast normally costs extra. For further information, contact the Romanian Tourist Office (see *Top Things To Do*) or see online (website: www.rotravel.com). **Grading:** Hotels are classified from **1** to **5 stars**.

BED & BREAKFAST:

 Accommodation of this type (also called *'Pensiune'*) is plentiful in Romania and in smaller towns or villages may be the only options. Private rooms tend to be cheaper than hotel rooms and will be basic but comfortable. Bed and Breakfast accommodation is classified from **1** to **3** daisies. For further information, contact the Romanian National Tourist Office (see *Top Things To Do*).

SELF-CATERING:

 Addresses of private accommodation and self-catering establishments are available from local tourist offices.

CAMPING/CARAVANNING:

 There are around 150 campsites in Romania. Prepaid tourist coupons valid from May to September are available from specialised travel agencies.

YOUTH HOSTELS:

 Most hostels are open in July and August although some are open year-round.

ACCOMMODATION INFORMATION

Youth Hostel Romania
Tel: (264) 586 616.
Website: www.hihostels-romania.ro

Top Things To See

- Discover the astonishing range of architecture of **Bucharest**, known as the 'Paris of the Balkans': the 19th-century **Roman Atheneum**, the **Palace of the CEC**, the **University**, the **Palace of Justice**, the **Town Hall** and the **Old Parliament Building**, built in 1907. Churches of interest include the 18th-century **Stravropoleos** and the 17th-century **Patriarchal Cathedral**.
- In Bucharest, admire the colossal size and exceptional facilities of the **Parliament Palace**, the second largest building in the world, after the Pentagon. Built in the 1989, it was initially called the **People's Palace**.
- The Romanian capital has many interesting museums such as **The Museum of the Romanian Peasant** which was awarded the 'European Museum of the Year' in 1994, **The Museum of History of Bucharest**, **The National History Museum of Romania**, **The Art Museum of Romania** (situated in the former royal palace), **The George Enescu Museum (Museum of Collections)** and the **National Museum Cotroceni** within the **Cotroceni Palace**.
- Beyond Bucharest, head for the palaces of **Mogosoaia**, **Buftea** and **Heresti** and old buildings and monasteries in **Snagov**, **Cernica**, **Pasarea**, **Caldarusani** and **Tiganesti**.
- On the Black Sea Coast, visit the Greek/Byzantine port of **Constanta**, founded in the sixth century BC; inland there are interesting archaeological sites including the ancient Greek city ruins of **Histria**, **Tomis** and **Callatis**. The area is inhabited by foxes, otters, wildcats and boars and in the migratory periods one can see over 300 species of birds. The **Danube Delta**, listed by UNESCO as a World Heritage Site, is a vast expanse of protected watery wilderness in the north of the Romania Black Sea Coast, also rich in wildlife. The **Danube Delta Museum** is worth a visit.
- Do not miss the **Hurezi Monastery**, in the Vâlcea county, listed by UNESCO as a World Heritage site.
- Get your imagination running at **Bran Castle**. It is here that the myth of Dracula, immortalised in Bram Stoker's famous novel, originated. The original Dracula was a medieval King known as 'Vlad the Impaler', owing to his unpleasant habits. One of Vlad's original abodes is Bran Castle; set in a commanding position, with its thick walls and peaked tower, it offers a dramatic view and a chilling atmosphere (tours are available to Bran Castle from the mountain resort of **Poiana**

Brasov, where it is possible to **ski** in winter and undertake **mountain climbing** and **walking** in summer).
- See Transylvania's numerous Saxon fortified churches, including the **Biertan Church**, which stands on top of a hill overlooking the village of **Biertan** and is a listed UNESCO World Heritage Site.
- **Traditional folk music** and **dancing** is still very much alive and shows can be seen in many hotels and restaurants.

Top Things To Do

- Wander around some of the most important streets in Bucharest: **Calea Victoriei (Victory Road)** which holds the **The Vernescu House** and Boulevards **Gh. Magheru**, **Carol I, Calea Mosilor, Calea Dorobantilor** and **Soseaua Kiseleff**.
- Enjoy a range of watersports or simply relax on the beaches of the **Black Sea Coast**. This coastline is the principal tourist area of Romania and ideal for family holidays. Its 70km (43 miles) of fine white sandy beaches boast many resorts, the main ones being **Constanta, Costinesti, Eforie Nord, Eforie Sud, Jupiter, Mamaia, Mangalia, Navodari, Neptun, Olimp, Saturn, Techirghiol, Venus** and **Aurora**.
- Feel rejuvenated by the curative properties of the salt waters and the mud from **Lake Techirghiol** (whose thermal springs have a year-round temperature of 24°C/75°F). **Mangalia, Eforie** and **Neptun** make the Romanian Riviera popular with those seeking spa treatments, especially for rheumatism. Transylvania holds many well-equipped spa towns, such as **Baile Felix, Baile Herculane, Covasna** and **Sovata**, some of which have facilities offering acupuncture, acupressure and slimming cures.
- In the **Carpathian Mountains**, a densely forested mountainous area, practice many sporting and leisure activities such as **skiing, bob-sleighing, horseriding** and **tennis**. Situated in picturesque valleys and on mountain slopes are many health and winter resorts, open all year round. The major resorts are: **Borsa, Busteni, Durau, Paltinis, Poiana Brasov** and **Predeal** (both of which have illuminated ski slopes), **Semenic** and **Sinaia** (bob-sleigh tracks). Spectacular mountain lakes are found in the **Fagaras** and **Retezat** ranges, and caves in the **Apuseni, Bihor** and **Mehedinti** regions.
- Purchase **regional crafts**: woodcarving, pottery and ceramics, wooden architecture and glass paintings can be found throughout the country.

TOURIST INFORMATION

Romanian National Tourist Office in UK
22 New Cavendish Street, London W1M 7LH, UK
Tel: (020) 7224 3692.
Website: www.romaniatourism.com *or* www.visitromania.com

Romanian National Tourist Office in the USA
355 Lexington Avenue, 19th Floor, New York, NY 10017, USA
Tel: (212) 545 8484.
Website: www.romaniatourism.com

Entertainment

FOOD & DRINK: The Romanians excel in full-bodied soups, some of the best being cream of mushroom, chicken, beef, vegetable and bean soup. Sour cream or eggs are also added to soups. Breakfasts almost always include eggs, either soft-boiled, hard-boiled, fried or scrambled. Omelettes, filled with either cheese, ham or mushrooms, are also frequently served. Vegetarians may have difficulties, as most local specialities are meat-based. Although there are inexpensive self-service snack bars, table service is the norm. There are no licensing hours, but the legal age for drinking in a bar is 18.

National specialities:
- Soups: *Ciorba de perisoare* (soup with meatballs), *ciorba tărănească* (vegetable soup with meat and rice balls served with sour cream), giblet soup and a variety of fish soups.
- Moldavian *parjoale* (flat meat patties, highly spiced and served with garnishes).
- *Mamaliga* (a staple of mashed cornmeal).
- *Nisetru la gratar* (grilled Black Sea sturgeon).
- *Pasca* (a sweet cheesecake).

National drinks:
- *Tuică* (plum brandy) and *Tuică de Bihor* (strong brandy, generally known as *palinca*).
- Wines: *Pinot Noir, Cabernet Sauvignon, Riesling, Pinot Gris* and *Chardonnay* from the Murfatlar vineyards. *Grasa* and *Feteasa* from Moldavia's Cotnari vineyards.
- Sparkling wines.
- *Glühwein* (mulled wine).

Tipping: A five to 10 per cent service tip is customary in restaurants. Porters, chambermaids and taxi drivers expect tips.

NIGHTLIFE: Bucharest has a growing number of discos and nightclubs with entertainment and live dancing. Restaurants at most major hotels double as nightclubs and there are also several Parisian-style cafes. Two casinos operate in the Calea

Victoriei. Opera is performed at the Romanian Opera House and the Romanian Athenaeum has two symphony orchestras. Folk entertainment is performed at the Rapsodia Romana Artistic Ensemble Hall and there are a number of theatres.

SHOPPING: Specialist purchases include embroideries, pottery, porcelain, silverware, carpets, ceramics, crystal, glassware, fabrics, wool jumpers, woodcarvings, metal, leather goods, rugs, glass paintings and silk dresses. **Shopping hours:** Mon-Sat 0900-1800, although this may vary according to season and area.

Business

- **GDP:** US$57 billion.
- **Main imports:** Machinery and equipment, fuels and minerals, chemicals, agricultural products, textiles and textile products and basic metals.
- **Main exports:** Textiles and footwear, metals and metal products, machinery and equipment, minerals and fuels, chemicals and agricultural products.
- **Main trade partners:** France, Germany, Italy, Russia, Turkey and UK.

ECONOMY: Romania is a major producer of wheat and maize, and grows vegetables, fruit, sugar beet and vegetable oil seeds; wine-making is still widespread and many farms also breed livestock. Communist-era economic policies favoured heavy industry and the agricultural sector has since found it difficult to catch up with European standards. Most land has now been transferred to private ownership. The previously neglected forestry and fishing industries are being developed under long-term programmes. Overall, the contribution of the agricultural sector to GDP has declined from about 33 per cent in 1990 to its present level of 14.8 per cent.
Post-communist industry has undergone a similar contraction, and now accounts for 28 per cent of GDP (down from nearly 60 per cent in 1990). Romanian industry produces industrial and transport equipment, metals, furniture, chemical products and manufactured consumer goods, but the most important sector is oil, natural gas and oil-derived products (petrochemicals, paints and varnishes). The mining industry produces coal, bauxite, copper, lead, zinc and iron ore. The Romanian economy was crippled under the Ceaucescu regime, not least by its leader's obsession with paying off the whole of the country's national debt (something rarely considered, let alone attempted, by most Governments). Since the 1989 revolution, successive Governments have concentrated on turning Romania into a market economy. Progress has been difficult, hampered by the economy's already weak condition and political instability. In the early- and mid-1990s, Romania came close to economic meltdown as the economy contracted by an average of seven per cent annually and inflation often reached 100 per cent. The situation has improved since 2000, when Romania registered positive growth. GDP is now increasing at an annual rate of five per cent; inflation is 22 per cent and official unemployment has fallen to eight per cent (although there is a large informal economy). IMF and World Bank support have been forthcoming under the usual conditions. Romania has also had access to loans from the European Bank for Reconstruction and Development to which it belongs as a 'country of operation'. The Romanians' ultimate objective is membership of the European Union, with whom it conducts over 60 per cent of its trade (Italy and Germany are the largest individual trade partners). The country originally hoped to join along with the 10 other countries that joined in May 2004. Unfortunately, it was unable to meet the accession criteria in time and now hopes to join, along with neighbouring Bulgaria, in 2007.

BUSINESS ETIQUETTE: A suit is essential at all business meetings and only on very hot days are shirtsleeves acceptable. English, German and French are used in business circles. Appointments are necessary and punctuality expected. Business cards are widely used. **Office hours:** Mon-Fri 0900-1530.

CONFERENCES/CONVENTIONS: For information on conferences and conventions, contact the Romanian Convention Bureau.

COMMERCIAL INFORMATION

The Chamber of Commerce and Industry of Romania
Bulevardul Octavian Goga 2, Sector 3, 030982 Bucharest, Romania
Tel: (1) 319 0114.
Website: www.ccir.ro

Romanian Convention Bureau
Calea Victoriei 118, 4th Floor, Suite 407, Sector 1, 70179 Bucharest, Romania
Tel: (21) 314 4100/4102.
Website: www.conventionbureau.ro

Russian Federation

Location: Eastern Europe/Asia.

Time: The Russian Federation is divided into 11 time zones.
Kaliningrad: GMT + 2 (GMT + 3 from last Sunday in March to last Sunday in October).
Moscow, St Petersburg, Astrakhan: GMT + 3 (GMT + 4 from last Sunday in March to last Sunday in October).
Izhevsk and Samara: GMT + 4 (GMT + 5 from last Sunday in March to last Sunday in October).
Perm, Ekaterinburg, Surgut: GMT + 5 (GMT + 6 from last Sunday in March to last Sunday in October).
Omsk and Novosibirsk: GMT + 6 (GMT + 7 from last Sunday in March to last Sunday in October).
Abakan, Norilsk, Tura: GMT + 7 (GMT + 8 from last Sunday in March to last Sunday in October).
Bratsk, Irkutsk, Ulan Ude: GMT + 8 (GMT + 9 from last Sunday in March to last Sunday in October).
Mirnyy, Tynda, Yakutsk: GMT + 9 (GMT + 10 from last Sunday in March to last Sunday in October).
Khabarovsk, Vladivostok, Yuzhno: GMT + 10 (GMT + 11 from last Sunday in March to last Sunday in October).
Magadan, Chirskiy: GMT + 11 (GMT + 12 from last Sunday in March to last Sunday in October).
Anadyr, Kamchatskiy, Petropavlosk: GMT + 12 (GMT + 13 from last Sunday in March to last Sunday in October).

Overview

The history of the Russian Federation is overwhelming. It is apparent on every corner of the country's staggeringly awesome cities, such as Moscow and St Petersburg, with their architectural marvels. But it also dwells in huge and remote expanses such as Siberia, filled with ancient forests and the world's deepest lake. Everything exists here on a mammoth level. Since the 15th century, when the Grand Prince of Moscow, Ivan III (the Great), annexed the rival principalities of Russia, Russia's ambitions have been as great as this first national sovereign's appellation. Names of rulers such as Peter the Great (1682-1725) and Catherine the Great (1762-96) roll of the tongue in easy familiarity. However, in the early 19th century, under Tsar Alexander I, the first steps were taken to dismantle the system of serfdom under which most people lived – and, by 1917, widespread strikes and rioting had forced the Tsar to abdicate. The liberal Provisional Government which took control was forced out by a Bolshevik coup under Vladimir Ilyich Ulyanov, better known as Lenin.
Lenin died in 1924 and was succeeded by Josef Stalin, who instituted a crash programme of industrialisation and the forced collectivisation of agriculture, an indiscriminately brutal process that caused mass starvation. Stalin begot purges in which thousands were shot or disappeared into the

vast network of concentration camps famously described as the 'gulag archipelago'. An estimated 20 million people then died driving out Hitler's armies in World War II – referred to as the Great Patriotic War. Yet by the time the war damage had been repaired, the USSR had become the world's second nuclear power, with a buffer zone of Communist-controlled Governments in Eastern Europe. Foreign policy was dominated by relations with the USA, which fluctuated from outright hostility (coming to the brink of nuclear war during the 1962 Cuban missile crisis) to the 'Cold Peace' of détente, fully actuated with the Presidency of Boris Yeltsin in 1991 and the dismantling of Communism.
But some incredibly tricky problems remain. The ruling class are now the security forces, the military, the so-called 'oligarchs' and regional Governors controlling fiefdoms; they have gotten more rich as the majority has suffered, despite economic improvements. The crisis surrounding Chechnya is another blot to be cleaned: Russo-Chechen relations are replete with warfare and large-scale brutality on both sides. A political solution is elusive.
Perhaps these are issues that come 'with the territory'. The Russian Federation's enormity has brought with it the 'nationalities problem'. Gone are the days of the 100-plus distinct ethnic groups in the Soviet Union – but the Russian Federation is still a melting pot, straddling two Continents, breathing both West and Eastern air, and sometimes undermining the cohesion and integrity of the nation in the process. Yet it is precisely because this country is so complex that it remains so endlessly fascinating. And it is in spite of it that it retains the simple truth of being so aesthetically beautiful.

General Information

AREA: 17,075,400 sq km (6,592,850 sq miles).
POPULATION: 141.5 million (UN, 2005).
POPULATION DENSITY: 8.28 per sq km.
CAPITAL: Moscow. **Population:** 8.3 million (2005).
GEOGRAPHY: The Russian Federation covers almost twice the area of the USA, and reaches from Moscow in the west over the Urals and the vast Siberian plains to the Sea of Okhotsk in the east. The border between European Russia and Siberia (Asia) is formed by the Ural Mountains, the Ural River and the Manych Depression. European Russia extends from the North Polar Sea across the Central Russian Uplands to the Black Sea, the Northern Caucasus and the Caspian Sea. Siberia stretches from the West Siberian Plain across the Central Siberian Plateau between Yenisey and Lena, including the Sayan, Yablonovy and Stanovoy ranges in the south to the East Siberian mountains between Lena and the Pacific coast, including the Chukotskiy and Kamchatka peninsulas.
Population figures: The following republics are part of the Russian Federation. Population figures were last verified in 2004.

Republic	Area (sq km)	Population (000's)	Capital
Adygheya	7600	446	Maikop
Altai	92,600	204	Gorno-Altaisk
Bashkortostan	143,600	4101	Ufa
Buryatia	351,300	1026	Ulan-Ude
Chechnyat*	N/A	609	Grozny
Chuvashia	18,300	1353	Cheboksary
Daghestan	50,300	2160	Makhachkala
Ingushetia*	N/A	460	Magas
Kabardino-Balkariya	12,500	783	Nalchik
Kalmykiya	75,900	314	Elista
Karachayevo-Cherkessiya	14,100	430	Cherkessk
Kareliya	172,400	717	Petrozavodsk
Khakassiya	61,900	578	Abakan
Komi	415,900	1126	Syktyvkar
Marii-El	23,200	755	Yoshkar-Ola

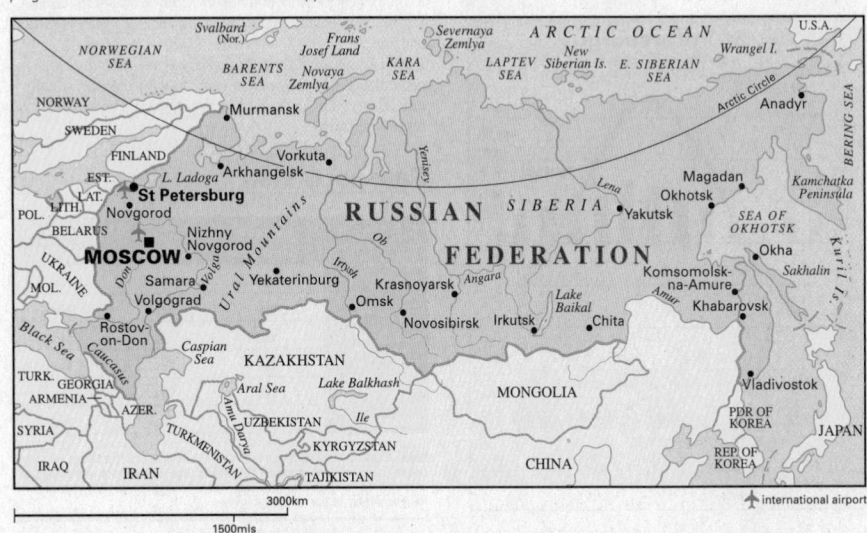

Mordoviya	26,200	919	Saransk
Northern Osetiya (Alaniya)	8000	677	Vladikavkaz
Sakha (Yakutiya)	3,103,200	986	Yakutsk
Tatarstan	68,000	3776	Kazan
Tyva	170,500	310	Kyzyl
Udmurtiya	42,100	1623	Izhevsk

*Until 1992, the territories of the Republic of Chechnya and the Ingush Republic were combined in the Chechen-Ingush autonomous republic (area 19,300 sq km).

GOVERNMENT: Republic since 1991. **Head of State:** President Vladimir Putin since 2000. **Head of Government:** Prime Minister Mikkail Fradkov. Recent history: Vladimir Putin was elected to a second term as Russian President in March 2004. His nearest opponent, the Communist candidate, only obtained 14 per cent of the votes. United Russia, the party backed by the President, won a landslide victory in Parliamentary elections in December 2003. Mr Putin has promised to continue to reform the economy. He has taken a very tough line against Chechen rebels.

LANGUAGE: Russian. English, French or German are spoken by some people.

RELIGION: Mainly Christian with the Russian Orthodox Church being the largest Christian community. Muslim, Buddhist and Jewish minorities also exist.

ELECTRICITY: 220 volts AC, 50Hz.

SOCIAL CONVENTIONS: It is customary to shake hands when greeting someone. Company or business gifts are well received. Each region has its own characteristic mode of dress. Conservative wear is suitable for most places and the seasonal weather should always be borne in mind. Smoking is acceptable unless stated otherwise. Avoid ostentatious displays of wealth; it is advisable to keep expensive jewellery, watches and cameras out of sight and take precautions against pickpocketing.

Photography: It is prohibited to take photographs of any military installation and/or establishments or sites of strategic importance. Failure to abide by this could result in police arrest.

Climate

Northern & Central European Russia: The most varied climate; mildest areas are along the Baltic coast. Summer sunshine may be nine hours a day, but winters can be very cold. **Siberia:** Very cold winters, but summers can be pleasant,

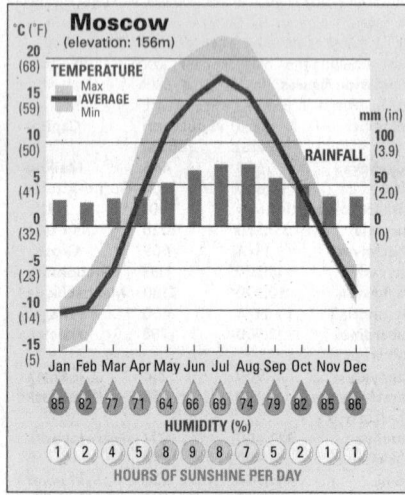

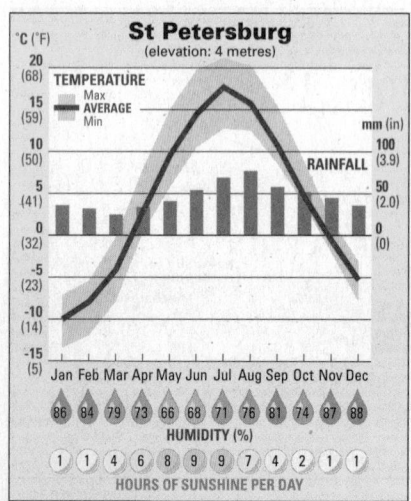

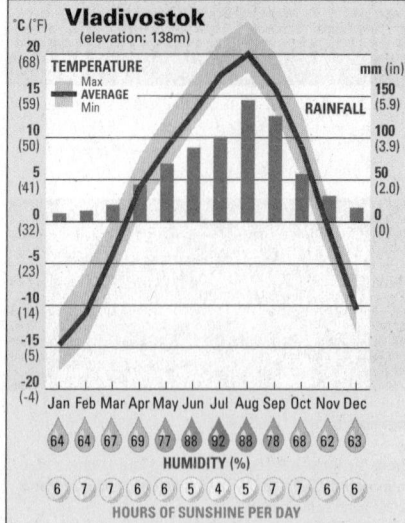

although they tend to be short and wet. There is considerable seasonal temperature variation. **Southern European Russia:** Winter is shorter than in the north. Steppes (in the southeast) have hot, dry summers and very cold winters. The north and northeastern Black Sea has mild winters, but heavy rainfall all the year round.

Communications

Telephone: IDD is available. Country code: 7. When dialling the Russian Federation from abroad, the 0 of the area code must *not* be omitted. Some Moscow hotels have telephone booths with IDD. For long-distance calls within the CIS, dial 8 then wait for the dial tone before proceeding with the call. Collect calls, calls placed using credit cards and calls from direct dial telephones in hotels can be extremely expensive. International calls can be made from phones in the street and phonecards are available from many shops and kiosks in the street. The emergency services can be reached as follows: fire – 01; police – 02; ambulance – 03. For enquiries regarding Moscow private telephone numbers, dial 09; for businesses, 927 0009. For national directory enquiries regarding Russian Federation and the CIS, dial 927 0009.

Mobile telephone: Roaming agreements exist with international mobile phone companies. All major cities are covered by at least one operator. Handsets can be hired from some companies.

Internet: Public access is available in hotels in larger cities and in Internet cafes.

Post: Airmail to Western Europe takes over 10 days. There are postboxes and post offices in every hotel. Inland surface mail is often slow. Post office hours: 0900-1900.

MEDIA: Over recent years, the Kremlin has secured greater control over Russia's media.

Press: The main dailies in the Russian Federation are *Izvestiya* (website: www.izvestia.ru) and *Komsomolskaya Pravda* (website: www.kp.ru), both published in Moscow. Newspapers and magazines are published in some 25 languages. Multilingual editions of the *Moscow News* (website: www.english.mn.ru) are available weekly. The *Moscow Times* (website: www.themoscowtimes.com) and *St Petersburg Times* are published in English. There is also a daily Internet newspaper, *Russia Today* (website: www.russiatoday.com).

TV: *Russia TV Channel* is state-owned. *NTV* is a national netowork owned by the gas company, Gazprom. *Centre TV* is a commerical network and *Russia Today* is an international English news channel. Other networks include *Channel One* and *Ren TV*.

Radio: *Radio Russia* and *Radio Mayak* are state-run networks. *Russkoye Radio* and *Moscow Echo* are privately run. *Voice of Russia* operates programmes in English and other languages.

Passport/Visa

	Passport Required?	Visa Required?	Return Ticket Required?
Full British	Yes	Yes	No
Australian	Yes	Yes	No
Canadian	Yes	Yes	No
USA	Yes	Yes	No
Other EU	Yes	Yes	No
Japanese	Yes	Yes	No

Note: *Regulations and requirements may be subject to change at short notice, and you are advised to contact the appropriate diplomatic or consular authority before finalising travel arrangements. Any numbers in the chart refer to the footnotes below.*

PASSPORTS: Valid 10-year passport required by all.
Note: Whilst in the country, visitors must carry ID at all times. Rather than carry original documents, it is advisable to carry photocopies of passports and visas, which will facilitate replacement should either be stolen.

VISAS: Required by all except the following, provided arriving from their country of origin:
(a) nationals of CIS countries (except nationals of Georgia and Turkmenistan who *do* require visas);
(b) nationals of Cuba for stays of up to 30 days;
(c) nationals of Mongolia, provided visiting for purposes of business and holding letter of invitation and return tickets, or travelling as tourists and holding prepaid hotel vouchers;
(d) transit passengers who are continuing their journey within 24 hours without leaving the transit area.

Types of visa and cost: *Tourist, Business, Private* and *Transit*: £30, if visa is processed in minimum eight working days. (Processing within three to five days costs £60; next-day processing £80; same-day processing £90; processing within one hour £120.) An additional £10 is payable for a double-entry visa. *Multiple-entry*: £100, standard six working days' processing (same-day processing costs £150). *Express*: £120.
All French passport holders younger than 18 years pay half rate.

Note: (a) Nationals of some countries may have to pay a consular fee in addition to the visa processing charges listed. Enquire at the Consulate or consular section of Embassy for a list of nationals and prices. (b) Transit visas are required by all except passengers remaining in the transit zone of Moscow Sheremetievo airport for less than 24 hours.

Validity: Dependent on purpose of trip. Transit visas are valid for up to three days. Tourist visas are valid for up to one month. Private visas are valid for up to 90 days.

Application to: Consulate (or consular section at Embassy); see *Passport/Visa Information.*

Application requirements: (a) Completed application form. (b) One recent passport-size photo stapled twice to upper-right corner of application form. (c) Passport valid for at least six months after visa expires, with at least two blank pages. (d) Fee, payable in cash only or postal orders for postal applications. (e) Postal applications must be accompanied by a large, pre-paid special delivery, self-addressed envelope. *Tourist*: (a)-(e) and, (f) Original tourist voucher (exchange order) issued by an authorised travel company stating their reference number, passenger names, dates of entry and exit, confirmation of payment, full itinerary, places to be visited, means of transportation and confirmation in Russian language. The voucher should be stamped and signed by an authorised person. (g) A standard tourist confirmation of acceptance (in the Russian language) issued by Russian tourist company or hotel accredited by the Ministry of Foreign Affairs in Russia, showing tourist reference number given by Russian Foreign Minister and names of applicants, full itinerary and dates of entry/exit. *Private* (for visiting relations or friends): (a)-(e) and, (f) Official original letter of invitation from Russian Ministry of Internal Affairs. *Business*: (a)-(e) and, (f) An official letter of invitation from company or organisation in the Russian Federation responsible for visit, certified by the local branch of Russian Ministry of Internal Affairs. (g) An introductory letter from applicant's company stating purpose of visit, itinerary, dates of entry and exit, assuming financial responsibility for the visit and stating the companies to be visited. *Transit*: (a)-(d) and, (e) Original and copy of confirmed air ticket to and from the Russian Federation. *Multiple-entry*: (a)-(e) and, (f) Original and a copy of your confirmed air ticket to and from Russia.

Note: (a) Those who are travelling in groups (standard package tours, coach tours, international competitions and cruises) should submit all documentation to the tour operator making the travel arrangements. For visits to relatives/friends in the CIS, enquire at the Consulate for details of application procedures. (b) All travellers staying in the Russian Federation for longer than three days must register their visas through their hotel or sponsor. Private visitors must register with local police on arrival. For travel to Tajikistan, your invitation should be confirmed by the Ministry of Foreign Affairs of the Republic of Tajikistan. (c) French nationals should also have their previous three months' bank statements, medical insurance and a copy of their tickets. (d) German nationals and all other Schengen country nationals, plus holders of Israeli or Estonian passports, should have travel insurance valid in the Russian Federation. (e) USA passport holders are required to fill out a special visa application form. (f) Since February 2003, every foreign citizen is given a migration card free of charge when they cross the Russian border. They must fill in their personal data, terms, purpose of visit and prospective place of residence and present the card when applying for registration within three days of arrival. The migration cards must be handed back upon departure.

Working days required: One to 12, depending on type of visa. Postal applications take at least eight to 12 days to process. Applications for visas may not be made earlier than three months before departure. Visas should be submitted 0900-1200; visas submitted 1500-1600 will be charged at the *Express Visa* fee.

Exit visas: Exit visas are required by all passengers who want to leave the country and are normally issued together with the entry visa. If the exit permit has not yet been issued by the representative of the Russian Federation which issued the visa, aliens should obtain it two days prior to departure at the latest from the *Intourist Service Bureau* in their hotel.

Temporary residence: Enquire at Embassy.

Money

Currency: Rouble (RUB) = 100 kopeks. Notes are in denominations of RUB1000, 500, 100, 50 and 10. Coins are in denominations of RUB10, 5, 2 and 1, and 50, 10, 5 and 1 kopeks.

Currency exchange: Foreign currency should only be exchanged at official bureaux and authorised banks, and all transactions must be recorded on the currency declaration form which is issued on arrival. It is wise to retain all exchange receipts. Bureaux de change are numerous and easy to locate. Large shops and hotels offer their own exchange facilities. US Dollars in pristine condition are the easiest currency to exchange. It is illegal to settle accounts in hard currency and to change money unofficially.

Credit & debit cards: Major European and international credit and debit cards, including Visa and Mastercard, are accepted in the larger hotels and at foreign currency shops and restaurants, but cash (in Roubles) is preferred. American Express cards may be turned down, but cash (in Roubles) is preferred. Check with your credit or debit card company for details of merchant acceptability and other services that might be available. ATM machines are widely available.

Traveller's cheques: Cash is preferred. To avoid additional exchange rate charges, travellers are advised to take traveller's cheques in US Dollars.

Currency restrictions: The import and export of local currency is prohibited. The import of foreign currency is US$10,000 but sums greater than US$3000 (or equivalent) must be declared. The export of foreign currency is limited to the amount declared on arrival.

Banking hours: Mon-Fri 0930-1730.

Exchange rate indicators:

Rate at time of publishing

£1.00=	RUB50.78
$1.00=	RUB28.67

Duty Free

Duty free regulations are liable to change at short notice. The following should be used as a guide only, and travellers are advised to contact the Embassy or Consulate for up-to-date information.

The following goods may be imported into the Russian Federation by persons aged 16 years and older without incurring customs duty:

200 cigarettes, 100 cigarillos, 50 cigars or 250g of tobacco products (over 18 years); 2l of alcoholic beverage (over 21 years); a reasonable quantity of perfume for personal use; gifts up to the value of US$10,000.

Note: On entering the country, tourists must complete a customs declaration form which must be retained until departure. This allows the import of articles intended for personal use, including currency and valuables which must be registered on the declaration form. Cameras, jewellery, computers and musical instruments should all be declared. Customs inspection can be long and detailed. It is advisable when shopping to ask for a certificate from the shop which states that goods have been paid for in hard currency. Presentation of such certificates should speed up customs formalities.

Prohibited imports: Photographs and printed matter directed against the Russian Federation, weapons and ammunition, radio electrical equipment, narcotics, fruit, vegetables, sturgeon of any species or sturgeon products, and live animals unless with a special permit.

Prohibited exports: Arms, works of art and antiques (unless permission has been granted by the Ministry of Culture), precious metals and furs.

Note: Up to 250g of caviar per person may be exported, provided a receipt is shown proving that it was bought at a store licensed to sell it to foreigners and a licence from the Ministry of Economical Development is presented.

Public Holidays

Below are listed Public Holidays for the January 2006-June 2007 period.

2006: Jan 1-2 New Year. **Jan 7** Russian Orthodox Christmas Day. **Mar 8** International Women's Day. **Apr 21** Orthodox Good Friday. **Apr 24** Orthodox Easter Monday. **May 1-2** Spring and Labour Day. **May 9** Victory in Europe Day. **Jun 12** Independence Day. **Nov 4** National Unity Day **Dec 12** Constitution Day.

2007: Jan 1-2 New Year. **Jan 7** Russian Orthodox Christmas Day. **Mar 8** International Women's Day. **Apr 6** Orthodox Good Friday. **Apr 9** Orthodox Easter Monday. **May 1-2** Spring and Labour Day. **May 9** Victory in Europe Day. **Jun 12** Independence Day.

Health

	Special Precautions?	Certificate Required?
Yellow Fever	No	No
Cholera	No	No
Typhoid & Polio	1	N/A
Malaria	No	N/A

Note: *Regulations and requirements may be subject to change at short notice, and you are advised to contact your doctor well in advance of your intended date of departure. Any numbers in the chart refer to the footnotes below.*

1: *Poliomyelitis* occurs. Immunisation is advisable.

Food & drink: All water should be regarded as being a potential health risk. Water used for drinking, brushing

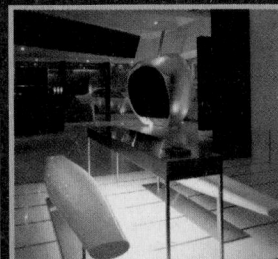

teeth or making ice should have first been boiled or otherwise sterilised. Contaminated tap water contains a high prevalence of *gastrointestinal* infections. The water supply in St Petersburg especially has been linked to *giardiasis*. Bottled water is widely available. Milk is pasteurised and dairy products are safe for consumption. Only eat well-cooked meat and fish, preferably served hot. Pork, salad and mayonnaise may carry increased risk. Vegetables should be cooked and fruit peeled.

Other risks: *Dysentery* is common throughout the country. *Hepatitis A* occurs. Widespread outbreaks of *diphtheria* have been reported. Consult a doctor regarding inoculation before travelling to the Russian Federation. *Tick-borne typhus* has been reported from east and central Siberia. *Tick-borne encephalitis* and *Lyme disease* occur in forested areas throughout the Russian Federation. Vaccination is advisable. Outbreaks of *Japanese encephalitis* have been reported from the southeast. *Leishmaniasis* can occur in the south. Outbreaks of *meningitis* have been reported from Volgograd.

Rabies is present and increasing. For those at high risk, vaccination before arrival should be considered. If you are bitten, seek medical advice without delay. For more information, consult the *Health* appendix.

Note: Visitors staying for more than three months must produce a certificate proving they are *HIV-negative*. The certification requirements are exacting and detailed; a medical examination may also be required. Foreign tests may be acceptable under certain conditions. Check details with the Embassy.

Health care: The highly developed health service provides free medical treatment for all citizens. If a traveller becomes ill during a booked tour, emergency treatment is free, with small sums to be paid for medicines and hospital treatment. If a longer stay than originally planned becomes necessary because of the illness, the visitor has to pay for all further treatment. This can be very expensive; air evacuation can cost up to £80,000. All visitors are strongly advised to have full medical cover that includes medical evacuation. It is advisable to take a supply of medicines that are likely to be required (check first that they may be imported legally). A reciprocal health care agreement is in operation between the UK and the Russian Federation, allowing citizens to receive free treatment. Private medical care can be expensive.

Note: There have been reports of outbreaks of *Avian Influenza* (*Bird Flu*) in a number of regions of Russia, including Tula, Tambov, Kurgan, Chelyabinsk and Novosibirsk. As a precaution, the European Union has banned the import of live birds and feathers from Russia. No human infections or deaths have been reported but travellers to the Russian Federation should consult their healthcare provider for travel medical advice before departure.

The risk from *Avian Influenza* is believed to be very low provided visitors avoid live animal markets, poultry farms and other places with close contact with domestic, caged or whild birds. Ensure poultry and egg dishes are throughly cooked.

Travel - International

AIR:

The national airline is *Aeroflot – Russian International Airlines* (SU) (website: www.aeroflot.com).

Approximate flight times: From Moscow to *London* is three hours 50 minutes, from St Petersburg to *London* is three hours 25 minutes. From Moscow to *Almaty* is four hours 40 minutes, to *Baku* is three hours 10 minutes, to *Bukhara* is three hours 40 minutes, to *Kiev* is one hour 45 minutes, to *Minsk* is one hour 20 minutes, to *Odessa* is two hours, to *Samarkand* is three hours 50 minutes and to *Yerevan* is two hours 50 minutes.

Main airports: *Moscow (SVO)* (Sheremetyevo) (website: www.sheremetyevo-airport.ru) is 35km (22 miles) northwest of the city. *To/from the airport:* Taxis are available at the airport to the city centre for approximately US$10-15 (travel time – 30 to 40 minutes). 'Autoline' fixed-route taxis and buses are also available. Express coaches depart for the city every 20 minutes (0545-0030). Coaches depart for the airport from the Central Air Terminal in Moscow, 37 Leningradsky Prospekt (travel time – 50 minutes for international flights). Express trains leave every 30 minutes. *Facilities:* Outgoing duty free shops, banks/bureaux de change, post office, car hire, restaurants and first aid. Moscow also has three primarily domestic airports: see *Travel – Internal* section.

St Petersburg (LED) (Pulkovo) (website: http://eng.pulkovo.ru) is 17km (10.5 miles) south of the city. *To/from the airport:* Buses are available to the city centre 0700-2000 every 10 minutes (travel time – 10 minutes). Taxis are available for roughly US$10 (travel time – 15 minutes). *Facilities:* Banks/bureaux de change, flight information, duty free shops, restaurant, bar, snack bar, left luggage and first aid.

Departure tax: None.

RAIL:

There are various connections from London. The main route is: London–Brussels–Cologne/Berlin –Moscow/St Petersburg. The journey from London to Brussels can be made by a variety of train and ferry services (including via *Eurostar*), or via the Channel Tunnel. There is a sleeper service from Cologne to Moscow. The *Moskva Express* runs from Berlin to Moscow (website: http://bahn.hafos.de). There are through trains or coaches from other Western and Eastern European cities, from CIS countries, and from China (PR), Iran, Mongolia and Turkey. See also *Trans-Siberian Express* in the *Travel – Internal* section.

ROAD:

Foreign tourists may drive their own cars or may hire cars (see *Travel – Internal*). Those entering by car should have their visas registered at the hotel, motel or campsite where they will stay for the first night, and must also ensure that the car registration number is recorded in the visa. Travellers driving their own vehicle will get a temporary permit from customs to be able to use their car legally in Russia. Travellers should also insure their vehicle with *Ingosstrakh*, which has offices at all crossing points and in most major cities, and to purchase service coupons at the border. The speed limit is 60kmph on minor roads, 90kmph on major roads and variable on highways. A road tax is payable upon entry to the country. The following crossing points between Finland and the Russian Federation are available: Vaalima–Torfianovska; Nuijamaa–Brusnichnoye and Rajajooseppi–Lotta. There are also crossing points between the Russian Federation and all neighbouring countries although, at present, there are restrictions on cross-border travel to Azerbaijan and Georgia. Plans to simplify this process are currently underway. Those entering by car should have their visas registered at the hotel, motel or campsite where they will stay for the first night, and must also ensure that the car registration number is recorded in the visa. Travellers driving their own vehicle will get a temporary permit from customs to be able to use their car legally in Russia. Travellers should also insure their vehicle with *Ingosstrakh*, which has offices at all crossing points and in most major cities, and to purchase service coupons at the border. Although motorcyclists can enter the Russian Federation, cyclists wishing to cross the Russian border should find out whether this is permissible from the Russian Embassy or their travel agent before departure. There are numerous and excellent road links with neighbouring countries: *Eurolines* (52 Grosvenor Gardens, London, SW1W 0AU; tel: (08705) 143 219; website: www.eurolines.com) and *National Express* (Ensign Court, 4 Vicarage Road, Edgbaston, Birmingham B15 3ES; tel: (08705) 808 080; website: www.nationalexpress.com) run regular coach services from the UK to the Russian Federation. Travellers can either choose Mini-Pass breaks or book a 15-, 30- or 60-day pass. The six Mini-Passes gave travellers the freedom to visit three cities, with prices starting from £55. Travellers can stay as long as they like in each city.

Travel - Internal

AIR:

The internal network radiates from Moscow's four airports. *Aeroflot* runs services from Moscow to most major cities. All-inclusive tours are available from specialist tour operators.

Note: In the 1990s, Aeroflot was broken up into many small airlines which led to a catalogue of air disasters earning it a reputation for poor safety. Thankfully, its safety record has improved in recent years.

Domestic airports: *Vnukovo Airport (VKO)* (website: www.vnukovo.ru) is 29.5km (18 miles) southwest of Moscow. *To/from the airport:* Coaches go to the airport from the Central Air Terminal (travel time – one hour 15 minutes). Taxis are available to the city. *Facilities:* Outgoing duty free.

Domodedovo (DME) (website: www.domodedovo.ru) is 48km (25 miles) southeast of Moscow. *To/from the airport:* An Aeroexpress train goes from Moscow to the airport (travel time - 40 to 50 minutes). Express buses and a 24 hour shuttle service are also available. Two official taxi firms operate at the airport. *Facilities:* Duty free, shops and restaurants.

Bykovo Airport (BKA) is the smallest of Moscow's airports, 35km from the city. *To/from the airport:* Coaches go to the airport from the Central Air Terminal.

Approximate flight times: From Moscow to *Bratsk* is six hours 45 minutes, to *Donetsk* is one hour 30 minutes, to *Irkutsk* is seven hours, to *Khabarovsk* is seven hours 30 minutes, to *Kharkov* is one hour 15 minutes, to *St Petersburg* is one hour 30 minutes, to *Volgograd* is one hour 50 minutes and to *Yalta* is two hours 15 minutes.

SEA:

Owing to its geographical position, the Russian Federation has ports on its Pacific and Baltic shores and in the south on the Black Sea.

Main ports: *Kaliningrad, Murmansk, Sochi* (website: www.moport-sochi.ru), *St Petersburg* and *Vladivostok* (website: www.vladcomport.ru).

RIVER:

Cruises and excursions are available on many of the Russian Federation's rivers. The most popular cruises are on the river Don and the Volga. Many companies offer cruises onboard comfortable, modern boats. The Volga towns, the Golden Ring and Moscow-St Petersburg are popular routes.

RAIL:

The railway is a vital part of the infrastructure of Russia because of the poor road system. The largest and busiest rail network in the world is predominantly for freight traffic. Only a few long-distance routes are open for travel by tourists, and reservations must be made on all journeys. Children under five years of age travel free. Children aged five to nine pay half fare. Rail travellers are advised to store valuables in the compartment under the bed or seat and not to leave the compartment unattended.

The *Trans-Siberian Express*, probably the most famous train in the world, is one of the best ways of seeing the interior of the country. It runs from St Petersburg to the Pacific coast of Siberia and on to Japan. There is a daily service, but the steamer from Nakhodka to Yokohama only sails approximately once a week. The through journey from Moscow to Yokohama takes 10 days. It is the world's longest continuous train journey, crossing seven time zones and 9745km (5778 miles) from Europe to the Pacific, with 91 stops from Vladivostok to Moscow. Bed linen and towels are provided in the 'Soft Class' (first-class) berths, and there is a toilet and washbasin at the end of each carriage. Second-class cabins have four berths. Attendants serve tea from samovars for a small charge and there is a restaurant car on every train where meals can be purchased (however, no alcohol is available on the train, so passengers are advised to bring their own if desired).

The *Trans-Manchurian Express* follows the same route, before heading southeast into China and down to Beijing. Another, slightly shorter but no less epic journey can be made on the *Trans-Mongolian Railway* to Beijing. It runs from Moscow to Irkutsk (Siberia), skirting Lake Baikal and then entering Mongolia. The journey to the Mongolian capital, Ulaan Baatar, is remarkable for its dramatic scenery. The journey concludes in Beijing.

ROAD:

The European part of the Russian Federation depends heavily on its road network. Generally, the few roads in Siberia and further east are impassable during the winter. It is a good idea to arrange motoring holidays through a reputable agency. It is also advisable to pre-plan the itinerary and accommodation requirements. On the majority of tourist routes, signposts are also written in the Latin alphabet. Travellers can take their own car (see *Travel – International*) or hire a vehicle; tariffs include the cost of insurance. Chauffeured cars are available in major cities. Sample distances: Moscow to St Petersburg: 692km (432 miles); Moscow to Minsk: 690km (429 miles); Moscow to Rostov-on-Don: 1198km (744 miles); Moscow to Odessa: 1347km (837 miles). **Bus:** Long-distance coach services have only recently become open to foreigners. They are a great way of seeing the country but patience is a necessity and getting lost is commonplace. **Traffic regulations:** Traffic drives on the right. Speeds are limited to 60kph (37mph) in built-up areas, 90kph (55mph) in non-built-up areas and 100kph (62mph) on highways (visiting motorists who have been driving for less than two years must not exceed 70kph (43mph)). Hooting the horn is forbidden except when to do so might prevent an accident. Motorists should avoid driving at night if possible. It is forbidden to carry unauthorised passengers or pick up hitch-hikers. Driving under the influence of drugs or alcohol is forbidden. Every car must display registration plates and stickers denoting the country of registration and be fitted with seat belts, a first-aid kit, a fire extinguisher and an emergency sign (triangle) or red light. In case of an accident, contact the nearest traffic inspection officer and make sure all participants fill in written statements, to be witnessed by a militia inspector. All repairs will be at the foreign motorist's expense. **Documentation:** An International Driving Permit and a national licence with authorised translations are necessary. Visitors travelling in their own cars must also possess the following documents at all times: passport and visa; itinerary card bearing visitor's name and citizenship, car registration number and full details of itinerary presented upon entry to the Russian Federation relating to the route to be taken and the date and place of stopovers; form provided by Customs on arrival guaranteeing that the car will be taken out of the Russian Federation on departure; petrol vouchers purchased at the border; and insurance cover documents. A road tax is payable upon entry to the country (see end of *Travel – International*). Motor insurance for travel within the Russian Federation should be arranged prior to departure, or upon entry to the Russian Federation at the offices of *Ingosstrakh*, the Russian Federation foreign insurance agency. Contact the Embassy or a specialist tour operator for further details.

URBAN:

Public transport in the cities is comprehensive and cheap. Many services are electric traction (metro, tramway, trolleybus). Stations on the Moscow and St Petersburg metros are always elegant and often palatial. Entry to the underground is by tokens, which are inserted into the ticket barrier. Fares are standard for the various forms of transport; weekly and monthly passes are available. Buses operate 0500-0000. Tickets are available in strips or booklets from people outside the metro station or from the drivers directly. Tickets must be punched in the machine provided on the bus. Taxis are also available; they can be hailed in the street, hired at a rank or booked by telephone. It is safer to use officially marked taxis; they are yellow with chequered signs on the doors. Taxis should not be shared with strangers.

Travel Times: The following chart gives approximate travel times (in hours and minutes) from **Moscow** to other major cities/towns in the Russian Federation:

	Air	Rail	Sea
Khabarovsk	7.30	-	-
St Petersburg	1.30	9.00	-
Irkutsk	7.00	88.00	-
Volgograd	1.30	-	-

Travel Advice

Because of the security situation in the North Caucasus, travellers are advised against all travel to Chechnya, Ingushetia, Dagestan and to the eastern and southern parts of Stavropol Krai that border Chechnya and Dagestan. Travellers are advised against all but essential travel to North Ossetia, Karachai-Cherkessia and Kabardino-Balkaria (including the Elbrus area).

There is a high threat from terrorism in Russia, including suicide bombings in public places. Attacks have occurred most frequently in Moscow and in the North Caucasus. Travellers should be vigilant at all times and also watch out for pickpockets and street crime, especially in large cities and in busy areas, eg railway concourses.

This advice is based on information provided by the Foreign and Commonwealth Office in the UK. It is correct at time of publishing. As the situation can change rapidly, visitors are advised to contact the following organisaions for the latest travel advice:

British Foreign and Commonwealth Office
Tel: (0845) 850 2829.
Website: www.fco.gov.uk

US Department of State
Website: http://travel.state.gov/travel

Accommodation

HOTELS:

There are over 2500 hotels in the Russian Federation, of which about 100 specialise in accommodating foreign guests. Some hotels meet international standards, whereas others are very basic. Direct reservations by clients are on the increase. Whatever class of accommodation, it is advisable not to leave valuables in hotel rooms and to lock the door before going to sleep.

BED & BREAKFAST:

Several companies provide bed & breakfast accommodation with English-speaking families in Moscow, St Petersburg and other cities.

CAMPING/CARAVANNING:

Camping holidays are now offered by a number of independent companies.

YOUTH HOSTELS:

There are currently seven hostels in the Russian Federation. Hostels tend to be safer and cleaner than hotels of similar prices. Reservations from outside the Russian Federation should be made at least three to four weeks in advance. Note there is no age restriction.

Note: Anyone travelling on a tourist visa to the Russian Federation must (officially at least) have accommodation arranged before arrival.

ACCOMMODATION INFORMATION

Russian Youth Hostel Association
St Petersburg International Hostel, 3rd Sovetskaya, 28, St Petersburg 193069, Russian Federation
Tel: (812) 329 8018.
Website: www.hostelling-russia.ru

Top Things To See

• The focal point of **Moscow** is the **Red Square**, on one side of which is the **Kremlin** surrounded by a thick red fortress wall containing 20 towers altogether. The **Sobakina Tower**, designed to withstand sieges, contains a secret escape passage. The **Tainitskaya Tower** translates as the 'Tower of Secrets', because it also had a secret subterranean passage leading to the river. The **Trinity Gate** is the tallest of the towers. The **Water-Hoist Tower** conveyed water to the Kremlin. The **Nabatnaya Tower** contained an alarm bell that was rung in times of danger. In the Kremlin grounds, the **Uspensky Cathedral** (1475-79), designed by the Italian architect Aristotle Fioravanti, contains three of the oldest Russian icons. The tsars were crowned here; Ivan the Terrible's throne is situated near the entrance. Also within the Kremlin stand the 14th-century **Grand Kremlin Palace** and the golden-domed **Belfry of Ivan the Great**. **St Basil's Cathedral** (built 1555-60), at another end of the square, famous for its brightly coloured domes. As the story goes, Ivan the Terrible was so overwhelmed by its beauty that he blinded the architect so that he could never create another building as impressive as this. Opposite St Basil's, the **Spassky** (**Redeemer's**) **Gate** is the main entrance to the Kremlin, built in 1491 by Pietro Antonio Solario. The **Blagoveshchensky** (**Annunciation**) **Cathedral** was built for Ivan III. It is extravagantly decorated, from its copper domes to its agate- and jasper-tiled floors. It contains 16th-century frescoes and a precious collection of icons. Although there is talk of finally burying Lenin's embalmed body, **Lenin's Mausoleum** is still open to the public on certain days. **Arbat Street** is the main thoroughfare of a traditionally bohemian quarter. Today it is a pedestrian zone with crafts and artists' stalls and street performers. **Novodevichy Convent** near **Sportivnaya metro station** houses a museum of rare and ancient Russian art, and is one of the finest examples of 16th- and 17th-century architecture in the city. The neighbouring **Ostozhenka** and **Prechistenka Streets** feature urban mansions and estates associated with many classic Russian authors, including Tolstoy. **Herzen Street** is one of the oldest in Moscow. A boat tour on the **Moskva River** is a pleasant way of discovering the city. Excursions start at the **Kutuzovskaya Pier**, accessible from **Kutuzovskaya Metro**. The river is a

superb vantage point to view the **White House** (the **Parliament Building**), scene of the dramatic siege of 1991, as well as many of the sights listed above.

• Several ancient towns of great historical, architectural and spiritual significance make up the **Golden Ring**, extending northeast from Moscow. They are a rich collection of kremlins (citadels), monasteries, cathedrals and fortresses. Since many were founded on river banks, a cruise is a pleasant way of discovering the region. Modern boats plying the **Volga** afford comfortable accommodation. In **Sofrin**, the literary and artistic museum of Abramtsevo houses paintings by Repin, Serov and Vrubel. The museum is surrounded by parkland and birch woods. Ornate traditional Russian huts are dotted around the estate. **Rostov Veliky**, founded in the ninth century, has a beautiful Kremlin and Cathedral of the Dormition, and overlooks the shores of the **Nero Lake**, surrounded by ancient monasteries. Neighbouring **Yaroslavl** lies on the banks of the Volga, and contains a host of ancient churches, most notably the **Transfiguration of the Saviour Cathedral**, built in the early 16th century. **Kostroma** is a renowned cheese-making centre. Its most outstanding building is the **Ipatievski Monastery-Fortress**. Built during the first half of the 14th century, it became the Romanovs' residence three centuries later. **Suzdal** is perhaps the most important town in the Golden Ring. It boasts 50 well-preserved examples of ancient architecture contained within a relatively small area, providing a wonderfully coherent vision of its past. The wives of tsars and boyars were exiled to the Blessed Virgin Convent. **Uglich** is another beautiful town on the banks of the Volga, notable for its Kremlin and the Chambers of Prince Dmitry. Prince Dmitry, son and heir of Ivan the Terrible drowned here, after accidentally being dropped in a river by his nurse.

• Spend some time in the Federation's second-largest city, 715km (444 miles) northwest of Moscow, and known both as a cultural centre and for its elegant buildings. **St Petersburg** is spread over 42 islands in the delta of the **River Neva** and, in comparison to Moscow, tends to be more Eastern in character. It was built by Peter the Great in 1703 and remained the capital for 200 years of Tsarist Russia. Known as Petrograd after the civil war, and Leningrad during the Soviet period, the city reverted to its original name in 1991 by popular demand. Wide boulevards, tranquil canals, bridges and some of the best examples of tsarist architecture gave rise to the epithet the 'Venice of the North'. Although badly damaged in World War II, much of it is now reconstructed. In June and July the city has the famous '**White Nights**', when darkness recedes to a brief twilight and the city is imbued with an unusual aura. The **Palace Square** and the **Winter Palace** are among the most popular attractions for followers of Russian history. **The Hermitage** houses the vast private collection of the tsars. While exploring the city the visitor will inevitably see the **Alexandrovskaya Column**. St **Isaac's Cathedral** is one of the biggest dome buildings of the world and, like the **Kazansky Cathedral**, houses a museum. The gorgeously decorated **Yusupov Mansion** was built for the Romanovs. Its rooms are sumptuously decorated in mid-19th-century style. The mansion's concert hall is now a venue for recitals, theatrical productions, opera and ballet. A waxwork exhibition commemorates Rasputin, who died in the building. The grand **Nevsky Prospekt**, dominated by the spire of the Admiralty Building, is one of the city's main thoroughfares and is lined by opulent buildings. These include the **Kazan Cathedral** and the **Church of the Resurrection**. The collection at the Russian Museum covers nearly 1000 years of Russian art history. Nevsky Prospect crosses the **Fontanka River** at **Anichkov Bridge**, and continues to **Palace Square**. The homes of Dostoyevsky, Pushkin, Anna Akhmatova and Rimsky-Korsakov serve as museums

dedicated to their former occupants. The cruiser *Aurora* is berthed on the Neva. A blank shot was fired from her bow to give a signal to start the assault on the Winter Palace in 1917. Lenin also announced the victory of the Revolution from here.

- The following palaces beyond the outskirts of St Petersburg are collectively known as the **Summer Palaces**. **Petrodvorets** is a former summer palace of Tsar Peter the Great and is known for its beautiful cascades and fountains. **Oranienbaum** was built as the summer residence of Alexander Menshikov, Peter the Great's associate. From here, Alexander oversaw the construction of the **Kronstadt naval fortress** on the nearby **Kotlin Island**. Its **Chinese** and **Sliding Hill Pavilions** are exceptionally beautiful. The **Grand Catherine Palace** at **Tsarskoye Selo** was built for Peter the Great's wife. The Scottish architect Charles Cameron designed some of the interiors, although a greater number by Bartholomeo Rastrelli survive. Cameron also designed the subtle buildings at nearby **Pavlovsk**, which were intended to complement the parkland's beauty. The park itself, designed by the Italian Gonzago, is one of the finest landscaped parks in Europe.
- Locate some of the Russian Federation's wonderful **wildlife**. The **Kursche Spit** is a beautiful sand peninsula extending nearly 100km (63 miles) along the coast, and is a rich habitat for plants and animals. Near **Vladivostok** is the **Ussuriysk taiga**, a unique habitat for plants of the pre-glacial period, as well as tigers, leopard, bison, boar and bears.
- Step back into a momentous time at **Volgograd**, formerly Stalingrad. The **Victory Museum** celebrates the victory over the Nazis, and the whole city is a monument to the year-long battle that took place there. Tours to the battlefields are available. The town stands at the confluence of the Volga and Don rivers. Visits to outlying **Cossack** and Volga-German villages provide a further glimpse of the region's history.
- Find utter isolation in **Siberia**, which covers an area of over 12,800,000 sq km (4,000,000 sq miles), containing unimaginably vast stretches of marshy forest (*taiga*). This 'sleeping land', the literal translation of its name, possesses a million lakes, 53,000 rivers and an enormous wealth of natural resources. Although the temperature in winter falls well below freezing point, the weather in summer can be very warm. Much of the region has been opened up, including **Sakhalin Island** and the **Chukchi Peninsula** just across the **Bering Strait** from Alaska. Air-hopping is one way of discovering the wilderness. A famous alternative is the *Trans-Siberian Railway*, the longest continuous railway in the world, a journey which is one of the greatest travel adventures. The line cuts through an area bigger than Western Europe, crossing a landscape which includes arctic wastes, tundra and steppe. The most scenic part of the journey is between **Irkutsk** and **Khabarovsk**.
- See the world's deepest lake, **Lake Baikal**, which is accessible from Irkutsk by hydrofoil during the summer. With a depth of 1637m (5371ft), it is the world's deepest lake. Its surface area equals that of Belgium and The Netherlands put together. It is 25 million years old, and it would take three months to walk around its 2000km (1243 mile) shoreline. The purity of its water is maintained by millions of tiny crayfish, providing a habitat for a wide variety of fish, including sturgeon, loach, grayling and omul (a type of salmon), one of many species unique to Baikal. Its shores are a feeding ground for wildfowl and the occasional bear. Freshwater seal colonies are found around the **Ushkan Islands** in the centre of the lake. **Olkhon Island** is the site of primitive rock drawings and a unique necropolis of an ancient Siberian tribe whose members are thought to have been ancestors of indigenous North Americans. The local climate is often harsh; the surface of the entire lake often freezes over in winter (trains were moved across the ice during the Russo-Japanese war). The *sarma* wind can sink boats and rip the roofs off buildings.
- Experience Buddhism in Russia – what many might consider to be a surreal sight. But many of the inhabitants of the Buryat Republic are, indeed, Buddhists. Dozens of picturesque **temples** (***datsans***) sprang up round Lake Baikal after Empress Elizabeth, Peter the Great's daughter, recognised the Buddhist religion in the Russian Federation. Although most *datsans* were destroyed during the 1930s, many of their treasures were preserved in the **Russian Orthodox church** in **Ulaan Ude**, the capital. The **Sandalwood Buddha**, on display in the town's Exhibition Hall, is said to have been made with the Buddha himself sitting as a model.

Top Things To Do

- Have a night out in **Moscow**, where you are spoiled for choice as to what to do. The world-famous **Bolshoi Opera and Ballet Theatre** at **Teatralnaya Square** dates from 1824 and has an interior colour scheme of red and gold. Alternatively, the **Moscow Circus** is equally – and justifiably – famous, with animal acts and clowns and more technical wonders.
- Discover the **handicrafts** of the Russian Federation. The **State Museum of Ceramics** in **Kuskovo**, 10km (6 miles) from the centre of Moscow, has a fascinating collection of Russian china, porcelain and glass. **Arkhangelskoye Estate**, a museum housed in a palace, exhibits European paintings and sculptures. **Zhostovo**, 30km (19 miles) from Moscow, is a centre renowned for its lacquered trays, and **Fedoskino**, 35km (22 miles) from Moscow, produces lacquer miniatures, brooches and other knick-knacks.
- Fly in a **MIG-29 aircraft**, a fighter capable of more than twice the speed of sound, that was once part of the formidable Soviet Air Force.
- Go **skiing** in the **Caucasus**, at **Teberda-Dombay** (west) and at **Baksan Elbrus** (north), and **Kamchatka**. **Cross-country skiing** is available outside the city at **Olgino** on the Gulf of Finland. **Heli-skiing** is now available in the Caucasus and Kamchatka where, it is claimed, the powder snow rivals that of Colorado and there is a guarantee of snow throughout the short season. Amid the wilds of **Karelia**, north of **St Petersburg**, **cross-country skiing** is routed through the *taiga* and over a terrain of frozen rivers and lakes including **Ladoga** and **Onega**.
- **Trekking** can climb to altitudes of 3200m (10,499ft), where the landscape changes en route from alpine meadows of red poppies to snow-capped peaks and scenic plateaux. Until recently, previously unexploited areas of the **Fan Mountains**, known as **Matcha**, had never been trodden by Western feet. **Perm** in the **Middle Ural Mountains** is home to some of the rarer birds of prey. The **Baseguy National Reserve** has been created on the **Kama River Basin** and ornithologists can get glimpses of eagle owls, great grey owls, Ural owls and golden eagles. The **Caucasus Mountains**, which stretch from the **Black Sea** to the **Caspian Sea**, separate Russia from Armenia and Georgia. Dominating the range is **Mount Elbrus**, at 5642m (18,510ft), the highest peak in Europe. The jagged peaks overlook a vast vegetation range from palm trees to deciduous forest and flower-carpeted valleys. Trekking, again strenuous, is possible across the beautiful scenery of the peak and its neighbours. Six-day Elbrus trekking circuits and three-summit climbs in the **Adyl-Su Valley** that include the Elbrus peak are also available.
- Siberia used to be associated with salt mines and permafrost, yet the **Altai region** of southern Siberia rivals Switzerland for rolling hills, snowy peaks, flowers and pine forests. Undiscovered areas of Siberia, on the borders of Kazakhstan and Mongolia where summer temperatures hit 22°C (71°F), are heady with the scents of its flowers, herbs and trees. **Mount Belukha** rises to 4506m (14,784ft) over a few scattered villages in an area where the bear population outnumbers the human. Not unsurprisingly, among tours offered are botany itineraries through June and July with safari camp accommodation.
- Go **ice skating** in St Petersburg's **Central Recreation Park**, a favourite among skaters, and also having a ski centre. Many other towns and cities have artificial ice-skating rinks for the summer but during the hard winters, frozen lakes and rivers ensure plenty of room for skating.
- Those interested in Russia's achievements in the field of space travel should visit **Star City**, just outside **Moscow**, which is a **cosmonaut training complex** open to visitors.
- Recreate on some of the Russian Federation's lovely **beaches** along the **Black Sea**. **Rostov-on-Don** contains several parks, four theatres, an orchestra and a racecourse, as well as a beach. **Sochi** is a popular resort with a subtropical climate and famous health spa, situated on the Black Sea's eastern coast beneath the dramatic **Caucasus Mountains**. For those who want a resort-based holiday, **Dagomys** is ideal. Overlooking the Black Sea, it is beautifully located amongst thickly wooded hills and subtropical greenery.

TOURIST INFORMATION

Russian National Tourist Office in the UK
70 Piccadilly, London W1J 8HP, UK
Tel: (020) 7495 7555.
Website: www.inntel-moscow.co.uk *or* www.visitrussia.org.uk

Intourist Ltd in the UK
7 Wellington Terrace, Notting Hill, London W2 4LW, UK
Tel: (020) 7727 4100 *or* (0870) 112 1232 (reservation line).
Website: www.intouristuk.com

Russian National Group in the USA
130 West 42nd Street, Suite 1804, New York, NY 10036, USA
Tel: (212) 575 3431 *or* (877) 221 7120 (toll-free in USA).
Website: www.russia-travel.com

Entertainment

FOOD & DRINK: The kind of food visitors will eat from day to day depends on which city they are visiting and the time of year. Breakfast is often similar to the Scandinavian, with cold meats, boiled eggs and bread served with Russian tea. For the midday and evening meal the food is often more traditional, again depending on the region.

National specialities:

- *Kasha* (porridge) is a staple breakfast dish, made with milk and oats, buckwheat or semolina.
- *Blini* (small pancakes filled with caviar, fish, melted butter or sour cream).
- *Ponchiki* (hot sugared doughnuts).
- *Pirozhky* (fried rolls with different fillings, usually meat).
- *Borshch*, a beetroot soup served hot with sour cream.
- *Pelmeni* (meat dumplings).

Things to know: City-centre bars close around midnight.

National drinks:

- *Chai* (sweet tea served without milk).
- Vodka (often flavoured and coloured with herbs and spices such as *zubrovka* (a kind of grass), *ryabinovka* (steeped with rowan-tree berries), *starka* (dark, smooth, aged vodka) and *pertsovka* (with hot pepper). *Posolskaya*, *Stolichnaya* and *Rossiskaya* are popular brands.
- *Krushon* (cold 'punch'; champagne, brandy and summer fruit are poured into a hollowed watermelon and chilled for several hours).
- *Nalivka* (sweet liqueur made with fruit or berries).
- *Nastoika* is a fortified wine made of herbs, leaves, flowers, fruit and roots of plants with medicinal properties.

Tipping: Hotels in Moscow and other large cities include a 10 to 15 per cent service charge. Otherwise 10 per cent is customary.

NIGHTLIFE: Theatre, circus, concert and variety performances are the main evening entertainments. Tickets are available in advance or from ticket booths immediately before performances. Visitors should note that prices for foreigners are usually much higher than those paid by Russian nationals. The repertoire of theatres provides a change of programme almost nightly. In the course of one month, 30 different productions may be presented by the *Bolshoi Opera and Ballet Company*. Details of performances can be obtained on arrival. Visitors should apply to the service bureau of their hotel. All of these establishments are open 0600-2200.

SHOPPING: A wide range of goods such as watches, cameras, wines and spirits, furs, ceramics and glass, jewellery and toys may be bought in Moscow and St Petersburg. Shops take payment in roubles and, occasionally, by credit card. It is necessary to allow extra time for souvenir hunting: shopping can be a time-consuming activity, owing to the relatively chaotic state of the retail trade in the Russian Federation. It is also advisable to shop around, as prices vary significantly. A good strategy is to choose your souvenirs in a department store such as *GUM* (on Red Square), and then buy them in a smaller, less centrally located shop. *Kholui* and *Palekh* lacquered boxes make attractive souvenirs. Traditional and satirical *Matryoshka* dolls (wooden dolls within dolls) are widely available. *Khokhloma* wooden cups, saucers and spoons are painted gold, red and black. *Dymkovskaya Igrushka* are pottery figurines based on popular folklore characters. Engraved amber, *Gzhel* porcelain, *Vologda* lace and *Fabergé* eggs and jewellery are highly sought after. A *samovar* makes a good souvenir. Antiquities, valuables, works of art and manuscripts other than those offered for sale in souvenir shops may not be taken out of the Russian Federation without an export licence. **Shopping hours:** Mon-Sat 0900-1900. Most food shops are also open on Sunday. Department stores and supermarkets are open throughout lunchtime. Stores which are open 24 hours a day are becoming more common.

Business

- **GDP:** US$613 billion.
- **Main imports:** Machinery and equipment, consumer goods, medicine, meat, sugar and semi-finished metal products.
- **Main exports:** Petroleum, petroleum products, natural gas, wood and wood products, chemicals and civilian and military manufactures.
- **Main trade partners:** China (PR), France, Germany, Italy, Japan, Kazakhstan, The Netherlands, Switzerland, Turkey, Ukraine and USA

ECONOMY: The Russian Federaion is blessed by an abundance of natural resources of every description. This includes rich agricultural land from which grain, potatoes and livestock are the main products. Land reform has been one of the most awkward problems facing Russia's post-communist Governments: much has been turned over to private ownership but a substantial proportion, especially in the more remote areas, is still owned collectively. Agriculture now accounts for 5 per cent of total economic output while employing 13 per cent of the workforce. Russia has huge deposits of oil and gas – its major export earners – as well as coal and minerals including gold, diamonds, nickel, manganese, copper, iron ore and phosphates. Further unexploited deposits have been located and there are undoubtedly more to be discovered, but they are often in areas (such as the permafrost-covered regions of Siberia and the Russian Far East) where exploitation is technically difficult and transport systems limited.

Energy products and heavy industry – production of vehicles, metal goods, construction materials and machinery – are the kernel of Russia's industrial sector. Textiles and chemicals are other important industries. By contrast, Russia's light industry – especially production of consumer goods– is paltry, accounting for just 2 per cent of total industrial production. The fastest growing part of the economy since 1990 has been the service sector. Here, banking, insurance and property have developed from a base close to nothing, and services now account for just over half of economic output. Both the industrial and service sectors have been hampered by the paucity of small and medium-sized businesses: this is a major flaw in the Russian economy. The sheer size and diversity of the country has made economic reform in the Russian Federation a gargantuan task, especially by comparison with its former East European allies and the other 14 Soviet republics. The economy underwent significant contraction after 1990: Russian economic statistics are notoriously unreliable but, by 1998, it is likely that GDP had declined by between 35 and 50 per cent. That year, a combination of internal and external factors led to the virtual collapse of the economy which was staved off by a large financial injection from the IMF (of the order of US$22 billion). Since then, the economy has undergone a significant recovery with average annual growth of 5 per cent in the last five years (the figure in 2004 was 7.1 per cent). The Government has got on top of the hyper-inflation which caused so much damage in the initial stages of the reform process. At 12 per cent, current inflation is high by recent Western standards but not unmanageable. The official unemployment rate is 8.3 per cent, with considerable underemployment. Russia hosts a substantial informal or 'grey' economy in which between 25 and 40 per cent of the workforce are engaged to some extent; however, 25 per cent of the population of Russia live below the poverty line. But there are some causes for optimism: the success of the Putin Government in stabilising the economy has boosted international confidence, especially given the difficult situation inherited from his predecessor, Boris Yeltsin. In what amounted to a firesale, the Yeltsin Government sold off the major components of the Russian economy – including the vital oil and gas sector – at knock-down prices to favoured bidders. This process gave rise to the so-called 'oligarchs', a small group of immensely rich individuals who – mostly by virtue of political contacts, good judgement and luck – now own the bulk of the Russian economy. (It is estimated that 20 conglomerates are now responsible for 70 per cent of Russia's GDP.) There is little Putin can do about corporate ownership, but there are other areas where the Government can make a difference. Perhaps the most important of these is modernisation of the national infrastructure: the Russian Federation suffers from insufficient and poor-quality transport networks as well as an erratic and antiquated telecommunications system. Moreover, neither commercial law nor the taxation system are functional and effective, with the result that operating conditions for most businesses are difficult. Organised crime thrives in such an environment: billions of dollars of international aid have simply disappeared. Moreover, the removal of exchange controls (as demanded by Western financial donors) has meant that there has also been a large legitimate exodus of money from Russia. In May 2004, five former Soviet bloc states and the three ex-Soviet Baltic republics joined the European Union. This development – unimaginable 15 years ago – presents both opportunities and dangers for the Russian Federation. On balance, the Russian economy will probably benefit from immediate proximity to the EU. Russia's trade patterns have gradually shifted towards Western industrialised nations (not least to meet their high energy demands).

BUSINESS ETIQUETTE: As a result of recent economic changes which have taken place in the Russian Federation, there are now many thousands of private companies in operation and international business relations have become active. The main business centres are Moscow, St Petersburg, Nizhny Novgorod, Novosibirsk and Vladivostock. **Office hours:** Mon-Fri 0900-1800.

COMMERCIAL INFORMATION

The Trade Delegation of the Russian Federation in the ULK
32/3 Highgate West Hill, London N6 6NL, UK
Tel: (020) 8340 1907 or 4491 or 3272.
Website: www.rustradeuk.org

Russo-British Chamber of Commerce in the UK
42 Southwark Street, London SE1 1UN, UK
Tel: (020) 7403 1706.
Website: www.rbcc.co.uk

Ministry for Economic Development and Trade for the Russian Federation – Department for Economic Co-operation with Europe
18/1 Ovchinnikovskaya nab, 113324 Moscow, Russian Federation
Tel: (095) 950 1779.
Website: www.economy.gov.ru

Chamber of Commerce and Industry of the Russian Federation
St. Ilyinka 6, 109012 Moscow, Russian Federation
Tel: (095) 929 0009.
Website: www.tpprf.ru

Intourist Travel Ltd
7 Wellington Terrace, Notting Hill, London W2 4LW, UK
Tel: (020) 7727 4100 (reservation line) or (0870) 112 1232 (general information).
Website: www.intouristuk.com

Rwanda

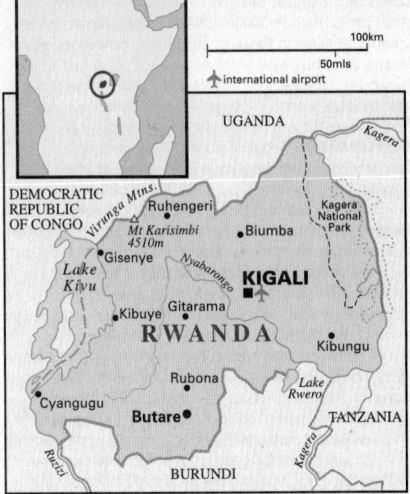

Location: Central Africa.

Time: GMT + 2.

Overview

Also known as 'the land of a thousand hills', Rwanda is a landlocked country of lovely and various landscapes. The Virunga volcanic mountains have high altitude-forests, world-famous mountain gorillas, and Lake Kivu offers beautiful beaches, jutting peninsulas and an archipelago of islands.

Many visitors have been surprised by the fact that Rwandans are now harmoniously living together only 10 years after the genocide that threatened to shatter the social fabric of the country. Reconciliation has not been easy. Upon assuming office, the Government of National Unity inherited a deeply scarred nation.

Sometimes, people cannot set Rwanda's recent history in a context. People need to go as far back as the late 13th century when pastoral Tutsi tribes arrived from the south and conquered the agricultural Hutu and hunter-gatherer Twa inhabitants of Rwanda, establishing a feudal kingdom. A unified state was established by King Kigeri Rwabuguri during the 19th century, but this lasted only until 1890 when Rwanda was annexed as a province of German East Africa. As part of the post-World War I settlement, Belgium was later granted the right to govern Rwanda-Urundi under a League of Nations mandate. The Belgians sponsored the continued dominance of the Tutsi minority at the expense of the Hutu but were forced, in the early 1960s, to concede internal autonomy and then Independence under majority Hutu rule. Intercommunal violence between Hutus and Tutsis continued and a Tutsi Government-in-exile was even established in the Ugandan capital, Kampala.

In 1973, Major-General Juvénal Habyarimana led a bloodless coup and established a Hutu-dominated military Government. A few years later, the country's sole political party was founded, dominated by Hutus. Sporadic fighting resumed in the early 1990s. Hutu extremists decided upon a 'final solution'. It required a single trigger: this was a plane crash which killed Hutu President Habyarimana in 1994. Encouraged by official broadcasts, armed militias set about the systematic murder of their ethnic and political opponents, largely Tutsis. The international community, and especially the UN, proved reluctant to intervene. There was particular opposition from the Americans, still scarred by their experience in Somalia, and the French, covertly backing the Habyarimana Government. The best estimate is that around 800,000 people were tragically and horrifically killed.

From their bases in Uganda, the Rwandan Patriotic Front launched a full-scale invasion, but the bulk of the Hutu militia had fled to the neighbouring Democratic Republic of Congo – a fact that has crafted a violent rift between the two countries.

Nevertheless, Rwandans are not only living together today but they are striving to be recognised as one people. Rwanda is a country of unimaginable beauty and such beauty defies its violent past: may it continue to defy it forever.

General Information

AREA: 26,338 sq km (10,169 sq miles).
POPULATION: 8.6 million (UN, 2005).
POPULATION DENSITY: 326.52 per sq km.
CAPITAL: Kigali. **Population:** 800,000 (estimate 2005).
GEOGRAPHY: Rwanda is a small mountainous country in central Africa, bordered to the north by Uganda, to the east by Tanzania, to the south by Burundi and to the west by the Democratic Republic of Congo. The country is divided by great peaks of up to 3000m (9842ft), which run across the country from north to south. The Virunga volcanoes, rising steeply from Lake Kivu in the west, slope down first to a hilly central plateau and further eastwards to an area of marshy lakes around the upper reaches of the A'Kagera River, where the A'Kagera National Park is situated.
GOVERNMENT: Republic since 1962. Gained independence from Belgium in 1962. **Head of State:** President Paul Kagame since 2000. **Head of Government:** Prime Minister Bernard Makuza since 2000. **Recent history:** Domestically, the Government faced a formidable task of reconstruction and reconciliation. The architects of the 1994 genocide have been (and still are being) tried before a UN- run tribunal based in Tanzania. Lesser offenders are dealt with in Rwanda. The Government, led by former army chief Paul Kagame, has a fairly impressive record under extremely difficult circumstances. The country relies heavily on western aid to sustain its economy. However, there are signs of an increasingly dictatorial attitude on the part of the Government, manifested in the Presidential and Parliamentary elections held in the summer of 2003: amid numerous allegations of intimidation and ballot rigging, Kagame and the Rwandan Patriotic Front won both polls with a huge majority. Given the Tutsi dominance of the RPF, there is a clear danger of a future repeat of the ethnic violence which has disfigured Rwanda since Independence.
Executive power is held by the President, who is directly elected to serve a seven-year term. The legislature is the bicameral National Assembly. This comprises the 80-member Umutwe w'Abadepite (Chamber of Deputies) and the 26-member Umutwe wa Sena (Senate). The Chamber of Deputies serves a five-year term: 53 members are elected by proportional representation, 24 seats are reserved for women, two for the National Youth Council and the remaining seat for the disabled. Members of the Senate serve an eight-year term: eight are appointed by the President; the remainder are indirectly elected.
LANGUAGE: The official languages are Kinyarwanda, French and English. Kiswahili is used for trade and commerce.
RELIGION: Animist (50 per cent), Christian (mostly Roman Catholic) and an Islamic minority.
ELECTRICITY: 220 volts AC, 50Hz.
SOCIAL CONVENTIONS: The traditional way of life is based on agriculture and cattle. The Rwandans settle in the fertile areas, but they do not form villages, each family being surrounded by its own fields. The majority of the population belong to the Hutu tribe. There is a significant Tutsi minority (15 per cent) and a smaller minority of Twa, a mixed race of traditional potters and hunters and said to be the country's first inhabitants. Normal social courtesies apply.

Climate

Despite its proximity to the Equator, the climate in Rwanda is cooled by the high altitude. It is warm throughout most of the country but cooler in the mountains. There are two rainy seasons: mid-January to April and mid-October to mid-December.
Required clothing: Lightweights are required for most of the year with warmer clothes for cooler upland evenings. Rainwear is advisable.

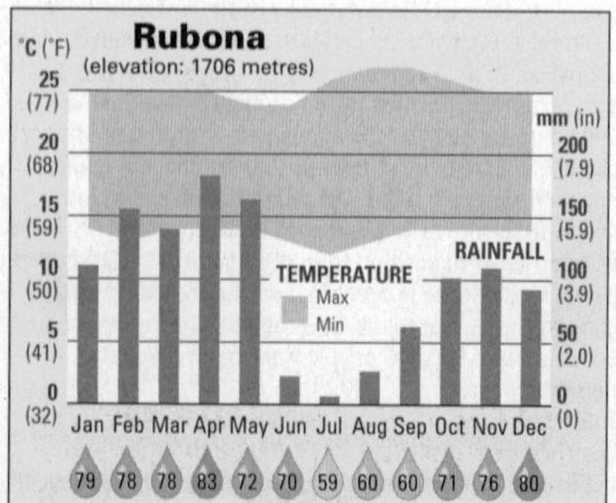

Communications

Telephone: There are no area codes. There is International Direct Dialling but this may be subject to occasional disruptions.
Mobile telephone: Roaming agreements exist with one international mobile phone company. Handsets can be hired. Coverage is quite unreliable.
Internet: There are Internet cafes in Kigali, including one at the airport.
Post: Post office hours (Kigali): Mon-Fri 0800-1200 and 1400-1700, Sat 0800-1200. Airmail to Western Europe takes approximately two weeks.
MEDIA: Many of Rwanda's broadcasters are Government owned. The first private radio station was launched in 2004.
Press: There is a growing number of English-language newspapers such as *The New Times, Rwanda Herald* and *Rwanda Newsline. Umesco* is a Kinyarwanda-language publication. Publications in French or Kinyarwanda are fortnightly or quarterly.
TV: *Télévision Rwandaise (TVR)* is state-owned.
Radio: *Radio Rwanda* is state-owned and operates in English, French, Kinyarwanda and Swahili. Priate radio stations include *Radio 10, Flash FM, Contact FM, City Radio, Radio Izuba and Radio Maria.*

Passport/Visa

	Passport Required?	Visa Required?	Return Ticket Required?
Full British	Yes	Yes/1	Yes
Australian	Yes	Yes	Yes
Canadian	Yes	Yes	Yes
USA	Yes	Yes	Yes
Other EU	Yes	Yes/1	Yes
Japanese	Yes	Yes	Yes

Note: *Regulations and requirements may be subject to change at short notice, and you are advised to contact the appropriate diplomatic or consular authority before finalising travel arrangements. Any numbers in the chart refer to the footnotes below.*

PASSPORTS: Passports valid for at least six months required by all.
VISAS: Required by all except transit passengers continuing their journey within 24 hours by the same or first connecting aircraft, provided holding onward or return documentation and not leaving the airport.
Note: (a) **1.** nationals of Canada, Congo (Dem Rep), Germany, Kenya, Mauritius, South Africa, Sweden, Tanzania, Uganda, the UK and the USA can receive a visa free of charge upon arrival for stays of up to three months. (b) nationals of Burundi and China (PR) (only if holding a Hong Kong (SAR) passport) receive a visa free of charge for stays up to one month upon arrival.
Types of visa and cost: *Single-entry/Multiple-entry*: £50.
Validity: Three months.
Application to: Consulate (or consular section at Embassy); see *Passport/Visa Information*.
Application requirements: (a) Valid passport. (b) Two passport-size photos. (c) Two completed application forms. (d) Company letters or guarantee for business trips. (e) Fee, payable by company certified cheque, postal order or cash. (f) A stamped, self-addressed registered envelope with all postal applications.
Working days required: 24 hours.
Temporary residence: Visas can be extended at the Immigration Office in Kigali.

PASSPORT/VISA INFORMATION

Embassy of the Republic of Rwanda in the UK
120-22 Seymour Place, London W1H 1NR, UK
Tel: (020) 7224 9832.
Website: www.ambarwanda.org.uk
Opening hours: Mon-Fri 0930-1730; 0930-1300 (visa section)

Embassy of the Republic of Rwanda in the USA
1714 New Hampshire Avenue, NW, Washington, DC 20009, USA
Tel: (202) 232 2882-4.
Website: www.rwandaembassy.org

Money

Currency: Rwanda Franc (RWF) = 100 centimes. Notes are in denominations of RWF5000, 1000, 500 and 100. Coins are in denominations of RWF50, 20, 10, 5, 2 and 1.
Credit & debit cards: Accepted at only a few hotels in Kigali. MasterCard is most widely accepted, with more limited use of Diners Club. Check with your credit or debit card company for details of merchant acceptability and other services that may be available.
Traveller's cheques: It may be difficult to change traveller's cheques outside Kigali.
Currency restrictions: The import and export of local currency is limited to RWF5000. The import and export of foreign currency is unlimited, provided declared on arrival.
Banking hours: Mon-Fri 0800-1200 and 1400-1800, Sat 0800-1300.
Exchange rate indicators:
Rate at time of publishing
£1.00= RWF986.04
$1.00= RWF557.88

Duty Free

The following items may be imported into Rwanda by persons over 16 years of age without incurring customs duty:
Two cartons of cigarettes and 2l of alcoholic beverages.
Note: Game trophies can only be exported with special permission of the Game Department.

Public Holidays

Below are listed Public Holidays for the January 2006-June 2007 period.
2006: Jan 1 New Year's Day. **Jan 28** Democracy Day. **Apr 7** Genocide Memorial Day. **May 1** Labour Day. **Jul 1** Independence Day. **Jul 4** Liberation Day. **Aug 1** Harvest Festival. **Aug 15** Assumption. **Sep 8** Culture Day. **Sep 25** Republic Day. **Dec 25** Christmas Day. **Dec 26** Boxing Day.
2007: Jan 1 New Year's Day. **Jan 28** Democracy Day. **Apr 7** Genocide Memorial Day. **May 1** Labour Day.

Health

	Special Precautions?	Certificate Required?
Yellow Fever	Yes	1
Cholera	Yes	2
Typhoid & Polio	3	N/A
Malaria	4	N/A

Note: *Regulations and requirements may be subject to change at short notice, and you are advised to contact your doctor well in advance of your intended date of departure. Any numbers in the chart refer to the footnotes below.*

Note: There is a constant danger of disease, owing to the lack of sanitation. The risk of epidemics is high.
1: A *yellow fever* vaccination certificate is required from all travellers over one year of age.
2: Following WHO guidelines issued in 1973, a *cholera* vaccination certificate is not a condition of entry to Rwanda. However, *cholera* is a serious risk in this country and precautions are essential. In early January 2006, there was an outbreak of *cholera* in Masaka, a suburb on the outskirts of Kigali. Seventeen people were reported to have died and 150 were hospitalised. Customs officials may demand to see some proof of immunisation. Up-to-date advice should be sought before deciding whether these precautions should include vaccination, as medical opinion is divided over its effectiveness; see the *Health* appendix for further information.
3: *Typhoid* is a risk, especially in rural areas.
4: *Malaria* risk exists all year throughout the country. The predominant, malignant *falciparum* strain is reported to be highly resistant to chloroquine and resistant to sulfadoxine-pyrimethamine.
Food & drink: Visitors are advised to bring their own supplies of food, bottled water and vitamins. Clean water is scarce, and all water should be regarded as being potentially contaminated. Water used for drinking, brushing teeth or making ice should have first been boiled or otherwise sterilised. Milk is unpasteurised and should be boiled. Powdered or tinned milk is available and is advised, but make sure that it is reconstituted with pure water. Avoid dairy products that are likely to have been made from unboiled milk. Only eat well-cooked meat and fish, preferably served hot. Pork, salad and mayonnaise may carry increased risk. Vegetables should be cooked and fruit peeled.
Other risks: *Bilharzia (schistosomiasis)* is present. Avoid swimming and paddling in fresh water; swimming pools that are well chlorinated and maintained are safe. *Dengue fever, filariasis, leishmaniasis* and *Rift Valley fever* are present. *Typhus fever, trypanosomiasis* (sleeping sickness), *onchocerciasis* (river blindness), *hepatitis A* and *E* are widespread; *hepatitis B* is highly endemic. *Menigococcal meningitis* and *TB* occur.
Rabies is present. For those at high risk, vaccination before arrival should be considered. If you are bitten, seek medical advice without delay. For more information, consult the *Health* appendix.
Health care: Medical facilities are severely limited and extremely overburdened. Almost all medical facilities in Kigali were destroyed during the civil war, but the situation

is now improving and most hospitals function to an acceptable level. However, medical insurance, including cover for emergency repatriation, is essential. Visitors are advised to bring their own personal medication.

Travel - International

AIR:

There is no direct commercial air service to Rwanda from the UK at present. The national carrier is *Rwandair Express* (website: www.rwandair.com).

Approximate flight times: From Kigali to *London* is 20 hours, including stopovers.

Main airports: *Kigali (KGL)* (Kigali International Airport), 12km (7.5 miles) east of Kigali (travel time – 25 minutes). *To/from the airport:* Bus and taxi services are available. *Facilities:* Bar, duty free shop, post office and currency exchange.

Departure tax: US$20 or equivalent in Rwanda Francs.

ROAD:

International routes are available from the surrounding countries of the Democratic Republic of Congo, Tanzania and Uganda. Visitors are advised to exercise extreme caution, owing to political instability. **Bus:** There are daily services from Kampala in Uganda and Bujumbura in Burundi to Kigali.

Travel - Internal

AIR:

Chartered planes are available but are usually expensive.
Departure tax: US$20.

ROAD:

Traffic drives on the right. Some local roads are not tarmacked and a 4-wheel drive vehicle would be advantageous. There can be landslides on some of the major roads during annual rainfall in spring and autumn. Extra care should be taken at night, as taxis use full headlights. The network is generally sparse; the roads linking the capital with Butare, Bugarana and the frontier posts are, however, good. Driving is not recommended and visitors are advised to exercise extreme caution. **Bus:** Minibuses and Government vehicles operate regular routes in Rwanda. Services are operated by the *Ministry of Transport and Communications*. A timetable and tariff booklet is available in Rwanda. **Taxi:** Available in Kigali and other large towns. Fares should be agreed in advance. Tipping is not expected. **Car hire:** Limited facilities in Rwanda. There are no international car hire firms operating, but there are local companies in Kigali. Fuel is expensive. **Documentation:** An International Driving Permit is required.

Travel Advice

Travellers are advised against all but essential travel to rural areas bordering Burundi and the Democratic Republic of the Congo. There remains a risk of indiscriminate attacks on Rwanda from rebel groups operating outside the country in the border regions with Burundi and the Democratic Republic of the Congo.
Travellers should be aware of the global risk of indiscriminate terrorist attacks, which could be against civilian targets, including places frequented by foreigners. This advice is based on information provided by the Foreign and Commonwealth Office in the UK. It is correct at time of publishing. As the situation can change rapidly, visitors are advised to contact the following organisations for the latest travel advice:

British Foreign and Commonwealth Office
Tel: (0845) 850 2829.
Website: www.fco.gov.uk

US Department of State
Website: http://travel.state.gov/travel

Accommodation

HOTELS:

Found mostly in Kigali; they are expensive. There are some cheaper new hotels of reasonable standard. Missions with dormitory accommodation are also available, particularly in remote districts and smaller towns. Ruhengeri and Gisenyi mission station hotels are excellent.

GUEST HOUSES:

Outside the main towns there are guest houses, which are generally cheaper than hotels. There is a solar-powered house at the edge of the A'Kagera National Park.

CAMPING:

Some safaris involve camping in East African style tents. Rest huts are available on the expedition route in the Virunga Volcanoes.

Top Things To See & Do

• Visit **Kigali**, the capital city. It is home to the **Genocide Museum**, which documents the 100-day massacre in 1994, and should serve as an important reminder why such events should never be allowed to repeat themselves again.

• **Kibungu (Umutara)**, in the east of the country, is in the centre of a region of lakes and waterfalls, including **Lake Mungesera** and the **Rusumo Falls**. **Gisenyi** is the main centre for excursions in the **Parc des Volcans**. Plane trips can be made from here to view the craters. Situated on the north of **Lake Kivu**, it also offers many opportunities for water sports or for excursions on the lake. **Kibuye**, further south, is another lakeside resort. Near **Cyangugu**, on the southern shores of the lake, are the spectacular grottoes of **Kaboza** and **Nyenji**, and the thermal waters at **Nyakabuye**. Nearby, the **Rugege Forest** is the home of many rare species of wildlife.

• Get close to some of Rwanda's fantastic **wildlife**. The **A'Kagera National Park** covers over 2500 sq km (1000 sq miles) of savannah to the west of the **A' Kagera River** (the frontier with Tanzania). The park has a variety of wildlife and is a habitat for over 500 species of birds. The major point of access is Kabarando. **Safaris** can also be undertaken at **Kabarando**; the park is devoted to game preservation and has lions, zebras, antelopes, hippos, buffalo, leopards, apes, impala, crested herons, fish eagles, cormorants, giraffes, elephants, elands and warthogs.

• Embark on a **gorilla trek** at the **Parc National des Volcans**. Military units currently guard the park and ensure the safety of visitors, particularly from poachers. This park is one of the last sanctuaries of the mountain gorilla and it is here that the well-known Diane Fossey spent 18 years studying them prior to her murder in 1985. The *ORTPN* bureau and some private companies in Kigali can organise guided tours or gorilla tracking for small parties; a permit is necessary but this should be organised through the *ORTPN*.

• Discover the intellectual capital of the country, **Butare**, which borders with Burundi. The most prominent tourist attraction in Butare is the superb **National Museum**, which houses perhaps the finest ethnographic collection in East Africa. Absorbing displays of traditional artefacts are illuminated by a fascinating selection of turn-of-the-century monochrome photographs, providing insight not only into pre-colonial lifestyles, but also into the subsequent development of Rwanda as a modern African state. Butare also boasts craft shops and a botanical garden. North of Butare is **Gitarama**, which has a good art museum; nearby is the cathedral town of **Kabgayi**; and at **Mushubati**, the grottoes of **Bihongori**.

• Climb the **Virunga Volcanoes** between Ruhengeri and Gisenyi. **Nyiragongo** in the Democratic Republic of Congo is the most commonly climbed volcano from Gisenyi. The **Parc National des Volcans** region is composed of volcanic mountains, of which two, **Nyamuragira** and **Nyiragongo**, across the frontier in the Democratic Republic of Congo, are still active. These are best **trekked** rather than climbed, and are still for the intrepid.

• Watch a performance of the **Rwanda National Ballet**, famous for its traditional dancing and singing.

TOURIST INFORMATION

Office Rwandais du Tourisme et des Parcs Nationaux (ORTPN)
Street address: Boulevard de la Révolution no.1, Kigali, Rwanda
Postal address: BP 905, Kigali, Rwanda
Tel: 576 514 *or* 573 396.
Website: www.rwandatourism.com

Entertainment

FOOD & DRINK: Hotels generally serve a reasonable choice of European dishes, while there are Chinese, Greek, Indian, Italian and Middle Eastern restaurants. Some restaurants also serve Franco-Belgian cuisine and African dishes. A fairly good selection of beers, spirits and wines is available. Beer is also brewed locally.
Tipping: 10 per cent is normal.
NIGHTLIFE: There are a few cinemas in Kigali. The *Rwanda National Ballet* is famous for its traditional dancing and singing and can be seen either at national ceremonies or sometimes on request in the villages. There are now several nightclubs, with African, Congolese and Western music; there are also some live music bars with food and dancing available. The French Cultural Centre runs a variety of activities.
SHOPPING: Special purchases include woven baskets with pointed lids, native clay statuettes, masks and charms. Do not buy souvenir gorilla skulls or hands; if they are offered, report the trader to the police. **Shopping hours:** Mon-Fri 0830-1300 and 1400-1730, Sat 0830-1230.

Business

• **GDP:** US$1.8 billion (2005).
• **Main imports:** Consumption goods, intermediate goods, capital goods and energy.
• **Main exports:** Tea, coffee, coltan, cassiterite and tin.
• **Main trade partners:** Belgium, France, Germany, Kenya and South Africa.

ECONOMY: Rwanda's economy, which is based on subsistence agriculture, was devastated by the massacres of 1994, the huge refugee populations that resulted, political upheaval and, since then, ongoing fighting in several parts of the country. Plantains, sweet potatoes, cassava and beans are grown for domestic consumption; tea and coffee are the principal cash crops and there is extensive livestock farming. Some rice and sugar plantations have also been developed. Rwanda has some mineral deposits – principally tin ores, but also several ores containing rare metals such as tungsten and tantalum, which are in heavy demand in the world market. Extraction of the large natural gas reserves discovered beneath Lake Kivu has begun, although it has been disrupted by local fighting. The industrial sector produces tobacco, metal goods, chemicals, rubber and plastics. In the service sector, the embryonic tourism industry (geared towards ecotourism) has had to restart from scratch as a result of the 1994 genocide and subsequent events. Given the political situation, exacerbated by a series of poor harvests during the late 1990s, it is hardly surprising therefore that Rwanda continues to rely heavily on international aid. A new Structural Adjustment Programme was begun in 1998, followed by an ambitious privatisation programme: both are being conducted under the supervision of the IMF and World Bank. In 2002, telecommunications and Government-owned tea plantations were put up for sale. The results so far have been quite good: the economy grew 3.8 per cent in 2004 and inflation was 10.8 per cent. But, like most sub-Saharan African economies, Rwanda is especially vulnerable to commodity price movements; these are presently at a very low level. Aid donors have also promised further assistance conditional on Rwanda pulling its troops out of the Democratic Republic of Congo. The main regional cooperation mechanism for Rwanda is the Common Market for Eastern and Southern Africa.
BUSINESS ETIQUETTE: Lightweight suits are advised and appointments are necessary. Best time to visit is from April to October or December to January. A knowledge of French is useful as only a few executives speak English.
Office hours: Mon-Fri 0800-1230 and 1330-1700.

COMMERCIAL INFORMATION

Chambre de Commerce et d'Industrie du Rwanda
BP 319, Kigali, Rwanda
Tel: 83538/41.
E-mail: frsp@rwanda1.com

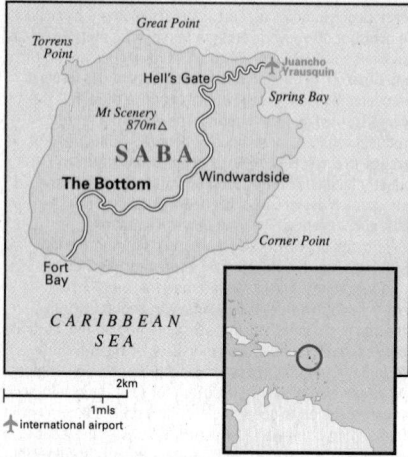

Location: Eastern Caribbean, Leeward Islands.

Time: GMT - 4.

Saba is part of the Netherlands Antilles and is represented abroad by Royal Netherlands Embassies – see *The Netherlands* section.

Overview

Saba is the peak of a submerged extinct volcano. With only one road ('The Road') and a population of less than 1500, Saba is the most unspoilt of The Netherlands Antilles; the inhabitants will claim that visitors are so few that each one is something of a celebrity. Until 50 years ago Saba was a secluded oasis, having neither an airport nor a sheltered harbour. There are four villages, until recently connected only by thousands of steps cut from the rock. A road now links the airport with the island's capital, The Bottom. The Bottom is situated 250m (820ft) above the ocean on a plateau surrounded by volcanic domes.

General Information

AREA: 13 sq km (5 sq miles).

POPULATION: 1466.

POPULATION DENSITY: 113 per sq km.

CAPITAL: The Bottom.

GEOGRAPHY: Saba is one of three Windward Islands in the Netherlands Antilles, although geographically it is part of the Leeward Group of the Lesser Antilles, lying 265km (165 miles) east of Puerto Rico, 44km (27 miles) south of St Maarten and 21km (13 miles) west of St Eustatius. Saba is the peak of a submerged extinct volcano. Mount Scenery is thick with forest and rises to almost 900m (3000ft) in less than 2km (1.2 miles).

GOVERNMENT: Part of the Netherlands Antilles; dependency of The Netherlands. Gained internal autonomy in 1954. **Head of State:** HM Queen Beatrix of The Netherlands, represented locally by Governor Dr Fritz M de los Santos Goedgedrag. **Head of Government:** Prime Minister Etienne Ys since 2004. **Recent history:** As part of the Netherlands Antilles, Saba gained partial independence from The Netherlands in 1954. The issue of the Antilles' constitutional status never left the political agenda, however, and was the subject of a referendum on the three Windward Islands in 1994. All three voted to remain within the Antilles but Saba registered the largest majority of 91 per cent. At the most recent general election for the *Staten* – the local governing body of the Antilles – held in January 2006, the *Partido Antia Restruktura* (PAR, Party for the Restructured Antilles) won the largest number of seats. PAR, which is based on the island of Curaçao, has dominated

Antilles' politics since its formation a decade ago. The leaders of the five Antilles islands agreed with the Dutch Government in late 2005 that each island would become an individual territory and that the federation would be broken up by July 2007. This time, Saba's residents had voted in a referendum to break away from the federation. Saba will become a Kingdom island, a newly-created status.

LANGUAGE: Dutch is the official language. *Papiamento* (a mixture of Portuguese, African, Spanish, Dutch and English) is the commonly used *lingua franca*. English and Spanish are also widely spoken.

RELIGION: Roman Catholic majority; also Anglican and Wesleyan.

ELECTRICITY: 110/220 volts AC, 60Hz.

SOCIAL CONVENTIONS: Dutch customs are still important throughout the Netherlands Antilles, but tourism on neighbouring St Maarten has brought some US influence to Saba (several businesses are US-owned). Dress is casual and lightweight cottons are advised.

Climate

Hot, but tempered by cooling trade winds. The annual mean temperature is 27°C (80°F), varying by no more than two or three degrees throughout the year; average rainfall is 1667mm. The temperature can drop to 16°C (60°F) on winter evenings. When climbing Mount Scenery, the temperature will drop by approximately 0.2°C (0.4°F) for each 100m (330ft) gained in altitude.

Required clothing: Lightweights and cottons are worn throughout the year. Umbrellas or light waterproofs are needed for the rainy season.

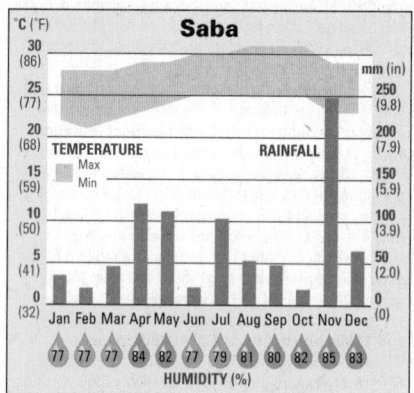

Communications

Telephone: Fully automatic system with good IDD. Country code: 599. Calls made through the operator are more expensive and include a 15 per cent tax. IDD is available μfrom hotels and some phone booths.

Mobile telephone: Analogue networks operated by *Windward Islands Cellular* and digital analogue network (system B) by *East Caribbean Cellular* (website: www.eastcaribbeancellular.com). Compatible with most US handsets but not with GSM handsets. Roaming agreements exist. Handsets can be hired at the company offices in The Bottom. GSM network is being developed and should now be in operation. Most US handsets can be used, and can be activated with a temporary number before or after arrival on the island. Visitors can also register online with ECC.

Internet: There is currently one Internet cafe on the island, in Windwardside.

Post: The post office is in The Bottom. Airmail to Europe takes four to six days, surface mail four to six weeks.

MEDIA: Press: The *Saba Herald* is published monthly in English.

TV: *Leeward Broadcasting Corporation*, St Maarten.

Radio: *Voice of Saba*.

Passport/Visa

	Passport Required?	Visa Required?	Return Ticket Required?
Full British	Yes	1	Yes
Australian	Yes	2	Yes
Canadian	Yes	2	Yes
USA	Yes	2	Yes
Other EU	Yes	1/2	Yes
Japanese	Yes	2	Yes

Note: *Regulations and requirements may be subject to change at short notice, and you are advised to contact the appropriate diplomatic or consular authority before finalising travel arrangements. Any numbers in the chart refer to the footnotes below.*

PASSPORTS: Passport or official travel documents valid for at least three months after intended return to home country required by all.

VISAS: Required by all except the following:
(a) **1.** nationals of Belgium, Bolivia, Burkina Faso, Chile, Costa Rica, Czech Republic, Ecuador, Germany, Hungary, Israel, Jamaica, Korea (Rep), Luxembourg, Malawi, Mauritius, The Netherlands, Niger, The Philippines, Poland, San Marino, Slovak Republic, Spain, Swaziland, Togo and the UK for touristic stays of up to three months;
(b) most nationals continuing to a third country within 24 hours by the same means of transportation and not leaving the airport and holding tickets with reserved seats and documents for their onward journey.
Note: (a) Nationals of the following countries must apply for a visa *before* entering the country even for touristic purposes: Albania, Bosnia & Herzegovina, Bulgaria, Cambodia, China (PR) (except Hong Kong SAR), CIS, Colombia, Cote d'Ivoire, Croatia, Cuba, Dominican Republic, Estonia, Ghana, Guinea-Bissau, Haiti, Kenya, Korea (DPR), Latvia, Libya, Lithuania, Macedonia (Former Yugoslav Republic), Mali, Nigeria, Romania, Serbia & Montenegro and Vietnam. (b) **2.** All other nationals may enter without a visa for touristic stays of up to 14 days. (c) All stays can be extended locally by the same period that they are valid for.

Types of visa and cost: All visas, regardless of duration of stay or number of entries permitted on visa, cost 35.

Validity: Visas are generally issued for as long as duration of stay, up until a maximum 90 days from date of issue.

Application requirements: (a) Passport or equivalent travel document valid for a minimum of three months after intended return to home country. Passports should contain a blank visa page and endorse residence permit. For minors (18 years and under), an approval of both parents or legal guardians with a copy of each parent's/guardian's passport is required. If passport is new, the old passport must also be submitted. (b) One fully completed application form. (c) One recent passport-size photo per person endorsed on passport, with daytime phone number and address written clearly on the back. More photos may be required. (d) Fee, payable by postal order (to Royal Netherlands Embassy) or cash. Cheques are not accepted. Visa handling fees may be charged on applications handed in, regardless of outcome, depending on Embassy/Consulate. (e) Evidence of sufficient funds amounting to a minimum of £30 for each day of stay (cash not accepted), eg original bank statements, credit card with credit limit statement, traveller's cheques. (f) A recent and original letter from employer, stating commencement date, with last payslip. If self-employed, submit letter from solicitor, accountant or company house. If unemployed, submit social benefit booklet. If in education, submit a recent and original letter from school/college/university, confirming attendance. (g) Valid medical or travel insurance. *Tourist:* (a)-(g) and, (h) Invitation from family or proof of accommodation. (i) Return or onward ticket(s), plus necessary documents for returning to country of origin. *Business:* (a)-(g) and, (h) Invitation from company that you are visiting.

Application to: Nearest Embassy of the Kingdom of The Netherlands. All further information about visa requirements may be obtained from The Royal Netherlands Embassies which formally represent the Netherlands Antilles; see *Passport/Visa Information* in *The Netherlands* section.

Working days required: Applications should be lodged at least one month prior to departure.

Temporary residence: Enquire at the office of the Lieutenant Governor of the Island Territory of Saba, The Bottom, Saba. In certain cases, Dutch Europeans may be permitted to reside in the Netherlands Antilles without having to apply for a residence permit. However, it is best to consult the nearest Dutch Embassy/Consulate in advance to ascertain whether this is applicable taking into consideration the individual circumstances of the traveller.

PASSPORT/VISA INFORMATION

Office of the Minister Plenipotentiary of the Netherlands Antilles
PO Box 90706, Badhuisweg 173-175, 2597 JP, The Hague, The Netherlands
Tel: (70) 306 6111.

Money

Currency: Netherlands Antilles Guilder or Florin (ANG) = 100 cents. Notes are in denominations of ANG250, 100, 50, 25, 10 and 5. Coins are in denominations of ANG5 and 1 and 50, 25, 10, 5 and 1 cents.

Note: The ANG is linked to the US Dollar.

Currency exchange: There are two banks on the island.
Credit & debit cards: MasterCard and Visa are accepted in larger establishments. Check with your credit or debit card company for details of merchant acceptability and other services that may be available.
Traveller's cheques: To avoid additional exchange rate charges, US Dollars are recommended.
Currency restrictions: There are no restrictions on the import and export of foreign or local currency. The import of Dutch or Surinam silver coins is prohibited.
Banking hours: Mon-Fri 0830-1130 and 1330-1630.
Exchange rate indicators:
Rate at time of publishing
£1.00=   ANG3.14
$1.00=   ANG1.78

Duty Free

The following items may be imported into Saba by tourists over 15 years of age only, without incurring customs duty:
200 cigarettes or 50 cigars or 100 cigarillos or 250g tobacco; 2l of alcoholic beverages; gifts to a value of ANG100.
Restricted items: The import of leather goods from Haiti is not advisable. If total value of goods exceeds ANG500, a declaration should be made at customs and cleared at the freight department.

Public Holidays

Below are listed Public Holidays for the January 2006-June 2007 period.
2006: Jan 1 New Year's Day. **Apr 14-17** Easter. **Apr 30** Queen's Birthday. **May 1** Labour Day. **May 25** Ascension. **Oct 21** Antillean Day. **Dec 4** Saba Day. **Dec 25** Christmas Day. **Dec 26** Boxing Day.
2007: Jan 1 New Year's Day. **Apr 6-9** Easter. **Apr 30** Queen's Birthday. **May 1** Labour Day. **May 17** Ascension. **Oct 21** Antillean Day. **Dec 3** Saba Day. **Dec 25** Christmas Day. **Dec 26** Boxing Day.

Health

	Special Precautions?	Certificate Required?
Yellow Fever	No	1
Cholera	No	No
Typhoid & Polio	No	N/A
Malaria	No	N/A

Note: *Regulations and requirements may be subject to change at short notice, and you are advised to contact your doctor well in advance of your intended date of departure. Any numbers in the chart refer to the footnotes below.*

1: A *yellow fever* certificate is required from travellers over six months of age arriving within six days of transiting countries with infected areas.
Food & drink: All mains water on the island is distilled from seawater and is therefore safe to drink. Bottled mineral water is widely available. Milk is pasteurised and dairy products are safe for consumption. Local meat, poultry, seafood, fruit and vegetables are generally considered safe to eat.
Other risks: Immunisation against *hepatitis A* is recommended. *TB* and *hepatitis B* might also occur in rural areas.
Health care: There is one hospital in The Bottom plus the University School of Medicine. Medical insurance is essential.

Travel - International

AIR:

Airlines serving Saba include *Winair* (website: www.fly-winair.com).
Approximate flight times: All international air travel is via St Maarten. From Saba to *London* (via St Maarten and Amsterdam) is 13 hours, to *Los Angeles* is 10 hours, to *New York* is six hours and to *Singapore* is 34 hours (these will vary considerably, depending on connections).
Main airports: *Juancho Yrausquin (SAB)* at Cove Bay. The runway, at 400m (1300ft), is one of the shortest in the world. There are daily STOL turboprop flights to St Eustatius and St Kitts (and thus the airport may be classified as 'international') and thrice daily to St Maarten. *To/from the airport:* Taxis are available.
Departure tax: US$7 to Netherlands Antilles, US$22 for all other destinations (due to exchange rates, prices may vary).
SEA:
Small boats operate from the Leo A Chance Pier at Fort Bay. There are regular ferry services to St Maarten (travel time – one hour). A weekly cargo boat brings groceries and other supplies from St Maarten. Cruise ships call occasionally.

Travel - Internal

ROAD:
Saba has one road, 15km (9.5 miles) long, bisecting the island from the airport to Fort Bay. Traffic drives on the right. **Taxis** are available.
Self-drive cars may be hired in Windwardside.
Documentation: A national driving licence is acceptable.

Travel Advice

Most visits to Saba are trouble-free but you should be aware of the global risk of indiscriminate international terrorist attacks, which could be against civilian targets, including places frequented by foreigners.
This advice is based on information provided by the Foreign and Commonwealth Office in the UK. It is correct at time of publishing. As the situation can change rapidly, visitors are advised to contact the following organisations for the latest travel advice:

British Foreign and Commonwealth Office
Tel: (0845) 850 2829.
Website: www.fco.gov.uk

US Department of State
Website: http://travel.state.gov/travel

Accommodation

There are various guest houses including *Caribe Guesthouse, The Cottage Club, Cranston's Antique Inn, Ecolodge Rendez-Vous, The Gate House, Juliana's, El Momo, Queen's Garden Resort, Scout's Place* and *Willard's of Saba*. Most have their own restaurant bar and swimming pool. Some apartments, cottages and villas are also available. A 5 per cent Government tax is added to bills.

Top Things To See & Do

• From the rocky beach at **Fort Bay**, there is a steep climb of 800 steps hewn out of the rock in order to gain access to the island. The island's four villages are mere clusters of ornate timber cottages perching on the flanks of the mountain. Vegetation becomes increasingly lush towards the summit and the crater itself holds a tropical rainforest scattered with exotic flowers – begonias, giant heliconias and orchids. Tours may be taken by taxi from the airport or pier, or on foot via the forest trails and thousands of stone-cut steps linking the villages.
• The **Harry L Johnson Memorial Museum** in **Windwardside** is the restored home of a Dutch sea captain. Windwardside also contains the **Tourist Office**, the island's two largest guest houses and most of its shops.
• In the capital, **The Bottom**, the **Artisan Foundation** exhibits early examples of 'Saba lace': intricate embroidery on linen that resembles lace.
• Although Saba has no beaches, the waters around Saba have been declared a protected marine park in recognition of the unique opportunities for **wall diving** they present to experienced divers. Visibility varies from 20 to 30m (75 to 100ft) with a water temperature of 30°C (86°F) in summer, whilst in winter visibility is up to 40m (125ft), with a water temperature of 24°C (75°F). The fragile coral reefs clinging to the submerged mountain slopes are teeming with colourful grazing fish, preyed on by sharks and barracuda. Giant sea turtles and humpback whales are seasonal visitors. Boats and diving equipment can be rented from dive shops. Qualified dive masters can provide tuition at all levels (beginners are confined to the shallow waters of Fort Bay).
Note: There are no beaches.
• Marked **hiking** trails lead up to **Mount Scenery**.

Entertainment

FOOD & DRINK: Fine local cuisine is offered at the island's guest houses and there are several public restaurants. Restaurants and bars are usually closed by midnight.
National specialities:
• Calaloo soup.
• Curried goat.
• Breadfruit.
• Soursop ice cream.
• Exotic fruit grown on the island – mangoes, papayas, figs, bananas and bitter mangoes.
National drinks:
• Saba has its own brand of rum – *Saba Spice*, a potent blend of rum, aniseed, cinnamon, orange peel, cloves, nutmeg, spice bush and brown sugar.
Tipping: A surcharge of 20 per cent is usually added to guest house and restaurant bills to cover Government tax and service. Elsewhere, 10 to 15 per cent is expected.
NIGHTLIFE: There are few visitors to the island and generally evenings are quiet, but on Friday and Saturday nights there is dancing at some restaurants and some guest houses have lively bars.
SHOPPING: By the middle of the last century, the decline in the world's demand for sugar and indigo had left Saba looking at a very bleak future; the plantations, the only source of employment, reverted to forest. Undaunted, the men built boats and became fishermen, the women stayed at home and embroidered napkins and table cloths using a technique remembered by Mary Gertrude Johnson from her days in a Venezuelan convent. The fishing industry is now marginal but the embroidery has become Saba's chief claim to fame. *The Saba Artisans' Foundation* (founded in 1972 with money from the United Nations' Development Programme) in The Bottom promotes local lacework, silk-screened fabrics and garments printed and handmade by Sabans, as does the *Island Craft Shop* in Windwardside.
Shopping hours: Mon-Sat 0800-1200 and 1400-1800.

Business

ECONOMY: Economic conditions vary widely between the different islands in the Netherlands Antilles group. Saba has some agriculture, producing sorghum, groundnuts, fruit and vegetables, as well as a modest fishing operation. There is no manufacturing industry other than textiles. Saba has very little of the Netherlands Antilles' recently developed 'offshore' financial services industry; tourism is the most important part of the service sector. Along with Bonaire and St Eustatius, Saba is a net beneficiary of the Netherlands Antilles central treasury. Saba has associate membership of the European Union, as an overseas territory of The Netherlands, and observer status at the Caribbean trading bloc, CARICOM.
Business is fairly formal and visitors should wear a suit. Appointments should be made and always kept as it is very discourteous to be late. **Office hours:** Mon-Fri 0730-1200 and 1330-1630.

St Eustatius

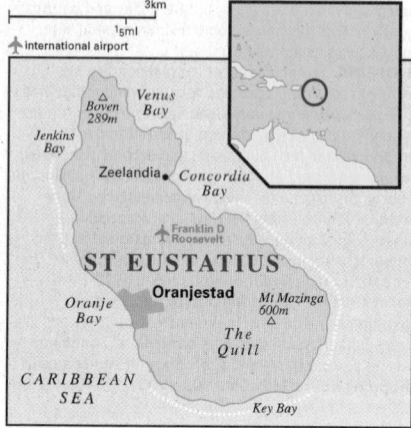

Location: Eastern Caribbean, Windward Islands.

Time: GMT - 4.

Overview

St Eustatius, popularly known as 'Statia', was a thriving transshipment port during the 17th and 18th centuries, becoming known throughout the Caribbean as 'The Golden Rock'. The subsequent decline of the island has only recently been halted by an influx of tourists. The foundations of the Dutch sea walls are now sunk beneath the clear waters of the bay. Scuba divers and snorkellers can see many of the submerged ruins. Other attractions on the island include walking up The Quill; surfing off the northeast coast; and fishing trips. The nightlife is centred on the main hotels and restaurants, including dancing and local live bands, which may play one of the two different indigenous blends of reggae and calypso - 'Pim Pim' and 'Hippy'.

General Information

AREA: 21 sq km (8 sq miles).

POPULATION: 2609 (official estimate 1996).

POPULATION DENSITY: 124 per sq km.

CAPITAL: Oranjestad.

GEOGRAPHY: Politically, St Eustatius is one of three Windward Islands in the Netherlands Antilles; geographically it is part of the Leeward Group of the Lesser Antilles. It lies 286km (178 miles) east of Puerto Rico, 171km (106 miles) east of St Croix, 56km (35 miles) due south of St Maarten and 14km (9 miles) northwest of St Kitts. On the south end of the island is an extinct volcano called The Quill, which has a lush rainforest in the crater. Twice a year, sea turtles clamber up onto the black volcanic sands that rim the island to lay their eggs; giant land crabs hunt on the beaches every night.

GOVERNMENT: Part of the Netherlands Antilles; dependency of The Netherlands since 1630. **Head of State:** Queen Beatrix of The Netherlands, represented locally by Governor Frits Goedgedrag since 2002. **Head of Government:** Prime Minister Etienne Ys since 2004. The Netherlands Antilles consist of Bonaire, Curaçao, Saba, St Eustatius and St Maarten. The capital of the island group is Willemstad, Curaçao. **Recent history:** As part of the Netherlands Antilles, St Eustatius (also known as Statia) gained partial independence from The Netherlands in 1954. The issue of the Antilles' constitutional status never left the political agenda, however, and was the subject of a referendum on the three Windward Islands in 1994. All three voted to remain within the Antilles, with St Eustatius registering a majority of 86 per cent. At the most recent general election for the Staten - the local governing body of the Antilles - held in January 2006, the Partido Antia

Restruktura (PAR, Party for the Restructured Antilles) won the largest number of seats. PAR, which is based on the island of Curaçao, has dominated Antilles' politics since its formation a decade ago.

The leaders of the five Antilles islands agreed with the Dutch Government in late 2005 that each island would become an individual territory and that the federation would be broken up by July 2007. St Eustatius will become a kingdom island, a newly-created status, though its inhabitants had voted in a referendum to maintain the status quo.

LANGUAGE: Dutch is the official language. Papiamento (a mixture of African, Dutch, English, Portuguese and Spanish) is, the commonly used *lingua franca*. English and Spanish are also widely spoken.

RELIGION: The majority are Protestant with a Roman Catholic minority.

ELECTRICITY: 110 volts AC, 60Hz. Plugs with two flat prongs are in use.

SOCIAL CONVENTIONS: Dutch customs are still important throughout the Netherlands Antilles, but US influences from the Virgin Islands nearby are dominant on St Eustatius. It is conventional to shake hands on meeting someone. Dress is casual and lightweight cottons are advised. Bathing suits should be confined to the beach and poolside areas only. It is common to dress up in the evening.

Climate

Hot, but tempered by cooling trade winds. The annual mean temperature is 27°C (80°F), varying by no more than two or three degrees throughout the year; the average rainfall is 1771mm (7 inches).

Required clothing: Tropical lightweights and cottons are worn throughout the year. Umbrellas or light waterproofs are also advisable.

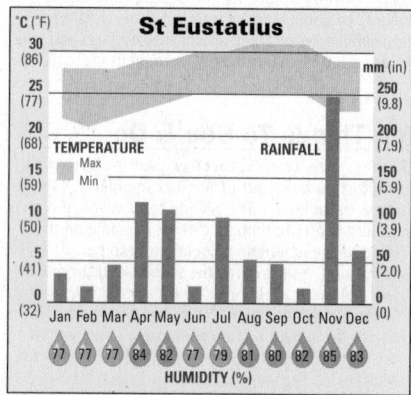

Communications

Telephone: Fully automatic system with good IDD connections. Country code: 599. Calls made through the operator are more expensive and include a 15 per cent tax.

Mobile telephone: Not compatible with GSM handsets but some US handsets can be used. Roaming agreements exist with international mobile phone companies.

Internet: Public access is available in the library.

Post: Airmail to Europe takes four to six days, surface mail four to six weeks. Main post office hours: Mon-Fri 0730-1600.

MEDIA: Press: No newspapers are published on St Eustatius, but English-language dailies, *Daily Herald* and *St Maarten Guardian*, are published on St Maarten. Most other newspapers in The Netherlands Antilles are published in Dutch or Papiamento.

TV: St Eustatius receives *TeleCuraçao* and programmes from the St Maarten-based *Leeward Broadcasting Corporation*.

Radio: The local station is *Radio Statia*.

Passport/Visa

	Passport Required?	Visa Required?	Return Ticket Required?
Full British	Yes	1	Yes
Australian	Yes	2	Yes
Canadian	Yes	2	Yes
USA	Yes	2	Yes
Other EU	Yes	1/2	Yes
Japanese	Yes	2	Yes

Note: *Regulations and requirements may be subject to change at short notice, and you are advised to contact the appropriate diplomatic or consular authority before finalising travel arrangements. Any numbers in the chart refer to the footnotes below.*

PASSPORTS: Passport valid for at least three months after intended return to home country required by all.

VISAS: Required by all except the following:

(a) **1.** nationals of Belgium, Bolivia, Burkina Faso, Chile, Costa Rica, Czech Republic, Ecuador, Germany, Hungary, Israel, Jamaica, Korea (Rep), Luxembourg, Malawi, Mauritius, The Netherlands, Niger, The Philippines, Poland, San Marino, Slovak Republic, Spain, Swaziland, Togo and the UK for touristic stays of up to three months;

(b) most nationals continuing to a third country within 24 hours by the same means of transportation and not leaving the airport and holding tickets with reserved seats and documents for their onward journey.

Note: (a) Nationals of the following countries must apply for a visa *before* entering the country even for touristic purposes: Albania, Bosnia & Herzegovina, Bulgaria, Cambodia, China (PR) (except Hong Kong SAR), CIS, Colombia, Cote d'Ivoire, Croatia, Cuba, Dominican Republic, Estonia, Ghana, Guinea-Bissau, Haiti, Kenya, Korea (DPR), Latvia, Libya, Lithuania, Macedonia (Former Yugoslav Republic), Mali, Nigeria, Romania, Serbia & Montenegro and Vietnam. (b) **2.** All other nationals may enter without a visa for touristic stays of up to 14 days. (c) All stays can be extended locally by the same period that they are valid for.

Types of visa and cost: All visas, regardless of duration of stay or number of entries permitted on visa, cost €35.

Validity: Visas are generally issued for as long as duration of stay, up until a maximum 90 days from date of issue.

Application requirements: (a) Passport or equivalent travel document valid for a minimum of three months after intended return to home country. Passports should contain a blank visa page and endorse residence permit. For minors (18 years and under), an approval of both parents or legal guardians with a copy of each parent's/guardian's passport is required. If passport is new, the old passport must also be submitted. (b) One fully completed application form. (c) One recent passport-size photo per person endorsed on passport, with daytime phone number and address written clearly on the back. More photos may be required. (d) Fee, payable by postal order (to Royal Netherlands Embassy) or cash. Cheques are not accepted. Visa handling fees may be charged on applications handed in, regardless of outcome, depending on Embassy/Consulate. (e) Evidence of sufficient funds amounting to a minimum of £30 for each day of stay (cash not accepted), eg original bank statements, credit card with credit limit statement, traveller's cheques. (f) A recent and original letter from employer, stating commencement date, with last payslip. If self-employed, submit letter from solicitor, accountant or company house. If unemployed, submit social benefit booklet. If in education, submit a recent and original letter from school/college/university, confirming attendance. (g) Valid medical or travel insurance. *Tourist:* (a)-(g) and, (h) Invitation from family or proof of accommodation. (i) Return or onward ticket(s), plus necessary documents for returning to country of origin. *Business:* (a)-(g) and, (h) Invitation from company that you are visiting.

Application to: Nearest Embassy of the Kingdom of The Netherlands. All further information about visa requirements may be obtained from The Royal Netherlands Embassies which formally represent the Netherlands Antilles; see *Passport/Visa Information* in *The Netherlands* section.

Working days required: Applications should be lodged at least one month prior to departure.

Temporary residence: Enquire at the office of the Lieutenant Governor of the Island Territory of St Eustatius, Oranjestad, St Eustatius. In certain cases, Dutch Europeans may be permitted to reside in the Netherlands Antilles without having to apply for a residence permit. However, it is best to consult the nearest Dutch Embassy/Consulate in advance to ascertain whether this is applicable taking into consideration the individual circumstances of the traveller.

PASSPORT/VISA INFORMATION

Office of the Minister Plenipotentiary of the Netherlands Antilles
PO Box 90706, Badhuisweg 173-175,
2597 JP The Hague, The Netherlands
Tel: (70) 306 6111.

Money

Currency: Netherlands Antilles Guilder or Florin (ANG) = 100 cents. Notes are in denominations of ANG250, 100, 50, 25, 10 and 5. Coins are in denominations of ANG5 and 1 and 50, 25, 10, 5 and 1 cents. The US Dollar is widely accepted.

Note: The Netherlands Antilles Guilder is linked to the US Dollar.

Currency exchange: There are three banks on the island. All major currencies can be exchanged.

Credit & debit cards: MasterCard and Visa are accepted in large establishments. Check with your credit or debit card company for details of merchant acceptability and other services which may be available.

Currency restrictions: There are no restrictions on the import and export of local or foreign currency, but the import and export of amounts of foreign currency exceeding ANG20,000 must declared. The import of Dutch or Surinam silver coins is prohibited.

Banking hours: Mon-Fri 0830-1130 and 1330-1630.

Exchange rate indicators:

Rate at time of publishing

£1.00=   ANG 3.14
$1.00=   ANG 1.78

Duty Free

The following may be imported into St Eustatius by tourists over 15 years of age only without incurring customs duty:

200 cigarettes or 50 cigars or 100 cigarillos or 250g tobacco; 2l of alcoholic beverages; gifts to a value of NAG100 (gifts over the value of NAG500 must be declared).

Restricted items: The import of souvenirs and leather goods from Haiti is not advisable.

Public Holidays

Below are listed Public Holidays for the January 2006-June 2007 period.

2006: Jan 1 New Year's Day. **Apr 14** Good Friday. **Apr 16-17** Easter. **Apr 30** Queen's Birthday. **May 1** Labour Day. **May 29** Ascension. **Jul 31** Carnival Monday. **Oct 21** Antilles Day. **Nov 16** Statia's Day. **Dec 25** Christmas Day. **Dec 26** Boxing Day.

2007: Jan 1 New Year's Day. **Apr 6** Good Friday. **Apr 8-9** Easter. **Apr 30** Queen's Birthday. **May 1** Labour Day. **May 17** Ascension.

Health

	Special Precautions?	Certificate Required?
Yellow Fever	No	1
Cholera	No	No
Typhoid & Polio	No	N/A
Malaria	No	N/A

Note: *Regulations and requirements may be subject to change at short notice, and you are advised to contact your doctor well in advance of your intended date of departure. Any numbers in the chart refer to the footnotes below.*

1: A yellow fever certificate is required from travellers over six months of age arriving within six days from infected areas.

Food & drink: Water on the island is considered safe to drink. Bottled mineral water is widely available. Milk is pasteurised and dairy products are safe for consumption. Local meat, poultry, seafood, fruit and vegetables are generally considered safe to eat.

Other risks: *Hepatitis A* and *rabies* occur.

Health care: There is one hospital on St Eustatius. Health insurance is advised.

Travel - International

AIR:

The national airline of The Netherlands Antilles is *ALM (LM)*. St Eustatius is served by *Winair* (website: www.fly-winair.com).

Approximate flight times: From St Eustatius to *London* (via St Maarten) is nine hours, to *Los Angeles* is seven hours, to *New York* is three hours 30 minutes and to *Singapore* is 33 hours (these times will vary considerably, depending on connections).

Main airports: *FD Roosevelt (EUX)* is 1km (0.6 miles) from Oranjestad. It is served by *Winair* (website: www.fly-winair.com) which runs scheduled flights from St Kitts & Nevis, from St Maarten six times daily (flight time – 17 minutes) and from Saba. *Golden Rock Airways* runs daily passenger charter flights to St Maarten and elsewhere. The runway is too small for jets.

Departure tax: US$5 to Netherlands Antilles; US$20 for international departures. Prices vary according to the airport. Transit passengers and children under two years of age are exempt.

SEA:

There are no ferry services operating on St Eustatius. Plans to develop a service are currently underway. The roll-on, roll-off pier at Oranjestad enables small cruise ships to dock on St Eustatius.

Travel - Internal

ROAD:

St Eustatius is a very small island and consequently has very few roads; a road of sorts runs right around the coast and a track leads up to the rim of *The Quill*, the extinct volcano in the south. The entire system can be walked in a few hours, but there are **car hire** and **taxi** companies in Oranjestad. Taxi drivers are not usually tipped. Traffic drives on the right.

Documentation: A national driving licence is acceptable.

Travel Advice

Most visits to St Eustatius are trouble-free but you should be aware of the global risk of indiscriminate international terrorist attacks, which could be against civilian targets, including places frequented by foreigners.

This advice is based on information provided by the Foreign and Commonwealth Office in the UK. It is correct at time of publishing. As the situation can change rapidly, visitors are advised to contact the following organisations for the latest travel advice:

British Foreign and Commonwealth Office
Tel: (0845) 850 2829.
Website: www.fco.gov.uk

US Department of State
Website: http://travel.state.gov/travel

Accommodation

HOTELS/GUEST HOUSES/APARTMENTS:

There are small hotels offering a total of approximately 50 beds, and several guest houses. There are also several fully equipped apartments available for weekly rental. Advance booking is advised. There is a 7 per cent service charge added to room rates. Information can be obtained from Statia Tourist Office (see *Top Things To See & Do*).

Top Things To See & Do

• St Eustatius, popularly known as 'Statia', is quiet and unhurried, with reminders of its bustling commercial past surviving only in the ruins of old warehouses, the weed-choked **Jewish Cemetery** (connected to **Synagogue Honen Dalim**, the second-oldest synagogue in the New World); colonial houses; **Fort Oranje**, built by the French in 1629 above the town; **Fort Amsterdam** on the Atlantic coast; and the foundations of the Dutch sea walls, now sunk beneath the clear waters of the bay.

• Other attractions of the island include the newly restored **Old Town**; walking up to **The Quill**, a dormant volcano surrounded by lush tropical rainforest; the **Miriam Schmidt Botanical Garden**; many beautiful and unspoilt beaches with unusual layers of black and tan sand.

• **Watersports:** These predominate, and for many visitors will form the central part of the holiday. **Snorkelling**, **windsurfing** and **water-skiing** are all available with facilities and tuition as necessary, but the island is perhaps becoming best-known as a centre for **scuba-diving**. Many wrecks lie on the black sand amid coral reefs and near the submerged old port just off Oranjestad, and these have long attracted a staggering variety of marine life. The fish have been joined by increasing numbers of expert divers, drawn by a unique combination of first-rate facilities, warm and clear water and coral, and – onshore – comfortable hotels and excellent cuisine. Dive centres on St Eustatius offer complete packages (PADI), resort courses, lessons, equipment hire and snorkel tours.

TOURIST INFORMATION

St Eustatius Tourism Development Foundation
Fort Oranje Street, St Eustatius, Netherlands Antilles
Tel: 318 2433.
Website: www.statiatourism.com

Caribbean Tourism Organisation in the UK
22 The Quadrant, Richmond, Surrey, TW9 1BP, UK
Tel: (020) 8948 0057.
Website: www.doitcaribbean.com *or*
www.onecaribbean.org

Entertainment

FOOD & DRINK: Despite the island's small size, there is a good range of restaurants offering different blends of imported and local cuisine. The hotel restaurants are probably the best – indeed the Mooshay Bay Dining Room at The Old Gin House, where Continental food is served on old pewter plates, has been given a 5-star rating by Gourmet Magazine – but the local Creole-style cooking is particularly suited for seafood dishes. The Chinese Restaurant offers authentic Cantonese cuisine; other restaurants also offer Cantonese dishes, together with French, US and local specialities.

Things to know: There are no licensing hours on the island (although most restaurants and bars are usually closed by midnight), and alcohol is virtually tax free. Most well-known brand names are available; a 'greenie' is a Heineken.

National specialities:
• Pickled conch shell meat.
• Grilled spicy fish.
• Lobster.

Tipping: Hotels add a 5 to 10 per cent government tax and 10 to 15 per cent service charge. Doormen and waiters expect a 10 per cent tip, but taxi drivers are not usually tipped.

NIGHTLIFE: Centred on the main hotels and restaurants, including dancing to both taped Western music and live local bands, that might play one of the two different indigenous blends of reggae and calypso – 'Pim Pim' and 'Hippy'.

SHOPPING: The reductions on duty free imports make the purchase of perfume, jewellery or alcohol worthwhile.

Shopping hours: Mon-Sat 0800-1200 and 1400-1800.

Business

ECONOMY: St Eustatius earns a modest income from agriculture and from a major petroleum transshipment programme, but it is tourism that dominates the economy. The island is also a net beneficiary from the central treasury of the Netherlands Antilles. There have been some efforts to develop the fishing industry but for the time being, government employment (in administration for the Netherlands Antilles group) is the most important source of regular employment. The Antilles group as a whole has Overseas Territory status at the EU and observer status at the Caribbean trading bloc CARICOM.

BUSINESS ETIQUETTE: Office hours: Mon-Fri 0730-1200 and 1330-1630.

COMMERCIAL INFORMATION

St Maarten Chamber of Commerce and Industry
PO Box 454, C A Cannegieter Street 11,
Philipsburg, St Maarten
Tel: 542 3590/5.
Website: www.sintmaarten.ne

St Kitts & Nevis

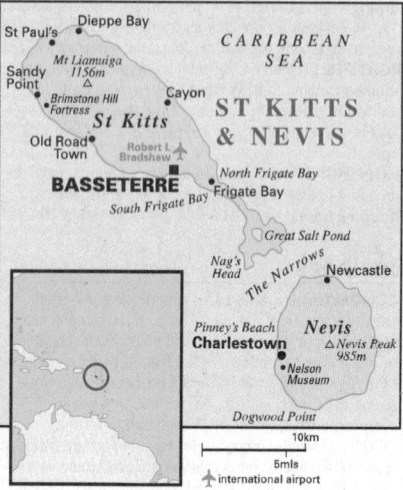

Location: Eastern Caribbean, Leeward Islands.

Time: GMT - 4.

Overview

The islands of St Kitts and Nevis were originally settled by Indians from South America. Although France and, to a lesser extent, Spain squabbled over possession throughout the 16th century, by 1623, the UK had prevailed and set about cultivating sugar on plantations worked by large numbers of slaves.

It was not until September 1983 that the islands became an independent state within the Commonwealth. Since then, the dominant issues for the nation have been the relative positions of the two islands of St Kitts & Nevis. The possibility of a merger with other Leeward Islands and the Virgin Islands has been debated, as has the growing problem of drug trafficking, in which St Kitts & Nevis, like most small Caribbean islands, has become involved. The people of Nevis are themselves deeply split, roughly between the population of the southern towns, which favour independence, and the rest of the island, which does not. Were Nevis to become independent, it would be the world's smallest sovereign state after the Vatican, which naturally gives rise to concerns about its economic viability. Commercialisation has not yet taken over and travellers will enjoy the easygoing, quiet way of life of the local people which remains almost unspoiled. The exotically beautiful island of St Kitts seems to embody a kind of lush tropical paradise usually associated with the South Pacific. The atmosphere here is palpably luxuriant. It is an intoxicating blend of sunlight, sea, air and fantastically abundant vegetation. At the centre of St Kitts stands the spectacular, cloud-fringed peak of Mount Liamuiga (pronounced *Lee-a-mweega*), a dormant volcano covered by a dense tropical forest.

Since the 18th century, Nevis has been known as the 'Queen of the Caribbean', and over the last 100 years, the island has become one of the world's most exclusive resorts and spas. Most of the original plantation owners lived on the island and it became renowned as a centre of elegant and gracious living. Although Nevis has lived through an earthquake and a tidal wave, which is claimed to have buried the former capital, the island is still dotted, as is St Kitts, with fascinating old buildings and historic sites, a delight for any traveller looking for their next Caribbean adventure.

General Information

AREA: St Kitts: 176.1 sq km (66.1 sq miles). **Nevis:** 93.3 sq km (36 sq miles). **Total:** 269.4 sq km (104 sq smiles).
POPULATION: 46,000 (UN, 2001).
POPULATION DENSITY: 170.74 per sq km.
CAPITAL: Basseterre. **Population:** 15,000.

GEOGRAPHY: St Kitts (officially known as St Christopher) lies in the northern part of the Leeward Islands in the eastern Caribbean. The high central body of the island is made up of three groups of rugged volcanic peaks split by deep ravines. The vegetation on the central mountain range is rainforest, thinning higher up to dense bushy cover. From here, the island's volcanic crater, Mount Liamuiga, rises to almost 1200m (4000ft). The foothills, particularly to the north, form a gently rolling landscape of sugar-cane plantations and grassland, while uncultivated lowland slopes are covered with thick tropical woodland and exotic fruits such as papaya, mangoes, avocados, bananas and breadfruit. To the southeast of the island, a low-lying peninsula, on which there are many excellent beaches, stretches towards Nevis.

Some 3km (2 miles) to the south and only minutes away by air or ferry across The Narrows channel is the smaller island of **Nevis**, which is almost circular in shape. The island is skirted by miles of silver-sand beaches, golden coconut groves and a calm, turquoise sea in which great brown pelicans dive for the rich harvest of fish. The central peak of the island, Nevis Peak, is 985m (3232ft) high and its tip is usually capped with white clouds. The mountain is flanked on the north and south sides by two lesser mountains, Saddle Hill and Hurricane Hill, which once served as look-out posts for Nelson's fleet. Hurricane Hill on the north side commands a view of St Kitts and Barbuda. On the island's west side, massed rows of palm trees form a coconut forest. There are pleasant coral beaches on the island's north and west coasts.

GOVERNMENT: Constitutional monarchy since 1983. Gained independence from the UK in 1983. **Head of State:** Queen Elizabeth II, represented locally by Governor General Sir Cuthbert Montroville Sebastian since 1996. **Head of Government:** Prime Minister Dr Denzil Douglas since 1995. **Recent history:** The Head of State of the Federation of St Christopher and Nevis (the islands' formal title) is the British monarch, represented locally by a Governor-General. Legislative power is vested in the Governor-General and the National Assembly, which has 11 members elected directly by universal suffrage for a five-year term and three appointed members. Nevis Island also has a separate legislature that, subject to certain conditions written into the constitution, may secede from the Government of the Federation.

Denzil Douglas was re-elected for a third consecutive term in October 2004. Tourism development and social projects are among his priorities. However, his Government has failed to rejuvenate the ailing sugar industry and deal with the country's large debt.

LANGUAGE: The official language is English.
RELIGION: Anglican and other Christian denominations.
ELECTRICITY: 230 volts AC, 60Hz (117 volts available in some hotels).
SOCIAL CONVENTIONS: All visitors to the islands are cordially welcomed; marriages are valid after two days' residence. Islanders maintain traditions of calypso dancing and music and this can be seen particularly during the summer months. Dress is informal at most hotels. Beach attire is not appropriate for around town, in shops or in restaurants. Nudity is not permitted on any beach. For more formal occasions and functions, a lightweight suit and tie is recommended. It is illegal to dress in camouflaged clothing. Homosexuality is illegal.

Climate

Hot and tropical climate tempered by trade winds throughout most of the year. The driest period is from January to April and there is increased rainfall in summer and towards the end of the year. The volume of rain varies according to altitude; rain showers can occur throughout the year. The average annual rainfall is about 125cm (50 inches) to 200cm (80 inches) with a wetter season from May to October. Like the other Leeward Islands, St Kitts lies in the track of violent tropical hurricanes which are most likely to develop between August and October.
Required clothing: Tropical lightweights, with light rainwear advisable all year round.

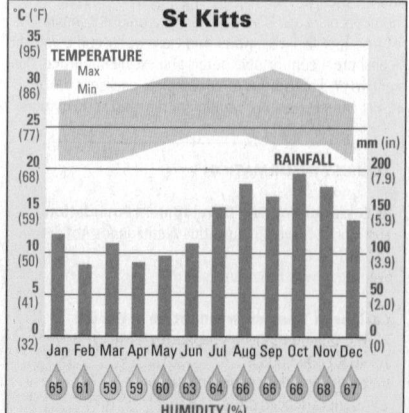

Communications

Telephone: IDD is available. Country code: 1 869.
Mobile telephone: Unregistered roaming is available – visitors with TDMA handsets can make calls without registering, provided they can give a credit card number.
Internet: Public access is available at many hotels and the Internet kiosk at the *Cable & Wireless* (website: www.candw.kn) offices in Basseterre, St Kitts.
Post: Airmail to Western Europe takes five to seven days. Post office hours: Mon-Wed, Fri and Sat 0800-1500, Thurs 0800-1100.
MEDIA: The Government operates national television and radio networks. There are several private radio stations. The main political parties publish weekly or fortnightly newspapers.
Press: Newspapers published in English include: *The Democrat* (website: www.pamdemocrat.org), *The St Kitts and Nevis Observer* (website: www.stkittsnevisobserver.com) (weekly) and *The Labour Spokesman* (website: www.sknlabourparty.org/spokesman) (twice weekly).
TV: *ZIZ Television* is a Government-owned TV channel.
Radio: *ZIZ* and *ZBC Radio* are Government-owned stations. *Winn FM*, *Voice of Nevis* (*VON*) and *Big Wave* are commercial stations.

Passport/Visa

	Passport Required?	Visa Required?	Return Ticket Required?
Full British	Yes	No/2	Yes
Australian	Yes	No	Yes
Canadian	1	No	Yes
USA	1	No	Yes
Other EU	Yes	No/2	Yes
Japanese	Yes	No	Yes

Note: *Regulations and requirements may be subject to change at short notice, and you are advised to contact the appropriate diplomatic or consular authority before finalising travel arrangements. Any numbers in the chart refer to the footnotes below.*

PASSPORTS: Passport valid for six months after date of return required by all except:
1. Antigua & Barbuda, Dominica, Grenada, St Lucia, St Vincent & The Grenadines, holders of British Dependent Territories Citizen or British Overseas Citizen Passport issued in Montserrat, nationals of Canada and the USA with valid photo ID.
VISAS: Required by all except the following for stays of up to three months:
(a) **2.** nationals of countries as indicated in the chart above, except nationals of Czech Republic, Estonia, Hungary, Latvia, Lithuania, Malta, Poland, Portugal, Slovak Republic and Slovenia who *do* require a visa; Holders of British passports issued to residents of Montserrat endorsed "British Overseas Territories Citizen" *or* "British Overseas Citizen" for stays of up to six months.
(b) nationals of Commonwealth countries (except nationals of Brunei, Cameroon, Mozambique, Pakistan, South Africa and Uganda who *do* require a visa). Nationals of Pakistan can obtain a visa on arrival for up to one month;
Nationals of Antigua & Barbuda, Dominica, Grenada, St Lucia, St Vincent & The Grenadines for stays of up to six months;
(c) nationals of Argentina, Bahrain, Bolivia, Brazil, Chile, Colombia, China (providing holding Hong Kong passport (SAR China), Costa Rica, Ecuador, Egypt, El Salvador, Guatemala, Honduras, Iceland, Israel, Jordan, Korea (Rep), Kuwait, Liechtenstein, Mexico, Monaco, Nicaragua, Norway, Oman, Panama, Paraguay, Peru, Qatar, Saudi Arabia, Taiwan (China), Turkey, United Arab Emirates, Uruguay, US Virgin Islands and Venezuela;
(d) those continuing their journey to a third country by the same aircraft within 24 hours without leaving the airport.
Types of visa and cost: *Ordinary*: US$50. Cost depends on nationality of applicant. Paid by cheque or postal order only.
Validity: Usually up to three months.
Application to: Consulate (or Consular section at Embassy or High Commission), *or* British Consulate in countries with no representation; see *Passport/Visa Information*.
Visa Requirements: (a) Passport valid for six months after the date of return. (b) Application form. (c) Fee. (d) Two colour passport photos. (e) Proof of adequate funds. (f) Proof of return journey.
Working days required: Two to three.
Temporary residence: Apply to the Ministry of Home Affairs, Basseterre, St Kitts.

PASSPORT/VISA INFORMATION

High Commission for St Kitts & Nevis in the UK
2nd Floor, 10 Kensington Court, London W8 5DL, UK
Tel: (020) 7937 9718.
Opening hours: Mon-Thurs 1000-1730, Fri 1000-1700.

Embassy of St Kitts & Nevis in the USA
3216 New Mexico Avenue, NW,
Washington, DC 20016, USA
Tel: (202) 686 2636.
Website: www.stkittsnevis.org

Money

Currency: Eastern Caribbean Dollar (XCD; symbol EC$) = 100 cents. Notes are in denominations of EC$100, 50, 20, 10 and 5. Coins are in denominations of EC$1, and 25, 10, 5, 2 and 1 cents. US Dollars are also legal tender on the islands.
Note: The Eastern Caribbean Dollar is tied to the US Dollar.
Currency exchange: Most major currencies can be exchanged at banks on the islands.
Credit & debit cards: All major cards are widely accepted. Check with your credit or debit card company for details of merchant acceptability and other services that may be available. ATMs are widely available.
Traveller's cheques: To avoid additional exchange rate charges, travellers are advised to take traveller's cheques in US Dollars.
Currency restrictions: There are no restrictions on the import of local or foreign currency, provided declared on arrival. Export of local and foreign currency is limited to the amount imported and declared.
Banking hours: Mon-Thurs 0800-1400, Fri 0800-1600.
Exchange rate indicators:
Rate at time of publishing
£1.00= EC$4.76
$1.00= EC$2.72

Duty Free

The following goods may be imported into St Kitts & Nevis by travellers aged 18 and over without incurring customs duty:
200 cigarettes or 50 cigars or 225g of tobacco; 0.95l of wine or spirits.

Public Holidays

Below are listed Public Holidays for the January 2006-June 2007 period.
2006: Jan 1 New Year's Day. **Jan 2** Carnival Day. **Apr 14** Good Friday. **Apr 17** Easter Monday. **May 1** May Day. **Jun 5** Whit Monday. **Jun 12** Queen's Birthday. **Aug 7** August Monday. **Sep 19** Independence Day. **Dec 25** Christmas Day. **Dec 26** Boxing Day.
2007: Jan 1 New Year's Day. **Jan 2** Carnival Day. **Apr 6** Good Friday. **Apr 9** Easter Monday. **May 1** May Day. **May 28** Whit Monday. **Jun 12** Queen's Birthday.

Health

	Special Precautions?	Certificate Required?
Yellow Fever	No	1
Cholera	No	No
Typhoid & Polio	No	N/A
Malaria	No	N/A

Note: *Regulations and requirements may be subject to change at short notice, and you are advised to contact your doctor well in advance of your intended date of departure. Any numbers in the chart refer to the footnotes below.*

1: A yellow fever vaccination certificate is required from travellers over one year of age arriving within six days from infected areas.
Food & drink: Mains water is chlorinated and safe. Bottled water is available and is advised for the first weeks of stay. Drinking water outside main cities and towns may be contaminated and sterilisation is advisable. Milk is pasteurised and dairy products are safe for consumption. Local meat, poultry, seafood, fruit and vegetables are generally considered safe to eat.
Other risks: *Hepatitis A, dengue fever* and *leptospirosis* occur.
Health care: There are large general hospitals in Basseterre and Charlestown, and a smaller public hospital at Sandy Point, St Kitts. There are no private hospitals, but several doctors and dentists are in private practice. Payment upfront will often be required, therefore health insurance is advised.

Travel - International

AIR:
Most international flights are via Antigua, Puerto Rico or St Maarten. *American Airlines* also has regular flights from the USA. *LIAT (LI)* (website: www.liatairline.com) runs several flights a week from Antigua and offers day-trip charters to St Maarten (for duty free shopping) and Antigua & Barbuda. Other airlines serving the islands include *American Eagle* (website: www.aa.com), *Caribbean Star* (website: www.flycaribbeanstar.com) and *Winair* (website: www.fly-winair.com).
Approximate flight times: From *London* to St Kitts is 12 hours, including stopover in Antigua. From *New York* to St Kitts is five hours.
Main airports: *St Kitts (SKB) (Robert Llewellyn Bradshaw,* formerly *Golden Rock Airport)* is 3.2km (2 miles) from Basseterre on St Kitts. *To/from the airport*: Taxi fares are regulated; fares from the airport to Basseterre are approximately EC$17 (50 cents is charged on each additional piece of luggage over one). *Facilities*: Tourist information, restaurant and duty-free shop.
Newcastle Airfield (NEV) is 11km (5 miles) from Charlestown on Nevis.
Departure tax: EC$41. Children under 12 years of age are exempt. An environment levy fee of EC$4 is also payable on departure.
SEA:
Main ports: *Basseterre*. This is a deep-water port capable of berthing ships up to 120m (400ft) and is regularly visited by cruise liners. Regular ferry services operate from St Kitts to St Maarten.

Travel - Internal

AIR:
Nevis Express (VF) which ran a daily round-trip from St Kitts to Nevis is no longer in operation.
SEA: There are regular passenger ferry services on the *MV Caribe Queen*, the *Sea Hustler* and the *Carib Breeze*, between Basseterre (St Kitts) and Charlestown (Nevis) with two to four sailings daily (travel time - 45 minutes). For information, contact the General Manager, St Kitts & Nevis Port Authority, Basseterre.
ROAD:
A good road network on both islands makes any area accessible within minutes. Driving is on the left. Extra care must be taken at night as roads are not well lit. **Bus:** There are privately run bus services, which are comfortable and make regular, but unscheduled, runs between villages. **Taxi:** Services on both islands have set rates. A schedule of taxi rates is obtainable at the government headquarters. There is a 50 per cent surcharge between 2200-0600. Taxi drivers expect a 10 per cent tip.
Car & moped hire: A selection of cars and mopeds can be hired from several companies. It is best to book cars through the airline well in advance. When hiring scooters safety equipment is not included in the price; those hiring these must bear this in mind as other road users do not usually give scooters due consideration. **Documentation:** Before driving any vehicle, including motorcycles, a local Temporary Driver's Licence must be obtained from the Police Traffic Department. This is readily issued on presentation of an International Driving Permit or national driving licence, and a fee of EC$125 for a licence valid for one year, or EC$62.50 for a licence valid for six months.
Travel times: The following chart gives travel times from **Basseterre**, St Kitts (in hours and minutes) to other major towns on the islands:

	Air	Road	Sea
Newcastle, Nevis	0.05	-	-
Charlestown, Nevis	-	-	0.45
Sandy Point	-	0.20	-
Frigate Bay	-	0.10	-
Cockleshell Bay	-	0.35	-

Travel Advice

Most visits to St Kitts and Nevis are trouble-free but you should be aware of the global risk of indiscriminate international terrorist attacks, which could be against civilian targets, including places frequented by foreigners. This advice is based on information provided by the Foreign and Commonwealth Office in the UK. It is correct at time of publishing. As the situation can change rapidly, visitors are advised to contact the following organisations for the latest travel advice:

British Foreign and Commonwealth Office
Tel: (0845) 850 2829.
Website: www.fco.gov.uk

US Department of State
Website: http://travel.state.gov/travel

Accommodation

In general, prices are considerably reduced in the low season (mid-April to mid-December). Group discounts and package rates are offered by most hotels on request. A government tax of 7 per cent is levied on all hotel bills and the hotels themselves add 10 per cent service charge, although this varies slightly between establishments.
HOTELS:
There is a good range of hotels on the two islands, the majority being on St Kitts; most are small and owner-managed, offering a high standard of facilities and comfort. Many are converted from the great houses and sugar mills on the old estates. A full list of hotels can be obtained from the Embassy, High Commission *or* Tourist Board (see *Top Things To See & Do*).
GUEST HOUSES:
There are several guest houses on both islands. A list is available from the St Kitts & Nevis Department of Tourism.
SELF-CATERING:
There are villas and apartments available. A list and full details are available from the St Kitts & Nevis Department of Tourism.

ACCOMMODATION INFORMATION

St Kitts & Nevis Hotel & Tourism Association (HTA)
PO Box 438, Liverpool Row, Basseterre, St Kitts
Tel: 465 5304.
E-mail: stkitnevhta@caribsurf.com

Credit: © St Kitts Tourism Authority

Top Things To See & Do

St Kitts
- **Basseterre**, the picturesque capital, located near the seabord of the west coast, retains the flavour of both French and British occupation, and there are many Georgian buildings surrounding **Independence Square**. Other sights in or near the capital include: **The Circus**, the public market, **St George's Church**, **Craft House**, **Brimstone Hill Fortress** (a UNESCO world heritage site), **Black Rocks**, **Romney Manor** and the **Caribelle Batik Factory**, the **Primate Research Centre**, **Frigate Bay Development**, the southeastern peninsula and **Mount Liamuiga**'s volcanic crater.
- At **Brimstone Hill**, set your eyes on one of the most impressive New World forts, built on the peak of a sulphuric prominence, known as 'The Gibraltar of the West Indies'. It commands the southern approach to what were the sugar mill plains, and boasts a splendid view of the nearby islands of Saba and St Eustatius. Built in 1690, Brimstone was the scene of a number of Franco-British battles during the 18th century.
- **Frigate Bay** is the main resort area on the island and has been designated a Tourist Area by the Government. It boasts two fine beaches, hotels, a golf course and a casino.

Nevis
- **Charlestown,** the capital is a delightful town, with weathered wooden buildings decorated like delicate gingerbread and great arches of brilliantly coloured bougainvillaea. The town contains several reminders of Nevisian history, such as the **Cotton Ginnery**, Alexander Hamilton's birthplace and museum, the **Court House**, the **War Memorial**, the **Alexandra Hospital** and the **Jewish Cemetery**. Some of the plantation houses have now been transformed into superb hotels, such as the famous **Nisbet**. Other sights in or near Charlestown include: **Nevis Philatelic Bureau**, the **Public Library**, the **Market**, **Bath House** (one of the oldest hotels in the Leeward Islands), Eva Wilkin's studio, Eden Brown's Great House, **Fig Tree Church**, **Nelson Museum**, **Bath Hot Springs**, the **Botanical Gardens of Nevis** and the **Newcastle Pottery**.
- North of Charlestown is **Pinney's Beach**, one of the best

on the island, an expanse of silver sand, backed by palm trees. Head further north still to **Black Sand Beach** and **Hurricane Hill,** which offer excellent views of both St Kitts and Barbuda.

- **Swimming** is excellent; most hotels have freshwater pools and some have their own beaches. **Scuba-diving** and **snorkelling** are catered for and beach hotels generally have equipment. Several Basseterre skippers are equipped to take scuba parties. There are dozens of unexplored wrecks around the islands. **Sailing** boats can be hired from beach hotels, although Nevis has very limited facilities. Fast boats and **water-skiing** equipment are available for hire. **Fishing** trips can be organised. Deep-sea fishing is a speciality.

- **Horseriding** in the rainforest or on the beach can be arranged through hotels.

- There are several **hiking** trails leading into the mountains or through the rainforest. Local guides can be arranged through hotels.

TOURIST INFORMATION

St Kitts Tourism Authority in the UK
10 Kensington Court, London W8 5DL, UK
Tel: (020) 7376 0881.
Website: www.stkitts-tourism.com

St Kitts Tourism Authority in the USA
414 East 75th Street, Suite 5, 75th Floor,
New York, NY 10021, USA
Tel: (212) 535 1234 *or* (800) 582 6208 (toll-free in USA).
Website: www.stkitts-tourism.com

Nevis Tourism Authority in the UK
c/o Nevis Island Estates, Elm House, Park Lane,
Lower Froyle, Alton, Hampshire GU34 4LT, UK
Tel: (01420) 520 810 *or* (0870) 200 1314.
Website: www.nevisisland.com

Nevis Tourism Authority in the USA
Tel: (866) 556 3847 (toll-free).

Caribbean Tourism Organisation in the UK
22 The Quadrant, Richmond, Surrey, TW9 1BP, UK
Tel: (020) 8948 0057.
Website: www.doitcaribbean.com *or* www.onecaribbean.org

Credit: © St Kitts Tourism Authority

Entertainment

FOOD & DRINK: St Kitts & Nevis has built up a widely established reputation for fine food, a reputation which the local restauranteurs guard zealously. Restaurants specialise in Chinese, Continental, Creole, French, Indian and West Indian cuisine. Most restaurants in St Kitts offer a continental menu with island variations. Nevis is less grand and Charlestown's small restaurants cater more to Nevisians than visitors. Fruit, including mangoes, papayas and bananas, is sold at the waterfront market. A wide range of imported drinks is available.

National specialities:
- Roast suckling pig.
- Spiny lobster.

- Crab back.
- Curries.
- *Roti,* thin pastry filled with curried potatoes, chickpeas and beef, chicken, goat, shrimp or vegetables.
- *Pelau,* rice, pigeon peas and meat, similar to paella.
- *Conch* (curried, soused or in salad).
- Turtle stews.
- Goat's water (mutton stew).
- Christophine, yams, breadfruit and papaya are also served.

National drinks:
- The locally produced *CSR* (cane spirit) is excellent.
- Local rums include Belmont Estate and Brinley Gold.

Tipping: 10 per cent service charge is added to hotel bills. In restaurants, leave 10 to 15 per cent.

NIGHTLIFE: Very low key. A number of hotels and inns have string or steel bands to dance to on Saturday nights in the peak season, and there is a disco called *J's Place* at the foot of the Brimstone Hill Fortress in St Kitts. *Reflections Night Club,* also in St Kitts, is open until the small hours. St Kitts has two casinos in Frigate Bay, complete with slot machines, roulette wheels and blackjack tables. In Nevis, *Club Trenim* is recommended. Otherwise, entertainment centres around the pleasant bars of the inns and hotels.

SHOPPING: Local crafts include carvings, batik, wall hangings, leather art and coconut work. Local textiles and designs are also available. Stamp collectors should note the excellent Philatelic Bureaux in Basseterre and Charlestown. Duty free shopping is relatively new to St Kitts and, as yet, only a few shops feature imported merchandise at substantial savings. Nevis' hot pepper sauce, ranked among the Caribbean's best, is a good take-home item and can be bought at the Main Street grocery in Charlestown. There are shopping malls on St Kitts these include TDC Mall and Pelican Mall. Friday and Saturday are the busy market days, and visitors should not miss the chance to witness this abundance of exotic food stalls, accompanied by lively local chatter. **Shopping hours:** Mon-Sat 0830-1200 and 1300-1600; some shops close early on Thursday.

Business

- **GDP:** US$403.9 million.
- **Main exports:** Foodstuffs, electronics, beverages and tobacco.
- **Main imports:** Machinery, manufactures goods, foods and fuel.
- **Main trade partners:** US, UK and CARICOM countries.

ECONOMY: St Kitts & Nevis has an agricultural economy, the mainstay of which is the sugar industry. As the world sugar price has been very low in the past few years and several sugar crops have been badly damaged by hurricanes and other adverse climatic conditions, St Kitts & Nevis has come to rely on regular injections of foreign aid to prevent economic collapse. The Government has responded by trying to broaden the base of the economy; bananas, yams and sweet potatoes are now important crops and the cultivation of rice and coffee is developing. Fishing is also growing in commercial importance. Manufacturing is dominated by sugar products, and textiles and drinks are also produced. A thriving electronics and data-processing sector is the principal success story from the Government's diversification policy, as is tourism which is developing rapidly, particularly on Nevis, and now brings about US$70 million a year into the economy. More recently, and especially on Nevis, an 'offshore' financial services industry has developed: there are now over 10,000 foreign businesses registered on the island and the government has been obliged to meet new international standards regarding the investigation of money-laundering. Unemployment is among the lowest in the Caribbean.

BUSINESS ETIQUETTE: Businesswear for men usually consists of a short- or long-sleeved shirt and tie, or open-neck tunic shirt or, alternatively, safari-type suits. **Office hours:** Mon-Fri 0800-1200 and 1300-1600.

CONFERENCES/CONVENTIONS: For further information on conferences and convention possibilities, contact the St Kitts & Nevis Hotel & Tourism Association (see *Accommodation Information*).

COMMERCIAL INFORMATION

St Kitts & Nevis Chamber of Industry and Commerce
PO Box 332, Horsford Road, Fortlands,
Basseterre, St Kitts
Tel: 465 2980.
Website: www.stkittsnevischamber.org

St Lucia

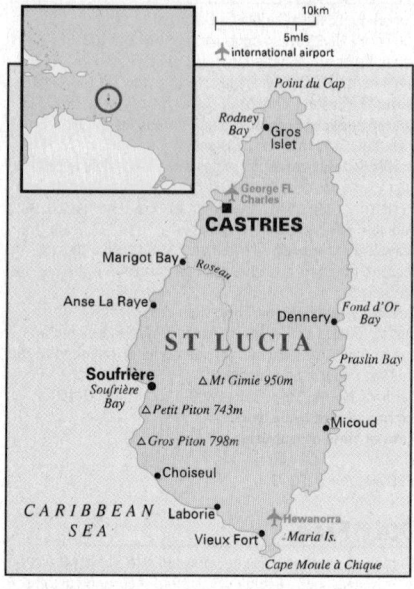

Location: Eastern Caribbean, Windward Islands.

Time: GMT - 4.

Overview

St Lucia is a beautiful volcanic island with lush rainforests, undulating agricultural land and unspoilt beaches. It is also one of the world's breeziest places, where the trade winds blow in from the sea to the southern shore.

Before the visitor influx, banana exports sustained St Lucia, especially after 1964 when it stopped producing sugar cane. Realising the island's potential as a tourist destination, the Government is now focusing its efforts on further diversification, principally directed towards the creation of a service sector based on tourism and financial services. There is indeed a lot on offer on the island: St Lucia has excellent beaches, mountain scenery, the Qualibou Volcano and its boiling sulphur springs, orchids and exotic plants, and tropical flower-lined roadsides. There is still considerable British and French influence felt on the island. Fierce resistance from the indigenous Carib Indians kept British and French colonists away from the island for 50 years. Then, between the signing of a peace treaty with the French in 1660 and the British takeover of the island in 1814, ownership changed no fewer than 14 times! The British maintained control until 1979, when St Lucia was granted independence. The French influence lives on in the patois spoken in the country.

Add the people's friendliness and hospitality, and any visitor to St Lucia will be able to relax and enjoy the islanders' leisurely lifestyle.

General Information

AREA: 616.3 sq km (238 sq miles).
POPULATION: 152,000 (UN, 2005).
POPULATION DENSITY: 246.63 km.
CAPITAL: Castries. **Population:** 67,000 (official estimate 2004).
GEOGRAPHY: St Lucia is the second-largest of the Windward Islands. It has some of the finest mountain scenery in the West Indies, rich with tropical vegetation. For such a small island, 43km (27 miles) by 23km (14 miles), St Lucia has a great variety of plant and animal life. Orchids and exotic plants of the genus *anthurium* grow wild in the rainforests and the roadsides are covered with many colourful tropical flowers. Flamboyant trees spread shade and blossom everywhere. Indigenous wildlife includes a species of ground lizard unique to St Lucia, and the *agouti*

and the *manicou*, two rodents, common throughout the island. The Amazona versicolor parrot is another, though more elusive, inhabitant of the deep interior rainforest. The highest peak is Mount Gimie at 950m (3117ft). Most spectacular are Gros Piton and Petit Piton, ancient, volcanic forest-covered cones which rise out of the sea on the west coast. Soufri (vents in a volcano which exude hydrogen sulphide, steam and other gases) and boiling waterpools can be seen here. The mountains are intersected by short rivers which in some areas form broad fertile valleys. The island has excellent beaches and is surrounded by a clear, warm sea.
GOVERNMENT: Constitutional monarchy. Gained independence from the UK in 1979. **Head of State:** Queen Elizabeth II, represented locally by Governor General Calliopa Pearlette Louisy since 1997. **Head of Government:** Prime Minister Kenny Davis Anthony since 1997. **Recent history:** Under the independence constitution, the Head of State is the British Monarch, represented by a Governor-General. Legislation is the responsibility of the 17-member House of Assembly, which is directly elected by universal adult suffrage for a 5-year term, and the 11-member Senate, composed of appointees of the Prime Minister (six nominations), the leader of the main opposition party (three nominations) and the Governor-General (two nominations). Kenny Anthony won a second term as Prime Minister in December 2001, the St Lucia Labour Party (SLP) gaining 14 of the 17 contested seats. The remaining seats were taken by the former ruling United Workers Party. His Government's biggest challenges are rising crime levels and high unemployment.
LANGUAGE: English and local French *patois*.
RELIGION: 78 per cent Roman Catholic; also Anglican, Methodist, Seventh Day Adventist and Baptist.
ELECTRICITY: 220 volts AC, 50Hz.
SOCIAL CONVENTIONS: Some French influences still remain alongside the West Indian style of life. The people are friendly and hospitable, and encourage visitors to relax and enjoy their leisurely lifestyle. The *madras* and *foulards* are not often seen in towns, but are sometimes worn at festivals such as the *Feast of St Rose of Lima* in August. Casual wear is acceptable, although some hotels and restaurants encourage guests to dress for dinner. Beachwear should not be worn in towns. It is an offence for anyone, including children, to dress in camouflage clothing. Certain homosexual acts are illegal.

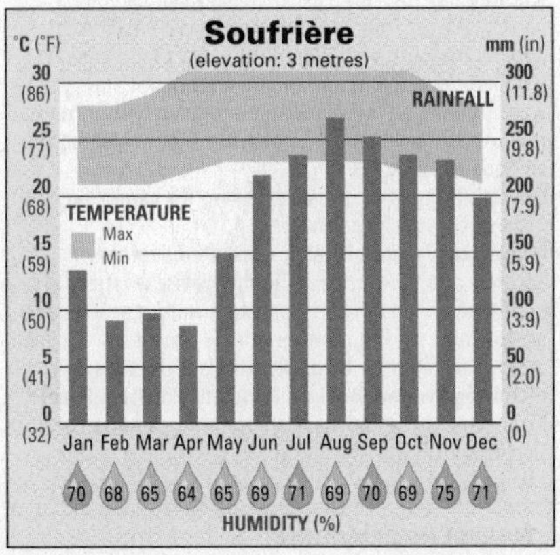
Soufrière
(elevation: 3 metres)
°C (°F)
mm (in)
RAINFALL
TEMPERATURE
Max
Min
30 (86)
25 (77)
20 (68)
15 (59)
10 (50)
5 (41)
0 (32)
300 (11.8)
250 (9.8)
200 (7.9)
150 (5.9)
100 (3.9)
50 (2.0)
0 (0)
Jan Feb Mar Apr May Jun Jul Aug Sep Oct Nov Dec
70 68 65 64 65 69 71 69 70 69 75 71
HUMIDITY (%)

Climate

Hot, tropical climate tempered by trade winds throughout most of the year. The driest period is from December to May and there is increased rainfall in summer and towards the end of the year (June to November).

Communications

Telephone: IDD is available.
Mobile telephone: Coverage is good. Mobile phones are available to hire. Operators on St Lucia have not yet declared roaming agreements with international mobile phone companies.
Internet: Public access is available at the Internet kiosk at Pointe Seraphine. Internet cafes are also run by *Cable & Wireless*.
Post: Airmail to Western Europe takes up to one week. Post office hours: Mon-Fri 0800-1630, Sat 0900-1330.
MEDIA: St Lucia's newspapers and broadcasters are mainly privately-owned. There are no daily newspapers. The government operates a radio network.
Press: The main newspapers are *The Crusader*, *The Mirror* (website: www.stluciamirroronline.com), *The Star* (website: www.stluciastar.com) and *The Voice of St Lucia*. *Visions Magazine* is published by the St Lucia Hotel and Tourism Association.
TV: *Helen Television Systems (HTS)*, *Daher Broadcasting Service* and *Catholic Broadcasting TV Network*.
Radio: *Radio Saint Lucia (RSL)* is a state-owned network. Other stations are *Radio Caribbean International*, *Radio 100* and *Hot FM*.

Passport/Visa

	Passport Required?	Visa Required?	Return Ticket Required?
Full British	Yes	No/1	Yes
Australian	Yes	No/2	Yes
Canadian	1	No/1	Yes
USA	1	No/1	Yes
Other EU	Yes	No/2	Yes
Japanese	Yes	No	Yes

Note: *Regulations and requirements may be subject to change at short notice, and you are advised to contact the appropriate diplomatic or consular authority before finalising travel arrangements. Any numbers in the chart refer to the footnotes below.*

PASSPORTS: Valid passport required by all except:
(a) **1.** nationals of Canada and the USA with valid proof of identity and holding return/onward tickets (for stays of up to six months);
(b) nationals of OECS countries (Antigua & Barbuda, Dominica, Grenada, St Kitts & Nevis and St Vincent & the Grenadines) with a valid National Identity Card;
(c) expired passports accompanied by photo ID issued to nationals of Antigua & Barbuda, Dominica, Grenada, St Kitts & Nevis, St Lucia, St Vincent & the Grenadines and the UK (regardless of endorsement in passport).
VISAS: Required by all except the following:
(a) nationals of Antigua & Barbuda, Dominica, Grenada, St Kitts & Nevis and St Vincent & the Grenadines for a maximum stay of six weeks;
(b) **1.** nationals of Canada, the UK and USA for a maximum stay of six weeks;
(c) **2.** nationals of EU countries (except nationals of Czech Republic, Estonia, Hungary, Latvia, Lithuania and Slovak Republic who *do* require a visa) and Hong Kong (SAR) for stays of up to 28 days;
(d) nationals of American Samoa, Andorra, Argentina, Bermuda, Botswana, Brazil, Brunei, Caricom Member States (except Haiti who have temporary visa restrictions), Cayman Islands, Chile, Costa Rica, Cuba, Ecuador, El Salvador, Faroe Island, French Guiana, French Polynesia, Gibralter, Greenland, Guadeloupe, Guam, Honduras, Israel, Korea (Rep), Lesotho, Malaysia, Marshall Islands, Martinique, Mayotte, Micronesia, Monaco, Netherlands Antilles, New Caledonia, New Zealand, Northern Marina Islands, Norway, Peru, Reunion, St Helena, St Martin, St Marteen, St Pierre & Miquelon, San Marino, Switzerland, Taiwan, Turks & Caicos Islands, Venezuela and Western Samoa, for stays of up to 28 days ;
(e) those continuing their journey to next destination by the same aircraft without leaving the airport.
Types of visa and cost: *Single-entry Tourist*: £35; *Business*: £40; *Student*: £30. These prices are for those applying in the UK. Cost depends on nationality of the applicant and the place of application. Postal applications must include an additional £5 postage fee.
Validity: Up to six weeks. Extensions to some visas can be made at the Immigration Department in St Lucia.
Application to: Consulate (or Consular section at Embassy or High Commission); see *Passport/Visa Information*.
Application requirements: (a) Passport valid for six months from date of return. (b) Completed application form. (c) Two passport-size photos. (d) Sufficient funds to cover duration of stay (e) proof of accommodation. (f) Copy of travel itinerary (g) letter of invitation with contact details (if invited by a friend or relative). (h) Fee, payable by cash (postal order for postal applications). (i) Valid return or onward ticket. *Students* also require a letter from the school, college or university. *Business* applicants also require a letter from employer.
Working days required: Two to three, depending on nationality of applicant.
Temporary residence: Refer applications or enquiries to Consulate, Embassy or High Commission. Processed through the Department of Immigration, St Lucia.

PASSPORT/VISA INFORMATION

St Lucia High Commission in the UK
1 Collingham Gardens, London SW5 0HW, UK
Tel: (020) 7370 7123.
Opening hours: Mon-Thurs 0930-1730, Fri 0930-1700.

Embassy of St Lucia in the USA
3216 New Mexico Avenue, NW,
Washington, DC 20016, USA
Tel: (202) 364 6792.
Website: www.sluonestop.com

Money

Currency: Eastern Caribbean Dollar (XCD; symbol EC$) = 100 cents. Notes are in denominations of EC$100, 50, 20, 10 and 5. Coins are in denominations of EC$1, and 50, 25, 10, 5, 2 and 1 cents. US Dollars are also accepted as legal tender.
Note: The Eastern Caribbean Dollar is tied to the US Dollar.
Currency exchange: US Dollars ensure a better exchange rate. Most banks have ATMs.
Credit & debit cards: American Express, Diners Club, MasterCard and Visa are accepted at all large shopping centre, restaurants, hotels etc. Check with your credit or debit card company for details of merchant acceptability and other services which may be available.
Traveller's cheques: Accepted. US Dollar cheques preferred and will help to avoid additional exchange rate charges.
Currency restrictions: There are no restrictions on the import and export of local or foreign currency.
Banking hours: Generally Mon-Thurs 0830-1500, Fri 0830-1700. Some banks at Rodney Bay Marina are open Sat 0800-1200
Exchange rate indicators: The following figures are included as a guide to the movements of the Eastern Caribbean Dollar against Sterling and the US Dollar:
Rate at time of publishing

£1.00=	EC$4.84
$1.00=	EC$2.73

Duty Free

The following items may be imported into St Lucia without incurring customs duty:
200 cigarettes or 250g tobacco products; 50 cigars; 1l of alcoholic beverage.

Public Holidays

Below are listed Public Holidays for the January 2006-June 2007 period.
2006: Jan 1-2 New Year. **Feb 22** Independence Day. **Apr 14** Good Friday. **Apr 16** Easter Sunday. **Apr 17** Easter Monday. **May 1** Labour Day. **Jun 5** Whit Monday. **Jun 15** Corpus Christi. **Aug 1** Emancipation Day. **Oct 2** Thanksgiving Day. **Dec 13** Festival of Lights and Renewal. **Dec 25-26** Christmas.
2007: Jan 1-2 New Year. **Feb 22** Independence Day. **Apr 6** Good Friday. **Apr 8** Easter Sunday. **Apr 9** Easter Monday. **May 1** Labour Day. **May 28** Whit Monday. **Jun 7** Corpus Christi.

Health

	Special Precautions?	Certificate Required?
Yellow Fever	No	1
Cholera	No	No
Typhoid & Polio	No/2	N/A
Malaria	No	N/A

Note: *Regulations and requirements may be subject to change at short notice, and you are advised to contact your doctor well in advance of your intended date of departure. Any numbers in the chart refer to the footnotes below.*

1: A yellow fever vaccination certificate is required from travellers over one year of age arriving within six days from infected areas.
2: *Typhoid* can be contracted through contaminated drinking water or food in the area. A vaccination is sometimes recommended.
Food & drink: Mains water is normally chlorinated, and whilst relatively safe, may cause mild abdominal upsets. Bottled water is available and is advised for the first few weeks of the stay. Milk is pasteurised and dairy products are safe for consumption. Local meat, poultry, seafood, fruit and vegetables are generally considered safe to eat.
Other risks: *Hepatitis A* occurs along with *dengue fever* and *leptospirosis*. *Bilharzia* (*schistosomiasis*) is present. Avoid swimming and paddling in fresh water; swimming pools which are well chlorinated and maintained are safe. Immunisation against *hepatitis B*, *diphtheria* and *tuberculosis* is sometimes advised.
Rabies is present. For those at high risk, vaccination before arrival should be considered. If you are bitten, seek medical advice without delay; for more information, see the *Health* appendix.
Health care: Costs of health care are high and full health insurance is essential

Travel - International

AIR:
St Lucia is served by many airlines including *Caribbean Star* (website: www.flycaribbeanstar.com) and *LIAT, the*

A B C D E F G H I J K L M N O P Q R S T U V W X Y Z

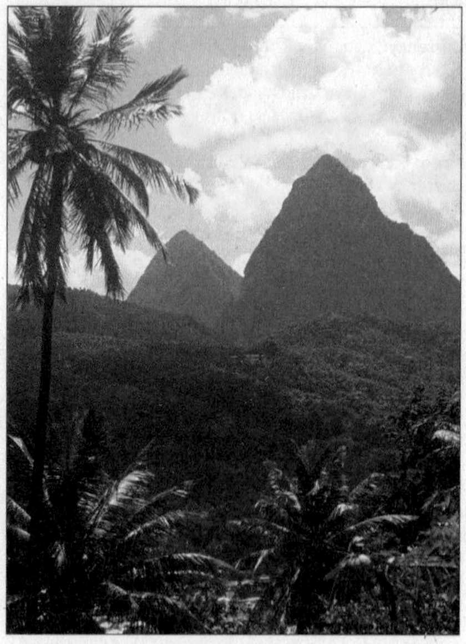

Credit: ©St Lucia Tourist Board

Caribbean Airline (website: www.liatairline.com).
Approximate flight times: From Castries to *London* is eight hours, to *Barbados* is 30 minutes, to *Los Angeles* is nine hours, to *New York* is four hours and to *Singapore* is 33 hours.
Main airports: *George F L Charles (SLU)* (services inter-island connections and small aircraft from Puerto Rico only) *To/from the airport*: Taxis or buses are available into Castries. *Facilities*: Bar/restaurant, a shop and car hire.
Hewanorra (UVF), 3km (2 miles) and 67km (42 miles) from Castries respectively. *To/from the airport*: Taxis or buses are available into Castries. *Facilities*: Bar/restaurant, left luggage and lockers, shops, tourist information, outgoing duty free shop and car hire.
Departure tax: EC$54. Transit passengers and children under 12 years of age are exempt.
SEA:
Main ports: *Castries, Soufrière* and *Vieux Fort. L'Express des Iles*, a high-speed catamaran service, operates between St Lucia and Dominica, calling at Martinique and Guadeloupe (travel times: St Lucia–Martinique – one hour 20 minutes; Martinique–Dominica – one hour 20 minutes). St Lucia is also served by a number of cruise lines as well as local passenger/freight lines. The duty free port at Pointe Seraphine offers two-berth cruise ship facilities, duty free shopping, restaurants and bars; it may be visited by anyone, although a valid passport and an airline ticket are required to make duty free purchases.
For information on airports and sea ports contact the Saint Lucia Air and Sea Ports Authority (SLASPA) (website: www.slaspa.com).

Travel - Internal

AIR:
Helicopter transfers operate between George F L Charles and Hewanorra airports.
SEA:
Boat charters are easily available at Castries, Marigot Bay and Rodney Bay.
ROAD:
All major centres are served by a reasonably good road network. The main cross-island route runs from Vieux Fort in the south of the island to Castries in the north. Roads are narrow and mountainous roads are steep, often with hairpin bends which are not marked. Traffic drives on the left. Seat belts must be worn at all times. Drinking and driving is against the law. **Car hire:** Cars can be obtained either in Castries, Soufrière and Vieux Fort, or through hotels. Hotels and local tour operators run coach trips for groups.
Documentation: On presentation of a national driving licence or International Driving Permit, a local licence will be issued by the police or car hire firm at a cost of US$20 or EC$54 (2005). **Bus:** Minibus services connect rural areas with the capital. There is a good service from Castries to Gros Islet in the north of the island with buses departing every 30 minutes during the day. Many services also operate on weekends and holidays. **Taxi:** Hiring a taxi is easy and cheap, with standard trips having fixed rates which should nevertheless be agreed upon beforehand, as tourists are vulnerable to being overcharged. When hiring a taxi at night care should be taken to hire a reputable company. Tipping is unnecessary.

Travel Advice

Most visits to St Lucia are trouble-free but you should be aware of the global risk of indiscriminate international terrorist attacks, which could be against civilian targets, including places frequented by foreigners.
You should not become complacent about safety and security; cases of robbery and other crimes do occur.
This advice is based on information provided by the Foreign and Commonwealth Office in the UK. It is correct at time of publishing. As the situation can change rapidly, visitors are advised to contact the following organisations for the latest travel advice:

British Foreign and Commonwealth Office
Tel: (0845) 850 2829.
Website: www.fco.gov.uk

US Department of State
Website: http://travel.state.gov/travel

Accommodation

HOTELS:
St Lucia has a range of accommodation to suit every taste and every budget, from deluxe hotels to self-catering apartments. All-inclusive holidays are also proving very popular and several hotels now offer this option. Most hotels provide some form of entertainment in the evening, from calypso music to the ever-popular limbo dancing. Details are available from hotels' reservation desks. A government tax of 8 per cent and service charge of 10 to 15 per cent are added to bills.
GUEST HOUSES:
A wide range is available; some offer self-catering facilities.
CAMPING AND CARAVANNING:
St Lucia's first campsite has recently been established at Anse La Liberte.

ACCOMMODATION INFORMATION

St Lucia Hotel and Tourism Association
PO Box 545, Castries, St Lucia
Tel: 452 5978 *or* 453 1811.
Website: www.stluciatravel.com.lc

The St Lucia Tourist Board also publishes an accommodation rate sheet (see *Top Things To See & Do*).

Top Things To See & Do

- **Castries** is one of the most beautifully situated Caribbean cities. Surrounded by hills, its large, safe harbour at the head of a wide bay is a constant hive of activity. Castries is also a major port of call for cruise ships, which dock at Pointe Seraphine. Head for the spacious **Derek Walcott Square** which features the 19th-century **Catholic Cathedral**, standing in the shade of a 400-year-old samaan tree. There is also a colourful, bustling market. **Morne Fortune**, 'hill of good luck', affords the visitor the chance to inspect the fortification which defends Castries. It also provides a magnificent panorama of the city and the surrounding area. **Heritage walks** are available through a range of tour operators.
- **Gros Islet**, on the northwest coast of the island, stages a street party every Friday. Nearby **Pigeon Island National Landmark** has a small museum telling the history of the island. It was from here that Admiral Rodney set sail in 1782 and destroyed the French Fleet in one of the most decisive engagements in European history. This end of the island is now being developed as a centre for tourism.
- **Anse La Raye**, on the west coast south of Castries, is a colourful fishing village where locals make boats from gum trees; every Friday evening, join the locals at the **Friday Night Fish Fry BBQ**. **Marigot Bay**, also on the west coast, is a secluded, palm-fringed yachtsman's paradise. Above Marigot Bay lies **Cul de Sac**, an area of three large banana plantations. From above, they look like gently moving oceans of green leaves. It was here that the original *Dr Doolittle* was filmed.
- **Soufrière** is the second-largest settlement on the island and takes its name from the volcano. This deep-water port stands at the foot of two extinct volcanoes, the **Pitons**. Rising to 798m (2619ft) above sea level, these are probably St Lucia's most famous landmarks. The town itself is typically West Indian, a cluster of brightly painted arcaded buildings set hard against the jungle.
- The road between Soufrière and Fond St Jacques runs eastwards through the rainforest; here are the **Diamond Waterfalls** in the **Diamond Botanical Gardens** and **Sulphur Springs** - St Lucia's 'drive-in volcano'.
- The picturesque little villages of **Choiseul** and **Laborie** are surrounded by splendid vegetation. The **Morne Coubaril Estate** is also worth a visit.
- On the east of the island, the headlands project into the ocean; a visit to the fishing villages of **Dennery** and **Micoud** is highly recommended.
- **Plantation tours** organised by a number of tour operators take visitors back in time to the colonial era. **Fond d'Or Nature Historic Park** is one tour which covers the Amerindian settlements and historic buildings of the sugar age and the tropical forest surrounding it.
- The sandy beach of **Anse de Sable** offers ideal **windsurfing** conditions for both novice and expert. The waves at **Cas en Bas** and **Vieux Fort** are a challenge even for the most experienced. The west coast, too, offers a selection of resorts and hotels geared to the special needs of the active watersports enthusiast, while elsewhere on the island guests can enjoy **water-skiing** and **para-sailing** above Rodney Bay. The natural and artificial coral makes St Lucia an ideal location for **snorkelling** and **scuba diving**. It is not uncommon to see turtles, nurse sharks and seahorse or even 'The Thing' (said to be St Lucia's Loch Ness Monster, it has been seen during the night around Anse Chastanet) whilst swimming in the clear blue waters. Snorkel equipment is available to hire from most hotels. Diving schools are spread throughout the island can accommodate for all levels of divers. Popular diving sites include **Anse Chastanet**, **Anse Le Raye**, **Coral Gardens** at the base of the Gros Piton, **Fairy Land** at the base of Anse Chastanet, **Lesleen M Shipwreck** and *Superman's* **Flight**. All west coast beaches have good **swimming**. The Atlantic coast has rugged surf and is not recommended to anyone with little experience and ability, and even an extremely proficient swimmer should not go unaccompanied. **Turtle and whale watching** is a great experience for all animal lovers. St Lucia is said to be one of the best places in the world to see whales because 20 species can be seen off the coast, including sperm whales, pilot whales and humpbacks.
- **Go sailing:** hotels offer hobbycats, dinghies and small speedboats by the hour or half-day; cost is dependent on the board basis of your hotel. From **Marigot Bay** and **Rodney Bay**, the more experienced sailor can hire a variety of craft from comparatively basic, small yachts to larger 12m (40ft) and 18m (60ft) vessels, with crew if required. Tour operators can also arrange for stays of a week or more on the island to be coupled with a 'free floating' holiday on board a chartered yacht visiting the neighbouring islands.
- Sea **fishing** trips are possible, fishing for barracuda, mackerel, kingfish and so on.
- **Nature trails and hikes:** *St Lucia Department of Forestry* and the *National Trust* organise a variety of rainforest, mountain and plantation walks. Local guides are available to help **climbers** tackle the Pitons. The main areas designated for **birdwatching** are the **Bois d'Orange Swamp**, **Boriel's Pond** and the **Rain Forest**. Arrangements can be made through the St Lucia Forestry Department.

TOURIST INFORMATION

St Lucia Tourist Board in the UK
1 Collingham Gardens, London SW5 0HW, UK
Tel: (0870) 900 7697.
Website: www.stlucia.org

St Lucia Tourist Board in the USA
9th Floor, 800 Second Avenue, New York, NY 10017, USA
Tel: (212) 867 2950 *or* (800) 456 3984 (toll-free).
Website: www.stlucia.org

Entertainment

FOOD & DRINK: St Lucian food is a combination of Creole with French and West Indian influences. Many imported spirits are available. Most hotels have restaurants, in addition to a wide range in the major towns serving many different types of food. Waiter service is the norm.
National specialities:
- Fresh seafood, including *langouste* (local lobster) cooked in a variety of ways.
- *Lambi* (conch).
- Green fig.
- Salt fish.
- Fried plantain.

National drinks:
- Rum, often served in punch and cocktails.
- Caribbean beer, including the locally brewed *Piton* and *Heineken*.
- Fresh fruit juices.

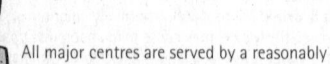

Tipping: An optional 10 to 12 per cent is sometimes added to bills. Taxi drivers do not expect tips.

NIGHTLIFE: Centres mainly in hotels and some restaurants. On Friday nights, the village of Gros Islet hosts a weekly 'jump up', popular with locals and visitors alike; Anse La Raye hold their *Friday Night Fish Fry BBQ*. Indies and *The Late Lime* are two of St Lucia's most popular nightclubs, both featuring live entertainment. During summer, there is little nightlife, but during the winter the resorts are lively, with plenty of local music and dance.

SHOPPING: Special purchases include unique batik and silkscreen designs made into shifts, sports shirts, table mats, cocktail napkins and shopping bags produced at a studio on the road between Castries and La Toc. Other craft outlets sell locally made bowls, beads, straw hats, flour-sack shirts, sisal rugs, bags, sandals and woodwork. Pointe Seraphine features over 30 duty free shops (open seven days a week), bars and restaurants placed around an open piazza. Another duty free shopping complex has recently been opened at La Place Carenage. Duty free shopping is available to all visitors, provided they present their passport or airline ticket when purchasing goods. **Shopping hours:** Mon-Fri 0830-1230 and 1330-1630, Sat 0830-1230 and 0900-2100 in shopping malls.

Credit: ©St Lucia Tourist Board

Business

- **GDP:** US$753 million (2004).
- **Main imports:** Food, fuel, manufactured goods, machinery and transport equipment.
- **Main exports:** Bananas, cocoa, vegetables, fruit, other agricultural products, oils and fats and manufactured goods.
- **Main trade partners:** Barbados, Japan, Trinidad and Tobago, UK and USA.

ECONOMY: St Lucia's economy still relies heavily on agriculture but has broadened during the last 15 years. Light industry has been a key part of this process: the establishment of export processing zones and the successful attraction of foreign investment has created a healthy sector producing plastic, textiles and industrial gases and assembling electronic components. There is also a significant construction industry. The main agricultural exports are bananas, coconuts and cocoa. The Government is focusing its efforts on further diversification, principally directed towards the creation of a service sector based on tourism and financial services. It has also affected various deregulation measures and privatisation of a number of major state-owned enterprises. St Lucia is a member of the regional trading bloc, CARICOM, and the region's principal political co-operative grouping, the Organisation of Eastern Caribbean States.

BUSINESS ETIQUETTE: Short- or long-sleeved shirt and tie or a light-weight suit are suitable for most business visits. **Office hours:** Mon-Fri 0800-1630, Sat 0830-1230.

CONFERENCES/CONVENTIONS: A number of hotels offer conference and back-up facilities, with seating for up to 200 persons. The St Lucia Tourist Board can provide details (see *Top Things To See & Do*).

COMMERCIAL INFORMATION

St Lucia Chamber of Commerce, Industry and Agriculture
PO Box 482, Vide Bouteille, Castries, St Lucia
Tel: 452 3165 *or* 453 1540.
Website: www.stluciachamber.org

Solar Tours and Travel (Information on Conferences/Conventions)
20 Bridge Street, PO Box 1519, Castries, St Lucia
Tel: 452 5898.
Website: www.solartoursandtravel.com

St Maarten

Credit: © St Lucia Tourist Board

Location: Eastern Caribbean, Windward Islands.

Time: GMT - 4.

Overview

Occupied since prehistory by Carib Indians, St Maarten was sighted by Christopher Columbus on St Maarten's day in 1493. However, the first European settlers were French and Dutch who, in 1648, partitioned the island. The island has remained under dual sovereignty ever since, the Dutch sector achieving partial independence from the Netherlands in 1954 with the establishment of the Netherlands Antilles. The most prominent physical feature in St Maarten is Mount Flagstaff, an extinct volcano, but the most important for visitors is the excellent beach that follows the south and west coasts. Beach activities and shopping at duty free centres satisfy most tourists. The island is also popular with sailing enthusiasts and divers.

General Information

AREA: 34 sq km (16 sq miles).
POPULATION: 36,231 (1996).
POPULATION DENSITY: 1066 per sq km.
CAPITAL: Philipsburg.
GEOGRAPHY: Politically, St Maarten is one of three Windward Islands in the Netherlands Antilles, although geographically it is part of the Leeward Group of the Lesser Antilles, and not strictly an island – it occupies just one-third of an island otherwise under French control (the French sector is called St Martin), lying 8km (5 miles) south of Anguilla, 232km (144 miles) east of Puerto Rico and 56km (35 miles) due north of St Eustatius. St Maarten is the southern sector, an area of wooded mountains rising from white sandy beaches. To the west, the mountains give way to lagoons and salt flats.
For information on the French sector (St Martin), see the *Guadeloupe* section.
GOVERNMENT: Part of the Netherlands Antilles; dependency of The Netherlands since 1630. **Head of State:** Queen Beatrix of The Netherlands, represented locally by Governor General Frits Goedgedrag. **Head of Government:** Prime Minister Etienne Ys since 2004. The Netherlands Antilles consist of Bonaire, Curaçao, Saba, St Eustatius and St Maarten. The capital of the island group is Willemstad, Curaçao. **Recent History:** As part of the Netherlands Antilles, St Maarten gained partial independence from The Netherlands in 1954. The issue of the Antilles' constitutional status never left the political agenda, however, and was the subject of a referendum on the three Windward Islands in 1994. All three voted to remain within the Antilles. At the most recent general election for the Staten – the local governing body of the Antilles – held in January 2006, the *Partido Antia Restruktura* (PAR, Party for the Restructured Antilles) won the largest number of seats. PAR, which is based on the island of Curaçao, has dominated Antilles' politics since its formation a decade ago.
The leaders of the five Antilles islands agreed with the Dutch Government in late 2005 that each island would become an individual territory and that the federation would be broken up by July 2007. St Maarten will become an autonomous territory of The Netherlands.
LANGUAGE: Dutch is the official language. Papiamento (a mixture of African, Dutch, English, Portuguese and Spanish) is the commonly used *lingua franca*. English and Spanish are also widely spoken.
RELIGION: Protestant, with Roman Catholic and Jewish minorities.
ELECTRICITY: 110/220 volts AC, 60Hz.
SOCIAL CONVENTIONS: Dutch customs are still important throughout the Netherlands Antilles, but tourism has brought increasing US influences and St Maarten is perhaps more easy-going than the southern islands. Dress is casual and lightweight cottons are advised, but it is common to dress up in the evening.

Climate

Hot but tempered by cooling trade winds. The annual mean temperature is 27°C (80°F), varying by no more than two or three degrees throughout the year; average rainfall is 1772mm (70 inches).
Required clothing: Tropicals and cottons are worn throughout the year. Umbrellas or light waterproofs are advisable.

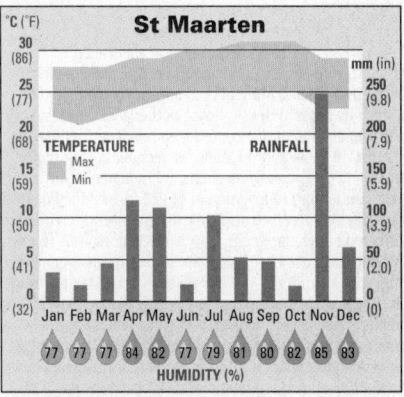
Credit: © St Lucia Tourist Board

Communications

Telephone: Fully automatic system with good IDD. Country code: 599. Calls made through the operator are more expensive and include a 15 per cent tax.
Mobile telephone: Compatible with most US handsets but not with GSM handsets. Phone hire is available at *Telcell's* customer care centre in Philipsburg. Roaming exists (member of the Pan American Roaming Corporation). Most US handsets can be used, and can be activated with a temporary number before or after arrival on the island. Visitors should register online or dial 0 when in an ECC coverage area. Handsets can be hired from ECC in Philipsburg.
Internet: ISPs include *TelNet* (website: www.sintmaarten.net).
Post: Airmail to Western Europe takes four to six days, surface mail takes four to six weeks.
MEDIA: Press: English-language dailies include the *Daily Herald* and *St Maarten Guardian*, published on St Maarten. Most other newspapers in the Netherlands Antilles are published in Dutch or Papiamento.
TV: The *Leeward Broadcasting Corporation* is based in St Maarten.
Radio: The local station is *Voice of St Maarten*.

Passport/Visa

	Passport Required?	Visa Required?	Return Ticket Required?
Full British	Yes	1	Yes
Australian	Yes	2	Yes
Canadian	Yes	2	Yes
USA	Yes	2	Yes
Other EU	Yes	1/2	Yes
Japanese	Yes	2	Yes

Note: *Regulations and requirements may be subject to change at short notice, and you are advised to contact the appropriate diplomatic or consular authority before finalising travel arrangements. Any numbers in the chart refer to the footnotes below.*

PASSPORTS: Passport or official travel documents valid for at least three months after intended return to home country required by all.

VISAS: Required by all except the following:
(a) **1.** nationals of Belgium, Bolivia, Burkina Faso, Chile, Costa Rica, Czech Republic, Ecuador, Germany, Hungary, Israel, Jamaica, Korea (Rep), Luxembourg, Malawi, Mauritius, The Netherlands, Niger, The Philippines, Poland, San Marino, Slovak Republic, Spain, Swaziland, Togo and the UK for touristic stays of up to three months;
(b) most nationals continuing to a third country within 24 hours by the same means of transportation and not leaving the airport and holding tickets with reserved seats and documents for their onward journey.

Note: (a) Nationals of the following countries must apply for a visa *before* entering the country even for touristic purposes: Albania, Bosnia & Herzegovina, Bulgaria, Cambodia, China (PR) (except Hong Kong SAR), CIS, Colombia, Cote d'Ivoire, Croatia, Cuba, Dominican Republic, Estonia, Ghana, Guinea-Bissau, Haiti, Kenya, Korea (DPR), Latvia, Libya, Lithuania, Macedonia (Former Yugoslav Republic of), Mali, Nigeria, Romania, Serbia & Montenegro and Vietnam. (b) **2.** All other nationals may enter without a visa for touristic stays of up to 14 days. (c) All stays can be extended locally by the same period that they are valid for.

Types of visa and cost: All visas, regardless of duration of stay or number of entries permitted on visa, cost 35.

Validity: Visas are generally issued for as long as duration of stay, up until a maximum 90 days from date of issue.

Application requirements: (a) Passport or equivalent travel document valid for a minimum of three months after intended return to home country. Passports should contain a blank visa page and endorse residence permit. For minors (18 years and under), an approval of both parents or legal guardians with a copy of each parent's/guardian's passport is required. If passport is new, the old passport must also be submitted. (b) One fully completed application form. (c) One recent passport-size photo per person endorsed on passport, with daytime phone number and address written clearly on the back. More photos may be required. (d) Fee, payable by postal order (to Royal Netherlands Embassy) or cash. Cheques are not accepted. Visa handling fees may be charged on applications handed in, regardless of outcome, depending on Embassy/Consulate. (e) Evidence of sufficient funds amounting to a minimum of £30 for each day of stay (cash not accepted), eg original bank statements, credit card with credit limit statement, traveller's cheques. (f) A recent and original letter from employer, stating commencement date, with last payslip. If self-employed, submit letter from solicitor, accountant or company house. If unemployed, submit social benefit booklet. If in education, submit a recent and original letter from school/college/university, confirming attendance. (g) Valid medical or travel insurance. *Tourist*: (a)-(g) and, (h) Invitation from family or proof of accommodation. (i) Return or onward ticket(s), plus necessary documents for returning to country of origin. *Business*: (a)-(g) and, (h) Invitation from company that you are visiting.

Application to: Nearest Embassy of the Kingdom of The Netherlands. All further information about visa requirements may be obtained from The Royal Netherlands Embassies which formally represent the Netherlands Antilles; see *Passport/Visa Information* in *The Netherlands* section.

Working days required: Applications should be lodged at least one month prior to departure.

Temporary residence: Enquire at the office of the Lieutenant Governor of the Island Territory of St Maarten, Philipsburg, St Maarten. In certain cases, Dutch Europeans may be permitted to reside in the Netherlands Antilles without having to apply for a residence permit. However, it is best to consult the nearest Dutch Embassy/Consulate in advance to ascertain whether this is applicable taking into consideration the individual circumstances of the traveller.

Credit: © St Maarten Tourist Bureau

PASSPORT/VISA INFORMATION

Office of the Minister Plenipotentiary of the Netherlands Antilles
PO Box 90706, Badhuisweg 173-175,
2597 JP
The Hague, The Netherlands
Tel: (70) 306 6111.
Website: www.doitcaribbean.com *or* www.onecaribbean.org

Money

Currency: Netherlands Antilles Guilder or Florin (ANG) = 100 cents. Notes are in denominations of ANG250, 100, 50, 25, 10 and 5. Coins are in denominations of ANG5 and 1, and 50, 25, 10, 5 and 1 cents. There are also a large number of commemorative coins which are legal tender. US Dollars are widely accepted, and prices are usually quoted in both Dollars and Guilders.

Note: The ANG is linked to the US Dollar.

Currency exchange: All major currencies can be exchanged at banks on the island.

Credit & debit cards: All major credit cards are widely accepted.

Traveller's cheques: Widely accepted. To avoid additional exchange rate charges, travellers are advised to take traveller's cheques in US Dollars.

Currency restrictions: There are no restrictions on the import and export of local or foreign currency, except the import and export of amounts of foreign currency exceeding ANG20,000 must be declared. The import of Dutch or Surinam silver coins is prohibited.

Banking hours: Mon-Fri 0830-1130 and 1330-1630. Some banks are also open on Saturday.

Exchange rate indicators:

Rate at time of publishing	
£1.00=	ANG3.14
$1.00	ANG1.78

Duty Free

The following may be imported into St Maarten by tourists over 15 years of age only without incurring customs duty:
200 cigarettes or 50 cigars or 100 cigarillos or 250g tobacco; 2l of alcoholic beverages; gifts to a value of ANG100.

Restricted items: The import of souvenirs and leather goods from Haiti is not advisable.

Public Holidays

Below are listed Public Holidays for the January 2006-June 2007 period.

2006: Jan 1 New Year's Day. **Apr 14** Good Friday. **Apr 16-17** Easter. **Apr 29** Carnival. **Apr 30** Queen's Birthday. **May 1** May Day. **May 25** Ascension. **Jul 21** Schoelcher Day (Abolition of Slavery). **Nov 1** All Saints' Day. **Nov 11** St Maarten Day. **Dec 15** Kingdom Day. **Dec 25** Christmas Day. **Dec 26** Boxing Day.

2007: Jan 1 New Year's Day. **Apr 6** Good Friday. **Apr 8-9** Easter. **Apr 29** Carnival. **Apr 30** Queen's Birthday. **May 1** May Day. **May 17** Ascension.

Health

	Special Precautions?	Certificate Required?
Yellow Fever	No	1
Cholera	No	No
Typhoid & Polio	No	N/A
Malaria	No	N/A

Note: *Regulations and requirements may be subject to change at short notice, and you are advised to contact your doctor well in advance of your intended date of departure. Any numbers in the chart refer to the footnotes below.*

1: A yellow fever vaccination certificate is required from travellers over six months of age arriving within six days of leaving or transiting infected areas.

Food & drink: Water on the island is considered safe to drink. Bottled mineral water is widely available. Milk is pasteurised and dairy products are safe for consumption. Local meat, poultry, seafood, fruit and vegetables are generally considered safe to eat.

Other risks: *Hepatitis A* may occur. *Rabies* occurs.

Health care: There is one general hospital, the St Maarten Medical Centre in Cayhill. Medical care is good. Medical insurance is advised.

Travel - International

AIR:

The national airline of the Netherlands Antilles is *ALM (LM)*. The Government-owned *Winair (WIA)*, based at Princess Juliana Airport, has scheduled flights to the Lesser Antilles, as well as charter flights to destinations throughout the Eastern Caribbean. Other airlines serving St Maarten include *Air France, American Airlines, BWIA, KLM, LIAT* and *TWA*.

Approximate flight times: From St Maarten to *London* (via Amsterdam) is 12 to 14 hours, to *Los Angeles* is nine hours, to *New York* is four hours 10 minutes, to *St Croix* is 45 minutes and to *Singapore* is 33 hours (all depending on connections).

Main airports: *Princess Juliana (SXM)*, 15km (9.5 miles) west of Philipsburg (travel time - 15 minutes), receives regular scheduled flights from other Caribbean islands, Europe and the USA. *To/from the airport*: Taxis are available. *Facilities*: Bank, a restaurant, refreshments, duty free shopping and car hire. In order to protect the livelihood of local taxi drivers, cars hired at the airport are delivered to guests' hotels.

Esperance (SFG), an airport in the French sector, is smaller and not equipped for jets.

Departure tax: US$6 to Netherlands Antilles; US$20 for international departures. Prices vary according to the airport. Transit passengers and children under two years of age are exempt.

SEA:

St Maarten is a leading port of call for cruise liners. Ferry services operate to Saba, St Barts and St Kitts & Nevis. Cruises operated by *Cunard, Holland America, Prince's Cruise* and *Royal Viking* regularly stop at Philipsburg.

Travel - Internal

SEA: Small boats may be chartered for fishing trips, scuba diving, water-skiing or visits to neighbouring islands. Daily ferries run to and from Anguilla, whilst a catamaran serves St Barts. There are marinas at Oyster Pond, Philipsburg and Simpson Bay Lagoon.

ROAD:

Most roads are good. Traffic drives on the right. **Bus:** These run regularly between Philipsburg and Marigot. Minibuses serve the more popular destinations. **Taxi:** There are good services on the island running from the airport, main hotels and towns. Taxis do not have meters but fares are fixed. There is a 50 per cent surcharge after midnight. There is a taxi station at Wathey Square. Taxi drivers do not expect a tip. **Car hire:** There are plenty of car hire firms in the city and at the airport. Chauffeur-driven cars are also available. **Documentation:** A national driving licence is acceptable.

Travel Advice

Most visits to St Maarten are trouble-free but you should be aware of the global risk of indiscriminate international terrorist attacks, which could be against civilian targets, including places frequented by foreigners.

This advice is based on information provided by the Foreign and Commonwealth Office in the UK. It is correct at time of publishing. As the situation can change rapidly, visitors are advised to contact the following organisations for the latest travel advice:

British Foreign and Commonwealth Office
Tel: (0845) 850 2829.
Website: www.fco.gov.uk

US Department of State
Website: http://travel.state.gov/travel

Accommodation

HOTELS:

St Maarten has long been a popular holiday destination and is well prepared for the year-round rush, with over 40 hotels offering a total of nearly 9000 beds. Luxury hotels are equipped with everything a visitor could ever need, from casinos to beauty parlours, and have extensive watersports facilities on the premises; even modest beachside establishments usually have their own swimming pool, restaurant and a few skis to lend. A Government tax of 5 per cent is levied on all hotel bills and many hotels add a 10 to 15 per cent service charge. Some even add a further 10 per cent as an energy surcharge.

GUEST HOUSES/APARTMENTS:

Several guest houses cater for the less demanding; apartments and villas may be rented.

ACCOMMODATION INFORMATION

St Maarten Hospitality and Trade Association
PO Box 486, Philipsburg, St Maarten
Tel: 542 0108.
Website: www.shta.com

Top Things To See & Do

- The only town of any size, **Philipsburg** is situated on a sand bar that separates **Great Salt Pond**, an *étang* or salt marsh, from the ocean. The entire town consists of two streets, *Voorstraat* (Front Street) and *Achterstraat* (Back Street), running the length of the isthmus and joined by short, narrow alleys. Land has been reclaimed from the marsh for the construction of a ring road. Many buildings do date back to the early colonial era, and despite the multitude of duty free shops, Philipsburg retains a predominantly colonial atmosphere. The nine shingled churches and the **Queen Wilhelmina Golden Jubilee Monument** are worth seeing. Nearby is **Fort Amsterdam**, dating from the time of the earliest settlers.
- Inland are the picturesque ruins of several plantation mansions, set in the wooded hills around Mount Flagstaff, and the **Border Monument**, celebrating 300 years of co-operation between the French and the Dutch.
- Across the border (no passports are required) is the charming market town of **Marigot**. Small boats are available for various watersports and fishing.
- **Sailing:** Enthusiasts are well catered for on **St Maarten**. The island is one of the Caribbean's leading sailing venues, hosting the *Heineken Regatta* every year. The island has around 12 marinas in beautiful settings. All kinds of vessels can be rented at marinas, from motorboats and yachts to canoes. For those not wishing to pilot their own boat, charter companies offer day trips to other islands, and 'picnic sails' take visitors to secluded bays and nearby uninhabited islands.
- Expeditions for **deep sea fishing** can be arranged, with half- and full-day charters available all year round. Bareboat charters are also available.
- Conditions are excellent for **diving**, with coral reefs located close to the shore. One of the most popular dive sites is the wreck of HMS Proselyte, a British man-of-war which sank in 1801. There are also many good sites for **snorkelling**. **Bodyboarding** is popular.
- Both **cycling** and **mountain biking** can be pursued on the coastal road and along the trails around **Paradise Peak**. There are excellent views.

Credit: © St Maarten Tourist Bureau

TOURIST INFORMATION

St Maarten Tourist Bureau
Vineyard Office Park Building,
WG Buncamper Road 33, Philipsburg, St Maarten
Tel: 542 2337.
Website: www.st-maarten.com

St Maarten Tourist Office in the USA
675 Third Avenue, Suite 1806,
New York, NY 10017, USA
Tel: (212) 953 2084 *or* (800) 786 2278 (toll-free in Canada and USA).
Website: www.st-maarten.com

Caribbean Tourism Organisation in the UK
22 The Quadrant, Richmond, Surrey, TW9 1BP, UK
Tel: (020) 8948 0057.
Website: www.doitcaribbean.com *or* www.onecaribbean.org

Entertainment

FOOD & DRINK: St Maarten's cuisine is as varied as its history, combining Creole, Dutch, English, French and, more recently, international influences. Seafood is, of course, a speciality. Duty on alcohol (and other goods) is low and prices in St Maarten are as cheap as duty free havens elsewhere. Most well-known brands are available.
Tipping: Hotel bills always include a government tax of 5 per cent and often a service charge of 10 to 15 per cent. Elsewhere, 10 to 15 per cent is acceptable for doormen, waiters and bar staff.
NIGHTLIFE: Many of the restaurants and bars have live entertainment and dancing until the early hours. All the large hotels have casinos.
SHOPPING: There is a good range of high-quality duty-free shopping available in Philipsburg. **Shopping hours:** Mon-Sat 0800-1200 and 1400-1800.

Credit: © St Maarten Tourist Bureau

Business

ECONOMY: Tourism dominates the economy; 70 per cent of all visitors to the Netherlands Antilles visit St Maarten, which results in around half a million tourists annually. Further investment in the tourism infrastructure is under way, including a new major port. Government service provides one of the few alternative sources of employment, while subsistence farming and fishing meet a fair proportion of the islands' domestic needs. St Maarten is the only island in the Antilles group apart from Curaçao which has achieved some success in developing an 'offshore' financial services industry. The Netherlands Antilles group enjoys Overseas Territory status at the EU and observer status at the Caribbean trading bloc CARICOM.
BUSINESS ETIQUETTE: Formality in business is expected in most of The Netherlands Antilles and lightweight tropical suits should be worn. Appointments should be made in advance and punctuality is taken very seriously. It is customary to shake hands. **Office hours:** Mon-Fri 0730-1200 and 1330-1630.

COMMERCIAL INFORMATION

St Maarten Chamber of Commerce and Industry
PO Box 454, C A Cannegieter Street 11, Philipsburg, St Maarten
Tel: 542 3590.
Website: www.sintmaartenchamber.org

Credit: © St Maarten Tourist Bureau

St Vincent and The Grenadines

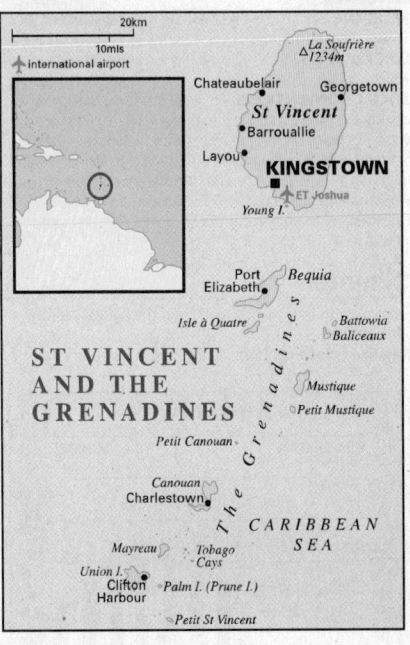

Location: Eastern Caribbean, Windward Islands.

Time: GMT - 4.

Overview

By the time St Vincent was discovered by Christopher Columbus in January 1498, the island had been occupied for nearly 200 years – by Carib Indians from South America, who had subjugated the original Arawak Indian inhabitants. The island remained a Spanish possession until 1627, when it was granted to the British Lord Carlisle. However, the Caribs fought furiously to keep possession of it. In 1783, the Treaty of Versailles restored St Vincent to Britain, after the French had temporarily taken it. Carib resistance was finally crushed in 1795, after which the settlement of St Vincent proceeded on more conventional lines. During the late 19th and 20th centuries, St Vincent endured a series of natural disasters: in 1812, the first recorded eruption of the La Soufrière volcano, during which many lives were lost; in 1896, floods; two years later, a hurricane; and in 1902, the second eruption of La Soufrière, killing 2000 inhabitants. The next eruptions, neither of which caused loss of life, occurred in the 1970s. Soon after World War II, the right to vote was extended to the entire adult population, after decades of restriction. This was an essential preparatory move towards independence – the key issue of the day. For small Caribbean islands like St Vincent & the Grenadines, a variety of proposals were studied during the 1960s, leading to St Vincent's adoption of Associate Statehood with the UK in 1969. Under this agreement the island was internally self-governing, while London looked after foreign and defence matters. It also gave St Vincent the right to declare full independence at any time, which it finally did in October 1979. The viability of St Vincent as a nation state has been the subject of constant debate ever since. St Vincent, like all the Windwards, is volcanic and mountainous with luxuriant vegetation and black sand beaches. The Grenadines are equally lush. Secluded coves, spectacular coral reefs, rainforest hiking and superb sailing conditions are among the main tourist attractions.

General Information

AREA: St Vincent: 344 sq km (133 sq miles). **Grenadines:** 45.3 sq km (17.3 sq miles). **Total:** 389.3 sq km (150.3 sq miles).
POPULATION: 119,000 (official estimate 2002).

POPULATION DENSITY: 305.7 per sq km (2002).
CAPITAL: Kingstown. **Population:** 13,526 (2001).
GEOGRAPHY: St Vincent & the Grenadines make up part of the Windward Islands and lie south of St Lucia. The highest peak of St Vincent, *La Soufrière* (1219m/4000ft), is volcanic, and deep down in the crater is a lake. The 'tail' of the comet of St Vincent (the Grenadines) is a string of islands and cays that splays south from Bequia (pronounced Beck-Way), Petit Nevis, Isle à Quatre and Pigeon Island to Battowia, Baliceaux, Mustique, Petit Mustique, Savan, Canouan, Petit Canouan, Mayreau and the Tobago Cays, Union Island, Palm Island and Petit St Vincent. All of the Grenadines are famous for their white beaches, clear waters and verdant scenery.
GOVERNMENT: Constitutional monarchy. Gained independence from the UK in 1979. **Head of State:** Queen Elizabeth II, represented locally by Governor General Frederick Ballantyne since 2002. **Head of Government:** Prime Minister Ralph Gonsalves since March 2001. **Recent History:** Gonsalves' Unity Labour Party won a second term in the elections held in December 2005. The Party secured 12 of the 15 seats in parliament. The remaining seats are held by the Democratic Party.
LANGUAGE: English.
RELIGION: Roman Catholic, Anglican, Methodist and other Christian denominations.
ELECTRICITY: 220/240 volts AC, 50Hz (except Petit St Vincent which has 110 volts AC, 60Hz).
SOCIAL CONVENTIONS: The Vincentians are fun-loving and easy-going people, and the informal and relaxed lifestyle combines many English influences with West Indian. The Saturday market in Kingstown is bustling with life, seemingly involving all islanders. All visitors are made welcome and casual wear is widely acceptable. Refrain, however, from wearing beachwear or mini shorts on the streets or while shopping.

Climate

Tropical, with trade winds tempering the hottest months, June and July.
Required clothing: Lightweights and waterproofs.

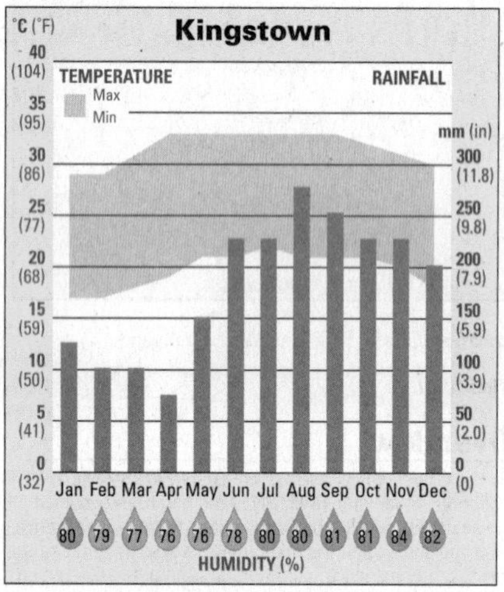

Communications

Telephone: IDD is available. Country code: 1 784.
Mobile telephone: Visitors from North America can use their mobile phones on all the islands.
Internet: Internet cafes are available.
Post: Airmail to Western Europe takes up to two weeks. Post office hours: Mon-Fri 0830-1500, Sat 0830-1130.
MEDIA: Press: All newspapers are in English and most are published weekly. The most popular papers are *The News*, *Searchlight* and *The Vincentian*; *The Herald* is published daily.
TV: *SVG Television* is operated by St Vincent and the *Grenadines Bradcasting Corporation*.
Radio: *NBC Radio* is a partly Government funded national station. private stations include *Hot 97* and *We FM*.

Passport/Visa

	Passport Required?	Visa Required?	Ticket Required?
Full British	1	No	Yes
Australian	Yes	No	Yes
Canadian	1	No	Yes
USA	1	No	Yes
Other EU	Yes	No	Yes
Japanese	Yes	No	Yes

Note: *Regulations and requirements may be subject to change at short notice, and you are advised to contact the appropriate diplomatic or consular authority before finalising travel arrangements. Any numbers in the chart refer to the footnotes below.*

PASSPORTS: Valid passport required by all except:
1. British subjects and nationals of Canada and the USA holding a driver's licence or birth certificate.
VISAS: Not required. Length of stay is determined by immigration authority on arrival, if necessary. Check with Consulate or High Commission before departure. A return or onward ticket is required by all visitors, as well as proof of accommodation and adequate funds.
Temporary residence: Refer applications or enquiries to the Prime Minister's Office in Kingstown.

PASSPORT/VISA INFORMATION

High Commission for St Vincent & the Grenadines
10 Kensington Court, London W8 5DL, UK
Tel: (020) 7565 2874.
Website: www.svghighcom.co.uk
Opening hours: Mon-Thurs 0930-1730, Fri 0930-1700.

Embassy of St Vincent & the Grenadines in the USA
3216 New Mexico Avenue, NW, Washington, DC 20016, USA
Tel: (202) 364 6730.
Website: www.embsvg.com

Money

Currency: Eastern Caribbean Dollar (XCD; symbol EC$) = 100 cents. Notes are in denominations of EC$100, 50, 20, 10 and 5. Coins are in denominations of EC$1, 50, 25, 10, 5, 2 and 1 cents.
Note: The Eastern Caribbean Dollar is tied to the US Dollar.
Currency exchange: All major currencies can be exchanged at banks and at the airport.
Credit & debit cards: All major credit and debit cards are widely accepted. Check with your credit or debit card company for details of merchant acceptability and other services that may be available.
Traveller's cheques: To avoid additional exchange rate charges, travellers are advised to take travellers cheques in US Dollars.
Currency restrictions: Free import of local and foreign currency, subject to declaration. Export of local and foreign currency is limited to the amount declared on import.
Banking hours: Mon-Thurs 0800-1500, Fri 0800-1700. The bank at *ET Joshua Airport* opens Mon-Sat 0700-1700 with additional extensions during the major festivals.
Exchange rate indicators:
Rate at time of publishing
£1.00= EC$4.69
$1.00= EC$2.66

Duty Free

The following items may be imported into St Vincent & the Grenadines without incurring customs duty:
200 cigarettes or 50 cigars or 225g of tobacco; 1.136l of alcoholic beverage.

Public Holidays

Below are listed Public Holidays for the January 2006-June 2007 period.
2006: Jan 1 New Year's Day. **Mar 14** National Heroes' Day. **Apr 14** Good Friday. **Apr 17** Easter Monday. **May 1** Labour Day. **Jun 5** Whit Monday. **Jul 3** Carnival Monday. **Jul 4** Carnival Tuesday. **Aug 1** Emancipation Day. **Oct 27** Independence Day. **Dec 25** Christmas Day. **Dec 26** Boxing Day.
2007: Jan 1 New Year's Day. **Mar 14** National Heroes' Day. **Apr 6** Good Friday. **Apr 9** Easter Monday. **May 1** Labour Day. **May 28** Whit Monday.
Note: If the above dates fall on a Sunday, the following Monday will be taken as a public holiday.

Health

	Special Precautions?	Certificate Required?
Yellow Fever	No	1
Cholera	No	No
Typhoid & Polio	No	N/A
Malaria	No	N/A

Note: *Regulations and requirements may be subject to change at short notice, and you are advised to contact your doctor well in advance of your intended date of departure. Any numbers in the chart refer to the footnotes below.*

1: A yellow fever vaccination certificate is required from travellers over one year of age arriving within six days from infected areas.

Food & drink: Mains water is normally chlorinated, and whilst relatively safe, may cause mild abdominal upsets. Bottled water is available. Milk is pasteurised and dairy products are safe for consumption. Local meat, poultry, seafood, fruit and vegetables are generally considered safe to eat.
Health care: There is one large hospital, the 207-bed Kingstown General Hospital. In addition, there are five district rural hospitals, 38 health centres and one medical laboratory. Visitors can get treatment at primary level, but need a referral for access to the main hospital. As facilities are limited, serious medical problems require evacuation to another island or the USA. Visitors would be expected to pay the full costs for services. Therefore health insurance with emergency repatriation is recommended. Visitors with Blue Cross or Blue Shield should have their cards with them and can obtain assistance through the Life of Barbados company.

Travel - International

AIR:
Travel to St Vincent & the Grenadines is via Barbados, Grenada, Martinique, St Lucia or Trinidad & Tobago, and then on to St Vincent & the Grenadines in a prop plane. *LIAT (LI)* is the main airline serving St Vincent & the Grenadines. Other airlines include *Air Martinique*, *BWEE Express*, *Caribbean Star*, *Mustique Airways* and *SVG Air*.
Approximate flight times: From St Vincent to *London* (via Barbados) is nine hours, to *Los Angeles* is nine hours, to *New York* is five hours and to *Singapore* is 33 hours.
Main airports: *ET Joshua (SVD)* is 3km (2 miles) southeast of Kingstown. *To/from the airport*: Buses and taxis go from the airport to the city. There are standard fares to a number of major hotels throughout the island. *Facilities*: Car hire, restaurant, bar and duty free shops. There are also small airports on Bequia, Canouan, Mustique and Union Island for light aircraft.
Departure tax: EC$35 on all international departures; children under 12 years of age and passengers staying for less than 24 hours are exempt.
SEA:
Some of the Grenadines are ports of call for a number of cruise lines: *Clipper Cruise Lines*, *Epirotiki*, *Festival Cruises*, *Fred Olsen*, *Hapag Lloyd*, *Holland America*, *Marline Universal*, *Seabourn* and *Sea Cloud Cruises*.

Travel - Internal

AIR:
Local and charter services are available. Small planes can be chartered for inter-island travel. *Mustique Air*, *SVG Air* and *TIA* run regular services to the Grenadines.
SEA:
Yacht chartering is easily arranged and is one of the best ways to explore the Grenadines. Yachts can be hired locally, with or without crew. Two ferries make frequent sailings to Bequia (travel time – 60 minutes). The rest of the Grenadines are served regularly by a mailboat. The Tourist Office can help with all details.
ROAD:
Traffic drives on the left. **Bus:** Services run regularly throughout St Vincent. Small minibuses run a shared *route-taxi* service with a standard fare anywhere along the route. Public transport is cheap but crowded. **Taxi:** These are shared and charge standard rates (fixed by the Government). taxis drivers do not expect a tip.
Car hire: Easily arranged through a number of national and international firms. **Documentation:** A local driving licence is essential and can be obtained on presentation of a valid national or international licence either at the airport or at the police station in Bay Street, Kingstown, or at the Licensing Authority in Halifax Street, Kingstown (Mon-Fri 0900-1500). The cost is around EC$75.

Travel Advice

Most visits to St Vincent and the Grenadines are trouble-free but you should be aware of the global risk of indiscriminate international terrorist attacks, which could be against civilian targets, including places frequented by foreigners.
This advice is based on information provided by the Foreign and Commonwealth Office in the UK. It is correct at time of publishing. As the situation can change rapidly, visitors are advised to contact the following organisations for the latest travel advice:

British Foreign and Commonwealth Office
Tel: (0845) 850 2829.
Website: www.fco.gov.uk

US Department of State
Website: http://travel.state.gov/travel

Accommodation

From casual and economical to elegant and exclusive, lodgings in St Vincent & the Grenadines offer something for every taste and budget. The choice ranges from a rustic cottage on the beach or an historic country hotel in the mountains, to a luxury resort with an island to itself. Young Island, an idyllic small island off the south coast of St Vincent, has a cottage community of separate huts including all modern facilities. All hotels are small and emphasise personal service. A list of rates is available from the St Vincent Department of Tourism and all its overseas offices. All rooms are subject to a 7 per cent hotel tax.

Grading: Many hotels in the Caribbean offer accommodation according to one of a number of plans. **FAP** (Full American Plan): room and all meals supplied (including afternoon tea, supper, etc); **AP** (American Plan): room and three meals supplied; **MAP** (Modified American Plan): breakfast and dinner included with the price of the room plus, in some places, British-style afternoon tea; **CP** (Continental Plan): room and breakfast only; **EP** (European Plan): room only. For further information regarding accommodation, contact the Department of Tourism (see *Top Things To See & Do*); or the St Vincent & the Grenadines Hotel Association (see *Accommodation Information*).

ACCOMMODATION INFORMATION

St Vincent & the Grenadines Hotel Association
PO Box 834, Kingston, St Vincent
Tel: 458 4379.
Website: www.svghotels.com

Top Things To See & Do

St Vincent

- **Kingstown**, the capital of St Vincent is a lively port and market town on the southern coast. The town contains 12 small blocks with a variety of shops and a busy dock area, which is the centre of commerce for the islands. The Saturday morning market, comprising many stalls piled high with fresh fruit and vegetables, brings everyone to town. In the centre of Kingstown, **St Mary's Roman Catholic Cathedral**, built of grey stone, is a graceful combination of several European architectural styles displaying Romanesque arches, Gothic spires and Moorish ornamentation. Its architecture has led Kingstown to become known as the City of Arches. The ruins of **Fort Charlotte** overlook a 180m (590ft) ridge north of town and offer a magnificent southward view of the Grenadines. The oldest **Botanical Gardens** in the Western hemisphere occupy 8.1 hectares (20 acres) to the north of Kingstown and contain a display of tropical trees, blossoms and plants, including a breadfruit tree descended from the original one brought to the island in 1765 by Captain Bligh.
- The **Falls of Baleine**, at the northern tip of St Vincent, are accessible only by boat. The 18m (59ft) freshwater falls stream from volcanic slopes and form a series of shallow pools at the base. A challenging **hike** for the more adventurous is the just over 5km (3 miles) journey up **La Soufrière**, St Vincent's northern volcano, which affords a wonderful bird's-eye view of the crater and its islands, and all of St Vincent.
- Strung along the western coast are the fishing villages of **Questelles**, **Layou**, **Barrouallie** and **Châteaubelair**, all of which have charming pastel-coloured cottages and excellent black-sand beaches from which fishermen set out daily in small brightly painted boats.
- Only 180m (590ft) off St Vincent, **Young Island** rises from the sea, a 10.1 hectare (25 acre) mountain blanketed with tropical foliage and blossoms. Young Island provides an excellent view of the procession of yachts sailing into the harbour of St Vincent. The entire island comprises one resort called *Young Island Resort*, which consists of 29 rustic cottages set on the beaches and hillsides. There is a freshwater pool and tennis courts hidden in the hilltop trees. Adjoining Young Island is the 18th-century **Fort Duvernette**, sculpted from an enormous rock, towering 60m (200ft) above the sea. A ferry, a smaller version of the African Queen, runs regularly between Young Island and St Vincent.

The Grenadines

- **Bequia:** This island lies 14km (9 miles) south of St Vincent and is the largest of the Grenadines, measuring 18 sq km (7 sq miles). Little changed by time, it is an island on which life is completely oriented to the sea. It can be reached by boat, although there is an airport, the **JF Mitchell**. Its seclusion has ensured it retained its age-old traditions of boat building and fishing. In the marine park, spearfishing, snares and nets are prohibited. The islanders themselves are the world's last hand-harpooners and their activities do not affect marine stocks, unlike the mechanised fishing of some fleets. The centre of the island is hilly and forested, providing a dramatic backdrop to the bays and beaches. **Admiralty Bay**, the island's natural harbour, is a favourite anchoring spot for yachtsmen from all over the world, and here visitors can watch men building their boats by hand on the shores. The attractive region around **Lower Bay** has good opportunities for swimming and other watersports. The quaint waterfront of **Port Elizabeth** is lined with bars, restaurants and craft shops. Bequia is encircled by gold-sand beaches, many of which disappear into coves, excellent for sailing, scuba diving and snorkelling. Lodgings vary from luxurious resort cottages to small, simple West Indian inns. Much of the nightlife centres on the hotels and beachside barbecues, invariably accompanied by a steel band.
- Heading south, the next port of call is **Mustique**, a gem in the ocean taking up only 4.5 sq km (2 sq miles). Mustique is privately owned, with a landscape as gentle as its lifestyle – verdant hills roll into soft white-sand beaches and turquoise waters. This island has long been a hiding place for the rich and famous, including members of the British Royal Family. A sprawling 18th-century plantation house has been converted into the island's only resort. Elegant accommodation is available in several stone houses, widely separated for seclusion. The public rooms of the **Main House** are beautifully decorated with antiques, and afternoon tea is served daily on the veranda. There is a hilltop swimming pool with a magnificent panorama, as well as tennis, horseriding, motorcycling and all watersports.
- **Canouan:** The island claims some of the best beaches in the Caribbean – long stretches of powder-white sands, wide shallows and coral. The island stretches over 11 sq km (7.9 sq miles).
- South of Canouan are the **Tobago Cays**, numerous islets and coves guarded by some of the most spectacular coral reefs in the world. Visitors can sail, snorkel and beachcomb in complete seclusion. The only way to get here is by chartered yacht.
- East of the Cays is **Mayreau**, one of the smaller Grenadines, which has few residents. The island can be reached by boat from Union Island.
- **Mount Parnassus** on **Union Island** soars 275m (900ft) from the sea – guarding the entrance to the southern Grenadines. The 850 hectare (2100 acre) mountainous island is fringed by superb beaches and is the stopping-off point for yachtsmen and visitors heading to some of the smaller Grenadines. **Clifton Harbour**, the main town, is small and commercial.
- The 44.5 hectare (110 acre) flat **Palm Island** acquired its name from the graceful coconut palms that line the beaches – 8000 in all. This private island has been turned into a resort, the *Palm Island Beach Club*, made up of 20 beachfront stone cottages. Here it is possible to dine in the open air and all watersports take place off the wide, white shores.
- The southernmost Grenadine governed by St Vincent is **Petit St Vincent**, a 45.7 hectare (113 acre) resort set on beaches. The luxuriant foliage and the 22 villas of Petit St Vincent offer guests the ultimate luxury and seclusion, including private patios and seaside vistas. Visitors gather for meals in beachfront pavilions and the ambience is carefree and festive.
- **Watersports:** These are a major pastime. Various **sailing** boats head south regularly through the Grenadines. For the novice, professionals are available to handle the sails. Visitors can, of course, bring their own yacht, or charter one, either with or without crew. Yachts are available for charter from Barefoot Yacht Charters (tel: 456 9526 or 9334; website: www.barefootyachts.com) or Sunsail St Vincent at the Lagoon Marina & Hotel (tel/fax: 458 4308; website: www.lagoonmarina.com). Other watersports, particularly **windsurfing** and **scuba diving**, can be arranged through some hotels. Dive sites around St Vincent include **New Guinea Reef**, where sea horses swim around an abundance of black coral; and **Bottle Reef**, so called because the sea bed is dotted with antique gin and rum bottles thrown into the sea from the English fort above in centuries past. **Deep-sea fishing** excursions are available.
- **Hiking:** This can be undertaken in the rainforest. Hiking to the **Soufrière volcano** (1200m/4000ft) in the north of the island is popular, though strenuous. The trip takes a full day.

TOURIST INFORMATION

St Vincent & the Grenadines Tourist Office in the UK
10 Kensington Court, London W8 5DL, UK
Tel: (020) 7937 6570.
Website: www.svgtourism.com

St Vincent & the Grenadines Tourist Office in the USA
801 Second Avenue, 21st Floor, New York, NY 10017, USA
Tel: (212) 687 4981 or (800) 729 1726 (toll-free).
Website: www.svgtourism.com

Entertainment

FOOD & DRINK: St Vincent is one of the few islands where good West Indian cuisine can almost always be enjoyed in hotels. Specialities include red snapper, kingfish, *lambi* (conch), *callalou* soup, *souse* (pickled meat or seafood) and sea-moss drink. In addition there is plenty of fresh fruit, vegetables and other seafood on offer. Lobster is available in season.

Vincentian beer and rum, a major ingredient in punch and cocktails, are the local drinks, as are a wide variety of local exotic fruit juices.

Tipping: 10 to 15 per cent service added to the bill.

NIGHTLIFE: Most evening events take place in hotels and it is best to ask at individual hotels for a calendar of events. Nightclubs include the *Aquatic* club and the *Buccama Club* on the Leeward Coast. *The Attic* in Kingstown features a wide variety of music during the week and live entertainment at weekends. There is one casino on the island, at Peniston, on the Leeward side.

SHOPPING: Designs on sea-island cottons can be bought and made up into clothes within a few days at a number of shops. Handicrafts and all varieties of straw-made items, grass rugs and other souvenirs can be bought at a number of workshops and gift shops. **Shopping hours:** Mon-Fri 0800-1200 and 1300-1600, Sat 0800-1200.

Business

ECONOMY: St Vincent & the Grenadines is poor by Eastern Caribbean standards, with agriculture the main source of income and export earnings. Bananas are the main crop, but St Vincent is also the world's leading producer of arrowroot and grows other exotic fruit, vegetables and root crops. Fishing has also been revitalised and a processing complex has been built with Japanese assistance. Agriculture is especially vulnerable to the unpredictable, often adverse weather patterns of the Caribbean.

Tourism is the other main component of the economy. By regional standards, this was relatively late to evolve and was initially hampered by the lack of a suitable infrastructure. This was addressed with the help of aid from the European Union and the industry is now growing rapidly: the most recent figures record its contribution to the economy at US$90 million. A small manufacturing sector and an embryonic 'offshore' financial services industry complete the country's economic inventory.

St Vincent is a member of the regional trading bloc CARICOM and the Organisation of Eastern Caribbean States, which is assuming a growing economic role. In addition to the USA and the UK, St Vincent's main trade links are with Trinidad & Tobago, Barbados, St Lucia and Martinique.

BUSINESS ETIQUETTE: Short- or long-sleeved shirt and tie or a safari suit are suitable for most business visits. **Government office hours:** These vary from department to department but generally Mon-Fri 0800-1615, with some opening for a few hours Saturday morning.

COMMERCIAL INFORMATION

St Vincent & the Grenadines Chamber of Industry and Commerce
PO Box 134, Coreas Building, Hillsborough Street, Kingstown, St Vincent
Tel: 457 1464.
Website: www.svgcic.com

For information on conferences and conventions, contact the St Vincent & the Grenadines Tourist Office (see *Top Things To See & Do*).

Samoa

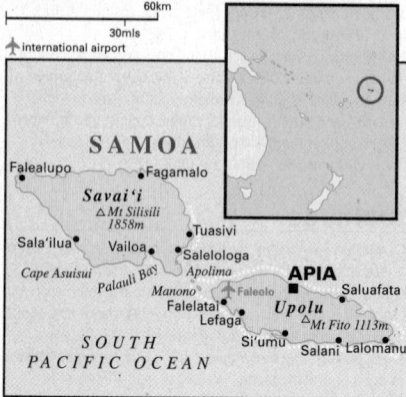

Location: South Pacific.

Time: GMT - 11.

Overview

Samoa consists of nine islands. Savai'i, the largest island, has been described as 'Polynesia at its truest'. Upolu is the second largest and most populous island. Apia, the capital, lies on the beautiful north coast of Upolu. Nearby at Vailima is the house built by the Scottish poet and novelist Robert Louis Stevenson, who lived there from 1889 until his death on 5 December 1894. The most beautiful part of Samoa is the Aleipata district where waterfalls and white-sand beaches dominate the landscape. From Apia, a 65km (40-mile) drive leads to the Falefa Falls, Mafa Pass and Fuipisia Falls. So why not give it a try and come and experience the *fa'a Samoa* (the Samoan way), arguably the most vibrant living culture in Polynesia?

General Information

AREA: 2831 sq km (1093 sq miles).

POPULATION: 182,000 (UN estimate 2005).

POPULATION DENSITY: 64.3 per sq km.

CAPITAL: Apia (Upolu Island). **Population:** 38,180 (2001).

GEOGRAPHY: Samoa consists of nine islands. The largest of these is Savai'i, which covers 1610 sq km (622 sq miles); fertile Upolu, the second largest (1120 sq km/433 sq miles), lies 13km (8 miles) to the southeast across the Apolima Strait. The islands are quiescent volcanoes and reach heights of up to 1858m (6097ft) on Savai'i and 1100m (3608ft) on Upolu. Volcanic activity has not occurred since 1911. The main city, Apia, is located in the north of Upolu.

GOVERNMENT: Constitutional monarchy. Gained independence from New Zealand in 1962. **Head of State:** HH Malietoa Tanumafili II since 1963. **Head of Government:** Prime Minister Tuila'epa Sailele Malielegaoi since 1998.

LANGUAGE: Samoan is the national language. In business and commerce, English is customary.

RELIGION: Congregational Church, Roman Catholic, Methodist, Latter Day Saints, Seventh Day Adventists, Assembly of God, Jehovah's Witness and Bahai Faith.

ELECTRICITY: 240 volts AC, 50Hz (110 volts AC in some hotels). Three-pronged plugs are in use as in Australia and New Zealand.

SOCIAL CONVENTIONS: Even more than their American Samoan neighbours, Samoans adhere to traditional moral and religious codes of behaviour. According to the Government, the Samoan is the purest surviving Polynesian type, with a reputation for being upright and dignified in character. Life in each village is still regulated by a council of chiefs with considerable financial and territorial power; this 'extended family' social system is intricately and unusually linked with the overall political system. Visitors should avoid walking through villages during evening prayer (usually between 1800 and 1900). Sunday is a day of peace and quiet, and visitors should behave quietly and travel slowly through villages. It is recommended for women to wear a *lavalava* (sarong) rather than shorts and pants; nude or topless bathing is prohibited. When entering a *fale*, shoes should be removed, visitors should never stand when elders are seated, and when sitting down, the soles of your feet should not be shown (the yogic cross-legged style is a good option). Permission should always be asked before taking photographs in a village. Visitors should not offer money to children, even when they ask. For access and fees to certain areas and villages, see *Top Things To Do*.

Climate

Samoa has a warm, tropical climate tempered by trade winds between May and September. Temperatures remain relatively constant throughout the year, becoming cooler at night. There are more than 2500 hours of sunshine annually. Rainfall is heaviest between December and April. Sea temperatures rarely fall below 24°C (75.2°F).

Required clothing: Lightweight cottons and linens with warmer clothes for evenings. Rainwear is advisable.

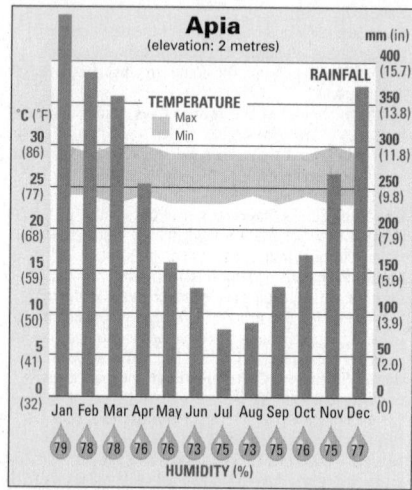

Communications

Telephone: Incoming IDD is available. Country code: 685. There are no area codes. Outgoing international calls must be made through the operator.

Mobile telephone: Samoa has its own analogue mobile phone system operated by Telecom Samoa. Visitors with analogue phones can be assigned a new number for the duration of their stay and calls will be charged to their credit card.

Internet: Internet and e-mail services are available in Apia and other locations around the islands.

Post: Main post office hours (located on Beach Road, Apia): Mon-Fri 0800-1630. Airmail to Europe takes about three weeks.

MEDIA: Samoa enjoys a 'generally free press'. **Press:** The main English-language newspapers are *Newsline*, *The Samoa Observer* and *Savali*.

TV: The Government operates to sole TV service, *Samoa Broadcasting Corporation* (SBC).

Radio: The *SBC* runs mediumwave and FM stations. Other stations include *Magik FM*, *K-Lite FM* and *Talofa FM*.

Passport/Visa

	Passport Required?	Visa Required?	Return Ticket Required?
Full British	Yes	1	Yes
Australian	Yes	1	Yes
Canadian	Yes	1	Yes
USA	Yes	1	Yes
Other EU	Yes	1	Yes
Japanese	Yes	1	Yes

Note: *Regulations and requirements may be subject to change at short notice, and you are advised to contact the appropriate diplomatic or consular authority before finalising travel arrangements. Any numbers in the chart refer to the footnotes below.*

PASSPORTS: Passport valid for six months beyond the date of departure from Samoa required by all.

VISAS: Required by all except:

1. nationals of any country visiting Samoa as a tourist will be issued with a free 60-day visa on arrival provided they hold confirmed onward tickets, a valid passport and proof of sufficient funds to support the stay. For longer stays, visas should be obtained before arrival or visa extensions can be applied for in Apia.

Types of visa and cost: *Visitor's Permit:* free on arrival. Other types of visa cost from €100-1200 and applicants should enquire directly with the Samoan Embassy.

Validity: Six months from date of issue.

Application to: Nearest Samoan Embassy or High Commission or the Immigration Division of the Prime Minister's Department in Apia (PO Box L1861).

Application requirements: (a) Two passport-size photos. (b) Completed application form. (c) Fee.

Working days required: Apply at least four weeks in advance.

Temporary residence: Costs from €100 depending on the purpose of your visit. Business and employment visas are 50 per cent cheaper if applied for outside Samoa. Each application is assessed on an individual basis and takes at least four weeks to process.

PASSPORT/VISA INFORMATION

Embassy of Samoa in Belgium
20, Avenue de l'Oree, B- 1000 Brussels , Belgium
Tel: (2) 660 8454.

Permanent Mission of Samoa to the United Nations
800 2nd Avenue, Suite 400J, New York, NY 10017, USA
Tel: (212) 599 6196.
Website: www.samoa.un.int

Money

Currency: Tala or Samoa Dollar (Tala) = 100 sene. Notes are in denominations of Tala100, 50, 20, 10, 5 and 2. Coins are in denominations of Tala1, and 50, 20, 10, 5, 2 and 1 sene.

Currency exchange: Available at the airport or through banks. There are four banks in Samoa: ANZ Bank Samoa Ltd, the National Bank of Samoa, Samoa Commercial Bank and Westpac. These have ATMs at many of their branches throughout Samoa.

Credit & debit cards: American Express, Cirrus, MasterCard and Visa are accepted on a limited basis. Check with your credit or debit card company for details of merchant acceptability and other services which may be available.

Traveller's cheques: Accepted in major hotels, banks and tourist shops. To avoid additional exchange rate charges, travellers are advised to take traveller's cheques in US Dollars or Pounds Sterling.

Currency restrictions: There are no restrictions on the import of local or foreign currency. Export of local currency is prohibited. Export of foreign currency is limited to the amount imported.

Banking hours: Mon-Fri 0900-1500; some banks open Sat 0900-1200 and may have slightly longer opening hours.

Exchange rate indicators:
Rate at time of publishing
£1.00=   Tala4.83
$1.00=   Tala2.74

Duty Free

The following items may be imported into Samoa by persons of 16 years of age or more without incurring customs duty:

200 cigarettes or 250g of cigars or tobacco; 1l of spirits; other goods for personal use up to Tala250.

Prohibited items: Firearms, ammunition, explosives, non-prescribed drugs and indecent publications. Live animals and plants (including seeds, fruit, soil, etc) may not be imported without prior permission from the Director of Agriculture.

Public Holidays

Below are listed Public Holidays for the January 2006-June 2007 period.

2006: Jan 1-2 New Year. Apr 14-17 Easter. Apr 25 ANZAC Day. May 14-15 Mother's Day. Jun 1 Independence Day. Aug 7 Labour Day. Aug 13-14 Father's Day. Oct 9 Lotu-a-Tamaiti (Day after White Sunday). Nov 3 Arbor Day. Dec 25 Christmas Day. Dec 26 Boxing Day.

2007: Jan 1-2 New Year. Apr 6-9 Easter. Apr 25 ANZAC Day. May 14-15 Mother's Day. Jun 1 Independence Day.

Credit: ©David Kirkland www.kirklandphotos.com

Health

	Special Precautions?	Certificate Required?
Yellow Fever	No	1
Cholera	No	No
Typhoid & Polio	2	N/A
Malaria	No	N/A

Note: Regulations and requirements may be subject to change at short notice, and you are advised to contact your doctor well in advance of your intended date of departure. Any numbers in the chart refer to the footnotes below.

1: A yellow fever vaccination certificate is required from travellers over one year of age arriving from infected areas.
2: Typhoid is present; polio has not been reported for three years.
Food & drink: Mains water is chlorinated, though bottled water may be preferable. Sterilisation is advisable. Milk is pasteurised and dairy products are safe for consumption. Local meat, poultry, seafood, fruit and vegetables are generally considered safe to eat.
Other risks: Hepatitis A occurs and hepatitis B is endemic.
Health care: Health insurance, while recommended, is not mandatory. All health services available to locals are accessible to foreigners usually at minimal cost to the traveller. Emergency medical facilities are available at Moto'otua Hospital, in Apia. Private medical and dental treatment is also available.

Travel - International

AIR:
 Samoa's national airline is Polynesian Airlines (PH) (website: www.polynesianairlines.co.nz). Others operating to the islands are Air New Zealand, Air Pacific, Polynesian Blue, Inter Island Airways and South Pacific Express.
Main airports: Apia (APW) (Faleolo) is 34km (21 miles) from the capital (travel time – 40 minutes). Airport facilities include banks/bureaux de change, post office, duty free shop and car hire (national firms). Buses and taxis operate to the city.
Departure tax: Tala40 for adults. Transit passengers and children under 12 years of age are exempt.

SEA:
 The international port is Apia, on Upolu. It is served by both cargo and passenger ships from Australia, Europe, Japan, New Zealand and the USA. There is also a weekly ferry service from Pago Pago on American Samoa.

Travel - Internal

AIR:
 Polynesian Airlines (PH) operates daily flights from Faleolo on Upolu to Maota and Asau on Savai'i. Charter and sightseeing flights are available.

SEA:
 There are passenger/vehicle ferries between Upolu (Apia) and Savai'i (travel time – 65 minutes). Check with Samoa Shipping Corporation for up-to-date schedules (tel: 20935/6).

ROAD:
Traffic drives on the right. Speed limits are 40kph (25mph) within the Apia area and 56kph (35mph) outside the Apia area. Drivers should be alert, especially at night, to the hazard of roaming pigs, dogs and people. **Bus:** Public transport covers most of the islands. There are no timetables; policepeople at the New Market Bus Stand in Apia have information on bus departures. **Taxi:** Cheap and readily available in Apia. They are not metered and prices should be negotiated in advance. There is a minimum charge of Tala2. Longer trips are at a higher rate but are Government regulated. **Car hire:** Available from several agencies. Deposit and insurance are usually required. **Bicycles** and **motor scooters** are also available. **Documentation:** An International Driving Permit for drivers over 21 years of age or a valid national licence. The Transport Ministry issues a local licence for a small fee. An International Driving Permit is required for car hire.

Travel Advice

Travellers should avoid driving out of built up areas at night. Serious crime is low and most visits to Samoa are trouble-free. You should be aware of the global risk of indiscriminate international terrorist attacks, which could be against civilian targets, including places frequented by foreigners.
This advice is based on information provided by the Foreign and Commonwealth Office in the UK. It is correct at time of publishing. As the situation can change rapidly, visitors are advised to contact the following organisations for the latest travel advice:

British Foreign and Commonwealth Office
Tel: (0845) 850 2829.
Website: www.fco.gov.uk

US Department of State
Website: http://travel.state.gov/travel

Accommodation

There is a Government-backed programme to improve and extend facilities for visitors. In recent years, a number of new hotels and resorts have opened, and the choice varies hugely.
HOTELS:
 There is a good selection of distinctive hotels in Samoa offering high standards at reasonable prices (some inclusive of meals). There are also hotels located in rural areas, including Upolu's south coast and Savai'i. For details, contact the Samoa Tourism Authority (see Top Things To Do).
SELF-CATERING:
 A village resort offers the opportunity for self-catering, although, if visitors prefer, a restaurant is also provided. There are many sporting and other facilities for guests. Beach cottages and fales are less expensive and offer fewer on-site facilities, though many of them can be found nearby.
Eco-Villages: Over recent years, the Samoa Tourism Authority has initiated a National Ecotourism Programme designed to encourage sustainable and environmentally aware tourism by actively involving visitors in their efforts to preserve the natural habitat and national culture. As a result, a number of eco-villages have been established. One recent resort development incorporates a number of these aims, and comes complete with composting toilet and outside open-air shower; an on-site work programme and other activities aim to recreate village life, as well as offering trips to other coastal resorts and eco-villages. For further details, contact the Samoa Tourism Authority (see Top Things To Do).

Credit: ©David Kirkland/www.kirklandphotos.com

Top Things To See

• **Upolu** is the most populous island. **Apia**, the capital and main commercial centre, lies on the beautiful north coast. Nearby **Vailima** is the house built by the Scottish poet and novelist Robert Louis Stevenson (the local name for him was Tusitala, meaning 'teller of tales'). From the lawn you can see his tomb on top of **Mount Vaea**. The house has been restored, and was officially opened as the **Robert Louis Stevenson Museum** in 1994 on the 100th anniversary of his death.
• The **Aleipata district** is the most beautiful part of

Samoa, with a landscape dominated by waterfalls, white-sand beaches and traditional villages. From Apia, a 65km (40 mile) drive leads to the **Falefa Falls**, **Fuipisia Falls** and **Mafa Pass**. Four offshore islands are within accessible distance.
• On the southwest coast, the attractive **Lefaga Village** can be reached by a cross-island road. The film Return to Paradise was filmed here in 1952.
• Just off the coast of Upolu, **Manono Island** was the inspiration for the legendary 'Bali Hai' in Rodgers and Hammerstein's musical, South Pacific.
• The largest island in the Samoan archipelago, **Savai'i** has been described as 'Polynesia at its truest'. There are scheduled flights and a regular car ferry from Apia on Upolu.
• The **Tafua Peninsula Rainforest Preserve** is ideal for seeing flying foxes and birdwatching; this Preserve is situated near the coastal village of Tafua.
• The **Tia Seu Ancient Mound** is an awe-inspiring 'pyramid' and the largest ancient structure in the whole of Polynesia at 12m (39ft) tall.
• **Mu Pagoa Waterfall**, along with the **Alofaaga Blowholes**, **lava caves** and **lava fields**, make for interesting sightseeing, as does the **Auala Green Turtle Conservation**, a programme managed by the women's committee, where guides show you turtles before they are released back into the wild.

Top Things To Do

• Samoa offers excellent **snorkelling** and **diving**. Good locations include the **Palolo Deep Marine Reserve** (open 0800-1800, on Upolu island) and the beaches from **Safotu** to **Manase** and between **Lesolo Point** and **Tuasivi (Savai'i island)**. Diving trips can be arranged via the Samoa Visitors Bureau.
• **Surfing** has recently become popular although, as the waves break directly on coral reefs, Samoan waters are for experienced surfers only. In some villages, surfing is not allowed on Sundays. On **Savai'i island**, the villages charge a daily surfing fee to help with school funding. There are currently two surfing resorts; surfing guides are available from the Samoa Visitors Bureau.
• There are many beautiful beaches and there is excellent freshwater **swimming** at **Falefa Falls, Fogaafu Falls, Papase'ea Sliding Rock** (a rock slide down a waterfall into a deep, cool, freshwater pool) and **Puila Cave Pool**. Boats can be hired for net, spear, deep-sea and snorkel **fishing**.
• **Hiking:** There are dozens of routes ranging from coastal walks to mountain treks. Trails tend to grow over rapidly and can sometimes be difficult to get through. Visitors should ask for local advice and permission before heading off or ask for a local guide from the Samoa Visitors Bureau.
• **Ecotourism:** Educational tours to Samoa's stretches of rainforest and conservation areas are available (one popular destination being **Tanumapua**, close to Apia). There are also several ecological research programmes and eco-lodges on offer (see also the Accommodation section).
Note: Visitors should respect Samoan village traditions (see Social Conventions in the General Information section). Almost all Samoan land (as well as lagoons and bays) is the communal property of a village, family or individual, and visitors should always find out whose land they are accessing (only 20 per cent of the land is not administered by a village). Villagers maintain the beaches, viewing areas and conservation areas and the decision to develop attractions is usually made by a council of chiefs. A small entry fee is payable for most beaches and other attractions. Fees are often indicated, but if no price is given, visitors should ask.

Entertainment

FOOD & DRINK: Among the local specialities are dishes cooked in the traditional Samoan oven, umu. A variety of Chinese food is also available in a few places and there are several snack and light meal restaurants in

Sidebar alphabet: A B C D E F G H I J K L M N O P Q R S T U V W X Y Z

Apia serving fast food and other Western food. Alcohol may not be purchased on Sundays except by hotel residents and their guests.

National specialities:
- Fresh seafood.
- Roast suckling pig.
- Chicken.
- Breadfruit and fruit.

National drinks:
- *Kava* is the national drink (see also the *American Samoa and Fiji* sections).

Tipping: Not customary.

NIGHTLIFE: Several nightclubs offer dancing and other entertainment. Several cinemas show English-language films and Chinese films with subtitles.

SHOPPING: Local items include *siapo* (tapa) cloth, made from mulberry bark and painted with native dyes; mats and baskets; *kava* drinking bowls, made of hardwood and polished to a high gloss; shell jewellery; and Samoan stamps, available from the Philatelic Bureau. **Shopping hours:** Mon-Fri 0800-1200 and 1330-1630, Sat 0800-1230. Some shops remain open during the lunch hour.

Business

ECONOMY: Most Samoans are involved in subsistence agriculture; some cash crops are also grown for export, the most important of which are coconut, cocoa and bananas. Timber is exported in small quantities. Fishing is another important source of income and employment. There is some small-scale manufacturing industry, mostly concerned with food-processing, textiles, woodworking and light engineering, and some small factories produce consumer goods for the domestic market. The Government has concentrated on tourism and export-oriented manufacturing in its efforts to develop the economy, although aspects of the climate – principally the country's annual cyclones – have made this difficult. Nonetheless, tourism has now expanded to the point where it contributes 17 per cent of GDP, based on the arrival of 90,000 visitors to the island group annually. The Government has also, with some success, sought to promote an offshore financial services industry. Further income comes from the remittances of Samoans working overseas – mostly in New Zealand and, to a lesser extent, in Australia; both these two countries also provide Samoa with a sizeable aid package. Tangible benefits from a 1996 trade agreement with the Chinese Government have become apparent. Meanwhile, a parallel programme of economic reforms won the approval and ensuing financial support of the World Bank, the Asian Development Bank and others. The economy is now growing at 5 per cent annually. Samoa is a member of both the South Pacific Forum and the South Pacific Commission. New Zealand, Australia, Singapore, Fiji, China (PR), Japan and the USA are the major trading partners.

BUSINESS ETIQUETTE: Shirt and smart trousers will suffice for business visits. Ties need only be worn for formal occasions. Best time to visit is from May to October.

Office hours: Mon-Fri 0800-1200 and 1300-1630.

COMMERCIAL INFORMATION

Ministry of Commerce, Industry and Labour
Level 4, ACB Building, Apia, Samoa
Tel: 20441 or 20442.
Website: www.mcilsamoa.ws

San Marino

Location: Western Europe, northeastern part of the Italian peninsula.

Time: GMT + 1 (GMT + 2 from last Sunday in March to Saturday before last Sunday in October).

Overview

San Marino is the only surviving Italian city-state. Like Andorra, Liechtenstein and Monaco, it is an anachronism, a reminder of the times when Europe – particularly Germany, Italy and the Pyrenees – was made up of tiny political units, often extending no further than a cannon could fire from a city's walls.

Of all the small European countries, San Marino's survival is the most surprising. Apart from the Vatican City (whose development followed a different course), it is the only one that is completely surrounded by one other country. Various treaties of friendship have been signed with Italy since the latter's unification, but San Marino proudly asserts its independence where possible. It has been a full member of the Council of Europe since 1988, and chaired the organisation during the first half of 1990.

In whatever part of the territory you go (61 km2), in particular at the peak of its mountain (750 meters high), your gaze is lost over a unique, dazzling panorama: the fertile soils of Emilia Romagna and the soft rolling hills of the Marche and Montefeltro, and on to the placid Adriatic sea. The Sammarinese territory is made up of nine ancient Citadels, including the capital, San Marino. These small centres arose as a result of the first human settlements; each offers something to be discovered and visited. The Fortresses are interconnected by a convenient urban network of rare beauty. The origins of San Marino are founded on the charming legend of the Saint, Founder of the community and of the Republic, when, in 301 A.D., Marino took refuge on Mt. Titano. The small capital holds a wealth of history, museums, and priceless architectural monuments. The annual destination of millions of tourists, it is a place of continuous discovery; a wealth of assorted crafts and souvenirs provide a vast, pleasant shopping experience.

General Information

AREA: 61.2 sq km (23.6 sq miles).
POPULATION: 28,753 (2002).

POPULATION DENSITY: 469.8 per sq km.
CAPITAL: San Marino. **Population:** 2,822 (UN estimate, 2000).
GEOGRAPHY: San Marino is a tiny state bordered by the Italian regions of Emilia-Romagna to the north and east and Marche to the south and west. The landscape is for the most part green with rolling hills, dominated by the three peaks of Mount Titano. Within San Marino lie the capital of the same name and eight villages.
GOVERNMENT: Republic since 1599. **Heads of State and Government:** The *Capitani Regenti* elected in October 2005 are Claudio Muccioli and Antonello Bacciocchi (2nd time). The Captains Regent are elected by the Great General Council every six months.
LANGUAGE: Italian.
RELIGION: Roman Catholic.
ELECTRICITY: 220 volts AC, 50Hz.
SOCIAL CONVENTIONS: Normal European courtesies and codes of conduct should be observed.

Climate

Temperate. Moderate snow in winter, some brief showers in summer. The atmosphere is clean, typical of low mountain and hill country with sea breezes.

Required clothing: Light- to mediumweights and rainwear are required.

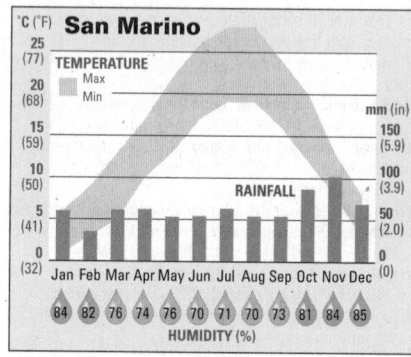

Communications

Telephone: IDD is available. Country code: 378. There are no area codes.
Mobile telephone: Roaming agreements exist with international mobile phone companies.
Internet: Internet cafes can be found in all main towns.
Post: Good postal service. Airmail to European destinations takes approximately four days.
MEDIA: Press: Daily newspapers published in San Marino are *La Tribuna Sanmerinese, Nuovo Corriere di Informazione Sammarinese* and *San Marino Oggi*; Italian and foreign newspapers are widely available.
TV/Radio: *San Marino RTV* is the state run radio and TV network.

Passport/Visa

Travellers will necessarily enter San Marino from Italy. As there are no frontier formalities imposed, any person visiting San Marino must comply with Italian passport/visa regulations; for details, see *Italy* section.

PASSPORT/VISA INFORMATION

Embassy of the Republic of San Marino in the UK
c/o Consulate of the Republic of San Marino
Flat 51, 162 Soane Street, London SW1 9BS
Tel: (020) 7823 4762

Money

Currency: The first Euro notes and coins were introduced in January 2002. For further information on currency, credit cards, travellers cheques, exchange rates and currency restrictions, see the *Italy* section.
Note: Since the early 1970s, San Marino has increased its production of indigenous gold and silver coins.
Currency exchange: Many banks offer differing exchange rates depending on the denominations of currency being bought or sold. Check with the banks for details and current rates.
Banking hours: Mon-Fri 0830-1330 and 1500-1630.

Duty Free

Visitors must comply with Italian customs regulations; see the *Italy* section.

Public Holidays

Below are listed Public Holidays for the January 2006–June 2007 period.
2006: Jan 1 New Year's Day. **Jan 6** Epiphany. **Feb 5** Anniversary of the Liberation of the Republic from the Alberoni Occupation and St Agatha's Day. **Mar 25** Anniversary of the Arengo. **Apr 1** Investiture of the new Captains Regent. **May 1** Labour Day. **Jun 15** Corpus Christi. **Jul 28** Anniversary of the Fall of Fascism. **Aug 15** Assumption. **Sep 3** San Marino's Day and Foundation of the Republic. **Oct 1** Investiture of the new Captains Regent. **Nov 1** All Saints' Day. **Nov 2** All Souls' Day. **Dec 8** Immaculate Conception. **Dec 24-26** Christmas. **Dec 31** New Year's Eve.
2007: Jan 1 New Year's Day. **Jan 6** Epiphany. **Feb 5** Anniversary of the Liberation of the Republic from the Alberoni Occupation and St Agatha's Day. **Mar 25** Anniversary of the Arengo. **Apr 1** Investiture of the new Captains Regent. **May 1** Labour Day. **Jun 7** Corpus Christi.
Note: If any of the above dates fall on a Sunday, the following Monday will be observed as a public holiday.

Health

The health regulations and recommendations are the same as for Italy; for details see the *Italy* section.

Travel - International

AIR:

The Italian national airline is *Alitalia (AZ)* (website: www.alitalia.it). **Approximate flight times:** From Bologna/Rimini to *London* is two hours 30 minutes. **Main airports:** *Bologna (BLQ)* is 125km (78 miles) from San Marino and *Rimini (RMI)* is 27km (17 miles) from San Marino. Good bus services are available to San Marino.

RAIL:

The nearest station is at Rimini. A funicular serves the capital and Borgo Maggiore. There are no internal railways.

ROAD:

Major cities in Italy are within easy reach by car. Rimini is only 24km (15 miles) away and connects to San Marino via the San Marino highway. From San Marino to Urbino is 55km (34 miles), to Ravenna is 70km (44 miles), to Forlì is 74km (46 miles), to Ancona is 130km (81 miles), to Bologna is 135km (84 miles), to Florence is 185km (116 miles), to Milan is 330km (206 miles) and to Rome is 350km (219 miles). **Documentation:** See *Italy* section.

Travel Advice

Most visits to San Marino are trouble-free but you should be aware of the global risk of indiscriminate international terrorist attacks, which could be against civilian targets, including places frequented by foreigners.
This advice is based on information provided by the Foreign and Commonwealth Office in the UK. It is correct at time of publishing. As the situation can change rapidly, visitors are advised to contact the following organisations for the latest travel advice:

British Foreign and Commonwealth Office
Tel: (0845) 850 2829.
Website: www.fco.gov.uk

US Department of State
Website: http://travel.state.gov/travel

Accommodation

All hotels in San Marino are comfortable and of a good standard. Every hotel allows special reductions for groups, children and large families. Full- and half-board arrangements are also available. For more information, contact the State Tourist Office (see *Top Things To See & Do*). **Grading:** Hotels in San Marino are classified in four categories, with 1/A category hotels at the luxury end of the market, 1/B category hotels being slightly more modest, and 2 and 3 category hotels for budget travellers.

Top Things To See & Do

• Set on the lower slopes of **Mount Titano**, the medieval centre of the city of **San Marino** has been perfectly preserved and must be explored on foot as cars are banned. The three peaks of the mountain behind are capped with fortified towers, linked by a system of walls and pathways that are accessible from the city below. The city itself is enclosed by three walls containing gateways, towers and ramparts. Inside the walls are narrow, winding streets, churches and medieval houses. Places worth visiting are the **Government Palace**; the **Basilica**; the **State Museum** and **Art Gallery**; **St Francis' Church**,

which also has a museum and art gallery; the **Capuccin Friars Church of St Quirino**; and the **Exhibition of San Marino Handicrafts**.
• Eight villages are scattered around the countryside outside the capital. Places of interest include **Malatesta Castle** at **Serravalle**; the modern church and the stamp and coin museum at **Borgo Maggiore**; the church and convent at **Valdragone**; and the fort at **Pennarossa**. Ancient ruins can be seen throughout the Republic. Attractions outside the city and villages include pine woods, springs, streams, lakes and fishing reserves. There is easy access to Italian beaches on the Adriatic coast nearby.
• Attend the *24 Ore di San Marino*, the country's main **sailing** regatta (held in July) or the *Gran Premio Formula 3000* (Formula One Grand Prix), one of several annual **motor racing** events.
• **Stamp-** and **coin-collecting** are popular in San Marino – probably because the country is the only one in the Italian area which issues legal tender gold coins (the famous *Scudi*), and San Marino's philatelic office has been offering information and a new issues and standing order service to collectors for over 40 years. For further information, contact the State Philatelic & Numismatic Office (tel: (0549) 882 365; website: www.aasfn.sm).

TOURIST INFORMATION

Ufficio di Stato per il Turismo (State Tourist Office)
Palazzo del Turismo, Contrada Omagnano 20, 47890 Republic of San Marino
Tel: (0549) 882 914.
Website: www.visitsanmarino.com

Entertainment

FOOD & DRINK: Italian cuisine is widely available. There is a wide selection of restaurants, both in the capital and in the outlying villages. Table service is customary, although a few restaurants are self-service.
National specialities:
• *Tortellini*, *tagliatelle*, *lasagne*, *ravioli* and *cannelloni*.
• *Passatelli* (broth).
• Roast rabbit with fennel.
• Bolognese veal cutlets, assorted 'mouthfuls' (three types of tender meat) and Roman veal escalopes.
• San Marino tart and *cacciatello* (similar to crème caramel) may be ordered for dessert.
National drinks:
• San Marino *muscat*, *biancale*, *albana* and *sangiovese* are all good-quality wines produced locally.
• *Mistra* is the local liqueur.
Tipping: Service charges are generally included in hotel bills. A 10 per cent tip is usual.
NIGHTLIFE: Revues, festivals and theatrical productions are popular.
SHOPPING: Special purchases include locally made ceramics; stamps and coins bought from the State Philatelic & Numismatic Office, local wines and liqueurs, local jewellery, playing cards and cigarettes. **Shopping hours:** Mon-Sat 0830-1300 and 1530-1930.

Business

ECONOMY: San Marino exports wine and cheese. Its other agricultural products are wheat, barley, maize, grapes and olive oil. Industrial production is concerned with cement, synthetic rubber, leather, textiles and ceramics. Light industries have been expanding quickly in recent years as the Government seeks to diversify the economy away from tourism. Nonetheless, tourism continues to provide much of the Republic's income, accounting for about half of GDP from around three million visitors each year. Quarried stone is an arcane though important export. Another unusual source of revenue is the sale of postage stamps and coins: both are popular with collectors and together account for over 10 per cent of government income. Statistical details of San Marino's external trade are included with those of Italy, with whom San Marino has a long-standing customs union. However, there are differences in taxation and regulatory structures which have afforded San Marino the status of a tax haven, as a growing number of non-resident deposits have been made in the principality's banks. In 2001 and 2002, the Government responded to OECD calls for tax haven economies to institute measures to tackle money-laundering.
Business Etiquette: A suit is recommended and prior appointments are absolutely essential. Avoid making appointments early in the morning or straight after lunch. A knowledge of Italian is useful.
CONFERENCES/CONVENTIONS: For information, contact the State Tourist Office (see *Top Things To See & Do*).

Location: West Africa, Gulf of Guinea.

Time: GMT.

Overview

The islands of São Tomé e Príncipe provide unspoiled beauty and isolation from the world now rarely found anywhere else. The islands lie on an alignment of once-active volcanoes, with rugged landscapes, dense forests and virgin and palm-fringed beaches. The history of the islands is dominated by the slave trade and slave-worked plantations. The town of São Tomé is picturesque, with colonial Portuguese architecture and attractive parks. There are several restaurants in the capital. Reservations are nearly always required, not for lack of space but to allow the proprietor to obtain sufficient food in advance!

General Information

AREA: 1001 sq km (386.5 sq miles).
POPULATION: 161,000 (official estimate 2003).
POPULATION DENSITY: 137.5 per sq km (census of 2001).
CAPITAL: São Tomé.
GEOGRAPHY: São Tomé e Príncipe comprises two main islands (São Tomé and Príncipe) and the islets Cabras, Gago Coutinho, Pedras Tinhosas and Ilheu dos Rolas (which is crossed by the Equator line). These lie approximately 200km (120 miles) off the west coast of Gabon, in the Gulf of Guinea. The country is rugged and has a great deal of forest cover and few natural resources. The landscape is varied, combining mountains, tropical forest and beaches.
GOVERNMENT: Republic. Gained independence from Portugal in 1975. **Head of State:** President Fradique de Menezes since 2001. **Head of Government:** Prime Minister Maria do Carmo Silveira (appointed June 2005).
LANGUAGE: Portuguese is the official language. Creole is also spoken. Some English is spoken, but French is more common.
RELIGION: Roman Catholic majority (82 per cent), with a number of other Christian denominations also represented.
ELECTRICITY: 220 volts AC.
SOCIAL CONVENTIONS: The Portuguese influence is very strong. People are friendly and courteous. Every greeting is accompanied by a handshake. Normal social courtesies should be observed. Alcohol is available and smoking is acceptable. **Photography:** Visitors wishing to photograph local people should ask permission first.

Climate

An equatorial climate with heavy rainfall, high temperatures and humidity. The south of the main island, being mountainous, is wetter than the north. The main dry season is from early June to late September. There is another dry season, the 'Pequenha Gravana', from the end of December to the start of February.
Required clothing: Tropicals and lightweight cottons throughout the year. Umbrellas or light waterproofs for the rainy season are advised.

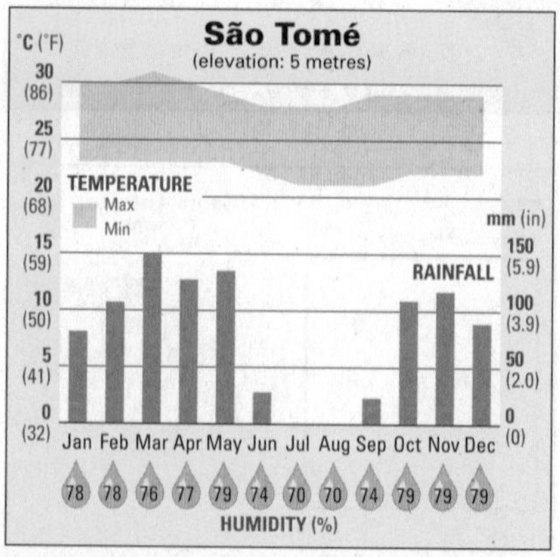

Passport/Visa

	Passport Required?	Visa Required?	Return Ticket Required?
Full British	Yes	Yes	Yes
Australian	Yes	Yes	Yes
Canadian	Yes	Yes	Yes
USA	Yes	Yes	Yes
Other EU	Yes	Yes	Yes
Japanese	Yes	Yes	Yes

Note: *Regulations and requirements may be subject to change at short notice, and you are advised to contact the appropriate diplomatic or consular authority before finalising travel arrangements. Any numbers in the chart refer to the footnotes below.*

PASSPORTS: Valid passport required by all.
VISAS: Required by all except transit passengers continuing their journey to another country by the same or first connecting aircraft within 24 hours provided holding valid onward or return documentation and not leaving the airport.
Types of visa and cost: *Tourist:* single-entry: US$60; mutiple-entry: US$70. *Business:* single-entry: US$80; multiple-entry: US$90. Visas processed immediately are available for an additional fee of US$5. Enquire at the Embassy for further details.
Validity: Three months from date of issue for single-entry; six months from date of issue for multiple-entry. Extensions are possible; apply at the Immigration Department in São Tomé.
Application requirements: (a) Valid passport. (b) Fee, payable by money order only. (c) One passport-size photo. (d) One application form. (e) Stamped addressed envelope to cover international postal charges. (f) Letter stating purpose of travel. (g) Yellow fever immunisation card "copy". *Business:* (a)-(g) and, (h) Company letter.
Application to: Consulate (or consular section at Embassy); see *Passport/Visa Information*. For applications in person, an appointment should be made with the Consulate (or consular section at Embassy) in advance.
Working days required: Two days (personal application); up to one week (postal applications).
Temporary residence: Enquire at Embassy (see *Passport/Visa Information*).

PASSPORT/VISA INFORMATION

Embassy of the Democratic Republic of São Tomé e Príncipe in Belgium
Square Montgommery, 175 Avenue de Tervuren, 1150 Brussels, Belgium
Tel: (2) 734 8966

Embassy of the Democratic Republic of São Tomé e Príncipe in the USA
400 Park Avenue, 7th Floor, New York, NY 10044, USA
Tel: (212) 317 0533.
Website: www.saotome.org

Money

Currency: Dobra (STD) = 100 cêntimos. Notes are in denominations of STD50,000, 20,000, 10,000 and 5000. Coins are in denominations of STD20, 10, 5, 2 and 1, and 50 cêntimos.
Currency exchange: Foreign currencies can be exchanged at banks and some hotels.
Traveller's cheques: Limited acceptance by banks and hotels. To avoid additional exchange rate charges travellers are advised to take traveller's cheques in US Dollars.
Currency restrictions: The import and export of local and foreign currency is unlimited, provided declared on arrival.
Banking hours: Mon-Fri 0730-1130.
Exchange rate indicators:
Rate at time of publishing
£1.00= STD13283.10
$1.00= STD7525.00

Duty Free

The following may be imported into São Tomé e Príncipe without incurring customs duty:
Reasonable quantities of tobacco products and perfume (opened).
Prohibited items: Alcoholic beverages and lottery tickets.

Public Holidays

Below are listed Public Holidays for the period January 2006-June 2007.
2006: Jan 1 New Year's Day. **Feb 3** Heroes' Day. **May 1** Labour Day. **Jul 12** Independence Day. **Sep 6** Armed Forces Day. **Sep 30** Agricultural Reform Day. **Nov 26** Argel Accord Day. **Dec 21** São Tomé Day (Catholic). **Dec 25** Christmas Day.
2007: Jan 1 New Year's Day. **Feb 3** Heroes' Day. **May 1** Labour Day.

Health

	Special Precautions?	Certificate Required?
Yellow Fever	Yes	1
Cholera	2	No
Typhoid & Polio	3	N/A
Malaria	4	N/A

Note: *Regulations and requirements may be subject to change at short notice, and you are advised to contact your doctor well in advance of your intended date of departure. Any numbers in the chart refer to the footnotes below.*

1: A *yellow fever* vaccination certificate is required from all travellers over one year of age. Travellers arriving from non-endemic zones should note that vaccination is strongly recommended for travel outside the urban areas, even if an outbreak of the disease has not been reported and they would normally not require a vaccination certificate to enter the country.
2: Following WHO guidelines issued in 1973, a *cholera* vaccination certificate is not a condition of entry to São Tomé e Príncipe. However, cholera is a risk in this country and precautions are essential. Up-to-date advice should be sought before deciding whether these precautions should include vaccination, as medical opinion is divided over its effectiveness; see the *Health* appendix for further information.
3: Vaccination against *typhoid* is advised.
4: *Malaria* risk, predominantly in the malignant *falciparum* form exists all year throughout the country. Chloroquine resistance has been reported.
Food & drink: All water should be regarded as being potentially contaminated. Water used for drinking, brushing teeth or making ice should have first been boiled or otherwise sterilised. Milk is unpasteurised and should be boiled. Powdered or tinned milk is available and is advised, but make sure that it is reconstituted with pure water. Avoid dairy products which are likely to have been made from unboiled milk. Only eat well-cooked meat and fish, preferably served hot. Pork, salad and mayonnaise may carry increased risk. Vegetables should be cooked and fruit peeled.
Other risks: *Bilharzia* (*schistosomiasis*) is present. Avoid swimming and paddling in fresh water; swimming pools which are well chlorinated and maintained are safe. *Hepatitis A* and *E* are also present; *hepatitis B* is endemic. *Meningococcal disease* may occur.
Rabies is present. For those at high risk, vaccination before arrival should be considered. If you are bitten, seek medical advice without delay. For more information, see the *Health* appendix.
Health care: The island has very basic medical facilities, with one hospital. It is important to carry a basic first aid kit. Health insurance is essential.

Travel - International

AIR:
The national airline is *Air São Tomé e Príncipe (KY)*, a subsidiary of *TAP Air Portugal*. It operates flights regularly between São Tomé and Libreville (Gabon), where they connect with ingoing or outgoing long-haul flights to or from Europe. *TAP Air Portugal* operates flights from Lisbon and there is also a scheduled flight from Angola.
Approximate flight times: From São Tomé to *London* is six hours 30 minutes (including stopover in Lisbon).
Main airports: *São Tomé (TMS)*, 5.5km (3.5 miles) from the town. Transport to the city centre is by airport bus, minibus or taxi. Airport facilities are fairly limited; left luggage, first aid and tourist information are available.
Departure tax: US$20 per adult, payable in cash on departure for all international flights. US$10 must be paid for children, except those under two years who are exempt.
SEA:
The main port is São Tomé, but this is not deep-water and few international cruise lines or other passenger ships call there; however, boats do sail there from Libreville and Doula.

Travel - Internal

AIR:
ASTP (*Air São Tomé e Príncipe*) runs regular flights between São Tomé and Príncipe (flight time - 40 minutes). Panoramic and charter flights are also available.
SEA:
A limited ferry service operates between São Tomé and Príncipe.
ROAD:
Traffic drives on the right. There are over 380km (236 miles) of roads, although in general these are deteriorating. Some of them are asphalted around São Tomé town, but 4-wheel drive vehicles are necessary to get further afield: animals on the road and potholes may cause problems. There is street lighting only in the capital. There is a **bus** network, and **share taxis** are also in operation. The only public transport on Príncipe is a minibus. **Car hire** can be arranged through the Miramar Hotel (see below). **Documentation:** An International Driving Permit is not legally required but is recommended.

Travel Advice

Crime rates are generally low, but armed robberies do happen. The threat from terrorism is low, but you should be aware of the global risk of indiscriminate terrorist attacks which could be against civilian targets, including places frequented by foreigners.
This advice is based on information provided by the Foreign and Commonwealth Office in the UK. It is correct at time of publishing. As the situation can change rapidly, visitors are advised to contact the following organisations for the latest travel advice:

British Foreign and Commonwealth Office
Tel: (0845) 850 2829.
Website: www.fco.gov.uk

US Department of State
Website: http://travel.state.gov/travel

Accommodation

HOTELS:
There are currently around 10 hotels in the country offering a total of 200 beds, including the *Miramar Hotel* in the capital São Tomé, the *Marlin Beach* hotel and the *Bom Bom Island Resort* on the northern coast of Príncipe. Apart from the hotels there is also a chain of state-run inns, operated at more modest levels of comfort. But tourism is high on the Government's agenda and a push to create more accommodation for this growing market is expected.
CAMPING:
This is possible on a number of deserted beaches.

Top Things To See & Do

- The island of São Tomé, with its capital of the same name, represents 90 per cent of the total surface of the country. **São Tomé** is a picturesque town, with colonial Portuguese architecture and attractive parks. There are a number of *roças* (cocoa plantations) on the island that are worth visiting: **Agostinho Neto**, the largest plantation in the country, is a clear example of São Tomé's colonial past; other *roças* are **Agua Izé**, where visitors can tour the plantation by train, **Monté Café** and **Ribeira Peixe**.
- Other attractions on the island include the **Boca de Inferno** (**Hell's Mouth**), a sea water fountain several metres high; the **Cascada São Nicoláu** waterfall near **Pousada Boa Vista**; the **Ilheu da Rolas** (**Turtledove Island**), a small island off São Tomé crossed by the equator; the **Pico de São Tomé**, the highest

mountain in the archipelago (2024m/6800ft); the **Porto Alegre**, on the southern tip of the island; the ancient fishing town of **São João dos Angolares**; and the fortress of **São Sebastião**, which also houses a museum with a collection of religious and colonial art.

- The small island of **Príncipe** is located 150km (94 miles) from São Tomé and its main town is **Santo Antonio**, which has preserved a distinctive colonial architecture and atmosphere. Dominated by two cocoa plantations, additional attractions for visitors are the **Ilheu Bom Bom**, a tiny island situated off Príncipe's northern coast, where one of the country's few tourist resorts is located; and the **Pico de Principe**, the island's summit (948m/3128ft).
- Saõ Tomé e Principe has some of the clearest waters on the western coast of Africa and is therefore ideal for **swimming**, **snorkelling** and **diving**. Beaches have white as well as black sand. **Lagoa Azul** (**Blue Lagoon**) on São Tomé is good for snorkelling (but there is only a rocky beach). Individual hotels can arrange diving trips as well equipment hire. Hotels and resorts can also organise deep-sea **fishing** trips, notably on **Bom Bom Island**.
- Visitors can also enjoy excellent **hiking** through São Tomé's **rainforest** as well as fascinating and varied **birdwatching**.
- Popular **theatre** has an important place in daily life and each island has its own form of traditional dance and mime. The *Auto de Floripes* (in São Tomé) and the *Tchiloli* (in Príncipe) date back to the 16th century and relate the *Tragedy of the Marquis of Mantua and the Emperor Charlemagne*. The roles are passed on from father to son while women usually remain spectators. There are also a number of religious processions dedicated to Catholic saints, and all the main Christian holidays are celebrated.

TOURIST INFORMATION

Tourism Office
CP40, Avenue Marginal 12 de Julho, São Tomé
Tel: (2) 21542.

Entertainment

FOOD & DRINK: There are several restaurants in the capital, augmented by a considerable number of more informal eating establishments patronised by the inhabitants. Reservations are nearly always required. Most dishes are highly spiced.
National specialities:
- Grilled fish and chicken.
- Fried fish.
- Tropical fruit are popular.

Tipping: Not always welcomed.

Business

ECONOMY: The economy is based on the export of agricultural products: cocoa, palm oil, bananas, coffee and coconuts. This concentration on cash crops, especially cocoa (most of which is exported) means that the country has to import most of its food. It also means the country's economy is overly dependent on favourable weather conditions and world commodity prices: by and large these have not been kind to São Tomé e Príncipe's economy in recent years. After the failure to develop an indigenous fishing industry in the 1980s, fishing rights were sold under licence to foreign fleets. Manufacturing industry is confined to a few food-processing plants and factories producing consumer goods for local consumption. A free trade zone has now been established on Príncipe island in an effort to boost the export economy. Since the late-1990s, economic policy has concentrated on promotion of the private sector and the removal of trade barriers. This has been carried out under the auspices of an IMF Structural Adjustment Programme. The country has also benefited from the IMF's Heavily Indebted Poor Countries Programme, which has eliminated a large slice of the foreign debt; nonetheless, the Government still considers elimination of its debt a high priority. It will be able to do this once revenues begin to flow from the oil and gas fields recently discovered (and as yet unexploited) in São Tomé's territorial waters. Exploration bids submitted in 2003 have already resulted in a windfall for the Government amounting to hundreds of millions of dollars. With its economy due for a radical transformation, the government is planning to construct a deepwater port and has suggested to the USA that it might consider establishing a naval base (not least to protect the oilfields). The Government also hopes to promote the currently minute tourism industry. Economic performance in recent years has been improving and is expected to get even better as revenue from oil starts to come in. Portugal and Angola supply most of the country's imports; The Netherlands is the main export market. São Tomé e Príncipe is a member of the African Development Bank and the CEEAC trade bloc.
Office hours: Mon-Fri 0800-1200 and 1500-1800, Sat 0800-1200.

COMMERCIAL INFORMATION

Ministry of Foreign Affairs and Co-operation
Avenue 12 July, CP 111, São Tomé
Tel: (2) 22662.

Saudi Arabia

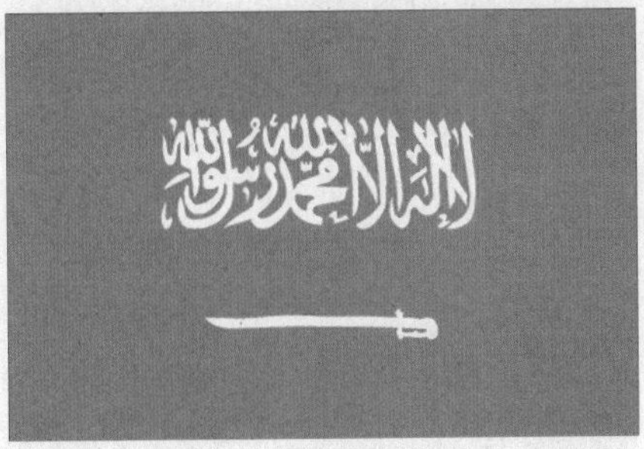

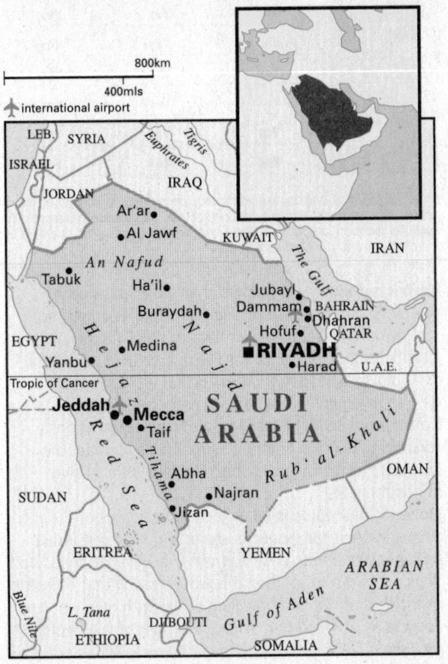

Location: Middle East.

Time: GMT + 3.

Overview

There is a veil hung over Saudi Arabia that distorts the reality that resides behind it. This is partly a two-way process, since Saudi Arabia does not permit touristic visits and exercises strict Islamic principles that non-Muslims might shy away from. Similarly, much media reportage of Saudi Arabia focuses solely on these Islamic-based laws, and equally focuses on its expanse of hot and repetitive desert, its archaic customs in dated cities.
Lift the veil, however, and you will find that many conceptions of Saudi Arabia are misconceptions. Saudi Arabia has many areas of beautiful oases and dramatic mountain-tops, beaches and rivers. Its cities, although having no nightlife, do have plenty of cafes and restaurants. There are also shops galore, from the souk to the huge department store. Indeed, Saudi Arabia's major cities are generally very modern, with amenities of a high standard. And, as long as you respect and abide by the viewpoints and customs of the country, you will find that you are treated cordially.
What has enabled Saudi Arabia to boast such steel-and-glass cities is oil. In 1933, the first explorations began for oil, vast deposits of which were discovered in the eastern part of the country. The oil search also brought the USA into contact with Saudi Arabia for the first time and they quickly became the country's principal Western ally. Nonetheless, there have been constant sources of friction between the two countries over the years - most notably, Israel. More current was the discovery that the bulk of the 9-11 terrorist hijackers were Saudi nationals and the fact that the recently appointed King Abdullah is generally less pro-American than was his father, takes a harder line on oil pricing.
Such oil might have brought modernising, then, but Saudi Arabia is still steeped in the most extraordinary history. In the year AD 622, Prophet Muhammad launched a successful campaign to recapture Mecca from the Persians, who had made it a province of their Empire. Afterwards, the Muslims would continue their expansion across the Arabian peninsula and into Syria, Mesopotamia (Iraq), Persia, and westwards into Egypt and North Africa.
This underlines one of the most important facts to consider about Saudi Arabia: as the birthplace of Muhammad, it contains the holiest cities of Islam. To be critical of any practices adopted in Saudi Arabia is to be neglectful of this fact, since the Saudis take the responsibility for protecting the integrity of this holy land with utmost seriousness, and Islamic laws are strictly enforced by the *mutawwa* (religious police). To the non-Islamic eye, Saudi Arabia also succeeds in being beautiful and praiseworthy, and in the current climate, this complex country will probably be a significant part of the worldwide map for some time.

General Information

AREA: 2,240,000 sq km (864,869 sq miles).
POPULATION: 25.6 million (UN, 2005).
POPULATION DENSITY: 11.4 per sq km.
CAPITAL: Riyadh (royal). **Population**: 4.7 million (UN estimate 2005). Jeddah (administrative). **Population:** 3,192,000 (UN estimate 2001; including suburbs).
GEOGRAPHY: Saudi Arabia occupies four-fifths of the Arabian peninsula. It is bordered to the northwest by Jordan, to the north by Iraq and Kuwait, to the east by the Gulf of Oman, Qatar, the United Arab Emirates and Oman, and to the south by Yemen. To the west lies the Red Sea. Along the Red Sea coast is a narrow coastal strip (*Tihama*) which becomes relatively hotter and more humid towards the south and has areas of extensive tidal flats and lava fields. Behind this coastal plain is a series of plateaux reaching up to 2000m (6560ft). The southern part of this range, *Asir*, has some peaks of over 3000m (9840ft). North of these mountains, in the far north, is *An Nafud*, a sand sea, and further south the landscape rises to *Najd*, a semi-desert area scattered with oases. Still further south the land falls away, levelling out to unremitting desert, the uninhabited 'Empty Quarter' or *Rub al Khali*. Along the Gulf coast is a low fertile plain giving way to limestone ridges inland.
GOVERNMENT: Absolute Monarchy since 1932. **Head of State and Government:** King Abdullah since the death of King Fahd Ibn Abd al-Aziz Al-Sa'ud on 1 August 2005. **Recent history:** In 2002, as the American Government geared up to launch operations in Afghanistan and Iraq, the Saudis made it clear that they would prefer the Americans to move elsewhere from their military base in Saudi Arabia. They did, and Qatar became the main command and control centre for these recent US military operations. The change in the Saudi position followed from a major shift in the country's domestic politics. Several factors were at work but the most important was the effective replacement of King Fahd, who after prolonged illness was effectively an invalid (and has since died, in August 2005), by Crown Prince Abdullah. The Crown Prince is generally less pro-American than Fahd.
Abdullah belongs to the generation of leaders who have governed Saudi Arabia since the death of Abdul Aziz, all of whom are now in their 70s: there is no clear line of succession and there may be a debilitating power struggle among the 6000 male descendants who make up the House of Saud. The most likely victors are the branch of the family descended from one of Ibn Saud's wives, bint Sudairi, who form a powerful clan within the group (commonly known as the 'Sudairi Seven'). Abdullah is not among them but all – and a number of their immediate relatives – occupy key ministerial, administrative and diplomatic posts. Abdullah has also taken some tentative steps towards relaxing the royal family's political stranglehold, mainly to appease international opinion and increasingly vocal domestic reformers.
Plans for municipal council elections were announced in October 2003. These elections were the first elections to a Government body in Saudi Arabia. Polling took place between February and April 2005.
Saudi Arabia is an absolute Monarchy with no political parties. The King appoints a Council of Ministers to run day-to-day affairs. A consultative council (*Majlis as-Shura*), numbering about 60, has been established to advise the Monarch; it has no formal powers.
LANGUAGE: Arabic. English is spoken in business circles.
RELIGION: The majority of Saudi Arabians follow Islam; around 90 per cent are Sunni Muslim, but Shia Muslims predominate in the Eastern Province.
ELECTRICITY: 127/220 volts AC, 60Hz.
SOCIAL CONVENTIONS: Saudi culture is based on Islam and the perfection of the Arabic language. The Saudi form of Islam is conservative and fundamentalist, based on the 18th-century revivalist movement of the Najdi leader Sheikh Muhammad Ibn Abdel-Wahhab. This still has a great effect on Saudi society, especially on the position of women, who are required by law only to leave the home totally covered in black robes (*abaya*) and masks, although there are regional variations of dress. The Najd and other remote areas remain true to Wahhabi tradition, but throughout the country this way of life is being altered by modernisation and rapid development. For more information, see the *World of Islam* appendix. Shaking hands is the customary form of greeting. Invitations to private homes are unusual. Entertaining is usually in hotels or restaurants and although the custom of eating with the right hand persists, it is more likely that knives and forks will be used. A small gift either promoting the company or representing your country will generally be well received. Women are expected to dress

A B C D E F G H I J K L M N O P Q R S T U V W X Y Z

modestly and it is best to do so to avoid offence. Men should not wear shorts in public or go without a shirt. The norms for public behaviour are extremely conservative and religious police, known as *Mutawwa'in*, are charged with enforcing these standards. Customs regarding smoking are the same as in Europe and non-smoking areas are indicated. During Ramadan, Muslims are not allowed to eat, smoke or drink during the day and it is illegal for a foreign visitor to do so in public.

Photography: Strictly speaking, photography is not permitted. However, many people do still take photos, but are careful to ask permission of the relevant authority before photographing people or any building.

Climate

Saudi Arabia has a desert climate. In Jeddah it is warm for most of the year. Riyadh, which is inland, is hotter in summer and colder in winter, when occasional heavy rainstorms occur. The *Rub al Khali* ('empty Quarter') seldom receives rain, making Saudi Arabia one of the driest countries in the world.

Required clothing: Tropical or lightweight clothing.

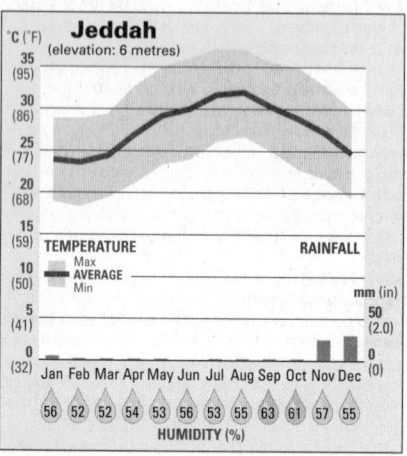

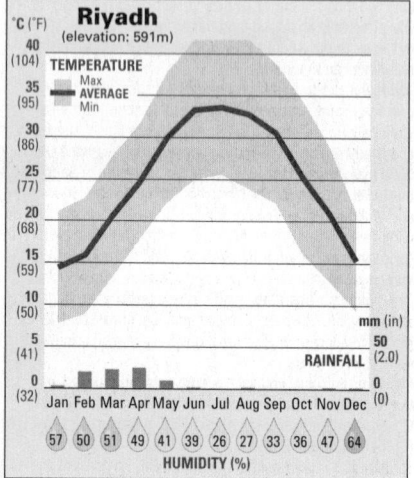

Communications

Telephone: A sophisticated telecommunications network and satellite, microwave and cable systems span the country. Full IDD is available.

Mobile telephone: International roaming agreements exist with some mobile phone companies. Coverage is mostly good.

Internet: The Ministry of Post, Telegraph and Telephones provides Internet facilities in most cities. E-mail can also be accessed from many hotels and Internet cafes.

Post: Internal and international services available from the Central Post Office. Post is delivered to box numbers. Airmail to Europe takes up to one week.

MEDIA: Saudi Arabia has a very tightly-controlled media environment and criticism of the Government, the royal family and religious tenets are not really tolerated - although there are signs of an increasing tolerance emerging. The state-run *Broadcasting Service of the Kingdom of Saudi Arabia* (BSKSA) is responsible for all broadcasting in the kingdom. The Minister of Culture and Information oversees radio and TV operations. Viewers in the country's east can pick up TV stations from more liberal Gulf neighbours. The Government blocks access to websites that it deems offensive.

Press: Saudi newspapers are created by royal decree, and there are 10 dailies and dozens of magazines. Pan-Arab papers, subject to censorship, are available. Newspapers tend to follow the lead of the state-run news agency on whether or not to publish stories on sensitive subjects. The main newspapers include *Al-Jazirah*, *Ar-Riyadh* and *Okaz*. English-language dailies include *Arab News*, *Riyadh Daily* and *Saudi Gazette*.

TV: The state-run Broadcasting Service of the Kingdom of Saudi Arabia (BSKSA) is responsible for all broadcasting in the Kingdom. It operates four TV networks, including the news channel *al-Ikhbariya*.

Radio: Private radio and TV stations cannot operate from Saudi soil. *Saudi Radio* is state-run.

Passport/Visa

	Passport Required?	Visa Required?	Return Ticket Required?
Full British	Yes	Yes	Yes
Australian	Yes	Yes	Yes
Canadian	Yes	Yes	Yes
USA	Yes	Yes	Yes
Other EU	Yes	Yes	Yes
Japanese	Yes	Yes	Yes

Note: *Regulations and requirements may be subject to change at short notice, and you are advised to contact the appropriate diplomatic or consular authority before finalising travel arrangements. Any numbers in the chart refer to the footnotes below.*

Restricted entry: (a) Holders of an Israeli passport or passports with Israeli stamps in them. (b) Passengers not complying with Saudi conventions of dress and behaviour, including those who appear to be in a state of intoxication, or who display inappropriate affection (especially between men and women) will be refused entry (see *Social Conventions* section). (c) There are special regulations concerning pilgrims entering Saudi Arabia. Contact the Consulate (or consular section at Embassy) for further information.

Note: (a) Unaccompanied women must be met at the airport by their sponsor or husband and have confirmed onward reservations as far as their final destination in Saudi Arabia. If met by a sponsor, it is worth noting that there are restrictions on women travelling by car with men who are not related by blood or marriage. However, it is acceptable for women visiting for business purposes to be accompanied and met at the airport by male business partners: further enquiries can be made at the Information Centre or Embassy. Women and under-aged children should be accompanied by a *Moharram* (close male family member). (b) No foreign passenger who is working as a domestic servant in Saudi Arabia should be transported to Saudi Arabia unless holding a valid non-refundable return ticket.

PASSPORTS: A passport valid for six months at time of entry is required by all except Muslim pilgrims holding Pilgrim Passes, tickets and other documents for their onward or return journey and entering the country via Jeddah or Medina - although sufficient evidence of Muslim faith must be provided (eg religious authenticated certificate). All passports must be valid for at least six months beyond the estimated stay in Saudi Arabia.

VISAS: Required by all except the following:
(a) nationals of Bahrain, Kuwait, Oman, Qatar, United Arab Emirates and Yemen;
(b) transit passengers continuing their journey by the same or first connecting aircraft within 18 hours, provided holding valid onward or return documentation, not leaving the airport and making no further landing in Saudi Arabia (except those travelling on Saudi Arabian Airlines who are permitted to make a second stop, and except nationals of Burkina Faso, Mali, Niger and Nigeria who *always* require a transit visa);
(c) holders of re-entry permits and 'Landing Permits' issued by the Saudi Arabian Ministry of Foreign Affairs (see *Passport/Visa Information*).

Types of visa and cost: *Family Visit:* £39. *Business:* £39; £96 (multiple-entry). *Work:* SAR50 (approximately £10), if paying at Embassy. Please consult the Consulate to confirm the exact amount as fluctuations occur due to exchange rates. *Residency:* £10. *Transit:* £10. *Pilgrim (Ummra):* no charge (one to three months for a maximum of 30 days).

Note: (a) The Pilgrim (*Ummra*) visa can only be obtained through an authorised '*Ummra* Agency', appointed by the Ministry of Foreign Affairs. Check with Embassy for a full list of appointed agents. Administrative fees may apply. (b) Transit passengers who stay in the King Abdulaziz International Airport, Jeddah Islamic Port or Prince Mohammed bin Abdulaziz Airport in Medina for over 24 hours can perform *Ummra* or visit a Holy Mosque, provided they withhold a signed agreement with one of the appointed *Ummra* agencies.

Validity: The visa stay period starts from the first day of

entry into Saudi Arabia within the visa's valid dates. *Ummra* visas are valid for 30 days for stays of up to two weeks.

Application to: Consulate (or consular section at Embassy); see *Passport/Visa Information*. Travellers are advised to apply well in advance. *Hajj* or *Umrah* visas are only available from the Consulate through an authorised travel agent. People visiting the Consulate directly for *Hajj* or *Umrah* visas will not be successful.

Application requirements: *Family/Residency:* (a) One application form. (b) One passport-size photo affixed to application form. Children travelling on parents' passport must have photos affixed on passport and endorsed by relevant authorities with photos attached on application form. Copies of birth certificate and marriage certificate of all accompanying children and spouses are also required. (c) Passport valid for at least six months. (d) Prepaid, self-addressed, recorded delivery envelope, if applying by post. If applying by post from Ireland (Rep), enclose a minimum of nine coupons. (e) Fee (payable in cash, by postal order or by banker's draft only). (f) Medical report, authenticated by the UK Foreign Office (for persons over 15 years of age). Applicants from Ireland (Rep) should legalise their medical report at the Irish Foreign Office in Dublin. (g) A copy a of marriage certificate showing the visitor is married to the person working in Saudi Arabia whom they intend to visit. These documents must be legalised through the British Foreign and Common Wealth Office or the Department of Foreign Affairs in Dublin. *Business:* (a)-(e) and, (f) Letter of invitation from Saudi host company endorsed by Saudi Chamber of Commerce (original and copy). (g) Letter from company or organisation in own country. *Work:* (a)-(d) and, (e) Letter of introduction from Saudi sponsor and copy of the employment contract. (f) Copies of academic qualifications and work experience in the field of job applied for. (g) A visa authorisation letter from the Ministry of Foreign Affairs, supplied by the Saudi Arabian employer. (h) Letter of *No Objection* if previously employed in Saudi Arabia. (i) An amount equivalent to SAR50 deposited at the Consulate's cashier desk. *Pilgrim:* (a)-(d) and, (e) Airline ticket with confirmed booking (both ways). The point of entry and departure must be Jeddah or Medina. (f) *Meningitis* immunisation certificate with validity for more than three years and vaccination issued no less than 10 days before travelling. A *Yellow Fever* certificate may be required, if travelling from an infected area. (g) ID card must be worn on wrist band and luggage must be clearly labelled: 'PILGRIM'. (h) Letter of approval issued by Saudi Ministry of *Hajj*, confirming that the authorised UK travel agent, tour operator and charities, through which the application for Hajj was submitted, have completed the necessary requirements regarding their pilgrims. (i) Proof of conversion to Islam may have to be submitted. *Transit:* (a)-(e) and, (f) Airline ticket reservation showing proof of leaving Saudi Arabia within 48 hours and visa valid for next destination if applicable.

Note: (a) An Exit Permit is required for most nationals, requiring a passport-size photo and must be issued by the Chief of Police (usually processed within three days after application). It is advised to enquire at the nearest Embassy for further information. (b) There are further requirements for *Ummra* applications, but these must be submitted by the endorsed travel agent or tour operator.

Working days required: At least two days. At least one week if applying by post. For information on processing time for all other types of visa, contact the Consulate (or consular section at Embassy).

PASSPORT/VISA INFORMATION

Royal Embassy of Saudi Arabia
30 Charles Street, London W1J 5DZ, UK
Visa section: 30-32 Charles Street, London W1J 5DZ, UK
Tel: (020) 7917 3000.
Website: www.saudiembassy.org.uk
Opening hours: Mon-Thurs 0900-1600, Fri 0900-1500.
Consular section: Mon-Thurs 0900-1130 (visa applications); 1400-1530 (passport collection), Fri 1330-1430.

Royal Embassy of Saudi Arabia
601 New Hampshire Avenue, NW, Washington, DC 20037, USA
Tel: 337 4076 (information section) *or* 944 3126 (visa section).
Website: www.saudiembassy.net

Money

Currency: Saudi Arabian Riyal (SAR) = 100 halala; 5 halala = 20 qurush. Notes are in denominations of SAR500, 200, 100, 50, 20, 10, 5 and 1. Coins are in denominations of 50, 25, 10, and 5 halala, and 10, 5, 2 and 1 qurush.

Currency exchange: Most foreign currencies can be exchanged at commercial banks and money-changers, which stay open longer.

Credit & debit cards: American Express, Diners Club, MasterCard and Visa are all widely accepted. Check with your credit or debit card company for details of merchant acceptability and other services which may be available.
Traveller's cheques: Widely accepted although they can be hard to change. To avoid additional exchange rate charges, travellers are advised to take traveller's cheques in Saudi Riyal, Euros, US Dollars or Pounds Sterling and to carry the purchase receipt.
Currency restrictions: Free import and export of both local and foreign currency. Import of Israeli currency is prohibited.
Banking hours: Sat-Wed 0800-1200 and 1700-2000; Thurs 0800-1200. Money-changers stay open longer.
Exchange rate indicators:
Rate at time of publishing

£1.00=	SAR6.62
$1.00=	SAR3.75

Duty Free

The following items may be imported into Saudi Arabia without incurring customs duty:
600 cigarettes or 100 cigars or 500g of tobacco; a reasonable amount of perfume; a reasonable amount of cultured pearls for personal use.
Note: Duty is levied on cameras and typewriters, but if these articles are re-exported within 90 days, the customs charges may be refunded. It is advisable not to put film into cameras.
Prohibited items: Alcohol, all edible goods, narcotics and drugs (except medicines for personal use accompanied by a prescription), pornography, religious books (besides the Qu'ran), pork, firearms, natural pearls, live animals and birds, all types of palm trees, most foods and items listed as prohibited by the Arab League (copy available from the Embassy).

Public Holidays

Below are listed Public Holidays for 2006.
2006: Jan 10 Eid al-Adha (Feast of the Sacrifice). **Sep 23** Saudi National Day. **Oct 22-24** Eid al-Fitr (End of Ramadan). **Dec 31** Eid al-Adha (Feast of the Sacrifice).
Note: Muslim festivals are timed according to local sightings of various phases of the moon and the dates given above are approximations. During the lunar month of Ramadan that precedes Eid al-Fitr, Muslims fast during the day and feast at night and normal business patterns may be interrupted. Some disruption may continue into Eid al-Fitr itself. Eid al-Fitr and Eid al-Adha may last anything from two to 10 days, depending on the region. During Hajj (when pilgrims visit Mecca) all government establishments and some businesses will be closed for 10 to 14 days. For more information, see the *World of Islam* appendix.

Health

	Special Precautions?	Certificate Required?
Yellow Fever	No	1
Cholera	No	No
Typhoid & Polio	2	N/A
Malaria	3	N/A

Note: Regulations and requirements may be subject to change at short notice, and you are advised to contact your doctor well in advance of your intended date of departure. Any numbers in the chart refer to the footnotes below.

1: A *yellow fever* vaccination certificate is required from all travellers arriving from countries of which any parts are infected.
2: Vaccination against *typhoid* is advised.
3: *Malaria* risk, predominantly in the malignant *falciparum* form, exists throughout the year in most of the Southern region, except the high altitude areas of Asir Province, and in certain rural areas of the Western Province. There is no risk in Jeddah, Mecca, Medina or Ta'if. Resistance to chloroquine has been reported. The recommended prophylaxis is chloroquine plus proguanil. *Cerebral Malaria* has also occurred, but solely in the Jizan region.
Food & drink: All water should be regarded as being potentially contaminated. Water used for drinking, brushing teeth or making ice should have first been boiled or otherwise sterilised. Milk is unpasteurised and should be boiled. Powdered or tinned milk is available and is advised, but make sure that it is reconstituted with pure water. Avoid dairy products which are likely to have been made from unboiled milk. Only eat well-cooked meat and fish, preferably served hot. Salad and mayonnaise may carry increased risk. Vegetables should be cooked and fruit peeled.
Note: During the *Hajj* (annual pilgrimage to Mecca), Saudi Arabia requires vaccination of pilgrims against *meningococcal meningitis*. Although this applies mainly to pilgrims, other travellers may find themselves affected, especially during the month of August.
Other risks: *Bilharzia* (*schistosomiasis*) is present. Avoid swimming and paddling in fresh water; swimming pools which are well chlorinated and maintained are safe. *Hepatitis A* is common and *hepatitis B* is endemic. *Visceral leishmaniasis* occurs in the southwest of the country. Cases of *Rift Valley Fever* have been reported, mostly in the Jizan area. *Rabies* is present. For those at high risk, vaccination before arrival should be considered. If you are bitten, seek medical advice without delay. For more information, consult the *Health* appendix.
Health care: Medical facilities are generally of a high standard, but treatment is expensive. Health insurance is essential.

Travel - International

AIR:

The national airline is *Saudi Arabian Airlines (SV)* (website: www.saudiairlines.com).
Approximate flight times: From *London* to Jeddah is five hours 50 minutes, to Riyadh is six hours 25 minutes, and to Dhahran is six hours 45 minutes. From *Los Angeles* to Jeddah is 18 hours 45 minutes and to Riyadh is 21 hours 15 minutes. From *New York* to Jeddah is 13 hours and to Riyadh is 16 hours. From *Singapore* to Jeddah is eight hours 25 minutes.
Main airports: *Riyadh (RUH)* (King Khaled International) Airport, 35km (22 miles) north of the city. *Facilities*: Car rental, bureaux de change, duty free, restaurant and snack bar.
Jeddah (JED) (King Abdul Aziz) Airport, 18km (11 miles) north of the city (travel time – 30 minutes). *To/from the airport*: Taxi and limousine services are available for Mecca, Medina and Taif. *Facilities*: Banks/bureaux de change, duty free shopping, car rental, restaurants and tourist information points.
Dammam (DMM) (King Fahd International) Airport, 30km (19) miles northwest of Dammam (travel time – 45 minutes). *To/from the airport*: Taxis are available from outside the airport. *Facilities*: Duty free shopping, gift shop, restaurant and cafe.
Dhahran (DHA) (Al Khobar) Airport, 13km (8 miles) southeast of Dhahran (travel time – 15 minutes).
Departure tax: SAR50. Children, *Hajj* and *Ummra* pilgrims and passengers accompanying human remains are exempt.

SEA:

Main ports: Dammam (Gulf), and Jeddah and Yanbu (Red Sea).

ROAD:

The principal international routes from Jordan are Amman to Dammam, Medina and Jeddah. There are also roads to Yemen (from Jeddah), Kuwait, Qatar and the United Arab Emirates. A causeway links Al Khobar with Bahrain. There are regular international buses between Saudi Arabia and Bahrain, Egypt, Jordan, Qatar, Syrian Arab Republic, Turkey and United Arab Emirates.

Travel - Internal

AIR:

There are many domestic airports and air travel is by far the most convenient way of travelling around the country. *Saudi Arabian Airlines (SV)* (website: www.saudiairlines.com) connects all main centres. *Arabian Express* economy class connects Jeddah with Riyadh in just over one hour and Riyadh with Dhahran in just under one hour. A boarding pass should be obtained the evening before departure. There are special flights for pilgrims arriving at or departing from Jeddah during the *Hajj*.

SEA:

A fast car ferry runs between Duba and Hurghada twice daily on Sundays, Tuesdays, Wednesdays and Fridays. Dhows may be chartered for outings on both coasts.

RAIL:

The railway is operated by the *Saudi Railways Organisation* (website: www.saudirailways.org). Children under four travel free. The main railway line is the 570km-long Riyadh–Dammam line, which links Dhahran, Abqaiq, Hofuf, Harad and Al Kharj. There is a daily service in air-conditioned trains with dining car. An additional line links Riyadh with Hofuf. The railway on the west coast made famous by Lawrence of Arabia's raid has long since been abandoned to the desert.

ROAD:

Traffic drives on the right. The road network is constantly being upgraded and expanded and, on the main routes, much of it is of the highest standard. The corniche that winds down the escarpment between Taif and Mecca is as spectacular a feat of engineering as may be seen anywhere, as is the King Fahed Gateway that links Saudi Arabia to Bahrain. However, standards of driving are erratic, particularly in the Eastern Province. As foreigners are tolerated rather than welcomed in Saudi Arabia, it is best to drive with extreme caution at all times. Women are not allowed to drive vehicles or ride bicycles on public roads. Non-Muslims may not enter Mecca or the immediate area; police are stationed to ensure that they turn off onto a specially built ring road, known amongst expatriates as the 'Christian Bypass'. **Bus:** Services have recently been developed by *SAPTCO* to serve inter-urban and local needs. Modern vehicles have been acquired, including air-conditioned double-deckers. All buses must have a screened-off section for the exclusive use of female passengers. **Taxi:** Available in all cities, but often very expensive. Some have meters, and fares should be negotiated in advance. **Car hire:** The major international car hire agencies have offices in Saudi Arabia. The minimum age is 25. **Documentation:** A national driving licence is valid for up to three months if accompanied by an officially sanctioned translation into Arabic. An International Driving Permit (with translation) is recommended, but not required by law. Women are not allowed to drive. There are also restrictions on women travelling by car with men who are not related by blood or marriage.

Travel Advice

There is a continuing high threat of terrorism in Saudi Arabia. It is believed that terrorists are planning further attacks, including against Westerners and places associated with Westerners in Saudi Arabia.
Travellers choosing to travel to, or remain in, Saudi Arabia should take all necessary steps to protect their safety and should make sure they have confidence in their individual security arrangements. Travellers should maintain a high level of vigilance, particularly in public places.
Travellers should remember that Islamic law is strictly enforced in Saudi Arabia.
This advice is based on information provided by the Foreign and Commonwealth Office in the UK. It is correct at time of publishing. As the situation can change rapidly, visitors are advised to contact the following organisations for the latest travel advice:

British Foreign and Commonwealth Office
Tel: (0845) 850 2829.
Website: www.fco.gov.uk

US Department of State
Website: http://travel.state.gov/travel

Accommodation

HOTELS:

There is a good range of hotel accommodation throughout the country. Accommodation is generally easy to find, except during the pilgrimage season when advance reservations are recommended. Service charges are fixed at 15 per cent for deluxe and first-category hotels and at 10 per cent for all others. Hotel charges double in Mecca and Medina during the pilgrimage season, and increase by 25 per cent during the summer months in resort areas such as Abha, Al-Baha, Kamis Mushait and Taif. For further information, contact the Saudi Arabian Ministry of Commerce. There are seven grades of hotel in Saudi Arabia: **deluxe**, **first-class A** and **B**, **second-class A** and **B**, and **third-class A** and **B**.

YOUTH HOSTELS:

There are around 20 youth hostels in Saudi Arabia.

Top Things To See & Do

- If you are Muslim, take the pilgrimage to **Mecca** – or *Hajj* – in January. Although concerns over overcrowding (many have perished due to crushing) persists, for Muslims, the pilgrimage remains a magnificent sight and, as long as you are able-bodied and can afford it, it is something that is required to be done at least once, according to Islamic tenet. Many symbolic ritual acts are performed at the *Hajj*, and completion of them is what nearly all Muslims strive towards. However, due to the impossibility of all Muslims travelling to Mecca, a quota system is in place, which means that for most Muslims, it really is an once-in-a-lifetime event. Places of significance to Muslims include the **Kaabah Enclosure**, the **Mountain of Light**, the **Plain of Arafat** and the **House of Abdullah Bin Abdul Muttalib**, where Muhammad was born. Non-Muslims are not allowed to enter holy cities such as Mecca and **Medina**, and until recently, such a crime was punishable by death by rioting.
- Saudi Arabia, somewhat surprisingly to some, boasts a multitude of fantastic **shops**, from traditional *souks* to large department stores and shopping complexes. This may be because there is such a huge demand for these facilities – since Saudi Arabia has no bars, casinos, nightclubs, theatres or cinemas, its shops are a much-loved way of passing the time.
- Visit the royal capital, **Riyadh** (**Ryad**), a modern city built on the site of the first town captured by Ibn Saud, when he stormed the **Masmak Fort** in 1902 (a spearhead embedded in the main door is said to be the one with which Ibn Saud killed the Turkish Governor). Apart from the fort and a few traditional **Najdi palaces** near **Deera Square**, little trace of the old town remains. However, this is a cosmopolitan city

A B C D E F G H I J K L M N O P Q R S T U V W X Y Z

that is well worth a visit, for the surprises it may give you.
- Watch the **King's Camel Race**, held near Riyadh in April or May. Camel racing was a traditional desert sport of Bedouin tribes. The annual King's Camel Race is one of the world's most important camel races, with something between 20,000 and 30,000 spectators, plus 2000 camels and riders, usually in attendance. The race itself is held on a track that stretches for around 14 miles. And it is all part of the national **Heritage and Cultural Festival** at **Jenadriyah**.
- Discover **Hofuf**, at the centre of the great **Al-Hasa oasis**, which has a strong Turkish influence and a very good **camel market**. Due to being at the centre of an oasis, the agriculture here thrives and the food is sensational. The area is also extraordinarily pretty.
- See the ragged, coral-coloured **Ottoman buildings** of the ancient city of **Jeddah**. If visiting, you should know that leisure facilities have increased and the corniche has a 'Brighton' feel about it. There is an **amusement park** and a wonderful creek allowing both **sailing** and **snorkelling**. Its hotels and restaurants are cosmopolitan and there are good fish and meat **markets**.
- For astonishing landscape and **wildlife**, head for **the Asir** (**Southern Region**), a range of coastal mountains and the only part of the kingdom where there is significant wild vegetation, mostly palms and evergreen bushes. Millet, wheat and dates are grown using largely traditional methods. The inhabitants are darker than other Saudis, being in part descended from African slaves. Baboon, gazelle, leopard, honey badger, mongoose and other 'African' species inhabit remoter areas. Unique to Asir are the ancient **gasaba towers**, phallus-shaped and of unknown purpose. Places to visit include the ancient caravan city of **Qaryat-al-Fau**, recently excavated; the great **dam** and **temple** at **Najran**; and nearby, amidst orchards of pomegranates, limes and bananas, the ornate ruins of the ancient cities of **Timna** and **Shiban**.
- **Obhir Creek**, 50km (30 miles) north of Jeddah, has good facilities for **swimming**, **water-skiing**, **fishing** and sailing, and there are similar **beaches** on the **Gulf coast** south of **Al Khobar**. Elsewhere, hotels and certain Embassies have swimming pools.
- Find some of Saudi Arabia's ancient **crafts** and **skills**, usually still in use and kept in the family. In **Jebel-al-Qara**, the potteries have been worked by eight generations of the same family. In **Abqaiq** there is a 5000-year-old saltmine, still in operation. And **Tarut Island** is the site of the oldest town on the peninsula, now a picturesque settlement of fishermen and weavers.
- As long as you are careful (Saudi Arabia does not boast great driving conditions and has a high incidence of car accidents), it is well worth taking a drive down the astounding modern **corniche road** that winds down the sheer cliffs of the **Taif escarpment** to the hot coastal plain. Look around you and you will see pink **palaces** inbetween the stunning cliff-tops. Such beauty – combined with its far milder climate – have made Taif the official summer capital.

TOURIST INFORMATION

Saudi Arabian Information Centre in the UK
18 Seymour Street, London W1H 7HU, UK
Tel: (020) 7486 3470.

Entertainment

FOOD & DRINK: Local food is often strongly flavoured and spicy. The most common meats are lamb and chicken, beef is rare and pork is proscribed under Islamic law. The main meat meal of the day is lunch. Foreign cooking is on offer in larger towns and the whole range of international cuisine, including fast food, is available in the oil-producing Eastern Province and in Jeddah.
Things to know: Eating, drinking and smoking in public during the fasting hours of Ramadan will incur strict penalties. Restaurants have table service. There are no bars. Alcohol is forbidden by law, and there are severe penalties for infringement; it is important to note that this applies to all nationals regardless of religion.
National specialities:
- The staple diet is *pitta* bread (flat, unleavened bread) which accompanies every dish.
- Rice, lentils, chick peas (*hummus*) and cracked wheat (*burghul*) are also common.
- *Kultra* (chicken or lamb on skewers) is popular for lunch.
- *Kebabs* served with soup and vegetables.
- *Mezze*, the equivalent of hôrs d'oeuvres, may include up to 40 dishes.
- Arabic cakes, cream desserts and rice pudding (*muhalabia*).

National drinks:
- Arabic coffee and fruit drinks are popular alternatives to alcohol.
- Alcohol-free beers and cocktails are served in hotel bars.

Tipping: The practice of tipping is becoming much more common and waiters, hotel porters and taxi drivers should be given 10 per cent.
NIGHTLIFE: Apart from restaurants and hotels there is no nightlife in the Western sense.
SHOPPING: *Souks* (markets) sell incense and incense burners, jewellery, bronze and brassware, richly decorated daggers and swords, and in the Eastern Province, huge brass-bonded chests. Bargaining is often expected, even for modern goods such as cameras and electrical equipment (which can be very good value). **Shopping hours:** Sat-Thurs 0900-1300 and 1630-2000 (Ramadan 2000-0100). These hours differ in various parts of the country.

Business

- **GDP:** US$215 billion.
- **Main exports:** Petroleum and petroleum products.
- **Main imports:** Machinery and equipment, foodstuffs, chemicals, motor vehicles and textiles.
- **Main trade partners:** USA, Japan, China (PR), Korea (Rep), UK, Taiwan (China) and Singapore.

ECONOMY: Saudi Arabia has the world's largest oil reserves – about 20 per cent of proven deposits – and is also currently the world's largest producer. Oil and natural gas products now account for 35 per cent of Saudi GDP, 75 per cent of Government revenue and 85 per cent of export income. The non-oil economy is devoted to agriculture and newly developed industries (considerable effort has been put into ensuring adequate irrigation and industrial water supplies in a country with extremely low rainfall). Agriculture, which supports a little over 10 per cent of the workforce, produces wheat, fruit, vegetables, barley, eggs and poultry, in most of which the Kingdom is now self-sufficient. In addition to oil and gas, there are other confirmed and exploitable mineral deposits including limestone, gypsum and marble plus phosphates, bauxite and gold.
The industrial sector produces petrochemicals, steel, engineering and construction materials and a wide range of consumer goods. The service sector is the fastest growing part of the economy at present, with finance and business services, consultancies and property services prominent.
The rapid expansion of the Saudi economy from the 1960s onwards stalled during the late 1980s as overstretched finances and persistently low world oil prices forced the Saudi exchequer to rein in its spending plans (Government debt is now nearly 100 per cent of GDP – much of which, such as US$40 billion of loans to Iraq, may not be recovered). This has had unfortunate consequences for the large body of foreign labour – an estimated 35 per cent of the workforce – upon which the Saudis rely for much of their technical, managerial and menial labour. Foreigners are now barred from a range of occupations as the Government seeks to tackle Saudi unemployment, which is estimated to be around 25 per cent. Meanwhile, the average Saudi income has fallen by around 40 per cent in the last 20 years. At present, the economy is picking up; annual GDP growth surged to 7.2 per cent in 2004 (IMF); inflation is only 0.1 per cent.
Since the late 1990s, the Saudis have gradually introduced economic reforms. A thriving private sector is viewed as essential to the Government's objective of diversifying the economy and reducing reliance on the oil and gas sector. Some state-owned businesses have been sold and a number of measures taken to deregulate the economy and open up domestic markets to foreign competition. To that end, a trade agreement has been signed with the European Union, and Saudi Arabia is expected to join the World Trade Organisation in due course. Saudi Arabia is the most influential member of the Organisation of Petroleum Exporting Countries (OPEC) and of the Islamic Development Bank.
BUSINESS ETIQUETTE: Appointments are necessary. Visiting cards printed in English with an Arab translation are usually exchanged. Men should wear suits for business meetings and formal social occasions. Thursday and Friday are official holidays. **Office hours:** Sat-Wed 0800-1200 and 1500-1800 (Ramadan 2000-0100), Thur 0800-1200, with some regional variation. **Government office hours:** Sat-Wed 0730-1430.

COMMERCIAL INFORMATION

Council of Saudi Chambers of Commerce & Industry
PO Box 16683, Riyadh 11474, Saudi Arabia
Tel: (1) 405 3200 *or* 7502.
Website: www.riyadhchamber.com

Riyadh Exhibitions Company Ltd (Information on Conferences/Conventions)
PO Box 56010, Riyadh 11554, Saudi Arabia
Tel: (1) 454 1448.
Website: www.recexpo.com

Saudi Arabian Ministry of Commerce (Information on Conferences/Conventions)
PO Box 1774, Airport Road, Riyadh, 11162, Saudi Arabia
Tel: (1) 401 2220 *or* 4708.
Website: www.commerce.gov.sa

Senegal

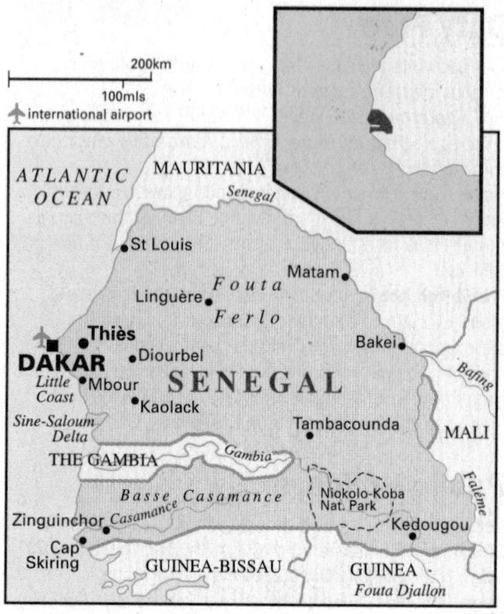

Location: West Africa.

Time: GMT.

Overview

Senegal is a country full of contradictions. Wide open to modernity and the outside world, Senegal, nevertheless, remains deeply rooted in its tradition based on *Diom* (honour), *Teranga* (hospitality), and respect for the elderly. From the great Leopold Sedar Senghor to Mariame BA, Senegal has produced some of the best African artists and still plays a key role in West Africa's arts, culture and politics, despite its small size and population. Senegalese music, particularly the *Mbalax*, has become well known internationally over the last couple of decades thanks to artists like Youssou N'dour and Baba Maal, and Senegalese food is considered among the best in Africa.
The country gained independence from France in 1960. Ever since, it has been held up as one of Africa's model democracies, with an established multi-party system and a tradition of civilian rule. Although Senegal is the most industrialised country in French West Africa after Côte d'Ivoire - poverty is still widespread, however, and unemployment high. The areas around the cities of Dakar and St Louis, colonised in the 1840s, were the earliest parts of the formal French empire in sub-Saharan Africa. Dakar, the capital of French West Africa from the early 1900s and the capital city of Senegal, is a bustling modern city and a major cruise ships port with good restaurants and shops. Tourism has been a growing industry in Senegal for well over a decade. In 2000, it was ranked as the country's second largest industry after fishing and before groundnuts and phosphates. The sector has created economic growth particularly in the Petite Côte, Senegal's principal tourist region where a resort originally built around a fishing village, Saly, has become an international tourist destination.
Senegal has a variety of first-rate natural assets that help make it an attractive destination: six national parks and four reserves, a variety of birds, some wildlife, and access to big game fishing and scuba diving. But it is its peoples, their music, culture and handicrafts that make Senegal what it is: a great, diverse and very colourful country.

General Information

AREA: 196,722 sq km (75,955 sq miles).
POPULATION: 10.6 million (UN, 2005).
POPULATION DENSITY: 53.88 per sq km.
CAPITAL: Dakar. **Population:** 2.51 million (est. 2005).
GEOGRAPHY: Senegal is bordered by Guinea Republic and

Guinea-Bissau to the south, Mali to the east and Mauritania to the north, and encloses the confederated state of The Gambia. To the west lies the Atlantic Ocean. Most land is less than 100m (330ft) above sea level, except for the Fouta Djallon foothills in the southeast and the Bambouk Mountains on the Mali border. On the coast between Dakar and St Louis is a strip of shifting dunes. South of Dakar there are shallow estuaries along the coastline, which is fringed by palm trees. In the northern part of the country, south of the Senegal Basin, lies the arid Fouta Ferlo, a hot dry Sahelian plain with little vegetation.

GOVERNMENT: Republic since 1963. Gained independence from France in 1960. **Head of State:** President Abdoulaye Wade since 2000. **Head of Government:** Prime Minister Macky Sall since 2004.

Recent history: The 40-year rule of Senegal's Socialist Party came to a peaceful end in elections in 2000, which were hailed as a rare democratic power transfer on a continent plagued by coups, conflict and election fraud. Veteran opposition leader Abdoulaye Wade won the Presidential elections, and he has since worked with four Prime Ministers. Senegal has had a good record on human rights, but in recent years some concern has been expressed over intimidation of journalists, and over the Ezzam amnesty law, passed on 7 January 2005, which provided for amnesty for politically motivated crimes between 1983 and 2004. President Wade has in recent years sought to strengthen Senegal's ties with the US. Since 1982, an armed separatist movement in the impoverished Casamance region of southern Senegal, known as the *Mouvement des Forces Démocratiques de Casamance*, has been fighting for independence. The conflict broke out over claims by the region's people that they were being marginalised by the *Wolof*, Senegal's main ethnic group. While much of what appears to be rebel activity is no more than banditry, the conflict has claimed hundreds of lives. A ceasefire was announced in December 2004 and a Peace Agreement was signed in early 2005, although there are reports of continuing low level banditry in the Casamance.

LANGUAGE: The official language is French. There are many local languages, the principal one being Wolof. Other groups include Peul, Serer and Diola.

RELIGION: Around 94 per cent Muslim, 4 per cent Christian (mostly Roman Catholic with some Protestants), and a minority holds traditional beliefs.

ELECTRICITY: 230 volts AC, 50Hz.

SOCIAL CONVENTIONS: Greetings are appropriate when coming across local people, especially in the bush, and the visitor should make the effort to learn these in one of the local languages. Handshaking on meeting, regardless of how many times a day one meets the person, is normal. When visiting a village, it is polite to call upon the village headman or schoolteacher to explain that you want to spend the night there or visit the area. They will often act as interpreter and will be helpful guides to the customs of the village and also in terms of money, ensuring that a traveller does not find himself in the embarrassing position of paying for hospitality that was given in friendship. Return hospitality with a gift of medicines, food or money for the community. It is not advisable to give money indiscriminately as tourists have encouraged the practice of begging. Casual wear is widely acceptable. Scanty swimwear should be reserved for the beach. Smoking is prohibited in some public places (especially mosques).

Credit: ©Ministère du Tourisme

Climate

Senegal is favoured by a warm climate. The dry season runs from December through to May with cool trade winds in coastal areas. Throughout the rest of the year, a hot monsoon wind blows from the south bringing the rainy season and hot, humid weather. Rainfall is heaviest in Casamance and in the southeast and slight in the Sahelian region in the north and northeast, where temperatures tend to be higher.

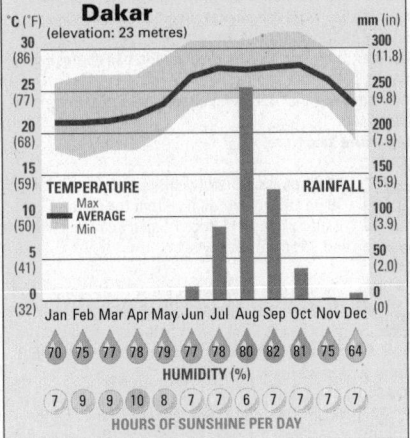

Dakar (elevation: 23 metres)

TEMPERATURE — Max, AVERAGE, Min
RAINFALL

HUMIDITY (%): Jan 70 Feb 75 Mar 77 Apr 78 May 79 Jun 77 Jul 78 Aug 80 Sep 82 Oct 81 Nov 75 Dec 64

HOURS OF SUNSHINE PER DAY: Jan 7 Feb 9 Mar 9 Apr 10 May 8 Jun 7 Jul 7 Aug 6 Sep 7 Oct 7 Nov 7 Dec 7

Communications

Telephone: IDD is available. Dial 17 (police) *or* 18 (fire brigade) *or* 821 3213 (emergency medical services).

Mobile telephone: Mobile phone coverage is limited to the main cities and tourist areas. Roaming agreements exist with some international mobile phone companies.

Internet: There are Internet cafes in Dakar, Saint Louis and other major towns.

Post: Airmail to Europe takes between seven and 10 days, and surface mail between two and six weeks.

MEDIA: Senegal's constitution guarantees freedom of the news media, although there are laws prohibiting reports that discredit the state or incite disorder. Still, the country has traditionally enjoyed a liberal media climate, and private media frequently criticise the Government. In recent years, however, there has been a number of attacks on journalists, and a *Radio France Internationale* correspondent covering the Casamance issue was expelled in 2004. Publications must be registered, but foreign publications circulate freely and multichannel pay-TV is readily available.

Press: *Le Soleil* (website: www.lesoleil.sn) is a state-owned daily, while *Sud Quotidien* (website: www.sudonline.sn), *L'Info*, *Wal Fadjri* (website: www.walf.sn) and *Le Matin* are privately published.

TV: *Radiodiffusion Television Senegalaise (RTS)* is the state-run national broadcaster that operates the *RTS1 TV* channel.

Radio: The *RTS* also operates the *Chaine Nationale* and *Chaine Internationale* networks, the capital's *94.5 FM* and *Dakar FM*, as well as four regional services. *Sud FM* is a private station available in Dakar and other cities. *Radio Nostalgie* is a Dakar-based private station. *Sept FM* is a private Dakar station operated by *Groupe Com 7*, while *Walf FM* is operated by *Groupe Wal Fadjri*. *BBC World Service* and *Radio France Internationale* are available on FM in Dakar.

Passport/Visa

	Passport Required?	Visa Required?	Return Ticket Required?
Full British	Yes	No	Yes
Australian	Yes	Yes	Yes
Canadian	Yes	No	Yes
USA	Yes	No	Yes
Other EU	Yes	No/1	Yes
Japanese	Yes	No	Yes

Note: *Regulations and requirements may be subject to change at short notice, and you are advised to contact the appropriate diplomatic or consular authority before finalising travel arrangements. Any numbers in the chart refer to the footnotes below.*

PASSPORTS: Passport valid for at least six months after date of entry required by all.

VISAS: Required by all except the following:
(a) nationals of countries referred to in the chart above (except **1.** nationals of Australia, Cyprus, Czech Republic, Estonia, Hungary, Latvia, Lithuania, Malta, Poland, Slovak Republic and Slovenia who *do* require a visa for stays of up to three months;

(b) nationals of Benin, Burkina Faso, Cape Verde, Côte d'Ivoire, The Gambia, Ghana, Guinea, Guinea-Bissau, Israel, Liberia, Mali, Niger, Nigeria, Sierra Leone, Taiwan (China) and Togo for stays of up to three months;

(c) transit passengers continuing their journey by the same or first connecting aircraft provided holding onward or return documentation and not leaving the airport.

Note: Applications from nationals of the following countries must be referred to the authorities in Dakar and will therefore take longer (up to 21 days): Afghanistan, Albania, Angola, Bosnia & Herzegovina, Cambodia, Chile, China (PR), Croatia, Cuba, Cyprus, Equatorial Guinea, Estonia, Guyana, Hong Kong (SAR), Iran, Iraq, Jordan, Korea (Dem Rep), Laos, Latvia, Lebanon, Libya, Lithuania, Maldives, Mozambique, Pakistan, Russian Federation, São Tomé e Príncipe, Serbia & Montenegro, Slovak Republic, Sudan, Syrian Arab Republic, Vietnam and Yemen.

Types of visa and cost: *Entry:* £3.15 (up to 15 days); £7.35 (15 to 30 days); £10.50 (up to 90 days). Cheques are not accepted.

Validity: Three months from the date of issue for stays of up to three months.

Application to: Consulate (or consular section at Embassy); see *Passport/Visa Information*. The visa section at the Embassy of Senegal in London is open 1000-1330 for lodging and 1300-1500 for collection.

Application requirements: (a) Valid passport. (b) Two passport-size photos. (c) Two completed application forms. (d) Letter of invitation or confirmed hotel booking, if applicable. (e) Self-addressed, stamped recorded delivery envelope for postal applications. (f) Evidence of return tickets. (g) Company letter for business trips.

Note: A WHO vaccination card, with current *Yellow Fever* and *Cholera* vaccinations, may be required if national is travelling from an endemic area.

Working days required: At least three. Nationals who must submit their applications to the authorities in Dakar prior to travel should submit their visa applications at least 21 days before the intended date of departure.

Temporary Residence: Enquire at Embassy (see *Passport/Visa Information*).

PASSPORT/VISA INFORMATION

Embassy of the Republic of Senegal in the UK
39 Marloes Road, London W8 6LA, UK
Tel: (020) 7937 7237 *or* 7938 4048.
Website: www.senegalembassy.co.uk
Opening hours: Mon-Fri 0900-1700; 0930-1300 (visa applications).

Embassy of the Republic of Senegal in the USA
2112 Wyoming Avenue, NW, Washington, DC 20008, USA
Tel: (202) 234 0540 *or* 0541.
Website: www.senegalembassy-us.org

Money

Currency: CFA (*Communauté Financiaire Africaine*) Franc (XOF) = 100 centimes. Notes are in denominations of XOF10,000, 5000, 2000 and 1000. Coins are in denominations of XOF500, 200, 100, 50, 25, 10, 5 and 1. Senegal is part of the French Monetary Area. Only currency issued by the *Banque des Etats de l'Afrique de l'Ouest* (Bank of West African States) is valid; currency issued by the *Banque des Etats de l'Afrique Centrale* (Bank of Central African States) is not. The CFA Franc is tied to the Euro.

Credit & debit cards: American Express is the most widely accepted, although Diners Club, MasterCard and Visa have limited use. Check with your credit or debit card company for details of merchant acceptability and other services which may be available. Commissions are added for the use of credit cards. There are ATMs in Dakar.

Traveller's cheques: Traveller's cheques are easy to cash in Dakar. To avoid additional exchange rate charges, travellers are advised to take them in Euros.

Currency restrictions: Import of local currency is unlimited; import of foreign currency is unlimited but subject to declaration. Export of local currency is restricted to XOF20,000. Export of foreign currency is limited to XOF50,000; for amounts exceeding this, the declaration issued on arrival must be presented.

Banking hours: Mon-Fri 0800-1100 and 1430-1600.

Exchange rate indicators:
Rate at time of publishing
£1.00= XOF958.81
$1.00= XOF542.39

Duty Free

The following may be imported into Senegal by persons over 18 years of age without incurring customs duty: *200 cigarettes or 50 cigars or 250g of tobacco; one bottle of wine, one bottle of alcohol, a reasonable quantity of* perfume for personal use; gifts up to the value of XOF5000.

Note: There is no free import of spirits.

Public Holidays

Below are listed Public Holidays for the January 2006-June 2007 period.

2006: Jan 1 New Year's Day. **Jan 10** Tabaski (Feast of the Sacrifice). **Jan 31** Tamkarit (Islamic New Year). **Apr 4** Independence Day. **Apr 10** Prophet Mohammed's Birthday. **Apr 17** Easter Monday. **May 1** Labour Day. **May 25** Ascension. **Jun 5** Whit Monday. **Aug 15** Assumption. **Nov 1** All Saints' Day. **Oct 22-24** Korité (End of Ramadan). **Dec 25** Christmas Day. **Dec 31** Tabaski. (Feast of the Sacrifice).

Jan 1 2007 New Year's Day. **Jan 20** Tamkarit (Islamic New Year). **Mar 31** Prophet Mohammed's Birthday. **Apr 4** Independence Day. **Apr 9** Easter Monday. **May 1** Labour Day. **May 17** Ascension. **May 28** Whit Monday.

Note: Muslim festivals are timed according to local sightings of various phases of the moon and the dates given above are approximations. During the lunar month of Ramadan that precedes Korité (Eid al-Fitr), Muslims fast during the day and feast at night and normal business patterns may be interrupted. Many restaurants are closed during the day and there may be restrictions on smoking and drinking. Some disruption may continue into Korité itself. Korité and Tabaski (Eid al-Adha) may last anything from two to 10 days, depending on the region. For more information, see the *World of Islam* appendix.

Health

	Special Precautions?	Certificate Required?
Yellow Fever	Yes	1
Cholera	Yes	2
Typhoid & Polio	3	N/A
Malaria	4	N/A

Note: *Regulations and requirements may be subject to change at short notice, and you are advised to contact your doctor well in advance of your intended date of departure. Any numbers in the chart refer to the footnotes below.*

1: A *yellow fever* vaccination certificate may be required from travellers over nine months coming from endemic areas. Enquire at nearest Embassy/Consulate prior to departure.

2: Following WHO guidelines issued in 1973, a *cholera* vaccination certificate is not a condition of entry to Senegal. However, *cholera* is a risk in this country and precautions are essential. Up-to-date advice should be sought before deciding whether these precautions should include vaccination, as medical opinion is divided over its effectiveness; see the *Health* appendix for more information.

3: Vaccination against *typhoid* is advised.

4: *Malaria* risk, predominantly in the malignant *falciparum* form, exists all year throughout the country; there is a lower risk in the central Western regions from January to June. Resistance to chloroquine and sulfadoxine-pyrimethamine has been reported. The recommended prophylaxis is mefloquine.

Food & drink: All water should be regarded as being potentially contaminated. Water used for drinking, brushing teeth or making ice should first be boiled or otherwise sterilised. Milk is unpasteurised and should be boiled. Powdered or tinned milk is available and is advised, but make sure that it is reconstituted with pure water. Avoid dairy products which are likely to have been made from unboiled milk. Only eat well-cooked meat and fish, preferably served hot. Pork, salad and mayonnaise may carry increased risk. Vegetables should be cooked and fruit peeled.

Other risks: Bilharzia (*schistosomiasis*) is present. Avoid swimming and paddling in fresh water; swimming pools which are well chlorinated and maintained are safe. *Sleeping sickness* (*trypanosomiasis*) is reported. *Hepatitis A* and *E* are widespread; *hepatitis B* is hyperendemic. *Meningococcal meningitis* risk exists, particularly during the dry season and in the savannah areas.

Dengue, filariasis, leishmaniasis and *onchocerciasis* (river blindness) are present. *Plague* occurs sporadically and *TB* is present.

Rabies is present. For those at high risk, vaccination before arrival should be considered. If you are bitten, seek medical advice without delay. For more information, see the *Health* appendix.

Health care: In Dakar, doctors are plentiful and most medicines are available. Up-country, however, facilities are minimal. Health insurance is essential.

Travel - International

AIR:

The national airline is *Air Senegal International (DS)* (website: www.air.senegal-international.com).

Approximate flight times: From Dakar to *Paris* is five hours 45 minutes, to *London* is seven hours and to *New York* is seven hours 40 minutes.

Main airports: *Dakar (DKR)* (Leopold Sedar Senghor) is 17km (10.5 miles) northwest of the city (travel time – 25 minutes). *To/from the airport*: Regular coach and bus services go to and from Dakar. Metered taxis are available. *Facilities:* Duty free shop, bar/restaurant, bank/bureau de change, post office and car hire.

There are two other operating airports in *Cap Skirring* and *Saint Louis*.

Departure tax: None.

SEA:

Main ports: *Dakar* (website: www.portdakar.sn). There are regular sailings from the Canary Islands, France, Morocco, Spain and several South American and West African ports.

RAIL:

There is one passenger train with restaurant and sleeping cars, running to/from Bamako, Mali. The train leaves Dakar every Saturday and Bamako every Wednesday. The journey can take 30 to 36 hours but expect four to 12 hour delays.

ROAD:

Roads from Mauritania are tarred and in good condition; the best place to cross the border is at Rosso. Roads from Guinea-Bissau are not yet tarred; there is a border crossing at São Domingo. There is a route from Senegal to Mali via Tambacounda. There is access across the Sahara by a 5500km (2120 mile) road that runs from Algeria via Mali. The trans-Gambian highway crosses the River Gambia by ferry. There is a good network of **buses** and **taxis** running across the major borders.

Travel - Internal

AIR:

Air Senegal runs services to all the main towns in Senegal. *Gambia Air Shuttle* offers flights from Dakar to Banjul (The Gambia).

There are aerodromes in Ziguinchor, Podor and Tamba.

Departure tax: None.

SEA:

It is often quicker to travel by sea than road. A replacement ferry from Dakar to Ziquinchor (travel time - 20 hours) had its maiden voyage in 2005 after the Joola Ferry disaster of 2002. Sea shuttles depart regularly from Dakar harbour to the Île de Gorée. An excellent new service, *L'Express du Senegal*, links Banjul, Dakar and Ziguinchor. Fares tend to be high.

RAIL:

The country has a network of about 1225km (761 miles) of rail track. Trains run from Dakar to towns en route for Bamako in Mali. There is an ongoing programme of upgrading and expansion. Children under three travel free. Children aged three to nine pay half fare.

ROAD:

Traffic drives on the right. There are approximately 3900km (2423 miles) of asphalt roads linking the major towns and the coastal region. The network of roads in the interior is rough (about 10,400km/6460 miles in total) and may become impassable during the rainy season; it is not advisable to drive at night. There are often police checkpoints at the entrance and exit to villages to enforce speed restrictions; fines are paid on the spot. **Bus:** There are many buses available for short distances as well as mini-buses (known locally as *car rapide*), which are cheaper if less efficient. Fares are usually up to XOF100. Long-distance services operate subject to demand only. **Taxi:** Available in most towns and fares are metered with a surcharge of XOF100. Rates increase after midnight. It is cheaper to hail a taxi in the street than arrange to be collected from the hotel. Bush taxis and estate cars are good for journeys into the interior. **Car hire:** Companies are found in Dakar and the main towns. **Documentation:** A French or International Driving Permit and Green Card are required.

URBAN:

Bus and minibus services operate in Dakar.

Travel Advice

Most visits to Senegal are trouble-free but you should be aware of the global risk of indiscriminate international terrorist attacks, which could be against civilian targets, including places frequented by foreigners.

Travellers are advised against road travel in the western Casamance, due to isolated incidents of banditry.

Pick pocketing and street crime is common in parts of Dakar. Travellers should take sensible precautions and avoid carrying valuables in public.

This advice is based on information provided by the Foreign and Commonwealth Office in the UK. It is correct at time of publishing. As the situation can change rapidly, visitors are advised to contact the following organisaions for the latest travel advice:

British Foreign and Commonwealth Office
Tel: (0845) 850 2829.
Website: www.fco.gov.uk

US Department of State
Website: http://travel.state.gov/travel

Accommodation

HOTELS:

The Government-controlled expansion of tourism has led to an increasing number of hotels. There are several of international standard, and more development is underway, including a number of hotels on the Petite Côte (the stretch of beaches between Dakar and Joal). In Casamance, some luxury resorts have been built. It is advisable to book accommodation in advance, particularly in Dakar where there is an increased demand during the tourist season, which lasts from December to May. Hotels in Dakar generally have air conditioning but tend to be expensive. In addition, visitors may choose the floating hotel in the River Region. Hotels are classified from 1 to 4 stars.

CAMPING: Government campsites (*campements*) provide a few beds, but no bedding. There are basic facilities for travellers who prefer to wander from the beaten track, although camping independently is strongly discouraged. Sometimes bungalows or grass huts are available; visitors must otherwise provide their own tents.

MISSIONS: Catholic missions will accommodate tourists only in cases of real need.

VILLAGE HUTS: A village will sometimes courteously offer a stranger one of the local huts as living accommodation, but it is necessary for visitors to provide their own bedding.

HOSTELS: For those on a budget there are two hostels in Senegal, one in Nianing and one in Mbour.

Top Things To See

- A visit to **Dakar**, a bustling modern city and major port situated at the tip of the Cap Vert peninsula, is recommended. The main museum is the **Institut Fondamental d'Afrique Noire (IFAN)**, which has a collection of masks, statues and musical instruments from West Africa. The **Galerie Nationale** is also worth a visit. The **Palais Présidentiel (Presidential Palace)** is a white building surrounded by luscious gardens. Visit Dakar's bustling **markets**. They include the **Kermel** and the **Sandaga**, the former selling mainly fruit, fabrics, clothing and souvenirs, the latter being the city's main fruit and fabrics market. A quite recent addition to the city is the monument **La Porte du 3ème Millénaire (the 3rd Millennium Gate)**, which was assembled in order to symbolise Senegal's entry into the third millennium, completed in 2001. The **Grande Mosquée**, the city's most famous mosque (noted for its **minaret**, which is lit at night), is closed to the public and located in **Médina**, which is off the tourist map.

- Head out to the **Soumbedioune Craft Village** by the ocean, on the Corniche Ouest just outside of the city, where intricate hand-woven fabrics, precious gold and silver jewellery, unique glass and sand painting, traditional basketry, leather work and pottery, wood carving and batik are on display.

- Head for the UNESCO World Heritage-listed **Île de Gorée (Gorée Island)** just 3km (1.8 miles) outside of the city. It used to be a slaving station and was one of the first French settlements on the continent. The island has many colonial-style houses, a small beach and several museums - the **Maison des Esclaves (Slaves' House)**, the **Historical Museum** in the **Fort d'Estrées**, the **Musée de la Mer** - everything concerning the sea, fishes and fishing, and the **Musée de la Femme**, which is all about Senegalese women.

- Go to the **fishing village** of **Cayar** and make sure to be there by the afternoon, in time for the spectacular return of the local fishermen from the high sea where they have spent the night. They bring tons of fish, shrimp, and lobsters in their brightly-coloured dugout canoes, and the beach is alive with buyers, families, and children.

- Travel the 30km (18 miles) north of Dakar to the **Retba Lake** (also called the **Lac Rose** or **Pink Lake** due to its pink colouring), a popular spot for picnics and weekend excursions. It is also the terminal for the **Paris-Dakar** motor rally.

- Further north along the coast is **St Louis**, a former slave settlement and once Senegal's capital. The city is partly located on the mainland, partly on an island and partly on the

Langue de Barbarie peninsula at the mouth of the River Senegal. It retains a nostalgic and provincial atmosphere reflected in its narrow streets flanked by beautiful colonial houses, balconies and verandas. The island can be reached via the **Pont Faidherbe**. There are some good **beaches**.
- Enjoy the **Petite Côte** (**Little Coast**) south of Dakar, which stretches for some 150km (94 miles) and is one of Senegal's best beach areas. The main tourist resorts in the area are **Mbour** and, slightly further north, **Saly Portudal**, which is set in a green park and has the highest concentration of luxury hotels as well as its own golf course.
- Visit the ruins of the old **Breton church** and the colonial settlement on the island of **Karaban**. However, travellers are currently advised to avoid this region while political instability continues.
- Explore Eastern Senegal, one of the best-kept secrets of the country, and visit the **Bedik**, **Bassari**, and **Tenda** people of the **Kedougou** area with their villages situated in the middle of breathtaking landscapes.

Credit: ©Ministère du Tourisme

Top Things To Do

- Explore the **Siné-Saloum delta** where the Saloum and Siné rivers flow into the Atlantic Ocean. This is a wild region of mangrove swamps, dunes and lagoons. Located largely within the **Parc National du Delta du Saloum**, the delta's myriad small islands are scattered between so-called *bolongs* (channels). Go on a trip in a **pirogue** (traditional African boat) out to the islands: some of the most beautiful include **Betani**, **Guior**, **Guissanor**, the **Île de Mars**, **Palmarin** and **Saloum**. The palm-fringed sandy **beaches** along the coast give way to dense vegetation populated by small villages of fishermen and groundnut farmers.
- Explore Senegal's **national parks**. The best time for visiting is usually between October and April. Accommodation is available, mostly in the form of campments or lodges. The only place to see large mammals in Senegal is the inland **Parc National de Niokolo Koba**, although some species, such as elephants, are now extremely rare. The park stretches over two geographical areas: the Sudanese savannah and the Guinea forest. Over 84 species live here, including Africa's largest lions, elephants, panthers, crocodiles and a variety of antelopes. **Birdwatchers** have more to be excited about. The parks and nature reserves in the coastal regions are renowned bird sanctuaries. **Parc National des Oiseaux de Djoudj** in the northeast, 60km (37 miles) from St Louis, at the southern edge of the Sahara, has 40,000 acres of water stretches and is one of the most important bird sanctuaries in the world. It is listed by UNESCO as a World Heritage Site. **Parc National de Basse Casamance** can be found in the very rainy extreme south of the country, and it benefits from the luxuriance of the Guinea forest with its kapok trees, oil palms and imposing parinarias. Basse Casamance is famous for its tropical vegetation and variety of wildlife, including the Derry Eland and Buffoon Cob antelope, as well as many species of monkey. The **Parc National Langue de Barbarie**, a narrow strip of sandy lands between the Atlantic and the River Senegal, is a refuge for birds and sea tortoises who come here to breed. Boat trips from St Louis are available. **Parc National du Delta du Saloum** is characterised by small islands, sand dunes and swamps providing a perfect habitat for hundreds of bird species, including pelicans, storks and pink flamingoes. Finally, the **Parc National de l'Île de la Madeleine** is a a protected marine park on a small archipelago west of Dakar, 3km (1.7 miles) from the coast.
- In addition to the national parks, Senegal boasts the following **natural reserves**: **Bandia** (900 hectares; 2224 acres); **Ferlo Nord** (a huge 487,000 hectares; 1,203,403 acres); **Guembuel** (special fauna extending over 720 hectares; 1779 acres); **Kalissaye** (an ornithological reserve created in 1987 and 16 hectares in size; 40 acres); **Ndiael** (a fauna reserve); and **Popenguine** (extending over 1009 hectares; 2493 acres).
- See a **play** at **The Daniel Sorano National Theatre** in the **Boulevard de la République** in **Dakar**, a popular venue for theatre, concerts and other arts performances. There are many cinemas showing the latest French films.
- Go on a **cruise** up the **River Senegal** and explore the interior of the country. Some of these cruises last for a week or more.
- There are plenty of good **beaches**, but swimming can be hazardous in some places; visitors are advised to enquire with their travel agent before booking a beach holiday. Dakar's main beaches include the **Plage Bel-Air** and the cleaner and safer **N'Gor** and **Yoff**. Other good beaches in the area are **Toubab Dialao** and **Yenn**, which are well known for their spectacular **red cliffs**. Other good areas for swimming include **Casamance**, **Hann Bay**, **N'Gor Beach** and **Petite Côte**.
- **Underwater** enthusiasts will find good **diving** waters all around the **Cap Vert Peninsula**, with February to April being the best months.
- **Water-skiing** facilities are available at **Dakar** alongside the **Children's Beach** on the lagoon between **N'Gor** and its island and at the **Hanns Bay marinas**. **Windsurfing** is possible, and both coastal and river **kayak trips** can be arranged.
- West Africa has a strong musical tradition, and Dakar is the best place to sample Senegal's vibrant **music** scene. Check out one of the numerous clubs and live venues. Villages also frequently put on musical performances for tourists.
- Try your luck with a rod and bait. From May through November, Senegal offers excellent sports **fishing**. Organised trips are available from fishing centres and hotels along the coast.
- The Senegalese are keen followers of traditional **Senegalese wrestling**. Join them and watch the matches every Sunday at the **Fass arena** and in the suburbs or at **the Iba Mar Diop Stadium** near the Great Mosque.
- Join an **ecotourism** programme in **Basse Casamance**. Travellers are advised to avoid this region while there is still a danger of political instability, but some villages offer traditional accommodations and activities for tourists in a programme that let the villagers use the income generated for development projects. This fertile, swampy region borders The Gambia in the north and Guinea-Bissau in the south and is well known for its traditional mud houses (also called *impluvium*), the most striking examples of which can be found in **Affinam** (on the north bank of the Casamance River) and **Enampor**.

Credit: ©Ministère du Tourisme

TOURIST INFORMATION

Ministère du Tourisme (Ministry of Tourism)
23 rue Calmette, BP 4049, Dakar, Senegal
Tel: 822 7366.
Website: www.tourisme-senegal.com

Bureau Sénégalais du Tourisme (Senegal Tourist Office) in the USA
350 Fifth Avenue, Suite 3118, New York, NY 10118, USA
Tel: (212) 279 1953.
Website: www.senegal-tourism.com

Entertainment

FOOD & DRINK: Senegalese food is considered among the best in Africa. The basis of many dishes is chicken or fish, but the distinctive taste is due to ingredients not found outside Africa. This food is served in many restaurants in Dakar. Provincial rest houses serve less sophisticated but delicious variations. There are bars in some hotels and clubs. Although Senegal is predominantly a Muslim country, alcohol is available.

National specialities:
- *Chicken au yassa* (chicken with lemon, pimento and onions).
- *Tiebou dienne* (rice and fish).
- *Maffe* (chicken or mutton in peanut sauce).
- *Dem à la St Louis* (stuffed mullet).
- *Accras* (a kind of fritter).

National drinks:
- *Toufam* (a kind of yoghurt thinned with sugared water).
- Mint tea, the first cup drunk slightly bitter, the second with more sugar and the third very sweet.
- Palm wine, which is drunk either fresh or fermented.
- Home-roasted coffee with pimento.

Tipping: A service charge of 10 to 15 per cent is included in all hotel and restaurant bills. Taxi drivers are not normally given a tip.

NIGHTLIFE: There are several nightclubs and music venues in Dakar, playing *mbalakh* (the local modern music), as well as a casino on the route to N'Gor. There are many cinemas showing the latest French films. The Daniel Sorano National Theatre in the Boulevard de la Republique is a popular venue for theatre, concerts and other arts performances.

SHOPPING: Visitors to Senegal must go to some of the many colourful markets. They are abundant with a range of bargins from food to handmade crafts and electronics. Most markets and centres sell traditional fabric, embroidery and costume, pottery, necklaces of clay beads and costume jewellery of wood or various seeds. At Soumbe-dionne, on the Corniche de Fann, is a craft village where the visitor can watch craftspeople at work and buy their handicrafts. Purchases include woodcarving in the form of African gaming boards, masks and statues; musical instruments; and metalwork, including copper pendants, bowls and statuettes. **Shopping hours:** Generally Mon-Sat 0830-1230 and 1530-1930. Some shops open Sunday morning, others are closed Monday.

Business

- **GDP:** US$7.4 billion (2004).
- **Main imports:** Food, consumer goods, petroleum, machinery, transport equipment, petroleum products and computer equipment.
- **Main exports:** Fish products, peanut products, phosphate products, cotton and petroleum products.
- **Main trade partners:** Cameroon, Côte d'Ivoire, France, Mali, Nigeria, Spain and USA.

ECONOMY: In a good year, Senegal is the world's leading producer of groundnuts, which are the country's main export commodity. The farming industry also produces millet, sorghum, maize, rice and vegetables for domestic consumption, but the country's vulnerability to extreme weather conditions have prevented it from reaching self-sufficiency in basic foodstuffs. Fish products have become an important export commodity, accounting for one-third of total export earnings, and the Government also accumulates revenues from the sale of fishing licences to other countries, mostly from the EU. Both farming and fisheries currently face severe problems - the former due to drought, the latter due to over-fishing by foreign fleets. Senegal is the most industrialised country in French West Africa after Côte d'Ivoire. Exploitable mineral deposits include phosphates (the chemical industry draws on sizeable deposits of lime phosphate and aluminium phosphate within Senegal). Some iron ore and gold deposits have been identified, and there are thought to be oil reserves both on- and offshore. The main industries – which are almost exclusively geared to domestic consumption – involve the processing of agricultural products and phosphates, milling, textiles, commercial vehicle assembly, food and drink, farming materials (implements, fertilisers), paint, asbestos, cement, printing and boat building. There is also, unusually in this part of Africa, a lively information technology sector.

Although the country remains dependent on foreign aid and its finances are weak, it has shown signs of recovery after a stagnant spell in the late 1990s. Current annual GDP growth is 6 per cent. In 1998, negotiations with the IMF led to the introduction of a Structural Adjustment Programme in exchange for financial support. Senegal is a member of the CFA Franc Zone and the West African trading bloc, ECOWAS.

BUSINESS ETIQUETTE: A lightweight suit is acceptable for business. French will generally be needed for meetings. Appointments should be made and punctuality is expected, despite the fact that a customer may be slightly late. Visiting cards are essential, preferably in French and English. The right hand should be used for shaking and to pass items. The period from July to October should be avoided for business visits, as many people are on holiday. **Office hours:** Mon-Fri 0800-1300 and 1400-1700. During Ramadan, some offices open 0730-1430.

CONFERENCES/CONVENTIONS: A number of hotels and conference centres offer facilities.

COMMERCIAL INFORMATION

Chambre de Commerce et d'Industrie et d'Agriculture de la Région de Dakar
BP 118, 1 place de l'Indépendance, Dakar, Senegal
Tel: 823 7189.
Email: cciad@telecom-plus.sn

Serbia & Montenegro

160km
80mls

✈ international airport

HUNGARY
Subotica
Sombor
Vojvodina
Zrenjanin
SLOVENIA
Novi Sad
ROMANIA
Pančevo
Šabac
Požarevac
Iron Gates Dam
BELGRADE
SERBIA & MONTENEGRO
BOSNIA & HERZEGOVINA
Negotin
Bor
Užice
Kragujevac
Kraljevo
Kruševac
Niš
Pljevlja
Novi Pazar
△Durmitor 2522m
Leskovac
BULGARIA
Nikšić
Mitrovica
MONTENEGRO
Kotor
Priština
Podgorica
Kosovo
Vranje
Cetinje
Gulf of Kotor
L. Scutari
Bar
ALBANIA
Bistra 2650m
FYR OF MACEDONIA
ADRIATIC SEA
Ulcinj

Location: Southern Central Europe.

Time: GMT + 1 (GMT + 2 from last Sunday in March to Saturday before last Sunday in October).

Overview

In June 1389, the Battle of Kosovo settled the fate of Yugoslavia and the Balkans for centuries to come, when an allied force of Serbs and Bosnians were defeated by the advancing Ottoman Turks. Another insurrection in 1876 led to another Serbian defeat but the Austrians offered the Serbs protection. However, by 1905, Serbian policy had become avowedly nationalist and anti-Austrian, both Serbia and Montenegro now recognized as Independent states.

The next few years leading to the outbreak of World War I brought a marked and rapid deterioration in the stability of the region. This issue of Albania, plus the Austrian presence in Bosnia & Herzegovina, was brought to a head in 1914 with the assassination of the Austrian Archduke Franz Ferdinand by a Serb revolutionary, and war was declared. After the end of the war, the 'Kingdom of Serbs, Croats and Slovenes' was formed, renamed Yugoslavia in 1929.

During World War II, Josip Broz (known as Tito) of the Communist Party of Yugoslavia took power. Following Tito's death in 1980, the rotating collective Presidency became increasingly concerned with holding the country together and preventing chronic economic decline. Such decline began in 1990 when Slovenia and Croatia returned Governments committed to the pursuit of outright Independence. The Yugoslav Republics staked out their positions: Montenegro backed Serbia; Macedonia pushed for Independence; and in Bosnia-Herzegovina, the three-way ethnic split (Muslim, Croat, Serb) gave rise to different aspirations.

In 1996, in Serbia, Slobodan Milosevic, former Communist Party apparatchik, won the Presidential election. However, in Kosovo, the once-autonomous province of Serbia which has a 90 per cent ethnic Albania population, autonomous status had been abolished by Belgrade. Kosovan Albanians were divided in their response between non-violent political opposition and armed insurrection. The hard line adopted by Belgrade drove most of the population to support armed struggle. However, it soon became clear that Milosevic was engaged in the ethnic cleansing of Kosovo. The USA

intervened with a bombing campaign against Serbia. By June 1999, much of the Serbs' infrastructure and key industrial complexes were in ruins and their forces were pulled out of Kosovo. Milosevic was later arrested and extradited to face the International war crimes tribunal in the Hague following election defeat in 2000. He died in March 2006 before the end of proceedings.

Serbia & Montenegro has slowly re-established itself in the international community, having rejoined the UN and other international bodies. Domestic progress has been difficult: the economy is still poor and organised crime is potent. The future status of Kosovo is also uncertain: currently, it is self-governing under UN mandate. And with the rebuilding of its global image has been an assertion of its touristic assets. From the thickly forested south to the flat, fertile farmland of the north, and from the mountainous Montenegro to the Adriatic coastline, this country offers vistas of beauty that have lingered and will linger far longer than any bullet-blasted walls.

General Information

As of February 2003, the Yugoslav Parliament ceased to be and the Union of Serbia & Montenegro was voted into existence. The Union has a federal Presidency and federal defence and foreign Ministries but the two republics are semi-independent states in charge of their own economies and with their own legislation. The union arrangement is to remain in place for a minimum of three years after which the two republics can hold referenda on whether to keep or scrap it. Kosovo is de facto an international protectorate but legally is part of Serbia. At the time of writing, all information is correct and up-to-date, but it may be subject to quick change and new events may alter various aspects of any of the following sections. All information should be double-checked with an official source.

AREA: Serbia & Montenegro comprises Serbia (including the provinces of Kosovo and Vojvodina) with 88,361 sq km (39,449 sq miles) and Montenegro with 13,812 sq km (5331 sq miles). These two were respectively the largest and smallest of the republics which made up the former Yugoslavia. The country officially covers 102,173 sq km (39,448 sq miles), or 40 per cent of the territory of the former federation (255,804 sq km/98,766 sq miles).

POPULATION: Together, Serbia & Montenegro have an estimated total population of 10.5 millon (UN, 2005).

POPULATION DENSITY: 41 per sq km.

CAPITAL: Belgrade is the capital of Serbia & Montenegro. **Population:** 1.5 million (census, 2002).

GEOGRAPHY: Roughly rectangular in shape and on a major European communications axis north-west and south-east, Serbia & Montenegro borders Hungary to the north, Romania to the northeast, Bulgaria to the southeast, the Kosovo region and Albania to the south, Bosnia & Herzegovina to the west and Croatia to the northwest. The province of Kosovo, now administered by the UN, is in the south, and shares borders with Macedonia (Former Yugoslav Republic of) and Albania. Serbia is dominated by the flat, fertile farmland of the Danube and Tisza valleys. The scenery varies from rich Alpine valleys, vast fertile plains and rolling green hills to bare, rocky gorges as much as 1140m (3800ft) deep, thick forests and gaunt limestone mountain regions. Belgrade, the capital, lies on the Danube. Montenegro is a small mountainous region on the Adriatic coast north of Albania, bordering Bosnia & Herzegovina to the west. Its small Adriatic coastline comprises the main ports of Bar and those in the Gulf of Kotor.

GOVERNMENT: Union of States since February 2003 (previously Federal Republic since 1992). First gained independence as the 'Kingdom of Serbs, Croats and Slovenes' in 1918 from the Austro-Hungarian Empire; renamed Yugoslavia in 1929. **Heads of State: Union of Serbia & Montenegro:** President Svetozar Marovic since 2003; **Serbia:** President Boris Tadic since 2004; **Montenegro:** President Filip Vujanovic since 2002. **Heads of Government:** Union of Serbia & Montenegro: Prime Minister Dragisa Pesic since 2001; **Serbia:** Prime Minister Vojislav Kostunica since 2004; **Montenegro:** Prime Minister Milo Djukanovic since 2003. **Recent history: Serbia & Montenegro.** A constitutional reorganisation brought a new series of elections which took place in February and December 2003, at which the electorate returned the nationalist Serb Radical Party as the largest party in the new Federal Assembly and the Serbian Assembly.

In Montenegro, both the 77-member legislature, the *Skupstina Republika Crne Gore* (Assembly of the republic of Montenegro), and the Executive President are elected to serve four-year terms.

In Serbia, the legislature, the *Narodna Skupstina Srbije* (Serbian National Assembly), has 250 members elected for a four-year term. An Executive President is directly elected for a five-year term.

Kosovo: The former Serbian autonomous region of

Kosovo is currently self-governing with the support of the UN Interim Administration Mission in Kosovo (UNMIK) under the authority of UN Security Council resolutions. **Recent History:** Ibrahim Rugova, the President of Kosovo, died on 21 January 2006. The Head of Parliament, Nexhat Daci, is expected to be named acting President until a new leader is chosen by Parliament. The future status of Kosovo is uncertain: for the time being, it is self-governing under UN mandate. Serbia & Montenegro is a Confederal Parliamentary Republic. At the federal level, the *Skupstina Srbije I Crne Gore* (Federal Assembly of Serbia and Montenegro) has 126 members directly elected for a four-year term: 91 from Serbia and 38 from Montenegro. The President, who is Head of State, is elected by the Federal Assembly and also serves a four-year term.

LANGUAGE: Serbian, which uses the Cyrillic script, Albanian and Hungarian.

RELIGION: Majority Eastern Orthodox Serbs, with a large Muslim ethnic Albanian minority (especially in the province of Kosovo), a Roman Catholic ethnic Serbian minority (mainly located in the province of Vojvodina) and a small Jewish community.

ELECTRICITY: 220 volts AC, 50Hz.

SOCIAL CONVENTIONS: Hitherto a relatively open, informal and secure society, Serbia & Montenegro is now changing for the worse following the impact of war. Once virtually non-existent, violent crime is now relatively common in the big cities. There are some restrictions on photography.

Climate

Serbia has a continental climate with cold winters and warm summers. Montenegro is largely the same, but with alpine conditions in the mountains and a Mediterranean climate on the Adriatic coast.

Required clothing: In winter, mediumweight clothing and heavy overcoat; in summer, lightweight clothing and raincoat required.

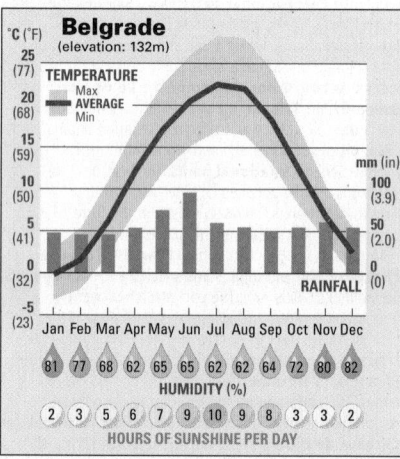

Belgrade (elevation: 132m)

°C (°F)
TEMPERATURE — Max, AVERAGE, Min
RAINFALL

HUMIDITY (%): 81 77 68 62 65 65 62 62 64 72 80 82

HOURS OF SUNSHINE PER DAY: 2 3 5 6 7 9 10 9 8 3 3 2

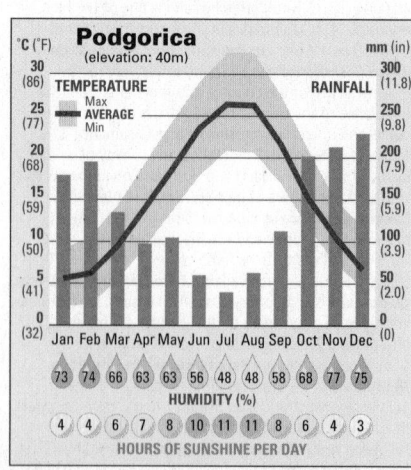

Podgorica (elevation: 40m)

°C (°F)
TEMPERATURE — Max, AVERAGE, Min
RAINFALL mm (in)

HUMIDITY (%): 73 74 66 63 63 56 48 48 58 68 77 75

HOURS OF SUNSHINE PER DAY: 4 4 6 7 8 10 11 11 8 6 4 3

Communications

Telephone: Telephone: IDD is available. Country code: 381.

Mobile telephone: GSM 900/1800 networks provide coverage in main towns. Roaming agreements exist with most international mobile phone companies.

Internet: Internet cafes can be found in the main urban centres.

Post: Postal services within Serbia and Montenegro are

reasonably good.

MEDIA: Press: Serbia: The main daily newspapers are *Vecernje Novosti* (website: www.novosti.co.yu), *Blic* (website: www.blic.co.yu) and *Politika* (website: www.politika.co.yu). **Montenegro:** Daily newspapers include *Vijesti* (website: www.vijesti.cg.yu), *Pobjeda* (website: www.pobjeda.co.yu) and *Dan* (website: www.dan.cy.yu).

TV: Serbia: *Serbia TV* is state-run, *B92 TV* and *TV Pink* are private. *Studio B TV* is run by Belgrade City Council. **Montenegro:** *Montenegrin TV* is state-run and *Montena TV* is private.

Note: *CNN* is also available via satellite (*Astra*) in a number of Belgrade and Montenegrin (Adriatic Coast) hotels.

Radio: Serbia: *Serbian Radio* is state-run, *B92* is private and the *Association of Independents Electronic Media* is a network of local broadcasting stations. **Montenegro:** *Montenegrin Radio* is state-run and *Radio Elmag* is privately operated.

Passport/Visa

	Passport Required?	Visa Required?	Return Ticket Required?
Full British	Yes	No/1	No
Australian	Yes	No/1	No
Canadian	Yes	No/1	No
USA	Yes	No/1	No
Other EU	Yes	No/1	No
Japanese	Yes	No/1	No

Note: *Regulations and requirements may be subject to change at short notice, and you are advised to contact the appropriate diplomatic or consular authority before finalising travel arrangements. Any numbers in the chart refer to the footnotes below.*

Restricted entry and transit: Nationals of Malaysia and Taiwan (China) will be refused admission and transit through the country.

PASSPORTS: Valid passport required by all.

VISAS: Required by all except the following:
(a) nationals of Mexico for up to 180 days;
(b) **1.** nationals mentioned in the chart above and nationals of Andorra, Argentina, Austria, Bolivia, Canada, Chile, Costa Rica, Croatia, Cuba, Iceland, Israel, Korea (Rep), Liechtenstein, Monaco, New Zealand, Norway, San Marino, Seychelles, Singapore, Switzerland, Tunisia and Vatican City for stays of up to 90 days for touristic purposes only;
(c) nationals of Armenia, Azerbaijan, China (PR), Georgia, Korea (Dem Rep), Mongolia, Russian Federation and Ukraine for business visits of up to 90 days;
(d) nationals of Macedonia (Former Yugoslav Republic) for stays of up to 60 days;
(e) nationals of Belarus, Bulgaria and Turkey for stays of up to 30 days;
(f) nationals of Hungary in the territory of the Republic of Montenegro, tourist passes and identity cards issued at the border crossings, for touristic stays of up to 90 days;
(g) nationals of Albania, Bosnia & Herzegovina, Croatia, Macedonia (Former Yugoslav Republic of), Russian Federation, Slovenia and Ukraine in the territory of the Republic of Montenegro, tourist passes and identity cards issued at the border crossings, for touristic stays of up to 30 days;
(h) nationals of Romania may transit Serbia and Montenegro without a visa during a maximum period of five days from date of entry, provided they possess a valid residence authorization in any EU country, Australia, Canada, Iceland, Norway, Switzerland or the USA, provided the duration of the transit is not longer than the duration of the authorization.
(i) nationals of Ukraine may transit Serbia and Montenegro without a visa during a maximum period not exceeding five days from the date of entry, provided they possess a residence authorization in any EU or Schengen country or Switzerland.

Types of visa and cost: *Visit*, *Business* and *Transit*. Fees vary according to nationality of applicant.

Validity: Visas are valid for one month from date of issue and cannot be postdated. Transit visas are valid for seven days (to be used within six months of issue).

Application to: Consular section at Embassy (see *Passport/Visa Information*). Tourist passes can be issued at the border, or on arrival, for all eligible nationals (see above). However, as regulations are subject to change, travellers are advised to check with the Embassy prior to departure.

Application requirements: (a) Completed application form (stating whether single- or double-entry or exit visa is required and giving the length of stay). (b) Valid passport. (c) Letter of invitation or an invitation/receipt or authorised tourist company certifying that the travel arrangement has been paid for, verified by the competent Serbian and Montenegrin authority. (d) Fee payable to Embassy in cash or by postal order. (e) Medical Insurance. (f) Return ticket (g) Proof of sufficient funds. *Business:* (a)-(g) and, (h) Letter of invitation from host company or evidence of self-employment.

Note: Visitors not staying at hotels must register with the police within 24 hours from arrival.

Working days required: 24 hours, unless application needs further referral.

Temporary residence: Enquire at Embassy.

Note: These regulations do not apply to the Kosovo area, which is currently under the administration of the UN. All nationals wishing to travel to Kosovo must present a valid passport and documentation supporting their reason for entry to the border police at their point of entry. Applicants granted entry may stay in Kosovo for up to 90 days and may extend their stay by applying to the Police Main Headquarters in Pristina.night.
On 1 July 2005, new entry control measures came into force for Kosovo. Visitors may now be required to provide documentary evidence (eg a letter of invitation giving a reason for their stay) to local authorities when entering Kosovo.

PASSPORT/VISA INFORMATION

Embassy of Serbia and Montenegro in the UK
28 Belgrave Square, London SW1X 8QB, UK
Tel: (020) 7235 9049.
Website: www.yugoslavembassy.org.uk
Opening hours: Mon-Fri 1000-1300 (visa section); 1400-1600 (visa telephone enquiries).

Embassy of Serbia and Montenegro in the USA
2134 Kalorama Road, NW, Washington, DC 20008, USA
Tel: (202) 332 0333 *or* 5974 (consular section).
Website: www.yuembusa.org
Opening hours: 0900-1700 Mon-Fri *or* 1000-1300 (consular section).

Money

Currency: The official currency in Serbia is the New Yugoslav Dinar. New Yugoslav Dinar (CSD) = 100 paras. Notes are in denominations of CSD5000, 1000, 200, 100, 50, 20 and 10. Coins are in denominations of CSD20, 10, 5, 2 and 1 and 50 paras.
The official currency in Montenegro is the Euro. Euro (€) = 100 cents. Notes are in denominations of €500, 200, 100, 50, 20, 10 and 5. Coins are in denominations of €2 and 1, and 50, 20, 10, 5, 2 and 1 cents.

Currency exchange: As elsewhere in the ex-Yugoslav republics, the only true repositories of value and frequently exchanged currencies are the Euro and the US Dollar (the Pound Sterling is rarely used in the republic). Money should be exchanged through official exchange offices only. There are very few ATMs that accept international bank cards. There are eight money-exchange machines in Belgrade (including one at the airport), accepting Sterling, American dollars and Euros, giving back Dinars. Scottish and Northern Irish pound sterling bank notes are not accepted.

Credit & debit cards: International credit cards such as Visa, Mastercard and Diners are accepted in most shops, hotels and restaurants in Serbia.

Traveller's cheques: Although acceptable in theory, in practice these can be very hard to exchange. It is advisable to take hard currency and credit or debit cards.

Currency restrictions: All visitors must complete the customs currency declaration form upon arrival and declare (including traveller's cheques) money in excess of €2000 or 120,000 Dinars. Any currency not declared on the form can be confiscated when leaving the country.

Banking hours: Mon-Sat 0600-1900. Some are open on Sunday.

Exchange rate indicators:
Rate at time of publishing (Serbia)
£1.00=   CSD128.82
$1.00=   CSD72.44
Rate at time of publishing (Montenegro)
£1.00=   €1.46
$1.00=   €0.82

Duty Free

The following items may be imported into Serbia & Montenegro without incurring customs duty:
200 cigarettes or 50 cigars or 250g of tobacco; 1l of wine and 750ml of spirits; 250ml of eau de toilette and a reasonable quantity of perfume; jewellery and clothing; two photo cameras, one movie camera (up to and including 16mm) or one video camera; one pair of binoculars; one pocket electronic calculator; camping equipment; one bicycle; one engine; sporting requisites (enquire for further details); if portable, one musical instrument, one record player, one radio receiver with or without a cassette recorder, one tape recorder and one typewriter.

Restricted imports: Weapons are prohibited, except if they are for hunting purposes and the hunt is organised by the Hunters Association of Serbia. Animals may be imported as long as there is proof of the health condition of the animal. Cats and dogs must have a vet certificate.

Public Holidays

Below are listed Public Holidays for the January 2006-June 2007 period.
2006: Jan 1 New Year's Day. **Jan 7** Orthodox Christmas Day. **Apr 21** Orthodox Good Friday. **Apr 24** Orthodox Easter Monday. **Apr 27** Statehood Day. **May 1-2** Labour Days. **May 9** Victory Day. **Nov 29** Republic Day.
2007: Jan 1 New Year's Day. **Jan 7** Orthodox Christmas Day. **Apr 6** Orthodox Good Friday. **Apr 9** Orthodox Easter Monday. **Apr 27** Statehood Day. **May 1-2** Labour Days. **May 9** Victory Day.
Note: Orthodox Christian holidays may also be celebrated in most parts.

Health

	Special Precautions?	Certificate Required?
Yellow Fever	No	No
Cholera	No	No
Typhoid & Polio	1	N/A
Malaria	No	N/A

Note: *Regulations and requirements may be subject to change at short notice, and you are advised to contact your doctor well in advance of your intended date of departure. Any numbers in the chart refer to the footnotes below.*

1: Vaccination against *typhoid* is sometimes advised.

Food & drink: Mains water is normally chlorinated and, whilst relatively safe, may cause mild abdominal upsets. Bottled water is available and is advised for the first few weeks of the stay. Milk is pasteurised and dairy products are safe for consumption. Local meat, poultry, seafood, fruit and vegetables are generally considered safe to eat.

Other risks: *Hepatitis A* and *B* may occur. *Tularaemia* has been reported recently in the Kosovo area and travellers are advised to boil all water and be cautious about food preparation. *Crimean congo haemorrhagic fever* is endemic in Kosovo. *Tick-borne encephalitis* and *typhus* occur.
Rabies is present. For those at high risk, vaccination before arrival should be considered. If you are bitten, seek medical advice without delay; for more information, see the *Health* appendix.

Healthcare: Doctors are well trained but medical facilities are limited. Many medicines and basic medical supplies are often unavailable. Hospitals usually require payment in hard currency. Prescribed medicines must be paid for. Health insurance with emergency repatriation is essential. Visitors may be asked to pay first and seek reimbursement later. Pharmacies are open 0800-2000 Mon-Fri, 0800-1500 Sat.

Travel - International

AIR:

The national airlines are *Yugoslav Airlines (JU)* (website: www.jatlondon.com) and *Montenegro Airlines* (website: www.montenegro-airlines.cg.yu).
Main airports: *Belgrade (BEG)* (Surcin) (website: www.airport-belgrade.co.yu) is 19km (12 miles) west of the city. *To/from the airport*: Buses and taxis are available into Belgrade. There are a number of car rental agencies at the airport. *Facilities*: Banks, bars, car hire and post offices.
Smaller airports exist elsewhere, such as *Podgorica (TGD)* (formerly Titograd) in Montenegro.
Departure tax: From Belgrade airport: CSD1000, payable at the airport. From Montenegro: €16.

SEA:

Main ports: *Bar* (website: www.lukabar.cg.yu) and *Kotor* (website: www.portofkotor.cg.yu) in Montenegro. Ferries link the Yugoslav Adriatic coast with Italy, operating between Bar and Bari and Ancona.

RAIL:
Rail services to Belgrade run from Bulgaria, Croatia, Greece, Romania and Turkey. Trains from western Europe travel via Budapest. For up-to-date information, contact *Rail Europe* (tel: (08705)

848 848; website: www.raileurope.co.uk). International trains have couchette coaches as well as bar and dining cars. On some lines, transport for cars is provided.
Note: Train travel should be undertaken with care as assaults and robberies have been reported.

ROAD:

The following frontier posts are open for road traffic:
From **Croatia:** Batrovci-Bajakovo.
From **Hungary:** Hercegszanto-Backi Breg (Bezdan); Tompa-Kelebija; Szeged Roszke-Horgos; Bacsalmas-Bajmok; and Tiszasziget-Djala (both crossings for nationals of Yugoslavia and Hungary only).
From **Romania:** Jimbolia-Srpska Crnja; Stamora Moravita-Vatin; Naidas-Kaludaerova (Bela Crkva); and Portile de Fier-(Turnu Severin)-Daerdap (Kladovo).
From **Bulgaria:** Bregovo-Mokranje (Negotin); Kula-Vrska Cuka (Zajecar); Kalotina-Gradina; Otomanci-Ribarci; Kjustendil-Deve Bair (Kriva Palanka); Blagoevgrad-Delcevo; and Petric-Novo Selo.
From **Albania:** Podgradec-Cafa Prusit; and Kukes-Vrbnica.
From **Macedonia (Former Yugoslav Republic of):** Presevo-Tabanovce; Globocica; Pohor Pcinjski; and Djeneral-Jankovic. Nearly all the passes mentioned above are open 24 hours a day. Delays between Kosovo and Macedonia are commonplace.
Bus: Connections are available to Belgrade from destinations including Budapest, Lyon, Munich, Paris, Thessaloniki and Zurich.

Travel - Internal

AIR:

Montenegro Airlines and *Yugoslav Airlines (JU)* both offer connections between Belgrade and Podgorica.
Departure tax: From Belgrade airport: CSD500. From Montenegro: €8.

RAIL:

Internal rail services are generally poor. Services are often overbooked, unreliable, unsafe and slow - especially in winter. Destinations accessible by rail include Bar, Belgrade, Nis, Novi Sad, Pristina and Subotica. For further information, contact Belgrade Bus Station (tel: (11) 636 299 (*reservations and information*); website: www.bas.co.yu).

ROAD:

Drivers should not rely on local petrol stations for fuel, owing to shortages of oil, although hard currency might otherwise be rationed and scarce petrol available. Spare parts are very difficult to obtain. Driving at night is not advisable, owing to the poor condition of the roads. There are several tollbooths along the motorways. Foreign-registered vehicles are charged at a higher toll then local vehicles. The toll also depends on the size of vehicle. Drivers should have at least €200/CSD15,000 (preferred) to pay in cash at the booths. **Coach:** Efficient and cheap coaches used to connect all towns. The fuel shortages have restricted the services severely. Two notoriously bad roads are the Ibarska Magistrala and the two-lane Moraca Canyon, and these should be avoided when possible. **Taxi:** Main cities have metered taxis. It is possible to negotiate a fare when the meters are not in use. In Kosovo, Pristina is able to provide taxis. Only use officially marked taxis. **Car hire:** Available from airports and main towns.
Regulations: Traffic drives on the right. Speed limits are 120kph (75mph) on motorways and 100kph (62mph) on other roads. Road signs may be poorly marked and new signs are likely to be in Cyrillic script in some areas of the country. Seatbelts must be worn at all times.
Documentation: International Driving License is required. No customs documents are required but car log books, a Green Card (not valid in Kosovo) and vehicle registration/ownership documents and locally valid insurance policy are necessary. Third-party insurance can be taken out at the border when travelling to Kosovo.

URBAN:

There are good bus services in the main towns, with tramways and trolleybuses in Belgrade. Multi-journey tickets are available and are sold in advance through tobacconists. The passenger punches the ticket in a machine on board. Fares paid to the driver are at double the pre-purchase prices.
Travel times: The following chart gives approximate travel times (in hours and minutes) from **Belgrade** to other major cities/towns in Serbia and Montenegro.

	Air	Road	Rail
Bar	-	7.00	6.00
Podgorica	0.30	6.00	5.30

Travel Advice

Travellers should exercise caution when travelling to Kosovo or within the Presevo and Bujanovac districts of South Serbia. Although the overall security situation in Kosovo remains calm, sporadic incidents including explosions continue to occur. It is recommended that travellers stay alert at all times and avoid any demonstrations or public gatherings.
While most visits are trouble-free, Serbia and Montenegro (including Kosovo shares with the rest of Europe a threat from international terrorism. Attacks could be indiscriminate and against civilian targets including places frequented by foreigners.
The Serbia and Montenegro Government does not recognise entry points from Kosovo or those on Kosovo's external borders with Albania or Macedonia.
There are still residual mines and other unexploded ordnance in some areas of Kosovo and some areas of South Serbia. Road conditions in Kosovo are poor and can be dangerous in bad weather. Travellers are advised against travelling at night.
This advice is based on information provided by the Foreign and Commonwealth Office in the UK. It is correct at time of publishing. As the situation can change rapidly, visitors are advised to contact the following organisations for the latest travel advice:

British Foreign and Commonwealth Office
Tel: (0845) 850 2829.
Website: www.fco.gov.uk

US Department of State
Website: http://travel.state.gov/travel

Accommodation

HOTELS AND INNS:

There are over 240,000 beds available in hotels across the country. Deluxe/A-class hotels are confined to Belgrade and a number of Montenegrin Adriatic resorts, most notably the exclusive island of Sveti Stefan. Further down the scale, and particularly in the smaller towns, services are poor. The best hotels are always heavily booked, so advance booking is essential. Prices are very high, and payable in hard currency for visiting foreign nationals. Also, the Montenegrin resorts may be overcrowded, following the closure of the Croatian coastline to all Serbian and Montenegrin nationals. Classification is from **deluxe** to **A**, **B**, **C** and **D class**.
Pensions: First-, second- and third-class pensions are available throughout the country. A *Hotel Directory* is available from the National Tourism Organisation of Montenegro (see *Top Things To See & Do*).
Inns: Motels are found on most main roads. Prices are set independently according to region, tourist season and the quality of service. There is a CSD60 per day residence charge.

GUEST HOUSES:

Many people offer rooms, often with meals, to visitors in villages without hotels. Discounts are available off-season. Contact tourist offices or travel agencies for details.

SELF-CATERING:

Holiday villages are available in many resorts as well as a selection of apartments and villas. Travel agencies and tourist offices have further information.

CAMPING/CARAVANNING:

Only available on official sites but there are over 20,000 camping units throughout the country. A permit from the local tourist office is required for off-site camping. A list is available from the National Tourism Organisation. *Alpine Club* mountain huts are available in all mountain areas. **Note:** Caravans are allowed in duty-free for up to one year.

YOUTH HOSTELS:

For information, contact the National Tourism Organisation of Serbia (NTOS) (see *Top Things To Do*) or Hostelling International Yugoslavia (See *Accomodation Infomation*)

ACCOMMODATION INFORMATION

Hostelling International Yugoslavia
E-mail: info@hostels.org.yu
Website: www.hostels.org.yu

Top Things To See & Do

- **Belgrade** is the capital of Serbia and the national capital. The **Kalemegdan Citadel (Belgrade Fortress)** straddles a hilltop overlooking the junction of the **Sava** and the **Danube**. Religious landmarks include the **Cathedral Church (Saborna Crkva)**. Go to the **National Museum**, the **Museum of Modern Art**, the **Museum of the Serbian Orthodox Church** and the **Ethnographical Museum**. Well worth a visit is the **Palace of Princess Ljubica** (1831) with a good collection of period furniture. **Skadarlija** is the 19th-century Bohemian quarter with cafes, street performers, art galleries and antique shops. Near **Kraljevo** is the restored **Monastery of Zica**, now painted bright red as it was in Medieval times. It was there that the Kings of Serbia were crowned. The **Kalenic Monastery** is a fine example of Serbian style.
- See **Novi Sad**, said to be the 'Serbian Athens.' It is a cultural centre with many museums, galleries, libraries and theatres.
- **Djerdap National Park** spans 64,000 hectares (158,146 acres), its main attraction is the **Djerdap Gorge**, a river valley made from four gorges: **Gornja Klisura**, **Gospodjin Vir**, **Veliki** and **Mali Kazan** and **Sipska**. A lake formed by a hydro-electric plant is one of the most visited tourist attractions in Serbia because of the diverse animal and plant life. Other national parks are **Sara**, **Fruska Gora**, **Kopaonik** and **Tara**. The **hiking** is particularly good in **Durmitor National Park**.
- Follow one of Serbia's numerous **wine routes**. The **Palic wine route** follows the trail of 'Wines from the Sands' because the entire region is on sandy soil. The wine-making tradition in this area is over two thousand years old. Specialities in this area are Italian Riesling, Rhine Riesling and Chardonnay. The region covers Mount Fruska Gora and the Danube River. Italian and Rhine Riesling, Sauvignon and Traminac are all all produced here. The **Knjazevac vineyards** date back to the Roman times, they are situated on the **Dzervin Hill** above Knjazevac. Black grape varieties found around this region are Red Burgundy, Prokupac and Plovdina; white varieties are Smederevka and Italian Riesling. Other wine routes in Serbia are: **Vrsac**, **Oplenac**, **Smederevo**, **Negotin** and **Zupa**.
- **Sail** along the coast of Montenegro, at the southern end of Yugoslavia's coastline, an area of spectacular mountain ranges with villages perched like eagles' nests on high peaks.
- Visit the bustling port of **Kotor**, with its picturesque old city quarter. The general architecture is mainly of Venetian origin, as this power dominated the region until 1797. Entering the city through the town gate brings the visitor to the square with the 17th-century **Clock Tower**, overshadowed by the twin towers of the **Cathedral of St Tiphun** (12th century). A visit to the **Naval Museum**, **the Drago**, **Bizanti**, **Pima** and **Grgurina Palaces** and the **Church of St Lucas** (1195) should not be missed.
- Drink some **olive oil** in the a place that is famous for it and also has the oldest **olive tree** in the world (which is two thousand years old): this is **Bar**, a cultural centre, port and popular tourist town on the **Adriatic coast**.
- **Herceg Novi** is a 700-year-old town with much to recommend. The **Savina Monastery** is a perfect example of baroque architecture and other cultural attractions include several galleries and exhibitions

which are on display throughout the year. On the **Herceg Hovi Riviera** are two beaches, **Zanjic** and **Borici**. Nearby is the town of **Topla** where the famous Montenegrin poet and bishop, Petar II Petrovic Njegos was educated; the old school building still stands today. Other religious sites include **St George's Church** and **St Salvation's Church**.

- **Ulcinj** is one of the oldest towns on the Adriatic coast, the **Balsica Tower** and **Renaissance Church Mosque** (where the **City Museum** is housed) must be seen. However, the 12km **Velika Plaza** fine sandy beach is also an attraction.
- **Birdwatch** in the **Scadar Lake** area, in the **Zetsko-Skadarska Valley**. Some 270 species, many endangered or rare, live there (including the curly pelican). The lake is also home to over 40 species of fish. Around the lake are 20 Monastery complexes and numerous islands: **Vranjina**, **Gvmozur**, **Starcevo Islet**, **Krajinski Archipelago** and **Beska Island**. Another good birdwatching site is in the **Biogradsko Lake and Primeval Forest National Park**, one of the last three jungles in Europe. It spans 5400 hectares (13,343 acres) between the **Lim** and **Tara Rivers**. Here, you can find eagles and 150 other bird species which inhabit the **Bjelasica Mountain region**.
- Stroll around the famous **Botanical Gardens** in **Kolasin**, which is situated in the wilderness of the **Bjelasica**, **Sinjajevina**, **Vucje** and **Kljuca mountains**, and holds many rare mountainous plants.

TOURIST INFORMATION

National Tourism Organisation of Serbia (NTOS)
Knez Michajlova Street 18, 11000 Belgrade, Serbia & Montenegro
Tel: (11) 629 992.
Website: www.serbia-tourism.org

National Tourism Organisation of Montenegro
Cetinjski put 66, Trg. Vektre, 81 000 Podgorica, Serbia & Montenegro
Tel: (81) 235 155-8.
Website: www.visit-montenegro.cg.yu

Entertainment

FOOD & DRINK: Cuisine varies greatly from one region to another. On the whole, the meat specialities are better than the fish dishes.
Things to know: Table service is usual in hotel restaurants. Bars and cafes have counter and table service. Most places serving alcohol close by 2200.
National specialities:
- *Pihtije* (jellied pork or duck).
- *Cevapcici* (charcoal-grilled minced meat).
- *Raznjici* (skewered meat).
- *Sarma* or *japrak* (vine or cabbage leaves stuffed with meat and rice).
- *Strukli* (nuts and plums stuffed into cheese balls and then boiled).
- *Alva* (nuts crushed in honey).
- *Lokum* (Turkish Delight).
National drinks:
- *Slivovica* (a potent plum brandy).
- *Loza* and *maraskino* (made of morello cherries).
- Wine: *Ljutomer*, *Traminer*, *Riesling* and *Vugava*.
Tipping: 10 per cent is expected by hotels, restaurants and taxis.
NIGHTLIFE: Cinemas stay open until 2300, restaurants until midnight and nightclubs until 0300. Belgrade has excellent nightlife with a range of performance arts to enjoy: Operas, concerts, theatre, many late-night cafes and clubs.
SHOPPING: Special purchases include embroidery, lace, leatherwork, *Pec* filigree work, metalwork and Turkish coffee sets. **Shopping hours:** Mon-Fri 0800-1200 and 1700-2000, Sat 0800-1500 (many shops are open all day Sat).

Business

- **GDP:** US$24 billion (2004).
- **Main imports:** Machinery and transport equipment, fuels and lubricants, manufactured goods, chemicals, food, live animals and raw materials.
- **Main exports:** Manufactured goods, food, live animals and raw materials.
- **Main trade partners:** Bosnia and Herzegovnia, Croatia, France, Germany, Hungary, Italy, Macedonia (Former Yugoslav Republic of), Russian Federation and Slovenia.

ECONOMY: Serbia & Montenegro were respectively the largest and smallest of the six constituent republics of the former Yugoslavia. Between 1990 and the overthrow of

Slobodan Milosevic in 2000, civil war followed by economic sanctions reduced their economies to less than half their previous output. Much of their infrastructure and industrial capacity was destroyed. Since 2000, the economic outlook has become much brighter. The lifting of sanctions has restored access to international markets and capital. Annual economic growth since 2000 has been between 10 and 15 per cent. Agriculture is now mainly geared to domestic consumption. Maize, wheat, sugar beet and potatoes are the main crops. Fruit and vegetables are also important. The mining industry – which has proved more resilient than the rest of the industrial economy – produces coal, copper ores and bauxite as well as smaller amounts of iron ore, zinc, oil and natural gas. However, service industries will be the future of the Union's economy. Tourism, which was the main component of the service sector, has recovered gradually after being all but wiped out; the latest official figures record that Serbia received two million visitors in 2002.

Although the two republics have been formally united since February 2003 in the 'State Union of Serbia and Montenegro', they follow distinct economic policies; there is no customs union or currency alignment. Both Governments have, however, embarked on reform programmes which have seen numerous companies privatised and various parts of the two economies opened up to competition. The process has drawn the broad approval of the IMF and the EU, which has supplied a $3 billion aid package to assist the reconstruction process. The policy divisions between Serbia & Montenegro are likely to cause difficulties in the near future, especially as regards the EU, which is firmly opposed to any future schisms in the Balkans. Despite that, Serbia and Montenegro hope to be able to join the group – which currently includes Romania, Bulgaria and Croatia – aiming for full EU membership in 2007.
BUSINESS ETIQUETTE: As with Croatia, but unlike Slovenia, things go very slowly or not at all on account of the cumbersome bureaucracy and general socio-economic collapse. Communication, however, is not a major problem, as English is popular as a second language. Office hours: Mon-Fri 0700/0800-1500/1600.

COMMERCIAL INFORMATION

Yugoslav Chamber of Commerce and Industry
Terazije 23, 11000 Belgrade, Serbia & Montenegro
Tel: (11) 324 8222 *or* 8123.
Website: www.pkj.co.yu

Serbian Chamber of Commerce and Industry
Resavska 13-15, 11000 Belgrade, Serbia & Montenegro
Tel: (11) 330 0900.
Website: www.pks.co.yu

Chamber of Economy of Montenegro
Foreign Economic Relations Sector, ul. Novaka Miloseva 11, 81000 Podgorica, Serbia & Montenegro
Tel: (81) 230 545 *or* 714
Website: www.pkcg.org

Belgrade Chamber of Commerce
Kneza Milosa 12, 11000 Belgrade, Serbia & Montenegro
Tel: (11) 2641 355.
Website: www.kombeg.org.yu

Seychelles

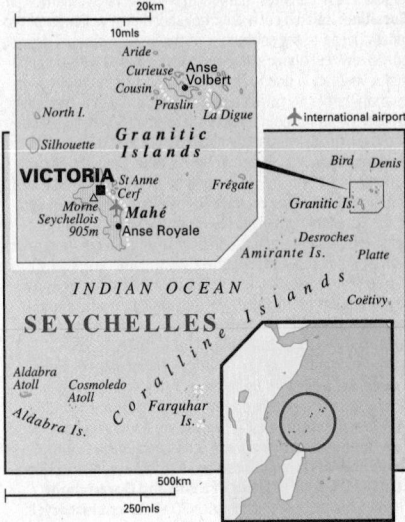

Location: Indian Ocean, 1600km (990 miles) east of Kenya.

Time: GMT + 4.

Overview

The Seychelles Archipelago contains 115 islands and islets. The first recorded sighting of the Seychelles was by the Portuguese navigator Vasco da Gama at the beginning of the 16th century. In 1756, French planters claimed Mahé and seven other islands for France. The islands, until then known as the Amirantes (Admiral da Gama had named them after himself), were re-named in honour of the French King's accountant, Vicomte Moreau de Séchelles. The Seychelles, annexed by Britain in 1794, were placed under the administration of Mauritius. Over the course of the 19th century, administration was handled by 'old India hands' – men and women with some experience of the tropics. For the next 150 years, isolated from the rest of the world and all but ignored by the major European powers, the Seychelles developed their own traditions, language and culture. The islands became a Crown Colony in 1903. Internal self-Government was granted in 1975 and independence a year later. Despite several coup attempts, multi-party democracy was restored in the Seychelles in 1991 under pressure from the country's main aid donors, particularly France and Britain.

The economy of this isolated island paradise relies heavily on tourism. Fine beaches, turquoise seas and warm weather are among the main draws for visitors. As a result of their extraordinary, isolated history, the Seychelles are also rich in rare plants which flourish nowhere else on the planet. 81 species are unique survivors from the luxuriant tropical forests that covered the islands until humanity's belated arrival two centuries ago. Outstanding amongst these is the coco-de-mer (sea coconut), native to Praslin, which grows in the Vallée de Mai. Its seed is the largest in nature, and gave rise to many legends when it was washed ashore on the coasts of Africa, India and Indonesia. Since the islands were unknown, the nuts were thought to have grown under the sea – hence the name.

The Seychelles are also a major attraction for birdwatchers. Millions of terns nest on the islands – among them that most beautiful of seabirds, the fairy tern. Up to two million sooty terns nest on Bird Island, and on Aride can be found the world's largest colonies of lesser noddies, roseate terns and other tropical birds. It was only some 30 years ago that active conservation of endangered species began in the Seychelles. Since then, with the establishment of island sanctuaries and nature reserves, much has been done to make the Seychelles a paradise for birds – and for those who love to watch them.

A B C D E F G H I J K L M N O P Q R S T U V W X Y Z

General Information

AREA: 455.3 sq km (176 sq miles).
POPULATION: 81,100 (official estimate 2005).
POPULATION DENSITY: 177.7 per sq km.
CAPITAL: Victoria (Mahé). **Population:** 71,000 (2005).
GEOGRAPHY: The Seychelles Archipelago occupies 400,000 sq km (150,000 sq miles) of the Indian Ocean northeast of Madagascar and contains 115 islands and islets. These fall into two groups of markedly different appearance, stemming from their distinct geologies:
Granitic: A dense cluster of 43 islands, the only mid-ocean group in the world with a granite rock formation. Their lush green vegetation is tropical in character, with a profusion of coconut palms, bananas, mangoes, yams, breadfruit and other tropical fruit. Indigenous forest exists on the higher slopes, where cinnamon and tea are planted. All, including the second largest, Praslin, are less than 65km (40 miles) from Mahé.
Coralline: Isolated coral outcrops speckling a vast area of the Indian Ocean to the southwest of the granitic group. They rise only a few feet above sea level but are covered with rich and dense vegetation due to fertilisation by copious amounts of guano. There is no permanent population. Aldabra, the largest atoll in the world, contains one-third of all Seychellois land and is a UNESCO-designated World Heritage Site.
The largest island in either group is **Mahé**, lying 4°S of the equator. It is 27km (17 miles) long by 8km (5 miles) wide and contains Victoria, the capital and main port, and 90 per cent of the population. Mahé is typical of the Granitic Islands, being mountainous and covered with jungle vegetation. Its highest point, indeed the highest point in the Seychelles, is Morne Seychellois (905m/2970ft). The isolated nature of the Seychelles has given rise to the evolution of many unique species of flora and fauna, including the coco-de-mer palm and unique varieties of orchid, giant tortoise, gecko, chameleon and 'flying fox' (fruitbat). National parks and reserves have been set up to protect this heritage. The Seychellois are descended from a mixture of French and British landowners, freed African slaves and a small number of Chinese and Indian immigrants, creating a unique culture.
GOVERNMENT: Republic since 1976. Gained independence from the UK in 1975. **Head of State and Government:** President James Alix Michel since 2004. **Recent history:** In April 2004, after more than a quarter of a century in power, Albert René retired and handed Presidency over to his Vice-President, James Michel. Mr Michel has promised to introduce a more open dialogue, particularly over economic matters, and to involve the private sector in the national economy.
LANGUAGE: Creole, English and French.
RELIGION: 83 per cent Roman Catholic with Anglican, Seventh Day Adventist, Muslim, Baha'i and other minorities.
ELECTRICITY: 240 volts AC, 50Hz. British three-pin plugs are in use.
SOCIAL CONVENTIONS: The people live a simple and unsophisticated island life and tourism is carefully controlled to protect the unspoilt charm of the islands. Before the international airport opened in 1971, the islands could be reached only by sea, and since they are miles from anywhere, visitors were few and far between and the people were little influenced by the outside world. They developed their own language and culture which – like so many things on the islands – are unique. Shaking hands is the customary form of greeting. The Seychellois are very hospitable and welcome guests into their homes. When visiting someone's home, a gift is acceptable. A mixture of imperial and metric systems operates. For example, petrol is dispensed in litres, whilst bars sell bottled and draught beer in half-pint measures. Casual wear is essential and formal clothes are only worn by churchgoers. Swimwear should only be worn on the beaches.

Climate

The islands lie outside the cyclone belt but receive monsoon rains from November to April with the northwest trade winds. This hot and humid season gives way to a period of cooler weather, though the temperature rarely falls below 23°C, and rougher seas when the trade winds blow from the southeast (May to October).

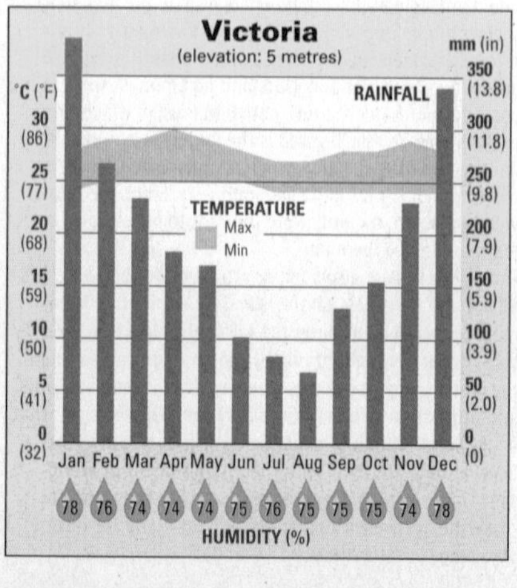

Required clothing: Tropical lightweights, with rainwear advisable during the rainy season. Sun hats and sunglasses essential all year round.

Communications

Telephone: IDD is available. Country code: 248. Phonecards are available. *SEYTELS* offers a 24-hour service via SEYTELS/Cable & Wireless Ltd, Francis Rachel Street, Victoria.
Mobile telephone: Roaming agreements exist with some international mobile phone companies.
Internet: There are several Internet cafes on Mahe. Most of the larger hotels have arrangements for visitors to obtain a temporary guest account.
Post: The main post office is in Victoria. Airmail collections are at 1500 weekdays and 1200 Saturdays; airmail to Western Europe normally takes up to one week. Post office hours: Mon-Fri 0800-1600, Sat 0800-1200.
MEDIA: The Government controls much of the islands' media, and operates the only radio and TV stations and the sole daily newspaper.
Press: *Seychelles Nation* is an English-language newspaper (morning daily except on Sundays); *Regar* is an opposition weekly publication.
TV: State-run *SBC TV* is operated by Seychelles Broadcasting Corporation (SBC).
Radio: SBC operates national mediumwave (AM) services and music station *Paradise FM*. The *BBC World Service* and *Radio France Internationale* are available via FM relays.

Passport/Visa

	Passport Required?	Visa Required?	Return Ticket Required?
Full British	Yes	No	Yes
Australian	Yes	No	Yes
Canadian	Yes	No	Yes
USA	Yes	No	Yes
Other EU	Yes	No	Yes
Japanese	Yes	No	Yes

Note: *Regulations and requirements may be subject to change at short notice, and you are advised to contact the appropriate diplomatic or consular authority before finalising travel arrangements. Any numbers in the chart refer to the footnotes below.*

PASSPORTS: Passport valid for six months from date of arrival in the Seychelles.
VISAS: Visa not required by any nationality as long as they have:
(a) onward or return ticket (if not, onward or return ticket must be purchased on arrival);
(b) proof of sufficient funds (between US$100-150 per day) and organised accommodation for the duration of the stay.
A visitor's permit, valid for up to one month, is issued on arrival, subject to possession of (a) and (b) as above; alternatively, a deposit may be made by 'security' bond in lieu. The permit may be renewed, provided the applicant holds a valid open return ticket and applies at least one week before the permit's expiry. For further information, contact the nearest Seychelles Tourist Office.
Transit: Passengers in transit must have tickets with reserved seats for their onward journey.
Temporary residence: Enquire at the High Commission. Additional information about temporary residence and visitor's permits may be obtained from the Immigration Division.

PASSPORT/VISA INFORMATION

The High Commission for Seychelles in France
51 avenue Mozart, 75016 Paris, France
Tel: (1) 4230 5747.
Email: ambsey@aol.com

Embassy of the Republic of Seychelles in the USA
Suite 400C, 4th Floor, 800 Second Avenue, New York, NY 10017, USA
Tel: (212) 972 1785.

Money

Currency: Seychelles Rupee (SCR) = 100 cents. Notes are in denominations of SCR100, 50, 25 and 10. Coins are in denominations of SCR5 and 1, and 25, 10 and 5 cents.
Note: Tourists must pay hotel bills in foreign currency (in the form of cash, traveller's cheques or credit or debit cards). Payment in local currency is only allowed if an exchange receipt can be shown as proof of the conversion from foreign currency into local currency. The duty free shop at the airport *only* accepts credit cards or foreign cash.
Currency exchange: Exchange facilities are available at the airport banks, which are open for all flight departures and arrivals. The following banks have branches in the Seychelles and will exchange traveller's cheques and foreign currency: *Barclays Bank, Bank of Baroda, Banque Française Commerciale, Central Bank of Seychelles, Development Bank of Seychelles, Habib Bank Ltd, Nouvo Banq* and *Seychelles Savings Bank*. Currency exchange receipts should be kept in order to facilitate re-exchange on departure. ATMs are available in Mahé and Praslin.
Credit & debit cards: Access, American Express, MasterCard and Visa are widely accepted; Diners Club has more limited use. Check with your credit or debit card company for details of merchant acceptability and other services which may be available.
Traveller's cheques: Accepted in most hotels, guest houses, restaurants and shops. To avoid additional exchange rate charges, travellers are advised to take traveller's cheques in US Dollars or Pounds Sterling.
Currency restrictions: The import and export of local and foreign currency is unlimited. The import and export of local currency is limited to SCR1000.
Banking hours: Mon-Fri 0830-1430, Sat 0830-1100.
Exchange rate indicators:

Rate at time of publishing	
£1.00=	SCR9.57
$1.00=	SCR5.56

Duty Free

The following items may be imported into the Seychelles by persons of 18 years or older without incurring customs duty:
400 cigarettes or 500g of tobacco; 2l of spirits or 2l of wine; 200ml of perfume or eau de toilette; other items not exceeding SCR3000; one video camera and one camera; musical instrument; portable electronic or electric equipment; sports requisites and other leisure equipment.
Prohibited items: The import of non-prescribed drugs and all firearms, including air pistols, air rifles and spearfishing guns, and plants and plant products, animals and animal products, radioactive substances and apparatus, dangerous drugs, biological specimens, fireworks and explosives, medicines and poisons are prohibited, unless prior authorisation has been granted. Video tapes must be declared and may be retained for security reasons. The import of animals and food and other agricultural produce is strictly controlled and subject to licensing.
Restricted exports: Shells, unprocessed coco-de-mer, processed or live fish and live tortoises may not be exported.

Public Holidays

Below are the Public Holidays for the January 2006-June 2007 period.
2006: Jan 1-2 New Year. **Apr 14** Good Friday. **Apr 17** Easter Monday. **May 1** Labour Day. **Jun 5** Liberation Day (Anniversary of 1977 Coup). **Jun 15** Corpus Christi. **Jun 18** National Day. **Jun 29** Independence Day. **Aug 15** Assumption/La Digue Festival. **Nov 1** All Saints' Day. **Dec 8** Immaculate Conception. **Dec 25** Christmas Day.
2007: Jan 1-2 New Year. **Apr 6** Good Friday. **Apr 9** Easter Monday. **May 1** Labour Day. **Jun 5** Liberation Day (Anniversary of 1977 Coup). **Jun 7** Corpus Christi. **Jun 18** National Day. **Jun 29** Independence Day.

Health

	Special Precautions?	Certificate Required?
Yellow Fever	No	1
Cholera	No	No
Typhoid & Polio	2	N/A
Malaria	No	N/A

Note: *Regulations and requirements may be subject to change at short notice, and you are advised to contact your doctor well in advance of your intended date of departure. Any numbers in the chart refer to the footnotes below.*

1: A *yellow fever* vaccination certificate is required by all travellers over one year arriving from infected areas or who have passed through partly or wholly endemic areas within the preceding six days.
2: *Typhoid* occurs in rural areas.
Food & drink: Mains water is normally chlorinated and, whilst relatively safe, may cause mild abdominal upsets. Bottled water is available and is advised for the first few weeks of the stay. Milk is pasteurised and dairy products are safe for consumption. Local meat, poultry, seafood, fruit and vegetables are generally considered safe to eat.
Other risks: *Hepatitis A* and *B* occur with occasional outbreaks of *dengue fever*. Visitors should beward of the effects of sunstroke or burning, since the Seychelles is close to the Equator.

Rabies may be present in certain areas. If you are bitten, seek medical advice without delay; for more information, see the *Health* appendix.
Health care: There is a large general hospital in Victoria and there are clinics elsewhere on La Digue, Mahé and Praslin, but medical facilities are limited. Visitors may obtain emergency treatment for a basic consultancy fee. Additional medical insurance is advised, including emergency repatriation. There are several pharmacies available in Victoria. On other islands, Government clinics are used. There are dental clinics available on Mahé, Praslin, and La Digue. Prices vary according to whether they are Government clinics, or private ones. A 24-hour doctor is on call for visitors at their hotels.

Travel - International

AIR:

The national airline is *Air Seychelles (HM)* (website: www.airseychelles.co.uk).
Approximate flight times: From Mahé to *London* is 12 hours (10 hours direct) and to *New York* is 20 hours and 40 minutes (via London).
Main airports: *Mahé Island (SEZ)* (Seychelles International) is 10km (6 miles) southeast from Victoria (travel time – 20 minutes). *To/from the airport*: Some coach services are provided by agents and taxis are available. *Facilities*: Duty free shop, banking and currency exchange facilities, car hire and restaurant/bar.
Departure tax: None. Tax is already included in the airline ticket.

SEA:

Cruise and cargo ships call at Mahé but there are no scheduled passenger services.

Travel - Internal

AIR:

Air Seychelles provides an efficient network of scheduled and chartered services from Mahé to Alphonse, Bird, Denis, Desroches Islands, Frégate and Praslin. *Helicopter (Seychelles) Ltd* (tel: 385 858; website: www.helicopterseychelles.com) provides an inter-island shuttle service and scenic flights. Charter flights can be arranged from any heli-stop.
Departure tax: None

SEA:

Privately owned schooners provide regular inter-island connections between Mahé, Praslin and La Digue. Boats can be chartered privately to get to the other islands.

ROAD:

Traffic drives on the left. There are paved roads only on La Digue, Mahé and Praslin; elsewhere the roads are sandy tracks. Visitors should be aware that Mahe is mountainous with narrow, winding roads, rarely with safety barriers. **Bus:** SPTC buses run on a regular basis on Mahé and Praslin from 0520-2130 (Mon-Sun). There are a number of 18-seater coaches for airport transfers and excursions. Prices for buses and coaches are very reasonable. **Taxi:** There are about 300 independently operated taxis on Mahé and Praslin, with a handful on La Digue, with Government-controlled rates. There is a surcharge for taxi fares on Praslin between 2200-0600. **Car hire:** There are over 550 cars or *Mini Mokes* for hire on Mahé, and a limited number on Praslin. It is advisable to make advance reservations, especially in the high season. Conditions of hire and insurance should be carefully checked. Hire is on an unlimited mileage basis and the price includes Third Party insurance and tax. Minimum age is 21. Petrol is approximately a third more expensive than in Europe. **Bicycles** may be hired on La Digue and Praslin.
Traffic regulations: There is a speed limit of 65kph (40mph) on the open road, decreasing to 40kph (25mph) in built-up areas and throughout Praslin. **Documentation:** A national driving licence is sufficient, for up to three months.
Travel Times: The following chart gives approximate travel times (in hours and minutes) from **Mahé** to other islands in the Seychelles.

	Air	Sea
Praslin	0.15	2.30
La Digue	-	3.15
Bird Is.	0.30	7.00
Denis Is.	0.30	6.00

Note: The ferry from Praslin to La Digue takes approximately 30 minutes.

Travel Advice

Most visits to the Seychelles are trouble-free but you should be aware of the global risk of indiscriminate international terrorist attacks, which could be against civilian targets, including places frequented by foreigners.
Please note that beaches are a favourite target for petty thieves.

This advice is based on information provided by the Foreign and Commonwealth Office in the UK. It is correct at time of publishing. As the situation can change rapidly, visitors are advised to contact the following organisations for the latest travel advice.

British Foreign and Commonwealth Office
Tel: (0845) 850 2829.
Website: www.fco.gov.uk

US Department of State
Website: http://travel.state.gov/travel

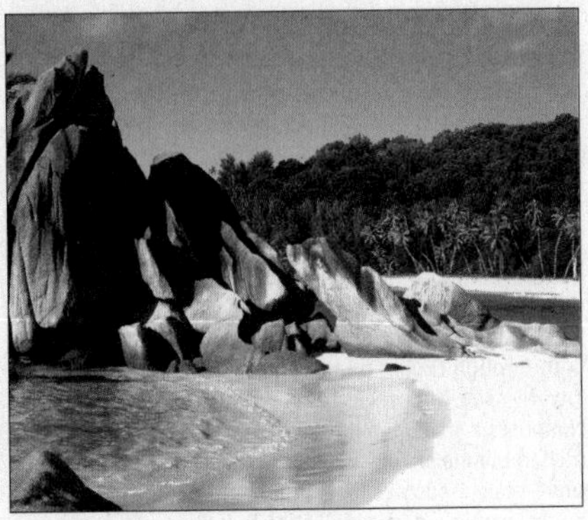

Credit: ©Paul Turcotte – Seychelles Tourism Marketing Authority

Accommodation

NOTE: Camping is not permitted throughout the Seychelles
Although the Seychelles have been a popular tourist destination for more than 10 years and now offer the full range of accommodation from self-catering apartments to luxury hotels, careful planning has ensured that the islands have retained the astonishing beauty and quiet charm that attracted the first tourists. Right from the start, the Government decreed that no new building could be higher than the surrounding palm trees, with the result that big-city levels of comfort and convenience have been achieved in thoroughly Seychellois settings. It is advisable to confirm reservations with a deposit, particularly during the high season from December to January and in July and August.

HOTELS & GUEST HOUSES:

All recently built hotels come well up to international standards and there are numerous large resort hotels equipped with air conditioning, private bathrooms, swimming pools and full sporting facilities. Older hotels and guest houses on the smaller islands may lack some sophistication, but their charming seclusion has long recommended them to those seeking complete peace and privacy: Somerset Maugham once sought out the quietest so that he could write a novel without interruption. Many hotels and guest houses are former plantation houses modestly modernised and run by the resident owner. Thatched-roof chalets and guest houses, built in the local style, are to be found mainly on outlying islands. The Seychelles Hotel Association comprises some 92 hotels on the islands. More information is available from the Association. For up-to-date prices, contact the Tourist Office (see *Top Things To Do*).

SELF-CATERING:

Self-catering units are available on the main islands. For details, contact the Tourist Office. Available at Mahé and Praslin.

ACCOMMODATION INFORMATION

Seychelles Hospitality and Tourism Association
1st Floor, Bodco Building, Harbour Trading Estate, Victoria, Seychelles
Tel: 610 210.
Website: www.shta-seychelles.com

Top Things To See

- To see many species of coral and fish, board a glass-bottomed boat from Victoria to nearby **St Anne Marine National Park**, which encloses the islands of **St Anne**, **Beacon** (classified as a nature reserve), **Cerf** (renowned for Creole food), **Long** (closed to the public), **Round** (reputed for its tuna steaks) and **Moyenne** (privately owned, but open to visiting tourists).
- Tour **Mahé** island by coach taking in such attractions as the market, the **Botanical Gardens** (with coco-de-mer palm, giant tortoises and orchids), and a replica of London's **Vauxhall Bridge Tower Clock** in **Victoria**, before setting off around the island to visit colonial-style mansions in graceful decline, old plantations of cinnamon and vanilla, and everywhere the greenest of vibrant green jungles.
- Discover fine displays depicting the history of spice cultivation in the **National Museum** in **Victoria,** which celebrates Seychellois history, folklore and music.
- In **Silhouette,** discover an old plantation house of traditional Seychellois timber construction.
- On **Praslin** island, the second-largest island, head for the famous **Vallée de Mai**, another UNESCO World Heritage Site, which contains the double-nutted coco-de-mer palm.
- In **La Digue,** just over three hours by schooner from Mahé or 30 minutes from Praslin, see the rare **black paradise flycatcher**. There are only 15 cars on the island and the ox-cart remains the principal means of transport (although bicycles may be hired). See beautiful old plantation houses, such as **Château Saint-Cloud**, as well as a vanilla plantation, copra factories and superb beaches.
- In **Frégate**, the most easterly and isolated of the granitic islands, look for the almost extinct **magpie robin**.
- Two hours by boat from Mahé, **Cousin** was bought (in 1968) by the International Council for Bird Protection, which operates it as a nature reserve. Amongst the rare bird species thus protected are the **brush warbler,** the **Seychelles toc-toc** and the **fairy tern**. The best time to visit is April or May, when 1.25 million birds nest on the island. All visits to the island must be made as part of an organised tour.
- In **Aride,** the most northerly of the granitic islands, see vast colonies of **seabirds** from October to the end of April.
- On **Bird** island, see the millions of **sooty terns** that migrate here to breed between May and October.
- Discover the **rock-pools** and **tortoise colony** of **Thérèse**, accessible from Port Glaud by a five-minute boat trip.
- On **Aldabra**, the world's largest atoll, and listed by UNESCO as a World Heritage Site, see the **giant land tortoises** (150,000 tortoises in total, reputedly five times more than on the Galapagos Islands). The atoll consists of 13 islands which make up about one-third of the Seychelles' land mass. Aldabra remains under strict supervision of the Seychelles Island Foundation (website: www.sif.sc or www.aldabra.org). Some tortoises have been exported to **Curieuse**, now a reserve for giant tortoises.

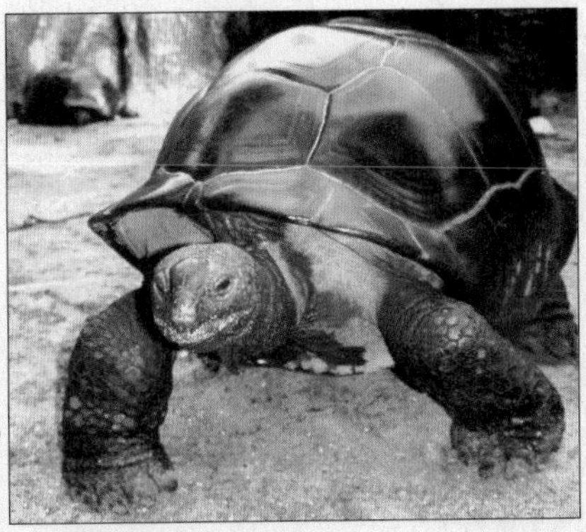

Credit: ©Tally & Lionel Pozzoli-Seychelles Tourism Marketing Authority

Top Things To Do

- Relax on **Mahé**'s numerous powdery white sandy **beaches** (there are almost 70 beaches on Mahé alone) while enjoying its lush vegetation, rising through plantations of coconut palms and cinnamon to forested peaks that afford unparalleled views of neighbouring islands.
- Go **water-skiing, windsurfing, sailing, fishing** and **scuba-diving** in **Desroches**, the largest of the Amirantes archipelago; water scooters may also be hired. The diving is particularly good: there are sea cliffs, tunnels and caves – and, of course, multitudes of fish of many different species. Visibility is best from September to May. A favourite location for **snorkelling** is the **St Anne National Marine Park**, which encompasses six islands off the coast of Mahé. Details about the Seychelles' best dive sites are available from the Seychelles Tourist Office (see *Tourist Information*).
- Go **deep sea fishing** in **Denis**. Marlin may be caught from October to December. The minimum stay is three days. The location of **Bird** island, at the edge of the Seychelles continental shelf (the sea floor drops rapidly to 2000m/5000ft), also makes it a favoured destination for fishermen. The best spots for salt water fly fishing are **Alphonse** and **Desroches** islands.
- The clear water of the Seychelles makes conditions perfect for **underwater photography**. The coastal

waters are a haven for 101 species of coral and over 920 species of fish. The annual *Subios* **underwater festival** is held in the Seychelles over a three-week period in November and attracts underwater experts from all over the world.

- Hire a **power boat, cabin cruiser** or **yacht** to explore the islands at your own pace. Vessels may be booked in advance by the day, week or month. Reservations may be made at local agents or through *The Marine Charter Association*, PO Box 204, Victoria, Mahé (tel: 224 679; website: www.seychelles.net/mca).

Entertainment

FOOD & DRINK: Seychellois Creole cuisine is influenced by African, Chinese, English, French and Indian traditions. The careful blending of spices is a major feature and much use is made of coconut milk and breadfruit. Breadfruit is prepared in similar ways to the potato (mashed, chipped, roasted and so on) but has a slightly sweeter taste. Other locally produced fruits and vegetables include aubergines, calabashes, choux choutes, patoles, *paw-paws* (papaya), bananas, mangoes, avocados, jackfruits, grapefruits, guavas, lychees, pineapples, melons, limes and golden apples. Lobster, octopus, pork and chicken are used more frequently than beef or lamb, which must be imported. Most restaurants offer a few items of what is termed 'international' cuisine, generally with a bias towards preparations of fresh fish and shellfish, as well as the Creole delicacies mentioned above. There are Italian and Chinese restaurants on Mahé. Some of the main hotels have bakeries and home-baked bread is also a feature of some of the small guest houses and lodges. Waiter service is the norm. All restaurants which are members of the *Seychelles Restaurateurs' Association* quote an average price per person for a three-course meal inclusive of two glasses of wine and coffee.
A wide range of wines, spirits and other alcoholic beverages is available in the Seychelles. The same company produces *Guinness* under licence and soft drinks.
Things To know: A hotel licence permits hotel residents to drink at any time. Alcohol can be sold to anyone between Mon-Fri 1400-1800, Sat 0800-1200 and 1400-1800. Other bars open 1130-1500 and 1800-2200. It is illegal to drink alcohol on any road or in public.
National specialities:
- *Kat-kat banane*.
- Coconut curries.
- *Chatini requin*.
- *Soupe de tectec*.
- *Bouillon brède*.
- *Chauve-souris* (fruitbat).
- *Salade de palmiste* (made from the 'heart' of the coconut palm and sometimes known as 'millionaire's salad').
- *Daube* (made from breadfruit, yams, cassavas and bananas).
National drinks:
- *Seybrew* (a German-style lager made locally).
- Local tea.
Tipping: Tips in restaurants, hotels, to taxi drivers, porters and so on are usually already included, as 5 to 10 per cent of the bill or fare. All hotel and restaurant tariffs include a service charge, but payment is not obligatory.
NIGHTLIFE: Largely undeveloped and unsophisticated. There is, however, much to be enjoyed in the evenings, and a speciality is the local *camtolet* music, often accompanied by dancers. Several hotels have evening barbecues and dinner dances. Theatre productions are often staged (in Creole, English and French) and there is one cinema in Victoria and casinos at *Beau Vallon Bay Hotel* and the *Plantation Club.*
SHOPPING: Local handicrafts include work with textiles (such as batik), fibres (such as basketwares, table-mats and hats) and wood (such as traditional furniture, ornaments and model boats). Pottery and paintings may also be bought. Special souvenirs might include jewellery made from green snail shells. Tea-growing and manufacturing in the Seychelles is done on a small scale. Local tea can be bought in the shops or when visiting the tea factory on Mahé, where many blends of tea may be sampled at the *Tea Tavern*. Vanilla is cultivated as a climbing plant around the base of trees as it can be pollinated by hand. Pods can be bought in shops and used as flavouring. Cinnamon grows wild on all the islands. It can be bought as oil or in quills made from dried bark which can be freshly grated before use. **Shopping hours:** Mon-Fri 0800-1700, Sat 0800-1200. Some shops close weekdays 1200-1300.

Business

ECONOMY: Tourism is the largest industry in the Seychelles' economy; it now accounts for over 20 per cent of GDP, and draws 70 per cent of foreign exchange earnings. The service sector as a whole covers three-quarters of the Seychelles' economy.
Despite a shortage of fertile land, the agricultural sector produces copra for export, a variety of cash crops including tea and vanilla, and staple foods like cassava and sweet potatoes for domestic consumption. Fishing became increasingly important from the 1980s onwards, both through expansion of domestic operations and the lucrative sale of licences to foreign fleets. Industry comprises a small mining sector which extracts guano (rich in minerals) and some natural gas, plus light and small-scale industries including food and drinks (notably a tuna-canning operation), boat-building, metals, chemicals, wood products and tobacco. There is also a thriving re-export business based on a recently established export-processing zone. Extensive searches for offshore oil and gas reserves have so far been unsuccessful. The economy's heavy dependence on tourism makes it especially vulnerable to external factors (such as the September 11 attacks on the USA). In 1995, in an attempt to diversify the service economy away from tourism, the Government started to promote the Seychelles as an 'offshore' financial services centre. This has been moderately successful, especially given that this is now a highly competitive and – because of concerns about fraud and money-laundering – controversial field. After several years of recession, the economy is growing slowly. The main financial problem is the size of the country's external debt. The Seychelles must import many essential products – an expensive process given the islands' location – and this consumes the bulk of the foreign exchange earned from tourism.
The Seychelles is a member of the African Development Bank and the Indian Ocean Commission (which provides for regional economic cooperation).
BUSINESS ETIQUETTE: Businessmen do not wear suits and ties, although a smart appearance is advised. Most executives speak English and/or French. **Office hours:** Mon-Fri 0800-1600.

Sierra Leone

Location: West Africa.

Time: GMT.

Overview

There was a time, not so long ago, when Sierra Leone attracted some 100,000 tourist arrivals a year, mainly Europeans. They came to enjoy the country's unique natural beauty, to sit on secluded white sandy beaches, to climb through unspoilt rainforests and to wade through refreshing waterfalls.
In some ways, nothing has changed. The people are still as receptive as ever to outsiders and the landscape remains a lush tropical paradise. Yet most of the visitors have now gone because of the former war, and much of the tourism infrastructure needs rebuilding after years of conflict. Sierra Leone emerged from a decade of civil war in early 2002, with the help of Britain, the former colonial power, and a large United Nations peacekeeping mission. More than 17,000 foreign troops disarmed tens of thousands of rebels and militia fighters in the biggest UN peacekeeping success in Africa for many years.
The Government is starting from scratch, going back to basics to entice foreign travellers to return to this small corner of Africa. A new tourism development act has been put in place, modelled after the one in the Gambia. The Ministry of Tourism and Culture is looking to create a solid and stable tourism climate, highlighting the country's unique cultural diversity.

General Information

AREA: 71,740 sq km (27,699 sq miles).
POPULATION: 4.76 million (UN estimate 2002).
POPULATION DENSITY: 66.4 per sq km.
CAPITAL: Freetown. **Population:** 837,000 (UN estimate 2001).
GEOGRAPHY: Sierra Leone is bordered to the northwest, north and northeast by Guinea Republic, and to the southeast by Liberia. To the south and southwest lies the Atlantic Ocean. A flat plain up to 110km (70 miles) wide stretches the length of the coast except for the Freetown peninsula, where the Sierra Lyoa Mountains rise to 1000m (3280ft). In some coastal areas, sand bars have formed that stretch out as far as 112km (70 miles). Behind the coastal plain is the central forested area, drained by eight principal rivers, which has been cleared for agriculture. The land rises in altitude eastwards to the

Guinea Highlands, a high plateau with peaks rising to over 1830m (6000ft) in the Loma Mountains and Tingi Hills area. The Mende tribe is prominent in the southeast and the Temne in the western and northern areas.

GOVERNMENT: Republic. Gained independence from the UK in 1961. **Head of State and Government:** President Ahmad Tejan Kabbah since 1996.

LANGUAGE: The official language is English. Krio is also widely spoken. Local dialects are Mende, Limba and Temne.

RELIGION: Animist (40 per cent), Islam (40 per cent) and Christian (20 per cent).

ELECTRICITY: 220/240 volts AC, 50Hz. Supply subject to fluctuations.

SOCIAL CONVENTIONS: The majority of people in Sierra Leone still live a traditional, agricultural way of life, with ruling chiefs, and religions which preserve social stability, as well as local music, dance, customs and traditions. Handshaking is the normal form of greeting. It is usual to be entertained in a hotel or restaurant, particularly for business visitors. Small tokens of appreciation are always welcome. Casual wear is suitable everywhere. Men are rarely expected to wear suits and ties.

Climate

Tropical and humid all year. Between November and April, it is very hot and dry, although the coastal areas are cooled by sea breezes. In December and January, the dry, dusty *Harmattan* wind blows from the Sahara. During the rainy season between May and November, rainfall can be torrential.

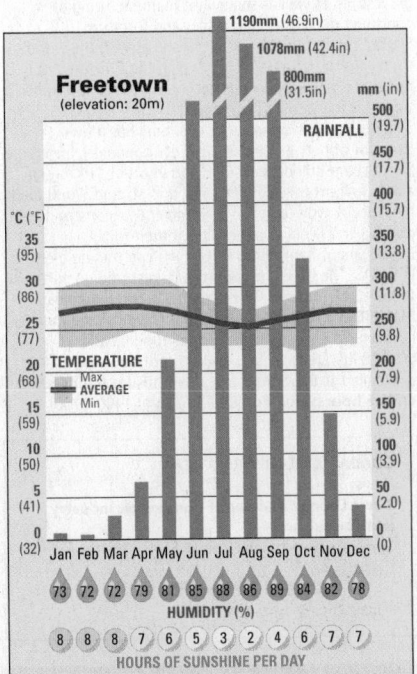

Credit: ©National Tourist Board of Sierra Leone

Communications

Telephone: IDD is available. Country code: 232.
Mobile telephone: Coverage limited to Freetown and environs.
Internet: Public access outlets are increasingly popping up, especially in Freetown where access is also available through the British Council.
Post: Airmail to Western Europe takes about five days.
MEDIA: Media freedom in Sierra Leone is limited, especially when it comes to reporting corruption; Broadcasters face many challenges, such as unreliable electricity supplies, a shortage of funds and a lack of advertising revenue. The UN Mission in Sierra Leone (Unmasil) operates some radio services, broadcasting news of UN activities and human rights information, as well as music and news.
Press: Newspapers include *Awoko*, *The Democrat* and *Concord Times*.
TV: *Sierra Leone Broadcasting Service* (*SLBS*) is a terrestrial network with limited coverage; *ABC TV* is private.
Radio: *Sierra Leone Broadcasting Service* (*SLBS*) is the national broadcaster. Private stations include *Kiss FM* and *SKYY FM*. FM relays of *BBC World Service* and *Radio France Internationale* are on the air in Freetown.

Passport/Visa

	Passport Required?	Visa Required?	Return Ticket Required?
Full British	Yes	Yes	Yes
Australian	Yes	Yes	Yes
Canadian	Yes	Yes	Yes
USA	Yes	Yes	Yes
Other EU	Yes	Yes	Yes
Japanese	Yes	Yes	Yes

Note: *Regulations and requirements may be subject to change at short notice, and you are advised to contact the appropriate diplomatic or consular authority before finalising travel arrangements. Any numbers in the chart refer to the footnotes below.*

Restricted entry: Nationals of Liberia need authorisation from the Government of Sierra Leone or they will be refused admission.

PASSPORTS: Passport valid for a minimum of six months required by all.

VISAS: Required by all except the following:
(a) nationals of Benin, Burkina Faso, Cape Verde, Côte d'Ivoire, The Gambia, Ghana, Guinea Republic, Guinea-Bissau, Liberia, Mali, Niger, Nigeria, Senegal and Togo;
(b) transit passengers continuing their journey by the same or first connecting aircraft within 24 hours provided holding onward or return documentation and not leaving the airport transit area.

Types of visa and cost: *Tourist:* £45 (single-entry); £90 (multiple-entry). *Express Tourist* and *Business:* £40 in addition to cost. *Business:* £60 (single-entry); £120 (multiple-entry: six months), £200 (multiple-entry: one year).

Validity: Entry Permits and visas generally are valid for three months and allow a stay of one month in Sierra Leone for single-entry only. An extension is possible by application to the Department of Immigration in Freetown. Multiple-entry tourist and visitor visas are valid for six months; a business multiple-entry visa is valid for up to one year.

Application to: Consulate (or consular section at Embassy or High Commission); see *Passport/Visa Information*.

Application requirements: (a) Completed application form. (b) Two passport-size photos. (c) Passport valid for six months. (d) Confirmation of hotel reservation for tourist visa. (e) Letter of invitation and company letter for *business* visa. (f) Vaccination against yellow fever, malaria and cholera are required in order to obtain a visa (see *Health* section). (g) Fee in cash or postal order for mail applications. (h) Evidence of sufficient funds.

Working days required: Three. Several weeks are required where referral to authorities in Sierra Leone is necessary. One day for Express visa.

PASSPORT/VISA INFORMATION

High Commission for the Republic of Sierra Leone in the UK
Oxford Circus House, 245 Oxford Street, London W1D 2LX, UK
Tel: (020) 7287 9884.
Website: www.slhc-uk.org.uk
Opening hours: Mon-Thurs 1000-1300 and 1430-1500; Fri 1000-1300.

Embassy of the Republic of Sierra Leone in the USA
1701 19th Street, NW, Washington, DC 20009, USA
Tel: (202) 939 9261.
Website: www.sierra-leone.org

Money

Currency: Leone (SLL) = 100 cents. Notes are in denominations of SLL5000, 2000, 1000, 500, 100, 50, 20, 10, 5, 2 and 1. Coins are in denominations of SLL100 and 50.
Credit & debit cards: These are not accepted.
Travellers cheques: These are generally not recommended.
Currency restrictions: The import and export of local currency is limited to SLL50,000. The import of foreign currency is unlimited subject to declaration; export of foreign currency is limited to the amount declared on arrival (amounts exceeding US$5000 must be authorised by the National Bank of Sierra Leone).
Banking hours: Mon-Thurs 0800-1330, Fri 0800-1400.
Exchange rate indicators:
Rate at time of publishing
£1.00= SLL4156.72
$1.00= SLL2355.00

Duty Free

The following may be imported into Sierra Leone without incurring customs duty:
200 cigarettes or 225g tobacco; 1.1l of wine or spirits.
Prohibited imports: Narcotics; firearms without a licence from the Commissioner of Police in Freetown.

Public Holidays

Below are listed Public Holidays for the January 2006-June 2007 period.
2006: Jan 1 New Year's Day. **Jan 10** Eid al-Adha (Feast of the Sacrifice). **Apr 11** Maulid-un-Nabi (Birth of the Prophet). **Apr 14** Good Friday. **Apr 17** Easter Monday. **Apr 27** Independence Day. **Oct 23** Eid al-Fitr (End of Ramadan). **Dec 25** Christmas Day. **Dec 26** Boxing Day. **Dec 31** Eid al-Adha (Feast of the Sacrifice).
2007: Jan 1 New Year's Day. **Mar 31** Maulid-un-Nabi (Birth of the Prophet). **Apr 6** Good Friday. **Apr 9** Easter Monday. **Apr 27** Independence Day.
Note: Muslim festivals are timed according to local sightings of various phases of the moon and the dates given above are approximations. During the lunar month of Ramadan that precedes Eid al-Fitr, Muslims fast during the day and feast at night and normal business patterns may be interrupted. Many restaurants are closed during the day and there may be restrictions on smoking and drinking. Some disruption may continue into Eid al-Fitr itself. Eid al-Fitr and Eid al-Adha may last anything from two to 10 days, depending on the region. For more information, see the *World of Islam* appendix.

Health

	Special Precautions?	Certificate Required?
Yellow Fever	Yes	1
Cholera	2	No
Typhoid & Polio	3	N/A
Malaria	4	N/A

Note: *Regulations and requirements may be subject to change at short notice, and you are advised to contact your doctor well in advance of your intended date of departure. Any numbers in the chart refer to the footnotes below.*

1: A *yellow fever* vaccination certificate is required of travellers arriving from infected areas. Travellers arriving from non-endemic zones should note that vaccination is strongly recommended for travel outside the urban areas, even if an outbreak of the disease has not been reported and they would normally not require a vaccination certificate to enter the country.
2: Following WHO guidelines issued in 1973, a *cholera* vaccination certificate is not a condition of entry to Sierra Leone. However, *cholera* is a serious risk in this country and precautions are essential. Up-to-date advice should be sought before deciding whether these precautions should include vaccination, as medical opinion is divided over its effectiveness; see the *Health* appendix for further details.
3: *Polio* and *typhoid* both occur.
4: *Malaria* risk exists, predominantly in the malignant *falciparum* form, throughout the country all year. Resistance to chloroquine has been reported. The recommended prophylaxis is mefloquine.
Food & drink: All water should be regarded as being potentially contaminated. Water used for drinking, brushing teeth or making ice should have first been boiled or otherwise sterilised. Milk is unpasteurised and should be boiled. Powdered or tinned milk is available and is advised, but make sure that it is reconstituted with pure water. Avoid dairy products which are likely to have been made from unboiled milk. Only eat well-cooked meat and fish, preferably served hot. Pork, salad and mayonnaise may carry increased risk. Vegetables should be cooked and fruit peeled.

Other risks: *Bilharzia* (*schistosomiasis*) is present. Avoid swimming and paddling in fresh water; swimming pools which are well chlorinated and maintained are safe. *Filariasis* and *dengue fever* are present. *Trachoma, hepatitis A* and *E, tungiasis* and *dysentery* are widespread. *Trypanosomiasis* (sleeping sickness) may be present and there is a significant risk of infection for travellers visiting or working in rural areas. *Meningococcal meningitis* and *TB* may occur. *Hepatitis B* is hyperendemic. *Lassa fever* can be contracted in Kenema and the east; the last widely publicised outbreak was in April 2004. There is a high incidence of *HIV/AIDS*.

Rabies is present. For those at high risk, vaccination before arrival should be considered. If you are bitten, seek medical advice without delay. For more information, consult the *Health* appendix.

Health care: Medical facilities are extremely limited and continuing to decline. According to UN estimates, Sierra Leone has the highest death rate and the second-highest infant mortality rate in the world (200 out of every 1000 infants die within one year of birth). Missions and foreign aid organisations provide some medical facilities. Health insurance is essential. It is advisable to take personal medical supplies.

Travel - International

AIR: Owing to political instability, some flights from Europe and the USA are still suspended or disrupted. The situation is likely to improve. Check with the relevant airlines, the Embassy or High Commission for up-to-date information. The only UK airline still flying to Sierra Leone is Astraeus Airlines (website: www.flyastraeus.com), which operates non-stop, twice-weekly scheduled services between London Gatwick and Freetown (Lungi) Airport.

Approximate flight times: From Freetown to *London* is 10 hours 30 minutes (including transit in Accra).

Main airports: *Freetown (FNA)* (Lungi) is 13km (8 miles) north of the city (travel time – 45 minutes). *To/from the airport*: There is a catamaran/ferry link as well as taxi and bus services to the city. A helicopter service is also available (travel time – six minutes). *Facilities*: Post office, bar, shops and currency exchange.

Departure tax: US$20 (payable in hard currency by all except nationals of Sierra Leone). Transit passengers and children under two years of age are exempt.

SEA: **Main ports:** *Freetown*. There are services to Guinea Republic and Liberia.

RAIL: There are no passenger services at present.

ROAD: There are routes from Guinea Republic and Liberia, but access depends on the prevailing political situation. Contact the Embassy or High Commission for up-to-date information.

Travel - Internal

AIR: *Sierra National Airlines (LJ)* does not operate internal flights. Private airlines can be chartered.

SEA: Ferries connect all coastal ports. For details, contact local authorities or the National Tourist Board of Sierra Leone (see *Top Things To See & Do*).

ROAD: Traffic drives on the right. Sierra Leone has over 10,000km (6214 miles) of roads. Although the principal highways have a tarred surface, the secondary roads are poorly maintained and often impassable during the rainy season. There are some roadblocks at night on major roads near centres of population. **Bus:** Local and long-distance bus services are operated by the *Sierra Leone Road Transport Corporation*. Buses are fast and cheap and connect all the major centres. **Documentation:** An International Driving Permit is required. **URBAN:** Limited bus services in Freetown are operated by the *Road Transport Corporation*, although a substantial part of the city's public transport is provided by minibuses and share-taxis.

Travel Advice

There is political unrest.
Visits to the Western Area of Sierra Leone, including Freetown are usually trouble-free.
Travel outside the Western Area can be difficult, as roads and infrastructure are poor.
Petty crime is common.
Travellers should take sensible precautions and maintain a high level of vigilance in public places.
The threat from terrorism is low, but you should be aware of the global risk of indiscriminate attacks, which could be against civilian targets including places frequented by foreigners.
This advice is based on information provided by the Foreign and Commonwealth Office in the UK. It is correct at time of publishing. As the situation can change rapidly, visitors are advised to contact the following organisations for the latest travel advice:

British Foreign and Commonwealth Office
Tel: (0845) 850 2829.
Website: www.fco.gov.uk

US Department of State
Website: http://travel.state.gov/travel

Accommodation

 There are several hotels in Freetown of international standard with air conditioning and swimming pools. It is always advisable to make reservations in advance. Additionally, there are three luxury hotels located on the peninsula at Lakka and Tokay. The YMCA in Freetown offers clean, cheap accommodation with shared bathroom and kitchen facilities at a reasonable rate. Hotels in the interior are rare, although in Bo there is now a hotel which is of international standard. There are also Government rest houses, for which application must be made to the Ministry of the Interior; guests must bring their own linen.

Top Things To See & Do

- The most accessible part of Sierra Leone is the **Freetown Peninsula**. From **Leicester Peak**, superb views of the city between the sea and the mountains unfold below, and a narrow, steep road through the mountains leads to the old Creole villages (dating from 1800) of **Leicester**, **Gloucester** and **Regent**. The area was chosen as a resettlement area for liberated slaves who built the villages of **Hastings**, **Kent**, **Sussex**, **Waterloo**, **Wellington** and **York**.
- **Freetown** itself, surrounded by thickly vegetated hills, is both a colourful and historic port. Attractions include a 500-year-old cotton tree; the museum; the **De Ruyter Stone**; **Government Wharf** and **'King's Yard'** (where freed slaves waited to be given land); **Fourah Bay College**, the oldest university in West Africa; **Marcon's Church**, built in 1820; and the **City Hotel**, immortalised in Graham Greene's novel *The Heart of the Matter*. The **King Jimmy Market** and the bazaars offer a colourful spectacle and interesting shopping.
- A boat trip up the **Rokel River** to **Bunce Island**, one of the first slave trading stations of West Africa, makes an interesting excursion.
- The **Outamba-Kilimi National Park** in northern Sierra Leone, which can be reached from Freetown by road or air, offers varied and spectacular scenery; at this and other reserves there are game animals such as elephants, chimpanzees and pigmy hippos.
- The **Sakanbiarwa** plant reserve has an extensive collection of orchids, which are at their best early in the year.

> **TOURIST INFORMATION**
>
> **National Tourist Board of Sierra Leone**
> *Street address*: Cape Sierra Hotel, Room 100, Aberdeen, Freetown, Sierra Leone
> *Postal address*: PO Box 1435, Aberdeen, Freetown, Sierra Leone
> Tel: (22) 236 620.

Entertainment

FOOD & DRINK: Restaurants in the capital serve Armenian, English, French and Lebanese food. African food is served in hotels.
National specialities:
- Excellent fish, lobster and prawns.
- Exotic fruit and vegetables.
Tipping: Most hotels and restaurants include a service charge of 10 to 15 per cent. Taxi drivers do not expect tips.
NIGHTLIFE: Freetown has nightclubs and two casinos and there is music, dancing and local entertainment arranged by the hotels along Lumley Beach in the Cape Sierra district. Some beachside clubs organise concerts by local pop bands.

SHOPPING: Shopping hours: Mon-Sat 0800-1200 and 1400-1700.

Business

- **GDP:** US$989 million (2003).
- **Main exports:** Diamonds, rutile, cocoa, coffee and fish.
- **Main imports:** Foodstuffs, machinery and equipment, fuels and lubricants.
- **Main trade partners:** EU and USA.

ECONOMY: Following what is hopefully a permanent end to the country's debilitating civil war, Sierra Leone can now start to rebuild its shattered economy. With an annual per capita income of just US$140, it is one of the world's poorest countries. It also recorded the lowest figure in the 2004 UN Human Development Index: in other words, it is the worst place in the world to live. The agricultural and mining sectors were particularly badly hit by the fighting. Agriculture employs over two-thirds of the workforce who grow coffee, cocoa, palm kernels, nuts and ginger as cash crops along with rice, bananas and cassava as staples. The fishing industry is also important. The principal industrial activity is mining: the country has some of the world's most valuable diamond mines, as well as deposits of gold, bauxite and titanium ore. Diamonds have proved as much a curse as a blessing, as much of the civil war fighting was motivated by control of the mines and both the Government and the rebel forces relied on the revenues to sustain their war efforts. The remainder of the industrial sector is devoted to mineral and ore processing, as well as some light manufacturing of consumer goods such as textiles and furniture.
Sierra Leone's other major economic asset is the world's third-largest natural harbour, which the Government is hoping to develop as a hub for international and transit trade for the whole of the region.
Since the end of the war, the economy has grown healthily at between 5 and 7 per cent annually. Inevitably, Sierra Leone still depends on large injections of foreign aid to support the economy, and the IMF and World Bank have been involved in the Government's reconstruction plans. Sierra Leone is a member of the African Development Bank and the West African trading bloc ECOWAS. The UK is the country's largest trading partner, followed by the USA, Germany and The Netherlands.
BUSINESS ETIQUETTE: English is the most common language in business circles. Appointments and punctuality are expected. Visiting cards are essential. September to June are the best months for business visits.
Office hours: Mon-Fri 0800-1200 and 1400-1700.

> **COMMERCIAL INFORMATION**
>
> **Sierra Leone Chamber of Commerce, Industry and Agriculture**
> Guma Building, Lamina Sankoh Street, Freetown, Sierra Leone
> Tel: (22) 226 305 *or* 220 904.
> E-mail: cocsl@sierratel.sl

Singapore

Credit: ©Singapore Tourism Board

Location: Southeast Asia.

Time: GMT + 8.

Overview

Singapore is the East's great melting pot, a cultural pot pourri that leaves the unsuspecting visitor dazzled. Sir Stamford Raffles, a British civil servant, brought the 'Lion City' to world prominence after searching for a trading station to counter the Dutch influence in the Straits of Malacca, and trade has remained the island's mainstay.

Centuries before Sir Stamford Raffles acquired it from the Sultan of Johor in 1819, Singapore had been virtually abandoned. However, within decades Singapore had become the main commercial and strategic centre for the region. In 1867, it became a British Crown Colony and housed one of the UK's most important naval bases. This status remained unchanged until 1942 when the Japanese army swept down through Malaya and occupied the colony. Three-and-a-half years later the Japanese surrendered in Singapore and the colony assumed its previous status. And with the dissolution of the British Empire came internal self-Government (1959). In 1963, Singapore joined the Federation of Malaysia, but later broke away in 1965 to become fully independent. The initial outlook was unpromising: Singapore is tiny and has no natural resources apart from a good harbour. However, Lee Kuan Yew (first elected Prime Minister in 1959 and re-elected eight times thereafter) managed to galvanise the population into building a strong, export-led manufacturing and service economy. Tourism for Singapore has also proven to be of good economic benefit. Culture lovers thrive in this fusion of Chinese, Malay and Indian cultures - the main ethnic groups - with its assortment of mosques, temples and synagogues. Singapore presents a happy collision of opposites – grand and expensive at the famed Raffles Hotel, but low-key and cheap in the food markets of Bugis Junction and Clarke Quay.

But even in the low-key and cheap areas, Singapore remains an incredibly clean city where nothing is allowed to dull the shine – even down to the banning of chewing gum. In the last few years there has been some pressure to relax the numerous laws that have given Singapore a reputation as a prosperous but rather antiseptic and pettily repressive city-state. More seriously, Singapore has the highest per capita rate of judicial execution in the world, and the Government is still highly intolerant of internal dissent. Abroad, Singapore has taken a more active role in regional affairs, mainly through the Association of South East Nations (ASEAN). There have also been improvements in relations between Singapore and Malaysia, between whom there are myriad disputes over access to air space, water resources and territorial boundaries. In addition, Singapore City's exciting riverside parade of bars and restaurants reveals that Singaporeans actually do know how to have fun – and plenty of it.

The natural world is never far away in Singapore, either: Bukit Timah Nature Reserve has a significant area of primary rainforest within its boundaries, while, for the adventurous, Sungei Buluh Nature Park offers the chance for trekking. Check out Pulau Ubin's mangrove forest, a bumboat's ride from Changi jetty, or Kusu site of Taoists' annual pilgrimage.

General Information

AREA: 659.9 sq km (254.8 sq miles).
POPULATION: 4.4 million (UN, 2005).
POPULATION DENSITY: 6,667.7 per sq km.
CAPITAL: Singapore City. **Population:** 4.2 million (2005).
GEOGRAPHY: The island of Singapore is situated off the southern extremity of the Malay Peninsula, to which it is joined by a causeway carrying a road, railway and waterpipe. The Johor Strait between the island and the mainland is about 1km (0.8 miles) wide. The Republic of Singapore includes some 64 islets. It is a mainly flat country with low hills, the highest being Bukit Timah at 163m (545ft). In the northeast of the island, large areas have been reclaimed, and much of the original jungle and swamp covering the low-lying areas has been cleared.
GOVERNMENT: Republic. Gained full independence from the UK in 1965. **Head of State:** President Sellapan Ramanathan since 1999, re-elected in 2005. **Head of Government:** Prime Minister Lee Hsien Loong since 2004. **Recent history:** In both January 1997 and September 2001, opposition parties decided to contest only a small proportion (about one-third) of the 83 seats. Not surprisingly, the People's Action Party (PAP) won both polls comfortably. Goh was widely expected to stand down in favour of Lee Junior and, indeed, finally did so in August 2004. In September 2005, Sellapan Ramanathan began his second six-year term as President of Singapore. He won the election after the other contenders were disqualified for not meeting the strict selection criteria.
The Parliament is unicameral; executive power nominally rests with the President, but is effectively wielded by the Prime Minister and the Cabinet: the Presidency is a largely ceremonial post whose incumbent is elected by Parliament to serve a six-year term. The 93-member Parliament is elected for a five-year term; apart from nine Presidential appointees, its members are elected under a constituency system.
LANGUAGE: Mandarin Chinese, English, Malay and Tamil. Mandarin, English, Malay and Tamil are the official languages. Most Singaporeans are bilingual and speak English, which is used as the main language of communication.
RELIGION: Taoist, Buddhist, Christian, Hindu and Muslim.
ELECTRICITY: 220/240 volts AC, 50Hz. Plug fittings of the three-pin square type are in use. Many hotels have 110-volt outlets.
SOCIAL CONVENTIONS: Handshaking is the usual form of greeting, regardless of race. Social courtesies are often fairly formal. When invited to a private home or entering a temple or mosque, remove your shoes. For private visits, a gift is appreciated and, if on business, a company souvenir is appropriate. Dress is informal. Most first-class restaurants and some hotel dining rooms expect men to wear a jacket and tie in the evenings; a smart appearance is expected for business meetings. Evening dress for local men and women is unusual. Each of the diverse racial groups in Singapore has retained its own cultural and religious identity while developing as an integral part of the Singapore community. Over 50 per cent of the population is under 20 years of age. Laws relating to jaywalking, littering and chewing gum are strictly enforced in urban areas. Smoking is widely discouraged and illegal in enclosed public places (including restaurants). Dropping a cigarette end in the street or smoking illegally can lead to an immediate fine of up to S$500.

Climate

Warm and fairly humid summer temperatures throughout the year (approximately 30ºC/86ºF during the day and 23ºC/74ºF in the evening). There is no distinct wet/dry season. Most rain falls during the northeast monsoon (November to January) and showers are usually sudden and heavy.
Required clothing: Lightweight cottons and linens.

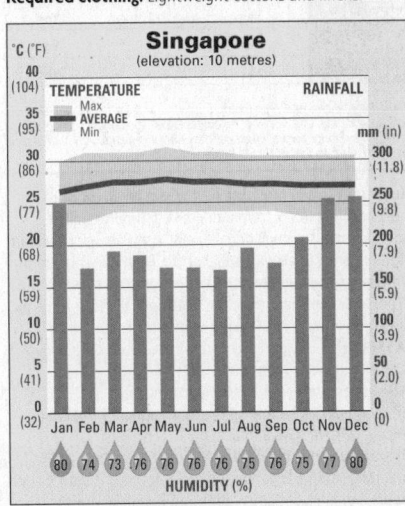

Communications

Telephone: Full IDD is available. Country code: 65. IDD calls made from hotels are free of surcharge.
Mobile telephone: Roaming agreements exist with international mobile phone companies. Coverage is good.
Internet: Internet cafes throughout Singapore provide public access to Internet and e-mail services.
Post: Airmail to Europe takes up to one week. There are limited postal facilities at many hotels. Post office hours: Mon-Fri 0830-1700, Sat 0830-1300. The airport and Orchard Point branches are open daily 0700-1900. The General Post Office on Fullerton Road (near the river) and the Comcentre near Orchard Road are open 24 hours.
MEDIA: Singapore's media environment has the shadow of Singaporean Government cast over it. Censorship is common; Internet access is regulated; and private ownership of satellite dishes is not allowed.
Press: Singapore Press Holdings, which has close links to the ruling party, has a virtual monopoly of the newspaper industry. The English-language dailies are *The Business Times* (website: http://business-times.asia1.com.sg), *The*

Credit: ©Singapore Tourism Board

New Paper, *The Straits Times* (website: http://straitstimes.asia1.com.sg) and *Today* (website: www.todayonline.com).

TV: *MediaCorp*, owned by a state investment agency, operates TV and radio stations.
MediaCorp operates *Channel 5* and *Channel 8*, which are entertainment-based channels, as well as the Malay-language channel, *Channel Suria*, Mandarin-language *Channel U* and *Channel NewsAsia*.

Radio: *MediaCorp* operates more than 12 stations in Singapore. *Unionworks* operates *WKRZ*, an English language station, and Mandarin station, *UFM*. *Radio Singapore International* operates broadcasts in four languages, including English.

Passport/Visa

	Passport Required?	Visa Required?	Return Ticket Required?
Full British	Yes	1	Yes
Australian	Yes	1	Yes
Canadian	Yes	1	Yes
USA	Yes	1	Yes
Other EU	Yes	1	Yes
Japanese	Yes	1	Yes

Note: *Regulations and requirements may be subject to change at short notice, and you are advised to contact the appropriate diplomatic or consular authority before finalising travel arrangements. Any numbers in the chart refer to the footnotes below.*

Note: (a) Women more than 24 weeks pregnant or more must obtain a letter from a doctor confirming that it is safe for them to travel and a Social Visit Pass For Expectant Mothers prior to arrival; apply at the High Commission or Embassy. (b) Severe penalties are imposed on those found in possession of narcotics; the death penalty is in force for those convicted of trafficking in heroin or morphine.
PASSPORTS: Passport valid for at least six months beyond date of departure required by all.
VISAS: Required *only* by the following:
(a) nationals of China (PR), CIS, Hong Kong (SAR), India, Macau (SAR) and Myanmar;
(b) nationals of Afghanistan, Algeria, Bangladesh, Egypt, Iran, Iraq, Jordan, Lebanon, Libya, Morocco, Pakistan, Saudi Arabia, Somalia, Sudan, Syrian Arab Republic, Tunisia, United Arab Emirates (temporary passport only) and Yemen.
Note: 1. All other nationals require a *Social Visit Pass*, which is issued on arrival, provided the traveller holds a valid passport, sufficient funds to cover stay in Singapore, confirmed onward/return tickets and entry documentation for further destinations. For nationals holding British and Irish passports, the maximum length of stay is 30 days, for other nationals, the maximum length of stay is 14 days. Visitors on a Social Visit Pass are not permitted to work in Singapore. Extentions of up to 90 days can be applied for at the time.
Types of visa and cost: *Entry Visa, Social Visit* (short- or long-term; S$20), *Business Visit* (£6.70), *Student's Pass* and *Transit*. For any extension of pass accumulating to a period of three months or more from the date of entry/issue and for every subsequent extension accumulating to three months or more, the cost is usually S$40. Payment by *NETS* or *CashCard* is preferable. Application packs with instructions and prevailing visa costs at the time of application are obtainable from the High Commission (see *Passport/Visa Information*).

Validity: At the discretion of the ICA.
Application to: Consulate (or Consular section at High Commission or Embassy); see *Passport/Visa Information*.
Application requirements: (a) Completed application form(s). (b) Two recent passport size photos. (c) Photocopies of valid passport. (d) Visa fee (payable by cash or postal order only. (e) Self-addressed, special delivery envelope if applicant wishes documents to be returned. (f) Letter of introduction form with signature of local sponsor (required by all except nationals of India and China (PR). *Business*: (a)-(f) and, (g) Printout of Singapore registered company's detailed business profile from ACRA. *Social Visit*: (a)-(f) and, (g) Local contact's Singapore identity card and photocopy. (h) Letter from the applicant's employer or unemployment booklet. *Student Pass*: (a)-(g) and (h) Applicant's birth certificate. (i) Applicant's highest education certificates. (j) Proof of financial means if applicant is from a country that always requires a visa.
Working days required: From two to four weeks for Level 2 nationals. Four working days for Level 1 nationals. However, it is still advisable to allow plenty of time. For those applying for *student* visas, allow two to six months.
Temporary residence: Apply to Consulate (or Consular section of High Commission or Embassy), who will forward application to the authorities in Singapore.

PASSPORT/VISA INFORMATION

High Commission for the Republic of Singapore in the UK
9 Wilton Crescent Belgravia, London SW1X 8SP, UK
Tel: (020) 7235 8315.
Website: www.mfa.gov.sg/london
Opening hours: Mon-Fri 0900-1700; 1000-1230 and 1400-1600 (visa section).

Embassy of the Republic of Singapore in the USA
3501 International Place, NW, Washington, DC 20008, USA
Tel: (202) 537 3100.
Website: www.mfa.gov.sg/washington

Money

Currency: Singapore Dollar (SGD; symbol S$) = 100 cents. Notes are in denominations of S$10,000, 1000, 500, 100, 50, 20, 10, 5 and 2. Coins are in denominations of S$1, and 50, 20, 10, 5 and 1 cents.
The currency of Brunei is also legal tender; 1 Brunei Dollar = 1 Singapore Dollar.
US Dollars, Australian Dollars, Yen and Pounds Sterling are also accepted at most major shopping centres in Singapore.
Currency exchange: Foreign currencies, traveller's cheques and cheques can be changed at most banks and licensed money changers; however, some do not offer this service on Saturday. ATMs are widespread.
Credit & debit cards: American Express, Diners Club, MasterCard and Visa are widely accepted. Check with your credit or debit card company for details of merchant acceptability and other facilities which may be available.
Traveller's cheques: To avoid additional exchange rate charges, travellers are advised to take traveller's cheques in Pounds Sterling. A passport is required when cashing traveller's cheques.
Currency restrictions: There is no restriction on the import and export of local or foreign currency.
Banking hours: Mon-Fri 1000-1500, Sat 0930-1300 (some are open until 1500). Branches of certain major banks on Orchard Road open Sun 0930-1500.

Exchange rate indicators:
Rate at time of publishing
£1.00=   S$2.89
$1.00=   S$1.63

Duty Free

The following goods may be imported into Singapore by persons aged 18 years and older without incurring customs duty:
1l of spirits, 1l of wine and 1l of beer.
Note: These allowances do not apply if arriving from Malaysia.
Restricted items: Fruit, vegetables, fish, arms, toy guns and weapons. Chewing gum and tobacco products must be declared upon arrival.
Prohibited items: Liquor or cigarettes with "Singapore duty not paid" on the label, carton or packet, cigarettes with the prefix 'E' printed on the packet, cigarette lighters of revolver or pistol shape, controlled drugs or psychotrophic substances, firecrackers, endangered species of wildlife and their byproducts, all pornographic films and literature, reproduction of copyright publications, videotapes, video compact discs, laser discs, records or cassettes.
Export permits are required for arms, ammunition, explosives, animals, telecommunications equipment, film and videotapes and discs, precious metals and stones, drugs and poisons.
The penalties for possession of narcotics are severe and visitors not complying with drug regulations do so at the risk of death.

Public Holidays

Below are listed Public Holidays for the January 2006-June 2007 period.
2006: Jan 1 New Year's Day. **Jan 10** Hari Raya Haji (Feast of the Sacrifice). **Jan 29-31** Chinese New Year. **Apr 14** Good Friday. **May 1** Labour Day. **May 13** Vesak (Birth of Buddha). **Aug 9** National Day. **Oct 21** Diwali. **Oct 22-24** Hari Raya Puasa (End of Ramadan). **Dec 25** Christmas Day. **Dec 31** Hari Raya Haji (Feast of the Sacrifice).
2007: Jan 1 New Year's Day. **Feb 18-20** Chinese New Year. **Apr 6** Good Friday. **May 1** Labour Day. **May 2** Vesak (Birth of Buddha).
Note: (a) Not all Muslim festivals listed above are national holidays, but all will affect Muslim businesses. Muslim festivals are timed according to local sightings of various phases of the moon and the dates given above are approximations. During the lunar month of Ramadan that precedes Hari Raya Puasa (Eid al-Fitr), Muslims fast during the day and feast at night and normal business patterns may be interrupted. Many restaurants are closed during the day and there may be restrictions on smoking and drinking. Some disruption may continue into Hari Raya Puasa itself. Hari Raya Puasa and Hari Raya Haji (Eid al-Adha) may last anything from two to 10 days, depending on the town. For more information, see the *World of Islam* appendix. (b) Hindu festivals are declared according to local astronomical observations and it is only possible to forecast the month of their occurrence.

Health

	Special Precautions?	Certificate Required?
Yellow Fever	No	1
Cholera	No	No
Typhoid & Polio	No	N/A
Malaria	No	N/A

Note: *Regulations and requirements may be subject to change at short notice, and you are advised to contact your doctor well in advance of your intended date of departure. Any numbers in the chart refer to the footnotes below.*

1: A *yellow fever* certificate of vaccination is required from persons over one year of age who have been in or passed through any country classified either partly or wholly as a *yellow fever* endemic zone within the previous six days. The countries formerly classified as endemic zones are considered by the Singapore authorities to be still infected.
Other risks: *Hepatitis A* and *E* are widespread; *hepatitis B* is hyperendemic.
Rabies is present. For those at high risk, vaccination before arrival should be considered. If you are bitten, seek medical advice without delay. For more information, consult the *Health* appendix.
HIV testing is required for workers who earn less than S$1250 per month and for applicants for permanent resident status. Foreign test results are not accepted.
Health care: Singapore General Hospital receives emergency cases and health care is exceptionally good. There is a large private sector. Health insurance is recommended, as there is no reciprocal health agreement with the UK.

Travel - International

AIR:

The national airline is *Singapore Airlines (SQ)* (website: www.singaporeair.com). Singapore is a major travel destination served by most major international airlines. There are direct flights to Singapore from a number of cities in Canada, the UK and USA.

Approximate flight times: From Singapore to *London* is 14 hours, to *Los Angeles* is 17 hours 25 minutes, to *New York* is 24 hours five minutes and to *Sydney* is nine hours 15 minutes.

Main airports: *Changi (SIN)* (website: www.changi.airport.com.sg) is 20km (12 miles) east of the city (travel time - 30 minutes). *To/from the airport:* Public transport is readily available to the city centre which is about 16km (10 miles) from the airport. Taxi fare is S$16-24 (there is a surcharge of S$3 for all fares from the airport, increasing to S$5 for fares between 1700-0000, Fri-Sat. The midnight surcharge, 0000-0600, is 50 per cent of the metered fare). There is a regular bus route between the airport and the train station. The Mass Rapid Transit train system now operates from the airport to the city centre and trains depart every 12 minutes. The Maxicab, a six-seater taxi shuttle, operates daily 0900-2300 and tickets cost S$7 (children: S$5); tickets must be bought in advance from the shuttle service counter in the arrivals hall. *Free New Asia – Singapore Tours* are available at no charge for transit passengers with a minimum layover of four hours. Passengers can sign up for a tour at a Free New Asia – Singapore Tour counter located in the airport's transit areas. *Facilities:* Fitness centre, swimming pool, supermarket, medical clinics and full banking services (including money changing) to business centres and transit hotels with private bathrooms (advance booking is recommended for the hotels). There are left luggage facilities, post offices, bars and restaurants, extensive duty free shops and car hire operators.

Departure tax: None.

SEA:

Main ports: *Singapore*. The world's busiest in terms of tonnage, it is served by a growing number of international passenger cruise lines. Cruising is one of the fastest-growing tourist development areas in Singapore and there are plans to considerably expand the already extensive port facilities. There is now also a number of international operators using Singapore as a base for cruises throughout South-East Asia. For further details, contact the Singapore Tourism Board (see *Top Things To See & Do*).

RAIL:

Trains run to Kuala Lumpur, Johor Bahru and Malacca (Malaysia) on a route which extends to Bangkok (Thailand). Services operate daily between Singapore and Kuala Lumpur; some offer air conditioning and dining cars. There are also overnight trains with sleepers. For more information on the railway between Thailand and Singapore, see online (website: www.ktmb.com.my). The *Eastern and Oriental Express* is a luxurious train travelling from Thailand and Malaysia to Singapore.

ROAD:

Singapore is connected to Malaysia and the mainland of Asia by two causeways: one which crosses the Johor Strait; the other linking Tuas in Singapore. Foreign motorists are required to pay a Vehicle Entry Permit (VEP) and a toll charge at the checkpoint upon entry into Singapore. Payment is to be paid using an electronic smartcard called an Autopass Card (sold at booths or VEP/toll offices at the checkpoint). Motorists need to show a valid road tax disc and an insurance certificate for the vehicle when buying the Autopass Card. A VEP costs S$20 per day, Mon-Fri, 0200-1700. Toll charges are payable upon arrival and departure from Singapore using the Tuas checkpoint (S$3.20 per trip) and on departure from Singapore at the Woodlands checkpoint (S$1.20). Bus and coach services operate to the Malaysian town of Johor Bahru and beyond. For required documentation, see *Travel – Internal* section. Buses arriving from Malaysia and Thailand terminate at the Lavender Street terminal.

Travel - Internal

AIR:

Sightseeing flights can be arranged locally through the *Republic of Singapore Flying Club* (Building 140-B, Piccadilly, Seletar Airbase, Eastcamp, Singapore 797754; tel: (065) 6481 0200; website: www.singaporeflyingclub.com).

SEA:

The Singapore Cruise Centre is located at the World Trade Centre, about 10 minutes' drive from the city centre. Harbour cruises and ferry services to Singapore's islands, Malaysia and the Indonesian Riau islands may be boarded at the ferry terminals located at the World Trade Centre and Tanah Merah Ferry Terminal at Changi. A ferry for Sentosa, the most popular offshore island, leaves every 20 minutes starting at 0730.

RAIL:

There are regular and well-maintained train services between all major cities and towns.

ROAD:

Bus: There is a well-developed system of local services run by two main companies. The service is cheap and efficient and operates 0600-0000 daily. Three *City Buzz* services loop the city 1000-2200 daily. Fares are priced at S$1 per trip or a City Buzz Pass Pack costs S$5 for a day's unlimited travel. A *SIA* hop-on, hop-off service operates daily 0900-1800. There are additional peak-hours-only shuttle and minibus services. A flat fare system operates on the one-man routes. A timetable and route map are available from bookstores. **Car hire:** There are several car hire/self-drive firms with offices at the airport and in hotels. Traffic drives on the left. All motorists driving into the city or travelling on some major roads are required to pay the ERP (Electronic Road Pricing). The cost is S$5 per day (some vehicles have a device fitted which means that payment is automatic). **Documentation:** A national driving licence is sufficient for stays up to one month. For visits beyond one month, an International Driving Permit is required.

URBAN:

Taxi: These are numerous and relatively cheap. They can be picked up from outside hotels and official ranks or flagged down in the streets. Taxis are metered. Some surcharges not shown on the metre include: S$1 for all luggage placed in the boot; 50 per cent of the metered fare for journeys between 0000 and 0600; S$3 for all journeys starting at the airport; S$1 for all trips starting in the Central Business District, Mon-Fri 1630-1900 and Sat 1130-1400. It is possible to negotiate hourly rates for round-island tours.

Metro: Singapore has one of the most advanced metro systems in the world. The trains operate 0530-0300 (0600-0000 on Sundays and public holidays) with stations being served on average every six minutes. Fares range from 70 cents to S$1.60. The *Mass Rapid Transit (MRT)* is a modern, comfortable, efficient and cheap way to explore Singapore. Operation hours are 0530-0000 and the train timetables are posted at each station. Over 40 stations link the city centre and suburbs, thus providing an opportunity to visit some of Singapore's attractions along the three main routes. The MRT system also extends out to Changi Airport (travel time from city centre - 27 minutes). '*A Quick Guide to the MRT Travel*' is available from MRT stations.

Trishaws: This traditional form of chauffeur-pedalled transport is a fun and exciting way to tour the streets of Singapore.

Travel Advice

Most visits to Singapore are trouble-free, but travellers should be aware that Singapore shares with the rest of South-East Asia a threat from terrorism. Attacks could be indiscriminate and against civilian targets, including places frequented by foreigners.

Travellers should not become involved with drugs of any kind: possession of even very small quantities can lead to imprisonment or the death penalty.

This advice is based on information provided by the Foreign and Commonwealth Office in the UK. It is correct at time of publishing. As the situation can change rapidly, visitors are advised to contact the following organisaions for the latest travel advice:

British Foreign and Commonwealth Office
Tel: (0845) 850 2829.
Website: www.fco.gov.uk

US Department of State
Website: http://travel.state.gov/travel

Accommodation

HOTELS:

There is a wide variety of accommodation, ranging from budget to modern high-class hotels. These have extensive facilities, including swimming pools, health clubs, several restaurants, full business services and shopping arcades. It is advisable to make advance reservations. All rooms are subject to 4 per cent tax and 10 per cent service charge. For further information on accommodation in Singapore, contact the Singapore Tourism Board (see *Top Things To See & Do*) who can supply the *Singapore Hotels Directory*. Some hotels are designated as being 'International Standard' with all modern conveniences such as swimming pools and air conditioning, and prices range from S$100 a night. However, there is no formal star system of grading.

GUEST HOUSES:

The majority of the guest houses are situated along Bencoolen Street and Beach Road. Although considerably cheaper than the main hotels, guest houses tend not to be good value for money; the price per night is usually between S$20 and S$30 for a small, ill-equipped room. Discounts are sometimes available when staying a few days.

YOUTH HOSTELS:

There are at least a dozen hostel-style establishments offering communal dormitory accommodation; the average price for a night's accommodation is S$10 or less. There is one YMCA international hostel in Singapore.

CAMPING:

The few campsites there are in Singapore are inconveniently located, making camping a difficult option. Campsites are: Changi Beach Park, East Coast Park, Pasir Ris Park, Sembawang Park and West Coast Park; permits are required to camp on a week-night. Tents can be rented from the Universal Adventure shop on Pulau Ubin, and can be pitched on open land on the island. The official campsite is called Jelutong; no permit is required.

ACCOMMODATION INFORMATION

Singapore Hotel Association
21 Bukit Batok Street 22, Singapore 659589
Tel: 6415 3588.
Website: www.sha.org.sg

Top Things To See & Do

- **Shop** in **Singapore City**'s **Orchard Road** - the 'Fifth Avenue' or 'Oxford Street' of Singapore, and just as bustling, with its vast luxury malls, shops ranging from megastores to vendors of souvenir tat, as well as cafes and restaurants. **Arab Street** is the centre of the Arabian quarter of Singapore, and is also a great place for shopping. Other streets with excellent shopping opportunities are **Baghdad Street** and **Bussorah Street**, while **Sultan Plaza** is a centre for cloth traders. The golden domes of the **Sultan Mosque**, Singapore's chief Muslim place of worship, dominate the area; nearby are two historic Muslim burial grounds. **Chinatown**, though somewhat overwhelmed by the growth of the **Financial District**, is another bustling and colourful area with shops, teahouses and restaurants, and also several temples such as the **Fuk Tak Ch'i in Telok Ayer Street** and the **Temple of the Calm Sea**. Ancient crafts of calligraphy, papermaking and fortune-telling are practised, and traditional goods and foodstuffs can be bought. The characteristic domestic architecture of Singapore – the shop-house with a moulded front, shuttered upper floor and an arcaded street front – is much in evidence.
- Prop up the bar at the **Raffles Hotel**, one of the most famous hotels in the world. A '**Singapore Sling**' (a head-spinningly good cocktail) in the **Long Bar** is almost de rigueur; to sober up, drop into the **Writers' Bar**, which provided inspiration for, amongst others, Noel Coward, Somerset Maugham and Joseph Conrad.
- Near the **Singapore River**, wander towards the **Parliament House**, the oldest Government building in the country, the core of which dates back to the 1820s.
- Explore the **National Orchid Garden** in Singapore's **Botanic Gardens**, which has the largest collection of orchids in the world. The Botanic Gardens have over 52 hectares (128 acres) of landscaped parkland and primary jungle and are situated to the west of the city (**Napier/Cluny Road**s), home to a wide range of animal and plant life. For more exotic treats of nature, venture into the **Bukit Timah Reserve**, established in 1883 and located northwest of the Botanic Gardens on **Bukit Timah Road**; it contains Singapore's last stretches of original and immaculately manicured rain forest. The nature reserve also consists of tropical vegetation with clearly marked trails which lead up to **Bukit Timah**, the highest hill in Singapore.
- View what was once an ancient fort of the Malay kings, covering 2.8 hectares (7 acres): **Fort Canning Park**, on **Fort Canning Rise**. The Colonial ruins of the **British citadel** can still be viewed, as can a 19th-century Christian cemetery. The **Battle Box** in the park is the old command bunker of the World War II defence of Singapore, now a museum open Tues-Sun 1000-1800, with a small admission fee charged.
- Buddhist and Hindu **temples**, **mosques** and Anglican and Catholic **cathedrals** are all likely to be encountered during a comparatively brief walk around some of the central areas of Singapore, such is its splendid diversity. **St Andrew's Cathedral**, the **Cathedral of the Good Shepherd**, the **Al-Abrar Mosque**, the vast and florid **Kong Meng Sang Phor Kark See Temple Complex**, the **Chettiar Hindu Temple** and the **Sri Mariamman Temple** are only a few of these.
- The **Jurong Bird Park** on **Jurong Hill** is home to South-

East Asia's largest collection of **birds**. There is also the world's largest walk-in **aviary**, a nocturnal house and several spectacular bird shows.

- The largest and best-known of Singapore's offshore islands is also one of the closest to the mainland. **Sentosa** is a multi-million dollar pleasure resort girdled by a monorail and offering a wide range of activities and attractions. These include the **Underwater World** and **Dolphin Lagoon**, **Images of Singapore**, the recently upgraded **Musical Fountain Show**, **The Merlion**, the **Butterfly Park & Insect Kingdom Museum**, **Sijori WonderGolf** and the **Carlsberg Sky Tower**. Lovely gardens, beautiful beaches and a plethora of restaurants and eating places all contribute to the island's popularity with tourists and locals alike. Many prefer to skip the theme park attractions and head straight for Sentosa's beaches – **Palawan**, **Siloso** and **Tanjong** – where a wide range of watersports is available. These were built with imported white sand and are often crowded, especially at weekends. There are bus, monorail and tram services linking Sentosa to the city centre, and the causeway bridge is open to foot traffic. An admission fee for entry to the island is charged and composite tickets can also be bought which give admission to some of the attractions.. Resort hotels, camping and other accommodation are available on the island.

- **Canoe** around the island - there are a number of operators hiring out canoes at **Changi point**, **East Coast** and **Sentosa Island**.

Credit: ©Singapore Tourism Board

TOURIST INFORMATION

Singapore Tourism Board in the UK
1st Floor, Carrington House, 126-130 Regent Street, London W1B 5JX, UK
Tel: (020) 7437 0033 or (08080) 656 565 (toll-free in the UK).
Website: www.visitsingapore.com

Singapore Tourism Board in the USA
1156 Avenue of the Americas Suite 702 New York NY 10036, USA
Tel: (212) 302 4861.
Website: www.visitsingapore.com

Entertainment

FOOD & DRINK: Singapore is a gourmet's paradise, ranging from humble street stalls to 5-star restaurants. There are over 30 different cooking styles, including various regional styles of Chinese cuisine, American, English, French, Indian, Indonesian, Italian, Japanese, Korean, Malay, Russian and Swiss. Malay cuisine is a favourite, famed for its use of spices and coconut milk.

Things to know: One of the best ways to eat in Singapore is in the open at one of the ubiquitous street foodstalls. Some are quiet and casual while others are in areas bustling with activity. All have a vast selection of cheap, mouthwatering food. Newton Circus and La Pau Sat are food centres where all types of Asian food can be sampled cheaply. Although there are many self-service establishments, waiter service is more common in restaurants. Bars/cocktail lounges often have table and counter service. There are no licensing hours. 'Happy hours' are usually from 1700-1900.

National specialities:
- *Beef rendang* (coconut milk beef curry).
- *Chicken sambal*.
- *Gado gado* (a fruit and vegetable salad in peanut sauce).
- *Satay* (skewers of marinated meat cooked over charcoal) served with peanut sauce, cucumber, onion and rice.

National drinks:
- *Singapore Sling* (cocktail containing gin, cherry liquor, cointreau, benedictine, pineapple juice, lime juice, grenadine and angostura bitters). It was founded in the early 20th century for the Raffles Hotel in Singapore.
- *Teh arak tarik* (ginger tea with milk).
- Soya bean milk.
- Sugar cane juice.

Tipping: Officially discouraged in restaurants, hotels and the airport. A 10 per cent service charge is included in restaurant bills.

NIGHTLIFE: Singapore has a vibrant and exciting nightlife. Entertainment ranges from bars, clubs, discos, karaoke pubs, street opera, night markets, river cruises, multiplex cinemas to theatre productions and international stage shows. Boat Quay and Clarke Quay are popular riverside landmarks that offer exclusive restaurants, alfresco dining and lively bars. Moored Chinese junks have been refurbished into floating bars and restaurants. Bugis Street, Changi Village and Holland Village, known as Holland V, are popular areas for food, drink and entertainment. Muhammad Sultan Road is one of the latest entertainment hubs in Singapore with a wide variety of pubs, nightclubs and wine bars, as is Club Street.

SHOPPING: The vast range of available goods and competitive prices have led to Singapore rightly being known as a shopper's paradise. Special purchases include Balinese, Chinese, Filipino, Indian and Malay antiques; batiks; cameras; Chinese, Indian and Persian carpets; imported or tailored clothing; jewellery and specialised items made of reptile and snake skins, including shoes, briefcases, handbags and wallets. Silks, perfumes, silverware and wigs are other favourite buys. The herding of shop owners from 'Chinatown' into multi-storey complexes lost some of the exciting shopping atmosphere, although these huge centres do provide an air-conditioned environment. Orchard Road is the main shopping street, although many of the large hotel complexes, such as Marina Square, have shopping centres attached. Although most outlets operate Western-style fixed pricing, bargains can still be made in some places but generally only after good research and shrewd negotiating. Electrical equipment of all types can be bought at Sungei Road, but caution is advised as there are many imitation products around. For more information on shopping in Singapore, see the *Singapore Shopping* brochure published by the Singapore Tourism Board.

Shopping hours: Mon-Fri 1000-2100, Sat 1000-2200. The Mustafa Centre in Little India is open 24-hours.

Note: A 5 per cent Goods and Services Tax (GST) is levied on most goods and services purchased from taxable retailers. Tourists whose purchases total S$100 or more from a single retailer participating in the Tourist Refund Scheme are eligible for a refund of the GST paid on goods not consumed in Singapore. Refunds may be received at the airport, prior to departure flights

Credit: ©Singapore Tourism Board

Business

- **GDP:** US$110 billion.
- **Main imports:** Machines and equipment, mineral fuels, chemicals and foodstuffs.
- **Main exports:** Machinery and equipment, consumer goods, chemicals and mineral fuels.
- **Main trade partners:** China (PR), Hong Kong (SAR), Japan, Korea (Rep), Malaysia, Taiwan (China), Thailand and USA.

ECONOMY: Singapore's economy relies on entrepôt trade, shipbuilding and repairing, oil refining, electronics and information technology, banking and finance and, to a lesser extent, tourism. From the late 1970s, the Government promoted export-oriented and service industries with the intention of making Singapore a regional economic hub. Singapore also derived some benefit from the decision of some companies to relocate following the reversion of Hong Kong to Chinese administration in 1997. High-technology manufacturing, particularly computer and telecommunications equipment, and financial services, mainly banking and insurance, form the kernel of the economy. There is also an important oil-refining industry. The newest addition to the economic portfolio is pharmaceuticals: on top of that, the Government is promoting Singapore as a centre for biotechnology, especially for stem cell research which has proved so controversial elsewhere. The importance of trade to the economy cannot be overstated: the total value of Singapore's trade is almost three times its GDP (compared with 17 per cent of GDP in the case of Japan). Vibrant economic activity more than compensates for Singapore's lack of natural resources. There is a little agriculture, with the cultivation of plants and vegetables, and some fishing; however, most foodstuffs and raw materials have to be imported. Singapore's only significant natural resource is its superb natural harbour, which is the busiest in the world after Rotterdam. This accounts in part for the high level of Singapore's re-export trade, which accounts for almost half of all trade.

Credit: ©Singapore Tourism Board

Singapore was less affected than many of its neighbours by the 1997 Asian financial crisis, owing to sound financial management, high savings and investment rates, and massive foreign exchange reserves. However, shortly afterwards the territory was plunged into its worst economic recession for 30 years, largely because of a sudden collapse of international demand in key industries, especially electronics. At the lowest point, Singapore's economy was contracting at an unprecedented rate of 6 per cent per annum. Industrial production fell by over 20 per cent during 2001. GDP growth was a paltry 0.8 per cent in 2003, but that figure rose to a robust 8.4 per cent in 2004. Current inflation is 1.7 per cent. Singapore is a member of the Association of South East Asian Nations (ASEAN) and of the Asian Pacific Economic Forum (APEC).

BUSINESS ETIQUETTE: English is widely spoken in business circles. Appointments should be made and punctuality is important. Chinese people should be addressed with their surnames first, while Malays do not have surnames but use the initial of their father's name before their own. Visiting cards are essential, although it is policy for Government officials not to use them.

Office hours: Mon-Fri 0900-1300 and 1400-1700, Sat 0900-1300.

CONFERENCES/CONVENTIONS: Singapore is the top convention city in Asia and ranks among the top 10 meetings destinations in the world. There are many hotels with extensive conference facilities, including the latest audio-visual equipment, secretarial services, translation and simultaneous interpretation systems, whilst Raffles City, a self-contained convention city, can accommodate up to 6000 delegates under one roof. Other popular venues for larger conventions and exhibitions include Suntec Singapore and Singapore Expo, the country's latest addition to conference venues. Full information on Singapore as a conference destination can be obtained from the Exhibition & Convention Bureau within the Singapore Tourism Board (see *Top Things To See & Do*). The Bureau is a non-profitmaking organisation with the dual objectives of marketing Singapore as an international exhibition and convention city and of assisting with the planning and staging of individual events.

COMMERCIAL INFORMATION

Singapore Indian Chamber of Commerce and Industry
101 Cecil Street, Tong Eng Building, Unit 23-01/04, Singapore 069533
Tel: 6224 2505 or 2855.
Website: www.sicci.com

Singapore International Chamber of Commerce
10-01 John Hancock Tower, 6 Raffles Quay, Singapore 048580
Tel: 6224 1255.
Website: www.sicc.com.sg

Credit: ©Slovak Tourist Board

Slovak Republic

Location: Central Europe.

Time: GMT + 2 (GMT + 1 from last Sunday in October to last Saturday in March).

Overview

The Slovak Republic was definitely the 'junior partner' throughout its 20th century alliance with the Czech Republic. Modernisation fell well behind that of the Czech Republic and the Czech's fairytale Prague is not wholly mirrored by the Slovak Republic's capital, Bratislava. However, Bratislava is vibrant, with a wonderful Old Town. In addition, it contains palaces bearing the architectural style of almost every age: Renaissance, Baroque, Rococo, Classical. There is much to indicate that tourism in the Slovak Republic is blossoming, and the infrastructure to abet that continually improves.

The separation of Czechoslovakia into its constituent parts – the Czech and Slovak Republics – on 1 January 1993 was one of the rare occasions in history that two nations have accomplished this peacefully. Indeed, it is not strictly fair to forge comparisons with neighbouring countries since, what proceeded this event were repeated attempts at invasion from the moment Slav peoples settled in the middle Danube region in the fifth and sixth centuries. Over the 10th century, marauding, nomadic Magyar tribes gradually settled in the region and created an embryonic Hungarian state. This period came to an end after a major military defeat in 1526 at the hands of the Ottoman Turks. Slovakia, however, resisted Ottoman occupation and allied itself with the Austrian Hapsburg monarchy. Between 1526 and 1784, Bratislava was nominated capital of the 'Kingdom of Hungary' and over a dozen Hapsburg monarchs were crowned in the city. The first nationalist movements began to emerge but the Slovak struggle for independence suffered a setback in 1867 when Austria gave the Hungarians free rein within its territories. With the end of World War I and the Austro-Hungarian Empire came the birth of Czechoslovakia. With the advent of Nazism in 1938, a dark period followed, with the country effectively under German control. After Alexander Dubcek's (then leader of the Communist Party of Czechoslovakia) 'socialism with a human face' and the Prague Spring came democratic socialism, finally yielding to democratic reforms in 1989. This led to the appointment of Václav Havel as President while the country introduced a pluralistic political system and a market economy. However, the Slovaks were worried about the crash liberalisation programme planned by Havel and his Finance Minister, Václav Klaus. It was then, in 1993, that the two nations parted amicably.

Such history pinpoints the crucial need to celebrate the Slovak Republic in its own right. It is a country that reaches its pinnacle of beauty in the Tatra Mountains and, indeed, teems with lowlands, canyons, caves and meadows; such a wide variation ensures that the Slovak Republic can provide both year-round beauty and year-round activities, from

hiking in the summer to skiing in the winter. Although Slovak history is one of immense Magyar cultural repression, the country emerged from more than a millennium of Hungarian serfdom with its language and identity largely intact, and cultural events and proud national demonstrations abound. Go with an open mind, and your expectations will surely be exceeded.

General Information

AREA: 49,033 sq km (18,932 sq miles).
POPULATION: 5.4 million (official estimate 2005).
POPULATION DENSITY: 110.1 per sq km.
CAPITAL: Bratislava. **Population:** 617,000 (2000).
GEOGRAPHY: The Slovak Republic is situated in Central Europe, sharing frontiers with the Czech Republic, Austria, Poland, Hungary and Ukraine. Mountains, lowlands, canyons, lakes, cave formations, forests and meadows provide many examples of the Slovak Republic's year-round natural beauty. The Slovak Republic is a small country but its terrain varies impressively from lowlands to mountain ranges. Almost half of the country is taken up by the Carpathian Arc, a range of mountains stretching across the north. The smaller ranges include the Lesser Carpathians, White Carpathians, Malá (Lesser) Fatra, Vel'ká (Greater) Fatra, High and Low Tatras and the Slovenské rudohorie Mountains (Slovak Ore Mountains).
GOVERNMENT: Republic since 1993. **Head of State:** President Ivan Gasparovic since 2004. **Head of Government:** Prime Minister Mikulás Dzurinda since 1998.
Recent history: Following the first democratic elections of June 1990 between the two republican Governments, the population voted for the 'sovereignty association' platform proposed by Vladimir Meciar.
The Slovak Republic ratified its first national constitution in September 1992, having agreed to all of the existing treaties and obligations of the former Republic. Under its terms, executive power lies with the Prime Minister and Ministers, the first being appointed by the President, who in turn is selected by the National Council. This is the country's supreme legislative body, which has 150 seats and is directly elected for a four-year term. The President is elected for a five-year term.

On 1 January 1993, the nation parted amicably with the Czech Republic. The following month, the former speaker of the Czechoslovak Parliament, Michal Kovac, was chosen by the country's new Parliament, the National Council (*Narodna Rada*), to take over the post of President. The party leader, Meciar, continued as Prime Minister at the Head of Movement for a Democratic Slovakia-dominated (*Hnutie za Demokratice Slovensko, HZDS*) Government. From then until the expiry of President Kovac's term of office in March 1998, Slovak politics were dominated by the feud between these two dominant political figures. Meciar was much lauded at the time as the principal architect of Slovakian nationhood. However, he was not a natural democrat, and his use of state agencies to suppress opponents and blatant tolerance of organised crime provoked strong international criticism. Nor was Meciar enthusiastic about the economic reforms which were equally essential to any EU aspiration. The struggle between Meciar and Kovac, a pro-European, pro-NATO liberal, reached extraordinary levels, but came to an end when Meciar was outmanoeuvred for control of both the Presidency (which was won by Rudolf Schuster) and the National Assembly. He tried to stage a comeback at the Parliamentary election held in 2002 but narrowly failed. Mikulas Dzurinda continued as Prime Minister at the head of a centre-right coalition set up specifically to keep the HZDS, which is still the country's largest political party, away from power. Under Schuster and Dzurinda, Slovakia made up for lost time, embarking on an economic reform programme and accelerating membership negotiations with the EU. By 2004, along with nine other countries, including most of its immediate neighbours, Slovakia joined the EU. However, Slovakia witnessed a dramatic Presidential clash between the controversial Meciar and Ivan Gasparovic only two weeks before Slovakia joined the EU, in late-April. Meciar, the hardline nationalist, was defeated; this was heralded as a victory for Slovakia's re-emergence on the global stage. However, some claimed that votes were cast against Meciar rather than in favour of Gasparovic; the elections witnessed an all-time-low turnout. It is still unclear whether Slovakia will succeed in moving forward under President Gasparovic's rule or whether Gasparovic will revert to the policies of Meciar that he once backed. Elections are scheduled to take place in 2006.
LANGUAGE: The official language is Slovak. Hungarian, Ruthenian, Ukrainian and German are spoken by ethnic minorities. English is also spoken.
RELIGION: The majority is Roman Catholic. Protestant churches comprise the remainder with Reformed, Lutheran, Methodist and Baptist denominations. There is also a Jewish minority. There is a Greek Orthodox minority in Eastern Slovak Republic.
ELECTRICITY: Generally 230 volts AC, 50Hz. Round two-pin plugs are in use. Lamp fittings are normally of the screw type.
SOCIAL CONVENTIONS: Shaking hands is the customary form of greeting. Punctuality is appreciated on social occasions. The minimum drinking age is 18.

Climate

The Slovak Republic lies in a moderate zone and possesses a continental climate with four distinct seasons. The average daily temperature in Bratislava in winter is -2°C (31 °F), rising to 21°C (70 °F) in the summer. January is the coldest month, the hottest being July and August. The highest peaks are snowcapped 130 days a year.

Required clothing: Mediumweights, heavy topcoat and overshoes for winter; lightweights for summer. Rainwear is advisable throughout the year.

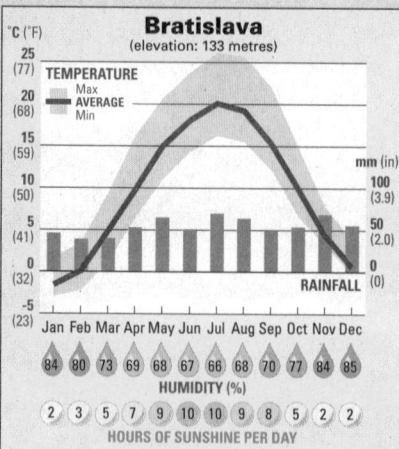

Bratislava
(elevation: 133 metres)

Communications

Telephone: IDD is available. Country code: 421. There are public telephone booths, including special kiosks for international calls. Surcharges can be quite high on long-distance calls from hotels. Dial 112 for all emergency services.

Mobile telephone: Roaming agreements exist with most international mobile phone companies. Coverage is good, extending over the whole country, with the exception of remote areas.

Internet: There are Internet cafes in main towns.

Post: Post office hours: Mon-Fri 0800-1800.

MEDIA: The constitution guarantees freedom of expression. All major daily newspapers are private and there are over 20 private radio stations. The introduction of commercial TV in the 1990s caused public broadcaster Slovak TV to lose a significant portion of its audience, with private TV broadcaster Markiza now claiming much of the audience. Cable and satellite TV are widely watched. Channels from neighbouring countries, such as the Czech Republic and Hungary, have a sizeable audience.

Press: The *Slovak Spectator*, the Slovak Republic's English-language newspaper, is published weekly; *Slovak Foreign Trade* is published monthly by the Slovak Chamber of Commerce. The principal dailies are *Novy Cas*, *Pravda* and *Sme*. Popular weekly Slovak magazines include *Plus 7 dni*, *Slovenka* and *Zivot*.

TV: *Slovak TV* is the public broadcaster: *TV Markiza*, *TA3* and *TV Joj* are all commercial networks.

Radio: *Slovak Radio* is a public broadcaster, operating five national networks and an external service. *Radio Expres*, *Radio Okey* and *Radio Twist* are all commercial stations, as is *Fun Radio*, a commercial News Agency

Passport/Visa

	Passport Required?	Visa Required?	Return Ticket Required?
Full British	1	No	No
Australian	Yes	No	No
Canadian	Yes	No	No
USA	Yes	No	No
Other EU	1	No/2	No
Japanese	Yes	No	No

Note: *Regulations and requirements may be subject to change at short notice, and you are advised to contact the appropriate diplomatic or consular authority before finalising travel arrangements. Any numbers in the chart refer to the footnotes below.*

Passport valid for at least three months beyond the length of stay required by all except:
(a) **1.** EU/EEA nationals (EU+ Iceland, Liechtenstein, Norway) and Swiss nationals holding a valid national ID card.
Note: EU and EEA nationals are only required to produce evidence of their EU/EEA nationality and identity in order to be admitted to any EU/EEA Member State. This evidence can take the form of a valid national passport *or* national identity card. Either is acceptable. Possession of a return ticket, any length of validity on their document, sufficient funds for the length of their proposed visit should *not* be imposed.
(b) nationals of Croatia holding a valid national ID card.

VISAS: Required by all except the following:
(a) EU nationals, nationals referred to in the chart above for stays of up to 90 days for tourist or transit purposes only

(except full British passport holders, who also do not need visas for business purposes for an indefinite period, and Italy, who are only visa exempt for up to 30 days);
(b) nationals of Andorra, Argentina, Aruba, Brazil, Brunei, Chile, El Salvador, Guatemala, Honduras, Hong Kong (SAR), Israel, Korea (Rep), Macau, Malaysia, Mexico, New Zealand, Nicaragua, Panama, Paraguay, Singapore, Switzerland, the Netherlands Antilles, Uruguay and Venezuela for stays of up to 90 days;
(c) **2.** nationals of Malta for stays of up to 180 days;
(d) nationals of Monaco for stays of up to three months;
(e) nationals of Bolivia, Bulgaria, Costa Rica, Holy See, Romania, San Marino and United Nations passport holders for stays of up to 30 days;
(f) holders of Refugee Travel Documents (Convention of 28 July 1951) are visa exempt, provided refugee status is given according to the Convention and status of EU states (*except* refugee status from Austria, Cyprus, Estonia, Greece, Hungary, Latvia, Lithuania, Poland, Slovak Republic and Slovenia), and from Iceland, Liechtenstein, Norway and Switzerland.
Note: (a) Visitors should have the equivalent funds of US$50 per person per day for their stay in the Slovak Republic; this may be checked by customs. (b) Further information is available from the Ministry of Foreign Affairs (website: www.foreign.gov.sk).

Types of visa and cost: *Tourist/Transit/Airport Transit*: £25 (single-entry); £52 (multiple-entry). *Transit*: £21 (two-way/return).
Note: (a) There is a processing fee of £2 per application.
(b) Visa cost continually fluctuates according to the exchange rate.
Validity: *Tourist*: *Single-entry*: up to 90 days; *Multiple-entry*: Unlimited number of 90-day stays during a 90-day period. *Transit*: Valid for 90 days for a maximum stay of five days (plus seven reserve days). *Airport Transit*: Three days within airport confines.
Note: *Tourist* visas can be issued a maximum 90 days before the intended start date.
Application to: Consular section at Embassy in person; see *Passport/Visa Information*.
Application requirements: (a) Passport valid beyond requested validity of visa, with one blank page. (b) Completed application form. (c) One passport-size photo. (d) Fee (including processing fee), payable by cash, cheque or postal order. (e) A stamped, self-addressed envelope for visas delivered by mail. (f) Valid health and travel insurance.
Working days required: Between one week to 30 days. However, all visa applications are referred to the Slovak Immigration Headquarters and local Embassies can not guarantee the time required for processing.
Temporary residence: Special application form required; enquire at the Embassy.

Credit: ©Slovak Tourist Board

PASSPORT/VISA INFORMATION

Embassy of the Slovak Republic in the UK
25 Kensington Palace Gardens, London W8 4QY, UK
Tel: (020) 7313 6470/1 *or* 313 6490 (consular section) *or* (09065) 508 956 (recorded visa information; calls cost £1 per minute).
Website: www.slovakembassy.co.uk
Opening hours: Mon-Fri 1000-1300.

Embassy of the Slovak Republicin the USA
3523 International Court, NW, Washington, DC 20008, USA
Tel: (202) 237 1054.
Website: www.slovakembassy-us.org

Money

Currency: Slovenská Koruna (SKK) = 100 halierov. Notes are in denominations of SKK5000, 1000, 500, 100, 50 and 20. Coins are in denominations of SKK10, 5, 2 and 1, and 50 halierov. Further information can be found online (website: www.nbs.sk).
Currency exchange: Foreign currency (including traveller's cheques) can be exchanged at bureaux de change, main hotels, all banks, road border crossings, as well as major travel agencies.
Credit & debit cards: Major credit cards (American Express, Diners Club, and MasterCard/Eurocard Visa) and debit cards (Eurocheque cards, Maestro and Visa Electron)

are widely accepted. Check with your credit or debit card company for details of merchant acceptability and other services which may be available.
Traveller's cheques: American Express, Thomas Cook and Visa traveller's cheques are accepted in banks and at bureaux de change. Exchange rate charges are at least 1 per cent of the nominal cheque value. To avoid additional charges, travellers are advised to take traveller's cheques in Euros, US Dollars or Pounds Sterling.
Currency restrictions: The import and export of local and foreign currency is permitted up to an amount equivalent of SKK150,000, which must be declared.
Banking hours: Generally Mon-Fri 0800-1800.
Exchange rate indicators:
Rate at Time of Publishing
£1.00=   SKK55.89
$1.00=   SKK32.12

Duty Free

The following goods may be imported into the Slovak Republic by visitors 18 years of age or older without incurring customs duty:
200 cigarettes, 100 cigarillos, 50 cigars and 250g of tobacco products; 1l of spirits and 2l of wine; 50g of perfume or 250ml of eau de toilette; gifts up to the value of €175; foodstuffs, fruits and flowers for personal use; medicine according to personal use.
Note: (a) All items of value, such as cameras and tents, must be declared at customs on entry in order to facilitate export clearance on departure. (b) Only half the above quantities are permitted if stay is less than two days. (c) Arms and ammunition require a licence. (d) House pets can only be transported with veterinary permission. (e) Objects of art and historical value need a licence and customs duty.
Abolition of duty free goods within the EU: On June 30 1999, the sale of duty free alcohol and tobacco at airports and at sea was abolished in all of the original 15 EU member states. Of the 10 new member states that joined the EU on May 1 2004, these rules already apply to Cyprus and Malta. There are transitional rules in place for visitors returning to one of the original 15 EU countries from one of the other new EU countries. But for the original 15, plus Cyprus and Malta, there are now no limits imposed on importing tobacco and alcohol products from one EU country to another (with the exceptions of Denmark, Finland and Sweden, where limits *are* imposed). Travellers should note that they may be required to prove at customs that the goods purchased are for personal use *only*.

Public Holidays

Below are Public Holidays for the January 2006-June 2007 period.
2006: Jan 1 New Year's Day and Independence Day of the Slovak Republic. **Jan 6** Catholic Epiphany. **Apr 14** Good Friday. **Apr 17** Easter Monday. **May 1** May Day. **May 8** Liberation of the Republic. **Jul 5** Day of the Apostles St Cyril and St Methodius. **Aug 29** Anniversary of the Slovak National Uprising. **Sep 1** Day of Constitution of the Slovak Republic. **Sep 15** Our Lady of the Seven Sorrows. **Nov 1** All Saints' Day. **Nov 17** Day of Freedom and Democracy of the Slovak Republic. **Dec 24-26** Christmas.
2007: Jan 1 New Year's Day and Independence Day of the Slovak Republic. **Jan 6** Catholic Epiphany. **Apr 6** Good Friday. **Apr 9** Easter Monday. **May 1** May Day. **May 8** Liberation of the Republic.

Health

	Special Precautions?	Certificate Required?
Yellow Fever	No	No
Cholera	No	No
Typhoid & Polio	No	N/A
Malaria	No	N/A

Note: *Regulations and requirements may be subject to change at short notice, and you are advised to contact your doctor well in advance of your intended date of departure. Any numbers in the chart refer to the footnotes below.*

Food & drink: Mains water is normally chlorinated and, whilst relatively safe, may cause mild abdominal upsets. Exercise caution in rural areas. Bottled mineral water is available in grocers' shops and restaurants. Milk is pasteurised and dairy products are safe for consumption.
Other risks: *Tick-borne encephalitis* is present in forested areas. Walkers and campers should take precautions against tick bites by wearing long trousers. Vaccination is advisable. *Lyme disease* is present.
Rabies is present. For those at high risk, vaccination should be considered. If you are bitten, seek medical advice without delay; for more information, consult the *Health* appendix.
Health care: European Economic Area (EEA) and Switzerland:

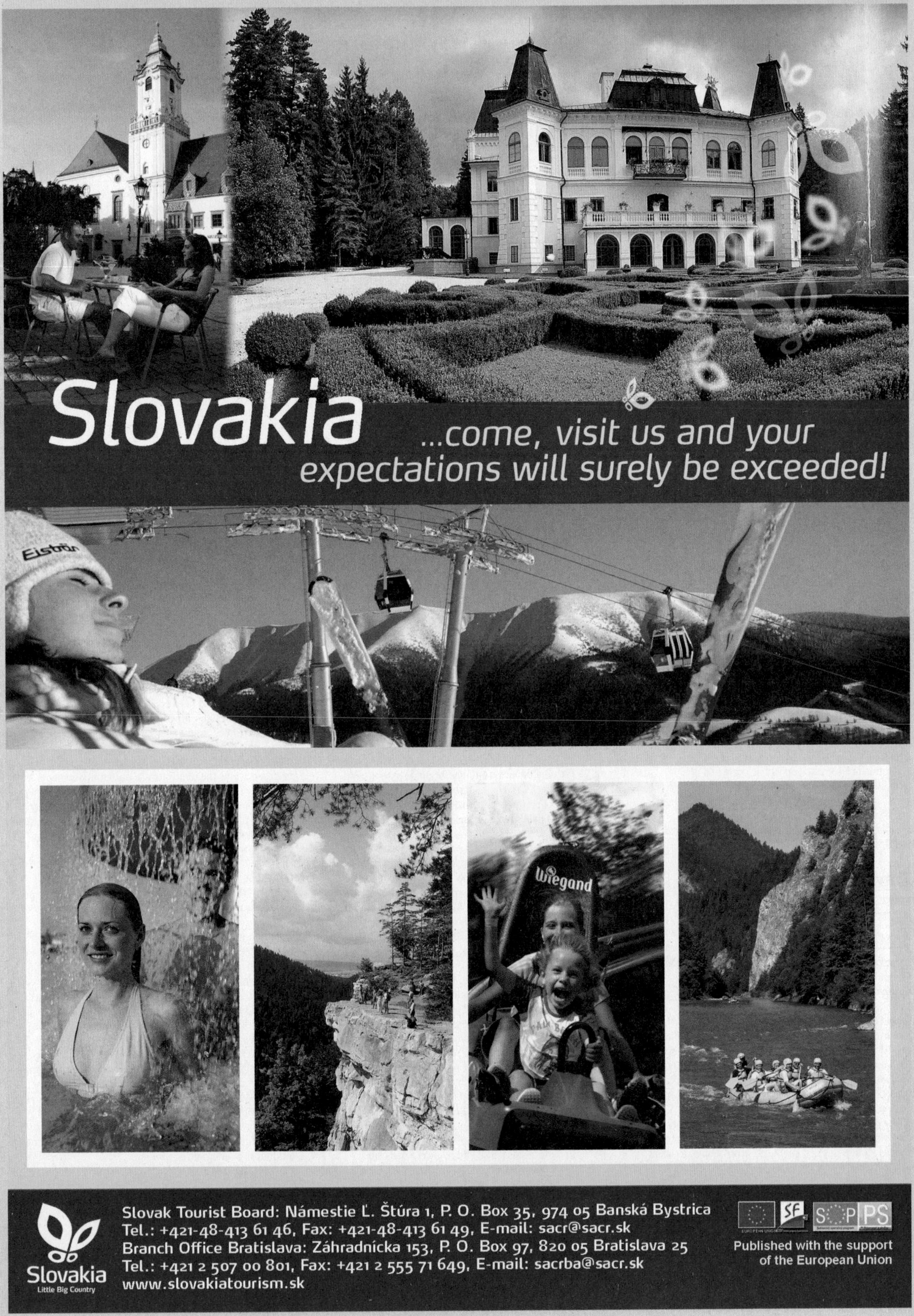

Credit: ©Slovak Tourist Board

If you or any of your dependants are suddenly taken ill or have an accident during a visit to an EEA country or Switzerland, free or reduced-cost necessary treatment is available – in most cases on production of a valid European Health Insurance Card (EHIC). Each country has different rules about state medical provision. In some, treatment is free. In many countries you will have to pay part or all of the cost, and then claim a full or partial refund. The EHIC gives access to state-provided medical treatment only and the scheme gives no entitlement to medical repatriation costs, nor does it cover ongoing illnesses of a non-urgent nature, so comprehensive travel insurance is advised. Note that the EHIC replaces the Form E111, which will no longer be valid after 31 December 2005. Some restrictions apply, depending on your nationality.

Medical insurance is mandatory for nationals of countries with no reciprocal health agreement: without this, entry may be refused. Make sure the doctor or dentist you see is contracted to the main health insurance company. You will have to pay a non-refundable contribution. If you do not have a European Health Insurance Card (EHIC), you will be charged for treatment and may not be able to get a refund. Some basic emergency dental treatment is available free of charge, but you will have to pay a non-refundable contribution. There is a non-refundable flat fee for each prescription, and you may have to contribute to the cost of the medicine itself. Pharmacies can give you a list of nationally subsidised drugs. A doctor can refer you to hospital, or you can go to the casualty ward of a hospital for emergency treatment. You will have to pay a daily charge (up to a maximum of 21 days) each time you are admitted. All other services and medicines are normally free, but there may be substantial non-refundable charges for complex procedures. If you go to hospital but are not admitted, you will also have to pay a fee. If a doctor asks for an ambulance for you, you will be charged a non-refundable fee. If the doctor does not think you need an ambulance, you will have to make your own arrangements. In a life-saving emergency, there is no charge for ambulance travel. More information can be obtained from the Slovak Ministry of Health (website: www.health.gov.sk).

Travel - International

AIR:

The Slovak Republic is served by its national airlines, *Air Slovakia (GM)* (website: www.airslovakia.sk) and *Slovak Airlines* (website: www.slovakairlines.sk). Low cost airlines *Sky Europe* (www.skyeurope.com) and *Ryanair* (www.ryanair.com) also fly to Slovakia.

Approximate flight times: From Bratislava to *London* is one hour 45 minutes.

Main airports: *Bratislava Airport (BTS)*, (M R Stefánik) (website: www.letiskobratislava.sk), is 9km (6 miles) from the city. *To/from the airport*: Buses run to the city (travel time – 30 minutes). Taxis are also available (travel time – 20 minutes). *Facilities*: Duty free shops, bank, post office, restaurant, bar, snack bar, flight information, left luggage, tourist information, first aid, disabled facilities and car hire.

Kosice Airport (KSC) is 10km (6 miles) south of the city (website: www.airportkosice.sk). *To/from the airport*: Taxis are available (travel time – 15 minutes). Buses are also available.

Tatry-Poprad Airport (TAT) is 5km (2.5 miles) from the city.

Vienna International Airport (VIE) (Schwechat) is 50km (31 miles) from Bratislava and can be used as a gateway for intercontinental travellers (website: www.viennaairport.com).

Departure tax: None.

RIVER: International connections from Austria are possible on the Danube which flows into the Black Sea, and is also linked with the Rhine and the Main. Services run as follows:
Bratislava–Vienna–Bratislava;
Bratislava–Hainburg–Bratislava; and
Vienna–Bratislava–Budapest, both ways.

RAIL:

The most convenient route to the Slovak Republic from Western Europe is via Prague or Vienna. The Slovak Republic's network also provides direct connections with Berlin, Bucharest, Budapest, Hamburg, Krakow, Kyiv, Lviv, Moscow, St Petersburg, Vilnius and Warsaw.

The *Inter-Rail* pass offers unlimited second-class train travel in up to 29 European countries (includes Morocco and Turkey) split into eight zones (A-H). Three different tickets are available: a ticket covering one zone (two to six countries, 16 days' validity), a ticket covering two zones (six to 10 countries, 22 days' validity) and an *All Zone Pass* (29 countries, ones month's validity). Ferry services between Italy and Greece are included. Passengers must be resident in Europe for at least six months before the pass is used. Travel is not allowed in the passenger's country of residence. Travellers under 26 years receive a reduction of about 30 per cent. Childrens' tickets are reduced by about 50 per cent. Supplements are required for some high-speed services, seat reservations and couchettes. Discounts are offered on *Eurostar* and some ferry routes. Available from *Inter Rail* (website: www.interailnet.com).

The *EuroDomino* pass enables holders anything from three to eight days' extensive travel within a one-month period on the entire rail network of their chosen country. It is valid in 28 European countries and North Africa, including the ferry service from Brindisi (Italy) to Igoumenitsa (Greece). To purchase a *EuroDomino* pass you must have been a resident in Europe for at least six months and a passport number is required at time of booking. It is not permitted to purchase a pass for travel within your own country of residence. To qualify for the youth rates, you must be under 26 years on the first date of validity of the pass. Children under four years travel for free.

Seat reservations, couchette and sleeper charges are not included in the cost of the pass and are payable at the normal rate. Passholder fares are payable on some services. Reservation/Supplement charges are payable on all trains within Spain.

Available from *Rail Europe* (website: www.raileurope.co.uk/eurodomino.htm).

ROAD:

The Slovak Republic can be entered via Austria, Czech Republic, Hungary, Poland or Ukraine. There is a motorway from Bratislava via Brno to Prague. There are *Eurolines* bus links from Bratislava and other important towns to major cities such as Cologne, London, Munich, Paris, Venice and Vienna. For further information, contact *Eurolines*, 52 Grosvenor Gardens, London SW1, UK (tel: (08705) 143 219; website: www.eurolines.com *or* www.nationalexpress.com).

Travel - Internal

AIR:

The domestic airlines are *Air Slovakia (GM)* (website: www.airslovakia.sk), *SkyEurope Airlines* (website: www.skyeurope.com) and *Slovak Airlines (9S)* (website: www.airslovakia.sk).

RIVER:

There are 2372 km of navigable waterways. The Danube is the main artery for transport by ship which is operated by *Slovak Shipping & Ports* (Pribinova 24, 815 24 Bratislava; tel: (2) 293 2226; website: www.lod.sk). Cruises covering historic and tourist interests are also operated. There is also regular passenger transport on the Danube.

RAIL:

The rail network is operated by *Railways of the Slovak Republic (ZSR)* (website: www.zsr.sk). There are several daily express trains between Bratislava and main cities and resorts. Reservations should be made in advance on major routes. Fares are low, but supplements are charged for travel by express trains. For further information, contact *ZSR*, Klemensová 8, 813 61 Bratislava (tel: (2) 5058 1111).

ROAD:

Traffic drives on the right. The major routes run from Bratislava to Presov and Kosice, via Kralovany and Poprad. The network of roads and supporting services (garages, petrol stations, restaurants, hotels and motels) is dense and reliable. Roads are standardised as motorways (200km), first- (3000km), second- (3500km) and third-class (11,000km) metalled roads, and are generally in good condition, particularly on the main arteries. Motorways are equipped with emergency telephones every half a mile or less. The *Slovakia* emergency system provides a fast and reliable network of garages, tow trucks and medical services. Road signs comply with European standards. **Bus:** The extensive network covers all areas and is efficient and comfortable. **Car hire:** Self-drive cars may be pre-booked through the tourist office in main towns and resorts. **Traffic regulations:** Seat belts are compulsory and drinking is absolutely prohibited. The speed limit in towns is 60kph (37mph); outside towns, 90kph (56mph); and on motorways, 130kph (81mph).

Documentation: Most hire companies require a valid international driving licence.

URBAN:

Buses, trolleybuses and trams exist in Bratislava and several other towns. All the cities operate flat-fare systems, and pre-purchase passes are available. Tickets should be punched in the appropriate machine on entering the tram or bus. A separate ticket is usually required when changing routes. There is a fine for fare evasion. Blue badges on tram and bus stops indicate an all-night service. **Taxi:** These are available in all the main towns and are metered and cheap; higher fares are charged at night.

Travel times: The following chart gives approximate travel times from **Bratislava** (in hours and minutes) to other major towns in the Slovak Republic.

	Air	Road	Rail
Poprad	**0.45**	**4.00**	**4.30**
Ko?ice	**1.00**	**5.30**	**5.00**
B. Bystrica	**-**	**2.30**	**4.10**
Pie?t'any Spa	**-**	**0.50**	**0.50**

Travel Advice

Most visits to the Slovak Republic are trouble-free but you should be aware of the global risk of indiscriminate international terrorist attacks, which could be against civilian targets, including places frequented by foreigners. This advice is based on information provided by the Foreign and Commonwealth Office in the UK. It is correct at time of publishing. As the situation can change rapidly, visitors are advised to contact the following organisations for the latest travel advice:

British Foreign and Commonwealth Office
Tel: (0845) 850 2829.
Website: www.fco.gov.uk

US Department of State
Website: http://travel.state.gov/travel

Accommodation

HOTELS:

There are over 1000 hotels in Slovakia. Prices compare very favourably with Western hotels, though services and facilities are often more limited. There is a shortage of accommodation in the peak seasons (May to October, but especially during July and August), and it is wise to pre-book. As yet, a relatively small portion of the hotel network is made up of intermediate and top-class establishments. At present, higher-standard hotels are to be found primarily in Bratislava, in regional towns (such as Banská Bystrica and Kosice), in spas of national and international significance and in major tourist resorts (such as the High Tatras). Future developments and investment will result in upward reclassification of many establishments. The international 5-star system has recently been introduced for hotel classification. The present system is: **5-star**, **4-star**, **3-star**, **2-star** and **1-star**. Visitors can expect rooms with a private bath or shower in hotels classified 3-star and upwards.

MOTELS:

Motels can be split into four classes. In cheaper motels, every room is provided with central heating and a washbasin with hot and cold water; on every floor there are separate bathrooms and WCs for men and women. The more expensive motels are provided with the following extras: a lift, a bathroom or shower with every room, a radio receiver and, in some cases, a TV set. Car parking facilities are available in both types.

PRIVATE HOUSES: The Slovak Union of Rural Tourism and Agrotourism can arrange stays in private houses in the Slovak Republic throughout the year.

SELF-CATERING:

Chalet communities in many parts of the country are available in three categories. The cheaper chalets offer drinking water, WC and heating in winter. Some may provide meals. The more expensive chalets have the following extras: electric lighting, flushing WC, washroom with running water, laundry facilities and an outdoor recreation area.

YOUTH HOSTELS:

There are a few hostels (mainly in Bratislava) affiliated to the International Youth Hostel Association in the Slovak Republic.

CAMPING/CARAVANNING:

Campsites are split into four classes and have all the usual facilities such as showers, cooking amenities, shops and, in some cases, caravans for hire. For further information, contact the Federation of Camping and Caravanning in the Slovak Republic. Camping outside official sites is limited. **Car camps:** In the lower classes these have a car park, fenced-in campsite, 24-hour

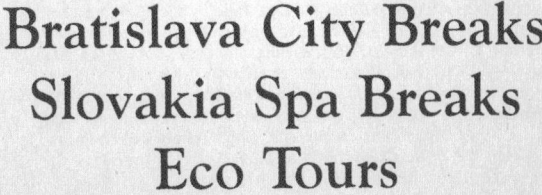

service, washroom, WC, drinking water and a roofed structure with cookers and washing-up equipment. Car camps in the higher classes are provided with the following extras: sale of refreshments, toiletries and souvenirs, showers with hot and cold water, flushing WC, laundry facilities, communal sitting room and a reception office.

ACCOMMODATION INFORMATION

Slovak Association of Hotels and Restaurants
Námestie Slobody 2, 974 01 Banská Bystrica, Slovak Republic
Tel: (48) 414 4669.
Website: www.zhr.sk/ang

Slovak Union of Rural Tourism and Agrotourism (Information on Private Houses)
Safarikovo nam. 4, 81102 Bratislava, Slovak Republic
Tel: (2).365 185.

Slovakia Youth Hostel Booking
Vysoka 32, 81445 Bratislava, Slovak Republic
Tel: (2) 5273 1024.

Federation of Camping and Caravanning in the Slovak Republic
Tel: (43) 589 8122.

Information on Hotels and Camping Accommodation online
Website: www.travelguide.sk

Bratislava Hotels
Website: www.bratislavahotels.com

International Youth Hostel Association in the Slovak Republic
Website: www.ckm.sk

Top Things To See

- **Bratislava**, the capital of the Slovak Republic, is the country's political, economic and cultural centre, located on the **River Danube** (**Dunaj** in Slovak). The centre of the **Old Town** (**Stavé Mesto**) is compact with much that is worth seeing near the **Old Town Square**; **Trinity Church** is noted for its magnificent *trompe l'oeil* frescos and the nearby **Corpus Christi Church** (**kaplnka Bozieho tela**) is now a museum packed with icons, jewellery and other aspects of ecclesiastical wealth. The **Town Hall** (**Stará radnica**) is a delightful mixture of Gothic, Renaissance and 19th-century styles, and the nearby **Jesuit Church** and the wonderful stucco decor of the **Mirbach Palace** are major tourist sites. The 15th-century **hrad** (**Bratislava Castle**), on the hill above the city, was burnt down by its own drunken soldiers in 1811; recently restored, it houses half of the **Slovak National Museum**, but visitors' time is better spent with the wonderful views across the Danube plain. The **Slovak National Gallery** on the waterfront houses Bratislava's most important art. The only other important site near the waterfront is Ödön Lechner's **Modr´y kostolic** (**Little Blue Church**), an Art Nouveau masterpiece dedicated to Bratislava's one important saint, Elizabeth, born in 1207. The controversial **Most SNP** (**Bridge of the Slovak National Uprising**) with its single support column dominates the area; views from the restaurant at the top are superb. Between the Old Town Square and the Bridge is the graceful boulevard, **Hviezdoslavolo námestie**; at the eastern end are the great late-19th-century **Slovak National Theatre** and the more **Sessionist Reduta Theatre**.
- See the famous **ruined castle**, **Devín**, 9km (6 miles) northwest from Bratislava. Near here the Germans were heavily defeated in 864 and 871 and the area is of immense Slovak Nationalist importance.
- Behold the relatively **intact medieval walls** of **Trnava**, which was the centre for Hungarian church administration from the 16th to the 18th century. Near the Polish border, **Bardejov** also offers the chance to gaze upon some almost perfectly preserved walls.
- Visit **Nitra**, the country's agricultural capital. Walk up to the ruined **hrad** (**castle**) where you will find statues of saints, a fine plague column and two enormous gateways. The Gothic **katedrála** (cathedral) at the **castle** contains the remains of two 10th-century saints; next door is the Baroque **Palace of the Bishop of Nitra**.
- The Slovak Republic's greatest tourist sites are its mountains: the **High Tatras** receive the most publicity, but the **Low Tatras** and **Malá Fatra**, although less monumental, are also quite developed. Although only 26km (16 miles) long, the **High Tatra Mountains** in the north are noted for impressive alpine features. The **High Tatra National Park** (**TANAP**) has an abundance of wildlife and over 13,000 species of alpine plants – due to the great differences in elevation from 900 to 2655m (2953 to 8710ft). There are more than 85 mountain lakes, of which **Great Hincovo Lake** is the largest. The park has a good selection of accommodation and sporting facilities, climatic spas and 350km (220 miles) of marked hiking trails. **Tatranská Lomnica** makes an ideal starting point for the eastern Tatras. Founded in 1892 as a State climatic spa, it nestles in the foothills of **Skalnaté Pleso** (1751m/5745ft) which boasts the Tatra's best downhill ski and bobsleigh tracks. The **Low Tatras National Park** covers the second-highest range within the western Carpathians. The park includes several ski and recreation resorts including **Jasna**, and the **Demänová Valley**, with its extensive ice-cave system. The **Pieniny National Park** is a bilateral national park shared with Poland, 30km (19 miles) northeast of the High Tatras. The **Malá Fatra National Park** is renowned for the scenic beauty of its valleys and gorges and its abundant wildlife. It is a favourite with hikers in both winter and summer; outside the park, the wooded spa town of **Rajecké Teplice** and the folk painted houses at **Cicmany** are important tourist sites.
- **Mining** and **coin minting** have played an important part in many of the Central Slovakian towns, with skilled German miners 'imported' in the 13th century. **Banská Bystrica** flourished as the capital of the seven 'Hungarian' (actually German) mining towns and was the centre for the failed 1944 uprising. The **Town Museum** in the Renaissance **Thurso Palace** and the 13th-century **Panna Márie** church with its Gothic altar by Master Pavol of Levoca are the most important tourist sites. **Banská Stiavnica** had the world's first **Mining University** (1762). The 11 buildings of the **Mining and Forestry Academy**, as well as a number of Renaissance **burghers' houses** are among its chief attractions. The mixed Gothic and Renaissance **hrad** (**town castle**), and the small **gallery houses** of the miners are the major sites in **Kremnica**, once the site of the richest gold seams in Europe.
- The **Spis** (**Zips**) region was resettled by Saxons after the 13th-century Tartar invasions; most villages combine Teutonic (including many Protestant churches) and Slovak traits. There are many religious sites to observe in this region. Here, you can see the world's highest Gothic altar (18.6m/61ft high and 6m/20ft wide) in the Gothic church of **sv Jakub** (**St James**), built by Master Pavol and complemented by 12 important side altars. **Kezmarok** is noted for its wooden **Protestant Church**, capable of seating 1500 worshipers. Walled **Spiská Kapitula** was the seat of provosts and later bishops from the 13th century. The Romanesque cathedral of **sv Martin** is featured in many postcards.
- Amble around **Spis Castle**; Dating from the 12th century, it is the biggest medieval castle in central Europe. Nearby, the walled town of **Levoca** became the wealthy capital of the Union of Zips Saxons in 1271.
- Southeast of **Poprad**, deep **canyons** cut through the **Slovensk´y raj** (**Slovak Paradise**) **National Park**. The pine forest landscape is riddled with basins and waterfalls, and the park contains Europe's oldest **ice-cave** at **Dobsiná** (**Dobsinská l'adová jaskyna**).
- The **Andrássy Mausoleum** at **Krásna Hôrka** is the Slovak Republic's finest Art Nouveau building, and is well worth a visit.
- **St Elizabeth's dóm** is the easternmost Gothic cathedral in Europe and is also one of the most beautiful.
- Northeast of **Kosice** is the **Herl'any Geyser**, which sprays cold mineral water as high as 30m (100ft) every 32 to 34 hours.

Top Things To Do

- Most towns have their own **folk festivals**, with dancing, local costumes and food. These tend to be in the summer months leading up to the harvest festivals in September.
- Europe's longest **cycling** route passes through the Slovak Republic, stretching from Passau in Germany along the Danube, through Vienna, Bratislava and on to Stúrovo. Cyclists can then continue their journey by taking a ferry across the Danube into Hungary. **Hrabusice-Podlesok** and **Cingov** are ideal starting points for the extensive hiking and biking trails.
- There is a very good network of marked **hiking/walking** trails in all mountain areas, and it is possible to plan a **walking tour** in advance. The **Small Carpathians** are a major walking area. **Kamzík** is the first major hill and the cafe, which offers superb views, can be reached either on foot or by chair lift.
- There are numerous **lakes** and **rivers** amidst the glacial landscape, offering excellent **fishing**, **canoeing**, **boating** and **swimming**. The primary watersports areas are at **Liptovská Mara**, **Orava**, **Sl'nava** and **Zemplínska Sírava**. **Rafting** is particularly good on the **Dunajec river** in the **Pieniny national park**.
- There are popular **skiing** centres in 30 mountain regions, the best of which are the **Tatra Mountains**, where over 40 ski tows and chairlifts are located. Other popular mountain areas include the **Slovensky raj** range, with its deep canyons, and the **Malá Fatra** range with its neighbouring **Vrátna dolina valley**. Wintersports resorts include **Smokovce** (including a climatic spa), **Strbské Pleso** and the picturesque Goral village of **Zdiar**, lying at the divide of the **Belianske Tatry** and the **Spiská Magura** mountain ranges.
- The country offers a great wealth of curative **springs**, **thermal spas**, **climatic health resorts** and **natural mineral waters**, renowned throughout the world. There are 23 spa towns officially recognised by the state authorities. **Bardejovské Kúpele** was already established as a health resort in the 13th century, once the playground of the Hungarian and Russian nobility. Its healing properties have been said to cure indigestion, disturbed metabolism and various respiratory problems. **Dudince**'s spring is rated among the best in the area with a mineral composition suitable for the curing of internal organs, neurological and vascular diseases. The world-famous thermal health resort of **Piestany** specialises in rheumatic treatment, with its opulent late 19th-century **Thermia Palace Hotel**. **Sliac**, first mentioned in 1244, is regarded as the most important spa for the treatment of cardiovascular disorders. **Trencianské Teplice**, established since 1488, is situated near a sulphuric spring and is suitable for the treatment of the motor neurone system; it is best reached by narrow-gauge railway. **Bojnice** is one of the most renowned spas for the treatment of rheumatism.
- The **Small Carpathians** stretch from Bratislava's northern suburbs to the Váh valley and are a major **wine-growing area**. **Modrá** is a major centre for wine and folk pottery.

TOURIST INFORMATION

Slovak Tourist Board
Slovenska agentura pre cestovny ruch, Namestie L.Stura 1, P.o. Box 35, 974 05 Banska Bystrica, Slovak Republic
Tel: (48) 413 6146.
Website: www.slovakiatourism.sk

Association of Information Centres in Slovakia
Namestie mieru 1 031 01 Liptovsky Mikulas, Slovak Republic
Tel.: (44) 551 4541.
E-mail: info@infoslovak.sk
Website: www.infoslovak.sk

Entertainment

FOOD & DRINK: Traditional Slovak eating and drinking habits date back to the old Slavic period influenced later by Austrian, German and Hungarian cooking. Slovak food is based on many different kinds of soups, gruels, boiled and stewed vegetables, roast and smoked meats and dairy products. The style of cooking varies from region to region. Slovak specialities include both sweet and savoury dishes made with flour, including dumplings. Popular drinks include Slovak beer, wine and mineral waters. are particular specialities, as are wine from the Tokay region and sparkling wine from the Bratislava region. Restaurants and other catering establishments are many and varied, including cafes, buffets, snack bars, inns, ale houses and wine taverns. All restaurants are graded according to quality. The main meal of the day is usually lunch, comprising soup, a main meal and desert.

National specialities:
- *Bryndzové haluisky* (small potato dumplings with sheep's cheese).
- Mutton with sauerkraut (flavoured with prunes, mushrooms and apples).
- Cabbage leaves filled with minced meat (served with a milky sauce).
- *Sulance* (potato dough turnovers filled with plum jam).

National drinks:
- *Borovicka* (strong gin).
- *Slivovica* (plum brandy).

Tipping: A 5 to 10 per cent tip is usual.

NIGHTLIFE: Theatre and opera are of a high standard. Much of the nightlife takes place in hotels, although nightclubs are to be found in major cities.

SHOPPING: Souvenirs include pottery, porcelain, woodcarvings, hand-embroidered clothing and food items. There are a number of excellent shops specialising in glass and crystal, while various associations of regional artists and artisans run their own retail outlets (pay in local currency). Other special purchases include folk ceramics from all regions of the Slovak Republic and woodcarvings from the eastern and central parts of the Slovak Republic (Kyjatice, Michalovce and Spijsská Belá). **Shopping hours:** Mon-Fri 0900-1800, Sat 0900-1200. Shopping centres open until 2100, with hypermarkets open 24 hours.

Business

- **GDP**: US$78.89 billion (2004).
- **Main exports**: Vehicles, machinery and transport equipment, base materials, plastics, chemicals and minerals.
- **Main imports**: Machinery and equipment, chemicals and fuels.
- **Main trade partners**: Germany, Italy, Czech Republic, Russian Federation, Poland and Australia.

ECONOMY: Of all the Soviet bloc economies, the former Czechoslovakia experienced the highest degree of state control. In the late-1960s, after the Prague Spring, the Soviet-backed Government revamped the economy to build up heavy industry at the expense of traditional strengths in light and craft-based industries, such as textiles, clothing, glass and ceramics. After the division of Czechoslovakia in 1993, the newly independent Slovak Government found these heavy industries to be something of a millstone, but they continue to play a central role in the economy. In a few cases, they have benefited from foreign investment. The other major economic problem was a dearth of natural resources: the most important of these, especially oil, were formerly available cheaply from the ex-Soviet Union but now had to be bought at market rates. The agricultural sector – almost all of which is now privately owned – produces wheat and grains, sugar beet, vegetables and livestock. However, its relative economic contribution (3.5 per cent of GDP, 5.8 per cent of the workforce) is not substantial. The bulk of the industrial economy has been transferred to the private sector, including the key areas of machinery and chemical industries, textiles, leather, shoes, glass, electronics, nuclear energy and car manufacturing. Slovak economic policy-makers chose a different path of development from their Czech neighbours, opting for a more gradual transition and retaining certain 'strategic' industries (notably the armaments industry) under state control. An estimated 85 per cent of the economy is now in private hands.

After the initial transition shock, the economy performed fairly well in the mid- and late 1990s, but then went into recession. Growth stagnated while the budget deficit, external debt and unemployment climbed to uncomfortably high levels. Since 2002, however, the situation has been brought under control. Growth is now at 5.3 per cent. Unemployment remains stubbornly high at 13.1 per cent; inflation in 2005 was 7.5 per cent.

Current Slovak economic policy is focused on turning the 15 per cent or so of the economy still controlled by the state over to private ownership, and reforming the republic's still rigid employment code. Both measures are integral to the Slovak Republic's forthcoming accession to the European Union. After signing an association agreement with the EU in October 1993, the country had fulfilled the membership criteria for the EU by the end of 2002. Along with nine other countries (including seven others from East and Central Europe), the Slovak Republic joined on May 1 2004, a decision endorsed by popular referendum during 2003.

Almost two-thirds of Slovak trade is now with the EU's 15 existing members. Otherwise, there remains important links with the other members of the Visegrad Group of central European states (Poland, the Czech Republic and Hungary – all of whom also joined the EU), as well as the Russian Federation and Ukraine.

BUSINESS ETIQUETTE: Businesspeople wear suits. A knowledge of German and English is useful. Long business lunches are usual. Office hours: Mon-Fri 0800-1700 (or longer).

COMMERCIAL INFORMATION

Slovak Chamber of Commerce and Industry
Gorkeho 9, 816 03 Bratislava, Slovak Republic
Tel: (2) 5443 3291.
Website www.scci.sk or www.sopk.sk

National Agency for the Development of Small and Medium Enterprises
Prievozska 30, 821 05 Bratislava, Slovak Republic
Tel: (2) 5557 1601.
Website: www.nadsme.sk

Slovak Investment & Trade Development Agency
Martincekova 17, 821 01 Bratislava, Slovak Republic
Tel: (2) 5826 0100. Website: www.sario.sk

Slovak Tourist Board's Congress & Convention Department
Tel: (2) 5070 0801.
E-mail: congress@sacr.sk

Slovenia

Location: Southern Central Europe.

Time: GMT + 1 (GMT + 2 from last Sunday in March to Saturday before last Sunday in October).

Overview

One of the smallest countries in Europe, Slovenia lies in an enviable geographical position between the majestic Alps and the Mediterranean. A country with spectacular mountains, thick forests and a short Adriatic coastline, Slovenia also enjoys substantial economic and political stability.

Following the destruction of the Austro-Hungarian Empire during World War I, Slovenia became a part of the new 'Kingdom of Serbs, Croats and Slovenes' in 1918 (renamed 'Yugoslavia' in 1929). In 1941, when the Axis powers dismembered Yugoslavia, Slovenia was carved up between Germany, Italy and Hungary. Local resistance, initially from non-communist nationalists, was hijacked by the Yugoslav Communist Party led by Josip Broz Tito, himself partly of Slovene origin. In 1945, Marshall Tito declared Socialist Yugoslavia, a a federation of six republics - Croatia, Montenegro, Serbia, Slovenia, Bosnia-Herzegovina, and Macedonia. After his death in 1980, the economic and political situation deteriorated in Yugoslavia. This ultimately led, ten years later to the end of the Socialist Federal Republic of Yugoslavia. The first clear demand for Slovene independence was made in 1987. Slovenia was the first republic to break away, achieving independence relatively peacefully in 1991, followed by full international recognition in January 1992. Slovenia has always been the most prosperous region of the former Yugoslavia and has found the transition from a socialist economy to the capitalist free market easier than most. It was the only one of the former Yugoslav republics to be in the first wave of candidates for membership of the European Union. It joined the union in May 2004.

Ljubljana, the capital is the starting point for a wide range of excursions. Situated in the heart of Slovenia, along the banks of the Ljubljanca River, the capital is within a two-hour drive of all the state borders. The old part of the town is particularly delightful.

General Information

AREA: 20,273 sq km (7827 sq miles).
POPULATION: 2 million (UN, 2005).
POPULATION DENSITY: 98.6 per sq km.
CAPITAL: Ljubljana. **Population:** 265,881 (2002).
GEOGRAPHY: This compact and strategically important country is dominated by mountains, rivers and major north-south and east-west transit routes. Slovenia borders Italy to the west, Austria to the north, Hungary to the northeast and Croatia to the southeast, with a 47km-

---

(30 mile-) Adriatic Sea coastline, where the main port is Koper.

GOVERNMENT: Republic since 1991. Gained independence from Yugoslavia (now Serbia and Montenegro) in 1992. **Head of State:** President Janez Drnovšek since 2002. **Head of Government:** Prime Minister Janez Jansa since 2004. **Recent history:** Former leader of the centre-left Liberal Democrats, Prime Minister Janez Drnovšek won the second round of presidential elections in December 2002. As President, he oversaw Slovenia's entry into the EU and Nato in 2004. Janez Jansa, the leader of the centre-right Slovenian Democratic Party, became Prime Minister in October 2004 in which his party almost doubled its vote. The party forged a coalition with three other parties: New Slovenia and the People's Party - both centre-right - and the centre-left Democratic Party of Pensioners. Mr Jansa's campaign was based on a promise to cut the costs of state administration and press ahead with privatisation in anticipation of Slovenia adopting the euro.

LANGUAGE: Slovene, which is closely related to Croat and Czech. Most Slovenes speak German, Hungarian or Italian, with English as a second language.

RELIGION: Most of the population is Roman Catholic (75 per cent), with small communities of other Christians including Eastern Orthodox; there are Muslim and Jewish minorities.

ELECTRICITY: 220 volts AC, 50Hz.

SOCIAL CONVENTIONS: Shaking hands is the normal form of greeting. Usual European social conventions apply and informal dress is widely acceptable. Smoking is prohibited on public transport, in cinemas, theatres, public offices and in waiting rooms.

Credit: ©Slovenian Tourist Board / B Kladnik

Climate

Continental climate with warm summers and cold winters (snowfalls in the Alps). Mediterranean climate on the coast.
Required clothing: Mediumweight clothing and heavy overcoats in winter; lightweight clothing and raincoats for the summer, particularly for the higher Alpine north.

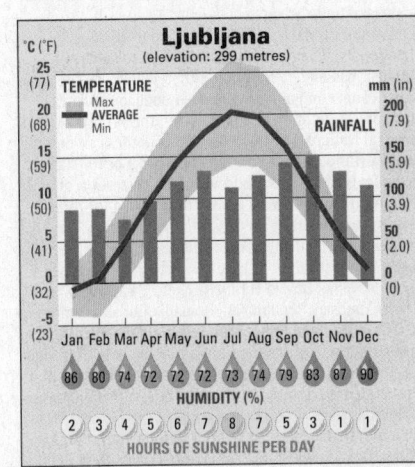

Communications

Telephone: IDD is available. Country code: 386. Calls can be made with magnetic phonecards, sold at post offices, newspaper kiosks and tobacco shops (website: www.telekom.si). For emergencies, dial 112 (ambulance service and fire brigade) or 113 (police).
Mobile telephone: Roaming agreements exist with international mobile phone companies. Good coverage.
Internet: Internet cafes are available in cities such as Ljubljana.

Post: Reasonable internal service. Stamps can be bought at bookstalls. Post office hours: Mon-Fri 0800-1800, Sat 0800-1200. The post office at Cigaletova 5, Ljubljana is open 24 hours.
MEDIA: The media scene is diverse and free, and the constitution supports freedom of expression. About two thirds of TV households are connected to cable or satellite.
Press: The main dailies are *Delo*, *Slovenske Novice* and *Dnevnik* (in Ljubljana). *Vecer* is a Maribor based daily. The state news agency, *STA*, produces material in English for international distribution on a daily basis. English-language publications include *Ars Vivendi*, *Slovenia Weekly*, *Slovenian Business Report* and *Slovenija*.
TV: *RTV Slovenia*, the public broadcaster, operates two national channels and regional services. *Pop TV* and *Kanal A* are commercial channels.
Radio: *RTV Slovenia*, the public broadcaster, operates national radio stations *A1*, *Val 202* and *Ars*, regional services and a tourist station with news in English and German. *Radio Hit* and *Radio City* are commercial stations.

Passport/Visa

	Passport Required?	Visa Required?	Return Ticket Required?
Full British	1	No	No
Australian	Yes	No	No
Canadian	Yes	No	No
USA	Yes	No	No
Other EU	1	No	No
Japanese	Yes	No	No

Note: Regulations and requirements may be subject to change at short notice, and you are advised to contact the appropriate diplomatic or consular authority before finalising travel arrangements. Any numbers in the chart refer to the footnotes below.

PASSPORTS: Passport valid for at least three months beyond the length of stay required by all except:
(a) **1.** EU/EEA nationals (EU+ Iceland, Liechtenstein, Norway) and Swiss nationals holding a valid national ID card.
Note: EU and EEA nationals are only required to produce evidence of their EU/EEA nationality and identity in order to be admitted to any EU/EEA Member State. This evidence can take the form of a valid national passport *or* national identity card. Either is acceptable. Possession of a return ticket, any length of validity on their document, sufficient funds for the length of their proposed visit should *not* be imposed.
(b) nationals of Croatia holding a valid national ID card.
VISAS: Required by all except the following:
(a) nationals of countries referred to in the chart above for stays of up to three months;
(b) nationals of Andorra, Argentina, Bolivia, Brazil, Brunei, Bulgaria, Chile, Costa Rica, Croatia, El Salvador, Gibraltar, Guatemala, Honduras, Hong Kong (SAR), Iceland, Israel, Korea (Rep), Liechtenstein, Macau (SAR), Mexico (one month only for business trips), Monaco, New Zealand, Nicaragua, Norway, Panama, Paraguay, Romania, San Marino, Switzerland, Uruguay, Vatican City and Venezuela for stays of up to 90 days;
(c) nationals of Malaysia for stays of up to 30 days;
(d) nationals of Singapore for stays of up to 14 days;
(e) transit passengers continuing their journey by the same or first connecting aircraft, provided holding onward or return documentation and not leaving the airport.
Note: (a) Nationals of the following countries can enter Slovenia without a visa for transit purposes or for stays of maximum 90 days, provided they are in possession of an EU/EFTA residents or work permit that is valid for three months from the date of entry into Slovenia *or* a *Schengen* visa (issued by one of the *Schengen* Member States) that is valid for at least one month beyond their stay in Slovenia: Bosnia & Herzegovina, Macedonia (Former Yugoslav Republic of), Romania (for a maximum of 10 days), Russian Federation, Serbia & Montenegro and Turkey. Nationals of these countries should note that their visa-free stay's duration depends on where they have a valid residence permit/visa, and may be less than 90 days.
(b) The following nationals require an airport transit visa if wishing to remain within the international transit area: nationals of Afghanistan, Bangladesh, Congo (Dem Rep), Ethiopia, Eritrea, Ghana, Iran, Iraq, Nigeria, Pakistan, Somalia and Sri Lanka.
Types of visa and cost: All visas, regardless of duration and number of entries, cost £25.
Validity: Visitor (single-, double- and multiple-entry): Either a single uninterrupted stay or collective duration over successive days not exceeding 90 days within a six-month period, starting from the first day of entry. Transit (single-, double- and occasionally multiple-transit): Up to five days.
Application to: Consulate (or consular section at Embassy); see *Passport/Visa Information*.
Application requirements: (a) Passport valid for at least three months longer than duration of stay. (b) Application form. (c) One passport-size photo. (d) Fee, payable by cash, cheque or postal order. (e) Medical travel insurance testifying the ability to cover urgent medical care whilst in Slovenia. (f) For private visits, an invitation from a person in Slovenia (letter of guarantee) authenticated by a notary, containing data guaranteeing accommodation and support for visit, and other possible costs. The letter must also contain a large amount of other data; please consult the nearest Embassy for further information. (g) For touristic travel, a voucher and confirmation from tourist agency or hotel. (h) For business travel, official invitation from company or organisation in Slovenia. (i) Additional documents, eg return ticket. (j) Letter from employer; contact the nearest Embassy for details.
Transit: (a)-(e) and, (f) Proof of permitted entry into next destination.
Working days required: Between three and 10 but depends on nationality.
Temporary residence: Enquire at Consulate (or consulate section at Embassy); see *Passport/Visa Information*.

PASSPORT/VISA INFORMATION

Embassy of the Republic of Slovenia in the UK
10 Little College Street, London SW1P 3SH, UK
Tel: (020) 7222 5400.
Website: www.gov.si/mzz/dkp/vlo/eng
Opening hours: Mon-Fri 0900-1700; 1000-1200 (consular section; for appointments in person).

Embassy of the Republic of Slovenia in the USA
1525 New Hampshire Avenue, NW, Washington, DC 20036, USA
Tel: (202) 667 5363.
Website: www.embassy.org/slovenia

Money

Currency: Slovene Tolar (SIT) = 100 stotins. Notes are in denominations of SIT10,000, 5000, 1000, 500, 200, 100, 50, 20 and 10. Coins are in denominations of SIT 50, 20,10, 5, 2 and 1, and 50, 20 and 10 stotins.
Currency exchange: The Tolar is fully convertible within Slovenia, but visitors are advised to exchange surplus amounts to the currency of their choice before leaving Slovenia, as it is not generally exchangeable elsewhere. Foreign currencies can be exchanged at banks and some hotels, supermarkets, petrol stations, tourist agencies and exchange bureaux.
Credit & debit cards: American Express, Diners, EuroCard, MasterCard and Visa are accepted at upmarket establishments; elsewhere cash is preferred. Credit cards can be used to get cash advances from banks.
Traveller's cheques: Widely accepted. To avoid additional exchange rate charges, travellers are advised to take traveller's cheques in Euros, US Dollars or Pounds Sterling.
Currency restrictions: The import and export of local currency is permitted, although amounts in excess of SIT3,000,000 must be declared to customs.
Banking hours: Mon-Fri 0830-1230 and 1400-1700; Sat 0830-1100/1200.
Exchange rate indicators:
Rate at time of publishing
£1.00= SIT353.73
$1.00= SIT199.55

Duty Free

The following goods can be imported into Slovenia by passengers over 17 years of age without incurring customs duty:
200 cigarettes or 50 cigars or 100 cigarillos or 250g of tobacco; 2l of wine and 1l of spirits; 50g perfume and 250ml of eau de toilette; listed items to not exceed €175 in value.
Note: An export licence is required for articles of archaeological, ethnographic, artistic, scientific or cultural value; or for articles over 100 years old.
Abolition of duty free goods within the EU: On June 30 1999, the sale of duty free alcohol and tobacco at airports and at sea was abolished in all of the original 15 EU member states. Of the 10 new member states that joined the EU on May 1 2004, these rules already apply to Cyprus and Malta. There are transitional rules in place for visitors returning to one of the original 15 EU countries from one of the other new EU countries. But for the original 15, plus Cyprus and Malta, there are now no limits imposed on importing tobacco and alcohol products from one EU country to another (with the exceptions of Denmark, Finland and Sweden, where limits are imposed). Travellers should note that they may be required to prove at customs that the goods purchased are for personal use only.

Credit: ©Slovenian Tourist Board / J Skok

Public Holidays

Below are listed Public Holidays for the January 2006-June 2007 period.
2006: Jan 1-2 New Year. **Feb 8** Preseren Day (Slovenian Cultural Holiday). **Apr 17** Easter Monday. **Apr 27** Resistance Day. **May 1-2** Labour Day Holiday. **Jun 11** Pentecost. **Jun 25** National Day. **Aug 15** Assumption.
Oct 31 Reformation Day. **Nov 1** All Saints' Day.
Dec 25 Christmas Day. **Dec 26** Independence Day.
2007: Jan 1-2 New Year. **Feb 8** Preseren Day (Slovenian Cultural Holiday). **Apr 9** Easter Monday. **Apr 27** Resistance Day. **May 1-2** Labour Day Holiday. **May 27** Pentecost. **Jun 25** National Day.

Health

	Special Precautions?	Certificate Required?
Yellow Fever	No	No
Cholera	No	No
Typhoid & Polio	1	N/A
Malaria	No	N/A

Note: Regulations and requirements may be subject to change at short notice, and you are advised to contact your doctor well in advance of your intended date of departure. Any numbers in the chart refer to the footnotes below.

1: Vaccination against typhoid is advised.
Food & drink: Mains water is considered safe and drinkable. However, bottled water is available and is advised for the first few weeks of the stay. Milk is pasteurised and dairy products are safe for consumption. Local meat, poultry, seafood, fruit and vegetables are generally considered safe to eat.
Other risks: *Hepatitis A* occurs. *Tick-borne encephalitis* is present in forested areas. Walkers and campers should take precautions against tick bites by wearing long trousers. Vaccination is advisable. Immunisation against *hepatitis B*, *diphtheria* and *tuberculosis* is sometimes advised.
Rabies is present. For those at high risk, vaccination before arrival should be considered. If you are bitten, seek medical advice without delay. For more information, consult the *Health* appendix.
Health care: European Economic Area (EEA) and Switzerland:
If you or any of your dependants are suddenly taken ill or have an accident during a visit to an EEA country or Switzerland, free or reduced-cost necessary treatment is available – in most cases on production of a valid European Health Insurance Card (EHIC). Each country has different rules about state medical provision. In some, treatment is free. In many countries you will have to pay part or all of the cost, and then claim a full or partial refund. The EHIC gives access to state-provided medical treatment only and the scheme gives no entitlement to medical repatriation costs, nor does it cover ongoing illnesses of a non-urgent nature, so comprehensive travel insurance is advised. Note that the EHIC replaces the Form E111, which is no longer valid since 31 December 2005. Some restrictions apply, depending on your nationality.
You can get free emergency medical treatment from a doctor in a public health institution, or from a private doctor who is contracted to the Health Insurance Institute of Slovenia (*Zavod za Zdravstveno Zavarovanje Slovenije* or *ZZZS*). If you see a doctor who is not contracted to the *ZZZS*, you will not be able to claim a refund. You can get emergency dental treatment from dentists contracted to the *ZZZS*. For some prescription drugs, you will have to pay 25 to 75 per cent of the cost; for others you will have to pay the full cost. These charges are not refundable. Some drugs are provided free of charge. A doctor will refer you to hospital if required. In an emergency, you can go to the emergency department of a hospital where you can get free treatment. If a doctor refers you to hospital, ambulance travel is free, otherwise you will have to pay 70 per cent of the cost. This is not refundable. More information can be obtained from the Health Insurance Institute of Slovenia (*ZZZS*) (website: www.zzzs.si).

Slovenia

Travel - International

AIR:

The national airline, *Adria Airways* (website: www.adria-airways.com), operates direct flights from London and most other European cities to Ljubljana.

Approximate flight times: From Ljubljana to *London* is two hour 30 minutes.

Main airports: *Ljubljana (LJU)* (Brnik) is 26km (16 miles) northwest of the city. *To/from the* airport: Buses are available to Kranj (travel time - 15 minutes) and to Ljubljana (travel time - 45 minutes) every 60 minutes, and every 120 minutes Sat-Sun. Taxis are also available (travel time - 20 minutes). *Facilities*: Bank, post office, duty free shop, restaurant, snack bar, shops, internet cafes, (www.neoplan.net) and car hire.

Maribor (MBX) and *Portoroz (POW)* also have some international connections.

Departure tax: None.

SEA:

Main ports: *Izola, Koper, Piran* and *Portoroz*. Between March and October, there are scheduled trips across the Adriatic on the *Prince of Venice* catamaran, which runs between Venice and Portoroz and Piran. The journey takes two hours. There are three marinas (Izola, Koper, Piran and Portoroz) to choose from for visitors arriving on private vessels.

RAIL:

Connections and through coaches are available from principal Eastern and Western European cities. The *Eurocity Mimara* train connects Ljubljana, Munich, Salzburg and Zagreb. There are direct trains to Slovenia from Austria (Vienna and Villach), Bulgaria, Croatia (Zagreb), Greece, Hungary (Budapest), Italy (Trieste and Venice), Macedonia (Former Yugoslav Republic of), Serbia and Montenegro and Switzerland. International trains have couchette coaches as well as bar and dining cars (website: www.slo-zeleznice.si). On some lines transport for cars is provided.

Rail passes: The *Inter-Rail* pass offers unlimited second-class train travel in up to 29 European countries (includes Morocco and Turkey) split into eight zones (A-H). Three different tickets are available: a ticket covering one zone (two to six countries, 16 days' validity), a ticket covering two zones (six to 10 countries, 22 days' validity) and an *All Zone Pass* (29 countries, one month's validity). Ferry services between Italy and Greece are included. Passengers must be resident in Europe for at least six months before the pass is used. Travel is not allowed in the passenger's country of residence. Travellers under 26 years receive a reduction of about 30 per cent. Children's tickets are reduced by about 50 per cent. Supplements are required for some high-speed services, seat reservations and couchettes. Discounts are offered on *Eurostar* and some ferry routes. Available from *Inter Rail* (website: www.interrailnet.com).

The *EuroDomino* pass enables holders anything from three to eight days' extensive travel within a one-month period on the entire rail network of their chosen country. It is valid in 28 European countries and North Africa, including the ferry service from Brindisi (Italy) to Igoumenitsa (Greece). To purchase a *EuroDomino* pass you must have been resident in Europe for at least six months and a passport number is required at time of booking. It is not permitted to purchase a pass for travel within your own country of residence. To qualify for the youth rates, you must be under 26 years on the first date of validity of the pass. Children aged four-11 years inclusive pay half the adult fares rounded up to the nearest pound. Children under four years travel for free. Seat reservations, couchette and sleeper charges are not included in the cost of the pass and are payable at the normal rate. Passholder fares are payable on some services. Reservation/supplement charges are payable on all trains within Spain. Available from *Rail Europe* (website: www.raileurope.co.uk/railpasses/eurodomino.htm).

ROAD:

The following are among the frontier posts open for road traffic:

From **Italy**: San Bartolomeo-Lazaret; Albaro Veskova- Skofije; Pesse-Kozina; Fernetti-Ferneteci (Sezana); Gorizia- Nova Gorica; Stupizza-Robic; Uccea-Uceja; Passo del Predil-Predel; and Fusine Laghi-Ratece.

From **Austria**: Wurzenpass (Villach)-Korensko Sedlo; Loibltunnel-Ljubelj; Seebergsattel-Jezersko; Grablach-Holmec; Rabenstein-Vic; Eibiswald-Radlji od Dravi; Langegg-Jurij; Spielfeld-Sentilj; Mureck- Trate; Sicheldorf- Gederovci; Radkersburg-Gornja Radgona; and Bonisdorf- Kuzma.

From **Hungary**: Bajansenye-Hodos.

From **Croatia**: Jelsane-Rupa. Nearly all the border crossings mentioned above are open 24 hours a day and are served by buses.

For information regarding **documentation** and **traffic regulations**, see the *Travel – Internal* section.

Travel - Internal

AIR:

Main airports: *Maribor (MBX)* in the east of the country and *Portoroz (POW)* on the Adriatic Coast.

SEA:

Slovenia has ports at *Izola, Koper, Piran* and *Portoroz*.

RAIL:

There are efficient Intercity and stopping services. Train travel is generally inexpensive.

ROAD:

Traffic drives on the right. There is a good network of high-quality roads in Slovenia. For further information, contact the national automobile club *Auto-Moto Zveza Slovenjie* (AMZS), Dunajska 128a, 1000 Ljubljana (tel: (1) 530 5300; website: www.amzs.si). There is a good **bus** network. The emergency roadside help and information service of AMZS is well organised and can be reached by dialling 1 987. **Traffic regulations:** Speed limits are 130kph (80mph) on motorways, 100kph (62mph) on roads reserved to motor traffic and 90kph (56mph) on roads outside residential areas. In cities it is 50kph (31mph). School buses cannot be overtaken. The alcohol limit is 0.05 per cent. Safety belts are compulsory (even in the back, if provided). Dimmed headlights must be turned on at all times while driving (even during the day). **Documentation:** Full national driving licences with a photograph are accepted. An International Green Card for non-EU members can be purchased at the border. International car insurance is mandatory.

URBAN:

Ljubljana has bus services and taxis are widely available.

Travel times: The following chart gives approximate travel times from **Ljubljana** (in hours and minutes) to other major cities/towns in Slovenia.

	Road	Rail
Portoroz	1.30	2.30
Maribor	2.00	2.30
Bled	0.45	1.15
Murska Sobota	3.00	3.30
Novo Mesto	1.00	1.30

Travel Advice

Most visits to Slovenia are trouble-free but you should be aware of the global risk of indiscriminate international terrorist attacks, which could be against civilian targets, including places frequented by foreigners.

This advice is based on information provided by the Foreign and Commonwealth Office in the UK. It is correct at time of publishing. As the situation can change rapidly, visitors are advised to contact the following organisations for the latest travel advice:

British Foreign and Commonwealth Office
Tel: (0845) 850 2829.
Website: www.fco.gov.uk

US Department of State
Website: http://travel.state.gov/travel

Accommodation

HOTELS:

Slovenia has over 190 hotels with 30,000 beds throughout the country. The hotel categories are **1** to **5 stars**.

PRIVATE ROOMS: These can be rented throughout Slovenia through local tourist offices. There are three categories: **I** (en suite), **II** (some en suite facilities – usually shower only) and **III** (shared facilities only). The Slovenian Tourist Board can provide more information (see *Top Things To Do*).

FARMHOUSES:

Visitors can choose between over 270 local farmhouses for an informal and welcoming stay close to nature.

YOUTH HOSTELS:

There are a dozen hostels in the country. The Youth Hostel International in Ljubljana is open from the end of June to the end of August and is located at Dijafki Pom Tabor, Vidovdanska 7, SI-1000, Ljubljana (tel: (1) 234 8840). There is also a youth hostel in Maribor.

CAMPING:

There are sites throughout the country. Most campsites are small but well equipped, with sports facilities and children's playgrounds. Contact the Slovenian Tourist Board for brochures and price lists (see *Top Things To Do*). Camping is not permitted outside campsites.

Credit: ©Slovenian Tourist Board / J Skok

ACCOMMODATION INFORMATION

Hotel Association of Slovenia
Vosnjakova 5, SI-1000, Ljubljana, Slovenia
Tel: (1) 430 7820.
Website: www.ntz-nta.si/slohotels

Association of Tourist Farms of Slovenia
Trnoveljska 1, SI-3000 Celje, Slovenia
Tel: (3) 491 6481.
E-mail: ztks@siol.net

Pocitniska Zveza Slovenije (Hostelling International Slovenia)
Gosposvetska 84, 2000 Maribor, Slovenia
Tel: (2) 234 2137.
Website: www.gaudeamus.si/hostelling

Top Things To See

- In the capital **Ljubljana**, cross the river towards to the **Town Hall** (1718) with its Baroque fountain and two open courtyards. Towering over the city are the twin towers of **Ljubljana Cathedral** (1708), which house some impressive frescoes. Then head for the **Castle**. Situated on a hill, splendid views of the city can be seen from the tower. The castle is currently undergoing repairs and only part of it is open to the public. On the eastern bank of the river is the **Town Museum** with an extensive collection of Roman artefacts. Near to the University is the **Ursuline Church** (1726) with an altar by Robba. The **National Museum**, the **National Gallery**, the **Municipal Gallery** and the **Modern Art Gallery** with the quiet Tivoli Gardens are all interesting.
- Discover the spectacular 20km cave of **Postojna**, only one hour's drive from the coast, which has been deemed one of the greatest sights of natural beauty, and features gigantic stalagmites and a cavernous hall which can hold over 10,000 people.
- In the port of **Koper**, explore the old town, entered through **Muda Gate** and enjoy various sights, clustered around the **Town Tower** (1480). Fine examples of the Venetian Gothic style are the 15th-century **Cathedral**, the **loggia** and the **Praetor's Palace**; also of interest is the Romanesque **Carmin Rotunda** (1317). Well worth a visit is the excellent **Provincial Museum**, which houses old maps of the area.
- To the south of Maribor, see the Roman remains and medieval centre of **Ptuj**, which is also the scene of traditional carnivals.
- In the mountain resort of **Bled**, see the neo-Gothic **Parish Church** (1904) with its interesting frescoes and **Bled Castle**, the former seat of the bishops of Brixen. Perching above a 100m (328ft) drop, the castle offers magnificent views over the city and lake.

Top Things To Do

- Relax in Slovenia's seaside resorts. **Portoroz** is the country's most popular resort, with numerous hotels and pavement cafes.
- Go **kayaking**, **canoeing** and **rafting** on the **Idrijca, Kolpa, Sava, Sava Bohinjka** and **Dolinka, Savinja** and **Soca** rivers.
- There is a wide range of good **skiing** resorts including those in **Bohinj, Bovec Pohorje** (which hosts international competitions), **Cerkno, Kranjska Gora, Krvavec, Zgornjesavska valley**, the **Rogla** and **Vogel**. The fashionable mountain resort of **Bled**, near the Austrian and Italian borders, is set on the idyllic **Lake Bled**, where **skating** and **curling** take place in winter, and **swimming** and **rowing** in summer. The trout and carp **fishing** are also very good.
- A popular **skiing** area in the winter, the **Julian Alps**, particularly the **Triglav National Park** is a great place for keen **trekkers** and visitors are attracted by the unusual tower on **Mount Triglav**.

A B C D E F G H I J K L M N O P Q R S T U V W X Y Z

- **Mountaineering** is a traditional Slovene sport – the **Julian and Kamnik Alps** are particularly popular. The Slovene Mountaineering Association organises adventure holidays (tel: (1) 434 5680; website: www.pzs.si). Slovenia's location south of the Alps means that **parachuting**, **paragliding** and **ballooning** are popular. **Hunting** is available.
- Feel revitalised at Slovenia's natural **spas**. In particular, the **Radenci Health Resort** (close to the Austrian border) is renowned for its 'three hearts' mineral water, said to have been served at the imperial court in Vienna and the papal court in the Vatican. At the **Rogaska Health Resort**, legend claims that the winged horse Pegasus created curative mineral waters with a magic blow of his hooves.
- Follow a **wine trail**. Worth visiting are the wine-growing hills of **Slovenske Gorice**, where a number of Slovenia's excellent white wines are produced.
- **Lipica** in the west of Slovenia is home to the *lippizaner* horse, bred by the Austro-Hungarian aristocracy of the 18th century. There are currently only 3000 of these horses left in the world. Take a tour of the stud farm, watch performances of classical riding or even ride the horses themselves.

Credit: ©Slovenian Tourist Board / A Fevžer

TOURIST INFORMATION

Slovenian Tourist Office in the UK
South Marlands, Itching Field, Horsham, West Sussex, R13 0NN, UK
Tel: (0870) 225 5305.
Website: www.slovenia-tourism.si

Slovenian Tourist Office in the USA
2929 East Commercial Boulevard, Suite 201, Fort Lauderdale, FL 33308
Tel: (954) 491 0112.
Website: www.slovenia-tourism.si

Entertainment

FOOD & DRINK: Slovenia's national cuisine shows an Austro-German influence with *sauerkraut*, grilled sausage and apple *strudel* often appearing on menus.
National specialities:
- The best-known Slovene foods are the breads made for special occasions, which appear in the form of braided loaves or wreathes: the *struklji* stuffed with sweet fillings, meat or vegetables.
- Another Slovene speciality is *potica*, a dessert prepared with a wide variety of fillings.

National drinks:
- The western and northeastern parts of Slovenia are known for their outstanding white wines (*Laski, Renski Rizling* and many others).
- The south is the homeland of the light, russet-coloured *cvicek* wine.
- The Adriatic Coast and the Karst region have mainly red *karstteran* wine.

Tipping: 10 per cent is generally expected.
SHOPPING: Attractive local gifts include bobbin lace, crystal glass and speciality wines. **Shopping hours:** Mon-Fri 0800-1900. Sat 0800-1300.
NIGHTLIFE: There is a wide selection of theatres, cinemas, casinos and nightclubs in the larger towns. Ljubljana also has a good opera house and the symphony orchestra plays regularly in the Big Hall of the Cultural and Congress Centre.

Business

- **GDP:** US$27.7 billion.
- **Main exports:** Manufactured goods, machinery and transport equipment, chemicals and food.
- **Main imports:** Machinery and transport equipment, manufactured goods, chemicals, fuels and lubricants and food.
- **Main trade partners:** Germany, Italy, Austria, France, Croatia and Bosnia & Herzegovina.

ECONOMY: Before the disintegration of Yugoslavia (now Serbia and Montenegro) that began in 1991, Slovenia was its richest and most industrialised republic. With few natural resources, Slovenia was initially seriously affected by the civil war and the collapse of the Yugoslav federal market. However, careful economic management enabled a solid recovery. GDP per capita is substantially higher than that of other transitional economies of central Europe. The agricultural sector is fairly small, growing cereals, sugar beet and potatoes, but the large areas of forest, covering about half the country, are an important natural resource. The mining industry is mostly concentrated on coal, but zinc and lead are also extracted along with small quantities of oil, gas and uranium. The manufacturing industry, which accounts for about 30 per cent of GDP, produces electrical equipment, textiles, wood-based products (including paper), chemicals and processed foods. The service sector is dominated by tourism and financial services. The tourism industry was almost annihilated during the early stages of the Yugoslav civil war when Slovenia was most heavily involved; it has since re-emerged.
Financial services are well developed, especially banking and insurance. Successive Governments have moved cautiously to reform the economy, introducing market-oriented reforms gradually and -for the most part - successfully. Inflation continued to decelerate, falling to 3.7 per cent in 2004, while the economy was growing moderately at 4 per cent in 2004. Unemployment is estimated to be at around 6 per cent (2004). Slovenia has joined the IMF, World Bank and the European Bank for Reconstruction and Development, and became a full member of the World Trade Organization in July 1995. In March 2004, Slovenia became the first transitional country to graduate from borrower status to donor partner at the World Bank. Slovenia is the only former Yugoslav republic to have been accepted for membership of the EU, which it joined in May 2004. Slovenia has agreed to adopt the Euro by 2007 and therefore must keep debt levels, budget deficits, interest rates and inflation levels within the EU's Maastrict criteria.

Credit: ©Slovenian Tourist Board / K Kunaver

BUSINESS ETIQUETTE: Smart dress is advised. Appointments are usual and visitors should be punctual. Visiting cards are essential. Slovenia is the most efficient and reliable of the ex-Yugoslav republics, being in many respects comparable to Austria and Germany. Executives will generally have a good knowledge of German, English and sometimes Italian. There is a well-developed network of local agents, advisers, consultants and lawyers willing to act for foreign companies. **Office hours:** Mon-Fri 0800-1600.
CONFERENCES/CONVENTIONS:
Slovenia's tradition as a meeting place goes back to 1821, when it played host to the Congress of the Holy Alliance. The main conference locations are Bled, Ljubljana, Portoroz, Radenci and Rogaska Slatina, where there are meeting facilities for up to 2000 participants.

COMMERCIAL INFORMATION

Chamber of Commerce and Industry of Slovenia
Dimiceva 13, SI-1504 Ljubljana, Slovenia
Tel: (1) 589 8000.
Website: www.gzs.si

Culture and Congress Centre (Information on Conferences/Conventions)
Cankarjev dom, Presernova 10, 1000 Ljubljana, Slovenia
Tel: (1) 241 7100.
Website: www.cd-cc.si

Conferences and Conventions Department of the Slovenian Tourist Board (see *Top Things To Do*)

Solomon Islands

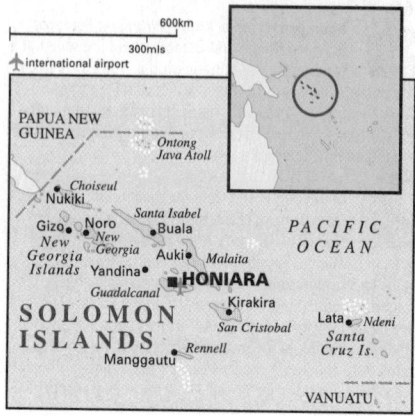

Location: Southwestern Pacific.

Time: GMT + 11.

Overview

The Solomon Islands archipelago is scattered in the southwestern Pacific, east of Papua New Guinea. The group comprises most of the Solomon Islands (those in the northwest are part of Papua New Guinea), the Ontong Java Islands, Rennell Island and the Santa Cruz Islands, which lie further to the east. The capital, Honiara, is situated on Guadalcanal Island, which also has the highest mountain, Mount Makarakombu, at 2447m (8028ft). The Solomon Islands are a remote and unspoilt travel destination, with a slowly developing tourist industry. The superb marine life in the surrounding waters makes the islands a diver's paradise. Guadalcanal, Malaita, Choiseul, New Georgia, San Cristobal and Santa Isabel are the main islands. Honiara, the capital on Guadalcanal, has a museum, botanical gardens and Chinatown. Villages and scenic drives are within easy reach. Popular tours include the World War II battlefields and various carving villages on the islands of Rennell and Bellona.

General Information

AREA: 27,556 sq km (10,639 sq miles).
POPULATION: 450,000 (estimate 2001).
POPULATION DENSITY: 16.3 per sq km (2001).
CAPITAL: Honiara. **Population:** 50,000 (2000).
GEOGRAPHY: The larger of the islands are 145 to 193km (90 to 120 miles) in length, while the smallest are no more than coral outcrops. The terrain is generally quite rugged, with foothills that rise gently to a peak and then fall away steeply to the sea on the other side. The capital Honiara is situated on Guadalcanal Island, which also has the highest mountain, Mount Makarakombu, at 2447m (8028ft). There are a number of dormant volcanoes scattered throughout the archipelago.
GOVERNMENT: Constitutional monarchy. Gained independence from the UK in 1978. **Head of State:** HM Queen Elizabeth II, represented locally by Governor-General Nathaniel Waena since 2004. **Head of Government:** Prime Minister Snyder Rini since April 2006.
LANGUAGE: English is the official language. Pidgin English and over 80 different local dialects are also spoken.
RELIGION: More than 95 per cent of the population are Christian; the rest mostly hold traditional beliefs.
ELECTRICITY: 230/240 volts AC, 50Hz. Australian-type flat three-pin plugs are in use.
SOCIAL CONVENTIONS: A casual atmosphere prevails

and European customs exist alongside local traditions. Informal wear is widely suitable although women often wear long dresses for evening functions. Men need never wear ties. Women, in general, should dress modestly and appropriately, noting that certain areas may be 'taboo' and exclusively reserved for men. It is customary to cover thighs. Visitors are discouraged from wearing beachwear and shorts around towns and villages. Swearing is a crime and can lead to huge compensation claims and even jail.

Climate

Semi-tropical, mainly hot and humid, with little annual variation in temperature. The wet season (November to April) can bring severe tropical storms.

Required clothing: Tropical, lightweights and cottons are recommended. Rainwear from November to April.

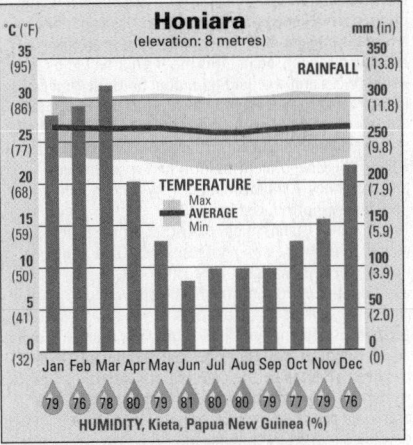

Honiara (elevation: 8 metres) — TEMPERATURE (Max / AVERAGE / Min), RAINFALL. HUMIDITY, Kieta, Papua New Guinea (%): Jan 79, Feb 76, Mar 78, Apr 80, May 79, Jun 81, Jul 80, Aug 80, Sep 79, Oct 77, Nov 79, Dec 76.

Communications

Telephone: IDD is available. Country code: 677. There are often technical problems with line connections.

Mobile telephone: GSM 900 network provided by *Solomon Telekom Company* (website: www.solomon.com.sb). Visitors can hire mobile phones on the islands; payment is preferred in cash (US/AUS/NZ currencies are accepted).

Internet: Public e-mail facilities are available in Gizo and Honiara.

Post: Airmail to Europe takes approximately seven days. Main post office hours (in Honiara): Mon-Fri 0900-1630, Sat 0900-1100. Other post office hours: Mon-Fri 0800-1630, Sat 0800-1200.

MEDIA: The *Solomon Islands Broadcasting Corporation (SIBC)*, a statutory body, operates a public radio service. There are no TV services based in the Solomon Islands, although Australia's *ABC Asia Pacific*, *BBC World* and other satellite TV channels can be received.

Press: The main newspapers are the daily English-language *Solomon Star* and *Solomons Voice*.

Radio: *Solomon Islands Broadcasting Corporation (SIBC)* operates national station *Radio Hapi Isles*, *Wantok FM* and provincial stations *Radio Hapi Lagun* and *Radio Temotu*. *Paoa FM* is a commercial station.

Passport/Visa

	Passport Required?	Visa Required?	Return Ticket Required?
Full British	Yes	No	Yes
Australian	Yes	No	Yes
Canadian	Yes	No	Yes
USA	Yes	No	Yes
Other EU	Yes	No	Yes
Japanese	Yes	No	Yes

Note: *Regulations and requirements may be subject to change at short notice, and you are advised to contact the appropriate diplomatic or consular authority before finalising travel arrangements. Any numbers in the chart refer to the footnotes below.*

PASSPORTS: Passport valid for at least six months required by all except nationals of Hong Kong (SAR) with a document of identity.

VISAS: A *Visitor's Permit* will be issued to most nationals on arrival at the airport (including those listed in the chart above). The permit allows stays of up to three months and the cost of the permit varies according to nationality.

Note: Visitors from the following countries need clearance from the Immigration Department 'and are required to give prior notice in order to obtain a visitor's permit:
(a) all African countries;
(b) all CIS countries (except Belarus);

(c) nationals of Afghanistan, Albania, Angola, Bahrain, Bangladesh, Benin, Bhutan, Bolivia, Bosnia & Herzegovina, Botswana, Bulgaria, Burkina Faso, Cambodia, Cameroon, Cape Verde, Chad, China (PR), Colombia, Comoros Islands, Congo (Dem Rep), Congo (Rep), Costa Rica, Côte d'Ivoire, Croatia, Cuba, Cyprus, Ecuador, El Salvador, Estonia, Guatemala, Haiti, Honduras, India, Indonesia, Iran, Iraq, Jamaica, Jordan, Korea (Dem Rep), Laos, Latvia, Lebanon, Lithuania, Macedonia (Former Yugoslav Republic of), Madagascar, Mauritius, Mexico, Mongolia, Myanmar, Nepal, Nicaragua, Oman, Pakistan, Panama, The Philippines, Qatar, Romania, Saudi Arabia, Seychelles, Sri Lanka, Syrian Arab Republic, Turkey, United Arab Emirates, Venezuela, Vietnam and Yemen.

Application to: Nearest Solomon Islands Consulate, High Commission or Embassy *or* Principal/Director of Immigration, Ministry of Commerce, Foreign Affairs and Tourism, PO Box G26, Honiara (E-mail: immigration@commerce.gov.sb).

Application requirements: *All visitors*: (a) Valid passport. (b) Onward or return tickets. (c) Proof of sufficient funds for the duration of stay. *Visitors requiring prior clearance*: (a)-(c) and, (d) Photocopy of passport. (e) Details of itinerary. (f) Reason for visit.

Working days required: Apply well in advance.

Temporary residence: Apply to the Labour Division, Ministry of Commerce, Foreign Affairs and Tourism (see address above).

PASSPORT/VISA INFORMATION

Embassy of the Solomon Islands in Belgium
Avenue Edouard Lacombrt 17, 1040 Brussels, Belgium
Tel: (2) 732 7085.

Permanent Mission of the Solomon Islands to the United Nations in the USA
Suite 400L, 800 2nd Avenue, New York, NY 10017, USA
Tel: (212) 599 6192.
Website: www.solomons.com

Money

Currency: Solomon Islands Dollar (SBD; symbol SI$) = 100 cents. Notes are in denominations of SI$50, 20, 10, 5 and 2. Coins are in denominations of SI$1, and 50, 20, 10, 5, 2 and 1 cents.

Currency exchange: Money can be changed at banks, bureaux de change, some hotels, and larger shops and restaurants. Automated foreign exchange machines and three ATMs are available in Honiara.

Credit & debit cards: All major credit cards are widely accepted in hotels and tourist resorts. Check with your credit, or debit, card company for details of merchant acceptability and other facilities which may be available.

Traveller's cheques: Can be exchanged at banks, of which there are three in the major towns. To avoid additional exchange rate charges, travellers are advised to take traveller's cheques in Australian Dollars or Pounds Sterling.

Currency restrictions: The import of local and foreign currency is unlimited provided declared on arrival. The export of local currency is limited to SI$250; the export of foreign currency is limited to the extent approved by the Solomon Islands' Monetary Authority.

Banking hours: Mon-Fri 0830-1500.

Exchange rate indicators:
Rate at time of publishing
£1.00=   SI$12.93
$1.00=   SI$7.33

Duty Free

The following items may be imported into the Solomon Islands without incurring customs duty for those aged 18 years and above:

200 cigarettes or 250g cigars or 250g of tobacco; 2l of spirits or equivalent; other dutiable goods up to a total value of SI$400.

Prohibited items: Unlicensed firearms or other weapons (without Police Permit) and offensive literature or pictures. Fruit and vegetables other than from New Zealand need an import permit.

Public Holidays

Below are listed Public Holidays for the January 2006-June 2007 period.
2006: Jan 1 New Year's Day. **Apr 14-17** Easter. **Jun 9** Queen's Birthday. **Jul 7** Independence Day. **Dec 25** Christmas Day. **Dec 26** National Day of Thanksgiving.
2007: Jan 1 New Year's Day. **Apr 6-9** Easter. **Jun 9** Queen's Birthday.

Note: Each part of the Solomon Islands has its own Province Day. These are listed below. If a Province Day falls on a Sunday, the following Monday is observed as a public holiday.
Feb 25 Choiseul. **Jun 2** Isable. **Jun 8** Temotu. **Jun 29** Central Island. **Jul 20** Rennell. **Aug 1** Guadalcanal. **Aug 3** Makira/Ulawa. **Aug 15** Malaita. **Dec 7** Western Province.

Health

	Special Precautions?	Certificate Required?
Yellow Fever	No	1
Cholera	No	No
Typhoid & Polio	2	N/A
Malaria	3	N/A

Note: *Regulations and requirements may be subject to change at short notice, and you are advised to contact your doctor well in advance of your intended date of departure. Any numbers in the chart refer to the footnotes below.*

1: A yellow fever vaccination certificate is required for travellers coming from infected areas.

2: Vaccination against typhoid is advised.

3: Malaria risk exists throughout the year except in some outlying islets in the east and south. The malignant *falciparum* strain is present and is reported to be resistant to chloroquine and sulfadoxine-pyrimethamine. The recommended prophylaxis is chloroquine plus proguanil.

Food & drink: All water should be regarded as being a potential health risk. Water used for drinking, brushing teeth or making ice should first be boiled or otherwise sterilised. Milk is unpasteurised and should be boiled. Powdered or tinned milk is available and is advised, but make sure that it is reconstituted with pure water. Avoid dairy products that are likely to have been made from unboiled milk. Only eat well-cooked meat and fish, preferably served hot. Pork, salad and mayonnaise may carry increased risk. Vegetables should be cooked and fruit peeled.

Other risks: Immunisation against *hepatitis A* is recommended. *Hepatitis B* is endemic. *Filariasis* occurs. *Dengue fever* is now a major health risk. There have also been reports of *Legionnaires Disease* from Auki in the Malaita Province. Coelenterates, poisonous fish and sea snakes are a hazard to bathers.

Health care: Medical facilities are very limited and there are drug shortages. There are eight hospitals, the largest being the Central Hospital in Honiara. Church missions provide medical facilities on outlying islands. Health insurance is essential. There are no decompression facilities.

Travel - International

AIR:

The national airline *Solomon Airlines (IE)* (website: www.solomonairlines.com.au) operates flights from Australia. *Qantas* offers three flights a week from Brisbane to Honiara. Other airlines serving the Solomon Islands include *Air Niugini* and *Air Pacific*.

The *Visit the South Pacific Pass* is valid for a number of airlines operating in the South Pacific, including *Air Caledonie*, *Air Marshall Islands*, *Air Nauru*, *Air Niugingi*, *Air Pacific*, *Air Vanuatu*, *Polynesian Airlines*, *Qantas*, *Royal Tongan Airlines* and *Solomon Airlines*. Offering reductions of up to 50 per cent on normal airfares, this sector-based pass allows for flexible island-hopping between the destinations of the Cook Islands, Fiji, Nauru, New Caledonia, Samoa, Tahiti, Tonga, Vanuatu and the more remote Melanesian and Micronesian islands, together with major cities in Australia (Brisbane, Melbourne and Sydney) and New Zealand (Wellington). The journey must be started outside the South Pacific and only one stopover in Australia is allowed. A minimum of two coupons must be bought before departure (a maximum of eight coupons can be purchased en route). For details and conditions, contact the South Pacific Tourism Organisation (see *Top Things To Do*).

Approximate flight times: From Honiara to *London* is 29 hours 45 minutes, excluding stopover in Brisbane.

Main airports: *Honiara (HIR)* (Henderson Field) on Guadalcanal Island, 13km (8 miles) east of Honiara (travel time – 20 minutes). *To/from the airport*: Bus and taxi services are available. *Facilities*: Bank/bureau de change, duty free shops (for scheduled international flights) and car hire.

Departure tax: SI$40. Transit passengers and children under two years are exempt.

SEA:

Main ports: *Honiara* (Guadalcanal Island), *Yandina* (Russel Islands) and *Noro* (New Georgia). The cargo line *Bank* offers a limited number of passenger places. It may also be possible to sail with a yacht from Australia or New Zealand as part of the crew.

Travel - Internal

AIR:

Domestic scheduled and charter services are run by *Solomon Airlines* from Henderson Field to most main islands and towns in the Solomons. The *Discover Solomons Pass* is a domestic airpass offering up to eight flights within the Solomon Islands over a period of 30 days. Flightseeing tours can also be arranged.

SEA:

Large and small ships, including *Malaita, Ramos, Western Province* and *Ysabel*, provide the best means of travelling between islands. Services are run by the Government and by a host of private operators; some of the Christian missions even have their own fleets. Cruises are also available with *World Discoverer*.

ROAD:

Traffic drives on the left. There are over 1300km (800 miles) of roads throughout the islands. About 455km (280 miles) are main roads and a further 800km (500 miles) are privately maintained roads for plantation use. Road maintenance is limited and the general condition of the roads is very poor, as are driving standards. Most of the roads are on Guadalcanal and Malaita. **Bus:** There are limited services on the islands. **Taxi:** Available in Auki and Honiara. It is advisable to agree the fare beforehand. **Car hire:** This is available through hotels in Honiara. **Documentation:** A national driving licence will suffice.

Travel Advice

Most visits to the Solomon Islands are trouble-free, but you should be aware of the global risk of indiscriminate terrorist attacks which could be against civilian targets, including places frequented by foreigners.
The Solomon Islands is in the Pacific 'Ring of Fire' and subject to earthquakes.
This advice is based on information provided by the Foreign and Commonwealth Office in the UK. It is correct at time of publishing. As the situation can change rapidly, visitors are advised to contact the following organisations for the latest travel advice:

British Foreign and Commonwealth Office
Tel: (0845) 850 2829.
Website: www.fco.gov.uk

US Department of State
Website: http://travel.state.gov/travel

Accommodation

HOTELS:

There are a number of hotels, motels and lodges in Honiara. Visitors are advised to make advance reservations. Accommodation is also available in Malaita, the Reef Islands and Western Solomons. A number of lodges and resorts on the islands offer a variety of leisure activities. A full list of accommodation and rates is available from the Ministry of Commerce, Employment and Tourism or the Solomon Islands Visitors Bureau (see *Top Things To Do*).

CAMPING:

Camping is rare and is best confined to more remote areas. Permission should always be obtained from the landowner, usually the village chief, before pitching a tent.

Top Things To See

• **Choiseul, Guadalcanal, Malaita, New Georgia, San Cristobal** and **Santa Isabel** are the main islands. They are up to 200km (120 miles) long and up to 50km (30 miles) wide. The **wildlife** on the islands is of great interest, consisting of a mixture of introduced and indigenous species. Most islands are populated with a range of reptiles (including turtles), as well as marsupials such as 'flying foxes' (fruit bats), *phalangers* and *opossums*. Hawks, cuckoos, waders and other often colourful birds exhibit the diversity of behaviour typical of island creatures. The buff-headed *coucal* is the world's largest cuckoo. The ubiquitous ants, beetles, spiders, moths, butterflies and frogs also come in a variety of forms. The ocean around the islands is crammed with exotic creatures.
• **Honiara**, the capital on Guadalcanal, has a **museum**, **botanical gardens** and **Chinatown**. There are relics of World War II in and around the town, and notice boards

indicate major battles and incidents that took place during the battle for Guadalcanal. Villages and scenic drives are within easy reach.
• Travel agencies can arrange excursions around **Guadalcanal** and other islands. Popular tours include the battlefields of World War II, the **Betikama carving centre**, and **Alite** and **Laulasi villages** on the island of Malaita, where shells are broken, rounded and, after further working, strung together. They are used to denote status and as gifts and items of barter in inter-tribal deals. The strings of shells can be worn as bracelets, necklaces, belts and earrings. They may also include animal and fish teeth and, in times past, the teeth of murderers. Collectively, these items are known as 'shell money'. Carvings for the tourist trade are made on **Bellona** and **Rennell**. Miniature daggers, spears and clubs are very popular. Other carvings show scenes from life on the Solomon Islands, both human and animal.

Top Things To Do

• The Solomon Islands consist of over 900 volcanic islands and coral atolls spread across the blue tropical waters. The superb marine life in the surrounding waters makes the islands an excellent destination for **swimming, diving** and **cruising** (please note that swimming is not recommended in the sea around Honiara because of sharks. Much of the best land-based diving is located in the Western Province on or near the islands of **Gizo** (the capital of the Western Province) and **New Georgia**. Well-known dive sites in the area include **Munda**, on the **Roviana Lagoon**, 15 minutes by plane from Gizo; and **Uepi Island**, on the north side of New Georgia, across the famous **Marovo Lagoon**. Diving tours to the numerous wrecks from World War II are also possible. All resorts offer a full range of diving facilities and most have resident dive instructors. Live-aboard diving tours are also available; for further information, see online (website: www.bilikiki.com or www.lalae.com.sb).
• There is also good **fishing** potential and enquiries may be made at the Point Cruz Yacht Club, which welcomes visitors.
• Tropical **rainforests** cover most of the archipelago and there are a number of dormant volcanoes. Exotic orchids, ferns and palms are widespread and butterflies are abundant. There are more than 70 species of reptiles. A variety of trees and shrubs have been introduced along with fruits and vegetables. Educational tours can be organised via the Solomon Islands Visitors Bureau (see *Tourist Information*). **Bushwalking** and **climbing** are also popular.

TOURIST INFORMATION

Solomon Islands Visitors Bureau
Street address: Mendana Avenue, Honiara, Solomon Islands
Postal address: PO Box 321, Honiara, Solomon Islands
Tel: 22442.
Website: www.visitsolomons.com.sb

South Pacific Tourism Organisation in Fiji
Street address: Level 3, FNPF Place, 343-359 Victoria Parade, Suva, Fiji
Postal address: PO Box 13-119, Suva, Fiji
Tel: (679) 330 4177.
Website: www.tcsp.com

Entertainment

FOOD & DRINK: There are a few restaurants outside the hotels in Honaria. Both Asian and European food is served and the cuisine is generally good. There are two Chinese restaurants in Honiara which are quite popular. Table service is normal. Spirits, wine and beer are available.
National specialities:
• *Tapioca* pudding.
• *Taro* roots with *taro* leaves.
Tipping: There is no tipping on the Solomon Islands and visitors are requested to honour this local custom.
NIGHTLIFE: Honiara is a comparatively quiet town, although there are a few clubs with music and dancing, the occasional film show, and snooker and darts. The clubs offer temporary membership to visitors.
SHOPPING: Local purchases include mother-of-pearl items, walking sticks, carved and inlaid wood, copper murals, conch shells and rare varieties of cowrie. New Georgia in the western district is known for carved fish, turtles and birds. Carvings in ebony, inlaid with shell, are unique. Duty free shopping is available at a number of stores in Honiara. **Shopping hours:** Mon-Fri 0800-1700, Sat 0800-1200.

Business

• **GDP:** SI$302 million (2005).
• **Main exports:** Timber, fish, palm oil and kernels and copra.
• **Main imports:** Machinery, transport equipment and mineral fuels.
• **Main trade partners:** Australia and Japan, UK, New Zealand, Korea (Rep), Thailand and Singapore.

ECONOMY: The economy depends on subsistence agriculture and fishing, which together employ about 90 per cent of the population. The agricultural sector produces coconuts, sweet potatoes, cassava, fruit and vegetables; livestock rearing has grown steadily. Copra is still produced in commercial quantities, but low world prices have reduced the income from this commodity. As a result, timber is now the islands' main source of revenue although, again, this has been affected by low world prices and a ceiling on production. The timber industry had grown very rapidly during the early-1990s but has been cut back drastically following international pressure (which included suspension of vital financial aid) on the Government to introduce a controlled logging policy. A moratorium of new timber-felling licences was introduced in 1998.
The Solomon Islands' main industrial prospect lies in its mostly undeveloped mineral resources. Gold mining is now important and is set for further expansion; in addition, there are confirmed deposits of copper, lead, zinc, silver, cobalt and other ores. In the service sector, there is a small and – initially – growing tourism industry which brings in around US$15 million annually, but this has been affected by the poor security situation. Despite its narrow economic base, the Government has so far eschewed the choice of some South Pacific neighbours to develop an 'offshore' finance industry. However, it has joined with fellow members of the Pacific Forum in establishing a free trade system in 2002, known as the Pacific Island Countries Trade Agreement (PICTA). The Solomon Islands continue to receive substantial overseas aid, although much of this is consumed by a large external debt. In 1998, following the Asian financial crisis, the Government also introduced a programme of structural reform under the auspices of the IMF.
BUSINESS ETIQUETTE: Shirt and smart trousers or skirt will suffice. English and French are widely spoken. The best time to visit is May to October. **Office hours:** Mon-Fri 0800-1200 and 1300-1630, Sat 0730-1200.

COMMERCIAL INFORMATION

Solomon Islands Chamber of Commerce and Industry
PO Box 650, Honiara, Solomon Islands
Tel: 39542.
E-mail: chamberc@solomon.com.sb

A B C D E F G H I J K L M N O P Q R S T U V W X Y Z

Somalia

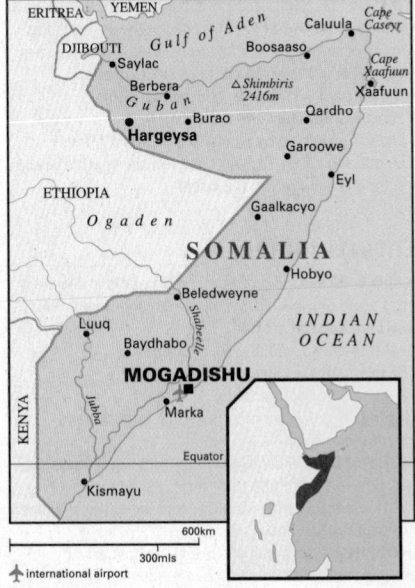

Location: East Africa.

Time: GMT + 3.

Overview

Somalia developed from a string of Arab sultanates along the northeast coast of Africa, which in turn had grown up from trading posts established from the 17th century onwards. As Arab influence waned, the British, French and Italians established protectorates on the Somali coast during the late-19th century. These were the subjects of various treaties, forged amid frequent border clashes between the colonial powers and the neighbouring Ethiopians, and between the European powers themselves.

Modern Somalia was created on 1 July 1960 from British and Italian Somalilands. Inherited tribal rivalries and territorial disputes have dominated the country's subsequent history.

Years of fighting between rival warlords and an inability to deal with famine and disease have led to the deaths of up to one million people.

The country has been without an effective central Government since President Siad Barre was overthrown in 1991. In the main part of the country, a Transitional National Government was elected in July 2000 by representatives of the country's major clans, political and religious movements. The Government is led by Abdullahi Yusuf Ahmed and Ali Mohamed Ghedi, who hold the titles of President and Prime Minister respectively. It has UN recognition but, if the 2004 accord holds, will be replaced under a new constitution.

General Information

AREA: 637,657 sq km (246,201 sq miles).
POPULATION: 9.38 million (UN estimate 2002).
POPULATION DENSITY: 14.9 per sq km.
CAPITAL: Mogadishu. **Population:** 1.21 million (UN, 2000, including suburbs).
GEOGRAPHY: Somalia is bordered to the north by the Gulf of Aden, to the south and west by Kenya, to the west by Ethiopia and to the northwest by Djibouti. To the east lies the Indian Ocean. Somalia is an arid country and the scenery includes mountains in the north, the flat semi-desert plains in the interior and the subtropical

region in the south. Separated from the sea by a narrow coastal plain, the mountains slope south and west to the central, almost waterless plateau which makes up most of the country. The beaches are protected by a coral reef that runs from Mogadishu to the Kenyan border in the south. They are among the longest in the world. There are only two rivers, the Jubba and the Shabeelle, and both rise in the Ogaden region of Ethiopia. Along their banks is most of the country's agricultural land. The Somali population is concentrated in the coastal towns, in the wetter, northern areas and in the south near the two rivers. A large nomadic population is scattered over the interior, although drought in recent years has led to many settling as farmers or fishermen in newly formed communities.

GOVERNMENT: Somalia gained independence from the UK and Italy in 1960. At the Arta Peace Conference in August 2000, an interim Parliament was established.
Executive President: Abdullahi Yusuf Ahmed since 2004. **Prime Minister:** Ali Mohamed Ghedi since 2004. The northern part of the country declared itself independent as the Republic of Somaliland with Dahir Riyale Kahin as acting President since 2002, although it has achived little international recognition.
LANGUAGE: Somali and Arabic are the official languages. Swahili is spoken, particularly in the south. English and Italian are also widely spoken.
RELIGION: The state religion is Islam and the majority of Somalis are Sunni Muslims. There is a small Christian community, mostly Roman Catholic.
ELECTRICITY: 220 volts AC, 50Hz.
SOCIAL CONVENTIONS: Traditional dance, music, song and craftsmanship flourish despite gradual modern development. Informal wear is acceptable and there is no objection to bikinis on the beach. Visitors should respect local customs.

Climate

The *Jilal* starts around January and is the harshest period, hot and very dry. *Gu* is the first rainy season lasting from March to June. *Hagaa*, during August, is a time of dry monsoon winds and dust clouds. The second rainy season is from September to December and is called *Dayr*.
Required clothing: Lightweights and rainwear.

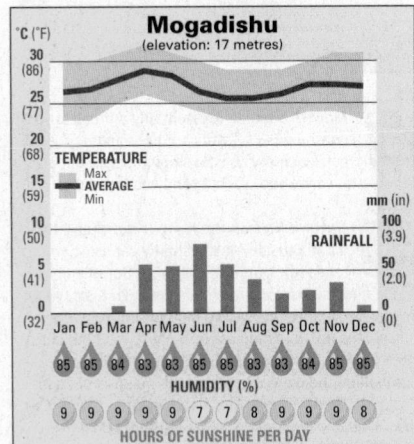

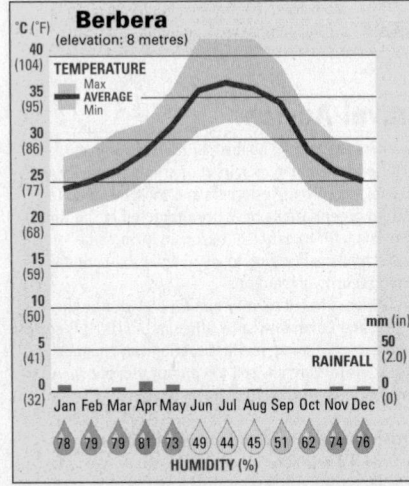

Communications

Telephone: IDD is available. Country code: 252. Outgoing international calls must be made via the operator.
Mobile telephone: GSM 900 network. Operators are *Hormuud Telecom Somalia Inc*, *Nationlink* (website: www.nationlinks.net) and *Telesom* (website: www.telesom.net).
Internet: Somalia's *SomaliNet* (website: www.somalinet.com) is one of the country's first ISPs. Internet facilities for visitors are yet to be fully established.
Post: Airmail to Europe takes up to two weeks.
MEDIA: Somalia's disintegration has been reflected in its media. Broadcasters and journalists operate in a dangerous environment and many Somalis rely on foreign broadcasts for their news.
Press: *Qaran*, *Xog-Ogaal* and *Ayaamaha* are Mogadishu based. *Somaliland Times – Hargeisa* is an English-language weekly publication.
TV: *Somali Telemedia Network (STN)* is a private channel, rebroadcasting Qatar-based *Al-Jazeera TV* and CNN. *Somali Broadcasting Corporation (SBC)* is a private network based in Puntland.
Radio: *Radio Mogadishu*, *Voice of the Republic of Somalia* is a FM station operated by the transitional Government. *Radio HornAfrik* is a widely-listened-to private FM station in Mogadishu, which rebroadcasts BBC programmes.

Passport/Visa

	Passport Required?	Visa Required?	Return Ticket Required?
Full British	Yes	Yes	Yes
Australian	Yes	Yes	Yes
Canadian	Yes	Yes	Yes
USA	Yes	Yes	Yes
Other EU	Yes	Yes	Yes
Japanese	Yes	Yes	Yes

Note: *Regulations and requirements may be subject to change at short notice, and you are advised to contact the appropriate diplomatic or consular authority before finalising travel arrangements. Any numbers in the chart refer to the footnotes below.*

Note: The Somali Embassy in London is closed at present owing to civil war in Somalia. Contact the Foreign Office (website: www.fco.gov.uk) for any information regarding entry into Somalia.
PASSPORTS: Valid passport required by all.
VISAS: Required by all except transit passengers continuing their journey by the same or first connecting aircraft, provided holding onward or return documentation and not leaving the airport.
Types of visa: *Tourist*, *Business* and *Transit*.
Validity: Dependent on nationality.
Application to: Contact the Somali Embassy in Addis Ababa, Ethiopia (tel: (1) 635 921/2; fax: (1) 627 847). The British Embassy in Ethiopia can also help with up-to-date information concerning travel to Somalia, available consular services, visa application requirements, visa costs and temporary residence.
Note: Upon arrival, all visitors - except those under 18 years of age - must exchange US$100 or equivalent into local currency. Please note that the exact amount to be exchanged may vary according to region.

PASSPORT/VISA INFORMATION

United Nations Development Programme for Somalia (UNDP)
Street address: Springette off lower Kabete Road, Spring Valley, Nairobi, Kenya
Postal address: PO Box 28832, Nairobi, 00200 Kenya
Tel: (20) 418 3640/2/3/4.
Website: www.unsomalia.net or www.so.undp.org

European Commission Somalia Unit (ECSU)
Street address: Union Building, Ragati Road, 00100 Nairobi, Kenya
Postal address: PO Box 45119, 00100 Nairobi, Kenya
Tel: (20) 271 2860 or 3250.
Website: www.delken.cec.eu.int

Money

Currency: Somali Shilling (SOS) = 100 cents. Notes are in denominations of SOS500, 100, 50, 20, 10 and 5. Coins are in denominations of SOS1, and 50, 10 and 5 cents.
Currency exchange: US Dollar bills are the easiest currency to exchange; hotels are the easiest and safest

places. Avoid money changers in crowded areas.

Credit & debit cards: Not accepted.

Traveller's cheques: US traveller's cheques are preferred but generally not recommended.

Currency restrictions: The import and export of local currency is limited to SOS200. The import of foreign currency is unlimited provided declared on arrival and exchanged at the national banks within five days after arrival. The export of foreign currency is limited to the amount declared on arrival. All foreign exchange transactions should be recorded on the official currency form which may be required prior to departure from Somalia.

Banking hours: Sat-Thurs 0800-1130.

Exchange rate indicators:

Rate at time of publishing

£1.00=	SOS3407.28
$1.00=	SOS1930.00

Duty Free

The following goods may be imported into Somalia without incurring customs duty:

400 cigarettes or 40 cigars or 400g of tobacco; one bottle of wine or spirits; a reasonable amount of perfume for personal use.

Public Holidays

Below are listed Public Holidays for the January 2006- June 2007 period.

2006: Jan 1 New Year's Day. **Jan 10** Eid al-Adha (Feast of the Sacrifice). **Feb 9** Ashoura. **Apr 11** Mouloud (Birth of the Prophet). **May 1** Labour Day. **Jun 26** Independence Day. **Jul 1** Foundation of the Republic. **Oct 23** Eid al-Fitr (End of Ramadan). **Dec 31** Eid al-Adha (Feast of the Sacrifice).

2007: Jan 1 New Year's Day. **Feb 9** Ashoura. **Mar 31** Mouloud (Birth of the Prophet). **May 1** Labour Day. **Jun 26** Independence Day.

Note: Muslim festivals are timed according to local sightings of various phases of the moon and the dates given above are approximations. During the lunar month of Ramadan that precedes Eid al-Fitr, Muslims fast during the day and feast at night and normal business patterns may be interrupted. Many restaurants are closed during the day and there may be restrictions on smoking and drinking. Some disruption may continue into Eid al-Fitr itself. Eid al-Fitr and Eid al-Adha may last anything from two to 10 days, depending on the region. For more information, see the *World of Islam* appendix.

Health

	Special Precautions?	Certificate Required?
Yellow Fever	Yes	1
Cholera	2	No
Typhoid & Polio	3	N/A
Malaria	4	N/A

Note: *Regulations and requirements may be subject to change at short notice, and you are advised to contact your doctor well in advance of your intended date of departure. Any numbers in the chart refer to the footnotes below.*

1: A *yellow fever* vaccination certificate is required from travellers arriving from infected areas. Travellers arriving from non-endemic zones should note that vaccination is strongly recommended for travel outside the urban areas, even if an outbreak of the disease has not been reported and they would normally not require a vaccination certificate to enter the country.

2: Following WHO guidelines issued in 1973, a *cholera* vaccination certificate is not a condition of entry to Somalia. However, at the beginning of 2000, an outbreak of cholera was reported, and precautions are recommended for those likely to be at risk. Up-to-date advice should be sought before deciding whether these precautions should include vaccination, as medical opinion is divided over its effectiveness; see the *Health* appendix.

3: Vaccination against *typhoid* is advised.

4: *Malaria* risk, predominantly in the malignant *falciparum* form, exists all year throughout the country. Resistance to chloroquine and sulfadoxine-pyrimethamine has been reported. The recommended prophylaxis is mefloquine.

Food & drink: Mains water is normally chlorinated and, whilst relatively safe, may cause mild abdominal upsets. Bottled water is available and is advised for the first few weeks of stay. Drinking water outside main cities and towns is likely to be contaminated and sterilisation is considered essential. Milk is unpasteurised and should be boiled. Powdered or tinned milk is available and is advised, but make sure that it is reconstituted with pure water. Avoid dairy products which are likely to have been made from unboiled milk. Only eat well-cooked meat and fish, preferably served hot. Pork, salad and mayonnaise may carry increased risk. Vegetables should be cooked and fruit peeled.

Other risks: *Bilharzia (schistosomiasis)* is present. Avoid swimming and paddling in fresh water; swimming pools which are well chlorinated and maintained are safe. *Hepatitis A* and *E* are widespread; *hepatitis B* is hyperendemic. *Meningococcal meningitis* may occur. *Rabies* is present. For those at high risk, vaccination before arrival should be considered. If you are bitten, seek medical advice without delay. For more information, see the *Health* appendix.

Health care: Medical facilities are very limited and visitors are advised to take their own medicines with them. Health insurance is essential. Medical treatment at government-run hospitals and dispensaries is free for Somalians and may sometimes be free for visitors.

Travel - International

AIR:

The national airline is *Somali Airlines*.

Approximate flight times: From Mogadishu to *London* is 15 hours, flying first to Dubai and then on to London with a stopover in Djibouti.

Main airports: *Mogadishu (MGQ)* is 6km (4 miles) west of the city. There is a taxi service to the city centre.

Departure tax: The equivalent of US$20. Transit passengers and children under two years are exempt.

SEA:

The principal ports are Berbera, Kismayu, Marka and Mogadishu.

ROAD:

There are routes to Somalia from Djibouti and Kenya. There is no border crossing with Ethiopia at present. Roads are underdeveloped, and travel requires suitable 4-wheel-drive desert vehicles.

Travel - Internal

AIR:

Somali Airlines run regular services to all major towns.

SEA:

Modern Somalia is essentially a broad strip of coastal desert. Roads are poor and consequently coastal shipping is an important form of transport, both socially and economically.

ROAD:

Traffic drives on the right. It is difficult to travel outside Mogadishu by car. Existing roads run from the capital to Burao and Baidoa and there are sealed roads between Kismayu and Mogadishu, and Hargeysa and Mogadishu. Passenger transport is restricted almost entirely to road haulage. There are few cars and buses, although there are reasonable bus services between the major centres in the south. **Taxi:** These are available in large towns. **Car hire:** Available in Mogadishu. **Documentation:** An International Driving Permit is required.

URBAN:

Minibuses and shared taxi-type services run in Mogadishu, but availability may be restricted outside normal working hours (Sat-Thurs 0700-1400).

Travel Advice

Travellers are advised against all travel to Somalia because of the dangerous level of criminal activity and internal insecurity. Westerners and those working for western organisations have been targeted in shootings. There is a high threat from terrorism in Somalia. Those travellers deciding to visit Somalia should take strong security precautions.

This advice is based on information provided by the Foreign and Commonwealth Office in the UK. It is correct at time of publishing. As the situation can change rapidly, visitors are advised to contact the following organisations for the latest travel advice:

British Foreign and Commonwealth Office
Tel: (0845) 850 2829.
Website: www.fco.gov.uk

US Department of State
Website: http://travel.state.gov/travel

Accommodation

HOTELS:

In the main cities of Hargeisa and Mogadishu, there are international-standard hotels. There are also hotels in Afgoi, Berbera, Borama, Burao, Kismayu and Marka.

REST HOUSES: Government-run rest houses are located in many places with dormitory accommodation for four to 10 people.

LODGES: There are tourist and hunting lodges in national parks at Lac Badana and Bush-Bush, as well as in other areas.

Top Things To See & Do

- **Kismayu National Park**, in the southwest, contains many common - and a few rare - East African species.
- **Hargeisa** in the north contains rarer species.
- A third park is located outside **Mogadishu**.
- Somalia's **beaches** line the Indian Ocean in the east and are protected by a coral reef running from Mogadishu to the Kenyan border in the south; they are among the longest in the world.

Entertainment

FOOD & DRINK: In peacetime, restaurants in the major cities serve Chinese, European, Italian and Somali food.

National specialities:

- Lobster, prawn, squid, crab, fresh tuna.
- Somali bananas, mangoes and papaya.
- Roast kid and spiced rice.

Tipping: 10 to 15 per cent is normal in hotels and restaurants.

NIGHTLIFE: Local bands playing African and European music perform at nightclubs. There are frequent traditional feasts with ritualistic and recreational dance, music and folk songs.

SHOPPING: Traditional crafts include gold, silver jewellery, woven cloth and baskets from the Benadir region, meerschaum and woodcarvings. **Shopping hours:** Sat-Thurs 0800-1230 and 1630-1900.

Business

ECONOMY: Somalia's economy has been seriously dislocated by years of fighting and political strife, as well as a severe long-term drought which has affected the whole of East Africa. Somalia now ranks among the poorest countries in the world. Subsistence agriculture and livestock rearing occupy most of the working population, although development is hampered by primitive techniques, poor soil and climatic conditions, and a chronic labour shortage. Bananas are the main cash crop and provide nearly half the country's export earnings; cotton, maize, sorghum and other crops are produced for domestic consumption. Animal products, particularly hides and skins, are another key source of revenue, mainly from Saudi Arabia. Fishing has dwindled to the level of individual small boats, but there are provisional plans to restore this to full commercial capacity. Oil and gas deposits have been located but their exploitation has been in abeyance due to the lack of an effective central government. There is little industry other than small-scale operations to meet domestic needs, mainly food-processing and oil refining. Most economic assets remain in the unstable hands of clan-based militias, with frequent competition for control of particular industries.

Over half the population relies on remittances from abroad as well as large injections of foreign aid, especially from the various United Nations relief organisations. These were disrupted by the closure in 2002 - at the behest of the US Government, which claimed links to terrorism - of the al-Barakat finance company which processed a large number of overseas payments; the company also had major interests in other parts of the economy, especially banking and telecommunications. Somalia is burdened by a huge foreign debt and its traditional trade relationships have largely been suspended due to payment problems.

BUSINESS ETIQUETTE: Wear lightweight suits or safari-style jackets without a tie in hot weather. The best time to visit is October to May. **Office hours:** Sat-Thurs 0800-1400.

South Africa

Location: Southern Africa.

Time: GMT + 2.

Overview

Covering a huge swathe of land, washed by the Atlantic and Indian oceans, South Africa has enormous wealth above and below ground, making it one of the richest natural storehouses on the planet.

In 1869, diamonds (and, later, gold) were discovered, attracting huge numbers of fortune hunters. President Paul Kruger of the Transvaal (now Gauteng) invoked strict franchise requirements. Britain's attempts at intervention resulted in the Anglo-Boer War; the British victory in 1902 established the Union of South Africa in 1910.

In 1948, the National Party came to power and cemented the policy of apartheid – officially, the separate development of all racial groups but, effectively, the creation of semi-autonomous 'homelands' for non-whites and the preservation of white supremacy. Four 'homelands' were created, comprising 13 per cent of all land in the country. Black opposition to apartheid was brutally repressed. In public, the international community reacted strongly against apartheid and maintained economic sanctions against South Africa, but there was largely clandestine support from the West for the South African Government.

In February 1989, FW De Klerk became national party President. South Africa's foreign creditors were also demanding wholesale changes in domestic policy to safeguard their investments. Apartheid no longer seemed viable, and it lost support from the white-dominated business world. The De Klerk Government removed the ban of anti-apartheid groups, and released the jailed ANC leadership including, after 27 years of imprisonment, its leader, Nelson Mandela.

By 1993, all three main parties (ANC, Inkatha and the National Party) had laid out a blueprint for a new constitutional future for South Africa, the centrepiece of which was the first genuinely inclusive national election in South Africa, held in 1994. Nelson Mandela became the country's President.

As the aatention shifted away from politics, the focus once again landed on South Africa's magnificent landscape; its desert dunes, savannah, subtropical forests and white-sand coast. Its game viewing equals the best in Africa: where else can you find both penguins and elephants? There are over 1000 bird species, and the Western Cape alone has one of the richest floral kingdoms in the world.

The country's fascinating human and cultural history does not just start in Apartheid, but stretches back to the aboriginal San (Bushmen) and Khoikhoi, through the black African peoples to the latest arrivals, the Afrikaans and British. Archbishop Desmond Tutu named the newly integrated South Africa 'the rainbow nation'. It is a fitting name for a country with 11 official languages and people of all colours, race and creed, living in a vividly coloured and sculpted landscape. No wonder its cities are so cosmopolitan. The South Africans are charming hosts; most speak English, and all have a fascinating story to tell.

General Information

AREA: 1,219,192 sq km (470,693 sq miles).

POPULATION: 46 million (UN, 2005).

POPULATION DENSITY: 36.8 per sq km.

CAPITAL: Pretoria (administrative). **Population:** 1.98 million (2001). Cape Town (legislative). **Population:** 2.89 million (2001). Bloemfontein (judicial). **Population:** 119,698 (2001).

GEOGRAPHY: The Republic of South Africa lies at the southern end of the African continent. It is bounded by the Indian Ocean to the east and the Atlantic Ocean to the west, and is bordered to the north by Namibia, Botswana, Zimbabwe, Mozambique and Swaziland and totally encloses Lesotho. South Africa has three major geographical regions, namely plateau, mountains and the coastal belt. The high plateau has sharp escarpments which rise above the plains, or *veld*. Despite two major river systems, the Limpopo and the Orange, most of the plateau lacks surface water. Along the coastline are sandy beaches and rocky coves, and the vegetation is shrublike. The mountainous regions which run along the coastline from the Cape of Good Hope to the Limpopo Valley in the northeast of the country are split into the Drakensberg, Nuweveldberg and Stormberg ranges. Following the 1994 elections, South Africa was organised into nine regions. These comprise the Western Cape with its provincial and national capital of Cape Town, the Eastern Cape with its provincial capital of Bisho, the Northern Cape with its provincial capital of Kimberley, KwaZulu-Natal with its provincial capital of Pietermaritzburg, the Free State with its provincial capital of Bloemfontein, the North West Province with its provincial capital of Mmabatho, Limpopo (formerly called the Northern Province) with its provincial capital of Polokwane (formerly called Pietersburg), Mpumalanga with its provincial capital of Nelspruit, and Gauteng with its provincial capital of Johannesburg.

GOVERNMENT: Republic. Gained independence from the UK in 1910. **Head of State and Government:** President Thabo Mvuyelwa Mbeki since 1999. **Recent history:** Under the terms of the new Constitution, which was adopted on 8 May 1996 and entered into force on 4 February 1997, legislative power is vested in a bicameral Parliament, comprising a National Assembly and a National Council of Provinces (formerly the Senate). The National Assembly is elected by universal adult suffrage under a system of proportional representation and has between 350 and 400 members. The 90-member National Council of Provinces comprises six permanent delegates and four special delegates from each of the provincial legislatures. The President, who is elected by the National Assembly from among its members, exercises executive power in consultation with the other members of the Cabinet. South Africa has held three successful national elections as well as local polls since the first genuinely inclusive national election in South Africa, which was held in February 1994. Thabo Mbeki was elected by Parliament to a second five-year term in April 2004, following the landslide general election victory of his ruling African National Congress (ANC). Mr Mbeki took over as President when Nelson Mandela stepped down in mid-1999. Mbeki's administration is struggling with two major domestic problems – a huge violent crime wave and an HIV-AIDS pandemic, which afflicts over 10 per cent of the adult population. Mbeki's persistent refusal to come to terms with the true nature of the HIV virus has drawn massive international criticism as well as being the subject of furious arguments between Mbeki and Mandela.

LANGUAGE: The official languages are Afrikaans, English, isiNdebele, isiXhosa, isiZulu, Sepedi, Sesotho, Setswana, Siswati, Tshivenda and Xitsonga.

RELIGION: Most inhabitants profess Christianity of some form and belong to either Catholic, Anglican and other protestant denominations, Afrikaner Calvinist churches or African independent churches. There are also significant Hindu, Muslim and Jewish communities, and traditional beliefs are still practised widely, sometimes in conjunction with Christianity.

ELECTRICITY: 220/240 volts AC; 250 volts AC (Pretoria), 50Hz. Three-pin round plugs are in use.

SOCIAL CONVENTIONS: Handshaking is the usual form of greeting. Normal courtesies should be shown when visiting someone's home. Casual wear is widely acceptable. Formal social functions often call for a dinner jacket and black tie for men and full-length dresses for women; this will be specified on the invitation. Smoking is prohibited in public buildings and on public transport.

Climate

South Africa's climate is generally sunny and pleasant. Winters are usually mild, although snow falls on the mountain ranges of the Cape and Natal and occasionally in lower-lying areas, when a brief cold spell can be expected throughout the country.

Required clothing: Lightweight cottons and linens and rainwear. Warmer clothes are needed for winter.

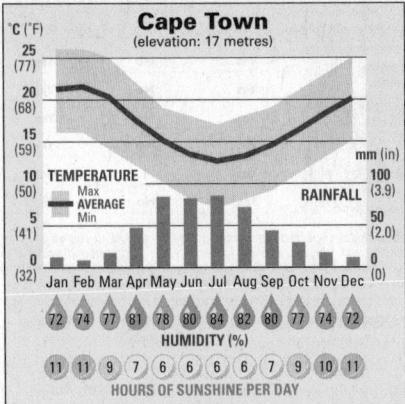

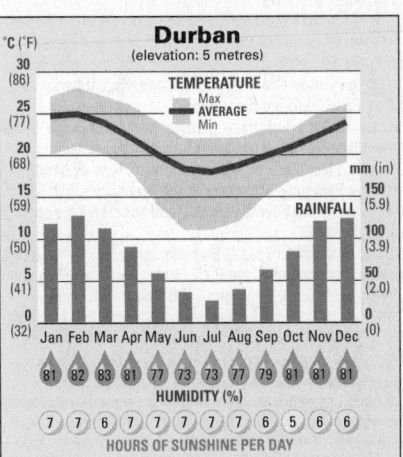

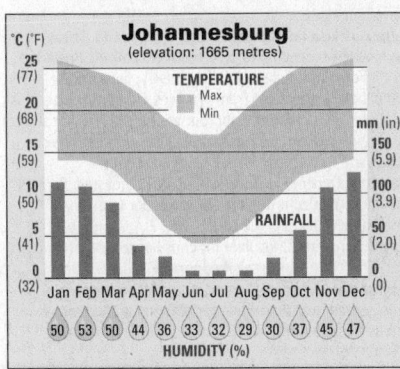

Communications

Telephone: IDD is available. Country code: 27.

Mobile telephone: Roaming agreements exist with international mobile phone companies. Coverage extends to most urban areas.

Internet: Internet cafes are present around the country.

Post: Airmail to Europe takes up to seven days. Post office hours: Generally Mon-Fri 0830-1630, Sat 0800-1130. Some transactions may not be carried out Mon-Fri after 1530 or Sat after 1100. The smaller post offices close for lunch 1300-1400.

MEDIA: South Africa's many broadcasters and publications reflect the diversity of the population as a whole. Well-established state-run and commercial TV networks broadcast nationally, and hundreds of thousands of viewers subscribe to pay-TV services operated by major cable and satellite company Multichoice. Deregulation in 1996 led to a proliferation of radio stations. The constitution provides for freedom of the press, and this is generally respected in practice.

Press: The main newspapers are in English and Afrikaans, and include *Cape Argus*, *The Citizen*, *Daily Dispatch*, *Mercury*, *Sowetan* and *The Star* (website: www.thestar.co.za).

TV: *SABC* is a state broadcaster operating three national TV networks; *E.tv* is a free-to-air commercial network; *M-Net* is a pay-TV network.
Radio: *SABC* is a state broadcaster with 20 regional and national services in 11 languages. Other radio channels are: *YFM*, *702 Talk Radio* and *Channel Africa*.

Passport/Visa

	Passport Required?	Visa Required?	Return Ticket Required?
Full British	Yes	No	Yes
Australian	Yes	No	Yes
Canadian	Yes	No	Yes
USA	Yes	No	Yes
Other EU	Yes	1	Yes
Japanese	Yes	No	Yes

Note: *Regulations and requirements may be subject to change at short notice, and you are advised to contact the appropriate diplomatic or consular authority before finalising travel arrangements. Any numbers in the chart refer to the footnotes below.*

PASSPORTS: Passport valid for at least 30 days after the intended date of departure required by all.
Note: All passengers must have a passport with at least one blank facing page (see *Application requirements* below).
VISAS: Required by all except the following for business and tourist purposes:
(a) **1.** nationals of countries referred to in the chart above for stays of up to 90 days, except nationals of Cyprus, Hungary, Poland and Slovak Republic who may stay for up to 30 days and nationals of Estonia, Latvia, Lithuania and Slovenia who *do* require a visa;
(b) nationals of Andorra, Argentina, Botswana, Brazil, British Virgin Islands, Bulgaria, Chile, Ecuador, Iceland, Israel, Jamaica, Liechtenstein, Mexico, Monaco, New Zealand, Norway, Paraguay, St Vincent & the Grenadines, San Marino, Singapore, Switzerland, Uruguay and Venezuela for stays of up to 90 days;
(d) nationals of Antigua & Barbuda, Barbados, Belize, Benin, Bolivia, Cape Verde, Costa Rica, Gabon, Guyana, Hong Kong (SAR) (Holders of Hong Kong British Nationals overseas passports and Hong Kong special passports), Jordan, Korea (Rep), Lesotho, Macau (SAR), Malawi, Malaysia, Maldives, Mauritius, Namibia, Peru, Seychelles, Swaziland, Thailand, Turkey and Zambia for stays of up to 30 days;
(e) transit passengers continuing their journey by the same or first connecting aircraft provided holding onward or return documentation and not leaving the airport.
Note: Unaccompanied children under the age of 18 years must hold written consent from their parents when travelling alone.
Types of visa and cost: *Visitors*, *Transit*: £35. *Study Permits*: £43 (depending on level of education). *Business*: £125. Some nationals (including the UK, India and Zimbabwe) are exempt from visa fees. Other nationals must apply for a visa with the appropriate fee. All fees are subject to change without notice; please check with Embassy or Consulate to confirm costs.
Validity: Dependent on length of stay requested. Permits may be extended if done so 30 days prior to expiry of original permit.
Application to: Consulate (or consular section at Embassy or High Commission); see *Passport/Visa Information*. Applicants in countries where South Africa is not represented may send their applications to the embassy in the nearest country.

Credit: ©South African Tourism

Application requirements: (a) Valid passport with at least one blank page. (b) Two passport-size photos (must be 45mm by 35mm). (c) One completed application form.
(d) Fee (payable by cash, bank draft or postal order). (e) A stamped self-addressed special delivery envelope if applying by post. (f) A valid vaccination certificate, if required by the Act. (g) Proof of sufficient funds to cover visit and return tickets. (h) Statement/documentation confirming purpose of visit. (i) Onward/return tickets. (j) Yellow fever certificate if travelling to, from or through the endemic zone. *Transit*: (a)-(j) and (k) Sufficient documentation for admission to destination.
Working days required: Four days. Up to 10 days for postal applications.
Temporary residence: Temporary residence permits encompass *Study*, *Work* or *Workseeker* Permits. Contact the nearest Consulate (or consular section at Embassy) for further details.

PASSPORT/VISA INFORMATION

South African High Commission in the UK
South Africa House, Trafalgar Square, London WC2N 5DP, UK
Tel: (020) 7451 7299.
Website: www.southafricahouse.com
Opening hours: Mon-Fri 0900-1700. (consular section): 0845-1245.

South African Consulate in the UK
15 Whitehall, London SW1A 2DD, UK
Tel: (020) 7925 8900/01/10.
Website: www.southafricahouse.com/Consulate.htm
Opening hours: Mon-Fri 0845-1245 (personal applications only).

Embassy of the Republic of South Africa in the USA
3051 Massachusetts Avenue, NW, Washington, DC 20008, USA
Tel: (202) 232 4400.
Website: www.saembassy.org

South African Consulate in the USA
Street address: 4301 Connecticut Ave, NW, Van Ness Building, Suite 220, Washington DC, 20008, USA
Postal Address: 3051 Massachusetts Ave, NW, Washington,DC 20008, USA
(202) 274 7991.
Opening hours: 0900-1200.

Money

Currency: Rand (ZAR) = 100 cents. Notes are in denominations of ZAR200, 100, 50, 20 and 10. Coins are in denominations of ZAR5, 2 and 1, and 50, 20, 10, 5, 2 and 1 cents.
Currency exchange: Money can be changed at banks, bureaux de change, some hotels, and larger shops and restaurants. Automated foreign exchange machines and ATMs are available at various locations. Proof of identify may be requested; therefore, it is advisable to carry a passport.
Credit & debit cards: MasterCard and Visa are preferred. American Express and Diners Club are also widely accepted. Some ATMs will give cash advances with credit cards. Credit cards are not accepted at petrol stations. Check with your credit or debit card company for details of merchant acceptability and other facilities which may be available.
Traveller's cheques: Valid at banks, hotels, restaurants and shops. To avoid additional exchange rate charges, travellers are advised to take traveller's cheques in Pounds Sterling or US Dollars.
Currency restrictions: The import of local currency is limited to ZAR5000 in cash. The export of local currency is limited to ZAR500 in cash. The import and export of foreign currency is unlimited provided it is declared upon arrival or departure.
Banking hours: Mon-Fri 0900-1530, Sat 0830-1100.
Exchange rate indicators:
Rate at time of publishing
£1.00= ZAR10.63
$1.00= ZAR6.03

Duty Free

The following goods may be imported into South Africa by passengers over 18 years of age without incurring customs duty:
200 cigarettes and 50 cigars and 250g of tobacco; 1l of spirits or liquor and 2l of wine; 50ml of perfume and 250ml of eau de toilette; other goods up to a value of ZAR3000.
Restricted items: Plants and plant material without import permit, including margarine, honey and other vegetable oils.

Prohibited goods: Narcotics; flick-knives; ammunition, explosives; meat, processed cheese and other dairy products; obscene literature.

Public Holidays

Below are listed the Public Holidays for the January 2006-June 2007 period.
2006: Jan 1 New Year's Day. **Mar 21** Human Rights Day. **Apr 14** Good Friday. **Apr 17** Family Day. **Apr 27** Freedom Day. **May 1** Workers' Day. **Jun 16** Youth Day. **Aug 9** National Women's Day. **Sep 24** Heritage Day. **Dec 16** Day of Reconciliation. **Dec 25** Christmas Day. **Dec 26** Day of Goodwill.
2007: Jan 1 New Year's Day. **Mar 21** Human Rights Day. **Apr 6** Good Friday. **Mar 28** Family Day. **Apr 27** Freedom Day. **May 1** Worker's Day. **June 16** Youth Day.
Note: Holidays falling on a Sunday are observed the following Monday.

Health

	Special Precautions?	Certificate Required?
Yellow Fever	No	1
Cholera	2	No
Typhoid & Polio	3	N/A
Malaria	4	N/A

Note: *Regulations and requirements may be subject to change at short notice, and you are advised to contact your doctor well in advance of your intended date of departure. Any numbers in the chart refer to the footnotes below.*

1: A *yellow fever* vaccination certificate is required from travellers over one year of age arriving from infected areas. African countries and the Americas formerly classified as endemic zones are considered by the South African authorities to be infected areas.
2: Visitors may wish to consider precautions against *cholera*, depending on the area in South Africa being visited.
3: Vaccination against typhoid is advised. An outbreak of typhoid occurred in the town of Delmas, Mpumulanga in September 2005.
4: *Malaria* risk, predominantly in the malignant *falciparum* form, exists throughout the year in the low altitude areas of Limpopo, Mpumalanga Province (including the Kruger National Park) and northeastern KwaZulu/Natal as far south as the Tugela River. The risk is highest from October to May. Resistance to chloroquine and sulfadoxine-pyrimethamine has been reported. It is strongly recommended that visitors to these areas take anti-malaria tablets before entering these zones. The recommended prophylaxis is mefloquine (World Health Organization) *or* chloroquine plus pyrimethamine (South African High Commission).
Food & drink: Mains water is considered safe to drink in urban areas but may be contaminated elsewhere and sterilisation is advisable. Milk is pasteurised and dairy products are safe for consumption. Local meat, poultry, seafood, fruit and vegetables are generally considered safe to eat.
Other risks: *Measels* has been present in the KwaZulu-Natal and Gauteng provinces. *Bilharzia (schistosomiasis)* is endemic in the north and east and may be present elsewhere. Avoid swimming and paddling in fresh water; swimming pools that are well chlorinated and maintained are safe. *Hepatitis A* occurs and *hepatitis B* is hyperendemic. *Dengue fever, onchocerciasis* (river blindness), *trypanosomiasis* (sleeping sickness) and *filariasis* are present.
Rabies may be present. For those at high risk, vaccination before arrival should be considered. If you are bitten, seek medical advice without delay. For more information, consult the *Health* appendix.
Health care: Medical facilities are good in urban areas but limited elsewhere. Doctors and hospitals often require immediate cash payment. Comprehensive health insurance is recommended. A leaflet on health precautions is available from the South African High Commission (see *Passport/Visa Information*).

Travel - International

AIR:

The national airline is *South African Airways (SA)* (website: www.flysaa.com). There are frequent direct and indirect flights by numerous major airlines from destinations throughout Europe and North America.
Approximate flight times: From Cape Town to *London* is 8 hours, from Durban is 12 hours 20 minutes and from Johannesburg is 11 hours 10 minutes. From Johannesburg to *New York* is 9 hours 50 minutes.
Main airports: *Cape Town (CPT)* (Cape Town International), 22km (16 miles) east of the city. *To/from*

EMPERORS PALACE
HOTEL CASINO AND CONVENTION RESORT

Welcome to Emperors Palace, a sensational resort that combines timeless classical elegance and sheer excitement, conveniently situated alongside Johannesburg International Airport.

The resort offers the deluxe five-star **D'oreale Grande** hotel as well as the cosy 80-key three-star select-services **Metcourt Laurel** hotel. The new 150-key three-star **Mondior Concorde** hotel is expected to open in February 2006.

A variety of outstanding cuisine can be enjoyed at nine uniquely themed **restaurants** and dazzling **entertainment** is showcased in the selection of showbars, theatres and nightclubs.

The Emperors Palace **Casino** is sure to offer players 24 hour fun, glamour, sophistication and excitement in gaming entertainment.

A must see is **The Ubunye Exhibition**, a commemoration of the historic multi-party talks which culminated in the birth of the new South Africa, while children are heartily entertained at **Chariots Entertainment World**, South Africa's most exciting in-door theme park.

Come to Emperors Palace ... Come to the Palace of Dreams!

EMPERORS
PALACE

FOR RESERVATIONS CALL +27 11 928 1928 . EMAIL RESERVATIONS@EMPERORSPALACE.COM . WEBSITE: WWW.EMPERORSPALACE.COM

PEERMONT GLOBAL HOTELS AND RESORTS

the airport: Inter-Cape buses run 24 hours and meet all incoming and outgoing flights. Courtesy buses are operated by some hotels. Taxis are available, with a surcharge after 2300 (travel time - 20 minutes); *Touch Down Taxis* are the officially authorised airport taxi firm. *Facilities:* Duty-free shop, car hire, bank/bureaux de change and restaurant/bar.
Bloemfontein (BFN) (Bloemfontein International), 10km (6 miles) east of the city (travel time - 15 minutes).
To/from the airport: There is an airport shuttle bus to the city centre (leaving from outside the airport building). Taxis are also available. *Facilities:* ATMs, restaurants, car hire and conference facilities.
Durban (DUR) (Durban International), 18km (11 miles) southwest of the city (travel time - 20 minutes). *To/from the airport:* Airport buses and taxis are available to the city. *Facilities:* Duty-free shop, car hire, bank/bureaux de change and bar/restaurant.
Johannesburg (JNB) (Johannesburg International), 22km (14 miles) east of the city (travel time - 35 minutes). *To/from the airport:* Bus services to Pretoria and Johannesburg are available. Buses link Kempton Park with Johannesburg. Taxis are available. Courtesy coaches are operated by some major hotels. *Facilities:* Duty-free shops, post office, car hire, bank/bureaux de change, medical clinic, conference facilities, restaurant and bar.
Port Elizabeth (PLZ) (Port Elizabeth International) is 5km (3 miles) west of the Capital Business District. *To/from the airport:* There is an airport shuttle bus to the main international hotels in Port Elizabeth upon request. Taxis are also available. *Facilities:* ATM, conference facilities, information desk (tel: (41) 507 7319), restaurants and pubs, shops, pharmacy, postal services, car hire.
For more information regarding airports, contact Airports Company South Africa (tel: (11) 723 1400; website: www.airports.co.za).
Departure tax: None.

SEA:
Main ports: *Cape Town, Durban, East London* and *Port Elizabeth*. Cruises are offered by various companies between South Africa and the Indian Ocean Islands.

RAIL:
The main routes are from South Africa to Zimbabwe, Botswana and Mozambique. Contact *South African Railways (SPOORNET)* (website: www.spoornet.co.za) for further information.

ROAD:
There are main routes into South Africa from Botswana (via Ramatlabama), Lesotho, Mozambique (now open after a long war - check with local police about state of road and safety), Namibia, Swaziland and Zimbabwe (via Beit Bridge).

Travel - Internal

AIR:
Daily flights link Bloemfontein, Cape Town, Durban, East London, Johannesburg, Kimberley, Port Elizabeth and Pretoria and with other connecting flights to provincial towns. *South African Airways* operates on the principal routes.
Flight discounts: An *Africa Explorer* fare is available to foreign visitors entering South Africa with an IATA airline. It offers a significant saving for anyone planning to use South African Airways' internal network. The fare is valid for a minimum of three days and a maximum of two months: travel may originate and terminate at any point within South Africa that is served by the airline. Travel is not permitted more than once in the same direction over any given sector. There is also a reduction of approximately 30 per cent on some standby fares. South African Airways has various other discount domestic fares including Apex, Slumber, Supersaver and Saver fares.

Credit: © South African Tourism

SEA:
Starlight Cruises offers links between major ports.

RAIL:
The principal intercity services are as follows: the *Blue Train* (website: www.bluetrain.co.za) is a luxury express offering routes between Pretoria and Cape Town; the *Trans-Oranje* between Cape Town and Durban via Kimberley and Bloemfontein (weekly); and the *Trans-Natal Express* between Durban and Johannesburg (daily, except Tuesday). *Rovos Rail* (website: www.rovas.co.za) offers luxury (partly steam) safaris from Pretonia to Cape Town. The *Transnet Museum* also offers various steam safaris around South Africa and Zimbabwe, and the *Trans-Karoo Express* travels between Cape Town, Johannesburg and Pretoria daily. All long-distance trains are equipped with sleeping compartments, included in fares, and most have restaurant cars. Reservations are recommended for principal trains and all overnight journeys. There are frequent local trains in the Cape Town and Pretoria/Johannesburg urban areas. All trains have first- and second-class accommodation. Children under two years of age travel free. Children aged two to 11 years pay half fare.

ROAD:
Traffic drives on the left. There is a well-maintained network of roads and motorways in populous regions. Around a third of roads are paved (with all major roads tarred to a high standard). In non-residential areas, speed limits are 120kph (75mph) and 60kph (35mph) in built up areas. Overtaking is permitted in any lane, including the hard shoulder. Fines for speeding are very heavy. It is illegal to carry petrol other than in built-in petrol tanks. Petrol stations are usually open all week 0700-1900. Some are open 24 hours. Petrol must be paid for in cash. **Bus/coach:** Various operators, such as *Greyhound, Intercape* and *Translux*, run intercity express links using modern air-conditioned coaches. On many of the intercity routes, passengers may break their journey at any scheduled stop en route by prior arrangement at time of booking and continue on a subsequent coach at no extra cost other than for additional accommodation. **Taxi:** Available throughout the country, at all towns, hotels and airports, with rates for distance and time. For long-distance travel, a quotation should be sought. **Car hire:** To hire a car, travellers must have held a valid driving licence for five years. Self-drive and chauffeur-driven cars are available at most airports and in major city centres. **Documentation:** An International Driving Permit is required. The minimum age is 23 (or 21 on presentation of an American Express/Diners card). Foreign licences in English are valid for up to 12 months; otherwise, British visitors who are planning to drive in South Africa should check with the *AA* or *RAC* prior to departure that they have all the correct documentation.

URBAN:
There are bus and suburban rail networks in all the main towns. Fares in Cape Town and Johannesburg are zonal, with payment in cash or with 10-ride pre-purchase 'clipcards' from kiosks. In Pretoria, there are various pre-purchase ticket systems, including a cheap pass for off-peak travel only. In Durban, conventional buses face stiff competition from minibuses and combi-taxis (both legal and illegal), which are also found in other South African towns. These, although cheap and very fast, should be used with care. For ordinary taxis, fares within the city areas are more expensive than long distances. Taxis do not cruise and must be called from a rank. Taxi drivers expect a 10 per cent tip.
Note: Avoid the Berea and Hillbrow areas of Johannesburg. There has been a number of muggings around the Rotunda Bus Terminal in the city. As a result of the high level of car hijacking in the Kruger Park, there is currently an increased police presence.
Travel Times: The following chart gives approximate travel times (in hours and minutes) from **Cape Town** to other major cities/towns in South Africa.

	Air	Road	Rail
Johannesburg	**2.00**	**15.00**	**24.00**
Durban	**2.00**	**18.00**	**38.00**
Pretoria	**2.00**	**16.00**	**26.00**
Port Elizabeth	**1.00**	**7.00**	**-**

Travel Advice

Most visits to South Africa are trouble-free but you should be aware of the global risk of indiscriminate international terrorist attacks, which could be against civilian targets, including places frequented by foreigners.
There is a high level of crime, but most occurs in townships and isolated areas away from tourist destinations.
The standard of driving is variable, and there are many fatal accidents.
This advice is based on information provided by the Foreign and Commonwealth Office in the UK. It is correct at time of publishing. As the situation can change rapidly, visitors are advised to contact the following organisations for the latest travel advice:

British Foreign and Commonwealth Office
Tel: (0845) 850 2829.
Website: www.fco.gov.uk

US Department of State
Website: http://travel.state.gov/travel

Accommodation

South Africa offers a wide range of accommodation from luxury 5-star hotels to thatched huts (*rondavels*) in game reserves. 'Time-sharing condominiums' are developing in popular resorts. Comprehensive accommodation guides giving details of facilities, including provision for the handicapped, are available at all SATOUR offices (see *Top Things To Do*) and from regional tourist offices.
Information covers hotels, motels, farm holidays, game park rest camps, caravan and campsites and supplementary accommodation such as beach cottages, holiday flats and bungalows. Rates should always be confirmed at time of booking. It is forbidden by law to levy service charges, although phone calls may be charged for.

EDITOR'S CHOICE: GAME RESERVES

Game reserve rest camps are protected enclosures within the confines of the park. Accommodation is usually in thatched huts known as *rondavels*, or in small cottages. Some camps have air-conditioned accommodation. Most *rondavels* and cottages are self-contained, with private baths and showers, and sometimes kitchens. Some camps have luxury air-conditioned accommodation. Conservation Corporation Africa (CCA) was founded in 1990 to develop sustainable wildlife reserves, achieved through low-density, high-quality tourism. Its lodges are bywords for luxury and elegance, but equally important is CCA's work to promote biodiversity, invest in the local rural economies and restore land.

FARM HOLIDAYS:
There is a wide range of guest farms open to tourists offering stays in various ecological regions. Opportunities exist for adventure activities such as horse riding, mountain-biking and fishing, as well as agricultural activities like bee-keeping and cattle-ranching. Full details can be obtained from SATOUR (see *Top Things To Do*).

BACKPACKER HOSTELS:
Located all over the country, hostels are cheap, clean and well-run places to stay. Buses often offer door-to-door services between hostels. Rooms are dorms with a shared shower. Self catering facilities are provided.

HOTELS:
All hotels are registered with the South African Tourism Board, which controls standards. 800 hotels are members of The Federated Hospitality Association of South Africa (FEDHASA).
Grading: Hotels are graded **1** to **5 stars** according to the range of facilities on offer, plus an optional classification band grading the level of services and hospitality:
Burgundy: Acceptable standard of services and hospitality in addition to the required facilities. **Silver:** Superior services, hospitality, quality and ambience.

GUEST HOUSES/BED & BREAKFAST:
There are very few towns that do not offer this type of accommodation. Advance bookings during the summer season (October to April) are becoming essential, especially in the Western Cape region.

SELF-CATERING:
Holiday flats, resorts and health spas are available along main routes, notably the Natal/Cape coasts and in Mpumalanga, limpopo and the Drakenberg. **Grading:** Self-catering accommodation is graded **1** to **5 stars** according to the facilities available and the level of services and hospitality.

CAMPING/CARAVANNING:
There are over 800 camp and caravan sites in the country; camping is not allowed outside of them. Caravan parks are to be found along all the tourist routes in South Africa, particularly at places favoured for recreation and sightseeing. The standard is usually high. Many caravan parks have campsites. A number of companies can arrange motor camper rentals, with a range of fully-equipped vehicles. **Grading:** Camp and caravan sites are classed as self-catering accommodation (see above).

ACCOMMODATION INFORMATION

The Federated Hospitality Association of South Africa (FEDHASA)
PO Box 71517, Brynston, South Africa
Tel: (11) 799 7676.
Website: www.fedhasa.co.za

Conservation Corporation Africa (CCA)
website: www.ccafrica.com

Top Things To See

- Stare out from the top of **Cape Town**'s **Table Mountain**, the famous flat-topped mountain with views out across the peninsula to the Atlantic and Indian Oceans. It is possible to walk up, but for the less intrepid, there is an excellent cable car.
- Walk around Cape Town's main hub, the **Victoria & Alfred Waterfront**, a beautifully restored old Victorian harbour which offers free entertainment, a wide variety of shops, museums - including the excellent **Aquarium** - taverns and restaurants. Boat trips leave from here for harbour tours or the notorious **Robben Island**, where Nelson Mandela and many other nationalist leaders were imprisoned. The relics of early colonial Government are centred on **Government Avenue**, with many fine old buildings and museums, including the **Parliament Buildings**; **Groote Kerk** (mother church of the Dutch Reformed faith); the **Cultural History Museum**; **National Museum**; **National Gallery**; **Bertram House**; and **Company's Garden**, planted in 1652 to provide food for passing sailors.
- See the only colony of **penguins** to live on the African mainland in **Simonstown**, a delightful Victorian town with a couple of interesting museums.
- Be astonished by South Africa's glorious patches of **flower** - South Africa has nearly 24,000 species of them. The **Kirstenbosch National Botanical Gardens**, created by Cecil Rhodes in 1895 on the lower slopes of Table Mountain, is one of the finest botanical gardens in the world, and open-air concerts are held there in the summer; the area between the **Cederberg mountains** and that which separates the west coast from the arid **Great Karoo Desert** bursts into a mass of flowers every October to November; **Elim** is a 19th-century Mission village whose principal profession is still growing and drying flowers; **Namaqualand** is a vast area of seemingly barren semi-desert, which secretly harbours a treasure-house of floral beauty that appears after sufficient winter rains, such as daisies, aloes, lilies, perennial herbs and many other flower species, best seen from July to September; and **Calvinia** and **Niewoudtville**, also good locations for flowers.
- South Africa is lucky enough to host some of the best opportunities to observe **wildlife** in its natural habitat in the world. Nature parks are noted more for their scenic beauty and hiking trails than for wildlife. Private game reserves offer a personalised game-viewing programme, while national game reserves are generally explored by tourists in their own vehicles. The **Addo Elephant National Park**, 72km (45 miles) north of **Port Elizabeth**, was created in 1931 to protect the last of the eastern Cape elephants. Recently massively expanded, it offers an excellent range of game, including black rhino, buffalo and antelope and more than 170 bird species. There are also several private reserves nearby, including the excellent **Shamwari** and **Kwandwe**, both of which have very upmarket accommodation and 'Big Five' (elephant, lion, leopard, rhino and buffalo) game viewing. **KwaZulu-Natal** covers five distinct ecosystems varying from dry thorn scrub to tropical forest is bordered by giant dunes, beaches and tropical reefs, and also has 'Big Five' game viewing - the only place in the world where hippos, crocodiles and sharks share the same lagoon. It also has superb birdwatching and diving and, outside the National Park, excellent fishing. The 96,000 hectare (237,120 acre) **Hluhluwe-Umfolozi National Park** offers a broad range of habitats, from rocky hillside to open savannah grass and thick woodland, supporting some 86 species of mammal and around 425 recorded bird species. This is the Eden of almost all white rhinos in the world, thanks to a carefully controlled breeding programme that has restocked much of the rest of Africa. **Mpumalanga** (the 'land of the rising sun') covers the highveld plains and mountains from **Gauteng** to the borders with Swaziland and Mozambique. This is one of the key tourist destinations in South Africa, home, with **Limpopo**, to the world-famous **Kruger National Park**, a massive reserve the size of Wales and among the best places in Africa to see the 'Big Five', as well as thousands of other species. Surrounding the park, in a series of linked game reserves called **Sabie Sand**, **Manyeleti**, **Klaserie**, **Timbavati** and the **Umbabat**, there are numerous private concessions, less crowded but considerably more expensive than the National Parks camps. These small, luxury camps provide

vehicles and guides, and offer facilities such as walks, night drives and off-road game-spotting not allowed within the park proper. As animals wander freely throughout the area, the game viewing is as good as in the main park. Safaris on foot follow a network of wilderness trails in the (compulsory) company of an armed ranger. The **Pilansberg Game Reserve** covers around 137,000 hectares (338,540 acres). Several farms and an extinct volcanic crater were included in one of the largest rehabilitation exercises ever carried out. This is now an excellent 'Big Five' reserve and the third-largest game park in South Africa. In the far north of the province, on the Botswana border, is the little-known **Madikwe National Park**, which offers excellent walking safaris. **Augrabies National Park** is home to many interesting species of desert plants while local animals include baboons, vervet monkeys, rhino and antelope.
- Watch the sun set spectacularly over the **Karoo**, a vast and beautiful upland area: drier, hotter and colder than the coasts.
- The town of **Graaff-Reinet**, situated in the heart of the **Karoo Nature Reserve** at the foot of the **Sneeuberg Mountains**, is one of the finest surviving Cape-Dutch towns in South Africa, with many attractive 18th- and 19th-century buildings, as well as parks and museums. Just 5km (3 miles) outside the town, it is possible for visitors to drive into the **Valley of Desolation** along a twisting single-track road that eventually climbs into the mountains.
- Take a walk in a forest of yellowwood, stinkwood and Cape chestnut trees along **Hogsback**, situated in the striking **Amatola Mountains**. On its trails can be found magical **waterfalls** - the most spectacular being the aptly-named **Bridal Veil** and **Madonna and Child**.
- Chill out in the closest thing South Africa has to a hippy hangout in the tourist town of **Port St Johns**. Both here and at various coves and rivermouths along the coast are small, hideaway lodges, perfect for those who want to relax or fish away from the crowds.
- Unveil some of South Africa's staggering natural phenomena. The **Royal Natal National Park** includes an **Amphitheatre**, an 8km- (5 mile-) long crescent-shaped curve in the main basalt wall. It is flanked by two impressive peaks, the **Sentinel** (3165m/10,384ft) and the **Eastern Buttress** (3047m/9997ft). Even higher is **Mont-aux-Sources** at 3284m (10,775ft). It is the source of the **Tugela River** which plummets 2000m (6562ft) over the edge of the plateau. Hikers should enjoy following the spectacular **Tugela Gorge**. In the **Escarpment**, just to the west of the Kruger boundary, the edge of the African continental plateau is marked with a series of dramatic mountains and plunging cliffs. The road along the rim of the escarpment provides spectacular views of the landscape below, including **The Pinnacle**, a massive, free-standing granite column; **God's Window**, a viewing point over the **Lowveld** 1000m (3300ft) below; **Lisbon Falls** and **Berlin Falls**. It then turns to run along the rim of the **Blyde Canyon** (26km/16 miles long and 350-800m/1050-2400ft deep), passing **Bourke's Luck Potholes**, a series of strange rock formations created by the swirling action of pebble-laden flood water. Meanwhile, **Sterkfontein**, in the **Magaliesberg mountains**, is home to the **Wonder Caves**, one of the world's most important prehistoric sites; 2.5 million-year-old *Australopithecus africanus* was first discovered here. Northwest of **Kimberley**, **Kuruman** was a missionary centre used by Robert Moffat and David Livingstone. It has a gushing spring known as the 'Eye of God' and is near the **Wonderwerk Cave**, an archaeological site of great importance where some of the earliest evidence of the use of fire has been found.
- For those with a penchant for history, the northern part of **KwaZulu-Natal** is mainly rolling grassland, spiked by occasional rocky *kopjies* (hills), which became the bloody frontline in a whole series of wars between the Zulus, Afrikaans and British (1830–1902). **Ladysmith** was the site of a devastating siege during the Anglo-Boer War. The **Town Hall** still shows the scars, while the old **Market Hall** next door is an excellent **Siege Museum**. The **Talana Museum**, in **Dundee**, is the site of the first battle of the Boer War. This is also the best place from which to visit **Isandlwana**, **Fugitive's Drift** and **Rorkes Drift**, where a devastating series of battles between the British and Zulus in January 1879 led to the desperate defence of Rorke's Drift mission station by a garrison of 139. Before

the battle began, 35 were already wounded. It resulted in the most Victoria Crosses in a single engagement in the history of British warfare and was filmed as *Zulu*, starring Michael Caine. The mission is now an interpretive and arts centre. Also nearby is the battlefield of **Blood River**, scene of a famous victory by the Afrikaaners over the Zulus in 1838. Further east, the little Afrikaaner town of **Vryheid** (**Freedom**) was founded in 1884. Today, it is still a pretty little town, with three small museums. Three major battles of the Anglo-Zulu War were fought nearby.
- Such places may spark off an interest in all things Zulu: if so, head for **Zululand**. In the mid-19th century, the Tugela River formed the boundary between British Natal and Zululand. **Eshowe** ('the sound of wind in the trees'), now a pretty little farming town, has a Zulu royal pedigree. **Fort Nongqayi** (1883) is now the Zululand Historical Museum, while the **Vukani Museum** has the world's largest collection of traditional Zulu arts and crafts. In the nearby hills are several Zulu cultural villages, including **Shakaland**, **Pobane**, **KwaBhekithunga**, **Stewart's Farm** and **Simunye**, all providing food and accommodation, a tour of a village, discussion of lifestyle and medicine and dance displays.. The site of the former royal capital, **Ondini**, is now the fascinating **KwaZulu Cultural Museum**.
- The vast and barren wilderness of the **Northern Cape** stretches from the west coast north to the Namibian and Botswana borders and east to the **Free State** and **North-West provinces**. The southwest features spectacular carpets of wild flowers in early spring, while the south is part of the **Great Karoo** and the north intrudes into the **Kalahari Desert**. It is here that, in 1866, a boy found a shiny 'pebble' at **Hopetown**, 128km (80 miles) south of **Kimberley**, allowing a primitive and sparsely populated settlement to become the diamond capital of the world. Kimberley attractions include the **Big Hole**, which is the largest humanmade excavation in the world, and the **Kimberley Mine Museum**, with its replicas of 19th-century Kimberley at the height of the gold rush. The **De Beers Hall Museum** houses a display of cut and uncut diamonds; here can be seen the famous '616' - at 616 carats, the largest uncut diamond in the world - and the 'Eureka' diamond, the first to be discovered in South Africa.

Top Things To Do

- South Africa's 13 major wine-producing regions have signposted **wine routes** that you simply must explore. The **Stellenbosch Wine Route** was the country's first, with all wineries situated within a 12km-/7.5 mile-radius of Stellenbosch. **Stellenbosch** is also one of South Africa's oldest villages with a great many attractive buildings, including the excellent **Village Museum**. The **Olifants Wine Route** is 200km/125 miles long, passing through the **Cederberg Mountains**, the unspoilt **West Coast** and Knersvlakte. The **Klein Karoo Wine Trust** is a 300km-/188mile-route through the eastern **Cape Winelands**. The **Swartland Wine Route** is a 40-minute drive away from **Cape Town**. The **Orange River Wine Trust** comprises the northern wine-making regions, irrigated by the **Orange**, **Vaal** and **Riet** rivers. The **Robertson Valley** is a two-hour drive from Cape Town, known particularly for Chardonnay. The winelands are a stunning region of vineyards, old Cape-Dutch villages and mansions. Many of the vineyards have excellent restaurants; most offer tastings and some provide bed and breakfast. Tiny **Franschhoek** originally hosted refugee Huguenots from France, who brought their wine-growing skills to South Africa. It now has an excellent **Huguenot Museum**. **Paarl** is home to several small museums and the **KWV Wine Cellars**. In the **Breede Valley** area, the charming little towns of **Tulbagh**, **Worcester**, **Wellington** and **Ceres** all have fine old buildings, interesting small museums, beautiful scenery, vineyards and fruit orchards.
- Enjoy some of South Africa's world-renowned **beaches**, such as: the horseshoe-shaped **Knysna Lagoon**; South Africa's trendiest resort, **Plettenberg Bay**; **East London**, built on the mouth of the **Buffalo River**, a popular seaside resort with a subtropical climate, fine beaches and some of the best surfing in South Africa; **Eastern Beach**; **Nahoon Beach**; **Orient Beach**; **Durban**'s city beaches, such as the **Golden Mile**, which actually stretches for 6km (4 miles) from the **Umgeni River** to the Point; the

Credit: © South African Tourism

South Coast beach resorts, such as **Amanzimtoti**, **Scottsburgh**, **Port Shepstone** and **Margate**, running together to create a ribbon of fun, sea and sand aimed at the family market, with plenty of timeshares, self-catering apartments and fast food; and **KwaZulu-Natal**'s startlingly beautiful coast, with silver sand beaches (shared with turtles), vast sand dunes and offshore coral reefs.

- South Africa has recently gained a reputation for **whale watching** and **shark-cage diving** (with great white sharks) on the Cape. Sharks migrate through the Cape's **False Bay** from June to August and move into the **Durban** area (**KwaZulu-Natal**) from October to January. For whale watching fans, the Western Cape Tourism Board has established a Cape Whale Route to observe southern right whales, which usually swim very close to the shore. The best time to spot them is from June to September, especially in **Walker Bay**, where a **Whale Festival** is held annually during the last week of September. **Hermanus**, however, is probably the best place in South Africa to go whale watching.

- South Africa's **diving** infrastructure and facilities are well developed. **Reef diving** is popular in **Sodwana Bay** (on the northern coast of KwaZulu-Natal), while **wreck diving** is widespread around the **Cape**. Popular inland diving sites include **Wondergat**, **Badgat** and **Miracle Water**. The offshore **Aliwal Shoal** and **Protea Banks** are some of the best dive sites in South Africa. The **Tsitsikamma Coastal Park** offers excellent opportunities for **underwater photography**.

- **Surfing** is a popular past-time in South Africa; one of the most well-known of locations is **Jeffrey's Bay** (**J-Bay**) near Cape Town. **Lambert's Bay** is another good surfing spot. The **Alexandria State Forest** is a reserve that runs along the coast and contains a hiking trail along the beach. East from here is **Dias Cross**, the location of one of Bartholemew Dias' stone crosses and a desolate paradise for beach lovers.

- One of the country's most popular sports, **fishing** can be practised along the coast or on the lakes and rivers in the game and nature reserves. One of the world's richest fishing grounds lies around the **Cape of Good Hope**, where the Atlantic and Indian Ocean currents meet and large shoals of tuna and swordfish draw increasing numbers of game fishing enthusiasts. The major trout fishing areas are the southern mountain ranges of the Western Cape and the foothills of the **Drakensberg Mountains** (in KwaZulu-Natal). **Fly fishing** is best in the mountain streams and along the coastline of the **Eastern Cape**. One highlight on South Africa's fishing calendar is the **Sardine Run**, in June, along the KwaZulu-Natal coast, where hordes of feeding game fish and sharks concentrate.

- South Africa is one of the few remaining countries where **steam locomotives** are still widely used. They range from the luxury *Pride of Africa* to small engines on narrow gauge railways like the *Midmar Steam Railway* near **Pietermaritzburg**. For those looking for a scenic ride, the famous *Outeniqua Choo-Tjoe* runs along the **Garden Route** on a day-trip from **George** and **Knysna** and the *Union Limited* crosses the famous **Kaaimans River Bridge**, one of the most photographed railway bridges in the world.

- **Bungee jump** from one of the world's highest drops – the bridge over the **Blaukrans River**, **Western Cape**. At 216m

(709ft), this jump is more than twice as high as the jump of the bridge linking Zambia and Zimbabwe across the Zambezi River near Victoria Falls. If you can, do not close your eyes though – the view is absolutely breathtaking.

- Go to the Victorian **Grahamstown**'s giant annual **arts festival**, held each July. The town has many fine buildings, amongst which the most interesting are the **Cathedral of St Michael and St George**, situated in the triangular **Church Square**, the **1820 Settlers Monument** (after the first British to settle the area), **Fort Selwyn**, and rows of shops and houses on **Church Square**, **Artificers' Square**, **Hill Street** and **MacDonald Street**.

- **The Drakensberg** is South Africa's largest mountain range and the official southern end of the **Great Rift Valley**, which slices north across Africa for 6000km (3728 miles). Its name, which means 'Dragon Mountains' in Afrikaans, stems from the jagged backbone of saw-toothed peaks. It is a refreshing place with cold mountain streams shaded by ferns and ancient yellowwood trees. The mountains are capped with snow in winter. The area provides good **walking**, **climbing** and **riding** while the peaks are the realm of eagles and bearded vultures. Popular climbs include **Champagne Castle**, **Cathkin Peak** and **Cathedral Peak**. In the nearby caves are good examples of the rock art of the Bushmen who, until a century ago, inhabited the area. The **Main Caves**, in the **Giant's Castle Game Reserve**, boast more than 500 rock paintings in a single shelter. The reserve, which flanks the border with Lesotho, is dominated by a massive basalt wall incorporating the peaks of **Giant's Castle** (3314m/10,873ft) and **Injasuti** (3459m/11,349ft) and is home to eland, other antelope and a variety of birds, including Cape vulture, jackal buzzard, black eagle and lammergeier.

Entertainment

FOOD & DRINK: A thriving agricultural sector yields excellent fresh produce, meat, fruit and wines and the long coastline produces very fresh and cheap. Bars/cocktail lounges have bartender service. 'Liquor stores' are open weekdays 0900-1800 and Sat 0900-1300, although alcohol is now available in supermarkets outside these hours and under certain circumstances on a Sunday.

National specialities:
- *Sosaties* (a type of kebab).
- *Potjiekos*, a casserole cooked for hours in an iron pot, usually outside.
- *Bredies* (meat, tomato and vegetable casseroles).
- *Biltong* (seasoned dried meat).
- *Poetoepap*, a sort of polenta made with white maize, is widely eaten with meat.
- Seafood including oysters, crayfish (or rock lobster) and linefish (examples of which are Kingklip, Kabbeljou, Cob and Red Roman).

National drinks:
- *Umqombothi*, a home-brewed sorghum beer.
- Excellent local red and white wines (including chardonnay), sherries, brandies and some unusual liqueurs.

Tipping: Normally 10 to 15 per cent if service is not included. It is customary to tip porters, waiters, taxi drivers, caddies and room service. By law, hotel rates do not include a service charge.

NIGHTLIFE: Cinemas show a variety of international films. In the large cities, there are regular plays, operas and symphony concerts. The local music scene is thriving, and there is a unique South African 'township' jazz style, exponents of which can be seen in all large cities. There are a number of nightclubs and discos open until late. The large hotels usually have live music or cabaret.

SHOPPING: Upmarket boutiques and supermarkets generally coexist with a mass of street traders selling arts, crafts and anything else profitable. Stores are modern. Special purchases include Swakara hand-crafted gold, coats, gold, diamond and semi-precious stone jewellery, leather, suede and fur goods, ceramics and crafts, of which there are now a bewildering variety including many from the rest of the continent. Local wine, brandy and liqueur are cheap and usually excellent.
Shopping hours: Mon-Fri 0900-1700, Sat 0900-1400, although there is an increasing trend to open later and all weekend in major tourist spots.

Business

- **GDP:** US$527.4 billion (2005 est) .
- **Main imports:** Machines, plastic products, chemicals and also vehicles.
- **Main exports:** Mineral raw materials (gold, diamonds, platinum), agricultural produce, chemical products, machinery, electric appliances and vehicles.
- **Main trade partners:** China, France, Germany, Iran, Japan, Netherlands, Saudi Arabia, UK and USA.

ECONOMY: The South African economy dominates the southern part of the African continent. Agriculture is strong enough to allow South Africa virtual self-sufficiency in foodstuffs: livestock is reared extensively, and sugar, maize and cereals are produced in large quantities. Specialised products such as wine and fruit are exported in large quantities. The industrial sector has traditionally been based on mining. The country has considerable deposits of common minerals such as coal, but also of valuable metals and ores which are in high demand but are scarce everywhere else except the Russian Federation: these include chromium, manganese, vanadium and platinum. Its most valuable minerals, however, are gold and diamonds, of which South Africa has long been both the world's largest producer and exporter. Gold alone accounts for one-third of the country's entire export income. The only key mineral that South Africa lacks is oil.

Recently, however, the traditional dominance of agriculture and mining has been supplanted by manufacturing and service industries. Manufacturing industry is concentrated in metal-based industries, mainly steel and heavy engineering, with machinery and transport equipment as the principal products. Manufacturing now accounts for around 20 per cent of total economic output. Some advanced technological industries have also emerged in recent years. In the service sector, both financial services and tourism have expanded rapidly and both are now mainstays of the South African economy.

The Mandela Government initially committed itself to a gradual economic transition through its Reconstruction and Development Programme, whose principal aim was to tackle the gross inequalities inherited from the apartheid regime. Progress was tempered, however, by the Government's insistence on fiscal restraint. The Government has since designed a scheme under which major economic assets – notably the mines – will be transferred to 'black empowerment entities' over a 10-year period. Inflation in 2005 was 3.1 per cent and annual growth was 4 per cent. Few inroads have been made into the high level of unemployment, officially at 26.2 per cent in 2004.

Perhaps the greatest long-term problem, especially as regards its impact on the workforce, is the very high level of HIV/AIDS infection in the country.

South Africa is the dominant member of the local Southern African Customs Union (with Botswana, Lesotho, Namibia and Swaziland); it has also joined the Southern African Development Community and the Organisation of African Unity.

BUSINESS ETIQUETTE: Suits are usually expected to be worn for meetings. Appointments are generally necessary and punctuality is expected. Business cards are widely used. **Office hours:** Mon-Fri 0830-1630.

CONFERENCES/CONVENTIONS: There are roughly 815 conference venues in South Africa. The main conference venues are in Pretoria and Johannesburg, though facilities exist in all other major towns, provided mainly by hotels and universities. The Conference and Incentive Promotions Division of SATOUR exists to promote South African venues and to ensure high standards of service and facilities for conference organisers. Contact SATOUR for details (see *Top Things To Do*).

Spain

Location: Western Europe.

Time: Mainland Spain/Balearics: GMT + 1 (GMT + 2 from last Sunday in March to Saturday before last Sunday in October).
The Canary Islands: GMT (GMT + 1 from last Sunday in March to Saturday before last Sunday in October).

Overview

Mediterranean beaches, sangria in the sun and paella by the plateful. Southern Spain has long been a popular place, but tourists are increasingly turning to the fascinations of another Spain, far removed from the high-rise developments lining the Costa del Sol.

Spain is a treasure chest of unforgettable scenery. Separating Spain from France, the snow-capped Pyrenees, as well as having breathtaking views, offer resorts like La Molina and Panticosa with plenty of opportunities for skiing. In the north, the winding rivers and lush, green forests of Galicia present a picture not usually associated with Spain, and in complete contrast to the Moorish-influenced south, Galician culture traces its routes to a Celtic origin. Everywhere are reminders of Spain's rich and varied past, from the Alhambra in Granada to Don Quixote's windmills in La Mancha.

Old mixes with new in cities such as Toledo, Barcelona, Salamanca and the capital, Madrid, as celebrated museums, galleries and Baroque churches rub shoulders with blaring bars and thumping discos.

What will never change is the Spaniards' passion for partying. Snack on tapas as you skip from bar to bar, before heading off to enjoy Spain's infamous nightlife. Then revitalise the senses - Spain's cultural heritage brims with flamenco, painting, opera, literature, sport, bullfighting and flamboyant, colourful fiestas.

Spain was a dictatorship under General Franco until his death in 1975. The authoritarian regime was then transformed into a democratic Government with King Juan Carlos I as Head of State. Modern Spain is a successful democracy with a lot of autonomy given to directly elected regional authorities, although the tension between the state and the separatist movement in the Basque region in the north remains a political problem.

As bargains abound amid intense airline competition, there has never been a better time to visit Spain. Just soak up the atmosphere - you won't be disappointed.

General Information

AREA: 505,988 sq km (195,363 sq miles); includes Spanish North Africa.

POPULATION: 44.1 million (official figures, 2005).
POPULATION DENSITY: 87.15 per sq km.
CAPITAL: Madrid. **Population:** 5.5 million (2005).
GEOGRAPHY: Spain shares the Iberian peninsula with Portugal and is bordered to the north by the Pyrenees, which separate Spain from France. The Balearic Islands (Mallorca, Menorca, Ibiza and Formentera), 193km (120 miles) southeast of Barcelona, and the Canary Islands off the west coast of Africa are part of Spain, as are the tiny enclaves of Ceuta and Melilla on the north African mainland. With the exception of Switzerland, mainland Spain is the highest and most mountainous country in Europe, with an average height of 610m (2000ft). The Pyrenees stretch roughly 400km (249 miles) from the Basque Country in the west to the Mediterranean Sea; at times the peaks rise to over 1524m (5000ft), the highest point being 3404m (11,169ft). The main physical feature of Spain is the vast central plateau, or *Meseta*, divided by several chains of sierras. The higher northern area includes Castile and León, the southern section comprises Castile/La Mancha and Extremadura. In the south, the plateau drops abruptly at the Sierra Morena, beyond which lies the valley of Guadalquivir. Southeast of Granada is the Sierra Nevada, part of the Betic Cordillera, which runs parallel to the Mediterranean, rising to 3481m (11,420ft) and the highest point on the Spanish peninsula (the Pico del Teide on Tenerife in the Canaries is the highest peak in Spain). The Mediterranean coastal area reaches from the French frontier in the northeast down to the Straits of Gibraltar, the narrow strip of water linking the Mediterranean with the Atlantic and separating Spain from North Africa.

GOVERNMENT: Parliamentary Monarchy since 1978.
Head of State: King Juan Carlos I since 1975. **Head of Government:** José Luis Rodríguez Zapatero since 2004.
Recent history: Spain's right-of-centre Popular Party (PP) won a clear majority in Parliament in 2000 and was comfortably ahead in the polls before the 2004 general elections. Three days before the elections, however, devastating terrorist attacks by Islamic extremists in Madrid killed 191 people and threw the political situation into turmoil. Unexpectedly, the Spanish Socialist Workers Party won the election and formed a minority Government under new Prime Minister Jose Luis Rodriguez Zapatero. In April, Zapatero was sworn in, and he immediately ordered Spanish troops to be withdrawn from Iraq. One of Spain's most serious domestic issues continues to be tension in the northern Basque region. The Supreme Court finally approved a Government request for a permanent ban on the Basque separatist party Batasuna in March 2003, despite the party's persistent denial that it is terrorist group ETA's political wing. In May 2005, the Government offered peace talks with ETA on condition that the group disarms.

LANGUAGE: Spanish (Castilian), Catalan (in the northeast), Galician (in the northwest) and Basque (in the north).

RELIGION: There is no official religion, but the majority of the population is Roman Catholic.

ELECTRICITY: 220 or 225 volts AC, 50Hz. Generally, round two-pin plugs and screw-type lamp fittings are in use.

SOCIAL CONVENTIONS: Spanish life has undergone rapid change in recent years and many of the stricter religious customs are giving way to more modern ways, particularly in the cities and among women. Nonetheless, many old customs, manners and traditions have not faded and hospitality, chivalry and courtesy remain important. Handshaking is the customary form of greeting. Normal social courtesies should be observed when visiting someone's home. If invited to a private home, a small gift is appreciated. Flowers are only sent for special celebrations. Conservative casual wear is widely acceptable. Some hotels and restaurants encourage men to wear jackets. A black tie is only necessary for very formal occasions and is usually specified if required. Outside resorts, scanty beachwear should be confined to beach or poolside. A new law banning smoking in offices, shops, schools, hospitals, cultural centres and on public transport was introduced on 1 January 2006. The evening meal is taken late, generally 2100-2200. The Spanish have two family names; in conversation only the first should be used. A new law banning smoking in offices, shops, schools, hospitals, cultural centres and on public transport was introduced on 1 January 2006.

Climate

Spain's climate varies from temperate in the north to dry and hot in the south. The best months are from April to October, although mid-summer (July to August) can be excessively hot throughout the country except the coastal regions. Madrid is best in late spring or autumn. The central plateau can be bitterly cold in winter.

Required clothing: Light- to mediumweights and rainwear, according to the season.

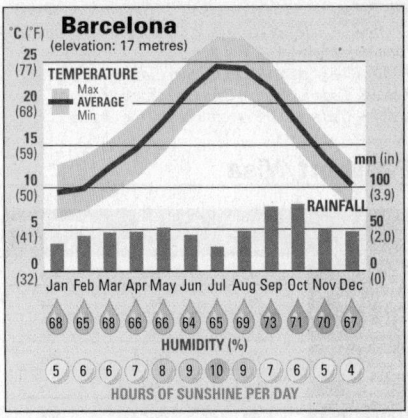

Barcelona (elevation: 17 metres)

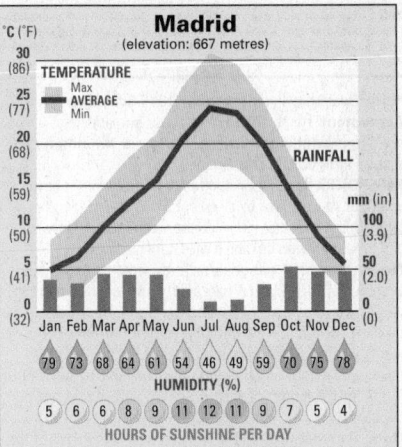

Madrid (elevation: 667 metres)

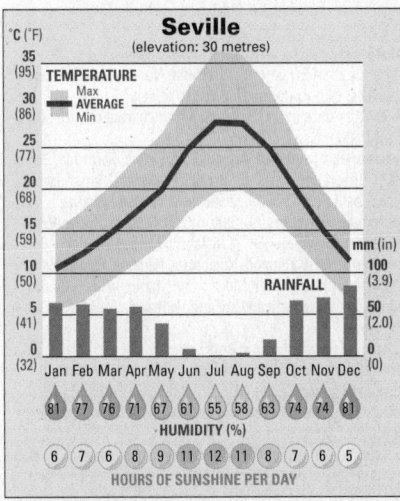

Seville (elevation: 30 metres)

Communications

Telephone: IDD is available. Country code: 34. Emergency calls: 112. Area codes are incorporated within a nine digit number. The following are a selection of codes for major centres: Madrid 91, Alicante 96, Balearic Islands 971, Barcelona 93, Benidorm 96, Bilbao 94, Granada 958, Málaga and Torremolinos 95, Las Palmas 928, Santander 942, Seville 95, Tenerife 922 and Valencia 96.

Mobile telephone: Roaming agreements exist with most international mobile phone companies. Coverage is good throughout most of the country.

Internet: There is a variety of Internet cafes in most urban areas.

Post: There are efficient internal and international postal services to all countries. Airmail within Europe usually takes around five days.

MEDIA: Broadcasting in Spain has witnessed a spectacular expansion in recent years with the emergence of new commercial operators and the launch of digital services.

Press: Local newspapers published in English include the *Costa Blanca News*, *Majorca Daily Bulletin* and the English-language edition of *Sur* (weekly). Spanish dailies with large circulations include *ABC* (website: www.abc.es), *El Marca* (sports only), *El Mundo* (website: www.elmundo.es), *El País* (website: www.elpais.es), *El Periodico de Catalunya* (website: www.elperiodico.com), *La Razon* (website: www.larazon.es) and *La Vanguardia* (website: www.lavanguardia.es).

A B C D E F G H I J K L M N O P Q R **S** T U V W X Y Z

A B C D E F G H I J K L M N O P Q R S T U V W X Y Z

TV: *TVE* operates *La Primera, La 2, TVE Internacionale* and *Channel 24. Tele Conco, Antena 3* and *Cuatro* are national, commercial networks.
Radio: *RNE* operates *Radio 1, Radio Clasica, Radio 3* and *Radio 5. Cadena SER* and *Onda Cero* are commercial stations. *Cadena COPE* is controlled by the church.

Passport/Visa

	Passport Required?	Visa Required?	Return Ticket Required?
Full British	1	No	Yes
Australian	Yes	No/2	Yes
Canadian	Yes	No/2	Yes
USA	Yes	No/2	Yes
Other EU	Yes/1	No	Yes
Japanese	Yes	No/2	Yes

Note: *Regulations and requirements may be subject to change at short notice, and you are advised to contact the appropriate diplomatic or consular authority before finalising travel arrangements. Any numbers in the chart refer to the footnotes below.*

Note: Spain is a signatory to the 1995 **Schengen Agreement**. For further details about passport/visa regulations within the Schengen area, see the introductory section *How to Use this Guide*.
PASSPORTS: Passport valid for at least three months beyond length of stay required by all except:
(a) **1.** EU/EEA nationals (EU + Iceland, Liechtenstein, Norway) and Swiss nationals holding a valid national ID card.
Note: EU and EEA nationals are only required to produce evidence of their EU/EEA nationality and identity in order to be admitted to any EU/EEA Member State. This evidence can take the form of a valid national passport *or* national identity card. Either is acceptable. Possession of a return ticket, any length of validity on their document, sufficient funds for the length of their proposed visit should *not* be imposed.
Note: The requested validity and precise requirements of the passport may vary according to nationality and these are subject to change at short notice; please consult nearest Embassy/Consulate for further details.
VISAS: Required by all except the following:
(a) nationals of EU countries, Iceland, Norway and Switzerland regardless of purpose and/or length of stay;
(b) **2.** other nationals referred to in the chart above for stays of up to 90 days;
(c) nationals of Andorra, Anguilla, Argentina, Bermuda, Bolivia, Brazil, British Virgin Islands, Brunei, Bulgaria, Cayman Islands, Chile, Costa Rica, Croatia, El Salvador, Falkland Islands, Guatemala, Honduras, Hong Kong (SAR), Israel, Korea (Rep), Liechtenstein, Macau (SAR), Malaysia, Mexico, Monaco, Montserrat, New Zealand, Nicaragua, Panama, Paraguay, Romania, St Helena, San Marino, Singapore, Turks & Caicos Islands, Uruguay, Vatican City and Venezuela for stays of up to 90 days;
(d) holders of travel documents issued by the Geneva convention of July 1951, by Belgium, Cyprus, Denmark, Germany, Iceland, Ireland, Liechtenstein, Luxembourg, The Netherlands, Norway, Spain, Sweden, Switzerland and the UK for stays of up to 90 days;
(e) nationals of any of the *Schengen* member states who hold permanent residency are entitled to re-enter the *Schengen* area without a visa, provided proof of residence and a valid passport are submitted;
(f) transit passengers continuing their journey by the same or first connecting aircraft provided holding valid onward or return documentation and not leaving the airport (except nationals of certain countries). Visitors are advised to check transit regulations with the relevant Embassy or Consulate before travelling.
Types of visa and cost: A uniform type of visa, the *Schengen* visa, is issued for tourist, business and private visits. Cost is £24.15.
Note: Spouses and children of EU nationals (providing spouse's passport and the original marriage or birth certificate is produced), and nationals of some other countries, receive their visas free of charge (enquire at Embassy for details).
Validity: *Short-stay* (single- and multiple-entry): valid for six months from date of issue for a stay of maximum 90 days per entry. *Transit* (single- and multiple-entry): valid for a maximum of five days per entry, including the day of arrival. Visas cannot be extended and a new application must be made each time.
Application to: In person (strictly only by appointment solicited in writing) to the appropriate Consulate (or consular section at Embassy) in the country of the passport holder. Postal applications are not accepted. Travellers visiting just one Schengen country should apply to the Consulate of that country; travellers visiting more than one Schengen country should apply to the Consulate of the country chosen as the main destination *or* the country they will enter first (if they have no main destination).
Note: Applicants will be seen by appointment only.
Application requirements: (a) Passport or travel document, valid for at least four months longer than requested visa with one full blank page. (b) Two completed application forms. (c) Two passport-size photos. (d) Fee, payable by cash or postal order only. (e) Letter from employer, school or college. (f) Bank statement. (g) Proof of purpose of visit. (h) Proof of medical insurance.
Working days required: Seven to ten days to obtain an appointment. After appointment, a visa will be issued in between two and three weeks dependent on nationality.
Temporary residence: Refer enquiries to Consulate (or consular section at Embassy).

PASSPORT/VISA INFORMATION

Spanish Embassy in the UK
39 Chesham Place, London SW1X 8SB, UK
Tel: (020) 7235 5555.
Website: www.mae.es

Spanish Consulate in the UK
20 Draycott Place, London SW3 2RZ, UK
Tel: (020) 7589 8989 *or* (0906) 550 8970 (recorded visa information; calls cost £1 per minute) *or* (0906) 526 6666 (to order visa applications; calls cost £1.50 per minute).
Website: www.conspalon.org
Opening hours: Mon-Fri 0915-1415 (closed Spanish national holidays; visa information by appointment only).

Embassy and Consulate of the Kingdom of Spain in the USA
2375 Pennsylvania Avenue, NW, Washington, DC 20037, USA
Tel: (202) 728 2330.
Website: www.spainemb.org

Money

Single European currency (Euro): The Euro is now the official currency of 12 EU member states (including Spain). The first Euro coins and notes were introduced in January 2002; the Spanish Peseta was still in circulation until 28 February 2002, when it was completely replaced by the Euro. Euro (€) = 100 cents. Notes are in denominations of €500, 200, 100, 50, 20, 10 and 5. Coins are in denominations of €2 and 1, and 50, 20, 10, 5, 2 and 1 cents.
Currency exchange: Money can be changed in any bank, and at most travel agencies, major hotels and airports. National Girobank Postcheques may be used to withdraw cash from UK accounts at main Spanish post offices.
Credit & debit cards: American Express, Diners Club, MasterCard and Visa are widely accepted, as well as Eurocheque cards. Check with your credit or debit card company for details of merchant acceptability and other facilities which may be available. ATMs are widely available.
Traveller's cheques: International traveller's cheques are widely accepted. To avoid additional exchange rate charges, travellers are advised to take traveller's cheques in Euros or Pounds Sterling. Traveller's cheques should be changed at banks or exchange bureaux.
Currency restrictions: The import and export of local currency is unlimited, but the export of amounts exceeding €6010 (in any currency) per person per journey must be declared. The export of cash notes and bearers-cheques, in any currency, exceeding €3050 per person per journey must also be declared.
Banking hours: 0900-1400.
Exchange rate indicators:
Rate at time of publishing
£1.00= €31.46
$1.00= €30.82

Duty Free

The following goods may be imported into Spain without incurring customs duty by passengers 17 years of age or older arriving from non-EU countries:
200 cigarettes or 100 cigarillos 50 cigars or 250g tobacco (300 cigarettes, 150 cigarillos, 70 cigars and 400g of tobacco for EU nationals); 1l of spirits if exceeding 22 per cent volume or 2l of alcoholic beverage not exceeding 22 per cent volume and 2l of wine (1.5l exceeding 22 per cent and 3l of up to 22 per cent and 5l of wine for EU nationals); 250ml eau de toilette and 50g of perfume; 500g of coffee or 200g of coffee extract (1000g of coffee and 4000g of coffee extract for EU nationals); 100g of tea or 40g of tea extract; gifts up to the value of approximately €37.26.
Abolition of duty free goods within the EU: On June 30 1999, the sale of duty free alcohol and tobacco at airports and at sea was abolished in all of the original 15 EU member states. Of the 10 new member states that joined the EU on May 1 2004, these rules already apply to Cyprus and Malta. There are transitional rules in place for visitors returning to one of the original 15 EU countries from one of the other new EU countries. But for the original 15, plus Cyprus and Malta, there are now no limits imposed on importing tobacco and alcohol products from one EU country to another (with the exceptions of Denmark, Finland and Sweden, where limits *are* imposed). Travellers should note that they may be required to prove at customs that the goods purchased are for personal use *only*.

Public Holidays

Below are listed Public Holidays for the January 2006-June 2007 period.
2006: Jan 1 New Year's Day. **Jan 6*** Epiphany. **Mar 19*** San Jose. **Apr 13*** Maundy Thursday. **Apr 14** Good Friday. **May 1** Labour Day. **Aug 15** Assumption. **Oct 12** National Day. **Nov 1** All Saints' Day. **Dec 6** Constitution Day. **Dec 8** Immaculate Conception. **Dec 25** Christmas Day.
2007: Jan 1 New Year's Day. **Jan 6*** Epiphany. **Mar 19*** San Jose. **Apr 5*** Maundy Thursday. **Apr 6** Good Friday. **May 1** Labour Day.
(a) *These holidays may be replaced by the autonomous communities with another date.
(b) The following dates are also celebrated as regional public holidays (within these regions, there are further public holidays peculiar to the various towns and cities):
Jan 29 Dia de la Convivencia (Ceuta). **Feb 28 Andalucía Day. Mar 1** Balearic Isles Day. **Apr 23** San Jorge (Aragon) and Day of the Region of Castilla y Leon. **May 2** San Segundo (Castilla y Leon) and Fiesta of the Communidad de Madrid. **May 17** Dia de las Letras Gallegas (Galicia). **May 30** Canaries Day. **May 31** Day of the Region of Castilla-La Mancha. **Jun 9** Day of the Region of Murcia and Day of La Rioja. **Sep 8** Asturias Day, Day of Extremadura and Nuestra la Virgen de la Victoria (Melilla). **Sep 11** National Day of Catalonia. **Sep 15** Nuestra Senora de la Bien Aparecida (Cantabria). **Sep 17** Commemoration of the Spanish Refounding of the City of Melilla. **Dec 26** San Esteban (Balearic Isles and Catalonia).
(c) Catalonia, Navarra, Pais Vasco (Basque Country) and Valenciana also celebrate Easter Monday (**Apr 17 2006** and **Apr 9 2007**).

Health

	Special Precautions?	Certificate Required?
Yellow Fever	No	No
Cholera	No	No
Typhoid & Polio	No	N/A
Malaria	No	N/A

Note: *Regulations and requirements may be subject to change at short notice, and you are advised to contact your doctor well in advance of your intended date of departure. Any numbers in the chart refer to the footnotes below.*

Other risks: *Leishmaniasis* is present and there have been some outbreaks of *Legionnaries Disease* in tourist resorts. *Rabies* is present. For those at high risk, vaccination before arrival should be considered. If you are bitten, seek medical advice without delay. For more information, consult the *Health* appendix.
Health care: European Economic Area (EEA) and Switzerland:
If you or any of your dependants are suddenly taken ill or have an accident during a visit to an EEA country or Switzerland, free or reduced-cost necessary treatment is available – in most cases on production of a valid European Health Insurance Card (EHIC). Each country has different rules about state medical provision. In some, treatment is free. In many countries you will have to pay part or all of the cost, and then claim a full or partial refund. The EHIC gives access to state-provided medical treatment only and the scheme gives no entitlement to medical repatriation costs, nor does it cover ongoing illnesses of a non-urgent nature, so comprehensive travel insurance is advised. Note that the EHIC replaces the Form E111, is no longer be valid since 31 December 2005. Some restrictions apply, depending on your nationality.
Make sure the practitioner you see works within the Spanish state health service. In some parts of the country, particularly the outlying islands, you may have to travel some distance to attend a state surgery (*consultorio*), health centre (*centro sanitario*) or hospital clinic (*ambulatorio*). If you need to call out a doctor in an emergency, make it clear that you have a European Health Insurance Card (EHIC) and that you want to be treated under the EU arrangements. Whenever you need treatment, show your EHIC. Dental

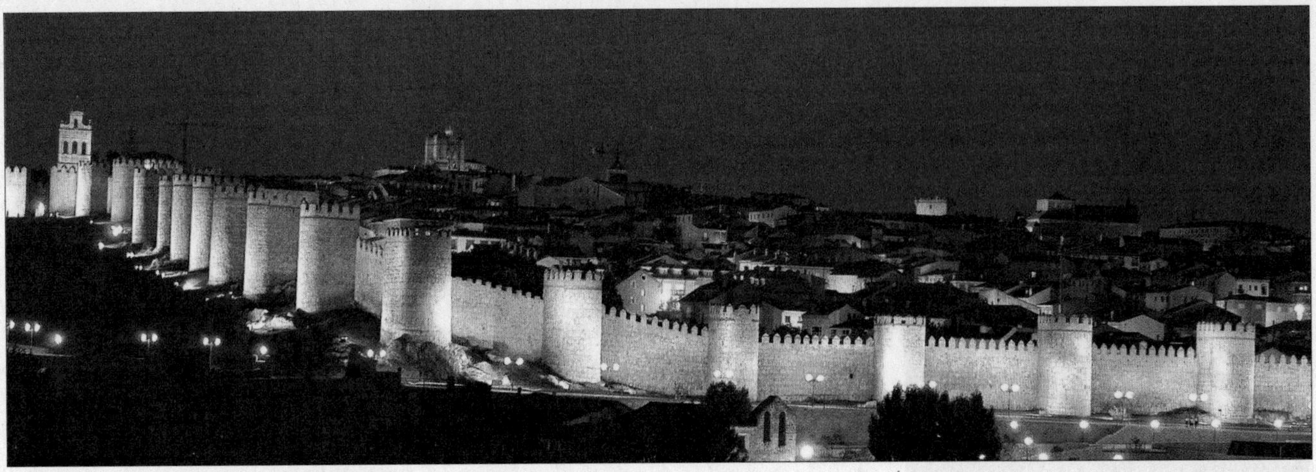

Credit: © Turespaña

treatment is not generally provided under the state system, and the costs will not be reimbursed. In Spain, doctors, health centres and hospitals have separate surgery times for private patients and those treated under the state health service. If you are asked to pay, you are not being treated under the Spanish health service and your EHIC will not be accepted. Medicines prescribed by health service practitioners can be obtained from any pharmacy (*farmacia*). You will have to pay up to 40 per cent of the cost unless you are an EEA pensioner, in which case the medicines will be free of charge. You must show proof that you are a state pensioner, otherwise you will be charged 40 per cent of the cost, which you can claim back on your return home. If a hospital says you need medicines after you are discharged, you must take the medical report to a GP, who will give you a prescription. A doctor will usually arrange any hospital treatment you may need. In an emergency, you can only get free treatment in a public ward at a public hospital. You must show your EHIC; if not, you will be charged as a private patient and will not get your money back. Under the strict terms of the Spanish health service, there are no refunds for private healthcare charges. Make sure you have private medical insurance in case you are treated in an emergency in a private hospital. Doctors in the emergency departments of state health service hospitals will prescribe medicines on the appropriate medical report, but do not issue official prescriptions. You must take the report to a primary care doctor who will issue the official prescription. More information can be obtained in Spain from the *Servicio Regional de Salud* (Regional Health Service Officers).

Travel - International

Note: For information on travel to and within the **Balearic Islands** and the **Canary Islands**, see the respective sections.

AIR:

The national airline is *IBERIA (IB)* (website: www.iberia.com). Many airlines operate to Spain, including an increasing number of low-cost airlines from the UK.

Approximate flight times: From Barcelona to *London* is two hours; from Ibiza is two hours 20 minutes; from Madrid is two hours 20 minutes and from Málaga is two hours 45 minutes. From Madrid to *Los Angeles* is 12 hours 20 minutes; to *New York* is eight hours 35 minutes; to *Sydney* is 30 hours.

Main airports: Spain boasts over 30 international airports. Information on the major airports follows; information on any of the others can be obtained from AENA (*Aeropuertos Espanoles y Navegación Aérea*), Calle Arturo Soria 109, Madrid 28043 (tel: (90) 240 4704 (customer service line); website: www.aena.es), which is the organisation responsible for running all of the Spanish airports.

Madrid (MAD) (Barajas) is 13km (8 miles) northeast of the city. *To/from the airport*: A bus service departs to the city around every 18 minutes on weekdays and every 19-23 minutes at weekends (0600-2325) and underground services run every four to seven minutes (0600-0200) costing €1. Taxi service is available. *Facilities*: Restaurants and bars, bank, several car hire offices, hotel reservation and tourist information desks, and outgoing duty free shop.

Barcelona (BCN) (el Prat) is 3km (2 miles) southwest of the city. *To/from the airport*: Bus service to the city departs Mon-Fri every 15 minutes, Sat every 30 mins and Sun every 20 mins (0600-0100). Rail service is every 20 minutes (0625-2350). Taxi service to the city is available, costing about €18 (travel time - 30 minutes). *Facilities*: A bank, restaurant, bar, several car hire companies, hotel reservation and tourist information desks and duty free shops.

Alicante (ALC) (Altet) is 12km (7 miles) southwest of the city. *To/from the airport*: Bus service runs to the city (0655-2310) every 10 to 40 minutes, costing €1. A taxi service is available to the city, costing about €12. There is a taxi connection between Alicante and Valencia Airport. *Facilities*: Duty free shop, bank, bureau de change, car hire, tourist information and restaurant.

Málaga (AGP) is 10km (6 miles) southwest of the city. *To/from the airport*: Buses run every 10 to 30 minutes (0700-0000). A train service runs every 30 minutes, costing 1.05-€1.15 (0700-0000). A taxi service to the city is available, costing €12. *Facilities*: Duty free shop, bank/bureau de change, restaurant and car hire.

Valencia (VLC) (Manises) is 8km (5 miles) west of the city. *To/from the airport*: An aero bus takes passengers into the city (0600-2200), costing €2.50. Other buses travel to the city every 15 minutes (0630-2345)). Taxis cost about €14 plus a €2.75 supplement. *Facilities*: Several car hire firms, bank/bureau de change, restaurant, bar and duty free shop.

Departure tax: None.

SEA:

Main ports: *Barcelona* (website: www.apb.es), *Cadiz* (website: www.puertocadiz.com), *Santander* (website: www.puertosantander.es), *Valencia* (website: www.valenciaport.com/cultures/es) and *Vigo* (website: www.apvigo.com).

Brittany Ferries (tel: (08703) 665 333; website: www.brittany-ferries.com) operates a service to Santander (on the north coast) from Plymouth (travel time - 18 hours), twice-weekly. *P&O European Ferries* (tel: (08705) 202020; website: www.poportsmouth.com) operates a twice-weekly service from Portsmouth to Bilbao (travel time - 35 hours).

RAIL:

The quickest route by train from the UK is through the Channel Tunnel with connections from Paris to Spain. *Eurostar* is a service by the railways of Belgium, the UK and France, operating direct high-speed trains from London (*Waterloo International*) to Paris *(Gare du Nord)* and to Brussels (*Midi/Zuid*). It takes two hours 40 minutes from London to Paris (via Lille) and two hours 20 minutes to Brussels. For further information and reservations, contact *Eurostar* (tel: (0870) 600 0792 (travel agents) *or* (08705) 186 186 (public; within the UK) or +44 (1233) 617 575 (public; outside the UK); a £5 booking fee applies to all telephone bookings; website: www.eurostar.com); *or* Rail Europe (tel: (08705) 848 848; website: www.raileurope.co.uk).

There are direct trains between Madrid-Paris and Madrid-Lisbon, as well as Barcelona-Paris, Barcelona-Zürich or Milan, Barcelona-Montpelier and Barcelona-Geneva. These services are called *Estrella*, *Talgo* or *Train-Hotel*. On other international services to and from Spain, a change of train is necessary. However, work on the *AVE* (high-velocity train) route between Madrid and Barcelona is expected to be completed in 2006, after which the French border connection is expected to be fully operational in 2010 and it will be possible to connect with the French *TGV* (high-velocity route) and the rest of the high-velocity routes in Europe. Motorail services run between Paris and Madrid. For more information, contact the Spanish Rail service (tel: (020) 7224 0345; website: www.spanish-rail.co.uk).

Rail passes: The *Inter-Rail* pass offers unlimited second-class train travel in up to 29 European countries (includes Morocco and Turkey) split into eight zones (A-H). Three different tickets are available: a ticket covering one zone (two to six countries, 16 days' validity), a ticket covering two zones (six to 10 countries, 22 days' validity) and an *All Zone Pass* (29 countries, one month's validity). Ferry services between Italy and Greece are included. Passengers must be resident in Europe for at least six months before the pass is used. Travel is not allowed in the passenger's country of residence. Travellers under 26 year receive a reduction of about 30 per cent. Children's tickets are reduced by about 50 per cent. Supplements are required for some high-speed services, seat reservations and couchettes. Discounts are offered on *Eurostar* and some ferry routes. Available from *Inter rail* (website:www.interrail.com).

The *Eurailpass* offers unlimited first-class train travel in 17 European countries. Tickets are valid for 15 days, 21 days, one month, two months or three months. The *Eurailpass Youth* ticket is available to those under 26 and offers unlimited second-class train travel. The *Eurailpass Flexi* allows either 10 or 15 travel days within a two-month period. The *Eurail Selectpass* is valid in three, four or five bordering countries and allows five, six, eight or 10 travel days (or 15 for five countries) in a two-month period. The *Eurail Regional Pass* allows four to 10 travel days in a two-month period in one of nine regions (usually two or more countries). Children receive a 50 per cent reduction. The passes cannot be sold to residents of Europe, Turkey, Morocco, Algeria, Tunisia or the Russian Federation. Available from *The Eurail Group* (website: www.eurail.com).

ROAD:

The main route from the UK is via France. The main motorways to Spain from France are via Bordeaux or Toulouse to Bilbao (northern Spain) and via Marseille or Toulouse to Barcelona (eastern Spain). There are numerous and excellent road links with neighbouring countries. *Eurolines* (52 Grosvenor Gardens, London SW1W 0AU; tel: (08705) 143 219; website: www.eurolines.com) and *National Express* (9 Ensign Court, 4 Vicarage road, Edgbaston, Birmingham B15 3ES; tel: 08705 808 080; website: www.nationalexpress.com) run regular coach services from the UK to Spain.

Travellers can either choose Mini-Pass breaks or book a 15-, 30- or 60-day pass. The six Mini-Passes give travellers the freedom to visit three cities, with prices starting from £55. Travellers can stay as long as they like in each city.

For information on **documentation** and **traffic regulations**, see *Travel – Internal* section.

Travel - Internal

AIR:

Domestic flights are run by *IBERIA (IB)* (website: www.iberia.com), *Air Europa* (website: www.air-europa.com), *Binter* (website: www.binternet.com and *Spanair* (website: www.spanair.com). Scheduled flights connect all main towns as well as the Balearic and Canary Islands and enclaves in North Africa. Air taxis are available at most airports. Reservations should be made well in advance.

SEA:

There are regular hydrofoil and car and passenger ferry sailings from Algeciras to Tangier and Ceuta (North African enclave); Málaga and Almeria to Melilla (North African enclave); Barcelona, Valencia and Alicante to the Balearic Islands; and Cádiz to the Canary Islands. There are also inter-island services, including a catamaran service linking Barcelona and Palma de Mallorca, which takes three hours and runs twice a day. For further information, contact *Trasmediterránea* c/o *Southern Ferries* (tel: (902) 454 645; website: www.trasmediterranea.es).

RAIL:

The state-owned company *RENFE* (website: www.renfe.es) operates a railway network connecting all the regions on the Iberian peninsula. It is mainly a radial network, with connections between Madrid and all the major cities. There are also some transversal services connecting the northwest coast with the Mediterranean coast, as well as services from the French border down the Mediterranean coast. Principal trains are air conditioned, and many have restaurant or buffet service. Reservations for passenger services in Spain may be made in the UK through the Spanish Rail service (see above), *European Rail Travel* (tel: (020) 7387 0444; website: www.europeanrail.com), *Freedom Rail* (tel: (0870)

Credit: © Turespaña

757 9898; website: www.freedomrail.com) and *Ultima Travel* (tel: (0151) 339 6171).

Discount Rail Travel: The Spanish rail system is one of the cheapest in Europe and various discounts are available. Travellers under 26 can purchase a RENFE *Tarjeta Explorerail*, which allows unlimited travel on all but some regional and fast trains. It can be bought in Spain, or in the UK from selected travel agents, and is available for seven-, 15- and 30-day periods. For more discount rail travel, See *Travel International* section.

Note: Seat reservations are required on all intercity trains. This ruling applies to the passes and cards mentioned above.

High-Speed Trains: The *Ave* service averages 300kph and connects Madrid and Seville in two hours 15 minutes, with 12 services each way via Córdoba. Some services also stop at Ciudad Real and Puerto Llano (La Mancha). The stretch from Madrid to Lleida has been in operation for several years. Planned completion of the Madrid to Barcelona leg is due in 2006, and the high-speed border connection with France in 2010. Also, in 2010, the stretches from Cordoba to Malaga, Madrid to Valencia and Madrid to Valladolid should be ready. The *Talgo 200* connects Madrid and Malaga thrice-daily in four hours 35 minutes. Holders of most of the cards and passes mentioned above qualify for discounts, albeit less substantial than the rates quoted above.

Tourist Trains: The *Andalus Express* and *Transcantábrico* offer a pleasant way of discovering their respective regions. There are also a number of privately-run narrow-gauge railways in Spain, located mainly in the north of Spain as well as the Mediterranean coast and the Balearic Islands, which run at a leisurely pace through picturesque scenery. For more information on tourist trains, contact the Spanish National Tourist Office (see *Top Things To Do*).

ROAD:

 Motorways are well-maintained and connect Spain north–south. Tolls are in operation on some sections and have to be paid in Euros. Trunk roads between major cities are generally fast and well-maintained. Rural roads are of differing quality.

Bus: There are bus lines which are efficient and cheap, operating between cities and towns. Departures are generally from a central terminal at which the operators will have individual booths selling tickets. Most places have a bus link of some kind, even the more remote villages.

Car hire: All major car hire companies are represented in major cities. Drivers must be over 21 to hire a car.

Motorcycles: No person under 18 may hire or ride a vehicle over 75cc. Crash helmets must be worn. **Regulations:** Traffic drives on the right. Side lights must be used at night in built-up areas. Spare bulbs and red hazard triangles must be kept in all vehicles. Traffic lights: two red lights mean 'No Entry'. Parking laws are rigorously enforced. The speed limit for motorways is 120kph (80mph) in general, but for buses and lorries the limit is 100kph (60mph); in built-up areas the limit is 50kph (30mph); for other roads it is 90kph (56mph).

Documentation: Most foreign licences including Canadian, EU and US are accepted. Third Party insurance is compulsory,

plus a Green Card if bringing your own car (available from insurance company).

URBAN:

 Traffic in Spanish cities is normally heavy, and urban driving takes some time to adjust to. City public transport facilities are generally good. Barcelona, Bilbao, Madrid and Valencia have metros as well as buses. Pre-purchase multi-journey tickets are sold. Other towns and resorts are well served by local buses. Metered taxis are available in most major cities and a 2 to 3 per cent tip is customary.

Travel Times: The following chart gives approximate travel times (in hours and minutes) from **Madrid** to other major cities and towns in Spain.

	Air	Road	Rail
Barcelona	1.00	8.00	8.00
Canary Is.	2.30	-	-
Mallorca	1.00	-	-
Palma	1.10	6.00*	5.00*

Note: *Plus nine hours by boat (three hours by catamaran).

Travel Advice

On 22 March 2006, the Basque terrorist organisation ETA announced a "permanent ceasefire", effective from 24 March 2006.

In March 2004, 192 people died and over 1400 were injured following bomb attacks on three trains in Madrid. A group purporting to represent Al Qaida claimed responsibility.

Visitors should be alerted to the existence of street crimes, especially in the larger cities.

Most visits to Spain are trouble-free but you should be aware of the global risk of indiscriminate international terrorist attacks, which could be against civilian targets, including places frequented by foreigners.

This advice is based on information provided by the Foreign and Commonwealth Office in the UK. It is correct at time of publishing. As the situation can change rapidly, visitors are advised to contact the following organisations for the latest travel advice:

British Foreign and Commonwealth Office
Tel: (0845) 850 2829.
Website: www.fco.gov.uk

US Department of State
Website: http://travel.state.gov/travel

Accommodation

HOTELS & HOSTELS:

 A variety of hotel-type accommodation is available including apartment-hotels, *hotel-residencias* and motels. The term *residencia* denotes an establishment where dining-room facilities are not provided, although there must be provisions for the serving of breakfast and a cafe. Further information on accommodation in Barcelona and Madrid can be obtained free of charge online (website: www.barcelona-on-line.com or www.madrid-on-line.com). **Grading:** Most accommodation in Spain is provided in hotels, classified from **1** to **5 stars** (the few exceptions have a Gran Lujo, Grande De Luxe category); or hostels and *pensiones*, classified from **1** to **3** stars. It is always advisable to book accommodation well in advance, particularly during festivals or at popular resorts on the coast from late spring to October.

GOVERNMENT LODGES: A chain of lodging places has been set up by the Ministry of Tourism in places of special interest or remote locations. These include attractive modern buildings and ancient monuments of historic interest, such as monasteries, convents, old palaces and castles. Standards are uniformly high, but not at the expense of individual charm and character.

PARADORES: National Tourist Inns, *Paradores*, are hotels with all modern amenities including rooms with private bathroom, hot and cold running water, central heating, telephone in every room, public sitting rooms, garages and complementary services. Many *Paradores* are restored

castles, convents or palaces in a scenic setting. Advance booking is advised.

GUEST HOUSES:

 Pensiones are common throughout Spain and vary in quality from austere to relatively luxurious. They are usually run by the family on the premises and provide bed and board only.

CAMPING/CARAVANNING:

 There are over 1000 campsites throughout the country, covering a wide quality and price range. Permission from the local police and landowner is essential for off-site camping and there may be no more than three tents/caravans or 10 campers in any one place. Regulations demand that off-site camping is in isolated areas only.

YOUTH HOSTELS:

 The *Spanish Youth Hostel Network (REAJ)* is the representative in Spain for the International Youth Hostel Federation and there are currently over 200 registered youth hostels throughout the whole of Spain. Most must be booked in Spain, but a couple can be booked from the UK.

ACCOMMODATION INFORMATION

Confederación Espanola de Hoteles y Alojamientos (CEHAT)
Calle Orense 32, 28020 Madrid, Spain
Tel: (91) 556 7112 *or* (90) 201 2141.
Website: www.cehat.com.

Paradores de Turismo
Calle Requena 3, Madrid 28013, Spain
Tel: (91) 516 6666.
Website: www.parador.es

Federación Espanola de Empresarios de Cámpings y Ciudades de Vacaciones (ANCE)
San Bernardo 97-99, 28015 Madrid, Spain
Tel: (91) 448 1234.
Website: www.fedcamping.com.

Spanish Youth Hostel Network (REAJ)
E-mail: info@reaj.com
Website: www.reaj.com

Turisme Juvenil de Catalunya in Barcelona
C/Rocafort 116-122, 08015 Barcelona, Spain
Tel: (934) 838 363.

Turisme Juvenil de Catalunya in Madrid
C/Castello 24, 1G, 28001 Madrid, Spain
Tel: (91) 522 7007.

YHA International in England
Tel: (01629) 592 600
Website: www.yha.org

Top Things To See

- **Madrid** is a paradise for art lovers. Explore the city's three superb art museums. The **Prado** has one of the most remarkable art collections in the world. The **Museo Nacional Centro de Arte Reina Sofia** focuses on modern art and is where Picasso's famous **Guernica** is on display. The **Museo Thyssen-Bornemisza** is one of the most important private collections of western paintings in the world. Discover Madrid's **Royal Palace**, which dates from the mid-18th century and has more than 20 rooms open to the public. Enjoy the atmosphere in the area around **Puerta del Sol**, the heart of the city, and on Madrid's most historic and popular square, the **Plaza Mayor**, completed in 1617 during the reign of Philip III.

- Travel the 30 kilometres from Madrid to **Alcalá de Henares**, a UNESCO World Heritage Site, and the birthplace of the writer Miguel de Cervantes and the English queen Catherine of Aragon. The main points of interest are the **university**, founded in the 16th century by Cardinal Cisneros, and the **oldest surviving public theatre** in Europe - as important to Spain as Shakespeare's Globe is to England.

Spain

- Absorb the lively atmosphere of **Barcelona**, Spain's second-largest city. A major commercial and industrial centre, it is graced by several of **Antoni Gaudí**'s architectural masterworks, the most famous being the still incomplete church of the **Sagrada Familia** (**Holy Family**). Visit the **Barri Gótic** (**Gothic quarter**), where the buildings date back to the 14th and 15th centuries. Highlights include the **Seu** (**old cathedral**), the **Episcopal Palace**, the **Palau de la Generalitat** and the **Plaça del Rei**. Take the funicular to **Tibidabo**, the highest of Barcelona's hills, or a cable car to **Montjuic** in the southern suburbs. Both offer spectacular views over the city and have funfairs at the summits. Barcelona's museums include the **Museo Picasso**, which focuses on the artist's formative years, but includes works from the Blue and Rose periods, the **Fundació Joan Miró** with works by another of Spain's most innovative 20th-century artists, the **Museum of Catalan Art**, the **Maritime Museum**, and the **Zoological Museum**.
- Frank Gehry's marvellous **Guggenheim Museum** has turned **Bilbao**, the main city of the Basque region, into a very successful tourist destination. The museum has been hailed as a masterpiece of 20th-century architecture. Bilbao's **Old Town** is quite extensive with a **Gothic Cathedral** and an attractive **Town Hall**.
- Check out the newest tourist attraction in **Valencia**, **Santiago Calatrava's City of Arts and Science Park**. The **Hemispheric**, an amazing glass structure, houses a planetarium, IMAX dome and laserium, and the **Palace of Arts** boasts the largest **oceanarium** in Europe. While in Valencia's, visit the **cathedral**. It claims possession of the Holy Grail. The **Fallas** (Mar 15-19) is a major festival culminating in the burning of papier-mâché effigies satirising famous Spanish figures and a magnificent fireworks display.
- Outside the fiesta season, **Pamplona**'s main attractions are its old **walled quarter**, **Renaissance cathedral** and imposing **citadel**.
- **Seville** is the romantic heart of Spain, the city of Carmen and Don Juan. Lovers of Gothic architecture should come here to see the **cathedral**, the largest Gothic building in the world. Christopher Columbus is buried here. The **bell tower**, known as the **Giralda** from its crowning weather vane, was originally a minaret and observatory. Seville bears numerous traces of the 500 years of Moorish occupation. Of great importance is the **Alcázar**, the palace-fortress of the Arab kings and one of the finest examples of *Mudéjar* (Moorish) architecture.
- Discover the magic of the **Alhambra**, the palace-fortress in **Granada** that was built by the Nasrid rulers in the 13th and 14th centuries. Highlights include: the **Palacios Nazariés**, its halls, courtyards and loggias decorated with painted enamel tiles, delicately fretted arches, stalactite vaulting, marble sculptures and stucco ornament; the **Alcazába**, an 11th-century hilltop fortress; and the **Generalife**, the gardens of the summer palace. The Alhambra is the most popular tourist attraction in Spain.
- To the south of Madrid is the ancient Spanish capital of **Toledo**. The city is dominated by the magnificent **cathedral** and **Alcazar**. Toledo is justly proud of its collection of paintings by El Greco, who lived and painted here. Go and see his most famous painting, The Burial of the *Count of Orgaz*, which is preserved in the **Santo Tomé Church**. There are more El Grecos as well as works by Goya and other artists in the **Hospital y Museo de Santa Cruz**, a magnificent Renaissance building with a Plateresque façade.
- Superbly situated on a plain overlooked by the Sierra de Gredos, **Avila** is a UNESCO World Heritage Site famous for its perfectly preserved 11th-century walls and for being the birthplace of the 16th-century mystic, St Teresa.
- The ancient university town **Salamanca**, 'European City of Culture' in 2002, is well worth a visit on account of its many superb Renaissance buildings, weathered to a golden-brown hue, and the unusual and absorbing **Museo Art Nouveau y Art Deco**, with its fascinating collections of objets d'art from the first half of the 20th century.

Top Things To Do

- Fancy a quick sprint through narrow, closed streets chased by a stampede of big bulls? In **Pamplona**, both locals and an increasing number of tourists indulge in this rather dangerous activity every year. The 'running of the bulls' at the **Festival of San Fermín** takes place in July and attracts huge numbers of tourists. If you fancy seeing a **bull fight** from the safety of your seat, go to **Madrid**, which is home to the imposing bullring of **Las Ventas**, also known as the '**Cathedral of Bullfighting**'.
- Feel the passion of **flamenco**, whose tragic lyrics and tones reflect the sufferings of the gypsy people. Gypsies say it is in the blood, but Spain's famous poet and writer Fredrico Garcia Lorca, called flamenco one of the greatest inventions of the Spanish people. Many flamenco or other regional dancing displays can be seen throughout Spain, particularly in Andalucia, Southern Spain.
- Follow the **Way of St James** to **Santiago de Compostela**, a centre of pilgrimage since the early middle ages and a UNESCO World Heritage Site. The focal point for all visits is the **Gothic Cathedral** completed in 1188. During the Middle Ages, the tomb of St James was regarded as one of the most holy sites in Christendom and thousands of pilgrims travelled through Spain each year to visit the shrine. This route, the Way of St James, was lined with monasteries, religious houses, chapels and hospices to cater for the pilgrims. The route began in Navarre, at Canfranc or Valcarlos; from there, travelling west, the main stopping places were Pamplona, Santo Domingo de la Calzada, Logroño, Burgos, León, Astorga and Santiago de Compostela.
- Explore Spain's natural beauty and abundant wildlife by visiting one of the **National Parks**. Walks, hiking trails and jeep excursions take visitors to marshes and wetlands, coastal dunes, isolated mountain peaks or Atlantic beaches. At certain times of the year, the skies are filled with migrating birds heading for North Africa and the parks are also the habitat of a wealth of indigenous flora and fauna. With a bit of luck it is possible to spot rare and endangered species like the royal eagle, the capercaillie (or European grouse) and the Pyrenean mountain goat. The major national parks in mainland Spain are: **Coto de Doñana** (provinces of **Seville** and **Huelva**), **Tablas de Daimiel** (**La Mancha**), **Ordesa** (**Huesca Pyrenees**), **Aigües Tortes** (**Lleida**) and **Montaña de Covadonga** (**Picos de Europa**).
- There are good opportunities for **rock climbing** in Spain's mountains. Well known, challenging climbs include the **Naranjo de Bulnes** in the **Picos de Europa** and **Monte Perdido** in **Ordesa National Park**.
- **Mountain biking** is becoming increasingly popular, and paths and tracks are plentiful.
- Explore Spain on **horseback**. Spain's long equestrian tradition means that horse riding can easily be arranged. Mountain trails, river valleys and wide plains can be accessed with the help of a horse.
- **Swimming**, **water-skiing**, and **windsurfing** facilities can be found at nearly all seaside resorts. Spain's premier windsurfing resort is **Tarifa**, on the Straits of Gibraltar, where the world championships are held. Inland lakes on the *meseta* in the regions of **Castilla** and **Extremadura** also have good facilities for windsurfing.
- **Whitewater rafting** and **canoeing** enthusiasts should head for the rapids in northern Spain. Centres are well equipped and have skilled staff.
- Spain is great for **sailing**, with over 4000km of coastline and plenty of harbours and sailing clubs.
- **Diving** is also popular; permits can be acquired from the relevant regional authorities.
- Excellent opportunities exist for all types of **fishing**. The rivers and streams of the Pyrenees and the Picos de Europa offer good freshwater game fishing, while trout is abundant throughout the country. The **Asturias** contain the best salmon rivers. Other catches include barbel, perch, pike and tench. Permits must be requested from the regional authorities.
- **Golf** is becoming increasingly popular, with **Costa del Sol** and **La Manga** emerging as two of Spain's premier golfing destinations. At present, Spain has over 200 golf courses, including courses designed by the likes of Robert Trent Jones, Severiano Ballesteros, Jack Niklaus and Jose María Olazabel. The **Valderrama** (near Madrid) is particularly well known.
- Spain offers great opportunities for **skiing** and there are many natural ski-runs and winter resorts, equipped with modern facilities, all blessed with the promise of warm sun and blue skies. There is also a wide range of hotels, inns and refuges from which to choose. There are five main skiing regions in Spain: the **Pyrenean Range**, the **Cantabrian Range**, the **Iberian Chain**, the **Central Chain** and the **Penibetic Chain**. They are all attractive for **mountaineering** in general and for **winter sports** in particular. Check out the upland area of the **Sierra Nevada**, south of Granada and only about 40km (25 miles) from the coast, a nice place for a holiday combining winter sports with coastal sunshine and watersports in the Mediterranean.

TOURIST INFORMATION

Spanish National Tourist Office in the UK
PO Box 4009, London, W1A 6NB, UK
Tel: (020) 7486 8077 *or* (0845) 940 0180 (24-hour brochure request line; calls cost 60p per minute).
Website: www.spain.info
Opening hours: Mon-Fri 0915-1615.

Spanish Tourist Office in the USA
666 Fifth Avenue, Btwn 52nd and 53rd Street, 35th Floor, New York, NY 10103, USA
Tel: (212) 265 8822.
Website: www.okspain.org

Entertainment

FOOD & DRINK: Eating out in Spain is often cheap and meals are substantial rather than gourmet. One of the best ways to sample Spanish food is to try *tapas*, or snacks, which are served at any time of day in local bars. These range from cheese and olives to squid or meat delicacies and are priced accordingly. Restaurants are classified by the Government and many offer tourist menus (*menu del dia*). Restaurants and cafes have table service. Cocktail lounges have table and/or counter service. There are no licensing hours.

National specialities:

- Seafood: cod *vizcaina* or cod *pil-pil* (Basque provinces); *Angulas*, the tasty baby eels (*Aguinaga*); shellfish and *hake à la Gallega* (Galicia); lobster Catalan (Catalonia); fresh anchovies (Andalucía).
- *Paella* based on meat or seafood (Eastern provinces).
- *Butifarra* sausage stewed with beans (Catalonia).
- Roast meats: lamb, beef, veal and suckling pig (Castile).
- *Gazpacho*, a delicious cold vegetable soup (Andalucía).
- *Jabugo* ham (Huelva).

National drinks:

- Sherry (there are four main types: *fino* (very pale and very dry), *amontillado* (dry, richer in body and darker in colour), *oloroso* (medium, full-bodied, fragrant and golden) and *dulce* (sweet)).
- Wine: *Rioja* (Logroñ); *Valdepeñas* (midway between Madrid and Cordóba); *Ampurdán*; *Chacolí* (Basque Country) and *Perelada* (Catalonia); *Cava* (sparkling wine): *Codorniú* and *Freixenet*.
- Spanish brandy: *Lanjarón, Vichy Catalan, Malavella* and *Font Vella*.

Tipping: Service charges and taxes are usually included in hotel bills, however in addition, a tip should be left for the chambermaid and porters should be tipped per bag. It is also customary to leave a tip for the waiter. Restaurants often include service in the bill so a tip is discretionary. In cafes and bars, it is 5 to 10 per cent. Tip taxis 10 to 15 per cent when metered.

NIGHTLIFE: Spaniards often start the evening with *el paseo*, a leisurely stroll through the main streets. A cafe terrace is an excellent vantage point to observe this tradition, or enjoy street theatre in the larger cities. The atmosphere is especially vibrant at fiesta time, or when the local football team has won, when celebrations are marked by a cacophony of car horns, firecrackers and a sea of flags and team regalia. *Tapas* bars offer delicious snacks in a relaxed, enjoyable setting and it is fun to try out several bars in one night. The nightclubs of Ibiza, Barcelona and Madrid have attracted the attention of the international media, but the variety on offer caters for most tastes. Things work up to *la marcha* (good fun) relatively late and it is possible to literally dance until dawn. Flamenco or other regional dancing displays provide an alternative for those who prefer to watch dancing.

SHOPPING: In Spain, the shopper can find items of high quality at a fair price, not only in the cities, but in the small towns as well. In Madrid, the Rastro Market is recommended, particularly on Sundays. Half of the market takes place in the open air and half in more permanent galleries, and it has a character all of its own. Catalonian textiles are internationally famous and there are mills throughout the region. Spanish leather goods are prized throughout the world, offering high-fashion originals at reasonable prices. Of note are the suede coats and jackets. In general, all leather goods, particularly those from Andalucía, combine excellent craftmanship with high-quality design. Fine, handcrafted wooden furniture is one of the outstanding products; Valencia is especially important in this field, and has a yearly international furniture fair. Alicante is an important centre for toy manufacturing. Shoe manufacturing is also of an especially high quality; the production centres are in Alicante and the Balearics. Fine rugs and carpets are made in Cáceres, Granada and Murcia. The numerous excellent sherries, wines and spirits produced in Spain make good souvenirs to take home. A seven per cent VAT is added to rates for all restaurants and hotel rooms. **Shopping hours:** Mon-Sat 0930-1330 and 1630-2000. However, most commercial stores and malls stay open from 1000-2100/2200.

Business

- **GDP:** US$955.1 billion.
- **Main imports:** Machinery and equipment, fuels, chemicals, semi-finished goods, foodstuffs, consumer goods, measuring and medical control instruments.
- **Main exports:** Machinery, motor vehicles, foodstuffs, pharmaceuticals, medicines and other consumer goods.
- **Main trade partners:** Germany, Italy, Japan, Netherlands, Portugal, UK and USA.

A B C D E F G H I J K L M N O P Q R S T U V W X Y Z

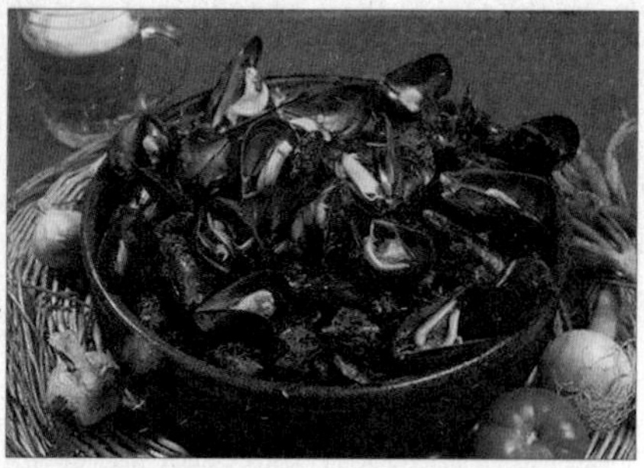

Credit: © Turespaña

ECONOMY: Until 1975, under the Franco regime, the Spanish economy developed almost in isolation, protected from foreign competition by tight import controls and high tariffs, and gradually evolved from an essentially agrarian economy to an industrial one. Spain joined the (then) European Community in 1986. The transition, which was expected to be very difficult, passed off remarkably well and the Spanish economy now ranks eighth in the world by output. Despite the decline of many of its traditional industries, such as shipbuilding, steel and textiles, Spain achieved the highest average growth rate in the Community during the 1980s and a steady performance throughout the 1990s. This was largely due to the growth of its service sector, which now accounts for two-thirds of economic output.

The only significant legacy of structural weaknesses in the Spanish economy which has not been fully tackled is unemployment, which remained stubbornly high at 11 per cent of the workforce in 2004. However, other economic indicators - such as interest rates and budget deficit - are within the limits that allowed Spain to join the European Monetary Union at the start of 1999. In common with most of its EU partners, the Spanish economy has slowed somewhat since 2000. The annual GDP growth at present is 3.5 per cent.

The agricultural sector produces cereals, vegetables, citrus fruit, olive oil and wine. The processed foods industry has also expanded rapidly. The fishing fleet, although reduced from its peak of a few decades ago, remains one of the world's largest. The relative importance of the agriculture, forestry and fisheries sectors has declined over the last decade and now accounts for less than 4 per cent of GDP. Energy requirements are met by indigenous coal and natural gas, imported oil (mostly from north Africa), and a sizeable nuclear power programme. In the manufacturing sector, the decline of older industries has been offset by rapid expansion in chemicals, electronics, information technology and industrial design. Spain has also become an important producer of motor vehicles; this industry alone accounts for 5 per cent of GDP and 80 per cent of all output is exported. In the service sector, Spain has a vast tourism industry mainly servicing visitors from northern Europe: in 2002, this brought an estimated $40 billion (about 7 per cent of GDP) into the economy. Financial services, transport, media and telecommunications have also undergone substantial growth.

BUSINESS ETIQUETTE: Businesspeople are generally expected to dress smartly. Although English is spoken, an interest in Spanish and an effort on the part of the visitor to speak even a few words will be appreciated. Business cards are exchanged frequently as a matter of courtesy and appointments should be made. Punctuality is important.

Office hours: Tend to vary considerably. Businesspeople are advised to check before making calls.

CONFERENCES/CONVENTIONS: Most large towns have dedicated convention centres in addition to the facilities provided by hotels. Seating capacity ranges from 540 in Jaca to 4200 in Palma de Mallorca; Madrid can seat up to 2650 persons.

COMMERCIAL INFORMATION

Consejo Superior de Cámaras de Comercio
Industria y Navegación de España, C/Ribera del Loira 12, 28042 Madrid, Spain
Tel: (90) 210 0096.
Website: www.camaras.org

Instituo Español de Comercio Exterior (ICEX) in the UK
2nd Floor, 66 Chiltern Street, London W1U 4LS, UK
Tel: (020) 7467 2330.
Website: www.mcx.es/londres

Spain Convention Bureau (FEMP)
Calle Nuncio 8, 28005 Madrid, Spain
Tel: (91) 364 3700.
Website: www.femp.es

Oficina de Congresos de Madrid (Information on Conferences/Conventions)
Calle Mayor 69, 28013 Madrid, Spain
Tel: (91) 588 2900.
Website: www.munimadrid.es/congresos

Balearic Islands

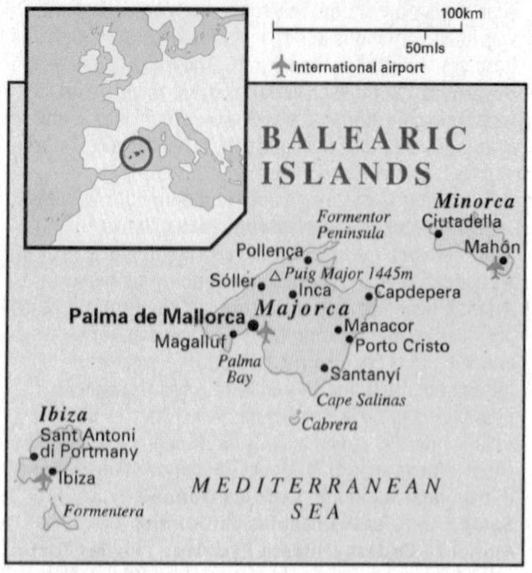
100km
50mls
International airport
BALEARIC ISLANDS
Minorca
Ciutadella
Mahón
Formentor Peninsula
Pollença
Sóller
Puig Major 1445m
Inca
Capdepera
Palma de Mallorca
Majorca
Manacor
Magalluf
Porto Cristo
Palma Bay
Santanyí
Cape Salinas
Cabrera
Ibiza
Sant Antoni di Portmany
Ibiza
Formentera
MEDITERRANEAN SEA

Location: Mediterranean, 240km (150 miles) due east of Valencia on the Spanish coast.

Time: GMT + 1 (GMT + 2 from last Sunday in March to Saturday before last Sunday in October).

Overview

The Balearics is the name given to the archipelago of four main islands off the Mediterranean coast of Spain (193km/120 miles south of Barcelona). Mallorca, Menorca and Ibiza are all popular tourist destinations, offering remarkably varied scenery as well as beach resorts that provide every kind of amenity. A narrow channel separates Ibiza from Formentera, the smallest inhabited island in the group.The largest town in the Balearics is Palma (Mallorca). Regular ferry services link Mallorca, Menorca, Ibiza and Formentera.

General Information

AREA: Mallorca: 3640 sq km (1405 sq miles). **Menorca:** 700 sq km (270 sq miles). **Ibiza:** 572 sq km (220 sq miles). **Formentera:** 100 sq km (38 sq miles). **Total:** 5014 sq km (1935 sq miles).

POPULATION: 878,627 (2006).

POPULATION DENSITY: 175.2 per sq km

CAPITAL: Palma de Mallorca. **Population:** 302,000 (2005).

GEOGRAPHY: Mallorca, Menorca and Ibiza are the main islands in this group, which is situated 193km (120 miles) south of Barcelona off the east coast of Spain. The landscape of these islands is characterised by woodlands, almond trees, fertile plains and magnificent coastlines with numerous sandy coves separated by craggy cliffs. The largest island, **Mallorca** (also known as the 'Isle of Dreams'), has a varied landscape: mountains and valleys, rocky coves and sandy beaches. The main geographical feature is the Sierra del Norte, a mountain range running along the northern coast. The island is covered with pines, and with olive and almond trees, which blanket the countryside with blossoms in springtime. **Menorca** has evidence of ancient history and a strong feeling of connection with Britain, owing to Admiral Nelson's stay on the island. Both the capital Mahón and the old town of Ciutadella at the north end of the island are set at the ends of deep inlets forming natural harbours. There are many bays and lovely beaches on the island. **Ibiza**, the third-largest island, has a rugged coastline with many fruit orchards and woods. The main town of the same name is situated above a busy harbour. A narrow channel separates Ibiza from **Formentera**, the smallest inhabited island in the group.

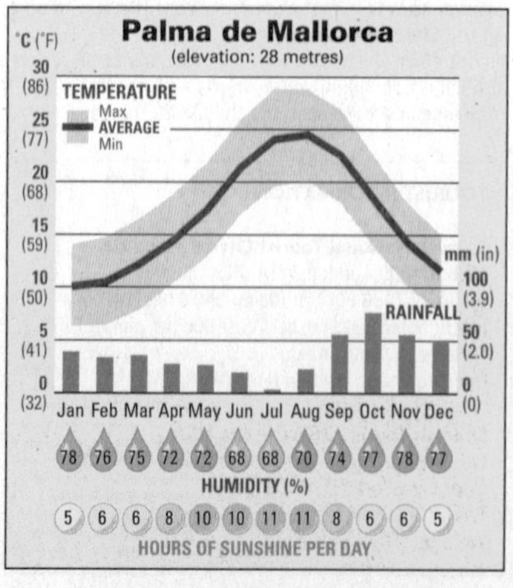
Palma de Mallorca
(elevation: 28 metres)
°C (°F)
30 (86)
25 (77)
20 (68)
15 (59)
10 (50)
5 (41)
0 (32)
TEMPERATURE
Max
AVERAGE
Min
mm (in)
100 (3.9)
RAINFALL
50 (2.0)
0 (0)
Jan Feb Mar Apr May Jun Jul Aug Sep Oct Nov Dec
78 76 75 72 72 68 68 70 74 77 78 77
HUMIDITY (%)
5 6 6 8 10 10 11 11 8 6 6 5
HOURS OF SUNSHINE PER DAY

Climate

The islands enjoy a temperate, Mediterranean climate. The maximum temperatures are not excessive, even in high summer, owing to the cooling influence of the sea. The climate during the winter is mild and dry, and temperatures below zero are practically unknown.

Communications

MEDIA: Press: *Diari de Balears* is a newspaper published in Catalan (website: www.diaridebalears.com) based in Palma de Mallorca. *Diario de Mallorca* is the main Spanish-language daily newspaper (website: www.diariodemallorca.es). The *Majorca Daily Bulletin* is Spain's oldest English-language daily newspaper, established in 1962. (website: www.majorcadailybulletin.es).

Radio: There are OM and FM radio stations on Mallorca, Menorca and Eivissa. (www.cope.es)

TV: *Televisió de les Illes Balears* (website: www.eprtvib.es).

Travel - International

AIR:

There are regular international flights to Mallorca, Menorca and Ibiza. Local flights run by IBERIA (IB) (website: www.iberia.com) link all the islands. Air Europa (website: www.air-europa.com) and Spanair (website: www.spanair.com) also fly between the islands and mainland Spain.

Approximate flight times: From *Palma de Mallorca* to London is two hours 15 minutes; from *Menorca* is two hours 20 minutes and from *Ibiza* is two hours 20 minutes.

Main airports: *Palma de Mallorca (PMI)* (Son San Juan) is 11km (7 miles) southeast of the city. *To/from the airport*: Buses to the city leave every 30 to 60 minutes (0705-0005; travel time - 30 minutes). Return is from Plaza España. Taxis to the city are also available. *Facilities*: Duty-free shop, first aid facilities, bank/bureau de change, bars, car hire, tourist information and post office.

Mahón (MAH) is 6km (4 miles) from Mahón. *To/from the airport*: Coaches or taxis are available to the town.

Ibiza (IBZ) is 8km (5 miles) from the town of Ibiza. *To/from the airport*: Buses to the city leave hourly (0700-2330). Taxis are available to the city.

SEA:

Main ports: *Palma* (Mallorca), *Mao* and *Ciutadella de Menorca* (Menorca) and *La Savina* (Formentera).

The following shipping lines run services to the Balearic Islands: *Balearia Eurolines Maritimes* (website: www.balearia.net); *Buquebus España SA*; *CNAN – Compagnie Nationale Algérienne de Navigation* (car ferry) from Algiers; and *Compañia Trasmediterránea* (car ferry) (website: www.trasmediterranea.es) from Alicante, Barcelona, Valencia and inter-island to Palma, Balearia.

Local: There is also a ferry service from Sète (France) to Palma. There are regular ferries from Ibiza to Formentera (travel time - 45 minutes).

RAIL:

On Mallorca, narrow-gauge trains run from Palma to Soller five times daily, and to Inca every hour. There is also a connection between Inca and Sa Poblem. Inter-Rail passes are not valid. There are no railways on any of the other islands.

ROAD:

There are generally good bus services on the islands connecting resorts with main towns. Car and scooter hire is generally available. The steep, narrow inland roads make it difficult for coaches and cars to pass each other (although there are special passing points). On Mallorca, three toll-free highways lead from Palma to Manova, Cala Blava and Inca. For travel by coach, it is best to check timetables before commencing your journey to avoid difficulties; hotels can often provide this information.

Accommodation

Note: The Balearic Government levies an 'eco tax' on people holidaying in the islands. This compulsory fee (equivalent to approximately €1 a day) is to be collected by accommodation providers and is, as yet, not generally included in travel agents'/brochure prices.

HOTELS:

Establishments of all categories exist in the Balearics, including hotels catering for around 230,000 visitors, chalets, apartments and bungalows. It is possible to rent furnished or unfurnished chalets for the season, although visitors must book in advance, owing to demand. Rates vary according to season and the standard of accommodation. Numerous packages are available.

CAMPING:
There are nine campsites in the Balearic Islands. For further information, contact the Spanish Tourist Office (see *Top Things To Do* in the main *Spain* section).

YOUTH HOSTELS:
The Spanish Youth Hostel Network (REAJ) runs a youth hostel in Palma. There is also a youth hostel in Alcúdia.

ACCOMMODATION INFORMATION

Spanish Youth Hostel Network (REAJ) in Palma
Costa Brava 13, 07610 Palma de Mallorca, Balearic Islands
Tel: (971) 260 892.
E-mail: reserves@tjove.caib.es

Spanish Youth Hostel Network (REAJ) in Alcudia
Ctra. Cap Pinar Km 407400, Alcudia 07400, Balearic Islands
Tel: (971) 545 395 *or* 542 *or* (902) 111 188 (information and booking).
E-mail: reserves@tjove.caib.e

Top Things To See & Do

- Go **yachting**. The Balearic Islands are an arrival point for many Mediterranean yacht cruises. Mooring fees in any of the yacht clubs (**Palma de Mallorca**, **Mahón**, **Ciudadela**, **Andraitx** and **Ibiza**) are reasonable.
- **Tennis** courts and **golf** courses are available through the big hotels around all the islands.
- **Bowling** enthusiasts will find American bowling alleys on all the islands.
- There are excellent facilities for **horseriding** in several places on the Balearic Islands.

Mallorca
- **Palma**, the capital of **Mallorca**, is a welcoming city with a history as a major Mediterranean port. The old city is beautifully situated on the **Bay of Palma** with modern developments to the east and west. Palma is overlooked by the 14th-century **Castle of Belver**, and other notable buildings include the golden sandstone **cathedral** (**La Seo**), the **Archbishop's Palace**, the **Monastery** and **Church of San Francisco** and the **Montesion Church**.
- **Mallorca**'s best scenery lies in the north of the island. One way to enjoy the mountains of the **Serra de Tramuntana** and the photogenic villages clinging to the lower slopes is to take the **antique tourist train** from **Palma** to **Sóller**. A tram takes visitors the short distance to the port and coastal resort of the same name.
- Make the trip to the beautifully sited **Monastery of Valldemossa**, where the composer Frederic Chopin spent the winter of 1838-9, trying, without success, to regain his health. He was accompanied by his mistress, George Sand, who later published a famous account of the disastrous visit.

Menorca
- **Mahón**, the capital of **Menorca**, has many buildings dating from the period of British occupation (1713-83) and is best explored on foot. The attractions include the **Town Hall** (**Casa Consistorial**), the **Church of Santa Maria** and the **Church of San Francisco**.
- A good highway links Mahón with the older town of **Ciudadela** (the former capital) on the opposite side of the island. It has a cathedral, partly dating from the 14th century, as well as several elegant palacios and medieval churches.
- Menorca also boasts prehistoric stone formations from the Talayot civilisation of the 2nd millennium BC. The most important site is **Talatí de Dalt**.

Ibiza
- **Ibiza Town** has a medieval **fortress**, and the **Dalt Vila** (**Upper Town**) with its narrow, cobbled streets, drawbridge and pretty main square is well worth exploring. Southwest of the town centre is the **Punic** **cemetery**, **Puig des Molins**.
- Go **clubbing**. Thanks largely to its frenetic nightlife, Ibiza has for the last decade or so been more popular than ever. The clubs specialising in house music are concentrated in **Ibiza Town** and **San Antonio**.
- Try **underwater fishing**. This is a popular activity, and there is plenty of sea bass, sole, dentex, dorado and sea bream to catch.
- **Sailing** is also available. There are facilities for different forms of sailing in the many sheltered bays.
- Facilities for other watersports, including **water-skiing**, **windsurfing**, **parasailing** and **diving**, are also available.

TOURIST INFORMATION

Oficina de Turismo de Mallorca
Plaza de la Reina 2, 07012 Palma, Mallorca, Spain
Tel: (971) 712 216.
Website: www.illesbalears.es

Oficina de Turismo de Mahón
Calle Molledelevant 2, 07701 Mahón, Menorca, Spain
Tel: (971) 352 674.
Website: www.e-menorca.org

Oficina de Turismo de Ibiza
OIT Antonio Riquer 2, Ibiza 07800, Eivissa, Spain
Tel: (971) 301 900.
Website: www.illesbalears.es

Entertainment

FOOD & DRINK:
Regional specialities:
- Mallorcan *ensaimada* (light, sweet pastry roll).
- *Escaldums* of chicken.
- Mallorcan soups.
- *St John's bread* (carob beans).
- Mayonnaise originates from Mahon.

Regional drinks:
- Aromatic liqueurs, such as *palo*, which is made from locally grown and *frigola*.
- Imported alcoholic and soft drinks are also widely available.

Tipping: 10 to 15 per cent in bars, restaurants and hotels.
NIGHTLIFE: Traditional fiestas provide a unique range of celebrations to help get to know the real culture. There are numerous nightclubs and discos (especially in Ibiza), some with open-air dancefloors overlooking the sea, floorshows, live bands and orchestras. There are also many cinemas, theatres, concerts and art exhibitions. Approximately 18km (11 miles) west of Palma, in Magaluf, there is an elegant casino with a large restaurant. For the latest news on the local nightlife, and details of current events, artistic and cultural, consult the local English-language newspaper, *The Bulletin*.
SHOPPING: On the Balearic Islands, there is a strong tradition of craftsmanship. Purchases include furniture, hand embroidered works, handpainted ceramics, carved olive-wood panels, wrought ironwork, glassware, items made from raffia and palm leaves, handmade shoes, the famous pearls made in Mallorca and other costume jewellery from Menorca. **Shopping hours:** Mon-Sat 0900-1300 and 1700-2000. Supermarkets and department stores are open 1000-2200.

Credit: ©Turespaña

Canary Islands

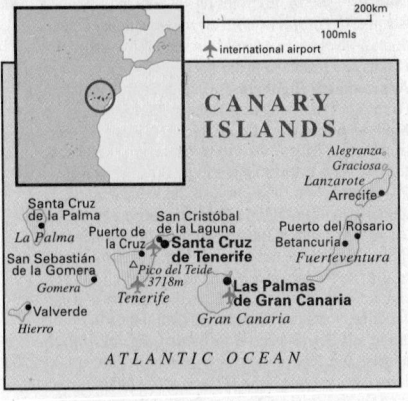

Location: North Atlantic, west of the African coast.

Time: GMT (GMT + 1 from last Sunday in March to Saturday before last Sunday in October).

Overview

The Canary Islands (*Islas Canarias*) are much closer to the coast of Africa than to mainland Spain and it is the mid-Atlantic location that accounts for the remarkably mild climate. While best known for their white, pristine beaches, the seven islands (Gran Canaria, Fuerteventura, Lanzarote, Tenerife, La Palma, Gomera and Hierro), all of volcanic origin, offer strikingly diverse landscapes: sub-tropical rainforests, arid plains, pine woods, sand dunes, mountain peaks and remarkable flora. The main tourist resorts are excellent for watersports, windsurfing, sailing, fishing, tennis, golf and so on. The local people take great pride in their folklore traditions and the carnival festivities are famous throughout Spain.

General Information

AREA: 7242 sq km (2796 sq miles).
POPULATION: 1.9 million (2004).
POPULATION DENSITY: 257 per sq km.
CAPITAL: Provincial capitals are Las Palmas de Gran Canaria: **Population:** 377,660 (2003); and Santa Cruz de Tenerife: **Population:** 220,033 (2003).
GEOGRAPHY: The Canary Islands are situated off the northwest coast of Africa and consist of seven islands which are divided into two provinces. **Las Palmas** comprises the islands of Gran Canaria, Fuerteventura and Lanzarote. **Santa Cruz de Tenerife** is made up of Tenerife, La Palma, Gomera and Hierro. All the islands are of volcanic origin and the climate is subtropical. The landscape is varied, and includes mountain ranges, valleys, deserts, cliffs, craters and forests.

Climate

The climate in the northern islands of the Canaries is subtropical; the south of the islands tends to be hotter and drier, although rainfall is generally low throughout the islands.

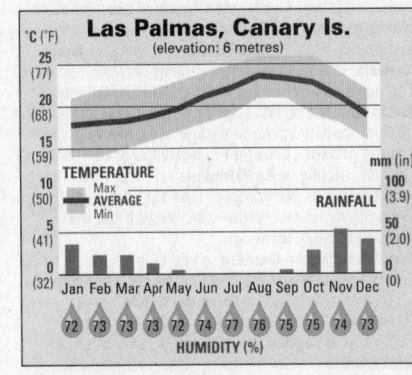

Communications

MEDIA: Press: *Tenerife News* is a fortnightly independent English-language newspaper with local and national news (www.tenerifenews.com).
Radio: *Power FM* broadcasts English-language news to all the islands. It is part of the Canaries' biggest radio network.
TV: *Televisión Canaria* (website: www.tvcanaria.tv).

Travel - International

AIR:

There are regular international flights to Tenerife, Lanzarote and Gran Canaria. Local flights run by *IBERIA (IB)* (website: www.iberia.com) link all the islands. *Air Europa* (website: www.air-europa.com) and *Spanair* (website: www.spanair.com) also fly between the islands and mainland Spain.

Approximate flight times: Flights from London to *Las Palmas* or *Tenerife* take four hours 15 minutes.

Main airports: *Gran Canaria (LPA)* is 22km (14 miles) south of Las Palmas. *To/from the airport:* Hotel coaches to the city leave every 30 minutes (0630-0200; travel time – 20 minutes). Return journey is from Iberia terminal (Hotel Iberia), Avenida Maritima. Public bus service to the city leaves every 30 minutes, operating a 24-hour service. Return is from the bus station, Parque de San Telmo. Taxis to the city are available. *Facilities:* Banks/bureaux de change, post office, chemists, medical service and car hire. *Tenerife-Norte Los Rodeos (TFN)*, in the north of the island, is 13km (8 miles) from Santa Cruz. *To/from the airport:* Bus service runs every 30 minutes from 0600-2300. *Tenerife-Sur Reina Sofia (TFS)*, in the south of the island, is used for resorts such as Playa de las Americas. *To/from airport:* A bus service is scheduled according to flight arrivals. Taxis are available.
La Gomera, 38km northwest of Valle Gran Rey and 34km from San Sebastian, offers regular connections with Gran Canaria and North Tenerife. *To/from the airport:* There are regular bus services to all towns on the island. For further information, contact La Gomera Airport (tel: (902) 404 714; website: www.aena.es).

SEA:

Main ports: *Las Palmas* and *Tenerife*.
The majority of cruise ships stop in the Canaries. Further details are available from the Spanish National Tourist Office. *Trasmediterránea* operates a weekly (Saturday) car ferry departing at 1800 from Cadiz-Tenerife-Las Palmas (tel: (902) 454 645; website: www.trasmediterranea.es).
All the islands are linked by regular car and passenger ferries. Day trips to the smaller islands are quickly and easily arranged.

ROAD:

There are bus services available. Cars may be hired.

Accommodation

HOTELS:

There is a large selection of hotels of all categories. There are also four *paradores* (tourist inns) as well as *pensiones* (guest houses), which are run by the family on the premises and provide bed and board.

CAMPING:

There are four campsites; three are in Las Palmas and one in Santa Cruz.

YOUTH HOSTELS:

There are two youth hostels in Gran Canaria, Falow Hostel and Hostel Alcaravaneras.

Top Things To See & Do

- Explore the cosmopolitan city of **Santa Cruz**, capital of **Tenerife**, the largest of the Canary Islands and enjoy its rich architecture, notably the **Church of San Francisco**, and its excellent art and history museums.
- Visit the lively city of **Las Palmas**, the capital of **Gran Canaria**, with its magnificent location between two bays. The sights include the Old Town, the Gothic Cathedral of **Santa Ana** and several museums. The city has a rich cultural life with opera, dance and music festivals.
- The city of **Santa Cruz** (not to be confused with Santa Cruz de Tenerife) on **La Palma** island (not to be confused with Las Palmas, the capital of Gran Canaria) is worth exploring for its 16th-century architecture and the **Natural History Museum**.
- **San Sebastián**, on **Gomera**, is interesting for its connections with the explorer Christopher Columbus, who is commemorated by the **Torre del Conde**, an old fortress and now a national monument.
- Take a trip to **Teguise**, the picturesque, old capital of **Lanzarote**, an intriguing town with aristocratic palaces, historic convents and churches and a castle built on a volcanic cone.
- On **Fuerteventura**, there is an interesting church in the town of **Betancuria**, the **Church of Santa María**, which is noted for its painted ceiling and murals.
- The Canary Islands offer plenty of opportunities for **walking** and exploration of the islands' various landscapes. There is a great number of large, volcanic territories. The **National Park of Timanfaya**, for instance, is a spectacular lava flow, awe-inspiring in its barren majesty and covering nearly one-third of Lanzarote. La Palma boasts one of the largest craters in the world, the **Caldera de Taburiente**, which is best viewed from the **La Cumbrecita** look-out point. Also on Tenerife, there is a gigantic crater. Most of these areas are accessible for walkers and offer wonderful views and many impressive sights.
- Visitors who are less keen to walk, can hire a camel instead. **Camel rides** to the volcanic region are a popular attraction on Lanzarote. **Malpaís de la Corona** has an immense volcanic cave called **Los Verdes**, 6km (3.5 miles) long; nearby is the **Jameo del Agua lagoon**.
- Take the cable car up to **La Rambleta**, the cable car terminal on **Mt Teide**. The mountain is Spain's highest, with its summit at 3718m (12,198ft). The cable car climbs up to 3550m (11,646ft). It is possible to walk to the summit, although this requires a written permit from the National Park office.
- The warm, clear sea is excellent for **underwater fishing**, **diving**, **snorkelling** and **swimming**. Facilities for **water-skiing** and **windsurfing** are available from beaches or from hotels.
- There are plenty of beaches that are perfect for sunbathing, like **Playa del Inglés** and **Maspalomas**, nearly 6km (4 miles) long.
- There are numerous **tennis** courts (often owned by the hotel or attached to apartments), **golf** courses and **riding** stables.

TOURIST INFORMATION

Tourist Board of the Government of the Canary Islands
Calle Joséde Zarate y Penchet, Centro Residencial Anaga, Office 206, 38001, Santa Cruz de Tenerife, Spain
Tel: (922) 240 038.
Website: www.canarias-turismo.com

Patronato de Turismo
Leon y Castillo 17, 35003 Las Palmas de Gran Canaria, Spain
Tel: (928) 219 600.
Website: www.grancanaria.com

Tourist Board of the Government of the Canary Islands
Calle Victor Hugo, 60 Bajo 35006, Las Palmas de Gran Canaria, Spain
Tel: (928) 293 698.
Website: www.canarias-turismo.com

Entertainment

FOOD & DRINK: In the main resorts, restaurants offer the full range of international cuisine, as well as local delicacies. Often restaurants cater for the tastes of particular nationalities. A full range of wines, spirits and liqueurs from throughout the world is available. Spanish wines and spirits are particularly good value. Local beers are pilsner-type lagers and, on the whole, rather weak.

Regional specialities:
- Watercress soup.
- *Sancocho canario*, a fish salad with a hot sauce.
- Local pastries: *tirijalas, bienmesabes, frangollo, bizcochos lustrados, quesadillas, rapaduras y marquesotes*
- Bananas, tomatoes, avocados and papayas are grown locally.

Regional drinks:
- Rum.
- Honey-rum.
- Malmsey wine.

SHOPPING: Besides the excellent duty-free shopping, there are numerous local items to tempt the visitor. Craftsmanship is represented mainly by skilled open-work and embroidery. Pottery, basket-work based on palm leaves, cane and reed and delicate woodcarvings are also popular. Tobacco produced here is excellent and world famous. Cigars from the Canary Islands are outstanding in quality.
Shopping hours: Mon-Sat 0900-1300 and 1600-2000. Large shopping centres are open all day.

Sri Lanka

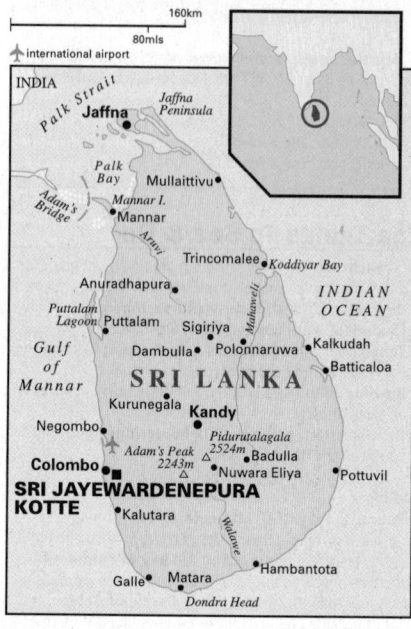

Location: South Asia.

Time: GMT + 6.

Overview

Depending on your viewpoint, Sri Lanka's shape resembles either a pearl or a teardrop, cast adrift in the Indian Ocean.

Those who consider this country a teardrop may do so because of its long history of troubles. The first Europeans to arrive in Sri Lanka were the Portuguese, quickly supplanted by the Dutch in the 17th century. The British acquired Sri Lanka (as Ceylon) from the Dutch in 1796, assuming full control in 1802. But once the country became a Republic in 1972, adopting a new constitution along with the Sinhala name, Sri Lanka, serious conflict arose from the Tamil minority's (occupying the north and east parts of Sri Lanka) demands for a separate Tamil state, with terrorist activity by the Liberation Tigers of Tamil Eelam prevalent since the 1970s. The Tamil are Hindu by religion and ethnically linked to the Tamils of southern India, in contrast to the majority (70 per cent) of Sri Lanka's population who are Buddhists of Sinhalese descent. The Indian Government became involved in this conflict, initially as official mediator but then, after the failure of an armistice in 1987, intervening militarily (on the Government's side). Its two-year military campaign ended with the death of over 1000 Indian soldiers and an ignominious retreat. The assassination of Indian premier Rajiv Ghandi in 1991 was the apotheosis of the Tigers' campaign of revenge. After that, the war entered a period of effective stalemate. Outside the Tiger-controlled areas in the north and east, the political environment was dominated by the struggle between the country's two main political groupings – the centre-right United National Party and the People's Alliance (a coalition of social-democratic and socialist parties). In 1995, the UNP's 17-year stranglehold on power was finally broken by the People's Alliance, under Chandrikha Kumaratunga. Kumaratunga was determined to resolve the Tamil conflict and a deal between the Government and the Tamil Tigers was finally concluded in early 2002. Despite scepticism, the ceasefire has more or less held, despite a serious feud between President Karamatunga and Prime Minister Wickremesinghe, which led in 2003 to suspension of Parliament and the dismissal of three ministers, seemingly catalysing a sudden resurgence in Tamil Tiger activity. As with any conflict of that length and hostility, many issues

Sri Lanka

remained to be resolved, not least the future Government of the Tamil-dominated northern and eastern parts of the island and the control of aid for reconstruction and rehabilitation. Being badly hit by the tsunami on December 26 2004, especially in Tamil-controlled areas, also escalated ethnic grievances.
Yet there is also much to champion Sri Lanka as a pearl: the Indians, Portuguese, Dutch and British have all left their marks in ancient architecture, and palm-fringed beaches are never far away from mountainous greenery in this jewel of an island. Indeed, Marco Polo proclaimed Sri Lanka as one of the best islands in the world.

General Information

AREA: 65,525 sq km (25,299 sq miles).
POPULATION: 19.4 million (UN, 2005).
POPULATION DENSITY: 296 per sq km.
CAPITAL: Sri Jayewardenepura Kotte (official).
Population: 115,826 (2001). Colombo (commercial).
Population: 2.2 million (2005). Sri Jayawardenepura Kotte is only 10km (6 miles) from Colombo.
GEOGRAPHY: Sri Lanka is an island off the southeast coast of the Indian state of Tamil Nadu. It is separated from India by the Indian Ocean, in which lies the chain of islands called Adam's Bridge. Sri Lanka has an irregular surface with low-lying coastal plains running inland from the northern and eastern shores. The central and southern areas slope into hills and mountains. The highest peak is Pidurutalagala (2524m/8281ft).
GOVERNMENT: Democratic Socialist Republic since 1978. Gained independence from the UK in 1948. **Head of State:** President Mahinda Rajapakse since November 2005. **Head of Government:** Prime Minister Ratnasiri Wickremanayake. **Recent history:** A deal between Sri Lanka's Government and the Tamil Tigers was finally concluded in early 2002. Despite scepticism from many quarters and a number of serious incidents, the ceasefire held. The island's sizeable Muslim population, who were persecuted by both sides throughout the two-decade-long conflict, was also brought into the settlement. However, as with any conflict of that length and hostility, many issues remained to be resolved, not least the future Government of the Tamil-dominated northern and eastern parts of the island and the control of aid (around $600 million has been pledged from various sources) for reconstruction and rehabilitation. All this was not helped by a serious feud between President Karamatunga and Prime Minister Wickremesinghe, which led in November 2003 to suspension of Parliament and the dismissal of three Ministers by President Karamatunga. This political turbulence seemed to catalyse a sudden resurgence in Tamil Tiger activity in early 2004, with the Renegade Tiger commander, Karuna, orchestrating a split in the rebel movement, going underground with his supporters. Unfortunately, this culminated in a suicide bomb blast in July 2004 in Colombo, shattering the infrastructure of the peace process negotiated in 2001. This followed the replacement of Wickremesinghe at the Assembly elections, with Mahinda Rajapakse becoming Prime Minister. Presidential elections in November 2005 were closely fought but Rajapakse won narrowly in an election which saw an almost total boycott in the Tamil areas. It remains to be seen how this Government, and Sri Lanka's highly polarised Parliament, continue to confront the difficult Tamil issue.
Executive power and legislative power are vested in the President and a single-chamber Assembly, respectively. The President is directly elected for a six-year term. The 255-member Assembly is elected by proportional representation.
LANGUAGE: Sinhala, Tamil and English.
RELIGION: Buddhist majority (70 per cent), with Hindu, Christian and Muslim minorities.
ELECTRICITY: 230 volts AC, 50Hz. Round three-pin plugs are usual, with bayonet lamp fittings.
SOCIAL CONVENTIONS: Shaking hands is the normal form of greeting. It is customary to be offered tea when visiting and it is considered impolite to refuse. Punctuality is appreciated. A small token of appreciation, such as a souvenir from home or company, is always welcomed. Informal, Western dress is suitable, except when visiting Buddhist temples, where modest clothing should be worn (eg no bare legs and uncovered heads). Visitors should be decently clothed when visiting any place of worship, and shoes and hats must be removed. Jackets and ties are not required by men in the evenings except for formal functions when lightweight suits should be worn.

Climate

Tropical climate. Upland areas are cooler and more temperate, and coastal areas are cooled by sea breezes. There are two monsoons, which occur May to July and December to January.
Required clothing: Lightweights and rainwear.

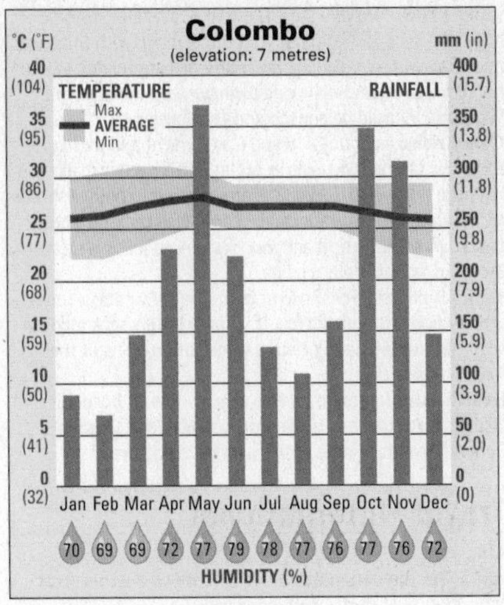
Colombo
(elevation: 7 metres)
°C (°F)
mm (in)
TEMPERATURE
RAINFALL
Max
AVERAGE
Min
40 (104)
35 (95)
30 (86)
25 (77)
20 (68)
15 (59)
10 (50)
5 (41)
0 (32)
400 (15.7)
350 (13.8)
300 (11.8)
250 (9.8)
200 (7.9)
150 (5.9)
100 (3.9)
50 (2.0)
0 (0)
Jan Feb Mar Apr May Jun Jul Aug Sep Oct Nov Dec
70 69 69 72 77 79 78 77 76 77 76 72
HUMIDITY (%)

Communications

Telephone: IDD facilities are available to the principal cities. Country code: 94. Phone cards are available at post offices and shops.
Mobile telephone: Roaming agreements exist with some international mobile phone companies. Coverage is average.
Internet: Internet is available in main towns and resorts; Internet cafes provide public access to Internet and e-mail services.
Post: Overseas mail usually takes 10 to 14 days. Post office hours: Mon-fri, 0830-1700, and Sat, 0830-1300. The main post office in Colombo is opposite the President's house: General Post Office, Janadhipathi Mawatha, Colombo 1, open 24-hours per day.
MEDIA: Press: The most popular daily newspapers published in English include the *Daily Mirror* (website: www.dailymirror.lk), *Daily News* (website: www.dailynews.lk), *Evening Observer*, *The Island* (website: www.island.lk) and *Lankadeepa* (website: www.lankadeepa.lk).
TV: *Sri Lanka Rupavahini Corporation (SLRC)* is a state-owned network that operates two channels, *Rupavahini* and *Channel Eye*. Private English-language stations include *MTV* and *TNL*.
Radio: *Sri Lanka Broadcasting Corporation (SLBC)* is a state-owned network that operates services in Sinhala, Tamil and English. Privately owned English radio stations include *TNL Radio*, *Sun FM* and *Yes FM*.

Passport/Visa

	Passport Required?	Visa Required?	Return Ticket Required?
Full British	Yes	No	Yes
Australian	Yes	No	Yes
Canadian	Yes	No	Yes
USA	Yes	No	Yes
Other EU	Yes	No/1	Yes
Japanese	Yes	No	Yes

Note: *Regulations and requirements may be subject to change at short notice, and you are advised to contact the appropriate diplomatic or consular authority before finalising travel arrangements. Any numbers in the chart refer to the footnotes below.*

PASSPORTS: Passport valid for at least six months from date of entry required by all.
VISAS: Required by all except nationals of the following countries, who will be issued with visas free of charge for a period of 30 days on arrival at Colombo Airport (for touristic visits only):
(a) nationals of those countries mentioned in the chart above (except **1.** nationals of Malta and the Slovak Republic who *do* require a visa);
(b) nationals of Albania, Bahrain, Bangladesh, Bhutan, Bosnia & Herzegovina, Brunei, Bulgaria, China (PR, including Hong Kong), Croatia, India, Indonesia, Iran, Israel, Korea (Rep), Kuwait, Macedonia, Malaysia, Maldives, Nepal, New Zealand, Norway, Oman, Pakistan, The Philippines, Qatar, Romania, Saudi Arabia, Serbia & Montenegro, Seychelles, Singapore, South Africa, Switzerland, Taiwan, Thailand, Turkey, United Arab Emirates and Vietnam;
(c) nationals of CIS countries.
Note: All business visitors require a visa.
Types of visa and cost: *Tourist* and *Business*: £38 (up to three months); fee given is for UK nationals. Fees vary according to nationality; contact the Consulate (or Consular section at Embassy or High Commission); see *Passport/Visa Information*. Multiple-entry visas cost £114 (three months) or £189 (12 months).
Validity: As above. Visitors can request to extend their stay by applying to the Department of Immigration & Emigration, 23 Station Road, Colombo 3 (tel: (1) 259 7513). This is issued at the discretion of the authorities who must be satisfied that the applicant has at least US$30 per day for the stay and holds an onward or return ticket for travel.
Application to: Consulate (or Consular section at Embassy or High Commission); see *Passport/Visa Information*. British nationals, travelling as tourists, may obtain a visa upon arrival, upon port of entry into Sri Lanka, for up to 30 days.
Application requirements: (a) Valid passport valid for six months from date of entry. (b) Completed application form. (c) Two passport-size photos signed on the back by applicant. (d) Visa fee, payable by cash (not if sending by post) or postal order/bank draft in favour of "Sri Lanka High Commission, London." (e) Self-addressed envelope, with appropriate cost of stamps necessary for returning passport by registered post. (f) Proof of sufficient funds (minimum US$30 per day) for duration of stay. (g) Return or onward ticket. *Business:* (a)-(g) and, (h) A letter from the company or organisation recommending the issue of visa and giving details of the status of the applicant, nature of business, duration of stay, sufficient funds and details of the party, if available in Sri Lanka, with whom the business is to be conducted, along with a letter from that company/organisation in Sri Lanka.
Working days required: At least three.
Temporary residence: Enquire at Embassy or High Commission.

PASSPORT/VISA INFORMATION

High Commission of Sri Lanka in the UK
13 Hyde Park Gardens, London W2 2LU, UK
Tel: (020) 7262 1841-7.
Website: www.slhclondon.org
Opening hours: Mon-Fri 0930-1700; 0930-1300 (visa section).

Embassy of Sri Lanka in the USA
2148 Wyoming Avenue, NW,
Washington, DC 20008, USA
Tel: (202) 483 4025-8.
Website: www.slembassyusa.org

Money

Currency: Sri Lanka Rupee (LKR) = 100 cents. Notes are in denominations of LKR1000, 500, 200, 100, 50, 20 and 10. Coins are in denominations of LKR10, 5, 2 and 1, and 50, 25, 10, 5, 2 and 1 cents. There are also large numbers of commemorative coins in circulation.
Currency exchange: Foreign currency must be changed only at authorised exchanges, banks and hotels, and these establishments must endorse such exchanges on the visitor's Exchange Control D form, which is issued on arrival and must usually be returned at the time of departure.
Credit & debit cards: American Express, MasterCard and Visa are widely accepted. Diners Club has more limited acceptance. Check with your credit or debit card company for details of merchant acceptability and other services which may be available.
Traveller's cheques: The rate of exchange for traveller's cheques is better than the rate of exchange for cash. To avoid additional exchange rate charges, travellers are advised to take traveller's cheques in US Dollars or Pounds Sterling.
Currency restrictions: The import and export of local currency is limited to LKR1000. The import of notes from India and Pakistan is not allowed. Otherwise, the import of foreign currency is not restricted but all amounts over US$5000 are subject to declaration. Export of foreign currency is limited to the amount declared on import.
Banking hours: Mon-Sat 0900-1300. Some city banks close at 1500, whilst some even have night bank facilities.
Exchange rate indicators:
Rate at time of publishing
£1.00= LKR177.53
$1.00= LKR102.03

Duty Free

The following items may be imported into Sri Lanka by persons over 18 years of age without incurring customs duty:
200 cigarettes or 50 cigars or 340g of tobacco; 2 bottles of wine and 1.5l of spirits; a small quantity of perfume and 250ml of eau de toilette.
Prohibited items: Firearms, explosives and dangerous weapons; ivory; antiques, statues and treasures; old books; animals/birds/reptiles (dead or alive) and parts; tea; rubber; coconut plants; dangerous drugs.

A B C D E F G H I J K L M N O P Q R S T U V W X Y Z

Note: (a) Only two members of the same family travelling together are entitled to free import allowances. (b) Valuable personal effects (including jewellery), must be declared on arrival in Sri Lanka. (c) There is no gift allowance. (d) Unused Sri Lankan currency should be reconverted to foreign currency upon departure. You are not permitted to leave Sri Lanka with currency in excess of Rs.250.

Public Holidays

Below are listed the Public Holidays for the January 2006-June 2007 period.

2006: Jan 1 New Year's Day. **Jan 10** Eid al-Adha (Hadji Festival Day). **Jan 14** Tamil Thai Pongal Day. **Feb 4** Independence Commemoration Day. **Feb 26** Mahasivaratri. **Apr 11** Milad un-Nabi (Birth of the Prophet). **Apr 13-14** Tamil and Sinhala New Year. **Apr 14** Good Friday. **May 1** May Day. **May 1-2** Vesak Poya Days. **Oct 21** Deepavali. **Oct 22-24** Eid al-Fitr (End of Ramadan). **Dec 25** Christmas Day. **Dec 31** Eid al-Adha (Hadji Festival Day).

2007: Jan 1 New Year's Day. **Jan 14** Tamil Thai Pongal Day. **Feb 4** Independence Commemoration Day. **Feb 16** Mahasivaratri. **Mar 31** Milad un-Nabi (Birth of the Prophet). **Apr 6** Good Friday. **Apr 13-14** Sinhala and Tamil New Year. **May 1** Labour Day.

Note: (a) Although not official public holidays, *Poya holidays* are often observed on the day of each full moon. In general, Hindu and Buddhist festivals are declared according to local astronomical observations and it is often only possible to forecast the approximate time of their occurrence. (b) Muslim festivals are timed according to local sightings of various phases of the moon and the dates given above are approximations. During the lunar month of Ramadan that precedes Eid al-Fitr, Muslims fast during the day and feast at night and normal business patterns may be interrupted; however, since Sri Lanka is not a predominantly Muslim country restrictions (which travellers may experience elsewhere) are unlikely to cause problems.

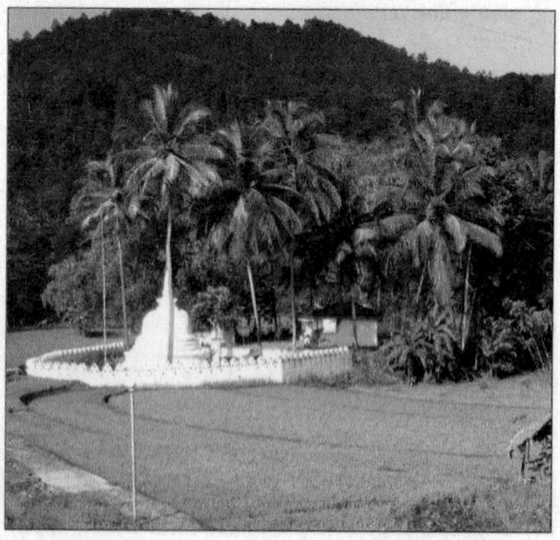

Credit: © Marie Peyre

Health

	Special Precautions?	Certificate Required?
Yellow Fever	No	1
Cholera	Yes	2
Typhoid & Polio	3	N/A
Malaria	4	N/A

Note: Regulations and requirements may be subject to change at short notice, and you are advised to contact your doctor well in advance of your intended date of departure. Any numbers in the chart refer to the footnotes below.

1: A yellow fever vaccination certificate is required from travellers over one year of age from infected areas.

2: Following WHO guidelines issued in 1973, a cholera vaccination certificate is not a condition of entry to Sri Lanka. However, cholera is a serious risk in this country and precautions are essential. Up-to-date advice should be sought before deciding whether these precautions should include vaccination as medical opinion is divided over its effectiveness; see the *Health* appendix.

3: Typhoid occurs in rural areas.

4: Malaria risk, predominantly in the benign *vivax* form, exists throughout the year, except in the districts of Colombo, Galle, Kalutara and Nuwara Eliya. The malignant *falciparum* strain is also present and is reported to be highly resistant to chloroquine and sulfadoxine-pyrimethamine. The recommended prophylaxis is chloroquine plus proguanil.

Food & drink: All water should be regarded as being potentially contaminated. Water used for drinking, brushing teeth or making ice should have first been boiled or otherwise sterilised. Bottled water and a variety of mineral waters are available at most hotels. Unpasteurised milk should be boiled. Powdered or tinned milk is available and is advised, but make sure that it is reconstituted with pure water. Pasteurised and sterilised milk is available in some hotels and shops. Avoid dairy products made with unboiled milk. Only eat well-cooked meat and fish, preferably served hot. Pork, salad and mayonnaise may carry increased risk. Vegetables should be cooked and fruit peeled.

Other risks: *Hepatitis A, B* and *E* are present and precautions should be taken. *Dengue fever* occurs and a haemorrhagic form has been discovered. *Filariasis* is present on the southwest coast of Sri Lanka. *Leptospirosis* can be contracted through water. *Leishmaniasis* is present and *Japanese encephalitis* is present except in mountainous regions.

Rabies is present. For those at high risk, vaccination before arrival should be considered. If you are bitten, seek medical advice without delay. For more information, consult the *Health* appendix.

Health care: Treatment is free at government hospitals and dispensaries; 24-hour treatment is available at Colombo General Hospital. Some hotels also have doctors.

Travel - International

AIR:

The national airline is *SriLankan Airlines (UL)* (website: www.srilankan.lk).

Approximate flight times: From Colombo to *London* is 12 hours, to *Hong Kong* is five hours 10 minutes, to the *Seychelles* is three hours 55 minutes and to *Tokyo* is nine hours.

Main airports: *Colombo Bandaranaike (CMB)* (Katunayake) is 29km (19 miles) north of the city. *To/from the airport:* Buses go to the city regularly and take 45 to 60 minutes. Taxis are available. There are trains to Maradana Station, located 1.6km (1 mile) from the city centre (travel time – 60 minutes). *Facilities:* Duty free shop, restaurant, bar, snack bar, bank, post office, tourist information and car hire.

Departure tax: None.

SEA:

Main ports: *Colombo, Galle, Hambantota, Kankasanthurai, Point Pedru* and *Trincomalee.* For more information on Sri Lankan ports, contact the Sri Lanka Port Authority, No.19, Chaithya Road, P.O Box 595, Colombo 01; tel: (1) 242 1201 *or* 1231; Website: www.slpa.lk.

Travel - Internal

AIR:

The major domestic airport is *Ratmalana* at Colombo. There are daily flights to smaller airports at Batticaloa, Gal Oya, Palali and Trincomalee. The airport at Jaffna is currently closed.

Departure tax: An embarkation tax of LKR1000 is payable at the Bandaranaike International Airport. Otherwise, none.

RAIL:

Trains connect Colombo with all tourist towns, but first-class carriages, air conditioning and dining cars are available on only a few. New fast services operate on the principal routes, including an inter-city express service between Colombo and Kandy, otherwise journeys are fairly leisurely.

Note: Rail services to Jaffna have ceased owing to the violent political disruptions in the northern area.

ROAD: Traffic drives on the left. Most roads are tarred, with a 56kph (35mph) speed limit in built-up areas and 75kph (45mph) outside towns. Flashing lights mean that the driver is asserting right of way, unlike in the UK. Avoid remote areas and travelling at night. **Bus:** An extensive network of services of reasonable quality is provided by the *Sri Lanka Central Transport Board.* Private bus drivers are paid according to the number of passengers and can often drive rather dangerously. **Taxi:** These have yellow tops and red and white plates. In Colombo, taxis are metered but it is advisable to agree a rate before setting off. Drivers expect a 10 per cent tip. **Car hire:** This is available from several international agencies. Air-conditioned minibuses are also available. Motorised rickshaws are also readily available for hire in towns and villages. Chauffeur-driven cars are less expensive and recommended. **Documentation:** In order to avoid bureaucratic formalities in Sri Lanka, an International Driving Permit should be obtained before departure. If not, a temporary licence to drive is obtainable on presentation of a valid national driving licence. This must be endorsed at the AA office in Colombo. The minimum age for driving a car is 18.

URBAN: Bus: The Central Transport Board provides intensive urban bus operations in Colombo, where there are also private buses and minibuses. Fares are generally collected by conductors. Services are often crowded.

Travel Times: The following chart gives approximate travel times (in hours and minutes) from **Colombo** to other major cities/towns in Sri Lanka.

	Air	Road	Rail
Matara	-	4.00	4.30
Badulla	-	9.30	9.00
Anuradhapura	0.45	5.30	6.00
Trincomalee 1.00	6.00	7.00	

Travel Advice

Travellers are advised against all but essential travel to the north or east of Sri Lanka.

Ongoing political violence and civil unrest, especially in the north and east, continues to escalate. Since December 2005, the security situation has deteriorated and there have been many fatal attacks. There is a threat from domestic terrorism. Travellers should follow local developments closely, be aware of their surroundings and alert to changing situations. Avoid political gatherings or demonstrations.

A state of emergency is in effect. This gives wide discretionary powers to the Sri Lankan Authorities. Travellers are strongly advised to comply with Government and security instructions.

You should be aware of the global risk of indiscriminate terrorist attacks which could be against civilian targets, including places frequented by foreigners.

This advice is based on information provided by the Foreign and Commonwealth Office in the UK. It is correct at time of publishing. As the situation can change rapidly, visitors are advised to contact the following organisations for the latest travel advice:

British Foreign and Commonwealth Office
Tel: (0845) 850 2829.
Website: www.fco.gov.uk

US Department of State
Website: http://travel.state.gov/travel

Accommodation

HOTELS:

Sri Lanka offers a wide choice of accommodation. There are seven international-class 5-star hotels with every modern facility. Hotels are classified from **1** to **5 stars**.

GUEST HOUSES:

Inns, guest houses and rest houses offer comfortable but informal accommodation.

PRIVATE HOMES: For visitors who would like to get to know the Sri Lankans and see how they live, arrangements can be made to stay in private homes or on a tea or rubber plantation.

PARK BUNGALOWS: There are also many park bungalows run by the Department of Wildlife Conservation, which are furnished and equipped for comfort rather than sophistication.

RESORTS: A network of domestic resorts in prime locations has been set up in Nuwara Eliya, Bandarawela, Anuradhapura, Kataragama and Bentota. Accommodation is comfortable and moderately priced.

ACCOMMODATION INFORMATION

Sri Lanka Tourist Hotels Association
50 Navam Mawatha, Colombo 2, Sri Lanka
Tel: (1) 245 2183 *or* 232 9143.
Website: www.chamber.lk

Ceylon Hotels Corporation
411 Galle Road, Bambalapitiya, Colombo 4, Sri Lanka
Tel: (1) 250 3497 *or* 259 8923.
Website: www.ceylonhotels.lk

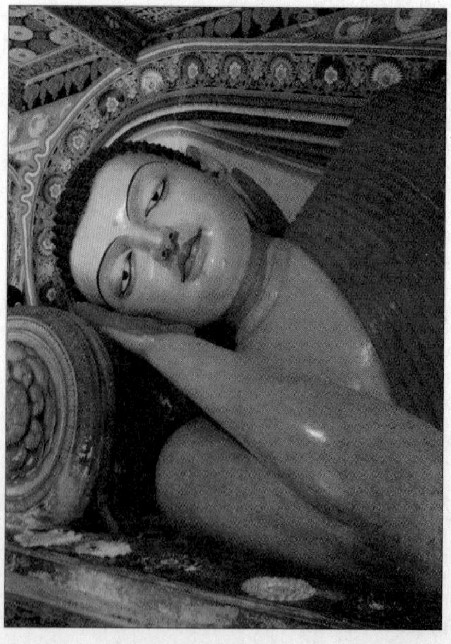

Credit: © Marie Peyre

Top Things To See & Do

- **Galle**; 116km (72 miles) from **Colombo**, Sri Lanka's capital city, is famous for its old **Dutch fort**, and is also a centre for **lace-making**, **ebony-carving** and **gem-polishing**.
- The **Vihara Maha Devi Park** in Colombo is named after the mother of one of Sri Lanka's greatest kings, and is noteworthy for its collection of beautiful flowering trees, a blossoming spectacle in March, April and early May. The park is open daily until 2100 and is well illuminated.
- Sri Lanka is replete with spectacular-looking sites of worship. There are numerous **Buddhist temples** scattered around Sri Lanka: **Kelani Rajamaha Viharaya**, 10km (6 miles) from **Fort**; the **Vajiraramaya** at **Bambalapitiya**, 6km (4 miles) from Fort; **Dipaduttaramaya** at **Kotahena**, 5km (3 miles) from Fort; and **Gotami Vihare** at **Borella**, 7km (4.5 miles) from Fort. Also worth visiting are the **Gangaramaya Bhikkhu Training Centre** and **Sima Malaka** at 61 Sri Jinaratana Road, Colombo, 3km (2 miles) from Fort; the **Purana Viharaya** at **Metharamaya**, Lauries Road, Colombo 4; and the **Purana Viharaya** at **Hendala**, 0.8km (0.5 miles) on the Colombo–Negombo road, en-route to the **Pegasus Reef Hotel**. Additionally, there are also some Hindu temples to explore: at **Kochikade Kotahena**, the **Pettah** and **Bambalapitiya**, Colombo 4; **Sri Siva Subramania Swami Kovil**, **Gintupitiya** – within walking distance of Sea Street, Colombo 11 (Pettah). Reflecting Sri Lanka's diverse communities, there are also mosques worth visiting in the **Davatagaha mosque** at **Union Place**, Colombo 2; and the **Afar Jumma mosque** in the Pettah.
- **Kandy**, a picturesque, naturally fortified town, 115km (72 miles) from Colombo, was the last stronghold of the Kandyan Kings. It withheld foreign conquest until 1815 when it was ceded by treaty to the British. It is now a cultural sanctuary where age-old customs, arts, crafts, rituals and ways of life are well preserved.
- See Sri Lanka's oldest and best-known fishing village, **Negombo**, 37km (32 miles) from Colombo, near Katunayake International Airport. It stands on a strand separating the sea from a lagoon. The seafood here, particularly the shellfish, is a speciality.
- Sri Lanka has approximately 1600km (1000 miles) of beautiful palm-shaded **beaches** as well as warm, pure seas and colourful coral reefs. The best time to visit Sri Lanka's southern beaches is from November to April. **Mount Lavinia**, 12km (7 miles) from Colombo, is a good beach resort close to Colombo and the domestic airport. Overlooking the area is what was **The Governors House**, built in 1805 by Sir Thomas Maitland, and now is the famous **Mount Lavinia Hotel**. **Beruwela**, 56km (35 miles) from Colombo, has good **bathing** in the bay all year round. **Bentota**, 64km (40 miles) from Colombo, is a pleasant self-contained resort destination, between the sea and the river. The Bentota resort is an interesting **diving** spot where multi-hued fish can be observed among myriad reef-dwellers. **Hikkaduwa**, 98km (61 miles) from Colombo, is a beautiful coral reef and beach. Regarded as a haven for **surfers**, watersports enthusiasts and **snorkellers**, this is a beautiful and colourful marine area, rife for exploration. **Tangale**, 195km (122 miles) from Colombo, is a beautiful bay and there is safe **swimming** all year round. The safe sea and wide sandy expanse always entice a multitude of sun-seeking visitors. At **Unawatuna** in Galle is a beach area acclaimed as being among the top-15 beaches in the world, with safe waters within a picturesque setting. Trincomalee, 257km (160 miles) from Colombo, is the ideal refuge for the beach addict. It boasts one of the finest natural harbours in the world and excellent beaches. All **watersports**, including **fishing**, are available here. There are many tempting underwater shipwrecks to explore for the intrepid diver. **Batticaloa**, 312km (195 miles) from Colombo, is famous for its 'singing fish' and the old Dutch fort. **Kalkudah**, 32km (20 miles) from Batticaloa, is ideal for bathing as the sea is clear, calm and reef-protected. **Passekudah**, close to **Kaludah**, is a fine bay, clear waters and safe swimming. **Arugam Bay**, 314km (196 miles) from Colombo, 3km (2 miles) from **Potuvil**, has a beautiful bay and good surfing. **Water-skiing** and **yachting** are available. **Windsurfing** is a sport that is gaining in popularity and facilities are located in Bentota, Beruwela, **Kalutara** and **Negombo**.
- For those searching for geological quirks, **Kundawella** is the scene of a large **blowhole** that operates as a natural spout, gushing water into the air and over the rocks of the beach.
- **Jaffna** is 396km (240 miles) from Colombo, at the country's northern tip, and is both city and seaport. It was once noted for its Hindu temples, Dutch forts, the **Keerimalai Baths**, the **tidal well** and the **Chundikulam Sanctuary**. Jaffna has many scenic beaches, the best known of which is **Casuarina Beach**.
- **Nilaveli**, 18km (11 miles) from Trincomalee, is very much a resort centre - all beach and watersports. **Whale**

watching is also one of its special attractions.
- There are a number of animal and bird sanctuaries and national parks where protected **wildlife** can be viewed. Several species are unique to the island, while some others have been introduced. Sri Lanka is well known for its elephants, sizeable numbers of which can be seen in **Gal Oya** and **Udawalawe National Parks** and at **Handapangala**. Other large mammals include leopards, deer and bears. Wild boars, porcupines and monkeys also exist, especially the Grey Langur which is common throughout the island. The native purple-faced Leaf Monkey is to be found in the higher hill regions. Of the 38 species of amphibian, 16 are unique to the island. Reptiles include two native crocodiles, the star tortoise, five species of turtle and many snakes. The five species of poisonous snake are rarely found in towns and villages. The island's **flora** varies greatly, ranging from temperate to tropical forests and from arid scrubland and plains to lush hills. There are rhododendron forests as well as tropical rainforests. Orchids and flowering trees can be seen in season.

Credit: © Marie Peyre

Entertainment

FOOD & DRINK: Standard foods are spicy and it is advised to approach curries with caution. There are many vegetables, fruits, meats and seafoods. Chinese, Continental, Indian and Japanese menus are available in Colombo. A speciality is basic curry, made with coconut milk, sliced onion, green chilli, aromatic spices such as cloves, nutmeg, cinnamon and saffron and aromatic leaves.

Things to know: Alcohol cannot be sold on *poya* holidays (which occur each lunar month on the day of the full moon).

National specialities:
- *Hoppers* is a cross between a muffin and a crumpet with a wafer-crisp edge, served with a fresh egg soft-baked on top.
- *Stringhoppers* are steamed circlets of rice flour, a little more delicate than noodles or spaghetti.
- *Jaggery* is a fudge made from the crystallised sap of the *kitul* palm.
- The *durian* fruit is considered a great delicacy.

National drinks:
- Tea is the national drink and thought to be amongst the best in the world.
- *Toddy* (sap of the palm tree).
- *Arrack* (fermented *Toddy* which comes in varying degrees of strength).

Tipping: Most hotels include a service charge of 10 per cent. Extra tipping is optional.

NIGHTLIFE: Some Colombo hotels have supper clubs with music for dancing. There are theatres in Colombo, cinemas showing films from the USA, ballet, concerts and theatre productions.

SHOPPING: Sri Lanka has several shopping malls, including Majestic City, Liberty Plaza, Crescat Boulevard, Odel Unlimited and JAIC Oberoi. Some 5-star hotels in Colombo also have shopping arcades. Special purchases include handicrafts and curios of silver, brass, bone, ceramics, wood and terracotta. Also cane baskets, straw hats, reed and coir mats and tea. Batik fabric, lace and lacquerware are also popular. Some of the masks, which are used in dance-dramas, in processions and on festival days, can be bought by tourists. The '18-disease' mask shows a demon in possession of a victim; he is surrounded by 18 faces – each of which cures a specific ailment. Versions produced for the tourist market are often of a high standard. Sri Lanka is also rich in gems. Fabrics include batiks, cottons, rayons, silks and fine lace. **Shopping hours:** Mon-Fri 0900-1730, Sat 0900-1300.

Business

ECONOMY: Although some parts of the economy have suffered severe dislocation as a result of the civil war – especially the once promising tourist industry – Sri Lanka has managed to accommodate the conflict to the extent that the economy performed reasonably well during the last five years. This was reflected in the GDP growth rate of over five per cent in 2004. In the first quarter of 2005, GDP growth rate fell to under five per cent and inflation rose to over 10 per cent. The tsunami, in December 2004, unfortunately slowed economic growth, despite incoming foreign aid and assistance from the International Monetary Fund. Agriculture sustains about one-third of the working population and directly contributes around 20 per cent of GDP. The main cash crops are tea, rubber and coconuts, which provide over 75 per cent of export earnings; rice is grown mainly for domestic consumption. Forestry and fishing are also important. The main industrial sectors are mining (gemstones and graphite being the principal minerals), and manufacturing. Iron ore, limestone, clay and uranium ore are also present in commercially exploitable quantities. Hydroelectricity is the main source of power, supplemented by imported oil. Important manufacturing industries include cement and textiles, both of which are valuable export earners.

In the service sector, the growth of tourism has been stunted by the civil war, but banking and insurance have both been performing well. Since the mid-1990s, successive Governments have followed the usual prescription of market-oriented policies – privatisation and deregulation – while seeking to build up potential export-earning industries. This strategy was slow to show results at first, but the Government persevered and some benefits are now beginning to materialise. The recent peace talks and ceasefire between Government and rebels has boosted business confidence both at home and abroad, and alleviated Sri Lanka's chronic shortage of investment capital. The Government is now hoping to consolidate its progress by further deregulation, fiscal reform, and privatisation: although it has all but pulled out of manufacturing, the state still owns 90 per cent of the island's land and the bulk of its utilities.

BUSINESS ETIQUETTE: Business attire is casual. English is widely spoken in business circles. Appointments are necessary and it is considered polite to arrive punctually. It is usual to exchange visiting cards on first introduction.
Office hours: Mon-Fri 0900-1700.

Credit: ©Marie Peyre

A
B
C
D
E
F
G
H
I
J
K
L
M
N
O
P
Q
R
S
T
U
V
W
X
Y
Z

Sudan

Location: Northeast Africa.

Time: GMT + 2.

Overview

Sudan is bordered by Egypt, the Red Sea, Ethiopia, Eritrea, Kenya, Uganda, the Democratic Republic of Congo, the Central African Republic, Chad and Libya. Sudan has only recently been developed as a tourist destination, and communications and facilities are still limited outside Khartoum. Travel restrictions are also in force in much of the country owing to the presence of separatist insurgents. There is currently a civil war in the south of the country and this, for obvious reasons, has negatively impacted upon the recent attempt to kickstart touristic growth in the country. Khartoum, the capital, is situated at the confluence of the Blue and White Niles. Among the tourist attractions here are the Omdurman camel market, the Arab souk and the National Museum. The main areas of archaeological interest include Bajrawiya, Naga and Meroe.
The Dinder National Park, on the Ethiopian border, is one of the largest in the world, and home to numerous species of wild animals. The Red Sea, with the transparency of its water, the variety of its fish and the charm of its marine gardens and coral reefs, is one of Sudan's main attractions.

General Information

AREA: 2,505,813 sq km (967,500 sq miles).
POPULATION: 32.9 million (UN estimate 2002).
POPULATION DENSITY: 13.1 per sq km.
CAPITAL: Khartoum. **Population:** 2.37 million (UN estimate 2002; including suburbs).
GEOGRAPHY: Sudan is bordered by Egypt to the north, the Red Sea to the northeast, Ethiopia and Eritrea to the east, Kenya, Uganda and the Democratic Republic of the Congo to the south, the Central African Republic and Chad to the west, and Libya to the northwest. There is a marked difference between the climate, culture and geography of northern and southern Sudan. The far north consists of the contiguous Libyan and Nubian deserts which extend as far south as the capital, Khartoum, and are barren except for small areas beside the Nile River and a few scattered oases. This gives way to the central steppes which cover the country between 15°N and 10°N, a region of short, coarse grass and bushes, turning to open savannah towards the south, largely flat to the east but rising to two large plateaux in the west and south, the Janub Darfur (3088m/10,131ft) and Janub Kordofan (500m/1640ft) respectively. Most of Sudan's agriculture occurs in these latitudes in a fertile pocket between the Blue and White Niles which meet at Khartoum. South of the steppes is a vast shallow basin traversed by the White Nile and its tributaries, with the Sudd, a 120,000 sq km (46,332 sq miles) marshland, in the centre. This gives way to equatorial forest towards the south, rising to jungle-clad mountains on the Ugandan border, the highest being Mount Kinyeti, at 3187m (10,456ft).
GOVERNMENT: Islamic Republic since 1986. Gained independence from the UK in 1956. **Head of State and Government:** President Omar Hassan Ahmad al-Bashir since 1989. **Recent History:** In January 2005, the Government and southern rebels signed a peace deal to end the long-running civil war. President Omar al-Bashir entered into a power-sharing administration in July 2005 with ex-rebel leader John Garang. Following Garang's death, his successor Salva Kiir is heading an interim administration in the southern party of the country. A referendum is planned in the south after six years of autonomy. Meanwhile, the ongoing crisis in the Darfur region has led to 2 million people fleeing their homes and tens of thousands of deaths
LANGUAGE: Arabic is the official language. English and many local dialects are widely spoken.
RELIGION: Muslim in the north; Christian and traditional animist beliefs in the south.
ELECTRICITY: 240 volts AC, 50Hz.
SOCIAL CONVENTIONS: In the north, Arab culture predominates, while the people in the more fertile south belong to many diverse tribes, each with their own lifestyle and beliefs. Because Sudan is largely Muslim and operates *Sharia*, women should not wear revealing clothing., although they are not expected to wear a veil or cover their heads. At official and social functions as well as in some restaurants, formal clothes are expected. The Sudanese have a great reputation for hospitality. A curfew operates in major cities from 0000-0400. **Photography:** There are many restrictions on photography: a photography permit can be obtained from the External Information Office at the Ministry of Information in Khartoum.

Climate

Extremely hot (less so November to March). Sandstorms blow across the Sahara from April to September. In the extreme north, there is little rain but the central region has some rainfall from July to August. The southern region has much higher rainfall, the wet season lasting May to October. Summers are very hot throughout the country, whilst winters are cooler in the north.
Required clothing: Tropical clothes all year, warmer clothes for cool mornings and evenings (especially in the desert).

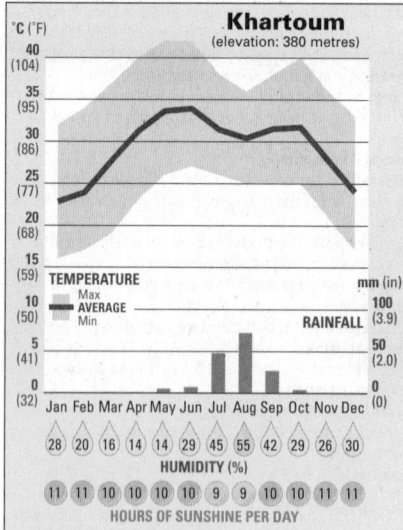

Communications

Telephone: IDD is available. Country code: 249. Outgoing international calls must go through the operator.
Mobile telephone: Roaming agreements exist with some international mobile phone companies. Coverage is available in main towns.
Internet: Internet access is available in main towns.
Post: Post office hours: Sat-Thurs 0830-1200 and 1730-1830. Airmail to Europe takes up to one week.
MEDIA: Press: Censorship is imposed on all press publications, following the 1989 coup. The main dailies are *Abbar al-Youm*, *Al-Rai al-Akhar* and *Al-wan* . The *Sudan Standard* is an English-language daily. There are English-language magazines entitled *New Horizon* and *Sudanow*.
TV: The Government run *Sudan National Broadcasting Corporation (SNBC)* operates two channels.

Radio: *SNBC* run national and regional netweoks, *Mango FM* is a Khartoum music station.

Passport/Visa

	Passport Required?	Visa Required?	Return Ticket Required?
Full British	Yes	Yes	Yes
Australian	Yes	Yes	Yes
Canadian	Yes	Yes	Yes
USA	Yes	Yes	Yes
Other EU	Yes	Yes	Yes
Japanese	Yes	Yes	Yes

Note: *Regulations and requirements may be subject to change at short notice, and you are advised to contact the appropriate diplomatic or consular authority before finalising travel arrangements. Any numbers in the chart refer to the footnotes below.*

Restricted entry: The Sudanese authorities refuse entry and transit to nationals of Israel and holders of passports that contain visas for Israel (either valid or expired).
PASSPORTS: Passport valid for at least six months required by all.
VISAS: Required by all except:
(a) nationals of the Syrian Arab Republic resident in the Syrian Arab Republic;
(b) those continuing their journey by the same or first connecting aircraft within six hours, provided holding confirmed onward tickets and documents.
Types of visa and cost: *Tourist*, *Business* or *Transit*: £53. Please note that the cost is £23 for Sudanese passport holders.
Validity: *Tourist* or *Business*: One month from the date of issue. *Transit*: One to seven days.
Visits may be extended through the Passport, Immigration and Nationality Office in Khartoum, Sudan.
Application to: Consular section at Embassy; see *Passport/Visa Information*.
Application requirements: (a) Three completed application forms (if applying for a transit visa, the country of destination after Sudan should be indicated, together with the anticipated date of arrival and departure from Sudan). (b) Three passport-size photos. (c) Fee, payable by postal order or company cheque only. (d) Letter or invitation from contact in Sudan.* (e) Passport valid for six months from date of entry, with no Israeli visas or immigration stamps affixed (if applying for a transit visa, applicant's passport should be duly endorsed for permission to enter the next country of destination after Sudan). (f) Cholera and yellow fever vaccinations are recommended. (g) A self-addressed envelope, if applicable. (h) Authentic documents from the travel agent proving reservations for a return ticket *or* a bank statement confirming financial capability for the trip *or* if travelling on business, a letter of invitation from the sponsoring company stating purpose of trip, duration of stay, financial responsibility and references in Sudan.
Note: *It is advisable that all business visitors have an invitation letter/fax from the Sudanese government when applying for a visa. A private company inviting an individual to work in Sudan needs to photocopy the first page of their passport and apply on their behalf with it to the Interior Ministry for initial approval. International Organisations need to get approval from the Foreign Affairs Ministry in Sudan. Contact the Consular section at Embassy for further information; see *Passport/Visa Information*.
Working days required: Up to four weeks.
Temporary residence: Enquire at Embassy.
Note: Special permits are required for all travel outside Khartoum. These can be obtained from the Passport and Immigration Office, Ministry of Interior, Khartoum. Travellers staying in Sudan for longer than three days must report to the police.

PASSPORT/VISA INFORMATION

Embassy of the Republic of Sudan in the UK
3 Cleveland Row, St James's, London SW1A 1DD, UK
Tel: (020) 7839 8080. Fax: (020) 7839 7560 *or* 7839 6009 (visa section).
Website: www.sudan-embassy.co.uk
Opening hours: Mon-Fri 0900-1600 (general enquiries); Mon-Fri 0930-1600 (visa section).

Embassy of the Republic of Sudan in the USA
2210 Massachusetts Avenue, NW, Washington, DC 20008, USA
Tel: (202) 338 8565.
Website: www.sudanembassy.org

Money

Currency: Sudanese Dinar (SDD) = 10 Sudanese Pounds; 1 Sudanese Pound = 100 piastres. Notes are in denominations of SDD1000, 500, 100, 50, 10 and 5. There are also a number of commemorative coins in circulation.

Note: The Sudanese Dinar is pegged to the Libyan Dinar. Exchange rates are liable to change significantly and rapidly. There is a black market with a premium of around 5000 per cent over the official rate.

Currency exchange: Currency should be exchanged only at official bureaux de change and banks, and receipts should be retained. There are severe penalties for changing money on the black market.

Credit & debit cards: Check with your credit or debit card company for merchant acceptability and other services which may be available. Due to recent conflicts, it is recommended to bring plenty of cash rather than rely on card transactions in Sudan.

Traveller's cheques: These are generally not recommended but should be in a major currency.

Currency restrictions: The import and export of local currency is prohibited. The import and export of foreign currency is unlimited, subject to declaration.

Banking hours: Sat-Thurs 0830-1200.

Exchange rate indicators:
Rate at time of publishing
£1.00=   SDD414.37
$1.00=   SDD234.69

Duty Free

The following items may be imported into Sudan by visitors over 20 years of age without incurring customs duty:
200 cigarettes or 50 cigars or 450g of tobacco; a reasonable amount of perfume and eau de toilette for personal use; a reasonable amount of gifts.

Prohibited items: The import of goods from Israel and South Africa is prohibited. Sudan also adheres to the list of prohibited goods drawn up by the Arab League and these include alcoholic beverages. Fresh fruit and vegetables and blank pro-forma invoices may not be imported. Firearms require a permit from the Ministry of Interior. Meat and fish products are prohibited without prior permission from the Ministry of Animal & Fish Resources.

Public Holidays

Below are listed Public Holidays for the January 2006-June 2007 period.

2006: Jan 1 Independence Day. Jan 10 Eid al-Adha (Feast of the Sacrifice). Jan 31 Islamic New Year. Mar 3 National Unity Day. Apr 6 Uprising Day. Apr 11 Al-Mowlid Al Nabawi (Birth of the Prophet). May 25 May Revolution Anniversary. Jun 30 Revolution Day. Oct 22-24 Eid al-Fitr (End of Ramadan). Dec 25 Christmas Day. Dec 31 Eid al-Adha (Feast of the Sacrifice).

2007: Jan 1 Independence Day. Jan 20 Islamic New Year. Mar 3 National Unity Day. Apr 6 Uprising Day. Mar 31 Al-Mowlid Al Nabawi (Birth of the Prophet). May 25 May Revolution Anniversary. Jun 30 Revolution Day.

Note: Muslim festivals are timed according to local sightings of various phases of the moon and the dates given above are approximations. During the lunar month of Ramadan that precedes Eid al-Fitr, Muslims fast during the day and feast at night and normal business patterns may be interrupted. Many restaurants are closed during the day and there may be restrictions on smoking and drinking. Some disruption may continue into Eid al-Fitr itself. Eid al-Fitr and Eid al-Adha may last anything from two to 10 days, depending on the region. For more information, see the *World of Islam* appendix.

Health

	Special Precautions?	Certificate Required?
Yellow Fever	Yes	1
Cholera	2	No
Typhoid & Polio	3	N/A
Malaria	4	N/A

Note: *Regulations and requirements may be subject to change at short notice, and you are advised to contact your doctor well in advance of your intended date of departure. Any numbers in the chart refer to the footnotes below.*

1: The risk of yellow fever is primarily in the equatorial south. A yellow fever vaccination certificate is required from travellers over one year of age from infected areas, and may be required from travellers leaving Sudan. Those countries and areas formerly classified as endemic zones are considered by the Sudanese authorities to be infected areas. Travellers arriving from non-endemic zones should note that vaccination is strongly recommended for travel outside the urban areas, even if an outbreak of the disease has not

been reported and they would normally not require a vaccination certificate to enter the country.

2: Following WHO guidelines issued in 1973, a cholera vaccination certificate is no longer a condition of entry to Sudan. However, cholera is a serious risk in the country and precautions are essential. Up-to-date advice should be sought before deciding whether these precautions should include vaccination as medical opinion is divided over its effectiveness; see the *Health* appendix.

3: Vaccination against typhoid is advised.

4: Malaria risk, predominantly in the malignant *falciparum* form, exists throughout the year throughout the country. In the north, the risk is seasonal and low. It is higher along the Nile south of Lake Nasser and in the central and southern part of the country. The Malaria risk on the Red Sea coast is very limited. High resistance to chloroquine and resistance to sulfadoxine-pyrimethamine has been reported. The recommended prophylaxis is mefloquine.

Food & drink: All water should be regarded as a potential health risk. Water used for drinking, brushing teeth or making ice should have first been boiled or otherwise sterilised. Milk is unpasteurised and should be boiled. Avoid dairy products which are likely to have been made from unboiled milk. Only eat well-cooked meat and fish, preferably served hot. Pork, salad and mayonnaise may carry increased risk. Vegetables should be cooked and fruit peeled.

Other risks: *Bilharzia* (schistosomiasis) is present. Avoid swimming and paddling in fresh water; swimming pools which are well chlorinated and maintained are safe. *Visceral leishmaniasis* especially occurs in eastern and southern Sudan. Vaccination is strongly recommended. The disease is transferred through sandflies which live mainly on river banks and in wooded areas.

The transmission rate of *trypanosomiasis* (sleeping sickness) is high, with a significant risk of infection for travellers visiting rural areas in the south of the country. *Hepatitis A, B and E, diphtheria* and *meningococcal meningitis* are also present. *Dracunculiasis* is prevalent in the south. *Shigellosis* was detected in North Dafur in June 2004, in the Abu Shoak Internally Displaced Persons (IDP) Camp, which has a population of 40,000: there were 11 deaths. *Ebola* was recently detected and contained in Yanbio in south Sudan. *Tetanus* and *Giardia Amoebiasis* also occur. *HIV/AIDS* is becoming an ever-growing problem. *Rabies* is present. For those at high risk, vaccination before arrival should be considered. If you are bitten, seek medical advice without delay. For more information, consult the *Health* appendix.

Health care: Medical treatment may be free at certain establishments but health insurance is essential and should include cover for emergency repatriation. Medical facilities are very limited, particularly outside Khartoum.

Travel - International

AIR:

 The national airline is *Sudan Airways (SD)*. Other airlines serving Sudan include *British Airways*, *Lufthansa* and *Syrian Arab Airlines*.

Approximate flight times: From Khartoum to *London* is eight hours, including stopover.

Main airports: *Khartoum (KRT)* (Civil) is 4km (2 miles) southeast of the city. *To/from the airport:* Taxi services are available. *Facilities:* Restaurants and duty-free shops.

Departure tax: US$20 (Sudanese nationals may pay in local currency). Transit passengers are exempt.

SEA:

 The only sea ports are Port Sudan and Suakin on the Red Sea. Piracy has been reported in the area.

RIVER:

There are car ferries from Aswan in Egypt to Wadi Halfa.

RAIL:

Rail links run from Cairo (Egypt) to Aswan High Dam and then by riverboat to Wadi Halfa.

ROAD:

 Entry to Sudan by road is at present only possible at Wadi Halfa on the Egypt/Sudan border.

Travel - Internal

Note: Travel outside of Khartoum is restricted; see *Passport/Visa* section.

AIR:

 Sudan Airways (SD) runs services to 20 airports, including Dongola, Juba, El Obeid and Port Sudan. The most reliable route is Port Sudan to Khartoum. There is also an air-taxi service operating twice weekly to Nyala, available from Khartoum.

Departure tax: SDD600.

RIVER:

 River steamers serve all towns on the Nile but conditions are mostly unsuitable for tourist travel. Services depend on fluctuating water

levels. It is wise to take food and water. Destinations include Dongola, Karima, Kosti and Juba. A 320km (200mile) navigable canal, the *Jonglei*, is under construction in the south.

RAIL:

 Sudan has an extensive rail network (5500km/3418 miles) but the service is in bad repair, extremely slow and uncomfortable. Travelling first class is advisable; second- and third-class compartments can get very crowded. Sleeping cars are available on main routes from Khartoum to Wau/Nyala, Khartoum to Kassala/Wadi Halfa and Port Sudan to Khartoum. There are a few air-conditioned carriages, for which a supplement is charged.

ROAD:

 Only major roads are asphalted; road conditions are poor outside towns, roads to the north are often closed during the rainy season (July to September) and street lights are non-existent. Owing to the bad conditions, a full set of spare parts should be carried for long journeys. Vehicles must be in good working condition. Traffic drives on the right.

Bus: Services run between the main towns and depart from the market places; however they are not entirely safe. *Souk* (market) lorries are a cheap but uncomfortable method of transport. **Taxi:** Also often unsafe, taxis can be found at ranks or hailed in the street. Taxis are not metered, fares must be agreed in advance. **Car hire:** Available in the main towns and at major hotels but charges are high. **Documentation:** *Carnet de Passage*, adequate finance and roadworthiness certificate (from the Embassy) are all needed. An International Driving Permit is recommended, although not legally required. A temporary driving licence is available from local police on presentation of a valid British or Northern Ireland driving licence, for a maximum period of three months. Women *are* allowed to drive in Sudan.

URBAN:

 Publicly operated bus services in Khartoum have of late become unreliable and irregular, which has led to the proliferation of private *bakassi* minibuses, nicknamed *boks*. They pick up and set down with no fixed stops. These operations are on the fringes of legality and should be used with care.

Travel Advice

Travellers are advised against all travel to the Eritrean border, and against all but essential travel to southern Sudan, Darfur and Kassala.

The Comprehensive Peace Agreement signed in January 2005 has effectively brought to an end the north-south civil war. The ruling National Congress Party and the SPLM/A have agreed to form a Government of National Unity, which includes representation from other political parties. However, some areas remain tense and travellers should remain vigilant and avoid demonstrations or similar large gatherings in public places.

Conflict continues in Darfur. Banditry is widespread and great caution is needed when travelling outside the major population centres or at night.

Travellers should be aware of the threat from terrorism.

This advice is based on information provided by the Foreign and Commonwealth Office in the UK. It is correct at time of publishing. As the situation can change rapidly, visitors are advised to contact the following organisations for the latest travel advice:

British Foreign and Commonwealth Office
Tel: (0845) 850 2829.
Website: www.fco.gov.uk

US Department of State
Website: http://travel.state.gov/travel

Accommodation

HOTELS:

 Accommodation is scarce outside Khartoum and Port Sudan. Khartoum has around 10 major hotels, including some of international standard, and Port Sudan also has several. There are a few smaller hotels in the main towns and several hostels.

YOUTH HOSTELS:

 Contact the Youth Hostels Association (see *Accommodation Information*).

ACCOMMODATION INFORMATION

Youth Hostels Association
PO Box 1705, House no. 66, Street no. 47,
Khartoum East,
Sudan
Tel: (11) 722 087.

Top Things To See & Do

• With **Omdurman**, the old national capital, and **Khartoum North**, the capital **Khartoum**, forms one unit called the 'three-towns capital'. Among the tourist attractions are the **Omdurman camel market** and the Arab **souk**. A good selection of Sudanese handicrafts is sold in several shops in the centre and in the reception halls of bigger hotels. Particularly noteworthy from a historical and artistic point of view is a visit to the well-organised **National Museum**, which contains archaeological treasures dating back to 4000 BC and earlier. A visit to the **Khalifa's House Museum** will reward those who are interested in Sudan's more recent history, especially the reign of the Mahdi (1881-1899).

• A visit to the **Gezira** model farm and a trip along the **Nile** to the dam at **Jebel Aulia**, where the Nile is especially rich in fish, are recommended. Sunset on the river is spectacular. The main areas of archaeological interest in Sudan are to be found beside the Nile north of Khartoum. They include **Bajrawiya**, **El Kurru**, **Meroe**, **Musawarat**, **Naga** and **Nuri**.

• Covering 6475 sq km (2500 sq miles) southeast of Khartoum on the Ethiopian border, the **Dinder National Park** is one of the largest in the world. There are many species of wild animals, including lion, giraffe, leopard, kudu, bushbuck and antelope, and birds such as guinea fowl, vulture, pelican, stork, kingfisher and the beautiful crown crane. Special three-day trips from Khartoum are organised in the high season (December to April).

• With the transparency of its water, the variety of its fish and the charm of its marine gardens and coral reefs, the **Red Sea** is one of Sudan's main tourist attractions. The busy **Port Sudan**, **Suakin**, famous during the Ottoman era, and the **Arous Tourist Village**, 50km (30 miles) north of Port Sudan, are just three centres from which to explore the coast. **Erkowit**, 1200m (3930ft) above sea level, is a beautiful resort in the coastal mountains and is famed for its evergreen vegetation.

• **Jebel Marra**, at more than 3088m (10,100ft), is the highest peak in the Darfur region of western Sudan. It is a region of outstanding scenic beauty, with waterfalls and volcanic lakes and a pleasant climate and, consequently, a favoured resort.

• The **Southern Provinces** are characterised by green forests, open parkland, waterfalls and treeless swamps abounding with birds and wild animals such as elephant, black and white rhino, common eland, Nile lechwe, lesser kudu, bisa oryx, zebra, crocodile, hippo, hyena, buffalo and the almost extinct shoebill. The **Gemmeiza Tourist Village**, situated in the heart of **East Equatoria**, is considered of special interest, owing to the abundance of game in that area.

Note: The people of the south are largely Christian and this has led to friction with the ruling Muslim factions in the north. Check with the Embassy before travelling if a visit to this region is intended.

Civil war and political instability prevent travellers from undertaking watersports activities at present, although there is normally great scope for them on the Red Sea coast, including **swimming**, **diving** on coral reefs and **fishing** for barracuda, sharks and grey cod.

TOURIST INFORMATION

Ministry of Tourism and National Heritage
P.O. box 13226, Khartoum, Sudan
Tel: (183) 472 604 *or* 471 329.

Entertainment

FOOD & DRINK: The staple diet is *fool*, a type of bean, and *dura*, cooked maize or millet, which are eaten with various vegetables. The hotel restaurants in Khartoum and Port Sudan serve international cuisine and there are a few Greek and Middle Eastern restaurants. If invited to a Sudanese home, more exotic food will usually be served. Alcohol is banned by the Islamic *Sharia* code.
Tipping: Not customary.
NIGHTLIFE: The best entertainment is found in Khartoum and Omdurman, with the national theatre, music hall, cinemas, open-air and hotel entertainment.
SHOPPING: The *souk* has stalls selling food, local crafts, spices, jewellery and silver. Special purchases include basketwork, ebony, gold and silver and assorted handicrafts. Visitors must not buy cheetah skins: the killing of cheetahs is prohibited and they are a protected species under the World Wildlife Act. **Shopping hours:** Sat-Thurs 0800-1330 and 1730-2000.

Business

ECONOMY: Once described as the bread basket of the Arab world, Sudan is a country of high, though largely unrealised, economic potential, which is presently crippled

---

by civil war, a foreign debt of around US$15 billion, and climatic effects which have brought both drought and flooding. Agriculture employs most of the workforce, producing cotton – the major export, wheat, groundnuts, sorghum and sugar cane. Production of gum arabic, once an important product, has declined through the introduction of synthetic substitutes and increasing competition, particularly from West Africa. Livestock breeding has suffered from persistent drought.

The manufacturing sector concentrates on processing the country's agricultural output – sugar, for example – and the production of textiles, cement and some consumer goods. There are some mineral deposits including marble, mica, chromite, gypsum and gold. There are also some onshore oil deposits: located in the mid-1990s, these came on stream in 1999 and have been of some help in easing Sudan's chronic power shortages. The government has announced a major dam project on the Nile and a new oil refinery that are intended to meet both electricity demand and the urgent need for planned water distribution.

Ultimately, Sudan relies on foreign aid to sustain its economy. Natural phenomena, compounded by the effects of the two-decade-long civil war, have made this more pressing than usual since 2000, as Sudan has needed two large injections of emergency food aid to stave off mass famine. Relations with the IMF have been rocky – Sudan was almost thrown out in the mid-1990s – but the Fund is now providing some financial support in exchange for a standard economic reform programme. Elsewhere, while the political posture of Sudan's Islamic government has alienated Western governments, it can still rely on support from wealthy Arab states, notably Saudi Arabia. Nonetheless, the Islamic government's economic programme has successfully achieved its principal targets of 5 to 6 per cent annual growth and inflation of below 5 per cent. Saudi Arabia is the largest exporter to Sudan, and is also a major recipient of Sudanese exports along with Egypt, Italy and Japan.

BUSINESS ETIQUETTE: Businessmen should wear a lightweight suit. Visiting businesspeople should respect Muslim customs. It should be clearly stated in advance if the visitor is female. English is widely spoken in business circles although knowledge of a few words of Arabic will be well received. Punctuality is less important than patience and politeness. Personal introductions are an advantage; business cards should have an Arabic translation on the reverse. **Office hours:** Sat-Thurs 0800-1430.

COMMERCIAL INFORMATION

Sudan Development Corporation (SDC)
PO Box 710, 21 al-Amarat, Khartoum, Sudan
Tel: (11) 472 186 *or* 472 195.

Sudan Chamber of Commerce
PO Box 81, Gamhoria Street, Khartoum 11114, Sudan
Tel: (11) 772 346 *or* 776 518.
Website: www.sudanchamber.org

Surinam

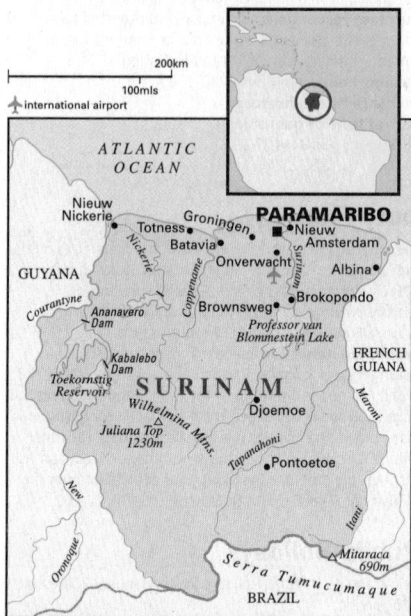

Location: North coast of South America.

Time: GMT - 3.

Overview

Surinam is bordered by the Atlantic Ocean, the Marowijne River, French Guiana and Brazil. By the time the Spanish arrived in the late 15th century, the Surinen (the original inhabitants of Surinam) had been driven out by other Amerindian groups. Fierce resistance to colonisation deterred most would-be occupiers from Europe, although the territory formally changed hands many times between the Dutch, English and French, before finally being confirmed as a Dutch possession by the terms of the 1815 Treaty of Vienna. At this time, the majority of the population were slaves, working on the plantations. Despite the abolition of slavery in 1863, conditions changed very little until the early 20th century and the discovery of large bauxite deposits, which brought about a major change in the economic - and consequently, political - complexion of the country.

In 1954, Surinam, with the Netherlands Antilles, became an autonomous region within the Kingdom of The Netherlands. Full independence was achieved in 1975.

While the 17th-century capital, Paramaribo, with its attractive colonial architecture, is a good starting point for any visitor, Surinam's main attraction is its tropical rainforest, which covers nearly 80 per cent of the country and is home to a huge variety of wildlife.

General Information

AREA: 163,265 sq km (63,037 sq miles).
POPULATION: 429,000 (UN estimate 2001).
POPULATION DENSITY: 2.6 per sq km.
CAPITAL: Paramaribo. **Population:** 214,000 (2000).
GEOGRAPHY: Surinam is bordered to the north by the Atlantic Ocean, to the east by the Marowijne River (which forms the border with French Guiana), to the west by the Corantijn River (which forms the border with Guyana), and to the south by forests, savannahs and mountains, which separate it from Brazil. In the northern part of the country are coastal lowlands covered with mangrove swamps. Further inland runs a narrow strip of savannah land. To the

---

south, the land becomes hilly and then mountainous, covered with dense tropical forest, and cut by numerous rivers and streams.

GOVERNMENT: Republic since 1987. Gained independence from The Netherlands in 1975. **Head of State:** President Runaldo Ronald Venetiaan since 2000.

LANGUAGE: Dutch is the official language. *Sranan Tongo*, originating in Creole, is the popular language. The main languages are Hindi and Javanese. English, Chinese, French and Spanish are also spoken.

RELIGION: Approximately 48 per cent Christian, 27 per cent Hindu and 20 per cent Muslim.

ELECTRICITY: 127 volts AC, 60Hz. European round two-pin plugs and screw-type lamp fittings are in use.

SOCIAL CONVENTIONS: Informal dress is suitable for most occasions. Guayabera or safari outfits are increasingly worn in place of jackets and ties. Women should wear long trousers on trips to the interior. Beachwear should be confined to the beach or poolside. **Photography:** It is inadvisable to photograph public places, particularly of a political or military nature (including police stations). There is a general sensitivity about the taking of photographs – it is advisable to seek prior permission.

Climate

Tropical and humid, cooled by the northeast trade winds. The best time to visit is February to April (short dry season) and August to October (long dry season). The rainy seasons last from November to January and from May to July. Surinam lies outside the hurricane zone and the most extreme weather condition is the *sibibusi* (forest broom), a heavy rain shower.

Required clothing: Lightweights and rainwear.

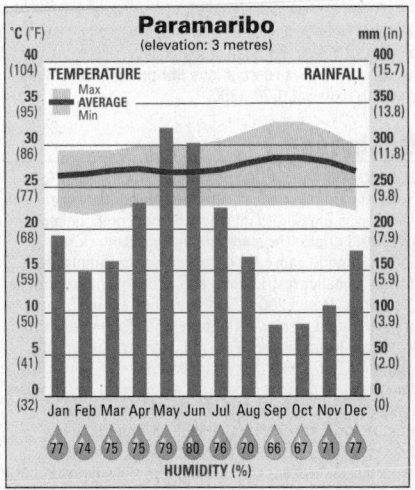

Paramaribo (elevation: 3 metres)

Communications

Telephone: IDD is available. Country code: 597. There are no area codes.

Mobile telephone: Roaming agreements exists with some international mobile phone operators. Coverage is mainly limited to Paramaribo.

Internet: Internet cafes are available.

Post: Post office hours: 0700 to mid-afternoon. Airmail to and from Europe usually takes about one week to arrive.

MEDIA: Press: Dutch-language dailies include *De Ware Tijd* and *De West*.

TV: *Algemene Televisie Verzorghy (ATV)* is Government-owned and broadcasts in Dutch, English, Portuguese, Spanish and local languages. *Surinaamse Televisie Stichting (STVS)* is also Government-owned.

Radio: *Stichting Radio Omroep Suriname* is Government -owned. Other commercial stations include *Radio Apintie*, *Radio Nickerie* and *Radio Paramaribo*.

Passport/Visa

	Passport Required?	Visa Required?	Return Ticket Required?
Full British	Yes	Yes	Yes
Australian	Yes	Yes	Yes
Canadian	Yes	Yes	Yes
USA	Yes	Yes	Yes
Other EU	Yes	Yes	Yes
Japanese	Yes	No	Yes

Note: *Regulations and requirements may be subject to change at short notice, and you are advised to contact the appropriate diplomatic or consular authority before finalising travel arrangements. Any numbers in the chart refer to the footnotes below.*

PASSPORTS: Passport valid for at least six months after arrival required by all.

VISAS: Required by all except the following:
(a) nationals of Antigua & Barbuda, Barbados, Belize, Brazil, Chile, Costa Rica, Dominica, Ecuador, The Gambia, Grenada, Guyana, Hong Kong (SAR), Israel, Jamaica, Japan, Korea (Rep), Malaysia, Netherlands Antilles (holding valid Netherlands passports), The Philippines, St Kitts & Nevis, St Lucia, St Vincent & the Grenadines, Singapore, Switzerland and Trinidad & Tobago;
(b) transit passengers continuing their journey by the same or first connecting aircraft within 24 hours, provided holding onward or return documentation and not leaving the airport.

Note: Nationals staying for more than 24 hours need to get a transit visa on arrival at the airport.

Types of visa and cost: *Single-entry Tourist*: US$30 (two months). *Multiple-entry Tourist*: US$60 (three to four months); US$90 (six months); US$175 (12 months). *Business*: US$45 (one month). *Multiple-entry Business*: US$90 (two months); US$270 (six months); US$540 (12 months).

Validity: Single-entry: two months; multiple-entry: up to one year.

Application to: Nearest Embassy (or Consular section at Embassy); see *Passport/Visa Information*.

Application requirements: (a) One completed, printed or typed, signed application form. (b) One current passport-size photo (in colour and current, no three-minute photos; for children with no individual passport, a colour photograph should be attached to the application form of the passport holder and their visa must also be paid for). (c) Valid passport. (d) Fee. (e) Self-addressed, stamped envelope with return postage for postal applications. (f) Photocopy of valid return ticket, if applicable. (g) For business trips, letter of invitation from company detailing purpose of trip, name of institute visited with contact details, plus approximate duration of stay, a completed business form and a guarantee or letter of reference.

Note: After arrival in Surinam, visitors are required to report to the Immigration Service within eight days at Police Precinct Nieuwe Haven, Van't Hogerhuysstraat, Paramaribo.

Working days required: At least one week before departure and no earlier than eight weeks. Applicants are encouraged to apply with plenty of time in case the application merits further scrutiny from official bodies. However, some applications may only take one day to be processed if a rush fee is paid of US$50, or equivalent.

PASSPORT/VISA INFORMATION

Embassy of the Republic of Surinam in the USA
4301 Connecticut Avenue, Suite 460, NW, Washington, DC 20008, USA
Tel: (202) 244 7488 *or* 244 7590/1/2.
Website: www.surinameembassy.org

Money

Currency: Surinam Dollar (SRD; symbol S$) = 100 cents. Notes are in denominations of S$100, 50, 20, 10 and 5. Coins are in denominations of 250, 100, 25, 10, 5 and 1 cents.

Note: On 1 January 2004, the Surinam Dollar replaced the Surinam Guilder as the new monetary system. The new currency will enable the Central Bank to re-value the present gulden system to a ratio of 1000 guldens per 1 Surinam Dollar, and not have to differentiate between old and new guldens. The existing gulden coins will not have to be re-issued but will maintain their value and be incorporated into the new system. Surinam Dollars are tied to US Dollars. The Government has kept the SRD exchange rate relatively stable since its inception, at around 2.7 SRD per U.S. dollar. Surinamese bank notes can only be exchanged at the Central Bank.
(Formerly, the monetary system in Surinam was: Surinam Guilder (SG) = 100 cents. Notes were in denominations of SG25,000, 10,000, 5000, 2000, 1000, 100, 25, 10 and 5. Coins are in denominations of 25, 10 and 5 cents.)

Currency exchange: Surinam Dollars are the only legal tender; since the introduction of the new monetary system from the former gulden system, gulden coins are still in circulation. However they have been re-valued to a ratio of 1000 guldens per 1 Surinam Dollar. The Central Bank is authorised to exchange money.

Credit & debit cards: American Express and MasterCard are the most widely accepted credit cards; Diners Club has limited acceptance. Check with your credit or debit card company for merchant acceptability and other facilities which may be available.

Traveller's cheques: Must be changed at banks. To avoid additional exchange rate charges, travellers are advised to take traveller's cheques in Pounds Sterling or US Dollars.

Currency restrictions: The import of foreign and local currency is unlimited, provided amounts in excess of US$10,000 are declared on arrival. On departure, the imported foreign currency can be exported again, up to the amount declared on arrival. The export of local currency is limited to S$1000.

Banking hours: Mon-Fri 0730-1400.

Exchange rate indicators: The following figures are included as a guide to the movements of the Surinam Dollar against Sterling and the US Dollar:

Date at time of publishing	
£1.00=	S$4.84
$1.00=	S$2.74

Duty Free

The following items may be imported into Surinam without incurring customs duty:
200 cigarettes or 200 cigarillos or 20 cigars or 500g of tobacco; 1l of spirits, 4l of wine and 8l of beer; 50g of perfume and 1l eau de toilette, lotions and eau-de-cologne; *other goods for personal use up to the value of US$500.*

Prohibited items: Fruit (except a reasonable quantity from The Netherlands), vegetables, coffee, plants, roots, bulbs, cocoa, rice, fish, meat and meat products (unless a valid health certificate is shown).

Public Holidays

Below are listed Public Holidays for the January 2006-June 2007 period.

2006: Jan 1 New Year's Day. **Mar 15*** Holi Phagwa. **Apr 14** Good Friday. **Apr 17** Easter Monday. **May 1** Labour Day. **Jul 1** Abolition of Slavery Day. **Oct 22-24** Eid al-Fitr (End of Ramadan). **Nov 25** Independence Day. **Dec 25-26** Christmas.

2007: Jan 1 New Year's Day. **Mar 3*** Holi Phagwa. **Apr 6** Good Friday. **Apr 9** Easter Monday. **May 1** Labour Day.

Note: (a) In addition, Chinese, Jewish and Indian businesses will be closed for their own religious holidays. (b) Muslim festivals are timed according to local sightings of various phases of the moon and the dates given above are approximations. During the lunar month of Ramadan that precedes Eid al-Fitr, Muslims fast during the day and feast at night and normal business patterns may be interrupted. Many restaurants are closed during the day and there may be restrictions on smoking and drinking. Some disruption may continue into Eid al-Fitr itself, which may last anything from two to 10 days, depending on the region. For more information, see the *World of Islam* appendix. (c) *Hindu festivals are declared according to local astronomical observations and it is only possible to forecast the approximate time of their occurrence.

Health

	Special Precautions?	Certificate Required?
Yellow Fever	Yes	1
Cholera	No	No
Typhoid & Polio	2	N/A
Malaria	3	N/A

Note: *Regulations and requirements may be subject to change at short notice, and you are advised to contact your doctor well in advance of your intended date of departure. Any numbers in the chart refer to the footnotes below.*

1: A yellow fever vaccination certificate is required from all travellers arriving within from infected areas.

2: Typhoid may occur (vaccination is advised); poliomyelitis is not reported.

3: Malaria risk, predominantly in the malignant *falciparum* form, exists throughout the year in the three southern districts of the country. In Paramaribo city and the seven coastal districts, transmission risk is low or negligible. The *falciparum* strain is reported to be resistant to chloroquine, sulfadoxine-pyrimethamine and some decline in sensitivity to quinine has been reported. Mefloquine is therefore the recommended prophylaxis.

Food & drink: Mains water is normally chlorinated and, whilst relatively safe, may cause mild abdominal upsets. Bottled water is available and is advised for the first few weeks of the stay. Drinking water outside main cities and towns is likely to be contaminated and sterilisation is considered essential. The *Melk Centrale* (Government Dairy Company) sells pasteurised milk but otherwise milk is unpasteurised and should be boiled. Powdered or tinned milk is available and is advised, but make sure that it is reconstituted with pure water. Avoid dairy products which are likely to have been made from unboiled milk. Only eat well-cooked meat and fish, preferably served hot. Pork, salad and mayonnaise may carry increased risk. Vegetables should be cooked and fruit peeled.

A B C D E F G H I J K L M N O P Q R S T U V W X Y Z

Other risks: *Bilharzia* (schistosomiasis) is present. Avoid swimming and paddling in fresh water; swimming pools which are well chlorinated and maintained are safe. *Hepatitis A* occurs; *hepatitis B* is highly endemic. *Myiasis* (botfly and screw worm) occurs in rural areas. *Dengue fever* is increasing. There is a high prevalence of the *HIV/AIDS* virus.
Rabies is present. For those at high risk, vaccination before arrival should be considered. If you are bitten, seek medical advice without delay. For more information, consult the *Health* appendix.
Health care: Health insurance is strongly recommended. Medical care is limited: there is only one emergency room in Paramaribo and there are few hospitals in outlying areas.

Travel - International

AIR:

The national airline is *Surinam Airways (PY)* (website: www.slm.firm.fr). *BWIA West Indies Airways* and *KLM* also fly to Surinam. There are direct flights from Amsterdam three to seven times a week.
Approximate flight times: From Paramaribo to *London* is 10 hours, excluding stopover time in Amsterdam or Miami, which may involve an overnight stay, owing to a lack of connecting flights.
Main airports: *Johan Adolf Pengel (PBM)* (Paramaribo) is 45km (28 miles) south of the city. *To/from the airport*: A coach meets all arrivals. There are also buses or taxis to the city (travel time - 45 minutes). *Facilities*: Duty free shop, bank, bar/restaurant and post office.
Departure tax: US$35. Transit passengers and children under two years of age are exempt.

SEA:

Main port: *Paramaribo. Surinam Shipping Line* sails from Mexico and New Orleans monthly. There are coastal services between ports and services to Germany and The Netherlands. The *Royal Netherlands Steamship Company* provides a service from Amsterdam to Surinam with limited passenger accommodation. There are regular car ferry services across the Surinam River and Marowijne River from Albina to St Laurent de Maroni (French Guiana), from Southdrain (Surinam) to Moleson Creek (Guyana), and across the Corantijn River from Nieuw Nickerie to Springlands (Guyana).

ROAD:

The coastal road from Paramaribo leads to the borders of French Guiana and Guyana.

Travel - Internal

Note: It is advisable to check the weather conditions before setting out for the interior, as heavy rains can cause delays.

AIR:

Domestic flights to towns in the interior are operated from Paramaribo (Zorg en Hoop airfield) by *Surinam Airways (PY)*. They also provide services from Paramaribo to the Nieuw Nickerie district, and maintain a charter service.

RIVER:

To visit the interior and some coastal areas, river transport is the least expensive and often most efficient option.

RAIL:

There are currently no services in operation.

ROAD:

Traffic drives on the left. There is a reasonable, largely paved, road network with some potholes. Drivers using their own cars should make sure they carry a full set of spares. **Bus:** There are services from the capital to most villages, with fixed routes at low prices. Buses tend to be very crowded and chaotic with loud music. **Taxi:** These are not metered, prices should be agreed before departure and tipping is not necessary. They can be hard to find after 2200 and on Sundays or holidays. **Car hire:** Available at the airport and in Paramaribo through main hotels. **Documentation:** International Driving Permit required.

Travel Advice

Most visits to Surinam are trouble-free but you should be aware of the global risk of indiscriminate international terrorist attacks, which could be against civilian targets, including places frequented by foreigners.
Burglary, armed robbery and violent crime occur with some frequency in Paramaribo and in outlying areas. This advice is based on information provided by the Foreign and Commonwealth Office in the UK. It is correct at time of publishing. As the situation can change rapidly, visitors are advised to contact the following organisations for the latest travel advice:

British Foreign and Commonwealth Office
Tel: (0845) 850 2829.
Website: www.fco.gov.uk
US Department of State
Website: http://travel.state.gov/travel

Accommodation

HOTELS:

Paramaribo has a number of modern hotels with air conditioning, but advance booking is essential owing to the limited number of beds. A 10 per cent service charge is added. There are several small guest houses and pensions in the city and elsewhere, but it is advisable to check with the tourist office for further information. Hotels and restaurants are rare outside the capital, and travellers are advised to bring their own hammock and food. For further information, contact Surinam Tourism Foundation or the Ministry of Transport, Communication and Tourism (see *Top Things To See & Do*).

APARTMENTS:

Furnished apartments with self-catering facilities can be rented.

CAMPING:

Blaka Watra, Cola Kreek, Republiek and Zandery are resorts with picnic grounds and camping/bathing facilities.

YOUTH HOSTELS:

There is a YMCA in Paramaribo (Heerenstraat).

Top Things To See & Do

- **Paramaribo,** the 17th-century capital is graced with attractive British, Dutch, French and Spanish colonial architecture. The nearby restored **Fort Zeelandia** houses the **Surinam Museum**. Other attractions include the 19th-century **Roman Catholic cathedral** (made entirely of wood - as is the 17th-century synagogue, which lies in stark contrast to the biggest mosque in the Caribbean), **Independence Square**, the **Presidential Palace** (with an attractive palm garden) and the lively waterfront and market districts. **Palmentuin** is a pleasant park, as is the **Cultuurtuin**, but the latter is a fair distance from the town.
- **Watersports:** Beaches are not of the highest standard and only a few are suitable for **swimming** (which is prohibited at some classified beaches within nature reserves). An unusual but popular location for swimming is **Colakreek**, a recreation area 50km (32 miles) south of Paramaribo consisting of numerous creeks with brown water in the small savannah belt behind the coastal plains. There are facilities for **sailing** at **Jachthaven Ornamibo**.
- **Ecotourism:** Nearly 80 per cent of the country is covered with tropical rainforest, which is protected by an efficient system of national parks and protected areas. Guided trips to **Raleighvallen/Voltzberg Nature Park** or **Natuurpark Brownsberg** (Brownsberg Nature Park) can be booked in Paramaribo. Some offer accommodation in lodges. Visits to indigenous village communities can also be organised and frequently involve **river tours**. One of the most popular is the five-day river tour of **Kumalu** and the **Awarra Dam** region. **Wildlife** enthusiasts can observe numerous mammals (including jaguars, pumas and ocelots), birds (such as flamingos and eagles), rare flowers (including orchids and *ixora*) as well as the black and blue morpho butterflies. Giant Leatherback sea turtles can be watched laying their eggs in the **Galibi Nature Reserve** (accessible by boat only). Further information can be obtained from the Foundation for Nature Preservation in Surinam, Cornelis Jongbawstraat 14, PO Box 12252, Paramaribo (tel: 427 102/3 *or* 476 597; website: www.stinasu.sr).

TOURIST INFORMATION

Surinam Tourism Foundation
Street address: Dr JF Nassylaan 2, Paramaribo, Surinam
Postal address: PO Box 656, Paramaribo, Surinam
Tel: 410 357.
Website: www.suriname-tourism.org

Entertainment

FOOD & DRINK: Owing to the diverse ethnic mixture of the population, Surinam offers a good variety of dishes including American, Chinese, Creole, European, Indian and Indonesian. Indonesian dishes are recommended, usually *rijsttafel* with rice (boiled or fried) and a number of spicy meat and vegetable side dishes, *nasi goreng* (Indonesian fried rice) and *bami goreng* (Indonesian fried noodles). Creole dishes include *pom* (ground tayer roots and poultry), *pastei* (chicken pie with various vegetables) and peanut soup. Indian dishes, such as *roti* (dough pancake) served with curried chicken and potatoes, and Chinese dishes, such as *chow-mein* and *chop suey*, are excellent. *Moksi meti* (various meats served on rice) is a local favourite.
Local drinks include the Indonesian *Dawet* (a coconut drink), *Gemberbier* (Creole ginger drink) and *Pilsener Parbo Bier*. There are some restaurants in Niew-Nickerie and Paramaribo, but they tend to be scarce outside the capital.
Tipping: Hotels include 10 to 15 per cent service charge and restaurants may also add 10 per cent to the bill.
NIGHTLIFE: There are several nightclubs in Paramaribo, often attached to a hotel, with live music and dancing. There are also a number of discos and several cinemas, including a drive-in. In general, it is best to stick to the hotels unless accompanied by locals who know the reputations of other nightspots, in particular those out of the town centre. The *Local Events Bulletin* lists all current activities and is usually available in hotels.
SHOPPING: Popular items include Maroon tribal woodcarvings, hand-carved and hand-painted trays and gourds, Amerindian bows and arrows, cotton hammocks, wicker and ceramic objects, gold and silver jewellery, Javanese bamboo and batik, as well as tobacco and liquor products. Chinese shops sell imported jade, silks, glass, dolls, needlework and wall decorations. **Shopping hours:** Mon-Fri 0730-1630, Sat 0730-1300.

Business

ECONOMY: Agricultural products include rice, citrus fruits, sugar and bananas, although this part of the economy is in poor financial condition, compounded by low world prices (the state banana company closed in 2002, although cause for optimism has been bolstered due to a smaller restructured banana company resuming business in March 2004). Shrimp fishing is both important and lucrative. The other main activities in this sector are livestock breeding and, most controversially, logging in Surinam's vast jungle interior. The timber is being exploited under a contract awarded to a Malaysian company, although the Government has come under pressure from the international environmental lobby to restrict the quantity. For the time being the most important industry is still mining, especially bauxite and, more recently, gold. There are also thought to be substantial reserves of iron ore, manganese, copper, nickel and platinum, as well as moderate onshore oil deposits. Apart from processing ores and food products, the industrial sector is largely devoted to the manufacture of cigarettes, drinks and chemicals.
Foreign aid, especially from The Netherlands (the former colonial power), has been essential to the economy but political disagreements between The Hague and especially the Bouterse government have meant that it has not always been forthcoming. Surinam became a full member of the Caribbean trading bloc CARICOM in 1995. Economic policy has become more austere since the accession of the Ventiaan administration which has sought to tackle Surinam's long-running fiscal and monetary difficulties under the supervision of the IMF and World Bank. The country's principal trading partners are the USA, The Netherlands, Trinidad & Tobago and Brazil.
BUSINESS ETIQUETTE: A suit is expected for business. All appointments should be honoured, though punctuality may be difficult owing to unpredictable transport. **Office hours:** Mon-Thurs 0700-1500, Fri 0700-1430.

COMMERCIAL INFORMATION

Surinam Chamber of Commerce and Industry
PO Box 149, Dr J C de Mirandastraat 10, Paramaribo, Surinam
Tel: 474 536.
E-mail: chamber@sr.net

Ministry of Foreign Affairs (Information on Conferences/ Conventions)
Lim A Postraat 25, Paramaribo, Surinam
Tel: 471 209.
E-mail: biza@sr.net

Swaziland

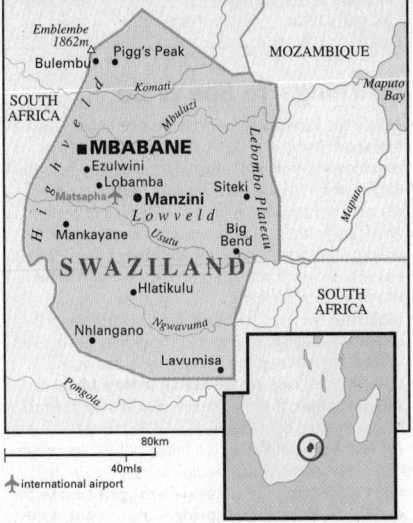

Location: Southern Africa.

Time: GMT + 2.

Overview

Swaziland is surrounded by South Africa to the north and west, and by Mozambique to the east. Although Swaziland has long been regarded as one of the most beautiful countries in Africa, it was not until an Italian and South African syndicate built southern Africa's first casino hotel on a prime valley site in the early 1990s that Swaziland geared itself towards tourism. The lush Ezulwini Valley is a miracle of nature and the seat of Swaziland's major tourist attractions, including the country's famous casino, the magnificent Royal Swazi golf course and the hot mineral spring known affectionately by locals and guests as the 'Cuddle Puddle'.

Swaziland has a number of protected nature reserves and game parks which are open for visitors and strong efforts have recently been made to bring wildlife back to the country. There are currently four Swaziland National Trust Commission (SNTC) nature reserves, namely Malolotja, Hawane, Mantenga and Mlawula, all of which are inhabited by a rich wildlife (including rare species such as the aardwolf or African finfoot) and a wide range of bird species. These reserves are characterised by some of the most beautiful landscapes in southern Africa. The SNTC has taken a number of once privately run game parks under its wing such as Mlilwane, the country's oldest established game sanctuary. Other game sanctuaries that have recently been proclaimed protected areas are Malolotsha, in the north near Piggs Peak; Hlane, in the shadow of the escarpment in the northeast; and Mkhaya. Hlane has wide open spaces supporting big herds of game where the visitor can see the old traditional scenes of Africa. Both Hlane and Malolotsha, which is situated on top of a mountain range and surrounded by steep canyons and waterfalls, are easily reached by road and different types of accommodation and tours are available. The industrial centre of Manzini lies east across the valley, a good half-hour's drive. On the way, visitors pass signposts to Swaziland's most famous waterfall, the Mantenga Falls. Throughout the year, a number of traditional festivals, dances and rituals are celebrated.

General Information

AREA: 17,363 sq km (6704 sq miles).
POPULATION: 980,722 (1997).

POPULATION DENSITY: 56.5 per sq km.
CAPITAL: Mbabane. **Population:** 73,000 (UN projection 2000).
GEOGRAPHY: Swaziland is surrounded to the north, west and south by the Mpumulanga of South Africa and to the east by Mozambique. There are four main topographical regions: the Highveld Inkangala, a wide ribbon of partly reforested, rugged country including the Usutu pine forest; the Peak Timbers in the northwest; the Middleveld, which rolls down from the Highveld through hills and fertile valleys; and the Lowveld, or bush country, with hills rising from 170 to 360m (560 to 1180ft). The Lubombo plateau is an escarpment along the eastern fringe of the Lowveld, comprising mainly cattle country and mixed farmland. One of the best-watered areas in southern Africa, Swaziland's four major rivers are the Komati, Usutu, Mbuluzi and Ngwavuma, flowing west–east to the Indian Ocean.
GOVERNMENT: Constitutional monarchy since 1973. Gained independence from the UK in 1968. **Head of State:** King Mswati III since 1986. **Head of Government:** Prime Minister Themba Dlamini since 2003. **Recent history:** In 1978, a new constitution concentrated political power in the hands of the Monarch, who appointed a Prime Minister and cabinet; the state of emergency remained in force, however. An elected Parliament, the Libandla, in which political parties remained illegal, was established, although its functions were restricted to conveying advice to the king and his principal advisory body, the Liqoqo (Supreme Council of State). The current Monarch, King Mswati III, was crowned in April 1986. Political stability continued to prove elusive during the late-1980s – the Mswati Monarchy was repeatedly threatened by plots organised by dissident members of the royal family and disaffected politicians but all were stifled with apparent ease.
The focus of opposition has been the People's United Democratic Movement (PUDEMO), which operated largely clandestinely until February 1992, when it declared itself a legal opposition party – in contravention of the Government ban on political association – and demanded a constitutional referendum. Although steady pressure has been exerted against the king from both inside and outside the country, he remains impervious to any entreaties and continues to be one of the world's few absolute monarchs. Prime Ministers who challenge or disobey royal commands are summarily dismissed. The current premier, who took up the post in 2003, is Themba Dlamini.
LANGUAGE: English and siSwati.
RELIGION: 60 per cent Christian, with most of the remainder adhering to traditional beliefs.
ELECTRICITY: 220/30 volts AC, 50Hz; 15-amp round pin plugs are in use.
SOCIAL CONVENTIONS: Traditional ways of life are still strong and Swazi culture in the form of religious music, dance, poetry and craftsmanship plays an important part in daily life. Casual wear is normal although more formal wear is customary at the casino and sophisticated hotels. Visitors wishing to camp near villages should first inform the headman. He can normally help with customs.
Photography: Permission to photograph individuals should always be sought. In some cases, a gratuity may be asked for (especially if the subject has gone to some effort to make a show – for example, by wearing traditional regalia). It is prohibited to photograph the Royal Palace, the Royal Family, uniformed police, army personnel, army vehicles or aircraft and bank buildings. Visitors wishing to photograph traditional ceremonies should first contact the Government Information Service, PO Box 451, Mbabane, Swaziland (tel: (40) 42761 or 43251; fax: (40) 43953).

Climate

Due to the variations in altitude the weather is changeable. Except in the lowland, it is rarely uncomfortably hot and nowhere very cold, although frosts occasionally occur in the Highveld which has a wetter, temperate climate. The Middleveld and Lubombo are drier and subtropical with most rain from October to March.

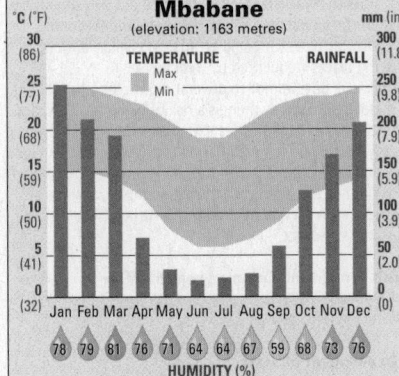

Mbabane (elevation: 1163 metres)
TEMPERATURE   RAINFALL
HUMIDITY (%)

Communications

Telephone: IDD is available. Country code: 268. Outgoing international calls must go through the international operator. Public telephones are available.
Mobile telephone: Roaming agreements exist with some international mobile phone operators. Coverage is mostly good, but can be patchy in rural areas.
Internet: There are Internet cafes in man towns.
Post: Post offices are in all main centres. Airmail to Europe is unreliable and can take from two weeks to two months. Post office hours: Mon-Fri 0800-1300 and 1400-1700, Sat 0800-1100.
MEDIA: Press: The English-language newspapers in Swaziland are *The Swazi Observer* and *The Times of Swaziland*.
TV: *Swazi TV* is a state-run channel operated by the *Swaziland Television Authority*.
Radio: State-run *Swaziland Broadcasting and Information Service* operates *The Siswati Channel*, *The English Channel* and *The Information Service*.

Passport/Visa

	Passport Required?	Visa Required? Required?	Return Ticket Required?
Full British	Yes	2/3	Yes
Australian	Yes	1	Yes
Canadian	Yes	1	Yes
USA	Yes	1	Yes
Other EU	Yes	2/3	Yes
Japanese	Yes	1	Yes

Note: *Regulations and requirements may be subject to change at short notice, and you are advised to contact the appropriate diplomatic or consular authority before finalising travel arrangements. Any numbers in the chart refer to the footnotes below.*

PASSPORTS: Passport valid for at least six months upon entry required by all.
VISAS: Required by all except the following:
(a) **1.** nationals of Australia, Canada, Japan and the USA for stays of up to two months;
(b) **2.** nationals of the EU for stays of up to two months* (except nationals of the Czech Republic, Estonia, Hungary, Latvia, Lithuania, Slovak Republic and Slovenia who *do* require a visa);
(c) nationals of Commonwealth countries for stays of up to two months (except nationals of Antigua & Barbuda, Bangladesh, Belize, Brunei, Cameroon, Dominica, India, Kiribati, Maldives, Mauritius, Mozambique, Nigeria, Pakistan, Sri Lanka, Tuvalu and Vanuatu who *do* require a visa);
(d) nationals of Iceland, Israel, Korea (Rep), Liechtenstein, Norway, San Marino, Turkey, Uruguay and Zimbabwe for stays of up to two months.
Note: * **3.** Nationals of Belgium, Denmark, Greece, Ireland, Luxembourg, The Netherlands and Portugal can also obtain a visa free of charge upon arrival and may remain in Swaziland longer than two months, at the discretion of the Immigration department. Nationals of the UK may also remain in Swaziland for an undisclosed amount of time.
Types of visa and cost: *Single-entry:* £16. *Multiple-entry:* £24 (three months); £38 (six months); £58 (nine months); £60 (12 months).
Note: Transit passengers should consult their carrying company when making reservations for up-to-date advice on whether a visa is required.
Validity: Three to six months from date of issue for stays of up to two months each. Applications for extensions should be submitted to the Chief Immigration Officer in Swaziland.
Application to: Consulate (or Consular section at Embassy or High Commission); see *Passport/Visa Information*.
Application requirements: (a) Application form. (b) Two passport-size photos. (c) Fee. (d) Valid passport. (e) Proof of means of support during stay. (f) Letter on headed paper confirming that the visitor holds return or onward tickets. (g) For all visitors except tourists, a letter of invitation from a Swazi national *or* for business trips, a letter from applicant's company giving details of the business and confirming the financial responsibility for the applicant.
Working days required: One or two unless authorisation is required, in which case the application could take several weeks.
Temporary residence: Apply to Chief Immigration Officer if staying longer than two months in Swaziland.

PASSPORT/VISA INFORMATION

Kingdom of Swaziland High Commission in the UK
20 Buckingham Gate, London SW1E 6LB, UK
Tel: (020) 7630 6611.
Website: www.swaziland.org.uk
Opening hours: Mon-Thurs 0900-1630, Fri 0900-1600 (by appointment only).

Embassy of the Kingdom of Swaziland in the USA
1712 New Hampshire Avenue, NW,
Washington, DC 20009, USA
Tel: (202) 234 5002.
E-mail: embassy@swaziland-usa.com

A B C D E F G H I J K L M N O P Q R S T U V W X Y Z

Money

Currency: Lilangeni (SZL) = 100 cents. The plural of Lilangeni is Emalangeni. Notes are in denominations of SZL200, 100, 50, 20 and 10. Coins are in denominations of SZL5, 2 and 1, and 100, 50, 20, 10, 5, 2 and 1 cents. The South African Rand is also accepted as legal tender (SZL1 = 1 Rand) although coins are not accepted.
Currency exchange: Visitors are advised to exchange Emalangeni back into their own currency before leaving Swaziland.
Credit & debit cards: American Express, MasterCard and Visa are widely accepted. Check with your credit or debit card company for details of merchant acceptability and other facilities which may be available.
Traveller's cheques: Widely accepted. Several banks will exchange travellers cheques, but to avoid additional exchange rate charges, travellers are advised to take them in Euros, Pounds Sterling or US Dollars.
Currency restrictions: The import and export of foreign and local currency is unrestricted.
Banking hours: Mon-Fri 0830-1430, Sat 0830-1100.
Exchange rate indicators:
Rate at time of publishing
£1.00= SZL11.71
$1.00= SZL6.63

Duty Free

The following items may be imported into Swaziland without incurring customs duty:
400 cigarettes and 50 cigars and 250g of tobacco; 1 bottle (max 750ml) of alcoholic beverage; 284ml of perfume per person; free export of souvenirs and presents.
Note: Married couples travelling together are allowed free import for one person only.

Public Holidays

Below are listed Public Holidays for the January 2006-June 2007 period.
2006: Jan 1 New Year's Day. **Apr 14** Good Friday. **Apr 17** Easter Monday. **Apr 19** Birthday of King Mswati. **Apr 25** National Flag Day. **May 1** Labour Day. **May 25** Ascension. **Jul 22** Birthday of the Late King Sobhuza. **Aug/Sep*** Umhlanga, Reed Dance Day. **Sep 6** Somhlolo Day (Independence Day). **Dec/Jan*** Incwala Ceremony. **Dec 25** Christmas Day. **Dec 26** Boxing Day.
2007: Jan 1 New Year's Day. **Apr 6** Good Friday. **Apr 9** Easter Monday. **Apr 19** Birthday of King Mswati. **Apr 25** National Flag Day. **May 1** Labour Day. **May 17** Ascension.
Note: *The dates of the Umhlanga and Incwala ceremonies vary according to local sightings of the moon. Contact the Embassy/High Commission for further details.

Health

	Special Precautions?	Certificate Required?
Yellow Fever	No	1
Cholera	Yes	2
Typhoid & Polio	3	N/A
Malaria	4	N/A

Note: *Regulations and requirements may be subject to change at short notice, and you are advised to contact your doctor well in advance of your intended date of departure. Any numbers in the chart refer to the footnotes below.*

1: A yellow fever vaccination certificate is required by travellers over one year of age arriving within six days from infected areas.
2: Following WHO guidelines issued in 1973, a cholera vaccination certificate is no longer a condition of entry to Swaziland. However, cholera is a risk in the country and precautions are essential. Up-to-date advice should be sought before deciding whether these precautions should include vaccination as medical opinion is divided over its effectiveness; see the *Health* appendix.
3: Vaccination against typhoid is advised.
4: Malaria risk exists throughout the year (particularly in the rainy season, from November to February) in all Lowveld areas, particularly Big Bend, Mhlume, Simunye and Tshaneni. The predominant *falciparum* strain is reported to be highly resistant to chloroquine.
Food & drink: Mains water is generally safe but bottled or sterilised water is preferable. Drinking water outside major cities and towns may be contaminated. Milk is pasteurised and dairy products are safe for consumption; exercise caution if milk is of uncertain provenance. Only eat well-cooked meat and fish, preferably served hot. Pork, salad and mayonnaise may carry increased risk. Vegetables should be cooked and fruit peeled.
Other risks: *Bilharzia* (schistosomiasis) is endemic. Avoid swimming and paddling in fresh water; swimming pools which are well chlorinated and maintained are safe.
Hepatitis A is present; *hepatitis B* is highly endemic and precautions should be taken.
Arthropod-borne diseases such as *Crimean-congo haemorrhagic fever, plague, relapsing fever, Rift valley fever* and *tick-bite fever* have been reported.
The humid climate may provoke *asthma* and other respiratory disorders.
Rabies is present.
Health care: Although medical facilities are generally limited in Swaziland, Mbabame Clinic is well-equipped to deal with minor problems. Most international visitors will use private services, frequently attached to the larger hotels. The public sector is improving and treatment is available at low cost. In emergency cases, where specialised treatment is required, the patient may be transported to a South African hospital. Health insurance is recommended. Personal medications may be brought into the country, but a doctor's note is advisable in case of questioning by authorities.

Travel - International

AIR:
The national airline is *Royal Swazi National Airways Corporation (ZC). Comair* operates flights to Johannesburg. *Swazi Airlink* runs a regular link between Manzini to Johannesburg.
Approximate flight times: From Manzini to *Johannesburg* is one hour; to *London* is 16 hours (including stopover).
Main airports: *Manzini (MTS)* (Matsapha) is 5km (3 miles) northwest of the city. *To/from the airport*: Taxi service to the city centre is available on all arrivals (travel time – 15 minutes). *Facilities*: Banks/bureaux de change, restaurants, car hire and snack bar.
Departure tax: SZL20; children under three years of age and direct transit passengers are exempt.
ROAD:
There are good roads from Johannesburg, Durban and northern KwaZulu-Natal as well as tourist buses running from KwaZulu-Natal and Mpumalanga. On crossing the border you will be required to show your passport and visa (if required). There is also a token road tax of E5 to be paid. **Bus:** There is a weekly service from Mbabane and Manzini to Johannesburg (travel time – eight hours), and a twice-weekly connection from Mbabane to Maputo.
RAIL:
A train service between Durban and Maputo travels through Swaziland stopping at Mpaka, 35km (22 miles) east of Manzini. Departures from Durban are twice weekly (travel time – 16 hours).

Travel - Internal

ROAD:
The road system is largely well developed, although there is little street lighting. Some roads are winding and roads can be rough in the bush. Small toll charges are set to be introduced on the new highway between Mbabane and Manzini. The maximum speed limit on all roads is 80kph (50mph). The legal blood alcohol limit is 0.15 per cent. Traffic drives on the left. **Bus:** There are numerous (not always entirely safe) buses connecting the different parts of the country, including non-stop buses. Minibus taxis run shorter routes at slightly higher prices than the buses. **Car hire:** There are a number of international car hire companies in Swaziland.
Documentation: An International Driving Permit is required.
Travel times: The following chart gives approximate travel times (in hours and minutes) from **Mbabane** to other major towns in Swaziland.

	Road
Manzini	**0.45**
Nhlangano	**2.00**
Piggs Peak	**1.00**
Siteki	**1.30**

Travel Advice

Most visits to Swaziland are trouble-free but you should be aware of the global risk of indiscriminate international terrorist attacks, which could be against civilian targets, including places frequented by foreigners.
Travellers are advised not to drive at night along the N4 and other isolated roads, as there is a risk of being hijacked, and livestock and unlit, parked vehicles pose additional hazards. This advice is based on information provided by the Foreign and Commonwealth Office in the UK. It is correct at time of publishing. As the situation can change rapidly, visitors are advised to contact the following organisations for the latest travel advice:

British Foreign and Commonwealth Office
Tel: (0845) 850 2829.
Website: www.fco.gov.uk

US Department of State
Website: http://travel.state.gov/travel

Accommodation

There are some good hotels in Swaziland, some of international standard, but it is necessary to book well in advance. Rates quoted are generally per person based on two people sharing. Expect prices to be significantly higher in peak season (December to January, and Easter). There are also smaller motels and inns, campsites and caravan parks outside the city. For further information, contact the Hotel and Tourism Association of Swaziland (see *Accommodation Information*). **Grading:** The star-grading system is in use.
CAMPING:
Camping is possible near almost every tourist attraction and in all the national parks.

ACCOMMODATION INFORMATION

Hotel and Tourism Association of Swaziland
PO Box 462, Oribi Court, Allister Miller Street,
Mbabane H100, Swaziland
Tel: (40) 42218.

Top Things To See & Do

- Attend the **Incwala** (a four-day fruit ceremony), which takes place every year at a time carefully chosen by astrologers (December/January). It culminates in a ritual during which the king eats the first fruit of the new season. The ceremony confers the blessing of their ancestors on the nation's consumption of these fruits. In August/ September, see the **Umhlanga** (Reed Dance), an event in which young women pay homage to the Queen Mother, Lombada.
- **Mbabane**, the capital of Swaziland, lies at the northern end of the Ezulwini Valley amid the granite peaks and valleys that make up the Dlangeni hills. The main attractions in town are the **Mall**, the **New Mall** and **Allister Miller**, the main street, named after the first European to be born there.
- The lush **Ezulwini Valley** is a miracle of nature and the seat of Swaziland's major tourist attractions. In the valley is the magnificent **Royal Swazi golf course**, the **casino**, the **hot mineral spring** – one of eight in the country – known affectionately by locals and guests as the 'Cuddle Puddle', a health studio and a cluster of fine hotels forming the **Holiday Valley** complex.
- In the heart of the Ezulwini Valley is Swaziland's royal valley, Lobamba, the spiritual and legislative capital of the kingdom. It is home to the royals' **Embo State Palace**. The **National Museum** is housed here, which offers displays on Swazi culture and has a traditional beehive village beside it.
- East across the valley is Swaziland's largest town and its commercial hub, **Manzini.** On the way here, visitors pass signposts to Swaziland's most famous waterfall, the **Mantenga Falls**, the thriving **Mantenga Arts & Crafts Centre**, the **Mlilwane Game Sanctuary**, Matsapha Airport and the industrial area of **Matsapha**, which produces everything from beer to television sets. There is an outstanding market every day except Sunday; dawn on Thursdays and Fridays is particularly worth a visit as it is when the rural people bring in their handicrafts to sell to retailers. Manzini's only other point of interest is its original Catholic mission, an elegant stone building opposite the new cathedral; it is not open to casual visitors. Unfortunately the city has little else to offer and is polluted with reckless drivers, city slickers and an ever-growing crime record.
- **Piggs Peak**, a small forestry town straggled along the main road, was named after a French prospector called William Pigg, who discovered gold nearby in 1884, where it was mined until the site was exhausted in 1954. Nearby, the **Ngwenya Glass Factory** is the origin of one of Swaziland's best-known exports, Ngwenya glass. Their products, which range from attractive wine glasses to endless trinkets in the shape of rotund animals, are made from recycled glass and are produced by highly skilled workers, who can be watched in action.
- **The South:** The scenery, particularly along the drive from Mahamba to Manzini through the Grand Valley, is superb, and the road passes near most of the historical sites of the Swazi royal house. **Big Bend** itself, dominated by a huge sugar mill, is only worth visiting for its hotel, the **New Bend Inn**. It is a slightly run-down colonial establishment with superb views of the valley and well-positioned bars; it is a lively Swazi haunt at weekends, when major parties take place. The area is currently being developed for tourism, and the first project has been the construction of another casino hotel at **Nhlangano**, about 120km (75 miles) south of Mbabane. The nearby **Mkondo River** twists its way through gorges and valleys, past waterfalls, pools and rapids and, in the distance, the

mountain ranges gleam brown, mauve and blue. Some of Swaziland's finest paintings are found in this area. Other indigenous paintings are located in the mountains north of Mbabane.

- **Whitewater rafting** trips are available on the **Great Usutu River** in the Mkhaya Game Reserve.
- **Hiking:** Popular hikes include the ascent to **Malolotsha Falls** at Piggs Peak; **Sibebe Mountain**, a huge granite outcrop that provides a scenic spot for a picnic; and the climb up **Emlembe**, Swaziland's highest peak.
- **Nature Reserves & Game Parks:**
- **Mkhaya Nature Reserve:** Roughly 30km (19 miles) north of **Big Bend** is Mkhaya Nature Reserve, situated along a turn-off from the brilliantly named village of **Phuzumoya** ('drink the wind') in classic lowveld scrubland, filled with acacia and thorn trees. Ted Reilly initially purchased Mkhaya to save the long-horned **Nguni cattle** when white beef-farmers regarded them as too puny and unproductive for their industry, and replaced them with imported stock. Today, the cattle graze alongside zebra, wildebeest and antelope, just as they always used to. Among the other endangered species at Mkhaya are the rare **black rhinos** and the near-extinct **roan antelope**.
- **Mlilwane Wildlife Sanctuary:** This reserve, near Lobamba, is in the heart of the Ezulwini Valley. Its name, **Mlilwane**, refers to the little fire that appears on occasion when lightning strikes the granite mountains. The wildlife is predominantly herbivorous, including antelope, giraffe and zebra, but crocodiles are not uncommon. Over 100km (62 miles) of road enables you to drive through the park to view game, or guided walks and drives can be arranged through the park office.
- **Mlawula Nature Reserve:** The **Lubombo Mountains** that run along the eastern border of Mlawula Nature Reserve provide fantastic views of both Swaziland and the western fringes of Mozambique. Unique species of **ironwood trees** and **cycads** grow on the slopes. There are well-organised trails through the reserve. The **Mlawula stream** and more substantial **Mbuluzi River** both flow through some spectacular valleys in this reserve, and early Stone Age tools over one million years old have been found along their beds.

For more information, contact the Swaziland National Trust Commission, PO Box 100, Lobamba, Swaziland (tel: (41) 61481/9 or 61179; website: www.sntc.org.sz); or the Ministry of Tourism (see *Tourist Information*).

Entertainment

FOOD & DRINK: Restaurants are found mainly in the larger centres and at hotels. Most serve international cuisine: Greek, Hungarian and Indian food is available. Food stalls in the local markets sell traditional Swazi meat stew and maize meal or stamped mealies and roasted corn on the cob (in season).
There is a good selection of spirits, beers and wines. Traditional Swazi beer can be tasted in rural areas. There are no formal licensing hours.
Tipping: 10 to 15 per cent of the bill is customary in restaurants and hotels.
NIGHTLIFE: In the main centres of Mbabane and Ezulwini Valley, there are nightclubs and discos, some with live music and cabaret. The main attraction in Ezulwini Valley is the casino at the Royal Swazi Hotel. There is also a cinema there.
SHOPPING: There is a modern shopping complex in Mbabane but local markets are always interesting places to shop. Purchases from craft centres include beadwork, basketry, grass and sisal mats, copperware, wooden bowls, local gemstone jewellery, wooden and soapstone carvings, calabashes, knobkerries, battleaxes, walking sticks, *karosses* (animal skin mats), drums, woven cloth and batik and tie-dye, which are often incorporated into traditional Swazi garments. **Shopping hours:** Mon-Fri 0800-1700, Sat 0800-1300.

Business

ECONOMY: The economy is dominated by and closely linked with that of South Africa, and the country is a member of the Southern African Customs Union (through which the Government receives around half its total revenue). Agriculture is by far the largest part of the economy, employing over 75 per cent of the working population. Sugar, cotton and fruit are the main cash crops. Tobacco and rice are recent additions to the country's produce, while livestock rearing is traditionally important. The industrial sector, which contributes over 40 per cent of GDP, is mainly concerned with processing agricultural products, largely food and wood products including paper, and also the production of textiles and metal goods. The country's mining industry produces coal, of which there are extensive reserves, and diamonds but the other main products of asbestos and iron ore have been in long-term decline due to falling export demand. The removal of sanctions against South Africa gave a boost to the Swazi economy but the gains have been undermined by a number of factors: drought, low commodity prices, the impact of widespread HIV/AIDS infection on the workforce, the low value of the South African rand (to which the Swazi currency is linked). Moreover, opposition from the business community to King Mswati's autocratic rule has made for a poor commercial environment. Unemployment remains at an estimated 40 per cent. The Government has made efforts to attract foreign capital to fund future development, notably through a number of prestige construction and infrastructure projects. Apart from South Africa, which dominates Swazi trade, the most important trading partners are the UK and France.
BUSINESS ETIQUETTE: Lightweight suits are generally expected for business. Appointments are necessary and business cards are exchanged. English is widely spoken in business circles. **Office hours:** Mon-Fri 0800-1300 and 1400-1645.
CONFERENCES/CONVENTIONS: The principal facilities are at the Royal Swazi Convention Centre in the Ezulwini Valley, which has seating for up to 600 people. Several hotels also have facilities for smaller numbers, with back-up services. The Ministry of Tourism (see *Top Things To See & Do*) can supply information.

Sweden

Location: Northeast Europe, Scandinavia.

Time: GMT + 1 (GMT + 2 from last Sunday in March to Saturday before last Sunday in October).

Overview

Sweden is a land of cultural contrast, from the Danish influence of the southwest to the nomadic Laplanders in the wild Arctic north. And while urban Sweden is stylish, modern and sophisticated, the countryside offers many simpler pleasures for those in search of tranquillity. Sweden's scenery has a gentler charm than that of neighbouring Norway's rugged coast. Much of Sweden is swathed in forest, and there are thousands of lakes, notably large stretches of water between Gothenburg and the capital, Stockholm. The lakeside resort of Östersund, in the centre of Sweden, is popular with Scandinavians, but most visitors opt first for the cities and the Baltic islands: the largest island, Gotland, with its array of ruined medieval churches, is a particular highlight. Another major attraction is the so-called 'Kingdom of Crystal', a forested area between Malmö and Stockholm boasting many fine glassworks.

Historically, Sweden has an interesting story. Its contacts with the outside world began in earnest during Viking times, when in addition to the well-documented raiding, there was extensive trading around the Baltic, primarily dealing in furs and weaponry.

Swedish connections with the other Scandinavian countries, Norway and Denmark, have been strong since late medieval times. The monarchies of all three are closely linked, and at various times, one king or queen has ruled over more than one of the countries. Many significant battles have been fought over control of the three dominions. Indeed, Norway only fully shed Swedish control

for the last time in the early years of the 20th Century. Although it did not gain a Parliament until the 19th Century, modern Sweden is known worldwide as a model of social democracy and tolerance. But there is a strong streak of independence, too; in common with the United Kingdom and Denmark, it has so far opted out of the common European Union currency system.

The land and its people have an air of reserved calm, and while best known for its automotive and musical exports – Volvo and Abba are pretty much household names – a strong historical undertone bubbles close beneath the surface. Nowhere is this more apparent than in Stockholm, where dozens of museums deal with all imaginable aspects of the past, and medieval and Baroque edifices housing boutiques and cafes overlook the attractive harbour.

General Information

AREA: 449,964 sq km (173,732 sq miles).

POPULATION: 8.9 million (UN, 2005).

POPULATION DENSITY: 19.7 per sq km.

CAPITAL: Stockholm. **Population:** 765,044 (2005).

GEOGRAPHY: Sweden is bordered by Norway to the west and Finland to the northeast, with a long Baltic coast to the east and south. Approximately half the country is forested and most of the many thousands of lakes are situated in the southern central area. The largest lake is Vänern, with an area of 5540 sq km (2140 sq miles). Swedish Lapland to the north is mountainous and extends into the Arctic Circle.

GOVERNMENT: Constitutional monarchy. Gained independence from Denmark in 1523. **Head of State:** King Carl XVI Gustaf since 1973. **Head of Government:** Prime Minister Göran Persson since 1996. **Recent history:** Two tragic events overshadow Sweden's recent past – the assassination of Prime Minister Olaf Palme (known on the world stage as a leading exponent of Scandinavian neutrality) in 1986, and the murder of Foreign Minister Anna Lindh in 2003, days before a national referendum rejected membership of the common European currency system. From the end of the Second World War, the nation has enjoyed increasing prosperity, and has developed an extremely supportive welfare state, funded by relatively high taxation. However, by the beginning of the 1990s, the economy was no longer performing as well as it had done and the centre-right coalition government of Carl Bildt, which took office in 1991, instituted an austerity programme. This was designed to reduce inflation, cut the budget deficit by reducing public expenditure and de-regulate and privatise much of Sweden's extensive public sector. Relations with the (then) European Community had become the major issue in Swedish politics, although with all the major political parties favouring membership, the issue was less than contentious. Negotiations for full membership began in 1993. These were completed by the September 1994 election, which was won by the SAP; Sweden joined the EU at the beginning of 1995. Sweden chose not to join the European single currency at its inception in 1999; public support was lacking and the government felt that economic conditions were not right. By 2003, the Government was prepared to sign on, but a referendum that September rejected the Euro. Another general election will take place during 2006.

LANGUAGE: Swedish. Lapp is spoken by the Sámi population in the north; there are also Finnish-speaking minorities. English is taught as the first foreign language from the age of nine.

RELIGION: Around 86 per cent of the population belong to the Church of Sweden (Evangelical Lutheran), which separated from the state in January 2000; other Protestant minorities constitute the majority of the remainder.

ELECTRICITY: 230 volts, three-phase AC, 50Hz. Two-pin continental plugs are used.

SOCIAL CONVENTIONS: Normal courtesies should be observed. It is customary for the guest to refrain from drinking until the host makes a toast. The guest should also thank the host for the meal with *Tack för maten*. Casual dress is acceptable for everyday occasions; smarter wear for social occasions, exclusive restaurants and clubs. Evening wear (black tie) will usually be specified when required. Smoking is prohibited on public transport and in most public buildings.

Climate

In spite of its northern position, Sweden has a relatively mild climate which varies greatly, owing to its length. The summers can be very hot but get shorter further north. The midnight sun can be seen between mid-May and mid-June above the Arctic Circle. Winters can be bitterly cold, especially in the north.

Required clothing: Light- to mediumweights for summer, heavyweights for winter and rainwear all year.

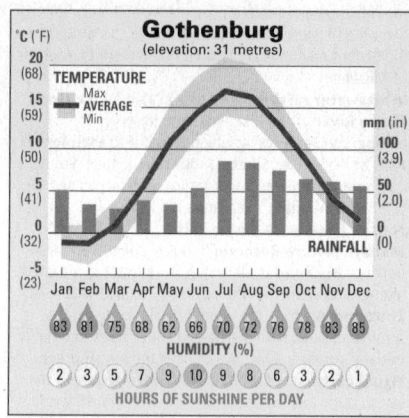

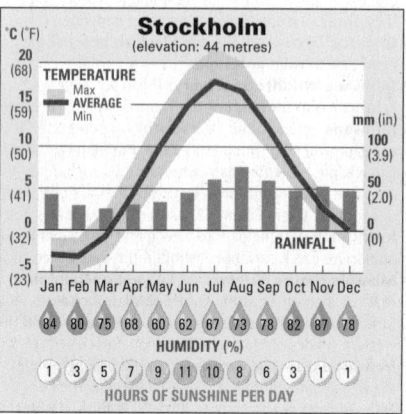

Communications

Telephone: Full IDD is available. Country code: 46. Coin-operated pay phones no longer exist and they are all now card-operated. Cards are readily available from kiosks and newsagents and instructions in English are displayed in most booths. Credit card phones (indicated by a 'CCC' sign) are widely available.

Mobile telephone: Coverage is available across most of the country.

Internet: Internet cafes exist in all main urban areas but are scarcer outside of these areas.

Post: Post office hours: Usually open during normal shopping hours (Mon-Fri 0800-2200, Sat 0900-1500). Some branches may be closed Saturday during July. Post boxes are yellow. Stamps and aerograms are on sale at post offices and also at most bookstalls and stationers. Airmail within Europe takes three to four days.

MEDIA: The Swedish public enjoys a wide variety of public and commercial broadcast services, though until relatively recently public TV and radio had a near-monopoly of the airwaves. Around 66 per cent of households have cable or satellite TV. Digital terrestrial broadcasting was launched by SVT in 1999. Swedes are among the top consumers of newspapers in the world.

Credit: www.imagebank.sweden.se ©Bo Lind/Swedish Travel and Tourism Council

Press: The provinces have their own newspapers which are widely read in their respective regions; the major dailies are confined largely to the capital and include such titles as *Aftonbladet* (website: www.aftonbladet.se), *Dagens Nyheter* (website: www.dn.se), *Expressen* (website: www.expressen.se) and *Svenska Dagbladet* (website: www.svd.se). Many papers are financed by political parties but independence and freedom of the press is firmly maintained. All papers are in Swedish. *The Local* (website: www.thelocal.se) provides English-language online news.

TV: *Sveriges Televison (SVT)* operates SVT1, SVT 2, SVT24 (news channel) and SVT Europa. *TV4, TV3, Kana; 5* and *ZTV* are other commerical channels available through satellite and/or cable.

Radio: *Sveriges Radio* operates *P1, P2, P3* and *P4. Radio Sweden International* broadcasts in a number of languages, including English. *Rix FM, NRJ, Mix Megapol* and *Radio Match* are commercial networks.

Passport/Visa

	Passport Required?	Visa Required?	Return Ticket Required?
Full British	1	No	No
Australian	Yes	No	No
Canadian	Yes	No	No
USA	Yes	No	No
Other EU	1/2	No	No
Japanese	Yes	No	No

Note: *Regulations and requirements may be subject to change at short notice, and you are advised to contact the appropriate diplomatic or consular authority before finalising travel arrangements. Any numbers in the chart refer to the footnotes below.*

Note: (a) Sweden is a signatory to the 1995 **Schengen Agreement.** For further details about passport/visa regulations within the Schengen area, see the introductory section *How to Use this Guide.* (b) Sweden does not recognise some Somali passports issued after 31st January 1991; check with Consulate or Consular section at Embassy for further details.

PASSPORTS: Passport valid for at least three months beyond length of stay required by all except:
(a) **1.** EU/EEA nationals (EU + Iceland, Liechtenstein, Norway) and Swiss nationals holding a valid national ID card.

Note: EU and EEA nationals are only required to produce evidence of their EU/EEA nationality and identity in order to be admitted to any EU/EEA Member State. This evidence can take the form of a valid national passport *or* national identity card. Either is acceptable. Possession of a return ticket, any length of validity on their document, sufficient funds for the length of their proposed visit should *not* be imposed.

(b) **2.** nationals of Denmark, Finland, Iceland and Norway, holding travel documents issued for travel between these countries.

VISAS: Required by all except the following:
(a) nationals of the countries referred to in the chart and listed under passport exemptions above for stays of up to three months (based on individual circumstances);
(b) nationals of Andorra, Argentina, Bolivia, Brazil, Brunei, Bulgaria, Chile, Costa Rica, Croatia, El Salvador, Guatemala, Honduras, Hong Kong (SAR), Israel, Korea (Rep), Liechtenstein, Macau (SAR), Malaysia, Mexico, Monaco, New Zealand, Nicaragua, Panama, Paraguay, San Marino, Singapore, Switzerland, Uruguay and Venezuela for stays of up to three months;
(c) those continuing their journey, holding tickets with confirmed reservations and required travel documents, arriving and departing from/to a Schengen country and not leaving the transit area.

Note: A transit visa is required by nationals of the following countries (if holding a visa valid for less than three months): Afghanistan, Bangladesh, Congo (Dem Rep), Eritrea, Ethiopia, Ghana, India, Iran, Iraq, Nigeria, Pakistan, Somalia and Sri Lanka.

Validity: One to 90 days.

Types of visa and cost: £25 (price is subject to change depending on the exchange rate). A uniform type of visa, the *Schengen* visa, is issued for tourist, business and private visits. Visa fees are non-refundable and payable on submission of the visa application.

Application to: Consulate (or Consular section at Embassy); see *Passport/Visa Information.* Travellers visiting just one Schengen country should apply to the Consulate of that country; travellers visiting more than one Schengen country should apply to the Consulate of the country chosen as the main destination *or* the country they will enter first (if they have no main destination).

Application requirements: (a) Valid passport with at least one blank page. (b) Two recent passport-size photos. (c) Fee, payable in cash or postal order (only if sent by post). (d) Completed, signed application form. (e) Proof of

occupation/student status. (f) Proof of purpose of visit (invitation letter from Swedish company/friend for business visas/private-visit visas, or evidence of pre-booked hotel accommodation. (g) Stamped, registered, self-addressed envelope for return of passport. (h) Health insurance covering 30,000, emergency treatment by a doctor, urgent ambulance transportation and transportation back to applicant's home. (i) Written consent from parents for minors. (j) Proof of means of support during stay may be required by some nationals. *Transit:* (a), (d) and (k) Copy of airline tickets.

Working days required: Seven to 60. However, applicants are advised to apply at least 30 days before the date of their intended departure.

Temporary residence: Enquire at Embassy.

Money

Currency: Swedish Krona (SEK) = 100 öre. Notes are in denominations of SEK1000, 500, 100, 50 and 20. Coins are in denominations of SEK10, 5, 2 and 1, and 50 öre.

Currency exchange: Currency can be converted at FOREX foreign exchange agencies; these are found in major cities, airports and ferry terminals etc. ATMs are widely available.

Credit & debit cards: American Express, Diners Club, MasterCard and Visa are all widely accepted, as well as Eurocheque cards. Most shops and restaurants require ID when paying with a credit card. Check with your credit or debit card company for details of merchant acceptability and other facilities which may be available.

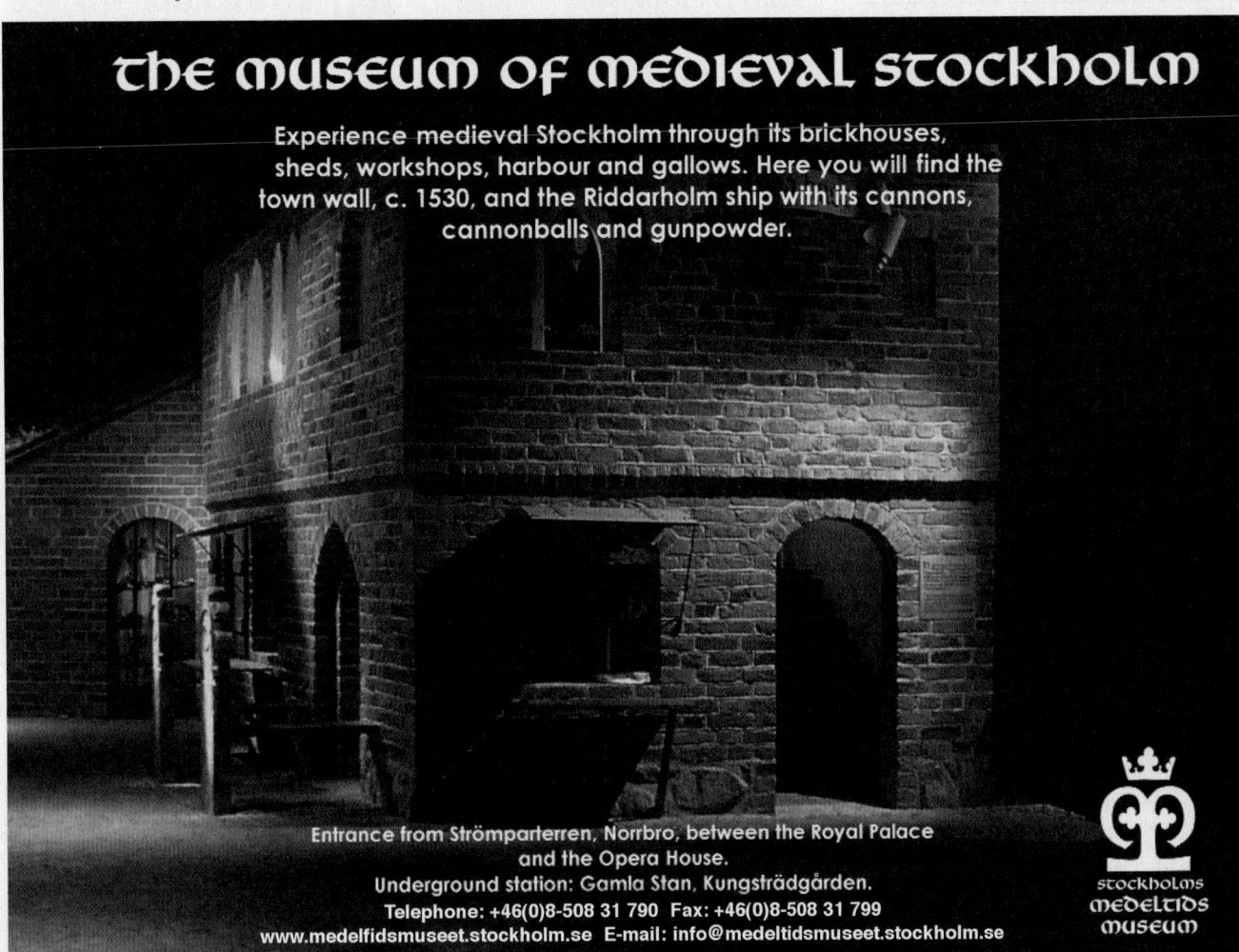

Traveller's cheques: Widely accepted. A nominal fee is charged when paying with traveller's cheques. To avoid additional exchange rate charges, travellers are advised to take traveller's cheques in Euros, Pounds Sterling or US Dollars.

Currency restrictions: There are no restrictions on the import or export of local or foreign currency.

Banking hours: Mon-Wed and Fri 1000-1500, Thurs 1000-1600/1730. Some banks in larger cities have longer opening hours and are open at weekends.

Exchange rate indicators:
Rate at time of publishing
£1.00= SEK13.63
$1.00= SEK7.73

Duty Free

The following items may be imported into Sweden without incurring customs duty:

200 cigarettes or 100 cigarillos or 50 cigars or 250g of tobacco*; 1l spirits over 22 per cent or 2l fortified or sparkling wine, 2l wine and 32l beer*; a reasonable quantity of perfume; gifts up to a value of SEK1700.

Note: *Travellers must be over 18 years of age to import any cigarettes or tobacco products; and over 20 years of age to import any alcoholic beverages. These regulations are strictly enforced.

Prohibited items: Narcotics, firearms, ammunition, weapons, most meat and dairy products, eggs, plants, potatoes from outside the EU, endangered species, fireworks and alcoholic beverages of over 60 per cent alcohol (120° proof).

Abolition of duty free goods within the EU: On 30 June 1999, the sale of duty-free alcohol and tobacco at airports and at sea was abolished in all of the original 15 EU member states. Of the 10 new member states that joined the EU on 1 May 2004, these rules already apply to Cyprus and Malta. There are transitional rules in place for visitors returning to one of the original 15 EU countries from one of the other new EU countries. But for the original 15, plus Cyprus and Malta, there are now no limits imposed on importing tobacco and alcohol products from one EU country to another (with the exceptions of Denmark, Finland and Sweden, where limits *are* imposed). Travellers should note that they may be required to prove at customs that the goods purchased are for personal use *only*.

Public Holidays

Below are listed Public Holidays for the January 2006-June 2007 period.

2006: Jan 1 New Year's Day. **Jan 5** Eve of Epiphany.* **Jan 6** Epiphany. **Apr 13** Maundy Thursday. **Apr 14** Good Friday. **Apr 17** Easter Monday. **Apr 30** Valborg's Eve.* **May 1** Labour Day. **May 25** Ascension. **Jun 5** Whit Monday. **Jun 23** Midsummer's Eve.* **Jun 24** Midsummer Holiday. **Nov 3** All Saint's Eve.* **Nov 4** All Saints' Day. **Dec 24** Christmas Eve.* **Dec 25** Christmas Day. **Dec 26** Boxing Day.
2007: Jan 1 New Year's Day. **Jan 5** Eve of Epiphany.* **Jan 6** Epiphany. **Apr 5** Maundy Thursday. **Apr 6** Good Friday. **Apr 9** Easter Monday. **Apr 30** Valborg's Eve.* **May 1** Labour Day. **May 17** Ascension. **May 28** Whit Monday.
Note: *Shops and offices will often close half a day early on the day before an official holiday.

Health

	Special Precautions?	Certificate Required?
Yellow Fever	No	No
Cholera	No	No
Typhoid & Polio	No	N/A
Malaria	No	N/A

Note: *Regulations and requirements may be subject to change at short notice, and you are advised to contact your doctor well in advance of your intended date of departure. Any numbers in the chart refer to the footnotes below.*

Other risks: *Lyme disease* is relatively common in the south of the country, especially during the summer months. *Tickbourne encephalitis,* a viral infection, is present. *Diphyllobothriasis* occurs rarely along the Baltic coast.

Health care: European Economic Area (EEA) and Switzerland: If you or any of your dependants are suddenly taken ill or have an accident during a visit to an EEA country or Switzerland, free or reduced-cost necessary treatment is available – in most cases on production of a valid European Health Insurance Card (EHIC). Each country has different rules about state medical provision. In some, treatment is free. In many countries you will have to pay part or all of the cost, and then claim a full or partial refund. The EHIC gives access to state-provided medical treatment only and the scheme gives no entitlement to medical repatriation costs, nor does it cover ongoing illnesses of a non-urgent nature, so comprehensive travel insurance is

advised. Note that the EHIC replaces the Form E111, which will no longer be valid after 31 December 2005. Some restrictions apply, depending on your nationality.

Health care standards in Sweden are good. Hospital services are provided at county and regional levels; the latter have a greater range of specialist fields. Make sure the doctor you see is affiliated to the public insurance scheme. You must show your European Health Insurance Card (EHIC), or you will be charged the full cost of the treatment. With an EHIC, you will still have to pay part of the cost, which is not refundable. You will also have to pay the full cost of dental treatment up to a fixed limit, and most of the cost above this limit. Any reductions will be made before you get your bill. Dental surgeries or clinics are indicated by *Tandläkare* or *Folktandvården* signs and emergency service is available in major cities out of hours. You will have to pay the full cost of any prescription drugs up to a limit, and part of any costs above this limit. If you are taking prescribed medicines, make sure you have an adequate supply before leaving for Sweden. You can go to any public hospital. In-patient care is free, but you will have to pay part of the cost of any outpatient care. There is a fixed, non-refundable daily charge. Health insurance is recommended to cover emergency evacuation. More information can be obtained in Sweden from the *Lokala Försäkringskassan* (local Social Insurance Office).

Travel - International

AIR:

The national airline is *SAS Scandinavian Airlines System (SK)* (website: www.sas.se).

Approximate flight times: From Stockholm to *London* is approximately two hours 30 minutes. From Gothenburg to *London* is two hours. From Stockholm to *Los Angeles* is 14 hours 10 minutes; to *New York* is 10 hours 10 minutes.

Main airports: *Stockholm (STO)* (Arlanda) (website: www.arlanda.lfv.se) is 42km (26 miles) north of the city. *To/from the airport:* There are frequent bus services operating between the airport and the city from 0625-2305 (travel time – 40 minutes). *Arlanda Express* trains leave for the city every 15 minutes between 0600-2359 (travel time – 20 minutes). Trains travel to a range of destinations, including Sundsvall, Falun, Mora and Uppsala from the airport. Taxi services are also available. *Facilities:* Duty free shop, car hire, banks/bureaux de change, cash dispenser, restaurant/bar, coffee shop and tourist information. There is a good selection of hotels within 10km of the airport.

Gothenburg (GOT) (Landvetter) (website: www.landvetter.lfv.se) is 24km (15 miles) east of the city (travel time – 25 minutes). *To/from the airport:* Coach services are frequent between the airport and the Central Station (every 15 minutes). Buses and taxis are available into Gothenburg, as well as to and from Copenhagen (travel time - 50 minutes). Car rental is also available. *Facilities:* Duty free shop, car hire, bank/bureau de change, restaurant/bar and coffee shop.

Malmö Sturup (MMX) (website: www.sturup.com) is 31km (20 miles) east of the city (travel time – 35 minutes). *To/from the airport:* Bus and taxi services go to the city. *Facilities:* Bureau de change and a duty-free shop.

Malmö City Hovercraft (HMA), 200m (650ft) from the Central Station, is now the city's main terminal for international air passengers using the hovercraft service operated by SAS which connects with flights at *Copenhagen Airport.* The terminal has its own duty free facilities. Taxi services are available.

For more information on airports, contact LFV (website: www.lfv.se).

SEA:

Main ports: *Gothenburg* (website: www.portgot.se), *Sundsvalls Hamn* (website: www.sundsvallshamn.se), *Hargs Hamn* (website: www.hargshamn.se) and *Trelleborg* (website: www.tralleborgshamn.se).

DFDS Seaways ferries sail all year round from Newcastle to Gothenburg (travel time – 24 hours). There are also ferry connections from Swedish ports to other destinations including Copenhagen, Gdansk, Helsingør, Kiel, Klaipeda, Oslo, Riga, St Petersburg and Tallinn.

RAIL:

One UK–Sweden route is from London (Victoria and Liverpool Street) to Hook of Holland or Ostend, and onwards via Copenhagen (travel time – 22-25 hours). There are connections by ferry from Denmark and through rail routes from Norway (Oslo, Narvik and Trondheim). However, the quickest route is to take the *Eurostar* train to Brussels, and then to catch a connection to Hamburg and on to Stockholm.

The Swedish high-speed train *x2000* travels from Oslo to Stockholm/Gothenburg.

Inlandsbanan (inland railway) is a 1300km route from Kristinehamn (Mid-Sweden) to Gällivare (North). It is a provately owned company offering tours during the summer months. Bicycles can be taken on the trains.

Connex AB operates trains from Stockholm to Gothenburg. Other destinations on the route include Kiruna, Luleå, Umeå and Sundsvall.

Rail passes: The *Inter-Rail* pass offers unlimited second-class train travel in up to 29 European countries (includes Morocco and Turkey) split into eight zones (A-H). Three different tickets are available: a ticket covering one zone (two to six countries, 16 days validity), a ticket covering two zones (six to 10 countries, 22 days' validity) and an *All Zone Pass* (29 countries, one month's validity). Ferry services between Italy and Greece are included. Passengers must be resident in Europe for at least six months before the pass is used. Travel is not allowed in the passenger's country of residence. Travellers under 26 years receive a reduction of about 30 per cent. Children's tickets are reduced by about 50 per cent. Supplements are required for some high-speed services, seat reservations and couchettes. Discounts are offered on *Eurostar* and some ferry routes. Available from *Inter Rail* (website: www.interrailnet.com).

The *Eurailpass* offers unlimited first-class train travel in 17 European countries. Tickets are valid for 15 days, 21 days, one month, two months or three months. The *Eurailpass Saver* ticket offers discounts for two or more people travelling together. The *Eurailpass Youth* ticket is available to those under 26 and offers unlimited second-class train travel. The *Eurailpass Flexi* allows either 10 or 15 travel days within a two-month period. The *Eurail Selectpass* is valid in three, four or five bordering countries and allows five, six, eight or 10 travel days (or 15 for five countries) in a two-month period. The *Eurail Regional Pass* allows four to 10 travel days in a two-month period in one of nine regions (usually two or more countries). Children receive a 50 per cent reduction. The passes cannot be sold to residents of Europe, Turkey, Morocco, Algeria, Tunisia or the Russian Federation. Available from *The Eurail Group* (website: www.eurail.com).

The *ScanRail* pass can be used for extensive travel of five or 10 days in two months or 21 consecutive days across Denmark, Finland, Norway and Sweden.

Payment of supplement if required on some trains. Seat reservation, couchette, sleeper or cabin charges are not included in the cost of the pass and are payable at the normal rate. The *ScanRail* pass also entitles holders to free travel on some ferry and buss routes as well as up to 50 per cent discount on ferries, buses and private railway throughout Scandinavia, free or discounted admission (up to 50 per cent off) to railway museums in Denmark, Finland, Norway and Sweden and reduced room rated at 160 hotels throughout Scandinavia. Available from *Rail Europe* (website: www.raileurope.co.uk/railpasses/scanrail.htm).

ROAD:

From the UK visitors can either drive to Sweden through Europe via Denmark or Germany, or catch a car ferry from Harwich (all year) to Gothenburg on the southwest coast (sailing time – 24 hours).

The Øresund Fixed Link, spanning 16km (10 miles) of waterway, joins the cities of Malmö (Sweden) and Copenhagen (Denmark). The link comprises a suspension bridge and an underwater tunnel, joined in the middle by an artificial island. It was designed to provide better connections between the Scandinavian peninsula and the European continent. **Coach:** There are services from London (Victoria), Dover and Folkstone to a number of Swedish cities throughout the year, taking approximately 30 hours (restricted service in winter). There are numerous and excellent road links with all neighbouring countries. *Eurolines* (52 Grosvenor Gardens, London, SW1W 0AU, UK; tel: (08705) 143 219; website: www.eurolines.com) and *National Express* (ensign Court, 4 Vicarage Road, Edgbaston, Birmingham B15 3ES; tel: (08705) 808 080; website: www.nationalexpress.com) run regular coach services from the UK to Sweden.

Travellers can either choose Mini-Pass breaks or book a 15-, 30- or 60-day pass. The six Mini-Passes give travellers the freedom to visit three cities, with prices starting at £55. Travellers can stay as long as they like in each city.

Øresund Runt Card: This pass enables visitors to travel on both sides of the Øresund River (Sweden and Denmark) on boats or trains. The ticket can be bought from the Malmo Tourism Office at Central Station.

Travel - Internal

AIR:

SAS serves over 30 local airports. Travel by air is relatively cheap and efficient and there are a number of reduced fares offered by *SAS*; contact the airline for further details.

SEA/LAKE:

Unlike Norway and Finland, there are few domestic ferry services in Sweden. The various archipelagos on the southeast coast are served by small ferries, the most comprehensive network being within the Stockholm archipelago, for which you can buy an island-hopping boat pass. The other major link is between the Baltic island of Gotland and the mainland at Nynäshamn and Oskarshamn, which are very popular routes in summer; booking ahead is strongly recommended. There are frequent coastal sailings to all ports and on the hundreds of lakes throughout the country, especially in the north. For details contact local authorities.

Canal: The Gota canal (served by vintage steamer; website: www.gotakanal.se) connects Gothenburg and Stockholm.

RAIL:

The excellent and extensive rail system is run by *Swedish State Railways* (SJ), SE-105 50 Stockholm (tel: (468) 762 20000; website: www.sj.se). The network is more concentrated in the populated south where hourly services run between the main cities, but routes extend to the forested and sparsely populated lake area of the north, which is a scenic and popular holiday destination. Restaurant cars and sleepers are provided on many trains. Reservations are essential for most express services. *x2000* high-speed trains travel from Stockholm to Gothenburg; other destinations on the route include Jönköping, Sundvall, Gävle, Malmö and Härnosand. Motorail car-sleeper services are operated during the summer on the long-distance routes from Malmö, Gothenburg and Västerås to Kiruna and Luleå.

Sweden Rail Pass: The pass offers unlimited travel for three to eight days in one month. Supplements for seat, sleepers, etc are not included in the pass. Up to two children under 16 can travel free with one adult and reduced fares are available for others.

The *Euro Domino* pass enables holders anything from three to eight days' extensive travel within a one-month period on the entire rail network of their chosen country. It is valid in 28 European countries and North Africa, including the ferry service from Brindisi (Italy) to Igoumenitsa (Greece). The purchase a *EuroDomino* pass you must have been a resident in Europe for at least six months and a passport number is required at time of booking. It is not permitted to purchase a pass for travel within your own country of residence.

To qualify for the youth rates, you must be under 26 years on the first date of validity of the pass. Children aged four-11 years inclusive pay half the adult fares rounded up to the nearest pound. Children under four years travel for free. Seat reservations, couchette and sleeper charges are not included in the cost of the pass and are payable at the normal rate. Passholder fares are payable on some services. Reservation/Supplement charges are payable on all trains within Spain. Available from *Rail Europe* (website: www.raileurope.co.uk/railpasses/eurodomino.htm).

ROAD:

Traffic drives on the right. Sweden's roads are well-maintained and relatively uncrowded, but watch out for animals crossing the road in remote areas. Credit and debit cards are becoming more acceptable as a means of payment at petrol stations. Most petrol stations have 24-hour automatic petrol pumps; they accept SKr100 and 20 notes. **Bus:** Express coach services and local buses are run by *Connex* (website: www.connex.com) and *Swebus* (website: www.swebus.se). Cheap and efficient links are available to all towns. Many coach operators do special offers on tickets on weekends (Friday to Sunday). Information is available in Sweden from local tourist offices. The *Gothenburg, Malmö* and *Stockholm Passes* (one-, two- or three-day) offer free public transport in those areas as well as free admission to selected museums and tourist attractions. Cards can be purchased from tourist information centres, train stations, camping sites or youth hostels. **Taxi:** Available in all towns and at airports. Intercity taxis are also available. Taxi drivers should be tipped around 10 per cent. **Car hire:** Available in most towns and cities. All international agencies are represented. **Regulations:** Speed limits outside built-up areas are 110, 90 or 70kph (68, 56 or 43mph) depending on road width and traffic density. In built-up areas the limit is 50kph (31mph) or 30kph (19mph) in school areas. Severe fines and sometimes prison sentences are imposed on drivers over the alcohol limit (0.02 per cent). There are on-the-spot fines for traffic offences. The use of dipped headlights is compulsory in the daytime for cars and motorcycles. Crash helmets are compulsory for motorcyclists. Seatbelts must be worn at all times. Children under seven may not travel in a car if it is not equipped with a special child restraint or a normal seat belt adapted for the child's use. Emergency warning triangles are obligatory. Studded tyres are only permitted from 1 November to the first Monday after the Easter holiday. **Documentation:** National driving licence is sufficient, but it must include a photo or it will not be recognised. The minimum age for car drivers is 18; for motorcyclists it is 17. The car's log book and written permission must be carried if driving someone else's car. A Green Card is not required by Swedish authorities, but it tops up the cover provided by a domestic policy. It is advisable to check the validity of insurance policies prior to departure.

URBAN:

Public transport is efficient, comprehensive and well-integrated. Stockholm has bus, trams, metro (*T-banan*) and local rail services. Pre-purchase multi-tickets and passes are sold, though single tickets can also be obtained on the bus. There are trams in Gothenburg and Norrköping. Taxis are widely available; large taxi companies are cheaper than independents. Several of the main cities, particularly Stockholm, have boat excursions and services.

Credit: www.imagebanksweden.se©Richard Ryan / Stockholm Visitors Board

Travel Times: The following chart gives approximate travel times (in hours and minutes) from **Stockholm** to other major cities/towns in Sweden.

	Air	Road	Rail
Gothenburg	**0.50**	**6.00**	**4.30**
Malmö	**1.05**	**8.00**	**6.45**
Luleå	**1.15**	**20.00**	**15.00**
Mora	**1.00**	**6.00**	**4.30**

Travel Advice

Most visits to Sweden are trouble-free but you should be aware of the global risk of indiscriminate international terrorist attacks, which could be against civilian targets, including places frequented by foreigners.

This advice is based on information provided by the Foreign and Commonwealth Office in the UK. It is correct at time of publishing. As the situation can change rapidly, visitors are advised to contact the following organisations for the latest travel advice:

British Foreign and Commonwealth Office
Tel: (0845) 850 2829.
Website: www.fco.gov.uk

US Department of State
Website: http://travel.state.gov/travel

Accommodation

HOTELS AND MOTELS:

Hotels are usually of a high standard. Most have a restaurant and/or cafe and a TV lounge, and many include a buffet breakfast in the price. Good first- and medium-class hotels are found in every Swedish town. They are mostly private but are, in many cases, operated by hotel groups and offer special reduced rates for the summer and weekends. Special packages are available throughout the year in Gothenburg, Malmö and Stockholm.

Scattered all over Sweden are country hotels, characterised by good food and attractive settings. Some are renovated and modernised manor houses or centuries-old farmhouses which have frequently been in the same family for generations. They are mostly independently owned and are often located in picturesque surroundings. Others are traditional old inns. During the summer many hotels offer facilities for swimming, fishing, boating, golf and flower-spotting or bird-watching excursions. There are also a number of mountain hotels which are ideal for those who want a peaceful holiday. They provide a good base for expeditions in the mountains and guided walks are often arranged, as well as other activities such as keep-fit classes, fishing and canoeing. Many are also popular skiing hotels in the winter. A comprehensive list of hotels can be found online (website: www.hotelsinsweden.net). The one- to five-star grading system was introduced in 2003. An *SHR* sign indicates that they belong to the *Swedish Hotel & Restaurant Association* (*SHR*), Sveriges Hotell & Restaurang Företagare, PO Box 1158, Kammarkargatan 39, 111 81 Stockholm (tel: (8) 762 7400; website: www.shr.se). Many Swedish hotels offer discounted rates throughout the summer and at weekends during the winter and some of the leading chains have special deals which can be booked in advance, including the *SARA Hotels Scandinavian Bonus Pass*, the *Scandic Hotel Cheque Scheme* and the *Sweden Hotel Pass*. Details of these offers and other (including family) discount schemes are contained in the annual guide *Hotels in Sweden*, obtainable from the Swedish Travel & Tourism Council (see *Top Things To Do*). Sweden also has a large number of motels, most of which are new, usually situated on the outskirts of towns or in the countryside. Parking is free. They may have swimming pools, a gymnasium and saunas, restaurants and self-service cafes.

FARMHOUSE ACCOMMODATION:

Working farms throughout Sweden offer accommodation, either in the main farmhouse or in an adjoining cottage. Accommodation is normally on a bed & breakfast basis, with self-catering facilities. Some farms offer full board. Accommodation can be booked through local tourist offices. For more information and bookings, see online (website: www.bopalantgard.org).

SELF-CATERING:

Forest cabins and chalets are available throughout the country, generally set in beautiful surroundings, near lakes, in quiet forest glades or on an island in some remote archipelago. Purpose-built chalets generally consist of a living room, two or three bedrooms, a well-equipped kitchen and a toilet. They can generally accommodate up to six people, and cooking utensils, cutlery, blankets and pillows are provided. Visitors only need to supply sheets and towels. Log cabins offer a slightly simpler type of accommodation. Renovated cottages and farm buildings are also available, usually in remote spots.

CHALET VILLAGES:

Sweden's many chalet villages offer the advantage of amenities such as a grocery, general shops, leisure facilities, restaurants, swimming pools, saunas, launderette, playgrounds, mini-golf, tennis, badminton or volleyball. Some have programmes of special activities such as music, dancing, barbecues, riding, fishing and walking trails. It is often possible to rent boats or bicycles. Information on rental of holiday cottages or flats can be obtained from specialist agencies, local tourist offices in Sweden or the Swedish Travel & Tourism Council.

CAMPING/CARAVANNING:

Family camping holidays are extremely popular in Sweden and there is a tremendous variety of attractive sites. Most are located in picturesque surroundings, often on a lakeside or by the sea with free bathing facilities close at hand. There are over 600 campsites, all officially approved and classified by the Swedish Travel & Tourism Council. Many offer facilities such as boat or bicycle rental, mini-golf, tennis, riding or saunas. Many campsites have facilities for the disabled. Most authorised sites are open with full service 1 Jun-15 Aug. Many sites are also open in April or May but the full range of ancillary facilities, such as the post office, may not be open. About 200 sites remain open in the winter, particularly in the winter sports areas in central and northern Sweden. All sites open during the winter have electric sockets for caravans. The price for one night for the whole family plus tent or caravan and use of services is one of the lowest rates in Europe, although at some sites there are small charges for the use of services like showers or launderette. A *Camping Card Scandinavia* is recommended. It can be bought beforehand and works as a credit card for site fees, allows a quicker check-in time, discounted petrol and provides

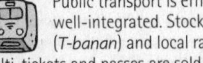

Credit: www.imagebank.sweden.se ©Peter Grant

accident insurance whilst on site. Contact Camping in Sweden for more details (website: www.camping.se). *Camping Cheques*, valid at more than 350 sites, can be purchased before the holiday but only as part of a package including a return car-ferry journey. Each cheque is valid for one night's fees for a family with car plus tent or caravan, but does not include additional services. Detailed information about camping in Sweden is contained in a pamphlet which is available free of charge from the Swedish Travel & Tourism Council; an abbreviated list of campsites is also available. Motor homes and caravans can be rented. *Camping Gaz* is not normally available in Sweden and visitors are recommended to take their own supplies. Only propane gas (eg Primus) is obtainable. This is widely available at more than 2000 Primus dealers along with the necessary equipment at reasonable prices. It is important to ensure that equipment designed to burn butane is not refilled with propane; this is both illegal and highly dangerous. It is possible to camp rough in areas away from other dwellings. A useful alternative to tent or caravan camping is to rent one of 4400 camping cabins which are available at 350 sites. These contain bunk beds and kitchen equipment but not sheets.

YOUTH HOSTELS:

There are more than 300 hostels that range from mansions to a renovated sailing ship, the *Af Chapman*, in the centre of Stockholm, as well as many purpose-built hostels. There are no restrictions on who may use Sweden's hostels. Hostels have two to four beds per room, or family rooms, plus self-catering facilities. The hostels are run by the *Swedish Tourist Federation (STF)* but members of the UK *Youth Hostels Federation* get a cheaper rate, on production of a membership card. All youth hostels are open during the summer and some for the whole year. They are closed during the day but are open to check in new guests 0800-0930 and 1700-2200. During the summer it is advisable to book in advance. A list of Swedish youth hostels can be ordered from STF (see *Top Things To Do*). The hostels are also listed in the International *Youth Hostel Handbook*, available through the YHA in the UK; see also online (website:

www.svenskaturistforeningen.se).

Swedish Tourist Federation: *STF* runs Sweden's youth hostels and several mountain stations in the north of the country and looks after the many mountain huts along the long-distance hiking trails. *STF* also publishes a list of guest harbours and issues guidance to hikers and canoeing enthusiasts. Membership is not required to stay at one of the hostels.

CASTLES AND MANORS: Many old buildings in Sweden are now being run as hotels. They provide a unique accommodation experience and are often situated on lakes or rivers with parklands and golf courses. Take advantage of the low weekend or summer prices. Package deals are also available.

ACCOMMODATION INFORMATION

Swedish Hotel & Restaurant Association (SHR)
Sveriges Hotell & Restaurang Företagare, PO Box 1158, Kammarkargatan 39, 111 81 Stockholm, Sweden
Tel: (8) 762 7400.
Website: www.shr.se

Top Things To See

- **Stockholm** is built on a number of islands. A highlight is the **Old Town**, a collection of well-preserved historic buildings lining cobbled streets. Its main streets, **Österlånggatan** and **Västerlånggatan**, are pedestrian precincts with a host of boutiques, handicrafts and antique shops. The Old Town has three churches of historic interest, **Storkyrkan** and **Riddarholm Church**, both dating from the 13th century and the **German Church** with its magnificent Baroque interior. Overlooking the harbour is the **Royal Palace** (website: www.royalcourt.se), which contains the State Apartments, the Crown Jewels, the Hall of State and Chapel Royal, Royal Armoury and **Palace Museum**. Close to the Old Town is the elegant **City Hall (Stadshuset)**.

- Cross by ferry to the **Djurgården Island** area, to see the **Nordic Museum (Nordiska Museet)** (website: www.nordiskamuseet.se), **Waldemarsudde House** (website: www.waldemarsudde.se), which was the home of the artist Prince Eugen until 1947, and **Liljevalchs Konsthall** (website: www.liljevalchs.com). The **Historical Museum (Historiska Museet)** (website: www.historiska.se) has prehistoric collections and medieval art. The **National Museum** houses the country's national fine arts collection. **Vasa Museum** (website: www.vasamuseet.se) contains a restored 360-year-old wooden warship, which was recovered from the harbour in 1961, while nearby is the **Skansen open-air folk museum** (website: www.skansen.se).

- Sweden's second city, **Gothenburg (Göteborg)**, is the 'home' of **Volvo** cars. Historically, though it has strong seafaring traditions. Visit the **Maritime Museum (Sjöfartsmuseet)** (website: www.sjofartsmuseum.goteborg.se) and the **Nordstaden Kronhuset** area, which houses the oldest building of the city, built in 1643 and now the **City Museum** (website: www.stadsmuseum.goteborg.se). Gothenburg was planned by the Dutch, and features a network of canals criss-crossing the city.

- Founded in the 13th century, **Malmö** (website: www.malmo.se) is Sweden's third largest city and offers a wealth of parks, gardens, restaurants and a beautiful beach. City sights include the main town squares, **Malmöhus Castle** and **St Petri Church**. The **Konsthallen** and **Rooseum museums** house art collections.

- Gotland and Öland are Sweden's biggest offshore islands, in the southeast of the country. On **Gotland** are the **Lummelunda Caves** (website: www.lummelundagrottan.se) with spectacular stalactites and stalagmites and a preserved medieval town at **Kattlundsgård**. **Öland** features the royal summer residence at **Solliden**; **Borgholm Castle** (website: www.borgholmsslott.se); a restored medieval church at **Gärdslösa**; a recently excavated fortified village at **Eketorp**; and many Viking stones and local windmills.

- German immigrants founded Sweden's crystal and glass-making industry in the southern province of **Småland**, and a total of 16 **glassworks** in the area are open to visitors.

- Head south to **Skåne**, which offers the medieval town of **Lund** with its 12th-century cathedral and 14th-century astronomical clock. There is also the spectacular **Öresund bridge**, the world's longest single bridge carrying both road and railway traffic between Denmark and Sweden.

- Sweden's Lakeland region comprises the nine provinces of **Dalsland**, **Värmland** and **Västergötland** in the west, **Dalarna**, **Närke** and **Västmanland** in the north, and **Östergötland**, **Södermanland** and **Uppland** to the east. These form a large part of Sweden with a mixture of open water, vast lakes, plains and meadows and large areas of wild natural scenery.

- Experience the '**ice beds**' and enjoy a well-earned thirst quencher in the Absolut Icebar at the sculpted **Ice Hotel** (website: www.icehotel.com) in the small northern village of **Jukkasjärvi**, **Lapland**. Constructed from tonnes of snow and ice cut from the **Torne River**, it is rebuilt every winter after the summer thaw and attracts many tourists.

- In **Jokkmokk**, there are collections of Lapp art and culture, and a **Lapp Staden**, an old village of 70 cone-shaped Lapp huts. **Arjeplog** has an interesting **Lapp museum**. Iron Age burial grounds and a medieval church are on the island of **Frösö**. The cable-car trip from **Åre** leads up to the summit of **Åreskutan**.

Top Things To Do

- Take a boat trip from the city centre through Stockholm's many islands to **Drottningholm Palace** (website: www.royalcourt.se), where the **Royal Theatre** has been preserved in its original 18th-century form and plays are still performed there in period costume. There is also a museum depicting the development of the theatre since the Renaissance period.

- If there are four days available to spare, take the classic boat journey through Sweden's **Great Lakes** and the historic **Göta Canal**. The tours start at both Stockholm and Gothenburg (website: www.gotakanal.se).

- Sweden has hundreds of miles of **beaches**, particularly on the west coast, and 96,000 lakes. There are numerous **water-skiing** and **windsurfing** centres on the coast and more accessible lakes.

- There are excellent facilities nationwide for **skating**, **tobogganing**, **snow-mobiling**, **ice-climbing** and **dog-sledging**.

- There are excellent **golf courses** and facilities provided for members and visitors. Sweden has over 400 courses. One situated north of the **Arctic Circle** enjoys 24-hour daylight during the summer months and many midsummer championships take place at midnight.

- Try to spot Sweden's only herd of musk ox in the

Härjedalen valley, southern Lapland, which also has abundant reindeer, buzzard, beaver and lynx. In winter, this region is also known for its **skiing**.

- Take to two wheels – **cycling** is a popular holiday recreation, particularly in the south. The Swedish Cycling Promotion Institute, in cooperation with regional tourist offices, offers scheduled cycling tours in almost every region.
- **Norrbotten** is a fisherman's paradise with plenty of mountain streams and excellent **sea fishing**. It is situated on the so-called **Midnight Sun Coast**, which is a 1500km (900 mile) stretch of Baltic coastline that runs all the way to the Finnish border.
- Take the kids to **Mora**, in the heart of the Swedish **Lakeland region**, where they can meet Father Christmas at the **Santaworld** theme park (website: www.santaworld.se).
- For those keen on the past, southwestern **Bohuslän** province is also one of the most important centres of ancient Swedish civilisation and there are many archaeological relics dating back to the Bronze Age and Viking times.

TOURIST INFORMATION

Swedish Travel & Tourism Council in the UK
Sweden House, 5 Upper Montagu Street,
London W1H 2AG, UK
Tel: (020) 7108 6168.

Swedish Travel & Tourism Council in the USA
Council PO Box 4649, Grand Central Station,
New York, NY 10163-4649, USA
Tel: (212) 885 9700.
Website: www.visitsweden.com

Entertainment

FOOD & DRINK: Swedes like straightforward meals, simply prepared from the freshest ingredients. As a seafaring country with many freshwater lakes, fish dishes are prominent on hotel or restaurant menus.
Things to know: Once on the open road the traveller is well catered for with picnic sites on the way, often with wooden tables and seats. Top-class restaurants in Sweden are usually fairly expensive, but even the smallest towns have reasonably priced self-service restaurants and grill bars. Many restaurants all over Sweden offer a special dish of the day at a reduced price which includes main course, salad, soft drink and coffee. Waiter service is common although there are many self-service snack bars. Wine, spirits and beer are sold through the state-owned monopoly, *Systembolaget*, open during normal shopping hours. Before 1300 on Sundays alcohol cannot be bought in bars, cafes or restaurants. After midnight alcohol can only be bought in nightclubs that stay open until between 0200-0500.
National specialities:
- *Smörgåsbord* (Scandinavian cold table. First pickled herring with boiled potatoes then perhaps a couple more fish courses, smoked salmon or anchovies followed by cold meat, pâté, sliced beef, stuffed veal or smoked reindeer).
- *Köttbullar* (small meatballs).
- Smoked reindeer from Lapland.

- *Gravlax* (salmon that has been specially prepared and marinated).
- Wild strawberries and cloudberries.
National drinks:
- *Snapps* (a Swedish liqueur which is traditionally drunk chilled with *smörgåsbord*, flavours vary from practically tasteless to sweetly spiced).
Minimum drinking age: 21 years, if buying alcohol in a shop; 18 years in a bar, restaurant or nightclub.
Tipping: Hotel prices include a service charge. Service in restaurants is not usually included in the bill; around 10 per cent should be added. Late at night the service charge is higher.
NIGHTLIFE: Stockholm has pubs, cafes, discos, restaurants, cinemas and theatres. In the more rural areas evenings tend to be tranquil. From August to June the *Royal Ballet* performs in Stockholm. Music and theatre productions take place in many cities during the summer at open air venues. Outside Stockholm in the 18th-century *Court Theatre of the Palace of Drottningholm* there are performances of 18th-century opera.
SHOPPING: VAT (*Moms*) is refundable to visitors who are resident in non-EU countries on goods bought at shops participating in the Tax-Free Shopping scheme. The refund is payable to the customer when departing from Sweden at either airports or customs offices at ports. There are many traditional markets and country fairs throughout Sweden. Special purchases include glassware and crystal, ceramics, stainless steel and silver, *hemslöjd* (cottage industry artefacts) and woodcarvings. Women's and children's clothes are good buys, especially handknitted Nordic sweaters. **Shopping hours:** Mon-Fri 0930-1800, Sat 0930-1400/1600. Some department stores stay open until 1900 or longer. In larger towns, some shops have longer opening hours and are also open Sundays 1200-1600. In rural areas, shops and petrol stations close by 1700/1800.

Business

- **GDP:** US$255.4 billion.
- **Main imports:** Machinery, motor vehicles, paper products, pulp and wood, iron and steel products and chemicals.
- **Main exports:** Machinery, petroleum and petroleum products, chemicals, motor vehicles, iron and steel, foodstuffs and clothing.
- **Main trade partners:** Belgium, Denmark, Finland, France, Germany, The Netherlands, Norway, the UK and USA.

ECONOMY: Sweden boasts one of Europe's most advanced industrial economies and one of the highest standards of social welfare in the world. It also boasts a relatively large number of world-class multinational companies (Ericsson, Volvo). A prolonged period of peace, which included a policy of neutrality during both World Wars, has contributed much to its economic development. Over half of the country is covered by forest, supplying raw material for the wood-based industries – paper, wood pulp and finished products such as furniture – which account for 20 per cent of Swedish material exports. Most of the country's agriculture is concentrated in the south and central regions and produces dairy products, meat, cereals and vegetables.

The agricultural and fisheries sector is, however, fairly insignificant today, accounting for just 2 per cent of GDP. Sweden has a strong industrial sector which produces a number of major exports including vehicles, office and telecommunications equipment, iron and steel, wood products and chemicals. The country is rich in mineral resources, which include 15 per cent of the world's known uranium deposits and large deposits of iron ore, copper, lead and zinc. Lacking fossil fuel deposits, Sweden has large nuclear power and hydroelectric programmes, which meet over 80 per cent of its energy needs.
Sweden was a long-standing member of the European Free Trade Association (EFTA), which linked most Western European economies outside the European Union, before it finally joined the EU in 1995. But there is a strong Euro-sceptic current: so far the Swedes have refused to join the Euro-zone, most recently at a national referendum in September 2003 (despite the endorsement of the national government).
Domestic economic policy has been mainly concerned with making the labour market more flexible and with addressing Sweden's large government debt. The economy was in recession between 1999 and 2002, but is now slowly recovering. Current annual GDP growth was 3.6 in 2004 and dropped to 2.1 in 2005. Both inflation and unemployment (0.6 and 5 per cent, respectively) are close to the EU average.
BUSINESS ETIQUETTE: Businesspeople are expected to dress smartly. English is widely spoken in business circles. Punctuality is important for business and social occasions. Business cards are commonly used. **Office hours:** Flexible working hours are a widespread practice, with lunch between 1200-1300.

COMMERCIAL INFORMATION

Stockholm Chamber of Commerce
Box 16050, 10321 Stockholm, Sweden
Tel: (8) 5551 0076.
Website: www.chamber.se
There are also chambers of commerce for other major towns and regions in Sweden.

**Stockholm Visitors Board
(Information on Conferences/Conventions)**
PO Box 16282, SE-103 25 Stockholm, Sweden
Tel: (8) 508 28500.
Website: www.stockholmtown.com

**Gothenburg Convention Centre
(Information on Conferences/Conventions)**
Mässans Gata 8, SE-412 51 Gothenburg, Sweden
Tel: (31) 708 8390.
Website: www.gcc.se

**Malmö Tourist Convention Bureau
(Information on Conferences/Conventions)**
Lugnagatan 84, SE-21159 Malmö, Sweden
Tel: (40) 342 204.
Website: www.malmo.se/conference
For a hotel and conference guide.

A B C D E F G H I J K L M N O P Q R S T U V W X Y Z

Switzerland

150km
100mls

✈ international airport

FRANCE

SWITZERLAND   GERMANY

Lake Constance
(Bodensee)

Winterthur

Basle   St Gall

Zurich   LIECH. AUSTRIA

Neuchâtel   Lucerne

Lake   Lake
Neuchâtel   Lucerne
Lake Thun   Rhine

■ BERNE   Davos

Lausanne   Interlaken   St
Andermatt   Moritz

Lake   Montreux   Rhône
Geneva

Geneva   Matterhorn
4478m   Lugano   Adda

Mont Blanc   Dufour-   Lake Como
4807m   spitze   Lake
4634m   Maggiore   ITALY

FRANCE

Location: Western Europe.

Time: GMT + 1 (GMT + 2 from last Sunday in March to Saturday before last Sunday in October).

Overview

Small, mountainous and wealthy, with a population of just seven million, Switzerland is renowned for its enviable quality of life in a country that ticks along like clockwork. Its products are sought after the world over, from dangerously delicious cheese and chocolate to luxurious watches whose timekeeping is as sharp as a Swiss army knife, another popular export from this clever little nation in the Alps.

Switzerland's famed political neutrality and isolated location, ring-fenced by mountains, have enabled it to play a safe but central role in European affairs. These factors also gave rise to the coveted Swiss bank account, whose anonymity, along with tax relief and what may be the safest banks in the world, have made Zürich one of Europe's major financial hubs. The conveniently central location in the middle of Europe has also made Switzerland a favourite meeting place for conventions and international conferences - Geneva, for instance, is home to the United Nations.

Switzerland is not only a place for professionals, though. As a stylish tourist destination it offers top ski resorts like Zermatt and celebrity-studded St Moritz, while the white peaks of mountains set against blue skies make a wonderful backdrop for summertime hiking. The ancient capital of Berne provides opportunities for sightseeing and elegant shopping, while nightlife can prove to be a lot of fun, too, since the Swiss like their food and folk music even in discotheques and nightclubs.

Switzerland's political model is based on consensus-building, and considering that the country consists of several culturally different groups speaking different languages, Swiss German, French, Italian and Rhaeto-Rumantsch, the country's peaceful domestic situation is admirable. And while the Swiss in practice have been neutral in foreign affairs for several centuries, there are signs that they are increasingly willing to get more deeply involved in world affairs and deploy on the international

stage the skills in democracy and diplomacy they have developed domestically. The most obvious sign is that Switzerland finally became a member of the United Nations in September 2002 .

General Information

AREA: 41,284 sq km (15,940 sq miles).

POPULATION: 7.4 million (official estimate 2005).

POPULATION DENSITY: 181 per sq km.

CAPITAL: Bern. **Population:** 127,000 (2005).

GEOGRAPHY: Switzerland is bordered by France to the west, Germany to the north, Austria to the east and Italy to the south. It has the highest mountains in Europe, with waterfalls and lakes set amid green pastures. The highest peaks are Dufour Peak, 4634m (15,217ft), on the Italian border; the Dom, 4545m (14,912ft); the Matterhorn, 4478m (14,692ft); and the Jungfrau, 4166m (13,669ft).

GOVERNMENT: Federal Republic since 1848. **Head of State and Government:** President Moritz Leuenberger since 2005. **Recent history:** Switzerland has long traditions of neutrality in its relations with the rest of the world, and it is not a member of the EU. There was a referendum in 2001 on whether to open talks about joining or not, and the result was negative. Nine years before membership of the European Economic Area was also rejected by referendum. Relations between Switzerland and the EU are now based on a wide range of bilateral agreements. There are signs that things may be slowly changing, however, as a referendum in 2005 supported membership of the EU, Schengen and Dublin agreements, bringing Switzerland into Europe's passport-free zone and increasing cooperation on crime and asylum issues. A further referendum the same year opened the job market to workers from the 10 newest EU member countries. On 10 December 2003, the National Assembly decided that the so-called 'Magic Formula' – in place since 1959 - regarding the composition of the Federal Council would have to change as a result of the right-wing Swiss People's Party's electoral success that same Autumn. There are seven seats in the Federal Council, and under the old formula, the four main parties divided these between them (two seats each for the Radicals, Christian Democrats and Social Democrats and one seat for the Swiss People's Party) in an effort to try to ensure that the main languages, religions and regions were represented in the Council. However, in 2003, the Swiss People's Party gained a seat at the expense of the Christian Democratic Party.

LANGUAGE: German in central and eastern areas, French in the west and Italian in the south. Raeto-Romansch is spoken in the southeast. English is spoken by many. Overlapping cultural influences characterise the country.

RELIGION: Roman Catholic (43 per cent) and Protestant (47 per cent).

ELECTRICITY: 220 volts AC, 50Hz.

SOCIAL CONVENTIONS: It is customary to give unwrapped flowers to the hostess when invited for a meal. Avoid red roses; never give chrysanthemums or white asters as they are considered funeral flowers. Informal wear is widely acceptable. First-class restaurants, hotel dining rooms and important social occasions may warrant jackets and ties. Black tie is usually specified when required.

Climate

The Alps cause many climatic variations throughout Switzerland. In the higher Alpine regions temperatures tend to be low, while the lower land of the northern area has higher temperatures and warm summers.

Required clothing: Warm clothes and rainwear; lightweights for summer.

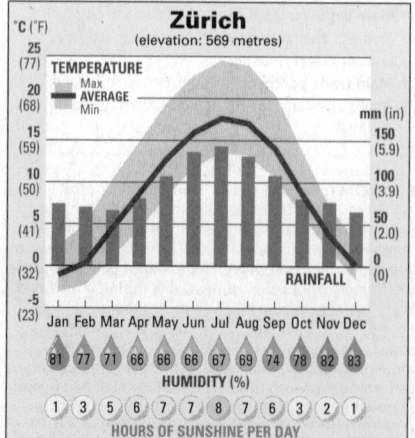

°C (°F)

Zürich
(elevation: 569 metres)

25
(77)

TEMPERATURE
Max
20   **AVERAGE**
(68)   Min

mm (in)

15   150
(59)   (5.9)

10   100
(50)   (3.9)

5   50
(41)   (2.0)

0   0
(32)   **RAINFALL**   (0)

-5
(23)   Jan Feb Mar Apr May Jun Jul Aug Sep Oct Nov Dec

81 77 71 66 66 66 67 69 74 78 82 83

HUMIDITY (%)

1 3 5 6 7 7 8 7 6 3 2 1

HOURS OF SUNSHINE PER DAY

Communications

Telephone: Full IDD is available. Country code: 41. Phonecards are available for use in payphones.

Mobile telephone: Roaming agreements exist with most international mobile phone companies. Coverage is good.

Internet: Internet access is available in Internet cafes and phone booths operated by *Swisscom*. Charges are payable by phonecard or credit card.

Post: Airmail within Europe takes three days. Post office hours: Mon-Fri 0730-1200 and 1345-1830. Saturday closing at 1100 except in major cities.

MEDIA: The main broadcaster in Switzerland is the public Swiss Broadcasting Corporation. It operates seven TV networks and 18 radio stations. Most of its funding comes from licence fee revenues, while a smaller proportion comes from TV advertising. Private TV and radio stations operate in the regions. Television stations from France, Germany and Italy are widely available, thanks in part to the very high take-up of multi-channel cable and satellite TV. Some German commercial broadcasters provide tailored versions of their channels for the Swiss market. Switzerland's press operates to a large extent along regional lines which reflect the country's linguistic divisions.

Press: The high level of interest in local politics throughout Switzerland has led to a large number of regional newspapers. However, the most popular dailies are *Corriere del Ticino* (Lugano-based), *Le Temps* (Geneva-based), *La Tribune de Geneve* (Geneva-based), *Neue Zürcher Zeitung* (Zurich-based), and *Tages-Anzeiger Zürich* (Zurich-based). European and international newspapers in English, including *The Herald Tribune* and *USA Today*, are also widely available.

TV: In addition to the Swiss public broadcaster, *Swiss Broadcasting Corporation*, there is *SF-DRS*, a German-language public broadcaster that operates three channels; *RTSI*, an Italian-language public broadcaster with two channels; and *TSR*, a French-language public broadcaster that similarly operates two channels.

Radio: *SR-DRS*, the German-language public broadcaster, operates five stations; *RSR*, the French-language public broadcaster, has four stations; *RSI*, Italian-language public broadcaster, broadcasts from three stations; *RR*, finally, is a Rumansch-language public radio station.

Passport/Visa

Note: The regulations below also apply to Liechtenstein (no border control between the two countries);

Passengers arriving at Basle or Geneva airports can enter either France or Switzerland, provided their documents for the country of entry are in order; Both airports have two different exits, one to France and one to Switzerland. Therefore passengers can exit to the French part of the airport with a valid French or Schengen visa, if required; The airport of Basle/Mulhouse is located on French territory; Part of Geneva airport is located by convention in France and some flights between France and Geneva are considered as domestic flights while others are considered international flights. In this case, passengers must hold proper entry documents for either of the destination countries.

	Passport Required?	Visa Required?	Return Ticket Required?
Full British	Yes	No	No
Australian	Yes	No	No
Canadian	Yes	No	No
USA	Yes	No	No
Other EU	1/2/3/4	No	No
Japanese	Yes	No	No

Note: *Regulations and requirements may be subject to change at short notice, and you are advised to contact the appropriate diplomatic or consular authority before finalising travel arrangements. Any numbers in the chart refer to the footnotes below.*

PASSPORTS: Passport valid for three months after intended period of stay required by all except:
(a) **1.** nationals of Austria, Belgium, Cyprus, Czech Republic, Finland, France, Germany, Greece, Hungary, Italy, Liechtenstein, Luxembourg, Malta, Monaco, The Netherlands, Portugal, San Marino, Slovak Republic, Slovenia, Spain and the UK holding a valid national identity card, providing not taking up employment and for stay up to three months;
(b) **2.** foreigners holding national Identity Cards issued by the governments of Belgium, France or Luxembourg, provided they are resident in one of these countries;
(c) **3.** nationals of Austria, Belgium, France, Liechtenstein, Luxembourg, Monaco, The Netherlands, Portugal, San Marino and Spain with normal passports, expired for up to five years, providing not taking up employment and for stay up to three months;
(d) **4.** nationals of Germany with passports expired for up to one year;

A B C D E F G H I J K L M N O P Q R S T U V W X Y Z

(e) nationals of Liechtenstein who may enter Switzerland without valid identity papers.

VISAS: Required by all except the following for stays of up to three months:

(a) nationals of countries referred to in the chart above;

(b) nationals of countries in South and North/Central America, including nationals of Caribbean island/West Indies states (except nationals of Belize, Bolivia, Colombia, Cuba, Dominican Republic, Ecuador, Haiti and Peru who *do* need a visa);

(c) nationals of Andorra, Brunei, Bulgaria, Croatia, Fiji, Hong Kong (SAR), Iceland, Israel, Kiribati, Korea (Rep), Liechtenstein, Malaysia, Monaco, New Zealand, Norway, Romania, San Marino, Singapore, Solomon Islands, South Africa, Tuvalu and Vatican City;

(d) nationals of Bahrain, Kuwait, Oman, Qatar, Saudi Arabia, Taiwan (China, PR), Thailand and United Arab Emirates, if in possession of passport valid for three months after leaving Switzerland, endorsed with a valid multiple-entry Schengen visa (valid for all Schengen states);

(e) nationals in direct transit travelling within 48 hours providing they hold all valid documents, except nationals of certain countries (see note).

Note: Stateless persons require a transit visa at all times. Nationals of Afghanistan, Angola, Bangladesh, Congo (Dem Rep), Ethiopia, Ghana, Guinea, India, Iran, Iraq, Lebanon, Nigeria, Pakistan, Sierra Leone, Somalia, Sri Lanka and Turkey require a transit visa unless they hold a visa or residence permit for an EU country, Canada, Iceland, Norway or the USA.

Tourists and business visitors who travel repeatedly to Switzerland but stay less than three months each time must apply for a residence permit if their total stay exceeds six months within a period of twelve months.

Types of visa and cost: *Tourist; Visitor; Business; Transit; Airport Transit.* All visas cost £25 (to be paid in cash only).

Validity: Three months. *Transit visas:* 48 hours.

Application to: Consulate (or Consular section at Embassy responsible for place of residence; see *Passport/Visa Information*) not more than three months before planned entry. Visa applications must be made in person; postal applications are not accepted.

Application requirements: *Tourist:* (a) Valid passport or travel document valid for three months after the intended visit to Switzerland. (b) One completed application form. (c) One recent passport-size photo (three for student visas). (d) Fee, payable in cash only. (e) Travel ticket to/from or via Switzerland to final destination. (f) Proof of sufficient funds in the form of a recent bank statement/travellers' cheques (£50 per day, £25 for students). (g) Hotel reservation. *Transit:* (a)-(e) and, (f) Proof of flight with an airline licensed in Switzerland. (i) Visa(s) for ongoing destination(s). (j) Valid ticket for the whole journey to the destination. *Visitor:* (a)-(e) and, (f) Invitation letter from Swiss resident sent directly to the Embassy, with a copy of their Swiss Passport/ID card or Resident Permit. In special cases, a 'declaration of guarantee' might be required which has to be approved by the Swiss authorities. *Business:* (a)-(e) and, (f) Invitation from Swiss company sent directly to the Embassy. *Student:* (a)-(f) and, (g) Student identity card or letter from university/college.

Working days required: Visas may be issued within 24 hours, but travellers are advised to apply at least one week prior to departure and no earlier than three months before proposed travel. Some applications may need to be referred to the Swiss authorities, which can take six to eight weeks for approval.

Temporary residence: Nationals of most European and some other countries do not require a visa if they intend to take up employment or residence in Switzerland; however, before entry they must obtain an *Assurance of a Residence Permit* from their employer in Switzerland.

PASSPORT/VISA INFORMATION

Embassy of Switzerland in the UK
16-18 Montagu Place, London W1H 2BQ, UK
Tel: (020) 7616 6000 *or* (09065) 508 909 (recorded visa information).
Website: www.swissembassy.org.uk
Opening hours: Mon-Fri 0900-1200 (for personal visa applications).

Embassy of Switzerland in the USA
2900 Cathedral Avenue, NW,
Washington, DC 20008, USA
Tel: (202) 745 7900.
Website: www.swissemb.org

Money

Currency: Swiss Franc (CHF) = 100 rappen or centimes. Notes are in denominations of CHF1000, 500, 200, 100, 50, 20 and 10. Coins are in denominations of CHF5, 2 and 1, and 50, 20, 10 and 5 centimes.

Eurocheques: Eurocheques are no longer guaranteed and and can not be accepted for encashments but may be useable for payments without the guarantee.

Currency exchange: Personal cheques within the Eurocheque system are accepted. ATMs provide a convenient means of obtaining Swiss Francs. There are Bureaux de Change at train stations and banks.

Credit & debit cards: American Express, Diners Club, MasterCard and Visa are widely accepted. Check with your credit or debit card company for details of merchant acceptability and other facilities which may be available.

Traveller's cheques: Pound Sterling, US Dollar, Euro or Swiss Franc cheques are accepted at airports, railway stations and banks. To avoid additional exchange rate charges, travellers are advised to take traveller's cheques in Pounds Sterling, Euros or US Dollars.

Currency restrictions: There are no restrictions on the import or export of local or foreign currencies.

Banking hours: Mon-Fri 0830-1630.

Exchange rate indicators:
Rate at time of publishing
£1.00=   CHF2.24
$1.00=   CHF1.27

Duty Free

The following items may be imported into Switzerland by persons over 17 years of age without incurring customs duty by:

(a) Visitors from European countries:
200 cigarettes or 50 cigars or 250g of tobacco; 2l of alcohol (up to 15 per cent) and 1l of alcohol (over 15 per cent); gifts up to a value of CHF300.

(b) Visitors from non-European countries:
400 cigarettes or 100 cigars or 500g of tobacco; 2l of alcohol (up to 15 per cent) and 1l of alcohol (over 15 per cent); gifts up to a value of CHF300.

Prohibited items: Most meat and processed meat, absinthe and narcotics are prohibited. There are strict regulations on importing animals and firearms.

Public Holidays

Below are listed Public Holidays for the January 2006-June 2007 period.
2006: Jan 1 New Year's Day. **Jan 2*** Berchtold's Day. **Apr 14*** Good Friday. **Apr 17*** Easter Monday. **May 25*** Ascension. **Jun 5*** Whit Monday. **Aug 1** National Day. **Dec 25** Christmas Day. **Dec 26** St Stephen's Day.
2007: Jan 1 New Year's Day. **Jan 2*** Berchtold's Day. **Apr 6*** Good Friday. **Apr 9*** Easter Monday. **May 17*** Ascension. **May 28*** Whit Monday.
Note: (a) *These holidays may not be observed in certain cantons. (b) There are additional regional holidays which are observed in certain cantons only.

Health

	Special Precautions?	Certificate Required?
Yellow Fever	No	No
Cholera	No	No
Typhoid & Polio	No	N/A
Malaria	No	N/A

Note: *Regulations and requirements may be subject to change at short notice, and you are advised to contact your doctor well in advance of your intended date of departure. Any numbers in the chart refer to the footnotes below.*

Other risks: *Rabies* is present. For those at high risk, vaccination before arrival should be considered. If you are bitten, seek medical advice without delay. For more information, see the *Health* appendix.

Health care: European Economic Area (EEA) and Switzerland:
If you or any of your dependants are suddenly taken ill or have an accident during a visit to an EEA country or Switzerland, free or reduced-cost necessary treatment is available - in most cases on production of a valid European Health Insurance Card (EHIC). Each country has different rules about state medical provision. In some, treatment is free. In many countries you will have to pay part or all of the cost, and then claim a full or partial refund. The EHIC gives access to state-provided medical treatment only and the scheme gives no entitlement to medical repatriation costs, nor does it cover ongoing illnesses of a non-urgent nature, so comprehensive travel insurance is advised. Note that the EHIC replaces the Form E111, which will no longer be valid after 31 December 2005. Some restrictions apply, depending on your nationality. Nationals of Cyprus, the Czech Republic, Estonia, Hungary, Iceland, Latvia, Liechtenstein, Lithuania, Malta, Norway, Poland, the Slovak Republic and Slovenia are not covered by the EHIC in Switzerland.

People who do not have UK, EU or EEA nationality are not covered.

Medical facilities in Switzerland are among the best in Europe, but treatment is expensive. You will normally have to pay the full costs for treatment and services and claim a refund afterwards. You will have to pay a fixed charge for each 30-day period of treatment. This is known as the 'excess charge' or 'patient's contribution' and is not refunded. It is recommended that all visitors take out adequate private travel insurance. Go to any doctor registered with the Swiss health insurance scheme. Dental treatment is not covered unless it results from serious illness or accident. If required, you will normally be referred to a public hospital by a doctor. In an emergency, go directly to the emergency department of any public hospital. In-patient treatment in a general ward of a public hospital is covered, but not in a semi-private or private ward, or in a private hospital. As well as the excess charge, you will have to pay a small, non-refundable, fixed daily in-patient charge for the cost of board and accommodation. You will have to pay 50 per cent of the costs of ambulance transport within Switzerland, including air ambulance. Various leaflets giving information on health spas and clinics are available from Switzerland Tourism (see *Top Things To Do*). More information can be obtained from *Gemeinsame Einrichtung KVG* (Common Institution), Gibelinstrasse 25, Postfach, CH-4503 Solothurn (tel: (32) 625 4820; fax: (32) 625 4829).

Travel - International

AIR:
The national airline is *Swiss (LX)* (website: www.swiss.com).
Approximate flight times: From Basle, Bern, Geneva or Zürich to *London* is one hour 50 minutes. From Geneva to *Los Angeles* is 17 hours and from Zürich is 14 hours 35 minutes. From Geneva to *New York* is nine hours 45 minutes and from Zürich is seven hours 20 minutes.

Main airports: *Zürich (ZRH) (Kloten)* (website: www.zurich-airport.com) is 11km (7 miles) from the city (travel time - 20 minutes). *To/from the airport:* Trains run every 10 to 15 minutes from under Terminal B. Regional and night buses are available. Passengers arriving in Switzerland by air can purchase a special *Fly-Rail Luggage* ticket from their airport of departure which will enable them to have their luggage delivered directly to a Swiss railway station. With the *Fly-Rail Baggage* service, passengers leaving Switzerland can check their bags in at the railway station up to 24 hours before their flight. Taxis to the city are available (travel time - 15-30 minutes). *Facilities:* Duty free shops, restaurants/bars, banks, bureau de change, nursery and car rental.

Geneva (GVA) (website: www.gva.ch) is 5km (3 miles) north of the city. *To/from the city:* Taxis to the city are available. There is a regular train service to Geneva Cornavin Station (travel time - six minutes). The no. 10 bus runs from the airport to the city centre.

Bern (BRN) (Belp) is 9km (5.5 miles) southeast of the city (travel time - 20-30 minutes). *To/from the airport:* Bus services are available to Bern station. A rail service runs from Bern to Zürich Airport. Taxis are also available.

Basle (BSL) (Basel-Mulhouse) is 12km (7 miles) from the city. *To/from the airport:* A bus runs to Basle SBB Luftreisebüro. Taxis are also available.

Departure tax: None.

RAIL:
Travelling from the UK, the quickest way is to travel by *Eurostar* through the Channel Tunnel to Paris (travel time - three hours) and, from there, to Switzerland. For further information and reservations contact *Eurostar* (tel: (0870) 0000 792 (travel agents) *or* (08705) 186 186 (public; within the UK) *or* (01233) 617 575 (public; outside the UK only); website: www.eurostar.com); *or Rail Europe* (tel: (08708) 371 371; website: www.raileurope.co.uk). General enquiries and information requests must be made by telephone.

Other connections from London via the main channel crossings are available (minimum travel time of about 14 to 15 hours to Basle and Lausanne, the main points of entry). There are also through trains from Spain, Italy and Germany.

Rail passes: The *Inter-Rail* pass offers unlimited second-class train travel in up to 29 countries (includes Morocco and Turkey) split into eight zones (A-H). Three different tickets are available: a ticket covering one zone (two to six countries, 16 days' validity), a ticket covering two zones (six to ten countries, 22 days' validity) and an *All Zone Pass* (29 countries, one month's validity). Ferry services between Italy and Greece are included. Passengers must be resident in Europe for at least six months before the pass is used. Travel is not allowed in the passenger's country of residence. Travellers under 26 years receive a reduction of about 30 per cent. Children's tickets are reduced by about 50 per cent. Supplements are required for some high speed services, seat reservations and couchettes. Discounts are offered on *Eurostar* and some ferry routes. Available from *Inter Rail* (website: www.interrailnet.com).

The *Eurailpass* offers unlimited first-class train travel in 17 European countries. Tickets are valid for 15 days, 21 days, one month, two months or three months. The *Eurailpass Saver* ticket offers discounts for two or more people travelling together. The *Eurailpass Youth* ticket is available to those aged under 26 and offers unlimited second-class train travel. The *Eurailpass Flexi* allows either 10 or 15 travel days within a two month period. The *Eurail Selectpass* is valid in three, four or five bordering countries and allows five, six, eight or 10 travel days (or 15 for five countries) in a two-month period. The *Eurail Regional Pass* allows four to 10 travel days in a two-month period in one of nine regions (usually two or more countries). Children receive a 50 per cent reduction. The passes cannot be sold to residents of Europe, Turkey, Morocco, Algeria, Tunisia, or the Russian Federation. Available from *The Eurail Group* (website: www.eurail.com).

ROAD:

Switzerland can be reached by road from Austria, France, Germany and Italy. Some approximate driving times to Geneva and Zürich by the most direct routes are: Calais– Geneva: 12-13 hours (747km/464 miles); Dunkirk–Geneva: 12-13 hours (732km/454 miles); Calais–Zürich: 13-14 hours (790km/490 miles); Dunkirk–Zürich: 14-15 hours (880km/ 546 miles). **Coach:** There are coach services to Switzerland as well as scheduled coach tour operators. Contact Switzerland Tourism for further details (see *Top Things To Do*). In the UK, *Eurolines*, departing from Victoria Coach Station in London, serves Zurich and Bern twice a week (travel time - 18 hours). For further information contact Eurolines (tel: (08705) 143 219; website: www.eurolines.com).

Travel - Internal

AIR:

All services are operated by *Swiss (LX)* (website: www.swiss.com). Domestic air travel is fast but expensive, and with the exception of the Geneva to Zürich flight (travel time - 45 minutes), many businesspeople prefer to travel by rail or road.

RAIL:

Rail transport is particularly well developed in Switzerland, with excellent services provided by *Schweizerische Bundesbahnen (SBB)* (website: www.sbb.ch) and many other operators. Use of the *Swiss Pass* (see below) is a superb way to view the scenery, although mainline services are geared to the needs of the hurried business traveller. Trains run at least hourly from the major centres and there is a country-wide timetable of regular services. There are dining cars on many trains, and snacks and refreshments are widely available. Independent railways, such as the *Rhätische Bahn* in the Grisons and the *Berner-Oberland-Bahn*, provide services in certain parts of the country. The *SBB* has introduced specialised cars for disabled people using wheelchairs. Facilities include a lift for wheelchairs, a specially adapted WC and radios adapted for people with hearing difficulties.

There is also a large number of mountain railways which are sometimes the only means of access to winter resorts. Some of these are attractions in their own right: the *Gornergrat-Bahn* in Zermatt is one of the oldest mountain railways and climbs to a height of over 3000m above sea level, offering a spectacular panorama of the Matterhorn and surrounding mountains.

Cheap fares: Available from Switzerland Tourism. The *Swiss Pass* gives unlimited travel on rail services, those of other main regional operators, boats, an extensive network of buses and city trams, as well as reduced price travel on other mountain railways not included in the full scheme. Tickets can be purchased for four, eight, 15, 22 or one month. An STS family card allows children up to 16 years of age free travel when accompanied by parents. There are also regional tickets for unlimited travel in different parts of Switzerland at various rates. Other offers include a *Swiss Transfer Ticket* allowing return travel from a Swiss border or airport to a selected destination. A leaflet describing all the schemes is available from Switzerland Tourism. A comprehensive timetable for all Swiss public transport can also be purchased. *InterRail* cards are valid.

The *EuroDomino* pass enables holders anything form three to eight days' extensive travel within a one-month period on the entire rail network of their chosen country. It is valid in 28 European countries and North Africa, including the ferry service from Brindisi (Italy) to Igoumenitsa (Greece). To purchase a *EuroDomino* pass you must have been a resident in Europe for at least six months and a passport number is required at time of booking. It is not permitted to purchase a pass for travel within your own country of residence. To qualify for the youth rates, you must be under 26 years on the first date of validity of the pass. Children aged four-eleven years inclusive pay half the adult fares rounded up to the nearest pound. Children under four years travel for free. Seat reservations, couchette and sleeper charges are not included in the cost of the pass and are payable at the normal rate. Passholder fares are payable on some services. Reservation/Supplement charges are payable on all trains within Spain. Available from *Rail Europe* (website: www.raileurope.co.uk/railpasses/eurodomino.htm).

ROAD:

Traffic drives on the right. Road quality is generally good. Many mountain roads are winding and narrow, and often closed in heavy winter conditions; otherwise chains and snow tyres may be necessary. Rail is often more efficient than driving. **Bus:** Postal motor coaches (website: www.post.ch) provide a service to even the remotest villages, but under the integrated national transport policy, few long-distance coaches are allowed to operate. **Taxi:** All taxis have meters for short and long trips, although it is advisable to agree the fare for longer distances out of town. **Car hire:** Available in all towns from hotels and airports and at all manned rail stations. All major European companies are represented. **Regulations:** The minimum driving age is 18. Seat belts are obligatory and children under 12 years must travel in the back of the car. Dipped headlights are compulsory during the day. Drink-driving fines are heavy. **Speed limits:** 80kph (50mph) on country lanes; max 120kph (75mph), min 60kph (37mph) on motorways; and 50kph (31mph) in towns. **Organisations:** The *AA* and *RAC* in the UK are linked with *TCS (Touring Club Suisse)* (website: www.tcs.ch) and *ACS (Automobil Club der Schweiz)*. Contact the *Automobil Club der Schweiz (ACS)*, Wasserwerkgasse 39, CH-3000 Bern 13 (tel: (31) 328 3111; website: www.acs.ch). In emergencies, there is a breakdown service offering assistance throughout Switzerland (tel: 140). **Motorway tax** (*vignette*): An annual road tax of CHF40 is levied on all cars and motorbikes using Swiss motorways. An additional fee of CHF40 applies to trailers and caravans. The *vignette* (sticker) is valid between 1 December of the year preceding and 31 January of the one following the year printed on the vignette. These permits, which are available at border crossings, are valid for multiple re-entry into Switzerland within the duration of the licensed period. To avoid hold-ups at the frontier, however, it is advisable to purchase the vignette in advance: call the Swiss Travel Centre (tel: (00800) 1002 0030) for more details. **Documentation:** A national driving licence is sufficient. Green Card insurance is advised - ordinary domestic insurance policies are valid but do not provide full cover. The Green Card tops the cover up to the level provided by the visitor's domestic policy.

URBAN:

Highly efficient and integrated urban public transport systems serve as a model for other countries. There are tramways and light rail services in Basle, Bern, Geneva, Neuchâtel and Zürich. These and a further dozen cities also have trolleybuses. Fares systems are generally automated with machines issuing single or multiple tickets at the roadside. Tickets are also available at enquiry offices. Fares are generally zonal. There is a day ticket for travel in one or more Swiss cities on any given day at a standard fare. Taxis are widely available and drivers expect a 15 per cent tip.

Travel times: The following chart gives approximate travel times (in hours and minutes) from **Zürich** to other major cities/towns in Switzerland.

	Air	Road	Rail
Basle	0.30	1.10	1.05
Bern	-	1.15	1.10
Geneva	0.40	2.45	2.55
Lugano	0.45	3.00	3.00

Travel Advice

Most visits to Switzerland are trouble-free but you should be aware of the global risk of indiscriminate international terrorist attacks, which could be against civilian targets, including places frequented by foreigners.

This advice is based on information provided by the Foreign and Commonwealth Office in the UK. It is correct at time of publishing. As the situation can change rapidly, visitors are advised to contact the following organisations for the latest travel advice:

British Foreign and Commonwealth Office
Tel: (0845) 850 2829.
Website: www.fco.gov.uk

US Department of State
Website: http://travel.state.gov/travel

Accommodation

HOTELS:

Hotels are of high quality and in high demand. All standards from luxury to family hotels and pensions are available. A service charge of 15 per cent is included in hotel bills, and an additional local tax may be payable (depending on the location). Most hotels in Switzerland are affiliated to the Schweizer Hotelier Verein (Swiss Hotels Association) (SHV). **Grading:** The SHV classifies all its hotels according to a 5-star rating system, which stipulates a range of facilities ranging from: **1-star (simple)** to **5-star (luxury)**.

Note: Membership of the SHV is voluntary, and there may be some first-class hotels which do not have a star rating. There are many hotels with no actual star classification that are recognised by, and members of, the SHV as well as Country Inns, Unique hotels, Aparthotels, Mountain Inns/Traveller's Lodges and Low Service hotels. The SHV issues an annual guide of around 2500 member hotels and pensions.

CHALETS & APARTMENTS:

Information regarding the rental of chalets, houses, flats and furnished apartments is available from local tourist offices and estate agents in Switzerland. A list of contacts is available from Switzerland Tourism (see Top Things To Do).

SPAS: Switzerland has about 22 different mineral springs for the treatment of various health conditions. A guide to Swiss spas, including hotels, is available from Switzerland Tourism.

PRIVATE CLINICS: Details of accommodation in private sanatoria and clinics is included in the publication *Private Clinics in Switzerland*, available from Switzerland Tourism.

CAMPING:

There are approximately 600 campsites in Switzerland. Camping on farmland is not permitted. Local area laws and fees vary. It is advisable to make advance reservations in the summer. Camping guides published by the *Swiss Camping Association* and the *Swiss Camping Federation* can be purchased from Switzerland Tourism. A list of campsites (produced in conjunction with the Swiss tourist board) is also available online (website: www.camping.ch).

YOUTH HOSTELS:

Visitors holding membership cards of a national organisation affiliated to the *International Youth Hostels Federation* are entitled to lower prices. To avoid disappointment, wardens of youth hostels should be given prior notice (at least five days) of arrival. An International Reply Paid Postcard (Youth Hostel Edition) should be used if confirmation is required. A list of Swiss youth hostels is obtainable from Switzerland Tourism.

ACCOMMODATION INFORMATION

Schweizer Hotelier Verein (Swiss Hotels Association) (SHV)
Monbijoustrasse 130,
Postfach 3001 Bern, Switzerland
Tel: (31) 370 4111.
Website: www.swisshotels.ch

The Swiss Camp Site Owners Association (VSC/ASC)
3800 Interlaken-Thunersee, Switzerland
Tel: (31) 852 0626.
Website: www.swisscamps.ch

Swiss Youth Hostels
Schaffhauserstrasse 14, 8042 Zürich, Switzerland
Tel: (1) 360 1414.
Website: www.youthhostel.ch

Top Things To See

- Explore **Zürich**, Switzerland's largest city, pleasantly set on its own lake, **Zürichsee**, on the banks of the **Limmat River**. The old part of the town (the **Altstadt**) is especially picturesque. Do not miss the Gothic **Basilica Fraumünster** (11th to 13th century) with its three naves and stained-glass windows by Marc Chagall. Across the river, the skyline is dominated by the **Grossmünster** with its twin towers. Other sights include the impressive **Town Hall**, a fine example from the late Renaissance (17th century), the **Swiss National Museum** and the modern art collections at the **Kunsthaus Zürich**.
- Visit the **Horological Museum** and **watch-making factories** at **La-Chaux-de-Fonds**. There are more factories at **Le Locle** nearby, all producing the precision watches Switzerland is so famous for.
- The university city of **Geneva**, situated on the Rhône-outlet of **Lake Geneva** (**Lac Léman**), has an old city centre that is best explored on foot. One of the finest examples of

Romanesque architecture is the **Cathédrale de St Pierre**. The **flower clock**, with over 6,500 blooms, near the lake in the **Jardin Anglais** pays homage to Geneva's watch industry.

- Cross over to the northern shore of the big lake to **Lausanne**, the capital of the canton of Vaud. Essential sights are the **Cathédrale Notre-Dame** in the **Cité**, the old centre, and the **Château St Maire** (1397-1431). A walk along the promenade of the old **Port d'Ouchy** reveals a slower pace of life. Take the **funicular** from Ouchy to the inner city of Lausanne.
- **Vaud** also boasts one of the country's most important historic buildings; head for the small town of **Romainmotier** to discover its 11th-century **Benedictine monastery**.
- The ancient capital of **Bern** is worth a visit. Experience its unique 11th-century **arcaded streets**. The medieval city centre is located on the Aare River between the 13th-century **clocktower** (**Zeitglockenturm**) and the striking copper spire of the **Nydegg church** (**Nydeggkirche**). Cross the **Nyddegg bridge** to see the ancient medieval **bear pits** (**Bärengraben**), a reminder of the city's ursine emblem seen throughout the town in the form of flags, statues, stained-glass windows and souvenirs.
- Enjoy the Baroque **Cathedral** and the famous **Abbey Library** (**Stiftsbibliothek**) in the courtyard of the old **Benedictine monastery** (incunabula and illuminated manuscripts), named a World Heritage Treasure by UNESCO, in **St Gallen**'s old city centre which is dominated by burgher houses from the 17th and 18th century.
- Head for **Neuchâtel**, attractively located beside a lake, and admire the striking **medieval yellow stone buildings** in town. They were once described by Alexander Dumas as 'carved from butter'. The town is celebrated for its cafe culture and first-class cuisine.
- The historic town of **Brig** in the Valais boasts the most important Baroque castle in Switzerland, the **Stockalperschloss**. Castle enthusiasts should also visit **Leuk**, **Martigny**, **Monthey** and **Sierre**.
- Explore the **Berner Oberland**, a major tourist area that includes spectacular scenery including famous peaks, mountain lakes, alpine streams and wild flowers, as well as **Europe's highest railway**. **Adelboden**, **Grindelwald** and **Lenk** were already famous with the European nobility and artists in the 19th century. From **Interlaken**, a network of roads and mountain railways such as the narrow-gauge **Berner-Oberland-Bahn** (**BOB**) serve the resorts in the Jungfrau region. **Jungfrau** (4158m/13,642ft), **Mönch** (4099m/13,448ft) and **Eiger** (3970m/13,024ft), whose dangerous, nearly perpendicular northern ascent was first climbed in 1938, are three of the most famous mountains in Switzerland. Their names mean the 'maiden', the 'monk' and the 'ogre'; together they are known as the **Finsteraarhorn Group**. **Finsteraarhorn** (4275m/14,026ft), the highest peak of the Berner Alps, is dominated by glaciers which stretch from the upper Aare and the Rhône valley to Lake Geneva. Also in the region, there are excursions up the **Schilthorn** mountain by funicular (made famous by James Bond in the movie *Her Majesty's Secret Service*); to the **waterfalls** at **Giessbach** and **Lauterbrunnen;** to the **Reichenbach falls** (where Sherlock Holmes fell to his fictional death); and to the Swiss **Open-Air Museum** at **Ballenberg**, with its charmingly preserved houses from all regions of the country displaying traditional crafts and trades, are all recommended. The castle at **Thun**, with its historical museum located at the top of the **Altstadt** (old town), should not be missed.
- Discover the ancient university and trading city of **Basle** (**Basel**). Straddling the Rhine between the Jura region, Alsace in France and Germany's Black Forest, it is a centre of art and research. The collection in the **Art Museum** ranges from Cranach and Holbein via Rembrandt to Monet, Picasso and Max Ernst. Visit the ancient red sandstone **cathedral** or **Münster** (parts date from the ninth to 13th century) and climb the tower for some impressive city vistas. Other sights include the **Spalentor** (1370), one of the original city wall's three remaining towers, and the **Church of St Peter** (15th century). Away from the town, mountain paths zigzag up the Jura mountains.
- Check out the 170m- (558ft-) long, covered wooden **Chapel Bridge** spanning the River Reuss in **Luzern** (known as Lucerne by the country's French-speaking citizens). It was the oldest in Switzerland (1333) until it was destroyed by a fire in 1993. It has since been reconstructed and is still worth seeing. Luzern's medieval old town (**Altstadt**) remains intact; important buildings include the **Hofkirche**, the old **Town Hall** (1602-1606) and the famous **Löwendenkmal**, a memorial to the city mascot, the 'dying Lion of Lucerne', carved out of a cliff.
- Head south through the **San Bernardino pass** to the lovely, Italian-speaking, southernmost tip of Switzerland, the region of **Ticino**. Here the climate is subtropical and the atmosphere Mediterranean. Follow the road from the Alpine valleys through **Bellinzona** with its three medieval castles and continue to the lake resorts of Southern Ticino. **Locarno**, on the shores of **Lago di Maggiore**, with its narrow streets, pavement cafes and lakeside lido is one of the most popular destinations, with a world-famous film festival

in August. Further south, the **health** and **holiday resort** of **Lugano** lies on the **Lago di Lugano** between the peaks of **Monte Bré** and **San Salvatore**. The largest city in Ticino, it is a favourite holiday destination for the Swiss. Piazzas, palazzos, palms, the **Cathedral of San Lorenzo** and the promenade along the lakeshore give the city a special flair.
- To get close to the highest mountains in Switzerland, take a trip to **Valais** ('The valley'), which stretches all the way from the **Rhône Glacier** past **Brig**, **Martigny** and **Sion** down to Lake Geneva. Glaciers can be found on all peaks of the Valais Alps, which include **Dufour Peak** (4634m/15,217ft), **Dom** (4545m/14,917ft), **Weisshorn** (4509m/14,793ft) and the **Matterhorn** (4478m/14,698ft). Small villages of weathered wooden-beamed houses, with flowers pouring out of the window boxes in summer, perch in clearings high on the slopes. High transverse valleys give access to their resorts at the foot of the alpine giants such as **Saas Fee** in the **Saas Valley** and **Zermatt** in the **Nikolai Valley**; the **Matterhorn** provides a magnificent backdrop for the latter. Any visit to the area should also include the **Rhône Glacier** and **grotto** at **Gletsch**.

Top Things To Do

- Join the Swiss in their favourite pastime and go **hiking**. Approximately 50,000km of trails lead through all kinds of terrain in this spectacularly beautiful country. Hiking times are given on the signposts, and trails are graded according to degree of difficulty. The organisation responsible for maintaining the trails and for co-ordinating local hiking associations is the Swiss Hiking Federation, Im Hirshalm 49, 4125 Riehen (tel: (61) 606 9340; website: www.swisshiking.ch). Guided walks, weekend trips and holidays are regularly organised by the Federation and the local associations and are open to individuals and groups. Most associations run at least one day's walk per week (usually on Sunday), and these do not need to be booked in advance. All trips are led by qualified volunteer guides. Details of the walks and addresses of local hiking associations are given in the free booklet *Switzerland on Foot*, available from Switzerland Tourism or directly from the Swiss Hiking Federation. Programmes of walks are also published on the Federation's website (see above). In addition to the above excursions, there are also 'Radio Walks', which are announced during the season every Sunday at 0655 on *Swiss Radio DRS* in the *Guten Morgen* programme. The meeting point, cost, timing and route can be found online (website: www.swisshiking.ch) and on the special telephone line of Swiss Hiking Trails (tel: (61) 606 9346). Participants need merely to turn up at the station or meeting point as announced.
- Enjoy the **mountain sports**. There are plenty of opportunities to go **climbing**, **ice climbing**, **ski touring**, **snow boarding**, **deep-snow skiing**, **heli-skiing** and **glacier walking**. The Swiss Association of Mountain Guides publishes a list of approved mountaineering centres as well as a list of approved guides. Further information can be obtained from Schweizerischer Bergführerverband, Hadlaubstrasse 49, 8006 Zurich (tel: (1) 360 5366; website: www.4000plus.ch) or from Switzerland Tourism. Accommodation is available in the mountains in the form of alpine huts or chalets. As these are open according to season, visitors should check availability with local tourist boards before arriving. It is often necessary to book in advance. In the south west, **Geneva** is the gateway to a variety of ski resorts. One especially extensive area well-suited to families but with excellent skiing for all abilities is **Portes du Soleil**, a cluster of small resorts forming a massive skiing circuit which straddles the French-Swiss border. Key Swiss resorts here include the pretty traditional village of **Champéry**, and the tranquil purpose-built mini resorts of **Champoussin** and **Les Crosets**. The main ski areas near Luzern include the attractive, traditional village of **Andermatt** with reliable snow and challenging skiing, and **Engelberg**, with a small ski area suitable for all abilities. Many of the country's top ski resorts are located in **Graubünden** including chic, expensive **Davos** and **Klosters**, with excellent skiing facilities and lots of varied and sophisticated après-ski, and glamorous **St Moritz** with its top-notch on- and off-piste activities (**snow-polo**, **horse-drawn sleighs**, the **Cresta run**), glitzy nightlife and luxury hotels. Smaller ski resorts in the area include the beautiful spa town of **Bad Scuol**, the smaller resorts of **Flims** and **Laax**, and beautiful **Arosa**, popular with downhill skiers of all levels and also for cross-country skiing. **Valais** contains some of Switzerland's most celebrated resorts including the picturesque car-free village of **Zermatt**, which offers excellent skiing for all abilities, lively nightlife and plenty of non-skiing activities. Trendy **Verbier** forms part of the extensive **Les Quatre Vallées** ski area, attracting serious skiers and snow-boarders to its challenging slopes and providing plenty of facilities for young people. The beautiful car-free village of **Saas Fee** has high, snow-sure slopes and is ideal for beginners and intermediates. The popular ski area of **Crans Montana** consists of chic **Crans sur Sierre** with its thriving nightlife,

and the more down-to-earth, restrained **Montana**. Smaller, more family-oriented resorts in the region include **Anzère**, **Bettmeralp**, **Riederalp** and **Zinal**. In the **Berner Oberland**, the popular year-round resorts of **Grindelwald**, **Mürren** and **Wengen** thrive during the winter ski and snowboard season (mid-December to late-March). Grindelwald is quite old-fashioned and quiet in the evenings but with excellent skiing, ideal for intermediates and beginners, and off-piste activities including tobogganing and winter walking trails. The ski network links up with the scenic ski village of **Wengen**, popular with British skiers, and with lots of long, gentle runs, ideal for intermediates. Nearby tiny, traffic-free **Mürren** counts among Switzerland's more rustic resorts, with limited but challenging skiing including the famous **Schilthorn run** where the British invented modern-day skiing. The quiet resort of **Kandersteg** is a good base for cross-country skiing. The popular winter resorts of **Adelboden**, **Lenk** and **Zweisimmen** are reached from Spiez on Lake Thun. The traditional village resort of **Gstaad** is an upmarket, glamorous destination for skiers with extensive slopes and a thriving après-ski scene. Smaller, more family-oriented winter resorts include **Château d'Oex**, **Leysin** and **Villars**.
- **Cycling** is not necessarily as strenuous as the mountainous terrain might indicate. There are 3300km (2046 miles) of well-marked interlinked trails, and most of them offer easy cycling. Hire a bicycle at a railway station and return it at any other station at the end of the tour. This is possible at most train stations. There are also inline **skating** routes throughout the country, varying in difficulty from easy to demanding.
- Lakes such as **Lake Geneva**, **Lugano**, and **Neuchâtel** offer **sailing**, **water-skiing** and **canoeing**. **Rowing** can be done on **Lake Zurich**.
- Go on a **cruise** or just take a **ferry trip** on one of Switzerland's many **lakes**. During the summer, **steamer cruises** on **Zürich's lake** are popular. The medieval castle at **Rapperswil**, on the bank of the lake, is well worth a visit. In the Lucerne area, ferries on the **Vierwaldstättersee** service the tiny villages surrounding the lake and connect with various mountain railways and cableways. Local ferries link Lugano with the scenic lakeside towns of **Gandria** and **Morcote**. During spring, the area is in full bloom with fig and olive trees, pomegranates and myrtle. On **Lake Constance**, boat trips to Konstanz and Lindau in Germany or to Bregenz in Austria are available. A boat trip on **Lake Geneva** is highly recommended. Dominated by the **Jet d'Eau**, a 145m- (476ft-) high fountain, the lake is generally alive with sailing boats. A crisp breeze, known as the *bise* (kiss), blows across the lake and there are facilities for all kinds of **watersports**, as well as **golf** and **riding** nearby.
- Enjoy a **theatre** production at the **Zürcher Schauspielhaus**, which is considered one of the most prestigious German-speaking theatres in the country.
- Go to **Basle** for the three days of the **Basler Fasnacht** (a pre-Lenten carnival), during which time no serious sightseeing should or can be done, as visitors are required to take part in grand masked parties and street parades with fancy costumes. There is even a **Fasnacht Fountain** in front of the **City Theatre**.
- Take the highest aerial **cablecar** in Europe at **Zermatt**, ascending the **Little Matterhorn**. The ski run from here back to Zermatt is the longest in Europe. The village is internationally known for not allowing cars. Transport is either on foot, by electric car or by horse and cart.
- If in Luzern, head south to the small town of **Engelberg**, where the world's first **revolving cable car** ascends **Mount Titlis**, the highest lookout-point in central Switzerland.
- The **Montreux International Jazz Festival** in July is always worth visiting as it constantly attracts the world's greatest jazz, blues and rhythm 'n' blues artists.
- Visit one of Switzerland's many climatic **health resorts**. The **Graubünden** resorts of **Arosa**, **Davos**, **Klosters** and **St Moritz** are renowned the world over. **Interlaken**, situated between the lakes of Brienz and Thun, is another renowned climatic health resort and the gateway to the **Berner Oberland**.
- **Geneva** is a traditional European centre for health and recuperation, and maintains state-of-the-art **sanatoria** such as the 100-year-old **Clinique Générale Beaulieu**, well worth a visit.

TOURIST INFORMATION

Switzerland Travel Centre in the UK
1st Floor, 30 Bedford Street, London WC2E 9ED, UK
Tel: (00800) 1002 0030 (toll-free in Europe) or (020) 7420 4900.
Website: www.myswitzerland.com

Switzerland Tourism in the USA
608 5th Avenue, Swiss Center, New York, NY 10020, USA
Tel: (212) 757 5944 or (877) 794 7795 (toll-free).
Website: www.myswitzerland.com

Entertainment

FOOD & DRINK: Swiss cuisine is varied. The great speciality is *fondue*, a delicious concoction of *Gruyère* and *Vacherin* cheese, melted and mixed with white wine, flour, Kirsch and a little garlic. Other cheese specialities are *Emmental* and *Tête de Moine*. Pork sausages or salami come in a variety of local recipes including *Beinwurst*, *Engadinerwurst*, *Kalbsleberwurst* (calf's liver pâté), *Knackerli*, *Landjäger* and *Leberwurst* (pâté). A great variety of Swiss wines are available throughout the country. Swiss beer of a lager type is also available. Bottled mineral water is an accepted beverage, with local brands including *Henniez*.

Things to know: Bars/cocktail lounges have table and/or counter service. Although there are many self-service snack bars, table service is normal.

National specialities:

- *Viande séchée* (dried beef or pork) from Valais and the Grisons where it is called *Bündnerfleisch,* served with spring or pickled onions.
- *Papet vaudoir* (leeks and potatoes).
- *Pieds de porc* (pigs' feet).
- *Rösti* (shredded fried potatoes).
- *Fondue Bourguignonne* (cubed meat with various sauces).
- *Leckerli* (spiced honey cakes topped with icing sugar, decorated in Bern with a white sugar bear).
- *Fasnachtküchli* (sugar-dusted pastries eaten during Carnival).
- *Gugelhopf* (a type of sponge cake with a hollow centre).
- *Schaffhausen* (cream-filled cakes).

National drinks:

- *Beer, Kirsch, Marc, Pflümli* and *Williams* (spirits).

Tipping: A service charge is included in all hotel, restaurant, cafe, bar, taxi and hairdressing services by law; further gratuities are not usually required.

NIGHTLIFE: Most major towns and resorts have nightclubs or discos with music and dancing, sometimes serving food. There are also cinemas and theatres, and some bars and restaurants have local folk entertainment.

SHOPPING: Special purchases include embroidery and linen, Bernese woodcarving, chocolate, cheese, Swiss army knives and luxury handmade clocks and watches. **Shopping hours:** Mon-Fri 0830-1200 and 1400-1830, Sat 0800-1200 and 1330-1600. Most shops are closed on Monday mornings.

Business

- **GDP**: US$251.9 billion.
- **Main exports**: Machinery, chocolate, watches, metals and chemicals.
- **Main imports**: Chemicals, textiles and minerals.
- **Main trade partners**: Germany, Austria, France, USA, UK, Spain, The Netherlands and Italy.

ECONOMY: Switzerland has a typical West European mixed economy with a bias towards light and craft-based industries: Swiss precision manufacturing such as watch-making is renowned throughout the world. The country is highly industrialised and heavily dependent on exports of finished goods (in total, exports are equivalent to just under half of Swiss GDP). Lacking raw materials of its own, almost all of these must be imported. In manufacturing, the machinery and equipment industry specialises in precision and advanced technology products: machine tools, printing and photographic equipment, electronic control and medical equipment. There is also a substantial chemical industry, employing 15 per cent of the workforce, which continues to grow steadily. Swiss firms have proved particularly adept at exploiting niche markets across a wide range of industries and products. Although half of the country's food is imported, the agricultural sector is a strong and major employer. The processed foods industry has a high international profile, particularly in such products as chocolate, cheese and baby foods.
The service sector is dominated by banking, where the particular reputation of the Swiss banking community for discretion has attracted large deposits. The Government has come under some pressure to allow disclosure in the course of criminal and other investigations: recognising the international climate, the Swiss authorities have generally responded more flexibly of late. Switzerland remains one of Europe's major financial centres. Among other service industries, tourism is of growing importance: Switzerland receives around 11 million visitors annually and the industry contributes around $12 billion to the national economy. The economy has been stagnant during the last two years, largely a reflection of conditions throughout continental Europe; the economy in 2005 was rather slow with growth at 1.8 per cent. Switzerland is not a member of the European Union, although nearly two-thirds of its exports are sold to EU countries. The government is in the process of negotiating a new set of bilateral agreements with the EU, but the prospect of it joining the Union is as remote as ever. A referendum rejected even membership of the European Economic Area – a body

created to reduce the economic barriers between the EU and the European Free Trade Association (EFTA), to which Switzerland does belong. In May 1992, Switzerland gained admission to the IMF and World Bank.

BUSINESS ETIQUETTE: Businesspeople are expected to wear suits. Although English is widely spoken, it is always appreciated if a visitor attempts to say a few words in the language of the host. When visiting a firm, a visiting card is essential. **Office hours:** Mon-Fri 0800-1200 and 1400-1700.

CONFERENCES/CONVENTIONS: The neutrality, stability and conveniently central location of Switzerland make the country a favourite meeting place for conventions and international organisations. It has an extensive and highly developed network of conference destinations with all the major cities and many of the smaller alpine and lake resorts offering hotels and convention centres which are fully equipped with a complete range of facilities including interpretation and audio-visual services. Each of Switzerland's main cities has its own Convention Bureau, whilst the Association of Swiss Convention Centres, Swiss Congress, oversees meetings activity throughout the country. The organisation is made up of the 19 leading congress locations in Switzerland and can help with the organisation of a meeting in any region of the country.

Syria

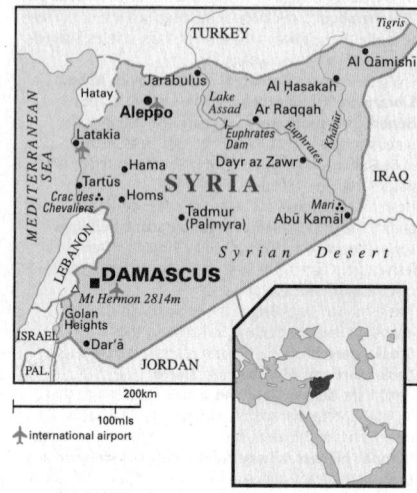

Location: Middle East.

Time: GMT + 2 (GMT + 3 from 1 April to 1 October).

Overview

The Syrian Arab Republic revels in its antiquity, having been inhabited for tens of thousands of years - and in the variation and cultural riches that such antiquity has brought it. This is a country that preserves scores of relics documenting the rise and fall of different civilisations, and which continues to welcome such diversity.

Syria was once regarded as a frontier region, bordered to the east by the Arabs and Persians. The Persian invasions were repulsed but Syria eventually fell to the Muslims in the mid-seventh century. From then on, Syria was to be firmly part of the Muslim world, although retaining Christian and Jewish populations. Muslim control of Syria was vital to the defeat of the Christians and their expulsion from Jerusalem. Even when the terrifying force of the 13th century Mongols was unleashed on Syria, their massive Hulagu army was eventually defeated at the Battle of Goliath's Well – a victory that, in retrospect, must be seen as one of the world's most decisive military engagements, preventing both the Muslim world – and the Christian one – from certain doom.

Today, Syria's Islamic identity is as central to the country as its Arab roots. Such doctrine over-spilled into Arab nationalism in the 1950s - indeed, Nasser's revolution in Egypt prompted Syria to join Egypt in the United Arab Republic. However, the alliance was short-lived, Syria seceding in 1961 to form the Syrian Arab Republic. Since then, Syria has been ruled at the head of a tightly controlled dictatorship. Even when General Hafez al-Assad of the Ba'ath Party (or Arab Socialist Renaissance) died in 2000, and his son Bashar assumed headship, Western hopes that the country would pursue a more pro-Western line proved misguided - in the vocabulary of the US Bush administration, the Syrian Arab Republic is a 'state of concern' (one level below the 'axis of evil'). Although Syria pulled its forces out of Lebanon in 2005 after being implicated by a UN report for the assassination of former Lebanese Premier, Rafik Hariri (Syrian troops have remained there ever since the 1973 Arab-Israeli war, in a (successful) attempt to prevent the expansion of Israel, and to counterbalance Israeli military might in the region), relations with numerous Western states remains fragile.

In short, the Syrian Arab Republic's long history is littered with dramatic episodes, from being subsumed into past Empires (Babylonians, Canaanites, Assyrians, Phoenicians, and so on) to more recent events, such as Napoleon's campaign in 1799/1800, the Egyptian invasion in the 1830s and the insurrection in 1860-61. However, such battles and scrambles over territory have translated into a catalogue of staggering cities full of stunning monuments, from the entire city of Damascus to the country's many mosques. The events have also failed to impair the character of the Syrian people who – surprisingly to some – exude friendliness and warmth, and are justly proud of their land.

General Information

AREA: 185,180 sq km (71,498 sq miles).

POPULATION: 18.6 million (UN, 2005).

POPULATION DENSITY: 100.4 per sq km.

CAPITAL: Damascus. **Population:** 3.5 million (official estimate 2003).

GEOGRAPHY: The country can be divided geographically into four main areas: the fertile plain in the northeast, the plateau, coastal and mountain areas in the west, the central plains, and the desert and steppe region in the central and southeastern areas. The Euphrates flows from Turkey in the north, through the Syrian Arab Republic, down to Iraq in the southeast. It is the longest river in the Syrian Arab Republic, the total length being 2330km (1450 miles), of which 600km (370 miles) pass through the Syrian Arab Republic. The Khabur River supports the al-Khabur Basin in the northeast.

GOVERNMENT: Republic since 1973. Gained independence in 1946. **Head of State:** President Bashar al-Assad since 2000. **Head of Government:** Prime Minister Muhammad Naji al-Otari since 2003. **Recent history:** In June 2000, after years of failing health, President Assad died. Having fallen out with his brother, Rifaat, some years earlier, and with the accidental death of his eldest son, Basil, in 1994, Assad had selected his second son, Bashar, as heir. While domestic policy has seen something of a relaxation under Bashar, Western hopes that the Syrian Arab Republic would pursue a more pro-Western line have proved misguided – in the vocabulary of the US Bush administration, the Syrian Arab Republic is a 'state of concern' (one level below the 'axis of evil'). The Syrians have provided some assistance to the Western 'War Against Terror' but were strongly opposed to the Anglo-American invasion of Iraq in 2003. Syria pulled its forces out of Lebanon in 2005, after coming under intense international pressure following a UN report that implicated the Syrian Arab Republic in the assassination of former Premier of Lebanon, Rafik Hariri. Both Syria and pro-Syria Lebanese officials were thought to be involved, although this has been strongly denied by Damascus.

The 1973 constitution allows for a single-chamber legislature, the 250-member People's Assembly. Executive power is vested in the President who is directly elected for a seven-year term.

LANGUAGE: Arabic, French and English. Kurdish is spoken by a small minority.

RELIGION: Over 80 per cent Muslim (mostly Sunni), with sizeable Christian (mostly Orthodox and Catholic) groups and Jewish minorities.

ELECTRICITY: 220 volts AC, 50Hz. European-style two-pin plugs.

SOCIAL CONVENTIONS: The Syrians take as much pride in their modern amenities as in their unique heritage and in the tradition of exquisite craftsmanship, and both should be appreciated. Visitors will enjoy the hospitality that is a deep-rooted Arab tradition and sharing the pleasures of an attractive Oriental way of life. It is customary to shake hands on meeting and on departure. A visitor will be treated with great courtesy and will frequently be offered refreshment, usually coffee. As a guest in someone's home or, more usually, in a restaurant, visitors should respect Arab customs and traditions. A souvenir from the visitor's home or company is well received. Conservative casual wear is suitable. Beachwear or shorts should not be worn away from the beach or poolside. Smoking follows Western habits and in most cases it is obvious where not to smoke. Smoking is prohibited in public from dawn to dusk during Ramadan.

Photography: No attempt should be made to photograph anything remotely connected with the armed forces or in the vicinity of defence installations, which even includes radio transmission aerials. It is wise to take a good look at what will be appearing in the background before pointing the camera.

Climate

The Syrian Arab Republic's climate is characterised by hot, dry summers and fairly cold winters. Nights are often cool.

Required clothing: Lightweights are essential in summer with protective headwear. Heavy winter clothing is advisable from November to March.

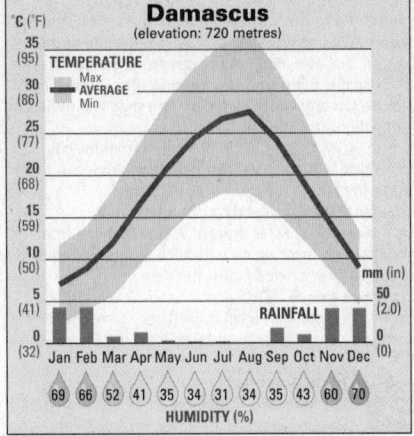

Damascus (elevation: 720 metres)

Communications

Telephone: IDD is available. Country code: 963. Public telephones are available.

Mobile telephone: International roaming agreements have been established. Coverage is good, covering 95 per cent of the populated areas.

Internet: Access to Internet services is available in universities and public offices.

Post: Airmail to Western Europe takes up to 10 days. Parcels sent from the Syrian Arab Republic should be packed at the post office. There are post offices in virtually all towns. Post office hours: Mon-Fri 0800-1400; larger branches are open longer.

MEDIA: The Government and Baath Party own and control much of the Syrian media. Criticism of the President and his family is not permitted and the domestic and foreign press are censored. Press freedom swelled after Bashar al-Assad became President in 2000, overseeing the licensing of the first private publications in almost 40 years. However, a subsequent press law imposed a range of restrictions. Publications had to obtain licences from the Prime Minister and could be suspended for violating content bans. Websites deemed to be offensive or anti-Syrian are banned by the Government.

Press: The *Syria Times* is published daily in English. All other newspapers are in Arabic (the most important ones being *Al-Baath*, *Al-Thawra* and *Tishrin*). International papers are also widely available.

TV: Many viewers have access to foreign TV broadcasts, as well as the three state-run networks. The use of satellite receivers is permitted. *Syrian TV* is state-run and operates domestic channels, plus a satellite service, broadcasting in Arabic, English and French.

Radio: Private, commercial FM broadcasters are currently being developed, but will be unable to transmit news or political content. The first of these private FM stations has already emerged: *Al-Madina FM*, launched in March 2005. *Syrian Arab Republic Radio* is a state-run service, as is *Radio Damascus*, although this is an external service (broadcasting in several languages, including English).

Passport/Visa

	Passport Required?	Visa Required?	Return Ticket Required?
Full British	Yes	Yes	Yes
Australian	Yes	Yes	Yes
Canadian	Yes	Yes	Yes
USA	Yes	Yes	Yes
Other EU	Yes	Yes	Yes
Japanese	Yes	Yes	Yes

Note: *Regulations and requirements may be subject to change at short notice, and you are advised to contact the appropriate diplomatic or consular authority before finalising travel arrangements. Any numbers in the chart refer to the footnotes below.*

Restricted entry and transit: The Government of Syria refuses entry and transit to holders of Israeli passports, any passenger holding a passport containing a visa (valid or expired) for Israel and those holding a stamp indicating an Israel-Jordan border crossing; nationals of Yemen Republic who hold a passport issued by the Democratic Republic of Yemen; *refused* entry to all female nationals of Afghanistan, Bangladesh, Mauritius, The Philippines, Sri Lanka and Thailand, unless they can show approval from immigration head office; females aged between 14 and 35 years unless accompanied by a father, husband or brother (and with proof of such status); and holders of passports bearing evidence of entry at Sharm El Sheikh, Rafha, Gaza or Nablus.

PASSPORTS: Passport valid for at least six months required by all except nationals of Lebanon holding valid national ID cards.

VISAS: Required by all except the following:
(a) nationals of Algeria, Bahrain, Egypt, Jordan, Kuwait, Lebanon, Libya, Mauritania, Oman, Qatar, Saudi Arabia, Somalia, Sudan, Tunisia, United Arab Emirates and Yemen Republic;
(b) nationals of Morocco, except females aged 18 to 25 who require special permission from the Syrian Chief of Immigration, unless married to a national of Syria and having proof of marriage;
(c) transit passengers continuing their journey by the same or first connecting aircraft within 24 hours provided holding onward or return documentation and not leaving the airport.

Types of visa and cost: *Single-entry:* £32. *Multiple-entry:* £50. *Transit.* Payable in cash or by postal order only. These fees are only for nationals of the UK. The cost of visas for other nationalities varies; consult the Embassy for further information.

Validity: Single-entry (three months from date of issue). Multiple-entry (six months from date of issue). Transit (three months from date of issue). Entry visas initially allow stays of up to 14 days. Extensions for up to three months are possible; apply at the Department of Immigration.

Application to: Consulate (or Consular section at the Embassy); see *Passport/Visa Information*. In countries where the Syrian Arab Republic does not have diplomatic representation, visitors should apply by post to the nearest Syrian Embassy.

Application requirements: (a) Two completed application forms. (b) Valid passport with at least one blank page. (c) Two passport-size photos. (d) Fee. (e) A stamped, self-addressed envelope for postal applications. (f) For a Business visa, a company letter on headed paper stating the nature of the business.

Working days required: Four.

Temporary residence: Applications to the Department of Immigration in Damascus.

Note: Those wishing to stay in the Syrian Arab Republic for a period exceeding one year must submit an AIDS test certificate.

PASSPORT/VISA INFORMATION

Embassy of the Syrian Arab Republic in the UK
8 Belgrave Square, London SW1X 8PH, UK
Tel: (020) 7245 9012 *or* 7201 8830/8831 (consular section).
Opening hours: Mon- Fri 1000-1200 (visa applications); 1400- 1500 (visa collection).
Website: www.syrianembassy.co.uk

Embassy of the Syrian Arab Republic in the USA
2215 Wyoming Avenue NW, Washington, DC 20008, USA
Tel: (202) 232 6313.
Website: www.syrianembassy.us

Money

Currency: Syrian Pound (SYP; symbol S£) = 100 piastres. Notes are in denominations of S£1000, 500, 200, 100, 50, 25, 10, 5 and 1. Coins are in denominations of S£25, 10, 5, 2 and 1.

Currency exchange: Syrian currency cannot generally be reconverted to hard currency. The country's banking system is state-owned, and there is at least one branch of the Commercial Bank of Syria in every main town. Hard currency can be exchanged for local currency in these branches.

Credit & debit cards: American Express and Diners Club are most readily accepted; some hotels will accept MasterCard. Tickets may be bought with credit cards. Check with your credit or debit card company for merchant acceptability and for other services which may be available.

Traveller's cheques: Can be difficult to exchange and are not generally recommended.

Currency restrictions: The export of local currency is limited to S£5000 by residents of Syria and US$5000 by foreigners. The amount of local currency imported is unlimited for residents of Syria and limited to US$5000 by foreigners.

Banking hours: Normally Sat-Thurs 0800-1400 (banks tend to close early on Thursdays).

Exchange rate indicators:
Rate at time of publishing
£1.00= S£92.81
$1.00= S£52.51

Duty Free

The following items may be imported into the Syrian Arab Republic without incurring customs duty (irrespective of passenger's age):

200 cigarettes or 50 cigarillos or 25 cigars or 250g of tobacco; 30g perfume for personal use; 570ml of spirits; 500ml of lotion and 500ml of eau de cologne; gifts worth up to S£250.
Prohibited items: Firearms and ammunition; live, frozen or stuffed birds, or any bird-derived products.

Public Holidays

Below are listed Publich Holidays for the January 2006-June 2007 period.
2006: Jan 1 New Year's Day. **Jan 10** Eid al-Adha (Feast of the Sacrifice). **Jan 31** Islamic New Year. **Mar 8** Revolution Day. **Mar 21** Mothers Day. **Apr 11** Mouloud (Birth of the Prophet). **Apr 17** Independence Day. **May 1** Labour Day. **May 6** Martyrs' Day. **Oct 6** October Liberation War. **Oct 22-24** Eid al-Fitr (End of Ramadan). **Dec 25** Christmas Day. **Dec 31** Eid al-Adha (Feast of the Sacrifice).
2007: Jan 1 New Year's Day. **Jan 20** Islamic New Year. **Mar 8** Revolution Day. **Mar 21** Mothers Day. **Mar 31** Mouloud (Birth of the Prophet). **Apr 17** Independence Day. **May 1** Labour Day. **May 6** Martyrs' Day.
Note: Muslim festivals are timed according to local sightings of various phases of the moon and the dates given above are approximations. During the lunar month of Ramadan that precedes Eid al-Fitr, Muslims fast during the day and feast at night and working hours are 0900-1400. Many restaurants are closed during the day and there may be restrictions on smoking and drinking. For more information, see the *World of Islam* appendix.

Health

	Special Precautions?	Certificate Required?
Yellow Fever	No	1
Cholera	2	No
Typhoid & Polio	3	N/A
Malaria	4	N/A

Note: Regulations and requirements may be subject to change at short notice, and you are advised to contact your doctor well in advance of your intended date of departure. Any numbers in the chart refer to the footnotes below.

1: A yellow fever vaccination certificate is required from travellers coming within six days from infected areas.
2: Following WHO guidelines issued in 1973, a cholera vaccination certificate is not a condition of entry to the Syrian Arab Republic. Up-to-date advice should be sought before deciding whether precautions should include vaccination, as medical opinion is divided over its effectiveness; see the *Health* appendix.
3: Vaccination against typhoid is advised.
4: Malaria risk, exclusively in the benign *vivax* form, exists along the northern border, in the El Hassaka province, from May through October.
Food & drink: Mains water is normally chlorinated and relatively safe. Bottled water is available and is advised for the first few weeks of the stay. Drinking water outside main cities and towns is likely to be contaminated and sterilisation is considered essential. Milk is unpasteurised and should be boiled. Powdered or tinned milk is available and is advised but make sure that it is reconstituted with pure water. Only eat well-cooked meat and fish, preferably served hot. Vegetables should be cooked and fruit peeled.
Other risks: *Hepatitis A* is common, so vaccination is recommended. *Hepatitis B* is endemic, and vaccination is recommended for those at high risk. *Bilharzia* (schistosomiasis) is present. Avoid swimming and paddling in fresh water; swimming pools which are well chlorinated and maintained are safe. *Visceral leishmaniasis* occurs in the north and there is increasing incidence of *cutaneous leishmaniasis*.
Rabies is present. For those at high risk, vaccination before arrival should be considered. If you are bitten, seek medical advice without delay. For more information, consult the *Health* appendix.
Health care: Health insurance is recommended. There is no reciprocal health agreement with the UK. Basic medical facilities exist in main cities but there are few outside them. Medical care is provided free of charge to those who cannot afford to pay. For more information, see the *Health* appendix.

Travel - International

AIR:
The Syrian Arab Republic's national airline is *Syrian Arab Airlines (RB)* (website: www.syrian-airlines.co.uk).
Approximate flight times: From Damascus to *London* is six hours and from Aleppo is four to five hours.
Main airports: *Damascus (DAM)*, 25km (18 miles) southeast of the city (travel time - 30 to 40 minutes). Two other international airports, *Aleppo* and *Latakia*, offer connections to *Amman* and *Beirut* airports. *To/from the airport*: A bus service runs to and from the city centre. Taxis are available, but it is advisable to negotiate fares beforehand if there is no taxi meter in the cab. *Facilities*: Bank, restaurants/snack bars, duty free shop and tourist information.
Aleppo (ALP) (Nejrab), 10km (6.5 miles) from the city (travel time - 20 minutes). *To/from the airport*: Bus and taxi services go to the city. *Facilities*: Bank, restaurants/snack bars and tourist information.
Latakia Airport (LTK) is situated 25km (16 miles) from the city. Although there are no scheduled flights serving this airport, some chartered flights run here.
Departure tax: S£200. Children under 10 years of age and transit passengers (continuing their journey within 24 hours and not leaving the customs zone) are exempt.
SEA:
Main ports: *Latakia* and *Tartus*. The nearest car ferry sails to Bodrum in western Turkey. Beirut (Lebanon), however, is served - from Alexandria, Cyprus and Greece - and Damascus can then be reached in a couple of hours by road. An attractive alternative is to take a ferry either from Italy (Ancona, Brindisi or Venice) or from Greece (Piraeus) and go as far as Turkey (Bodrum, Izmir or Kusadasi). From any of these ports it is easy to join the main road south via Aydin, Dinar, Antalya, and the steep rugged coast through Alanya, Anamur, Mersin, Tarsus, Iskenderun, Antakya, to Aleppo or Latakia. Three days should be allowed for the sea crossing and another three for the drive. Certain lines offer a mixture of cruise and car ferry; the return journey could be made via Bodrum, Heraklion, Rhodes, Santorini and Piraeus. Cruise ferries are organised by Cypriot, Greek, Italian and Turkish companies and their programmes vary year by year. Contact a travel agent for details.
RAIL:
Links go via Ankara (Turkey) and Istanbul. Change at Ankara for the *Taurus Express* to Aleppo.
ROAD:
The principal international routes are from Istanbul, via the E5 road to Adana, Ankara and Iskenderun in Turkey. Enter at Bab-al-Hawa for Aleppo, or at Kassab for Latakia. From the east, the best routes are from Aqaba on the Red Sea in Jordan. **Bus:** Services are available across the desert, with routes from Aleppo and Damascus to Istanbul; Damascus to Amman; Damascus to Beirut and Tripoli; and Damascus to Riyadh.
Documentation: To enter the Syrian Arab Republic with a car, a customs certificate must be produced; it is obtainable from Automobile Clubs and Touring Clubs against a deposit. An international driving permit can also be obtained from these organisations, which is obligatory for holders of licences which do not use the Latin alphabet.

Travel - Internal

AIR:
Syrian Arab Airlines flies to Aleppo, Deir ez Zor, Latakia, Palmyra and Qamishli. In general, fares are exceedingly cheap.
RAIL:
The railway extends 2200km (1364 miles). A service operates between Damascas-Aleppo-Deirez-Zar-Hassakeh-Kamechli. A second line runs between Aleppo-Latakia-Banias-Tartous-Homs-Damascas-Deraa. First-class carriages are air conditioned.
ROAD:
There are 25,887km (16,086 miles) of roads. Traffic systems are poor and there are numerous accidents. Second-class roads are unreliable during the wet season. The principal route is Aleppo to Damascus and Dar'a (north-south axis). Traffic drives on the right. **Bus:** Services run from Damascus and Aleppo to most towns and are cheap, widely used, efficient and comfortable. There are orange-and-white air-conditioned *Karnak (*Government-operated) buses and buses run by *Transtour*. Reservations should be made well in advance. Karnak bus routes serve their own terminals, which are usually in or near the city centres. There are also privately-run bus and microbus services, which started recently all over the Syrian Arab Republic. **Taxi:** Shared taxis are available to all parts of the country. Service taxis (old limousines) run on major routes and cost 50 to 70 per cent more than Karnak buses.
Documentation: International Driving Permit required. Green Cards are not yet accepted in the Syrian Arab Republic. Insurance is required by law and a customs certificate is needed. These are available from touring and automobile clubs.
URBAN:
Publicly owned bus services operate in all major towns and cities. Most buses outside the capital, however, have no signs in a European script to indicate destination or stops, which can make travelling rather difficult. Taxis are widely available. Fares should be agreed in advance and according to the meter in the cities.
Travel times: The following chart gives approximate travel times (in hours and minutes) from **Damascus** to other major cities/towns in the Syrian Arab Republic.

	Air	Road
Aleppo	1.00	5.30
Latakia	1.00	5.00
Deir ez Zor	1.00	8.00
Al Hasakah	-	8.00

Travel Advice

Developments in the region may trigger public unrest. Travellers should be particularly vigilant in public places. There is a continuing threat from terrorism in Syria. Travellers should not attempt to enter Iraq via the Syrian border, which is subject to restrictions on both sides.
This advice is based on information provided by the Foreign and Commonwealth Office in the UK. It is correct at time of publishing. As the situation can change rapidly, visitors are advised to contact the following organisations for the latest travel advice:

British Foreign and Commonwealth Office
Tel: (0845) 850 2829.
Website: www.fco.gov.uk

US Department of State
Website: http://travel.state.gov/travel

Accommodation

HOTELS:
While accommodation can generally be arranged on arrival from November to March, reservations are highly recommended throughout the year. Particularly during exhibitions, up-market hotels in Aleppo and Damascus are often fully booked. Tariffs are the same throughout the year. All rates are subject to a 15 per cent service charge. Hotels range from fairly low grade to luxurious 5-star accommodation. The best-quality hotels are found in Damascus, though Aleppo, Hama, Homs, Latakia and Palmyra also have luxury hotels. For further information, contact the Ministry of Tourism *or* the Tourist Information, Centre (see *Top Things To Do*).
GUEST HOUSES:
Available in Aleppo, Bosra, Damascus, Dar'a, Idlib and Zabadani. *Cités Universitaires* offer summer accommodation.
CAMPING AND CARAVANNING:
There are official campsites in Aleppo, Latakia, Palmyra and Tartus. There are also campsites at many of the summer coastal resorts.
APARTMENTS AND SELF CATERING:
There are self-catering apartments available for hire in most of the main towns.

Top Things To See

- Navigate through the world's oldest inhabited city: **Damascus**. A central feature of this cluttered and clamorous city is the **Ummayyad Mosque**, entered by passing through the **Al-Hamidiyah Bazaar**. The history of the mosque in many ways traces the history of Damascus; built on the site of a temple to the ancient Aramean god Haddad, the original temple was adapted and enlarged by the Romans and used as a temple to Jupiter. It was later knocked down by the Byzantines, who replaced the pagan temple with the Cathedral of John the Baptist, which was subsequently converted into a mosque to accommodate the Islamic teachings brought by the Arabs in AD 636. The mosque houses the **Tomb of St John the Baptist**. The **Tikiyeh Mosque**, built in the mid-16th century, stands out by its two elegant minarets and great dome. The 18th-century **Al Azem Palace** is now a national museum, where there are, amongst other examples of Islamic art, beautifully illuminated copies of the Koran. Situated in old Damascus, a little way off the famous **Via Recta**, or the 'Street called Straight', is the **House of Hanania**, where St Paul hid, using the underground chapel for worship. The church in the **Damascus Wall** from where St Paul escaped in a basket is also still preserved. Other attractions include the **Sayyida Zainab Shrine** (the granddaughter of the Prophet Mohammad), the **Tomb of Saladin** at the back of the Ummayyad Mosque, and the outskirts of Damascus, especially **Dummar**, with seasonal entertainment and restaurants. **Ghota**, the fruit orchards surrounding Damascus, is at its best during the blooming of apricot, plums, cherries and other trees in early spring.

- See some of the oldest **minarets** in the whole of Islam in **Bosra**, the first city in the Syrian Arab Republic to become Muslim. As a stopover on the pilgrimage route to Mecca, Bosra was a prosperous city until the 17th century. By then the region was becoming unsafe and the pilgrims began to take a less dangerous route further west. The **Mosque of Omar** in the centre of the town (called **Jami-al Arouss**, 'the bridal mosque', by the Bosriots), used to be a pagan temple and now stands as the only mosque surviving from the early-Islamic period that has preserved its original facades.

- To find a whole new meaning to the phrase 'girl power', head to **Palmyra**, a town set in a desert oasis, and where the legendary Queen Zenobia ruled and stood against the two great empires of the Romans and the Persians. Zenobia was taken captive to Rome when the Emperor Aurelian conquered and destroyed the city in AD 272. The ruins of the **Valley of Tombs**, the **Hypogeum of the Three Brothers**, the **Great Temple of Bel** and the **Monumental Arch**, now a world UNESCO Heritage Site, are some of the fine remains found over a wide area of the city, prized as containing some of the most famous monuments to the Classical period in the Middle East. **Halabiyé** and **Zalabiya**, situated 40km (25 miles) from **Deir ez Zor**, also contain ruins that bear witness to an important military role during the reign of Queen Zenobia.

- Visit **Crac des Chevaliers**, the most famous crusader castle in the world. A stronghold of the Hospitallers during the days of the Latin Kingdom of Jerusalem (1100-1290), it maintained a garrison of several thousand soldiers in peacetime. The castle, rising from an altitude of 670m (2200ft), was protected by watchtowers and supplied with food from the surrounding fertile countryside. The crusader castles of **Salaheddin**, near **Latakia**, and **Markab**, near **Banyas**, also merit a visit.

- Situated on the **River Orontes**, 45km (28 miles) from **Homs**, **Hama** dates back to beyond 5000 BC. See the aesthetic spectacle of the *norias*, gigantic wooden waterwheels, which are Hama's unique feature, still used to provide water for the city and to irrigate the many public gardens. The **orchards**, the **Great Mosque** and the **Al Azem Palace's Museum** are also of interest.

- Be gobsmacked by **Aleppo**, older possibly even than Damascus, and containing a massive **Citadel** that stands on the site of a **Hittite acropolis**. This UNESCO Heritage Site is one of the most magnificent examples of Islamic Arab military architecture in the Syrian Arab Republic. There is an impressive number of mosques in the city.

- See the 'pearl of the **Euphrates**' – that great and legendary river – at **Deir ez Zor**, located on the right bank of the river. The garden and orchards along the banks of the Euphrates harmonise beautifully with the golden desert hues and the silver thread of the river.

- Stroll around **Mari**'s **Royal Palace**, built by **Zimrilim**, ruler of this important city-state 2000 years ago, and boasting 300 rooms and halls. It was rediscovered in the course of excavations during the 1930s and is now protected by a modern roof. Mari itself was built at a strategic point on the trade routes from the Syrian Arab Republic to Mesopotamia. The town's oldest ruins date back 5000 years.

Top Things To Do

- Be stunned by the bright colours of Syrian cities during the annual **Silk Road Festival** (usually held in September), commemorating the country's meeting of myriad nationalities and communities by harking back to when the Syrian Arab Republic was the meeting place for the Silk Road caravans from around the world. Syrian cities are usually also awash with artistic and cultural activities during this time.

- Attend a musical festival, held every two years, at **Bosra**'s well-preserved Roman amphitheatre (with room for 15,000 spectators). The eastern exit to the town is one of the gorgeous amphitheatre's last surviving vestiges of a pre-Roman civilisation. The remains of an archway dating from the first century – the Nabatean period, of which nearly all traces are now lost – are unique in the Syrian Arab Republic.

- Browse around one of the Syrian Arab Republic's many **souks** (markets). Particularly recommended is the one at **Aleppo**, made up of 16km (10 miles) of meandering low

corridors lined with shops and bustling with activity. **Damascus' Long Souk** is also wonderful.

- Get a back-rub in the Syrian Arab Republic's well-preserved *hammams*, or public baths. There are some lovely ancient *khans* (rest houses) to unwind in.

- Relax on the Syrian Arab Republic's Mediterranean coast, such as in the spot of **Latakia**, a major holiday resort. The city stands at the foot of the forested chain of mountains overlooking the coastal strip on one side and the edge of the **Fertile Plains** (the 'Cradle of Civilisation') on the other. There are a number of antiquities, including the ruined **Temple of Bacchus** and a **triumphal arch**. **Tartus** also has some lovely beaches and mountains. Near Tartus, 10km (6 miles) inland, are the **Drekish Mountains**, famous for the purity of their water. Most of the Mediterranean resorts offer **canoeing**, **scuba diving** and other **watersports**.

TOURIST INFORMATION

Ministry of Tourism
Shukry El-Qutly Street,
Damascus, Syrian Arab Republic
Tel: (11) 221 0122 *or* 5916.
Website: www.syriatourism.org

Entertainment

FOOD & DRINK: There are numerous restaurants in Aleppo and Damascus serving a variety of Oriental and European dishes.

Things to know: Table service is the norm and a meal is paid for afterwards. There are bars serving a wide range of alcoholic drinks. Alcohol is permitted but restrictions are imposed during Ramadan when it is illegal to drink in public from dawn to dusk, even for non-Muslims.

National specialities:

- *Kubbeh* (minced semolina and meat formed in balls and stuffed with minced meat, onion and nuts).
- *Yabrak* (vine leaves stuffed with rice and minced meat), *ouzi* (pastry stuffed with rice and minced meat) and a variety of vegetables cooked with meat and tomato sauce, usually presented on separate plates and eaten by mixing it with cooked rice.
- *Mensaf* (pieces of lamb on rice and pine nuts).
- Main vegetables are okra, French beans and *malukhiyya*.
- *Baklava* is a favourite dessert made from flaky pastry filled with honey and nuts.

National drinks:

- Tea and coffee.
- Local beers include *Al-Sharq*, brewed in Aleppo, and *Barada*, from Damascus.

Tipping: Often expected, especially in more expensive establishments; 10 per cent is generally acceptable.

SHOPPING: *Souks* (markets) are the best places for shopping, notably those in Aleppo. Local handicrafts in the Syrian Arab Republic are numerous and precious, including mother-of-pearl items (such as backgammon boards), olive-wood carvings, weaving and embroidery, leather goods and gold and silver jewellery. **Shopping hours:** Sat-Thurs 0930-1400 and 1630-2200 (summer); Sat-Thurs 0930-1400 and 1600-2000 (winter).

Business

- **GDP:** US$22.2 billion (2004).
- **Main exports:** Petroleum, textiles, phosphates, antiques, fruit and vegetables, and cotton.
- **Main imports:** Foodstuffs, metal and metal products, machinery, textiles and petroleum.
- **Main trade partners:** Germany, Italy, France, Lebanon and Saudi Arabia.

ECONOMY: The main components of the Syrian economy are agriculture and oil. In the agricultural sector, cotton is the principal commodity and a key export. Wheat, barley, fruit and vegetables are the other main products, the bulk of which are grown for domestic consumption. Oil is the main industry and provides two-thirds of Syrian export earnings, although the future of the sector is limited by the relatively small size of the Syrian Arab Republic's reserves (which are already over half-exhausted). There are also reserves of phosphates (another export earner), iron ore and natural gas. The rest of the industrial economy is divided roughly between three areas: chemicals, rubber and plastics; textiles and leather goods; and food and drink. The service economy is relatively under-developed but expanding rapidly: tourism especially has seen exceptional growth to the extent that the Syrian Arab Republic now receives over one million visitors annually. A particular problem for the Syrian economy in a very arid region is the availability of water. The Syrians have concluded a long-term agreement with Turkey over use of the northern part of Tigris/Euphrates river system (which also serves Iraq), but this is still a highly sensitive issue.

The Government of Basil al-Assad has set a high priority on economic reform. Much of the economy is still state-owned and highly regulated. Some measures have been introduced to promote private enterprise and attract foreign investment; fiscal policy has focused on an overhaul and simplification of the convoluted tax system. The new cabinet installed in May 2003 - and reshuffled again in 2004 - has been tasked to accelerate the economic reform process, although it is likely to encounter many of the same obstacles as its predecessors in the form of well-entrenched vested interests and monopolies. The Government must also tackle the problem of unemployment (officially 10.8 per cent but almost certainly higher). Annual GDP growth in 2004 was 1.7 per cent. The Syrian Arab Republic's trade patterns have shifted since the demise of the Soviet bloc, with which it traded extensively. It is now more vulnerable to attitudes in Washington: under the Bush administration, the Syrian Arab Republic is classed as a 'rogue state' and since November 2003 has been subject to partial economic sanctions. This has a knock-on effect on trade with other countries.

BUSINESS ETIQUETTE: Formal suits are necessary for business. Business people generally speak English and French. Appointments are necessary and visiting cards are widely used. Arabs often discuss business with more than one person at a time. A list of notarised translators is available from the British Embassy. Hotels with conference facilities can be found in Damascus (Cham Palace, Ebla-Cham, Omayyad and The Sheraton), in Aleppo (Shahba-Cham), in Latakia (the Cote d'Azure) and in Hama (Apamee-Cham). **Office hours:** Sat-Thurs 0800-1400. All government offices, banks and Muslim firms close Friday and remain open Sunday; Christian firms are generally open Friday and closed Sunday. During the month of Ramadan, government offices start work one hour later than usual.

COMMERCIAL INFORMATION

Damascus Chamber of Commerce
PO Box 1040, 126 rue Mou'awiah,
Damascus, Syrian Arab Republic
Tel: (11) 211 339.
Website: www.dcc-sy.com

Federation of Syrian Chambers of Commerce
PO Box 5909, rue Mousa Ben Nousair,
Damascus, Syrian Arab Republic
Tel: (11) 337 344.
Website: www.fedcommsyr.org

A B C D E F G H I J K L M N O P Q R **S** T U V W X Y Z

Tahiti and Her Islands

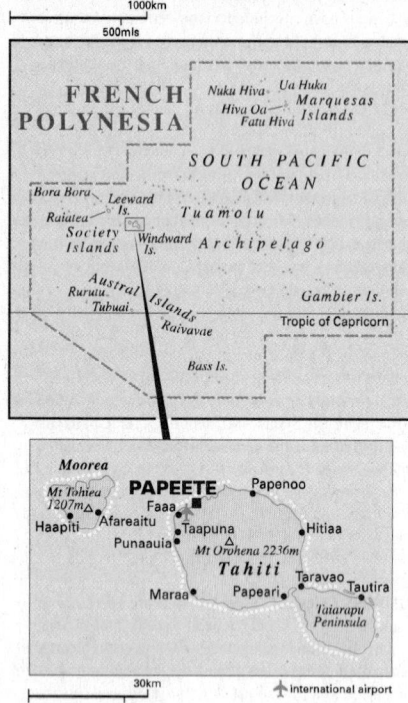

Location: South Pacific.

Time: Tahiti and Her Islands span three time zones.
Gambier Islands: GMT - 9.
Marquesas Islands: GMT - 9.5.
Society Archipelago, Tubuai Islands, Tuamotu Archipelago (except Gambier Islands), Tahiti: GMT - 10.

Overview

The first Europeans to arrive on the island groups were 16th-century Spanish and Portuguese explorers. The British, notably Captain Cook and later Captain Bligh (of 'HMS Bounty' notoriety), and then the French, took control of the islands in the 18th century. Tahiti, the largest island in French Polynesia, dominated by Mount Orohena at 2236m (7337ft) and Mount Aorai at 2068m (6786ft), and characterised by its spectacular tropical scenery, banana groves, plantations and flowers, was made a French protectorate in 1842 and a colony in 1880. The other islands were annexed by the turn of the century. This status quo remained until 1957, when Polynesia was made an Overseas Territory. A revised constitution, introduced in 1977, ceded greater autonomy. For the next 20 years, the islands' politics were dominated by the French nuclear testing programme. By the time the programme ended in 1996, 150 separate explosions had been detonated, mainly on the atoll of Mururoa. In general, the French government was able to rely on the firm backing of most of French public opinion and an often ambivalent attitude on the part of the inhabitants of French Polynesia, who were well aware of the considerable benefits of the test programme to the otherwise threadbare local economy. The tests had begun in 1966, but it was not until the 1980s that opposition to them began to assume significant proportions, following the terrorist attack by French special forces on the Greenpeace vessel *Rainbow Warrior*.
By the time of the final series of tests in 1995/6, Tahiti had become the focus of opposition from throughout the South Pacific, and several riots occurred. Although the protesters failed to stop the tests, their campaign had an important political effect by linking the anti-nuclear movement and the burgeoning pro-independence movement which had so

far been largely unrepresented in any political forum, despite the support of a large proportion (possibly the majority) of the population. The politics of the territory had been dominated for the previous decade by the centre-right *Tahoeraa Huiratira* (TH) party, led by Gaston Flosse, allied to the French Gaullist *Rassemblement pour la République* (RPR), which backed French rule and nuclear testing. However, in recent years, changes have been afoot: Tahiti and her Islands gained Overseas Country status in 2004, and pro-independence leader Oscar Temaru was elected by the territory's assembly in March 2005. It only remains to be seen whether these changes result in imminent and full independence.
What hasn't changed is the ambience on Tahiti and Her Islands, which exudes a laid-back tranquillity, as romantic sunsets send giant curls of turquoise breaking over the islands' reefs. Remote and pristine, Tahiti and Her Islands is really a place where nature dominates, and it is nature that matters.

General Information

AREA: 4167 sq km (1609 sq miles).
POPULATION: 252,000 (UN, 2005).
POPULATION DENSITY: 60.48 per sq km.
CAPITAL: Papeete (Tahiti Island). **Population:** 26,181 (2002).
GEOGRAPHY: French Polynesia comprises 120 islands divided into five archipelagos: the Society Archipelago, Tuamotu Archipelago, Marquesas Islands, Austral Islands and Mangreva Islands. The Windward and Leeward Islands, collectively called the Society Archipelago, are mountainous with coastal plains. Tahiti, the largest of the Windward group, is dominated by Mount Orohena at 2236m (7337ft) and Mount Aorai at 2068m (6786ft). Moorea lies next to Tahiti, a picturesque volcanic island with white sand beaches. The Leeward Islands to the west are generally lower in altitude. The largest islands are Raiatea and Bora Bora. Tuamotu Archipelago comprises 80 coral atolls, located 298km (185 miles) east of Tahiti. The Marquesas Islands lie 1497km (930 miles) northeast of Tahiti and are made up of two clusters of volcanic islands divided into a southern and northern group. The grass-covered Austral Islands south of Tahiti are scattered in a chain from east to west over a distance of 499km (310 miles).
GOVERNMENT: French Overseas Territory since 1946.
Head of State: President Jacques Chirac since 1995, represented locally by High Commissioner Michel Mathieu since 2001. **Head of Government:** Oscar Temaru, President of the Council of Ministers since 2005. **Recent history:** Tahiti and her Islands gained *Overseas Country* status in 2004. Pro-independence leader Oscar Temaru was elected by the territory's assembly in March 2005. It was the third change in leadership in 12 months and followed months of wrangling between Mr Temaru and pro-France rival, Gaston Flosse. Mr Flosse's Government lost a vote of confidence on February 2005, precipitating the poll in which Mr Temaru defeated the pro-France candidate, Gaston Tang Sang by 29 votes to 26.
The French Government is represented by a High Commissioner who controls foreign affairs, defence and justice. In other spheres, the islands have enjoyed internal autonomy since July 1977, which is exercised by an elected Government. This comprises a legislature, the 57-member Territorial Assembly which is directly elected for a five-year term, and an Executive President and Council of Ministers, all of whom are chosen from among the membership of the Assembly.
LANGUAGE: The official languages are French and Tahitian. Other Polynesian languages are spoken by the indigenous population. English is widely understood, mainly by islanders accustomed to dealing with foreign visitors.
RELIGION: Approximately 55 per cent Protestant and 34 per cent Catholic.
ELECTRICITY: 110/220 volts AC, 60Hz. US-style two-pin plugs are in use.
SOCIAL CONVENTIONS: The basic lifestyle of the islands is represented by the simple Tahitian fares built of bamboo with *pandanus* roofs. Local women dress in bright *pareos* and men in the male equivalent, but casual dress is expected of the visitor (except in Papeete, where bathing suits and shorts are not considered suitable dress). Traditional dances are still performed mostly in hotels, with Western dance styles mainly in tourist centres. Normal social courtesies are important.

Climate

Temperate, but cooled by sea breezes. Two main seasons: humid (hot and wet) from November to March, cool and dry from April to October.
Required clothing: Lightweight cottons and linens are worn, with a warm layer for cooler evenings. Rainwear is advisable.

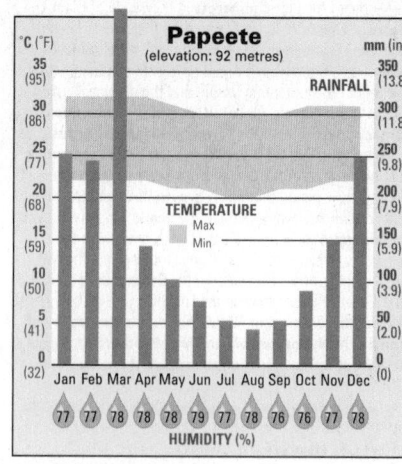

Communications

Telephone: IDD is available. Country code: 689. Operator assistance may be required for international calls. There are many phone booths which operate using cards (*Telecarte*) that can be purchased at the airport, bars, magazine stands and the post office. Hotel telephone charges are extremely high.
Mobile telephone: The GSM 900 network is not compatible with US mobile phones. Mobile phones are available to rent, which offer better rates than roaming fees.
Internet: There are Internet cafes in Papeete and Moorea.
Post: Airmail to Western Europe takes around six to eight days. The central post office hours (in Papeete): Mon-Fri 0700-1800, Sat-Sun 0800-1100 (outside Papeete, there is a restricted service in the afternoons and at weekends).
MEDIA: Press: There is an English-language weekly, the *Tahiti Beach Press*.
TV: RFO Polynesie is a public service, operated by Reseau France Outre-Mer, that provides two channels. Tahiti Nui TV is Government-operated.
Radio: *RFO Polynesie* is a public radio broadcaster, operated by Reseau France Outre-Mer. Private FM stations include *Radio 1* and *Radio Bleue*.

Passport/Visa

	Passport Required?	Visa Required?	Return Ticket Required?
Full British	Yes	No/2	No
Australian	Yes	No/2	Yes
Canadian	Yes	No/3	Yes
USA	Yes	No/3	Yes
Other EU	Yes/1	No/4/5	No/4
Japanese	Yes	No/3	Yes

Note: *Regulations and requirements may be subject to change at short notice, and you are advised to contact the appropriate diplomatic or consular authority before finalising travel arrangements. Any numbers in the chart refer to the footnotes below.*

PASSPORTS: Passport valid for at least three months beyond applicant's last day of stay required by all except the following:
1. nationals of France, providing they are travelling from other French Overseas Territories in the Pacific with a National Identity Card or an expired passport (maximum five years).
VISAS: Required by all except the following:
(a) nationals of countries referred to in the chart above: **2.** for stays up to three months; **3.** for stays of up to one month; **4.** for stays of up to three months; except **5.** nationals of France who can stay for an unlimited period;
(b) nationals of Andorra, Brazil, Bulgaria, Holy See, Hong Kong (SAR), Iceland, Liechtenstein, Macau (SAR), Monaco, Norway, San Marino and Switzerland for stays of up to three months;
(c) nationals of Argentina, Bolivia, Brunei, Chile, Costa Rica, Croatia, El Salvador, Guatemala, Honduras, Korea (Rep), Malaysia, Mexico, New Zealand, Nicaragua, Panama, Paraguay, Singapore and Uruguay for up to one month;
(d) transit passengers continuing their journey by the same or first connecting aircraft, provided holding valid onward or return documentation and not leaving the airport.
Types of visa and cost: All visas, regardless of duration of stay and number of entries permitted, cost €35. In most circumstances, no fee applies to students, recipients of government fellowships and citizens of the EU and their family members.
Validity: *Short-stay* visas (up to 30 days): valid for

two months (single- and multiple-entry). *Short stay visas* (31 to 90 days and double- or multiple-entry): valid for a maximum of six months from date of issue. *Transit visas:* valid for single- or multiple-entries of maximum five days per entry, including the day of arrival.

Application to: French Consulate General (for personal visas), or Consular section at Embassy (for diplomatic or service visas); see *Passport/Visa Information*. All applications must be made in person.

Application requirements: (a) Valid passport with blank page to affix the visa. Minors travelling alone must submit notarised parental authorisation, signed by both parents, plus one copy. (b) Up to two completed application forms. (c) One passport-size photo on each form. (d) Fee, to be paid in cash or credit card (American Express and Diners Club are not accepted). (e) Evidence of sufficient funds for stay. (f) Letter from employer, or proof of stay in country of residence. (g) Proof of address. (h) Medical insurance. (i) Return ticket and travel documents for remaining journey. (j) Proof of accommodation during stay. (k) Detailed itinerary, including reservations and round-trip airline tickets (only required when visa is issued), plus one copy. (l) Proof of employment (eg last payslip or letter from employer). (m) Proof of valid health/travel insurance with worldwide coverage, plus copy. *Business:* (a)-(m) and, (n) Business invitation guaranteeing payment of travel expenses, plus one copy.

Working days required: One day to three weeks depending on nationality.

Temporary residence: If intending to work or stay for longer than 90 days, nationals should contact the long stay visa section of the Consulate General or Embassy (tel: (020) 7073 1248).

PASSPORT/VISA INFORMATION

Embassy of The French Republic in the UK
58 Knightsbridge, London SW1X 7JT, UK
Tel: (020) 7073 1000.
Website: www.ambafrance-uk.org

French Consulate General in the UK
21 Cromwell Road, London SW7 2EN, UK
Visa section: 6A Cromwell Place,
London SW7 2EW, UK
Tel: (020) 7073 1200 (consular section) *or* 1250 (visa section) *or* 7073 1295 (visa applications in progress; 1500-1700 only) *or* (09065) 508 940 (visa information service; calls cost £1 per minute) *or* 266 654 (24-hour visa application form request service; calls cost £1.50 per minute) *or* 540 700 (24-hour automated visa appointment booking service).
Website: www.ambafrance-uk.org *or* www.consulfrance-londres.org

Embassy of the French Republic in the USA
4101 Reservoir Road, NW,
Washington, DC 20007, USA
Tel: (202) 944 6195.
Website: www.ambafrance-us.org *or* www.consulfrance-washington.org (consular section)

Money

Currency: French Pacific Franc (XPF) = 100 centimes. Notes are in denominations of XPF10,000, 5000, 1000 and 500. Coins are in denominations of XPF100, 50, 20, 10, 5, 2 and 1. The French Pacific Franc is tied to the Euro.
Currency exchange: Exchange facilities are available at the airport, major banks and at authorised hotels and shops in Papeete.
Credit & debit cards: American Express, Diners Club, MasterCard and Visa are all accepted. Check with your credit or debit card company for details of merchant acceptability and other services which may be available. ATMs are common on Tahiti, with a few on the smaller islands.
Traveller's cheques: The recommended means of importing foreign currency. To avoid additional exchange rate charges, travellers are advised to take traveller's cheques in US Dollars or Euros.
Currency restrictions: See *France* section.
Banking hours: Mon-Fri 0745-1530. Some are open Saturday 0745-1130.
Exchange rate indicators:
Rate at time of publishing
£1.00= XPF175.53
$1.00= XPF98.30

Duty Free

The following items may be imported into Tahiti by passengers 17 years and over without incurring customs duty:
200 cigarettes or 100 cigarillos or 50 cigars or 200g of

tobacco; 2l of still wine and 1l of spirits over 22 per cent or 2l of spirits up to 22 per cent; 50g of perfume and 250ml of eau de toilette; goods up to a value of XPF5000 (XPF2500 for passengers up to 15 years of age).*
Prohibited Items: All food products of animal origin.
Note: (a) Plants, fruit, weapons, ammunition and drugs may not be imported. (b) All baggage coming from Fiji and Samoa is collected for compulsory fumigation on arrival in Papeete; allow two hours.

Public Holidays

Below are listed Public Holidays for the January 2006-June 2007 period.
2006: Jan 1 New Year's Day. **Mar 5** Missionary Day. **Apr 14** Good Friday. **Apr 17** Easter Monday. **May 1** Labour Day. **May 8** Victory Day. **May 25** Ascension. **Jun 5** Whit Monday. **Jun 29** Anniversary of Internal Autonomy. **Jul 14*** Fall of the Bastille. **Aug 15** Assumption. **Sep 8** Internal Autonomy Day. **Nov 1** All Saints' Day. **Nov 11** Armistice Day. **Dec 25** Christmas Day.
2007: Jan 1 New Year's Day. **Mar 5** Missionary Day. **Apr 6** Good Friday. **Apr 9** Easter Monday. **May 1** Labour Day. **May 8** Victory Day. **May 17** Ascension. **May 28** Whit Monday. **Jun 29** Anniversary of Internal Autonomy.
Note: *Celebrations continue for up to 10 days.

Health

	Special Precautions?	Certificate Required?
Yellow Fever	No	1
Cholera	No	No
Typhoid & Polio	2	N/A
Malaria	No	N/A

Note: *Regulations and requirements may be subject to change at short notice, and you are advised to contact your doctor well in advance of your intended date of departure. Any numbers in the chart refer to the footnotes below.*

1: A yellow fever vaccination certificate is required by travellers over one year of age arriving within six days from infected areas.
2: Vaccination against typhoid is advised.
Food & drink: Mains water is normally chlorinated and, whilst relatively safe, may cause mild abdominal upsets. Bottled water is available and is advised for the first few weeks of the stay. Drinking water outside main cities and towns may be contaminated and sterilisation is advisable. Milk is pasteurised and dairy products are safe for consumption. Local meat, poultry, seafood, fruit and vegetables are generally considered safe to eat.
Other risks: Immunisation against *hepatitis A* and *B* is recommended. *Dengue fever* and *filariasis* occur.
Health care: Medical facilites are good on the major islands. Private medical insurance is recommended.

Travel - International

AIR:
 Air Tahiti Nui (TN) (website: www.airtahitinui.com) is the only Tahiti-based international carrier.
Air passes: The *Visit the South Pacific Pass* is valid for many airlines operating in the South Pacific, including most of the larger ones, such as *Air Caledonie, Air Marshall Islands, Air Nauru, Air Niugini, Air Pacific, Air Vanuatu, Polynesian Airlines, Qantas, Royal Tongan Airlines* and *Solomon Airlines*. Offering reductions of up to 40 per cent on normal airfares, this sector-based pass allows for flexible island-hopping between the destinations of the Cook Islands, Fiji, Nauru, New Caledonia, Samoa, Tahiti, Tonga, Vanuatu and the more remote Melanesian and Micronesian islands, together with major cities in Australia (Brisbane, Melbourne and Sydney) and New Zealand (Auckland, Christchurch and Wellington). It is only available for people resident outside of the South Pacific. The journey must be started outside the South Pacific and only one stopover in Australia is allowed. A minimum of two sectors must be bought before departure (extra sectors can be purchased en route). There is a maximum of one pass per person, and passes must be used within six months of the first day of travel. Children under 12 years of age pay 75 per cent of the adult fare. For details and conditions, contact the South Pacific Tourism Organisation (see *Top Things To Do*).
Approximate flight times: From Papeete to *Auckland* is five hours, to *Honolulu* is five hours, to *London* is 19 hours 20 minutes, to *Los Angeles* is seven hours 30 minutes, to *New York* is 16 hours and to *Sydney* is eight hours.
Main airports: *Papeete (PPT)* (Faaa), on Tahiti, is 6km (4 miles) from the city (travel time - 15 minutes).
To/from the airport: Le Truck buses run regularly. Metered taxis are also available, but are expensive.
Facilities: Bank/bureau de change, post office, duty free

shop, left luggage, news-stand, restaurant, bar, light refreshments, car hire, cyber point and tourist information.
Departure tax: None.
SEA:
 Main ports: *Papeete.* The port is served by *Cunard, Holland America, P&O, Princess* and *Radisson Seven Seas*.

Travel - Internal

AIR:
 Domestic flights run by *Air Tahiti (VT)* (website: www.airtahiti.aero) connect Tahiti with neighbouring islands (Bora Bora, Huahine, Maupiti, Moorea and Raiatea) and remote archipelagos (Tuamotu East and North with Manihi, Rangiroa, Takapoto and Tikehau; Austral Islands of Rurutu and Tubuai; Marquesas Islands of Hiva Oa and Nuku Hiva).
SEA:
There are inter-island connections on the many ferries, catamarans, copra boats and schooners that make regular trips throughout the islands. Daily connections exist between Bora Bora, Huahine, Moorea, Papeete and Raiatea. Yacht and sailboat charter is available at most of the major islands. Some come complete with a captain and crew.
ROAD:
Traffic drives on the right. **Bus:** Open-air buses, known as *le truck*, and RTC white coaches operate frequently in Papeete and the other islands, offering an inexpensive method of travel. Le truck leave from the central market in Papeete town centre, travelling to all destinations. No schedule is operated. Bus stops along the way are indicated by blue signs illustrating the *le truck*, from where a wave of the hand will prompt them to stop. **Taxi:** Available in Bora Bora, Huahine, Moorea, Raiatea and Tahiti. **Car hire:** Major and local agencies hire out cars on the main islands. **Documentation:** A national driving licence is sufficient.

Travel Advice

Most visits to French Polynesia are trouble-free but you should be aware of the global risk of indiscriminate international terrorist attacks, which could be against civilian targets, including places frequented by foreigners.
This advice is based on information provided by the Foreign and Commonwealth Office in the UK. It is correct at time of publishing. As the situation can change rapidly, visitors are advised to contact the following organisations for the latest travel advice:

British Foreign and Commonwealth Office
Tel: (0845) 850 2829.
Website: www.fco.gov.uk

US Department of State
Website: http://travel.state.gov/travel

Accommodation

HOTELS/BUNGALOWS/PENSIONS:
 Accommodation varies from air-conditioned, carpeted, deluxe rooms with telephones and room service, to thatched-roofed bungalows (Tahitian *pensions* where the bathroom is shared and may be outdoors with cold showers). In the outer islands, resort hotels normally have individual gardens and over-water bungalows and rooms, many built of bamboo; shows and dance bands are often laid on in the evening. A tax of 7 per cent is added to the cost of all hotel rooms, but this does not apply to pensions or family lodgings. There is a youth hostel in Papeete. It is possible to rent a room in a family home through GIE Tahiti Tourisme (see *Top Things To See & Do*) for a more genuine experience. There are two campsites on Tahiti; camping is also possible in the grounds of some pensions.

Top Things To See & Do

- Wander around **Papeete**'s (the capital of the island, **Tahiti**) public **market**, **Le Marché**. The market is open all week but really comes to life on Sunday mornings when out-of-town merchants come to sell their wares. Flowers, spices, fabrics and fresh produce are all on offer.
- See some of Tahiti's impressive watery wonders, from the **Blowhole of Arahoho**, which throws water skywards, to the **Faarumai** and **Vaipahi waterfalls**.
- Lap up the beach-life that Tahiti and Her Islands offers: relax on the island of **Moorea**'s dazzling white-sand beaches and clear lagoons, ideal for **swimming**, **diving**

and **snorkelling**, and surrounded by volcanic peaks and a winning mixture of tradition and touristic entertainment; and discover the **Leeward Islands**, sheltered by the surrounding coral reef, the coastal waters and lagoons, all good for encountering the local aquatic life; go **deep-sea fishing**, **scuba-diving**, snorkelling or swimming on a nearby *motu* (small sandy atoll within a reef), or take a trip by **glass-bottomed boat** around the lagoons of **Bora Bora**. The sea around the South Pacific islands is excellent for scuba diving, providing visibility that often reaches 40 metres (130ft). There are plenty of diving clubs in Tahiti which are members of the French Diving Federation and which are open all year round. Equipment can be hired and charter boats can take divers to the best areas. Complete certification courses or resort courses are available. Other popular and well-provided-for watersports include **windsurfing**, **water-skiing**, **surfing** (highly rated at the **Avo Moía Pass** and in **Teahupoo**) and **kite surfing**.

- Visit the beautiful **Opunohu Valley** on Moorea, an ancient dwelling place, uninhabited for 150 years, with 500 ancient structures including temples or *marae*, some of which have been restored. The marae used to be sacred buildings, or funerary sites, of a rectangular shape on which religious and social ceremonies would be performed. The marae (open-air temple) of **Mahaiatea**, on Tahiti, is also worth a visit.
- Inhale the faintly sweet aroma that lingers on the 'Vanilla Island' of **Tahaa**. The breeze constantly carries the aroma of vanilla, from the island's numerous vanilla plantations. The island also shares a coral reef with the island of **Raiatea**, and offers a tranquil and relaxed lifestyle.
- Ascend the two **mountains** of **Otemanu** and **Pahia** on the island of Bora Bora, and find yourself a wonderful lookout point across this most famous of the Leeward Islands, still only 45 minutes from Tahiti by plane. Club Alpin in **Arue** also provides information and assistance for climbing **Mount Aorai**, with a shelter at 1798m (5900ft) and **Mount Diademe**.
- Visit the burial spots of both Paul Gauguin and Jacques Brel on the **Marquesas Islands**. Both are buried on **Hiva Oa**. For greater insight into the life of Gauguin, the famous French Post-Impressionist painter of the 19th century, visit the **Paul Gauguin Museum** on Tahiti.
- Go **horse riding** between the numerous valleys of **Ua Huka**. Hourly and day-long horse riding tours can be arranged through Club Equestre de Tahiti and Centre de Tourisme Equestre de Tahiti, both at the Hippodrome, Pirae, Tahiti. For more equine-related fun, **Tahitian-style horse racing** can be seen at the Hippodrome in Pirae.
- Cherish one of Tahiti and Her Islands' most beautiful locations: the island of **Fatu Hiva**, with its valley of **Hanavare**, hidden between volcanic rock on the **Bay of Virgins**. This also contains the important archaeological site of **Puamau**, with its intact 2.1m- (7ft-) high *tiki* (a male figure in Polynesian myth), the largest on the Marquesas.
- Come across some of the amazing life that lurks beneath the lovely waters of Tahiti and Her Islands. There are **shark** and **ray feeding demonstrations** on Moorea and Bora Bora, and **humpback whale watching** is possible between July and October in the waters of **Rurutu**.

TOURIST INFORMATION

Tahiti Tourisme in the UK
c/o Synergy, 48 Westminster Palace Gardens, Artillery Row, London SW1P 1RR, UK
Tel: (020) 7222 1311.
Website: www.tahiti-tourisme.co.uk

South Pacific Tourism Organisation (SPTO) in Fiji
Street address: Level 3, FNPF Place, 343-359 Victoria Parade, Suva, Fiji
Postal address: PO Box 13119, Suva, Fiji
Tel: (679) 330 4177.
Website: www.spto.org

Entertainment

FOOD & DRINK: All the classified hotels have good restaurants. Chinese, French, Italian and Vietnamese food is served, as well as the Polynesian specialities; Papeete is noted for Chinese and French cuisine. Tahitian food can be found in some hotels. *Trucs* or lunch wagons parked on the waterfront sell steak, chips, chicken, *poisson cru*, *brochettes* and *shish kebabs*. A full range of alcoholic drinks are available.
Things to know: A key to how expensive a restaurant will be is often indicated by dollar signs; for instance,

$$$$ will indicate an expensive restaurant, whereas $ will indicate a budget restaurant.
National specialities:
- Smoked breadfruit.
- Mountain bananas.
- *Fafa* (spinach) served with young suckling pig.
- *Poisson cru* (marinated fish; for example raw tuna served with coconut cream and limes).
- *Poe* (starchy pudding made of papaya, mango and banana).
National drinks:
- *Noni Juice* comes from the Noni tree and is famous for its health-enhancing effects.
- *Hinano* is the beer of Tahiti.
Tipping: In general tolerate but not practised, since it is contrary to the Tahitian idea of hospitality.
NIGHTLIFE: Papeete is full of life in the evenings with many restaurants and nightclubs. Most hotels feature Tahitian dance shows, bands and other traditional entertainment.
SHOPPING: Facilities are concentrated in Papeete. Special purchases include Marquesan woodcarvings, dancing costumes, shell jewellery, Tahitian perfumes, *Monoi Tiare Tahiti* (coconut oil scented with Tahiti's national flower), vanilla beans and brightly patterned *pareu* fabrics that make the traditional Tahitian *pareo*.
Shopping hours: Mon-Fri 0800-1200 and 1330-1700/1730, Sat 0800-1100. Shops will sometimes close for lunch, anytime between 1100-1400. Some shopping centres in the suburbs of Tahiti are open 0730-2200

Business

- **GDP:** US$4.58 billion (2003 estimate).
- **Main exports:** Cultured black pearls, fish and coconut products.
- **Main imports:** Fuels, foodstuffs, machinery and equipment.
- **Main trade partners:** France, USA, Japan, Australia and New Zealand.

ECONOMY: The traditional Polynesian economy was agricultural, but that sector now accounts for less than 5 per cent of total output and employment. Coconuts are the principal cash crop and vanilla, coffee and citrus fruit are also produced in quantity. There is a substantial fishing industry, based on tuna, most of the income of which is derived from licences granted to foreign fleets. Manufacturing is mainly devoted to processing agricultural products and a small mining industry has evolved following the recent discovery of phosphate and cobalt deposits.
French Polynesia as a whole has suffered from a serious unemployment problem since the end of French nuclear testing in the mid-1990s; although much disliked by local governments and the majority of their peoples, the tests provided many construction and service jobs. As a result, Tahiti now depends heavily on remittances from migrant workers. The Government believes that tourism offers the best, and perhaps the only, prospect for a self-supporting economy. At present, French Polynesia as a whole receives around 230,000 visitors annually, and the industry is worth over US$400 million annually. The territory suffers from a serious trade deficit - imports exceed exports by a factor of 10 - so that considerable aid is needed from the French to balance the country's finances.
BUSINESS ETIQUETTE: Informal in atmosphere. Literature will be in French, but English is understood in some business circles, particularly those connected with tourism. **Office hours:** Mon-Fri 0800-1200 and 1330-1730, Sat 0800-1200.

COMMERCIAL INFORMATION

Chambre de Commerce, d'Industrie, des Services et des Métiers Polynésie Française (CCISM)
BP 118, Papeete, Tahiti
Tel: 472 700.
E-mail: mailto:cci.tahiti@mail.pf

Taiwan – China

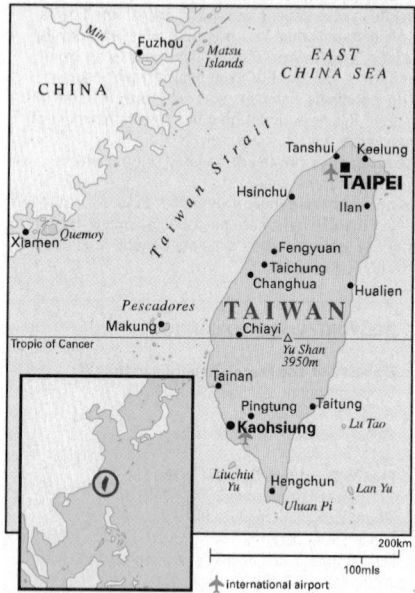

Location: Between the South and East China Seas, off the southeast coast of the People's Republic of China.

Time: GMT + 8.

Overview

Think of Taiwan and the first thing that will spring to mind is probably the 'Made in Taiwan' labels attached to so many clothes purchased in the Western world, which will have no doubt contributed to the perception of Taiwan as some industrial landscape defined by hundreds of factories and warehouses, and precious little else to offer visitors. Taiwan might have been known as one of the 'tiger' economies of Asia, but few people, until recently at least, thought of this small island off the southeast coast of China as a potential tourist destination.
Formerly called 'Formosa' (Portuguese for 'beautiful'), Taiwan was originally inhabited by mainland Chinese until the 17th century, before being occupied by the Dutch and Spanish for a while. It then fell under Chinese rule again for a couple of centuries, before being occupied by the Japanese from 1895 until the end of WW2.
The Chinese Civil War, which had already been in progress for some years, came to a head in 1948. The nationalist forces of Chiang Kai-Shek were defeated by Mao's Communists, and the nationalist leadership, along with thousands of supporters, fled to Taiwan. Here, their political vehicle, the *Kuo Min-Tang* (*KMT*) rapidly came to dominate Taiwanese politics. The KMT was spectacularly successful at developing the economy and, in less than a century, Taiwan made a successful transition from an agricultural-based economy to an industrial one. In March 2000, however, the main opposition party, the *Democratic Progressive Party* (*DPP*), gained control of the Presidency through its candidate Chen Shui-Bian, and for the first time, the KMT was completely excluded from political power.
For all practical purposes, Taiwan has been independent for half a century, but the fledgling democracy is still regarded by China as a renegade province that must be reunited with the mainland. The political issue of its relationship with China remains a sticking point in international relations, with both sides prone to exchanging rhetoric and political point-scoring on a regular basis. More than 700 Chinese missiles are aimed at the island but the military threat is

partly offset by the pivotal relationship between Taipei and Washington (the US, which has no diplomatic ties with Taiwan, is nevertheless the main provider of arms to the island - one of the world's big arms purchasers).
2004 was the Year of Tourism in Taiwan and, since then, the country has focused on promoting its historical and cultural treasures in a bid to attract more tourists. Taiwan certainly has plenty to offer, from truly unique scenery to exciting sporting activities and colourful festivals, not to mention the most varied Chinese food on earth (Taipei is a gourmet's paradise, boasting cuisine from every region of China). Boutique hotels and trendy bars have sprung up in a flurry of construction, which culminated in the opening of the 'world's tallest building', Taipei 101.
Taiwan is relatively small (only a little over half of Sri Lanka's size), but its population numbers almost 23 million, making its population density second only to Bangladesh. A gateway to the massive Chinese market, it has a strong relationship with the West and is keen to increase links with Europe.

General Information

AREA: 36,188 sq km (13,972 sq miles).
POPULATION: 22.7 million (2004, Government statistics).
POPULATION DENSITY: 627.27 per sq km.
CAPITAL: Taipei. **Population:** 2.6 million (2004).
GEOGRAPHY: Taiwan (China) is the main island of a group of 86 islands. It is dominated by the Central Mountain Range covering 69 per cent of its land area and running its full length north to south on the eastern seaboard. Over 200 peaks exceed 3000m (9850ft), the highest being Yu Shan (Jade Mountain) at 3952m (13,042ft), and most are heavily forested. About 31 per cent of the country is alluvial plain, most of it on the coastal strip. The Pescadores (Fisherman's Isles), which the Chinese call Penghu, comprise 64 islands west of Taiwan (China, PR) with a total area of 127 sq km (49 sq miles). The offshore island fortress of Quemoy (Kinmen) and Matsu forms part of the mainland province of Fukien.
GOVERNMENT: Republic since 1912. **Head of State:** President Chen Shui-bian since 2000. **Head of Government:** Premier Su Tseng-chang since 2006. **Recent history:** President Chen Shui-bian, from the Democratic Progressive Party (DPP), was elected in 2000, ending more than 50 years of Nationalist (Kuomintang) rule. He was reelected by a very narrow margin in March 2004, after a campaign focusing on formal independence for Taiwan. As a result, Beijing, which sees constitutional change as a dangerous step towards formal statehood for Taiwan, refuses to deal with Mr Chen.
Domestic opposition has plagued Mr Chen in his second term. The Nationalist Party (Kuomintang) and its allies, who favour closer ties with Beijing, have given his DPP a drubbing in local and parliamentary polls. But the president received a boost when a reform allowing the public to vote on constitutional changes was approved in 2005. Mr Chen says a vote that could pave the way for a new charter may be held by 2007.
President Chen Shui-bian chose Su Tseng-chang, his former Chief of Staff, to replace Prime Minister Frank Hsieh, who resigned in January 2006, after less than a year in the post. Frank Hsieh, the former Premier, resigned after accepting blame for the DPP's defeat in local Government elections. Su Tseng-chang is the fifth Premier to be appointed by President Chen in the past six years, and many analysts believe that his room for manoeuvre will be limited, especially since the opposition parties have a Parliamentary majority. Mr Su, a possible Presidential candidate for 2008, has named a new Cabinet made up of a mix of old and new political faces.
Under the amended 1947 constitution, Taiwan has an executive who is Head of State and is directly elected for a four-year term. The Parliament has two chambers. The Li Fa Yuan (Legislative Yuan) has 225 members – 168 elected for a three-year term in multi-seat constituencies, 41 elected by proportional representation, eight representing ethnic minorities, and six representing the overseas Chinese community. After six constitutional amendments between April 1991 and 2000, the National Assembly is now a non-standing body and its delegates are nominated by political parties on the basis of proportional representation. Most of its original functions have been transferred to the Legislative Yuan.
A 300-member non-standing body will be selected by proportional representation according to laws to be passed by the Legislative Yuan. The National Assembly's functions will be limited to voting on constitutional amendments, presidential impeachment, or alteration of national boundaries as proposed by the Legislative Yuan. Its former powers have been transferred to the Legislative Yuan.
LANGUAGE: The official language is Northern Chinese (Mandarin). Taiwanese is widely spoken, and English is taught as the first foreign language in schools.
RELIGION: Buddhism; also Taoism, Christianity and Islam.
ELECTRICITY: 110 volts AC, 60Hz.
SOCIAL CONVENTIONS: Handshaking is common. Casual wear is widely acceptable. Ancient festivals and customs are celebrated enthusiastically and traditional holidays are important. Entertainment is usually offered in restaurants, not at home. Visitors are not expected to entertain. Chinese culture in the form of drama, opera and art is very strong. Despite rapid industrialisation and development, the way of life is very much Chinese, steeped in tradition and old values.

Climate

A subtropical climate with moderate temperatures in the north, where there is a winter season. The southern areas, where temperatures are slightly higher, enjoy sunshine every day, and there is no winter season. The typhoon season is from June to October.
Required clothing: Light- to mediumweights, with rainwear advised.

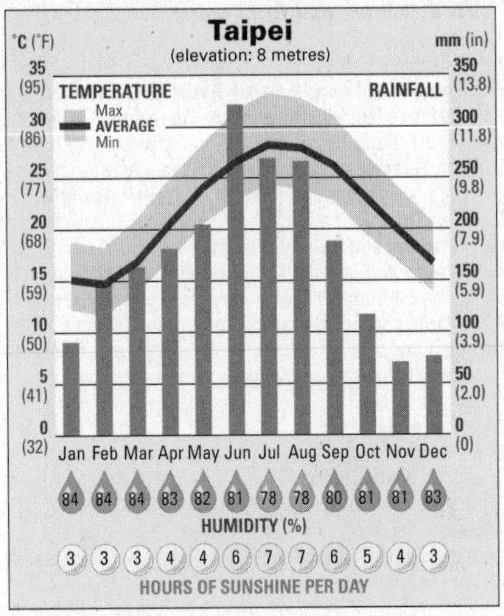

Communications

Telephone: Full IDD is available. Country code: 886. There is an extensive internal telephone system.
Mobile telephone: Roaming agreements exist with international mobile phone companies.
Internet: Internet cafes provide public access to Internet and e-mail services.
Post: Airmail to Western Europe takes up to 10 days.
MEDIA: Press: Daily Chinese-language papers include the *United Daily News*, the *Central Daily News*, *China Times*, *Taiwan Daily* and *Liberty Times*. English-language dailies include *The China Post*, *Taipei Times* and *Taiwan News*.
TV: *Public Television Service (PTS)* is the only non-profit public broadcaster. Commercial networks include *China Television Company (CTV)*, *Chinese Television System (CTS)*, *Taiwan Television Enterprise (TTV)* and *Formosa Television (FTV)*.
Radio: *Broadcasting Corporation of China (BCC)* has national and regional networks, while *CBS-Radio Taiwan International*, the national broadcaster, also beams services to mainland China and the rest of the world with programmes in various languages and Chinese dialects. *Public Radio System (PRS)* is Government-run and broadcasts travel, weather and social information. *International Community Radio Taipei (ICRT)* is the biggest English-language FM station.

Passport/Visa

	Passport Required?	Visa Required?	Return Ticket Required?
Full British	Yes	No/1	Yes
Australian	Yes	No/1	Yes
Canadian	Yes	No/1	Yes
USA	Yes	No/1	Yes
Other EU	Yes	No/1	Yes
Japanese	Yes	No/1	Yes

Note: *Regulations and requirements may be subject to change at short notice, and you are advised to contact the appropriate diplomatic or consular authority before finalising travel arrangements. Any numbers in the chart refer to the footnotes below.*

Restricted entry and transit: Nationals of China (PR) are not currently permitted to enter Taiwan unless on business.
PASSPORTS: Passport valid for at least six months required by all.
VISAS: Required by all except the following, provided they have no criminal record, have a confirmed return air ticket or air ticket and visa for next destination, and seat reservation for departure:
nationals of countries referred to in the chart above (except **1.** nationals of Cyprus, Czech Republic, Estonia, Hungary, Latvia, Lithuania, Poland, Slovak Republic and Slovenia who *do* require a visa), and nationals of Brunei, Costa Rica, Iceland, Korea (Rep), Liechtenstein, Malaysia, Monaco, New Zealand, Norway, Singapore and Switzerland for stays of up to 30 days (this period cannot be extended).
Note: (a) Nationals of Czech Republic, Hungary and Poland are eligible to apply for a Landing visa on arrival at CKS International Airport or Kaohsiung International Airport, on condition that they are holding tickets for an onward destination, and have no criminal record. The Landing visa is valid for 30 days and cannot be extended. They must provide a passport-size photo of themselves with a completed application form and pay a fee of TWD1200, plus a handling fee of TWD800. Nationals from countries who have a reciprocal agreement with Taiwan receive this visa free of charge.
(b) Passengers arriving at Kaohsiung International Airport (including passengers arriving from China (PR), may apply for a temporary entry permit at the Kaohsiung Station Aviation Police Bureau. They must convert the permit into a visa at the Bureau of Consular Affairs or its Kaohsiung Office within three days. If they fail to do so, they will be subject to a fine.
(c) Nationals holding Hong Kong (SAR), British National (overseas) or Macau (SAR) passports, if born in Hong Kong or Macau or if having previously visited Taiwan, may obtain a visa on arrival, valid for up to 14 days.
(d) Passengers arriving at CKS International Airport may apply for a landing visa at the Visa Office at CKS International Airport, Bureau of Consular Affairs *or* the Ministry of Foreign Affairs.
Types of visa and cost: *Single-entry visitor*: £25. *Multiple-entry visitor*: £50. *Landing*: TWD1200, plus TWD800 handling fee. Multiple-entry visas are issued for business purposes only and require a document from your employer regarding the purpose of visit.
Validity: *Single-entry visitor*: up to three months; up to two extensions of 60 days each may be granted by local police stations for certain applicants, if they have stayed in Taiwan for an initial period of at least 60 days and documents have been submitted that provide evidence for the necessity of an extension. These visas are valid for three months from date of issue. *Multiple-entry visitor* (business purposes only): six months from date of issue. *Landing*: 30 days. A visa is not required by travellers continuing their journey by the same or connecting aircraft on the same day, provided holding confirmed onward tickets and the necessary travel documentation and provided not departing from the transit lounge.
Note: Travellers intending to stay more than three months in Taiwan will be required to take an AIDS test. If the test is positive, they will be required to leave the country.
Application to: Visa section of Taipei Representative Office (see *Passport/Visa Information*).
Application requirements: (a) Application form. (b) Two passport-size photos. (c) Passport (valid for at least six months). (d) Documents verifying purpose of visit, or most recent bank statement, or letter from a sponsor in Taiwan (if appropriate). (e) Fee payable in cash, company cheque, by postal order or banker's draft (cheques should be made payable to 'Taipei Representative Office in the UK' and include applicant's name, address and telephone number, as well as a cheque guarantee card number, all written on the back. Personal cheques are not accepted). (f) For a postal application, a registered, stamped-addressed envelope. (g) Confirmed return air ticket and visa for next destination and confirmed seat reservation. (h) Cholera and yellow fever vaccinations are required if arriving from an infected area.
Working days required: One. However, some visa applications may be subject to delay. Applicants who have paid rush handling fees may collect their visas at 1630 on the same day.
Temporary residence: Those wishing to stay more than six months must apply for a Resident visa. Contact the Taipei Representative Office for further information (see *Passport/Visa Information*).

PASSPORT/VISA INFORMATION

Taipei Representative Office in the UK
50 Grosvenor Gardens, London SW1 0EB, UK
Tel: (020) 7881 2650 *or* 2654 (visa section).
Website: www.tro-taiwan.roc.org.uk
Opening hours: Mon-Fri 0930-1230 (visa section).

Taipei Economic and Cultural Representative Office (TECRO) in the USA
4201 Wisconsin Avenue, NW, Washington, DC 20016, USA
Tel: (202) 895 1800.
Website: www.tecro.org

Money

Currency: New Taiwan Dollar (TWD) = 100 cents. Notes are in denominations of TWD2000, 1000, 500, 200 and 100. Coins are in denominations of TWD50, 20, 10, 5 and 1.
Currency exchange: All travellers are required to make a currency declaration in writing together with the baggage declaration. Unused currency can be reconverted on departure, on production of exchange receipts.
Credit & debit cards: American Express, Mastercard, Visa and Diners Club are accepted in most hotels, restaurants and shops.
Traveller's cheques: Cashed in most hotels, restaurants and shops. To avoid additional exchange rate charges, travellers are advised to take traveller's cheques in US Dollars.
Currency restrictions: The import and export of local currency is limited to TWD40,000 and a permit from the Ministry of Finance is required for amounts over TWD8000. The import and export of foreign currency is unlimited, although amounts over TWD10,000 must be declared on arrival. All exchange receipts must be retained.
Banking hours: Mon-Fri 0900-1530.
Exchange rate indicators:
Rate at time of publishing
£1.00= TWD56.55
$1.00= TWD32.04

Duty Free

The following items may be imported by persons over 20 years of age without incurring customs duty: *200 cigarettes or 25 cigars or 454g of tobacco; 1 bottle (not more than 1l) of alcoholic beverage; reasonable quantities of perfume; other goods for personal use up to the value of TWD 20,000 (TWD 10,000 for passengers under 20 years of age).*
Prohibited items: Narcotics, arms, ammunition, gambling articles, non-canned meat products, fresh fruit and toy pistols. Publications promoting communism are prohibited, as are items originating in Albania, Bulgaria, Cambodia, China (PR), Cuba, Korea (Dem Rep), Laos, Romania, Vietnam and members of the CIS. All baggage must be itemised and declared in writing.

Public Holidays

Below are listed Public Holidays for the January 2006-June 2007 period.
2006: Jan 1-3 Founding of the Republic of China and New Year's Day. **Jan 29-31** Chinese New Year. **Feb 28** Peace Memorial Day. **Mar 29** Youth Day. **Apr 4** Women's/Children's Day and Tomb-Sweeping Day. **May 1** Labour Day. **May 8** Mother's Day. **May 31** Dragon Boat Festival. **Aug 8** Father's Day. **Sep 3** Armed Forces Day. **Sep 7** Ghost Festival. **Sep 28** Teacher's Day (Confucius' Birthday). **Oct 6** Mid-Autumn Moon Festival. **Oct 10** National Day. **Oct 25** Taiwan's Retrocession Day. **Nov 12** Birthday of Dr Sun Yat-sen. **Dec 25** Constitution Day.
2007: Jan 1-3 Founding of the Republic of China and New Year's Day. **Feb 18-20** Chinese New Year. **Feb 28** Peace Memorial Day. **Mar 29** Youth Day. **Apr 4** Women's/Children's Day and Tomb-Sweeping Day. **May 1** Labour Day. **May 8** Mother's Day. **Jun 19** (5th Day, 5th Moon) Dragon Boat Festival.

Health

	Special Precautions?	Certificate Required?
Yellow Fever	No	1
Cholera	Yes	2
Typhoid & Polio	3	N/A
Malaria	No	N/A

Note: Regulations and requirements may be subject to change at short notice, and you are advised to contact your doctor well in advance of your intended date of departure. Any numbers in the chart refer to the footnotes below.

1: A yellow fever vaccination certificate is required of travellers arriving from infected areas.
2: A cholera vaccination certificate is a condition of entry if arriving or having passed through an infected area.
3: Vaccination against typhoid is advised.
Food & drink: All water should be regarded as being potentially contaminated. Water used for drinking, brushing teeth or making ice should have first been boiled or otherwise sterilised. Milk is unpasteurised and should be boiled. Powdered or tinned milk is available and is advised, but make sure that it is reconstituted with pure water. Avoid dairy products which are likely to have been made from unboiled milk. Only eat well-cooked meat and fish, preferably served hot. Pork, salad and mayonnaise may carry increased risk. Vegetables should be cooked and fruit peeled.
Other risks: Immunisation against *hepatitis A, B, diphtheria* and *tuberculosis* is recommended. *Japanese encephalitis, dengue fever, filariasis, influenza* and *visceral leishmaniasis* occur. Rhesus negative blood is rare.
Rabies is present. If you are bitten, seek medical advice without delay. For more information, consult the *Health* appendix.
Notes: Outbreaks of *Severe Acute Pulmonary Syndrome (SARS)* occured in Taiwan in 2003.
Avian influenza (bird flu) is present in China.
Healthcare: Healthcare facilities are good and doctors are well-trained. Imported medicines are expensive, but locally produced and manufactured medicines are plentiful. Health insurance is recommended.

Travel - International

AIR:
The national airline is *China Airlines (CI)* (website: www.china-airlines.com).
Approximate flight times: From Taipei to *London* is approximately 15 hours including a stop in Hong Kong, Bangkok or Tokyo.
Main airports: *Chiang Kai-shek-Taipei (TPE)* is 40km (25 miles) south of the city (travel time - 30 minutes). *To/from the airport*: Buses depart every 15 to 20 minutes for both Sung Shan (domestic) airport and the main railway station. Taxis and buses are available to the city centre. *Facilities*: Duty free shop, post office, car hire, bank/bureau de change, bar/restaurant and tourist information.
Kaohsiung International (KHH) (website: www.kia.gov.tw) is 9km (4 miles) from the town centre. *To/from the airport*: A regular bus service is available (travel time - 30 minutes). There is a taxi service to the town. *Facilities*: Duty free shop, car hire, bank/bureau de change, post office and bar/restaurant.
Departure tax: None.
SEA:
Main ports: *Keelung* and *Kaohsiung* (website: www.khb.gov.tw).
Ferries run regularly between Keelung and Kaohsiung ports (Taiwan) and Okinawa (Japan). There are also sea links between Kaosiung and Macau.

Travel - Internal

AIR:
Far Eastern Air Transport (website: www.fat.com.tw), *Mandarin Airlines* (website: www.mandarin-airlines.com), *Transasia Airways* (website: www.tna.com.tw) and *Uni Air* (website: www.uniair.com.tw) are amongst the domestic airlines that run services to local destinations from Sung Shan Airport, Taipei.
SEA:
There are currently connections between Keelung and Okinawa. Services are also available between Taiwan and the islets.
RAIL:
Services are provided to destinations all over the island by the *Taiwan Railway Administration* (website: www.railway.gov.tw). The main tourist routes are Taipei-Taichung-Chiayi-Tainan-Kaohsiung (a top-class service), Taipei-Taichung-Sun Moon Lake (with the last leg of the journey by bus), Chiayi-Alishan (with spectacular mountain scenery) and Taipei-New Hualian-Taitung (scenic coastal route). Air-conditioned electric trains run at least hourly from Taipei to Kaohsiung; some trains have restaurant cars. Children under three travel free; children aged three to 13 pay half fare. Train tickets can be purchased at many major hotels in Taipei, as well as at the main railway station.
ROAD:
Traffic drives on the right. There is an adequate road system joining all major cities. A highway links Taipei and Kaohsiung. Some main streets have English signs. Congestion can be a problem, and mudslides may block mountain roads. **Bus:** There are both local and long-distance bus and coach services. Long-distant buses are provided by *Guo-Guang Bus Corporation, Union Bus, Dragon Bus, Free Go Bus Corporation* and *Aloha Bus*. Reserve tickets 14 days in advance of travel date. Travellers should not take illegal highway buses provided by unlicensed companies. Taipei, Taichung and Kaohsiung are the main transferring stops.
Taxi: These are plentiful and inexpensive (metered). Rates are charged at TWD70 for the first 1.5km and TWD5 for every 300m after that. A 20 per cent surcharge is charged 2300-0600. An extra TWD10 is needed for a taxi ordered over the phone and for luggage put in the trunk. The destination may have to be written in Chinese for the driver. It is not customary to tip taxi drivers. **Car hire:** This is available in major towns. Most rental fees do not include insurance. Seatbelts must be worn by the driver and the front seat passenger. Travellers are recommended to hire a car with a driver. **Documentation:** An International Driving Permit is required.
URBAN:
A number of private bus companies provide extensive services in Taipei. The Mass Rapid Transit (MRT) system, a monorail train, serves Taipei and its suburbs. Open 0600-0000, there are currently five lines in operation with stations situated by all major tourist attractions. Ticket prices range from NT$20 to NT$65 and a day pass costs NT$150. Metered taxis are available in Taipei; tipping is not expected, but it is starting to come into practice.
Travel times: The following chart gives approximate travel times (in hours and minutes) from **Taipei** to other major cities/towns:

	Air	Road	Rail
Kaohsiung	0.40	5.30	4.40
Tainan	0.40	4.30	4.10
Taitung	0.50	10.00	5.30
Makung	0.40	-	-

Travel Advice

Most visits to Taiwan are trouble-free but you should be aware of the global risk of indiscriminate international terrorist attacks, which could be against civilian targets, including places frequented by foreigners.
Travellers should take sensible precautions against small-scale and petty crimes which are sometimes carried out against foreigners.
Earthquakes (mostly minor) occur regularly and typhoons and tropical storms are a risk: visitors are advised to learn about emergency procedures for such events on arrival.
This advice is based on information provided by the Foreign and Commonwealth Office in the UK. It is correct at time of publishing. As the situation can change rapidly, visitors are advised to contact the following organisations for the latest travel advice:

British Foreign and Commonwealth Office
Tel: (0845) 850 2829.
Website: www.fco.gov.uk

US Department of State
Website: http://travel.state.gov/travel

Accommodation

HOTELS:
There are over 500 tourist hotels in the country offering a broad range of accommodation and services. Prices range from US$30-50 a day for smaller hotels, with US$90-150 a day being average. For details, contact the Press Division of the Taipei Representative Office in the UK or the Taiwan Visitors Bureau. Hotels are rated on a scale of **1 to 5 'Plum Blossoms'**, using a system equivalent to the more familiar 5-star system.
CAMPING/CARAVANNING:
Campsites are available.
YOUTH HOSTELS:
Dormitory and non-dormitory rooms are available in major cities and in scenic areas.

ACCOMMODATION INFORMATION

International Tourist Hotel Association of Taipei
Tel: (2) 2721 7379.

Chinese Taipei Youth Hostel Association
808, 8 Floor, No. 206, Sungchiang Road,
Taipei, Taiwan
Website: www.yh.org.tw

Hostelling International
13 Floor-10, No. 50, Sec.1, Zhongxiao West Road,
Taipei 100, Taiwan
Tel: (2) 2388 0885.
Website: www.yhtaiwan.com

Top Things To See

- Admire the view from the top of **Taipei 101**, the world's tallest building. You can take a lift (the fastest of its kind in the world) up to **The Observatory** on the top floor for the ultimate city vista.
- Take the **northeast coastal road**, which goes through a national scenic area and offers spectacular panoramas passing the foothills of the **Central Mountain Range** and overlooking the East China Sea and the Pacific Ocean. You will travel through many small villages, the lifestyles of whose inhabitants have changed little with the advent of high technology. Make sure you see the spectacular

A B C D E F G H I J K L M N O P Q R S T U V W X Y Z

Taroko Gorge, Taiwan's best-known natural attraction, a ravine with towering cliffs shot through with extensive marble deposits.

- Go **bird watching**: Taiwan is home to about 460 different species of birds, including rare endemic species such as the Formosan blue magpie, and the Swinhoe's and Mikado pheasants. There is also a big concentration of land mammal species, the best-known of which is the Formosan rock-monkey, and about 400 species of butterflies.
- Visit **Tainan**, the oldest city on the island, which is known as the 'City of 100 Temples'; there are, in fact, 220, and amongst them some of the best examples of Confucian temple architecture in Taiwan.
- Check out Taipei's **National Palace Museum**, which contains the world's largest collection of Chinese artefacts.
- Discover the **East Rift Valley**, where the world's largest continental plate, the Eurasian plate, and the largest oceanic plate (the Philippine plate) meet. This is Taiwan's largest fault line, a geologist's paradise - but also a fertile area rich in sediments that has earned the area the tag of the 'land of milk and honey'.
- Learn about the aboriginal Yami, one of the world's last surviving hunter-gatherer tribes, on their island, **Lanyu** (**Orchid Island**), off the southeast coast.
- Admire the astonishing basalt rock formations of the **Penghu archipelago**, a group of islands in the middle of the **Taiwan Straits**. The columns were formed when lava erupting from deep into the earth cooled and contracted, and were then carved by wind and wave erosion.
- Take a look at the **Chiang Kai-Shek Memorial Hall**, an imposing tomb and shrine to Taipei's most famous leader, which also houses Taipei's main venues for the performing arts, the **National Theatre** and **National Opera House**, in its large grounds.
- Chill out for a day or two in **Kenting National Park**, a popular forest recreation area boasting fine beaches, coral lakes and a bird sanctuary, as well as facilities for watersports and golf, all set amidst tropical coastal forest.

Top Things To Do

- Eat out: Taiwan is a gourmet paradise, and Taipei is the best place on earth to taste a full range of **cuisines** from mainland China, as well as some local delicacies.
- Join in the celebrations for one of many festivals taking place in the capital, and gain an insight into the island's culture. The **Chinese New Year**, the **Dragon Boat Festival** and the **Mid-Autumn Moon Festival** are all colourful affairs that really bring the streets to life.
- Attend a **glove puppet show**: these shows, which feature finely wrought puppets with gorgeous costumes, are popular with all ages, and great to break the language barrier.
- Soak in a hot spring: Taiwan's volcanic past has left abundant reserves of geothermal energy all over the island, and there are over 100 **hot mineral springs** scattered around the island, many of which are in the **Datun Mountains** of the **Yangmingshan National Park**.
- Gawp at jars of pickled snakes and demonstrations with live pythons at **Taipei**'s **Huahsi Night Market**, known locally as **Snake Alley**.
- **Dive** or **snorkel** in the waters around **Green Island**, off the southeast coast: there are splendid forests of corals to admire, and, what's more, visibility is good all-year-round here.
- Try **paragliding**: Taiwan's precipitous terrain and steady winds offer perfect opportunities for **hang-gliding** and paragliding at all skill levels. **Green Bay** on the **North Shore** and the **Luye Plateau** in **Taitung County** in the southeast offer inspiring scenery to boot.
- **Hike** in one of Taiwan's many national parks, or climb **Yu Shan** (**Jade Mountain**), at 3,952m, the highest peak in North-East Asia. It is the symbol of Taiwan's spirit and a favourite target for **mountain climbers**.
- **Shop** for unusual souvenirs: malls and markets alike have plenty of exciting goods on offer, among them bamboo wares, paper umbrellas, aboriginal handicrafts, glass art, candied fruit and, of course, tea.

Entertainment

FOOD & DRINK: The Chinese, never at a loss for vivid description, refer to their cuisine as an 'ancient art of ultimate harmony: pleasing to the eye; mouth-watering; and a delight to the palate'. Culinary styles come from all over China including Canton, Hunan, Mongolia, Peking, Shanghai, Szechuan and Taiwan. Most hotels have restaurants offering both Western and Chinese cuisine and some of the larger hotels offer several styles of Chinese cooking (the Chinese word for hotel, *fan-dien*, means 'eating place').

Things to know: Restaurants almost always have table service although some hotels have buffet/barbecue lunches. Most bars have counter service. There are no set licensing hours and alcohol is widely available.

National specialities:
- Cantonese food: Fried shrimp with cashews and deep-fried spring rolls and tarts.
- Pekinese food: *Peking duck*, steamed prawns, eels with pepper sauce and ham marrow sauce.
- Szechuan food: *Mother Ma's bean curd*, aubergine with garlic sauce, fried prawns with pepper sauce, minced chicken with *Gingko* nuts and fried breads.
- Shanghai food: Shark's fin in chicken, mushroom with crab meat, *ningpo* (fried eel), shark's fin soup and West Lake fish.
- Hunan food: Steamed ham and honey sauce, diced chicken with peanuts and smoked duck.
- Mongolian food: *Huoguo* ('firepot' - meat dipped in a sauce based on sesame paste, shrimp oil, ginger juice and bean paste) and barbecue (various slices of meat and vegetables cooked on an iron grill and eaten in a sesame bun).
- Taiwanese food: Spring rolls with peanut butter, sweet-and-sour spare ribs, bean curd in red sauce, oyster omelette and numerous excellent seafoods.

Tipping: Tipping is not an established custom, although it is on the increase. Taipei hotels and restaurants add 10 per cent service charge and extra tipping is not expected. The standard tip for porters is TWD50 per piece of luggage.

NIGHTLIFE: Taiwan has an abundance of nightlife, and Taipei in particular is lively at night. Western-style entertainment can be found in hotels, and in the many discos, clubs, restaurants and cinemas in Taipei. Popular amongst local people are KTVs, a type of sing-along club modelled on Japanese karaoke bars; and beer houses, which sell draught beer and snacks. The northern district of Tienmu contains a street of open-air beer houses. The visitor can also sample both traditional and modern tea houses, open all day and in the evening. In the tea-growing countryside around Mucha, it is possible to visit all-night tea houses and sip locally produced teas such as 'iron Buddha' *tiehkuanyin* tea. High-quality meals and snacks are also provided. These tea houses are popular with local families, particularly on special occasions. Back in Taipei, there are night markets selling a variety of items, both modern and traditional. These are bustling with browsers and bargain hunters, whose persistence can be spectacularly rewarded. It is advisable to take a pen and paper to assist in the bargaining process, as most vendors speak only Chinese. Taipei's largest night market is probably *Shihlin Night Market*, famous for its good-value clothing and food. Snacks such as oyster omelettes, pork liver soup and papaya milkshakes are available. Many shops are open at night.

SHOPPING: One of the best ways to shop is to visit the night markets (see above). Purchases include Formosan sea-grass mats, hats, handbags and slippers, bamboo items, Chinese musical instruments, various dolls in costume, handpainted palace lanterns made from silk, lacquerware, ceramics, teak furniture, coral, veinstone and jade items, *ramie* fibre rugs, brassware, handmade shoes, fabrics and chopsticks (decorated, personalised sticks of wood or marble).
Shopping hours: Mon-Sat 1000-2200. Some convenience stores are open 24 hours per day.

Business

ECONOMY: Taiwan was one of the first 'tiger economies' of the Pacific basin. After phenomenal growth from the 1950s onwards, Taiwan had by 1980 become one of the top 20 trading nations in the world and until the mid-1990s grew at an average annual rate of 8 per cent (much higher than most industrialised countries). Taiwan's success was built on a policy of rapid industrialisation coupled with low overheads and labour costs, which allowed Taiwanese products to compete successfully on world markets. This achievement has been all the more impressive, considering the island's dearth of raw materials (excepting small quantities of coal and marble). Massive foreign currency reserves accumulated over the years have since helped Taiwan to minimise the effects of turbulence in the world economy: this was amply illustrated by the 1997 Asian financial crisis in which Taiwan suffered the least damage of any major economy in the region. However, the crisis drew attention to structural problems in the economy, especially an urgent need for reform of the tax and banking systems. Taiwan's principal industries are textiles, shipbuilding, metals, plywood, furniture and petrochemicals. Agriculture and fisheries, though declining in relative terms, are large enough to allow Taiwan considerable self-sufficiency in basic foodstuffs such as rice, sugar cane, maize and sweet potatoes; fishing is of comparatively minor significance. After a brief recession in 2000/01, the economy is now growing steadily at around 3.8 per cent annually. Unemployment was a manageable 4.7 per cent in 2005, while inflation is currently 1.6 per cent. Export volumes are once again on the increase, and Taiwan runs a healthy trade surplus.

The performance of the Taiwanese economy is significantly affected by external political and economic conditions, especially in China (PR). Despite the 2004 re-election victory of the Sino-Sceptic President Chen, trade volumes with the mainland - already over US$50 billion annually - have increased sharply. Bilateral trade between Taiwan and the mainland rose from $41.01 billion in 2002 to $58 billion in 2003 and is expected to have passed $70 billion in 2004. In January 2002, Taiwan was admitted to the World Trade Organization.

Office Hours: Mon-Fri 0830/0900-1730.
CONFERENCES/CONVENTIONS: There is a wide range of convention facilities, including the vast Taipei World Trade Center Complex which houses the Exhibition Hall, the Grand Hyatt Taipei, the International Trade Building and the Taipei International Convention Center. Hotels offer a comprehensive range of facilities and there are some with seating for 1000 and over.

Tajikistan

200km
100mls
✈ international airport

KAZAKHSTAN   KAZ.

UZBEK-
ISTAN   KYRGYZSTAN

Khudzand
Ura-
Tyube   A l a i   Lenin Peak 7134m

Penjikent Novabad Surkhob   CHINA

DUSHANBE Mt Garmo   Lake
7495m   Kara-Kul

TAJIKISTAN P A M I R Murgab

Kulyab

Kurgan-
Tyube   Khorog

AFGHANISTAN   Wakhan Corridor

PAKISTAN

Location: Central Asia.

Time: GMT + 5.

Overview

The Tajiks come from an ancient stock – the inhabitants of the Pamir Mountains claim to be the only pure descendants of the Aryan tribes who invaded India over 4000 years ago, and that the Saxon tribes of Western Europe also originated there. Tajikistan's inaccessibility has protected it from most invaders, although Alexander the Great founded a city on the site of modern-day Khojand, calling it *Alexandria Eskate* (Alexandria the Furthest).

Tajikistan was established as a sovereign state in 1991, following the dissolution of the Soviet Union. The ensuing power struggle led to civil war in late 1992, resulting in about 30,000 deaths. In 1994, Russian troops were brought in at the request of the beleaguered regime. Moscow also brokered negotiations between the Government and the United Tajik Opposition (UTO). By 1997, the government and opposition had gradually put together a workable deal, under which the UTO accepted a 30 per cent share of administrative responsibilities and integrated some of its units into the army. The Government would, for its part, legalise the main opposition political parties that were previously banned.

It is now nine years since the opposing parties signed the 1997 peace agreement that brought the Tajik civil war to an end and the political situation is currently stable. Tajikistan was never well equipped with a comprehensive infrastructure for tourists, and some sites were destroyed in the civil war at the end of 1992. However, there is still much to see. The country's mountainous terrain is ideally suited to the adventurous trekker, while the ancient Silk Road routes, incorporating some of Tajikistan's most stunning landscapes, offer a glimpse into a more prosperous era.

General Information

AREA: 143,100 sq km (55,251 sq miles).
POPULATION: 6.3 million (UN estimate 2005).
POPULATION DENSITY: 44 per sq km.
CAPITAL: Dushanbe. **Population:** 575,900 (2002).
GEOGRAPHY: Tajikistan is bordered by Kyrgyzstan and Uzbekistan to the north, Afghanistan to the south and China (PR) to the east. 93 per cent of the republic is occupied by mountains, most notably by the sparsely populated Pamir Mountains, which include Mount Garmo (formerly Pik Kommunizma; 7495m/24,590ft), the highest point of the former Soviet Union. The mountainous terrain means that in winter it is impossible to reach the east or the north of the country by road without taking a detour through Uzbekistan and Kyrgyzstan. In the fertile plains of the southwest, cotton dominates the agriculture. In the

north, in the Khudzand (formerly Leninabad) region, cotton and silk are the main crops.

GOVERNMENT: Republic. Gained independence from the Soviet Union in 1991. **Head of State:** President Imamali S Rahmonov since 1992. **Head of Government:** Prime Minister Oqil Ghaybulloyevich Oqilov. **Recent history:** In February 2005, Parliamentary elections were held in Tajikistan which were condemned by the OSCE as falling short of international standards in some areas. Mr Rahmonov's People's Democratic Party won virtually all 63 seats in the lower house of Parliament. The opposition Islamic and Communist parties won just a handful between them.

LANGUAGE: Tajik is the official language, an ancient Persian language similar to the languages of Iran and Afghanistan. In the Pamir Mountains, there are at least five different languages, all related to an even more ancient form of Iranian. Russian is widely used (35 per cent of the population speak Russian fluently), and discrimination against Russian speakers is prohibited by law. English is sometimes spoken by those involved in tourism.

RELIGION: Predominantly Sunni Muslim (80 per cent) with a small Shi'ite Muslim minority (5 per cent). A large Ishmaeli minority exists in the Pamirs. There is also a smaller and shrinking Russian Orthodox minority and a small Jewish community.

ELECTRICITY: 220 volts AC, 50Hz. Round, two-pin continental plugs are standard.

SOCIAL CONVENTIONS: *Lipioshka* (bread) should never be laid upside down, and it is normal to remove shoes, but not socks, when entering someone's house. Shorts are rarely seen in Tajikistan and, if worn by females, are likely to provoke unwelcome attention from the local male population.

Climate

In Dushanbe, temperatures vary between a minimum -13°C (8°F) in December/January to a maximum 33°C (91°F) in July/August. Humidity is generally low. In the mountains, it can reach -45°C (-49°F) when the wind chill factor is taken into consideration, and rise to 20°C (68°F) in summer. In the Pamir Mountains, the climate is semi-arid to polar.

Required clothing: Warm clothing should be taken by anyone intending to visit the mountains. Those intending to visit the southwest in summer should bring light, loose clothing.

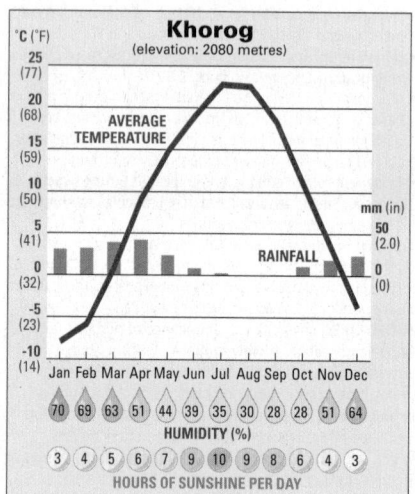

°C (°F)   **Khorog**
(elevation: 2080 metres)
25 (77)
20 (68)   AVERAGE
15 (59)   TEMPERATURE
10 (50)
mm (in)
5 (41)   50 (2.0)
0 (32)   RAINFALL   0 (0)
-5 (23)
-10 (14)

Jan Feb Mar Apr May Jun Jul Aug Sep Oct Nov Dec
70 69 63 51 44 39 35 30 28 28 51 64
HUMIDITY (%)
3 4 5 6 7 9 10 9 8 6 4 3
HOURS OF SUNSHINE PER DAY

Communications

Telephone: IDD to Tajikistan is available but services are unreliable. Country code: 992 (followed by 372 for Dushanbe). International telephone calls can be made from telephone offices which will usually be found attached to a post office (in Dushanbe, on Prospekt Rudaki). There are now also some new, private telephone offices in Dushanbe. International, operator-routed calls can also be ordered from some hotels such as the Hotel Tajikistan and the Hotel Independence. Direct-dial calls within the CIS are obtained by dialling 8 and waiting for another dial tone and then dialling the city code. Calls within the city limits are free of charge.

Mobile telephone: Roaming agreements exist with most international mobile phone companies. Coverage is limited to urban areas.

Internet: There are Internet cafes in the main cities. Some will allow you to plug in your own computer.

Post: Mail to Western Europe and the USA can take between two weeks and two months. Stamped envelopes can be bought from post offices. Addresses should be laid out in the following order: country, postcode, city, street, house number and, lastly, the person's name. Postal services available include registered mail, restricted delivery, special delivery and Express mail (in Dushanbe only). Both surface and air mail are

available for parcels. Post office hours: Mon-Fri 0800-1800, Sat: 0900-1700. Visitors can also use the post offices located within the major hotels.

MEDIA: Press freedom is provided for in the constitution, but is not widely respected; independent journalists are said to come under huge pressure from the state. The Government controls the editorial policy of the state-owned media and state-operated radio and TV dominate broadcasting. There are over 30 local and regional private TV stations and more than 200 registered newspapers. Some are government-owned; others are connected to political parties and movements. There are no dailies. A few private radio stations exist. Dushanbe's first private station opened in September 2002, after waiting four years for a licence.

Press: All the main newspapers are printed in Dushanbe and include *Narodnaya Gazeta* (Russian), *Jumhuriyat* and *Tojikiston Ovozi* (Tajik).

TV: *Tajik TV* is a nationwide state-run channel, while *Soghd TV* and *Khatlon TV* are state-operated regional channels in the south.

Radio: *Tajik Radio* is state-run and operates two national networks. Private stations include *Asia-Plus* (Dushanbe's first private station), *Radio Vatan* and *Radio Tiroz*.

Passport/Visa

	Passport Required?	Visa Required?	Return Ticket Required?
Full British	Yes	Yes	Yes
Australian	Yes	Yes	Yes
Canadian	Yes	Yes	Yes
USA	Yes	Yes	Yes
Other EU	Yes	Yes	Yes
Japanese	Yes	Yes	Yes

Note: *Regulations and requirements may be subject to change at short notice, and you are advised to contact the appropriate diplomatic or consular authority before finalising travel arrangements. Any numbers in the chart refer to the footnotes below.*

Note: Passport and visa regulations for all the CIS states are liable to change at short notice. All travellers are advised to contact the nearest Tajikistan Embassy or Consulate for up-to-date details. Countries where Tajikistan has diplomatic representation currently include Austria, China (PR), Germany, Iran and Turkey.

PASSPORTS: Passport valid for at least six months after date of departure required by all.

VISAS: Required by all except nationals of CIS member states (Belarus, Kazakhstan, Kyrgyzstan and the Russian Federation).

Types of visa and cost: *Standard:* €35 for seven days; €45 for 15 days; €50 for 30 days; €70 for 90 days. Express visas (processed on same day) cost double the given fee.

Validity: Dependent on purpose of trip.

Note: An invitation, either official or private, is necessary for visits to Tajikistan. The length of stay should be specified on the invitation, which must be endorsed by the Ministry of Foreign Affairs in Tajikistan. A visa can then be issued by the nearest Tajikistan Embassy. Special visas must also be obtained by those wishing to visit the Gorno-Babakhshan region (the Pamir Mountains). Tourists can apply for a letter of invitation from the State National Travel Agency, 14 Pushkin Street, Dushanbe, Tajikistan 734 095 (tel/fax: (372) 231 401).

Application requirements: (a) Two completed application forms. (b) Two recent passport-size photos. (c) Valid passport. (d) A letter, telex, fax or other confirmation of acceptance of invitation (see above) from the Ministry of Foreign Affairs. (e) Fee. (f) Postal applications must be accompanied by a large, stamped, self-addressed envelope.

Note: (a) All visitors are required to register with the authorities within 72 hours of arrival. Hotels will usually arrange this; however, independent travellers will need to go to the Ministry of Foreign Affairs or the local OVIR office themselves. (b) An HIV test is required by all foreigners planning to stay longer than 90 days. Foreign tests may be acceptable.

Working days required: 10 (for Standard visas). Express visas are issued on the same day.

PASSPORT/VISA INFORMATION

Embassy of the Tajikistan Republic in Germany
Otto-Suhr-Allee 84, 10585 Berlin, Germany
Tel: (30) 347 9300.
Website: www.embassy-tajikistan.de

Embassy of the Tajikistan Republic in the USA
1005 New Hampshire Avenue, NW, Washington, DC 20037, USA
Tel: (202) 223 6090.
Website: www.tjus.org

Money

Currency: Tajik Somoni (TJS) = 100 diram. Notes are in denominations of TJS100, 50, 20, 10, 5 and 1, and 50, 20, 5 and 1 diram.

Currency exchange: The preferred hard currency is the US Dollar, although other hard currencies are in theory also acceptable. All bills are normally settled in cash, and tourists must pay in hard currency for accommodation in hotels, although these are normally included in the price of organised tours. Owing to a shortage of change, a supply of small notes should be carried. International banking services are not available. All money should be changed at the official bureaux de change and the receipts should be kept. However, this law is not rigidly enforced.

Credit & debit cards: Not accepted.

Traveller's cheques: Limited acceptance.

Currency restrictions: The import of local and foreign currency is unlimited, subject to declaration on arrival. The export of local currency is prohibited except by Tajikistan residents and the export of foreign currency is limited to the amount declared on arrival. All currency must be declared on arrival and a customs declaration form obtained.

Banking hours: Mon-Fri 0800-1700.

Exchange rate indicators:
Rate at time of publishing
£1.00=   TJS4.92
$1.00=   TJS2.79

Duty Free

Reasonable quantities of goods for personal use may be imported into Tajikistan by persons of 18 years of age or older without incurring customs duty; however, certain items attract a 10 per cent import duty.

Note: A detailed customs declaration form must be filled in and retained by all travellers.

Public Holidays

Below are Public Holidays listed for the January 2006-June 2007 period.
2006: Jan 1 New Year's Day. **Jan 10** Eid-i-Kurbon (Feast of the Sacrifice). **Mar 8** International Women's Day. **Mar 20-22** Navrus (Persian New Year). **May 1** International Labour Day. **May 9** Victory Day. **Sep 9** Independence Day. **Oct 22-24** Eid-i-Ramazon (End of Ramadan). **Nov 6** Constitution Day. **Dec 31** Eid-i-Kurbon (Feast of the Sacrifice).
2007: Jan 1 New Year's Day. **Mar 8** International Women's Day. **March 20-22** Navrus (Persian New Year). **May 1** International Labour Day. **May 9** Victory Day. **Sep 9** Independence Day.

Health

	Special Precautions?	Certificate Required?
Yellow Fever	No	No
Cholera	1	No
Typhoid & Polio	2	N/A
Malaria	3	N/A

Note: *Regulations and requirements may be subject to change at short notice, and you are advised to contact your doctor well in advance of your intended date of departure. Any numbers in the chart refer to the footnotes below.*

1: Following WHO guidelines issued in 1973, a cholera vaccination certificate is not a condition of entry to Tajikistan. However, cholera is a serious risk in this country and precautions are essential. Up-to-date advice should be sought before deciding whether these precautions should include vaccination, as medical opinion is divided over its effectiveness; see the *Health* appendix for more information.
2: Vaccination against typhoid is advised.
3: Cases of malaria, predominantly in the benign *vivax* form, have been reported in some central, western and northern areas of Tajikistan and particularly on the southern border (Khatlon area) between June and October. Those wishing to visit the area should bring suitable medication with them. Resistance to chloroquine is suspected.
Note: Travellers planning to stay in Tajikistan more than 90 days must present a medical certificate indicating that they are HIV-free.

Food & drink: All water should be regarded as being a potential health risk. Water used for drinking, brushing teeth or making ice should have first been boiled or otherwise sterilised. Milk is pasteurised and dairy products are safe for consumption. Only eat well-cooked meat and fish, preferably served hot. Pork, salad and mayonnaise may carry increased risk. Vegetables should be cooked and fruit peeled.

Other risks: There is a *diphtheria* epidemic in Tajikistan and medical advice should be sought before travelling. *Hepatitis A, B* and *E* occur. Rare occurrences of *plague* have been reported. *Trachoma* is common, *Crimean Congo haemorrhagic fever, typhus, leishmaniasis, sand-fly fever, tick-borne relapsing fever, brucellosis, plague* and *echinococcosis* all occur but risks to the traveller are low. *Rabies* is present. For those at high risk, vaccination before arrival should be considered. If you are bitten, seek medical advice without delay. For more information, consult the *Health* appendix.

Health care: Standards of health care are low. As the domestic health service is plagued by shortages of medicines and drugs, travellers are advised to take antibiotics and any prescription medicines, contact lens solutions and a first-aid kit containing basic medicines and water treatment tablets. There is no reciprocal health agreement with the UK. Although fees for health services are low, health insurance is recommended.

Travel - International

AIR:

 The national airline is *Tajikistan Airlines* (website: www.tajikistan-airlines.com). **Approximate flight times:** From Dushanbe to *Moscow* is four hours, to *Karachi* is two hours and to *Delhi* is one hour 30 minutes.

Main airports: *Dushanbe Airport (DYU)* is 1 mile (2km) south of the city. *To/from the airport:* Bus nos. 3 and 12, and trains 3 and 4, run to the city centre 0600-1800 (travel time - 20 minutes). Taxis are also available 0800-2000 (travel time - five minutes). *Facilities:* First aid, left luggage, chemist, post office, restaurants, snack bars, tourist information and nursery.

RAIL:

 Trains are the most reliable way of reaching Dushanbe for those not arriving by air. Passenger railways are, however, restricted at present. Dushanbe is connected to a spur of the Trans-Caspian Railway which winds down to the Afghan border in Uzbekistan before heading north towards Dushanbe. Travellers are advised to sit with their back to the engine, as throwing rocks at the windows of passing trains seems to be a popular pastime among local children. The journey from Tashkent to Dushanbe takes approximately 22 hours; from Moscow it takes approximately four days. Khojand in the north of the country can be reached directly from Samarkand in Uzbekistan. There is also a train service between Dushanbe and Volgograd in the Russian Federation.

ROAD:

 Tajikistan can be approached by road from Uzbekistan, subject to occasional unannounced border closures and snow. Cars with a Tajik registration, however, are not allowed to enter Uzbekistan, unless the vehicle belongs to a government body. It is not advisable to attempt to cross the border from Kyrgyzstan at present. A road has recently been built into China (PR). The border between Tajikistan and Afghanistan is officially closed. **Bus:** Services have been severely disrupted by border closures and should not be relied upon. A service normally operates connecting Dushanbe with Tashkent and Samarkand.

Travel - Internal

AIR:

 The domestic airline is *Tajik Air*, offering internal flights to Khorog in Gorno-Badakhshan (one of the most technically demanding regularly scheduled flights in the world), Khojand and less frequently to Kulyab. All flights are subject to the weather and the endemic fuel shortages of the region. Flights from Dushanbe to Khorog take one hour, to Khojand one hour and to Kulyab 30 minutes. Internal services are subject to cancellations, long delays and overloading of passengers.

RAIL:

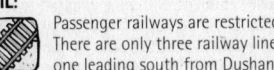 Passenger railways are restricted at present. There are only three railway lines in Tajikistan: one leading south from Dushanbe through Kurgan-Tyube and Shaartuz to the Uzbek/Afghan border at Termez; one that leads due south from Dushanbe, through Kurgan-Tyube to Tugul on the Afghan border; and one in the northern region which runs from Samarkand, through Khojand to the Fergana Valley. A branch from Kulyab to Kurgan-Tyube is currently under construction.

Note: Travellers are advised to store their valuables in the compartment under the bed/seats, to ensure the door is securely shut from the inside by tying it closed with wire or strong cord, and not to leave the compartment unattended.

ROAD:

 There is a reasonable road network in Tajikistan, though some parts may be seasonally impassable. During the winter (October to

March), three of the four main roads from the capital and the southwest of the country (east to Khorog via Khalaikum, northeast to Osh via the Garm valley, and north to Khojand via the Anzob Pass and Ayni) are all closed by snow. The only way of reaching these areas is through Uzbekistan. The road between Osh (in Kyrgyzstan) and Khorog is kept open all year round and traverses one of the most beautiful and unspoilt regions in the world, the Pamir Mountains. Recent political and economic troubles have meant that road maintenance has been widely neglected. Foreigners are, in theory, allowed to go anywhere except border zones - it is worth noting that the road from Dushanbe to Khorog is in a border zone for much of its length - without having to get special permission (other than an endorsement on their visas). Tourists should inform their tour operator of their plans. If travelling independently, it is worth getting as many official-looking documents as possible in order to negotiate the many checkpoints. Traffic drives on the right. **Bus:** There are services between the major towns when the roads are open. In the south, buses go to Kurgan-Tyrube and Kulyab and as far down as Pyanj and Ayvadaz. Buses to the east reach only around 100km (60 miles), as far as Komsomolabad. Information on timetables and fares can be found at the bus station, or *autovokzal*.
Taxi: These and chauffeur-driven cars for hire can be found in all major towns. Many are unlicensed and travellers are advised to agree a fare in advance. Officially marked taxis are safe, but sharing with strangers should be avoided. As many of the street names have changed since independence, it is also advisable to ascertain both the old and the new street names when asking directions. **Car hire:** Self-drive car hire is not currently available.
Documentation: It is in theory possible to bring, or buy, one's own transport: drivers should have an International Driving Permit and have arranged insurance before departure.

Travel Advice

Travellers are advised to avoid all but essential travel to areas immediately adjoining the Afghan border due to the continuing threat from terrorism and unrest in Afghanistan. Travellers should take particular care in the Garm valley and off-road areas which may be mined along the Uzbek and Kyrgyz borders.
Travellers should be aware of the continuing threat from terrorism which Tajikistan shares with other countries in Central Asia.
The overall security situation in Tajikistan is currently stable.
The tourism, health and transport infrastructure of Tajikistan is poor and travel within the country requires careful planning. Travellers should observe strict hygiene practices and take particular care over food and drink preparation.
This advice is based on information provided by the Foreign and Commonwealth Office in the UK. It is correct at time of publishing. As the situation can change rapidly, visitors are advised to contact the following organisations for the latest travel advice:

British Foreign and Commonwealth Office
Tel: (0845) 850 2829.
Website: www.fco.gov.uk

US Department of State
Website: http://travel.state.gov/travel

Accommodation

HOTELS:

 Tajikistan is not well supplied with hotels. Although there are no restrictions on where visitors may stay, hotels other than the main hotels are unused to accommodating foreigners and all but the most insistent visitors may find it difficult to obtain a room. The main hotels are clean and friendly, although it is difficult to get a room in the Oktyabrskaya, which houses both the US and Russian embassies. Outside the capital, accommodation is very hard to find. For further information, contact the State National Tourism Company of the Republic of Tajikistan (see *Top Things To See & Do*).
DACHAS: It is possible to stay in the government dachas in Khorog, but standards of comfort, amenities and cleanliness vary.

Top Things To See & Do

- Visit the Tajik capital, **Dushanbe**, which lies in the **Hissar valley** in the southwest of the country only three hours from the border with Afghanistan. Known primarily for its Monday market (the name Dushanbe is derived from the Tajik word for Monday), it was no more than a village until the Trans-Caspian Railway reached it in 1929. Soviet power had only been established in the region for

A B C D E F G H I J K L M N O P Q R S T U V W X Y Z

six years and, somewhat unoriginally, the city was renamed **Stalinabad** and proclaimed capital of the new Soviet Socialist Republic of Tajikistan. It was from here that Brezhnev launched his invasion of Afghanistan in 1979. The main points of interest all lie on, or are close to **Prospekt Rudaki**, which runs from the railway station in the south to the bus station in the north. As well as the principal mosque, this area boasts a synagogue that dates back to the late-19th century, a Russian church and a columned opera house. Other features in the city include the **Tajikistan Unified Museum**, situated just north of the railway station in **Ploshchad Aym**, which has stuffed snow leopards and Marco Polo sheep amongst its exhibits. The **ethnographic museum** is on ulitsa Somoni, not far from the **Hotel Tajikistan**.

- Uncover the history of the **Hissar Port**, 16km (10 miles) west of Dushanbe. The site was built between the 16th and 19th centuries and contains, among other things, a ruined **citadel**, two **madrassahs** (Islamic seminaries), a **caravanserai** and a mausoleum.
- Further west, at **Penjikent** on the Uzbek border, lie the remains of a Sogdian fort that are only now being excavated. The frescoes in Penjikent are reputed to be extremely fine.
- Marvel at the kaleidoscopic colours of the **Muragazor Lakes**, South of Penjikent, a system of seven lakes whose colours change as the light alters.
- View the remains of Buddhist temples near **Kurgan-Tyube** in the south, from which the biggest Buddha in Central Asia was recovered and is now stored, ignominiously carved up into 60 pieces, in Dushanbe.
- The **Pamirs** are at the hub of Asia. Often described as the **Roof of the World**, these mountains form one of the most unexplored regions on earth. High, cold and remote, they have attracted climbers and hunters from the former Soviet Union for years, but only now are they opening up for the rest of the world. The bulk of the Pamir lies in the semi-autonomous region of Gorno-Badakhshan and visitors should be aware that some elements have been conducting an armed campaign to gain even more autonomy. However, the campaign has been confined to a number of well-defined theatres, most of which are well away from areas likely to interest visitors; the road between Dushanbe and Khorog is the exception.
- The only town of any significance on the **Pamir Highway**, which stretches from Dushanbe into Kyrgyzstan, is **Khorog**. The capital of the eastern Tajik region of **Gorno-Badakhshan**, Khorog is a small one-street town with a museum containing stuffed animals and a display of photographs of Lenin. The flight into Khorog from the Tajik capital is said to be the most difficult in the world.
- **Lake Sareskoye**, in the heart of the Pamirs, was formed in 1911 when the side of a mountain was dislodged by an earthquake and fell into the path of a mountain river.
- In the north of the Pamirs, **Lake Kara-Kul**, formed by a meteor 10 million years ago, is 3915m (12,844ft) above sea-level and hence too high for any aquatic life.
- **Pik Lenina** and **Mount Garmo** (formerly Pik Kommunizma) are to the northwest and west respectively of Lake Kara-Kul. At well over 7000m (22,966ft), these two peaks tower over Tajikistan and the neighbouring republic of Kyrgyzstan to the north. Helicopter flights are available for those wishing to climb them. Some people are convinced that **yetis** are alive and thriving in this remote wilderness.
- **The Silk Road:** This ancient trading route was used by silk merchants from the second century until its decline in the 14th century, and is open in parts to tourists, stretching from northern China, through bleak and foreboding desert and mountainous terrain, to the ports on either the Caspian Sea or Mediterranean Sea. For further details of the route, see *Silk Road* in the *China* section. The main highlight for travellers along the Silk Road in Tajikistan is its stunning natural scenery set against the Pamir and Fan mountains and incorporating lush valleys and turquoise lakes. **Trekking** trips are best arranged from Samarkand (Uzbekistan). Travel along the Silk Road can be quite difficult due to the terrain, harsh climate and lack of developed infrastructure. Visitors to the region are advised to travel with an organised tour company or travel agent.
- Explore the mountains by foot: tour operators offer a number of set **hiking** itineraries, mostly in the southwest of the country and its surrounding mountains, generally during the summer months. The trips generally start in Moscow and include a 14-day trekking trip around the ancient **Sogdian lakes** such as **Iskander-kul**, north of Dushanbe and the **Muragazor lakes**, finishing in **Samarkand** in Uzbekistan; and a trip to the mountain passes of the **Kara-Tak**, north of Dushanbe, walking 8 to 10km (5 to 6 miles) per day, with baggage being carried by donkeys, and staying in mountain villages. Some operators will organise itineraries to suit individual tastes.
- The national sport is **wrestling**, called *Gushtin Geri*. *Bushkashi* is a team game in which the two mounted teams attempt to deliver a headless and legless goat's carcass weighing 30 to 40kg over the opposition's goal line. Players are allowed to wrestle the goat from an opponent, but physical assault is frowned upon.
- There is **skiing** and **hunting** in the hills behind Dushanbe.

TOURIST INFORMATION

State National Tourism Company of the Republic of Tajikistan (SAYOH)
Prospekt Rudaki 42, Dushanbe, Tajikistan
Tel: (372) 211 808.
Website: www.tajiktour.tajnet.com

Entertainment

FOOD & DRINK: Traditional Tajik meals start with sweet dishes such as *halwa* and tea and then progress to soups and meat before finishing with *plov*.

National specialities:

- *Plov* is made up of scraps of mutton, shredded yellow turnip and rice, fried in a large wok, and is a staple dish in all the Central Asian republics.
- *Shashlyk* (skewered chunks of mutton grilled over charcoal, served with raw sliced onions) and *lipioshka* (round unleavened bread) are often sold on street corners and served in restaurants: the Vastoychny bar restaurant in Dushanbe (on Prospekt Rudaki near the Hotel Tajikistan) serves particularly good *shashlyk*.
- *Manty* (large noodle sacks of meat), *samsa* (samosas) and *chiburekki* (deep-fried dough cakes) are all popular as snacks.
- *Shorpur* is a meat and vegetable soup; *laghman* is similar to *shorpur*, but comes with noodles.
- In the summer, Tajikistan is awash with fruit: its grapes and melons were famous throughout the former Soviet Union. The bazaars also sell pomegranates, apricots, plums, figs and persimmons.
- *Strogan* is the local equivalent of beef *Stroganoff*.
- *Pirmeni*, originating in Ukraine, are small boiled noodle sacks of meat and vegetables similar to ravioli, sometimes in a vegetable soup, sometimes not.

National drinks:

- Tea or *chai* is the most widespread drink on offer and can be obtained almost anywhere.
- Beer, wine, vodka, brandy and sparkling wine (*shampanski*) are intermittently available in many restaurants. If the restaurant is unable to supply it, it is acceptable to bring your own.
- *Kefir*, a thick drinking yoghurt, is often served with breakfast.

NIGHTLIFE: There are no restaurants operating in the evenings except for the one in the Hotel Oktyabrskaya which shuts at 2200. There is a dollar bar in the basement of the Hotel Tajikistan which is open some evenings. The Ayni opera and ballet theatre on Prospekt Rudaki is still operating, albeit with a reduced programme of matinees. The streets of Dushanbe are usually deserted by 2000.

SHOPPING: Shortages are the norm in Tajikistan; there is a bazaar and street market behind the Hotel Tajikistan where it is possible to buy food and sometimes handicrafts. Shokhmansur (also known as Zilyoni) Bazaar near Ploshchad Ayni also sells food. There is a souvenir shop on the corner of Prospekt Rudaki and ulitsa Ismail Somoni, under an art gallery which exhibits and sells the work of local artists. **Shopping hours:** Food shops open Mon-Sat 0900-1700.

Business

ECONOMY: Tajikistan is the poorest of the five former Soviet Central Asian republics, with an estimated four-fifths of the population living below the poverty line. Basic services and infrastructure are poor to non-existent. Although less than 10 per cent of the country's land can be cultivated, Tajikistan has a sizeable agricultural sector accounting for one-quarter of GDP and employing half the workforce. Large quantities of cotton are produced under ecologically ruinous schemes established during the Soviet era. Grain, fruit and vegetables are also grown. In recent years, the country has been badly hit by a regional drought, an earthquake and a series of mudslides (caused by poor land use) which forced the Government to make several appeals for international food aid.

Tajikistan's economic prospects lie with exploitation of its mineral resources, which include gold, aluminium, iron, lead, tin and mercury ores. There are coal deposits as well as small amounts of natural gas, which together with hydroelectric schemes meet the bulk of the country's energy needs. There is little heavy industry other than mineral processing (mainly aluminium); light industry is concentrated in food processing and textiles. The Tajik economy suffered severely during the 1990s from the dislocations caused by the break-up of the Soviet Union followed by two outbreaks of civil war. It has recovered slowly since the 1997 peace accord but some positive results are now showing: the hyper-inflation which blighted the economy during the civil war has now been cut to around 10 per cent. Annual GDP growth in 2005 was a healthy 10 per cent. The Government's economic reform programme, which is now being implemented, comprises a typical recipe of privatisation, deregulation and fiscal reform. Tajikistan secured membership of the IMF and World Bank in 1993; it also belongs to the European Bank for Reconstruction and Development as a 'Country of Operation'. It has received substantial aid from Middle Eastern donors, including Saudi Arabia, Kuwait and the Islamic Development Bank. External donors now supply around 60 per cent of Tajik government income.

Tajikistan now has its own currency, the Somoni, which was introduced in October 2000 to replace the five-year-old Tajik rouble. In April 1998, Tajikistan was admitted to the Customs Union of the Commonwealth of Independent States, a loose federation of former Soviet republics, whose members continue to dominate Tajik trade. Further afield, The Netherlands and the UK are important trading partners. In July 2001, Tajikistan acquired observer status at the World Trade Organisation.

BUSINESS ETIQUETTE: Tajikistan is looking for foreign investment in a number of sectors, particularly in aluminium processing, which needs extensive modernisation. Foreign businesses are not barred from any economic sphere: although land, livestock and mineral resources are owned by the Government, it is possible to lease them. Foreign concerns are allowed to participate in the privatisation programme. Foreign investments in certain priority areas, which are as yet undefined, are eligible for tax holidays - including import and export duties - although, in effect, each foreign investor negotiates his or her own terms and many are better than the standard laid down in law. All foreign investors must be registered with the Ministry of External Economic Affairs. **Office hours:** Mon-Fri 0800-1700.

COMMERCIAL INFORMATION

Ministry of Economy and Foreign Economic Relations
42 Rudaki Street, Dushanbe 734002, Tajikistan
Tel: (372) 232 944.
Fax: (372) 210 404.

US Department of Commerce
Business Information Service for the Newly Independent States
USA Trade Center, Stop R-Binis,
1401 Constitution Avenue, NW,
Washington, DC 20230, USA
Tel: (202) 482 4655.
E-mail: bisnis@ita.doc.gov

Tanzania

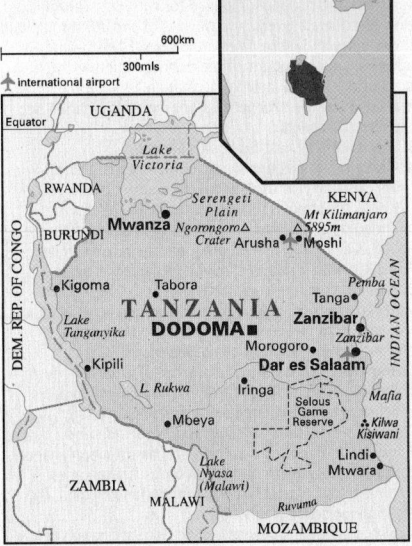

Location: East Africa.

Time: GMT + 3.

Overview

The United Republic of Tanzania became independent in 1961 and merged with Zanzibar in 1964. Mainland Tanzania has on the whole been – and still is - peaceful and stable with few tribal or regional divisions. It stands out as a stable democracy in a region that has witnessed some of the most vicious civil conflicts in Africa. It could be said, however, that 15 years after the introduction of multi-party politics, ruling party *Chama cha Mapinduzi* (*CCM*) still behaves as if the country were a one-party state. Particularly on Zanzibar, which has its own Parliament and President, the political situation has been more volatile since multi-party politics were introduced, with occasional violent conflict between opposition parties and the Government.

Tourism has steadily been growing in importance and ranks as the second highest foreign exchange earner after agriculture. According to 2002 figures, tourism was worth about US$1 billion to the Tanzanian economy, but the industry has suffered a serious downturn in recent years as a result of international terrorism.

Tanzania's popularity is not surprising for a country that boasts Kilimanjaro, the Serengeti, the Ngorongoro Crater and Zanzibar. Tanzania is definitely a country to be recognised both in terms of wildlife and beauty. For many, it is the ultimate safari destination. With national parks extending over some 33,660 sq km (13,000 sq miles), Tanzania has more land devoted to national parks and game reserves than any other wildlife destination in the world. Everything from pristine coral reefs to the Crater Highlands, remote game reserves and the famous national parks are protected by government law. The Serengeti National Park is a plain-dwellers' stronghold of 14,763 sq km (5678 sq miles), claimed to be the finest in Africa. Here are 35 species of big mammals, including wildebeest and zebra, and also an extensive selection of birdlife. The Selous Game Reserve is larger than Switzerland and covers one-sixth of Tanzania's land surface.

The capital city and also a major port, Dar es Salaam is the natural starting point for trips in Tanzania. It is near Mount Kilimanjaro, Dodoma and Zanzibar, and many beautiful beaches are within easy reach of the city, such as those at Kunduchi, Mjimwena and Mbwa Maji. Mount Kilimanjaro, at 5895m (19,341ft), is Africa's highest mountain and the most famous tourist attraction in Tanzania.

As a contrast to the exciting game areas and the mountain, Zanzibar is a beautiful jewel in the Indian Ocean with a fascinating spice and slaving legacy.

In addition to its beautiful landscape, Tanzania is home to approximately 120 tribal groups. Tribal diversity is prized and far from being a source of division; Tanzanians place a high value on their country's multicultural heritage. Over the past few years, cultural tourism has become an increasing attraction for visitors and visits to tribal villages are often a highlight of safari itineraries. The Masaai are perhaps the most well known of Tanzania's tribes and inhabit the northern regions of the country. Masaai tribal life revolves around protecting and caring for their herds of cattle and finding ample grazing land in their region. The 'Spice Islands' of the Zanzibar Archipelago, Pemba, Mafia, and the entire Tanzanian coast is home to the Swahili people, a vibrant mix of Arab, Indian and Bantu origins who historically based their livelihoods around Indian Ocean trade. The Swahili Coast, as the region is called, is a predominantly Islamic region with old mosques and coral palaces found throughout the area. Swahili culture centres around the *dhow*, a wooden sailing boat powered by the seasonal wind. Fishing remains a mainstay of coastal income in small villages throughout the area, and coconut and spice plantations continue to form an important source of export. Whether you enjoy the tranquillity of the Swahili coast or the challenge of ascending Mount Kilimanjaro, Tanzania has it all.

General Information

AREA: 945,087 sq km (364,900 sq miles).

POPULATION: 38.4 million (UN estimate 2005).

POPULATION DENSITY: 40.6 per sq km.

CAPITAL: Dodoma. **Population:** 1,692,025 (2002).

GEOGRAPHY: The United Republic of Tanzania lies on the east coast of Africa and is bordered by Kenya and Uganda to the north; by Burundi, Rwanda and the Democratic Republic of Congo to the west; by the Indian Ocean to the east; and by Zambia, Malawi and Mozambique to the south. The Tanzanian mainland is divided into several clearly defined regions: the coastal plains, which vary in width from 16 to 64km (10 to 39 miles) and have lush, tropical vegetation; the Masai Steppe in the north, 213 to 1067m (698 to 3500ft) above sea level; and a high plateau in the southern area towards Zambia and Lake Nyasa (Lake Malawi). Savannah and bush cover over half the country, and semi-desert accounts for the remaining land area, with the exception of the coastal plains. Over 53,000 sq km (20,463 sq miles) is inland water, mostly lakes formed in the Rift Valley. The United Republic of Tanzania includes the islands of Zanzibar and Pemba, about 45km (28 miles) off the coast to the northeast of the country.

GOVERNMENT: Federal Republic since 1964. Tanganyika gained independence from the UK in 1961. In 1964, Tanganyika joined with Zanzibar, which had been a British protectorate until 1963, and became Tanzania. **Head of State:** President Jakaya Kikwete since 2005. **Head of Government:** Prime Minister Edward Lowassa since 2005. **Note:** Zanzibar is semi-autonomous and has its own Parliament and President. **President of Zanzibar:** Amani Karume. **Recent history:** Following constitutional changes implemented in 1995, legislative power rests with the unicameral National Assembly (*Bunge*), which is elected every five years. The *Bunge* has 274 members of whom 232 are directly elected, 37 are reserved for women appointed by the President and five allocated to members of the regional Zanzibar Assembly. Executive power belongs to the President, who is directly elected every five years. Ruling party Chama cha Mapinduzi (CCM) remains the overwhelmingly dominant force in Tanzanian mainland politics. President Benjamin Mkapa was elected with 62 per cent of the vote in Tanzania's first multi-party elections in 1995. He was re-elected in 2000 with 67 per cent of the vote and stood down in 2005. He was succeeded by the long-serving Foreign Minister Jakaya Kikwete who secured 80 per cent of the vote against a weak and divided opposition. The Civic United Front (CUF), with a strong power base on Zanzibar (most notably the island of Pemba), managed to secure 19 parliamentary seats there. Elections on the island have been closely contested between CCM and CUF and marred by violence, intimidation and serious allegations of rigging. After some thirty demonstrators were killed by the security forces during an opposition demonstration on Pemba island in 2001, reconciliation talks culminated in the signing of an agreement between CCM and CUF providing for an inquiry into the January 2001 violence; the dropping of charges against CUF members; by-elections to fill the 16 seats left vacant by CUF and the establishment of a permanent voter register for 2005 and reform of the Zanzibar Electoral Commission (ZEC). There were elections throughout Tanzania, including Zanzibar, on 14 December 2005. In Zanzibar, Zanzibar's Electoral Commission (ZEC) had declared Amani Abeid Karume on 1 November 2005 as the winner of the Presidential poll, held amid tension and violence, particularly in the capital, Stone Town. However, the results were disputed with claims that Sharif Hamad of the Civic United Front (CUF) won the majority of votes. There have been many reports of demonstrations by CUF supporters on the island, who have alleged widespread fraud in the proceedings: claims denied by the electoral commission. The elections were marred by controversy from the very beginning, since nationwide voting across Tanzania had been postponed due to the death of opposition Vice-Presidential candidate, Jumbe Rajab Jumb; postponement that Zanzibar did not adhere to. These incidents only serve to underscore Zanzibar's increasing dislocation from the rest of Tanzania and what many perceive as a drive for autonomy amongst some islanders.

LANGUAGE: Kiswahili and English are the official languages. The terms Swahili and Kiswahili are used interchangeably, though the term Swahili normally refers to the people while Kiswahili refers to the language. Originating along the coast, Kiswahili is a Bantu language with many words derived from Arabic. Other African languages such as Bantu and those of Nilo-Hamitic and Khoisan origin are also spoken.

RELIGION: Muslim, Christian, Hindu and traditional beliefs.

ELECTRICITY: 230 volts AC, 50Hz. Plugs may be round or square three-pin, fused or unfused.

SOCIAL CONVENTIONS: When meeting and parting, hands are always shaken; this applies throughout the country in both rural and urban areas. It is the convention to use the right hand, not the left, to shake hands or pass or receive anything. The standard greeting when addressing an individual is *Jambo* to which the reply is also *Jambo*. The greeting for a group is *Hamjambo* to which the reply is *Hatujambo*. People are delighted if visitors can greet them in Kiswahili. There is no fixed protocol to do with hospitality. Dress is smart and a good appearance is highly regarded. Suits and ties or safari suits are worn by men and suits or dresses by women. Ashtrays are usually an indication of permission for a visitor to smoke. Smoking is prohibited in cinemas and on public transport. **Photography:** In some places, a charge will be levied on visitors wishing to take photographs; elsewhere a permit may be required.

Climate

The climate is tropical and coastal areas are hot and humid. The rainy season lasts from March to June. The central plateau is dry and arid. The northwestern highlands are cool and temperate and the rainy season here lasts from November to December and February to May.

Required clothing: Tropical clothing is worn throughout the year, but in the cooler season, from June to September, jackets and sweaters may be needed, especially in the evenings.

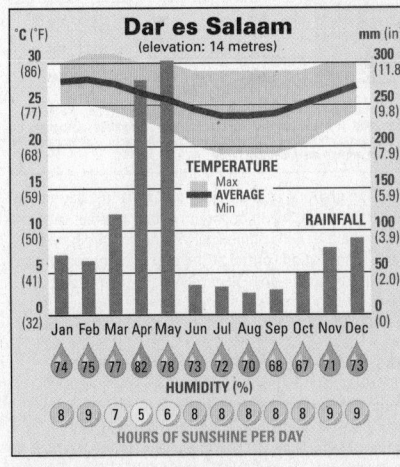

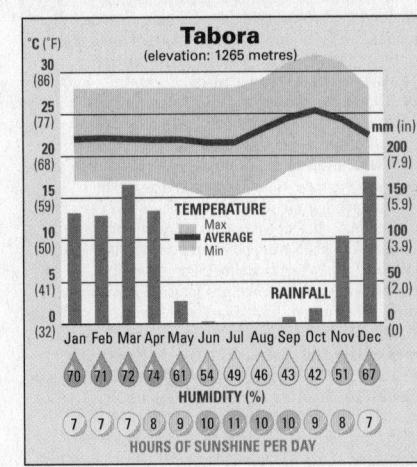

Communications

Telephone: Country code: 255. IDD is available. In some rural areas, international calls must go through the operator. There are many public call boxes in post offices and main towns.

Mobile telephone: Roaming agreements exist with most international mobile phone companies. Coverage is limited to main urban areas.

Internet: E-mail can be accessed in Internet cafes in main urban areas.

Post: Airmail to Europe takes one week. Courier services take less than 24 hours.

MEDIA: Until the 1990s, Tanzania's media were largely state-controlled. Founding President Julius Nyerere believed television would increase the divide between rich and poor. It was only in 1994 that the first private station was launched, and in 2001 that state-run TV was first broadcast. Numerous private radio stations are on the air. Liberalisation laws were brought into force in 2001, but these do not apply to Zanzibar. There are no private broadcasters or newspapers in Zanzibar, though many locals can receive mainland broadcasters and read the mainland press.

Press: Newspapers in Tanzania include the Government-owned *Daily News*, which is Tanzania's oldest newspaper; *Uhuru*, which is also owned by the government and published in Swahili; the private English-language newspapers *The Guardian* and *Daily Mail*; the private Swahili-language newspapers *Nipashe* and *Alasiri*; and the private weeklies *Business Times, The Express* and *Arusha Times*.

TV: Channels include state-run *Televisheni ya Taifa (TVT)* and private networks *Independent Television, Dar es Salaam Television* and *Coastal Television Network*. *TV Zanzibar* is state-run.

Radio: State-run stations include *Radio Tanzania Dar es Salaam, Parapanda Radio Tanzania* and *Voice of Tanzania-Zanzibar*. There are dozens of private FM radio stations, most of them operating in urban areas. Among the private networks are *Radio Free Africa, Radio One* and *Radio Uhuru*. News bulletins from international radio stations - including the *BBC, Voice of America* and Germany's *Deutsche Welle*, are carried by many stations.

Passport/Visa

	Passport Required?	Visa Required?	Return Ticket Required?
Full British	Yes	Yes	Yes
Australian	Yes	Yes	Yes
Canadian	Yes	Yes	Yes
USA	Yes	Yes	Yes
Other EU	Yes	Yes/1	Yes
Japanese	Yes	Yes	Yes

Note: *Regulations and requirements may be subject to change at short notice, and you are advised to contact the appropriate diplomatic or consular authority before finalising travel arrangements. Any numbers in the chart refer to the footnotes below.*

Note: The granting of a visa does not guarantee permission to enter Tanzania. The Immigration Officer reserves the right to grant or deny admission. Visa holders are subject to normal immigration control at the port of entry and should carry with them, for possible presentation to Immigration Officers, the documents submitted with their applications.

PASSPORTS: Passport valid for at least six months required by all.

VISAS: Required by all nationals except the following:
(a) nationals of Antigua & Barbuda, Barbados, Belize, Bermuda, Botswana, Brunei, Cyprus, Dominica, Grenada, Jamaica, Kenya, Kiribati, Lesotho, Malaysia, Malawi, Maldives, Malta, Namibia, Nauru, St Kitts & Nevis, St Lucia, St Vincent & the Grenadines, Seychelles, Singapore, Solomon Islands, Swaziland, Tonga, Tuvalu, Uganda, Vanuatu, Zambia and Zimbabwe for stays of up to three months and issued with a visitor's pass on arrival;
(b) **1.** nationals of Cyprus and Malta.

Note: Nationals who do not require visas for stays of up to three months, may still need entry permit clearance, except nationals of Kenya and Uganda. All other nationals must obtain visas in advance except nationals coming from a country where there is no Tanzania Embassy, High Commission or Consulate to issue a visa. In this case, these nationals may obtain a visa on arrival at one of the following four main entry points, provided all immigration and health requirements are met: Dar es Salaam International Airport, Kilimanjaro International Airport, Namanga Entry Point (Tanzania-Kenya border crossing) and Zanzibar International Airport.

Types of visa and cost: *Tourist:* £38 (single-entry). *Business:* £50 (single-entry). Cost of Tourist Visa depends on nationality of applicant. The above prices are for UK nationals; Irish nationals always pay £5. For postal applications, fees must be paid to the Tanzania High Commission at any Barclays Bank branch. Please note that

once visas are processed, fees are non-refundable.

Validity: Single-entry: Three months from date of issue; Multiple-entry: Six months from date of issue.

Application to: Consulate (or Consular section at High Commission or Embassy); see *Passport/Visa Information*.

Application requirements: (a) One completed application form. (b) Two recent passport-size photos. (c) Valid passport. (d) Fee, payable in cash if the application is made in person, or paid to the Tanzania High Commission at any Barclays Bank branch for postal applications. The pay-in slip must be enclosed with the application form. (e) Pre-paid, self-addressed, stamped envelope for postal applications. (f) For business visitors, a letter indicating the nature of the trip and the business contact in Tanzania.

Note: All nationals may be asked to attend an interview and/or supply further documents.

Working days required: Normally three working days. Up to 10 working days for postal applications.

Temporary residence: Enquire at High Commission or Embassy.

PASSPORT/VISA INFORMATION

High Commission for the United Republic of Tanzania in the UK
3 Stratford Place, London WC1 1AS, UK
Tel: (020) 7569 1470.
Website: www.tanzania-online.gov.uk
Opening hours: Mon-Fri 1000-1230 (visa section) and 1500-1600 (visa collection only).

Embassy of the United Republic of Tanzania in the USA
2139 R Street, NW, Washington, DC 20008, USA
Tel: (202) 939 6123/5/7.
Website: www.tanzaniaembassy-us.org

Money

Currency: Tanzanian Shilling (TZS) = 100 cents. Notes are in denominations of TZS10,000, 5000, 2000, 1000 and 500. Coins are in denominations of TZS200, 100, 50, 20, 10, 5 and 1, and 50, 10 and 5 cents.

Currency exchange: Money may be changed at banks, authorised dealers and bureaux de change. A receipt should be obtained and kept until departure.

Credit & debit cards: Major credit cards are accepted in larger hotels. Check with your credit or debit card company for details of merchant acceptability and other facilities which may be available. Cash can be withdrawn from some ATMs using Visa or Mastercard.

Traveller's cheques: May be cashed with authorised dealers or bureaux de change. To avoid additional exchange rate charges, travellers are advised to take traveller's cheques in US Dollars or Pounds Sterling.

Currency restrictions: The import and export of local currency is prohibited. The import of foreign currency is unlimited, subject to declaration. The export of foreign currency is limited to the amount declared on arrival.

Banking hours: Mon-Fri 0830-1230 (some places are open until 1600), Sat 0830-1300.

Exchange rate indicators:
Rate at time of publishing
£1.00= TZS2101.82
$1.00= TZS1180.38

Duty Free

The following items may be imported into Tanzania without incurring customs duty:
200 cigarettes or 50 cigars or 250g of tobacco; one bottle of alcoholic beverages; 570ml of perfume.

Public Holidays

Below are listed Public Holidays for the January 2006-June 2007 period.
2006: Jan 1 New Year's Day. **Jan 12** Zanzibar Revolution Day. **Jan 10** Eid al-Kebir. **Apr 14** Good Friday. **Apr 17** Easter Monday. **Apr 26** Union Day. **May 1** International Labour Day. **Jul 7** Saba Saba (Industry's Day). **Aug 8** Nane Nane (Farmer's Day). **Oct 22-24** Eid al-Fitr (Ramadan). **Dec 9** Independence and Republic Day. **Dec 25** Christmas Day. **Dec 26** Boxing Day. **Dec 31** Eid al-Kebir.
2007: Jan 1 New Year's Day. **Jan 12** Zanzibar Revolution Day. **Apr 6** Good Friday. **Apr 9** Easter Monday. **Apr 26** Union Day. **May 1** International Labour Day.

Note: Muslim festivals are timed according to local sightings of various phases of the moon and the dates given above are approximations. During the lunar month of Ramadan that precedes Eid al-Fitr, Muslims fast during the day and feast at night and normal business patterns may be disrupted slightly. Some disruption may continue into Eid al-Fitr itself. Eid al-Fitr and Eid al-Kebir (Eid al-Adha) may last anything from two to 10 days, depending on the region. For more information, see the *World of Islam* appendix.

Health

	Special Precautions?	Certificate Required?
Yellow Fever	Yes	1
Cholera	Yes	2
Typhoid & Polio	3	N/A
Malaria	4	N/A

Note: *Regulations and requirements may be subject to change at short notice, and you are advised to contact your doctor well in advance of your intended date of departure. Any numbers in the chart refer to the footnotes below.*

1: A *yellow fever* vaccination certificate is required of all travellers over one year of age travelling from infected areas and travellers coming from countries considered to be endemic by the Tanzanian authorities. The risk of yellow fever is highest in northwestern forest areas.

2: According to 1973 WHO guidelines, a *cholera* vaccination is no longer required for entry into Tanzania. However, there are regular outbreaks of *cholera* throughout the country and precautions are essential. Up-to-date advice should be sought before deciding whether these precautions should include vaccination as medical opinion is divided over its effectiveness. For more information, see the *Health* appendix.

3: Vaccination against *typhoid* is advised.

4: *Malaria* risk, predominantly in the malignant *falciparum* form, exists all year throughout the country below 1800m (5906ft). The strain is reported to be highly resistant to chloroquine and sulfadoxine-pyrimethamine. Mefloquine, doxycycline or atovaquone/proguanil are recommended.

Food & drink: All water should be regarded as being potentially contaminated. Travellers should use bottled water for drinking, brushing teeth, washing vegetables and reconstituting powdered milk. Other food hygiene precautions should be strictly observed.

Other risks: *Bilharzia (schistosomiasis)* is present. Avoid swimming and paddling in fresh water; swimming pools which are well chlorinated and maintained are safe. *Sleeping sickness* (trypanosomiasis) occurs. *Hepatitis A* and *E* also occur; *hepatitis B* is endemic. Immunisation against *diphtheria, meningitis* and *tuberculosis* is sometimes recommended. *Plague* is present in the Tanga region. There is a high incidence of *HIV/AIDS*.
Rabies is present. For those at high risk, vaccination before arrival should be considered. If you are bitten, seek medical advice without delay. For more information, see the *Health* appendix.

Healthcare: Private health insurance is recommended. There are over 2000 hospitals and clinics and some Christian missions also provide medical treatment; however, facilities are limited outside Dar es Salaam and medicines are often unavailable. All treatment must be paid for.

Travel - International

 AIR: The national airline is *Air Tanzania (TC)* (website: www.airtanzania.com). *British Airways* flies to Dar es Salaam from London.

Approximate flight times: From Dar es Salaam to London is 10 hours 10 minutes.

Main airports: *Dar es Salaam International (DAR)* is 13km (8 miles) southwest of the city (travel time - 25 to 30 minutes). *To/from the airport:* A shuttle bus service and taxi services are available to the city. *Facilities:* Outgoing duty free shop, car hire, post office, banking and currency exchange facilities, a bar and restaurants.
Kilimanjaro International Airport (JRO) is 50km (31 miles) from Arusha. *To/from the airport:* Shuttle bus services and taxis are available to Arusha from Kilimanjaro. *Facilities:* Shops, post office, bar and restaurant.
Zanzibar Airport (ZNZ) is 8km (5 miles) from Kisauni.

Departure tax: None, except Zanzibar Airport, which charges US$25.

SEA/LAKE:
 Main ports: *Dar es Salaam* port is served by ocean freighters and passenger liners. Other ports include *Mtwara, Tanga, Zanzibar* and the Indian Ocean ports of *Kilwa, Lindi* and *Mafia*. Ferries operate between Dar es Salaam and Mombasa (Kenya). Passenger services run on Lake Tanganyika to Bujumbura (Burundi), Congo (Dem Rep of) and Mpulunga (Zambia); Lake Victoria connecting Tanzania with Kenya and Uganda; and Lake Nyasa linking Tanzania with Malawi and Mozambique.

RAIL:
There is a twice-weekly restaurant car service by *Tanzania - Zambia Railway Authority (Tazara)* (website: www.tazara.com.tz) from Dar es Salaam to Kapiri Mposhi (Zambia). *Tanzania Railways Corporation (TRC)* (website: www.trctz.com) provides services between Tanzania, Burundi, Congo (Dem Rep), Kenya, Rwanda and Uganda. Trains may get very crowded but officials can be readily persuaded to find seats for tourists. Travellers should take special care of their baggage. It is unwise to forward luggage.

ROAD:

 The tarmac road connecting Tanzania with Zambia is in good condition, as is the road north to Kenya. From Lusaka in Zambia, the Great North Road is paved all the way to Dar es Salaam. Road links from Rwanda and Mozambique are poor. **Coach:** *Scandinavia Express* (website: www.scandinaviagroup.com) runs coaches from Dar es Salaam to Nairobi (Kenya) and Kampala (Uganda), and from Dar es Salaam to Lusaka (Zambia).

Travel - Internal

AIR:

 Air Tanzania (TC) (website: www.airtanzania.com), *Coastal Aviation* (website: www.coastal.cc) and *Precision Air* (website: www.precisionairtz.com) run regular services to all main towns. Check with the airline office before leaving for the airport. All national parks have airstrips and there are several charter companies operating single- and twin-engine aircraft to any town or bush airfield or airstrip in the country.

Departure tax: For all departures from Zanzibar to destinations within Tanzania, the tax is TZS5000.

SEA/LAKE:

 Azam Marine runs comfortable, air-conditioned ferry services daily between Dar es Salaam and Zanzibar (travel time - about two hours). Alternatively, the faster *Sea Express*, a hydrofoil, and the *Flying Horse*, a large catamaran, make this connection. There is also a crossing from Zanzibar to Pemba Island. Timetables and tickets can be obtained at the booking office at the main passenger port. Both Lake Tanganyika and Lake Victoria have steamer services. First-, second- and third-class seating is available on both services; first class has more comfortable seats and is likely to be less crowded. The service on Lake Victoria calls at the ports of Bukoba, Musoma and Mwanza.

RAIL:

 Tanzania Railways Corporation (TRC) (tel: 211 7833; website: www.trctz.com) provides the principal services, including routes to northern Tanzania, while those on the route to Zambia are run by *Tazara* (website: www.tazara.co.tz). *TRC* runs a daily service from Dar es Salaam to Mwanza on Lake Victoria and Kigoma on Lake Tanganyika with a restaurant car.

ROAD:

 Traffic drives on the left. Tanzania has a good network of tarmac and all-weather roads connecting all major towns. Most minor roads are not all-weather, becoming impassable to all except 4-wheel-drive vehicles during the long rains in April and May. It is not advisable to drive at night because of wild animals, cattle and goats on the road. There are often petrol shortages and spare parts for vehicles can be hard to find. There are a large number of road accidents. **Bus:** Inexpensive buses connect most places; for example, there are services from Dar es Salaam to Arusha, Morogoro and Moshi. Visitors should avoid travelling by bus during the April/May rains. *Scandinavia Express* (www.scandinaviagroup.com) is one of the more reliable and comfortable intercity operators. **Car hire:** Self-drive car hire is available in major cities, although it can be expensive. Vehicles with drivers are also available. **Documentation:** An International Driving Permit is required for car hire and must be endorsed by the police on arrival. Otherwise an International Driving Permit is recommended although it is not legally required. A temporary licence to drive is available from the police on presentation of a valid national driving licence.

URBAN:

 Buses and minibuses operate in Dar es Salaam on a flat-fare basis. Services are often crowded. Taxi services are available. It is advisable to use authorised taxis.

Travel Advice

Most visits to Tanzania are trouble-free, but travellers should be aware of the high threat from terrorism in Tanzania, including Zanzibar. Armed robberies, especially at remote sites, are increasing. Travellers to the area bordering Burundi should exercise caution. This advice is based on information provided by the Foreign and Commonwealth Office in the UK. It is correct at time of publishing. As the situation can change rapidly, visitors are advised to contact the following organisations for the latest travel advice:

British Foreign and Commonwealth Office
Tel: (0845) 850 2829.
Website: www.fco.gov.uk

US Department of State
Website: http://travel.state.gov/travel

Accommodation

HOTELS:

 Tanzania has a range of accommodation from very good, expensive hotels to cheaper hotels which, although adequate, lack comfort.

Although accommodation is on the expensive side, it is often possible for two people to share a single room except in top hotels. The less expensive hotels are often fully booked. The island of Zanzibar has a full range of accommodation, from luxury resorts to beach bungalows to budget hotels. For more information, contact Tanzania Tourist Board (see *Top Things To Do*).

WILDLIFE LODGES:

 There are wildlife lodges in all national parks. Reservations can be made through specialist tour operators or by contacting the lodges.

GUEST HOUSES:

 These are often offshoots of local bars and provide cheap accommodation, but there may be problems with drunken behaviour and theft. Sharing a room is advisable and special attention to possessions should be paid while staying there. These can not be booked in advance. Prices are higher in the larger towns, but in general the quality can be assessed from the tariffs.

CAMPING/CARAVANNING:

There are public campsites in many of the national parks. Some have standard facilities, including taps, toilets, bivouac huts and firewood; others are more basic. Permits for entry to each park and also for photography and filming must be obtained before arrival. It is advisable to check the prices and site procedure before arrival. A list of public and private campsites is available on the Tanzania National Parks website, and further information on camping can be obtained from *Wildlife Explorer Ltd* in the UK (see *Accommodation Information*).

YOUTH HOSTELS:

There are youth hostels in Lake Manyara National Park (primarily educational groups) and Mikumi National Park, YMCA hostels in Dar es Salaam and Moshi, and a YWCA hostel, which takes couples as well as women, in Dar es Salaam.

ACCOMMODATION INFORMATION

Tanzania National Parks
PO Box 3134, Arusha, Tanzania
Tel: (27) 250 3471.
Website: www.tanzaniaparks.com

Wildlife Explorer Ltd
Website: www.wildlife-explorer.co.uk

Top Things To See

- Once the capital city (this function has now moved to Dodoma), the major port of **Dar es Salaam** is the natural starting point for trips to various parts of Tanzania. It is near the island of Zanzibar (see below). Parts of Dar es Salaam have a tranquil air that belies industrial and commercial growth. Attractions include the **National Museum**, housing the 1.7 million years old skull of **Nutcracker Man**; **Observation Hill**, which contains the campus and facilities of the University of Dar es Salaam; and the **Village Museum**, with exhibits of traditional housing and crafts.
- Head for the atmospheric fishing village of **Msasani**, only 8km (5 miles) from Dar es Salaam. It contains interesting tombs dating back to the 17th century. Further south, at **Kilwa Klsiwani**, there are ruins of Portuguese and Arab architecture.
- If you go north, visit **Kunduchi**, 24km (15 miles) from the city, a fishing village with nearby ruins of Persian tombs and mosques.
- Travel further north to **Bagamoyo**, 72km (45 mile) from Dar es Salaam. It is a one-time slave port and terminus for the trade caravans. This tiny township is the nearest mainland point to Zanzibar and possesses sandy beaches set in a beautiful bay. Livingstone's body rested in the tiny chapel of the convent here on its way back to London. The town mosque and Arab tombs date from the 18th and 19th centuries. Just 5km (3 miles) to the south is the village of **Kaole**, near which are the ruins of a mosque and pillars believed to be 800 years old.
- Carry on north from Bagamoyo to **Tanga**, the country's second port near the Kenyan border. It is a town with a quiet, laid-back feel to it. Along the older sections of the town, examples of old colonial architecture and a few Arab houses still give testament to the area's importance during the heyday of the Indian Ocean trade.
- Travellers on their way to the heartland of Tanzania might consider paying the capital **Dodoma** a visit. It is situated on the eastern edge of the southern highlands and is surrounded by a rich agricultural area. Tanzania's national assembly moved to Dodoma in 1996. The area around the city constitutes the centre of Tanzania's growing wine industry.
- Visit **Musoma** on the shores of Lake Victoria in the north of Tanzania, very near the Kenyan border. Located near Butaiama, the hometown of the first President of Tanzania, the city houses the **Mwalimu Julius K. Nyerere Museum**. Exhibits document the rise of nationalism, the independence movement, and the early history of Tanzania. On display are various items of interest that belonged to the late leader, including a copy of Plato's *Republic*, which he translated into Kiswahili by hand. Musoma is a vibrant town with a lively waterfront. Do not miss the spectacle that is **market day**, when women from the surrounding area bring their crops of mangoes and green leafy vegetables, ripe avocados and bunches of bright yellow bananas, to sell on brown canvas spread over the ground.
- The small town of **Mtwara** is located on the coast of south-eastern Tanzania, along the rugged patch of coastline that leads to the country's border with Mozambique. The town has one site of particular interest, **St. Paul's Church**, which houses some remarkable murals of Biblical scenes painted by German priests.
- Explore and enjoy the island of **Zanzibar**, once the metropolis of East Africa, variously ruled by Shirazi Persians, the Portuguese, the Omani Arabs and British colonials. Zanzibar's old **Stone Town** is a labyrinth of narrow, winding streets lined with exotic shops, bazaars, colonial mansions, mosques and squares. Visit the **house** where **Dr Livingstone** lived. The Anglican **Cathedral Church of Christ** stands on the site of the **Old Slave Market**, off Creek Road, while on the seafront are the **palace of the former sultan** and the towering **Beit-el-Ajaib (The House of Wonders)**. Zanzibar is a fascinating place with palaces, forts, stone aqueducts and baths; its history as a cosmopolitan centre of trade gives it a unique atmosphere.

Note: Visitors to Zanzibar should observe Muslim conventions regarding dress when away from the beach. For more information, see the World of Islam appendix.

Top Things To Do

- Walk to the very top of Africa. It is a bit of a trek, but it is possible to climb Africa's highest mountain, **Mount Kilimanjaro** (5895m/19,341ft), in three days or so. It is essential to have the right equipment (such as warm clothing, boots, gloves and a hat) and some experience. Be aware that guides and porters are essential even for the lower peaks. Organised climbs with food and staff can be arranged at some cost through selected hotels. It is advisable to book well in advance. Alternatively, climbers can bring their own supplies and hire staff and equipment (arctic sleeping bags and extra trousers) at the park gate. Although Kilimanjaro may be attempted by any strong mountain walker, visitors should be aware of the dangers of high altitude sickness which, in extreme cases, can be fatal.
- Tanzania has 804km (503 miles) of coastline with superb **beaches**. Enjoying one of them is definitely among the most relaxing and pleasant activities the country has to offer. Many beautiful beaches are within easy reach of Dar es Salaam, such as those at **Kunduchi**, **Mbwa Maji** and **Mjimwena**.
- Go **scuba diving** and **snorkelling** around the islands of **Mafia** and **Zanzibar**, which have recently gained a high reputation amongst divers. Mafia's **Chloe Bay** is part of a protected marine park, with an unbroken reef running the length of the island. There are also many secluded beaches. Offshore from Zanzibar are several islands ringed with coral reefs.
- Try **big-game fishing** from the island of **Mafia**. Some 40 minutes' flight south of Dar es Salaam, the island is renowned for the big catches made in its waters. Power boats and tackle are available for hire. **Zanzibar** also offers good fishing. The main fishing season is from September to March.
- For those who fancy watching the creatures of the sea rather than catching them, **Dolphin safaris** are on offer from **Zanzibar**. **Dhow trips** are also popular.
- Discover Zanzibar's **spice** and **fruit plantations**. Organised tours are available all over the **'Spice Island'** (as Zanzibar is also known). Along the way, visitors will be invited to taste and buy spices, herbs and fruit. Sadly, because of a decline in world prices, the spice industry and, particularly, its mainstay product - cloves - is now near collapse.
- Visit the **Sukuma** (or **Bujora**) **Museum**, 15km (9 miles) east of Mwanza. It stages weekly performances of the traditional dances of the Wasukuma tribe, including the **Bugobobobo** (**Sukuma Snake Dance**).
- Watch traditional **bull-fighting** on the island of **Pemba**. The sport – which does not involve killing the bulls - is a hangover from the days of Portuguese rule in the 16th and 17th centuries.
- Join a **boat trip** on **Lake Victoria**, the largest lake in Africa. It has some spectacular varieties of freshwater tropical fish, many of which are exported to aquariums all over the world. Its shores are peaceful and pristine and offer a quiet alternative to the constant movement and bustle of a safari itinerary.
- Go on **safari** and explore Tanzania's **national parks** and **game reserves**. Tanzania's national parks extend over some 33,660 sq km (13,000 sq miles). In addition, there is the unique Ngorongoro Conservation Area, in which wildlife is protected and where the Masai tribespeople also live and herd their cattle. There are also some 10 game reserves where government-approved hunting safaris operate under licence and about 40 controlled areas where the hunting of game is controlled by a quota system. Numerous tour operators can organise tailor-made safaris, either by vehicle, on foot, on horseback or by balloon.

NATIONAL PARKS

- **Serengeti National Park**: The endless plains of the Serengeti National Park is where one of the world's great natural spectacles, the annual migration of some two million wildebeests followed by their predators, can be observed. This is a plain-dwellers' stronghold of 14,763 sq km (5678 sq miles) reaching up to the Kenyan border and claimed to be the finest in Africa. Here are 35 species of animals, including wildebeest, zebra, gazelle, cheetah and lion and also an extensive selection of birdlife. Probably the best time to see the migrating herds is from November to May.
- **Ngorongoro Conservation Area**: Rising high above the plains of the Serengeti, this vast protected area stretches from **Lake Natron** in the northeast (the breeding ground for east Africa's flamingos) to **Lake Enaysi** in the south and **Lake Manyara** in the east. The area includes the still active volcano **Ol Doinyo Lengai** (**Mountain of God**), which last erupted in 1983. The park's centrepiece is the **Ngorongoro Crater**, a collapsed volcano forming a crater that is 610m (2000 ft) deep, 20km (12.5 miles) in diameter, covering an area of 311 sq km (122 sq miles). The crater accounts for just one-tenth of the conservation area, which is home to almost every species of African plains mammal (except for the impala, topi and giraffe) and particularly well known for the endangered black rhino. It also has the densest population of predators in Africa. The rich birdlife includes flamingos which are attracted by the soda content in **Lake Magadi** on the crater floor. **Lake Manyara National Park**: Famous for its elephants and tree-climbing lions. The wall of the **Great Rift Valley** forms a backdrop to the park, before which lies forest, open grassland, swamp and the soda lake. Wildlife includes lions, herds of buffaloes, baboons, elephants, rhinos, impalas, giraffes, leopards, zebras, bushbucks, reedbucks, waterbucks and blue and vervet monkeys. Manyara is also noted for its birdlife, particularly the flamingos.
- **Arusha National Park**: This park lies within the **Ngurdoto Crater**, a volcano that has probably been extinct for a quarter of a million years. Visitors are able to see buffalos, rhinos, elephants, giraffes and warthogs.
- **Mikumi National Park**: This park, 1300 sq km (500 sq miles) in area, offers a chance to see lions, zebras, hippos, leopards, cheetahs, giraffes, impalas, wildebeests and warthogs. A popular spot for visitors is the **Kikaboga Hippo Pool**. Although December to March is the ideal time for viewing at Mikumi, there are animals throughout the year.
- **Tarangire National Park**: Only 130km (80 miles) from Arusha and 8km (5 miles) off the Great Cape to Cairo road, it is nonetheless an area which compares favourably with the Serengeti in terms of wildlife density.
- **Ruaha National Park**: Tanzania's second-largest and wildest park and the world's largest elephant sanctuary, Ruaha is located 118km (73 miles) from Iringa in the Southern Highlands along an all-weather road. The park affords views of unparalleled scenery along the **Ruaha Gorge**, with many sightings of antelopes. Iringa is also connected with Dar es Salaam and other centres by air and bus service. The best time to visit is from July to November.
- **Selous Game Reserve**: The Selous Game Reserve in southern Tanzania covers an area larger than Switzerland (about one-sixth of Tanzania's land surface), making it one of the biggest in the world, with a massive elephant population. There is also a high concentration of stalking lions and other game. UNESCO declared the game reserve a World Heritage Site in 1982. The Selous Game Reserve is inaccessible during the rainy season (from March to May) owing to floods.
- **Gombe National Park**: This park is near Kigoma on the shores of **Lake Tanganyika** and is home to about 200 chimpanzees, more easily seen here in their natural habitat than anywhere else in the world. This is the place where Jane Goodall devoted her life to recording chimpanzee ethology in a 37-year study.
- **Other national parks**: These include **Katavi**, **Mahale Mountains**, **Rubondo** and **Udzungura Mountains**. There are also marine parks at **Kilwa Reserve**, **Latham Island Reserve**, **Rufigi Delta** and **Tanga Coral Gardens**. Further information can be obtained from Tanzania National Parks, PO Box 3134, Arusha (tel: (27) 250 1930 or 250 3471).

TOURIST INFORMATION

Tanzania Tourist Board
PO Box 2485, Dar es Salaam, Tanzania
Tel: (22) 211 1244/5.
Website: www.tanzaniatouristboard.com

Entertainment

FOOD & DRINK: Most hotels serve local Tanzanian food while the major hotels offer Western and other international food.
Things to know: Table service is normal in restaurants. Bars generally have counter service. Tanzania is a secular state and alcohol is not prohibited. Zanzibar's population is predominantly Muslim. Alcohol is available in some tourist hotels and restaurants, but should not be drunk in public.
National specialities:
- Seafood such as prawns and lobsters.
- Tropical fruit such as coconuts, pawpaws, mangoes, pineapples and bananas.

National drinks:
- A good lager, *Safari*, is produced locally.
- *Konyagi* is a popular gin.
- A chocolate and coconut liqueur called *Afrikoko*.
- A wine called *Dodoma*, which comes in red or rosé.

Tipping: Not generally encouraged, though waiters and porters in tourist hotels and restaurants may expect to be tipped.
NIGHTLIFE: In Dar es Salaam, there are several nightclubs, cabarets and cinemas. Generally, the nightlife centres are in the top tourist hotels and restaurants.
SHOPPING: The city and town centres usually have markets which sell curios such as African drums, old brass and copper, carved chess sets, jewellery, and a speciality, large wooden salad bowls carved from a single piece of teak, *mninga* or ebony. Haggling is accepted, indeed often expected. **Shopping hours:** Mon-Fri 0830-1200 and 1400-1800, Sat 0830-1230. Some shops open on Sunday.

Business

- **GDP:** US$10.1 billion (2004).
- **Main exports:** Cotton, coffee, tea, sisal, cashew nuts, tobacco, minerals, manufactured goods, horticultural products and services.
- **Main imports:** Petroleum, consumer goods, machinery and transport equipment, used clothing, chemicals and pharmaceuticals.
- **Main trade partners:** UK, South Africa, India, Japan, China (PR), Kenya and the United Arab Emirates.

ECONOMY: Agriculture employs around 80 per cent of the working population. Cash crops are the country's main export earners, although depressed prices have kept Tanzanian revenues at a static level despite increases in production. There is an expanding mineral sector: diamonds are mined commercially, as are other gemstones and gold. Coal, phosphates, gypsum, tin and other ores are also extracted. Reserves of uranium, nickel, silver and natural gas have been located. The Government granted oil and gas exploration in the mid-1990s, and some small projects are under way, such as natural gas from the Rufiji delta. The industrial sector is small and concentrated in agricultural processing and light consumer goods: sugar processing, brewing, textiles and the manufacture of cigarettes are the most important.

The Government had pinned much of its hopes on development of its service industries, especially transport and tourism. Tanzania's relatively poor road network is the subject of a major programme of maintenance and construction, mainly financed by the EU. Tourism, which according to 2002 figures was worth about US$1 billion to the Tanzanian economy, has suffered a serious downturn as a result of international terrorism.

The Government had privatised several key industries, including the national airline and the main chain of hotels, in anticipation of a growing tourist market (Tanzania received 500,000 visitors in 2002). Both, along with a number of flagship industries, were bought by South African interests which are establishing a strong presence in Tanzania. Liberalisation of trade and the financial sector were also implemented as part of an IMF-supported structural adjustment programme.

On the whole, the economy has performed fairly well since the mid-1990s, but Tanzania remains one of the world's poorest countries. GDP growth in 2004 was 6.7 per cent. Tanzania is a recipient of foreign aid from both bilateral and multilateral donors, and some efforts have been made to tackle its large foreign debt. In 2000 the country benefited to the tune of US$2 billion from the Heavily Indebted Poor Countries initiative. In July 2003, Tanzania's Poverty Reduction and Growth Facility arrangement with the International Monetary Fund was extended for three years. Total external debt is now US$7.5 billion. The country remains heavily dependent on foreign aid. Tanzania is a member of the African Development Bank, the Southern African Development Community and the East African Community (EAC). After a failed attempt in 1977, an East African Customs Union was established with Kenya and Uganda in 2005.

BUSINESS ETIQUETTE: Normal courtesies should be shown when visiting local businesspeople. Almost all executives speak English. **Office hours:** Mon-Fri 0800-1200 and 1400-1630, Sat 0800-1230. **Government office hours:** Mon-Fri 0730-1530.

COMMERCIAL INFORMATION

Tanzania Chamber of Commerce, Industry and Agriculture
PO Box 9713, Dar es Salaam, Tanzania
Tel: (22) 211 9436.
Website: www.tccia.co.tz

Arusha International Conference Centre (AICC)
PO Box 3081, Arusha, Tanzania
Tel: (27) 250 2593/5 or 8008.
Website: www.aicc.co.tz

Thailand

Location: South-East Asia.

Time: GMT + 7.

Overview

Thailand has a rich and colourful culture, and many exotic and exciting monuments testify to this. In recent decades, Thailand has rightfully transformed itself from primarily a backpacker destination into one of the world's top tourist 'honeypots', catering for all tastes and budgets. There is certainly no shortage of things for the visitor to enjoy. Where else but Thailand can you cruise on a converted rice barge, roar upriver in a long-tail boat and take a white-knuckle ride on a bamboo raft, then stay in jungle tree houses as guests in the homes of hilltribe villagers, or on rafthouses floating on a river? Equally memorable are the trails leading deep into the rainforest past cooling waterfalls, and the simple beauty of the translucent sea lapping onto endless white, soft sand.

A holiday in Thailand can combine the beauty of the Golden Triangle's temples and remote hill tribes north of Chiang Mai, the beaches of Pattaya and more pristine Krabi, and the dynamic capital Bangkok with its futuristic high-rise buildings juxtaposed against the exquisite beauty of the gleaming Grand Palace. In every town and city, bargain-hunters thrive in the street markets crammed with all manner of goods, where good-natured bartering is the norm.

Early morning is when the saffron-robed monks leave the sanctuary of their *wats* to receive alms from the people, be it in a dusty village or on crowded city streets. Buddhism is a way of life here and with the reverence the people have for the Monarchy, a dynasty that has maintained the Independence of the country for centuries; the result for the Thais is a blend of tradition with contemporary living. Thailand's distinctive character is largely shaped by the combined influences of strong Monarchy and a powerful military. Formerly known as Siam, the country has been ruled by the Chakri Dynasty, of which the current King, Bhumibol Adulyadej, is a member, since the late 18th century. Although the nation is now a constitutional Monarchy (which it became in 1932 following a bloodless coup), he remains a powerful figure.

The country adopted its current name (which means 'Land of the Free') in 1939. This became something of a misnomer two years later when Japanese forces invaded, and Thailand became embroiled in the Second World War. Following this, in 1947, a military coup seized power, which it would retain until the early 1970s, and the subsequent tale of natural disaster, collapsed Governments, further coups and corruption allegations has continued to dog Thailand's leaders. For all this, it has become a hugely popular destination on the long-haul tourist trail, possessed as it is of great natural beauty and a very rich cultural heritage.

General Information

AREA: 513,115 sq km (198,115 sq miles).
POPULATION: 63.1 million (2003).
POPULATION DENSITY: 122.9 per sq km.
CAPITAL: Bangkok. **Population:** 7.5 million, including Thon Buri (UN estimate 2001).
GEOGRAPHY: Thailand is bordered to the west by Myanmar and the Indian Ocean, to the south and east by Malaysia and the Gulf of Thailand, to the east by Cambodia, and to the north and east by Laos. Central Thailand is dominated by the Chao Phraya River.
GOVERNMENT: Constitutional monarchy since 1973.
Head of State: HM King Bhumibol Adulyadej (Rama IX) since 1946. **Head of Government:** Prime Minister Thaksin Shinawatra since 2001. **Recent history:** Thailand's recent past has been characterised by economic boom and bust, unstable Government, unrest in the Muslim south and, of course, in common with other countries in the region, the effects of the December 2004 tsunami disaster. After a quarter of a century of military rule, civilian Government was restored to Thailand following student riots in Bangkok, but this was to last only three years before the military took over again in 1976. This eventually became a civilian Government again in 1983, but eight years later yet another military coup took place. This time, though, a civilian Prime Minister was installed, and following this, despite various Government collapses and allegations of corruption in high places, Parliamentary democracy has prevailed. Thailand was one of the 'Asian Tiger' economies in the 1980s and 1990s, but suffered with the regional economic collapse of 1997. Recovery began a couple of years later, and things have gradually picked up since then. In 2001, newly-elected Prime Minister Thaksin Shinawatra overcame accusations of corruption, and he remains in power following re-election in 2005. However, during his term of office, he has been forced to address growing unrest in the Muslim south of the country, as well as the devastation caused by the Tsunami. He has also presided over controversial crackdowns on the drugs industry, in which many people were killed.

Under the most recent version of the constitution, finalised in October 1997, the legislature is the bicameral *Ratha Sapha* (National Assembly). The 393-member *Saphaphuthan Ratsadon* (House of Representatives) is elected for a four-year term. Executive power is vested in the Prime Minister and Cabinet of Ministers, with the former drawn from the ranks of the *Ratha Sapha* – normally the leader of the largest party (or largest party in the governing coalition).
LANGUAGE: Thai is the official language. English is widely spoken, especially in establishments catering for tourists.
RELIGION: The vast majority adhere to Buddhism (Theravada form), 5 per cent are Muslim and there are Christian minorities.
ELECTRICITY: 220 volts AC, 50Hz. American- and European-style two-pin plugs are in use.
SOCIAL CONVENTIONS: Present-day Thai society is the result of centuries of cultural interchange, particularly with China and India, but more recently with the West. Western visitors will generally receive a handshake on meeting someone. A Thai will be greeted with the traditional closed hands and a slight bow of the head, the *wai*. Buddhist monks are always greeted in this way. The Thai Royal Family is regarded with an almost religious reverence. Visitors should respect this. It is very bad manners to make public displays of anger, as Thais regard such behaviour as boorish and a loss of 'face'. Public displays of affection between men and women are also frowned upon, and it is considered rude to touch anyone on the head or to point one's feet at someone. Shoes should be removed before entering someone's home or a temple. Informal dress is widely acceptable and men are seldom, if ever, expected to wear suits. A traditional Thai shirt is the most suitable attire for men at any official function. Beachwear should be confined to the beach and topless sunbathing is frowned upon. Smoking is widely acceptable.

Climate

Generally hot, particularly between March and May. The monsoon season runs from June to October, when the climate is still hot and humid with torrential rains. The best time for travelling is November to February (cool season).
Required clothing: Lightweights and rainwear are advised.

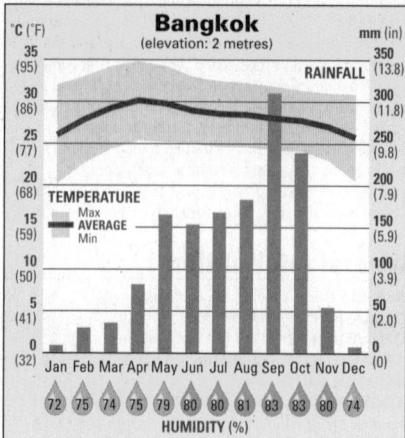

Bangkok
(elevation: 2 metres)

HUMIDITY (%)
72 75 74 75 79 80 80 81 83 83 80 74

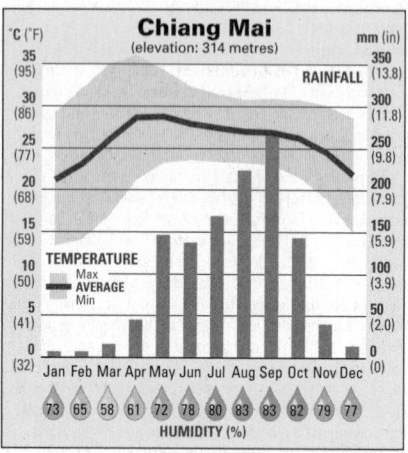

Chiang Mai
(elevation: 314 metres)

HUMIDITY (%)
73 65 58 61 72 78 80 83 83 82 79 77

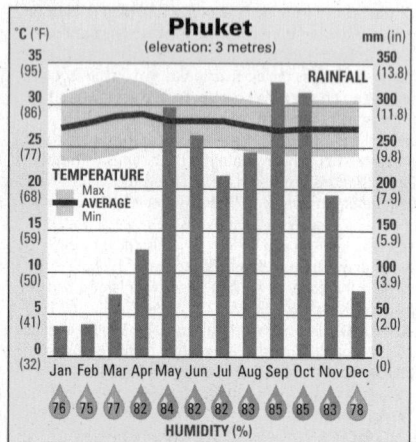

Phuket
(elevation: 3 metres)

HUMIDITY (%)
76 75 77 82 84 82 82 83 85 85 83 78

Communications

Telephone: IDD is available. Country code: 66.
Mobile telephone: Roaming agreements exist with international mobile phone companies. There is good coverage especially around main towns.
Internet: Internet cafes provide public access to Internet and e-mail services.
Post: Airmail to Europe takes up to one week. The General Post Office in Bangkok (on Charoen Krung Road) hours: Mon-Fri 0800-2000, Sat-Sun and holidays 0800-1300. Post offices up-country are open Mon-Fri 0800-1630, Sat 0900-1200.
MEDIA: While the Government and military are controlling nearly all the national terrestrial TV networks and operating many of Thailand's radio networks, the print media are largely privately run.
Press: Many daily and weekly Thai newspapers are available, including *Thairath*. Other English-language dailies are *Bangkok Post*, *The Nation* and *Thailand Times*.
TV: Thai TV stations are variously controlled by the Government and the army. They include *TV3*, *TV5*, *BBTV Channel 7* and *Television of Thailand*. Even *Independent Television* is part-owned by the Prime Minister's office.
Radio: *Radio Thailand* and *MCOT* are operated by Government agencies, while *Army Radio* is controlled by the Royal Thai Army.

Passport/Visa

	Passport Required?	Visa Required?	Return Ticket Required?
Full British	Yes	No	Yes
Australian	Yes	No	Yes
Canadian	Yes	No	Yes
USA	Yes	No	Yes
Other EU	Yes	No/1/2	Yes
Japanese	Yes	No	Yes

Note: *Regulations and requirements may be subject to change at short notice, and you are advised to contact the appropriate diplomatic or consular authority before finalising travel arrangements. Any numbers in the chart refer to the footnotes below.*

Restricted entry: Nationals of Afghanistan and Iraq will be refused (except for business purposes).
PASSPORTS: Passport valid for six months beyond intended length of stay required by all except the following: (a) holders of a Hong Kong (SAR) certificate of identity issued to residents of Hong Kong (transit only); (b) holders of a Singapore certificate of identity with a visa; (c) holders of South African temporary passports; (d) holders of a UN laissez-passer and Macau (SAR) China Travel Permits.
VISAS: Required by all except the following nationals for touristic stays, provided they hold valid passports, sufficient funds and confirmed tickets to leave Thailand within 30 days:
(a) nationals of the countries referred to in the chart above, except **1.** nationals of Cyprus, Czech Republic, Estonia, Hungary, Latvia, Lithuania, Malta, Poland, Slovak Republic and Slovenia, who *do* need a visa;
(b) nationals of Bahrain, Brazil, Brunei, Hong Kong (SAR), Indonesia, Israel, Korea (Rep), Kuwait, Laos, Malaysia, New Zealand, Norway, Oman, Peru, The Philippines, Qatar, Singapore, South Africa, Switzerland, Turkey, United Arab Emirates and Vietnam;
(c) transit passengers continuing their journey, provided holding confirmed tickets and other documents for an onward journey and they do not leave the transit lounge.
Note: (a) **2.** The following nationals can obtain an entry visa on arrival at 23 designated immigration checkpoints throughout Thailand (consult nearest Embassy/Consulate for further information), provided holding a confirmed ticket to leave within 15 days, proof of sufficient funds, application form with recent photo, a valid passport and that their visit is for tourist purposes only: Bhutan, China (PR), Cyprus, Czech Republic, Hungary, India, Kazakhstan, Maldives, Mauritius, Oman, Poland, Russian Federation, Saudi Arabia and Ukraine. The fee for this service is approximately 300 Baht; note that this is subject to frequent change. Travellers should also note that there are normally long queues at the immigration checkpoints. (b) Visitors who enter the Kingdom with Visa on Arrival generally cannot file an application for extension of stay except in special cases such as illness which prevents them from travelling, etc. They should submit their application to the Office of Immigration Bureau, Immigration Division 1, Soi Suan Plu, South Sathorn Road, Bangkok 10120. Tel. (662) 287-3127 *or* 3101-10 ext. 2264-5; website www.police.go.th/frconten.htm).
Types of visa and cost: *Tourist*: £25 (single-entry); *Non-immigrant* (for activities such as business or study): £40 (single-entry), £90 (multiple-entry); *Transit*: £15 (single-entry; also issued to those participating in sports activities in Thailand or crew members of a conveyance entering Thailand).
Validity: *Tourist*: 60 days. *Non-immigrant*: 90 days. *Transit*: Three days, 15 days (crew members) or 30 days (those participating in sports activities). All visas must be used within three months of date of issue, except multiple-entry non-immigration visas which are valid for up to six months. Extensions are available from the Immigration Bureau in Bangkok.
Application to: Consulate (or Consular section at Embassy); see *Passport/Visa Information*.
Application requirements: (a) Passport with validity not less than six months. (b) One completed application form. (c) Two recent passport-size photos (4 x 5cm). (d) Fee (cash only). (e) Proof of sufficient funds to cover stay (Bt20,000 per person, Bt40,000 per family). (f) Confirmed onward or return ticket paid in full. *Non-immigrant*: (a)-(f) and, (g) Copy of passport. (h) For a business visit, a letter from the employer in country of origin and from the business partner in Thailand explaining the purpose of the visit is required. Other documents may also be required, depending on purpose of visit. *Transit*: (a)-(g), (h) Visa for next destination in passport or travel document and, (i) Letter of invitation stating the application's participation in sports activities in the Kingdom.
Note: (a) The Royal Thai Embassy in London does not accept visa applications by post. (b) Nationals of Algeria, Bangladesh, Egypt, India, Iran, Lebanon, Libya, Nepal, Pakistan, Palestinian Authority passport holders, Sri Lanka,

Sudan, Syrian Arab Republic and Yemen must fill in three application forms with three photographs when applying for a Thai visa and must provide additional information. Contact Consulate for details. (c) Nationals of China, Korea (Democratic People's Republic of) and Saudi Arabia must fill in three application forms with three photographs when applying for a Thai visa at the Royal Thai Embassy in London or Royal Thai Consulates across the UK and Ireland (d) Yellow fever vaccination certificates are required for applicants who have visited or come from an affected area. Other vaccinations may also be requested by the Immigration Doctor and compliance is essential.
Working days required: Two days if submitted in person, approximately one week plus mailing time if applying by post.
Temporary residence: This must be applied for at the Office of Immigration (tel: (662) 287 3101-10) or at a Consular office in the home country (only for certain nationals: see *Note*.

PASSPORT/VISA INFORMATION

Royal Thai Embassy in the UK
29-30 Queens Gate, London SW7 5JB, UK
Tel: (020) 7589 2944 (ext. 115/119).
Website: www.thaiembassyuk.org.uk
Opening hours: Mon-Fri 0930-1230 (consular section); Mon-Fri 1400-1700 (telephone enquiries).

Royal Thai Embassy in the USA
1024 Wisconsin Avenue, Suite 401, NW, Washington, DC 20007, USA
Tel: (202) 944 3600 *or* 3608 (consular section).
Website: www.thaiembdc.org

Royal Thai Consulate General in the USA
351 East 52nd Street, New York, NY 10022, USA
Tel: (212) 754 1770 *or* 2536-8 *or* 1896.
Website: www.thaiembdc.org

Money

Currency: Baht (THB) = 100 satang. Notes are in denominations of THB1000, 500, 100, 50, 20 and 10. Coins are in denominations of THB10, 5 and 1, and 50 and 25 satang. In addition, there are a vast number of commemorative coins which are also legal tender.
Currency exchange: Foreign currencies can be exchanged at banks (which have the best rates), hotels (which charge high commissions) and, in larger towns, bureaux de change (generally open 0800-2000). Outside large towns and tourist areas, notes higher than THB500 may be difficult to exchange, so visitors are advised to carry small change.
Credit & debit cards: American Express, MasterCard and Visa are widely accepted. Check with your credit or debit card company for details of merchant acceptability and other facilities which may be available.
Traveller's cheques: Accepted by all banks and large hotels and shops. To avoid additional exchange rate charges, travellers are advised to take traveller's cheques in US Dollars, Euros or Pounds Sterling.
Currency restrictions: Foreign visitors may bring in an unlimited amount of Thai currency. For travellers leaving Thailand, both Thais and foreigners, the maximum amount permitted to take out without prior authorisation is THB50,000 per person or, if visiting a neighbouring country, THB500,000 per person. The import and export of foreign currency is unlimited.
Banking hours: Mon-Fri 0830-1530.
Exchange rate indicators:
Rate at time of publishing
£1.00=   THB69.90
$1.00=   THB39.59

Duty Free

The following goods may be imported into Thailand without incurring customs duty by any person, irrespective of age:
200 cigarettes or 250g of tobacco or equal weight of cigars; 1l of alcoholic liquor; one still camera with five rolls of film or one movie camera with three rolls of 8mm or 16mm film.
Restricted exports: There are restrictions on the import of non-prescribed drugs and all firearms and ammunition, and the export of items of archaeological interest or historical value, without a certificate of authorisation from the Department of Fine Arts in Thailand. The export of images of the Buddha and other religious artefacts is also subject to this ruling. Radio transceiver equipment, plant and living materials, live animals or products, medicines and chemicals also require a permit from the relevant Government agency. Cameras, video cameras and portable computers must be declared to the Customs Officer. Jewellery and ornaments are required to go through the Customs formalities at the Outbound section.

Prohibited items: Gold bullion must be declared on arrival and can be left at the airport of entry to be retrieved on departure. The import of meat from any country affected by Bovine Spongiform Encephalopathy (BSE) ('mad cow disease') and foot and mouth diseases is prohibited; the measure covers meat from all 15 EU countries and any other infected country. Pornographic material and protected wild animals or products are also prohibited.
Warning: Any drug-related offences are severely punished and may result in life imprisonment or even the death penalty.

Public Holidays

Below are listed Public Holidays for the January 2006-June 2007 period.
2006: Jan 1 New Year's Day. **Feb 12** Magha Bucha Day. **Apr 6** Chakri Day. **Apr 13-15** Songkran (Thai New Year). **May 1** Labour Day. **May 5** Coronation Day. **May 12*** Visakha Bucha. **Jul 1** Mid Year Bank Holiday. **Jul 12*** Khao Phansa Day (Buddhist Lent). **Aug 12** HM The Queen's Birthday. **Oct 23** Chulalongkorn Day. **Dec 5** HM The King's Birthday. **Dec 10** Constitution Day. **Dec 31** New Year's Eve.
2007: Jan 1 New Year's Day. **Mar 3** Magha Bucha Day. **Apr 6** Chakri Day. **Apr 13-15** Songkran (Thai New Year). **May 1** Labour Day. **May 5** Coronation Day. **May 31*** Visakha Bucha.
Note: * The religious festivals are determined by the Buddhist lunar calendar and therefore are difficult to predict. The dates provided here are estimates.

Health

	Special Precautions?	Certificate Required?
Yellow Fever	No	1
Cholera	2	No
Typhoid & Polio	3	No
Malaria	4	No

Note: *Regulations and requirements may be subject to change at short notice, and you are advised to contact your doctor well in advance of your intended date of departure. Any numbers in the chart refer to the footnotes below.*

1: A yellow fever vaccination certificate is required from travellers over one year of age arriving from infected areas. Countries and areas included in endemic zones are considered to be infected areas.
2: Following WHO guidelines issued in 1973, a cholera vaccination certificate is not a condition of entry to Thailand. However, cholera is a serious risk in this country and precautions are essential. Up-to-date advice should be sought before deciding whether these precautions should include vaccination, as medical opinion is divided over its effectiveness; see the *Health* appendix.
3: Vaccination against typhoid is advised.
4: Malaria risk exists throughout the year in rural areas throughout the country, especially in forested and hilly areas and around the international borders. There is no risk in cities and the main tourist resorts, eg Bangkok, Chiang Mai, Pattaya, Phuket and Samui. The malignant *falciparum* form is present and is reported to be highly resistant to chloroquine and resistant to sulfadoxine-pyrimethamine. Resistance to mefloquine and to quinine has been reported from areas near the borders with Myanmar and Cambodia.
Food & drink: Food and water-borne diseases are common. Use only bottled or otherwise sterilised (eg boiled) water for drinking, brushing teeth or making ice. Unpasteurised milk should also be boiled, although pasteurised or homogenised milk is available from some dairies. Tinned or powdered milk is safe as long as it is reconstituted with sterile water. Beware of dairy products that may have been made with unboiled milk. Stick to meat and fish that have been well cooked, preferably served hot, but not reheated. Avoid raw vegetables and unpeeled fruit.
Other risks: *Amoebic* and *bacillary dysentery* and *hepatitis A* and *E* may occur. *Hepatitis B* is highly endemic and *trachoma* is also reported. *Japanese encephalitis* may occur, particularly in rural areas. A vaccine is available, and travellers are advised to consult their doctor prior to departure. Precautions should be taken to guard against mosquito bites due to the risk of this disease and *dengue fever*. There has been an increase in the reported cases of *dengue fever* since January 2005, especially in Southern Thailand and areas bordering Malaysia. The Thai Ministry of Public Health issued a nationwide dengue fever epidemic alert on 9 May 2005. There were outbreaks of Avian Influenza (bird flu) amongst poultry in Thailand in 2004 and 2005, when there were a number of human fatalities. There have been no new cases in 2006. Travellers to Thailand are unlikely to be affected by Avian Influenza, but should avoid visiting live animal markets, poultry farms and other places where they may come into close contact with wild or caged birds; and ensure poultry dishes are thoroughly cooked. *HIV* infection is rife in Thailand, especially among prostitutes in Bangkok and Chiang Mai. Rare cases of *Bengal Cholera* have been reported and an outbreak of *leptospiros* in the northeast of the country, following flooding in 1999 caused a number of deaths.
Rabies is present. For those at high risk, vaccination before arrival should be considered. If you are bitten, seek medical advice without delay. For more information, consult the *Health* appendix.
Note: Those suspected or confirmed of carrying AIDS will be refused entry.
Health care: Health insurance is recommended. Medical facilities are good in main centres. All major hotels have doctors on call.

Travel - International

AIR:
The national airline is *Thai Airways International* (website: www.thaiairways.com).
Bangkok is the main entry point into Thailand, as well as being a major access point for travel to Cambodia, Laos, Myanmar, Nepal and Vietnam.
Approximate flight times: From Bangkok to *London* is 12 hours; to *Manila* is three hours; to *Singapore* is two hours 15 minutes and to *Sydney* is nine hours.
Main airports: *Bangkok International (BKK)* (Don Muang) (website: www.airportthai.co.th) is 24km (15 miles) north of the city (travel time - 40 to 60 minutes). *To/from the airport*: There are four airport bus routes to the city and buses leave from each terminal every 20 minutes from 0500 to 0030. There are also three regular public bus routes and four air-conditioned bus routes to Bangkok railways station, the southern and eastern bus terminals and to the city centre. Trains also run to the city centre (from 0606-2007). Limousines are available at all hours. Taxis are also available. There is a direct coach service to Pattaya at 0900, 1200 and 1900, returning at 0630, 1400 and 1830. *Facilities*: Left luggage, first aid, chemist, duty free shop, banks/bureaux de change, restaurant, bar and snack bars post office, car hire, accommodation reservations, Internet and telephone rental.
Chiang Mai International Airport (CNX), 15km (9 miles) southwest of the city (travel time - 20 minutes). *To/from the airport*: Taxi and limousine services are available to the city centre. *Facilities*: Car hire, banks/bureaux de change, restaurant, shops and bar.
Phuket International Airport (HKT) is 35km (22 miles) northwest of Phuket. *To/from the airport*: Taxis and limousines are available to the city centre. *Facilities*: Left luggage, duty free shops, first aid, banks, bureau de change, post office, restaurant and snack bars, car hire and tourist information.
Hat Yai International (HDY) has recently been opened; so far it is only used for flights to Asian destinations and domestic flights. The nearest town is Songkhla (approximately 20km/12.5 miles away). *To/from the airport*: Taxis, bus and train services are available. *Facilities*: Duty free shop, restaurant, car hire, tourist information and post office.
Suvarnabhumi International Airport (SBI) (website: www.suvarnabhumiairport.com/th/index.htm) is 25 km (14 miles) east of Bangkok's city centre. The construction of the new airport is almost complete. The airport will open for full commercial operations between June and October 2006. When it opens, it will replace *Don Muang* airport. *To/from the airport*: A city-link-connection is under construction.
Departure tax: THB500 for all international departures. Transit passengers and children under two years of age are exempt.
SEA:
Main port: *Bangkok*. Limited passenger services are available. There are passenger crossings between Thailand and Laos at several points along the Mekong river. Cruise lines calling at Thailand include *Orient Lines*, *Princess*, *Radisson Seven Seas* and *Seabourn*.
RAIL:
Through trains operate to Kuala Lumpur, with daily connections to Singapore, Malaysia and to the borders with Cambodia (at Aranyaprathet) and Laos (at Nong Khai). The opulent Eastern and Oriental Express runs directly from Bangkok to Singapore but it is expensive.
ROAD:
There are international roads from Cambodia, Malaysia and Laos. Roads into Myanmar are not officially open to tourist traffic.

Travel - Internal

AIR:
Thai Airways International (TG) (website: www.thaiairways.com) runs services to all major towns, using a total of 22 airports.
Bangkok Airways (PG) (website: www.bangkokair.com) flies seven additional routes. Discounts are available in off-peak seasons and during special promotional periods.
PB Air and *Phuket Air* also fly domestically.
Departure tax: THB50 for all domestic flights, THB400 for domestic flights from Samui Airport. Children under two years are exempt.
RIVER:
Thailand has, depending on the season, up to 1600km (1000 miles) of navigable inland waterway. Services operate between Thanon Tok and Nonthaburi, and luxury cruises are available on the *Oriental Queen*. Long-tailed motorboats and taxi-boat ferries also operate. Strong competition on all of the major routes ensures that fares are kept low. Reduced services operate during the monsoon season from May through to October along the east coast and Andaman coast, and from November until January on the Gulf coast. The more remote spots become inaccessible in these periods.
RAIL:
The excellent railway network extends over 4600km (2860 miles), linking all major towns with the exception of Phuket. It is run by *State Railways of Thailand*. It has recently been extended to serve centres on the east coast. There are four main trunk routes to the northern, eastern, southern and northeastern regions, and also a line serving Thon Buri, River Kwai Bridge and Nam Tok. There are several daily services on each route, with air-conditioned, sleeping and restaurant cars on the principal trains. The journeys are leisurely and comfortable, and travelling by train is certainly one of the best ways to get around the country. The *Southern Line Express* stops at Surat Thani for those who wish to continue by bus and ferry to the islands off the east coast. Most railway timetables are published in English.
ROAD:
There is a reasonable road network comprising many highways and 52,000km (32,300 miles) of national and provincial roads. All major roads are paved. Traffic drives on the left. **Bus:** There are inter-urban routes to all provinces. Fares are very cheap and buses very crowded. Privately owned air-conditioned buses (seats bookable) are comfortable and moderately priced. **Taxi:** There are plenty of taxis, which operate day and night. There are three types: *taxi-meter*; *taxis* which are unmetered; and 3-wheeled, open-air *tuk-tuks*. Where there is no meter, fares should be agreed before departure. It is sometimes possible to agree fares for longer trips even in taxi-meters. It is also possible to take a *motorbike taxi*. These are especially useful in Bangkok's horrendous rush-hour traffic. Taxi drivers do not always carry change, so it is important to have the correct amount. Passengers are also expected to pay for any motorway tolls. **Car hire:** Available in all main cities. Passports may be held as a form of deposit. **Motorcycle** hire is also available, especially on the larger islands. **Documentation:** International Driving Permit required. IDPs are valid for three months, after which a Thai driving licence is required.
URBAN:
Conventional bus services in Bangkok are operated by the *Government Mass Transit Authority*, but there are also extensive private minibus operations and passenger-carrying trucks. Premium fares are charged for air-conditioned (white and blue buses) and express buses. The ordinary buses are red or blue and charge a flat rate regardless of distance travelled. Fares are generally low and are collected by conductors. In Bangkok, taxis displaying the TAXI-METER sign are metered. *Samlors* or *tuk-tuks* are three wheeled taxis without a meter; the fare must be negotiated before the journey commences. These are cheaper than taxis but are only suitable for short distances. There are express, rapid and ordinary motorboat services on the Chao Phraya river between Nanthaburi pier to the north of Bangkok to Wat Ratcha Singkhon pier in southern Bangkok. The express boats, marked with a yellow flag, are more expensive than the rapid orange flag flying boats. The ordinary flagless boats are the cheapest. Bus maps of the city are available, on arrival, from the tourist office at Don Muang Airport. The *Skytrain (BTS)*, an elevated mass transit system in Bangkok, runs from 0600-0000. The *Metro (MRT)* runs from Hua Lamphang to Bang Sue with 16 stations inbetween. Trains leave every three to five minutes between 0600 and 0000.
Travel Times: The following chart gives approximate travel times (In hours and minutes) from **Bangkok** to other major cities/towns in Thailand.

	Air	Road	Rail
Chiang Mai	1.00	10.00	14.00
Pattaya	-	3.00	-
Phuket	1.20	10.45	-
Samui	1.20	13.00	14.00

Credit: ©Tourism Authority of Thailand

Travel Advice

Travellers are advised against all but essential travel to, or through, the far southern provinces of Pattani, Yala, Narathiwat and Songkhla, where there is continuing violence due to insurgency and civil unrest. Since January 2004, there have been regular attacks including bombings and shootings. The Thai Government has declared a serious state of emergency in the provinces of Pattani, Yala and Narathiwat.

There is a high threat from terrorism throughout Thailand. Attacks could be indiscriminate and against places frequented by foreigners.

Penalties for possession, distribution or manufacture of drugs are severe and can include the death penalty.

Outbreaks of Avian Influenza (Bird Flu) in Thailand have resulted in a small number of human fatalities. As a precaution, travellers should avoid live animal markets, poultry farms and other places where they may come into close contact with domestic, caged or wild birds; and ensure poultry and egg dishes are thoroughly cooked.

British Foreign and Commonwealth Office
Tel: (0845) 850 2829.
Website: www.fco.gov.uk

US Department of State
Website: http://travel.state.gov/travel

Accommodation

HOTELS:

Bangkok has some of Asia's finest hotels, with thousands of rooms meeting international standards. Many hotels belong to the large international chains. All luxury hotels have swimming pools, 24-hour room service, air conditioning and a high staff-to-guest ratio.

Accommodation styles cover every range, however, and the budget traveller is also well catered for. Bang'lampoo in Bangkok is the main area for cheap accommodation. Hotels outside the capital and developed tourist areas are less lavish but are extremely economical. Member hotels of the Thai Hotels Association can be booked on arrival at the counter of Bangkok's Don Muang Airport, and at similar counters in some provincial airports. There is no official system of grading hotels, but prices generally give a good indication of standards. The Tourism Authority of Thailand publishes regional accommodation guides, which give comprehensive details on pricing and facilities.

GUEST HOUSES:

Guest houses are cheap and popular with tourists, as are bungalows, which also often have cafes and English-speaking staff.

SELF-CATERING:

Holiday villas and flats can be rented. For details, look for advertisements in the English-language newspapers.

CAMPING/CARAVANNING:

In general, visitors will find that camping in Thailand is not popular, as other accommodation is available at such reasonable prices. Most of Thailand's campsites are in the area of the National Parks, which are under the management of the Department of Forestry; there are also some private tourist resorts which provide camping facilities. Camping is allowed on nearly all of the islands and beaches, many of which are National Parks in their own rights. Some national parks rent out tents at a reasonable price.

YOUTH HOSTELS:

YMCA, YWCA and small, cheap hotels are available all over the country.

ACCOMMODATION INFORMATION

Thai Hotels Association (THA)
203-209/3 Ratchadamnoen Klang Avenue,
Bowonniwet Bangkok 10200, Thailand
Tel: (2) 281 9496.
Website: www.thaihotels.org

Thai Youth Hostels Association
25/14 Phitsanulok Road, Dusit, Bangkok 10300, Thailand
Tel: (2) 6287 413-5.
Website: www.tyha.org

Top Things To See

- Marvel at Bangkok's **Grand Palace** (website: www.palaces.thai.net/gp) which, covering a huge area, is one of the major attractions. Here also is **Wat Phra Kaeo**, a temple complex housing the **Emerald Buddha**. This Buddha statue is not covered in emeralds, as the name suggests, but is made of translucent green jade. Upriver from the Grand Palace are the **Royal Barges**. These richly ornamented barges are still used today for special processions on the **Chao Phraya River**.

- One of the largest temple complexes in the country is **Wat Pho**. Altogether, there are over 30 individual temples here, among which the **Temple of the Reclining Buddha** is the largest. The Buddha's statue is enormous, an amazing 47.5m (156ft) long and 15m (49ft) high. The gardens surrounding the temples offer an escape from the hectic pace of the surrounding city.

- Other Bangkok sights include **Lak Muang (the city stone)**, the **Erawan Shrine**, where local offerings are made daily, and the **National Museum** (website: www.thailandmuseum.com). Housed in the **Suan Pakkad Palace** (website: www.suanpakkad.com) is a collection of precious antiques. Also interesting is the former home of the American silk-dealer **Jim Thompson** who vanished without a trace in 1967 (website: www.jimthompsonhouse.com). Today, the house is a craft museum with a shop selling high-quality silks at reasonable prices.

- For a rather different type of sightseeing, witness Bangkok's notorious **Patpong** 'red light' district, centre of the city's seedier attractions, but a lively night-time venue for those of a less sensitive nature. It has cleaned up its act somewhat in recent years, and is surrounded by nightclubs and restaurants.

- In the far north is **Chiang Mai**, Thailand's second-largest city and a centre for excursions to the region's ancient and beautiful temples, the teak forests and their working elephants, caves and waterfalls, and journeys to visit the northern hill tribes. The main attractions are the **Doi Suthep temple** and **elephant trekking** in the surrounding countryside.

- For those keen on history, there are some excellent historic Khmer sites in the northeast, including **Lopburi, Phanom Rung** and **Pimai**.

- In the **Mae Sa Valley**, there is an **elephant training school** and, nearby, an **orchid farm**; longer trips can be made to the **Doi Inthanon National Park** and to **Chiang Rai**, from where the Mekong River and the Golden Triangle can be reached. Another interesting route to take is the road to **Mae-Hong-Son** near the border with Myanmar.

- In central Thailand, **Phitsanulok** makes a convenient base for excursions. The town is also the site of the **Wat Phra Si Rattana Mahathat**. This important monastery houses the well-known **Phra Buddha Chinnarat**, reputedly one of the most beautiful Buddha images in Thailand. From Phitsanulok, one can visit the ancient city kingdoms of **Kamphaeng**.

- Areas of the southern coastal region were ravaged by the tsunami of December 2004, but **Phang Nga Bay**, easily reached from Phuket, boasts one of the world's most stunning seascapes; the area was featured in the James Bond film *The Man with the Golden Gun*. Approximately 3500 islands (*ko*) are scattered in the bay.

- Spend a day out at the **Ancient City**, a vast private park to the east of Bangkok, with models, some full sized, some reduced, of most of Thailand's historic monuments and the temple ruins of the Khmer Empire, situated near the Cambodian border.

Top Things To Do

- Take a day excursion from Bangkok for a train trip across the notorious **River Kwai bridge** at **Kanchanaburi**, which was built by Allied prisoners under the direction of the Japanese during the Second World War (website: www.kanchanaburi-info.com). Also outside the city is the **Rose Garden Country Resort** with daily performances of traditional Thai music, dance, games and ceremonies (website: www.rose-garden.com).

- **Horse races** are held every two weeks at the **Royal Bangkok Sports Club** on Saturday and at the **Royal Turf Club** on Sunday. Another spectator sport is *takraw*, also sometimes called Siamese football, in which a small woven rattan ball is kicked around by players standing in a circle and often performing spectacular moves. The aim of the game is to keep the ball off the ground, and to do this any part of the body can be used except for the hands.

- Braver souls can try **Thai kick-boxing**. Also known as **muay thai**, this traditional sport can be seen every day of the year at the major stadiums in both Bangkok and the provinces. Thai boxing matches are preceded by elaborate ceremonies and accompanied by lively music. Thailand has over 60,000 full-time boxers. Foreigners may enrol at a traditional *muay* training camp, some of which specialise in training westerners.

- Cast off your cares through traditional **meditation**. Thailand has dozens of temples and meditation centres specialising in *vipassana* (insight) meditation. Instruction and accommodation is usually free, though donations are expected. Different meditation techniques and dress codes apply to different centres.

- The northeast of the country offers a number of special festival celebrations, one of the most exciting being the **elephant roundup** at **Surin** each November.

- Go **walking** in the countryside. The best trails are in northern Thailand, particularly the remote provinces of **Chiang Mai, Chiang Rai** and **Mae Hong Son**. This is also the region of the infamous **Golden Triangle**, where Thailand, Laos and Myanmar meet and from where much of the world's opium originates.

- Thailand's 2710km (1694 miles) of coastline, on both the Indian and the Pacific Oceans, as well as its many offshore islands, make it a popular destination for watersports, particularly **diving** and **snorkelling**. **Sea canoeing** and **kayaking** have become increasingly popular in recent years, the coastal limestone islands in **Phang Nga Bay**, north of Phuket, being the favourite destination, also offering the chance to explore the half-submerged cave systems known as *hongs*.

- The presence of big game fish, such as barracuda, tuna, *wahoo*, swordfish or marlin, attracts many **game fishing** enthusiasts, who can charter fully crewed boats from most major coastal resorts.

- Take a tour from Chiang Mai to the **Mae Sa Valley**, where there is an elephant training school and, nearby, an orchid farm; longer trips can be made to the **Doi Inthanon National Park** and to **Chiang Rai**, from where the **Mekong River** and the **Golden Triangle** can be reached.

- Take a **boat trip** through **Bangkok**'s **Floating Market**, or along the *klongs*, a network of canals leading off the river, and lined with dwellings opening directly on to the water.

TOURIST INFORMATION

Tourism Authority of Thailand in the UK
3rd Floor, Brook House, 98-99 Jermyn Street,
London SW1Y 6EE, UK
Tel: (09063) 640 666 (consumer enquiries; calls cost 60p per minute) *or* (0870) 900 2007 (brochure request line) *or* (020) 7925 2511 (trade enquiries).
Website: www.thaismile.co.uk
Opening hours: Mon-Fri 0930-1700 (personal callers).

Tourism Authority of Thailand in the USA
61 Broadway, Suite 2810, New York, NY 10006, USA
Tel: (212) 432 0433.
Website: www.tourismthailand.org

Credit: ©Bruce Logan

Entertainment

FOOD & DRINK: There are many Asian and European restaurants. Thai food is hot and spicy, but most tourist restaurants tone down the food for Western palates. *Pri-kee-noo*, a tiny red or green pepper, is one of the hot ingredients that might best be avoided. These are generally served on a side plate in a vinaigrette with the main course. Popular fruits are *papaya, jackfruit, mangosteens, rambutans, pomelos* (similar to grapefruits) and, above all, *durians*, which *farangs* (foreigners) either love or hate. Owing to the strong smell of durians, the majority of hotels do not allow them onto the premises.

Things to know: Bars have counter or table service. There are no licensing laws.

National specialities:
- *Tom yam* (a coconut-milk soup prepared with makroot leaves, ginger, lemon grass, prawns or chicken).
- *Gang pet* (hot 'red' curry with coconut milk, herbs, garlic, chillies, shrimp paste, coriander and seasoning) served with rice.
- *Kaeng khiaw* ('green' curry with baby aubergines, beef or chicken) served with rice and *gai yang* (barbecued chicken).
- *Kao pat* (fried rice with pieces of crab meat, chicken, pork, onion, egg and saffron) served with onions, cucumber, soy sauce and chillies.
- Desserts include *salim* (sweet noodles in coconut milk).
- *Songkaya* (pudding of coconut milk, eggs and sugar often served in a coconut shell).
- Well worth trying is sticky rice and mangoes (rice cooked in coconut milk served with slices of mango). This is a favourite breakfast dish in the mango harvest season (March to May).

National drinks:
- Local whisky, either *Mekhong* or *SamSong*.
- Coconut milk straight from the shell during the harvest season.

Tipping: Most hotels and restaurants will add 10 per cent service charge and 7 per cent Government tax to the bill.

NIGHTLIFE: Bangkok offers a wide range of entertainment venues, from nightclubs, pubs, bars, cinemas and restaurants (many of which are open air), to massage parlours, pool halls and cocktail lounges. Performances of traditional religious and court dances can be seen at the Thai Cultural Centre. Elsewhere on the mainland, nightlife takes the form of traditional dances. The islands are renowned for their nightlife, and attendance is almost exclusively by foreigners. The *full moon parties* are notorious and continue well into the following morning.

SHOPPING: Good buys include Thai silks and cottons, batiks, silver, pottery with *celadon* green glaze, precious and semiprecious stones, dolls, masks, lacquerware, pewterware, bamboo artefacts and bronzeware. The weekend market at *Chatuchuk Park* in Bangkok is a regular cornucopia with items ranging from genuine antiques to fighting fish. Tailor-made clothes are also good value and can be made in a matter of days. **Shopping hours:** Mon-Sun 1000-2100; department stores 1000-2200.

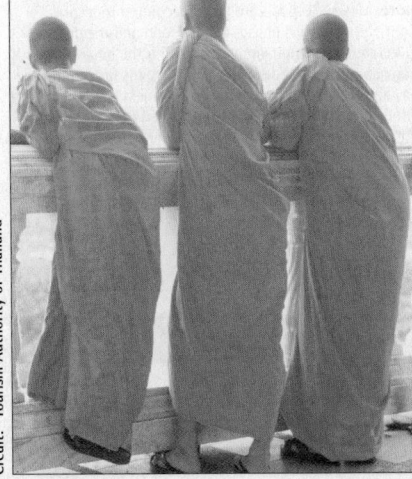
Credit: ©Tourism Authority of Thailand

Business

- **GDP:** US$163.5 billion (2004).
- **Main exports:** Food and live animals, office equipment, textiles and clothing, and rubber.
- **Main imports:** Cars, machinery and electrical machinery, and plastics
- **Main trade partners:** USA, Japan, China (PR), Singapore, Malaysia, Hong Kong (SAR), Indonesia and UK.

ECONOMY: The Thai economy expanded very rapidly during the 1980s and early to mid-1990s; average annual GDP growth between 1990 and 1996 was 8.5 per cent. Nevertheless, certain aspects of its economic performance during this period gave cause for concern, notably the foreign debt, shortcomings in the taxation system and the weakness of the country's financial institutions. The economy was already slowing down when the Asian currency crisis struck in the late summer of 1997. In 1998, the economy contracted by 11 per cent. After a strong initial recovery, the Thai economy stuttered in 2001/2 but recovered to 6.1 per cent in 2004. However, following the tsunami in December 2004, growth is expected to have slowed to around 4 per cent in 2005. Before Thailand assumed its position as one of the Asian tiger economies, agriculture had been the main economic activity: this has declined in relative importance as the industrial and service base has expanded and developed. The sector remains important nonetheless: the main crops are rice (of which Thailand is the world's leading exporter), sugar, cassava, maize, rubber, cotton and tobacco. Fishing is also significant, especially for prawns, which have become one of the country's largest exports. Another important natural resource, timber, was highly lucrative until, under international pressure, a logging ban was introduced in 1989. However, illegal logging continues - especially on the Thai-Myanmar border where much of the best quality timber may be found. The country's other principal natural resources are minerals, and gemstones are the most lucrative (again, there is much illegal activity in this industry), but there are also major deposits of tin and lead, plus copper, gold, zinc and iron, and rare metal ores containing antimony, manganese and tungsten. Natural gas and oil fields have been located offshore and are now being developed. In the industrial sector, Thailand manufactures cement, electronics, jewellery and refined sugar; there is also an important oil refinery. In the service sector, Thailand has a large tourism industry, worth billions to the economy. Thai companies are also highly active in transport, telecommunications, finance and the media. Thailand is a member of the Association of South East Asian Nations (and as such will participate in the planned Free Trade Area), as well as the Asian Development Bank and the Colombo Plan (a cooperative trading body covering South Asia).

BUSINESS ETIQUETTE: Most people in senior management speak English, but in very small companies, or those situated outside the industrial belt of Bangkok, English is not as widely spoken. Most businesses of substantial size prefer visitors to make appointments. Visiting cards are essential. Punctuality is advisable.
Office hours: Mon-Fri 0830-1700. **Government office hours:** Mon-Fri 0830-1200 and 1300-1630.
CONFERENCES/CONVENTIONS: The Thailand Incentive and Convention Association has 191 members representing all sectors of business interested in conventions and incentives. Members include hotels, airlines, publishing houses, advertising agencies, cruise operators, travel agents, lawyers, equipment suppliers and banks. The aim of the association is to provide help with every possible query that an organiser may have, as well as providing practical assistance. It publishes a quarterly newsletter, an annual guide, a gift-ideas catalogue and a social programme. The Bangkok Convention Centre is the largest venue in the country, but there are many other venues (including hotels) in Bangkok and elsewhere. The largest markets for delegates in 1988 were Malaysia, Japan, the USA, Taiwan and Australia, though interest from Canada and Germany showed a considerable increase. In October 1991, Thailand hosted the annual meeting of the World Bank and International Monetary Fund attended by 15,000 delegates.

COMMERCIAL INFORMATION

Department of Export Promotion
22/77 Rachadapisek Road, Chatuchak,
Bangkok 10900, Thailand
Tel: (2) 511 5066.
Website: www.thaitrade.com

Thai Chamber of Commerce
150 Rajbopit Road, 2146, 10200 Bangkok, Thailand
Tel: (2) 622 1860.
Website: www.thaiechamber.com

Thailand Incentive and Convention Association (TICA) (Information on Conferences/Conventions)
99/7 Soi Ladprao 8, Ladyao, Chatuchak,
Bangkok 10900, Thailand
Tel: (2) 938 6590.
Website: www.tica.or.th

Togo

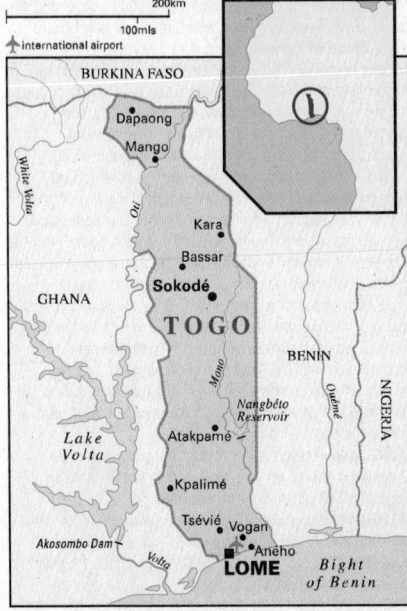

Location: West Africa.

Time: GMT.

Overview

Togo seems to be squashed in between neighbouring Ghana, Burkina Faso and Benin. Yet this tiny sliver of a country manages to squeeze in dense forests, savannah, coastal lagoons, long sandy beaches and swampy plains.

Togo formed part of the Slave Coast, from where captives were shipped abroad by European slavers during the 17th century. In 1922, the country was divided into a French-controlled eastern region and a British-occupied western sector, each of which was governed under a League of Nations mandate. After a UN-sponsored referendum in 1956, the British sector merged with the neighbouring colony of Gold Coast to form Ghana, while later in the year, the French part chose to become the autonomous Republic of Togo. It was granted full independence in 1960.

Since 1967, when a military coup brought Lieutenant-Colonel Etienne Gnassingbe Eyadema to power until his death in February 2005, the country has suffered from this ruler's authoritarian style of Government which has spawned numerous opponents and several coup attempts. When Etienne Gnassingbe Eyadema died, the military's immediate installation of his son, Faure Gnassingbe, as President provoked widespread international condemnation. After standing down, Mr Faure won the elections two months later, which led to renewed questions about Togo's commitment to democracy.

Despite its uncertain political situation, the country boasts captivating wonders and offers a nice succession of landscapes. The capital city Lomé lies on the Gulf of Benin and is the only capital in the world situated right next to a border. Modern hotels line the beach, while the city's past can be uncovered among the pockets of colonial architecture and its traditions discovered in the famous fetish market, which sells traditional remedies and carved figures to ward off evil. Togo's national parks are home to buffaloes, elephants and antelope, as well as numerous tropical bird species. Coffee and cocoa farms, waterfalls and palm plantations characterise the country's plateau, which rises behind the coast. In northeastern Togo, the traditional mud-tower settlements of the Batammariba in the Koutammakou landscape gained UNESCO World Heritage status in 2004.

General Information

AREA: 56,785 sq km (21,925 sq miles).

POPULATION: 5.1 million (UN estimate 2005).

POPULATION DENSITY: 89.81 per sq km.

CAPITAL: Lomé. **Population:** 732,000 (official estimate 2001).

GEOGRAPHY: Togo shares borders with Burkina Faso to the north, Benin to the east and Ghana to the west, with a short coast on the Atlantic in the south. The country is a narrow strip, rising behind coastal lagoons and swampy plains to an undulating plateau. Northwards, the plateau descends to a wide plain irrigated by the River Oti. The central area is covered by deciduous forest, while savannah stretches to the north and south. In the east, the River Mono runs to the sea; long sandy beaches shaded by palms characterise the coastline between Lomé and Cotonou in Benin.

GOVERNMENT: Republic since 1967. Gained independence from France in 1960. **Head of State:** President Faure Gnassingbe since April 2005 (succeeded his father, Gnassingbe Eyadema, after his death in February 2005). **Head of Government:** Prime Minister Edem Kodjo.

Recent history: When President Eyadema unexpectedly died in February 2005, the constitution was hastily changed and his son, Faure, initially assumed power. This was condemned both at home and by the international community and led to violent protests between rival political parties. Amid rising violence, Faure reluctantly stepped down and scheduled Presidential elections for April of that year. Against a backdrop of political violence and accusations of vote rigging and intimidation, Faure won the Presidential election and was sworn in as the new President in May 2005. However, the political situation remained tense with opposition parties calling for the appointment not to be recognised. Up to 500 people were killed in the political violence surrounding the Presidential poll, according to the UN. Around 40,000 Togolese fled to neighbouring countries. The internal situation remains uncertain but there has been a sustained period of relative calm since then.

LANGUAGE: French is the official language, while Ewe, Watchi and Kabiyé are the most widely spoken African languages. Very little English is spoken.

RELIGION: 50 per cent traditional or animist, 35 per cent Christian and 15 per cent Muslim.

ELECTRICITY: 220 volts AC, 50Hz single phase. Plugs are square or round two-pin.

SOCIAL CONVENTIONS: Music and dance are the most popular forms of culture. The Togolese have had a varied colonial heritage which has resulted in the variety of Christian denominations and European languages; the voodoo religion is a strong influence in the country and many young girls, after fulfilling an initiation period, will devote their lives to serving the religion and the voodoo village priest. Practical, casual clothes are suitable. Beachwear should not be worn away from the beach or poolside.

Climate

From December to January, the *Harmattan* wind blows from the north. The rainy season lasts from April to July. Short rains occur from October to November. The driest and hottest months are February and March.

Required clothing: Tropical lightweights. Rainwear for the rainy season.

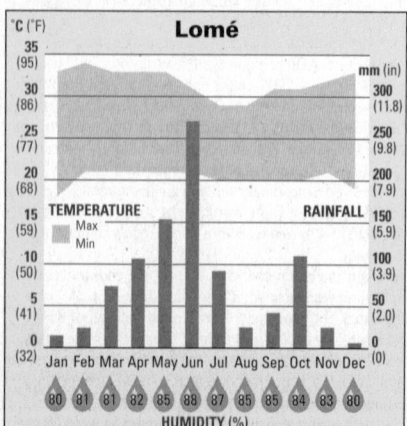

Communications

Telephone: IDD is available to main cities. Country code: 228. There are no area codes.

Mobile telephone: Roaming agreements exist with most international mobile phone companies. Coverage is good around urban areas and patchy elsewhere.

Internet: Public access is available in Internet cafes all over the country.

Post: Postal facilities are limited to main towns. Airmail to Western Europe takes at least two weeks.

MEDIA: Freedom of the press is provided for in the constitution, but is not respected in practice. The major television channel is Government-owned, as is the only daily newspaper and some of the private radio stations. Journalists writing for the private weeklies are subject to harassment and legal action. Several private radio and TV stations which had criticised the military-backed succession of Faure Gnassingbe as President were closed in 2005. Press offences cannot be punished by imprisonment.

Press: The main newspaper is the Government-owned *Togo-Presse*, published in French, *Ewe* and *Kabiyé*. *Le Regard* is an independent weekly.

TV: *Television Togolaise (TUT)* is a state-run television channel. *Media Plus* is a pay-TV operator.

Radio: *Radio Lomé* is a state-run radio station and *Radio Zephyr* is a privately-run station.

Passport/Visa

	Passport Required?	Visa Required?	Return Ticket Required?
Full British	Yes	Yes	Yes
Australian	Yes	Yes	Yes
Canadian	Yes	Yes	Yes
USA	Yes	Yes	Yes
Other EU	Yes	Yes	Yes
Japanese	Yes	Yes	Yes

Note: *Regulations and requirements may be subject to change at short notice, and you are advised to contact the appropriate diplomatic or consular authority before finalising travel arrangements. Any numbers in the chart refer to the footnotes below.*

PASSPORTS: Valid passport required by all, except nationals of the following with a National Identity Card: Benin, Burkina Faso, Cape Verde, Central African Republic, Chad, Côte d'Ivoire, Ghana, Guinea, Mali, Mauritania, Niger, Nigeria and Senegal.

VISAS: Required by all except the following for stays of up to 90 days:

(a) nationals of Benin, Burkina Faso, Cape Verde, Central African Republic, Chad, Côte d'Ivoire, Gambia, Ghana, Guinea, Guinea-Bissau, Liberia, Mali, Mauritania, Niger, Nigeria, Senegal and Sierra Leone;

(b) transit passengers continuing their journey by the same or first connecting aircraft within 24 hours, provided not leaving the airport;

(c) children under 15 if accompanied by their parents.

Note: All nationals can obtain an entry visa on arrival in Togo for a maximum stay of up to seven days. Passports need to be handed in on arrival and collected along with the visa from the police station the following day.

Types of visa and cost: *Entry* and *Residence*: fee depends on nationality. All nationals of the USA will be issued a visa for a maximum stay of 12 months for a fee of approximately US$100.

Validity: *Entry visas:* Up to 90 days. Visas can be extended on arrival in Lomé at the Direction Générale de la Police Nationale. For stays exceeding 90 days, a residence visa (*visa de séjour*) will be issued.

Application to: Consulate (or Consular section at Embassy); see *Passport/Visa Information*.

Application requirements: (a) A valid passport. (b) Two completed application forms. (c) Three passport-size photos. (d) Yellow fever vaccination certificate for travellers over one year of age. (e) Fee. (f) A letter from employer confirming the applicant will return to country of residence to resume duties after the visit *or* a letter from the airline or travel organisation guaranteeing onward or return air tickets. (g) A stamped addressed envelope if applying by post. (h) Company letter for business trips.

Working days required: Three.

PASSPORT/VISA INFORMATION

Embassy of the Republic of Togo in France
8 rue Alfred Roll, 75017 Paris, France
Tel: (1) 4380 1213.

Embassy of the Republic of Togo in the USA
2208 Massachusetts Avenue, NW,
Washington, DC 20008, USA
Tel: (202) 234 4212.

Money

Currency: CFA (*Communauté Financiaire Africaine*) Franc (XOF) = 100 centimes. Notes are in denominations of XOF10,000, 5000, 2500, 2000, 1000 and 500. Coins are in denominations of XOF250, 100, 50, 25, 10, 5 and 1. Togo is part of the French Monetary Area. Only currency issued by the *Banque des Etats de l'Afrique de l'Ouest* (Bank of West African States) is valid; currency issued by the *Banque des Etats de l'Afrique Centrale* (Bank of Central African States) is not. The CFA Franc is tied to the Euro.

Currency exchange: Foreign currencies can be exchanged at banks and bureaux de change in Lomé and other major cities. The main branch of the Togolese Central Bank in Lomé (BTCI) can give cash withdrawals against a Visa card.

Credit & debit cards: American Express is widely accepted, with more limited use of Diners Club, MasterCard and Visa. Check with your credit or debit card company for details of merchant acceptability and other facilities which may be available.

Traveller's cheques: International traveller's cheques are accepted in Lomé and other major cities.

Currency restrictions: The import of local currency is limited to XOF1 million, the export to XOF25,000. The import of foreign currency is limited to the equivalent of XOF1 million which should be declared on arrival. The export of foreign currency is limited to the amount declared on entry.

Banking hours: Mon-Fri 0800-1600.

Exchange rate indicators:

Rate at time of publishing

£1.00=	XOF961.81
$1.00=	XOF551.18

Duty Free

The following goods may be imported into Togo by persons over 15 years of age without incurring customs duty:
100 cigarettes or 100 cigarillos or 50 cigars or 100g of tobacco; one bottle of spirits and one bottle of wine; 500ml of eau de toilette and 250ml of perfume.

Public Holidays

Below are listed Public Holidays for the January 2006-June 2007 period.

2006: Jan 1 New Year's Day. **Jan 10** Tabaski (Feast of the Sacrifice). **Jan 13** Liberation Day. **Apr 11** Mouloud (Anniversary of Buddha's birthday). **Apr 17** Easter Monday. **Apr 27** Independence Day. **May 1** Labour Day. **May 25** Ascension. **Jun 5** Whit Monday. **Jun 21** Day of the Martyrs. **Aug 15** Assumption. **Sep 24** Anniversary of the Failed Attack on Lomé. **Oct 22-24** Eid al-Fitr (End of Ramadan). **Nov 1** All Saints' Day. **Dec 25** Christmas Day. **Dec 31** Tabaski (Feast of the Sacrifice).

2007: Jan 1 New Year's Day. **Jan 13** Liberation Day. **Mar 31** Mouloud (Anniversary of Buddha's birthday). **Apr 9** Easter Monday. **Apr 27** Independence Day. **May 1** Labour Day. **May 17** Ascension. **May 28** Whit Monday. **Jun 21** Day of the Martyrs.

Note: Muslim festivals are timed according to local sightings of various phases of the moon and the dates given above are approximations. During the lunar month of Ramadan that precedes Eid al-Fitr, Muslims fast during the day and feast at night and normal business patterns may be interrupted. Many restaurants are closed during the day and there may be restrictions on smoking and drinking. Some disruption may continue into Eid al-Fitr itself. Eid al-Fitr and Tabaski (Eid al-Adha) may last anything from two to 10 days, depending on the region. For more information, see the *World of Islam* appendix.

Health

	Special Precautions?	Certificate Required?
Yellow Fever	Yes	1
Cholera	2	No
Typhoid & Polio	3	N/A
Malaria	4	N/A

Note: *Regulations and requirements may be subject to change at short notice, and you are advised to contact your doctor well in advance of your intended date of departure. Any numbers in the chart refer to the footnotes below.*

1: A *yellow fever* vaccination certificate is required from all travellers over one year of age.

2: Following WHO guidelines issued in 1973, a *cholera* vaccination certificate is not a condition of entry to Togo. However, *cholera* is a serious risk in this country and precautions are essential. Up-to-date advice should be sought before deciding whether these precautions should include vaccination, as medical opinion is divided over its effectiveness. See the *Health* appendix for more information.

3: Vaccination against *typhoid* is advised.
4: *Malaria* risk exists throughout the year in the whole country. The predominant malignant *falciparum* form is reported to be resistant to chloroquine. The recommended prophylaxis is mefloquine.
Food & drink: All water should be regarded as a potential health risk. Water used for drinking, brushing teeth or making ice should have first been boiled or otherwise sterilised. Milk is unpasteurised and should be boiled. Powdered or tinned milk is available and is advised but make sure that it is reconstituted with pure water. Avoid dairy products which are likely to have been made from unboiled milk. Only eat well-cooked meat and fish, preferably served hot. Pork, salad and mayonnaise may carry increased risk. Vegetables should be cooked and fruit peeled.
Other risks: *Bilharzia* (*schistosomiasis*) is present. Avoid swimming and paddling in fresh water; swimming pools which are well chlorinated and maintained are safe. *Trypanosomiasis* (sleeping sickness) is reported, as are *hepatitis A*, *B* and *E* and *meningococcal meningitis*. *Dracuncaliasis* is common in the indigenous population, but unlikely to pose a significant threat to travellers. *Dengue fever*, *filariasis* (*elephantitis*), *leishmaniasis*, *onchocerciasis* (river blindness) and *plague* also occur sporadically. *Rabies* is present. For those at high risk, vaccination before arrival should be considered. If you are bitten, seek medical advice without delay. For more information, consult the *Health* appendix.
Health care: Limited medical services are provided by the state. Most towns have either a hospital or a dispensary, but these are usually overcrowded and lack adequate supplies. Visitors who get seriously ill are advised to contact their Embassy, which can refer them to a specialist or arrange evacuation. Health insurance and a good supply of personal medical provisions are recommended. There is no reciprocal health agreement with the UK or USA. It is important to carry a basic first aid kit.

Travel - International

AIR:
The main airline running services to Togo is *Air Afrique (RK)* (website: www.flyafriqiyah.com), in which Togo is a shareholder. Flights are available from London, Brussels, Geneva, Paris and many African destinations. Togo has become an important transit point for air travel in Africa. There are frequent flights to major African destinations.
Approximate flight times: From Lomé to *London* is 7 hours.
Main airports: *Aéroport International Gnassingbé Eyadema (AIGE)* is 6km (4 miles) northeast of the city. *To/from the airport*: Taxis operate to the city centre. *Facilities*: Bar, restaurant, snack bar, shops, bank, post office, duty free shop and car hire.
Departure tax: None.
SEA:
Main ports: *Lomé*. Ferries from Benin and Ghana call at Lomé and coastal ports. For details, contact the port authorities (website: www.togoport.tg/index.html)
ROAD:
There are routes from Benin, Burkina Faso and Ghana (a coastal route runs from Benin through Lomé to Ghana) but conditions are unreliable. The border with Ghana is closed periodically.

Travel - Internal

AIR:
Air Togo runs services to Sokodé, Mango, Dapango, Lama-Kara, Lomé and Niamtougou.
SEA:
Ferries run along the coast. For details, contact the port authorities.
RAIL:
There are services between Atakpamé, Blitta and Lomé; Kpalimé and Lomé; and Aného and Lomé. Trains run at least daily on each route.
ROAD:
Traffic drives on the right. Tarred roads run to the border countries and the major northern route is called 'The Highway of Unity'. There are roads linking most settlements, but these are largely impassable during the rainy season. Police checkpoints are frequent and may cause delays. It is advisable to keep windows rolled up and doors locked. **Bus/taxi:** National bus, minibus and taxi systems are reasonably efficient and cheap. Taxis and minibuses are widely available in Lomé and shared taxis are available between towns. There is a surcharge for luggage. Drivers do not expect a tip. **Cycling:** Bicycles can be rented in large towns and often incur less delays than cars. **Car hire:** This is available in Lomé; elsewhere the cost of car hire is very high and it is usually better to hire a taxi. **Documentation:** An International Driving Permit is required.

Travel Advice

Following the Presidential elections on 24 April 2005, there was a period of political unrest, particularly in Lomé, including attacks on Westerners. The internal situation remains uncertain but there has been a sustained period of relative calm. Travellers should avoid crowds and keep a low profile in case the situation deteriorates.
Extra caution is advised if moving around after dark. Entry and exit points at borders are being opened and closed without warning.
Crime is common in some areas of Lomé. Car-jackings have also been reported.
The threat from terrorism is low, but you should be aware of the global risk of indiscriminate terrorist attacks, which could be against civilian targets, including places frequented by foreigners.
This advice is based on information provided by the Foreign and Commonwealth Office in the UK. It is correct at time of publishing. As the situation can change rapidly, visitors are advised to contact the following organisations for the latest travel advice:

British Foreign and Commonwealth Office
Tel: (0845) 850 2829.
Website: www.fco.gov.uk

US Department of State
Website: http://travel.state.gov/travel

Accommodation

HOTELS:
Only Lama-Kara and Lomé have international-class accommodation but there are hotels in all the main towns. There is a severe shortage of accommodation, so it is advisable to book in advance. For further information, contact the Office National Togolais du Tourisme (see *Top Things To See & Do*).
CAMPING:
This is available free of charge though not recommended. Check with rangers before camping in National Parks.

Top Things To See & Do

- Togo's capital, **Lomé**, is the only capital in the world situated right next to a border. The city itself is a mixture of the traditional, especially around the **Grand Marché**, and the modern. Wander round the **fetish market**, with its intriguing voodoo charms, lotions and potions, and the **Village Artisanal**. The coast is rather disappointing and visitors have to leave the city well behind to find a nice spot.
- Visit **Togoville**, where the colonial treaty between the Germans and the ruler Mlapa III was signed. The chief still shows copies of the treaty to visitors. In the village itself, there are numerous **voodoo shrines** and the **Roman Catholic Cathedral**, built by the Germans.
- Discover historical **Aného**, Togo's colonial capital until 1920, which has preserved a distinctively colonial atmosphere, reflected in such attractions as the 19th-century **Peter and Paul Church**, the **Protestant Church** and the **German Cemetery**.
- Explore the short coastline, home to several small **fishing villages**, sometimes with examples of colonial architecture.
- Spot wildlife in the **Fazao National Park** outside **Sokodé**, the **Kéran National Park** near **Kara** and the **Fosse aux Lions** (**Lions' Den**) southwest of **Dapaong**.
- See the traditional mud Takienta tower-houses in **Koutammakou**, home to the Batammariba and a UNESCO World Heritage site since 2004.
- Enjoy watersports in **Lake Togo**.
- **Swim** in West Africa's biggest pool (the olympic-sized pool at Hotel Sarkawa) or cool off at the lakeside resort of **Porto Seguro**, which has **water-skiing** and **sailing** facilities.
- Relax on the **beaches** surrounding Lomé. (Beaches are unsafe for all but the best swimmers, but there are several pools along the beach.)
- Go **whale-watching** in the Gulf of Benin. Whales can be seen here every October.
- **Hike** in the scenic hill country around **Kapilmé**.

TOURIST INFORMATION

Office National Togolais du Tourisme (Togo National Tourist Office)
BP 1289, route d'Aného, Lomé, Togo
Tel: 215 652 *or* 214 313.
Website: www.togo-tourisme.com

Entertainment

FOOD & DRINK: Togolese food is particularly good. Most restaurants catering for visitors tend to be French-orientated, although some do serve African dishes. In Lomé in particular, there are many small cafes serving local food. Meat, poultry and seafoods are plentiful and well prepared, as are the local fruit and vegetables. A good selection of alcoholic drinks is available.
National specialities:
- *Pâtes* or *akume*, maize flour mixed with water served with different sauces usually made with vegetables such as okra, spinach or meat.
- *Fufu*, mashed yam eaten with sauces made from groundnut, goat or palm nut.
- *Riz sauce arachide* - rice with peanut sauce.

National drinks:
- Palm wine.
- *Tchakpallo* (fermented millet), produced locally.

Tipping: When not included, a tip of about 10 per cent is customary.
NIGHTLIFE: There are numerous nightclubs, particularly in Lomé. Most serve food and are open until the early hours for dancing to a mixture of West African and Western popular music. There are also cinemas showing French and English-language films.
SHOPPING: Market purchases include wax prints, indigo cloth, Kente and dye-stamped Adinkira cloth from Ghana, embroideries, batik and lace from The Netherlands, locally made heavy marble ashtrays, gold and silver jewellery, traditional masks, wood sculpture and religious statuettes. Voodoo stalls display an extraordinary range of items used in magic, among them, cowrie shells. **Shopping hours:** Mon-Fri 0800-1730, Sat 0730-1230.

Business

- **GDP:** US$1.4 billion.
- **Main exports:** Cocoa, phosphate, coffee and cotton.
- **Main imports:** Consumer goods including foodstuffs, fabrics, clothes, vehicles and equipment.
- **Main trade partners:** EU (mainly France and The Netherlands), China, Ghana and other francophone West African countries (Benin and Burkina Faso).

ECONOMY: About two-thirds of the working population is employed in agriculture: a wide range of crops are produced, including cotton, cocoa and coffee (the main cash crops) and basic foodstuffs including cassava, maize, yams and sorghum. Togo's other major principal exports are the ores from the country's phosphate mines, although revenues have been hit recently by slack demand and low world prices. Limestone and marble deposits have also been exploited. Togo's mines contain some of the world's richest calcium deposits. Most of Togo's other industry is based on the processing of these agricultural and mineral products, apart from a handful of factories engaged in the production of textiles and consumer goods for domestic consumption. A successful export processing zone, now entering its second decade of operation, has attracted numerous manufacturers from across the world. The service sector is small and tourism negligible.
The country's main economic problems are a huge foreign debt and declining revenues due to low world commodity prices. A typical programme of structural adjustment has been undertaken under the supervision of the IMF and World Bank. Current annual GDP growth is 2 per cent while deflation is 0.4 per cent. Togo is a member of the CFA Franc Zone, the West African trading bloc ECOWAS and various international commodity organisations.
BUSINESS ETIQUETTE: It is acceptable for visiting businesspeople to wear a safari suit except on very formal business and social occasions. Business is conducted in French, only a few executives speak English. Appointments should be made and business cards should be carried.
Office hours: Mon-Fri 0700-1730.

COMMERCIAL INFORMATION

Chambre de Commerce et d'Industrie du Togo (CCAIT)
BP 360, avenue Georges Pompidou, Lomé, Togo
Tel: 221 7065 *or* 221 2065.
Website: www.ccit.tg

Tonga

Location: South Pacific.

Time: GMT + 13.

Overview

Tonga's 176 islands range from steep, active volcanoes to low coral forms, most of which are uninhabited. The islands were first visited by the Dutch in the early 17th century, and later by the British seafarer Captain Cook, who dubbed the archipelago the 'friendly islands' in 1773. The adoption of Christianity by the ruling family – which followed the arrival of Methodist missionaries in the 1820s – and an overall policy of accommodation with the British - then the principal imperial power in the area - meant that the islands were not formally colonised. The ruling family of Tonga, the last remaining Polynesian Kingdom, can be traced back more than 1000 years.

Sightseeing highlights include the Royal Palace on the waterfront in Nuku'alofa, the Mala'ekula (Royal Tombs) and the Anahulu Cave, an underground cavern of stalactites and stalagmites. The islanders enjoy a laidback pace of life which visitors find easy to adopt, whether relaxing on one of the magnificent white sand beaches, diving among the stunning coral reefs or watching the migratory whales return to their breeding grounds from June to November.

General Information

AREA: 748 sq km (289 sq miles).

POPULATION: 106,000 (UN estimate 2005).

POPULATION DENSITY: 141.7 per sq km.

CAPITAL: Nuku'alofa. **Population:** 22,400 (1996).

GEOGRAPHY: Tonga is an archipelago of 176 islands in the South Pacific, most of which are uninhabited, covering an area of 7700 sq km (3000 sq miles). The major island groups are 'Eua, Ha'apai, the Niuas, Tongatapu and Vava'u. Tonga's high volcanic and low coral forms give the islands a unique character. Some volcanoes are still active and Falcon Island in the Vava'u group is a submerged volcano that erupts periodically, its lava and ash rising above sea level and forming a visible island which disappears when the eruption is over. Nuku'alofa, on Tongatapu Island, has a reef-protected harbour lined with palms. The island is flat with a large lagoon, but no running streams, and many surrounding smaller islands. 'Eua Island is hilly and forested

with high cliffs and beautiful beaches. The Ha'apai Islands, a curving archipelago 160km (100 miles) north of Tongatapu, have excellent beaches. Tofua, the largest island in the group, is an active volcano with a hot steaming lake in its crater. The Vava'u Islands, 90km (50 miles) north of Ha'apai, are hilly, densely wooded and interspersed with a maze of narrow channels. They are known for their stalagmite-filled caves.

GOVERNMENT: Constitutional monarchy. Gained full independence within the Commonwealth in 1970. **Head of State:** King Taufa'ahau Tupou IV since 1965. **Head of Government:** Prime Minister HRH Prince 'Ulukalala-Lavaka-Ata since 2000. **Recent history:** There has been little by way of a threat to the dominant political position of the King. The Legislative Assembly, which meets once a year, does little more than ratify the edicts of the monarch. Critics of the regime continue to risk arrest and imprisonment. The Human Rights and Democracy Movement, formed in 1992, began to apply consistent pressure on the King to democratise. So far, he has proved disinclined to do so at more than the most sedentary pace. Changes are afoot, however: the King, who is in his 80s, is in poor health. Both traditionalists and reformers are preparing for the post-Taufa'ahau era, and, so far, the traditionalists have stolen a march: constitutional changes were put into effect in 2003 giving greater powers to the monarch and imposing strict limits on political opposition. In the most recent general election in March 2005, however, six of the nine people's representatives seats contested were won by pro-democracy candidates, suggesting the Movement is gaining momentum.

LANGUAGE: Tongan and English.

RELIGION: Wesleyan Church, Roman Catholic and Anglican. Small denominations of Muslim, Baha'i and Mormon faiths.

ELECTRICITY: 240 volts AC, 50Hz.

SOCIAL CONVENTIONS: Shaking hands is a suitable form of greeting. Although by Western standards Tongan people are by no means rich, meals served to visitors will usually be memorable. A token of appreciation, while not expected, is always welcome, especially gifts from the visitor's homeland. Casual wear is acceptable, but beachwear should be confined to the beach. It is illegal for both men and women to go shirtless in public. Sunday is regarded as a sacred day, an aspect of Tongan life thrown into sharp relief by the controversy surrounding the so-called 'Tongan loop'. The International Date Line forms a loop around the islands, thereby making them a day ahead of Samoa, even though Samoa is almost due north of Tonga. Members of the Seventh Day Adventist Church therefore maintain that a Tongan Sunday is really a Saturday, and are unwilling to attend church on a day which is only a Sunday because of an apparently arbitrary manifestation of international law. This complex and almost insoluble problem may cause visitors a certain amount of confusion, but travellers to Tonga are advised to respect the religious beliefs of the islanders.

Climate

Tonga's climate is marginally cooler than most tropical areas. The best time to visit is from May to November. Heavy rains occur from December to March.

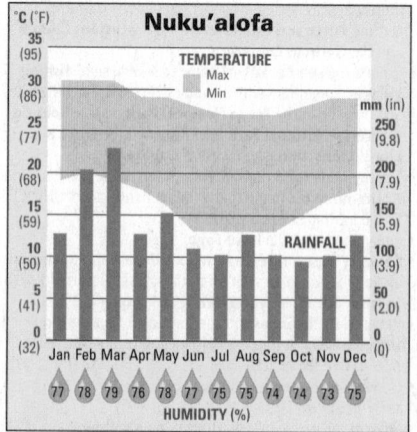

Communications

Telephone: IDD is available. Country code: 676. There are no area codes.

Mobile telephone: Coverage is limited to Nuku'alofa. No roaming agreements exist.

Internet: There are Internet cafes in Nuku'alofa.

Post: Main post office hours (located in the centre of Nuku'alofa): Mon-Fri 0830-1600. All mail must be collected from the post office. Airmail to Europe takes approximately

10 days. There are branch offices on Ha'apai and Vava'u.

MEDIA: The state's control of the media increased following an amendment to the constitution in 2003 which limited the right of the courts to review royal decisions. State-owned radio and TV are usually biased towards Government policy, while private broadcasters offer little independent coverage. Although some privately-owned newspapers carry opposition views, journalists have been known to face harassment and threats of criminal charges.

Press: The *Matangi Tonga*, *The Times of Tonga* (New Zealand-based) and *Tonga Chronicle* are the English-language newspapers.

TV: *Television Tonga* is state-run. Private networks include *TV7* and *Friendly Island Broadcasting Network* (Vava'u). *Tonfon TV* is a pay-TV service.

Radio: State-run A3Z Radio Tonga operates *Radio Tonga 1* and *Kool 90FM*. Private stations include *Radio 2000*, *Radio Nuku'alofa* and Christian station *93FM*.

Passport/Visa

	Passport Required?	Visa Required?	Return Ticket Required?
Full British	Yes	No	Yes
Australian	Yes	No	Yes
Canadian	Yes	No	Yes
USA	Yes	No	Yes
Other EU	Yes	No/1	Yes
Japanese	Yes	No	Yes

Note: *Regulations and requirements may be subject to change at short notice, and you are advised to contact the appropriate diplomatic or consular authority before finalising travel arrangements. Any numbers in the chart refer to the footnotes below.*

PASSPORTS: Passport valid for at least six months required by all.

Note: Ordinary, diplomatic or official Tongan or Tonga National passport holders may enter the Kingdom with passports valid for the date of arrival in Tonga.

VISAS: Visas required by all except the following who can obtain a visitor's visa free of charge on arrival entitling the holder of stays of up to 31 days:

(a) **1.** nationals of countries mentioned in the table above (except nationals of the Czech Republic, Estonia, Hungary, Latvia, Lithuania, Poland, Slovak Republic and Slovenia who *do* need a visa);

(b) nationals of The Bahamas, Barbados, Brazil, Brunei, Cook Islands, Dominica, Fiji, Kiribati, Malaysia, Marshall Islands, Micronesia (Federated States of), Monaco, Nauru, New Caledonia, New Zealand, Niue, Norway, Palau, Papua New Guinea, Russian Federation, St Kitts & Nevis, St Lucia, St Vincent & Grenadines, Samoa, Seychelles, Singapore, Solomon Islands, Switzerland, Tahiti and Her Islands, Turkey, Tuvalu, Ukraine, Vanuatu and Wallis & Futuna, provided holding a valid return ticket to a country where they have citizenship or a valid endorsement in their passport, granting them residency in a country that is not their country of nationality;

(c) those continuing their journey by the same or first connecting flight within less than 24 hours and not leaving the airport.

Note: Visas, valid on arrival and allowing multiple entry into Tonga, are required by all non-Tongan passport holders who are travelling on a one-way ticket, except for the following:

(a) holders of ordinary, diplomatic or official Tongan passports; (b) holders of Tongan National passports; (c) holders of a letter of authority issued by one of Tonga's overseas diplomatic missions and bearing the official stamp of that Tongan diplomatic mission, or a letter of authority issued by the Immigration Division, Ministry of Foreign Affairs of the Government of Tonga, bearing the official stamp of either the Ministry of Foreign Affairs or the Principal Immigration Officer.

Types of visa and cost: *Visitors:* TOP40 per month. *Business:* TOP200. *Employment:* TOP150. *Transit:* If transit period exceeds 24 hours, an airport tax of TOP25 is payable by all nationals over two years of age.

Note: Companies and businesses registered and operating in Tonga may bring non-nationals into the country on an employment visa, provided that the said non-citizen holds a specialised skill. Persons undertaking voluntary and charitable work in Tonga are also required to hold an employment visa.

Validity: Visitors are allowed stays of up to 31 days. Extensions for a maximum of three months or in exceptional circumstances six months require permission from the Principal Immigration Officer. Business/employment visas are valid for up to two years and are renewable.

Application to: Applications for visas must be made prior to arrival. For enquiries, contact the Consulate (or Consular section at Embassy or High Commission) *or* the Visa Section, Immigration Division at the Ministry of Foreign

Affairs Headquarters in Nuku'alofa (fax: 26970 *or* 23360).
Application requirements: (a) Valid Passport. (b) Two passport-size photos. (c) Completed application form. (d) Fee, if applicable, accompanied by letter permitting entry into the kingdom and permission to obtain a visa. (e) Onward or return tickets with reserved seats, including valid visa for onward destination if applicable. (f) Proof of adequate funds for duration of stay.
Business/Employment: (a)-(d) and, (e) Medical certificate issued by a doctor specified by the Immigration Division. (f) Two character references. (g) Police certificate from national's own country of residence.
Working days required: Approximately two to three.

PASSPORT/VISA INFORMATION

Tonga High Commission in the UK
36 Molyneux Street, London W1H 5BQ, UK
Tel: (020) 7724 5828.
Opening hours: Mon-Fri 0900-1700.

Tonga Consulate General in the USA
360 Post Street, Suite 604,
San Francisco, CA 94108, USA
Tel: (415) 781 0365.
E-mail: tania@sfconsulate.gov.to

Money

Currency: Pa'anga (TOP) = 100 seniti. Notes are in denominations of TOP50, 20, 10, 5, 2 and 1. Coins are in denominations of 50, 20, 10, 5, 2 and 1 seniti.
Currency exchange: Foreign exchange is available at banks and at major hotels.
Credit & debit cards: Limited use of both Diners Club and Visa.
Traveller's cheques: Accepted at banks and at some hotels and tourist shops. To avoid additional exchange rate charges, travellers are advised to take traveller's cheques in Australian Dollars or Pounds Sterling.
Currency restrictions: There are no restrictions on the import or export of foreign or local currencies.
Banking hours: Mon-Fri 0900-1600, Sat 0830-1130.
Exchange rate indicators:
Rate at time of publishing
£1.00=   TOP3.50
$1.00=   TOP1.99

Duty Free

The following goods may be imported into Tonga without incurring customs duty by persons over 18 years of age only:
200 cigarettes or 250g of cigars or 250g of tobacco; 1l of alcoholic liquor (only for persons 21 years and over); reasonable quantity of perfume; one camera and personal belongings.
Note: (a) The import of arms, ammunition and pornography is prohibited. (b) Birds, animals, fruit and plants are subject to quarantine regulations. (c) The export of valuable artefacts and certain flora and fauna is restricted.

Public Holidays

Below are listed Public Holidays for the January 2006-June 2007 period.
2006: Jan 1 New Year's Day. **Apr 14** Good Friday. **Apr 17** Easter Monday. **Apr 25** ANZAC Day. **May 4** HRH the Crown Prince's Birthday. **Jun 4** Independence Day. **Jul 4** HM King Taufa'ahau Tupou IV's Birthday. **Nov 4** Constitution Day. **Dec 4** Tupou I Day. **Dec 25** Christmas Day. **Dec 26** Boxing Day.
2007: Jan 1 New Year's Day. **Apr 6** Good Friday. **Apr 9** Easter Monday. **Apr 25** ANZAC Day. **May 4** HRH the Crown Prince's Birthday. **Jun 4** Independence Day.

Health

	Special Precautions?	Certificate Required?
Yellow Fever	No	1
Cholera	No	No
Typhoid & Polio	2	N/A
Malaria	No	N/A

Note: *Regulations and requirements may be subject to change at short notice, and you are advised to contact your doctor well in advance of your intended date of departure. Any numbers in the chart refer to the footnotes below.*

1: A yellow fever vaccination certificate is required from travellers over one year of age arriving from infected areas.
2: Vaccination against typhoid is advised.

Credit: ©Tonga Visitors Bureau

Food & drink: Mains water is chlorinated and safe to drink in the main towns. Elsewhere, drinking water should be considered a potential health risk and sterilisation is advisable. Bottled water is available and is advised for the first few weeks of the stay. Milk is pasteurised and dairy products are safe for consumption. Local meat, poultry and seafood are generally considered safe to eat. To prevent serious stomach ailments, wash vegetables and fruit with boiled water and boil any questionable drinking water before use.
Other risks: *Hepatitis A* and *B* occur. Sporadic outbreaks of *Japanese encephalitis* occur; *dengue fever* may also occur.
Health care: The Government provides comprehensive medical and dental facilities for residents and visitors. There are hospitals in Vaiola (Tongatapu), Hihifo (Ha'apai) and Neiafu (Vava'u), which will treat minor ailments and dispense medicines. There are also clinics, dispensaries, chemists and pharmacies. However, serious medical problems should be taken to Australia, Hawaii, New Zealand or Pago Pago (American Samoa). Visitors only pay a token fee for medicines. There are also competent private medical practitioners. Health insurance is recommended. For emergency services, dial 911.

Travel - International

AIR:

The main airline serving Tonga is *Air Pacific* (website: www.airpacific.com) (*Royal Tongan Airlines* collapsed in 2005). *Air New Zealand* and *Polynesian Airlines* also serve the country.
Air passes: The *Visit the South Pacific Pass* is valid for many airlines operating in the South Pacific, including most of the larger ones, such as *Air Caledonie, Air Marshall Islands, Air Nauru, Air Niugini, Air Pacific, Air Vanuatu, Polynesian Airlines, Qantas* and *Solomon Airlines*. Offering reductions of up to 40 per cent on normal airfares, this sector-based pass allows for flexible island-hopping between the destinations of the Cook Islands, Fiji, Nauru, New Caledonia, Samoa, Tahiti, Tonga, Vanuatu and the more remote Melanesian and Micronesian islands, together with major cities in Australia (Brisbane, Melbourne and Sydney) and New Zealand (Auckland, Christchurch and Wellington). It is only available for people resident outside of the South Pacific. The journey must be started outside the South Pacific and only one stopover in Australia is allowed. A minimum of two sectors must be bought before departure (extra sectors can be purchased en route). There is a maximum of one pass per person, and passes must be used within six months of the first day of travel. Children under 12 years of age pay 75 per cent of the adult fare. For details and conditions, contact the South Pacific Tourist Organisation.
Approximate flight times: From Nuku'alofa to *London* is 20 hours.
Main airports: *Fua'Amotu (TBU)* is 13km (8 miles) from Nuku'alofa. *To/from the airport:* Transport by taxi and bus is available. *Facilities:* There are car hire services (*Avis*), bars, bank/bureau de change, shops, tourist information and a duty free shop.
Departure tax: TOP25 for all passengers; children under 12 years of age and transit passengers are exempt.
SEA:

Main ports: *Neiafu, Niuatoputapu, Nuku'alofa* and *Pangai*. There are no regular passenger services, but berths may be available on cruise ships.

Travel - Internal

AIR:

Domestic carriers *Peau Vava'u* (PVL) (website: www.peauvavau.to) and *Airlines Tonga* (website: www.airlinestonga.com) provide inter-island services.
SEA:

Local ferries sail between all the island groups. There are regular sailings from Faua Wharf in Nuku'alofa to Ha'apai and Vava'u. Ferry schedules are subject to change according to demand or the weather.
ROAD:

Traffic drives on the left. There is a good network of metalled roads, although with some potholes. Horses are often used. The low speed limits are strictly obeyed. **Bus:** Minibus services are available throughout Tongatapu. **Taxi:** Saloon-car taxis, minimokes and mini-buses are available. **Car hire:** May be arranged through various agencies. Self-drive or chauffeur-driven cars are available. **Documentation:** A current local driving licence is required, available from the Police Traffic Department in Nuku'alofa on production of a valid national or international licence, the fee and a passport. The minimum driving age is 18.
Travel times: The following chart gives approximate travel times (in hours and minutes) from **Nuku'alofa** to other major centres on Tonga.

	Air	Sea
Neiafu (Vava'u)	1.00	24.00
Pangai (Ha'apai)	0.30	18.00
'Eua	0.10	3.00

Travel Advice

Incidences of robbery and theft have recently increased in Tonga. There have also been some incidences of violent assault. Foreign tourists may be at risk and should take particular care at night.
The threat of terrorism in Tonga is low, but you should be aware of the global risk of indiscriminate terrorist attacks which could be against civilian targets, including places frequented by foreigners.
This advice is based on information provided by the Foreign and Commonwealth Office in the UK. It is correct at time of publishing. As the situation can change rapidly, visitors are advised to contact the following organisations for the latest travel advice:

British Foreign and Commonwealth Office
Tel: (0845) 850 2829.
Website: www.fco.gov.uk

US Department of State
Website: http://travel.state.gov/travel

Accommodation

HOTELS:

There are excellent hotels, guest houses, and island and beach resorts made up of Tongan-style houses. Traditional boarding houses are also very popular with tourists. There is a growing selection of accommodation and capacity is expected to increase to 900 rooms. A government tax of 7.5 per cent plus service charge is added to hotel bills. For a complete list of available accommodation, contact the Tonga Visitors' Bureau (see *Top Things To See & Do*).

CAMPING:
Niu-akalo Hotel offers camping grounds.

Top Things To See & Do

Tongatapu Group
- In **Nuku'alofa**, the capital, sightseeing itineraries should include the white Victorian **Royal Palace** on the waterfront, just beyond **Vuna Wharf**. The Palace was completed in 1867. When HM King Taufa'ahau Tupou is in residence, the royal standard flies from the Palace. The grounds are decorated with tropical shrubs and flowers. While visitors are not allowed to enter the Palace or gardens, there are good views from the low surrounding walls. The **Mala'ekula** (Royal Tombs) are situated in the southern part of the business district along Taufa'ahau Road. The tombs have been a burial place for Tongan royalty since 1893.
- One of the most impressive sights in Tonga are the **Blow Holes**, found along the coastline at **Houma**, 14.5km (9 miles) from Nuku'alofa. Waves send sea water spurting some 18m (60ft) into the air through holes in the coral reef. This stretch of coastline is known as the **Mapu 'a Vaea** (the Chief's Whistle) by Tongans because of the whistling sound made by the geyser-like spouts.
- At **Kolovai**, 18km (11 miles) west of Nuku'alofa, visitors can find the rare **flying foxes**, dark brown fruitbats, some with wingspans of up to 1m (3ft). The **Ha'atafu** and **Monotapu** beaches are also situated at the western end of the island; they are easily accessible and well protected.
- On the eastern end of the island are the **Langi** (Terraced Tombs), 9.5km (6 miles) from the Ha'amonga Trilithon towards Nuku'alofa. The tombs form quadrilateral mounds faced with huge blocks of stone rising in terraces to heights of 4m (13ft), built for the old *Tu'i tonga* (Spiritual Kings). The stones are of coral, built around AD 1200, possibly carried from **Wallis Island** on large canoes known as *lomipeau*.
- **Ha'amonga Trilithon** is a massive stone arch possibly used as a seasonal calendar, erected at the same time as the Terraced Tombs and again made from coral. Each stone is thought to weigh in the region of 40,000kg (about 39 tons). The **Anahulu Cave** is an underground cavern of stalactites and stalagmites near the beach of the same name, about 24km (15 miles) from the capital. **Oholei Beach** is good for swimming.
- The island of **'Eua**, a 10-minute flight away from Tongatapu, has a blend of modern comfort (the island has one hotel and a motel) and the traditional South Sea island lifestyle. Many species of exotic bird live on the island.

Outlying Islands
- **Ha'apai Group:** This group of 68 small islands forms the geological and geographical centre of Tonga and is characterised by white sandy beaches, pristine water and spectacular coral reefs. The group's main island, also named **Ha'apai**, has the quaint old town of **Pangai** as its centre. Most of the 68 islands are small, low-lying coral atolls, the exception being the volcanic islands of **Tofua** (whose volcano is still active) and the extinct **Kao** to the

West. The famous mutiny on the HMS Bounty in 1789 is said to have taken place in the waters surrounding these islands and it was from here that Captain William Bligh and his loyal men began their epic 6500km (4063 mile) journey to Timor - in a rowing boat. Captain James Cook used these islands as a place of rest and relaxation, making stopovers at **Nomuka** in 1774 and 1777 and visiting **Lifuka** in 1783. During April, a week-long festival culminates with the crowning of the local beauty queen. In 1995, the entire Ha'apai group was declared a Conservation Area with a view to protect the fragile ecosystems and coral reefs.
- **Vava'u Group:** Lying 240km (150 miles) north of Tongatapu, this cluster of 50 or so thickly wooded islands has one hotel, one motel, one beach resort and four guest houses. There is a daily one-hour flight from the capital and a weekly ferry service; private cruisers and ferries also operate from the harbour at **Neiafu**, the main town. There is excellent diving, with visibility often as much as 30m (100ft). Other attractions include the Fangatongo Royal Residence, the view from **Mount Talau** and **Sailoame Market** in Neiafu.
- **Watersports:** Tongan coral reefs provide great beauty and variety for **scuba diving** and **snorkelling**; fully-equipped boats, scuba diving and snorkelling equipment can be hired. Contact the Tonga Visitors Bureau for information. There are sandy beaches and excellent **swimming** throughout the islands, with pools at some hotels. There is a world-standard **surfing** beach on the island of **'Eua**, 11km (7 miles) from Tongatapu. Niutoua Beach, on the main island, and Ha'apai and Vava'u islands are also good for surfing.
- Tongan waters are excellent for **fishing**. There are plentiful game fish including barracuda, tuna, marlin and sailfish. Charter boats are available.
- **Whale watching:** Humpback whales arrive in Tongan waters from around June through to November to calf and to mate. Special speakers for whale watching are plugged into a hydrophone installed on board the Phoenix catamaran based at Neiafu; only the male whales sing.
- **Horse riding:** Horses are still a means of transportation on all the main island groups. Hotels and tour operators can make arrangements for hiring horses.

TOURIST INFORMATION

Tonga Visitors' Bureau
PO Box 37, Vuna Road, Nuku'alofa, Tonga
Tel: 25334.
Website: www.tongaholiday.com

South Pacific Tourism Organisation in Fiji
Street address: Level 3, FNPF Place,
343-359 Victoria Parade, Suva, Fiji
Postal address: PO Box 13119, Suva, Fiji
Tel: 330 4177.
Website: www.spto.org

Entertainment

FOOD & DRINK: Restaurants have table service, and are found mainly in hotels. Apart from hotel dining rooms, there are restaurants featuring Tongan, French, German, Italian, Japanese and Taiwanese cuisine.
National specialities:
- *'Ufi* (a large white yam).
- *Taro*.
- *Lu pulu* (meat and onions, marinated in coconut milk, baked in taro leaves in an underground oven).
- *Feke* (grilled octopus or squid in coconut sauce).
- Devilled clams, *'ota* (raw fish marinated in lemon juice) and lobster.
- Tropical fruits and salads are excellent.
- Feasts play a major role in the Tongan lifestyle. Up to 30 different dishes may be served on a *pola* (a long tray of plaited coconut fronds), and will typically include suckling pig, crayfish, chicken, octopus, pork and vegetables steamed in an *umu* (underground oven), with a variety of tropical fruits.
Tipping: Not encouraged, but no offence is caused if services are rewarded in this way.
NIGHTLIFE: Nightlife is sedate, limited to music and dancing in the hotels, clubs and occasionally at the *Yacht Club*. Floorshows are held on some nights in the main hotels and the Tongan National Centre. Tongan feasts and entertainment are also organised.
SHOPPING: Special purchases are hand-decorated and woven *tapa* cloth, woven floor coverings, *Ta'ovala pandanus* mats, woven *pandanus* baskets, 'Ali Baba' laundry baskets, polished coconut-shell goblets and ashtrays, model outrigger canoes, tortoiseshell ornaments, brooches, earrings, rings and silver-inlaid knives. Tongan stamps and coins are collectors' items; complete sets are on sale at the philatelic section of the Tongan Treasury. There are duty free shops on Tongatapu and Vava'u. A government tax of 5 per cent is added to all bills for goods and services. **Shopping hours:** Mon-Fri 0800-1700, Sat 0800-1200.

Business

ECONOMY: Agriculture is the strongest part of Tonga's economy, producing coconuts, vanilla and pumpkins as cash crops, and a variety of fruit, vegetables and nuts for domestic consumption. The fishing industry was relatively underdeveloped and has been a focus of government plans to expand the economy. Industrial activity is mostly light and small-scale: textiles, handicrafts, brewing and the production of furniture and construction materials predominate. More recently, these have been joined by enterprises engaged in small manufacturing operations and food processing. The search for oil, which has been licensed to foreign consortia, continues offshore despite lack of success so far. Tonga's own energy requirements are met from renewable sources, principally wave and solar power. Most of the growth in the economy and the best immediate prospect for Tonga's economic future lie in tourism which has been expanded under a recently completed 10-year development programme. The industry is now worth $10 million annually to the Tongan economy. Nonetheless, the Government is constantly looking for other projects to diversify the island's economy. A further vital source of revenue is remittances from the many thousands of Tongans working abroad, mainly in New Zealand and Australia. Current annual GDP growth is around 1.5 per cent but inflation is a staggering 12 per cent. Tonga is a member of the South Pacific Forum and the South Pacific Commission. A regional free-trade accord, known as the Pacific Island Countries Trade Agreement, was signed among a group of Pacific governments in 2002. Australia, New Zealand, the USA, Fiji and Japan are Tonga's main trading partners. Some UK exports appear in Tonga as re-exported products from Australia and New Zealand.
BUSINESS ETIQUETTE: Shirts and ties will suffice for business visits. English is widely spoken followed by French. **Office hours:** Mon-Fri 0830-1630.
CONFERENCES/CONVENTIONS: For advice, contact the Tonga Visitors' Bureau (see *Top Things To See & Do* section).

COMMERCIAL INFORMATION

Ministry of Labour, Commerce and Industries
PO Box 110, Nuku'alofa, Tonga
Tel: 23688.
E-mail: Tongatrade@candw.to

Tonga Chamber of Commerce and Industry
Taufa'ahau Road, PO Box 1704, Nuku'alofa, Tonga
Tel: 25168.
E-mail: chamber@kalianet.to

Credit: ©Tonga Visitors Bureau

Trinidad & Tobago

CARIBBEAN SEA

Charlotteville
Roxborough
Scarborough · *Tobago*
Crown Point

TRINIDAD & TOBAGO

Toco
Galera Point
VENEZUELA **PORT OF SPAIN**
Mt Aripo △ 949m
Dragon's Mouths · Piarco · Arima
Caroni · Matura Bay
Chaguanas · Sangre Grande
Gulf of Paria · *Trinidad* · Cocos Bay
San Fernando · *Ortoire* · Mayaro Bay
Point Fortin · *Pitch Lake*
Moruga · *Galeota Point*
Icacos Point
ATLANTIC OCEAN

60km
30mls
✈ international airport

Location: Southern Caribbean, off Venezuelan coast.

Time: GMT - 4.

Overview

The history of Trinidad & Tobago has been one of invasion and conquest since its discovery by Christopher Columbus, who claimed it for Spain in 1498. In 1888, Tobago was amalgamated with Trinidad and administered as a single colony thereafter. The British sponsored the West Indies Federation as a potential post-colonial model, in the belief that most of the Caribbean islands would be unable to survive politically or economically on their own. The Caribbean peoples thought otherwise and the Federation collapsed in the early-1960s. By this time, Trinidad & Tobago had already been granted internal self-government and achieved full independence in 1962.

The home of carnival, steel bands, calypso and limbo dancing, Trinidad & Tobago's blend of different cultures gives them an air of cosmopolitan excitement. *Liming,* or talking for talking's sake, is a popular pastime, as is chatting about, watching and playing cricket. Trinidad and Tobago is one of the wealthiest countries in the Caribbean, thanks to its considerable reserves of oil and gas. Along the north of

Trinidad runs the Northern Range of mountains, looming over the country's capital, Port of Spain. On the north and east coasts lie beautiful beaches. Port of Spain, surrounded by lush green hills, is the capital and business hub of oil-rich Trinidad. Bazaars throng beneath modern skyscrapers and mosques rub shoulders with cathedrals. San Fernando is the island's second town and the main commercial centre in the south. Close by is the fascinating natural phenomenon of the Pitch Lake, a 90-acre (36.4 hectares) lake of asphalt which constantly replenishes itself.

Tobago is very different from her sister isle 32km (20 miles) away. The island is so beautiful and fertile that just about every western European colonial power has fought to have it. It is a tranquil island with calm waters and a number of fine beaches, each with their own flavour. They include Pigeon Point on the southwest coast. Buccoo Reef, an extensive coral reef, lies offshore.

The only shadow on the paradisiacal image of the islands, is the negative impact of drugs. As with other nations in the region, Trinidad and Tobago - a major transshipment point for cocaine - has become ridden with drugs, gang-related violence and corruption, which is threatening the increasingly important tourism industry.

General Information

AREA: Total: 5128 sq km (1980 sq miles). **Trinidad:** 4828 sq km (1864 sq miles). **Tobago:** 300 sq km (116 sq miles).
POPULATION: 1.3 million (UN, 2005).
POPULATION DENSITY: 253.5 per sq km.
CAPITAL: Port of Spain. **Population:** 49,031 (2000).
GEOGRAPHY: Trinidad and her tiny sister island of Tobago lie off the Venezuelan coast. Along the north of Trinidad runs the Northern Range of mountains, looming over the country's capital, Port of Spain. South of Port of Spain on the west coast the terrain is low, and the Caroni Swamps contain a magnificent bird sanctuary largely inhabited by the scarlet ibis. On the north and east coasts lie beautiful beaches. Central Trinidad is flat and largely given over to agriculture.
GOVERNMENT: Republic. Gained independence from the UK in 1962. **Head of State:** President Maxwell Richards since 2003. **Head of Government:** Prime Minister Patrick Manning since 2002. **Recent history:** In the election of December 2000, the Asian United National Congress (UNC) came out on top with a small majority, under the leadership of Basdeo Panday. Panday continued as Prime Minister but his Government was brought down by a serious corruption scandal (the UNC has been persistently dogged by such allegations) after less than a year. At the December 2001 poll, the UNC and Patrick Manning's People's National Movement (PNM) were tied on 18 seats each. After 12 months of almost paralysed Government, the country went to the polls once again, in October 2002. This time, the PNM, with Patrick Manning still at the helm, was returned with a small working majority.
The President is the constitutional Head of State. Executive power is vested in a Prime Minister and a Cabinet drawn from the largest parties in the bicameral Parliament. This comprises the Senate, with 31 appointed members, and the House of Representatives, with 36 members elected by universal adult suffrage. Since 1980, Tobago has had its own 15-seat House of Assembly, with 12 members elected and three selected by the ruling party. Tobago was granted full internal self-Government by the national Government in January 1987.
LANGUAGE: The official language is English. French, Spanish, Hindi and Chinese are also spoken.
RELIGION: 30 per cent Roman Catholic, 29 per cent other Christian denominations, 24 per cent Hindu, 11 per cent Anglican, and 6 per cent Muslim.
ELECTRICITY: 110/220 volts AC, 60Hz. US pattern twin plus

earth plugs are standard, though variations may be found.
SOCIAL CONVENTIONS: Many local attitudes are often reflected in the lyrics of the *calypso,* the accepted medium for political and social satire since pre-emancipation days. Hospitality is important and entertaining is commonly done at home. Casual wear is usual, with shirt sleeves generally accepted for business and social gatherings, but beachwear is not worn in towns.

Climate

The tropical climate is tempered by northeast trade winds. The dry season is from November to May, but it is hottest between June and October. The climate in Tobago is pleasant most of the year and although May, June and July can be wet at times, the differentiation between the wet and dry seasons is much less acute.
Required clothing: Tropical lightweights are required. Rainwear is advisable, especially for the wet season.

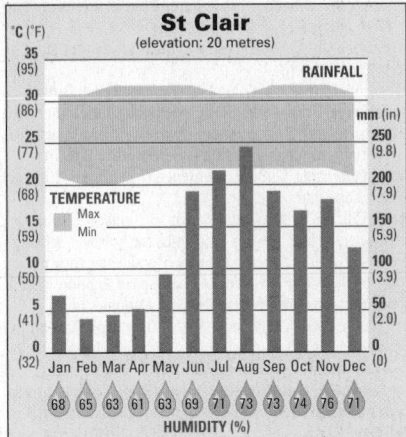

St Clair (elevation: 20 metres)

°C (°F) / RAINFALL / mm (in)
TEMPERATURE — Max / Min
HUMIDITY (%)
Jan Feb Mar Apr May Jun Jul Aug Sep Oct Nov Dec
68 65 63 61 63 69 71 73 73 74 76 71

Communications

Telephone: IDD is available. Country code: 1 868. There are no area codes. In Tobago, international telephone calls can be made from the TSTT building on Wilson Road in Scarborough. Many public phone booths take phonecards which can be bought from local shops and the TSTT building.
Mobile telephone: Roaming agreements exist with international mobile phone companies. Coverage is available in most of Trinidad & Tobago.
Internet: There are numerous Internet cafes on the islands.
Post: The main post office is on Wrightson Road, Port of Spain. Airmail to Western Europe takes up to two weeks; incoming mail can take much longer. The main post office in Tobago is in Market Square, Scarborough.
MEDIA: The former public broadcaster NBN, which operated two TV and four radio stations, closed in January 2005 after more than 40 years on the air. A new state-owned company, the Caribbean News Media Network, is expected to launch. Privately-run *TV6* dominates the ratings in Trinidad and Tobago.
Press: English-language dailies include *Newsday, The Trinidad Guardian* and *Trinidad & Tobago Express.* As well as these dailies and numerous weekly publications such as *The Bomb* and *The Punch,* Tobago has its own weekly paper, *Tobago News.*
TV: *TV6* is a private channel owned by Caribbean Communications Network (CCN); *Gayelle* is a private channel; *NCC TV* is operated by National Carnival Commission.
Radio: Trinidad Broadcasting Company operates *Radio Trinidad, Sangeet 106.1 FM* and several other stations; *Radio 90.5* broadcasts Indian music; *Ebony 104* broadcasts Creole music and culture; Other stations include *WEFM* and *i95.5 FM.*

Passport/Visa

	Passport Required?	Visa Required?	Return Ticket Required?
Full British	Yes	No/2	Yes
Australian	Yes	Yes/3	Yes
Canadian	Yes	No/1	Yes
USA	Yes	No/1	Yes
Other EU	Yes	No/2	Yes
Japanese	Yes	Yes	Yes

Note: *Regulations and requirements may be subject to change at short notice, and you are advised to contact the appropriate diplomatic or consular authority before finalising travel arrangements. Any numbers in the chart refer to the footnotes below.*

Credit: The Republic of Trinidad & Tobago Tourist Board

A B C D E F G H I J K L M N O P Q R S T U V W X Y Z

PASSPORTS: Valid passport required by all persons aged 16 years and over. Passport must be valid for at least six months from date of return.
Note: All visitors must be in possession of a valid return ticket to their country of residence or citizenship and sufficient funds to maintain themselves whilst in Trinidad & Tobago. Visitors must also provide a proper local address in Trinidad & Tobago, and complete an Immigration E/D card (form 1).
VISAS: Required by all except:
(a) **1.** nationals of Canada and the USA for stays not exceeding three months;
(b) **2.** nationals of EU countries for stays not exceeding three months, except nationals of the Czech Republic, Estonia, Hungary, Latvia, Lithuania, Poland, the Slovak Republic and Slovenia who can stay visa free for one month;
(c) **3.** nationals of Commonwealth countries (except Australia, Cameroon, India, Mozambique, New Zealand, Nigeria, Papua New Guinea, South Africa, Sri Lanka, Tanzania and Uganda, who *do* require a visa) for stays of up to three months;
(d) nationals of Brazil, Iceland and Liechtenstein for stays of up to three months;
(e) nationals of Aruba, Colombia, Curacao, French Guiana, Guadeloupe, Israel, Korea (Rep), Martinique, the Netherlands Antilles, Norway, Saba, Surinam, Switzerland and Venezuela;
(f) nationals of Albania, Bosnia & Herzegovina, Bulgaria, Croatia, Romania, Serbia & Montenegro and Turkey for stays of up to one month.
Note: Citizens who do require visas for Trinidad & Tobago must apply before arrival at the Embassy; however, where there is no Embassy in the country of residence, they may apply on arrival for a waiver of visa, subject to prior approval by the Immigration Division. Nationals of Cameroon, Cuba, China, India, Korea (Dem Rep), Macedonia (Former Yugoslav Republic of), Mozambique, Nigeria, Papua New Guinea, Sri Lanka, Tanzania, Uganda and Vietnam always require a visa and may not apply for a waiver of visa.
Types of visa: £8.50 (single-entry); £17 (Double-entry).
Validity: 90 days.
Application requirements: (a) Completed application form. (b) One passport-size photograph. (c) Valid passport with at least one empty page. (d) Reason for visit. (e) Letter of invitation or letter from employer. (f) Proper local address in Trinidad and Tobago. (g) Proof of sufficient funds. (h) Proof of return ticket. (i) Fee (payable by cash or postal order only).
Application to: Consulate (or Consular section at Embassy or High Commission); see *Passport/Visa Information*.
Working days required: Tourist visas will normally be issued within 10 working days. Applications from nationals of the following countries may take up to four weeks: Albania, China, Cuba, Korea (Dem Rep), Serbia & Montenegro and Vietnam.
Temporary residence: Enquire at Embassy or High Commission.

PASSPORT/VISA INFORMATION

High Commission of the Republic of Trinidad & Tobago in the UK
42 Belgrave Square, London SW1X 8NT, UK
Tel: (020) 7245 9351.
Website: www.immigration.gov.tt
Opening hours: Mon-Fri 0900-1700; Mon-Fri 1000-1400 (visa applications).

Embassy of the Republic of Trinidad & Tobago in the USA
1708 Massachusetts Avenue, NW,
Washington, DC 20036, USA
Tel: (202) 467 6490.
E-mail: embttgo@erols.com

Money

Currency: Trinidad & Tobago Dollar (TTD; symbol TT$) = 100 cents. Notes are in denominations of TT$100, 20, 10, 5 and 1. Coins are in denominations of 50, 25, 10, 5 and 1 cents.
Currency exchange: Foreign currency can only be exchanged at authorised banks and some hotels. There are ATMs taking cash cards and credit cards in both Trinidad and Tobago (Scarborough only).
Credit & debit cards: American Express, Diners Club, MasterCard and Visa are accepted by most banks, shops and tourist facilities. Many traders charge 5 per cent for the use of credit cards. Check with your credit or debit card company for details of merchant acceptability and other services which may be available.
Traveller's cheques: These are very widely accepted and will often prove the most convenient means of transaction. Banks charge a fee for exchanging traveller's cheques. Check for the best rates. To avoid additional exchange rate charges, travellers are advised to take traveller's cheques in US Dollars or Pounds Sterling.
Currency restrictions: The import of local currency is unlimited, provided declared on arrival. The export of local currency is limited to TT$200. There is free import of foreign currency, subject to declaration. The export of foreign currency is limited to the equivalent of TT$2500 per year.
Banking hours: Mon-Thurs 0800-1400, Fri 0900-1200 and 1500-1700.
Exchange rate indicators:
Rate at time of publishing

£1.00=	TT$11.19
$1.00=	TT$6.30

Duty Free

The following goods may be imported into Trinidad & Tobago by persons over 17 years of age without incurring customs duty:
200 cigarettes or 50 cigars or 250g of tobacco; 1.5l of wine or spirits in opened bottles; a reasonable quantity of perfume; gifts up to the value of US$200.

Public Holidays

Below are listed Public Holidays for the January 2006-June 2007 period.
2006: Jan 1 New Year's Day. **Mar 30** Spiritual Baptist Shouters' Liberation Day. **Apr 14** Good Friday. **Apr 17** Easter Monday. **May 30** Indian Arrival Day. **Jun 15** Corpus Christi. **Jun 19** Labour Day. **Aug 1** Emancipation Day. **Aug 31** Independence Day. **Sep 24** Republic Day. **Oct 21** Divali. **Oct 22-24** Eid ul Fitr. **Dec 25** Christmas Day. **Dec 26** Boxing Day.
2007: Jan 1 New Year's Day. **Mar 30** Spiritual Baptist Shouters' Liberation Day. **Apr 6** Good Friday. **Apr 9** Easter Monday. **May 30** Indian Arrival Day. **Jun 7** Corpus Christi. **Jun 19** Labour Day.
Note: Hindu festivals are declared according to local astronomical observations and variations may occur. Muslim festivals are timed according to local sightings of various phases of the moon and the dates given above are approximations.
When a public holiday falls on a Sunday, the holiday will be observed on the Monday following immediately. When two public holidays fall on the same date the following date is also given as a public holiday (website: www.gov.tt/events/publicholidays.asp).

Health

	Special Precautions?	Certificate Required?
Yellow Fever	Yes	1
Cholera	No	No
Typhoid & Polio	No	N/A
Malaria	No	N/A

Note: *Regulations and requirements may be subject to change at short notice, and you are advised to contact your doctor well in advance of your intended date of departure. Any numbers in the chart refer to the footnotes below.*

1: A *yellow fever* vaccination certificate is required from travellers over one year of age arriving from infected areas. Although no human cases have been recorded, *yellow fever* vaccination is recommended. The *yellow fever* virus is present in monkeys. Mosquitoes that bite these monkeys are then a risk to humans.
Food & drink: Mains water in Tobago is safe to drink, though bottled water is available in supermarkets. Drinking water outside main cities and towns may be contaminated and sterilisation is advisable. Milk is pasteurised and dairy products are safe for consumption. Local meat, poultry, seafood, fruit and vegetables throughout both islands are generally safe to eat. The authorities advise caution, however, during carnival time when buying food from the 'hawker' stalls in Port of Spain.
Other risks: *Hepatitis A* occurs and vaccination is recommended. *Hepatitis B* is present and vaccination is recommended for those in intimate contact with locals or who are staying for more than six months. Mosquitoes can be inconvenient anywhere just before and after dusk. Visitors are advised to carry insect repellent and bite cream. The incidence of *dengue fever* is rising.
Rabies is present. For those at high risk, vaccination before arrival should be considered. If you are bitten, seek medical advice without delay. Bats are a problem as far as the transmission of rabies is concerned. For more information, consult the *Health* appendix.
Health care: Although there is no reciprocal health agreement with the UK, public sector health care is free. However, health insurance is recommended as Tobago's health care provision is basic, with limited supplies and medication.

Travel - International

AIR:
The national airline is *BWIA (BW)* (website: www.bwee.com), which flies to other Caribbean islands and to several towns on the North and South American coasts. BWIA operates frequent services from London (Heathrow), Miami and New York to Port of Spain.
Approximate flight times: From Port of Spain to *Barbados* is 50 minutes; to *London* is 10 hours (flying BWIA; with a further 30-minute flight to Crown Point, Tobago); to *New York* is six hours 30 minutes; and to *St Lucia* is two hours 10 minutes (including stop at Barbados).
Main airports: *Piarco International Airport (POS)* is 25km (16 miles) east of Port of Spain. *To/from the airport*: Buses are available to the city (travel time - 25 minutes). There are taxis to the city for hotels throughout the island with set fares posted in taxis. Fares increase after midnight. Sharing taxis is an accepted practice. *Facilities*: Duty free shops, banks, ATMs, car hire, restaurants, light refreshments, shops and tourist information.
Crown Point (TAB) is 13km (8 miles) from Scarborough and very close to most of the main hotels. *To/from the airport*: Taxis are available (prices for standard journeys are published in the airport arrival lounge). *Facilities*: Bank, bureau de change, shops, restaurant, duty free shop, snack and car hire.
For more information on airports, contact the Airports Authority of Trinidad and Tobago (website: www.tntislands.com).
Departure tax: TT$100 (payable in local currency only). Transit passengers, passengers over 60 and children under five years of age are exempt.
SEA:
Main ports: *Port of Spain* and *Scarborough*. Cruise lines that stop at Port of Spain include *Princess* (website: www.princess.com) and *Silversea* (website: www.silversea.com).

Travel - Internal

AIR:
There are flights twice daily run by *Caribbean Star* (website: www.flycaribbeanstar.com) from Piarco (Port of Spain) to Tobago (Crown Point). During peak seasons (especially Carnival time), these are often heavily booked. *Tobago Express* also links Tobago and Port of Spain.
SEA:
There is a daily (except Saturday) car ferry/passenger service from Port of Spain to Tobago (Scarborough) (travel time - approximately six hours). The day journey (from Port of Spain around 1400) gives a good view of the two islands; the night journey (from Scarborough around 2300) can be uncomfortable. Ferry fares are around TT$160 (return). Return by plane to Port of Spain is recommended.
ROAD:
Traffic drives on the left. The road network in Trinidad between major towns is good, but traffic around Port of Spain can be difficult during rush hour and around Independence Square at any time. Two major highways run north-south and east-west. Roads which run off major routes can be very unpredictable, and are susceptible to poor weather conditions. In Tobago, the roads, though narrow in parts, are improving dramatically and most of the island is easy to reach. There is a major highway (Claude Noel Highway) running west-east. Tourists should have no qualms about driving around Tobago at any time of the day or night, although caution should be exercised in more rural areas where chickens and sheep may wander across roads. Hand signals, which may be unfamiliar, are often used. **Bus:** Services are operated by the state *Public Service Corporation (PTSC)*. In the absence of a railway, the main towns are served by bus but although these are cheap, they are crowded and unreliable. The use of shared taxis has increased due to the shortcomings of the bus network; these are available both outside and within Port of Spain. In Tobago, there are regular bus services between Scarborough bus station and Crown Point, Buccoo, Plymouth and Roxborough. **Taxi:** All official taxis have registration 'H'. Hiring a private taxi is much more expensive but gives the freedom to go where you like. Though there are fixed rates for certain journeys, it is best to establish this before you start your journey. The quickest and most cost-effective way to get around is by Route taxis and Maxi taxis which serve standard routes within Trinidad, particularly around Port of Spain, starting their route from, in or near Independence Square. These have fixed rates. In Tobago, Route taxis (H registered and unregistered) are plentiful along most major routes during the day and can be stopped anywhere along them. Drivers will indicate they have room by sounding their horn. **Car hire:** Cars and motorcycles are available in Port of Spain or Scarborough, and can be arranged via hotels and in

Tobago at the airport or through the hotels. Trailbikes are becoming more popular in Tobago, but mopeds are more advisable for the inexperienced rider. **Bicycle hire:** In Tobago, there are a number of places in the Lowlands (southeast) where you can hire bicycles. **Documentation:** Visitors in possession of a valid driving permit issued in any of the countries listed below may drive in Trinidad & Tobago for a period of up to three months. They are, however, entitled to drive only a motor vehicle of the class specified on their permit. Drivers must at all times have in their possession: (a) their International Driving Permit or equivalent; and, (b) any travel document on which is certified their date of arrival in Trinidad & Tobago. Visitors whose stay exceeds the three-month period are requested to apply to the Licensing Department, Wrightson Road, Port of Spain, for a local Driving Permit. The above information applies to all signatories to the Convention on International Driver's Permits including The Bahamas, Canada, France, Germany, the UK and the USA. *Excluded*: China, South Africa and Vietnam, whose nationals require a passport, International Driving Permit and national licence.

URBAN:

 Owing to the deterioration of bus services, most public transport journeys in Port of Spain are now made by shared taxis (see above).

Travel Advice

While most visits to Trinidad and Tobago are trouble-free, visitors should be aware that there are increasing levels of violent crime, especially shootings and kidnappings. Visitors should be aware of the global risk of indiscriminate terrorist attacks which could be against civilian targets, including places frequented by foreigners.
This advice is based on information provided by the Foreign and Commonwealth Office in the UK. It is correct at time of publishing. As the situation can change rapidly, visitors are advised to contact the following organisations for the latest travel advice:

British Foreign and Commonwealth Office
Tel: (0845) 850 2829.
Website: www.fco.gov.uk

US Department of State
Website: http://travel.state.gov/travel

Accommodation

HOTELS:
 There are major international chain hotels in Port of Spain, and a number of smaller hotels in the surrounding areas. In Tobago, there is a growing number of international-standard resort hotels as well as many smaller private hotels and guest houses. There is a wide range of prices. A 10 per cent government room tax and VAT are levied.

GUEST HOUSES:
 The Tourism and Industrial Development Company Ltd publishes a list of guest houses found throughout Trinidad & Tobago (see *Accommodation Information*).

HOUSES/APARTMENTS:
 There is a growing number of apartments and houses available for rent in Tobago, ranging from the very luxurious to the plain and simple.
Though many are located in the west in the main tourist part of the island around Crown Point and Shirvan Road, there are many other more secluded and unspoilt areas where there are properties of all standards to rent. Information is available from local sources.
Note: All types of accommodation must be booked well in advance for the *Carnival*.

ACCOMMODATION INFORMATION

Tourism and Industrial Development Company Ltd (TIDCO)
Level 1, Maritime Centre, 29 Thames Avenue, Barataria, Trinidad
Tel: 675 7034/5/6/7
Website: www.visittnt.com

Trinidad Hotels, Restaurants and Tourism Association
c/o Trinidad & Tobago Hospitality and Tourism Institute,
Airway Road, Chaguaramas, PO Box 243,
Port of Spain, Trinidad
Tel: 634 1174/5
Website: www.tnthotels.com

Top Things To See

Trinidad
• **Port of Spain**, surrounded by the lush green hills of the **Northern Range**, is the capital and business hub of oil-rich Trinidad. The city captures the variety of Trinidadian life, with bazaars thronging beneath modern skyscrapers and mosques rubbing shoulders with cathedrals. The architecture of the city incorporates a mixture of styles: these include Victorian houses with gingerbread fretwork; the German Renaissance **Queen's Royal College**; **Stollmeyer's Castle**, an imitation of a Bavarian Castle; the **President of the Republic's residence** and the Prime Minister's office at **Whitehall** (both built in Moorish style); and the 19th-century Gothic **Holy Trinity Cathedral**. Places of interest include the shopping district centred on **Frederick Street**; the **Royal Botanic Gardens**; the **Red House** (a stately colonial building, now the seat of Government) and the **National Museum** and **Art Gallery**.
• Head for the magnificent **Queen's Park Savannah**, to the north of the capital, at the foot of the Northern Range. A mixture of natural and manmade beauty, with attractive trees and shrubs (including the African Tulip, or 'Flame of the Forest'), it forms a backdrop to playing fields and elaborate mansions, now mostly Government offices and embassies.
• On the outskirts of the city is **Fort George**. Built in 1804, it offers an excellent view of Port of Spain and the mountains of northern Venezuela.
• **Maracas Bay**, **Las Cuevas** and **Chaguaramas** are the nearest beaches to Port of Spain. Maracas tends to be the place to go after Carnival has finished.
• Approximately 13km (8 miles) to the south of the capital by road and boat is the **Caroni Bird Sanctuary**, home of the Scarlet Ibis.
• At the **Diego Mountain Valley**, 16km (10 miles) from Port of Spain, see one of the island's most beautiful **water wheels**.
• **Arima**, the third-largest town on the island, has an **Amerindian Museum** at the **Cleaver Woods Recreation Centre** in the west of town and the nation's new **horse racing track**.
• About 13km (8 miles) north is the **Asa Wright Nature Centre** at **Blanchisseuse**, containing a collection of rare specimens such as the **Oilbird** or **Guacharo**.
• The **Aripo Caves** are noted for their stalactites and stalagmites.
• **Asa Wright** is a must for birdwatching enthusiasts.
• Travel to **Valencia** on the east coast, a lush tropical forest near the **Hollis Reservoir**. **Cocal** and **Mayaro** are also worth visiting.
• **San Fernando** is the island's second town and the main commercial centre in the south. Close by, be fascinated by the natural phenomenon of the **Pitch Lake**, a 36.4 hectare (90 acre) lake of asphalt which constantly replenishes itself.

Tobago
• The capital, **Scarborough**, has many quaint houses which spill down from the hilltop to the waterside, as well as interesting **Botanical Gardens**. It is overshadowed by the **Fort King George** built in 1779 during the many struggles between the French and the English, an excellent point from which to view the sunset. The **Court House** built in 1825 is today used as the meeting place for the Tobago House of Assembly, while the **Tobago Museum** showcases artefacts from Tobago's early American Indian and colonial days.
• There are a number of fine beaches throughout the island, each with their own flavour. They include **Pigeon Point** on the northwest coast (admission is charged for use of facilities); **Store Bay** and **Turtle Beach**, where brown pelicans can be seen diving into the waters to catch fish; **Man O'War Bay**, at the opposite end of the island; and **Mount Irvine** and **Bacolet Bays. Buccoo Reef** is an extensive coral reef lying a mile offshore from Pigeon Point. Excursions can be made in glass-bottomed boats and it is an excellent place for snorkelling. These trips run from Store Bay or Pigeon Point, leaving every day at around 1100.
• At **Fort James**, there is a well-maintained red brick building, and at **Whim**, a large plantation house. **Arnos Vale Hotel** is a former sugar plantation, now a hotel; a disused sugar mill fitted out with formidable crushing wheels, made in 1857, is still on the grounds. **Englishman's Bay** is an excellent place for a day trip. **Birdwatching** is a favourite pastime here. The hotel offers tea to non-residents during the late afternoon on the balcony above the gardens. This is a must for birdwatchers and needs to be booked by phone first.
• Be puzzled by a mystery tombstone with inscriptions dating from 1700 in the fishing village of **Plymouth**.
• **Charlotteville** is a fishing town commanding precipitous views of the headlands. Looming above the town is **Pigeon Peak**, the highest point on the island. There are good swimming beaches, including **Pirate's Bay**, which can only be reached by boat.
• **Tobago Forest Reserve** in the east has many trails which

Credit: ©The Republic of Trinidad & Tobago Tourist Board

provide excellent long **hikes** for the more active visitor.
• On the Atlantic (windward) side of the island are many tiny villages including **Mesopotamia** and **Goldsborough**, the town of **Roxborough** and several beautiful bays.
• **Speyside** is a colourful beach settlement, from which can be seen tiny **Goat Island** and **Little Tobago**, a 182 hectare (450 acre) **bird sanctuary**. Speyside offers excellent **snorkelling** and **scuba diving**. Windward beaches are wilder but just as picturesque as those on the Caribbean.
• On the north coast are the beautiful villages of **Castara** and **Parlatuvier**.

Top Things To Do

• A vast mixture of races has led to a varied cultural life, the diversity of which is reflected in costume, religion, architecture, music, dance and place names. The major event in Trinidad is the **Carnival**, renowned throughout the Caribbean and the rest of the world. The festivities climax at the beginning of Lent, on the two days immediately preceding Ash Wednesday, although the run-up to Carnival starts immediately after Christmas when the Calypso tents open and the Calypsonians perform their latest compositions and arrangements. During Carnival, normal life grinds to a halt and the whole of Trinidad & Tobago is absorbed in the festivities. A week before the Carnival proper, **Panorama** is staged. This is the Grand Steel Drum (pan) tournament; all the big steel bands parade their skills around the Savannah, the large park in the north of Port of Spain. The Panorama preliminaries and local finals in Tobago are worth visiting, as are the pan yards as the bands practise for the big event. **Hosay**, coinciding with the Muslim New Year, sees the Muslim population of Port of Spain, San Fernando and Tunapuna take to the streets in a festival of their own. Contact the Tourism and Industrial Development Company Ltd (see *Tourist Information*) for more information and exact dates of the above.

- In the rapidly expanding town of **Chaguanas**, sample a wide range of **West Indian culinary specialities**, particularly East Indian fare.
- There are good facilities for all types of **watersports**, especially at the beaches along the north and east coasts of Trinidad, and all around Tobago. **Buccoo Reef,** just off the southwest coast of Tobago, and **Speyside** offer exciting **scuba diving** with magnificent coral formations and abundant marine life. Trips in glass-bottomed boats are very popular. Tobago has some of the finest reefs in the Caribbean and many scuba schools located at **Speyside** and **Store Bay**.
- All kinds of **fishing** - from deep-sea to inland - are widely available and usually rewarding on and off both islands. Kingfish, Spanish mackerel, wahoo, bonito, dolphin fish and yellow tuna are the usual catches, with grouper, salmon and snapper are also to be found off the west and north coasts of Trinidad. In Tobago, there is an increasing number of boats available for hire.
- **Birdwatching and wildlife:** The islands boast no fewer than 622 species of butterfly and over 700 species of orchid. The latter are perhaps best seen in Trinidad's **Botanic Gardens** in Port of Spain (along with a wide selection of indigenous trees, shrubs, ferns and cacti). The **Emperor Valley Zoo** has a similarly representative selection of local wildlife - reptile as well as mammal. Birdwatchers on Trinidad should head for the **Nariva Swamp, the Aripo Savannah** and **the Asa Wright Nature Centre** and look out in particular for the national bird, the scarlet ibis, conserved in the **Caroni Bird Sanctuary**. While on Tobago a visit to **Little Tobago Island** is recommended, particularly if you are keen on birds. Boats leave from Speyside. Hummingbirds are ubiquitous on Tobago; there are 19 recorded species, seven of which are unique to the island. There are specialist birdwatching tours and nature trips available, details of which can be provided by any hotel.
- **Cricket** is the major spectator sport and the season runs from February to June. The best national and international matches can be seen at the Queen's Park Oval, in Port of Spain. Trinidadians are keen on **racing**, and the **Arima Velodrome** hosts a number of major meetings, particularly around New Year and Easter.

TOURIST INFORMATION

Trinidad & Tobago Tourism Office in the UK
Albany House, Albany Crescent, Claygate,
Surrey KT10 0PF, UK
Tel: (0800) 804 8787.
Website: www.visittnt.com

Caribbean Tourism Organisation in the UK
22 The Quadrant, Richmond, Surrey TW9 1BP, UK
Tel: (020) 8948 0057.
Website: www.doitcaribbean.com *or*
www.onecaribbean.org

Entertainment

FOOD & DRINK: Bars and restaurants open until late, with a very wide choice of local and Western food and drink. Chinese, Indian and West Indian cooking is available on both islands. Tobago also offers some notable seafood specialities and all types of fried fish.

National specialities:
- Creole soups, the best being *sans coche, calaloo* and peppery pigeon pea soup.
- *Tatoo* (armadillo).
- *Manicou* (opossum).
- Pork souse, pork boiled and served cold in a salty sauce with lime, cucumber, pepper, and onion slices.
- *Tum-tum* (mashed green plantains).
- *Lappe* (island rabbit).
- *Pastelles:* meat folded into cornmeal and wrapped in a banana leaf - a speciality generally available over Christmas.
- Seafood in Trinidad includes bean-sized oysters and *chip-chip* (tiny shellfish similar in taste to clams).
- Freshwater fish *cascadou*.
- Indian dishes on both islands include *roti* (dahlpuri bread stuffed with chicken, fish, goat or vegetables).
- *Palhouri*, fritters made with split peas, and hot curries.

National drinks:
- Excellent rums and Angostura bitters are used to make rum punch.
- The local beers are *Carib* and *Stag*.

Tipping: Most hotels and guest houses add 10 per cent service charge to the bill, otherwise a 10 to 15 per cent tip is usual in hotels and restaurants.

NIGHTLIFE: Trinidad has a wide and varied nightlife including hotel entertainment and nightclubs with calypso, limbo dancers and steel bands. During the carnival season (from New Year to Carnival, held 2 days before Ash Wednesday), both islands are alive with live music in the calypso tents and pan (steel band) yards. In Tobago, the main Calypsonians from Trinidad travel over to perform at Shaw Park, Scarborough and Roxborough. There is something happening most nights of the week at this time - details available from the locals and the *Tobago News*.

SHOPPING: Goods from all over the world can be found in Port of Spain, but local goods are always available. Special purchases include Calypso records, steel drums, leather bags and sandals, ceramics and woodcarvings. Gold and silver jewellery can be good value, as can Indian silks and fabrics. Rum should also be considered. Bright, printed fabrics and other summer garments are available in Trinidad & Tobago, particularly in Port of Spain.

Shopping hours: Mon-Thurs 0800-1600, Fri 0800-1800 and Sat 0800-1300. Some shops stay open later in Port of Spain, and malls are often open till 2100. Shops close on public holidays, especially during Carnival.

Business

- **GDP:** US$13.79 billion (2005).
- **Main exports:** Petroleum and petroleum products, natural gas, chemicals, steel products, fertiliser, sugar, cocoa, coffee, citrus and flowers.
- **Main imports:** Machinery, transport equipment, manufactured goods, food and live animals.
- **Main trade partners:** USA, Venezuela, Germany, Brazil, Jamaica, Spain, Italy and France.

ECONOMY: The oil and gas industry has been the most important in Trinidad & Tobago for some time. It had been in long-term decline from the 1980s due to falling yields and low world prices. More recently, however, new discoveries, increased foreign investment and a steady increase in world prices have reversed the trend. In the summer of 2003, Trinidad signed a landmark agreement with nearby Venezuela, one of the world's largest producers, to collaborate in all aspects of the oil and gas industries. This should ensure the long-term future of the sector for Trinidad. Apart from oil and gas, Trinidad has the world's largest deposits of asphalt.

The non-oil industrial sector is concentrated in relatively new industries established with oil and gas revenues, such as plastics and electronics. The agricultural sector is small, with sugar cane, coffee, cocoa and citrus fruits as the main commodities. Once a net exporter of foodstuffs, Trinidad now imports the bulk of its requirements. The Government has also sought to address historic under-investment in the tourism industry, a promising part of the economy which has undergone steady growth. The islands now cater to about 400,000 visitors annually; the industry is worth about US$275 million to the Trinidadian economy. Trinidad & Tobago formerly had the most heavily regulated economy in the region but the state-controlled edifice was dismantled during the 1990s as part of an IMF-approved package of privatisation, fiscal and trade liberalisation. The external debt has been substantially reduced while growth and inflation are both close to 5 per cent; unemployment has been cut to 13 per cent from higher levels during the 1990s. As ever, this was achieved at the cost of reductions in social provision and lower than average incomes for the bulk of the population. Trinidad & Tobago is a member of the Caribbean trading bloc, CARICOM.

BUSINESS ETIQUETTE: Lightweight suits or 'shirt jacks' should be worn. It is normal to shake hands and exchange business cards. The best time to visit is from December to April, except during the Christmas festivities. **Office hours:** Mon-Fri 0800-1630.

COMMERCIAL INFORMATION

Trinidad and Tobago Chamber of Industry and Commerce (Inc)
Columbus Circle, Westmoorings, PO Box 499,
Port of Spain, Trinidad
Tel: 637 6966.
Website: www.chamber.org.tt

Tunisia

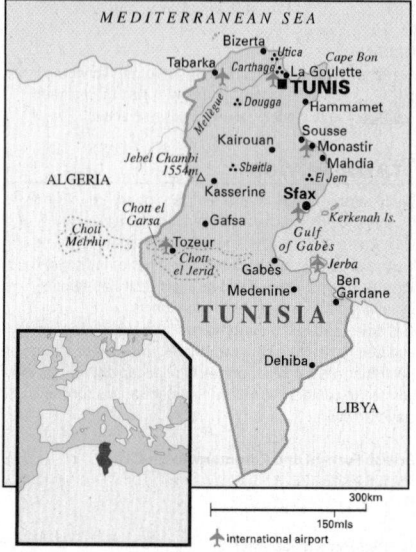

Location: North Africa.

Time: GMT + 1.

Overview

For such a tiny country – the smallest in North Africa – Tunisia packs a lot in. It is a truly kaleidoscopic nation, ranging from Mediterranean beaches to the Sahara desert, from ancient souks to Star Wars film sets. This Arab-Berber nation is one of the most liberal in the Islamic world; alcohol is freely available and women need not feel intimidated.

The capital, Tunis, reflects the country's diversity. Its French colonial past has a far-reaching influence (it only gained independence in 1956), most obviously in its cuisine that blends sophisticated French styles with Arab spice. Older history is evident in the remains of what was Roman Carthage, while the Roman ruins at Dougga and El Jem are some of the finest in Africa.

Since independence, Tunisia, first under the 30-year rule of Habib Bourgiba, and now under a government led by Zine El Abidine Ben Ali, now in his fourth five-year term as President, has pursued a policy aimed at prevention of Islamic fundamentalism. It is also one of the most advanced Arab nations in terms of women's rights, and has by far the most successful economy in the region. This is bolstered by an annual influx of millions of tourists.

Despite its location, edging the Sahara, Tunisia is a surprisingly fertile land. It has six National Parks; that around Lac Ichkeul is one of only two UNESCO-protected Biosphere Reserves in the world. If you are feeling energetic, the view from the near-deserted village of Takrouna over the mountainous north is stunning. Alternatively, visit a central desert oasis like Zaafrane, Tozeur or Kebili with its hot pools. Finally, when you tire of culture, history and nature, simply lie on the beach and relax at some point along its 1400km (875 miles) stretch of Mediterranean coastline.

General Information

AREA: 163,610 sq km (63,170 sq miles).
POPULATION: 10.7 million (official estimate 2005).
POPULATION DENSITY: 63 per sq km.
CAPITAL: Tunis. **Population:** 700 thousand (official estimate 2003 [excluding suburbs]).
GEOGRAPHY: The Republic of Tunisia lies on the Mediterranean coast of Africa, 130km (80 miles) southwest

Credit: ©The Tunisian National Tourist Office/www.fotoseeker.com

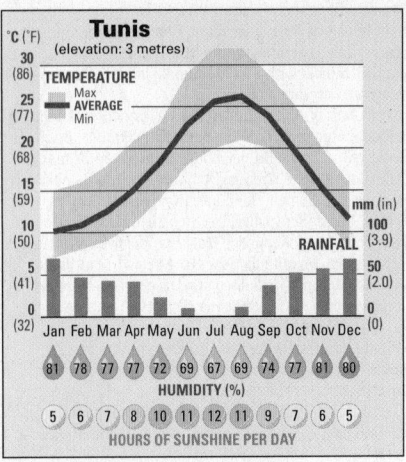

Tunis (elevation: 3 metres)

°C (°F) 30 (86), 25 (77), 20 (68), 15 (59), 10 (50), 5 (41), 0 (32)

TEMPERATURE — Max, AVERAGE, Min

mm (in) 100 (3.9), 50 (2.0), 0 (0)

RAINFALL

Jan Feb Mar Apr May Jun Jul Aug Sep Oct Nov Dec

HUMIDITY (%): 81 78 77 77 72 69 67 69 74 77 81 80

HOURS OF SUNSHINE PER DAY: 5 6 7 8 10 11 12 11 9 7 6 5

of Sicily and 160km (100 miles) due south of Sardinia. It is bordered by Algeria to the west and Libya to the southeast. The landscape varies from the cliffs of the north coast to the woodlands of the interior, from deep valleys of rich arable land to desert, and from towering mountains to salt pans lower than sea level. South of Gafsa and Gabès is the Sahara desert. The 1100km (700 miles) of coastline is dotted with small islands, notably Jerba in the south and Kerkennah in the east, and from the northwest to the southeast the coastline is backed successively by pine-clad hills, lush pasture, orchards, vineyards and olive groves.
GOVERNMENT: Republic since 1959. Gained independence from France in 1956. **Head of State:** President Zine Al-Abidine Ben Ali since 1987. **Head of Government:** Prime Minister Mohamed Ghannouchi since 1999. **Recent history:** Celebrating 50 years of independence from France during 2006, Tunisia has so far had only two Presidents. The 'Founding Father' of the independent country, Habib Bourgiba, ruled from 1956 until he was judged senile and unable to continue in power in 1987, when the current incumbent, Zine El Abidine Ben Ali assumed power in a bloodless coup. The *Rassemblement Constitutionel Démocratique* (RCD) continues to hold a substantial majority in the *Majlis al-Nuwaab* (Chamber of Deputies). A Presidential poll was held in March 1994 and Ben Ali was 're-elected' with 99.9 per cent of the vote. At legislative elections held at the same time, half of the 19 seats reserved for the opposition were allocated to the Democratic Socialists and the others divided between the *Mouvement de la Renovation* (formerly the Communists), the *Parti de l'Unité Populaire* and the *Union Démocratique Unioniste*. The 1999 Presidential vote produced a similar result, giving Ben Ali a third consecutive term. Strictly speaking, a fourth term was forbidden by the constitution but a Referendum in 2002 allowed Ali to stand for up to another two terms. Unsurprisingly, Ali won the controversial fourth term in 2004 with the main opposition party withdrawing two days prior to the vote stating that their participation would only serve to legitimise a rigged election.
Under the 1959 constitution, legislation is the responsibility of the unicameral Chamber of Deputies, whose 163 members are elected by universal adult suffrage for five years. All but 19 seats, which are reserved for opposition parties under a system of proportional representation, are elected under a simple majority system. The President, who is also elected by universal suffrage for a five-year term, is Head of State and appoints a Prime Minister and Council of Ministers who exercise executive power under his leadership. There are also various advisory bodies – the State Council, the Social and Economic Council, the Constitutional Council and the Higher Islamic Council.
LANGUAGE: The official language is Arabic. French is the second language, Italian is spoken in major cities, and English and German mainly in tourist resorts.
RELIGION: The principal religion is Islam; there are small Roman Catholic, Protestant and Jewish minorities.
ELECTRICITY: 220/110 volts AC, 50Hz. A two-pin continental plug/adaptor is needed.
SOCIAL CONVENTIONS: Arabic in culture and tradition, Tunisia is nevertheless one of the more liberal and tolerant Muslim countries. The nomadic Bedouin still follow their traditional way of life in the southern desert. The Tunisians' varied origins are shown in the architecture, crafts, music and regional folk dances. Tunisia has also developed an international reputation as an intellectual and cultural centre. Shaking hands is the usual form of greeting. Hospitality is very important and a small gift in appreciation of hospitality or as a token of friendship is always appreciated. Dress can be informal but should respect the conventions of Islam when visiting religious monuments, ie shoulders and knees must be covered. Outside tourist resorts, scanty beachwear should not be worn.

Climate

Tunisia has a warm climate all year. Best periods are spring and autumn. Temperatures can be extremely high inland. Winter is mild and has the highest rainfall.
Required clothing: Lightweights in summer, mediumweights and rainwear in winter. Sunglasses are advised.

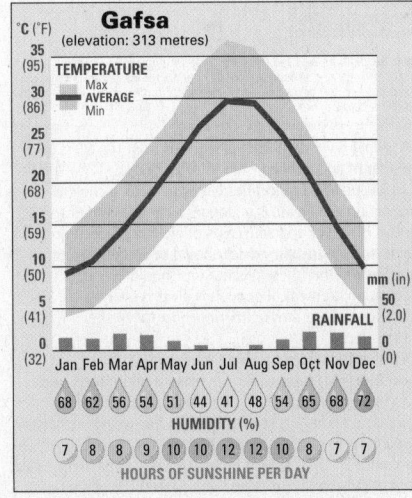

Gafsa (elevation: 313 metres)

°C (°F) 35 (95), 30 (86), 25 (77), 20 (68), 15 (59), 10 (50), 5 (41), 0 (32)

TEMPERATURE — Max, AVERAGE, Min

mm (in) 100 (3.9), 50 (2.0), 0 (0)

RAINFALL

Jan Feb Mar Apr May Jun Jul Aug Sep Oct Nov Dec

HUMIDITY (%): 68 62 56 54 51 44 41 48 54 65 68 72

HOURS OF SUNSHINE PER DAY: 7 8 8 9 10 10 12 12 10 8 7 7

Communications

Telephone: Full IDD is available. Country code: 216. Automatic dialling extends to almost every part of the country and covers direct international calls.
Mobile telephone: Roaming agreements with international mobile phone companies exist.
Internet: E-mail can be accessed from Internet cafes in Tunis, Nabeul, Sousse and Tahar ben Amar.
Post: Airmail to Europe takes three to five days; an express service guarantees delivery in four days or under. Post office hours: Mon-Sat 0730-1330 (summer); Mon-Fri 0830-1300 and 1500-1745, Sat 0830-1330 (winter); Mon-Thur 0830-1430, Fri-Sat 0830-1430 and 0830-1330 (during Ramadan).
MEDIA: The government retains a tight hold on local broadcasting and the press, despite freedom of information being 'guaranteed' by the constitution. The internet is also monitored – making the choice of Tunisia for the November 2005 Global Information conference a somewhat controversial one.
Press: Daily newspapers are printed in Arabic or French, the most popular being *As-Sabah*, *La Presse de Tunisie*, *Le Temps* and *Tunisia Daily*.
TV: *ERTT* is the state-run broadcaster, owning the stations *Tunis 7* and *Canal 21*. The country's first privately-run commercial station is *Hannibal TV*, while many satellite channels are popular, particularly those broadcast from Egypt
Radio: State-run *Tunisian Radio* and privately-owned *Radio Mosaique* are the principal radio broadcasters.

Passport/Visa

	Passport Required?	Visa Required?	Return Ticket Required?
Full British	Yes	No	Yes
Australian	Yes	Yes/2	Yes
Canadian	Yes	No	Yes
USA	Yes	No	Yes
Other EU	Yes	No/1	Yes
Japanese	Yes	No	Yes

Note: *Regulations and requirements may be subject to change at short notice, and you are advised to contact the appropriate diplomatic or consular authority before finalising travel arrangements. Any numbers in the chart refer to the footnotes below.*

PASSPORTS: Passport valid six months after return date required by all.
VISAS: Required by all except the following:
(a) **1.** nationals referred to in the chart above for stays of up to three months (up to four months for nationals of the USA), except nationals of Australia who *do* need a visa, and nationals of the Czech Republic, Hungary, Latvia, Lithuania, Poland and the Slovak Republic, who must travel on a recognised package holiday, and nationals of Cyprus and

Estonia who *do* need a visa;
(b) nationals of Austria, Belgium, Finland, France, Germany, Greece, Italy, Luxembourg, The Netherlands, Portugal, Spain and Switzerland with a valid National Identity Card on a recognised package holiday;
(c) nationals of Algeria (unlimited stay), Andorra, Antigua & Barbuda, Argentina, Bahrain, Barbados, Bermuda, Bosnia & Herzegovina, Brazil, Brunei, Bulgaria (two months max.), Chile, Côte d'Ivoire, Croatia, Dominica, Fiji, The Gambia* (see *Note* below), Guinea, Honduras, Hong Kong (SAR), Iceland, Kiribati, Korea (Rep), Libya, Liechtenstein, Macedonia (Former Yugoslav Republic), Malaysia, Maldives, Mali* (see *Note* below), Mauritania* (see *Note* below), Mauritius, Monaco, Morocco (unlimited stay), Niger* (see *Note* below), Norway, Oman, Qatar, Romania, St Kitts & Nevis, St Lucia, San Marino, Senegal, Serbia & Montenegro, Seychelles, Solomon Islands, Switzerland, Turkey and Vatican City;
Note: Providing holding a sufficient amount of foreign currency to cover their stay.
(d) nationals of the CIS and Turkmenistan for package holidays only, except nationals of Armenia who *do* need a visa;
(e) transit passengers, provided holding valid onward or return documentation and not leaving the airport or ship. Nationals of Lebanon and Syria must continue by the same or first connecting aircraft within 24 hours after arrival; nationals of other countries must continue their journey within 48 hours of arrival; nationals of Bolivia, China, Colombia, Ghana, Iran, Israel, New Zealand, Peru, Philippines, Singapore and Sri Lanka need a visa at all times.
Note: 2. Nationals of Australia and South Africa, who *do* need a visa, can obtain it on arrival at the point of entry. Check with the Embassy for details of length of stay.
Types of visa and cost: *Short-stay* and *Transit*: £20.
Validity: *Short-stay* usually for stays of up to three months. *Transit*: three days. For up-to-date lengths of stay, contact nearest Consulate.
Application to: Consulate (or Consular section at Embassy); see *Passport/Visa Information*.
Application requirements: (a) Valid passport. (b) Photocopy of first five pages of passport and any stamps. (c) Three application forms completed in black ink and capital letters. (d) Two passport-size photos with full name printed on back. (e) Fee (payable by postal order or cash; cheques are not accepted). (f) Registered, stamped, self-addressed envelope for postal application (please ensure that cost of return postage comes to £4.25).
Working days required: Approximately three weeks, for both postal and personal applications.
Temporary residence: For more information, contact the visa section of the Tunisian Embassy (see *Passport/Visa Information*).

PASSPORT/VISA INFORMATION

Embassy of the Republic of Tunisia in the UK
29 Prince's Gate, London SW7 1QG, UK
Tel: (020) 7584 8117 (for enquiries) *or* (09065) 508 977 (24-hour visa information line; calls cost £1 a minute).
Opening hours: Mon-Fri 0900-1700; 0930-1300 (consular section); Mon-Thurs 0930-1300 (visa submissions).

Embassy of the Republic of Tunisia in the USA
1515 Massachusetts Avenue, NW,
Washington, DC 20005, USA
Tel: (202) 862 1850 *or* 680 6006 (tourism enquiries).
Website: www.tunisiaonline.com

Money

Currency: Tunisian Dinar (TND) = 1000 millimes. Notes are in denominations of TND30, 20, 10 and 5. Coins are in denominations of TND1, and 500, 100, 50, 20, 10 and 5 millimes.
Currency exchange: All banks change money, as do most hotels of three stars and above.
Credit & debit cards: American Express, Diners Club, MasterCard and Visa are widely accepted. Check with your credit or debit card company for details of merchant acceptability and other services which may be available. There are ATMs in every large town and tourist destination.
Traveller's cheques: Readily cashed in banks and the usual authorised establishments; to avoid additional exchange rates, travellers are advised to bring traveller's cheques in US Dollars.
Currency restrictions: The import and export of local currency is strictly prohibited. The import of foreign currency is unlimited. The export of foreign currency is limited to the amount imported although re-exchange of local into foreign currency must be only up to 30 per cent of the total imported, up to a maximum of TND100. All currency documentation must be retained.
Banking hours: Mon-Thurs 0800-1100 and 1400-1615; Fri 0800-1100 and 1300-1615 (winter); Mon-Fri 0730-1130 (summer).
Exchange rate indicators:
Rate at time of publishing
£1.00= TND2.37
$1.00= TND1.36

Duty Free

The following goods may be imported into Tunisia by anyone, irrespective of age, without incurring customs duty:
200 cigarettes or 50 cigars or 400g of tobacco; 1l of alcoholic beverages; a reasonable quantity of perfume; gifts up to a value of TD100.
Restricted items: The export of antiques is subject to a permit from the Ministry of Cultural Affairs. Pets must have a health certificate from the Veterinary authorities, stating they are free from any diseases.
Prohibited items: Firearms (unless for hunting), explosives, narcotics, walkie-talkies, obscene publications, any other items which may be regarded as dangerous to public security, health, morality and so on.

Public Holidays

Below are Public Holidays for the January 2006-June 2007 period.
2006: Jan 1 New Year's Day. **Jan 10** Eid al-Idha (Feast of the Sacrifice). **Jan 31** Hegire (Islamic New Year). **Mar 20** Independence Day. **Mar 21** Youth Day. **Apr 9** Martyr's Day. **Apr 11** Mouled (Prophet's Anniversary). **May 1** Labour Day. **July 25** Republic Day. **Aug 13** Women's Day. **Oct 22-24** Eid al-Fitr (End of Ramadam). **Nov 7** New Era Day. **Dec 31** Eid al-Idha (Feast of the Sacrifice).
2007: Jan 1 New Year's Day. **Jan 20** Hegire (Islamic New Year). **Mar 20** Independence Day. **Mar 21** Youth Day. **Mar 31** Mouled (Prophet's Anniversary). **Apr 9** Martyr's Day. **May 1** Labour Day.
Note: Muslim festivals are timed according to local sightings of various phases of the moon and the dates given above are approximations. During the lunar month of Ramadan that precedes Eid al-Fitr, Muslims fast during the day and feast at night and normal business patterns may be interrupted. Many restaurants are closed during the day and there may be restrictions on smoking and drinking. Some disruption may continue into Eid al-Fitr itself. Eid al-Fitr and Eid al-Idha may last for two days. For more information, see the *World of Islam* appendix.

Health

	Special Precautions?	Certificate Required?
Yellow Fever	Yes	1
Cholera	Yes	2
Typhoid & Polio	3	No
Malaria	No	No

Note: *Regulations and requirements may be subject to change at short notice, and you are advised to contact your doctor well in advance of your intended date of departure. Any numbers in the chart refer to the footnotes below.*

1: A yellow fever certificate is required from travellers over one year of age arriving from infected areas.
2: Following WHO guidelines issued in 1973, a cholera vaccination certificate is no longer a condition of entry to Tunisia. However, sporadic cases of cholera do occur in this region and up-to-date advice should be sought before deciding whether these precautions should include vaccination, as medical opinion is divided over its effectiveness; see the *Health* appendix for further information.
3: Vaccination against typhoid is advised.
Food & drink: Mains water is normally chlorinated, and whilst safe may cause mild abdominal upsets. Bottled water is available and is advised for the first few weeks of the stay. Drinking water outside main cities and towns may be contaminated. Milk should be boiled when unpasteurised (ie if not commercially processed and packed). Powdered or tinned milk is available and is advised but make sure that it is reconstituted with pure water. Avoid dairy products which are likely to have been made from unboiled milk. Only eat well-cooked meat and fish, preferably served hot. Salad and mayonnaise may carry increased risk. Vegetables should be cooked and fruit peeled. These precautions should include western-style buffets.
Other risks: *Dysenteries* and *diarrhoeal diseases* are common in this region. *Hepatitis A* is present and *hepatitis E* is endemic in some areas; precautions should be taken. *Lassa fever* occurs in rural areas. *Mediterranean spotted fever* has been reported. *Tungiasis* is present.
Rabies is present. For those at high risk, vaccination before arrival should be considered. If you are bitten, seek medical advice without delay. For more information, see the *Health* appendix.
Health care: Health insurance is recommended. Tunisia has a well-developed, if somewhat limited, public health service. There are a few private 'polyclinics' available in the larger towns, which function as hospitals and provide a range of procedures. Some doctors and hospitals expect immediate cash payments before treatment.

Travel - International

AIR:
The national airline is *Tunis Air (TU)* (website: www.tunisair.com). There are regular direct flights to Tunisia from all over Europe, but no direct flights from Asia, Australasia, South America or the USA. *Air France*, *British Airways* and *Lufthansa* fly regularly to Tunisia.
Approximate flight times: From *London* to Tunis is two hours 30 minutes, to Djerba is three hours, to Monastir is three hours and to Sfax is three hours 15 minutes.
Main airports: *Tunis (TUN)* (*Carthage International*) is 8km (5 miles) northeast of the city (travel time - 15 to 30 minutes). *To/from the airport*: An airport-city coach and buses are available. Return is from Hotel Africa Meridien (city air terminal). Taxis are available; a surcharge is levied at night. *Facilities*: Duty free shop, banks/bureau de change, restaurant and car hire.
Djerba (DJE) (*Melita*) is 8km (5 miles) from the city.
Monastir (MIR) (*Skanes*) is 8km (5 miles) west of the city. *To/from the airport*: Buses are available to the city centre.
Sfax (SFA) is 15km (9 miles) from the city.
Tabarka (TBJ) is 2km (1.25 miles) from the city.
Tozeur (TOE) (*Nefta*) is 10km (6 miles) from the city.
To/from the airport: Taxis are available at all the airports. *Facilities*: All the above airports have bars, restaurants, both incoming and outgoing duty free shops, bank and car hire.
Note: A new airport at Enfidha, 100km (62 miles) south of Tunis, is scheduled for completion soon.
Note: Tunisian currency is *not* valid in duty free shops.
Departure tax: None.
SEA:
Tunisia has seven major ports. *SNCM (Ferry Terranée)* runs ferry services from France and Italy to Tunisia. For more information, contact their main office in France (tel: (8) 2588 8088; website: www.sncm.fr). The major routes are *Marseilles- Tunis* (travel time - 23 hours) and *Genoa-Tunis* (travel time - 23 hours). A hydrofoil service is available from Sicily between May and September. *Costa Cruises* (website: www.costacruises.com) offer summer cruises from Savoa to Tunisia.
ROAD:
Theoretically, there are several points of entry by road from Algeria, normally served by buses and long-distance taxis: Annaba (in Algeria) to Tabarka (following the coast road); Souk Ahras (in Algeria) to Ghardimaou and El Oued (Algeria) to Gafsa. However, political unrest means that it is difficult for tourists to cross the border. Entry by road from Libya is via the coast road at Gabès, via Ben Gardane and Ras Ajdir.

Travel - Internal

AIR:
Tuninter runs regular services seven to eight times a day between Tunis and Djerba airports (flight time - approximately one hour). There is a daily flight to Sfax from Tunis Tuesday to Friday, with two flights on Monday. There are flights to Tozeur on most weekdays. Tuninter is represented internationally by *Tunis Air* (tel: (020) 7734 7644). Prices are reasonable and services are normally heavily subscribed, so it is advisable to book ahead.
SEA:
Ferries operate between Sfax and the Kerkennah Islands twice daily, and between Jorf and Jerba Island regularly during the day.
RAIL:
Regular trains (run by SNCFT) connect Tunis with major towns. The main route is between Tunis and Gabès, via Sousse, Sfax and Gafsa. It is essential to purchase a ticket before boarding the train or double the fare may be charged. Several daily trains run on each route, many with air-conditioned accommodation and a buffet. The superb views of the Selja Gorge can be seen from the *Lezard Rouge* (Red Lizard), a restored old-fashioned train that runs daily between Metaloui and Redeyef. It is highly advisable to book in advance, if possible, especially for the more popular air-conditioned routes.
ROAD:
Tunisia has an extensive road network. In case of breakdown, the *Garde Nationale* (National Guard) will assist free of charge (they usually contact the nearest garage). Traffic drives on the right. **Bus:** The green and yellow coloured national buses, run by SNTRI,

are air conditioned and travel daily to most towns across the country. Other services include the intercity buses which are cheap and reasonably comfortable. The destination is written in French and Arabic on the front of the bus. Passengers are allowed 10kg of luggage without additional charge. Each piece of luggage must, however, be registered. **Taxi:** Long-distance taxis (usually large Mercedes or similar), called *louages*, are authorised to carry five passengers. They have no fixed schedule and leave their respective departure points when full. They serve the whole of Tunisia. This is the quickest form of public road transport. There are many *louage* stations and prices are similar to those of buses and trains. **Car hire:** This can be very expensive. To rent a self-drive car, the driver must be over 21 years of age. A full driving licence, which has been valid for at least one year, is acceptable. **Speed limits:** 50kph (30mph) in towns; 110kph (60mph) on major highways. **Documentation:** Log books, valid national driving licences and insurance are essential. Both the AA and RAC are affiliated to the National Automobile Club (NACT) based in Tunis. Insurance valid for up to 21 days can be purchased at the border.
Note: For safety reasons, it is forbidden to drive a car in the Sahara without first contacting the National Guard post at the nearest town, giving the planned itinerary and the expected point of exit from the area. Full provisions, a suitable vehicle and an experienced guide are necessary for any travel in the Sahara.

URBAN:
A suburban train line (TGM) links Tunis with the northern suburbs. Tunis and Sousse also have a modern and convenient tram system (*métro léger*). **Taxi:** Within Tunis and other cities, city taxis are numbered and have meters. The price on the meter is what you should pay. There is a 50 per cent surcharge on night fares. **Bicycle:** Bicycles and motorcycles are available for hire in most major towns and do not require a licence.
Travel times: The following chart gives approximate travel times (in hours and minutes) from **Tunis** to other major cities/towns in Tunisia.

	Air	Road	Rail
Monastir	0.35	3.00	3.00
Sfax	0.50	4.00	4.00
Djerba	0.60	7.00	-
Tozeur	1.10	6.00	-

Note: Travellers to Port el Kantaoui are advised to take the train to Sousse, and travel the remaining 7km (4 miles) by taxi. For Monastir they should change in Sousse for the Metro Leger. For Jerba, they should take the train to Gabès and then the shuttle-bus.

Travel Advice

Most visits to Tunisia are trouble-free, but you should be aware of a high threat from terrorism. There was a serious attack on a synagogue in Djerba in 2002, for which Al Qaeda claimed responsibility.
There is little violent crime, but visitors should watch out for petty criminals such as pickpockets, particularly in crowded market places.
This advice is based on information provided by the Foreign and Commonwealth Office in the UK. It is correct at time of publishing. As the situation can change rapidly, visitors are advised to contact the following organisations for the latest travel advice:

British Foreign and Commonwealth Office
Tel: (0845) 850 2829.
Website: www.fco.gov.uk

US Department of State
Website: http://travel.state.gov/travel

Accommodation

HOTELS:
Tunisia has several vacation villages within each area. There is a luxury resort in Tabarka which hosts the International Coral Festival of Underwater Photography. Hotel accommodation is classified by a star system ranging from deluxe (**5-star**) to clean but simple (**1-star**).

MARHALAS:
Marhalas are converted caravanserais and often consist of several connected underground houses (in *Matmata* and *Ksars* - ancient granaries), where sleeping quarters and communal bathing and toilet facilities have been installed. They also have their own simple, but clean and adequate, restaurants. There are *Marhalas* at Houmt Souk, Nefta and Kairouan.

CAMPING/CARAVANNING:
Tents can be pitched or trailers parked on beaches and in parks with permission from the property owner or from the nearest police or National Guard station. The major campsites are *Le Moulin Bleu* (Blue Mill) at Hammam-Plage, 20km (12 miles) from Tunis; *L'Auberge des Jasmins* (Jasmin Inn) at Nabeul, 65km (40 miles) from Tunis, equipped with showers, wash-basins, toilets, hot and cold running water, shop, restaurant and outdoor theatre in an orange grove; *L'Idéal Camping* at Hammamet, 60km (35 miles) from Tunis, with restaurant facilities; *Sonia Camping & Caravan Site* at Zarzis, 505km (313 miles) from Tunis; and *The Youth Centre of Gabès*, 404km (251 miles) from Tunis (summer only).

Credit: ©The Tunisian National Tourist Office/www.fotoseeker.com

YOUTH HOSTELS:
Available at Djerba, Hammamet, Nabeul and Monastir. Youth Hostels are open to all young people who are members of the *International Youth Hostel Association*. It is recommended to make reservations well in advance, especially for groups. For details, contact the Tunisian National Tourist Office (see *Top Things To Do*).

Top Things To See

- Tunisia's main appeal, aside from its seaside resorts, is based on its many historical monuments, which reflect the Punic, Roman, Byzantine and Islamic influences. **Tunis**, the capital, is dominated by the **Zitouna Mosque**, which is accessible to non-Moslems. The **Bardo Museum** (website: www.di.com.tn/museebardo) is a major tourist attraction, housing one of the world's greatest collections of Roman mosaics. Situated in a former palace belonging to the Husaynid beys who ruled Tunisia in the 18th and 19th centuries, the museum includes archaeological treasures from the Carthaginian, Roman, early Christian and Islamic eras. Another popular museum - the **National Museum of Carthage** - is located on the outskirts of the city near the airport.
- Don't miss the country's leading site of interest: founded by the Phoenicians in 814 BC, **Carthage** thrived as a maritime centre and later became the third-largest city in the Roman Empire before being destroyed by the Arabs in AD 692.
- **Bizerte** has been a major port since Phoenician times when it was known as Hippo Zarytus. Under French rule in the late 19th century, it became a naval base and has remained Tunisia's biggest military centre ever since. At the heart of the town is the picturesque **Vieux Port** (**Old Port**), surrounded by shops and cafes and usually dotted with dozens of multi-coloured fishing boats. The **Kasbah** dates mainly from the 17th century. Within its walls is a mini-town of narrow, winding alleys. • Known as the Garden of Tunisia, the **Cap Bon** peninsula combines sleepy villages, rolling green fields and vineyards with the biggest and most cosmopolitan resort in the country.
- **El Haouaria** is best-known for its annual June **falconry festival**. On the outskirts of the village, opposite the island of **Zembra**, is a spectacular series of Roman caves. Nearby, **Les Grottes des Chauves-Souris** are home to thousands of bats.
- **Monastir**'s most impressive landmark is the golden-domed **Bourguiba Mosque** - final resting place of the founder of modern-day Tunisia and its first president, Habib Bourguiba. The town's **Ribat** supposedly dates from the eighth century but it has been restored so many times that little of the original structure is left.
- Within the **medina** at **Kairouan**, there are more than 50 mosques, the **Great Mosque** of **Sidi Oqba** being the star attraction. Originally constructed in AD 671, the existing building was built by the Aghlabids in AD 863.
- For Tunisia's best preserved Roman ruins, take an excursion to **Dougga**, which enjoys a lofty setting 96km (60 miles) southwest of Tunis. Formerly known as Thugga under the Numidian King Massinissa in the second century BC, under Roman rule, Dougga had a population of up to 10,000.
- Some 8km (5 miles) north of Kelibia are the remarkable remains of **Kerkouane**, a Punic town. Destroyed in 236 BC, it was unearthed in 1952 and is listed by UNESCO as a World Heritage Site.
- Spend a day in **Sousse**, Tunisia's third-largest city, 8km (5 miles) south of **Port El Kantaoui**. Sousse was one of the Phoenicians' great coastal cities but it fell to Arab invaders in the seventh century. In AD 790, the foundations of a new city were laid and several remnants of that time still remain, including the **Great Mosque** and its **Ribat** - one of a chain of fortresses which stretched along the Mediterranean coast.

Top Things To Do

- Follow the stars to the sands. Tunisia's desert near **Tozeur** has featured in numerous films, most notably in The English Patient and Star Wars. An increasing number of tour operators now offer **desert safaris** to the locations where these famous blockbuster movies were shot.
- Go **desert trekking** from **Douz**, either by camel or in 4-wheel-drive vehicles. Anyone planning a desert safari needs to inform the National Guard and ensure their vehicle is equipped with a full tool kit and handbook, spare tyres, fuel and water, a compass and emergency rations. It is also advisable to hire a local driver.
- Experience the wilderness: the focal point of Tunisia's desert tourism industry, **Chott El Jerid** is one of a series of large salt lakes which lie lifeless in summer but fill during the winter to create inland seas.
- Pamper yourself. There are about 100 **hot-spring spas** throughout Tunisia - mostly in the north of the country. Many of the spas have been used for this purpose since Roman and Punic times.
- Take a stroll along the bustling trading street of **Rue Djamaa Ez-Zitouna** in Tunis, or practise your haggling skills in the 13th-century **Souk el Attarine** (the perfume-makers' market), which still sells scents and oils.
- Play a round of **golf** - there are excellent courses at **Port el Kantaoui** near Sousse, **Monastir**, **Tabarka**, **Carthage** at Tunis, **Tozeur** and **Djerba Hammamet**. Players of all abilities will find very high-quality facilities.
- Tunisia's clear waters, coral beds and diverse sea life make it a popular destination for **scuba diving**. **Tabarka Yachting Club** and the **International Diving Centre** at **Port el Kantaoui** are prime venues.
- Cross the causeway or take a ferry to the island of **Djerba**. **Houmt Souk**, the main town, means 'marketplace' and this remains the town's primary purpose although it also benefits from tourism.
- Cross from the coast near the city of **Sfax** to **Kerkennah**, which makes a pleasant day trip, and for those seeking to get away from it all, it is also worth considering staying several days.
- If the beach appeals, head for **Mahdia**, one of Tunisia's newest tourist towns, which has been expanding rapidly since the creation of a tourist zone 5km (3 miles) west of the town centre. It is where the best beaches can be found.

TOURIST INFORMATION

Tunisian National Tourist Office in the UK
77A Wigmore Street, London W1U 1QF, UK
Tel: (020) 7224 5561 *or* 5598 (press).
Website: www.cometotunisia.co.uk

Entertainment

FOOD & DRINK: Tunisian food is well prepared and delicious. Tunisian dishes are cooked with olive oil, spiced with aniseed, coriander, cumin, caraway, cinnamon or saffron and flavoured with mint, orange blossom or rose

Credit: ©Nigel Tansley

water. Restaurants catering for tourists tend to serve rather bland dishes and 'international' cuisine, and visitors are advised to try the smaller restaurants. Prices vary enormously, and higher prices do not necessarily mean better meals. Tunis and the main cities also have French, Italian and other international restaurants. Self-service may sometimes be found but table service is more common. Moorish cafes, with their traditional decor, serve excellent Turkish coffee.

Things to know: Although Tunisia is an Islamic country, alcohol is not prohibited. Tunisia produces a range of excellent table wines, sparkling wines, beers, aperitifs and local liqueurs.

National specialities:
• *Dorado* (bream).
• Couscous.
• *Tajine* (a fish dish).
• *Brik* or *brik à l'oeuf* (egg and a tasty filling fried in an envelope of pastry).

National drinks:
• Mint tea with pine nuts.
• *Boukha* (wine, distilled from figs).
• *Thibarine* (wine).

Tipping: 10 per cent for all services.

NIGHTLIFE: In Tunisia, the theatre season lasts from October to June when local and foreign (especially French) companies put on productions and concerts. International groups appear at the *Tunis Theatre* and in the towns of Hammamet and Sousse. There are numerous cinemas in the larger cities. There are nightclubs in the major tourist resorts and at most beach hotels, as well as in the big city hotels. Belly dancing is a common cabaret feature and lively local bands often play traditional music. Casinos are also availabe in Tunis, Yasmine, Hammamet, Sousse and Djerba.

SHOPPING: Special purchases include copperware (engraved trays, ashtrays and other utensils); articles sculpted in olive wood; leather goods (wallets, purses, handbags); clothing (kaftans, jelabas, burnuses); pottery and ceramics; dolls in traditional dress; beautiful embroidery; fine silverware and enamelled jewellery. Among the most valuable of Tunisia's products are carpets. The two major types are woven (non-pile) and knotted (pile). The quality of all carpets is strictly controlled by the National Handicrafts Office, so be sure to check the ONA seal before buying.

Shopping hours: Mon-Sat 0730-1330 and 1500-1900 (summer); Mon-Sat 0900-1200 and 1500-1900 (winter).

Weekly markets: A source of good purchases are the markets which are set up on certain days in many Tunisian towns and villages. All the products of the region are displayed, including handicrafts, farm produce and secondhand goods. Haggling is expected and shopkeepers are pro-active in attracting your custom. There are ONA workshops and stores throughout the country where visitors can buy items at fixed prices. ONA stores make a reduction of 10 per cent on the price of goods purchased in foreign currency. No duty is payable on articles up to £900 in value which are shipped to EU countries, only if accompanied by an EUR1 form. Visitors who make a purchase of more than TND5, anywhere in Tunisia, should ask for a sales slip and keep all sales slips, along with bank receipts for any currency exchanged, for customs inspection.

Business

• **GDP**: US$70.8 billion.
• **Main exports**: Textiles, mechanical goods, phosphates, chemicals, hydrocarbons and agricultural products.
• **Main imports**: Textiles, chemicals and foodstuff.
• **Main trade partners**: France, Italy, Spain and Germany.

ECONOMY: Tunisia lacks the vast natural resources of its North African neighbours, but careful and successful economic management has brought the country reasonable prosperity. Annual GDP growth is just over 5 per cent and current inflation is 4.1 per cent. Only unemployment at 13.8 per cent is a cause for concern. Agriculture and mining are the foundations of the economy. The main agricultural products are wheat, barley, olive oil, wine and fruit, but other foodstuffs have to be imported. Large quantities of phosphate ores are mined along with iron, lead, aluminium fluoride and zinc. Tunisia is also a modest oil exporter, although this industry is in decline; natural gas reserves are likely to last longer. There is a small manufacturing sector involved in processing organic chemicals derived from petroleum and purification of phosphate ore. Other industries produce textiles, construction materials, machinery, chemicals, paper and wood. Tourism dominates the service sector, though the industry is sensitive both to the regional political climate and, more recently, international terrorism: the latter in particular has led to a recent downturn. According to the most recent figures, over five million people visited the country in 2002, contributing nearly US$2 billion to the Tunisian economy.
Government economic policy during the last decade has followed the path of deregulation, including abolition of trade controls, privatisation and making the Tunisian Dinar fully convertible. Tunisia's most important trade links are with the EU whose members (principally France and Germany) account for three-quarters of all the country's trade. Economic relations were strengthened during 1995 by the signing of a free trade agreement with the EU, which is being introduced over a 12-year period ending in 2010. This is similar in content to the association agreements signed by would-be members. Although a considerable diplomatic coup for the Tunisian Government, the agreement was part of a wider trend of growing trade links between the southern part of the EU and the rest of the Mediterranean basin. Tunisia is a member of the Union of the Arab Maghreb, the main North African political and economic bloc, and of various pan-Arab economic organisations.

BUSINESS ETIQUETTE: Arabic and French are the most widely used languages in business circles and a knowledge of either is useful. Interpreter services are available. Appointments are required. **Office hours:** Mon-Fri 0830-1300 and 1500-1745 (winter); Mon-Sat 0830-1300 (summer). Government office opening hours may vary by half an hour.

COMMERCIAL INFORMATION

Agence de Promotion de l'Industrie (API)
63 rue de Syrie, 1002 Tunis, Tunisia
Tel: (71) 792 144.
Website: www.tunisieindustrie.nat.tn

Chambre de Commerce et d'Industrie de Tunis
1 rue des Entrepreneurs, 1000 Tunis, Tunisia
Tel: (71) 359 300.
E-mail: ccitunis@planet.tn

Credit: ©The Tunisian National Tourist Office/www.fotoseeker.com

Turkey

Location: Southeastern Europe/Asia Minor.

Time: GMT + 2 (GMT + 3 from last Sunday in March to Saturday before last Sunday in October).

Overview

Knocking at Europe's door yet on the threshold of Asia, Turkey is truly a land of contrasts. Here you can scale the icy heights of remote Mount Ararat in search of Noah's Ark, cross the historic Euphrates and Tigris rivers, follow in the footsteps of St Paul or simply relax on the golden Mediterranean sands of Patara beach. Vibrant Istanbul, straddling the blue waters of the Bosphorus separating Europe from Asia, beckons with its skyline pierced by countless minarets, chaotic bazaars and a history redolent with harem intrigue and despotic Sultans.

In Turkey, you can also cruise along more than 1000km (620 miles) of Mediterranean coastline, past secluded coves, rocky headlands and pretty fishing villages, or explore a hinterland rich in the wonderfully preserved remains of Graeco-Roman cities such as Ephesus. For the adventurous, the austere beauty of the Anatolian plateau, the surreal rock-chimney landscape of Cappadocia and the atmospheric ruins of the enigmatic Hittites await discovery. Here, too, is the unique experience of watching the dervishes whirl in pious Konya.

With a code of hospitality nurtured by their Islamic beliefs yet with a remarkable tolerance of other customs, the Turks offer a warm welcome wherever you travel – be it sipping sweet black tea or thick coffee with friendly villagers or sharing a bottle of *raki* over *mezes* (hors d'oeuvres) with cosmopolitan Istanbul 'city slickers'.

The modern Republic of Turkey was established in the 1920s by nationalist leader Kemal Ataturk. His ambition and achievement was to transform Turkey into a modern, secular state, and his legacy of political secularism was guarded throughout the 20th century by the powerful Turkish military, which has intervened in national politics whenever it has deemed the country's stability to be at risk. In recent years, however, as Ankara has set its sights firmly on European Union membership, the military has kept a lower profile in public life.

Turkey became an official EU candidate country in 1999, whereupon it initiated a series of important human rights and economic reforms in accordance with EU requirements. The death penalty was done away with, tougher measures against torture were introduced and the penal code was revised. There were also important reforms in the areas of women's rights and Kurdish culture, language education and broadcasting. Membership talks with the EU started in 2005. Both culturally and politically, Turkey is a fascinating society - a modern, westernised country, with a largely Muslim population, cautiously spanning the divide between religions and cultures.

General Information

AREA: 779,452 sq km (300,948 sq miles).
POPULATION: 73.3 million (UN estimate 2005).
POPULATION DENSITY: 94.04 per sq km.
CAPITAL: Ankara. **Population:** 3.5 million (2005 estimate).
GEOGRAPHY: Turkey borders the Black Sea and Georgia and Armenia to the northeast, Iran to the east, Iraq to the southeast, the Syrian Arab Republic and the Mediterranean to the south, the Aegean Sea to the west and Greece and Bulgaria to the northwest. Asia Minor (or Anatolia) accounts for 97 per cent of the country and forms a long, wide peninsula 1650km (1025 miles) from east to west and 650km (400 miles) from north to south. Two east-west mountain ranges, the Black Sea Mountains in the north and the Taurus in the south, enclose the central Anatolian plateau, but converge in a vast mountainous region in the far east of the country. It is here that the ancient Tigris and Euphrates rivers rise.
GOVERNMENT: Republic since 1923. **Head of State:** President Ahmet Necdet Sezer since 2000. **Head of Government:** Prime Minister Recep Tayyip Erdogan since 2002. **Recent history:** After a period of economic crisis in 2001 nearly brought Turkey's economy to collapse, the country agreed a recovery programme with the IMF in 2002 and has since made good progress, with impressive economic growth and decreased inflation. The conservative and Islamist-based Justice and Development Party (AKP) won the General Elections in 2002 and had its domestic position consolidated when it won 42 per cent of the vote in local elections in 2004. Recep Tayyip Erdogan has been Prime Minister since 2002, and although his party has Islamist roots, Mr Erdogan insists that it is committed to secularism. He sees EU entry as a top priority and introduced reforms which paved the way for the opening of membership talks in October 2005. Accession negotiations are expected to take about 10 years. In November 2003, Turkey suffered four major terrorist attacks which targeted two synagogues, the British Consulate-General and the HSBC bank, all in Istanbul. In summer 2004, Kurdish secessionists called off a five-year ceasefire following what they called annihilation operations against their fighters by the Turkish authorities. There have since been clashes between Kurdish fighters and Turkish forces in the south-east.
LANGUAGE: Turkish. Kurdish is also spoken by a minority in the southeast. French, German and English are widely spoken in cities and tourist areas.
RELIGION: Muslim with a small Christian minority. Turkey is a secular state which guarantees complete freedom of worship to non-Muslims.
ELECTRICITY: 220 volts AC, 50Hz.
SOCIAL CONVENTIONS: Shaking hands is the normal form of greeting. Hospitality is very important and visitors should respect Islamic customs. Informal wear is acceptable, but beachwear should be confined to the beach or poolside. Smoking is widely acceptable but prohibited in cinemas, theatres, city buses and *dolmuses* (collective taxis).

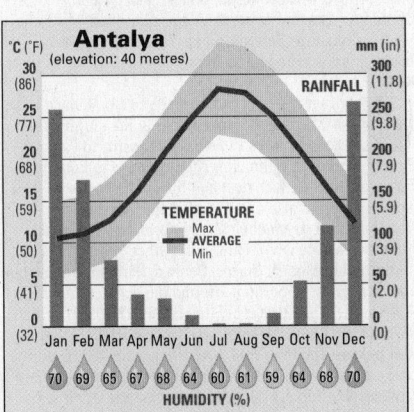

Antalya (elevation: 40 metres)

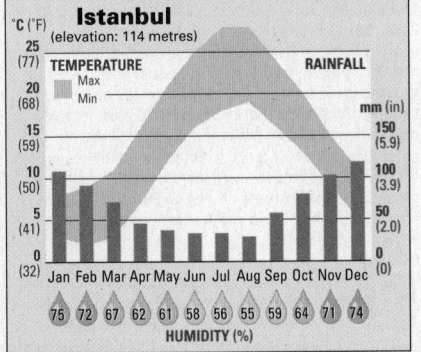

Istanbul (elevation: 114 metres)

Climate

Temperatures in Ankara vary between -4°C (25°F) and 30°C (86°F). Marmara and the Aegean and Mediterranean coasts have a typical Mediterranean climate with hot summers and mild winters.
Required clothing: Light- to medium-weights and rainwear.

Communications

Telephone: Country code: 90. The cheapest way to make calls is from PTT telephone booths, which are found in all areas. Telephone cards are available for these.
Mobile telephone: Roaming agreements exist with international mobile phone companies. Coverage is mostly good, but can be patchy in some rural areas.
Internet: Internet cafes exist in main urban areas.
Post: Turkish post offices are recognisable by their yellow *PTT* signs. Post office hours: major outlets Mon-Sat 0800-2400, Sun 0900-1900; smaller post offices have the same opening hours as Government offices.
MEDIA: *Turkish Radio and Television* (TRT), the state broadcaster, runs four national television networks as well as a number of radio stations. Competing with TRT are around 300 private TV stations and over 1000 private radio stations. Although some of the most repressive sanctions have been lifted to enable Turkey to meet EU entry requirements, there are still reports from independent international observers of journalists being imprisoned, or attacked by police. Kurdish-language broadcasts have been introduced in order to meet EU criteria on minorities.
Press: The main newspapers are *Hürriyet*, *Milliyet*, *Sabah* and *Zamam*. English-language daily newspapers include *The Turkish Daily News*.
TV: Four state-run channels are operated by TRT. Private channels include *Kanal D, Show TV and Star TV. CNN Türk* is the Turkish channel of news network CNN.
Radio: TRT stations include *TRT 1* (cultural and educational), *TRT 3* (popular music) and *TRT 4* (folk and classical music). *Show Radyo* and *Capital Radio* are commercial stations, while *Radyo Foreks* broadcasts news.

Passport/Visa

	Passport Required?	Visa Required?	Return Ticket Required?
Full British	Yes	4	Yes
Australian	Yes	4	Yes
Canadian	Yes	4	Yes
USA	Yes	4	Yes
Other EU	1	2/4/5	Yes
Japanese	Yes	3	Yes

Note: Regulations and requirements may be subject to change at short notice, and you are advised to contact the appropriate diplomatic or consular authority before finalising travel arrangements. Any numbers in the chart refer to the footnotes below.

PASSPORTS: Passport valid for at least six months from date of arrival in Turkey required by all, except the following nationals:
1. Belgium, France, Germany, Greece, Italy, Liechtenstein, Luxembourg, Malta, The Netherlands, Spain and Switzerland, who can enter with a national ID card (which must have a validity of one year).
VISAS: Required by all except the following:
(a) **2.** nationals of EU countries for stays of up to three months (except those listed under notes **4** and **5** below in *Sticker-type entry visas*);
(b) **3.** nationals of Argentina, Bolivia, Brazil, Bulgaria* (see *Note* below), Chile, Ecuador, El Salvador, Guatemala, Honduras, Hong Kong (SAR), Iceland, Iran (providing they have a minimun of US$100 per day while entering Turkey), Israel, Japan, Korea (Rep), Liechtenstein, Malaysia, Monaco, Morocco, New Zealand, Nicaragua, San Marino, Singapore, Switzerland, Trinidad & Tobago, Tunisia, Turkish Republic of Northern Cyprus, Uruguay and Vatican City for stays of up to three months;
(c) nationals of Bosnia & Herzegovina, Croatia and Macedonia (Former Yugoslav Republic) for stays of up to two months;
(d) nationals of Costa Rica, Kazakhstan, Kyrgyzstan and Macau (SAR) for stays of up to one month;
(e) transit passengers continuing their journey by the same of first connecting aircraft within 24 hours, provided not leaving the airport and in possession of confirmed onward tickets. If you travel by sea or land via Turkey, you will need a visa. The procedure is the same as for a tourist visa.
Note: (a) Visa exemption for Bulgarians does not apply to those who enter Turkey through certain custom points (contact Consulate for details). Bulgarians must always obtain a visa for transit passages.
Sticker-type entry visas: Tourists and business visitors from the following countries *do* require visas and can obtain a sticker-type entry visa at the point of entry for a fee. Prices are dependent on nationality (for British nationals, the cost is £10 [£36 if obtained prior to arrival], and for US nationals, the cost is US$45):

(a) **4.** Armenia, Australia, Austria, Azerbaijan, Belarus, Belgium, Canada, Estonia, Hungary, Ireland, Italy, Jordan, Latvia, Lithuania, Malta, Moldova, The Netherlands, Norway, Poland, Portugal, Russian Federation, Serbia & Montenegro, Slovak Republic, Spain, Tajikistan, Turkmenistan, Ukraine and the UK* (see *Note* below) and USA for stays not exceeding three months;
(b) Albania for stays not exceeding two months;
(b) **5.** Greek Cypriot Administrative Region and Romania for stays not exceeding one month;
(c) Georgia for stays not exceeding 15 days (providing they have a minimun of US$50 per day while entering Turkey).
Note: British National Overseas passport holders should contact the visa section of the Consulate General before travelling.
Types of visa and cost: Prices vary according to nationality. *Tourist* (multiple-entry, up to three months): £36. *Single transit* (up to three months): £27. *Study* (up to one year): £72. *Work* (up to one year): £75. Some visas must be obtained in advance. Contact the Consulate (or Consular section at Embassy); see *Passport/Visa Information*.
Validity: Multiple entry: three months, two years or five years.
Application to: Consulate (or Consular section at Embassy); see *Passport/Visa Information*. Applicants must now pre-book an appointment with the relevant Consulate. An online appointment system is available (website: www.turkishconsulate.org.uk/en/visa).
Application requirements: (a) Valid passport. (b) One recent passport-size photo. (c) Application form. (d) Latest bank statement and photocopy. (e) Fee (varies for different nationals), payable by postal order, company cheque and cash only. (f) £5 administrative fee. (g) Registered, pre-paid, self-addressed, special delivery envelope if applying by post. (h) Sufficient funds (exact amount required varies according to nationality).
Note: Application requirements may vary according to nationality and type of visa sought.
Working days required: Usually three, but dependent on nationality of applicant. Some applications may be referred to the Ministry of Foreign Affairs in Ankara, which may take much longer (minimum six to eight weeks).
Temporary residence: Apply to the Turkish Consulate General (see *Passport/Visa Information*) or to the Turkish Diplomatic Mission in the country of residence.

PASSPORT/VISA INFORMATION

Embassy of the Republic of Turkey in the UK
43 Belgrave Square, London SW1X 8PA, UK
Tel: (020) 7393 0202.
Website: www.turkishembassylondon.org
Opening Hours: Mon-Fri 0900-1730.

Turkish Consulate General in the UK
Rutland Lodge, Rutland Gardens,
London SW7 1BW, UK
Tel: (020) 7591 6900 *or* (09068) 347 348 (recorded visa information; calls cost 60p per minute).
Website: www.turkishconsulate.org.uk
Opening hours: Mon-Fri 0900-1230 (visas).

Embassy of the Republic of Turkey in the USA
2525 Massachusetts Avenue, NW,
Washington, DC 20008, USA
Tel: (202) 612 6700 *or* 6740 (consular section).
Website: www.turkishembassy.org

Money

Currency: The New Turkish Lira (TRY) was introduced on January 1 2005. The old Turkish Lira (TL) was withdrawn from circulation on January 1 2006. It is now only possible to exchange old Turkish Lira for New Turkish Lira at the Central Bank until December 31 2015. 1TRY = 1,000,000TL. Notes are in denominations of TRY100, 50, 20, 10, 5 and 1. Coins are in denominations of TRY1 and 50, 25, 10, 5 and 1 New Kuruº (Ykr).
Currency exchange: Cash can usually be exchanged commission free in bureaux de change, banks or hotels. Traveller's cheques can only be exchanged in banks. ATMs are available in most areas. Travellers planning to exchange currency back before leaving Turkey, or making a major purchase which may need to be declared to customs, must retain transaction receipts to prove that the currency was legally exchanged.
Credit & debit cards: American Express, Diners Club, MasterCard and Visa are accepted. Check with your credit or debit card company for details of merchant acceptability and other services which may be available.
Traveller's cheques: Traveller's cheques can only be exchanged in banks. To avoid additional exchange rate charges, travellers are advised to take traveller's cheques in Pounds Sterling or US Dollars.
Currency restrictions: There are no restrictions on the import of local or foreign currency, though visitors bringing in a large amount of foreign currency should declare it, and have it specified in their passport upon arrival to avoid

difficulties on departure. No more than the equivalent of US$5000 in local or foreign currency may be exported. It must be shown that this has been obtained from authorised banks.

Banking hours: Mon-Fri 0830-1200 and 1330-1700. Some banks in tourist areas are open daily.

Exchange rate indicators:

Rate at time of publishing

£1.00=	TRY2.39
$1.00=	TRY1.35

Duty Free

The following goods may be imported into Turkey without incurring customs duty:

200 cigarettes and 50 cigars or 200g of tobacco and 200 cigarette papers or 50g of chewing tobacco or 200g of pipe tobacco or 200g of snuff tobacco* (see Note below); five bottles (1l) or seven bottles (700ml) of wine and/or spirits; reasonable amounts of coffee and tea; five bottles (up to 120ml each) of perfume; gifts up to a value of €255.65 (or equivalent); electronic articles up to a value of €255.65 (or equivalent).

Note: (a)* A further 400 cigarettes, 100 cigars and 500g of pipe tobacco may be imported if purchased on arrival at a duty free shop. (b) Very specific amounts and categories of personal belongings may be imported duty free, according to a list available from the Turkish Embassy, Financial and Customs Counsellor's Office.

Prohibited imports: Narcotics, sharp implements, weapons and more than one set of cards.

Restricted exports: (a) The export of souvenirs such as carpets is subject to customs regulations regarding age and value. (b) The export of antiques is forbidden, according to a list available from the Turkish Embassy, Finance and Customs Counsellor's Office. (c) Minerals may only be exported under licence from the General Directorate of Mining Exploration & Research.

Public Holidays

Below are listed Public Holidays for the January 2006-June 2007 period.

2006: Jan 1 New Year's Day. **Jan 9-13** (9th is a half-day holiday for the public sector) Kurban Bayrami (Feast of the Sacrifice). **Apr 23** National Sovereignty and Children's Day. **May 19** Commemoration of Atatürk and Youth and Sports Day. **Aug 30** Victory Day. **Oct 22-24** (22nd is a half-day holiday for the public sector) Ramazan Bayrami (End of Ramadan). **Oct 28-29** (28th is a half-day) Republic Day. **30 Dec 2006-3 Jan 2007** (30th is a half-day holiday for the public sector) Kurban Bayrami (Feast of the Sacrifice). **2007: Jan 1** New Year's Day. **Apr 23** National Sovereignty and Children's Day. **May 19** Commemoration of Atatürk and Youth and Sports Day.

Note: Muslim festivals are timed according to local sightings of various phases of the moon and the dates given above are approximations. During the lunar month of Ramadan that precedes Ramazan Bayrami, Muslims fast during the day and feast at night and normal business patterns may be interrupted. Some restaurants are closed during the day and there may be restrictions on smoking and drinking. Generally, centres of tourism are unaffected. Some disruption may continue into Ramazan Bayrami itself. Ramazan Bayrami and Kurban Bayrami may last anything from two to 10 days, depending on the region. For more information, see the *World of Islam* appendix.

Health

	Special Precautions?	Certificate Required?
Yellow Fever	No	No
Cholera	No	No
Typhoid & Polio	1	N/A
Malaria	2	N/A

Note: *Regulations and requirements may be subject to change at short notice, and you are advised to contact your doctor well in advance of your intended date of departure. Any numbers in the chart refer to the footnotes below.*

1: Outbreaks of *typhoid* may occur in rural areas.

2: Potential *malaria* risk (exclusively in the benign *vivax* form) exists from May to the end of October in the Çukorova/Amikova areas and in southeast Anatolia, Adana and Antalya (Side). There is no malaria risk in the main tourist areas in the west and southwest of the country.

Food & drink: Mains water is usually chlorinated in larger towns and cities, but should not be assumed to have been so treated: if used for drinking or making ice it should have first been boiled or otherwise sterilised. If a water source bears the words *içilmez*, it means that it is not for drinking; sources labelled *içilir, içme suyu* or *içilebilir* are safe to drink. Bottled spring water is widely available. Milk is pasteurised. Eat only well-cooked meat and fish, preferably served hot.

Other risks: *Hepatitis A, B* and *C* are present. *Cutaneous* and *visceral leishmaniasis, meningitis* and *TB* occur. The first cases of the human form of *avian flu* were reported in Turkey in early 2006. See *Travel Advice.* *Rabies* is present. For those at high risk, vaccination before arrival should be considered. If you are bitten, seek medical advice without delay. For more information, see the *Health* appendix.

Health care: Turkey has a large health sector. A great number of Turkish doctors and dentists speak a foreign language, particularly at major hospitals. Private health insurance is recommended; ensure that it covers Asiatic as well as European Turkey.

Travel - International

AIR:

The national airline is *Turkish Airlines (TK)* (website: www.turkishairlines.com).

Approximate flight times: From Istanbul to *Frankfurt/M* is three hours five minutes, to *London* is four hours and to *New York* is 11 hours 15 minutes.

Main airports: *Ankara (ESB)* (Esenboga) is 35km (22 miles) northeast of the city. *To/from the airport:* Havas buses (website: www.havas.net) go from the city centre to the airport every 30 minutes between 0430-2400 and leave the airport after flight arrivals (travel time - 45 minutes). There is a taxi service available into the city. *Facilities:* Duty free shops, bank/bureau de change, and restaurants and bars. *Istanbul (IST)* (Atatürk, formerly Yesilkoy) is 24km (15 miles) west of the city (travel time - 30 to 50 minutes). *To/from the airport:* A Havas coach travels to and from the airport and the city centre at 0500, then every 30 minutes between 0600-2300. There are taxi services to the city. *Facilities:* Duty free shops, bank/bureau de change, bar, restaurant, and car hire.

Izmir (IZM) (Adnan Menderes). *To/from the airport:* Havas buses meet domestic flights and travel from the city centre once an hour on the hour. *Facilities:* Bank/bureau de change, bar and restaurant.

Sabiha Gökçen (SAW) is 40km (25 miles) from Istanbul, on the Asian side. *To/from the airport:* There are shuttle bus services to the city (travel time - 30 to 45 minutes) and to Atatürk International Airport (travel time - 60 to 70 minutes). Taxis are available 24 hours a day. *Facilities:* Duty free shops, bank, ATMs, business centre and restaurants/cafes.

There are other international airports at *Adana, Antalya, Dalaman* and *Trabzon.*

Departure tax: US$50 is levied only on Turkish nationals, not resident overseas departing from Turkey.

SEA:

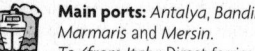

Main ports: *Antalya, Bandirma, Istanbul, Izmir, Marmaris* and *Mersin.*

To/from Italy: Direct ferries operate in the summer between Ancona-Cesme and Brindisi-Cesme (website: www.marmaralines.com or www.mesline.com). There are currently no direct ferries between Venice and Turkey; passengers must travel via Greece and the Greek Islands. *To/from Cyprus:* Three routes exist on which sea buses, together with car and passenger ferries, operate: Alanya-Girne, Tasucu-Girne, Gazimagusa-Mersin. *To/from Greece:* There are privately operated ferry lines between Turkey and the Greek islands: Lesbos-Ayvalik, Chios-Cesme, Samos-Kusadasi, Cos-Bodrum, Rhodes-Bodrum, Rhodes-Marmaris and Rhodes-Fethiye. Cos-Bodrum is the only winter car ferry route. *To/from Ukraine:* Ferries operate between Odessa-Istanbul (website: www.ukrferry.com).

Note: All ships, including private yachts, arriving in Turkish waters must go to one of the following ports of entry: Akcay, Alanya, Anamur, Antalya, Ayvalik, Bandirma, Bodrum, Botas (Adana), Canakkale, Cesme, Datca, Derince, Didim, Dikili, Fethiye, Finike, Giresun, Güllük, Hopa (Artvin), Iskenderun, Istanbul, Izmir, Kas, Kemer, Kusadasi, Marmaris, Mersin, Ordu, Rize, Samsun, Sinop, Söke, Tasucu (Silifke), Tekirdag, Trabzon and Zonguldak.

RAIL:

Train journeys can be made to Istanbul via some of the major European cities. The journey from London takes three days: *Eurostar* to Paris, *Orient Express* to Vienna (overnight), *Avala* to Budapest, overnight *Ister* to Bucharest and finally the *Bosfor* to Istanbul. There is also a less comfortable couchette car from Budapest to Istanbul. More information is available from the website www.seat61.com. Other international rail routes go to Bulgaria, Greece, Georgia, Germany and Serbia and Montenegro. For more information contact *Turkish Railways (TCDD)* in Istanbul (tel: (212) 527 0050/1 *or* 520 6575 (reservations); website: www.tcdd.gov.tr).

Rail passes: The *Inter-Rail* pass offers unlimited second-class train travel in up to 29 European countries (includes Morocco and Turkey) split into eight zones (A-H). Three different tickets are available: a ticket covering one zone (two to six countries, 16 days' validity), a ticket covering two zones (six to 10 countries, 22 days' validity) and an *All Zone Pass* (29 countries, one month's validity). Ferry services between Italy and Greece are included. Passengers must be resident in Europe for at least six months before the pass is used. Travel is not allowed in the passenger's country of residence. Travellers under 26 years receive a reduction of about 30 per cent. Children's tickets are reduced by about 50 per cent. Supplements are required for some high-speed services, seat reservations and couchettes. Discounts are offered on *Eurostar* and some ferry routes. Available from *Inter Rail* (website: www.interrailnet.com).

ROAD:

There are roads from Bulgaria, the CIS, Greece and Iran. From London, drivers may either choose the northern route of Belgium-Germany-Austria-Hungary-Romania-Bulgaria, or the southern route through

Credit: ©Bruce Logan

Belgium-Austria-Italy with a car-ferry connection to Turkey.
Coach: There are regular services between Turkey and Austria, France, Germany, Greece and Switzerland, as well as Jordan, Iran, Saudi Arabia and the Syrian Arab Republic. It is possible to travel by coach from London to Istanbul, changing in Frankfurt (travel time - approximately 70 hours). Tickets are available from *National Express* (tel: (08705) 808 080; www.nationalexpress.com).

Travel - Internal

Note: Road conditions and driving standards in Turkey can be poor. Serious road accidents are common. All visitors should be extra careful when travelling around Turkey's road network.

AIR:

Turkish Airlines (tel: (020) 7766 9300 (UK office); website: www.turkishairlines.com) provides an important network of internal flights from Istanbul, Ankara, Adana, Antalya, Dalaman, Izmir and Trabzon to all of the major Turkish cities.

SEA:

A frequent car ferry crosses the Dardenelles at Gallipoli, from Canakkale to Eceabat and Gelibolu to Lapseki. *Istanbul Fast Ferries* (tel: (212) 444 3436; website: www.ido.com.tr) operates frequent seabus services from Bostanci, Kadiköy, Kartal, Yalova and Büyükada Island to Auça, Bakirköy, Karaköy and Yenikapi. *Turkish Maritime Lines* used to operate the Black Sea service and the Istanbul-Izmir route, but the company recently went out of business. It is hoped a new operator will take over the routes.

RAIL:

Many trains of the *Turkish Railways (TCDD)* (website: www.tcdd.gov.tr) have sleeping cars, couchettes and restaurant cars. Some are now air-conditioned. Fares are comparatively low, but are more expensive for express trains. Discounts of 20 per cent are available for students (though a Turkish student card may be required), groups, round-trips and passengers over 60. Children aged seven and under travel free. Tickets can be purchased at *TCDD* offices at railway stations and *TCDD*-appointed agents. The journey from Istanbul to Ankara takes five to nine hours, depending on the type of train.

ROAD:

There is currently huge investment in road building. Traffic drives on the right. In case of an accident, contact the Turkish Touring and Automobile Club (*Turkiye Turing ve Otomobil Kurumu*), 1 Oto Sanayi Sitesi Yani, 4 Levent, Istanbul (tel: (212) 282 8140; website: www.turing.org.tr). **Coach:** Many private companies provide frequent day and night services between all Turkish cities. Services are often faster than trains and competition between operators has led to lower fares. Tickets are sold at the bus or coach companies' branch offices either at stations or in town centres. One should shop around for the best prices. Coaches depart from the bus stations (*otogar*) in large towns and from the town centre in small towns. **Car hire:** Both chauffeur-driven and self-drive cars are available in all large towns. All international companies are represented. **Documentation:** An International Driving Permit is required for visits of over three months. Green Card International Insurance, endorsed for Turkish territory in both Europe and Asia, and Turkish third-party insurance (obtainable from insurance agencies at frontier posts) are also required. Cars can be brought into Turkey for a maximum of six months in one year. On entering, an entry-exit form is filled out. For longer stays, it is necessary to apply to either the Ministry of Finance and Customs or the Turkish Touring and Automobile Club.

URBAN:

Bus and trolleybus: Extensive conventional bus (and some trolleybus) services operate in Istanbul, Ankara and Izmir. There are buses in all other large towns. These are generally reliable, modern and easy to use. Tickets are bought in advance from kiosks and dropped into a box by the driver. **Taxi:** There are many types of taxi, share-taxi and minibus in operation. Taxis are numerous in all Turkish cities and towns and are recognisable by their chequered black and yellow bands. Metered taxis are available. For longer journeys, the fare should be agreed beforehand. A *dolmus* is a collective taxi which follows specific routes and is recognisable by its yellow band. Each passenger pays according to the distance travelled to specific stops. The fares are fixed by the municipality. The *dolmus* provides services within large cities to suburbs, airports and often to neighbouring towns. This is a very practical means of transport and much cheaper than a taxi. Taxis may turn into a *dolmus* and vice versa according to demand. **Ferry:** There are extensive cross-Bosphorus and short-hop ferries between the parts of Istanbul. **Metro:** Ankara has a two-line metro system. Further expansion is planned.
Travel times: The following chart gives approximate travel times (in hours and minutes) from **Ankara** to other major cities/towns in Turkey.

	Air	Road	Rail
Istanbul	0.45	6.00	7.00
Izmir	0.50	7.00	10.00
Antalya	1.00	8.00	-
Erzurum	1.15	11.00	18.00

Travel Advice

There is a high threat from terrorism in Turkey. International terrorist groups, as well as indigenous ones, are believed to be currently active in Turkey. Further attacks, including in tourist areas, could well occur. On 16 July 2005, an explosion on a minibus in the western Turkish resort of Kusadasi killed five people. On 11 July 2005, an explosion in the coastal resort of Cesme, western Turkey, injured 20 people.
Four people have died from H5N1 avian influenza in Turkey since December 2005. Others have been treated for the virus. Outbreaks of avian influenza in poultry have occurred across Turkey, including in Istanbul, Ankara and the Aegean coast region. As a precaution, visitors should avoid live animal markets, poultry farms and other places where they may come into contact with domestic, caged or wild birds; and ensure that poultry and egg dishes are thoroughly cooked.
This advice is based on information provided by the Foreign and Commonwealth Office in the UK. It is correct at time of publishing. As the situation can change rapidly, visitors are advised to contact the following organisations for the latest travel advice:

British Foreign and Commonwealth Office
Tel: (0845) 850 2829.
Website: www.fco.gov.uk

US Department of State
Website: http://travel.state.gov/travel

Accommodation

EDITOR'S CHOICE: CAPPADOCIAN CAVE HOTELS/INNS

The early Christians sought refuge in the caves of Cappadocia, living and worshipping underground. Some of these cave dwellings have now been converted into hotels with all the mod cons: air conditioning, heating and private bathrooms.

HOTELS:

In recent years, Turkey has made a considerable effort to develop its hotel facilities. **Grading:** Hotels registered with the Ministry of Tourism are graded from **1 star** (1 *yildizli*) to **5 stars** (5 *yildizli*). Classification is based on the standard of service and facilities. Motels and holiday villas are **first class** (1 *sinif*) or **second class** (2 *sinif*). There are other establishments registered with local authorities, and these too correspond to a certain standard in regard to facilities and services. There is also a national hotel association: TUROB (see *Accommodation Information* below).

GUEST HOUSES:

Guest houses (pensions) can be found in holiday resorts and major towns.

SELF-CATERING:

Villas and apartments can be rented, especially on the Aegean and Mediterranean coasts.

CAMPING/CARAVANNING:

There are numerous sites, but facilities are generally limited.

YOUTH HOSTELS:

There are a number of excellent youth hostels in Turkey. The *Yücelt Interyouth Hostel* in Istanbul (see *Accommodation Information*) is a member of Hostelling International.

ACCOMMODATION INFORMATION

TUROB (Touristic Hotels and Investors Association)
Cumhuriyet Cad. Pak Apt. Kat 6 D: 12, Harbiye (Divan Oteli Yani), 33437 Sisli-Istanbul, Turkey
Tel: (212) 296 2464.
Website: www.turob.org

Yücelt Interyouth Hostel
Caferiye Sok No 6/1, Sultanahmet, Istanbul 34400, Turkey
Tel: (212) 513 6150/1.
Website: www.yucelthostel.com

Top Things To See

- Discover **Istanbul**, the only city in the world to span two continents and a bustling, cosmopolitan place officially founded by Emperor Constantine in AD 326 on the back of a much older village. The capital of the Byzantine and Ottoman empires right up until 1923, its illustrious past has left a rich legacy of mosques, churches, museums and magnificent palaces, coupled with bustling bazaars and a vibrant street life. Istanbul is made up of three distinct cities. Head for the **old city** of Istanbul with its parks and gardens. Amongst hundreds of fascinating sights, the main attractions include **Topkapi**, the sumptuous palace of the Ottoman sultans overlooking the Sea of Marmara and the Bosphorus; the delicately decorated **Blue Mosque**, the only mosque in the world with six minarets; the vast dome of **Aya Sophia**, built in 536 as a Byzantine cathedral, later a mosque and now a museum and, underground, the **Yerebatan Sarayi**, a vast Byzantine cistern supported by 336 Corinthian columns. Nearby, the commercial heart of the city, the **Grand Bazaar**, is still a captivating sight for shoppers and window-shoppers alike, while further along the narrow inlet of the **Golden Horn**, the **Kariye Camii** has some of the finest Byzantine mosaics to survive today. Cross the Golden Horn to **Beyoglu**, 'modern' Istanbul, which dates back to the foreign cantonments of the 13th century. This is where you find the restaurants, hotels, and modern shops, while the truly modern areas around **Taksim** are home to cultural centres, exhibition halls and office blocks.
- Experience the historically and symbolically significant **Bosphorous**, the narrow strait that divides Europe from Asia. Two massive suspension bridges now span these overcrowded waters, in which tour boats, ferries, supertankers and fishing vessels vie for space. From all of them you see the Istanbul skyline, one of the most dramatic in the world. Tours up the Bosphorous include several notable buildings, including the Sultans' 19th-century **Dolmabahçe Palace**. On the far, Asian shores lie **Uskudar** (**Scutari**), where Florence Nightingale nursed the wounded during the Crimean War; the charming Ottoman summer palace of **Beylerbeyi**; and a whole series of delightful villages full of fish restaurants and fine old mansions, built by the 19th-century aristocracy. Looming at each other across the water are several Byzantine and Ottoman castles, including **Anadoluhisar** and **Rumelihisar**.
- Explore the **Dardanelles**, the narrow straits leading through to the Mediterranean. This was the site of the infamous Gallipoli landings during World War I, which led to the deaths of nearly 250,000 British, Turkish and Anzac troops and shot Turkish General Mustafa Kemal (later known as Ataturk) to fame. Inland, the cities of **Edirne**, in Thrace, and **Bursa**, in Marmara, are both fascinating historic towns with a wide range of magnificent architecture, such as the **Selimiye Camii** in Edirne, said to be the masterwork of Turkish imperial architect Mimar Sinan. Make a short trip south from Gallipoli and discover the ruins of ancient **Troy**. Of the nine levels of the excavated settlement mound, the sixth is supposed to be the Troy depicted in Homer's Iliad.
- **Izmir**, the birthplace of Homer, is Turkey's third city and an important port on the Aegean coast. It is a modern metropolis set in a curving bay surrounded by terraced hillsides. As a result of earthquakes and a great fire, there are only a few reminders of **old Smyrna - Kadifekale**, the fourth-century fortress situated on top of Mount Pagos. The fortress affords a superb view of the city, and of the **Gulf of Izmir**, the **Roman agora** with some well-preserved porticos and Statues of Poseidon and Artemis.
- Take in the grandeur of the remains of the Hellenistic and Roman city of **Ephesus** (modern **Selçuk**). Alleged to have been founded in the 13th century BC, it has been carefully restored and is now one of the most spectacular ancient cities in the world. Top sights within the huge archaeological area include the **Grand Theatre**, where St Paul preached to the Ephesians, the second-century **Temple of Serapi**, the elegant façades of the **Temple of Hadrian** and the **Library of Celsus**. Also visit the site of **Meryemana**, reputed to be the house of the Virgin Mary and located very close to Ephesus in the small vale of **Mount Bulbul Dagi (Nightingale Mountain)**.
- Visit **Bodrum** (birthplace of Herodotus, known as the father of history), one of the finest resorts on the South Agean coast. Dominating the town from its position between the two harbours is the magnificent 15th-century Crusader **Castle of St Peter**. It now houses a fascinating **Museum of Underwater Archaeology**. Another Bodrum attraction is the **Mausoleum of Halicarnassus**, the crumbling remains of one of the Seven Wonders of the Ancient World.
- Experience the charm of **Antalya**, the popular resort situated on a cliff promontory on the Western Mediterranean coast. It boasts a picturesque walled **old town** and **harbour**, **Kaleiçi**, the monumental **Hadrian's Gate**, **Kesik Minare** and **Yivli Minare** mosques and **Hidirlik Kulesi**, the round Roman tower, and a superb **Archaeological Museum**. Admire Turkey's finest Roman **aqueduct** north of the city.
- Head for the prosperous city of **Adana** in the middle of the flat **Cukurova plain**. It is the centre of Turkey's cotton

industry and home to an imposingly huge modern **mosque**. The massive **Taskopru Bridge**, built by Hadrian in the second century, the **ancient covered bazaar** and nearby **Crusader castles** and **Hittite settlements** are all interesting sites.
- The historic town of **Safranbolu**, a short distance inland from the Black Sea Coast, is a UNESCO World Heritage site and renowned for its traditional Ottoman architecture. Explore the **30 mosques**, **180 fountains** and **15 bridges** in the area.

Credit: ©Bruce Logan

- Visit the spectacular 14th-century **Monastery of the Black Virgin** at **Sumala**, 54km (34 miles) from Trabzon. It is set into the face of a sheer cliff, 300m (1000ft) above the valley floor, and contains some magnificent **frescoes**.
- Travel south from Ankara, past the vast **salt lake** of **Tuz Gölü**, to **Konya**, a former Selçuk capital and one of the great religious centres of Turkey. The town is home to the **Mevlana Tekkesi**, the **monastery** and **mausoleum of Mevlana Celâddin Rumi**, one of Islam's most celebrated mystics and founder of the Order of Whirling Dervishes. Explore the 13th-century **Alâeddin Mosque**, the **Karatay Medrese** (now an excellent **Ceramics and Tile Museum**) and the **Iplikci Mosque**, Konya's oldest structure. South of the city, **Catalhöyük** is the second-oldest town in the world, dating back to the sixth millennium BC.
- A visit to **Cappadocia**, southeast of Ankara, is a must. Marvel at the spectacular, almost surreal landscape of rock and cones, capped pinnacles and fretted ravines where dwellings have been hewn from the soft, volcanic rock since 400 BC and the elaborate cave systems have sheltered generations of persecuted settlers. Check out the impressive UNESCO-listed **Göreme** national park in Cappadocia, with over 30 magnificently **frescoed Byzantine rock churches** open to the public. There are over 400 **underground cities** in the area; two of the biggest and most exciting are **Kaymakli** and **Derinkuyu**, with up to eight floors and complex systems of apartments, public rooms and streets that could house literally hundreds of people.

Top Things To Do

- Go **skiing**. Turkey may not be the obvious ski destination, but it does have a number of winter sports resorts, generally located up in its forested mountains. The core season is from January to March. The following ski centres are easily accessible by road or Turkish Airlines domestic flights: **Erciyes**: 25km (15 miles) from Kayseri (Cappadocia); **Koroglu**: on the Istanbul-Ankara highway, 50km (30 miles) from Bolu and the Black Sea coast; **Palandoken**: 5km (4 miles) from Erzurum (central-eastern Anatolia); **Saklikent**: 48km (30 miles) north of Antalya, in the Bakirli Dagi mountain range (Mediterranean Coast); **Sarikamis**: near Kars (far eastern Anatolia); **Uludag**: 36km (22 miles) south of Bursa (Marmara).
- Turkey is great for **mountaineering**, containing a number of mountain ranges with peaks ranging from heights of 3250m (10,660ft) to the 5165m (16,945ft) of **Mount Agri** (**Ararat**), the highest mountain in Anatolia, which provide excellent climbing possibilities for both novice and expert climbers. Make sure you get the required permission from the Turkish Mountaineering Club.
- Enjoy your favourite watersport in the Mediterranean. The coast, particularly **Izmir**, has very warm waters and the watersports on offer are virtually unlimited, from plain **swimming** and **diving** to **windsurfing**, **water skiing**, **sailing** and beyond.
- Turkey's vast interior of unspoilt nature, mountains, plateaux, villages and ancient ruins is perfect for exploring on foot. Try the long-distance footpath, the **Lycian Way**, which stretches for 500 kilometres between Fethiye and Antalya providing a month's walking through some of Turkey's most spectacular scenery.
- It is not very well known, but Turkey has some excellent rivers for **whitewater rafting**, one of which is rated by professional rafters as one of the top ten in the world, the **Coruh River**. Rivers that are commercially rafted in Turkey include the **Dalaman River**, the **Köprü River**, the **Coruh River**, and the **Zamanti River**.
- Take a **boat trip** on the **Aegean Sea** in a *gulet*, a traditional and locally produced wooden ship.
- Have a **Turkish bath**. A visit to one of Turkey's historical *hamams*, for instance, is likely to be a memorable experience. In Istanbul, the most popular are the historic **Galatasaray Hamam** in **Beyoglu** and **Cagaloglu Hamam** in **Sultanahmet**, though local baths are often just as good.
- Catch a ceremony by the renowned **Whirling Dervishes**, the members of the Mevlevi Order performing the famous whirling dance (*Sema*). It is an amazing ceremony, reflecting how all life revolves, and can be seen in Konya, where the Order originated, or in Istanbul.
- There are currently five championship **golf courses** in Turkey. One of them is at the **Klassis** resort close to Istanbul; the other four are in the resort of **Belek** in the Antalya region.
- Have a bath in the mineral waters at **Pamukkale**. The Romans considered the site sacred for its magic healing waters, and the spa has been used for its therapeutic powers ever since. Pamukkale was the capital of Phrygia during the reign of Constantin the Great, and later become the bishops' centre during the Byzantine Period. Roman architecture dominates the city. It is cited on the list of World Heritage of UNESCO. It also contains the ruins of the Roman city of **Hierapolis**.
- Attend the **Aspendos International Opera and Ballet Festival** in June and July, during which the city's remarkable second-century AD amphitheatre is used for the various performances.

TOURIST INFORMATION

Turkish Culture and Tourism Office in the UK
4th Floor, 29-30 St James's Street,
London SW1A 1HB, UK
Tel: (020) 7839 7778.
Website: www.gototurkey.co.uk

Turkish Tourist Office in the USA
821 UN Plaza, New York, NY 10017, USA
Tel: (212) 687 2194.
Website: www.tourismturkey.org

Entertainment

FOOD & DRINK: Turkish food combines culinary traditions of a pastoral people originating from Central Asia and the influences of the Mediterranean regions. Guests are usually able to go into a kitchen and choose from the pots if they cannot understand the names of the dishes.
Things to know: Turkey is a secular state and alcohol is permitted, although during Ramadan it is considered polite for the visitor to avoid drinking alcohol.
National specialities:
- *Shish kebab* (pieces of meat threaded on a skewer and grilled).
- *Doner kebab* (pieces of lamb packed tightly round a revolving spit).
- *Barbunya* (red mullet) and *kiliç baligi* (swordfish).
- *Dolma* (vine leaves stuffed with nuts and currants).
- *Karniyarik* (aubergine stuffed with minced meat).
- *Turkish Delight* (originally made from dates, honey, roses and jasmine bound by Arabic gum and designed to sweeten the breath after coffee).

National drinks:
- *Raki* (anisette), known as 'lion's milk', which clouds when water is added. Drinking *raki* is a ritual and is traditionally accompanied by a variety of *meze* (hors d'oeuvres).
- *Ayran* (a refreshing yoghurt drink).
- Tea.
- Strong black Turkish coffee.
- Turkish beer, red and white wines.

Tipping: A service charge is included in hotel and restaurant bills.
NIGHTLIFE: There are nightclubs in most main centres, either Western or Oriental, with music and dancing. There are theatres with concerts in Ankara, Istanbul and Izmir and most towns have cinemas. Turkish baths (*hamam*) are popular.
SHOPPING: Istanbul's *Kapali Carsi Bazaar* has jewellery, carpets and antiques for sale. Turkish handicrafts include a rich variety of textiles and embroideries, articles of copper, onyx and tile, mother-of-pearl, inlaid articles, leather and suede products, jewellery and, above all, carpets and *kilims*.
Shopping hours: Daily 0930-1900 in tourist areas. Closing hours vary, with some shops staying open until midnight. Outside tourist areas shops may close at lunchtime and on Sundays. Istanbul covered market: Mon-Sat 0800-1900 (closed Sunday).

Business

- **GDP:** US$356.7 billion.
- **Main exports:** Clothing and textiles, road vehicles, iron and steel, electrical machinery and fruit and vegetables.
- **Main imports:** Machinery, appliances and parts, mineral fuels and oil, road vehicles, iron and steel products and plastics and products.
- **Main trade partners:** Exports to: Germany, UK and USA. Imports from: Germany, Russia and Italy.

ECONOMY: Turkey is self-sufficient in basic foodstuffs including maize, sugar, wheat and barley. Cotton, tobacco, fruit, vegetables and nuts are grown for both domestic consumption and export. A variety of livestock is reared. The agricultural sector still accounts for around 12 per cent of total economic output and is a major employer, especially of women in the workforce, 60 per cent of whom work on the land. There is a sizeable mining industry producing copper, chromium, borax and, to a lesser extent, bauxite and coal. Manufacturing and services are the most important sectors. Manufacturing has grown significantly, in particular the production of textiles and clothing, road vehicles and electronic goods.
The service sector too has seen steady growth. Tourism dominates this sector and is the second biggest revenue earner in the country.
Economic performance between 1998 and 2002 was poor with negative GDP growth during most of the period (9 per cent during 2001), while inflation was between 40 and 65 per cent. There was improvement in 2003, when inflation was cut to near 20 per cent, and in 2004, when it was cut to 10 per cent. Growth of about five per cent is predicted for 2005 and 2006. Unemployment has remained steady at just over 10 per cent since 2002. Relations with the international financial community have been difficult. Successive governments have agreed reform programmes based on the usual diet of deregulation and privatisation. However, political instability has undermined Government attempts to sell utilities and key industries (including banking and food-processing). Turkey has long harboured an aspiration to join the European Union, having lodged its original application in 1963. Poor economic management, the unresolved situation in Cyprus, perennial disputes with Greece and a bad human-rights record have combined to thwart any prospect of EU membership in the past. However, official EU membership talks finally began in October 2005. Europe has increasing influence over the country; Turkish trade patterns have shifted from the Middle East in favour of Europe, and hundreds of thousands of Turkish workers are employed across the EU.
BUSINESS ETIQUETTE: A formal suit or jacket and tie should always be worn for business. English is widely spoken in business circles, although an effort by the visitor to speak a little Turkish is appreciated. The majority of people in business value punctuality and visiting cards are widely used.
Office hours: Mon-Fri 0830-1200 and 1330-1730.
Summer: In the Aegean and Mediterranean regions of Turkey, government offices and many other establishments are closed during the afternoon in the summer months. The summer hours are fixed each year by the provincial Governors.
CONFERENCES/CONVENTIONS: Istanbul and Antalya are the most popular venues, followed by Ankara, Marmaris and Bodrum. There are many 4- and 5-star hotels, which provide facilities and can host conferences and meetings to international standards. The *Crowne Plaza Istanbul* has a conference centre with facilities for up to 1000 people.

COMMERCIAL INFORMATION

Union of Chambers and Commodity Exchanges of Turkey
TOBB Atatürk Bulvari, 149 Bakanliklar 06640,
Ankara, Turkey
Tel: (312) 413 8000.
Website: www.tobb.org.tr

Istanbul Convention and Exhibition Centre
Harbiye 80230, Istanbul, Turkey
Tel: (212) 296 3055.
Website: www.icec.org

Crowne Plaza Istanbul (Information on Conferences/Conventions)
Tel: (212) 560 8110.
Website: http://istanbul.crowneplaza.com

A B C D E F G H I J K L M N O P Q R S T U V W X Y Z

Turkmenistan

Location: Central Asia.

Time: GMT + 5.

Overview

The territory of what is now Turkmenistan provided the bedrock for many of the most powerful empires of their age. The Parthians, the Seljuks and the Khans of Khoresm all based their empires at various points on the edge of the Kara-Kum Desert, while Alexander the Great conquered the region during his epic campaign of the fourth century BC. The influence of Islam dates from the seventh century AD, when the region was under Arab control. Modern-day Turkmen are descended from tribes that migrated to the area in the 10th century from the northeast.

Turkmenistan's harsh desert conditions and terrain mean that tourism has been relatively undeveloped. Another reason is that since independence from the Soviet Union in 1991, the country has remained largely closed to the outside world under the rule of President Niyazov. It is effectively a one-party state, governed by Niyazov's Democratic Party of Turkmenistan, which comprises mostly former communists. Although the country benefits from from its oil and gas deposits, its economy remains underdeveloped due to the low presence of foreign investors.

Almost all the attractions lie around the fringes of the desert and in ancient ruins such as Merv (now Mary). The capital, Ashgabat, is a modern city. It replaced the one founded in 1881, which was destroyed in an earthquake in 1948. The Sunday market here is the best place to buy Turkmen carpets. Mary, due east of Ashgabat, is Turkmenistan's second city and lies near the remains of Merv, which was once the second city of Islam until Ghengis Khan's son Toloi reduced it to rubble in 1221.

General Information

AREA: 488,100 sq km (188,456 sq miles).

POPULATION: 5 million (UN estimate 2005).

POPULATION DENSITY: 10.2 per sq km.

CAPITAL: Ashgabat. **Population:** 605,000 (official estimate 1999).

GEOGRAPHY: Turkmenistan shares borders with Kazakhstan to the north, Uzbekistan to the east, Afghanistan to the southeast and Iran to the south. To the west is the Caspian Sea. Nearly 80 per cent of the country is taken up by the Kara-Kum (Black Sand) Desert, the largest in the CIS. The longest irrigation canal in the world stretches 1100km (687 miles), from the Amu-Darya River in the east, through Ashgabat, before being piped the rest of the way to the Caspian Sea.

GOVERNMENT: Republic. Gained independence from the Soviet Union in 1991. **Head of State and Government:**

President Saparmyrat Niyazov (Türkmenbashy) since 1992.

Recent history: The current President has acquired the honorific title of *Türkmenbashy* – leader of all Turkmen – which conveys something of a spiritual, as well as political, leader. In 1999, he was made President for life. 'Türkmenbashy' has evolved a cult of personality to rival any in the world – it has reportedly extended to renaming calendar months in honour of him and assorted relatives. Opposition has been quickly and brutally suppressed, especially in the wake of a reported assassination attempt against Niyazov in late 2002. This peculiar and unpleasant regime is tolerated by the international community for two main reasons – the country's strategic position and its enormous (and, as yet, largely undeveloped) reserves of oil, gas and precious metals.

LANGUAGE: Turkmen is the official state language, and is closer to Turkish, Azeri and Crimean Tartar than those of its neighbours Uzbekistan and Kazakhstan. The Turkmen script was changed from Latin to Cyrillic in 1940, but the process of changing back to the Turkish version of the Latin script is underway.

RELIGION: Predominantly Sunni Muslim with a small Russian Orthodox minority. Turkmenistan shares the Central Asian Sufi tradition.

ELECTRICITY: 220 volts AC, 50Hz. Round two-pin continental plugs are standard.

SOCIAL CONVENTIONS: *Lipioshka* (bread) should never be laid upside down, and it is normal to remove shoes, but not socks, when entering someone's house. Shorts are rarely seen in Turkmenistan and, if worn by females, are likely to provoke unwelcome attention from the local male population.

Climate

Turkmenistan has an extreme continental climate: temperatures in Ashgabat vary between 46°C (114°F) in summer and -5°C (23°F) in winter, although it has been known to reach -22°C (-8°F) in extremity. Temperatures in the desert in summer can reach 50°C (122°F) during the day before falling rapidly at night. During the winter, it can reach -10° to -15°C (14° to 15°F).

Required clothing: For those intending to visit the desert in summer, lightweights are vital for the day with warmer clothing for those intending to spend the night in the open. Heavyweights should be taken for winter visits.

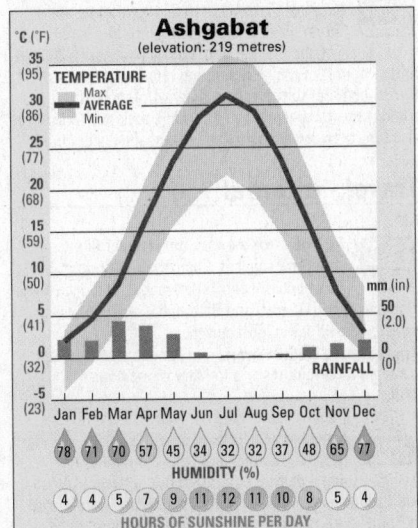

Communications

Telephone: Country code: 993. Area code for Ashgabat: 12.

Mobile telephone: Roaming agreements exist with some international mobile phone companies. Coverage is limited to Ashgabat.

Internet: All Internet cafes were closed by the Government. The state strictly controls Internet access.

Post: Letters to Western Europe and the USA can take between two weeks and two months. Stamped envelopes can be bought from post offices. Mail addresses should be laid out in the following order: country, postcode, city, street, house number and lastly the person's name. Post office hours: Mon-Fri 0900-1800. The main Post Office in Ashgabat is open until 1900.

MEDIA: Turkmenistan has an incredibly poor record when it comes to press freedom. Reporters Without Frontiers has said the President uses the media solely to 'promote his own glory'. The Turkmen Government controls all media, monitoring media outlets, operating printing presses and laying down editorial policies. Programmes from Russian TV stations are censored. The Government controls Internet access, banning or censoring what it considers inappropriate sites and restricting use.

Press: The main newspapers in Ashgabat are *Turkmenistan* and *Vatan* (both in Turkmen) and *Neitralnyi Turkmenistan* (Russian).

TV: State-owned *Turkmen TV* operates four channels.

Radio: Two stations are operated by state-owned *Turkmen radio*.

Passport/Visa

	Passport Required?	Visa Required?	Return Ticket Required?
Full British	Yes	Yes	No
Australian	Yes	Yes	No
Canadian	Yes	Yes	No
USA	Yes	Yes	No
Other EU	Yes	Yes	No
Japanese	Yes	Yes	No

Note: *Regulations and requirements may be subject to change at short notice, and you are advised to contact the appropriate diplomatic or consular authority before finalising travel arrangements. Any numbers in the chart refer to the footnotes below.*

Note: Visa regulations within the CIS are liable to change at short notice. Prospective travellers are advised to contact the nearest Turkmenistan Embassy well in advance of intended date of departure.

PASSPORTS: Valid passport required by all.

VISAS: Visa required by all.

Note: Special permission must be sought by those wishing to visit border zones.

Types of visa and cost: Dependent upon nationality and duration of stay, contact the Embassy for details of prices (see *Passport/Visa Information*).

Validity: Subject to the nature of the visit and the discretion of the authorities in Turkmenistan.

Application to: Consulate (or Consular section at Embassy); see *Passport/Visa Information*.

Note: a) For those coming from countries without Embassies or Consulates of Turkmenistan, entry visas may be obtained for a maximum of 10 days on arrival, provided holding an invitation from a company in Turkmenistan; (b) Tourists should normally book through a recognised tour operator, who will obtain visas on their behalf; (c) Visitors intending to stay for more than three months must produce a certificate stating that they are HIV-negative.

Application requirements: (a) Two completed application forms; (b) Two passport-size photos; (c) Passport with at least one blank page, valid for six months from date of departure from Turkmenistan; (d) Covering letter explaining purpose of visit; (e) Fee; (f) Stamped, self-addressed envelope; (g) Letter of invitation approved by the Ministry of Foreign Affairs in Turkmenistan (not needed by visitors seeking a transit visa only).

Working days required: Three to seven.

Temporary residence: Applications for temporary residence to carry out business are handled by the Interior Ministry; those wishing to obtain temporary residence for other reasons should apply to the Consular Affairs Office at the Foreign Ministry.

PASSPORT/VISA INFORMATION

Embassy of Turkmenistan in the UK
2nd Floor, St George's House, 14-17 Wells Street, London W1T 3PD, UK
Tel: (020) 7255 1071.
Opening hours: Mon-Fri 1000-1800; 1000-1700 (visa section).

Embassy of Turkmenistan in the USA
2207 Massachusetts Avenue, NW, Washington, DC 20008, USA
Tel: (202) 588 1500.
Website: www.turkmenistanembassy.org

Money

Currency: Turkmen Manat (TMM) = 100 tenge. Notes are in denominations of TMM10,000, 5000, 1000, 500, 100, 50, 10, 5 and 1. Coins are in denominations of 50, 20, 10, 5 and 1 tenge.

Currency exchange: The preferred hard currency is US Dollars and visitors carrying other currencies may find it hard to change them. It is advisable to take new, clean US Dollar notes in small denominations. Foreign currency can be changed at banks and major hotels. Foreigners are expected to pay all travel and hotel bills in hard currency, and prices bear little relation to what locals are expected to pay. Most packages are all-inclusive and extra payment for accommodation and meals is unnecessary.

Credit & debit cards: Not generally accepted.

Traveller's cheques: Should be in US currency, but are generally not accepted.

A B C D E F G H I J K L M N O P Q R S T U V W X Y Z

Currency restrictions: The import and export of local currency is prohibited for foreigners. Import of foreign currency is unlimited subject to declaration, and export is limited to the amount declared on import.
Banking hours: Mon-Fri 0930-1730.
Exchange rate indicators:
Rate at time of publishing
£1.00= TMM9185.19
$1.00= TMM5200.05

Duty Free

Import regulations in Turkmenistan are subject to change at short notice, and travellers should contact the Embassy before departure for up-to-date information.
The following goods may be imported into Turkmenistan by passengers aged 16 and over:
200 cigarettes or 200g of tobacco; 2l of any alcoholic beverage (passengers aged 21 and over); personal belongings up to a reasonable value.
Note: On entering the country, tourists must complete a customs declaration form which must be retained until departure. This allows the import of articles intended for personal use, including currency and valuables which must be registered on the declaration form. Customs inspection can be long and detailed. It is advisable when shopping to ask for a certificate from the shop which states that goods have been paid for in hard currency. Presentation of such certificates should speed up customs formalities.
Prohibited items: Military weapons, ammunition and narcotics may not be imported or exported. Works of art and antiques may not be exported (unless permission has been granted by the Ministry of Culture).

Public Holidays

Below are listed Public Holidays for the January 2006-June 2007 period.
2006: Jan 1 New Year's Day. **Jan 10** Kurban Bairam (Feast of the Sacrifice). **Jan 12** Remembrance Day. **Feb 18** President's Birthday. **Feb 19** National Flag Day. **Mar 8** International Women's Day. **Mar 20** Novruz Bairam (Turkmen New Year). **May 9** Victory Day. **May 18** Constitution Day. **Jun 21** Day of Election of First President. **Oct 6** Remembrance Day (Anniversary of the 1948 Earthquake). **Oct 22-24** Ramadan Bairam (End of Ramadan). **Oct 28** Independence Day. **Dec 12** Neutrality Day. **Dec 31** Kurban Bairam (Feast of the Sacrifice).
2007: Jan 1 New Year's Day. **Jan 12** Remembrance Day. **Feb 18** President's Birthday. **Feb 19** National Flag Day. **Mar 8** International Women's Day. **Mar 20** Novruz Bairam (Turkmen New Year). **May 9** Victory Day. **May 18** Constitution Day. **Jun 21** Day of Election of First President.
Note: Muslim festivals (End of Ramadan and Feast of the Sacrifice) are timed according to the phases of the moon and the dates given are approximations. For more information, see the *World of Islam* appendix.

Health

	Special Precautions?	Certificate Required?
Yellow Fever	No	No
Cholera	No	No
Typhoid & Polio	1	N/A
Malaria	2	N/A

Note: Regulations and requirements may be subject to change at short notice, and you are advised to contact your doctor well in advance of your intended date of departure. Any numbers in the chart refer to the footnotes below.

1: Vaccination against typhoid is essential. Typhoid is endemic.
2: Malaria risk exclusively in the benign (*P vivax*) form exists from June to October in some villages located in the southeastern part of the country, mainly in the Mary district.
Food & drink: All water should be regarded as a potential health risk. Water used for drinking, brushing teeth or making ice should have been boiled or otherwise sterilised. Milk is pasteurised and dairy products are safe for consumption. Only eat well-cooked meat and fish, preferably served hot. Pork, salad and mayonnaise may carry increased risk. Vegetables should be cooked and fruit peeled.
Other risks: *Diphtheria* and *tuberculosis* outbreaks are reported, and suitable precautions should be taken. *Hepatitis B* and *E* occur. *Hepatitis A* is endemic and inoculation is essential. *Plague* and *trachoma* occur rarely. Because the climate is very hot and dry, precautions should also be taken against *dehydration*. It is important to drink plenty of (boiled or bottled) water.
Rabies is present. For those at high risk, vaccination should be considered. If you are bitten, seek medical advice without delay. For more information, consult the *Health* appendix.
Health care: Medical insurance, including cover for emergency repatriation, is highly recommended. Medical facilities are poor, high levels of disease have been reported. Travellers are advised to take a well-equipped first aid kit with them containing basic medicines and any prescriptions that they may need.

Travel - International

AIR:
The national airline is *Turkmenistan Airlines (T5)*. All flight tickets bought by foreigners within Turkmenistan must be paid for in hard currency. The prices tend to be 10 times as much as those that locals pay.
Approximate flight times: From *London* to Ashbagat is six hours 30 minutes, from *Karachi* is four hours 30 minutes, from *Moscow* is three hours 30 minutes, from *Istanbul* is two hours 30 minutes, from *Abu Dhabi* is two hours, from *Tashkent* is two hours, from *Kyiv* is two hours and from *Tehran* is one hour.
Main airports: *Ashgabat Airport (ASB)* is approximately 13km (8 miles) northwest of the city centre. *To/from the airport:* The airport is served by buses and taxis.
Departure tax: US$25. Nationals of CIS countries pay US$15 and nationals of Turkmenistan pay US$5.
SEA:
There are ferries to Turkmenbashi (formerly Krasnovodsk) from Baku (Azerbaijan) and an irregular service to Astrakhan (Russian Federation). It is theoretically possible to travel from Moscow to Turkmenbashi via the Volga River and the Caspian Sea without setting foot on dry land.
RAIL:
The *Trans-Caspian Railway* connects Turkmenistan with the rest of the Central Asian republics and thence to Moscow and the rest of the CIS. The terminus is in Turkmenbashi on the Caspian Sea, from where it runs through Ashgabat before it crosses into Uzbekistan near the city of Chardzhou.
Approximate rail times: From Turkmenbashi to Tashkent is 24 hours, to Dushanbe is 36 hours and to Moscow is three days. There is a rail link to the Iranian network, enabling train travel from Turkmenistan to Turkey (Istanbul).
ROAD:
Turkmenistan is connected by road to Kazakhstan, Uzbekistan and to Mashad and Tehran in Iran. The crossing into Iran is only open to nationals of the CIS and Iran. **Bus:** Services are available to the capitals of the neighbouring republics, and north across the Kara-Kum desert to Kunya-Urgench with connections to Urgench and Khiva in Uzbekistan. A service also runs between Ashgabat and Mashhad (eastern Iran).

Travel - Internal

AIR:
Turkmenistan Airlines runs regular flights between Ashgabat, Chardzhou, Dashoguz, Mary, Turkmenbashi and Turkmenabat, and once daily flights to Kerki (far east) and Balkanabat. All flight tickets have to be paid for in local currency.
Approximate flight times: From Ashgabat to Chardzhou is one hour 30 minutes and to Mary is one hour.
RAIL:
There is a daytime and overnight train between Ashgabat and Turkmenbashi; two daily overnight trains to Turkmenabat, one continuing to Dashgouz; and a daily overnight service between Ashgabat and Gushgi via Mary (although Gushgi is off limits due to its border with Afghanistan). The *Trans-Caspian Railway* runs from Turkmenbashi (formerly Krasnovodsk) in the west, through Ashgabat and Mary to Chardzhou in the east before continuing to Bukhara in Uzbekistan.
ROAD:
Traffic drives on the right. Conditions can be dangerous. The main road in Turkmenistan runs along the route of the *Trans-Caspian Railway* (see above). There is also a road that runs north from Ashgabat to Tashauz and Kunya-Urgench before crossing into Uzbekistan. This road crosses 500km (311 miles) of the Kara-Kum desert. **Bus:** Cheap services are available within all the major towns. Modern and comfortable long-distance buses also operate to Dashgouz, Mary, Turkmenabashi and Turkmenabat from Ashgabat. **Taxi:** Taxis and chauffeur-driven cars for hire can be found in all major towns. Many are unlicensed and travellers are advised to agree the fare in advance. As many of the street names have changed since independence, it is also advisable to ascertain both the old and the new street names when asking directions.
Car hire: Self-drive hire is available from a few large hotels. Traffic regulations: Drinking and driving is strictly forbidden. **Documentation:** An International Driving Permit, or national licence with authorised translation, is required.

Travel Advice

Travellers should be aware of the global risk of indiscriminate terrorist attacks which could be against civilian targets including places frequented by foreigners. Travellers should carry an identity document at all times. Requests to produce proof of identity, for example by the police, are frequent.
Travellers should not overstay their visa. They should also register with the State Service of Turkmenistan for the Registration of Foreign Nationals if staying for more than three days.
This advice is based on information provided by the Foreign and Commonwealth Office in the UK. It is correct at time of publishing. As the situation can change rapidly, visitors are advised to contact the following organisations for the latest travel advice:

British Foreign and Commonwealth Office
Tel: (0845) 850 2829.
Website: www.fco.gov.uk

US Department of State
Website: http://travel.state.gov/travel

Accommodation

HOTELS:
There are no restrictions on where foreigners can stay in Turkmenistan. When Turkmenistan gained independence, there was an acute shortage of hotel accommodation, a situation which the Turkmen are working hard to rectify, with feverish hotel construction underway in Ashgabat. A row of luxury hotels has recently been built on the edge of town along a road known locally as the 'Miracle Mile'. These are small hotels with between 15 to 40 rooms that are owned and run by various ministries and governmental organisations. Architectural motifs are mosques, palaces and fortresses. Every provincial centre has at least one hotel, but visitors should not expect Western standards of comfort and amenities. The exception is a new hotel which recently opened in Turkmenbashi; however, as it only has 40 rooms, it is advisable to contact a recognised Turkmen tour company for a reservation. Accommodation and services in hotels are payable in local currency or US Dollars.
REST HOUSES:
Dom Otdykha (literally 'rest houses') were built on the shores of the Caspian Sea by co-operatives and other concerns for fatigued workers. It is sometimes possible for travellers to obtain accommodation in them.
CAMPING:
There are campsites on the shores of the Caspian Sea, and the facilities are gradually improving.

Top Things To See & Do

- Visit **Ashgabat**, the capital, on the southern rim of the **Kara-Kum** desert. Some of the more recent additions to the modern city include the **Arch of Neutrality**, a 75m- (246ft-) high monument with a revolving 12m- (39ft-) tall golden statue of President Niyazov at its peak. At the base of the monument, there is a cafe and lifts which can be taken to the viewing platforms. Nearby stands the magnificent white marble **Palace of Turkmenbashi**, decorated with gold-mirrored glass together with an Islamic-motif dome. There are a number of museums, including a fine-art museum and the **National Museum of Turkmenistan**. There is a small carpet museum attached to the carpet factory on Ulitsa Kuragli (formerly Piervomaiskaya), which houses the world's largest handwoven rug. The **Tolkuchka bazaar** (Sunday market) in Ashgabat is the best place anywhere to buy Turkmen carpets, mistakenly called Bukhara carpets in the West.
- Discover the remains of **Old Nisa**, the capital of the Parthian kings who ruled from the third century BC to the third century AD over an empire which included Iraq and stretched as far as the Syrian Arab Republic.
- View pure-bred **Akhal-Teke** horses at the national **Turkmenbashi Stud Farm**, which is 10km (6 miles) from Ashgabat. Trips are best organised through a local travel agency.
- See the ruins of the famous mosque (revered for its striking mosaic tiles and 8m- (26ft-) long dragons) at the modern town of **Anau**, once the site of the destroyed 15th-century city, 20km (12 miles) east of Ashgabat.
- Enjoy the natural splendour of **Chuli**, a popular mountain resort reached by taxi or private car through a picturesque gorge. Climbing and hiking trips can be arranged, and visitors can stay here.
- Take a day trip to **Bakharden**, 90km (56 miles) west of Ashgabat. The underground mineral lake (known in Turkmen as **Kov Ata** which means 'father of lakes') is

fed by hot springs and has a constant temperature of 37°C (97°F). Bathing is permitted although there is an admission fee. Accommodation is not available.

- Head east of Ashgabat to **Mary**, Turkmenistan's second city. A large industrial centre, Mary has little to recommend it other than its interesting **Regional Museum**. However, it lies near the remains of the city of **Merv**, which was once the second city of Islam and known as the 'Queen of Cities' until Ghengis Khan's son, Toloi, reduced it to rubble and reportedly killed a million of its inhabitants in 1221. The ruins of Merv and of the many that both preceded it and succeeded it are spread over a large area. Most of what remains are the brick-built mausolea of rulers and holy men - including the impressive **Mausoleum of Sultan Sanjar**, completed in 1140. Time, weather and invasions have taken their toll on the mud-built cities of the Turkmen.
- **Dashgouz** is the largest city in the northern region of Turkmenistan, on a direct train route, 500km (311 miles) from Ashgabat, across the Kara-Kum desert. Although there are a few places to stay and eat, the main sights lie outside the city. The ruins of **Konye-Urgench**, an ancient fortress town with relics dating back to the 14th century, are well worth visiting. Entry is approximately US$2, payable in Manat. Things to see include the **Kutlug Timur Minaret**, one of the tallest minarets in Asia at 67m (220ft) high and built in the 1320s; the **Sultan Tekesh**, **Turabeg Khanym** and **Najm-ed-din Kubra Mausoleums**.
- Situated to the west of Ashgabat, **Turkmenbashi** was known as Krasnovodsk, but it was renamed in honour of President Saparmurat Niyazov, who has been given the title 'Turkmenbashi' or 'leader of all the Turkmen'. Situated on the shores of the Caspian Sea, it is a Russian creation, built as a bridgehead for the campaign to subdue Central Asia, and later to become the terminal for the **Trans-Caspian Railway**. There are some panoramic views from the mountainside surrounding the town and visitors can enjoy some good beaches and swimming a little further out of town. The **Museum of Regional History and Natural History** makes an interesting visit.
- Step back in time and uncover the delights of **The Silk Road**: this ancient trading route was used by silk merchants from the second century AD until its decline in the 14th century, and is open in parts to tourists, stretching from northern China, through bleak and foreboding desert and mountainous terrain to the ports on either the Caspian or Mediterranean Sea. For further details of the route, see *The Silk Road* in the *China* section. Among the many silk route attractions worth seeing in Turkmenistan are the vibrant Sunday **Tolkuchka market** in **Ashgabat** (selling such wares as traditional carpets, camels and pistachio nuts), the historical silk road cities of **Konye-Urgench** and **Merv** (including **Kyz-Kala**, a windowless castle known locally as the 'House of the Maiden Tears' and the mausoleum of Mohammed Ibn-Zeida) and the **Kugitang Nature Reserve** which reportedly bears impressions of hundreds of dinosaur footprints. Travel along the silk road can be quite difficult due to the terrain, harsh climate and lack of developed infrastructure. Visitors to the region are advised to travel with an organised tour company or travel agent.
- Explore the countryside on **horseback**: Turkmenistan is home to the *Akhal-Teke* horse, a special breed known for its speed and intelligence. These horses occupy a special place in Turkmen culture and are a source of great national pride. An old Turkmen saying goes, 'Getting up in the morning, greet your father and then see your horse.' Rides can be arranged through local tour operators or through travel agents specialising in Turkmenistan. Rides can be done just outside Ashgabat through the gorges of the Firuza River and to the local hot springs, and in other parts of the country.
- Spend a day at the races: in spring and autumn, **horse races** are held at the **Hippodrome** in Ashgabat, and 10km (6 miles) south of Ashgabat is the **Turkmenbashi Stud Farm** where the Akhal-Teke horses are bred.

TOURIST INFORMATION

State Committee of Turkmenistan for Tourism and Sport
17 1984/Pushkin Street,
744000 Ashgabat, Turkmenistan
Tel: (12) 354 777 *or* 397 606 *or* 771 *or* 390 065 *or* 396 740.
Website: www.tourism-sport.gov.tm

Entertainment

FOOD & DRINK: Turkmen food is similar to that of the rest of Central Asia. There are a number of good Western-standard restaurants in Ashgabat, although they rarely have an extensive menu. In general, hotel food shows strong Russian influence: *borcht* is cabbage soup, *entrecôte* is a well-done steak, *cutlet* are grilled meat balls, and *strogan* is the local equivalent of beef Stroganoff. *Pirmeni*, originating in Ukraine, are small boiled dumplings of meat and vegetables similar to ravioli, sometimes served in a vegetable soup.

National specialities:
- *Plov* - pronounced 'plof' - is the staple food for everyday (but is also served at celebrations) and consists of chunks of mutton, shredded yellow turnip and rice fried in a large wok.
- *Shashlyk* (skewered chunks of mutton grilled over charcoal which come with raw sliced onions) and *lipioshka* (rounds of unleavened bread) are served in restaurants and are often sold in the street
- Manty are larger noodle dumplings filled with meat.
- *Shorpa* is a meat and vegetable soup.
- *Ka'urma* is mutton deep-fried in its own fat and *churban churpa* is mutton fat dissolved in green tea.
- *Ishkiykli* are dough balls filled with meat and onion which are traditionally cooked in sand that has been heated by a fire.
- On the shores of the Caspian Sea, seafood is often substituted for mutton in traditional dishes such as plov.
- In the west of Turkmenistan, there is a speciality in which mutton is roasted in a clay oven fired with aromatic woods.

National drinks:
- Green tea is very popular and can be obtained almost anywhere.
- Beer, wine, vodka, brandy and sparkling wine (*shampanski*) are all widely available in restaurants.
- *Kefir*, a thick drinking yoghurt, is often served with breakfast.

NIGHTLIFE: Ashgabat has an opera and ballet theatre, which shows both Russian and European works and a drama theatre. There are also a few restaurants offering dancing.

SHOPPING: The Sunday market is the best place in the world to buy the misleadingly named Bukhara rugs, which are actually made in Turkmenistan. There is a shop in the Art Gallery which sells traditional Turkmen handicrafts, silver and costumes including the distinctive Turkmen sheepskin hats. The central bazaar in Ashgabat is a good place to buy food and curiosities.
Shopping hours: Mon-Fri 0900-1800. Bazaars open at dawn.

Business

ECONOMY: Although 90 per cent of the land is occupied by the Kara-Kum desert, agriculture is important to the Turkmen economy. Substantial quantities of cotton - the country is the world's 10th-largest producer - are also produced under ecologically ruinous schemes established during the Soviet era. Grain, fruit and vegetables are widely grown and livestock breeding is an important source of employment. The other mainstay of the economy and its best prospect for the future is an abundance of oil and natural gas deposits, the scale of which rivals anything in the Persian and Mexican Gulfs. New pipelines are planned to supplement the sole existing one, which transports the products via Russia. Other commercially viable reserves include bromine, iodine salts and various other minerals. Most of Turkmenistan's industry is devoted to processing the country's principal raw materials: textiles are a key export industry and much of the extracted oil is refined within the country. Oil and gas account for 85 per cent of Turkmenistan's export income (under long-term contracts, 80 per cent of the gas goes to the Ukraine while 60 per cent of the oil is bought by Italy). As one of the poorest republics of the former Soviet Union, Turkmenistan suffered considerable economic disruption and hardship after its demise in 1991 (GDP declined by 10 per cent per year between 1993 and 1998); the increasing inability of many of its former trade partners to pay for its products has also caused serious difficulties. The Government responded by seeking out new markets. In 1992, Turkmenistan joined the IMF and the World Bank, then the European Bank for Reconstruction and Development (as a 'Country of Operation') and the Islamic Development Bank. The following year a new national currency, the Manat, was introduced. In 1996, the Government introduced an economic reform programme aimed at controlling persistent inflation and promoting foreign investment, especially in the oil and gas sector. This has met with some success; inflation is now 11.6 per cent, while current annual GDP growth is 12 per cent. The government has also concentrated resources in developing Turkmenistan's previously poor infrastructure, especially the road network. Some aspects of the reform programme have been delayed, including land reform in which the major role was to be assumed by the private sector. Turkmenistan is a member of the Economic Co-operation Organisation, which brings together the former republics of the southern Soviet Union with Romania, Bulgaria, Albania, Greece and Turkey.

BUSINESS ETIQUETTE: The Government is particularly interested in encouraging foreign investment in a number of areas, including oil and gas production and refining; agricultural production and processing (particularly in cotton); consumer goods; export-orientated products; research and development; environmental protection and infrastructure. The Turkmen government has put a number of measures in place to encourage foreign investment. Free Enterprise Economic Zones - one in each of the eight *velayat* (regions) - have been created with special incentives for companies that invest in them. These include: no import duties, a three-year tax holiday from the start of production, with a further 13 years of reduced taxes; full-profit repatriation and a swifter licensing procedure. Concerns which are 100 per cent foreign owned must be sited in Free Enterprise Economic Zones, but joint ventures may be set up anywhere. All foreign investments are protected by government guarantee from expropriation. All foreign companies and individuals wishing to invest in Turkmenistan must go through the Commission for International Economic Affairs of the Office of the President of Turkmenistan. Business is conducted formally and smart dress is required. **Office hours:** Mon-Fri 0900-1800.

COMMERCIAL INFORMATION

Chamber of Commerce and Industry
B Karryev Street 17, Ashgabat 744000, Turkmenistan
Tel: (12) 354 717 *or* 355 594.
E-mail: expo@online.tm

US Department of Commerce
Business Information Service for the Newly Independent States
USA Trade Center, Stop R-Binis,
Ronald Reagan Building, 1401 Constitution Avenue,
NW, Washington, DC 20230, USA
Tel: (202) 482 4655.
Website: www.bisnis.doc.gov

A B C D E F G H I J K L M N O P Q R S **T** U V W X Y Z

Turks & Caicos

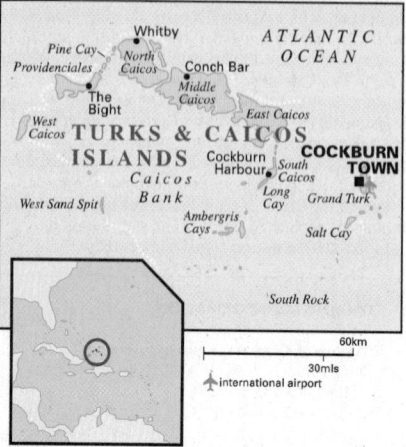

Location: Caribbean, southeast of The Bahamas.

Time: GMT - 5 (GMT - 4 from first Sunday in April to Saturday before last Sunday in October).

The Turks & Caicos Islands are a British Overseas Territory and are formally represented abroad by British diplomatic missions.

Overview

The name Turks is derived after the indigenous Turk's Head 'fez' cactus, and the name Caicos is a Lucayan term 'caya hico', meaning string of islands. Columbus was said to have discovered the islands in 1492, but some still argue that Ponce de Leon arrived first.

Whoever first discovered the islands, in 1962, having been a Jamaican dependency for some 75 years, the Turks & Caicos Islands became a separate British Colony – a status that it retains to this day.

The islands are a spectacular destination for those who wish to get away from it all. One of the most valuable possessions of the Turks & Caicos Islands are their pristine white sandy beaches, which are complemented with crystal clear turquoise waters. In addition, there are numerous national parks, nature preserves, sanctuaries and historical sites.

Despite an increase in tourist numbers - tourism is the islands' main source of revenue the islands remain largely uncommercialised and unspoilt with small, personal places to stay and a heavy emphasis on ecotourism. In addition to tourism, the Turks and Caicos economy is based on fishing and offshore financial services.

People on the islands known as 'Belongers' are known for their friendly spirit, which will ensure this is a destination that will help people de-stress, feel comfortable and truly relax.

General Information

AREA: 430 sq km (166 sq miles).
POPULATION: 26,000 (2005 census estimate).
POPULATION DENSITY: 44.2 per sq km.
CAPITAL: Grand Turk. **Population:** 3720 (official estimate 2003).
GEOGRAPHY: The Turks & Caicos Islands are an archipelago of 40 islands (8 of which are inhabited) forming the southeastern end of the Bahamas chain. There are two principal groups, each surrounded by a continuous coral reef. Caicos is the larger group and includes Providenciales, Middle (or Grand) Caicos, and the islands of North, South, East and West Caicos, plus numerous small cays, some of which are inhabited. The Turks group, separated by a 35km- (22 mile-) wide channel of water, consists of Grand Turk, Salt Cay and a number of small uninhabited cays.
GOVERNMENT: British Overseas Territory since 1670.

Gained internal autonomy in 1962. **Head of State:** HM Queen Elizabeth II, represented locally by His Excellency Richard Tauwhare (with effect from 11 July 2005). **Head of Government:** Chief Minister Michael Eugene Misick since 2003. **Recent history:** The British Monarch is Head of State, represented locally by a Governor who is responsible for defence and foreign affairs as well as internal security. The internal Government comprises Legislative and Executive Councils. The former consists of a speaker, three ex-officio members of the Executive Council, three appointees, and 11 members elected by universal adult suffrage. The Executive Council consists of a Chief Minister and four other Ministers drawn from the Legislative Council, plus three appointees to the posts of Chief Secretary, Financial Secretary and Attorney-General.

The ruling People's Democratic Party (PDM) won a third term at the general elections on 24 April 2003. However, the opposition Progressive National Party (PNP) filed election petitions against the results in two of the thirteen constituencies. On 19 June 2003, the Chief Justice declared the results in both districts void. As a result, a fresh election was required in each one. This put the governing PDM in a minority in the Legislative Council. The Chief Minister, the Hon Derek Taylor, asked the Governor to dissolve the Legislative Council and to call a new general election. The Governor, acting in accordance with the Constitution, told the leaders of both parties on 23 June 2003 that he was denying both the PDM's request for a new general election and the PNP's request for the immediate appointment of their Leader as Chief Minister, and that he would issue writs for by-elections in the two constituencies affected to be held on 7 August 2003. The PNP won both seats in the by-elections giving them a majority of 8-5 in the Legislative Council. Derek Taylor resigned as Chief Minister on 15 August 2003. Michael Misick was sworn in as Chief Minister on the same day.

LANGUAGE: The official language is English. Some Creole is spoken.

RELIGION: Roman Catholic, Anglican, Methodist, Baptist, Seventh Day Adventist and Pentecostal.

ELECTRICITY: 120/240 volts AC, 60 Hz.

SOCIAL CONVENTIONS: Shaking hands is the normal form of greeting. Hospitality is important and, when visiting someone's home, normal social courtesies should be observed - if possible, a return invitation should be made. A souvenir from home is well received. Informal dress is accepted for most events, but beachwear should be confined to the beach.

Climate

Tropical; tempered by trade winds, generally pleasant. Cool nights. Rain in winter. Hurricanes and tropical storms (with flooding) can strike between July to November.

Required clothing: Tropical lightweights. Light sweaters are advised for evenings.

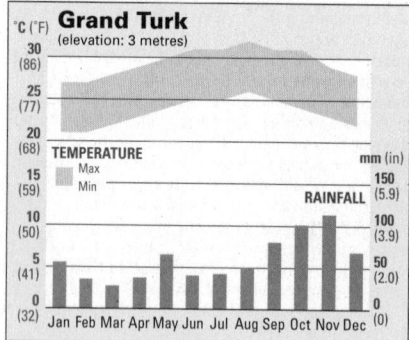

Communications

Telephone: IDD is available. Country code: 1 649. There is a good communications network run by *Cable & Wireless Ltd*, with automatic exchange on all the islands. The local telephone directory lists charges for international calls. There is a 10 per cent tax on all calls. Public card-phones are in operation on all the islands; phonecards are available from *Cable & Wireless* and outlets near phone booths. Cheap rates are in operation Mon-Fri 1900-0600 and Sat-Sun all day.

Mobile telephone: Roaming agreements exist with international mobile phone companies.

Internet: Public access is available in Internet kiosks located at the airport and in Internet cafes around the islands.

Post: The General Post Office is on Grand Turk, with sub-offices in South Caicos, Salt Cay and Providenciales. Airmail to Western Europe takes 5 days. Post office hours: Mon-Thurs 0800-1630, Fri 0800-1600.

MEDIA: Press: The *Turks & Caicos Free Press, Turks & Caicos Press* and *The Turks & Caicos Weekly News* are

published weekly, and *The Times of the Islands Magazine* quarterly. *Where, When, How* is a travel magazine which appears monthly.

TV: There are no TV broadcasters based in the territory, although cable and satellite TV is available and stations from the Bahamas can be picked up.

Radio: *Radio Turks and Caicos* is Government-run.

Passport/Visa

	Passport Required?	Visa Required?	Return Ticket Required?
Full British	Yes	No	Yes
Australian	Yes	No	Yes
Canadian	1	No	Yes
USA	1	No	Yes
Other EU	Yes	No/2	Yes
Japanese	Yes	No	Yes

Note: Regulations and requirements may be subject to change at short notice, and you are advised to contact the appropriate diplomatic or consular authority before finalising travel arrangements. Any numbers in the chart refer to the footnotes below.

PASSPORTS: Passport valid for a minimum of six months required by all except:
1. nationals of Canada and the USA, provided holding proof of identity (birth certificate and photo ID).

VISAS: Required by all except the following for stays of up to 30 days:
(a) nationals of countries referred to in the chart above (**2.** except nationals of Czech Republic, Estonia, Latvia, Lithuania, Slovak Republic and Slovenia whmo *do* require a visa);
(b) nationals of Commonwealth countries (except nationals of Cameroon, Jamaica, Mozambique and Namibia);
(c) nationals of Anguilla, Argentina, Bahrain, Bermuda, Bolivia, Brazil, British Virgin Islands, Bulgaria, Cayman Islands, Chile, China (PR), Costa Rica, Côte d'Ivoire, Ecuador, Hong Kong (SAR), Iceland, Israel, Korea (Rep), Kuwait, the Leeward Islands, Liechtenstein, Mexico, Monaco, Montserrat, Nicaragua, Norway, Oman, Panama, Paraguay, Peru, Qatar, San Marino, Saudi Arabia, Senegal, Surinam, Switzerland, the Syrian Arab Republic, Taiwan (China), Tunisia, Turkey, United Arab Emirates, United States Pacific Territories, Uruguay, Vatican City, Venezuela, Vietnam, Western Samoa, Yemen, Zaire and Zimbabwe;
(d) nationals of countries not specified above who are lawful residents of the UK, the USA or Canada, or who are holders of a valid visa permitting their travel to the UK, the USA or Canada may be granted leave to enter Turks and Caicos without a visa;
(e) most transit passengers continuing their journey by the same or first connecting aircraft, provided holding onward or return documentation and not leaving the airport.
Nationals of a few countries may require a transit visa. Check with the UK Passport Service before departure.
Types of visa and cost: *Tourist, Business* and *Transit:* £28.
Validity: Three months.
Application to: UK Passport Service.
Application requirements: (a) Passport with six months remaining validity. (b) Return or onward ticket. (c) Evidence of sufficient funds for the duration of stay.
Working days required: Applications generally have to be referred to Grand Turk, which takes one month.
Temporary residence: Work and residence permits are required; apply to the Chief Immigration Officer, Government Buildings, Grand Turk.

PASSPORT/VISA INFORMATION

Governor's Office
Governor's House, Waterloo, Grand Turk, Turks & Caicos
Tel: (649) 946 2309/2910.
E-mail: Governor_Office@gov.tc

UK Passport Service
London Passport Office, Globe House, 89 Ecclestone Square, London SW1V 1PN, UK
Tel: (0870) 521 0410 (24-hour passport advice line).
Website: www.passport.gov.uk *or* www.ukpa.gov.uk
Opening hours: Mon-Fri 0745-1845, Sat 0900-1500 (appointment only).

Money

Currency: US Dollar (USD; symbol US$) = 100 cents. Notes are in denominations of US$100, 50, 20, 10, 5, 2 and 1. Coins are in denominations of 50, 25, 10, 5 and 1 cents.

Credit & debit cards: MasterCard and Visa are widely accepted. Check with your credit or debit card company for details of merchant acceptability and other services which may be available.

Traveller's cheques: Accepted by most hotels, shops, restaurants, banks and taxi services.
Currency restrictions: None.
Banking hours: Mon-Thurs 0830-1430, Fri 0830-1630.
Exchange rate indicators:
Rate at time of publishing
£1.00=   US$1.77

Duty Free

The following items may be imported into the Turks & Caicos Islands without incurring customs duty: *200 cigarettes or 50 cigars or 125g tobacco; 1l of spirits or 2l of wine or perfume for personal use.*
Restricted items: Spearguns and Hawaiian slings. Firearms require a police permit.
Prohibited items: Drugs and pornography.

Public Holidays

Below are listed Public Holidays for the January 2006-June 2007 period.
2006: Jan 1 New Year's Day. **Mar 13** Commonwealth Day. **Apr 14** Good Friday. **Apr 17** Easter Monday. **May 22** National Heroes' Day. **Jun 12** HM The Queen's Birthday. **Aug 1** Emancipation Day. **Sep 29** National Youth Day. **Oct 9** Columbus Day. **Dec 25** Christmas Day. **Dec 26** Boxing Day. **2007:** Jan 1 New Year's Day. **Mar 12** Commonwealth Day. **Apr 6** Good Friday. **Apr 9** Easter Monday. **May 21** National Heroes' Day. **Jun 12** HM The Queen's Birthday.

Health

	Special Precautions?	Certificate Required?
Yellow Fever	1	No
Cholera	No	No
Typhoid & Polio	2	N/A
Malaria	No	N/A

Note: *Regulations and requirements may be subject to change at short notice, and you are advised to contact your doctor well in advance of your intended date of departure. Any numbers in the chart refer to the footnotes below.*

1: A yellow fever vaccination certificate is required from travellers over one year of age arriving from infected areas.
2: A small risk of typhoid exists in rural areas.
Food & drink: All water should be regarded as being potentially contaminated. Water used for drinking, brushing teeth or making ice should have first been boiled or otherwise sterilised. Powdered or tinned milk is available and is advised, but make sure that it is reconstituted with pure water. Only eat well-cooked meat and fish, preferably served hot. Pork, salad and mayonnaise may carry increased risk. Vegetables should be cooked and fruit peeled.
Other risks: A low risk of *dengue fever. Hepatitis A, B and C* occur.
Rabies is present. For those at high risk, vaccination before arrival should be considered. If you are bitten, seek medical advice without delay; for more information, see the *Health* appendix.
Health care: There is a reciprocal health agreement with the UK. On presentation of proof of residence in the UK (NHS card, driving licence, etc), those under 16 or over 65 receive all medical and dental treatment free of charge. Other UK residents are entitled to free treatment as follows: on *Grand Turk*, dental treatment, prescribed medicines and ambulance travel; on the *outer islands*, medical treatment at Government clinics and prescribed medicines. There are community clinics on all islands. There is a small hospital on Grand Turk and a number of private practitioners, and also an emergency care facility.

Travel - International

AIR:

 The main airline is *Air Turks & Caicos (QW)* (tel: 941 5481; website: www.airturksandcaicos.com).
Approximate flight times: From Grand Turk to *London*, via the USA or Jamaica, is approximately 13 hours 30 minutes, to *Miami* is one hour 15 minutes, and to *New York* is three hours. From Providenciales to *Miami* is one hour 20 minutes, and to *New York* is five hours 50 minutes (via Miami). It takes three hours 30 minutes to get to Boston. There are direct flights from the UK, Canada, The Bahamas, Jamaica, Dominican Republic and Haiti.
Main airports: *Grand Turk (GDT)* is 3.2km (2 miles) south of Cockburn Town (travel time - five minutes). *To/from the airport:* There is a taxi service from Grand Turk to hotels; prices vary. *Facilities:* Left luggage, first aid, bars and restaurants. There are international airstrips on *Providenciales (PLS)* and *South Caicos (XSC)*.
Departure tax: US$35. Children under two are exempt.

SEA:

 Main ports: *Cockburn Harbour (South Caicos), Grand Turk, Providenciales* and *Salt Cay.* Harbour facilities on South Caicos are currently being improved. There are plans to build a new port on North Caicos.
The archipelago is off the beaten track for most major cruise lines. However, *Fred Olsen Cruises* sail to the islands. Boats can be chartered to sail to islands in the Bahamas or Haiti.

Travel - Internal

AIR:

 In addition to the international airports on *Grand Turk*, *Providenciales* and *South Caicos*, there are landing strips on Middle Caicos, North Caicos, Parrot Cay, Pine Cay and Salt Cay. *Turks & Caicos Airways* runs a regular air-taxi service to all the inhabited islands, as well as flights to Cap Haïtien, Nassau and Puerto Plata. Charter flights are also available.
SEA:

 Limited coast-hopping and inter-island services. Boats may be chartered at most of the inhabited islands.
ROAD:

There are over 120km (75 miles) of roads on the islands, of which about one-fifth are sealed. Traffic drives on the left. Speed limits are 20 mph (32 kph) in town and 40 mph (64 kph) elsewhere. If possible, driving at night in Providenciales should be avoided. **Taxi:** Available at most airports, but the supply may be limited and sharing is often necessary. Negotiate on the fare beforehand. **Car hire:** Available from some local firms on Grand Turk, Providenciales, and North and South Caicos.
Regulations: Seatbelts must be worn at all times. Driving under the influence of alcohol is illegal. **Documentation:** Local licence available for a fee if holding a national driving licence or an International Driving Permit. A tax of US$10 is levied on all rentals.
Travel times: The following chart gives approximate travel times (in hours and minutes) from **Grand Turk** to other major cities/towns on the islands:

	Air
Salt Cay	0.05
Middle Caicos	0.20
North Caicos	0.25
Providenciales	0.30

Travel Advice

Most visits to the Turks & Caicos Islands are trouble-free but you should be aware of the global risk of indiscriminate international terrorist attacks, which could be against civilian targets, including places frequented by foreigners. The hurricane season runs from 1 June to 30 November. This advice is based on information provided by the Foreign and Commonwealth Office in the UK. It is correct at time of publishing. As the situation can change rapidly, visitors are advised to contact the following organisations for the latest travel advice:

British Foreign and Commonwealth Office
Tel: (0845) 850 2829.
Website: www.fco.gov.uk

US Department of State
Website: http://travel.state.gov/travel

Accommodation

There is accommodation on Grand Turk, North, Middle and South Caicos, Salt Cay, Providenciales and Pine Cay, including hotels, inns, a guest house and self-catering apartment complexes. The standard is high, and many have beach frontage, private gardens, swimming pool and extensive watersports facilities. On Providenciales, there is a *Club Med Turkoise*. All rooms are subject to 8 per cent tax and 10 per cent service charge. Advance reservation is necessary. For further details, contact the Turks & Caicos Islands Tourist Office (see *Top Things To See & Do*).

Top Things To See & Do

The Caicos Group
- **West Caicos:** The westernmost island has an abrupt coastline leading to deep water that is ideal for **fishing** and **scuba diving**. Uninhabited, it is currently only visited by sailors, fishermen and thousands of seabirds. An ideal place to see a variety of **birdlife** is Lake Catherine. Ruins of **Yankee Town**, a railroad and a steam engine are remnants of the time when the island was habited.
- **Providenciales:** This island is the centre of the country's major tourist development. There are beautiful white beaches, a coral reef and an abundance of aquatic life. The main tourist centre lies around **Turtle Cove**, with its

---

peaceful yacht basin, and **Grace Bay**. Grace Bay has a 12 mile beach and the **Princess Alexandra Marine Park**; also popular are the **Sea Centre, Bamboo Gallery** (an art centre) and the **Ports of Call** shopping area. Explore **Blight** and **Blue Hills**, the two main and oldest settlements on the island. **Chalk Sound** is a large turquoise lake in the south of Providenciales. Once a month the waters around the island light up with **glow** worms; take a cruise along the waters to see this magical display.
- **Little Water Cay:** Known for its variety of birdlife, this small cay is being developed as a nature resort.
- **Pine Cay** is inhabited mostly by tropical birds and iguanas, and has one of the most beautiful beaches in the Caicos Islands, if not the whole Caribbean. The northern end has many freshwater lakes with species of saltwater fish brought here by Hurricane Donna in 1960. Part of the **Caicos Cays National Underwater Park** is located here. The reefs of the Caicos bank, with their rich variety of corals and vividly coloured fish, are a must-see.
- **Parrot Cay** lies between Providenciales and North Caicos. Once a private island which used to be a hideout for legendary pirates such as Annie Bonnie and Mary Reid, it is now being developed into a modern resort.
- The fertile soils and water of **North Caicos**, known as the 'Emerald Isle' of the Caicos, provide good farmland. It has miles of deserted white sand beaches, along which hotels provide luxurious and peaceful accommodation. Flamingos, ospreys, iguanas and various other wildlife can be seen at the island's nature reserve.
- Also known as Grand Caicos, **Middle Caicos** is undeveloped. The three main settlements on the island are **Conch Bar, Banbarra** and **Lorimers**. Blessed with a lovely coastline, to the west of **Conch Bar**, the shoreline dips in and out with bluffs and small coves. The north and south coasts could not be more different; in the north are limestone cliffs and sandy beaches, in the south is swampland and tidal flats. Do not miss the island's spectacular caves. There is a trail linking Middle Caicos and North Caicos; in the low tide, it is safe to walk across it.
- **East Caicos** is uninhabited but when flying to South Caicos, look down for the salmon in the translucent green water. Some of the most beautiful beaches in the Caribbean are to be found here. Turtles come and lay their eggs on the 17 mile beach on the north coast. In the northwest of the island, at **Jacksonville**, there is a series of caves with evidence of early petroglyphs.
- **South Caicos:** The town of **Cockburn Harbour** is situated on a small ridge at the extreme southwest of the island of South Caicos. It was once the chief port for the shipment of salt from the islands. The town is a quiet and pleasant place to potter around in the evening. During the day, there are numerous beaches to explore and, as everywhere in the Turks & Caicos group, there is superb **diving, yachting** and **big-game fishing**.

The Turks Group
- A few minutes from South Caicos by air, with the small metropolis of **Cockburn Town, Grand Turk** is the islands' seat of government and commerce, as well as their historic and cultural centre. The **Turks & Caicos National Museum**, situated on the waterfront, tells the story of the Molasses shipwreck discovered in the Americas and exhibits rare prints and manuscripts from all of the islands. **Front Street** has a number of colonial buildings, dating from the early 19th century. They have imposing entrances in the high, whitewashed walls that surround their gardens. The **Lighthouse** overlooking North Creek on the north coast was shipped to Grand Turk from the UK in pieces in the 19th-century and re-assembled. There are many delightful bays on the eastern shores of Grand Turk. The island is also a fine base for **diving** and **fishing**. **Heritage walks** and **guided tours** are available.
- Go to **Salt Cay**, the most charming and atmospheric of all the Salt Islands. There are fine beaches and also still-productive salt ponds. The island is dominated by a great white house, built in the 1830s in solid Bermudian style. Salt Cay also hosts relics of the now defunct whaling industry. In the winter, spot gigantic humpback whales.
- During February, March and April, **whale-watching** enthusiasts are able to observe large numbers of the North Atlantic humpback whale population passing through very close to the western shores of Grand Turk and Salt Cay en route to their breeding grounds at Mouchoir Bank nearby. During this period, divers can listen to an underwater concert of whale songs. Encounters with **dolphins** are also frequent. The *JoJo Dolphin Project* is one of numerous regional nature conservation programmes, which encourage tourists to respect the environment. Other marine species that can be observed include turtles, spotted eagle rays and manta rays. **Birdwatching** is widespread as rare birds and butterflies are found throughout the islands.

Entertainment

FOOD & DRINK: As well as traditional foods, continental dishes are also available as are US/European snacks such as hot dogs and hamburgers.

Things to know: With rare exceptions, dining takes place in hotels. Although some establishments have buffet-style serveries, table service is common. Alcohol is freely available, a wide selection of imported beer, wines and spirits can be found in most bars.

National specialities:
• *Hominy*; cooked with peas or dried conch.
• Whelk soup.
• Conch chowder.
• Lobster and special types of fresh fish.

National drinks:
• Rum-based punch and cocktails.

Tipping: There is no tipping in hotels on any of the islands, 15 per cent is added to all bills. In restaurants, tip 15 per cent.

NIGHTLIFE: There are nightclubs and discos, and hotels arrange beach parties and other entertainments. Events are broadcast in advance on local radio.

SHOPPING: Fairly expensive. The islands' small shops sell locally made baskets, jewellery, ceramics, shells, sponges, hand-screened cloth, souvenir T-shirts and rare conch pearls (although the latter is discouraged because of problems of over fishing).

Business

• **GDP:** US$297 million (2003).
• **Main imports:** Foods and beverages, tobacco, clothing, manufactures and construction materials.
• **Main exports:** Lobster, dried and fresh conch and conch shells.
• **Main trade partners:** UK and USA.

ECONOMY: Since salt mining went into decline in the mid-1960s, and finally ceased during the 1990s, the Turks & Caicos Islands have relied on tourism and offshore financial services for most of their income. There is little agriculture but the sizeable fishing industry is both a major contributor to the islands' food requirements and a valuable export earner - particularly from the USA, which buys much of the catch. The only other notable industry is construction, which is largely geared towards improving tourism infrastructure. In the mid-1980s, measures were introduced by the Government to attract an offshore financial services industry and these have met with reasonable success. Unfortunately, it brought laundered money and illicit capital fleeing from elsewhere. Under pressure from London and, more publicly, the Organisation for Economic Cooperation and Development, the Government has now introduced a tighter regulatory structure to prevent fraud and money-laundering. Meanwhile, it has refocused on tourism as the key to the islands' future economic well-being. The sector is now worth about US$500 million to the islands' economy.

Despite receipts from tourism and financial service, some aid from the UK is still needed to balance the budget and fund capital projects.

BUSINESS ETIQUETTE: The informal relaxed atmosphere prevails even in business circles. A lightweight suit will be the most needed. Best months to visit are from April to October. **Office hours:** Mon-Fri 0800-1300 and 1400-1630.

CONFERENCES/CONVENTIONS: 40 per cent of visitors to Turks and Caicos are business travellers. The Williams Auditorium offers facilites for 1000 people. *Allegro* and *Beaches* also offer conference facilities.

Tuvalu

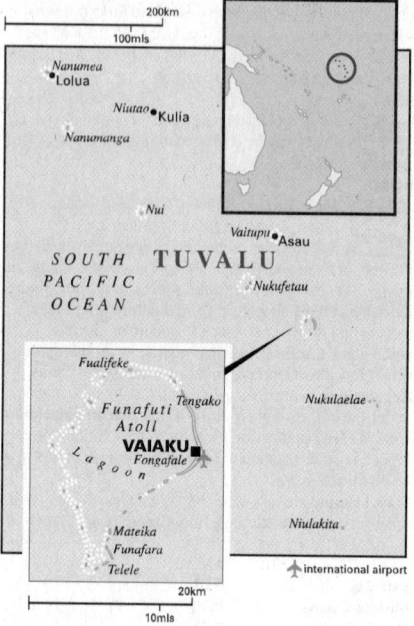

Location: West Pacific.

Time: GMT + 12.

Overview

Tuvalu, the world's second-smallest country and, according to the United Nations, one of the least developed, fulfils the classic image of a South Sea paradise. Visitors come to the islands to enjoy the peaceful atmosphere and palm-fringed beaches. Pandanus, papaya, banana, breadfruit and coconut palms are typical. Most activity is centred in the capital, Funafuti, where the greatest attraction is the enormous Funafuti Lagoon. The lagoon is 14km (9 miles) wide and about 18km (11 miles) long and is excellent for swimming and snorkelling. The second most populated island in the atoll is Funafala, which can be visited by hopping aboard the Funafuti Island Council's catamaran. There are no shops whatsoever in Funafala, so visitors should take their own provisions. Traditional buildings with thatched roofs can be seen virtually everywhere on the islands.

General Information

AREA: 26 sq km (10 sq miles).
POPULATION: 10,880 (2002).
POPULATION DENSITY: 418.5 per sq km.
CAPITAL: Funafuti. **Population:** 4,590 (2000).
GEOGRAPHY: Tuvalu (formerly the Ellice Islands) is a scattered group of nine small atolls in the western Pacific Ocean extending about 560km (350 miles) from north to south. Nearest neighbours are Fiji (to the south), Kiribati (north) and the Solomon Islands (west). The main island, Funafuti, is also the capital and lies 1920km (1200 miles) north of Suva, Fiji.
GOVERNMENT: Constitutional monarchy. Gained independence from the UK in 1978. **Head of State:** HM Queen Elizabeth II, represented locally by Governor-General Filoimea Telito. **Head of Government:** Prime Minister Maatia Toafa since 2004. **Recent history:** Following the resignation of Saufatu Sopoanga, Maatia Toafa won a Parliamentary vote in October 2004 by eight votes to seven. The Prime Minister has undertaken a review of the constitution and says he aims to hold a referendum on whether to replace the British Monarch as Head of State. Tuvalu has no political parties. Allegiances revolve around personalities and geography.

LANGUAGE: Tuvaluan and English are the main languages.
RELIGION: Approximately 98 per cent Protestant.
ELECTRICITY: 220/240 volts AC, 60Hz (Funafuti only).
SOCIAL CONVENTIONS: Traditional values continue to dominate Tuvaluan culture. Footwear should be removed when entering a church, a village meeting house (*manepa*) or private house. Religion plays an important part in daily life. Sunday is a day of rest and church-going for the locals, when visitors are advised to choose activities which do not cause too much disruption. There are limits imposed on the consumption of alcohol outside licensed premises. Whilst dress is usually casual, it is customary for women to keep their thighs covered and beachwear should be confined to the beach or poolside. There are procedures which should be followed by those invited to a feast and visitors should take local advice about this and other matters. It is customary not to speak a foreign language in the presence of a person who does not know it, so apparent indications of a desire to hold a private or confidential conversation should be interpreted as simple courtesy to fellow islanders. Visitors are welcome to join in the numerous local festivals and celebrations with feasting and traditional entertainment.

Climate

The climate is humid and hot with a mean annual temperature of 30°C (86°F) and comparatively little seasonal variation. March to October tends to be cooler and more pleasant, whilst some discomfort may be experienced during the wet season from November to February.
Required clothing: Lightweight for summer, rainwear for the wet season.

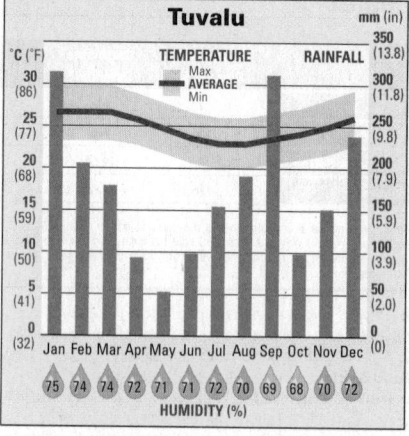

Communications

Telephone: IDD service is available. Country code: 688. There are no area codes. Tuvalu has recently acquired satellite communications technology and international phone calls can be made from most of the islands.
Mobile telephone: Tuvalu has no mobile phone network.
Internet: ISPs include *Tuvalu.TV*.
Post: Airmail services to Europe take between five and 10 days to arrive, but can be erratic. Tuvalu stamps are among the most sought after in the world.
MEDIA: Media freedom is respected in Tuvalu.
Press: The Government Broadcasting and Information Division publishes *Tuvalu Echoes* (in English, on a fortnightly basis).
TV: There is no Tuvalu-based station, but many islanders have satellite dishes to receive foreign channels.
Radio: *Radio Tuvalu* is Government-operated.

Passport/Visa

	Passport Required?	Visa Required?	Return Ticket Required?
Full British	Yes	No	Yes
Australian	Yes	No	Yes
Canadian	Yes	No	Yes
USA	Yes	2	Yes
Other EU	Yes	No/1	Yes
Japanese	Yes	Yes	Yes

Note: *Regulations and requirements may be subject to change at short notice, and you are advised to contact the appropriate diplomatic or consular authority before finalising travel arrangements. Any numbers in the chart refer to the footnotes below.*

PASSPORTS: Valid passport required by all.
VISAS: Required by all except the following:
(a) **1.** nationals listed in the chart above (except nationals of Cyprus, Czech Republic, Estonia, Hungary, Latvia, Lithuania, Malta, Poland, Slovak Republic and Slovenia who *do* require a visa);

(b) nationals of Commonwealth countries (except nationals of Brunei, Cameroon, Mozambique, Namibia, St Kitts & Nevis and South Africa, who *do* require a visa);
(c) nationals of Iceland, Liechtenstein, San Marino, Switzerland, Tunisia, Turkey and Uruguay;
(d) **2.** nationals of the USA (*only* if the passport is issued by the Marshall Islands);
(e) transit passengers continuing their journey on the same or first connecting aircraft within 24 hours provided holding required travel documents for onward destination and not leaving the airport transit lounge.
Note: Entry permits are issued on arrival providing nationals can provide a valid passport, sufficient funds, proof of accommodation and a return/onward ticket.
Types of visa and cost: Visitor and work permits issued free of charge.
Validity: Visitors are normally permitted to remain in Tuvalu for up to one month, after meeting entry requirements; their visit may then be extended for a maximum of three months at a cost of £10.
Application to: British Consulates, Tuvalu representatives abroad or the Principal Immigration Officer, Office of the Chief of Police, Funafuti, Tuvalu.

PASSPORT/VISA INFORMATION

Consulate of Tuvalu in the UK
230 Worple Road, London SW20 8RH, UK
Tel: (020) 8879 0985.
E-mail: tuvaluconsulate@netscape.net
Opening hours: Mon-Fri 1000-1730.

Money

Currency: Australian and Tuvaluan currency are both in use, but transactions over A$1 are always conducted in Australian Dollars. For details of Australian Dollar denominations and exchange rates, see the *Australia* section.
Tuvaluan Dollar (TVD; symbol TV$) = 100 cents. Coins are in denominations of TV$1, and 500, 200, 100, 50, 20, 10 and 5 cents.
Credit & debit cards: Credit cards are not accepted, but MasterCard may be used at the National Bank of Tuvalu for cash advances.
Traveller's cheques: Australian Dollars are recommended.
Currency restrictions: There are no restrictions on the import and export of foreign or local currency.
Banking hours: Mon-Thurs 0930-1300, Fri 0830-1200.

Duty Free

The following items may be imported into Tuvalu by visitors without incurring customs duty:
200 cigarettes or 225g of tobacco or cigars (for all visitors irrespective of age); 1l of spirits and 1l of wine (for visitors aged 18 years and over).
Prohibited items: Pornography, pure alcohol, narcotics, arms and ammunition. All plant and animal material must be declared and quarantined. The following items are duty free but must be declared upon arrival: one pair of binoculars, one still camera and six rolls of unexposed film, one cine camera and 200m of unexposed film, one portable radio, one broadcast receiver, one portable tape recorder, one portable typewriter and a reasonable quantity of sports equipment.

Public Holidays

Below are listed Public Holidays for the January 2006-June 2007 period.
2006: Jan 1 New Year's Day. **Mar 13** Commonwealth Day.
Apr 14 Good Friday. **Apr 17** Easter Monday. **Jun 12** Queen's Official Birthday. **Aug 5** National Children's Day. **Oct 1-2** Tuvalu Days (Anniversary of Independence). **Nov 11** Prince of Wales's Birthday. **Dec 25-26** Christmas.
2007: Jan 1 New Year's Day. **Mar 12** Commonwealth Day.
Apr 6 Good Friday. **Apr 9** Easter Monday. **Jun 12** Queen's Official Birthday.

Health

	Special Precautions?	Certificate Required?
Yellow Fever	No	No
Cholera	No	No
Typhoid & Polio	No	N/A
Malaria	No	N/A

Note: *Regulations and requirements may be subject to change at short notice, and you are advised to contact your doctor well in advance of your intended date of departure. Any numbers in the chart refer to the footnotes below.*

Food & drink: All water is stored in tanks and supply is limited so visitors are advised to use water sparingly and take local advice.

Other risks: *Hepatitis A* occurs; *hepatitis B* is endemic. *Dengue fever* and *filariasis* are also present. There is a threat of *tuberculosis*. Poisonous fish and sea snakes can be a potential hazard to bathers.
Health care: Visitors are advised to bring antiseptic cream as cuts are inclined to turn septic but, apart from this precaution, there are no serious health risks. The mosquitoes are non-malarial, but the visitor may nevertheless wish to take protective measures. There are no reciprocal agreements with the UK or USA and travellers are recommended to take out full medical insurance before departure. Tuvalu's only hospital is in Funafuti; the outer islands only have trained nurses. More serious and complicated problems may require medicinal evacuation to Fiji or Australia.

Travel - International

AIR:

There are plans to establish a national airline in the near future. Presently *Air Marshall Islands (CW)*, the airline of the Marshall Islands, offers return flights to Funafuti from *Majuro* (Marshall Islands) via *Tarawa* (Kiribati), from *Nadi* (Fiji) and from *Suva* (Fiji). *Air Fiji* also flies between Suva (Fiji) and Funafuti. It is advisable to book in advance.
The *Visit the South Pacific Pass* is valid for many airlines operating in the South Pacific, including most of the larger ones, such as *Air Caledonie, Air Marshall Islands, Air Nauru, Air Niugini, Air Pacific, Air Vanuatu, Polynesian Airlines, Qantas* and *Solomon Airlines*. Offering reductions of up to 40 per cent on normal airfares, this sector-based pass allows for flexible island-hopping between the destinations of the Cook Islands, Fiji, Nauru, New Caledonia, Samoa, Tahiti, Tonga, Vanuatu and the more remote Melanesian and Micronesian islands, together with major cities in Australia (Brisbane, Melbourne and Sydney) and New Zealand (Auckland, Christchurch and Wellington). It is only available for people resident outside of the South Pacific. The journey must be started outside the South Pacific and only one stopover in Australia is allowed. A minimum of two sectors must be bought before departure (extra sectors can be purchased en route). There is a maximum of one pass per person, and passes must be used within six months of the first day of travel. Children under 12 years of age pay 75 per cent of the adult fare. For details and conditions, contact the South Pacific Tourism Organisation.
Main airports: *Funafuti International (FUN). To/from the airport:* Buses run 0500-2359 (travel time - 30 minutes). Taxis are also available. There is a pick-up service to the only hotel. *Facilities:* VIP lounge, left luggage and lockers, bank, bureaux de change, restaurant, snack bars, bars, chemist, post office and shops.
Departure tax: A$10. Children under three years of age and transit passengers are exempt.
SEA:

Shipping services operate from Fiji, Australia and New Zealand, calling at the main port of Funafuti. Adventure cruises organised by tour operators also call from time to time.

Travel - Internal

AIR:

The only airstrip is at Funafuti. There is no internal air service.

SEA:

The islands are served by a passenger and cargo vessel, the *Nivaga II*, based at Funafuti, which occasionally calls at Suva (Fiji).

ROAD:
There are a few roads, constructed from impacted coral, and several dirt tracks that span the islands. There are **taxis**, but limited transport service is also provided by privately operated **minibuses**. The usual forms of transport on the islands are small **pick-up trucks**, **motorcycles** and **bicycles**, which can be hired at the hotel.

Travel Advice

Most visits to Tuvalu are trouble-free but you should be aware of the global risk of indiscriminate international terrorist attacks, which could be against civilian targets, including places frequented by foreigners.
This advice is based on information provided by the Foreign and Commonwealth Office in the UK. It is correct at time of publishing. As the situation can change rapidly, visitors are advised to contact the following organisations for the latest travel advice:

British Foreign and Commonwealth Office
Tel: (0845) 850 2829.
Website: www.fco.gov.uk

US Department of State
Website: http://travel.state.gov/travel

Accommodation

Tuvalu's remote location and lack of amenities have limited the development of tourism. There is one hotel, the Government-owned *Vaiaku Lagi Hotel*, which overlooks the beautiful Funafuti lagoon. The 17 rooms all have lagoon views and private shower. All-inclusive packages are available. There is also one motel, the *Island Breeze Motel*. Several guest houses and lodges (including *Filamona Lodge*, *Hideaway Guest House*, *Laisinis Guest House* and *Su's Place Guest House*) provide simple accommodation with meals. There are no camping grounds.

Top Things To See & Do

- Begin in the capital, **Funafuti**, where the greatest attraction is the enormous **Funafuti Lagoon**. The lagoon is 14km (9 miles) wide and about 18km (11 miles) long and is excellent for **swimming** and **snorkelling**.
- Admire the abundant sea and wildlife in the **Funafuti Marine Conservation Area**. This protected marine park, consisting of six tiny islets, is home to numerous tropical fish, sea birds and turtles. Access is by private or chartered boat. Privately owned boats are available for hire and trips can be made to the many beautiful uninhabited islets in the Funafuti atoll.
- Buy locally crafted goods at the **Women's Handicraft Centre**, a short distance from the Vaiaku Lagi Hotel (see *Entertainment* section).
- Visit the **Philatelic Bureau**, which provides stamps to collectors all over the world, and the **University of the South Pacific Centre**, which sells a range of books relating to Tuvalu and the surrounding region.
- Stand on the spot that made Tuvalu the focus of international scientific attention almost 100 years ago, when an expedition was sent from London to drill far into the ground to prove Charles Darwin's theory on the formation of coral atolls.
- Head to **Funafala**, the second most populated island in the atoll, which can be visited by taking the Funafuti Island Council's catamaran (three times a week for a stop of two hours). There are no shops in Funafala, so visitors should take their own provisions. Traditional buildings with thatched roofs can be seen virtually everywhere on the islands.
- **Dive** or **game fish**; equipment is available in Funafuti. Visitors interested in **watersports** should bring their own equipment as there is little for hire. **Swimmers** should wear sand shoes as stonefish are an occasional hazard. Owing to the strong tide, swimming in the ocean is very dangerous. Swimming in the lagoon is considered fairly safe.
- Watch a game of **kilikiti**, a local version of cricket, or **te ano**, a much-loved traditional ball game reminiscent of volleyball.

TOURIST INFORMATION

Ministry of Tourism, Trade and Commerce
Private Mail Bag, Vaiaku, Funafuti, Tuvalu
Tel: 20840 *or* 20408.
Website: www.timelesstuvalu.com

South Pacific Tourism Organisation in Fiji
Street address: Level 3, FNPF Place, 343-359 Victoria Parade, Suva, Fiji
Postal address: PO Box 13119, Suva, Fiji
Tel: 330 4177.
Website: www.spto.org

Entertainment

FOOD & DRINK: The *Vaiaku Lagi Hotel*, *Su's* and *Kai Restaurants* have fully licensed bars and dining facilities, where a good variety of food is served, with an emphasis on fish and local food. In addition, the Vaiaku Lagi Hotel has a barbecue in the courtyard once a fortnight. There is also a number of privately owned snackfood shops and two restaurants on Funafuti's main island with licensed bars and a good variety of food. Beer is imported. **Tipping:** Optional, but not expected.
NIGHTLIFE: There are fortnightly discos ('twists') at the *Vaiaku Lagi Hotel*. Groups of entertainers perform traditional dances for a small fee.
SHOPPING: A range of shops, including food, souvenir and clothing shops, are available, mainly on Funafuti. However, the range of merchandise is limited and not designed with the visitor in mind - for example, there is no film-processing service. For local crafts, including Tuvalu

weaving, shell jewellery and the traditional lidded wooden boxes (*tulumas*) used by fishermen, the *Women's Handicraft Centre* near the main hotel is excellent. There are no shops on Funafala. **Shopping hours:** Mon-Sat 0600-0000.

Business

ECONOMY: Tuvalu relies on a number of standard and unusual sources of income to sustain its economy. Remittances from abroad, especially Nauru where large numbers of Tuvaluans work in the phosphate industry, are vital. In a less orthodox vein, the sale of stamps (mostly to collectors) is a valuable foreign currency earner. A new source of income was identified when a regional telecommunications operator sought to lease Tuvalu's national telephone code and recover its costs from companies offering 'premium rate' services. The Government agreed and now acquires 10 per cent of its annual budget from this source. It has since made a similar arrangement with its Internet domain suffix, '.tv.' Another important revenue stream comes from the sale of fishing licences to US and Japanese fleets. Fishing is also an important activity in the local economy. Exploration is currently underway to locate mineral resources suspected to lie within Tuvalu's territorial limit. On land, copra is the only significant export: most of the soil is of unsuitable quality for agriculture, which is confined to subsistence activities. There is some small-scale industrial activity producing coconut-based products and handicrafts.

Much of the income from these various sources, plus subventions from the country's major aid donors, has been lodged in a Trust Fund established to generate income for development projects from foreign investment and provide some guarantees against a very uncertain economic future. Tuvalu is a member of the South Pacific Commission and the South Pacific Forum. In 2002, Tuvalu joined the Pacific Island Countries Trade Association (PICTA), a free-trade zone established by the South Pacific Forum. Australia, New Zealand and Fiji are the main trading partners, while the UK provides an aid package mainly to assist the development of the island's infrastructure. **BUSINESS ETIQUETTE:** A high standard of business ethics is to be expected, given that the overwhelming majority of the population is Congregationalist. **Office hours:** Mon-Thurs 0730-1615 and Fri 0730-1245.

COMMERCIAL INFORMATION

Tuvalu Cooperative Society Ltd
PO Box 11, Funafuti, Tuvalu
Tel: 20634 *or* 20642 *or* 20747.
Fax: 20748.

Uganda

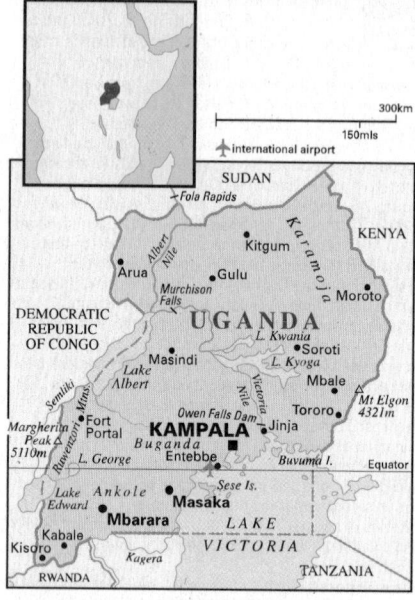

Location: Central/East Africa.

Time: GMT + 3.

Overview

Uganda's great natural beauty led Winston Churchill to call it 'the pearl of Africa'. From the moment the visitor lands at Entebbe's international airport, with its breathtaking equatorial location on the forested shore of island-strewn Lake Victoria, it is clear that Uganda is no ordinary safari destination. Dominated by an expansive golf course leading down to the lakeshore, and a century-old botanical garden alive with the chatter of acrobatic monkeys and colourful tropical birds, Entebbe itself is the least obviously urban of all comparably sized African towns. Just 40km distant, sprawled across seven hills, there is the capital Kampala. The bright modern feel of this bustling, cosmopolitan city reflects the ongoing economic growth and political stability that has characterised Uganda since 1986. Since the late 1980s, Uganda has managed to move on from the abyss of civil war and the economic catastrophe of the Idi Amin days and the return to power of Milton Obote. Human rights have greatly improved and the country has launched a successful campaign to fight the AIDS virus. However, military action and tentative peace talks have not halted the massacres and mutilations perpetrated by the Lord's Resistance Army against civilians in the north which has resulted in the displacement of more than 1.6 million people and the killing and kidnapping of tens of thousands in the course of nearly two decades.

Ecologically, Uganda is where the East African savannah meets the West African jungle. Abundant wildlife (including the famous mountain gorillas) and an excellent climate contribute to the attractions here and, although visitor facilities cannot yet compete with those of neighbouring Kenya, the annual number of tourists to Uganda is rising steadily. Where else but in this lush country can one observe lions prowling the open plains in the morning and track chimpanzees through the rainforest undergrowth the same afternoon, then the next day navigate tropical channels teeming with hippos and crocs before setting off into the misty mountains to stare deep into the eyes of a mountain gorilla?

General Information

AREA: 241,139 sq km (93,104 sq miles).
POPULATION: 27.6 million (UN, 2005).

POPULATION DENSITY: 114.5 per sq km.
CAPITAL: Kampala. **Population:** 1.2 million (2002).
GEOGRAPHY: Uganda shares borders with Sudan to the north, Kenya to the east, Lake Victoria to the southeast, Tanzania and Rwanda to the south and the Democratic Republic of Congo to the west. Kampala is on the shores of Lake Victoria, and the White Nile flowing out of the lake traverses much of the country. The varied scenery includes tropical forest and tea plantations on the slopes of the snow-capped Ruwenzori Mountains, the arid plains of the Karamoja, the lush, heavily populated Buganda, the rolling savannah of Acholi, Bunyoro, Tororo and Ankole, and the fertile cotton area of Teso.
GOVERNMENT: Republic. Gained independence from the UK in 1962. **Head of State:** President Yoweri Kaguta Museveni since 1986. **Head of Government:** Prime Minister Apolo Nsibambi since 1999. **Recent history:** Yoweri Museveni, Uganda's leader since 1986, was declared the winner of the Presidential elections in February 2006, the first multi-party poll in 25 years. He is reported to have taken 59 per cent of the vote, compared with the 37 per cent share of his main rival, Kizza Besigye from the opposition Forum for Democratic Change. Observers said the conduct of the poll was an improvement on the 2001 vote, but critics accused the Government of intimidating the opposition in the run-up. Parliament abolished a constitutional limit on Presidential terms in 2005.
LANGUAGE: English is the official language, with Luganda and Swahili also widely spoken.
RELIGION: 60 per cent Christian, 32 per cent animist and 5 per cent Muslim.
ELECTRICITY: 240 volts AC, 50Hz.
SOCIAL CONVENTIONS: Shaking hands is the normal form of greeting. Casual dress is usual for most occasions in the daytime or evening. Ugandans have adopted a socially conservative culture and homosexuality and drug abuse is illegal and widely condemned. **Photography:** Since 1992, photography has been allowed in all areas with the exception of airports or military installations. However, some areas are still sensitive and it is advisable to take local advice. Commercial photographers should consult the Ministry of Information for a permit.

Climate

The temperature, usually ranging between 21-25°C, can be quite cool in some parts of the country owing to the country's high altitude, despite its position on the equator. The mountain areas become much cooler and the top of Mount Elgon is often covered with snow. Other parts of the country are much warmer. There is heavy rain between March and May and between October and November.
Required clothing: Lightweights and rainwear, with warm wraps for the evenings are advised.

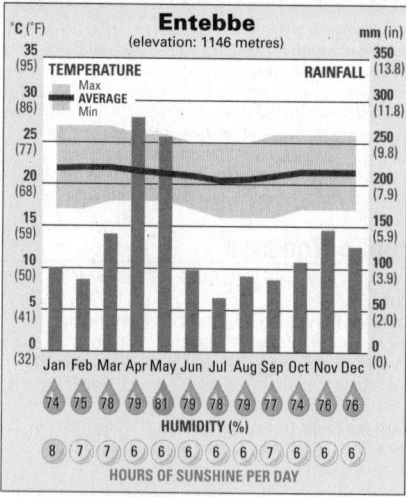

Communications

Telephone: IDD is available to and from principal towns in Uganda. Country code: 256. Service for local calls is unreliable. Phone shops are available in towns.
Mobile telephone: Coverage extends to all major towns and international roaming agreements exist with international mobile phone companies.
Internet: There are Internet cafes in most large towns.
Post: Airmail to Europe can take from three days to several weeks. Post office hours: Mon-Fri 0830-1230 and 1400-1730. Some post offices are open Sat 0830-1300.
MEDIA: Private radio and television stations have thrived since the government loosened its control of the media in 1993.
Press: The English-language papers include *The Economy*, *Financial Times*, *Guide*, *The Monitor*, *New Vision* and *The Star*.
TV: *Uganda Television* is the public broadcaster; *WBS* and

Channel Television are private channels.
Radio: Radio Uganda is a publicly run station that operates five stations in Uganda. It can be heard across the country in English and vernacular languages. Radio Simba, Capital Radio and KFM are private stations. BBC World Service is widely available on FM, and Radio France Internationale operates on FM in Kampala.

Passport/Visa

	Passport Required?	Visa Required?	Return Ticket Required?
Full British	Yes	Yes	Yes
Australian	Yes	Yes	Yes
Canadian	Yes	Yes	Yes
USA	Yes	Yes	Yes
Other EU	Yes	Yes/1	Yes
Japanese	Yes	Yes	Yes

Note: Regulations and requirements may be subject to change at short notice, and you are advised to contact the appropriate diplomatic or consular authority before finalising travel arrangements. Any numbers in the chart refer to the footnotes below.

Restricted entry: Entry may be refused to passengers not holding sufficient funds, return or onward tickets, and other necessary travel documents.

PASSPORTS: Passport valid past the date of expected departure from Uganda required by all.

VISAS: Required by all except the following:
(a) **1**. nationals of Malta and Ireland (Rep);
(b) nationals of Angola, Antigua & Barbuda, The Bahamas, Barbados, Belize, Burundi, Comoros, Cyprus, Eritrea, Fiji, The Gambia, Grenada, Jamaica, Kenya, Lesotho, Madagascar, Malawi, Mauritius, Rwanda, St Vincent & the Grenadines, Seychelles, Sierra Leone, Singapore, Solomon Islands, Swaziland, Tanzania, Tonga, Vanuatu, Zambia and Zimbabwe.

Note: Although transit passengers do require a visa, they are able to obtain one on entry provided they are continuing to a third country by the same or first connecting flight within 24 hours, they are holding confirmed tickets and travel documents and not leaving the airport.

Some nationals requiring visas may be issued with them on arrival to Uganda; check with your local Embassy for further details.

Types of visa and cost: Single-entry: £25 (three months). Transit: £15. Student: £15 (three months).

Validity: Single-entry: Three months from date of issue; Transit: 24 hours from the time of arrival.

Application to: Consulate (or Consular section at High Commission or Embassy); see Passport/Visa Information. Transit visas are issued at the airport.

Application requirements: (a) Passport valid past the date of your expected departure from Uganda. (b) Completed application form. (c) Two recent passport-size photos (with full name printed on the back of one). (d) Fee (cash or postal orders only). (e) Registered self-addressed envelope, if applying by post. Business: (a)-(e) and, (f) Letter of invitation/introduction. Transit: Applicants must have an entry visa for the country of final destination and evidence of onward travel.

Note: Working journalists require a letter of accreditation issued by the Secretary of the Media Council, Department of Information, Po Box 23780, Lugard Road, UTV Premises, Kampala, Uganda (tel: (41) 230367; email: ljoykar@yahoo.com).

Working days required: Three.

Temporary residence: Enquire at Embassy or High Commission.

PASSPORT/VISA INFORMATION

High Commission for the Republic of Uganda in the UK
Uganda House, 58-59 Trafalgar Square,
London WC2N 5DX, UK
Tel: (020) 7839 5783.
Website: www.ugandahighcommission.co.uk
Opening hours: Mon-Fri 0930-1300, 1400-1730;
1000-1300 (visa section).

Embassy of the Republic of Uganda in the USA
5911 16th Street, NW, Washington, DC 20011, USA
Tel: (202) 726 7100.
Website: www.ugandaembassy.com
Opening hours: Mon- Fri 0900 1500 (consular section).

Money

Currency: Uganda Shilling (UGX). Notes are in denominations of UGX10,000, 5000 and 1000. Coins are in denominations of UGX500, 200, 100 and 50.

Currency exchange: Foreign currency may be exchanged at the Central Bank, commercial banks and foreign exchange bureaux.

Credit & debit cards: American Express, Diners, MasterCard and Visa are accepted but not widely used. Some large hotels, restaurants, travel agencies and shops in urban areas accept credit cards. Check with your credit or debit card company for details of merchant acceptability and other services which may be available.

Traveller's cheques: Traveller's cheques are not widely accepted outside Kampala. To avoid additional exchange rate charges, travellers are advised to take traveller's cheques in US Dollars or Pounds Sterling. It is advised that travellers bring sufficient US dollars in cash in case of emergencies.

Currency restrictions: The import and export of local currency is prohibited. Free import of foreign currency if declared on arrival. Export of foreign currency is unlimited, up to the amount declared on arrival. It is imperative to obtain a currency declaration form on arrival in Uganda. Unspent shillings can be reconverted to foreign currency.

Banking hours: Generally Mon-Fri 0830-1400, Sat 0900-1200. Forex bureaux are open until 1700 and able to do electronic transfers to and from overseas.

Exchange rate indicators:
Rate at time of publishing
£1.00= UGX3246.45
$1.00= UGX1825.72

Duty Free

The following items may be imported into Uganda by visitors over 17 years without incurring customs duty (except from Kenya and Tanzania):
200 cigarettes or 225g of tobacco or a combination thereof; one bottle of spirits or wine; 568ml of perfume.
Restricted exports: A special permit is required to export game trophies.

Public Holidays

Below are listed Public Holidays for the January 2006-June 2007 period.
2006: Jan 1 New Year's Day. **Jan 10** Eid al-Adha (Feast of the Sacrifice). **Jan 26** Liberation Day. **Mar 8** International Women's Day. **Apr 14** Good Friday. **Apr 17** Easter Monday. **May 1** Labour Day. **Jun 3** Martyrs' Day. **Jun 9** National Heroes' Day. **Oct 9** Independence Day. **Oct 22-24** Eid al-Fitr (End of Ramadan). **Dec 25** Christmas Day. **Dec 26** Boxing Day. **Dec 31** Eid al-Adha (Feast of the Sacrifice).
2007: Jan 1 New Year's Day. **Jan 26** Liberation Day. **Mar 8** International Women's Day. **Apr 6** Good Friday. **Apr 9** Easter Monday. **May 1** Labour Day. **Jun 3** Martyrs' Day. **Jun 9** National Heroes' Day.

Note: Muslim festivals are timed according to local sightings of various phases of the moon and the dates given above are approximations. During the lunar month of Ramadan that precedes Eid al-Fitr, Muslims fast during the day and feast at night and normal business patterns may be interrupted. Many restaurants are closed during the day and there may be restrictions on smoking and drinking. Some disruption may continue into Eid al-Fitr itself. Eid al-Fitr and Eid al-Adha may last anything from two to 10 days, depending on the region. For more information, see the World of Islam appendix.

Health

	Special Precautions?	Certificate Required?
Yellow Fever	Yes	Yes/1
Cholera	Yes	No/2
Typhoid & Polio	3	N/A
Malaria	4	N/A

Note: Regulations and requirements may be subject to change at short notice, and you are advised to contact your doctor well in advance of your intended date of departure. Any numbers in the chart refer to the footnotes below.

1: A yellow fever vaccination certificate is required from travellers over one year of age arriving from infected areas. Travellers arriving from non-endemic zones should note that vaccination is strongly recommended for travel outside the urban areas, even if an outbreak of the disease has not been reported and they would normally not require a vaccination certificate to enter the country.
2: Following WHO guidelines issued in 1973, a cholera vaccination certificate is not a condition of entry to Uganda. However, cholera is a serious risk in this country and precautions are essential. Up-to-date advice should be sought before deciding whether these precautions should include vaccination, as medical opinion is divided over its effectiveness; see the Health appendix for more information.
3: Typhoid and poliomyelitis are widespread and immunisation is advised.

4: Malaria risk, predominantly in the malignant falciparum form, occurs all year throughout the country, including the main towns of Fort Portal, Jinja, Kampala, Mbale and parts of Kigezi. Resistance to chloroquine and sulfadoxine-pyrimethamine has been reported. The recommended prophylaxis is mefloquine.

Food & drink: All water should be regarded as being a potential health risk. Water used for drinking, brushing teeth or making ice should have first been boiled or otherwise sterilised. Milk is unpasteurised and should be boiled. Powdered or tinned milk is available and is advised, but make sure that it is reconstituted with pure water. Avoid dairy products which are likely to have been made from unboiled milk. Only eat well-cooked meat and fish, preferably served hot. Pork, salad and mayonnaise may carry increased risk. Vegetables should be cooked and fruit peeled.

Other risks: Bilharzia (schistosomiasis) is present. Avoid swimming and paddling in fresh water; swimming pools which are well chlorinated and maintained are safe. Meningitis risk exists, depending on area visited and time of year. Hepatitis E occurs. Vaccination against Hepatitis A is advised and Hepatitis B and tuberculosis for those at high risk. Rabies is also present. For those at high risk, vaccination before arrival should be considered. If you are bitten, seek medical advice without delay. For more information, consult the Health appendix. Sleeping sickness (trypanosomiasis) is reported. HIV/AIDS is widespread.

Health care: Visitors should bring personal supplies of medicines that are likely to be needed, but enquire first at the Embassy or High Commission whether such supplies may be freely imported. Comprehensive health insurance is essential and should include cover for emergency air repatriation in case of serious accident or illness. The Ugandan health service has still not recovered from the mass departure of foreign personnel in 1972 and there are medical facilities of a reasonable standard only in large towns and cities.

Travel - International

AIR: The main airline, Uganda Airlines (QU), is no longer in operation. Several airlines are now vying to replace the defunct carrier. Other airlines serving Uganda include British Airways (website: www.britishairways.com) which flies three times a week from London, Emirates (website: www.emirates.com) and Kenya Airways (website: www.kenya-airways.com) which flies from London, Nairobi and Amsterdam.

Approximate flight times: From Kampala to London is eight hours.

Main airports: Entebbe (EBB) is 40km (22 miles) southwest of Kampala (travel time – 30 minutes). To/from the airport: There are bus services to Kampala. Most hotels in Kampala and Entebbe will arrange airport transfers. Taxis are also available. Facilities: Duty free shops, restaurants, banks/bureaux de change, car hire and hotel reservations.

Departure tax: No airport tax is levied on passengers upon embarking at the airport (service charge is included in the ticket).

Note: All airline tickets purchased in Uganda must be paid for in hard currency.

LAKE: Between Kampala in Uganda and Mwanza in Tanzania, it is possible to catch a boat on Lake Victoria.

RAIL: Uganda Railways do not operate passenger services at present.

ROAD: There are connections with all neighbouring countries, although borders are not always open. However, travellers should take local advice before crossing the border with Rwanda, and should not attempt to cross the border with the Democratic Republic of Congo. **Bus:** There is a daily bus service between Kampala and Nairobi, Arusha and Dar-es-Salaam.

Travel - Internal

AIR: Eagle Air and United Airlines offer flights from Entebbe to most major towns. Charter flights are also available.

LAKE: Local boat services link Entebbe to the Ssese Islands.

ROAD: Traffic drives on the left. The road network extends over 28,332km (17,605 miles). The roads are of variable quality and radiate from Kampala, although the network is sparse in the north. There are still some army and police check points on roads and railways. The speed limit is 50 mph (80 kph) or 62 mph (100 kmh) on highways. Always keep vehicle doors locked. **Bus:** Services run between most parts of Uganda but are unreliable and often very crowded. Scheduled services operate between Entebbe and Kampala (travel time – one hour) and to and from the airport. An extensive network of minibuses, known as *Matatus*, runs to most parts of the country and they are a quick and convenient form of transport, but very overcrowded. However, there is a law against overloading on buses and if this occurs, the driver and passengers are liable to pay a fine. Post-bus services operate Monday to Saturday from Kampala to main towns. There are also special **taxis**, identifiable by their black and white stripes, which take passengers to wherever they want to go but are more expensive than *Matatas*. **Documentation:** An International Driving Permit and adequate third-party insurance is required. UK driving licences are accepted. Drivers must carry their vehicle log books and must pay for a temporary road licence.

Note: There have been a number of serious accidents involving long distance buses services between Kampala, Nairobi, Kigali and Dar es Salam. There have also been incidents on overnight buses between Nairobi and Kampala when bandits posing as passengers have forced buses to stop and have robbed the passengers. Visitors are advised not to travel on these overnight long distance buses.

Travel Advice

Most visits to Uganda are trouble-free. Kampala is a relatively safe city but visitors should take the usual precautions against crime and when going out at night. Uganda shares with neighbouring countries a threat of terrorism.

Visitors are advised against all travel to northern and north eastern Uganda because of rebel insurgency and tribal clashes.

There was an armed attack on a vehicle in the Murchison Falls National Park in November 2005, in which a British national was killed. Travellers are advised not to visit this park.

All travel to the region known as West Nile (Nebbi, Arua, Moyo and Yumbe districts in Uganda's far north west) is advised against, with the exception of trips to Arua town. Arua town should only be visited by air and visitors should remain within the confines of the town.

Travel by road at night is advised against except in central Kampala, and between Kampala and the airport at Entebbe.

Between 19 and 22 January 2006, there were clashes between dissidents and Government troops in North Kivu, in the east of the Congo (Dem Rep), close to the Bwindi and Mgahinga National Parks in Uganda. As a result of the fighting, thousands of civilians crossed the border into Uganda, although many have now gone back to the Congo (Dem Rep). Anyone planning to visit this south-west corner of Uganda, including the national parks, should exercise caution and seek local advice before embarking on their journey.

This advice is based on information provided by the Foreign and Commonwealth Office in the UK. It is correct at time of publishing. As the situation can change rapidly, visitors are advised to contact the following organisations for the latest travel advice:

British Foreign and Commonwealth Office
Tel: (0845) 850 2829.
Website: www.fco.gov.uk

US Department of State
Website: http://travel.state.gov/travel

Accommodation

There are international-standard hotels in Entebbe and Kampala. In smaller towns, hotels are generally of a more limited quality and they may not take traveller's cheques or credit cards. Camping, rustic bush camps and guest houses are also available. Information can be obtained from the Uganda Tourist Board (see *Top Things To See & Do*). All of the major national parks offer accommodation in game lodges. Note that most places will add 10 per cent service charge and 20 per cent VAT to any bill.

CAMPING AND CARAVANNING:
Most national parks and major tourist spots have camping sites, but campers should be well prepared and take the necessary precautions.

Top Things To See & Do

- **Kampala**, the capital, is set among hills with fine modern architecture, tree-lined avenues, cathedrals, mosques and palaces of the old Kingdom of Buganda, and the **Uganda Museum**. The **Kabaka Tombs** are on **Kasubi Hill**. Shoes must be removed before entering the buildings.
- **Jinja**, the second-largest town in Uganda, lies on the shores of **Lake Victoria**. Though somewhat underpopulated, there is a very lively **Saturday market**. See the source of the **Nile** at the nearby **Owen Falls Dam**.
- The major gateway to Uganda for air travellers, **Entebbe** has fine botanical gardens and a lakeside beach, although bathing is not advisable because of the dangers of *bilharzia* (see *Health* section).
- **Fort Portal** is a good base for exploring the **Ruwenzori Mountains**, the hot springs at **Bundibugyo** and the **Semluke Wildlife Reserve**.
- **Kisoro** is the starting point for **climbing** expeditions to **Mounts Muhavura** and **Mgahinga**. There are seven **lakes** in the vicinity, which offer **fishing** and possible duck shooting. See mountain gorillas in the **Bwindi Forest**.
- Uganda has 10 **national parks**, 10 **wildlife reserves** and seven **wildlife sanctuaries**, some of which are acclaimed as being amongst Africa's best. The country's main wildlife attraction for foreign visitors is the rare mountain gorilla, found in **Bwindi Impenetrable National Park** and **Mgahinga Gorilla National Park**, both in the southwest of the country. Many other species of primates can also be seen, including chimpanzees and monkeys. **Kibale National Park** alone contains 12 different types of primate, while **Ruwenzori National Park** is regarded as one of the most spectacular in Africa. Other wildlife is present in abundance.
- The Uganda Forest Department has set up several forest **ecotourism** projects at rainforest sites on popular tourist routes around the country. Camping facilities or traditional African *bandas* are available to accommodate travellers, and the sites are staffed by rangers and guides who can design programmes and provide information (charges are made for these services). Sites developed so far are the **Budongo Forest Reserve**, the largest mahogany forest in East Africa, situated near Masindi on the road to Lake Albert; the **Mabira Forest**, between Jinja and Kampala; the **Mpanga Forest**, containing abundant birdlife and a drum-making village, situated near Kampala; the **Kasyoha Kitomi Forest**, 1.5km (0.9 miles) from the main Mbarara to Kasese highway, near the Albertine Rift Valley; and the **Kalinzu Forest Reserve**, in the southwest of the country.
- Go **trekking:** The wide range of ecosystems in the country includes high mountains, lush hills, wetlands and arid lands. Many national parks have extensive nature trails, and several of Uganda's lakes have trails leading along the banks. Park rangers are available to advise visitors. It is usually best to be accompanied by a local guide. Popular treks include the **Karamoja**, the foothills of the mountains (the **Central Circuit trail**) and the **Sasa River Trail** on **Mount Elgon**. Set in fertile and lush country near **Mount Elgon**, **Mbale** is popular with **hikers** and inexperienced mountaineers. For further information, contact the Uganda Wildlife Authority, Plot 3, Kintu Road, Nakasero, PO Box 3530, Kampala (tel: (41) 346 287-8; website: www.uwa.or.ug).
- **Mount Elgon**, the **Rwenzoris** and the **Virungas** attract experienced **mountaineers** for easy and medium climbs.
- Specialist operators take groups of visitors to the rapids of the **White Nile** which provide thrilling **whitewater rafting**. Huge waves surge around heavily forested islands, the volume of water in this area being equivalent to 10 times that of the Zambezi. Hippos, crocodiles and monkeys are among the creatures that can be seen on the way. **Bujagali Falls** has grade 5 rapids. For more information, contact the Uganda Wildlife Authority (see above) *or* the Uganda Tourist Board.
- There is excellent **fishing** in numerous inland waters. There is a great opportunity for sport fishing at **Murchison Falls National Park**.

TOURIST INFORMATION

Uganda Tourist Board
PO Box 7211, 13-15 Kimathi Avenue, Impala House, Kampala, Uganda
Tel: (41) 342 196/7.
Website: www.visituganda.com

Entertainment

FOOD & DRINK: There are restaurants in and around Kampala. Many hotels serve local food.

National specialities:
- *Matoke* (a staple made from bananas).
- Millet bread.
- *Cassava*, a root that is commonly made into flour.
- Sweet potatoes.
- Chicken and beef stews.
- Freshwater fish.

National drinks:
- *Waragi*, a banana gin, popular among visitors as a cocktail base.

Tipping: Although always appreciated, it is not standard practice. It is normal to tip 5 to 10 per cent at tourist orientated restaurants. Guides and drivers should also be tipped.

SHOPPING: Purchases include bangles, necklaces and bracelets, woodcarvings, basketry, tea, coffee and ceramics. **Shopping hours:** Mon-Sat 0800-1700 some shops may close earlier on Saturdays.

Business

- **GDP:** US$6 billion (2003).
- **Main exports:** Coffee, fish and fish products, tea, tobacco, cotton, corn, beans and sesame.
- **Main imports:** Manufactured goods, machinery, transport equipment, chemicals and fuels.
- **Main trade partners:** Kenya, UK, South Africa and India.

ECONOMY: Agriculture dominates the Ugandan economy, accounting for half of total output and employing over 80 per cent of the workforce. Livestock rearing and a wide range of subsistence crops meet local needs; coffee is the main export commodity. Tobacco, tea, sugar cane and cocoa are also grown for export, and some processing of these is now carried out locally. The industrial sector produces textiles, cement, fertilisers, metal goods and a variety of household items. There are large deposits of copper and cobalt, the mining of which has been disrupted by civil wars and insurgency. In addition, there are known deposits of tin, tungsten, beryllium and tantalum ores. The relatively small tourism industry has suffered from the worldwide downturn since 2002. That year, Uganda received 350,000 visitors; the sector was worth US$250 million to the economy.

The economy recorded fairly steady economic growth throughout most of the last decade (averaging six per cent annual growth between 1998 and 2003) and, in contrast with much of the rest of Africa, has enjoyed a series of good harvests. The most pressing problem has been the country's debt burden. Uganda has benefited from several cancellations of long-term debt under a programme operated by the Paris Club of major donors and, more recently, the Heavily Indebted Poor Countries relief programme. Its total external debt now stands at just under US$4 billion. In exchange, the Government has been obliged to introduce a series of economic reforms, principally the removal of price controls and trade restrictions and a reduction in government spending.

Uganda is a member of the African Development Bank and of the Common Market for Eastern and Southern Africa (COMESA). In 2003, Uganda joined with neighbouring Kenya and Tanzania in a plan to revive the East African Customs Union (a previous attempt folded in 1977).

BUSINESS ETIQUETTE: A suit and tie are best worn by men for business meetings. English is used for all business discussions. Appointments should always be made. **Office hours:** Mon-Fri 0800-1230/1300 and 1400-1630/1700.

CONFERENCES/CONVENTIONS: The Uganda International Conference Centre with its main auditorium and three committee rooms has seating for up to 2000 persons. It is adjacent to the 4-star Nile Hotel and is 3km (2 miles) from the centre of Kampala. The Speke Resort & Country Lodge Munyayo, with 10 state-of-the-art conference rooms with modern facilities, has a capacity of over 3000 people. For further information, contact the Uganda Tourist Board (see *Top Things To See & Do*).

COMMERCIAL INFORMATION

Uganda Investment Authority
PO Box 7418, Investment Centre, Plot 28, Kampala Road, Kampala, Uganda
Tel: (41) 301 000 *or* (81) 251 562 *or* (75) 251 562.
Website: www.ugandainvest.com

Ukraine

Location: Central Eastern Europe.

Time: GMT + 2 (GMT + 3 from last Sunday in March to Saturday before last Sunday in October).

Overview

Ukraine came to international attention in late 2004 when 10 days of mass protests over electoral fraud led to a re-run of the Presidential election and the eventual declaration of Viktor Yushchenko as President. The people's 'Orange Revolution' undoubtedly raised Ukraine's profile abroad and the country is beginning to find its place on the tourist map.

Ukraine first came under Russian suzerainty in the 1650s, as an alternative to invasion by the Poles. Although part of Ukraine was annexed by Poland shortly afterwards, the whole of Ukraine was taken over by Russia after the partition of Poland at the end of the 18th century. When the empire of the Tsar collapsed in 1917, Bolshevik forces consolidated their control over Ukraine and the republic was incorporated into the Soviet Union. The failed Moscow coup of August 1991 spelt the end for the USSR; shortly afterwards the Ukrainian Supreme Soviet made a declaration of full independence. The dominant figure in Ukrainian politics used to be Leonid Kuchma, who held the Presidency from 1994 to 2004. However, Kuchma's increasingly autocratic and repressive leadership style and rapidly deteriorating relationship with Parliament reached the point where he was on the verge of declaring a state of emergency in 2003.

Constitutionally barred from standing at the November 2004 Presidential poll, he concentrated on making life as difficult as possible for his probable successor - Viktor Yushchenko. The poll itself was surrounded in controversy with Yushchenko narrowly surviving a dioxin poison attack during the run-up. The country came to the brink of collapse when Yushchenko's opponent, Viktor Yanukovych, seemed to have won the Presidential elections. This instigated mass protests on both sides and the so-called Orange Revolution.

Going back further in time, the country's rich history and its natural beauty are two of the biggest attractions. More than 500 of the cities date back some 900 years. Cities such as these – as well as many others which are only a few hundred years behind them – are enriched with monuments, buildings, archaeological sites and incredible palaces. Ukraine's capital, Kyiv, is the origin of the Kyiv Rus State, founded in the eighth and ninth centuries and the third-largest city in the CIS. Striking examples of Baroque

and Renaissance architecture can be found in Lviv, one of Europe's oldest cities, while Odessa is probably best known for the Potemkin Stairway, but is also home to one of the world's largest opera houses. Ukraine is a varied country whose landscapes range from the spectacular Carpathian Mountains in the west to the central plains to the stunning Black Sea views in the south. The coastal resorts of the Crimea were once a favourite destination for Kremlin leaders; Yalta, the 'Pearl of the Crimea', attracts the bulk of summer visitors, while the nearby vineyards provide plenty of wine tasting opportunities.

General Information

AREA: 603,700 sq km (233,090 sq miles).
POPULATION: 47.8 million (UN estimate 2005).
POPULATION DENSITY: 79.2 per sq km.
CAPITAL: Kyiv. **Population:** 2.67 million (official estimate 2005).
GEOGRAPHY: Ukraine is bordered by the Russian Federation to the north and east; Belarus to the north; Poland, the Slovak Republic and Hungary to the west; and Romania and Moldova to the southwest. It is a varied country with mountains in the west, plains in the centre and the Black Sea views to the south. The north of the state is dominated by forests. Its other two main features are wooded steppe with beech and oak forests and the treeless steppe. The River Dnieper divides Ukraine roughly in half, and flows into the Black Sea.
GOVERNMENT: Republic. Gained independence from the Soviet Union in 1991. **Head of State:** President Viktor Yushchenko since 2005. **Head of Government:** Prime Minister Yuri Yekhanurov since September 2005. **Recent history:** Following the elections in late 2004 when he lost to the candidate backed by outgoing President Leonid Kuchma, Mr Yushchenko and his supporters took to the streets to protest that the vote had been rigged. After 10 days of peaceful but dramatic demonstrations dubbed the 'Orange Revolution', a rerun was ordered and Mr Yushchenko won. Viktor Yuschenko's first year in Government has been far from smooth. The heady days of the Orange Revolution have faded, no thanks to a slowing economy and rising prices. In early September 2005, Yushchenko sacked his Government following resignations and corruption claims. Yushchenko's close ally Yuri Yekhanurov succeeded Yuliya Tymoshenko as Prime Minister later that month. However, the deal negotiated to end the dispute with Russia over gas prices in January 2006 resulted in Parliament passing a vote of no-confidence in Yekhanurov's Government. Parliament claimed too much had been yielded to Russia. Meanwhile, Yushchenko is consulting lawyers over the legality of this move and the sacked Government remains in power.
LANGUAGE: Ukrainian is the sole official state language. A member of the eastern Slav languages and similar to Russian, it was discouraged for centuries by Tsarist and Soviet authorities. It is still widely spoken in western and central Ukraine, although Russian is spoken by virtually everyone. Russian is the main language spoken in Kyiv, eastern Ukraine and Crimea. The present Government uses every opportunity to promote the revival of Ukrainian, particularly in schools. There are 12 million ethnic Russians in Ukraine, 500,000 Jews and more than 250,000 Crimean Tatars.

RELIGION: There are about 35 million Ukrainian Orthodox faithful, although the church is divided into a traditional pro-Moscow and a breakaway pro-Kyiv faction. 5 million Eastern-rite (Uniate) Catholics, subservient to Rome, are concentrated in western Ukraine and it is now several years since a Stalin-era ban on their church was lifted. There are also Protestant and Muslim minorities. Mass emigration has reduced the numbers of Jews, concentrated in Kyiv, Lviv and Odessa.
ELECTRICITY: 220 volts AC, 50Hz.
SOCIAL CONVENTIONS: Ukrainian people are warm and particularly friendly to visitors. It is not at all uncommon for Ukrainians to invite strangers into their own homes. People on the street are friendly despite the rigours of post-Soviet life. Formal attire is rarely required, though people dress smartly for the theatre. Visitors should avoid ostentatious displays of wealth in public places.

Climate

Temperate with warm summers; crisp, sunny autumns; and cold, snowy winters.
Required clothing: Lightweight clothes needed in summer, light- to mediumweight in the spring and autumn and heavyweight in the winter.

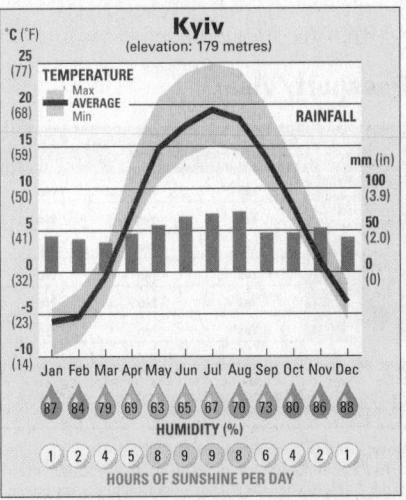

Communications

Telephone: Ukraine has reliable communications with the West, and most major cities provide IDD facilities and can be dialled from abroad. Country code: 380. Telephone cards for public payphones can be bought in post offices.
Mobile telephone: Roaming agreements exist with most international mobile phone companies. Coverage is limited to main urban areas.
Internet: Internet cafes are available in major cities.
Post: Services are erratic. Letters to Western Europe can take two weeks or more. The main post office in Kyiv is located at Khreshchatik 22 and is open 24 hours. Telephone

Credit: ©Bruce Logan

calls can be made here and faxes can be sent. Post office hours: Generally 0800-1700.
MEDIA: Prior to the November 2004 Presidential elections, state-run TV tended to toe the Government line. However, during the dispute that followed the election, balanced reports were broadcast for the first time in years. Following his election, Viktor Yushchenko declared his belief in press freedom, in contrast to his predecessor, who suppressed the opposition press. Under President Kuchma, several opposition newspapers were closed and a number of journalists investigating high-profile crimes died in mysterious circumstances. The most famous of these was Georgiy Gongadze, who disappeared in 2000 and whose body was found a year later. A Parliamentary commission investigating the case believes Kuchma to be one of the organisers of the abduction, an allegation which he denies.
Press: The most widely read include the daily *Fakty i Kommentarii, Kievskiye Vedomosti, Silski Visti* and *Vecherniye Vesti*. The Russian press is also widely available. The *Kyiv Post* is a daily English-language newspaper. Western newspapers are available in Kyiv.
TV: The state-run *National TV Company of Ukraine* operates *UT1, UT2* and *UT3*. Commercial channels include *ICTV, Inter TV, 5 Kanal, STB, Novy Canal* and *Studio 1+1*.
Radio: Three networks are operated by the state-run *National Radio Company of Ukraine*, while commercial stations include *Europa Plus, Hit FM, Nashe FM* and *Russkoye Radio*.

Passport/Visa

	Passport Required?	Visa Required?	Return Ticket Required?
Full British	Yes	No	No
Australian	Yes	Yes	No
Canadian	Yes	No	No
USA	Yes	No	No
Other EU	Yes	No	No
Japanese	Yes	No	No

Note: *Regulations and requirements may be subject to change at short notice, and you are advised to contact the appropriate diplomatic or consular authority before finalising travel arrangements. Any numbers in the chart refer to the footnotes below.*

Note: (a) Ukrainian visas are *not* valid in the Russian Federation, and Russian Federation visas are *not* valid in Ukraine. (b) As a general rule, visitors requiring visas should apply before travelling.
PASSPORTS: Passport valid for at least one month beyond return date required by all.
VISAS: Required by all except the following:
(a) nationals of countries referred to in the chart above;
(b) nationals of all CIS countries (except nationals of Turkmenistan who *do* need a visa);
(c) nationals of Andorra, Hungary, Iceland, Liechtenstein, Monaco, Mongolia, Norway, Poland, Romania, San Marino, Switzerland and Vatican City.
Types of visa and cost: *Tourist*: £20 (single-entry); £35 (double-entry); *Business/Private*: £20 (single-entry); £40 (double-entry); £110 (multiple-entry). *Student*: £10 (single-entry). *Transit*: £10 (double-entry); £50 (multiple-entry, business only).
US citizens: £63 (single-entry); £69 (double-entry); £104 (multiple entry) (inclusive of handling fee).
Note: A handling charge of £20 is also required from the Embassy for each application.
Validity: *Single-entry*: Valid for stays of up to 90 days within six months after first trip to Ukraine; *Double-entry/Multiple-entry*: Six to 12 months; *Transit*: Five days for each entry.
Application to: Consulate (or Consular section at Embassy); see *Passport/Visa Information*.
Application requirements: (a) Valid passport/travel document with at least one blank page. (b) One completed application form. (c) Two recent passport-size photos. (d) Fee (postal order or company cheque only; if applying by post, enclose two separate postal orders or company cheques covering the handling charge and visa fee). (e) A contact telephone number. (f) Recorded, registered, self-addressed envelope for postal applications. *Tourism*: (a)-(f) and, (g) Tourist voucher with confirmation of hotel booking. *Business*: (a)-(f) and, (g) Letter of invitation from Ukrainian company or organisation stating purpose of the visit (*see note below). (h) Copy of registration certificate of company or office in Ukraine. (i) For *multiple-entry* visas, detailed letters from Ukrainian company and company in home country explaining necessity for multiple-entry visa (*see note below). *Private*: (a)-(f) and, (g) Letter of invitation from Ukraine (faxed copy is acceptable) issued by the Passport and Immigration Department of a local Police Station in Ukraine (*see note below). *Student*: (a)-(f) and, (g) The original invitation letter from the Ministry of Education of Ukraine or from the University/College. *Transit*: (a)-(f) and, (g) Photocopy of the visa (if required) of the country of destination.
Note: *Nationals of Canada, the EU, Japan, Switzerland, Turkey and the USA applying for business or private visas *do not* require a letter of invitation.
Working days required: 10 if submitted by post; three if submitted in person. This applies only to nationals of Turkey. For all other nationals, processing will always take approximately 10 days.

PASSPORT/VISA INFORMATION

Embassy of Ukraine in the UK
60 Holland Park, London W11 3SJ, UK
Tel: (020) 7727 6312.
Website: www.ukremb.org.uk
Opening hours: Mon-Thurs 0900-1300, 1430-1830; Fri 0900-1300, 1430-1715.
Not open to personal callers.
Consular section: Ground Floor, 78 Kensington Park Road, London W11 2PL, UK
Tel: (020) 7243 8923 *or* (0906) 550 8955 (information line).
Opening hours: Mon-Fri 0930-1200.

Embassy of Ukraine in the USA
3350 M Street, NW, Washington, DC 20007, USA
Tel: (202) 333 0606.
Website: www.ukraine.info.us

Consulate General of Ukraine in the USA
240 East 49 Street, New York, NY 10017, USA
Tel: (212) 371 5690.
Opening hours: Mon-Fri 0915-1200.
Website: www.ukrconsul.org

Money

Currency: Hryvnya (UAH) = 100 kopiyok (singular: kopiyka). Notes are in denominations of UAH200, 100, 50, 20, 10, 5, 2 and 1. Coins are in denominations of 50, 25, 10, 5, 2 and 1 kopiyok.
Currency exchange: Money should only be changed at currency booths on the street or in banks. It is advisable to keep receipts showing money changed. Changing money with black-market traders is not recommended and can be dangerous.
Credit & debit cards: Not readily accepted. Only a few restaurants and hotels will accept them. Travellers should be aware there is a high level of credit card fraud.
Traveller's cheques: Not generally advised. If taken, they should be made out in US Dollars.
Currency restrictions: The import of local currency is limited to UAH1000. The export of local currency is limited to UAH10,000. Amounts over UAH1000 require a customs form. The import of foreign currency is limited to US$10,000 and any amounts exceeding US$1000 require a special customs form. The export of foreign currency is limited to US$5000. Amounts over US$1000 must be declared on a customs form. Any higher amounts can be exported with special permission from the National Bank of Ukraine.
Banking hours: Mon-Fri 0930-1730.
Exchange rate indicators:
Rate at time of publishing
£1.00= UAH8.86
$1.00= UAH5.05

Duty Free

The following items may be imported into Ukraine without incurring customs duty:
200 cigarettes or 50 cigars or 250g of tobacco products; 1l of spirits and 2l of wine (persons over 20 years of age only); goods for personal use, provided holding proof of their export, or imported under conditions of transit (toiletries and personal effects); gifts up to the value of €200.
Prohibited: Means of transportation that are five or more years old for permanent use in Ukraine, for selling or breaking into parts; strong, poisonous, radioactive or explosive substances or other objects that can harm the population and animals or contaminate the environment; printed materials, films, negatives, photos, movies, videos, computer disks, scripts, records and other audio recordings, drawings, and other printed materials that contain propaganda of war, racism or genocide; food products without the relevant certificate; seeds and plants. Animals require veterinary certificates issued by relevant Ukrainian authorities. Contact the Embassy of Ukraine for further details.

Public Holidays

Below are listed Public Holidays for the January 2006-June 2007 period.
2006: Jan 1 New Year's Day. **Jan 7** Orthodox Christmas Day. **Mar 8** International Women's Day. **Apr 16-17** Easter. **May 1-2** Labour Days. **May 9** Victory Day. **Jun 7** Trinity Day. **Jun 28** Constitution Day. **Aug 24** Ukrainian Independence Day.
2007: Jan 1 New Year's Day. **Jan 7** Orthodox Christmas Day. **Mar 8** International Women's Day. **Apr 8-9**. Easter **May 1-2** Labour Days. **May 9** Victory Day. **Jun 7** Trinity Day. **Jun 28** Constitution Day.
Note: If a holiday falls on Thursday, then Friday and Saturday may also be holidays. If a holiday falls on a Saturday or Sunday, then Monday is considered a holiday as well.

Health

	Special Precautions?	Certificate Required?
Yellow Fever	No	No
Cholera	No	No
Typhoid & Polio	1	N/A
Malaria	No	N/A

Note: *Regulations and requirements may be subject to change at short notice, and you are advised to contact your doctor well in advance of your intended date of departure. Any numbers in the chart refer to the footnotes below.*

1: *Typhoid* may occur in rural areas.
Food & drink: All water should be regarded as a potential health risk. Water used for drinking, brushing teeth or making ice should have first been boiled or otherwise sterilised. Milk is pasteurised and dairy products are safe for consumption. Only eat well-cooked meat and fish, preferably served hot. Pork, salad and mayonnaise may carry increased risk. Vegetables should be cooked and fruit peeled.
Other risks: Widespread outbreaks of *diphtheria* have been reported in recent years. *Tick-borne encephalitis* occurs in forested areas. Visitors are advised to seek medical advice about immunisation and precautionary measures. Good personal hygiene and care with water and food supplies are essential. *Hepatitis A* may occur and precautions should be taken. Travellers may wish to consider immunisation against *rabies*. There have been cases of *avian flu* in the Crimean peninsula, but no human cases have been reported.
Health care: The health service does, in theory, provide free medical treatment for all citizens and travellers who become ill. However, as in most parts of the former Soviet Union, health care is a serious problem. For minor difficulties, visitors are advised to ask the management at their hotels for help. For major problems, visitors are well advised to seek help outside the country. The UK and Ukraine have a bilateral agreement on emergency medical treatment, so UK travellers should not need to pay an insurance levy on arrival. Travel insurance is strongly recommended, however. It is advisable to take a supply of those medicines that are likely to be required (but check first that they may be legally imported) as medicines can prove difficult to obtain. Travellers are advised to contact their Embassy, in the first instance, for advice on where to get medical help.

Travel - International

AIR:
Ukraine International Airlines (PS) (website: www.ukraine-international.com/eng) links Kyiv with Amsterdam, Barcelona, Berlin, Brussels, Frankfurt/M, Helsinki, Lisbon, London, Madrid, Paris, Rome, Vienna and Zürich. *Aerosvit (VV)* (website: www.aerosvit.ua/eng) operates domestic routes as well as serving a number of international destinations.
Approximate flight times: From Kyiv to *London* is three hours 30 minutes, to *Moscow* is one hour 35 minutes and to *Vienna* is two hours.
Main airports: *Kyiv – Borispol International (KBP)* is approximately 34km (21 miles) from central Kyiv. *To/from the airport:* Buses run to the city centre every 20 to 30 minutes for most of the day (travel time - approximately one hour). The arrival/departure point in central Kyiv is the central railway station. Taxis usually cost about UAH100. *Facilities:* Banks/bureaux de change, duty free shops, restaurants, pubs, child facilities, left luggage and car hire.
Departure tax: None.
SEA/RIVER:
Main ports: *Ilyichevsk, Izmail* and *Odessa*. *UkrFerry* (website: www.ukrferry.com) operates ferries from Odessa to Istanbul, Turkey; from Ilyichevsk to Poti and Batumi, Georgia; from Ilyichevsk to Varna, Bulgaria; and from Ilyichevsk to Derince, Turkey. Ferries are available to the Russian Federation ports of Novorossiysk and Sochi. The Republic's most important internal waterway is the River Dnieper. Several companies offer Black Sea cruises around the Crimean peninsula.
RAIL:
The 22,730km (14,207 miles) of railway track link most towns and cities within the republic and further links extend from Kyiv to all other CIS member states. The main stations are Kyiv and Lviv. Regular daily services connect these stations with Moscow. There are international trains to many other major European cities. Fast '*firmeny*' trains are the most rapid, modern and comfortable trains. Tickets are cheap by UK standards. If travelling by overnight train, do not leave the compartment

unattended. Timetables for trains within CIS states, including trains to Ukraine, are available in English from the website www.poezda.net. The fastest train from Kyiv to Moscow takes 10 hours 30 minutes and to St Petersburg 25 hours 30 minutes.

ROAD:

 Outside urban areas, roads can be badly lit and in poor condition. Border points are at Chop, Mostiska and Uzhgorod. A road tax is payable at the border. Petrol stations and repair garages are becoming more common, but it is recommended to carry spare parts. Leaded and unleaded petrol are available. Cash is usually required at petrol stations. Insurance cover can be difficult to arrange. See *Travel – Internal* for information on **traffic regulations** and **documentation**. **Coach:** *Eurolines* (52 Grosvenor Gardens, London SW1W 0AU; tel: (08705) 143 219; website: www.eurolines.com) and National Express (Ensign Court, 4 Vicarage Road, Edgbaston, Birmingham B15 3ES; tel: 08705 808 080; website: www.nationalexpress.com) run regular coach services from the UK to Ukraine and other European cities. **Passes:** Travellers can either choose Mini-Pass breaks or book a 15-, 30- or 60-day pass. The six Mini-Passes give travellers the freedom to visit three cities, with prices starting from £55. Travellers can stay as long as they like in each city. **Bus:** A few buses run daily services from Karkiv to Moscow.

Travel - Internal

AIR:

 Domestic flights in Kyiv depart from both *Borispol airport (KBP)* and from *Zhulany airport (IEV)*. *Aerosvit* (website: www.aerosvit.ua/eng) is one of the main domestic carriers.

RIVER:

 Cruises between Kyiv, Odessa and Sevastopol are very popular and can be booked through various tour operators.

RAIL:

 Trains are more reliable than air travel in winter, when aircraft are sometimes grounded. Timetables for trains in CIS states, including trains within Ukraine, are available in English from the website www.poezda.net. The Ukrainian Railways website ww.uz.gov.ua also publishes information, but is not available in English.

ROAD:

 Bus: There are services to most cities and towns. One of the most modern and comfortable fleets of buses is operated by *Autolux* (website: www.autolux.com.ua). The company runs coaches to all the major cities and publishes its website in English. **Taxi:** Hiring a driver for a long-distance destination is a realistic option. **Car hire:** Self-drive hire cars are gradually becoming more available. **Regulations:** Speed limits are 60kph (37mph) in built-up areas, 90kph (55mph) in outside areas and 130kph (80mph) on the motorways. Traffic drives on the right; righthand-drive cars are prohibited. Drinking and driving is strictly prohibited. The limit of alcohol allowed in drivers' blood is zero. Heavy fines are imposed if traffic police smell alcohol on a driver's breath. **Documentation:** An International Driving Permit is necessary.

URBAN:

 Kharkiv, Kyiv and Dnipropetrovsk have clean, efficient and cheap metro systems, where tickets can be purchased at vending machines inside the stations. Buses and trolleybuses are extremely crowded and are best avoided. Taxis are easy to find in the cities. Official taxis have yellow and black signs on the roof and are metered. Fares should be negotiated in advance for private taxis. Some shared taxis and minibuses exist on fixed routes. Hitchhiking is very common, although not recommended. Travellers can indicate the need for a lift and the driver will take them to their destination cheaply by Western standards, but prices should be agreed in advance. There are no public transport services from 0100-0500.

Travel Advice

Most visits to Ukraine are trouble-free but you should be aware of the global risk of indiscriminate international terrorist attacks, which could be against civilian targets, including places frequented by foreigners.
Travellers should be aware of petty crime, particularly in crowded areas, tourist spots and on public transport.
This advice is based on information provided by the Foreign and Commonwealth Office in the UK. It is correct at time of publishing. As the situation can change rapidly, visitors are advised to contact the following organisations for the latest travel advice:

British Foreign and Commonwealth Office
Tel: (0845) 850 2829.
Website: www.fco.gov.uk

US Department of State
Website: http://travel.state.gov/travel

Credit: ©Bruce Logan

Accommodation

HOTELS:

 Standards are lower than in countries where the tourist industry is more developed. The best hotels are in Kyiv, Odessa and the seaside resort Yalta.

PRIVATE ROOMS: A room in a private home is an excellent accommodation option in Ukraine as the people are friendly and hospitable, and prices tend to be far more reasonable. However, there is no organisation as such that arranges rooms in private homes. Visitors can, however, ask around, as the savings and greater comfort may be well worth the effort (as long as due caution is observed).

APARTMENTS AND SELF CATERING:

 Apartments are available for short-term let in larger cities, in particular in Kyiv and Odessa.

YOUTH HOSTELS:

 The *Youth Hostel Association of Ukraine* (see *Accommodation Information*) runs several hostels in Kyiv, Lviv and Balaclava (Sevastopol).

CAMPING/CARAVANNING:

 Campsites are available on the outskirts of cities.

ACCOMMODATION INFORMATION

Youth Hostel Association of Ukraine
PO Box 156, Kyiv 01025, Ukraine
Tel: (44) 331 0260.
Website: www.hihostels.com.ua

Top Things To See

- Visit **Kyiv**, the capital of Ukraine and the third-largest city in the CIS. It is also the cradle of Russian civilisation, the origin of the Kyiv Rus State founded in the eighth and ninth centuries and the city from which the Orthodox faith spread throughout Eastern Europe. The **Golden Gate of Kyiv** is the last remnant of the 10th-century walls built to defend the city.
- Discover Kyiv's religious heritage. The **Caves Monastery** in the city centre is the focal point of the early Orthodox church. Visitors have to carry candles to see the church relics, which are set in a maze of catacombs. It is the headquarters of the pro-Russian Orthodox church. The 11th-century **St Sofia Cathedral** contains splendid icons and frescoes and is situated in beautiful grounds. The **Cathedral of St Vladimir** is the headquarters of the rival pro-Ukrainian church.
- Enjoy a spot of culture at Kyiv's **Opera House**, the **Museum of Ukrainian Art** (with its collection of the work of regional artists from the 16th century to the present) and the **Historical Museum of Ukraine**.
- Wander up **Andreyev Hill**, a restored cobbled street in central Kyiv now used by artists to sell their wares. There are a lot of cafes and restaurants in this area. Alternatively, people-watch in **Khreshchatik Street** and **Independence Square**, Kyiv's main thoroughfares. The square is particularly elegant with its chestnut trees and fountains.
- **Martinsky Palace and Parliament** in Kyiv is the official residence of Ukraine's President. The nearby **Park of Glory** is a war memorial, with a vast and controversial monument of a woman with a sword and shield overlooking the river.
- Explore **Lviv**, a city of striking Baroque and Renaissance architecture, and the focal point of Ukrainian national culture. The **City Castle** was the first building to fly Ukraine's blue-and-yellow national flag. Located by the foothills of the picturesque Carpathians, it is one of the oldest and most unusual cities in Europe. The **National Museum**, **Museum of History**, **Art Gallery**, **Antique Armoury** (City Arsenal) and **Museum of Ethnography and Crafts** are famous for their collections. Development of the pharmaceutical trade in Ukraine is represented by the collection of the **Pharmaceutical Museum** – the oldest functioning pharmacy of Lviv (established in 1735).
- Lviv itself is often called 'the open-air museum'. The highlight of its architecture is doubtlessly **Market Square**, connected for more than 600 years with local history. The Market Square of the old city performed the function of an economic, political and administrative centre up to the end of the 19th century. The area housed members of the urban nobility and wealthy merchant class, building many mansions and commercial properties. Today, Market Square is the core of the historical and architectural preservation area, consisting of 45 buildings. They reflect elements of many architectural traditions, such as Gothic, Baroque, Renaissance and Rococo.
- Head to **Odessa**, the site of the famous 192 steps of the **Potemkin stairway** from Sergei Eisenstein's film, *Battleship Potemkin*. In addition, Odessa is also a centre

of renewal of Jewish culture, with a community of 45,000. There is a vast **Opera House** – one of the world's largest. The ceiling is decorated with scenes from the plays of Shakespeare. Also worth visiting is the **Statue of the Duke of Richelieu**, the **Vorontsov Palace** on the waterfront and the **Archaeological Museum** with exhibits from the Black Sea area and Egypt.

• **The Crimea** was once a summer playground for Kremlin leaders. Hotels and services are relatively cheap for Westerners, and the place is a favourite with German tourists. The region's dusty capital of **Simferopol** has few tourist sights. It is **Yalta**, the 'Pearl of the Crimea', which draws visitors. Former Communist Party spas have now been turned into resort centres. The **Vorontsov Palace** was designed by Edward Blore, one of the architects of Buckingham Palace. **Nikitsky Gardens**, just outside of Yalta, is a good afternoon's excursion. Industry is centred on **Massandra**, above Yalta. **Livada** is where Roosevelt, Churchill and Stalin met in the **Livada Palace** in 1945. **Foros** is where Gorbachev was held for three days during the 1991 coup.

Top Things To Do

• Watch a **theatre** or **opera** performance in Lviv. Several theatre companies perform in Lviv. The **Opera House** of Ivan Franko is a source of great pride to locals. Extravagantly built, with richly decorated façade and interior, its architecture leads Lviv Opera to be classed among the best theatres in Europe.

• **Taste wine** in the **Crimea**. The region's vineyards produce good-quality wine which can be tasted locally quite cheaply. The **Wine Tasting Hall** in Yalta is as good a place as any.

• **Ski** or **snowboard** in the **Carpathian Mountains** in the west. The leading resorts are **Bukovel**, **Slavsko**, **Drahobrat** and **Tysovets**. Bukovel is the only resort of international standard. Drahobrat is the highest resort in the country and has the most reliable snow.

• The **Carpathians** are ideal for **walking** holidays in spring and summer.

• **Cycling** is becoming increasingly popular. Although the city streets are not particularly cyclist-friendly, there are several parks and forests in and around Kyiv which make excellent day trips. It is possible to hire bicycles in **Kyiv** for one or more days. Ukraine's countryside offers quieter roads and lanes for rural cycling. Travellers can take bicycles on trains as long as they are in a cover.

• Take part in the **Kyiv Days** celebrations, held annually during the last weekend of May. Events include performances by actors and musicians, as well as fireworks displays.

• Join the locals, who go **swimming** in summer in the **Dnieper River** in Kyiv and climb onto its ice in winter to fish. It is possible to take boat trips on the river. There is a park and a beach on **Trukhaniv Island**.

TOURIST INFORMATION

Intourist Travel Ltd in the UK
7 Princedale Road, Holland Park, London W11 4NW, UK
Tel: (020) 7792 5240 *or* (0870) 112 1232 (general enquiries).
Website: www.intouristuk.com

Entertainment

FOOD & DRINK: Visitors now have a wide choice of cuisines (including French, Indian, Italian, Japanese or Thai), particularly in Kyiv.
National specialities:
• *Borshch* (beetroot soup).
• *Varenniki* (dough containing cheese, meat or fruit).
• *Holubtsi* (cabbage rolls).
• Chicken Kiev exists but is better known in the West.
National drinks:
• Crimean wines are excellent, especially dessert wines such as *Krasny Kamen* ('Red Stone').
• *Abrau* and *Miskhako* are excellent brands of cabernet.
• *Artyomov* champagne (bottled in eastern Ukraine).
• Fortified wines from Massandra, particularly one named 'Black Doctor'.
Tipping: Tips and, if appropriate, small gifts are appreciated. Service is sometimes included in first-class restaurants and hotel bills.
NIGHTLIFE: Opera is performed in the ornate theatres of Kyiv, Lviv and Odessa. Ukrainians have a deep-rooted musical tradition and singing is very popular. Most cities also have good musical comedy, puppet-theatre and troupes performing theatrical works in Ukrainian and Russian. Tickets are cheap by Western standards and readily available on the day of performance at the box offices. Prominent visiting artists most often perform in Kyiv's vast Ukraine Theatre, where prices are higher.

SHOPPING: Artwork is the best buy. Top-quality paintings, ceramics and jewellery may be purchased quite cheaply at galleries or direct from artists on the street. Avoid the state shops, which have dull merchandise. **Shopping hours:** Large state or department stores tend to open Mon-Fri 0800-1900, whereas small boutiques are generally open 0900-1800.Some shops stay open as late as 2000. Smaller shops may close for an hour at lunch, usually from 1300-1400 or 1

Business

• **GDP:** US$67.28 billion (2004).
• **Main exports:** Ferrous and nonferrous metals, fuel and petroleum products, chemicals, machinery and transport equipment and food products.
• **Main imports:** Energy, machinery and equipment and chemicals.
• **Main trade partners:** Russia, Germany, Turkey, Turkmenistan, Italy and USA.

ECONOMY: Ukraine has large areas of very fertile land, which gave it its reputation as the 'bread basket' of the former Soviet Union. Grain, sugar beet and vegetables are the main crops and there is extensive livestock farming. The country is also blessed with mineral resources, particularly coal in the huge Donbass fields, as well as iron ore, manganese and titanium. There are a few reserves of gas and oil but Ukraine has to import over three-quarters of its requirements of these products from elsewhere, mainly from the Russian Federation and Turkmenistan. Much of this is still needed to fuel the heavy industries that dominate the country's manufacturing economy. Metalworking, engineering products (especially machinery and transport equipment) and chemicals are the most important of these. A large proportion of industry was previously devoted to military production but this has sharply declined since the demise of the Soviet Union and drastic cuts in defence budgets.
With some reluctance, Ukraine began to dismantle its highly centralised command economy in 1992 and introduce market mechanisms under the guidance of the IMF, which the country joined, along with the World Bank, in the same year. Key elements of the programme were privatisation, price reform, trade liberalisation and, as a necessary adjunct, the introduction of a fully convertible currency – the Hryvnya – which came into use in 1995. Throughout this period, and for some years after, the Ukrainian economy contracted at about 12 per cent per year, as well as suffering very high inflation which occasionally touched 400 per cent. The reform programme has continued to make slow progress in the face of opposition from entrenched interests, fear of foreign competition and disagreements amongst the pro-reformers over the pace of change. After a difficult first 10 years, the post-Soviet economy is now fairly stable: annual GDP growth is now 12 per cent (2004), while inflation has been reduced to a more manageable 12.3 per cent (2004). Officially, unemployment is 2.9 per cent of the workforce (2005), but a large 'grey' economy has evolved, which some estimates put at half the size of the legitimate economy. Ukraine also belongs to the European Bank for Reconstruction and Development as a 'Country of Operation'. Negotiations for Ukraine's membership of the World Trade Organisation are ongoing. Several of Ukraine's neighbours will be joining the European Union in the near future. Ukraine itself is far from a condition in which it might be accepted for EU membership, but this is bound to have a major impact on the country's economic policy-making.
BUSINESS ETIQUETTE: Suits, and ties for men, are required for official business. Exchange of business cards is extremely common and visitors are advised to bring company cards. **Office hours:** Mon-Fri 0900-1700/1800. Lunch tends to be at least one-and-a-half hours.

COMMERCIAL INFORMATION

Chamber of Commerce and Industry
33 vul. Velyka Zhytomyrska , 01601 Kyiv, Ukraine
Tel: (44) 272 2911
Website: www.ucci.org.ua

Ministry of Economy
12/2 Grushevskogo Str, 01008 Kyiv, Ukraine
Tel: (44) 253 9394.
Website: www.me.gov.ua

Economic and Commercial Section/Trade and Economic Mission
Embassy of Ukraine in the UK
60 Holland Park, London W11 3SJ, UK
Tel: (020) 7221 0589.

United Arab Emirates

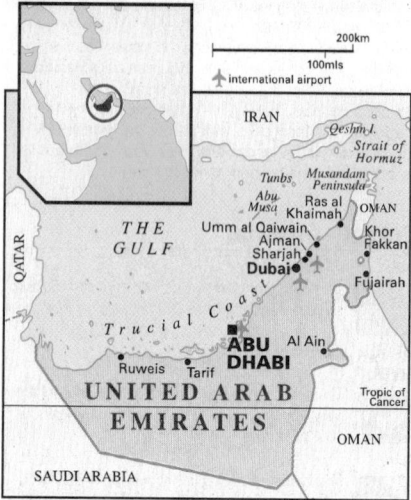

Location: Middle East.

Time: GMT + 4.

Overview

This group of small sheikhdoms on the coastline of the Persian Gulf was a backwater of the Islamic civilisation that prospered in the Middle East from the seventh century onwards. After attacks on British-owned shipping by pirates operating in the Gulf region, they were brought under British suzerainty in the 19th Century. The sheikhdoms – which became known as the Trucial States – carried on largely unmolested and ignored until the 1950s when the British started to relinquish control as part of its post-imperial retrenchment. The British plan for the Trucial States was to weld its seven distinct regimes into a single administrative bloc. The discovery of oil in 1966, which gave the local economy a sudden and rapid boost, helped to ease the process and soon transformed the emirate and its way of life. Dubai's first oil exports in 1969 were followed by a period of rapid development that laid the foundations for today's modern society.
The United Arab Emirates (UAE) is a federation of seven states - Abu Dhabi, Dubai, Ajman, Fujairah, Ras al Khaimah, Sharjah and Umm al Qaiwain - formed in 1971 after independence from Britain. Although internal politics are prone to instability, because of the uncertain nature of the federation and boundary disputes, the ruling families in the two main emirates, Dubai and Abu Dhabi, have managed to stabilise the federation.
From the timeless tranquillity of the desert to the lively bustle of the *souk*, Dubai offers a kaleidoscope of attractions for visitors. The emirate embraces a wide variety of scenery in a very small area. In a single day, the tourist can experience everything from rugged mountains and awe-inspiring sand dunes to sandy beaches and lush green parks, from dusty villages and ancient houses with windtowers to luxurious residential districts and from the colourful *souks* to ultra-modern shopping malls. Indeed, one of Dubai's greatest visitor attractions is its superb shopping. As an open port with low import duties, Dubai's retail prices are reasonable and the variety of products available is virtually unrivalled. Whatever the visitor's tastes - be it couture from Paris or Milan, hi-tech electronics from Japan, or a piece of silver Bedouin jewellery - he or she will find it at the right price in Dubai.
Sometimes called the 'Manhattan of the Middle East', Abu Dhabi City is essentially a modern and sleek city, filled with skyscrapers. The United Arab Emirates' capital, located on an island connected to the mainland by two bridges, is often accused of being a rather soulless place, but it does have its attractions: the Petroleum Exhibition and the Heritage Village, the beautiful Corniche (beach), the Al Hisn Fort, the

old *souk* (market), the Breakwater Island and Sheikh Zayed's palace. The most picturesque place is undeniably the Batin, the oldest part of the town, where the small harbours receive the daily catch brought by the fishing *dhows*.

Credit: ©The Government of Dubai, Department of Tourism and Commerce Marketing

General Information

AREA: 77,700 sq km (30,000 sq miles).
POPULATION: 4.3 million (official estimate 2004).
POPULATION DENSITY: 55.3 per sq km.
CAPITAL: Abu Dhabi. **Population:** 1.7 million (2004 figure for entire Emirate).
GEOGRAPHY: The Emirates are bordered to the north by the Gulf and the Musandam Peninsula, to the east by Oman, to the south and west by Saudi Arabia and to the northwest by Qatar. They comprise a federation of seven small former sheikhdoms. Abu Dhabi is the largest Emirate, and the remainder (Ajman, Dubai, Fujairah, Ras al-Khaimah, Sharjah and Umm al Qaiwain) are known collectively as the Northern States. The land is mountainous and mostly desert. Abu Dhabi is flat and sandy, and within its boundaries is the Buraimi Oasis. Dubai has a 16km (10 mile) deep-water creek, giving it the popular name of 'Pearl of the Gulf'. Sharjah has a deep-water port on the Batinah coast at Khor Fakkan, facing the Indian Ocean. Ras al-Khaimah is the fourth emirate in size. Fujairah, one of the three smaller sheikhdoms located on the Batinah coast, has agricultural potential, while Ajman and Umm al Qaiwain were once small coastal fishing villages.
GOVERNMENT: Federation of seven autonomous Emirates. The highest federal authority is the Supreme Council of Rulers comprising the absolute rulers of the seven Emirates. Decisions reached by the Council must have the agreement of at least five members, including Abu Dhabi and Dubai, the two largest members. The council appoints a President to act as Head of State. There are no political parties. **Head of State:** President Sheikh Khalifa since 2004. **Head of Government:** Prime Minister of the United Arab Emirates and Ruler of Dubai Crown Prince Sheikh Mohammed bin Rashid Al Maktoum since January 2006. **Recent history:** Following the sudden death of Sheikh Maktoum bin Rashid Al-Maktoum, who had been Prime Minister and Emir of Dubai since 1990, Crown Prince Sheikh Mohammed bin Rashid Al Maktoum, his brother, succeeded him in January 2006. Sheikh Mohammed had been the UAE Defence Minister since 1971 and heir apparent to the throne of Dubai since 1995.
LANGUAGE: Arabic is the official language. English is widely spoken and used as a second language in commerce.
RELIGION: Mostly Muslim, of which 16 per cent are Shiite and the remainder Sunni.
ELECTRICITY: 220/240 volts AC, 50Hz. Square three-pin plugs are widespread.
SOCIAL CONVENTIONS: Muslim religious laws should be observed. Women are expected to dress modestly and men should dress formally for most occasions. Alcohol is tolerated, with non-Muslims allowed to drink alcohol in the city's bars, restaurants, clubs and hotels. Smoking is the same as in Europe and in most cases it is obvious where not to smoke, except during Ramadan when it is illegal to eat, drink or smoke in public.

Climate

The best time to visit is between October and May. The hottest time is from June to September with little rainfall.
Required clothing: Lightweights, with mediumweights from November to March; warmer clothes for evening.

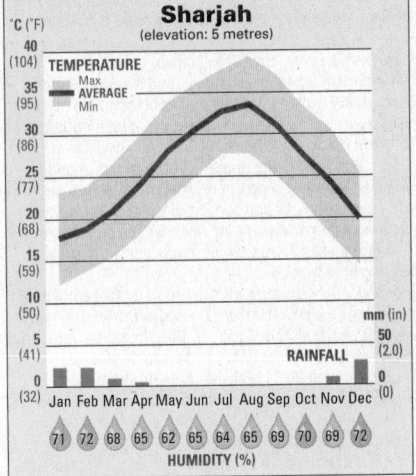

Sharjah
(elevation: 5 metres)

Month	Jan	Feb	Mar	Apr	May	Jun	Jul	Aug	Sep	Oct	Nov	Dec
HUMIDITY (%)	71	72	68	65	62	65	64	65	69	70	69	72

Communications

Telephone: Country code: 971. Main area codes: Abu Dhabi 2; Ajman, Sharjah and Umm al Quwain 6; Al Ain 3; Dubai 4; Fujairah 9; Jebel Ali 4 and Ras al-Khaimah 7. There is a good local telephone network. Telephone calls *within* each state are free.
Mobile telephone: Roaming agreements exist with most international mobile phone operators. Coverage is excellent.
Internet: There are numerous Internet cafes in the UAE.
Post: Airmail letters and parcels take about five days to reach Europe.
MEDIA: The UAE, and in particular Dubai, is trying to establish itself as a regional media hub. A number of pan-Arab broadcasters operate from the UAE and major media organisations such as *Reuters* and *Sony* have moved in, drawn by tax incentives and freedom of speech. Although the constitution provides for freedom of speech, media content is controlled to some extent. There are some restrictions as to what are considered acceptable subjects of reporting. Foreign publications may be censored before distribution.
Press: English-language daily newspapers include *7 Days*, *Gulf News* and *Khaleej Times*. Foreign newspapers are available in hotel bookshops and supermarkets.
TV: Channels include *Emirates Dubai TV*, *Abu Dhabi TV*, *MBC* (all pan-Arab broadcasters), *Ajman TV*, *Sharjah TV* and news channel *Al-Arabiya* (run by MBC).
Radio: Stations include *Abu Dhabi Radio*, *Radio Asia*, *Ras al Khaimah Radio*, *Al-Arabya FM*, English-language *Dubai 92* and Arabic-language *Dubai 93.9*.

Passport/Visa

	Passport Required?	Visa Required?	Return Ticket Required?
Full British	Yes	No	Yes
Australian	Yes	No	Yes
Canadian	Yes	No	Yes
USA	Yes	No	Yes
Other EU	Yes	No/1	Yes
Japanese	Yes	No	Yes

Note: Regulations and requirements may be subject to change at short notice, and you are advised to contact the appropriate diplomatic or consular authority before finalising travel arrangements. Any numbers in the chart refer to the footnotes below.

Restricted entry and transit: The Government of the United Arab Emirates refuses entry and transit to those holding transit documents issued from Lebanon or the Syrian Arab Republic, and travel documents issued by the Coalition Authority in Iraq, should their visas be obtained through an associate in the UAE.
Note: No problems in entering the UAE occur for those travelling with an Israeli stamp endorsement.
PASSPORTS: Passport valid for a minimum of three months from date of arrival (six months for business travel) required. Often a sponsor will hold a visitor's passport. In these cases a receipt will be issued. This will generally be accepted in place of a passport where a transaction may require one.
VISAS: Required by all except the following:
(a) nationals of countries referred to in the chart above (UK

nationals must travel with a passport reading 'British Citizen' as national status), except **1.** nationals of Cyprus, Czech Republic, Estonia, Hungary, Latvia, Lithuania, Malta, Poland, Slovak Republic and Slovenia, who *do* need a visa for touristic or business stays of up to 30 days;
(b) nationals of Andorra, Brunei, Hong Kong (SAR), Iceland, Korea (Rep), Liechtenstein, Malaysia, Monaco, New Zealand, Norway, San Marino, Singapore, Switzerland, and Vatican City for stays of up to 30 days;
(c) nationals of Gulf Co-operation Council countries (Bahrain, Kuwait, Qatar, Oman and Saudi Arabia);
(d) transit passengers, provided holding valid onward or return documentation and not leaving the airport for up to 12 hours.
Note: The Embassy only issues visas for diplomatic or certain business visits. For routine travel, visas for tourists, travellers (intending to visit family) and business travellers must be arranged via the *sponsor* (the hotel/package tour operator or UAE resident/company concerned). This includes transit visas. To obtain approval, the sponsor will require the visitor's proposed flight and passport details in advance. Business visits are made by invitation only and proof of company trading licence is required. The sponsor will then confirm to the visitor that a visa has been arranged, usually by fax, and that she/he will be met at the airport.
Types of visa and cost: *Visitor* and *Business*: £20. Price given is for UK nationals but price is dependent on nationality. Multiple-entry visas are only issued in very special circumstances. In case of visa being arranged by a sponsor, the request for multiple-entry should be marked clearly.
Validity: 30 days from date of entry and two months from date of issue. It may be possible to extend visas on request for up to a maximum of 90 days at the local immigration office.
Application to: Sponsor (as described above).
Application requirements: (a) Valid passport. (b) One passport-size photo. (c) Duplicate application form. (d) Letter from applicant's company/organisation (with extra copy) stipulating position held and purpose of visit. (e) Proof of sponsorship (often in the form of a fax). (f) Fee, payable in cash only. (g) Sponsor's name, address, telephone number and occupation (business activity if a company). Contact local sponsor for details of individual requirements.
Working days required: Between one and five when arranged through a sponsor. However, allowances should be made for possible delays in approval procedure. It is strongly advised to apply well in advance of departure date.

PASSPORT/VISA INFORMATION

Embassy of the United Arab Emirates in the UK
30 Princes Gate, London SW7 1PT, UK
Tel: (020) 7581 1281.
Website: www.uaeembassyuk.net
Opening hours: Mon-Fri 0900-1500.

Consulate of the United Arab Emirates in the UK
48 Princes Gate, London SW7 2QA, UK
Tel: (020) 7581 1281 *or* (0906) 550 4550.
Website: www.uaeembassyuk.net
Opening hours: Mon-Fri 0930-1300 (visa applications); 1330-1430 (visa collection).

Embassy of the United Arab Emirates in the USA
3522 International Court, NW,
Washington, DC 20008, USA
Tel: (202) 243 2400 *or* (800) 823 6911 (toll-free).
Website: www.uae-embassy.org

Money

Currency: UAE Dirham (AED) = 100 fils. Notes are in denominations of AED1000, 500, 200, 100, 50, 20, 10 and 5. Coins are in denominations of AED1, and 50, 25, 10 and 5 fils (10 and 5 fils coins are rarely used).
Note: The Dirham is tied to the US Dollar.
Currency exchange: Most hotels will handle the exchange of foreign currency.
Credit & debit cards: American Express, Diners Club, MasterCard and Visa are widely accepted. Check with your credit or debit card company for details of merchant acceptability and other services which may be available.
Traveller's cheques: These are widely accepted. To avoid additional exchange rate charges, travellers are advised to take traveller's cheques in US Dollars or Pounds Sterling.
Currency restrictions: The import and export of both local and foreign currency are unrestricted. Amounts over AED40,000 must be declared at the Customs Counter at Dubai International Airport.
Banking hours: Sat-Wed 0800-1300, Thurs 0800-1200. Some also open Sat-Wed 1630-1800.
Exchange rate indicators:
Rate at time of publishing
£1.00=   AED6.48
$1.00=   AED3.67

Duty Free

The following items may be imported into the United Arab Emirates without incurring customs duty:
2000 cigarettes and 400 cigars and 2kg of tobacco; 2l of spirits of more than 22 per cent alcohol, and 2l of wine (non-Muslims over 18 years only); a reasonable amount of perfume for personal use.
Note: It is prohibited to bring alcohol into Sharjah and usually not allowed if entering the UAE by land.
Prohibited items: Firearms and dangerous weapons, religious propaganda, unstrung pearls except for personal use, raw seafood (only when visiting Dubai and/or Sharjah), fruit and vegetables from cholera-infected areas.

Public Holidays

Below are listed Public Holidays for the January 2006-June 2007 period:
2006: Jan 1 New Year's Day. **Jan 10** Eid al-Adha (Feast of the Sacrifice). **Jan 31** Al-Hijra (Islamic New Year). **Apr 11** Mouloud (Birth of the Prophet). **Aug 6** Accession of HH Sheikh Zayed. **Aug 22** Leilat al-Meiraj (Ascension of the Prophet). **Oct 22-24** Eid al-Fitr (End of Ramadan). **Dec 2** National Day. **Dec 31** Eid al-Adha (Feast of the Sacrifice).
2007: Jan 1 New Year's Day. **Jan 20** Al-Hijra (Islamic New Year). **Mar 31** Mouloud (Birth of the Prophet).
Note: Muslim festivals are timed according to local sightings of various phases of the moon and the dates given above are approximations. During the lunar month of Ramadan that precedes Eid al-Fitr, Muslims fast during the day and feast at night and normal business patterns may be interrupted. Many restaurants are closed during the day and there may be restrictions on smoking and drinking. Some disruption may continue into Eid al-Fitr itself. Eid al-Fitr and Eid al-Adha may last anything from two to 10 days, depending on the region. For more information, see the *World of Islam* appendix.

Health

	Special Precautions?	Certificate Required?
Yellow Fever	No	No
Cholera	No	No
Typhoid & Polio	1	N/A
Malaria	No	N/A

Note: *Regulations and requirements may be subject to change at short notice, and you are advised to contact your doctor well in advance of your intended date of departure. Any numbers in the chart refer to the footnotes below.*

1: Immunisation against *polio* is sometimes advised; *typhoid* occurs in rural areas.
Food & drink: Mains water in major cities is safe to drink, but in small villages it should be filtered, or bottled water should be used. Water used for drinking, brushing teeth or making ice should have first been boiled or otherwise sterilised. Milk is unpasteurised and should be boiled. Powdered or tinned milk is available and is advised, but make sure that it is reconstituted with pure water. Avoid dairy products which are likely to have been made from unboiled milk. Only eat well-cooked meat and fish, preferably served hot. Salad and mayonnaise may carry increased risk. Vegetables should be cooked and fruit peeled.
Other risks: *Cutaneous leishmaniasis* and *tick-borne typhus* may occur; avoid mosquito, sandfly and tick bites. Wear shoes to avoid soil-borne parasites. Take precautions against heat exhaustion and sunstroke. Immunisation against *hepatitis A* is recommended. *Hepatitis B* is endemic.
Rabies is present close to the border with Oman. For those at high risk, vaccination before arrival should be considered. If you are bitten, seek medical advice without delay. For more information, consult the *Health* appendix.
Health care: Medical facilities are of a very high quality but are extremely expensive. Private health insurance is essential.

Travel - International

AIR:
The national airlines are *Emirates (EK)* (website: www.emirates.com) and *Gulf Air (GF)* (website: www.gulfairco.com). *Emirates* operates international flights to and from Dubai; *Gulf Air* serves all UAE airports. Many other airlines operate scheduled services to Dubai.
Approximate flight times: From *London* to Abu Dhabi or Dubai is seven hours; from *Frankfurt/M* to Dubai is six hours; from *Hong Kong* to Dubai is nine hours 15 minutes and from *Sydney* to Dubai is 14 hours 45 minutes.
Main airports: *Abu Dhabi (AUH)* (website: www.dcaauh.gov.ae) is 32km (20 miles) east of the city (travel time – 40 minutes). *To/from the airport:* Buses and taxis are available at the airport. *Al Ghazal* taxis operate a fixed-rate service. *Facilities:* Duty free shop, bank, bar, snack bar, bureau de change, post office and car hire.
Al Ain International Airport (AAN) (website: www.alain-airport.gov.ae) is 13km (8 miles) northwest of Al Ain. *To/from the airport: Al Ghazal* taxis operate a fixed-rate service to the city centre. Public buses serve the airport. *Facilities:* Bank, bureau de change, ATM, restaurants, coffee shop, 24-hour cafe, duty free complex, children's playground in landscaped gardens, and medical centre.
Dubai (DXB) (website: www.dubaiairport.com) is 4km (2.5 miles) southeast of the city (travel time – 10 minutes). *To/from the airport:* Taxis and buses are available at the airport. Bus stations are opposite both Terminal 1 and 2. *Facilities:* Duty free shops, bank, post office, shops, car hire, restaurant, snack bar and bar. The airport consists of two terminals. Expansion plans are underway to provide a new third Terminal and two new passenger concourses, due to be completed by 2006.
Sharjah (SHJ) (website: www.shj-airport.gov.ae) is 10km (6 miles) from the city. *To/from the airport:* Taxis are available at the airport. *Facilities:* Duty free shop, car hire, restaurants, snack bars, ATM and bureau de change.
Ras al-Khaimah (RKT) (website: www.rakairport.com) is 15km (9 miles) from the city. *To/from the airport:* Taxis are available at the airport. *Facilities:* Duty free shop and restaurant/snack bar.
There is also an airport at *Fujairah* with duty free facilities.
Departure tax: None.
SEA:
Main ports: *Jebel Ali, Rashid* and *Zayed* (Abu Dhabi), *Khalid* (Sharjah), *Saqr* (Ras al-Khaimah) and *Fujairah*. Cruises call at Abu Dhabi and the cruise terminal in Dubai, and there are passenger/cargo services to the USA, the Far East, Australia and Europe. There are regular sailings between Sharjah and Bandar-é-Abbas (Iran).
ROAD:
There is a good road into Oman and a good one into Saudi Arabia that connects with the Trans-Arabian Highway on the overland route to Europe. Buses run daily between Dubai or Abu Dhabi and Oman. There are also services between Dubai or Abu Dhabi and Saudi Arabia and between Abu Dhabi and Egypt, Jordan, Lebanon and Syria.

Travel - Internal

AIR:
Daily flights link Abu Dhabi and Dubai. Flights can also be chartered and there are small landing fields throughout the United Arab Emirates.
SEA:
Commercial and passenger services serve all coastal ports. A water taxi travels between Dubai and Deira across the creek.
ROAD:
There are good tarmac roads running along the west coast between Abu Dhabi and Dubai, Sharjah and Ras al Khaimah; between Sharjah and Dhaid; and linking Dubai with other Northern States and the interior. Traffic drives on the right and the speed limit in built-up areas is 60 to 80kph (37-50mph) and 100 to 120kph (62 to 74mph) elsewhere. **Bus:** Limited services link most towns. However, most hotels run their own scheduled bus services to the airport, city centre and beach resorts. **Taxi:** Available in all towns. In Abu Dhabi and Al-Ain, urban journey fares are metered, whilst fares for longer journeys should be agreed in advance. There is a surcharge for air-conditioned taxis. Many travellers find taxis to be the quickest and most convenient method of travel from Abu Dhabi to Dubai. **Car hire:** Most international car hire companies have offices at airports or hotels. A passport and either a valid international or national licence are necessary. **Documentation:** An International Driving Permit is recommended, although it is not legally required. A local driving licence can be issued on presentation of a valid national driving licence, two photos and a passport.

Travel Advice

There is a high threat from terrorism. Al Qaeda continues to issue statements threatening to carry out attacks in the Gulf region. These include references to attacks on Western interests, including residential compounds, military, oil, transport and aviation interests.
Travellers should review their security arrangements carefully. They should remain vigilant, particularly in public places.
This advice is based on information provided by the Foreign and Commonwealth Office in the UK. It is correct at time of publishing. As the situation can change rapidly, visitors are advised to contact the following organisations for the latest travel advice:

British Foreign and Commonwealth Office
Tel: (0845) 850 2829.
Website: www.fco.gov.uk

US Department of State
Website: http://travel.state.gov/travel

Accommodation

HOTELS:
There is an excellent selection of hotel accommodation, with regular new openings competing to outdo each other. Rates tend to be cheaper in summer. Most of the major international hotel chains are represented, eg Hilton, Hyatt, Inter-Continental, Marriott, Ramada and Sheraton. There are also top-class beach resort hotels at Jebel Ali and Jumeirah Beach in Dubai and a mountain resort hotel at Hatta Fort. The stunning all-suite Burj Al Arab is probably the most deluxe. Contact the Ministry of Information and Culture (see *Top Things To Do*) for more information.
YOUTH HOSTELS:
The *United Arab Emirates Youth Hostel Association* (part of the Hostelling International network) runs hostels in Dubai (two hostels), Sharjah, Kourfakkan and Fujairah. See below for contact details.

Credit: ©The Government of Dubai, Dept of Tourism and Commerce Marketing

ACCOMMODATION INFORMATION

United Arab Emirates Youth Hostel Association
39 Al Nahda Road, Al Nahda 2 area, PO Box 94141, Dubai, UAE
Tel: (971) 4298 8151.
Website: www.uaeyha.com

Top Things To See

Abu Dhabi
- A predominantly modern city, **Abu Dhabi** nevertheless retains some of its ancient past. See the **Diwan Amiri (White Fort)**, built in 1793, the many mosques, from the massive **blue mosque** on the corner of the **Corniche** to the tiny one in the centre of **Khalifa Street Roundabout**, surrounded by trees, and the **museum**. The oldest part of the town is the **Batin** area, served daily by the fishing *dhows* bringing their catch of Gulf prawns and other fish to the small harbours. The old building yards demonstrate craftspeople's skills that have remained unchanged for centuries. Discover the city's ancient burial mounds at **Um al Nar**.
- **Al Ain**, 100km (60 miles) from Abu Dhabi, is an oasis and former caravan stop, built on a huge fertile plain. There is spectacular scenery along the journey from Abu Dhabi. The resort includes a **camel market**, **zoo** and **museum** containing old and new artefacts and Mesopotamian pottery.
- There is also a water spring at **Ain Faidha**, 14km (9 miles) from Al Ain.
- Explore the important archaeological digs at **Hili**, 10km (6 miles) from Al Ain. The stone tombs, including the famous **Great Sepulchre**, date back 5000 years. Head for the **Hafit Mountain**, south of Al Ain, containing ancient tombs, pottery and swords.
- There are more ancient sites worth visiting at **Um Al Nar** and **Badi'i Bent Saud**.
- A fun park is situated at **Al-Hir** and majestic sand seas are to be seen at **Liwa**.
- Other areas of great scenic beauty include **Qarn Island**, **Belghilam Island** (famous for its gazelle breeding), near to **Sadiyat Island**, and **Abul-Abyadh Island**.

Dubai
- The 'Pearl of the Arabian Gulf' grew up as a seafaring settlement along either side of the Creek, a natural harbour for *dhow* traders, pearl divers and fishermen. Deira on the northern bank and Bur Dubai to the south are connected by a tunnel and two bridges and can also be reached by *abra* (water taxi). **Bur Dubai** has substantial areas of old buildings, atmospheric alleyways

and souks (markets), including the world-famous **Gold Souk** and colourful **Spice Souk**. Gain fascinating glimpses of the past from **Al Fahidi Fort**, the **Dubai Museum** (which houses, among other things, artefacts recovered from the ancient graves at Al-Ghusais), the traditional windtower houses of the nearby Bastakiya district and, at the mouth of the Creek, the magnificently restored **Sheikh Saeed's Palace**, as well as the diving and heritage villages. The **Deira** side of the creek is cosmopolitan and lively, with many attractive gardens and first-class shopping facilities, ranging from Western-style shops to the ancient *souks* where spices, perfume, clothing, antiques, handicrafts and jewels are available.

- Marvel at the **Palm Islands**, said to be visible from the moon and forming the largest manmade islands in the world. The **Palm Jumeirah** will feature a number of hotels as well as private residences when it opens in 2006. The **Palm Jebel Ali** is slated to have more leisure facilities, including an aquatic theme park, when it opens in 2008. The third of the islands, **Palm Deira**, will be more geared towards residential use with over 7,000 villas, and will be the largest of the trio when it opens in 2009. New bridges will connect the islands to the mainland in one of the largest construction projects ever undertaken by man. The three islands are going to be accompanied by **'The World'**, all very Dubai, an ambitious attempt to recreate the shape of the world on 300 offshore islands, slated to open in 2008. Watching these outlandish projects take shape has become one of Dubai's main attractions, with the view perhaps best from the Burj al Arab hotel.

- Discover the ancient fortressed villages of **Hatta** and **Wadi Hatta**, a lush and attractive valley in the foothills of the **Hajar Mountains** with superb desert scenery, on the journey from Dubai.

The rest of the Emirates

- The **desert** offfers a spectacular and varied wilderness of magnificent red dunes and stark mountains with pockets of green oases. Meet the nomadic *Bedu* folk, whose hospitality is famous, and watch camel races at dawn. **Admire** the stunning white sand dunes at **Awir**, where there is a national park. There is a selection of 'safari' holidays available.

- On the **East Coast**, visit the resorts of **Dibba** and **Fujairah**, where there is a museum, a Necropolis, an old fort and, nearby, many small mountain villages.

- The **Northern Emirates** is a region which has undergone a dramatic transformation since the discovery of natural gas in 1980 and there has been a considerable amount of expansion in the commercial sector. **Sharjah** is an excellent shopping centre, with its new *souk* containing hundreds of shops. There is also an ancient fort and heritage museum. Go on an excursion to **Ras al-Khaimah**, where there is an old seaport with spectacular views over the coast and the **Hajar Mountains**; and also to the **Dhaid** and **Khatt** oases, the latter with mineral springs. There are also trips available to the natural harbour at **Dibba** and the beautiful **Khor Kalba**, one of the most famous shell beaches in the world. The archaeological site at **Mileiha** (in Sharjah itself) dates back to the 4th century BC; 80-million-year-old fossils are to be seen here. Other archaeological sites include **Dur** at **Umm al-Qaiwain** where Hellenic ruins can be seen (210-100 BC), the **Drabhaniya** ruins in **Ras al-Khaimah** and the **Zaura** ruins in **Ajman**.

Top Things To Do

- Dubai has been declared the number-one **golf** destination worldwide, by the International Golf Tour Operators Association. The Emirates Golf Club, Dubai, which opened in 1988, was the first grass golf course in the Gulf. In addition, there is also the Abu Dhabi Golf Club (whose facilities include two 18-hole grass courses and a floodlit driving range), Dubai Creek Golf Club and the Nad Al Shiba Golf and Racing Club.

- **Watersports:** Boats and **water-skiing** equipment are available for hire. **Sailing** and **windsurfing** are popular around Dubai and boats are available for hire. The waters off Dubai are considered among the best areas in the world for **diving**. There are sub-aqua clubs in main centres and an extensive range of equipment is available for hire. **Swimming** is possible in the many hotel pools or beaches. Much of the long expanse of **Jumeirah Beach** in Dubai is dominated by luxury hotels and their facilities. However, there is a stretch of public beach available, with clean white sand, crystal clear seawater and bath-temperature surf. Some of the hotels allow non-guests to use their pools and stretches of beach if they buy lunch or pay a nominal fee. In the Northern Emirates, important resort areas are **Khor Fakkan**, which has excellent beaches and watersports facilities and **Khalid Lagoon** (an aquatic park with several islands and a miniature theme park). The **East Coast** is an impressive stretch of lush coastline, with steep mountains, unspoilt sandy bays and beaches, ancient fortresses and date palm groves sloping down to the edge of the Indian Ocean with its host of

marine life. **Scuba diving** and **snorkelling** are very popular here.

- There is an abundance of game fish in the Gulf. Fully-equipped boats with crew can be hired from the Jebel Ali Hotel marina for **deep-sea fishing** trips.

- The emirate has many well-qualified tour companies offering such activities as **desert safaris** by 4-wheel drive, **sand-skiing**, **moonlit bedouin barbeques**, **camel riding** and *dhow* cruises. Attend the **Dubai World Cup** (the world's richest horse race), the **PGA Desert Classic Golf Tournament**, the **Dubai Shopping Festival** or one of the 80 or so major trade exhibitions held in Dubai each year.

- Opened in 2002, at **Dubai Creekside Park**, **Children's City** is proving a big hit with both local and international youngsters. The 7,700 sq-m (82,882 sq-ft) development takes young minds on a journey through the human body, science and space, with the help of different 'zones'. With plenty of hands-on action to keep even the most demanding children occupied, this is no dull old museum. All exhibits are in English as well as Arabic.

- **Skiing** and **snowboarding** are now possible at the new **Ski Dubai** indoor snowsports centre (opened December 2005) which includes the world's first indoor black run.

Credit: ©The Government of Dubai, Department of Tourism and Commerce Marketing

Entertainment

FOOD & DRINK: Local fruit and vegetables are increasingly available and there is excellent local fish. Hotels serve both Arab and European food and there is also a number of Chinese, Indian and other restaurants.
Things to know: All the Emirates, with the exception of Sharjah, permit the consumption of alcohol by non-Muslims. It is illegal to drink alcohol in the street or to buy it for a UAE citizen.
National specialities:
- *Hummus* (chickpea and sesame paste).
- *Tabbouleh* (bulghur wheat with mint and parsley).
- *Ghuzi* (roast lamb with rice and nuts).
- *Warak enab* (stuffed vine leaves).
- *Koussa mashi* (stuffed courgettes).
- *Makbous* (spicy lamb with rice).
- Seafood with spicy rice are also popular.
National drinks:
- *Ayran* (a refreshing yoghurt drink).
- Strong black coffee.
Tipping: Most hotels, restaurants and clubs add fairly high service charges to the bill, therefore tipping is not necessary. Taxi drivers are not tipped.
NIGHTLIFE: There are several nightclubs located in major centres and entertainment ranges from Arabic singers and

dancers to international pop stars. Bars are found in all top hotels and range from sophisticated cocktail lounges to English-style pubs. Some hotels also have discos. Traditional dances are performed on public holidays. Most large towns have cinemas showing English-language films.
SHOPPING: Customs duties are low and therefore luxury goods are cheaper than in most countries. The Dubai duty-free shop is one of the cheapest in the world. *Souks* sell traditional Emirate leather goods, gold, brass and silverware. **Shopping hours:** Daily 0900-1300 and 1600-2100, but many shops are open all day. Shops close for prayers Fri 1130-1330.

Business

- **GDP:** US$104.2 billion (2004 estimate).
- **Main exports:** Crude oil, natural gas, re exports, dried fish and dates.
- **Main imports:** Machinery and transport equipment, chemicals and food.
- **Main trade partners:** Exports to: Japan, Korea (Rep), India and Thailand. Imports from: China, India, Japan, Germany, UK, France and USA.

ECONOMY: Oil and gas are the Emirates' main industries, and underpin the country's considerable prosperity. Outside the oil and gas sector, which includes refining and the production of oil-derived chemicals, most economic activity is government sponsored, and designed to diversify the economy and reduce dependence on oil. This strategy has been reasonably successful and the oil sector's contribution to GDP is now down to about 45 per cent. Chemicals, aluminium and steel production are the most important of the new industries. Other newly established industries produce consumer goods for the domestic market. There is some agriculture, mostly livestock rearing, in what is an unfavourable climate; fishing is also significant.
The economy has boomed in recent years. GDP growth for 2005 was estimated to be 28.5 per cent. At the end of 2005, the International Monetary Fund predicted the UAE's economy would become the third largest in East and Central Asia. By 2006, the GDP is expected to reach US$150.9 billion. Most of the country's economic development has been concentrated in the two richest and most powerful of the seven Emirates, Abu Dhabi and Dubai; the remainder are relatively underdeveloped. UAE is a member of OPEC, and of the Gulf Co-operation Council which is increasingly concerning itself with regional economic collaboration. Plans to establish a customs union among the six member states are well advanced, and the GCC has sought advice from the EU on the creation of a single currency.
BUSINESS ETIQUETTE: Business entertaining will often be lavish. Suits should be worn and prior appointments are essential. English is widely spoken in business circles, but translation services are likely to be available. **Office hours:** Sat-Wed 0800-1300 and 1500/1600-1800/1900 and Thurs 0800-1200. **Government office hours:** Sat-Wed 0730-1330, Thurs 0730-1200. All offices are closed every afternoon during the month of Ramadan.
CONFERENCES/CONVENTIONS: The Dubai International Congress Centre can accommodate 10,000 delegates. At Port Rashid in Dubai, the cruise terminal has a wide range of facilities including a business centre with Internet access and a conference room. Dubai World Trade Centre hosts a multitude of events (including car rallies and tennis exhibitions). Many hotels in the UAE offer high-standard conference and meeting facilities.

United Kingdom

Location: Northwest Europe.

Time: GMT (GMT + 1 from last Sunday in March to Saturday before last Sunday in October).

Overview

Despite its relatively small size, the United Kingdom is one of the most culturally diverse countries on Earth, peopled by four main 'native' nationalities, plus later arrivals from all over the world. The United Kingdom consists of Great Britain (England, Scotland and Wales), plus the six counties of Northern Ireland. The Isle of Man and the Channel Islands (principally Jersey and Guernsey) are also parts of the British Isles, but somewhat confusingly not officially part of the UK.

Topographically, the British mainland is broadly divisible into two main regions: the relatively low-lying south and the highland regions of the north and west. Scotland, Wales, and the northern areas of England occupy the latter, which are in general much more sparsely populated than the more prosperous southeast of England.

London is perennially the principal British attraction for overseas visitors, with its historic landmarks such as the Palace of Westminster (the Houses of Parliament), Buckingham Palace, Westminster Abbey, St. Paul's Cathedral and the Tower of London. They also flock to the many West End theatres and the shopping areas of Knightsbridge, Oxford Street and Regent Street.

Within easy day-trip distance of London are the university cities of Oxford and Cambridge, the picturesque Cotswolds with their many pretty villages, Stratford-upon-Avon (home of William Shakespeare), the cathedral at Canterbury and the seaside attractions of Brighton.

Further afield lie delights like Cornwall (to the southwest), Yorkshire, Durham, Northumberland and Cumbria (a large part of which constitutes the Lake District).

Wales adjoins England to the west, and offers, in addition to its populous southern cities, a diverse range of historic castles, spectacular coastline and impressive mountain landscapes. The majority of Scotland's population lives in the busy central belt, a lowland region in which the main centres of Glasgow, Stirling, and the Scottish capital, Edinburgh, lie. But equally as popular as the cities is the dramatic scenery of the Highlands to the north and west, location of Britain's highest mountains and a bewildering array of offshore islands, notably Skye, Orkney and Shetland.

Halfway to Ireland in the Irish Sea sits the Isle of Man, a scenic island with Norse traditions. And west again is Northern Ireland, whose vibrant capital Belfast is a lively option for the visitor. North of the city are the spectacular Antrim Glens, while to the west is the lush 'lakeland' of Fermanagh.

The Channel Islands are closer to France than England, situated a short distance off the Normandy coastline.

General Information

The United Kingdom of Great Britain and Northern Ireland consists of *England*, *Scotland*, *Wales* and *Northern Ireland*. Although they form one administrative unit (with regional exceptions), they have had separate cultures, languages and political histories. The *United Kingdom* section consists of a general introduction (covering the aspects that the four countries have in common), sections devoted to the four constituent countries. The Channel Islands (Alderney, Guernsey, Jersey and Sark and Herm) and the Isle of Man are dependencies of the British Crown, which are also included for convenience of reference.

AREA: 242,514 sq km (93,788 sq miles).

POPULATION: 59.8 million (official estimate 2004).

POPULATION DENSITY: 244.2 per sq km.

CAPITAL: London. **Population:** 7.43 million (official estimate 2004).

GEOGRAPHY: The British landscape can be divided roughly into two kinds of terrain – highland and lowland. The highland area comprises the mountainous regions of Scotland, Northern Ireland, northern England and North Wales. The English Lake District in the northwest contains lakes and fells. The lowland area is broken up by sandstone and limestone hills, long valleys and basins such as the Wash on the east coast. In the southeast, the North and South Downs culminate in the White Cliffs of Dover. The coastline includes fjord-like inlets in the northwest of Scotland, spectacular cliffs and wild sandy beaches on the east coast and, further south, beaches of rock, shale and sand sometimes backed by dunes, and large areas of fenland in East Anglia.

More detailed geographical descriptions of the various countries may be found under the respective entries.

GOVERNMENT: Constitutional Monarchy. The United Kingdom is an hereditary Monarchy, with real power being held by the Prime Minister, who is the leader of the largest Parliamentary party and the head of the Cabinet. The two main political parties are the Conservatives (Tories) and Labour, although a centre party (the Liberal-SDP Alliance, later merged as the Liberal Democrats) threatened to disturb this old balance in the mid-1980s. The absence of proportional representation in Parliamentary elections does not encourage the prosperity of smaller parties in Britain. Elections must be held every five years, though the timing is at the discretion of the Prime Minister. The legislature is bicameral; the House of Commons is elected, while the House of Lords is a peculiar mixture of appointed members, judges, bishops and hereditary peers. Britain is almost unique in the world in having no written constitution, and the political and administrative machine is powered by a mixture of common and statute law, judicial decisions and archaic convention; the royal assent to an Act of Parliament, for instance, is still proclaimed in Norman French.

Head of State: HM Queen Elizabeth II since 1953. **Head of Government:** Prime Minister Tony Blair since 1997.

Recent history: Since his instalment as Prime Minister in 1997, Tony Blair has become the longest-serving Labour Premier of all time, but his tenure has been characterised by a number of controversies as well as what he would claim as achievements.

Blair has enjoyed huge Parliamentary majorities for his party in the face of largely ineffective opposition from the Conservatives, who have undergone a number of leadership changes since the resignation of Margaret Thatcher in 1990, and have failed to regain power since the election defeat of 1997. It remains to be seen how the latest incumbent, David Cameron, will fare since becoming leader in December 2005. One of the principal problems facing Blair at present is the ongoing Iraq situation. His decision to support the US invasion of the Middle Eastern country deeply divided the UK, and opinion as to the wisdom of the action remains polarised.

Related to events in the Middle East, terrorist attacks in July 2005 brought London to a standstill, and security continues to be tight: immigration controls are rigorous, and certain sections of both sides of the political divide are eager to introduce a system of compulsory identity cards for UK citizens, something that rubs against the grain for many people. The debate continues, and is likely to do so for some time.

On the positive side, the Blair Government would claim some credit for Northern Ireland's current more or less peaceful environment, which has prevailed since the 'Good Friday Agreement' of 1998, which established the conditions for the ongoing cease-fire between the Republican and Loyalist factions. The two sides are still unable to agree on a basis for governing the Province, though, and direct rule from London is still in force.

Another achievement of the Blair Government was the 1999 introduction of devolved power for Scotland and Wales, giving the two nations a far greater say in matters directly affecting their parts of the UK. Controversy has dogged even this, though, with the much feted new Scottish Parliament building in Edinburgh running vastly over budget, to the consternation of many north of the Border. Europe, and the UK's place within the EU, continues to be another source of headaches for politicians, who are deeply divided on how far the country should commit itself to the institution, and indeed the Euro.

It is also uncertain whether Blair will remain as Prime Minister for the full five-year term of this Government, and speculation is rife as to when he will hand over the reins to Chancellor and Labour Party rival, Gordon Brown.

LANGUAGE: English. Some Welsh is spoken in parts of Wales, Gaelic in parts of Scotland and Northern Ireland, and French and Norman French in the Channel Islands. The many ethnic minorities within the UK also speak their own languages (eg Cantonese, Greek, Hindi, Mandarin, Turkish, Urdu, etc).

RELIGION: Predominantly Protestant (Church of England), but many other Christian denominations also: Roman Catholic, Church of Scotland, Baptist, Methodist and other free churches. There are sizeable Hindu, Jewish and Muslim minorities.

ELECTRICITY: 240 volts AC, 50Hz. Square three-pin plugs are standard and the visitor is unlikely to come across the older round three-pin type.

SOCIAL CONVENTIONS: The Monarchy, though now only symbolic, is a powerful and often subconscious unifying force. Members of the Royal family are the subject of unceasing fascination, with their every move avidly followed and reported by the popular press, both in Britain and abroad. Handshaking is customary when introduced to someone for the first time. Normal social courtesies should be observed when visiting someone's home and a small present such as flowers or chocolates is appreciated. It is polite to wait until everyone has been served before eating. **Clothing:** A tie, trousers and shoes (as opposed to jeans and trainers) are necessary for entry to some nightclubs and restaurants, otherwise casual wear is widely acceptable. **Use of public places:** Topless sunbathing is allowed on certain beaches and tolerated in some parks. Smoking or non-smoking areas will usually be clearly marked. A complete ban on smoking in bars, restaurants, clubs, pubs and offices come into force in Scotland on 26 March 2006 and a ban is being implemented in Northern Ireland from April 2007. MPs have also voted by a huge margin to ban smoking from all pubs and private members' clubs in England. The change is expected to take effect in summer 2007. Cigarettes should not legally be sold to children under 16 years of age.

Climate

Owing to it being an island, the UK is subject to very changeable weather. Extremes of temperature are rare but snow, hail, heavy rain and heatwaves can occur. For detailed descriptions, see *Climate* in the respective country sections.

Required clothing: Waterproofing throughout the year. Warm clothing is advisable at all times, and is essential for any visits to upland areas.

Communications

Telephone: Country code: 44. There are numerous public call boxes. Some boxes take coins, others phonecards or credit cards.

Mobile telephone: Roaming agreements exist with most international mobile phone operators. Coverage is mostly good, but can be patchy in rural areas.

Internet: There are Internet cafes and centres in most urban areas. Some multimedia phone booths, often located at main railway stations and airports, offer touch-screen access.

Post: Stamps are available from post offices and many shops and stores. There are stamp machines outside some post offices. Post boxes are red. First-class internal mail normally reaches its destination the day after posting (except in remote areas of Scotland), and most second-class mail the day after that. International postal connections are good. Post office hours: Mon-Fri 0900-1730 and Sat 0900-1230, although some post offices are open much longer hours.

MEDIA: The UK has a strong tradition of public-service broadcasting and an international reputation for creative programme-making. The *BBC* began daily radio broadcasts in 1922 and quickly came to play a pivotal role in national life. The Empire Service, which became the *BBC World Service*, established a reputation worldwide. The *BBC* is funded by a licence fee, which all households with a TV set must pay. There is no advertising on *BBC1* and *BBC2*. Commercial TV began in 1955 with the launch of *ITV*.

Press: Dominated by about 10 major newspapers, UK circulation figures are amongst the highest in the world.

The most influential newspapers are *The Daily Telegraph*, *The Financial Times*, *The Guardian*, *The Independent*, *The Observer* (on Sunday) and *The Times*. The more popular 'tabloid' newspapers are *The Daily Express*, *The Daily Mail*, *The Daily Mirror* and *The Sun*. Most papers have an associated Sunday newspaper, though there are some independents. There are also daily regional newspapers, particularly in Scotland and the north. The London *Evening Standard* is produced in several editions daily, the first being at midday.

TV: *BBC TV* operates *BBC1*, *BBC2* and digital services including *BBC News 24* and *BBC World*, a commercially-funded international news channel. *ITV* is a major commercial network, organised around regional franchises. *Channel 4* is a commercially funded but publicly owned national station. *Five* is a national commercial channel. *Independent Television News (ITN)* supplies news to *ITV* and *Channel 4*. *British Sky Broadcasting (BSkyB)* operates digital satellite TV platform, *Sky*, and provides film, entertainment channels and news channel *Sky News*. There are many other privately-owned TV channels.

Radio: *BBC Radio*'s national services include music station *Radio 1*, adult music station *Radio 2*, cultural network *Radio 3*, flagship speech station *Radio 4* and news and sport station *Five Live*. *BBC Radio* also has regional broadcasts (see individual country). *BBC Asian Network* targets Asian communities in the UK. *BBC World Service* can be heard worldwide via shortwave and increasingly on FM relays; it has programmes in more than 40 languages. Commercial radios include music station *Virgin Radio*, commercial sports station *Talk Sport and* commercial classical music station *Classic FM*. There are hundreds of privately-owned radio stations.

Passport/Visa

	Passport Required?	Visa Required?	Return Ticket Required?
Full British	N/A	N/A	N/A
Australian	Yes	No	No
Canadian	Yes	No	No
USA	Yes	No	No
Other EU	1	No	No
Japanese	Yes	No	No

Note: *Regulations and requirements may be subject to change at short notice, and you are advised to contact the appropriate diplomatic or consular authority before finalising travel arrangements. Any numbers in the chart refer to the footnotes below.*

PASSPORTS: Passport valid for at least three months beyond length of stay required by all except:
1. EU/EEA nationals (EU + Iceland, Liechtenstein, Norway) and Swiss nationals holding a valid national ID card.
Note: EU and EEA nationals are only required to produce evidence of their EU/EEA nationality and identity in order to be admitted to any EU/EEA Member State. This evidence can take the form of a valid national passport *or* national identity card. Either is acceptable. Possession of a return ticket, any length of validity on their document, sufficient funds for the length of their proposed visit should *not* be imposed.
Note: (a) A passport is not required for travel between Great Britain and Ireland, Northern Ireland, the Channel Islands or the Isle of Man. (b) Passengers transiting the UK destined for the Republic of Ireland are advised to hold return tickets to avoid delay and interrogation.
VISAS: Required by all except the following:
(a) nationals listed in the chart above;
(b) nationals of Commonwealth countries (except nationals of Bangladesh, Cameroon, Fiji, The Gambia, Ghana, Guyana, India, Jamaica, Kenya, Mozambique, Nigeria, Pakistan, Sierra Leone, Sri Lanka, Tanzania, Uganda and Zambia who *do* need a visa);
(c) nationals of American Samoa, Andorra, Argentina, Aruba, Bolivia, Bonaire, Brazil, Chile, Cook Islands, Costa Rica, Croatia, Curacao, East Timor, El Salvador, Federated States of Micronesia, French Guiana, Greenland, Guadeloupe, Guam, Guatemala, Honduras, Hong Kong (SAR), Iceland, Israel, Korea (Rep), Liechtenstein, Macau (SAR), Marshall Islands, Martinique, Mexico, Monaco, New Caledonia, Nicaragua, Niue, Norway, Palau, Panama, Paraguay, Puerto Rico, Reunion, Saba, St Eustatius, St Maarten, San Marino, Switzerland, Tahiti and her Islands, Uruguay, US Virgin Islands, Vatican City (not with service and emergency passports) and Venezuela;
(d) those in transit, provided arriving and departing by air within 24 hours and holding all necessary onward documentation.
Important Note: *Direct Airside Transit visas* are required by nationals of the following countries, even if not entering the UK or changing airports during transit: Afghanistan, Albania, Algeria, Angola, Bangladesh, Belarus, Burundi, Cameroon, China (PR), Colombia, Congo (Dem Rep), Congo (Rep), Côte d'Ivoire, Ecuador, Eritrea, Ethiopia, The Gambia, Ghana, Guinea, Guinea-Bissau, India, Iran, Iraq, Kenya, Lebanon, Liberia, Macedonia, Moldova, Mongolia, Myanmar, Nepal, Nigeria, Pakistan, Palestinian Territories, Rwanda, Senegal, Serbia & Montenegro (including documents issued by the United Nations Mission in Kosovo), Sierra Leone, Somalia, Sri Lanka, Sudan, Tanzania, Turkey, Turkish Republic of Northern Cyprus, Uganda, Vietnam and Zimbabwe.

Credit: ©Darren Small

Note: (a) Entry clearance in the form of a passport sticker is required for all non-visa nationals and British nationals and nationals of non-EEA member states who intend to stay in the UK for more than six months. This must be obtained from a diplomatic mission before travelling. (b) Nationals not requiring visas are advised to be in possession of either a return ticket or, if arriving on a one-way ticket, proof of sufficient funds to accommodate and support themselves for the duration of stay. (c) Applicants in Bangkok (including applicants from Cambodia or Laos) applying for a visa valid for longer than six months must provide with their visa application a certificate confirming they are free from infectious tuberculosis (TB).
Types of visa and cost: *Direct Airside Transit* and *Visitors In Transit Visa*: £30. *Single, Double and Multiple Visit Visa*: £50. *Longer Term Validity Visit Visa*: £85. Handling applications on behalf of Commonwealth countries costs £30.

Validity: *Direct Airside Transit*: 24 hours. *In Transit Visa*: 48 hours. *Single, Double and Multiple Visit Visa*: Up to six months. *Longer Term Validity Visit Visa*: Anything over six months.
Application to: Nearest British Consulate (or consular section at Embassy or High Commission); see *Passport/Visa Information*.
Application requirements: (a) Passport valid for entire visit. (b) Passport-size photo (some nationals may require additional photos). (c) Completed application form (some nationals may be required to fill out an additional form). (d) Fee (postal applications must be accompanied by bank draft, postal or money order only). The supplementary documentation required will vary depending on the type of application, but in all cases it is advisable to also provide: (e) Evidence of funds (bank statements or pay slips) and projected food and accommodation expenses whilst in the UK. (f) Letter of invitation (if applicable). (g) Evidence of sponsor's funds (if applicable). (h) Proof of intention to leave the UK following end of allocated visit.
Working days required: Dependent on nationality of applicant. Applications usually take between one and 10 working days. Applications that are referred to the Home Office may take up to 13 weeks. Nationals should apply with plenty of time but no more than three months in advance of travel.
Note: It is possible that nationals may be asked to attend an interview in order to process their application.
Temporary residence: Enquiries can be made at nearest British Consulate, Embassy or High Commission.

PASSPORT/VISA INFORMATION

UK Visas
Foreign and Commonwealth Office,
King Charles Street, London SW1A 2AH, UK
Tel: (020) 7008 8438.
Website: www.ukvisas.gov.uk
Opening Hours: Mon-Fri 0930-1330

British Embassy in the USA
3100 Massachusetts Avenue, NW,
Washington, DC 20008, USA
Tel: (202) 588 7800.
Website: www.britainusa.com

British Consulate in the USA
845 Third Avenue, New York, NY 10022, USA
Tel: (212) 745 0200.
Website: www.britainusa.com

Money

Note: See the individual *Money* sections within the *Jersey*, *Guernsey*, *Isle of Man* and *Northern Ireland* sections for information on currency specific to these regions.
Currency: Pound (GBP; symbol £) = 100 pence. Notes are in denominations of £50, 20, 10 and 5. Additional bank notes issued by Scottish banks (including £1 notes) are legal tender in all parts of the UK. Coins are in denominations of £2 and 1, and 50, 20, 10, 5, 2 and 1 pence.
Currency exchange: Money can be exchanged in banks, exchange bureaux and many hotels. The exchange bureaux are often open outside banking hours but charge higher commission rates. All major currencies can be exchanged. Cash can be obtained from a multitude of ATMs available across the country.
Credit & debit cards: American Express, MasterCard and Visa are all widely accepted. Check with your credit or debit card company for details of merchant acceptability and other services which may be available.
Traveller's cheques: Widely accepted. To avoid additional exchange rate charges, travellers are advised to take traveller's cheques in Pounds Sterling.
Currency restrictions: There are no restrictions on the import or export of either local or foreign currency.
Banking hours: Mon-Fri 0930-1630 (there may be some variations in closing times). Some branches of certain banks are open Saturday morning; some all-day Saturday.
Exchange rate indicators
Rate at time of publishing
$1.00= $0.57

Duty Free

Note: The Channel Islands are treated as being outside of the EU for the Duty Free section.
The following items may be imported into the UK without incurring customs duty by travellers aged 17 years and over arriving from non-EU countries:
200 cigarettes or 100 cigarillos or 50 cigars or 250g of tobacco; 2l of table wine; 1l of alcoholic beverages stronger than 22 per cent or 2l of fortified or sparkling wine or other liqueurs; 60ml of perfume and 250ml of eau de toilette; other goods including souvenirs up to the value of £145. Goods obtained duty and tax paid in the EU are unlimited.
Prohibited/restricted items: Prohibited items include unlicensed drugs, offensive weapons, indecent and obscene material featuring children, counterfeit and pirated goods, meat, dairy and other animal products and pornography. Restricted items include firearms, explosives and ammunition, live animals, endangered species, certain plants and their produce and radio transmitters.
The UK is one of the few regions of the world completely free of rabies and, until recently, all cats and dogs imported into the country had to spend six months in quarantine. To bring animals and birds into the UK, an import licence must be obtained at least six months in advance. Some animals may now qualify for the PET Travel Scheme (PETS) and can be brought into the UK without being put into quarantine. At present, this is limited to certain travel carriers and animals. Severe penalties are imposed on persons attempting to smuggle domestic animals into the country. An illegally imported animal is liable to be destroyed.
For further information about importing animals, contact the Department for the Environment, Food and Rural Affairs, Area 207, 1A Page Street, London SWIP 4PQ (website: www.defra.gov.uk/animalh/quarantine/index.htm); *or* the PETS helpline (tel: (0870) 241 1710; e-mail: pets.helpline@defra.gsi.gov.uk) *or* the nearest British mission abroad.
Abolition of duty free goods within the EU: On 30 June 1999, the sale of duty free alcohol and tobacco at airports and at sea was abolished in all of the original 15 EU member states. Of the 10 new member states that joined the EU on 1 May 2004, these rules already apply to Cyprus and Malta. There are transitional rules in place for visitors returning to one of the original 15 EU countries from one of the other new EU countries. But for the original 15, plus Cyprus and Malta, there are now no limits imposed on importing tobacco and alcohol products from one EU country to another (with the exceptions of Denmark, Finland and Sweden, where limits *are* imposed). Travellers should note that they may be required to prove at customs that the goods purchased are for personal use *only*.

Public Holidays

Below are listed Public Holidays for the January 2006-June 2007 period.
2006: Jan 1-2 New Year's Day. **Apr 14** Good Friday. **Apr 17** Easter Monday (*except Scotland*). **May 1** Early May Bank Holiday. **May 29** Spring Bank Holiday. **Aug 28** Summer Bank Holiday (*except Scotland*). **Dec 25** Christmas Day. **Dec 26** Boxing Day.
2007: Jan 1 New Year's Day. **Apr 6** Good Friday. **Apr 9** Easter Monday (*except Scotland*). **May 7** Early May Bank Holiday. **May 28** Spring Bank Holiday.
Note: Public holidays are usually referred to as 'bank holidays' in the UK.
Note: Please see the individual *Public Holiday* sections for details of additional holidays in each country.

Health

	Special Precautions?	Certificate Required?
Yellow Fever	No	No
Cholera	No	No
Typhoid & Polio	No	N/A
Malaria	No	N/A

Note: Regulations and requirements may be subject to change at short notice, and you are advised to contact your doctor well in advance of your intended date of departure. Any numbers in the chart refer to the footnotes below.

Health care: European Economic Area (EEA) and Switzerland: If you or any of your dependants are suddenly taken ill or have an accident during a visit to an EEA country or Switzerland, free or reduced-cost necessary treatment is available - in most cases on production of a valid European Health Insurance Card (EHIC). Each country has different rules about state medical provision. In some, treatment is free. In many countries you will have to pay part or all of the cost, and then claim a full or partial refund. The EHIC gives access to state-provided medical treatment only and the scheme gives no entitlement to medical repatriation costs, nor does it cover ongoing illnesses of a non-urgent nature, so comprehensive travel insurance is advised. Note that the EHIC replaces the Form E111, which will no longer be valid after 31 December 2005. Some restrictions apply, depending on your nationality.
The National Health Service provides free medical treatment (at hospitals and general surgeries) to all who are ordinarily resident in the UK, but requires payment for dental treatment, prescriptions and spectacles. Immediate first aid/emergency treatment is free for all visitors, after which charges are made unless the visitor's country has a reciprocal health agreement with the UK. The following have signed such agreements: all EU countries (but Danish residents of the Faroe Islands are not covered), Anguilla, Australia, Barbados, British Virgin Islands, Bulgaria, Channel Islands (applies only if the visitor is staying less than three months), CIS countries, Falkland Islands, Iceland, Isle of Man, Montserrat, New Zealand, Norway, Romania, Russian Federation, St Helena, Serbia & Montenegro, and Turks & Caicos Islands. The agreements provide differing degrees of exemption for different nationalities; full details of individual agreements are available from the Department of Health (website: www.dh.gov.uk).

Travel - International

AIR:
The principal national airline is *British Airways (BA)* (tel: (0870) 850 9850; website: www.britishairways.com).
Approximate flight times: From London to *Paris* is one hour 15 minutes; to *New York* is seven hours 45 minutes; to *Los Angeles* is 11 hours; to *Singapore* is 12 hours 35 minutes; to *Sydney* is 21 hours 45 minutes.
For approximate durations of other international flights from London, see the *Travel – International* section of the destination country.
For flights from regional airports in the United Kingdom, see *Travel-International* in each country section.
Main airports: See *Travel – International* in the relevant country sections for information on UK airports.
Departure tax: None.
SEA:
There are many ports offering ferry connections between the UK and mainland Europe, Ireland, the Channel Islands, the Isle of Wight, the Scilly Isles and the Isle of Man.
Main ports: *Dover, Harwich, Holyhead* and *Portsmouth*.
UK ferry operators include: *Brittany Ferries* (tel: (08703) 665 333; website: www.brittany-ferries.co.uk); *Caledonian MacBrayne* (tel: (0870) 650 000; website: www.calmac.co.uk); *Condor Ferries* (tel: (0845) 243 5140; website: www.condorferries.co.uk); *DFDS Seaways* (tel: (08702) 520 524; website: www.dfdsseaways.co.uk); *Fjord Line* (tel: (0870) 143 9669; website: www.fjordline.co.uk); *Irish Ferries* (tel: (08705) 171 717; website: www.irishferries.com); *Isle of Man Steam Packet Co* (tel: (08705) 523 523; website: www.steam-packet.com); *Isles of Scilly Travel* (tel: (0845) 710 5555; website: www.islesofscilly-travel.co.uk); *Norse Merchant Ferries* (tel: (0870) 600 4321; website: www.norsemerchant.com); *P&O Ferries* (tel: (08705) 980 333; website: www.poferries.com); *Red Funnel* (tel: (0870) 444 8898; website: www.redfunnel.co.uk); *Superfast* (tel: (0870) 234 0870 *or* 2211 (travel agents); website: www.superfast.com); *Stena Line* (tel: (08705) 707 070; website: www.stenaline.com); *Swansea–Cork Ferries* (tel: (01792) 456 116; website: www.swanseacorkferries.com); and *Wightlink* (tel: (0870) 582 7744; website: www.wightlink.co.uk). A map of ferry routes is available on VisitBritain's website: www.visitbritain.com.
RAIL:
Trains meet connecting ferries at Dover, Newhaven, Portsmouth and Weymouth, sailing for Belgium, France, Germany and Spain (board at Victoria Station or Waterloo (for Portsmouth and Weymouth) in London); and at Harwich, sailing for Germany, The Netherlands and Scandinavia (board at Liverpool Street). See also the *Channel Tunnel* and *Eurostar* sections below.
The Channel Tunnel: *Eurotunnel* runs shuttle trains for cars, bicycles, motorcycles, coaches, minibuses, caravans, campervans and other vehicles over 1.85m (6.07ft) between Folkestone in Kent, with direct road access from the M20, and Calais, with links to the A16/A26 motorway (Exit 13). All road vehicles are carried through the tunnel in shuttle trains running between the two terminals. Terminals and shuttles are well-equipped for disabled passengers. Passenger Terminal buildings contain a variety of shops, restaurants, bureaux de change and other amenities. The journey takes about 35 minutes from platform to platform and around one hour from motorway to motorway. There are up to four passenger shuttles per hour at peak times, 24 hours per day and services run every day of the year. Motorists pass through customs and immigration before they board, with no further checks on arrival. Fares are charged according to length of stay and time of year and whether or not you have a reservation. The price applies to the car, regardless of the number of passengers or size of the car. Promotional deals are frequently available, especially outside the peak holiday seasons. Tickets may be purchased in advance from travel agents, or from Eurotunnel Customer Services in France or the UK with a credit card. For further information, brochures and reservations, contact *Eurotunnel Customer Services UK*, Customer Relations Department, Saint Martin's Plain,

A B C D E F G H I J K L M N O P Q R S T U V W X Y Z

Cheriton, Folkestone, Kent CT19 4QD (tel: (08705) 353 535; website: www.eurotunnel.com). For further information about departure times of shuttles at the French terminal, contact *Eurotunnel Customer Information* in Coquelles (tel: France +33 (3) 2100 6543).

Eurostar: *Eurostar* is a service provided by the railways of Belgium, the UK and France, operating direct high-speed trains from London (*Waterloo International*) to Paris (*Gare du Nord*) and to Brussels (*Midi/Zuid*). It takes two hours 40 minutes from London to Paris (via Lille) and two hours 20 minutes to Brussels. For further information and reservations, contact *Eurostar* (tel: (0870) 600 0792 (travel agents) or (08705) 186 186 (public; within the UK) or +44 (1233) 617 575 (public; outside the UK); a £5 booking fee applies to all telephone bookings; website: www.eurostar.com); *or Rail Europe* (tel: (08705) 848 848; website: www.raileurope.co.uk). Work on the UK section of the high-speed rail line is being done in two stages. Stage 1 (from the Channel Tunnel through Kent to the outskirts of London) has been completed. Stage 2, to be completed in January 2007, will take the route to a new terminal at St Pancras. When it is completed, the transit times between London St Pancras and Brussels will be just two hours and between London St Pancras and Paris just two hours 15 minutes.

ROAD:

 Eurolines (52 Grosvenor Gardens, London SW1W 0AU; tel: (08705) 143 219; website: www.eurolines.com) and *National Express* (Ensign Court, 4 Vicarage Road, Edgbaston, Birmingham B15 3ES; tel: 08705 808 080; website: www.nationalexpress.com) run regular coach services from the UK to numerous European cities.

Passes: Travellers can either choose Mini-Pass breaks or book a 15-, 30- or 60-day pass. The six Mini-Passes give travellers the freedom to visit three cities, with prices starting from £55. Travellers can stay as long as they like in each city. Few formalities are encountered when driving between Northern Ireland and the Republic of Ireland.

Travel - Internal

Note: This section is a general introduction to transport within the UK. Further information is given in the individual *Travel* sections for England, Scotland, Wales, Northern Ireland, the Channel Islands and the Isle of Man.

AIR:

 British Airways operates a shuttle service from London to Edinburgh, Glasgow, Manchester and Newcastle amongst other cities. Other internal operators include *bmi (BD)* (website: www.flybmi.com), *flybe (BE)* (website: www.flybe.com), *easyJet (EZY)* (website: www.easyjet.com), and *Ryanair (FR)* (website: www.ryanair.com).

Approximate flight times: From London to *Aberdeen* is one hour 30 minutes; to *Belfast* is one hour 15 minutes; to *Edinburgh* is one hour 20 minutes; to *Glasgow* is one hour 20 minutes; to *Jersey* is one hour; to *Manchester* is 55 minutes; and to *Newcastle* is one hour and 10 minutes.

SEA:

 Information on travel to the Channel Islands, Ireland, the Isle of Man and the Scottish islands are given in the relevant *Travel* sections for those countries.

RAIL:

 The UK is served by an excellent network of railways. *Intercity* lines provide fast services between London and major cities, and there are services to the southeast and to major cities in the Midlands, the north and south Wales and between Edinburgh and Glasgow. Some rural areas are less well served (eg the north coast of the west country, parts of East Anglia, Northern Ireland, Northumberland and North Yorkshire, parts of inland Wales, and southern and northern Scotland), although local rail services are generally fairly comprehensive.

Rail passes: There are many discretionary fares, and visitors using trains may like to consider one of the all-line *BritRail* range of passes giving unlimited travel. This is available to visitors from overseas and is not available in the UK; tickets must be purchased in the visitor's home country, although tickets can be collected in the UK. Further details can be obtained from *BritRail* (website: www.britrail.com). The *Inter-Rail* pass offers unlimited second-class train travel in up to 29 European countries (includes Morocco and Turkey) split into eight zones (A-H). Three different tickets are available: a ticket covering one zone (two to six countries, 16 days' validity), a ticket covering two zones (six to 10 countries, 22 days' validity) and an *All Zone Pass* (29 countries, one month's validity). Ferry services between Italy and Greece are included. Passengers must be resident in Europe for at least six months before the pass is used. Travel is not allowed in the passenger's country of residence. Travellers under 26 years receive a reduction of about 30 per cent. Children's tickets are reduced by about 50 per cent. Supplements are required for some high-speed

services, seat reservations and couchettes. Discounts are offered on *Eurostar* and some ferry routes. Available from *Inter Rail* (website: www.interrailnet.com).

For information about UK train services and fares, contact *National Rail Enquiries* (tel: (08457) 484 950; website: www.nationalrail.co.uk). It can be much cheaper to purchase rail tickets in advance. Disabled travellers are also entitled to discounted train fares; see the *Disabled Traveller* appendix.

ROAD:

 There are trunk roads ('A' roads) linking all major towns and cities in the UK. Roads in rural areas ('B' roads) can be slow and winding, and in upland areas may become impassable in winter. Motorways radiate from London and there is also a good east–west and north–south network in the north and the Midlands. The M25 motorway circles London and connects at various junctions with the M1, M3, M4, M10, M11 and M40. The only motorway that leaves England is the M4 from London to South Wales. Access to Scotland is by the A1/A1(M) or the A68 to Edinburgh, or the M6 to Carlisle followed by the A74 to Glasgow. Within Scotland, motorways link Edinburgh, Glasgow and Perth. In Northern Ireland, motorways run from Belfast to Dungannon and from Belfast to Antrim. For further information on roads within each country, see the respective *Travel* sections. **Coach:** Every major city has a coach terminus: in London, it is Victoria Coach station, about 1km (0.7 miles) from the train station. There are coach services to all parts of the country. Many coaches have onboard toilets and refreshments. Private coaches may be hired by groups wishing to tour the UK; these can be booked in advance and will visit most major tourist attractions. Many of these destinations now have coach parks nearby. The main carrier is *National Express* (website: www.nationalexpress.com). **Traffic regulations:** Traffic drives on the left. Speed limits are 30mph (48kph) in urban areas, 70mph (113kph) on motorways and dual carriageways, elsewhere 50mph (80kph) or 60mph (97kph) as marked. Unleaded petrol and diesel are sold at all petrol stations. LPG (liquified petroleum gas) is increasingly available. Seatbelts must be worn by the driver and front seat passenger. Where rear seat belts have been fitted, they must also be worn. It is illegal to use a hand-held mobile phone while driving. The minimum driving age is 17. **Documentation:** National driving licences are valid for one year. Drivers must have Third Party insurance and vehicle registration documents. **Automobile associations:** The AA (website: www.theaa.com) and RAC (website: www.rac.co.uk) are able to provide a full range of services to UK members touring the UK. These organisations can also assist people who are travelling from abroad with maps, tourist information and specially marked routes to major events or places of interest.

URBAN:

 All cities and towns have bus services of varying efficiency and cost. Glasgow, Liverpool, London and Newcastle have underground railways. London and Glasgow's date back to the 19th century. The urban areas of Birmingham, Cardiff, Glasgow, Liverpool and Manchester are also well served by local railway trains. Manchester has an efficient modern tram service. **Taxis:** Licensed taxi operators are generally metered; small supplements may be charged for weekends, bank holidays, excess baggage and late-night travel. In the larger cities, unlicensed operators offer a cheaper (but less efficient and knowledgeable) unmetered service with fares based loosely on elapsed clock mileage; these taxis are called mini-cabs and can be summoned by telephone.

Travel Advice

Most visits to the UK are trouble-free but you should be aware of the global risk of indiscriminate international terrorist attacks, which could be against civilian targets, including places frequented by foreigners.

This advice is correct at time of publishing. As the situation can change rapidly, visitors are advised to contact the following organisations for the latest travel advice:

US Department of State
Website: http://travel.state.gov/travel

The Ministry of Foreign Affairs in your home country.

Accommodation

> **EDITOR'S CHOICE:** *The Landmark Trust* (see *Accommodation Information*) is a charity which restores historic buildings and lets them for holidays. Among the more unusual properties are *Fort Clonque*, a 19th-century coastal fort on Alderney in the Channel Islands; and *The Pineapple*, near Falkirk in Scotland, which was built in 1761 and features a pineapple-shaped roof.

HOTELS:

 These range from budget chain hotels to boutique city hotels to luxurious country house manors. Hotels tend to be more expensive in large cities, especially London. From 2006, a new common grading system comes into effect, replacing the different classification schemes formerly used by each country. This will be phased in completely by 2008.

GUEST HOUSES:

 There are guest houses and bed & breakfast facilities throughout the country.

SELF-CATERING:

 Cottages can be rented in many areas and self-catering apartments are available in cities. For information, contact the local tourist board, or consult the relevant section in local and national papers.

CAMPING AND CARAVANNING:

 There are camping and caravan sites throughout the UK, for short and long stays. Some sites hire out tents or caravans to those without their own equipment. Most sites offer basic facilities, while some have playgrounds, clubs, shops, phones and sports areas.

HOLIDAY CAMPS: These offer accommodation, food and a full range of leisure activities generally at an all-inclusive price. They provide good holidays for families, and some run babysitting and children's clubs.

YOUTH HOSTELS: There are over 300 youth hostels in the UK. Standards vary greatly, from very basic night-time accommodation for hikers and cyclists, to modern hostels and motels which are often used by families and groups. Prices are very reasonable.

ACCOMMODATION INFORMATION

VisitBritain
Thames Tower, Blacks Road, Hammersmith, London W6 9EL, UK
Website: www.visitbritain.com
VisitBritain's website has a comprehensive accommodation search facility.

The Landmark Trust
Shottesbrooke, Maidenhead, Berkshire SL6 3SW, UK
Tel: (01628) 825 925.
Website: www.landmarktrust.org.uk

Top Things To See & Do

Details of resorts and places of interest throughout the UK may be found by consulting the respective sections for England, the Isle of Man, Northern Ireland, Scotland and Wales. There is also a separate section for the individual Channel Islands (Alderney, Guernsey, Jersey and Sark & Herm).

TOURIST INFORMATION

VisitBritain
Thames Tower, Blacks Road, Hammersmith, London W6 9EL, UK
Tel: (020) 8846 9000.
Website: www.visitbritain.com

Visit Britain in the USA
551 Fifth Avenue, Suite 701, New York, NY 10176, USA
Tel: (800) 462 2748 (general information line, toll-free in the USA) or (212) 986 2266 (executive offices).
Website: www.visitbritain.com/usa

Entertainment

Each of the countries of the United Kingdom has its own particular national dishes and drinks, festivals and other events of interest, its own attractions for shoppers and its own nightlife and other entertainments. Details may be found by consulting the individual country sections.

Tipping: In hotels, a service charge of 10 to 12 per cent is usual, which may be added to the bill. 10 to 15 per cent is usual for restaurants and it too is often added to the bill, in which case, a further tip is not required. 10 to 15 per cent is also usual for taxi drivers and hairdressers but this is not included in the bill. There is no legal requirement to pay service charges that have been added to bills and if the service has been unsatisfactory, it may be deducted by the customer. Travellers should remember, however, that, in the UK, wage levels for catering staff are set at a deliberately low level in the expectation that tips will make up the difference.

Business

- **GDP:** US$2.213 trillion.
- **Main exports:** Manufactured goods, machinery and transport, chemicals, and services.
- **Main imports:** Finished manufactured goods, food, beverages, tobacco, machinery and transport equipment, chemicals, fuels, clothing and footwear.
- **Main trade partners:** Germany, USA and France.

ECONOMY: The UK is a member of the G7 group of the world's leading industrial nations. Since the end of World War II, the UK has followed the trend among all major economies away from industrial production towards service industries, that now account for three-quarters of national income. The transition has often been painful, and although the UK is not unique in this respect – most Western European economies have undergone a similar process during the past 20 years – a worse situation might have occurred without the cushion of revenues from North Sea oil. The UK's traditionally strong agricultural sector has suffered a number of serious setbacks, including two major outbreaks of disease (BSE and foot-and-mouth) which caused havoc in the industry and the loss of billions of pounds in export income. Engineering (especially of military products), chemicals, electronics, construction and textiles are the main components of the industrial sector. Among service industries, tourism, media, retail, financial services, telecommunications and computer services are the most important and have undergone rapid growth, while heavy industries have suffered relative decline. The Conservative administration of the 1980s and early 1990s was the first in Western Europe to dismantle the mixed economy of private and state-owned industries that had become the standard model for members of the EU. Many former state-owned industries including oil, telecommunications, gas and electricity, were sold to private shareholders, while the Government imposed tight fiscal controls and enacted pro-business legislation. Controls on trade and on the movement of capital were removed. The model has since been adopted throughout both the industrialised and developing worlds; it has been maintained and then extended by the Labour administration, which took office in 1997.
Britain's economic performance in the last few years has been reasonable, although some cracks are beginning to show as the Government has been forced to plan for a much higher level of borrowing than anticipated. Unemployment remained stable and among the lowest in the EU at 1.43 million in 2005 (4.7 per cent of the workforce). GDP growth dropped to 1.5 per cent during 2005, rising to 1.7 per cent in the third quarter. Inflation reached 1.9 per cent, the highest in seven years. The UK's external economic relations are now dominated by the EU (which accounts for 70 per cent of all UK trade), although there are other important trade links with the USA, the Far East and with members of the Commonwealth. Nonetheless, Europe dominates the economic agenda and the overriding issue facing present and future Governments is the extent to which they are willing to integrate into the European economy. The argument is now focused on whether Britain should adopt the single European currency, the Euro. Although the economy met the necessary criteria, the Government chose not to join up when the currency was introduced in 1999. The Government has since remained firmly on the fence; while many political and business leaders favour membership, there is huge opposition in the country at large. The conclusion of the debate may be decisive to Britain's economic future.
BUSINESS ETIQUETTE: Businesspeople are generally expected to dress smartly (suits are the norm). Appointments should be made and the exchange of business cards is customary. A knowledge of English is essential. **Office hours:** Mon-Fri 0900/0930-1700/1730.
CONFERENCES/CONVENTIONS: The UK conference scene is well organised with several publications comprehensively listing every possible kind of venue (including dedicated centres, hotels, universities, football grounds, race courses, manor houses, castles and theatres). In addition, regional and local tourist boards promote their own areas vigorously. Birmingham and London have an international reputation; there are several excellent conference venues. There are other towns with facilities of near comparable size, and comprehensive back-up services are available everywhere. Bristol, Glasgow, Manchester and Newcastle are among the cities offering a variety of venues, whilst smaller towns such as Chester, Inverness, Llandudno, Salisbury and York offer uniquely attractive environments without sacrificing efficiency. The large political parties of the UK traditionally hold their conferences in seaside towns during the winter; locations include Blackpool (the famous Winter Gardens), Bournemouth and Brighton. Those looking for conventional venues will find the maximum seating capacity (19,000 persons) in London; however, if organisers wished to book Wembley Stadium they could probably do it, so, effectively, there is no upper limit. All parts of the UK are easily accessible by rail and air from London. The *British Conference Destinations Directory* gives brief regional details and is published by the British Association of Conference Destinations, VisitBritain has a venue search facility on its website www.visitbritain.com/business.

COMMERCIAL INFORMATION

The British Chambers of Commerce
65 Petty France, St James's Park, London SW1H 9EU, UK
Tel: (020) 7654 5800.
Website: www.chamberonline.co.uk

British Association of Conference Destinations
6th Floor, Charles House, 148-149 Great Charles Street, Birmingham B3 3HT (tel: (0121) 212 1400; website: www.bacd.org.uk).

England

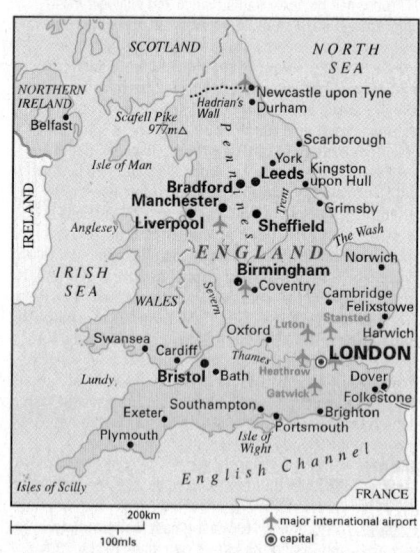

Location: Great Britain.

Overview

England's eventful history and scenic diversity render it one of the world's most popular visitor destinations. United as a single nation little over years ago, its origins go back to the dawn of civilisation, and the variety of interest it offers reflects this.
From prehistoric Stonehenge to 21st-century attractions like London's Millennium Eye, its inhabitants have contributed much to the appeal of the UK's largest constituent country. This is not restricted to a material legacy either – England's cultural mix is rich, thanks to the many invaders, settlers and immigrants who have arrived on it's shores through the millennia. Countless others around the globe share aspects of customs, language and history with the English themselves.
England's heritage, and therefore its appeal as a destination, is many faceted and deeply rooted, ranging from the literary genius of Shakespeare to 'everyday' pageantry in the changing of the guard at Buckingham Palace.
The variety and contrast in the nation's countryside is enormous too, and is often a source of surprise to many visitors venturing beyond the cities for the first time – as is the vast range of visitor attractions, resorts and sights to see and enjoy. England is a country of patchwork landscapes: from the rugged coastlines and golden beaches of Devon and Cornwall, to the craggy mountains of the Peak District, the ancient forests riddled with folklore, to the picturesque Lake District, to great cities and centuries-old villages. Woven into its fabric lies a rich-veined 'Englishness', earthed in a heritage of stone circles, Arthurian legend, Shakespeare, the triumphalist ego of a crumbling aristocracy, and the cocky independence of an island nation.
England today is welcoming, friendly, fascinating and fun, where pomp and circumstance balance the often bizarre idiosyncrasies of its people, and a sense of humour is the passport to certain acceptance.

General Information

For information on Government, religion, electricity, social conventions, passport and visa, money, duty free, health and business, see the main *United Kingdom* section.
AREA: 130,281 sq km (50,356 sq miles).
POPULATION: 50.1 million (official estimate 2004).
POPULATION DENSITY: 384.6 per sq km.
CAPITAL: London. **Population:** 7.43 million (Greater London; official estimate 2004).
GEOGRAPHY: Much of the countryside is relatively flat, consisting of fertile plains and gentle hills. Mountains, moors and steeper hills are found mainly in the north and the west; the Lake District (Cumbria) and the northwest are divided from the Yorkshire Dales, and the northeast, by the (relatively) high-rising Pennines, 'the backbone of England'. The eastern part of the country, particularly East Anglia, is the lowest lying. The coastline is varied, and ranges from long stretches of sandy beaches to steep cliffs and isolated rocky coves.
LANGUAGE: English. The multiplicity of local dialects throughout the country, overlaid with class, and town and country accents, makes English a language of astonishing diversity – words and forms of syntax which are obsolete in the southeast may often be found elsewhere. In the larger cities, particularly London, there are many communities who do not speak English as a first language (or who have a *patois* – originating outside of this country – which adds yet more variety to the English language).

Climate

The climate is temperate with warm wet summers and cool wet winters. Weather varies from day to day and throughout the country as a whole. The west coast and mountainous areas receive the most rain; the east coast, particularly in the north, is colder and windier. The southeast is sunnier than the north with less rain and a climate approaching the continental. The southwest has the mildest climate overall.
Required clothing: European according to season, plus rainwear.

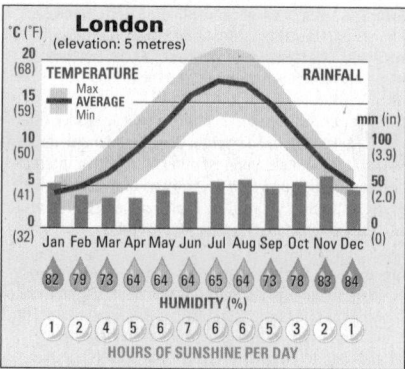

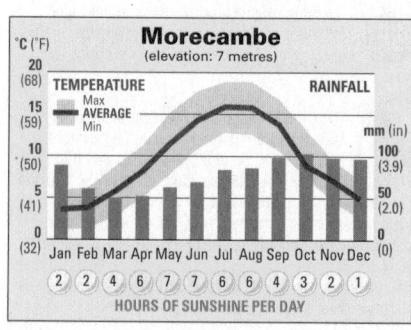

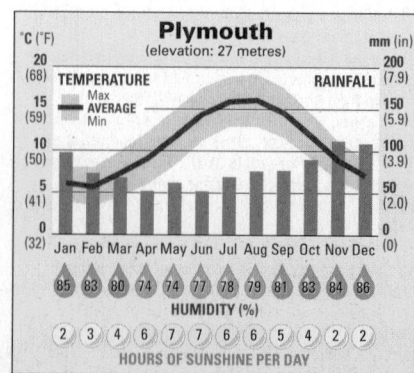

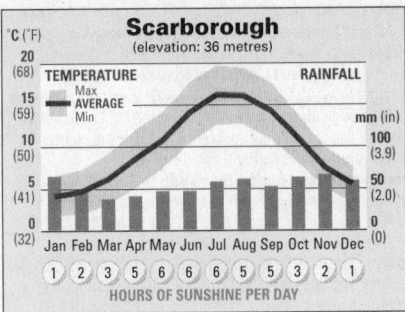

Scarborough
(elevation: 36 metres)

°C (°F)
TEMPERATURE
— Max
— AVERAGE
— Min

RAINFALL

mm (in)

HOURS OF SUNSHINE PER DAY
1 2 3 5 6 6 6 5 5 3 2 1

Communications

MEDIA: Press: All the major UK national newspapers are published in England, primarily out of London. However, there is a plethora of regional and local papers, some published on a daily basis. Major players in this sector include the *Evening Standard* (London), the *Yorkshire Post* (Leeds), the *Evening News* (Manchester) and the *Birmingham Post*. There are additionally a number of non-English dailies, primarily available in the major cities.
TV: Both the *BBC* and *ITV* (the commercial network) offer extensive localised news and current affairs programming around the country – this is usually broadcast immediately before or after main national news bulletins. Some local general interest programming is also available.
Radio: As well as its national channels, the *BBC* has an extensive network of local radio stations, normally broadcasting to a specific county. There are also many commercial stations, normally offering musical output and some local news coverage.
See also the main *United Kingdom* section.

Public Holidays

Note: Public holidays observed in England are the same as those observed in the rest of the UK (see the main United Kingdom section).

Travel - International

AIR:
There are numerous international flights operating from English airports.
Approximate flight times: From Birmingham or Manchester to *Paris* is one hour 30 minutes and to *New York* is seven hours 45 minutes. For approximate durations of international flights from London, see the *Travel - International* section of the destination country.
Main airports: *Heathrow (LHR)* (tel: (0870) 000 0123; website: www.heathrowairport.com) is located 24km (15 miles) west of central London. The airport has three passenger terminals grouped together in the airport's central area. The fourth terminal is a short distance from the main complex. A fifth terminal is under construction and is due to open in 2008.
To/from the airport: **Underground:** The airport is linked to the entire Greater London area by the underground railway network. Stations for Heathrow Terminals 1, 2, 3 and 4 are on the Piccadilly Line. Note: A replacement bus service is operating between Terminal 4 and Terminals 1, 2 and 3 until September 2006. The travel time to the West End is 45 minutes, and to the mainline stations, King's Cross and St Pancras, 55 minutes. All other mainline stations can be reached with only one change of train in central London. Services run Mon-Sat 0513-0022, and Sun 0557-2355. 24-hour information is available from Transport for London (tel: (020) 7222 1234; website: www.tfl.gov.uk). **Train:** The *Heathrow Express* (tel: (0845) 600 1515; website: www.heathrowexpress.com) is a fast service from London Paddington to Heathrow. Trains depart every 15 minutes (travel time – 15 to 20 minutes). The *Heathrow Connect* (tel: (0845) 678 6975; website: www.heathrowconnect.com) is a stopping train from London Paddington to Heathrow, leaving every half hour (travel time – 25 minutes). There are *Railair* buses, with frequent services connecting Heathrow with trains at Feltham, Reading, Watford and Woking stations. Details are available in each terminal. **Coach:** *National Express* (tel: (08705) 808 080; website: www.nationalexpress.com) runs two to three buses an hour from Heathrow to London Victoria coach station (travel time – 50 to 60 minutes), operating 0535-2135. It also runs services every 15 to 30 minutes (almost 24 hours a day) to Gatwick (travel time – one hour 5 minutes) and to Stansted airport once or twice an hour (travel time – one hour 25 minutes), operating 0330-2340. It runs direct services from Heathrow to many parts of the UK including Birmingham (travel time – two hours 20 minutes), Bristol (travel time – two hours), Cardiff (travel time – three hours 10 minutes) and Leeds (travel time – five hours 20 minutes), as well as connecting services to other cities. The *Oxford Bus Company*

(tel: (01865) 785 400; website: www.oxfordbus.co.uk) runs a service directly between Heathrow and Oxford at half-hourly intervals during the day and two-hourly intervals throughout the night. *Green Line* coach/bus services (724) (website: www.greenline.co.uk) run to Watford, St Albans, Hatfield, Welwyn Garden City, Hertford and Harlow. **Local bus:** *Transport for London* (tel: (020) 7222 1234; website: www.tfl.gov.uk) operates numerous local bus services from Heathrow Central bus station, including the N9 night bus to central London. **Taxi:** Available for hire outside each airport terminal. Each terminal has its own taxi rank and the information desk can give an indication of fares. **Car hire:** Self-drive and chauffeur-driven cars can be hired from desks in each airport terminal. To central London takes 30 minutes to one hour. **Private car:** Heathrow is reached either through the tunnel of the M4 motorway spur or from the A4 (Bath) road. It is also close to the M25 orbital motorway, making journeys to virtually all parts of the country relatively simple. It is advisable to avoid the area during peak times (0700-1000 and 1600-1900). Unloading but no waiting is allowed outside terminals. Short- and long-term car parking is available; there are coach connections from the long-term car park to all terminals.
Gatwick (LGW) (tel: (0870) 000 2468; website: www.gatwickairport.com) is located 45km (28 miles) south of central London.
To/from the airport: **Train:** *Gatwick Express* (tel: (0845) 850 1530; website: www.gatwickexpress.co.uk) operates a nonstop service from Victoria Station at 15-minute intervals from 0500-0030 and also trains at 0330 and 0430 (travel time – 30 minutes). There are also cheaper stopping trains from Victoria (travel time – 35 minutes) as well as regular services from London Bridge Station (travel time – 30 minutes). There are fast and frequent trains from Gatwick, which connect with mainline stations throughout southeast England. There are direct trains daily between Gatwick and many other cities nationwide. For further information, contact National Rail Enquiries (tel: (08457) 484 950). **Coach:** *National Express* (tel: 08705 808 080; website: www.nationalexpress.com) runs coaches to Victoria Coach Station hourly 0515-2215 (travel time to Victoria – one hour 25 minutes). Services run to Stansted Airport at 0205 and 0405 then once or twice an hour from 0525-2150. Coaches to Heathrow run at 0205 and 0405 then every 15 to 30 minutes until 2345 (travel time – one hour 10 minutes). There are direct coach services to many parts of the UK including Birmingham (approximate travel time – four hours); Brighton (approximate travel time – 45 minutes); Cardiff (approximate travel time – four hours 35 minutes); and Leicester (approximate travel time – four hours five minutes). Certain charter tour operators also provide coaches from Gatwick for arriving passengers. Check with relevant tour operator. **Taxi:** Available outside the terminal (travel time to central London – one hour. **Car hire:** Self-drive and chauffeur-driven cars can be hired from desks in the arrivals hall. **Private car:** Gatwick can be reached from London on the A23/M23. It is also close to the M25 orbital motorway, linking all main routes from London. There are ample parking facilities for short and long stays. For fee enquiries, telephone (0870) 000 1000.
London City Airport (LCY) (tel: (020) 7646 0088; website: www.londoncityairport.com) is located 10km (6 miles) east of the City of London. This airport, situated at the Royal Docks in the London Borough of Newham, provides frequent scheduled air services linking the City of London

with many European cities. Check-in time is usually about 10 minutes.
To/from the airport: **Train/Underground:** A new Docklands Light Railway station opened at the airport in December 2005. Frequent services run to Bank, Canary Wharf and Canning Town. The nearest Underground connection is at Canning Town (Jubilee Line). Silvertown Station, on the Silverlink Metro line, is 328m (300 yards) from the airport terminal; trains run to various stations in north and west London. More details are available from Transport for London (tel: (020) 7222 1234; website: www.tfl.gov.uk). **Coach/Bus:** A shuttle bus operates every 10 minutes from the terminal to Canary Wharf (Docklands Light Railway and Jubilee Line) and Liverpool Street Station (London Underground and mainline trains to the east of England). The service operates approximately Mon-Fri 0655-2120, Sat 0645-1315 and Sun 1230-2020. Local buses 69, 473 and 474 stop at the terminal, linking it with nearby Docklands Light Railway and Silverlink Metro stations. **Taxi:** There is taxi rank outside the terminal. **Car hire:** Self-drive and chauffeur-driven cars can be hired from desks in the arrivals hall. **Private car:** The airport is reached from the City via Commercial Road/East India Dock Road (A13) over the Canning Town Flyover, turning right into Prince Regent Lane, or via Tower Hill along The Highway (A1203) and Silvertown Way (travel time – 30 minutes); from the M25 via the M11 and North Circular (A406) or the A13. Access from the City of London will usually present no problems provided the morning and evening rush hours are avoided. London City Airport has ample car parking space located just outside the terminal building.
Stansted (STN) (tel: (0870) 000 0303; website: www.stanstedairport.com) is located 48km (30 miles) northeast of central London.
To/from the airport: **Train:** The *Stansted Express* (tel: (0845) 600 7245; website: www.stanstedexpress.co.uk) runs every 15 minutes (Fri-Mon 0430-2325; Tues-Thurs 0455-2255) from London Liverpool Street to Stansted (travel time – 45 minutes). There are also services from Stansted to Cambridge and the North. Further information is available from National Rail Enquiries (tel: (08457) 484 950). **Coach:** *National Express* connects Stansted with London Victoria Coach Station. Coaches run every 10 to 20 minutes during the day and every 20 to 30 minutes at night (travel time – one hour 30 minutes). Services run every two hours between Stansted, Heathrow and Gatwick. National Express also operates direct buses to Birmingham, Oxford and Norwich. *Terravision* runs coaches to Liverpool Street Station and to Victoria Coach Station. *First* runs buses to Chelmsford, Southend and Colchester. A number of local operators serve other towns and villages in East Anglia. **Taxi:** To central London takes one hour 30 minutes. **Car hire:** Cars can be hired from desks in the terminal building. For air taxis/business aviation services, contact *Artac Air Chartering Service* (tel: (01376) 566 000; website: www.artac.com). **Private car:** The airport is easily accessible by road on the M25/M11 from London. The Midlands and the North are reached via the A1, A604 and M11. Long- and short-term car parking space is available.
Luton (LTN) (tel: (01582) 405 100; website: www.london-luton.co.uk) is located 51km (32 miles) northeast of London.
To/from the airport: **Train:** Access to Luton Airport is via Luton Airport Parkway station. A courtesy shuttle service operates between the station and airport terminal. Luton is on the *Thameslink* line which runs from Bedford via

Credit: ©Darren Small

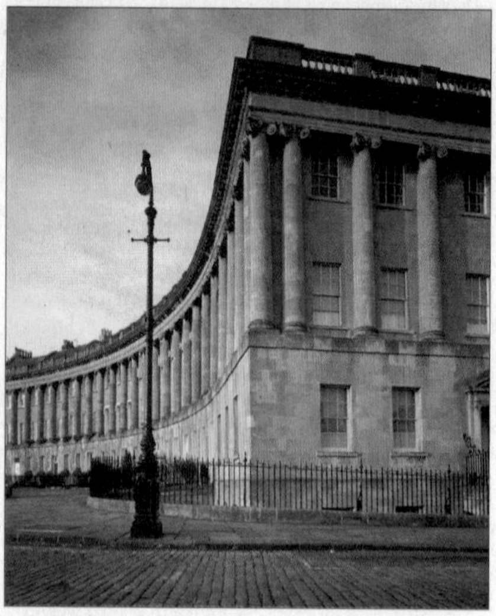

Credit: ©Bath Tourism Plus

London (stopping at King's Cross and London Bridge stations) and Gatwick Airport to Brighton. *Midland Mainline* services connect Luton with the Midlands and the North. Trains run direct to Leicester, Nottingham, Derby and Sheffield (website: www.midlandmainline.com). National Rail Enquiries (tel: (08457) 484 950). **Coach:** *National Express* (tel: (08705) 808 080) runs daily services to Birmingham. Services also run to many other parts of the UK. Direct services connect Luton Airport with Stansted, Heathrow and Gatwick. *Greenline* 757 (website: www.greenline.co.uk) runs daily from the airport to Luton and on to central London. Buses run half-hourly during the day and hourly in the evening (half-hourly all day Sunday). *easyBus* (website: www.easybus.co.uk) runs an express minibus to central London (Baker Street) daily every 30 to 60 minutes. **Local bus:** Buses run from the airport to Luton bus and rail stations, with frequent services during the day, and hourly evening services (Mon to Sat). **Taxi:** Can be hired from the rank immediately outside the terminal building. **Car hire:** Major car hire companies have desks in the terminal building. **Private car:** The airport can be reached on the M1 exiting at Junction 10. Access to the airport from the east is via the A505 dual carriageway from Hitchin. The M25 connects all motorways and the airport can therefore be accessed from the East, South and West via M25, M4, M11 and M23. Travelling from the west also provides several routes from the Dunstable area through Luton. Airport signs should be followed throughout. Long- and short-term car parking is available within the airport boundary.

Birmingham (BHX) (tel: (0870) 733 5511: website: www.bhx.co.uk) is located 13km (8 miles) southeast of the city centre.

To/from the airport: **Train:** The main terminal is linked to Birmingham International Station and the National Exhibition Centre (NEC) by the *Air-Rail Link* courtesy bus service. Birmingham International is connected to the Intercity network and regional lines and has a fast service to London Euston every 30 minutes (travel time - one hour 20 minutes). Further information is available from National Rail Enquiries, Birmingham New Street Station, in the city centre, is 10 minutes away by Intercity or local services and provides interchange for services throughout the rest of the country.(tel: (08457) 484 950). **Coach/Bus:** *Travel West Midlands* operates local services into the suburbs. Service 900 from the airport to the NEC and various locations around the city centre, operates every 20 to 30 minutes (0500-2100). *National Express* (tel: (08705) 808 080; website: www.nationalexpress.com) offers frequent, daily services to central Birmingham, Coventry, Manchester, Northampton and all the London airports. Frequent coaches run to and from Birmingham from London Victoria and most major cities and towns throughout the country. **Taxi:** Taxis are available outside the terminals (travel time to city centre - 25 minutes). **Car hire:** Major car hire companies have desks in the terminal building. **Private car:** The M1, M5, M6, M40 and M42 are the main routes to Birmingham. The airport is well signposted from the city. There is multi-storey and open-air parking at the airport. For further details, contact National Car Parks (NCP) (tel: (0870) 606 7050).

Manchester (MAN) (tel: (0161) 489 3000; website: www.manchesterairport.co.uk) is located 17km (10 miles) southwest of the city centre.

To/from the airport: **Train:** Manchester Airport station links the airport to Manchester city centre, with trains departing daily every five to 20 minutes (travel time - 15 to 20 minutes). Fast trains to all parts of the country leave from Manchester Airport station and there are connections for further services at Manchester Piccadilly and Manchester Victoria (tel: (08457) 484 950; website: www.nationalrail.co.uk). **Coach/Bus:** *National Express* (tel: (08705) 808 080; website: www.nationalexpress.com) runs daily services to most parts of the UK including Scotland. *Skyline* operates buses to the airport's station and on to Manchester, Altrincham and Stockport. Bus 43 runs as often as every 10 minutes to the city centre. For more detailed information on times and frequency of local bus services, contact *Greater Manchester Passenger Transport Authority* (tel: (0161) 228 7811; website: www.gmpte.com). **Taxi:** There are taxi ranks situated outside the arrivals halls at each terminal and at the station (travel time to the city centre - 25 minutes). **Car hire:** Major car hire companies have have booking offices in Terminals 1, 2 and 3. **Private car:** The airport is at the heart of the country's motorway network and a specially constructed spur from the M56 runs directly into the terminal building. Road connections serve Greater Manchester, Merseyside, Lancashire, Cheshire, the Midlands and West and South Yorkshire. There is car parking space within the airport boundary.

Newcastle (NCL) (tel: (0870) 122 1488; website: www.newcastleairport.com) is located 10km (6 miles) northwest of the city centre.

To/from the airport: **Metro:** The Tyne and Wear Metro (website: www.tyneandwearmetro.co.uk) connects the whole of the Newcastle area with the airport. It runs to Newcastle city centre, across the River Tyne to Gateshead and South Shields and to Tynemouth and the coast. For information, call Traveline (tel: (0870) 608 2608). **Train:** The nearest railway station is Newcastle Central, 11km (7 miles) from the airport, linked by the Metro. For further information, contact *National Rail Enquiries* (tel: (08457) 484 950). **Coach:** *National Express* operates services to the airport from several cities including Durham, Edinburgh, Leeds and Manchester. **Local bus:** Services 75, 76, 77 and 79 run from Eldon Square bus concourse, in the centre of Newcastle. These stop on the main road at the airport entrance (travel time - 20 minutes). **Taxi:** A taxi rank is situated outside the railway station, and at the Haymarket near the Eldon Square bus concourse in Newcastle city centre (travel time to city centre - 15 to 20 minutes). Only licensed taxi cabs are allowed to pick up at the airport. **Car hire:** Major car hire companies have desks in the terminal building. **Private car:** The airport can be reached from the south by the A1(M) north, then the A696 Jedburgh trunk road, and from the north by the A1 south, then the A696 Jedburgh trunk road. Open-air long- and short-term parking facilities are available (advance booking recommended during busy periods).

Facilities: The airports listed above are all of a high international standard and include bank/bureaux de change, duty free shops, restaurants and bars.

SEA:

There are many ports offering ferry connections between England and mainland Europe, Ireland, the Channel Islands, the Isle of Wight, the Channel Isles and the Isle of Man. See *Travel - International* in the main *United Kingdom* section for a list of operators.

RAIL:

The *Intercity* network serves all main cities in the UK mainland. All routes radiate from London. For all rail information, call National Rail Enquiries (tel: (08457) 484 950; website: www.nationalrail.co.uk). Rail services are operated by numerous private companies. Terminus stations in London serve the following regions:

Southern England and South London: *Charing Cross, London Bridge, Victoria* and *Waterloo*.

East Anglia, Essex, North-East and East London: *Liverpool Street*.

South Midlands, West of England, South Wales and West London: *Paddington*.

East and West Midlands, North Wales, North-West England, West Coast of Scotland and North-West London: *Euston, Marylebone* and *St Pancras*.

East and North-East England, East Coast of Scotland and North London: *King's Cross*.

There are also many smaller lines that operate less frequently. There are services to the Republic of Ireland via *Fishguard* and *Holyhead*, and to Northern Ireland.

ROAD:

England is served by a good network of motorways and trunk roads that connect all the main cities and towns.

The main motorways are: **M1:** London, Luton, Leicester, Sheffield, Leeds. **M2/A2:** London to Dover. **M3:** London to Winchester. **M4:** London, Reading, Bristol, Newport, Cardiff, Swansea. **M5:** Birmingham, Gloucester, Bristol, Exeter. **M6:** Coventry, Birmingham, Stoke, Warrington (connecting with the M62 for Liverpool and Manchester), Preston (connecting with the M55 for Blackpool), Morecambe, Carlisle. **M11:** London to Cambridge. **M20/A20:** London to Folkestone. **M25:** London orbital. **M40:** London to Birmingham. **M62:** Liverpool, Warrington, Manchester, Huddersfield, Leeds, Hull. The main trunk roads are: **A1/A1(M)** (motorway in parts): London, Peterborough, Doncaster, Darlington, Newcastle, Edinburgh. **A3:** London, Guildford, Portsmouth. **A5:** London, St Albans, Nuneaton, Birmingham area, Shrewsbury, across inland north Wales to Holyhead. **A6:** London, Bedford, Leicester, Manchester. **A11:** London to Norwich. **A12:** London, Ipswich, Great Yarmouth. **A23:** London to Brighton. **A30:** London, Basingstoke, Yeovil, Exeter, Penzance. **A40:** London, Oxford (M40), Gloucester, Cheltenham, across inland south Wales to Fishguard.

Distances from London (by road): To Birmingham 169km (105 miles), Manchester 299km (186 miles), Liverpool 325km (202 miles), Exeter 278km (173 miles), Penzance 452km (281 miles), Bristol 185km (115 miles), Carlisle 484km (301 miles), Newcastle 441km (274 miles), Sheffield 257km (160 miles), York 311km (193 miles), Cambridge 89km (55 miles), Southampton 124km (77 miles), Dover 114km (71 miles), Oxford 92km (57 miles), Norwich 182km (113 miles), Portsmouth 113km (70 miles) and Harwich 122km (76 miles).

Coach: Many coach companies offer express and stopping services throughout England and the rest of the UK. The main operator, *National Express* (tel: (08705) 808 080; website: www.nationalexpress.com), provides nationwide coach information.

Urban transport in London: The Underground: London has a comprehensive metro service known as the 'Underground' or, colloquially, as the 'tube'. The tube is the oldest and one of the most extensive underground railway networks in the world. There are 13 lines, including the *Docklands Light Railway*, and some - such as the *Central* and the *Metropolitan* - extend well into the surrounding suburbs. Each line has its own colour on the network map, copies of which are widely available and can also be downloaded from Transport for London's website: www.tfl.gov.uk. Some lines operate certain sections during peak hours and some stations close altogether in the evenings or at weekends. There is also an extensive network of overground rail services in the London area, particularly in the southeast, many of which connect with Underground services. All of the railway terminus stations connect with at least one Underground line, with the exception of Fenchurch Street (which is, however, virtually adjacent to Tower Hill station on the District Line). Various travel discounts are available. The one-day, three-day or weekly *Travelcard* offers unlimited travel on bus, Underground and overground rail services in one or more zones; it is one of the best methods for visitors to travel throughout London. Monthly and annual Travelcards require a passport-size photograph. Travelcards can be stored electronically on *Oystercards*. It is also possible to purchase pre-pay Oystercards, for which money is deducted on each journey, usually saving on the cost of a full fare. For 24-hour enquiries on bus and underground travel, contact Transport for London (tel: (020) 7222 1234; website: www.tfl.gov.uk). For enquiries about rail services, contact National Rail Enquiries (tel: (08457) 484 950). Maps and leaflets are widely available, although it should be remembered that the maps of the Underground and overground rail networks are diagrammatic, and do not indicate the relative distances between stations. **Bus:** London is served by an excellent network of buses (over 700 routes). There has been huge investment over the past few years, resulting in new buses, improved service frequency and increasing numbers of 24-hour services. During rush hours, bus travel in central London can become agonisingly slow, although the introduction of bus lanes and 'red routes' on many roads has partly improved this situation. There is a good timetabled network of night bus services; all routes passing through central London call at Trafalgar Square. In central London, bus tickets must be purchased from machines before boarding. Saver bus tickets and pre-pay Oystercards offer discounts. The historic Routemaster buses have been gradually withdrawn from service, with the last route switching to modern buses in December 2005, but the Routemaster can still be seen on 'heritage' routes 9 and 15 in central London. **Taxi/Car hire:** Black cabs can be hailed in the street or ordered by phone. Fares are metered but surcharges are levied for extra passengers, large amounts of luggage, travel at night, and on Sundays or public holidays. Thousands of black cabs have facilities for wheelchair-bound passengers. Mini-cabs and cars for hire are also available; numbers are listed in the Yellow Pages telephone directory. **River transport:** Leisure and commuter services on the River Thames are run by a variety of private companies, including *Thames Clippers* (website: www.thamesclippers.com). The main commuter service is between Chelsea Harbour and Embankment. At weekends, there are a variety of cruises and pleasure trips. For further information, contact Transport for London (tel: (020) 7222 1234; website: www.tfl.gov.uk). There are three tram routes in South London (website: www.tfl.gov.uk/trams): Wimbledon - Croydon - Elmers End; Croydon - Beckenham Junction and Croydon - New Addington.

Urban transport: Elsewhere: All towns and cities have bus services. In addition, the areas of Birmingham, Liverpool, Manchester and the cities in South Yorkshire and Newcastle have suburban rail services. Newcastle also has a metro, which consists of a circular line with three branches. It connects with Newcastle Central, Manors and Heworth railway stations and terminates at South Shields (ferry connection to North Shields, also on the metro), St James, South Hylton and Newcastle Airport. Manchester has a fast metrolink tram service running on former railway lines from Bury in the north to Altrincham in the south and from Eccles in the west via Salford Quays to the city centre. All cities have taxi services, many using black cabs. Taxi ranks are usually placed near bus stations, railway stations and town centres. Local telephone directories give the numbers of mini-cabs and hire cars.

Accommodation

Accommodation is available at hotels, motels and posthouses, guest houses, farmhouses, inns and self-catering establishments and on campsites.

HOTELS:

It is rare to find a town in England, however small, which does not have at least one hotel; in villages, very often doubling as the local pub. Some London hotels, for example the *Savoy*, are famous the world over but there are many newer first-class hotels. In addition, there are many smaller hotels throughout the larger cities; in London, Earl's Court and the area around King's Cross are famous for their many streets of small hotels bearing such names as the *Albany*, *Apollo* or *Victoria*. **Grading:** VisitBritain, the AA and RAC (as well as the Wales Tourist Board and VisitScotland) have now agreed common standards for quality assessment, which come into force from 2006. Hotels and guesthouses are classified by use of a star-rating system. A comprehensive accommodation search facility is available on the VisitBritain website (see *Accommodation Information*).

GUEST HOUSES:

There are guest houses and bed & breakfast facilities throughout the country. Under the new quality standards, guest houses, inns and farmhouses providing bed & breakfast services are classified by a star-rating system. (The old diamond-rating system may still be in place in some areas while the new standards are being phased in.)

SELF-CATERING:

Cottages and bungalows can be rented in many areas. For information, contact VisitBritain or look in the relevant section in local and national papers. Standards may vary.

CAMPING/CARAVANNING:

There are camping and caravan sites throughout the UK, for short and long stays. Some sites hire out tents or caravans. Most sites offer basic facilities, while some have playgrounds, clubs, shops, phones and sporting areas.

HOLIDAY CAMPS: Offer accommodation, food and a full range of leisure activities generally at an all-inclusive price.

YOUTH HOSTELS:

Standards vary greatly, from very basic night-time accommodation for hikers and cyclists, to modern hostels often used by families and groups. Prices are very reasonable.

ACCOMMODATION INFORMATION

VisitBritain
Thames Tower, Blacks Road, Hammersmith,
London W6 9EL, UK
Website: www.visitbritain.com
The VisitBritain's website has a comprehensive accommodation search facility.

Youth Hostel Association of England and Wales
Trevelyan House, Dimple Road,
Matlock, Derbyshire DE4 3YH, UK
Tel: (01629) 592 700 *or* (0870) 770 8868 (UK only).
Website: www.yha.org.uk

Top Things To See

There is so much packed into England that it is impossible to do more than scratch the surface: the immense variety of landscapes and widely differing urban environments means that the old tourism cliché 'something for everyone' really does apply here.

- **London** is the natural starting point for most visitors, offering such classic sights as the **Houses of Parliament** (website: www.parliament.uk), **Westminster Abbey** (website: www.westminster-abbey.org), **Trafalgar Square** (website: www.london.gov.uk/mayor/trafalgar_square), the **Tower of London** (website: www.hrp.org.uk/webcode/tower_home.asp) and **St. Paul's Cathedral** (www.stpauls.co.uk). But it is worth escaping the crowds for a quiet stroll in one of the royal parks, including **Hyde Park** and **St. James's Park** (website: www.royalparks.gov.uk).
- Immediately at the southern end of Westminster Bridge stands the former **County Hall**, now redeveloped to include the **London Aquarium** (website: www.londonaquarium.co.uk), one of Europe's largest. The **South Bank Arts Centre** (website: www.southbankcentre.org.uk), near Waterloo Station, is among the most famous attractions south of the river. It comprises the **Royal National Theatre** (website: www.nationaltheatre.org.uk) and the **Royal Festival Hall** (website: www.rfh.org.uk). In Southwark there is an authentic reconstruction of the famous **Shakespeare Globe Theatre** (website: www.shakespeares-globe.org). The redeveloped Bankside Power Station houses the **Tate Modern** gallery (website: www.tate.org.uk/modern). Its collection includes major works by Monet, Picasso and Warhol.
- Great views over the capital are to be had by taking a ride on the **London Eye** (website: www.londoneye.com), located on the south bank of the Thames opposite Westminster.
- On the London outskirts, revisit the time of Henry VIII at **Hampton Court Palace** (website: www.hrp.org.uk/webcode/hampton_home.asp) by the bank of the Thames to the west, or take a boat trip east to see the **Thames Flood Barrier** (website: www.greenwich.gov.uk/Greenwich/LeisureCulture/Attractions/eg-at-thamesbarrier-content1.htm) and the **Royal Observatory** at **Greenwich** (website: www.rog.nmm.ac.uk), location of the Meridian, 0° longitude.
- Take a day trip to one of England's most historic university cities, both **Oxford** (website: www.oxford.gov.uk) and **Cambridge** (website: www.visitcambridge.org) are within easy reach of the capital.
- Away from the London area, a visit to the delightful Georgian city of **Bath** (website: www.visitbath.co.uk) is an experience not to be missed. The 5000-year-old stone circle at nearby **Stonehenge** is one of the world's great ancient monuments.
- The Midlands towns of **Warwick** and **Stratford-upon-Avon** (website: www.stratford.co.uk) offer those in a hurry a chance to see one of the great English castles (website: www.warwick-castle.co.uk) and learn all about the life of Shakespeare in a single day.
- Marvel at the medieval architecture of **York** (website: www.york-tourism.co.uk), with its magnificent **Minster** (largest church in northern Europe), almost complete city walls and Viking past.
- The eastern side of England is notable for a number of other fine medieval cathedrals, including those of **Norwich** (website: www.cathedral.org.uk), **Lincoln** (website: www.lincolncathedral.com) and **Durham** (website: www.durhamcathedral.co.uk).
- World-renowned china and porcelain manufacturers are based in and around **Stoke-on-Trent** (known as the 'Potteries'). **Spode** and **Wedgwood** both have major visitor centres, and factory tours are available (website: www.visitstoke.co.uk).
- Experience early 20thcentury life in industrial northeast England at **Beamish** open air museum (website: www.beamish.org.uk), **County Durham**.

Top Things To Do

- **London**'s huge range of museums and galleries are guaranteed to appeal to all ages. Highlights include the **Natural History Museum** (website: www.nhm.ac.uk), the **Victoria & Albert Museum** (website: www.vam.ac.uk), the **Science Museum** (website: www.sciencemuseum.org.uk) and the **National Gallery** (website: www.nationalgallery.org.uk), whose collection is one of the world's best. **London Zoo** (website: www.zsl.org) is another popular family attraction.
- A popular Sunday pursuit is a visit to **Petticoat Lane market**, in the **City of London**. Other street markets in tha capital include **Brick Lane** in the **East End**, and **Portobello Road** in **Notting Hill**, famous for antiques (website: www.londontown.com/London/General_Street_Markets).
- **Notting Hill** is also famous for its **Carnival** in the late August holiday weekend.
- Head for **London's West End**, which contains many of the principal theatres, cinemas, restaurants, cafes, hotels and nightclubs, as well as the best-known shopping areas, like **Oxford**, **Regent** and **Bond Street**, as well as **Covent Garden**. Other famous shopping streets include **King's Road** and **Knightsbridge**, site of **Harrods**. The **Royal Albert Hall**, home of the summer **Promenade Concerts**, is also here.
- Keen garderners will be spoilt at the **Chelsea Flower Show**. Every year, for five days during May, the grounds of the Royal Hospital in Chelsea are transformed into a plant paradise with thousands of glorious blooms, a selection of spectacular show gardens and the finest examples of horticultural excellence in the world (website: www.rhs.org.uk/chelsea).
- **Football** (soccer) is a major sport in England, with clubs like **Chelsea** and **Arsenal** in London, **Liverpool**, **Manchester United**, and **Newcastle United** being household names around the world. A visit to a top game makes an excellent afternoon or evening out (website: www.premierleague.com).
- English sporting events are often characterised by their traditional atmosphere and valued as much for the social opportunities which accompany them as for the sporting action. Many of the most famous events are patronised by the Royal family, and a certain style of dress is *de rigeur*. The main **horse races** attract a huge following and include **Aintree**, **Ascot** (famous for the extravagant hats worn by women on Ladies' Day) and the **Grand National** (the nation's premier event, prompting bets worth millions of pounds).
- **Rowing** is another traditional sport which provides fans of English culture with a chance to observe some age-old rituals. The year's most prestigious event is the **Henley Regatta**, held at Henley-on-Thames in late June. Boaters and blazers are worn by the men, while women often wear dresses and hats. Rowing eights from all over the world come to compete. The Oxford vs Cambridge **Boat Race** takes place in March or April. Eights from England's two oldest universities race along the Thames in London from Putney to Mortlake. Nowadays, there are races for women as well as for men.
- In the summer months, there is nothing quite so English to enjoy as a day at the **cricket**. **Lord's Cricket Ground** (website: www.lords.org) in northwest London is known as the world headquarters of this popular sport.
- Do not miss one of the world's great sporting events, the **Wimbledon Tennis** Championships (website: www.wimbledon.org), held every June/July in southwest London.
- Although not normally associated with such a warm-weather sport, England boasts a major **surfing** resort, **Newquay**, in **Cornwall** (website: www.newquay.com).
- Attend a Royal Shakespeare Company performance at the **Royal Shakespeare Theatre**, in **Stratford-upon-Avon** (website: www.rsc.org.uk). Once home to William Shakespeare (1564-1616), Stratford draws visitors in their millions. Attractions associated with the Bard include **Shakespeare's Birthplace**, **Anne Hathaway's Cottage**, (former home of his wife), **Mary Arden's House**, (home of the playwright's mother), and **Holy Trinity Church**, where he and his family lie buried.

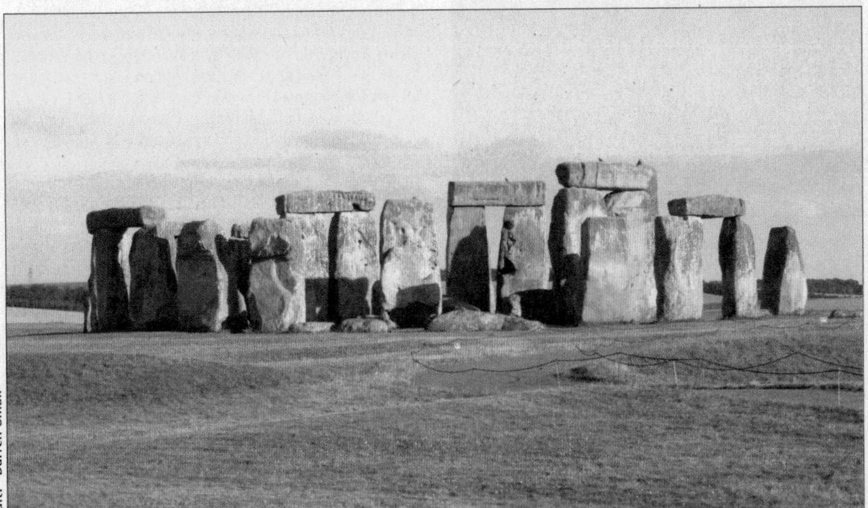

Credit: ©Darren Small

- Spend a day in **Windsor**, the jewel in Berkshire's crown. Windsor's massive castle is one of the Queen's official residences as well as being open to visitors. It has been a royal home for nearly 900 years since the time of William I. Guided tours of the town are available, as well as bus tours and river cruises. Nearby is the 19 sq km (7.3 sq miles) **Windsor Great Park**. Some 3km (2 miles) outside the town is **Legoland**, a major family attraction.
- If rural scenery appeals, escape to **Cumbria** (website: www.cumbria-the-lake-district.co.uk), where the **Lake District** is dominated by England's tallest mountains, or walk along 1800-year-old **Hadrian's Wall** (website: www.hadrians-wall.org), which spans England from west of the border city of **Carlisle** (website: www.historic-carlisle.org.uk) to **Newcastle** (website: www.visitnewcastlegateshead.com), marking the northern boundary of the Roman Empire. Keen **walkers** can also enjoy the **Pennine Way** (website: www.thepennineway.co.uk), which stretches 270 miles (430km) from the north Midlands to the Scottish border.
- Those with an interest in matters nautical will find much to occupy them in **Portsmouth** (website: www.visitportsmouth.co.uk), including Nelson's flagship **HMS Victory**.
- Canals, a legacy of the industrial revolution, criss-cross the English landscape, and a **narrowboat trip**, whether just for the day or over an extended period, is a fine way to experience a quieter side of English life (website: www.britishwaterways.co.uk).
- Attend one of England's regular major events such as the **British Motor Show** and **Cruft's Dog Show** which take place at the **National Exhibition Centre**, Birmingham (website: www.necgroup.co.uk/whatson).

TOURIST INFORMATION

VisitBritain
Thames Tower, Blacks Road, Hammersmith,
London W6 9EL, UK
Tel: (020) 8846 9000.
Website: www.visitbritain.com (international visitors) *or* www.enjoyengland.com (UK visitors)

Visit Britain in the USA
551 Fifth Avenue, Suite 701, New York, NY 10176, USA
Tel: (800) 462 2748 (general information line, toll-free in the USA) *or* (212) 986 2266 (executive offices)
Website: www.visitbritain.com/usa

Entertainment

FOOD & DRINK: Good English cooking is superb and there are some restaurants specialising in old English dishes. In general, the north of the country tends to offer more substantial and traditional food, at more reasonable prices than the south. Every region, however, will have its own speciality. For those who want variety, London and the larger cities offer every type of ethnic food imaginable,

Credit: ©Darren Small

Chinese and Indian being particularly popular and good value for money.

Things to know: Table service in restaurants is usual but there are self-service snack bars. Set-price lunches, especially on Sundays, with a choice of about three dishes, are particularly good value, as is pub food. The British pub is nothing short of a national institution and even the smallest village in the remotest corner of the country will usually have at least one. There are about as many beers in England as there are cheeses in France and the recent revival of real ale has greatly improved the range and qualities of brews available. Look out for the sign 'Free House' outside a pub, meaning that beer from more than one brewery will be sold there. Wine bars and cocktail bars are now common in the larger cities and towns, and the latter will often have a 'happy hour' (when prices are reduced) in the early evening. Under 18s will not be served alcohol and children under 16 are not generally allowed into pubs, although they may sit in the garden. Licensing hours vary between towns, but many pubs, especially in main centres, are open typically 1100-2300; the visitor should not be surprised, however, if they find a pub closing for a period in the afternoon. On Sunday, hours are 1200-2230. Private clubs often have an extension into the early hours. A new law came into force in November 2005 under which pubs can apply for licences allowing 24-hour opening. MPs have also voted to ban smoking from all pubs and private members' clubs in England. The change is expected to take effect in summer 2007.

Regional specialities:
- Roast beef and Yorkshire pudding.
- Game or venison pies.
- *Apple crumble* (slices of cooked apple with sweet crumble).
- *Spotted dick* (suet pudding with currants and raisins).
- *Syllabub* (a medieval dish consisting of double cream, white wine and lemon juice).
- English cream tea, particularly in south-coast seaside resorts, consisting of scones, jam, butter, clotted or double cream and, of course, tea.
- Regional varieties of baking such as *Bakewell tart*, a pastry base covered with jam, almond filling and topped with icing; and breads of all description.
- *Cheddar* and *Stilton* are the most famous British cheeses.

Regional drinks:
- Beer - bitter and lager are the most popular, but stout, pale ale and brown ale are also widely drunk.
- Cider.
- Tea.
- Gin.
- Pimm's, a refreshing gin-based drink, usually mixed with lemonade, fruit and mint, and especially popular in summer.
- English wines are becoming increasingly popular.

Tipping: A service charge (usually 12.5 per cent) might be included in the prices stated on the menu but it is more likely to be added to the bill at the end. This is technically an optional charge but it would be very unusual to ask for it to be removed. Where 'service is not included', a tip of at least 10 per cent is expected, although 12 to 15 per cent is becoming more common. Diners should check the bill thoroughly, as tipping is not required on top of a service charge. Tipping is not usual in bars and pubs if ordering at the bar.

NIGHTLIFE: The main cities, London in particular, have a vast range to choose from: theatre (including open-air in the summer), opera, ballet, concerts, films, restaurants, nightclubs and discos, as well as, of course, pubs. The weekly magazine, *Time Out*, publishes a comprehensive guide to events in the capital.

SHOPPING: Cutting-edge fashion from top labels such as *Burberry* or designer Stella McCartney can be bought in major cities. China and porcelain from *Wedgwood*, *Crown Derby*, *Royal Doulton* and *Royal Worcester* are good buys, as are luxury food and chocolates. Antiques are to be found all over the country. In London, Charing Cross Road is famous for bookshops, and there are several street markets: Petticoat Lane for clothes and Bermondsey for antiques, to name just two. **Tax-free shopping:** Many shops throughout the country now operate a tax-free shopping scheme for overseas visitors. The store will provide a form that should be completed at the time of purchase. Upon arrival at Customs, present the goods and the forms (within three months) to the Customs Officer, who will stamp the vouchers certifying that the goods are being exported, and that you will be entitled to a refund of Value Added Tax (VAT). For further information, contact VisitBritain.

Shopping hours: In major cities, Mon-Sat 0900/0930-1730; in London's West End and other large shopping centres, shops stay open to 2000. Most cities have at least one night a week of late night shopping until 2000, usually on Thursday. Many local shops stay open to 1900 or 2000 and some even later; many of these are open on Sunday morning or all day. Larger shops will open Sun 1000/1100-1600/1700. Some towns and areas of cities may have early closing one day a week, usually Wednesday or Thursday.

Scotland

200km
100mls

✈ major international airport
◉ capital

Location: Northern part of Great Britain.

Overview

Scotland is famous primarily for its spectacular scenery, but it also offers a rich historical and cultural heritage, together with a wide range of activities. The populous central belt is the focus of most economic activity, centred primarily on the major cities, Glasgow and the Scottish capital Edinburgh. Scotland's scenery is as varied as it is beautiful. Rugged mountain peaks sweep down to breathtaking lochs glistening in remote glens like Glen Affric near Inverness and Loch Trool in Galloway. A straggling coastline, with white sandy beaches, sheltered bays and rocky cliffs looks out to the remote islands of the Atlantic. To the south, the rolling hills of the Borders, lush lowland pastures and extensive woodlands present a softer beauty.

Scotland's capital, Edinburgh, is among the outstanding cities of the world, where the Medieval Old Town contrasts with the elegant Georgian New Town. Other towns, notably Glasgow, display a wealth of Victorian architecture. Everywhere you can find ancient castles and houses. Prehistoric forts, stone circles and burial mounds can be explored, particularly at the Neolithic Heart of Orkney, Scotland's latest World Heritage Site.

Scotland's rich musical heritage has feet tapping to bagpipes, fiddles and accordions. The best Celtic music can be heard at either the *Girvan Traditional Folk Festival* in May or the *Newcastleton Festival* in July.

Scotland is a paradise for outdoor enthusiasts. Play golf on the world's most famous course at St Andrews. Go fishing, sailing, diving, or join the walkers, cyclists and climbers on the hills, in woodlands and on deserted country lanes. Finally, at the end of the day, relax with Scotland's greatest export, a dram of fine malt *whisky*.

General Information

For information on time, religion, electricity, passport & visa, money, duty free and health, see the main *United Kingdom* section.
AREA: 77,925 sq km (30,086 sq miles).
POPULATION: 5.08 million (official estimate 2004).
POPULATION DENSITY: 65.2 per sq km.
CAPITAL: Edinburgh. **Population:** 449,000 (official estimate 2001).
GEOGRAPHY: The country consists of the southern Lowland area, a region of moorland and pastoral scenery – where most of the population is concentrated – and the northern Highlands, dominated by the Grampian Mountains and Ben Nevis (1344m/4140ft), the highest peak in the British Isles. The whole of the exceedingly beautiful coastline is indented with lochs (particularly in the north and west). Off the west coast there are many islands, the largest of which are Skye and Lewis, the latter being part of the Outer Hebrides. The Orkney and Shetland Islands lie to the northeast of the Scottish mainland, across the Pentland Firth from John O'Groats.
GOVERNMENT: Head of State: HM Queen Elizabeth II.
Head of Parliament: First Minister Jack McConnell since 2002. **Recent history:** Despite Scotland's absorption into Britain following the 1707 Treaty (or Act) of Union, there

has always been a strong streak of independence in the nation, and the regaining of independence has always been the aim of many Scots. The North Sea oil boom of the late 1960s served partly to fuel resentments as well, some arguing that the vast revenues generated by the new offshore industry should be channelled into Scotland rather than the UK as a whole. Scotland did, however, achieve a much greater degree of autonomy from the UK Government in 1999, when for the first time in three centuries it regained its own Parliament as part of the devolution process. The Scottish Parliament has control over matters such as education and health, and has its own tax-raising powers. The UK Government maintains control over issues such as defence and foreign policy. Scotland's Parliament is housed in a new purpose-built building adjacent to the Palace of Holyrood House in Edinburgh – a source of some controversy due to immense cost over-runs.
LANGUAGE: English. Gaelic is still spoken by some, mostly in the West and Highlands.

Climate

Scotland is generally colder than the rest of the UK, especially in the more northerly regions. The west tends to be wetter and warmer than the cool, dry east. In upland areas, snow is common in winter, and fog and mist may occur at any time of year.
Required clothing: Similar to the rest of the UK, according to season. Waterproofing advised throughout the year and warm clothing for the Highlands.

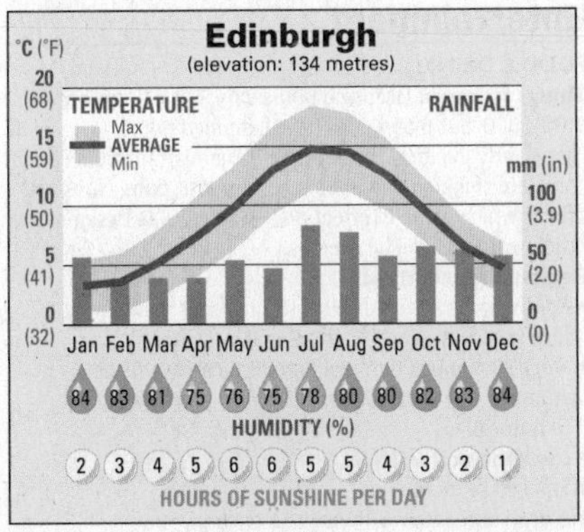

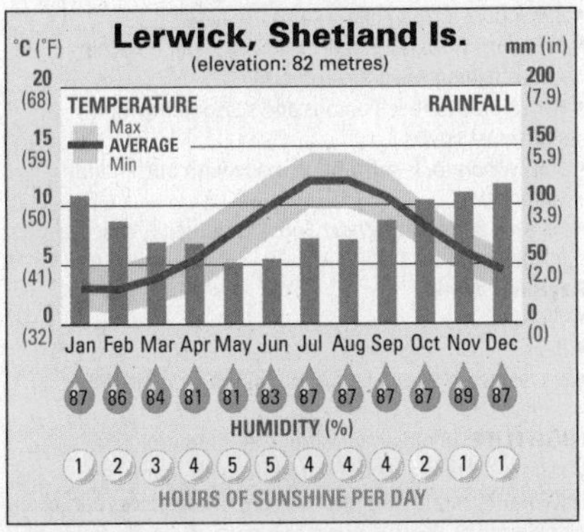

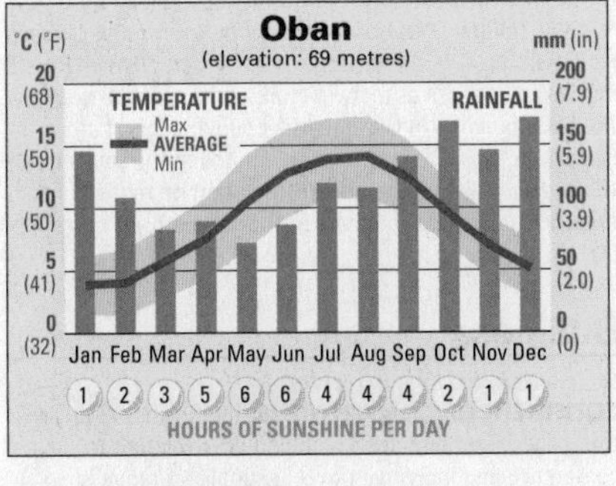

Communications

MEDIA: Press: Scotland's main national newspapers include *The Scotsman*, *The Herald*, and the tabloid *Daily Record*. *Scotland on Sunday* and the *Sunday Herald* are major Sunday titles, while there are numerous local daily evening papers.
TV: All UK networks broadcast in Scotland, with substantial national Scottish input, mainly in the news, sport and current affairs sectors. Major broadcasters include *BBC Scotland*, *Scottish Television* and *Grampian TV*.
Radio: *BBC Radio Scotland* is the major national English language station, but all UK national BBC stations are also available throughout the country, in addition to its Gaelic service, *Radio Nan Gaidheal*. Commercial stations include *Radio Forth* (Edinburgh), *Radio Clyde* (Glasgow), and *Central FM* (Stirling).

Public Holidays

Below are listed Public Holidays for the January 2006-June 2007 period.
Public holidays observed in Scotland are the same as those observed in the rest of the UK (see the main *United Kingdom* section) with the addition of:
2006: Jan 3 New Year Bank Holiday. **Aug 7** Summer Bank Holiday.
2007: Jan 2 New Year Bank Holiday. **Aug 6** Summer Bank Holiday.

Travel - International

AIR:
Continental Airlines flies from Edinburgh and Glasgow to the USA (website: www.continental.com). *British Airways* flies from London, Birmingham, Bristol, Manchester and Southampton to Edinburgh and Glasgow (website: www.britishairways.com); a number of low-cost airlines such as *easyjet* (website: www.easyjet.com) and *bmi* (website: www.flybmi.com) also fly to Scotland.
Approximate flight times: From Edinburgh to *New York* is seven hours 45 minutes and from Glasgow to *New York* is seven hours 40 minutes.
Main airports: *Edinburgh (EDI)* (tel: (0870) 040 0007; website: www.edinburghairport.com) is located 12km (8 miles) west of the city centre. *To/from the airport:* **Train/bus:** *Lothian Buses* (tel: (0131) 555 6363; website: www.lothianbuses.co.uk) operates service 100 between the airport and Waverley Bridge (in the city centre, opposite the main railway station), Mon to Sat every 20 minutes 0450-0650, then at least every 10 minutes until 0020. Sunday services run every 15 to 30 minutes 0450-0925, then at least every 10 minutes until 0020. The N22 night bus runs once an hour daily 0045-0345. **Taxi:** Available from the rank outside the airport (travel time to city centre – 25 minutes). **Car hire:** Self-drive and chauffeur-driven cars can be hired from desks within the terminal. **Private car:** The A8 runs directly to the airport from the city centre. If coming from the west or north, follow the signs on the M9, M8 and A90. Short- and long-stay parking is available.
Glasgow (GLA) (tel: (0870) 040 0008; website: www.glasgowairport.com) is located 14km (9 miles) west of the city centre. *To/from the airport:* **Train:** Paisley's Gilmour Street station is 3km (2 miles) from the airport. It is easily reached by taxi or bus and offers connections to Glasgow Central and other regional stations. For further information, contact *National Rail Enquiries* (tel: (08457) 484 950). **Bus/Coach:** All buses depart from outside the main airport terminal. *Scottish Citylink* (tel: (08705) 505 050; website: www.citylink.co.uk) runs regular services to the city centre via Queen Street railway station and Buchanan bus station (bus no 905), Mon-Sat 0600-0000 and Sun 0700-0000. Scottish Citylink's coach services also operate between the airport, Greenock and Gourock, as well as to Fort William, Kyle of Lochalsh and Portree, Skye. **Taxi:** To the city centre is 20 minutes; to Paisley station is five minutes. Taxis are available from the rank on the terminal forecourt. **Car hire:** Major car hire companies have desks next to Domestic Arrivals. **Private car:** The M8 runs direct to the airport from the city centre. Short- and long-stay parking is available.
Facilities: Edinburgh and Glasgow airports are both of a high international standard and include bank/bureaux de change, duty free shops, restaurants and bars.
Other airports: *Aberdeen (ABZ)* (tel: (0870) 040 0006; website: www.aberdeenairport.com) is located 11km (7 miles) northwest of the city centre. *To/from the airport:* **Train:** Aberdeen and Inverness trains stop at Dyce station, which is a short taxi ride from the airport. **Bus:** There are frequent bus services from the city centre to the airport. For details, contact *First* (tel: (01224) 650 065). **Coach:** *Stagecoach Bluebird* services also run to the airport (tel: (01224) 212 266). **Taxi:** Available from the airport (travel time to city centre – 20 minutes). **Car hire:** Major car hire companies have desks at the airport. **Private car:** Signs for the airport should be followed from the A96 Aberdeen to Inverness road. Short- and long-stay parking is available.
Facilities: These include bureau de change, tax-free shopping, restaurants and bars.
Inverness (INV) is the major airport serving the Highlands, with transfer connections available to airports in the north of Scotland. It is located 14km (9 miles) east of the city centre and is served by taxis and buses. *Facilities:* ATM, bar/restaurant and bookshop.
There are several smaller airports in the north of Scotland that are served by flights from Glasgow and, in some cases, from Aberdeen, Inverness and Edinburgh as well. These include *Barra*, *Benbecula*, *Kirkwall* (Orkney), *Sumburgh* (Shetland), *Stornoway* and *Tiree*. For further information, contact Glasgow Airport (see above).
SEA:
Main ports: *Aberdeen*, *Cairnryan*, *Lerwick*, *Oban*, *Rosyth* and *Stranraer*.
Ferry services operate between the mainland and all the Scottish islands but some of these may be infrequent. *Caledonian MacBrayne* (tel: (08705) 650 000; website: www.calmac.co.uk) operates the largest network of ferries on the river Clyde and west coast, serving many islands, including the Inner and Outer Hebrides. During the summer, services often operate hourly or half-hourly but in the winter they are less frequent. *Northlink Ferries* (tel: (0845) 600 0449; website: www.northlinkferries.co.uk) operates services to Orkney and Shetland; from Aberdeen to Lerwick daily, more often in summer (travel time – 12 hours); and from Scrabster to Stromness daily, more often in summer (travel time – 90 minutes).
Other routes include *P&O Irish Sea* ferry service between Cairnryan and Larne (travel time – one hour; tel: (0870) 242 4777; website: www.poirishsea.com); and *Stena Line's* service between Stranraer and Belfast (travel time – one hour 45 minutes (fast ferry); tel: (08705) 707 070; website: www.stenaline.com).
Smyril Lines (tel: (01595) 690 845; website: www.smyril-line.com) runs a weekly service between Hanstholm (Denmark) and Lerwick, continuing to the Faroe Islands and Iceland. The ferry goes via Bergen (Norway) in the summer.
Superfast Ferries (tel: (0870) 234 0870; website: www.superfast.com) operates three services a week between Rosyth (just outside Edinburgh) and Zeebrugge (Belgium).
RAIL:
There are two main-line routes into Scotland from England: from London Euston up the west coast to Glasgow Central and beyond to Perth and Inverness; and from London King's Cross up the east coast to Edinburgh and beyond to Dundee and Aberdeen. For details, contact *National Rail Enquiries* (tel: (08457) 484 950; website: www.nationalrail.co.uk). There are good services connecting all the main towns, particularly in the Edinburgh–Glasgow area. Many of the routes that pass through the Highlands (such as: Perth-Inverness; Inverness-Kyle of Lochalsh; Glasgow-Fort William-Mallaig) are very spectacular. The network extends right up to Thurso and Wick in the extreme north of the country. Sleeper services are available on *First Scotrail's Caledonian Sleeper* (connecting London Euston with Edinburgh, Glasgow, Aberdeen, Inverness and Fort William nightly; tel: (0845) 601 5929; website: www.firstscotrail.com).
ROAD:
Scotland is connected to the main UK road network by good trunk roads, and has several internal motorways. Main access from England is via the A74/M74 (Carlisle to Glasgow), the A696/A68 (Newcastle to Edinburgh via the Cheviots) and the A1 (Newcastle to Edinburgh via the coast). The main motorways within Scotland connect Edinburgh with Glasgow (M8), Edinburgh with Stirling (M9), and the Forth Bridge, near Edinburgh, with Perth (M90). In general, the internal trunk road network is better and more direct on the east coast, and roads north of Inverness tend to be slower and often single track. Snow is common in winter, especially in the Highlands, and motorists are advised to follow local advice concerning weather conditions. The main cross-country road, the A9, connects Perth with Inverness and Thurso. **Car hire:** Self-drive cars are widely available in the major centres.
Distances: *From London*: Edinburgh 663km (412 miles), Glasgow 654km (406 miles), Aberdeen 884km (549 miles), Inverness 923km (573 miles), Fort William 828km (514 miles), Perth 696km (433 miles) and Thurso 1066km (663 miles). *From Edinburgh*: Glasgow 72km (45 miles), Aberdeen 211km (131 miles), Inverness 261km (162 miles), Fort William 231km (138 miles), Perth 69km (43 miles) and Thurso 439km (273 miles).
URBAN:
All the major towns and cities have bus services. Glasgow also has an underground and a suburban train network.

Accommodation

There is a wide range of accommodation available in Scotland, comprising guest houses, bed & breakfasts, hotels, international resort hotels, self-catering, campsites, serviced apartments, lodges, inns, restaurants with rooms and campus accommodation. More than 1000 hotels, guest houses and bed & breakfasts are members of the 'Walkers Welcome' initiative and make special efforts to meet the needs of walkers. Over 1000 accommodation providers are members of the cyclist-friendly 'Cyclists Welcome' scheme.
Grading: VisitScotland, VisitBritain, the Wales Tourist Board, the AA and RAC have recently agreed common standards for accommodation quality assessment. Accommodation is classified using a star rating system of one to five stars.

ACCOMMODATION INFORMATION

VisitScotland publishes a series of accommodation guides covering hotels and guest houses, bed & breakfast, self-catering and camping and caravanning, for which there is a charge, plus postage and packing.(See *Top Things To Do* for contact details).

Scottish Youth Hostels Association
7 Glebe Crescent, Stirling FK8 2JA, UK
Tel: (01786) 891 400 (general enquiries) *or* (0870) 155 3255 (reservations).
Website: www.syha.org.uk

Top Things To See

- Scotland's most visited tourist attraction is the massive **Edinburgh Castle** (website: www.historic-scotland.gov.uk), which dominates the city skyline from its position atop a volcanic crag. Stroll downhill along the historic **Royal Mile** past the new **Scottish Parliament** building (website: www.scottish.parliament.uk/vli) to the **Palace of Holyrood House**, the Queen's official Edinburgh residence (website: www.royal.gov.uk).
- The capital is also the home of most of the country's major museums and galleries, including the **Royal Museum** and **Museum of Scotland** (website: www.nms.ac.uk) and the **National Gallery** (website: www.natgalscot.ac.uk).
- In **Glasgow**, whet the cultural tastebuds at the world-famous **Burrell Collection** (website: www.glasgowmuseums.com), where more than 9000 assorted paintings, tapestries and antique furniture are on view. For a more modern approach, the **Glasgow Science Centre** (website: www.glasgowsciencecentre.org) features interactive attractions and the 127m (416ft) revolving **Glasgow Tower**. Also on Clydeside is **Clydebuilt** (website: www.scottishmaritimemuseum.org), the **Maritime Museum** telling the story of Glasgow's shipbuilding industry.
- **Stirling Castle** (website: www.historic-scotland.gov.uk), a former home of Mary Queen of Scots, is another essential venue for visitors to central Scotland, while the nearby **Old Town Gaol** (website: www.oldtownjail.com) gives an unpleasant insight into life in a Victorian prison. Nearby at **Bridge of Allan**, the imposing **Wallace Monument** (website: www.nationalwallacemonument.com) commemorates **William 'Braveheart' Wallace**, 13th century scourge of the English. Climb the spiral staircase to the top for wonderful views across the **Forth Valley**.
- Outside the main cities, the **Highlands** is perhaps the most famous region in Scotland. On the southern fringes at **Callander**, the **Rob Roy Visitor Centre** (website: www.robroyvisitorcentre.com) tells the story of another Scottish folk hero. And the views from the road north out of Callander are among the finest in the country.
- Further northwest lie the seaside towns of **Oban**, from where the ferry leaves for **Mull** and **Iona** (Scotland's first Christian settlement), and **Fort William**, the latter overshadowed by Britain's highest mountain, **Ben Nevis**. From Fort William the road turns northeast along the **Great Glen**, location of the infamous **Loch Ness** and its legendary monster. You can learn all about 'Nessie' at the **Loch Ness 2000 visitor centre**, Drumnadrochit (website: www.loch-ness-scotland.com).

- At the eastern end of Loch Ness lies the small and attractive city of **Inverness**. Between here and Aberdeen, on the east coast, are situated many of Scotland's best-known **whisky distilleries** (website: www.maltwhiskytrail.com).
- Further down the east coast at **Dundee**, step aboard the **Discovery** (website: www.rrsdiscovery.com), on which Captain Scott made his ill-fated Antarctic voyage.
- In southern Scotland, be sure to see **Dumfries**, former home of **Robert Burns**, Scotland's most celebrated poet. See his very own chair at the **Globe Inn** (website: www.globeinndumfries.co.uk) in the centre of town.

Top Things To Do

- Take an open-top **'hop on/hop off' bus tour** around all the main sights in **Edinburgh** (website: www.edinburghtour.com), **relax** on a sunny day in the central **Princes Street Gardens**, or **browse the shops** along **Princes Street** itself.
- The annual **Edinburgh Festival**, which runs during the last two weeks of August and the first week of September (the *Fringe* starts and finishes a week earlier), is among the world's biggest arts events (website: www.eif.co.uk). Almost every room in the city large enough to hold an audience is in use during this time, and it is possible to see as many as 10 shows in one day; these might range from a short open-air concert to a full-scale production by the Royal Shakespeare Company or the London Symphony Orchestra. Accommodation in Edinburgh is booked up months in advance at this time.
- Another major summer event in the capital is the **Edinburgh Tattoo** (website: www.edinburgh-tattoo.co.uk), a spectacular military show held in the large forecourt of Edinburgh Castle.
- In **Glasgow**, sports fans should make the pilgrimage to **Hampden Park**, the national Scottish football (soccer) stadium. Guided tours are available (website: www.hampdenpark.co.uk).
- **Island-hopping** is a popular pursuit for visitors to Scotland. Regular ferry services link the mainland with the many **Hebrides** (to the west), including **Skye**, **Lewis**, **Harris** and many more, and with the **Orkneys** and **Shetlands** to the north.
- For those who like outdoor pursuits, Scotland is a haven for **walkers**, **climbers** and many other sporting pursuits including (snow permitting) **skiing**, which is centred on **Aviemore** in the **Grampians**.
- **Boating** of all types is another popular activity – tour boats run on many lochs, including **Loch Lomond**, **Loch Ness** and **Loch Katrine**.
- Scotland has an extensive network of signposted **cycling** routes and off-road trails for mountain biking. On small country roads there is often little traffic. Bicycle hire and cycling tours are available throughout the country.
- There are extensive **sailing** possibilities, together with **canoeing** and **whitewater rafting**, the latter on the fast-moving **Highland rivers**.
- Many Scottish rivers offer excellent **salmon fishing** – permits can be bought, but prices can vary considerably. **Sea angling**, particularly off the west coast, is also good.
- **Golfers** will be in their element in Scotland, which offers some 500 courses nationwide, among them the **Old Course** at St Andrews 'the ('Home of Golf'), and further top championship courses at **Carnoustie**, **Turnberry**, **Royal Troon** and **Muirfield**.
- **Wildlife** abounds in Scotland's more sparsely inhabited areas. Red deer, golden eagles, peregrine falcons and wildcat are some of the creatures inhabiting mountainous

regions, while the lower slopes of the central Highlands provide sanctuary for red squirrel, capercaillie and pine marten.
- Do not miss the **Highland Games** if in Scotland during the summer season. The biggest and best-known event is at **Braemar**, on the first Saturday every September (website: www.braemargathering.org).

TOURIST INFORMATION

VisitScotland
Ocean Point One, 94 Ocean Drive, Leith, Edinburgh EH6 6JH, UK
Tel: (0131) 472 2222 (marketing and media enquiries only).

For holiday enquiries or brochure requests, please contact:
VisitScotland.com
Fairways Business Park, Deer Park Avenue, Livingston EH54 8AF, UK
Tel: (0845) 225 5121 (within the UK) *or* (01506) 832 121 (outside the UK).
Website: www.visitscotland.com

VisitBritain in New York deals with enquiries relating to Scotland (see United Kingdom section).

Entertainment

FOOD & DRINK:
Things to know: Licensing hours vary; basic hours are 1100-2300, but many pubs have extended hours, particularly in cities. The Scottish Parliament introduced a complete smoking ban in bars, restaurants, pubs, clubs and offices which came in effect on 6 March 2006. Designated hotel bedrooms will be exempt.
Regional specialities:
- *Porridge*, a traditional Scottish breakfast made from locally grown oats and either milk or water.
- *Haggis* (chopped oatmeal and offal cooked in the stomach of a sheep), *neeps* (turnips) and *tatties* (potatoes).
- *Cullen skink* (fish soup).
- Smoked salmon.
- *Partan bree* (crab with rice and cream).
- Drop scones (scotch pancakes),
- *Black bun*, a fruit cake on a pastry base.
- *Arbroath smokies* (haddock smoked over oak chips in the Angus fishing town of Arbroath).
- *Forfar bridies* (beef, onions and seasoning with a shortcrust cover).
- *Selkirk bannock* (a fruit bun made with butter and sultanas).
- *Hawick Balls* and *Jethart Snails* (traditional boiled sweets in the Borders).
Regional drinks:
- Whisky.
- Beer.
- *Irn Bru* (carbonated soft drink said to be made from girders!).
NIGHTLIFE: In major cities, such as Edinburgh and Glasgow, there is a vibrant nightlife, with many bars, restaurants, nightclubs and cinemas. These places also offer a fine array of theatre, opera and music concerts. Some of the main venues for drama performances include the *Festival Theatre*, *Playhouse*, *Assembly Rooms* and *Queen's Hall* in Edinburgh, the *Citizen's Theatre* and *Theatre Royal* in Glasgow, as well as many picturesque regional theatres. The SECC building in Glasgow is a popular concert arena for live bands. Nightlife may be more limited in the smaller villages and islands. For more information on musical and theatrical events, contact VisitScotland (see *Top Things To Do*).

Business

See main *United Kingdom* entry.
CONFERENCES/CONVENTIONS: The Business Tourism Unit of VisitScotland deals with enquiries relating to conference and incentive travel. It supplies a range of publications and guides to help the meeting or incentive planner.

COMMERCIAL INFORMATION

VisitScotland - Business Tourism Unit
Ocean Point One, 94 Ocean Drive, Leith, Edinburgh EH6 6JH, UK
Tel: (0131) 472 2355.
Website: www.conventionscotland.com

Wales

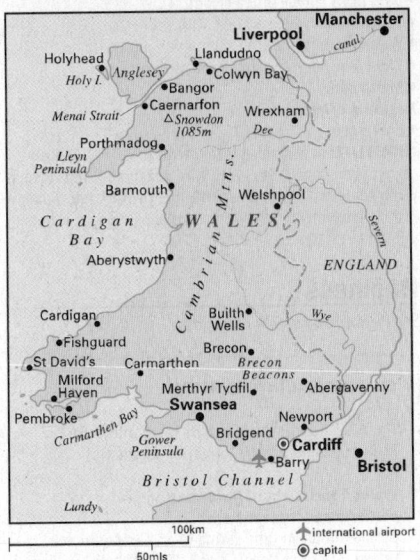

Location: Western Great Britain.

Overview

Wales is a historic land of castles and mountains, sweeping beaches and strong national identity dating back to pre-Norman times and reinforced in 1999, when Wales was granted its own Assembly.

The Welsh economy suffered badly following the demise of the coal-mining industry during the 1980s, but the areas affected, primarily in the south of the country, are now enjoying better times. Cardiff in particular has seen extensive regeneration of late, both in the city centre and the nearby Cardiff Bay area, which is now seen as a major entertainment and administrative centre. In the rural north, farming and tourism continue to be the main sources of income.

Populous South Wales incorporates the capital Cardiff, the cities of Swansea and Newport, Carmarthen Bay and two national parks, Pembrokeshire Coast and Brecon Beacons. The Cambrian Mountains and the attractive coastal resorts of Cardigan Bay are highlights of mid-Wales, while the North has popular seaside resorts like Llandudno and Rhyl, the island of Anglesey and the scenic delights of Snowdonia National Park.

General Information

For information on time, electricity, passport/visa, money, duty free and health, see the main *United Kingdom* section.
AREA: 20,732 sq km (8004 sq miles).
POPULATION: 2.95 million (official estimate 2004).
POPULATION DENSITY: 142.3 per sq km.
CAPITAL: Cardiff. **Population:** 305,353 (2001).
GEOGRAPHY: Wales is a country of great geographical variation with many long stretches of attractive and often rugged coastline. South Wales is mainly known for its industrial heritage but the western part of the coast between Carmarthen Bay and St David's is similar to that of the more pastoral west country of England, and backed by some equally beautiful countryside. The scenery of mid-Wales includes rich farming valleys, the broad sandy sweep of Cardigan Bay and rolling hill country. North Wales is one of the most popular tourist areas in the British Isles, with many lively coastal resorts. Inland, the region of Snowdonia has long been popular with walkers and climbers. Much of the central inland area of the country is mountainous, with some breathtaking scenery.
GOVERNMENT: Head of State: HM Queen Elizabeth II.
Head of Government: First Minister Rhodri Morgan since 2000. **Recent history:** Following a referendum in May 1999, Wales was granted its own Assembly with a considerable degree of autonomy. The Welsh Assembly does not have a similar level of power and responsibility as that enjoyed by the Scottish Parliament, in that it cannot raise taxes, but it does give the Welsh considerably more say in their own destiny than in the previous nine centuries.
LANGUAGE: English and Welsh are the official languages. Welsh is taught in all schools, and at least one-fifth of the population speaks it.
SOCIAL CONVENTIONS:
A smoking ban is to be implemented in all enclosed public spaces, including pubs and restaurants, in summer 2007.

Climate

Wales tends to be wetter than England, with slightly less sunshine. The coastal areas, however, can be very warm in summer. Conditions in upland areas can be dangerous and changeable at all times of the year.
Required clothing: Similar to the rest of the UK, according to season. Waterproofing advised throughout the year, and warm clothes are required for upland areas.

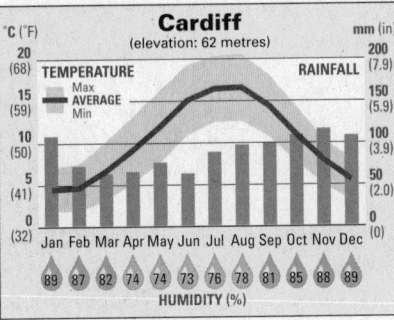

Communications

MEDIA: Press: Wales' major daily newspaper is the *Western Mail*, published in Cardiff. All the UK national papers are generally available, as are numerous local papers.
TV: All the national UK channels are available throughout Wales. In addition, *S4C* broadcasts Welsh language programming.
Radio: *BBC Radio Wales* caters for the English-speaking sector, while *BBC Cymru* broadcasts in Welsh. All national stations are also available. A number of local commercial stations offer output in both languages.

Public Holidays

Note: Public holidays observed in Wales are the same as those observed in the rest of the UK (see the main *United Kingdom* section).

Travel - International

AIR:
Main airports: *Cardiff International Airport (CWL)* (tel: (01446) 711 111; website: www.cwlfly.com) is 19km (12 miles) from Cardiff.
To/from the airport: **Train:** A rail link connects the airport with Cardiff Central station. (A shuttle bus takes passengers from the terminal to the station.) Trains run once an hour. Cardiff Central is served by the Intercity network and regional lines, including a fast service to London Paddington.
Coach: Regular coach services operate to Cardiff Central Bus Station from London Victoria and other major destinations with connections to the rest of the country.
Local bus: The 'Airbus Xpress' bus X91 runs between Cardiff city centre and the airport every 30 minutes Mon-Fri and hourly Sat-Sun. **Taxi:** Available through local operator *Cardiff Airport Taxis* (tel: (01446) 710 693). **Car hire:** Major firms have offices at the airport. **Private car:** Cardiff is reached on the M4 from London, exiting at Junction 33 and following the signs. Short- and long-stay parking is available. *Facilities:* Restaurants, shops, bureaux de change, ATMs, children's play area and executive lounge.

SEA:
Main ports: *Fishguard*, *Holyhead* (Anglesey), *Pembroke* and *Swansea*, all of which have ferry connections to the Republic of Ireland.

RAIL:
There are two main line routes into Wales. One runs from London Paddington to Fishguard along the South Wales coast (branching at Whitland to serve Haverford West and Milford Haven), while the other links Holyhead with Chester and northwest England. In addition, the line from Cardiff to Chester (via Newport, Hereford and Shrewsbury) links the south Wales cities with Abergavenny in Gwent and Wrexham in Clwyd. There are also two smaller cross-country lines: these run from Shrewsbury to Welshpool, Barmouth, Harlech, Porthmadog and Pwllheli; from Shrewsbury via Welshpool to Aberystwyth; and from Craven Arms (on the Shrewsbury–Ludlow line) through Llandrindod Wells and Llandovery down to Swansea. There are also a large number of local steam railways, rescued by railway enthusiasts during the Beeching era, known collectively as **The Great Little Trains of Wales**. The most famous of these is the one at Ffestiniog, Porthmadog in Snowdonia, which has lovingly restored locomotives and carriages from the last century. Others include the *Welshpool and Llanfair Railway* (in north Powys), the *Talyllyn Railway* (near Barmouth in Cardigan Bay) and the *Bala Lake Railway*. Passport tickets are available, giving access to all the

railways for the whole season. For further information, contact The Great Little Trains of Wales (tel: (01286) 870 549; website: www.greatlittletrainsofwales.co.uk).
ROAD:
The best road approach to Wales from southern England is via the M4 motorway, which runs from west London to Newport, Cardiff and Swansea, almost to Carmarthen. The A5 links London and the Midlands with the ferry port of Holyhead, and the A55 links Holyhead with Chester. The best cross-country road is probably the A44/A470 from Oxford to Aberystwyth. Many of the smaller roads are slow, and in upland areas may become impassable during bad weather. The latest traffic information is available from *Traffic Wales* (tel: 0845 602 6020; website: www.traffic-wales.com).
Distances: From London to *Cardiff* is 249km (155 miles), to *Fishguard* is 425km (264 miles), to *Holyhead* is 476km (296 miles) and to *Aberystwyth* is 394km (245 miles).
URBAN:
All the main cities have local bus services. There is a good network of local train services radiating from Cardiff.

Accommodation

HOTELS:
The Wales Tourist Board also produces an annual 'Where to Stay' brochure. For a selection of Wales' finest hotels, contact *Welsh Rarebits* (see *Accommodation Information*).
Grading: The Wales Tourist Board, VisitScotland, VisitBritain, the AA and RAC have now agreed common standards for quality assessment, which come into force from 2006. Hotels and guesthouses are classified by use of a star-rating system.
BED & BREAKFAST:
Bed & breakfasts are available throughout Wales. The Wales Tourist Board has listings on its website and in its 'Where to Stay' brochure.
SELF-CATERING:
There is a wide variety of self-catering accommodation, ranging from holiday villages in or near popular coastal resorts to remote cottages in the mountains of Snowdonia. Contact the tourist board for more details.
CAMPING/CARAVANNING:
There are hundreds of campsites and caravan parks in the country, and all sites referred to in accommodation lists or brochures supplied by tourist offices will meet certain minimum requirements.

ACCOMMODATION INFORMATION

Welsh Rarebits
Prince's Square, Montgomery SY15 6PZ, UK
Tel: (01686) 668030 (UK bookings) *or* (800) 873 7140 (toll-free in the USA).
Website: www.rarebits.co.uk

A comprehensive hotel search facility is available on the Wales Tourist Board's website (see Top Things To Do).

Credit: ©Wales Tourist Board

Credit: ©Wales Tourist Board

Top Things To See

- **Cardiff Castle** (website: www.cardiffcastle.com) is a must. Despite extensive rebuilding in the 19th century, parts date back to the Middle Ages. Also enjoy the **National Museum and Gallery** (website: www.museumwales.ac.uk), which has collections of Welsh archaeology, arts and crafts, as well as European paintings.
- The **Millennium Stadium** (website: www.millenniumstadium.com), recently-built home of Welsh Rugby Union, is an imposing attraction open for guided tours on non-matchdays.
- The **Cardiff Bay** area, about 2km (1.5 miles) south of the centre, offers diverse activities ranging from boat trips to the impressive **Barrage** (which now seals the Bay off from the open sea), to the **Techniquest Science Discovery Centre** (website: www.techniquest.org), which is great for the kids. It is also the location of the new **Welsh National Assembly**.
- Five miles (8km) west of Cardiff, experience historical Welsh Culture at **St Fagans** with its open-air **National History Museum** (website: www.museumwales.ac.uk/en/stfagans).
- Sample a taste of South Wales' days as an industrial powerhouse in the former coal-producing **Valleys** inland from Cardiff. **Blaenafon** (a UNESCO World Heritage Site) offers industrial heritage attractions in the shape of **Big Pit Mining Museum** and the **Ironworks** (website: www.museumwales.ac.uk/en/bigpit).
- On the northern tip of **Cardigan Bay** is Harlech (website: www.harlech.com), famous for both its castle that overlooks the peaks of Snowdonia, and for the stirring song, Men of Harlech, referring to the 15th-century defence of the castle.
- Across the Menai Strait, the island of **Anglesey**, known as **Ynys Môn** locally, is notable for the remarkable **Menai Bridge**, the **Anglesey Sea Zoo** (website: www.angleseyseazoo.co.uk) at **Brynsiencyn**, and **Llanfairpwllgwyngyllgogerychwyrndrobwllllantysiliogogogoch** (commonly called Llanfair PG), which boasts the UK's longest place name.
- Dotted along the North Wales coastline are a number of traditional seaside resorts, among them **Rhyl** and **Llandudno**, all with an array of family-oriented attractions.
- Learn about Wales' ancient Celtic heritage at **Celtica** in **Machynlleth** (website: www.celticawales.com). This interesting town also boasts the **Centre for Alternative Technology** (website: www.cat.org.uk), which highlights environmental issues and sustainable energy use, and **Senedd-Dy Owain Glyndwr** (the 15th-century Welsh Parliament building).
- See the filming location of the cult 1960s TV series *The Prisoner* at the fantasy village of **Portmeirion** (website: www.portmeirion-village.com), near Porthmadog in north Wales.

Top Things To Do

- Welsh heritage and culture is to the fore at the annual **National Eisteddfod** (website: www.eisteddfod.org.uk), a festival of the country's arts staged at different locations each year in late July/early August.
- Whether buying or merely window-shopping, **Cardiff**'s numerous **Victorian arcades** are an attractive environment in which to pass the time.
- Enjoy the natural surroundings at South Wales' biggest inland draw, **Brecon Beacons National Park**, whose main touring bases are **Brecon** and **Abergavenny**. The narrow-gauge **Brecon Mountain Railway** runs through the hills from Merthyr Tydfil.
- Spend a day on the beach at one of the numerous **resorts** lining the coast between Cardiff and Swansea, including **Aberavon**, **Barry** and **Porthcawl**. Others, further west along the **Gower Peninsula**, include **Oxwich** and **Port Eynon**.
- **Swansea** is probably best known as the birthplace of Dylan Thomas (1914-1953). A city centre walking trail begins at the **Dylan Thomas Centre** (website: www.dylanthomas.com), and leads visitors around sites associated with the poet and playwright.
- Experience nature and history in the former county of **Pembrokeshire**, in the southwest, which has many castles as well as the **Pembrokeshire Coast National Park**. The best-known religious building in the area is the **cathedral** of **St David**, Britain's smallest city.
- **Ride** on one of North and mid-Wales' numerous **narrow-gauge steam railways** (website: www.greatlittletrainsofwales.co.uk). Among them, the **Ffestiniog Railway** passes through glorious scenery in the Snowdonia National Park, while the **Welshpool** and **Llanfair** railway passes through gentler countryside close to the English border. Another, the **Snowdon Mountain Railway**, (website: www.snowdonrailway.co.uk), climbs to the summit of Wales' highest peak.
- The Welsh national sport is **Rugby Union**, and there are hundreds of clubs around the country. The venue for the big matches is the **Millennium Stadium** (see *Top Things To See*).
- Also for the sportingly inclined, Wales has many **golf** courses, **tennis** courts and sports centres throughout the country.
- **Sea fishing** is good off all coasts and there are also many opportunities for **coarse** and **game fishing** inland; **Brecon**, **Snowdonia** and the **River Teifi** (**Cardigan**) are among the most popular.
- **Whitewater rafting**, **rock-climbing** and other adventurous pursuits are available in many parts of the country, whose landscape is ideal for these.

TOURIST INFORMATION

Wales Tourist Board/Bwrdd Croeso Cymru
Brunel House, 2 Fitzalan Road, Cardiff CF24 0UY, UK
Tel: (08708) 300 306.
Website: www.visitwales.com

Wales Tourist Board/Bwrdd Croeso Cymru in the USA
551 Fifth Avenue, 7th Floor, New York, NY 10176, USA
Tel: (800) 462 2748 (toll-free in the USA).
Website: www.visitwales.com

Entertainment

FOOD & DRINK:
Regional specialities:
- *Welsh rarebit* (cheese on toast).
- *Bara brith* (a type of tea bread).
- *Laver bread*, which is made with seaweed.
- Welsh cakes (made with sultanas or currants).
- Welsh *cawl* (a meat and vegetable broth).
- Marsh lamb.

Regional drinks:
- *Brains* beer.

NIGHTLIFE: In general, it is similar to that of an English town of comparable size, with bars, restaurants and cinemas being common in the cities and large towns. A smoking ban is to be implemented in all enclosed public spaces, including pubs and restaurants, in summer 2007.

Business

See main *United Kingdom* section.

COMMERCIAL INFORMATION

The Wales Tourist Board publishes a Conference Planner brochure. For information, contact:

Wales Tourist Board (Information on conferences/conventions)
Business Tourism Unit, Bwrdd Croso CyrmruBrunel House, 2 Fitzalan Road, Cardiff CF24 0YU, UK
Tel: (029) 2047 5202.
Website: www.meetings.visitwales.com

Northern Ireland

Location: Northern Ireland.

Overview

Occupying the northeastern corner of an island brimming with superlatives, Northern Ireland contains many hidden facets of the Emerald Isle. This small province enjoys a diverse terrain, with a dramatic coastline, gently rolling fields and the lush Mountains of Mourne. The capital, Belfast, is a vibrant city with ornate Victorian architecture and lively nightlife. Central Derry contains one of the finest walled towns in Europe. Both have been too long overshadowed by the 'Troubles', but seem at last to be enjoying a more peaceful present.

The Antrim Coast is one of the most scenic shorelines in Britain, winding past towering cliffs, sandy beaches, picturesque harbours and family resorts. You can hike deep into the glacier-carved Glens of Antrim or walk along the amazing volcanic columns of the Giant's Causeway. Inland lies Lough Neagh, the largest lake in the British Isles, and the Fermanagh lakelands, sprinkled with tiny islands, wooded parks and monastic ruins.

The six counties of Northern Ireland belonged to the ancient and powerful kingdom of Ulster. Tales of legendary heroes intertwine with those of St Patrick, who spread Christianity from his base near Downpatrick. The Ulster American Folk Park near Omagh, Old Bushmill's whiskey distillery, the Belleek pottery, crumbling castle ruins and the stately mansions of the Anglo-Irish aristocracy offer more history and culture in a friendly, easy-going country that is a delight to explore.

General Information

For information on time, religion, electricity, passport & visa, health and duty free, see the main *United Kingdom* section.
AREA: 13,576 sq km (5242 sq miles).
POPULATION: 1.7 million (official estimate 2004).
POPULATION DENSITY: 125.2 per sq km.
CAPITAL: Belfast. **Population:** 269,000 (official estimate 2004).
GEOGRAPHY: Northern Ireland contains some beautiful scenery, from the rugged coastline in the north and northeast to the gentle fruit-growing regions of Armagh. To the west are the Sperrin Mountains and the lake of Fermanagh, where the winding River Erne provides excellent fishing. The high moorland plateau of Antrim in the northeast gives way to the glens further south and to the Drumlin country of County Down; further south still, the Mountains of Mourne stretch down to the sea.
GOVERNMENT: Head of State: HM Queen Elizabeth II. **Head of Government:** Prime Minister Tony Blair. **Recent history:** Following a quarter of a century of well-publicised 'troubles' focusing on differences between the Nationalist and Unionist communities, relative peace descended on Northern Ireland during the early 1990s. Deep divisions and mistrust between the two factions still exist, but the atmosphere is now one of at least attempted reconciliation rather than open conflict.
Today's disputes are political, rather than violent, but much work remains to be done before satisfactory Government can return to the Northern Ireland Assembly at Stormont. A short-lived return to autonomous rule came to an end in 2002 following continued inability on the part of the two main parties to co operate, and a scandal involving alleged 'spying' at the Northern Ireland Office. Following the cessation of overt hostilities, two major political parties have emerged as successors to the previously dominant Ulster Unionists and SDLP (the mainly nationalist party). Sinn Fein, under the leadership of Gerry Adams, and Ian Paisley's Democratic Unionists, are now the main protagonists in Northern Ireland politics, and they are considerably more hardline in their approaches than their predecessors. But discussions continue in an attempt to restore devolved Government to the province, which has enjoyed a dramatic economic upturn since the advent of peace. Huge investment has gone into Northern Ireland in the past decade, and the tourism industry has also experienced a major upturn – fruits of the so-called 'Peace Dividend'.
LANGUAGE: English. Irish is spoken by a minority.
SOCIAL CONVENTIONS: Due to the political situation in Northern Ireland, visitors should take care when visiting certain parts of the main cities and the border area. No problems should arise, provided the visitor follows local advice and avoids expressing dogmatic opinions on political or religious topics.

Climate

In general the weather is similar to the rest of the UK, but Northern Ireland tends to have less sunshine and more rain. Extremes of temperature are rare but conditions can be changeable.
Required clothing: Similar to the rest of the UK, according to season. Waterproofs are advisable throughout the year.

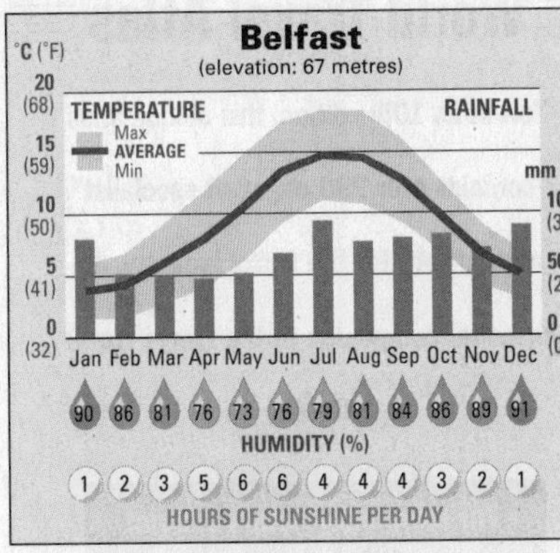

Communications

MEDIA: Press: The main Northern Irish daily newspapers are the *Belfast Telegraph* and the *Irish News*. There are numerous local newspapers produced in larger towns around the Province. UK national and Republic of Ireland newspapers are also readily available, some produced in localised editions.
TV: All the national UK stations are available in Northern Ireland, together with Republic of Ireland output from RTE (the state broadcaster) and commercial programming.
Radio: As elsewhere in the UK, the BBC is the main provider. As well as the national stations, it offers *Radio Ulster* (Belfast) and *Radio Foyle* (Londonderry). Commercial stations include *Downtown Radio* (Belfast) and *Cool FM*.

Money

For information on currency, credit cards, traveller's cheques, exchange rates and currency restrictions, see the main *United Kingdom* section.
Note: For travelling around and staying at small hotels, cash is needed. Elsewhere, as in England, cheques backed by a banker's card are widely accepted. Some hotels will change money but banks and bureaux de change give the best rate of exchange.
Banking hours: Mon-Fri 0900-1600. In very small villages, the bank may open two or three days a week only, so aim to get cash in the bigger centres.

Public Holidays

Below are listed Public Holidays for the January 2006-June 2007 period.
Public holidays observed in Northern Ireland are the same as those observed in the rest of the UK (see the main *United Kingdom* section) with the addition of:
2006: Mar 17 St Patrick's Day. **Jul 12** Battle of the Boyne (Orangemen's Day).
2007: Mar 17 St Patrick's Day.

Travel - International

AIR:
There are frequent direct flights to Belfast from London airports as well as other major regional UK airports. Airlines that serve Northern Ireland from the UK include *bmibaby*, *British Airways*, *easyJet* and *flybe*. From North America, *Aer Lingus* operates flights to Shannon and Dublin. There are direct flights from Canada to Belfast with *Zoom Airlines* (website: www,flyzoom.com). Other major airlines operate services from the USA and Canada to Belfast via London, Glasgow and Manchester.
Approximate flight times: From Belfast to *London* is one hour 15 minutes and from Belfast to *Glasgow* is 45 minutes.
Main airports: *Belfast International Airport (BFS)* (tel: (028) 9448 4848; website: www.belfastairport.com) is located 29km (18 miles) northwest of Belfast city centre. *To/from the airport*: **Train:** There is at present no direct rail link to Belfast International Airport, but trains run from Londonderry (Derry), Lisburn and Belfast to Antrim (10km/6 miles away) from where a taxi may be hired, or a shuttle bus can be taken to the airport. Trains to and from Dublin are via Belfast Central Station, which has its own *Airbus* stop. A rail timetable is on display at the main exit from the terminal. **Bus:** *Airbus* runs to the city centre Mon to Fri every 20 to 30 minutes, Sat every 30 minutes and Sun every 30 to 60 minutes (tel: (028) 9066 6630). *The Airporter* coaches (tel: (028) 7126 9996) travel to the airport from Londonderry (Derry). **Taxi:** Travel time to city centre – 30 minutes. Taxis are available for hire outside the main airport building. **Car hire:** Major car hire companies are represented at the airport. **Private car:** The M1 provides the main link with Fermanagh and the west of the Province whilst forming part of the journey to and from Dublin and the east coast of Ireland. The M2 is the airport's main link with the centre of Belfast and to Londonderry (Derry), 116km (72 miles) to the northwest. There is nearby car parking for short and long stays. Access is from the M1 and M2 (parking is available) or by train to Antrim and then taxi.
Facilities: Bureau de change, ATMs, shops and restaurants. There is also an executive lounge at the airport, which costs £9.50-12 to use, depending on your carrier.
Belfast City Airport (BHD) (tel: (028) 9093 9093; website: www.belfastcityairport.com) at *Belfast Harbour* is handy for flights to most regional airports. Regular train and bus services run to the city centre.
Departure tax: None.
SEA:
Main ports: *Belfast*. When travelling via Great Britain to Northern Ireland there is a choice of several services across the Irish Sea: *P&O Irish Sea* (tel: (0870) 242 4777; website: www.poirishsea.com) offers frequent daily services between Cairnryan (southern Scotland) to Larne (travel time – one hour 45 minutes), and a summer service between Troon and Larne (travel time – one hour 49 minutes); *Stena Line* (tel: (08705) 707 070; website: www.stenaline.co.uk) operates frequent daily services between Stranraer (southern Scotland) and Belfast (travel time – one hour 45 minutes) and services between Fleetwood and Larne (travel time – eight hours). An overnight service and daily services are offered on the Liverpool to Belfast route and Liverpool to Dublin route by *Norse Merchant Ferries* (travel time – eight hours; tel: (0870) 600 4321; website: www.norsemerchant.com). The *Isle of Man Steam Packet Company* (tel: (08705) 523 523 *or* (01624) 645 620; website: www.steam-packet.com) runs a seacat crossing from Douglas (Isle of Man) to Belfast (travel time – two hours and 45 minutes). *Irish Ferries* operates services from Great Britain to the Republic of Ireland, including a service between Rosslare and Pembroke (travel time – three hours 45 minutes) and a service between Dublin and Holyhead (travel time – one hour 49 minutes). *Irish Ferries* (tel: (08705) 171 717; website: www.irishferries.com) also operates between Cherbourg, Roscoff and Rosslare (approximate travel time – 19 hours). *Brittany Ferries* operates the Roscoff-Cork route with one departure per week in each direction from March to early November only (travel time – 14 hours). For more information, contact *Brittany Ferries* in Cork (tel: (0053) 2142 77801; website: www.brittanyferries.com). Northern Ireland's only inhabited island is Rathlin, a few kilometres off the north coast. *Caledonian MacBrayne* (tel: (08705) 650 000; website: www.calmac.co.uk) operates regular services between Ballycastle and Rathlin.
RAIL:
There are four main rail routes from Belfast Central Station: north to Londonderry via Ballymena and Coleraine; north east to the port of Larne; east to Bangor along the shores of Belfast Lough; south to Dublin, in the Irish Republic, via Newry. The Belfast–Dublin non-stop express takes approximately two hours. There are eight trains daily in both directions (only five on Sunday). The busiest times are holiday weekends and the first and last trains on Friday and Sunday, when it is best to reserve seats. *Freedom of Northern Ireland* passes are available for unlimited travel on trains and buses (costing £13 for one day; £32 for three days and £47 for seven days, to be used within eight days of purchase) and are available from main Northern Ireland railway stations. For information on timetables for *all* rail services, contact *Translink* (tel: (028) 9066 6630; website: www.translink.co.uk).
ROAD:
Bus: Northern Ireland has an excellent bus network and there are particularly good bus links between those towns which are not served by rail. *Translink* operates both *Metro*, which provides services in Belfast, and *Ulsterbus*, which is responsible for all other services in Northern Ireland. Belfast has three main bus stations: Europa Buscentre at Great Victoria Street, Laganside Buscentre and Newtonabbey. *Centrelink* provides a link between Belfast's principal rail and bus stations, as well as main shopping centres and the Waterfront Hall. *Metro* operates over 12 high-frequency arterial routes, as well as branch routes in and around the capital, and eight nightlink services that depart from Donegal Square West, Sun 0100-0200. Ulsterbus operates a comprehensive network of services across the rest of the country, including some scenic routes such as the *Antrim Coaster* (Belfast–Antrim Coast–Portrush–Coleraine), the *Lakeland Express* (Enniskillen–Belfast) and the *Orchard Express* (Belfast–Portadown–Armagh). For more information on any of these services, timetables or prices, contact Translink (tel: (028) 9066 6630; website: www.translink.co.uk).
Traffic regulations: Traffic drives on the left. The speed limit is 30mph (48kph) in towns and cities unless signs show 40mph (64kph) or 50mph (80kph). On country roads, the limit is 60mph (96kph); on dual carriageways, trunk roads and motorways, 70mph (112kph), unless signs show otherwise.
Breakdowns: If the car is rented, contact the rental company. Members of the continental equivalent of the *Automobile Association (AA)* (tel: (0870) 600 0371: website: www.theaa.com) can contact their 24-hour breakdown service. The *Royal Automobile Club (RAC)* (tel: (0800) 919 700; website: www.rac.co.uk) provides a similar service. They can be contacted from their roadside phones or from any call box. Non-members should consult the Yellow Pages for breakdown services.
Parking: Permitted where there is a blue 'P' sign, which indicates a car park in towns or a lay-by at the roadside outside towns. Drivers can park elsewhere on the street except when there is a single yellow line, when parking is permitted only at the times shown on the yellow signs nearby; or when there is a double yellow line, which prohibits all parking. Control Zones, which are usually in town centres, are indicated by yellow signs: 'Control Zone. No Unattended Parking'. An unattended car in a Control Zone is treated as a security risk. Never park on zigzag markings near pedestrian crossings.
Taxi: Available at main stations, ports and Belfast International Airport and are also bookable by telephone in larger towns and cities.
Car hire: The main firms operate in Northern Ireland and have desks at Belfast International Airport with cars available on the spot. There is also a host of smaller firms.

Accommodation

HOTELS:
A wide range of accommodation is available in Northern Ireland. Most establishments belong to the *Northern Ireland Hotels Federation* (see *Accommodation Information*). **Grading:** The Northern Irish Tourist Board operates a 'star' classification system, rating hotels from one to five stars.

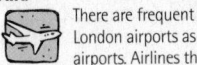

GUESTHOUSES/BED AND BREAKFAST:
There are numerous bed and breakfasts and guesthouses listed on the Northern Ireland Tourist Board's website.

FARM & COUNTRY HOUSE HOLIDAYS:
This is one of the most popular forms of holidaying in Northern Ireland. The *Northern Ireland Farm & Country Holidays Association* (see *Accommodation Information*) produces an accommodation voucher, valid for bed & breakfast for one night. Visitors can enjoy home-baking and home-cooked meals and may have the chance to help feed the animals or watch the milking.

SELF-CATERING:
There are self-catering establishments in all of Northern Ireland's six counties. For further information, contact the Northern Ireland Tourist Board *or* the *Northern Ireland Self Catering Holiday Association* (see *Accommodation Information*). *Cottages in Ireland* also provides a range of self-catering cottages in rural locations (see *Accommodation Information*).

CAMPING/CARAVANNING:
The Northern Ireland Tourist Board lists details of over 60 caravan and campsites on its website. The *Forest Service* (see *Accommodation Information*) issues permits for camping in forest areas.

YOUTH HOSTELS:
Hostelling International Northern Ireland (see *Accommodation Information*) runs six youth hostels throughout the six counties of Northern Ireland, including Armagh City youth hostel and Belfast International youth hostel.

ACCOMMODATION INFORMATION

Northern Ireland Hotels Federation
The Midland Building, Whitla Street, Belfast BT15 1JP, UK
Tel: (028) 9035 1110.
Website: www.nihf.co.uk

Northern Ireland Farm & Country Holidays Association
Tel: (028) 8284 1325.
Website: www.nifcha.com

Northern Ireland Self Catering Holidays Association
Tel: (028) 9077 6174.
Website: www.nischa.com

Cottages in Ireland
Tel: (0870) 236 1630.
Website: www.cottagesinireland.com

Forest Service
Dundonald House, Upper Newtownards Road, Belfast BT4 3SB, UK
Tel: (028) 9052 4480.
Website: www.forestserviceni.gov.uk

Hostelling International Northern Ireland
22-32 Donegall Road, Belfast BT12 5JN, UK
Tel: (028) 9032 4733.
Website: www.hini.org.uk

The Northern Ireland Tourist Board's website has a comprehensive accommodation search facility (see Top Things to See & Do).

Top Things To See & Do

- Northern Ireland is very compact – nothing is more than a couple of hours by road from **Belfast**, so the city is an excellent base from which to explore the Ulster countryside. Take a guided coach tour around the focal points of Belfast's troubled recent history, including the **Shankill** and **Falls Roads** to see the famous Republican and Unionist **wall murals** (website: www.belfast.net/mo/tours.htm).
- Experience Northern Ireland's best art, archaeology and natural history collections at Belfast's **Ulster Museum** (website: www.ulstermuseum.org.uk), or climb to the summit of **Cave Hill** for superb views over the city.
- Enjoy a pint of Guinness in the National Trust-owned **Crown Liquor Saloon** (website: www.crownbar.com), an ornate Victorian public house opposite Belfast's **Grand Opera House** (website: www.goh.co.uk).
- One of Ireland's most famous natural attractions is located on the **Antrim coastline** to the northwest of Belfast – the remarkable **Giant's Causeway** (website: www.giantscausewayofficialguide.com), whose hexagonal volcanic formations have fascinated visitors for centuries, and have taken their place in Irish legend. Close by in the village of **Bushmills** is the famous **whiskey distillery** of

---

the same name (website: www.bushmills.com), while also along this stretch of coastline stand the massive cliff top ruins of **Dunluce Castle** (website: www.northantrim.com/dunlucecastle.htm).
- Also to the north of Belfast, the nine **Glens of Antrim** are renowned for their beauty, and run inland from the rugged and spectacular eastern coast.
- To the south, in **County Down**, escape to the tranquillity of the **Silent Valley** (website: www.newryandmourne.gov.uk/tourism/activities/forest/silent_valley.asp) and the remarkable **Mountains of Mourne**.
- Visit what is alleged to be **St. Patrick's Grave** at **Down Cathedral** (website: www.downcathedral.org), **Downpatrick**.
- Northern Ireland, like the rest of the island, is a haven for **golfers**. The best courses can be found on the coastline, including **Royal Portrush** (website: www.royalportrush.com) and **Royal County Down** at **Newcastle** (website: www.royalcountydown.org).
- **Boat trips** to the monastic ruins of **Devenish Island**, and excellent **fishing** are highlights for visitors to **Enniskillen** and **Lough Erne** in **County Fermanagh** (website: www.fermanaghlakelands.com), to the southwest of the province.
- The unusual experience of an **underground boat trip** through magnificent caverns is offered at **Marble Arch Caves**, **Florencecourt** (website: www.marblearchcaves.net).

TOURIST INFORMATION

Northern Ireland Tourist Board
59 North Street, Belfast BT1 1NB, UK
Tel: (028) 9023 1221.
Website: www.discovernorthernireland.com

Tourism Ireland in the UK
Nations House, 103 Wigmore Street, London W1U 1QS, UK
Tel: (020) 7518 0800 (trade enquiries only) *or* (0800) 039 7000 (brochure request line and enquiries).
Website: www.tourismireland.com

Tourism Ireland in the USA
345 Park Avenue, 51st Street, 17th Floor, New York, NY 10154, USA
Tel: (800) 223 6470 (tourist information) *or* (800) 669 9967 (travel agents) *or* (212) 418 0800 (corporate offices).
Website: www.tourismireland.com

Entertainment

FOOD & DRINK:
Regional specialities:
- An Ulster fry – eggs, sausages, ham or fish with chips.
- Shellfish.
- Homemade vegetable soups.
- Irish stew.
- Dried seaweed.
- Home-baked cakes and pastries.

Regional drinks:
- *Guinness* – a dark heavy stout with a creamy head.
- Irish whiskey, often drunk along with a bottle of stout.
- *Hilden* – real ale produced at Lisburn.

The pubs are open all day Mon-Sat 1130-2300 and Sun 1230-2200 with half an hour 'drinking-up' time. Pubs in Belfast often stay open until 0100 Thurs-Sat. **Note:** A smoking ban is to be implemented in all enclosed public spaces, including pubs and restaurants, in April 2007.

NIGHTLIFE: Northern Ireland has a strong tradition for musical entertainment, from the toe-tapping live folk bands playing in crowded pubs to the soulful lyrics of Van Morrison and the world-famous talent of flautist James Galway. Visitors will be able to find something to suit, from the latest dance music in nightclubs to opera or classical concerts. Traditional Irish music in 'singing pubs' provides a good evening's entertainment in many places, particularly Belfast and Londonderry. Special musical events include the summer *Jazz and Blues Festival* in Londonderry and Limavady and the October *Ards Guitar Festival* held in Newtownards. There is also a wealth of theatres and art galleries located in and around Belfast, including the famous *Lyric Theatre*, where Liam Neeson started his career. There are summer theatres in Newcastle and Portrush, plus the *Riverside Theatre* at Coleraine. The *Belfast Festival at Queen's* (three weeks in November each year) is Ireland's biggest international festival. Other main venues for drama performances and concerts are the *Grand Opera House*, *Ulster Hall*, *King's Hall* and the *Waterfront Hall* (all in Belfast), the *Armagh Theatre and Arts Centre* and the *Millennium Forum* theatre in Derry and numerous regional theatres. Further information can be obtained from the Northern Ireland's Arts Council's monthly magazine *art.ie* or from the Northern Ireland Tourist Board (see *Top Things To See & Do*).

SHOPPING: Ulster is well known for its pure Irish linen; cut-glass goblets, decanters and bowls; creamy Belleek pottery; handwoven tweed; pure wool jumpers and cardigans hand-knitted in traditional patterns; hand-embroidered wall hangings; Carrickmacross lace and silver jewellery. **Shopping hours:** Shops are generally open Mon-Sat 0900-1800, Sun 1300-1800 (late-night shopping on Thursday in Belfast city centre until 2100). Other cities and towns close for a half-day one day a week (it differs from town to town). Modern shopping centres on the outskirts of towns have late-night shopping Thurs to Fri to 2100.

Business

ECONOMY: The 25-plus years of the Troubles had a profound impact on the economy of Northern Ireland. Historically, the province's main economic strengths were manufacturing, concentrated on the shipbuilding and aerospace industries in the eastern part of the province, and agriculture, which is prevalent throughout. However, manufacturing has, in common with the rest of the UK, been in long-term decline, although a steady stream of Government contracts has enabled it to survive in a reduced form. Agriculture has performed steadily, underpinned by the policies of the European Union. The public sector is now the largest single part of the economy and subventions from the British Government in one form or another account for the bulk of the province's income. The political settlement in the province has presented a number of new opportunities for Northern Ireland's economy, as well as a number of problems. The most important of these is tourism, which is particularly sensitive to political circumstances in the province and has been largely depressed until recently. However, Northern Ireland and the Republic of Ireland now market themselves jointly overseas under the Tourism Ireland banner and tourism in Northern Ireland has seen growth in recent years. Similar considerations apply to foreign investment that the province is seeking to attract – especially in view of the success enjoyed by the Irish Government during the 1990s. Indeed, the growing economic links between Northern Ireland and the Republic may offer the best prospects for the future development of the province's economy. Along with the rest of the UK, the Republic of Ireland already accounts for the bulk of Northern Ireland's external trade.

CONFERENCES/CONVENTIONS:
For information on conferences/conventions, contact the Northern Ireland Tourist Board (website: www.discovernorthernireland.com/convention).

COMMERCIAL INFORMATION

Northern Ireland Chamber of Commerce and Industry
22 Great Victoria Street, Belfast BT2 7BJ, UK
Tel: (028) 9024 4113.
Website: www.northernirelandchamber.com

Isle of Man

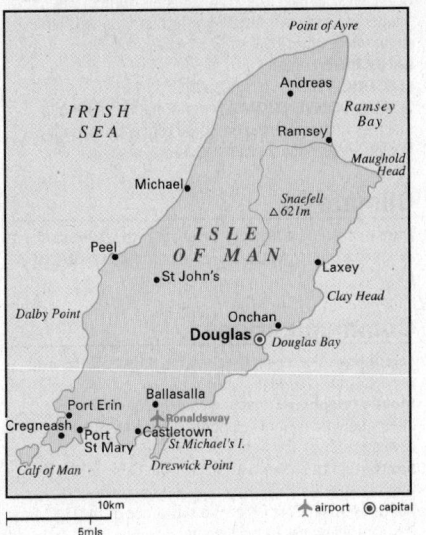

Location: Irish Sea.

Time: GMT (GMT + 1 from last Sunday in March to last Saturday in October).

Overview

Viking and Celtic heritage combine to create unusual interest on this charismatic island. Numerous attractions reflect this rich historic mix, branded by Manx National Heritage (website: www.gov.im/mnh) as the Story of Man, an umbrella name applied to sites ranging from prehistoric tombs to multimedia exhibitions, and to which English Heritage and National Trust members gain free entry.
Also important are Man's Victorian narrow-gauge railways: the Steam Railway linking Douglas and Port Erin; the Manx Electric Tramway, running north to Ramsey; and the Snaefell Mountain Railway, which climbs 620m (2034ft) above sea level from Laxey. A smaller line operates on the cliffs at Groudle Glen.
The island is also famous for hosting the annual *TT Races* and other motorsport events.
Scenic highlights include 17 picturesque National Glens, the south coast bays, and Snaefell itself, from which England, Scotland, Ireland and Wales are all visible on a clear day.

General Information

For information on religion, social conventions, passport and visa and duty free, see the main *United Kingdom* section.
AREA: 572 sq km (221 sq miles).
POPULATION: 76,315 (2001).
POPULATION DENSITY: 133.4 per sq km.
CAPITAL: Douglas. **Population:** 25,347 (2001).
GEOGRAPHY: The Isle of Man is situated in the Irish Sea, 114km (71 miles) from Liverpool and 133km (83 miles) from Dublin. The island has a mountain range down the middle, the highest peak being *Snaefell* at 620m (2036ft) and a flat northern plain to the Point of Ayre, the most northerly point. The Calf of Man, an islet off the southwest coast, is administered as a nature reserve and bird sanctuary by the Manx Museum and National Trust.
GOVERNMENT: Crown Dependency with own Parliament. The Isle of Man is not constitutionally part of the UK; it is a self-governed dependency of the Crown within the British Commonwealth. The Parliamentary institution of *Tynwald* (a word which comes from the Old Norse 'thing' meaning assembly and 'vollr' meaning field) comprises the Legislative Council and the 24 elected members of the House of Keys legislates for the island, levies taxation and has control of the island's finances. A contribution is paid annually to the UK Treasury. The Acts of Tynwald require the royal assent, and are proclaimed to the people in July each year at the open-air assembly on Tynwald Hill at St John's, thus maintaining the Norse tradition. The Government of the Isle of Man maintains its own education, health, national insurance, social security, police, postal and other public services. **Head of State:** HM Queen Elizabeth II, represented locally by Lieutenant-Governor Ian MacFadyen since 2000. **Head of Government:** Chief Minister Donald Gelling since 2004.
Recent history: Recent years have brought two major

economic successes to the Isle of Man, whose economy is surprisingly strong. Formerly largely reliant on mining, fishing, farming and tourism, the island has lately capitalised on its independent status to build up a thriving offshore banking and financial services sector, which has brought with it much wealth and employment. Another major success came in the film industry – in 1995, the island's Government decided to enter films in a big way, and Man is now one of the busiest production areas in the UK. Many major movies and TV programmes have been filmed on location there, and the island also boasts a large sound stage facility. Following an outbreak of foot and mouth disease on the UK mainland in 2001, the Manx Government made the difficult decision to cancel that year's TT motorcycle races, an event that temporarily more than doubles the population in June each year. The measure worked, as the disease did not reach the island. Also in 2001, a new primary school teaching purely in the Manx language was established, as part of efforts to revive the island's branch of Gaelic. This too has been a success, and more than 40 children now study at the school.
LANGUAGE: Manx Gaelic, the indigenous language, is related to Scots and Irish Gaelic. At one time spoken by all the Manx, the tongue was replaced by English during the last century, and now only 600 or so people speak it to some degree. On Tynwald Day, summaries of the new laws are read out in Manx and English. Manx Gaelic evening classes are regularly held, and a weekly radio programme and newspaper column appear in the language.
ELECTRICITY: 240 volts AC, 50Hz.

Climate

The climate of the Isle of Man is temperate. There is a considerable variation in rainfall over the island, the driest parts being in the extreme south and over the northern plain, the wettest being the hilly interior. Frost and snow occur much less frequently than in other parts of the British Isles.

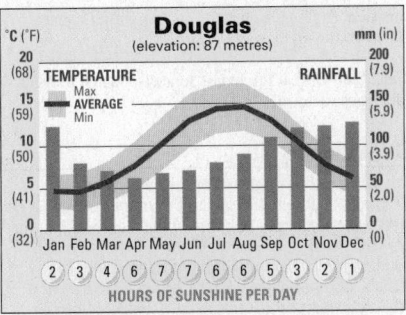

Communications

Telephone: To telephone the Isle of Man from the UK, the STD (area) code is 01624.
Mobile telephone: Roaming agreements exist with most international mobile phone companies. Coverage is good.
Internet: There are a number of Internet cafes on the island.
Post: Services are administered by Isle of Man Post which issues its own postage stamps. Post office opening hours vary, but most are open Mon-Fri 0900-1730 and Sat 0900-1230. Some have half days on Wed or Thurs.
MEDIA: Press: Local papers include the *Isle of Man Courier*, the *Manx Independent* and the *Isle of Man Examiner*.
TV: There are no stations based on the Isle of Man. Residents can receive UK channels.
Radio: Local stations include *Manx Radio, Energy FM* and *3FM*.

Money

Currency: The Isle of Man Government issues its own decimal coinage, and currency notes of £50, 20, 10, 5 and 1, and coins of £5, 2 and 1, and 50, 20, 10, 5, 2 and 1 pence, all of which are on a par with the UK equivalents. The coins and notes of England, Scotland and Northern Ireland circulate freely on the island.
Banking hours: Mon-Fri 0930-1630. Some are open Sat 1000-1200.

Public Holidays

Below are listed Public Holidays for the January 2006-June 2007 period.
Public holidays observed in the Isle of Man are the same as those observed in the rest of the UK (see the main *United Kingdom* section) with the addition of:
2006: Jun 9 TT Senior Race Day. **Jul 5 2006** Tynwald Day (National Day).
2007: Jun 8 TT Senior Race Day.

Health

No vaccination certificates are required to enter the Isle of Man. There is a reciprocal health agreement with the UK, allowing all visitors from the mainland free medical treatment. Dental treatment and prescribed medicines must be paid for. No proof of UK residence is required to benefit from the agreement. A new hospital opened in 2003 and there are many dental practices.

Travel - International

AIR: *British Airways (BA)* (website: www.britishairways.com) operates year-round services between the Isle of Man and London Gatwick, Glasgow, Luton and Manchester. *Euromanx* (www.euromanx.com), *flybe (BE)* (www.flybe.com)and *British Northwest Airlines* (website: www.flybnwa.co.uk) also operate services to the Isle of Man.
Main airports: *Ronaldsway (IOM)* (tel: (01624) 821 600; website: www.iom-airport.com) is 16km (10 miles) from Douglas. *To/from the airport:* A local bus operates approximately half-hourly at peak times and hourly at other times. Taxis and car hire are also available. Short- and long-stay parking is available. *Facilities:* Restaurant, buffet, bar, shops, bureau de change and ATMs. Wireless Internet access is available in the departure lounge and buffet area.
Departure tax: None.
SEA: **Main ports:** *Douglas*. Sailings are run by the *Isle of Man Steam Packet Company* (tel: (08705) 523 523 *or* (01624) 661 661; website: www.steam-packet.com) daily from Douglas to Heysham, Belfast, Dublin and Liverpool, although crossings to Belfast are not scheduled in the winter months.
RAIL: Horse trams run along the 3km (2 miles) of the Douglas Promenade during the summer. The *Steam Railway* operates from Douglas to Port Erin and the *Manx Electric Railway* runs from Douglas to Ramsey. Other services include the unique *Snaefell Mountain Railway*, which runs to the summit of Snaefell mountain, and the *Groudle Glen Railway* (a narrow gauge system), which provides a limited service along a scenic track near Douglas in the summer months.
ROAD: The island is served by *Isle of Man National Transport* **buses** throughout the year. There are also a number of coach operators who operate full- and half-day excursions. Private **taxis** operate all year round and there are a number of **car hire** firms. **Bicycles** are available for hire in the summer months. **Regulations:** Traffic drives on the left. There used to be no maximum speed limit except in built-up areas. However, this is under review. There are proposals to introduce a 60mph limit across the island.
Documentation: Full UK driving licence is acceptable.

Accommodation

 Hotel, guest house and self-catering accommodation is available, but pre-booking is necessary in the summer months. Grading of accommodation follows UK standards and ranges from basic to deluxe. Camping is only permitted on official campsites. The importation of caravans is prohibited.

Top Things To See & Do

- The Isle of Man's colourful past as Norse stronghold, Scottish outpost and latterly English protectorate has left a rich legacy of historic interest. The best place to begin finding out about the island, its history and culture is the **Manx Museum** (website: http://www.gov.im/mnh/heritage/museums/manxmuseum.xml) in **Douglas**, where interactive displays explain the Isle of Man's background. A new art gallery has recently been added to the complex.
- Other prime sites include **The House of Manannan** in **Peel**, **Peel Castle**, **Castle Rushen**, **Cregneash Village** and the **Tynwald Hill**, site of the world's longest continuously running Parliament.
- Another major attraction is the world's biggest working **water wheel**, at the now-disused **Laxey lead mines**.
- No visit to the Isle of Man is complete without a ride on the island's narrow-gauge railways (website: www.isleofman.com/gettingaround) The Isle of Man **Steam Railway** runs from Douglas to Port Erin in the south. The **Manx Electric Railway** connects Douglas with Laxey, from where the rack and pinion **Snaefell Mountain Railway** makes a steep climb to the 2,036 ft (620m) summit of the island's central peak. The **horse-drawn trams** of **Douglas** seafront are a related diversion.
- The Isle of Man stages many road races, notably the world-famous summer **TT** (**Tourist Trophy**) **motorcycle** event (website: www.iomtt.com). Competitors from all over the world race around a special circuit on the island's

Credit: ©Isle of Man Department of Tourism and Leisure

roads, and an atmosphere of celebration prevails. Races and rallies for modern and vintage cars take place throughout the summer on the island's roads, and include the **Manx National Car Rally**, the **Manx International Car Rally** (considered one of the most challenging races in the UK), the **International Hill Climb Championships** and the **Manx Classic** (especially for vintage cars). The varied terrain, sometimes mountainous and with sharp bends, adds to the challenge and excitement of the races.

• The Island is also popular for **sailing** and **walking**, and is famous for its **kippers** (smoked herring), to which **Peel's Moore's Museum** (website: www.isleofman.com/whattodo/shopping/moores) is dedicated.

TOURIST INFORMATION

Isle of Man Department of Tourism and Leisure
Sea Terminal Buildings, Douglas, IM1 2RG, Isle of Man
Tel: (01624) 686 801.
Website: www.visitisleofman.com

Entertainment

FOOD & DRINK:
Things to know: Drinks are cheaper than in the UK.
Licensing hours: Pubs usually open Mon-Thurs 1000-2300, Fri-Sat 1000-2400. On Sunday, pubs open 1200-2300. These times can vary according to individual pubs, as 24-hour licensing is now permitted. Special opening hours apply to the Easter and Christmas/New Year periods.
Regional specialities:
• *Queenies* (small scallops).
• Manx kippers (smoked herring).
• *Bonnag* (a type of bread).
• Davison's ice cream, made in Peel.
Regional drinks:
• Real Manx Ale.
• Manx whiskey, gin and vodka.
• *Kella* whiskey.
SHOPPING: VAT is at the same rate as the UK and prices are in general similar to those in the UK. Special purchases include Manx tartan, crafts and pottery. **Shopping hours:** Mon-Sat 0900-1730. Early closing Thursday during the winter months.

Business

• **GDP:** US$2.1 billion (2003 estimate).
• **Main exports:** Tweeds, herring, processed shellfish, beef and lamb.
• **Main imports:** Timber, fertilisers and fish.
• **Main trade partners:** UK

ECONOMY: The island's economy relies principally on tourism and financial services attracted by banking secrecy laws that render assets deposited on the island less vulnerable to disclosure requirements than those on the mainland. Taxation rates are also, on the whole, lower than those of the UK. There is a small agricultural sector but very little industry. Financial incentives offered to film and television producers has seen an increase in the number of major productions shot on the island in recent years.
BUSINESS ETIQUETTE: See the main *United Kingdom* section.
CONFERENCES/CONVENTIONS: Seating is available for up to 1500 persons, although facilities on the island lend themselves very well to meetings of 100 persons or less. All conference hotels have superb back-up services. For further information, contact the Department of Tourism (see *Top Things to See & Do*).

COMMERCIAL INFORMATION

Isle of Man Chamber of Commerce
17 Drinkwater Street, Douglas IM1 1PP, Isle of Man
Tel: (01624) 674 941.

Channel Islands

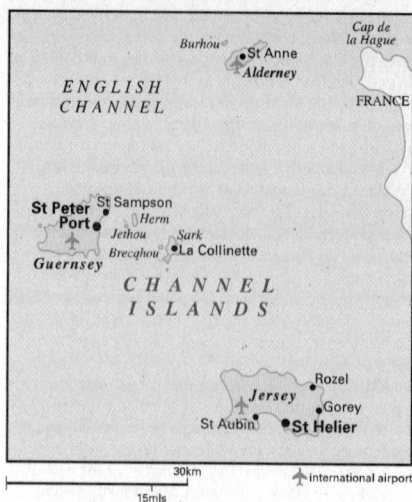

Alderney, Guernsey, Jersey and Sark & Herm.

There are other, very small islands in the group, but these are not normally open to visitors.

Alderney

Location: English Channel, the northernmost Channel Island; off the north coast of France.

Time: GMT (GMT + 1 from last Sunday in March to last Saturday in October).

Overview

Alderney, the third-largest of the Channel Islands, has pledged allegiance to the English Crown for close on 1000 years and is frequently described as the most British of the Channel Islands. Yet, Alderney (*Aurigny* in French) has a distinctly French flavour, which is not surprising as the island's closest neighbour, France, is only 8 miles away. A little oasis where time seems to have stopped, Alderney offers the perfect ingredients for a short or long holiday, at any time of the year. Unlike the other Channel Islands, Alderney has not been affected by mainstream tourism. Travellers will be able to wind down and enjoy Alderney's quality of life, hospitality and gastronomy. In fact, there is something for everyone every week of the year. This little island boasts over 30 social, sporting and cultural clubs and associations who, between them, provide a busy diary of events throughout the year. From golf, tennis, fishing, walks across the common and the rugged cliffs, sandy and quiet beaches and an abundance of flora and fauna (including wild pheasants, black rabbits and 'blond' hedgehogs), Alderney has a lot to offer.

General Information

AREA: 7.9 sq km (3.1 sq miles).
POPULATION: 2,294 (2001).
POPULATION DENSITY: 290.0 per sq km.
CAPITAL: St Anne.
GEOGRAPHY: The most northerly of the Channel Islands, Alderney lies 12km (8 miles) off the coast of Normandy in France and some 32km (20 miles) from Guernsey. The central part of the island is a plateau varying in height from 76 to 90m (250 to 296ft). The land is flat to the edge of the southern and southwestern cliffs, where it falls abruptly to the sea. On the northern, eastern and southeastern sides, it slopes gradually towards rocky and sandy bays and quiet beaches.
GOVERNMENT: Dependency of the British Crown with considerable internal autonomy. **Head of State:** HM Queen Elizabeth II represented locally by Lieutenant-Governor Sir Fabian Malbon. **Head of Government:** Sir Norman Browse. **Recent history:** The States of Alderney (the Legislature) consists of a President and ten States Members. The President serves as the civic head and has responsibility for the administration of the island, with the exception of the police, public health and education, which are presided over by the Lieutenant-Governor of Guernsey. The President of Alderney is elected for a four-year term by universal adult suffrage of residents of Alderney. The President chairs the monthly States Meetings and stands

for election every four years. Following the decision of Jon Kay-Mouat, Alderney's longest serving President, to retire from office in January 2002, Sir Norman Browse was elected President of the States on 19 January 2002 to serve until December 2004.
At the Presidential Elections in 2004 Sir Norman was unopposed and re-instated for a further four-year term ending December 2008.
LANGUAGE: English.
ELECTRICITY: 240 volts AC, 50Hz.
SOCIAL CONVENTIONS: For information relating to Alderney on people, religion, social conventions, business, tipping and economy, see the *Guernsey* section.

Climate

The island enjoys a temperate climate with warm summers and milder winter temperatures than those experienced in the UK.

Communications

Telephone: Alderney is linked to the British STD service; the area code is 01481.
Mobile telephone: Roaming agreements exist with internationational mobile phone companies. Good mobile coverage.
Internet: Information is available from Cable & Wireless Guernsey (website: www.cw.com/guernsey/index.html).
Post: Alderney's Post Office is a sub-office of the Guernsey Post Office and has its own stamps which is used on postage mailed from the island. Post office hours: Mon-Fri 08.30-17.00pm and Sat 08.30-12.00pm.
MEDIA: Press: UK national newspapers and some foreign papers are available on the Island, together with the *Alderney Journal*, *Guernsey Press*, *Guernsey Globe* and the *Jersey Evening Post*.
TV: *Channel TV* is the local ITV provider and ITV's *Channel 4* (but not Channel 5) and *BBC 1* and *2* are also available.
Radio: *BBC* local radio and the commercial station *Island FM* are also received on the island.

Passport/Visa

No passports are required for travel between the UK, the other Channel Islands and Alderney. See *Passport/Visa* in the main *United Kingdom* section.

Money

Currency: Pound (GBP; symbol £) = 100 pence. UK notes and coins are legal tender and circulate together with Channel Islands issue, which are in the same denominations. Channel Islands notes can be reconverted at parity in UK banks, although they are not accepted as legal tender in the UK.
Credit & debit cards & ATMs: All major credit cards are accepted. HSBC and Lloyds/TSB have cash dispensers on Victoria Street.
Traveller's cheques: Traveller's cheques are widely accepted.
Banking hours: Mon-Fri 0930-1300 and 1430-1530 (Lloyds/TSB 0930-1230 and 1330-1600, Fri 1300-1800).

Duty Free

As Alderney falls under the authority of the Bailiwick of Guernsey, customs regulations are the same; see the *Guernsey* section.

Public Holidays

Below are listed Public Holidays for the January 2006-June 2007 period.
Note: Public Holidays observed in the Channel Islands are the same as those observed in the rest of the UK (see the main *United Kingdom* section) with the addition of:
Aug 7 2006 Summer Bank Holiday and **Dec 15 2006** Homecoming Day.

Health

No vaccination certificates are required to enter Alderney. There is a reciprocal health agreement with the UK, allowing all short-stay visitors (three months maximum) from the mainland free immediate and necessary medical treatment and free emergency dental treatment. Visitors should nevertheless be aware that the NHS does not operate in the Balliwick (Guernsey, Alderney, Sark & Herm) under routine circumstances. Doctor's visits, ambulance services and prescribed medicines must be paid for. Proof of UK residence (driving licence, NHS card and so on) is required to benefit from the agreement. The island has a small hospital, two medical practices and one dental practice. Visitors are advised to obtain health insurance cover prior to their trip.

Travel - International

AIR:

Aurigny Air Services (GR) offers flights to Guernsey (flight time – 15 minutes) and Southampton (flight time – 45 minutes). For further information, contact Aurigny Air Services, Alderney (tel: (01481) 822 886 (reservations); website: www.aurigny.com). There are also daily direct services from *Rockhopper.aero* (from/to Bournemouth, Brighton, Jersey and Guernsey), plus thousands of private aviators.

Main airports: *Alderney Airport* (ACI) (website: www.flyalderney.com/airport.html) is famous for its sun dial outside the building and its 'knit-while-you-wait' box in the departure lounge, which invites passengers to help knit squares towards making blankets to send to poverty-stricken countries. *To/from the airport*: Travellers can walk the short distance from the airport to the island's capital of St. Anne's or hire a taxi. *Facilities:* Buffet, duty free shop and taxis (from rank adjacent to terminal building).

Departure tax: None.

SEA:

There is a regular passenger ferry service from Dielette (Normandy) and Guernsey to Alderney, provided by *Manche Iles Express* (tel: (01481) 822 881). Other ferry services operated include *Condor Ferries*, *It Ferries*, *Lady Maris* and *Voyager*. For further information, contact the States of Alderney Tourism Office (see *Top Things To Do*).

RAIL:

For information on rail travel, contact *Alderney Railway*, PO Box 75, Alderney.

ROAD:

Caravans may not be imported to Alderney. **Regulations:** Traffic drives on the left. Maximum speed limit is 35mph (56kph). **Documentation:** Valid national driving licences are accepted.

Travel - Internal

ROAD:

Getting around Alderney is easy as everything is within walking distance. **Bus:** During the summer months, an internal bus service operates on the island running from St Anne's to the five main beaches. **Taxi:** Private taxi companies operate on the island. **Car hire:** There are several car hire companies on the island and two garages which have hire cars. **Bicycle hire:** There are several bike hire firms that rent out bicycles at daily or weekly rates. There are also guided **coach** and **boat** tours. Alderney also has its own version of the Orient Express, the famous *Alderney Railway*, which features a diesel engine **train** pulling along old converted London Underground carriages (tel: (01481) 823 580).

Travel Advice

Most visits to Alderney are trouble-free but you should be aware of the global risk of indiscriminate international terrorist attacks, which could be against civilian targets, including places frequented by foreigners.

This advice is correct at time of publishing. As the situation can change rapidly, visitors are advised to contact the following organisations for the latest travel advice:

US Department of State
Website: http://travel.state.gov/travel

The Ministry of Foreign Affairs in your home country.

Accommodation

HOTELS, GUEST HOUSES, SELF CATERING:

Available, but pre-booking is necessary in the summer months.

CAMPING:

Only permitted on the one official campsite. The import of caravans is prohibited.

For further information, contact the States of Alderney Tourism Office (see *Top Things To See & Do*).

Top Things To See & Do

- The island's town, **St Anne**, dates back to the 15th century and has numerous shops and inns lining its cobbled streets. Principal visitor attractions include **St Anne's Church**, often referred to as the 'Cathedral of the Channel Islands' and the **Alderney Society Museum**. Located in the High Street, the museum documents the island's history from neolithic times. It is open daily in summer.
- The quaint, traditional **Alderney Cinema** is another highlight. Seats are bookable in advance, as are drinks at nearby pubs for the half-time break when the projectionist changes the film reel.
- Guided tours up a 32m- (96ft-) high **historic lighthouse** are available at the eastern end of the island near **Quesnard Point** at weekends. The lighthouse is accessible either on foot or on the 150-year-old narrow-gauge **Alderney Railway**.
- All parts of the island can be reached on foot and there are some interesting **panoramic walks** along the cliffs. The recently formed **Alderney Wildlife Trust** has published a series of recommended walks and also offers guided tours throughout the main season. For details, contact the Alderney Tourism and Wildlife Trust Information Centre in Victoria Street (tel: (01481) 823 737).
- Alderney is well located for **sailing excursions** to the other Channel Islands and France (which is only 12km/8 miles away). The Sailing Club organises several annual events and races, including the *Alderney International Sailing Regatta* (usually held in July). For further details (including boat hire and sailing classes), contact the Alderney Sailing Club, The Harbour (tel: (01481) 822 959; E-mail: info@sailalderney.com).

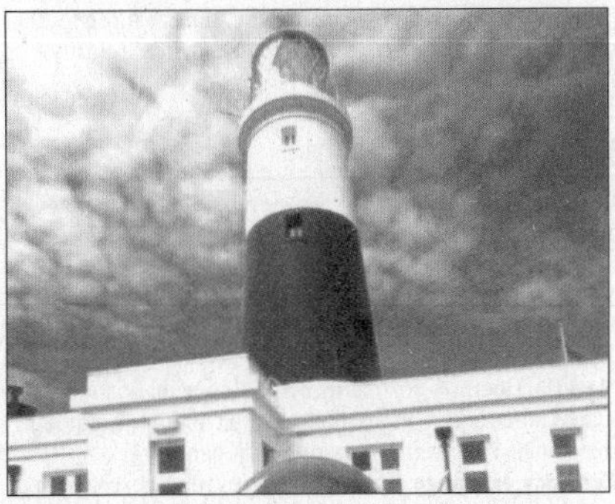

Credit: ©States of Alderney

- Alderney is surrounded by numerous sandy beaches suitable for **swimming** and **windsurfing**. Surf/sail boards are available for hire on the island. Dogs are banned from most of the islands' beaches between May and September. Some of the best beaches can be found on **Arch Bay**, **Braye Bay** (also popular for water-skiing), **Clonque** (a beach for naturalists), **Corblets** (one of the best swimming beaches and also recommended for board surfing), **Longis Bay** (next to Longis Common, which offers good birdwatching), **Platte Saline** (also for naturalists; swimming is not recommended due to strong undercurrents) and **Say** (pronounced 'Soy').
- **Fishing** is well catered for: no permission is needed to fish anywhere from the coastline or the harbour and the local shop offers equipment and advice. The **Angling Festival** is held annually in October. **Sea fishing** enthusiasts are able to charter small boats.
- There is a well-maintained 9-hole **golf** course with a bowling green. Green fees are comparatively low compared to the rest of the Channel Islands. For information, contact the *Alderney Golf Club* (tel: (01481) 822 835). Facilities are available on the island for both **squash** and **tennis**.

TOURIST INFORMATION

States of Alderney Tourism Office
The Island Hole, Royal Connaught Square, Alderney, Channel Islands, GY9 3AA
Tel: (01481) 823 737 (brochure hotline) *or* 822 811 (general enquiries).
Website: www.alderney.net

Entertainment

FOOD & DRINK: Cuisine is largely French influenced. The local speciality is shellfish. A wide variety of alcoholic beverages is available. Spirits, beers and wines are cheaper than on the mainland.

SHOPPING: Alderney has its own duty free retail outlets where visitors can purchase spirits and tobacco at exceptionally low prices prior to their departure. There is no VAT, but a Guernsey Bailiwick tax is imposed on certain goods such as spirits, wines, beers and tobacco. Prices on luxury goods are lower than in the UK, although the overall cost of foodstuffs is higher. Special purchases include Alderney pullovers, local pottery and crafts. **Shopping hours:** These vary, but the majority of shops open Mon-Sat 0900-1730. Shops generally close for lunch and on Wednesday afternoons. Shops may open on Sundays during the high season.

Business

See main *United Kingdom* section.

Guernsey

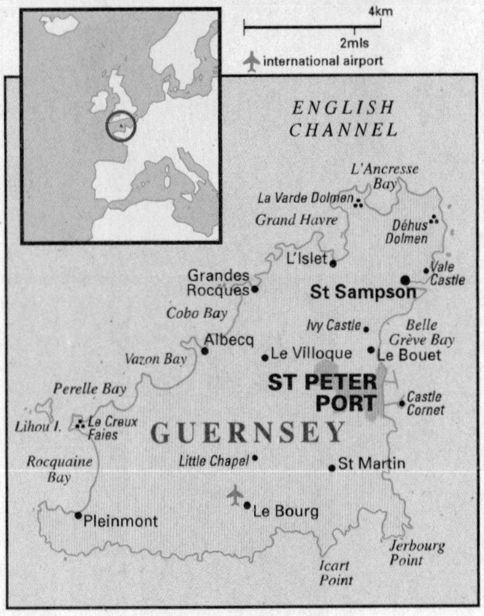

Location: English Channel, off the northern coast of France.

Time: GMT (GMT + 1 from the last Sunday in March to last Sunday in October).

Guernsey is a Dependency of the British Crown represented abroad by British Embassies – see *United Kingdom* section.

Overview

Think all the quiet charm of Jersey with fewer of the trappings of mass tourism, and what you have is the tranquil island of Guernsey. Indeed, 'tranquil', in this case, really does mean bucolic: wooded valleys, sunsets over the Atlantic Ocean, botanical gardens, secret coves and cliff-top walks are amongst the island gems that will guarantee that you relax. And this is all available with the added bonus that Guernsey is incredibly child-friendly; perfect news to anyone frustratingly trying to find the ideal family holiday location. Safe beaches with gorgeously blue water await you.

For those who feel that they might tire of beach-related pursuits, Guernsey has wonderful facilities for activities such as cycling and golf. It also has oodles of history. As far back as the 11th century, the Channel Islands (*les Isles Normandes*), of which Guernsey is one, were part of the Duchy of Normandy. When William, Duke of Normandy, conquered England, the Channel Islands were incorporated into the combined realm of both England and Normandy. King John of England lost mainland Normandy to the French 140 years later but the Channel Islands stayed loyal to England. The French made many subsequent attempts, all of which were repelled, over the ensuing centuries to capture the islands. The Germans were more successful, albeit briefly, during World War II, when much of the island's population was evacuated to England. But, today, Guernsey enjoys a large degree of internal self-government, having developed its own legal and political institutions, and is also responsible for the government of neighbouring Alderney.

Such history is apparent all around Guernsey. Evidence of Neolithic man is everywhere, in burial chambers and defensive earth works, long excavated and unveiled. Fortifications, testament to Guernsey's many attempts throughout history to repel invasion, can be seen in edifices like Castle Cornet, now housing an excellent museum. More modern history has, sadly, left its mark in 20th-century, Second-World-War bulwarks and buttresses.

Guernsey's sea air encourages a hearty appetite, and the island's fertile sea and soil provides the island's cuisine with a host of ingredients, from seafood to locally grown vegetables. Whether you decide to eat in Guernsey's gourmet restaurants or simply at a beach kiosk, you will be very well catered for.

General Information

AREA: 63.1 sq km (24.3 sq miles).
POPULATION: 65,228 (2005).
POPULATION DENSITY: 1033.7 per sq km.
CAPITAL: St Peter Port.
GEOGRAPHY: Guernsey is situated in the Gulf of St Malo, 50km (30 miles) from the coast of France and 130km (80 miles) from the south coast of England. The cliffs on the south coast rise to 80m (270ft), from which the land slopes away gradually to the north. Guernsey is an ideal centre for excursions to the other Channel Islands and France. The islands of Alderney, Brecqhou, Herm, Jethou, Lihou and Sark are dependencies of Guernsey.

Credit: ©VisitGuernsey

GOVERNMENT: Dependency of the British Crown. Although Guernsey is British, its history and constitution mean that it is not part of the United Kingdom or the European Union. Internally, Guernsey is self governing with its own Parliament (the States of Guernsey) and its own laws. Only foreign affairs and defence are handled by the UK, although there are arrangements by which Guernsey laws are approved by the crown. **Head of State:** HM Queen Elizabeth II, represented locally by Lieutenant-Governor Sir John Foley since 2000. **Head of Government:** Bailiff De Vic Graham Carey since 1999. **Recent history:** The most recent elections were held in 2000. No political parties are represented at Guernsey elections. The British Monarch is Head of State, represented locally by a Lieutenant Governor. Internal affairs are governed by the island's Parliament, the States of Deliberation. The 'States', as it is commonly known, has 57 members divided into three groups: 45 deputies elected directly by universal suffrage; 10 representatives of the *douzaines* or parish councils and two representatives from the small neighbouring island of Alderney.
LANGUAGE: English is the official language. Norman *patois* is spoken in some parishes.
RELIGION: Church of England, Presbyterian, Baptist, Congregational and Methodist.
ELECTRICITY: 240 volts AC, 50Hz. Three-pin plugs in use.
SOCIAL CONVENTIONS: Handshaking is the customary form of greeting and normal social courtesies should be observed when visiting someone's home. It is not usual to start eating until everyone is served. If invited to someone's home, a small present such as flowers or chocolates is appreciated. Casual wear is acceptable in most places. A ban on smoking in enclosed public places comes into force on 1 July 2006.

Climate

The most popular holiday season is from Easter to October, with temperatures averaging 20-21°C (68-70°F). These months give an average of 200 and 260 hours of sunshine. Rainfall is mainly during the cooler months. The sea is 17°C (63°F) on average during the summer.
Required clothing: Normal beach and holiday wear for summer, with some warmer clothing as there are often sea breezes. Warm winter wear and rainwear are advised.

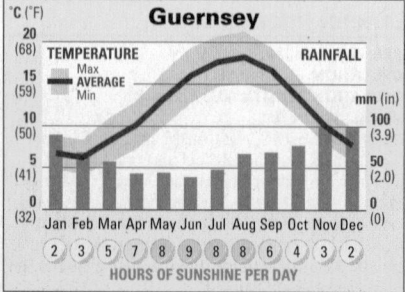

Guernsey — temperature and rainfall chart. Hours of sunshine per day: Jan 2, Feb 3, Mar 5, Apr 7, May 8, Jun 8, Jul 9, Aug 8, Sep 6, Oct 4, Nov 3, Dec 2.

Communications

Telephone: Country code: 44, followed by (0)1481.
Mobile telephone: Roaming agreements exist with international mobile phone companies. Handsets can be hired.
Internet: Public access is available at Internet cafes and in libraries. Coverage is good.
Post: Only Guernsey stamps will be accepted on outgoing mail. The main post office is at Smith Street, St Peter Port. Post boxes are painted blue.
MEDIA: Press: The local newspapers are *The Guernsey Press and Star* and *The Guernsey Weekly Press*. English, French, German, Dutch and Italian newspapers are also available at newsagents. All the main British newspapers are available in Guernsey on the day of publication.
TV: *Channel Television* is popular. For more information, see the *United Kingdom* section.
Radio: *BBC Radio Guernsey* operates. Commercial radio is in its infancy but so far includes *104.7 Island FM*.

Passport/Visa

Passport and Visa requirements are the same as those for the rest of the UK; see the *United Kingdom* section for further information.

Money

Currency: Guernsey has its own currency but all UK notes and coins are legal tender, and circulate with the Channel Islands issue. Pound Sterling (GBP; symbol £) = 100 pence. Notes are in denominations of £50, 20, 10, 5 and 1. Coins are in denominations of £2 (special issue) and 1, and 50, 20, 10, 5, 2 and 1 pence.
Note: (a) Guernsey still has its own £1 note. (b) Channel Islands notes and coins are not accepted in the UK, although they can be reconverted at parity in UK banks.
Currency exchange: Foreign currencies can be exchanged at bureaux de change, in banks and at many hotels.
Credit & debit cards: American Express, Diners Club, MasterCard and Visa are all widely accepted. Check with your credit or debit card company for details of merchant acceptability and other services which may be available.
Traveller's cheques: Widely accepted.
Banking hours: Mon-Fri 0930-1530. Some banks open earlier and close later on weekdays.
Exchange rates: See the *United Kingdom* section.

Duty Free

The following goods may be imported into Guernsey by persons over 18 years of age without incurring customs duty: *200 cigarettes or 100 cigarillos or 50 cigars or 250g of tobacco; 2l of still table wine; 1l of alcoholic beverages over 22 per cent proof or 2l of fortified wine/sparkling wine/liqueurs or an additional 2l of still table wine; other goods to a value of £145.*
Note: (a) Certain animals may be imported into the Channel Islands under the 'Pet Passport' scheme. For further details, contact an official source. (b) Commercial goods, prohibited and restricted goods, or goods in excess of the personal allowance must be declared. (c) Guernsey is not part of the EU and therefore normal restrictions apply.
Prohibited goods: Unlicensed drugs; offensive weapons; obscene or pornographic material; counterfeit goods.
Restricted items: Firearms, explosives and ammunition; animals and birds; uncooked meats and poultry; certain plants.

Public Holidays

Guernsey observes all the Public Holidays observed in the UK (see *United Kingdom* section) and, in addition, the beneath Public Holidays listed for the January 2006-June 2007 period.
2006 and 2007: May 9 Liberation Day (commemorating the arrival of the British Forces at the end of World War II).

Health

	Special Precautions?	Certificate Required?
Yellow Fever	No	No
Cholera	No	No
Typhoid & Polio	No	N/A
Malaria	No	N/A

Note: *Regulations and requirements may be subject to change at short notice, and you are advised to contact your doctor well in advance of your intended date of departure. Any numbers in the chart refer to the footnotes below.*

Health care: Most doctors and dentists are in private practice and patients are required to pay for any treatment by a GP. This can be at a surgery, at a temporary residence or in the Accident and Emergency Department at the Princess Elizabeth Hospital (PEH) which is operated by the Board of Health, as these services are provided by GPs in private practice. However, the Reciprocal Health Agreement only provides for immediately necessary treatment, such as urgently needed treatment for conditions which may arise during a stay. Hospital accommodation and medical services are provided free of charge to UK visitors under the act. There is also a charge for the ambulance service. Medical insurance is strongly recommended.

Travel - International

AIR:
Guernsey can be reached all year round from various locations on mainland Britain, Dinard, Zurich and Amsterdam and at weekends during the summer from Rotterdam, Dortmund and Hanover. Airlines serving Guernsey include *Aurigny Air Services* (website: www.aurigny.com), *British Airways Express*, *Flybe* and *Swiss*.
Approximate flight times: From Guernsey to *London* is one hour.
Main airports: Guernsey (GCI) is 6km (4 miles) from St Peter Port. *To/from the airport:* Bus and taxi services are available to the town (travel time – 15 minutes). *Facilities:* ATM, car hire, tourist information, first aid room, shops (including duty free shop in departure lounge) and light refreshments.
Departure tax: None.
SEA:
Condor Ferries (website: www.condorferries.co.uk) operates car/passenger catamaran services to Guernsey from Poole (travel time – two hours 30 minutes), Weymouth (travel time – two hours) and St Malo (travel time – two hours). A car ferry operates to Portsmouth (travel time – 10 hours 30 minutes). Services also operate from Jersey. *Manche Iles Express* (website: www.manche-iles-express.com) operates from various French ports and from Jersey. Day excursions are available daily to Herm, Jersey and Sark by boat. Inter-island services are also available from *Aurigny Air Services*, *Condor Ferries* and *Manche Iles Express*.

Travel - Internal

ROAD:
Bus: A comprehensive bus service serves all parts of the island. A variety of island tours are also available during the summer. **Car hire**: There are many car hire companies available on Guernsey, with rates that compare favourably with the UK. There is an unlimited mileage allowance. Coach hire for large parties is also available. **Bicycle hire:** Available from various firms for daily or weekly hire. **Regulations:** Driving is on the left. Maximum speed limit is 35mph (56kph). Parking is free, although time limits are imposed. If these are exceeded, fines are levied. **Documentation:** A full national driving licence is required.
Travel times: The following chart gives approximate travel times (in hours and minutes) from **St Peter Port** to the neighbouring Channel Islands.

	Air	Sea
Alderney	0.15	-
Herm Island	-	0.20
Jersey	0.15	1.00
Sark Island	-	0.40

Travel Advice

Most visits to Guernsey are trouble-free but you should be aware of the global risk of indiscriminate international terrorist attacks, which could be against civilian targets, including places frequented by foreigners.
This advice is correct at time of publishing. As the situation can change rapidly, visitors are advised to contact the following organisations for the latest travel advice:

US Department of State
Website: http://travel.state.gov/travel

The Ministry of Foreign Affairs in your home country.

Accommodation

HOTELS:
A large selection of well-maintained hotels, offering facilities for the single or group visitor, is available. The Guernsey Government has a scheme for the compulsory inspection and grading of hotels to ensure standards of accommodation are maintained and improved. All hotels being given a number of stars (with 5 stars given as the highest grade) according to the facilities offered. Over 94 per cent of rooms have en suite facilities. All have at least a washbasin. Advance booking is advisable during the summer period.
GUEST HOUSES:
These are normally family-run establishments, providing a good standard of accommodation in a homely atmosphere. This can be based on full-

board, half-board or bed & breakfast, according to the visitor's requirements. A number of these have residential liquor licences. All are graded under the Diamond Scheme with 5 diamonds offering the best service and 1 diamond offering basic comfort.

SELF-CATERING:

Units are graded 5 stars to 1 star according to size, number of persons accommodated, standards and amenities offered.

CAMPING/CARAVANNING:

There are five official campsites at various locations around the island. Full details are available from the Tourist Office. Visitors are not permitted to bring caravans into Guernsey.

ACCOMMODATION INFORMATION

Guernsey Hotel and Tourism Association (GHATA)
c/o Guernsey Chamber of Commerce, Suite 3,
16 Glategny Esplanade,
St Peter Port GY1 1WN, Guernsey
Tel: (01481) 713 583.
Website: www.ghata.com

A full-colour brochure of all accommodation is available from Visit Guernsey (see *Top Things To See & Do*).

Top Things To See & Do

- **St Peter Port** is the island's capital and retains much of the character of a traditional fishing village. The church dates in part from the 12th century, while the 17th-century oldest house, now a National Trust shop, stands in **Cornet Street**. The **Priaulx Library** contains a large browse-friendly collection of historical records. Nearby, **Castle Cornet** overlooks the harbour. Built during the reign of King Stephen, it bears influences from many eras, through to the German occupation of World War II. It also contains the **Royal Guernsey Militia Museum**, a **Maritime Museum** and attractive gardens. **Hauteville House**, on the south side of St Peter Port at the top of the hill, was once the home of Victor Hugo. It was here that he wrote *The Toilers of the Sea* (which is set in St Sampson). His statue stands in **Candie Gardens**, as does the main **Island Museum**, and some small **botanical gardens**.
- Guernsey has an extensive array of **beaches** ranged all around its coastline. Within walking distance of St Peter Port are those of **Havelet Bay** and **Belle Grève Bay**. In the north of the island are **L'Ancresse Bay** and **Grande Havre**, both with big sandy beaches. Further afield, and popular with surfers, is the northwest-facing **Vazon Bay**, with its huge sweeping sands. At the western end lies **Roquaine Bay**, which boasts two beaches as well as the **Fort Grey Maritime Museum**, focusing on the many shipwrecks that have occurred off Guernsey. At the northern end of the bay, **Lihou Island** is home to flocks of seabirds, and is accessible to walkers at low tide. On the south coast, steep steps reach the beach at **Petit Bôt**, and **Moulin Huet Bay** is a sheltered location for sunbathers. The cliff paths around the island make for interesting walks. The **Water Lanes** leading to the shore, particularly at Moulin Huet and Petit Bôt, are highlights among these. The beach at **Cobo** is also very good.
- **Fortifications** are scattered all around the coast – among them are **Ivy Castle** near **Le Bouet**, a Norman stronghold, and **Vale Castle** at **St Sampson**. On the West Coast lies **Fortress Rousse**, an 18th-century tower now open to the public. **Dolmens** (Neolithic tombs) are common on Guernsey. Among them are **Déhus Dolmen**, near the yacht marina in the Vale, and **La Catioroc**, on a mound overlooking **Perelle Bay** (reputedly once a witches' meeting place).
- Go to the wartime **German Underground Hospital** at **St Andrew**, or the **German Occupation Museum** at **Forest**, which both give an insight into island life during World War II German occupation. Also located in German tunnels is the island's **Aquarium**.
- The **Little Chapel** at **Les Vauxbelets** is thought to be the smallest church in the world, with space for a priest and a congregation of two.
- Visit Guernsey's only stately home open to the public: **Sausmarez Manor** at **St Martin**.
- Eat delicious cuisine at very cheap prices by attending **Tennerfest** (website: www.tennerfest.com). You can probably guess from the title of the festival how much selected restaurants around the island will charge you for feasting well. You may save pounds in your bank account but, be warned, you may gain a few around your waist!
- Guernsey's location and mild climate provide good opportunities for **watersports**, particularly **swimming** and **sailing**. **Diving** excursions and courses are offered by the Guernsey School of Diving/Sarnia Skin Divers (tel: (01481) 722 884) and other organisations; contact Visit Guernsey for details (see *Tourist Information*).
- Attend the **Guernsey Eisteddfod Society Annual Festival**. This festival celebrates the best of arts and academic events, and culminates in an exhibition at the end of March (the festival as a whole begins in January).

TOURIST INFORMATION

Visit Guernsey
PO Box 23, St Peter Port GY1 3AN, Guernsey
Tel: (01481) 723 552.
Website: www.visitguernsey.com

Entertainment

FOOD & DRINK: Guernsey is famous for its food and the island has a wide variety of restaurants ranging from traditional French and English cuisine to Italian, Indian and Chinese. There are two self-service restaurants in St Peter Port. A wide variety of alcoholic beverages are available and spirits, beers and wines are relatively cheap compared to the mainland.

Things to know: Table service is normal in restaurants, with counter service in bars. Eating out is also excellent value for money as there is no VAT. After a recent change in the licensing laws, pubs in Guernsey are now able to stay open until 0045 seven nights a week.

Local specialities:

- Shellfish, with freshly caught lobsters, crabs and scallops forming the basis of many dishes.
- *Guernsey gâche* - pronounced 'gosh' (a fruit loaf usually served with local butter).
- *Gâche melée* (a local apple cake).

Tipping: 10 to 12 per cent is normal, except where a service charge is included.

NIGHTLIFE: Discos are located in St Peter Port, whilst live music and cabarets are organised by some hotels during the summer season. The Beau Sejour Leisure Centre at St Peter Port contains a cinema, theatre, bars and cafe.

SHOPPING: There is no VAT but a Guernsey Bailiwick tax is imposed on certain goods such as spirits, wines, beers and tobacco. Prices of luxury goods are cheaper than in the UK, although the overall cost of foodstuffs is higher. Special purchases include Guernsey's local pottery, knitted sweaters, crafts, gold and silver jewellery and candles. **Shopping hours:** Mon-Sat 0900-1730 (there may be limited Sunday opening).

Business

- **GDP:** US$2.59 billion (2003 estimate).
- **Main imports:** Coal, petrol, oil, machinery and equipment.
- **Main exports:** Cut flowers and tomatoes.
- **Main trade partners:** UK.

ECONOMY: Finance, tourism and light industry are the main components of Guernsey's economy. The island has gradually been developed as an offshore financial centre and the financial sector now accounts for 60 per cent of government revenues. Various institutions are incorporated on the island to take advantage of its favourable tax and corporate disclosure requirements. However, along with Jersey, the island's government agreed in 2002 to join an EU-wide campaign to improve international financial transparency and stamp out tax evasion.

Flowers and tomatoes are the main horticultural exports and enjoy international recognition. Tourism's relative importance has been far outstripped by the financial sector.

BUSINESS ETIQUETTE: Businesspeople are generally expected to dress smartly, with a suit and tie for men. Appointments should be made and business cards are customary. Business is conducted in English. **Office hours:** Mon-Fri 0900-1700.

CONFERENCES/CONVENTIONS: Guernsey's main conference venue, the Beau Sejour Centre, has a maximum seating capacity of 1500 with 2646 sq m (28,482 sq ft) of exhibition space and banqueting for 900 people or a reception area for 2000 people. Many hotels also offer conference space.

COMMERCIAL INFORMATION

Guernsey Chamber of Commerce
Suite 3, 16 Glategny Esplanade,
St Peter Port GY1 1WN, Guernsey
Tel: (01481) 727 483.
Website: www.chamber.guernsey.net

Meet Guernsey
Tel: (01481) 234 567.
Website: www.conferenceguernsey.gg

Jersey

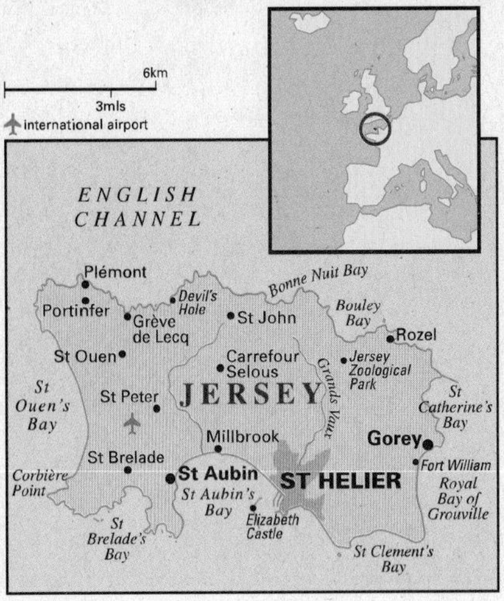

Location: English Channel, off the northern coast of France.

Time: GMT (GMT + 1 from last Sunday in March to Saturday before last Sunday in October).

Jersey is a Dependency of the British Crown represented abroad by British Embassies – see *United Kingdom* section.

Overview

The largest of the Channel Islands, Jersey has been inhabited for many thousands of years, as can be seen from the neolithic tomb at *La Hougue Bie*. The Normans made the greatest impact on the Channel Islands, annexing them to the Duchy of Normandy during the 10th century. When William of Normandy gained the English crown in 1066, the Channel Islands became part of the Anglo-Norman realm; they were retained after the loss of Normandy in 1204. As a mark of his gratitude for their loyalty, King John granted Jersey its own constitution; this has been ratified by every successive monarch and the connection between the island and the English throne is expressed in the flag, which contains a crest surmounted by the Plantagenet crown.

Like its neighbours, Jersey has at various times been a haven for smugglers and pirates, and is also vulnerable to attack due to its proximity to France, so often Britain's enemy in the past. The mixture of languages – English, French and Norman-French – reflects the history of the island.

Jersey is highly developed for tourism. It boasts a formidable array, for its small size, of modern attractions and special events catering for its huge number of visitors. The island does not neglect its natural and historical heritage though – there is plenty of historical interest as well as many beautiful scenic attractions.

General Information

AREA: 116 sq km (45 sq miles).

POPULATION: 90,800 (2005).

POPULATION DENSITY: 753 per sq km.

CAPITAL: St Helier. **Population**: 28,310 (2001).

GEOGRAPHY: Jersey is the largest of the Channel Islands, lying approximately 160km (100 miles) south of the coast of England and 23km (14 miles) from the coast of Normandy in France. The island is roughly 14.5km (9 miles) by 8km (5 miles). It slopes from north to south and often appears to visitors to be largely composed of pink granite. Jersey has over 20 bays, many small harbours and magnificent beaches bathed by the warm waters of the Gulf Stream.

GOVERNMENT: Dependency of the British Crown. **Head of State**: Queen Elizabeth II, represented locally by the Lieutenant-Governor Sir John Cheshire. **Head of Government**: Bailiff Sir Philip Bailhache since 1995.

Recent history: As a direct dependency of the British crown, Jersey has its own legislative and taxation systems which are an intriguing blend of Norman and English. The Jersey States Assembly, one of the oldest legislative bodies in the world, is composed of 12 Constables, 12 Senators and 29 Deputies (none of whom receives any remuneration for their services), as well as several non-voting officials, some of whom are appointed by the crown. The island's laws are subject to ratification by the Privy Council, although this is little more than a formality. Jersey has jealously guarded its independence since the war, manifested in strict criteria governing rights of residency and a marked reluctance to accept controls over its thriving financial services industry.

Credit: ©Jersey Tourism/Pete Marsden & Skydive Jersey Ltd

In recent years, however, under pressure from the Organisation for Economic Cooperation and Development, the Jersey authorities have been forced to cede some controls over the industry. The island's antique political system has also come under scrutiny. A process of public consultation began in November 2003; this is intended to produce a more democratic system, including a blueprint for a wider franchise and a wholly elected government.

LANGUAGE: English is the official language. A dialect of Norman-French is still spoken by some people. French is still used in courts.

RELIGION: Each of Jersey's parishes has its own Anglican church, but some parishes, particularly St Helier, have been subdivided to provide more than one centre for Church of England worship. There are 12 Roman Catholic and 18 Methodist churches, as well as a wide range of free churches.

ELECTRICITY: 240 volts AC, 50Hz.

SOCIAL CONVENTIONS: Similar to the UK, with French influences (see the *United Kingdom* section).

Climate

The most popular holiday season is from May until the end of September, with temperatures averaging 20-21°C (68-70°F). Rainfall averages 33 inches a year, most of which falls during the cooler months. Sea temperatures average over 17°C (63°F) in deep water during the summer.

Required clothing: Normal beach and holidaywear for summer, with a jumper or similar as there are often sea breezes. Warm winterwear and rainwear are advised.

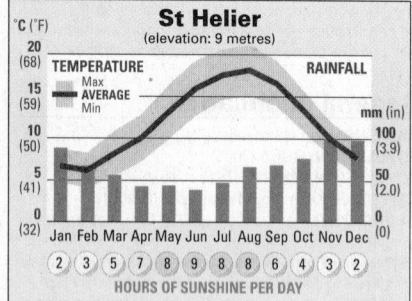

St Helier
(elevation: 9 metres)

TEMPERATURE — Max, AVERAGE, Min — RAINFALL

HOURS OF SUNSHINE PER DAY: Jan 2, Feb 3, Mar 5, Apr 7, May 8, Jun 8, Jul 8, Aug 7, Sep 6, Oct 4, Nov 3, Dec 2

Communications

Telephone: Country code: 44 (not necessary when dialling from the UK), followed by (0)1534.

Mobile telephone: Roaming agreements exist with most international mobile phone companies. 'Pay As You Go' phones will *not* work in Jersey.

Internet: There are a number of Internet cafes, like City Bar on Halkett Place, Murray's cafe in St Aubins, St Helier, and Cafe JAC at the Jersey Arts Centre. Internet service and training is also available at the Jersey Library.

Post: There is a standard one-price rate to the UK, which is, in general, as good as a first-class UK service, although the prices are lower than UK first class. There is also one rate for internal mail. UK stamps are not valid in Jersey. The main post office is in Broad Street, St Helier. Post office hours: Mon-Fri 0900-1730, Sat 0900-1230.

MEDIA: Press: Newspapers published in Jersey are the *Jersey Evening Post* and the *Jersey Weekly Post*.

TV: Jersey has two local television stations. *Channel TV*, La Pouquelaye, St. Helier, broadcasts at 1800 and 2320. *Spotlight Channel Islands* broadcasts at 1830 and 2230 on BBC 1. Cable - *Newtel Cable Ltd* - and satellite channels are available. French television is also available in Jersey. A French aerial is needed to receive the broadcasts.

Radio: There is a plethora of radio stations to select from. On the local front, *Radio Jersey* offers running commentary on Island life; *Channel 103* is a commercial radio station that plays Top of the Pops hits. Guernsey: *Radio Guernsey* keeps listeners posted on events in the neighbouring island of Guernsey. From the UK: *Radio One* plays current chart hits; *Radio Two* offers easy listening; *Radio Three* offers a variety of classical and jazz tunes; *Radio Four* is a talk radio format that provides commentary on current affairs. There is also a large choice of French radio stations to choose from.

Passport/Visa

Passport and visa requirements are the same as those for the rest of the UK. See the *United Kingdom* section for further information.

Money

Currency: Jersey has its own currency but all UK notes and coins are legal tender, and circulate with the Channel Islands issue. Pound Sterling (JEP; symbol £) = 100 pence. Notes are in denominations of £50, 20, 10 and 5. Coins are in denominations of £2, £1, 50, 20, 10, 5, 2 and 1 pence.

Note: Channel Islands notes and coins are not accepted in the UK, although they can be reconverted at parity in UK banks.

Exchange rates: For exchange rates and currency restrictions, see the *United Kingdom* section.

Currency exchange: Foreign currencies can be exchanged at bureaux de change, in banks and at many hotels. ATMs are available.

Credit & debit cards: American Express, Diners Club, MasterCard and Visa are all widely accepted. Check with your credit or debit card company for details of merchant acceptability and other services which may be available.

Traveller's cheques: Widely accepted.

Banking hours: Mon-Fri 0930-1530. Some banks are open later on weekdays and Saturday mornings.

Duty Free

The Channel Islands are a low-duty zone. The following goods may be imported into Jersey by persons over 17 years of age without incurring customs duty:

200 cigarettes or 50 cigars or 100 cigarillos or 350g of tobacco; 2l of still table wine; 1l of spirits or 2l of alcoholic beverages under 22 per cent or 2l of sparkling or fortified wine; 60g (2 fl oz) perfume and 250ml eau de toilette; other goods to a value of £145.

Public Holidays

Below are listed Public Holidays for the January 2006-June 2007 period.

Public Holidays are as for the UK (see *United Kingdom* section) with the following date also observed:

May 9: Liberation Day (commemorating the arrival of the British Forces at the end of World War II).

Health

	Special Precautions?	Certificate Required?
Yellow Fever	No	No
Cholera	No	No
Typhoid & Polio	No	N/A
Malaria	No	N/A

Note: *Regulations and requirements may be subject to change at short notice, and you are advised to contact your doctor well in advance of your intended date of departure. Any numbers in the chart refer to the footnotes below.*

Health care: There is a reciprocal health agreement with the UK. Providing the visitor has been in Jersey for six months or less, on presenting proof of UK residence (driving licence, NHS card, etc), they can obtain free in- and out-patient treatment at the General Hospital, Gloucester Street, St Helier (tel: (01534) 622 125) and at the Morning Medical Centre, Woodville Avenue, St Helier (Mon-Fri 0830-1630; tel: (01534) 616 833). The agreement does not cover the costs of medical treatment at a doctor's surgery (but there is a free GP-style surgery most mornings in Newgate Street, St Helier), prescribed medicines, or dental treatment, but travel by ambulance is free. Despite the agreement, private medical insurance is advised for UK residents on long visits in case emergency repatriation is necessary and to cover the cost of prescribed medicines and dental treatment. All visitors should bring the name and address of their family doctor in case of a serious accident or illness.

Travel - International

AIR:

Jersey can be reached by air from London and most other major cities in the UK. There are also direct flights to Jersey from Antwerp and Zurich. Major airlines operating to Jersey include *British Airways* (website: www.ba.com), *British Midland* and *Flybe.com* (website: www.flybe.com) (from London and major UK cities) and *VLM* (website: www.flyvlm.com) (from London). Airlines operating to Jersey from the French coast include *Aurigny Air Services* (website: www.aurigny.com) (from Dinan).

Approximate flight times: From Jersey to *London* is 50 minutes.

Main airports: *St Peters (JER)* is 8km (5 miles) from St Helier. *To/from the airport:* Taxis are available and the local bus leaves for St Helier centre every 20 minutes. *Facilities:* Low-tariff shopping, restaurant and bar, car hire, ATMs, business facilities and provision for the disabled.

Departure tax: None.

SEA:

There are several sea routes to Jersey from abroad:

From the UK: Crossings are by catamaran (car/passenger) from Poole (travel time – three hours 45 minutes) and Weymouth (travel time – three hours 30 minutes). Catamarans for foot passengers only operate to St Malo (travel time – one hour 10 minutes). A car ferry operates from Portsmouth (travel time – 10 hours 30 minutes). Crossings are more frequent between April and October. For further information, contact Condor Ferries (tel: (0845) 345 2000; website: www.condorferries.co.uk).

From France: From St Malo: car/passenger and passenger crossings with *Emeraude Lines*; passenger crossings with *Condor Ferries*. From Granville: passenger crossings with *Emeraude Lines* and *Granville Island Sea*. From Carteret: *Alizés Côtes des Iles* and *Emeraude Lines*.

From Guernsey: *Condor Ferries* and *Emeraude Lines* operate between Jersey and Guernsey. Services are also available from the other Channel Islands.

Visitors bringing speedboats, surfboards or sailboards into Jersey *must* register at the Harbour Office on arrival. Third party insurance is required.

Travel - Internal

ROAD:

Traffic drives on the left. There is a speed limit of 64kph (40mph). **Bus:** These operate throughout the island; the network centres on the bus and coach station at Weighbridge, St Helier. Explorer tickets are valid for one, three, five and seven days (prices range from £6.00 to £31.50), available from *Connex* in St Helier, and cannot be purchased prior to arrival. **Car hire:** Available in St Helier. This is fairly priced, and so is petrol. Persons wishing to hire a car must: (a) be over 21 years of age; (b) have had a full licence for at least one year; and (c) have a valid full licence with no endorsements or disqualifications for dangerous driving or driving over the alcohol limit within the previous five years. **Bicycle hire:** Available in St Helier, with one in Millbrook and one in St Ouen. **Mopeds:** Can also be hired from a number of companies in St Helier. Crash helmets must be worn. Addresses and telephone numbers of all these companies can be obtained from Jersey

Tourism (see *Top Things To Do*). **Documentation**: Visitors who wish to drive must have a valid Certificate of Insurance or an International Green Card, and a valid driving licence or International (not UK International) Driving Permit (not photocopies). Nationality plates must be displayed. **Motor caravans** and **trailers** may not be imported.

Travel Advice

Most visits to Jersey are trouble-free but you should be aware of the global risk of indiscriminate international terrorist attacks, which could be against civilian targets, including places frequented by foreigners.
This advice is correct at time of publishing. As the situation can change rapidly, visitors are advised to contact the following organisations for the latest travel advice:

US Department of State
Website: http://travel.state.gov/travel

The Ministry of Foreign Affairs in your home country.

Accommodation

HOTELS:

The official consumer information pack, compiled by the Jersey Hospitality Association, is available from Jersey Tourism (see *Top Things To Do*). Jersey has its own hotel and guest house grading scheme. Hotels are graded from **1 to 5 suns** and guest houses are graded from **1 to 3 diamonds**. The greater the number of suns or diamonds, the higher the grade achieved. All hotels are inspected and graded annually.

GUEST-HOUSES:

There are more than 200 guest houses on the island, some offering bed, breakfast and evening meals, others just bed and breakfast. Despite the large number of establishments, advance booking is recommended as many guest houses are not open throughout the whole year.

SELF-CATERING:

There is limited self-catering accommodation registered with the Tourism Department. Premises taking less than six people do not have to register and are not inspected. This type of accommodation is available through a number of handling agents. Furnished flats, bungalows, chalets and villas are not generally available, owing to the acute shortage of housing for permanent residents. Some units do, however, become available at various times and advertisements can be placed in the local newspaper. Contact the *Jersey Evening Post*, Advertisement Department for details.

CAMPING:

Camping is only permitted on recognised campsites, of which there are four. Owing to limited capacity, advance booking is essential. There are no caravan sites on Jersey.

YOUTH HOSTELS:

There are no youth hostels in Jersey.

ACCOMMODATION INFORMATION

The booklet *Jersey – Open House*, available from Jersey Tourism (see *Top Things To Do*), gives comprehensive information on all types of accommodation on the island.

Jersey Hospitality Association
La rue le Masurier, St Helier,
Jersey JE2 4YE, Channel Islands
Tel: (01534) 721 421.
Website: www.jerseyhols.com

Jersey Evening Post
Advertisement Department, PO Box 582, Five Oaks,
St Saviour, Jersey JE4 8XQ, Channel Islands
Tel: (01534) 611 611.
Website: www.thisisjersey.com

Top Things To See

- In **St Helier**, by far the biggest town on the island, admire **Elizabeth Castle**, which stands on an island on the bay, accessible by causeway at low tide. This imposing fortress withstood Cromwell's forces for seven weeks in 1651, and housed occupying Germans during World War II. On an outcrop above the town, **Fort Regent** is now a leisure complex with sports and conference facilities. The former castle's ramparts offer excellent views across the town and the bay. Go to the award-winning **Jersey Museum**, the **Maritime Museum** and the **Occupation Tapestry Gallery**.

- Enjoy fine views from Jersey's **'Points'**, clifftop headlands overlooking the sea. Most of these are on the northern side of the island, notably those at **Grosnez** and **Plemont** on the northwest corner. Further east are **Belle Hougue**, **Ronez**, **Sorel** and **Vicard Points**, while on the southwest tip, **Corbière Point** is another popular sightseeing port of call.

- Visitor attractions dotted around the coastline include mighty **Mont Orgeuil** castle at **Gorey**, as well as a number of restored military bunkers in various locations.

- Discover many endangered species at the **Jersey Zoological Park**, in **Trinity**, the headquarters of the **Jersey Wildlife Preservation Trust**, founded by the late Gerald Durrell.

- At **La Grève de Lecq**, visit the **British Army Barracks Museum.**

- Marvel at the spectacle of flower-festooned floats and entertainers at the **Battle of Flowers** festival in August. The museum in **St Ouen** displays floats entered in the Battle of Flowers.

- Traditional crafts are a feature of the island, and many of the workshops are open to visitors. Leatherwork at **L'Etacq** (**St Ouen**) and stoneground flour from locally grown corn at **Le Moulin de Quetivel**, **St Peter's Valley**, are among these, while in **Grouville** at **Jersey Pottery**, also renowned for its restaurant and gardens, one is able to visit the workshops and retail area.

- **La Mare Vineyards**, close to **Devil's Hole**, has vineyards set in the grounds of an 18th-century farmhouse. Enjoy displays from the local cider industry and homemade products are on sale.

- Go to **St Peter**, the home of the 24-lane **Jersey Bowl** bowling centre, and the award-winning **Living Legend Village** attraction.

- At **La Hougue Bie** in **Grouville**, a museum housed in a massive neolithic tomb dating back 5000 years has exhibitions on the agriculture, archaeology, geology and history of the island.

- Chill out in **Howard Davis Park** in **St Saviour**, an attractive public garden with many subtropical plants flourishing in the mild climate.

- In the **St Lawrence** parish, St Peter's Valley, remember the history of the island by paying a visit to the **Jersey War Tunnels**, an underground hospital, which contains displays of photographs and documents, and a collection of firearms, daggers and memorabilia from World War II. The tunnel complex was hewn out of the rock by forced labour during the occupation of Jersey by German Forces (website: www.jerseywartunnels.com).

Top Things To Do

- On the south side of the island, and on either side of St Helier, extensive beaches stretch 5km (3 miles) west around **St Aubin's Bay**, and east to **La Roque Point**. **Portelet**, a secluded sandy bay; **St Brelade's Bay**, regarded as one of the island's most beautiful beaches and popular for **windsurfing** and **water-skiing**; and **Beauport**, a small bay flanked by towering rocks of pink granite, are situated to the west of **St Aubin**. Both east and west seaboards are dominated by long, sweeping beaches - the **Royal Bay of Grouville** and **St Catherine's Bay** flanking the town of **Gorey** to the east, and the 8km- (5mile-) beach on **St Ouen's Bay**, which forms almost the entirety of the west coast. This area is particularly good for **surfers**. There are fewer beaches on the north coast, but **Plémont**, with its rock pools and caves, is particularly attractive. **Bouley Bay** is popular with sub-aqua enthusiasts and **anglers**; and **Rozel**, on the northeast coast, is a fishing harbour with an old fort and a small sandy beach.
Note: Bathers and fishermen should beware, however, as Jersey has some of the largest tidal movements in the world, with as much as 12m (40ft) between low and high tide, causing very strong currents.

- **Walk** or **cycle** round the island. The north has the highest land and the most rugged scenery, but gentler walks are possible inland and in the south. One suggested route follows the line of the old Jersey Railway – now a traffic-free public path – which runs from St Aubin to the lighthouse at Corbière on the island's southwestern tip. Jersey's network of 'Green Lanes', which have a 24kph (15mph) speed limit, are ideal for cyclists.

- Jersey has two 18-hole **golf** courses open to visitors who are members of a recognised golf club. Both courses are well-known throughout the golfing world: **La Moye** in St Brelade and **Royal Jersey** in Grouville (website: www.royaljersey.com); both courses require proof of handicap or membership. Golfers who do not belong to a club can play at the 18-hole **Les Mielles** or **Les Ormes** courses and either of the two 9-hole courses at **Wheatlands** or **Greve D'Azette**, where no handicap is needed. For further details, contact Jersey Tourism (see *Tourist Information*).

- Go on a **pottery, candle-making** or **leatherwork course**, which are very popular in Jersey.

TOURIST INFORMATION

Jersey Tourism
Liberation Square, St Helier, Jersey JE1 1BB, Channel Islands
Tel: (01534) 500 700 *or* 500 777 (general visitor enquiries) *or* 500 800 (brochure line) *or* 500 888 (accommodation reservations).
Website: www.jersey.com

Jersey Tourism (Trade Information Office) in the UK
7 Lower Grosvenor Place, London SW1W 0EN, UK
Tel: (020) 7233 7474.
Website: www.jersey.com

VisitBritain in the USA
551 Fifth Avenue, 7th Floor, Suite 701,
New York, NY 10176, USA
Tel: (1-800) 462 2748 (toll-free in the US only) *or* (212) 986 2266 (PR and trade enquiries only).
Website: www.jersey.com

Entertainment

FOOD & DRINK: Jersey has an excellent range of restaurants to cater for every taste. Seafood is very popular and a wide selection of home-grown produce is available; scallops, oysters, spider crabs and lobster are particularly good. Fresh seafood can be bought from the local fish market. Jersey cows are renowned for their rich and creamy milk. The island has an enviable reputation for good cuisine whether in small pubs, wine bars or high-class restaurants.
National specialities:
- *Bean crock* (dried beans with onions, herbs and pig trotters).
- *Fiottes* (balls of flour, sugar and eggs, cooked in milk).
- *La soupe d'anguilles* (conger eel soup).
- Cream tea (served with strawberries).
Licensing hours: Restaurants: 0900-2300; Pubs/bars: 1100-2300.
Tipping: In general, this follows UK practice.
SHOPPING: The island is a low-duty area and there is no VAT. As well as St Helier (where there are two covered markets), there are shopping areas such as Red Houses, St Brelade and Gorey, St Martin. Luxury items such as spirits, cigarettes, jewellery and perfumes are popular buys. Local products such as knitwear, pottery, woodcrafts and even flowers are good value. **Shopping hours**: Mon-Sat 0900-1730. The markets and some shops are closed on Thursday afternoons. During the summer months, many shops are open in the evenings.

Credit: ©Jersey Tourism

A B C D E F G H I J K L M N O P Q R S T **U** V W X Y Z

Business

- **GDP**: US$3.6 billion.
- **Main exports**: Foodstuff, textiles, light industrial and electrical goods.
- **Main imports**: Machinery and transport equipment, manufactured goods, foodstuff, mineral fuels and chemicals.
- **Main trade partners**: UK.

ECONOMY: Although agriculture is still important as a source of employment and prestige – Jersey cows are renowned throughout the world – offshore banking and tourism are the mainstays of the economy: the former because of the island's exemption from the UK tax system and the latter through continental influence and a benign climate. Finance and banking account for more than half of the GDP and are largely responsible for Jersey's unemployment rate of less than one per cent. New and highly regulated legislation designed to tighten up some of the less salubrious aspects of Jersey's financial environment should serve to strengthen its reputation in an era when offshore finance is coming under growing political pressure through its implication in money-laundering. In the last few years, Jersey has signed up to several international initiatives designed to tackle the problem while improving financial transparency.

BUSINESS ETIQUETTE: Businesspeople are generally expected to dress smartly (suits are usual apart from Fridays when office workers generally 'dress down'). Appointments should be made and the exchange of business cards is customary. A knowledge of English is essential. **Office hours**: Mon-Fri 0900/0930-1700/1730.

CONFERENCES/CONVENTIONS: Jersey plays host each year to a large number of conferences; the main period is from October to May.

COMMERCIAL INFORMATION

Jersey Chamber of Commerce
Chamber House, 25 Pier Road,
JE1 4HF St Helier, Jersey
Tel: (01534) 871 031 or 724 536.
Website: www.jerseychamber.com

Jersey Conference Bureau
Liberation Square, JE1 1BB St Helier, Jersey
Tel: (01534) 733 449.
Website: www.jerseyconferences.co.uk

Sark and Herm

Location: English Channel.

Time: GMT (GMT + 1 from last Sunday in March to last Saturday in October).

Overview

Sark is a feudal state ruled by a *Seigneur*, who is also a member of the autonomous Parliament called the Chief Pleas. The island's countryside is characterised by its granite cliffs topped with flowered fields known as *cotils*. Whilst only 5km (3 miles) long, and 2.5km (1.5 miles) wide, it boasts 65km (40 miles) of picturesque coastlines. There are no cars, giving Sark an enchantment which is quite unique. After World War II, Herm was left derelict and abandoned until the Guernsey authorities bought it from the Crown for an undisclosed fee. Today, Herm is privately leased, and run as a resort island. It relies heavily on visitors coming to the island via Guernsey. Herm Island is a destination for day visitors from other Channel Islands, as well as a favourite with 'locals' from Guernsey, Jersey, Alderney and Sark. It offers unspoilt beaches and a safe, clean pollution free environment. There are no cars, no crowds and definitely no stress. Herm is the perfect place to stay for a truly relaxing island holiday, offering peace, comfort, natural beauty and relaxation.

General Information

For information on electricity, religion, duty free, public holidays, health, entertainment and business, see the *Guernsey* section.
AREA: Sark: 5.5 sq km (2.1 sq miles). **Herm:** 2 sq km (0.8 sq miles).
POPULATION: Sark: 600 (2005 estimate). **Herm:** 97 (2001, including Jethou).

POPULATION DENSITY: Sark: 109 per sq km. **Herm:** 48.5 per sq km.
GEOGRAPHY: Sark is a 45-minute boat journey east of Guernsey. It is almost two islands, the two parts being joined by a narrow isthmus known as *La Coupée*. The island is a plateau, with a collection of animals and plants unique to Sark. In the spring and autumn, the island becomes home to an unusual selection of migratory birds. The main village is situated at La Collinette. The coastline is rugged, with many cliffs and caves. **Herm** lies between Guernsey and Sark. It has lush and varied scenery, with meadows, unusual wild flowers and steep cliffs overlooking secluded coves and pounding surf.
GOVERNMENT: Dependencies of the British Crown with considerable internal autonomy.
Sark has a hierarchical system. The island of Sark is a personal *fief* held by the Seigneur direct from the British Crown. Below him is the island's Parliament, the Chief Pleas, with the right to a suspensory veto on its ordinances. The *Seigneur* appoints a Seneschal of Sark (subject to the approval of the Lieutenant-Governor of Guernsey) who is President of the Chief Pleas and Chairman of Sark's local Court of Justice, the Seneschal's Court. The present *Seigneur* is Michael Beaumont and the Seneschal (or President of the Chief Pleas) is Lt-Col R J Guille. Guernsey leases the island of Herm to Adrian and Pennie Heyworth, who are under contract as tenants to be responsible for certain administrative duties on the island.
Head of State: HM Queen Elizabeth II. **Head of Government:** Seigneur Michael Beaumont (Sark).
LANGUAGE: Local *patois*, a type of old Norman French, and English.

Climate

These islands enjoy a temperate climate with warm summers and milder winter temperatures than those experienced in the UK.

Communications

Telephone: Sark and Herm are connected to the UK STD telephone network; area code: 01481.
Mobile telephone: Roaming agreements exist with most international mobile phone companies. Coverage is excellent.
Internet: There is an Internet cafe on Sark.
Post: There is a post office on Sark.
MEDIA: See *Guernsey* section for more information.

Passport/Visa

See main *United Kingdom* section.

Money

Currency: Both Sark and Herm use Sterling as currency. UK mainland banks can be found on Sark.

Duty Free

For information on *Duty Free*, *Public Holidays*, *Health*, *Entertainment* and *Business*, see the *United Kingdom* section.

Travel - International

SEA:

Sark can be reached by sea from Guernsey and Jersey. Herm can be reached from Guernsey.
Sark: The main harbour is at *Maseline*. All visitors arriving from the UK must transfer at Guernsey. Sailings from the UK are with *Condor Ferries* (tel: (0870) 243 5140; website: www.condorferries.co.uk) departing from *Poole*, *Portsmouth* or *Weymouth*. Condor Ferries also operates sailings from France to Guernsey departing from *Saint Malo*. The *Isle of Sark Shipping Company* (tel: (01481) 832 450; website: http://sarkshipping.guernsey.net) runs daily services between Guernsey and Sark in summer (travel time – 45 to 50 minutes), with a more limited service in winter. *Manches Iles Express* runs a service from Jersey to Sark (website: www.manche-iles-express.com).
Herm: There is a ferry service daily between Guernsey and Herm (travel time – 20 minutes). Ferries leave every 30 minutes from Guernsey to Herm and faster catamarans can be chartered. Carriers include: *Herm Seaway Express* (tel: (01481) 724 161), *Herm Travel Trident* (tel: (01481) 721 379) and *Island RIB Voyages* (tel: (01481 713031; website: www.islandribvoyages.com).
ROAD:

No cars are allowed on either island. The Sark 'taxi' is a horse-drawn carriage which takes visitors around the island. Bicycles can also be hired on Sark. Herm has only a few essential tractors and an emergency 4-wheel drive vehicle.
Note: There is a landing tax for all visitors to Sark.

Accommodation

There are several hotels, many guest houses and self-catering cottages and apartments on Sark. Herm has one hotel, the *White House Hotel*, which has a tennis court, croquet lawn and outdoor swimming pool, and several self-catering cottages. There is also a campsite, the *Seagull* campsite, at the top of the island. For further information, contact the Sark Tourism Office or Herm Island Administration Office (see *Top Things To See & Do* section).

Top Things To See & Do

- **Sark Island** stands high out of the sea and its jagged coast and rocky cliffs occasionally harbour small sandy beaches where **swimming** is possible, notably at **Dixcart Bay**. Enjoy the island's rock pools, including the **Venus Pool** (a 6.1m (20ft) tidal pool) and **Adonis Pool**; most of which are only accessible at low tide. **Herm Island** has long sandy beaches on its northern shore which are suitable for swimming and **snorkelling**. **Diving** is also available (a certificate to show proof of qualification is normally required).
- **Sailing:** The islands of Sark and Herm both welcome visiting yachts and boats, though permission should be obtained from the harbour administration offices. Herm Harbour charges no fee for mooring. For details, contact Herm Island Administration Office (see *Tourist Information*).
- Sark and Herm are car-free islands, with the exception of a few farm tractors, which makes **walking** around them all the more pleasant. The islands offer numerous scenic walks along the cliffs, and a guide with pathways can be obtained from the tourist offices. It is possible to walk around Herm in less than two hours.

Credit: ©VisitGuernsey

- The islands are a treat for **birdwatchers**.
- **Creux Harbour** on Sark is tiny but picturesque – boat passengers come ashore through cliff-cut tunnels.
- At the northernmost point of the Sark lies the **Bec du Nez** or 'Oystercatcher's Rock'– a stretch of rock that juts out to sea, commanding a breathtaking view.
- At low tide, it is possible to take a boat trip around the coastline of Sark to visit caves including the **Boutique Caves** - according to legend, a past haunt of smugglers.
- A popular attraction for visitors in Sark are the gardens of **La Seigneurie**, which has been the home of Sark's *Seigneurs* since 1730. It has a large Victorian watchtower and is one of the best formal gardens in the Channel Islands.
- Other attractions in Sark include the 19th-century **windowless prison** (still occasionally used to keep disorderly drunkards for a night or two); **Le Manoir** (an 18th-century manor house built by the first Seigneur of Sark); and the ancient **windmill**, standing at the highest point in the Channel Islands.
- Cross **La Coupée**, a very high isthmus (79.2m/260ft above sea level) carrying a narrow road above the sea, which links Sark with **Little Sark**. Before it gained railings, people used to cross it on their hands and knees when there were high winds; even now, cyclists and horse carriage passengers must dismount.
- Attractions on **Herm** include a **Tom Thumb village** restored from derelict houses, a restored chapel, woods, caves, swimming in rock pools and the **shell beach** – covered by countless shells deposited by the Gulf Stream, some from as far away as Mexico.
- **The Mermaid Tavern** is Herm's only pub and the island's social hub.

TOURIST INFORMATION

Sark Tourism Office
Harbour Hill, Sark, GY9 0SB, Channel Islands
Tel: (01481) 832 345.
Website: www.sark.info

Herm Island Administration Office
Herm Island via Guernsey, GY1 3HR, Channel Islands
Tel: (01481) 722 377.
Website: www.herm-island.com

United States of America

Location: North America.

Time: The USA is divided into six time zones:
Eastern Standard Time: GMT - 5 (GMT - 4 from first Sunday in April to last Sunday in October). **Central Standard Time:** GMT - 6 (GMT - 5 from first Sunday in April to last Sunday in October). **Mountain Standard Time:** GMT - 7 (GMT - 6 from first Sunday in April to last Sunday in October).
Pacific Standard Time: GMT - 8 (GMT - 7 from first Sunday in April to last Sunday in October). **Alaska:** GMT - 9 (GMT - 8 from first Sunday in April to last Sunday in October).
Hawaii: GMT - 10.
When calculating travel times, bear in mind the adoption of *Daylight Saving Time (DST)* by most States in summer. From the first Sunday in April to the last Sunday in October, clocks are put forward one hour, changing at 0200 hours local time. Regions not observing *DST* include most of Indiana, all of Arizona and Hawaii.

Overview

Mickey Mouse, Miami Vice, Sleepless in Seattle... thanks to cinema and TV we all have impressions of the United States of America. Yet nothing can prepare you for your first glimpse of Manhattan's unforgettable skyline, your first ride in a yellow cab, the ubiquitous hamburger joints, the vast expanses of prairie, the sweet strains of New Orleans jazz or the neon-lit excesses of Las Vegas.

The USA is a huge country to explore, with 50 states to choose from, flanked by two oceans and covering an incredibly varied terrain. For five centuries, since the 'New World' discoveries of Christopher Columbus, people from every corner of the globe have come here in search of 'the American Dream'. Between them, they have created the richest, most powerful country on earth, and a fascinating melting pot of cultures and traditions.

Before the arrival of Christopher Columbus in North America in 1492, the continent was inhabited by peoples thought to have been descended from nomadic Mongolian tribes who had travelled across the Barents Sea. The first wave of European settlers, mainly English, French and Dutch, crossed the Atlantic in the 17th century and colonised the Eastern Seaboard. The restrictions on political rights and the punitive taxation which the British Government imposed on the American colonists led to the American War of Independence (1775–1783), with the Declaration of Independence being signed in 1776. The outcome was a humiliating defeat for the English King, George III. The American Constitution born of this victory has been imitated by many other countries. By 1853, the boundaries of the United States were, with the exception of Alaska and Hawaii, as they are today. Economic activity in the southern States centred on plantation agriculture dependent on slavery. Attempts by liberally inclined Republicans, led by Abraham Lincoln, to end slavery were fiercely opposed. The election of Lincoln to the Presidency in 1861 precipitated a political crisis in which seven southern States (joined later by three others) seceded from the Union, leading to the American Civil War. The more powerful and better equipped Union forces prevailed over the rebel Confederacy after four years of fighting. After the war, the country entered a period of consolidation, building up an industrial economy and settling the vast interior region of America known as the Midwest.

The terrorist attacks on the World Trade Centre and the Pentagon on 11 September 2001, which claimed over 3000 lives, made for a defining moment in American history. The impact on the American people and its body politic was immense. The country demanded action, and President George W Bush immediately despatched a substantial force to tackle and destroy the perpetrators: the al-Qaeda movement headed by Osama bin Laden and its hosts, the Taleban regime in Afghanistan. The Taleban were brought down within weeks. Some senior al-Qaeda personnel were captured, including Kahlid Sheikh Mohammed, the alleged organiser of '9/11', but others, including Bin Laden himself, eluded capture. The Bush administration now turned its sights upon the Iraqi regime of Saddam Hussein. With support from Britain and others, the Americans sought to use Saddam's possession of 'weapons of mass destruction' – a phrase encompassing nuclear, chemical and biological armaments – to justify an invasion of Iraq. This was completed in March 2003 after three weeks of fighting. However, no 'weapons of mass destruction' have been found, a fact which has since caused some political embarrassment for Bush and his allies. The Iraq campaign was an undoubted military success. Most of the leading figures from Iraq's brutal Ba'athist regime were captured, including Saddam Hussein himself, or killed. But American and allied forces have since been confronted with a dogged insurgency which, using paramilitary tactics, has claimed hundreds of soldiers' lives and continues to destabilise efforts to rebuild Iraq according to the American blueprint.

More recently, the country suffered from major changes in the weather patterns. In August 2005, Hurricane Katrina caused widespread damage in the states of Florida, Louisiana, Mississippi and Alabama. Communications and the transport infrastructure were badly affected. There were a number of casualties. Some infrastructure damages are still being repaired but most tourist parts of the states are now ready for visitors.

General Information

Information on the USA is provided in two parts: a general overview and individual State profiles, each of which has its own section.
AREA: 9,809,155 sq km (3,787,319 sq miles).
POPULATION: 296 million (official estimate 2005).
POPULATION DENSITY: 32.5 per sq km.
CAPITAL: Washington, DC. **Population:** 550,521 (official estimate 2005). 20 other cities have a population larger than that of Washington, DC. New York is the largest city, with a population of over 8 million. Chicago, Dallas, Houston, Los Angeles, Philadelphia, Phoenix, San Antonio and San Diego, had populations of over 1 million in 2000.
GEOGRAPHY: Covering a large part of the North American continent, the USA shares borders with Canada to the north and Mexico to the south and has coasts on the Atlantic, Pacific and Arctic oceans, the Caribbean Sea and the Gulf of Mexico. The State of Alaska, in the northwest corner of the continent, is separated from the rest of the country by Canada, and Hawaii lies in the central Pacific Ocean. The third-largest country in the world (after the Russian Federation and Canada), the USA has an enormous diversity of geographical features. The climate ranges from subtropical to Arctic, with a corresponding breadth of flora and fauna. For a more detailed description of each region's geographical characteristics, see the individual State sections.
GOVERNMENT: Federal Republic since 1789. Gained independence from the UK in 1776. The USA is a Federal Republic with 50 States and the District of Columbia (as in 'Washington, DC'), which lies between Maryland and Virginia. The Constitution (the final arbiters of which are the members of the Supreme Court) ensures that the powers of the executive, legislature, judiciary, presidency and the individual states are balanced by constitutional procedures.

The President is elected by an electoral college system, based on universal adult suffrage, every four years. No president may be elected to serve more than two full terms of office. The legislature is bicameral; the Senate has two members from each state while the larger House of Representatives allocates seats on the basis of population. Collectively these two bodies are known as Congress. Each state enjoys a fairly high degree of self-government. **Head of State and Government:** President George W Bush since 2001.
Recent history: Conditions in Iraq, and national security generally, are a major issue for Bush junior, who secured a second term at the Presidential election in November 2004. Republics tightened their grip on the Senate, kept control of the House of Representatives, and also presided over the possibility of further changes in the Supreme Court. It seems that Americans were keen to preserve stability in the White House whilst their nation remained in the midst of its 'War on Terror'. It remains to be seen how Bush junior will act in such a 'War' while in his final term as President - and, also, how the President will respond to domestic affairs and criticism of his persistent snubbing of environmental concerns, which culminated in him refusing to sign the Kyoto Protocol on greenhouse emissions.
LANGUAGE: English, with significant Spanish-speaking minorities.
RELIGION: Protestant majority with Roman Catholic, Jewish and many ethnic minorities.
ELECTRICITY: 110 volts AC, 60Hz. Plugs are of the flat two-pin type. European electrical appliances not fitted with dual-voltage capabilities will require a plug adaptor, which is best purchased before arrival in the USA. The television system is NTSC I/II and is not compatible with the PAL and SECAM systems used in Asia and Europe, although cassettes can be converted.
SOCIAL CONVENTIONS: The wide variety of national origins and the USA's relatively short history has resulted in numerous cultural and traditional customs living alongside each other. In large cities, people of the same ethnic background often live within defined communities. Shaking hands is the usual form of greeting. A relaxed and informal atmosphere is usually the norm. As long as the fundamental rules of courtesy are observed, there need be no fear of offending anyone of any background. Americans are renowned for their openness and friendliness to visitors. Gifts are appreciated if one is invited to a private home. As a rule, dress is casual. Smart restaurants, hotels and clubs insist on suits and ties or long dresses. Smoking is becoming increasingly unpopular in the US and is often considered offensive; it is essential to ask permission from all present before lighting up. Smoking is forbidden on city transport

and often restricted or forbidden in public buildings. There will usually be a notice where no smoking is requested and most restaurants have smoking and non-smoking sections. Smoking is banned in all restaurants in California and New York City.

Climate

See the individual State sections.

Communications

Telephone: Full IDD is available. Country code: 1. For emergency police, fire or medical services in major cities, dial 911. The following area codes denote toll-free (freephone) numbers: 800, 855, 866, 877 and 888. Telephone numbers with the prefix 900 are usually expensive.

Mobile telephone: Most foreign mobile telephones, unless tri-band, do not work in the USA and charges are high. Most visitors choose to hire a mobile telephone.

Internet: There are Internet cafes in most urban areas. Many of the international airports offer Internet access too.

Post: There are numerous post offices throughout the States. Stamps can also be bought at stamp machines in hotels and shops and at ATMs, at an extra cost. Airmail to Europe takes up to one week. Post office hours: Mon-Fri 0900-1700 (24 hours at main offices in larger cities).

MEDIA: Press: The most influential papers are the *Los Angeles Times*, *The New York Times*, *The Wall Street Journal*, *USA Today*, and the *Washington Post*. Owing to the high degree of self-government of each State, newspapers tend to be region specific, although recent economic pressures have resulted in large-scale mergers. Even so, the USA publishes more newspapers than any other country, and has perhaps the bulkiest Sunday newspapers in the world, particularly the Sunday edition of *The New York Times*.

TV: The top television networks are *ABC* (*American Broadcasting Corp*), *CBS* (*Columbia Broadcasting System*), *CNN* (*Cable News Network*), *FOX* (*Fox Television Network*), and *NBC* (*National Broadcasting Corp*).

Radio: Among the national radio networks are *ABC Radio Networks*, *American Radio Network* (operated by *CBS*), *National Public Radio* and *Westwood One* (operated by *CBS*).

Passport/Visa

	Passport Required?	Visa Required?	Return Ticket Required?
Full British	Yes	No/2/3	Yes
Australian	Yes	No/2	Yes
Canadian	Yes	No/1	No
USA	N/A	N/A	N/A
Other EU	Yes	No/2	Yes
Japanese	Yes	No/2	Yes

Note: *Regulations and requirements may be subject to change at short notice, and you are advised to contact the appropriate diplomatic or consular authority before finalising travel arrangements. Any numbers in the chart refer to the footnotes below.*

Restricted entry: The following are not eligible to receive a USA entry visa:
(a) people afflicted with certain serious communicable diseases or disorders deemed threatening to the property, safety or welfare of others;
(b) anyone who has been arrested (except for very minor driving offences) or who has a criminal record;
(c) narcotics addicts or abusers and drug traffickers;
(d) anyone who has been deported from or denied admission to the USA.

Note: Those who are ineligible may be eligible for a waiver of ineligibility.

PASSPORTS: Valid passport required by all; validity varies - for most countries it is required for the duration of the stay; check with the Embassy (see *Passport/Visa Information*).

New Requirements for Travellers: The US Intelligence Reform and Terrorism Prevention Act of 2004 requires that by January 1,2008, travellers to and from the Caribbean, Bermuda, Panama, Mexico and Canada have a passport or other secure, accepted document to enter or re-enter the United States. In order to facilitate the implementation of this requirement, the Administration is proposing to complete it in phases following a proposed timeline, which will be published in the Federal Register in the near future. This is a change from prior travel requirements and will affect all United States citizens entering the United States from countries within the Western Hemisphere who do not currently possess valid passports. This new requirement will also affect certain foreign nationals who currently are not required to present a passport to travel to the United States. Most Canadian citizens, citizens of the British Overseas Territory of Bermuda, and to a lesser degree, Mexican

citizens will be affected by the implementation of this requirement.
For further details about the Western Hemisphere Travel Initiative, visit the website of the US Department of State: http://travel.state.gov/travel/cbpmc/cbpmc_2223.html).

Note: (a) For nationals included in the Visa Waiver Program (see below), passports must be valid for at least 90 days from date of entry (except for nationals of Andorra, Brunei and San Marino, who must hold passports valid for at least six months beyond the intended date of departure from the USA).
(b) All travellers entering the USA under the Visa Waiver Program now require individual machine-readable passports. Children included on a parent's passport also now require their own machine-readable passport. Travellers not in possession of machine-readable passports will require a valid USA entry visa.
(c) Passports issued on or after 26 October 2005 need to have a biometric identifier in order for the holder to travel visa free under the Visa Waiver Program (VWP). Machine-readable passports issued between 26 October 2005 and 25 October 2006 require a digital photograph printed on the data page or an integrated chip with information from the data page. Machine-readable passports issued on or after 26 October 2006 require an integrated chip with information from the data page (e-passport).

VISAS: Required by all except the following:
(a) citizens of countries under the Visa Waiver Program (see **2.** below);
(b) **1.** nationals of Bermuda and Canada, provided holding valid passports;
(c) nationals of Mexico, provided holding a valid passport and a US Border Crossing Card.

Note: (a) Landed Immigrants of Canada and British residents of Bermuda who are citizens of, and have valid passports from, Commonwealth countries or Ireland are no longer eligible to enter the USA without a visa. (b) The Transit Without Visa (TWOV) and International-to-International (ITI) transit programs have been indefinitely suspended as of 2 August 2003. All passengers using US airports for transit purposes are now required to obtain a transit visa. This does not affect qualified travellers travelling visa free under the Visa Waiver Program (see below).

Visa Waiver Program: (a) **2.** The following nationals, upon presentation of a valid passport (see **Note** above), do not require a visa under the Visa Waiver Program: Andorra, Australia, Brunei, EU countries (except nationals of Cyprus, Czech Republic, Estonia, Greece, Hungary, Latvia, Lithuania, Malta, Poland and Slovak Republic, who *do* require a visa), Iceland, Japan, Liechtenstein, Monaco, New Zealand, Norway, San Marino, Singapore and Switzerland.
To qualify for visa-free travel under the Visa Waiver Program, nationals must travel on a valid passport (see **Note** above), for holiday, transit or business purposes only and for a stay not exceeding 90 days.
If entering the USA by air or sea, passengers must hold a return or onward ticket or itinerary (if onward tickets terminate in Bermuda, Canada, Mexico or the Caribbean Islands, travellers must be legal permanent residents of those countries), hold a completed form I-94W and enter aboard an air or sea carrier participating in the Visa Waiver Program (lists of participating air or sea carriers are available from most travel agents or the carriers themselves).
If entering the USA by land from Canada or Mexico, hold a completed form I-94W* issued by Immigration at the port of entry and a US$6 fee (only payable in US Dollars).

Note*: (a) Passengers must have the full address and ZIP code of where they are staying in the USA to be able to fully complete the I-94W form. (b) Members of Visa Waiver Program countries who want to work, study or remain more than 90 days in the USA must apply for a visa before travelling, as should those who have been previously refused a visa, have a criminal record, or are in any way ineligible for an unrestricted visa. (c) **3.** Holders of UK passports with the endorsement British Subject, British Dependent Territories Citizen, British Protected Person, British Overseas Citizen or British National (Overseas) Citizen do not qualify for the Visa Waiver Program. Persons unsure about visa requirements (including those defined in 'Restricted Entry' above) should contact the US Consulate General *or* the Visa Department of the US Embassy (see *Passport/Visa Information*).

Types of visa and cost: *Tourist, Business, Transit* and *Student.* Other types of visa are also available, contact the US Embassy (website: www.usembassy.org.uk) for further details. The visa application fee is US$100 (currently equivalent to £63), regardless of whether the visa is issued or denied and regardless of the duration of the visa or entries required. The Embassy will provide a paying-in slip, which is attached to the application form DS-156. The fee must be paid in cash at a bank prior to submitting a visa application to the US Embassy, and the bank will issue a receipt of payment, which must be attached to the application form. The fee receipt, once paid, is valid for one

year. Some nationals may also have to pay a reciprocal visa issuance fee – details are available from the State Department (website: www.travel.state.gov).

Validity: Visas may be used for travel to the USA until the date it expires, or, if marked 'valid indefinitely', for up to 10 years. Some visas are valid for multiple entries. The length of stay in the USA is determined by US immigration officials at the time of entry but is generally six months; there is, however, no set time.

Note: (a) The Embassy no longer issues visas valid indefinitely. Any new B-1/B-2 visa issued will be valid for a maximum of 10 years. (b) A visa does not expire with the expiry of the holder's passport. An unexpired, endorsed visa in an expired passport may be presented for entry into the USA, as long as the visa itself has not been cancelled, is undamaged, is less than 10 years old and is presented with a valid non-expired passport, provided that both passports are for the same nationality.

Application to: Visa branches at Consulates General. Those residing in England, Scotland or Wales should apply to the Embassy in London (see *Passport/Visa Information*).

Application requirements: (a) Completed visa application form DS-156 and form DS-157, if required. (b) Valid passport (validity dependant upon nationality) and with at least one blank page. (c) One recent passport-size photo. (d) Embassy copy of the fee receipt endorsed by the bank. (e) Evidence of sufficient funds to cover all expenses while in the USA. (f) Documentation of intent to return to country of residence. (g) Supporting documents (such as purpose of visit) and/or issuance fees, where relevant. (h) Stamped self-addressed, special delivery envelope, for return by post. Business: (a)-(h) and, (i) Evidence of intended business activities in the USA, such as a letter from their employer.

Important Note: All applicants aged 14 to 79 are required to schedule an appointment for an interview (tel: (09055) 444 546; Mon-Fri 0900-1600). Applicants under the age of 14 and those 80 and over may be eligible to apply for a visa by mail. Also note *Restricted Entry*.

Note: Additional processing requirements and information are required for: (a) males aged 16-45; (b) nationals of Cuba, Iran, Korea (Dem Rep), Libya, Sudan and the Syrian Arab Republic. (c) nationals of China (PR), Northen Cyprus, the Russian Federation, Somalia and Vietnam. Please note that requirements are subject to change at short notice and any applicant should check with the US Embassy (website: www.usembassy.org.uk).

Working days required: Varies with each embassy; interview appointment waiting time is usually 25 to 30 days (27 days for London Embassy), and visa processing time is usually five to seven working days (three days for London Embassy). It is important to allow sufficient time for processing the visa, and final travel plans should not be made until a visa has been issued. Applications lodged during the peak travel season may take longer.

Temporary residence: The law in the USA is complex for those wishing to take up residence. More information may be obtained from the Embassy (see *Passport/Visa Information*).

PASSPORT/VISA INFORMATION

Embassy of the United States of America in the UK
24 Grosvenor Square, London W1A 1AE, UK
Tel: (020) 7499 9000.
Website: www.usembassy.org.uk
Opening hours: Mon–Fri 0830-1730.
Consulates in: Belfast and Edinburgh.

American Embassy in the UK - Visa Services
Tel: (09068) 200 290 (24-hour visa information line; calls cost 60p per minute, UK only; identical information is available on the embassy website at no cost) *or* (09055) 444 546 (operator-assisted visa information)

Money

Currency: US Dollar (US$) = 100 cents. Notes are in denominations of US$100, 50, 20, 10, 5, 2 and 1. Coins are in denominations of US$1, and 50, 25, 10, 5 and 1 cents.

Currency exchange: Hotels do not, as a rule, exchange currency and only a few major banks will exchange foreign currency, so it is advisable to arrive with US Dollars.

Credit & debit cards: Most major credit cards are accepted throughout the USA, including American Express, Diners Club, MasterCard and Visa. Check with your credit or debit card company for details of merchant acceptability and other services that may be available. Visitors are advised to carry at least one major credit card, as it is common to request prepayment or a credit card imprint for hotel rooms and car hire, even when final payment is not by credit card.

Traveller's cheques: Widely accepted in hotels, stores and restaurants, provided they are US Dollar cheques; Sterling traveller's cheques are not acceptable and few banks will

change these. Change is issued in US Dollars. It should be noted that many banks do not have the facility to cash traveller's cheques (the US banking system differs greatly from that of the UK) and those that do are likely to charge a high commission. One or (in some cases) two items of identification (passport, credit card, driving licence) may also be required. To avoid additional exchange rate charges, travellers are advised to take traveller's cheques in US Dollars.
Currency restrictions: There are no limits on the import or export of either foreign or local currency. However, amounts in excess of US$10,000 or the equivalent (including foreign currency, traveller's cheques, money orders and 'bearer bonds') must be registered with US Customs on Form 4790. Failure to do so may result in civil and criminal prosecution, including seizure of the money. There is an embargo on transactions of US currency with Cuba, Iran, Iraq, Libya and Korea (Democratic People's Republic of).
Banking hours: Variable, but generally Mon-Fri 0900-1500.
Exchange rate indicators:
Rate at time of publishing
£1.00= US$1.74

Duty Free

The following goods may be imported by visitors over 21 years of age into the USA without incurring customs duty: *200 cigarettes or 50 cigars or 2kg of smoking tobacco or proportionate amounts of each; 0.95l (1qt) of alcoholic beverage; gifts or articles up to a value of US$100.*
Note: (a) Items should not be gift-wrapped, as they must be available for customs inspection. (b) The alcoholic beverage allowance (see above) is the national maximum; certain States allow less and if arriving in those States, the excess will be taxed or withheld. (c) For information about the importation of pets, refer to the brochure *Pets, Wildlife – US Customs*, available at US Embassies and Consulates. (d) Further information on US customs regulations is available online (website: www.customs.ustreas.gov).
Prohibited and restricted items: The following are either banned or may only be imported under licence:
(a) Narcotics and dangerous drugs, unless for medical purposes (doctor's certificate required). (b) Absinthe, biological materials, some seeds, fruits and plants (including endangered species of plants and vegetables and their products). (c) Firearms and ammunition (with some exceptions – consult Customs' website). (d) Hazardous articles (fireworks, toxic materials), including matches and match books (unless packed tightly in a closed container). (e) Meat and poultry products – fresh, dried or canned. (f) Any fish (unless certified as disease free) or their eggs, unless canned, pickled or smoked. (g) Dairy products and eggs. (h) Cuban cigars, brought from any country. (i) Wildlife and endangered species, including crustaceans, molluscs, eggs, game and hunting trophies and crafted articles of any part thereof. (j) Dog and cat fur. (k) Some art and artefacts (such as Pre-Columbian monumental and architectural sculpture and murals from South America). (l) Imports from Iran and leather souvenirs from Haiti (eg drums). (m) Some automobiles. (n) More than one article (limited to once every 30 days) displaying a counterfeit or confusingly similar logo to trademarked and copyrighted articles. (o) Merchandise from embargoed countries: Afghanistan, Cuba, Iran, Iraq, Libya, Serbia & Montenegro and Sudan; information materials (pamphlets, books, tapes, films and recordings) are permitted, except from Iraq.
Note: Gold coins, medals and bullion, formerly prohibited, may be brought into the USA, except from embargoed countries (see above).

Public Holidays

Below are listed Public Holidays for the January 2006-June 2007 period.
2006: Jan 2 New Year's Day. **Jan 16** Martin Luther King Day. **Feb 20** Presidents' Day. **May 29** Memorial Day. **Jul 4** Independence Day. **Sep 4** Labor Day. **Oct 9** Columbus Day. **Nov 10** Veterans' Day. **Nov 23** Thanksgiving Day. **Dec 25** Christmas Day.
2007: Jan 1 New Year's Day. **Jan 15** Martin Luther King Day. **Feb 19** Presidents' Day. **May 28** Memorial Day.

Health

	Special Precautions?	Certificate Required?
Yellow Fever	No	No
Cholera	No	No
Typhoid & Polio	No	N/A
Malaria	No	N/A

Note: *Regulations and requirements may be subject to change at short notice, and you are advised to contact your doctor well in advance of your intended date of departure. Any numbers in the chart refer to the footnotes below.*

Credit: ©New York State Division of Tourism

Other risks: *Rabies* may be present in wildlife. For those at high risk, vaccination before arrival should be considered. If you are bitten, seek medical advice without delay. For more information, consult the *Health* appendix.
Health care: Medical insurance providing cover up to at least US$500,000 is strongly advised. Only emergency cases are treated without prior payment and treatment will often be refused without evidence of insurance or a deposit. All receipts must be kept in order to make a claim. Medical facilities are generally of an extremely high standard. Many medications available over the counter in other countries require a prescription in the US. Those visiting the USA for long periods with school-age children should be aware that school entry requirements include proof of immunisation against *diphtheria*, *measles*, *poliomyelitis* and *rubella* throughout the USA, and schools in many States also require immunisation against *tetanus*, *pertussis* and *mumps*. *HIV*-positive visitors must apply at the Embassy for a waiver of inadmissibility before entry.

Travel - International

AIR:
The principal US airlines operating international services are: *American Airlines (AA)* (website: www.aa.com), *Continental Airlines* (website: www.continental.com), *Delta Air* (website: www.delta.com), *Northwest Airlines* (website: www.nwa.com) and *United Airlines* (website: www.ual.com). Many other airlines operate services from all over the world to the USA.
Main airports: The busiest airports in the USA include *Hartsfield-Jackson Atlanta International (ATL)* (website: www.atlanta-airport.com), *Chicago O'Hare International (ORD)* (website: www.ohare.com/ohare/home/asp), *Los Angeles International (LAX)* (website: www.lawa.org/lax), *Dallas/Fort Worth International (DFW)* (website: www.dfwairport.com), and *Las Vegas McCarran International (LAS)* (website: www.mccarran.com). For further details, consult the individual State sections.
Approximate flight times: From *London* to Miami is nine hours 45 minutes, to New York is seven hours 50 minutes, to San Francisco is 11 hours 10 minutes, to Seattle is nine hours 50 minutes and to Washington DC is eight hours 25 minutes (all times are by non-stop flight).
Note: Return flights to Europe from the east coast of the USA take approximately 30 to 40 minutes less than outward westbound flights, and from the west coast of the USA approximately 60 minutes less. Visitors arriving in the USA via international airports may be subject to serious delays. A stringent new security system, which requires all visitors with visas to be photographed and fingerprinted upon entry, was put into operation in January 2004, as part of US anti-terrorism measures. Experts warn that this heightened state of alert could prevail for the next few years.
Departure tax: None.
SEA:
The top ports of call are *Port of Anchorage* (www.muni.org/port), *Honolulu*, State of Hawaii, Harbor Division (www.state.hi.us/dot/harbors), *Port of New Orleans* (www.portno.com), *New York*, The Port Authority on NY & NJ (www.panynj.gov/aviation.html), and *Tampa Port Authority* (www.tampaport.com). Numerous cruise lines sail from ports worldwide to both the east and west coasts; contact a travel agent for fares and details.
RAIL:
The US and Mexican rail networks connect at Yuma, El Paso and Del Rio, with limited scheduled passenger services. There are several connections with the Canadian network, including New York–Montréal, Chicago–Toronto and Seattle–Vancouver services. For further information, contact *Amtrak* (tel: (800) 872 7245 (toll-free in USA) *or* (212) 582 6875 (New York); website: www.amtrak.com). In the UK, contact *Leisurail* (tel: (0800) 698 7545 *or* (0870) 750 0222).
ROAD:
There are many crossing points from Canada to the USA. The major road routes are: New York to Montréal/ Ottawa, Detroit to Toronto/Hamilton, Minneapolis to Winnipeg and Seattle to Vancouver/Edmonton/Calgary. There are road links to Mexican destinations from El Paso, San Diego, Tucson and San Antonio. **Bus:** *Greyhound* offers services to many destinations in Canada and some destinations in Mexico (tel: (800) 231 2222 (toll-free in USA); website: www.greyhound.com).

Travel - Internal

AIR:
The USA may be crossed within five hours from east to west and within two hours from north to south. Strong competition between airlines has resulted in a wide difference between fares. Categories of fares include first-class, economy, excursion and discount. Night flights are generally cheaper.
Cheap fares: Money-saving schemes for overseas visitors include discounts on internal flights with the *Visit USA (VUSA) Airpass*, offered by the principal US airlines (often in conjunction with *British Airways*) and can be purchased in advance. (Delta offers a similar scheme branded as *Discover America*.) These passes are offered as a minimum of three and a maximum of 10 coupons entitling the passenger to that number of flights within the USA at a discounted fare; price is based on the number of flight segments. A number of restrictions usually apply, including: (a) the pass must be booked in conjunction with a round-trip flight to the USA (although this can, in some cases, be on a different carrier); (b) tickets must be purchased outside North America and are not available to US, Canadian and some Caribbean residents; (c) tickets must often be purchased before a specified time (eg 21 days in advance); (d) the traveller must utilise the first coupon within a specified time period (usually within 60 days of arrival in the USA) and use all the coupons within 180 days of arrival. Agents are advised to contact the offices of individual airlines once a basic itinerary has been organised, as terms may vary.
Note: Baggage allowance is often determined by number and size in addition to weight.
SEA/LAKE/RIVER:
There are extensive water communications both along the coastline and along the great rivers and lakes. The Ohio River carries more water traffic than any other inland waterway in the world. Tour ships and passenger and freight lines crisscross all the Great Lakes from ports in Duluth, Sault Sainte Marie, Milwaukee, Chicago, Detroit, Buffalo, Rochester, Cleveland and Toronto.
RAIL:
Nearly all the long-distance trains are operated by Amtrak, which serves more than 500 communities in 45 States over a 35,000km (22,000 mile) route system. Even so, rail is not considered the best or fastest way to travel within the USA, as trains can be slow and infrequent, as well as expensive. Some services, however, are popular and reliable. Services along the northeast corridor exist between Boston, New York and Washington. The 'Acela Express' high-speed rail service along the northeast corridor is capable of travelling up to 240kph (150mph), reducing the current three-hour trip between Washington, DC and New York by 30 minutes and the New York to Boston journey from four hours 30 minutes to three hours. Other routes from Washington, DC

Credit: ©Larry Geddis

run south to Miami and New Orleans, and from Boston, New York or Washington, DC to Chicago. From Chicago, daily services radiate to Seattle, Portland, Oakland, San Francisco, Los Angeles, New Orleans and San Antonio (via Fort Worth). Connections also exist between Los Angeles and San Diego, Los Angeles and San Francisco, San Francisco and Bakersfield, San Francisco and Seattle (via Portland), San Antonio and Oklahoma City, New Orleans and Atlanta, and Kansas City and St Louis, amongst others. A coast-to-coast train service is provided between Jacksonville and Los Angeles via Tucson, El Paso, San Antonio, Houston and New Orleans. Prices and timetables are subject to change without notice.

A variety of State and municipal bodies operate short-distance and commuter rail lines around various urban centres, many connected to stops on the Amtrak lines. Amtrak also operates a Thruway bus service, which connects to some cities and towns not on the Amtrak grid. A number of independent companies offer short routes, often in scenic locations, onboard vintage trains. These routes are often a good idea for travellers wishing to reach wilderness locations that are off the beaten track.

Amtrak contact details: For up-to-date information, contact Amtrak (tel: (800) 872 7245 (toll-free in USA); website: www.amtrak.com); in the UK, contact *Leisurail* (tel: (0800) 698 7545 or (0870) 750 0222). US travel agents can also obtain information on Amtrak train services, schedules and travel packages through the Western Folder Distribution Company Travel Information Network by entering their ARC number online (website: www.travelinfonetwork.com). **Facilities and services:** Nearly all trains have coach seating and air conditioning, with a variety of sleeping accommodation available for a supplemental charge. All long-distance trains have waiter-staffed, seated dining facilities. Cafe cars on shorter trips provide snacks and beverages that guests can take back to their seats.

Tour packages: Amtrak offers a variety of tour packages throughout the USA flexible to any budget. Full details are provided in the *Amtrak Travel Planner*, which is widely available. A great deal of the USA's beautiful scenery and historical sites can only be viewed by train. Passenger trains continue to attract a discerning and ever-increasing clientele. Indeed, rail travel in the USA – as in many other countries – has undergone a considerable revival in recent years, and the trend continues. It is therefore advisable for passengers to reserve well in advance, as some routes are often booked out.

Cheap fares: The *USA Rail Pass* is specifically designed for international travellers from outside the USA or Canada and offers 15 or 30 days of unlimited travel either on a national or regional basis.

The *National USA Rail Pass* offers travel on the whole Amtrak network in the USA and Canada (excluding Auto Train, Metroliner and Acela Express between Boston, New York and Washington). It costs US$440 (US$295 off-peak) per person for 15 days and US$550 (US$385 off-peak) for 30 days. The peak season is from 28 May to 1 September and off-peak fares are in effect for the remainder of the year. Children under 2 years of age travel free and those aged 2 to 15 pay half the adult fare.

The following *Regional USA Rail Passes* are also available: The *Northeast Rail Pass* is valid on trains from Newport News (Virginia) north to Boston (Massachusetts), Burlington (Vermont) and Montréal (Canada), west from Philadelphia to Harrisburg (both Pennsylvania), west from New York City to Niagara Falls (New York State), and all stations in between; the *East Rail Pass* covers the region east of Chicago (Illinois) and New Orleans (Louisiana) up to Montréal; the *West Rail Pass* covers the region west of Chicago to Seattle (Washington State), Portland (Oregon), San Francisco and Los Angeles (both California); the *Far West Rail Pass* covers the region from Denver (Colorado) to Seattle, San Francisco and Los Angeles; and the *Coastal Rail Pass* covers the west coast and from Seattle to San Diego (California). Prices for these passes vary between US$205 for the 15-day Northeast Rail Pass and US$405 for the 30-day West Rail Pass (with a 20 to 30 per cent reduction during off-peak season). The *Northeast Rail Pass* also provides the option of purchasing a 5-day pass for US$149 during the peak and off-peak seasons. Passes can be purchased prior to travel to the USA or at Amtrak stations, upon presentation of a valid passport issued outside Canada or the USA. Passports and passes must be presented for the issuance of rail tickets. The passes cover coach-class travel tickets and seat reservations on Amtrak passenger services. However, rail passes act as a form of payment for seats only – to guarantee a seat on a specific train, a reservation must be made well in advance; cancellation fees may apply. Travellers should contact Amtrak (tel: (800) 872 7245) to find out whether reservations are required on specific journeys they wish to make. For journeys where reservations are required, train times should be reconfirmed 24 hours prior to departure. Travellers planning to travel during peak times should make reservations well in advance. Further information on prices and timetables is available from Amtrak (for contact details, see above). A list of international sales representatives can be found online (website: www.amtrak.com/international/salesreps.html).

ROAD:

Driving is a marvellous way to see the USA, although the distances between cities can be enormous (eg 4716km (2930 miles) between San Francisco and New York City). A realistic evaluation of travel times should be made to avoid over-strenuous itineraries. Driving conditions are excellent and the road system reaches every town. Petrol (gas) is cheaper than in Europe. *AAA* (American Automobile Association; website: www.aaa.com) offers touring services, maps and travel advice to affiliate auto club members. Some *AAA* clubs offer referrals to companies for vehicle insurance policies, which are compulsory in all States, even for hire cars. *AAA* basic benefits are offered as a courtesy to affiliate auto club members who present their valid membership card (eg AA membership for the UK) while visiting in the USA. For further information, Americans should contact their local *AAA* club office (listed in the local telephone directory), while visitors to the USA should contact their own national association for information on the *AAA* before departure.

Bus: *Greyhound* is the main national coach carrier and covers the whole of the USA. This 24-hour service is supplemented by over 11,000 other tour lines, covering the country with reasonably priced and regular services. Some Greyhound services are available to Canada and Mexico. There are express bus services between major cities. Air conditioning, toilets and reclining seats are available on all buses. Meals are not provided, however, food and drink (non-alcoholic) may be consumed on board and there are regular meal stops on longer routes. Unlimited stopovers are allowed for unrestricted fares. Reservations are not accepted (although may be required if connecting to another carrier) and seating is on a first-come, first-served basis; passengers are advised to arrive at the terminal approximately one hour before the scheduled departure. For information on fares and schedules, contact *Greyhound* (tel: (800) 231 2222 (toll-free in USA) or (214) 849 8100 (international callers); website: www.greyhound.com).

Cheap fares: Greyhound offers a range of *Discovery Pass* programmes, valid for 4 to 60 days in the USA and/or Canada, which can be purchased by US, Canadian and overseas travellers. The *International Ameripass* is 10 to 15 per cent cheaper than the domestic version, but must be purchased outside the USA and Canada. The *Ameripass*, which gives seven, 10, 15, 21, 30, 45 or 60 days unlimited travel throughout the USA and some points within Mexico, costs US$229-609 for domestic purchasers (US$219-559 for international). A four-day pass is also available for US$165, but only to overseas visitors. Passes are validated at the ticket counter at the beginning of the trip and identification must be shown; individual tickets are not necessary. The pass is valid for a continuous period (depending on which pass is purchased) starting from validation. Unlimited stops are allowed.

Discounted fares are available for children aged 2 to 12 years, passengers over 62 years old and students enrolled in undergraduate or postgraduate study. A variety of regional discounts are also available.

For further details, contact *Greyhound* on one of their *Discovery Pass* numbers (tel: (888) 454 7277 (if purchased in the USA) *or* (888) 661 8747 (if purchased in Canada) *or* (402) 330 8552 or 330 8584 (if purchased overseas)).

Car hire: Major international companies have offices at all gateway airports and in most cities. There are excellent discounts available for foreign visitors. US$160 per week is an acceptable budget rate and drivers should make sure that free unlimited mileage is included. A drop-off charge will most likely be added if the car is deposited in a different city from the one in which it was hired. Credit-card deposits and inclusive rates are generally required. As a guide to car sizes, an 'Economy' or 'Compact' refers to a car the size of a standard European car, while a 'Standard' refers to a car nearly the size of a limousine. Minimum ages for hirers vary according to the rental company, pick-up point and method of payment. Agents are advised to contact the individual companies for information on drivers under 25 years of age.

Those looking to hire a car in the USA can save money through fly-drive deals and by booking a car in advance (obtaining written confirmation of the price is recommended).

Drive away: *Auto Driveaway* provides a service enabling the traveller to drive cars to and from a given point, only paying the price of petrol. A deposit is often required and time and mileage limits are set for delivery, which leaves very little time for sightseeing (there are heavy financial penalties for those who exceed the limits). Drivers should also check the car beforehand, so as not to incur any unnecessary repair costs. Some companies allow the driver to finish the journey in Canada. Details are published under *Automobile & Truck Transporting* in the US Yellow Pages. For further information, contact *Auto Driveaway* (tel: (312) 341 1900; website: www.autodriveaway.com).

Campers/motorhomes: The hire of self-drive campers or motorhomes, which are called 'recreational vehicles' or RVs in the USA, is easy and provides a good means of getting around. For more information contact *The Recreational Vehicle Dealers Association* (tel: (480) 464 7300; website: www.cruiseamerica.com).

Documentation and insurance: An International Driving Permit is recommended, although it is not legally required (it is often very useful as an additional proof of identity). A full national driving licence is accepted for up to one year. All travellers intending to hire or drive cars or motorhomes in the USA are strongly advised to ensure that the insurance policy covers their total requirements, covering all drivers and passengers against injury or accidental death. A yellow 'non-resident, interstate liability insurance card', which acts as evidence of financial responsibility, is available through motor insurance agents. Additional Collision Damage Waiver covering the car itself is also strongly recommended; in some states this extra insurance is included in hire rates by law.

Traffic regulations: Traffic drives on the right. The speed limit is usually 55mph (89kph) on motorways, but varies from State to State. Speed limits are clearly indicated along highways and are strictly enforced, with heavy fines imposed. Note that it is illegal to pass a school bus that has stopped to unload its passengers (using indicators and warning lights) and all vehicles must stop until the bus has moved back into the traffic stream. It is illegal for drivers not to have their licences immediately to hand. If stopped, do not attempt to pay a driving fine on the spot (unless it is demanded), as it may be interpreted as an attempt to bribe.

Note: There are extremely tough laws against drinking and driving throughout the USA. These laws are strictly enforced.

URBAN:

Some US cities now have good public transport services following a 'transit renaissance' after the energy crises of the 1970s. There are numerous underground train systems in operation in major cities including New York (subway), Washington, DC (metro), Boston ('T'), Chicago (train) and San Francisco (BART – Bay Area Rapid Transit); others are being planned or built. There are also several tramway and trolleybus systems, including the much-loved antique trams found in San Francisco.

Note: Many of the underground train systems are dangerous during off-peak hours (the New York subway, in particular, has acquired an almost gothic reputation for violence, although this has been much exaggerated), but they offer cheap, quick and efficient travel during the working day, particularly in New York, Boston and Chicago. Travel by any other means during the day is likely to be slow and arduous.

Travel Advice

Most visits to the USA are trouble-free but visitors should be aware of the global risk of indiscriminate international terrorist attacks, which could be against civilian targets, including places frequented by foreigners.

The US Government remains concerned about continued threats. Since the terrorist attacks on 11 September 2001, the US Government has issued a number of warnings of potential further terrorist attacks in the US. The US domestic threat level stands at "elevated" (yellow).

Visitors should expect stringent security checks at airports and public buildings.

Visitors should be alert to the dangers of car and street crime in cities.

This advice is based on information provided by the Foreign and Commonwealth Office in the UK. It is correct at time of publishing. As the situation can change rapidly, visitors are advised to contact the following organisations for the latest travel advice:

British Foreign and Commonwealth Office
Tel: (0845) 850 2829.
Website: www.fco.gov.uk

US Department of State
Website: http://travel.state.gov/travel

Accommodation

HOTELS/MOTELS:

There are many good traditional hotels. However, the majority are modern and part of national and international chains, often with standard prices. Motels are hotels situated along main roads, away from the city centre and towns. In general, the quality of accommodation is high, with facilities such as televisions and telephones in each room. Hotels expect payment in advance and reservations are held until around 1800, unless a late arrival is requested.
Grading: Basic categories fall into **Super, Deluxe, Standard, Moderate** and **Inexpensive**. Prices vary according to standards.
Pre-paid voucher schemes: Several companies offer a pre-paid voucher scheme for use at various hotel and motel chains throughout the USA.

BED & BREAKFAST:

This long established tradition in the UK is now spreading across the USA. B&B signs are not generally displayed by individual homes, but most homes offering this service are listed in directories, which may be purchased by interested travellers. 'B&B inns' have up to 20 or so rooms, and are distinguished from 'country inns' in that the latter offer meals in addition to breakfast.
RANCH HOLIDAYS: There are ranches all over the southern and western States offering riding, participation in cattle drives, and activity holidays in mountain and lakeland settings.

CAMPING/CARAVANNING:

This is extremely popular, especially in the Rocky Mountains and New England. The camping season in the north lasts from mid-May to mid-September; reservations are recommended if camping during the high season. Camping alongside highways and in undesignated areas is prohibited.
The 24,000-plus campsites fall into two general categories:
Public sites: Usually linked with National or State Parks and Forests, offering modest but comfortable facilities from US$10-22 per night. Most of them will have toilet blocks, electricity hook-ups and picnic areas. Campsites are usually operated on a first-come, first-served basis and will often restrict the length of stay. Advance reservations are possible at some national parks.
Privately run sites: These range from basic to resort luxury. Most have laundry and drying facilities, entertainment and information services. Reservations can be made through a central reservation office in the USA. Fees range from around US$20-40. Camping in the **backcountry** (a general term for areas inaccessible by road) requires a permit, available free of charge. Visitors are advised not to drink water from rivers and streams without boiling it for at least five minutes. It is also advisable to check fire regulations and inform a park ranger of the itinerary before setting out to a backcountry area.

YMCA/YOUTH HOSTELS:

There are over 2400 YMCA centres throughout the USA. Membership is not necessary but reservations should be made two days prior to arrival via the Head Offices. The YMCA offers centrally located accommodation at attractive rates, coast to coast throughout the USA. Most centres offer single and double accommodation for both men and women and many also have sports facilities. Youth hostels offer their members simple, inexpensive overnight accommodation usually located in scenic, historical or cultural places. HI-AYH (Hostelling International - American Youth Hostels) operates some 150 hostels in both urban and rural locations. Membership is open to everyone, with no age limit, with free group and youth (under 18 years) memberships. European visitors should take out membership before travelling.

SELF-CATERING:

Self-catering facilities, known in the USA as 'apartments', 'condominiums' (or 'condos'), 'efficiencies' or 'villas', are also available.
HOME EXCHANGE: There are several agents who offer home exchange programmes between the UK and USA.

ACCOMMODATION INFORMATION

American Hotel & Lodging Association
1201 New York Avenue, NW, Suite 600,
Washington, DC 20005, USA
Tel: (202) 289 3100.
Website: www.ahla.com

Professional Association of Innkeepers International
Website: www.paii.org
There are also numerous national and regional B&B associations.

Kampgrounds of America (KOA)
Tel: (406) 248 7444.
Website: www.koa.com

YMCA of the USA
101 North Wacker Drive, Chicago, IL 60606, USA
Tel: (312) 977 0031.
Website: www.ymca.net

Hostelling International - American Youth Hostels (HI-AYH)
8401 Colesville Road, Suite 600,
Silver Spring, MD 20910, USA
Tel: (301) 495 1240.
Website: www.hiayh.org or www.hihostels.com

Top Things To See & Do

For details on resorts, excursions, places of interest and tourist attractions in the USA, see the individual State sections.

Entertainment

FOOD & DRINK: In large cities, restaurants are mostly modern and very clean, offering a vast range of cuisines, prices and facilities. Restaurants come in all shapes and sizes, ranging from fast-food, self-service and counter service to drive-in and table service. The 'diner' is an integral part of the US way of life; consisting of a driveway, neon lights and simple food served from the counter; these are generally located in or just outside smaller towns. See Food & Drink in the individual State sections for further details on regional specialities.
Things to know: There are also many types of bars, ranging from the smart cocktail lounge, cafe-style, high 'saloon' style bars and imitations of English pubs to the 'regular' bar. Generally speaking, waiter/waitress service costs more. Drinking laws are set by the individual States, counties, municipalities and towns, although traditionally closing time in bars is between midnight and 0300. **Legal Drinking Age:** The legal age for drinking also varies from 18 to 21 from State to State and the laws on the availability of alcohol run from New Orleans' policy of anytime, anywhere and to anyone, to localities, such as in Utah, where drinking is strictly prohibited.
National specialities:
• Fried chicken.
• Hamburgers.
• Apple pie.
National drinks:
• Coca-Cola.
• Espresso.
• Regional wines.
• Microbrewery beer.
Tipping: Widely practised, as service charges are not usually included in the bill and waiters depend heavily on tips for their income. Waiters generally expect 15 to 20 per cent, as do taxi drivers and hairdressers. It should be noted that a cover charge is for admission to an establishment, not a tip for service. Porters generally expect US$1 per bag.
NIGHTLIFE: Clubs generally stay open until the early hours in cities, where one can find music and theatre of all descriptions. Theatre tickets for Broadway, New York's equivalent of London's West End 'Theatreland', can be booked through the Group Sales Box Office, 226 West 47th Street, 10th Floor, New York, NY 10036, USA (tel: (800) 223 7565 or (212) 398 8383; website: www.bestofbroadway.com). Special discounts for group bookings are available. Tickets must be paid for in advance and will be mailed out or kept at the theatre box office for collection on the night of the performance. Gambling is only allowed in licensed casinos and the legal age for gamblers is 21 years of age or over.
SHOPPING: Variety, late opening hours, competitive prices and an abundance of modern goods typify US shopping. Many small stores, specialist food shops and hypermarkets are open 24 hours a day. Clothes and electronic goods can be bought direct from factories. Retail outlets range from flea markets and bargain stores to large chain department stores. Malls are a popular way of shopping in the USA and consist of a cluster of different kinds of shops in one

---

Credit: ©Alaska Division of Tourism

building, often a few storeys high, connected by an indoor plaza. Note that a sales tax is levied on most or all items in most States and the addition is not included on the price label; sales tax can be anywhere from 3 to 15 per cent, depending on the State; some States have no sales tax at all. **Shopping hours:** Mon-Sat 0900/0930-1730/1800. There may be late-night shopping one or two evenings a week. Some States permit Sunday trading.

Business

ECONOMY: The US economy is the world's largest, most powerful and most diverse. The roots of this lie in the physical expansion and development of the country during the 19th century. As a result, the USA benefited from a unique combination of mass immigration, technological and marketing innovations, exploitation of natural resources, the expansion of international trade, historical fortune (hugely destructive wars that caused immense damage to other world powers but left the USA virtually untouched) and the fostering of a political and economic system well designed to exploit them. The enormous influence of US-based multinational companies in the world economy has not only afforded unique global influence to the US Government but also allowed its currency to acquire unique international status. Large areas of the USA, particularly in the Midwest, are under cultivation and produce a wide range of commodities: the most important of these are cotton, cereals and tobacco, all of which are exported on a large scale. The principal mining operations produce oil and gas, coal, copper, iron, uranium and silver. The US manufacturing industry is a world leader in many fields including steel, vehicles, aerospace, telecommunications, chemicals, electronics and consumer goods. Since the late-1970s, however, the biggest employer has been the service sector, particularly finance (including banking, insurance and equities), leisure and tourism. Services now account for three quarters of output and employment. New computer-based industries associated with the Internet, which began revolutionising lifestyles and commerce during the late-1990s, rose quickly, burned brightly and died suddenly. Toward the close of 2000, many of these 'dot-com' industries plunged into bankruptcy. The USA's technology sector went into decline and the country found itself in recession. Annual growth averaged around 4 to 5 per cent during the late-1990s, but slipped to 2.2 per cent as the economy slowed

down. The events of September 2001 added to the pessimistic outlook for the economy, as several industries (notably civil aviation and tourism) suffered a sudden fall in demand. In addition to important IT and telecommunications industries, traditional manufacturing industries, such as steel, were also depressed. Toward the end of 2003, a BSE scare caused a major upheaval in the USA's meat industry, particularly affecting its exports (mainly to Japan). The internationally controversial war on Iraq has also threatened many trade friendships and lowered the value of the US Dollar (US$1 in 1990 had the same buying power as US$1.42 in 2003), although the USA's economic might has been maintained.
Unemployment reached 5.9 per cent in November 2003, although productivity increased by 9.4 per cent in the third quarter of 2003.
The USA's most important trade relationship is with Canada (which accounts for approximately 20 per cent of all US trade). The two countries concluded a free trade agreement in 1989: this accord formed the basis for the North American Free Trade Agreement (NAFTA), to which Mexico became a signatory in 1992. (NAFTA is of similar proportions to the EU in terms of population and economic output.) Other major trading partners are Japan, the UK and Germany, followed by other members of the EU.
BUSINESS ETIQUETTE: Businesspeople are generally expected to dress smartly, although a man may wear a short-sleeved shirt under his suit in hot weather. Normal business courtesies should be observed, although Americans tend to be less formal than Europeans. Appointments and punctuality are normal procedure and business cards are widely used. Dates in America are written month-day-year: 4 July 2006 would thus be abbreviated as 7/4/06. Write out the month in full to avoid confusion. **Office hours:** Mon-Fri 0900-1730.
CONFERENCES/CONVENTIONS: If for no other reason than its role in the world economy, the USA is an important conference destination; there are State, city and regional travel and convention organisations in every part of the country, each actively promoting its own assets. With so much information available, the real problem for the organiser is to find some way of getting through it all. There are several magazines aimed at helping the conference organiser; they include *Meeting & Conventions Magazine* (website: www.meetings-conventions.com), *Successful Meetings Magazine* (website: www.successmtgs.com) and *Corporate Meetings and Incentive Magazine* (website: www.meetingsnet.com). Home to three of the 10 largest convention venues in the USA, Las Vegas was the most popular US trade show venue in 2004, hosting some 174 shows, followed by New York City, Chicago, Atlanta, Dallas, Orlando, New Orleans, San Diego, San Francisco and Washington, DC. Organisers interested in US venues should contact the US Travel Industry Association or the travel organisations listed in the individual State sections. In addition to the State organisations, addresses of travel and convention organisations for cities and counties are also included.

COMMERCIAL INFORMATION

The Partnership for New York City
1 Battery Park Plaza, 5th Floor,
New York, NY 10004, USA
Tel: (212) 493 7400.
Website: www.nycp.org

The US Chamber of Commerce
1615 H Street, NW, Washington, DC 20062, USA
Tel: (202) 659 6000 *or* (800) 638 6583.
Website: www.uschamber.org

The Trade Information Center - US Department of Commerce
Tel: (800) 872 8723.
Website: www.tradeinfo.doc.gov

The National Foreign Trade Council
1625 K Street, NW, Suite 200,
Washington, DC 20006, USA
Tel: (202) 887 0278.
Website: www.nftc.org

British American Business Inc
52 Vanderbilt Avenue, 20th Floor,
New York, NY 10017, USA
Tel: (212) 661 4060.

British American Business Inc in the UK
75 Brook Street, London W1K 4AD, UK
Tel: (020) 7467 7400.
Website: www.babinc.org

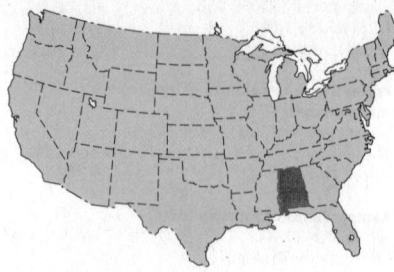

Alabama

Time: Central (GMT - 6). *Daylight Saving Time* is observed.

Overview

Alabama, which means 'tribal town' in the Creek Indian language, offers mountains, lakes, caverns, woodland and beaches. Montgomery was the first capital of the Confederacy, and the First White House of the Confederacy, home to Jefferson Davis, first President of the provisional Government. Alabama played a key role in the American civil rights movement in the 1950s and 1960s. The Reverend Martin Luther King Jr first preached at the Dexter Avenue King Memorial Baptist Church in Montgomery, a National Historic Landmark, and sites commemorating the struggle can be found across the State.
Mobile is a major seaport. The city is famed for its diverse architecture resulting from English, French and Spanish rule, notably in the Church Street Historic District. Alabama was hit hard by Hurricane Katrina in 2005 but much of the infrastructure and attractions have been repaired and are open to visitors.

General Information

Nickname: The Heart of Dixie.
State bird: Yellowhammer (Flicker).
State flower: Camellia.
CAPITAL: Montgomery.
Date of admission to the Union: 14 Dec 1819.
POPULATION: 4.56 million (official estimate 2005).
POPULATION DENSITY: 33.6 per sq km.
2004 total overseas arrivals/US ranking: 72,000/29.

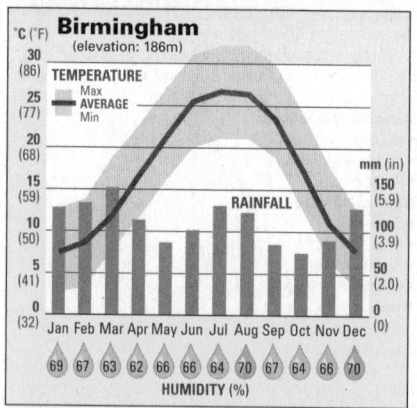

Credit: ©Dan Brothers

Climate

Hot and humid in summer months. Mild in winter months and cooler in the mountains. Temperatures range from a January high of 10°C (50°F) and a low of 0°C (32°F) to a July high of 33°C (90°F) and a low of 21°C (70°F).
Required clothing: Lightweight cotton clothes and rainwear. Warm clothing for evenings in the spring and autumn, during the winter season and in mountain areas.

Top Things To See & Do

• **Birmingham** is Alabama's largest city. Attractions include the **VisionLand** theme park and **McWane Center** (a hands-on science adventure) and **IMAX theatre**; the **Birmingham Museum of Art**; and the **Alabama Sports Hall of Fame (ASHOF)**, founded in 1967 and dedicated to sporting legends such as Jesse Owens and Joe Louis.
• **Montgomery** was the first capital of the Confederacy. Visit the **First White House of the Confederacy**, home to Jefferson Davis, first President of the provisional Government. Country music lovers from across the USA make pilgrimages to the **Hank Williams Memorial** in the Oakwood Cemetery Annex. Fans lay flowers next to the huge cowboy hat that lies on his gravestone. Attend the **Alabama Shakespeare Festival**, the fifth-largest Shakespeare festival in the world, which attracts around 170,000 visitors every year between August and November, and is staged at the **Carolyn Blount Theatre**. Some 200 years of American art is covered in the **Montgomery Museum of Fine Arts**.
• The Reverend Martin Luther King Jr first preached at the **Dexter Avenue King Memorial Baptist Church** in Montgomery, a National Historic Landmark, and sites commemorating the struggle can be found across the State. These include the statues in Birmingham's **Kelly Ingram Park**, the **National Voting Rights Museum and Institute** in **Selma**, and the **Civil Rights Memorial** in **Montgomery**. In Birmingham, visitors can go on the **Black Heritage Tour** of the city centre and visit the **Birmingham Civil Rights Institute (BCRI)** with its impressive display of African-American history. **Tuskegee** is just an hour's drive from Montgomery. A former slave, Booker T Washington, founded the **Tuskegee Institute** to improve educational opportunities for blacks. Take a guided tour of the thriving university and a restored version of Washington's home, another National Historic Landmark.
• Head for **Mobile**, a major seaport, home to the **Mobile Museum of Art** and a lively **Family Mardi Gras** celebration (January-February); carnival costumes are on display in the **Museum of Mobile**. Admire the city's diverse architecture resulting from English, French and Spanish rule, notably in the **Church Street Historic District**. For children, there is the **Gulf Coast Exploreum** and the **Phoenix Fire Museum**, which includes antique fire engines.
• Other Alabama tourist destinations and attractions include the **US Space & Rocket Center** in **Huntsville**; the **Robert Trent Jones Golf Trail**; the **Russell Cave National Monument** in **Bridgeport**; and the resort towns of **Gulf Shores** and **Orange Beach**.

TOURIST INFORMATION

Alabama Bureau of Tourism & Travel
Suite 126, Alabama Center for Commerce,
401 Adams Ave, Montgomery, AL 36104 , USA
Tel: (334) 242 4169 *or* (800) 252 2262 (toll-free).
Website: www.800alabama.com

Greater Birmingham CVB
2200 Ninth Avenue North, Birmingham, AL 35203, USA
Tel: (205) 458 8000 *or* (800) 458 8085 (toll-free).
Website: www.birminghamal.org

Alaska

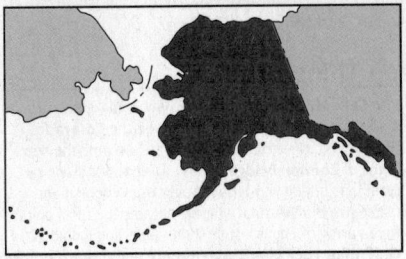

Time: Alaska (GMT - 9) in the greater part of the State; Hawaii-Aleutian (GMT - 10) west of 169° 30'. *Daylight Saving Time* is observed in the greater part of the State, but not west of 169° 30'.

Overview

The largest state in the USA, Alaska is a sparsely populated land of immense natural beauty. At one-fifth the size of the lower 48 States, Alaska has 3 million lakes, over 3000 rivers, 17 of the USA's 20 highest peaks, 100,000 glaciers and 15 national parks, preserves and monuments.

Anchorage - Alaska's largest city is both a popular tourist destination and the centre of commerce and transportation for the region; 40 per cent of the State's population lives here. Fairbanks - Alaska's second-largest city, situated at the northern end of the Alaska Highway, is a trade and transportation centre for the Interior and Far North regions. From mid-May through to July, visitors can enjoy more than 20 hours of sunlight a day.

General Information

Nickname: The Last Frontier.
State bird: Willow Ptarmigan.
State flower: Forget-Me-Not.
CAPITAL: Juneau.
Date of admission to the Union: 3 Jan 1959.
POPULATION: 663,661 (official estimate 2005).
POPULATION DENSITY: 0.4 per sq km.
2004 total overseas arrivals/US ranking: Under 38,000.

Climate

The climate varies widely throughout the State. Anchorage's summer weather is pleasant and the winters are mild. Fairbanks, the Interior and parts of the Bush region experience Alaska's most extreme weather conditions with average temperatures ranging from 22°C (72°F) in high summer to -28°C (-19°F) in winter.

Required clothing: In the Anchorage area, a layered wardrobe is the best option, with a light jacket in summer and a warm coat in winter. Elsewhere, very warm winter clothing is required in the coldest months. Lightweight clothing is advisable during the summer.

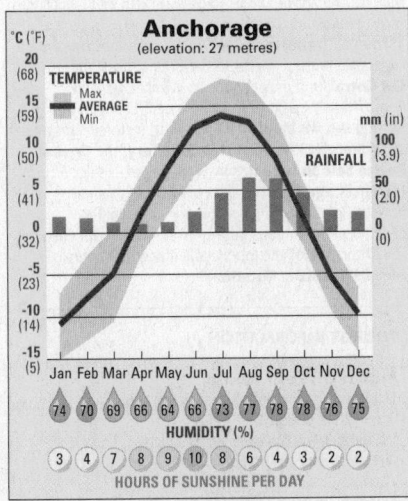

Travel - International

AIR:

 Ted Stevens Anchorage International (ANC) (website: www.dot.state.ak.us/anc) is served by seven international carriers and 15 domestic carriers.

Fairbanks International (FBK) (website: www.dot.state.ak.us/faiiap) is the state's second-largest airport and has direct services from a number of North American gateways.

Ketchikan International (KTN) sits on Gravina Island just across from the city; a small ferry runs from the airport to just above the State ferry dock.

Juneau International (JNU) is located 14km (9 miles) north of Juneau.

Domestic airports: Most in-State flights are on jet or turboprop aircraft. Several airlines, largely based at Anchorage, operate scheduled air-taxi and air-charter services to almost every Alaskan village. *Alaska Airlines* (tel: (800) 252 7522; website: www.alaskaair.com) flies to Alaska's largest cities (Anchorage, Fairbanks, Juneau and Ketchikan), as well as a number of bush communities throughout the state. A number of smaller, regional airlines provide statewide services.

SEA:

 The *Alaska Marine Highway System* (website: www.dot.state.ak.us/amhs) provides a practical ferry service on four separate routes: Inside Passage/Southeast, Southwest and Southcentral. Cross-Gulf route. Visitors can board the ferry at Bellingham (Washington) and travel up to Skagway on the Inside Passage/Southeast route; the Southwest route connects the Kenai Peninsula and Prince William Sound to the Aleutians Islands; the new Kennicott ferry runs an infrequent Southcentral service (once a month during summer), linking the two routes (running between Juneau and Seward).

RAIL:

The scenic, historic and expensive *Alaska Railroad* (website: www.alaskarailroad.com) operates daily between Anchorage, Fairbanks, Grandview, Hurricane and Seward. At the southern end of the rail corridor, connections with the State ferry system can be made at Seward and Whittier. Except for the Anchorage–Seward and Anchorage–Grandview routes, the railway operates all year round, with reduced services from September to May.

ROAD:

The famous *Alaska Highway* covers a staggering 2647km (1645 miles) from Delta Junction, near Fairbanks, to Dawson Creek (British Columbia, Canada). Drivers should note that weather conditions can be hazardous, and create visibility and navigational challenges. The road system is in good condition, however, and if drivers use common sense and are prepared for changes in the weather, the Alaska Highway is an ideal way to explore the State. Other roads only reach a quarter of the State's vast area, and treacherous weather conditions can make driving a hazardous option. Further information and suggested itineraries may be found online courtesy of 'North to Alaska' (website: www.northtoalaska.com).

Bus: *Alaska Direct Bus Line* (tel: (907) 277 6652 or (800) 770 6652 (toll-free); website: www.akinformation.com/data/general/akdirect.htm) offers bus services from Anchorage to Whitehorse, Canada (travel time – 16 to 18 hours) and from Fairbanks to Whitehorse (travel time – 13 to 15 hours), thrice weekly in summer, weekly in winter. From Whitehorse, *Greyhound Canada* (website: www.greyhound.ca) offers thrice-weekly connections to Vancouver, British Columbia (travel time – 40 hours 30 minutes). The total travel time from Alaska to the lower 48 States can take up to 5 days and involve a number of connections. Greyhound Canada also has daily connections from Prince George, British Columbia to Prince Rupert, British Columbia (travel time - 10 hours 30 minutes), from where a ferry may be taken to Alaska. This trip follows the impressive *Yellowhead Highway* as it heads along to the coast.

URBAN:

 Cars are available for hire statewide, with major chains featured in most cities.

Top Things To See

- Delight in the wealth of local history that can be seen at the **Heritage Library and Museum**, the **Anchorage Museum of History and Art** (www.anchoragemuseum.org), the **Oscar Anderson House Museum**, and the **Alaska Native Heritage Center**.
- Take a short trip north of Anchorage leading to the **Eagle River Visitor Center** and the alpine beauty of **Chugach State Park** (website: www.dnr.state.ak.us/parks/umts/chugach).
- Behold the most sought after winter attraction, the **aurora borealis**, which lights up the northern skies (best from December to March).
- Experience the most popular excursion - **Columbia Glacier**, a 6km-(4mile-) wide piece of ice. This fastest moving glacier in the world can be reached via day cruises, charter boat, flight-seeing tours and the State ferry.
- Explore **Denali National Park & Preserve** (website: www.alaskatravel.com/denali-park), famous for its panoramic views of **Mount McKinley** and the **Alaska Range**. A popular day excursion takes tourists on a

shuttle bus through the wilderness to see caribou, grizzly bears, wolves and moose.
- Enjoy the **Totem Bight State Historical Park** (website: www.dnr.state.ak.us/parks/units/totembgh.htm) with its collection of replica totem poles and a tribal house. The park overlooks the **Tongass National Forest** (website: www.fs.fed.us/r10/tongass), the largest in the USA and home to more than 50 species of birds, mountain goats, orca whales and glacier bear. Excursions include a boat or plane trip into the **Misty Fiords National Monument** (website: www.mistyfiords.org).
- Visit **Kodiak Island** (website: www.kodiakisland.org), the home of Alaska's largest fishing fleet. The legacy of Russian influence can be found at the **Baranov Museum** (website: www.baranov.us), while the culture of the island's native people can be explored in the little **Alutiiq Museum** (website: www.alutiiqmuseum.com). The **Kodiak National Wildlife Refuge** (website: www.kodiak.fws.gov) covers two-thirds of the island, offering a protected habitat for Kodiak brown bears, which are the largest carnivores in North America.

Top Things To Do

- Tour the local wildlife museums including the **Alaska Zoo** (website: www.alaskazoo.org), the **Imaginarium** (website: www.imaginarium.org), and **Potter's Marsh**, where up to 130 species of waterfowl can be viewed from a boardwalk.
- View the geographical reminders of the 1964 Good Friday Earthquake (North America's strongest) seen at **Earthquake Park**, while admission to the Alaska **Experience Center** (website: www.alaskaexperiencetheatre.com) includes a film on this devastating event.
- Try your luck panning for gold nuggets at **Crow Creek Mine**.
- Visit **Pioneer Park** (formerly Alaskaland Theme Park) (website: http://fairbanks-alaska.com/alaskaland.htm), a 18 hectare (44-acre) park built for the Alaska 1967 Centennial Exposition. Among the attractions are three museums, a 12m (40-foot) antique carousel and an old-time saloon.
- Hike in **Juneau**. It is also famed for the great outdoors and its many hiking trails, as well as opportunities to view whales, bears and eagles.
- Take part in one of the many outdoor pursuits available (such as **hiking**, **rafting** and **fishing**) in **Valdez**, situated on the edge of the **Prince William Sound**.
- Partake in **sled-dog racing**. The official sport of Alaska **dog mushing**. Visitors can take a team of spirited huskies on a sled-dog tour or watch the experts at work in one of the many annual sled-dog races.
- Cheer on your favorite sled team during the annual **Yukon Quest International Sled Dog Race** held every February. Covering 1000 miles between Whitehorse, Yukon Territory and Fairbanks during the depths of the Arctic Winter, the Yukon Quest is the 'Toughest Sled Dog Race in the World' (website: www.yukonquest.com).

TOURIST INFORMATION

Alaska Travel Industry Association
2600 Cordova Street, Suite 201, Anchorage, AK 99503, USA
Tel: (907) 929 2842.
Website: www.travelalaska.com or www.alaskatia.org
Provides tourist information to visitors and trade.

Alaska Public Lands Information Center
605 West Fourth Avenue, Suite 105, Anchorage, AK 99501, USA
Tel: (907) 271 27 42.
Website: www.nps.gov/aplic
Other offices in Fairbanks, Ketchikon and Tok.

Entertainment

FOOD & DRINK: To enjoy Alaskan cuisine one must love fish. Salmon, halibut and trout feature heavily on most menus.

Regional specialities:
- Smoked salmon.
- Caribou stew.

NIGHTLIFE: Live music is very popular in Alaska. Many bars offer a wide choice of late-night sounds, ranging from rock to jazz and blues.

SHOPPING: Unique Alaskan products and crafts include gold nugget jewellery; items carved from ivory and jade; handmade clothing and toys; items made from skin, fur or bone; and woven baskets of beach grass, bark and baleen. Native sea-oil candles, beaded mittens, fur mukluks and miniature hand-carved totem poles are also popular souvenirs. The 'Made in Alaska' logo indicates that an item has been genuinely manufactured in Alaska, and the 'silver hand' logo identifies Native Alaskan handicrafts.

Arizona

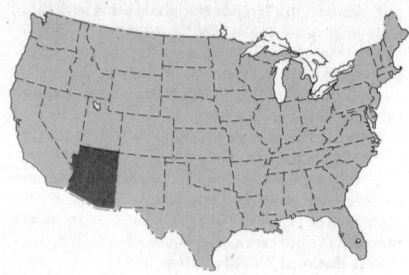

Time: Mountain (GMT - 7). *Daylight Saving Time* is not observed.

Overview

Arizona contains some of the most spectacular scenery in the whole of the USA. The Grand Canyon, the Painted Desert National Park and Petrified Forest National Park (comprising the Painted Desert in the north and Rainbow Forest in the south) are just some of the highlights. Phoenix, the largest city in the State, shares borders with Scottsdale, the primary resort destination in Arizona. Both cities have a variety of accommodations and attractions, unique shopping, fine art galleries and many cultural events. The sixth-largest city in the USA and the capital of Arizona, Phoenix has enjoyed a growth in popularity recently, thanks to its improved airport facilities and a large investment in extensive urban redevelopment. Today, it claims to have more 5-star hotels than any other US city. Tombstone is the site of the infamous shoot-out at the OK Corral..

General Information

Nickname: Grand Canyon State.
State bird: Cactus Wren.
State flower: Saguaro Cactus Blossom.
CAPITAL: Phoenix.
Date of admission to the Union: 14 Feb 1912.
POPULATION: 5.94 million (official estimate 2005).
POPULATION DENSITY: 20 per sq km.
2004 total overseas arrivals/US ranking: 487,000/12

Climate

Mostly warm and comfortable all year round. Mountainous areas, such as Flagstaff at 2134m (7000ft), are colder, particularly in winter, and in summer, there are cool mountain breezes. Desert temperatures range from hot during the day to cold at night.
Required clothing: Lightweight cotton clothing for all seasons, with a wrap for cool nights. Warmer clothing is needed in the mountains, especially in the ski areas.

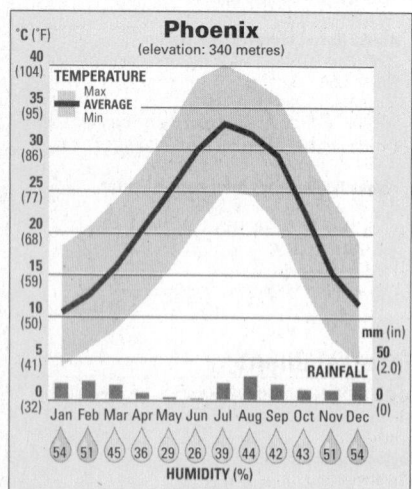

Phoenix
(elevation: 340 metres)

Travel - International

AIR:

Phoenix Sky Harbor International (PHX) (website: www.phoenix.gov/AVIATION) is 6km (4 miles) from the city centre. *To/from the airport:* The airport is linked by a Valley Metro bus service that runs every 25 minutes 0600-1830 (travel time – 22 minutes). Taxis are available 24 hours a day, as is a door-to-door limousine service and a super-shuttle service; the latter departs every 15 minutes (0900-2100), less frequently at night. *Facilities:* ATMs and car hire.
Tucson International (TUS) (website: www.tucsonairport.com) is 16km (10 miles) from the city centre. *To/from the airport:* Taxis and shared-ride vans that travel door-to-door run 24 hours a day; a local Sun Tran bus service is also available, although these are slow. *Facilities:* Bank, business services and car hire.
Approximate flight times: From Phoenix to *Los Angeles* is one hour 25 minutes, to *Miami* is four hours 10 minutes and to *New York* is four hours 30 minutes.

RAIL:

Three *Amtrak* (tel: (800) 872 7245 (toll-free); website: www.amtrak.com) trains run a weekly service from downtown Tucson, on the 'Sunset Limited' line between Los Angeles and New Orleans. There is no rail link between Tucson and Phoenix, although an *Amtrak* Thruway bus service connects the cities. There is a daily service from Flagstaff on the 'Southwest Chief' line between Los Angeles and Chicago. The *West Rail Pass* is available for 15 or 30 days unlimited travel between the Pacific Coast and as far east as Chicago and New Orleans. The *Far West Rail Pass* is also available for 15 or 30 days travel, covering the region from the Pacific Coast as far east as Alburquerque (New Mexico) and El Paso (Texas). First-class sleeping cars can be reserved for an additional fee.

ROAD:

Most major routes run east-west. **Bus:** Greyhound buses (tel: (800) 231 2222 (toll-free); website: www.greyhound.com) are available to many destinations throughout the USA. *Gray Line* (www.graylinearizona.com), with offices in Phoenix, Tucson and Flagstaff, offers two-hour to two-day local sightseeing tours.
Approximate driving times: From Phoenix to *Tucson* is two hours, to *Las Vegas* is five hours 30 minutes, and to *Albuquerque* is nine hours.
Approximate bus journey times: From Phoenix to *Los Angeles* is seven hours, to *El Paso* is seven hours 45 minutes, and to *San Diego* is eight hours.

URBAN:

Bus: *Phoenix Valley Metro* (website: www.valleymetro.org) buses run every 30 minutes throughout the day and every 10 to 20 minutes during peak traffic hours, although stops are spaced far apart; schedules are available at the downtown terminal, at First Avenue and Washington Street. Tickets for local and costlier express fares are sold in books of 10; daily and monthly local passes are available. A free *DASH* bus service runs Mon-Fri 0630-2300 between the Arizona Center and the State Capitol (downtown). A bus service links Phoenix and Scottsdale, and special dial-a-ride services operate in both cities Mon-Sat 0630-1000. Tucson also has a local bus network. **Car hire:** Easily available in Phoenix and other major cities, with many car hire firms offering special weekend or weekly rates.

Top Things To See

- Tour the recently expanded **Heard Museum** (website: www.heard.org). Founded in 1929, the museum is devoted to the art, anthropology, history and Native American culture of Arizona.
- See the home and workshop of the famous architect Frank Lloyd Wright at **Taliesin West**.
- Be dazzled, if not alarmed, by the gargantuan bubble that is **Biosphere 2** (website: www.bio2.com) - a Plexiglas bubble laboratory containing five separate and self-contained ecosystems. It was designed to help scientists colonise Mars but a series of mishaps has plagued this project; even sightseers do not come in their crowds any more (during the early-1990s it was one of the State's most popular attractions). It is nevertheless worth a look, if only from afar. Guided tours are available.
- Discover Arizona's most visited State Historic Park, the **Yuma Territorial Prison** (website: www.desertusa.com/yuma/du_yumatp.html), with its cells carved out of the rock. From 1876 to 1909, it housed many of Arizona's most dangerous and notorious criminals.
- See the **Tonto National Monument** (website: www.nps.gov/tont). The monument features well-preserved cliff dwellings occupied 500 years ago by the Salado Indians and examples of their weavings, jewellery, weapons and tools.
- Journey through the **Navajo Reservation**. It spreads over more than 64,750 sq km (25,000 sq miles) and is home to 250,000 Navajos. They traditionally lived in hogans (dome-shaped houses of log and adobe) in small, scattered settlements. Nowadays, visitors are more likely to meet a Navajo as a guide on a horseback ride in the **Canyon de Chelly National Monument** (website: www.nps.gov/cach) or on one of the jeep tours through **Monument Valley** (www.desertusa.com/monvalley), where a number of John Wayne films were shot.

- See the **Hopi Reservation**, comprising 6475 sq km (2500 sq miles) and accommodating 7000 Hopis. They have lived in the region for 1500 years and are known for their amazing agricultural talents in farming dry and difficult land. The Hopis live in snug pueblo-style villages on top of three mesas. This area is treasured for its outstanding natural beauty.

Top Things To Do

- Visit **Lake Havasu City** (website: www.golakehavasu.com) nestled amidst rugged desert peaks on the **Colorado River**. This city with a small-town feel became the new home of **London Bridge** in 1971. Dismantled stone by stone, the bridge was brought over from England and reassembled in Arizona, where it became the focal point for an array of English-style shops, pubs and lodgings.
- **Golf**, **hike**, **rock climb**, **play tennis**, and **mountain bike** in the **Lake Havasu** area, as well as take **jeep tours** in the nearby **Sonoran Desert** (website: www.desertusa.com/du_sonoran.html) and **Mojave** (website: www.desertusa.com/du_mojave.html) or **Chemehuevi Mountains**.
- Explore the beautiful **Oak Creek Canyon** (website: www.visitsedona.com). The canyon provides lush scenery, and there are prehistoric Native American ruins to be seen nearby. **Jeep tours**, hiking and **mountain biking** are also available.
- Spend some time in **Tucson** (website: www.ci.tucson.az.us), one of the fastest-growing resort cities in the USA. Surrounded by a ring of five mountain ranges in the Sonoran Desert, it is known for its constant sunshine; and its location, only 160km (100 miles) from the Mexican border, is apparent in its architecture, cuisine, lively fiestas and cultural festivals.
- Travel the **Apache Trail** (website: www.americansouthwest.net/arizona/apache_trail), an extraordinary scenic drive. Attractions include **Goldfield Ghost Town and Mine Tours** (website: www.goldfieldghosttown.com), **Superstition Mountain Museum**, **Lost Dutchman State Park** and **Tortilla Flat** (an old stagecoach stop offering 'killer' chili and prickly-pear cactus ice cream).
- Experience the jewel of the National Park Service and a UNESCO World Heritage Site, the **Grand Canyon**. The impact is awe-inspiring. This massive rend in the earth may be experienced in a variety of different ways: by aeroplane or helicopter, from the back of a mule, on foot or aboard a raft. For those wanting to catch a memorable sunrise or sunset, it is worth booking accommodations at one of the hotels in and around the canyon. As the area is far from any city, those wanting to save time and see it all can take a 'flightseeing' trip over the canyon. Further information is available from the Grand Canyon Chamber of Commerce (tel: (928) 638 2901; website: www.grandcanyonchamber.org).
- Hire a houseboat and float serenely past the scenic wonderland of red rocks on **Lake Powell**. Many tour boats ply the waters of the second-largest man-made lake in the USA. Well worth seeing is the **Rainbow Bridge**, a spectacular natural stone bridge on the Navajo Reservation, which most visitors travel to by boat. Information is available from Lake Powell Resorts & Marinas (tel: (800) 528 6145 or (928) 645 2433 website: www.visitlakepowell.com).
- Encounter **Tombstone** (website: www.tombstone.org). It owes its enduring appeal to the brief showdown at the **OK Corral**, and movies such as *Wyatt Earp* and *Tombstone* mean that it has retained its popularity. This notorious town plays on its past with restored sites and attractions like the **Boot Hill Cemetery**, the **Crystal Palace Saloon** (website: www.crystalpalacesaloon.com), the **Bird Cage Theatre** and even has its original newspaper, named the *Tombstone Epitaph*. Re-enactments of famous gunfights are played out each day.
- Tee off on one of the more challenging golf courses in **Mesa**, **Phoenix** or **Tucson**.

Entertainment

FOOD & DRINK: Most restaurants serve American or American/Continental food but Mexican, Chinese and Italian cuisine is also available, sometimes as a 'Southwest style' fusion using Mexican spices.

Regional specialities:

• Salsa.

• Frijoles.

NIGHTLIFE: Phoenix and Tucson have various nightclubs, and there is evening entertainment at many resorts in the area. Scottsdale's nightlife is more concentrated, while the university crowd go out in Tempe, where there are good jazz clubs on Mill Avenue.

SHOPPING: Phoenix has excellent shopping facilities, including **Biltmore Fashion Park** and the **Arizona Center**. Other good shopping centres in the metro area are at the **Scottsdale Fashion Square** and the upscale Italian-style **Borgata**, also in Scottsdale, and along pedestrianised **Mill Avenue** and at the **Arizona Mills** mall in Tempe. Special buys in Arizona include Navajo silver and turquoise jewellery, sand paintings, rug weaving, Hopi silver jewellery, kachina carvings, pottery, basketry and paintings. Tucson is a good place to pick up many of these items, as well as reasonably priced goods from Mexican import stores.

Arkansas

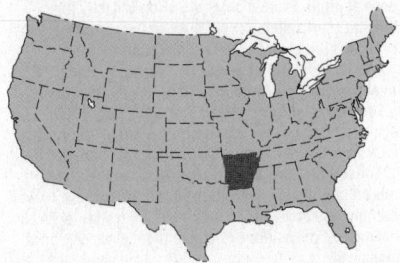

Time: Central (GMT - 6). *Daylight Saving Time* is observed.

Overview

Arkansas has a varied landscape of plains, mountains, forests, rivers, cattle farms, industrial centres and oil wells. The main claims to fame of this State are the beauty of its outdoors and that former President Bill Clinton was the Governor in Little Rock before moving to the White House – there are museums and exhibits dedicated to his life. One of Arkansas' earliest settlements, Little Rock is a thriving place filled with museums, art exhibitions and parks. The glorious Ozark Mountains stretch from southern Missouri through northern Arkansas.

General Information

Nickname: The Natural State.
State bird: Mockingbird.
State flower: Apple Blossom.
CAPITAL: Little Rock.
Date of admission to the Union: 15 Jun 1836.
POPULATION: 2.78 million (official estimate 2005).
POPULATION DENSITY: 20.2 per sq km.
2004 total overseas arrivals: Under 38,000.

Climate

The region has the most continental climate of any area in the USA. Winters are cold and summers warm.
Required clothing: Lightweights for the summer and heavyweights for the winter.

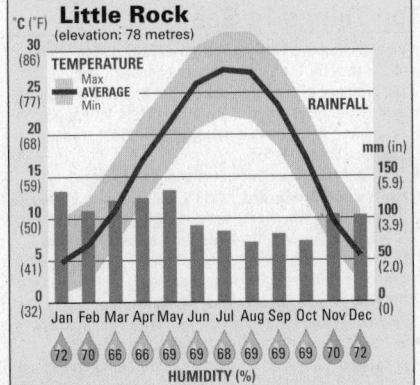

Little Rock (elevation: 78 metres)

Credit: ©Arkansas Department of Parks & Tourism

Top Things To See & Do

• Visit **Little Rock**, one of Arkansas' earliest settlements, and a thriving place filled with museums, art exhibitions and parks. Attractions include the **Decorative Arts Museum**; **River Market District**; **the Governor's Mansion**; **Historic Arkansas Museum**; **Arkansas Arts Center**; and the **Museum of Discovery**. The **William J Clinton Presidential Center** houses the largest Presidential archive. The centre is situated in a 30-acre park and includes the **Presidential Library and Museum**, the renovated **Choctaw Station**, originally built in 1899 and the **Rock Island Railroad Bridge**, which is also being renovated. The best time to visit Little Rock is during *Riverfest* on the last evening of *Memorial Day* weekend, when the locals celebrate in style at **Julius Breckling Riverfront Park** with bands, dancing and a fireworks display.

• Enjoy the glorious scenery of the **Ozark Mountains**, which stretch from southern Missouri through northern Arkansas. The village of **Mountain View** is a musical mecca, home to the **Ozark Folk Center** and events such as the *Arkansas Folk Festival* in April and the *Arkansas State Old-Time Fiddle Championships* in September. Fishing in the **White River** is another option, but before casting out, a fishing licence must be obtained from one of the local stores. Excursions can be taken to **Buffalo National River**, which is a great spot for canoeing, or to the **Blanchard Springs Caverns** on the south border of the **Ozark National Forest**, which covers 0.5 million hectares (1.2 million acres) and is home to **Mount Magazine**, the tallest mountain in the State.

• Head to **Eureka Springs,** which draws millions of tourists to its *Great Passion Play* outdoor drama and the *Christ of the Ozarks* statue, which stands 1.8m (6ft) high and was completed in 1966.

• Soothe away your worries at **Hot Springs National Park**, where visitors can relax in a choice of bathhouses, cheer on thoroughbreds or fish and swim at three great lakes.

• Explore the **Museum of Regional History** in Texarkana, which lies on the border with Texas. There is an exhibition devoted to Scott Joplin (the African-American ragtime pianist and composer), a famous former resident of the town.

• Other State attractions include the **Crater of Diamonds State Park**, where visitors can dig for diamonds, **Fort Smith National Historic Site** and **Toltec Mounds Archaeological State Park**.

TOURIST INFORMATION

Arkansas Department of Parks & Tourism
1 Capitol Mall, Little Rock, AR 72201, USA
Tel: (501) 682 7777 *or* (800) 628 8725 (toll-free).
Website: www.arkansas.com

Little Rock CVB
Street address: Robinson Center, Markham, Little Rock, AR 72201, USA
Postal address: PO Box 3232, Little Rock, AR 72203, USA
Tel: (501) 376 4781 *or* (800) 844 4781 (toll-free).
Website: www.littlerock.com

California

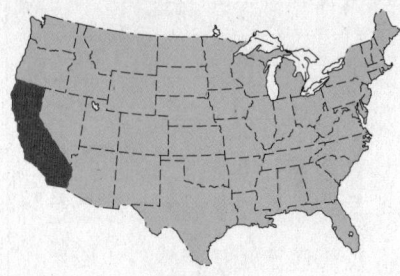

Time: Pacific (GMT - 8). *Daylight Saving Time* is observed.

Overview

'The Golden State' of California has it all: snow-capped mountains, vast deserts, lush forests and long stretches of golden beach. The most populous state in the USA, California can be divided into 12 tourist regions: the Central Coast, Los Angeles County, Orange County, the North Coast, San Diego County, the San Francisco Bay Area, Shasta Cascade, Gold Country, the Central Valley, the High Sierra, the Deserts and the Inland Empire. Known as 'the Middle Kingdom', the Central Coast extends from the Bay Area to Los Angeles County, along the Pacific coast and to the vineyards of the valleys around Santa Barbara. The Monterey Peninsula and Big Sur are tranquil areas of great natural beauty with some of the most scenic drives in the country. No trip to California is complete without a visit to the second-biggest city in the USA: Los Angeles, the 'City of Angels'. It lives up to its reputation as 'the entertainment capital of the world', offering the best in theatre, symphony and ballet as well as the chance to spot stars in Hollywood. Orange County is home to one of the world's most famous attractions, Disneyland Resort. As well as the theme parks, resorts and shopping, the county offers 67km (42 miles) of beaches and the charming rural communities of the Santa Ana Mountains. The North Coast is a land of rugged shoreline, redwood forests and vineyards.

The San Francisco Bay Area is one of the world's most popular destinations. San Francisco is a cosmopolitan city, whose cable cars and Golden Gate Bridge are instantly recognisable.

In the northeastern corner of the State lies one of the country's most beautiful and unspoiled regions – the Shasta Cascade. The region's waterfalls, whitewater rivers, forests, icy lakes and towering mountains – including the California Cascade range – provide stunning vistas. Gold Country is where the California Gold Rush, which forever changed the State – and the country – began in 1849. The beautiful wilderness of the High Sierra, immortalised in the photography of Ansel Adams, is an outdoor enthusiast's delight.

The Deserts region, in the southeast, features expansive landscapes, brilliant skies, traces of pioneer history and glittering resort cities. Natural phenomena include the isolated Death Valley National Park and the vast Joshua Tree National Park.

The Inland Empire is the fastest-growing metropolitan region in the USA. Only one hour from Los Angeles, its varied landscape – from snow-capped mountains to sand dunes and farmlands – makes it an ideal film location, and the region is known as 'Hollywood's largest backlot'.

General Information

Nickname: Golden State.
State bird: California Valley Quail.
State flower: California or Golden Poppy.
CAPITAL: Sacramento.
Date of admission to the Union: 9 Sep 1850.
POPULATION: 36.12 million (official estimate 2005).
POPULATION DENSITY: 85.2 per sq km.
2004 total overseas arrivals/US ranking: 1.37 million/5.

Climate

Summers are very warm, with cool evenings, while the spring and autumn months are mild, with cool evenings. The winter 'rainy season' is gentle and occurs between January and March.
Required clothing: Lightweight during the summer with warmer wear for the cooler winter period.

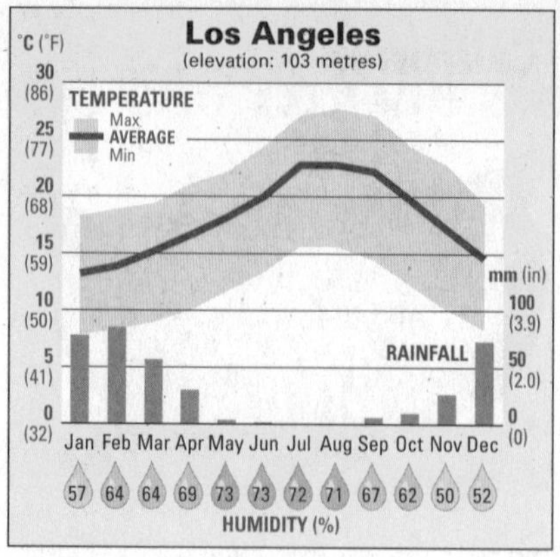

Los Angeles
(elevation: 103 metres)
°C (°F)
TEMPERATURE
Max
AVERAGE
Min
30 (86)
25 (77)
20 (68)
15 (59)
10 (50)
5 (41)
0 (32)
mm (in)
100 (3.9)
50 (2.0)
0 (0)
RAINFALL
Jan Feb Mar Apr May Jun Jul Aug Sep Oct Nov Dec
57 64 64 69 73 73 72 71 67 62 50 52
HUMIDITY (%)

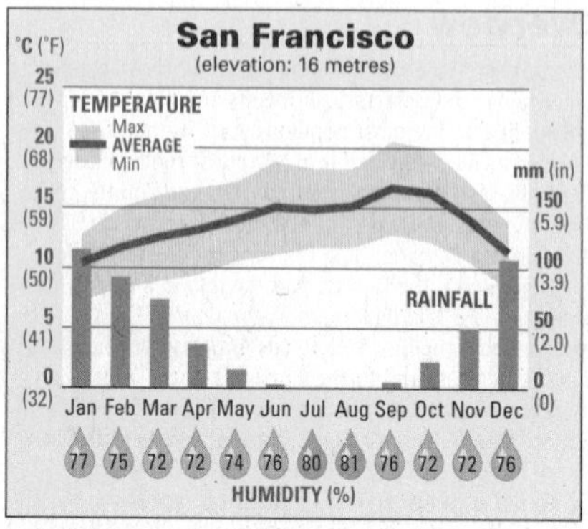

San Francisco
(elevation: 16 metres)
°C (°F)
TEMPERATURE
Max
AVERAGE
Min
25 (77)
20 (68)
15 (59)
10 (50)
5 (41)
0 (32)
mm (in)
150 (5.9)
100 (3.9)
50 (2.0)
0 (0)
RAINFALL
Jan Feb Mar Apr May Jun Jul Aug Sep Oct Nov Dec
77 75 72 72 74 76 80 81 76 72 72 76
HUMIDITY (%)

Travel - International

AIR:

Main airports: *Los Angeles International (LAX)* (website: www.lawa.org/lax) serves more than 80 passenger airlines. Located on Santa Monica Bay, 24km (15 miles) from the city centre, it is the world's fifth-busiest airport and third-busiest in the USA (2003 total passenger rankings), handling all international arrivals (some 14.8 million) and three-quarters of domestic arrivals to the Southern California region. *To/from the airport*: The airport is located 26km (16 miles) southwest of downtown Los Angeles; a free 24-hour shuttle service is available to the LAX Transit Center, where there are local buses to the city center (travel time - 30 to 45 minutes). Coaches provide reasonably priced services to all major locations in the city centre, as well as many surrounding areas such as Hollywood. Various door-to-door shuttle services are also available.

San Francisco International (SFO) (website: www.sfoairport.com) is 25km (15 miles) southeast of the city (travel time - 30 minutes). The airport handles over 7 million international arrivals per year and is ranked 11th busiest in the USA (2002 2003 total passenger rankings). *To/from the airport*: *SamTrans* buses leave every 30 minutes (travel time - 30 minutes to 1 one hour). The *SFO Airporter* bus departs every 15 minutes. Limousine, taxi and various shuttle services are also available. *Oakland International (OAK)* (website: www.flyoakland.com) is located across the Bay 32km (20 miles) from central San Francisco and receives international charter flights and US domestic flights. *To/from the airport*: Airporter buses link the airport with central Oakland and San Francisco International Airport. *AirBART* buses connect with the *BART* rapid transit (underground) system at Coliseum/Oakland International Airport station every 15 minutes, giving access to central San Francisco.

Domestic airports: *The Bob Hope Airport in Burbank (BUR)* (website: www.burbankairport.com) is about 20km (13 miles) from central Los Angeles, and receives US domestic services only. Burbank is the nearest airport for access to Hollywood.

San Diego International (SAN) (website: www.san.org), 5km (3 miles) west of San Diego city centre, is primarily a gateway to southern California for domestic traffic.

Approximate flight times: From Los Angeles to *Anchorage* is five hours 40 minutes, to *Honolulu* is five hours 40 minutes, and to *London* is 10 hours 15 minutes. From San Francisco to *Miami* is five hours, to *New York* is five hours 15 minutes, and to *Washington, DC* is four hours 50 minutes.

SEA:

A ferry service links **San Francisco** with the Bay communities of Sausalito, Larkspur (in Marin County), Tiburon, Vallejo, Oakland and Alameda. San Francisco departure is from Pier 1, adjoining the Ferry Building at the foot of Market Street, or from Fisherman's Wharf. In the **Los Angeles** area, there is a daily, low-fare cruise service from **Long Beach** to **Catalina Island**.

RAIL:

The *Amtrak* terminal in **Los Angeles** is Union Station, at 800 North Alameda Street, on the edge of the business district. It is at the western end of several major routes across the southern Rockies, is the southern terminus of the West Coast line to Seattle (although there are frequent shuttle services heading further south to San Diego), and at the western end of east-west routes from Chicago, St Louis and New Orleans. In **San Francisco**, the *Embarcadero BART* station and the *Transbay Terminal*, at 425 Mission Street, are used only for limited suburban services. The *Amtrak Terminal* at Oakland, across the Bay, is the central node on the West Coast line and also the western terminus of a line running across the high Rockies to Salt Lake City and beyond. *Amtrak* provides free shuttles between their Oakland station and the Transbay Terminal. **San Diego** is served by *Amtrak* trains from Los Angeles, with a station located downtown, on 4005 Taylor Street. For information on train schedules and reservations, contact *Amtrak* (tel: (800) 872 7245 (toll-free); website: www.amtrak.com).

Approximate rail travel times: From **Los Angeles** to *Phoenix* is eight hours, to *Dallas* is 39 hours, and to *Chicago* is 61 hours.

From **Oakland** to *Reno* is six hours, to *Salt Lake City* is 16 hours, and to *Denver* is 31 hours

ROAD:

Greyhound (tel: (800) 231 2222 (toll-free); website: www.greyhound.com), runs a reliable and frequent service to and from every major city in the USA, as well as locations in Canada and Mexico. There are six *Greyhound* bus stations in Los Angeles; the main station is at 1716 East Seventh Street. In San Francisco, *Greyhound* buses use the Transbay Terminal (see above), while San Diego has a downtown terminal at Broadway and First Avenue 120 West Broadway.

Approximate driving times: From **Los Angeles** to *Las Vegas* is six hours, to *Dallas* is 29 hours, and to *Miami* is 58 hours. From **San Francisco** to *Reno* is four hours, to *Seattle* is 16 hours, and to *New York* is 61 hours. All times are based on non-stop driving at or below the applicable speed limits.

Approximate bus travel times: From **Los Angeles** to *San Diego* is two hours 30 minutes, to *Las Vegas* is five hours 30 minutes, to *San Francisco* is seven hours 30 minutes, to *Phoenix* is eight hours 30 minutes, to *Yosemite* is 10 hours 15 minutes, to *Sacramento* is 12 hours 30 minutes, to *Albuquerque* is 17 hours 30 minutes and to *Portland* (Oregon) is 22 hours.

From **San Francisco** to *Sacramento* is two hours, to *Lake Tahoe* is five hours, to *Reno* is five hours 30 minutes, to *Los Angeles* is seven hours 30 minutes, to *Yosemite* is seven hours 30 minutes and to *Portland* (Oregon) is 16 hours.

URBAN:

Los Angeles: The distances between the city's various attractions can be intimidating at first but it is a relatively easy city to get around quickly, provided the visitor has a car. The freeways are well marked, though congested during rush hours. Leading car hire and motor camper rental agencies have offices at the airport and in the city centre. Local radio stations broadcast frequent traffic reports from 0600-1000 and 1500-1900. Many southern Californian freeways have designated car-pool lanes, known as HOVs. Do not merge into an HOV lane if your car is not carrying the specified number of passengers as fines are levied. *LA County Metropolitan Transit Authority (MTA)* buses run approximately every 15 minutes (0500-0200) on major routes, with a reduced service at night. Express buses are also available. The *Metrorail* train system covers three routes: downtown to Long Beach (blue); between Union Station to North Hollywood (red); and Hawthorne to Norwalk (green).

Travel beyond Los Angeles: Within Los Angeles County, the *Southern California Rapid Transit District (RTD)* provides a good bus service. For trips beyond Los Angeles, the *Orange County Transit District* accepts transfers from *RTD* for services throughout suburban Orange County. Buses are reasonably priced but travellers may have to wait some time to catch one. Though taxis are readily available, the large size of Los Angeles makes them expensive and impractical.

San Diego: The *Metropolitan Transit System* is operated by *San Diego Transit Corporation*, a consortium of companies providing a good and extensive bus service at moderate prices. The *San Diego Trolley* runs a 26km (16 mile) route from the Santa Fe Depot to San Ysidro, on the Mexican border (travel time - 45 minutes). Taxis are expensive. Car hire is readily available.

San Francisco: Public transport, operated by *MUNI*, is excellent. The network of buses (including night buses), streetcars and cable cars is the most economical way to get to destinations beyond walking distance. The basic fare includes transfers between the different forms of transport, except for cable cars, which have a separate fare structure. Passengers must have exact change when they board as drivers carry no change; the MUNI Passport travel passes (one-, three- or seven-day) are available and allow for travel on all *MUNI* and *BART* systems within the city. Taxis are readily available in most of the central area and other major streets. Because San Francisco occupies a comparatively small area, taxi fares tend to be lower than in most other major cities. All major national car hire agencies are represented in San Francisco; motor campers may also be hired. For information on local companies, look in the San Francisco *Classified Telephone Directory*. Buses and streetcars also provide services from the centre to more distant points in the city, including Golden Gate Park, Twin Peaks, Seal Rocks, Mission Dolores, the Presidio and Golden Gate Bridge. The clean and efficient *Bay Area Rapid Transit (BART)* subway and surface-rail system links San Francisco with communities on the east side of sprawling San Francisco Bay, including Oakland, Alameda, Fremont, Richmond and Berkeley, site of the prestigious University of California campus.

Top Things To See

- View the famous **Hollywood** sign. Nestled in the hills above the city, the sign stands as a constant reminder of the presence of the film industry. The streets and beaches are often used as locations, though most of it happens behind the well-guarded gates of the various studios scattered across the city.
- See other Hollywood area attractions including **Hollywood Boulevard**, with its 'walk of fame' etched in the pavement; the world-famous **Hollywood Bowl**, 2301 N. Highland Avenue; the **Hollywood Bowl Museum** (www.hollywoodbowl.org/event/museum.cfm) featuring changing exhibits on performing arts in Los Angeles; and the **Hollywood Entertainment Museum** (www.hollywoodmuseum) honouring the film industry.
- See one of San Francisco's principal attractions, its network of 130-year-old cable cars, the USA's only mobile National Historic Landmark. In the **San Francisco Cable**

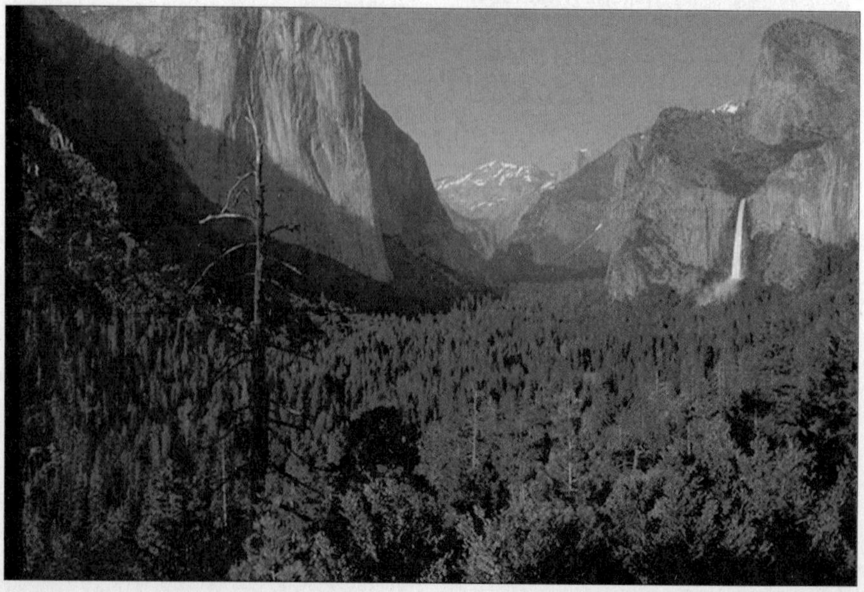
Credit: ©Robert Holmes/California Tourism

Car Museum (www.cablecarmuseum.org), visitors can view the actual cable-winding machinery as it reels 17km (11 miles) of steel at a steady pace of 15km (9.5 miles) per hour.

- Visit the **Roy Rogers-Dale Evans Museum**, a frontier fortress full of mementoes from the Western stars' films and television shows, and the **Route 66 Museum** (www.califrt66museum.org), displaying a collection of artefacts and photographs related to the famous highway.
- Enjoy the **San Diego Maritime Museum** (www.sdmaritime.com) anchored along Harbour Drive, a good place to begin an exploration of the waterfront. Here, visitors can look at the **Star of India** (a century-old windjammer), the steam ferry Berkeley, and the luxury yacht **Medea**. The cruise ship terminal is a popular waterfront destination and excursion boats leaving from Pier B can take visitors on a tour of the bay.
- View the famous 1920s sardine factory, **Cannery Row** (www.canneryrow.com) and **Fisherman's Wharf** (www.montereywharf.com) in historic Monterey.
- Discover that the **Golden Gate Bridge** (www.goldengatebridge.org) is not actually gold at all. It is painted orange, is resistant to harsh weather conditions and is at its most visible through fog. The 1017 acres of **Golden Gate Park** (www.nps.gov/goga) encompass meadows, lakes, rose gardens, an arboretum, a rhododendron dell, an open-air music concourse, a children's playground, a buffalo paddock and the tallest artificial waterfall in the West.
- Experience the **Sequoia** and **Kings Canyon National Parks** (www.nps.gov/seki), famed for their forests of giant sequoia trees, the largest trees on earth. The 2500-year-old **General Sherman Tree** (www.nps.gov/seki/shrm_pic.htm) in **Giant Forest** is the largest tree in the world (by volume) with a circumference of 31.1m (102.6feet). **Kings Canyon** is the deepest canyon in the USA.
- Enjoy the **Yosemite National Park** (www.nps.gov/yose) which contains the world's best-known glacier-carved valley, spectacular waterfalls and granite monoliths, and the **Mariposa Grove of Giant Sequoias** www.redwoodsinyosemite.com/sequoias.htm).
- **Glacier Point** (www.yosemitefun.com/glacier_point.htm) offers some of the best views of the area. Attractions in **Yosemite Village** include the **Yosemite Museum** (www.museumsusa.org/musuems/info) with a Native American cultural exhibit, the **Museum Gallery** with historical works of art, and the **Ansel Adams Gallery**, which has a large selection of limited-edition and signed photographs, prints and posters.
- Tour the famed **J Paul Getty Museum** (www.getty.edu/museum), an exact replica of a Roman country villa, housing one of the world's largest and most valued art collections.
- See where James Marshall discovered the first Californian gold at **Sutter's Mill** (www.sfmuseum.org/hist2/gold.html) in Coloma. Visitors can see where the gold rush began and pan for gold at the **Marshall Gold Discovery State Historic Park** (www.parks.ca.gov/parkindex), which has a museum and both original and restored buildings.
- Try to escape from **Alcatraz** (www.nps.gov/alcatraz). Once the site of the USA's toughest maximum security prison, it is now a National Park.
- Encounter the **Stearns Wharf** (www.stearnswharf.org), once part-owned by the film star James Cagney and his brothers, and the oldest active working pier in California. It offers gifts and souvenirs, wine tasting and a seafood market. Views of the mountains and the ocean are spectacular from here.
- Discover the **Mojave National Scenic Preserve** (www.nps.gov/moja). It offers a remote slice of the Old West, featuring spectacular natural landscapes and history. Another eerily remote area is the **Joshua Tree National Park** (www.nps/gov/jotr) - 220 sq km (850 sq miles) of protected land with many opportunities for hiking and rock climbing.
- Enjoy the revered **Redwood National Park** (www.nps.gov/redw) covering 45,000 hectares (110,000 acres) of land and including three State Parks, the world's tallest tree, stunning shorelines and the world's largest free-roaming herd of Roosevelt elk. It also features two of the most scenic panoramas on the West Coast: the **Crescent City Overlook** (www.redwood.national-park.com/sights.htm) and the **Klamath River Overlook**. Much of the Redwood National Park is located in the county, as is the **Avenue of the Giants** (www.humboldtredwoods.org), a 53km (33-mile) scenic route with hiking and picnicking.

Top Things To Do

- Capture an insider's view of the industry - tour the **NBC, Warner Bros or Universal Studios Hollywood** (website: www.seeing-stars.com/studiotours). The Universal tour is the most popular artificial attraction in America after the Disney theme parks.
- Explore West Hollywood where more post-Oscar parties are hosted than in any other city. Over 70 percent of all filming in **West Hollywood** is on the Sunset Strip. Major films shot in the area include *Get Shorty*, *Casper*, *Heat* and *Leaving Las Vegas*. West Hollywood is best known for its sophisticated shopping and exciting and varied nightlife. The city is home to illustrious clubs, mostly found along the Sunset Strip, which are frequented by the rich and famous.
- Shop **Beverly Hills** (websiste: www.beverlyhills.org). It is home to the most famous shopping district in the world and is also home to the LA branch of the **Museum of Television and Radio** (website: www.mtr.org), which allows visitors to gain access to 75 years of programming history.
- Walk the **Santa Monica Pier** (website: www.santamonicapier.org), the city's most famous landmark. Having undergone a phased US$45 million restoration, the West Coast's oldest pleasure pier, built in 1908 during the height of the city's popularity as a seaside resort, is now home to **Pacific Park** (website: www.pacpark.com). The park features a 17m (55ft) roller coaster and a giant Ferris wheel as well as many other rides. The old pier's carousel, with hand-crafted gilt and painted horses, offers rides each day. Additional features here include the newly renovated **Boat House**, pubs, restaurants, shops and a fresh fish market.
- Be a kid again at **Disneyland** (website: www.disney.go.com). The park continues to be hugely popular. *Tomorrowland* brings a new generation 3-D experience, with a high-speed journey throughout the land upon rocket cars of the future, an interactive pavilion of technology and the landmark *Astro Orbitor* attraction. Other attractions include *Honey, I Shrunk the Audience*, *Innoventions*, the ever-popular *Star Tours*, and the thrill rides, such as *Splash Mountain* and the *Matterhorn*. *Disneyland* is open every day of the year.
- Visit **Little Saigon**, the largest Vietnamese business district in the USA. The area features a wide variety of French, Vietnamese and Asian shops and restaurants as well as an **Asian Garden**.
- Tee off on one of the greens at **Pebble Beach** (website: www.pebblebeach.com), home of the *AT&T National Pro-Am Golf Tournament*. Pebble Beach is a world-class resort with two full service resort hotels, four golf courses and, of course, the famed 17-Mile Drive on which sits the oft-photographed **Lone Cypress Tree**.
- Explore the world-famous **San Diego Zoo** (website: www.sandiegozoo.org), which houses 800 different species. The entire zoo is designed as a 40-hectare (100-acre) tropical garden, which can be visited on foot or on a guided bus tour.
- Head to **Laguna Beach** (website: www.lagunabeachinfo.org), the 'Riviera of the West Coast'. It is considered by many to be the jewel of Southern Californian beach cities. Part of Laguna's charm is its seaside village atmosphere; the strand flows seamlessly into the town, which is filled with bistros, shops and art galleries. Heisler Park, on a bluff overlooking the Pacific, is a great place for a picnic or barbecue and has stairs leading directly down to the beach. Laguna Beach is also home to more than 70 art galleries, including the famous **Laguna Art Museum**.
- Explore 'The Lake in the Sky,' **Tahoe** (website: www.sierratahoe.com). Situated over 1800m (6000ft) above sea level in a stunning alpine setting, it is not hard to see why. Tahoe has clear blue skies, snow-capped mountains and an array of cultural and historical riches. The 115km (72-mile) drive around the lake affords impressive views of the basin. Lake cruises are also available – the *MS Dixie II* and *Tahoe Queen* paddle-wheelers cruise from **South Shore** to **Emerald Bay**, with views straight into the clear waters. This world-famous skiing destination has a great selection of high-quality resorts, including **Alpine Meadows** (website: www.skialpine.com), **Diamond Peak** (website: www.diamondpeak.com), **Heavenly Ski Resort** (website: www.skiheavenly.com), and **Homewood Mountain Resort** (website: www.skihomewood.com). There are plenty of activities for non-skiers, ranging from ice skating, swimming, hot tubbing and snow-tubing at **Squaw Valley** to sleigh rides and snowmobiling at **Northstar-at-Tahoe**.
- Hang out at one of Los Angeles famous beaches. One can bask in the sun in a quiet cove in **Malibu**, see the day sailors of **Marina del Rey** (website: www.visitthemarina.com), or watch the volleyball players on **Manhattan Beach** (website: www.ci.manhattan-beach.ca.us). For a classic Los Angeles experience, a visit to **Venice Beach** (website: www.venicebeach.com), where the body-beautiful skate by and street performers attract crowds every day, is a must. Also a part of Venice is **Muscle Beach** (website: www.healthandfitness.com/musclebeach), where local hunks flex their pecs for bystanders.
- Fish for bass at **Clear Lake**. With more than 160km (100 miles) of shoreline, it is the largest natural freshwater lake in California, known as the 'bass capital of the world.' There are opportunities in Lake County for attending one of the many festivals as well as water-skiing, fishing, swimming, boating, cycling, birdwatching and rock hounding.
- Experience **Big Sur** (website: www.bigsurcalifornia.org), offering vast stretches of sun-baked sand beaches and a wide variety of recreational activities. While there take time to explore the **Bixby Bridge** (website: www.caviews.com/bixbybri.htm), and **Julia Pfeiffer State Park** (website: www.parks.ca.gov).
- Journey through the **Shasta Cascade Region**. Roughly the size of Belgium, the region contains some of California's most breathtaking natural wonders. The 'Three Shastas' include the huge **Shasta Dam**, (website: www.shastalake.com/shastadam), the beautiful **Shasta Lake** (website: www.shastalake.com), and the dramatic, snow-capped **Mount Shasta** (website: www.mtshastachamber.com), one of the nation's tallest mountains at 4248m (14,162ft). The region contains seven national forests, several national and state parks, six wild and scenic rivers, the State's largest lakes, the **Trinity Alps** (website: www.trinitycounty.com), and the **California Cascade Range** (website: www.shastacascade.org). It is an outdoor enthusiast's dream, offering an endless range of activities in summer or winter.
- Play **golf** where there are 330 days of sunshine in **Palm Springs** (website: www.palm-springs.org), a year-round paradise for lovers of the outdoors. This 19th-century desert resort area now features no fewer than 10,000 swimming pools, 600 tennis courts and 90 golf courses. Visitors can shop, watch polo matches, tour museums and art galleries, attend the theatre or dance the night away. More adventurous travellers can go horse riding or hiking through the historic **Indian Canyons** (website: www.indian-canyons.com), be whisked from sea level to the top of 3300m (10,800ft) Mount San Jacinto (website: www.parks.ca.gov) via an aerial tramway or hover above the **Coachella Valley** in a hot-air balloon.

TOURIST INFORMATION

California Tourism
980 Ninth Street, Suite 480, Sacramento, CA 95814, USA
Tel: (916) 444 4429 *or* (800) 862 2543 (toll-free).
Website: www.visitcalifornia.com

California Tourism Office in the UK
McCluskey International, 4 Vencourt Plaza, Hammersmith, London W6 9NU, UK
Tel: (020) 8237 7979.
Website: www.visitcalifornia.com *or* www.mccluskeyinternational.co.uk
Trade enquiries only.

California State Parks
PO Box 942896, Sacramento, CA 94296, USA
Tel: (916) 653 6995 *or* (800) 777 0369 (toll-free).
Website: www.parks.ca.gov

LA Inc (The CVB)
333 South Hope Street, 18th Floor, Los Angeles, CA 90071, USA
Tel: (213) 624 7300 *or* (800) 228 2452 (toll-free).
Website: www.seemyLA.com

San Francisco CVB
201 Third Street, Suite 900, San Francisco, CA 94103, USA
Tel: (415) 974 6900 *or* 391 2000 (visitor information).
Website: www.sfvisitor.org

Entertainment

FOOD & DRINK: California has always been a social melting pot, and this is reflected in its modern, cosmopolitan cuisine with an endless variety of ethnic influences.

Regional specialities:

- Steak.
- Seafood.

NIGHTLIFE: There are few places in the world that can rival California's nightlife. Los Angeles is home to an array of illustrious clubs with rich and famous patrons. San Francisco, with its young, lively population, is known around the world as a great party town.

SHOPPING: Some visitors come to California just for the shopping. Whether they are after the latest fashions or quaint handicrafts, the State's vast range of shops and malls will satisfy any consumer. The boutiques and department stores of Los Angeles are famous worldwide. The city of Ontario, east of Los Angeles, is home to California's largest entertainment and outlet mall. Orange County and Santa Barbara are also known for the quality and variety of their shopping.

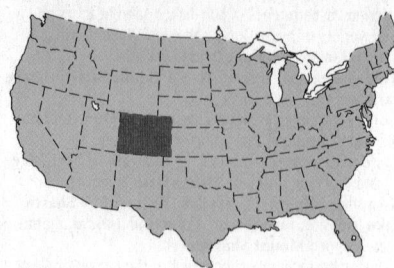

Colorado

Time: Mountain (GMT - 7). *Daylight Saving Time* is observed.

Overview

Colorado is known for its famous Rocky Mountains and is a year-round destination that boasts spectacular national parks, forests, gold-rush ghost towns and Native American ruins. The capital, Denver, is the gateway to numerous ski resorts and is home to many museums, parks, gardens and a restored Victorian square. Located at 1609m (5280ft) above sea level, on high rolling plains at the foot of the Rocky Mountains, Denver, known as the Mile High City, has a population of 500,000 people and is the largest city within a 1000km (625-mile) radius. Founded as a gold-mining camp in 1859, Denver was the centre of the Old West, filled with wagon trains, cowboys, Native Americans, gamblers and gunfighters.

General Information

Nickname: Centennial State.
State bird: Lark Bunting.
State flower: Rocky Mountain Columbine.
CAPITAL: Denver.
Date of admission to the Union: 1 Aug 1876.
POPULATION: 4,67 million (official estimate 2005)
POPULATION DENSITY: 17.1 per sq km
2004 total overseas arrivals/US ranking: 372,588/15

Climate

The capital, Denver, has a mild, dry climate with an average of 300 sunny days a year. Spring is mild with warm days and cool evenings; summer has very warm days with low humidity and cool evening breezes. Denver often enjoys an Indian Summer right into November, while winter is cold, sunny and crisp, with some snowfall. The mountains enjoy warm summer days with cool evenings. Autumn arrives early in the high ground, with abundant snowfall from December to April and temperatures around freezing point.
Required clothing: Warm clothing, especially in the mountains, from November to March/April. Cottons and linens during the summer months.

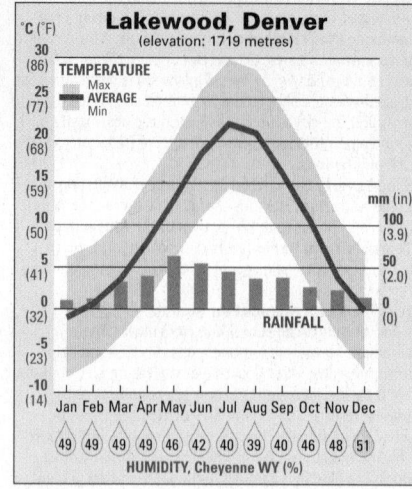

Lakewood, Denver
(elevation: 1719 metres)

TEMPERATURE
Max
AVERAGE
Min

RAINFALL

Jan Feb Mar Apr May Jun Jul Aug Sep Oct Nov Dec

49 49 49 49 46 42 40 39 40 46 48 51

HUMIDITY, Cheyenne WY (%)

Travel - International

AIR:

Main airports: *Denver International (DEN)* (website: www.flydenver.com) is one of the largest airports in the world. It covers 137 sq km (53 sq miles), which is twice the size of Manhattan Island. The airport is located 38km (24 miles) northeast of Denver (travel time – 30 minutes). *British Airways* operates direct flights to Denver from London Heathrow. *To/from the airport*: SkyRide buses run to downtown Denver and Boulder. Taxis, shuttle buses, public buses and limousines are available to the city. There are also many shuttles that operate services to Colorado's various resorts, such as Aspen, Colorado Springs, Estes Park (Rocky Mountain National Park), Steamboat Springs, Summit County and Winter Park. Advance booking is recommended. *Facilities*: ATMs, car hire and post office.
Domestic airports: The major ski resorts are all served by their own airports with domestic flights from many major centres in the USA. Airports include *Aspen/Pitkin County, Colorado Springs, Durango/La Plata, Gunnison County, Vail/Eagle County* and *Yampa Valley* (for Steamboat).
Approximate flight times: From Denver to *London* is 10 hours, to *New York* is three hours 40 minutes, and to *Washington, DC* is three hours 40 minutes.

RAIL:

Denver's growth is historically linked to its importance as a rail centre. It is a hub on the major *Amtrak* east–west route (tel: (800) 872 7245 (toll-free); website: www.amtrak.com), with daily services to Chicago and San Francisco on the 'California Zephyr'. Westbound trains pass through Glenwood Canyon, which is one of the most beautiful railway routes in the USA. The 'Southwest Chief', which links Chicago with Los Angeles, passes through the southeast corner of the State, where a bus link to Denver is available. The *Ski Train* (tel: (303) 296 4754; website: www.skitrain.com) makes a scenic

two-hour journey through the Rockies during the skiing season and on Saturdays in summer.
Approximate rail travel times: From Denver to *Salt Lake City* is 15 hours 30 minutes, to *Chicago* is 20 hours five minutes, and to *San Francisco* is 33 hours 55 minutes.

ROAD:

Greyhound (tel: (800) 229 9424 (toll-free); website: www.greyhound.com) has a terminal in downtown Denver, at 1055 19th Street.
Approximate driving times: From Denver to *Albuquerque* is nine hours, to *Salt Lake City* is 10 hours, to *Dallas* is 16 hours, to *St Louis* is 17 hours 10 minutes, to *Minneapolis* is 17 hours 30 minutes, to *Chicago* is 20 hours 20 minutes, to *Los Angeles* is 23 hours 50 minutes, to *Seattle* is 28 hours 30 minutes and to *New York* is 37 hours.
Approximate bus travel times: From Denver to *Cheyenne* is two hours 30 minutes, to *Albuquerque* is nine hours 30 minutes, to *Amarillo* is 10 hours 30 minutes, to *Kansas City* is 13 hours and to *Las Vegas* is 16 hours.

URBAN:

Denver is well served with buses and a light rail system run by *RTD* (website: www.rtd-denver.com), as well as taxis. The *16th Street Mall Shuttle* provides free transport every 90 seconds, Mon-Fri 0600-0900, along the 1.6km- (1 mile-) long pedestrian mall in the city centre. During summer (June to September), the *Cultural Connection Trolley* takes passengers around Denver's main attractions, departing every 30 minutes, 0930-2200. Car hire is readily available.

Top Things To See

- View the skyline from the **Colorado State Capitol** (website: www.milehighcity.com/capitol), with its spectacular genuine gold roof and sweeping views over the city and the Rockies.
- See the **US Mint**, the second-largest storehouse of gold bullion in the USA after Fort Knox in Alaska.
- Experience the **Denver Botanic Gardens** (website: www.botanicgardens.org). They are comprised of water gardens, a Japanese garden, a rock alpine garden and a conservatory housing a collection of orchids and bromeliads.
- View the red sandstone pinnacles of the **Garden of the Gods** (website: www.gardenofthegods.com).
- Experience **Mesa Verde National Park** (website: www.nps.gov/meve), located in the high plateau country of southwestern Colorado. The 21,044-hectare (52,000-acre) park is designated as a World Heritage Site and contains some of the largest and most impressive examples of the dramatic Anasazi culture's cliff dwellings. Built over 700 years ago, these amazing structures have as many as 200 rooms. The park has paved roads offering views over the major ruins. There is a museum that attempts to explain the riddle of why the Native Americans built their villages in caves, and why, by the year 1300, they had completely abandoned the Mesa Verde plateau.
- Explore the **Rocky Mountain National Park** (website: www.nps.gov/romo), located 104km (65 miles) northwest of Denver, and Colorado's most popular attraction. Reaching heights of 3736m (12,183ft), **Trail Ridge Road** crosses the park and forms one of the highest continuous highways in North America. Massive peaks, rugged canyons, flower-strewn meadows, peaceful lakes and thundering waterfalls combine to offer the visitor over 640km (400 miles) of spectacular wilderness. With its majestic mountain backdrop and picturesque main street, the resort village of **Estes Park** (website: www.estesparkresort.com), on the edge of Rocky Mountain National Park, is very popular with visitors.
- Discover the **Black Canyon of the Gunnison National Park** (website: www.nps.gov/blca). It preserves the most spectacular 19km (12-mile) stretch of the 85km (53-mile) gorge carved by the **Gunnison River**. A paved road circles the rim of the canyon, which at some points is nearly half a mile deep.
- See the **Colorado National Monument**, an area of fantastic red rock canyons, monoliths, pillars and cliffs; while **Dinosaur National Monument** (website: www.nps.gov/dino) is a plateau cut by two rivers and is home to one of the world's richest deposits of dinosaur and reptile fossils.
- Visit the **Great Sand Dunes National Monument** (website: www.nps.gov/grsa), with some of the highest inland sand dunes in North America. **Hovenweep National Monument** features the ruins of an ancient civilisation, with prehistoric towers, pueblos and cliff dwellings dating back almost 900 years.

Top Things To Do

- Explore the **16th Street Mall**, a tree-lined promenade in the heart of the city, running between downtown Denver and Union Station. Popular with shoppers, it is always alive with pedestrians, cafes, street performers and fountains.

- Enjoy an American football game. Watch the **Denver Broncos** (website: www.denverbroncos.com) play on **Invesco Field** at **Mile High Stadium**.
- Travel on the **Manitou & Pikes Peak Cog Railway**, (website: www.cograilway.com) offering views of the Continental Divide.
- Ski the **Rocky Mountains** (website: www.nps.gov/romo), renowned the world over for unparalleled skiing. In recent years, the region has gained considerable popularity with European ski enthusiasts as well as visitors from within the USA, and the range of facilities and accommodation is unrivalled.
- Enjoy the snow at **Aspen** (website: www.aspenchamber.org), located 256km (160 miles) west of Denver. The resort attracts the rich and famous from all over the world and is perhaps America's most sophisticated ski resort, offering a full range of winter and summer activities and countless restaurants and shops.
- Visit **Vail** (website: www.vail.snow.com), two hours west of Denver. This resort town is among the top ski destinations in the nation and built in a Tyrolean style.
- Ski or snowboard in **Summit County**, home to the popular ski resorts of **Keystone** (website: www.keystone.snow.com) (with the longest ski season in the State), **Arapahoe Basin** (website: www.arapahoebasin.com), **Copper Mountain** (website: www.coppercolorado.com), and **Breckenridge** (website: www.breckenridge.snow.com).
- Plan a ski trip to one of these popular resorts: **Beaver Creek Resort** (website: www.beavercreek.snow.com) (suitable for families), **Howelsen Ski Area** (the oldest ski area in Colorado and home to the most complete ski-jumping complex), **Silver Creek** (website: www.silvercreek-resort.com) (affordable family skiing), **Steamboat** (website: www.steamboat.com) (with its nickname Ski Town USA and its distinctly Western heritage), or **Ski Sunlight** (website: www.sunlightmtn.com) (with the world's largest hot springs pool at Glenwood Springs). All the resorts offer reliable amounts of snow and an extensive range of accommodation and other facilities.

TOURIST INFORMATION

Colorado Tourism Office
1625 Broadway, Suite 1700, Denver, CO 80202, USA
Tel: (303) 892 3885 or (800) 265 6723 (toll-free) or (303) 892 3850 (international inquiries).
Website: www.colorado.com

Colorado Tourism Office in the UK
c/o Cellet Travel Services Ltd, 47 High Street, Henley-in-Arden, Warwickshire B95 5AA, UK
Tel: (01564) 794 999.
Website: www.cellet.co.uk

Entertainment

FOOD & DRINK: There are restaurants offering Southeast Asian cuisine, innovative *New Southwestern* cuisine and international cuisines in every price range. For a distinctly Colorado-style meal, visitors can visit Denver, Boulder and many mountain towns, which offer freshly-brewed local beer and delicious food.
Regional specialities:
- Fresh rainbow trout.
- Buffalo and elk steaks.

NIGHTLIFE: The **Denver Performing Arts Complex** houses seven theatres including the **Boettcher Concert Hall**. Among the other varied entertainments in the city, there are smaller venues staging theatre, popular music, jazz, dance, comedy and country & western music. For detailed information on scheduled events, visitors can consult The *Denver Post* or the *Rocky Mountain News*. Many of the ski resorts, notably Aspen and Vail, have countless restaurants, bars and other *après-ski* diversions.

SHOPPING: Denver offers extensive shopping facilities. **Cherry Creek Shopping Center**, the **Denver Pavillions** (located on 16th Street Mall), **Park Meadows Center** (the first shopping centre in the USA that resembles a beautiful mountain lodge) and **Larimer Square** all offer a pleasant shopping environment. Denver now has three factory outlet shopping centres: **Castle Rock** (situated 20 minutes south of Denver), **Silverthorne** in Summit County and **Rocky Mountain Factory Outlets** at Loveland. The **Colorado Mills** complex is located in Lakewood, near Denver, and has been described as 'Disneyland meets outlet mall'. Aspen in the Rocky Mountains has an unsurpassed range of shops and upmarket boutiques selling top designer lines. Special buys in Colorado include gold earrings and necklaces, Native American jewellery, Navajo rugs, and handicrafts such as pottery, wind chimes and wildlife sculptures.

Connecticut

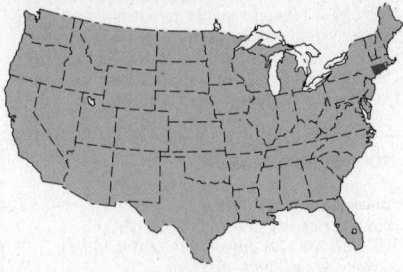

Time: Eastern (GMT - 5). *Daylight Saving Time* is observed.

Overview

Connecticut is a mixture of town and country; beyond the towns and major cities inhabited by New York commuters are quiet colonial villages set in a rural landscape. The third-smallest State in the USA, Connecticut has a rich literary history. Hartford was the home of Mark Twain, and tourists can visit The Mark Twain House, at Nook Farm, where he wrote his greatest work, *The Adventures of Huckleberry Finn*, in 1884. Next door is the cottage in which the author of *Uncle Tom's Cabin*, Harriet Beecher Stowe, lived until her death in 1896, also open for tours.

General Information

Nickname: Constitution State.
State bird: American Robin.
State flower: Mountain Laurel.
CAPITAL: Hartford.
Date of admission to the Union: 9 Jan 1788 (original 13 States; date of ratification of the Constitution).
POPULATION: 3.51 million (official estimate 2005).
POPULATION DENSITY: 244 per sq km
2004 total overseas arrivals/US ranking: 252,000/18

Climate

In winter, temperatures generally average -5-2.8°C (23-37°F). Summer temperatures range from 18.9-27.8°C (66-82°F).
Required clothing: Cottons, linens and a light jacket for the summer months. Heavyweight clothing with extra bundling for the winter months.

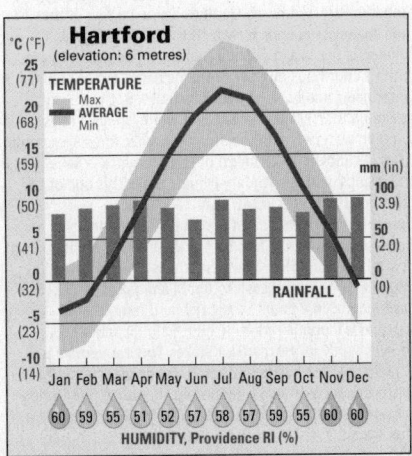

Hartford (elevation: 6 metres)
TEMPERATURE — Max, AVERAGE, Min
RAINFALL
HUMIDITY, Providence RI (%)
Jan 60 Feb 59 Mar 55 Apr 51 May 52 Jun 57 Jul 58 Aug 57 Sep 59 Oct 55 Nov 60 Dec 60

Top Things To See & Do

- Visit **Hartford**, the home of Mark Twain. **The Mark Twain House**, at Nook Farm, is where he wrote his greatest work, *The Adventures of Huckleberry Finn*, in 1884. Next door, visitors can tour the cottage in which the author of *Uncle Tom's Cabin*, Harriet Beecher Stowe, lived. For children, there is the delightful **Bushnell Park Carousel**, which was built in 1914 in one of the first public US parks. Other Hartford attractions include the oldest public art museum in the country, **Wadsworth Atheneum**, the **Museum of Connecticut History**, and the **Old State House**, which housed the State government until 1914.
- Explore **New Haven**, the site of **Yale University**, the **Peabody Museum of Natural History**, the **Center for**

British Art, and **Yale University Art Gallery**. The Art Gallery houses a fine collection, including American decorative arts, pre-Colombian pieces and works by European masters such as Van Gogh. More modern fare can be viewed at the **Neon Garage**. The town is also known for its theatre; famous names to have trodden New Haven's boards include Jodie Foster, Glenn Close and Meryl Streep. *The New Haven Symphony Orchestra* and the *Yale Repertory Theater* have their homes here.
- Discover Connecticut's maritime past at **Mystic Seaport**. There is a display of wooden ships, a maritime museum, shops, and art and craft collections. Marvel at the sharks, dolphins and seals at **Mystic Aquarium**. Shop and dine in the New England Colonial setting of **Olde Mistick Village**. Some 8km (5 miles) east of Mystic, **Stonington Borough** is a delightful old fishing village, which boasts a number of antique shops and a **Lighthouse Museum**.
- Other attractions in the State include the entertainment complexes and casinos of **Foxwoods Resort** and the **Mashantucket Pequot Museum and Research Center** in Mashantucket, the **Mohegan Sun** in Uncasville, the **Haight Vineyards** in **Litchfield** and the **Ocean Beach Park**, with a sand beach and wooden boardwalk, in **New London**.

TOURIST INFORMATION

Connecticut Office of Tourism
505 Hudson Street, Hartford, CT 06106, USA
Tel: (860) 270 8080 or (800) 282 6863 (toll-free).
Website: www.ctbound.org

Greater New Haven CVB
59 Elm Street, New Haven, CT 06510, USA
Tel: (203) 777 8550 or (800) 332 7829 (toll-free).
Website: www.newhavencvb.org

Credit: ©Connecticut Commission on Culture and Tourism

Delaware

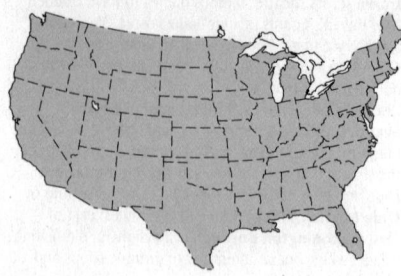

Time: Eastern (GMT - 5). *Daylight Saving Time* is observed.

Overview

This small State's administrative and commercial centre is Wilmington. Founded in 1638, the city includes museums, galleries, a port and a trolley car system modelled on the world-famous cable cars in San Francisco. Fort Christina Historic Park is the site of Delaware's first permanent settlement when Finns and Swedes landed here in 1638. The rest of the State is mostly rural. Lewes is a quaint seaside historic town with some delightful beaches. Cape Henlopen State Park is Delaware's largest State Park, with its seabird nesting colony and white sand dunes.

General Information

Nickname: Diamond State.
State bird: Blue Hen Chicken.
State flower: Peach Blossom.
CAPITAL: Dover.
Date of admission to the Union: 7 Dec 1787 (original 13 States; date of ratification of the Constitution).
POPULATION: 843,524 (official estimate 2005).
POPULATION DENSITY: 130.8 per sq km.
2004 total overseas arrivals: Under 38,000.

Climate

Delaware has a humid, temperate climate. Winter temperatures average 1.7°C (35°F). Average summer temperature is 24°C (75°F).
Required clothing: Lightweights for the summer with cover-up for cool nights and more ample weights for the winter.

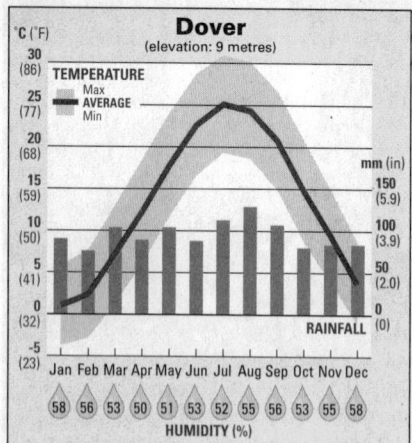

Top Things To See & Do

• Explore the museums, galleries and port of **Wilmington**.
• Visit Delaware's first permanent settlement, **Fort Christina Historic Park**.
• View the permanent collection of 19th- and 20th-century American art and Pre-Raphaelite English art of the 19th century at the **Delaware Art Museum**, including works by Edward Hopper, Howard Pyle and Andrew Wyeth.
• Head to nearby **Brandywine Valley**, home to the Du Pont mansions, as well as the Hagley Museum, which explains how this powerful family's fortune was made.
• Explore the capital, **Dover**, home to numerous museums, including the **Air Mobility Command Museum**, which exhibits planes and military artefacts.
• Relax on the beaches in the historic seaside town of **Lewes**. East of Lewes is the **Cape Henlopen State Park**, Delaware's largest State Park.
• Enjoy a family day out at **Rehoboth Beach**, a seaside

resort popular for its amusement park, 1.6km- (1 mile-) long boardwalk, fine restaurants and shops. Bargain hunters will be enticed by the retail outlet shopping that is available in the vicinity.
• Go clubbing in **Dewey Beach**, a lively holiday spot with plenty of bars and clubs to keep youthful holidaymakers happy, as well as opportunities for watersports.
• Sightsee in historic **New Castle**, which includes some wonderfully preserved buildings, such as the 1732 Old Court House, which served as the first state capitol, and the Colonial style **George Read II House**.

TOURIST INFORMATION

Delaware Tourism Office
99 Kings Highway, Dover, DE 19901, USA
Tel: (302) 739 4271 *or* (866) 284 7483 (toll-free).
Website: www.visitdelaware.com

Greater Wilmington CVB
100 West 10th Street, Suite 20,
Wilmington, DE 19801, USA
Tel: (302) 652 4088 *or* (800) 489 6664 (toll-free).
Website: www.visitwilmingtonde.com

Florida

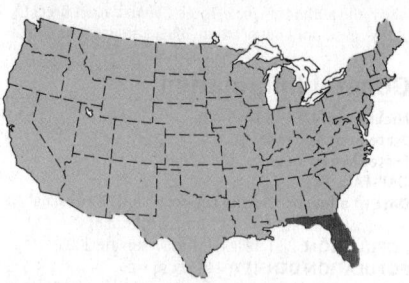

Time: The Eastern part of Florida (which includes all the major towns and cities) falls in the Eastern Time Zone (GMT -5) and the Western part of the Florida panhandle falls in the Central Time Zone (GMT -6).
Daylight Saving Time is observed in both.

Overview

Florida is one of the most popular tourist destinations in the world, with visitors heading to 'The Sunshine State' in search of fun, sun and thrills. Walt Disney World, Magic Kingdom Park and Busch Gardens are just a few of the man-made attractions for which the State is famed. Orlando is the face of Florida that most people recognise, with its enormous number of theme parks, movie studios, water parks and entertainment facilities. But there is more to Florida than Mickey Mouse and white-knuckle rides. Winding waterways, freshwater lakes, hills, forests, exciting cities, 13,560km (8426 miles) of coast, countless bays, inlets and islands, and a legendary climate make this one of the most popular States in the USA.
Florida is divided into eight geographical regions: Northwest; North Central; Northeast; Central West; Central; Central East; Southwest; and Southeast Florida & the Keys. Situated on the southeastern tip, Miami and Miami Beach have long been a haunt of the rich and famous, and star-spotting is a popular pastime here. Palm Beach scores equally highly in the glamour stakes. Fort Lauderdale is a popular spot for families, offering a wide assortment of sports and recreational activities. To the south, the Florida Keys offers a tropical climate, beautiful beaches and clear blue waters.
The capital of Florida, Tallahassee, is geographically closer to Atlanta than Miami and is strictly Southern in tone. It was chosen as the State capital in 1823, as a compromise between Pensacola and St Augustine, which had both been vying for the honour. Today, it is often described as 'The Other Florida' with its rolling hills, oak forests, cool climate and distinctly Southern feel.
Tampa and St Petersburg are the main cities in the Central West region. Sarasota is the cultural capital of the region, thanks to John Ringling and his wife who amassed an impressive art collection, which is today displayed in their restored mansion. The southwestern region is home to Naples, a popular seaside retreat. Just off the mainland, Marco Island stands as a model of ecological preservation.
In the northeastern corner of Florida stands Jacksonville, named after General Andrew Jackson. Nearby St Augustine is known as 'America's Oldest City' and is home to more

than 60 historic sites. Amelia Island, often called the 'Isle of Eight Flags', is the only site in the country to have been governed by eight different countries during its history. At its heart lies Fernandina Beach, the nation's second-oldest city. Daytona is located in the slender Central East region. The beach is the city's main attraction, with a 510m (1700ft) boardwalk brimming with amusements, rides and snack bars.

General Information

Nickname: Sunshine State.
State bird: Mockingbird.
State flower: Orange Blossom.
CAPITAL: Tallahassee.
Date of admission to the Union: 3 Mar 1845.
POPULATION: 17.79 million (official estimate 2004).
POPULATION DENSITY: 104.5 per sq km.
2004 total overseas arrivals/US ranking: 4.3 milion/1.

Climate

Summers throughout the state are long, warm and fairly humid. Winters are mild with periodic invasions of cool to occasionally cold air. Coastal areas in all sections of Florida average slightly warmer temperatures in winter and cooler ones in summer.
Required clothing: Lightweight cotton and sun hats are recommended for summer. Light jackets are fine for cooler evenings and winter.

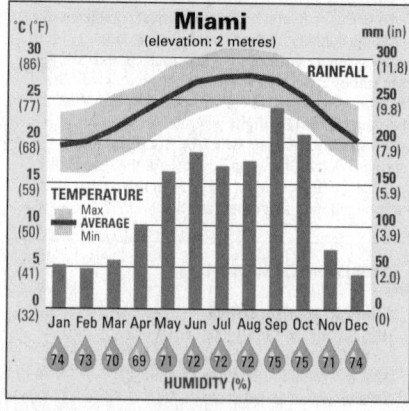

Travel - International

AIR:

 Main airports: *Miami International Airport (MIA)* (website: www.miami-airport.com) is 9km (6 miles) west of Miami (travel time – 25 minutes). *To/from airport:* There is a 24-hour shuttle service to the central bus station and hotels on request. Public buses are also available to the city. Taxi, van and limousine services are also available; fares are fixed.
Greyhound (tel: (800) 231 2222 (toll-free); website: www.greyhound.com) runs daily services throughout the Florida Keys and to destinations in the north. *Facilities:* ATMs, car hire and currency exchange.
Tampa International Airport (TPA) (website: www.tampaairport.com) is 8km (5 miles) northwest of Tampa (travel time – 15 minutes). *To/from the airport:* A bus service runs into the city; limousine and taxi services are also available. *Facilities:* ATMs, car hire and currency exchange.
Orlando International (OIA) (website: www.state.fl.us/goaa), is 15km (9 miles) south of Orlando (travel time – 15 minutes). Scheduled flights from the UK arrive here . *To/from the airport:* There is a 24-hour shuttle service available to any hotel in Orlando. Coach, bus, taxi and limousine services are available. *Facilities:* ATMs, car hire and currency exchange.
Fort Lauderdale-Hollywood (FLL) (website: www.fll.net) is 8km (5 miles) from Fort Lauderdale (travel time – 10 minutes). *To/from to airport:* Limousines, taxis and bus services are available, with rail connections to the surrounding counties. *Facilities:* ATMs, car hire and currency exchange.
St Petersburg-Clearwater International Airport (PIE) (www.fly2pie.com). *To/from to airport:* Limousines, taxis and bus services are available. *Facilities:* ATMs and car hire.
Approximate flight times: From Miami to *Barbados* is three hours 25 minutes, to *Honolulu* is 12 hours 15 minutes, and to *London* is eight hours 10 minutes. From Tampa to *London* is 10 hours (direct flight), to *Miami* is 55 minutes and to *New York* is two hours 40 minutes. From Orlando to *London* is nine hours, to *New York* is two hours 30 minutes and to *Washington, DC* is two hours five minutes.

A B C D E F G H I J K L M N O P Q R S T U V W X Y Z

SEA:

Main ports: *Miami, Fort Lauderdale, Port Everglades, Port Canaveral, Port of Palm Beach, St Petersburg* and *Tampa*. The port of Miami has been called the 'Cruise Capital of the World' and offers ocean liners for business meetings, weekend getaways and extended luxury cruises. The port of Fort Lauderdale, Port Everglades, is the second most important cruise port in Florida. Other cruise ports on the east coast include Port Canaveral and Port of Palm Beach. The main West Coast cruise ports include St Petersburg and Tampa. Major cruise lines in Florida include *Carnival, Commodore, Cunard, Princess, Radisson Seven Seas* and *Royal Caribbean*.

RAIL:

Amtrak (tel: (800) 872 7245; website: www.amtrak.com) is the rail service provider. Amtrak's Miami Station is 11km (7 miles) northwest of the city centre. It is the southernmost point on the network, marking the southern end of the main east coast line from New York (and ultimately Boston). Amtrak also serves Jacksonville, with services running through Orlando to Tampa (a branch line terminates at Sarasota, a few miles south of Tampa on the Gulf of Mexico), and west through Pensacola.

ROAD:

The best major routes through Florida are: Daytona Beach to St Petersburg (I-4), Jacksonville to the Alabama border (I-10), St Petersburg to Tampa (I-275), the lower West Coast to Fort Lauderdale (I-75), the North-South highway (I-95) or (I-75) and the East-West cross-state highway from Clearwater to Vero Beach (State 60). Florida's Turnpike is a 723km (449 mile) system of limited-access toll highways, which passes through 11 counties from north Miami to a junction with I-75 in north central Florida. Most roads are excellent throughout the State.

Approximate driving times: From **Orlando** to *Fort Lauderdale* is four houirs 30 minutes, to *Key West* is eight hours 45 minutes, and to *St Petersburg* is two hours and 30 minutes.. All times are based on non-stop driving at or below the applicable speed limits.

Approximate Greyhound travel times: From **Miami** to *Jacksonville* is 11 hours 15 minutes, to *Tampa* is eight hours 15 minutes, and to *Tallahassee* is 14 hours.

URBAN:

Miami's transport system includes an elevated *Metrorail* system running a north-south route through the city. The *Downtown Metromover* combines the fun of a theme park with the convenience of above-street-level travel. Metrobuses operate frequently through most areas of Greater Miami. Fares are moderate and transfers are available. Taxis can be expensive in the Miami area; one can usually hail them but delays may be encountered at rush hours. Taxis can also be booked by telephone. Most major car hire and motor camper hire firms have offices at the airport or in central Miami. Many provide a drop-off service in other parts of the State. Major hotels can often arrange immediate car hire. Road signs marked with an orange sun on a blue background indicate routes to major tourist attractions.

Top Things To See

- Tour **St. Augustine**, the USA's oldest city, a time capsule capturing nearly 500 years of fascinating history. Situated on the uppermost Atlantic Coast of Florida, the water's-edge colonial village has 144 blocks of historic houses listed on the National Register of Historic Places. The **Castillo de San Marcos** (website: www.nps.gov/casa) endures as the nation's oldest and only remaining 17th-century masonry fort. Now a National Monument, the Spanish-built bastion guarded the mouth of **Matanzas Bay** from British invaders. The **Spanish Quarter Living Museum** (website: www.historicstaugustine.com) is a village where actors portraying Spanish soldiers and settlers in traditional costume re-enact 18th-century crafts.
- Visit **St Petersburg**, home to world-class museums, including the **Salvador Dali Museum** (website: www.salvadordalimuseum.org), which contains the world's most comprehensive collection by this famous Spanish surrealist.
- Explore the **Florida International Museum** (website: www.floridamuseum.org), which was named a **Smithsonian Institution** affiliate and is home to the largest private collection of John F Kennedy memorabilia, including a recreation of JFK's Oval Office.
- Experience the **Florida Holocaust Museum** (website: www.flholocaustmuseum.com). The museum is one of the largest in the country and is dedicated to the memory of millions of innocent people who died or suffered in the Holocaust.
- See the **Ringling Museum Complex** in **Sarasota** (website: www.ringling.org), the official **State Museum of Florida**. It is a major attraction with superb old masterpieces and a fine contemporary collection.
- Pay a small fee and visitors can still take their cars on part of **Daytona Beach**, but the top speed now allowed is just 16kmph (10mph). Real speed is confined to the **Daytona International Speedway** (website: www.daytonainternationalspeedway.com), which hosts the famous *Daytona 500* race each February. The *Pepsi 400 NASCAR Winston Cup* Series takes place in the summer. The speedway also houses a huge collection of racing memorabilia and early racing films and conducts 30-minute tours on days with no races.
- Journey to **Cape Canaveral** – home of the US Space Program. All of NASA's shuttle flights take off from the **Kennedy Space Center**. The **Kennedy Space Center Visitor Complex** (website: www.kennedyspacecenter.com) runs continuous tours of the complex where visitors see the actual launchpads and astronaut training centres as well as museums and exhibits. IMAX presentations give visitors the illusion of space travel. Tours take in the **Apollo/ Saturn Visitors' Center**, the **Launch Complex 39 Observation Gantry** and the **International Space Station Center**, which highlight the past, present and future of the USA's Space Program. Visitors should plan to spend at least an hour at each of these facilities.
- Explore **Marco Island** (website: www.marco-island-florida.com), located at the southernmost tip of Florida's **Gulf Coast** and nearly lost amongst the **Ten Thousand Islands**, a maze of mangrove isles that stretch from Naples to the Florida Keys. It is an area of stunning beauty. Marco Island, the largest and only inhabited isle, is a retreat for the wealthy.
- Experience Florida's famous **Everglades National Park** (website: www.nps.gov/ever). Its pampered perfection complements the tangled wildness and sweeping sawgrass prairies. The Everglades is the USA's third-largest national park. Several excursions offer a glimpse of the country's only subtropical region, by means of airboat tours, nature trails and safari vans. The unassuming fishing hamlets of **Everglades City** and **Chokoloskee Island**, both locked in time, offer visitors an interactive eco-adventure in the inspirational beauty of Florida's final frontier.
- Visit **Biscayne National Park** (website: www.nps.gov/bisc). The park offers glass-bottomed boat rides through mangroves and islands and out to tropical coral reefs rising 8m (25ft).
- Discover the **Riverwalk** (website: www.goriverwalk.com) in **Fort Lauderdale**, a linear park linking hotels, restaurants and attractions along the banks of the **New River**, leading to the **Broward Center for the Performing Arts**. Water taxis ply Fort Lauderdale's canals and the Intracoastal Waterway.
- Venture to the **Florida Keys**. Stretching from **Key Largo** (website: www.fla-keys.com/keylargo) at the northern end to **Key West** (website: www.fla-keys/com/keywest) in the south, 45 of the over 800 islands of the Florida Keys, once known as the Cayos, are linked by Overseas Highway 1. Enjoy **Key Largo**, the longest island of the Keys chain and the site where Humphrey Bogart and Lauren Bacall battled with both Edward G Robinson and the elements in the movie *Hurricane*. Key Largo's star attractions are **John Pennekamp Coral Reef State Park** – the first underwater preserve in the USA – and the adjacent **Key Largo National Marine Sanctuary**. These two refuges feature 55 varieties of delicate corals and almost 500 different species of fish. Key Largo also features the world's first **underwater hotel**, where guests can spend the evening in the midst of the marine life of the Keys.
- Tour the pre-Civil War mansion in **Key West** where Ernest Hemingway (website: www.hemingwayhome.com) lived for 10 years while writing some of his best-known novels. His legend remains and visitors continue to seek out his home – now a museum – and his favourite bar. In the evening, visitors gather at **Mallory Square** (website: www.mallorysquare.com) to 'call it a day'. The daily 'Sunset Celebration' is a tradition that Key Westers share with visitors. While musicians, jugglers, mime artists and an occasional fire-eater provide the entertainment, the sun sinks slowly below the horizon.

Top Things To Do

- Cast out your line at the 'World's Luckiest Fishing Village', Destin's **East Pass**. Harbouring the largest and most elaborately equipped charter-boat fleet in Florida, more billfish are caught on the Northern Gulf each year than by all the other Gulf ports combined. There is also a wider variety of game fish than elsewhere, from cobia and scampi to triggerfish and king mackerel. Numerous deep-sea excursions are available for both first-time fishers and the more experienced angler.
- Venture to **Busch Gardens** (website: www.buschgardens.com), a huge amusement park featuring African wildlife. Giraffes, zebras and antelope roam freely through the park's 24-hectare (60-acre) plain, next to thrilling rides such as the Kumba.
- Experience the terrifying attack of a Great White shark on

Credit: ©Visit Florida

the *Jaws Ride* at **Universal Studios, Florida** (website: www.universalorlando.com).
- Plan the family holiday for **Walt Disney World Resort** (website: www.disney.go.com). The resort is the biggest, and arguably the best, amusement park in the world. It contains four sections: the **Magic Kingdom**, with seven theme regions; **Epcot Center**, a science and world exhibition centre; **Disney MGM Studios**, a movie and theme park; and **Animal Kingdom**, an adventure and safari park featuring wild animals, exotic landscapes and thrill rides. Popular attractions include a 13-storey free-fall plunge on the *Twilight Zone Tower of Terror* at Disney MGM Studios; Epcot's *Mission:SPACE*, which recreates space travel and pushes the boundaries of entertainment technology; and *Stitch's Great Escape* at *Tomorrowland* in the Magic Kingdom. **Blizzard Beach**, Disney's largest water park, is set in a faux snow-capped mountain range featuring Florida's only chairlift, which carries guests to the tip of *Mount Gushmore*. A number of water slides challenge visitors, including *Summit Plummet*, the tallest, fastest water slide in the world. More high-speed rides can be found at **Typhoon Lagoon**.
- Meet the newest family member, Baby Shamu, at **SeaWorld Orlando** (website: www.seaworld.com), southwest of Orlando (travel time – 19 minutes) and one of the country's largest marine parks featuring whales, dolphins, sea lions, seals and otters. The most popular shows are the ones starring the killer whale, Shamu.
- Take a swim at **New Smyrna Beach** (website: www.nsbfla.com). Billed as the 'World's Safest Bathing Beach,' it is also the beach closest to the popular Orlando area and Central Florida attractions and an attraction in itself. Only a short drive from Orlando and Daytona Beach International Airports, New Smyrna Beach lays claim to the best Florida offers - excellent backwater fishing, fresh seafood and seasons of sunshine. As the second-oldest settled city in Florida, **New Smyrna** offers visitors tours of several historical sites and museums.
- Get away to **Fort Myers Beach** (website: www.fortmeyersbeach.org), ideal for family holidays with its safe, gently sloping shoreline and numerous activities.
- Take advantage , golfers, of the fact that Southwest Florida has more **golf** holes per capita than any other destination in the USA.
- Relax in **Naples** (website: www.naples-florida.com), a charming city with an atmosphere of understated elegance. Home to cosy beach cottages and 5-star resorts, Naples is also known for its pristine shoreline and abundant wildlife.
- Dive in and experience the different watersports offered at **Miami Beach** (website: www.miamibeachfl.gov). Equipment for kayaking, windsurfing, boogie boarding, and scuba diving is available for rent. Boating activities are also available.
- Fish **The Keys** (website: www.fla-keys.com). They boast

more sportfishing world records than any other fishing destination in the world. Anglers can find sailfish, marlin, kingfish, snapper, barracuda and grouper.

TOURIST INFORMATION

Visit Florida (the Official Tourism Marketing Corporation for the State of Florida)
Street address: 661 East Jefferson Street, Suite 300, Tallahassee, FL 32301, USA
Postal address: PO Box 1100, Tallahassee, FL 32302, USA
Tel: (850) 488 5607.
Website: www.visitflorida.org or www.visitflorida.com

Visit Florida in the UK
28 Eccleston Square, London SW1V 1NZ, UK
Tel: (020) 7932 2406 or (01737) 644 882 (brochure request).
Website: www.flausa.com/uk
This office is not open to the public.

Central Florida Visitors & Convention Bureau
600 North Broadway, Suite 300, Bartow, FL 33830, USA
Tel: (863) 298 7565 or (800) 828 7655 (toll-free).
Website: www.sunsational.org

Greater Miami CVB
701 Brickell Avenue, Suite 2700, Miami, FL 33131, USA
Tel: (305) 539 3000 or (800) 933 8448 (toll-free).
Website: www.miamiandbeaches.com or www.gmcvb.com

Orlando/Orange County CVB
6700 Forum Drive, Suite 100, Orlando, FL 32821, USA
Visitor Centre: 8723 International Drive, Orlando, FL 32819, USA
Tel: (407) 363 5872 or (800) 215 2213 (toll-free) or (407) 972 3304 (visitor centre).
Website: www.orlandoinfo.com

Entertainment

FOOD & DRINK: Miami/Miami Beach: There are more than 300 fine restaurants, and most hotels maintain excellent dining rooms. Some gourmet eateries are expensive but many popular restaurants have economy prices. Cuban and Mexican food is very popular in Miami, and because Florida is surrounded almost entirely by water, seafood is a State speciality. Fresh stone crabs are not available anywhere else in the USA. **Orlando:** International Drive is the centre of a variety of restaurants that include Chinese, tapas, Cuban, Asian/Pacific rim and even fondue. **Tampa:** There is a clear emphasis on Latin cuisine in Tampa but all tastes are catered for, with everything from international restaurants to fast food.
Regional specialities:
• Seafood.
• Key Lime pie.
NIGHTLIFE: Miami/Miami Beach: Nightclubs exist in most hotels and resorts. The Coconut Grove area, with its trendy nightclubs and cocktail bars, offers a swinging nightlife both inside the clubs and on the streets where many people just come for a stroll, in order to be where the action is. The most lavish and lively clubs are Cuban supper clubs. **Les Folies** and **Les Violons**, both on Biscayne Boulevard, are highly recommended and feature spectacular shows and excellent food. **Orlando: Pleasure Island** is a high-energy, nighttime entertainment complex featuring seven themed nightclubs, stage shows and live concerts, plus a giant New Year's Eve celebration every night of the week. It is located in an area known as **Downtown Disney**, along with such restaurants as **Wolfgang Puck**, **House of Blues** and the **Cuban-style Bongo's Cafe**. **Tampa:** The best nightlife on the Gulf Coast can be found in Ybor City, which is Tampa's lively and historic Latin quarter. The action centres on Seventh Avenue, which closes to traffic at weekends to allow the party atmosphere to spill out on to the streets.
SHOPPING: Miami: The city's main shopping streets are **Flagler Street**, between Biscayne Bay and Miami Avenue; and **Biscayne Boulevard**, between Flagler Street and north to 16th Street. Luxury and designer shops can be found at **Village of Merrick Park** in Coral Gables, south of Miami. **Miami Beach:** The principal shopping area is **Lincoln Road** *Mall*. Just north of Miami Beach is the **Bal Harbour Shopping District**. **Fort Lauderdale:** The famous **Sawgrass Mills Factory Outlet Mall** is located on the northwest edge of the city and many boutiques can be found near the waterfront. **Tampa:** The main shopping area is around **Franklin Street Mall**. **Orlando:** Shoppers can take advantage of a huge range of retail outlets from factory outlet malls such as **Lake Buena Vista Factory Stores** to designer malls such as **Orlando Premium Outlets and the Mall at Millenia**.

Georgia

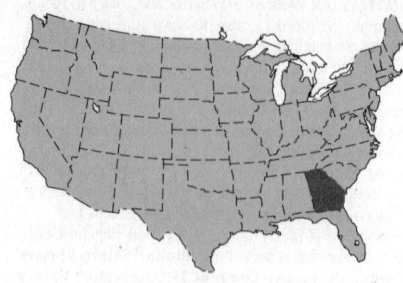

Time: Eastern (GMT – 5). *Daylight Saving Time* is observed.

Overview

Georgia is the largest State east of the Mississippi River, and was founded in 1735 by James Oglethorpe, an Englishman who landed in Savannah and established the 13th colony in the New World. Georgia is the only State to be named after a British Monarch. It is geographically diverse, with landscapes ranging from mountains in the northeast to the mysterious, low-lying Okefenokee Swamp in the south, called the land of the 'trembling earth' by the region's Native American tribes. It was in this State that gold was first struck in North America in the early part of the 19th century, and the gold rush that followed centered around the town of Dahlonega.
Now a booming services-industry centre with a population of over 400,000 (and a metro population topping 4 million), Atlanta – known as 'The City in a Forest' – most dramatically expresses the transition from Old South to New. Along its residential streets, magnolia and dogwood trees surround handsome Georgian-style homes, yet only blocks away, some of the country's most dazzling contemporary buildings are rising at record speed to add to Atlanta's ever-growing skyline.
Georgia's varied climate ranges from the low humidity of the Blue Ridge Mountains to the subtropical southern coastal region.

General Information

Nickname: Peach State.
State bird: Brown Thrasher.
State flower: Cherokee Rose.
CAPITAL: Atlanta.
Date of admission to the Union: 2 Jan 1788 (original 13 States; date of ratification of the Constitution).
POPULATION: 9.97 million (official estimate 2005).
POPULATION DENSITY: 58.9 per sq km.
2004 total overseas arrivals/US ranking: 571,269/10.

Climate

Hot/humid in summer; mild in winter. Cooler in the northern mountains. Temperatures range from a January high of 10°C (50°F) and a low of 0°C (32°F) to a July high of 33°C (90°F) and a low of 21°C (70°F).
Required clothing: Lightweight cotton clothes and rainwear. Warm clothing for evenings in the spring and autumn, during the winter season and in mountain areas.

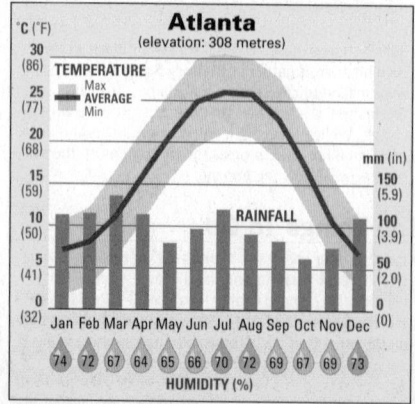

Travel - International

AIR:

 Main airports: *Hartsfield-Jackson Atlanta International (ATL)* (website: www.atlanta-airport.com) is 16km (10 miles) south of the city

(travel time – 20 minutes). With almost 80 million passengers using the airport in 2002, the airport is the busiest in the world (2002 passenger rankings), although most of those passengers are domestic. *To/from the airport:* The *Metropolitan Atlanta Rapid Transport Authority (MARTA)* operates rapid rail services every 10 minutes (0430-0100), from the airport to the city centre (travel time - 15 minutes) and throughout the metropolitan area. Taxis, shuttle vans, and limousines are also available. *Facilities:* Business centre, car hire and currency exchange.
Approximate flight times: From Atlanta to *London* is nine hours, to *New York* is two hours 10 minutes and to *Washington, DC* is one hour 40 minutes.
RAIL:

 The *Amtrak* (tel: (800) 872 7245 (toll-free); website: www.amtrak.com) 'Crescent' service, linking New York City with New Orleans, stops in Atlanta, while the 'Silver Service/Palmetto' service between New York City and Miami stops in Savannah; see the *New York* section for approximate travel times on these lines. Bus 23 runs to the Amtrak station in Atlanta, 1688 Peachtree Street; a taxi is required to get to the Amtrak station in Savannah, which is situated some 5 km (3 miles) southwest of the city, at 2611 Seaboard Coastline Drive.
ROAD:

 Greyhound (tel: (800) 231 2222 (toll-free); website: www.greyhound.com) has terminals in Atlanta, Hapeville, Marietta and Norcross.
Approximate driving times: From Atlanta to *Dallas* is six hours, to *New Orleans* is nine hours, and to *Seattle* is 53 hours. All times are based on non-stop driving at or below the applicable speed limits.
Approximate bus travel times: From **Atlanta** to *Chattanooga* is two to four hours, to *Mobile* is six to 10 hours, to *St Petersburg* is 12 to 16 hours.
URBAN:

The public transport system in Atlanta is excellent. The most economical transport is the *Metropolitan Atlanta Rapid Transport Authority (MARTA)* (website: www.itsmarta.com), which consists of 74km (46 miles) of rapid rail and 2373km (1475 miles) of bus lines operating Mon-Sat 0500-0100 and Sun 0630-0030. Daily and weekly travel passes are available. **Car hire:** Cars and motorcampers can be hired for touring the Atlanta area. Local companies can be contacted through the Atlanta classified telephone directory.

Top Things To See

• Tour the **Georgia State Capitol** on Washington Street, Capitol Square, **Atlanta**. It also houses the **Georgia Hall of Fame** and the **Hall of Flags**.
• Visit the **Tomb of Martin Luther King**, located at the **Ebenezer Baptist Church** in Atlanta.
• Visit **Madison**, a historic town that was spared from ruin during Sherman's March in 1864.
• Travel to the **Pine Mountain** (website: www.pinemountain.org) area; noted for its **Callaway Gardens** (website: www.callawaygardens.com) and for President Franklin D Roosevelt's **Little White House** (website: www.fdr-littlewhitehouse.org) at **Warm Springs**.
• Explore **Savannah**, the USA's first planned city. It has become the greatest urban historic preservation site in the USA. Much of Savannah's original beauty remains, and more than a thousand of its buildings are historically important, including the Regency-style **Owens-Thomas House** designed by William Jay, and **Davenport House**

Credit: ©Suzanne Anderson for the Buckhead Life Restaurant Group

(website: www.davenporthousemuseum.org), one of the best examples of Georgian architecture in the New World.
- Encounter **Fort Pulaski** (website: www.telfair.org/buildings), one of Savannah's five forts open to the public, named after the Polish hero of the American Revolution.
- Journey through **Waycross**, one of three gateways to the **Okefenokee Swamp** (website: www.okefenokee.com), one of the country's most beautiful wilderness areas. The swamp is a refuge of exotic plant and animal life, including alligators.
- Witness golfing history during the **Masters Golf Tournament** (website: www.masters.org) held at the **Augusta National Golf Club** every year.

Top Things To Do

- Play a game of **golf** on one of over 400 golf courses in the State. Georgia is a paradise for outdoor enthusiasts due to its temperate climate.
- Shop in **Underground Atlanta** (website: www.undergroundatlanta.com), a restored four-square block shopping and entertainment area, located near the business centre of Atlanta and home to the **Zero Mile Post**, which marks the city's birthplace.
- See the wildlife at the **Atlanta Zoo** (website: www.zooatlanta.org) in **Grant Park**. While at the park, tour the restored **Confederate Fort Walker**, and the **Cyclorama**, a world-famous 123m (406ft) circumference painting of the Battle of Atlanta.
- Climb or ride the cable car to the top of **Stone Mountain** (website: www.stonemountainpark.com), where gigantic representations of three Confederate heroes – Robert E Lee, Jefferson Davis and Thomas 'Stonewall' Jackson – have been carved into a cliff-face. A climb takes approximately 45 minutes to an hour, while the cable car is an easier option of getting to the top.
- Pan for gold in **Dahlonega** (website: www.dahlonega.org), an old mining town.
- Spend the day at **Tybee Island** (website: www.tybeeisland.com) featuring sands, fishing piers and a marine science centre. The city is also home to the celebrated *Savannah Jazz Festival* in September.
- Fish, play tennis, golf or just enjoy the beaches in the resort area of the **Golden Isles** (website: www.bgivb.com).
- Have a holiday on **Jekyll Island** (website: www.jekyllisland.com), an ideal destination for bird watchers, golfers and history enthusiasts. It can be reached within an hour's drive from either Savannah or Jacksonville, Florida. The resort island is known for its natural beauty and a deep sense of history. From 1886 to 1942, Jekyll was the winter sanctuary of some of the US's wealthiest industrialists, such as William Rockefeller and Richard Crane. The beautifully restored **Victorian Clubhouse** and the historic district are perfect examples of this bygone era.
- Taste colas from around the globe at the **World of Coca-Cola** (website: www.woccatlanta.com). Coke was created in Atlanta in 1886 and the museum houses the largest collection of the drink memorabilia.

TOURIST INFORMATION

Georgia Department of Economic Development
Street address: Tourism Division, 75 Fifth Street NW, Suite 1200, Atlanta, GA 30308, USA
Postal address: Tourism Division, PO Box 1776, Atlanta, GA 30301, USA
Tel: (404) 962 4000 *or* (800) 847 4842 (toll-free).
Website: www.georgia.org

Georgia Tourism in the UK
woodlands, Park Street, hitchin, Hertfordshire, SG4 9AH, UK
Tel: (01293) 560 848.
Website: www.georgia.org

Entertainment

FOOD & DRINK: Atlanta offers an extensive choice of food, its restaurants covering a wide variety of cuisine, from Continental to Thai, or Ethiopian.
Regional specialities:
- Barbeque.
- Peaches in any dishes.
- Crab cakes.
- Grits.

NIGHTLIFE: Nightlife varies from intimate piano bars and dinner theatres to the underground music clubs of Atlanta. The *Buckhead* and *Virginia-Highlands* communities in Atlanta have a thriving nightlife.
SHOPPING: Lenox Square Mall and **Phipps Plaza**, both shopping centres in Buckhead, can be reached by *MARTA* bus and rail.

Hawaii

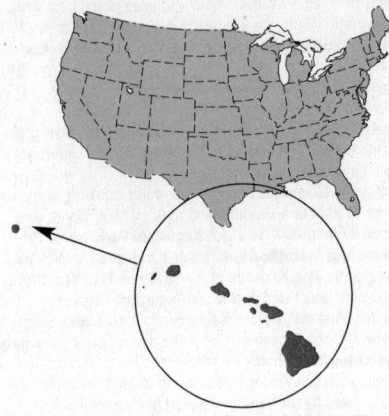

Time: Hawaii-Aleutian (GMT - 10). *Daylight Saving Time* is not observed.

Overview

The island group of Hawaii lies 3860km (2400 miles) off mainland USA, comprised of 132 islands and atolls. The state of Hawaii consists of eight islands, of which seven are inhabited and six allow visitors. Oahu contains the capital, Honolulu, and is the most commercialised, while Hawaii is the biggest island. Oahu has two diagonal mountain ranges (the Waianae and Koolau), with many beautiful waterfalls. Hawaii is cloaked in macadamia orchards and coffee plantations. The islands support rainforest, green flatlands and a variety of other climates – in fact, of 13 climatic regions, Hawaii has all but two.
Physically and psychologically, Hawaii stands apart from the USA, with an ethnically diverse population and a rich Polynesian heritage.
When Captain James Cook landed here in the 18th century, Oahu had been untouched by the West. It achieved prominence when the volume of Honolulu's commercial traffic increased and the US Navy acquired rights to Pearl Harbor.

General Information

Nickname: Aloha State.
State bird: The Nene (Hawaiian Goose).
State flower: Yellow Hibiscus.
CAPITAL: Honolulu.
Date of admission to the Union: 21 August 1959.
POPULATION: 1.28 million (official estimate 2005).
POPULATION DENSITY: 45per sq km.
2004 total overseas arrivals/US ranking: 1.31 million/14.

Climate

Warm throughout the year, with an average temperature of 24-29°C (75-85°F), and no appreciable difference between 'summer' and 'winter'. Heavy rainfall can occur in some mountainous areas from December to February, but most areas only receive short showers, while others remain totally arid.
Required clothing: Lightweights are advised throughout the year, with warmer clothes for winter. Beachwear is popular, and protection from the midday sun, such as sunglasses and sun hats, is advisable.

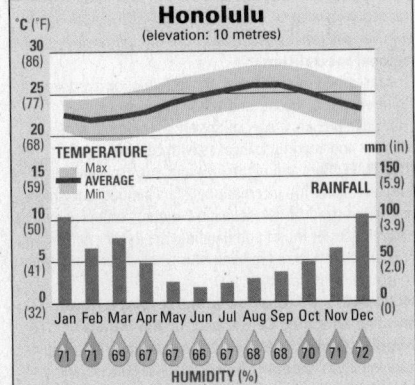

Honolulu (elevation: 10 metres)

	°C (°F)		mm (in)
	30 (86)		
	25 (77)		
	20 (68)	TEMPERATURE	150 (5.9)
	15 (59)	Max / AVERAGE / Min — RAINFALL	100 (3.9)
	10 (50)		50 (2.0)
	5 (41)		
	0 (32)	Jan Feb Mar Apr May Jun Jul Aug Sep Oct Nov Dec	0 (0)

HUMIDITY (%): 71 71 69 67 66 67 67 68 68 70 71 72

Travel - International

AIR:

Main airports: *Honolulu International Airport (HNL)* (website: www.hawaii.gov/dot/airports/oahu/hnl) is about 13km (8 miles) northwest of the city (14.5km/9 miles from Waikiki). Almost a quarter of the arrivals at the airport are international. *To/from the airport*: City bus services 19 and 20 run every 30 minutes (travel time – 30 minutes). However luggage is not allowed on city buses. Various shuttles and coaches to Waikiki hotels meet all flight arrivals during the day (travel time – approximately 25 minutes). Taxis are also available (travel time - 20 minutes) and cost about US$25-35. *Facilities*: Business centre and car hire.
Other international airports are *Hilo International Airport* and *Kana International Airport*.
Domestic airports: Hawaii: *Waimea-Kohala*. Kauai: *Lihue*. Lanai: *Lanai Airport*. Maui: *Hana, Kahului, Kapalua-West, Maui*. Molokai: *Ho'olehua* and *Kalaupapa*. Oahu: *Dillingham Airfield, Kalaeloa*.
Frequent inter-island services are offered by *Aloha Airlines* and *Hawaiian Airlines*, which also sells passes offering unlimited inter-island flying; coupon books for these are available from local travel agents. All-island passes are typically available in increments of five, seven, 10 and 14 days.
Approximate flight times: From Honolulu to *Anchorage* is five hours 40 minutes, to *London* is 17-19 hours (including stopover, and depending on route taken), and to *New York*.

SEA:

Main ports: Hawaii: *Hilo, Kawaihae*. Kauai: *Nawiliwili, Port Allen*. Maui: *Kahului*. Molokai: *Kaunakakai*. Oahu: *Honolulu, Kalaeloa Barber's Point, Kewalo Basin*. Cruise lines running to Hawaii include *Carnival Cruises, Celebrity Cruises, Norwegian Cruise Lines, P&O Cruises (Honolulu), Princess Cruises* and *Royal Caribbean. Norwegian Cruise Lines* also operates inter-island cruises. Ferries run between Maui, Lanai and Molokai.

RAIL:

The *Hawaiian Railway Society* (www.hawaiianrailway.com) on Oahu offers 90-minute journeys on a historical diesel-electric locomotive formerly used to haul sugar cane from Ewa Plantation Village to Ko'olina, available on Sundays. On Maui, the *Lahaina-Kaanapali & Pacific Railroad* (www.sugarcanetrain.com), also known as the *Sugarcane Train*, offers daily 30-minute rides between Old Town Lahaina and Kaanapali Beach Resort.

Credit: ©Maui Visitors Bureau (MVB) and Ron Dahlquist Photography

Credit: ©Maui Visitors Bureau (MVB) and Ron Dahlquist Photography

ROAD:

Driving is on the right-hand side of the road. Right-hand turns are permitted in the right lane at a 'stop' light unless otherwise indicated. Pedestrians are given the right of way most of the time. **Bus:** Deluxe modern tour buses operate on all islands. **Taxi:** Metered taxis are available throughout the main islands. **Car hire:** Available through local and international agencies. Drivers must be over 21 years of age for car hire. **Documentation:** Foreign driving licence required.

URBAN:

Good local bus services are provided on Oahu by *TheBus* (website: www.thebus.org), which covers the entire island with over 60 routes. An exact flat-fare system operates and free transfers are available on request. For further information, telephone the *Bus Information Line* (tel: (808) 848 5555). On other islands, taxis are available and car hire is possible. Limited public bus services operate on Kauai and Hawaii.

Top Things To See

• Tour the **National Cemetery of the Pacific** (www.cem.va.gov/nchp/nmcp/htm) or **Punchbowl** in Honolulu, a memorial and cemetery for US military veterans.

• View the fine collection of Asian art at the **Honolulu Academy of Arts** (www.honoluluacademy.org).

• Experience **Oahu's** most visited attraction - **Pearl Harbor** (www.pearlharbor.navy.mil) and the **USS Arizona Memorial** (www.nps.gov/usar) (open daily 0730-1700), the scene of Japan's surprise attack which brought the USA into World War II. Free tours take visitors by boat to the memorial spanning the wreck of the Battleship Arizona where 1177 men died; it is recommended to arrive early as the last boat leaves at 1500.

• Partake in the **Circle Island Tour**, which takes in the whole of Oahu. Allow at least a day for the tour. Attractions en route include **Waimea Falls Park,** (www.hawaiiweb.com/oahu/beaches), Pearl Harbor, the **Polynesian Cultural Centre** (www.polynesia.com), **Sea Life Park** (www.sealifepark.dolphindiscovery.com) (swim with the dolphins), the **Waialua Coffee Visitors' Center** (on a former plantation), and **Sunset Beach** (www.hawaiiweb.com/oahu/beaches).

• Explore the **Hawaii Volcanoes National Park** (www.nps.gov/havo), one of the natural wonders of the world. At 4103m (13,677ft), **Mauna Loa** is the largest single mountain mass in the world, while at 1200m (4000ft), the still-active **Kilauea's** steaming vents and frequent eruptions provide an unusual (and safe) spectator sport. The volcano is continuously erupting, and can be seen entering the ocean at sea-level.

• See **Mount Haleakala** (www.nps.gov/hale) in Maui, a massive volcanic crater whose name translates as 'The House of the Sun'.

• Discover Maui's **Ka'eleku Caverns** (www.mauicave.com), which are located beneath the **Hana Rainforest**, and are now open to the public for guided tours.

• Delight in the spectacular natural attractions of **Lanai Island** (www.lanaicity.com). They include the dramatic **Shipwreck Beach** or **Kaiolohia** with its petroglyph rock carvings and the mystical **Garden of the Gods** at Kanepu'u.

• Discover **Molokai** (www.molokai-hawaii.com), 'Hawaiian by Nature'. The island offers wide open vistas, an easy-going ambience and a lively local community. Attractions include the harbour town of **Kaunakakai**, with its quaint and colourful shops, **Mount Kamakou**, and the **Moaulu Falls**.

Top Things To Do

• Visit **The Leeward Coast** (www.visit-Oahu.com/gd_leeward.aspx) on the western side of Oahu Island. In recent years a certain amount of development has taken place and new residential areas, golf courses, parks, a shopping centre and an amusement park (**Hawaiian Waterways Adventure Park**) have sprung up.

• Relax at **Waikiki Beach** on Oahu Island. The area is a

particularly popular resort region and is currently undergoing a US$300 million rejuvenation programme, including construction of new walkways, traffic calming measures, and picnic and entertainment areas. Some 436 hotel rooms will be lost during phase one alone; phase two, which is slated for commencement in 2006, will spell the end for three of Waikiki's hotels, to be replaced by a single 890-room venue. Waikiki Beach is probably the most famous **surfing** beach in the world; learners are welcome here.

• Explore the **Aloha Tower Marketplace** (www.alohatower.com), an attractive and modern waterfront development in Honolulu. It is one of the major attractions in the area, with shopping plazas, restaurants and pavement entertainers.

• Enjoy the **Honolulu Zoo** (www.honoluluzoo.org), home to over 1230 mammals, birds, and reptiles. Meet Violet, the female orangutan. Nearby is **Kapiolani Park**, where the **Honolulu Marathon** is concluded annually. The park was created by King Kalakaua in the 1870's and is a beautiful 500-acre park listed on the state's Historic Register.

• Watch the whales. From November to April, **Lanai**, once known as the 'Pineapple Isle', is the perfect place for **whale watching**, as humpback whales make the waters around the island their winter breeding and calving grounds.

• Be amazed by the beauty of **Kauai** (www.kauai-hawaii.com), 'Hawaii's Island of Discovery', (some say it is the most outstanding in the archipelago), with staggering mountains and miles of sandy beaches. It is ideal for the visitor who does not care for crowded beaches or high-rise hotels. Local attractions include **Mount Waialeale**, the **Wailua River**, and the nearby temple of **Holoholoku Heiau**. **Hanakapiai Beach** is 2 miles inland and there is a stupendous waterfall 2 miles up in the **Hanakapiai Valley**.

• Take part in **deep-sea fishing**. It is very popular off Hawaii's **Big Island**.

• Engage in **boating**. For would-be yachtspeople, one-week yachting charters are available, with or without crews. All boats are equipped with Coast-Guard-approved safety equipment and are under Coast Guard supervision.

• Go **snorkelling**. It is especially popular near the **Molokini Crater** off Maui, as well as at various sites around each of the islands.

TOURIST INFORMATION

Hawaii Tourism Authority
1801 Kalakaua Avenue, Honolulu, HI 96815, USA
Tel: (808) 973 2255.
Website: www.hawaiitourismauthority.org

Hawaii Visitors & Convention Bureau
2270 Kalakaua Avenue, 8th floor,
Honolulu, HI 96815, USA
Tel: (808) 923 1811 *or* (800) 464 2924 (toll free).
Website: www.gohawaii.com

Hawaii Hotel & Lodging Association
2250 Kalakaua Avenue, Suite 404-4,
Honolulu, HI 96815, USA
Tel: (808) 923 0407.
Website: www.hawaiihotels.org

Entertainment

FOOD & DRINK: Hawaiian food offers the best of 'Pacific Rim' and 'New American' cooking styles, influenced by Chinese, Mediterranean, Mexican and other Asian countries. Many dishes are based on chicken, pork, seafood and local fruit and vegetables cooked using traditional methods. The classic traditional Hawaiian feast is the *luau* based around a *puaa kalua* (whole pig) that has been shaved and rubbed with rock salt on the inside. It is then placed on chicken wire, filled with hot stones from the fire, and cooked in an *imu* (pit) along with sweet potatoes, plantains and sometimes *laulau* (pork, butterfish and spinach-like taro shoots wrapped in leaves and steamed). Served with traditional Hawai'ian *poi* (thick paste made from ground taro).
Regional specialities:
• Local seafood includes *moi* (mullet) *ulua*, *opakapaka* (pink snapper), lobster and yellowfin tuna.
• Hawaiian breakfast specialities are macadamia nuts and banana and coconut pancakes with coconut syrup.
NIGHTLIFE: Bars and nightclubs abound, especially on Oahu and Maui. Top international stars are booked, whilst *luau* shows (traditional Hawaiian banquets followed by live performances of music and dancing) are in themselves a great attraction. Jazz, big band music, tea dances and hula groups are all available.
SHOPPING: The **Aloha Tower Marketplace**, **Royal Hawaiian Shopping Center** and the **Ala Moana Shopping Center** in Waikiki Beach, Honolulu, are popular shopping areas. **Opening hours:** Mon-Sat 0900-2100. Some shops may open Sun 0830-1800.

Idaho

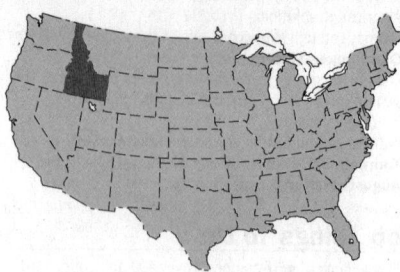

Time: Mountain (GMT - 7) in the greater part of the State; Pacific (GMT - 8) in the north. *Daylight Saving Time* is observed.

Overview

Idaho's history is rich in texture, from the early preeminence of American Indians to the pioneer fur trappers, miners, loggers, railroad builders, and farmers who later settled the territory. Traces of Idaho history can still be viewed today in many parts of the state. Northern Idaho has the greatest concentration of lakes in the West and evergreen forests abound. The Salmon River bisects the rugged Frank Church River of No Return Wilderness and provides some of the best whitewater kayaking and rafting in the world. The Sawtooth Wilderness Area and the White Cloud peaks provide additional recreational opportunities. World-famous Sun Valley is located between these mountain ranges. Hells Canyon, the deepest river gorge in North America, lies on the state's western border, overlooked by the Seven Devils Mountains. In Idaho's southwestern corner are the tallest sand dunes on the continent. In the south central region is the Craters of the Moon National Monument, where America's astronauts trained for moonwalks. Idaho has 16 alpine ski areas, over 320km (200 miles) of groomed nordic trails, over 11,500km (7,200 miles) of groomed snowmobile trails, 187,800-hectares (464,000-acres) of lakes and reservoirs, 41,000km (26,000 miles) of fishing streams, 3916km (2,433 miles) of floatable rivers, 25 state parks and 15 national forests, a haven for outdoor enthusiasts.

General Information

Nickname: Gem State.
State bird: Mountain Bluebird.
State flower: Syringa.
CAPITAL: Boise.
Date of admission to the Union: 3 Jul 1890.
POPULATION: 1.43 million (official estimate 2005).
POPULATION DENSITY: 6.6 per sq km.
2004 total overseas arrivals: Under 38,000.

Climate

In summer, the days are hot, with cool nights. In winter, the temperatures are low with snow in the mountains. The climate varies from north to south.
Required clothing: Lightweights for the summer with cover-up for cool nights and heavyweights for the winter. Travellers will need extra clothes when travelling in the mountains in summer or winter.

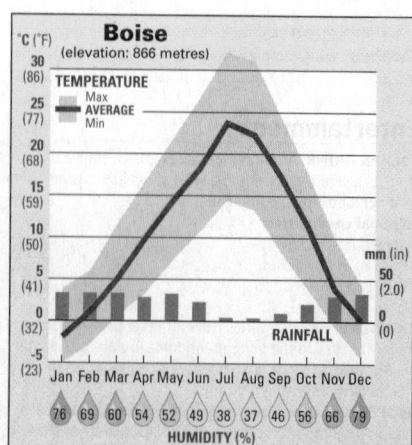

Top Things To See & Do

- The contrasting terrain of Idaho includes **Hell's Canyon National Recreational Area**, the deepest river gorge in North America and home to the **Snake**, **Salmon** and **Rapid rivers**; **Clearwater National Forest**; and two of the finest big-game hunting areas in the USA – **Chamberlain Basin** and **Selway-Bitterroot Wilderness**.
- Attend the lively festival and the **Western Idaho Fair** held in August in **Boise**, the State capital. It is also home to the **World Center for Birds of Prey**; the **Basque Museum & Cultural Center** and the **Boise Art Museum**.
- Attractions to the southeast include the massive **Shoshone Falls**; the **Shoshone Indian Ice Caves**; and historic **Fort Hall**.
- The upmarket **Sun Valley** resort area in the centre of the State offers **skiing** and wintersports, as well as a range of summer activities. In the nearby hills is a wide choice of hot springs, including the **Warfield Hot Spring** and **Russian John Hot Spring**.
- See the **Craters of the Moon National Monument & Preserve**, a huge lava field with a maze of tunnels and caves. There are plenty of campsites available nearby.
- **Sawtooth National Recreation Area** is home to the **Sawtooth** and **White Cloud mountains** and the **Smokey** and **Boulder ranges**. Further north, the **Lewis and Clark Scenic Byway** offers travellers a chance to trace the 'Corps of Discovery' expedition route along the **Clearwater** and **Lochsa rivers**, in the land of the Nez Perce Indians, who are recalled by the **Nez Perce National Historical Park**.
- In the north of the State, the resort town of **Coeur d'Alene** is home to the world's only **floating golf green**, which is situated on a lake where visitors can also hire canoes or take a boat cruise.
- Visit the **Wallace District Mining Museum**, situated to the east of Coeur d'Alene. Also on offer in this area is the **Sierra Silver Mine Tour** and the **Oasis Bordello Museum**. Visitors can also ride up **Silver Mountain** on the world's longest **single-stage gondola**.

TOURIST INFORMATION

Idaho Department of Commerce, Division of Tourist Development
Street address: 700 West State Street, Boise, ID 83720, USA
Postal address: PO Box 83720, Boise, ID 83720, USA
Tel: (208) 334 2470 *or* (800) 635 7820 (toll-free).
Website: www.tourism.idaho.gov

Rocky Mountain International in the UK
Woodpeckers End, 93 Burridge Road, Burridge, Southampton, Hampshire SO31 1BY, UK
Tel: (09063) 640 655 (customer request line; 60p per minute).
Website: www.rmi-realamerica.com

Illinois

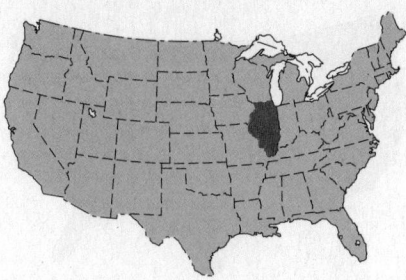

Time: Central (GMT − 6). *Daylight Saving Time* is observed.

Overview

Illinois, stretching from Lake Michigan to the Mississippi River, embraces vast, rich farmlands, the giant city of Chicago, rolling glacial plains and, to the south, the hills and valleys of the Illinois Ozarks. Illinois boasts 6900km (4300 miles) of scenic shoreline, 1100 historic sites and half a million acres of state parks. Abraham Lincoln, the 16th US President, spent most of his professional (he was a lawyer) and political life here. Nicknamed the 'Windy City', Chicago is one of the world's giant trade, industry and transportation centres and the birthplace of the skyscraper. In contrast, its Lake Michigan shoreline is dotted with sandy beaches, hundred of parks, harbors, zoos and vast expanses of forest reserve. It is one of the USA's largest cities and the hub of the Midwest. The inhabitants in the 'Chicagoland' area speak more than 50 languages, making it the most ethnically diverse city in the USA. For visitors to the USA, it is the gateway to the farmlands and cities of Illinois and Indiana, and the recreation areas of Wisconsin.

General Information

Nickname: Land of Lincoln.
State bird: Springfield Cardinal.
State flower: Native Violet.
CAPITAL: Springfield.
Date of admission to the Union: 3 Dec 1818.
POPULATION: 12.71 million (official estimate 2005).
POPULATION DENSITY: 84.8 per sq km.
2004 total overseas arrivals/US ranking: 978,929/6.

Climate

Wide variation between hot summers and freezing winters, especially in the north of the State. The highest humidity is in the summer near the Great Lakes.
Required clothing: Warm winter clothes are needed in the coldest months. Light- to mediumweights are advised for the summer. Rainwear may be useful.

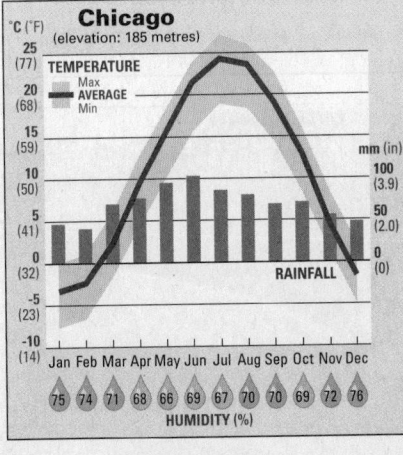

Travel - International

AIR:
 Main airports: *Chicago O'Hare International (ORD)* (website: www.ohare.com/ohare/home/asp), 27km (17 miles) northwest of downtown Chicago, is considered the world's busiest airport averaging over 180,000 passengers a day. Lower-level pedestrian passageways inside the airport terminals lead directly to the *Chicago Transit Authority* (CTA) station; the free *Airport Transit System* (ATS) also links the terminals and station. *To/from the airport:* The

CTA Blue Line train provides a 24-hour service between central Chicago and O'Hare (travel time – approximately 40 minutes). Taxis and limousines are also widely available, as are shuttle buses and buses serving regional destinations. Connections from *O'Hare* to *Midway International* (see below) are provided by the *Omega Airport Shuttle* bus, which operates an airport transfer service every hour 0700-2200 (travel time - 30 minutes to one hour), and *Coach USA Wisconsin*, with an hourly service between the airports from 0800-2200. *Facilities:* Car hire, restaurants, and full-service business support.
Domestic airports: *Midway International (MDW)* (website: www.ohare.com/midway/home.asp), 16km (10 miles) southwest from downtown Chicago, handles regional and local flights. *To/from the airport:* Transport to the city is available on the *CTA's Orange Line* (travel time – 20 to 30 minutes), which connects with other CTA rail and bus routes serving the city and 40 suburban communities. *Continental Airport Express* shuttles run between *Midway International* and downtown Chicago and the northern suburbs every 15 minutes daily 0600-2330. Taxis are also readily available; a number of other buses serve regional destinations. *Facilities:* Car hire, restaurants and shops.
Approximate flight times: From Chicago to *London* is eight hours 40 minutes, to *Los Angeles* is four hours 20 minutes, to *New York* is two hours, and to *Washington, DC* is one hour 50 minutes.
RAIL:
 Downtown Chicago's *Union Station* is the focal point of the *Amtrak* rail passenger network (tel: (800) 872 7245 (toll-free); website: www.amtrak.com); three of the four transcontinental lines converge here and it is also the northern terminus of north-south lines to San Antonio and New Orleans. A sixth line runs northeast to Toronto (Canada), with connections to Montreal. Services to neighboring cities are limited.
Approximate rail travel times: From Chicago on the 'Pennsylvanian' to *New York* is 21 hours; on the 'Capitol' to *Washington, DC* is 17 hours 45 minutes. Approximate times for Chicago-Los Angeles and Chicago-Oakland (San Francisco) services may be found in the *California* section.
ROAD:
Long-distance bus companies operating in the State include *Greyhound* (tel: (800) 231 2222 (toll-free); website: www.greyhound.com), with services across the USA, and *Trailways* (tel: (800) 992 4618 (toll-free); website: www.trailways.com, with services to neighboring states. There is a 24-hour bus terminal at 603 West Harrison Street in Chicago.
Approximate driving times: From Chicago to *New York* is 16 hours, and to *Los Angeles* is 44 hours. All times are based on non-stop driving at or below the applicable speed limits.
Approximate bus travel times: From Chicago to *St Louis* is five to seven hours and to *New York City* is 17 hours.
URBAN:
A wide network of bus routes run by the *Chicago Transit Authority* (CTA) (tel: (312) 836 7000; website: (www.transitchicago.com) covers the city on the major north-south and east-west streets. **Train:** The CTA runs both subway trains and elevated trains from 'The Loop' in downtown Chicago to the suburbs. The CTA system uses a transit card system for fare payment, there are available at all elevated train stations. Commuter rail services are run by *METRA*. **Car hire:** Cars and motor campers are available.

Top Things To See

- Visit the **Chicago Pumping Station**; a landmark that survived the Great Chicago Fire of 1871, which houses a tourist information centre; open daily.
- View the skyline from one of Chicago's many soaring skyscrapers' observation towers, including the **Sears Tower**

Credit: ©City of Chicago/Mark Montgomery

(website: www.thesearstower.com) and the **John Hancock Center** (website: www.hancock-observatory.com).

- Take a walk along the **Navy Pier** (website: www.navypier.com), the largest recreational pier in the USA. Attractions include an **open-air theatre**, **botanical gardens**, the **Chicago Children's Museum** (website: www.chichildrensmuseum.org), plus a giant **Ferris Wheel** standing 15 storeys high and offering the best view of the famous Chicago skyline.
- Tour the **Cahokia Mounds** (website: www.cahokiamounds.com), a relic of the most sophisticated prehistoric Native American civilization community north of Mexico.
- Look in on **Springfield**, the capital of Illinois. It was here that Abraham Lincoln married and began his legal career. Attractions include **Lincoln's Tomb** (a State Historical Site) and the **Illinois State Museum** (website: www.museum.state.il.us).
- Travel back in time at the **New Salem State Park** (website: www.lincolnsnewsalem.com). It is a recreation of the pioneer community as it was in Lincoln's day.

Top Things To Do

- Attend an American Football game. The **Chicago Bears** (website: www.chicagobears.com) play from September to December at **Soldier Field**.
- Take in a baseball game. The baseball teams, **Chicago Cubs** (website: www.chicago.cubs.mlb.com) and **Chicago White Sox** (website: www.chicago.whitesox.mlb.com), play during the summer months at **Wrigley Field** and **U.S. Cellular Park**.
- Enjoy the fast-paced action when the **Chicago Bulls** (website: www.nba.com/bulls) take to the basketball court from January to April at the **United Center**, which is also home to the ice hockey team, the **Chicago Blackhawks** (website: www.chicagoblackhawks.com).
- Tee off on one of the many **golf** courses. Illinois has the highest number of public and championship golf courses in the USA; there are 700 of these, 200 of which can be found in the immediate 'Chicagoland' area.
- Enjoy the music at the **23rd Annual Chicago Blues Festival** held in June (website: www.chicagobluesfestival.org). International, national and local artists will perform on over five stages at the largest free-admission blues festival in the world.
- Take time to enjoy more than 2000 exhibits at **The Museum of Science & Industry** (website: www.msichicago.org) in Chicago. The pedestrianised Museum Campus is the site of three museums surrounded by one continuous park. These are the **Field Museum of Natural History**, which spans the development of the universe from 4.5 billion years ago to the present day; the **John G Shedd Aquarium and Oceanarium**; and the **Adler Planetarium**, which houses the **Sky Dome**.
- For art lovers, Chicago has a number of **outdoor sculptures** by artists such as Picasso, Miro, Moore, Chagall and Calder.
- Ride one of the twelve roller coasters at **Six Flags Great America Amusement Park** (website: www.sixflags.com/park/greatamerica/index.asp) in Chicago or cool down in the **Six Flags Hurricane Harbor**.

Entertainment

FOOD & DRINK: Chicago is packed with some 7000 restaurants of all types, serving food from around the world.
Regional specialities:
- Prime rib steaks.
- Deep pan Chicago pizza.

NIGHTLIFE: Chicago boasts everything from nightclubs, jazz spots, cinemas and discos to belly dancing, rock bands and folk music. It is the home of 'urban blues', a form developed by such greats as Muddy Waters and Elmore James, continued today in Chicago and around the world by performers such as Buddy Guy and Robert Cray.

SHOPPING: The main shopping areas in Chicago include **State Street**, North Michigan Avenue's **Magnificent Mile**, **Woodfield Mall** and the quaint speciality stores in Old Town, Lincoln Avenue and New Town.

Indiana

Time: Eastern (GMT - 5) in the greater part of the State; Central (GMT - 6) in the west; Eastern (GMT - 5) in the east. *Daylight Saving Time* is not observed in the greater part of the State, but is observed in the west and east.

Overview

Adjoining Lake Michigan to the north, Indiana features deep valleys, cornfields, foothills and vast farmlands. Amid the rolling plains stands Indianapolis, the State capital and national centre for industry, commerce and culture. The business sector lies at the heart of the city; however, many of the tourist attractions are situated on the outskirts.

General Information

Nickname: Hoosier State.
State bird: Cardinal.
State flower: Peony.
CAPITAL: Indianapolis.
Date of admission to the Union: 11 Dec 1816.
POPULATION: 6.27 million (official estimate 2005).
POPULATION DENSITY: 66.5 per sq km.
2004 total overseas arrivals/US ranking: 144,000/26.

Climate

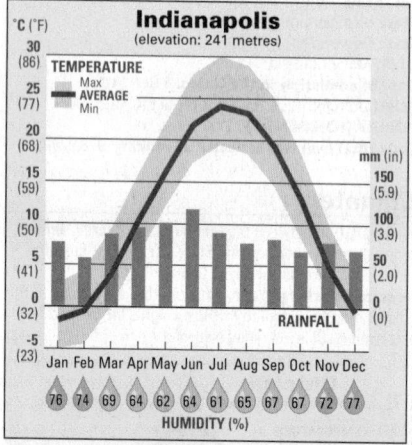

Mild to cold winters and hot summers.
Required clothing: Lightweights for the summer and heavyweights for the winter.

Top Things To See & Do

- Visit the State capital, **Indianapolis**. Located downtown are the **Eiteljorg Museum of American Indians and Western Art** and the **Indianapolis Zoo**, which is renowned for its large collection of dolphins and whales. Further out are the **Indianapolis Museum of Art** and the **Krannert Pavillion**, with an extensive display of modern art. A must for families is the **Children's Museum of Indianapolis**. Indianapolis also offers a selection of musical entertainment to suit all tastes: the **Madame Walker Theatre Center** has seen the likes of Louis Armstrong grace its stage, while every June the city hosts the *Indy Jazz Fest*. The *Indianapolis Symphony Orchestra* and *Indianapolis Opera* are other popular options. The most famous sporting event to hit the city is the *Indianapolis 500* speedway race on Memorial Day Weekend; a month of shows, exhibitions and parades in May leads up to the main event. The other big motorsport events are the *Brickyard 400* race in August, and the US *Grand Prix Formula One* race, held in late September.
- Spot wolves at **Wolf Park**, an hour northwest of Indianapolis near **Lafayette**. The creatures wander freely and, even when they can not be seen, their piercing howls announce their presence.
- Head south to **Bloomington**, which reaches bursting point during its *Fourth Street Festival of the Arts & Crafts* in August. Other local highlights are the **Bloomington Antique Mall**, **Indiana University Art Museum** and **Lake Monroe**, which lies just south of the town.
- Enjoy many of the other State attractions, which include the **Indiana Dunes National Lakeshore**; **Amish Acres**, a restored 19th-century Amish community at Nappanee; the **Conner Prairie Pioneer Settlement**; the **Squire Boone Caves**; the **James Dean Memorial Gallery** in **Fairmount**, 16km (10 miles) south of his birthplace, **Marion**, on 8 Feb 1931; and **Fort Wayne**, Indiana's second-largest city and the scene of many bloody battles. Fort Wayne is home to the **Lincoln Museum**, which depicts the life story of the USA's 16th president.

Credit: ©Indiana Office of Tourism Development

Iowa

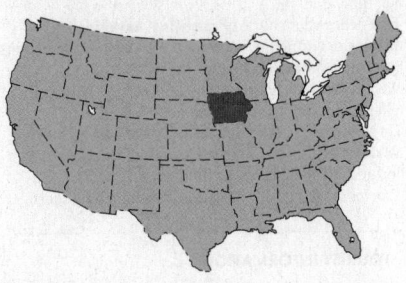

Time: Central (GMT - 6). *Daylight Saving Time* is observed.

Overview

Almost 95 per cent of Iowa's gently undulating land is given over to agriculture, but dotted across the landscape are many scenic parks, lakes and recreation areas, such as East Okoboji, West Okoboji (Iowa's deepest natural lake), Spirit Lake and Clear Lake. Its rich cultural heritage can be seen in the German Amana Colonies, with their many historic sites and museums. The tulips of Pella reflect the town's Dutch past and Des Moines, Iowa's capital, was clearly named by French explorers.

General Information

Nickname: Hawkeye State.
State bird: Eastern Goldfinch.
State flower: Wild Rose.
CAPITAL: Des Moines.
Date of admission to the Union: 28 Dec 1846.
POPULATION: 2.97 million (official estimate 2004).
POPULATION DENSITY: 20 per sq km.
2004 total overseas arrivals: Under 38,000.

Climate

Hot, moist summer and cold generally dry winters. Although most of the annual rain falls in the warm months, snowstorms and occasional blizzards occur during the winter.
Required clothing: Cottons and linens for the summer. Heavyweights and extra bundling for the winter months.

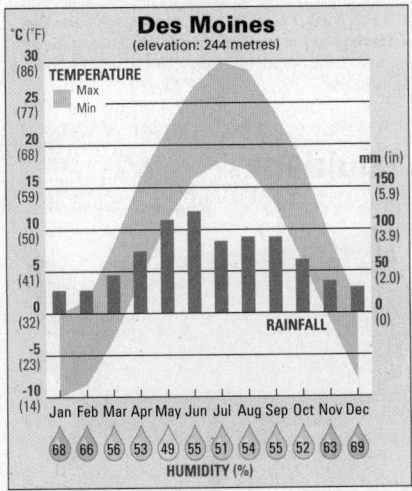

Top Things To See & Do

- Explore the State capital, **Des Moines**. It has a great selection of amusements for children including the **Science Center of Iowa**, which transports visitors out of this world with impressive laser shows and simulated space shuttle flights. Other sights in Des Moines are the **State Historical Museum and Archives**, **Botanical Center**, **Des Moines Art Center** and **Jordan House** in **West Des Moines**. The city also hosts a number of annual events such as the *Iowa State Fair* in August and a *Jazz in July* celebration, with free daily jazz concerts throughout the city. Just out of town, the community of **Indianola** is the setting for the **National Balloon Museum**, which holds the colourful *National Balloon Classic* in August.
- Visit **Iowa City**, dominated by the **University of Iowa** campus. The city also boasts the beautiful **Old Capitol** building among the cluster of historic buildings called

Credit: ©Iowa Tourism Office

the Pentacrest. Museums include the **Museum of Natural History** and the **Medical Museum** in the University of Iowa Hospitals and Clinics. The **Amana Colonies** are seven villages situated along the Iowa River. They welcome tourists to the **Museum of Amana History**, **Community Church**, **Communal Kitchen Museum** and the **Cooper Shop Museum**. They are renowned for their friendly nature, and their German heritage is evident in the local restaurants, which serve family-style portions of traditional dishes. The **South Amana Barn Museum** in **South Amana** is an unusual museum that depicts the history of rural USA in miniature.

- Make the most of Iowa's other attractions, such as the **Boone and Scenic Valley Railroad**; **Effigy Mounds National Monument**, with its relics of ancient Native American culture; and **Fort Museum**, a replica of the town of **Fort Dodge** in the 19th century. Also worth a visit are Iowa's two national scenic byways: the **Loose Hills Scenic Byway** along the **Missouri River** in western Iowa and the **Great River Road** along the **Mississippi River** on Iowa's eastern border.

TOURIST INFORMATION

Iowa Tourism Office
200 East Grand Avenue, Des Moines, IA 50309, USA
Tel: (515) 242 4705 *or* (888) 345 4692 (toll-free).
Website: www.traveliowa.com

Greater Des Moines CVB
400 Locust Street, Suite 265, Des Moines, IA 50309, USA
Tel: (515) 286 4960 *or* (800) 451 2625 (toll-free).
Website: www.seedesmoines.com

Kansas

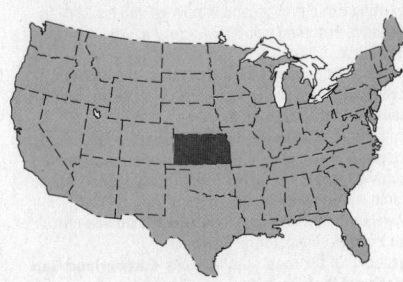

Time: Central (GMT - 6) in the greater part of the State; Mountain (GMT - 7) in four Western counties. *Daylight Saving Time* is observed.

Overview

The geographical centre of North America, Kansas is a major agricultural area, with vast areas of farmland. As highway signs remind travellers, 'Every Kansas farmer feeds 75 people – and you.'
It was through Kansas that families on the Oregon and Santa Fe trails drove their wagons westwards in search of new homesteads, while cowboys on the Chisholm Trail drove vast herds of longhorns north in search of the railroads. To cater for the new population, cowtowns like

Abilene and Dodge City were born, and as whites forced Native Americans to move westwards, fierce battles over land erupted. Later, feuds over Kansas's maintenance of slavery gave rise to the term 'Bleeding Kansas'. Today, the State boasts many monuments to its Old West past, as well as numerous recreation centres, reservoirs and rivers offering all kinds of outdoor pursuits.

General Information

Nickname: Sunflower State.
State bird: Western Meadowlark.
State flower: Sunflower.
CAPITAL: Topeka.
Date of admission to the Union: 29 Jan 1861.
POPULATION: 2.74 million (official estimate 2005).
POPULATION DENSITY: 12.9 per sq km.
2004 total overseas arrivals: Under 38,000.

Climate

The region has a continental climate with cold winters and hot summers.
Required clothing: Lightweights for the summer and heavyweights for the winter.

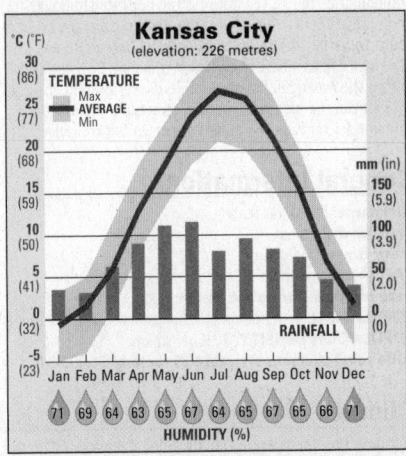

Top Things To See & Do

- Step back in time in the restored cattle town of **Dodge City**. Here, it is worth visiting the **Boot Hill Museum** which recreates the Boot Hill Cemetery and Front Street as they looked in the 1870s. Near Boot Hill is the **Gunfighter Wax Museum**, located in the **Kansas Teachers' Hall of Fame**.
- Tour the **Eisenhower Center** in **Abilene**, which houses the Eisenhower family home from 1898 to 1946, as well as a museum and library.
- Explore the museums of **Wichita**, the largest city in Kansas, famed today for aircraft manufacture, and home to the **Museums on the River District**, which includes an art museum and a botanical garden. Particularly worth a visit are the **Old Cowtown Museum**, which introduces visitors to the cattle days of the 1870s with an open-air history exhibit, the **Mid-America All-Indian Center Museum**, where traditional and modern works by Native American artists are on display, and **Exploration Place**, with its many fascinating discovery exhibits. Wichita is also home to **Sedgwick County Zoo**, one of Kansas's top tourist attractions.
- Visit Kansas's capital, **Topeka**, boasting the **Kansas Museum of History**, the **Kansas State Capitol**, dating back to 1866, and the **Topeka Zoological Park**.
- Stand at the geographical centre point of the entire USA, marked by the stone monument 3km (2 miles) northwest of **Lebanon** on the northern border of the State.

TOURIST INFORMATION

Kansas Travel & Tourism
1000 SW Jackson Street, Suite 100, Topeka, KS 66612, USA
Tel: (785) 296 2009 *or* (800) 252 6727 (toll-free).
Website: www.travelks.com

Greater Wichita CVB
100 South Main Street, Suite 100, Wichita, KS 67202, USA
Tel: (316) 265 2800 *or* (800) 288 9424 (toll-free).
Website: www.visitwichita.com

Kentucky

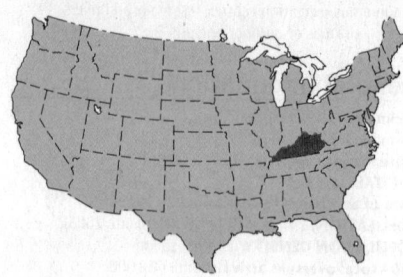

Time: Eastern (GMT - 5) in the eastern part of the State; Central (GMT - 6) in the west. *Daylight Saving Time* is observed.

Overview

Kentucky is best known for horses, bourbon, fried chicken and bluegrass music. Lexington is the horse-breeding centre and many of its surrounding farms welcome visitors on free tours. Louisville was founded by General George Rogers Clark in 1778 as a base from which to harass British troops during the American Revolution. Today, restored historic sites sit side-by-side with modern structures and visitors can wander through the quaint streets in Old Louisville.

General Information

Nickname: Bluegrass State.
State bird: Cardinal.
State flower: Goldenrod.
CAPITAL: Frankfort.
Date of admission to the Union: 1 Jun 1792.
POPULATION: 4.17 million (official estimate 2005).
POPULATION DENSITY: 39.9 per sq km.
2004 total overseas arrivals/US ranking: 71,000/34.

Climate

Kentucky has a temperate climate. Annual rainfall is 122cm (48 inches), including an average snowfall of 34.8cm (13.7 inches). The wettest seasons are spring and summer, and the driest is autumn.
Required clothing: Spring and autumn usually require light wraps, especially during the evening. Summer can be very warm, but cool evenings are not unusual.

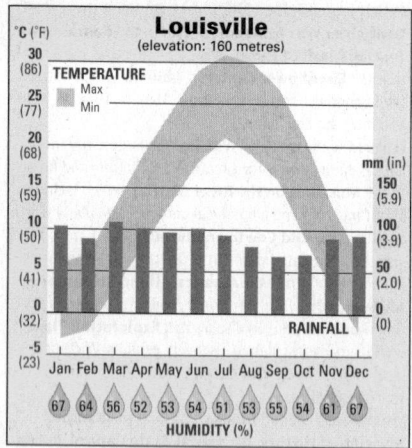

Louisville
(elevation: 160 metres)

Travel - International

AIR:
 Main airports: *Cincinnati/Northern Kentucky International (CVG)* (website: www.cvgairport.com) is located in Northern Kentucky, 20km (12 miles) from Cincinnati, Ohio. *To/from the airport:* Buses, shuttles and taxis are available to Cincinnati. *Facilities:* ATMs, car hire and Internet access. *Louisville International (SDF)* (website: www.louintlairport.com) is situated 8km (5 miles) south of the city. *To/from the airport:* Buses, taxis, shuttles and limousines provide transportation to the city centre. *Facilities:* ATMs, car hire, and Internet access.
RAIL:
 There is a daily *Amtrak* (tel: (800) 872 7245 (toll-free); website: www.amtrak.com) service between Chicago and New Orleans, which stops at Fulton. Three trains a week run between New York Union Station

and Chicago, serving Ashland, South Portsmouth and Mayville. There is no service to Louisville, although *Amtrak Thruway* buses connect daily with Chicago.
ROAD:
 The main service provider is *Greyhound* (tel: (800) 229 9424 (toll-free); website: www.greyhound.com).
Approximate bus travel times: From Louisville to *Cincinnati* is two hours, to *Nashville* is three hours and to *Chicago* is six hours. From Lexington to *Cincinnati* is one hour and to *Knoxville* is three hours.
URBAN:
In Louisville, there is an extensive system of buses serving most of the metropolitan area, and a trolley service from the east side of Fourth Street to the Riverfront Wharf. The Toonville II Trolley serves Third, Fourth and Fifth Street, while the Main Street Trolley has stops on Main Street and Market Street.

Top Things To See

- Visit the **Kentucky Horse Park** (website: www.imh.org), a working horse farm in Lexington. The park provides an educational look at the State's equestrian history. Visitors can watch films about horseracing and breeding, and demonstrations of horseshoeing and harness making. The **International Museum of the Horse** and the **American Saddle Horse Museum** are also located here.
- See the Falls of the **Ohio State Park** (website: www.fallsoftheohio.org), where visitors can walk onto the world's largest exposed Devonian fossil bed.
- Tour **Shaker Village of Pleasant Hill** (website: www.shakervillageky.org). Members of the 19th-century Shaker religious sect lived a simple life here, and, today, visitors can tour their 2024-hectare (5000-acre) farm and living history museum.
- Travel to **Harrodsburg**, the oldest permanent English settlement west of the Alleghenies. **Old Fort Harrod State Park** (website: www.parks.ky.gov/stateparks/fh) contains part of the replica 1774 fort. Actors dressed in 18th-century costume demonstrate skills, such as blacksmithing and quilting.
- Visit **Hodgenville**, the birthplace of Abraham Lincoln. The Lincoln family lived at the **Sinking Spring Farm** for more than two years before moving to **Knob Creek**. **Lincoln's Boyhood Home** (website: www.nps.gov/liho) is a reproduction cabin located on the original site where he lived until he was eight years old. The **Abraham Lincoln Birthplace National Historic Site** (website: www.nps.gov/abli) has 56 steps, one for each year of his life. The 47-hectare (116-acre) park traces the history of the President's humble roots.
- Observe over 66 exhibits of fresh and saltwater fish from around the world at the **Newport Aquarium** (website: www.newportaquarium.com), open daily.
- Explore the vast **Daniel Boone National Forest** (website: www.fs.fed.us/r8/boone), with its magnificent **Red River Gorge** that runs through the entire region. Two of Kentucky's most beautiful lakes, **Cave Run Lake** and **Laurel River Lake**, lie at each end of the forest.
- View the **Big South Fork National River and Recreation Area** (website: www.nps.gov/biso), a national park wilderness straddling the Kentucky–Tennessee border.

Top Things To Do

- Take the family to the **Lexington Children's Museum** (website: www.explorium.com). It has a number of exciting exhibits that can be touched and explored by children, including a *Bubble Factory* and the *Science Station X*.
- Ride on the nation's oldest steamboat, the **Belle of Louisville** (website: www.belleoflouisville.org), which still sails along the **Ohio River**.
- Enjoy time in Louisville during the two weeks of Derby celebrations leading up to the most important date on Louisville's calendar – the first Saturday in May, when the famous **Kentucky Derby** (website: www.kentuckyderby.com) at **Churchill Downs** provides an exciting climax to the festivities.
- Visit one of the most popular areas, **Cumberland Gap National Park** (website: www.nps.gov/cugo), with its breathtaking views of the **Appalachian Mountains**. The Cumberland Falls are known as the 'Niagara of the South' and this is one of the few places in the world where you can see a 'moonbow' on a regular basis. Canoeing and rafting trips are very popular in this area.
- Take a tour through **Mammoth Cave** (website: www.nps.gov/maca); the largest known network of natural caves and underground passageways in the world, with more than 560km (350 miles) of explored passageways. Many species of animals and different types of cave formation can be found within the national park. Park rangers lead tours of varying length from 30 minutes to six hours 30 minutes. Above ground, the park offers miles of hiking trails, including a wheelchair access route.
- Hike or backpack over two major trails, the **Sheltowee**

Trace National Recreation Trail (website: www.sheltoweetrace.com) and the **Jenny Wiley National Recreation Trail** (website: www.parks.ky.gov/resortparks/jw). They provide routes through the scenic forested highlands of Eastern Kentucky.
- Experience your choice of **canoeing**, **kayaking** and **rafting** opportunities in one of the 14 major river systems in Kentucky. **Rockcastle** (website: www.rockcastlekytourism.com) is one of the most popular whitewater canoe runs in the USA.
- Go to the races at the **Kentucky Speedway** (website: www.kentuckyspeedway.com), a motor racing circuit located 18km (30 miles) south of the *Cincinnati/Northern Kentucky International* airport.

Entertainment

FOOD & DRINK: Kentucky is home to the famous 'Kentucky Fried Chicken,' which consists of chicken fried in a secret original recipe involving a blend of 11 herbs.
Regional specialities:
- Kentucky Fried Chicken.
- Country ham, which is usually cured for a few years to strengthen its flavour.
NIGHTLIFE: Country music is very popular in many of the bars and clubs in Kentucky, which is not surprising for a State that has produced stars such as Billy Ray Cyrus, Crystal Gayle, Loretta Lynn and Dwight Yoakam. Jazz performances take place at Glassworks on Market Street, Louisville.
SHOPPING: Berea is Kentucky's arts and craft capital. Local shops sell pottery, woodwork, jewellery, quilts and weaving. The largest hand-weaving studio in the USA, **The Churchill Weavers** produces a quality collection of ladies accessories, blankets and neckties. Louisville is great for antique shopping. Popular antique shops in Louisville include **Den of Steven** and **Joe Ley Antiques**. In Western and Northern Kentucky, there is a variety of outlet malls in which to shop for bargains.

Louisiana

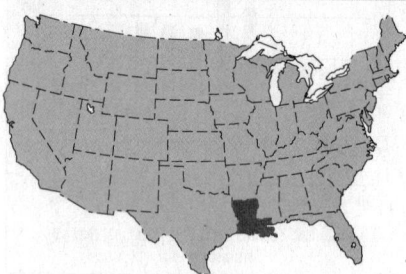

Time: Central (GMT - 6). *Daylight Saving Time* is observed.

Overview

Louisiana's marshy Mississippi Valley is one of the most attractive areas of the USA. New Orleans, its largest city, is one of the country's major tourist destinations. It is famed for Dixieland jazz, architecture, superb cuisine and its unique French Quarter. The city also boasts a wide choice of museums and galleries. Other places to see in the State include Lafayette, a city of magnificent gardens and the start of the 40km (25 mile) Azalea Trail; the Atchafalaya Basin, the largest and most remote swamp in the USA; the huge salt domes of Avery; and Alexandria, surrounded by forests and parks. The 138m- (452ft-) high marble and limestone Capitol Building is situated in Baton Rouge. Louisiana was hit hard by Hurricane Katrina in 2005, but most of the tourism attractions and infrastructure have been repaired and are open to visitors. It is always wise to check before visiting a site however.

United States of America: Louisiana

General Information

Nickname: Pelican State.
State bird: Brown Pelican.
State flower: Magnolia Grandiflora.
CAPITAL: Baton Rouge.
Date of admission to the Union: 30 Apr 1812.
POPULATION: 4.52 million (official estimate 2005).
POPULATION DENSITY: 33.7 per sq km.
2004 total overseas arrivals/US ranking: 150,000/29.

Climate

Humid and subtropical. Milder in spring, autumn and winter.
Required clothing: Lightweight cotton clothing for summer, with sweaters and jackets for winter. Rainwear or an umbrella is advised for all seasons.

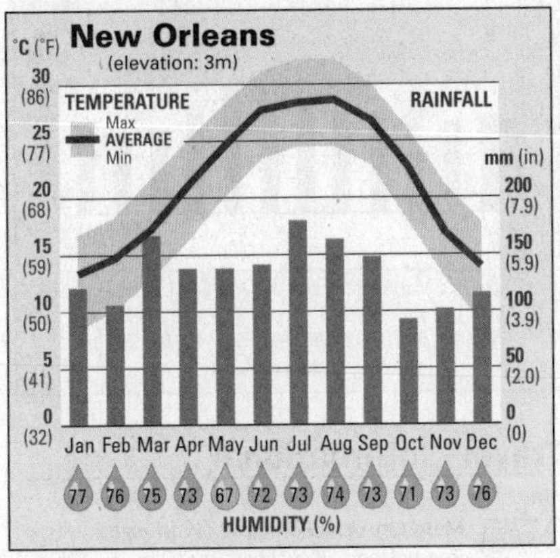
New Orleans
(elevation: 3m)
°C (°F)
TEMPERATURE
Max
AVERAGE
Min
RAINFALL
mm (in)
30 (86)
25 (77)
20 (68)
15 (59)
10 (50)
5 (41)
0 (32)
200 (7.9)
150 (5.9)
100 (3.9)
50 (2.0)
0 (0)
Jan Feb Mar Apr May Jun Jul Aug Sep Oct Nov Dec
77 76 75 73 67 72 73 74 73 71 73 76
HUMIDITY (%)

Travel - International

Note: If you are travelling out of Louis Armstrong International in the post Katrina era, the following is recommended: (1) Arrive two hours prior to your scheduled departure time – staffing levels are reduced, causing delays in security procedures. (2) Book your flight early, as flights out of New Orleans are operating at or near capacity.

AIR:

Main airports: *Louis Armstrong New Orleans International (MSY)* (website: www.flymsy.com) is located 29km (18 miles) from New Orleans' city centre (travel time – 20 to 30 minutes). *To/from the airport*: Shuttles, public buses, taxis and limousines are available at the airport. *Greyhound* (see below) also has buses from the airport to many destinations. *Facilities:* Bank, car hire and post office.

Approximate flight times: From New Orleans to *Atlanta* is one hour 25 minutes, to *Los Angeles* is four hours 10 minutes, and to *New York* is two hours 50 minutes.

RIVER:

The Delta Queen Steamboat Company (tel: (504) 586 0631 *or* (800) 543 1949 (toll-free); website: www.deltaqueen.com) runs scheduled paddlewheel cruises up and down the Mississippi River, stopping at several cities. *The New Orleans Steamboat Company* (tel: (504) 586 8777 *or* (800) 233 2628 (toll-free); website: www.steamboatnatchez.com) offers a number of harbour cruise options. Information and tickets are available at booths behind Jackson Brewery and the aquarium in New Orleans.

RAIL:

Amtrak trains serve New Orleans (tel: (800) 872 7245 (toll-free); website: www.amtrak.com). Services include the 'Crescent', which links New Orleans with New York via Atlanta (Georgia); and the 'City of New Orleans', which heads north from New Orleans to Chicago via Memphis (Tennessee). Trains depart from New Orleans Union Passenger Terminal, located at 1001 Loyola Avenue.

ROAD:

Greyhound buses connect all Louisiana's major towns and cities with destinations throughout the USA (tel: (800) 231 2222 (toll-free); website: www.greyhound.com). Buses stop at New Orleans Union Passenger Terminal (see above). (**Note:** Greyhound bus services to and from New Orleans are limited due to damage from Hurricane Katrina.)

Approximate driving times: From New Orleans to *Houston* is six hours, to *Birmingham* is seven hours and to *Memphis* is eight hours. All times are based on nonstop driving at or below the applicable speed limits.

Approximate bus travel times: From New Orleans to *Mobile* is three hours, and to *Memphis* is 10 hours.

URBAN:

Bus: The famous 'Streetcar Named Desire' that Blanche Dubois dreamt of has been replaced, rather prosaically, by a bus. However, bus services are extensive and available throughout the city. The *Regional Transit Authority* offers a *VisiTour* pass allowing unlimited rides on buses and streetcars all day. **Streetcar:** These still run a 24-hour service (with a reduced service at night) on St Charles Avenue and Carrollton in New Orleans, starting from Canal Street. A streetcar runs every 15 minutes Mon-Fri 0600-2300 and Sat-Sun 0700-2300, along the riverfront between the Convention Center and Esplanade Avenue. **Car hire:** A national driving licence and a major credit card are needed to hire a car. **Horsecab:** Horse-drawn carriages offer a scenic means of transport through the French Quarter.

Top Things To See

- Explore the **Warehouse District** that has been revitalised by galleries, restaurants and shops that display the crafts of local artists.
- Tour the **Louisiana State Museum** (website: http://lsm.crt.state.la.us) on **Jackson Square**, which includes exhibitions on Mardi Gras and jazz.
- The collection of French works at the **New Orleans Museum of Art** (website: www.noma.org) is renowned throughout the world.
- At the **Louisiana Children's Museum** website: www.lcm.org), kids of all ages can pretend to star in their own TV show or shop in a recreated mini-mart.
- Explore the **Global Wildlife Center** (website: www.globalwildlife.com). Visitors can enjoy horseback riding among the exotic animals that roam the 364-hectare (900-acre) park.
- Tour **Rivertown USA** (website: www.rivertownkenner.com), which is a combination of historical sites and family attractions in a Victorian setting. (**Note:** At time of publishing, the museums at Rivertown were closed for restoration. Check the website for opening dates.)
- View the **Capitol Building**, in **Baton Rouge**. It is a 34-storey building with a viewing platform overlooking 11 hectares (27 acres) of formal gardens in the Capitol grounds.
- Tour the **LSU Rural Life Museum** (website: http://rurallife.lsu.edu), an outdoor museum located in the grounds of a former plantation, showing the type of work done in a 19th-century plantation community.
- Enjoy **Houma** (website: www.houmatourism.com), a bayou town. The town is known for its many swamp tours, where alligators, wading birds and myriad other forms of swamplife thrive.
- Journey to **New Iberia** (website: www.cityofnewiberia.com), home of the world-famous Tabasco sauce. The city offers tours of subtropical gardens, stately antebellum homes, rice mills and the hot sauce and pepper plant farms.
- Explore **Natchitoches** (website: www.natchitoches.net). The oldest town in Louisiana, perched on **Cane River Lake**, was first established as a fort and trading post in 1714 to prevent the Spanish from encroaching on French territory. It is now a charming lake town and farm centre.
- Stop by the **RW Norton Museum** (website: www.rwnaf.org). It features Old West artists Frederic Remington and Charles M Russell.
- Smell the **American Rose Center** (website: www.ars.org/ARC/gardens.htm). The centre is a famous garden showplace with 42 acres of roses featuring the "What's New" garden with the national newest rose varieties.
- View the **Poverty Point State Historic Site** (website: www.nps.gov/popo), an ancient Native American religious area dating from 1700 BC and one of the most important archaeological finds in the USA.

Top Things To Do

- Listen to the Music, an integral part of the unique atmosphere of New Orleans. Old-line musicians play classic tunes during brunch and dinner, street musicians huddle in doorways at dusk to perform, and free concerts are offered weekly in the **French Quarter**. Louis Armstrong, Harry Connick Jr, Fats Domino, Pete Fountain, the Neville Brothers and Jelly Roll Morton are all part of the city's rich musical heritage. (**Note**: Most of the nightclubs are open but in the rebuilding status due to damage from Hurricane Katrina.)
- Hear traditional jazz at its best, visit **Bourbon Street**. (**Note:** Most of the businesses are back up and running after damage from Hurricane Katrina.)
- Attend the biggest party of the year - **New Orleans' Mardi Gras**. It rocks the whole city during the three weeks leading up to Ash Wednesday. Colourful parades, masquerade balls and street parties make the festival one of the loudest and liveliest celebrations in the world.
- Experience a Bayou/swamp tour. They offer Cajun storytellers, food, music and an opportunity to go crawfish harvesting with the locals.
- Ferries provide transport across the **Mississippi River**, including one departing from the levée at the foot of Canal Street. One-day cruises are available: **Steamboat Natchez** (website: www.steamboatnatchez.com) has harbour, dinner and jazz cruises.
- Travel the swamp at **Honey Island Swamp** (website: www.honeyislandswamp.com); boat tours are available. **Louisiana Swamp Tours** (website: www.louisianaswamp.com) offers a selection of special cruises through the Louisiana swamps, including buffet and dinner cruises.
- Enjoy the animals at the **Baton Rouge Zoo** (website: www.brzoo.org). It has 57 hectares (140 acres) of walk-through areas and forest settings for over 400 animals.
- See the quiet and elegant town of **St Martinville**, once known as 'Le Petit Paris' for its luxurious balls, operas and highlife. Its Cajun museum and church are well worth visiting. On the **Creole Nature Trail** (website: www.creolenaturetrail.org), near **Lake Charles**, ducks, geese, alligators, nutria and muskrats run rampant.
- Walk around **Shreve Square** (website: www.shreveport-bossier.org). It has an attractive cluster of nightclubs, restaurants and shops.
- Fish at the region known as 'Sportman's Paradise' for its many forests and lakes offering opportunities for fishing, hunting, canoeing and hiking. An annual fishing tournament takes place at **Toledo Bend**.
- Place your bet at **Louisiana Downs Thoroughbred Racetrack**, across the **Red River** in **Bossier City**, open for racing from late spring until the autumn.

TOURIST INFORMATION

Louisiana Office of Tourism
Street address: 1051 North Third Street, Baton Rouge, LA 70802, USA
Postal address: PO Box 94291, Baton Rouge, LA 70804, USA
Tel: (225) 342 8100 *or* (800) 677 4082 (toll-free).
Website: www.louisianatravel.com

Louisana Office of Tourism in the UK
PO Box 815, Bromley, Kent BR1 9WS, UK
Tel: (020) 460 8473 *or* (0800) 652 8251 (brochure request line).
Website: www.louisianatravel.com

Entertainment

FOOD & DRINK: New Orleans is justly renowned for its superb gourmet restaurants which offer Creole specialities. One can savour a breakfast of *beignets* and *café au lait*, dine while overlooking the city or the riverfront, or travel to the seafood houses out by the lake. *Southern Cookin'*, found in the Crossroads region in northern Louisiana, is savoured for its delicious fried chicken, barbecued meat, cornbread and peach pie.
Regional specialities:
- Creole cooking.
- Seafood: fresh fish, shrimp, crabs, oysters and crayfish.

NIGHTLIFE: Nightlife is especially lively in New Orleans. The shows and cabarets of **Bourbon Street** are renowned – every third door on this famous street is a nightclub.
SHOPPING: Louisiana offers tax-free shopping to international visitors for items sold by a participating merchant. A tax refund voucher can be requested from any *Louisiana Tax Free Shopping (LTFS)* participator and the tax can be refunded at the LTFS centre at New Orleans airport on presentation of voucher, receipt, passport and travel ticket. Refunds can also be obtained by mail if sent with voucher, receipts, travel ticket and a notarised statement explaining why vouchers were not redeemed at the airport as well as the present whereabouts of the merchandise.
Among the cities of this State, New Orleans has many excellent shopping opportunities. Souvenirs are plentiful, and other good buys include Creole pecan pralines, Mardi Gras masks, beautifully bottled and hand-mixed perfumes, and various antiques on sale in shops on **Royal Street**. In addition, fine retail shops can be found at **Jackson Brewery**. The **French Market** is the USA's oldest city market and offers a mix of speciality shops, chain stores and restaurants. For second-hand items, the **Community Flea Market** is located nearby.

A B C D E F G H I J K L M N O P Q R S T U V W X Y Z

Maine

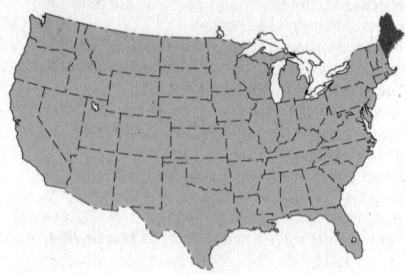

Time: Eastern (GMT - 5). *Daylight Saving Time* is observed.

Overview

Nothing ever changes much in the State of Maine. Forests and lakes still cover 90 per cent of the land, just as they did when Leif Ericson and his band of Viking explorers first set foot on the coast. The length of the Maine coast from Kittery to Lubec still testifies to two vigorous traditions: fishing and shipbuilding. Lobsters are plentiful here and lobster pounds dot the coastline.

General Information

Nickname: Pine Tree State.
State bird: Chickadee.
State flower: White Pine Cone and Tassel.
CAPITAL: Augusta.
Date of admission to the Union: 15 Mar 1820.
POPULATION: 1.32 million (official estimate 2005).
POPULATION DENSITY: 14.4 per sq km.
2004 total overseas arrivals/US ranking: 115,000/31.

Climate

Warm and sunny from May to October, followed by cold winters with abundant snowfall from December to April and temperatures around freezing point.
Required clothing: Heavyweight clothing from November to March/April. Cottons and linens during the summer months.

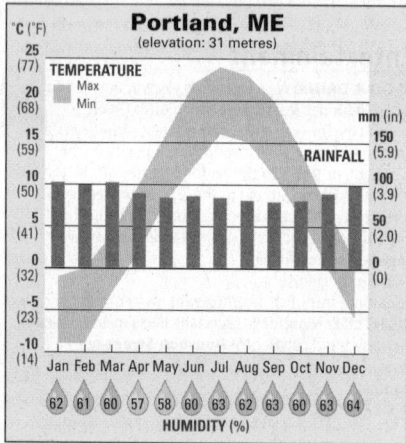

Top Things To See & Do

- Discover **Portland**, Maine's largest city, which features a Victorian reconstruction in what is now called the **Old Port Exchange**. Ferries run to the nearby **Casco Bay Islands**.
- Water-ski on **Sebago Lake**.
- Shop for bargains in **Freeport**.
- Potter round the many bookshops and art galleries of **Kennebunk**, a few miles south of Portland, and a popular haunt for authors and artists. To the east is the town's coastal counterpart, **Kennebunkport**, the summer home of former US President George Bush and family.
- In the summer head to **Camden**, 161km (100 miles) northeast of Portland. The **Camden Hills State Park** offers more than 40km (25 miles) of trails and a harbour view. In **Belfast**, north of Camden, travellers can enjoy antique sales and flea markets.
- Take a boating excursion from forested **Deer Isle** to **Isle au Haut**, part of **Acadia National Park**, boasting 47,633 acres (19,277 hectares) of lakes, woodlands, ponds and mountains. The pretty village of **Bar Harbor** makes a good base to visit the carriage roads and hiking trails of the park's main sector on **Mount Desert Island**.

Credit: ©Maine Office of Tourism

TOURIST INFORMATION

Maine Office of Tourism
59 State House Station, Augusta, ME 04333, USA
Tel: (207) 624 7483 *or* (888) 624 6345 (toll-free).
Website: www.visitmaine.com

CVB of Greater Portland
245 Commercial Street, Portland, ME 04101, USA
Tel: (207) 772 5800.
Website: www.visitportland.com

Maryland

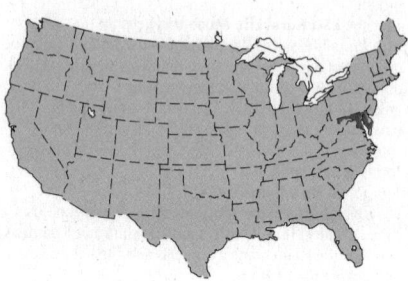

Time: Eastern (GMT - 5). *Daylight Saving Time* is observed.

Overview

Maryland, one of the original 13 States of the USA, was founded by Lord Baltimore in 1634. Its Atlantic Plain, divided by Chesapeake Bay, rises through the rolling hills and scenic farmland of the State's heartland to the Allegheny Mountains of the northwest. Its tourist destinations range from the 16km (10 miles) of white, sandy beaches at Ocean City to Baltimore's bustling Inner Harbor. Chesapeake Bay's 6400km (4000 miles) of shoreline, including its tributaries, separate the Eastern Shore area of Maryland from the rest of the State. The twin-spanned Chesapeake Bay Bridge is the major link between the two sections. The distance between Baltimore and Washington, DC is only about 60km (40 miles).

General Information

Nickname: Old Line State *or* Free State.
State bird: Baltimore Oriole.
State flower: Black-eyed Susan.
CAPITAL: Annapolis.
Date of admission to the Union: 28 Apr 1788 (original 13

Credit: ©Tim Tadder

States; date of ratification of the Constitution).
POPULATION: 5.6 million (official estimate 2005).
POPULATION DENSITY: 174 per sq km.
2004 total overseas arrivals/US ranking: 197,000/23

Climate

Hot, humid summers and mild, damp winters.
Required clothing: Lightweight cotton clothes for summer with light jackets for winter.

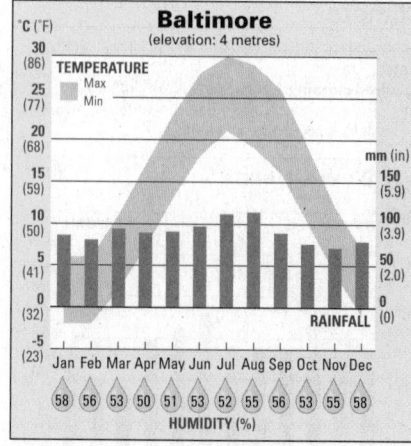

Travel - International

AIR:
 Main airports: *Baltimore/Washington International (BWI)* (website: www.bwiairport.com) is 16km (10 miles) south of Baltimore and 40km (25 miles) northeast of Washington, DC. *To/from the airport:* MTA light-rail services depart every 17 minutes to Baltimore (travel time - approximately 25 minutes), while airport shuttles run every 20 minutes (travel time - 30 minutes). *MARC* commuter trains run hourly on weekdays between Washington, DC, and Baltimore Pennsylvania Station via the airport. Fast and frequent shuttle buses and rail services are also available to Washington, DC. Taxis and limousines are also available. *Facilities:* Bank, car hire and post office.
Approximate flight times: From Baltimore to *London* is seven hours 30 minutes, to *Los Angeles* is five hours 45 minutes and to *New York* is one hour 15 minutes.

RAIL:
 Baltimore is on the main East Coast *Amtrak* line (tel: (800) 872 7245 (toll-free); website: www.amtrak.com) and consequently receives frequent direct services from as far afield as New Orleans and Miami. There are also frequent shuttles to Washington, DC, New York and Boston. For approximate travel times on this line, see the *New York* section. Trains arrive at Pennsylvania Station, 1525 North Charles Street.

ROAD:
 Greyhound (tel: (800) 229 9424 (toll-free); website: www.greyhound.com) buses stop at the Greyhound Bus Station, 2110 Haines Street, in downtown Baltimore.
Approximate driving times: From Baltimore to *Washington, DC* is 50 minutes, to *Miami* is 23 hours and to *Los Angeles* is 56 hours. All times are based on non-stop driving at or below the applicable speed limits.
Approximate driving travel times: From Baltimore to *Washington*, DC is 50 minutes, to *Miami* is 23 hours, to *Los Angeles* is 56 hours. All times are based on non-stop driving at or below the applicable speed limits.
Approximate bus travel times: From Baltimore to *Philadelphia* is two hours 30 minutes and to *New York* is four hours.

URBAN:
 The entire Baltimore metropolitan area is covered by the *Maryland Transit Administration* (website: www.mtamaryland.com), which runs buses, light rail and the metro. Services run 0600-0000 (weekdays) and 0700-0000 (weekends); exact change is required on buses. Water taxis provide regular cross-harbour services, including a route between the National Aquarium and Fell's Point. Taxis can be hailed easily on the street in major tourism areas, and in front of major hotels, or ordered by phone. Cars and motorhomes can be hired.

Top Things To See

- Look at the skyline from the Top of the World **Observation Level** at the **World Trade Center**.
- Tour the art museums including the **Baltimore Museum of Art** (website: www.artbma.org), **Walters Art Museum** (website: www.thewalters.org) and the **American**

Visionary Art Museum (website: www.avam.org).
- View the star-shaped, brick-built **Fort McHenry National Monument** (website: www.nps.gov/fomc), whose bombardment in 1814 inspired the writing of 'The Star-Spangled Banner' and where special drills and military ceremonies are performed.
- Begin in **Frederick** (website: www.fredericktourism.org) for a tour of Civil War sites. A town of quaint brick buildings and parks, it is an excellent starting point to view the historic sites found in and around the city.
- Observe the outstanding panoramic views from the Catoctin peaks in **Gambrill State Park**.
- See **Camp David Presidential Retreat**, near Thurmont. It is the traditional retreat for US Presidents. The public is not allowed inside, but visitors can experience the same lovely landscape in **Catoctin Mountain Park** (website: www.nps.gov/cato), which surrounds it.
- Motor over the famous **Bay Bridge** (website: www.cbbt.com). The bridge leads to **St Michaels**, a quaint town that highlights life along **Chesapeake Bay**, **Crisfield** and **Smith Island**, home to huge populations of Maryland blue crabs.

Top Things To Do

- Tour the **National Aquarium** (website: www.aqua.org), home to more than 560 species of animals.
- Listen to the music at the beautiful **Pier Six Concert Pavilion** (website: www.piersixconcertpavilion.com) where concerts are hosted during the summer months (June to late September).
- Climb the **Washington Monument** (website: www.nps.gov/wamo) for a panoramic view.
- Take a water taxi ride to the neighbourhoods of **Fell's Point** (www.fellspoint.us) and **Little Italy** (website: www.littleitalymd.com).
- Soak up the sun at **Ocean City**, a lovely beach resort boasting an expansive white sand beach, a 5km- (3 mile-) long boardwalk, amusements, tram rides, boating and deep-sea fishing.
- Travel through the **Chesapeake & Ohio Canal National Historic Park** (website: www.nps.gov/choh), stretching 295km (184 miles) from Washington, DC to Cumberland in Western Maryland, where the young Lieutenant-Colonel George Washington began his military career. His headquarters can still be seen here. The canal was once a major avenue of commerce. The towpath for mule-drawn barges now serves as a popular hiking and biking trail.
- Enjoy the different water-based activities at **Deep Creek Lake** (website: www.deepcreeklake.com), the State's four-season resort. Golf and skiing is also available.
- Take part in the weeklong activities celebrating the annual running of the **Preakness Stakes** (website: www.preakness celebration.org) held every May. It is the second event in thoroughbred racing's prestigious triple crown.

TOURIST INFORMATION

Maryland Office of Tourism Development
217 East Redwood Street, 9th Floor, Baltimore, MD 21202, USA
Tel: (410) 767 3400 *or* (800) 634 7386 (toll-free).
Website: www.mdisfun.org

Annapolis & Anne Arundel County CVB
26 West Street, Annapolis, MD 21401, USA
Tel: (410) 280 0445.
Website: www.visit-annapolis.org

Entertainment

FOOD & DRINK: Maryland is well known for its many outstanding restaurants offering fresh seafood caught in Chesapeake Bay.
Regional specialities:
- Maryland Blue Crabs.
NIGHTLIFE: Baltimore's **Fell's Point** district is a historic waterfront neighbourhood that was once a shipbuilding centre. Today, it is home to a variety of restaurants and pubs known for their lively atmosphere. The nearby neighbourhood of **Canton** is rapidly gaining a similar reputation.
SHOPPING: Shopaholics will want to visit **Harborplace** and **The Gallery**, three buildings filled with clothing shops, gift boutiques and eating places located in the heart of the Inner Harbor. Antique lovers should head to **Howard Street**, better known as **Antique Row**. About 20 minutes outside of Baltimore, there is a huge array of assorted shops along the main street of Ellicott City. **Towson Town Center**, north of Baltimore, is a popular mall. **Arundel Mills**, near Baltimore/Washington International Airport, offers discounted merchandise and entertainment facilities.

Massachusetts

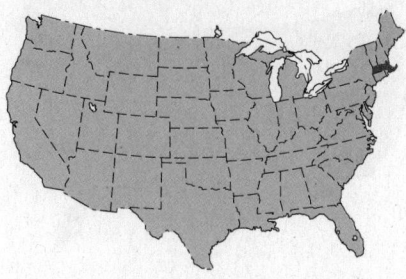

Time: Eastern (GMT - 5). *Daylight Saving Time* is observed.

Overview

The gateway to New England, Massachusetts was the destination of the *Mayflower* in 1620 and is one of the original 13 States. It is very diverse, offering everything from cobblestoned streets and village greens to space-age technology centres. The Berkshire Hills cut across its western corner. To the east the land rolls down to the sea, embracing the State capital, Boston, and the beaches of Cape Cod. Massachusetts has been named by the WWF as one of the world's top 10 whale watching spots, with a variety of species of whales found just 40km (25 miles) off the coast. Whale watching cruises operate from April to October.

General Information

Nickname: Bay State.
State bird: Chickadee.
State flower: Mayflower.
CAPITAL: Boston.
Date of admission to the Union: 6 Feb 1788 (original 13 States; date of ratification of the Constitution).
POPULATION: 6.4 million (official estimate 2005).
POPULATION DENSITY: 234 per sq km.
2004 total overseas arrivals/US ranking: 379,258/13.

Climate

Warm and sunny from May to October, followed by cold winters. The autumn is spectacular: the climate and variety of hardwoods produce vibrant colours, attracting visitors worldwide. Foliage season begins in mid- to late-September, with peak colour often coinciding with the Columbus Day weekend in mid-October.
Required clothing: Warm winter clothes are needed in the coldest months. Light- to mediumweights are advised for the summer.

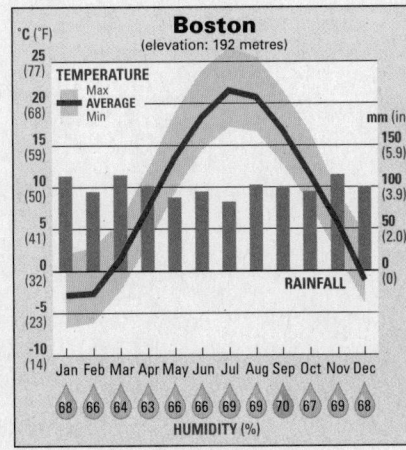

Boston
(elevation: 192 metres)

°C (°F) / mm (in)

TEMPERATURE — Max / AVERAGE / Min
RAINFALL

HUMIDITY (%): 68 66 64 63 66 66 69 69 70 67 69 68

Travel - International

AIR:

 Main airports: *Boston Logan International (BOS)* (website: www.massport.com), 6km (4 miles) from the city centre, is the largest airport in New England; it received almost 4 million international passengers in 2004. *To/from the airport:* A free shuttle bus (marked *Massport*), runs 0530-0100, stopping at each airline terminal, the Water Transportation Terminal, Satellite Parking and the *MBTA* subway station, which has a service (blue line) every eight to 12 minutes to downtown Boston

(travel time - 15 minutes). Buses are available to destinations all over the State, and a commuter rail link is available from Boston to various points in Massachusetts. Taxis and limousines are also available (travel time - 20 minutes). *Massport Airport Water Shuttle*, serviced by a separate bus, offers a boat ride from the airport to Rowes Wharf in downtown Boston (travel time ~seven minutes). *Facilities:* Banking services, car hire and Internet access.
Approximate flight times: From Boston to *London* is six hours 30 minutes, to *Miami* is three hours 30 minutes and to *New York City* is one hour 15 minutes.
RAIL:

 Amtrak (tel: (800) 872 7245 (toll-free); website: www.amtrak.com) links Boston with New York (Pennsylvania Station), Philadelphia and Washington, DC, on the 'Acela Express', and the 'Federal' line runs daily from Boston to New York City, Philadelphia, Baltimore and Washington, DC, while the 'Regional' line covers many stops between Boston and Newport News (Virginia). There are four stations in Boston: North Station, 135 Causeway Street, South Station, Atlantic Avenue and Summer Streets, or Back Bay Station and Route 128 Station. Car hire is available at most stations.
Approximate rail travel times: From Boston to *New York City* is four hours 15 minutes, however, with the *Acela* high-speed train, travel time from Boston to New York City is three hours 30 minutes. *Amtrak* operates around a dozen *Acela Express* roundtrip trains daily between Boston, New York City and Washington, DC.
ROAD:

 Long-distance bus companies operating in the state include *Greyhound* (tel: (800) 231 2222 (toll-free); website: www.greyhound.com) and *Peter Pan Bus Lines* (website: www.peterpanbus.com).
Approximate driving times: From Boston to *Providence* is one hour, to *Dallas* is 37 hours, and to *Seattle* is 63 hours. All times are based on non-stop driving at or below the applicable speed limits.
Approximate bus travel times: From Boston to *Portland*, Maine is two hours, to *Chicago* is 22 hours, and to *Los Angeles* is 68 hours.
URBAN:

Massachusetts Bay Transportation Authority (MBTA) (website: www.mbta.com) operates Boston's subway system (known as the 'T'), as well as bus, trolleybus and train services throughout the city and surrounding towns. The subway system is the oldest in the USA and runs daily 0500-0100. Fares are moderate and passengers can transfer easily between surface and underground transportation. The *Boston Visitor Pass* allows for daily, three-day or weekly travel on all subway and local buses. Suburban buses and commuter trains extend travel beyond the immediate city, to destinations such as Concord, Ipswich and Salem. Taxis can be hailed throughout the city, but delays can be experienced during rush hours; taxis can also be hired by telephone. Car hire is available.

Top Things To See

- Survey the **Boston Skyline** from the **Skywalk Observatory** at the **Prudential Tower** (website: www.prudentialcenter.com). It is a viewing platform on the 52nd floor (open daily 1000-0800), offering a spectacular view over the city.
- Also in Boston, see the **1822 USS Constitution** at **Charlestown Navy Shipyard**, the **Museum of Fine Arts** (website: www.mfa.org), the famous **Museum of Science** (website: www.mos.org), the **John F Kennedy Library and Museum** (website: www.jfklibrary.org), the **Old North Church** (website: www.oldnorth.com), **Faneuil Hall** (website: www.faneuilhall.com), and the **Cheers Bar**, upon which the popular TV series was based.
- Tour **Harvard University** in **Cambridge**, (website: www.harvard.edu), the USA's oldest university (1636).
- Dare to visit **Salem** (website: www.salemweb.com), famous for the 1692 witch trials and its seafaring history.
- Visit **Concord** (website: www.concordma.com), one of the most historic and beautiful towns in the USA. Its **Old North Bridge** was the site of the 'shot heard round the world' in the opening engagement of the American War of Independence. The engagement commenced on what is now called Battle Road in **Lexington** on 15 April 1775.
- See **Battleship Cove** (website: www.battleshipcove.org) in **Fall River**. The cove harbours 20th-century US Navy vessels and is the largest complex of its kind in the country.
- Experience the restored whaling community of **New Bedford** (website: www.newbedford.com). It has the **Seamen's Bethel**, which inspired Herman Melville's description in *Moby Dick*, and the **New Bedford Whaling Museum** (website: www.whalingmuseum.org), which displays the skeleton of a rare, 20m (66ft) blue whale.

A B C D E F G H I J K L M N O P Q R S T U V W X Y Z

- Enjoy the **Higgins Armory** (website: www.higgins.org) in Worcester. Set in a Gothic-style castle, it contains the largest on-display collection of medieval and Renaissance armour in the western hemisphere.

Top Things To Do

- Travel the **Freedom Trail**, which is marked by signs and a red pavement line. It is a 5km (3-mile) walk that passes 16 points of historical interest, some of which are in the **Boston National Historical Park** (website: www.nps.gov/bost).
- Explore **Marblehead** (www.marblehead.com). It is one of the east coast's premier sailing centres; its old town is full of 18th- and 19th-century homes of fishermen, merchants and artisans.
- Travel back in time to **Plimoth Plantation** (website: www.plimoth.org) in **Plymouth**. It is an open-air museum recreating a 1627 Pilgrim village. The Mayflower II, also in Plymouth, is a full-scale reproduction of the ship in which the Pilgrims made their harrowing 66-day voyage from England.
- Linger in **Cape Cod**. It has some 400km (250 miles) of beautiful beaches, and 21 seaside towns and fishing villages, making it one of the USA's prime resort areas. The **Cape Cod National Seashore** (website: www.nps.gov/caco) stretches over 10,927 hectares (27,000 acres) and features expanses of unspoilt sandy beach and stunning desert-like sand dunes.
- Relax on **Nantucket Island**, once a great whaling port, now a popular sun resort. Nantucket and **Martha's Vineyard** (website: www.mvy.com), a picture-postcard island, both lie off the coast of Cape Cod. They are accessible by air from Boston, Hyannis, New Bedford, New York City and Providence (Rhode Island), and by ferry from Hyannis and Woods Hole – booking well ahead for ferry and air services is strongly advised in the summertime.
- Experience **Old Sturbridge Village** (website: www.osv.org) in central Massachusetts; a living history museum recreating an 1830s New England town.
- Travel the **Mohawk Trail** (website: www.mohawktrail.com). The legendary Native American trail winds through 202,347 hectares (500,000 acres) of State parks, forests and reservations. It is very popular for foliage viewing in the autumn.
- Hear a performance of **The Boston Symphony Orchestra** (website: www.bso.org), one of the greatest of all international ensembles. The orchestra has a full schedule of autumn and winter concerts, and makes its summer home at **Tanglewood** in the Berkshires (in western Massachusetts). 'Boston Pops' concerts are staged in the spring and summer, as well as at Christmas.

TOURIST INFORMATION

Massachusetts Office of Travel & Tourism
10 Park Plaza, Suite 4510, Boston, MA 02116, USA
Tel: (617) 973 8500 *or* (800) 227 6277 (toll-free).
Website: www.massvacation.com

Massachusetts Office of Travel & Tourism in the UK
c/o First Public Relations, Molasses House, Clove Hitch Quay, Plantation Wharf, London SW11 3TN, UK
Tel: (020) 7978 5233.
Website: www.massvacation.com *or* www.firstpr.co.uk

Entertainment

FOOD & DRINK: There is a wide variety of very good restaurants. Boston has many ethnic communities, and culinary opportunities range from Greek and Portuguese to Chinese and Syrian. Seafood is a speciality throughout Massachusetts, including local lobster, scallops, scrod and delicious clam chowder. The legal age for the purchase of alcohol is 21 (with valid identification).
Regional specialities:
- New England seafood.
- Orchard fruits and farm produce.
- Maple syrup.
NIGHTLIFE: Boston offers a variety of jazz clubs, dance clubs and intimate piano bar lounges, as well as pubs such as the **Bull & Finch Pub**, the inspiration for the TV show *Cheers*.
SHOPPING: The high-fashion district in Boston is **Newbury Street** in **Back Bay**. Two shopping and restaurant complexes near Newbury Street are **Copley Place** and **The Shops at Prudential Center**. Department stores and **Filene's Basement** are in the town centre. **Faneuil Hall Marketplace**, which is similar to London's Covent Garden, contains shops and restaurants. Statewide, there are a number of factory-outlet stores that offer designer and other items at bargain prices.
SPORT: The famous Boston *Red Sox* baseball team plays at the eccentric yet cosy **Fenway Park** stadium.

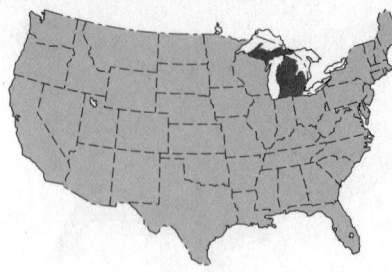

Michigan

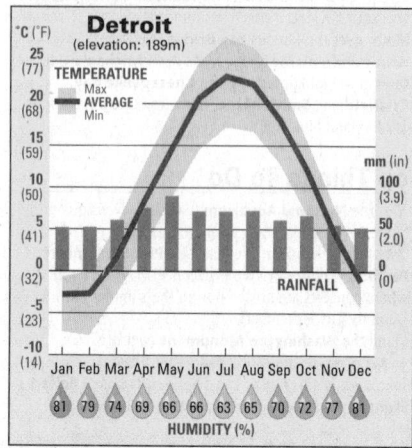

Time: Eastern (GMT - 5) in the greater part of the State; Central (GMT - 6) in Dickinson, Gogebic, Iron and Menominee Counties. *Daylight Saving Time* is observed.

Overview

Michigan comprises two peninsulas. These are divided by Lake Michigan, and linked by one of the world's longest suspension bridges across the Straits of Mackinac. Lakes Superior, Huron and Erie also form the State's shorelines. The Lower Peninsula, mainly agricultural and industrial, contains inland lakes, meadows and sandy beaches, as well as the 'Motor City' of Detroit. The Upper Peninsula is more rugged, and boasts forests, white beaches, trout streams and winter ski resorts.

General Information

Nickname: Great Lakes State.
State bird: Michigan Robin.

State flower: Apple Blossom.
CAPITAL: Lansing.
Date of admission to the Union: 26 Jan 1837.
POPULATION: 10.12 million (official estimate 2005).
POPULATION DENSITY: 40.4 per sq km.
2004 total overseas arrivals/US ranking: 372,588/15.

Climate

Summers are warm with cool nights. Winters are cold, especially around the Great Lakes where conditions can be severe (however, there are good conditions for wintersports).
Required clothing: Warm winter clothes are needed in the coldest months. Light-to-medium weights are advised for the summer.

Credit: ©Dietrick Floeter

Travel - International

AIR:

Main airports: *Detroit Metro (DTW)* (website: www.metroairport.com) is 32km (20 miles) west of the city centre. The airport is the USA's 10th busiest for total passenger numbers (2005) and also receives a sizeable share of international arrivals (372,588 in 2005) in 2002). *To/from the airport:* Metropolitan shuttles and taxis are available to downtown areas. *Facilities:* ATMs, car hire, and currency exchange.

Approximate flight times: From Detroit to *London* is 7 hours 30 minutes, to *Los Angeles* is 5 hours 10 minutes, and to *New York City* is 1 hour 40 minutes.

RAIL:

Detroit is on the *Amtrak* 'Michigan Services' Chicago–Toronto line, which runs from Chicago to Toronto, (tel: (800) 872 7245 (toll-free); website: www.amtrak.com); see the *Illinois* section for approximate travel times. The station is located at 11 West Baltimore Avenue; car hire is available.

ROAD:

Greyhound (tel: (800) 231 2222 (toll-free); website: www.greyhound.com) buses are most frequent in the south; only a few buses serve the Upper Peninsula.

Approximate driving times: From Detroit to *Buffalo* is six hours, to *Dallas* is 24 hours, and to *Seattle* is 49 hours. All times are based on non-stop driving at or below the applicable speed limits.

Approximate bus travel times: From Detroit to *Chicago* is 6 hours, to *Duluth* is 19 hours 15 minutes and to *Los Angeles* is 32 hours.

URBAN:

Most larger communities have bus and taxi services. Detroit also has a city-centre rapid rail system, the *People Mover*, which connects 13 stations in downtown Detroit. *DOT* and *SMART* buses serve the city centre and suburbs respectively.

Top Things To See

- Hear the music of Motown at **Hitsville USA** (now home to Motown Historical Museum; website: www.motownmuseum.com) in **Detroit**; where the sounds of Diana Ross, The Temptations, and The Four Tops are immortalised.
- Spend a day at the **Cultural Center** featuring the **Detroit Historical Museum** (website: www.detroithistorical.org), the **Detroit Institute of Arts** (the fifth-largest art museum in the USA) and the **Charles H Wright Museum of African-American History** (the largest museum of its kind).
- Drive through the Detroit suburb of **Dearborn** where The **Henry Ford Museum** (website: www.hfmgv.org) and **Greenfield Village** (website: www.hfmgv.org) can be found. The 5 hectare (12 acre) indoor museum focuses on America's industrial development and the 33 hectare (81 acre) village comprises more than 80 buildings, a train and a riverboat.
- Tour the **Automotive Hall of Fame** (website: www.automotivehalloffame.org), **Spirit of Ford** and **Henry Ford's Fair Lane Estate** (website: www.henryfordestate.org), also in Dearborn.
- Escape to **Mackinac Island** (website: www.mackinacisland.org), a well-known summer resort. Cars are not allowed and visitors must walk, cycle or use horse-drawn carriages. Attractions include the impressive **Grand Hotel** (website: www.grandhotel.com) and **Fort Mackinac** (website: www.mackinacparks.com), a restored 18th-century military outpost.
- Travel through the **Isle Royale National Park** (website: www.nps.gov/isro). The park is a beautiful wilderness island in Lake Superior.

Top Things To Do

- Dine while visiting the **Renaissance Center**. It houses dozens of restaurants, a 1400-room hotel and a variety of shops, as well as being General Motors' world headquarters.
- Ride a bike at **Belle Isle**, the nation's largest urban island park. It also offers canoeing, an aquarium and the **Dossin Great Lakes Museum**.
- Explore the **Detroit Zoological Park** (website: www.detroitzoo.org), containing more than 5000 animals in natural settings, which can be toured by tractor-train.
- Enjoy **Greektown** where Greek food, entertainment and speciality shops are offered.
- Get your feet wet travelling along **Michigan's Great Lakes coastline**. The 60,000 km (36,000 miles) of rivers and 11000 inland lakes offers great boating, canoeing, fishing and watersports opportunities.
- Visit **Ann Arbor**, the home of the **University of Michigan** (website: www.umich.edu), which has a multitude of bookstores and cozy cafes.
- Head for **Traverse City**. This heart of a recreational haven features sand dunes, resorts, golf and skiing.

TOURIST INFORMATION

Travel Michigan
300 North Washington Square, 2nd Floor, Lansing, MI 48913, USA
Tel: (517) 373 0670 *or* (888) 784 7328 (toll-free):
Website: www.michigan.org

Great Lakes of North America (UK Office)
c/o Cellet Travel Services Ltd, 47 High Street, Henley-in-Arden, Warwickshire B95 5AA, UK
Tel: (01564) 794 999 *or* (08700) 503 410 (brochure request).
Website: www.cellet.co.uk

Entertainment

FOOD & DRINK: The State has a wide variety of US and ethnic restaurants.

Regional specialities:
- Steak.
- Seafood.

NIGHTLIFE: There is a variety of nightlife, including supper clubs with star entertainment. Clubs offer a variety of music, ranging from 'Motown' soul music, which originated in Detroit, to blues (this is the hometown of John Lee Hooker) and classical music.

SHOPPING: Detroit's main shopping areas include the **Renaissance Center**, **Greektown** and suburban malls. Resorts have speciality shops and gallery districts. The nation's first shopping mall, **Northland**, opened in Southfield in 1954.

Minnesota

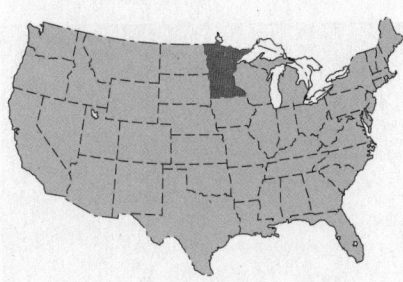

Time: Central (GMT - 6). *Daylight Saving Time* is observed.

Overview

Minnesota, the second northernmost State in the USA (after Alaska), is one of the nation's leading outdoor tourist destinations, with 68 State parks, 55 State forests and more than 12,000 lakes. The State borders Canada, the upper Midwest States and Lake Superior, the largest freshwater lake in the world.

Minneapolis and St Paul adjoin each other on either side of the Mississippi River and have a metropolitan area population of nearly 3 million. They are known as the Twin Cities and began as frontier towns, with German, Irish and Scandinavian immigrants.

General Information

Nickname: North Star State.
State bird: Common Loon.
State flower: Showy Pink and White Lady's Slipper.
CAPITAL: St Paul.
Date of admission to the Union: 11 May 1858.
POPULATION: 5.13 million (official estimate 2005).
POPULATION DENSITY: 22.8 per sq km.
2004 total overseas arrivals/US ranking: 90,000/29

Climate

Winters are cold with adequate snow for skiing, skating, snowmobiling, ice fishing and sledding. Summers are warm, with adequate rainfall for crop growth, and are conducive to summer sports, including swimming, fishing, camping and hiking. Minnesota only rarely experiences heat waves or drought.

Required clothing: Warm winter clothes are needed in the coldest months. Light- to mediumweights are advised for the summer.

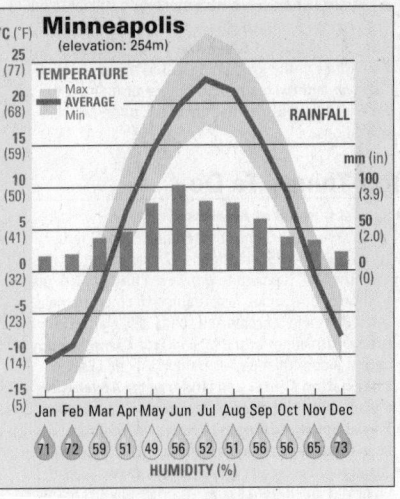

°C (°F) **Minneapolis**
(elevation: 254m)

TEMPERATURE
Max
AVERAGE
Min
RAINFALL

	Jan	Feb	Mar	Apr	May	Jun	Jul	Aug	Sep	Oct	Nov	Dec
HUMIDITY (%)	71	72	59	51	49	56	52	51	56	56	65	73

Travel - International

AIR:

Main airports: *Minneapolis-St Paul International (MSP)* (website: www.mspairport.com) is 16km (10 miles) from the cities (which are contiguous). A US$2.6 billion expansion plan is underway to accommodate the growing number of passengers, expected to reach 40 million per year by the time the improvements are completed in 2010. *To/from the airport:* There is a free shuttle bus between terminals, and *Airport Express* shuttles run to hotels in Minneapolis and St Paul, while buses connect with cities in the surrounding area. An airport limousine service and taxis are available. *Facilities:* ATMs, car hire and currency exchange.

Approximate flight times: From Minneapolis/St Paul to *London* is eight hours five minutes, to *Los Angeles* is four hours, and to *Miami* is three hours 30 minutes

RAIL:

Minneapolis/St Paul is on the *Amtrak* Chicago–Seattle line (tel: (800) 872 7245 (toll-free); website: www.amtrak.com); for approximate travel times, see the *Illinois* section. The station is at a location equidistant to Minneapolis and St Paul, at 730 Transfer Road.

ROAD:

Greyhound (tel: (800) 231 2222 (toll-free); website: www.greyhound.com) provides a long-distance bus service. Terminals are located in both downtown Minneapolis (950 Hawthorne Street) and St Paul (166 West University Avenue).

Approximate driving times: From Minneapolis/St Paul to *Denver* is 17 hours, to *Dallas* is 19 hours, and to *Los Angeles* is 41 hours. All times are based on non-stop driving at or below the applicable speed limits.

Approximate bus travel times: From Minneapolis/St Paul to *Milwaukee* is eight hours, to *New York City* is 18 hours, and to *Miami* is 43 hours.

URBAN:

Local bus services in Minneapolis/St Paul are operated by *Metropolitan Council Transit Operations* (website: www.metrotransit.org). Trolleys serve the downtown locations in both Minneapolis and St Paul.

Top Things To See

- Tour the **Walker Art Center** (website: www.walkerart.org) The center stages contemporary art exhibitions, concerts and lectures, and also features an **Outdoor Sculpture Garden**, which is the largest of its kind in the USA. It is open all year round and is one of the State's top tourist attractions.
- Visit **Minnehaha Falls** (website: www.nps.gov/miss/maps/model/minnehaha.html), made famous in Longfellow's poem, The *Song of Hiawatha*.
- View the **Landmark Center** (website: www.landmarkcenter.org), which houses the **Minnesota Museum of American Art** (website: www.mmaa.org). Its distinguished history includes the trials of several famous gangsters in the 1930s, when it was the **Federal Court House**.
- Tour the **St. Louis County Heritage & Arts Center**, known locally as **The Depot** (website: www.duluthdepot.org). It houses exhibits by four different museums.
- See the **Split Rock Lighthouse State Park** (website: www.mnhs.org/places/sites/srl). It preserves one of the most scenic lighthouses in the USA.
- Stop by the **Mississippi River Visitor Center** (website:

www.mississippirivervisitorcenter.org), a collaboration between the National Park Service and the Science Museum. The **Great River Road** that runs south from the Twin Cities to the Iowa border offers magnificent views of the river and the many bird species, including the American Bald Eagle, that travel this route on their migrations.

Top Things To Do

- Shop at the **Mall of America** (website: www.mallof america.com). The largest entertainment and retail complex in the USA, it attracts 42 million visitors each year. The Mall is poised to grow even further, with plans for hotels, new shops, restaurants and entertainment attractions and a fitness and spa facility planned for the future. Attractions at the Mall include **Camp Snoopy** (the largest indoor theme park in the USA), the **LEGO Imagination Center** and **Underwater Adventures**, a 5.4 million-litre (1.2 million gallons) walk-through aquarium.
- Play at **Spirit Mountain** (website: www.spiritmt.com), a year-round holiday and outdoor recreation centre.
- Travel the spectacular **North Shore Drive** (website: www.lakesuperiordrive.com) (US Highway 61) following the north shore of Lake Superior for 240km (150 miles) from Duluth to the Canadian border. It was designated an 'All American Road' for its unique, scenic beauty.
- Stay at one of the major resort areas. They include the towns of Bemidji, Brainerd, Detroit Lakes and Grand Rapids, as well as the Lake Mille Lacs area.
- Take in a Broadway show. The Twin Cities offer more theatres than any other US metropolitan area outside New York City, with more than 100 theatre companies. Broadway shows and theatrical events are performed at the restored Historic Orpheum Theatre, Historic State Theatre and the Historic Pantages Theatre in the Hennepin Theater District (website: www.hennepintheaterdistrict.org) in downtown Minneapolis.
- Canoe in the **Boundary Waters Canoe Area Wilderness** (website: www.bwcaw.org) in the **Superior Natural Forest**.
- Enjoy the **wintersports** well provided for, abetted by the

State's strategic northern location. Skiing, ice-skating, sledging, ice fishing, dog sledging and snowmobiling are all available.

TOURIST INFORMATION

Minnesota Office of Tourism
100 Metro Square, 121 7th Place East, St Paul, MN 55101, USA
Tel: (651) 296 5029 *or* (800) 657 3700 (toll-free).
Website: www.exploreminnesota.com

Greater Minneapolis Convention & Visitors Association
250 Marquette Avenue South, Suite 1300, Minneapolis, MN 55401, USA
Tel: (612) 767 800 *or* (888) 676 6757 (toll-free).
Website: www.minneapolis.org

Entertainment

FOOD & DRINK: The Twin Cities have many excellent restaurants, notably steakhouses; however, international cuisine as diverse as Greek and Japanese is also widely available.

Regional specialities:
- Freshwater fish.

NIGHTLIFE: The State's nightclubs offer rock groups, jazz combos and musical comedy. Popular gathering places are the **Loon** and the **Fine Line Music Cafe** in the Warehouse District of Minneapolis, and the **Dakota Bar & Grill** in St Paul. **America Live!** is a nightclub collective in the Mall of America.

SHOPPING: The **Mall of America** stands 15 minutes south of downtown Minneapolis at Bloomington. It is home to more than 520 stores, dozens of restaurants (including the first **Rainforest Cafe**), nine nightclubs, 14 cinemas, an indoor roller coaster and a walk-through aquarium. At each corner of the mall are the major department stores – **Bloomingdale's**, **Macy's**, **Nordstrom** and **Sears**.

Mississippi

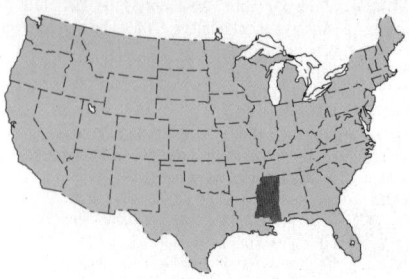

Time: Central (GMT - 6). *Daylight Saving Time* is observed.

Overview

The beautiful 'Magnolia State' is a land of great variety, with wide-open spaces, white sand beaches, bustling cities, quaint little towns and a real feel of the Deep South. This is the State where the key battle of the American Civil War was fought (at Vicksburg in 1863) and where racial strife erupted with terrifying force in the 1960s. It is also the State whose geographical beauty and rich atmosphere have inspired a wealth of artistic talent, from William Faulkner, Eudora Welty and Tennessee Williams to Elvis Presley, Jimmie Rodgers and B B King. As well, the mighty Mississippi River, thousands of acres of lush parkland and the Gulf of Mexico coastline combine to make Mississippi a popular outdoor destination.

Mississippi was hit hard by Hurricane Katrina in 2005 but much of the infrastructure and attractions have been repaired and are open to visitors.

General Information

Nickname: Magnolia State.
State bird: Mockingbird.
State flower: Magnolia Blossom.
CAPITAL: Jackson.
Date of admission to the Union: 10 Dec 1817.
POPULATION: 2.92 million (official estimate 2005).
POPULATION DENSITY: 23.3 per sq km.
2004 total overseas arrivals: Under 38,000.

Climate

Mississippi's climate is moderate, with January's temperature reaching 10°C (50°F) and summers sometimes stretching to 32°C (90°F). The year-round average is 18°C (64°F).

Required clothing: Summer months require light cottons and linens. Heavier weight clothing is needed for the winter months.

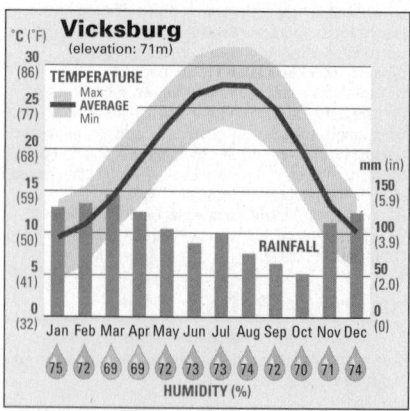

Travel - International

AIR:

Main airports: Jackson International (JAN) (website: www.jmaa.com) lies to the east of the city. *To/from the airport*: Buses, taxis, and limousines are available. *Facilities*: ATMs and car hire. There are further airports at *Greenville, Gulf Coast (Biloxi), Hattiesburg, Meridian* and *Tupelo*.

RIVER:

The *Delta Queen Steamboat Company* (tel: (800) 543 1949 (toll-free); website: www.deltaqueen.com), runs scheduled paddlewheel cruises up and down the Mississippi River, stopping at several Mississippi cities, and travelling as far upriver as Minneapolis/St

Credit: ©Explore Minnesota Tourism Photo

Paul. A similar journey is available on a European-style hotel barge operated by *RiverBarge Excursion Lines* (tel: (888) 456 2206 (toll-free); website: www.riverbarge.com).

RAIL:

Two *Amtrak* (tel: (800) 872 7245 (toll-free); website: www.amtrak.com) lines traverse Mississippi: the 'City of New Orleans' passes through Jackson on its way north to Chicago, and the 'Crescent' cuts through the southeast corner of the State (stopping at Meridian, Laurel, Hattiesburg and Picavune) on its way from New Orleans to Atlanta, Washington, DC and New York City.

Approximate rail travel times: From Jackson to *New Orleans* is four hours 30 minutes, to *Memphis* is four hours 30 minutes, and to *Chicago* is 10 hours 25 minutes.

ROAD:

The speed limit on interstate highways in Mississippi is 70mph (112kmph) unless otherwise stated. *Greyhound* buses (tel: (800) 231 2222 (toll-free); website: www.greyhound.com) are frequent along the coast of Mississippi; services north and into the Delta are infrequent.

Approximate bus travel times: From Jackson to *Memphis* is four hours, to *Montgomery* is seven hours, and to *Dallas* is 10 hours.

URBAN:

Jackson Transit System (JATRAN) runs buses throughout the city; services run until 1800. Bus schedules and maps are posted at most bus stops and are available at *JATRAN* headquarters, 1025 Terry Road, Jackson (tel: (601) 948 3840).

Top Things To See

- Travel the historic **Natchez Trace Parkway** (website: www.nps.gov/natr) that winds 640km (400 miles) through Mississippi, ending up at Natchez in the southwest and, as one writer put it, is 'what God meant a highway to be.' Free of billboard advertising and commercial traffic, and with a speed limit of 50mph (80kmph), the parkway provides a scenic introduction to the delights of Mississippi and leads visitors down paths once trekked by buffalo, Native Americans and frontiersmen.
- Visit **Tupelo**, best known for its native son, Elvis Presley. Visitors can stop at **Elvis Presley's Birthplace** (website: www.elvispresleybirthplace.com), the humble two-room house where 'the King' was born, and the adjacent museum which contains rare photos, memorabilia and a statue of Elvis aged 13.
- Sample Mississippi's vibrant blues tradition at the **Delta Blues Museum** (website: www.deltabluesmuseum.org) in Clarksdale.
- Explore the **Old Capitol Historical Museum** (website: www.mdah.state.ms.us/museum/ocmuseum.html), containing exhibits chronicling the Civil Rights movement, while the **Smith Robertson Museum** (website: www.city.jackson.ms.us/CityHall/robertson.htm) houses displays on African-American Mississippian history and heritage.
- Take the family to **Leland**'s (website: www.lelandms.org) *Birthplace of the Frog* exhibition where the childhood of Jim Henson, creator of the *Sesame Street* and *Muppets* characters, can be remembered.
- Enjoy the sounds of music at the **Highway 61 Blues Museum** (website: www.highway61blues.com) in downtown **Leland**.
- Visit the **Canton Movie Museum** (website: www.cantontourism.com) and the **Canton Multi-Cultural Center and Museum**, with topics ranging from slavery and civil rights to family and music. Local Canton residents are featured at the oral history kiosk.

Top Things To Do

- Explore the **Tupelo Buffalo Park** (website: www.tupelobuffalopark.com), featuring a herd of buffalo, which can be viewed from aboard the Monster Bison Bus.
- Tour the **Corinth Civil War Interpretative Center**. The centre chronicles the Battle of Corinth and its significance in Civil War history.
- Visit **Oxford**, the picturesque town captured forever in the writings of William Faulkner. **Rowan Oak**, Faulkner's house, can be visited today and remains much as the literary giant left it, with the outline of his novel, *A Fable*, scrawled on his study wall. Audio walking tours of the town are available from the tourism council.
- Explore **Vicksburg National Military Park** (website: www.nps.gov/vick) where some of the bloodiest battles of the Civil War took place. Here, on 4 July 1863, the Union victory helped the Yankees gain control of the Mississippi River, a crucial element in winning the war. Living history demonstrations and battle re-enactments every summer provide a fascinating insight into this dramatic period.
- Discover **Natchez** (website: www.natchez.ms.us). It was spared major destruction in the Civil War. Today, over 500 historic buildings still stand, including mansions, churches and public buildings, providing a wonderful glimpse of pre-war life in the Deep South. Many of these graceful mansions contain original furnishings, while a good number offer bed & breakfast accommodation. **Natchez-under-the-Hill**, once notorious for its riverside gambling, is now a colourful area of pubs, gift shops, restaurants and dockside gaming.
- Make Natchez your starting point for the **Deep South Antique & Wine Trail** (website: www.deepsouthantiqueandwinetrail.com), which is a co-operative endeavour between the States of Mississippi and Louisiana and covers 322km (200 miles) and six counties, with over 100 antique shops en route.
- Enjoy the famous **All-American Rose Garden** in Hattiesburg (website: www.hattiesburg.org), which features 740 patented bushes.
- Relax at the **Pearl River Resort** (website: www.pearlriverresort.com) in Choctaw. The resort features gaming and entertainment facilities, two hotels, and a golf club. New additions, slated for completion in 2006, include a recreational complex, a fitness and wellness centre, a lake-side hotel, exposition hall, a Choctaw memorial and a labyrinth.

TOURIST INFORMATION

Mississippi Development Authority/Tourism Development Division
Street address: 501 North West Street, Jackson, MS 39201, USA
Postal address: PO Box 849, Jackson, MS 39205, USA
Tel: (601) 359 3297 *or* (866) 733 6477.
Website: www.visitmississippi.org or www.mississippi.org

Mississippi Tourist Information UK
Lofthouse Enterprises, Woodlands Park Street, Hitchin, Herts SG4 9AH, UK
Tel: (01293) 560 848.
Website: www.deep-south-usa.com

Entertainment

FOOD & DRINK: The tiny Delta town of Belzoni claims to be the catfish capital of the world. The highlight of the year is the Catfish Festival, which sees the crowning of the Catfish Queen and a catfish-eating contest.

Regional specialities:

- Farm-raised catfish.
- Fried Chicken.

NIGHTLIFE: Las Vegas-style entertainment casinos abound, especially in Greenville, Natchez, Philadelphia, Tunica, Vicksburg, and along the Mississippi Gulf Coast. Vicksburg has the *Bottleneck Blues Bar*, decorated in a 1930s delta-style.

SHOPPING: Antique shops and malls are plentiful. The **Canton Flea Market**, held in May and October, is ever-popular. In Port Gibson the 'Pieces and Strings' market runs from the last weekend in March to the end of April and features African- and European-American quilts and quilting demonstrations.

Missouri

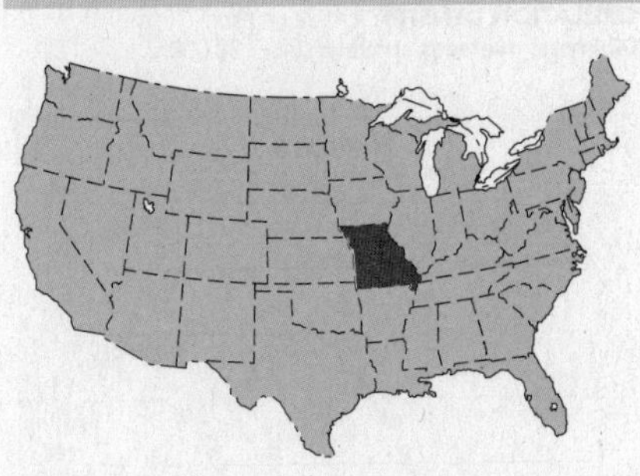

Time: Central (GMT - 6). *Daylight Saving Time* is observed.

Overview

Missouri, in the heart of the USA, is a blend of frontier West, gracious South, the sophisticated East and industrial North. The Missouri Valley was a major pioneer route, with St. Louis known as 'The Gateway to the West.' It is bounded by the Mississippi River in the east. Prairies lie north of the Missouri River (the longest in the USA), with great plains to the west, rolling hills in the south and the Southern-style cotton lands to the southeast. The State's riverboat culture was immortalised by Mark Twain in *Life on the Mississippi* and in his tales of *Tom Sawyer* and *Huckleberry Finn*. The largest city in Missouri and one of the US's largest inland ports, St. Louis was once a booming centre for fur traders and explorers opening up 'The West.' It is now a modern communications, commercial, industrial and cultural centre. It still retains its love affair with the Mississippi River, on whose banks can be heard ragtime, blues and Dixieland jazz.

General Information

Nickname: Show Me State.
State bird: Bluebird.
State flower: Hawthorn Flower.
CAPITAL: Jefferson City.
Date of admission to the Union: 10 Aug 1821.
POPULATION: 5.8 million (official estimate 2005).
POPULATION DENSITY: 32.1 per sq km
2004 total overseas arrivals/US ranking: 91,000/29

Climate

The region has the most continental climate of any area in the USA. Winters are cold and summers warm, with frequent heatwaves.

Required clothing: Warm winter clothes are needed in the coldest months. Light-to-medium weights are advised for summer.

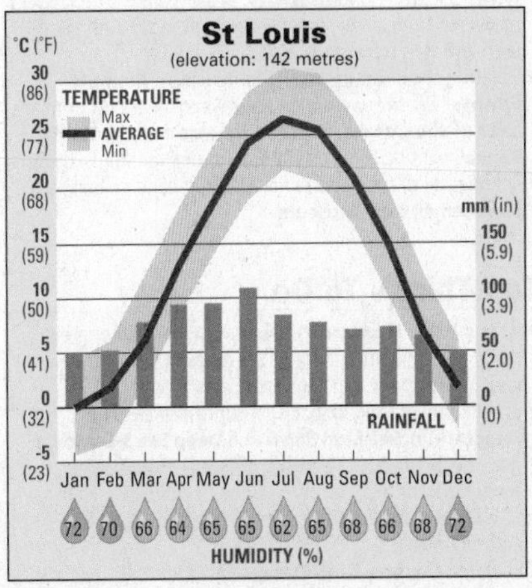

Travel - International

AIR:

Main airports: *Lambert St Louis International (STL)* (website: www.lambert-stlouis.com) is 21km (13 miles) northwest of central St Louis (travel time - 30 minutes). *To/from the airport*: The *Metro Link* light-rail system connects the airport with downtown St. Louis. Taxis and airport limousines are available. *Greyhound* buses (see below) stop at the airport, providing a route to further flung destinations. *Facilities*: ATMs, car hire and restaurants.

Kansas City International (KCI) (website: www.flykci.com) is 32km (20 miles) northwest from the city centre (travel time - 40 minutes). *To/from the airport*: Shuttle buses run every 30 minutes (0600-0000) to hotels in Kansas City and Westport. Taxis are also available. *Facilities*: ATMs, car hire and restaurants.

Approximate flight times: From London to *St. Louis* is eight hours five minutes and to *Kansas City* is 13 hours 20 minutes (including stopover).

RAIL:

St Louis is a stopping point on *Amtrak*'s daily 'Texas Eagle' service from Chicago to San Antonio, which continues thrice weekly to Los Angeles. Trains on the daily 'Southwest Chief Service' from Chicago to Los Angeles stop in Kansas City; the station is located at 30 West Pershing. For approximate travel times on the former line, see the *Illinois* section; for the latter, see the *California* section. There are also twice daily services from Kansas City to St Louis (one of which continues to Chicago) and an additional daily St Louis–Chicago service. The St Louis station is located at 550 South 16th Street. For more information, contact *Amtrak* (tel: (800) 872 7245 (toll-free); website: www.amtrak.com).

ROAD:

Long-distance bus companies operating in the State include *Greyhound* (tel: (800) 231 2222 (toll-free); website: www.greyhound.com) and *Jefferson Lines* (tel: (800) 451 5333 (toll-free); website: www.jeffersonlines.com), with services from Kansas City.

Approximate driving times: From St Louis to *Chicago* is five hours, to *Nashville* is six hours, and to *Seattle* is 45 hours. From Kansas City to *Topeka* is two hours, to *Little Rock* is seven hours, and to *Los Angeles* is 34 hours. All times are based on nonstop driving at or below the applicable speed limits.

Approximate bus travel times: From St. Louis to *Indianapolis* is five hours, and to *Tulsa* is nine hours. From Kansas City to *Omaha* is five hours and to *Denver* is 13 hours.

URBAN:

The *Metro Link* light-rail system in St Louis (website: www.metrolouis.org) is complemented by a network of BSTS public bus routes; the Metro Link is free in downtown St Louis Mon-Fri 1100-1330. There are public bus services around Kansas City and surrounding suburbs (website: www.kcata.org). Car hire and taxis are readily available in both cities.

Top Things To See

- Adventure up the **Gateway Arch** (website: www.stlouisarch.com) on **St Louis**'s riverfront. At 192m (630ft) it is the nation's tallest memorial. It honours St Louis as the starting point for settlers who began their trek to the western frontier from the city and contains an observation deck and exhibits on the American West.
- Tour **Hannibal**, Mark Twain's hometown during the 19th century. Many museums and shows celebrate the author's life and works, including the **Mark Twain Boyhood Home** and the **New Mark Twain Museum** (website: www.marktwainmuseum.org).
- Tour the **Arabia Steamboat Museum** (website: www.1856.com) in **Kansas City**. Displayed are artefacts recovered from a steamboat which sank in the Mississippi with 200 tons of cargo in 1856.
- Visit one of three outstanding State parks – **Bennett Springs** (website: www.mostateparks.com/bennett.htm), the **Lake of the Ozarks** (website: www.odd.net) and **Ha Ha Tonka** (website: www.mostateparks.com/hahatonka.htm).
- See the site of the nation's first daylight bank robbery; the **Jesse James Bank Museum**.

Top Things To Do

- Get soaked in **Hurricane Harbor** waterpark, among the many rides and attractions at **Six Flags St. Louis** theme park (website: www.sixflags.com/parks/stlouis) .
- Explore the St. Louis **Zoo**. Exhibits included are **The Insectarium**, **Sea Lion Show** and **Deep Sea 3-D Movie**.
- Take the family to the **Worlds of Fun** (website: www.worldsoffun.com) entertainment complex in Kansas City. It has more than 120 rides, rollercoasters and live entertainment.
- Shop the **Country Club Plaza** (website: www.countryclubplaza.com) in Kansas City, the nation's oldest shopping centre established in 1922.
- Journey to the **Lake of the Ozarks** (website: www.oddnet) in central Missouri. It has more than 1600km (1000 miles) of forested shoreline and offers watersports, canoeing, golfing, tennis, caves, shows and museums, as well as the recently renovated **Timber Falls Indoor Water Park** (website: www.timberridgeresort.com).
- Explore **Branson** (website: www.cityofbranson.org). The city first became popular at the turn of the 20th century, when Harold Bell Wright's *The Shepherd of the Hills*, with its colourful depiction of life in the Ozarks, was published. Today, the area is known as a live entertainment capital offering pop, swing, rock and roll, country and gospel music performances at around 40 theatres, with more than 90 daily shows, and attracts legends of the entertainment world, such as Andy Williams and Mel Tillis. The city is also known for its three picturesque lakes, **Lake Taneycomo**, **Table Rock Lake** and **Bull Shoals Lake**, which provide excellent opportunities for fishing and water activities.
- Spend the day at Branson's best-known attraction; **Silver Dollar City** (website: www.silverdollarcity.com). Explore the turn-of-the-century crafts village with daily music shows and rides like the *Thunderation Rollercoaster*, the *Lost River Water Ride* and the *Buzz Saw Falls*.

TOURIST INFORMATION

Missouri Division of Tourism
301 West High, Jefferson City, MO 65101, USA
Tel: (573) 751 4133 *or* (800) 519 2300 (toll-free).
Website: www.visitmo.com

Missouri Division of Tourism in the UK
c/o Cellet Travel Services Ltd, 47 High Street, Henley-in-Arden, Warwickshire B95 5AA, UK
Tel: (01564) 794 999.
Website: www.cellet.co.uk

Entertainment

FOOD & DRINK: Everything from elegant downtown restaurants to more casual eating places serve traditional ethnic fare in St. Louis.
Regional specialities:
- Steaks.
- Barbecues.

NIGHTLIFE: There are many nightclubs and restaurants on the riverfront in St Louis, where jazz and ragtime music is performed nightly and discos can be found in most modern hotels. There are four full-gaming casinos located within 15 minutes of downtown Kansas City, whose historic *Westport* district is home to great blues, jazz and R&B.

SHOPPING: Two of the St. Louis area's most elegant regional shopping malls are **Plaza Frontenac** and the **St. Louis Galleria**. The new St. Louis Mills mall combines shopping with a NASCAR Speedcar track, a skatepark and an ice rink (the new practice ground for the St. Louis Blues NHL ice hockey team). The city's neighbourhoods are also filled with fashionable boutiques, speciality shops, gourmet delicatessens and antique stores.

Soulard Market in south St. Louis is a colourful and amusing place to shop on Saturdays. The market was established in 1779 and today offers fresh goods, such as meat and home-baked items, as soon as they arrive in the city. **Union Station**, the city's historic Victorian railroad station, has been redeveloped as a festival marketplace, with more than 100 shops and restaurants, and numerous nightclubs. Branson is also becoming a popular shopping destination, with three outlet malls, and unique craft and gift stores throughout the city. Kansas City has nationally-known stores, plus hundreds of shops and boutiques to be found off the beaten path.

Montana

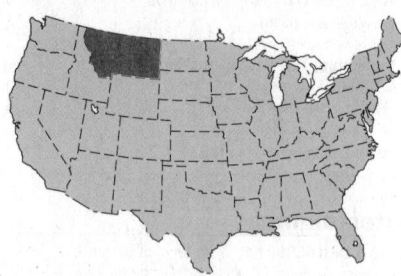

Time: Mountain (GMT - 7). Daylight Saving Time is observed.

Overview

Montana is the fourth-largest State, after Alaska, Texas and California, covering 38 million hectares (94 million acres). Almost a quarter of Montana is national forest or public lands, with almost 2 million hectares (5 million acres) protected as wilderness areas. Elk, deer, antelope, wolves and bears are just a few of the 500 species of wildlife that can be seen in Montana.

General Information

Nickname: Treasure State.
State bird: Western Meadowlark.
State flower: Bitterroot.
CAPITAL: Helena.
Date of admission to the Union: 8 Nov 1889.
POPULATION: 935,670 (official estimate 2005).
POPULATION DENSITY: 2.45 per sq km.
2004 total overseas arrivals: Under 38,000.

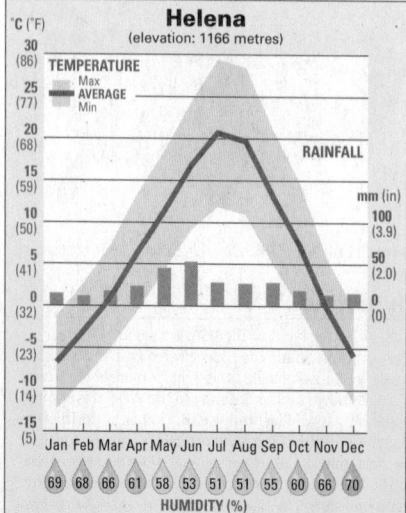

Helena
(elevation: 1166 metres)

Credit: ©Travel Montana/Donnie Sexton

Climate

Summer temperatures average between 14.4°C-30°C (58°F-86°F). Seasonal extremes are greater to the East of the Continental Divide. The Great Plains are subject to waves of frigid arctic air 6 to 12 times each winter. Winter temperatures average -10.6°C to -0.6°C (13°F to 31°F).
Required clothing: Lightweights for the summer and heavyweights with extra bundling for the winter.

Top Things To See & Do

- See bisons roam free in the **National Bison Range**, just north of Missoula. This high plains refuge was established in 1908 to protect the animal from extinction. Today, the park is home to around 450 bisons. Between May and October, when all the routes are open, there is a small per-vehicle charge to access the range and view the magnificent creatures.
- **Waterton-Glacier International Peace Park** is home to many endangered bears, big horn sheep, mountain goats, moose and grey wolves. The park is divided into two areas: **Waterton Lakes National Park** in Alberta (Canada) and the larger **Glacier National Park** in Montana. The 84km (52 mile) **Going-to-the-Sun Road** crosses the park's spectacular alpine landscape and is one of America's most scenic drives. Hiking is a popular option, with over 1200km (750 miles) of trails to follow, many offering back-country camping opportunities. There are also special routes for cyclists and horses, and many of the larger lakes have tour boat services. Anyone who enters the park is advised to take park rangers' warnings and advice about encounters with bears very seriously.
- Other recreation areas include the **Bob Marshall Wilderness Area**, the huge **Charles M Russell National Wildlife Refuge** and **Yellowstone National Park**, which is shared with Idaho and Wyoming, and is the oldest national park in the world, dating back to 1872.
- **Billings**, with nearly 100,000 residents, is Montana's largest city and a regional business/service centre. The area around Billings offers great opportunities for fishing, hiking and western adventures, such as guest ranches and cattle drives. The outdoor recreation department at **Montana State University – Billings** offers canoeing classes and other outdoor activities. The highlights of the town's calendar are the *Billings Summer Fair* (third weekend of July), *Big SkyFest* hot air balloon festival (late July/early August) and the Montana Fair (August), in addition to an active year-round cultural scene.
- Head for **Little Bighorn Battlefield National Monument**, which lies an hour southeast of Billings. General George Armstrong Custer and his men made their last stand here on 25 June 1876 against the Sioux and Cheyenne warriors. A tour takes visitors through the battle movements of both sides and the visitors' centre houses a museum that displays weapons used in the battle. **Helena**, the State capital, offers fine 19th-century architecture, museums and the Gothic-style **St Helena Cathedral**, modelled on the cathedral in Cologne, Germany.

TOURIST INFORMATION

Montana Promotional Division
Department of Commerce, 301 South Park Avenue, Helena, MT 59620, USA
Tel: (406) 841 2870 *or* (800) 847 4868 (toll-free).
Website: www.visitmt.com

Information about Montana's seven convention and visitors bureaus, communities and chambers of commerce is available on the Montana Promotional Division's website or in their free publications, *The Montana Travel Planner* and *Montana Vacation Guide*.

Rocky Mountain International in the UK
7 Thornton Avenue, Warsash, Southampton, Hampshire SO31 96D, UK
Tel: (01489) 557 533 (trade enquiries only) *or* (09063) 640 655 (consumer request line; 60p per minute).
Website: www.rmi-realamerica.com

Nebraska

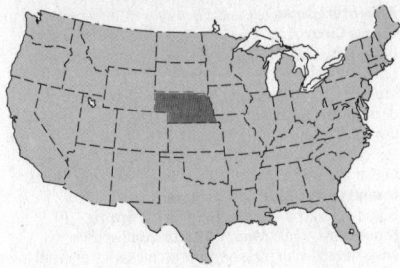

Time: Central (GMT - 6) in the greater part of the State; Mountain (GMT - 7) in the west. *Daylight Saving Time* is observed.

Overview

Nebraska rises from the Missouri prairie lands to the Great Plains and foothills of the Rocky Mountains. Omaha, its largest city, is one of the State's major tourist destinations. Girls and Boys Town, the famous homeless boys' community, is situated nearby. Originally founded as 'Boys Town' by Father Edward Flanagan, the home for unwanted and distressed boys is still thriving, and, today, girls also enjoy the care and protection it offers.

Lincoln is one of the most stunning State capitals in the USA. The State Capitol Building, known as the 'Tower on the Plains', is as impressive inside as it looks from the street; for an unsurpassed view of the city, take the elevator to the top floor.

General Information

Nickname: Cornhusker State.
State bird: Western Meadowlark.
State flower: Goldenrod.
CAPITAL: Lincoln.

Omaha
(elevation: 332 metres)

°C (°F)
TEMPERATURE
Max
AVERAGE
Min
mm (in)
RAINFALL

HUMIDITY (%)
74 72 65 64 64 67 64 66 67 64 70 75
Jan Feb Mar Apr May Jun Jul Aug Sep Oct Nov Dec

Date of admission to the Union: 1 Mar 1867.
POPULATION: 1.76 million (official estimate 2005).
POPULATION DENSITY: 8.7 per sq km.
2004 total overseas arrivals: Under 38,000.

Climate

The region has the most continental climate of any area in the USA. Winters are cold and summers warm.
Required clothing: Lightweights for the summer and heavyweights for the winter.

Top Things To See & Do

- Visit **Omaha**, the State's largest city. Nearby is **Girls and Boys Town**, the famous homeless boys' community. The attraction that draws the most visitors through its gates, however, is the **Henry Doorly Zoo**, which contains **Lied Jungle**, the largest indoor tropical rainforest in the world. In contrast to the zoo's popular **Scott Kingdoms of the Seas Aquarium**, where brown sharks swim ominously close to onlookers, the **Desert Dome** houses three distinct desert climates in one biosphere. Located just underneath is **The Kingdoms of the Night** nocturnal exhibit, which houses animals that live in dark habitats. The city's varied nightlife ranges from punk to opera, while theatre lovers can take advantage of the free **Shakespeare on the Green (Nebraska Shakespeare) festival**, which takes place in late June and early July in **Elmwood Park**.
- Explore the State capital, **Lincoln**. Enjoy spectacular views from the top floor of **The State Capitol Building**. Other city sights include the **Museum of Nebraska History**, which has a moving exhibit on the history of the Plains Native Americans; **Mueller Planetarium**; **Sheldon Memorial Art Gallery**, including a collection of Warhol Pop Art; and the **University of Nebraska State Museum**, which boasts the largest mounted mammoth in a US museum.
- Tour the **Strategic Air & Space Museum**, near **Ashland**, which features exhibitions and displays of aircraft and missiles, and is regarded as one of the best in the USA.
- Discover other State attractions such as the **Homestead National Monument of America**; the pioneer landmarks of **Scotts Bluff National Monument** and **Chimney Rock**; **Fort Robinson State Park**, where Chief Crazy Horse surrendered in 1877; and the **Buffalo Bill State Park**.

TOURIST INFORMATION

Nebraska Division of Travel & Tourism
PO Box 98907, Lincoln, NE 68509, USA
Tel: (402) 471 3796 *or* (877) 6327 2752 (toll-free).
Website: www.visitnebraska.org

Greater Omaha CVB
1001 Farnham-on-the-Mall, Suite 200, Omaha, NE 68102, USA
Tel: (402) 444 4660 *or* (866) 9376 6242 (toll-free).
Website: www.visitomaha.com

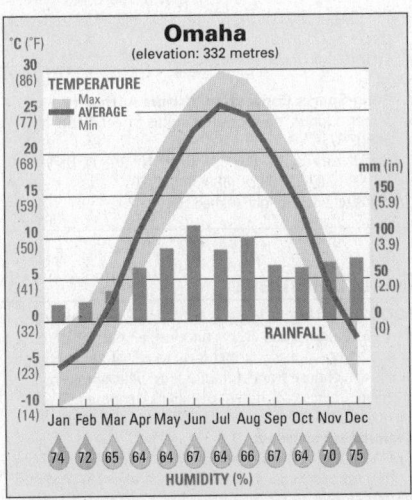
Credit: © J Nabb

Nevada

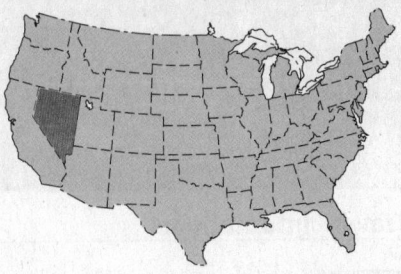

Time: Pacific (GMT - 8). *Daylight Saving Time* is observed.

Overview

Explorer John C Fremont's 1844/5 expedition with legendary scout Kit Carson opened up the region called Nevada, previously part of Mexico. The name 'Nevada', meaning 'snow-capped' in Spanish, was adopted in 1861 when the territory was established. The State has since been sectioned off into 'territories'. The Cowboy Country, found along the I-80 corridor across northern Nevada, was once the main trail across the State, used by thousands of pioneers on horseback and in covered wagons. The Reno-Tahoe Territory, situated on the eastern slopes of the Sierra Nevada, contains many of Nevada's most scenic and historic sights. The Pony Express Territory, named after the famous riders, offers one of the last opportunities to experience the Old West. In the Pioneer Territory, which encompasses south central Nevada, visitors can trace the story of Nevada's rich mining history.

Las Vegas, Nevada's largest city, is one of the major gambling and entertainment centres of the world. Las Vegas is probably the easiest place in the world in which to get married. Around 230 marriage licences are issued per day.

Reno, another entertainment and casino city, is known for its quiet residential areas, and surrounding historic and natural attractions.

General Information

Nickname: Silver State.
State bird: Mountain Bluebird.
State flower: Sagebrush.
CAPITAL: Carson City.
Date of admission to the Union: 31 Oct 1864.
POPULATION: 2.41 million (official estimate 2005).
POPULATION DENSITY: 8.2 per sq km.
2004 total overseas arrivals/US ranking: 1.37 million/5.

Climate

Nevada is basin and range country, with about 250 mountain ranges running north–south. Base elevation ranges from 1365m (4500ft) to 1880m (6200ft); altitudes vary from over 3945m (13,000ft) to less than 152m (500ft). The climate in Nevada is arid with abundant sunshine, light rainfall and snow. Average temperatures vary from about 21°C (70°F) in the south to 7°C (45°F) in the north.
Required clothing: To the south, lightweights with extra covering for evenings are suggested. In the northern areas, heavier weight clothing is recommended.

Reno
(elevation: 1342 metres)

°C (°F)
TEMPERATURE
Max
AVERAGE
Min
mm (in)
RAINFALL

HUMIDITY (%)
69 65 57 51 47 43 38 38 44 51 58 70
Jan Feb Mar Apr May Jun Jul Aug Sep Oct Nov Dec

Travel - International

Air:

Main airports: *McCarran International (LAS)* (website: www.mccarran.com) is situated 1.6km (1 mile) from the Strip, 8km (5 miles) from central Las Vegas. The airport is one of the USA's busiest. *To/from the airport*: The *Citizens Area Transit (CTA)*, a service of the Regional Transportation Commission of Clark County, operates bus services to and from the airport. Routes 108 and 109 have direct access to the airport and stop on Zero Level, directly outside the arrivals and baggage claim area. CAT *Paratransit Services* is a shared public transport service in small buses for persons with disabilities who cannot independently use the regular CAT bus. There is no CAT bus service from the airport to the Strip. *CLS Transportation* and *Gray Line* both provide a reasonably priced service to the Strip and downtown hotels. *Bell Trans* (website: www.belltrans.com) operates a minibus service to the Strip and downtown Las Vegas, with *Las Vegas Limousine* and *Showtime Shuttle* operating similar services. The *Airport Shuttle* provides a door-to-door service. Shuttle/limo companies are located on the east side of baggage claim; hotel shuttles are often free for guests. Shuttle services to and from communities outside Las Vegas are also available; reservations are often required. Taxis are available on the west side of baggage claim. *Facilities*: ATMs, business service centre, and car hire.

Reno/Tahoe International (RNO) (website: www.renoairport.com) is located 6.5km (4 miles) southeast of the centre of Reno. *To/from the airport*: Local bus route 24 takes travellers into the city (travel time - 20 minutes). Taxis and limousines are available. *Facilities*: ATMs and car hire.

Approximate flight times: From Las Vegas to *Chicago* is three hours 25 minutes, to *Los Angeles* is one hour 10 minutes, and to *New York* is five hours.

RAIL:

Amtrak (tel: (800) 872 7245 (toll-free); website: www.amtrak.com) trains stop at Reno, 135 East Commercial Row, on the 'California Zephyr' line, which links Chicago with Emeryville (California). There is no Amtrak service to Las Vegas, although a Thruway bus service operates from the airport station (from the Charter Bus Area) and the Greyhound Station, 200 South Main Street.

ROAD:

There is a total of 79,520km (49,700 miles) of streets and highways, of which 64,830km (40,520 miles) are county roads. *Citizen's Area Transit, Gray Line Tours of Southern Nevada, Greyhound, K-T Services* and *Ray & Ross Transport* offer daily bus services.

Approximate bus travel times: From Las Vegas to *San Francisco* is 14 hours 20 minutes, to *New Orleans* is 46 hours 20 minutes and to *Miami* is 60 hours 25 minutes.

URBAN:

Buses are operated by the *Citizens Area Transit – CAT* (tel: (702) 228 7433); routes 301 and 302 run to the Strip from downtown Las Vegas. Privately run trolley services are also available. The *Las Vegas Strip Trolley* (tel: (702) 382 1404) runs the length of the Strip every 15 minutes (0930-0130) and costs US$1.75 per journey. The *Downtown Trolley* (tel: (702) 229 6024), serving the downtown casinos, runs every 15 to 20 minutes (0800-2130) and costs US$0.50 per journey. The *Meadows Mall Express Trolley* (tel: (702) 229 6024) runs a downtown route, popular with shoppers, from 1030 to 1700 Monday to Saturday; the fare is US$1.75 per journey. The *Robert N Broadbent Las Vegas Monorail* takes passengers along the 6km (4-mile) route from the MGM Grand Hotel & Casino to Sahara Avenue, stopping at a number of stations en route (travel time - 15 minutes). The second line, extending to Fremont Street in downtown Las Vegas, will be completed by 2007. Taxis and limousines are also available in Las Vegas, and all major car hire companies are represented.

Top Things To See

- Tour the **Western Folklife Center** in **Elko**. It is dedicated to the preservation of Western ranch culture and known for the *Cowboy Poetry Gathering*.
- Explore where the steep eastern slopes of the **Sierra Nevada** rise up to contain **Lake Tahoe** (website: www.tahoe.com). **Carson City** is only 14.4km (9 miles) away, but is nearly 500m (1500ft) below. The lake not only hangs over the State capital, but also the towns of **Minden** and **Gardnerville**, which are almost directly below it.
- Visit the **Nevada Historical Society Museum** (website: www.nevadaculture.org) in Reno, excellent for those wishing to learn about Nevada's history.
- Experience the famous **Death Valley National Park** (website: www.nps.gov/deva), where visitors will witness unique geological features in the extremes of the desert. • Discover one of Nevada's own parks, the **Berlin-Icthyosaur State Park** (website: www.parks.nv.gov/bi.htm), home to the well-preserved and greatly detailed ghost town of **Berlin**.
- See the mining town of **Goldfield** (website: www.ghosttowns.com/states/nv/goldfield.html). It was founded in 1902, and contains the beautiful **Goldfield Hotel** and the **Esmeralda County Courthouse**, as well as the old mining district.
- Enjoy the **Fremont Street Experience** (website: www.vegasexperience.com), a pedestrian mall in Las Vegas dominated by gaming with a spectacular light show every night.
- Visit the **Liberace Museum** (website: www.liberace.org), also in Las Vegas. The museum contains memorabilia from the world-famous pianist.
- Watch the stunning **Fountains of Bellagio** display of over 1000 fountains, choreographed with light and sound at Las Vegas' **Bellagio Resort** (website: www.bellagio.com) (Mon-Fri every 30 minutes 1500-1900 and every 15 minutes 1900-2400; Sat and Sun every 30 minutes 1200-1900, and every 15 minutes 1900-2400).
- Spend time at **Lake Mead** and **Lake Mohave**. They are contained in the vast (600,000-hectare/1.5-million-acre) **Lake Mead National Recreation Area** (website: www.nps.gov/lame).
- See the fascinating landscape of naturally carved red sandstone in the **Valley of Fire State Park** (website: www.parks.nv.gov/vf.htm) at the north of Lake Mead.
- Delight in the **Desert National Wildlife Refuge** (website: www.fws.gov/desertcomplex/desertrange) complex, incorporating the **Pahranagat National Wildlife Refuge** (website: www.fws.gov/desertcomplex/pahranagat), **Ash Meadows National Wildlife Refuge** (website: www.fws.gov/desertcomplex/ashmeadows) and **Moapa Valley National Wildlife Refuge** (website: www.fws.gov/desertcomplex/moapavalley). It is the largest wildlife refuge in the USA. Moapa Valley was the site of Nevada's first city.
- Stop first at the **Hoover Dam**'s (website: www.usbr.gov/lc/hooverdam) new **visitor centre**, where tourists can see right over the edge of the **Black Canyon** precipice. **Hoover Dam** itself was completed in 1935, and is the highest dam in the western hemisphere. The **Boulder City/Hoover Dam Museum** (website: www.bcmha.org) houses historical artefacts relating to the workers, and construction of the dam and Boulder City.

Top Things To Do

- Gamble at one of the many casinos lined up along the **Las Vegas Strip** (website: www.visitlasvegas.com). The Strip is best seen at dusk when it is lit up in neon lights. (see Entertainment section for casinos.)
- Get married in Vegas. More than 45 wedding chapels operate throughout the metropolitan area, including some in major hotels in the city. The **Little White Chapel** (website: www.alittlewhitechapel.com), 1301 Las Vegas Boulevard South, where Joan Collins was married, has a 24-hour drive-through window.
- See where **Reno** was founded, where **Myron Lake's** bridge crossed the **Truckee River**. A whitewater park on the river is a popular attraction with kayakers and thrill seekers; the park also includes an amphitheatre, picnic facilities and river access for boaters.
- Travel to **Reno**, self-proclaimed as 'The Biggest Little City in the World'. Many casinos are to be found downtown on **Virginia Street** including Harrah's (website: www.harrahs.com), the Eldorado (website: www.eldoradoreno.com), the Golden Phoenix (website: www.goldenphoenixreno.com), Circus Circus (website: www.circusreno.com), Silver Legacy (website: www.silverlegacyreno.com), Fitzgerald's (website: www.fitzgeralds.com), and the Sands Regency (website: www.sandsregency.com).
- Enjoy the outdoors at **Lake Tahoe** (website: www.tahoe.com), a top-class skiing resort with a vibrant nightlife, and home to the *Shakespeare at Sand Harbor Festival*, which takes place in the summer. The spectacular scenery can be seen from the lake's excursion boats.
- Stop at **Scotty's Castle** (website: www.nps.gov/deva/scottys1.htm), a popular, if slightly odd, century-old desert guest ranch.
- Discover **Laughlin** (website: www.visitlaughlin.com), the second most popular holiday destination in Nevada, owing largely to the reasonably priced accommodation and restaurants, and the fact that it has unusually sunny summers and mild winters considering its location. A US$100 million development has begun on the **Laughlin Bay Marina** (website: www.laughlinbaymarina.com), opened in 2005 and the hub of entertainment in the Laughlin area.
- Ride the Canyon Blaster roller coaster at **Adventuredome** (website: www.adventuredome.com) in **Circus Circus**, Las Vegas. You can also see circus acts daily from 1100-2400 (free of charge) and experience other thrilling theme park rides.
- View the Las Vegas skyline from one of the observation decks of the **Stratosphere Tower** (website: www.stratospherehotel.com). At 1,149 foot high, it is said to be America's tallest freestanding tower. Be sure to try one of the world's three highest thrill rides: **Big Shot!, Insanity - the Ride** or **X Scream**.
- Go on a backcountry adventure in the **Spring Mountains**, while **Mount Charleston** (website: www.nevadawilderness.org/southern/charleston.htm) is good for wintersports and is home to the **Las Vegas Ski and Snowboard Resort** (website: www.skilasvegas.com).
- Take the **Black Canyon River Raft Tour** (website: www.grandcanyontourcompany.com/heloraft.htm) in **Boulder City**. The tour is a 19km (12-mile) rapid-free raft trip, beginning at **Hoover Dam**.
- Hike the **River Mountain Hiking Trail**, an 8km (5-mile) round-trip route with spectacular views of Lake Mead and Las Vegas Valley.

TOURIST INFORMATION

Nevada Commission on Tourism
401 North Carson Street, Carson City, NV 89701, USA
Tel: (775) 687 4322 *or* (800) 638 2328 (toll-free).
Website: www.travelnevada.com

Nevada Commission on Tourism in the UK
c/o Cellet Travel Services Ltd, 47 High Street, Henley-in-Arden, Warwickshire B95 5JY, UK
Tel: (01564) 794 999 *or* (0870) 523 8832 (brochure request line).
Website: www.travelnevada.com *or* www.cellet.co.uk

Las Vegas Convention Visitors Authority
3150 Paradise Road, Las Vegas, NV 89109, USA
Tel: (702) 892 0711 *or* 7575 *or* (877) 847 4858 (toll-free).
Website: www.visitlasvegas.com

Reno-Sparks Convention Visitors Authority
Street address: 4590 South Virginia Street, Reno, NV 89502, USA
Postal address: PO Box 837, Reno, NV 89504, USA
Tel: (775) 827 7600 *or* (888) 448 7366.
Website: www.renolaketahoe.com

Entertainment

FOOD & DRINK: Las Vegas is becoming world-renowned for its restaurants and every conceivable taste is catered for, from a seven-course gourmet meal to a custom hamburger. Diners can choose from seafood, steak, Southwestern, Brazilian, Chinese, Continental, Italian, Japanese and Mexican cuisines.

Regional specialities:

- Las Vegas buffet - an amazing array of foods of all types, often for a low cost.
- Steak.
- Cocktails.

NIGHTLIFE: Las Vegas is known for its elaborate entertainment as much as for gambling. Visitors have their pick of being entertained by some of the biggest stars in the business - Céline Dion, Julio Iglesias, Liza Minnelli, Wayne Newton, illusionists Penn & Teller and a collection of lesser known entertainers among whom may be the next rising star.
Hotels & Casinos: The 3044-room **Mirage Hotel-Casino** displays a man-made volcano. Nearby, the **Treasure Island** features Buccaneer Bay with a full-scale pirate ship and British frigate engaged in battle. The **MGM Grand Hotel & Theme Park** is the largest resort hotel in the world. **New York, New York** duplicates the Big Apple's skyline, while the **Las Vegas Hilton Hotel & Casino** offers an interactive Star Trek experience with virtual reality stations, a themed bar and Star Trek memorabilia. There is also **The Excalibur**, with 4008 rooms, built in the style of a medieval castle, and the Egyptian-themed **Luxor**, a full-scale pyramid watched over by a sphinx. The US$2.7 billion **Wynn Las Vegas** opened its doors in 2005.

SHOPPING: Vast malls display a wide range of products: the **Forum Shops** at Caesars Palace, the **Fashion Show Mall**, the **Desert Passage** at the Aladdin Resort, the **Grand Canal Shoppes** at the Venetian Resort (includes a reproduction of Venice's Grand Canal – complete with gondolas), the **Boulevard Mall** (the largest shopping centre in Nevada), the **Meadows Mall** (with 140 shops and restaurants), and the **Belz Factory Outlet World** are all popular. The **Fashion Outlet Stores** (south of Belz Factory Outlet World) in Primm are also worth visiting.

A B C D E F G H I J K L M N O P Q R S T U V W X Y Z

New Hampshire

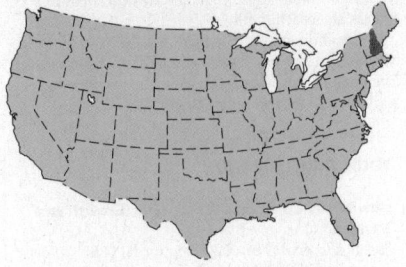

Time: Eastern (GMT - 5). *Daylight Saving Time* is observed.

Overview

New Hampshire was named for Hampshire, England, by Captain John Mason. New Hampshire is noted for its scenic beauty, from Mount Washington in the northern White Mountains to the ocean beaches near Hampton. The State is sometimes referred to as the 'Mother of Rivers' and is also known as the 'Granite State' as five of the great streams of New England originate in its granite hills.

General Information

Nickname: Granite State.
State bird: Purple Finch.
State flower: Purple Lilac.
CAPITAL: Concord.
Date of admission to the Union: 21 Jun 1788 (original 13 States; date of ratification of the Constitution).
POPULATION: 1.31 million (official estimate 2005).
POPULATION DENSITY: 53.7 per sq km.
2004 total overseas arrivals/US ranking: 90,000/28.

Climate

Warm and sunny from May to October, followed by cold winters with abundant snowfall from December to April and temperatures around freezing point.
Required clothing: Required Clothing: Heavyweight clothing from November to March/April. Cottons and linens during the summer months.

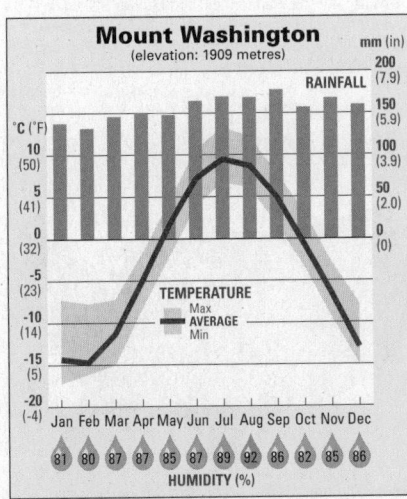

Top Things To See & Do

- Take the **Cog Railway** ride to the top of **Mount Washington** to enjoy panoramic views of Canada and the neighbouring States.
- The Mount Washington **Observatory** has played an important part in recording and researching weather for more than 50 years, and at the new **Weather Discovery Center** in **North Conway**, visitors can use hands-on, interactive exhibits to learn about the weather and its effects.
- If you feel adventurous, climb to the top along **Tuckerman Ravine Trail**. At the summit, there is a museum, information centre and a snack bar where visitors can sit down and rest their weary feet.
- **Franconia Notch State Park**, a dramatic 13km (8 mile) gorge nearby, is one of New England's most acclaimed beauty spots. It was formed by glacial movements that began during an ice age 400 million years ago. Franconia is best known for the '**Old Man of the Mountain**', a huge human profile formed by five ledges of stone.

- The **Basin Waterfall** is another of the park's most popular attractions. Major ski resorts in Franconia include **Cannon Mountain**, **Loon Mountain** and **Waterville Valley**.
- New Hampshire also attracts visitors for its tax-free outlet shopping. In **North Conway**, most major clothing labels can be snapped up for a fraction of the normal price at one of the many factory outlet shops.
- The town of **Laconia**, between **Lake Winnipesaukee** and **Lake Winnisquam**, is another popular tourist destination.

TOURIST INFORMATION

New Hampshire Division of Travel and Tourism Development
172 Pembroke Road, PO Box 1856, Concord, NH 03302, USA
Tel: (603) 271 2665 *or* (800) 386 4664 (toll-free).
Website: www.visitnh.gov

New Hampshire Lodging & Restaurant Association
Street address: 14 Dixon Avenue, Suite 208, Concord, NH 03301, USA
Postal address: PO Box 1175, Concord, NH 03302, USA
Tel: (603) 228 9585.
Website: www.nhlra.com

New Jersey

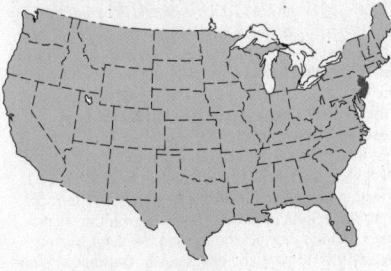

Time: Eastern (GMT - 5). *Daylight Saving Time* is observed.

Overview

New Jersey, one of the Mid-Atlantic States, is bordered by the Atlantic Ocean to the east and the Delaware River to the west. Small in size, the State nonetheless features hundreds of miles of rolling countryside and natural parkland set amidst mountains, lakes and forests. In increasing numbers, tourists from around the world are discovering that New Jersey is more than just a gateway to the United States – it is America in miniature, with an abundance of tourist attractions to suit every taste. These include beautiful beaches, exciting nightlife and many award-winning cultural attractions. While sections of the State such as Atlantic City and the Jersey Shore are world-renowned, there is also a wealth of lesser-known historic landmarks, national parks and cultural events on offer.

General Information

Nickname: Garden State.
State bird: Eastern Goldfinch.
State flower: Purple Violet.
CAPITAL: Trenton.
Date of admission to the Union: 18 Dec 1787 (original 13 States; date of ratification of the Constitution).
POPULATION: 8.72 million (official estimate 2005).
POPULATION DENSITY: 385.9 per sq km.
2004 total overseas arrivals/US ranking: 685,000/10.

Climate

The State's temperature ranges from a July average of 23°C (74°F) to -1°C (30°F) in January, with a more pronounced difference between north and south in the winter. There is moderate rainfall throughout the year.
Required clothing: Required Clothing: Heavyweights with extra bundling for the winter months. Lightweights for the summer. Raingear might come in handy.

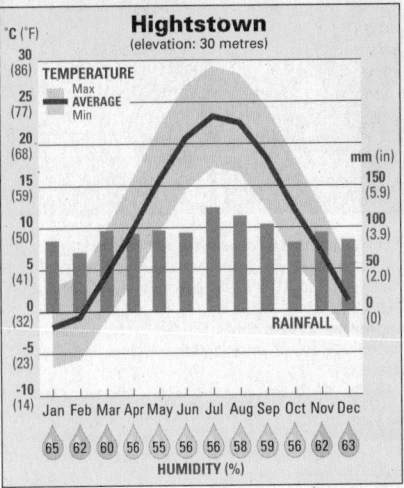

Travel - International

AIR:

 Main airports: *Atlantic City International Airport (ACY)* (website: www.acairport.com) is 16km (10 miles) from Atlantic City. *To/from the airport*: A regular shuttle service runs to Atlantic City (cost: US$25) and taxis are available to the city for around US$40. Limousine service is also available at the terminal building. *Facilities*: ATMs and car hire.
Philadelphia International Airport (PHI) is one hour's drive from Atlantic City via the Atlantic City Expressway (see the *Pennsylvania* section).
Newark Liberty International Airport (EWR) (website: www.newarkairport.com), 27km (16 miles) southwest of midtown Manhattan, is the major hub for international arrivals to the State, although many travellers head to nearby Manhattan, which is connected by bus services (travel time - 30 minutes). *To/from the airport*: Taxis, buses (both local and those serving regional destinations), shuttles and limousines are available at all three terminals. *NJ Transit* operates bus routes to and from the airport; buses 40 and 62 stop at Newark Airport Terminal B. Newark is linked to Princeton by the *Princeton Airporter*, which runs an hourly service 0700-2100 (cost US$24). Taxi fares to the city of Newark are determined by zone, and cost US$15-20.
The *Newark Airport AirTrain* is a monorail service that connects the airport terminals with the *Newark Liberty International Airport Station*, serviced by Amtrak and NJ Transit trains, which travel to Newark Penn Station (with connections to buses, trains to southern New Jersey, and the PATH rapid-transit system (website: www.pathrail.com) to Manhattan), Hoboken (connections to northern and western New Jersey) and New York Penn Station in Midtown Manhattan. For further information, contact the New Jersey Transit Information Center (tel: (800) 772 2222; website: www.njtransit.com). *Facilities*: The airport has extensive facilities, including banks, shops and duty-free shops, restaurants, bars and coffee shops, a nursery and car hire.
TRANSPORT TO NEW YORK CITY: Rail services to Manhattan are available at Newark Liberty International Airport Station and Newark Penn Station (see above).
Newark Liberty Airport Express runs frequent bus services 0400-2345 to Midtown Manhattan, stopping at the Port Authority Bus Terminal and Grand Central Station Terminal (both of which are also served by New York Airport Service express buses running to JFK and La Guardia airports – see *New York* section) and Penn Station (travel time – 30-60 minutes); the fare is US$14. *NJ Transit* buses from Newark arrive at the Port Authority Terminal in Manhattan. Shared minibuses that stop on demand are run by *Express Shuttle USA*, which serves the area between 23rd and 63rd Streets (0600-2300) for US$15 per person, and *SuperShuttle Manhattan*, which stops anywhere south of 227th Street (24 hours) for US$15-19. *Gray Line Air Shuttles* run from Newark to Manhattan 0700-2330 and cost around US$18-23. Taxis to downtown and midtown Manhattan cost US$40-60, plus tolls.
Inter-airport transfers: There are direct bus services from Newark to JFK 0600-2030 on the *Princeton Airporter* for US$27, and to La Guardia on the *ETS Air Shuttle* for US$25.

A B C D E F G H I J K L M N O P Q R S T **U** V W X Y Z

There is a scheduled helicopter service between the airports, and limousine service is also available. The flat-rate taxi fare from Newark to JFK is US$60 plus tolls; to La Guardia, the fare is US$50 plus tolls.

Approximate flight times: See flight times in *New York* section, as they are almost exactly the same.

SEA:

Circle Line Tours operates a year-round ferry service to the Statue of Liberty and Ellis Island from Liberty State Park in Jersey City. *Hoboken Ferry Service, TNT Hydrolines* and *Port Imperial Ferry* operate services to and from New York City. *Cape May-Lewes Ferry* operates a service to and from Cape May to the State of Delaware.

RAIL:

Penn Station in Newark serves *NJ Transit* trains as well as most *Amtrak* (tel: (800) 872 7245 (toll-free); website: www.amtrak.com) services along the New York–Philadelphia–Washington corridor, including high-speed Acela Express trains. For train times on these routes, see the *New York* section; trains from Newark to New York take 15 to 20 minutes. Trains between Atlantic City and Philadelphia are operated by *NJ Transit* and *Amtrak*.

ROAD:

Travel from New Jersey to New York City is across the George Washington Bridge or through the Lincoln and Holland Tunnels. Bridges connecting to Philadelphia are the Walt Whitman Bridge, Betsy Ross Bridge and the Benjamin Franklin Bridge. The Delaware Memorial Bridge connects New Jersey with Delaware. The New Jersey Turnpike runs north and south through the State, while the Garden State Parkway takes travellers to the shore points. **Bus:** Penn Station (McCarter Highway/Market Street, Newark) handles long-distance and regional buses. Greyhound (tel: (800) 231 2222 (toll-free); website: www.greyhound.com) is the main long-distance carrier.

Approximate driving times: From Newark to *Washington, DC* is four hours 30 minutes, to *Miami* is 26 hours 30 minutes, and to *Los Angeles* is 57 hours. All times are based on non-stop driving at or below the applicable speed limits.

Approximate bus travel times: From New Jersey to *Philadelphia* is one hour 40 minutes, to *Boston* is four hours 45 minutes, and to *Cleveland* is nine hours 30 minutes.

Top Things To See

• Tour the **Newark Museum** (website: www.newarkmuseum.com). It is considered one of the nation's most comprehensive fine arts museums and the largest museum complex in the State, with 80 galleries of art (ancient and modern) and science, a planetarium and a mini-zoo.

• Visit **Branch Brook Park** (website: www.branchbrookpark.org) in Newark, which has more cherry blossoms than Washington, DC in the springtime, and plays host to an annual cherry blossom festival.

• Tour the **Liberty Science Center** (website: www.lsc.org), one of New Jersey's leading attractions. The center is located in **Liberty State Park** in **Jersey City**. It offers a hands-on science museum with an IMAX Dome Theater, as well as exhibits on inventions, technology, environment and health.

• See the **Edison National Historic Site** (website: www.nps.gov/edis) in **West Orange**. Tours of Thomas Edison's home, laboratory and library are offered. It also displays the equipment and chemicals with which Edison invented the first incandescent lightbulb, photograph and motion picture. • Tour the **Old Barracks Museum** (website: www.barracks.org) on **Barracks Street** in **Trenton**. It is the site of the famous day-after-Christmas battle during the Revolutionary War and includes restored soldiers' quarters, 18th-century period rooms and antiques.

• Examine New Jersey's history (dating back to 500 BC) at the **New Jersey State Planetarium and Museum** (website: www.state.nj.us/state/museum) in Trenton.

• In **Camden**, climb aboard the **USS New Jersey Museum** (website: www.battleshipnewjersey.com), located in one of the most decorated battleships in US naval history.

• Explore **Morristown National Historic Park** (website: www.nps.gov/morr). This historic park is the site of George Washington's winter encampments and the **Ford Mansion**, now a museum. Battle re-enactments take place throughout the year.

• Taste the grapes from one of the oldest vineyards in the USA – the **Renault Winery** (www.renaultwinery.com) in **Egg Harbor**. The **Glass Museum** is also featured.

• Head for **Princeton**. It is a charming, historic town, home of the world-renowned **Princeton University** (website: www.princeton.edu). The town offers excellent art exhibitions and music, as well as dance and theatre performances, exclusive shops and restaurants. Walking tours take visitors to **Princeton University** and the battlefield where Washington's army defeated the British in 1777.

• View **Einstein's House** (website: www.princetoninfo.com/einstein.html). Eisntein was a Princeton University lecturer. He lived at 112 Mercer Street from the time he left Germany and joined the Institute for Advanced Study until his death in 1955.

Top Things To Do

• Ride the **Circle Line ferry** (website: www.statueoflibertyferry.com) to the **Statue of Liberty** (website: www.nps.gov/stli), east of Newark and **Ellis Island** (website: www.nps.gov/elis). The ferry services operate from **Liberty State Park** (website: www.libertystatepark.com) in **Jersey City**.

• Explore **Palisades Interstate Park** (website: www.njpalisades.org). Located north of Newark, the park has 2500 acres of scenic roads, stunning views, picnic areas, a historic museum and nature sanctuary, and hiking and skiing trails, plus an enormous children's fun park.

• Play at the **Atlantic City Boardwalk** (www.atlantic.citynj.som). Lined with dazzling casinos, amusement rides, games and shops on one side and by 10km (6 miles) of sand beach and surf on the other, it is an attraction in itself.

• When in Atlantic City, experience the notorious **Trump Plaza Hotel** (www.trumpplaza.com) and Trump **Taj Mahal Casino** (www.trumptaj.com) (one of the largest in the world).

• Discover the **Adventure Aquarium** (website: www.adventureaquarium.com) on the Camden waterfront, which combines entertainment, science and cutting-edge technology with some 5000 aquatic animals and over 80 individual fresh and salt water exhibits. Some of the exhibits include *Touch-A-Shark, Penguin Island* and *West African River Experience*.

• Camp, canoe, swim, fish, ride horses or hike in a venture out to the **Pine Barrens** (website: www.pineypower.com), the largest wilderness area east of the Mississippi River. Designated the **New Jersey Pinelands National Reserve** (website: www.nps.gov/pine) in 1978, it was the first national reserve to be created in the USA, and was recognised by UNESCO as a Biosphere Reserve in 1983.

• Spend some time in the **Shore Region** (home to rock stars Bruce Springsteen and Jon Bon Jovi). The region boasts white sandy beaches, rolling farmland, quaint seaside resort towns and historic sites. Dotting the shore are exciting towns like **Seaside Heights** and **Point Pleasant**, which are home to boardwalk amusement rides and games, while quieter towns like **Spring Lake** and **Ocean Grove** offer charming bed & breakfast inns.

• Ride the exciting amusement rides and see the world's largest safari park at **Six Flags Great Adventure and Wild Safari** (website: www.sixflags.com/parks/greatadventure) in **Jackson**. The park also features **Hurricane Harbor** waterpark.

• Spend the day at **Allaire State Park** in **Farmingdale**. The park is a restored 18th-century bog-iron mining village that offers period shops, bakeries and churches, as well as the **Pinecreek Railroad** train, craft and antique shows and square-dancing on weekends.

• Cruise aboard the *River Belle* or *River Queen*, large sternwheelers that ply the waters off Point **Pleasant Beach** (website: www.pointpleasantbeach.com). Deep-sea fishing boats are also available.

• Ski in **Mountain Creek** (website: www.mountaincreek.com). The resort offers skiing and snowboarding for all skill levels.

• Enjoy camping, hiking and watersports in the summer at the **Delaware Water Gap National Recreation Area** (website: www.nps.gov/dewa).

• Visit the **Land of Make Believe** (www.Lomb.com) in **Hope**. This 30-acre park fulfills childhood fantasies with rides, attractions and a waterpark.

• River raft on the **Delaware River**. Rafting, along with hiking, canoeing, and fishing, can be organised during the summer, and ice-skating, tobogganing, snowmobiling, skiing and ice fishing are available during the winter.

• Visit the **Wildwoods** (website: www.wildwoodsnj.com) and **Ocean City** (website: www.oceancityvacation.com) boardwalks that buzz with excitement, in contrast to the quieter retreats of **Stone Harbor** (website: www.stoneharbor-resort.com) and **Avalon** (website: www.avalonbeach.com).

• Vacation at the popular Victorian seaside town of **Cape May** (website: www.capemay.com). This National Historic Landmark has many bed & breakfast inns, trolley tours and the superb **Cape May County Zoo**.

Entertainment

FOOD & DRINK: New Jersey offers everything from gourmet cuisine to 'home-cooking' country food, in settings ranging from restaurants to diners.
Regional specialities:
• Seafood.
• Steaks.

NIGHTLIFE: Atlantic City's nightclubs are open until the small hours and there is round-the-clock gambling available at the casinos. Some of the oceanfront towns have clubs and entertainment centres with a lively atmosphere along the boardwalks into the evenings.

SHOPPING: Shopping in New Jersey appeals to all tastes and budgets. **Jersey Gardens Mall** in Elizabeth is the State's largest outlet shopping mall, while upmarket shopping malls feature the famous department stores of **Macy's**, **Bloomingdales** and **Saks Fifth Avenue**. Bargains on brand-name merchandise can be found at the **Secaucus Outlet Center** in Secaucus. **Liberty Village** and **Turntable Junction** outlet centres in Flemington offer equally attractive deals. Antique stores fill small New Jersey towns like Chester, Haddonfield and Mullica Hill, while outdoor flea markets offer an eclectic array of jewellery, clothing, housewares, furniture and more. There is no sales tax on clothing in New Jersey.

New Mexico

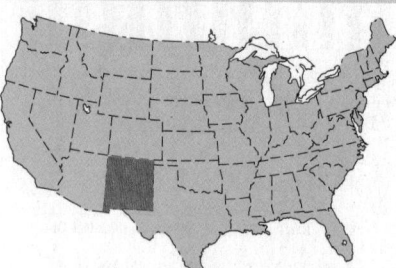

Time: Mountain (GMT - 7). *Daylight Saving Time* is observed.

Overview

New Mexico is graced with deserts, forests, cities, lakes and mountains. Its Pueblo Native American and Spanish cultures are still very much alive. Albuquerque, the largest city, has an international airport, and its Old Town, museums and cultural centres make it an important tourist destination and a good base for travelling through the State. Santa Fe, with its adobe architecture, is the USA's oldest State capital.

General Information

Nickname: Land of Enchantment.
State bird: Roadrunner.
State flower: Yucca Flower.
CAPITAL: Santa Fe.
Date of admission to the Union: 6 Jan 1912.
POPULATION: 1.93 million (official estimate 2005).
POPULATION DENSITY: 61.2 per sq km.
2004 total overseas arrivals/US ranking: 90,000/29.

Credit: ©Dan Monaghan

Climate

Before 'Land of Enchantment' became the official State description, New Mexico was known as 'The Sunshine State' because it receives well above the average national levels of sunshine each year. But with a State as large and varied as New Mexico, the climate differs considerably from one place to the next. In villages and cities such as Angel Fire and Las Vegas, which are 1.5km (1 mile) above sea level, temperatures above 37.7°C (100°F) are not uncommon. In winter, snow falling in the lowlands frequently melts by midday, but ski areas maintain good bases from late November into mid-April.

Required clothing: Covers a wide gamut. Warm winter clothes are required in cold snowy areas, while cool summer cotton is preferred for warmer climes. Check for weather details before visiting a section of the State.

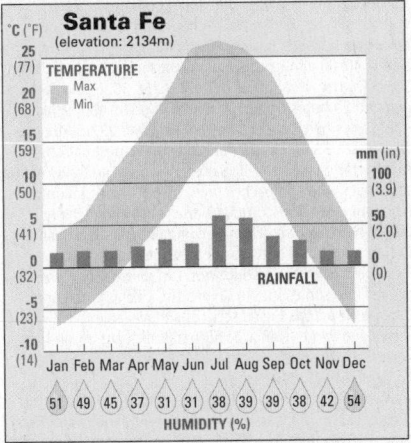

Travel - International

AIR:

Main airports: *Albuquerque International Airport (ABQ)* (website: www.cabq.gov/airport) is located 6km (4 miles) southeast of the city centre. *To/from the airport:* Taxis, limousines and shuttle buses are available to Albuquerque and Santa Fe (travel time - 70 minutes) and regional buses serve other destinations in the State. *Facilities:* ATMs, car hire and shops.

El Paso Airport (ELP) (website: www.elpasointernationalairport.com) also serves as a gateway into southern New Mexico – see the *Texas* section.

RAIL:

Amtrak (tel: (800) 872 7245 (toll-free); website: www.amtrak.com) serves New Mexico on two routes: the 'Southwest Chief', connecting Chicago to Los Angeles, and the thrice-weekly 'Sunset Limited', connecting Orlando and New Orleans to Los Angeles.

ROAD:

The main **bus** companies operating in New Mexico are *TNM&O* and *Greyhound* (tel: (800) 231 2222 (toll-free); website: www.greyhound.com). There are four daily buses to Santa Fe and Taos from the modern bus terminal in Albuquerque, 300 Second Street SW.

Approximate bus travel times: From Albuquerque to *Santa Fe* is one hour 15 minutes, to *Phoenix* is nine hours, and to *Los Angeles* is 18 hours.

URBAN:

In Albuquerque, most buses run Mon-Sat 0600-1800. Santa Fe has seven routes running throughout the city.

Top Things To See

- Explore the **Coronado State Monument** (website: www.nmmonuments.org) where Spanish explorer, Coronado, and his men stayed while searching for the seven cities of gold.
- Visit the **Indian Pueblo Cultural Center** (website: www.indianpueblo.org) tracing the history of the State's 19 Native American Pueblos. Exhibits feature contemporary works by pueblo artists and seasonal and traditional dances are performed.
- Tour **Santa Fe**, the 'City of the Holy Faith'. The oldest and highest capital in the country, it boasts more than 150 art galleries, most of which are within easy walking distance of the city centre. These include the **Museum of New Mexico** (website: www.museumofnewmexico.com) and the **Wheelwright Museum of the American Indian** (website: www.wheelwright.org), which displays jewellery, weavings, pottery and paintings of Native American cultures.
- Travel along the **Santa Fe Trail** (website: www.nps.gov/safe) and visit the **San Miguel Mission**,

one of the oldest churches in the country, and Loretto Chapel (website: www.lorettochapel.com), with its 'Miraculous Stairway'. Further down the trail is the State Capitol, one of the newest capitol buildings in the country. Its unique design is modelled after the Zia sun symbol on the State flag.
- Experience the Old West in **Taos** at the home of 19th-century scout, Kit Carson (website: www.nmculture.org), and in the nearby house where Carson's brother-in-law and Governor of New Mexico Territory was murdered. The Governor's wife and children escaped by digging through the wall of their adobe home with kitchen utensils.
- Observe the country's largest reservation – the **Navajo**. The **Navajo** are noted for their beautiful silver and turquoise jewellery, sand paintings and other crafts.
- Uncover the world's largest gypsum sand dunes at **White Sands National Monument** (website: www.nps.gov/whsa) in the **Tularosa Basin**. They were formed when rainwater dissolved gypsum in a nearby mountain and then collected in the basin's **Lake Lucero**. As the desert weather evaporated the lake water, the gypsum crystals were left behind and eventually formed the continually growing sand dunes.

Top Things To Do

- Ski one of the nine major skiing areas in the State. The high mountains and dry air make for great downhill and cross-country skiing.
- Experience **whitewater rafting** on the **Rio Grande** or **Rio Chama** river.
- Ride the **Sandia Peak Aerial Tramway** (website: www.sandiapeak.com) which takes tourists 4.3km (2.7 miles) above the deep canyons of **Albuquerque**. It is the world's longest single-span tramway and should be avoided by those who do not have a head for heights.
- Be lifted high into the Albuquerque skyline aboard 'The Cliff Hanger', one of the many thrill rides at **Cliff's Amusement Park** (website: www.cliffs.net).
- Travel along the popular **Turquoise Trail** (website: www.turquoisetrail.org) where former mining towns such as **Madrid** and **Golden** were left deserted when supplies of gold, turquoise and coal mines ran dry.
- Descend 250m (830ft) into the **Carlsbad Caverns** down a steep, slippery path, before touring the many chambers and passages. The world-famous caverns were explored in 1922 and declared a national monument by President Calvin Coolidge a year later; they were re-designated as part of **Carlsbad Caverns National Park** (website: www.nps.gov/cave) in 1930.
- Cast your line in the **Animas** and **San Juan** rivers known to provide some of the best trout fishing in the nation.
- Enjoy the **Traditions** festival marketplace dedicated to selling products and services made in New Mexico. Performances and exhibitions in the outdoor plaza and gazebo showcase New Mexico culture.

TOURIST INFORMATION

New Mexico Department of Tourism
Street address: 491 Old Santa Fe Trail, Santa Fe, NM 87503, USA
Postal address: PO Box 20002, Santa Fe, NM 87501, USA
Tel: (505) 827 7400 *or* (800) 733 6396 (toll-free).
Website: www.newmexico.org

Albuquerque CVB
Street address: 20 First Plaza, NW, Suite 601, Albuquerque, NM 87102, USA
Postal address: PO Box 26866, Albuquerque, NM 87125, USA
Tel: (505) 842 9918 *or* (800) 733 9918 (toll-free).
Website: www.itsatrip.org

Entertainment

FOOD & DRINK:
Regional specialities:
- Most menus feature *tortillas*, which are flat discs of Mexican bread made of wheat flour or cornmeal and baked on a hot dry griddle.
- Native American *fry-bread* is deep-fried wheat bread, often eaten with honey or served as the base of a Navajo taco.

NIGHTLIFE: Santa Fe has an active theatre scene and lively music venues with top-class acts. The *Santa Fe Opera* performs beneath the stars against a beautiful mountain backdrop. In Albuquerque, performing arts range from ballet to Spanish folk operetta, and from medieval music to barbershop choruses.

SHOPPING: Silver jewellery is a great buy. Native American craftspeople often use turquoise streaked with threads of silver or gold. Other popular gemstones include coral, *lapis lazuli* (dark blue), *malachite* (green), jet and pink shell. A small animal shape carved from stone is called a 'fetish', and may be strung with beads on a necklace. Each pueblo has characteristic styles and colours of pottery ranging from brightly coloured pots to plain clay ones. Other special buys include Navajo rugs; wooden dolls; *retablos*, which are wooden boards painted with an image of Christ or a saint; and painted carvings called *bultos*.

New York

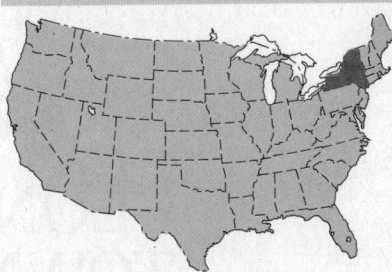

Time: Eastern (GMT - 5). *Daylight Saving Time* is observed.

Overview

New York State can be divided into 11 holiday regions: The Adirondacks, Capital-Saratoga, The Catskills, Central-Leatherstocking, Chautauqua-Allegheny, Finger Lakes, Greater Niagara, Hudson Valley, Long Island, New York City and Thousand Islands-Seaway.

There is only one New York City. No other US metropolis even comes close to it in terms of population, diversity of culture, entertainment, business and commerce. Yet within a day's drive, visitors can find fine beaches and seascapes; quiet, forested mountains; quaint, small towns; and plenty of historical sightseeing.

Long Island, a short train ride east of Manhattan, is the largest island adjoining the continental USA. A popular destination for native city dwellers, Long Island boasts some beautiful white sand beaches, as well as the celebrated seaside resort of the Hamptons.

To the north of the city lie the Hudson River Valley and the resort area of The Catskills. Many visitors have compared the Hudson River with the Rhine – both feature busy boat traffic, dramatic cliffs, green hills and magnificent mansions. The Catskills, situated almost in New York City's backyard, are among the State's leading resort areas.

New York State's capital, Albany, lies in the Capital-Saratoga region, north of the Hudson Valley. Saratoga Springs has been a leading spa and horseracing centre since the late-19th century and is the 'summer home away from home' for the *New York City Opera/Ballet* and *Philadelphia Orchestra*.

A B C D E F G H I J K L M N O P Q R S T **U** V W X Y Z

The Finger Lakes region in Central New York is dotted with resorts, campsites, water recreation areas, fine lakes and woodland scenery. Gouged into the land by the action of prehistoric glaciers, 11 slender lakes extend from north to south like the fingers of a hand. The area used to be famous for the quality of its glass, and today is known as the State's prime wine-producing region.

The Greater Niagara region is home to the State's second-largest city, Buffalo, a major industrial centre with a strong sense of history. It is a good base from which to plan an excursion to the most celebrated natural attraction in New York State, the 56m (184ft) Niagara Falls, which can be visited on foot, by boat or by helicopter.

The lakes and rivers of the Chautauqua-Allegheny region offer a range of outdoor recreational activities. Visitors can also tour Amish communities, Native American reservations and wineries- the region is the largest grape-growing area outside California. Adirondack Park is the largest State park in the USA at 2.4 million hectares (6 million acres). The region is known for its woodland cabins, luxurious lakeside resort hotels and the prospect of canoeing, salmon fishing and big-game hunting. The adjacent Thousand Islands-Seaway region offers a host of summer activities, including cruises among the many picturesque islands. More than 320km (200 miles) of spectacular coastline can be seen from the famous Seaway Trail byway, a scenic route stretching 700km (454 miles) past Lake Erie, the Niagara River, Lake Ontario and the St Lawrence River.

General Information

Nickname: Empire State.
State bird: Bluebird.
State flower: Rose.
CAPITAL: Albany.
Date of admission to the Union: 26 Jul 1788 (original 13 States; date of ratification of the Constitution).
POPULATION: 19.25 million (official estimate 2005).
POPULATION DENSITY: 136.4 per sq km.
2004 total overseas arrivals/US ranking: 4.2 million/2.

Climate

Warm and sunny from May to October, followed by cold winters.
Required clothing: Lightweight cottons and linens for summer months. Heavyweight with extra bundling for the winter.

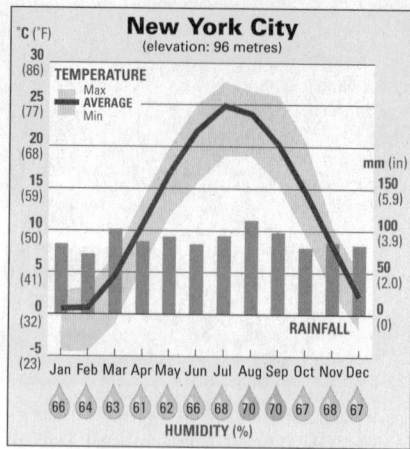

New York City
(elevation: 96 metres)
TEMPERATURE — Max, AVERAGE, Min
RAINFALL

HUMIDITY (%)
Jan 66 Feb 64 Mar 63 Apr 61 May 62 Jun 66 Jul 68 Aug 70 Sep 70 Oct 67 Nov 68 Dec 67

Travel - International

AIR:

 The three airports serving New York City are operated by the Port Authority of *New York* and *New Jersey* (website: www.panynj.gov).
Main airports: *John F Kennedy (JFK), La Guardia (LGA)* and *Newark Liberty International (EWR)*; all of these airports handle domestic and international flights, but most international flights into New York arrive at *JFK*. Flights from or via London to New York land at *JFK* and *EWR*. Some transfer connections via continental Europe land at *LGA*, but the airport's primary function is to handle internal US flights. For further information on timetables, transport and details of travel to New York City, contact the New York Port Authority. Travellers from Europe arriving at *JFK* will generally make their onward connection from there. Connections to smaller locations, and connections for travellers arriving at *EWR*, may have to be made by transferring to *LGA*.
John F Kennedy International (JFK) (website: www.panynj.gov/aviation/jfkframe.HTM) is located in Queens, 24km (15 miles) southeast of midtown Manhattan (travel time – 50-60 minutes). The airport receives the most

international passengers in the USA (15.3 million in 2004), over half of its total passenger count. *To/from the airport:* For transport into the city, a free *Airport Shuttle Bus* labelled *'Long Term Parking Lot'* takes travellers to Howard Beach Station; from there, a subway connection on the 'A' train (which runs every 10 to 15 minutes) takes approximately 90 minutes to central Manhattan, stopping at a number of stations with further connections on the way. The *AirTrain* light rail system also connects the airport with Howard Beach Station, as well as Jamaica Station (for the Long Island Railroad and the 'E' and 'J/Z' subway trains.) Tickets cost US$5. An express bus service, the *New York Airport Service Express Bus*, is offered by New York Airport Service to the Port Authority Bus Terminal (Manhattan West Side) or Grand Central Station (Manhattan East Side). A single fare is US$15; buses operate every 15 to 30 minutes from 0600-0000 (travel time 45-90 minutes depending on traffic). *Airlink* (tel: (718) 560 3900) operates a shared minibus service on demand 24 hours a day, which goes anywhere between Battery Park and 125th Street (travel time – 40-60 minutes, including stops at all major hotels). *SuperShuttle Manhattan* (tel: (212) 258 3826), available on demand 24 hours a day, is a shared door-to-door service going anywhere between Battery Park and 227th Street. Taxis cost US$45 plus tolls and tips for all destinations on Manhattan island. Travellers are advised not to travel with a taxi driver who approaches them first. Always find out the standard rate as unscrupulous drivers may overcharge. Uniformed taxi dispatchers (recommended) are available during peak hours and provide information on fares.
Transport to other destinations: Limousine services are available to some cities in Connecticut, Long Island and upstate New York. Coach services are available to New Jersey and Pennsylvania. *Facilities:* Bank, car hire, and currency exchange.
La Guardia (LGA) (website: www.panynj.gov/aviation/lgaframe.HTM) is located in Queens, 13km (8 miles) east of midtown Manhattan (travel time – 30-45 minutes). *To/from the airport:* For transport into the city, the M60 *MTA* bus goes over Triborough Bridge and intersects with all subway lines as it crosses to the Upper West Side of Manhattan; exact change (US$2) or a 'MetroCard' (an electronic fare card in use on all MTA buses and most subway stages) is required plus an additional US$2 if changing to the subway. The 24-hour *Triboro Coach* services Q33 and Q47 run from the airport to Manhattan and Queens, connecting with local buses and various subway lines. Frequent express bus services are provided by *Airlink, New York Airport Service Express Bus* and *SuperShuttle*. Private limousines and vans are available. From summer 2006, *Circle Line Harbor Cruises* plans to begin running a ferry service to East 34th Street and Pier 11 on Wall Street in downtown Manhattan (travel time – 30-45 minutes). Yellow taxis are readily available from designated taxi stands. *Facilities:* Bank, car hire and currency exchange.
Newark Liberty International Airport (EWR) (website: www.newarkairport.com) is located across the river in New Jersey. For details, see the *New Jersey* section. *To/from the airport:* Newark Liberty Airport Express offers links between EWR and Manhattan. *Facilities:* ATMs, car hire and currency exchange.
Inter-Airport transfers: Regular helicopter transfers are available on *New York Helicopter (HD)* between New York airports and to Newark Airport Terminal 'C'. Coach transfers are available between all three New York airports, though it may be necessary to change at Port Authority Bus Terminal in Manhattan. *New York Airport Express* Service offers links between JFK and LGA (journey time - 45 minutes), as well as services between Manhattan and the airports. The *Princeton Airporter* offers a frequent service between JFK and EWR; *Olympia Trails* provides links between all three airports, 0600-2400. A limousine service is available to Newark Airport. Taxis are also available.
Approximate flight times: From New York to *London* is six hours 50 minutes, to *Los Angeles* is six hours, to *Miami* is three hours 10 minutes, and to *Washington, DC* is one hour 10 minutes.
SEA/LAKE:
 The *Staten Island Ferry* (departing from Battery Park) operates between Lower Manhattan and Staten Island. The *Circle Line Ferry* (departing from Battery Park) sails to the Statue of Liberty and Ellis Island. *Circle Line Sightseeing Cruises* provide guided tours around Manhattan Island and along the Hudson River (departing from Pier 83, West 42nd Street). Frequent ferry services also run from Manhattan to Brooklyn, New Jersey and Queens. Operators include *NY Waterway* (website: www.nywaterway.com) and *Seastreak* (website: www.seastreakusa.com). *Lake Champlain Ferries* (website: www.ferries.com) provide several crossings on Lake Champlain, between New York State and Vermont. Routes include: Plattsburg NY–Grande Isle; Port Kent NY–Burlington and Essex NY–Charlotte. Wolfe Island, Ontario, is connected to Cape Vincent in New York by a ferry service which operates daily during the summer (website: www.wolfeisland.com). A service from Wolfe Island to Kingston, Ontario, operates daily throughout the year.

RAIL:

Pennsylvania Station, at Seventh Avenue and 33rd Street, serves both the *Long Island Railroad*, with routes to Long Island, *NJ Transit*, with routes to New Jersey, and *Amtrak*, nationwide (tel: (800) 872 7245 (toll-free); website: www.amtrak.com). Grand Central Station, at 42nd Street and Park Avenue, is the terminus for services to upstate New York (*Metro North*) and Connecticut. There are two daily trains to Montréal and one to Toronto.

Approximate rail travel times: From New York on the 'Maple Leaf' to *Niagara Falls* is nine hours; on the 'Silver Meteor' to Orlando (Disney World) is 21 hours; and on the 'Crescent' to *Atlanta* is 16 hours. There are frequent shuttles to *Washington, DC* and *Boston*, taking three hours 15 minutes and four hours 30 minutes respectively.

ROAD:

Travel from Manhattan to New Jersey is across George Washington Bridge or through the Lincoln or Holland Tunnels. The Verrazano-Narrows Bridge connects Brooklyn with Staten Island. Queensborough Bridge links Manhattan and Queens. Take Triborough Bridge for upstate New York and the New England Thruway and Bruckner Expressway to New England. Bus: The Port Authority Bus Terminal, at 42nd Street and Eighth Avenue, handles long-distance and regional buses, including *Greyhound* services (tel: (800) 231 2222 (toll-free); website: www.greyhound.com).

Approximate driving times: From New York to *Washington, DC* is five hours, to *Dallas* is 33 hours, and to *San Francisco* is 61 hours. All times are based on non-stop driving at or below the applicable speed limits.

Approximate bus travel times: New York to *Philadelphia* is two hours 20 minutes, to *Boston* is four hours 45 minutes, and to *Pittsburgh* is nine hours.

URBAN:

Public transport (buses and subway) in New York is run by *Metropolitan Transportation Authority (MTA) – New York City Transit* (tel: (718) 330 1234; website: www.mta.nyc.ny.us), whose services are cheaper and more efficient than those of the private companies also operating. **Subway:** Despite its reputation, the New York City subway is fast, air conditioned, cheap and runs 24 hours a day, seven days a week. Moreover, the latest statistics show that crime on the subway has declined considerably. Express trains run between major stops and local trains stop at every station. Subway maps are posted in each subway car and pocket maps are available from token booths. Prepaid MetroCards can be purchased from subway booths, vending machines or some newsagents and can be used on buses. There are reduced fares for senior citizens and the disabled. **Bus:** Services are extensive and are run mostly by *MTA New York City Transit*. MetroCards are valid, or one may pay the driver; the exact fare is required, change will not be given. Three-quarters of the city's buses are equipped with wheelchair lifts at the rear door. **Taxi:** The standard yellow cab is metered and reasonably cheap. There is no charge for extra passengers, but there is a 50-cent surcharge between 2000 and 0600. **Hansom cabs:** Horse-drawn carriages line up at 59th Street and Fifth Avenue, just outside the *Plaza Hotel*. **Car hire:** All the major national car hire companies are represented in New York City and many have offices at the city's airports.

Top Things To See

- View New York's most famous image: the 46.5m- (151ft-) high **Statue of Liberty** (website: www.nps.gov/stli), located on **Liberty Island**, which may be reached by boat from **Battery Park** on Manhattan's southern tip. A lift and staircase inside the Statue take visitors up to an observation platform. The Liberty/Ellis Island Ferry departs from the historic **Castle Clinton** (website: www.nps.gov/cacl) at Battery Park every 30 minutes and also stops at **Ellis Island** (website: www.nps.gov/elis), the gateway for the massive numbers of immigrants arriving in New York between 1892 and 1954. On the island, the **Wall of Honor** (website: www.wallofhonor.com), the world's longest wall of names, commemorates over 600,000 immigrants, and the **Ellis Island Immigration Museum** (website: www.ellisisland.com) offers an interesting insight into the lives of New York's early immigrants.
- Walk through the **Financial District**, containing the famous **Wall Street** and the **New York Stock Exchange**, where visitors have access to a public gallery to catch a glimpse of the frenetic trading action.
- Encounter one of New York's landmark buildings - the 102-storey **Empire State Building** (website: www.esbnyc.com), completed in 1931. Ride a lift up to the observatory on the 86th floor where you can see for approximately 80km (50 miles).
- Enjoy the now 'family-friendly' **Times Square** (website: www.timessquarenyc.org), with the renovated **Biltmore Theater**, and the world's largest toy store, home to a 60ft Ferris wheel and life-size Barbie house.
- Walk across **Brooklyn Bridge**, which is particularly striking at night, and usually bustling with people during the day. Having crossed the bridge, visitors arrive in **Brooklyn Heights**, a good area to explore by foot.
- Discover **Staten Island** (website: www.statenislandusa.com). Visitors to the island often do so mainly to enjoy the view of the classic New York skyline from the **Staten Island Ferry**, which operates from Battery Park (downtown) past the Statue of Liberty and Ellis Island to Staten Island. The Verrazano-**Narrows Bridge** connects Staten Island with Brooklyn.
- Get wet at **Niagara Falls** (website: www.niagara-usa.com), one of the most outstanding spectacles on the North American continent. There are three main waterfalls, **American, Bridal Veil** and **Canadian (Horseshoe) Falls**, each in a different stream of the Niagara River. The **Niagara River** rapids, just above the Falls, and the **Niagara Gorge**, below the Falls, offer beautiful scenery and many opportunities for sightseeing. Visitors can take the **Maid of the Mist Boat Tour** (website: www.maidofthemist.com) that travels into the spray of the Falls, or explore the **Cave of the Winds**, on **Goat Island**, in the middle of the river above the Falls. The **Niagara Whirlpool**, on the river beneath the Falls, can be visited by jet boat.
- Tour **Lockport** (website: www.elockport.com), known for its five enormous locks on the **Erie Canal**. The **Lockport Cave Tour** takes visitors along the locks, through a tunnel blasted out of rock in the 19th century, and ends in an underground boat ride.
- View the **George Eastman House** (website: www.eastmanhouse.org), a national historical landmark in **Rochester**. George Eastman, inventor in 1892 of roll film and the Kodak camera, lived here. Also tour the outstanding **International Museum of Photography**, detailing the development of the art from the time of Daguerre to the satellite photos of the space age.
- Encounter the site of the most famous rock concert in history - the 1969 *Woodstock Music and Arts Festival*, commemorated at the **Bethel Woodstock Museum** at **Kauneonga Lake**. Today, Woodstock is a haven of art and craft galleries and shops.
- Spend time in the city of **Albany** (website: www.albany.org). The city stands beside the Hudson River north of New York City and makes a good base from which to explore 'upstate New York'. Albany is dominated by the US$2 billion **Rockefeller Empire State Plaza**, a striking 10-building complex that includes the 44-storey **Corning Tower**, the venerable **State Capitol** and the city's performing arts theatre (nicknamed 'The Egg' for its unusual shape).
- Tour Albany's **New York State Museum** (website: www.nysm.nysed.gov), the country's oldest and largest State Museum, portrays the urbanisation of New York City and has lifelike dioramas among the exhibits on Native Americans, gems and birds.
- Discover what the **Catskills** (website: www.catskillregiontoday.com) have to offer. From the lush greenery of the southern Catskills to the dramatic, unspoiled peaks of the north, there is plenty to occupy visitors, whether they are seeking excitement or the perfect spot for a tranquil stay.
- Play ball! For more than 50 years the name **Cooperstown** (website: www.cooperstownchamber.org) has been synonymous with baseball. Home of the **National Baseball Hall of Fame and Museum**, **Doubleday Field** and numerous trading card and memorabilia shops, this vibrant village is situated on the shore of **Otesgo Lake**.
- Tour the **Metropolitan Museum of Art** (website: www.metmuseum.org), one of the greatest museums in the world. Egyptian, Roman and Greek Art along with Oriental paintings, modern art and ancient glass are some of the museum's many collections.

Top Things To Do

- Visit **Chinatown** (website: www.chinatownnyc.com), Manhattan's most thriving ethnic neighbourhood. It extends from Canal Street into **Little Italy** (website: www.littleitalynyc.com) and east into the **Lower East Side**. This labyrinth of narrow streets, crammed with Chinese stores and restaurants, is home to over 100,000 residents.
- Enjoy **Greenwich Village** (website: www.nycgv.com), a melting pot for art, literature and music for decades, though its legendary bohemian feel has partly been replaced by upmarket beatnik chic. South of Greenwich Village is **SoHo** (South of Houston) (website: www.sohonyc.com), which has become synonymous with art since the 1960s, and retains its arty, avant-garde character, with plenty of galleries, cafes, boutiques and loft spaces fronted by interesting cast-iron façades.
- See the **Rockefeller Center** (website: www.rockefellercenter.com), famous for its (winter-only) ice skating rink. It is also the home of NBC Studios, which can be visited. Head up to the **Top of the Rock** observation deck for unobstructed views of the Brooklyn Bridge, the Chrysler Building and Central Park.
- Grab some candyfloss at **Coney Island** (website: www.coneyisland.com) or try any of the other attractions such as the museum, rides or circus sideshows. Walk along **Brighton Beach** (website: www.brightonbeach.com), full of Russian shops and restaurants.
- Explore the world-famous **Bronx Zoo** (website: www.bronxzoo.com). See the Polar Bear, King of Ice or any of the many other exhibits. Go for a stroll in **New York Botanical Garden** (website: www.nybg.org). The garden encompasses over 250 acres with 50 gardens and a landmark conservatory.
- See New York's most famous park, **Central Park** (website: www.centralparknyc.org), created in 1856, when officials set aside 341 hectares (843 acres) of land between Fifth and Eighth Avenues and 59th and 110th Streets. John Lennon fans may pay their respects at **Strawberry Fields**, the area of the park dedicated to his memory. Also within the park is the **Central Park Wildlife Center**, a small but interesting zoo. During summer, the park hosts afternoon and evening concerts. Additions to the park include the **Dana Discovery Center** and fishing pond (with free poles and bait). Visitors should note that it is not advisable to visit Central Park after dark.
- Experience the **Hudson River Valley** (website: www.hudsonrivervalley.com). It was originally inhabited by Native Americans over 3000 years ago, before being settled by the Dutch in the early 17th century. The Hudson Valley has a long tradition as a holiday destination. In the mid- to late-19th century, it served as a retreat for wealthy industrialists from New York City such as the Vanderbilts and Rockefellers, who built the elaborate estates along the shores of the Hudson known as 'Millionaires' Row'. Today, the area continues to offer year-round opportunities for many outdoor activities such as boating, camping, hiking, hunting, skiing, bicycling, rock climbing and canoeing.
- Enjoy your holiday in **Westchester County** (website: www.westchestertourism.com). The county is bordered on the west by the Hudson River and on the east by the **Long Island Sound**. It offers plenty of opportunities for boating, sailing and watersports. The county is home to 40 private and public golf courses and top-name department stores, discount malls and exclusive boutiques. The city's historic roots go deep and are reflected in the many museums, historic sites and other attractions.
- Have lunch at the **Culinary Institute of America** (website: www.ciachef.edu), one of the world's great cookery schools. Visitors can sample the cuisine at one of the three restaurants on its campus, the **American Bounty Restaurant**, **Caterina de Medici** or **Escoffier Room**, as well as two cafes.
- Experience the USA's largest wilderness reserve outside Alaska and one of the most successful conservation efforts in history, the **Adirondack Park** (website: www.apa.state.ny.us). Created in 1882 to preserve the **Great North Woods** of New York State, the 2.5-million-hectare (6-million-acre) natural sanctuary is protected under the State Constitution. There are miles of sandy beaches and thousands of secluded swimming holes, broad lakes for windsurfing and boating, and nearly every species of freshwater fish to challenge fishing enthusiasts. The Adirondacks are a winter playground, with more than nine different ski areas and thousands of trails for cross-country skiing and snowshoeing.
- Ski **Lake Placid** (website: www.lakeplacid.com). This winter playground provides you with natural wonders, Olympic venues for the sports enthusiast, museums, shops and plenty of other activities.
- Enjoy the snow at **Hunter Mountain** (website: www.huntermtn.com) ski resort, known as 'the snowmaking capital of the world', ensuring plenty of snow throughout the winter. With 53 trails on three mountains, the resort caters for everyone from beginners to experienced skiers. In the summer months, a 1.5km (1 mile) chairlift takes visitors up to a summit lodge. Night skiing is one of the attractions at the resort of **Ski Windham** (website: www.windhammountain.com).
- Head to **Saratoga Springs** (website: www.saratoga.com). It has been a leading spa and horseracing centre since the late-19th century and the streets are lined with regal Victorian mansions. Walking tours of the city's historic districts are available from the *Saratoga Urban Cultural Park Visitors Center*. Popular attractions include the **Saratoga Raceway** and the **Saratoga Race Course**. The raceway is known as the world's most beautiful harness track and features races nine months a year. The race course hosts the country's most prestigious thoroughbred racing during late July and August. Spectators are welcome at the polo matches held during the summer. For those in the mood for something other than horses, a drive over to nearby **Saratoga Spa State Park**, with its 890 hectares (2200 acres) of woods, manicured lawns, Georgian architecture and pavilions, mineral bathhouses and recreational facilities is recommended. Activities on

A B C D E F G H I J K L M N O P Q R S T U V W X Y Z

offer include sunrise and sunset hot-air balloon flights.
- Travel to **The Hamptons** (website: www.hamptons.com), offering a mix of culture, restaurants, historic sites, nightlife, shops and recreational activities. Long Island's Native American heritage can be explored in **Southampton**, where the Shinnecock Indians maintain a reservation and present a public pow-wow in early September. The region features the seaside resort of **Montauk**, fishing villages and beaches, one of which, in **East Hampton**, was rated the second most beautiful in the northeastern USA.
- See the largest State Park in New York; **Allegany State Park** (website: www.nysparks.com) occupies 26,000 hectares (64,000 acres) and offers excellent facilities for both summer and winter recreation including camping, hiking, fishing and cross-country skiing. The **Allegany Reservoir** provides excellent canoeing and watersports.
- New York is renowed orlwide for its **shopping**, **entertainment** (**Broadway**) and **dinning out** facilities (see *Entertainment*).

TOURIST INFORMATION

New York State Division of Tourism
Street address: 30 South Pearl Street, Albany, NY 12245, USA
Postal address: PO Box 2603, Albany, NY 12220, USA
Tel: (518) 292 5361 *or* (800) 225 5697 (toll-free).
Website: www.iloveny.com

New York State Division of Tourism in the UK
3 Lonsdale Road, London, NW6 6RA, UK
Tel: (020) 7629 6891.
Website: www.nylovesu.co.uk

Long Island CVB and Sports Commission
330 Motor Parkway, Suite 203, Hauppauge, Long Island, NY 11788, USA
Tel: (631) 951 3440 *or* (877) 386 6654 (toll-free).
Website: www.funonli.com

NYC & Company
810 Seventh Avenue, New York, NY 10019, USA
Tel: (212) 484 1200 *or* (800) 692 8474 (toll-free).
Website: www.nycvisit.com
Provides information on New York City.

Niagara County Tourism
Niagara Office Building, 345 Third Street, Suite 605, Niagara Falls, NY 14303, USA
Tel: (716) 282 8992 *or* (800) 338 7890 (toll-free).
Website: www.niagara-usa.com

Entertainment

FOOD & DRINK: New York is packed with thousands of restaurants of all types, serving food from around the world.
Regional specialities:
- Wine.
- Steaks.
- Seafood.

NIGHTLIFE: From theatre and film to comedy and dance clubs to jazz, blues and rock, there's a nightlife here for everyone's tastes. Clubs generally stay open until the early hours. Theatre tickets for Broadway can be booked through the Group Sales Box Office, 226 West 47th Street, 10th Floor, New York, NY 10036 (tel: (800) 223 7565 *or* (212) 398 8383; website: www.bestofbroadway.com). Special discounts for group bookings are available. Tickets must be paid for in advance and will be mailed out or kept at the theatre box office for collection on the night of the performance. Half-price tickets are available on the day of performance from the *tkts* booths in Times Square and South Street Seaport.
SHOPPING: Fifth Avenue, New York City's most glamorous thoroughfare, is filled with luxury shops and department stores. No trip to New York is complete without stopping by **Bloomingdale's** (1000 Third Avenue at 59th Street), **Lord and Taylor** (Fifth Avenue at 38th Street) and **Saks Fifth Avenue** (611 Fifth Avenue at 50th Street). Don't forget **Macy's**, known as the world's largest store, 131 West 34th Street at Herald Square. **Woodbury Common**, one hour's drive from Manhattan, is the largest discount designer outlet in the world. **Long Island** offers a variety of ever increasing shopping opportunities – from indoor shopping malls such as **Roosevelt Field** in **Garden City**, the East Coast's largest shopping centre, to quaint visitor-oriented shopping villages on historic main streets in places like **Huntington**, **Sea Cliff**, **Stony Brook** and **Syosset**. **Manhattan Mall** in Midtown Manhattan has an eight-floor mall with 60 shops.

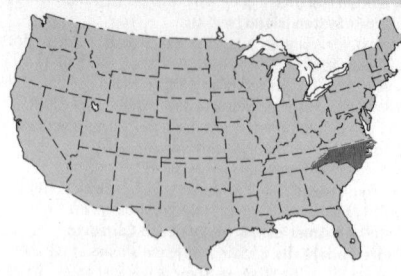

North Carolina

Time: Eastern (GMT - 5). *Daylight Saving Time* is observed.

Overview

Natural attractions in North Carolina range from sandy beaches in the east to high mountain ranges in the west. Fringed by 480km (300 miles) of beaches, islands and inlets, the North Carolina coast is renowned for its fishing, boating and other recreational opportunities. The Heartland, often referred to as 'the Piedmont', is composed of gently rolling plains that host picturesque golf courses, lakes and farmland, as well as the State's largest urban areas. Charlotte, the largest city, is a thriving convention and entertainment centre. The Outer Banks Barrier Islands along the coast include resorts, fishing villages and stretches of national seashore. Cape Hatteras National Seashore also boasts areas of undeveloped beach. Western North Carolina is bounded by two ranges of the southern Appalachians, the Blue Ridge Mountains and the Great Smoky Mountains, with peaks exceeding 1800m (6000ft). Other attractions include Raleigh, with its fine architecture and cultural centres, and the Qualla Boundary Cherokee Indian Reservation.

General Information

Nickname: Tar Heel State.
State bird: Cardinal.
State bird/flower: Flowering Dogwood.
CAPITAL: Raleigh.
Date of admission to the Union: 21 Nov 1789 (original 13 States; date of ratification of the Constitution).
POPULATION: 8.68 million (official estimate 2005).
POPULATION DENSITY: 47.4 per sq km.
2004 total overseas arrivals/US ranking: 252,000/18.

Climate

North Carolina has a moderate climate with an average year-round temperature of 16°C (61°F). The climate varies sharply with altitude, with the State's Atlantic coastline naturally warmer than the mountains in the west.
Required clothing: Lightweight cotton clothes and rainwear. Warm clothing for evenings in the spring and autumn, during the winter season and in mountain areas.

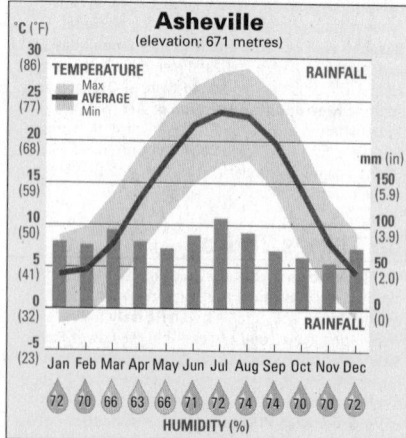

Asheville
(elevation: 671 metres)

TEMPERATURE / RAINFALL

°C (°F)
30 (86)
25 (77)
20 (68)
15 (59)
10 (50)
5 (41)
0 (32)
-5 (23)

mm (in)
150 (5.9)
100 (3.9)
50 (2.0)
(0)

RAINFALL

Jan Feb Mar Apr May Jun Jul Aug Sep Oct Nov Dec

72 70 66 63 66 71 72 74 74 70 70 72
HUMIDITY (%)

Travel - International

AIR:

Main airports: *Charlotte/Douglas International (CLT)* (website: www.charlotteairport.com), 13km (8 miles) west of Charlotte, offers direct domestic and international services to more than 150 cities, with over 500 daily flights.
To/from the airport: The *Carolina Transportation Airport Express* shuttle service operates to the uptown area, major

hotels and most business districts. Fixed-fare taxis are also available. *Facilities:* Banking services, car hire and postal/shipping.
Raleigh-Durham International (RDU) (website: www.rdu.com) is situated 6km (4 miles) from the Research Triangle Park. *To/from the airport:* The Raleigh/Durham Shuttle leaves every 30 minutes to the city centre (travel time - 15 minutes). Taxis are also available. *Facilities:* Car hire, currency exchange and internet access.

RAIL:

A number of *Amtrak* (tel: (800) 872 7245 (toll-free); website: www.amtrak.com) routes pass through the State, including a daily New York–Miami (via Orlando). The 'Piedmont' provides a daily passenger train service from Raleigh to Charlotte. The station in Raleigh is located at 320 West Cabarrus Street, while the Charlotte station can be found at 1914 North Tryon Street.

ROAD:

North Carolina has a good road network of highways and scenic byways allowing easy access to all parts of the State. *Interstate 40* is the major east–west artery, crossing the State from Wilmington on the Atlantic Coast to the Great Smoky Mountains, via Raleigh, Durham and Winston-Salem. A State-wide system of designated Bicycling Highways covers 4830km (3000 miles) of roads. There are many bus companies serving the area, including *Greyhound* (tel: (800) 229 9424 (toll-free); website: www.greyhound.com) services, with stops at many destinations within the State, including Chapel Hill, Charlotte, Durham, Raleigh and Winston-Salem.

Approximate bus travel times: From Raleigh to *Richmond* is three to four hours and to *North Charleston* is eight hours. From *Durham* to *Chapel Hill* is 35 minutes and to *Washington, DC* is six hours.

URBAN:

The *Triangle Transit Authority* (website: www.ridetta.org) provides a bus service between the metropolitan areas of Raleigh, Durham, Cary and Chapel Hill.

Top Things To See

- See where the Wright brothers made the first powered flight in 1903, commemorated at the **Wright Brothers Memorial** (website: www.nps.gov/wrbr) at **Kitty Hawk**.
- View the attractions along the **Cape Hatteras National Seashore** (website: www.nps.gov/caha) including the **Outer Banks ponies**, **Bodie Island** and the **Hatteras lighthouses**, which are among the oldest in the country.
- Tour the restored **New Bern's Tryon Palace** (website: www.tryonpalace.org) and surrounding buildings, which transport visitors back to the 18th century.
- Visit New Bern's **Fireman's Museum** (website: www.newbernmuseums.com), formed by the two oldest continuously operated fire companies in the USA. Included in the exhibits is 'Fire Horse Fred', who pulled the fire-hose wagon for 17 years. He died in 1925 while pulling the fire wagon to a false alarm.
- In **Cotton Exchange**, look across the river to where the **USS North Carolina Battleship Memorial** sits, a World War II battleship (website: www.battleshipnc.com). Her story is told on summer nights in 'The Immortal Showboat', a spectacular sound and light show.
- View the works by Botticelli, Monet, Raphael and Rubens at the **North Carolina Museum of Art** (website: www.ncartmuseum.org) in **Raleigh**.
- Visit **Durham**, known as 'The City of Medicine'. The city is

Credit: ©NC Division of Tourism, Film and Sports Development. Bill Russ. Photographer.

the home of the world-famous **Research Triangle Park** (website: www.rtp.org) and **Duke University** (website: www.duke.edu) with its lovely chapel and gardens.
• Journey through the **Morehead Planetarium** (www.moreheadplanetarium.org) in Raleigh where more than 100 of the USA's astronauts trained before venturing into space.

Top Things To Do

• Explore the **Crystal Coast** (website: www.crystalcoast.com) area, which includes the deep-sea port of **Morehead City**, the historic waterfront town of **Beaufort** and many beautiful beaches.
• Visit **Wilmington**, North Carolina's largest seaport. The **Cotton Exchange** (website: www.shopcottonexchange.com) a 19th-century structure converted into shops and boutiques, once exported more cotton than any other port in the world.
• In **Raleigh**, explore the **North Carolina Botanical Gardens** (website: www.ncbg.unc.edu), containing almost every plant found in the State.
• Ride the thrill rides at the State's biggest theme park, **Carowinds** (website: www.carowinds.com), 10 minutes south of **Charlotte**. It pays tribute to the film *Wayne's World* with a white-knuckle, wooden roller coaster ride called *Hurler*.
• Visit **Old Salem**, a preserved and restored 18th-century Moravian village. Attractions include the new US$10 million **Old Salem Visitor Center** (website: www.oldsalem.org) offering tours of the districts, the **St Philips Moravian Church** (the oldest extant African-American church in North Carolina), the **Old Salem Toy Museum** and the restored **Herbst House**.
• Explore the magnificent North Carolina Mountains, including **Mount Mitchell** (2040m/6684ft), the highest peak in Eastern America. Two hundred peaks in the **Appalachian Mountain chain** reach more than 1.6km (1 mile) high.
• Travel along the scenic **Blue Ridge Parkway** (website: www.nps.gov/blri), which winds along the spine of the **Blue Ridge** and **Great Smoky Mountains**.
• Enjoy a ride on the **Tweetsie Railroad** (website: www.tweetsie.com), a steam locomotive that carries passengers through mountain passes and a frontier village.
• Tour George Vanderbilt's elaborate 225-room **Biltmore Estate** (website: www.biltmoreestate.com) located in **Ashville**. The estate includes a winery with a visitor centre, tasting room and shop where bottles of the local vintage are sold.
• Experience **Grove Park Inn Resort** (website: www.groveparkinn.com). The list of people who have stayed at this high-class hotel includes Thomas Edison, F Scott Fitzgerald, Henry Ford, Franklin D Roosevelt and Woodrow Wilson.

TOURIST INFORMATION

North Carolina Division of Tourism
301 North Wilmington Street, Raleigh, NC 27699, USA
Tel: (919) 733 4171 *or* (800) 847 4862 (brochure requests; toll-free).
Website: www.visitnc.com

North Carolina Division of Tourism in the UK Office
c/o Hills Balfour, Notcutt House, 36 Southwark Bridge Road, London SE1 9EU, UK
Tel: (020) 7922 1100.
Website: www.hillsbalfour.co.uk

Entertainment

FOOD & DRINK: Numerous festivals are held annually in North Carolina in honour of favourite foods, including apples, watermelons, seafood, turkey, pickles and collard greens.
Regional specialities:
• Sweet potato pie.
• Barbecue.
NIGHTLIFE: Student bars dominate the university towns of Chapel Hill, Durham and Raleigh; top rock bands appear at the **Cat's Cradle Club** in Carroboro. Charlotte offers a wide range of entertainment, including nightclubs and bars around the **Uptown Entertainment District**.
SHOPPING: North Carolina's aquariums offer workshops for coastal crafts and include shops selling unusual gifts. They are located in Manteo on Roanoke Island, Kure Beach and Pine Knoll Shores. Brevard is also popular for its many craft centres and shops. The world's largest furniture market is located in High Point near Winston-Salem. **Concord Mills**, just north of Charlotte, has over 200 outlets and speciality shops, restaurants and a 24-screen cinema.

North Dakota

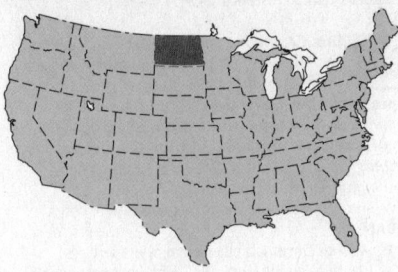

Time: Central (GMT - 6) in the greater part of the State; Mountain (GMT - 7) in the west. *Daylight Saving Time* is observed.

Overview

North Dakota, one of the most rural States in the USA, is famous for its scenery and Old West heritage. Visitors will be able to enjoy the western experience and to pick up the trail of some of America's greatest legends like Lewis and Clark, Sakakawea, Theodore Roosevelt, Custer and Sitting Bull and others. North Dakota is also famous among outdoor adventurers for its world-class walleye and perch fishing to unbeatable upland game, waterfowl and big game.

General Information

Nickname: Peace Garden State.
State bird: Western Meadowlark.
State flower: Wild Prairie Rose.
CAPITAL: Bismarck.
Date of admission to the Union: 2 Nov 1889.
POPULATION: 636,677 (official estimate 2005).
POPULATION DENSITY: 3.5 per sq km.
2004 total overseas arrivals: Under 38,000.

Climate

General: Winters are cold with adequate snow for winter sports. Summers are warm, with adequate rainfall for crop growth, and are conducive to summer sports.
Required clothing: Lightweights for the summer and heavyweights for the winter.

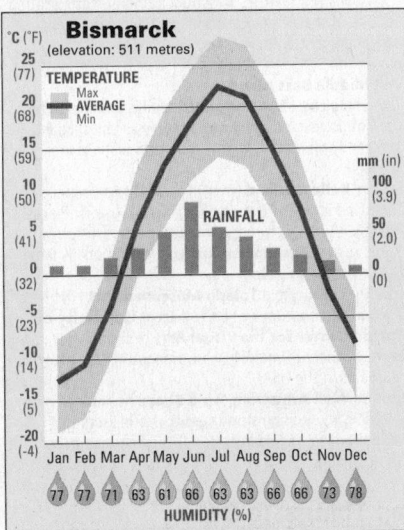

Top Things To See & Do

• Visit the State's largest city, **Fargo**, on the eastern border. The metropolitan area of **Fargo-Moorhead** is a prime tourist destination.
• The 28,329 hectare (70,000 acre) **Theodore Roosevelt National Park** set in the Badlands of western North Dakota offers spectacular views and includes the restored cow-town of **Medora**. The park takes its name from Theodore Roosevelt, who bought Elkorn Ranch here after his wife and his mother died on the same day on 14 February 1884. He found inspiration among the quiet canyons of 'rough-rider country', famously declaring 'I never would have been President if it weren't for my experiences in North Dakota'.
• Head for **Fort Abraham Lincoln**, south of **Mandan**. The fort was the final command and home of Lt Colonel

Credit: ©North Dakota Tourism/Jason Lindsey

George Custer, where he and his Seventh Cavalry departed for the Battle of Little Bighorn. On 25 June 1876, Custer's entire command of 265 men was wiped out in a 20-minute battle with the Sioux, led by Sitting Bull, Gall and Crazy Horse. It is still possible to see **Custer's house** and inspect the commissary and barracks of this famous fort.
• Outdoor activities are very popular in North Dakota. The State has many world-class **fishing** waters as well as **hunting** opportunities.

TOURIST INFORMATION

North Dakota Tourism Division
Century Center, 1600 East Century Avenue, Suite 2, Bismarck, ND 58503, USA
Tel: (701) 328 2525 *or* (800) 435 5663 (toll-free).
Website: www.ndtourism.com

Fargo-Moorhead CVB
2001 44th Street, SW, Fargo, ND 58103, USA
Tel: (701) 282 3653 *or* (800) 235 7654 (toll-free).
Website: www.fargomoorhead.org

Ohio

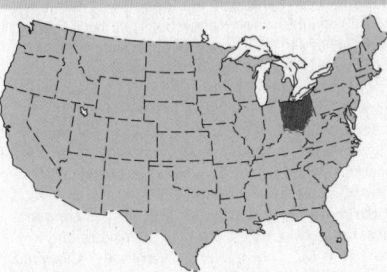

Time: Eastern (GMT - 5). *Daylight Saving Time* is observed.

Overview

Ohio, birthplace of eight US Presidents, is located in the heart of the Midwest. The sandy shores of Lake Erie mark the State's northern border and the long and winding Ohio River marks its southern border. The State's expanse of fertile farmland is dotted with industrial centres, but also embraces the rolling hills overlooking the Scioto River Valley in the north. The landscape becomes wilder and steeper as it reaches the foothills of the Appalachian mountain chain, and the thick forest lands full of waterfalls and sandstone cliffs in the south. The Cuyahoga Valley National Recreation area in the northeast near Cleveland has rugged terrain with river valleys and steep, forested hills. The State also has 40,869km (25,543 miles) of waterways, including the Mohican and Tuscarawas rivers. Columbus is Ohio's capital and is the largest city in both area and population – it is the 15th-largest city in the USA.

General Information

Nickname: Buckeye State.
State bird: Cardinal.
State flower: Scarlet Carnation.
CAPITAL: Columbus.
Date of admission to the Union: 1 Mar 1803.
POPULATION: 11.46 million (official estimate 2005).
POPULATION DENSITY: 98.7 per sq km.
2004 total overseas arrivals/US ranking: 323,000/16.

Climate

Mild to cold winters and hot summers.
Required clothing: Lightweights for the summer and heavyweights for the winter.

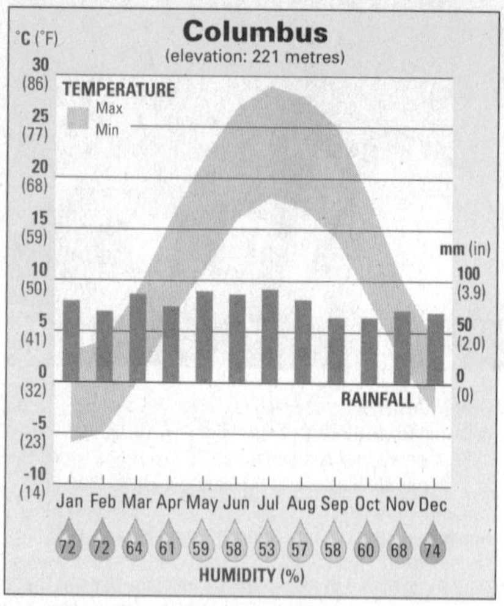
Columbus
(elevation: 221 metres)
°C (°F)
TEMPERATURE
Max
Min
mm (in)
RAINFALL
30 (86) 25 (77) 20 (68) 15 (59) 10 (50) 5 (41) 0 (32) -5 (23) -10 (14)
100 (3.9) 50 (2.0) 0 (0)
Jan Feb Mar Apr May Jun Jul Aug Sep Oct Nov Dec
72 72 64 61 59 58 53 57 58 60 68 74
HUMIDITY (%)

Travel - International

AIR:

Main airports: *Cincinnati/Northern Kentucky (CVG)* (website: www.cvgairport.com) is 19km (12 miles) southwest of the city centre (travel time - 15 minutes). *To/from the airport*: *TANK* public buses (website: www.tankbus.org) run between the airport and downtown Cincinnati and Covington daily (0500-0000; travel time - 30 minutes); buses stop outside Terminals 1 and 3. *Airport Executive Shuttle* buses serve the city centre and the Kentucky side of the river; drop-offs at various points en route can be arranged. Taxis and limousine services are also available. *Facilities*: ATMs, business services and car hire.

Cleveland Hopkins International Airport (CLE) (website: www.clevelandairport.com) is 18km (10 miles) southwest of the city centre (travel time - 20 minutes). *To/from the airport*: The *Greater Cleveland Regional Transit Authority (RTA)* offers a rapid transit service departing every 15 minutes between the airport and Tower City Center (travel time - 20 minutes), where connections to other bus and rail services are available. Taxis and limousines are available. *Facilities:* ATMs, business services and car hire.

Port Columbus International Airport (CMH) (website: www.port-columbus.com) is located 11km (7 miles) northeast of downtown Columbus. *To/from the airport*: Taxis, limousines and shuttle buses to the city centre are available, as is the *Capital City Flyer* bus, operated by *Central Ohio Transit Authority (COTA)*.

Approximate flight times: From Cincinnati to *London* is nine hours, to *New York* is one hour 30 minutes, and to *Washington, DC* is one hour. From Cleveland to *Cincinnati* is one hour 15 minutes, and to *New York* is one hour 40 minutes.

RIVER:

There are over 1600km (1000 miles) of canals in Ohio and there are many canal boat excursions available.

RAIL:

A number of *Amtrak* (tel: (800) 872 7245 (toll-free); website: www.amtrak.com) services run west-east across the State, starting from Chicago. A parallel line from Chicago to Pittsburgh passes through Akron daily. The Chicago to Washington, DC service via Indianapolis and Cincinnati only runs three days a week. For journey times, see the *Illinois* section. Ohio also offers a number of scenic railway excursions run by private operators, often on historic trains.

ROAD:

Bus: *Greyhound* (tel: (800) 231 2222 (toll-free); website: www.greyhound.com) offers services throughout the State.

Approximate bus travel times: From Cincinnati to *Louisville* is two hours, to *Indianapolis* is two hours 30 minutes, and to *New York* is 15 hours. From Cleveland to *Pittsburgh* is three hours, to *Detroit* is 4 hours, and to *Washington, DC* is nine hours. From Columbus to *Cleveland* is three hours and to *St Louis* is nine hours.

URBAN:

The Cincinnati bus system offers services throughout Hamilton County and portions of Clermont County. In addition to numerous bus routes, Cleveland's *Regional Transit Authority* has three rapid-transit lines that meet at downtown's *Tower City Center Station*. Taxis are available in the major cities.

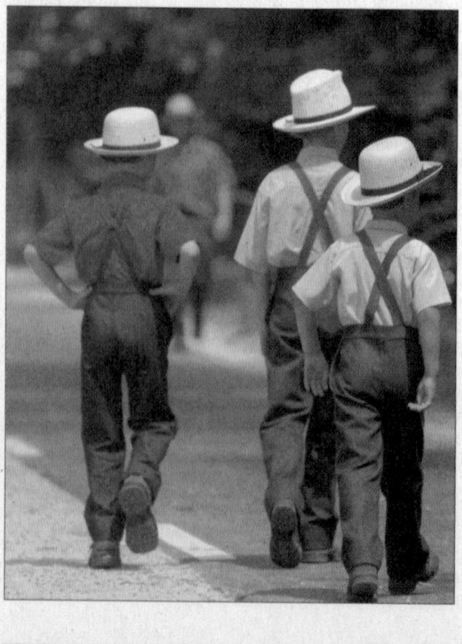
Credit: ©Ohio Division of Travel & Tourism

Top Things To See

- Tour **Cincinnati's National Underground Railroad Freedom Center** (website: www.freedomcenter.org) focusing on the struggle for freedom experienced by runaway slaves. It is the first of its kind in the USA and features five history galleries, a changing exhibits gallery, a theatre, and research and education centres, as well as the Underground Railroad Children's Exhibit and Slave Jail.
- Visit the **Museum Center** (website: www.cincymuseum.org) at **Cincinnati Union Terminal**, where the **Cincinnati Historical Museum** and the **Cincinnati Museum of Natural History** are housed in an Art Deco train station and a 'Baseball as America' exhibition will delight sports fans.
- Tour the **Holden Arboretum** (website: www.holdenarb.org), the largest in the USA. The arboretum, located east of **Cleveland**, has been connecting visitors with nature for over 75 years.
- In the southeast, explore **Hocking Hills State Park** (website: www.hockinghills.com), home to **Ash Cave** (Ohio's largest recess cave, with a 27m- (90ft-) high waterfall). Also visit the **Rock House** (a series of large rooms mysteriously carved into the side of a cliff), the 46m- (150ft-) high **Cantwell Cliffs** and **Hocking Forest**, where rock climbing is permitted.
- Situated in the picturesque north central region, **Ashland** is Ohio's apple country. The **Johnny Appleseed Heritage Center & Outdoor Historical Drama** (website: www.jahci.org) features an outdoor amphitheatre seating 1600 to host this musical drama and a research and education centre. There is also an orchard, garden and nature trail.
- Visit **Middle Bass Island** (website: www.middlebassisland.org). The island is dominated by the Gothic castle of the **Lonz Winery**, established in 1860 and still making wine - tours and tastings are available.
- Explore **Kelleys Island** (website: www.kelleysisland.com). The island is on the National Register of Historic Places. Along with old, picturesque homes, it offers historical sights such as **Inscription Rock**, an exceptionally large Native American pictograph.
- Tour the century-old **Toledo Museum of Art** (website: www.toledomuseum.org) and adjacent **University of Toledo Center for the Visual Arts** (website: www.cva.utoledo.edu). They are among the top 10 art museums in the USA.
- Visit the **Neil Armstrong Air & Space Museum** (website: www.ohiohistory.org/places/armstron) in **Wapakoneta** named in honor of the first man to set foot on the moon.

Top Things To Do

- Experience Cleveland's **African Safari Wildlife Park** (website: www.africansafariwildlifepark.com), the Midwest's only drive-through safari, while **Cleveland Metroparks Zoo** (website: www.clemetzoo.com) and the **Rainforest**, south of the city centre, is the seventh-oldest zoo in the country, with more than 3300 animals. The Rainforest features animals and insects in realistic habitats, with simulated tropical thunderstorms and an 8m- (25ft-) high waterfall.
- Spend some time at two of the most interesting neighbourhoods: the lavishly restored **German Village** (website: www.germanvillage.org) in **Columbus**, with superb architecture, fine restaurants and taverns, and the 27-acre **Brewery District** (website: www.brewerydistrict.org), the vintage beer-making factories which now contain restaurants, speciality shops and taverns.
- Take a narrated ride on a sternwheeler in **Zanesville**. Also visit the **National Road/Zane Grey Museum** (website: www.ohiohistory.org/places/natlroad) with information about the building of America's first highway and Zanesville's famous Western writer.
- Visit the world's largest Amish population residing in the northeast's **Holmes**, **Stark**, **Tuscarawas** and **Wayne** counties. There are country shops selling everything from handwoven baskets, handmade quilts and antiques to homemade cornmeal. For a glimpse into the Amish lifestyle, the **Yoder's Amish Home** (website: www.yodersamishhome.com) in Holmes County offers two reproduction Amish farmhouses and buggy rides for children.
- Journey through the 33,000-acre **Cuyahoga Valley National Recreation Area** (website: www.nps.gov/cuva) which encompasses a 35km- (22 mile-) long river surrounded by steep, forested hills, sandstone gorges and hidden waterfalls popular with birdwatchers and hikers. Within this area is also the **Hale Farm and Village**, a living-history museum depicting life in the mid-19th century.
- Spend the day at **Cedar Point Amusement Park** (website: www.cedarpoint.com), one of the largest in the USA and celebrated for its rollercoasters, most notably the Top Thrill Dragster, the highest in the world. In the park's popular **Soak City** water park, the **Splash Zone** includes waterslides, chutes, geysers and over 100 watery gadgets to enjoy. A giant bucket, some 48 ft high, continuously douses visitors to the zone. An **Indoor Waterpark Resort** for winter water fun opened in November 2004. The park has recived a number of awards in recent years.
- Take the family to **Paramount's Kings Island Theme Park** (website: www.pki.com). The park offers Broadway-style shows and big-name stars, as well as a 15-acre water park and thrill rides. Most exciting, however, is the unveiling of the **Boomerang Bay 'Down Under'** resort, featuring over 50 wet and wild activities and 30 slides.
- Near Locust Grove, explore **Serpent Mound State Memorial** (website: www.ohiohistory.org/places/serpent), a giant snake effigy mound, one-quarter of a mile long and 6m/20ft wide, created by the Adena Native Americans over 2000 years ago.
- Grab a hotdog and watch a ballgame. The State's pro baseball teams are the **Cincinnati Reds** (website: www.cincinnati.red.mlb.com) and the **Cleveland Indians** (website: www.cleveland.indians.mlb.com). The **Indians** play at **Jacobs Field (The Jake)** and the **Reds** play at the **Great American Ballpark**.
- **Fishing**, **swimming**, **watersports** and **boating** can be enjoyed on **Lake Erie**, the main attraction in the northwest.

TOURIST INFORMATION

Ohio Division of Travel & Tourism
Street address: 77 South High Street, 29th Floor, Columbus, OH 43216, USA
Postal address: PO Box 1001, Columbus, OH 43216, USA
Tel: (614) 466 8844 *or* (800) 282 5393 *or* 848 1300 (toll-free).
Website: www.ohiotourism.com

CVB of Greater Cleveland
50 Public Square, 3100 Terminal Tower, Cleveland, OH 44113, USA
Tel: (216) 621 4110 *or* (800) 321 1001 (toll-free).
Website: www.travelcleveland.com

Entertainment

FOOD & DRINK: Ohio is farm country, with fresh local produce and big wholesome meals.

Regional specialities:
- Corn.
- Fried chicken.

NIGHTLIFE: The Flats in Cleveland is a popular nightlife entertainment area. The **Short North District, German Village** and the **Brewery District** in Columbus have excellent nightlife. Nightlife areas in Cincinnati include **The Wharf** at Covington Landing and the **Oldenberg Brewery Complex**. Dayton is known for its jazz clubs, while the blues can be enjoyed at Cleveland's new **House of Blues** venue.

SHOPPING: Major outlet shopping centres include **Ohio Factory Shops**, 58km (36 miles) south of Columbus; **Jeffersonville Outlet Center** in Jeffersonville; **Aurora Farms Factory Outlets**; **Lake Erie Factory Outlet Center** in Milan, and **JC Penney Outlet Store** and **Brice Outlet Mall** in Columbus. The **Easton Town Centre** in Columbus features shops, restaurants and a 30-screen cinema. The towns of Lebanon and Waynesville are known as the **'Antiques Capital of the Midwest.'** For speciality Amish buys, the best areas for shopping are the 8km- (5 mile-) radius around Fredericksburg in Wayne County and the area between Charm and Farmerstown in Holmes County.

Oklahoma

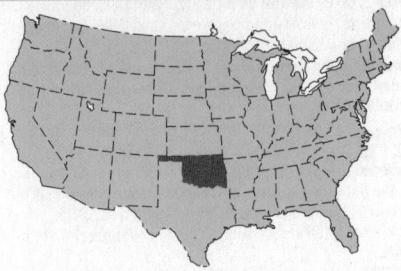

Time: Central (GMT - 6). *Daylight Saving Time* is observed.

Overview

Oklahoma is home to more Native American tribes than any other State except California, with 39 tribal headquarters and members of at least 67 tribes. While Native Americans have lived in Oklahoma for thousands of years, many tribes were forcibly relocated to this land (many dying from starvation and disease along the way on the infamous 'trails of tears') when it was established as Indian Territory in the early 19th century. Today, visitors will find Native American art galleries, museums, historic sites, pow wows, dances and festivals. Oklahoma is also home to the longest driveable stretch of Route 66, with nearly 643km (400 miles) of 'America's Main Street'.

General Information

Nickname: Sooner State.
State bird: Scissor-tailed Flycatcher.
State flower: Mistletoe.
CAPITAL: Oklahoma City.
Date of admission to the Union: 16 Nov 1907.
POPULATION: 3.55 million (official estimate 2005).
POPULATION DENSITY: 19.6 per sq km.
2004 total overseas arrivals: 38,000/38.

Climate

The region has a continental climate with cold winters and hot summers.
Required clothing: Lightweights for the summer and heavyweights for the winter.

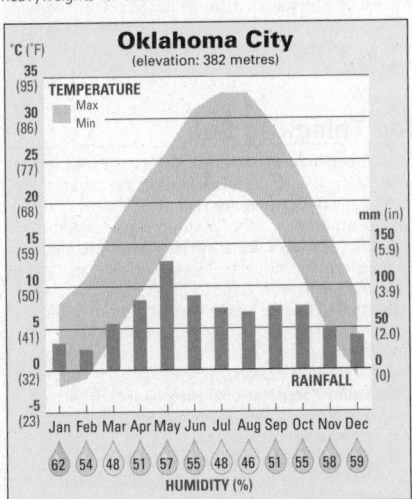

Credit: ©Oklahoma Tourism

Top Things To See & Do

- Get an insight into Native American culture at the **Cherokee Heritage Center** (outside **Tahlequah**), the **Cheyenne Cultural Center** (in **Clinton**) and the **Five Civilized Tribes Museum** (in **Muskogee**). There are numerous other sites in the State.
- Drive on the longest driveable stretch of **Route 66**. Along an older route, the State saw cowboys and cattle drives on the **Chisholm Trail**. A life-size statue of a cattle drive, entitled 'On the Chisholm Trail', is located outside the **Chisholm Trail Heritage Center**, in **Duncan**, as a monument to the US cowboy.
- Cattle are still transported along the Chisholm Trail route, nowadays in trucks, heading for the largest cattle auction in the USA, located in **Oklahoma City's Stockyards City**. Here, visitors will find shops selling authentic western wear and gear.
- Oklahoma City is also home to the **National Cowboy &**

Western Heritage Museum, showcasing Western and Native American art and artefacts, the **Oklahoma City National Memorial Museum**, and the **Myriad Botanical Gardens & Crystal Bridge Tropical Conservatory**.
- Attend the annual **Red Earth Native American Cultural Festival**, an enormous celebration of art, music and dance held each spring. Other aspects of the State's heritage are apparent at the **Oklahoma Prison Rodeo** in **McAlester** to the east, the **Oklahoma International Bluegrass Festival** in **Guthrie** to the north, and in many unique rural festivals, such as the **Okra Festival**, the **Rattlesnake Roundups**, the **Kolache Festival**, **Strawberry Festival** and the **Watonga Cheese Festival**.
- Fortunes made in oilfields left a legacy in northeastern Oklahoma that includes mansions, museums, art galleries and Art Deco architecture. The **Gilcrease Museum** in **Tulsa** contains the world's most comprehensive collection of art of the American West. The Rodgers and Hammerstein musical *Oklahoma!* is still running at **Discoveryland**, in **Sand Springs** (outside Tulsa).
- Some 50 State parks and many other natural havens showcase Oklahoma's 11 distinct ecoregions and plentiful unspoilt beauty, including **Robbers Cave State Park**, **Greenleaf State Park**, **Beavers Bend State Resort Park**, **Roman Nose State Park**, the **Wichita Mountains National Wildlife Refuge**, **Alabaster Caverns State Park**, the **Tallgrass Prairie Preserve** and the **Talimena Scenic Drive** through the **Ouachita National Forest**.

TOURIST INFORMATION

Oklahoma Tourism & Recreation Department (Travel & Tourism Division)
Street address: 15 North Robinson, Suite 100, 6th Floor, Oklahoma City, OK 73102, USA
Postal address: PO Box 52002, Oklahoma City, OK 73152, USA
Tel: (405) 521 2406 *or* (800) 652 6552 (toll-free).
Website: www.travelok.com

Tulsa CVB
2 West Second Street, Williams Tower II, Suite 150, Tulsa, OK 74103, USA
Tel: (918) 585 1201 *or* 560 0263 *or* (800) 558 3311 (toll-free).
Website: www.visittulsa.com

Oregon

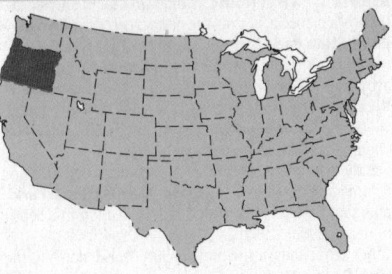

Time: Pacific (GMT - 8) in the greater part of the State; Mountain (GMT - 7) in most of Malheur county. *Daylight Saving Time* is observed.

Overview

Visitors are drawn to the scenic beauty of Oregon, which combines historic towns, sleepy fishing villages, ski resorts and wineries. The landscape is rich in diversity from its nearly 400 miles of coastline and mountains to lakes, rivers and streams, deserts and forests (nearly half of Oregon's total area is forested).

General Information

Nickname: Beaver State.
State bird: Western Meadowlark.
State flower: Oregon Grape (Holly Grape).
CAPITAL: Salem.
Date of admission to the Union: 14 Feb 1859.
POPULATION: 3.64 million (official estimate 2005).
POPULATION DENSITY: 14.3 per sq km.
2004 total overseas arrivals/US ranking: 162,000/24.

Climate

Summers can be quite warm, with temperatures reaching 30°C (90s °F). Winter months reach 4°C (40s °F) during the day and fall back into the low to -1°C (30s °F) at night. Most of the yearly rainfall occurs from October to May.
Required clothing: Light cotton and linens during the summer months. Rainwear and heavyweight clothing suggested for the winter months.

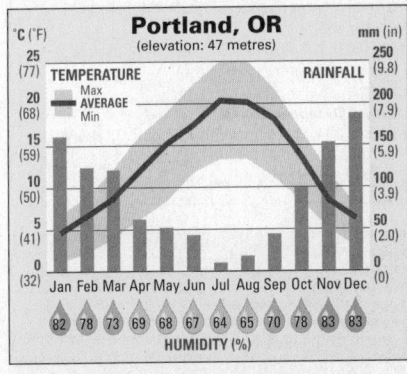

Top Things To See

- In the northeast, deep gorges vie for attention with the craggy beauty of the towering **Wallowa Mountains**.
- Outdoor types will also be drawn to the southeast's huge and desolate **Steens Mountain Wilderness Area**, as well as the **Oregon Dunes National Recreation Area** along the coast.
- **Salem** is the capital of Oregon and the State's third-largest city; Visit its many fine museums, gardens and parks, including the **Mission Mill Museum**, **Old Aurora Colony Museum**, **Bush House Museum** and **Oregon Garden**, which contains the **Frank Lloyd Wright House**.
- The more urbane should consider **Portland**, the 'City of Roses', which boasts gardens, restaurants, shops, concerts, jazz festivals, theatres and first-class hotels. It is possible to see the best of the city's vibrant dramatic and visual arts scene on the first Thursday of each month when the small galleries in the Southwest and Northwest districts remain open until 2100. The **Portland Art Museum** houses paintings and sculptures from the 1350s to the 1950s. The city also boasts the **American Advertising Museum**, the **Oregon Museum of Science and Industry**, **Pittock Mansion**, **Oregon Zoo** and the renovated **PGE Park**.
- Head for the stunning **Columbia River Gorge**, an hour

from Portland. Here, the Columbia furrows its way through a canyon 300m- (1000ft-) deep, plunging between hills and sheer cliff faces.

- The **Columbia River Maritime Museum** can be found in **Astoria**. The **Vista House**, completed as a memorial to Oregon's pioneers, acts as the visitors centre in **Crown Point State Park**. East of Crown Point, a string of waterfalls, including the mighty **Multnomah Falls**, attracts 2 million visitors per year. The towns of **Hood River** and **The Dalles** offer visitor services in the gorge; whilst the **Columbia River** itself, with its 50kph (30mph) winds, is a windsurfing paradise.
- See the nation's deepest lake, located in southern Oregon. It forms the centrepiece of **Crater Lake National Park**, plunging from an 1800m- (6000ft-) elevation to a depth of nearly 600m (1932ft).
- Other attractions in the State include **Bend**, home to the **High Desert Museum**; **Eugene**, with the renovated **Hult Center for the Performing Arts**; and **Baker City**, offering the **National Historic Trail Interpretive Center**.

Top Things To Do

- Go **skiing** in the **Willamette Pass** and **Hoodoo Ski Areas**.
- On the Idaho border lies North America's deepest gorge – **Hells Canyon**. In some places, the walls drop 1650m (7900ft) to the **Snake River** below. A quick flit through on a **jet boat** or a leisurely drift by **raft** are two ways of viewing this mighty wonder.
- For those heading towards the coast, the renowned **US Highway 101** hugs the Pacific shore with a stretch lying between the coastal towns, where hundreds of miles of State parks offer direct connections with the beach. Some of Oregon's most famous cheeses are nurtured on the shore of **Tillamook Bay** and those who hunger for a hunk of cheese should visit the **Tillamook Cheese Visitor's Center**. **Newport** offers the sights and smells of a classic seaport, including an **Aquarium**, whilst connoisseurs of ale can sample local favourites across the bay bridge at the **Rogue Ale Brewery**. Both the **Oregon Coast Aquarium** and **Oregon State University Hatfield Marine Science Visitor Center** are located here, providing unique and educational views of coastal wildlife and the environment.

TOURIST INFORMATION

Oregon Tourism Commission
670 Hawthorne Avenue, SE, Suite 240, Salem, OR 97301, USA
Tel: (503) 378 8850 *or* (800) 547 7842 (toll-free).
Website: www.traveloregon.com

Travel Oregon in the UK
PO Box 184, Mawman Smith, Falmouth, TR11 5FA, UK
Tel: (01326) 250213.
Website: www.traveloregon.com

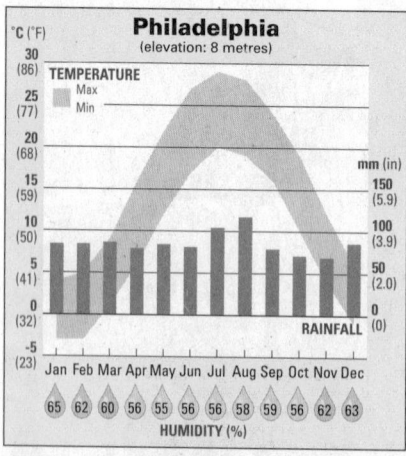

Credit: ©Steve Terrill

Pennsylvania

Time: Eastern (GMT - 5). *Daylight Saving Time* is observed.

Overview

Pennsylvania is a region steeped in colourful history. It started out as the 'Holy Experiment' of Quaker activist William Penn, Jr. Granted a charter by King Charles II to develop a colony in the New World, Penn selected a lush wooded portion of the countryside, where he vowed to welcome anyone who believed in God. Less than a century later, the country's Founding Fathers signed the Declaration of Independence and the Constitution at Independence Hall in Philadelphia – now one of the largest cities in the USA – and the American nation was born. Pennsylvania boasts 20 State and one National Forests, 116 State Parks, one Great Lake (Lake Erie), 50 other natural lakes, 2500 man-made lakes, along with thousands of miles of rivers and streams. The State is also something of a cultural mecca, with many world-class museums, while its citizens represent a rich mix of cultural and ethnic backgrounds.

General Information

Nickname: Keystone State.
State bird: Ruffed Grouse.
State flower: Mountain Laurel.
CAPITAL: Harrisburg.
Date of admission to the Union: 12 Dec 1787 (original 13 States; date of ratification of the Constitution).
POPULATION: 12.43 million (official estimate 2005).
POPULATION DENSITY: 104 per sq km.
2004 total overseas arrivals/US ranking: 613,000/11.

Climate

The weather can be changeable, with moderate amounts of rain throughout the year. Summers are warm with occasional heat waves. Winters can be cold with periods of snowfall, especially in the western part of the State.
Required clothing: Warm winter clothes are needed in the coldest months. Light-to-medium weights are advised for the summer.

Philadelphia
(elevation: 8 metres)

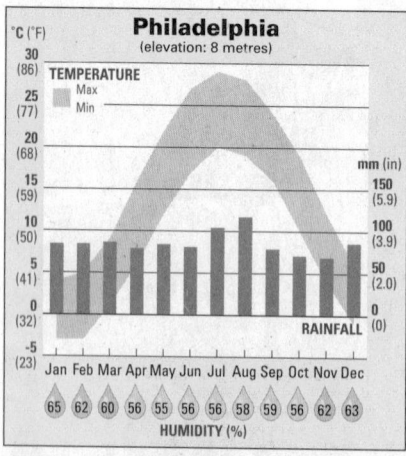

Travel - International

AIR:

Main airports: *Philadelphia International Airport (PHL)* (website: www.phl.org) is 13km (8 miles) southwest of the city (travel time – 25 minutes). *To/from the airport:* The cheapest way to reach the city centre is the *SEPTA Airport Express Train*, running every 30 minutes to all three city centre stations, 0600-2400 daily. Taxis and limousine services are also available. *Facilities:* Bank, car hire and post office.
Greater Pittsburgh Airport (PIT) (website: www.pitairport.com) is 22.5km (14 miles) west of the city

---

centre. *To/from the airport:* Port Authority Transit public buses run approximately every 20 minutes daily 0500-2400 to Oakland via Robinson and downtown Pittsburgh. The *Airlines Transportation* shuttle runs every hour daily 0700-2200 to downtown Pittsburgh and Oakland. Limousine services and taxis are also available. *Facilities:* Bank, car hire and post office.
Approximate flight times: From *London* to Philadelphia is eight hours 20 minutes and to *Pittsburgh* is nine hours.

LAKE/RIVER:

Pennsylvania has three of the country's busiest ports within its borders. Philadelphia is the largest freshwater port in the world. Erie is one of the major Great Lakes ports and Pittsburgh is one of the nation's largest inland ports, providing access to the extensive 1400km (900 mile) US inland waterway system.

RAIL:

Pennsylvania has dozens of passenger railroads (website: www.parailways.com) in addition to mainline *Amtrak* (tel: (800) 872 7245 (toll-free); website: www.amtrak.com) services. Philadelphia is home to one of Amtrak's busiest stations, at 30th Street, which is served by the 'Acela Express' service linking Washington, DC (travel time – one hour 35 minutes) with New York City (travel time - one hour 10 minutes) and Boston (travel time - five hours). Free transfers to the urban transportation system, run by *SEPTA*, are available to *Amtrak* passengers (request upon ticket purchase). Pittsburgh has daily *Amtrak* services to Chicago, New York City, Philadelphia and Washington, DC. See the *Illinois* and *New York* sections for examples of travel times on several services passing through these cities.

ROAD:
Bus: *Greyhound* (tel: (800) 231 2222 (toll-free); website: www.greyhound.com) is the main service provider.
Approximate driving times: From Philadelphia to *New York* is two hours, to *Washington, DC* is three hours, and to *Pittsburgh* is six hours. From Pittsburgh to *Niagara Falls* is four hours and to *Chicago* is eight hours. All times are based on non-stop driving at or below the applicable speed limits.
Approximate bus travel times: From Philadelphia to *Miami* is 30 hours, to *Dallas* is 37 hours, and to *Seattle* is 74 hours.

URBAN:
In Philadelphia, the *Southeastern Pennsylvania Transportation Authority (SEPTA)* (tel: (215) 580 7800; website: www.septa.org) has interconnecting buses, trolleys (streetcars), subways and elevated railways. The distinctive *PHLASH* buses connect most of the city's major attractions. Exact change is required on all services. Pittsburgh has an efficient network of buses serving the various districts. The *PAT* subway service is rather modest but is free in downtown Pittsburgh.

Top Things To See

- Visit **Independence National Historical Park** (website: www.nps.gov/inde) in **Philadelphia**. In the centre of the park stands **Independence Hall** where the Declaration of Independence and the Constitution were signed in 1776. The **National Constitution Center** (website: www.constitutioncenter.org) is the first museum dedicated to honouring the US Constitution. The glass **Liberty Bell Center** houses the bell that was sounded at the first public reading of the Declaration of Independence and features indoor and outdoor areas with interpretive exhibits.
- Tour **Valley Forge National Historical Park** (website: www.nps.gov/vafo), one of the most revered shrines of the American Revolution.
- Spend time at the **Fairmount Park** (website: www.fairmountpark.org), by the **Schuylkill River**, one of the USA's largest city parks. Visitors can learn all about the river in the neo-classical **Fairmount Water Works Interpretive Center** (website: www.fairmountwaterworks.com) on **Waterworks Drive**.
- Explore the **Point State Park Fountain** in the **Golden Triangle** area of central **Pittsburgh**. It symbolises the creation of the **Ohio River** at the meeting of the **Monongahela** and **Allegheny** rivers.
- Tour **Gettysburg**, the famous Civil War battle site, featuring the **Gettysburg National Military Park** (website: www.nps.gov/gett) and the **Eisenhower National Historic Site** (website: www.nps.gov/eise).
- Discover the **Pocono Mountains** (website: www.800poconos.com) and their neighbours to the west – the **Endless Mountains** (website: www.endlessmountains.org). Popular with honeymooners since the early-19th century, the mountains offer breathtaking scenery as well as historical interest.
- Stop at **Steamtown** (website: www.nps.gov/stea). The National Historic Site features dozens of antique railroad cars and interpretive displays.

Top Things To Do

- Plunge into whitewater on the **Youghiogheny river**. With its Class III and IV rapids, it provides some of the best rafting in the East.
- Journey back in time at **Old Bedford Village** (website: www.oldbedfordvillage.com). It offers a living history of the pioneer era, with costumed guides, crafts demonstrations and 40 authentic buildings. The area is also home to two of Frank Lloyd Wright's masterpieces: **Kentuck Knob** (website: www.kentuckknob.com) and the spectacular **Fallingwater** (website: www.paconserve.org).
- Experience the life of the Pennsylvania Dutch (website: www.padutch.com). The town of **Lancaster** is closely associated but the centre of tourism is the town of **Intercourse**, where, at **The People's Place**, films, crafts and interpreters weave the story of these settlers. Detours down side roads are rewarded with glimpses of horse-drawn ploughs and buggies, auctions, antique shops and the occasional private home where the exquisite Amish quilts and crafts are sold.
- Indulge your sweet tooth in nearby **Hershey** (website: www.hersheypa.com), home of the world's largest chocolate factory, 'Chocolatetown USA', with a visitor's centre, shopping outlets and an amusement park.
- Descend 76m (250ft) below the earth to **Lackawanna Coal Mine** (website: www.thecoalminetour.com). Former miners lead visitors on tours through the mines for a first-hand account of the lives and times of the miners. Explore further the culture of coal miners at Eckley Miners' Village (website: www.eckleyminers.org), an authentic coal-mining town.
- See the **Allegheny National Forest** (website: www.fs.fed.us/r9/forests/allegheny), which offers a vast area of woodlands, virgin timber, rivers and beautiful vistas. Wintersports enthusiasts can explore 480km (300 miles) of snowmobiling trails and seven cross-country ski trails.
- Explore the **Pennsylvania Grand Canyon** (website: www.visittiogapa.com/grandcanyon.html), a 300m- (1000ft-) deep gorge that twists along 80km (50 miles) of **Pine Creek** and embraces 121,000 hectares (300,000 acres) of forest. It can be explored on foot, horseback, canoe or river raft.
- Fish, boat or swim. Bordering **Lake Erie**, one of the Great Lakes, the northwestern corner of the State features 32,000 acres of lakes, as well as hundreds of miles of rivers.

TOURIST INFORMATION

Pennsylvania Tourism Office
Department of Community & Economic Development, 4th Floor, Commonwealth Keystone Building, 400 North Street, Harrisburg, PA 17120, USA
Tel: (717) 787 5453 *or* (800) 847 4872 (toll-free, brochure request).
Website: www.visitpa.com

Pennsylvania Tourism in the UK
c/o Destination Marketing, Power Road Studios, 114 Power Road, Chiswick, London W4 5PY, UK
Tel: (020) 8994 0978.
Website: www.visitpa.com

Entertainment

FOOD & DRINK: Various regions in Pennsylvania have their own specialities.
Regional specialities:
- Mountain trout - Pocono Mountains area.
- Pennsylvania Dutch food, a unique variation of German cuisine including shoo-fly pie (a sweet dessert made with molasses) – Lancaster area.
NIGHTLIFE: There are numerous dinner theatres, nightclubs, jazz clubs and ethnic entertainment throughout Pennsylvania's towns and cities.
SHOPPING: Philadelphia and Pittsburgh have always been famous for antiques and handicrafts. The main shopping areas in Philadelphia include the **Bourse**, **Head House Square** and **New Market**. The second-largest shopping complex in the USA, **The Plaza & The Court at King of Prussia**, lies to the north of the city. For budget shoppers, **Franklin Mills** (just outside Philadelphia), **Grove City** (north of Pittsburgh) and **Reading** have hundreds of factory outlets, offering the chance to pick up name-brands at reduced prices. In addition, there is no sales tax on clothing and shoes in Pennsylvania. Antiques buffs should stop in **Adamstown**, where over 1500 dealers display their wares every Sunday.

Rhode Island

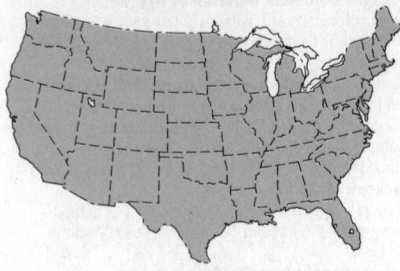

Time: Eastern (GMT - 5). *Daylight Saving Time* is observed.

Overview

Although it takes just 45 minutes to drive from one end of Rhode Island to the other, the smallest State of the union offers more than 640km (400 miles) of coastline, broad sandy beaches, parks, cities and a wealth of historic attractions. It was also the first State to declare independence from Great Britain on 4 May 1776 and the first that passed laws against slavery in 1774. Providence underwent a major facelift in the 1990s that has resulted in the renaissance of Rhode Island's capital city. The revitalisation project included the rerouting of two rivers and the building of beautifully landscaped pedestrian walkways and Venetian-style footbridges.
Newport, a top sailing spot, is an all-seasons resort offering a beautiful harbour that is rich in colonial history, as well as white beaches and some splendid scenery. Newport was the setting for the marriage of John F Kennedy to Jacqueline Bouvier and hosted the Americas Cup race for 53 years.

General Information

Nickname: Ocean State.
State bird: Rhode Island Red.
State flower: Violet.
CAPITAL: Providence.
Date of admission to the Union: 29 May 1790 (original 13 States; date of ratification of the Constitution).
POPULATION: 1.08 million (official estimate 2005).
POPULATION DENSITY: 26.9 per sq km.
2004 total overseas arrivals: 72,000/34.

Climate

Rhode Island's climate is milder than that of the other New England states. Winters are relatively cold with temperatures ranging from -6.1-2.2 °C (21-36° F) and summer temperatures averaging between 17.2-27.2°C (63-81° F). Precipitation is fairly evenly distributed throughout the year.
Required clothing: Cottons and linens for summer months and heavyweights with extra bundling for the winter months.

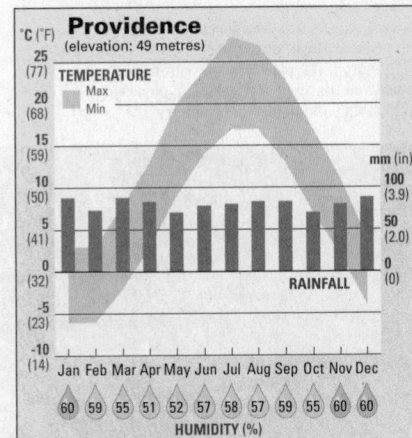

Top Things To See & Do

- Visit the State capital, **Providence**. Wander through **Waterplace Park**, a 1.6-hectare (4-acre) urban park that surrounds a tidal basin. The **East Side** is filled with many fine restored homes, and **Brown University** includes several 18th-century buildings. The **Museum of Natural History and Planetarium** is one of a kind in the State, with collections containing over 24,000 archaeological and ethnographic specimens, with the focus on Native American and Pacific Island heritage. Other highlights

include the **RISD Museum**, an art museum which houses 80,000 works of art and boasts an interesting Japanese collection; while in the adjacent city of **Pawtucket**, the **Slater Mill Historic Site**, the birthplace of the American Industrial Revolution, is also open for tours.
- Sail into the pretty harbour at **Newport**. Many of the town's magnificent mansions (including those built by the Vanderbilts and the Astors) are open to the public. Other sights include the **Touro Synagogue**, which has been restored to its former glory, and the **White Horse Tavern**, built in 1673 by a pirate.
- Be entertained at one of Newport's summer jazz and folk festivals. Classical music takes centre stage in July during the *Newport Music Festival*, while the following month sees the arrival of the *Apple & Eve Newport Folk Festival*. Also in August, the *JVC Jazz Festival* in Newport, one of the oldest and best known in the country, draws music-lovers to **Fort Adams State Park**.
- Take the one-hour ferry trip from **Point Judith** to **Block Island** to see the **National Wildlife Refuge** and the magnificent 60m- (200ft-) high **Mohegan Bluffs**.
- Head to the State's scenic centrepiece, **Narragansett Bay**, home to yachting regattas as well as a thriving fishing industry.

TOURIST INFORMATION

Rhode Island Tourism Division
1 West Exchange Street, Providence, RI 02903, USA
Tel: (401) 222 2601 *or* (800) 556 2484 (toll-free; 24 hours).
Website: www.visitrhodeisland.com

Newport County CVB
23 America's Cup Avenue, Newport, RI 02840, USA
Tel: (401) 849 8048 *or* 845 9123 (visitor information) *or* (800) 326 6030 (toll-free).
Website: www.gonewport.com

South Carolina

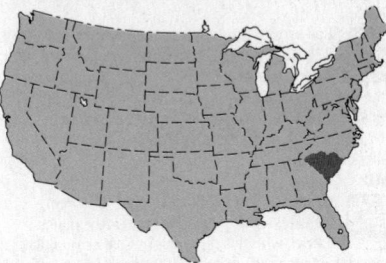

Time: Eastern (GMT - 5). *Daylight Saving Time* is observed.

Overview

South Carolina has beautiful scenery, from the rolling hills of the Upcountry to the glistening lakes of the midlands to the wide, white sandy beaches of the 320km (200-mile) Atlantic coastline. The State has a rich history documented by attractive plantations and the northwestern foothills where fierce battles were fought during the Civil War. Charleston, situated on the coast, is one of its best-known tourist destinations, being the site of the first permanent English settlement. Myrtle Beach, a popular resort city famous for its golf, centred on the sun-drenched 95km (60mile) stretch of coastline on the northern border, and Hilton Head, which has 20km (12 miles) of beautiful beaches, unspoilt forest and golf courses, are among the other top attractions.

General Information

Nickname: Palmetto State.
State bird: Carolina Wren.
State flower: Carolina Yellow Jasmine.
CAPITAL: Columbia.
Date of admission to the Union: 23 May 1788 (original 13 States; date of ratification of the Constitution).
POPULATION: 4.26 million (official estimate 2005).
POPULATION DENSITY: 51.3 per sq km.
2004 total overseas arrivals/US ranking: 144,000/26

Climate

South Carolina has a temperate climate. Spring and autumn are the most pleasant seasons. In winter, temperatures generally average 5-7°C (40-45°F) in inland areas, and 12-15°C (55-60°F) by the shore. Summer temperatures, modified by mountains in some areas and by sea breezes in others, range from 24–29°C (75–85°F), and can reach as high as 32°C (90°F) and above.

Required clothing: Lightweights are advised throughout the year, with warmer clothes for winter. Beachwear is popular, and protection from the midday sun, such as sunglasses and sun hats, is advisable.

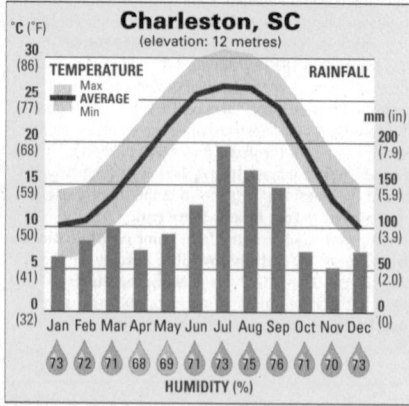

Charleston, SC
(elevation: 12 metres)

TEMPERATURE — Max / AVERAGE / Min — RAINFALL

HUMIDITY (%): 73 72 71 68 69 71 73 75 76 71 70 73

Travel - International

AIR:

Main airport: *Charleston International Airport* (website: www.chs-airport.com) is located 19km (12 miles) north of downtown Charleston. The State is accessible from several international gateways, including Atlanta, Charlotte, Cincinnati, New York, Philadelphia and Raleigh/Durham airports, with connecting services to domestic airports (see below). *To/from the airport:* A shuttle service and taxis are available to downtown Charleston. *Facilities:* ATMs, business centre and car hire.

Domestic airports: A number of national and regional carriers serve the airports in Charleston, Columbia, Florence, Greenville/Spartanburg, Hilton Head Island and Myrtle Beach. Hilton Head Island is also served by *Savannah (Georgia) International Airport*.

RAIL:

Rail service through America's *Amtrak* (tel: (800) 872 7245 (toll-free); website: www.amtrak.com) system is available to Charleston and Columbia on the main New York–Washington–Miami routes, and to Greenville on the New York–Washington–New Orleans route. Trains on these routes also stop at a number of smaller centres.

ROAD:

Greyhound (tel: (800) 231 2222 (toll-free); website: www.greyhound.com) is the main carrier, with bus terminals in Charleston (3610 Dorchester Road) and Greenville (100 West. McBee Avenue).

Approximate bus travel times: From Charleston to *Savannah* is three hours, and to *Charlotte* is six hours. From Columbia to *Savannah* is two hours, to *Washington, DC* is 10 hours, and to *Miami* is 13 hours.

URBAN:

The *Coastal Rapid Public Transit Authority* serves Myrtle Beach and Conway. In Myrtle Beach, the *Great American Trolley* travels from the central beach area to Broadway at the beach via Myrtle Square Mall. *CARTA* runs a reliable bus service within Charleston, while *Downtown Area Shuttles (DASH)* operates a frequent service from the tourist information point.

Top Things To See

- Tour some of the many churches that dot the streets of **Charleston**, nicknamed 'The Holy City'. Among the most historic are the **First Baptist Church** (website: www.fbcharleston.org), **French Huguenot Church** (website: www.frenchhuguenotchurch.org), **St Philip's Episcopal Church** (website: www.stphilipschurchsc.org) and the **Unitarian Church** (website: www.charlestonuu.org).
- Take a guided tram tour at **Charles Towne Landing** (website: www.charlestowne.org). It is an unusual park located on the first permanent English settlement in South Carolina. The tour takes you around the original 1670 fortification. You can board a replica of a 17th-century trading ketch, or explore 11km (7 miles) of pathways through beautiful English park gardens.
- View the **Spirit of South Carolina** (website: www.scmaritime.org), a replica tall ship docked at the north end of Union Terminal Pier.
- Explore **Fort Sumter** (website: www.nps.gov/fosu), possibly the most important historic military site in the nation; the first shots of the Civil War were fired at

Fort Sumter from Fort Johnson in 1861. Boat tours to Fort Sumter leave from **Liberty Square** and **Patriots Point Maritime Museum** (website: www.patriotspoint.org).
- Tour the **Columbia Museum of Art** (website: www.colmusart.org), where contemporary art shares the spotlight with masterpieces of the Baroque and Renaissance.
- Visit the **Confederate Relic Room and Museum** (website: www.state.sc.us/crr) in Columbia. The museum features weapons and memorabilia, including flags, newspapers, clothing, pictures and money.
- Trace the history of the American soldier at the **Fort Jackson Museum** (website: www.jackson.army.mil/museum). A special exhibit focuses on the life and times of President Andrew Jackson.
- Explore **Brookgreen Gardens** (website: www.thewebstation.com/brookgreen). Located halfway between Myrtle Beach and Georgetown, the gardens are a showplace of art and nature developed in the 1930s by Archer and Anna Hyatt Huntington on the site of four colonial rice plantations. Amongst the 2000 species of plants, visitors can view around 550 of America's finest 19th- and 20th-century sculptures by artists such as Frederic Remington and Daniel Chester French, as well as many by Anna Hyatt Huntington herself.
- Visit the **South Carolina Hall of Fame** in **Myrtle Beach** (website: www.myrtlebeachinfo.com/chamber/aboutarea/halloffame). It has interactive video displays that salute outstanding citizens of South Carolina.

Top Things To Do

- Relax at a Charleston beach resort. These include **Fairfield Ocean Ridge** (website: www.fairfieldvacations.com) at **Edisto Island**, **Seabrook Island Resort** (website: www.discoverseabrook.com), **Wild Dunes Resort** (website: www.wilddunes.com) on the **Isle of Palms**, and **Kiawah Island** (website: www.kiawahresort.com).
- Spend the day at the **Riverbanks Zoo and Garden** (website: www.riverbanks.org) in Columbia. Ranked among the top 10 zoos in the nation, the zoo uses water and light to create the illusion of privacy and wild, unlimited space for the 2000 animals.
- Entertain the children at any of the popular attractions in and around Myrtle Beach (website: www.lovingmyrtlebeach.com/attractions). They include the **Myrtle Beach National Wax Museum**; **Myrtle Beach Pavilion Amusement Park**, which boasts a giant **German Pipe Organ** dating from 1900; **NASCAR Speedpark**; and **Ripley's Aquarium**.
- Get wet on any one of the fun water rides at **Myrtle Waves Water Park** (website: www.lovingmyrtlebeach.com/attractions) and **Wild Water and Wheels** (website: www.wild-water.com) in **Surfside Beach**. The **Family Kingdom Amusement Park** (website: www.family-kingdom.com) boasts *Swamp Fox*, a legendary wooden rollercoaster.
- Spend the day at the oceanfront **Huntington Beach State Park** (website: www.discoversouthcarolina.com/stateparks). It is also home to **Atalaya**, once the castle-like studio of Mrs Huntington. The park offers a visitors' centre, boardwalk, nature trails, camping, picnicking, sunbathing and nature programmes.

- See what all the excitement is about and visit **Myrtle Beach State Park** (website: www.discoversouthcarolina.com/stateparks). It is one of the most popular parks in the State with cabins, camping, swimming and pier fishing.
- Rent an old beach house on **Pawley's Island** (website: www.townofpawleysisland.com). One of the oldest resorts on the Atlantic Coast, the island was once a refuge for colonial rice planters' families wishing to avoid malaria. The original Pawley's Island rope hammocks have long been handmade in this area.
- Camp at **Table Rock State Park** (website: www.discoversouthcarolina.com/stateparks), one of the State's oldest and most popular parks. Boating, fishing, swimming, nature trails and summit hikes have drawn record numbers of visitors.
- Tee off on one of over 335 **golf** courses statewide. The Low Country offers more than 100 championship courses, several of which are frequented by renowned master players – the *Kiawah Island Resort* is ranked as one of the top courses in the USA.
- Visit **Hilton Head** (website: www.treasuredcoast.com), considered a golfer's paradise with its miles of dazzling white sand beaches, bike trails, beaches, tennis courts, and some of the nation's premier golf courses.

TOURIST INFORMATION

South Carolina Department of Parks, Recreation & Tourism
1205 Pendleton Street, Columbia, SC 29201, USA
Tel: (803) 734 1700 *or* (888) 727 6453 (toll-free).
Website: www.discoversouthcarolina.com

Myrtle Beach Area Chamber of Commerce and Information Center
Street address: 1200 North Oak Street, Myrtle Beach, SC 29577, USA
Postal address: PO Box 2115, Myrtle Beach, SC 29578, USA
Tel: (843) 626 7444 *or* (800) 356 3016 (toll-free).
Website: www.myrtlebeachinfo.com

Entertainment

FOOD & DRINK: Charleston boasts a number of fine seafood restaurants. There are more than 1700 restaurants on the Grand Strand in Myrtle Beach, offering every type of food imaginable.

Regional specialities:
- Shrimp with grits.
- Charleston she-crab soup.

NIGHTLIFE: The liveliest spot in South Carolina is Myrtle Beach, where the nightclubs are open for business every night of the week. Choices range from country music venues to high-energy dance clubs. In Charleston, fun-seekers should head for the trendy new **Terrace** at **Merion Square** or the eclectic **Tristan** in the city's French Quarter.

SHOPPING: Popular places to shop for bargains include the **Waccamaw Outlet Park**, the **Factory Outlet Shops**, the variety of shops at **Barefoot Landing** and numerous golf and sporting goods shops. A popular purchase is the Pawley's Island hammock, which visitors can watch being made at the **Hammock Shop** on Pawley's Island. Myrtle Beach also offers good shopping opportunities at the **Tanger Outlet Center** and the massive **Mall of South Carolina** in Myrtle Beach.

Credit: ©S.C. Department of Parks, Recreation & Tourism, DiscoverSouthCarolina.com

South Dakota

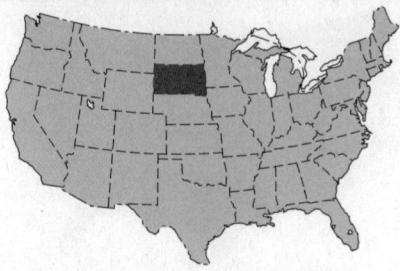

Time: Central (GMT - 6) in the eastern part of the State; Mountain (GMT - 7) in the west. *Daylight Saving Time* is observed.

Overview

Tucked into the heart of the USA, the 'Mount Rushmore State' offers untouched nature in abundance, vast stretches of fertile prairies and early pioneer towns. Near the eastern border, Sioux Falls is the largest city in the region, and boasts its namesake waterfall. On the opposite side of the State, Rapid City is the gateway to the Black Hills, with mountains, caves, forests and lakes. Also in South Dakota's southwest corner is its biggest tourist attraction by far, the Mount Rushmore National Memorial, where the 18m- (60ft-) high heads of four US presidents (George Washington, Thomas Jefferson, Theodore Roosevelt and Abraham Lincoln) have been blasted and carved out of the mountain. In the Black Hills, the Crazy Horse Memorial, a privately funded monument, is the world's largest mountain sculpture in progress. The upper half of the 22-storey-high horse's head is a memorial honouring the North American Indian, standing 171m- (563ft-) high and 195m- (641ft-) long.

General Information

Nickname: Mount Rushmore State.
State bird: Ring-necked Pheasant.
State flower: American Pasque Flower.
CAPITAL: Pierre.
Date of admission to the Union: 2 Nov 1889.
POPULATION: 776,000 (official estimate 2005).
POPULATION DENSITY: 18 per sq km.
2004 total overseas arrivals: Under 38,000.

Climate

Winters are cold with adequate snow for winter sports. Summers are warm, with adequate rainfall for crop growth, and are conducive to summer sports.
Required clothing: Lightweights for the summer and heavyweights for the winter.

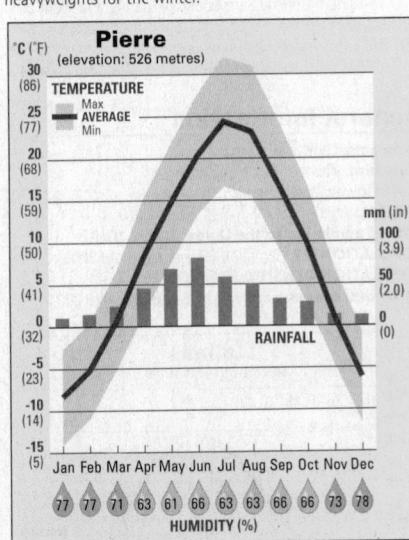

Top Things To See & Do

- Visit **Sioux Falls**. As well as its namesake waterfall, visit the **Center for Western Studies**, the **Old Courthouse Museum**, **St Joseph's Cathedral** and the **Washington Pavilion of Arts and Science**.
- Discover the natural beauty of the **Black Hills**, **Wind Cave National Park** and **Custer State Park**, with its herd of over 1500 bison.
- Explore **Jewel Cave National Monument**, the third-

longest cave in the world, also located at Custer.
- Gaze up at four former presidents at **Mount Rushmore National Memorial**. Work began on this massive 'Shrine of Democracy' in 1927 and took 14 years to complete.
- See a work in progress at the **Crazy Horse Memorial** in the Black Hills. The excellent **Indian Museum of North America** is located here and is well worth a visit.
- Dip in the waters of **Evans Plunge**, the world's largest naturally heated swimming pool, in the community of **Hot Springs**. The town is also home to **The Mammoth Site**, the world's largest concentration of Columbian and woolly mammoth bones discovered in their primary context (ie where they died).
- Marvel at the scenery of **Badlands National Park**, which encompasses 98,785 hectares (244,000 acres) of striking rock formations – steep canyons, jagged spires, bands of colourful rocks – blended with mixed-grass prairies. Campgrounds and cabins are available to visitors.
- Enjoy the numerous attractions of **Pierre**, the capital of South Dakota, including the **South Dakota Cultural Heritage Center**, **South Dakota National Guard Museum**, **South Dakota State Capitol** and the **South Dakota World War II Memorial**. Some 48km (30 miles) north of **Fort Pierre** is **Triple U Buffalo Ranch**, the location of many scenes in the film *Dances with Wolves*.

TOURIST INFORMATION

South Dakota Department of Tourism
711 East Wells Avenue, Pierre, SD 57501, USA
Tel: (605) 773 3301 *or* (800) 732 5682 (toll-free).
Website: www.travelsd.com

Rocky Mountain International in the UK
18 Church Road, Warsash, Southampton, Hampshire SO31 9GD, UK
Tel: (01489) 557 533 (trade enquiries only) *or* (09063) 640 655 (customer request line; calls cost 60p per minute).
Website: www.rmi-realamerica.com

Tennessee

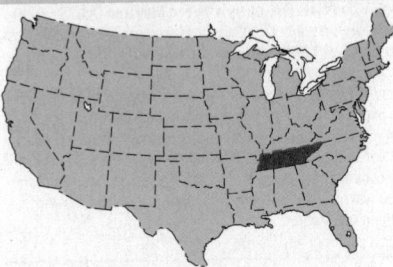

Time: Eastern (GMT - 5) in the eastern part of the State; Central (GMT - 6) in the west. *Daylight Saving Time* is observed.

Overview

Located in the southeast region of the USA, Tennessee is unique in that it shares a border with eight States. Tennessee has always been a melting pot of musical styles. From the eastern mountains came Appalachian folk songs and bluegrass, while country music flowered in Nashville. Gospel, blues, rockabilly, and ultimately, rock 'n' roll, all stemmed from the Mississippi belt.
Nashville is a major music performance and recording centre and also boasts a host of fine colleges and churches. To the southwest is Memphis, home of the blues and the birthplace of rock 'n' roll, near the Mississippi border. Tennessee's largest city and a major trading centre, Memphis is known chiefly for being the location of Graceland, the home of Elvis Presley.
Over on the southeastern side of the State, perched next to the Tennessee River, is Chattanooga. This bustling city, with its train, was made famous by Glenn Miller's song 'Chattanooga Choo Choo.'
More than half of Tennessee is forested, and great tracts have been set aside as State and National parks, forests, wilderness areas and game preserves. Gatlinburg and Pigeon Forge are the starting points for trips into the Great Smoky Mountains National Park.

General Information

Nickname: Volunteer State.
State bird: Mockingbird.
State flower: Iris.
CAPITAL: Nashville.

Date of admission to the Union: 1 Jun 1796.
POPULATION: 5.96 million (official estimate 2005).
POPULATION DENSITY: 54.6 per sq km.
2004 total overseas arrivals/US ranking: 162,000/24.

Climate

Tennessee has a generally mild climate year round, but still enjoys four distinct seasons. The average high temperature in winter is 9.4°C (49°F) and the average low is -1°C (30°F). In the summer, the average high temperature is 31.7°C (89°F) and the average low is 19.4°C (67°F). The average annual rainfall in Tennessee is 124.7cm (49.7 inches).
Required clothing: Cottons and linens for the summer months and more substantial clothing for the winter.

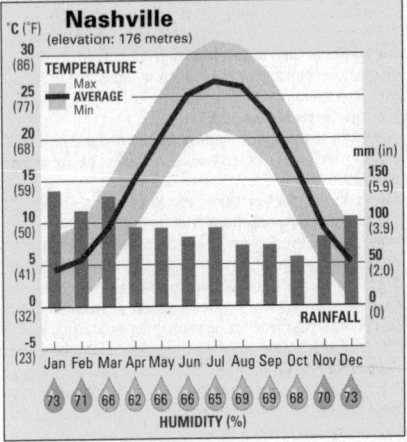

Travel - International

AIR:

 Main airports: *Memphis International Airport (MEM)* (website: www.mscaa.com) is 16km (10 miles) southeast of the city (travel time – 20 minutes). *To/from the airport:* Taxis, limousines and hotel shuttles are available to the city centre, as is the hourly *Memphis Area Transit Authority (MATA)* local bus, which departs near Terminal C. An out-of-town shuttle bus operates from the airport to Arkansas (Little Rock and Jonesboro) and to Mississippi (Oxford). *Facilities:* ATMs, business service centre and car hire.
Nashville International Airport (BNA) (website: www.nashintl.com *or* www.flynashville.com) is located 13km (8 miles) southeast of the city. *To/from the airport:* The *Metropolitan Transit Authority (MTA)* bus 18 leaves the airport nine times a day (Mon-Fri) and four times a day at the weekend. The *Anytime-Transport Shuttle Service* (website: www.anytimetransportshuttleservice.com) runs to destinations in suburban Nashville, Middle Tennessee, and Bowling Green (Kentucky). Limousine services, car hire and taxis are widely available. *Gray Line* operates a van service to hotels in central Nashville every 15 minutes 0600-2300 (travel time – 30 minutes). *Greyhound* operates services to Fort Campbell, Knoxville and Memphis several times a day; the *Express Shuttle* service travels to Chattanooga seven times a day; and the *K-Town Shuttle* serves Knoxville four times a day.
Domestic airports: *Chattanooga Metropolitan Airport (CHA)* (website: www.chattairport.com), 5km (3 miles) east of the city, serves the greater Chattanooga area including southeast Tennessee, north Georgia, and northeast Alabama. *To/from the airport:* Taxi and limousine services are available. *Facilities:* ATMs and car hire.
McGhee Tyson Airport (TYS) (website: www.tys.org) is located 7.5km (12 miles) south of central Knoxville. *To/from the airport:* Limousines and taxis are available at the airport; the *Airport Express Shuttle* provides connections to the city centre. *Facilities:* ATMs and car hire.
RAIL:

 Memphis and Newbern-Dyersberg, on the Chicago-New Orleans line, are the only stations on the national *Amtrak* rail network (tel: (800) 872 7245 (toll-free); website: www.amtrak.com). Nashville and Chattanooga have connecting Thruway bus services (operated by *Greyhound*) to Atlanta, which is on the New Orleans-Washington, DC-New York City route. Car hire is available at the Memphis station. The Tennessee Valley Railroad runs a 10km (6-mile) round trip from Chattanooga.
ROAD:
Bus: *Greyhound* (tel: (800) 231 2222 (toll-free); website: www.greyhound.com) is the main service provider, with bus terminals at Chattanooga, Knoxville, Memphis and Nashville.

Top Things To See

- Enjoy the bald eagles at **Reelfoot Lake** (website: www.reelfootlake.com), the recreational opportunities of **Kentucky Lake** (website: www.kentuckylake.org), or the quiet, sombre atmosphere of the battlefields at **Shiloh National Military Park** (website: www.nps.gov/shil).

- Visit the **West Tennessee Delta Heritage Center** in **Brownsville**. It showcases the region's heritage and provides a good introduction to the area. Its five major exhibitions include the **Tennessee Room**, which highlights West Tennessee towns and attractions, the **West Tennessee Music Museum**, the **Scenic Hatchie River Museum**, the **Cotton Museum**, and **Sleepy John Estes' House**, a tribute to this big man of the blues.
- Pay respect to the King – **Elvis Presley**. His beloved **Memphis** home, **Graceland** (website: www.elvis.com/graceland), is a mecca to the pilgrims of rock 'n' roll. The impressive **Trophy Room** effectively documents his impact on the music industry as a singer and entertainer.
- Encounter Memphis' legendary past as a Delta city and a civil rights centre. It was at the Lorraine Motel at 450 Mulberry Street that Martin Luther King Jr was assassinated. The **National Civil Rights Museum** housed at the site is an effective reminder of the courage of thousands of African-Americans.
- Tour the **Carter House** (website: www.state.tn.us/environment/hist/stateown/carterho.php) in Franklin. The bullet-pocked walls bear witness to one of the deadliest battles of the American Civil War.
- Experience the military history as well as the macabre on the **Tennessee Antebellum Trail** (website: www.state.tn.us/environment/hist/PathDivided/heritagemap.php). Daily tours to seven historic sites are offered, including the blood-stained floors of **Carnton Mansion** (website: www.carnton.org), where, after the battle at **Franklin**, the bodies of five Confederate generals once lay. Starting in Nashville, this 145km- (90 mile-) loop drive also takes in the **Rippavilla Plantation** (website: www.rippavilla.org), dating from 1852, where the five generals ate their last breakfast.
- View the magnificent arched ceiling of stained glass in the **Union Station Hotel** (website: www.wyndham.com/hotels/BNAUS/main.wnt) at 1001 Broadway, **Nashville**.
- Explore the many galleries and museums which reflect Tennessee's Antebellum and plantation history, including the **Carl Van Vechten Gallery** in Nashville, which exhibits collections by Cézanne, Picasso and Renoir as well as displays of work by Georgia O'Keeffe and Alfred Steiglitz.
- Tour the **Hermitage** (website: www.thehermitage.com), President Andrew Jackson's manor house, 19km (12 miles) from downtown Nashville. Admission includes a visit to nearby **Tulip Grove Mansion**.
- Visit the **Bicentennial Mall State Park** (website: www.state.tn.us/environment/parks/parks/Bicentennial) which was built in Nashville to honour the State's founding in 1776.
- Explore the **Rock City Gardens** (website: www.seerockcity.com) in **Chattanooga**. The subterranean black-lit gnome dioramas and Mother Goose theme areas are constructed around several interesting rock formations.
- Experience Chattanooga's **Ruby Falls** (website: www.rubyfalls.com), a spectacular 44m- (145ft-) high underground waterfall which flows 341m (1120ft) below the surface of Lookout Mountain.
- Visit the **Blount Mansion** (website: www.blountmansion.org) in **Knoxville**, the 1792 frame house of Governor William Blount. The mansion is a National Historic Landmark.
- Walk through **James White's Fort** (website: www.discoveret.org/jwf). The fort still exhibits portions of the original stockade built in 1786 by Knoxville's founder.
- Visit the ancient **Cumberland Plateau**, which forms a natural boundary between Middle and East Tennessee. Waterfalls, deep river canyons, parks and resorts characterise this historic region.

Top Things To Do

- See where critics claim that the blues were born, on **Beale Street** (website: www.bealestreet.com) in **Memphis**. A legendary piece published by the 'Father of the Blues,' W C Handy, in 1912, successfully proclaimed its power and authenticity. Beale Street includes restaurants, gift shops, boutiques, parks and nightclubs, as well as the **Beale Street Police Museum** and **A Schwab's Dry Goods Store**, a small department store which has been in the same family since 1876 and still offers old-fashioned bargains.
- Head to 'Music City USA' – **Nashville**. The centre of Nashville's music industry is **Music Row**, around Division and Demonbreun streets. Spanning an entire city block, the **Country Music Hall of Fame** (website: www.countrymusichalloffame.com) is located in the revitalised entertainment district of central Nashville.
- Journey on **The Delta**, an indoor, quarter-mile river, complete with four 25-passenger flatboats featured inside Nashville's award-winning **Opryland Hotel and Convention Center** (website: www.gaylordhotels.com/gaylordopryland).
- View the process of bourbon-making at the famous **Jack Daniel Distillery** (website: www.jackdaniels.com/tour), 120km (75 miles) southeast of Nashville. Much insight into Mister Jack's famous distilling process is offered during the daily guided tours (0900-1630).
- Hear good ole country music at the **Grand Ole Opry** (website: www.opry.com) in Nashville. The opry is the setting for the nation's longest-running live radio show, which moved here in 1976 (the original setting, **Ryman**, has been renovated and is also open to the public) and is the place to hear country music on Friday and Saturday nights.
- View denizens of the deep at the **Tennessee Aquarium** (website: www.tennis.org) in **Chattanooga**. The aquarium houses one of the world's largest collections of freshwater marine life.
- Ride the **Incline**, also in Chattanooga, which propels its passengers up a stomach-churning gradient of 72.7° – the world's record-holding, steepest passenger railway. The journey is worthwhile, especially on a clear day, when the territories of seven States are visible from **Lookout Mountain** (website: www.lookoutmountain.com).
- Try the authentic tastes of Appalachia at the **Farmer's Market**, 24km (15 miles) from downtown **Knoxville**. The pavilion sells local produce, plants, jams, jellies, arts and crafts.
- Take a trip to **Gatlinburg** (website: www.gatlinburg.com). At the base of the **Great Smoky Mountains, Gatlinburg** offers miniature golf courses, haunted houses, restaurants, the *Ripley's Aquarium*, and more.
- Experience the **Great Smoky Mountains** (website: www.nps.gov/grsm). The largest wilderness area in the USA, this national park extends over202,000 hectates (half a million acres) of the **Appalachian Mountains**, bordered by North Carolina and the Tennessee valleys. The park is home to bears, white-tailed deer, wild turkeys and more than 1500 species of flowering plants. Conifer forests are to be found at elevations of more than 1800m (6000ft). The mountains are beautiful in all seasons, but perhaps the best time to see them is in October when they are showered in colour. The park has three visitor centres, *Cades Cove, Oconaluftee Visitor Centre* and *Sugarlands*. There are also 10 campgrounds, each with tent sites, trailer space, water and tables. There are over 1400km (900 miles) of hiking trails and 270km (170 miles) of road throughout the park. Rangers at the visitor centres can assist with trip planning.
- Spend the day at **Dollywood** (website: www.dollywood.com). Die-hard country fans will want to visit this all-American attraction in the Tennessee hills, created by the Queen of Country herself – Dolly Parton. Dollywood is usually open between May and October 1000-1900, and in winter for Christmas specials. The park's newest attraction is **Timber Tower**, the first and only ride of its kind in North America.
- Stay in **Pigeon Forge** (website: www.mypigeonforge.com). In addition to Dollywood, miniature raceways, arcades, *Boyds Bear Country* (where you can make your own bear), major shopping outlet malls and more are available. The city celebrates the culture of the East Tennessee mountains and you will find craftspeople demonstrating their skills and selling their wares.

TOURIST INFORMATION

Tennessee Department of Tourism Development
312 8th Avenue North, 25th Floor,
Nashville, TN 37243, USA
Tel: (615) 741 2159 *or* (800) 462 8366 (toll-free).
Website: www.tnvacation.com *or* www.tntourism.com

Tennessee Tourism in the UK
Lofthouse Enterprises, Woodlands Park Street, Hitchin,
Herts SG4 9AH, UK
Tel: (01462) 440784.
Website: www.deep-south-usa.com

Entertainment

FOOD & DRINK:
Regional specialities:
- Barbecue.
- Country ham.
- Blackberry cobbler.

NIGHTLIFE: In Nashville, good venues for live music include **Caffé Milano** (jazz, bluegrass and rock), **Henry's Coffee House**, with acoustic performances, and **Canyon Country Saloon**, which features up and coming artists. **Lucy's Record Shop** sells music during the day, but on Friday and Saturday hosts the latest alternative performers, and the funky **Radio Cafe**, an old pharmacy, features national artists playing blues, country, jazz and rock. *The Nashville Scene* or the *Tennessean* newspapers list all live music events. Memphis has many nightclubs along Beale Street.
SHOPPING: Pigeon Forge is known for its many major outlet malls. **Opry Mills** is a shopping and entertainment resort covering more than 750 acres on the site of former Opryland USA.

Texas

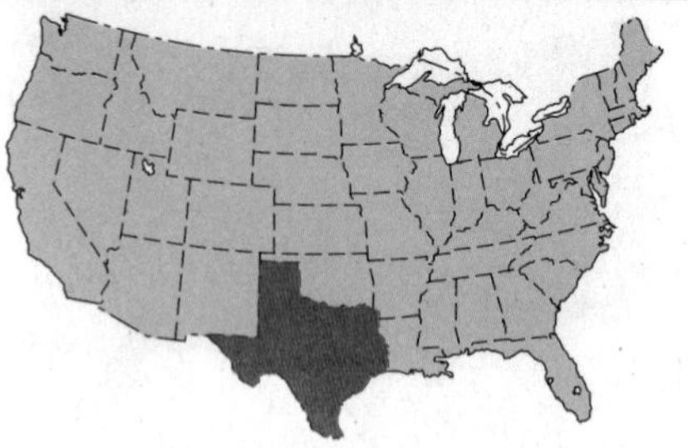

Time: Central (GMT - 6). *Daylight Saving Time* is observed.

Overview

Texas, the 'Lone Star State,' is the second-largest state in the USA, covering more than 695,676 sq km (268,600 sq miles). Spain was the first European power to lay claim to Texas; the State also flew the flags of France and Mexico before gaining its independence in 1836. Texas borders Mexico along the Rio Grande and embraces vast mountain ranges and canyons to the west. Lakes, plantations and pine forests are found to the east; broad plains to the north; citrus groves, Gulf of Mexico beaches and low-lying alluvial plains to the south; and rolling hill country and clear natural springs at its heart. Its great wealth stems from its vast oil reserves. It has several booming cities: Dallas, El Paso, Fort Worth, Houston, San Antonio, and its capital city, Austin.
Originally a trading post, Dallas has grown into an important centre for commerce and fashion. It has a glittering high-rise skyline, elegant stores, fine restaurants and a rich cultural life. Located in the Prairies and Lakes region, Dallas is a modern sophisticated city, yet still possesses the much-renowned Texan hospitality and southwestern charm. It is increasingly recognised for its cosmopolitan spirit and entrepreneurial flair.
Dallas is a city rich in historical sites and futuristic sights. The downtown area features shimmering glass towers and angled spires, whereas in the West End Historic District there are 100-year-old buildings now occupied by lively shops, restaurants and museums.
Much more 'Western' in spirit, Fort Worth started as a military outpost and then became a cow town where cattlemen brought their herds to be shipped. Much of the Old West is preserved in Fort Worth today and it continues to be a centre for the cattle industry.
The fourth-largest city in the USA and the largest in Texas, Houston has a population of more than 1.9 million (its metro population of 4.7 million falls short of the 5.2 million in the Dallas/Fort Worth area, however). Houston has been the centre of the US oil industry ever since 'black gold' was discovered at nearby Beaumont in 1901. The city is named after Texas hero General Sam Houston, the first President of the Republic of Texas. It is also the space headquarters of the USA and a thriving international port, being connected to the Gulf of Mexico by the 80km (50-mile) Houston Ship Channel.

General Information

Nickname: Lone Star State.
State bird: Western Mockingbird.
State flower: Bluebonnet.
CAPITAL: Austin.
Date of admission to the Union: 29 Dec 1845.
POPULATION: 22.86 million (official estimate 2005).
POPULATION DENSITY: 32.9 per sq km.
2004 total overseas arrivals/US ranking: 829,000/7.

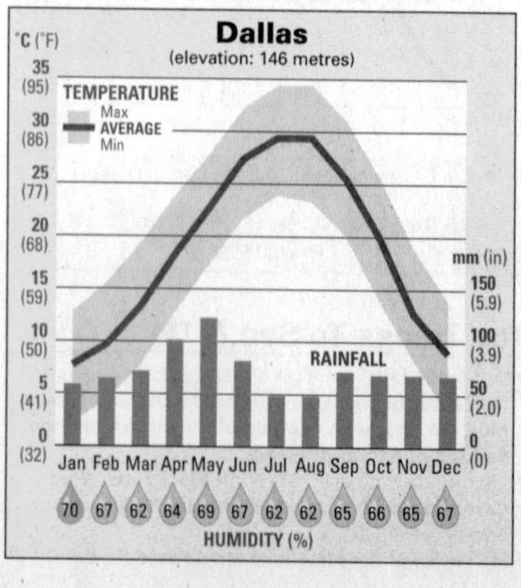

A B C D E F G H I J K L M N O P Q R S T U V W X Y Z

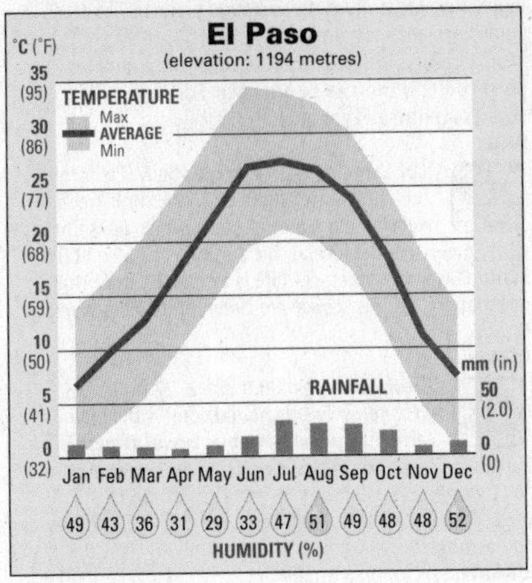
El Paso
(elevation: 1194 metres)
°C (°F)
35 (95)
30 (86)
25 (77)
20 (68)
15 (59)
10 (50)
5 (41)
0 (32)
TEMPERATURE
Max
AVERAGE
Min
RAINFALL
mm (in)
50 (2.0)
0 (0)
Jan Feb Mar Apr May Jun Jul Aug Sep Oct Nov Dec
49 43 36 31 29 33 47 51 49 48 48 52
HUMIDITY (%)

Climate

Average temperature: 34-36°C (93-96°F) during summer; 12-14°C (54-57°F) during winter; and 19-22°C (66-72°F) for coastal winter temperatures.

Required clothing: Lightweights are advised throughout the year, with warmer clothes for the winter.

Travel - International

AIR:

Main airports: *Dallas/Fort Worth International (DFW)* (website: www.dfwairport.com) is 27km (17 miles) from both cities (travel time - 35 minutes). The airport is the fourth-busiest in the USA and sixth-busiest in the world (2002 passenger rankings), annually serving over 52 million passengers. The airport itself is the size of Manhattan. *To/from the airport*: Passenger shuttle vans provide a free transit link between terminals. The *Dallas Area Rapid Transit (DART)* no 202 express bus runs from the North Shuttle Parking Lot to downtown; a free shuttle service is provided to the North Shuttle Parking Lot from all terminals. There are also free shuttles to the *Trinity Railway Express* commuter line, which links Dallas, Fort Worth and the airport. The *Yellow Checker Shuttle Co* Airporter van runs to the city every 30 minutes. Taxis, shared-ride shuttles, limousines, and courtesy cars are also available. *Facilities:* Car hire, currency exchange and postal services.

George Bush Intercontinental Airport Houston (IAH) (website: www.fly2houston.com) is 32km (20 miles) north of the city (travel time - 30 minutes). *To/from the airport:* The *Airport Express* shuttle travels to the Galleria and downtown hotels (travel time - 45 minutes). Metro bus route 102 operates every 30 minutes approximately 0500-2400 daily, dropping passengers off in downtown Houston. Taxis are also available, but expensive. *Facilities:* ATMs, car hire and currency exchange.

El Paso International Airport (ELP) (website: www.elpasointernationalairport.com) is 13km (8 miles) east of the city; it serves as a gateway to western Texas, southern New Mexico, and northern Mexico. *To/from the airport*: Sun Metro runs daily bus services to the airport on route 33. Many hotels offer a complimentary shuttle service. *Facilities*: ATMs, business centre and car hire.

San Antonio International Airport (SAT) (website: www.sanantonio.gov/aviation) is 14km (8.5 miles) from the city, with flights from Latin America and major US cities. *To/From the airport*: Public buses and the more expensive *SA Trans Shuttle* run to the city centre (travel times - 1 hour and 20 minutes respectively). Taxis are also available. *Facilities*: ATMs, business centre and car hire.

Domestic airports: *Dallas Love Field (DAL)* (website: www.dallas-lovefield.com) is 9.5km (6 miles) from Dallas city centre. The airport is a hub for *Southwest Airlines*. *To/from the airport*: DART buses travel to downtown Dallas; shuttles and taxis are also available. *Facilities*: ATMs and car hire.

Approximate flight times: From Dallas/Fort Worth to *London* is nine hours, to *Miami* is two hours 40 minutes, and to *New York* is three hours 30 minutes. Flight times from Houston are similar.

RAIL:

Amtrak (tel: (800) 872 7245 (toll-free); website: www.amtrak.com) journeys between main cities are difficult and (except for Dallas to Fort Worth) can only be made on the long-distance trains. The daily 'Texas Eagle' service from Chicago passes through Dallas and Fort Worth on its way to San Antonio, where transfers to Los Angeles are possible on the thrice-weekly 'Sunset Limited', which arrives from Orlando via New Orleans and Houston. The daily 'Heartland Flyer' links Oklahoma City and Fort Worth.

ROAD:

Greyhound (tel: (800) 231 2222 (toll-free); website: www.greyhound.com) runs frequent services connecting Dallas, Fort Worth, Houston, San Antonio and other major towns and cities in Texas and further afield. Bus services off the main routes are not highly developed.

Approximate bus travel times: From Dallas/Fort Worth to *Houston* is four hours 30 minutes, to *Memphis* is 13 hours 30 minutes, and to *El Paso* is 13 hours. From Houston to *San Antonio* is four hours, to *Dallas* is four hours 30 minutes and to *New Orleans* is eight hours 30 minutes.

Approximate driving times: From Dallas/Fort Worth to *Little Rock* is seven hours, to *Mexico City* is 24 hours, to *Miami* is 28 hours, and to *Los Angeles* is 29 hours. From Houston to *El Paso* is 15 hours, to *Chicago* is 24 hours, and to *Miami* is 25 hours. All times are based on non-stop driving at or below the applicable speed limits.

URBAN:

Dallas Area Rapid Transit (DART) (website: www.dart.org) provides a convenient light-rail service with two north-south lines passing through the city centre. *DART* also runs the *Trinity Railway Express* commuter rail line between Dallas and Fort Worth; buses between the cities are operated by *Greyhound* (see above). *DART* also operates the city's local bus network, which is well run and reasonably priced. *DART* services run daily 0500-0030. In Fort Worth, *The T* operates both the bus network and the *Longhorn Trolley* service, which runs between various tourist attractions and hotels. Most major car hire companies have offices in both cities and motor campers are available for hire. Houston's *Metropolitan Transport Authority (METRO)* (website: www.ridemetro.org) provides reasonably priced bus services. The *METRORail* light-rail system runs 12km (7.5 miles) from downtown Houston to south of Reliant Park. The train serves 16 stations with transfers to *METRO* buses available. Taxis are readily available, but can be impractical and expensive for short distances. Car hire is the best way to get around, but visitors are advised to make advance reservations as the demand is high.

Top Things To See

- Tour the **Old City Park** (website: www.oldcitypark.org), a pioneer community in **Dallas** featuring homes, a church, a schoolhouse and Main Street as it was in the days of the original settlers.
- See **Dealey Plaza** (website: www.jfk.org), the site of President John F Kennedy's Dallas assassination. There is a dramatic exhibit of the event at the **Sixth Floor Museum**. The John F Kennedy Memorial at Main and Market Streets is open all year round.
- Go and see the famous **Southfork Ranch** (website: www.southforkranch.com), home of the famous TV series' Ewing clan. The ranch is open daily, year-round for guided tours.
- Explore **Fair Park** (website: www.fairpark.org), home to the **Age of Steam Museum**, **Dallas Aquarium**, the **Museum of Natural History** (with a superb dinosaur exhibition), the **Texas Hall of State**, and **The Women's Museum: An Institute for the Future**.
- View the **Historic Stockyards** (website: www.fortworthstockyards.org) in **Fort Worth**. They still retain the flavour of the Old West. Daily cattle drives take place along **Exchange Avenue**.
- Visit the 300-acre (121-hectare) **University of Texas** (website: www.utexas.edu) campus in Austin, which offers the **Lyndon B Johnson Presidential Library** (website: www.lbjlib.utexas.edu).
- Relax in **Tranquility Park**. The park in **Houston** was dedicated to the Sea of Tranquility where astronaut Neil Armstrong said the first words from the moon on July 20, 1969. 'Houston, Tranquility base here. The eagle has landed.'
- See the veteran, pre-World War I battleship, *Texas*. It is moored on the **San Jacinto River** near the **Battleground Monument** (website: www.tpwd.state.tx.us/parks), which marks the 1836 battle for Texan independence.
- Tour the **Lyndon B Johnson Space Center** (website: www.nasa.gov/centers/johnson) in Houston. The centre has exhibitions of space technology and stages regular film shows explaining the US space programme.
- Experience the **Alamo** (website: www.thealamo.org). In 1836, it was the site of a furious battle between a handful of independence-seeking Texans (led by Davy Crockett) and a large Mexican army. Today it is a shrine to Texan courage and patriotism. The six-storey-high *IMAX Theater* tells the whole story of the Alamo in a gripping film.
- Visit the **San Antonio Missions National Historic Park** (website: www.nps.gov/saan), which comprised four Spanish missions, while the **Institute of Texan Cultures** (website: www.texancultures.utsa.edu/public) tells the story of the region's multicultural heritage.
- Bird watch at the **Santa Ana National Wildlife Refuge** (website: www.fws.gov/southwest/refuges/texas/santana.html), one of the top 10 birding sites in the USA, boasting a record count of species.
- Time warp back to the frontier days. Visit **Buffalo Gap Historic Village** (website: www.buffalogap.com), a reconstructed frontier settlement.
- View **The Meteor Crater**, 16km (10 miles) west of the city of **Odessa**. Approximately 168m (550 feet) in diameter, it is the second-largest meteor crater in the USA and was created when a barrage of meteors crashed to the earth between 20,000 and 30,000 years ago.
- Visit **Midland**. The city is home to the **Commemorative Air Force Museum** (website: www.commemorativeairforce.org), which houses WWII artifacts and memorabiliia, and the **Petroleum Museum** (website: www.petroleummuseum.org), which contains one of the most complete collections of the petroleum industry in the nation.

Top Things To Do

- Visit the **West End Historic District** in **Dallas** (website: www.dallaswestend.org). There are 100-year-old buildings now occupied by lively shops, restaurants and museums.
- Ride the glass-elevator to the top of the 50-storey **Reunion Tower**. It has observation terraces and a revolving restaurant with nighttime dancing.
- Win a teddy bear at one of the skill games while you spend the day at **Six Flags Over Texas** theme park (website: www.sixflags.com/parks).
- Engage in one of the activities at **Sundance Square** (website: www.sundancesquare.com) located in downtown **Fort Worth**. The square is a vibrant entertainment district with a fine collection of hotels, shops, restaurants, live music clubs, theatres, movies and an exciting nightlife. There is also a log-cabin village, a zoological park and a Japanese garden.
- Fish, boat, and swim at **Highland Lakes** (website: www.highlandlakes.com). A day trip into the scenic hill country, where several award-winning wineries are located, is well worthwhile.
- Wear your swimsuits to **Six Flags Splashtown** (www.sixflags.com/parks), a water recreation park with dozens of splashy water rides, slides, chutes and floats.
- Tour **San Antonio**'s **Paseo del Rio** (Riverwalk) (website: www.thesanantonioriverwalk.com), a unique shopping and entertainment area.
- Delight in the world's largest marine-life park, **Sea World of Texas** (website: www.seaworld.com).
- Become a cowboy. Working ranch holidays are widely available in the hill country to the west of San Antonio, near **Bandera** (website: www.banderacowboycapital.com), the 'Cowboy Capital of the World'.
- Discover **Padre Island** (website: www.nps.gov/pais), a narrow 170km (95-mile) barrier island with watersports, fishing centres and an impressive expanse of protected National Seashore, wildlife refuges and birdlife sites; it is connected to Corpus Christi by a causeway.
- Experience **Galveston Island** (website: www.galveston.com). It is further up the coast near Houston. The island is rich in history and pirate lore and noted for its sandy beaches, fishing, watersports and turn-of-the-century architecture.
- Visit **Palo Duro Canyon State Park** (website: www.paloduroCanyon.com), near **Amarillo.** The park has startling scenery and facilities for hiking, picnicking, camping and horse riding.
- See spectacular views of stark desert, forests, mountains and canyons carved by the Rio Grande at **Big Bend National Park** (website: www.nps.gov/bibe), south of El Paso. Hiking and rafting, especially in the Santa Elena canyon, are popular.

- **Golf** on one of the many courses available in and around Austin, Houston, Fort Worth, Dallas, Irving and San Antonio.
- Explore the **Space Center Houston** (website: www.spacecenter.org) – the official visitor center of **NASA's Johnson Space Center**. Climb aboard a computer simulator, touch a moon rock, see a full-size space shuttle replica or visit any one of the many other exhibits.

TOURIST INFORMATION

Texas Economic Development, Tourism Division
221 East 11th Street, 4th Floor, Austin, TX 78701, USA
Tel: (512) 936 0101.
Website: www.traveltex.com

State of Texas Tourism Office in the UK
c/o First Public Relations, Molasses House,
Clove Hitch Quay, Plantation Wharf,
London SW11 3TN, UK
Tel: (020) 7978 5233.
Website: www.firstpr.co.uk

Austin CVB
301 Congress, Suite 200, Austin, TX 78701, USA
Tel: (512) 474 5171 or (800) 926 2282 (toll-free).
Website: www.austintexas.org

Dallas CVB
325 North St Paul, Suite 700, Dallas, TX 75201, USA
Tel: (214) 571 1000 or 1301 (tourist information).
Website: www.visitdallas.com

Greater Houston Convention and Visitors Bureau
901 Bagby, Suite 100, Houston, TX 77002, USA
Tel: (713) 437 5200 or (800) 446 8786 (toll-free).
Website: www.visithoustontexas.com

Entertainment

FOOD & DRINK: Beef is widely featured – this being cattle country – but there is also a great variety of international cuisine including Chinese, French, Italian, Mexican and Spanish.
Regional specialities:
- Steak.
- Tex-Mex dishes.
NIGHTLIFE: Dallas has clubs, cabarets, discos, singles bars and corner pubs, with music ranging from classical to jazz and from country to contemporary rock. Some clubs are listed as 'private' – they are located in a 'dry' area and membership (usually available for a nominal fee) is required to be served alcohol. There are also some comedy clubs sprinkled throughout the city and others offer comedy and drama while customers dine. Fort Worth also has a number of nightclubs, but the musical emphasis here is on country & western music. **Billy Bob's Texas**, the world's largest honky-tonk nightclub, with a 6000-person capacity, plays host to some of the biggest names in country music in addition to having live bull riding. For an authentic Old West experience, the **White Elephant Saloon** offers live western entertainment. Houston's many nightspots range from big-name entertainment to supper club revues, pavement cafes, discos and singles bars. **Bayou Place** in downtown Houston is a popular night spot. Austin is noted for its nightly live music venues. Historic 6th Street takes on a lively atmosphere in the evenings as people go pub-crawling between venues catering for country & western, soul, R&B, rock 'n' roll and jazz music. San Antonio offers all sorts of musical entertainment, including traditional 'Tejano' sounds, Dixieland jazz, symphony concerts, country & western and college music. The **Paseo del Rio** is the centre for much of the city's nightlife.
SHOPPING: Dallas has more shopping centres per capita than any other US city and some of the largest shopping malls in the southwest. The elegant and original **Neiman Marcus** department store is now a popular tourist attraction. **Dallas Market Center** is one of the world's largest wholesale trade shopping centres and also offers fine restaurants. Both Dallas and Fort Worth have fine speciality shops. Nearby **Grapevine Mills Outlet Mall** sells discounted merchandise. World-class shopping is available in more than 300 stores at the **Galleria** shopping centre in Houston. The best buys are Western-style clothes, hats, boots, saddles and riding equipment. **Katy Mills Outlet Mall** carries discount name-brand fashions. Authentic Mexican folk art can be found throughout San Antonio, especially at **El Mercado**, patterned after an authentic Mexican market. Between San Antonio and Austin lies San Marcos, where the **Prime Outlet Mall** and **Tanger Outlet Mall** offer plenty of bargains.

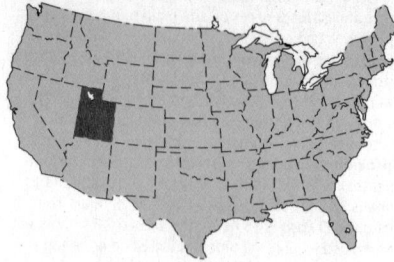

Utah

Time: Mountain (GMT - 7). *Daylight Saving Time* is observed.

Overview

Utah's attractions include canyons, colourful towns and breathtaking national parks. Salt Lake City is the world centre of The Church of Jesus Christ of Latter-day Saints. Utah, surrounded by the Wasatch Mountains, boasts historic buildings, churches, museums, science exhibitions and arts festivals. Other State attractions include Zion National Park around the Virgin River Canyon, with its temple-like rock formations; Canyonlands, Arches and Capitol Reef national parks; Timpanogos Cave; and the Dinosaur National Monument near Vernal. Utah has five national parks.

General Information

Nickname: Beehive State.
State bird: California Gull/Sea Gull.
State flower: Sego Lily.
CAPITAL: Salt Lake City.
Date of admission to the Union: 4 Jan 1896.
POPULATION: 2.47 million (official estimate 2005).
POPULATION DENSITY: 11.2 per sq km.
2004 total overseas arrivals/US ranking: 252,000/18

Climate

Utah enjoys a distinct four-season climate. In summer the days are hot, with cool nights. In winter, the temperatures are low with snow in the north. The climate varies from north to south and from desert to mountain. Summer days are hot in the desert but temperatures drop dramatically at night.
Required clothing: Heavyweight clothing for the winter months and lightweights (cottons and linens) for the summer months. Travellers will need extra clothes when travelling in the mountains in summer or winter.

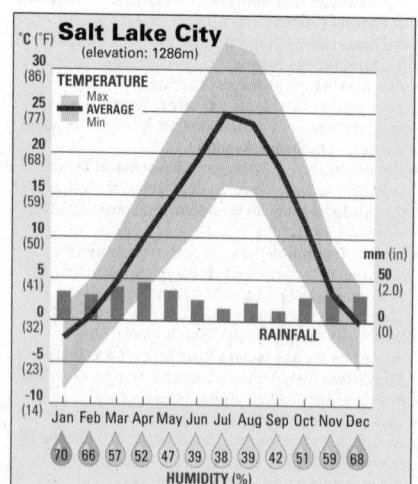

Travel - International

AIR:

 Main airports: *Salt Lake City International Airport (SLC)* (website: www.slcairport.com) is located 6km (4 miles) west of the city centre and 4 minutes west of Temple Square. *To/from the airport:* The Utah Transit Authority (website: www.utabus.com) operates a daily service (route 50) between the city centre and South and West Temple via the airport; other bus services are also available: route 53 runs between the city centre and Tooele/Grantsville via the airport, while route 56 runs from the airport to West Valley. *Redtail Aviation* offers

flights into Moab from the surrounding areas. Taxis, limousines and vans are readily available. There are Ground Transportation Information desks in both terminals, where hotel courtesy cars can be arranged. *Facilities:* ATMs, business centre and car hire.
RAIL:

 Salt Lake City is on *Amtrak's* daily 'California Zephyr' line (tel: (800) 872 7245 (toll-free); website: www.amtrak.com), which links Chicago with Emeryville (California). The station is located at 340 South 600 Street West; car hire is available. Other Utah destinations on this service are Green River, Helper and Provo.
ROAD:

 Greyhound (tel: (800) 231 2222 (toll-free); website: www.greyhound.com) is the main carrier. **Approximate bus travel times:** From Salt Lake City to *Las Vegas* is eight hours 30 minutes, and to *Los Angeles* is 15 hours 30 minutes. From Cedar City (near Zion National Park) to *Salt Lake City* is five hours, and to *Los Angeles* is 10 hours.
URBAN:

 In Salt Lake City, the *Utah Transit Authority (UTA)* (website: www.utabus.com) offers frequent bus services to the University of Utah campus, to Ogden, the suburbs, the airport and east to the mountain canyons and Provo. Journeys within downtown areas are free. Maps are available at libraries and the Visitors' Bureau. *UTA* also runs the *TRAX* tram system. A number of taxi companies operate in the city.

Top Things To See

- See the largest lake west of the Mississippi River, the **Great Salt Lake** (website: http://ut.water.usgs.gov/greatsaltlake). It is the second saltiest body of water in the world, after the Dead Sea. It stretches 148km (92 miles) north to south and is about 77km (48 miles) wide. Visit the **Great Lake State Park** (www.utah.com/stateparks/greatsaltlake.htm) to explore the area.
- Experience the natural scenic wonders of the **Wasatch-Cache National Forest** (website: www.fs.fed.us/r4/wcnf), the **East Canyon State Park** (website: www.utah.com/stateparks/east_canyon.htm), the **Willard Bay State Park** (website: www.utah.com/stateparks/willard_bay.htm), the **Lost Creek State Park** (website: www.utah.com/stateparks/lost_creek.htm), and the **Antelope Island State Park** (website: www.utah.com/stateparks/antelope_island.htm).
- Visit the 1500-year-old **Jardine Juniper**, the oldest juniper in the **Rocky Mountains**, 19km (12 miles) from **Logan** in **Logan Canyon** (website: www.utah.com/cities/logan.htm), and a short hike from **Wood Camp Campground** (website: www.go-utah.com/wood-camp-campground).
- Tour the **Museum of Church History and Art** (website: www.lds.org/churchhistory/museum) in **Salt Lake City**. The museum houses Mormon historical memorabilia, fine art sculptures and paintings.
- Also in the city, view the **Utah State History Museum** that houses State historical exhibits, featuring hundreds of photographs, some 3500 artefacts and other works of art. Other attractions include the **Marmalade Historic Hill District** (website: www.utah.com/culture/marmalade_district.htm), where many of the original pioneer homes can be found; the **Pioneer Memorial Museum** (website: www.dupinternational.org); and the **Utah Museum of Natural History** (website: www.umnh.utah.edu) at the **University of Utah**.
- Explore the **Timpanogos Cave National Monument** (website: www.nps.gov/tica) on the north slope of **Mount Timpanogos**. The monument's cave systems consist of three spectacularly decorated caves.
- Explore the **Drive-Through-the-Ages Geological Area** (website: www.go-utah.com/uintas-scenic-byway) that has rock layers that were laid down during a period of more than a billion years.
- Discover the **Dinosaur National Monument** (website: www.nps.gov/dino) sprawled across eastern Utah and into Colorado. Pittsburgh palaeontologist Earl Douglass began scouring the area for bones in 1908 and the quarry he excavated lies at the west end of the park.
- See the **Little Sahara Recreation Area** (website: www.utah.com/playgrounds/little_sahara.htm). It has more than 20,000 acres (8092 hectares) of free-moving sand dunes.
- Delight in **Navajo Lake** (website: www.goutah.com/Navajo-Lake) and the 421-hectare (1040-acre) **Joshua Tree Natural Area** near the Arizona border.
- Take the family through **Bryce Canyon National Park** (website: www.nps.gov/brca). The park shows thousands of delicately carved spires rising in brilliant colours from amphitheatres.

- Explore the **Canyonland National Park** (website: www.nps.gov/cany), which is divided, into three sections by the Green and Colorado rivers. The **Needles Region** contains spires, arches and canyons and Native American ruins. The **Island in the Sky** (website: www.nps.gov/cany/island) offers breathtaking views of the surrounding mountains and canyons. The most remote district of the park is the rugged **Maze** area.

Top Things To Do

- Tour the **American West Heritage Center** (website: www.americanwestcenter.org), at the foot of the **Wellsville Mountains**, which includes the **Man and His Bread Museum** and the **Ronald V Jensen Living Historical Farm**, an authentic Mormon pioneer farm. Daily activities here are performed exactly as they would have been in 1917. The centre is currently a massive 65 hectares (160 acres) and intends to add another 71 hectares (175 acres).
- See **Salt Lake Temple** (website: www.ldschurchtemples.com). The temple occupies a full city block in Salt Lake City. It houses the Mormon Tabernacle, Assembly Hall, various statues, monuments and two visitor centres.
- Explore **Salt Lake City** (website: www.visitsaltlake.com). The city is a thriving modern city whose proximity to the mountains and lakes makes it a popular base for outdoor enthusiasts. The city is also the spiritual centre of The Church of Jesus Christ of Latter-day Saints and home to the *Mormon Tabernacle Choir* (website: www.mormontabernaclechoir.org).
- Ride the year-round **Snowbird Tram** (website: www.snowbird.com) that rises 870m (2854ft) to the top of the 3300m (10827ft) **Hidden Peak** with its 360-degree view of Utah's mountain ranges and valleys.
- Drive the **Alpine Loop Scenic Byway** (website: www.utah.com/byways/alpine_loop.htm). It is one of Utah's most popular summer drive destinations.
- Experience the **Flaming Gorge National Recreation Area** (website: www.utah.com/nationalsites/flaming_gorge.htm) which stretches from **Ashley National Forest** (www.fs.fed.us/r4/ashley) to the south Wyoming desert. Recreational activities available include fishing, boating and hiking.
- Journey to the **Glen Canyon National Recreation Area** (website: www.nps.gov/glca). Some of the outdoor recreation available is boating, fishing, swimming, backcountry hiking and 4-wheel drive trips.
- Visit one of the nation's oldest national parks, **Zion National Park** (website: www.nps.gov/zion), offering miles of trails. The park has over593 sq km (229 sq miles) of canyons and soaring cliffs. It is a place of plant and animal diversity.
- Start off your trip in **Moab** (website: www.discovermoab.com), a great base for exploring Utah's southeast. The town boasts the **Hole 'n the Rock** (website: www.moab-utah.com/holeintherock), a 14-room house carved out of a sandstone cliff; the **Dan O'Laurie Museum** (website: www.moab-utah.com/danolaurie/museum.html); and **Pale Creek Ranch**, which offers trail rides into the **La Sal Mountains** (website: www.go-utah.com/la_sal_mountains).
- Ski at one of the resorts in Utah. The State has 14 ski resorts, seven of which are less than an hour's drive from Salt Lake City. These include **Alta Ski Resort** (website: www.alta.com), **Beaver Mountain** (website: www.skithebeav.com), **Snowbird Ski and Summer Resort** (website: www.snowbird.com), **Park City Mountain Resort** (website: www.parkcitymountain.com), **The Canyons** (website: www.thecanyons.com), and **Deer Valley Resort** (website: www.deervalley.com). Seven snowmobile complexes are located across the State, linking hundreds of miles of trails systems.

TOURIST INFORMATION

Utah Office of Tourism
300 North State Street, Capitol Hill,
Salt Lake City, UT 84114, USA
Tel: (801) 538 1030 *or* (800) 200 1160 (toll-free).
Website: www.utah.com *or* www.utah.gov

Utah State Parks and Recreation
1594 West North Temple, Suite 116,
Salt Lake City, UT 84114, USA
Tel: (801) 538 7220 *or* (800) 322 7220 (toll-free; reservations).
Website: www.stateparks.utah.gov

Entertainment

FOOD & DRINK: The centre of Salt Lake City offers a variety of ethnic restaurants, with inexpensive eateries on the outer fringe. Each community has its share of interesting restaurants with varied cuisine.
Regional specialities:
- Sushi.
- Steak.
- Cappuccino.
NIGHTLIFE: Salt Lake City and Park City offer many restaurants and clubs with live music. Night skiing is also a popular activity in Utah. Slopes are lit at night and used by skiers of all ages. The annual *Sundance Film Festival* in January in Park City and surrounding venues draws many celebrities and others. In Salt Lake City, the *Mormon Tabernacle Choir* presents free weekly performances of inspirational music and thought in the acoustically unique Mormon Tabernacle in Temple Square.
SHOPPING: Salt Lake City has one of the country's largest downtown covered shopping malls, **Crossroads Plaza**, with four floors of restaurants and boutiques. **The Cooperative Mercantile Institution** in Salt Lake City was the first department store in the West, developed out of Brigham Young's efforts to organise city merchants. Speciality shops are abundant in many Utah towns. Ski shops also can be found in major skiing areas.

Vermont

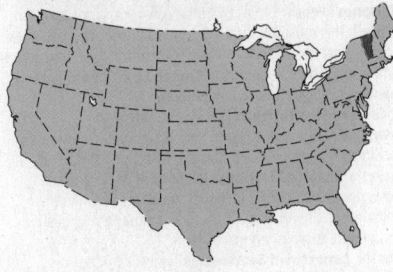

Time: Eastern (GMT - 5). *Daylight Saving Time* is observed.

Overview

Vermont is a State that is best enjoyed outdoors. Although it is the only New England State without a seashore, its border with Lake Champlain more than compensates. The largest city, Burlington, affords magnificent views of the water, and has many sporting and recreation areas. Vermont is the USA's third-largest ski State, with 16 alpine resorts and just under 30 for cross-country skiing.

General Information

Nickname: Green Mountain State.
State bird: Hermit Thrush.
State flower: Red Clover.
CAPITAL: Montpelier.
Date of admission to the Union: 4 Mar 1791.
POPULATION: 623,050 (official estimate 2005).
POPULATION DENSITY: 25 per sq km.
2004 total overseas arrivals/US rating: Under 72,000/36.

Climate

Sunny and warm summers, followed by cold winters with abundant snowfall.
Required clothing: Heavyweight clothing from November to March/April. Cottons and linens during the summer months.

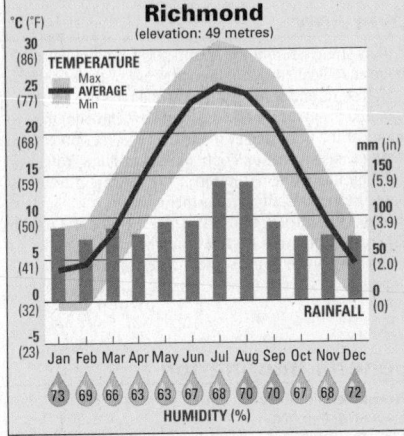

Richmond (elevation: 49 metres)

Top Things To See & Do

- Visit **Burlington**, the State's largest city. Wander along the lively waterfront, cycle by the shore, or take advantage of the many watersports on offer.
- Enjoy beautiful **Lake Champlain**. There are three different ferries crossing from points in Vermont to New York and back departing two to three times per hour each day. **Missisquoi National Wildlife Refuge** and **Burton Island State Park** lie at the northern end of the lake and offer great camping and hiking opportunities. The best views, however, are to the south at **Mount Philo State Park**, Vermont's oldest State park, which affords magnificent views of the water, and has many sporting and recreation areas.
- Ski Vermont's highest peak, **Mount Mansfield**, the location of the area's most popular ski resort, **Stowe**, which offers a choice of slopes suitable for both beginners and thrill-seekers. In the summer, skis are exchanged for mountain bikes and hiking boots. Fishing is also a hugely popular pastime, with rods and reels available to hire locally.
- Take to the water at **Brattleboro**, in southeast Vermont, where the sporting action revolves around the West and Connecticut rivers. Canoeing is the best way to explore the lush green countryside. Other less energetic attractions include the **Brattleboro Museum & Art Center**, and the **Shelburne Museum**, heading back up lake towards Burlington.
- Discover other State attractions including **Shelburne Heritage Park**, with its early New England buildings; **Green Mountain National Forest**, with its historical trails and drives; and the ski destinations of **Mount Snow**, **Jay Peak**, **Smugglers' Notch** and **Sugarbush**.

TOURIST INFORMATION

Vermont Department of Tourism and Marketing
6 Baldwin Street, Drawer 33, Montpelier, VT 05633, USA
Tel: (802) 828 3676 *or* (800) 837 6668 (toll-free).
Website: www.vermontvacation.com

Discover New England in the UK
c/o Cellet PR, 16 Dover Street, London, W1S 4LR, UK
Tel: (020) 7491 1112 *or* (01564) 794 999 (brochure request).
Website: www.discovernewengleand.org *or* www.vermont-uk.com

Virginia

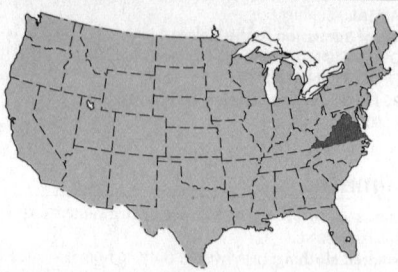

Time: Eastern (GMT - 5). *Daylight Saving Time* is observed.

Overview

Virginia stretches from the Atlantic Ocean to the Blue Ridge and Allegheny Mountains. It is one of the country's most historic and scenic States. Driving trails link more than 250 Civil War sites across Virginia. Richmond, the capital of the Confederacy in the Civil War, has many fine old buildings and cultural options. Williamsburg, Yorktown and Jamestown (the birthplace of the USA) are three of its most historic sites, situated further east.

Shenandoah Valley, with its caverns, waterfalls and popular resorts, is to the west. Norfolk is an important Atlantic seaport and home to the world's largest naval base. Virginia boasts nearly 60 wineries offering tastings and tours.

General Information

Nickname: Old Dominion State.
State bird: Cardinal.
State flower: Dogwood.
CAPITAL: Richmond.
Date of admission to the Union: 25 Jun 1788 (original 13 States; date of ratification of the Constitution).
POPULATION: 7.57 million.
POPULATION DENSITY: 68.3 per sq km.
2004 total overseas arrivals/US ranking: 235,000/21.

Climate

Generally speaking, Virginia enjoys pleasantly hot summers and relatively mild but crisp winters, with moderate rainfall throughout the year. Average coastal temperatures in July and August rarely exceed 90°F (32°C), while in winter there is often snow. The mountainous areas in the west of the region provide welcome respite from the higher temperatures of summer.

Required clothing: Warm winter clothes are needed in the coldest months. Light-to-medium weights are advised for the summer. Rainwear may be useful.

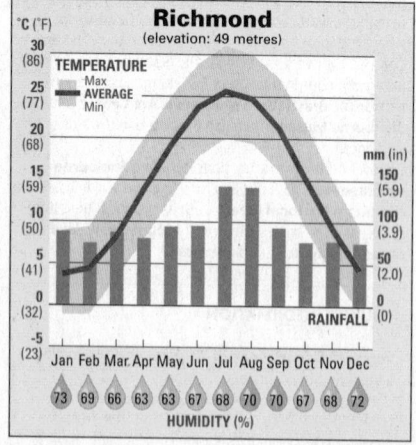

Travel - International

AIR:

Main airports: There are flights from US and major European cities into Virginia's *Washington Dulles International Airport (IAD)* (website: www.metwashairports.com) and Maryland's *Baltimore/Washington International Airport (BWI)* (website: www.bwiairport.com). Washington, DC is also served by North American flights via its *Ronald Reagan Washington National Airport* (website: www.metwashairports.com); see the *Washington, DC* section for airport details and flight times.

Norfolk International Airport (ORF) (website: www.norfolkairport.com) is located 8km (5 miles) northeast of downtown Norfolk with domestic departures to a number of cities throughout the USA. *To/from the airports:* Shuttle bus service and taxis are available. *Facilities:* ATMs, business services and car hire.

RAIL:

Amtrak (tel: (800) 872 7245 (toll-free); website: www.amtrak.com) rail service passes through Virginia on two main north–south routes, linking New Orleans (via Atlanta and Charlottesville) and Miami (via Richmond) with Washington, DC and New York City. A couple of services (originating in Newport News) continue on to Boston.

Approximate rail travel times: From Richmond to *Washington, DC* is two hours 10 minutes, to *New York* is six hours 30 minutes, and to *Boston* is 10 hours 20 minutes.

ROAD:

Located mid-way between New York and Miami, Virginia boasts well-maintained major highways as well as some of the nation's oldest and most scenic byways.

Bus: *Greyhound* (tel: (800) 231 2222 (toll-free); website: www.greyhound.com) buses run from most larger towns to destinations across the USA. A number of East Coast routes are run in partnership with *Carolina Trailways*.

Approximate bus travel times: From Richmond to *Norfolk* is two hours 30 minutes, to *Baltimore* is three hours 45 minutes, and to *Philadelphia* is four hours 45 minutes.

Top Things To See

- Visit **Arlington National Cemetery** (website: www.arlingtonnationalcemetery.org), where an eternal flame burns at the gravesite of John F Kennedy.
- See the **Iwo Jima Marine Memorial** (website: www.nps.gov/gwmp/usmc.htm), dedicated to all Marines who have given their lives in defence of the USA.
- Tour George Washington's **Mount Vernon Estate** (website: www.mountvernon.org). Enjoy the gardens that overlook the **Potomac River**.
- Explore the intriguing **Edgar Allan Poe Museum** (website: www.poemuseum.org) in **Richmond**. The museum highlights his life and career with photos, relics and writings.
- View some of the beautiful mansions in the state of Virginia. Thomas Jefferson's beloved **Monticello** (website: www.monticello.org), the graceful, domed mansion he lived in for 40 years, can be visited at **Charlottesville**. Minutes away is **Ash Lawn** (website: www.ashlawnhighland.org), the 216-hectare (535-acre) plantation which belonged to President James Monroe. The mansion and grounds of **Montpelier** (website: www.montpelier.org), where James Madison, 'Father of the US Constitution', lived with his wife, Dolley, can be found in **Orange County**.
- Explore **Cumberland Gap National Historical Park** (website: www.nps.gov/cuga). Here, the adventurous Daniel Boone travelled the famous pass to the west.
- Stop at the **Birthplace of Country Music Alliance Museum** (website: www.birthplaceofcountrymusic.org) in **Bristol**. This museum provides a good introduction to the rich musical heritage of this region heard in local barns and rural music sheds such as the **Carter Family Fold** (website: www.carterfamilyfold.org) in **Hiltons**.
- Follow the **Blue Ridge Parkway** (website: www.blueridgeparkway.org). This drive, one of America's most scenic, takes visitors through lush farmland.
- View the **Colonial National Historical Park** (website: www.nps.gov/colo) and archaeological dig at Jamestown. You will see the remains of the first permanent English settlement, established in 1607.
- See the **Jamestown Settlement** (website:

www.historyisfun.org). It has a full-scale replica of **James Fort** on display, along with reproductions of three 17th-century ships that brought the English settlers to Virginia.
- Enter the **Virginia Air and Space Center** (website: www.vasc.org) and come face-to-face with the Apollo 12 Command Module and a D-9 passenger jet.
- Travel back in time to **'Colonial Williamsburg'** (website: www.history.org). Formerly the State capital, Williamsburg is the largest restored 18th-century town in America and is home to **William and Mary** (website:www.wm.edu), the second-oldest college in the USA.
- Follow the **Chesapeake Bay Bridge-Tunnel** (website: www.cbbt.com). It leads to Virginia's Eastern Shore, a 112km- (70 mile-) long peninsula that is bordered by the Atlantic on one side and **Chesapeake Bay** on the other.

Top Things To Do

- Take a cruise on the **Potomac River**. Trips afford scenic views of Alexandria, Washington, DC and the Mount Vernon Estate.
- Take a walking tour of **Richmond**. It is the State capital and was also the Capital of the Confederacy. This compact city is ideal for walking tours of historic districts and is ringed by Civil War battlegrounds.
- Spend the day at **Paramount's Kings Dominion** theme park (website: www.kingsdominion.com), 32km (20 miles) north of Richmond. New for 2006, is the *Italian Job Turbo Coaster*.
- Travel the **Skyline Drive**, which runs through **Shenandoah National Park** and across the crests of the **Blue Ridge Mountains** (website: www.nps.gov/blri). A wide range of outdoor activities, from hiking and canoeing to horse riding and special naturalist programmes, are on offer in and around the park.
- Enjoy the fun and sun at **Virginia Beach** (website: www.vbfun.com), a popular seaside town offering a range of attractions and facilities.
- Visit **First Landing/Seashore State Park** (website: www.dcr.state.va.us/parks). The park offers miles of seashore, picnic areas, camping and a beautiful biking trail.
- Experience **False Cape State Park** (website: www.dcr.state.va.us/parks), an ocean-to-freshwater bay habitat, accessible only by boat or an 8km (5-mile) bike ride, and offers excellent opportunities for walking and camping.
- Ride the new *Curse of DarKastle* thrill ride at **Busch Gardens** (website: www.buschgardens.org) in Williamsburg.
- Try whitewater canoeing, popular on the **Shenandoah, Maury** and **James** rivers. Rapids as high as Class IV are found along urban Richmond's stretch of the **James River**.

TOURIST INFORMATION

Virginia Tourism Corporation
901 East Byrd Street, 19th Floor, Richmond, VA 23219, USA
Tel: (804) 786 2051 *or* (800) 847 4882 (toll-free).
Website: www.virginia.org

Virginia Tourism Corporation in the UK
1st Floor, 182-184 Addington Road, South Croydon, Surrey CR2 8LB, UK
Tel: (020) 8651 4743.
Website: www.virginia.org

Entertainment

FOOD & DRINK: The region excels in local seafood and in the traditional cuisine of the cities.
Regional specialities:
- Oysters.
- Blue Crabs.

NIGHTLIFE: Richmond's comedy clubs, theatres, rock and jazz venues and pubs offer a diverse nightlife. In Virginia Beach, **Peabody's** and **Hot Tuna** are popular clubs.

SHOPPING: Among the top attractions for visitors to Virginia are the quality and the quantity of its shopping, particularly in the discount and outlet categories. A wide range of shops is found in the malls throughout Virginia, notably at **The Fashion Center at Pentagon City** in Arlington, **Tysons Corner Center** and the **Potomac Mills** outlet mall in Woodbridge.

Richmond
(elevation: 49 metres)

Washington, DC

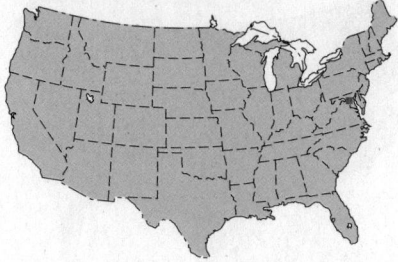

Time: Eastern (GMT - 5). *Daylight Saving Time* is observed.

Overview

"DC" stands for 'District of Columbia', not a state but an administrative district created specifically to avoid having the capital city in any one state. Washington, DC is a city of green parks, wide tree-lined streets, white marble buildings and, surprising for a US city, no skyscrapers, which gives it a more European air. It is the centre for visiting diplomats and has one of the largest concentrations of hotel and motel rooms in the country. Tourism is the leading private industry and business interests are increasingly attracted by the many light-industrial, high-tech and research companies now moving into the region. The 'Metro area' refers to the District of Columbia and surrounding counties and cities in Maryland and Virginia.

General Information

Nickname: None.
State bird: Wood Thrush.
State flower: American Beauty Rose.
CAPITAL: N/A.
Senate appoval date of the federal city:: 1 July 1790.
POPULATION: 550,521 (official estimate 2005).
POPULATION DENSITY: 3110 per sq km.
2004 Total overseas arrivals/US ranking: 578,376/9.

Climate

Summers are very warm, with highs in July of 21-32°C (75-90°F). Although generally mild, winter temperatures can be quite low, ranging from -4-4°C (24-40°F) in January. Rainfall is moderate throughout the year.

Required clothing: Heavy clothing and extra bundling for the winter months. Cottons and linens advised for the summer months. Rain gear might be advisable.

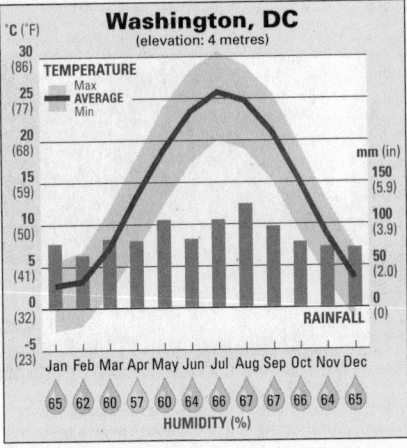

Travel - International

AIR:

 Main airports: *Washington-Dulles International (IAD)* (website: www.metwashairports.com) is 43km (27 miles) from the city (in Virginia; travel time – 50 minutes). *To/from the airport:* The *Washington Flyer Coach Service* operates every 30 minutes daily 0545-2215 (with a reduced service at the weekend) between the airport and the West Falls Church *Metrorail* (subway) station. Tickets may be purchased from the airport's Ground Transportation Center ticket counter; the bus departs from the Main Terminal (door 4). A *Metrobus* service is available at the station to areas not served by Metrorail. Taxis are also available. *Facilities:* ATMs, car hire, and currency exchange.
Baltimore-Washington International Airport (BWI) (website: www.bwiairport.com) is located 48km (30 miles) from Washington, DC (travel time – 38 minutes). *To/from the airport:* A frequent shuttle train service is provided between the airport terminal and the airport's own rail station (BWI Rail Station), where *Amtrak* and *MARC* services to the city are available. *MARC* trains also run to a number of other destinations. A *SuperShuttle* bus departs every hour from the lower level; tickets can be bought from the Ground Transportation Desk; services to other destinations are also available. Metrobus express route B30 runs every 40 minutes daily to Green Belt *Metrorail* station for US$3. The Greenbelt *Metrorail* station connects to other stations throughout the city, as well as Virginia, Montgomery and Prince George Counties. A daily light-rail service is available to downtown Baltimore and Hunt Valley. The *Airport Shuttle* offers a door-to-door service in the State of Maryland. Taxi services are available on the lower level near each exit; average fares are US$63 (to Washington, DC) and US$103 (to Washington-Dulles International Airport). Limousines and luxury sedans are also available at the airport. *Facilities:* ATMs, car hire and currency exchange.

Domestic airports: *Ronald Reagan Washington National (DCA)* (website: www.metwashairports.com) receives transfer connections from other US gateways. It is 5km (3 miles) southwest of the city. *To/from the airport:* *Metrorail*, the region's rapid transit system, operates frequent subway trains from its National Airport station (opposite terminals B and C) to a variety of stops in both the city and the Maryland and Virginia suburbs. *Metrobus* services are also available at the *Metrorail* station, to areas not served by the train. *SuperShuttle* operates a service to Union Station. Taxi and limousine are also available. *Facilities:* ATMs, car hire, and currency exchange.
Approximate flight times: From Washington, DC to *Honolulu* is 13 hours 40 minutes, to *London* is six hours 50 minutes, and to *Los Angeles* is five hours 40 minutes.

RAIL:

 Amtrak (tel: (800) 872 7245 (toll-free); website: www.amtrak.com) operates long-distance services through Washington, DC. The principal corridor is the New York–Philadelphia–Baltimore–Washington, DC route, with frequent fast trains. There are also routes to Chicago via Pittsburgh or Cincinnati; New Orleans via Charlotte and Atlanta; and Miami via Raleigh or Charleston. There are also local trains to the Philadelphia area. The travel time to New York is three hours by *Metroliner* or two hours 45 minutes on the *Amtrak Acela Express*. The main station is Union Station, 50 Massachusetts Avenue NE.

ROAD:

 Greyhound (tel: (800) 231 2222 (toll-free); website: www.greyhound.com) services arrive and depart from the modern bus terminal at 1005 First Street NE.
Approximate driving times: From Washington, DC to Miami is 22 hours, to Dallas is 28 hours, and to Seattle is 58 hours. All times are based on non-stop driving at or below the applicable speed limits.
Approximate bus travel times: From Washington, DC to *Philadelphia* is three hours 30 minutes, to *New York* is four hours 30 minutes, and to *Knoxville* is 12 hours 30 minutes. The main service provider is *Greyhound*.

URBAN:

 The *Washington Metropolitan Area Transit Authority (WMATA)* (website: www.wmata.com) provides bus and rail transit service in Washington, DC and neighbouring communities. The Metro (subway) system offers quick and comfortable transport within the city centre; fares are zonal with a surcharge during peak hours. Lines extend into the suburban areas of Maryland and northern Virginia. There are also suburban and central bus services. It is possible to transfer from Metro to bus without additional charge (except during rush hour), but not from bus to Metro. Taxis are available within the city area; fares are again zonal (and comparatively cheap by big-city standards). Most major car rental and motor camper rental agencies have offices in Washington, DC.

Travel Advice

Following the terrorist attack on the Pentagon of 11 September 2001 and then subsequent anthrax alerts and sniper attacks in 2002, security throughout the capital is on heightened alert. Travellers may experience extensive waits or cancellations of tours around sensitive public buildings. General information can be obtained from the nearest US embassy or from the Foreign Commonwealth Office (website: www.fco.gov.uk); the Washington, DC Convention and Tourism Corporation (website: www.washington.org) and from the District of Columbia's (website: www.dc.gov), which highlights specific closure of federal buildings and the status of different tours.

Credit: ©JakeMcGuire.com / Washington, DC Convention & Tourism Corporation (WCTC)

Credit: ©JakeMcGuire.com/
Washington, DC Convention & Tourism Corporation (WCTC)

Top Things To See

- See the **White House** (website: www.whitehouse.gov), which has been the home of every US President since 1800 and is visited by more than 1 million people every year.
- Visit the **Tidal Basin** (website: www.nps.gov/nacc/cherry/indexB.htm), a beautiful lake famous for its Japanese cherry trees, lying just to the southwest.
- View the **Lincoln Memorial** (website: www.nps.gov/linc), dedicated to President Abraham Lincoln. The Gettysburg Address is inscribed on the south wall of the monument.
- See the **Jefferson Memorial** (website: www.nps.gov/thje). This monument is in tribute to President Thomas Jefferson, the author of the Declaration of Independence. Open-air concerts are held at the Jefferson Memorial in the summer.
- Climb the **Washington Monument** (website: www.nps.gov/wamo), which, at 169m/555ft, is the tallest masonry structure in the world. This monument was built for President George Washington, 'Father of his Country'.
- See the modern **National Gallery of Art**, with its stunning East Building designed by the world-famous architect I M Pei and its beautiful six-acre sculpture garden.
- Tour the **Capitol** (website: www.aoc.gov), where Senators and Representatives meet under a magnificent 55m (180ft) dome to shape US legislative policy.
- Inspect the **Arlington National Cemetery** (website: www.arlingtoncemetery.org). It contains the graves of 175,000 US soldiers who fought in wars from the American Revolution onwards.
- See the **J Edgar Hoover Building** (the FBI's headquarters) at Ninth Street and Pennsylvania Avenue.
- Explore **Rock Creek Park** (website: www.nps.gov/rock), established in 1890 'for the benefit and enjoyment of the people of the United States'. Visitors can enjoy a picnic, hiking, playing soccer, and biking along with other outdoor activities. While at the park, view **The Old Stone House**, a museum formed to celebrate the everyday life of middle class colonial America.
- Encounter the **US Supreme Court** (website: www.supremecourtus.gov), the highest court in the country.

Top Things To Do

- Explore the **Smithsonian Institution** (website: www.si.edu), which includes the old **Museum of Natural History**.
- Spend the day at The **National Zoo** (website:www.nationalzoo.si.edu). Enjoy over 5000 species of animals including Tai Shan, the baby panda bear.
- Experience many recreational activities, including boat trips, on the **Potomac River** (the jetty is to the south of the Lincoln Memorial).
- Explore the **Constitution Gardens** (website:www.nps.gov/coga), with more than 50 acres of trees and lawns.
- Step into the **International Spy Museum** (website: www.spymuseum.org) with its collection of treason and other historical espionage.
- Head for picturesque **Georgetown** (website: www.georgetowndc.com). The area is one of DC's liveliest spots, and the cobblestone streets, cafes and lovely riverside walk make this a pleasant area in which to wander.

- Take in a programme at the **National Theatre** (website: www.nationaltheatre.org) or the **Ford Theatre** (website: www.nps.gov/foth).
- Enjoy a play at the **John F Kennedy Center for the Performing Arts** (website: www.kennedy-center.org). It stands at the foot of New Hampshire Avenue, overlooking the Potomac River. Here there are four theatres for live performances of opera, concerts, musical plays, drama and festival occasions; free performances are held every day of the year from 6pm at the **Millennium Stage**. A fifth theatre houses the **American Film Institute**.
- Listen to one of the US military bands play free concerts at the **Washington Monument**, the **Capitol**, and the **Navy Memorial** during the summer.

TOURIST INFORMATION

Washington, DC Convention & Tourism Corporation
901 Seventh Street NW, 4th Floor, Washington, DC 20001, USA
Tel: (202) 789 7000 or (800) 422 8644 (toll-free).
Website: www.washington.org

Entertainment

FOOD & DRINK: Washington, DC has a renowned selection of excellent restaurants and almost any national cuisine can be found.
Regional specialities:
- Sushi.
- Steaks.
- Cappucino.
NIGHTLIFE: Washington DC enjoys a growing number of nightclubs with live entertainment. There are, however, numerous bars and discos in central Washington, Adams-Morgan, Georgetown and the suburbs.
SHOPPING: There are several shopping areas in Washington, DC. A collection of self-contained shops known as the '**Shops at National Place**' can be found off F Street, between 11th and 15th Streets; Connecticut Avenue (between K Street and Dupont Circle) has many speciality shops; and Georgetown offers a wide range of boutiques, bookshops, antique dealers, arts and crafts shops, and pavement stalls as well as a very attractive mall on M Street. More traditional malls include the Pentagon City Mall, located in Arlington, VA (15 minutes by Metro from the downtown area), and the Mazza Gallerie, at the corner of Wisconsin and Western Avenues. Some of the Government buildings offer unique souvenirs in gift shops open to the public.

Credit: ©JakeMcGuire.com/
Washington, DC Convention
& Tourism Corporation (WCTC)

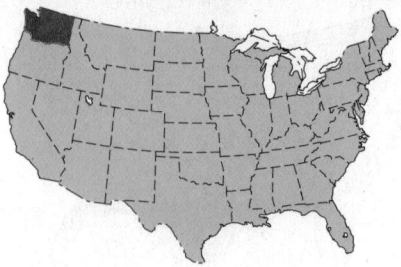

Washington State

Time: Pacific (GMT – 8), *Daylight Saving Time* is observed.

Overview

Washington State, bordering Canada and the Pacific Ocean, offers some of the nation's finest scenery for outdoor recreation. It has the second-highest population of any western State, yet visitors can travel from any city centre to peaceful countryside within minutes. The Snake and Columbia rivers flow through eastern Washington before joining to cut a passage through the Cascades, the north–south mountain range that dominates the centre of the State, rising to 4392m (14,411ft) at Mount Rainier. There are many fine beaches and small resorts on the Pacific coast. Much of the State is covered by coniferous forest. Holiday highlights include yachting on Puget Sound, hiking along the Pacific Crest National Scenic Trail and mountain climbing in the Cascades and the Olympic Mountains.

General Information

Nickname: Evergreen State.
State bird: Willow Goldfinch.
State flower: Coast Rhododendron.
CAPITAL: Olympia.
Date of admission to the Union: 11 Nov 1889.
POPULATION: 6.29 million (population estimate 2005).
POPULATION DENSITY: 34 per sq km.
2004 total overseas arrivals/US ranking: 300,000/15.

Climate

Washington has two distinct climate zones. Summer days west of the Cascades rarely rise above 26°C (79°F), and winter days seldom drop below 8°C (46°F) while the east of the State has warm summers and cool winters.
Required clothing: Warm winter clothes are needed in the coldest months. Light-to-medium weights are advised for the summer. An umbrella can come in handy any time of year.

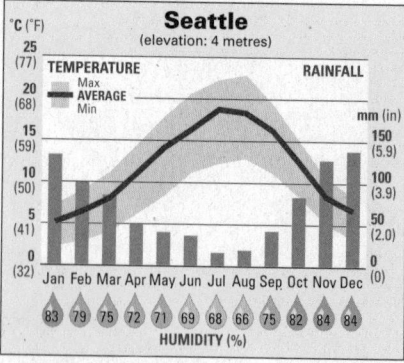

Travel - International

AIR:

Main airport: *Seattle-Tacoma International (SEA)* (website: www.portseattle.org/seatac) is 22km (14 miles) south of the city (travel time – 20 minutes). *To/from the airport*: Shuttles and buses link the airport to points throughout the city, running continuously 24-hours; a door-to-door service is available from *Shuttle Express*, serving a variety of destinations, including Seattle and Tacoma. The *Airport Express Gray Line* departs twice an hour to downtown Seattle hotels. *Metro Transit* offers a public bus service to Seattle, while *Sound Transit* has regional services. The Downtown Seattle Transit Tunnel closed for two years in September 2005 to build *Link* light rail between SeaTac and downtown Seattle. All buses normally operating in the tunnel will move to surface streets in downtown Seattle. Taxis are available. The airport Ground Transportation Information desk is located

on the third floor of the parking garage. *Facilities:* Car hire, currency exchange, and Internet access.
Approximate flight times: From Seattle to *London* is nine hours five minutes, and to *San Francisco* is one hour 50 minutes. .

SEA:

 Washington State Ferries (website: www.wsdot.wa.gov/ferries) link Seattle with the Olympic Peninsula, Bainbridge Island and other points in the region. The *Victoria Clipper* (website: www.victoriaclipper.com) links Victoria and Vancouver (British Columbia, Canada) to Seattle via high-speed catamarans.

RAIL:

 Three *Amtrak* (tel: (800) 872 7245 (toll-free); website: www.amtrak.com) lines cross the State. The daily 'Empire Builder' from Chicago splits at Spokane, with onward services to Seattle and Portland (Oregon). There are four trains daily from Seattle to Portland; the 'Coast Starlight' continues on to Los Angeles, while the daily 'Amtrak Cascades' service comes from Eugene-Springfield (Oregon) and heads north to Vancouver, British Columbia via Tacoma (travel time – four hours); see the *California* and *Illinois* sections for other travel times. The Seattle station is located at 303 South Jackson Street; most major car hire firms are available.

ROAD:

 Greyhound (tel: (800) 231 2222 (toll-free); website: www.greyhound.com) is the main carrier. **Approximate driving times:** From Seattle to *Portland* is three hours, to *Los Angeles* is 44 hours, and to *Miami* is 69 hours.
Approximate bus travel times: From Seattle to *Spokane* is seven hours.

URBAN:

 Seattle has an excellent bus system. An underground bus tunnel operates through central Seattle from the International District to the *Convention Center*, with stops at Pioneer Square, the financial district and the *Westlake Center*. A high-speed monorail links the city centre with the *Seattle Center*. Public transport is free in the centre of downtown. Taxis and car hire are also available.

Top Things To See

- Visit **Seattle** (website: www.seeseattle.org). The State's largest city is surrounded by the waters of **Lake Washington** and **Puget Sound** and enjoys spectacular views of **The Cascades** and the **Olympic Mountains**. The waterfront area is known for its seafood restaurants, shops and water excursions.
- Tour **Pioneer Square** (website: www.pioneersquare.org), a 17-square-block **National Historic District** showcasing Seattle's early history with shops, art galleries, restaurants and a unique underground tour.
- Shop at **Pike Place Public Market** (website: www.pikeplacemarket.org) situated just above the waterfront. The oldest continually operating farmers' market in the USA features abundant seafood and produce, as well as handcrafted items from the Pacific Northwest.
- Enjoy glacier-studded mountains, rainforests, lakes, streams and miles of unspoiled coastline at **Olympic National Park** (website: www.nps.gov/olym).
- See **Mount St Helens** in Gifford Pinchot National Park (website: www.fs.fed.us.gpnf), the site of the infamous volcanic eruption of 1980, which left a gigantic crater in the mountain's north flank. It is possible to take short trips by light aircraft over the summit.

Top Things To Do

- Take in a show at the **Seattle Center** (website: www.seattlecenter.com). Built for the 1962 World Fair, it is the city's cultural heart, the home of opera, symphony, ballet and repertory theatre companies. It also contains the 185m- (605ft-) tall **Space Needle** (website: www.spaceneedle.com) with an observation deck, restaurant and cocktail bar.
- Hop on an excursion to **Tillicum Village** (website: www.tillicumvillage.com), 13km (8 miles) from downtown Seattle. Harbour tours and fishing excursions are easily available.
- Spend the day at **Woodland Park Zoo** (website: www.zoo.org) in Seattle. The zoo houses over 300 types of wildlife and is highly regarded for its 'natural' displays and habitats for its wildlife.
- Interact with juvenile rockfish, sea stars, and plankton on a 13-ft wet table at the **Seattle Aquarium** (website: www.seattleaquarium.org). Other exhibits include the *Underwater Dome*, *Marine Mammals* and *Puget Sound Orcas: Family Activity Center*.
- Explore **Mount Rainier National Park** (website: www.nps.gov/mora). It offers breathtaking views, skiing and other wintersports.
- Ride the historic 1909 Looff Carrousel at **Riverfront Park**

(website: www.spokaneriverfrontpark.com) in **Spokane**. Other attractions include an **IMAX Theatre**, an **Ice Palace**, **Clock Tower** and different thrill rides.
- Taste the grapes of the heart of the region's wine country in the cities of **Kennewick**, **Pasco**, **Richland** and **Yakima**.
- Watch a ball game at Safeco Field when the **Seattle Mariners** (website: http://seattle.mariners.mlb.com) baseball team takes to the plate.

TOURIST INFORMATION

Washington State Tourism
PO Box 42525, Olympia, WA 98504, USA
Tel: (360) 725-4028 *or* (800) 544 1800 (toll-free).
Website: www.experiencewashington.com

Washington State Information in the UK
c/o First Public Relations, Molasses House, Clove Hitch Quay, Plantation Wharf, London SW11 3TN, UK
Tel: (020) 7978 5233.
Website: www.firstpr.co.uk

Entertainment

FOOD & DRINK: Seattle has more than 2000 restaurants serving many different types of cuisine.
Regional specialities:
- Seafood.
NIGHTLIFE: Jazz spots, nightclubs and discos are scattered throughout Seattle.
SHOPPING: Westlake Center, Nordstrom, the Bon Marché and Pacific Palace are among the major malls and department stores located in the heart of Seattle's retail district. Other interesting shopping areas include **Pioneer Square**, the **Waterfront** and **Pike Place Market**.

West Virginia

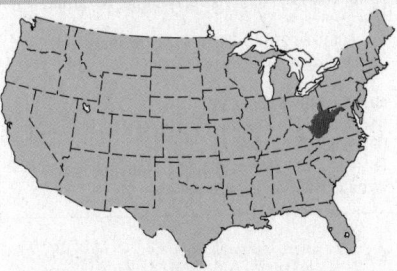

Time: Eastern (GMT - 5). *Daylight Saving Time* is observed.

Overview

Surrounded by the Appalachians, the mountain State of West Virginia has a history of poverty and physical isolation. Today, however, tourists flock to this beautiful region to enjoy historic sightseeing and an abundance of recreational sports, including skiing and other wintersports, mountain-biking, whitewater rafting, hiking and fishing.

General Information

Nickname: Mountain State.
State bird: Cardinal.
State flower: Rosebay Rhododendron.
CAPITAL: Charleston.
Date of admission to the Union: 20 June 1863.

POPULATION: 1.82 million (official estimate 2005).
POPULATION DENSITY: 28.9 per sq km.
2004 total overseas arrivals: Under 38,000.

Climate

West Virginia enjoys pleasantly hot summers and relatively mild but crisp winters, with moderate rainfall throughout the year. Average temperatures in July and August rarely exceed 32°C (90°F), while in winter there is often snow.
Required clothing: Lightweights for the summer and heavyweights for the winter.

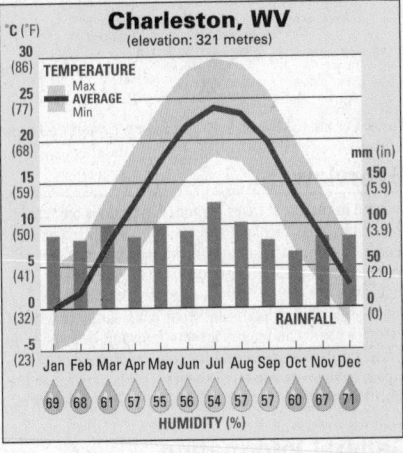

Top Things To See & Do

- At the historic town of **Harper's Ferry**, the site of John Brown's rebellion in 1859, numerous fine museums run exhibits on slavery and the Civil War. More than 200 festivals, fairs, special events, tournaments and races celebrate and showcase the culture and heritage of West Virginia.
- **Whitewater rafting** is a favourite activity at the **New River Gorge National River**, which winds its way through the Appalachians.
- The **Monongahela National Forest** occupies a vast area in the eastern part of the State and includes the **Spruce Knob-Seneca Rocks National Recreation Area**. Home to bears and deer, Monongahela offers over 500 campsites and miles of **hiking** trails.
- West Virginia also boasts some of the nation's best **State parks**, with good naturalist programmes and recreational facilities. These include four resort State parks, complete with lodges, cabins, swimming pools, championship golf courses, restaurants and additional amenities.
- Other attractions include the **State Capitol** in **Charleston**, one of the finest Italian Renaissance buildings in the USA.

TOURIST INFORMATION

West Virginia Division of Tourism
90 MacCorkle Avenue, SW, South Charleston, WV 25303, USA
Tel: (304) 558 2200 *or* (800) 225 5982 (toll-free).
Website: www.wvtourism.com

West Virginia Tourism in the UK
c/o Destination Marketing, Power Road Studios, 114 Power Road, Chiswick, London W4 5PY, UK
Tel: (020) 8994 0978.
Website: www.callwva.com

Wisconsin

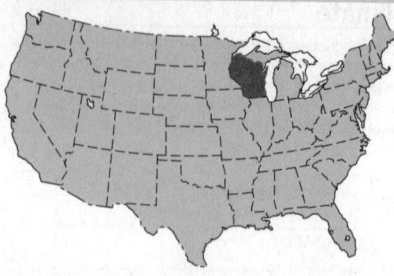

Time: Central (GMT - 6). *Daylight Saving Time* is observed.

Overview

Located in the Great Lakes Region, Wisconsin is bordered to the east by Lake Michigan and the north by Michigan, and separated from Canada in the north west by Lake Superior. This is a beautiful State, with over 15,000 lakes and thousands of miles of rivers and streams. Its varied countryside also includes sandstone cliffs, sandy beaches, northern forests and rich, southern farmland. Wisconsin is famed for its hospitality and friendly atmosphere and is known as the beer capital of the nation. Milwaukee, on the southeast shores of Lake Michigan, is the State's largest city.

General Information

Nickname: Badger State.
State bird: Robin.
State flower: Wood Violet.
CAPITAL: Madison.
Date of admission to the Union: 29 May 1848.
POPULATION: 5.54 million (official estimate 2005).
POPULATION DENSITY: 33 per sq km.
2004 total overseas arrivals/US ranking: 108,000/28.

Climate

Summers are warm with cool nights. Winters are cold, especially around the Great Lakes where conditions can be severe (however, there are good conditions for wintersports).
Required clothing: Lightweights for the summer with cover-up for cool nights. Heavyweights for the winter and extra bundling for wintersports.

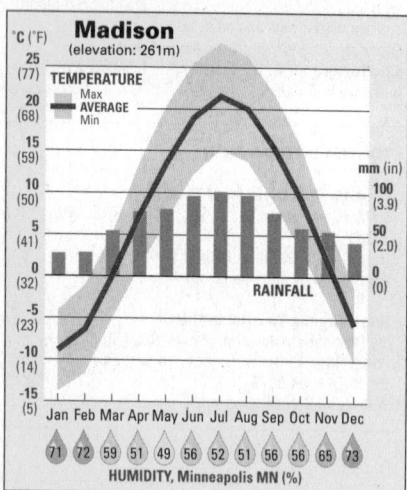

Top Things To See & Do

- **Milwaukee**, on the southwest shores of Lake Michigan, is well known for its German heritage and beer industry; the city boasts over 1500 bars and taverns. Many festivals are held throughout the summer, the most lavish of which is the *Summerfest* in late-June. The **Charles Allis Art Museum** and the lakefront **Milwaukee Art Museum** offer fine collections of art.
- West of Milwaukee, **Madison**, the State capital, is located on an isthmus between **Lake Mendota** and **Lake Monona**. This gracious city is the site of the **University of Wisconsin**, and student culture thrives, with lively coffee shops, secondhand (thrift) shops and bicycle paths.
- Also in Madison is the impressive **State Capitol**, with its outstanding ceiling frescoes, and, in nearby **Baraboo**, the **Circus World Museum**, former home of the Ringling Brothers' Circus.

- Wisconsin's **Door County** is a peninsula comprising 403km (250 miles) of beautiful coastline that extends into Lake Michigan. The scenery here is breathtaking, with lighthouses, picturesque villages, art galleries and miles of sandy beaches. Camping is plentiful, as is Door County cuisine, such as 'fish boils' and cherry pie.
- Other State attractions include the 21 **Apostle Islands** on Lake Superior, home to the largest collection of lighthouses in the USA, as well as fine sandy beaches, caves, forests, black bears and bald eagles. Especially popular is **Madeline Island**, with its fine beaches and unspoilt landscape.

> **TOURIST INFORMATION**
>
> **Wisconsin Department of Tourism**
> *Street address*: 201 West Washington Avenue, Madison, WI 53703, USA
> *Postal address*: PO Box 8690, Madison, WI 53708, USA
> Tel: (608) 266 2161 *or* (800) 432 8747 (toll-free).
> Website: www.travelwisconsin.com
>
> **Greater Milwaukee CVB**
> 648 North Plankinton Avenue, Suite 425, Milwaukee, WI 53203, USA
> Tel: (414) 273 7222 *or* (800) 554 1448 (toll-free).
> Website: www.visitmilwaukee.org

Wyoming

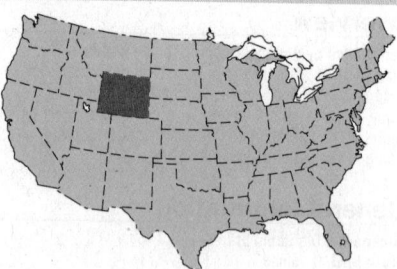

Time: Mountain (GMT - 7). *Daylight Saving Time* is observed.

Overview

In the heart of the Rockies, Wyoming is known as the 'Cowboy State' and was the home of 'Buffalo Bill' Cody. It is the ninth-largest State in the USA and has the smallest population. The spirit of the Wild West is alive and kicking in Wyoming, with its open spaces, rugged country and breathtaking scenery. Geographical attractions include 11 major mountain ranges, prairies, grasslands, parks, forests, lakes and rivers.

General Information

Nickname: Equality State/Cowboy State.
State bird: Western Meadowlark.
State flower: Indian Paintbrush.
CAPITAL: Cheyenne.
Date of admission to the Union: 10 July 1890.
POPULATION: 509,294 (official estimate 2005).
POPULATION DENSITY: 2 per sq km.
2004 total overseas arrivals/US ranking: Under 57,000/37.

Climate

Generally cold, semi-arid climate. Summers are short and hot while winters are cold and relatively long. Differences between summer and winter are extreme.
Required clothing: Cottons and linens during the summer months and heavyweight clothing for the winter.

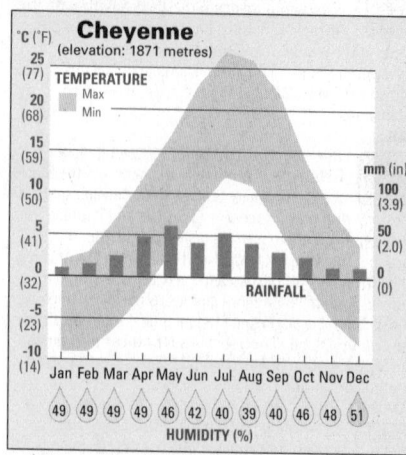

Top Things To See & Do

- Ranching is still a major industry here, and one of the world's largest rodeos – **Cheyenne Frontier Days**, held annually in July – has drawn visitors to the State capital since 1897.
- Spend time at one of the many guest or **working ranches** and experience at first hand Wyoming's special frontier heritage.
- Visit the world's first national park, the huge **Yellowstone National Park** (website: www.nps.gov/yell), located on top of one of the earth's few 'hot spots' – a place where the earth's crust is so thin that the hot, molten core can influence surface conditions.
- Yellowstone's violent volcanic history has resulted in a unique environment of geysers, bubbling hot pools, alpine lakes and great canyons. **Old Faithful Geyser**, the park's most famous attraction, erupts almost hourly, sending jets of boiling water into the air.
- Just south of Yellowstone is the beautiful **Grand Teton National Park**, with ample hiking, cycling and horseriding opportunities; and the mountain valley town of **Jackson**, which in winter becomes one of the world's premier ski spots.
- South of Jackson is **Bridger-Teton National Forest**. The Shoshone and Arapaho Native American tribes live east of this forest, on the **Wind River Indian Reservation**.
- Heading northeast, **Cody**, Buffalo Bill's hometown, is best known for the **Buffalo Bill Historical Center** – often called 'The Smithsonian of the West'. Cody is also home to **Old Trail Town**, a collection of pioneer buildings and relics of the Big Horn Basin area.
- Further east, view the dramatic **Big Horn Mountains**, with the charming towns of **Buffalo** and **Sheridan** nestled at the base of the range.
- At Buffalo, the **Jim Gatchell Museum of the West** offers fascinating insights into frontier history.
- In the northeast, the majestic **Devil's Tower National Monument** rises over 360m (1200ft) from the valley and attracts thousands of climbers.
- Head back towards the centre of the State, to the **National Historic Trails Interpretative Center** in **Casper**, which chronicles the great westward emigration of the 19th century.

> **TOURIST INFORMATION**
>
> **Wyoming Business Council – Tourism Office**
> I-25 at College Drive, Cheyenne, WY 82002, USA
> Tel: (307) 777 7777 *or* (800) 225 5996 (toll-free).
> Website: www.wyomingtourism.org
> *The Tourism Office has a full list of local tourist offices on their website.*
>
> **Rocky Mountain International in the UK**
> Woodpeckers End, 93 Burridge Road, Burridge, Southampton, Hampshire SO31 1BY, UK
> Tel: (09063) 640 655 (customer request line; 60p per minute).
> Website: www.rmi-realamerica.com

US External Territories

This section includes basic facts on a number of the US External Territories: **Baker & Howland Islands**, **Jarvis Island**, **Johnston Atoll**, **Kingman Reef**, **Midway Islands**, **Navassa Island**, **Palmyra** and **Wake Island**. For more information on these islands, contact a US Embassy; see *USA* section.

The following countries all have their own sections in the *World Travel Guide*:

American Samoa, **Guam**, **US Virgin Islands**. For **Palau** and the **Northern Mariana Islands**, see the *Pacific Islands of Micronesia* section.

Baker & Howland Islands and Jarvis Island

Location: Central Pacific Ocean.

Time: GMT - 12.
Area: Baker Island: 1.63 sq km (0.62 sq mile) surrounded by 123.44 sq km (47.66 sq mile) of submerged land. **Howland Island:** 1.84 sq km (0.71 sq mile) surrounded by 129.79 sq km (50 sq mile) of submerged land. **Jarvis Island:** 4.39 sq km (1.69 sq mile) surrounded by 143.24 sq km (55.30 sq mile) of submerged land.
Population: Currently uninhabited. **Geography:** Baker & Howland Islands are two low-lying coral atolls located about 2575km (1600 miles) southwest of Honolulu, Hawaii. There are no lagoons on the islands. Jarvis Island is a low-lying coral island about 2090km (1300 miles) south of Hawaii. **History:** The Islands were originally settled by the USA in 1935, but were subsequently evacuated during World War II. In 1974, the Islands were registered as national wildlife refuges to be administered by the US Fish & Wildlife Service and visitors wishing to land on the islands must seek permission from this organisation (for address, see *Contact Information*). In 1990, Congress passed legislation for the Islands to be included within the boundaries of the State of Hawaii.

Johnston Atoll

Location: Pacific Ocean.

Time: GMT - 10.

Area: 2.6 sq km (1 sq mile). **Population:** Uninhabited.
Geography: Located 1319km (820 miles) west-southwest of Honolulu, Johnston Atoll consists of Johnston Island, Sand Island and two manmade islands, East (Hikina) and North (Akau). **History:** The USA began a chemical disposal facility on Johnston Atoll in 1985, but it was not until 1989 that it gained the world's attention when the USA agreed to destroy 400 tons of nerve gas here after transporting it from the Federal Republic of Germany. Complaints were lodged by the South Pacific Forum nations and various environmental groups, which resulted in the USA sending a group of scientists to monitor the safety of the disposal facilities activities. Today the Atoll is no longer a storage or disposal site for chemical weapons; by 2004, the site was completely cleaned and closed. An oasis for reef and birdlife, nowadays, the Atoll is jointly administered by the Department of the Interior, the US Fish and Wildlife Service and the US Department of Defense, Johnston Atoll (for address, see *Contact Information*).

Kingman Reef

Location: Pacific Ocean.

Geography: Located 1500km (925 miles) southwest of Hawaii, Kingman Reef consists of a reef and shoal measuring 8km (5 miles) by 15km (9.5 miles). **History:** The reef is closed to public access and was a Naval Defense Sea Area and Airspace Reservation administered by the US Department of Defense. In 1990, Congress passed legislation for the reef to be included within the boundaries of the State of Hawaii. In January 2001, the waters around the reef were designated a

National Wildlife Refuge. For further information, contact the US Fish & Wildlife Service – Pacific Islands, see *Contact Information*.

Midway Islands

Location: Northern Pacific Ocean.

Time: GMT - 11.

Area: 5 sq km (2 sq miles). **Population:** 40 (2002).
Geography: Located 1850km (1150 miles) northwest of Hawaii, the Midway Islands consist of Sand Island, Eastern Island and several small islets within the reef. **History:** The Islands' administration transferred from the US Department of Defense to the Department of the Interior in 1996 (for address, see *Contact Information*). Limited tourism is now permitted; the Islands are a national wildlife refuge (contact Midway Atoll National Wildlife Refuge; for address, see *Contact Information*). However, regularly scheduled trips to Midway are currently not available, attempts are being made to re-establish these. In 1990, Congress passed legislation for the Territory to be included within the boundaries of the State of Hawaii.

Navassa Island

Location: Caribbean Sea.

Time: GMT - 5.

Area: 5.2 sq km (2 sq miles). **Population:** Uninhabited.
Geography: Navassa Island is a raised coral island with a limestone plateau and lies 160km (100 miles) south of Guatánamo Bay, Cuba and 65km (40 miles) west of Haiti. **History:** In 1857, Navassa became a US Insular Area and was mined for guano until operations ceased in 1898. In 1997, the Office of Insular Affairs, under the control of the US Department of the Interior, took responsibility of the island. Reports in 1998 showed that a variety of unique plant and animal species existed on Navassa and visits to the island were subsequently prohibited. The US Department of the Interior and US Fish and Wildlife Service (for address, see *Contact Information*) took command in 1999 and it became a National Wildlife Refuge.

Palmyra

Location: Pacific Ocean.

Time: GMT - 11.

Area: 100 hectares (247 acres). **Population:** Uninhabited.
Geography: Palmyra is made up of approximately 50 low-lying islets about 1600km (1000 miles) south of Honolulu. **History:** Administered by the US Department of the Interior since 1961, Palmyra was included within the boundaries of the State of Hawaii after legislation in 1990. In 1996, it became known that the Hawaiian owners of the islands were to sell the atoll to a US company which was allegedly planning to establish a nuclear waste storage facility. The Government of Kiribati protested at these moves and reiterated its attempts to include the atoll within its own national boundaries. However, the original designs for the island were abandoned and, in November 2000, the atoll was sold to the Nature Conservancy (website: http://nature.org) for approximately US$30 million. The lagoons and surrounding waters were later transferred to the US Fish & Wildlife Service (for address, see *Contact Information*)) in January 2001, and it was designated a National Wildlife Refuge.

Wake Island

Location: Pacific Ocean.

Time: GMT + 12.

Area: 8 sq km (3 sq miles). **Population:** 200 (2005 estimate).
Geography: Wake Island lies in the Pacific Ocean and consists of three islets, Wake, Wilkes and Peale, approximately 2060km (1280 miles) east of Guam and 500km (310 miles) north of the Marshall Islands. The location (not the size) of this island makes it of major importance to the US Government. **History:** A protectorate island of the USA, the US flag having been formally raised over the island in 1898, its strategic location has led in the past to its use as a trans-Pacific telegraph relay station and a stopover for flights in the days before jet flight became universal. From 1941-44, it was occupied by the Japanese. In 1990, Congress proposed that the islands should be included within the boundaries of Guam. This sparked off a reaction from the Republic of the Marshall Islands, which also claimed rights to the island. The island has been a military air force base since 1972 and is administered by the US Department of Defense (for address, see *Contact Information*).

CONTACT INFORMATION

US Fish and Wildlife Service – Pacific Islands
PO Box 50167, Room 5-231, 300 Ala Moana Boulevard, Honolulu, Hawaii, HI 96850, USA
Tel: (808) 792 9540.
Website: www.fws.gov/pacific

US Department of the Interior
1849 C Street, NW, Washington, DC 20240, USA
Tel: (202) 208 3100.
Website: www.doi.gov

US Department of Defense
Department of the Air Force, The Pentagon, Washington, DC 20330, USA
Tel: (703) 545 6700.
Website: www.defenselink.mil

US Department of Defense, Johnston Atoll (FCDNA)
Commander, APO San Francisco, CA 96035, USA
Website: www.defenselink.mil

Midway Atoll National Wildlife Refuge
PO Box 29460, Honolulu HI 96820-1860, USA
Tel: (808) 674 8237.
Website: http://midway.fws.gov

US Virgin Islands

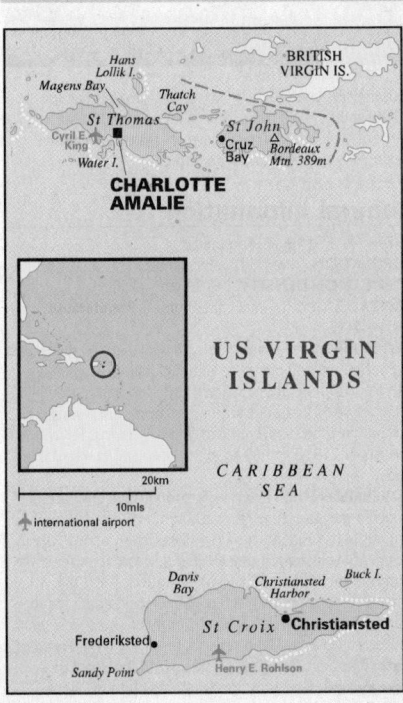

Location: Caribbean, Leeward Islands.

Time: GMT - 4.

Overview

The US Virgin Islands were first inhabited by Carib and Arawak Indians but, in common with the rest of the Caribbean, they endured various waves of European invasion and settlement from the 1490s onwards, finally becoming part of the Danish West Indies. The US Government purchased the Islands in 1917 and they are now an unincorporated territory of the USA. A measure of self-Government was introduced in 1954, along with the introduction of an elected Senate.

The result of the Islands' history and location is a unique blend of Danish heritage and American modernity combined with a relaxed and friendly attitude typical of the Caribbean. Add to this miles of glistening beaches, first-class diving facilities and verdant tropical vegetation, and there is more than enough to seduce any visitor.

The Danes' legacy is evident in Christiansted, on the largest island, St Croix, whose historic sites include Fort Christiansværn (dating from 1774) and the Old Custom House. St Thomas too retains much of its Danish influence; in the capital, Charlotte Amalie, converted warehouses now

Credit: ©US Virgin Islands Department of Tourism / Steven Simonsen

house stylish boutiques. Those seeking unspoilt natural beauty should head to St John. With no airport, and two-thirds of the island's deep valleys set aside as a National Park, this is an ideal Caribbean retreat.

General Information

AREA: 347.1 sq km (134 sq miles).
POPULATION: 108,708 (2005 estimate).
POPULATION DENSITY: 313.18 per sq km.
CAPITAL: Charlotte Amalie (St Thomas). **Population:** 18,914 (2005).
GEOGRAPHY: The islands are situated 64km (40 miles) east of Puerto Rico and comprise some 50 islands covered with lush tropical vegetation. St Thomas is long and narrow, rising abruptly to a ridge with an excellent deep-water harbour. St John is covered partly in bay forests. St Croix consists of 215 sq km (83 sq miles) of rolling ex-plantation land.
GOVERNMENT: US External Territory (Unincorporated). Gained a measure of self-Government in 1954. Although US Virgin Islands residents are US citizens, they cannot vote in Presidential elections – one elected delegate represents the islands in the US House of Representatives. The 1954 Organic Act created an elected 15-member Senate for the islands. Since 1970, executive authority has been vested in an elected Governor who serves a four-year term. **Head of State:** President George W Bush since 2001. **Head of Government:** Governor Charles Wesley Turnbull since 1999. **Recent history:** Politics on the islands follow the Republican-Democrat division of the USA itself. From the evidence of gubernatorial elections, the political complexion of the islands was distinctly Republican from 1970 until 1982. This is when the Governorship passed to the Democrats, who held the post until Roy Schneider, representing the Independent Citizens' Movement, was elected in 1994. Despite the fact that the Republicans did not even put up a candidate, Schneider's efforts to secure a second term failed when he was defeated by Democrat Charles Turnbull at the November 1998 poll. At the most recent elections in November 2002, Turnbull secured a second term of office, while simultaneous elections for the Senate returned the Democrats with a majority of a single seat.
LANGUAGE: English is the official language. Spanish and Creole are also widely spoken.
RELIGION: Christian, mainly Protestant.
ELECTRICITY: 120 volts AC, 60Hz.
SOCIAL CONVENTIONS: The US Virgin Islanders are overwhelmingly friendly and helpful and the pace of life is very relaxed. Shaking hands is the normal form of greeting and the appropriate time of day (good morning/afternoon/evening) is usually uttered at every encounter. Politeness and courtesy is expected. Dress is informal for most occasions apart from the formal requirements of some hotels.

Climate

Hot throughout the year, cooled by the eastern trade winds. Lowland areas have fairly evenly distributed rainfall, with August to October being the wettest time.
Required clothing: Lightweight clothes throughout the year. Umbrella or light waterproof clothing is useful.

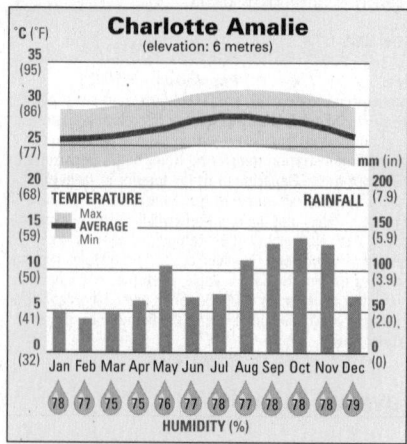

Charlotte Amalie (elevation: 6 metres)

TEMPERATURE — Max / AVERAGE / Min
RAINFALL

HUMIDITY (%): Jan 78, Feb 77, Mar 75, Apr 75, May 76, Jun 77, Jul 78, Aug 77, Sep 78, Oct 78, Nov 78, Dec 79

Communications

Telephone: IDD is available. Country code: 1 340. The USA (including most toll-free numbers) can be dialled directly from the islands. Efficient overseas cable and telephone services are in operation.
Mobile telephone: Roaming agreements exist with most international mobile phone operators.
Internet: Internet cafes are available.
Post: Airmail to Europe takes up to one week. The postage is the same as in the USA. First-class post to the USA automatically travels by air through the US postal service. Post office hours: Mon-Fri 0900-1700, Sat 0900-1200.
MEDIA: Press: Daily newspapers include *St Croix Avis* and *Virgin Islands Daily News*.
TV: Channels include local *ABC* network *WSVI TV 8* (Channel 8) and local *NBC* network *WVGN TV 14* (Channel 11).
Radio: *WSTA AM 1340* has been on air since the 1950s.

Passport/Visa

Immigration requirements for the US Virgin Islands are the same as for the USA; see the *USA* section.
Passport/Visa Information: The US Virgin Islands are a United States External Territory represented abroad by US Embassies. For addresses, see the *USA* section.

Money

Currency: US Dollar (USD; symbol US$) = 100 cents. See the *USA* section for information on currency exchange, exchange rates, credit and debit cards and so on.
Traveller's cheques: To avoid additional exchange rate charges, travellers are advised to take traveller's cheques in US Dollars.
Currency restrictions: Import and export of amounts in excess of US$10,000 must be declared.
Banking hours: Mon-Thurs 0900-1430, Fri 0900-1400 and 1530-1700.

Duty Free

Duty must be paid on all gifts and alcohol brought in from abroad. Other customs regulations, duty free exemptions and prohibitions are as for the USA; see *Duty Free* in the *USA* section.

Public Holidays

Below are listed Public Holidays for the January 2006-June 2007 period.
2006: Jan 1 New Year's Day. **Jan 6** Three Kings' Day. **Jan 19** Martin Luther King Day. **Feb 13** Presidents' Day. **Apr 13** Holy Thursday. **Apr 14** Good Friday. **Apr 17** Easter Monday. **May 22** Memorial Day. **Jul 3** Danish West Indies Emancipation Day. **Jul 4** US Independence Day. **Jul 25** Hurricane Supplication Day. **Sep 4** Labor Day. **Oct 9** Columbus Day. **Oct 17** Virgin Islands Thanksgiving Day. **Nov 1** D Hamilton Jackson Day. **Nov 11** Veterans' Day. **Nov 23** US Thanksgiving Day. **Dec 25** Christmas Day.
2007: Jan 1 New Year's Day. **Jan 6** Three Kings' Day. **Jan 19** Martin Luther King Day. **Feb 12** Presidents' Day. **Apr 5** Holy Thursday. **Apr 6** Good Friday. **Apr 9** Easter Monday. **May 21** Memorial Day.

Health

	Special Precautions?	Certificate Required?
Yellow Fever	No	No
Cholera	No	No
Typhoid & Polio	1	N/A
Malaria	No	N/A

Note: *Regulations and requirements may be subject to change at short notice, and you are advised to contact your doctor well in advance of your intended date of departure. Any numbers in the chart refer to the footnotes below.*

1: Vaccination against *typhoid* and *poliomyelitis* is advised.
Food & drink: Water precautions are advised outside the main centres. Mains water is considered safe to drink. Milk is pasteurised and dairy products are safe for consumption. Local meat, poultry, seafood, fruit and vegetables are generally considered safe to eat.
Other risks: *Bilharzia (schistosomiasis)* may be present in some fresh water; swimming pools that are well chlorinated and maintained are safe. *Leptospirosis* is a risk. Visitors should enquire locally. Immunisation against *hepatitis A* should be considered. *Rabies* is present; if you are bitten, seek medical advice without delay. For more information, consult the *Health* appendix.
Health care: Medical costs are very high and health insurance is essential. Medical facilities are of a similar standard to those in the USA. There are hospitals on St Croix and St Thomas; a clinic is located on St John.

Travel - International

AIR:

US Airways (US) (website: www.usairways.com) has daily direct flights to St Thomas and St Croix. *American Airlines (AA)* (website: www.aa.com) offers daily, direct services from New York (*JFK*) and Miami to St Thomas and St Croix. Services from the US mainland to the Virgin Islands are available through *Air Sunshine* (website: www.airsunshine.com), *American Eagle* (website: www.aa.com) and *Cape Air* (website: www.flycapeair.com). Seaplanes connect St Thomas and St Croix several times a day. For more information contact *Seabourne Airlines* (website: www.seabourneairlines.com).
Approximate flight times: From St Croix to *London* is 10 hours 50 minutes (excluding stopover), to *New York* is three hours 45 minutes, to *Miami* is two hours 30 minutes, to *St Maarten* is 45 minutes, to *St Thomas* is 30 minutes and to *San Juan* is 30 minutes.
Main airports: *St Thomas (STT) (Cyril E King)* is 5km (3 miles) west of Charlotte Amalie. *To/from the airport:* A bus service operates from Charlotte Amalie.
St Croix (STX) (Henry E Rohlsen) is about 14km (9 miles) southwest of Christiansted. *To/from the airport:* A bus service operates to the cities. Taxis are also available.
Facilities: Cafe and car hire facilities.
Departure tax: None.
SEA:

Main ports: *Charlotte Amalie* (St Thomas), *Frederiksted* (St Croix), *Cruz Bay* (St John) and *Christiansted* (St Croix). Regular ferries sail between St Thomas and St John and the British Virgin Islands and Fajardo (Puerto Rico). Ferries leave from Charlotte Amalie and Red Hook Dock on St Thomas, for Cruz Bay on St John. The *Virgin Islands Fast Ferry* operates a service from St Croix to St Thomas from November to May. Booking is advised (tel: (877) 733 9425 (toll-free) ; website: www.virginislandsfastferry.com). A number of cruise lines operating out of Miami and San Juan includes the US Virgin Islands in their itineraries around the Caribbean. For more information on cruise ships to the US Virgin Islands, contact the US Virgin Islands Department of Tourism (see *Top Things To See & Do*) or consult the 'Cruise Ship Schedules' online (website: www.ships.vi).
ROAD:

Well-maintained roads connect all main towns. Speed limit is 35kph (20mph) in towns and 55kph (35mph) elsewhere. Driving is on the left.
Bus: Public services operate on St Thomas from Charlotte Amalie to Red Hook and Bordeaux, and St Croix has a taxi-van service between Christiansted and Frederiksted (Mon-Sat 0530-2130). St John has a bus service running from Cruz Bay to Coral Bay. It costs $1 each way. **Taxi:** Available on all the islands. These follow standard routes between various points, and the fares for these are published. Sharing taxis is a common practice. **Car hire:** There are several international car hire agencies at the airports and in the main towns on St Croix, St John and St Thomas. Jeeps or mini-mokes are popular modes of travel and these too can be hired. **Documentation:** National licences are accepted; an International Driving Permit is not required.
Travel times: The following chart gives approximate travel times (in hours and minutes) from **Charlotte Amalie** to

other major cities/towns in the US Virgin Islands.

	Air	Road	Sea
Chris'sted, SC	0.25	-	-
Cruz Bay, SJ	-	-	0.45
Magens Bay	-	0.20	-
Coral World	-	0.40	-

Note: SC = St Croix; **SJ** = St John.

Travel Advice

Most visits to the US Virgin Islands are trouble-free but visitors should be aware of the global risk of indiscriminate international terrorist attacks, which could be against civilian targets, including places frequented by foreigners. This advice is based on information provided by the Foreign and Commonwealth Office in the UK. It is correct at time of publishing. As the situation can change rapidly, visitors are advised to contact the following organisations for the latest travel advice:

British Foreign and Commonwealth Office
Tel: (0845) 850 2829.
Website: www.fco.gov.uk

US Department of State
Website: http://travel.state.gov/travel

Accommodation

HOTELS:

The islands have more hotels per square mile than anywhere in the Caribbean. Costs vary according to standard, but are generally quite high compared to other Caribbean islands. The islands' hotel association has a counter at the airport to assist with reservations. A variety of guest houses, condominiums and villas are also available on St John and St Thomas.

CAMPING:

There are two main campsites, both on the island of St John. One of the main sites, Cinnamon Bay Camp, is located inside the 11,560 acre St John National Park. Inexpensive bare plots, plots with tents already set up and cottages are available for a maximum stay of two weeks. The site is very popular, so reservations should be made well in advance. The other campsite is at Maho Bay near a beautiful beach. So-called 'eco-tents', which are part of the tourist authorities' wish to encourage 'sustainable tourism' and rustic cabins are also available.

BOATING EXCURSIONS: St Thomas is the US Virgin Islands' boating capital. Visitors can take bare boat or crewed chartered yachts for a week-long journey.

ACCOMMODATION INFORMATION

St Thomas & St John Hotel & Tourism Association
PO Box 2300, St Thomas, VI 00803, US Virgin Islands
Tel: 774 6835.
Website: www.sttstjhta.com or www.virgin-islands-hotels.com

St Croix Hotel & Tourism Association
PO Box 24238, Gallows Bay, St Croix, VI 00824, US Virgin Islands
Tel: 773 7117.
Website: www.stcroixhotelandtourism.com

Cinnamon Bay Camp
PO Box 720, Cruz Bay, St John, VI 00831, US Virgin Islands
Tel: 776 6330.
Website: www.cinnamonbay.com

Maho Bay Camp
PO Box 310, Cruz Bay, St John, VI 00830, US Virgin Islands
Tel: 715 0501.
Website: www.maho.org

Top Things To See & Do

- Explore **St Croix**, the largest of the US Virgin Islands. **Christiansted** is one of the two major towns showing early Danish influence. **Fort Christiansværn** (dating from 1774), **Government House**, the **Old Custom House and Art Gallery** and the **wharf** area are among its historic sites. Outside of Christiansted, on **West Airport Road**, is the **Cruz Rum Distillery** where visitors can taste the islands' rum and watch it being made. On the way to **Frederiksted** is **Whim Greathouse**, portraying plantation life in the 18th century. Frederiksted is also of Danish origin and has a 15-acre tropical rainforest nearby. **St George Village Botanical Gardens** and **Croix Aquarium** are both worth a visit.
- Sail to the much smaller **Buck Island**, easily reached via the 10km (6 mile) channel that separates it from Christiansted. Offshore is one of the world's most impressive marine gardens, maintained by the National Park Service as an underwater protected reef.

- Head to cosmopolitan **St Thomas**, the second-largest of this chain of islands. Like St Croix, it has many associations with the Danes and retains much Danish influence. The main town, **Charlotte Amalie**, is the group's capital. Imported goods from all over the world make it a marvellous shopping centre and stores tucked into remodelled Danish warehouses line each side of the picturesque **Main Street**. Cobblestoned alleys with numerous boutiques lead down to the waterfront. **Blackbeard's Castle** is the earliest fortification in the US Virgin Islands. Other attractions include **Fort Christian**, built in 1672; the **Coral World Observatory**; the **Frederick Lutheran Church** of 1850; **Government House** on **Government Hill** (1866); **Venus Pillar** on **Magnolia Hill**; **Bluebeard's Tower**, the 19th-century pirate's one-time abode; and the **Synagogue** on **Crystal Gade**, one of the oldest in the western hemisphere. On the northern coast is **Magens Bay**, claimed to be one of the world's top 10 beaches.
- Escape the crowds on **St John**, the most 'unspoilt' of the islands. It has no airport, and two-thirds of the island's deep valleys and most of its shoreline have been set aside as the **Virgin Islands National Park**. **Cruz Bay** is a small town offering excellent gift shops and dive centres. **Trunk Bay** is a beautiful beach, and the diving is very good. Accommodation on the island is limited. **Caneel Bay** is a luxurious resort. **Cinnamon Bay** and **Maho Bay** have campsites. Cottages can also be rented.
- **Sail** around the territory's myriad islands. Visitors can hire sailing boats or powerboats, with or without a skipper. A list of operators can be obtained from the US Virgin Islands Department of Tourism (see *Tourist Information*). **Boat races** take place all year round, including the **Rolex Cup Regatta** (on St Thomas) and the **Mumm's Cup Regatta** (on St Croix). Guided **kayak** tours through **Mangrove Lagoon** and **St Thomas' Marine Sanctuary** provide the opportunity to see egrets, herons and other wildlife.
- **Dive** or **snorkel** among the stunning coral reefs. Warm and calm seas, a rich marine life and excellent visibility are the main attractions for divers of all abilities. Facilities are well-developed. The diving season is busiest from December through April. Some of the best dive sites include **Andreas Reef** (on St Thomas, known for its variety of tropical fish); **Buck Island Reef National Monument** (a protected area on St Croix with markers describing marine life); **Carval Rock** (for advanced divers, on St John); **Salt River Canyon** (one of the most popular sites, also on St Croix); and **Submarine Alley** (an advanced dive site, also on St Thomas, with large coral islands).
- **Fish** for blue and white marlin, sailfish and wahoo; the **North Drop** (accessible from St John or St Thomas) is the best-known spot. Sport fishing charters with experienced skippers are widely available. Local fishermen are keen to encourage the 'catch-and-release' method in order to preserve fish species. Fishing competitions, such as the **Bastille Day Kingfish Tournament** or the **Open Atlantic Blue Marlin Tournament** attract amateurs and professionals from all over the world.

TOURIST INFORMATION

US Virgin Islands Department of Tourism in the UK
c/o Destination Marketing, Power Road Studios, 114 Power Road, Chiswick, London W4 5PY, UK
Tel: (020) 8994 0978.
Website: www.usvitourism.vi

US Virgin Islands Department of Tourism in the USA
One Penn Plaza, Suite 3525, New York, NY 10019, USA
Tel: (212) 502 5300.
Website: www.usvitourism.vi

Caribbean Tourism Organisation in the UK
22 The Quadrant, Richmond, Surrey TW9 1BP, UK
Tel: (020) 8948 0057.
Website: www.doitcaribbean.com or www.onecaribbean.org

Entertainment

FOOD & DRINK: High-quality restaurants serve everything from French and Italian to Chinese cuisine. Island specialities include fresh fish and lobster. Dining out is casual and there is an increasing number of eateries on the main islands offering seafood, burgers, steaks and local fare.
National specialities:
- *Kallaloo* (a stew of okra, meat, seafood, local greens and spices).
- *Sause* (lime-flavoured stock of pig's head, tail and feet).
- *Fungi* (cornmeal and okra side dish that accompanies fried or boiled fish).
- Seafood: lobster, *wahoo*, grouper, *mahi-mahi* and tuna.
National drinks:
- *Cruzan* rum is strong and distinctive.

Credit: ©US Virgin Islands Department of Tourism / Alex Cerulli

Tipping: All hotels add 8 per cent room tax and 10 to 15 per cent service charge. Restaurants will either add a 10 to 15 per cent service charge or expect the equivalent tip.
NIGHTLIFE: Steel bands, folk singing, calypso and limbo dancing are popular. Discos are also available. St Thomas has several nightclubs; many hotels also offer entertainment. Cinemas on St Croix and St Thomas show English-language films. There is a casino on St Croix.
SHOPPING: All luxury items up to US$1200 are cheap as they are duty free. Charlotte Amalie on St Thomas is the best shopping centre. Best buys include watches, cameras, fine jewellery, china, leather goods, perfume, spirits and designer clothing. **Shopping hours:** Mon-Sat 0900-1700. When cruise ships are in port, some larger shops open on Sunday.

Business

- **GDP:** US$1.9 billion.
- **Main imports:** Crude oil, foodstuffs, consumer goods and building materials.
- **Main exports:** Petroleum products and rum.
- **Main trade partners:** Puerto Rico and USA.

ECONOMY: When Denmark sold the islands to the US government in 1917, they insisted that the existing privileges of the inhabitants be respected. A result of this is that the Virgin Islands are not part of the Federal Customs Area, a state of affairs that affords various advantages. This, in turn, has allowed the islands to support a high standard of living that they are naturally reluctant to relinquish. Tourism is a key industry, contributing around US$1.2 billion annually to the economy. The manufacturing industry is relatively new and thriving, producing pharmaceuticals, electronics and textiles. In addition, the islands have one of the world's largest oil refineries and a thriving trade in rum. Agriculture is confined to producing for local consumption; there are no significant natural resources. Transhipment and financial services are the islands' other main sources of revenue.
CONFERENCES/CONVENTIONS: The US Virgin Islands are an idyllic place to hold a conference or convention. In St Croix, facilities are available in four major hotels for up to 200 people and in two beach resorts for up to 125. In St John, facilities are available at the Hyatt Regency for up to 350 persons and in the National Park for 50 persons. St Thomas has meeting facilities in two hotels for up to 300 persons and in seven beach resorts for up to 850 persons. For further information on conference/convention facilities in the US Virgin Islands, contact the US Virgin Islands Department of Tourism (see *Top Things To See & Do*).

COMMERCIAL INFORMATION

St Croix Chamber of Commerce
PO Box 3009, Orange Grove, Suite 12, Christiansted, VI 00820, US Virgin Islands
Tel: 773 1435.
Website: www.stxchamber.org

St Thomas–St John Chamber of Commerce
PO Box 324, 6-7 Main Street, St Thomas, VI 00804, US Virgin Islands
Tel: 776 0100.
Website: www.usvichamber.com

Location: South America.

Time: GMT - 3 (GMT -2 from the second Sunday in October to the second Sunday in March).

Overview

Known as the 'Oriental Republic' because of its location on the eastern bank of the Rio de la Plata, Uruguay is one of the smallest of the South American republics. Parts of the territory which is now Uruguay were settled by the Spanish in the 1620s and the Portuguese in the 1680s; as a result, Uruguay became a major bone of contention between these rival European powers. The Spanish prevailed in the early 18th century, after the establishment of a settlement at San Felipe de Montevideo (which eventually became the Uruguayan capital) in 1726. The formal creation of the Uruguayan state took place in 1828. Throughout much of this early 19th-century period, the future Uruguay was occupied by Portuguese troops from neighbouring Brazil; interventions – military and otherwise – by its larger neighbouring powers were to become a recurrent feature of Uruguay's political history. The conjunction between internal and external forces became apparent during the Great War of 1843-52, which centred on the siege of Montevideo, then under Colorado control, by Blanco forces. The war, which was eventually won by the Colorados, established the pattern whereby Argentina and Brazil became the guarantors of Uruguayan independence, with the intervention of global powers on occasion – Britain and France in the 19th century, the USA in the 20th century. Today, the country's economic health still relies heavily on its two large neighbours and main trading partners. Although the tourism industry only brings in under US$1 billion annually, Uruguay is drawing increasingly more visitors each year, and for good reasons. The country enjoys 500km (300 miles) of fine sandy beaches on the Atlantic and the Río de la Plata, woods, hills, hot springs, hotels, casinos, art festivals and numerous opportunities for sport and entertainment. Montevideo, the capital, contains more than half of Uruguay's population. Located on the River Plate, which has been one of the essential elements for the development of the territory, Montevideo is also the country's natural trading centre. It is a delight for lovers of culture. Museums, theatres, exhibitions, shows, popular feasts... there is an intense agenda all year round and the city itself is a collection of art and history.

General Information

AREA: 176,215 sq km (68,037 sq miles).

POPULATION: 3.5 million (UN estimate 2005).

POPULATION DENSITY: 19.9 per sq km.

CAPITAL: Montevideo. **Population:** 1.33 million (2004).

GEOGRAPHY: Uruguay is bordered to the north by Brazil, to the southeast by the Atlantic, and is separated from Argentina in the west and south by the River Uruguay, which widens out into the Rio de la Plata estuary. The landscape is made up of hilly meadows broken by streams and rivers. There is a string of beaches along the coast. Most of the country is grazing land for sheep and cattle. Montevideo, the most southern point of the nation, accommodates more than half of the population. About 90 per cent of the land is suitable for agriculture, although only 12 per cent is used in this way.

GOVERNMENT: Republic since 1967. Formerly declared independence from Spain in 1825 and officially recognised in 1928. **Head of State and Government:** President Tabare Vazquez since 2005. **Recent history:** Tabare Vazquez from the *Frente Amplio* coalition was elected as President in 2005, becoming the first leftist leader to become the Uruguayan Head of State. On being elected, Vazquez vowed to alleviate poverty and to build better relations with Uruguay's neighbours, Brazil and Argentina. He has restored diplomatic ties with Cuba, which had been broken under the Batlle Presidency. It is thought that Uruguay's 2002 economic crisis and a disenchantment with free-market policies may have influenced this dramatic political shift. The *Frente Amplio* had further success in the mayoral elections of May 2005, winning seats in the interior for the first time ever. Eight leftist Mayors took office in July 2005.

LANGUAGE: Spanish. Some English is spoken in tourist resorts.

RELIGION: Roman Catholic is the predominant religion.

ELECTRICITY: 220 volts AC, 50Hz. Continental flat three-pin or round two-pin plugs.

SOCIAL CONVENTIONS: Shaking hands is the normal form of greeting. Uruguayans are very hospitable and like to entertain both at home and in restaurants. Normal courtesies should be observed. Smoking is not allowed in cinemas or theatres or on public transport.

Climate

Uruguay has an exceptionally fine temperate climate, with mild summers and winters. Summer is from December to March and is the most pleasant time; the climate during other seasons offers bright, sunny days and cool nights.

Required clothing: Mediumweight clothing for winter; lightweight clothing and raincoat required.

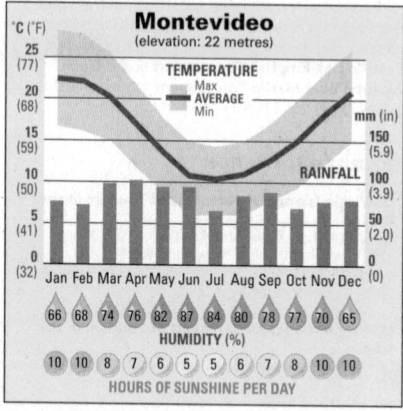

Communications

Telephone: Country code: 598. The local telephone service, which is operated by the Government, is good.

Mobile telephone: Roaming agreements exist with some international mobile phone operators. Visitors should check with their service provider before travelling. Coverage is good in urban areas and patchy elsewhere.

Internet: There are Internet cafes in main urban areas.

Post: Post office hours: 0800-1800 (main post office in the old city, Montevideo: 0900-1900). Airmail to Europe takes three to five days.

MEDIA: The Uruguayan constitution guarantees a free press and freedom of speech. There are over 100 private newspapers, more than 100 radio stations and around 20 television channels. State-run radio and television broadcasts are operated by *SODRE*.

Press: All newspapers are in Spanish; the most popular dailies include *El Observador*, *El País*, *La República* and *Ultimas Noticias*.

TV: Among the major channels are *Monte Carlo TV*, *Saeta TV Canal 10*, *Teledoce*, *TV Ciudad*, and government-run *Tveo TV Nacional*.

Radio: Stations include *AM Libre*, state-owned *Radiodifusion Nacional SODRE* and *Radio El Espectador*.

Passport/Visa

	Passport Required?	Visa Required?	Return Ticket Required?
Full British	Yes	No	Yes
Australian	Yes	No	Yes
Canadian	Yes	No	Yes
USA	Yes	No	Yes
Other EU	Yes	No/1	Yes
Japanese	Yes	No	Yes

Note: *Regulations and requirements may be subject to change at short notice, and you are advised to contact the appropriate diplomatic or consular authority before finalising travel arrangements. Any numbers in the chart refer to the footnotes below.*

PASSPORTS: Valid passport required by all except:
(a) nationals of Uruguay who arrive from Argentina, Brazil, Chile or Paraguay with a national identity card;
(b) nationals of Argentina, Bolivia, Brazil, Chile, Colombia, Costa Rica, Dominican Republic, Ecuador, Guatemala, Honduras and Paraguay with a national identity card for stays of up to 90 days.

VISAS: Required by all except the following:
(a) nationals of countries referred to in the chart above, except **1.** nationals of Estonia who *do* need a visa (please note that nationals of Canada, Ireland, Malta and the USA are only permitted visa-free stays of up to three months);
(b) nationals of Andorra, Argentina, The Bahamas, Barbados, Belize, Bolivia, Brazil, Bulgaria, Chile, Colombia, Costa Rica, Croatia, Ecuador, El Salvador, Guatemala, Honduras, Hong Kong (SAR), Iceland, Israel, Jamaica, Mexico, New Zealand, Nicaragua, Norway, Panama, Paraguay, Peru, Romania, South Africa, Switzerland, Trinidad & Tobago and Venezuela;
(c) nationals of Dominican Republic, Liechtenstein and Turkey for stays of up to three months;
(d) nationals of Korea (Rep) and Malaysia for up to 30 days;
(e) holders of a re-entry permit issued by Uruguayan officials.

Types of visa and cost: *Tourist:* £27. *Business* and *Tourist:* Enquire at Consulate (or Consular section at Embassy) for cost as it may vary with the exchange rate.

Validity: Visas are usually for stays of up to three months, but check with the Consulate, as this is dependent on nationality. Extensions for a further three months are possible; apply at the Immigration Office in Uruguay.

Application to: Consulate (or consular section at Embassy); see *Passport/Visa Information.*

Application requirements: (a) Valid passport. (b) One passport-size photo. (c) Completed application form. (d) References in Uruguay (name, address and phone number) or hotel booking confirmation. (e) Return ticket and travel documentation (including the flight number and the dates of arrival and departure). (f) Postal applications should be accompanied by a stamped, self-addressed envelope. (g) For business visits, a letter from the company in the country of origin.

Working days required: 21.

Temporary residence: Enquire at Embassy.

PASSPORT/VISA INFORMATION

Embassy of Uruguay in the UK
2nd Floor, 140 Brompton Road, London SW3 1HY, UK
Tel: (020) 7589 8835 *or* 7589 8735 (visa section).
Opening hours: Mon-Fri 1000-1700.
Visa section: Mon-Fri 1000-1230 (appointment only).

Embassy of Uruguay in the USA
1913 Eye Street, NW, Washington, DC 20006, USA
Tel: (202) 331 1313 *or* 331 4219 (consular section).
Website: www.uruwashi.org

Money

Currency: Peso Uruguayo (UYU) = 100 centécimos. Notes are in the denominations of UYU2000, 1000, 500, 200, 100, 50, 20, 10 and 5. Coins are in denominations of UYU10, 5, 2 and 1 and 50 centécimos.

Currency exchange: Visitors are advised to buy local currency at banks and exchange shops, as hotels tend to give unfavourable rates. Inflation in Uruguay, though less severe than in other Latin American countries, leads to frequent fluctuations in the exchange rate.

Credit & debit cards: American Express, Diners Club, MasterCard and Visa are the most commonly used. Check with your credit or debit card company for details of merchant acceptability and other services which may be available. ATMs may reject European or US credit cards.

Traveller's cheques: Sterling traveller's cheques can only

be changed at The Bank of London & South America; visitors are therefore advised to carry US Dollar traveller's cheques (US$50 and US$100 denominations only).
Currency restrictions: There are no restrictions on the import or export of either local or foreign currency.
Banking hours: Mon-Fri 1300-1700.
Exchange rate indicators:
Rate at time of publishing
£1.00= **UYU42.37**
$1.00= **UYU24.05**

Duty Free

The following items may be imported into Uruguay without incurring customs duty (50 per cent of these allowances for persons under 18 years of age):
(a) Residents of Uruguay arriving from Argentina, Bolivia, Brazil, Chile or Paraguay (maximum once a month):
200 cigarettes or 25 cigars or 250g of tobacco; 1l of alcohol; 2kg of foodstuffs.
Total value of exempted imports not to exceed US$300 if arriving by sea or air or US$150 if arriving by land.
(b) Residents of Uruguay arriving from other countries (once a year):
400 cigarettes or 50 cigars or 500g of tobacco; 2l of alcohol; 5kg of foodstuffs.
Total value of exempted imports not to exceed US$500 if arriving by sea or air.
(c) All other nationals:
400 cigarettes or 50 cigars or 500g of tobacco; 2l of alcohol; 5kg of foodstuffs; two articles of the following electrical, optical and electronic equipment: portable radio, photo camera, movie camera, movie projector, typewriter and slide projector.
Restricted: All plants and plant derivatives must be accompanied by a sanitary certificate.

Public Holidays

Below are listed Public Holidays for the January 2006-June 2007 period.
2006: Jan 1 New Year's Day. **Jan 6** Epiphany. **Feb 27-28** Carnival. **Apr 13** Maundy Thursday. **Apr 14** Good Friday. **Apr 19** Landing of the 33 Patriots. **May 1** Labour Day. **May 18** Battle of Las Piedras. **Jun 19** Birth of General Artigas. **Jul 18** Constitution Day. **Aug 25** National Independence Day. **Oct 12** Discovery of America. **Nov 2** All Souls' Day. **Dec 25** Christmas Day.
2007: Jan 1 New Year's Day. **Jan 6** Epiphany. **Feb** Carnival. **Apr 5** Maundy Thursday. **Apr 6** Good Friday. **Apr 19** Landing of the 33 Patriots. **May 1** Labour Day. **May 18** Battle of Las Piedras. **Jun 19** Birth of General Artigas.
Note: Many businesses close during Carnival Week and during Tourist Week (Easter).

Health

	Special Precautions?	Certificate Required?
Yellow Fever	No	2
Cholera	No	No
Typhoid & Polio	1	N/A
Malaria	No	N/A

Note: Regulations and requirements may be subject to change at short notice, and you are advised to contact your doctor well in advance of your intended date of departure. Any numbers in the chart refer to the footnotes below.

1: There is a slight risk of *typhoid fever* but no cases of *polio* have been reported in Uruguay in recent years; vaccination against *typhoid* is advised.
2: A *yellow fever* certificate is required for travellers coming from endemic areas and from infected countries according to the epidemiological situation and the risk evaluation.
Other risks: There are occasional outbreaks of *hepatitis A*.
Food & drink: Mains water is considered safe to drink. Drinking water outside main cities and towns may be contaminated and sterilisation is advisable. Milk is pasteurised and dairy products are safe for consumption. Local meat, poultry, seafood, fruit and vegetables are generally considered safe to eat.
Health care: Uruguay has an excellent medical service. Private health insurance is recommended.

Travel - International

AIR:
The national airline is *PLUNA* (PU) (website: www.pluna.com.uy), which operates flights to various destinations in Argentina, Brazil, Chile and Paraguay.
Approximate flight times: From Montevideo to *London* is 15 hours 40 minutes (including one hour 40 minutes' stopover in Madrid) and to *New York* is 14 hours.
Main airports: *Montevideo (MVD)* (Carrasco) (website: www.aic.com.uy) is 19km (12 miles) from the city (travel time - 35 minutes). *To/from the airport:* There is an airport bus to the city centre. Taxis are also available. *Facilities:* Duty free shop, post office, restaurants, car hire, pharmacy, travel agencies, ATMs and a bureau de change.
Air passes: The *Mercosur Airpass* is valid within Argentina, Brazil, Chile (except Easter Island), Paraguay and Uruguay. Participating airlines include *TAM Mercosur* (PZ), *Pluna* (PU), *TAM Linhas Aéreas* (JJ) and *VARIG* (RG). The pass can only be purchased by passengers who live outside South America, who have a return ticket. Only eight flight coupons are allowed with a maximum of four coupons for each country and it is valid for seven to a maximum of 30 days. At least two countries must be visited and the flight route cannot be changed. A maximum of two stopovers is allowed per country.
The *Visit South America Pass* is valid within Argentina, Bolivia, Brazil, Colombia, Chile (except Easter Island), Ecuador, Paraguay, Peru, Uruguay and Venezuela. Participating airlines include *Aer Lingus* (EI), *American Airlines* (AA), *British Airways* (BA), *Cathay Pacific* (CX), *Finnair* (AY), *Iberia* (IB), *LAN* (LA) and *Qantas* (QF). The pass must be bought outside South America in country of residence. It allows unlimited travel to 34 cities. A minimum of three flights must be booked, with no maximum; the maximum stay is 60 days, with no minimum, and prices depend on the number of flight zones. For further details, contact one of the participating airlines.
Departure tax: US$26 is levied on international departures (US$14 to Buenos Aires), if departing from Carrasco International Airport. US$22 is levied on international and domestic departures from Laguna del Sauce Airport (Punta del Este). There is no departure tax on other domestic flights.
SEA:
Main ports: *Montevideo*, the main international port, is served by cargo lines from the USA and Europe. There is a night-ferry service from Buenos Aires to Montevideo (travel time - 10 hours). High-speed ferries (called 'planes' due to their speed) also operate between Montevideo and Buenos Aires (travel time - three hours; website: www.buquebus.com). There are also services from *Colonia* (160km/100 miles west of Montevideo) to Buenos Aires by ferry and a thrice-daily hydrofoil service. A port departure tax may be levied.
ROAD:
Coaches and buses travel regularly between Brazil and Uruguay - these are modern coaches with bar, TV, WC and radio. The travel time between Montevideo and Porto Alegre (Brazil) is 11 hours 30 minutes; to Rio de Janeiro (Brazil) is 59 hours. Buses depart link Montevideo with Asunción and Iguazú Falls in Paraguay, as well as with Florianópolis, Rio de Janeiro and Santiago in Brazil and with northern and southern regions of Argentina. More information is available from the website www.trescruces.com.uy.

Travel - Internal

AIR:
The only internal flights available since *TAMU*, a branch of the Uruguayan Air Force, suspended its services, are the domestic legs of international flights from Punta del Este via Montevideo to Brazil.
SEA/RIVER:
There are no scheduled boat services along the principal rivers but the River Uruguay is navigable from Colonia to Salto, and the Río Negro (flowing across the country from northeast to northwest) is navigable as far as the port of Mercedes.
RAIL:
A few local services run between villages. These are not usually used by tourists and are under threat of closure.
ROAD:
Traffic drives on the right. There are 45,000km (28,000 miles) of roads in Uruguay, 90 per cent of which are paved or otherwise improved for all-weather use. However, the conditions of roads varies. Traffic is often disorganised. **Bus:** The bus service is good: two main bus lines (*COPSA* and *COT*) provide services throughout the country, connecting all towns and the Brazilian border points. More information is available from the website www.trescruces.com.uy. **Car hire:** Available in Montevideo. **Documentation:** An International Driving Permit or UK licence is required. A temporary licence to drive in Uruguay, valid for 90 days, must be obtained from the Town Hall (*Municipio*).
URBAN:
Extensive bus services operate in Montevideo and the suburbs. There are flat fares for the central area and suburban services. Metered taxis are available in all cities and from the airport. Drivers carry a list of fares. A surcharge is made for each item of baggage and between 2400-0600. Within city limits, taxis may be hired by the hour at an agreed rate. Taxi drivers expect a tip.

Travel Advice

Most visits to Uruguay are trouble-free but you should be aware of the global risk of indiscriminate international terrorist attacks, which could be against civilian targets, including places frequented by foreigners.
The risk of crime is generally low throughout Uruguay, but travellers should show greater awareness in and around Montevideo.
This advice is based on information provided by the Foreign and Commonwealth Office in the UK. It is correct at time of publishing. As the situation can change rapidly, visitors are advised to contact the following organisations for the latest travel advice:

British Foreign and Commonwealth Office
Tel: (0845) 850 2829.
Website: www.fco.gov.uk

US Department of State
Website: http://travel.state.gov/travel

Accommodation

HOTELS:
There are numerous first-class hotels in Montevideo and along Uruguay's coastal resorts, where rates are usually a little higher. It is essential to book during the summer and during carnival week in Montevideo. There are several lower-priced hotels in the city for more basic accommodation. The Ministry of Tourism has a hotel listing page on its website (see *Top Things To See & Do*). **Grading:** A star rating system of one to five stars is used. Prices tend to be higher during the tourist season. There is a 23 per cent value-added tax in Montevideo. At the beaches, many hotels offer only US-plan terms (full board).
CAMPING:
Allowed at numerous designated sites throughout the country; elsewhere it is necessary to get police permission. Campsites are listed on the Ministry of Tourism's website (see *Top Things To See & Do*).
YOUTH HOSTELS:
Uruguay is a member of the International Youth Hostel Federation and there are several youth hostels throughout Uruguay offering cheap accommodation, run by Asociación de Alberguistas del Uruguay (see *Accommodation Information*).

ACCOMMODATION INFORMATION

Asociación de Alberguistas del Uruguay (Hostelling International Uruguay)
Canelones 935, PO Box 10680, CP 11100, Montevideo, Uruguay
Tel: (2) 900 5749.
Website: www.hosteluruguay.org

Top Things To See & Do

- The architecture of **Montevideo**, the capital, combines colonial, European and modern influences. Head for the old inner city, known as the **Ciudad Vieja** (**Old Town**), a small peninsula surrounded by the sea near the metropolitan port. The **Cabildo** (the Old Town **Council Hall**), the **Cathedral**, the **Plaza Matriz**, the **Plaza Zabala** and the **Port Market** are fine examples of Uruguay's colonial past. The Old Town, also a centre for antique shops, contrasts dramatically with the rising number of modern buildings and office blocks surrounding the area. The most interesting entrance to the city is via the **Puerta de la Ciudadela** (**Door to the Citadel**), part of the **old wall** that still surrounds Montevideo leading on, via the **Plaza Independencia**, to the popular and lively city centre. The suburbs have restaurants, nightclubs and hotels.
- To the west of Montevideo is **Colonia Suiza** ('**The Swiss Colony**'), reached by hydrofoil from the capital. Visit its delightful **old quarter**.
- Be charmed by the picturesque river ports of **Carmelo** on the **River Uruguay** and **Mercedes** on the **Rio Negro** (a tributary); further up Uruguay is **Salto**, one of the country's largest cities.
- **Fray Bentos**, near Mercedes, gave its name to the famous processed meat company.
- The journey north through **Florida** and **Durazno** to **Tacuarembó** on the Brazilian border takes one through the heart of the country's agricultural lands.
- The beautiful hills surrounding the town of **Minas** are

well worth a visit, as is **Colonia del Sacramento**, which has been rebuilt in its original 18th-century style.

- The Atlantic coast resorts are popular from December to April, and have fine beaches. Most fashionable of these is **Punta del Este**, 145km (90 miles) from Montevideo. It has two main beaches and offers **water-skiing**, **fishing**, **surfing** and **yachting**; there is also a **golf** course. Villas and chalets can be rented in the wooded area on the edge of town. Two nearby islands, **Gorniti** and **Lobos**, are worth a visit. Other beach resorts along the Uruguayan coast include **Atlántida**, **Piriápolis** and the fishing port of **La Paloma**. There are nine major bathing beaches in Montevideo, the best of which are **Carrasco**, **Malvin**, **Miramar**, and **Pocitos**. Note that some of the 'metropolitan' beaches tend to be dirty and unsuitable for bathing. Those along the Atlantic coast are, however, clean and are suitable for swimming.

- **Boating** is a favourite Uruguayan pastime. **Santiago Vazquez** on the **St Lucia River** is one of several popular centres. Arrangements can be made for hire of motor or sailing boats in Montevideo and elsewhere. The mineral baths at **Minas** are also worth a visit.

- There are three **fishing** areas: along **the Rio de la Plata** from **Colonia** to **Piriápolis** for surf-casting; from **Piriápolis** to **Punta del Este** (considered one of the best fishing areas in the world); and along the **Atlantic Coast** towards the Brazilian border. Boats and tackle can be hired in fishing clubs in Fray Bentos, Montevideo, Mercedes, Paysandú, Punta del Este and Salto.

- Attend a **horserace** at the **Hipodromo de Maroñas** on Saturday and Sunday afternoons.

- **Football** is the most popular spectator sport; matches are played regularly throughout the country.

- **Dune walking** is increasingly popular in Cabo Palonia.

- See how the Uruguayans master **tango**.

- Have fun during **Carnival Week** (usually in February). Although this 'fiesta' is officially only for the Monday and Tuesday preceding Ash Wednesday, most shops and businesses close for the entire week. Houses and streets are appropriately decorated and humorous shows are staged at open-air theatres. La **Semana Criolla**, or Holy Week (April), offers traditional activities like *asados* (barbecues), folk music and horseriding/cowboy stunt riding. For a complete list of special events, contact the Ministerio de Turismo (see *Tourist Information*).

TOURIST INFORMATION

Ministerio de Turismo del Uruguay (Ministry of Tourism)
Rambla 25 de Agosto de 1825 esq, Yacaré, S/N (plano), Montevideo, Uruguay
Tel: (2) 188 5100.
Website: www.turismo.gub.uy

Entertainment

FOOD & DRINK: The majority of Uruguayan restaurants are *parrilladas* (grill-rooms). Table service is usual in restaurants. Cafes or bars have either table and/or counter service.
National specialities:
- *Bife de chorrizo* (rump steak).
- *Cazuela* (stew), usually served with *mondongo* (tripe).
- *Morcilla dulce* (sweet black sausage made from blood, orange peel and walnuts) and *morcilla salada* (salty sausage).
- *Dulce de leche* (milk sweets).
- *Chaja* (ball-shaped sponge cake filled with cream and jam).
National drinks:
- Uruguayan wines are of good quality. A popular drink is *medio-medio* (half dry white wine and half champagne).
- Beers are very good.
- Local spirits are *caña*, *grappa* and locally distilled whisky and gin.
There are no set licensing hours. **Tipping:** 10 per cent when no service charge is added.
NIGHTLIFE: Theatre, ballet and symphonic concerts are staged in Montevideo from March to January. Tango is nearly as popular as in Argentina. There are discos in the Carrasco area. There are several dinner-dance places in Montevideo. Large Montevideo hotels have good bars. When there is music for dancing, the price of drinks increases quite considerably. There are also several casinos.
SHOPPING: Special purchases include suede jackets, amethyst jewellery and paintings. The Tristan Narvaja Market is famous for its antiques and there are many antique shops in the Old Town. **Shopping hours:** Mon-Fri 0900-1200 and 1400-1900, Sat 0900-1230.

Business

- **GDP:** US$13.2 million (2004).
- **Main exports:** Meat, wool, hides, leather, wool products, fish, rice and furs.
- **Main imports:** Machinery, chemicals, fuel and vehicles.
- **Main trade partners:** USA, Brazil, Germany and Argentina.

ECONOMY: Uruguay is one of the more prosperous Latin American countries. The economy has a traditionally strong agricultural sector, with beef and wool being the most important products; dairy exports to other Latin American countries are substantial. Crop farming is widespread, producing mostly cereals, rice, fruit and vegetables. Manufacturing is concentrated in oil and coal-derived products, chemicals, textiles, transport equipment and leather products. The oil and coal, both for manufacturing and energy consumption (the latter supplemented by Uruguay's own hydroelectricity stations), are imported. Mining is confined to small-scale extraction of building materials, industrial minerals and some gold. The tourism industry brings in just under US$1 billion annually. Uruguay's economic health depends heavily on that of its two large neighbours, Argentina and Brazil. Both Latin American giants have been in the doldrums since the turn of the millennium, then, in August 2002, both Argentina and, to a lesser extent, Brazil were gripped by financial crises. This led to a collapse in the cross-border trade upon which Uruguay is heavily dependent. The government was forced to take emergency measures in the form of currency devaluation, loan rescheduling and, in an unusually drastic move, closing down the country's entire financial system as it approached meltdown. It also appealed for support from the IMF, which responded with a US$3 billion package. With the worst of the crisis past, Uruguay is now returning to something approaching economic health. Annual growth reached 12.3 per cent in 2004, while 5 to 7 per cent growth was expected in 2005. Inflation in 2004 was 7.6 per cent. Uruguay is a member of Mercosur, the principal regional trade bloc, as well as the Asociación Latinoamericana de Integración (ALADI) and the Inter-American Development Bank.
BUSINESS ETIQUETTE: Businessmen should wear conservative suits and ties. As far as communication is concerned, some knowledge of Spanish will prove invaluable, although English may be spoken by many in business and tourist circles. Appointments are necessary and punctuality is expected. Business cards are essential and it would be an advantage to have the reverse printed in Spanish. Avoid visits during Carnival week. **Office hours:** Mon-Fri 0830-1200 and 1430-1830.

COMMERCIAL INFORMATION

Cámara Nacional de Comercio y Servicios del Uruguay
Rincón 454, Piso 2, CP 11000, Montevideo, Uruguay
Tel: (2) 916 1277.
Website: www.cncs.com.uy

Uruguayan American Chamber of Commerce
1710 First Avenue, Suite 333, New York, NY 10128, USA
Tel: (212) 722 3306.
Website: www.uruguaychamber.com

Uzbekistan

Location: Central Asia.

Time: GMT + 5.

Overview

The territory of modern-day Uzbekistan and its close neighbours have seen many empires rise and fall. The Sogdians, the Macedonians, the Huns, the Mongolians, the Seljuks, the Timurids and the Khanates of Samarkand, Bukhara Khiva and Khorezm all held sway here at one time or another. Central Asia really came of age with the development of the Silk Road from China to the West. Samarkand and Bukhara lay astride this, the most valuable trading route of its day. The riches that it brought were used to build fabulous mosques and madrassars, most of which were destroyed by the Mongol hordes in the 13th century. Much of the damage was repaired and new cities were built by Timur the Lame in the 14th century.
The Russians had had their eyes on the lands over their southern border since Peter the Great sent his first military mission to Khiva in 1717. It was to be another 150 years before they started to make any considerable headway. In 1865, General Kaufmann took Tashkent and signed agreements with the Khans. There were Russian client Khans in Khiva until 1920. The Bolsheviks were resisted in Central Asia by bands known as Basmachi until the 1930s; they were finally suppressed and Moscow took control. Uzbekistan declared independence from the Soviet Union in 1991.
Today Uzbekistan is bordered by Afghanistan, Turkmenistan, Kazakhstan, Kyrgyzstan and Tajikistan. The country boasts some of the finest architectural jewels among the Silk Road countries, featuring intricate Islamic tile work, turquoise domes, minarets and preserved relics from the time when Central Asia was a centre of empire and learning. Good examples of this architecture can be found in the ancient walled city of Khiva in Urgench, the winding narrow streets of the old town of Bukhara and Samarkand, known locally as the 'Rome of the Orient'. The Ferghana Valley, surrounded by the Tian Shan and Pamir mountains, still produces silk and is well worth visiting for its friendly bazaars and landscape of cotton fields, mulberry trees and fruit orchards. Uzbekistan's mountain ranges attract hikers, cyclists and backcountry skiers, while experienced mountaineers come to climb some of the world's highest peaks.
Owing to the difficulties of touring independently, travellers with limited time are advised to buy a package and make use of the services of a recognised tour company.

General Information

AREA: 447,400 sq km (172,740 sq miles).
POPULATION: 26.9 million (UN, 2005).
POPULATION DENSITY: 60.1 per sq km.
CAPITAL: Tashkent. **Population:** 2.2 million (UN estimate 2001; including suburbs).
GEOGRAPHY: Uzbekistan is bordered by Afghanistan to the south, Turkmenistan to the west, Kazakhstan to the north,

Kyrgyzstan to the northeast and Tajikistan to the east. The country has a colourful and varied countryside. The south and east are dominated by the Tien-Shan and Pamir-Alai mountain ranges and the Kyzyl Kum Desert lies to the northeast. The northwestern autonomous region of Karakalpakstan is bordered by the Aral Sea and the sparsely populated Ustyurt Plateau with its vast cotton fields.

GOVERNMENT: Republic. Declared independence from the Soviet Union in 1991. **Head of State:** President Islam Karimov since 1991. **Head of Government:** Prime Minister Shavkat Mirziyayev since 2003. **Recent history:** Islam Karimov took over as head of the Uzbek Communist party (now the People's Democratic Party of Uzbekistan, PDPU). In 1989 Uzbekistan assumed independence in 1991 upon the break up of the Soviet Union. The PRPU, with Karimov at its head, has held power continuously ever since, occasionally in alliance with allied parties such as the Progress of the Fatherland party. He has been re-elected several times, most recently in 2000, with overwhelming majorities and against nominal opposition. In April 2002, Karimov won a referendum to extend the length of his current term from five to eight years, guaranteeing that he will remain in power until at least 2008. Domestic opposition is divided between secular democratic forces and Islamic parties. *Erk* (Freedom), *Birlik* (Democracy), and a third organisation, *Adolat* (Justice), comprising the secular opposition, have combined in the Democratic Opposition Co-ordinating Council. All three are currently banned, although a more relaxed attitude recently on the part of the Government has allowed them to organise openly. Uzbekistan has played a valuable role in recent American military campaigns in Afghanistan (with whom it shares a border) and Iraq: the American military now have a relatively small but permanent and growing presence in the country. This has been of some concern to the Russians, who have military bases in most of the former Soviet republics but not Uzbekistan. In November 2005, Russia and Uzbekistan signed an agreement paving the way for much closer military cooperation.

LANGUAGE: The official language is Uzbek, a Turkic tongue closely related to Kazakh and Kyrgyz. There is a small Russian-speaking minority. Many people involved with tourism speak English. The Government has stated its intention to change the Cyrillic script to the Latin.

RELIGION: Predominantly Sunni Muslim, with Shia (15 per cent), Russian Orthodox and Jewish minorities.

ELECTRICITY: 220 volts AC, 50Hz. Round two-pin continental plugs are standard.

SOCIAL CONVENTIONS: *Lipioshka* (bread) should never be laid upside down and should never be put on the ground, even if it is in a bag. It is normal to remove shoes but not socks when entering someone's house or sitting down in a *chai-khana*. Shorts are rarely seen in Uzbekistan and, worn by women, are likely to provoke unwelcome attention from the local male population. Avoid ostentatious displays of wealth (eg jewellery) in public places. Homosexuality is illegal.

Photography: Photography near airports, military barracks and police stations can upset the authorities.

Climate

Uzbekistan has an extreme continental climate. It is generally warmest in the south and coldest in the north. Temperatures in December average -8°C (18°F) in the north and 0°C (32°F) in the south. However, extreme fluctuations can take temperatures as low as -35°C (-31°F). During the summer months, temperatures can climb to 45°C (113°F) and above. Humidity is low. The best time to visit is during the spring and autumn.

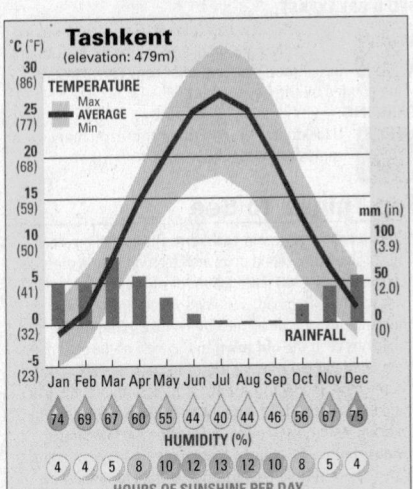

Communications

Telephone: Country code: 998. Area code for Tashkent: 71. IDD is available, but calls from hotel rooms still need to be booked either from reception or from the floor attendant.

International calls can also be made from main post offices (in Tashkent on Prospekt Navoi). Direct-dial calls within the CIS are obtained by dialling 8 and waiting for another dial tone and then dialling the city code. Calls within the city limits are free of charge.

Mobile telephone: Roaming agreements exist with most international mobile phone operators. Coverage is limited to populated areas.

Internet: Internet cafes exist in Tashkent.

Post: Letters to Western Europe and the USA can take between two weeks and two months. Stamped envelopes can be bought from post offices. Addresses should be laid out in the following order: country, postcode, city, street, house number and, lastly, the person's name. Post office hours: Mon-Fri 0900-1800. The Main Post Office in Tashkent (see above) is open until 1900. Visitors can also use the post offices situated in the major hotels. There are a number of international courier services based in Tashkent.

MEDIA: Press freedom is guaranteed and a constitutional ban on censorship exists, but these are frequently ignored in Uzbekistan, where the state maintains a tight grip on the media. International media rights bodies have reported that the use of violence against journalists and disinformation by the authorities are commonplace. Pre-publication self-censorship remains widespread. Following deadly unrest in Andijan in 2005, journalists were expelled from the area and foreign TV news broadcasts were blocked. Private TV and radio stations broadcast alongside state-run networks. Foreign channels operate via cable TV, which is widely available.

Press: There are no independent daily newspapers in Uzbekistan. The main editions are published in Tashkent and include *Khalk Suzi* and *Narodnoye Slovo* (in Russian and Uzbek), *Hurriyat* (published by a Government agency) and *Uzbekistan Ovizi*.

TV: *Uzbek State Television and Radio Company* operates two networks. Private channels include *MTRK, Bekabad TV, Samarkand TV* and *Orbita TV*.

Radio: The *Uzbek State Television and Radio Company* operates state-run radio services. Private stations include *Oriat FM, Uzbegim Taronasi* and *Radio Grand*.

Passport/Visa

	Passport Required?	Visa Required?	Return Ticket Required?
Full British	Yes	Yes	No
Australian	Yes	Yes	No
Canadian	Yes	Yes	No
USA	Yes	Yes/1	No
Other EU	Yes	Yes	No
Japanese	Yes	Yes	No

Note: *Regulations and requirements may be subject to change at short notice, and you are advised to contact the appropriate diplomatic or consular authority before finalising travel arrangements. Any numbers in the chart refer to the footnotes below.*

PASSPORTS: Passport valid for six months after departure date required by all.

VISAS: Required by all except the following:
(a) nationals of the CIS (except nationals of Kyrgyzstan, Tajikistan and Turkmenistan who *do* require a visa);
(b) transit passengers continuing their journey within 24 hours by the same or first connecting aircraft provided holding valid onward or return documentation and not leaving the transit area.

Types of visa and cost: *Tourist* and *Business*. *Single-entry*: US$40 (seven days); US$50 (15 days); US$60 (30 days); US$80 (three months); US$120 (six months); US$160 (one year). *Multiple-entry*: US$60 (one month); US$150 (six months); US$250 (one year). *Group*: US$15 per person (15 days); US$25 per person (30 days). *Transit*: US$20 (24 hours); US$25 (48 hours); US$30 (72 hours); US$40 (double-entry).

Note: (a) **1.** US nationals can obtain multiple-entry business or tourist visas issued for up to four years for a cost of US$100 and transit visas for a cost of US$25. (b) Visa applications are subject to a US$20 service charge (US$10 for transit visas). (c) Visa regulations within the CIS are liable to change at short notice.

Validity: Tourist visas are normally single-entry/exit and are valid for the duration of the tour. Business visas are multiple-entry, valid for six months in the first instance and extendable. Nationals of Austria, Belgium, France, Germany, Italy, Japan, Spain, Switzerland and the UK can obtain a multiple-entry visa for touristic/business stays of up to one month; nationals of the USA can obtain such visas for stays of up to four years. Visas should be used within one month of date of issue.

Application to: Uzbek Embassies where they exist.

Application requirements: (a) Valid passport valid for entire period of stay with at least one blank page to affix the visa. (b) Two completed and signed application forms. (c) Two passport-size photos. (d) Fee, payable by cheque in Pounds Sterling on collection of visa. (e) Pre-paid, stamped,

self-addressed envelope, if applying by post. *Tourist:* (a)-(e) and, (f) Letter of invitation from inviting partners in Uzbekistan. Applications are usually made through a travel agent. *Business:* (a)-(e) and, (f) Business invitation from Uzbekistan giving details of activities to be undertaken and length of stay in Uzbekistan. This letter can be sent directly to the Ministry of Foreign Affairs in Uzbekistan, who will then contact the Embassy directly, giving permission for the stay. *Private visits:* (a)-(e) and, (f) Letter of invitation from friends/relatives endorsed by the immigration department of the Ministry of Internal Affairs in Uzbekistan. *Transit:* (a)-(e) and, (f) Air ticket to onward destination.

Note: (a) Tourists (other than nationals of Austria, Belgium, France, Germany, Italy, Japan, Spain, Switzerland and USA, who also do not need to submit letters of invitation as part of their visa application requirement) will normally have their visa application completed by their travel agent. (b) A personal interview may be required before a visa can be issued. (c) Visitors staying longer than three days must register with the Ministry of Internal Affairs within three working days. However, most hotels will automatically do this on behalf of the visitor. (d) Before applying by post, applicants should first contact the Consular section of the Embassy (except for nationals of Austria, Belgium, France, Germany, Italy, Japan, Spain, Switzerland and USA).

Working days required: 10. For nationals of Austria, Belgium, France, Germany, Italy, Japan, Spain, Switzerland, the UK and USA, allow two days.

Temporary residence: It is possible to apply for temporary residence. The government of Uzbekistan officially requires visitors to carry a medical certificate proving they are free of HIV, but this is rarely enforced.

PASSPORT/VISA INFORMATION

Embassy of the Republic of Uzbekistan in the UK
41 Holland Park, London W11 3RP, UK
Tel: (020) 7229 7679.
Website: www.uzbekembassy.org
Opening hours: Mon-Fri 0900-1800; Mon-Wed and Fri 1000-1300 (consular section).

Embassy of the Republic of Uzbekistan in the USA
1746 Massachusetts Avenue, NW, Washington, DC 20036-1903, USA
Tel: (202) 887 5300.
Website: www.uzbekistan.org

Consulate General of the Republic of Uzbekistan in the USA
801 2nd Avenue, 20th Floor, New York, NY 10017, USA
Tel: (212) 754 7403/4718.
Opening Hours: Mon-Wed 1000-1300; Thurs (collection of documents only).

Money

Currency: Uzbek Sum (UZS) = 100 tiyn. Notes are in denominations of UZS1000, 500, 200, 100 and 50. Coins are denominations of UZS50, 25, 10, 5 and 1, and 50, 25, 10, 5 and 1 tiyn.

Currency exchange: Tourists and businesspeople without special status have to pay for hotels, hotel services and transport in hard currency; US Dollars are the most widely acceptable. All bills are normally settled in cash. It is illegal to change money on the black market and penalties can be harsh. Banks and the currency exchange bureaux in major hotels will change at the official rates.

Credit & debit cards: Acceptable in some of the major hotels in tourist centres. Uzbekistan has said that it intends to introduce its own Visa card in the near future.

Traveller's cheques: Limited acceptance.

Currency restrictions: The import of foreign currency is unlimited, but should be declared on arrival. Travellers importing sums in excess of US$1000 may be subject to a body search. The export of foreign currency is permitted. Travellers who have imported sums in excess of US$2000 are required to provide proof of lawful exchange into Sum, otherwise a fine of 30 per cent of the amount imported will be payable. The import and export of local currency is unlimited.

Banking hours: Mon-Fri 0900-1800. Some banks open Sat 0900-1500.

Exchange rate indicators:
Rate at time of publishing
£1.00= UZS2046.63
$1.00= UZS1161.06

Duty Free

The following goods may be imported into Uzbekistan by visitors over 16 years without incurring customs duty:
1000 cigarettes or 1kg of tobacco products; 1.5l of alcoholic beverages and 2l of wine; a reasonable quantity

of perfume for personal use; other goods for personal use up to a value of US$10,000.

Note: All valuable items such as jewellery, cameras and computers should be declared on arrival.

Prohibited imports: Firearms, ammunition, drugs, photographs and printed matter directed against the country, live animals (without special permit) and fruit or vegetables.

Prohibited exports: Items more than 100 years old and those of special cultural importance require special permission for export. When buying items that may be more than 100 years old, ask for a certificate stating the age of the item(s). Precious metals, stones, furs, arms and ammunition, antiquities and art objects (subject to duty and special permit from the Ministry of Culture) are also prohibited.

Public Holidays

Below are listed Public Holidays for the January 2006–June 2007 period.

2006: Jan 1 New Year's Day. **Jan 10** Kurban Khait (Feast of the Sacrifice). **Mar 8** International Women's Day. **Mar 21** Navrus. **Apr 11** Prophet's Birthday. **May 1** Labour Day. **May 9** Day of Memory and Respect. **Sep 1** Independence Day. **Oct 24** Ramadan Khait (End of Ramadan). **Nov 18** Flag Day. **Dec 8** Constitution Day. **Dec 31** Kurban Khait (Feast of the Sacrifice).

2007: Jan 1 New Year's Day. **Mar 8** International Women's Day. **Mar 21** Navrus. **Mar 31** Prophet's Birthday. **May 1** Labour Day. **May 9** Day of Memory and Respect.

Note: Muslim festivals are timed according to local sightings of various phases of the moon and the dates given above are approximations. For further information, consult the *World of Islam* appendix.

Health

	Special Precautions?	Certificate Required?
Yellow Fever	No	No
Cholera	Yes	1
Typhoid & Polio	2	N/A
Malaria	No/3	N/A

Note: *Regulations and requirements may be subject to change at short notice, and you are advised to contact your doctor well in advance of your intended date of departure. Any numbers in the chart refer to the footnotes below.*

1: Following WHO guidelines issued in 1973, a *cholera* vaccination certificate is not a condition of entry to Uzbekistan. However, *cholera* is a serious risk in this country and precautions are essential. Up-to-date advice should be sought before deciding whether these precautions should include vaccination, as medical opinion is divided over its effectiveness; see the *Health appendix* for more information.

2: Vaccination against *typhoid* is advised.

3: Although *malaria* is not considered a problem, there have been sporadic cases reported in the Uzunskiy, Sariassiskiy and Shurchinskiy districts (Surkhanda-Rinskaya region). It is recommended that travellers take chloroquine as their anti malarial drug.

Food & drink: All water, particularly outside main centres, should be regarded as being a potential health risk. Water used for drinking, brushing teeth or making ice should have first been boiled or otherwise sterilised. Milk is pasteurised and dairy products are safe for consumption. Only eat well-cooked meat and fish, preferably served hot. Pork, salad and mayonnaise may carry increased risk. Vegetables should be cooked and fruit peeled.

Other risks: Immunisation against *hepatitis A* and *meningococcal meningitis* is advised. *Hepatitis B* and *E* occur. *Trachoma* is quite common. *Tickborne encephalitis* and *diphtheria* also occur.

Rabies is present. For those at high risk, vaccination before arrival should be considered. If you are bitten, seek medical advice without delay. For more information, consult the *Health* appendix.

Health care: Emergency health care is available free of charge for visitors although, as in most parts of the former Soviet Union, medical care in Uzbekistan is inadequate and there are extreme financial problems. Doctors and hospitals often expect cash payment for health services. There is a severe shortage of basic medical supplies, including disposable needles, anaesthetics, antibiotics and vaccines. Travellers are therefore advised to take a well-equipped first-aid kit with them containing basic medicines and any prescriptions that they may need. For minor difficulties, visitors are advised to ask the management at their hotel for help. In case of emergency, travellers should get a referral from either the Tashkent International Medical Clinic or from the appropriate Embassy, since foreigners are strongly advised not to approach local health care facilities without somebody who knows local conditions and the

language. For major problems, visitors are well advised to seek help outside the country. Travel insurance is essential.

Travel - International

AIR:

 The national airline, *Uzbekistan Airways (HY)* (website: www.uzairways.com), currently flies from London, Athens, Bangkok, Bahrain, Birmingham, Delhi, Frankfurt, Hoshemin, Istanbul, Kiev, Kuala Lumpur, Moscow, New York, Osaka, Paris, Rome, Seoul, Sharjah and Tel Aviv. It also flies to most destinations within the CIS. Flights to Tajikistan have been suspended since the Tajik civil war at the end of 1992.

Approximate flight times: From Tashkent to *London* is seven hours (direct), to *Bangkok* is six hours 30 minutes, to *Frankfurt* is six hours, to *Beijing* is five hours 30 minutes, to *Tel Aviv* is four hours 30 minutes, to *Delhi* is three hours 30 minutes, to *Istanbul* is three hours 30 minutes and to *Moscow* is three hours 30 minutes.

Main airports: *Tashkent International Airport (TAS)* is in the south of the town, about 11km (seven miles) from the centre. *To/from the airport:* Buses run frequently to the city centre (travel time – 30 to 60 minutes). Trains and tolley buses connect the airport with the centre (travel time – 10 to 20 minutes) and taxis are available (travel time – 15 to 20 minutes). *Facilities:* Bureau de change, duty free shops, restaurants and bars.

Departure tax: US$10.

RAIL:

 Tashkent is the nodal point for rail services from Central Asia. Lines lead west to Ashgabat (Turkmenistan), south to Samarkand and on to Dushanbe (Tajikistan), east to Bishkek (Kyrgyzstan) and Almaty (Kazakhstan) and north to Moscow (Russian Federation). From Tashkent, along the *Saratov-Syr Darya Line*, the journey to Moscow takes nearly three days. There is also a spur line to the Fergana Valley in the east of the country, which leads to Osh in Kyrgyzstan. It is possible to connect to China through Almaty; and to Iran and the Middle East (via Turkmenistan). Foreigners have to pay for rail tickets in hard currency, preferably US Dollars, but it is still a cheap option by Western standards.

ROAD:

 Uzbekistan has road connections to all its neighbours. The border between Afghanistan and Uzbekistan is closed to all except Uzbek and Afghan nationals. Travellers should exercise caution around the Kyrgyz–Uzbek border as some violent incidents have occured. It is not advisable to bring your own car. Contact your local Embassy for details. **Bus:** There are services to all the neighbouring countries, although the occasional border closures between Uzbekistan and Tajikistan make this route unreliable. Long-distance buses leave from the Tashkent bus station near the metro station. Foreigners have to pay for tickets in hard currency. **Car hire:** It is possible to hire cars with drivers for long journeys; they will normally ask to be paid in US Dollars. The best place to look for these is at the long-distance bus and train stations.

Travel - Internal

AIR:

 Uzbekistan Airways (HY) (website: uzairways.com) flies to all the major towns and cities in Uzbekistan on a regular basis. Destinations include Andijan, Karshi, Namangan, Navoi (which is 45 minutes by bus from Bukhara), Nukus, Samarkand, Tashkent and Termez. Tickets can be bought at the *Uzbekistan Airways* ticket agency opposite the Hotel Russia on Shota Rustaveli in Tashkent or at the departure terminal of the airport. International flights booked in Tashkent should be paid for in US Dollars although some credit cards are accepted. It is preferable to pay for domestic flights in Sum.

Approximate flight times: From Tashkent to *Termez* is one hour 20 minutes, to *Nukus* is two hours, to *Samarkand* is 40 minutes, to *Navoi* is one hour and to *Namangan* is one hour 40 minutes.

RAIL:

There are 3400km (2113 miles) of railways linking Termez, Samarkand, Bukhara, the Fergana Valley and Nukus. There are two railway stations in Tashkent – North and South. The *Trans-Caspian Railway* traverses the country from Chardzhou in Turkmenistan via Kagan (near Bukhara), Samarkand and Dzhizak, where the railway branches off to serve the capital, Tashkent. Passengers should store valuables under the bed or seat, and should not leave the compartment unattended. Tickets can be bought on the ground floor of the Hotel Locomotif or at the OVIR office at the station.

ROAD:

The Republic of Uzbekistan is served by a reasonable road network. Traffic drives on the right. **Bus:** Services connect all the major towns within Uzbekistan and are cheap and fairly reliable. **Taxi:**

Taxis and cars for hire can be found in all major towns. It is safer to use officially marked taxis, although many taxis are unlicensed. Travellers are advised to agree a fare in advance, and not to share taxis with strangers. As many of the street names have changed since independence, it is also advisable to ascertain both the old and the new street names when asking directions. Cars can be hired by the trip, by the hour or by the day or week. **Documentation:** An International Driving Permit will be required when car hire facilities have been introduced.

URBAN:

Tashkent is served by taxis, buses, trolleybuses, trams and the only underground in Central Asia. The underground network has been expanded making it 47km (19 miles) long. There are now three lines: *Chilanzar, Uzbekistan* and *Yunusabad*. Public transport is cheap and generally reliable. There are regular bus services to all major towns in Uzbekistan.

Note: Visitors wishing to travel to Termez and other areas of the Surkhandarya region require a permit from the Ministry of Foreign Affairs in Tashkent. They usually take five days to process.

Travel Advice

Travellers should avoid all but essential travel to areas bordering Afghanistan, Tajikistan and Kyrgyzstan other than via authorised crossing points.

There is a high threat from terrorism in Uzbekistan. Travellers should be aware of the potential risk of indiscriminate attacks which could be against civilian targets, including places frequented by foreigners. Travellers should be particularly vigilant in public places and should pay attention to any security announcements by the Uzbek authorities.

This advice is based on information provided by the Foreign and Commonwealth Office in the UK. It is correct at time of publishing. As the situation can change rapidly, visitors are advised to contact the following organisations for the latest travel advice:

British Foreign and Commonwealth Office
Tel: (0845) 850 2829.
Website: www.fco.gov.uk

US Department of State
Website: http://travel.state.gov/travel

Accommodation

HOTELS:

Tourists are still required to stay in hotels that are licensed by Uzbektourism (see *Top Things To Do*), and most hotels are run by them. However, a growing number of independent hotels are now being licensed. It is necessary for visitors to have a slip of paper stamped by the hotel to prove that they have stayed there. Services and facilities are not generally up to Western standards, but efforts are being made to improve them and there is a growing number of western-style hotels owned by foreign companies. Most tourist hotel rooms have a shower and WC ensuite, although supplies of soap and toilet paper can be unreliable. All regional capitals have at least one Uzbektourism hotel that will accept foreigners. Many tourists will have booked tours which include accommodation, others will have to pay in US Dollars, unless they have special exemptions.

BED & BREAKFAST:

There are a few bed & breakfast hotels springing up, but they are small and can be difficult to get into. A new association of bed & breakfasts is being created by the Government.

CAMPING:

Uzbektourism runs a number of temporary campsites in the mountains.

Top Things To See

- Compare old and new in **Tashkent**. The capital preserves only a small proportion of its architectural past. A massive earthquake in 1966 flattened much of the old city and it was rebuilt with broad, tree-lined streets and the new buildings are of little architectural interest. The earlier buildings lie in the **old town** to the west of the centre. A myriad of narrow winding alleys, it stands in stark contrast to the more modern Tashkent. Of interest among the older buildings are the 16th-century **Kukeldash Madrasa**, which is being restored as a museum, and the **Kaffali-Shash Mausoleum**. Many of the Islamic sites in Tashkent are not open to non-Muslims, and visitors should always ask permission before entering a mosque or other religious building. Tashkent houses many museums of Uzbek and pre-Uzbek culture. These include the **State Art Museum**, which houses a collection of paintings, ceramics and the Bukharan royal robes. The **Museum of Decorative and Applied Arts** exhibits embroidered wall hangings and reproduction antique jewellery. As important historical figures, such as Amir Timur – better known as Tamerlane in the West – are being given greater prominence, the exhibits and perspective of the museums are also changing.

- See the site of Alexander the Great's slaying of his friend Cleitos at **Samarkand**, the pivot of the Silk Road and the city transformed by Timur in the 14th century into one of the world's greatest capitals. Much of its past glory survives or has been restored. The centre of the historical town is the **Registan Square**, where three huge madrassas (Islamic seminaries) – including **Shir-Dor** and **Tillya-Kari** – built between the 15th and 17th centuries, dominate the area. Decorated with blue tiles and intricate mosaics, they give some idea of the grandeur that marked Samarkand in its heyday. The **Bibi Khanym Mosque**, not far from the Registan, is testimony to Timur's love for his wife. Now it is a pale shadow of its former self, having been partly destroyed in the 1897 earthquake, and seems permanently under repair. Timur himself is buried in the **Gur Emir**. On the ground floor, under the massive cupola, lie the ceremonial graves of Timur and his descendants. The stone that commemorates Timur is reputed to be the largest chunk of Nephrite (jade) in the world. The actual bodies are situated in the basement, which unfortunately is not open to the public.
- The **Shah-i-Zinda** is a collection of the graves of some of Samarkand's dignitaries. The oldest date from the 14th century as Samarkand was starting to recover from the depredations of the Mongol hordes of the 13th century.
- Other sites of interest in Samarkand include the **Observatory of Ulug Beg**, Timur's grandson, which was the most advanced astronomical observatory of its day. There is also the **Afrasiab Museum**, not far from the observatory, containing a frieze dating from the sixth century, which shows a train of gifts for the Sogdian ruler of the day.
- Visit **Bukhara**, West of Samarkand, which was once a centre of learning renowned throughout the Islamic world. It was here that the great Sheikh Bahautdin Nakshbandi lived. He was a central figure in the development of the mystical Sufi approach to philosophy, religion and Islam. In Bukhara, there are more than 350 mosques and 100 religious colleges. The centre of historical Bukhara is the **Shakristan**, which contains the **Ark**, or palace complex of the Emirs. Much of this was destroyed by fire in the 1920s, but the surviving gatehouse gives an impression of what the whole must have been like. Near the gatehouse is the **Zindan** or jail of the Emirs, which has a display of some of the torture methods employed by the Emirs against their enemies. Not far from the Ark, the 47m- (154ft) high **Kalyan Minaret**, or tower of death, was built in 1127 and, with the **Ishmael Samani Mausoleum**, is almost the only structure to have survived the Mongols. It was from here that convicted criminals were thrown to their deaths. Other sites of interest in Bukhara include the **Kalyan Mosque**, which is open to non-Muslims, the **Ulug Beg Madrasa** – the oldest in Central Asia – and, opposite, the **Abdul Aziz Madrasa**.
- Explore **Khiva**, northeast of Bukhara, near the modern and uninteresting city of **Urgench**. Khiva is younger and better preserved than either Samarkand or Bukhara. The city still lies within the original city walls, and has changed little since the 18th century. Part of its attraction is its completeness; although it has been turned into a museum town and is hardly inhabited, it is possible to imagine what it was like in its prime when it was a market for captured Russian and Persian slaves.
- View the best collection of Russian avant-garde art outside St Petersburg at the **Art Gallery** in **Nukus**, the capital of Karakalpakstan, in the west of the country.
- Keep an eye out for snow tigers, the rare Tian-Shan grey bear and the Berkut eagle in the **Chatkalsky Reserve**, a narrow unspoilt gorge in the western Tian-Shan.

Top Things To Do

- **Trek** in the mountains in the south of the country. There are high peaks for those wanting a challenge, while easier treks can be done in the foothills and on the plateaux. The best time to go is between March and November. There is superb hiking along the spurs and gorges of the **Chatkal Range** to the ancient silver mine in the **Chatkal Natiore Preserve**.
- **Climb** 7000m-(22,965ft-) high mountains. There are many opportunities for serious **mountaineering**, and Uzbekistan contains some of the world's highest peaks, including **Peak Pobeda** (7439m/24,399ft), **Peak Korzhenevskaya** (7105m/23,304ft) and **Peak Khan-Tengri** (6995m/22,943ft). Equipment can be transported to base camps by helicopter.
- Go **ice climbing** in the **Gissar, Matcha** and **Turkestan** ridges. Vertical rock faces for **rock climbing** can be found in the Fan mountains (at **Bodkhana, Chapdara, Maria-Mirali** and **Zamok**) and on the **Matchi Ridge** (at **Aksu, Asan-Usan** and **Sabakh**).

- **Ski** in the mountains above Tashkent.
- Explore the deepest **caves** in Asia at **Boi-Bulok** (1415m/4641ft) and **Kievskaya** (990m/3247ft). These are suitable for experienced cavers only. Beautiful gypsum formations can be seen at the **Kugitang** cave, while the caves of **Baisuntau** contain mummified bears and those in western **Tian Shan** feature underground rivers and lakes.
- Cycle the **Silk Road** from Tashkent via Lake Aidarkul to Khiva. Easier rides can be done in the **Ferghana Valley** and around **Tashkent**, where lake and mountain scenery can be enjoyed. Organised tours are available.
- **Raft** or **kayak** on the **Angren, Chatkal, Pskem, Syr Darya** and **Ugen** river, the best time being September to October.

TOURIST INFORMATION

Uzbektourism
47 Horezmskaya Street, 7000 Tashkent, Uzbekistan
Tel: (71) 133 5414.
Website: www.uzbektourism.uz

Entertainment

FOOD & DRINK: Uzbek food is similar to that of the rest of Central Asia. During the summer and autumn, there is a wide variety of fruit: grapes, pomegranates, apricots – which are also dried and sold at other times of the year – and, dwarfing them all, mountains of honeydew and watermelons. Uzbeks pride themselves on the quality and variety of their bread. In general, hotel food shows a strong Russian influence. There are a number of restaurants that serve both European and Korean food (Stalin transported many Koreans from their home in the east of the former Soviet Union, believing them to be a security threat). There is a hard-currency restaurant at the top of the Hotel Uzbekistan in Tashkent that serves Chinese and Korean food. Beer, wine, vodka, brandy and are all widely available in restaurants.

National specialities:
- *Plov* is the staple food for both every day and celebrations, and usually consists of chunks of mutton, shredded red and yellow carrot and rice fried in a cast iron or aluminium pot. There are dozens of variations of this dish.
- *Shashlyk* (skewered chunks of mutton barbecued over charcoal – kebabs – served with sliced raw onions).
- *Lipioshka* (rounds of unleavened bread) are served in restaurants and are often sold on street corners and make an appetising meal.
- *Samsa* (samosas) are also sold in the street, but the quality is variable.
- *Manty* are large boiled dumplings stuffed with meat.
- *Shorpa* is a meat and vegetable soup.
- *Strogan* is the local equivalent of Beef Stroganoff.
- *Pirmeni* originated in Ukraine and are small boiled dumplings of meat and vegetables, similar to ravioli, sometimes served in a vegetable soup.

National drinks:
- Tea is the staple drink of Central Asia, and *chai-khanas* (tea houses) can be found almost everywhere in Uzbekistan, full of old men chatting the afternoon away with a pot of tea in the shade.
- *Shampanski*, sparkling wine.
- *Kefir*, a thick drinking yoghurt, is often served with breakfast.

Tipping: It is usual to tip 5 to 10 per cent in restaurants, bars and nightclubs. Restaurants in international hotels usually include service in the bill.

NIGHTLIFE: Tashkent has a variety of theatres that show everything from European operas to traditional Uzbek dancing and music. The Navoi theatre, opposite the Tashkent Hotel in Tashkent, shows opera and ballet. The prices are low by Western standards; shows generally start at 1800. There is also a number of themed Western-style bars, restaurants and discos.

SHOPPING: The best place to experience Central Asia is in the bazaars. The bazaars of Tashkent and Samarkand offer goods ranging from herbs and spices to Central Asian carpets. In the Alaiski Bazaar in Tashkent, it is possible to buy decorated Uzbek knives. Silk is still produced in the country and well-priced silks can be bought at large department stores. Many museums have small shops which sell a variety of modern reproductions and some original items. It is possible to buy carpets and embroidered wall hangings. Bukhara is famous for its gold embroidery, and visitors can buy elaborately embroidered traditional Uzbek hats. Visitors should be aware that it is illegal to export anything more than 100 years old or items which have a cultural significance.

Shopping hours: Food shops open 0800-1700, all others open 0900-1900.

Business

- **GDP:** US$17.1 billion (World Bank estimate).
- **Main exports:** Cotton, gold, natural gas, mineral fertilisers, ferrous metals, textiles and motor vehicles.
- **Main imports:** Machinery and equipment, foodstuffs, chemicals and metals.
- **Main trade partners:** Russian Federation, Germany, Switzerland, UK, Kazakhstan, Tajikistan, Korea (Rep of) and Japan.

ECONOMY: Agriculture is the main component of Uzbekistan's economy. Livestock is reared in the steppes while a variety of crops, including grains, fruit and vegetables, are grown in the more fertile valleys. In addition, vast quantities of cotton are produced in formerly arid areas fed by artificial irrigation schemes. Uzbekistan continues to consume over three-quarters of the water available to the ex-Soviet Central Asian Republics. The result of this ill-conceived plan has been one of the world's greatest ecological catastrophes in the Aral Sea, once among the world's largest inland seas, which has been deprived of the bulk of its river sources and has consequently contracted to one-third of its original size. The country has substantial natural resources - especially natural gas, which is an important export earner - and oil. Uzbekistan also boasts the world's largest opencast gold mine and has deposits of silver, uranium, copper, lead, zinc and tungsten. Machinery and vehicles account for the bulk of manufacturing output.

Self-sufficiency in food and energy products meant that Uzbekistan did not suffer as badly as other republics from the collapse of the Soviet Union and its economic system. In principle, this made reform a somewhat easier prospect than for many of Uzbekistan's neighbours. In 1992, Uzbekistan joined the IMF, the World Bank, and the European Bank for Reconstruction and Development (as a 'Country of Operation'). A new currency – the Sum – was introduced in 1996. Economic reform began in earnest in 1994 but the Government has since blown hot and cold over putting it into effect. Much of the economy has now been transferred into private ownership, but key sectors remain under state control and the financial crises of 1997/98 in Asia and the Russian Federation persuaded the Government to put many reform plans on hold. Currency and export controls were introduced in an attempt to insulate the economy, as far as possible, from external influence (although the Government now plans to make the Sum fully convertible in the near future). The lack of reform has also deterred many potential foreign investors. Uzbekistan's recent economic performance has been patchy. Current annual GDP growth is 4.2 per cent. There are no reliable inflation figures available. Uzbekistan has joined the Economic Co-operation Organisation of ex-Soviet republics and former socialist countries. In April 2004, the European Bank of Reconstruction and Development curbed its investment programme due to the lack of progress by Uzbekistan on political and economical benchmarks set by the bank. Until there is more clarity on the legal issues and efficiency in the banking sector, foreign investors will face a difficult environment.

BUSINESS ETIQUETTE: Uzbekistan's Government is actively encouraging foreign investment, particularly in the processing industries for its raw material output. The January 1994 decree put into law a number of tax incentives for foreign investors, formally laid out guarantees for property protection, and promised a faster and less bureaucratic method of registration for foreign concerns. Other areas in which the Uzbeks would like to encourage foreign investment include the financial sector, energy production, extraction and processing of mineral raw materials, textiles, telecommunications, tourism and ecology. All foreign companies currently have to be registered with the Ministry of Foreign Economic Relations. **Office hours:** Mon-Fri 0900-1800.

COMMERCIAL INFORMATION

Agency for Foreign Economic Relations
Ulitsa. T Shevchenko 1, 700029 Tashkent, Uzbekistan
Tel: (71) 138 5000 *or* 5123/5.
Website: www.mfer.uz

Uzbekistan Exhibition Centre
107 Amir Temur Street, 700084 Tashkent, Uzbekistan
Tel: (71) 134 4545 *or* 135 0973.
Website: www.uzexpocentre.uz.

Business Information Service for the Newly Independent States
US Department of Commerce, USA Trade Center, Stop R*BISNIS, 1401 Constitution Avenue, NW, Washington, DC 20230, USA
Tel: (202) 482 4655.
Website: www.bisnis.doc.gov

Vanuatu

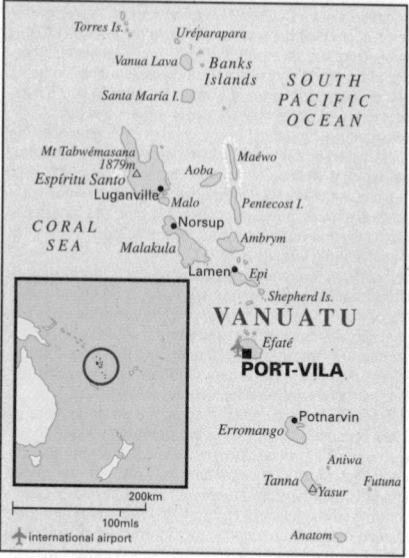

Location: Southwest Pacific.

Time: GMT + 11.

Overview

The island group of which Vanuatu is a part has been settled since BC 500. Up to and beyond the 13th century AD, it was at the heart of the empire of Tonga. During the 19th century, the islands making up Vanuatu (then called the New Hebrides) were settled by British and French missionaries, planters and traders. The UK and France eventually agreed on a condominium over the two islands. After World War II, a complex power struggle began between the indigenous islanders and the dual colonial interests over the future political and economic course of the islands. The constitutional position was settled in 1977, at a conference between British, French and New Hebridean representatives in Paris, and the islands became fully independent in 1980.

A drive since then to encourage overseas tourists to travel to Vanuatu has led to ever-increasing numbers of visitors. It is easy to see why they come. The islands are an adventure enthusiast's paradise. The geologically active archipelago is a natural playground of colourful reefs, bubbling volcanoes and lush jungle. Visitors can drive up to the crater of Yasur, cited as the most accessible active volcano in the world, sea kayak round the islands' shorelines, explore underwater World War II relics, or hike and bike through coconut plantations and tropical rainforest. Those less inclined to exert themselves can relax on the many beautiful beaches, sample the multicultural cuisine in the capital, Port-Vila, or charter a boat from one island to the next. Tourism is centred on the islands of Efaté, Tanna and Espiritu Santo. International visitors arrive in Port-Vila, on Efaté, and from here can travel by boat or plane to explore the rest of the country.

General Information

AREA: 12,190 sq km (4707 sq miles).
POPULATION: 222,000 (UN estimate 2005).
POPULATION DENSITY: 18.2 per sq km.
CAPITAL: Port-Vila (Island of Efaté). **Population:** 30,139 (1999).
GEOGRAPHY: Vanuatu, formerly called the New Hebrides, forms an incomplete double chain of islands stretching north to southeast for some 900km (560 miles). They are situated approximately 2250km (1407 miles) northeast of Sydney, Australia, and 800km (500 miles) west of Fiji. Together with the Banks and Torres islands, the chains comprise about 40 mountainous islands and 40 islets and rocks. The islands are volcanic in origin and there are five active volcanoes. The Ambrym and Lopevi volcanoes are permanently active and highly dangerous. Lopevi was extinct for many years but became active 50 years ago. Further to the south, on the island of Tanna, is Yasur, cited as the most accessible active volcano in the world and a major tourist attraction. Geophysical activity is under constant monitoring by the French scientific organisation, IRD (Institut de Recherche pour le Développement). Most of the islands are densely forested and mountainous with narrow bands of cultivated land along the coasts.
GOVERNMENT: Republic. Gained independence from the UK/France in 1980. **Head of State:** President Kalkot Mataskelekele since 2004. **Head of Government:** Prime Minister Ham Lini since 2004. **Recent history:** In July 2004, Serge Vohor became Prime Minister (for the third time), only to be ousted on a vote of no confidence in December 2004, following a controversial move on Vohor's part to attempt to switch diplomatic recognition from China to Taiwan without even first (reputedly) consulting his Ministers. He was quickly replaced by Ham Lini, who swiftly revoked the agreements with Taiwan that had been signed. Kalkot Mataskelekele's post as President has been, by comparison, highly stable. However, parties in Vanuatu have been subject to splits and factional disputes and these have dogged Vanuatu's politics throughout the last decade.
LANGUAGE: English and French are the official languages. Bislama (Pidgin English), the most widely used day-to-day language, is a Melanesian mixture of French and English. French and English are widely spoken and both English and French names exist for all towns. There are more than 115 local dialects.
RELIGION: Mostly Christian, including Presbyterian, Anglican, Roman Catholic and several other denominations.
ELECTRICITY: 240 volts AC. Australian three-pin plugs are in use.
SOCIAL CONVENTIONS: Informal wear is suitable for most occasions. Some establishments appreciate men wearing long trousers in the evenings. Life goes at its own pace and while modern influences can be seen in the main centres, in the hill villages and outlying islands, age-old customs continue. Those hiking or exploring must be aware that Vanuatu has strict and sensitive land ownership regulations.

Climate

Subtropical. Trade winds occur from May to October. Warm, humid and wet between November and April. Rain is moderate. Cyclones are possible between December and April.

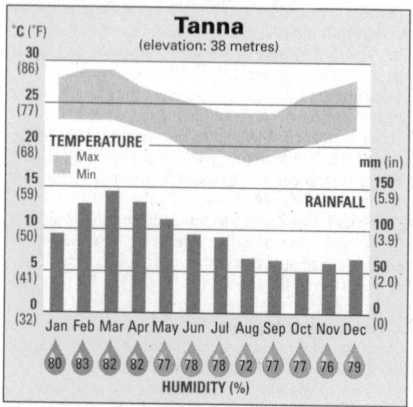

Communications

Telephone: Country code: 678. There are no area codes. Outgoing international calls must go through the international operator. There are public telephones at airports and post offices. Phone cards can be purchased in local currency from the post office. For emergency services, dial: 22333 for fire services; 22222 for police; 22100 for an ambulance.
Mobile telephone: Roaming agreements exist with a few international mobile phone companies. Coverage is good.
Internet: There is an Internet cafe in Port-Vila and Luganville. Internet facilities are also available at some post offices.
Post: Post offices are located on the main streets in Port-Vila and Luganville, on Espiritu Santo. Airmail to Europe takes about seven days. Post office hours: Mon-Fri 0730-1630.
MEDIA: Vanuatu's only TV channel was established with the help of Radio France Overseas (RFO) and broadcasts in French and English. Radio Vanuatu runs a shortwave and mediumwave (AM) service, and a commercial FM station. Vanuatu Weekly is a Government newspaper, existing alongside a handful of privately-owned papers.
Press: Port Vila Presse is published daily in English and French, the Vanuatu Daily Post in English and the Vanuatu Weekly in English, French and Bislama. The monthly Pacific Island Profile is published in English and French. For tourist information, see the quarterly publication, Hapi Tumas Long Vanuatu.
TV: Television Blong Vanuatu is run by the state-owned Vanuatu Broadcasting and Television Corporation (VBTC).
Radio: VBTC operates Radio Vanuatu.

Passport/Visa

	Passport Required?	Visa Required?	Return Ticket Required?
Full British	Yes	No	Yes
Australian	Yes	No	Yes
Canadian	Yes	No	Yes
USA	Yes	No	Yes
Other EU	Yes	No	Yes
Japanese	Yes	No	Yes

Note: Regulations and requirements may be subject to change at short notice, and you are advised to contact the appropriate diplomatic or consular authority before finalising travel arrangements. Any numbers in the chart refer to the footnotes below.

PASSPORTS: Passport valid for a minimum of four months beyond date of arrival required by all.
VISAS: Required by all except the following, provided they are in possession of confirmed onward travel documents and have proof of sufficient funds for visit, for stays of up to 30 days:
(a) nationals of countries listed in the chart above;
(b) nationals of Commonwealth countries, and dependencies of the United Kingdom;

Credit: ©Kirklandphotos.com

(c) nationals of Bermuda, Brazil, Chile, China (PR), Cuba, Hong Kong (SAR), Korea (Rep), Kuwait, Marshall Islands, Mexico, Micronesia (Federated States), Morocco, Norway, Palau, Peru, The Philippines, Russian Federation, Switzerland, Taiwan, Thailand, Tunisia, United Arab Emirates, Vatican City and Zimbabwe;
(d) transit passengers continuing their journey by the same or first connecting aircraft, provided holding valid onward or return documentation and not leaving the airport.
Types of visa and cost: *Visitor* (for tourist and business purposes): VUV2500.
Validity: A maximum of 30 days with the possibility of extensions of up to four months in any period of one year.
Application to: Principal Immigration Officer, Private Bag 9092, Port-Vila, Vanuatu (tel: 22354; fax: 25492).
Application requirements: (a) Passport valid for six months at time of application. (b) Two passport-size photos. (c) Proof of sufficient funds and/or accompanying business letter. (d) Return or onward tickets, and other necessary documents for onward destination.
Working days required: One to two.

PASSPORT/VISA INFORMATION

Honorary Consulate of Vanuatu in France
9 rue Daru, 75008 Paris, France
Tel: (1) 4053 8225.

Money

Currency: Vatu (VUV) = 100 centimes. Notes are in denominations of VUV5000, 1000, 500 and 200. Coins are in denominations of VUV100, 50, 20, 10, 5, 2 and 1. Australian Dollars are also accepted in some shops and restaurants.
Currency exchange: Exchange facilities are available at the airport and trade banks. It is advisable to exchange foreign currency after arriving in Vanuatu. Australian Dollars are accepted by many shops, restaurants and hotels in Port-Vila, but rarely outside major towns. There are ATMs at the ANZ Bank and supermarket.
Credit & debit cards: MasterCard and Visa are quite widely accepted, American Express and Diners Club less so. Check with your credit or debit card company for details of merchant acceptability and other services which may be available.
Traveller's cheques: These are widely accepted.
Currency restrictions: There are no restrictions on the import or export of either local or foreign currency.
Banking hours: Generally Mon-Fri 0800-1500, except Westpac Bank: Mon-Fri 0830-1600. Bureaux de change open Mon-Fri 0800-1730/1800, Sat-Sun 0830-1600.
Exchange rate indicators:
Rate at time of publishing

£1.00=	VUV199.48
$1.00=	VUV114.41

Duty Free

The following items may be imported into Vanuatu by passengers aged 15 and over without incurring customs duty: *Personal effects and clothes, used or worn and for own use; 200 cigarettes or 100 cigarillos or 50 cigars or 250g of tobacco; 1.5l of spirits and 2l of wine; 250ml of eau de toilette and 100ml of perfume; other articles up to a value of VUV20,000.*

Public Holidays

Below are listed Public Holidays for the January 2006-June 2007 period.
2006: Jan 1 New Year's Day. **Feb 21** Father Lini Day. **Mar 5** Custom Chief's Day. **Apr 14** Good Friday. **Apr 17** Easter Monday. **May 1** Labour Day. **May 25** Holy Thursday (Ascension). **Jul 24** Children's Day. **Jul 30** Independence Day. **Aug 15** Assumption. **Oct 5** Constitution Day. **Nov 29** Unity Day. **Dec 25** Christmas Day. **Dec 26** Family Day.
2007: Jan 1 New Year's Day. **Feb 21** Father Lini Day. **Mar 5** Custom Chief's Day. **Apr 6** Good Friday. **Apr 9** Easter Monday. **May 1** Labour Day. **May 17** Holy Thursday (Ascension).

Health

	Special Precautions?	Certificate Required?
Yellow Fever	No	No
Cholera	No	No
Typhoid & Polio	1	N/A
Malaria	2	N/A

Note: *Regulations and requirements may be subject to change at short notice, and you are advised to contact your doctor well in advance of your intended date of departure. Any numbers in the chart refer to the footnotes below.*

1: *Typhoid* is present and vaccination is advised. No cases of *poliomyelitis* have been reported in recent years.
2: A low to moderate risk of *malaria*, predominantly in the malignant *falciparum* form, exists throughout the year everywhere. The strain is reported to be resistant to chloroquine and sulfadoxine-pyrimethamine. The *vivax* strain is, in some cases, resistant to chloroquine. The recommended prophylaxis is chloroquine plus proguanil.
Food & drink: Mains water is normally chlorinated and, whilst relatively safe, may cause mild abdominal upsets. Bottled water is available and is advised for the first few weeks of the stay. Milk is pasteurised and dairy products are safe for consumption. Local meat, poultry, seafood, fruit and vegetables are generally considered safe to eat.
Other risks: *Hepatitis A, dengue fever* and *typhoid fever* exist throughout the islands. *Hepatitis B* is endemic. Poisonous fish and sea snakes can be a hazard to bathers. *Rabies* is present. For those at high risk, vaccination before arrival should be considered. If you are bitten, seek medical advice without delay. For more information, consult the *Health* appendix.
Health care: There are hospitals in Aoba, Epi, Espiritu, Malekula, Port-Vila, Santo and Tanna as well as smaller clinics and medical dispensaries on the smaller islands. Health insurance is advised.

Travel - International

AIR:
The national airline is *Air Vanuatu (NF)* (website: www.airvanuatu.com), which offers regular services between Port-Vila and Brisbane, Melbourne and Sydney (Australia), and Auckland (New Zealand).
Approximate flight times: From Vanuatu to *London* is 30 hours.
Main airports: *Port-Vila (VLI) (Bauerfield)* is 6km (4 miles) from Port-Vila (travel time - 15 minutes). *To/from the airport*: Buses and taxis are available. *Facilities*: Bank/bureaux de change, left luggage, duty free shops, bars, restaurant and club lounge for business class passengers.
Air passes: The *Visit the South Pacific Pass* is valid for many airlines operating in the South Pacific, including most of the larger ones, such as *Air Caledonie, Air Marshall Islands, Air Nauru, Air Niugini, Air Pacific, Air Vanuatu, Polynesian Airlines, Qantas, Royal Tongan Airlines* and *Solomon Airlines*. Offering reductions of up to 40 per cent on normal airfares, this sector-based pass allows for flexible island-hopping between the destinations of the Cook Islands, Fiji, Nauru, New Caledonia, Samoa, Tahiti, Tonga, Vanuatu and the more remote Melanesian and Micronesian islands, together with major cities in Australia (Brisbane, Melbourne and Sydney) and New Zealand (Auckland, Christchurch and Wellington). It is only available for people resident outside of the South Pacific. The journey must be started outside the South Pacific and only one stopover in Australia is allowed. A minimum of two sectors must be bought before departure (extra sectors can be purchased en route). There is a maximum of one pass per person, and passes must be used within six months of the first day of travel. Children under 12 years of age pay 75 per cent of the adult fare. For details and conditions, contact the South Pacific Tourist Organisation.
Departure tax: VUV2500. Children under 12 years of age are exempt. The departure tax must be paid in cash and in local currency (Vatu) only.
Note: The departure tax is often included in airfares: please check with your travel agent when booking.

Travel - Internal

AIR:
Domestic services are provided by *Vanair*, under the umbrella of *Air Vanuatu Ltd* as *Air Vanuatu* domestic. It offers scheduled services to 29 destinations within the archipelago. However, it is very expensive and is an occasionally unreliable air service. *Unity Airlines* (website: www.unity-airlines.com) and *Air Club Vila* (website: www.airclubvila.com) offer charter flights.
Vanair deducts 20% from the standard domestic airfare to travellers with an international ticket issued outside of Vanuatu. It also offers the *Vanuatu Pass* which allows four flights to any destination for US$236.
Departure Tax: VUV400. Children under 12 years of age are exempt. The departure tax must be paid in cash and in local currency (Vatu) only.
Note: The departure tax is often included in airfares: please check with your travel agent when booking.
A separate departure fee has been launched which charges visitors and locals VUV200 from any Shefa province domestic airport. This applies to every leg where a passenger departs from the following domestic airports: Bauerfield- Port-Vila, Swio Airport- Emae, Pele Airport-Tongoa, Valesdir Airport- Epi and Laman Bay Airport- Epi.

SEA:
Inter-island ferries infrequently operate from Port-Vila and Espiritu Santo to the northern and southern islands. Boats can also be chartered.
ROAD:
Traffic drives on the right. Of the 1130km (702 miles) of road, 54km (32 miles) are paved. Roads are either compacted coral or dirt tracks. The road around the island of Efate is currently open but visitors should check with their hotel or the police whether the road is open before attempting to drive around the island. There is no public transport. **Bus:** Private buses serve the town centre and the airport in Port-Vila. **Minibus:** Frequent services available. As there are no timetables, the most common way to catch a minibus is to flag one down and tell the driver where to go. **Taxi:** These are plentiful and all are metered, although a fixed rate can be agreed. **Car hire:** Major car hire operators have offices in Port-Vila. Cars, 4-wheel drive vehicles and jeeps are available.
Documentation: A national driving licence is acceptable.

Travel Advice

Visitors are advised not to travel to the island of Ambae, where in November 2005, the Mount Manaro volcano became highly active resulting in 3000 people being evacuated from the centre of the island.
Caution is advised when considering travel to the islands of Ambrym and Tanna, which can be affected by volcanic activity.
Vanuatu is in an earthquake zone and suffers frequent tremors and shocks. Three earthquakes measuring between 6.2mw and 5.6mw hit Vanuatu on 25 and 26 September 2005. No serious injuries or damage were reported.
Most visits to Vanuatu are trouble-free but you should be aware of the global risk of indiscriminate international terrorist attacks, which could be against civilian targets, including places frequented by foreigners.
Violent crime is increasing and travellers should avoid visiting isolated locations alone.
This advice is based on information provided by the Foreign and Commonwealth Office in the UK. It is correct at time of publishing. As the situation can change rapidly, visitors are advised to contact the following organisations for the latest travel advice:

British Foreign and Commonwealth Office
Tel: (0845) 850 2829.
Website: www.fco.gov.uk

US Department of State
Website: http://travel.state.gov/travel

Accommodation

Vanuatu has several international-standard resorts based in Port-Vila, including luxury/superior resorts such as *Chantillys on the Bay, Mangoes Resort, Erakor Island Resort*, and luxury/superior hotels such as *Breakas Beach Resort, Harbour Villa* and *The Melanesian Port Vila*. There are also plenty of standard hotels and adventure lodges on Port-Vila. A number of smaller resorts with simpler facilities are located on Efaté, Espiritu Santo, Malekula, Tanna and other islands. Conventional hotel-style accommodation as well as self-contained studio apartments, bungalows, guest houses and lodges are available in all resorts. There is no hotel tax or service charge. Full details are available from the Vanuatu National Tourism Office (see *Top Things To See & Do*) or the Vanuatu Hotel and Resort Association (see *Accommodation Information*).
CAMPING/CARAVANNING:
Camping is available on Efaté and Nguna Island and some of the outer islands. For a complete list of campsites, contact the Vanuatu National Tourism Office (see *Top Things To See & Do*).

ACCOMMODATION INFORMATION

Vanuatu Hotel and Resort Association
PO Box 1359, Port-Vila, Vanuatu
Tel: 23456.
E-mail: fatumaru@vanuatu.com.vu

Credit: ©Kirklandphotos.com

Credit: ©Kirklandphotos.com

Top Things To See & Do

- Visit the capital, **Port-Vila**, on **Efaté Island**; its **Cultural Centre** has one of the most extensive Pacific artefact collections in the world. There are also plenty of opportunities for active visitors, especially those interested in watersports.
- Drive to the summit of the world's most accessible active volcano, **Yasur**, on **Tanna Island**. Peer into the crater at a seething mass of bubbling lava. The village of the **John Frum** cargo cult can also be visited; it began with the arrival of an American soldier in World War II and believers wait for him to return with great riches.
- Discover James A Michener's inspiration for *South Pacific*, **Espiritu Santo Island**. Here, scuba divers can see where the liner *President Coolidge* and the destroyer *USS Tucker* rest on the seabed.
- Watch men perform the **Naghol** (a ritual leap) during April and May on **Pentecost Island**. To ensure a bountiful yam harvest; they tie vines to their ankles and leap from a 30m (100ft) tower, falling head first. Only the vine saves them from death. Only recently, this ceremony was opened to the public and the fee goes towards local projects. Visitors who are interested should contact the National Tourism Office of Vanuatu well in advance.
- Explore Vanuatu's underwater world. The good visibility and warm temperature of Vanuatu's waters ensure excellent conditions for **scuba-diving**, which can be practised all year round. Most dive operators are located in **Port-Vila**, on the island of **Efaté**, and on **Espiritu Santo**, Vanuatu's largest island. Numerous World War II shipwrecks, usually in fairly deep waters, lie scattered around the islands, one of the most famous being the *SS President Coolidge*. The **Million Dollar Point**, where military equipment was dumped at the end of the war, can also be visited by divers. The seabed around the offshore islands of North Efaté is renowned for its deep canyons. For further information on diving, contact the Vanuatu Scuba Association (VSA), Tranquility Island Dive Base, PO Box 991, Port-Vila, Vanuatu (tel: 22209).
- Enjoy the numerous other **watersports** on offer. There are many beautiful beaches suitable for **swimming** and most hotels have pools. **Kayaking**, **game fishing**, **sailing**, **windsurfing** and **water-skiing** are also popular.
- Spot Vanuatu's prolific and varied **birdlife**. One of the best times to view birds is during the breeding season (September to January), particularly in the southern islands.
- Go **hiking** through the rainforest and in the mountains.

TOURIST INFORMATION

Vanuatu National Tourism Office
PO Box 209, Ground Floor, Pilioka House, Port-Vila, Vanuatu
Tel: 22515 *or* 22685 *or* 22813.
Website: www.vanuatutourism.com

South Pacific Tourism Organisation (SPTO) in Fiji
Street address: Level 3 FNPF Place, 343-359 Victoria Parade, Suva, Fiji
Postal address: PO Box 13119, Suva, Fiji
Tel: (679) 330 4177.
Website: www.spto.org

Entertainment

FOOD & DRINK: There are many restaurants in the main tourist areas. Seafood features strongly on hotel and restaurant menus in Port-Vila and the main towns. The numerous ethnic backgrounds of the inhabitants of Vanuatu are reflected in different styles of cooking. Chinese and French influences are the strongest. Food is generally excellent everywhere. French cheese, pâtés, bread, cognac and wine are available in Port-Vila's two major shops. Local fruit is excellent.
National specialities:
- *Lap Lap* - grated yam, banana or manioc smothered in coconut cream and cooked in an earth oven.
- Coconut crab.

National drinks:
- *Kava*, a soporific drink made from the root of a plant related to the pepper tree. Vanuatu kava is the strongest in the world. It is non-alcoholic but is intoxicating.
Tipping: Not expected or encouraged, as it goes against local tradition.
NIGHTLIFE: Port-Vila has several nightclubs with music and dancing. There is also a cinema. Evening cruises are organised with wine, snacks and island music. Traditional music and dancing take place at various island festivities to which visitors are welcome, and some hotels put on evening entertainment and dancing. Details are available from the Vanuatu National Tourism Office (see *Top Things To See & Do*).
SHOPPING: Special purchases include grass skirts from Futuna and Tanna, baskets and mats from Futuna and Pentecost, carved forms and masks from Ambrym and Malekula, woodwork from Tongoa and Santo, and pig tusks and necklaces made of shells or colourful seeds from villages near Port-Vila. Duty free shops sell a selection of luxury items.
Shopping hours: Mon-Fri 0700-2000. Shops open Saturday mornings. Chinese stores also open Sunday mornings from 0800 and in the evenings. Most shops close from 1130-1330 (except restaurants, banks, supermarkets and the Post Office). The market in the town centre is open every day (except Sunday) for flowers, fruit, vegetables and handicrafts.

Business

- **GDP:** US$37.2 million (2003).
- **Main exports:** Cocoa, beef and veal, copra, timber, kava and coffee.
- **Main imports:** Machinery and transport equipment, foodstuffs, fuel, basic manufactured goods and chemicals.
- **Main trade partners:** Australia, New Zealand, Indonesia and the EU.

ECONOMY: Agriculture and fishing occupy 40 per cent of the working population. Fruit and vegetables are grown for domestic consumption while coffee, copra, beef and veal are the main export commodities. The sale of fishing licences to foreign fleets is another important source of revenue. There is also a sizeable timber industry, originally encouraged by the Government but now strictly regulated in the wake of international pressure. The industrial sector is mostly concerned with food processing and construction. Identified mineral resources, including manganese, gold and copper, have yet to be exploited on a commercial scale. While mineral deposits may be of future value to the Vanuatu economy, the Government's recent efforts to diversify the economy have been focused on the service sector. The most important of these is tourism – backed by the construction of new hotels and airport improvements, allied to a focus on 'ecotourism' – and 'offshore' financial services. Tourism is worth about US$55 million to the economy annually. Visitor numbers have increased significantly over the last 12 months. A 'flag of convenience' shipping register was also created. Despite these efforts, the economy is still vulnerable to its geographical circumstances; a severe earthquake followed by a tsunami in late 1999 caused considerable damage to several islands. Meanwhile, offshore finance has run into trouble. In April 2002, Vanuatu was one of seven countries 'named and shamed' by the Organisation for Economic Cooperation and Development (OECD) and threatened with sanctions for its failure to take adequate measures against money-laundering. Since then, the Vanuatu authorities have tightened their financial services regulatory regime. Foreign aid remains essential to sustain the economy, which is currently growing at 2.4 per cent annually. In 2002, Vanuatu signed up to the newly-established regional trade bloc created under the Pacific Island Countries Trade Agreement (PICTA). Australia, New Zealand, Japan, the UK and France are the principal donors.
BUSINESS ETIQUETTE: A casual approach to business prevails. Shirts and smart trousers will suffice – ties are only necessary for the most formal occasions. Business is conducted in Pidgin English or French. **Office hours:** Mon-Fri 0730-1130 and 1330-1630.

COMMERCIAL INFORMATION

Vanuatu Chamber of Commerce
PO Box 189, Port-Vila, Vanuatu
Tel: 27543.
Fax: 27542.

Vanuatu Investment Promotion Authority
1st Floor, Pilioko House, Port-Vila, Vanuatu
Tel: 24096.
Website: www.investinvanuatu.com

Vatican City

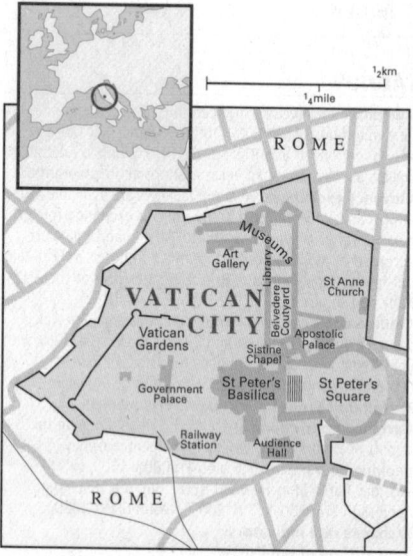

Location: Europe, Italy (Rome).

Time: GMT + 1 (GMT + 2 from last Sunday in March to Saturday before last Sunday in September).

Italian State Tourist Offices can provide advice and information on visiting the Vatican City. For addresses, see *Italy* section.

Overview

The Vatican City is situated entirely within the city of Rome, sprawling over a hill west of the River Tiber, and separated from the rest of the city by a wall. Vatican City comprises St Peter's Church, St Peter's Square, the Vatican and the Vatican Gardens. The Vatican City is famous for its magnificent St Peter's Basilica. Near St Peter's stands the Vatican Palace, the Pope's residence. Among the principal features of the Palace are the Stanze, the Sistine Chapel and the Vatican Museum, containing major works of art and valuable pictures.

General Information

AREA: 0.44 sq km (0.17 sq miles).
POPULATION: 900 (2002).
POPULATION DENSITY: 2045.5 per sq km.
GEOGRAPHY: The Vatican City is situated entirely within the city of Rome, sprawling over a hill west of the River Tiber, and separated from the rest of the city by a wall. Vatican City comprises St Peter's Church, St Peter's Square, the Vatican and the Vatican Gardens.
GOVERNMENT: The State of the Vatican City came into existence in 1929. **Head of State and Government:** His Holiness Pope Benedict XVI since 2005.
LANGUAGE: Italian and Latin are the official languages, though most international languages are spoken to some extent.
ELECTRICITY: 220 volts, 50Hz.

Climate

See *Italy* section.

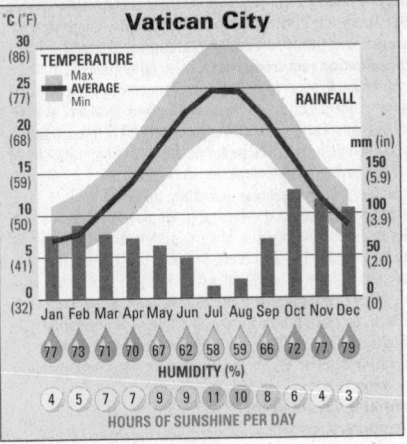

Vatican City — TEMPERATURE (Max, AVERAGE, Min), RAINFALL chart. HUMIDITY (%): 77 73 71 70 67 62 58 59 66 72 77 79. HOURS OF SUNSHINE PER DAY: 4 5 7 7 9 11 10 8 6 4 3

Communications

Telephone: The international dialling code is that for Italy (39), plus 06. The Vatican has its own telephone network.
Post: Stamps issued in the Vatican City are valid only within its boundaries.
MEDIA: Press: The daily newspaper published in the Vatican City is *L'Osservatore Romano*, with weekly editions in English and other international languages.
Radio: *Vatican Radio* broadcasts worldwide on a daily basis. Programmes are offered in 34 languages and are sent out from the Vatican on short wave, medium wave, FM, and satellite. For frequencies, see online (website: www.vatican.va).

Passport/Visa

There are no formalities required to enter the Vatican City, but entry will always be via Rome, and Italian regulations must therefore be complied with (see *Passport/Visa* in the *Italy* section).
There is free access only to certain areas of the Vatican City; these include St Peter's Church, St Peter's Square, the Vatican Museum and the Vatican Gardens. Special permission is required to visit areas other than those mentioned.
Passport/Visa Information: See *Italy* section for Italian embassy and consulate addresses.

Money

Currency: Vatican coins are similar in value, size and denomination to those of Italy, although the monetary system is separate from that of Italy; the Euro is, however, legal tender in the Vatican City (see *Money* in the *Italy* section). Vatican coins are the Gold Lire 100 (nominal); Silver Lire 500; 'Acmonital' Lire 100 and 50; 'Italma' Lire 10, 5 and 1; and 'Bronzital' Lire 20.
The first Euro coins and notes were introduced in January 2002 (see *Money* in the *Italy* section).

Duty Free

There are no taxes and no customs/excise in the Vatican City. For Italian duty free allowances, see *Duty Free* in the *Italy* section.

Public Holidays

See *Italy* section.

Health

See *Italy* section.

Travel - International

The Vatican City has its own small railway, which runs from the Vatican into Italy. For travel in Rome, see the *Italy* section. There is a speed limit of 30kph (20mph) in the Vatican City.

Travel Advice

Most visits to the Vatican City are trouble-free but you should be aware of the global risk of indiscriminate international terrorist attacks, which could be against civilian targets, including places frequented by foreigners. This advice is based on information provided by the Foreign and Commonwealth Office in the UK. It is correct at time of publishing. As the situation can change rapidly, visitors are advised to contact the following organisations for the latest travel advice:

British Foreign and Commonwealth Office
Tel: (0845) 850 2829.
Website: www.fco.gov.uk

US Department of State
Website: http://travel.state.gov/travel

Accommodation

Board and lodging is not available to members of the general public in the Vatican City itself; for information on accommodation in Rome, see the *Italy* section.

Top Things To See & Do

- The Vatican City is best known to tourists and students of architecture for the magnificent **St Peter's Basilica**. Visitors are normally admitted to the dome, 0800-1700.
- **The Museum & Treasure House** is open 0845-1300 in winter and 0845-1600 during the summer months.
- Leading up to it is the 17th-century **St Peter's Square**, a superb creation by Bernini. On either side are semicircular colonnades, and in the centre of the square is an Egyptian obelisk hewn in the reign of Caligula.
- It is also possible to visit the **Necropoli Precostantiniana**, the excavations under St Peter's, although permission has to be obtained in advance and is usually granted only to students and teachers with a professional interest in the work being carried out. Contact the Tourist Information Office in St Peter's Square.
- The **Vatican Gardens** can only be visited by those on guided tours or bus tours. Tickets are available from the Tourist Information Office in St Peter's Square; it is advisable to apply two days in advance. There is a restaurant in the museum and a bar and cafeteria on the roof of St Peter's.
- To the right of St Peter's stands the **Vatican Palace**, the Pope's residence. Among the principal features of the Palace are the **Stanze**, the **Sistine Chapel**, the **Garden House** or **Belvedere**, the **Vatican Library** and the **Vatican Collections**, containing major works of art and valuable pictures. The **Museum & Treasure House** includes the **Collection of Antiquities**, **Museo Pio-Clementino**, the **Egyptian Museum**, the **Etruscan Museum** and the **Museum of Modern Religious Art**.

TOURIST INFORMATION

Note: Italian State Tourist Offices can provide advice and information on visiting the Vatican City. For addresses, see *Italy* section.

Apostolic Nunciature in the UK
54 Parkside, Wimbledon, London SW19 5NE, UK
Tel: (020) 8944 7189.
Opening hours: Mon-Fri 1000-1700.

Apostolic Nunciature in the USA
3339 Massachusetts Avenue, NW, Washington, DC 20008, USA
Tel: (202) 333 7121.

Business

ECONOMY: The Vatican has three main sources of income: the *Instituto per le Opere di Religione* (IOR, Institute of Religious Works), voluntary contributions known as 'Peter's Pence' and the interest on the Vatican's investments. The IOR – the Vatican Bank – has attracted some controversy in recent years through the emergence of huge debts and allegations of corruption. Nonetheless, as the heart of a worldwide entity with millions of adherents, the Vatican continues to wield immense financial influence. The Vatican produces little other than religious artefacts, and its material requirements are largely met from Italian sources.

COMMERCIAL INFORMATION

Prefecture of the Economic Affairs of the Holy See
Palazzo delle Congregazioni, Largo del Colonnato 3, 00120 Rome, Italy
Tel: (06) 6988 4263.

Instituto per le Opere di Religione (IOR)
00120 Città del Vaticano, Rome, Italy
Tel: (06) 6988 3354.

Venezuela

Location: South America.

Time: GMT - 4

Overview

Originally inhabited by Carib and Arawak Indians, Venezuela was claimed as a Spanish territory by Christopher Columbus in 1498. Spanish rule was administered from a distance, leaving the various regions to develop separately from the capital, Caracas, which was founded by Diego de Losada in 1567. In the 18th century, an attempt to inject a measure of unification by the Spanish was met with widespread resistance and uprisings led by Simón Bolívar (after whom the currency is named). In 1830, Venezuela became a sovereign state, led by José Paéz.
Today's politics are dominated by President Hugo Chávez, the leader of a coup attempt in 1992, who formed his own party and, drawing on the support of millions of disaffected poor people, won the 1998 Presidential election. Despite attempts by the opposition to remove him, Chávez's position remains secure for now. In the 2005 Parliamentary elections, his party won a majority of seats in the National Assembly.
Venezuela offers a myriad of landscapes and experiences - tropical beaches, immense plains, enormous rivers, forests, jungle, waterfalls and great mountains. The clear, warm waters of its Caribbean coastline are ideal for snorkelling and diving, while numerous islands off the coast invite visitors to explore. The tropical lowlands hide a huge array of wildlife, lush vegetation and dramatic waterfalls, yet within the same country lie high Andean peaks, providing a challenge to trekkers and mountaineers.
The country is home to the world's highest waterfall, Angel Falls (about 16 times higher than Niagara Falls), and the world's longest and highest cable car, whisking tourists from the university town of Mérida to the 4765m- (15,629ft-) high 'Pico Espejo. The capital, Caracas, boasts fine historical monuments, an excellent collection of museums and art galleries, and contrasting examples of old and new architecture.
Visitors to this country have the choice of a relaxing resort experience, a cultural city break or a wealth of adventurous activities. Whether they wish to experience one, or all of the above, Venezuela has more than enough to offer on all counts.

General Information

AREA: 916,445 sq km (353,841 sq miles).
POPULATION: 26.6 million (UN, 2005).
POPULATION DENSITY: 29.02 per sq km.
CAPITAL: Caracas. **Population:** 3.6 million (metropolitan area, 2004).

Venezuela

GEOGRAPHY: Venezuela is bordered to the north by the Caribbean, to the east by Guyana and the Atlantic Ocean, to the south by Brazil, and to the west and southwest by Colombia. The country consists of four distinctive regions: the Venezuelan Highlands in the west; the Maracaibo Lowlands in the north; the vast central plain of the Llanos around the Orinoco; and the Guiana Highlands, which take up about half of the country.

GOVERNMENT: Republic. Gained independence from Spain in 1830. **Head of State and Government:** President Hugo Chávez Frías since 1998. **Recent history:** Venezuelans either love or loathe Hugo Chávez. In August 2004, the opposition gathered enough names for a petition demanding a referendum on Chávez's rule. Chávez won the ballot, with 59 per cent of people agreeing that he should serve out his remaining two-and-a-half years of term. The opposition is driven exclusively by its dislike of Chávez: with his removal, the alliance of business, unions, the old political parties and assorted interest groups will fragment. However, for now, Chávez's future is secured. In the 2005 Parliamentary elections, Chávez's party won 114 seats in the 167-seat National Assembly. Voter turnout was low and the main opposition parties boycotted the elections, protesting against what they perceived to be a biased electoral board. However, despite the opposition's doubts regarding the election's legitimacy, a two-thirds majority in Parliament now paves the way for Chavez to alter the constitution, which currently limits a President to two terms in office.

LANGUAGE: Spanish is the official language. English, French, German and Portuguese are also spoken by some sections of the community.

RELIGION: 86 per cent Roman Catholic.

ELECTRICITY: 110 volts AC, 60Hz. US-style two-pin plugs are the most commonly used fittings.

SOCIAL CONVENTIONS: Shaking hands or using the local *abrazo*, a cross between a hug and a handshake, are the normal forms of greeting. In Caracas, conservative casual wear is the norm. Men are expected to wear suits for business, and jackets and ties are usual for dining out and social functions. Dress on the coast is less formal but beachwear and shorts should not be worn away from the beach or pool. Smoking follows European habits and in most cases it is obvious where not to smoke. Some public buildings are also non-smoking areas.

Climate

The climate varies according to altitude. Lowland areas have a tropical climate. The dry season is from December to April and the rainy season from May to December. During the rainy season, there is the possibility of flooding in certain low-lying areas, such as the Llanos and in some valley of the Andes. Various parts of Venezuela, including Caracas and the eastern part of Sucre, are vulnerable to earthquakes, although there have been no serious earthquakes for many years. The best time to visit is between January and April.

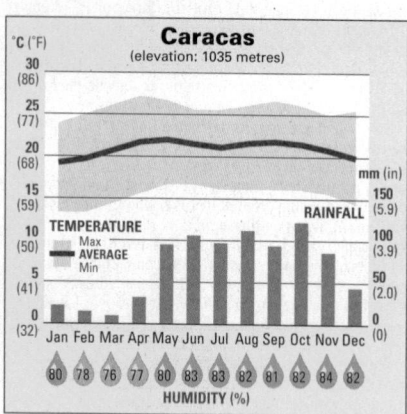

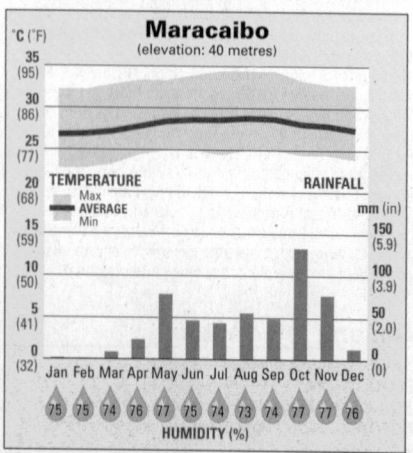

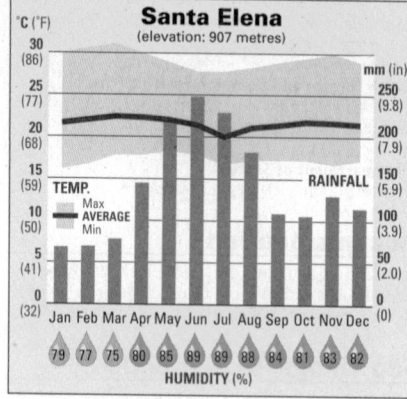

Communications

Telephone: IDD is available. Country code: 58.

Mobile telephone: Roaming agreements exist with some international mobile phone companies. Coverage is limited to around Caracas and major cities.

Internet: There are Internet cafes in most urban areas.

Post: There is an efficient mail service from Venezuela to the USA and Europe. Airmail to Europe takes three to seven days. Internal mail can sometimes take longer. Surface mail to Europe takes at least one month.

MEDIA: President Chávez's attitudes towards the media have attracted criticism from external watchdogs. A 2005 media law banned the inappropriate airing of scenes of sex and violence, as well as material deemed harmful to national security. Opponents of the bill claimed it was an attempt to silence media criticism. Both private and state-owned broadcasters operate in the country. President Chávez has his own weekly TV and radio programme.

Press: The English-language daily newspaper is *The Daily Journal*, published in Caracas. Spanish-language dailies include *El Nacional* (website: www.el-nacional.com), *El Mundo* (website: www.elmundo.com.ve), *El Universal* (website: www.eluniversal.com) and *Ultimas Noticias* (website: www.ultimasnoticias.com.ve).

TV: *Venezolana de Television* is Government-run. Other channels include Caracas-based *Radio Caracas Television (RCTV)*, private networks *Televen* and *Venevision* and 24-hour news channel *Globovision*. *Telesur* is a pan-American broadcaster based in Caracas.

Radio: *Radio Nacional de Venezuela* is a state broadcaster with 15 stations. *Union Radio Noticias* is a commercial news network.

Passport/Visa

	Passport Required?	Visa Required?	Return Ticket Required?
Full British	Yes	No/2	Yes
Australian	Yes	No/2	Yes
Canadian	Yes	No/2	Yes
USA	Yes	No/2	Yes
Other EU	Yes	No/1/2	Yes
Japanese	Yes	No/2	Yes

Note: *Regulations and requirements may be subject to change at short notice, and you are advised to contact the appropriate diplomatic or consular authority before finalising travel arrangements. Any numbers in the chart refer to the footnotes below.*

PASSPORTS: Passport valid for at least six months (if entering with a visa) or for the duration of stay (if entering with a Tourist Entry Card) required by all.

VISAS: Required by all except the following, who do, however, require a Tourist Entry Card (DEX-2), which is issued free of charge by an authorised air carrier on presentation of valid air tickets (including return or onward ticket) for stays of maximum 90 days (non-extendable):

(a) nationals of countries mentioned in the chart above, except **1.** nationals of Cyprus, Estonia, Latvia and Malta who *do* need a visa;

2. (b) nationals of Andorra, Antigua & Barbuda, Argentina, Barbados, Belize, Brazil, Bulgaria, Chile, Costa Rica, Croatia, Grenada, Guatemala, Hong Kong (SAR), Iceland, Jamaica, Liechtenstein, Malaysia, Mexico, Monaco, Netherlands Antilles, New Zealand, Norway, Panama, Paraguay, Romania, San Marino, St Kitts & Nevis, St Lucia, St Vincent & the Grenadines, South Africa, Switzerland, Taiwan, Trinidad & Tobago and Uruguay.

Types of visa and cost: *Tourist Entry Card:* Free of charge (single-entry). *Tourist:* £21.90 (multiple-entry). *Business:* £43.80 (multiple-entry). *Student:* £43.80 (multiple entry). *Transit:* £21.90 (single-entry).

Validity: *Tourist*/Tourist Entry Cards: 90 days (tourist visas are valid for up to one year but only permit entry for 90 days in any one period). *Business:* 180 days. *Transit:* up to 72 hours.

Application to: Consulate (or consular section at Embassy); see *Passport/Visa Information*. Tourist Entry Cards are available at the airport check-in desk prior to departure.

Application requirements: *Tourist:* (a) Completed and signed application form. (b) Two recent colour passport-size photos. (c) Passport with at least six months' validity at time of visa application. (d) Fee (postal order). (e) Self-addressed, recorded delivery envelope for postal applications. (f) A letter of employment from employer, stating date of commencement, position and salary. (g) Latest bank statement. *Business:* (a)-(e) and (f) Employer's reference and letter confirming purpose of visit. (g) Reference from company to be contacted in Venezuela. *Student:* (a)-(e) and, (f) Letter of admission from educational institution. (g) Proof of academic degrees/attestations. *Transit:* (a) Ticket confirming you will be continuing to a third country. (b) Name of airline carrier. (c) Flight number. (d) Date you will be entering and departing Venezuela. (e) Name of entry and departing Venezuelan port or airport.

Working days required: Three.

Temporary residence: Special authorisation is required from the Ministry of Internal Affairs in Caracas.

PASSPORT/VISA INFORMATION

Embassy of the Republic of Venezuela in the UK
1 Cromwell Road, London SW7 2HR, UK
Tel: (020) 7584 4206/7.
Website: www.venezlon.co.uk
Opening hours: Mon-Fri 0900-1600.

Embassy of the Republic of Venezuela (Consular Section) in the UK
56 Grafton Way, London W1P 5LB, UK
Tel: (020) 7387 6727.
Website: www.venezlon.co.uk
Opening hours: Mon-Fri 1000-1300.

Embassy of the Bolivarian Republic of Venezuela in the USA
1099 30th Street, NW, Washington, DC 20007, USA
Tel: (202) 342 2214.
Website: www.embavenez-us.org

Money

Currency: Bolívar (VEB) = 100 céntimos. Notes are in denominations of VEB50,000, 20,000, 10,000, 5000, 2000, 1000, 500, 100, 50, 20, 10 and 5. Coins are in denominations of VEB500, 100, 50, 25, 5, 2 and 1, and 50, 20, 10 and 5 céntimos.

Currency exchange: Banks will change cheques and cash, and *cambios* will change cash only; as will hotels, although often at a less favourable rate. Travellers are advised to bring currency in US Dollars.

Credit & debit cards: American Express, MasterCard and Visa are accepted in main cities and tourist centres; Diners Club has more limited acceptance. Check with your credit or debit card company for details of merchant acceptability and for other facilities which may be available.

Traveller's cheques: Widely accepted, although one may be asked to produce a receipt of purchase when changing them in Venezuela. Exchange is more difficult in some places than others. Some kinds of traveller's cheques are not accepted; seek advice before travelling. To avoid additional exchange rate charges, travellers are advised to take traveller's cheques in US Dollars.

Currency restrictions: The import and export of local and foreign currency is unlimited.

Banking hours: Mon-Fri 0830-1530.

Exchange rate indicators:
Rate at time of publishing
£1.00=   VEB3783.71
$1.00=   VEB2149.88
Note: The above rates are the official rates for non-commercial transactions. 'Essential Import' and 'Preferential' rates are also used.

Duty Free

The following items may be imported into Venezuela without incurring customs duty:
200 cigarettes and 25 cigars; 2l of alcoholic beverages; four small bottles of perfume; new goods up to a value of US$1000.

Prohibited Items: Flowers, fruit, meat and meat products, live plants and birds or bird products or bird by-products from Chile.

Public Holidays

Below are listed Public Holidays for the January 2006-June 2007 period.

2006: Jan 1 New Year's Day. **Feb 27-28** Carnival. **Apr 13** Holy Thursday. **Apr 14** Good Friday. **Apr 19** Declaration of Independence. **May 1** Labour Day. **Jun 24** Battle of Carabobo. **Jul 5** Independence Day. **Jul 24** Birth of Simón Bolívar. **Oct 12** Columbus Day. **Dec 25** Christmas Day. **Dec 31** New Year's Eve.

2007: Jan 1 New Year's Day. **Feb 19-20**Carnival. **Apr 5** Holy Thursday. **Apr 6** Good Friday. **Apr 19** Declaration of Independence. **May 1** Labour Day. **Jun 24** Battle of Carabobo.

Note: There are some additional regional holidays; enquire at the Corporación de Turismo de Venezuela (see *Top Things To Do* section).

Health

	Special Precautions?	Certificate Required?
Yellow Fever	Yes	1
Cholera	2	No
Typhoid & Polio	3	N/A
Malaria	4	N/A

Note: *Regulations and requirements may be subject to change at short notice, and you are advised to contact your doctor well in advance of your intended date of departure. Any numbers in the chart refer to the footnotes below.*

1: A *yellow fever* vaccination certificate is required from travellers over nine months old, except in the northern coastal area. The cities of Caracas and Valencia are not in the endemic zone. The last outbreaks of *yellow fever* were in September 2004, when one person died in the municipality of Sucre, Merida State. Sporadic cases are, however, under control due to a countrywide vaccination and surveillance programme.

2: Cases of autochthonous *cholera* were reported in 1996. Visitors are advised to take necessary precautions. Up-to-date advice should be sought before deciding whether these precautions should include vaccination as medical opinion is divided over its effectiveness. See the *Health* appendix for more information.

3: Vaccination against *typhoid* is advised.

4: *Malaria* risk in the benign *vivax* form exists throughout the year in some rural areas of Apure, Amazonas, Barinas, Bolívar, Sucre and Táchira states. The malignant *falciparum* form is restricted to certain jungle areas of Amazonas (Atabapo), Bolívar (Cedeño, Gran Sabana, Raul Leoni, Sifontes and Sucre) and Delta Amacuro (Antonia Diaz, Casacoima and Pedernales) states and is reported to be highly resistant to chloroquine in the interior of Amazonas state. The recommended prophylaxis is chloroquine in *vivax* risk areas and mefloquine in *falciparum* risk areas.

Food & drink: Mains water is not drinkable and should be boiled or filtered. Bottled water is available and is advised for the first few weeks of the stay. Drinking water outside main cities and towns may be contaminated and sterilisation is advisable. Milk is pasteurised and dairy products are safe for consumption. Local meat, poultry, seafood, fruit and vegetables are generally considered safe to eat.

Other risks: *Bilharzia* (*schistosomiasis*) is present in north-central Venezuela. Avoid swimming and paddling in fresh water; swimming pools that are well chlorinated and maintained are safe. *Paragonimiasis* (oriental lung fluke) has been reported. *Hepatitis A* also occurs; *hepatitis B* and *D* (delta hepatitis) are highly endemic. *Cutaneous* and *mucocutaneous leishmaniasis* occur in rural areas. *Visceral leishmaniasis* is rarer. In the southeast, some deaths have been caused by mercury in the river water. *Dengue fever* is increasingly common and there are epidemics of *viral encephalitis* at times. *Brucellosis* has occasionally been acquired by travellers through eating or drinking contaminated milk products. *Filariasis, onchocerciasis* and *American trypanosomiasis* (chagas disease) are present. *Rabies* has been reported. For those at high risk, vaccination before arrival should be considered. If you are bitten, seek medical advice without delay. For more information, consult the *Health* appendix.

Health care: The best-equipped hospitals are in the state capitals. Emergency treatment is free and most hospitals have intensive care units. However, private hospitals are of a much higher standard, and although health insurance is not mandatory, it is recommended.

Travel - International

AIR:

The national airlines are *Aeropostal (Alas de Venezuela) (VH)* (website: www.aeropostal.com), and *Avensa and Servivensa (VC)* (website: www.avensa.com.ve), which no longer flies to Europe.

Approximate flight times: From Caracas to *London* is 13 hours (indirect), to *Los Angeles* is 10 hours 45 minutes and to *New York* is five hours.

Main airports: *Caracas (CCS)* (Simon Bolívar) is 20km (12 miles) from the city (travel time - 30 to 45 minutes). *To/from the airport*: There is a coach service to the city every 60 minutes (0530-2359). Buses (*littoral*) are available to the city every 60 minutes (0600-1800). Taxis to the city are available on ranks. *Facilities*: Duty free shop, bank/bureau de change, bar/restaurant, tourist information and car hire.

Departure tax: VEB73,000 on international flights from all international airports. Transit passengers and children under two years are exempt.

The Visit South America Pass: The *Visit South America* pass is valid within Argentina, Bolivia, Brazil, Colombia, Chile (except Easter Island), Ecuador, Paraguay, Peru, Uruguay and Venezuela. Participating airlines include *Aer Lingus* (EI), *American Airlines* (AA), *British Airways* (BA), *Cathay Pacific* (CX), *Finnair* (AY), *Iberia* (IB), *LAN* (LA) and *Qantas* (QF). The pass must be bought outside South America in the country of residence. It allows unlimited travel to 34 cities. A minimum of three flights must be booked, with no maximum; the maximum stay is 60 days, with no minimum, and prices depend on the amount of flight zones. For further details, contact one of the participating airlines.

SEA:

Main ports: *La Guaira* (website: www.plcsa.gov.ve), *Puerto Cabello* (website: www.ipapc.gov.ve), *Maracaibo* (website: www.puertodemaracaibo.com), *Guanta, Porlamar* and *Ciudad Bolívar* (on the Orinoco River). The principal shipping lines operating to Venezuela are: from the USA: *Venezuelan Line*; from European ports: *French Line, Hamburg Süd, Hapag Lloyd, Polish Ocean Lines* and the Spanish ships, 'Cabo San Juan' and 'Cabo San Roque'. Cruise ships often make Caracas a port of call.

Exit tax: Exit tax on all air and sea departures, regardless of nationality, of VEB29,400.

RAIL:

There are no international rail links with neighbouring countries.

ROAD:

Road access is from Colombia (Barranquilla and Medellin) to Maracaibo, and from the Amazon territory of Brazil (Manaus) to Caracas.

Travel - Internal

AIR:

Almost all large towns are connected with scheduled services operated by domestic airlines, including *Aeropostal* (website: www.aeropostal.com), *Aerotuy* (website: www.tuy.com) and *Avensa and Servivensa*. There are various discount tickets offered by *Avensa and Servivensa*, including special student and family prices. For further information, contact your local travel agency. Air travel is the best means of internal transport but services are often overbooked and even confirmation does not always ensure a seat. Travellers are advised to arrive at the airport well before the minimum check-in time in order to obtain confirmed seats. Schedule changes and flight cancellations with no advance warning are also likely.

Departure tax: VEB14,700.

SEA:

Ferries link *Puerto La Cruz* with Margarita Island (travel time - two hours 45 minutes).

RAIL:

The East-West Railway travels between Acarigua and Maturin. It is for both passengers and cargo.

ROAD:

On 5 January 2006, the Venezuelan authorities closed the main motorway linking Maiquetia International Airport with Caracas due to the risk of a collapsed bridge. At the time of publishing, it is not clear how long it will remain closed.

Traffic drives on the right. Internal roads between principal cities are of a high standard, with 17,050km (10,595 miles) of paved motorways, 13,500km (8400 miles) of macadam highways and 5850km (3635 miles) of other roads. All vehicles must carry a spare tyre, wheel block, jack wrench and special reflector triangle. The quality of roads is variable but the main roads in Caracas and to the interior are good. Some routes have many potholes that have not been filled; on these roads a 4-wheel drive is recommended. In the event of an accident, both vehicles must remain in the position of the accident until a Traffic Police Officer arrives, otherwise insurance companies will be unable to pay claims. Drivers routinely ignore red lights. Petrol pump attendants expect a tip. **Bus:** There are fairly cheap interurban bus services; quality of travel varies a lot however. **Car hire:** Self-drive cars are available at the airport and in major city centres but are expensive. **Documentation:** National driving licences are valid for one year. International Driving Permits are also valid. Drivers must have their licence and insurance documents with them at all times when driving.

URBAN:

Caracas has a 35-station metro, which is comfortable and inexpensive. Conventional **bus** services have badly deteriorated in recent years and there has been a rapid growth in the use of *por puestos* (share-taxis). These are operated by minibus companies and tend to serve as the main form of public transport in Caracas and major cities. Fares charged are in general similar to those on the buses, although they are higher during the evenings and at weekends. **Taxis** in Caracas are metered but the fare can nonetheless be negotiated with the driver. It is customary not to use meters after midnight; the fare should be agreed before setting out. Taxi fares double after 2000. Taxi rates are posted at the airport. Drivers are not tipped unless they carry suitcases. Travellers are recommended to only take white taxis with yellow number plates or the Black Explorers from the airport. Many hotels book or supply their own limousine service. Motorcycles may not be used in Caracas after 2200.

Travel times: The following chart gives approximate travel times (in hours and minutes) from **Caracas** to other major cities/towns in Venezuela.

	Air
Porlamar	0.45
Canaima	1.15
Cumana	0.45
Maracaibo	1.00

Travel Advice

The incidence of street crime in Venezuela is high and rising. There have been muggings and kidnappings by bogus taxi operators at Caracas International Airport (Maiquetia).

Political demonstrations may occur at any time in the major cities, possibly leading to localised violence.

Travellers should be aware of the global risk of indiscriminate terrorist attacks, which could be against civilian targets, including places frequented by foreigners.

This advice is based on information provided by the Foreign and Commonwealth Office in the UK. It is correct at time of publishing. As the situation can change rapidly, visitors are advised to contact the following organisations for the latest travel advice:

British Foreign and Commonwealth Office
Tel: (0845) 850 2829.
Website: www.fco.gov.uk

US Department of State
Website: http://travel.state.gov/travel

Accommodation

HOTELS:

There are many excellent hotels in Caracas. Numerous smaller hotels are open throughout the country but it is essential to make reservations at both these and the larger international hotels well in advance. It normally follows that the more expensive the hotel, the better the facilities. Hotels do not add a service charge, and generally there is no variation in seasonal rates. Hotels outside the capital tend to be cheaper and the standard may not be as high. Hotels in Venezuela have been graded **3-star** to **5-star**.

YOUTH HOSTELS:

There are a number of youth hostels in Venezuela.

CAMPING/CARAVANNING:

Camping in Venezuela can involve spending a weekend at the beach, on the islands, in the Llanos or in the mountains. Camping can also be arranged with companies who run jungle expeditions. As in much of South America, however, good facilities are not widespread and camping is not used by travellers as a substitute for hotels on the main highways. No special campsites are yet provided for this purpose.

ACCOMMODATION INFORMATION

Hostelling International
Avenida Lecuna Partque Central, Edifizio Tajamar, Nivel OFC 1, Oficina. 107, Caracas, Venezuela
Tel: (212) 576 4493.
E-mail: hostellingven@cantv.net

Idiomas Vivos s.r.l. (Information on Youth Hostels)
Residencia La Hacienda, Local 1-4T, Final Avenida ppal. de las Mercedes, Apartado. 80160, Caracas 1080, Venezuela.
Tel: (212) 993 6082.
Website: www.ividiomas.com

Top Things To See

- Begin in the capital, **Caracas**, typical of the 'new Venezuela', despite being one of the oldest established cities in the country (founded in 1567). The city is constantly growing and changing but, among the new developments, there are still areas of the old town intact – **San José** and **La Pastora**, for example. Other periods of the country's history have left substantial monuments; these include the **Plaza Bolívar**, flanked by the old cathedral and the Archbishop's residence, the **Casa Amarilla** and the **Capitol** (the National Congress) building, erected in 1873 in just 114 days, which has a fine mural depicting Venezuelan military exploits. Other places worth visiting include the **Panteon Nacional** (which contains the body of Simon Bolívar), the **Jardín Botánico**, the **Parque Nacional del Este**, and, for recreation, the **Country Club**.
- Tour the capital's museums, including the **Museo de Bellas Artes**, the **Museo del Arte Colonial**, the **Museo del Arte Contemporáneo**, the **Museo de Transporte** and the **Casa Natal del Libertador** (a reconstruction of the house where Bolívar was born; the first was destroyed in an earthquake).
- Visit the old town in **La Guaira**, the main port for Caracas.
- Explore **Maracay**, with its **opera house**, **bullring** and **Gomez Mausoleum**. Excursions run to **Lake Valencia** and Gomez's country house, the **Rancho Grande**.
- Catch a rodeo or a display of **Joropo**, Venezuela's national dance, in the **Llanos**. The area is the heart of the Venezuelan cattle country and the landscape is mostly flat. It is veined by numerous slow-running rivers, forested along their banks. The swamps are the home of egrets, parrots, alligators and monkeys.
- See the modern cathedral in **Barquisimeto**, one of the oldest settlements in Venezuela, which is now the country's fourth-largest city and capital of the Llanos.
- Take a sightseeing tour from **Maracaibo** to the peninsula of **Guajira** to the north, where the Motilone and Guajiro Indians live. Their lifestyle has changed little since the days of the first Spanish settlers. Their houses are raised above the lake on stilts and are in fact the original inspiration for naming the country Venezuela, or 'Little Venice'.
- See the university town of **Mérida**, whose sights include the **Valle Grande**, the **Flower Clock**, **Los Chorros de Milla**, the **Lagoons of Mucubaji**, **Los Anteojos**, **Tabay**, **Pogal**, **Los Patos**, **San-say** and the famous **Black Lagoon**. A mountain railway runs from the town to **Pico Espejo**.
- Visit **Ciudad Bolívar**, formerly known as **Angostura**, and the home of Angostura bitters, an old city on the south bank of the Orinoco which still bears traces of its colonial past.
- See the extraordinary array of wildlife in the **Gran Sabana National Reserve**, the largest of the Venezuelan plateaux.

Top Things To Do

- Take a **scenic flight** or **motorised canoe trip** to the foot of **Angel Falls** (**Salto Angel**), the world's highest waterfall, in the southeast. The falls have an uninterrupted drop of 979m (3212ft), which is about 16 times the height of Niagara Falls. Access to the falls is fairly difficult (there is no road link) and involves a flight to **Canaima** first (the main tourist base, some 50km (31.5 miles) northwest of the falls). The canoe trip operates from June to November, the rainy season, and takes approximately two days.
- Explore Venezuela's parks. There are over 40 national parks and around 20 nature reserves (*monumentos naturales*). **Parque Nacional El Avila** includes around 200km (125 miles) of fairly easy, signposted trails, as well as numerous camping grounds.
- Try **mountain trekking** or **rock climbing** in the **Sierra Nevada de Mérida**, where several of the country's highest peaks (such as the **Pico Bolívar** or the **Pico Humboldt**) and the magnificent **Parque Nacional Sierra Nevada** are located. Experienced guides and equipment can be hired in **Mérida**, the regional tourist hub. Other popular trekking destinations in the area include **Los Nevados** (reached via an easy trek along a beautiful mountain track); **Pico El Aguila** (accessible from **Valera**, which can be reached on a bus ride from Mérida along Venezuela's highest road); and the **Sierra de la Culata** (particularly known for its desert-like landscapes).
- Board the world's longest and highest **cable car** (*teleferico*), which runs for 12.6km (7.9 miles) from Mérida to the top of **Pico Espejo** (4765m/15,629ft), and provides easy access to starting points for mountain treks.
- **Swim**, **surf**, **snorkel** or **dive** at **Isla de Margarita**, some 40km (25 miles) off the mainland north of **Cumaná**. Another good spot is the **Parque Nacional Mochima**, consisting of a wealth of islands and islets, some of which, such as the **Isla de Plata** (the most developed), are surrounded by coral reefs.
- Take a **boat trip** through the mangrove *caños* (channels) of **Parque Nacional Morroy** in the northwest, or sail to the park's islands (two of the best known are **Cayo Sombrero** and **Chichiriviche**). The **fishing**, both fresh- and salt-water, is good.
- Head underground to the **Cueva del Guácharo**, the most spectacular of Venezuela's many cave systems, located three hours by bus from Cumaná.
- Enjoy the novelty of **skiing** in the tropics. The **Cordillera de Mérida** are the only peaks in the country with a permanent snowline. The **Sierra Nevada National Park** offers opportunities to ski between November and June but, at an altitude of 4270m (14,000ft), this is recommended only for the hardiest and most dedicated.
- Climb **Mount Roraima**, suggested as the site of Conan Doyle's *Lost World*. A fortnight's supplies and full camping equipment should be taken as the trip can take up to two weeks.
- Spend a day at the races. Caracas has South America's largest and most modern horse racing track – **La Rinconada** – open Saturday and Sunday.
- Head for the **Caribbean** coastal resorts. **Maiquetia** is one of the best and most popular, offering wide beaches, an extensive range of watersports and some of the best fishing (including an international competition for the giant blue sailfish). There are daily air-shuttles from Maiquetia to **Porlamar**, on **Margarita Island**. Also to the west of Caracas are **Macuto**, **Marbella**, **Naiguata**, **Carabelleda**, **Leguna** and **Oriaco**, all of which boast excellent beaches. To the north of Maiquetia are the idyllic islands of **Los Roques**.
- Pass through the 1130m (3710ft) **Portachuelo Pass** to the coastal resorts of **Ocumare de la Costa** and **Cata**. The coastline here is dotted with fine beaches and islands, many inhabited only by flamingos and scarlet ibis. Most can be reached by hired boat. **Morrocoy**, off the coast from **Tucacas**, is the most spectacular of these – hundreds of coral reefs with palm beaches ideal for **scuba diving** and **fishing**.
- Enjoy the popular coastal resort of **Puerto la Cruz**, a good centre for travelling to remoter beaches. There is the **Morro marina** development in the **Lecherías** area adjacent to Puerto la Cruz, and the attractive town of **Pueblo Viejo** with 'old' Caribbean architecture and a Venetian lagoon layout – boats are the only means of transport.

TOURIST INFORMATION

Nacional Instituto de Turismo (INATUR)
Mexico Avenue, Caracas Hilton Hotel, South Tower, Floors 1 and 2, Caracas, Venezuela
Tel: (212) 576 1193 *or* 9032.

Entertainment

FOOD & DRINK: Cumin and saffron are used in many dishes but the distinctive and delicate flavour of most of the popular dishes comes from the use of local roots and vegetables. There is no good local wine, although foreign wines are bottled locally. There are several good local beers, mineral waters, gin and excellent rum.

Things to know: Bars have either table or counter service. A *lisa* is a glass of draught beer and a *tercio* a bottled beer. Most bars are open very late and there are no licensing laws. Table service is the norm and opening hours are 2100-2300.

National specialities:

- *Arepas* (the native bread made from primitive ground corn, water and salt).
- *Pabellón criollo* (hash made with shredded meat and served with fried plantains and black beans on rice).
- *Hallaca* (cornmeal is combined with beef, pork, ham and green peppers, wrapped in individual pieces of banana leaves and cooked in boiling water, traditionally eaten at Christmas and New Year).
- *Parrilla criolla* is beef marinated and cooked over a charcoal grill.
- *Hervido* (soup made with chunks of beef, chicken or fish and native vegetables or roots).

National drinks:

- Coffee.
- *Merengada* (fruit pulp, ice, milk and sugar).
- *Pousse-café* is an after-dinner liqueur.

Tipping: Tips are discretionary but in the majority of bars and restaurants, 10 per cent is added to the bill and it is customary to leave another 10 per cent on the table. Bellboys and chambermaids should be tipped and, in Caracas, tips are higher than elsewhere.

NIGHTLIFE: There are many nightclubs and discos in the major cities of Venezuela. The National and Municipal Theatres offer a variety of concerts, ballet, plays, operas and operettas. There are other theatres - some of which are open-air - in Caracas, as well as several cinemas.

SHOPPING: There are many handicrafts unique to Venezuela that are made by local Indian tribes. Good purchases are gems and jewellery, *cacique* coins, gold, pearls, pompom slippers, seed necklaces, shoes and handbags, Indian bows, arrows, mats, pipes and baskets, *alpargatas* (traditional local footwear of the Campesinos), *chinchorros* (local hammocks) and many other Indian goods. **Shopping hours:** Mon-Sat 0900-1300 and 1500-1900.

Business

- **GDP:** US$118 billion (2005).
- **Main imports:** Machinery and transport equipment, manufactured goods and construction materials.
- **Main exports:** Petroleum, aluminium, steel, chemical products, iron ore, cigarettes, plastics, fish and cement and paper products.
- **Main trade partners:** Brazil, Colombia, Cuba, Japan and USA.

ECONOMY: Venezuela was a primarily agricultural country until the discovery and extraction of oil began in the 1920s. Oil is now dominant, providing 50 per cent of government revenue and 70 per cent of export earnings. The national oil corporation, *PDVSA*, is one of the world's largest companies. Venezuela has some of the largest known reserves in the world. There are long-term plans to introduce greater diversity into the economy but little change in its basic structure may be expected in the near future.
Agriculture's share of the workforce has now fallen to 4 per cent of GDP, but the sector remains important by providing a non-oil export income in the form of its dairy and beef produce. Some cash crops – mostly rice, sugar and coffee – are grown. Most of the other farming activity is devoted to staple crops for domestic consumption. As well as oil, Venezuela has substantial deposits of iron and aluminium ores, plus gas, coal, diamonds, gold, zinc, copper, titanium, lead, silver, phosphates and manganese. The processing of these ores and the country's agricultural products account for the bulk of the industrial sector. However, over-dependence on oil income has meant that Venezuela's industries are suffering from a historic failure to modernise. Venezuela was a prominent founding member of the Organisation of Petroleum Exporting Countries (OPEC) and the current President, Hugo Chávez, has played a leading role in the revival of the organisation's fortunes since the late 1990s. Since the beginning of 2002, Venezuela's recent economic performance has been severely affected by the turbulent political situation. After the currency crisis of February 2002 came an attempted coup. Then in December large parts of the economy – including the all-important oil industry – were affected by a two-month-long strike. This had a devastating impact: the economy is believed to have contracted by around 10 per cent during 2003. In 2004, the decline was reversed with a growth rate of 17.4 per cent. Venezuela belongs to the *Asociación Latinoamericana de Integración* (ALADI), which seeks to promote a common market for Latin America, and to the Inter-American Development Bank.

BUSINESS ETIQUETTE: English is becoming more widely spoken in business circles, particularly at executive level. Nevertheless, Spanish is essential for most business discussions. Appointments are necessary and a business visitor should be punctual. It is common to exchange visiting cards. **Office hours:** Mon-Fri 0800-1800 with a long midday break.

CONFERENCES/CONVENTIONS: Larger hotels have facilities. For further information, contact the INATUR (see *Top Things To Do*).

COMMERCIAL INFORMATION

Consejo Nacional de Promoción de Invensiones, CONAPRI (National Council for Investment Promotion)
Edificio Forum, Local LC-A (planta baja), Calle Guaicaipuro, El Rosal, Caracas 1060, Venezuela
Tel: (212) 951 6507.
Website: www.conapri.org

Federación Venezolana de Cámaras y Asociaciones de Comercio y Producción, FEDECAMARAS (Federation of Chambers of Commerce and Industry)
Apartado 2568, Edificio Fedecámaras, Pent-House 2, Avenida El Empalme, El Bosque, Caracas, Venezuela
Tel: (212) 731 1711.
Website: www.fedecamaras.org.ve

Vietnam

400km
200mls

★ international airport

Location: South-East Asia.

Time: GMT + 7.

Overview

Vietnam, a name too long associated with the horrors of war, has finally won its last battle – to capture the imagination of the travelling public. Elegant Hanoi now vies with its dynamic sister, Ho Chi Minh City (still fondly called Saigon by the locals), for the attention of visitors drawn by the eclectic mix of old and new. More modern than other Vietnamese cities, Ho Chi Minh City has also retained its French colonial influences. Its vibrancy is maintained by the ever-entrepreneurial Saigonese who have taken the Government reforms to heart and re-embraced the capitalist ethic with unrestrained enthusiasm. The streets are jam-packed with mopeds and scooters, often carrying whole families. The markets are chaotically busy.
Elsewhere, the scenes are timeless. Early morning on the Mekong Delta brings the daily floating markets where fruit and vegetables are peddled. Everywhere the green patchwork of rice paddies stretches into the distance, broken only by the silhouette of water buffalo and conical-hatted peasants bending down to tend the young plants. The soaring mountains in the north of the country tower over tiny villages where life continues much as it has done for centuries, with traditional costumes still proudly worn. Old French hill stations survive throughout the country, offering welcome respite from the heat of the plains below. And, in the South China Sea, the 3000 chalk islands in Ha Long Bay are not to be missed.
The ancient former imperial capital, Hue, takes you back to a time of concubines and eunuchs. In every town, young women wearing the simple but feminine national dress, the *Ao Dai*, weave their way through the traffic at the controls of a motorbike.
Only in Vietnam could the past and the present be encapsulated so perfectly.

General Information

AREA: 329,247 sq km (127,123 sq miles).
POPULATION: 83.6 million (UN estimate 2005).
POPULATION DENSITY: 253.9 per sq km.
CAPITAL: Hanoi. **Population:** 3.08 million (official estimate 2004).

GEOGRAPHY: Vietnam shares borders to the north with the People's Republic of China and to the west with Laos and Cambodia. The South China Sea lies to the east and south. The land is principally agricultural with a central tropical rainforest.
GOVERNMENT: Socialist republic since 1980. Gained independence from France in 1954. **Head of State:** President Tran Duc Luong since 1997. **Head of Government:** Prime Minister Phan Van Khai since 1997. **Recent history:** Reforms have resulted in rapid economic growth in the last decade (see *Economy*) but there has been no parallel development in the country's political environment: the Communist Party has no intention of relaxing its hold on political power for the time being. The present constitution, promulgated in 1992, asserts the political supremacy of the Communist Party of Vietnam. The 496-member National Assembly is responsible for legislation. The Assembly is elected every five years from candidates proposed by the CPV. Executive power is exercised by the Council of Ministers. The Assembly elects a President, who acts as Head of State and also appoints a Prime Minister from among the members of the Assembly. The Prime Minister leads the Council of Ministers, the members of which hold executive power. In April 2001, the party chose a new Secretary General in Nong Duc Manh, who consequently began a crackdown on dissident and 'unauthorised' literature. Nong is one of the triumvirate that now govern Vietnam, along with Prime Minister Phan Van Khai and President Tran Duc Luong. The party is concerned by corruption among senior officials as well as the growth of religious fervour among the population.
LANGUAGE: Vietnamese is the official language. English, French, Chinese and occasionally Russian and German are spoken.
RELIGION: Buddhist majority. There are also Taoist, Confucian, Hoa Hao, Caodaist and Christian (predominantly Roman Catholic) minorities.
ELECTRICITY: 220/110 volts AC, 50Hz; plugs are mostly flat pin.
SOCIAL CONVENTIONS: Handshaking and a vocal greeting is normal. Clothing should be kept simple, informal and discreet. Avoid shorts if possible as they are usually only worn by children. Footwear should be removed when entering Buddhist pagodas. Vietnamese people should not be touched on the head. **Photography:** There are restrictions at ports, airports and harbours, and in similar areas elsewhere. It is courteous to ask permission first before taking photographs of people.

Climate

Because of its geography, the climate in Vietnam varies greatly from north to south. Tropical monsoons occur from May to October. It is almost totally dry throughout the rest of the year.

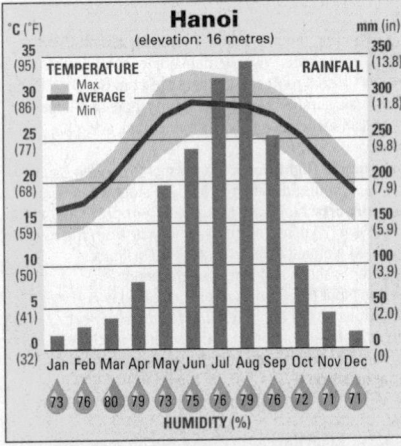

Hanoi (elevation: 16 metres)

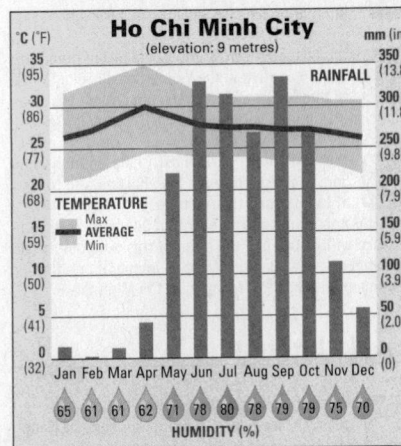

Ho Chi Minh City (elevation: 9 metres)

Required clothing: Tropicals and washable cottons are worn all year. Rainwear is essential during the rainy season.

Communications

Telephone: Country code: 84. IDD is available.
Mobile telephone: Coverage is largely limited to main urban areas.
Internet: E-mail can be accessed from Internet cafes in Hanoi and Ho Chi Minh City.
Post: Postal services can be slow. Airmail to Europe can take up to three weeks.
MEDIA: The media is controlled by the Communist Party. Newspapers straying beyond restrictive Government reporting guidelines are shut down. Internet access is tightly controlled. Web content is subject to Government approval and sites deemed unacceptable are blocked.
Press: Daily and weekly newspapers in Vietnam include *Lao Dong*, *Nhan Dan* (The People) and *Quan Doi Nhan Dan*. The *Vietnam Economic Times*, *Vietnam Investment Review*, *Saigon Times* and *Vietnam News* are published in English. *Le Courrier du Vietnam* is published in French.
TV: *VTV* is the national television service. Regional stations also exist and some foreign cable channels are broadcast.
Radio: *Voice of Vietnam (VoV)* is state operated. *VoV 5* broadcasts programmes in English, French and Russian.

Passport/Visa

	Passport Required?	Visa Required?	Return Ticket Required?
Full British	Yes	Yes	No
Australian	Yes	Yes	No
Canadian	Yes	Yes	No
USA	Yes	Yes	No
Other EU	Yes	Yes/1	No
Japanese	Yes	No/1	No

Note: *Regulations and requirements may be subject to change at short notice, and you are advised to contact the appropriate diplomatic or consular authority before finalising travel arrangements. Any numbers in the chart refer to the footnotes below.*

PASSPORTS: Passport valid for at least one month after expiration of visa required by all.
VISAS: Required by all except:
(a) nationals of Bulgaria, China (PR) (AB passport), Cuba, Korea (Dem Rep), Mongolia (AB, AC or AO passport), Romania, Russian Federation and Ukraine (AB passport);
(b) nationals of Indonesia, Laos, Malaysia, Singapore and Thailand for stays of up to 30 days;
(c) nationals of The Philippines for stays of up to 21 days;
(d) **1.** nationals of Denmark, Finland, Japan, Korea (Rep), Norway and Sweden for stays of up to 15 days;
(e) transit passengers continuing their journey within 24 hours, provided holding valid return or onward tickets. At present, visas can be issued for either groups or individuals.
Note: For security reasons, it is advisable to carry copies of documents rather than originals when in Vietnam.
Types of visa and cost: *Tourist*: £38 (single-entry); £55 (express service); £70 (multiple-entry). *Single-entry Business*: £40. *Multiple-entry Business*: £70 (one month); £90 (three months); £140 (six months or more).
Validity: Tourist visas are valid for one month from proposed date of entry. Visas can usually be extended for another month, at extra cost, in the larger towns.
Note: All regulations, including those concerning which counties require visas, cost of visas and validity of visas, are very complex and subject to frequent change. It is therefore advisable to contact the consular section at the Embassy before any travel to Vietnam.
Application to: Consulate (or consular section at Embassy); see *Passport/Visa Information*.
Application requirements: (a) Completed application form. (b) One recent passport-size photo. (c) Valid passport. (d) Fee (non-refundable), payable by cash, bank draft or postal order. (e) To have your passport returned by post, please add £5 and include a stamped self-addressed envelope. *Business*: (a)-(e), and (f) Approval obtained through a Vietnamese sponsor.
Working days required: Two (tourist visa express application); five (tourist visa). Entry visas can be applied for in person up to six months prior to date of travel.

PASSPORT/VISA INFORMATION

Embassy of the Socialist Republic of Vietnam in the UK
12 Victoria Road, London W8 5RD, UK
Tel: (020) 7937 1912.
Website: www.vietnamembassy.org.uk
Opening hours: Mon-Fri 0900-1700; 0930-1230 (visa section).

Embassy of the Socialist Republic of Vietnam in the USA
1233 20th Street, NW, Suite 400, Washington, DC 20036, USA
Tel: (202) 861 0737 *or* 2293 (consular section).
Website: www.vietnamembassy-usa.org

Money

Currency: New Dông (VND). Notes are in denominations of VND500,000, 100,000, 50,000, 20,000, 10,000, 5000, 2000, 1000, 500, 200 and 100. Coins are in denominations of VND5000, 2000, 1000, 500 and 200.
Currency exchange: The US Dollar is the most favoured foreign currency. Australian, British, Japanese, Singaporean and Thai currency, as well as the Euro, can usually be changed in the larger cities; great difficulty may be encountered in trying to exchange any other currencies. There is a charge for changing money in banks.
Credit & debit cards: An increasing number of outlets accept MasterCard and Visa. However, outside main centres, it is wise to carry cash. Check with your credit or debit card company for details of merchant acceptability and other services which may be available.
Traveller's cheques: These are widely accepted in hotels and banks. To avoid additional exchange rate charges, travellers are advised to take traveller's cheques in US Dollars or Euros.
Currency restrictions: Import and export of local currency is prohibited. Import and export of foreign currency over US$3000 is subject to declaration. Proof of all expenses should be kept.
Banking hours: Mon-Fri 0730/0800-1130 and 1300-1600.
Exchange rate indicators:
Rate at time of publishing
£1.00= VND28,021.34
$1.00= VND15,906.00

Duty Free

The following items may be freely imported into Vietnam by foreign visitors without incurring customs duty:
400 cigarettes; 100 cigars or 500g of tobacco; up to 5kg of tea and up to 3kg of coffee; 1.5l of liquor at 22 per cent and above, and 2l of liquor below this amount, and 3l of all other alcoholic beverages; a reasonable quantity of perfume and personal belongings; other goods not exceeding VND5 million.
Prohibited items: The importation of non-prescribed drugs, firearms and pornography is prohibited.

Public Holidays

Below are listed Public Holidays for the January 2006-June 2007 period.
2006: Jan 1 New Year's Day. **Jan 29-31*** Têt, Lunar New Year. **Apr 30** Liberation of Saigon. **May 1** May Day. **Sep 2** National Day.
2007: Jan 1 New Year's Day. **Feb 18-20*** Têt, Lunar New Year. **Apr 30** Liberation of Saigon. **May 1** May Day.
Note: *Check with the Embassy for the exact date. Visitors may experience difficulties during this period as shops, restaurants and public services close and prices tend to go up in the few shops that remain open.

Health

	Special Precautions?	Certificate Required?
Yellow Fever	Yes	1
Cholera	Yes	2
Typhoid & Polio	3	N/A
Malaria	4	N/A

Note: Regulations and requirements may be subject to change at short notice, and you are advised to contact your doctor well in advance of your intended date of departure. Any numbers in the chart refer to the footnotes below.

1: A *yellow fever* vaccination certificate is required from travellers over one arriving from infected areas.
2: Following WHO guidelines issued in 1973, a *cholera* vaccination certificate is not an official condition of entry to Vietnam. However, *cholera* is a serious risk in this country and precautions are essential. Up-to-date advice should be sought before deciding whether these precautions should include vaccination, as medical opinion is divided over its effectiveness. For more information, see the *Health* appendix.
3: Vaccination against *typhoid* is advised.
4: *Malaria* risk exists, predominantly in the *falciparum* form, throughout the year everywhere except urban areas, the Red River delta and the coastal plains of Central Vietnam. The risk is highest in the three central highlands provinces of Dak Lak, Gia Lai and Kon Tum, as well as the southern provinces of Ca Mau, Bac Lieu and Tay Ninh. The malignant *falciparum* form is reported to be highly resistant to chloroquine and sulfadoxine-pyrimethamine. The recommended prophylaxis is mefloquine, doxycycline or atovaquone/proguanil, depending on the specific area visited.
Food & drink: All water should be regarded as being potentially contaminated. Water used for drinking, brushing teeth or making ice should have first been boiled or otherwise sterilised. Milk is unpasteurised and should be boiled. Powdered or tinned milk is available and is advised, but make sure that it is reconstituted with pure water. Avoid dairy products that are likely to have been made from unboiled milk. Only eat well-cooked meat and fish, preferably served hot. Pork, salad and mayonnaise may carry increased risk. Vegetables should be cooked and fruit peeled.
Other risks: *Bilharzia (schistosomiasis)* is present in the delta of the Mekong River. Avoid swimming and paddling in fresh water; swimming pools which are chlorinated and well maintained are safe.
Japanese encephalitis is a risk in Hanoi and in rural areas. A vaccine is available and travellers are advised to consult their doctor prior to departure. *Hepatitis A, B* and *E* occur; precautions should be taken. *Dengue fever* can be epidemic and *filariasis* is endemic in some rural areas. *Typhoid fever, amoebic* and *bacillary dysentry* can occur. *Trachoma* and *plague* occur rarely. There have been renewed outbreaks of *avian influenza*, although the number infected is still minimal. All visitors are advised against close contact with, and under-cooked consumption of, poultry.
Rabies is present. For those at high risk, vaccination before arrival should be considered. If you are bitten, seek medical advice without delay. For more information, consult the *Health* appendix.
Health care: There are hospitals in major towns and cities, and health care centres in all provinces, but facilities are limited everywhere and there is a lack of medicines. Health insurance is essential and should include cover for emergency repatriation by air. Immediate cash payment is expected for services.

Travel - International

AIR:
The national airline is *Vietnam Airlines (VN)* (website: www.vietnamairlines.com). The most usual routes to Vietnam are from Bangkok, Hong Kong, Kuala Lumpur, Manila, Paris, Singapore and Taipei. Most Asian carriers have flights to Vietnam, as do *Air France* and *Qantas*.
Approximate flight times: From Hanoi to *London* is approximately 17 hours, including two hours' stopover in Bangkok.
Main airports: *Noi Bai International Airport (HAN)* at Noi Bai is 45km (28 miles) north of Hanoi. *To/from the airport:* Buses and metered taxis are available. *Facilities:* Restaurants, shops and bureaux de change.
Tan Son Nhat International Airport (SGN) is 7km (4.5 miles) from Ho Chi Minh City. *To/from the airport:* Metered taxis and limousines are available. *Facilities:* Snack bar, duty free and bureaux de change.
Departure tax: US$14 (Ho Chi Minh City), US$12 (Hanoi) and US$8 (Da Nang), payable in US Dollars or new Dông.
SEA:
Main ports: *Ho Chi Minh City, Vung Tau, Haiphong, Da Nang* and *Binh Thuy*. International cruise facilities are available.
RAIL:
It is possible to cross into China by rail from Lao Cai to Kunming in the Yunnan province of China or through Lang Son to Nanning. There are trains from Beijing-Dong Dang-Hanoi and back twice weekly.
ROAD:
There are routes to Guangxi, China through Lang Son, Cambodia through Moc Bai and also to Laos at Lao Bao and Cau Trieu.
Note: It is important to remember that all Vietnamese visas are issued with a specified exit point. If this exit point needs to be altered, it must be done so at an immigration office or through a travel agent in Hanoi or Ho Chi Minh City.

Travel - Internal

AIR:
Vietnam Airlines (VN) operates daily flights between Hanoi, Ho Chi Minh City, Hue, Da Nang and Nha Trang. Regular services are also provided between Hanoi and Ho Chi Minh City to Buon Ma Thuot, Dalat, Na San, Phu Quoc, Pleiku, Qui Nhon and Vinh. *The Northern Airport Flight Service Company* operates flights by helicopter to Halong Bay from Hanoi.
SEA:
A local network operates between ports. Details of ferry services can be found on the Vietnam National Tourism Administration website (see *Top Things To Do*). Cruise facilities are available. Contact the Embassy before departure.
RAIL:
Visitors may use the rail transport system independently or as part of a rail tour. Long-distance trains are more expensive but are faster, more reliable and more comfortable. Although a few carriages now have air conditioning, facilities are still short of international standards, and foreigners' rates are comparable to the air fares. The main rail route connects Hanoi and Ho Chi Minh City and the journey can take between 30 and 40 hours. There are also services from Hanoi to Haiphong, Dong Dang, Lao Cai, Thai Nguyen and from Yen Vien to Ha Long. Contact Vietnam Railways (website: www.vr.com.vn) for more information.
ROAD:
There is a reasonable road network. Traffic drives on the right. Roads, especially in the north, are often in a bad state of repair and may be impassable during the rainy season. Driving in Vietnam can be a hair-raising experience as the normal rules of highway discipline are rarely followed by the majority of drivers. There is a good highway from Hanoi to Ho Chi Minh City.
Bus: Services are often poor and overcrowded, although long-distance buses are sometimes more modern and air-conditioned. Minibuses often run between tourist hotels in the major towns. **Car hire:** It is possible to hire chauffeur-driven cars. Self-drive car hire is non-existent.
Documentation: An International Driving Permit and a test (taken in Vietnam) are required.
URBAN:
There are local bus services in Ho Chi Minh City and in Hanoi, which also has a tramway. It is also possible to travel by taxi, motorbike or *cyclo* (cycle rickshaw; motorised version also exists); the last of these options can leave the traveller vulnerable to theft from opportunistic passers-by and the Government is trying to phase them out. When travelling by taxi, it is advisable to note down the driver's registration number (displayed on rear side of taxi) for security reasons.

Travel Advice

There have been renewed outbreaks of avian influenza (bird flu) amongst poultry throughout Vietnam, with a number of human fatalities in this latest outbreak. The World Health Organisation is still investigating the possibility of human-to-human transmission. Travellers should avoid visiting live animal markets, poultry farms and other places where they may come into close contact with wild or caged birds; and ensure poultry dishes are thoroughly cooked.
Most visits to Vietnam are trouble-free but you should be aware of the global risk of indiscriminate international terrorist attacks, which could be against civilian targets, including places frequented by foreigners.
Serious or violent crimes against foreigners in Vietnam are rare, but travellers should remain vigilant for petty or opportunistic theft.
This advice is based on information provided by the Foreign & Commonwealth Office in the UK. It is correct at time of publishing. As the situation can change rapidly, visitors are advised to contact the following organisations for the latest travel advice:

British Foreign and Commonwealth Office
Tel: (0845) 850 2829.
Website: www.fco.gov.uk

US Department of State
Website: http://travel.state.gov/travel

Accommodation

Tourist facilities have vastly improved in the last few years and most towns have small hotels and guest-houses. In the major towns, there is a full range of accommodation to suit all budgets. For information, contact a travel operator that specialises in Vietnam *or* the Vietnam National Administration of Tourism (see *Top Things To Do*).

Top Things To See

- The capital, **Hanoi**, sprawls on the banks of the **Red River**. It is a beautiful city that retains an air of French colonial elegance with pretty yellow stucco buildings lining leafy streets. In the middle of the city lies the peaceful **Hoan Kiem Lake** (Lake of the Restored Sword) with the 18th-century **Ngoc Son Temple** (Jade Mountain Temple) sitting on an island in its centre. The temple can be reached by **The Huc Bridge** (Rising Sun Bridge). Wander round the **Old Quarter**, a fascinating maze of small antiquated streets lined with markets and pavement restaurants and cafes, to the north of Hoan Kiem Lake. Discover the former **Ville Française**, west of the Old Quarter and south of the West Lake . This is the old French administrative centre and is characterised by enormous colonial-era châteaux and wide spacious boulevards. It also houses Hanoi's most popular attraction, the **Ho Chi Minh Mausoleum**. Ho Chi Minh was the father of the modern state and is still held in reverential regard. His house, built in 1958, is also on public view. Other museums in Hanoi include the **Bao Tang Lich Su** (History Museum), the **Bao Tang Quan Doi** (Army Museum), **Ho Chi Minh Museum**, **Bao Tang My Thuat** (Fine Arts Museum), **Bao Tang Cach Manh** (Revolutionary Museum) and **Independence Museum**. There are a number of interesting pagodas in Hanoi. The **One Pillar Pagoda**, first constructed in 1049 (subsequently destroyed by the French just before they were ejected from the city and then rebuilt by the new Government), was built to resemble a lotus flower – the symbol of purity rising out of a sea of sorrow. The **Temple of Literature** built in 1076 was the first university in Vietnam. It is a graceful complex of small intricate buildings and peaceful courtyards. To the northwest of the **Citadel** is the **West Lake**, which is about 13km (9 miles) in circumference. Picnic on the shores of the lake. The lake also contains the wreckage of a crashed American B52 bomber.

- About 160km (100 miles) from Hanoi, near the port of **Haiphong**, is **Ha Long Bay**. Be amazed by this complex of 3000 chalk islands rising out of the South China Sea. The area is strange, eerie and very beautiful. Many of the islands contain bizarre cave formations and grottoes.
- Visit **Catba Island**, near Ha Long Bay, a designated National Park and a rich repository of plants and wildlife.
- About 250km (155 miles) north of Hanoi, high in the **Hoang Lien Mountains**, is the old hill station of **Sapa**. This area is inhabited by the Hmong and Zhao hill tribes. Every weekend there is a market when the local tribespeople come into town to trade. In the evening, they celebrate with huge amounts of potent rice alcohol. It is absolutely vital that when visiting this area tourists are sensitive to local culture and traditions. Follow the road from Sapa 200km (125 miles) further into the mountains (this can only realistically be attempted by jeep), to reach **Dien Bien Phu**, scene of the humiliating defeat of the French by the Viet Minh that finally put paid to French colonial occupation in Indochina. This is a wild, beautiful and remote region.
- Discover the beautiful imperial architecture of **Hue** (although a great deal of this was destroyed during the Tet offensive in 1968), the former capital of the emperors of Vietnam. **The Perfume River** forms the border between the city itself and the former 'Forbidden Purple City', the mighty **Citadel**. This 'city within a city' with its tombs, pagodas and lakes covered in lotus flowers was largely destroyed during the Vietnam War, but one can still see evidence of its former magnificence. Within easy reach of the city are the tombs of several of Vietnam's emperors. Most interesting, perhaps, are the **Tomb of Minh Mang** and the **Tomb of Tu Duc**. The city also houses fine examples of Buddhist pagodas and other temples, such as the **Thien Mu Pagoda**.
- Near Hue is **Da Nang**, city of **China Beach**, the **Marble Mountains** and the **Cham Museum**, which houses magnificent examples of the art of the Indianised Cham civilisation. Approximately 20km (12 miles) from Da Nang is **Hoi An**. This is a delightful small town replete with temple and pagodas.
- Head for **Nha Trang**, a day's drive from Hoi An, through some of Vietnam's most breathtaking scenery. This is a pleasant resort with a good beach. From here it is easy to reach the town of **Da Lat** in the Central Highlands, evocative of a typical French town, which is popular among domestic tourists for its cool climate and alpine scenery.
- Set back from the delta formed by the Mekong River, **Ho Chi Minh City** (formerly **Saigon**) is the main commercial centre of the southern part of Vietnam, named in honour of the leader who successfully led the nation against both France and the USA. There is a lot to see in Ho Chi Minh City. The colourful **Emperor of Jade Pagoda** is an excellent example of a Chinese temple. The hustle and bustle of trading is best observed in the markets of **Cholon**, the ancient Chinese quarter. The **Hôtel de Ville** is a wonderful example of French colonial architecture. The twin towers of **Notre Dame Cathedral** have been a familiar landmark in Ho Chi Minh City since the 1880s. The **War Remnants Museum** bears witness to the suffering inflicted on the Vietnamese people during the Vietnam War in the 1960s and 1970s. Other sites relevant to that era are **Re-Unification Hall** and the former US Embassy.
- Go to **Tay Ninh**, northwest of Ho Chi Minh City. This is an interesting destination as it is the home of the Caodai religion, a purely Vietnamese sect formed this century, which takes teachings and precepts from most of the world's major religions. Tay Ninh is the site of the largest **Caodaist temple** in Vietnam. This structure is colourful and unique.
- South of Ho Chi Minh city, see the flat, verdant plains of the **Mekong Delta**, where much of Vietnam's rice crop is grown. There are several towns in this region from which the visitor can take boat trips on the many tributaries of the Mekong.

Top Things To Do

- Vietnam is ideal for long-distance **cycling** as much of the country is flat and the shortage of vehicles makes for light traffic. Caution is needed, however, especially on busier roads as traffic can be very undisciplined. Bicycle hire is widely available.
- In total, Vietnam has 3260km (2021 miles) of coastline. The most popular beaches are **Vung Tau**, just north of the Mekong Delta; and **Nha Trang**, near Da Lat, where the clear, turquoise waters offer good **snorkelling** and **scuba diving**. Other good beaches can be found at **Phan Thiet** (southcentral coast); **Mui Ne** (noted for its large sand dunes); and the magnificent **Ha Long Bay**, where some 3000 islands, covered in lush vegetation and dotted with beaches and grottoes, rise out of the Gulf of Tonkin. Access to the islands is by boats, which can be hired in Ha Long City.
- Go **hiking** or **horse riding** in the beautiful countryside around **Da Lat**. Guides are recommended and can be hired locally. Generally, the northwest is the best region for hiking. Other good destinations include **Bach Ma National Park**, **Cuc Phuong National Park** (near Hanoi) and **Lang Bian Mountain** (in Da Lat), where guides are compulsory. In the north, **Ba Be Lake National Park** (which contains several lakes, waterfalls and caves) and **Cat Ba National Park** on Cat Ba Island also offer beautiful scenery.
- **Caving** enthusiasts may head for the spectacular **Pong Nha** river caves, northwest of Dong Hoi.
- **Boat trips** are particularly popular in the **Mekong Delta**, Vietnam's southernmost region, which consists of an intricate network of rice paddies, swamps and forests interlaced with canals and rivers. River cruises also operate on the **Saigon River** (a good way to see Ho Chi Minh City) or the **Perfume River** (near Hue).
- See some of the **Vietnam War sights**. It is possible to walk part of the **Ho Chi Minh Trail**, a series of roads, trails and paths used as supply routes by the North Vietnamese during the war. It ran from North Vietnam southward through the Truong Son mountains and into western Laos. The claustrophobic network of tunnels used by villagers and guerrillas during the war at **Cu Chi** (35km/22 miles from Ho Chi Minh City) and **Vinh Moc** can also be visited.

TOURIST INFORMATION

Vietnam National Administration of Tourism
80 Quan Su, Hanoi, Vietnam
Tel: (4) 942 3998.
Website: www.vietnamtourism.com

Entertainment

FOOD & DRINK: Vietnamese cooking is varied and usually very good. It is a mixture of Vietnamese, Chinese and French traditions, with a plethora of regional specialities. As in all countries of the region, rice or noodles usually provide the basis of a meal. Not surprisingly, fish is plentiful.
National specialities:
- Breakfast is generally noodle soup locally known as *pho* (pronounced 'fur').
- French-style baguettes are available throughout Vietnam.
- *Nem* (pork mixed with noodles, eggs and mushrooms wrapped in rice paper, fried and served hot).
- *Banh chung* (glutinous rice, pork and onions wrapped in large leaves and cooked for up to 48 hours, to be eaten cold at any time).
- Vietnamese dishes are not complete without *nuoc mam* (a fish sauce) or *mam tom* (a shrimp sauce).
National drinks:
- Green tea is refreshing and available everywhere.
- The French culinary legacy embraces rich, fresh, filter coffee, usually brewed on the table in front of the customer.
- *Bia Hoi*, a local draught beer available at street stalls in Hanoi. It is not only cheap, but free of additives.
- *Rice wine* is also a favourite throughout the country. It is generally extremely potent.
Tipping: Tipping is not customary, but is becoming more usual in tourist areas, especially in the south. Upscale restaurants and hotels may add a 5 to 10 per cent service charge to the bill. Taxi drivers do not expect to be tipped.

SHOPPING: Local specialities include lacquer painting, reed mats, embroidery, tailor-made *ao dais* (female national costume) and mother-of-pearl inlay on ornaments and furniture, not to mention the ubiquitous conical hat.
Shopping hours: Daily 0800/0830-2100/2200.

Business

- **GDP:** US$51.6 billion (2005 estimate).
- **Main exports:** Crude oil, textiles and garments, footwear, rice, coffee and fish.
- **Main imports:** Machinery and equipment, refined petroleum and steel.
- **Main trade partners:** Exports to: USA, Japan, China and Australia. Imports from: China, Korea (Rep), Japan and Singapore.

ECONOMY: The economy of Vietnam was devastated by 30 years of war up to 1975, after which policy errors and a USA-enforced trade boycott combined to stifle development. Since the end of the boycott in 1994, and the introduction of liberalising and deregulating measures by the Government, the Vietnamese economy underwent significant growth of around 8 to 9 per cent annually. The 1997 Asian financial crisis put a temporary brake on the economy but annual growth has since recovered to 8.4 per cent in 2005; average inflation was 4.4 per cent between 2001 and 2005, and unemployment has hovered around 6 or 7 per cent in the past few years.
Agriculture remains the principal employer in Vietnam and produces 23 per cent of total output. Rice, of which Vietnam is the world's second-largest exporter (after Thailand), is the staple crop. Other cash crops include sugar cane, coffee, rubber, tea, cotton and groundnuts. Timber was once exploited on a large scale but the industry was cut back throughout the 1990s prior to a total ban in 1997. Oil, coal and natural gas are present in significant quantities, along with deposits of tin, zinc, antimony, chromium and gold. The oil and gas fields are mostly offshore and of relatively low quality, but after steady growth during the 1990s, it accounted for 26 per cent of Vietnam's industrial output by 2000. The remainder of the industrial sector is devoted to the production of textiles, chemicals, processed foods and machinery. The industrial sector, whose annual growth has averaged over 10 per cent since 1995, accounts for 39 per cent of GDP.
The ending of the US embargo in 1994 allowed Vietnam to join institutions such as the World Bank and IMF, as well as giving access to the wider international financial system. The banking and finance sector has undergone rapid growth in the last few years, and the Government has belatedly realised the importance of modernising what is a fairly primitive system. Similar considerations apply to Vietnam's relatively poor infrastructure and the archaic condition of many of its state-owned industries. Vietnam is a member of the Asian Development Bank and has signed the ASEAN Free Trade Agreement. The country's accession to the World Trade Organisation is expected to take place in 2006.
BUSINESS ETIQUETTE: Smart lightweight casuals would usually be worn for meetings as suits are needed for only the most formal occasions. English is not spoken by all officials and a knowledge of French will be useful. Business cards should have a Vietnamese translation on the back.
Office hours: Mon-Sat 0730-1200 and 1300-1630.

COMMERCIAL INFORMATION

Vietnam Chamber of Commerce and Industry
4th Floor, 9 Dao Duy Anh Street, Hanoi, Vietnam
Tel: (4) 574 3985
Website: www.vcci.com.vn

Yemen

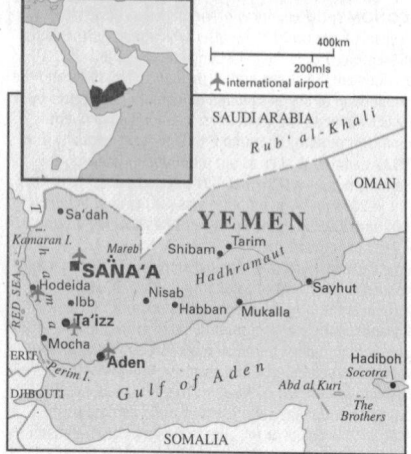

```
                    400km
              200mls
        ✈ international airport

        SAUDI ARABIA
            Rub' al-Khali

                           OMAN
  • Sa'dah
Kamaran I.  Mareb      YEMEN
         • Shibam • Tarim
   SANA'A       Hadhramaut
Hodeida              • Sayhut
   • Ibb  Nisab
  • Ta'izz  Habban Mukalla
  • Mocha
ERIT  Perim I.  Aden        Hadiboh
DJIBOUTI  Gulf of Aden  Abd al Kuri  Socotra
                                   The
                                   Brothers
              SOMALIA
```

Location: Middle East, Arabian Peninsula.

Time: GMT + 3.

Overview

To the Romans, Yemen was Arabia Felix, whose mountains and fertile areas distinguished it from the barren desert of the rest of the Arabian peninsula. After the fall of the Roman Empire, Yemen came into the seventh century under the influence of Islam. It remained within the orbit of various regional powers until, in the 15th century, it became a flashpoint in the struggle between the Egyptians and the Ottoman Empire. During the early 17th and early 19th centuries, the struggle for control was between the Europeans and the Ottomans.

Protection of the Suez sea route was imperative for the British, who occupied the port of Aden in 1839. The Yemeni hinterland was mostly under the loose control of the Ottoman Empire throughout the 19th century, until 1918, when the Imam Yahya took power in what became the Yemen Arab Republic (YAR). Aden and its surroundings, meanwhile, were firmly established as a British colony. Yahya was assassinated in 1948 and his son Ahmed took

Credit: ©Yemen Tourism Promotion Board

over. From 1958 to 1961, the YAR was federated with Egypt and Syria in the United Arab States. Ahmed died in 1962 and an army coup led to civil war.

By this time, in the south, the British colonial forces faced armed opposition from both the leftist National Liberation Front (NLF) and the Front for the Liberation of Occupied South Yemen (FLOSY). In 1967, just before the formation of the Yemen Democratic People's Republic in the south by the victorious NLF forces, a Republican Government took control in the north. There was intermittent warfare between the two Yemens throughout the late 1960s and early 1970s and political instability in the north throughout the 1970s.

In 1978, Lieutenant-Colonel Ali Abdullah Saleh became Head of State in the north. In the same year, Ali Nasser Muhammad became Head of State in the south. In 1986, civil war between rival elements within the armed forces broke out. A new Government was formed under Haydar Abu Bakr al-Attas. The long-promised merger of the two Yemens took place in 1990 and Ali Abdullah Saleh became leader of the unified country.

Since then Yemen has established itself as a tourist destination, attracting travellers with its striking scenery, spectacular Islamic and pre-Islamic architecture and the deep sense of the past. Yemen boasts hugely varied landscapes, from magnificent mountains to lush fruit-growing valleys to semi-arid plains and wide sandy beaches. The towns and cities hide souks and spice markets, mosques and ancient city walls. The country is home to numerous significant archeological sites, while adventure travellers can enjoy camping and trekking in the unique Socotra archipelago, which counts over 270 endemic species among its enormous range of wildlife and plantlife.

General Information

AREA: 536,869 sq km (207,286 sq miles).

POPULATION: 21.5 million (UN, 2005).

POPULATION DENSITY: 40.04 per sq km

CAPITAL: Sana'a. **Population:** 1 million (2005 estimate).

GEOGRAPHY: The Republic of Yemen is bordered in the northwest, north and northeast by Saudi Arabia, in the east by Oman and in the south by the Gulf of Aden. To the west lies the Red Sea. The islands of Perim and Karam in the southern Red Sea are also part of the Republic. Yemen is predominantly mountainous, supporting terraced agriculture. The Hadramaut is a range of high mountains in the centre of the country. Highlands rise steeply in central Yemen, ranging in height from approximately 200m (656ft) to the 4000m (13,123ft) peak of Jabal Nabi Shuaib. In contrast is *Tihama*, a flat semi-desert coastal plain to the west, 50 to 100km (30 to 60 miles) wide. Surface water flows down from the mountains through the valleys during the rainy season and the area is cultivated for cotton and grain. In the east, the mountains drop away to the *Rub al-Khali* or 'Empty Quarter' of the Arabian Peninsula, a vast sea of sand. The arid coastal plains are fringed with sandy beaches.

GOVERNMENT: Republic since 1990. **Head of State:** President Ali Abdullah Saleh since 1990. **Head of Government:** Prime Minister Abd-al-Qadir Abd-al-Rahman Ba-Jammal since 2001. **Recent history:** In April 2003, at the most recent election for the House of Representatives, the General People's Congress (GPC) took an overall majority with 238 seats; most of the remainder were taken by Al-Islah. The next Presidential elections are due in 2006, but President Ali Abdullah Saleh does not plan to stand. Executive power is held by the President who is directly elected for a five-year term and appoints a Prime Minister and Council of Ministers. Legislative power is held by the 301-member *Majlis al-Nuwaab* (House of Representatives), which is also directly elected.

LANGUAGE: Arabic. English is widely spoken as a second language.

RELIGION: Sunni Muslim (especially in the north) and Shia Muslim, with some small Christian and Hindu communities. There is also a small Jewish minority.

ELECTRICITY: 220/230 volts AC, 50Hz.

SOCIAL CONVENTIONS: Traditional values are still very much part of everyday life and visitors will be treated with traditional courtesies and hospitality. Many of the population work in agriculture, with several thousand dependent on fishing. The rest live and work in towns and there is a small nomadic minority living along the northern edges of the desert. Guns become more noticeable further north, slung over the shoulder and carried in addition to the traditional *jambia*. In towns, women are veiled with black or coloured cloth, while in the villages such customs are not observed. Yemenis commonly chew *qat*, a locally grown shrub bearing shoots that have a stimulant effect (similar to caffeine), chewed in markets and cafes but more stylishly sitting on cushions in a guestroom or *mafrai* at the top of a multi-storeyed Yemeni house. For the visitor, conservative casual clothes are suitable; visiting businesspeople are expected to wear suits. Men need to wear a jacket and tie for formal occasions and in smart dining rooms. Women are expected to dress modestly and

beachwear and shorts should be confined to the beach or poolside. Smoking is forbidden during Ramadan. Foreigners are requested not to smoke, eat or drink in public.

Photography: Tourists should not take photos of women, military places, police personnel or installations.

Climate

The climate varies according to altitude. The coastal plain is hot and dusty throughout most of the year. The highlands are warm in summer and, during winter, from October to March, nights can be very cold in the mountains. Annual rainfall is extremely low and temperatures, particularly in summer, are very high. The most pleasant time is from October to April.

Required clothing: Lightweight clothes are worn in the coastal plain all year. Warmer clothes are needed from November to April in the highlands.

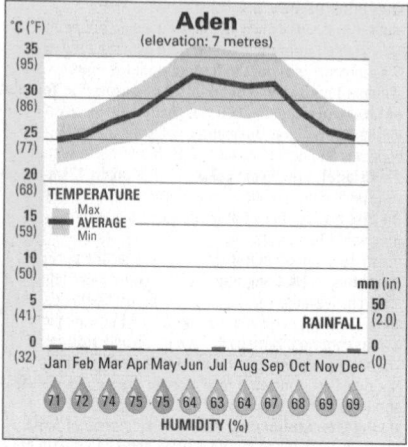

```
°C (°F)          Aden
  35        (elevation: 7 metres)
 (95)
  30
 (86)
  25
 (77)
  20
 (68)   TEMPERATURE
  15       Max
 (59)      AVERAGE
           Min
  10
 (50)
   5                          mm (in)
 (41)                     RAINFALL  50 (2.0)
   0                              0
 (32) Jan Feb Mar Apr May Jun Jul Aug Sep Oct Nov Dec  (0)

     71  72  74  75  75  64  63  64  67  68  69  69
                  HUMIDITY (%)
```

Communications

Telephone: Country code: 967. IDD is available in parts of the country.

Mobile telephone: Roaming agreements exist with most international mobile phone operators. Coverage is good in the west and in coastal areas of the east.

Internet: There are Internet cafes throughout Yemen.

Post: Airmail to Western Europe from Sana'a takes about four days; mail to and from other towns may take longer. Post office hours: Sat-Thurs 0800-1400 and 1600-2000.

MEDIA: All broadcasting is controlled by the Ministry of Information through the Public Corporation for Radio and Television. The Ministry also funds some newspapers and retains a tight control over the press. TV and radio stations from Oman and Saudi Arabia are available.

Press: Daily and weekly Arabic newspapers include *26 September*, *Al-Jumhuriaya* and *Al-Thawra*. The *Yemen Observer* and *The Yemen Times* are published in English.

TV: State-run *Republic of Yemen Television* operates two channels.

Radio: *Republic of Yemen Radio* is also state-run, and operates two stations.

Passport/Visa

	Passport Required?	Visa Required?	Return Ticket Required?
Full British	Yes	Yes	No
Australian	Yes	Yes	No
Canadian	Yes	Yes	No
USA	Yes	Yes	No
Other EU	Yes	Yes	No
Japanese	Yes	Yes	No

Note: *Regulations and requirements may be subject to change at short notice, and you are advised to contact the appropriate diplomatic or consular authority before finalising travel arrangements. Any numbers in the chart refer to the footnotes below.*

Restricted entry and transit: The Government of the Republic of Yemen refuses entry and transit facilities to holders of Israeli passports, or holders of passports containing visas valid or expired for Israel or any indication, such as entry or exit stamps, that the holder has visited Israel. Entry is also refused to nationals of Algeria, Egypt, Libya, Sudan and Tunisia if their journey does not originate from their home country.

PASSPORTS: Passport valid for at least six months after date of departure required by all.

VISAS: Required by all except the following:
(a) nationals of Egypt, Iraq, Jordan and the Syrian Arab Republic;
(b) nationals of members of the Arab Gulf Co-operative

Council (Bahrain, Kuwait, Oman, Qatar, Saudi Arabia and United Arab Emirates);
(c) transit passengers continuing their journey by the same or first connecting aircraft within 168 hours, provided holding valid onward or return documentation and not leaving the airport.
Types of visa and cost: *Tourist/Visitor* (Single-entry): £40. *Business*: £50 (Single-entry); £120 (six month Multiple-entry); £220 (one year Multiple-entry). *Transit*: £30.
Validity: *Single-entry*: two months from date of issue for stays of up to one month; *Multiple-entry*: six months *or* one year from date of issue for stays of up to one month each.
Application to: Consulate (or consular section at Embassy); see *Passport/Visa Information*.
Application requirements: (a) Two completed application forms. (b) Two passport-size photos. (c) Return air ticket. (d) Valid passport. (e) Fee (if applying in the UK, the fee must be paid at a branch of HSBC and proof of payment must be presented with visa application). (f) An airline ticket in and out of Yemen. (g) Stamped, self-addressed envelope for postal applications. (h) For tourist visits, letter from travel company organising the trip. Group travel must be organised through a travel company in Yemen. (i) For business visits, a letter from applicant's company explaining the purpose of the visit and nature of their business.
Working days required: Three. If applying by post, processing will normally take five days.

PASSPORT/VISA INFORMATION

Embassy of the Republic of Yemen in the UK
57 Cromwell Road, London SW7 2ED, UK
Tel: (020) 7584 6607 *or* 7581 4039 (consular section).
Website: www.yemenembassy.org.uk
Opening hours: Mon-Fri 0900-1600; 1000-1400 (visa section).

Embassy of the Republic of Yemen in the USA
2319 Wyoming Avenue, NW, Washington, DC 20008, USA
Tel: (202) 965 4760.
Website: www.yemenembassy.org

Money

Currency: Yemeni Riyal (YER) = 100 fils. Notes are in denominations of YER1000, 500, 200, 100, 50 and 20. Coins are in denominations of YER10, 5 and 1.
Currency exchange: Local currency can easily be reconverted at banks, bureaux de change and hotels. There are very few ATMs. US Dollars in cash are the easiest convertible currency.
Credit & debit cards: Cards generally have limited acceptance; American Express and Diners Club are the most widely accepted. Check with your credit or debit card company for details of merchant acceptability and other services which may be available.
Traveller's cheques: Can be exchanged at some banks and hotels. To avoid additional exchange rate charges, travellers are advised to take traveller's cheques in Pounds Sterling.
Currency restrictions: Import and export of local currency up to YER2000 for residents, and prohibited for non-residents. There are no restrictions on the import of foreign currencies but amounts exceeding US$3000 should be declared on arrival. Export of foreign currency is permitted up to the amount imported and declared.
Banking hours: Sat-Wed 0830-1200, Thurs 0800-1130.
Exchange rate indicators:
Rate at time of publishing
£1.00= YER344.11
$1.00= YER195.88

Duty Free

The following items may be imported into the Republic of Yemen without incurring customs duty:
600 cigarettes or 60 cigars or 450g of tobacco; two bottles of alcoholic beverages (non-Muslims only); one bottle of perfume or eau de toilette; gifts up to a value of YER100,000; gold ornaments (women only) weighing up to 350g.
Prohibited items: Firearms, illegal drugs, obscene literature, all products of Israeli origin.

Public Holidays

Below are listed Public Holidays for the January 2006-June 2007 period.
2006: Jan 1 New Year's Day. **Jan 10** Eid al-Adha (Feast of the Sacrifice). **Jan 31** Muharram (Islamic New Year). **Apr 11** Mouloud (Birth of the Prophet). **May 1** Labour Day. **May 22** National Unity Day. **Sep 26** Revolution Day. **Oct 14** National Day. **Oct 22-24** Eid al-Fitr (End of Ramadan). **Nov 30** Independence Day. **Dec 31** Eid al-Adha (Feast of the Sacrifice).
2007: Jan 1 New Year's Day. **Jan 20** Muharram (Islamic New Year). **Mar 31** Mouloud (Birth of the Prophet). **May 1** Labour Day. **May 22** National Unity Day.
Note: Muslim festivals are timed according to local sightings of various phases of the moon and the dates given above are approximations. During the lunar month of Ramadan that precedes Eid al-Fitr, Muslims fast during the day and feast at night and normal business patterns may be interrupted. Many restaurants are closed during the day and there may be restrictions on smoking and drinking. Some disruption may continue into Eid al-Fitr itself. Eid al-Fitr and Eid al-Adha may last anything from two to 10 days, depending on the region. For more information, see the *World of Islam* appendix.

Health

	Special Precautions?	Certificate Required?
Yellow Fever	No	1
Cholera	No	No
Typhoid & Polio	2	N/A
Malaria	3	N/A

Note: *Regulations and requirements may be subject to change at short notice, and you are advised to contact your doctor well in advance of your intended date of departure. Any numbers in the chart refer to the footnotes below.*

1: A *yellow fever* vaccination certificate is required from travellers over one year of age arriving from infected areas.
2: Vaccination against *typhoid* is advised. In 2005, Yemen had its first outbreak of *polio* since 1996.
3: *Malaria* risk, almost exclusively in the malignant *falciparum* form, exists throughout the year (but mainly from September through February) in the whole country below 2000m. However, there is no risk in Sana'a City. Resistance to chloroquine has been reported. Chloroquine plus proguanil is recommended.
Food & drink: Where mains water is chlorinated, it may cause mild abdominal upsets; supplies in Sana'a are said to be safe. Bottled water is available and is advised for the first few weeks of the stay. Drinking water outside main cities and towns is likely to be contaminated and sterilisation is considered essential. Water used for drinking, brushing teeth or making ice should have first been boiled or otherwise sterilised. Milk is unpasteurised and should be boiled. Avoid dairy products that are likely to have been made from unboiled milk. Only eat well-cooked meat and fish, preferably served hot. Salad and mayonnaise may carry increased risk. Vegetables should be cooked and fruit peeled.
Other risks: *Cutaneous leishmaniasis* exists throughout the area and *visceral leishmaniasis* may occur in the west of Yemen. *Bilharzia* (*schistosomiasis*) is present. Avoid swimming and paddling in fresh water; swimming pools which are well chlorinated and maintained are safe.
Typhoid fever, *tuberculosis*, *dracunculiasis*, *onchocerciasis*, *lymphatic filariasis* and *hepatitis A* occur; *hepatitis B* is endemic. The altitude may cause health problems.
Rabies is present. For those at high risk, vaccination before arrival should be considered. If you are bitten, seek medical advice without delay. For more information, see the *Health* appendix.
Health care: Health care facilities are relatively poor, especially outside major cities. The major hospitals in Sana'a are: Al Jumhuriyya, Al Kuwait and Al Thawra. In Aden, there is the Al Jumhuriyya, the Saudi Hospital and the Refinery Hospital. Most large cities have a general hospital. There is no reciprocal health agreement with the UK. Medical insurance is essential.

Travel - International

AIR:

The national airline is *Yemen Airways (Yemenia) (IY)* (website: www.yemenia.com).
Approximate flight times: From London to *Sana'a* is eight hours and to *Aden* is eight hours.
Main airports: *Sana'a (SAH)* (El-Rahaba) is 13km (8 miles) north of the city (travel time - 30 minutes). *To/from the airport*: Transport to the city centre is by taxi. *Facilities*: Bank/bureau de change, duty free shop, baggage facilities, restaurants and car hire.
Taiz (TAI) (al-Janad) is 4km (2.5 miles) from the city (travel time - 10 minutes). *To/from the airport*:Taxis, buses and car hire are available.
Hodaidah (HOD) is 8km (5 miles) from the city. *To/from the airport*: Taxis, buses and car hire are available.
Aden (ADE) (Khormaksar) is 11km (7 miles) from the city (travel time - 20 minutes). *To/from the airport*: Limited bus and taxi services available.
Departure tax: None.

SEA:

Main ports: *Aden* (website: www.portofaden.com), *Hodeida*, *Mocha*, *Mukalla* and *Nashton*. Cargo vessels with passenger berths call at Hodeida.

ROAD:

Driving to Yemen is not recommended but the main border crossing points are Haradh and Al Bura' in the North from Saudi Arabia and Hadnut in the East from Oman.

Travel - Internal

AIR:

Yemen Airways (IY) (website: www.yemenia.com) operates services between Sana'a, Ta'izz and Hodeida. There are also flights from Aden. It is advisable to double-check flight reservations and times before departure.
Departure tax: None.

SEA:

Local ferries connect local ports. For details, contact port authorities. Mariners should be aware that there is the possibility of attacks against ships and, in particular, yachts off the Yemen coast, especially in the Gulf of Aden. Travellers are advised against yachting in this area.

ROAD:

There are approximately 5000km (3125 miles) of asphalt roads and 20,000km (12,500 miles) of feeder roads. Road conditions and driving standards are quite poor and many roads are in a state of disrepair, with mountain roads particularly hazardous. The Ministry of Housing, Construction and Urban Planning is now supervising a redevelopment and reconstruction plan for Yemen's road network. Within Sana'a and from Ta'izz to Mokha, the roads are reliable. From Aden to Ta'izz is three to five hours' driving time. A road links Aden and Sana'a, otherwise the road network is mainly limited to desert tracks. Use of 4-wheel-drive vehicles and a guide is recommended. There is a road from Aden to Mukalla of 500km (310 miles). Traffic drives on the right but sometimes drivers travel on the left. **Bus:** There are regular intercity bus services. **Taxi:** Recognisable by yellow licence plates. Taxi-sharing is the cheapest transport between cities. There are minimum charges within main cities but fares should be negotiated beforehand for intercity journeys. **Car hire:** Available in main towns; 4-wheel drive is recommended. Chauffeur-driven cars are also available. **Regulations:** The maximum speed limit is 100km/h (62mph) but this is rarely enforced. Driving under the influence of alcohol or drugs can result in a fine or prison sentence. **Documentation:** An International Driving Permit is required. A temporary licence valid for three months is available from local authorities on presentation of a valid national licence.
Travel times: The following chart gives approximate travel times (in hours and minutes) from **Sana'a** to other major cities/towns in the Republic of Yemen.

	Air	Road
Ta'izz	**0.45**	**3.30**
Hodeida	**0.40**	**3.00**
Aden	**0.45**	**4.30**

Travel Advice

All travel to the area around Saada in northern Yemen is advised against, primarily due to heavy fighting that has occurred there since 20 June 2004. The Yemen Tourist Police are discouraging individual travel outside Sana'a and require all such travellers to apply for permission.
There have been a small number of kidnappings, now all resolved, of foreigners in the Shabwa region for which the motive remains unclear. Travellers are advised against all but essential travel to this region until the situation becomes clearer.
There is a high threat from terrorism and evidence that terrorists may target Western interests in Yemen. Visitors should consider whether their personal security arrangements are adequate. Travellers should be particularly vigilant in places frequented by foreigners, such as hotels. Foreigners wishing to travel to the governorates north of

Credit: ©Yemen Tourism Promotion Board

Sana'a and to Hadhramaut will need prior permission from the Yemen Tourist Police.
This advice is based on information provided by the Foreign and Commonwealth Office in the UK. It is correct at time of publishing. As the situation can change rapidly, visitors are advised to contact the following organisations for the latest travel advice:

British Foreign and Commonwealth Office
Tel: (0845) 850 2829.
Website: www.fco.gov.uk

US Department of State
Website: http://travel.state.gov/travel

Accommodation

HOTELS:
Accommodation varies from ancient palace hotels and modern luxury hotels to *funduks* and tribal huts. It is necessary to book in advance and to receive a written confirmation. Winter and summer rates are the same. All bills are subject to a 10 to 15 per cent service charge. Standards range from basic to 5-star. The best hotels are located in Hodeida, Mareb, Sana'a, Ta'izz and Tawahi (Aden). There are also hotels at Jaar, Mukalla (al-Shaab), Mukheiras, Seiyyum (al-Salaam) and Shihr (al-Sharq). Outside the main centres, facilities are limited. Contact a travel agent *or* the General Authority of Tourism for further details (see *Top Things To See & Do*).
CAMPING:
Khokha and Mokha have campsites; details may be obtained from local travel agents in Sana'a.

Top Things To See

- Wander through **Sana'a**, the modern capital and long an important citadel along the trade route between Aden and Mecca. The citadel, **Qasr al-Silah**, was rebuilt after the arrival of Islam in the seventh century and is still intact. The old centre is surrounded by the remains of the city walls, which can be seen in the south along **Zuberi Street** before **Bab al-Yemen**, in the east along **Mount Nugum** starting from the walls of the citadel, and in the north on the road from **Bab Sha'oob** to **Taherir Square**.
- See the **Great Mosque of Sana'a**, the oldest and largest of the mosques in Sana'a and one of the oldest in the Muslim world, constructed in the lifetime of the Prophet and enlarged in AD 705.
- Tour the **National Museum** in Taherir Square in **Dar al-Shukr** (or the 'Palace of Gratefulness'); it contains engravings of pre-Islamic times, bronze statues, a beautiful **mashrabia** (cooling place for water) and several examples of folk art. It offers a good view of Taherir Square and the **Muttawakelite Estate** from the roof.
- Visit **Rawdha**, some 8km (5 miles) north of Sana'a, a garden city famous for its sweet grapes, the **mosque** built by Ahmed ibn al-Qasim and the **Rawdha Palace**, now used as a hotel.
- **Amran**, north of Rawdha, lies on the edge of the fertile basin of **al-Bawn**. The city is surrounded by the old clay city walls of pre-Islamic, Sabean origin.
- Travel to **Hajjah,** a day's journey to the west of Sana'a. The countryside is made up of high mountains and large valleys, including the **Wadi Sherez**, 1000m (3280ft), and **Kohlan**, 2400m (7875ft). Hajjah itself is a citadel, situated on the central hill of Hajjah, famous for underground prison cells used by the Imams.
- Discover the city of **Ta'izz**, which lies in the south at an altitude of 1400m (4590ft). The old city has been all but swallowed up by the fast-growing modern city around it but beautiful old houses and mosques remain within the line of the 13th-century city wall, which is still intact along the southern side. To the north, only the gates of **Bab Musa** and **al-Bab al-Kabir** remain. The southern wall offers a splendid view of Ta'izz. **Al-Qahera**, within the city walls, is the fortress and the oldest part of the city. **Al-Ashrafiya** and **al-Mudhaffar** are two of the most beautiful mosques in Yemen. The museum in the **Palace of Imam Ahmed** contains the personal effects of the last Imam, and has preserved the spirit of Yemen from before the beginning of the Republic. The **Salah Palace**, to the east just outside the city, is another museum of the royal family. The **Souk Ta'izz** sells a variety of goods, including silverware and carpets. **Mount Saber** is 18km (11 miles) from Ta'izz and offers a breathtaking view of the city and the Ta'izz basin. The mountain rises to an altitude of 3000m (9840ft).
- Explore **Mokha,** an old Himyarite port on the Red Sea. In the 17th and 18th centuries, Mokha enjoyed a boom period exporting coffee, which was becoming fashionable in Europe (particularly Amsterdam and Venice, where the first coffee houses were opened). Coffee was later cultivated elsewhere and Mokha fell into decline. In recent years, the Government has improved the harbour and communications within Mokha in an attempt to resurrect this once-prosperous city.
- Visit the modern Red Sea port of **Hodeida** and see the **fish market**, where fishing boats have been built from wood in the same way for hundreds of years.
- Take the Sana'a to Ta'izz road, which runs through extremely mountainous countryside and passes the towns of **Dhofar**, the ancient capital of the Himyarites (115 BC–AD 525), and **Ibb**, a once-important stopping point on the Sana'a to Ta'izz road. Remains of the city walls and an aqueduct can still be seen. The **Sumara Pass**, at an altitude of 2700m (8860ft), gives a spectacular panoramic view over the **Yarim** and **Dhamar** basins.
- Tour the walled city of **Sa'dah**. The **al-Hadi Mosque** is still an important institution for education in Zaydism. It is possible to walk along the top of the city walls, which afford good views of the city. The **Najran Gate** in the north is the most interesting of the gates, protected by an alleyway leading to the doors. The **Great Mosque** is the central building in the city. The market sells traditional stone necklaces and some fine silverware. The **Sa'dah Fortress** is the seat of the provincial government, thickly walled, and once the Imam's residence. Outside the city is the **Zaydi Graveyard**, filled with some of the most beautiful gravestones in Yemen.
- Step back in time and see the ancient **Mareb Dam**, used thousands of years ago to irrigate the surrounding land. The dam fell into disuse around AD 570, after which large numbers of people emigrated northwards. The stonework is impressive, measuring 600m (1968ft) wide and 18m (60ft) deep.
- Visit the port of **Aden**, whose history goes back a long way; it is mentioned in the Biblical *Book of Ezekiel* (c. 6th century BC). There is a collection of pre-Islamic artefacts in the **National Museum of Antiquities** near Tawahi Harbour. **Crater**, the oldest part of the city, lies in the crater of an extinct volcano and is where the most ancient constructions in Aden may be seen. These are the **Aden Tanks**, manmade reservoirs, partly cut out of the rock, with a storage capacity of 50 million litres. Also in Crater may be found the **Ethnographical Museum** and the **Military Museum**. The 14th-century **Mosque of Sayyid Abdullah al-Aidrus** commemorates the patron saint of Aden. In **Ma'allah**, see traditional Arab boats.

Top Things To Do

- Shop for souvenirs in **Sana'a**'s 1000-year-old **Bab al-Yemen Market**, which is divided into 40 different crafts and trades. The spice market is one of the best to visit. Other markets include the **Souk al-Nahaas**, once the copper market, now selling embroidered head-dresses, belts and **jambias** (curved daggers).
- Enjoy the subtropical climate of **Wadi Wa'aar**, lying between Sana'a and Sa'dah in the north. Out of this rises the **Shahara**, a huge mountain massif, the highest point being nearly 3000m (9840ft) above sea level. This can be **climbed** by foot or by 4-wheel drive car. **Shahara Bridge**, built in the 17th century, connects two mountains and can still be crossed by foot.
- To the south of Aden is **Little Aden**, also in the crater of an extinct volcano; this is an area of small fishing villages in sheltered bays, with several superb beaches fringing the Indian Ocean.
- **Hike** and **camp** on **Socotra Island**; the island's remarkable landscape is home to a huge array of wildlife and plants.
- Along a route, running roughly parallel to the Red Sea coast, **Beit al-Faqih**, 60km (37 miles) inland from Hodeida, has a good craft market. **Manakha**, once a road station for the Ottoman Turks, is situated on a saddle of the **Haraz Mountains**. Traditional Ismaeli villages lie to the east. This area is exceptionally good for **hiking**.
- Take a day trip. **Hadda Mountain**, south of Sana'a, is dotted with villages and orchards growing apricots, peaches, walnuts and almonds. The village of Hadda has two old Turkish mills. **Wadi Dhar**, 10km (6 miles) from Sana'a, is an idyllic valley filled with grapes, pomegranates and citrus fruits, surrounded by a barren plateau. **Shibam**, 36km (22 miles) from Sana'a, is a pre-Islamic settlement, protected by the great fortification of **Koukaban**.
- The **Sad'ah Basin** is strikingly fertile, providing Yemen's early crops of grapes, and is excellent for **walking** and **hiking**.
- **Diving** is increasingly popular in the **Red** and **Arabian seas**, as is **sailing**. **Fishing** is also a possibility.

TOURIST INFORMATION

Yemen Tourism Promotion Board
48 Hadda Street, PO Box 5607, Sana'a, Republic of Yemen
Tel: (1) 510 794/5/6.
Website: www.yementourism.com

Entertainment

FOOD & DRINK: Hotel restaurants serve both Oriental and Western dishes, particularly Chinese and Indian. There are a few independent restaurants serving international and Arab cuisine.
Things to know: Alcohol is not generally available but may be served in hotels. It is illegal to buy alcohol for a Yemeni citizen. Tourists are advised to respect Muslim customs and traditions.
National specialities:
- Seafood.
- *Haradha* (a mincemeat and pepper dish).
- *Marag lahm* (meat soup).
- *Hanid* (lamb meat cooked in typical oven with spices).
- *Kabsa* (rice with lamb meat).

Tipping: The practice of tipping is becoming more common. Waiters and taxi drivers should be tipped 10 to 15 per cent.
NIGHTLIFE: This is generally centred on the major hotels.
SHOPPING: *Souks* (markets) are interesting places to shop and buy handicrafts. Purchases include *foutah* (national costume), leather goods, *jambia* (daggers), candlesticks, scarves (woven with gold thread), amber beads, brightly coloured cushions and ceramics. Other items include gold- and silverwork, spice, perfume, *bukhur* incense with charcoal and pottery containers in which to burn it, coloured mats and sharks' teeth. **Shopping hours:** Sun-Thurs 0800-1300 and 1600-2100.

Business

- **GDP:** US$12.8 billion.
- **Main imports:** Petroleum products, cereal, feed grains, food, machinery, transport equipment, iron, sugar and honey.
- **Main exports:** Crude petroleum, refined oil products, seafood, fruit, vegetables, hides and tobacco products.
- **Main trade partners:** China, France, India, Indonesia, Korea (Rep), Kuwait, Saudi Arabia, Singapore, Switzerland, Thailand, United Arab Emirates and USA.

ECONOMY: Yemen is one of the poorest countries in the Arab world, and among the principal motivations behind the unification of Yemen in 1990 was the prospect of economic transformation and expansion. However, it is only in the last few years that the economy has started to show sporadic signs of improvement. Under IMF auspices, the Government has implemented a programme of structural reforms involving privatisation and an overhaul of the financial system. In exchange, the Yemenis received financial support and some relief of Yemen's US$5 billion foreign debt. The economy is now growing at around 5 per cent, and inflation eased to 11 per cent, after a rapid increase in previous years. Large-scale unemployment persists; an estimated 30 per cent of the workforce are out of work and there is serious under-employment.
Agriculture is concentrated in the fertile northern part of the country. The principal cash crops are cereals, cotton, coffee, fruit, vegetables and *qat* (a narcotic leaf); sorghum, potatoes, wheat and barley are grown for local consumption. Livestock rearing and fishing, both of which occur throughout the country, are also important. The manufacturing industry is mainly involved in the production of construction materials, processed foods, tobacco, drinks and chemicals. However, the most important industrial activity is oil and gas production. Yemeni reserves are modest by regional standards but since the opening of the refining complex at Aden in 1994 and new fields coming on stream, the sector accounts for the majority of export earnings. Aden also hosts a newly established free-trade zone. Other mineral deposits, which are concentrated in the south, include copper, gold, lead, zinc and molybdenum.
BUSINESS ETIQUETTE: Businesspeople are expected to dress smartly for meetings and formal social occasions. English is commonly used in business circles. Appointments are needed and visitors should be punctual. Business cards are often exchanged. Do not be surprised during a meeting if Yemeni businessmen chew *qat*. **Office hours:** Sat-Wed 0800-1500, during Ramadan 1000-1500.

COMMERCIAL INFORMATION

General Investment Authority
Al-Quds Street, Southern Safya, PO Box 19022, Republic of Yemen
Tel: (1) 262 962/3.
Website: www.giay.gov.ye

principal roads or near towns. It is advisable to book in advance and to obtain confirmation in writing. All bills are subject to a 10 per cent service charge in lieu of tips and 20 per cent sales tax. Tipping in hotels is not permitted by law. Hotels are graded according to a 5-star system.

LODGES & CAMPS IN NATIONAL PARKS:
All lodges and many camps in the parks are offered on a fully catered basis. As the quality of accommodation and associated facilities varies enormously from one place to another, visitors intending to stay should contact the relevant tour operator/tourist office for detailed information.

LODGES:

These are generally stone buildings with thatched roofs designed to complement the natural environment, housing a maximum of 40 beds.

CAMPS:

The most common and most widely used type of accommodation for safaris. In general, standard facilities include hot and cold running water, electricity and waterborne sanitation plus the basic accoutrements for comfortable living. For instance, Luangwa's camps have beds, clean linen, refrigerators, crockery, cutlery, mosquito nets, lamps, toilets and showers. At non-catered camps, visitors must bring their own food and drink. Some are open all year round while others open from June to October or November.

GRZ-HOSTELS:

These are available throughout the provinces. They have a small capacity, rising in exceptional cases to 24 rooms. Government rest houses are available in many centres but they are very basic.

CAMPING/CARAVANNING:

Sites are available at most of the tourist centres, including several national parks. It is best to make reservations well in advance. If booking is more than four weeks in advance, some operators charge a 15 per cent deposit. Prices may increase during peak periods.

ACCOMMODATION INFORMATION

Hotel and Catering Association of Zambia
PO Box 30815, Lusaka, Zambia
Tel: (1) 252 779.
Website: www.zambiatourism.com

Top Things To See

- Located on the southernmost edge of Zambia bordering Zimbabwe, the astonishing **Victoria Falls** are the mightiest cataracts in the world – the 2.5km- (1.5 mile-) wide Zambezi River drops 100m (330ft) into a narrow chasm at a rate of 550 million litres every minute. The spray can be seen 30km (20 miles) away. **Knife Edge Bridge** is the best place to view the eastern cataract, the main falls and the boiling pot (where the river turns and heads down the Batoka Gorge). **Victoria Falls Bridge** is a railway bridge, from one side there is a view down the gorge, from the other there is a view through the falls. Scenic flights in **micro-light aircraft** offering aerial views of the falls are also available.
- Attractions in the capital, **Lusaka**, the **Kabwata Cultural Village** (devoted to the preservation of indigenous arts and crafts and displays of traditional dancing), the **Cathedral of the Holy Cross**, the **Munda Wanga Botanical Gardens and Zoo** and the **Lusaka National Museum**.
- Situated 320km (137miles) from the capital, **Ndola** is an important commercial centre and the gateway to the mineral producing region of Zambia. In the town, visit the **Copperbelt Museum**. Outside are two sunken lakes, **Lake Chilengwa** and **Lake Kashiba**, the latter is especially good for **birdwatching**. Travel to the border with Zaire to the **Dag Hammerskjold Memorial site** marking the spot where the UN Secretary General was killed in a plane crash during the Katanga Crisis in Zaire in 1961.
- As the second largest city in Zambia, **Kitwe** owes a lot of its importance to copper; however, it has now become a location for a number of industries. See the **Mindolo Dam** which is 7km (4.5 miles) away and the **Makwera Falls and Lake**, located 9km (5.5miles) from the city. Visitors can take a tour down a number of **mines** that are in the area.
- In **Luanshya**, discover the oldest **copper mine** in Zambia.
- **Livingstone**, the 'Tourist Capital of Zambia', has several luxury hotels, a casino, and the **Livingstone Museum**, housing Livingstone memorabilia and anthropological exhibits.

Top Things To Do

- See **wildlife** in the **Kafue National Park**. Situated in the centre of the southern half of the country, Kafue

encompasses a huge area (22,500 sq km/8687 sq miles) and is the second largest National Park in the world. Noted for its beauty, the park is bisected by the **Kafue River**, which attracts hundreds of species of birds and offers good **game fishing**. The principal attraction is the prolific wildlife. Accommodation is provided throughout the year at **Mukambi Lodge** (no guided safaris during the rainy season, November to April), and the **Musungwa Lodges**, and at **New Kalala Camp** (full catering) and others. There are also several seasonal non-catered camps.
- In the **South Luangwa National Park**, see a huge variety of animals such as elephants, hippo, lions, zebras, giraffes, antelopes, buffaloes, monkeys and wild dogs. Blossoming trees and exotic flowers set the scene. The main rainy season runs from November/December to May. There are lodges at **Chichele**, **Kapani**, **Mfuwe** (all year) and **Tundwe** (dry season), and catered camps at **Chibembe**, **Kaingo Camp**, **Tena Tena** (dry season) and **Chinzombo** (all year). There are also several non-catered camps.
- The **North Luangwa National Park** is one of Africa's most spectacular surviving wilderness areas. It covers 4636 sq km (1790 sq miles) of primarily woodland park with numerous small rivers, including the beautiful **Mwaleshi** which all play an important role. The park is particularly noted for its huge herds of buffalo. Walking safaris here will also reveal elephants, leopards, wildcat, hyena, puku, impala, zebra, baboon and velvet monkey. Over 350 bird species are found here, including the crested leorie, crowned crane, carmine bee-eater and giant eagle owl.
- The **Lochinvar National Park** offers exceptional diversity of birdlife (over 420 recorded species). The park is situated on the southern edge of the **Kafue Flats**, a wide floodplain of the Kafu river, famous for its large herds of lechwe, an antelope unique to the Kafue Flats. There is one lodge, open throughout the year.
- **Sumbu National Park:** The sandy shorelines of **Lake Tanganyika** provide the setting for three all-year beach resorts: at **Kasaba**, **Ndole** and **Nkamba** bays. There is also a small non-catered camp at Ndole Bay. Activities include **swimming**, **boat rides** and **freshwater big-game fishing** for the Goliath tigerfish (up to 35kg), giant catfish and the Nile perch (both up to 50kg and more). It is possible to arrange visits into the surrounding bush to watch game. **Kasaba Lodge** boasts an afternoon tea service, a bar and beach barbecues. **Nkamba Bay Lodge** offers exactly the same facilities as Kasaba but facilities are housed in rondavels.
- The **Mosi-oa-Tunya National Park** close to the **Victoria Falls** is small by Zambian standards but is home to most of Zambia's more common wild animals.
- The **Kasanka National Park** is one of Zambia's smallest parks, with an area of 450 sq km (280 miles). It encompasses eight lakes and four rivers, the largest being the beautiful **Luwombwa**. Animals include elephant, hippo, reedbuck, waterbuck, hyena, warthog, baboon, jackal, leopard and the rare blue monkey, which can be found in the forests that flank Kasanka's rivers.
- The **Lower Zambezi National Park** lies along the **Zambezi River**, 100 km (62 miles) downstream of the Victoria Falls. It has abundant wildlife, including elephant, hippo, buffalo, zebra, lion and leopard together with a great variety of birds. Game drives and walks will often reveal big cats and, on occasion, the cheetah. **Canoe safaris**, **fishing** for tiger fish, bottle-nose fish or bream and **birdwatching** activities are available.
- Zambia's centre for **adventure sports** is **Livingstone**. In addition to **bungee jumping** off the 111m- (364ft-) bridge linking Zambia and Zimbabwe across the **River Zambezi**, you can now **abseil** down the gorge or **high-wire** across it – the latter involving a gravity-defying trip in a body harness attached to a cable spanning the chasm.
- **Whitewater rafting** trips on the **Zambezi** are considered particularly wild. Longer and quieter river trips lasting from one to seven days usually follow the **Victoria Falls–Lake Kariba** itinerary, with **Lake Kariba** also offering the possibility to relax for a week on a luxurious **houseboat**.

TOURIST INFORMATION

Zambia National Tourist Board in the UK
2 Palace Gate, London W8 5NG, UK
Tel: (020) 7589 6655.
Website: www.zambiatourism.com
Opening hours: Mon-Fri 0930-1300 and 1400-1700.

Entertainment

FOOD & DRINK: Owing to the liberalisation of the economy, there is now plenty of food in the shops. Local and imported beers, spirits and assorted soft drinks are available.

National specialities:
- Freshwater fish: bream from the Kafue, Luapula and Zambezi rivers, Nile perch and lake salmon.

National drinks:
- *Mosi* and *Rhino* lager.

Tipping: A 10 per cent sales tax is added to all bills. Tipping in hotels has been abolished by law but a 10 per cent tip may be expected or included in bills elsewhere.

NIGHTLIFE: Lusaka has dancing and floorshows in the main hotels, cinemas and theatres. The Copperbelt and Livingstone areas offer a variety of entertainments including casinos and nightclubs.

SHOPPING: Lusaka has modern shops, supermarkets and open-air markets. Special purchases include African carvings, pottery and copperware, beadwork and local gemstones. **Shopping hours:** Mon-Fri 0800-1700 and Sat 0800-1300 (some stay open until 1700).

Business

- **GDP:** US$4.3 billion.
- **Main imports:** Crude oil, refined petroleum products, manufactured goods, machinery, transport equipment and foodstuffs.
- **Main exports:** Copper, cobalt, lead, zinc, cut vegetables and cotton.
- **Main trade partners:** Japan, Malawi, South Africa, Tanzania and the UK.

ECONOMY: The Zambian economy relies heavily on the country's mineral wealth, particularly copper (of which Zambia is one of the world's largest producers), and also cobalt and zinc. These account for the bulk of export earnings and provide essential raw materials for Zambia's manufacturing industry, which accounts for over one-third of national output. Apart from raw material processing, the manufacturing sector includes vehicle assembly and oil refining as well as the production of fertilisers, textiles, construction materials and a variety of consumer products. Despite the role played by industry (unusually high by African standards), export earnings were steadily declining throughout the 1990s, mainly as a result of persistently low commodity prices. One stark illustration of the trend was the closure in 2002 of the Konkola copper mine – the country's largest and a major source of Government revenue – as being no longer viable. Agriculture produces 14 per cent of GDP and employs 85 per cent of the population. Maize and cattle are the main earners; other crops (cassava, millet, sorghum and beans) are produced mainly for domestic consumption but have to be supplemented by substantial food imports. Zambia's hydroelectric projects have allowed it self-sufficiency in energy.
Economic policy changed radically during the 1990s when the Government sought the backing of the IMF in tackling Zambia's serious financial problems. With some difficulty, many of the IMF-imposed measures were put into effect. More recently, Zambia has been a beneficiary of the Heavily Indebted Poor Countries programme to reduce the external debts of the world's poorest countries, but still owes over US$6 billion. The IMF is still involved with Zambia, although the current Zambian administration has proved reluctant to implement some of its demands, particularly privatisation of remaining state assets. The economy has been growing (5.1 per cent in 2004) but inflation (21 per cent) and unemployment (estimated at 50 per cent) remain high. Zambia is a member of the Southern African Development Council (SADC).

BUSINESS ETIQUETTE: Formal dress is acceptable for people at business meetings. English is widely used in business circles. **Office hours:** Mon-Fri 0800-1300 and 1400-1700.

COMMERCIAL INFORMATION

Ministry of Commerce, Trade and Industry
PO Box 31968, Kwacha Annex, Cairo Road, Lusaka, Zambia
Tel: (1) 228 301.
E-mail: comtrade@zamnet.zm

Zambia Chamber of Commerce and Industry
Showgrounds, Great East Road, Box 30844, Lusaka, Zambia
Tel: (1) 255 046 or 253 020 or 252 369.

Mulungushi International Conference Centre
PO Box 33200, Lusaka, Zambia
Tel: (1) 290 506 or 291 229.
E-mail: micc@zamtel.zm

Zimbabwe

Location: Southern Africa.

Time: GMT + 2.

Overview

Present-day Zimbabwe was the site of a large and complex African civilisation in the 13th and 14th centuries. It was populated by descendants of the Bantu tribes, who had migrated from the north around the 10th century. Evidence of their mainly pastoral lifestyle may still be seen in the ruins of Great Zimbabwe, near the present-day town of Masvingo. The first contact with Europeans was with the Portuguese at the end of the 15th century. Relations between the two were fairly stable – the Portuguese were largely concerned with ensuring communications between their colonies in Angola and Mozambique on either side of Zimbabwe – until the 1830s, when the region was thrown into upheaval by the northward migration of the Ndebele people from South Africa. At this point, a new aggressive breed of colonists arrived in the form of British mining interests led by Cecil Rhodes' British South Africa Company (BSAC). The BSAC took control of the country – which they called 'Southern Rhodesia' – until 1923, when it became, nominally, a British colony. From 1953–63, Southern Rhodesia formed part of the Central African Federation with neighbouring Northern Rhodesia (now Zambia) and Nyasaland (now Malawi). In 1965, to resist decolonisation, the settlers – with South African support – issued a Unilateral Declaration of Independence (UDI). This triggered a bitter civil war between the white minority Government and fighters for African independence, ending only in 1980, with the granting of independence and the holding of a general election under British auspices, which was won decisively by Robert Mugabe's ZANU party.
Modern Zimbabwe is in a terrible state. The economy has all but collapsed. There is widespread famine, which has been cynically manipulated by the Government so opposition strongholds suffer the most. The Government lacks the resources or machinery to deal with the ravages of the HIV/AIDS pandemic, which affects an estimated one-quarter of the population. With all this and the forced and violent removal of white farmers in a brutal land redistribution programme, President Mugabe has earned himself widespread scorn from the international arena.
It is a shame that the country has gained such a bad reputation as it boasts some amazing natural sites. The Victoria Falls are without a doubt one of the world's grandest natural spectacles and every viewpoint reveals something new. Running from northeast to southwest down the centre of the country, and connecting its two largest cities, is the Highveld, a chain of low mountains and Zimbabwe's most populous area.
Zimbabwe also offers some of the best wildlife parks in southern Africa. From the forested mountains of the Eastern highlands to the sun-washed grasslands of Hwange

National Park, from the hot Mopani Forest to the shores of Lake Kariba, more than 11 per cent of Zimbabwe's land – 44,688 sq km (17,254 sq miles) – has been set aside as parks and wildlife estates. There are also several botanical gardens, sanctuaries and more than a dozen national safari areas for hunting (an activity that helps to finance the conservation programme and is strictly controlled).

General Information

AREA: 390,757 sq km (150,872 sq miles).
POPULATION: 12.9 million (UN, 2005).
POPULATION DENSITY: 33.01 per sq km.
CAPITAL: Harare. **Population:** 1.5 million (2005).
GEOGRAPHY: Zimbabwe is bordered by Zambia to the northwest, Mozambique to the north and east, South Africa to the south and Botswana to the southwest. The central zone of hills gives rise to many rivers, which drain into the manmade Lake Kariba to the northwest, the marshes of Botswana to the west or into the Zambezi River to the northeast. The *highveld* landscape is dotted with *kopjes* (massive granite outcrops). Along the eastern border for some 350km (220 miles) is a high mountainous region of great scenic beauty, rising to 2592m (8504ft) at Mount Inyangani, the country's highest point.
GOVERNMENT: Republic. Gained independence from the UK in 1980. **Head of State and Government:** President Robert Mugabe (Head of Government since 1980 and Head of State since 1987). **Recent history:** Elections for a new Senate in November 2005 were largely boycotted by the opposition. Mugabe's party won 24 of the 31 constituencies where elections were held amid low voter turnout. Most controversial has been Mugabe's urban slum demolition drive. The UN estimates 700,000 people have been left without jobs or homes as a result. It seems that only the removal of Mugabe will halt the spiral of decline. The President is now in his 80s and is coming under pressure to retire from other regional Heads of State (including South Africa's Thabo Mbeki, Mugabe's only significant ally) and, more discreetly, from senior figures in ZANU-PF. Either way, Zimbabwe is shortly to reach a critical stage in its post-independence history.
LANGUAGE: The official language is English, with Shona and Sindebele dialects.
RELIGION: Christianity, with traditional beliefs in rural areas, and some Hindu, Muslim and Jewish minorities.
ELECTRICITY: 220/230 volts AC, 50Hz.
SOCIAL CONVENTIONS: Urban culture in Zimbabwe is greatly influenced by Western culture and education but, in rural areas, traditional values and crafts continue. Shaking hands is the customary form of greeting. European courtesies and codes of practice should be observed when visiting someone's home. Return invitations are appreciated. Giving a token of appreciation is optional. It is an offence to make derogatory or insulting comments about President Mugabe. Visitors should be aware that an open hand is the political symbol of the main opposition political party, the Movement for Democratic Change, and that a friendly wave may therefore be interpreted as a provocative political gesture. Casual wear is suitable for daytime and men are only expected to wear suits and ties for business meetings. Smart restaurants or hotel bars require male guests to wear a jacket and tie. Smoking is common, although it is prohibited on public transport and in some public buildings. There are laws against indecency which equates to homosexual activity being illegal.
Photography: The local authorities are very sensitive about taking pictures of governmental buildings, military installations and embassies. A permit can be granted by the Government office.

Climate

Although located in the tropics, temperate conditions prevail all year, as the climate is moderated by altitude and

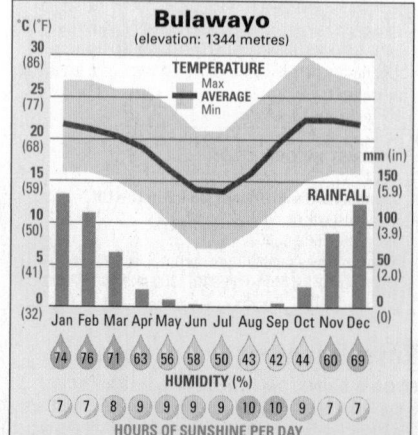

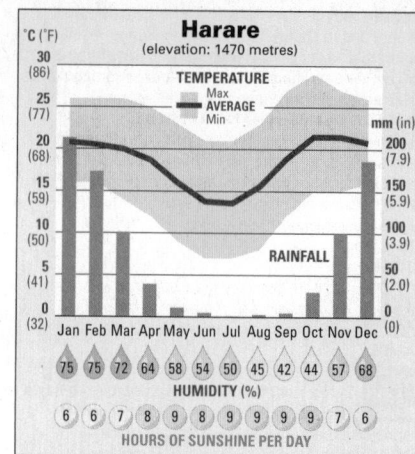

the inland position of the country. The hot and dry season is from August to October, and the rainy season from November to March. The best months to visit are April to May and August to September. Night-time temperatures can fall below freezing.
Required clothing: Light- to mediumweights with warmer clothes for evenings and rainwear for the wet season.

Communications

Telephone: Full IDD is available.
Mobile telephone: Coverage is limited to a few urban areas.
Internet: There are Internet cafes in Harare and in Mashonaland.
Post: Airmail to Europe takes up to one week.
MEDIA: All broadcasters transmitting from Zimbabwe and the main newspapers are state-controlled and follow the Government line. The private press has come under severe pressure. The only privately-owned daily, the *Daily News*, is subject to a publication ban. The paper and the Government had waged war in the courts.
Press: The main English-language newspapers are *The Chronicle* (website: www.chronicle.co.zw), *The Financial Gazette* (website: www.fingaz.co.zw), *The Herald* (website: www.herald.co.zw), *The Sunday Mail* and *The Sunday News*. Visitors should note that the carrying of the main independent newspapers (*The Financial Gazette, The Independent* and *The Standard* (website: www.thestandard.co.zw) can provoke a hostile reaction from *ZANU* (PF) supporters.
TV: *Zimbabwe Broadcasting Corporation* is state-run.
Radio: *Zimbabwe Broadcasting Corporation (ZBC)* is state-run and has four networks.

Passport/Visa

	Passport Required?	Visa Required?	Return Ticket Required?
Full British	Yes	2	Yes
Australian	Yes	2	Yes
Canadian	Yes	2	Yes
USA	Yes	2	Yes
Other EU	Yes	1/2	Yes
Japanese	Yes	2	Yes

Note: *Regulations and requirements may be subject to change at short notice, and you are advised to contact the appropriate diplomatic or consular authority before finalising travel arrangements. Any numbers in the chart refer to the footnotes below.*

PASSPORTS: Passport valid for at least six months beyond date of departure required by all.
VISAS: Required by all except the following:
(a) **1.** nationals of Cyprus, Ireland and Malta;
(b) nationals of Antigua and Barbuda, Aruba, The Bahamas, Barbados, Belize, Bermuda, Botswana, Cayman Islands, Congo (DRC), Fiji, Grenada, Hong Kong (SAR), Jamaica, Kenya, Kiribati, Leeward Islands, Lesotho, Malawi, Malaysia, Maldives, Mauritius, Montserrat, Namibia, Nauru, New Zealand, St Kitts & Nevis, St Lucia, St Vincent & the Grenadines, Singapore, Solomon Islands, Swaziland, Tanzania, Tonga, Trinidad & Tobago, Turks & Caicos Islands, Tuvalu, Uganda, Vanuatu, Western Samoa and Zambia;
(c) passengers continuing their journey to a third country within 6 hours by the same or connecting flight, provided holding tickets with reserved seats and documents for onward travel and not leaving the transit area.
Note: 2. Nationals of the following countries may obtain visas valid for up to 90 days on arrival in Zimbabwe, provided holding tickets and documents for return or onward travel and sufficient funds for their stay: Argentina,

Australia, Austria, Belgium, Brazil, Brunei, Canada, Cook Islands, Denmark, Dominican Republic, Egypt, Finland, France, Germany, Ghana (gratis visa; free-of-charge), Greece, Iceland, Indonesia, Israel, Italy, Japan, Korea (Rep), Kuwait, Liechtenstein, Luxembourg, Monaco, The Netherlands, New Zealand, Norway, Palau, Palestinian Authority Region (State Of), Papua New Guinea, Poland, Portugal, Puerto Rico (USA), Seychelles, South Africa (gratis visa; free-of-charge), Spain, Sweden, Switzerland, United Arab Emirates, United Kingdom, Uruguay, USA, US Virgin Islands and Vatican City.

Types of visa and cost: Visa at port of entry: cost dependent on nationality, British nationals £36; contact consular section at Embassy or High Commission for further details. Cost of visa from Embassy: single-entry £40; double-entry £50. Multiple-entry visas only issued when in Zimbabwe.

Validity: Six months from date of issue.

Application to: Consular section at Embassy; see *Passport/Visa Information*. For Multiple-entry visas, travellers must apply direct to the Chief Immigration Officer in Harare, Zimbabwe.

Application requirements: (a) Completed application form. (b) Passport valid for at least six months beyond date of departure. (c) Fee, payable by cash or banker's draft (cheques are not accepted). (d) Two passport photographs. (e) Letter of invitation or an itinerary. (f) Return ticket and proof of sufficient funds (this requirement applies to all visitors, including those who may enter visa-free).

Note: All visitors to Zimbabwe must be in possession of return tickets (or funds in lieu) and sufficient funds to support themselves. The granting of a visa is not a guarantee of entry.

Working days required: Usually seven; minimum of 48 hours from receipt of application.

Temporary residence: Apply to Chief Immigration Officer, Private Bag 77717, Causeway, Harare, Zimbabwe.

PASSPORT/VISA INFORMATION

Embassy of the Republic of Zimbabwe in the UK
Zimbabwe House, 429 Strand, London WC2R 0JR, UK
Tel: (020) 7836 7755.
Website: www.zimbabweembassy-uk.com
Opening hours: Mon-Fri 0900-1700; 0900-1230 (visa section).

Embassy of Zimbabwe in the USA
1608 New Hampshire Avenue, NW, Washington, DC 20009, USA
Tel: (202) 332 7100.
Website: www.zimbabwe-embassy.us
Openign hours: Mon-Fri 0900-1200 (consular section).

Money

Currency: Zimbabwe Dollar (ZWD; symbol Z$) = 100 cents. Notes are in denominations of Z$100, 50, 20, 10, 5 and 2. Coins are in denominations of Z$5, 2 and 1, and 50, 20, 10, 5 and 1 cents.

Currency exchange: Major foreign currencies can be exchanged at bureaux de change, banks and major hotels at the official exchange rate.

Credit & debit cards: American Express, Diners Club and Visa are widely accepted, whilst MasterCard has more limited use. Some ATMs accept credit cards. Check with your credit or debit card company for details of merchant acceptability and other services which may be available.

Traveller's cheques: Banks and major hotels will exchange these. To avoid additional exchange rate charges, travellers are advised to take traveller's cheques in US Dollars or Pounds Sterling.

Currency restrictions: The import and export of local currency is limited to Z$15,000. The import of foreign currency is unlimited. The export of foreign currency is unlimited as long as supported by the visitor's currency declaration form.

Banking hours: Mon-Tues and Thurs-Fri 0800-1500, Wed 0800-1300 and Sat 0800-1130.

Exchange rate indicators:
Rate at time of publishing
£1.00= Z$176466
$1.00= Z$99838

Duty Free

The following items may be imported into Zimbabwe without incurring customs duty:
Goods up to a value of US$250 per person, inclusive of tobacco, perfume and gifts; for persons of 18 years of age or older, 5l of alcoholic beverages (up to 2l of which may be spirits).

Note: (a) The import of drugs, honey, pornographic or obscene literature, toy firearms, flick knives and lockable knives is prohibited. (b) Permits are issued on arrival for firearms and ammunition. (c) Agricultural products including seeds, bulbs, fresh meat and drugs require an import licence.

Public Holidays

Below are listed Public Holidays for the January 2006-June 2007 period.
2006: Jan 1 New Year's Day. **Apr 14** Good Friday. **Apr 17** Easter Monday. **Apr 18** Independence Day. **May 1** Workers' Day. **May 25** Africa Day. **Aug 7** Heroes' Day. **Aug 8** Defence Forces Day. **Dec 22** Unity Day. **Dec 25-26** Christmas.
2007: Jan 1 New Year's Day. **Apr 6** Good Friday. **Apr 9** Easter Monday. **Apr 18** Independence Day. **May 1** Workers' Day. **May 25** Africa Day.

Health

	Special Precautions?	Certificate Required?
Yellow Fever	No	1
Cholera	Yes	2
Typhoid & Polio	3	N/A
Malaria	4	N/A

Note: Regulations and requirements may be subject to change at short notice, and you are advised to contact your doctor well in advance of your intended date of departure. Any numbers in the chart refer to the footnotes below.

1: A yellow fever vaccination certificate is required from travellers over one year arriving from infected areas.
2: Following WHO guidelines issued in 1973, a cholera vaccination certificate is not a condition of entry to Zimbabwe. However, cholera is a risk in this country and precautions are advisable. Up-to-date advice should be sought before deciding whether these precautions should include vaccination, as medical opinion is divided over its effectiveness.
3: Vaccination against typhoid is advised.
4: Malaria risk, predominantly in the malignant *falciparum* form, exists from November to June in all areas below 1200m (3937ft) and throughout the year in the Zambezi Valley although there is negligible risk in Harare and Bulawayo. Resistance to chloroquine has been reported. The recommended prophylaxis is mefloquine.

Food & drink: All water should be regarded as being a potential health risk. Water used for drinking, brushing teeth or making ice should have first been boiled or otherwise sterilised.

Other risks: *Bilharzia (schistosomiasis)* is present. Avoid swimming and paddling in fresh water; swimming pools which are well chlorinated and maintained are safe. *Human trypanosomiasis* (sleeping sickness) has been reported. *Trachoma* and *hepatitis A* and *E* are widespread. *Hepatitis B* is hyperendemic. Epidemics of *meningoccal meningitis* may occur, particularly in the savannah areas during the dry season. There may be a small risk of plague in rural areas, especially Matabeleland.
Dengue, filariasis, leishmaniasis and *onchocerciasis* (river blindness) are present.
Rabies is present. For those at high risk, vaccination before arrival should be considered. If you are bitten, seek medical advice without delay. For more information, consult the *Health* appendix.
HIV/AIDS is a high risk throughout the country (around 25 per cent of the adult population are infected) and precautions should be taken.

Health care: Medical facilities are good in the major towns and there are well-equipped clinics in most outlying areas, although medical costs can be high. There may be drugs shortages in public hospitals. There is no reciprocal agreement with the UK. Health insurance is essential; adequate medical provision is often only provided privately, especially in urban areas. Private hospitals may require health insurance or a cash payment before admission.

Travel - International

AIR:
 The national airline is *Air Zimbabwe (UM)* (website: www.airzim.co.zw). **Approximate flight times:** From Harare to *London* is 10 hours 30 minutes. There are direct flights connecting London with Victoria Falls. Connections from the capital to Bulawayo take approximately one hour.
Main airports: The Civil Aviation Authority of Zimbabwe (website: www.caaz.co.zm) is responsible for air travel and airports in Zimbabwe.
Harare (HRE) is 14km (9 miles) southeast of the city. *To/from the airport:* Coaches run at regular intervals to the city (travel time – 20 minutes). Taxis are available. *Facilities:* Post office, restaurant, duty free shop and bank/bureau de change.

Bulawayo (BUQ) is 24km (15 miles) from the city. *To/from the airport:* Limited bus and taxi services are available. *Victoria Falls (VFA)* is 22km (13 miles) from the town. *To/from the airport:* Bus and taxi services are available. *Facilities:* Bureau de change, duty free shop, bars, restaurant and car rental.
Departure tax: US$20 (non-residents); US$20 or Z$1100 (residents). Children under two years and transit passengers are exempt.

RAIL:
 There are train connections from South Africa, Botswana, Mozambique and Zambia.

ROAD:
 There are roads from Botswana, Malawi, Mozambique, South Africa, Tanzania and Zambia. Off the main routes (Beitbridge and Victoria Falls), travel conditions are often difficult during heavy rains. Border posts are generally open from 0600-1800, although the more popular route through Beitbridge is open from 0600-2230. For details, contact the Embassy or High Commission (see *Passport/Visa Information*).

Travel - Internal

AIR:
 Connections to Buffalo Range, Bulawayo, Gweru, Hwange, Kariba, Masvingo and Victoria Falls are run by *Air Zimbabwe* and other airlines. There are also special light-aircraft services at Kariba and Victoria Falls offering sightseeing and game-viewing flights.

RAIL:
 There are daily trains between Bulawayo, Chiredzi, Harare, Labatse, Mutare, Plumtree, Triangle and Victoria Falls run by *National Railways of Zimbabwe* (website: www.planet.nu/sunshinecity/nrz). The rail system is under-developed and poorly maintained.

ROAD:
 There is an excellent road network, with paved roads connecting all major towns and many rural areas. Traffic drives on the left. There are often fuel shortages, even in the main cities, and therefore it is wise to drive with a full tank of petrol when possible and be aware that public transport may be cancelled. **Bus/coach:** There are a number of buses, minibuses and coach services serving most of the country. However, buses are not recommended since they are often overcrowded and inadequately maintained. *Blue Arrow Luxury Coaches* provides bus services to principal destinations including Harare-Bulawayo (via Chivhu and Kwe Kwe). For more details, contact the Zimbabwe Tourism Authority (see *Top Things To Do*). **Car hire:** Available at airports and main hotels. **Documentation:** International Driving Permit or national licence; if not in English, it must be accompanied by a certificate of authority or translation of text. Valid for 90 days. **Regulations:** Speed limits are 40km/h (25mph) in National Parks, 120km/h (75mph) on open roads and 60-80km/h (40-50mph) on other roads. Police road blocks are common and it is an offence to continue driving when the President's motorcade passes.

URBAN:
 A reasonable bus service is provided in Harare by a subsidiary of the *Zimbabwe Omnibus Company*. Tickets are bought in advance from booths. There is also a local bus network in Bulawayo.

WATER:
 Ferries run on Lake Kariba from Kariba to Binga and Mlibizi.

Travel Advice

There has been an increase in tension in urban areas and a general increase in the level of violent crime. There is a continuing risk of violence at political demonstrations, but main tourist areas have been largely unaffected by political and social unrest.
Most visits to Zimbabwe are trouble free. Travel with organised tour operators to well-established destinations is recommended. Independent travel, particularly backpacking, is strongly advised against.
Travel to the high-density suburbs is advised against; the Government of Zimbabwe's 'clean up' campaign has increased tension in these areas. Travellers should avoid engaging in overtly partisan political activity, or in activities that could be construed as such.
This advice is based on information provided by the Foreign and Commonwealth Office in the UK. It is correct at time of publishing. As the situation can change rapidly, visitors are advised to contact the following organisations for the latest travel advice:

British Foreign and Commonwealth Office
Tel: (0845) 850 2829.
Website: www.fco.gov.uk
US Department of State
Website: http://travel.state.gov/travel

Accommodation

HOTELS:

There are hotels and lodges (which are similar to guest houses and provide bed and breakfast). A list of registered hotels is available from the Zimbabwe Tourism Authority (see *Top Things To Do*). Non-residents must pay hotel bills in foreign currency (usually US Dollars) or by credit card. Local currency is not acceptable, even on presentation of exchange certificates. All hotels are graded on a 5-star system, with those classified 1-star or above being registered with the Zimbabwe Tourism Authority. Over 70 hotels are registered.

CAMPING/CARAVANNING:

Most centres and tourist areas have caravan parks and campsites.

ACCOMMODATION INFORMATION

Hospitality Association of Zimbabwe (HAZ)
PO Box CY 398, Causeway, Harare, Zimbabwe
Tel: (4) 733 211.
Website: www.haz.co.zw

Top Things To See

• Formerly Salisbury, **Harare**, the capital, is Zimbabwe's commercial and industrial centre and also the usual starting point for any visit. It is a clean and sophisticated city, characterised by flowering trees, colourful parks and contemporary architecture. Local sightseeing includes the modern museum and art gallery, the **Robert McIlwaine Recreational Park**, which has a lake and game reserve, the **Lion & Cheetah Park**, the **Larvon Bird Gardens** and the landscaped gardens of aloes and cycads at **Ewanrigg Botanical Gardens**. Due to its pleasant climate, Harare is known as the 'Sunshine City'.

• **Bulawayo**, Zimbabwe's second city, is a major commercial, industrial and tourist centre. The city is rich in historical associations and is the home of the **National Museum**. Nearby are the ancient **Khami ruins**, while to the south is the **Rhodes Matopos National Park**, notable for its exotic formations of huge granite boulders. Dams with excellent fishing, caves with rock paintings, **Cecil Rhodes' grave** and a well-stocked game park make this area popular with visitors.

• A holiday in Zimbabwe would be incomplete without a visit to the **Great Zimbabwe National Monument**, the largest complex of ruins in Africa south of the pyramids in Egypt. The **Main Enclosure**, or **Temple**, has walls over 9m (30ft) tall, 4m (14ft) thick and over 228m (250 yards) in circumference, giving approximately 485,521 cubic metres (635,000 cubic ft) of hand-trimmed mortarless stonework. The remains are what is left of a city-state that flourished between the 13th and 15th centuries, trading in gold. **Lake Kyle National Park** is not far away; there is a well-organised campsite close to the lake.

• Do not miss the **Victoria Falls**. 120km (75 miles) from the Hwange National Park are the largest waterfalls in the world – at 2.5km (1.5 miles) wide, 550 million litres of water plunge 100m (330ft) into a narrow chasm every minute; the spray can be seen 30km (20 miles) away. To gain an overall impression of the Falls, the 'Flight of the Angels' light plane trip is a must, as is a cruise up the mighty **Zambezi River**. It is possible to walk across to Zambia (with the minimum of formalities) to view from the other side.

Top Things To Do

• Formerly Wankie National Park, **Hwange National Park** is one of Zimbabwe's largest parks, both in size, 14,620 sq km (5644 sq miles), and in the variety of animals and birds that may be seen. Hwange is one of the last of the great elephant sanctuaries in Africa, with over 40,000 living in the national park.

• Not far from the Victoria Falls is the **Zambezi National Park**, where sable antelopes and other exotic animals graze in a parkland setting.

• **Mana Pools National Park** is one of Zimbabwe's most beautiful national parks, occupying 2196 sq km (848 sq miles) of forest along the shores of the Zambezi River. The animal population includes hippo, elephant, rhino, buffalo and many types of antelope. Game-viewing on foot is allowed. The birdlife along the river and in the bush is particularly prolific. It is possible to fish for tigerfish, bream and the giant vundu.

• Situated in the northwest of the country on the Zambian border, **Lake Kariba** covers 7770 sq km (3000 sq miles) and holds a million gallons of water. Game can be viewed from the comfort of various safari camps, or from well-appointed cruise vessels and self-contained safari-crafts.

• Located close to Bulawayo, Zimbabwe's second major city, **Matobo National Park** is noted for its spectacular

granite rock formations and its wealth of ancient rock paintings. Cecil Rhodes' tomb can be visited at Malindidzimu (View of the World). The Nswatugi and Pomongwe caves are worth visiting.

• Situated in the mountain range that covers the eastern part of Zimbabwe, **Nyanga National Park** is an area of high grasslands, evergreen forests, waterfalls, cliffs and lakeside cottages. Trout fishing is very popular and the trout hatchery is well worth a visit.

• Apart from the traditional way of driving along the parks' game viewing roads, **canoeing** and **boat safaris** are popular alternatives. At **Lake Kariba**, which has abundant elephant, buffalo, rhino and smaller game living on its banks, boats can be hired for a day or for over a week. Canoeing safaris ranging from three to 10 days are especially popular between April and November along the **Zambezi River** past the **Mana Pools** flood plains.

• At the mighty **Victoria Falls**, the 111m- (364ft-) bridge linking Zimbabwe to Zambia offers one of the world's highest **bungee jumps**. **Whitewater rafting** through the Zambezi Gorge is at its wildest between July and August. **Canoeing** and **kayaking** can be practised on the more subdued river stretches above the falls.

• The string of mountains and the lush countryside in Zimbabwe's **Eastern Highlands**, which form a natural border with neighbouring Mozambique, are particularly sought after by **walkers** and **trekkers**. Climbing Zimbabwe's highest mountain, **Mt Nyangani**, takes around one hour 30 minutes. The **World's View** offers a panoramic view across northern Zimbabwe. From here, a steep footpath leads to the road to **Nyanga village** with its English gardens, village common and church.

• Zimbabwe offers excellent **freshwater fishing**, the best locations being **Lake Kariba** (famous for its tigerfish), the **Zambezi River** above the Victoria Falls (known for its giant catfish), the streams of the **Eastern Highlands** and the many lakes.

• There are around 40 **golf clubs**, most of which have 18-hole courses. The Eastern Highlands have the highest concentration of courses. The Zimbabwe Open is an annual competition attracting world-class players.

TOURIST INFORMATION

Zimbabwe Tourism Office in the UK
Zimbabwe House, 429 Strand, London WC2R 0JR, UK
Tel: (020) 7836 7755.
Website: www.zimbabwetourism.co.zw

Zimbabwe Tourism Office in the USA
128 East 56th Street, New York, NY 10022, USA
Tel: (212) 486 3444.
Website: www.zimbabwetourism.co.zw

Department of National Parks and Wildlife
Borrowdale Road, PO Box CY 140, Causeway,
Harare, Zimbabwe
Tel: (4) 707 624 *or* 724 027 *or* 792 786.

Zimbabwe Association of Tour and Safari Operators
PO Box 7240, Harare, Zimbabwe
Tel: (4) 708 878-9.

Central Reservations for Lodges
Tel: (4) 706 077/8.

Entertainment

FOOD & DRINK: Zimbabwe is a cosmopolitan society and enjoys both local and international cuisine. Eating out is popular and comparatively cheap. Beer is the most widely consumed alcoholic beverage. Imported wines, spirits and liqueurs are available in hotels.

Things to know: Table service is the norm in restaurants. Public bars are almost always part of a hotel. Licensing hours in Zimbabwe are 1030-1500 and 1630-2300. Major hotels have 24-hour bars and room service.

National specialities:
• *Sadza* (a stiff maize meal) eaten with meat and/or gravy and a relish.
• *Nhedzi soup* (wild mushroom).
• Game meat, including ostrich, warthog and crocodile tail.
National drinks:
• *Whawha* (traditional maize beer).
Tipping: A 10 to 15 per cent tip is usual.
NIGHTLIFE: Rather limited outside the cities with emphasis on eating and discos, but larger cities have nightclubs, cinemas and repertory theatres. The three main tourist areas have casinos.
SHOPPING: A sales tax of 10 to 22 per cent is added to all purchases, the higher rate being on luxury items, except those which are to be exported. Special purchases are copper, wooden and soapstone carvings, gameskin and leather products, pottery and basketwork. **Shopping hours:** Mon-Fri 0800-1700 and Sat 0800-1300.

Business

• **GDP:** US$8.3 billion (2005).
• **Main imports:** Machinery and transport equipment, other machines, chemicals and fuels.
• **Main exports:** Cotton, tobacco, gold, ferroalloys, textiles and clothing.
• **Main trade partners:** China, Germany and South Africa.

ECONOMY: Zimbabwe's economy is now in freefall. Half the workforce is unemployed; hyper-inflation was 252 per cent in 2004 and the GDP contracted by 13 per cent in the same year. There are four main reasons: a catastrophic decline in the value of the Zimbabwean Dollar; the chaos in the vital agricultural and agro-industrial sectors caused by Government policies on land redistribution; the drought that is afflicting the entire region; and the growing impact of the very high rates of HIV/AIDS infection on the workforce. Approximately two-thirds of the population face food shortages. The situation is now extremely serious and the immediate prospects of recovery are virtually zero without radical political change. Under other circumstances, Zimbabwe would have one of the most diverse and best-performing economies on the African continent.
The agricultural base relies on tobacco and other cash crops, including sugar, coffee, cotton and maize, as the main export earners. Livestock rearing is also important. The mining industry produces gold and nickel, mainly for export, as well as smaller quantities of a host of other minerals including silver, emeralds, lithium, tin, iron ore, manganese, cobalt, coal, diamonds and a number of rare metals. Large coal deposits and hydroelectric plants supply the country's power stations. Manufacturing industry was well developed by regional standards: food processing, metals, chemicals and textiles were the main components. In the service sector, tourism grew rapidly in the period after independence but the industry has all but vanished. Zimbabwe is better developed than many of its neighbours (especially as regards basic infrastructure such as roads, telecommunications, water and electricity), much of this benefit has been squandered or allowed to disintegrate through neglect. Zimbabwe's economy remains heavily dependent on South Africa. The South Africans have been more sympathetic to the Zimbabwean Government than most of the international community; all the major donors in Europe and North America have now suspended grants and loans to Zimbabwe, further depressing economic prospects. The IMF has expelled Zimbabwe, as has the Commonwealth (formerly a valuable source of aid). Although Zimbabwe is a member of the Southern African Development Community and has signed up to the Common Market for Eastern and Southern Africa, these are of marginal assistance in present circumstances. Zimbabwe's once thriving trade patterns have been all but wrecked as the country has become isolated internationally.
BUSINESS ETIQUETTE: Normal courtesies should be observed and men should wear a suit and tie. The atmosphere will generally be less formal than in many European countries. **Office hours:** Mon-Fri 0800-1630.

COMMERCIAL INFORMATION

Ministry of Industry & International Trade
Private Bag 7708, 13th Floor, Mukwati Building,
Fourth Street, Causeway, Harare, Zimbabwe
Tel: (4) 702 731.

Zimbabwe National Chambers of Commerce (ZNCC)
P.O. Box 1934, ZNCC Business House, 42 Harare Street, Harare, Zimbabwe
Tel: (4) 749 335 *or* 749 737.
Website: www.zncc.co.zw

Appendices

Travel Trade Associations

Members' Handbook

ABTA

In 2005, visits abroad by UK residents rose to reach a record 66.3 million, according to national statistics conducted by Census (website: www.statistics.gov.uk). Such statistics augment sustained growth in UK travel and tourism over the last few years, hinting at the overcoming of global deterrents, such as 9/11 in New York and the subsequent 'War on Terror', which initially blighted UK confidence in overseas travel. To summarise, more UK nationals are travelling abroad than ever before. All of which puts a big responsibility on the organisation that represents the vast majority of tour operators and travel agents in Britain – the Association of British Travel Agents (ABTA). Indeed, ABTA recently announced record data for online searches in January 2006: its website logged over 135,000 visits, a figure that doubles the amount recorded the previous year. January is a notorious peak period for people researching holidays, but it appears that more people are choosing to research their holidays through recognised and trusted associations, and ABTA's profile continues to expand, particularly since the appointment of its new President, Martin Wellings, in 2004. It is for all these reasons that the Association strives so hard to ensure consistently high standards of trading practice for the benefit of consumers and the travel industry. ABTA's principal duties are to create as favourable a business environment as possible for its members, while ensuring that standards of service and business throughout its membership are of the highest calibre. This is all good news for the holidaymaker, to whom ABTA's famous symbol has come to represent choice, value and protection.

ABTA was formed in 1950 with just 100 members, at a time that coincided with the dawn of a new era for British travellers. World War II had set in motion huge advances in aviation technology, and the advent of the jet aircraft brought foreign travel within the scope of a far wider group than ever before. Foreign travel came to be seen as a temporary escape from the drabness of post-war Britain and the mass-market holiday boom began. So how does ABTA work?

- ABTA is a self-regulatory body that is run by its membership. The Board of Directors and committees, appointed by members, make up the policy-making and enforcing machinery of the Association and help to ensure that ABTA remains in close touch with the whole of its membership, plus dealing with the many areas of specific interest to the industry.

  As well as their year-round work to raise standards and improve conditions throughout the industry, ABTA's Board and committees are also active behind the scenes. This action takes the form of liaison and negotiation with other trade bodies and representatives of government in the UK and overseas – for example, to reduce delays at airports, put pressure on governments to avert air traffic control strikes, improve insurance cover recommended by ABTA travel agents and protest at the ever-increasing range of taxes on travellers.

- ABTA shall continue to lobby, on behalf of its members and general public, on any issue which could be detrimental to travel prospects. ABTA is also expected to continue parliamentary lobbying regarding issues such as airport expansion and the introduction of a comprehensive financial protection scheme to cover all travel arrangements. ABTA has also just overseen successful lobbying of the review of US entry procedure; the necessity for biometric passport data requirements has now been delayed until October 2006.

- The members of ABTA are required to adhere to strict rules that govern their business practice. These are contained in ABTA's Code of Conduct that regulates all aspects of tour operators' and travel agents' relationships with their customers (and between themselves), and which have been drawn up by specialists in the travel industry in conjunction with the Office of Fair Trading. In 2005 ABTA received Stage 2 approval from the OFT for the Code, one of only five trade associations to do so.

- The Code of Conduct lays down in detail the minimum standards on brochures, requiring that they contain clear, comprehensive and accurate descriptions of such things as the type of travel, destination, nature of accommodation and meal facilities offered. It details rules that govern booking conditions in brochures as they relate, for example, to the cancellation or alteration of tours, holidays or other travel arrangements by the tour operator. It also contains strict rules about dealing with complaints promptly and efficiently. The Code also regulates the conduct between tour operators and travel agents. The Code regulates all aspects of members' relationships with their customers, and covers their responsibility with regard to the standard of service they provide and the information they are responsible for giving – for example, regarding insurance facilities, passport, visa and health requirements or alterations to travel arrangements. It also lays down rules concerning members' trading relationships with each other.

- Members of ABTA are required to adhere to precise financial specifications monitored by ABTA's Financial Services Department, which regularly checks all members' accounts.

- ABTA administers a comprehensive system of financial protection, the purpose of which is to ensure that if an ABTA member fails financially, ABTA is able to arrange for customers whose holidays or other travel arrangements are in progress at the time of the failure to continue their holidays, as far as possible as originally planned, and, in any event, to make certain that customers abroad are returned to the UK. ABTA also reimburses customers whose holidays have not yet started to enable them to make alternative holiday arrangements.

- Tour operator- and travel agent-members of ABTA are required to provide bonds or other suitable protection to secure their customers in the event of financial failure. In addition, there are funds which cover all members and provide a 'second line of defence' to back up the extensive bonding system.

- There are one or two exceptions to this wide-ranging protection scheme. It should be noted that it does not apply in the event of financial failure of a non-ABTA company or firm, even if the booking was made through an ABTA travel agent. Completed holidays or contracts that have been terminated or broken at the time of financial failure are also not covered by this financial protection.

  If an ABTA travel agent fails, no refund will be made if no booking has been made with a supplier.

  In line with the law, non package holiday tour operators are not required by ABTA to provide financial protection.

- In addition to a comprehensive advice service offered to pre- and post-departure queries, the Association provides a low-cost independent arbitration service to members' clients who have failed to get their dispute settled. It is administered by the Chartered Institute of Arbitrators, and the costs are subsidised by ABTA. The scheme provides for a simple and inexpensive method of arbitration on documents alone, with the ruling of the Arbitrator being legally binding. A client may elect against using this service and may prefer to resolve a dispute through the courts.

For further information, contact: ABTA, 68-71 Newman Street, London W1T 3AH, UK (tel: (020) 7637 2444 or (0901) 201 5050 (travel information line; UK callers only; 50p per minute) or (020) 7307 1900 (press enquiries); website: www.abta.com). Contact: Keith Betton/Frances Tuke.

ACTA

The Association of Canadian Travel Agencies (ACTA) is a national non-profit trade association, which was established in 1977.

ACTA's mission is to represent the interests of its members - primarily retail travel agents - to the public, to governments, to suppliers and other bodies, assisting them in maximising their economic objectives. ACTA's core functions include advocacy, information and research, public relations and the development of membership for the purposes of strengthening the association's effectiveness as the voice of the industry.

As members of Canada's largest, not-for-profit retail travel association, members benefit from the following:

- Information on travel industry developments;
- Input into the association's advocacy agenda;
- Invitations to regional and national events, conferences and tradeshows;
- International industry representation through alliances with affiliated associations in other countries;
- Member-discounted rates for various products and services;
- Research and information on consumer and market trends.

For further information, contact: ACTA, 350 Sparks Street, Suite 510, Ottawa, Ontario, K1R 7S8 Canada (tel: (613) 237 3657; website: www.acta.travel).

AFTA

The Australian Federation of Travel Agents Limited (AFTA) is the representative body for Australia's travel agents with its Head Office located in Pitt Street, Sydney, and was founded in 1957. AFTA represents the majority of travel agents in Australia.

AFTA provides financial, legal and marketing benefits, education and training, and develops policies and strategies critical to the retail travel sector. AFTA also has membership of the World Travel Agents Associations Alliance (WTAAA), ensuring that AFTA is listened to at international forums.

AFTA's role as industry watchdog ensures that the viewpoint of the agent is transmitted through media outlets and through lobbying activities. AFTA policies are established by a national Board of Directors in conjunction with the Chief Executive, and AFTA provides a unique forum of industry networking.

Major Activities:

- The Australian Travel Professionals Program (ATPP), established by AFTA to 'enhance professionalism through education', has over 2900 members from both retail and wholesale sectors of our industry. The Program helps meet the needs of consumers and the travel industry for professional standards and quality service.
- The AFTA Travel & Tourism Colleges. Support for the colleges is given by the travel and tourism industry through on-the-job training and employment of graduates. The AFTA Colleges produce graduates of exceptionally high calibre. Colleges are located in four major cities: Adelaide, Brisbane, Perth and Sydney. There is also an External Studies Program for those wishing to gain entry into the industry.
- AFTA Traveller Magazine is the official magazine of AFTA, published quarterly.
- AFTA Business Insurance for AFTA travel Agents.
- Credit Card Fee Rates: AFTA has negotiated various Merchant Fee Rates on behalf of AFTA Members.
- Industry and Government relations.
- Consumer grievance and ethics service.
- Conciliation process for industry disputes.

For further information, contact: AFTA Limited, 3rd Floor, 309 Pitt Street, Sydney NSW 2000, Australia (tel: (02) 9264 3299 or (1300) 326 416; website: www.afta.com.au).

ANTOR

ANTOR (the Association of National Tourist Office Representatives) is the principal lobbying organisation for the world's tourist offices. Its UK membership comprises more than 60 national and regional tourist offices represented in Britain.

A voluntary, non-political organisation founded in 1951, ANTOR UK aims to provide a fraternal forum for members to meet and exchange ideas; it is committed to playing a leading role in encouraging responsible tourism; and it is available to provide media comment on a wide range of issues affecting worldwide travel and tourism.

ANTOR UK works in close partnership with other important industry bodies including ABTA, AITO (Association of Independent Tour Operators) and the FTO (Federation of Tour Operators). It is also a member of the Travel Advice Review Group established by the British Foreign and Commonwealth Office.

There are other ANTOR bodies in Belgium & Luxembourg, France, Sweden, Canada and Australia, but they have no formal links with ANTOR UK.

For further information, contact: ANTOR UK, PO Box 5017, Hove, East Sussex BN23 3ZD, UK (tel: (44) 870 241 9084; website: www.antor.com).

Contact: Peter Lilley, Executive Secretary.

Worldwide Membership Directory

ASTA

The international travel and tourism industry transcends borders. Business colleagues and customers are situated all over the world. The challenge is often to find a way to expand the focus beyond the community and promote services to those colleagues on the other side of the world. The American Society of Travel Agents (ASTA) aims to provide that opportunity. Members of ASTA gain access to the following international membership benefits:

Industry Integrity and Consumer Awareness:

- ASTA Logo: Consumers and US travel agents look for the ASTA logo because they prefer to do business with firms they can trust. ASTA members adhere to the strong Code of Ethics and Bylaws, thus assuring that ASTA members are reputable companies. Members receive exclusive use of the ASTA logo on their letterhead, storefronts, websites, etc.
- International Photo ID Membership Card: US suppliers and travel agents worldwide recognise the international Photo Membership Card as a sign of professionalism and 'integrity in travel'.

ASTAnet:

- Industry Information: ASTAnet is a major information resource available 24 hours a day. ASTAnet contains information on business practices, commission levels, up-to-the-minute information, and more.
- Web Exchange: The Web Exchange is similar to a virtual bulletin board listing travel and supplier specials, important commission notices and other needs by ASTA agents and suppliers. Many postings concern the need for receptive agents all over the world.
- Directory Listing: ASTA members receive a free listing on ASTAnet's online member directory. The listing includes a link to the member's e-mail address and an optional link to their website, providing exposure to other members and consumers worldwide.
- Trip Request Service: ASTA's Trip Request Service offers members exclusive access to potential business from consumers. Anywhere from US$500,000 to US$1 million in business awaits each day.

Education and Business Service:

- ASTA's International Destination Expo (IDE) is a new show designed to immerse travel professionals in the culture, attractions and travel business of each year's chosen international destination, providing extensive in-country training. Visit the website www.ASTAnet.com for dates and locations.
- THE TRADE SHOW (Travel Retailing and Destination Expo) is a new three-day event connecting thousands of consumers, travel agents and travel suppliers from every segment of the industry in one convenient location. The show will occur every year during the second week in September, alternating between Orlando in even years and Las Vegas in odd years. Visit the website www.THETRADESHOW.org for dates and locations.
- Global Discussion Groups: An automated e-mail tool for interactive discussions on topics of common interest with travel agents around the world.
- ASTA offers home-study courses for agents which focus on various specialisations such as the Model Agency Program, Cuba Travel Specialist Course, USA Travel Expert Program, Family Travel Specialist Course, Niche Travel Specialist Course, Mature Adult Travel Specialist Course, Travel Marketing Specialist Course and North American Rail Travel Specialist.

For more information, contact: ASTA, 1101 King Street, Suite 200, Alexandria, Virginia 22314, USA (tel: (703) 739 2782; website: www.astanet.com).

Institute of Travel & Tourism

ITT

The Institute of Travel & Tourism (ITT) was inaugurated in 1956 when the package tourism industry was in its infancy. Its original members were a handful of professionals who recognised the need for an organisation to set, maintain and improve standards within the travel and tourism industry.

The aim of ITT is 'to develop the professionalism of its members within the industry'. This may seem a high ideal for an industry that is fragmented and has traditionally prided itself on its entrepreneurial spirit. There are many in the travel industry who, with no formal training, are justifiably proud of their achievements, earned by hard work on the job. However, today's travel market is sophisticated, highly competitive and requires the use of complex information technology. Imagination and common sense are not always enough, and everyone involved in the travel business needs to be competent and well trained – in short, a professional. Consequently, ITT aims to help practising and potential managers develop and maintain their professional knowledge and skills. The awarding of a recognised professional qualification entitles members to use designatory letters within their title: A Inst TT, M Inst TT, F Inst TT. ITT ensures that these designations are recognised as a mark of professional achievement.

ITT acknowledges the importance of education and training at every level of experience and seniority. Many young people follow full-time courses of study at colleges around the UK. ITT accredits college courses that offer comprehensive and high-quality teaching, equipment and facilities. Students attending Institute-approved colleges are assured of the highest-quality education and preparation for a career in the travel industry. This accreditation process has now been extended to include in-company skills training courses. The accreditation of in-house management-level training will be developed in the near future.

Formal qualifications are essential in establishing a minimum level of knowledge and expertise, but ITT recognises that continuing professional development is crucial. To this end, ITT runs a series of one-day seminars each year, on subjects as diverse as travel legislation and the law, brochure production, technology, time management, presentation skills, negotiating skills, sales skills, management skills, business development and financial management and control. These seminars are offered both as open courses or in-house courses for companies, which can be tailored or developed to meet the specific needs of individual firms.

ITT arranges regular meetings for members, providing a forum for discussion of current issues, such as market conditions and legislation. ITT also organises an annual conference, which gives members the opportunity to probe issues affecting the industry, and to hear the views of senior industry figures and opinion formers. In 2006, the annual conference takes place from 12 to 14 June in Muscat, Oman. ITT is also hosting its third annual conference for aspiring travel professionals, ASPIRE 06 at Butlins Bognor Regis Resort, UK. Product knowledge is essential too, and educational tours to destinations such as Disneyland Paris, The Gambia and India have been organised for members in recent years.

ITT is managed by a Chairman and a Board of Directors, comprised of senior travel industry professionals.

For further information, contact: ITT, PO Box 217, Ware, Hertfordshire SG12 8WY, UK (tel: (0870) 770 7960; website: www.itt.co.uk).

UFTAA

UFTAA, founded in 1966, is the United Federation of Travel Agents' Associations and the highest world body representing the travel industry. In 2003, UFTAA became a Confederation comprising nine regions worldwide. The national associations are thus members through their respective regions. In addition to the National Associations, UFTAA highly values the individual membership and support of a large number of individual travel agents, tour operators, wholesalers, travel partners and others allied to the tourist industry. UFTAA represents some 100 national associations. The 2006 UFTAA Congress is to be held from 15 to 19 September in Delhi, India.

The Federation's objectives are:

- To provide an international forum where worldwide travel issues are addressed.
- To unite and reinforce national associations of travel agents and thereby encourage the establishment of associations in countries where they do not exist.
- To represent and promote the interests of the trade to governments, suppliers and other international bodies and take any initiative that can help, stimulate and develop the travel and tourism sector throughout the world.
- To serve, help and advise members, to see to their protection and development within economic, legal and social spheres, and take the necessary steps to standardise norms of professional ethics.
- To encourage and maintain efficient communication between members.
- To preserve human and natural environments and a harmonious co-existence of all sectors of travel and tourism.
- To study and disseminate legislation relating to travel trade activities, particularly those that overlap national borders.

UFTAA also operates a training programme taught by authorised centres and a Professional Travel Agents' ID-Card Programme offering added values at national level. Additionally, UFTAA offers professional assistance through the Travel Agency Commissioners, as well as legal and litigation services.

For further information, contact: UFTAA, 1 avenue des Castelans, Stade Louis II, Entrée H, MC-98000 Monaco (tel: (377) 9205 2829; website: www.uftaa.travel).

WATA

WATA, the World Association of Travel Agencies, is a non-profit-making organisation created by independent travel agents for the benefit of all travel agencies around the world. It helps locally respected agencies combine their personal touch with the influence gained by global recognition. Since its foundation in 1949, WATA has become a truly well-respected name in the travel industry worldwide. With over 100 members in 50 countries, WATA has today established an international network of travel agents who enjoy some unique privileges and benefits.

WATA's basic idea is to bring local (preferably privately owned) travel agencies into an international network, so that every member is offered all the facilities and advantages of being associated with an international body – in addition to enjoying local prominence. As a consequence, a substantial increase in the volume of business to the agency's turnover can be expected.

By becoming a WATA member, a travel agency/tour operator can rely on:

- Business opportunities: WATA insures business increase, visibility of the member's products and business support.
- Exclusivity: Striving for recognition and credibility on the market.
- Dynamism: Members are proactive, exchanging ideas, experience and expertise.
- Prestige and quality: Assurance of a high quality of service.

In addition to having 100 members worldwide and respectability within the tourism industry, WATA is launching a full E-Business platform to promote and sell the incoming services of its members worldwide.

Membership of WATA is open to any travel agency, preferably privately owned, which can prove a sound financial structure, and that adheres to the highest professional standards expected in the industry, enjoying a prominent standing in the local community. WATA membership is exclusive on a per-city basis so a strong selection is made.

Please apply for an application form and a copy of the Articles of Association.

For further information, contact: Administrative Manager, WATA, 11 rue Riant Coteau, 1196 GLAND, Switzerland (tel: (22) 995 1545; website: www.wata.net).

International Organisations

Listed below are major international organisations concerned with economics and trade.

Asia-Pacific Economic Co-operation – APEC

35 Heng Mui Keng Terrace, Singapore 119616

Tel: (65) 6775 6012.

Website: www.apec.org

Members: Australia, Brunei, Canada, Chile, China (PR), Chinese Taipei, Hong Kong (SAR), Indonesia, Japan, Korea (Rep), Malaysia, Mexico, New Zealand, Papua New Guinea, Peru, The Philippines, Russian Federation, Singapore, Thailand, USA and Vietnam.

Asociación Latinoamericana de Integración – ALADI

(Latin American Integration Association – LAIA)

Cebollatí 1461, Montevideo 11200, Uruguay

Tel: (2) 410 1121.

Website: www.aladi.org

Members: Argentina, Bolivia, Brazil, Chile, Colombia, Cuba, Ecuador, Mexico, Paraguay, Peru, Uruguay and Venezuela.

Association of Southeast Asian Nations – ASEAN

70A Jalan Sisingamangaraja, Jakarta 12110, Indonesia

Tel: (21) 726 2991 or 724 3372.

Website: www.aseansec.org

Members: Brunei, Cambodia, Indonesia, Laos, Malaysia, Myanmar, The Philippines, Singapore, Thailand and Vietnam.

Caribbean Community & Common Market – CARICOM

Street Address: 3rd Floor, Bank of Guyana Building, 1 Avenue of the Republic, Georgetown, Guyana

Postal Address: PO Box 10827, Georgetown, Guyana

Tel: (22) 2000 175.

Website: www.caricom.org

Members: Antigua & Barbuda, The Bahamas, Barbados, Belize, Dominica, Grenada, Guyana, Haiti, Jamaica, Montserrat, St Kitts & Nevis, St Lucia, St Vincent & The Grenadines, Surinam and Trinidad & Tobago.

Associate Members: Anguilla, Bermuda, British Virgin Islands, Cayman Islands and Turks & Caicos Islands.

Observers: Aruba, Colombia, Dominican Republic, Mexico, The Netherlands Antilles, Puerto Rico and Venezuela.

The Colombo Plan for Co-operative Economic & Social Development in Asia and the Pacific

13th Floor, Bank of Ceylon, Merchant Tower, 28 St Michael's Road, Colombo 3, Sri Lanka

Tel: (11) 256 4448.

Website: www.colombo-plan.org

Members: Afghanistan, Australia, Bangladesh, Bhutan, Fiji, India, Indonesia, Iran, Japan, Korea (Rep), Laos, Malaysia, Maldives, Mongolia, Myanmar, Nepal, New Zealand, Pakistan, Papua New Guinea, The Philippines, Singapore, Sri Lanka, Thailand, USA and Vietnam.

Commonwealth

Commonwealth Secretariat, Marlborough House, Pall Mall, London SW1Y 5HX, UK

Tel: (020) 7747 6500.

Website: www.thecommonwealth.org

Members: Antigua & Barbuda, Australia, The Bahamas, Bangladesh, Barbados, Belize, Botswana, Brunei, Cameroon, Canada, Cyprus, Dominica, Fiji, The Gambia, Ghana, Grenada, Guyana, India, Jamaica, Kenya, Kiribati, Lesotho, Malawi, Malaysia, Maldives, Malta, Mauritius, Mozambique, Namibia, Nauru, New Zealand, Nigeria, Pakistan, Papua New Guinea, St Kitts & Nevis, St Lucia, St Vincent & The Grenadines, Samoa, Seychelles, Sierra Leone, Singapore, Solomon Islands, South Africa, Sri Lanka, Swaziland, Tonga, Trinidad & Tobago, Tuvalu, Uganda, United Kingdom, United Republic of Tanzania, Vanuatu and Zambia.

Dependencies & Associated States: Australia: Ashmore & Cartier Islands, Australian Antarctic Territory, Christmas Island (Pacific), Cocos (Keeling) Island, Coral Sea Islands Territory, Heard & McDonald Islands and Norfolk Island; New Zealand: Cook Islands, Niue, Ross Dependency and Tokelau Islands; United Kingdom: Anguilla, Bermuda, British Antarctic Territory, British Indian Ocean Territory, British Virgin Islands, Cayman Islands, Channel Islands, Ducie & Oeno Islands, Falkland Islands, Gibraltar, Henderson, Isle of Man, Montserrat, Pitcairn, St Helena and Dependencies (Ascension Island and Tristan da Cunha), South Georgia, South Sandwich Islands and Turks & Caicos Islands.

Commonwealth of Independent States – CIS

17 Kirova Street, 220050 Minsk, Belarus

Tel: (17) 222 3517.

Website: www.cis.minsk.by

Members: Armenia, Azerbaijan, Belarus, Georgia, Kazakhstan, Kyrgyzstan, Moldova, Russian Federation, Tajikistan, Turkmenistan, Ukraine and Uzbekistan.

Co-operation Council for the Arab States of the Gulf

PO Box 7153, 11462, Riyadh, Saudi Arabia

Tel: (1) 482 7777 (ext 1245).

Website: www.gcc-sg.org

Members: Bahrain, Kuwait, Oman, Qatar, Saudi Arabia and United Arab Emirates.

Council of Arab Economic Unity

Street Address: General Secretariat, 1113 Cornishe El-Nil Street, 4th Floor, Cairo, Egypt

Postal Address: PO Box (1) Mohammed Farid 11518, Cairo, Egypt

Tel: (2) 575 5321 or 575 4252 or 575 5045.

Website: www.caeu.org.eg

Members: Egypt, Iraq, Jordan, Kuwait, Libya, Mauritania, Palestine National Authority, Somalia, Sudan, the Syrian Arab Republic and Yemen.

Council of Europe

Avenue de l'Europe, 67075 Strasbourg CEDEX, France

Tel: (3) 8841 2000 (general) or 8841 2033 (information point).

Website: www.coe.int

Economic Community of West African States – ECOWAS

60 Yakubu Gowon Crescent, Asokoro District, PMB 401, Abuja, Nigeria

Tel: (09) 314 7647-9.

Website: www.sec.ecowas.int

Members: Benin, Burkina Faso, Cape Verde, Côte d'Ivoire, The Gambia, Ghana, Guinea, Guinea-Bissau, Liberia, Mali, Niger, Nigeria, Senegal, Sierra Leone and Togo.

European Union – EU

Brey 12th Floor, Office 100, B-1049 Brussels, Belgium

Tel: 00 800 6789 1011

Website: www.europa.eu.int

Meetings of the principal organs take place in Brussels, Luxembourg and Strasbourg.

Members: Austria, Belgium, Cyprus, Czech Republic, Denmark, Estonia, Finland, France, Germany, Greece, Hungary, Ireland, Italy, Latvia, Lithuania, Luxembourg, The Netherlands, Malta, Poland, Portugal, Slovak Republic, Slovenia, Spain, Sweden and United Kingdom.

European Central Bank – ECB

Street Address: Kaiserstrasse 29, D-60311, Frankfurt-am-Main, Germany

Postal Address: Postfach 16 03 19, D-60066, Frankfurt-am-Main, Germany

Tel: (69) 13440.

Website: www.ecb.int

European Free Trade Association – EFTA

9-11 rue de Varembé, CH-1211 Geneva 20, Switzerland

Tel: (22) 332 2626.

Website: www.efta.int

Members: Iceland, Liechtenstein, Norway and Switzerland.

Franc Zone

Direction Générale des Services Etrangers (Service de la Zone Franc), Banque de France, 31 rue Croix-des-Petits-Champs, BP 75001, Paris, France

Tel: (1) 4292 4292 or 6480 2020.

Website: www.banque-france.fr

Members: Benin, Burkina Faso, Cameroon, Central African Republic, Chad, Comoros Islands, Congo (Rep), Côte d'Ivoire, Equatorial Guinea, Gabon, Guinea-Bissau, Mali, Niger, Senegal and Togo.

League of Arab States

Arab League Building, PO Box 11642, Medan, Tahrir Square, Cairo, Egypt

Tel: (2) 575 0511.

Website: www.arableagueonline.org

Members: Algeria, Bahrain, Comoro Islands, Djibouti, Egypt, Iraq, Jordan, Kuwait, Lebanon, Libya, Mauritania, Morocco, Oman, Palestine National Authority, Qatar, Saudi Arabia, Somalia, Sudan, Syrian Arab Republic, Tunisia, United Arab Emirates and Yemen.

Nordic Council

Store Strandstræde 18, DK 1255, Copenhagen, Denmark

Tel: (33) 960 200.

Website: www.norden.org

Members: Denmark (with the autonomous territories of the Faroe Islands and Greenland), Finland (with the autonomous territory of the Åland Islands), Iceland, Norway and Sweden.

Organisation for Economic Co-operation & Development – OECD

2 rue André Pascal, F-75775, Paris Cedex 16, France

Tel: (1) 4524 8200.

Website: www.oecd.org

Members: Australia, Austria, Belgium, Canada, Czech Republic, Denmark, Finland, France, Germany, Greece, Hungary, Iceland, Ireland, Italy, Japan, Korea (Rep), Luxembourg, Mexico, The Netherlands, New Zealand, Norway, Poland, Portugal, Slovak Republic, Spain, Sweden, Switzerland, Turkey, United Kingdom and USA.

African Union - AU

Street Address: Roosevelt Street (Old Airport Area) W21 K19, Addis Ababa, Ethiopia

Postal Address: PO Box 3243, W21 K19, Addis Ababa, Ethiopia

Tel: (1) 517 700.

Website: www.africa-union.org

Members: Algeria, Angola, Benin, Botswana, Burkina Faso, Burundi, Cameroon, Cape Verde, Central African Republic, Chad, Comoros Islands, Congo (Dem Rep), Congo (Rep), Côte d'Ivoire, Djibouti, Egypt, Equatorial Guinea, Eritrea, Ethiopia, Gabon, The Gambia, Ghana, Guinea, Guinea-Bissau, Kenya, Lesotho, Liberia, Libya, Madagascar, Malawi, Mali, Mauritania, Mauritius, Mozambique, Namibia, Niger, Nigeria, Rwanda, Saharan Arab Democratic Republic, São Tomé & Principe, Senegal, Seychelles, Sierra Leone, Somalia, South Africa, Sudan, Swaziland, Tanzania, Togo, Tunisia, Uganda, Zambia and Zimbabwe.

Organisation of American States – OAS

17th Street & Constitution Avenue, NW, Washington, DC 20006, USA

Tel: (202) 458 3000.

Website: www.oas.org

Members: Antigua & Barbuda, Argentina, The Bahamas, Barbados, Belize, Bolivia, Brazil, Canada, Chile, Colombia, Costa Rica, Cuba*, Dominica, Dominican Republic, Ecuador, El Salvador, Grenada, Guatemala, Guyana, Haiti, Honduras, Jamaica, Mexico, Nicaragua, Panama, Paraguay, Peru, St Kitts & Nevis, St Lucia, St Vincent & the Grenadines, Surinam, Trinidad & Tobago, Uruguay, USA and Venezuela.

Note: *The Cuban Government was suspended from OAS activities in 1962.

Organisation of the Petroleum Exporting Countries – OPEC

Obere Donaustrasse 93, A-1020 Vienna, Austria

Tel: (1) 2111 2279.

Website: www.opec.org

Members: Algeria, Indonesia, Iran, Iraq, Kuwait, Libya, Nigeria, Qatar, Saudi Arabia, United Arab Emirates and Venezuela.

Secretariat of Central American Economic Integration – SIECA

Secretaria de Integración Económica Centroamericana, formerly known as MCCA – Mercado Común Centroamericano

4a Avenida 10-25, Zona 14, Apartado Postal 1237, 01901 Guatemala City, Guatemala

Tel: (3) 682 151/4.

Website: www.sieca.org.gt

Members: Costa Rica, Guatemala, El Salvador, Honduras and Nicaragua.

South Pacific Forum

The Secretary General, Forum Secretariat, Private Mail Bag, Suva, Fiji

Tel: 331 2600.

Website: www.forumsec.org.fj

Members: Australia, Cook Islands, Fiji, Kiribati, Marshall Islands, Micronesia (Federated States of), Nauru, New Zealand, Niue, Palau, Papua New Guinea, Samoa, Solomon Islands, Tonga, Tuvalu and Vanuatu.

Southern African Development Community – SADC

SADC House, Private Bag 0095, Gaborone, Botswana

Tel: 395 1863.

Website: www.sadc.int

Members: Angola, Botswana, Congo (Dem Rep), Lesotho, Madagascar, Malawi, Mauritius, Mozambique, Namibia, South Africa, Swaziland, Tanzania, Zambia and Zimbabwe.

Union of the Arab Maghreb

14 Rue Zalagh, Agdal, Rabat, Morocco

Tel: (37) 671 274/8 or 280 or 278 or 285.

Website: www.maghrebarabe.org

The location of the Union's Secretariat rotates with the chairmanship.

Members: Algeria, Libya, Mauritania, Morocco and Tunisia.

United Nations

United Nations Headquarters, First Avenue at 46th Street, New York, NY 10017, USA

Tel: (212) 963 7112 or 963 4475 (public enquiries).

Website: www.un.org

Members: The UN currently has 191 Member States.

United Nations Conference on Trade and Development – UNCTAD

Palais des Nations, 8-14 Avenue de la Paix, 1211 Geneva 10, Switzerland

Tel: (22) 917 5809.

Website: www.unctad.org

UN International Monetary Fund (IMF)

700 19th Street, NW, Washington, DC 20431, USA

Tel: (202) 623 7000.

Website: www.imf.org

World Bank Group

1818 H Street, NW, Washington, DC 20433, USA

Tel: (202) 473 1000.

Website: www.worldbank.org

World Trade Organization

Centre William Rappard, 154 rue de Lausanne, CH-1211 Geneva 21, Switzerland

Tel: (22) 739 5111.

Website: www.wto.org

Calendar of Events

April 2006 - March 2007

APRIL 2006

Mar 28-2	IFWTO (International Federation of Women's Travel Organisation) 37th Annual Conference, Athens, Greece
3-5	The Beijing International Travel & Tourism Market, Beijing, China
10-12	6th Global Travel & Tourism Summit, Washington, DC, USA
19-22	28th International Fair of Tourism, Belgrade, Serbia & Montenegro
20-22	AITF 2006 (Azerbaijan International Tourism Fair), Baku, Azerbaijan
23-27	55th PATA Annual Conference, Pattaya, Thailand
25-29	8th Caribbean Conference on Sustainable Tourism Development, Puerto Rico
27-29	The International Tourism Exhibition – Fair of the Silk Road Countries, Tbilisi Georgia
27-29	KITF 2006 (Kazakhstan International 'Tourism & Travel'), Almaty, Kazakhstan
30-May 5	ATA 30th International Congress, Accra, Ghana

MAY 2006

2-5	Arabian Travel Market (ATM), Dubai, United Arab Emirates
3-4	EyeforTravel: Revenue Management & Pricing in Travel, Las Vegas, USA
6-9	Indaba 2006, Durban, South Africa
17-19	2nd Kyrgyzstan International Travel & Tourism Exhibition, Bishkek, Kyrgyzstan
19-21	ITEX 2006, Kuala Lumpur, Malaysia
25-29	IGLTA (International Gay & Lesbian Travel Association) World Convention, Washington, DC, USA
30-Jun 1	IMEX 2006 (Worldwide Exhibition for Incentive Travel, Meetings & Events), Frankfurt, Germany

JUNE 2006

5-6	EyeforTravel: Travel Distribution Summit Europe, London, UK
6-7	AIME, Melbourne, Australia
12-14	ITT Annual Conference, Muscat, Oman
15-18	20th International Travel Expo, Hong Kong (SAR), China (PR)
17-27	Australia Tourism Exchange, Adelaide, Australia
20-22	LACIME 2006: Latin America & Caribbean Incentive & Meetings Exhibition, Sao Paulo, Brazil
22-23	5th International Symposium on Aspects of Tourism, Eastbourne, UK
22-24	Beijing International Tourism Expo, Beijing, China (PR)

JULY 2006

16-19	NBTA International Convention Exposition, Chicago, USA
19-22	92nd Annual Convention, Destination Marketing Association International (formerly IACVB), Texas, USA

AUGUST 2006

27-Sep 1	AIEST 2006 (56th Congress), Moscow, Russia

SEPTEMBER 2006

5-7	Mediterranean Travel Fair (MTF), Cairo, Egypt
5-7	Business Travel Show, Dusseldorf, Germany
6-8	La Cumbre 2006, The Americas Summit, Houston, USA
10-13	The Trade Show, Orlando, USA
12-15	PATA Travel Mart, Hong Kong (SAR), China
19-23	51st Annual IFEA Convention & Expo, Ottawa, Canada
21-23	Top Resa Deauville: Travel & Tourism Trade Show, Deauville, France

21-24	14th International Travel Show, Warsaw, Poland
22-24	JATA World Travel Fair, Tokyo, Japan
27	World Tourism Day

OCTOBER 2006

4-5	EyeforTravel: Travel Distribution Summit USA, Chicago, USA
4-6	CIS Travel Market, St Petersburg, Russia
7-9	Envie De Partir, Paris, France
7-13	World Youth & Student Travel Conference, Melbourne, Australia
11-13	The International Hotel Conference, Rome, Italy
15-20	Skal International World Congress, Pattaya, Thailand
18-20	Seatrade Mediterranean Cruise & Ferry Convention, Naples, Italy
25-28	Tour Salon 2006 (International Exhibition of Tourism), Poznan, Poland
25-29	ABAV 2006 (The Fair of Americas), Rio de Janeiro, Brazil
29-Nov 1	ICCA Exhibition, Rhodes, Greece
30-Nov 1	45th ICCA Congress & Exhibition, Rhodes, Greece

NOVEMBER 2006

2-4	MADI Travel Trade, Prague, Czech Republic
2-5	Philoxenia 2006, Thessaloniki, Greece
3-7	NTA Annual Convention, Salt Lake City, USA
6-9	World Travel Market (WTM), London, UK
10-12	SITV Travel & Tourism Fair, Comar, France
10-12	12th Backpacker & Adventure Travel Expo, Sydney, Australia
20-2	International Golf Travel Market (IGTM), Andalucía, Spain
23-26	ABTA Convention, Athens, Greece
26-28	Arabian Tourism Bureau 2006 (ATB3), Damascus, Syria
28-30	EIBTM, Barcelona, Spain

DECEMBER 2006

11-14	International Luxury Travel Market (ILTM), Cannes, France

JANUARY 2007

1	International Fair for Holidays, Travel & Leisure, Vienna, Austria
9-14	Vakantiebeurs, Utrecht, The Netherlands
12-14	Adventure Travel & Sports Show, London, UK
12-15	ESPO, Zurich, Switzerland
18-21	ITF Slovakia Tour (International Travel Fair), Bratislava, Slovak Republic
31-Feb 4	FITUR International Tourism Trade Fair, Madrid, Spain
TBC	BTL (Lisboa Travel Market), Lisbon, Portugal

FEBRUARY 2007

2-3	Intourfest Moscow, Moscow, Russian Federation
7-11	Reisen Hamburg 2006, Hamburg, Germany
13-15	Business Travel Show, London, UK
TBC	Vacances, Sport et Loisirs (Travel Trade Fair), Geneva, Switzerland

MARCH 2007

14-15	BTTF (British Travel Trade Fair), Birmingham, UK
25-29	ASTA International Destination Expo, JeJu Island, Korea
TBC	Salon Mondial du Tourisme, Versailles, France
TBC	4rd International Institute for Peace through Tourism Summit, Pattaya, Thailand

Weather

The following gives an indication of the way in which weather conditions affect people. The comfort or discomfort felt in different conditions depends on temperature, humidity and wind. For information on specific weather conditions in each country, see the relevant country entry.

Humidity

Humidity, expressed as a percentage, is the amount of moisture in the air. A relative humidity of 100 per cent is the maximum possible moisture content held at any given temperature. As air can hold more moisture at greater heat, so 100 per cent humidity at 26°C (79°F) holds more moisture than 100 per cent humidity at 10°C (50°F). Low humidity results in rapid evaporation; perspiration evaporates easily and wet clothes dry quickly. Such conditions prevail in hot and dry climates, where one experiences far less discomfort and can endure relatively high temperatures. In a hot climate with high humidity conditions, perspiration cannot evaporate easily and clothes dry slowly. One feels hot and uncomfortable as heat loss through perspiration is minimised. A breeze can sometimes relieve the discomfort associated with high humidity. Below freezing point the air can hold very little moisture and humidity has little effect. Although damp (raw) cold is less pleasant than dry cold in temperatures above freezing point, wind is a more important factor.

Wind

One feels cooler in wind because air movement around the body has the effect of carrying body heat away. In hot weather the body temperature is regulated chiefly by the evaporation of perspiration. When the air temperature exceeds normal skin temperature (about 34°C; 93°F), in a dry climate, the cooling power of wind becomes critical. In low temperatures, the wind speed is equally critical. A temperature of 0°C (32°F) with a wind speed of 50kmph (30mph) feels colder than the lower temperature of -20°C (4°F) in calm conditions. High wind speeds can increase the risk of frostbite. Many regions have particular winds which occur at certain times of the day or seasons of the year, and there are general rules; for instance, winds generally drop at night and increase by day (especially on the coast). Wind speed almost always increases with altitude. However, average wind statistics are almost impossible to supply, although forecasts are given in some countries, such as the USA, on TV and radio or in newspapers.

Wind-chill factor

Wind-chill factor does not indicate actual temperature; rather, it gives an indication of outdoor conditions by estimating the temperature a suitably dressed person would feel outside. It can be deduced from wind speeds and average temperatures. In less extreme conditions, a sunny day will produce extra warmth. The rate of heat loss from the body can be measured in kilogram calories per square metre of body surface per hour. The wind-chill factor is often given in weather bulletins.

Temperature range

This can be estimated by measuring the difference between the maximum and minimum temperatures, which usually occur just after midday and just before dawn. In cloudy, rainy areas, the range may be quite small, but in very sunny, dry climates such as deserts or mountainous regions, there may be a large range with surprisingly cold nights. As a general rule, the greatest range is inland and the lowest on the coast.

Precipitation

Precipitation includes all forms of moisture falling on the ground (rain, snow, sleet, hail or fog drip). Generally, this is rain, but on high mountains, or in countries with very cold winters such as Canada, the Russian Federation and parts of China (PR), Scandinavia and the USA, it may well fall as snow. All forms are measured as the melted equivalent of rain, with one foot of snow being roughly equivalent to one inch of rain. Generally, below 2°C (36°F), snow or sleet are as likely as rain. At freezing point or below, snow is most likely. Rain falling below freezing point, although rare, is very dangerous, especially on roads.

Precautions

Height above sea level: The general fall in temperature is at the rate of 0.6°C for every 100m (1°F for every 300ft), especially in cloud. Higher altitudes can also mean a wide range of day and nighttime temperatures. Atmosphere becomes thinner over 1800m (6000ft), the sun's rays are more powerful, and breathing and exertion become more difficult. Adequate clothing should always be taken when walking or climbing.

Heat

In high temperatures the body keeps cool by sweating. However, if the humidity is too low or evaporation is increased by wind, the body may not sweat fast enough to match the rate of evaporation. In such conditions the risk of heat exhaustion or heatstroke increases.
Heat exhaustion: Symptoms are loss of appetite, lassitude and general discomfort, with possible hallucinations and vomiting. The sufferer should be moved to a cool place and made to drink salty water to replace moisture and salt lost in perspiration.
Heatstroke: When the body's cooling mechanism stops, the body becomes dry and temperature rises. The symptoms are burning sensations and dry skin followed by feverishness, sometimes developing into headache and confusion. Immediate medical attention is essential as heatstroke may be fatal. The patient should be cooled as fast as possible, preferably put in a cool place,

splashed with cold or iced water, wrapped in a wet sheet with a fan directed onto the body; vigorous massage can also help. Prevention: In a very hot country, do not over-exert until after about a week's acclimatisation, especially after air travel. (Air conditioning delays the process of acclimatisation.) Drink plenty of liquids (not too much alcohol) and take salt. Avoid sunburn and wear light, comfortable clothing.

Cold

Body heat can be generated by physical activity and maintained by wearing suitable clothing. The danger occurs if one stops moving, becomes tired or if one remains in a strong wind below freezing point.
Hypothermia: Also known as 'exposure'. The body temperature falls, which can be fatal. Risks of hypothermia usually occur through lack of adequate clothing in mountainous regions or at sea, especially at night and if clothes become wet (evaporation from wet clothing causes the body to lose heat more rapidly). Rain and snow with a strong wind increases the danger; old people are particularly susceptible. Hypothermia becomes critical at a very low level of body temperature, around 25°-28°C (77°-82°F). The body should be re-warmed rapidly, preferably in a bath of 40°-45°C (104°-113°F). Artificial respiration and cardiac massage are required if breathing has stopped.
Frostbite: Affects flesh exposed to extreme cold, usually the face, hands and feet. The flesh freezes and this can result in a loss of limbs. The affected parts should be re-warmed slowly as soon as possible, preferably in water no hotter than 40°-44°C (104°-111°F). Do not bandage, massage or rub frostbitten skin.

Climate Graph Conversions

Easy-to-use and informative climate charts are provided within each country's entry.

Health

The health of travellers abroad may not be protected by services and legislation well-established at home. Changes in food and water may bring unexpected problems, as may insects and insect-borne diseases, especially in hot countries. Few have at their fingertips the current detailed knowledge needed to advise those travelling to a particular country, and personal reminiscences may not always reflect current or common problems. A danger of generalising is that it may be forgotten, for example, that malaria is a risk in Turkey, poliomyelitis occurs in Europe, and hepatitis A virus occurs worldwide and is not destroyed by many methods of purifying drinking water. Specific advice on which diseases are present in countries to be visited is likely to be complicated. A practical starting point for the traveller seeking advice is to consider which diseases can be prevented by immunisation, prophylactic tablets, or other measures, and decide whether it is appropriate to do so.

An unpredictable environment is especially a problem for the overland traveller who plans their own journey and needs greater knowledge of disease prevention and management than the traveller in an aeroplane or on a sea cruise, whose environment, food and drink are largely in the hands of the operator. Unforeseen changes in timetables may lead to stays in accommodation that are not of the expected standard. Delays at airports can take place in overcrowded and unhygienic conditions, where the facilities have not kept pace with increased demand and insect-borne diseases may also be contracted. Jet lag and exhaustion may prompt a traveller to take risks with food and drink. More experienced travellers tend to have fewer health problems. Better planning, immunisation and experience in prevention may all play a part, as well as salutary lessons learnt on previous occasions.

A questionnaire survey of returning travellers (most of whom had been to Europe, especially the Mediterranean countries) showed that half had had diarrhoea or respiratory symptoms while abroad. Excessive alcohol, sun and late nights can add to the problems. About one in 100 package holidaymakers who take out a health insurance policy make a claim. Diarrhoea and sunburn are principal reasons but accidents are also common. Injuries occur especially in and around swimming pools, to pedestrians forgetting that traffic drives on the opposite side to home, and from unfamiliar equipment such as gates on lifts. Sexually transmitted diseases are a big problem in certain destinations and cases could require urgent treatment. Long-stay travellers may adapt to these initial problems but then find themselves suffering from diseases endemic in their chosen country, such as malaria, hepatitis, diarrhoea and skin problems. Two per cent of British Voluntary Service overseas personnel contract hepatitis A within eight months if they are not protected. Car accidents occur while driving on non-metal roads, and some emotional problems may be resolved only by an early return home.

The traveller should be insured against medical expenses and most policies include the cost of emergency repatriation where appropriate. Such insurance, however, rarely covers a service overseas that is similar to that available at home. Language and administrative differences are likely to present problems. Leaflet T6, issued annually by the Department of Health, describes the free or reduced-cost medical treatments available in other countries and the documents (passport, NHS medical card, European Health Insurance Card - EHIC) that the traveller has to have with them. Reciprocal arrangements between countries differ and fees may have to be paid and then reclaimed in the visited country itself, which can be time-consuming. Extra provision should be made for such emergencies. Any reciprocal arrangement between the UK and a country is mentioned in each country's entry. The EHIC, which replaced form E111 in January 2006, is needed in some countries of the European Union. Only a 'small' supply of medicines for personal use may be taken out of the UK, unless Home Office permission is obtained.

Immunisation

Yellow Fever

This disease is caused by a virus that circulates in animals indigenous to certain tropical forested areas. It mainly infects monkeys, but if a person enters these areas the virus may be transmitted to them by mosquitoes whose normal hosts are monkeys: this is jungle yellow fever. It occurs haphazardly and is clearly related to a person's habits. If, from an animal source, the virus begins to circulate between a person and his own mosquitoes, primarily Aedes aegypti, epidemics of urban yellow fever result. Immunisation protects the individual and is effective in preventing the spread of the virus to countries where Aedes aegypti is prevalent. It is therefore reasonable for such countries to request a certificate of vaccination from all travellers from areas where human cases are occurring. Many national administrations, however, require immunisation of all travellers over one year of age from all countries, or else all travellers over one year from countries where endemic (enzootic) foci occur. A map indicating yellow fever endemic zones can be found in this appendix. Immunisation is clearly not required when travelling outside the enzootic zones. Within the zones, if it is not compulsory, it is not always necessary. For instance, in the absence of an epidemic of yellow fever, a business trip within the confines of Nairobi would be perfectly safe. Nevertheless, local and current knowledge of cases is required for such decisions to be made, so, in practice, immunisation is recommended to all travellers within enzootic zones. Immunisation in the UK is undertaken only at recognised yellow fever vaccination centres. A current list of vaccination centres within the UK can be found online: (website: www.info.doh.gov.uk/doh/yellcode.nsf/pages/Help?open). Once immunised (a single vaccination is used), the vaccination certificate becomes valid for 10 years after 10 days. It is not recommended for pregnant women and children under nine months of age.

Cholera

IIn 1973, the World Health Organization (WHO), recognising that immunisation cannot stop the spread of cholera among countries, deleted the requirement of cholera immunisation as a condition of admission to any country from the International Health Regulations. In 1990, the WHO stated that immunisation against cholera was ineffective and not recommended. In 1991, the WHO confirmed that certification was no longer required by any country or territory. For a small number of countries, however, a cholera vaccination certificate is still a condition of entry; in this case, advice should be sought from a medical professional.

Typhoid Fever

Typhoid fever is endemic worldwide and is usually spread faecal-orally. The risk of infection is increased in areas of high carriage rates and poor hygiene. The risk is not significantly increased for the traveller to areas with public health standards similar to those of the UK - namely Australia, Canada, northern Europe, Japan, New Zealand and the USA - and immunisation for these areas is not necessary. Outside these areas the risks reflect not only local hygiene and carriage rates but also lifestyle. Travelling or living rough, living in rural areas, or 'eating out' makes transmission more likely. The risks are therefore small for the air traveller with full board at a reputable hotel, and immunisation is unnecessary. On the other hand, overland travel to Australia would be a clear indication for immunisation. Between these extremes there are many circumstances for which risks cannot be precisely defined. Typhoid vaccination is now no longer routinely recommended for the millions of tourists to southern Europe each year, although it may still be advisable, not only for those whose lifestyle or occupation increase the risk of such exposure, but also during local outbreaks.

Hepatitis A

The hepatitis A virus is endemic worldwide and spread faecal-orally. Protection from symptomatic infection can be provided by active immunisation or passively acquired immunoglobulin. The virus circulates freely in our own population however, and many travellers will be immune already. Protection should be offered to the same groups as are offered typhoid immunisation, as exposure to one infection would imply the risk of exposure to the other. The recurrent tropical traveller may have his antibodies against hepatitis A checked. If antibodies are present, that person is immune. If antibodies are absent, inactivated hepatitis A vaccine should be given. Hepatitis A in children is usually mild and more often asymptomatic, so immunisation is not essential. Hepatitis A vaccine is available for use in children over the age of 12 months.

Poliomyelitis

A survey undertaken in Scotland in 1989 showed that 20 per cent of the tested population did not have antibodies to all three serotypes of poliovirus. Hence a consultation about travel abroad is an opportunity to complete primary courses or boost immunisations that are nationally recommended. Although the number of polomyelitis cases has fallen greatly worldwide, some vaccine-derived outbreaks have recently developed and immunisation is still advised. Oral poliomyelitis vaccine is given, but supplies of inactivated polio vaccine are available if oral vaccine is contraindicated.

Tetanus

As with poliomyelitis, all individuals should gain or maintain immunity to tetanus. It is firmly recommended for life in the UK, as well as for travel abroad. A preparation combined with low-dose diphtheria toxoid is recommended for travellers when immunity requires boosting.

Special Rare Diseases

Avian Flu

As of 13 February 2006, 169 people have caught the disease and of these 91 have died. Human cases have been confirmed in Vietnam, Thailand, Cambodia, Indonesia, China, Iraq and Turkey.

In a bid to prevent the spread of the virus, millions of birds in the affected countries have been culled.

WHO is now very concerned that the disease may mutate into a form that is more easily transmitted between humans. Governments around the world are being urged to prepare contingency plans in case of an outbreak.

SARS

Severe Acute Respiratory Syndrome (SARS) is a respiratory illness caused by a novel coronavirus (SARS-CoV). It began in Guangdong Province, China (PR), in November 2002. The disease was first recognised in Asia in February 2003, and spread to more than two-dozen countries in Asia, Europe and North and South America over the following months. There were over 8000 confirmed cases of the disease and international travel was a significant factor in the worldwide spread of the disease. There have been no reported cases since early in 2004 and experts announced in February 2005 that another SARS outbreak on the scale of that in 2002-03 is highly unlikely. Nevertheless, travellers should pay attention to reports of any further outbreaks. Additionally, it would be prudent for travellers to China to avoid visiting live food markets and avoid direct contact with civets and other wildlife from these markets.

SARS is an airborne illness and can be transmitted from person to person. The incubation period for SARS is typically two to seven days. The illness generally begins with a prodrome of fever. The fever is often high, sometimes associated with chills and rigors and might be accompanied by other symptoms such as headache, malaise, and muscle pain. At the onset of illness, some persons have mild respiratory symptoms. After three to seven days, a lower respiratory phase begins with the onset of a dry, non-productive cough. In 10 to 20 per cent of cases, the respiratory illness is severe enough to require hospitalisation and mechanical ventilation. The severity of illness is highly variable, ranging from mild illness to death. To date, there is no available immunisation against the coronavirus/SARS.

BSE

Bovine Spongiform Encephalopathy (BSE) is an illness caused by an unconventional transmissible agent, causing fatal brain disease with unusually long incubation periods, measured in years. Strong evidence has accumulated indicating a causal relationship between BSE or 'mad cow disease' and a disease in humans called variant Creutzfeldt-Jakob disease (vCJD). BSE in cattle caused a huge epidemic in the UK, with over 180,000 cases reported since 1987, with a peak in 1992.

Bioassays have identified the BSE agent in the brain, spinal cord, retina, distal root ganglia, ileum and bone marrow of cattle experimentally infected orally. To reduce any risk of acquiring vCJD from food, travellers to Europe, the UK, and other areas with indigenous cases of BSE, may consider avoiding beef and beef products altogether.

The current risk of acquiring vCJD from eating beef (muscle meat), and beef products produced from cattle in countries with a possible increased risk of BSE, cannot be determined precisely.

Sporadic cases of BSE were reported in many countries in Europe, including in the UK, and a few outside Europe, in 2005.

Rabies

Most doctors do not think it necessary to immunise the average traveller visiting areas where rabies is endemic, although this may be advisable for those in remote areas who would be many days' travel away from a source of vaccine and rabies immunoglobulin if infected. However, all travellers should avoid contact with animals, especially cats and dogs. If they do get bitten, wounds should be promptly washed with copious soap and water followed by the application of alcohol (spirits like gin and whisky can be used). If the animal's owner is available, ask whether the animal has been vaccinated against rabies (check certification). A forwarding address or telephone number should be left to enable contact should the animal become unwell over the next two weeks. Seek local medical advice promptly and give details of the incident to local police. On return, the traveller's medical practitioner should be informed and further check-ups and treatment may be necessary.

Diphtheria

Diphtheria is endemic worldwide. Most morbidity and mortality occur in children and they should be immunised as nationally recommended (initial primary course and booster on school entry and school leaving). Adult travellers with a high risk of infection are those in contact with children in poorer areas – for example, health workers and teachers. Travellers may have their immunity boosted by a low-dose preparation of diphtheria toxoid. A preparation combined with tetanus toxoid is now also available.

Meningococcal Meningitis

Although the bacteria responsible for this illness circulates widely throughout the world, certain areas, like the dry areas bordering the southern Sahara, are renowned for recurrent epidemics and many areas suffer occasional epidemics, as in Brazil, India and Nepal. Immunisation is recommended for travellers to such areas with outbreaks, particularly those staying long-term. Travellers heading to remote areas should check for the latest disease outbreaks.

Tick-borne Encephalitis

Tick-borne encephalitis is caused by an arbovirus, transmitted by the bite of an infected tick. Its distribution is confined to warm and low-forested areas in parts of Central Europe and Scandinavia, particularly Austria, Czech Republic, Germany, Slovak Republic and throughout all the republics of the former Yugoslavia (Bosnia & Herzegovina, Croatia, Macedonia, Serbia & Montenegro and Slovenia). The forests are usually deciduous with heavy undergrowth. Those normally at risk are foresters and those clearing such areas, but increasing contact will occur with increased recreational use, such as camping and walking. Most human illness occurs in late-spring and early-summer. Tick bites are best avoided by limiting contact with such areas, wearing clothing to cover most of the skin surface and using insect repellents on outer clothes and socks. Where prolonged contact is necessary, a killed vaccine is essential.

Japanese B Encephalitis

This virus infection is transmitted by mosquitoes in certain rural areas of eastern Asia, the Indian subcontinent and a few Pacific islands. Occasional larger outbreaks develop and this infection tends to have a higher mortality rate than the many other similar viruses that can cause encephalitis. If planning to sleep in rural areas with a high risk or an active outbreak, immunisation should be considered; this is available from Sanofi Pasteur MSD (tel: (0800) 085 5511-freephone); website: www.apmsd.co.uk). Considerable protection is offered by avoiding mosquito bites (see the Malaria Prophylaxis section) and staying indoors at night in rural areas where known cases are occurring.

West Nile Virus

West Nile Virus is a rare infection spread by the bite of an infected mosquito. It can affect people, horses, many types of birds and some other animals. There is no evidence to suggest that West Nile Virus can be spread from person to person or directly from an animal to person.

There was a severe outbreak of the virus in the US in 2003, when there were 1764 reported human cases of West Nile Virus in 34 states. 31 of these cases were fatal.

In 2005, avian, animal or mosquito West Nile Virus infections as well as human cases were reported in many states.

It is best evaded by avoiding mosquito bites; use an insect repellent - preferably one containing DEET - on clothes or exposed skin.

Plague

Plague is an infection of wild rodents transmitted by fleas. It exists in many rural areas of Africa, Asia and the Americas. The risk to the traveller from the bite of an infected flea is low. Routine immunisation is not recommended. In enzootic areas (usually rural and hilly), contact with rodents should be discouraged by preventing their access to food and waste, avoiding dead rodents and rodent burrows. Fleas can be discouraged by insect repellents. The most recent outbreak was in the Democratic Republic of Congo in 2005. There is an incubation period of between three and seven days and persons usually show 'flu-like' symptoms. Early diagnosis and treatment is essential.

Hepatitis B

Vaccination should be considered for groups such as medical, nursing and laboratory staff planning to work among populations with high HBsAg carriage rates. The recommended regimen consists of three doses, the boosters given at one month and six months after the initial dose. Immunity is predicted to last about five years but those at high risk should have antibodies checked three months after completion of course. Quicker regimens are used but are less effective and should be boosted again at six to 12 months. A combined hepatitis A and B vaccine is available.

Other Considerations

HIV

People infected with HIV (human immunodeficiency virus), who may appear perfectly well, pass on the infection by sexual intercourse or if their blood is inoculated into other people, as in the sharing of needles by drug users, the transfusion of untested blood, or the reuse of injection needles without sterilisation between patients. Certain areas of the world, such as parts of tropical Africa, Asia and South America have a higher number of carriers of HIV. However, the potential for infection exists worldwide and precautions should always be taken, whether at home or abroad. The use of condoms and spermicidal cream during sexual intercourse should reduce the level of risk. Thought must also be given to the need for blood transfusions, where blood is not tested for HIV antibodies, and the need for injections where there is doubt about the sterility of the needles (these may be sterilised by placing in boiling water for 20 minutes). Kits containing appropriate needles and syringes are available. Travellers should know their blood group. The World Health Organization (WHO) is vigorously opposed to any country requiring travellers to present a certificate stating that they are free from HIV infection. Besides being against International Health Regulations, it is both clinically unsound and epidemiologically unjustifiable as a means of limiting infection. However, at least 40 countries have introduced restrictions, such as compulsory HIV testing or refusal of entry for 'suspicious' visitors, though mostly those planning to stay, work or study long-term.

Malaria Prophylaxis

Malaria is widespread in tropical and subtropical areas of the world and is spread by the bite of a female anopheline mosquito that has been infected by the malaria parasite. The increasing mobility of the population, especially through air travel, brings a further hazard since travellers may be bitten by mosquitoes at airports en route as well as in the countries where they stay. The speed of travel means that first symptoms may occur in a country and in a context where the disease will not be immediately considered. Mosquitoes may even be brought by aeroplanes to non-endemic areas and infect, for example, airport staff or travellers' relatives. Infection also occurs through blood transfusion (cold storage does not destroy the parasites) and the sharing of needles by drug users.

The life-threatening form of malaria is caused by Plasmodium falciparum. Because of the travelling habits of those living in the UK, this form of malaria is usually imported from Africa, but also from Asia. Prevention is primarily aimed at this parasite. Nevertheless, the same advice is given to those likely to be exposed to the less dangerous P vivax, P malariae and P ovale, partly to prevent an unpleasant illness but also because P falciparum infection can never be presumed to be absent in any malarious area. There is no immediate prospect of an effective vaccine, so regular ingestion of prophylactic tablets is necessary. This requires habits that some find difficult or even distasteful, and because of increasing resistance to these tablets, they can no longer guarantee protection from illness. Bites must be avoided or reduced (see below) and any flu-like illness with fever and shivers lasting more than two days should be promptly diagnosed. If such symptoms develop after return, even months afterwards, the attending doctor should be reminded of the date and place of travel.

Note: A map showing areas of malarial risk and areas where chloroquine resistance has been reported is printed in this appendix (source: WHO, Geneva).

Personal precautions against malaria:

- Avoid mosquito bites, especially after sunset, when the anopheline mosquitoes responsible for transmitting malaria are most active. Long trousers, sleeves and dresses, netting on windows, and mosquito nets over beds help to prevent mosquito bites.
- Insect repellents may be used on exposed skin, and insecticides inside buildings or on breeding sites. Repellent-impregnated wrist and ankle bands, and electrical insecticide vaporisers may also be used.
- Mosquitoes should not be encouraged to breed by leaving stagnant water – for example, in blocked drains or around plant pots.
- Prophylactic tablets are necessary because the above measures, although valuable, are unlikely to be fully effective.

Precautions against malaria before travel:

- Start most tablets two weeks before departure to confirm tolerance and obtain adequate blood concentrations before exposure.
- Take the tablets with absolute regularity, according to the doctor's instructions. Prophylactic doses of drugs are not normally curative should infection get established.
- Prophylaxis is usually continued for four weeks after leaving an endemic area, though the new antimalarial, Malarone, only needs to be taken for one week after leaving such areas. All forms of the parasite develop first in the liver and only later re-enter the blood, where most prophylactic drugs take effect.
- Seek advice on which type of tablet to take from an advice centre (see table).

Deep Vein Thrombosis (DVT)

Travelling which involves any long periods of inactivity, either by land or air, can cause deep vein thrombosis (DVT) in predisposed individuals. This is when a blood clot (thrombus) forms within a vein that accompanies an artery (deep vein) and remains there. This, in turn, leads to a risk of pulmonary embolus (PE), where the clot travels from its original site to another part of the body, which can be potentially life threatening.

There are some identifiable groups of people who are at an increased risk of DVT. These include people who have:

- A previous history of DVT/PE
- Obesity
- Recently had major surgery
- Congestive heart failure
- Malignant disease
- Paralysis of the legs
- Pregnant women
- Women taking oral contraception

The risks can be reduced by frequently exercising the lower limbs and walking whenever possible, taking deep-breathing exercises and preventing dehydration by drinking lots of water and avoiding excess alcohol or caffeine.

Children

As children begin to crawl and walk they become more vulnerable to faecal-oral infections and hazards such as bites, accidents and burns. Open wounds should be kept clean and covered with dressings until healed. Deaths from scorpion bites are unusual but mostly occur in children under two years of age. Allowing toddlers to play outside unattended can be particularly hazardous.

Taking adequate malarial prophylaxis should not encourage the traveller to ignore the risks from other mosquito-borne diseases such as dengue fever, which can be more severe in children. Protection from mosquito bites is also important in those children who are strongly allergic to them. Appropriate clothes and bed or window netting at night are usually more valuable in the long term than insect repellents.

Pregnancy

Live vaccinations are best not given during pregnancy, although if someone unprotected against yellow fever is going to live in a high-risk area, the theoretical risk of vaccination is outweighed by the serious nature of the illness. If the vaccine is not given, a doctor's letter endorsed with a health board or authority stamp to say the inoculation is contraindicated is usually accepted. Inactivated poliomyelitis vaccine may be used instead of oral live vaccine.

A mother immunised against tetanus passes on protection to her baby over the neonatal period and a booster can be given during pregnancy if necessary. Hepatitis A in pregnancy may be more severe and also result in premature labour. Prevention is generally encouraged for those at risk. Malarial prophylaxis should be maintained throughout pregnancy but the risks of some drugs have to be balanced against the type of malaria and likelihood of its transmission in different areas; specialist advice should be sought.

Contraception

Those using oral contraceptives should be aware that absorption could be affected during gastrointestinal illnesses, that some brands may not be available locally, and that they may be continued over the usual break in the cycle if menstruation is going to occur at an inconvenient time, such as during a long journey. They may contribute to the fluid retention that some people experience in hot climates. Reliable condoms are not available in all localities abroad.

QUICK GUIDE TO VACCINATION/PROPHYLAXIS
Requirements & Programmes

When time permits, immunisation should be started well in advance so that adequate intervals between doses can be maintained. If notice to travel is short, a rapid course or single dose may be given but the immunity provided will not be as effective. Children should be up-to-date with the routine UK vaccination schedule. Extra consideration should be given to the need for vaccinating pregnant women. If it is known that a full initial (primary) course of any of these vaccines has been given, then only single booster doses are necessary.

Against	No. of injections in primary course (inc. period of protection)	Validity of certificate	Revaccination	Other details
Yellow Fever	1 injection gives protection for 10 years.	10 days after inoculation for 10 years.	Every 10 years validity taking immediate effect.*	Reactions to vaccination are rare, although some discomfort might be experienced. Not for infants under 9 months or pregnant women.
Diphtheria	If over 10 years, 3 doses of low-dose vaccine at monthly intervals. Usually given as DTP to children under 10 years.	Not applicable.	Low-dose booster combined with tetanus toxoid every 10 years.	Only mild reactions expected.
Typhoid Fever				
(a) Vi vaccine	1 injection.	Not applicable.	Single booster every 3 years.	Only mild local and systemic reactions. Not for children under 18 months of age. A combined preparation with Hepatitis A vaccine is now available.
(b) Oral	1 capsule on alternate days for 3 doses.	Not applicable.	Annual 3-dose booster for recurrent travellers.	Only mild reactions expected. To be kept refrigerated. Do not use with antibiotics within 12 hours of mefloquine, in pregnant or immuno-compromised, or concurrent oral polio vaccine. Not for children under 6 years of age. More expensive.
Hepatitis A	1 injection will provide protection for 6 months to 1 year	Not applicable.	Single booster at 6 months to 1 year can be expected to provide 10 years' protection.	Half-dose preparation now available for ages 1 to 15 years. Combined preparation vaccines are now available with Typhoid Vi or hepatitis A.
Poliomyelitis	3 oral doses given at 4 weekly intervals.	Not applicable.	Single booster every 10 years.	Different (inactivated) vaccine available for pregnant women.
Tetanus	3 injections given at 4 weekly intervals.	Not applicable.	Single booster every 10 years. Now combined with low-dose diphtheria toxoid to boost both.	Local tenderness, swelling and redness may occur.
Malaria	Tablets should be taken 2 weeks prior to departure and continued regularly while in malarial zone. It is essential to continue taking tablets for 4 weeks after leaving zone – except Malarone.	Not applicable.	Not applicable.	Pregnant women and newborn infants require special consideration. Malarone is effective when given for 2 days before, during, and only 7 days after travel. It is expensive and not licensed for trips longer than 4 weeks.

* If vaccination is recorded on a new certificate, travellers are advised to retain their old certificate until their new certificate is valid.

Publications

HEALTH ADVICE FOR TRAVELLERS (T7) – DEPARTMENT OF HEALTH

Available free online (website: www.dh.gov.uk/PolicyAndGuidance/HealthAdviceForTravellers/fs/en) or from the Department of Health, PO Box 777, London SE1 6XH, UK (tel: (08701) 555 455).

This is a yearly publication containing advice on how to reduce health risks, with a list, by country, of compulsory and recommended immunisations. It advises about travel insurance and entitlement to reduced-cost medical treatment for UK nationals in other countries.

INTERNATIONAL TRAVEL AND HEALTH – WORLD HEALTH ORGANIZATION, GENEVA

This lists, by country, compulsory immunisations and malaria risk, and gives the distribution by geographical area of other health risks with appropriate advice. Previously published as a handbook (last published 2005), the information is now available and frequently updated online (website: www.who.int/ith).

ABC OF HEALTHY TRAVEL (FIFTH EDITION)

E Walker, G Williams, F Raeside & L Calvert, British Medical Journal, 1997.

An easy-to-read guide to the health problems of travel, intended for the general practitioner and informed lay person.

HEALTH INFORMATION FOR INTERNATIONAL TRAVEL 2005-2006

Available from the Public Health Foundation, PO Box 753, Walford MD 20604, USA (tel: (877) 252 1200 (toll-free); website: http://bookstore.phf.org).

Although written primarily for healthcare providers, this book contains information that could be useful for any traveller.

ROUGH GUIDE TO TRAVEL HEALTH

2004, Rough Guides (website: www.roughguides.com).

Contains pre-planning information, safety tips for active travel and an A-Z Health section.

THE TRAVELLERS' GOOD HEALTH GUIDE 2nd Edition 2002

T Lankester, Sheldon Press.

Contains clear, concise information on all you need to know to stay healthy abroad.

YOUR CHILD'S HEALTH ABROAD – A MANUAL FOR TRAVELLING PARENTS (2ND EDITION)

Dr J W Howorth & Dr M Ellis, Bradt Publications, 2004.

A down-to-earth guide for anyone travelling overseas with children.

TRAVEL WITH CHILDREN (4TH EDITION)

Cathy Lanigan, 2002, Lonely Planet (website: www.lonelyplanet.com).

Contains practical information and tips for travelling with children.

LONELY PLANET HEALTHY TRAVEL GUIDES

Destination-specific pocket guides offering practical advice; see online (website: www.lonelyplanet.com).

STAYING HEALTHY IN ASIA, AFRICA AND LATIN AMERICA

D G Schroeder ScD, MPH, Moon Publications, 1995; updated 2000.

An informative handbook providing information on staying healthy whilst visiting, or living in, developing countries.

Advice Centres

Note: *Members of the public should be aware that personal medical advice cannot necessarily be obtained from organisations listed in this section. In many cases their own medical practitioner will be in the best position to take account of relevant personal factors. Where specialist advice is supplied to members of the public (very often for a fee), this has been noted. Some addresses, however, are provided to particularly assist professionals in the travel trade who wish to keep abreast of developments in the rapidly changing medical world.*

UNITED KINGDOM

DEPARTMENT OF HEALTH

Public Enquiries Office: Richmond House, 79 Whitehall, London SW1A 2NL

Tel: (020) 7210 4850. Minicom: (020) 7210 5025.

Website: www.dh.gov.uk.

Public Health Protection Agency: Website: www.phls.co.uk.

LONDON SCHOOL OF HYGIENE AND TROPICAL MEDICINE

Keppel Street, London WC1E 7HT

Main Switchboard: Tel: (020) 7636 8636.

Malaria Information Healthline: Tel: (09065) 508 908 (24 hours; calls cost £1 per minute).

Website: www.lshtm.ac.uk.

MEDICAL ADVISORY SERVICE FOR TRAVELLERS ABROAD –(MASTA)

Masta Travellers Healthline: Tel: (0906) 8224 100 (calls cost 60p per minute).

Validated by the London School of Hygiene and Tropical Medicine, this is a 24-hour, regularly updated advice line (with interactive technology) for travellers seeking information about vaccinations etc, in most countries and regions.

HOSPITAL FOR TROPICAL DISEASES (HTD)

Mortimer Market Centre, 2nd Floor, Capper Street, London WC1E 6AU

Tel: (020) 7387 9300 or 4411.

Website: www.thehtd.org.

Travellers Healthline Advisory Service: Tel: (09061) 337 733 (calls cost 50p per minute, which also links to a fax-back service costing £1.50 per minute). Fax: (09061) 991 992 (no fax modems; ordinary fax machines only).

MASTA TRAVEL LOCATION LINE

30 clinics nationwide.

Tel: (020) 7291 9333.

Website: www.masta.org

SCOTTISH CENTRE FOR INFECTION AND ENVIRONMENTAL HEALTH

Part of Health Protection Scotland (HPS).

Clifton House, Clifton Place, Glasgow G3 7LN

Travel Medicine Clinic: Tel: (0141) 300 1100.

Website: www.show.scot.nhs.uk/scieh/.

LIVERPOOL SCHOOL OF TROPICAL MEDICINE

Pembroke Place, Liverpool L3 5QA

Tel: (0151) 708 9393.

Website: www.liv.ac.uk/lstm.

NHS WALK-IN CENTRE

There are 66 walk-in centres nationwide; more are currently being developed.

Tel: 0845 4647 (NHS Direct).

Website: www.nhs.uk

DIABETES UK

10 Parkway, London NW1 7AA

Tel: (020) 7424 1000.

Website: www.diabetes.org.uk.

Issues leaflets and travel guides to the more popular countries with advice pertinent to the diabetic.

ROYAL ASSOCIATION FOR DISABILITY AND REHABILITATION (RADAR)

12 City Forum, 250 City Road, London EC1V 8AF

Tel: (020) 7250 3222. Minicom: (020) 7250 4119.

Website: www.radar.org.uk.

A wide range of leaflets and services are available to help disabled people arrange, insure and enjoy their travels. (See separate appendix in The Disabled Traveller.)

SWITZERLAND

WORLD HEALTH ORGANIZATION (WHO)

Avenue Appia 20, 1211 Geneva 27

Tel: (22) 791 2111.

Website: www.who.int.

USA

US DEPARTMENT OF HEALTH AND HUMAN SERVICES

200 Independence Avenue, SW, Washington, DC 20201

Tel: (202) 619 0257 or (877) 696 6775 (toll-free in the USA).

Website: www.os.dhhs.gov.

INTERNATIONAL ASSOCIATION FOR MEDICAL ASSISTANCE TO TRAVELLERS (IAMAT)

1623 Military Road, #279, Niagara Falls, NY 14304-1745

Tel: (716) 754 4883.

Website: www.iamat.org.

A non-profit organisation dedicated to the gathering and dissemination of health and hygiene information worldwide.

CENTER FOR DISEASE CONTROL AND PREVENTION (CDC)

National Center for Infectious Diseases: Mailstop C-14, 1600 Clifton Road, Atlanta, GA 30333.

Tel: (404) 639 3311 (information line) or 3534 (public enquiries) or (800) 311 3435.

Website: www.cdc.gov.

Travellers Health Section: Contact via online form; Website: www.cdc.gov/netinfo.htm

Website: www.cdc.gov/travel (general information).

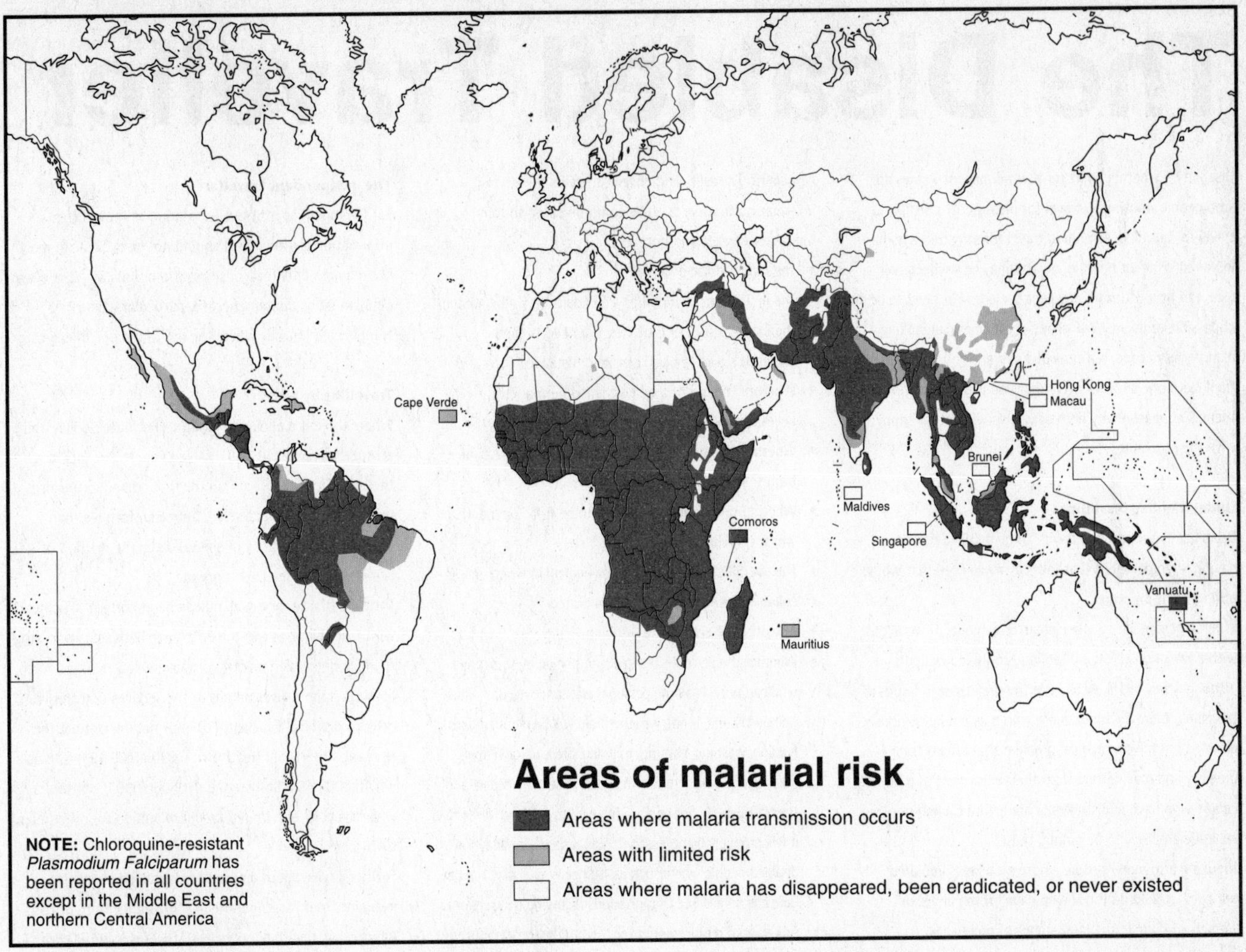

Areas of malarial risk

- ■ Areas where malaria transmission occurs
- ■ Areas with limited risk
- □ Areas where malaria has disappeared, been eradicated, or never existed

NOTE: Chloroquine-resistant *Plasmodium Falciparum* has been reported in all countries except in the Middle East and northern Central America

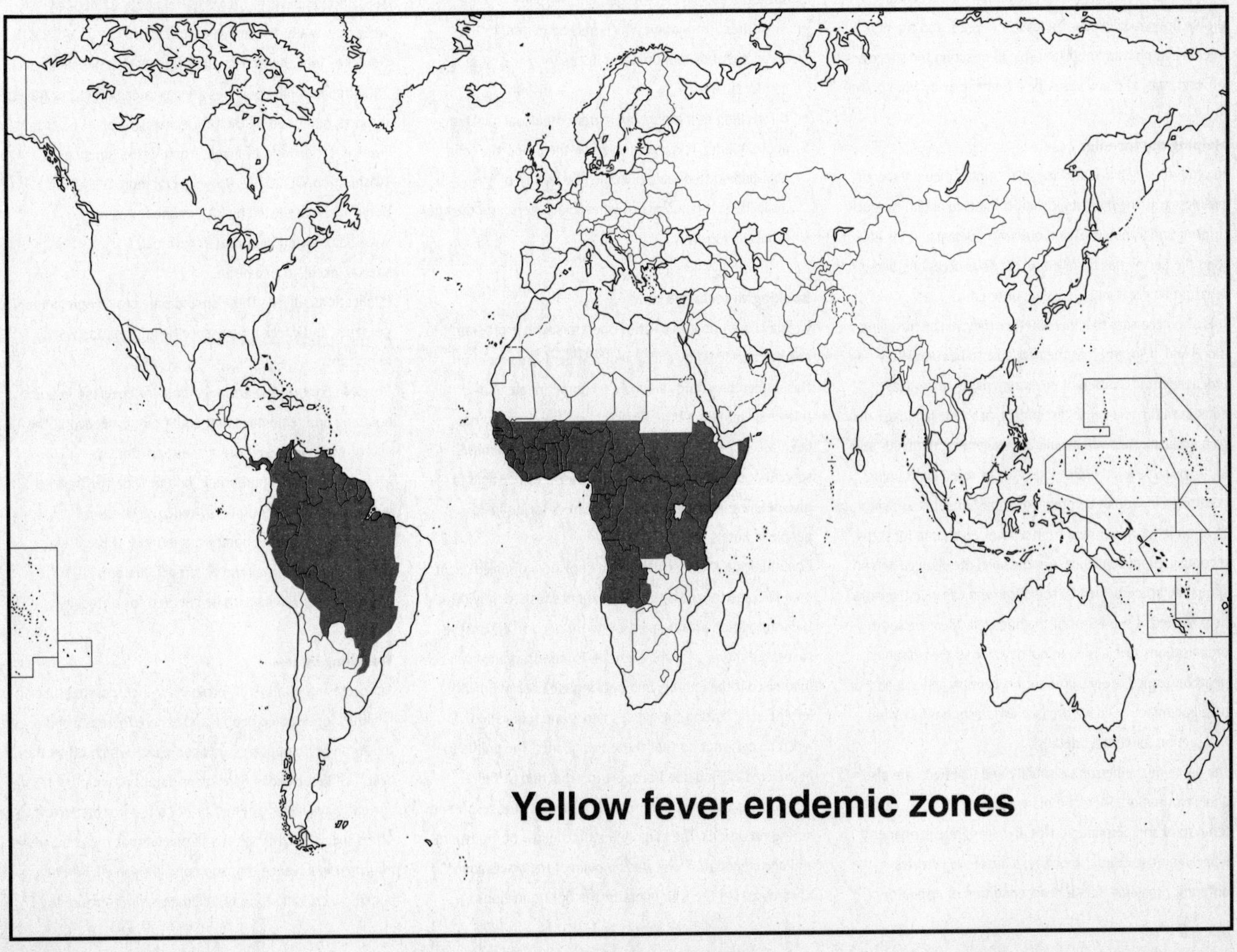

Cape Verde

Comoros

Maldives

Singapore

Hong Kong

Macau

Brunei

Mauritius

Vanuatu

Yellow fever endemic zones

The Disabled Traveller

Disability – whether short term or permanent – does not stop people wanting to travel for pleasure, or needing to travel for business. Arranging travel for someone who has impaired vision or hearing, or who may be a wheelchair user, can be a daunting prospect but does not need to be an impossible problem. Careful and sometimes painstaking planning is needed, but provided you and your client are frank with one another over what you can and cannot do, there is no reason why both of you should not be happy with the outcome.

Understanding disability

Disability can take many forms: to be disabled means having an impairment that takes away abilities that would otherwise be enjoyed.

When a person uses a wheelchair, or can only move about with a walking aid, their disability is only too evident. Although they are likely to have the greatest difficulties in travelling, there are many more who may not be obviously disabled but have a medical problem that affects their mobility and may detract from their enjoyment of a holiday. People who have had strokes or are arthritic, blind or epileptic are likely to be among these.

There are also many people whose mobility is impaired temporarily, such as those who have broken limbs, or women who are in the later stages of pregnancy. Opportunities and choice for the disabled traveller have grown dramatically over the past few years, and travel agents can play an important role in ensuring the success of what may, in many cases, be a first trip away from home.

Helping the traveller

In order to help a disabled traveller to plan their holiday or business trip, the most important thing is to obtain as much information as possible. Find out when, where and for how long the person has travelled on previous occasions, and what problems, if any, were encountered.

It is also necessary to know whether they will be travelling alone and, if so, whether they are able to be completely independent in a different environment, an unfamiliar climate that could cause discomfort, or where language may be a problem. Help will usually be available at terminals and in hotels but should not be expected or relied upon unless confirmed in writing beforehand. Sometimes it is sufficient to arrange for minor help from a hotel, eg a ramp for steps. If complete independence is impossible, the disabled person should be accompanied by someone who can give the extra help needed. If this is out of the question, there are some organisations specialising in holidays for severely disabled unaccompanied people, both in this country and abroad. For details, contact Holiday Care (see *Organisations* following this section for contact details).

The name of the person's disability and its effects are also vital information. There are many kinds of disability, both temporary and permanent. Not all necessitate permanent wheelchair use or limit mobility; a broken leg creates different problems than a heart condition or respiratory complaint. The following checklist covers the kind of information that needs to be communicated to tour operators, carriers and hoteliers:

- The name of the disability
- The limitations to mobility – eg ability to walk unaided, the use of a stick or crutches, the need to hold someone's arm to help over long distances
- Whether the use of a wheelchair is permanent, necessary most of the time, or for distance only
- Whether transfer from a wheelchair into a coach, air or train seat is easy or difficult
- Whether one or both legs need to be fully extended whilst travelling
- The overall dimensions of the wheelchair, whether it is collapsible and if it is battery operated
- Any other effects of the disability
- Whether the person is being accompanied by someone who can provide all the personal assistance needed whilst on holiday and, if not, whether help will be required with feeding, washing, bathing, toileting, dressing or simply pushing the wheelchair. If this kind of help is needed, and the traveller will not be accompanied by a friend or relative, it will probably be necessary to join a special holiday for disabled people where such assistance is available: Holiday Care has details (see Organisations following this section)
- Any special requirements for the holiday or the journey, such as a special diet, oxygen or other aids
- Any other information which may be helpful to the travel agent or tour operator in ensuring the most comfortable trip
- If travelling as a group, apart from the usual questions about budget, it is useful to know the proportion of able-bodied to disabled people; the nature of the disabilities; the number of wheelchair users; and the age groups involved

Booking an inclusive tour

Holiday Care provides a list of operators whose programmes can be considered by a disabled traveller (some mention this in their brochures and give a contact name and telephone number). If a particular country or resort has been asked for, the service can tell you which operators serve that destination and, in some cases, will be able to give detailed information about facilities for disabled people in hotels there.

Communication is essential when booking a disabled client on a package tour. It is the travel agent's task to provide all the information a tour operator might need to ensure the success of the trip for the client. Misunderstandings will be minimised if the enquiry and booking are backed up with a letter clearly stating the client's needs and requesting written confirmation that these can be met. The points to be covered will include transport to, from and at the destination; accommodation; and facilities at the resort and during excursions. The paragraphs that follow on transport and accommodation will also help direct the travel agent towards asking the tour operator the right questions.

The independent traveller

For the independent traveller, as long as the necessary information is available, it should not be difficult to meet the requirements for a business trip or holiday – but every detail must be double-checked, particularly on a complicated journey where the risk of a problem is greater.

Travelling by air

Where there is a choice of airlines, check their policy and attitude towards carrying disabled people; the facilities they have for them (both on the ground and in the air); the type of aircraft (some are more comfortable than others); the availability of special diets; the method of boarding and disembarkation; etc.

The time of day for travelling can be important to someone with a disability, as can the difference between a non-stop flight or one which involves stopovers.

Each UK airport gives details of the services that they can offer to disabled travellers. For information, contact the relevant airport (tel: Heathrow: (0870) 0000 123; Gatwick: (0870) 0002 468; Stansted: (0870) 0000 303; website: www.baa.com; see *United Kingdom* section for other main UK airports).

Further advice about air travel for disabled people is available from Passenger Medical Clearance Unit, British Airways Plc, Health Services (HMAG), Waterside, PO Box 365, Harmondsworth UB7 0GB (tel: (020) 8738 5444; website: www.britishairways.com/health).

Details of facilities and services for disabled people at over 280 airports in 40 countries are contained in Access Travel; Airports, published by the US Department of Transportation, and available from Access America, Washington, DC 20202, USA. Several more relevant publications are listed by BAA online (website: www.baa.com/main/airports/heathrow/special_needs_frame.html).

Publications such as these should only provide preliminary guidance and checking any specific information is still important.

Check to confirm the arrangements for checking in and boarding and remember that equal care is needed at the end of the journey; ensure any airport transfer arrangements are appropriate, and provide the traveller with the telephone numbers needed to confirm arrangements for the homeward journey. If there is a change in the time, airline or airport, the new arrangements will have to be checked for suitability.

Travelling by sea

An increasing number of ferries have incorporated special facilities for disabled people and, where there is a choice of routes and/or companies, you can check which offers the best facilities. Holiday Care keeps details of what is currently available; whether or not a ferry or hovercraft offers special facilities, it is still crucial that the company is informed in advance that someone is disabled. When booking a crossing for a disabled passenger, ensure the company knows the nature of the disability and the sort of help needed during the journey.

Cruises can be especially attractive to older and disabled people, and most shipping lines offering cruises or fly/cruises are used to carrying disabled passengers. However, the following potential problems should be considered:

- A cruise may not be feasible for someone who cannot walk at all and is unaccompanied
- Shore excursions may not be possible, especially if tendering is involved and passengers have to board launches
- Coaches on shore excursions are unlikely to have any special facility for a disabled person
- Bad weather can be distressing for everyone, but especially so for someone not too steady on their feet or a wheelchair user

When booking a wheelchair user on a cruise, obtain the following information before making definite reservations:

- Width of lift floors and whether they offer access to all parts of the ship
- Width of cabin and toilet/bathroom doors; whether the doors open outwards and, if not, whether they block the plumbing; whether any existing steps at the doorways can be ramped temporarily
- Whether any cabins have an extra basin in the room to save some trips to the bathroom; where they are located; how much they cost; and their location in relation to lifts, etc
- Whether a wheelchair user is excluded from any part of the ship because of stairs, narrow doorways or other obstacles
- Which excursions ashore require a launch to be used and whether help would be available if the stairs down to the launch cannot be used; whether the gangplank used by passengers is too steep for a wheelchair user; and whether the one used by the crew is any lower and could be used instead
- What special arrangements might be needed at the beginning and end of the cruise
- Any restrictions on the type of wheelchair used
- Availability of laundry and/or launderette facilities

Travelling by road and rail

The provision of facilities for disabled travellers in coaches, taxis, hire cars and trains varies considerably from country to country. Even where there are specially adapted vehicles, as in the UK, these may not be available on all routes or at more than a few locations; check with the relevant carrier for further information. However, rail companies in the UK have recently done much to improve the service offered to disabled passengers.

The Disabled Person's Railcard gives discounts to holders and is available to people with a variety of disabilities; for information, ask for the Disabled Person's Railcard leaflet at stations, travel centres and post offices, which gives details and includes an application form. Application forms can also be obtained online (website: www.nationalrail.co.uk). Visually impaired travellers who do not have a Disabled Person's Railcard (website: www.disabledpersons-railcard.co.uk) are entitled to discounts on standard and season tickets. Disabled travellers may be accompanied by one companion, who will be entitled to the same discounts.

Guide dogs accompanying blind people are always conveyed free of charge.

Rail companies can give various types of assistance to disabled travellers, provided it is arranged in advance. Disabled travellers can contact their local station or ring National Rail Enquiries (tel: (08457) 484 950). For full details, ask for the Rail Travel for Disabled Passengers leaflet, free from all stations and travel centres. The leaflet can also be obtained by post from the Association of Train Operating Companies (ATOC), 40 Bernard Street, London WC1N 1BY.

Note: All new licensed London cabs have been equipped to carry wheelchairs. There are now approximately 4000 cabs that are capable of this and it is hoped that soon all cabs in service will be able to take wheelchairs on board. These cabs are available from cab ranks at stations, airports and hotels across London and can be hailed in the normal way. The Disability Discrimination Act stipulates that all trains, trams and tube trains brought into use after 31 December 1998 should be accessible to disabled people and allow them to travel in safety and reasonable comfort. The Act, passed in 1995, means that travel for disabled people on all types of public transport is becoming easier.

Where there are no special facilities, it may still be possible for a disabled person to travel by road or rail, always ensuring that prior notification is given to the operator, giving precise details of route and timing. Where appropriate, help may then be provided.

Car hire

Some international car hire firms have cars equipped with hand controls for drivers with lower-limb disability. For further details, contact individual car hire companies.

Accommodation

The nature and degree of the disability will dictate the type of accommodation required. The points covered are important and particularly relevant to wheelchair users; however, when booking, ask what facilities will be needed for minimum and maximum comfort, request these facilities, back up your request with a letter and ask for confirmation in writing that they are available.

Access

For wheelchair access, entrance or side doors need to be ramped or level, with a minimum width of 80cm (32in). Interior doors also need to be at least this width, with no steps leading into public rooms (restaurant, lounge, bar, toilets, etc).

There are many disabled people who do not use wheelchairs but are unable to use steps or stairs. A number of accommodation guides - details of which can be obtained from Holiday Care - show where there are ground-floor bedrooms. Most of these also show where there is a lift available, so even if there are no ground-floor bedrooms, access may be just as feasible due to the lift. If making enquiries about a hotel or guest house with a lift, ensure that the bedroom is as near to the lift as possible, and do ask whether there are any steps in the corridor between the lift doors and the bedroom.

General facilities

If ground-floor bedrooms are not available, there should be a lift large enough to take a wheelchair, ie at least 140cm (55in) deep by 1100cm (43in) wide.

Bedroom

The door should be at least 80cm (32in wide); there should be sufficient turning space for a wheelchair, ie 140cm (55in) by 140cm (55in), and free width of at least 80cm (32in) to one side of the bed.

Bathroom

The door should be at least 80cm (32in) wide; enough room is needed to enter in a wheelchair and close the door, with space beside the WC for a wheelchair to enable sideways transfer; support rails near the bath and WC are also needed.

Outside

There should be a route without steps and with a firm smooth surface which wheelchairs can use; this would ideally facilitate access to the swimming pool or beach without needing to negotiate steps; the availability (or otherwise) of a swimming pool hoist should be indicated; the accommodation should be in a central position with shopping and entertainment facilities within easy reach, since otherwise, specially arranged transport would be needed to enable disabled travellers to go on trips or excursions.

The Accessible Symbol

Tourism for All, whose members include the Association of British Travel Agents, VisitBritain and the British Hospitality Association, has drawn up a range of minimum standards that must be met by an establishment before the Accessible Symbol can be awarded. Requirements for the symbol are as follows:

- A public entrance to the building must be accessible to disabled people from a setting-down or car-parking point
- Where an establishment has a car park, a parking space must be reserved for a disabled guest on request
- Disabled people must have access to the following areas (if provided): reception, restaurant or dining room, lounge, TV lounge (unless TV is provided in the bedroom) and bar
- A minimum of one guest room with bath or shower and WC facilities en suite, which is suitable for a wheelchair user, should be provided. Where these facilities are not en suite, a unisex WC compartment and a bath or shower room suitable for a wheelchair user must be provided on the same floor level

Useful Publications

Access to Air Travel, available from RADAR
Door to Door – A Guide to Transport for Disabled People, available from RADAR

Useful Contacts

Disabled Living Foundation, 380-384 Harrow Road, London W9 2HU (tel: (020) 7289 6111 (main switchboard) or (0845) 130 9177 (helpline, open Mon-Fri 1000-1600); minicom: (020) 7432 8009; website: www.dlf.org.uk).

Organisations

Holiday Care

7th Floor, Sunley House, 4 Bedford Park, Croydon, Surrey CR0 2AP

Tel: (0845) 124 9971 (information) or 9974 (admin) or 9973 (reservations; UK only) or (20) 8760 0072 (outside UK). Minicom: (0845) 124 9976.

Website: www.holidaycare.org.uk

Holiday Care, which was established as a registered charity in 1981, is the UK's central source of holiday information for people whose disability makes it difficult for them to find a holiday. An entirely non-commercial organisation, it provides details of accommodation, transport, facilities or publications that are most appropriate to the person's needs. At present, the following areas of information are covered by the service; new topics are continually being added.

UK holidays for disabled people: Specialist commercial and voluntary operators; access, accommodation and catering guides; self-catering accommodation; hotels and guest houses; special interest and activity holidays; farm holidays; specially-adapted accommodation; group facilities; university and college accommodation; holiday camps and centres; accommodation where personal or nursing care is provided; boating holidays; coach, rail, taxi and ambulance information; car hire; non-smoking accommodation; holidays suitable for those with epilepsy; holidays for people with learning difficulties; opportunities for those with mental health needs; escorts; financial assistance; information for deaf and/or blind people; various holidays for physically, mentally and/or sensorily disabled children; use of oxygen on holiday.

It is vital that adequate insurance cover is arranged. One of the biggest problems disabled people have faced in the past has been the inclusion in policies of a 'pre-existing medical condition' exclusion clause. These still appear in the policies offered by quite a number of tour operators. Do check very carefully that the policy offered does not have this clause. Even those who exclude nothing often require that a 'fitness to travel' certificate is obtained from a doctor beforehand. Holiday Care offers information on insurance for disabled travellers. Recommended companies include VentureSure (tel: (0845) 230 3521; website: www.venturesure.co.uk) which can provide travel insurance for disabled or terminally ill people.

RADAR

(Royal Association for Disability and Rehabilitation) 12 City Forum, 250 City Road, London EC1V 8AF

Tel: (020) 7250 3222. Minicom: (020) 7250 4119.

Website: www.radar.org.uk

RADAR is a national organisation run by and for disabled people. It acts as a pressure group to improve the environment for disabled people, campaigning for their rights and needs and challenging negative attitudes and stereotypes. Information and advice is given on a variety of subjects that affects the daily lives of disabled people. The organisation publishes Holidays in Britain & Ireland – A Guide For Disabled People.

BREAK

Davison House, 1 Montague Road, Sheringham, Norfolk NR26 8WN

Tel: (01263) 822 161.

Website: www.break-charity.org

BREAK provides holidays, short breaks and respite care for children, adults and families with special needs at two centres on the picturesque North Norfolk coast, so that while guests enjoy a seaside holiday, those who regularly care for them can have a much needed rest. There is also a wheelchair-friendly self-catering chalet in the West Country for families on low incomes.

British Red Cross

44 Moorfields, London EC2Y 9AL

Tel: 0870 170 7000.

Website: www.redcross.org.uk

The British Red Cross can provide regional contact addresses and telephone numbers for local organisations that are able to offer help and support. The British Red Cross also has international offices where people can obtain useful equipment, such as wheelchairs, whilst on holiday. An information pack can be supplied on request.

Tripscope

The Vassall Centre, Gill Avenue, Bristol BS16 2QQ

Tel/Minicom: (0845) 758 5641 (helpline; from within the UK) or (117) 939 7782 (from outside the UK).

Website: www.tripscope.org.uk

Tripscope is a travel and transport information service for disabled and elderly people, and can advise on planning local, long-distance and international journeys.

Access Travel

6 The Hillock, Astley, Manchester M29 7GW

Tel: (01942) 888 844.

Website: www.access-travel.co.uk

Access Travel was founded in 1991 and is a tour operator that deals specifically with disabled travellers - in particular, wheelchair users. The company personally inspects accommodation and can therefore recommend suitable lodgings according to the traveller's individual needs. They can also assist with consumer protection; quotes and discounts on airfare; special aids; nursing and care services; adapted vehicles; and disabled-friendly car hire.

Religion

BUDDHISM

Introduction

Buddhism was founded by Siddhartha Gotama, who lived in and around the Ganges Plain during the fifth and sixth centuries BC. Heir to the throne of the Sakyan kingdom, at the age of 29, Siddhartha renounced his royal heritage to search for a means of ending the sense of dissatisfaction and futility of which he had become acutely aware.

Having tried and discarded all the then-available approaches to spiritual practice, he discovered a radically different path: a middle way between the extremes of indulgence and asceticism. This brought him the enlightenment he sought and he became known thereafter as 'the Buddha' - the enlightened one.

The Buddha summarised his teaching in four statements known as the noble truths: life in the relative world is fundamentally unsatisfactory and, although happiness can be found in the world, all things that give rise to it — possessions, people, wealth, desirable mental states — inevitably age, decay and die; our sense of dissatisfaction is not something that falls upon us out of the blue, rather, we become dissatisfied whenever we want life to be different from the way it is right now; there is an ending to all dissatisfaction, suffering and distress, known as Nirvana or Enlightenment; this goal is attained by following the Buddhist path, which comprises the perfection of ethical conduct, meditation and wisdom. (For a lucid modern exposition of the Buddha's path to enlightenment, see The Buddhist Path, by Sangharakshita, Windhorse Publications.)

Having established itself in northern India during the fifth century BC, Buddhism was contained within the subcontinent for about 100 years. The teaching spread to Nepal by the fourth century BC, and reached Kashmir, Sri Lanka and Central Asia by the second century BC. The later spread of the religion occurred partly along trade routes and partly due to the work of missionaries. By the time of the birth of Christ, Buddhism was established in China, and reached Korea by the end of the third century. Increased trade in the Far East at this time gave greater impetus to the spread of the religion, and by the seventh century, Buddhists were to be found in Japan, Java, Myanmar, Sumatra, Thailand and Tibet. Further westward expansion was halted by Islamic conquests, but conversion persisted; Buddhism did not reach Bhutan until the ninth century but today it is one of the most strongly Buddhist countries in the world.

Strands of Buddhism

The spread of Buddhism over a period of over 1500 years led to the development of many different strands of Buddhism. The countries listed below are where the religion is most commonly practised or where it originated; these (and other) strands of Buddhism are followed by millions of people all over the world, including in Western countries.

Theravada Buddhism

(In Cambodia, Laos, Myanmar, Sri Lanka and Thailand.) Theravada has approximately 100 million followers worldwide. Theravada draws its inspiration from the earliest surviving records of the Buddha's teachings. The ideal is a person who attains liberation by purifying themselves of all defilements and desires; thus it is focused heavily on mediation and concentration. Orange or yellow robes distinguish the monks.

Mahayana Buddhism

(In China, Japan, Korea and Vietnam.) Mahayana emerged in the first century BC. Mahayanans attempted to reformulate the teachings of Buddha to accommodate a greater number of people; they completed the conversion of Buddhism from a philosophy to a religion. The chief religious ideal is the bodhisattva ('being of wisdom') - any being destined for or intent on enlightenment; this is an attainable goal for lay and monastic Buddhists alike. The priests wear brown, grey or black robes.

Vajrayana Buddhism

(In Bhutan, Mongolia, Nepal, Sikkim and Tibet.) This is also known as Tibetan Buddhism. Vajrayana derived from Mahayana. Much of its ritual is based on the mysticism of the primitive, animistic religion of Tibet, and on Tantra (rituals and yoga used in conjunction with mantras to unify the devotee with their chosen deity). The monks wear maroon robes.

Buddhism is not a centralised religion with centralised institutions, although it does have a hierarchical form of organisation within each of the three main strands. In countries such as Bhutan, Sri Lanka and Thailand, where the Government and a large part of the population is Buddhist, the state is very closely associated with religion and its organisation and institutions tend to be more formal. In other countries, such as Japan, the religion exists within a looser framework.

Festivals

Visitors are welcome to attend the many festivals that are an integral part of Buddhist life. However, as they are scheduled by the lunar calendar and often take place on a full moon, the dates the festivals are held change annually; in addition, each country also has its own individual festivals. For further information, consult the relevant country's Public Holidays section, or contact an embassy or tourist board (listed in Passport/Visa Information and Tourist Information sections for each entry). The main festivals celebrated annually include:

Wesak (Buddha Day): Commemorates the Buddha's Enlightenment (as well as his Birthday and Death). It is celebrated in the Theravada countries around the full moon in May. Houses and streets are decorated and roads are packed with processions. Long lines of monks and worshippers throng the temples either meditating or listening to religious discourses.

Tooth Ceremony: Takes place annually in Kandy, Sri Lanka, lasting for about a week in July or August. Up to 100 elephants take part.

Songkran: Celebrated in Thailand during April; the three-day festival involves water-splashing, the freeing of fish, fighting kites and dancing.

Hana Matsuri (Flower Festival), Jodo-e and Nehan-e: (April, December and February, respectively.) Celebrated in Japan to commemorate, respectively, the Birth, Enlightenment and Death of Buddha.

Chinese New Year: The main festival celebrated in China (PR), the Vajrayana countries and by the Chinese populations in Hawaii, Hong Kong (SAR), Malaysia, Taiwan (China), and also many Western countries. This is actually a pre-Buddhist festival to mark the beginning of spring. It usually falls in late January or February and lasts for up to a week. The third day is the Feast of Lanterns, when long, painted dragons dance in the streets. Vajrayana countries also have very colourful festivals and ceremonies, with demon dancing and the blowing of enormous long horns by brightly-hatted monks.

Further Information

The FWBO Communications Office, 16-20 Turner Street, Manchester M4 1DZ UK (tel: (0161) 839 9579; website: www.fwbo.org; opening hours: 1000-1700) or see online (website: www.buddhanet.net).

CHRISTIANITY

Belief

The Bible consists of the Old Testament (inherited from Judaism) and the New Testament (which tells the story of Jesus and his apostles), and also contains letters written to Christian communities, especially those by St Paul.

The New Testament story

The Christian belief is based on the life and teachings of Jesus who, as recorded in the gospels of Matthew, Mark, Luke and John, travelled through Palestine for three years declaring his message and performing miracles until he was arrested, accused of being a rebel against the occupying Roman authorities, and crucified. The Jewish authorities were particularly upset by his claim to be the Son of God and therefore the long-awaited Messiah. According to believers, three days after his crucifixion, Jesus rose from the dead and for the next few weeks appeared several times to his followers. He then 'ascended' to heaven.

Subsequent to his death, resurrection and Ascension, his apostles (see below) and other disciples travelled throughout the Roman Empire preaching and gaining converts. Of these converts, St Paul, who was originally fanatically anti-Christian, is perhaps the most important; many Christian doctrines are based on his letters to the various Christian communities.

The miracles

In the gospels, Jesus is often portrayed as reluctant to carry out miracles, performing them only out of compassion, with a reminder that people should not believe in him for his miracles. The miracles most often mentioned involve making the lame walk and the blind see, from others he 'casts out devils' (a phrase now given a psychological slant by many). A few seem to have a mystical or symbolic significance: turning water to wine at a wedding in Cana; feeding 5000 people with two loaves and three fishes; and calming the storm on Lake Galilee seem to fall into this category.

The parables

The miracles are often a prelude to a discussion in which a parable (sometimes several) are told. Jesus is not primarily someone who lays down moral laws; it is the approach to life and attitude of his listeners that he targets. Taken collectively, the parables form a set of yardsticks against which the Christian can measure himself. As they are stories, rather than codes of behaviour, their origin many years ago in a largely pastoral and Roman-occupied Middle East does not confine and date them. The parables emphasise ethical precepts central to Christianity: returning good for evil; forgiveness; welcoming the sinner; and valuing a person for what they are, not who they are. The most direct statements of Christian ethics in the Bible are perhaps to be found in the Beatitudes, the most famous being 'Blessed are the meek for they shall inherit the Earth'.

The apostles

The 12 apostles were disciples who were particularly close to Jesus; several were fishermen. Notable among the apostles was Peter (meaning 'stone'), who, through force of character and conviction, was able to overcome his weaknesses. Another apostle, Matthew, symbolises the universal nature of the Christian appeal; he had been a tax-collector (a corrupt and despised profession in the Roman Empire). Most notorious was Judas Iscariot, who betrayed Jesus to the authorities; throughout the centuries, his actions, and those of the priests he assisted, have been used as a justification for persecution of the Jewish people.

The gospels

John's Gospel is accepted as being the closest eyewitness account of the events of Jesus' life. The visionary nature of his work, however, inclines many interpreters against being over-literal. The other Gospels are collectively called the 'synoptic' Gospels; though there are differences between them, they draw on the same source material. Mark's, the earliest, is a bald 'no frills' narrative; the aim is clearly to bring the material together and put it in writing. Matthew's is written from a Jewish perspective and has a clear emphasis on putting the story into the context of Jewish tradition. Luke, on the other hand, as a gentile convert, emphasises the universal elements of the story. From Luke also comes the Acts of the Apostles, an account of the early days of

Christianity, which significantly gives us a picture of the second major progenitor of Christianity: St Paul.

Practices

Whilst Christian denominations vary radically in their practices, virtually all perform the Act of Holy Communion and hold services on Sunday (the day of the Resurrection, traditionally the Christian day of rest), though such activities are not necessarily confined to Sunday. A prayer ('grace') is often said at table before meals, especially the evening meal. It may be read or memorised and may also give mention to preoccupations or current events. It is customary for persons in attendance to lower their eyes, bow their head and clasp their hands in front of them or hold the hand of the persons sitting next to them. The prayer always finishes with the word 'Amen' (meaning 'so be it'), at which time those attending can resume their normal posture and begin their meal. It is a breach of manners to begin eating before the prayer is completed.

In general, practising Christians are definably members of a community centred on their church; originally, the act of baptism symbolised the acceptance of a Christian as a full member, but it is now performed at so young an age (in most denominations) that there is usually some other recognised form of acceptance which occurs when a person is old enough to take responsibility for his actions. The nature of this form of acceptance varies greatly, but what is centrally important is that individuals are offered the choice of whether or not to accept it.

Communion

At the Last Supper, when Jesus celebrated the Jewish Passover immediately before being taken prisoner and crucified, he broke bread and drank wine with his apostles, saying: 'Do this in remembrance of me'. This has become the Christian sacrament of Communion whereby, in re-enacting this event, Christians renew their relationship with God. There is no particular time or place for this sacrament, though over the centuries, many rites and practices have grown around it, mostly in the Roman Catholic Mass.

The Christian calendar

The most important event in the Christian calendar is Easter, which celebrates the death and resurrection of Jesus: Good Friday, the day when hope was lost; Easter Sunday, the day it was restored. Second in importance is Christmas, which celebrates the birth of Jesus. The Christmas tradition of exchanging gifts and family celebration is a secular affair and not rooted in any Christian doctrine. The older European tradition is to celebrate on St Nicholas' Day (6 December), whilst other churches prefer to commemorate the arrival of the Magi with their gifts. Many other events in the life of Jesus are celebrated in the Christian calendar. The most important dates are as follows:

Christmas: (25 December; Orthodox: 6 January.) Celebrates the Birth of Jesus; see above.

Epiphany: (6 January, 12 days after Christmas.) The coming of the wise men with their gifts.

Ash Wednesday: (46 days before Easter.) Commencement of Lent, traditionally a period of fasting and self-denial leading up to Easter.

Palm Sunday: (One week before Easter.) Celebrates the arrival into Jerusalem of Jesus riding on a mule.

Good Friday: (Two days before Easter.) Traditionally referred to as three days before Easter Sunday, this commemorates the crucifixion.

Easter Sunday: (A moveable Feast which usually occurs in March or April; Western and Orthodox churches determine its date according to different calendars.) The day of the Resurrection; see above.

Ascension Day: (39 days after Easter.) The day Jesus ascended to heaven on a cloud following his resurrection and last appearances on Earth.

Whit Sunday: (Seven weeks after Easter.) Marking the day the Holy Spirit entered the disciples left behind and the beginning of their ministry.

Virtually all Christian churches mark the above dates; Orthodox and Catholic churches, in particular, also mark other occasions, such as Noah's Flood (Orthodox) and the Immaculate Conception (Roman Catholic).

Doctrines

It is difficult to set out a list of 'the definitive' Christian doctrines; the following beliefs are held, with differing degrees of literalness, by most Christians:

- There is only one God
- Jesus is his son
- He was born of the Virgin Mary
- He lived, was crucified, resurrected from the dead and ascended to heaven (the meaning of this is explained separately, see below)
- Through the working of the Holy Spirit, his apostles were moved to preach in the name of Jesus, and establish the church as we know it
- God, Jesus and the Holy Spirit are not three entities but one and the same (the complex doctrine of the Trinity)
- The Bible, including the Jewish Old Testament, seen in the light of the New Testament, represents the word of God to his people
- God remains in commune with his church and its members

There is a broad range of attitudes to these beliefs, from the Roman Catholics' insistence on orthodoxy to the Quakers' belief in the 'still, small voice'.

The significance of the Resurrection

To Christians, the significance of the Resurrection is essentially about personal and collective redemption through the self-sacrifice of one man. According to the New Testament, the story of Jesus is the story of a man who preached an emphasis on the importance of spiritual guiding values as opposed to the primacy of tradition or law as defined by man. According to the Gospels, he was angered by hypocrisy, relished debate, spoke of forgiveness and returning love for hate and, ultimately, was betrayed and abandoned by those closest to him. In the Resurrection, Jesus joins humanity again, but this time with his divinity in the ascendant. For a Christian, the belief in the resurrection of Christ is the belief in the potential redemption of both the individual, and the redemption of humankind as a whole.

Denominations

The following is a list of some of the main Christian denominations worldwide, together with a brief description of their particular customs.

Roman Catholic

(Worldwide, especially in Europe and Latin countries.) Roman Catholics believe that the Pope inherits supreme authority within the church directly from St Peter. Elaborate rituals are performed and the role of the priest is central; it is his responsibility to listen to Confession, assign penances and give absolution (forgiveness). Many saints are venerated and countries with large Roman Catholic denominations are often noted for their fiestas on Saints' Days; spectacular carnivals before or after Easter also occur. Modesty in dress when visiting churches is required (eg covering the head for women).

Orthodox

(Central Europe, the Middle East and Russia.) Orthodox churches are similar to Catholic ones in the elaborate style of their liturgies and rituals (called 'Greek Rite'). Services are long, with the congregation standing throughout; stress is laid on the importance of the Ascension, and saints are highly regarded. In some places, icons (usually miniature religious paintings on small pieces of wood) are used as an aid to contemplation. Each province has its own Patriarch and, whilst there is no overriding central control, the Patriarch of Istanbul is recognised as the most senior. Modesty in dress when visiting churches is required (eg covering the head for women).

Anglican & Episcopalian

(English-speaking countries.) The Church of England parted from the Roman Catholic Church in the 16th century. Many of its rites are similar to those of the Catholic Church, although, over the centuries, the influences of Puritanism and non-conformity have, for the most part, tended to concentrate worship on the main doctrines and away from

the veneration of saints, etc. The priest is also less of an intermediary between his congregation and God. Anglican and Episcopalian churches throughout the world have forms of service derived from that of the Church of England. The church is broad and 'high' churches tend to be similar in character to Roman Catholicism, whilst 'low' churches look more to non-conformist influences. Requirements on dress are not as strict as those of Catholic and Orthodox churches, but respect is always appreciated.

Methodist, Presbyterian & Congregationalist

(English-speaking countries and the Pacific.) Industriousness, temperance (meaning more than just sobriety), straightforwardness and honesty are the values of these churches; qualities which the New Testament sums up in the concept of 'stewardship'. In form of service, some are similar to the 'low' church of the Church of England, whilst others are more austere and Calvinistic (putting emphasis on the man–God relationship, strongly opposing the role of priest as mediator).

Baptist

(CIS, Europe, parts of the Far East and the USA.) Most churches practise baptism within a few weeks of birth; for Baptists, 'believer's baptism' is practised, which means the (adult) consent of the baptised is essential if the rite is to be significant. Congregations are autonomous and independent of each other though each belongs to a national union. Other beliefs are similar to those described above under Methodist (above).

Pentecostal

(Caribbean and the USA.) These are the most exuberant churches of all, with much community singing and uninhibited celebration; 'speaking in tongues' and dancing often enter into church services. Beliefs are usually fundamentalist.

Seventh Day Adventist

(The Pacific and the USA.) This Fundamentalist church celebrates the Sabbath on Saturday (the 'seventh day'). Church members look forward to the 'Second Coming' when Jesus will return to Earth and there is a heavy emphasis on the Old Testament.

Evangelical

Many churches have evangelical congregations and this is an area in which the Pentecostal church has been influential. The importance of the gospel is central and proclaiming God's word is emphasised.

The growth of Christianity

The history of Christianity is central to the history of the modern world and pervades every aspect of philosophy, politics and culture, especially in Europe. Space here does not permit more than a brief survey and it should be remembered that, although originally a Middle Eastern religion, it was in Europe that Christianity most firmly took root and flourished. The following survey has been written largely from a Western European viewpoint; this is not to belittle the achievements of the many founding fathers of the Church, many of whom lived in Syria and North Africa. The early church, initially small groups converted by the remaining apostles and St Paul, grew rapidly in the Roman Empire but suffered considerable persecution and also many heresies and schisms. The remarkable spread of the religion culminated in the reign of the Emperor Constantine (306-337), who became a Christian himself and summoned the first Ecumenical council of the Church (325) in an attempt to settle the matter of the Arian heresy, the first sign of a split between the eastern and western churches that was never subsequently healed. The church was at this time organised under the leadership of several patriarchs (at Alexandria, Antioch, Constantinople, Jerusalem and Rome), with the latter accorded a somewhat vague primacy. Christianity spread rapidly throughout Europe during the Dark Ages (although parts of eastern and northeastern Europe were not converted until the 11/12th centuries), a growth mirroring the breakdown of secular power. The propensity of

Christianity to produce schismatic groups in no way abated during this period, eventually leading to the establishment of many diverse Christian groups, such as the Coptics and Maronites, which still survive to this day. The rapid and dramatic spread of Islam in the seventh century resulted in many Christian lands (such as Spain and almost all of the Middle East) being overrun; the conquest of Jerusalem was in particular keenly felt, the city being revered by Christians, as well as by Muslims and Jews.

The career of Charlemagne (771-814) produced a revival both of Christianity and of secular power, and his coronation as Holy Roman Emperor in Rome on Christmas Day 800 – thus recreating the Roman Empire in the West and formalising the concept of Christendom – was an event of enormous significance, not least because it brought into sharp focus the conflicting aspirations of the Church and State. It was widely believed that Constantine had granted the Church ultimate supremacy in earthly affairs (the so-called 'Donation of Constantine', later proved to be a forgery), and this dispute rumbled on throughout the Middle Ages, often flaring into armed conflict. The launching of the Crusades in 1096 was motivated not only by a desire to reinforce ecclesiastical supremacy in the West, but also to come to the aid of the Byzantine Empire which had come consistently under attack. There existed also the fainter hope of producing a reconciliation between Rome and Constantinople. The astounding success of the First Crusade, which led to the establishment of Christian states in the Middle East for almost 200 years, brought Christianity, Judaism and Islam into sharp and violent conflict. The triumph of Islam in the East was assured after the conquest of Constantinople in 1453; the Eastern (Orthodox) church retained its hold in Greece and Russia, and also in many isolated (and often heretical) communities in the Middle East. Shortly afterwards, the 'seamless robe of Christ' was split still further by the Reformation and the teachings of Luther, Calvin and Zwingli. By the end of the 16th century, despite the work of the Counter-Reformation and the Council of Trent, much of northern Europe had turned to Protestantism. Increasingly, the religious split in Europe manifested itself in many of the wars of the period – the French Wars of Religion, the Dutch War of Independence and the English Civil War and Revolution, for instance – culminating in the gruesome politico-religious violence of the Thirty Years' War (1618-1648).

By this time, most of the major European powers had started to establish overseas empires, exporting religion at the same time and, by the 18th century, Christianity had established itself as the most widely spread faith in the world. Methodism was the last of the major Christian denominations to take root and, by that time, most of the established churches in Europe had achieved a more tranquil modus vivendi with their secular counterparts by the rationalism of the Enlightenment. From this time on, the most zealous Christians, from the Jesuits to Evangelicals, were finding that the most fertile ground for their teaching lay in the colonies: during the 19th century, the work of conversion in all parts of the world proceeded apace. The 20th century has seen the Christian Church in Europe holding a smaller constituency and relying more on moral and ethical, rather than theological, influence on the life of its adherents. Certainly, the increasing power and sophistication of the state has, in our century, resolved the ancient Church and State dispute very firmly in favour of the secular arm. The foundation of the ecumenical World Council of Churches in 1948 can be seen partly as an attempt to bury old differences between the denominations.

Despite the increasing drift away from religion in the West, revivals, often of a dramatic nature, have taken place throughout the century, and one should in particular cite the recent rise of fundamentalist preachers in the USA. Two other events are worthy of particular mention. Firstly, the work of the Second Vatican Council in the 1960s, an attempt to bring the Catholic Church in line with the needs of the modern world: it has been said that, convened 500 years earlier, it would certainly have prevented the Reformation. Secondly, the spread of the so-called 'liberation theology' in the Third World and Eastern Europe, born of an attempt to use the moral authority and teachings of the Church to aid the struggle against political and social oppression. Although in many ways a return to the fundamental teaching of Christ, the development is viewed with alarm by the Vatican and, to a lesser extent, by other Church leaders. The legacy of Christianity to the world is incalculable: almost every work of literature, art and music before about 1600 – and many after this date – were inspired by the faith, while the soaring cathedrals of both Western and Eastern Europe rank among the greatest achievements of mankind. Certainly, the religion will continue to guide, comfort and inspire countless millions across the globe, although it seems unlikely to spawn any further major global changes.

Futher information
A local church or the Christian Enquiry Agency, 27 Tavistock Square, London WC1H 9HH, UK (tel: (020) 7387 3659; website: www.christianity.org.uk).

ISLAM

Introduction
Muhammad, the Prophet of Islam, was born in AD 570, the posthumous son of a Hashemite from Mecca. His mother died when he was about six, his grandfather died when he was just eight, after which he was brought up by his uncle, Abu Talib, who had set him up as a merchant by the time he was 25 years old. His teachings began around 610, but despite gaining some followers, he was rejected by the townspeople and was forced to leave for Medina in 622. For the next decade he organised the Islamic Community, creating a community based on the will of God. His activities led to persecution of the early Muslims, followed by years of conflict, mainly with the Meccans, as the number of Muslims increased. By his death in 632, many Arabian tribes had either joined or been subdued by the Muslims.

Within a year of the Prophet's death, the Muslims had advanced into Iraq and, by the early eighth century, had reached the River Indus and the Pyrenees. In the context of this remarkable expansion, the victory of Charles Martel at Tours (732) must rank as one of the most decisive in history: most of the countries which were conquered during this period still remain Islamic or else have large Muslim populations.

The history of Islam and its influence on Christian Europe, with which it coexisted uneasily for centuries, repays careful study. Certain European countries, notably Spain, Portugal and Sicily, have fascinating reminders of both cultures; it is also worth remembering that, during the Middle Ages, the Islamic world was far advanced compared with that of the West in the fields of philosophy, medicine, science, geography, poetry and music. Many classical works survived only because they were translated into Arabic during the Dark Ages before being brought to Western Europe in the 12th century; the rediscovery of the works of Aristotle in this way was of fundamental importance to the development of Western philosophy. During the Crusades (1100-1290), armies of Christian Europe and Islam came into violent conflict. In recent years, an understanding of Islam has often been obscured by political complexities, and the following section is an attempt to explain some of the important tenets of the faith. Anyone planning to visit a Muslim country should familiarise themselves with at least a little of the history, culture and beliefs of this increasingly influential religion.

Belief
The Islamic religion is based on the 'submission to the will of God (Allah)'. Islam has teachings for the mind, body and spirit; also laws on education, economy, politics, science, crime and punishment, human behaviour and all aspects of morality in daily life for individuals (men and women of any race), families, governments and whole societies anywhere in the world.

The Qur'an (Koran) and Sunnah are the two basic sources of Islamic teachings, law and order. The Qur'an is the main religious book for Muslims; it is the spoken word of Allah (God) and is subdivided into 30 equal parts containing 114 chapters (or Sura) in Arabic. The Sunnah is complementary to the Qur'an; it contains the sayings of the Prophet Muhammad and documents his way of life.

The Prophet received the spoken word of Allah containing the foundation of the faith (the Qur'an) while in Mecca in the seventh century AD; the city is now Islam's principal holy city. Medina, also in Saudi Arabia, a little over 300km (200 miles) due north of Mecca, is second only to Mecca in importance. It was to Medina that Muhammad and his followers moved after his monotheistic beliefs were given a hostile reception by some Meccans. The journey from Mecca to Medina (Hijra) is celebrated each year, the event being taken as the starting point of the Islamic calendar (Ah 1). The prophet spent 10 years in Medina before returning to Mecca with his followers.

Islamic sects
After Muhammad's death in AD 632, temporal authority was assumed by a series of Khalifahs, with various sects developing. The two strongest sects within Islam (that is, those with the most followers) arose shortly after the time of Muhammad's death. Both sects agree on the core fundamentals of Islam – the Five Pillars – and recognise each other as Muslims.

Sunni
(Mainly in Bangladesh, Egypt, the Gulf States, India, Indonesia, parts of Lebanon, Malaysia, North Africa, Pakistan, Saudi Arabia, the Syrian Arab Republic and large parts of Turkey.) Sunni's make up between 85 to 90 per cent of the worlds Muslims. At the time of Muhammad's death, they believed that the succeeding Caliph (leader of Islam) should be popularly chosen according to merit. Today, the Caliphate has been abolished and Sunnis do not have a formal clergy, just scholars and jurists who may offer non-binding opinions.

Shi'a
(Mainly in Afghanistan, parts of India, Iran, the greater part of Iraq, southern Lebanon and Pakistan). The Shi'as separated from the main sect in 661, believing that the succeeding Caliphate should pass down only to direct descendents of Muhammad. Muhammad's son-in-law, Ali, became the fourth Caliph after Muhammad; one of the main tenements of Shi'a is the illegitimacy of all Caliphates after him. When the line of Muhammad became extinct in the seventh century, a council of 12 scholars selected an Imam, a spiritual guide with a similar function to the Caliph, who has come to be imbued with a Pope-like infallibility; the best-known modern Imam was Ayatollah Khomeini. Shi'as' are generally considered more 'fundamentalist' than their Sunni counterparts.

The Five Pillars of Islam
There are five basic religious tenets, generally called the Five Pillars of Islam:
Shahadah: The profession of faith: 'I testify there is no God but Allah and Muhammad is the Messenger of Allah'.
Salah: The faithful must turn towards Mecca and recite a prescribed prayer five times daily; at dawn, just after midday, asr (mid-afternoon), just after sunset and before midnight. In some Muslim countries the activities of the day stop at the time of prayer. The muezzin calls to prayer, chanting from the minaret of each mosque. For obvious practical reasons, not all Muslims go to a mosque for prayer. Shopkeepers and businesspeople will offer prayers on their premises, usually on a mat set to one side. Muslims must always pray facing towards Mecca.
The most important prayer is the Friday prayer, delivered from a pulpit of the mosque by a prayer leader. In many Muslim countries, Friday is a holiday, with banks and shops closed all day.
Zakah: A compulsory payment from a Muslim's annual savings. It literally means 'purification', and is an annual payment of 2.5 per cent of the value of cash, jewellery and precious metals above a specified minimum amount (a separate rate applies to animals, crops and minerals). Zakah is used for helping the poor and needy, the disabled, the oppressed, debtors and other welfare purposes as defined in the Qur'an and Sunnah.
Ramadan: All Muslims are required to fast during the Holy Month of Ramadan (a lunar month of 29 or 30 days, which falls 11 days earlier each year, depending on sightings of the moon). All Muslims abstain totally from food, drink, sex and tobacco from dawn to sunset. Non-Muslims should respect

this practice and, wherever possible, avoid infringing these laws in front of Muslims, since this would be considered an insult. Often, shops and restaurants will open much earlier and close during the afternoons and, in smaller towns, some will close altogether, but some businesses do open at night. Straight after sunset most, if not all, Muslims will break their fast, and little business or travel will be practical for the visitor at this time.

Originally the festival celebrated the month during which the Qur'an was first revealed and, later, when Muhammad's followers won a great victory over opponents to his faith in Mecca. Eid al-Fitr, an official holiday in some Muslim countries of three or more days, takes place after the end of Ramadan. It is a celebratory feast when those luxuries that have been denied are enjoyed with relish.

The Hajj: The pilgrimage to Mecca. Every Muslim who can afford it and is fit enough must make the journey at least once in their life, although some Muslims make the pilgrimage more than once. At the time of the pilgrimage, the pilgrim (Hajji/Hajja) enters the holy precincts of Mecca wearing a white, seamless garment (ihram) and performs the sevenfold circumambulation of the Ka'aba (the black stone housed in the centre of the Holy Mosque) and the sevenfold course between the little hills of Safa and Marwah near the Ka'aba. Muslims perform this in memory of Hagar who is mentioned in the Old Testament, who ran seven times between Safa and Marwah seeking a spring for her thirsty son. The Hajj lasts from the eighth to the 13th day of Dhu-al-Hijja. On the ninth day, pilgrims stand praying on the plain of Arafat - an essential part of the ritual of the Hajj. The Hajj culminates with Eid al-Adha (Feast of the Sacrifice) on the 10th day in which a sheep, cow or camel is sacrificed and the meat distributed among the poor. There are three further days of Hajj called Tashriq. The days from the 10th to the 13th are usually an official holiday. After shaving the head (which is performed only by men), the ihram is discarded and normal dress (ihlal) resumed. As long as the hajji/hajja is in ihram (sanctified state), he/she must refrain from sexual intercourse, the shedding of blood, hunting and the uprooting of plants. All of the different activities of the Hajj are symbolic and have stories associated with them.

Social customs

Muslims regard Islam as an integral part of daily life, resulting in an ordered society in which a person's social, spiritual and economic status is clearly defined. This way of life is, for the most part, drawn from the Qur'an. Greetings and replies in particular are formal and stylised. Manners and courtesy reflect a deeply held convention of hospitality and mutual respect. It is customary for Muslim households to extend hospitality to people whom Western society would disregard socially. For instance, tradition dictates that anyone who appears at meal times must be invited to share the meal, and this would apply as much to strangers or tradespeople, whatever the reason for their call, as it would to friends or relatives. Hospitality was a part of Arab culture before Islam and the laws and teaching of Islam reinforced it. Subjects such as illness or death are not surrounded by taboo as they are in many Western societies, and are discussed frankly by all. Muslims are encouraged to have close relationships, have an open heart and an understanding of others, and to try and help with others' problems.

The label of a family can cover any number of individuals rather than only those related by blood ties. Arab families are close-knit, and the importance of family unity cannot be stressed too strongly. Inter-family disputes are a cause for public shame and require immediate attention.

Women and Islam

Possibly the aspect of Islam most deeply criticised by non-Muslims is the treatment of women. That men and women should dress and behave modestly is seen by Muslims as symbolic of the importance and value placed on women as mothers and guardians of the family. The Prophet encouraged monogamy, although polygamy was allowed,

provided that the husband was in a position to provide for all wives (a maximum of four is allowed) and treated them equally. Polygamy may also occur in special circumstances, such as when the number of women in society is larger than the number of men, or when a wife is chronically ill or sterile. Today, monogamy is more common, polygamy being allowed but not encouraged. Many, but not all, royal families have employed polygamy to ensure succession, and for practical reasons such as providing ministers and administrators – but, otherwise, it is not the norm.

The theory behind modest dress and veil for women is to preserve respect, dignity and virginity, and to safeguard them from interference or abuse by men, although for some time this tradition has been slowly relaxed in many countries through contact with non-Islamic cultures. Women are allowed to work in some cases, especially when the need arises, but the Islamic code of dress and modesty must always be observed. In some jobs it is obligatory to have female teachers or doctors, for example when dealing with Muslim girls or women. Today in the Arab and Muslim world, many Muslim women are working because of financial need and because of the liberalising of religious practice and observance. Women invariably rule the household and the family; given the importance of the family, this affords older women considerable influence. Younger women, however, hold no such position and although many Islamic countries have relaxed restrictions and women have begun to play an active part in many spheres of activity (particularly in medicine, education, public services and the media), a number of countries still follow strict traditional practices. Fundamentalism, enjoying a resurgence in many Islamic countries, is as much an articulation of the resentment felt at the interference of stronger foreign economies in their internal affairs as anything else, and the introduction of Western culture into traditional life. However, this can often manifest itself in a retreat back to almost medieval traditions as a positive form of disapproval of the decadence of the West. Thus, in many countries, the position of women can be protected and their role in society appreciated, whilst at the same time, their ability to control their own lives is largely denied.

Note: The above account of women and Islam, which describes widely held beliefs and customs, should not be taken as conclusive.

Social Conventions

Forms of address: The Arabic equivalent of 'Mr' is Sayyid (for Muslims) and Khawaja (for Christians), while married women should be addressed as Sayyida or Sitt, and girls as Anissa. In Islam it is also encouraged to call a Muslim man 'my brother' and a Muslim woman 'my sister'. Islam regards men as equal, but social conventions, hospitality and politeness of Islamic societies prevent over familiarity.

Greeting: There follows a short list of Arabic greetings and phrases. The transliterations are phonetic and intended to assist pronunciation.

Marharba	-	Hello
Markhabtain	-	Hello (reply)
Ma'a Salama	-	Goodbye
Ahlan wa sahlan	-	Welcome
Ahlan feekum	-	Welcome (reply)
Sabah al-khir	-	Good morning
Sabah innoor	-	Good morning (reply)

These were all originally purely Arabic greetings. In Islam, the common greeting still widely used is Assalaamu Alaykum ('Peace be with you').

Note: Throughout the Arab world, English is widely spoken in business, and it is not essential for English speakers to learn Arabic. However, attempts to say even a few words and phrases in Arabic are generally very much appreciated. Business: This must always be conducted on a personal introduction or invitation basis only. Without invitations or introductions, a business visit, while being courteously received, will ultimately amount to nothing. Honesty is the basis of all business dealings in Islamic countries and a word

is a bond. Arguing and haggling over prices is the norm and an Arabic tradition of buying and selling. Once a bargain has been struck, the deal cannot be renegotiated or cancelled unless either party cannot raise the money.

Clothing conventions: These are derived in part from religious beliefs and in part from climatic necessity. Western business suits are only practical during the summer if they are lightweight. Businessmen will be accepted if they wear open-necked shirts, as long as they are well turned out. Women are advised not to wear revealing clothes as this will attract unwelcome attention or ridicule at best, and resentment and hostility at worst. Women should also cover their heads when entering a Mosque. Depending on which country, Muslim women are sometimes advised to show face and hands only.

Do not sit in a position that points the soles of the feet towards anyone, as this is considered a deliberate insult. Shoes should be removed upon entering a Mosque or a house.

Sexual politics: Remember the position that women hold in Islam (see above) and that some gestures considered normal by westerners might be interpreted as serious insults. Divorce and marriage are considered civil matters, and while divorce is not a common practice, it is relatively easy. Adultery is considered an insult to Allah and society and severely punished, often by flogging, or sometimes by stoning the guilty parties to death.

Giving and receiving: Always use the right hand. To offer gifts with the left hand is considered an insult.

Drug use: Drugs are not culturally acceptable and, in the majority of countries, the possession, use, or trading of illegal substances is severely punished. Drug abuse is not permitted in Islam, particularly hard drugs such as heroin, morphine or cocaine, but also any drug which interferes with the consciousness, reasoning or judgement, affecting work, study or family life.

Alcohol: The consumption of alcohol is forbidden by (Qur'anic) law. Many non-practising Muslims will, however, drink alcohol and will offer drinks to guests when outside their own country. Most Islamic countries (with the exception of Kuwait, Libya and Saudi Arabia) permit the sale and consumption of alcohol by non-Muslims. Generally, the sale of alcohol will be confined to international hotels, but visitors may, in some cases, buy alcohol from wholesalers with a permit from their company or local Embassy. Bars are usually closed during Ramadan. Never drink alcohol while eating. Drunkenness is considered disgraceful; the visitor is advised against excessive consumption.

Gambling: This is considered by most Islamic countries to be an evil, and is strictly outlawed.

Smoking: This is also discouraged in Islam because of the health hazards associated with it. However, do not refuse a cigarette unless you are an ardent non-smoker, as an offer of a cigarette is often a compliment, especially from one's host. If invited to smoke a narghileh (hookah), do not refuse and follow the ritual behaviour exhibited. This social activity is popular in some, but by no means all, Arab countries.

Food: Pork is forbidden by Islamic law and all meat is killed by cutting the animal's throat and draining the blood; this is called halal meat. It is customary for the host/hostess to cut up whole items of food (especially with mezze, the Arabic equivalent of hors d'oeuvres) and distribute them. It is also customary to offer guests the most succulent parts of the meal, often the entrails or eyes; to refuse these is considered an insult. In restaurants, the person who makes the invitation pays the bill and it is considered an insult to contravene.

Note: Etiquette in all Islamic countries is complicated and highly evolved, and all those wishing to learn more are advised to do further research on the subject.

The Islamic calendar

The Islamic calendar is lunar, with the first of each month coinciding with the date of the actual New Moon. During a 30-year period, there are 19 Common and 11 Kabishah years; in 'Common' years of 354 days, the months are alternately 30 and 29 days long; in the 'Kabishah' year of 355 days, the last month has 30 days. The ninth month is Ramadan. The Islamic months are: Muharram, Safar, Rabi (1), Rabi (2), Jumada (1), Jumada (2), Rajab, Sha'ban, Ramadan, Shawwal, Dhu al-Qa'da and Dhu al-Hijja. These months are especially used in Saudi Arabia.

Further information

The Muslim Educational Trust, 130 Stroud Green Road, London N4 3RZ, UK (tel: (020) 7272 8502; website: www.muslim-ed-trust.org.uk).

JUDAISM

Introduction

The history of Judaism dates back over 5000 years to the Bible. In a somewhat dramatic moment, Abraham, at the age of 99, entered into a covenant with God and became Jewish after circumcising himself; he was chosen as the first Jew because of his righteousness and so began the religion and its many customs, traditions and laws. Years later came Moses, who was given the opportunity by God to receive his commandments. While most people remember the Ten Commandments, Moses actually received 613 on Mount Sinai. These commandments shape the Jewish faith today. Jews believe that there is only one God, and that the Bible, known as the Tanakh, consists only of the Old Testament. Of that, the first five books, known as the Five Books of Moses, or the Torah, are the most important.

Today there are approximately 14 million Jews in the world, with around 350,000 living in the UK. Other countries with a large Jewish population naturally include Israel, as well as Argentina, Australia, Belgium, Brazil, Canada, France, Holland, South Africa and the USA.

The different levels

All Jews fall into one of two categories, depending on their family origins; Ashkenazi Jews are of East-European extraction, while Sephardic hail from Spain, Mediterranean and Middle-Eastern countries. However, there are many different movements within Judaism, all of which interpret and adapt the traditional laws and customs in contrasting ways. The main movements are listed below.

Orthodox

This is one of the world's biggest Jewish movements. Orthodox Jews regard the Torah and the Talmud (Jewish laws) as being given directly to them by God, hence they are held in the highest authority.

Within Orthodoxy, there are different strands. These include: Ultra Orthodox, who follow the religion very strictly and may remove themselves as far as possible from the modern world; some even steer clear of television and newspapers due to the influence that these may have on their social standards and moral viewpoints. They may also live in separate communities from other Jewish people and follow their own customs, which could include specific dress codes.

Modern Orthodox Jews will usually participate in social and secular activities, such as going to a sports game or watching TV, provided it does not conflict with Jewish laws or impact on their religious life. On a religious level, they will observe the Sabbath, festivals, dietary laws (Kashrut) and other Jewish commandments.

The basic principles of Orthodox Judaism have not changed since Biblical times.

Reform

This movement was founded in Germany in the 19th century after Jews were liberated from their ghettos and began to integrate back into society – the feeling was that the religion would lose members if it did not move with the times. Members of the Reform movement take a more modern approach towards Judaism while seeking to retain its traditional principles and morals. Unlike Orthodox movements, women can be ordained as Rabbis, men and

women sit together in the synagogue (place of worship) and, on death, cremation is allowed.

Liberal

Like Reform, the liberal movement adopts a modern approach to Judaism. Liberal Jews believe that the Torah was God-inspired and is an interpretation of his words. They do not observe the faith in the same way an Orthodox Jew would. For example, Orthodox Jews will have a head covering, usually a kipah or yarmulke, which shows respect for God; liberal Jews do not believe this is necessary. They may also not be as stringent when it comes to keeping food laws – many will eat meat from such animals as pigs. For them, dietary laws and many other Jewish rituals that the Orthodox practises are not as important to them. However, some Liberal Jews will follow the laws of Kashrut – in this Jewish movement, the emphasis is put on personal choice. There are other movements within Judaism, including Conservatives (a group who essentially grew out of the tension between Orthodoxy and Reform; they believe that Jewish law should change and adapt, absorbing aspects of the predominant culture while remaining true to Judaism's values) and groups such as Jews for Jesus (who believe that Jewishness is cultural and inherited; they are Jews by birthright and Christian in belief).

The importance of the Jewish Sabbath

The Jewish Sabbath (Shabbat) commemorates God's resting on the seventh day of creation, after he had spent the previous six days creating the heavens and the earth, and is considered by Jews to be the holiest day of the week. The Sabbath begins at sundown on Friday and lasts until sunset on Saturday night and, during that time, Jews are prohibited from doing any form of work that could be seen as changing the world from how it was before the start of the Sabbath. Taken in a modern context, Orthodox Jews generally refrain from such activities as cooking, driving, watching television or using other electronic equipment, switching lights on and off, handling money and carrying anything outside of the home, even in their pockets (very religious Jews will generally attach their front door keys to an item of clothing). Jewish shops and businesses are closed on the Sabbath.

As well as attending the Friday night service at synagogue, Jews traditionally welcome the Sabbath by lighting candles and making Kiddush (traditional Friday night blessings over wine and challah bread), bestowing special blessings upon children in their household, and eating a celebratory meal. After a further synagogue service on the Saturday morning, during which a portion of the Torah is recited (known as the Reading Of The Law) and seven male congregants are called up to the reading and blessed, the day's formal religious proceedings are over, but the remainder of the day is traditionally spent resting or spending time with family members.

At sunset on Saturday night, the Sabbath is brought to a close with a ceremony known as Havdalah, which is performed at the evening service in synagogue but can also be performed at home – this involves making blessings over wine and a special plaited candle with a double wick, and is concluded by extinguishing the candle in a saucer of the wine. Following this, normal activities may be resumed.

Synagogue etiquette

Orthodox Jews generally attend synagogue daily for morning, afternoon and evening services (Shacharit, Mincha and Maariv respectively), although the latter two are frequently recited together. They also attend these on the Sabbath and festivals. Those who are less orthodox may attend less frequently. A minimum of 10 men over Bar Mitzvah age (13) is required to conduct a service – this is known as a Minyan.

Synagogue etiquette varies depending on the denomination of Judaism to which a person belongs. In Orthodox synagogues men and women sit separately – the women's area often consists of an upstairs gallery, or they will sit in a

different part of the building closed off by a curtain. Men wear the traditional head covering (kipah or yarmulke) – married women also cover their heads with hats or scarves, and are expected to dress modestly. At Reform and Liberal synagogues, men and women will often sit together.

Jewish festivals

The Jewish calendar is full of festivals and special days, either commemorating a major event in Jewish history or celebrating a certain time of year (such as Jewish New Year). Festival days are known as Yom Tovim and many of these days are marked by Jews refraining from working; however, unlike the Sabbath, cooking (for the day ahead only) and carrying items outside of the home are both permitted. Except where stated, all of the following festivals are guided by these laws. The main festivals are as follows:

Purim: This one-day festival takes place four weeks before Passover and usually falls in February or early March. It recalls the story of Esther, a Queen who foiled a plot by one of her advisors, Haman, to kill all Jews. As well as the story being read in synagogue in a book called the Megillah, it is a day for parties and celebrations (fancy dress is traditional). Pastries called Hamentaschen are also eaten – these are triangular (the same shape as Haman's hat, supposedly) and filled with poppy seeds, jam or fruit. Normal work and activities are permitted on Purim.

Pesach (Passover): This takes place around March/April, and commemorates Moses freeing the Israelites from their enslavement under the Pharaoh in Egypt. The festival lasts for eight days and, during that time, no 'leavened' food (food containing wheat or any type of grain) may be consumed (including bread, cereals, whisky and beer); Jews who come from the Middle East will eat rice and pulses, but European Jews will not. The reason for eating no leavened food is to remember when the Israelites had to leave Egypt in a hurry and did not have time to prepare proper food for themselves – their bread did not rise in time and so was considered 'unleavened' and tasted more like crackers. This is symbolised on Pesach by eating Matzah – unleavened bread.

On the first two nights, a service known as a Seder (order) is held at home – this tells the story of the Passover and the Jewish exodus from Egypt, chronicled in a book called the Haggadah. It is customary for those attending to lean to their left to show that they are no longer bound by the restrictions of slavery imposed by the Pharaoh of Egypt and may sit however they please. Four cups of wine are also drunk during the service, and a celebratory meal is eaten. A four-day period follows when normal work activities may be resumed, although leavened food is still forbidden. The final two days of the festival, like the first, are Yom Tovim. The festival finishes at sundown on the eighth day.

A great deal of preparation is required for Passover as not only are Jews not allowed to eat leavened food (known as chametz), they are not allowed to own it either, and must clear their houses of it before the festival begins. These days, people will get a rabbi to sell on their chametz for a token sum of money to a non-Jew, which can be redeemed after the festival is over. It is also customary to use different crockery, cutlery and cookware, which have not been used to cook foods containing chametz, for the duration of the festival.

Shavuot (Pentecost): Shavuot takes place seven weeks after Passover (usually around late May/early June) and commemorates Moses being given the Ten Commandments by God, following the Exodus from Egypt. The festival lasts for two days and requires relatively little advance preparation. However, it is traditional to eat dairy products, as when the Jews were awaiting the arrival of their commandments and were unsure as to what their new dietary laws would be, they ate only dairy products and vegetables, to avoid eating the meat of any animals that might be forbidden. The synagogue is decorated with flowers for the festival's duration in celebration of the giving of the commandments. Some ultra-Orthodox Jews often stay up on the first night to study the Bible.

Rosh Hashanah (Jewish New Year): The Jewish New Year takes place around September/October, and is considered one of the most important and serious holidays (or high holy days) in the Jewish calendar. As well as being a time for celebration it is also a time for reflection and repentance for sins committed in the previous year. In synagogue, people pray to God to forgive them for their wrongdoings and to give them a good year – during the service, a Shofar, or ram's horn, is blown to alert congregants to the seriousness of the festival and the fact that God is deciding their fates for the coming year – which will be sealed on the Day Of Atonement 10 days later. This period is known as The Ten Days Of Repentance and is traditionally a solemn time. However, Rosh Hashanah is also a time for celebration – other traditions include eating apples dipped in honey in the hope that this will lead to a sweet year.

Yom Kippur (Day Of Atonement): The Ten Days Of Repentance end with Yom Kippur, the Jewish Day Of Atonement, which is the day on which the fates of all Jews are sealed for the coming year. This high holy day is the most solemn and serious day in the Jewish calendar, which involves praying for forgiveness of sins and afflicting oneself as punishment for those committed in the past year. Jews fast (refraining from any food or drink) for 25 hours from sundown on the previous evening until sundown the next night, and are not allowed to work, bathe or wear leather shoes. The fast begins with a special evening service known as Kol Nidre (All Vows), and synagogue services last for the whole of the following day until the Fast ends.

Although it is a solemn day, Yom Kippur is also thought of as a happy day because it is a time for Jews to cleanse themselves of wrongdoings and reach a spiritual high. Fasting is not only done as a means of affliction but also because nothing is supposed to detract congregants from their prayers on the day. However, children below Bar Mitzvah or Bat Mitzvah age, pregnant women and diabetics are discouraged from fasting, as is anybody whose health is likely to be seriously affected by the 25-hour abstinence.

Succot (Tabernacles): This festival begins five days after the end of Yom Kippur and commemorates the booths the Israelites constructed in the wilderness and lived in after their exodus from Egypt. During the eight-day festival, Jews are supposed to live in a similar booth known as a Succah (dwelling) – the walls are made of wood and the ceiling of greenery to leave the stars visible. In countries such as Israel, where the climate permits, many people sleep in the Succah, but elsewhere it is used mainly for meals.

In synagogue, each congregant says a blessing over four different species of plants – a palm branch (lulav), citron (esrog), myrtle branch and willow twig – which are representative of the four different types of Jewish person. The middle four days of the festival are regular working days – although the fourth of these, Hoshana Rabba (Save Us), is treated as one final chance to purge the soul of sins committed in the previous year. The eighth day of the festival is called Shemini Atzeret (The Eighth Day Of Solemn Assembly), when a prayer for rain is said during the synagogue service.

Simchat Torah (Rejoicing Of The Law): Following immediately on from Succot is Simchat Torah, which celebrates the end of the reading of the Torah in synagogue – and the fact that it can now be read from the beginning again. This is one of the happiest festivals in the Jewish calendar – it is celebrated by making seven circuits of the synagogue, which are punctuated with dancing and singing of traditional Hebrew songs. Children are given flags to hold on the circuits, and many synagogues hold parties after the service.

Chanukah: Another eight-day festival, which takes place in December. The story of Chanukah hails back to a period in history when Jews were forbidden to follow their faith and many were forcibly converted or killed for not converting. Eventually, a band of Jews called the Maccabees gathered an army and revolted against the Greeks and won the battle, although their temple and way of life was all but destroyed. This band of men sought to clean up the temple and restore the faith, but in order to light the temple, a special seven-branch candelabra (Menorah) was needed, and only enough oil could be found to keep it alight for one day. However, a miracle occurred and the Menorah continued to remain alight for seven days until new oil could be made to keep the light going.

Traditions of Chanukah include lighting candles on a Menorah every night for eight nights in the home, eating food cooked in oil (doughnuts, potato pancakes), giving presents, holding parties and celebrations, and playing games with a dreidel, a traditional spinning top. As with Purim, normal work and activities are permitted on Chanukah.

Keeping kosher

The Jewish dietary laws, known as Kashrut, cover the way in which meat is ritually killed and prepared, as well as which foods can and cannot be eaten.

For an animal to be kosher, the Torah dictates it must chew the cud and have cloven hooves – as such, Jews may eat beef, lamb and any other products from cows or sheep. Most poultry, including chicken, turkey, duck and goose, is permitted; birds of prey are not.

Animals killed for meat are ritually slaughtered in the quickest and cleanest way possible by a specially trained person known as a schochet. Jews are not permitted to consume the blood of an animal, so the meat has to be 'koshered' (to have all the blood removed), which is normally done by the kosher butcher selling the product. Poultry is killed and prepared in the same way. Fish does not have to undergo any specific treatment for it to be kosher, but it must have fins and scales; shellfish is not permitted.

Jews are forbidden to consume milk and meat in the same meal, because according to the Bible: "Thou shalt not seethe a kid in its mother's milk". Many Jews wait until three hours after eating meat or poultry before consuming any dairy products, although some ultra-Orthodox may wait up to six hours. Foods that contain neither meat nor dairy products are referred to as parev.

Animal by-products – such as eggs and dairy products – are all permitted, provided they come from an animal which is kosher, although more religious Jews may only consume the latter if they have been made with milk from a supervised kosher dairy. If a speck of blood is found in an egg, it is considered non-kosher and must not be used. Jews should also be wary of animal products in processed foods.

When it comes to eating out, special care and attention is placed on establishments that are specially supervised. Just like pre-made food, restaurants need to have supervision. Many Orthodox Jews will only eat out in a restaurant that is supervised by a Jewish authority; however, less Orthodox Jews may feel comfortable eating in a restaurant which is not supervised, provided they are not offered any product which conflicts with basic dietary laws.

The Jewish life cycle

As well as festivals and Sabbaths, the life of a practising Jew is marked by certain other key events that are steeped in tradition.

Brit Milah (Circumcision): Baby boys are circumcised when they are eight days old, in accordance with the covenant made between God and Abraham in the Bible. This is done by a mohel (who has special medical training), and is often accompanied by a party or celebration. The baby is also officially named and given their Hebrew name at this ceremony. If the child is premature or unwell, Brit Milah may be carried out at a later date.

Bar Mitzvah: A Jewish boy officially becomes a man on his 13th birthday; in other words, he is now old enough to form part of the Minyan in synagogue and also to be called to the Reading Of The Law on Sabbath and festivals. This is a big event in many families – in synagogue, the boy will be called up to the Torah for the first time on the Sabbath closest to his birthday, and the ceremony will be marked by parties and celebrations afterwards.

Bat Mitzvah: The female equivalent of a Bar Mitzvah. As a rule, girls are not called to the Reading Of The Law in synagogues (although, within liberal and reform movements, this is possible), but still take part in a special synagogue ceremony to honour their own coming-of-age; again, parties and celebrations are also traditional but they may be lower-key than those held for Bar Mitzvah boys. A Bat Mitzvah usually takes place when the girl is around 12 years old.

Marriage: Jews are married underneath a special canopy known as a chupa, and traditions associated with the ceremony include the bride circling the groom, and the groom smashing a glass with his foot (wearing shoes) as a symbol to never forget that while this is a happy time, it is still sad that the Temple in Jerusalem was destroyed.

Death: Jews are buried quickly; usually a day or so after death takes place. In the event of the death of a close relative (parent, child, brother or sister), the mourners enter a seven-day period known as shiva – they are not allowed to leave the house (except to go to synagogue) or engage in any work for seven days, and must sit on low chairs to receive visitors. Mirrors must also be covered up. This is a solemn and dignified time, for both the deceased and their family. Jews in mourning also display their grief by tearing an item of clothing that they will wear for the entire seven-day period.

After the initial week is finished, a longer mourning period begins, lasting 30 days in the case of a sibling's death, or 12 months in the case of a parent, child or spouse, during which time, many Jews will not attend parties or celebrations; men are not allowed to shave for a minimum period of 30 days, although many will not shave for the entire year. After a year, the official mourning period ends but the person's death is remembered on each anniversary by lighting a memorial light known as a Yahrzeit candle.

Jewish terms

The following is a guide to the most common Jewish terms and phrases:

Shalom	–	Hello, goodbye, peace
Mazel 'Tov	–	congratulations, well done
Mitzvah	–	good deed
Tzedakah	–	charity
Chutzpah	–	cheek
Nachos	–	joy (often used when congratulating someone on the birth of a child, "may you have much nachos from them")
Kosher	–	fit for consumption
Shabbat Shalom	–	traditional Sabbath greeting
H'ag Samaech	–	greeting traditionally used on festivals

The Jewish calendar

The western year 2006 coincides with the Jewish year 5766; 2007 will coincide with 5767 and so on.

The following is a list of months in the Jewish calendar and when each occurs in the Western calendar, together with notable festivals that month. Although it neither concurs with the start of the Jewish or Western New Year, the months are traditionally listed in this order.

Nissan	(March/April), Pesach
Iyar	(April/May)
Sivan	(May/June), Shavuot
Tamuz	(June/July)
Av	(July/August)
Elul	(August/September)
Tishri	(September/October), Rosh Hashanah/Yom Kippur/Succot/Simchat Torah
Cheshvan	(October/November)
Kislev	(November/December), Chanukah
Tevet	(December/January)
Shevat	(January/February)
Adar	(February/March)

In leap years, an extra month, called Adar Sheni, is included.

Further information

See online (website: www.jewish.co.uk or www.jewish.net).